国家出版基金项目
NATIONAL PUBLICATION FOUNDATION

海上絲綢之路文獻集成

總主編　陳支平　陳春聲

科技與文化編

85

主編　王揚宗　葉　農

海峽出版發行集團
THE STRAITS PUBLISHING & DISTRIBUTING GROUP
福建人民出版社

本册目次

福建方言字典［一］

（*A Dictionary of the Hok-këèn Dialect of the Chinese Language, According to the Reading and Colloquial Idioms*）

〔英〕麥都思（Walter Henry Medhurst）編

《福建方言字典》，英國麥都思編。麥都思（Walter Henry Medhurst，一七九六—一八五七），英國倫敦會傳教士。一八一六年入倫敦會所屬印刷廠而被派往馬六甲，習得馬來語及多種漢語方言。一八三四年抵穗，一八四三年赴滬，創建墨海書館。著者自一八一八年起依清人謝秀嵐《彙集雅俗通十五音》學習南洋通行之閩南語，並據所編《閩南語詞彙集》修訂補充而成是書，所用羅馬拼音法對後世閩南語字典編纂頗具啓發。全書收漢字一萬兩千餘，逐字注音，並以英文釋義，所引例句，多出中國古典名著。據一八三二年澳門版影印。

福建方言字典

A

DICTIONARY

OF THE

HOK-KËÈN DIALECT

OF THE

CHINESE LANGUAGE,

ACCORDING TO THE READING AND COLLOQUIAL IDIOMS:

CONTAINING ABOUT 12,000 *CHARACTERS,*

THE SOUNDS AND TONES OF WHICH ARE ACCURATELY MARKED;—AND VARIOUS EXAMPLES OF THEIR USE,

TAKEN GENERALLY FROM APPROVED CHINESE AUTHORS.

ACCOMPANIED BY

A SHORT HISTORICAL AND STATISTICAL ACCOUNT OF

HOK-KËÈN;

A TREATISE ON THE ORTHOGRAPHY OF THE HOK-KËÈN DIALECT; THE NECESSARY INDEXES, &c.

BY W. H. MEDHURST,

BATAVIA.

MACAO, CHINA:

PRINTED AT THE HONORABLE EAST INDIA COMPANY'S PRESS,

BY G. J. STEYN AND BROTHER.

1832.

TO THE

COURT OF DIRECTORS

OF THE

HONORABLE EAST INDIA COMPANY,

AND TO THE

SELECT COMMITTEE

FOR THE MANAGEMENT OF THEIR AFFAIRS IN CHINA,

UNDER WHOSE PATRONAGE, AND BY WHOSE LIBERALITY,

THE FOLLOWING WORK IS PRINTED,

IT IS NOW MOST RESPECTFULLY INSCRIBED,

BY THEIR MUCH OBLIGED,

AND OBEDIENT HUMBLE SERVANT,

BATAVIA,

JULY 20th. 1831.

THE AUTHOR.

ADVERTISEMENT.

In the absence of the author of this Dictionary, a note explanatory of the delay in its publication seems necessary. The printing of it was commenced at the press of the Hon. E. I. Company in 1831, and continued with some interruptions until their charter expired in April, 1834, when the work stopped at the 320th page. It remained untouched until December, 1835, when Mr. Medhurst, being in China, circulated a subscription paper to procure funds to complete the printing, and obtained upwards of one hundred names. Messrs. Olyphant & Co. of Canton advanced the necessary funds on the guaranty of this subscription, and the printing was immediately resumed, the Company having loaned the use of their font of Chinese types for the purpose.

It is probable that the student will discover some errors in the work, but at present, a full table of errata cannot be made out. The following, however, have been noticed.

Page 16, for 淯 Beáou, read 消.
Page 48, for 笊 Chaou, read 笊.
Page 87, for 穄 Chèy, read 穄.
Page 95, for 漆 *Ch'hat*, read 柒.
Page 127, for 牀 Ch'hông, read 牀.
Page 144, for 侳 Choè, read 做.
Page 221, for 棪 Hëem, read 稴.
Page 241, for 候 Hoê, read 侯.
Page 252, for 璜 Hông, read 瑝.
Page 266, for 還 Hwân, read 還.
Page 274, for 痕 Hwûn, read 痕.
Page 276, for 袚 Hwut, read 祓.

Page 328, for 犴 Köen, also read 豣.
Page 332, for 鍥 read Këet, 鍥.
Page 351, for 殻 K'hák, read 殼.
Page 354, for 噭 K'haðu, read 礉.
Page 357, for 欹 K'he, read 攲.
Page 388, for 軓 K'hwúy, read 軌.
Page 436, for 呂 Lē, transpose 侶.
Page 541, for 發 P'hwat, read 癹.
Page 542, for 箟 Pin, read 篦.
Page 577, for 二 Sëáng, read 二.
Page 611, for 梭 Soe, read 廋.
Page 675, for 堂 *T'heⁿa*, read 廳.

Some errors in marking the tones, and in distinguishing the reading sounds from the colloquial, may also be found; but when the circumstances attending the printing of the work are considered, it is hoped these imperfections will not be severely criticised.

S. WELLS WILLIAMS.

Macao, June 1, 1837.

PREFACE.

AFTER the numerous and elaborate works on Chinese Philology already before the Public, the presentation of a new one would seem almost to need an apology, were it not that the object of the present Dictionary is not so much to elucidate the Chinese language generally, as that of one of its dialects, in particular. Previous efforts have been confined to the Mandarin or Court dialect, with the exception of a Canton Vocabulary published in 1828, and (so far as the Author's information extends) nothing has yet been done to elucidate the Hok-këèn or Emoey tongue.

The Mandarin tongue is partially understood throughout the whole Empire, by the better informed part of the inhabitants, and, in some central districts, it is said to be the current language of the people, but, in the southern provinces, the vulgar dialects differ more or less from the Court language, and in Hok-këèn, where the difference is most marked, the cultivation of the Mandarin tongue is less general. The author, having never visited China, has had little opportunity of conversing with the higher ranks of the Chinese, but from a constant intercourse with the middling and lower classes who emigrate to the Eastern Islands, his uniform experience for the last fourteen years has been, that not one man in five hundred knows any thing of the Mandarin tongue, or can carry on a conversation of more than ten words in it. In Hok-këèn, a doctor, a fortune-teller, a stage-player, or a police officer may sometimes be

b

met with, who having travelled into other provinces, or been employed about Government offices, will perhaps be able to converse a little in the Court dialect; but, in most cases, the people are totally unacquainted with it, and never think of studying it till, having succeeded at the literary examinations, and got a prospect of preferment or employment, they go to a regular school for the study of the Mandarin, and acquire it almost as they would a new language. Indeed, instances have been known of literary graduates of considerable standing giving up the prospect of Government situations, rather than take the trouble of studying the Court dialect.

Not only does the Mandarin tongue differ from the vulgar idioms, but these provincial dialects differ considerably from each other, so that an inhabitant of Hok-këèn will not be able to understand a native of Canton,—and the author has frequently had occasion to interpret for two Chinese from adjoining provinces, who could not understand each other. Even in the same province, the difference of dialect is sometimes so great, that people divided by a mountain, a river, or twenty miles of country, are by no means intelligible to each other. In the ten counties of Hok-këèn, there are certainly as many different dialects, and if the same obtains throughout every one of the eighteen provinces of China, the different dialects in that Empire will be nearly two hundred.

A person who contemplates learning the Chinese language, without much prospect of verbal intercourse with the people, or who will be generally conversant with the higher classes and Government officers, throughout all the Provinces, would certainly do well to study the Mandarin dialect;—but he whose intercourse will probably be confined to one district, and who will have to do with the great mass of the people residing in it, would do better to study the vulgar dialect of that particular place.

The author, on commencing the study of Chinese, attended solely to the Mandarin, but, finding that it was not understood by the mass of emigrants in the Malayan archipelago, he turned his attention, in the year 1818, to the Hok-këèn dialect. In 1820, a small Vocabulary was drawn up, and a few sheets of it printed at Malacca; in 1823, this work was enlarged, and sent to Singapore, to be printed under the patronage of the Singapore Institution, the Committee of which offered to publish it at their own expence. The affairs of that Institution, however, not having prospered, the Manuscript lay untouched for several years, was since sent to Malacca and Penang, and, in the year 1829, came back untouched into the author's hands. Considerable advancement having in the mean time been made in the knowledge of the language, and the Select

Committee for managing the affairs of the Honorable East India Company, in China, having generously offered to bring the work through the press, the author undertook to re-compose it entirely, to enlarge it by the addition of several thousand characters, and to illustrate the meaning of each principal word by a quotation from some respectable Chinese author.

The present work is founded on a native Dictionary of the Hok-këèn dialect, published in the year 1818, called the 十五音 Sip gnoé yim, or "fifteen sounds," which contains both the Reading and Colloquial idiom, with the sounds and tones very accurately defined. The inhabitants of Hok-këèn have a method of expressing themselves in common conversation, very different from the style in which their books are written; and this variation appears, not only in the substitution of more easy and familiar words for the abstruse and difficult terms used in books, but also in the inflection and alteration of even common words, giving them sometimes a nasal or contracted termination, and sometimes completely changing their sound and tone. This has given rise to the distinction between the Reading and Colloquial forms of speech, which, in the native Dictionaries, are distinguished, by having the former printed in red, and the latter in black ink; while the same is attempted to be marked in the following work, by putting the Colloquial in italics, and printing the Reading idiom in roman letters.

The Chinese have a method of spelling their words, by dividing them into initials and finals, and taking the initial of one word and the final of another, they form a third by the conjunction. In the native Dictionary above alluded to, fifteen initials (hence the name) and fifty finals are employed, to express all the possible variations in sound, of which the Hok-këèn dialect is capable. These initials and finals are hereafter described, and attempted to be expressed in European letters; the system of orthography which has been adopted to elucidate these sounds may not possibly be the best, and no doubt they would be differently expressed by others; but whatever may be the faults or deficiencies of his system, the author flatters himself that it is uniform, and that any given word will be found to bear the same orthography throughout the work. Walker's and Sheridan's pronouncing Dictionaries have been consulted, but it was found impossible to adopt their systems in every instance, as the Hok-këèn dialect contains sounds, which neither of those orthoëpists had ever occasion to illustrate. The nasals, in particular, can be accurately expressed by no possible system of European orthography, and if twenty people had to define them, they would no doubt write them in as many different ways; the author has therefore adopted that mode of spelling which appeared to him the best, following, in most instances, the orthography of Dr. Morrison, in his Dictionary of the Mandarin tongue, where the sounds at all resembled each other;—and having once adopted it, he has found it necessary to adhere to the same throughout the work, in order to prevent mistakes and confusion.

In addition to the sounds formed by the junction of the fifteen initials and fifty finals, the inhabitants of Hok-këèn have a method of multiplying their few monosyllables, by the application of various tones, which, while the word retains the same form of spelling, produce an alteration of the intonation, by a variation of the accent. Respecting these tones of the Chinese language, some difference of opinion has obtained, and while some have considered them of the first importance, others have paid them little or no attention. The author inclines decidedly to the former opinion; having found, from uniform experience, that without strict attention to the tones, it is impossible for a person to make himself understood in Hok-këèn. Chinese children, as soon as they begin to speak, learn the tones, as speedily as they do the sounds themselves, and the poorest people invariably observe the minutest regard to the tones; so that the author has never heard a real native of Hok-këèn make the slightest mistake in the tones, even in the hurried conversation of common life. Indeed a Chinese is more likely to make a mistake in the orthography than in the accent of a word, and when charged with pronouncing *tëem* instead of *lëem*, will defend himself, by saying that, at any rate the words are in the same tone, and therefore there cannot be much difference between them. A horse in Hok-këèn is *báy*, in the upper tone, with an acute accent, but the Chinese, in speaking of a horse, would as soon think of changing the orthography into *báng*, as of altering the accent into *bây*, which is in the lower even tone, with a circumflex over it. In the native Dictionary which is made the basis of the present work, the tones are most particularly defined, and the arrangement of each section is more according to the tone than the orthography; for instance, the first section contains all the words of the even tone, under a certain final, as connected with the different initials, and not a single upper tone is brought forward, till all the even tones of that final are given; the second section then contains all the words under the upper tone of the same final, and so on; so that *kwun* in the even tone will be found under one section, and *kwún*, in the upper tone under another. This arrangement, in which the accent is regarded more than the spelling, is peculiar to the Chinese, and shews what great stress they lay on a difference of tone, even more so than on a difference of orthography. In the following pages, this arrangement has been reversed, and the words are classed according to their alphabetical order, yet the author has endeavoured to mark, *in every instance*, the peculiar tone to be affixed to each word, and that not only in the words placed for reference at the head of each line, but also in the examples adduced; so that, with the exception of typographical errors, each word will be found to have, not only the same mode of spelling, but also a uniform intonation, throughout the book.

It is possible that, in the meaning given to each particular word, some dissimilarity may be observed between the present work and the Dictionary published by Dr. Morrison; if such should be the case, the author would not be understood as intentionally differing from his indefatigable predecessor, whose elaborate work he has seldom or ever consulted for the meaning of words; but, having followed an entirely independant authority, and having adopted the meanings assigned in native Dictionaries, and illustrated in the quotations referred to, it is not unlikely but some trifling discrepancy may arise. Fewer meanings may also be found in this, than in the Doctor's work; but it must be remembered, that the present undertaking is on a much smaller scale than the preceding one, and to have given all the meanings of each word, and proofs of their being used in every several sense, from Chinese authors, would have swelled this Dictionary to too great a size, particularly as it is designed to illustrate, not so much the language, as a single dialect of it. However, the most common and approved sense of each word is generally given.

The quotations adduced are most of them from Chinese authors of the best reputation, viz. from the Five Classics, the Four Books, authentic Histories, and approved Odes, being generally the same which are quoted in the Imperial Dictionary, under the characters referred to. A few vulgar phrases may be found here and there, and some quotations from novels and unauthorized productions; but good authors, however ancient, have generally been preferred, both as being held in greater respect among the Chinese themselves, and as giving the most appoved sense of the characters in question. It may be that the author has mistaken the meaning of some passages, and has awkwardly expressed the sense of others, while published translations of the works quoted from may be brought, in triumphant proof of alledged ignorance or carelessness;—but it must be remembered, that a person giving the sense of an isolated passage is very likely to express himself differently from one who translates the book in detail; and that some variation or amplification is indeed necessary in a quotation, in order to give the reader a correct idea of the sentence, which would be less requisite where the passage stood in its proper connection. If it be asked,—why not give sentences from modern authors, or examples of every-day conversation, in illustration of each character? the answer may be, that there are no modern authors, of any reputation, but what are built upon, and imitators of ancient writings; and to manufacture sentences for the occasion would be

c

liable to this very serious objection, that such sentences may or may not be good Chinese, according to the proficiency or unskilfullness of the Compiler; and to adduce ungrammatical or un-idiomatical sentences in elucidation, would be to lead the mind astray, and to retard instead of promote the progress of the student. Should the author be spared to compose the Second Part of this Dictionary, viz. the English and Chinese, it is his intention to adduce, under each important word, a phrase from some English author, and to give the sense of it in Chinese, by which means the student will be enabled to judge of the familiar way of writing and speaking Chinese, and of the method of rendering English composition into it.

For the short historical and statistical account of Hok-këèn, the author is indebted to Chinese histories and geographical works, to Malte Brun's Universal Geography, and to an account of the Dutch embassy to Hok-këèn in the seventeenth century. These productions are most of them old, yet, as China remains long stationary, the present state of the province differs perhaps little from what it was formerly. In estimating the population of Hok-këèn, a different opinion is hazarded from what Dr. Morrison has given, in his View of China for Philological Purposes: it is however proposed with diffidence, and not without being substantiated by two independant authorities. Hok-këèn contains ten counties, of which only one, viz. 漳州 Chëang chew, near the port of Emöey, is the identical spot where the dialect illustrated in this Dictionary is spoken in its purity; in the adjoining county to the east, viz. 泉州 Chwâŭ chew, the dialect differs very little; and in the neighbouring county on the opposite side, viz. 潮州 Teâou chew, in the province of Canton, the dialect differs a little more, but still the inhabitants of each district are mutually intelligible to each other. Of the dialects of the northern counties, of 汀州 T'heng chew, and 延平 Yêên pêng, as well as of the north-eastern counties of 興化 Hin hwà, and 福州 Hok chew, the author is unable to speak with any degree of decision.

For any typographical errors, which may creep in during the excution of the work, the author hopes for the indulgence of the public, as, the work being printed at the distance of nearly two thousand miles from his place of abode, it is impossible for him to correct the sheets as they are put to press, or to mark out any errors which might have inadvertently dropped from his pen in the composition. To the Rev. Dr. Morrison and his son, who have kindly undertaken the revision of the proofs, the author would express his unfeigned obligations, and his earnest hopes that they may succeed, in the difficult task of reading and comparing the very minute distinctions, of accent as well as sound, which the author has found it necessary to employ in the work, and that they may send it forth to the public, as correct as his best wishes could desire.

To the Directors of the Honorable East India Company, and to the Gentlemen of the Select Committee for the management of their affairs in China, the author acknowledges himself as under great and manifold obligations, for their kind notice and patronage of the work, and for their munificent liberality, in printing it, free of expence, at their own press in China.

May the present feeble undertaking be rendered eminently serviceable in the promotion of Chinese literature, and may students of the language, whether for civil or religious purposes, derive essential benefit therefrom! and to that God who has granted health for the undertaking, and ability to bring it to a conclusion, shall be all the glory.

W. H. M.

Batavia, July 29th. 1831.

A SHORT HISTORICAL AND STATISTICAL ACCOUNT OF THE PROVINCE OF HOK-KËÈN.

(COMPILED FROM EUROPEAN AND CHINESE AUTHORS.)

THE PROVINCE of 福建 Hok-këèn, 'happy establishment,' lies in the S. E. quarter of the Empire of China. The latitude of its Capital, 福州 Hok-chew, 'happy region,' is 26° 3' N. and its Longitude 1° 30' E. from Peking. The account given of it by Malte Brun is as follows:

"Fou-kien (or Hok-këèn) is one of the smallest, yet richest, provinces of the Empire. Its situation "is favourable for fishing, navigation, and trade. The air is very warm, but pure and healthy. The fields "are watered with an infinity of rivers, which come from the mountains, and which the labourers manage with "great dexterity, for watering their rice-grounds. Black tea is the principal product. It also contains musk, "precious stones, iron, tin, and quicksilver mines; silk, hemp, and cotton are manufactured; steel is prepared, both "in the form of bars, and ready-made articles of hardware; and among the delicious and abundant fruits which it "produces, the oranges are remarkable for the flavour of muscat grapes which they possess. Fou-chew-fou (Hok-"chew-hoó), the capital of the province, is, above all, celebrated for its situation, for the great trade which it pos-"sesses, for the multitude of its men of learning, for the beauty of its rivers, which bear the great barks of China "to its very walls, and, finally, for an admirable bridge, thrown over the gulf, consisting of a hundred arches, and "entirely built of a beautiful white stone. Yen-peng-fou (Yëên-pêng-hoó), situated on the declivity of a mountain, "at the foot of which flows the river Min-ho, is not large, but it is considered as one of the handsomest towns in "the Empire. Tchang-chew-fou (Chëang-chew-hoó) is near the port of Emouy (Āy-moôi[ng]), a great emporium of "trade, frequented by the Spaniards from Manilla."

The Hok-këèn province was formerly called the Bân 閩 country: the following notices respecting its early history are taken from the 綱鑑易知 Kong kàm ē te, or "History of China."

As early as the first year of 秦始皇 Chin-sé-hông, B. C. 215, we find mention made of the Bân country. The Empire being then divided into 36 districts, or 郡 Kwûn, to which were added four others from the 粤 Wat country, namely, 閩中 Bân-tëung, or Hok-këèn; 南海 Lâm-hae, or Canton; 桂林 Kwùy-lîm, Cochin China; and 象郡 Sëāng-kwûn (perhaps Siam.)

d

In the 30th year of 漢武帝 Hàn-boó-tey, B. C. 105, the people of 東越 Tong-wat slew 王餘善 Ông-ê-sëën, and tendered their submission to the Government. In the preceding year, 王餘善 Ông-ê-sëën had rebelled, and the Emperor sent his General 陽僕 Yâng-pok to subdue the country; after which he transplanted the people to the region between the 江 Kang and 淮 Hwaê rivers. The Emperor having considered that the country of 閩 Bân was full of dangerous defiles, and the people ever disposed to revolt, which would be likely to occasion endless trouble to future ages, resolved on completely removing the inhabitants to another region, leaving their own country desolate.

In the period of the 唐 Tông dynasty, in the 12th year of 宣宗 Swan-chong, A. D. 849, the Emperor appointed 于延陵 Ê-Yëên-lêng to be the ruler of 建州 Këën-chew. When Yëên-lêng came in to return thanks for the appointment, his Majesty asked, how far Këën-chew was from the Capital? Eight thousand lé, was the reply. Upon which the Emperor said, "As soon as you come thither, whether your government be good or bad, I shall be fully acquainted with it: do not say to yourself, it is far off, for ten thousand lé are as near to me as the steps of my throne. Do you know this?"

In the 5th year of 懿宗 E-chong, A. D. 853, it is said that many of the eunuchs of the palace were natives of Hok-këën, and had great influence at court.

In the 4th year of 僖宗 Hé-chong, A. D. 868, Hok-chew 福州 was taken by the rebel Hông-chaôu 黄巢 (*Wuîng-chaôu*). In the 7th year of the same reign, A. D. 871, arose the rebel 王緒 Ông-sē: he was a native of 壽州 Sēw-chew, in the province of 江南 Kang-lâm, and by trade a butcher. Having collected a company of about 500 men, he seized upon the government of his native district; and about a month afterwards got possession of 光州 Kong-chew, when his adherents swelled to the number of 10,000. There was a magistrate of 固始 Koè-sé district, in the neighbourhood of 光州 Kong-chew, by the name of 王潮 Ông-teaôu, who, together with his younger brethren, 審知 Sim-te, and 審邽 Sim-kwuy, was alike distinguished for courage and spirit. 王緒 Ông-sē made this 王潮 Ông-teaôu his Lieutenant-General, and placed much confidence in him.

In the 11th year of 僖宗 Hé-chong, A. D. 875, 王緒 Ông-sē took possession of 汀州 Theng-chew and 漳州 Chëang-chew, both in the province of 福建 Hok-këën. About this time 秦宗權 Chîn-Chong-kwân, who had been appointed by the Emperor to be Governor of 光州 Kong-chew, demanded the taxes due from that district; and 王緒 Ông-sē refusing to pay them, 宗權 Chong-kwân was enraged, and marched an army to attack him. Ông-sē, in his fright, collected the troops of both the 壽 Sēw and 光 Kong districts, about 5000 men, and crossing the river, seized upon the three districts of 江 Kang, 洪 Hong, and 虔 K'hëen, and the same month took possession of the two districts of 汀 T'heng and 漳 Chëang, but could not keep them long.

In the autumn of the same year, 王緒 Ông-sē came to 漳州 Cheang-chew, and because the road was dangerous and provisions scarce, gave orders throughout the army, that no one should be permitted to bring their old and feeble relatives along with them, on pain of death. But 王潮 Ông-teâou and his brethren ventured to carry with them their aged mother. Ông-sē reproved them, saying, "All armies have laws, and there are no armies without them; you have now disobeyed my laws, and if I do not punish you, it will be the same as if we had no laws." Ông-teâou and his brethren replied, "All men have mothers, and there are no men without them; how is it that your Excellency would have us to throw away our mother." Ông-sē was enraged, and ordered them to behead the old woman; but Ông-teâou and his brethren interfered, saying, "We must serve our mother, as much as our general; if you kill the mother, what will be the use of the sons? we beg therefore to die first." The troops then interposed, and the matter was passed over. A certain fortune-teller told Ông-se, that there was in the army an individual, who would one day become a king; whereupon Ông-sē put to death all those soldiers who appeared to have the least spark of bravery, or any disposition to assume command. This rendered the troops uneasy, and when they came as far as Lâm-an 南安 (*Lâm-wⁿa*); in the district of 泉州 Chwân-chew, Ông-teâou directed the commander of the advanced guard to conceal some stout fellows among the bamboo bushes, in order to seize Ông-sē, and binding him, expose him to public scorn. Upon this Ông-teâou was made general, and led his troops to the siege of 泉州 Chwân-chew.

In the 5th year of 昭宗 Chēaou-chong, A. D. 883, 王潮 Ông-teâou took possession of 福州 Hok-chew. About this time 陳巖 Tîn-gâm, the Governor of 福建 Hok-kēēn, was sick, and summoned 王潮 Ông-teâou, the ruler of 泉州 Chwân-chew, in order to deliver over to him the command of the district, but died before his arrival. His Lieutenant, 范暉 Hwàn-hwūy, immediately appointed himself to succeed, and sent out troops to oppose Ông-teâou, but upon Ông-teâou's attacking 福州 Hok-chew, Hwàn-hwūy gave up the city and fled: Ông-teaôu then succeeded to the Government. In the winter of the same year, Ông-teâou was regularly invested, by the Emperor, with the dignity of Governor of 福建 Hok-kēēn province; from which period is dated the elevation of his family to independent sway in that part of China.

In the 9th year of 昭宗 Chēaou-chong, A. D. 888, Ông-teâou died. Before his death he had elevated his brother 王審知 Ông-Sim-te to the rank of Lieutenant-Governor, and on one occasion, for some error which he had committed, had struck him with his staff; Sim-te did not however take offence at this; and Ông-teâou, in his last illness, set aside his own son, and ordered Sim-te to superintend the affairs of the province. This 審知 Sim-te is still worshipped by the Hok-kēēn people, as being the founder of their state.

In the 3rd year of 梁太祖 Lēâng-T'haè-choé, A. D. 900, 王審知 Ông-Sim-te was appointed, by the Emperor, to be King of 閩 Bân. He was a man of economical and sparing habits, wore hempen shoes, and dwelt in a mean abode, without ever thinking of enlarging or beautifying the place of his residence. He was gentle in punishments, and sparing in exactions, so that all ranks became rich and happy, and his whole territory was tranquil.

In the 2nd year of 唐莊宗 Tông-Chông-chong, A. D. 915, 王審知 Ông-Sim-te, the ruler of 閩 Bân, died, and was succeeded by his son 延翰 Yëên-hān. In the following year, 王延稟 Ông-Yëên-pín, the adopted son of 王審知 Ông-Sim-te, slew 延翰 Yëên-hān, and set up his younger brother, 延鈞 Yëên-kin, in his stead.

In the 2nd year of 唐明宗 Tông-Bêng-chong, A. D. 918, the Emperor appointed 王延鈞 Ông-Yëên-kin to be king of 閩 Bân. In the 7th year of the same reign, A. D. 923, 王延鈞 Ông-Yëên-kin assumed the title of Emperor of 閩 Bân, and altered his name to 璘 Lîn.

In the 1st year of 唐廢帝 Tông-Hwùy-tèy, A. D. 935, 李倣 Lé-hông, of the 閩 Bân country, murdered his sovereign 王璘 Ông-Lîn, and set up in his stead 福王 Hok-ông, 'the King of happiness,' called 繼鵬 Kèy-pêng, and altered his name to 昶 Ch'hëáng.

In the 3d year of 晉高祖 Chìn-Ko-choé, A. D. 931, 王曦 Ông-he, of the 閩 Bân country, murdered his nephew and sovereign 昶 Ch'hëáng, and set up himself in his room; acknowledging fealty to 晉 Chìn. In the 5th year of the same sovereign, A. D. 933, 王曦 Ông-he, of the 閩 Bân country, took the title of Emperor.

In the 1st year of 晉齊王 Chìn-Chêy-ông, A. D. 937, 王延政 Ông-Yëên-chèng, of the district of 富沙 Hoò-say, styled himself Emperor, and called his country 殷 Yin. This 王延政 Ông-Yëên-chèng was the younger brother of 王曦 Ông-he; and he had 潘承祐 Hwan-Sîn-yew, to be his President of the board of appointments, and 楊思恭 Yâng-Soo-këung, to be his President of the military board, and to be associated with him in the government of the state. The country was small and the people poor, while the troops had no rest: hence 思恭 Soo-këung sought to ingratiate himself with his Prince, by collecting as much revenue as possible, and therefore increased the taxes on fields and arable lands, even to fish, salt, vegetables, and fruit; nothing was left without having a double tax levied on it; insomuch that the people of the country called him "skin-flint."

In the 2nd year of the same Emperor, A. D. 938, 朱文進 Choo-bûn-chìn, a military officer of the 閩 Bân country, murdered his prince 曦 He, and set himself up in his stead. In the same year, 朱文進 Choo-bûn-chìn yielded subjection to the 晉 Chìn dynasty, and was dignified with the title of 閩王 Bân-ông, the king of Bân. Upon which the state of 殷 Yin marched to the attack of 朱文進 Choo-bûn-chìn, and the Chinese government sent troops to attack 殷 Yin. The people of 閩 Bân, however, put 朱文進 Choo-bûn-chìn to death, and sent his head to 建州 Këèn chew.

In the following year, A. D. 939, the state of 殷 Yin altered its designation to 閩 Bân, after which the Emperor's troops contended with those of 閩 Bân, and the latter were routed; whereupon the Emperor's troops entered 建州 Këèn-chew, and 延政 Yëên-chèng came out and surrendered. Thus the country of 閩 Bân fell into the hands of the Chinese.

REMARKS

ON THE POPULATION OF HOK-KEÈN.

IN THE statement given to Sir G. Staunton, in 1795, by Chew-ta-jin, a mandarin of high rank, the population of Hok-këèn is rated at 15,000,000, and that of the whole Empire at 333,000,000. This estimate has been by many thought to be exaggerated, but in the appendix to the Report of the Anglochinese College, for 1829, it is stated (on the authority of the 大清會典 Taē-Ch'heng hwūy tëèn, or "Collection of statutes of the Taē-Ch'heng dynasty," in 261 volumes), that the Emperor 乾隆 Këen-lëûng in his 57th year, 1792, found the amount of the whole population to be 307,467,200.

In Morrison's "View of China for Philological purposes,"—which follows the 大清一通志 Taē-Ch'heng yit t'hong chè, or "Complete statistical account of the Empire of the Taē-Ch'heng dynasty,"—the population Hok-këèn, in 1790, is stated to be 1,684,328, while that of the whole Empire is rated at less than 150,000,000. This statement has been preferred by many, on account of its moderation, but it seems to assign very disproportionate numbers to several particular provinces, giving in some instances *more than* is found in the largest estimate and assigning in others only a few hundred thousands to districts, which, according to every other statement, are peopled by millions.

In the possession of the author is a work called the 欽定大清會典 K'him tēng Taē-Ch'heng hwūy tëèn, "Collection of statutes of the Taē-Ch'heng dynasty, as fixed by authority," in 16 volumes, published in the 28th year of 乾隆 Këen-lëûng, 1763. According to this, the number of *men*, between the ages of 16 and 60 is stated to be upwards of 100,000,000 throughout the whole Empire, and 4,710,399 in Hok-këèn. Now if we reckon as many women, infants, and superannuated people, as able-bodied men, we shall have an aggregate of 200,000,000 as the probable population of China.

With this agrees the account published by Father Allerstein, in 1743, as quoted by Malte Brun, which rates the whole population at 198,218,485, and that of Hok-këèn at 8,063,671. The comparative statements are as follow:—

Names of the Provinces.	According to Sir G. Staunton.	According to Dr. Morrison.	According to a work in the possession of the Author.	According to Allerstein.
盛京 Sēng-keng	—	{390,714 / 95,929}	221,742	668,852
直隸 Tit-ley	38,000,000	3,504,038	9,374,217	15,222,940
山東 San-tong	24,000,000	25,447,633	12,769,872	25,180,734
山西 San-sey	27,000,000	1,860,816	5,162,351	9,768,189
河南 Hô-lâm	25,000,000	2,662,969	7,114,346	16,332,507
江蘇 Kang-soe }	32,000,000	{ 28,967,235	12,618,987	22,761,030
安徽 An-hway }		1,433,023	12,435,361	23,161,409
江西 Kang-sey	19,000,000	5,922,160	5,055,251	11,006,604
福建 Hok-këën	15,000,000	1,684,528	4,710,399	8,063,671
浙江 Chëet-kang	21,000,000	18,975,099	8,662,808	15,429,690
湖北 Hoê-pok	14,000,000	21,604,369	4,568,860	8,080,603
湖南 Hoê-lâm	13,000,000	9,098,010	4,336,332	8,829,820
陝西 Sëem-sey	18,000,000	257,704	3,851,043	7,287,443
甘肅 Kam-sëuk	12,000,000	340,086	2,133,222	7,412,014
四川 Soò-ch'hwan	27,000,000	7,789,782	1,368,496	2,782,976
廣東 Kóng-tong	21,000,000	1,491,271	3,969,248	6,782,975
廣西 Kóng-sey	10,000,000	2,569,518	1,975,619	3,947,414
雲南 Yîn-lâm	8,000,000	3,083,459	1,003,058	2,078,892
貴州 Kwùy-chew	9,000,000	2,941,391	1,718,848	3,420,722
			103,050,060 *males.*	
			100,000,000 *females.*	
	333,000,000	143,124,734	203,050,060	198,218,483

From a comparison of the above accounts, we may perhaps conclude, that the first is rather exaggerated, and the second disproportionate in the numbers assigned to the various provinces; but the third (allowing the numbers to be doubled on account of the females) and the fourth agree so nearly together, in circumstantials and generals, that it cannot be venturing too much, to consider them as affording a true statement of the population of China; particularly as it regards the provinces of Hok-këën and Canton (the most known to Europeans). For each of these,—judging from the immense number of emigrants, who, from the two provinces alone, amount, it is said, to half a million,—also considering the dense population of the city of Canton,—and taking into account the universal testimony of the Hok-këën people themselves, that the inhabitants of their native province exceed the ants in number,—the sum of six or eight millions would seem to approach nearer the truth, than the million and a half of Dr. Morrison's account, or the fifteen and twenty millions of Sir G. Staunton's. The following extract from the 大清會典 Taē-Ch'heng hwŭy tëén is found in the appendix to the College Report above alluded to, which abundantly confirms the supposed populousness of these two provinces. In the 5th year of 雍正 Yung-chêng, 1727, it was declared that the population of Hok-këën was so dense, that the abundance of commerce must be brought in to aid effects of agriculture; and therefore the people of that province were allowed to trade to the nations of the south, in the China sea and the same privilege was extended to Canton, "which is a narrow territory, with a numerous population.

In order to ascertain the value of each province in China, and of Hok-këen in particular the following comparative view of the land in cultivation, and the revenue derived therefrom in the 18th year of 乾隆 Këen lëûng (A. D. 1753), is submitted:

Names of the Provinces.	*Area in Sq. Miles.*	*Quantity of land, in English acres.*	*Quan. of land in cultivation, in Eng. acres.*	*Revenue in Taels.*	*Measures of grain, each 133lbs avoir:*	*Bundles of straw.*	*Measures of grain expended in the provinces.*	*Measures of grain sent to Peking.*
盛京 Sĕng-keng	—	—	501,864	38,110	76,206	—	—	—
直隷 Tit-ley	58,949	37,727,360	18,143,837	2,411,286	191,229	94,404	—	—
山東 San-tong	65,104	41,666,560	19,421,081	3,346,257	507,680	—	158,902	348,77[illegible]
山西 San-sey	55,268	35,871,520	6,591,724	2,970,266	[illegible],246	—	—	—
河南 Hô-lâm	65,101	41,666,560	14,456,407	3,303,080	[illegible]	—	28,991	[illegible]
江蘇 Kang-soe }	92,961	59,495,040	13,797,689	3,371,334	[illegible]	—	138,132	[illegible]
安徽 An-hwuy }			6,762,418	1,688,000	[illegible],248	—	278,971	[illegible]
江西 Kang-sey	72,176	46,192,640	9,585,412	1,879,810	[illegible]99,632	—	129,499	[illegible]
福建 Hok-këèn	53,480	34,227,200	2,565,417	1,177,899	168,453	—	—	—
浙江 Chëet-kàng	39,150	25,056,000	9,195,754	2,812,449	[illegible]	—	273,742	[illegible]
湖北 Hoê-pok	144,770	92,652,800	11,338,269	1,108,158	286,354	—	154,150	[illegible]
湖南 Hoê-lâm			6,245,759	1,163,063	277,641	—	143,897	[illegible]
陝西 Sëem-sey	154,008	98,565,120	5,047,420	1,530,907	168,453	—	—	—
甘肅 Kam-sëuk			3,556,626	257,723	503,476	5,051,174	—	
四川 Soò-ch'hwan	166,800	106,752,000	9,182,9[illegible]	659,075	14,329	—	—	—
廣東 Kóng long	79,456	50,851,840	6,576,658	1,257,286	348,095	—	—	
廣西 Kóng-sey	78,250	50,080,000	1,748,012	332,597	130,375	—	—	
雲南 Yin-lâm	107,969	69,100,160	1,389,996	153,750	2[illegible]0,348	—	—	—
貴州 Kwùy-chew	64,554	41,314,560	513,835	10[illegible],156	154,590	—	—	—
	[illegible]	830,719,360	141,624,111	29,311,2[illegible]	8,41[illegible],422	5,145,575	1,606,284	4,754,8[illegible]

OF THE DIVISIONS AND SUBDIVISIONS OF HOK-KËÈN.

The province of Hok-këen is divided into ten larger and two smaller counties. The names of the former are as follow:

Hok-chew 福州, the happy region.
Hin-hwà 興化, flourishing renovation.
Chwân-chew 泉州, the fountain region.
Chëang-chew 漳州, the region of the river Cheang.

Yëên-pêng 延平, lengthened pacification.
Keen-lêng 建寧, established tranquillity.
Seaòu-boó 邵武, awakened military ardour.
T'heng-chew 汀州, the region of the river T'heng.
Hok-lêng 福寧, happy tranquillity.
Taê-wan 臺灣, terraced harbour, — Formosa.

The two smaller counties are, —

E'ng-ch'hun 永春, eternal spring.
Lëûng-gâm 龍巖, dragon precipice.

The seat of government is in 福州 Hok-chew.

The whole province is bounded on the north by 浙江 Chëet-kang and 江西 Kang-sey; and on the west by 江西 Kang-sey and 廣東 Kóng-tong (Canton); while to the south and east it is bounded by the ocean. The rivers and mountains of this province are picturesque and beautiful, and the inhabitants are generally distinguished for their literary talents.

The county of 福州 Hok-chew contains ten districts, as follow:

Bîn-hëën 閩縣, *Bân-kwān*, the Bân district.
Hoê-kwan 侯官, *Kaôu-kw^na*, noble officer.
Hok-ch'heng 福清, *Hok-ch'hē^na*, happy clearness.
Koé-tëên 古田, *Kóe-ch'hân*, ancient field.
Tëâng-lòk 長樂, *Tëô-lôh*, constant delight.
E'ng-hok 永福, ——, eternal happiness.
Bân-ch'heng 閩清, *Bân-ch'hē^na*, the clear flow of Bân.
Lëên-kang 連江, ——, the connected river.
Lô-gwân 羅源, ——, the netted fountain.
Pîn-lâm 屏南, ——, the screen of the south.

The seat of Government is in 閩縣 Bân-kwān, and 侯官 Kaôu-kw^na.

This county is bordered on the west by the ocean, on the east it joins 延平 Yëên-pêng, to the north it is bounded by 建寧 Këên-lêng, and to the south by 興化 Hin-hwà. The inhabitants are economical, but litigious and superstitious; every family is a school, and every man a scholar. The superior class are fond of literature, and the common people are obedient to the laws. — The most celebrated mountains are the 九仙 Kéw-sëen, "nine fairies," and the 大鵬 Taē-pêng, "great ostrich;" there is also a "remarkable rocky monastery," and "a marsh-mallow cave," the scenery about which is said to be enchanting. The river 鰲 Gô, "leviathan," surrounds the district flowing towards the east, and there is a celebrated pool called the 浴鳳 Yëuk-hōng, "phœnix bath." Of palaces may be enumerated the 長春 Tëâng-ch'hun, "constant spring," and 水晶 Súy-ch'heng, "water chrystal;" while of temples may be particularized the 松風 Sëûng-hong, "fir tree breeze," and the 眉壽 Bê-sēw, "eye-brow longevity." — This county has been the residence of several famous men, among whom 蔡襄 Ch'haê-sëang may be mentioned, as having taught the common people propriety; and 眞德秀 Chin-tek-sēw, as having greatly promoted the general welfare. In the 唐 Tông dynasty lived 周朴 Chew-p'hok, who would not submit to 黄巢 Hông-chaôu; and in the 宋 Sòng dynasty flourished four learned men, who were called the four teachers of Bân; besides various others celebrated for their talents and worth, who all belonged to this district.—The city of 福州 Hok-chew lies about fifteen leagues westerly from the sea, on the southern shore of the river 閩 Bân, which falls with a wide mouth into the sea, and admits vessels of considerable burden up to the city walls. The convenience of this river makes the town very populous, and the trade thereof brisk; the city is adorned with many beautiful buildings, and has a large suburb annexed, called 南臺 Lâm-taê, with many idol Temples. Across the bay, near 南臺 Lâm-taê, lies a stone bridge, 150 rods long, and one and a half broad, built of white free stone, resting on 100 very high arches; provided with rails and benches at the top, and adorned at equal distances with stone lions, neatly carved. The river at this place is about half a league in breadth, separated into small arms by several islands, which are all united by bridges, the principal one of which is that described above. Near this bridge, at the south end, stands a large temple. Another bridge, not unlike this, being about 100 rods long, may be seen at the city 福清 Hok-ch'heng; and many more about the principal cities. About three leagues from 福州 Hok-chew, stands a temple, reckoned to be the largest in the province.

The county of 興化 Hin-hwà, contains two districts, viz:—

P'hoê-tëên 莆田, *P'hoê-ch'hân*, the field at the water's edge; and

Sëen-yêw 仙遊, ———, the fairy ramble.

The seat of government is in 莆田 P'hoê-tëên.

This is a small but fruitful county, bordered on the south-east by the sea on the south it skirts 泉州 Chwân-chew, on the west 永春 E'ng-ch'hun, and to the north it is bounded by 福州 Hok-chew.—Here, every house has a scholar, and clever men spring up like trees in a forest; in this respect it is quite a literary district, and considered the crown of all Hok-këèn.—The land and water carriage in this county are both good.—the roads being a rod in breadth, and paved with square free-stone; and the number of rivulets with which it abounds, affording a great facility for inland navigation; while heavier goods may be easily transported by the sea, which partly surrounds this region. It contains two celebrated hills, called 壺公 Hoê-kong, and 何嶺 Hô-léng, both of which are the fabled residence of fairies, and the subject of much observation by the Chinese mountain-gazers. At the foot of the 壺公 Hoê-kong hill, south-eastward from 興化 Hin-hwà, lies a village, in the splendour and size of its buildings resembling a great city, but it has neither walls nor privileges belonging to it; yet many rich merchants reside there, and traffic throughout all China. Here is a well called the 蠏井 Haê-chéng, "crab-fish well," the tides of which are said to correspond to the sea. The noted rivers of this county are, the 九溪 Kéw-chêy, and the 木蘭 Bòk-lân; the last received its name from a young woman, of the name of 錢木蘭 Chëên-bòk-lân, who, grieved at the constant bursting of a flood-gate (by which the lands were deprived of irrigation, and the waters designed for that purpose were lost in the sea), threw herself into the stream, out of vexation, and was drowned. Some time after this, a literary graduate, of the name of 王十鵬 Ông-sip-p'hêng, passing by this place, observed the troubled state of the waters, and asked the reason of it: the boatmen told him the foregoing tale, adding that the waters were troubled, because the soul of the deceased was

f

not yet appeased, and it was likely never would be, as she died a virgin, and had left no posterity, to sacrifice to her manes. The graduate then made a vow, that if he should succeed in the approaching literary examination, he would return and marry the soul of this 錢木蘭 Chēěn-bok-lân, in order to procure her posterity. He succeeded accordingly, and soon returned to fulfil his vow, which he did, by causing a tablet to be made, with the name of the deceased engraven on it, and to this tablet he was regularly married; but as it bore him no children, he married a second wife, and gave the son of this second marriage to 木蘭 Bok-lân, to be her heir and successor. This lad, when grown up, regularly sacrificed to 木蘭 Bok-lân, as his mother; and thus (the Chinese say), her soul was appeased, and the waters became still. It is added, that subsequently, in the reign of 正德 Chêng-tek, of the 明 Bêng dynasty (A. D. 1510), the Emperor effectually repaired this flood-gate, at the suggestion of an old woman called 陳婆 *Tân-pô*, by which means a great quantity of land was brought under cultivation, much to the comfort of the people, and the benefit of the revenue.—There has been a conflux of famous officers, in this county, celebrated as well for their talents as fidelity, risking their situations rather than flinch from duty, and scorning to flatter, while they persevered in equity.—This is the birth-place of 媽祖 Má-choé, the sailor's goddess, who was dignified with the title of 天妃 T'hēen-hwuy, "Queen of Heaven," by the present dynasty, and who is said to be able to foretell the happiness or misery of mankind. Almost every ship bears an image of this goddess in its stern, and Chinese seamen scarcely ever venture to sea without her. In this county lived a man, of the family name of 何 Hô, who sought out the philosopher's stone, and when his alchymic preparations had succeeded, is said to have mounted on a carp fish and sailed away.—The productions of this county are grass-cloth, silks, and cottons, Le-che fruit, snail-shells, &c.

The county of 泉州 Chwân-chew, contains five districts, as follow:—

Chìn-kang 晉江, ———, the district of the Chìn river.
Lâm-an 南安, *Lâm-wⁿa*, southern ease.
Tông-an 同安, *Tâng-wⁿa*, similar ease.
Hwŭy-an 惠安, *Hwŭy-wⁿa*, kind ease.
An-k'hey 安溪, ———, the peaceful stream.

The seat of government is in 晉江 Chìn-kang.

This county is bounded on the south and east by the sea, on the west by 漳州 Chëang-chew, and on the north by 永春 E'ng-ch'hŭn. The city of 晉江 Chìn-kang, its capital, lies near the sea, in a delightful plain, and, by a large bay, admits the greatest ships to ride close under its walls; and that on both sides of the city, for it is built on a promontory, encompassed with water, except on the north and south-east sides. On the opposite shore are many populous trading towns, chiefly in a place towards the north-west, called 洛陽 Lok-yâng. Here is the famous bridge called the 洛陽橋 Lok-yâng-këô, which has been deservedly considered one of the wonders of China; it is built of a black kind of stone, supported by about 250 strong columns or buttresses, 125 on each side. These columns are sharpened towards the upper part, in order the better to break the impetuous egress and regress of the current; they are capped with five stones, of an equal breadth, each twenty feet long, and two broad, which successively touch one another, at each buttress, and thus form a path-way to walk upon, at least 2500 feet in length; on each side, rails of the same kind of stone are put for safety, adorned with lions and other images. It is certainly wonderful where so many large stones of equal size could have been procured, and how they could have been conveyed to, and constructed across, such a wide and impetuous stream of water. Before the bridge was built, the people used to cross this part of the river in boats; but many vessels being every year destroyed by the violence of the tide, squalls, and other accidents, a man of the name of 蔡襄 Ch'haè-sëang resolved, for the safety of passengers, to build a bridge. The tradition respecting it, as related by the Chinese, is as follows:—Formerly, in crossing this sheet of water, many boats were upset, and a number of lives were lost: popular credulity soon invented a cause for these numerous disasters, which were imagined to originate in two fairies or elfs, one of whom was a tortoise, and the other a snake; these wicked elfs had formerly inspired a certain butcher, and prompted him to destroy much animal life, and practise other enormities; till the butcher, determined on reformation, and desirous of obtaining a new heart, ripped himself open, and threw his old stomach and bowels into this stream; where they remained, in the shape of a tortoise and snake, doing great mischief, while the butcher himself became a god. He is still worshipped by the people of Hok-këen, under the title of 玄天上帝 Heên-t'hëen-sëăng-tèy, "the high Emperor of the darkened Heavens," and is represented standing with one foot on a tortoise, and the other on a snake, the two elfs which formerly excited him to do so much mischief. In order to carry on their wicked designs, the Chinese fable, that the tortoise elf used to transform himself into a boat, and the snake elf into a boatman, and thus appearing at the side of the stream, offered to assist passengers in crossing it. When arrived at the middle of the river, a storm generally arose, the boat sunk, and the two elfs, assuming their own shapes, devoured the victims at their leisure. On one occasion, it is related, that when the boat full of passengers was arrived at the middle of the stream, a storm arose, —the prelude to a disaster; but suddenly a noise was heard from heaven, saying, Ch'haè taē jîn chaē ch'hwân, put k'hó tëêm 蔡大人在船.不可沉, *Ch'hwà twā lâng tē chûn, ām t'hang tëêm*,—"The Magnate Ch'haè being aboard, let not the vessel sink;"—whereupon the storm abated, and all escaped safe to land. On going ashore, the passengers enquired one of another, who among them was called by the family name of Ch'haè; but when none appeared, a woman of the company said, that though she did not belong to that clan herself, she had been lately married to a man of the name of Ch'haè, and was now pregnant by him: upon which they all concluded, that the infant in her womb must be the person for whom the celestial voice was sent. The woman accordingly made a vow, that if her child of which she was then pregnant should prove to be a boy, and should afterwards become a magnate, she would insist on his making a bridge over this river. The child proved to be a boy, and was called 蔡襄 Ch'haè-sëang; he prospered in learning, and rose to the dignity of Twān-bêng-tëen Taē-hak-soō 斷明殿大學士, "Great Doctor of the decidedly clear Hall." Arrived at this pitch of greatness, he was reminded of his mother's vow; and judging that if he remained at court, the thing would never be done, he fell upon a plan of getting himself appointed to the government of his native district, which on ordinary occasions was not allowed. He flourished in the reign of 仁宗 Jîn-chong, of the 宋 Sòng dynasty (A. D. 1050), and observing the Emperor one day about to go abroad, he previously rubbed some honey on the stump of a tree, in order to tempt the ants to swarm there, contriving it so that the ants should form lines to imitate certain Chinese characters. The Emperor observing the ants thus swarming in a peculiar manner, went up, and read the characters thus curiously formed, which sounded as follows:—蔡斷.蔡斷.本府作官 Ch'haè-twan, Ch'haè-twan, pún hoó chok kwan, "Ch'haè-twan! Ch'haè-twan! be thou an officer in thy native district."—This sentence was no sooner out of the Emperor's mouth, than Ch'haè-sëang pretended to take it for a positive order, and fell down at his Majesty's feet, thanking him for his appointment. The Emperor not liking to retract his words, because 天子不虛言 T'hëen choó put he gân, the son of Heaven never speaks in vain, confirmed the decree, and he was accordingly appointed to the office. Upon his arrival at 泉州 Chwân-chew, his native district, he spared neither expence nor labour, to execute the task assigned him; but he made very little progress, at first, and the three years of his officiate were likely to close before the work could be completed. The principal difficulty was to carry the bridge across the deepest part of the stream; and no hope could be entertained of success, unless the tide retired remarkably low, and the bed of the river was left unusually dry. In order to obtain this, he thought it best to apply to the dragon king of the deep, and, with this intention, he drew up a letter to the Chinese Neptune, but was at a loss how to send it:—in this perplexity, he cried out one day in the midst of the hall, 誰人下得海 Sûy jîn hāy tek haé, "who is there that can descend into the sea?"—Upon uttering these words, a servant whose name was 下得海 Hāy-tek-haé, thinking himself called, promptly answered, "Here;" and the magistrate taking his answer for an assent, insisted upon his going. The poor man finding there was no resource, took the letter in his bosom, and went to sleep close by the sea side, when it was quite low water, thinking that when the tide rose, the sea would cover him, and he could then deliver his message. On awaking in the morning, however, he found himself still in the same place, and the letter in his bosom changed for another in a yellow envelope, which he immediately took to his master. On opening this letter, only one character was found written in it, viz. 醋 Ch'hoè, "vinegar." For some time he was at a loss to know what to make of this communication; but on analyzing the character, he found it composed of four others, which ran thus, 廿一日酉 Jëep-yit jit yéw, "the 21st day, in the evening,"—at which time he imagined the water would be nearly dry. Accordingly he prepared materials and workmen against the appointed period, when the water was indeed unusually low; and having laid the foundation of the central buttresses, before the water rose again, he was enabled to proceed with the work without interruption. Four million taels of silver are said to have been expended on this stupendous work.

The people of this county are peaceful and economical, while for literature and poesy they have been always celebrated.—To the south of the capital of 泉州 Chwân-chew, is a mountain called 寶蓋 Pó-kaè, "precious covering," which has on its top a turret of nine galleries, serving as a land-mark for seamen: there are also various other hills and mountains, the windings and forms of which are very romantic. Off the coast lie the 彭湖 P'heng-hoê, or Piscadores; and from the interior flow the 洛陽 Lók-yâng and 晉江 Chìn-kang rivers, with some other smaller rivulets. In this county 朱文公 Choo-bûn-kong, the celebrated commentator on the Four Books, established his school of learning, and hosts of literati flocked to hear his doctrines. Here, also, 游酢 Yêw-choè purified the minds of his pupils, and 德秀 Tek-sèw emptied the prisons, by the clear justice of his punishments. There were others, also, celebrated for their acquaintance with ancient laws, and for their firm and public spirited conduct, all of whom were brought up in this neighbourhood.

The county of 漳州 Chëang-chew is divided into seven districts, as follow:—

Lëûng-k'hey 龍溪, ——— the dragon stream.
Chëang-p'hóe 漳浦, *Chëo^ng-p'hóe*, the banks of the river Cheang.
Lâm-chēng 南靖, ——— the southern stillness.
Tëâng-t'haê 長泰, *Tëo^ng-twà*, lengthened greatness.
Pêng-hô 平和, ——— peaceful harmony.
Chëàou-an 詔安, ——— decided ease.
Haé-têng 海澄, ——— the limpid ocean.

The seat of government is at 龍溪 Lëûng-k'hey.

This county is bordered on the east by 泉州 Chwân-chew, on the south by the sea, on the west by part of the province of Canton, and on the north by 永春 E'ng-ch'hun and 汀州 T'heng-chew. The inhabitants attend to their callings, and study plainness, employing their strength in agriculture and fishing; their manners, however, are rough, and the people obstinate and fierce, being violent and difficult to manage. Of the notable hills in this county, may be particularized,—the 大武 Taē-boó, "great warrior," and the 梁山 Lëâng-san, "bridge hill," near the district of 漳浦 Chëang-p'hoé.—The side of the 龍巖 Lëûng-gâm, or "dragon precipice," is beautifully variegated in its appearance; while the rocky islet of 丹霞 Tan-hây, "red mist," alternately wears a different colour every morning and evening. On the east side of the capital of Chëang-chew is a mountain, on which stands a stone of five rods high, which (according to the Chinese) shivers and shakes like a tree blown by the wind, before rain or tempestuous weather; nearer the city lies another mountain, called 九龍 Kéw-lëûng, "the nine dragons," which joins the former; and is remarkable for a crystal fountain. On the summit of the 南峯 Lâm-hong, "southern peak," is always seen the happy omen of crimson clouds; and from the heights of the 天官 T'hëen-kwan, "celestial magistrate," is constantly heard the sound of the pipe and flute. The cavern of the 龍門 Lëûng-bûn, "dragon gate," is warm in winter and cold in summer; while the enchanting grotto of the 天柱 T'hën-chē, "the pillar of heaven," is enough to tempt people to forsake the world and lead a hermit's life.—The river 漳 Chëang, from which this county is named, takes its rise near the city of 龍巖 Lëûng-gâm, runs eastward towards the city of 漳平 Chëang-pêng, and then takes a southerly direction past 長泰 Tëâng-t'hae, into the sea, into which it empties itself by two mouths. More to the south glides the 石滕 Sek-seng, "stone-bank stream," which flows from west to east, and loses itself in the sea, to the northward of the garrison of 銅山 Tông-san. On the south side of the capital of 漳州 Chëang-chew, is a large bridge of hewn stone, with thirty-six high arches, and so broad, that on each side are tradesmen's shops and mechanic's stalls.—Of the remarkable people which this county has produced, may be enumerated 康仙 K'hong-sëen, a conjurer, who sold medicines, and was afterwards honoured as a god; also, 周匡物 Chew-k'hong-bùt, of the 唐 Tông dynasty, in whose time the people of this region first began to understand learning; and 顏師魯 Gân-soo-loé, of the 宋 Sông dynasty, who was so esteemed, that the people of 泉州 Chwân-chew made an image of him, and worshipped it. Besides, there were 陳淳 Tin-sûn, who read every book, and examined every substance; 朱熹 Choo-hé, the great philosopher and commentator; and 吳解 Goê-haē, whose appearance, and mind, studies, and style of composition were all of an ancient cast. Besides these famous men, fable speaks of some supernatural individuals, such as 潛翁 Chëem-ong, who melted a stone wall, and brought up a white toad to follow him; and

E

劉希岳 Lêw-he-gak, who flew away in the shape of a cockchafer, and was delivered from the body. — The chief productions of this county are silver, iron, and shark's-fins.

The county of 延平 Yëën-pêng is divided into the six following districts:—

Lâm-pêng	南平,	*Lam-pat ng*, southern pacification.
Chëang-lòk	將樂,	——— future bliss.
Say-hëën	沙縣,	*Swa-kwān*, the sandy district.
Yëw-k'hey	尤溪,	——— blame-worthy stream.
Sûn-ch'hëang	順昌,	——— obedient fulness.
E'ng-an	永安,	——— eternal ease.

The seat of government is 南平 Lâm-pêng.

This county lies in the centre of the Province of Hok-këën; and is bounded, on the east by 福州 Hok-chew, on the south by 永春 E'ng-ch'hun; on the west by 汀州 T'heng-chew, and on the north by 邵武 Sëaòu-boó and 建寧 Këën-lêng. The capital city lies on the western shore of the river 閩 Bân, from whence the buildings rise gently up the hill, presenting a delightful prospect to those who pass by; and, though none of the largest, it is reckoned the handsomest town in Hok-këën. The walls tower above the neighbouring heights, which, on the outside, are reckoned inaccessible, making the city very strong, and the key to the whole territory. The city is a league long, but not above a mile and a half broad, full of large and handsome edifices. Every house is furnished with water, conveyed from the mountains in cane pipes, the like of which is not to be seen elsewhere, throughout all China. Provisions are to be had there in great abundance, and at a cheap rate, the streets and houses being thronged with inhabitants. On the east side of the city, two great rivers, the 閩 Bân, and the 西 Sey, uniting their waters, form a great lake, through which vessels come thither, from all parts of the adjacent country. Each of these rivers is furnished with a handsome bridge. In the city there are three beautiful temples. Most of the coarse Chinese paper is made here; and the people boast, that they speak a purer mandarin dialect than is spoken in any other part of Hok-këën. The town of 沙 Say lies on the north shore of the river (though it formerly stood on the southern shore), the old city having been pulled down by Imperial command, because that in it a young man had murdered his father. To the north-east of the capital city lies a high mountain, from whose top the sun may be seen rising over all the other hills; and to the south of the same is an ascent, called 越王 Wat-ông, on which the ancient kings of Wat used to have many palaces, to serve as retiring places from the heat of summer. More southerly are the mountains 九仙 Kew-sëen, "nine fairies," and 七星 Ch'hit-seng, "seven stars." Here is also an over-hanging precipice, one hundred fathoms in height; and the 孤峰 Koe-hong, "orphan peak," which thrusts itself high up into the clouds. — The river 閩 Bân, above-mentioned, rises in the borders, between 福建 Hok-këën and 浙江 Chëet-kang, near the city 龍泉 Lëûng-chwân, in 處州 Ch'hè-chew, from whence it passes southerly,—then westward, by the cities of 浦城 P'hoe-sêng and 建寧 Këën-lêng,—after that east, by the city of 延平 Yëën-pêng (where it receives the 西溪 Sey-k'hey); and from thence, still continuing eastward, it enters the county of 福州 Hok-chew, and at last disembogues itself into the sea, in about the twenty-sixth degree of north latitude. After passing the city 浦城 P'hoé-sêng, the river flows with great rapidity, through vallies, and among rocks and cliffs; but further on it glides along more slowly: the general force of the current, however, may be calculated by this, that vessels go from 浦城 P'hoé-sêng to the metropolis, 福州 Hok-chew, with the stream, in three days, while they are fifteen in towing up against it. In some places, it is dangerous, on account of the swift current, the multiplicity of rocks, and the narrowness of the channel, which is frequently no wider than to permit a small Chinese vessel to pass through; hence it often happens, that boats are broken to pieces. The 西溪 Sey-k'hey rises in the north, in the territory of 汀州 T'heng-chew, and first takes a southerly course,—then an easterly, when it enters the county of 延平 Yëên-pêng, and unites with the river 閩 Bân: in the Sey are many waterfalls and dangerous shoals, in passing by which, the boatmen, to prevent accidents, tie trusses of straw before the bows of the vessels; by this means they bear off the violence, of the blows, should they happen to strike. The river 尤溪 Yêw-k'hey, which rises in this county, takes its course eastward, by the city of 尤溪 Yêw-k'hey, and turning to the north, falls into the river 閩 Bân.—The people of this county encourage one another in the study of the classics and odes, while the poorer sort attend to ploughing and weaving. Among the government officers who have been employed in this district, may be mentioned 朱松 Choo-sëûng, the father of the celebrated philosopher, of whom 李侗 Lé-tōng, was the instructor; 陳瓘 Tîn-hwân was distinguished for his steady upright conduct; and 張若谷 Teâng-jëak-kok for his exertions in opposing banditti. The productions of this county are silver, iron, marble, white grass-cloth, musk, and rock salt.

The county of 建寧 Këèn-lêng, contains seven districts, as follow:—

Këèn-an	建安,	established ease.
Aou-lêng	甌寧,	tea-cup tranquility.
Këèn-yâng	建陽,	established vigour.
Chông-an	崇安,	exalted ease.
P'hoé-sêng	浦城,	the river-side citadel.
Chèng-hô	政和,	regulated harmony.
Sëûng-k'hey	松溪,	the fir tree stream.

The seat of government is in the two districts Këèn-an and Aou-lêng.

This county is bordered, on the north and north-east, by part of the province of 浙江 Cheet-kang, on the east by 福寧 Hok-lêng, on the south by 福州 Hok-chew and 延平 Yëên-pêng, on the west by 邵武 Sëâou-boô, and on the north-west and north by part of the province of 江西 Kang-sey. The capital city, lying on the eastern shore of the river 閩 Bân, is not much inferior, either in beauty or size, to the metropolis of Hok-këèn. In the last war with the Tartars, it suffered much damage; for, having revolted from the 大清 Taè-ch'heng dynasty, it was taken, after a long siege, and laid in ashes, most of the inhabitants being put to the sword. On this occasion the fire consumed a bridge over the swift river 閩 Bân, the pillars whereof were built of free stone, to a great height, and finished on the top with wood; it was also adorned with houses and shops on each side; being now rebuilt, the town has regained something of its former lustre. Beyond the bridge, on the opposite shore, stands a stately pagoda; and near the city is another handsome bridge, also furnished with shops and houses, on both sides. The city of 建寧 Këèn-lêng is a place of great trade, for all those commodities which come either up or down the river must pass through it. The city itself is larger than 延平 Yëên-pêng, but not so closely built, having several corn-fields within the walls. The streets are all paved with pebbles, and are very full of inhabitants, who get their living by the manufacture of coarse paper. Farther up the river 閩 Bân, is the city 浦城 P'hoé-sêng, beyond which the river is no longer navigable; here the merchandise is taken out of the vessels, and carried by porters over high mountains and deep vallies, a distance of four days journey, into the province of Chěet-kang. The whole way, as far as the art or labour of man can make it, is levelled, and paved with square stones, being provided at intervals with houses and villages, for the entertainment of travellers. The goods to be transported over the mountains are first weighed, and delivered to a head man, who, for a certain gratuity, sends them, by porters, to other places, where the merchant receives them without any trouble: if any thing happens to be lost, the head man is bound to make it good. It is said, that there are always about 10,000 porters ready at the spot, waiting to receive goods, and carry them over the mountains. A toll-house is erected at the head of the road, for the levying of a small duty, which is employed in keeping the road in repair. This county is celebrated for its mountains, among which are the famous 武彝 Boó-ê hills, near the city of 崇安 Chông-an, which produce a superior sort of tea, called *Bohea*; this hill is divided into nine peaks, and has a rivulet running between them called the 璜溪 Hông-k'hey, "pearly stream," which is highly spoken of, for the beautiful winding of its waters. Here are to be seen a number of temples and monasteries, on the hill-tops, the residence of priests and hermits; the scenery about this region is, also, so picturesque, that many noblemen and officers of government, retiring from the world, select this as the residence in which they desire to end their days. Near the city of 浦城 P'hoé-sêng, is a hill called 漁梁 Gê-lëâng, which is reckoned one of the ten great mountains of China. The river 閩 Bân, which runs through this county has been already spoken of in the description of 延平 Yëên-pêng county; in addition to this, is the 東溪 Tong-k'hey, which rises in the mountains between the provinces of 浙江 Chëet-kang and 福建 Hok-këên, and running southward, falls into the 閩 Bân, below the city of 建寧 Këên-lêng: also, the brook 九脚 Kéw-këak, which begins in the 武彝 Boó-ê mountains, runs from thence south-westward, and, after passing by the city of 建陽 Këên-yâng, falls at last into the river 閩 Bân, near the city of 建寧 Këên-lêng. The Chinese speak also of cataracts, a hundred fathoms deep, the spray of which dashes about like falling pearls; and of old grottoes, with their stone doors, which are to be met with in this romantic district. Here the people are said to be incessantly addicted to study, every family being possessed of a library, and every village acquainted with righteousness, while the chanting of odes and reciting of books may be heard, throughout all the district: here flourished another Orpheus, who played upon an iron flute, and produced sounds that penetrated the clouds, and split the soild rocks; and here dwelt a self-denying philosopher, who, as long as his clothes would hold together by a hundred patches, despised all the silks and satins of the whole province. This county has had several distinguished officers, some celebrated for the suppression of banditti, others for the preservation of human life; others, again, discoursed learnedly on the fate of empires, and testified against the vices of the age. Among the distinguished natives may be mentioned 蔡元定 Ch'haè-gwân-têng, who taught his disciples independence of character, and contempt of the world; this man applied to 朱文公 Choo-bûn-kong, the celebrated philosopher, to be received as his pupil; but the latter declined that honour, saying, Goê tong é ló yëw soō che, put tong chaē tëy choó che lëet 吾當以老友事之.不當在弟子之列, "I ought to serve him with the respect due to an old friend, but cannot think of classing him among my disciples." His son, 蔡沈 Ch'haè-sím, subsequently became the disciple of the great commentator; and assisted him in writing a commentary on the 尚書 Sëāng se. Besides these, the county of 建寧 Këên-lêng, has produced a famous man called 胡安國

Hoĕ-an-kok, who wrote a commentary on the 春秋 Ch'hun-ch'hew, and who was dignified with the title of the evergreen fir tree of literature: which shews, say the Chinese, that celebrated regions never fail to produce extraordinary men. Besides these literary characters, the Chinese fable of a superhuman genius, called "the true man of the hazy atmosphere," who,—with a bald head and bare feet,—living on air and devouring mists,—used to point with a smile to the deepest recess of the 武彝 Boó-ê hills, covered with white clouds, and say, there is my residence. The natural productions of this county are, the silver of 浦城 P'hoe-sêng, the iron of 建安 Hông-an, the tea of 武彝 Boó-ê, and the books of 建陽 Këèn-yâog, which have been always sought after by merchants.

The county of 邵武 Seàou-boó contains the following districts:—

Seàou-boó 邵武, awakened military ardour.
Kong-tek 光澤, bright favour.
T'haè-lêng 泰寧, great tranquillity.
Këèn-lêng 建寧, established tranquillity.

The seat of government is in 邵武 Seàou-boó.

This county is bounded on the east by 建寧 Këèn-lêng, on the south by 延平 Yêèn-pêng and 汀州 T'heng-chew, and on the west and north by the province of 江西 Kang-sey. The capital city of this region was anciently a mean place, and was first fortified and enfranchised in the 唐 Tông dynasty. This county possessing a firm and profitable soil, and being on the borders of the province, it is fortified with several garrisons. The people of this region are sturdy agriculturists, and elegant scholars, easily moved, and with difficulty pacified; the climate here is healthy, and the air pure and cold. The most celebrated mountain in this county is the 七臺 Ch'hit-taê, "seven terraces:" and of rivers may be specified the 樵溪 Chĕaou-k'hey, which begins in the mountain of 烏君 Oe-kwun, "black prince," and glides from thence southward, then eastward by the city of 邵武 Seàou-boó; thence bending to the south, in the county of 延平 Yêèn-pêng, it falls into the 西溪 Sey-k'hey, near 將樂 Chĕang-lok, from whence both streams run easterly, and pour their waters into the 閩 Bân. The most remarkable city is 烏坂 Oe-pán, "the black mound," and the most distinguished village is that of 白鼠 Pek-ch'hé, "the white mouse." Of public officers, 蘇爲政 Soe-wûy-chèng was remarkable for his purity and decision, and 尹洙一 Yin-ch'oo-yit for his improvement of the public morals; 秀綱 Lé-kong and 施宜生 Se-gê-seng were distinguished, in the 宋 Sòng dynasty, for their services to the state; and 黃中 Hông-tëung with 李閎祖 Lé-hông-choé were equally celebrated for their deep erudition, as a proof of which, the great philosopher 朱文公 Choo-bûn-kong acknowledged the one for his teacher and the other for his friend. The natural productions of this county are said to be, silver, iron, copper, and tea.

The county of 汀州 T'heng-chew contains the following districts:—

Tëâng-t'heng 長汀, the lengthened district watered by the T'heng.
Lêng-hwà 寧化, peaceful renovation.
Sëāng-hâng 上杭, the upper Hâng district.
Boó-pêng 武平, *Boó-paiⁿᵍ*, pacified military ardour.
Ch'heng-lêw 清流, *Ch'haiⁿᵍ-laôu*, the pure flow.

h

Lëën-sêng 連城, the connected citadel.
Kwuy-hwà 歸化, a returning to complete renovation.
E'ng-tēng 永定, eternal settlement.

The seat of government is in 長汀 Tëâng-t'heng.

This county is bordered on the east by 延平 Yëën-pêng, on the south-east by 龍巖 Lëûng-gâm, on the south by part of the province of Canton, on the west by that of 江西 Kang-sëy, and on the north by 邵武 Seàou-bóó. The manners and demeanour of the people of this district resemble, in some respects, those of the middle regions of China; they are bold and courageous, fond of fighting, but at the same time honest and upright. The picturesque scenery about the 臥龍 Gô-lëûng ("sleeping dragon") hill is well worthy of being sketched; while the 龍門 Lëûng-bûn, "dragon gate," a hill to the westward of the city of 寧化 Lêng-hwà, appears as if it were piled up into the clouds; the green freshness of the 金山 Kim-san, "golden hill," would please the admirer of landscapes, but the precious metals therein contained would tempt more strongly the cupidity of the multitude; the gold mines discovered in this hill were first worked in the dynasty 宋 Sòng; it lies south of the capital of 汀州 T'heng-chew, near the city of 上杭 Sëäng-hâng, on the eastern shore of the river 汀 T'heng; upon it there are three little lakes, which, the Chinese say, turn the iron that is thrown therein into copper. The river 汀 T'heng commences in the territory of 汀州 T'heng-chew, and proceeding southward by the city of 上杭 Sëäng-hâng, enters the county of 潮州 Tëâou-chew, in the province of Canton, where continuing its southerly course, it discharges itself into the sea. The Chinese remark on it as singular, that, while all the other streams of this province flow easterly, this alone should have a direct southerly course. Of the distinguished natives of this county, some have been celebrated for their abstinence and uprightness, others for their learning and poesy; so that the county has not been left destitute of talent. This region has abundance of all things requisite for the sustenance of mankind, notwithstanding it is so mountainous; and possesses at the same time gold, silver, copper, tin, and iron mines: it produces likewise wax, grass-cloth, and various medicinal herbs.

The county of 福寧 Hok-lêng contains the following districts:

Hây-p'hoé 霞浦, the misty water's edge.
Hok-téng 福鼎, the happy caldron.
Hok-an 福安, the happy rest.
Lêng-tek 寧德, tranquil virtue.
Sēw-lêng 壽寧, long-lived tranquillity.

The seat of government is in 霞浦 Hây-p'hoé.

This county is bordered on the east and south-east by the sea, on the south and south-west by 福州 Hok-chew, on the west by 建寧 Këën-lêng, and on the north by the province of 浙江 Chëet-kang. This county is very mountainous, and the ways across the hills are scarcely passable, especially towards the north and north-east; hence the literary examiner proceeds to this region, from 福州 Hok-chew, by water. The city of 福寧 Hok-lêng is fair and large, lying near the sea, to its great commercial advantage. A little above this city rises the hill 龍首 Lëûng-sêw, "dragon head;" south of the same appears the high mountain 洪山

Hŏng-san; on the same side is the hill 南金 Lâm-kim, "southern gold;" and north-east thereof stretches the mountain 大姥 Taē-ló, with its six high precipices. The river 藍 Lâm rises in a mountain of that name, and running from north to south, through the territory of 福寧 Hok-lêng, empties itself into the sea. This county is not celebrated for the possession of many famous men; but the hills are said to yield silver.

The county of 臺灣 Taē-wan contains the following districts:

Taē-wan 臺灣, terraced harbour.
Hŏng-san 鳳山, phenix hill.
Choo-lô 諸羅, diverse nets.
Chëang-hwà 彰化, variegated renovation.

This county is commonly called Formosa, by Europeans. on account of the beauty of its scenery; it is situated opposite to the main land of the province of Hok-këěn, and is governed by officers sent from China. This island was originally in the possession of several savage tribes, resembling the Malays in complexion, but speaking a different language; the first Europeans who visited this country were the Spaniards and Portuguese; next to them, the Dutch took it, and finding it advantageously situated for their Japanese and Chinese trade, formed a considerable settlement upon it; and in 1632 built there a strong fort, called the castle of Zealandia, surrounded with a double wall, and provided with redoubts and ramparts: this fort was taken in 1661 by Coxinga the famous Chinese pirate, whose adherents afterwards submitting to the Tartar dynasty, the city and territory surrounding it have since remained in the possession of the Chinese. "Formosa," says Malte Brun, "has a Chinese Government, with a garrison of 10,000 men; but its authority is limited to the west side. The city of Taē-wan, is populous and wealthy; the streets, in straight lines, and covered with awnings for seven or eight months in the year, to protect them from the heat of the sun, lined with storehouses and elegant shops, where silks, porcelain, varnished and other wares are arranged with admirable art, so as to give the appearance of so many charming galleries, would be delightful to walk in, if less crowded with passengers and better paved. This city is defended by a good fortress, which was built by the Dutch. The harbour is spacious and deep, but the entrances of it are extremely narrow, and only eight or twelve feet deep. Between the port of Taē-wan and the coast of China, the little archipelago of the islands of 澎湖 P'hêng-hoē, or Piscadores (Fishermen's islands), affords good anchorage, and a station which, with a suitable navy, might command the channel of "Formosa." The Dutch, however, complain that they could obtain no fresh water there. The Chinese say, that the inhabitants of Formosa were a set of savage fishermen, but now having submitted to the Celestial Empire, they have left off their barbarous customs, and bid fair to become a civilized people.

The smaller county of 永春 Eng-ch'hun contains, besides the capital, the two following districts

Tek-hwà 德化, virtuous renovation.
Taē-tëĕn 大田, *Twā-ch'hân*, great rice field.

The other small county of 龍巖 Lëûng-gâm contains also two districts, viz

Chëang-pêng 漳平, the plain of the river Chëang.
Lêng-yâng 寧洋, tranquillized ocean.

These two inferior counties, being lately separated from the larger counties of 泉州 Chwân-chew and 漳州 Chëang-chew, exhibit nothing worthy of remark, beyond what has been already specified in speaking of the above-named counties themselves.

ON THE ORTHOGRAPHY

OF THE

HOK-KËÈN DIALECT.

THE inhabitants of Hok-këèn, having no alphabet, distinguish the sounds of their dialect into initials and finals, the knowledge of which is the key to the whole dialect.

I. OF THE INITIALS.

The initials, called by them Joō-t'hoê 字頭, *Jē-t'haôu*, "head characters," are fifteen in number, as follow:—

1. Léw 柳	6. P'hó 頗	11. Eng 英
2. Pëen 邊	7. T'hⁿa 他	12. Bûn 門
3. Kêw 求	8. Cheng 曾	13. Gé 語
4. Khè 去	9. Jip 入	14. Ch'hut 出
5. Tēy 地	10. Sê 時	15. Hé 喜

1. Léw 柳 gives the initial sound of *l*, in its combination with all those sounds which are not nasal; but when it is joined to a nasal final, the power of the *l* is in a great measure merged in the nasal, in which case it acquires a sound something similar to *n*.

2. Pëen 邊 gives invariably the initial sound of *p*.

3. Kêw 求 affords the initial sound of *k*.

4. K'hè 去 affords the initial sound of *k'h*, which is the *k* aspirated, to be pronounced with a strong emission of the breath, between the enunciation of the *k*, and the utterance of the succeeding vowel.

5. Tēy 地 gives the initial sound of *t*.

6. P'hó 頗 gives the initial sound of *p'h*, which is the *p* strongly aspirated; an apostrophe is inserted between the *p* and the *h*, to shew that the *p* is not softened by the *h*, as in our word *Philip*, but that, while retaining its natural sound, the *h* is to be strongly aspirated before the utterance of the succeeding vowel.

7. T'hⁿa 他 gives the initial sound of *t'h*, which is the *t* strongly aspirated, as explained above. In this initial, the *t* is not softened by the succeeding *h*, as in our word *thing*, but something like that word as attempted to be pronounced by a German or Hollander, just beginning to learn English.

8. Cheng 曾 conveys the initial sound of *ch* as in *cheap*.

9. Jip 入 gives the sound of *j* very much softened, as the *j* in French, or like the sound of *s*, in the English words *pleasure, precision, crosier*, &c.

10. Sê 時 has the common sound of *s*.

11. Eng 英 is a negative initial, denoting that the finals arranged under it retain the sounds of the latter part of the final, without any addition; except in those finals which contain two divided vowels, beginning with *e*, expressed or understood, to which the letter *y* is generally affixed as an initial. Thus under this initial will be found words beginning with *a, e, i, o, u, w*, and *y*.

12. Bûn 門 gives the initial *b*; except when connected with a nasal final, in which case it drops the sound of *b*, and takes that of *m*, as has been already observed under the first initial.

13. Gé 語 conveys the initial sound of *g* hard; except in nasal words, when it acquires the sound of *gn*, pronounced with a nasal twang.

14. Ch'hut 出 gives the initial *ch'h*, which is the *ch* strongly aspirated, to be pronounced with a whizzing noise between the *ch* and the vowel.

15. Hé 喜 gives the initial *h*, but more strongly aspirated than is usual in English words. In its conjunction with the 1st, 4th, 7th, 10th, 11th, 27th, and 43d finals, being followed by *w*, or *o*, it approaches nearly to the sound of *f*.

Thus, the fifteen initials, when expressed by our orthography, are as follow:—

l, and *n*,	*k'h*, or *k* aspirated,	*t'h*, or *t* aspirated,	*s*,	*g*, and *gn*.
p,	*t*,	*ch*,	*a, e, i, o, u, w*, and *y*,	*ch'h*, or *ch* aspirated,
k,	*p'h*, or *p* aspirated,	*j*,	*b*, and *m*,	*h*.

These comprise, in all, twenty-four distinct initial sounds; which, arranged according to the English alphabet, stand thus;—*a, b, ch, ch'h, e, g, gn, h, i, j, k, k'h, l, m, n, o, p, p'h, s, t, t'h, u, w*, and *y*.

In this arrangement it will be seen, that the soft *c, d, f, q, r, v*, and *x*, are wanting. However, if we consider that the soft *c* may be expressed by *s*, the hard *c* by *k*, and the *q* by *kw*, the Hok-këèn dialect will be found to want only the *d, f, r, v, x*, and *z*, of our alphabet, which letters are never found in any Hok-këèn word, neither can the natives of that province easily pronounce any word beginning with them.

II. Of the Finals.

The finals used in the Hok-këèn dialect, and called Joō-boé 字母 *Jé-boé*, "mother characters," are fifty in number, as follow.—

i

1.	Kwun	君	11.	Koe	沽	21.	Kang	江	31.	*Kai*^{ng}	更	41.	K^{n}oe	姑
2.	Këen	堅	12.	Këaou	嬌	22.	Këem	兼	32.	*Kwui*^{ng}	褌	42.	*Ū*^{m}	姆
3.	Kim	金	13.	Key	稽	23.	Kaou	交	33.	*Këo*	茄	43.	*Kwang*	光
4.	Kwuy	規	14.	Këung	恭	24.	Këa	迦	34.	*Kee*^{ng}	梔	44.	*Kwae*^{ng}	閂
5.	Kay	嘉	15.	Ko	高	25.	Köey	檜	35.	*Këo*^{ng}	薑	45.	*Möey*	糜
6.	Kan	干	16.	Kae	皆	26.	*K*^{n}*a*	監	36.	*Kë*^{n}*a*	驚	46.	*K*^{n}*ëaou*	嘄
7.	Kong	公	17.	Kin	巾	27.	Koo	艍	37.	*Kw*^{n}*a*	官	47.	Chom	箴
8.	Kwae	乖	18.	Këang	姜	28.	*Ka*	膠	38.	*Ke*^{ng}	鋼	48.	Gnaou	爻
9.	Keng	經	19.	Kam	甘	29.	Ke	居	39.	*Käy*	伽	49.	K^{n}o	扛
10.	Kwan	觀	20.	Kwa	瓜	30.	Kew	丩	40.	*Kae*^{ng}	閒	50.	Gnew	牛

1. Kwun 君 is pronounced something like *Koo-un*, enunciated as one syllable.

2. Këen 堅 is a divided sound, as denoted by the diœresis on the first vowel; thus it must be pronounced *Ke-en*, or *Ke-yen*, and is by some thought to sound almost like *Ke-ăn*.

3. Kim 金 is sounded like the *kim* in *kimbo;* and is by some pronounced as if written *Ke-im*, enunciated rapidly, as one syllable.

4. Kwuy 規 is like *qui*, in the English word *quiet*, or sometimes pronounced a little longer, as if written *Koo-wy*, though still but one syllable.

5. Kay 嘉; the *a* in this word is like the sound of *a* in *care*, or like the *ea* in *bear*, *wear*, &c.

6. Kan 干 is to be pronounced with the Italian sound of the *a*, as in *far*, *father*, &c.

7. Kong 公 is pronounced like *cong*, in the word *congress*.

8. Kwae 乖 is sounded as *Koo-wae*, pronounced in the time of one syllable, with the Italian *a*, as in *far*.

9. Keng 經 rhymes with *leng* in *lengthen*, and is sometimes a little drawled out, so as to appear to sound like *ke-eng*, though still but one syllable.

10. Kwan 觀 is pronounced as *Koo-wan*, or like *coo*, to cry as a dove, and the word *wan*, "pale," thus, *coo-wan*, pronounced as one syllable.

11. Koe 沽 rhymes with our English words *toe*, and *hoe*, but differs from them in being pronounced with a full mouth, as if written *ko-oo*.

12. Keaou 嬌 is a diphthong, as containing three separate vowels, viz. *e* as in *me*, *a* as in *far*, and *u* as in *bull*, all of which, though uttered like *ke-yaou*, form but one syllable.

13. Key 稽 is a peculiar sound, sometimes a little drawled out as *Ke-ay*, but generally pronounced short as the French *e*, or as the *ey* in *dey*, or *bey*, when these words are applied to the governors of Algiers and Tunis. It is to be distinguished from the 5th final *Kay*, which is a flat sound like the *a* in *care*, and from the 39th final *Kay*, which sounds like the *a* in *fate*.

14. Këung 恭 is a sound that rhymes with *young*, but is by some persons written *këong*, and made to rhyme with *song*.

15. Ko 高 is precisely like the sound of *co*, in *co-equal*.

16. Kae 皆; in this final the *a* is sounded as in *far*, and the *e* as in *me*,—thus making together the sound of *Ka-e*, pronounced as one syllable.

福建方言字典

17. Kin 巾 sounds like the English word *kin;* though occasionally drawled out, so as nearly to resemble *ke-yin.*

18. Këang 姜; in this sound the vowels are divided, as if written *ke-yang,* or as if the word *key* were connected with the first syllable of the word *anger,* thus *key-ang.*

19. Kam 甘 is pronounced like the word *kam,* "crooked," or like *cam,* in "camlet."

20. Kwa 瓜 is pronounced as if written *koo-a,* short, with the final *a* as in *papa.*

21. Kang 江 is sounded with the *a* as in *far.*

22. Këem 兼 contains a double vowel, and is pronounced as if written *ke-yem,* or according to some *ke-yăm;* an idea may be formed of this sound by taking the word *key,* and *'em,* the contraction of *them,* and pronouncing them rapidly together, thus *key-'em.*

23. Kaou 交; the *a* in this word is sounded as in *far,* and the *ou* as in *pound;* some idea may be formed of it, if the word *cow* had an *a* introduced, and were to be pronounced *ca-ow,* but rapid, as a monosyllable.

24. Këa 迦; in this final the vowels are divided, and must be distinctly pronounced, as if written *ke-ya;* the *a* being sounded as in *far.*

25. Köey 檜; in this final the vowels are also distinctly expressed, as if written *ko-wey* and have together the sound of *co-a* in *co-agent,* pronounced with a peculiar turn of the mouth.

26. $K^{n}a$ 監; this is a nasal sound, with the *a* as in *far;* pronounced with the full sound of the *k,* but the *n* is only slightly heard: like the *ca* in *carpet,* enunciated as if coming chiefly from the nose. It has been described as an attempt to pronounce a syllable through the nose, while the nose is shut.

27. Koo 艍 is pronounced exactly like the word *coo,* to cry as a dove.

28. *Ka* 膠 is a sound similar to *ca,* in *cart.*

29. Ke 居 is sounded like *kee,* in *keep.*

30. Kew 丩 is a sound like that which is attached to the letter *q,* in English: and is pronounced like *eu* in *curious,* or as if written *ke-yew,* though but one syllable.

31. Kai^{ng} 更; this sound is similar to the 5th final, *koy,* turned into a nasal: hence the *ng* are written above, to intimate that they are not to retain their full sound, but to be pronounced through the nose; the *a* to be sounded as in *care,* and the *i* as in *marine.*

32. $Kwui^{ng}$ 褌; this sound is similar to the 4th final, *kwuy,* only terminating in a strong nasal, and is seemingly lost in the nose. It may also be written $kooi^{ng},$ the small letters ^{ng} not possessing their full sound, but intimating the presence of a nasal; and the *i* to be pronounced as in *marine.*

33. *Këo* 茄; in this sound the vowels are distinctly divided, as if written *ke-yo,* and pronounced as in the syllable *gëo,* in *gëometry:*

34. Kee^{ng} 梔 is like the 29th final, *ke,* only turned into a nasal.

35. $K\ddot{e}o^{ng}$ 薑 resembles the 33d final, *këo,* converted into a nasal, as if written $ke\text{-}y\ddot{e}o^{ng}.$

36. $K\ddot{e}^{n}a$ 驚 is similar to the 24th final, *këa,* with a nasal sound introduced. NB. This must not be sounded with the full power of the *n,* as *ke-na,* but like *këa,* or $ke\text{-}y^{n}a$ pronounced through the nose.

37. $Kw^{n}a$ 官 is the same with the 20th final, *kwa,* only pronounced with a strong nasal termination: as if written $koo\text{-}w^{n}a.$

38. *Ke^{ng}* 鋼; this sound is by some written *ko^{ng}*, and by others *ku^{ng}*, but the difference is immaterial, as the word is sounded as if attempted to be pronounced without any vowel, thus *k^{ng}*. The vowel is inserted principally for the purpose of bearing the accent.

39. *Kay* 伽 is a sound so much resembling the 5th final, that when this Dictionary was commenced the same letters were employed for expressing both; but closer examination has discovered a difference; the sound of the 5th final resembling the flat *a* in care, and that of the 39th, the *a* in *fate*, to rhyme with *gay*, *may*, &c.

40. *Kae^{ng}* 閒 is like the 16th final, *kae*, but terminating in a nasal.

41. K^{n}oe 沽 is the same with the 11th final, *koe*, converted into a nasal.

42. *Ū^{m}* 姆 is a sound attempted to be formed without opening the lips; something like the contracted *'m* in *take 'm*. It is in fact merely the sound of *m*, without any vowel either before or after it, or like the reply of an indifferent person, when too lazy to open his mouth.

43. *Kwang* 光 is a sound borrowed from the Mandarin dialect, and may be sounded *koo-wang*, pronounced as a monosyllable.

44. Kwae^{ng} 閂 resembles the 8th final, *kwae*, converted into a nasal as if written *koo-wae^{ng}*.

45. *Mŏey* 隟 is something similar to the 25th final, *kŏey*, only beginning with a nasal.

46. *K^{n}eaou* 嘄 is the same with the 12th final, *keaou*, turned into a nasal.

47. Chom 箴; in this sound the *o* is full, as in *chop*, and rhyming with *sŏm* in *sombre*, but pronounced as though the mouth was quite full.

48. Gnaôu 爻 resembles the 23d final, *kaou*, only commencing with a nasal.

49. K^{n}o 扛 is like the 15th final, *ko* with a nasal introduced.

50. Gnêw 牛 is a sound resembling the 30th final, *kew*, beginning with a nasal.

All these finals, with the exception of five, begin with a *k*, which being dropped, the remainder of the word is what properly constitutes the final. Of the other five, those beginning with *ch*, *m*, and *g*, drop those letters, and leave the rest of the word for the final; while *u^{m}* having no initial consonant, is a final as it stands. The finals without the initial letters are as follow:—

1. *wun*, or *oo-un*	11. *oe*, or *o-oo*	21. *ang*	31. *ai^{ng}*	41. *^{n}oe*
2. *ĕen*, or *e-yen*	12. *eaou*, or *e-yaou*	22. *ëem*, or *e-yem*	32. *wuing*, or *ooi^{ng}*	42. *u^{m}*
3. *im*, or *e-im*	13. *ey*, or *e-ay*	23. *aou*	33. *ëo*, or *e-yo*	43. *wang*, or *oo-wang*
4. *wuy*, or *oo-wy*	14. *ëung*, or *ëong*	24. *ëa*, or *e-ya*	34. *ee^{ng}*	44. *wae^{ng}*, or *oo-wae^{ng}*
5. *ay*	15. *o*	25. *ŏey*, or *o-wey*	35. *ëo^{ng}*, or *e-yëo^{ng}*.	45. *^{m}ŏey*
6. *an*	16. *ae*	26. *^{n}a*	36. *e^{n}a*, or *e-y^{n}a*	46. *^{n}eaou*, or *^{n}e-yaou*
7. *ong*	17. *in*, or *e-yin*	27. *oo*	37. *w^{n}a*, or *oo-w^{n}a*	47. *om*
8. *wae*, or *oo-wae*	18. *ëang*, or *e-yang*	28. *a*	38. *e^{ng}*, or *u^{ng}*	48. *^{n}aou*
9. *eng*, or *e-eng*	19. *am*	29. *e*	39. *ay*	49 *^{n}o*
10. *wan*, or *oo-won*.	20. *wa*, or *oo-a*.	30. *ew*, or *e-yew*.	40. *ae^{ng}*.	50. *^{n}ew*, or *^{n}e-yew*.

Of these fifty finals, thirty-three are plain, and seventeen nasal sounds. The plain sounds consist of—

Three simple vowels,	28.	*a*, as in *far*.
	29.	*e*, as in *me*.
	15.	*o*, as in *go*.
Eight diphthongs,	11.	*oe*, as in *hoe*.
	16.	*ae*; something like *i*.
	5.	*ay*, as *a* flat, in *care*.
	39.	*ay*, as *a* slender, in *gay*.
	13.	*ey*, as in *they*.
	27.	*oo*, as in *coo*.
	30.	*ew*, as in *yew*.
	23.	*aou*.
Three double vowels, divided by a diœrhesis,	24.	*ëa*.
	33.	*ëo*.
	25.	*öey*.
One triple vowel, divided by a diœrhesis,	12.	*ëaou*.
Five syllables consisting of a vowel and a consonant,	19.	*am*.
	6.	*an*.
	3.	*im*.
	17.	*in*.
	47.	*om*.
Three syllables containing a vowel and two consonants,	21.	*ang*.
	9.	*eng*.
	7.	*ong*.
Two syllables containing a double vowel and a consonant,	22.	*ëem*.
	2.	*ëen*.
Two syllables with a double vowel and a double consonant,	18.	*ëang*.
	14.	*ëung*.
Six syllables, beginning with a *w*,	20.	*wa*.
	8.	*wae*.
	10.	*wan*.
	43.	*wang*.
	1.	*wun*.
	4.	*wuy*.

The nasals are formed from the plain sounds, by attempting to pronounce them through the nose or by giving them a nasal twang in the termination; and are expressed by an *n*, *m*, or *ng*, being prefixed, inserted, or affixed, above the line. Of the nasals there are three kinds; first, those in which single vowels or diphthongs take, a nasal sound, which are denoted by a small *n* preceding the nasal vowel. 2dly, Those formed by a half-expressed *ng* terminating the word, and communicating its nasal sound to the whole. 3dly, Those formed by the letter *m*, in which the sound of the *m* is so prevalent, as to communicate its force to the whole word.

k

Of the first sort of nasals, there are eight, as follow:—

26.	^{n}a,	formed from	28. *a*	46.	$^{n}\breve{e}aou$,	formed from	12. *ĕaou*
36.	$\breve{e}^{n}a$,	———	24. *ëa*	48.	^{n}aou,	———	23. *aou*
37.	$w^{n}a$,	———	20. *wa*	49.	^{n}o,	———	15. *o*
41.	^{n}oe,	———	11. *oe*	50.	^{n}ew,	———	30. *ew.*

In these instances all the letters after the ^{n} are nasal, though the ^{n} does not so fully alter the sound, as to deserve notice in an alphabetical arrangement. Hence in the following Dictionary, the nasal sound ^{n}a follows immediately after the plain *a*, and is not reserved to be inserted under the letter *n*; except where one of the initials *l*, *b*, or *g* is joined to any of the above nasal finals, in which case the power of these letters is merged into that of *n*, *m*, and *gn*, which are then written large, and arranged under their proper places in the alphabet.

Of the second sort of nasals, there are seven as follow:—

31.	ai^{ng},	formed from	5. *ay*	35.	$\breve{e}o^{ng}$,	formed from	33. *ĕo*
32.	wui^{ng},	———	4. *wuy*	38.	e^{ng},	———	7. *'ong*
34.	ee^{ng},	———	29. *e*	40.	ae^{ng},	———	16. *ae*
44.	wae^{ng},	———	8. *wae.*				

In these cases the ^{ng} is so clearly discernible in the pronunciation of the word, that although it has not seemed necessary to write the ^{ng} large, yet attention has been paid to these letters in the alphabetical arrangement.

Of the third sort of nasals, there are two, as follow:—

42. u^{m} 45. *mŏey.*

The number of these finals is increased by the contracted tones formed from them. These appear to the Chinese to make only a difference in the intonation, but in European writing they require a variation in the orthography. These contracted tones do not always terminate in the same letter, but vary according to the orthography of the several finals; thus finals ending in a vowel, whether nasal or plain, form the contracted tone by adding a rapid *h* to the end of the word, with a short mark on the preceding vowel, as *ka*, *kăh*; the presence of this *h* however, does not intimate that the latter part of the word is aspirated, but only that it is contracted, and suddenly stopped, before the full sound of the word is completed. Finals terminating in *n*, form *t* in the contracted sound; those in *m* form *p*; and those in *ng* form *k*; according to the following table.

1.	*Kwun* forms	*kwut*	11.	*Koe* forms	none	21.	*Kang* forms	*kak*	31.	Kai^{ng} forms	$ka\breve{i}^{ng}h$
2.	*Kĕen*	*kĕet*	12.	*Keaou,*	*keaoŭh*	22.	*Kĕem*	*kĕep*	32.	$Kwui^{ng}$	none
3.	*Kim*	*kip*	13.	*Key*	none	23.	*Kaou*	*kaoŭh*	33.	*Kĕo*	*kĕŏh*
4.	*Kwuy*	none	14.	*Kĕung*	*kĕuk*	24.	*Kĕa*	*kĕăh*	34.	Kee^{ng}	$ke\breve{e}^{ng}h$
5.	*Kay*	*kăyh*	15.	*Ko*	*kŏh*	25.	*Kŏey*	*kŏĕyh*	35.	$K\breve{e}o^{ng}$	none
6.	*Kan*	*kat*	16.	*Kae*	none	26.	$K^{n}a$	$k^{n}\breve{a}h$	36.	$K\breve{e}^{n}a$	none
7.	*Kong*	*kok*	17.	*Kan*	*kat*	27.	*Koe*	*koŏh*	37.	$Kw^{n}a$	none
8.	*Kwae*	*kwaĕh*	18.	*Kĕang*	*kĕak*	28.	*Ka*	*kăh*	38.	Ke^{ng}	none
9.	*Keng*	*kek*	19.	*Kam*	*kap*	29.	*Ke*	*keĕh*	39.	*Kay*	*kăyh*
10.	*Kwan*	*kwat*	20.	*Kwa*	*kwăh*	30.	*Kew*	none	40.	Kae^{ng}	none

41.	*K^{n}oe*	forms	none	44.	*Kwae^{ng}*	forms	*kwaĕ^{ngh}*	47.	*Chom*	forms	*chŏmh*
42.	*U^{m}*		none	45.	*Möey*		none	48.	*Gneaou*		none
43.	*Kwang*		*kwak*	46.	*K^{n}eaou*		*k^{n}eaoŭh*	49.	*K^{n}o*		*k^{n}ŏh*

50. *Gnew* —— none.

The fifty finals, with the thirty-four contracted sounds, if arranged alphabetically, would be as follow:—

a	*aĭ^{ngh}*	*aoŭh*	*e*	*^{n}ëaou*	*eĕ^{ngh}*	*ëŏh*	*im*	*^{n}oe*	*om*	*w^{n}a*	*wan*
^{n}a	*ak*	*ap*	*ëa*	*ëaoŭh*	*eep*	*ëo^{ng}*	*in*	*öey*	*ŏmh*	*wae*	*wang*
ae	*am*	*at*	*ë^{n}a*	*^{n}ëaoŭh*	*ĕet*	*ëuk*	*ip*	*^{m}öey*	*ong*	*waĕh*	*wat*
ae^{ng}	*an*	*ay*	*ëăh*	*eĕh*	*ek*	*ëu^{ng}*	*it*	*oĕyh*	*oo*	*wae^{ng}*	*wui^{ng}*
ăh	*ang*	*ay*	*ëak*	*eem*	*eng*	*ew*	*o*	*ŏh*	*oŏh*	*waĕ^{ngh}*	*wun*
^{n}ăh	*aou*	*ăyh*	*ëang*	*een*	*e^{ng}*	*^{n}ew*	*^{n}o*	*^{n}ŏh*	*u^{m}*	*wăh*	*wut*
ai^{ng}	*^{n}aou*	*ăyh*	*ëaou*	*ee^{ng}*	*ëo*	*ey*	*oe*	*ok*	*wa*	*wak*	*wuy*

These eighty-four finals, annexed to the fifteen initials, would produce one thousand two hundred and sixty distinct sounds, but many of the possible sounds according to this scheme of orthography are not used, and by a reference to the following table, it will be found that about nine hundred sounds are all that the Hok-këĕn people actually employ.

TABLE OF THE SOUNDS IN THE HOK-KEÈN, DIALECT.

A	bak	bëo	bwan	chăyh	che^{ng}	ch'hap	ch'heep
^{n}a	bam	bew	bwat	che	chëo	ch'hat	ch'hëet
ae	ban	bey	bwuy	chëa	chëŏh	ch'hay	ch'hek
ah	bang	bin		chë^{n}a	chëo^{ng}	ch'hăyh	ch'heng
ak	baou	bit	Cha	chëah	chëuk	ch'he	ch'he^{ng}
am	baoŭh	bo	chae	chëak	chëung	ch'hëa	ch'hëo
an	bat	boe	chăh	chëang	chew	ch'hë^{n}a	ch'hëŏh
ang	bay	böey	chai^{ng}	cheaou	chey	ch'hëăh	ch'hëo^{ng}
aou	bayh	böĕyh	chak	cheaŏuh	ch'ha	ch'hëak	ch'hëuk
ap	be	bŏh	cham	cheĕh	ch'hae	ch'hëang	ch'hëung
at	bëa	bok	chan	chëem	ch'hah	ch'heaou	ch'hew
ay	beaou	bong	chang	chëen	ch'hai^{ng}	ch'heaoŭh	ch'hey
ăyh	beĕh	boo	chaou	chee^{ng}	ch'hak	ch'heĕh	ch'him
	bëen	bun	chaouh	chëep	ch'ham	ch'hëem	ch'hin
Ba	bëet	but	chap	chëet	ch'han	ch'hëen	ch'hip
bae	bek	bwa	chat	chek	ch'hang	ch'hee^{ng}	ch'hit
băh	beng	bwăh	chay	cheng	ch'haou	ch'heĕ^{ngh}	ch'ho

ch'hoe
ch'höey
ch'höĕyh
ch'hok
ch'hong
ch'hoo
ch'hoŏh
ch'hui^{ng}
ch'hun
ch'hut
ch'huy
ch'hwa
ch'hw^{n}a
ch'hwăh
ch'hwan
ch'hwat
chim
chin
chip
chit
cho
choe
chöey
chŏh
chok
chom
chŏmh
chong
choo
chui^{ng}
chun
chut
chuy
chwa
chw^{n}a
chwae
chwăh
chwan
chwat

E
ee^{ng}
eĕh
ek
eng
e^{ng}
ey

Ga
gae
gak
gam
gan
gang
gaou
gap
gat
gay
ge
gëa
g^{n}ëa
gëăh
gëak
gëang
geaou
gëem
gëen
gëep
gëet
gek
geng
gëo
gëuk
gëung
gey
gim
gin
gip
git
gnae
gnaou
gnay
gnayh
gneaou
gneaoŭh
gnew
gno
gnoe
go
goe
göey
göĕyh
gok
gong
goo
gwa
gwae
gwan
gwat
gwut
gwuy

Ha
hae
ha^{n}e
hăh
hak
ham
han
hang
haou
hap
hat
hay
hăyh
he
hëa
hë^{n}a
hëăh
hëak
hëang
hëaou
heĕh
hëem
hëen
hee^{ng}
hëep
hëet
hek
heng
he^{ng}
hëo
hëŏh
hëo^{ng}
hëuk
hëung
hew
hey
him
hin
hip
hit
h^{n}aou
ho
h^{n}o
hoe
höey
höĕyh
hŏh
hok
hong
hoo
hu^{m}
hwa
hw^{n}a
hwae
hwăh
hwan
hwat
hwui^{ng}
hwun
hwut
hwuy

Jé
jëa
jëak
jëang
jeaou
jeĕh
jëem
jëen
jee^{ng}
jëep
jëet
jek
jeng
jëo
jëŏh
jëuk
jëung
jew
jim
jin
jip
jit
jöey
joo
jun
jwa
jwăh
jwan
jwuy

Ka
k^{n}a
kae
kae^{ng}
kăh
kai^{ng}
kak
kam
kan
kang
kaou
kaoŭh
kap
kat
kay
kăyh
ke
këa
kë^{n}a
këăh
këak
këang
keaou
keaoŭh
keĕh
këem
këen
kee^{ng}
këep
këet
kek
keng
ke^{ng}
këo
këŏh
këo^{ng}
këuk
këung
kew
key
k'ha
k'h^{n}a
k'hae
k'hae^{ng}
k'hăh
k'hai^{ng}
k'hăi^{ngh}
k'hak
k'ham
k'han
k'hang
k'haou
k'haoŭh
k'hap
k'hat
k'hay
k'hăyh
k'he
k'hëa
k'hë^{n}a
k'hëăh
k'hëak
k'hëang
k'heaou
k'heaoŭh
k'heĕh
k'hëem
k'hëen
k'hee^{ng}
k'hëep
k'hëet
k'hek
k'heng
k'he^{ng}
k'hëo
k'hëŏh
k'hëo^{ng}
k'hëuk
k'hëung
k'hew
k'hey
k'him
k'hin
k'hip
k'hit
k'ho
k'hoe
k'höey
k'höĕyh
k'hok
k'hom
k'hong
k'hoo
k'hwa
k'hw^{n}a
k'hwae
k'hwăh
k'hwan
k'hwat
k'hwui^{ng}
k'hwun
k'hwut
k'hwuy
kim
kin
kip
kit
ko
koe
köey
köĕyh
kŏh
kok
kong
koo
koŏh
kwa
kw^{n}a
kwae
kwae^{ng}
kwăh
kwan
kwang
kwat
kwui^{ng}
kwun
kwut
kwuy

La
lae
lăh
lak
lam
lan
lang
laou
lap
lat
lay
lăyh
le
lëa
lëăh
lëak
lëang
leaou
leaoŭh
leĕh
lëem
lëen
lëep
lëet
lek
leng
lëo
lëŏh
lëuk
lëung
lew
ley
lim
lin
lip
lit
lo
loe
löey
lŏh
lok
long
loo
loŏh
lun
lut
luy
lwa
lwăh
lwan
lwat

Ma
mäe
mai^{ng}
mai^{ngh}
maou
me
më^{n}a
mee^{ng}
meĕ^{ngh}
mo
möey
mŏh
mooi^{ng}
mw^{n}a

Na
nae
nai^{ng}
naou
ne
në^{n}a
neaou
nee^{ng}
nee^{ngh}
nëo^{ng}

ne^{ng}
new
no
noe
nooi^{ng}
nw^{n}a

O
oe
öey
ŏĕyh
ŏh
ok
ong
oo
ŏoh

Pa
pae
pai^{ng}
pak
pan
pang
paou
paoŏh
pat
pay
păyh
pe
pë^{n}a
pëăh
pëak
peang
peaou
peĕh
pëen
pee^{ng}
pee^{ng}h
pëet
pek
peng

pe^{ng}
pëo
pëung
pew
pey
p'ha
p'h^{n}a
p'hae
p'hae^{ng}
p'hăh
p'hai^{ng}
p'hak
p'han
p'hang
p'haou
p'haŏuh
p'hat
p'hay
p'he
p'hë^{n}a
p'hëăh
p'hëang
p'heaou
p'hëen
p'hee^{ng}
p'hëet
p'hek
p'heng
p'hëo
p'hew
p'hey
p'hin
p'hit
p'ho
p'hoe
p'höey
p'höĕyh
p'hŏh
p'hok
p'hong
p'hoo

p'hoŏh
p'hooi^{ng}
p'hun
p'hut
p'hwa
p'hw^{n}a
p'hwăh
p'hwan
p'hwat
p'hwuy
pin
pit
po
poe
pöey
pŏh
pok
pong
poo
poŏh
pooi^{ng}
pun
put
pwa
pw^{n}a
pwae
pwăh
pwan
pwat
pwuy

Sa
s^{n}a
sae
săh
s^{n}ăh
sai^{ng}
sak
sam
san
sang

saou
sap
sat
say
săyh
se
sëa
së^{n}a
sëăh
sëak
sëang
seaou
seĕh
sëem
sëen
see^{ng}
sëep
sëet
sek
seng
se^{ng}
sëo
sëŏh
sëo^{ng}
sëuk
sëung
sew
sey
sim
sin
sip
sit
so
soe
söey
söĕyh
sŏh
sok
som
song
soo

sun
süt
suy
swa
sw^{n}a
swae^{ng}
swaĕ^{ng}h
swăh
swan
swat
swüi^{ng}

Ta
t^{n}a
tae
tăh
tai^{ng}
tak
tam
tan
tang
taou
tap
tat
tay
tayh
te
tëa
të^{n}a
tëăh
tëang
teaou
teĕh
tëem
tëen
tee^{ng}
tëep
tëet
tek
teng
te^{ng}

tëo
tëŏh
tëo^{ng}
tëuk
tëung
tew
tey
t'ha
t'h^{n}a
t'hae
t'hăh
t'hai^{ng}
t'hak
t'ham
t'han
t'hang
t'haou
t'hap
t'hat
t'hay
t'hăyh
t'he
t'hë^{n}a
t'hëăh
t'hëang
t'heaou
t'heĕh
t'hëem
t'hëen
t'hee^{ng}
t'hëep
t'hëet
t'hek
t'heng
t'he^{ng}
t'hëo
t'hëuk
t'hëung
t'hew
t'hey
t'him

t'hin
t'hit
t'ho
t'hoe
t'höey
t'hŏh
t'hok
t'hong
t'hoo
t'hooi^{ng}
t'hun
t'hut
t'huy
t'hwa
t'hw^{n}a
t'hwăh
t'hwan
t'hwat
tim
tin
tip
tit
to
toe
töey
tŏh
tok
tong
too
toŏh
tooi^{ng}
tun
tut
tuy
twa
tw^{n}a
twăh
twan
twat

Ūm

u^{n}

Wa
w^{n}a
wae
wae^{ng}
waĕh
waĕ^{ng}h
wăh
wan
wat
wöey
wöĕyh
woo
wui^{ng}
wun
wut
wuy

Yang
yaou
yëa
yë^{n}a
yëăh
yëak
yëem
yëen
yëep
yëet
yëo
yëŏh
yëo^{ng}
yëuk
yew
yim
yin
yip
yit
yung

ON THE CONJUNCTION OF INITIALS AND FINALS.

The initials and finals are joined by the first letter of an initial being substituted in the place of the first letter of the final. The Hok-këèn people are accustomed to join them, by first naming the final, then enumerating each initial in order, they drop the first letter of the final, and substitute the first letter of the initial in its stead. Thus:—

I

1. Kwun connects itself with its initials in the following manner:

K,wun	*l,ëw*	*p,ëen*	*k,ëw*	*k'h,è*	*t,ëy*	*p'h,ó*	*t'h,^{n}a*	*ch,eng*	*j,ip*	*s,ê*	*,eng*	*b,ûn*	*g,ê*	*ch'h,ut*	*h,ê*
	lun	*pun*	*kwun*	*k'hwun*	*tun*	*p'hun*	*t'hun*	*chun*	*jun*	*sun*	*wun*	*bun*	none	*ch'hun*	*hwun.*

According to this scheme, the *w* of the final is omitted in its connection with several of the initials, but if the final be sounded *koo-wun*, that omission will not be discernible, thus:

Koo,-wun	*l,ëw*	*p,ëen*	*k,ëw*	*k'h,è*	*t,ëy*	*p'h,ó*	*t'h,^{n}a*	*ch,eng*	*jip*	*s,ê*	*,eng,*	*&c.*
	loo-wun	*poo-wun*	*koo-wun*	*k'hoo-wun*	*too-wun*	*p'hoo-wun*	*t'hoo-wun*	*choo-wun*	*joo-wun*	*soo-wun*	*oo-wun,*	*&c.*

These sounds however must not be too much lengthened out, but pronounced rapidly as monosyllables. The 4th, 8th, 10th, 20th, 33d, 37th, 43d, and 44th finals, all beginning with *w*, may have that *w* preceded by, or changed into *oo*, and thus be joined with their initials in the same way as above.

2. Këen connects itself with its initials as follows:—

K,ëen	*l,ëw*	*p,ëen*	*k,ëw*	*k'h,è*	*t,ëy*	*p'hó*	*t'h,^{n}a*	*ch,eng*	*j,ip*	*s,ê*	*,eng*	*b,un*	*g,ê*	*ch'h,ut*	*h,ê*
	lëen	*pëen*	*këen*	*k'hëen*	*tëen*	*p'hëen*	*t'hëen*	*chëen*	*jëen*	*sëen*	*yëen*	*bëen*	*gëen*	*ch'hëen*	*hëen*

Here a *y* is inserted under the 11th initial, and will be found prefixed to the same initial, in its conjunction with all those finals which have *e* followed by a vowel or diphthong. This is done on account of the lengthening of the *e*, the consonant *y* being equivalent to *ee*, and being formed by placing the organs in the position of *e*, and squeezing the tongue against the roof of the mouth. The 2d, 12th, 14th, 18th, 22d, 24th, 30th, 33d, 35th, 36th, 46th, and 50th finals are included under this rule. The 3d and 17th finals, though beginning with *i*, yet, as they have a slight sound of *e* connected with them, are included under the same rule. Under all the other finals, the conjunction with the 11th initial is formed merely by leaving out the first letter of the final.

3. Kim connects itself with its initials as follows:—

K,im	*l,ëw*	*p,ëen*	*k,ëw*	*k'hè*	*t,ëy*	*p'h,ó*	*t'h,^{n}a*	*ch,eng*	*j,ip*	*s,ê*	*,eng*	*b,ûn*	*g,ê*	*ch'h,ut*	*h,ê*
	lim	none	*kim*	*k'him*	*tim*	none	*t'him*	*chim*	*jim*	*sim*	*yim*	none	*gim*	*ch'him*	*him*

For the *y* under the 11th initial, see rule under the 2d final.

4. Kwuy is joined with its initials in the following manner:—

Kwuy	*l,ëw*	*p,ëen*	*k,ëw*	*k'h,è*	*t,ëy*	*p'h,ó*	*t'h,^{n}a*	*ch,eng*	*j,ip*	*s,ê*	*,eng*	*b,ûn*	*g,ê*	*ch'h,ut*	*h,è*
	luy	*pwuy*	*kwuy*	*k'hwuy*	*tuy*	*p'hwuy*	*t'huy*	*chuy*	*jwuy*	*suy*	*wuy*	*bwuy*	*gwuy*	*ch'hwuy*	*hwuy*

For the omission of the *w* in connection with some initials, see remarks under the 1st final.

5. Kay is thus joined with its initials:—

Kay	*l,ëw*	*p,ëen*	*k,ëw*	*k'h,è*	*t,ëy*	*p'hó*	*t'h,^{n}a*	*ch,eng*	*j,ip*	*s,ê*	*,eng*	*b,ûn*	*g,è*	*ch'h,ut*	*h,ê*
	lay	*pay*	*kay*	*k'hay*	*tay*	*p'hay*	*t'hay*	*chay*	none	*say*	*ay*	*bay*	*gay*	*ch'hay*	*hay*

The 6th, 7th, 9th, 11th, 13th, 15th, 16th, 19th, 21st, 23d, 25th, 26th, 27th, 28th, 29th, 31st, 34th, 35th 39th, 40th, 41st, 42d, 45th, 47th, 48th, 49th, and 50th finals are all joined in the same manner, without any variation. The 5th, 10th, 20th, 33d, 37th, 43d, and 44th, may also be referred to this example, which is the usual method of joining initials with finals.

6. Kan is thus joined with its initials:

Kan	*l,ëw*	*p,ëen*	*k,ëw*	*k'h,è*	*t,ëy*	*p'h,ó*	*t'h,^{n}a*	*ch,eng*	*j,ip*	*s,ë*	*,eng*	*b,ûn*	*g,ë*	*ch'h,ut*	*h,e*
	lan	*pan*	*kan*	*k'han*	*tan*	*p'han*	*t'han*	*chan*	none	*san*	*an*	*ban*	*gan*	*ch'han*	*han*

7. Kong forms its junction with its initials in a similar manner, thus:

Kong	*l,ëw*	*p,ëen*	*k,ëw*	*k'h,è*	*t,ëy*	*p'h,ó*	*t'h,^{n}a*	*ch,eng*	*j,ip*	*s,ë*	*,eng*	*bûn*	*g,ë*	*ch'h,ut*	*h,é*
	long	*pong*	*kong*	*k'hong*	*tong*	*p'hong*	*t'hong*	*chong*	none	*song*	*ong*	*bong*	*gong*	*ch'hong*	*hong*

8. Kwae joins with its initials thus:

Kwae	*l,ëw*	*p,ëen*	*k,ëw*	*k'h,è*	*tëy*	*p'hó*	*t'h^{n}a*	*ch,eng*	*j,ip*	*së*	*,eng*	*b,ûn*	*g,e*	*ch'h,ut*	*h,è*
	none	*pwae*	*kwae*	*k'hwae*	none	none	none	*chwae*	none	none	*wae*	*bwae*	*gwae*	none	*hwae*

9. Keng is thus joined with its initials:—

Keng	*l,ëw*	*p,ëen*	*k,ëw*	*k'h,è*	*t,ëy*	*p'h,ó*	*t'h,^{n}a*	*ch,eng*	*j,ip*	*s,ë*	*,eng*	*b,ûn*	*g,e*	*ch'h,ut*	*h,è*
	leng	*peng*	*keng*	*k'heng*	*teng*	*p'heng*	*t'heng*	*cheng*	*jeng*	*seng*	*eng*	*beng*	*geng*	*ch'heng*	*heng*

10. Kwan unites thus with its initials:

K,wan	*l,ëw*	*p,ëen*	*k,ëw*	*k'h,è*	*t,ëy*	*p'h,ó*	*t'h,^{n}a*	*ch,eng*	*j,ip*	*s,ë*	*,eng*	*b,ûn*	*g,e*	*ch'h,ut*	*h,é*
	lwan	*pwan*	*kwan*	*k'hwan*	*twan*	*p'hwan*	*t'hwan*	*chwan*	*jwan*	*swan*	*wan*	*bwan*	*gwan*	*ch'hwan*	*hwan*

11. Koe connects itself thus with its initials:

K,oe	*l,ëw*	*p,ëen*	*k,ëw*	*k'h,è*	*t,ëy*	*p'h,ó*	*t'h,^{n}a*	*ch,eng*	*j,ip*	*s,ë*	*,eng*	*b,ûn*	*g,e*	*ch'h,ut*	*h,e*
	loe	*poe*	*koe*	*k'hoe*	*toe*	*p'hoe*	*t'hoe*	*choe*	none	*soe*	*oe*	*boe*	*goe*	*ch'h*[illegible]	*hoe*

12. 'Këaou is thus joined with its initials:—see the note under the 2d final.

Keaou	*l,ëw*	*p,ëen*	*k,ëw*	*k'h,è*	*t,ëy*	*p'h,ó*	*t'h,^{n}a*	*ch,eng*	*j,ip*	*s,ë*	*,eng*	*b,ûn*	*g,e*	*ch,h,ut*	[illegible]
	lëaou	*pëaou*	*këaou*	*k'hëaou*	*tëaou*	*p'hëaou*	*t'hëaou*	*chëaou*	*jëaou*	*seaou*	*yaou*	*bëaou*	*geaou*	*ch'hëaou*	*hëaou*

13. Key is thus united with its initials:

Key	*l,ëw*	*p,ëen*	*k,ëw*	*k'h,è*	*t,ëy*	*p'hó*	*t'h,^{n}a*	*ch,eng*	*j,ip*	*s,ë*	*,eng*	*b,ûn*	*g,ë*	*ch'h,ut*	*h,ë*
	ley	*pey*	*key*	*k'hey*	*tey*	*p'hey*	*t'hey*	*chey*	none	*sey*	*ey*	*bey*	*gey*	*ch'hey*	*hey*

14. Këung unites thus with its initials:—see the note under the 2d final.

Këung	*l,ëw*	*p,ëen*	*k,ëw*	*k'h,è*	*t,ëy*	*p'h,ó*	*t'h,^{n}a*	*ch,eng*	*j,ip*	*s,ë*	*,eng*	*b,ûn*	*g,ë*	*ch'h,ut*	*h,è*
	lëung	*pëung*	*këung*	*k'hëung*	*tëung*	none	*t'hëung*	*chëung*	*jëung*	*sëung*	*yung*	none	*gëung*	*ch'hëung*	*hëung*

15. Ko unites thus with its initials:

Ko	*l,ëw*	*p,ëen*	*k,ëw*	*k'h,è*	*t,ëy*	*p'hó*	*t'h,^{n}a*	*ch,eng*	*j,ip*	*s,ë*	*,eng*	*b,ûn*	*g,ë*	*ch'h,ut*	*h,è*
	lo	*po*	*ko*	*k'ho*	*to*	*p'ho*	*t'ho*	*cho*	none	*so*	*o*	*bo*	*go*	*ch'ho*	*ho*

16. Kae connects itself with its initials thus:

Kae	*l,ëw*	*p,ëen*	*k,ëw*	*k'h,è*	*t,ëy*	*p'h,ó*	*t'h,^{n}a*	*ch,eng*	*j,ip*	*s,ë*	*,eng*	*b,ûn*	*g,è*	*ch'h,ut*	*h,è*
	lae	*pae*	*kae*	*k'hae*	*tae*	*p'hae*	*t'hae*	*chae*	none	*sae*	*ae*	*bae*	*gae*	*ch'hae*	*hae*

17. Kin connects itself thus with its initials: — see the note under the 2d final.

Kin	*l,êw*	*p,ëen*	*k,êw*	*k'h,è*	*t,ëy*	*p'h,ó*	*t'h,^{n}a*	*ch,eng*	*j,ip*	*s,ê*	*,eng*	*b,ûn*	*g,ê*	*ch'h,ut*	*h,e*
	lin	*pin*	*kin*	*k'hin*	*tin*	*p'hin*	*t'hin*	*chin*	*jin*	*sin*	*yin*	*bin*	*gin*	*ch'hin*	*hin*

18. Këang joins thus with its initials: — see the note above.

Këang	*l,êw*	*p,ëen*	*k,êw*	*k'h,è*	*t,ëy*	*p'h,ó*	*t'h,^{n}a*	*ch,eng*	*j,ip*	*s,ê*	*,eng*	*b,ûn*	*g,ê*	*ch'h,ut*	*h,ê*
	lëang	*pëang*	*këang*	*k'hëang*	*tëang*	*p'hëang*	*t'hëang*	*chëang*	*jëang*	*sëang*	*yang*	none	*gëang*	*ch'hëang*	*hëang*

19. Kam joins with its initials in the usual way, thus: —

Kam	*l,êw*	*p,ëen*	*k,êw*	*k'h,è*	*t,ëy*	*p'h,ó*	*t'h,^{n}a*	*ch,eng*	*j,ip*	*s,ê*	*,eng*	*b,ûn*	*g,ê*	*ch'h,ut*	*h,ê*
	lam	none	*kam*	*k'ham*	*tam*	none	*t'ham*	*cham*	none	*sam*	*am*	*bam*	*gam*	*ch'ham*	*ham*

20. Kwa unites with its initials thus: —

Kwa	*l,êw*	*p,ëen*	*k,êw*	*k'h,è*	*t,ëy*	*p'h,ó*	*t'h,^{n}a*	*ch,eng*	*j,ip*	*s,ê*	*,eng*	*b,ûn*	*g,ê*	*ch'h,ut*	*h,ê*
	lwa	*pwa*	*kwa*	*k'hwa*	*twa*	*p'hwa*	*t'hwa*	*chwa*	*jwa*	*swa*	*wa*	*bwa*	*gwa*	*ch'hwa*	*hwa*

21. Kang joins with its initials as follows: —

Kang	*l,êw*	*p,ëen*	*k'êw*	*k'h,è*	*t,ëy*	*p'h,ó*	*t'h,^{n}a*	*ch,eng*	*j,ip*	*s,ê*	*,eng*	*b,ûn*	*g,ê*	*ch'h,ut*	*h,ê*
	lang	*pang*	*kang*	*k'hang*	*tang*	*p'hang*	*t'hang*	*chang*	none	*sang*	*ang*	*bang*	*gang*	*ch'hang*	*hang*

22. Këem is thus connected with its initials: — see note under the 2d final.

Këem	*l,êw*	*p,ëen*	*k,êw*	*k'h,è*	*t,ëy*	*p'h,ó*	*t'h,^{n}a*	*ch,eng*	*j,ip*	*s,ê*	*,eng*	*b,ûn*	*g,ê*	*ch'h,ut*	*h,ê*
	lëem	none	*këem*	*k'hëem*	*tëem*	none	*t'hëem*	*chëem*	*jëem*	*sëem*	*yëem*	none	*gëem*	*ch'hëem*	*hëem*

23. Kaou is joined thus with its initials: —

Kaou	*l,êw*	*p,ëen*	*k,êw*	*k'h,è*	*t,ëy*	*p'h,ó*	*t'h,^{n}a*	*ch,eng*	*j,ip*	*s,ê*	*,eng*	*b,ûn*	*g,ê*	*ch'h,ut*	*h,ê*
	laou	*paou*	*kaou*	*k'haou*	*taou*	*p'haou*	*t'haou*	*chaou*	none	*saou*	*aou*	*baou*	*gaou*	*ch'haou*	*haou*

24. Këa unites with its initials thus; see the note under the 2d final.

Këa	*l,êw*	*p,ëen*	*k,êw*	*k'h,è*	*t,ëy*	*p'h,ó*	*t'h,^{n}a*	*ch,eng*	*j,ip*	*s,ê*	*,eng*	*b,ûn*	*g,ê*	*ch'hut*	*h'ê*
	lëa	none	*këa*	*k'hëa*	*tëa*	none	none	*chëa*	*jëa*	*sëa*	*yëa*	*bëa*	*gëa*	*ch'hëa*	*hëa*

25. Köey unites thus with its initials.

Köey	*l,êw*	*p,ëen*	*k,êw*	*k'hè*	*t,ëy*	*p'h,ó*	*t'h,^{n}a*	*ch,eng*	*j,ip*	*s,ê*	*,eng*	*b,ûn*	*g,ê*	*ch'h,ut*	*h.ê*
	löey	*pöey*	*köey*	*k'höey*	*töey*	*p'höey*	*t'höey*	*chöey*	*jöey*	*söey*	*öey*	*böey*	*göey*	*ch'höey*	*höey*

N. B. *öey* is sometimes written *wöey*, because this final *köey* has something of the sound of a *w* in it, and may be pronounced *ko-wey.*

26. K^{n}a joins thus with its initials.

K^{n}a	*l,êw*	*pëen*	*k'êw*	*k'h,è*	*t,ëy*	*p'h,ó*	*t'h,^{n}a*	*ch,eng*	*j,ip*	*s,ê*	*,eng*	*b,ûn*	*gê*	*ch'h,ut*	*hê.*
	na	none	*k^{n}a*	*k'h^{n}a*	*t^{n}a*	*p'h^{n}a*	*t'h^{n}a*	*ch^{n}a*	none	*s^{n}a*	*^{n}a*	*ma*	none	none	none.

This being the first of the nasals, it becomes necessary to notice the variation of some of the initials, when connected with nasal finals; such as the 1st, the 12th, and sometimes the 13th, initials, which lose in a great measure their original sounds, and merge into those of the nasals; thus *l* becomes *n* or l^{n}, *b* becomes *m*, and *g* is converted into *gn*. Indeed, so much is the sound of the initial letter lost in the nasal, that to a learner's ear the words under the above initials appear to have the sound of *n*, *m*, and *gn* full; and thus it has been thought advisable to write them in the following dictionary: but a little closer attention to the sound of the 1st initial when connected with a nasal final, will convince the student that the *l* is not altogether lost, but enters in some measure into the sound of the word, as though *na* were written l^{na}, but pronounced through the nose, with a little more stress laid on the *n* than on the *l*. The sound of *b*, in the 12th initial is more completely merged into that of *m*, yet pronounced with a whining noise, like a child crying *ma*. The sound of *g*, when connected with a nasal final, is more evidently preserved than the other two, and is pronounced as though written *gn* full, with a strong nasal sound.

27. Koo is joined thus with its initials:

Koo	*l,éw*	*p,ëen*	*k,éw*	*k'h,è*	*t,ëy*	*p'h,ó*	*t'h,^{n}a*	*ch,eng*	*j,ip*	*s,é*	*,eng*	*b,un*	*g,é*	*ch'h,ut*	*h,é*
	loo	*poo*	*koo*	*k'hoo*	*too*	*p'hoo*	*t'hoo*	*choo*	*joo*	*soo*	*oo*	*boo*	*goo*	*ch'hoo*	*hoo*

The sound of *oo* under the 11th initial is sometimes written *woo*, because this final has something of the sound of *w* in it, as though drawled out into *koo-woo;* and this latter form has usually been followed in the succeeding pages.

28. Ka joins thus with its initials:

Ka	*l,éw*	*p,ëen*	*k,éw*	*k'h,è*	*t,ëy*	*p'h,ó*	*t'h,^{n}a*	*ch,eng*	*j,ip*	*s,é*	*,eng*	*b,ún*	*g,é*	*ch'h,ut*	*h,é*
	la	*pa*	*ka*	*k'ha*	*ta*	*p'ha*	*t'ha*	*chạ*	none	*sa*	*a*	*ba*	*ga*	*ch'ha*	*ha*

29. Ke unites with its initials in the usual way:

Ke	*l,éw*	*p,ëen*	*k,éw*	*k'h,è*	*t,ëy*	*p'h,ó*	*t'h,^{n}a*	*ch,eng*	*j,ip*	*s,é*	*,eng*	*b,ún*	*g,é*	*ch'h,ut*	*h,é*
	le	*pe*	*ke*	*k'he*	*te*	*p'he*	*t'he*	*che*	*je*	*se*	*e*	*be*	*ge*	*ch'he*	*he*

30. Kew connects itself thus with its initials:—see the rule under the 2d final.

Kew	*l,éw*	*p,ëen*	*k,éw*	*k'h,è*	*t,ëy*	*p'h,ó*	*t'h,^{n}a*	*ch,eng*	*j,ip*	*s,é*	*,eng*	*b,ún*	*g,é*	*ch'h,ut*	*h,é*
	lew	*pew*	*kew*	*k'hew*	*tẹw*	*p'hew*	*t'hew*	*chew*	*jew*	*sew*	*yew*	*bew*	*gew*	*ch'hew*	*hew*

31. Kai^{ng} joins with its initials thus:

Kai^{ng}	*l,éw*	*p,ëen*	*k,éw*	*k'h,è*	*t,ëy*	*p'h,ó*	*t'h,^{n}a*	*ch,eng*	*j,ip*	*s,é*	*,eng*	*b,un*	*g,é*	*ch'h,ut*	*h,é*
	nai^{ng}	*pai^{ng}*	*kai^{ng}*	*k'hai^{ng}*	*tai^{ng}*	*p'hai^{ng}*	*t'hai^{ng}*	*chai^{ng}*	none	*sai^{ng}*	*ai^{ng}*	*mai^{ng}*	*gnay*	*ch'hai^{ng}*	*hai^{ng}*

This being a nasal final, the 1st and 12th initials in connection with it are changed from *l* and *b*, to *n* and *m;* and the 13th initial *g* is written *gn*, with the omission of the final *ng*, the *i* being changed into *y;* though it must be remembered that this sound is to be pronounced through the nose, retaining the full power of both the *g* and *n*, at the beginning of the word.

32. Kwui^{ng} connects itself thus with its initials;

Kwui^{ng}	*l,éw*	*p,ëen*	*k,éw*	*k'h,è*	*t,ëy*	*p'h,ó*	*t'h,^{n}a*	*ch,eng*	*s,é*	*,eng*	*b,un*	*g,é*	*ch'h,ut*	*h,é*
	nooi^{ng}	*pooi^{ng}*	*kwui^{ng}*	*k'hwui^{ng}*	*tooi^{ng}*	*p'hooi^{ng}*	*t'hooi^{ng}*	*chui^{ng}*	*swui^{ng}*	*wui^{ng}*	*mooi^{ng}*	none	*ch'hui^{ng}*	*hui^{ng}*

This final being nasal, the 1st and 12th initials undergo an alteration as mentioned under the 26th final; but

m

there are also changes in the vowels, which make a difference in appearance while there is none in reality, the vowels being changed only to acommodate the vowel sound to the different consonants of the initials, but if the final be written *koo-i*^{ng}, the whole will correspond. See under the 1st final.

33. Këo unites thus with its initials:—see the note under the 2d final.

Këo	*l,ěw*	*p,ëen*	*k,ěw*	*k'h,è*	*t,ēy*	*p'h,ó*	*t'h,*^{n}*a*	*ch,eng*	*j,ip*	*s,ě*	*,eng*	*b,ŭn*	*g,ě*	*ch'h,ut*	*h,ě*
	lëo	*pëo*	*këo*	*k'hëo*	*tëo*	*p'hëo*	*t'hëo*	*chëo*	*jëo*	*sëo*	*yëo*	*bëo*	*gëo*	*ch'hëo*	*hëo*

34. Kee^{ng} joins thus with its initials:—see under the 26th and 31st finals.

Kee^{ng}	*l,ěw*	*p,ëen*	*k,ěw*	*k'h,è*	*t,ēy*	*p'h,ó*	*t'h,*^{n}*a*	*ch,eng*	*j,ip*	*s,ě*	*,eng*	*b,ún*	*g,ě*	*ch'h,ut*	*h,ě*
	nee^{ng}	*pee*^{ng}	*kee*^{ng}	*k'hee*^{ng}	*tec*^{ng}	*p'hee*^{ng}	*t'hee*^{ng}	*chee*^{ng}	*jee*^{ng}	*see*^{ng}	*ee*^{ng}	*mee*^{ng}	none	*ch'hee*^{ng}	*hee*^{ng}

35. Këo^{ng} unites thus with its initials:—see remarks under the 2d, 26th and 31st finals.

Këo^{ng}	*l,ěw*	*p,ëen*	*k,ěw*	*k'h,è*	*t,ēy*	*p'h,ó*	*t'h,*^{n}*a*	*ch,eng*	*j,ip*	*s,ě*	*,eng*	*b,un*	*g,ě*	*ch'h,ut*	*h,ě*
	nëo^{ng}	none	*këo*^{ng}	*k'hëo*^{ng}	*tëo*^{ng}	none	none	*chëo*^{ng}	none	*sëo*^{ng}	*yëo*^{ng}	none	none	*ch'hëo*^{ng}	*hëo*^{ng}

36. Kë^{n}a joins thus with its initials:—see remarks under the 2d, 26th, and 31st finals.

Kë^{n}*a*	*l,ěw*	*p,ëen*	*k,ěw*	*k'h,è*	*t,ēy*	*p'h,ó*	*t'h,*^{n}*a*	*ch,eng*	*j,ip*	*s,ě*	*,eng*	*b,ŭn*	*g,ě*	*ch'h,ut*	*h,ě*
	na	*pë*^{n}*a*	*;ë*^{n}*a*	*h'hë*^{n}*a*	*të*^{n}*a*	*p'hë*^{n}*a*	*t'hë*^{n}*a*	*chë*^{n}*a*	none	*së*^{n}*a*	*yë*^{n}*a*	*mëa*	*g*^{n}*ëa*	*ch'hë*^{n}*a*	*hë*^{n}*a*

Here the little ^{n}, denoting the nasal, is omitted under the 1st and 12th initials as unnecessary, it being contained in the *n* and *m* at the beginning of the words; under the 13th initial it is retained.

37. Kw^{n}a connects thus with its initials:—see under the 26th and 31st finals.

Kw^{n}*a*	*l,ěw*	*p,ëen*	*k,ěw*	*k'h,è*	*t,ēy*	*p'h,ó*	*t'h,*^{n}*a*	*ch,eng*	*j,ip*	*s,ě*	*,eng*	*b,ún*	*g,ě*	*ch'h,ut*	*h,ě*
	nw^{n}*a*	*pw*^{n}*a*	*kw*^{n}*a*	*k'hw*^{n}*a*	*tw*^{n}*a*	*p'hw*^{n}*a*	*t'hw*^{n}*a*	*chw*^{n}*a*	none	*sw*^{n}*a*	*w*^{n}*u*	*mw*^{n}*a*	none	*ch'hw*^{n}*a*	*hw*^{n}*a*

38. Ke^{ng} joins thus with its initials:—see remarks under the 26th and 31st finals.

Ke^{ng}	*l,ěw*	*p,ëen*	*k,ěw*	*k'h,è*	*t,ēy*	*p'h,ó*	*t'h,*^{n}*a*	*ch,eng*	*j,ip*	*s,ě*	*,eng*	*b,ŭn*	*g,ě*	*ch'h,ut*	*h,ě*
	ne^{ng}	*pe*^{ng}	*he*^{ng}	*k'he*^{ng}	*te*^{ng}	none	*t'he*^{ng}	*che*^{ng}	none	*se*^{ng}	*e*^{ng}	none	none	*ch'he*^{ng}	*he*^{ng}

39. Kay unites thus with its initials:

Kay	*l,ěw*	*p,ëen*	*k,ěw*	*k'h,è*	*t,ēy*	*p'h,ó*	*t'h,*^{n}*a*	*ch,eng*	*j,ip*	*s,ě*	*,eng*	*b,ŭn*	*g,ě*	*ch'h,ut*	*h,ě*
	lay	none	*kay*	*k'hay*	*tay*	none	*t'hay*	*chay*	none	*say*	*ay*	*bay*	*gay*	*ch'hay*	*hay*

40. Kae^{ng} joins with its initials thus:—see under the 26th and 31st finals.

Kae^{ng}	*l,ěw*	*k,ěw*	*k'h,è*	*p'h,ó*	*ch,eng*	*s,ě*	*b,ŭn*	*g,ě*	*h,ě*
	nae	*kae*^{ng}	*k'hae*^{ng}	*p'hae*^{ng}	*chae*^{ng}	*sae*^{ng}	*mae*	*gnae*	*hae*^{ng}

Under this final the *l*, *b*, and *g*, are changed by the nasal as noticed under the 26th and 31st finals, but the small ^{ngs} are omitted, as being included in the nasal at the beginning of the word, though care must still be taken to pronounce the whole as coming from the nose.

41. K^{n}oe is found connected with only three initials thus:—

K^{n}*oe*	*l,ěw*	*k,ěw*	*g,ě*
	noe	*k*^{n}*oe*	*gnoe*

42. Um is found in connection with only two initials thus:—*Um*

Um	*,eng*	*h,é*
	um	*hum*

This final um is found in connection with only these two initials, the first of which resembles the sound of *um* and the latter *hum*, both attempted to be pronounced without opening the mouth.

43. Kwang is found united with only three initials thus:—*Kwang*

Kwang	*k,éw*	*,eng*	*h,é*
	kwang	*wang*	*hwang*

44. Kaeng is found connected with only four initials:—*Kwaeng*

Kwaeng	*k,éw*	*s,é*	*,eng*	*b,ŭn*
	kwaeng	*swaeng*	*waeng*	*bwaeng*

45. Möey is found connected with only one initial; as *b,ŭn,—möey.*

46. Kneaou is connected with only three initials, thus:—*Kneaou*

Kneaou	*l,éw*	*k,éw*	*g,é*
	neaou	*kneaou*	*gneaou*

47. Chom is found connected with four initials, thus:—*Chom*

Chom	*k'h,è*	*t,ēy*	*ch,eng*	*s,é*
	k'hom	*tom*	*chom*	*som*

48. Gnaou is connected with only four initials, thus:—*Gnaou*

Gnaou	*l,éw*	*b,ŭn*	*g,é*	*h,é*
	naou	*maou*	*gnaou*	*hnaou*

49. Kno is found in connection with five initials, thus:—*Kno*

Kno	*l,éw*	*k,éw*	*b,ŭn*	*g,é*	*h,é*
	no	*kno*	*mo*	*gno*	*hno*

50. Gnêw is found connected with only two initials, thus:—*Gnêw*

Gnêw	*l,éw*	*g,é*
	new	*gnew*

For a complete view of the initials and finals, with the method of joining them, see the following table.

A TABLE OF THE INITIALS AND FINALS OF THE HOK-

FINALS.	柳 L-éw	邊 P-ëen	求 K-êw	去 K'h-è	地 T-ēy	頗 P'h-ó	他 T'h-^{n}a
1 君 K,wun	縮 *lun*	分 *pun*	君 kwun	坤 k'hwun	敦 tun	奔 p'hun	吞 t'hun
2 堅 K,ëen	嗹 lëen	邊 pëen	堅 këen	愆 k'hëen	顛 tëen	偏 p'hëen	天 t'hëen
3 金 K,im	凛 lím	〇 pim	金 kim	欽 k'him	髟 tim	〇 p'him	琛 t'him
4 規 K,wuy̍	腄 luy	悲 pwuy	規 kwuy	虧 k'hwuy	追 tuy	屁 *p'hwùy*	推 t'huy
5 嘉 K,ay	詉 lây	皎 *pay*	嘉 kay	呿 k'hay	茶 tây	帕 *p'hày*	衾 t'hay
6 干 K,an	跰 *lan*	班 pan	干 kan	看 k'han	丹 tan	扳 p'han	灘 t'han
7 公 K,ong	鼜 *long*	梆 póng	公 kong	空 k'hong	東 tong	磅 p'hong	通 t'hong
8 乖 K,wae	〇 lwae	扒 pwaè	乖 kwae	㧟 k'hwae	〇 twae	〇 p'hwae	〇 t'hwae
9 經 K,eng	乳 *leng*	兵 peng	經 keng	傾 k'heng	丁 teng	烹 p,heng	聽 t'heng
10 觀 K,wan	煖 lwán	般 pwan	觀 kwan	寬 k'hwan	端 twan	拌 p'hwan	湍 t'hwan
11 沽 K,oe	魯 loé	晡 poe	沽 koe	箍 k'hoe	都 toe	菩 p'hoe	偷 t'hoe
12 嬌 K,eaou	瘶 leaou	標 peaou	嬌 keaou	橇 k'heaou	朝 teaou	僄 p'heaou	挑 t'heaou
13 稽 K,ey	禮 léy	篦 pey	稽 key	溪 k'hey	低 tey	批 p'hey	梯 t'hey
14 恭 K,ëung	龍 lëûng	餴 pëung	恭 këung	穹 k'hëung	中 tëung	〇 p'hëung	衷 t'hëung
15 高 K,o	覶 lo	褒 po	高 ko	科 k'ho	刀 to	波 p'ho	拖 t'ho
16 皆 K,ae	來 laê	擺 paé	皆 kae	開 k'hae	懛 tae	𨟠 p'hae	台 t'hae
17 巾 K,in	蠶 lin	賓 pin	巾 kin	欣 k'hin	珍 tin	繽 p'hin	趁 t'hìn
18 姜 K,ëang	良 lëâng	乒 pëàng	姜 këang	腔 k'hëang	張 tëang	塴 p'hëang	暢 t'hëàng
19 甘 K,am	婪 lam	〇 pam	甘 kam	堪 k'ham	擔 tam	〇 p'ham	探 t'ham
20 瓜 K,wa	瀨 lwà	簸 *pwà*	瓜 kwa	誇 k'hwa	帶 *twà*	鯊 *p'hwa*	泰 *t'hwà*
21 江 K,ang	硠 *lang*	邦 pang	江 kang	空 *k'hang*	東 *tang*	香 *p'hang*	窗 *t'hang*
22 兼 K,ëem	拈 lëem	〇 pëem	兼 këem	謙 k'hëem	沾 tëem	〇 p'hëem	添 t'hëem
23 交 K,aou	佬 laou	包 paou	交 kaou	敲 k'haou	兜 taou	抛 p'haou	偷 *t'haou*
24 迦 K,ëa	臛 lëa	〇 *pëa*	迦 këa	奇 *k'hëa*	爹 *tëa*	〇 *p'hëa*	〇 *t'hëa*
25 檜 K,öey	內 löēy	杯 pöey	檜 köey	魁 k'höey	對 *töèy*	坯 p'höey	焠 t'höey
26 監 *K,^{n}a*	拏 ná	〇 p^{n}a	監 *k^{n}a*	坩 *k'h^{n}a*	今 *t^{n}a*	粃 *p'h^{n}à*	他 t'h^{n}a
27 艍 K,oo	汝 *loó*	斧 *poó*	艍 koo	丘 *k'hoo*	蛛 too	哱 *p'hoo*	筯 *t'hoo*
28 膠 *K,a*	拉 *la*	巴 pa	膠 *ka*	脚 *k'ha*	乾 *ta*	瞟 *p'ha*	奓 *t'hà*
29 居 K,e	飈 le	悲 pe	居 ke	欺 k'he	知 te	丕 p'he	笞 t'he
30 丩 K,ew	飫 lew	彪 pew	丩 kew	丘 k'hew	丟 tew	夢 p'hew	抽 t'hew
31 更 *K,ai^{ng}*	嬣 *nai^{ng}*	拼 *pai^{ng}*	更 *kai^{ng}*	坑 *k'hai^{ng}*	瞠 *tai^{ng}*	摒 *p'hai^{ng}*	撐 *t'hai^{ng}*
32 褌 *K,wui^{ng}*	軁 *nooi^{ng}*	方 *pooi^{ng}*	褌 *kwui^{ng}*	勸 *k'hwui^{ng}*	轉 *tooi^{ng}*	鐇 *p'hooi^{ng}*	傳 *t'hooi^{ng}*
33 茄 *K,ëo*	蜊 *lëó*	標 *pëo*	茄 *këo*	徼 *k'hëò*	釣 *tëò*	票 *p'hëò*	挑 *t'hëo*
34 梔 *K,ee^{ng}*	拈 *nee^{ng}*	邊 *pee^{ng}*	梔 *kee^{ng}*	鉗 *k'heè^{ng}*	甜 *tee^{ng}*	篇 *p'hee^{ng}*	天 *t'hee^{ng}*

KËÈN DIALECT, WITH THE METHOD OF JOINING THEM.

曾 Ch-eng	入 J-ip	時 S-ê	英 E-ng	門 B-ûn	語 G-é	出 Ch-hut	喜 H-[illegible]
尊 chun	潤 jūn	孫 sun	温 wun	門 bûn	○ gwun	春 ch'hun	分 hw[illegible]
亶 chëen	然 jëên	先 süen	烟 yëen	免 bëén	研 gëên	千 ch'hëen	軒 hi[illegible]
斟 chim	王 jîm	心 sim	音 yim	○ bim	吟 gîm	深 ch'him	欣 hi[illegible]
錐 chuy	葰 jwûy	雖 suy	威 wuy	溦 bwuy	危 gwuy	推 ch'huy	飛 hwu[illegible]
查 chay	○ jay	沙 say	亞 ay	馬 *báy*	牙 gây	差 ch'hay	蝦 hay
繒 chan	○ jan	山 san	安 an	曼 bân	言 gân	餐 ch'han	頇 h[illegible]
宗 chong	○ jong	喪 song	翁 ong	摸 *bong*	昂 gông	倉 ch'hong	風 h[illegible]
揣 chwae	○ jwae	○ swae	歪 wae	○ bwae	㕦 gwae	○ ch'hwae	蠣 hw[illegible]
曾 cheng	仍 jêng	生 seng	英 eng	明 bêng	迎 gêng	清 ch'heng	兄 he[illegible]
專 chwan	軟 jwán	宣 swan	冤 wan	瞞 bwân	元 gwân	川 ch'hwan	歡 hwa[illegible]
䣜 choe	○ joe	穌 soe	烏 oe	謨 boê	吾 goê	粗 ch'hoe	呼 h[illegible]
焦 cheaou	爪 jeáou	消 seaou	夭 yaou	苗 beâou	堯 ge[illegible]ou	鍬 ch'heaou	囂 h[illegible]
儕 chey	○ jey	西 sey	挨 *ey*	迷 be[illegible]y	倪 g[illegible]y	妻 ch'hey	溪 [illegible]
終 chëung	娀 jëûng	嵩 sëung	雍 yung	○ bëung	卬 g[illegible]ung	充 ch'hëun[illegible]	凶 [illegible]
侳 cho	○ jo	搔 so	阿 o	無 *bô*	莪 go	磋 ch'ho	訶 [illegible]
哉 chae	○ jae	獅 sae	哀 ae	埋 baê	涯 gaê	猜 ch'hae	參 [illegible]
真 chin	人 jîn	身 sin	因 yin	民 bîn	銀 gîn	親 ch'hin	興 [illegible]
章 chëang	壤 jëáng	相 söang	央 yang	○ bëang	研 gëang	昌 ch'hëang	香 [illegible]
簪 cham	○ jam	三 sam	庵 am	餡 bám	儼 [illegible]am	參 ch'ham	[illegible]
紙 *chwá*	若 *jwā*	搓 swa	話 *wā*	磨 *bwâ*	外 *gwā*	門 ch'hwa	咧 [illegible]
椶 *chang*	○ jang	雙 *sang*	翁 *ang*	龐 bâng	仰 g[illegible]ng	葱 *ch'hang*	烘 [illegible]
占 chëem	染 jëêm	纖 sëem	奄 yëem	○ beem	嚴 g[illegible]em	僉 ch[illegible]m	欣 [illegible]
糟 *chaou*	○ jaou	捎 saou	歐 aou	卯 baôu	爻 *gaou*	鈔 ch'h[illegible]ou	哮 [illegible]
遮 chëa	遮 *jëa*	賒 sëa	也 yëá	乜 bëá	蜈 *gëâ*	車 *ch'hia*	靴 [illegible]
罪 chōëy	綏 jōêy	衰 söey	喂 öey	尾 *böëy*	外 göëy	吹 *ch'h[illegible]y*	灰 h[illegible]
蹔 *ch^{n}á*	○ *j^{n}a*	衫 *s^{n}a*	㘝 ^{n}á	馬 má	○ g^{n}a	○ ch'^{n}a	○ [illegible]
朱 choo	字 joō	思 soo	污 oo	無 boô	牛 *goô*	雌 ch'hoo	夫 [illegible]
查 *cha*	○ ja	些 sa	啞 a	羓 *ba*	髿 ga	叉 ch'ha	㗇 h[illegible]
之 che	乳 jé	施 se	伊 e	迷 *be*	嗅 ge	雌 ch'he	希 h[illegible]
舟 chew	蹂 jew	修 sew	憂 yew	繆 bêw	嶤 gëw	秋 ch'hew	休 h[illegible]
爭 *chai^{ng}*	○ *jai^{ng}*	生 *sai^{ng}*	嬰 *ai^{ng}*	槭 *mai^{ng}*	䛂 *gnay*	星 *ch'hai^{ng}*	哮 *h*[illegible]
磚 *chui^{ng}*	○ *jui^{ng}*	孫 *swui^{ng}*	捐 *wui^{ng}*	糜 *mooi^{ng}*	○ *gnui^{ng}*	川 *ch'hui^{ng}*	荒 *h*[illegible]
蕉 *chëo*	尿 *jëō*	燒 *sëo*	腰 *yëo*	描 *bëô*	蟯 *gëô*	鵲 *ch'hëo*	喝 h[illegible]
淵 *chee^{ng}*	爾 jee^{ng}	兹 *see^{ng}*	䨶 ee^{ng}	彌 *mee^{ng}*	○ *gnee^{ng}*	鮮 *ch'hee^{ng}*	哼 *he*[illegible]

n

A TABLE OF THE INITIALS AND FINALS OF THE HOK-

FINALS.	柳 L-éw	邊 P-ëen	求 K-êw	去 K'h-è	地 T-ēy	頗 P'h-ó	他 T'h-^{n}a
35 薑 *K,ëo*^{ng}	两 *nëó*^{ng}	○ pëo^{ng}	薑 *këo*^{ng}	腔 *k'hëo*^{ng}	張 *tëo*^{ng}	○ *p'hëo*^{ng}	○ t'hëo^{ng}
36 驚 *K,ë*^{n}*a*	領 *në*^{n}*á*	兵 *pë*^{n}*a*	驚 *kë*^{n}*a*	慶 *k'hë*^{n}*à*	朾 *të*^{n}*a*	硑 *p'hë*^{n}*a*	聽 *t'hë*^{n}*a*
37 官 *K,w*^{n}*a*	爛 *nw*^{n}*ā*	般 *pw*^{n}*a*	官 *kw*^{n}*a*	寬 *k'hw*^{n}*a*	單 *tw*^{n}*a*	潘 *p'hw*^{n}*a*	歎 *t'hw*^{n}*a*
38 鋼 *K,e*^{ng}	郎 *né*^{ng}	榜 *pé*^{ng}	鋼 *ke*^{ng}	康 *k'he*^{ng}	當 *te*^{ng}	○ *p'he*^{ng}	湯 *t'he*^{ng}
39 伽 *K,ay*	詉 *lây*	○ *pay*	伽 *kay*	伽 k'hay	㚖 tay	○ p'hay	胎 *t'hay*
40 間 *K,ae*^{ng}	乃 naé	○ pae^{ng}	間 *kae*^{ng}	嗙 k'hae^{ng}	○ *tae*^{ng}	夕 *p'haé*^{ng}	○ t'hae^{ng}
41 姑 *K,*^{n}*oe*	奴 noê	○ p^{n}oe	姑 *k*^{n}*oe*	○ k'h^{n}oe	○ t^{n}oe	○ p'h^{n}oe	○ t'h^{n}oe
42 姆 *U*^{m}	○ nu^{m}	○ pu^{m}	○ *ku*^{m}	○ k'hu^{m}	○ tu^{m}	○ p'hu^{m}	○ t'hu^{m}
43 光 *K,wang*	○ lwang	○ pwang	光 *kwang*	○ k'hwang	○ twang	○ p'hwang	○ t'hwang
44 閂 K,wae^{ng}	○ nwae^{ng}	○ pwae^{ng}	閂 kwae^{ng}	○ k'hwae^{ng}	○ twae^{ng}	○ p'hwae^{ng}	○ t'hwae^{ng}
45 糜 *M,öey*	○ nöey	○ p^{n}öey	○ *k*^{n}*öey*	○ k'h^{n}öey	○ t^{n}öey	○ p'h^{n}öey	○ t'h^{n}öey
46 嘄 K,^{n}eaou	猫 *neaou*	○ p^{n}eaou	嘄 k^{n}eaou	○ k'h^{n}eaou	○ t^{n}eaou	○ p'h^{n}eaou	○ t'h^{n}eaou
47 箴 *C,hom*	○ lom	○ pom	○ kom	嗛 k'hom	丼 *tôm*	○ p'hom	○ t'hom
48 爻 *G,naôu*	撓 naôu	○ p^{n}aou	○ k^{n}aou	○ k'h^{n}aou	○ t^{n}aou	○ p'h^{n}aou	○ t'h^{n}aou
49 扛 *K,*^{n}*o*	娜 nó	○ p^{n}o	扛 *k*^{n}*o*	○ k'h^{n}o	○ t^{n}o	○ p'h^{n}o	○ t'h^{n}o
50 牛 *G,néw*	肘 néw	○ p^{n}ew	○ k^{n}ew	○ k'h^{n}ew	○ t^{n}ew	○ p'h^{n}ew	○ t'h^{n}ew

ON THE TONES.

THE paucity of words, or of orthographical variations in the Chinese language, has rendered a system of tones necessary. The language spoken at court, (commonly called the *mandarin* dialect,) contains four hundred and eleven different monosyllables, each of which is increased by the application of four tones;* the Hok-këèn comprises more than double that number, which are severally varied by almost double the number of tones. The four tones of the court dialect are the 平 Pêng, 上 Söäng, 去 K'hè, and 入 Jip, or the 'even,' 'high,'

* The following verse, taken from the Chinese Imperial Dictionary, will serve to explain the powers of these tones:

平聲平道莫低昂 Pêng seng pêng tō, bók te gâng;
上聲高呼猛烈強 Söäng seng ko hoe, béng lëét këâng;
去聲分明哀遠道 K'hè seng hwun bêng, ae wán tō;
入聲短促急收藏 Jip seng twán chëuk, kip sew chông.

KËÈN DIALECT, WITH THE METHOD OF JOINING THEM.

曾 Ch-eng	入 J-ip.	時 S-ê	英 E-ng	門 B-ûn	語 G-é	出 Ch-hut	喜 H-é
章 *chëo*^{ng}	○ jëo^{ng}	相 *sëo*^{ng}	鴦 *yëo*^{ng}	○ mëo^{ng}	○ gnëo^{ng}	菖 *ch'hëo*^{ng}	香 *hëo*^{ng}
正 *chë*^{n}*a*	○ jëna	聲 *së*^{n}*a*	纓 *yë*^{n}*á*	名 *më*^{n}*â*	迎 *gë*^{n}*â*	䗁 ch'hë^{n}a	兄 *hë*^{n}*a*
煎 *chw*^{n}*a*	○ jw^{n}a	山 *sw*^{n}*a*	安 *w*^{n}*a*	槾 *mw*^{n}*a*	○ gw^{n}a	槾 *ch'hw*^{n}*a*	歡 *hw*^{n}*a*
莊 *che*^{ng}	○ je^{ng}	喪 *se*^{ng}	央 *e*^{ng}	○ me^{ng}	○ gne^{ng}	倉 *ch'he*^{ng}	方 *he*^{ng}
遮 chay	○ jay	閣 say	肥 ay	賣 *bāy*	个 *gây*	坐 *ch'hāy*	係 hāy
截 *chae*^{ng}	○ jae^{ng}	褯 sae^{ng}	○ ae^{ng}	買 maé	芠 gnaē	○ ch'hae^{ng}	歆 *haè*^{ng}
○ ch^{n}oe	○ j^{n}oe	○ s^{n}oe	○ ^{n}oe	○ moe	五 gnoé	○ ch'h^{n}oe	○ h^{n}oe
○ chu^{m}	○ ju^{m}	○ su^{m}	姆 *ú*^{m}	○ bu^{m}	○ gu^{m}	○ ch'hu^{m}	媒 *hû*^{m}
○ chwang	○ jwang	○ swang	嚾 wang	○ bwang	○ gwang	○ ch'hwang	鈁 *hwáng*
○ chwae^{ng}	○ jwae^{ng}	樣 *swaë*^{ng}	閂 *wae*^{ng}	○ bwae^{ng}	○ gwae^{ng}	○ ch'hwae^{ng}	○ hwae^{ng}
○ ch^{n}öey	○ j^{n}öey	○ s^{n}öey	○ ^{n}öey	糜 *möêy*	○ gnöey	○ ch'h^{n}öey	○ h^{n}öey
○ ch^{n}eaou	○ j^{n}eaou	○ s^{n}eaou	○ y^{n}eaou	○ meaou	㗊 gneàou	○ ch'h^{n}eaou	○ h^{n}eaou
箴 chom	○ jom	森 som	○ om	○ mom	○ gom	○ ch'hom	○ hom
○ ch^{n}aou	○ j^{n}aou	○ s^{n}aou	○ ^{n}aou	矛 maôu	爻 gnaôu	○ ch'h^{n}aou	欲 h^{n}aôu
○ ch^{n}o	○ j^{n}o	○ s^{n}o	○ ^{n}o	茵 *mo*	我 gnó	○ ch'h^{n}o	訶 h^{n}o
○ ch^{n}ew	○ j^{n}ew	○ s^{n}ew	○ ^{n}ew	○ mew	牛 gnêw	○ ch'h^{n}ew	○ h^{n}ew

---

'departing,' and 'entering' tones; these in Hok-këèn are multiplied by dividing them into high and low, or into a first and second series, such as:—

First series:

Sëāng pêng, 上平 *chëō*^{ng} *pat*^{ng}, the upper (or first) even tone;

Sëāng sëāng, 上上, the upper (or first) high tone; called more generally the Sëāng seng, 上聲 *sëāng së*^{n}*a*, the high tone;

Sëāng k'hè, 上去 *chëō*^{ng} *k'hè*, the upper (or first) departing tone;

Sëāng jip, 上入 *chëō*^{ng} *jip*, the upper (or first) entering tone.

"The even tone travels on a level road, neither elevated nor depressed;
"The high tone exclaims aloud, being fierce, violent, and strong;
"The departing tone is distinct and clear, gruffly traveling to a distance;
"The entering tone is short and contracted, being hastily gathered up."

Second series:

Hāy pêng, 下平 *āy paing*, the lower (or second) even tone;

Hāy sëāng 下上 *āy sëāng*, the lower (or second) high tone;

This being always like the first high tone, goes by the same name of sëāng seng, 上聲 *seang sëna*, the high tone.

Hāy k'hè, 下去 *āy k'hè*, the lower (or second) departing tone;

Hāy jip, 下入 *āy jip*, the lower (or second) entering tone.

These are the names given them by the Chinese; it is for us to describe and designate them according to our method of accentuation.

1. The Sëāng pêng, 上平 *chëōng paing*, "upper (or first) even tone," is, as the name denotes, a smooth even tone, gently flowing from the lips, without any effort, and is most commonly pronounced with a musical note. It has neither rise nor deflection, and is therefore left without any accent, being the natural unconstrained expression of the voice; thus kwun.

2. The Sëāng sëāng, 上上, "upper high tone," or simply Sëāng seng, 上聲 *sëāng sëna*, "the high tone," is, as the name imports, a high, shrill tone of the voice, pronounced with strength and rapidity, and is therefore denoted by the acute accent; thus kwún.

3. The Sëāng k'hè, 上去 *chëōng k'hè*, "upper (or first) departing tone," is a low gruff tone of the voice, which seems to come immediately from the throat, and to be lengthened out while proceeding slowly from it. The Chinese call it a departing tone, because they say it goes away like the flowing of water, never to return. It is marked with the grave accent; thus kwùn.

4. The Sëāng jip, 上入 *chëōng jip*, "upper (or first) entering tone," is a short contracted sound as if terminated abruptly, and has at the same time a rapid utterance, something like the Sëāng seng, 上聲 *sëāng sëna*: it is therefore distinguished by a short mark ˘, followed by a final h, in all those words ending in a vowel, as *ko*, *kŏh*; but in words ending with a consonant, the entering tone is marked by changing the long consonant into a corresponding abrupt one; thus words ending in *n*, take the letter *t*, as *kwun*, *kwut*; those in *ng*, take the letter *k*, as *keng*, *kek*; and those ending in *m*, take the letter *p*, as *kam*, *kap*. The Chinese consider this to be nothing more than a variation in tone, and as making no alteration in the orthography of a word; which is indeed true with respect to all those words ending in a vowel or diphthong, where the entering tones are merely abrupt terminations of the vowel sound of the other tones; as if a person about to pronounce *ko* long, should be suddenly taken with a hiccup, and stop short before the *o* was well out of his mouth, thus forming a rapid *kŏ* or *kŏh* instead of *ko*: so also with respect to those words ending in the consonants *n*, *ng*, and *m*; by considering the organic formation of those letters, we shall find, that "the entering sound" is nothing more than an abrupt termination of them. Thus, the final *n* is formed by pressing the tip of the tongue against the gums of the upper teeth, while a person breathes through the nose, with his mouth open; now the final *t* is produced by a similar process, with the exception of the nasal breathing. So also, the final *ng* is formed by pressing the middle of the tongue to the roof of the mouth near the throat, while the voice passes principally through the nose; and this, it may be observed, is precisely the case with the final *k*, without the nasal emission. Further, the final *m* is produced by closing the lips till the breath is collected, and then letting the voice issue by the

nose: the like process is necessary in order to enunciate the final *p*, except that the sound terminates abruptly on closing the lips.

5. The Hāy pêng, 下平 *āy pa*^{ng}, "lower (or second) even tone," is an inflected sound, beginning low and ending high, being dwelt upon a moment during the enunciation, and then turned to another tone before coming to a close.. It may be exemplified by the drawling tone given to some words when spoken ironically, or to the word "*indeed!*" when used as an exclamation. It should have been marked by a rising circumflex, thus *kwǔn;* but that being rarely met with in printing offices, it has, for the sake of convenience, been designated by the falling circumflex; thus kwûn.

6. The Hāy sëāng, 下上, "lower (or second) high tone," is precisely the same as the Sëāng sëāng, 上上, "upper (or first) high tone;" and is therefore also generally designated the Sëāng seng, 上聲 *sëāng sē*^{n}*a*, "high tone;" which see.

7. The Hāy k'hè, 下去 *āy k'hè*, "lower (or second) departing tone," is a low, protracted, monotonous sound, something like the "upper (or first) departing tone," but not so gruff and guttural; it is therefore marked by a horizontal line, as a long sound; thus kwūn.

8. The Hāy jip, 下入 *āy jip*, "lower (or second) entering tone," is a combination of two tones, having an abrupt sound, like the "upper entering tone," with the addition of an inflected intonation of the vowel, similar to that just described under the "lower (or second) even tone." For this tone, as far as it regards the abrupt termination of the words, the same letters and marks are employed as notified under the "upper entering tone," but the inflected intonation is marked by a perpendicular stroke either in the middle of the short mark over the vowel, or when followed by an abrupt consonant over the vowel alone; thus kăh, kát, káp, kwát.

The power of these intonations may be seen at one view, together with the manner of their proceeding from the mouth, and the use of the signs employed, by the following eight figures.

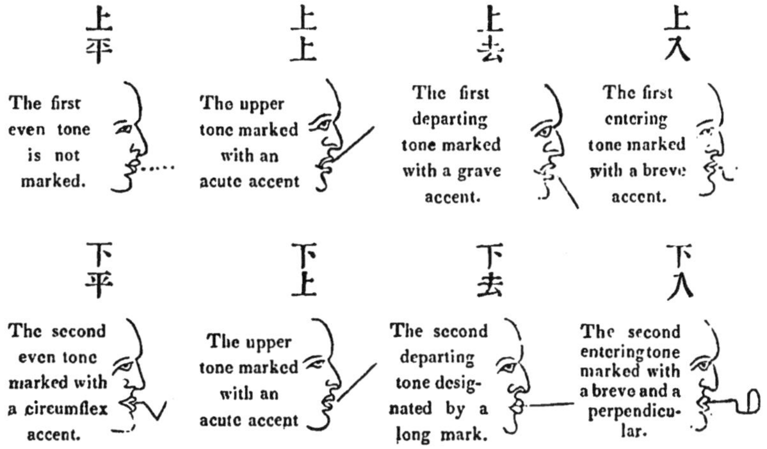

9

None of these accents have anything to do with stress or emphasis, always retaining their peculiar force, whether at the beginning or end of a sentence — when interrogating or affirming — in angry or in soothing words— when speaking aloud, or when whispering: they remain ever the same.

The poorer class of people and young children, who are unacquainted with letters, and know not the names of the accents, or the rules by which the language is governed, are yet most exact in their accentuation of Chinese words; and generally speaking, the more ignorant they are of letters, and the methods of defining speech, the more particular they are in distinguishing the accents. In order to converse intelligibly with the common people in the Hok-këèn dialect, it is indispensably necessary to attend to the accentuation, particularly as a slight variation of accent not only makes a difference in the grammatical inflection of words, but also quite alters their sense, and makes them mean very different things. This may be seen from the following short sentences, which are put together merely to show the necessity of distinguishing the accent, in words which have precisely the same orthography.

Sek yéw ló jîn,	昔有老人	*chá woō laōu lâng,*
Bēng pók chêng hoē,	命蒲情厚	*më^{n}ā pǒh, chéng kaōu;*
Yëúk maé t'hëet koe,	欲買鐵鈎	*aè báy t'heĕh kaou,*
Hëêm ehëên boô koè,	嫌錢無够	*hëêm cheé^{ng} bô kaòu;*
Höêy k'han oe koé,	回牽烏狗	*tooî^{ng} k'han oe kaóu,*
Gē chëak pék hoê,	遇着白猴	*toó tëŏh păyh kaôu;*
Koé hwūy hoê hoé,	狗吠猴吼	*kaóu pwūy kaôu haóu:*
Put te,	不知	*ū^{m} chae,*
Sē koé wùy hoê,	是狗畏猴	*sē kaóu kë^{n}a kaôu,*
Hék hoê wùy koé,	或猴畏狗	*á sē kaóu kë^{n}a kaóu.*

"Formerly there was an old man,
"Whose lot was poor, but his disposition liberal;
"And he desired to purchase an iron hook,
"But found that his money was not sufficient;
"Returning, he led after him a black dog,
"And accidentally met a white monkey;
"The dog barked, and the monkey screamed:
"So that it could not be known,
"Whether the dog was afraid of the monkey,
"Or the monkey afraid of the dog."

In these few lines there are five words written with the same letters — *kaou* — which, according to the common system of orthography, would all be pronounced in the same way; but in tone as well as in sense, they severally differ from one another; thus, there are:

Kaou, in the first even tone, meaning 'a hook;'
Kaóu, in the high tone, translated 'a dog;'
Kaòu, in the first departing tone, denoting 'sufficient;'
Kaôu, in the second even tone, signifying 'a monkey;'
Kaōu, in the second departing tone, meaning 'liberal.'

These, without a particular attention to the variation of the tones, could not be distinguished, and without being distinguished, such a sentence, and very many like it, would not be understood. Another sentence is adduced to show how all the eight tones may sometimes occur in connection, each requiring to be very accurately discriminated in order to have the speaker intelligible.

Yéw tek che kay,	有德之家	*woō tek ây kay,*	"A family possessing virtue,
Chin jê boô káy,	眞而無假	*chin yĕá bô káy,*	"True, and without deceit,
Soo tē taē kày,	斯値大價	*chĕy tàt twā kày,*	"This is of great price,
K'hwaè e sim kek,	快於心膈	*k'hwaè tē sim kăyh;*	"And grateful to the heart;
Hwān chöēy taè kây,	犯罪帶枷	*hwān chöēy gĕâ kây,*	"But criminals wearing the wooden collar,
Yit bē yaòu káy,	一味要假	*chit bē böĕyh káy,*	"Who are altogether deceitful,
Soò bîn che hāy,	四民之下	*sè bín ây kāy,*	"Are the lowest dregs of the people,
T'hëen jîn kae gèk,	天人皆逆	*t'heeng lâng kae kăyh,*	"Alike opposed by Providence and men."

Here the closing words of each line are expressed by the same letters, (with the addition of a final *h* in the 4th, and 8th lines, to denote the abrupt termination of the sound,) but by the various inflections they produce seven different tones: as

Kay, the first even tone, denoting 'a family;'
Káy, the upper tone, translated 'deceitful;'
Kày, the first departing tone, meaning 'a price;'
Kăyh, the first entering tone, which means 'the breast;'
Kây, the second even tone, denoting a 'cangue, or wooden collar;'
Kāy, the second departing tone, signifying 'low;'
Kâyh, the second entering tone, which means 'to oppose.'

Now without a due attention to the tones, a person in uttering the above sentence, would be likely to call 'a family,' a 'wooden collar;'—to confound 'price' with 'low,' and 'deceitful;'—or to use the substantive 'breast' in place of the verb 'to oppose;' which would render mutual conversation difficult, and the best ideas frequently unintelligible.

A TABLE,

Exhibiting the fifty Joō boé, 字母 *jē boé*, as divided into eight Tones.

The reading of these characters with a Chinese teacher would enable the student soon to distinguish between them.

	1	2	3	4	5	6	7	8	9	10
上平	君 kwun	堅 këen	金 kim	規 kwuy	嘉 kay	干 kan	公 kong	乖 kwae	經 keng	觀 kwan
上声	滾 kwún	蹇 këén	錦 kím	鬼 kwúy	假 káy	柬 kán	廣 kóng	拐 kwaé	景 kéng	琯 kwán
上去	棍 kwùn	見 këèn	禁 kìm	季 kwùy	嫁 kày	澗 kàn	貢 kòng	怪 kwaè	敬 kèng	貫 kwàn
上入	骨 kwut	結 këet	急 kip	○ —	骼 kăyh	葛 kat	國 kok	○ —	格 kek	决 kwat
下平	群 kwûn	○ këên	○ kîm	葵 kwûy	枷 kây	○ kân	狂 kông	○ kwaê	煢 kêng	權 kwân
下声	滾 kwún	蹇 këén	錦 kím	鬼 kwúy	假 káy	柬 kán	廣 kóng	拐 kwaé	景 kéng	琯 kwán
下去	郡 kwūn	健 këēn	㦗 kīm	櫃 kwūy	下 *kāy*	○ kān	狅 kōng	○ kwaē	梗 kēng	倦 kwān
下入	滑 kwút	傑 këét	及 kíp	○ —	逆 *kăyh*	○ kát	咯 kók	○ —	極 kék	橜 kwát

	11	12	13	14	15	16	17	18	19	20
上平	沽 koe	嬌 keaou	稽 key	恭 këung	高 ko	皆 kae	巾 kin	姜 këang	甘 kam	瓜 kwa
上声	古 koé	皎 keáou	改 *kéy*	拱 këúng	果 kó	改 kaé	謹 kín	襁 këáng	敢 kám	○ kwá
上去	固 koè	叫 keàou	計 kèy	供 këùng	過 kò	介 kaè	艮 kìn	○ këàng	鑑 kàm	卦 kwà
上入	○ —	勪 *keaŏuh*	莢 *kĕyh*	菊 këuk	閣 *kŏh*	○ —	吉 kit	脚 këak	鴿 kap	啯 kwăh
下平	糊 *koê*	橋 keâou	鮭 kêy	窮 këûng	翗 kô	○ kaê	○ kîn	強 këâng	銜 *kâm*	○ kwâ
下声	古 koé	皎 keáou	改 *kéy*	拱 këúng	果 kó	改 kaé	謹 kín	襁 këáng	敢 kám	○ kwá
下去	怙 koē	轎 keāou	易 *kēy*	共 këūng	膏 kō	○ kaē	近 kīn	倞 këāng	艦 *kām*	○ kwā
下入	○ —	噭 *keaŏuh*	○ *kĕyh*	局 këúk	○ *kŏh*	○ —	糭 *kit*	矍 këák	○ káp	○ kwăh

	21	22	23	24	25	26	27	28	29	30
上平	江 kang	兼 këem	交 kaou	迦 këa	檜 köey	監 k^n*a*	艍 koo	膠 *ka*	居 ke	丩 kew
上声	港 káng	檢 këém	狡 kaóu	○ këá	粿 *köéy*	敢 k^n*á*	韭 *koó*	絞 *ká*	已 ké	久 kéw
上去	降 kàng	劍 këèm	教 kaòu	寄 *këà*	檜 köèy	酵 k^n*à*	句 koò	教 *kà*	既 kè	救 kèw
上入	角 kak	夾 këep	餃 *kaŏuh*	○ këăh	郭 *köĕyh*	○ —	欱 *koŏh*	甲 *kăh*	築 *kĕĕh*	○ —
下平	○ kâng	鹹 *këêm*	候 *kaôu*	伽 këâ	葵 *köêy*	擥 k^n*â*	錁 koô	○ kâ	期 kê	求 kêw
下声	港 káng	檢 këém	狡 kaóu	○ këá	粿 *köéy*	敢 k^n*á*	韭 *koó*	絞 *ká*	已 ké	久 kéw
下去	共 *kāng*	鐱 këēm	厚 *kaōu*	崎 *këā*	跪 *köēy*	○ k^n*ā*	舅 *koō*	齩 *kā*	具 kē	舊 kēw
下入	磔 *kák*	○ *këép*	○ *kaŏuh*	屐 *këăh*	饋 *köĕyh*	○ —	○ koŏh	○ *kăh*	○ *kĕĕh*	○ —

A TABLE, &c.—Continued.

	31	32	33	34	35	36	37	38	39	40
上平	更 kai^{ng}	褌 kwui^{ng}	茄 këo	梔 kee^{ng}	薑 këo^{ng}	驚 kë^{n}a	官 kw^{n}a	鋼 ke^{ng}	伽 kay	間 kae^{ng}
上聲	耞 kaí^{ng}	捲 kwuí^{ng}	○ këó	○ keé^{ng}	○ —	子 kë^{n}á	寡 kw^{n}á	○ ké^{ng}	○ —	醶 kaé^{ng}
上去	徑 kaì^{ng}	卷 kwuì^{ng}	叫 këò	見 keè^{ng}	○ —	鏡 kë^{n}à	觀 kw^{n}à	槓 kè^{ng}	○ --	○ —
上入	○ —	○ —	脚 këŏh	○ —	○ —	○ —	○ —	○ —	莢 kăyh	○ —
下平	○ kaî^{ng}	○ —	茄 këô	墘 keê^{ng}	强 këô^{ng}	行 kë^{n}â	寒 kw^{n}â	○ —	瘸 kây	○ —
上聲	耞 kaí^{ng}	捲 kwuí^{ng}	○ —	○ —	○ —	子 kë^{n}á	寡 kw^{n}á	○ —	○ —	醶 kaé^{ng}
下去	○ kaī^{ng}	○ —	轎 këō	○ —	[illegible] këō^{ng}	件 kë^{n}ā	汗 kw^{n}ā	○ —	○ —	○ —
下入	○ —	○ —	○ —	○ —	○ —	○ —	○ —	○ —	○ —	○ —

	41	42	43	44	45	46	47	48	49	50
上平	姑 k^{n}oe	姆 u^{m}	光 kwang	閂 kwae^{ng}	糜 möey	嘄 k^{n}eaou	筬 chom	爻 gnaou	扛 k^{n}o	牛 gnew
上去	○ —	○ —	○ —	○ —	○ —	○ —	譖 chòm	○ —	○ —	○
下平	○ —	○ —	○ —	○ —	○ —	○ —	○ —	○ -	○ —	牛 gnew
下入	○ —	○ —	咉 kwăk	○ —	○ —	○ —	○ —	○ —	○ —	○

The fifty finals multiplied by the fifteen initials would produce 750 sounds; these diversified by the seven tones, amount to 5250. About half of theso have no characters attached to them, and there are only 2500 distinct enunciations actually in use among the Hok-këèn people. The characters to which these are applied in the following Dictionary amount to 12,000; on the average about five characters to each enunciation. The distribution, however, is very irregular; some enunciations having only one character, and others including many; one simple enunciation (kê,) having fifty-six characters applied to it. In Morrison's alphabetical Dictionary, two hundred and forty-seven characters appear under the same letters.

ON THE DIFFERENCE BETWEEN THE COLLOQUIAL AND READING DIALECTS.

In the Hok-këèn dialect there are two distinct forms of speech, called the Reading and Colloquial (or vulgar). These differ from one another, not only in the more compact or diffuse construction of the sentences, but even in the sounds of many of the words. The Chinese language admitting of a very contracted as well as of a more dilated style, and the books being generally composed in the former, they require

P

frequently to be commented on, and paraphrased in order to be readily understood. This has given rise to the distinction between the reading and vulgar forms of speech. This distinction prevails to some extent in the mandarin tongue; in which, after reading over a passage, it is generally thought necessary to dilate upon it, for the sake of elucidation and explanation. But in the Hok-keĕn dialect this proceeds to an unusual extent; the explanation of any literary composition being not only much extended and varied, but the words themselves frequently differing in their termination and sometimes in their whole construction. So great is the distinction between these two forms of speech, that a person well acquainted with the reading dialect, would not be able to understand a conversation in the vulgar tongue; nor could a person fully proficient in the latter be able to make out the meaning of any passage recited from a book not previously familiar to him. In the following pages the colloquial is distinguished from the reading dialect by being put in italics, and the spoken sound of particular characters is denoted by the word *Vulg.* being prefixed. The examples hereafter adduced will be sufficient to show how the sentences are extended and varied, but the alterations in particular words will need a more distinct notice.

The variations between the reading and colloquial may be generally referred to two heads; namely, *regular* and *irregular*.

1. The *regular* variations consist in changes in the termination, and may be arranged according to the order of the finals: though it must be remembered that but a *few* of the characters in the reading dialect are changed according to this system, and those only which are of every day occurrence.

Characters falling under the 1st final kwun form *kwui*^{ng} in the colloquial; as kwun, *kwui*^{ng}; tun, *tooi*^{ng}; sun, *swui*^{ng}; wun, *wui*^{ng}; bun, *mooi*^{ng}; ch'hun, *ch'hui*^{ng}; hwun, *hwui*^{ng}.

Words under the 2d final këen form *kee*^{ng} in the colloquial; as lëen, *nee*^{ng}; pëen, *pee*^{ng}; këen, *kee*^{ng}; tëen, *tee*^{ng}; t'hëen, *t'hee*^{ng}; p'hëen, *p'hee*^{ng}; chëen, *chee*^{ng}; sëen, *see*^{ng}; bëen, *mee*^{ng}; ch'hëen, *ch'hee*^{ng}; hëen, *hee*^{ng}. Words in the entering tone këet form *keĕh* in the colloquial; as lëet, *leĕh*; pëet, *peĕh*; tëet, *teĕh*; sëet, *seĕh*; bëet, *beĕh*; &c.

Words under the 3d and 4th finals kim and kwuy are irregular in their formation of the colloquial.

Words under the 5th final kay are also irregular, except in the first and second entering tones, which are generally vulgarisms, formed from the entering tone of the 9th final; which see.

Words under the 6th final kan form *kw*^{n}*a* in the colloquial; as lan, *nw*^{n}*a*; kan, *kw*^{n}*a*; k'han, *k'hw*^{n}*a*; tan, *tw*^{n}*a*; t'han, *t'hw*^{n}*a*; chan, *chw*^{n}*a*; san, *sw*^{n}*a*; an, *w*^{n}*a*; ban, *mw*^{n}*a*; han, *hw*^{n}*a*.

Words under the 7th final kong form *kang* and *keng* in the colloquial; as:

long, { *lang* / *ne*^{ng} } pong, { *pang* / *pe*^{ng} } kong, { *kang* / *ke*^{ng} } k'hong, { *k'hang* / *k'he*^{ng} } tong, { *tang* / *te*^{ng} } t'hong, { *t'hang* / *t'he*^{ng} }

chong, { *chang* / *che*^{ng} } song, { *sang* / *se*^{ng} } ong, { *ang* / *e*^{ng} } bong, - - *bang*; ch'hong, { *ch'hang* / *ch'he*^{ng} } hong, { *hang* / *he*^{ng} }

Words in the entering tone kok form *kŏh* in the colloquial; as lok, *lŏh*; pok, *pŏh*; kok, *kŏh*; tok, *tŏh*; chok, *chŏh*; ok, *ŏh*; bok, *bŏh*; hok, *hŏh*.

Words occurring under the 8th final kwae are seldom formed into the colloquial with any degree of regularity.

Words under the 9th final keng form *kai*^{ng} and *kë*^{n}*a* in the colloquial; as:

leng, { *nai*^{ng} / *në*^{n}*a* } peng, { *pai*^{ng} / *pë*^{n}*a* } keng, { *kai*^{ng} / *kë*^{n}*a* } k'heng, { *k'hai*^{ng} / *k'hë*^{n}*a* } teng, { *tai*^{ng} / *të*^{n}*a* } p'heng, { *p'hai*^{ng} / *p'hë*^{n}*a* } eng, { *ai*^{ng} / *yë*^{n}*a* }

t'heng, { *t'hai*^{ng} / *t'hë*^{n}*a* } cheng, { *chai*^{ng} / *chë*^{n}*a* } seng, { *sai*^{ng} / *së*^{n}*a* } ch'heng, { *ch'hai*^{ng} / *ch'hë*^{n}*a* } beng, - - *më*^{n}*a;* heng, { *hai*^{ng} / *hë*^{n}*a* }

Words under this final, in the entering tone kek, form *kăyh* in the colloquial; as lek, *láyh;* pek, *păyh;* kek, *kăyh;* k'hek, *k'hăyh;* t'hek, *t'háyh;* chek, *chăyh;* ek, *áyh;* bek, *băyh;* ch'hek, *ch'hăyh;* hek, *hăyh.*

Words under the 10th final kwan form *kw*^{n}*a* and *kwui*^{ng} in the colloquial; as:

pwan, - *pw*^{n}*a;* kwan, { *kw*^{n}*a* / *kwui*^{ng} } k'hwan, { *k'hw*^{n}*a* / *k'hwui*^{ng} } twan, - *tooi*^{ng}*;* p'hwan, - *p'hwui*^{ng}*;* chwan, { *chw*^{n}*a* / *chwui*^{ng} }

swan, - - *swui*^{ng}*;* wan, { *w*^{n}*a* / *wui*^{ng} } bwan { *mw*^{n}*a* / *mooi*^{ng} } ch'hwan, { *ch'hw*^{n}*a* / *ch'hwui*^{ng} } hwan, { *hw*^{n}*a* / *hwui*^{ng} }

Sometimes words under this final, in the entering tone kwat, form *köĕyh* in the colloquial; as, kwat, *köĕyh;* k'hwat, *k'höĕyh;* swat, *söĕyh;* ch'hwat, *ch'höĕyh;* gwat, *göĕyh.*

Words under the 11th final koe form *kaou* in the colloquial; as loe, *laou;* koe, *kaou;* toe, *taou;* t'hoe, *t'haou;* choe, *chaou;* soe, *saou;* oe, *aou.*

Words under tho 12th final keaou form *këo* in the colloquial; as leaou, *lëo;* peaou, *pëo;* keaou, *këo;* teaou, *tëo;* p'heaou, *p'hëo;* cheaou, *chëo;* jeaou, *jëo;* seaou, *sëo;* yaou, *yëo;* beaou, *bëo;* geaou, *gëo;* ch'heaou, *ch'hëo.*

Words under the 13th final key seldom change into the colloquial; but sometimes colloquial words are found under this final derived principally from the 16th final kae; which see.

Words under the 14th final këung form *keng* in the colloquial; as lëung, *leng;* këung, *keng;* tëung, *teng;* chëung, *cheng;* jëung, *jeng;* yung, *eng;* ch'hëung, *ch'heng;* hëung, *heng.* Sometimes the entering tone of this final këuk forms *kek;* as lëuk, *lek;* këuk, *kek;* k'hëuk, *k'hek;* tëuk, *tek;* chëuk, *chek;* jëuk, *jek;* sëuk, *sek;* yëuk, *ek;* gëuk, *gek.*

Words under the 15th final ko form *köey, kaou,* and *kwa* in the colloquial; as:

lo, { *laou* / *lwa* } cho, - - *chaou;* ko, { *köey* / *kwa* } p'ho, { *p'höey* / *p'hwa* } so, { *söey* / *saou* / *swa* } o, *öey;* ch'ho, *ch'haou;* mo, *bwa;* gno, *gwa;* ho, *höey.*

Words under the 16th final kae sometimes form *key,* and sometimes *kwa,* in the colloquial; as lae, *lwa;* kae, *key* and *kwa;* tae, *twa;* t'hae, *t'hwa;* ch'hae, *ch'hwa;* mae, *bey;* hae, *hey.*

Words under the 17th final kin seldom change into the colloquial with any degree of regularity.

Words under the 18th final këang form *këo*^{ng} in the colloquial; as lëang, *nëo*^{ng}*;* këang, *këo*^{ng}*;* tëang, *tëo*^{ng}*;* chëang, *chëo*^{ng}*;* sëang, *sëo*^{ng}*;* yang, *yëo*^{ng}*;* ch'hëang, *ch'hëo*^{ng}*;* hëang, *hëo*^{ng}*.*

Words occurring under the 19th final kam form *k*^{n}*a* in the colloquial; as, lam, *na;* kam, *k*^{n}*a;* tam, *t*^{n}*a;* sam, *s*^{n}*a.*

Words under the 20th final kwa are generally in the colloquial, formed from ko and kan; which see.

Words under the 21st final kang are principally colloquial, and are derived from kong; which see.

Words under the 22d final këem sometimes form the colloquial into *kee^ng*; as lëem, *nee^ng*; këem, *kee^ng*; k'hëem, *k'hee^ng*; tëem, *tee^ng*; t'hëem, *t'hee^ng*; but the words under this final are principally in the reading dialect,

Words under the 23d final kaou are partly colloquial, derived from ko, and koe; which see: but there are still many reading words under this final which form *ka*, in the colloquial; as laou, *la*; paou, *pa*; kaou, *ka*; k'haou, *k'ha*; p'haou, *p'ha*; chaou, *cha*; aou, *a*; haou, *ha*.

Words under the 24th final këa are principaly in the reading form, seldom changing into the colloquial with any regularity; there are also under this final a few colloquial words, formod from ke; which see. The entering sound këak is chiefly colloquial, and formed from kek; which see.

Words under the 25th final köey are principally in the reading form; but there are some colloquials formed from ko; which see: and words in the entering tone *köĕyh* are generally formed from kwat; which see.

Words under the 26th final $k^{n}a$ are partly in the reading form, and partly in the colloquial, formed from kam; which see.

Words under the 27th final koo are principally reading words, changing irregularly into the colloquial; and some colloquial words formed at random from the reading.

Words under the 28th final ka are partly in the reading form, which sometimes form into the colloquial by changing pa into *pay*; p'ha into *p'hay*: but more frequently words under this final are colloquialisms, formed from kaou; which see.

Words under the 29th final ke are principally in the reading form, but sometimes form *këa* in the colloquial; as ke, *këa*; k'he, *k'hëa*; ge, *gëa*; in the entering tone *keĕh*, there are some colloquial words formed from këet; which see.

Words under the 30th final kew are principally in the reading form, without any particular changes into the colloquial.

Words under the 31st final *kai^ng* are all colloquial, formed from keng; which see.

Words under the 32d final *kwui^ng* are also all colloquial, formed principally from kwun and kwan; which see.

Words under the 33d final *këo* are colloquial, formed generally from keaou; which see.

Words under the 34th final *kee^ng* are all colloquial, formed principally from këen; but sometimes also from këem; which see.

Words under the 35th final *këo^ng* are colloquial, and derived from këang; which see.

Words under the 36th final *kë^na* are generally colloquial, derived from keng; which see.

Words under the 37th final *kw^na* are principally colloquial, derived from kan and kwan; which see.

Words under the 38th final *ke^ng* are colloquial, derived mostly from kong; which see.

Words under the 39th final kay are sometimes colloquial, formed from kae, and kwuy.

Words occurring under the 40th to the 50th finals are few and irregular.

Thus, taking the summary of the above, the regular formations from the reading dialect into the colloquial are generally as follows:

kwun	forms	*kwui^{ng}*	kok	forms	*kŏh*	koe	forms	*kaou*	kae	forms	*kwa* / *kay*
këen	"	*kee^{ng}*	keng	"	*kai^{ng}* / *kë^{n}a*	kwat	"	*köĕyh*	këang	"	*këo^{ng}*
këet	"	*keĕh*	kek	"	*kăyh*	keaou	"	*këo*	kam	"	*k^{n}a*
kan	"	*kw^{n}a*	kwan	"	*kw^{n}a* / *kwui^{ng}*	këung	"	*keng*	këem	"	*kee^{ng}*
kong	"	*kang* / *ke^{ng}*				ko	"	*köey* / *kwa* / *kaou*	kaou	"	*ka*
									këuk	"	*kek*

There are some variations from the reading into the colloquial made by changing the initial; which may be arranged according to the order of the initials; thus,

Under the	first	initial,	noe becomes *loe;* and neaou becomes *cheaou.*		
Under the	third	initial,	kim	"	*gim.*
Under the	seventh	initial,	t'huy	"	*ch'huy.*
Under the	eighth	initial,	chëa	"	*jëa.*
Under the	ninth	initial,	jé	"	*lé;* jun, *lun;* jé, *hē.*
Under the	tenth	initial,	sae	"	*t'hae;* sun, *chun;* sim, *chim;* suy, *chuy;* sëuk, *chëuk;* sew, *chëw;* sè, *ch'hè.*
Under the	thirteenth	initial,	gê	"	*hê.*
Under the	fourteenth	initial,	ch'he	"	*k'he.*
Under the	fifteenth	initial,	hāy	"	*āy;* hoê, *oé;* hâm, *âm.*
			hwun	"	*pun;* hwuy, *pwuy;* hoô, *poô,*
			hay	"	*kay;* hoe, *koe;* hok, *kŏh.*
			hëuk	"	*t'hëuk.*

II. The *irregular* variations include a change of both initial and final; and sometimes give a word in the colloquial quite different from the reading; as:

Sin, 伸 *ch'hun.*	Choē, 助 *chān.*	Sëûng, 松 *ch'hêng.*	Bút, 物 *mei^{ng}h.*
Ché, 紙 *chwá.*	Lék, 力 *lát.*	Hwân, 還 *hêng.*	Gnêw, 牛 *goô.*
Soé, 瘦 *sán.*	Boê, 掼 *bong.*	Chō, 坐 *chēy.*	

Among those reading words which are totally altered in the colloquial, may be adduced the following:

Jím, 忍 *lún.*	Hé, 許 *k'hoé.*	Hák, 學 *ŏh.*	Hëên, 賢 *gaôu.*
Hoō, 父 *pāy.*	Toé, 賭 *keáou.*	Sëā, 射 *chöh.*	Hoê, 猴 *kaóu.*
Sek, 塞 *t'hat.*	Chō, 柱 *t'heāou.*	Te, 知 *chae.*	Tan, 單 *k'hëa.*
Sit, 識 *bat.*	Sëuk, 縮 *lun.*	Sat, 殺 *t'haé.*	Taê, 抬 *gëâ.*
Tëên, 田 *ch'hân.*	E', 雨 *hoē.*	Jëém, 染 *bàk.*	Wá, 瓦 *hëā.*
Bòk, 木 *ch'hâ.*	To, 多 *chēy.*	Jîn, 人 *lâng.*	Gé, 蟻 *hëā.*
Jé, 乳 *leng.*	Lêng, 能 *ēy.*	Hwaē, 壞 *k'hëep.*	Sit, 食 *chëāh.*
Hông, 虹 *k'hēng.*	Lân, 難 *ŏh.*	Tò, 到 *kaòu.*	Ná, 拏 *lëāh.*

q

Kwan,	冠	*kŏèy.*	Kan,	乾	*ta.*	Choó,	子	*kē^{n}á.*	Ok,	屋	*ch'hoŏ.*
Yaŏu,	要	*bŏĕyh.*	T^{n}á,	打	*p'hăh.*	Ok,	惡	*p'ha^{n}ĕ.*	Kēak,	脚	*k'ha.*
Sîm,	辱	*ch'hŏēy.*	Jēúk,	肉	*băh.*	Put,	不	*ū^{m}.*	Hêy,	携	*kw^{n}ā.*
Kim,	今	*t^{n}a.*	Yēā,	夜	*mai^{ng}.*	Bōêy,	媒	*hâ^{m}.*	E',	與	*hoē.*
Lîm,	林	*nâ.*	Sèk,	石	*chēŏh.*	Ko,	高	*kwân.*	Sip,	濕	*tâm.*
Yéw,	有	*woō.*	Sē,	寺	*eē^{ng}.*	Twán,	短	*têy.*	Se,	書	*ch'hăyh.*

Besides all these, there are a number of words in the colloquial, some of which are not to be met with in the following pages, and some do not appear to have any corresponding sounds in the reading dialect, being probably introduced from some foreign language, or which were indigenous to the province of Hok-kēèn before its union with the empire of China.

I. PARTICLES.

Ch'hin ch'haé,	*Any how.*	T'hēém-chaé â, K'hēém-chaé á,	*Perhaps.*
Chin chaē,	*Very.*	Lēem pee^{ng},	*Immediately.*
Chin chē^{n}â,	*Truly.*	Toó toó,	*Just now.*
Ka la koó á,	*By and bye.*	An nēy,	*Thus.*
An chw^{n}á,	*How?*	An nēy sai^{ng},	*In that way.*
Chŏ neē^{ng},	*In what way?*	S^{n}á meē^{ngh},	*What?*
Chw^{n}á kóng,	*How is it?*	S^{n}á soō,	*What's the matter?*
Hēŏ^{ng} pêng,	*On that side.*	K'hăh chāy,	*More.*
Chéy pêng,	*On this side.*	Kwúy lēep,	*A little.*
Hit lêy, Hwut lêy,	*That.*	Twā lim,	*Very much.*
Chit lêy, Chêy lêy,	*This.*	Kap,	*With, and.*
Ché taōu,	*Here.*	Tek k'hak,	*Certainly.*
Hé taōu,	*There.*	Aōu sin,	*Afterwards.*
Hwut taōu,	*In that place.*	Nā,	*If.*
Chun á,	*Just like.*	Chēā,	*Then.*
Ch'hin chēō^{ng},	*Like as.*	Lóng,	*Altogether.*
Chit pw^{n}a,	*The same.*	Lóng chóng,	*The whole.*
Kŏh yēō^{ng},	*Different.*	Tē,	*At.*
Lâm sám,	*Disorderly.*	Tē tit,	*At present.*
Kín kín,	*Speedily.*	Taē seng,	*Previously.*
K'hăh mai^{ngh}, Tam mai^{ngh},	*More speedily.*	Kăh kwaè,	*So strange!*
		Chŏ poĕ,	*All at once.*
		Chŏ hōēy,	*Together.*

Tùy aōn,	*Afterwards.*
Há yëâ,	*Alas!*
Chë^{n}â tīn,	*By the troop.*
Kwà,	*And, also.*
Chë^{n}â ch'heng,	*By the thousand.*
Bô taē wâ,	*No resource.*
Hwat lâng taē wâ,	*To be a match for one.*
Le le á,	*A little.*
Tâk paé,	*Several times.*
Saé saé,	*What need?*
Bóng,	*So so.*
Bóng kë^{n}â kë^{n}â,	*Just walking about.*
Bóng kōèy,	*Getting on so so.*
Bóng kóng,	*Talking in jest.*
Cha hwui^{ng},	*Yesterday.*
Maī^{ng}h chaē,	*This morning.*
Mîn á chaē,	*To-morrow.*
Kaôu hëăh twā,	*So great!*
Kăh lê lê,	*How widely different!*
A',	*Also.*
Jwā chēy,	} *How many?*
Lwā chēy,	
Tá lôh k'hè,	} *Where are you going?*
Kà k'hè,	
Tóh tooí^{ng},	*Back again.*
Téng bīn,	*Above.*
Āy téy,	*Below.*
Lëŏh lëŏh á,	*A little.*
Chëō^{ng} lôh,	*Up and down.*
Sëó k'hwá,	*In a small degree.*
Chëó k'höëyh,	*Very few.*
Kë^{n}a ne,	*Lest.*
Chóng sē,	*After all.*
Böëyh chaé ëy,	*How can?*
Oō ch'hun,	*Over and above.*
Sëō^{ng},	*Very, extreme.*
Tòk tòk,	*Only.*
Chá k'hé,	*Early in the morning.*
K'hé t'haôu,	*In the beginning.*
Swăh böéy,	*At the end.*

II. VERBS.

Aōu bân,	*To oppress, to injure.*
Ūm t'hang,	*Do not.*
T'hang,	*Ought.*
Soō nëô^{ng},	*To consult.*
T'hek kak,	} *To throw away.*
Hëet,	
Hoē,	*To give.*
Hwat lîn tooí^{ng},	*To turn around.*
Tè,	*To wear on the head.*
Twā,	*To rest in.*
Twā tē,	*To dwell at.*
K'hëā,	*To reside.*
Gaôu chëèn,	*To play.*
Gaôu kwún,	*To sport.*
T'hit t'hô,	} *To ramble.*
Ch'hit t'hô,	
Lëăh chò,	*To consider.*
Kwăh tēw,	*To cut down corn.*
Sëep sēy,	*To flatter.*
Chò hwà sē,	*To have a lucky hit.*
Sëō^{ng} lôh kày,	*To repent.*
Tŏh,	*To burn as fire.*
Seáou léy,	*To be ashamed.*
T'hó,	*To take.*
Tin tāng,	*To move.*
Peè^{ng} kaôu lâng,	*To juggle.*
Kè tit,	*To remember.*
Sēw k'hè,	*To be angry.*
T'hëùng lòk,	*To be joyful.*
Toó tëŏh,	*To meet with.*
E wá,	*To rely on.*
P'hăh hwa,	*To put out (fire).*

Laôu bák chaé,	*To weep.*
Têêm lôh chúy,	*To drown.*
Wut chut,	*To be grieved.*
T'hun lún,	*To be patient.*
Ū^{m} keè^{ng},	*To lose.*
Wá lwā,	*To rely on.*
Ēy, *Can; and*	Bēy, *cannot.*
Ka laŏuh,	*To fall down.*
Têô^{ng} tê,	*To take care.*
Köèy è,	*To be pleased.*
Sèy jē,	*To be careful.*
Ū^{m} teè^{ng}h,	*To refuse.*
Têŏh bwâ,	*To be troubled.*
Pwăh keáou,	*To game.*
Têô,	*To jump.*
Chŏh ch'hân,	*To plough.*
Gaôu k'hëëni,	*To be stingy.*
O ló,	*To praise.*

III. NOUNS & ADJECTIVES.

Pak t'hăyh,	*Naked.*
Ch'héw wuí^{ng},	*A sleeve.*
Lâ sâm,	*Dirty.*
Ta po,	*A male.*
Cha boé,	*A female.*
Nëô^{ng} pāy,	*A father.*
Nëô^{ng} léy,	*A mother.*
Hăng, *a sort;*	Chit hăng, *one sort.*
Wun koo,	*Humpbacked.*
Tang e^{ng},	*The middle.*
Kip kèy,	*Diligent.*
Teâou tit,	*Exact, true.*
Hăm bān,	*Dull, stupid.*
Sèy ê,	*A concubine.*
Ch'hin ch'haí^{ng},	*Handsome.*
Laóu á,	*A rogue.*
Kā tō,	*One's self.*
Ch'haí^{ng} hwun,	*Unaccustomed.*
Kwàn sè,	*Accustomed.*
Nooí^{ng} chë^{n}á,	*Weak.*
Ch'haí^{ng} maí^{ng},	*Blind.*
Ka chëăh,	*The back.*
Ka ch'hui^{ng},	*The buttocks.*
Chaê teâou,	*Talent.*
Haōu sai^{ng},	*A son.*
Hwân ló,	*Troubled.*
P'hún tw^{n}ā,	*Lazy.*
Lân san,	*A few, odd.*
Àm koe chây,	*A cockchaffer.*
Kaou seâou,	*A cheat.*
Gîn á,	*A servant boy, a slave.*
Thaè ko pai^{ng},	*The leprosy.*
Sè kak,	*Four-square.*
Sè twa,	*Great men.*
Sè sèy,	*The lower ranks of men.*
Sin nëô^{ng},	*A bride.*
Sin kë^{n}â saè,	*A bridegroom.*
Nw^{n}â t'hoê,	*Mud.*
Keaou t'haôu,	*Proud.*
Chaē sit lé,	*A virgin.*
So chaē, *or* gāy,	*A place.*
T'haôu sai^{ng},	*An animal.*
Sông hëung,	*Poor.*
Tang,	*A reason.*
Bit pô,	*A bat.*
Pan gê,	*Cheap.*
Böéy yëăh,	*A butterfly.*
Lō k'hëet,	*Deep, cunning.*
Ch'hek, *corn;*	Ong, *a flame.*
Kaou é, *a chair;*	Chē chūy, *who?*
Cheâou chwuí^{ng},	*Complete.*
T'haôu chang böéy,	*A cue of hair.*
Ay,	*Sign of the possessive.*
Á,	*A diminutive.*

A

DICTIONARY

OF THE

HOK-KËÈN DIALECT

OF THE CHINESE LANGUAGE.

CHINESE AND ENGLISH.

A

上平

A 鴉 A crow. Oe a 烏鴉, a black crow. A hwuy put tò san 鴉飛不到山, *oe a pöey bëy kadu sw^{n}a*, a crow could not fly to that hill. When Lé kóng 李廣 went to subjugate the Tan e 單于 nation, he came to a hill, and on asking the name of it, was informed, that it was called "the hill which crows could not fly over:" for as soon as the crows came to the place, their feathers dropped off, so as to prevent their flying.

A 丫 A hwân 丫鬟, *a t'habu*, a slave girl.

A 亞 A p'hëèn 亞片, Opium. A p'hëèn kong soo 亞片公司, *a p'hëèn kong se*, the Opium farm.

A 啞 Dumb; Ē jëăng t'hun t'hàn wûy a 豫讓呑炭爲啞, *Ē jëăng t'hun höey t'hw^{n}à chò ây kâou*. Ē jëăng swallowed charcoal to make himself dumb (or to change his voice).

B

上聲

A' 阿 A prefix to a man's name. A' soo 阿四, *á sè*, a fourth son; á heng 阿兄, *á hë^{n}a*, Brother! an appellation generally given to the inhabitants of Tëâou-chew 潮州, *Tëô chew*.

上去

`A 亞 One second in order, inferior in rank: à sèng 亞聖, a secondary sage; Bēng choó 孟子, the Philosopher Mencius, was so called.

K'hóng Bēng che à 孔孟之亞, second only to Confucius and Mencius.

`A 婭 Yin à 姻婭, a familiar epithet used between persons related by marriage: Só só yin à 瑣瑣姻婭, distant relatives and connections.

`A 俹 To rely on, to depend upon.

去
Ā **諾** Read Lok: an affirmative; an expression of assent.

去
ⁿA **㰳** The noise made by an ox, or an ass: a nasal sound.

去
ⁿĀ **餡** Minced meat. Péng tëung jëuk ^{n}ā 餅中肉餡, *pē^{n}à tëung bāh ^{n}ā*, the minced meat in pies; Köéy ^{n}ā 粿餡, minced meat for pastry.

平
Ae **哀** To lament, lamentable: Lok jê put yîm, ae jê put sëang 樂而不淫哀而不傷, *t'hëùng lok yëá bēy yîm lwān, pē ae yëá bēy sëang haē*; "Pleasing without wantonness, sad without wounding." Said of the 關雎 Kwan ch'he ode.

Ae t'hòng ch'hám t'hat 哀痛慘怛, *ae t'hē^{n}à ch'hám t'hat*, sadly pained and grieved. Hé noē ae kē aè oè yëuk, wat ch'hit chêng 喜怒哀懼愛惡欲曰七情, Joy, anger, sorrow, fear, love, hatred, and desire, are called the seven passions.

Ae **埃** Dust; small particles of dust.

上
Aé **餲** Turned sour: soō ē jê aé 食饐而餲, rice injured by heat and damp, till it turns sour. See the Lûn gé 論語.

Aé **藹** Collected, gathered together: aé aé hèw yew yew, ch'hun kwuy sip jē lêw 藹藹復悠悠春歸十二樓, when the clouds are collected together, and again drifted about;—in the season of spring—we can return to the twelve-storied gallery. See Tông se 唐詩, the odes of the Tông Dynasty.

Aé **靄** A collection of clouds.

Aé **靉** Aé taè 靉靆, a dark appearance of the clouds.

Aé **矮** Vulg: *ây*: short: jîn aé aé 人矮矮 *lâng ây ây*, a short man.

去
Aè **愛** Vulg: *sëŏh*: to love, to pity; affection, attachment.

Sim hoē aè è 心乎愛矣, When we love any at heart.

Hây put wūy è 遐不謂矣, Distance is not considered:

Tëung sim chông che 中心藏之, Being laid up in our affections,

Hô jit bông che 何日忘之, When can we forget them? See the 詩經 Se keng.

Goê hô aè yit gnêw 吾何愛一牛, *gwá k'ham t'he^{n}à chit chëăh goô*, Do you think I am sparing of a single ox? See 孟子 Beng choō.

Aè **隘** Narrow minded. Pek-ê aè, Léw-hāy-hwūy put këung; aè é put këung, kwun chóo put yêw yëá 伯夷隘柳下惠不恭 隘與不恭君子不由也 Pek-ê was narrow minded. Léw-hāy-hwūy was disrespectful; but both narrow-mindedness and disrespect, are what the good man would not adopt.

Hëém aè 險隘, a narrow pass, a dangerous defile.

Aè **阨** Distressed.

福建方言字典

Aè 僾 A disturbed, distressed appearance.

Aè 縊 To hang, to throttle: choō aè jê soò 自縊而死, *ka tē jeĕh teaòu jê sè*, to strangle one's-self and die. Geùk tēung aè soó 獄中縊死, *kⁿa k'hoe laē ká sè*, he was strangled in the prison.

丟

Aē 噫 To belch. Tⁿá aē 打噫, *p'hăh oŏh*, to throw out wind.

Paóu sit k'hè bwán jê aē 飽食氣滿而噫, *chēăh pá k'hè mwⁿá jê p'hăh aĭh*, having eaten to the full, the wind rises and is ejected.

夫

A'h 押 To guard, to control. Ch'heĕm ăh 簽押, to take care of the slips of bamboo used by the Mandarins: ch'heĕm ăh taē yêâ 簽押大爺, the officer who takes care of these slips of bamboo.

A'h sòng 押送, ăh sàng, to guard, to escort. A'h wûn 押韻, to agree in sound, to rhyme with, to rhyme.

A'h 鴨 A duck; a tame duck: Sat key sat ăh 殺鷄殺鴨, *t'haĕ key t'haĕ ăh*, to kill fowls and ducks. Soò gwăt jé ăh seng 四月乳鴨生, *sē gōĕy'h sèy chēăh ăh ch'hut sè*, in the fourth month, the young ducks come out of the shell.

Gô ch'hùy ăh lēuk 鵝翠鴨綠, (the hills looked) grey as geese, and green as ducks.

夭

A'h 匣 A chest, a casket. Kim kwùy geūk ăh 金匱玉匣, golden chests and pearly caskets.

T'haè-o ch'hut ăh 太阿出匣, the celebrated *T'haè-o* sword came out of its sheath spontaneously.

夫

Ak 沃 To water, to irrigate, to fructify: Ak tēĕn 沃田, ak ch'hân, to water the rice fields. Kwân ak 灌沃, to pour out. Ak t'hoè 沃土, *pwûy tēy*, fertile land. A surname.

Ak 偓 Ak chak 偓促, restricted, limited.

Ak 握 Chēáng ak 掌握, to hold in the hand: Séw ak peng kwân 手握兵權, *ch'hèw gīm peng ây kwân*, to seize on the military power.

Ak 幄 A curtain; Wûy ak 幃幄, *poè lēĕm*, a curtain, a tent.

Wŭn têw wûy ak tēung 運籌幃幄中, to be planning schemes in the tent.

Ak 喔 The cackling of a fowl: the sound of loud laughing.

Ak 渥 To drip: Tēem ak 霑渥, the rain dripping through

Hông yin tēem ak 皇恩霑渥, *hông tèy ây yin sip lok k'hè*, the Imperial favour distilling on the people.

Ak 齷 Ak chak 齷齪, the teeth near to each other; closely set; impelled.

Ak 鋈 Ak kim 鋈金, to lay on gold; to gild.

夭

Ak 籆 A spindle, a distaff.

上平

Am 庵 A straw shed; Am bëäou 庵廟, *am bëō*, a temple, a monastery.

Am 腌 Am cham 腌臢, *a sâm*, unclean, impure, filthy.

Am 腤 Flesh boiled and preserved.

Am 闇 To understand; Bē am 未闇, *bōëy hëäou tit*, I do not understand.

Am kan t'hëen wūy 闇干天位, to have designs upon the Imperial dignity.

Am 諳 To remember, to recollect: all, every. Am lëën ch'him 諳練深, in every thing deeply experienced.

上声

A'm 闇 Dark, closed doors.

A'm 黯 An appearance of great grief, also grief at parting.

A'm jëën seaou hwûn chëá, wûy pëet jê é è, 黯然銷魂者惟別而已矣, *ch'hám ây yëōⁿᵍ, kaòu kwûn seaou k'hè, chóng sē sëo pëèt lëⁿā lëⁿā*, greatly grieved, till my soul is consumed, I can only take my leave, and no more. See the Kang yëem pëet chip 江淹別集.

A'm 渰 The appearance of disturbed water, bubbling up: also the water in which the cocoons of the silk worms have been boiled.

上去

Am 闇 All, every one; to understand.

ˋAm 暗 Dark, dismal, no light: Jit boô kong wûy àm 日無光爲暗, *jit bô kwuiⁿᵍ chò àm*, when the sun does not shine, it is dark. Pwàn bêng pwàn àm che soô 半明半暗之辭, *pwⁿà bêng pwⁿà àm ây wā*, half clear and half dark sentences.

下平

Âm 頷 Âm k'hang 頷控, a drain, a spout. Súy âm 水頷, *Chúy âm*, an aqueduct.

下去

Ām 頷 Ām kēng 頷頸 *ām kwún á*, the neck, the back-part of the neck. Ām kwut sûy 頷骨垂, the neck bending forwards.

上平

An 安 Peace, rest, quietness, cessation:—how? in what way? A surname.

Chēng jê hoē lêng an 靜而後能安 *chēng jëên aōu ēy an*, Being tranquil, then we may be at ease. See the 大學 Tāe hak.

Pêng an 平安, peaceful and at rest. T'hó an 妥安, secure & quiet. An lêng sêng hoē 安能成乎, *an chwⁿà ēy chēⁿà*, how can it succeed?

An 鞍 Vulgarly *wⁿa*: a saddle; má an 馬鞍, *báy wⁿa*, a horse's saddle.

Pek má k'hwà kim an, k'hê ch'hut bān jîn k'hàn 白馬掛金鞍騎出萬人看, *pāyh báy k'hwà kim wⁿa, k'hëà ch'hut bān lâng k'hwⁿà*, Riding out on a white horse, harnessed with a golden saddle, myriads of people will look at us.

An 侒 Yëèn an 宴侒, unemployed, indolent.

An 鵪 An sûn 鵪鶉, *yëen ch'hun* a quail.

福建方言字典

去

'An 按 Vulg: wⁿà: to place, to put down, to put the hand on.

'An 案 Vulg: wⁿà: a table; àn tok 案桌, wⁿà tŏh, a table, a magistrate's bench.

P'hwàn àn 判案, p'hwⁿà àn, a judgment seat.

'An 晏 Vulg: wⁿà: late: Jëĕm-choó t'höèy tëâou, Choó wát, hô àn yëá 冉子退朝子曰何晏也, Jëĕm-choó t'hèy teâou, Hoo choó kóng, sⁿa sŏo kaòu heah wⁿa. Jëĕm choó came back from court, when Confucius asked him, why are you so late? See the 下論 hāy lūn. A surname.

'An 唵 An oath. This character is commonly used in novels.

平

Ân 掞 Tight: pok ân 縛掞, pak ân ân, tie it tight.

Ân 閒 Vulg: êng: leisure: chwân jit boô ân 全日無閒, chwatⁿᵍ jit bô êng, no leisure throughout the whole day.

Sip hoé che kan hêy, song chëá hân hân hêy 十畝之間兮桑者閑閑兮 chàp hoè têy ây tëung kan, bàn seⁿᵍ ây lâng ân ân, in a field of ten acres wide, the mulberry-leaf gatherers go leisurely to work. See the 詩經 Se keng, book of odes.

去

Ān 限 A limit, a boundary; yéw ān 有限, oō ān, limited. Yit jîn che chéng sîn yéw ān 一人之精神有限, chit lâng ây cheng sîn oō ān, one man's spirits and vigour are but limited.

Ān 㞡 Bûn ān 門㞡, mûotⁿᵍ têng, the threshold of a door.

o

去

Ang 尪 Read ong: an idol, a god: ong sîn 尪神, ang sîn, a god: ong koong 尪公, ang kong, a divinity: gêng ong 迎尪, gēⁿá ang, to carry an idol in procession; paé ong 拜尪 paè ang, to worship the gods. Loé jîn p'hok ong 魯人暴尪, Loé ây lâng p'hak ang, the people of the Loé country dried their gods in the sun; this was in a time of drought, when the people thought to force their gods to give them rain, by putting their images under a burning sun. See the 左傳, chó twān.

Ang 汪 Read ong: A surname: also, overflowing, vast as the ocean. Chëûng goé seng é ong yâng 從吾生以汪洋, chëûng gwá chit sè lâng è ang yëōⁿᵍ, to spend one's whole life on the vast Ocean.

Ang 翁 Read ong: a husband, an old man; ong pô 翁婆, ang pô, husband and wife. A surname.

上

A'ng 㣕 A'ng lang 㣕㑣, Disorderly outrageous.

去

'Ang 甕 Read òng a jar; súy ong 水甕, chuy àng, a water jar. 'Ong wūy koe jîn k'hae 甕爲故人開, chëw àng tëŏh yin wūy koè lâng k'hway, the liquor jar should be opened for an old friend. See the 薛家傳 Sëet kay twān.

'Ang 塕 'Ong sêng 塕城, ang seⁿa, the vacant space between the outer and inner city gates. Read òng.

'Ang 䙲 Read òng: the leg or upper part of a stocking; bëet òng 襪䙲, bŏëyh àng the leg of a stocking.

'Ang 鞥 Hëa àng, 靴鞥, the top part of a boot.

Ang 齆 *P'hcè^{ng} àng* 鼻齆, the inside of the nose, a disease in the nose.

平

Âng 洪 Read hông: a surname.

Âng 紅 Read hông: Red; of a red colour: a surname: hông sam 紅衫, *âng s^{n}a.* a red coat.
Yit tëém hông hwa kwun ch'háe khé, yēw lâe chim pëen swat yin e 一點紅花君採去.又來枕邊說因依, *chìt tëèm âng hwa, lè t'hàyh k'hè, kŏh lâe chim t'haŏu pee^{ng} kóng yin e,* "one speck of a red flower (a drop of blood), you have already taken away, and now you come to the side of my pillow to whisper and hum." A couplet on the mosquito, made by 蘇妹 Sŏe-moēy.

去

Āng 籠 Read ōng: A basket: t'hoé ōng 土籠, *t'hoê āng,* a basket of earth.

平

Aou 歐 Read oé: A surname. Also aou yâng 歐陽, a double surname.

Aou 甌 A cup: tây aou 茶甌, a tea cup. Aou k'héng c'hëak sëet hëang 甌傾雀舌香, *aou têy chīn sē chăyh cheĕh p'hang,* the bottom of the cup was strongly scented with the smell of the sparrow's-tongue tea.

Aou 坳 Uneven, an unevenness in the ground.

Aou 凹 Tēy aou 地凹, a hollow place in the ground. Koé hëēn bê aou chē bek to 古硯微凹聚墨多, *koé chá ây hëe^{ng} k'hwut á k'hëŏh bak chēy,* the hollow place in an old ink stone, collects the ink in abundance.

Aou 曉 Deep and hollow eyes; the eyes turned inward.

声

Aóu 拗 To twist; séw aóu 手拗, *ch'hèw aóu,* to twist with the hand.

Aóu 毆 Aóu t^{n}á 毆打, *phăh láng,* to beat people.

Aóu 媼 Ló áou 老媼, an old woman: an epithet for the terrestrial gods.

Aóu 嘔 Read oé: to vomit: oé t'hoê 嘔吐, *aòu t'hoē,* to vomit up any thing. Oé hông 嘔紅, *aóu hŏëyh,* to vomit blood.

Aóu 糿 Oé néw 糿紐, *aóu laóu,* to rumple up any thing. Ché oé néw 紙糿紐, *chwá aóu laóu,* to roll up paper into a ball.

去

Aòu 拗 To hold fast: chip aòu 執拗, to adhere to one's own opinion. Ông-keng-kong chip aòu 王荆公執拗, ông-keng-kong obstinately adhered to his own opinion.

Aòu 砌 Aòu, sek put pêng yëá 砌.石不平也, *aòu, sĕ chëŏh ū^{m} pat^{ng} yëá,* aòu means a stony uneven place.

Aòu 殉 Read oè: stinking, rotten, not fresh. But oè k'hè 物殉去, *meè^{n}h aòu k'hè,* any thing turned, as meat.

Aòu 懊 Aòu náou 懊惱, sour, surly, stubborn.

平

Aôu 喉 Read hoê: the throat: yëen hoê 咽喉, *nâ aôu,* the gullet.

Pá yëen hoĕ ch'hè 把咽喉處, *páy ná aŏu ây wūy,* to guard the important passes of a country.

玉

Aōu 諾 Read lo̍k: to assent to. Put k'heng hé lo̍k 不輕許諾, *ūm k'hin k'hwaè hé aŏu,* not easily assenting to any thing.

Aōu 後 Read hoē: after, afterwards, behind. Chëĕn hoē 前後, *chêng aōu,* before and behind, first and last.

Tùy hoē 對後, *tùy aōu,* behind; hoē laê 後來, *aōu laê,* afterwards.

大

Ap 姶 Beautiful, fair, handsome.

Ap 哈 Shortness of breath.

Ap 唈 Read yip: to swallow down; to gobble. Gê ap sûy 魚唈水, *hê ap chúy,* the fishes swallow down water.

Ap 厭 To be moistened; ap yip hêng loē 厭浥行露 to be moistened by falling dew. See the 國風 Kok hong.

Ap 壓 To repress, to press down, to descend. Tòng chëet, k'hëúng yëw hok ap che gê 棟折恐有覆壓之虞, *tàng â chëĕh kënna ne woā tāyh lâng ây kan lân,* if the beam should break, it is to be feared some one may be crushed by the accident.

火

Àp 盍 Why not? àp, hô put yëá 盍何不也, *àp, sé sⁿa soō ūm,* àp means why not?

Choó wat, àp kok gân jé ché 子曰盍各言爾志, *Hoo choó kóng, sⁿa soō ūm sûy lâng kóng lé ây sim ché,* Confucius said, why do you not each one tell us of your views? See the 上論 Seāng lūn.

Àp 盒 A casket; Pwân àp 盤盒, *pwⁿâ àh,* a tray for carrying presents on.

Àp 柙 A cage for wild beasts; hoé soō ch'hut è àp 虎兕出於柙, *hoé kap yëá goô ch'hut àh,* the tiger and wild cow broke out of their cages. See the 下論 hāy lūn.

Àp 狎 Familiar, nearly related. Këèn choo sōey chëá, suy àp pit pëèn 見齊衰者雖狎必變, *k'hwⁿà keèng twā seng hâ ây lâng, sûy sē ch'hin kïn, yëá tëŏh pëèn sek,* on seeing a person in mourning, although a familiar friend, he would change colour (i. e. put on a sad countenance): Said of Confucius.

Àp 嗑 To eat, to unite; also verbose. Yéw hám kē àp 有噞其嗑, *taē kay taè chëăh,* let us all eat together.

Sē àp, kwà bêng 噬嗑卦名, *sē àp, sē kwà ây mêⁿâ,* Sē àp, is the name of one of the diagrams.

大

At 乙 A black kind of bird; also, at at 乙乙, difficult to get out.

At 遏 To restrain; at ché 遏止, to repress, to forbid. Boô k'hëuk hông, boô at tek 無曲防·無遏糴, *ūm t'hang ch'hòng wan k'hwut chúy chàh, yëw ūm t'hang at chè lâng tëăh bé,* do not turn aside the aqueducts, and do not repress the selling of rice. See 下孟 Hāy bēng.

At 揠 Vulg: *payh*: to pull up. Sōng jîn yéw bin kē bëâou che put tëáng jê at che chëá 宋人有憫其苗之不長而揠之者, *Sòng ây lâng woō hwân ló e ây pò ch'hē â ây ūm tëâng twā, jê pàyh e k'hè laê,* a man of the Sòng country was grieved that his corn would not grow fast enough, so he pulled it up (to make it longer).

At 頞 Pit at 鼻頞, *p'heèng at*, the bridge of the nose. Ké chit séw, ch'hëuk at 舉疾首蹙頞, *chò poó t'hâou kak t'hë"à, p'heèng t'haôu gnëaôu gnëaôu*, they all got head-aches, and drew up the skin of their foreheads (by frowning). See 孟子 Bëng choó.

At 圠 The unevenness of mountains.

㞢

Ay 窒 Ay tay 窒窊, *këaou ây yëō"g*, the appearance of pride.

Ay 涇 Ch'him ay 深涇, deepness of water.

Ay 腽 Ay k'hay 腽骴, a contraction of the limbs.

㞢

A'y 瘂 A'y k'hoé 瘂口, *ây kaóu*, dumb, unable to speak. Ch'hêng bêng ây k'hoé 睛瞑瘂口, *ch'hai"g mai"g ây kaóu*, blind and dumb; said of those who can neither write nor read.— "Are you dumb, that you cannot speak?" jé sē áy k'hoé, put lêng gân hoê 爾是瘂口不能言乎, *lé k'ham sē ây kaóu, bēy hëáou kóng wā.*

A'y 啞 Mute: áy jêên jê ch'heàou 啞然而笑, *ây kaóu tân ch'hëò*, he was mute, and did nothing but laugh.

Áy 矮 Read wúy: short, dwarfish: T'hoé-hêng-sun wúy choó, put bwán soò ch'hek 土行孫矮仔不滿四尺, *T'hoé-hêng-sun sē ây á kē"á, bô mw"á sè ch'hëŏh kwân*, Thoé-hêng-sun was a dwarf; not above four spans high. See the 封神傳 Hong sîn twān.

㞢

Ây 下 Read hāy: below, under; hāy téy 下底, *āy tèy*, underneath. T'hëen hāy kok kay 天下國家, *t'hee"g āy kok kay*, the Empire, with the different states and families. See 孟子 Bëng choó.

T'hëen kàng. hāy bîn 天降下民 *t'hee"g kàng āy tèy āy pay'h sai"g*, Heaven has sent down into being the lower classes of people.

夫

Ăyh 阨 Read ek: calamity; *chae ăyh* 災阨, affliction, straits. Ek këûng jê put bín, 阨窮而不憫, *wōō chae ăyh kap sòng hëung, yëá bô hwân ló*, being in affliction and poverty, he still was not grieved. Said of Léw-hāy bwūy 柳下惠, in 孟子 Bëng chóo.

Ăyh 軛 Read ek: a yoke: pok ek é kày gnêw 縛軛以駕牛 *pak ăyh á è kày goô*, to bind on the yoke, in order to yoke in the oxen.

Ăyh 厄 Read ek: straits, difficulties. Kwun choó che ek, ê Tîn Ch'haè che kan 君子之厄於陳蔡之間, *kwun choó woō ăyh wūn, tē Tîn kok Ch'haè kok āy tëung kan*, the good man (meaning Confucius) was in straits between the countries of Tîn and Ch'haè. See 下孟 hāy bēng.

Ăyh 噫 Read aē: t"á aē 打噫 *p'hăh ăyh*, to belch.

夾

Ăyh 狹 Read hëep: narrow, confined. Tëâng twán kóng hëep 長短廣狹 *tê"g tèy k'hwăh ăyh*, long and short, broad and narrow.

Loē hëep lân hêng 路狹難行 *loē ăyh ŏh kē"á*, the road is narrow and difficult to travel.

Koē loē hēep aè 固陋狹隘, *koē chip p'hēăh, sim kwⁿa āyh,* obstinate and narrow-minded.

A'yh 噎 A noise in the throat, made by belching

B

上平

Ba 疤 Read pa: a scar, a mark of a wound.

Ba 膗 Jēuk ba 肉膗, *băh ba,* a rising of the flesh, an inflammation.

下平

Bâ 媌 Read bēâou: a prostitute; *ch'hēang bâ* 娼媌, a bad woman. Bân jîn hoe kê wûy bēâou 閩人呼妓爲媌, *Bân lâng kēò kê sē bâ,* the Hok-kēèn people call a prostitute Bâ.

Bâ 痳 Bâ hong 痳瘋, the leprosy. Bâ hong put k'hó e 痳瘋不可醫, *bâ hong bô Chang wuy,* the leprosy is incurable.

Bâ 蝥 Read mâou: pan mâou 蟹蝥, *pan bâ,* cantharides: also, pitted with the small pox.

Bâ 貓 Read beâou; as, beâou lê 貓貍, *bâ lê,* a fox. Beâou lê yéw hēet 貓貍有穴, *bâ lê woō k'hang,* the foxes have holes. Gēuk bēēn bēâou 玉面貓, *gēuk bīn bâ,* a pearly faced fox, a white fox.

下去

Bā 峇 Bā bā 峇峇, a country-born Chinese. Bā bā put sit Tông san kwuy ké 峇峇不識唐山規矩, *bā bā ūm bat Tēng swⁿa kwuy kè,* half-caste Chinese are not acquainted with the customs of China.

Bā 盼 Hwun hwun bā bā 紛紛份盼, sometimes confused and sometimes clear.

上聲

Baé 惡 Read ok: bad, corrupt, wicked. Ok kwúy 惡鬼, *baé kwúy,* a bad devil; ok joō 惡字, *baé jē,* a foul word; ok bůt 惡物, *baé meēⁿh,* a worthless thing; ok jîn 惡人, *baé lâng,* a wicked man.

Baé 炑 Dull, not bright. Chēak hⁿó put baé 灼火不炑, *chìh chēak hóey bēy baé,* a little fire will not burn brightly. See 列女傳 *Lēēt lè twān.*

下平

Baê 埋 Vulg. *taê:* To bury, to inter, to hide under ground; also, the name of a sacrifice.

Gnóc hoê baê kim ê kim lêng 五胡埋金於金陵, *goē āy hoê taê kim twā tē kim lêng,* the five Hoê's (or foreign states) buried gold at Kim-lêng.

Chòng baê hoō bóe 葬埋父母, *chòng taê pāy bóe,* to bury one's parents.

Soō tēy kê wàt, ê baê 祀地祇日瘞埋, *ch'haê tēy sin kông, è bâe,* to sacrifice to the terrestrial gods is called, ê baê.

Baê 霾 Rain following wind. Chöung hong ch'hēⁿá baê, hwūy jēên k'hêng laê 終風且霾惠然肯來, *chìt jìt woō hong kwà hoê, yin hwūy kaòu k'hêng laê,* after a whole day's wind and rain, he was so kind as to be willing to come.

Baê 眉 Read bê: the eye-brows; bók bê 目眉, *bák baê,* the eye-brows. Kwan-é yéw gō ch'hâm bê 關羽有臥蠶眉,

Kwan-é woō gō ch'hêng ây baē, Kwan-é (the Mars of China) had eye-brows like sleeping silkworms.

Baê **楣** Read bê: the lintel; bûn bê 門楣, *mooi^ng baê*, the lintel of a door.
Sūy k'hè êng bê 瑞氣盈楣, *seāng sūy ây k'hè êng mw^n á lé ây mooi^ng baê*, may happy influences replenish the lintel of your door.

夫

Băh **肉** Read jëuk: flesh: te jëuk 豬肉, *te băh*, pork; yâng jëuk 羊肉, *yëō^ng băh*, mutton; gnêw jëuk 牛肉, *goô băh*, beef.
Jëuk suy to, put soó sìn soō k'hè 肉雖多·不使勝食氣, *băh suy chëy, bô hoē e yē^n á pooī^ng ây k'hè*, although he had much flesh, yet he would not let it exceed the quantity of rice at a meal. Said of Confucius, in the 上論 sëāng lūn.

夫

Bak **染** Read jëém: to defile, to soil. Jëém woo 染污 bak lâ sâm, to defile with dirt.
Put jëém sëuk k'hè 不染俗氣, *ū^m t'hang bak tëöh loé sëuk ây k'hè*, don't defile yourself with a common vulgar spirit.
Tông-Lé-koē bōng léw chëep jëém p'haôu 唐李固夢柳汁染袍, *Tông teâou ây Lé-koē bāng kee^ng lëw chëep bak tëöh e ây p'haôu*, Lé-koē of the Tông dynasty dreamt that the juice of a willow tree spotted his gown, (and he afterwards attained to the highest literary honours). See the 廣事類賦 kóng soō lūy hoò.

夭

Bak **目** Read bok: the eye; vulg: *bak chew*, the eye. Bê, bok, pit, k'hoé, 眉目鼻口, *baê, bak, p'hee^ng, ch'hùy*, the eye-brows, eyes, nose, and mouth.

Bé bok p'hàn hêy 美目盼兮, *ch'hin ch'hai^ng ây bak chew, oe pāyh pun k'hè hwun bêng*, beautiful eyes, with the white and black clearly divided. See the 上論 sëāng lūn.

Bak **木** Read bok: wood; sē bok 樹木, *ch'hēw bak*, timber. Bok ch'hëāng 木匠, *bak ch'hëō^ng*, a carpenter.
Yëên bok kêw gê 緣木求魚, *pāyh chëō^ng ch'hēw bak ch'hūy hê*, to climb a tree in order to seek for fish; (representing the unsuitableness of the means to the end). See 孟子 Bēng choó.

Bak **茉** Read bwat; as bwat lē hwa 茉莉花, *bak neē^ng hwa*, the jessamine flower.

Bak **墨** Read bek: ink; bek hëën 墨硯, *bak hee^ng*, an ink stone. Bûn bek che pöèy 文墨之輩, *bûn bak ây poèy*, learned men.
Tong p'hek toê se hoó, sey wân hān bek lim 東壁圖書府·西園翰墨林, *tang ây pëăh wôo toê ch'hāyh ây hoó, sae ây hwui^ng wôo hān bak ây lim*, within the eastern wall is the palace of books and maps, and towards the western garden is the forest of learned men.

声

Bám **餡** A way of calling infants.

声

Bán **挽** Read bwán: to drag, to pull; k'han bwán 牽挽, *k'han bán*, to pull along. Bwán hwûy t'hëen è 挽回天意, *bán tooi^ng t'hee^ng ây è*, to pull back (to reverse) the decrees of heaven.

Bán **折** Read chëet: to pluck, to pick; chëet hwa 折花, *bán hwa*, to pick flowers. Wûy tëäng chëá chëet che 爲長者折枝, *wuy sè twā lâng bán ch'hēw kè*, to pluck a branch at the command of a superior. See 孟子 Bēng choó.

平

Bân 曼 Distant, a far journey.

Bân 墁 The plaster of a wall. Hwûy wá ék bân 毀瓦畫墁, *p'hāh p'hwā ây ch'hoò hēā, wā wā ây ch'hëŏ^ng pēāh*, broken tiles and scratched walls; (a reproachful expression intimating, a bad execution of work).

Bân 漫 The wide and vast appearance of water; an inundation.

Bân 饅 A cake; bân t'hôe 饅頭, *bûn t'hâou*, a loaf of bread. Pok sè chwân sit bân t'hôe 北勢全食饅頭, *pak sè chwân chēāh bûn t'hâou*, in the north country, they eat nothing but bread.

Bân 鰻 Vulg. *mwⁿâ*: an eel; haé bân 海鰻, *haè mwⁿâ*, a sea eel, a congar eel.

Bân 蠻 A foreigner, a barbarian; bân bek 蠻貊, uncivilized people. Gân tëung sìn, hêng tok kèng, suy bân bek che pang, hêng é, 言忠信行篤敬.雖蠻貊之邦行矣, *kóng wā laōu sit, chò soō chîn kèng, suy kaòu bân bek ây pang kok, yēá ēy kēⁿâ*, when a men's words are sincere, and his conduct respectful, even into barbarous countries, he may safely travel.

Bân 閩 The province of Hok-këèn. Hok-këèn wat Bân sêng 福建曰閩省, *Hok-këèn kēò Bân saiⁿᵍ*, Hok-këèn is called the Bân province

Yâng-bûn-kông cheng lâm bân sip pat tōng 楊文廣征南閩十八洞, *Yëôⁿᵍ-bûn-kông k'hè cheng hwat lâm bân saiⁿᵍ ây chap pāyh tōng*, Yëôⁿᵍ-bûn-kông conquered the eighteen caves of the southern Bân. See the 宋史 Song soò. History of the Sòng dynasty.

去

Bān 萬 A myriad, ten thousand; also, a surname. Bān söèy yëâ 萬歲爺, the lord of ten thousand years; an appellation given to the Emperor, similar to "Long live the king!"

Bān sēw boô këang 萬壽無疆, *chēⁿâ bān neēⁿᵍ bô këûng chīn*, ten thousand years of life without limitation; used as a wish of congratulation on the Emperor's birth-day.

Bān 曼 Not yet: also used as an expletive.

Bān 蔓 Luxuriant, wild, spreading as weeds. Bān ch'hó lân toê 蔓草難圖, *bān yëên ây ch'hâou ôh tê kaòu ch'heng k'hè*, weeds widely spread are with difficulty cleared away. See the 左傳 chó twān.

Bān 幔 A curtain; wûy bān 幃幔, a tent curtain.

Bān 嫚 To slight, to despise.

Bān 縵 Inelegant, ravelled; also, the string of a guitar. K'heng yin lān hêy, kew bān bān 卿雲爛兮糺縵縵, the hanging clouds broken and dispersed, seem intertwined and ravelled together.

Bān 僈 Slowly, leisurely; bān bān 僈僈 very slow. Ch'hēⁿa bān 且僈, stop a little.

Bān 謾 An expletive, a particle. also, and.

Bān 慢 To despise to slight, to neglect; boo bān 侮慢 to contemn. Tōng yûng māou, soo wān pó bān 動容貌.

斯遠暴慢, *tín tāng lân ây yûng maōu tëŏh, chēă ēy hwui^{ng} k'hè pò bān,* by regulating properly the motion of our countenance, we shall be able to avoid insult and neglect.

Bān 漫 To be inundated by water.

Bān 命 The same as bān 慢, to slight. Also read bēng, a decree. Këèn hëên jê put lêng ké, ké jê put lêng sëèn, bān yëá, 見賢而不能舉.舉而不能先.命也, *k'hw^{n}à gâou lâng jê bēy kè yūng, kè yūng jê bēy hoē c taè seng, chèy sē taē bān yēā,* if on seeing clever people, we cannot employ them; and in employing them if we do not prefer them, this is really slighting them. See the 大學 Taē hak.

Bān 蠆 A sting, the sting of a bee, or other insect. Bān bé yéw tok 蠆尾有毒, *bān bōēy wōo tok,* in the tail of a stinging insect there is poison.

声

Báng 蚊 Read bún, a musquito, a small gnat. Bún tëàng 蚊帳, *bûng tà;* musquito curtains. Pē bún gëet soó 被蚊齧死, *hōe bùng kā sè,* to be bitten to death by musquitoes.

Báng 網 Read bóng: a head-kerchief; bóng kin 網巾, *báng kin,* a kerchief formerly worn by officers, to keep their hair tied closely together.

平

Bâng 厖 Exuberant, great, abundant.

Bâng 尨 A dog with long shaggy hair. Boô soò bâng hwūy 無使尨吠, *ū^{m} t'hang hōe kaôu pwūy,* don't set the dogs a-barking.

Bâng 哤 To talk incoherently.

Bâng 龐 A surname; Bâng-t'hông 龐統, a celebrated man in the 三國 Sam kok.

去

Bāng 望 Read bōng: to hope, to expect; kè bōng 冀望, *kè bāng,* to hope for. Bōng tō jê bē che këèn 望道而未之見, *bāng tō chun á yeā bōey ēy k'hw^{n}à,* he looked towards virtue as one that had not yet come within sight of it. Said of 文王 Bûn ông, in the 下孟 hāy bēng.

Bāng 夢 Read bōng: to dream; a dream, a vision of the night. Kéw è, goé put hēw bōng këèn Chew-kong 久矣.吾不復夢見周公, *koó è, gwá bô kōh bāng keè^{ng} Chew-kong,* it is now a long time since I have dreamed about Chew-kong. Said by K'hông-choó 孔子, Confucius, in the 上論 sëāng lūn.

Bāng 網 Read bóng: a net; a fishing net. Koé chëá bóng koé, yūng soò ch'hùn che bok 古者網罟用四寸之目, *koé lâng ây bāng, yūng sè ch'hùn ây bak,* "The ancients in their nets used meshes of four inches square:" in order to allow the smaller fishes to escape, that they might grow larger. See the commentary of the 上孟 sëāng bēng.

声

Baóu 卯 One of the horary characters, used by the Chinese in reckoning years, months, days, and hours. Sip gwat che kaou, sok jit sin baóu 十月之交.朔日辛卯, *chap gōēyh ây kaou chōēyh, ch'hey yit sē sin baóu,* upon the change of the tenth moon, the first day will be denoted by the characters sin baóu.

Baóu 昴 One of the 28 constellations; the Plëiades.

Baóu 茆 A water plant, a certain vegetable. Soo lo̍k p'hwàn súy, gân ch'haé kê baóu 思樂泮水.言採其茆, sëö^{ng} k'hè p'hwⁿà këung ây chúy, kóng büëyh bán e ây baóu ch'haè, thinking of going to the pond before the prince's school, and talking about picking the baóu vegetable there. See the 大雅 Taē gnáy odes.

灭

Baŏuh 貿 Read boē: to bargain; to bargain for any thing in the lump. Boē kó choó 貿菓子, baŏuh kwúy chè, to bargain for the whole of a man's fruit.

夫

Bat 識 Read sit: to know, to be acquainted with. Sëang sit 相識, sëo bat, to be mutually acquainted with.
Sit joō 識字, bat jē, to know letters.
Sëang koè boô sëang sit 相顧無相識, sëo k'hwⁿà bô sëo bat, to look at one another, without knowing each other. See the 唐詩 Tông se.

灭

Ba̍t 密 Read bi̍t: secret, close, concealed, near, not distant. Ji̍p lîm, wûy k'hëúng put bi̍t 入林惟恐不密, ji̍p ch'ëw nâ, wûy këⁿa nē ūm bat, when a man enters the forest [to secrete himself] he is only afraid lest it should not be close and secret enough;—(Said of those learned men who retire from the world in disgust).

虐

Báy 馬 Read má: a horse: a surname. K'hê má 騎馬, k'hëâ báy, to ride on a horse. Hwuy kám hoē yëá, má put chìn yëá 非敢後也.馬不進也, ūm sē gwá kⁿà tùy aōu, sē báy bëy këⁿâ, it is not that I dare to be behind-hand, but because my horse cannot get forward. See the 上論 Sëäng lūn. Said by Confucius, when he was last in flight.

E

Báy 碼 Read má: a water dam, built of stones: a farm of the taxes. Se̍k má 石碼, chëŏh báy, a stone dam or mound.
Má choó 碼仔, báy á, a farm of the taxes: keàou má choó 叫碼仔 këà báy á, to let out the farms; chéw má choó 酒碼仔, chéw báy á, the arrack farm; a p'hëèn má choó 鴉片碼仔, a p'hëèn báy á, the opium farm.

Báy 瑪 Má lô se̍k 瑪瑙石, báy lô chëŏh, the cornelian stone.

Báy 買 Read maé: to buy, to purchase. Ê hwa këem tëe̍p chè, maé se̍k jeáou yîn laê 移花兼蝶至.買石繞雲來, sw̌á hwa lëën bōey yëăh kaòu, báy chëŏh teⁿ hwûn kăh sē laê, removing a flower, the butterfly comes along with it, and buying a stone, even the surrounding clouds accompany it. See the 唐詩 Tông se.

歪

Bāy 賣 Read maē: to sell, to dispose of. Chò maé maē 做買賣, chò báy bāy, to buy and sell.
Maē to maé to̍k 賣刀買犢, bāy to báy goô á, to sell a knife, in order to buy a heifer.

灭

Bǎyh 麥 Read be̍k: wheat; a surname. Tāe be̍k 大麥, twā bǎyh, barley; hwan be̍k 番麥, hwan bǎyh, Indian corn.
Bēng hāy che gwa̍t, be̍k ch'hew chè 孟夏之月麥秋至, k'hè t'haôu hāy ây goëyh bǎyh tang kaòu, in the first months of summer, the wheat harvest comes in. See the 禮記 Léy kè.

奉

Be 迷 Read bêy: to secrete one's-self.

上聲

Bé 米 Rice; a surname. Bé kwùy 米貴, the rice is dear. Bé ch'hëuk hwuy put to yëá 米粟非不多也, *bè ch'hek ūm sè ūm chēy*, it is not because the rice and paddy are insufficient. See the 上孟 Sëāng bēng. Bé tëen paè sek 米顛拜石, *bè tëen paè chëŏh*, the fool Bé used to worship stones. This was a man of the Sòng Dynasty, who possessed great talents, and rose very high in office, but he had this failing, that whenever he saw a stone, he could not help worshipping it; hence he was called a fool. Query, Do not many of his countrymen merit the same appellation?

Bé 敉 To soothe, to pacify. Bé lêng boó 敉寧武, *an lêng boò ây soō*, to still and pacify warlike concerns. See the 上書, sëōng se.

Bé 眯 Any thing got into the eye.

Bé 弭 To stop, to put a stop to. Kwùy-k'hong-choó bé tō 季康子弭盜, *Kwùy-k'hong-choó bè bô tō ch'hat*, Kwùy-k'hong-choó exterminated the robbers.

Bé 亹 Unwearied, not feeling tired. Sit che ch'him ch'him, tat che bé bé 息之深深 達之亹亹, *swāh e ây sè, sëōng tëŏh ch'him ch'him, kaòu bat e chëw sëōng bēy yëà*, on giving up the study of any thing, we think it difficult, but if we persevere till we understand it, we shall feel no disposition to be tired. See the 禮記 Léy kè.

Bé 彌 To stop, to put a stop to.

Bé 尾 Vulg: bōèy: a tail, an end; t'hoê bé 頭尾, *t'haôu bōèy*, head and tail. Wùy séw wùy bé 畏首畏尾, *kë a t'haôu kë a bōèy*, to be afraid of both beginning and ending; to be irresolute.

Séw bé put lêng sëang koè 首尾不能相顧, *t'haôu bōèy bēy ēy sëo koè*, not to be able to look after both head and tail, i. e. mind two things at once.

Bé 咩 The bleating of sheep.

Bé 芊 A surname, common in the 楚 Ch'hoé country.

Bé 美 Vulg: súy: Beautiful, fine, elegant, good, handsome: Choó wūy seäou chīn bé è 子謂韶盡美矣, *K'hóng-choó kóng, Sùn ây gak chīn chaē súy*, Confucius said, that the music of Sùn was very fine.

Sey hong bé jîn 西方美人, *sae heng ây gâou lâng*, the clever man of the west.

Sey-se chōng maōu bé lēy 西施狀貌美麗, *Sae-se ây chēng maōu súy kwà ch'hin ch'haing*, Sae-se's appearance was beautiful and engaging.

Bé 靡 Beautiful, wanton, overturned; not, a negative particle. Tēng wöēy che yim, bé bān che yim yëá 鄭衛之音, 靡曼之音也, *têng wöēy ây sëna, sè bé bān ây yim*, the expression of amorous ditties have generally a wanton sound.

Bé séy té ché 靡所底止, *bô sèy t'hang swāh*, that which cannot be stopped.

平

Bê 薇 A kind of vegetable; also, a flower. Ch'haé bê jê sit 採薇而食, *bán bê â jê chëāh*, they picked the Bê vegetable, and ate of it;—said of Pek-ê and Sëuk-chēy, who wandered into the mountains, and lived on wild vegetables, rather than eat the rice of the 周 Chew dynasty.

Ch'hëâng bê hwa 薔薇花, *ch'hëô^ng bê hwa*, a rose.

Bê 眉 Vulg: *baě:* the eye-brows; bòk bê 目眉, *bàk baě*, the eye brows. Also written 睂 bê.

Chîn séw gô bê 螓首蛾眉, *chîn t'haôu gô baě*, a head like the Chîn insect, and eye-brows like the silkworm.

Bê 楣 Bûn bê 門楣, *mooi^ng baě*, the lintel of a door. Ch'hun sek êng bê 春色盈楣, *ch'hun t'hee^ng ây sek êng mw^nâ mooi^ng baě*, may the beauties of spring replenish the lintel of your door;—a good wish pasted up on people's doors.

Bê 嵋 Gô bê 峨嵋, the name of a hill.

Bê 彌 Very, more, extensive. Hoo-choô che tō, gëâng che bê ko, chwàn che bê këen 夫子之道.仰之彌高.鑽之彌堅, *Hoo-choô ây tō, t^na k'hè k'hw^nà nā kwân, chwui^ng e nā têng*, with respect to the doctrine of Confucius, the more it is looked up to, the higher it appears, and the more it is bored into, the harder it seems. See the 上論 Sëang lun.

Bê 瀰 Full, overflowing, abundant. Hô súy bê bê 河水瀰瀰, *kâng chúy bê mw^nâ*, the waters of the river were full and overflowing. See the 國風 Kok hong.

Bê 湄 The brink of water, the water's edge. Chaē súy che bê 在水之湄, *tē chúy ây bê*, on the water's edge. See the same.

Bê 堳 A mound or altar of earth.

Bê 郿 The name of a place. Ch'hëen toe Bê-oe 遷都郿塢, he removed the capital to Bê-oe.

Bê 微 Small, diminutive, worthless, trifling. Taē jin put tëuk sèy bê che soō 大人不逐細微之事, *twā lâng bô tē tëuk sèy bê ây soō*, great men are not particular about small, trifling things.

Ch'hit ch'hek bê k'he, ê sew hoō bóe 七尺微軀貽羞父母, *ch'hit ch'hëŏh sèy sèy ây hin sin, lûy tëŏh seâou lèy ê pāy bóe*, "my seven-span-long, diminutive body, has only involved my parents in disgrace,"— an expression of humility.

Bê 薇 Tôe bê hwa 荼薇花, the name of a flower.

Bê 麋 A large kind of stag; also, a doe. Koè hông gān bê lòk 顧鴻鴈麋鹿, *k'hw^nà twā chëăh ây gān, kap twā chëăh ây lòk*, looking at the large wild geese, and the larger stags. See the 上孟 Sëang bēng.

Bê 劘 To divide, to part.

Bê 糜 Vulg: *mōëy:* Rice-water, congee, rice gruel: a surname. Bê chëuk 糜粥, *âm mōëy*, congee.

Leâng-hwūy-ông é t'hoé tëy che koè bê lân kè bin jê chëen che 梁惠王以土地之故.糜爛其民.而戰之, *Lëâng-hwūy-ông ê t'hoè tëy ây yëên koè, bê lân e ây pàyh sai^ng, jê hôe e k'hè sëo t'haě*, Lëâng-hwūy-ông merely on account of extension of territory, harassed his people (literally, boiled them down into gruel), and drove them to war.

Bê 獼 Bê hoê 獼猴, a kind of monkey.

Bê 縻 To drag, to influence. Gnó yéw h^nó chëak, goê é choô bê che 我有好爵.吾與子縻之, *gwá woō hó ây chëak wūy, gwá hoē lè bê e*, I have an eligible office, which I will give to you, to draw it into your influence. See the 易經 Yĕăh keng

Bê 虆 Plants growing in the water.

Bê 㗘 The noise made in calling ducks; bê bê, something similar to the "dill, dilly," of English housewives.

去

Bē 未 Vulg: *böĕy:* not yet; not; also, one of the horary characters. Bē laê 未來, *böĕy laê*, not yet come.

Hwân bê sêng 還未成, *yĕâ böĕy chĕnā*, not yet completed.

Bē lêng soō jîn, yëen lêng soō kwúy 未能事人.焉能事鬼, *böĕy ēy hok saē lâng, böĕyh chaê ēy hok saē kwúy*, not being able to do your duty to men, how can you serve spiritual beings? See the 下論 Hāy lūn.

Bē 味 Taste. Gnóe bē 五味, the five tastes; choo bē 滋味, a taste. Sam gwat put te jëuk bē 三月不知肉味, *sⁿa göĕyh jît ūᵐ chae bâh āy chòo bē*, for three months he did not know the taste of flesh;—Said of Confucius, when he was trying to learn the music of Sùn; so ardent was he in his desire to get acquainted with it. See the 上論 Sëāng lūn.

Bē 寐 To sleep, to retire to rest. Gnō bē kêw che 寤寐求之, *k'hwùn k'hè yĕâ kêw e*, waking and sleeping he sought her. See the 國風 Kok hong.

Sëuk hin yëā bē 夙興夜寐, *châ sè k'hè, âm chĕw k'hwùn.* Early to bed and early to rise. See the 詩經 Se keng.

Bē 謎 A riddle; a dark saying. Chò bē kip jîn ch'haé 做謎給人猜, *chò bē hoē lâng ch'haê*, to make riddles, and set people to unravel them.

平

Bëâ 乜 A slanting look; read bëá, a surname.

声

Beáou 渺 The flowing appearance of water.

Beáou 緲 The diminutive appearance of things, when viewed at a distance.

Beáou 淼 The expansiveness of water.

Beáou 杳 Dark, indistinct, distant, enlarged. Koè hëang beáou boô chêy 故鄉杳無際, *koō āy hëoⁿᵍ lê beáou hwuīⁿᵍ bô chêy*, to be removed from one's native village, to an unlimited distance. See the 唐詩 Tông se.

Beáou 邈 Distant, indistinct; also, to look lightly on. Beáou hōe put te sëy che 邈乎不知所之, *hwuīⁿᵍ hwuīⁿᵍ, ūᵐ chae kaôu tá lŏh wūy*, distant, to an unknown extent.

Beáou 窔 The south-east corner of a house.

Beáou 皛 Clear, evident, manifest.

Beáou 渹 Dark, unfathomable.

Beáou 窅 Deep and distant. Wùy jëên jê cheng, beáou jëên jê ch'him 蔚然而靜.窅然而深, quiet and still, deep and profound. See 莊子 Chung-chóó.

Beáou 藐 K'heng beáou 輕藐, *khin beaou*, to slight and despise.

Beáou 眇 Blind of one eye, dim-sighted. P'hó léng lé, beáou lêng sè 跛能履眇能視, *kŏēy k'ha ēy kēⁿá*, *ch'hai^{ng} mai^{ng} ēy k'hwⁿà*, the lame can walk, and the dim-sighted can see. See the 易經 Yĕăh keng.

Beáou 杪 The furthest end of any thing, bók beáou 木杪, the extremity of a tree.
Lēên beáou sŭèy boé 年杪歲暮 *nēe^{ng} bŏèy hŏèy àm*, the end of the year, and the close of the season.

Beáou 秒 Hô beáou 禾秒, *ch'hëuk mai^{ng}*, the blade of corn.

Beáou 龍龍龍 The appearance of flying dragons.

Beáou 仯 A little child; also, to be alarmed, and frightened.

下平

Beâou 描 Vulg: *bëŏ:* to copy any thing by writing over the original. Beâou joō 描字, *bëŏ jē*, to copy or decypher characters; to trace writing.

Beâou 貓 Vulg: *neaou:* a cat, a common cat. Beâou ch'hé tông jé 貓鼠同乳, *neaou kap neaou ch'hé tâng chëăh leng*, "a cat and a rat sucking the same mother." This was a singular circumstance, which occurred in the Hàn dynasty, and was considered as a bad omen.

Beâou 苗 Hô beâou 禾苗, *pò ch'hē á*, the young shoots of corn; a surname. Kok che sé seng, wat beâou 穀之始生曰苗, *ch'hek ây toō toō á sai^{ng} kóng beâou*, when the grain is beginning to grow it is called beâou.
Ông te hoo beâou hōe 王知夫苗乎, *ông lè chae pò ch'hē á ū^m*, does your Majesty know any thing about the young shooting corn? See 孟子 Bēng choó.
Hāy lap wat beâou 夏獵曰苗, *hōy t'hee^{ng} p'hăh lăh kóng beâou*, the summer hunt is called beâou.

上去

Beāou 妙 Wonderful, deep, mysterious, excellent; also, young. Sîn hwà put ch'hek wūy che beāou 神化不測謂之妙, *sîn ây peèn hwà bô t'hang ch'hek*, *kóng kēò beāou*, Divine transformations, unsearchable in their nature, are called beāou.
Bê beāou 微妙, wonderful, minute.
Beāou sīm 妙甚, very good; excellent!
Lēên beāou 年妙, *neē^{ng} hŏēy k'hăh chee^{ng}*, young in years.

Beāou 玅 Fine, minute, excellent.

Beāou 廟 Vulg: *bēō:* a temple, a place of idolatrous worship. Chong beāou 宗廟, *choé chong ây bēō*, an ancestorial temple.
K'hóng-choó jip taē beāou, bŏéy soō būn 孔子入大廟每事問, *K'hóng-choó jip twā bēō, tak hâng mooī^{ng}*, Confucius entered the great temple, and enquired about every thing he saw. See the 論語 Lūn gé.—Also written 庿 beāou.

下入

Beĕh 篾 Read bēet, basket work, wicker-work. Bēet lâm 篾籃, *beĕh nâ*, a wicker basket.
Bēet sek 篾席, *beĕh ch'hĕŏh*, a rush mat.

声

Bëén 免 To avoid, to do without, to escape, to conclude. Bëén chit 免職, to be put out of office.

Yâng-sê chëûng Ch'haè-keng yêw, bē bëén pek p'hek yéw tëèm 楊時從蔡京遊·未免白璧有玷, *Yëō^{ng}-sê t'hàn Ch'hwà-keng yêw, bēy bëèn păyh p'hek woō tëèm*, Yëō^{ng}-sê following Ch'hwà-keng in his peregrinations, could not avoid the evil of the white gem being spotted, i. e. he could not avoid contamination. See the 宋史 Sŏng-soó, History of the Sŏng dynasty.

Bëén 丏 A low wall to protect people from archery; also, invisible.

Bëén 沔 The name of a stream. Bëén pé lêw súy, teâou chong ê haé 沔彼流水·朝宗於海, *Bëén hwut lêy laôu chúy, k'hè teâou chong ê hae*, the flowing waters of the Bëén stream go to pay their respects to the sea. See the 小雅 Seáou gnáy.

Bëén 勉 To urge, to spur on, to animate, to exert. Choó pit bëén che 子必勉之, *lé tek k'hak teŏh bëén lëy e*, Sir! you must exert yourself in it.

Bëén 娩 To bring forth children, to bear young. Hwun bëén 分娩 to be delivered of a child.

Bëén 鮸 The name of a fish, a kind of John Dory.

Bëén 冕 A crown, an Emperor's cap. Bān kok e kwan paè bëén lêw 萬國衣冠拜冕旒, *bān kok ây s^{n}ā kin teŏh paè bëén lêw*, the robes and coronets of all nations must pay reverence to the Emperor's crown. See the 唐詩 Tông se.

Bëén 湎 To be drowned, to be overwhelmed. But pëēn naé soo bîn bëén ê chéw 勿辨乃司民湎於酒, *s^{n}a soō ū^{m} pëēn bêng yêw soō kw^{n}a kap păyh sai^{ng} tîm bëèn ê chéw*, why do you not enquire into the officers' and people's being drowned in wine. See the 尚書 Sëō^{ng} se.

Bëén 緬 Distant; also, bëén sëáng 緬想, *bëén sëō^{ng}*, to think.

Bëén 愍 Bëén kè 愍忌, a sacrifice offered on every birth-day of a deceased relative: read bín.

平

Bëên 棉 Bok bëên 木棉, the silky cotton tree: the name of a tree which has flowers like cotton, and of which they make cloth.

Bok bëên, Kang-lâm to yéw che 木棉江南多有之, *ch'hâ mee^{ng}, tē Kang-lâm chēy woō*, of the silky cotton, there is an abundance in Kang-lâm.

Bëên hwa 棉花, *mee^{ng} hwa*, the cotton tree; cotton.

Bëên 綿 Cotton; wool; also, soft and yielding; also, unbroken, uninterrupted; also, close and continuous, as weeds and creeping plants.

Bëên yâng 綿羊, *mee^{ng} yëō^{ng}*, a wool goat, a sheep.

Bëên bëên kat lúy 綿綿葛藟, intertwined and uninterrupted, like the tendrils of creeping plants.

Bëên 眠 Vulg: *bîn:* to sleep, to rest; to lie down. T'hëen chok kím p'hē, tēy chok chöen, gwat lé sëûng gô p'hwān gnó bëên 天作錦被·地作氈·月裡孀娥伴我眠, *t'hee^{ng} chò kim p'hōēy, tēy chò chee^{ng} teâou, goēyh lāe ây sëûng gô p'hw^{n}ā* *gwá k'hwùn*, "the heaven forms my canopy, and the earth my carpet, while the nymphs of the moon sleep by my side." A couplet made by the founder of the 明 Bêng dynasty, when, in the utmost poverty, he commenced his career.

Beēn 聯 Connected, uninterrupted. Lân kwùy bêēn hong 蘭桂聯芳, *lân hwa kwùy hwa sëo swà p'hang*, "the lân flower and cassia blossoms are successively fragrant;"—(used with respect to those whose sons and grandsons advance successively to literary honors).

Bëën tùy 聯對 *lëën tùy*, a pair of antithetical sentences, generally written on boards, and stuck up on each side of a room.

Bēēn 宀 The covering of a house.

Bēēn 櫋 The eaves of a roof.

Bēēn 緡 Bëën bân 緡蠻, the noise of a bird: also, cotton threads.

丟

Bēēn 面 Vulg: *bïn*: The face, the front, the countenance. Jîn sim jê bëën 人心如面, *lâng ây sim ch'hin chëō^ng lâng ây bïn*, people's minds are like their faces; i. e. varying.

Yung yëá, k'hó soó lâm bëën 雍也可使南面, *Yung yëá, t'hang saé e bïn ^n à lâm*, Yung may be employed in facing the south; (i. e. in ruling the people; — because all rulers bëën lâm 面南, *bïn ^n à lâm*, face the south, and all subjects bëën pak 面北, *bïn ^n à pak*, face the north).

Bēēn 偭 To turn the back on. Bëën kwuy pöëy ké 偭規背矩, *sëo pöëy kwuy kè*, to act contrary to establish-ed customs.

Bëēn 麵 Vulg: *meē^ng*: flour made of wheat. bëën paou 麵包, *bïn paou*, bread. Bëën paou kan 麵包干, *bïn paou kw^n a*, biscuit.

E bëën wûy he seng 以麵爲犧牲, *t'hó meē^ng chò t'haou sai^ng*, "to use wheaten flour instead of animals in sacrifice." This was done by 武帝 Boó-têy, of the 梁 Lëâng dynasty, out of compassion. See 下孟註 Hây bēng choò.

Bëēn 湎 To drink wine to excess.

灭

Bëet 篾 Vulg: *bëëh*: wicker-work, basket-work. bëët lâm 篾籃, *bëëh nâ*, a wicker basket.

Bëet 蔑 Not, nothing, diminutive; to slight.

Bëet 衊 Black blood.

Bëet 滅 To exterminate, to overthrow, to annihilate, to extinguish, finish. Bëët kok chëá gnóe sip 滅國者五十, *bëët kok göe chap*, he overcame fifty states. See the 上孟 Sëäng bēng.

Kê tëëm êng teng, bëët hëw bêng 幾點螢燈滅復明, *kwúy tëëm ây höëy kim ch'hai^ng bëët bó yëw kóh kwui^ng*, just like a few spots of fire-fly lamps, at one time extinguished, and then bright again: — Said of composition which is in some parts dark and in others clear.

Bëet kêw chok 滅九族, *bëët káou ây chok* to exterminate all a man's nine relations.

Bëet 烕 To exterminate.

Beet 韈 Vulg: *böëyh*: stockings; ch'hwàn bëet 穿韈, *ch'hèng böëyh*, to wear stockings.

灭

Bek 陌 Tëen bek 田陌, *ch'hân hwⁿā*, the elevated paths between the rice fields. Sëang-yâng k'hae ch'hëen bek 商映開阡陌, *Sëang-yâng k'hwuy ch'hân hwⁿā*, Sëang-yâng (of the 秦 Chin dynasty) recommended the enlarging of the paths between the rice fields. See the 戰國策 Chëen kok ch'hek.

Bek 脈 Hëet bek 血脈, *höeÿh maiⁿh*, the pulse, the arteries. Also written 脉 bek.
Hëet bek kwàn t'hong 血脈貫通, *höeÿh maiⁿh kwàn t'hong*, the blood of the arteries runs through the whole frame.

Bek 万 Bek kê 万俟, a double surname.

Bek 嶕 Bek p'hek 嶕帕, secret, close.

Bek 瀎 Shallow water.

Bek 幎 A veil, a covering for the eyes. Bek bok yŭng choo 幎目用緇, *tà bīn ày kìn yŭng oe ây*, the veil that covers the eyes should be black. See the 儀禮 Gê léy.

Bek 冪 A cloth used for covering over food.

Bek 冖 To cover over any thing; one of the radicals.

Bek 幦 The covering of a carriage; bek 幭 has the same meaning.

Bek 塓 To plaister: bek kwán këung sit 塓館宮室, *bwăh ŏh kwán kap këung sit*, to plaister the school and house. See the 左傳 Chó twān.

Bek 蟔 The name of an insect.

Bek 覓 Sim bek 尋覓, *sīm ch'höey*, to seek for any thing. Sëep chew k'hong, jê bek loē 涉舟航而覓路, *tăh chûn köey chûy jê ch'höey loē*, he crossed the water in a boat, and sought out for the road. Said of 晉武帝 Chin Boó-tèy, in his wanderings.

Bek 虩 A white tiger.

Bek 貊 The barbarians of the north. Suy bān bek che pang, hēng è 雖蠻貊之邦行矣 *suy jëën bān bek ây pang kok, yëâ këⁿā*, even among the most barbarous nations, (if we possess sincerity), we may safely travel. See the 下論 Hāy lūn.

Bek 霢 Small rain; ek che é bek bok 益之以霢霂, *t'hëeⁿg che-é sèy hoē*, added to which there was a drizzling rain. See the 小雅 Seáou gnáy.

Bek 霡 The same as the preceding.

Bek 驀 An excellent horse; to surpass.

福建方言字典

Bĕk 糸 Small threads of silk.

Bĕk 墨 Vulg: *bák*: ink; bĕk teâou 墨條, *bák teâou*, a stick of ink, commonly called Indian ink; bĕk súy 墨水, *bák chúy*, liquid ink.
Bûn bĕk che pōèy 文墨之輩, *bûn bák ây lâng*, the literati.
Hëung boô pwàn tëēm bĕk 胸無半點墨, *heng k'hàm bô pwⁿà tëēm ây bák chúy*, "on his breast there is not half a dot of ink;" — (entimating an entire want of liarning).

Bĕk 默 Silent, to meditate, to refrain from speaking. Bĕk bĕk put gân 默默不言, *tëèm tëèm bô kóng wā*, silent, without speaking.
Bĕk jê chè che 默而識之, *tëèm tëèm jê ka tē bat e*, to meditate silently and gain a knowledge of a thing. See the 上論 Sëāng lūn.

Bĕk 麥 Vulg: *báyh*: wheat: taē bĕk 大麥, *twā báyh*, barley. Hwan bĕk 番麥 *hwan báyh*, Indian corn.
Kim hoo boê bĕk, pò chëūng jê yew che 今夫辨麥. 播種而耰之, *tⁿa hwut lëy báyh, yëà chê jê k'haou ch'hâou*, now with respect to the wheat, when it is sown and harrowed, &c. See the 下孟 Hāy bēng.

Bĕk 帞 A veil for the head.

Bĕk 絔 A cloth for wrapping up any thing.

去

Béng 猛 Bold, fierce, ferocious, courageous, strong, daring. Yúng béng 勇猛, strong and ferocious.
O chèng gëēm ê béng hoé 苛政嚴於猛虎, *o chèng k'hăh gëēm ê béng hoé*, tyrannical government is severer than a fierce tiger.

Béng 艋 A small kind of boat.

Béng 酩 Béng téng 酩酊, very drunk.

Béng 茗 Fine tea, plucked late from the tree; béng gâm 茗巖, fine tea.

Béng 佲 Good, fine.

Béng 皿 A vessel for containing any thing. Seng sat, k'hè béng, e hok, put pē, put kám é chèy 牲殺. 器皿. 衣服. 不備. 不敢以祭, *t'hâou saiⁿᵍ, k'hè bêng, yìn chëôⁿᵍ, bô cheâou pē, ūᵐ kⁿá ê chèy*, when the sacrificial animals, the vessels, and the apparel, were not ready prepared, he did not dare to sacrifice. See the 上孟 Sëāng bēng.

平

Bêng 明 Clear, bright; to illustrate, to illumine, to display, to distinguish; bêng pĕk 明白, to understand clearly.
Bêng bêng chaē sëāng, hek hek chaē hāy 明明在上. 赫赫在下, *bêng kwuiⁿᵍ tē tëng bīn, oe âm tē āy téy*, clear and bright above, dark and dreary below. See the 大雅 Taē gnáy.
Bêng gwăt sëûng kan chëàou 明月松間照, *bêng gōëyh sëûng kan chëò*, the clear moon shining among the firs.

Bêng 明 To survey, to behold: a surname.

G

Bêng 儚 Dark and dreary. Also written 儚 bêng, dim, obscure.

Bêng 盲 Blind, the pupil of the eye destroyed. Bok bêng 目盲, *bak chew ch'hai^{ng} mai^{ng}*, the eyes blinded.
K'hae bêng jîn bok 開盲人目, *k'hwuy ch'hai^{ng} mai^{ng} lâng ây bak chew*, to open the eyes of the blind.

Bêng 盟 An oath, a conspiracy. Ch'hap hëet é këet bêng 歃血以結盟, *ch'hap höëyh è kat bêng*, to smear with blood, in order to bind with an oath.
Hwân-kong yéw gnóe bêng che kìm 桓公有五盟之禁, *Hwân-kong woō goē bêng ây kìm*, Hwân-kong had five things which he interdicted on oath.

Bêng 萌 To sprout out, to shoot forth. Bêng gây 萌芽, *paoùh eè^{ng}*, to bud. Ch'hun sé seng, jê bêng che 春始生而萌之, *ch'hun t'hee^{ng} k'hè t'hâou sai^{ng} jê paoùh k'hè laê*, in the spring they begin to grow, and bud forth.

Bêng 名 Vulg: *mê^{n}â*: a name, a designation, fame: bêng seng 名聲, *mê^{n}â sê^{n}a*, reputation.
Bêng é bêng che 名以命之, *hoē e chît lêy mê^{n}â, é këò è*, to give a person a name, in order to call him by. See the 禮記 Léy kè.

Bêng 銘 To remember, to record the merits of a person deceased. Téng bêng 鼎銘, *tê^{n}á bêng*, a sculptured tripod.
Bêng seng 銘旌, a flag recording the merits of deceased persons.

Bêng 冥 Dark, dismal: bêng hwun 冥昏, *mai^{ng} hwui^{ng}*, the evening. Boô chëang taē ke, wûy tîn bêng bêng 無將大車.維塵冥冥, *bô chëang twā ch'hëa, tok woō tîn ae. bêng bêng*, nothing was seen of the great chariot, but a cloud of dust, dark and impenetrable. See the 小雅 Seáou gnây. Hong é höey bêng 風雨晦明, *hong kap hoē, oe oe àm àm*, with the storm of wind and rain, it was dark and dismal.

Bêng 溟 Small rain; also, the sea. Bit é bêng bok 密雨溟沐, *bat ây hoē bêng bòk*, the close rain drizzled down.
Pok bêng yéw gê 北溟有魚, *pak haē woō hê*, in the northern sea there are fishes.

Bêng 暝 A name; dark.

Bêng 瞑 To open the eyes without seeing any light: dimness of sight; closing the eyes in death.
Kê sè bêng bêng 共視瞑瞑, *e k'hw^{n}à ch'hai^{ng} mai^{ng}*, he looked dimly.
Kam sim bêng bok 甘心瞑目, *kam sim k'hâyh bak chew*, he contentedly closed his eyes in death.

Bêng 蓂 Bêng këep ch'hó 蓂莢草, *bêng këep ch'hâou*, a kind of sensitive plant, which was said to put forth a leaf on the first day of the moon, and to continue producing one leaf a day till the full; at which time the leaves began to fall, till by the end of the moon they were all gone. Spoken of in the 綱鑑 Kóng kàm.

Bêng 螟 The name of an insect, that lends its chrysalis to another, to be brought up as its own.
Bêng-lêng yéw choó 螟蛉有子, *bêng-lêng woō kê^{n}á*, "the bêng-lêng insect has its chrysalis," which is stolen by another.

Bêng 蝱 A flying insect, that stings people.

Bêng 鏋 A kind of dart or sharp weapon. Hàn-Kong-boó chok bwuy bêng kong ch'hek bê chek 漢光武作飛鏋光赤眉賊, *Hàn-Kong-boó chok hwuy bêng kong ch'hek bê ây ch'hat*, the Emperor Kong-boó of the Hàn dynasty made a kind of flying dart, to oppose the red eye-browed robbers.

Bêng 鳴 The cry of a bird, or any cry or noise; the crowing of a cock, or ringing of a bell, or any other kind of sound; vulg: *tân*, to ring, or *t'hê*, to crow, or *haóu*, to cry or call.
Key bêng koé hwūy būn ê tëung kok 鷄鳴狗吠聞於中國, *key t'hê kaóu pwūy tit t'hē^{n}a ê t'hong tëung kok*, the crowing of cocks, and barking of dogs, were heard throughout all the middle country (i. e. China). See 孟子 Bēng choó.
Sam lëên put bêng, bêng chek keng jîn 三年不鳴.鳴則驚人, *s^{n}a neē^{ng} bô tân, tân chēw hoē lâng kē^{n}a*, it did not sound once in three years, but when it did sound, it alarmed people.

Bêng 甍 A beam, a rafter.

Bêng 粺 Clear, fine rice.

Bêng 榠 The pith of a tree; also, the name of a tree.

丟

Bēng 命 A command, a decree, the decree of heaven; fate; to order, to command. Chëang bēng chëá ch'hut hoē 將命者出戶, *t'hui^{ng} bēng lêng ây lâng ch'hut mooî^{ng}*, the bearer of the message went out at the door. See the 下論 Hāy lūn.
T'hëen bēng yéw chaē, kê wûy Chew-Bûn-ông hoê 天命有在.其爲周文王乎, *t'hee^{ng} ây bēng woō tē tit, e chò ch'hin chëō^{ng} Chew-Bûn-ông hoê*, "The decree of heaven being fixed, let him do as Bûn-ông of the Chew dynasty." Said by Chó-ch'hò 曹操, when he wanted his son to assume the title of Emperor. See the 三國 Sam kok.
Sê wūn put chêy, bēng toê to ch'hwan 時運不齊.命途多舛, *sê wūn ū^{m} chêy chwui^{ng}, mē^{n}ā toê chêy ch'hwan ch'hok*, the revolution of times and seasons is not equal, and the way of fate is full of errors. Said by 王勃海 Ông-put-haé.

Bēng 孟 The beginning of any thing; applied to the beginning of the four quarters of the year; also, a surname.
Soò sê kae yéw bēng gwat 四時皆有孟月, *sì sê chò poô woō bēng göēyh*, the four seasons, have each their commencing months.
Bēng boé sam ch'hëen kàou choó 孟母三遷教子, *Bēng-choó ây nëō^{ng} lêy s^{n}a kwùy pw^{n}a ch'hoò böēyh kà e ây kē^{n}ā*, the mother of Mencius thrice removed her dwelling, in order to instruct her son.

Bēng 甯 Any thing wished, or desired: a surname.

Bēng 甯 A surname: Bēng-boó-choó, pang yéw tō, chek tê 甯武子邦有道則知, *Bēng-boó-choó, pang kok woō to ây sê chëet, chek tê*, Bēng-boó-choó, when a country possessed the right way, displayed wisdom. See the 上論 Chëō^{ng} lūn.

Bēng 瞑 To open one's eyes; also, dark.

Bēng 瞢 Sorrowful. Put é ê höēy, ek boô bēng yēen 不與於會.亦無瞢焉, *bô hōe gwá, chò hōēy bēng yĕá bô hwân lô*, if you do not admit me to a share of the confederacy, I shall not be grieved. See the 左傳 Chó twān.

平

Bēô 描 Read beâou; to transcribe, to copy; beâou joō 描字, *bēô jē*, to trace writing.

Beâou sēá put chin 描寫不眞, *bēô sēá ūm chin*, to copy incorrectly.

去

Bēō 廟 Read beâou: a temple: Taē-pek-kong beâou 大伯公廟, *Twā-pāyh-kong bēō*, an idol temple; the temple of the "old great uncle."

Chong beâou che soō 宗廟之事, *chong bēō āy soō*, the business of the ancestorial temple.

平

Bêw 繆 Intertwined, twisted, plaited together. Têw bêw yéw hoè 綢繆牖戶, *têw bêw t'hang moiⁿᵍ*, "to twist straw about the windows and doors," — said of the birds who thus form their nests. See the 國風 Kok hong.

去

Bēw 繆 Erroneous, confused: hô é ch'hok bēw chè ch'hoó 何以錯繆至此, *an chwⁿá ch'hò bēw kaôu an nèy saiⁿᵍ*, how is it become wrong and confused to so great a degree? Said by 于定國 É-tēng-kok.

Bēw 謬 Wrong, false, erroneous, wandering. Ch'ha che hô lê, bēw é ch'hēen lé 差之毫釐.謬以千里, *ch'hay goē āy hô lê, ēy bēw kaôu chēⁿá ch'heng lé*, a difference of only a hair's breath will afterwards lead to an error of a thousand furlongs.

声

Béy 買 Read maé: to buy, to purchase. Seáou chaé t'hèng maé maē, é chit chēy 小宰聽買賣以質劑, *sēô chaé āy kwⁿa t'hēⁿa lâng bēy bēy, ē chit pat ⁿᵍ chēⁿà*, the under governor attended to people's buying and selling, in order to promote equity. See the 周禮 Chew léy.

平

Bêy 迷 To be deceived, to err, to wander; bēy loē 迷路, to go the wrong way, Bêy toê bē wán 迷途未遠, *bēy āy loē bōēy woō hēá hwuiⁿᵍ*, we have not yet wandered far out of the way. Said by 陶淵明 Tō-yēen-bêng.

去

Bēy 袂 The sleeve of a coat, a cuff. Sēet kêw tēâng, twán yēw bēy 褻裘長.短右袂, *sae k'hēa āy sⁿa tēôh tēⁿᵍ, ch'hòng tèy chēⁿà ch'hèw āy ch'hèw wuiⁿᵍ*, his private dress was long, with the right hand sleeve short. Said of Confucius, in the 上論 Chēōⁿᵍ lūn.

Bēy 賣 Read maē: to sell, to dispose of. Māe to maé tok 賣刀買犢, *bēy to, k'hè bèy goô á*, to sell a knife, in order to buy a heifer.

声

Bín 黽 To urge, to strive, to exert one's-self. Bin bēén chēūng soō 黽免從事, to exert one's self in a person's service.

Bín 敏 Clever, diligent, intelligent. Gnó suy put bín, ch'héng sēâng sè che 我雖不敏.請嘗試之, *gwá suy bēy bín, ch'hēⁿá bóng ch'hè k'hwⁿà*, although I am not clever, yet I request the trial to be made. See the 上孟 Sēāng bēng.

Bín jê hⁿó hak 敏而好學, *bín kwà aè t'hak ch'hāyh*, intelligent and fond of learning.

Bín 僶 To force one's-self to any thing, against the will and power.

Bín 閔 A surname: Bín-choô sē ch'hek 閔子侍側, *Bín-choô k'hēā ē sin peeⁿᵍ*, Bín-choô was standing by the side (of Confucius). See the 下論 Hāy lūn.

Bín 憫 To be silently grieved, to be displeased and sorrowful. Ek kēūng jê put bín 阨窮而不憫, *ăyh kwà kêng jê bēy bin,* in affliction and poverty, and yet not grieved. See the 上孟 Sëāng bēng.

Bín 慜 To be sorrowful, to lament, to pity. Gôe taē jē choô bín ê 吾代二子慜矣, *gwá t'hèy lē nō lâng hwân ló,* I am distressed for both of you. See the 左傳 Chó twān.

Bín 泯 To be annihilated, to be thrown into confusion. Bîn ê taē bín lwān 民彝大泯亂, *păyh sai^ng ây ê lûn twā bín lwān,* the moral relations of the people were thrown into the greatest confusion. See the 尚書 Sëōng se.

Bín 湣 A disapproving name, or codemnatory epithet, given to some kings after their death. Such as 周湣王 Chew-Bín-ông, the confused king of Chew; and 宋湣公 Sòng-Bín-kong, the stupid duke of the Sòng country.

Bín 刡 To rub, to scrape, to brush; a brush.

平

Bîn 民 The people; the common people; tē bîn 治民, to rule the people. Bîn boô lêng bêng yëen 民無能名焉, *păyh sai^ng bô chit lêy mē^nâ t'hang kèò,* "the people had no name by which they could designate him." Said of Sûn, who was above all praise. Bîn chêng taē k'hó këèn ê 民情大可見矣, *păyh sai^ng ây sèng chêng twā t'hang k'hwnà,* the dispositions of the people could be extensively seen. See the 古文 Koé bûn.

Bîn 岷 The common people, the horde. Bîn che ch'he ch'he 氓之蚩蚩, *păyh sai^ng gōng gōng,* the common horde are stupid as grubs. See the 國風 Kok hong.

Bîn 岷 The name of a hill. Bîn san tō Kang 岷山導江, *tē Bîn sw^na ch'hwā Kang chúy,* from the Bîn hill he led the waters of the Kang:"— Said of 禹 E', who 治水 tê súy, regulated the waters.

Bîn 珉 A fine kind of stone. Bîn gëük put pëēn 珉玉不辨, *chēōh kap gëük bô hwun pëēn,* not distinguishing between stones and gems.

Bîn 玟 The same as the foregoing.

Bîn 痻 Sickness, a disease; to gnó koe bîn 多我覯痻, *chēy lâng kap gwá k'hw^nà pai^ng,* many came to visit me in my sickness. See the 大雅 Taē gnáy.

Bîn 忞 To constrain one's-self.

Bîn 緡 A thread, a string: the string on which small coins are strung. Also written 緍 bîn. Kê tcàou wûy hô, wûy se e bîn 其釣維何.維絲伊緡, *e tëò hé yūng s^nà meē^nh, tok se kap su^nà,* "what did he use in angling? nothing but silk and thread." See the 國風 Kok hong.

去

Bīn 面 Read bëēn: the face, the countenance; a surface; to face, to front. Jé boô bëēn chêng, t'höey yéw hoē gân 汝無面從.退有後言, *lé ū^m t'hang bīn t'hàn, kaòu t'hèy ch'hëd woō aōu wā,* you must not merely comply before one's face, and then on retiring bring up some after words. See the 尚書 Sëōng se.

入

Bit 宓 To rest, to be silent: a surname: Chin-bit 秦宓, a man famous in the Sam-kok.

H

Bi̍t 苾 A kind of grass.

Bi̍t 蜜 Honey: bi̍t hong 蜜蜂 *bi̍t p'hang*, a honey bee. Kê kam jê bi̍t 其甘如蜜, *kê tee^ng ch'hîn chëō^ng bi̍t*, as sweet as honey.

Bi̍t 謐 Silent whispers; quiet, peaceful. Lōēy gōēy chek bi̍t 內外寂謐, *laē gwā chek bi̍t*, within and without, peaceful and quiet. See the 漢書 Hàn se.

Bi̍t 密 Vulg: *bat:* secret, close, concealed, retired. Chông k'hè bi̍t bi̍t 藏去密密 *k'hè^ng k'hè bat bat*, secretly hidden. Bi̍t yîn pu̍t ê, choō gnó sey kaou 密雲不雨自我西郊, *bat hwân ū^m lŏh hoē, choō gwân sae kaou*, close clouds without rain, coming from our western border. See the 易經 *Yĕăh keng*.

Bi̍t 汨 Dusty and muddy; also, deep and hidden.

Bi̍t 樒 Fragrant wood; a name for cassia; cinnamon. Kaou-chew yéw bi̍t hëang sē 交州有樒香樹, *Kaou-chew woō bi̍t hëo^ng ch'hēw*, in the district of Kaou-chew, there exists the fragrant bi̍t tree, — chek kim che tîm hëang yĕá 卽今之沉香也, *chek sē tong kim ây tîm hëo^ng*, which is the cinnamon of the present day.

Bi̍t 蠠 To urge, to exert one's-self.

声

Bó 拇 The thumb; taē hó ché 大拇指, *twā pó bó*, the great thumb.

Bó 踇 The great toe.

Bó 嬤 Bó bó 嬤嬤, a common appellation for mother.

Bó 母 Vulg: *nëô^ng lêy:* mother; hoō bó 父母, *pāy bó*, father and mother. Wûy t'hëen tēy bān bu̍t hoō bó 惟天地萬物父母, *wûy t'hee^ng tēy chò bān mee^nh ây pāy bó*, Heaven and earth are the parents of all things. See the 尙書 Sëō^ng se.

平

Bô 無 Read boô: not, not at all. Boô put kèng 無不敬, *bô ū^m kèng*, unfailing respect. T'hëen hāy boô put sē che hoō bó 天下無不是之父母, *t'hee^ng āy bô ū^m tëŏh ây pāy bó*, "under the whole Heavens there are no faulty parents;" — meaning that children should never suppose their parents to be in the wrong.

去

Bō 帽 A cap, a hat: Po̍k-taē-hoē é bō se t'hêy Bûn-tèy 薄大后以帽絮提文帝, *Po̍k-taē-hoē t'hó chi̍t lêy bō se hoē Bûn-tèy*, the great Empress Po̍k took a silken cap, and gave it to (her son) the Emperor Bûn.

Bō 磨 A mill. Súy bō 水磨, *chúy bō*, a water mill. Jê gé swân bō 如蟻旋磨, *ch'hîn chëō^ng hëā pwan swân tē bō chëŏh*, "like an ant going round a mill stone." The Chinese say, that an ant always travels round a mill-stone in an opposite direction to that in which the stone is turned; from which the ancients obtained their ideas of the motion of the heavenly bodies. See the 天文志 Thëen bûn chè.

声

Boé 畝 An acre: tëên boé 畝田, *ch'hân boé*, an acre of ground. Gnoé boé che t'hek, sē che é song 五畝之宅樹之以桑, *goē boé ây t'hâyh, chèng e ê se^ng*, let every plot of five acres be planted with the mulberry tree. See the 上孟 *Chëō^ng bēng*.

Boé 畆 The same as the preceding.

Boé 牡 The male of domestic animals; the name of a flower. Boé-tan, hwa che hoō kwùy chēá yēá 牡丹花之富貴者也, *boé-tan sē hwa ây k'hăh poò kwùy ây*, the Moutan is the richest and noblest of flowers.

Boé 姥 An old woman: t'hēen boé san 天姥山, *t'hee^{ng} boé sw^{n}a*, the name of a hill.

Boé 母 Vulg: *nĕō^{ng} lēy*: a mother: boé choó 母子, *boé kē^{n}á*, mother and child. K'hēĕn goē hoō yēá, k'hwun goē boé yēá 乾吾父也.坤吾母也, *t'hee^{ng} sē gwán ay nĕō^{ng} pāy, tēy sē gwán ây nĕō^{ng} lēy*, heaven is our father, and the earth is our mother. See the 西銘 Sey bēng.

Boé 姆 An instructress; an uncle's wife: gak boé 岳姆, *tēo^{ng} ú^{m}*, a mother-in-law. Sēūk hoe pek che ch'hey wûy boé 俗呼伯之妻爲姆, *sēùk kēò pāyh ây boé sē ú^{m}*, in common conversation we call an uncle's wife, aunt.

Boé 某 Any one, such an one, a certain person. Choó kò che wat, boé chaē soo, boé chaē soo 子告之曰.某在斯.某在斯, "Confucius informed him saying, this is such an one, and that is such an one;" said of his introducing his friends to a blind man who waited on him. See the 下論 Hāy lūn.

Boé 厶 The same as the preceding; also, one of the radicals.

Boé 栂 Kang boé 江栂, the name of a tree, the wood of which yields excellent potash.

平

Boê 謀 To scheme, to contrive, to plan, key boê 計謀, a plan, a sheme. Wûy jîn boê, jê put tëung hoē 爲人謀而不忠乎, *wûy lâng soā nēō^{ng}, jê ú^{m} tëung hoē*, in consulting people's interests, are we unfaithful? See the 上論 Sēāng lūn. Boê chong chek chēûng 謀臧則從, *boê hó chēw thàn e*, if the plan is good, then follow it. See the 大雅 Taē gnáy.

Boê 侔 Even, equal to, alike. K'hê ê jîn, jê boê ê t'hēen 畸於人而侔於天, *k'hăh twā ê lâng, jê kap t'hee^{ng} pat^{ng} twā*, greater than men, and equal to heaven.

Boê 牟 Boê nê 牟尼, a name of Buddha: also, to take, to win; the noise of a bull. Sēāng kan choó sim, hāy boê pek sèng 上干主心.下牟百姓, *lēng bīn kan kēw choó kong ây sim kw^{n}a, āy lēy boê ch'hé pāyh sai^{ng}*, above he sought to win the heart of the chief, and below to captivate the affections of the people. See the 戰國策 Chēēn kok ch'hek.

Boê 眸 Bòk boê 目眸, *bak ang á*, the pupil of the eye. Chûn hoē jîn chēá, bòk lēāng ê boê choó 存乎人者莫良於眸子, *chûn twā tē lâng, bô k'hăh hó ê bak ang á*, (to know) what is retained in a man's mind, there is no better sign than the pupil of the eye. See the 下孟 Hāy bēng.

Boê 模 Kwuy boê 規模, a pattern, a rule, a manner, a plan. Sēw chwân boê ê choó ch'hēang 受全模於梓匠, *sēw chwui^{ng} hó ây kwuy boê ê bak ch'hēō^{ng}*, "to receive a complete plan from the head carpenter;"—an expression of 左思 Chó-soo.

Boê 嫫 Boê-boé 嫫母 was a very ugly woman, the wife of 黃帝 Hông-tèy; hence it has become a bye-word for any ugly female.

Boê 膜 Vulg: *mŏh:* the thin skin under the outer skin: the epidermis. Tē jëuk, tê kê kin boê, ch'hé hⁿó cheĕ 治肉.除其筋膜.取好者, *ch'hòng bǎh hëet ê ây kǒn mih, t'hǎyh hó ây,* in preparing meat, take away the tendons and inner skin, and select the best of it. See the 爾雅 Jé gnáy.

Boê 摸 Vulg: *bong:* to feel, to touch with the hand. 'Am boê boê loē 暗摸無路, *àm bong bô loē,* it is so dark that we cannot feel our way.

Boê 摹 To feel: the same as the preceding.

Boê 謨 To scheme, to plan: the same as 謀 boê. Gwān Sëen-seng bông ch'hoó wán boê 願先生弘此遠謨, *gwān Sin-saiⁿᵍ ch'hòng k'hǎh twā chèy lêy hwuīⁿᵍ boê,* I beseech you, Sir, to enlarge this distant plan. See the 漢書 Hàn se.

Boê 脢 The back; the flesh of the back.

Boê 漠 Tam boê 淡漠, quiet and still: the name of a place. Pok hong yéw Sa-boê che tēy 北方有沙漠之地, *pak heⁿᵍ woō Swa-boê ây têy,* in the northern region is the desert of Sha-mŏh.

Boê 蟊 An insect that eats the roots of grain.

Boê 麰 A large kind of wheat: ê gnó laê boê 貽我來麰, *sàng gwá laê ây twā bǎyh,* he presented me with some large wheat. See the 小雅 Seâou gnáy.

亖

Boē 戊 One of the horary characters; also, lucky, fortunate. Kit jit wûy boē 吉日爲戊, *hó jit chò boē,* a lucky day is called boē.

Boē 懋 To praise, to admire; also, to urge, to exert. Ê boē naé tek 予懋乃德, *gwá o ló lê ây tek,* I applaud your virtue.

Boē 儆 Niggardly, parsimonious.

Boē 募 To call, to summons.

Boē 幕 A tent, a curtain: wûy boē che tëung 帷幕之中, *wûy boē ây tang eⁿᵍ,* within the tent;— in the tented field.

Boē 慕 To think of, to long after, to desire: a surname: wàn boē 怨慕, to fret after.

Jîn seàou chek boē hoō boé 人少則慕父母, *lâng sèy chĕw boē lëem pāy boé,* when people are young they long after their parents. See 孟子書 Bēng-choó se.

Yit kok che séy boē, t'bëen hāy boē che 一國之所慕.天下慕之, *chit kok ây sèy boē, t'heeⁿᵍ āy boē e,* he that is desired by a whole country, will be desired by the whole Empire.

Boē-yûng 慕容, a double surname.

Boē 墓 Hwûn boē 墳墓, *hwûn bōng,* a grave, a tomb. Koé put sew boē 古不修墓, *koé ây lâng bô sew chêng bōng,* the ancients did not ornament their tombs. See the 禮記 Léy kè.

Ek boē hwuy koé yëá 易墓非古也, *wⁿâ bōng ūᵐ sē koé chá ây lêy,* to remove a tomb is not according to the practice of the ancients.

Boē **暮** The evening, dark, dusk: teaou boē 朝暮, morning and evening. Jit boē ch'hwa hwun koé 日暮撾昏鼓, *jit àm p'hăh mai^{ng} hwui^{ng} koé*, at the decline of day, beat the evening drum.

Boē **貿** Vulg. *baoūh*: to exchange, to barter, to trade; boē ek 貿易, trade, commerce. Boē ch'hëen yéw boô 貿遷有無, *boe ch'hēen woō bô ây mee^{n}h*, to exchange what we have, for that which we have not. See the 尙書 Sëāng se.

Boē **茂** Luxuriant, abundant; boē sèng 茂盛 luxuriant foliage. Jê sëûng pek che boē 如松栢之茂, *ch'hin chëō^{ng} ch'hêng păyh ây boē*, like the luxuriance of the fir tree.

去

Böéy **每** Every, each, all; böéy böéy 每每, constantly, frequently. Böéy jîn jê wat che, jit ek put chëok è 每人而悅之日亦不足矣, *tak lâng hoē o'hw^{n}a hé, jit bô kàou yëá*, if you wanted to please every body, the day would not be long enough. See 孟子 Bēng choó.
Böéy yéw lëāng pêng 每有良朋, *tak paē woō hó pêng*, constantly meeting with a good friend. See the 小雅 Seáou gnáy.
Böéy jit 每日, *tak jit*, every day; böéy jîn 每人, *tak lâng*, every man.

Böéy **浼** To pollute, to defile; jé yëen lêng böéy gnó chae 爾焉能浼我哉, *lé an chw^{n}á ēy bak lâ tâm gwá chae*, how can you defile me (by your presence)? See the 上孟 Sëāng bēng.

Böéy **渼** The name of a place; also, of a river.

Böéy **尾** Read bé: the tail, the end, the termination; thoê bé 頭尾 *t'hâou böéy*, the head and tail.

Só hêy, bé hêy, lêw lê che choó 瑣兮尾兮流離之子, *sèy hêy, böéy hêy, lêw lê ây kē^{n}á*, diminished and reduced to extremities, like a vagabond and abandoned person. See the 國風 Kok hong.

Böêy **杪** Read beáou: the end or extremity of any thing. Söêy bwat wat beáou 歲末曰杪, *nëe^{ng} böêy kóng böêy*, the end of the year is called *böêy*.
Bok sèy che, wūy che beáou 木細枝謂之杪, *ch'hêw bak ây sèy ke kóng këō böêy*, the small branches of a tree are called *böêy*.

平

Böêy **梅** Vulg: *ûm*: A prune, a plum; a surname. Jëak chok hô keng, jé wûy yeêm böêy 若作和羹爾惟鹽梅, *nā böêyh chò teaou hô ây kai^{ng}, lé thang chò e ây sëe^{ng} ûm á*, "if we want to make a mixed broth, you can be the salted prunes in it."—Said to a clever man, whose services were valuable to the state. See the 尙書 *Sëō^{ng} se*.

Böêy **脢** The flesh of the back.

Böêy **酶** The best of the wine; Böêy, chéw boé yëá 酶酒母也, *böêy se chéw ây k'hăh kāou yëá*, the böêy is the strongest (literally the mother) of the wine.

Böêy **莓** Moss; the name of a plant. Sûy è chō böêy t'hae 隨意坐莓苔, *sûy è chēy lē boêy t'hê*, leisurely sitting down upon the moss.

Böêy **囮** To translate; also, a decoy or trap for birds and beasts. Neáou böêy 鳥囮, *cheáou böêy*, a decoy for birds, where a living bird is used, to decoy others into the net.

Böêy **媒** Böêy chëak 媒妁, *hûm lâng*, a go-between, to make up marriages. Put t'haē hoō boé che bēng, böêy chëak che gân 不待父母之命·媒妁之言, *ūm têng t'haē pāy boè ây bēng lēng, hûm lâng ây wā*, "without waiting for the command of parents, or the mediation of the match-maker." Said of young people who venture upon premature marriages, without consulting their friends. See the 上孟 Sëāng bēng.

Böêy **煤** A collection of soot, böêy t'hàn 煤炭, *boēy t'hwⁿà*, coals.

Böêy **禖** The sacrifice offered by an Emperor, when seeking for a son. E' t'haē lô soō ê Ko-böêy 以太牢祠于高禖, *yūng t'haē lô ch'haē ê Ko-böêy*, "to sacrifice with the principal animals to Ko-böêy," in order to obtain children; because Ko-böêy is said to have been the first who brought forth children. See the 禮記 Léy kè.

Böêy **黴** The green and black appearance which any thing wears that has been long in the rain; mouldiness.

Böêy **枚** A stem: the 十枝 sip che, ten branches, of the horary characters, are called 條 tëâou; and the 十二幹 sip jē kàn, twelve stems of the same, are called 枚 böêy. Ē ê tëâou böêy 施於條枚, *twā tē tëâou böêy*, twining about both branches and stem. See the 大雅 Tae gnáy.
Also, a numeral, employed in reckoning: kè böêy 幾枚, *kwúy böêy*, how many stalks? Böêy pok kong sîn 枚卜功臣, to reckon up meritorious servants.
Also, a piece of wood held in the mouth, to keep people from talking; a gag: má k'hè kim, jîn hâm böêy 馬棄企·人銜枚, *báy k'hè kim, lâng hâm böêy*, "the horses were deprived of their metal ornaments, and the men held the wooden gag in their mouths," in order to keep them from talking, that they might march in silence, and surprise the enemy. See the 三國 Sam kok.

Böêy **霉** Vernal showers: böêy ê sëen woo e hòk 霉雨善汙衣服, *ūm â ây hoē gâou bak lâ sâm sⁿa k'hoè*, the vernal showers are very apt to soil the clothes.

Böêy **鋂** A double ring; a great lock or chain.

Böêy **鶥** The same as 囮 böêy, a decoy for birds.

丟 Böēy **未** Read bē: Not yet, not arrived at, unattained. Hak se hoê, tùy wat, bē yëá 學詩乎.對曰.未也, *woō t'hak se á bô, yìn e kóng, yëá böēy*, "has he studied the odes? He answered, not yet."

夭 Böēyh **要** Read yaôu: to want, to desire: kéw yaòu, put bông pêng seng che gân 久要不忘平生之言, *koó böēyh, ūm p'hàh bēy kè, chit sè lâng ây wā*, I have long desired it, and have not forgotten the protestations of my whole life.

天 Böēyh **襪** Read bëet: a stocking, clothing for the legs. Chëak haê, chëak bëet 着鞋着襪, *ch'hëung ây, ch'hëung böēyh*, to wear shoes and stockings.

天 Bŏh **莫** Read bòk: not, do not. Bòk wūy, kim jit put hak, hwân yéw laê jit, 莫謂今日不學.還有來日, *bŏh kóng, kin á jit ūm t'hak, yëá woō laê jit*, don't say you will not learn to day, thinking that another day may come.

天 Bok **木** Vulg: *bak*: Wood: sē bok 樹木, *ch'hēw bak*, a tree. Vulg: *ch'hâ*, fire-wood. Bok ch'hëāng 木匠, *bak ch'hëōⁿᵍ*, a carpenter.

Bo̍k chëûng sîn chek chèng, hoē chëûng kàn chek sèng 木從繩則正. 后從諫則聖, *bak t'hàn sŏh chēw chē^{n}à, kwun t'hàn t^{n}à chēw sē^{n}à*, when wood (is cut) according to the line, it becomes straight, and when a prince (acts) according to advice, he becomes wise. See the 尙書 *Sëō^{ng} se.*

Bo̍k 沐 To wash the head, to bathe, to wet, to drench. K'hóng-choó bo̍k yëuk jê tëâou 孔子沐浴而朝, *K'hóng-hoo-choó chăng ek chēw tëâou keè^{ng} ông*, Confucius used to bathe before going to court. See the 下論 Hāy lūn.

Chëet hong bo̍k é 櫛風沐雨, *ch'hōey tëŏh hong, ak tëŏh hoē*, to be exposed to the wind, and drenched in the rain.

Bo̍k 霂 Bek bo̍k 霢霂, a gentle shower, a drizzling rain.

Bo̍k 目 Vulg: *bak chew:* the eye; bo̍k lëuk, 目錄, a table of contents. Bo̍k put sè hwuy léy che sek 目不視非禮之色, *bak chew ūm thong k'hw^{n}à hwuy lèy ây sek*, let not the eyes look upon improper beauty.

Si̍p bo̍k séy sè 十目所視, *chap ây bak chew sèy k'hw^{n}à*, that which ten eyes have seen, (i. e. exposed to public view).

Bo̍k 苜 A kind of grass, sometimes used for food. Má sē bo̍k sëuk, chek hwûy 馬嗜苜蓿則肥, *bèy chëăh bok sëuk ây ch'hâou, chēw pwûy*, when horses feed upon the bo̍k sëuk grass, they become fat.

Bo̍k 睦 Harmonious, amicable, friendly: hô bo̍k 和睦, peaceful. Kéw chok kè bo̍k 九族旣睦, the nine relations living in amity.

Bo̍k 穆 Harmonious, obedient, elegant, deep and distant. A surname. Kit-hoó chok sëūng, bo̍k jê ch'heng hong 吉甫作誦. 穆如淸風, when Kit-hoó recited his verses, they were harmonious as the pure and gentle breeze. See the 大雅 Taē gnáy.

T'hëen choó bo̍k bo̍k 天子穆穆, *Hóng tèy bo̍k bo̍k*, the Emperor put on a deep and thoughtful appearance. See the 上論 Sëāng lūn.

Bo̍k 繆 A bad epithet given after death. A surname.

Cheaou bo̍k 昭繆, a succession of generations,—the father's line being ranged under the cheaou, the son's under the bo̍k, and so on.

Sē é cheaou bo̍k 序以昭繆, arranged according to the cheaou and bo̍k.

Bo̍k 牧 A shepherd, a pastor; bo̍k chëá 牧者 may be applied both to those who keep sheep, and to those who take the oversight of men; a ruler of a province. A surname.

Kim yéw sēw jîn che gnêw yâng, jê wūy che bo̍k che chëá 今有受人之牛羊. 而爲之牧之者, *t^{n}a woō sēw lâng ây goô yeô^{ng}, jê kap e è^{n}g e ây lâng*, now suppose a man had received another's sheep and oxen, and had undertaken to feed them, &c. See the 上孟 Sëāng bēng.

Bo̍k 莫 Vulg: *bŏh:* not, do not: bo̍k gnó te yëá hoē 莫我知也乎, *bô lâng chae gwá*, nobody knows me; bo̍k put chun ch'hin 莫不尊親, *bô ūm chun kèng pāy boē*, thus there will be none who do not honour their parents. A surname.

Bo̍k 寞 Che̍k to̍k 寂寞, silent, quiet, still. Teàou ê che̍k bo̍k che hëang 釣於寂寞之鄉, *tëò hê twā tē chēng chēng ây hëo^{ng} lé*, to angle in a quiet and retired village. See the 韓文 Hân bûn.

Bo̍k 瘼 Sick; pain, sickness.

Bok 鏌 Bok-yëâ 鏌鋣, the name of a sword.

Bok 漠 Sa-bok che tēy 沙漠之地, the desert of Sha-mǒ. Also,—wide, distant: bōng che bok bok jëĕn yëâ 望之漠漠然也, *bāng khwⁿâ e, chun â hwuīⁿᵍ hwuīⁿᵍ*, looking after him he appeared far off.

Bok 勛 Diligent; seldom used.

Bok 豋 A different name for pulse, or beans.

Bong 摸 Read boē, to feel: séw boē 手摸 *ch'hëw bong*, to feel with the hand.

Bóng 莽 The appearance of deep grass: chaē yëâ, wat ch'hó bóng che sîn 在野曰草莽之臣, *twā tē yëâ, kóng ch'haóu bóng ây, jîn sîn*, dwelling in the wilderness, one is called an officer of the long wild grass. See 孟子 Bēng-chóó.

Bóng 莽 Careless, rough, slovenly. Kwun wûy chèng yëen bût ló bóng 君爲政焉勿鹵莽, *kwun chò chèng soō, ūᵐ t'hang ló bóng*, in the management of the affairs of government, be not rough and slovenly. See 莊子 Chōng-chóó.

Bóng 儚 Pē bóng 備儚, not to flatter.

Bóng 网 The old form of 網 bóng, a net.

Bóng 罔 To deceive; ignorant, stupid. Sē bóng bîn yëá 是罔民也, *sē p'hëĕn pāyh saiⁿᵍ*, this is to deceive the people.
Hak jê put soo chek bóng 學而不思則罔, *t'hak jê bô sëōⁿᵍ kóng bóng*, to learn without thinking engenders stupidity. See the 上論 Sëāng lūn.

Bóng 網 Vulg: *bāng*: a net for catching fish or birds. Chok këet sîn, jê wûy bóng koé, é tëĕn é gê 作結繩而爲網罟以佃以漁, *chò kat sŏh, jê ch'hòng bāng, è phăh lăh kwà lëăh hê*, they tied knots in cords, and made nets, to hunt and fish with. See the 易經 *Yëăh keng*.

Bóng 惘 Having lost one's aim: disappointed.

Bóng 輞 An outer ring put to the wheel of the Emperor's carriage when employed in hunting.

Bóng 魍 Bóng lëáng 魍魎, spirits inhabiting marshes and damp places, said to be like little children of three years old, of a dark red colour.

Bóng 蟒 A large kind of serpent.

Bóng 漭 The appearance of wide extensive water: also, not clear.

Bóng 矇 Not clear; a dark day, without much light from the sun.

Bóng 鋂 A kind of smoothing iron: koé bóng t'hâm 鈷鋂潭, a round pool or pond in shape like a Chinese smoothing iron.

Bóng 崃 Tông bóng 嵣崃, a hilly appearance.

去

Bòng 恾 Cunning, artful.

Bòng 悻 To be deceived, to be wrought upon, to be tempted.

平

Bông 亡 To flee away; to lose, to be lost, to die, to be out of existence. Bông jîn boô é wûy pó, jîn ch'hin é wûy pó 亡人無以爲寶.人親以爲寶 *ch'hut bóng ây lâng, bô è s^{n}à mcē^{n}h wûy pó, jîn aè pāy boè è wûy pó*, a fugitive like myself does not consider anything of value, except the love of one's parents, which is of real value.

Ch'hëûng yëuk t'hoe an, bông boô jit è 縱慾偷安.亡無日矣, *t'hàn soo yëuk t'haou an jëên, lông pöëy bô tē^{n}ā tëôh jit*, when a man complies with his carnal desires, and pilfers self-indulgent ease, the day of his ruin is uncertain (i. e. it is near).

Bông 忘 To forget, to slight, to miss, to lose, bông kè 忘記, *bēy kè tit*, to forget. È kay naé tek, wat tok put bông 予嘉乃德曰篤不忘, *gwà o lô lè ây tek kòng tok ū^{m} k^{n}á bēy kè tit*, I applaud your virtue, and promise not to forget it. See the 尚書 *Sëō^{ng} se*.

Bông 芒 The appearance of grass; abundant.

Bông 茫 The wide expansive appearance of water.

Bông 邙 Pok bông san 北邙山, *pak bông swⁿa*, the name of a hill, in the 河南 Hô-lâm province.

Bông 崈 The name of a hill.

Bông 冡 To cover over any thing.

Bông 鋩 Vulg: *mai^{ng}*: sharp, sharp-pointed. Hëûng kek yāou bông 雄戟耀鋩, *hëûng bêng ây käyh, yāou kwui^{ng} kwà mai^{ng}*, the martial spears, were gleaming and sharp.

Bông 忙 Hurried, hasty, in a bustle. Boē hwun, sîn kò pëet, boô naé t'haè ch'hong bông hoē 暮婚晨告別.無乃大息忙乎, *mai^{ng} hwui^{ng} hwun yëen, mai^{n}h chaē kò sëo pëet, bô naè t'haè ch'hong bông hoē*, to marry in the evening, and depart the next morning, is it not too hurried and hasty? See 杜甫詩 Toē-hoó se.

Bông 蒙 To receive, to be acted on; to be thankful for; youth, the time of youth. To bông 多蒙, to be thankful for. A surname.

Bông é yáng chèng, sèng kong yëá 蒙以養正聖功也, *sedou lëên yáng chē^{n}à, sèng jin ây kong lô*, when from youth a person is brought up in the right way, he will display the merits of a sage. See the 易經 *Yëàh keng*.

Bông 㠓 The name of a hill.

Bông 望 Chëem bông 瞻望, to look towards.

Bông 幪 To cover over: a cloth for covering.

Bông 濛 Small drizzling rain; also the name of a river.

Bông 曚 The appearance of the sky before sun-rise.

Bông 朦 The appearance of the sky after the moon is gone down.

Bông 矇 Blind; having lost the pupil of the eye.

Bông 蠓 A small kind of insect, that flies in swarms.

Bông 艨 Bông tông 艨艟, a war-boat, a vessel of war.

Bông 罞 A net for catching stags: also, the motion of the eyes.

Bông 䍚 A net for covering over any thing: also, a pig.

Bông 雺 The vapours of heaven descending, when not answered by the corresponding mists of the earth.

Bông 硭 Bông seaou 硭硝, a kind of medicine, something like saltpetre.

Bông 幪 A great cloth, a large napkin.

[illegible]

Bōng 望 Vulg: *bāng:* to look towards, to look up to, to hope for, to expect. Kè bōng 冀望, *kè bāng,* to hope, to anticipate.

Bōng bōng jëên k'hè che, jëak chëang böéy yëen 望望然去之.若將浼焉, *bōng bōng jëên k'hè e, chun á chëang bak e lâ sâm,* looking towards them, he got out of their way, as though he would have been defiled by them. See 孟子 Bēng-choó.

Sè bîn jê sëang, bōng tō jê bē che këên 視民如傷.望道如未之見, *k'hw*^{n}*à păyh sai*^{ng} *ch'hin chëō*^{ng} *woō sëang haē, bāng tō chun á yëá böēy ēy keè*^{ng}, he viewed the people as though they had been injured by him, and looked towards virtue as if he had not yet come in sight of it. Said of 文王 Bûn-ông.

Bōng 朢 The full of the moon.

Bōng 妄 Disorderly, corrupt: vulg. *lâm sám,* out of all order. Kim che bōng jê yëá bōng 今之命儒也妄, *t*^{n}*a ây kóng këò t'hak ch'hăyh lâng, lâm sám,* those who are now called learned men, are corrupt and disorderly. See the 禮記 Léy kè. Ch'hoú ek bōng jîn yëá é è 此亦妄人也已矣, *chéy yëá sē lâm sám ây lâng tē*^{n}*ā tē*^{n}*ā,* this then is a disorderly, worthless fellow.

Bōng 夢 Read *bāng:* a dream; bōng këèn 夢見 *bāng keè*^{ng}, to see in a dream. Chong-chew bōng wûy hoê tëep 莊周夢爲蝴蝶, *Chong-chew bāng chò böèy yëăh,* Chong-chew dreamed that he was a butterfly.

Bōng tèy laē ê lëâng pit 夢帝賚予良弼, *bāng sëāng tèy sàng gwá hó ây hoò pit,* I dreamed that the high Emperor presented me with a good assistant in the government. See the 尙書 *Sëō*^{ng} *se.*

Bōng 夣 The same as the preceding.

Bōng 懞 Dark, as when the sun and moon do not shine; confused.

Bōng 墓 Read boē: a grave: paè boē 拜墓, *paè bōng*, to worship at the tombs. Kò boē seng ae 過墓生哀, *kòèy hwûn bōng sai^ng ae ch'hâm*, on passing a tomb, we feel melancholy.

上聲

Boó 武 Martial, military, brave. A surname. Kéw kéw boó hoo, kong hoê kan sêng 糾糾武夫.公侯干城, *bêng bêng ây boó hoo, kong hoê ây kan sëⁿâ*, brave military men, are the clubs and forts of princes. See the 國風 Kok hong. Bûn k'hó keng pang, boó k'hó têng kok 文可經邦武可定國, *e ây bûn t'hang keng pang, e ây boó t'hang tëⁿā kok*, his literary talents are sufficient to regulate a state, and his military acquirements equal to establish a nation. Said of 郭諸宜 Kok-choo-gê.

Boó 娬 Boó mē 娬媚 soft, effeminate.

Boó 碔 Boó hoo 碔砆 a fine kind of stone, resembling a gem.

Boó 侮 Boó bān, to insult, to despise, to revile. Boó k'héy t'hëúng lâp hoó 無啓寵納侮, *ûⁿ t'hang k'hè t'hâou t'hëúng aè, këⁿa nê lâp boó bān*, do not begin to shew favour, lest you should receive insult. See the 尚書 *Sëōⁿᵍ se*.

Boó 憮 To love: boó jëên 憮然, vacant, not self-possessed. Also written 儛 boó.

Boó 撫 To soothe, to pacify. Also read hoó.

Boó 嫵 The same as 娬 boó; soft, effeminate.

Boó 廡 Side chambers, round a court: a yard.

Boó 膴 Thick, fat, fine, elegant. Chew gwân boó boó 周原膴膴, *Chew ây gwân têy boó boó*, the original territory of the Chew dynasty was fertile and fat. See the 大雅 Taē gnáy.

Boó 舞 To gambol, to frisk, to throw about the arms. Also written 儛 boó. Boó këèm 舞劍, to brandish a sword. Boó kan é ê lëāng kae 舞干羽于兩階, *boó t'hây kap cheáou mô tē sëāng pêng gîm kay*, they brandished their clubs and feathers on both sides of the stairs. See the 尚書 *Sëōⁿᵍ se*. Chëuk tō sew boó 足蹈手舞, *k'ha tō ch'hèw boó*, frisking and gamboling with the arms and legs.

Boó 鵡 Eng boó 鸚鵡, a parrot, a cockatoo. Eng boó lêng gân, put lê hwúy neáou, 鸚鵡能言不離飛鳥, *eng boó ëy kóng wā, sëāng âm lê ê pwuy cheáou*, a parrot is able to talk, but still it is nothing more than a bird. See the 禮記 Léy kè.

Boó 潕 The name of a hill.

Boó 侮 The same as 侮 boó, to slight, to insult, to despise. Boó sêng jîn che gan 侮聖人之言, *boó sêng jîn ây wā*, to despise the words of the sages.

平

Boô 无 The ancient form of 無 boô, not; boô kēw 无咎 *bô chöēy*, faultless.

Boô 亡 Also used for 無 boô, not; boô jê wûy yéw 亡而爲有, bô jê chò woō, to pretend the existence of things that do not exist.

Boô 無 Vulg. *bô*: no, not, not in existence, do not. Boô yéw put jê ké 無友不如已, *ām t'hang woō pêng yéw ām tăh lëŏh ka tē,* don't have a friend who is not equal to yourself. See the 上論 Sëang lŭn.
Kwun choó boô séy cheng 君子無所爭, *kwun choó bô sëy chai^ng*, a good man has nothing that he strives about. See the 上論 Sëang lŭn.

Boô 蕪 Overgrown with weeds, and grass. Ae sè ch'hó che hoo wöèy 哀庶草之蕪穢, *ac sè ch'háou ây boô wöèy,* lamenting to see the grass and weeds so overgrown.

Boô 毋 Not, do not, an interdiction. A surname. Boô put kèng 毋不敬, *bô ām kèng,* be not in any case disrespectful. See the 禮記 Léy kè.

Boô 巫 A conjurer, a necromancer, one who performs incantations. A surname. Jin jê boô hêng, put k'hó é chok boô e 人而無恒不可以作巫醫, *lâng nā bô hêng sim, ām t'hang chò sae kong kwà e seng,* if a man does not possess a persevering mind, he can neither be a necromancer, nor a physician. See the 下論 Hāy lŭn.

Boô 誣 To deceive, to cheat. Kwun choó che tō, yeën k'hó boô yëá 君子之道焉可誣也, *kwun choó ây tō, an chw^nâ ëy p'hëèn tit,* the way of a good man, how can it be deceitful! See the 上論 Sëang lŭn.

Boô 罞 A sort of net: near-sighted.

Boô 譕 A deceitful expression; not; also used for 謀 boê, to consult.

丟

Boō 務 To attend to any thing, to employ all one's powers in any thing. Soō boō 事務, business.
Kwun choó boō pún 君子務本, *kwun choó chwan yūng k'hwùy lat ê kin pún,* the good man attends sedulously to the principal thing. See the 上論 Sëang lŭn.

Boō 霧 A fog, a mist: yin boō 雲霧 clouds and mist; bōng hoō 濛霧, a mist.
Lók hây é koe boō chêy hwuy 落霞與孤霧齊飛, *lân lŏh ây hây, kap koe kw^nâ ây boō chò poô tit pwuy,* scattered hazes and solitary mists flying about together. See the 王勃文 Ong-put bûn.

Boō 瞀 To look with the eyes downwards, dim-sighted, near-sighted. Hoo boō sè cheá, é hây wûy ch'hek 夫瞀視者以黈爲赤, *kīn sè ây lâng lëăh wui^ng chò ch'hëăh,* near-sighted people take yellow for red.

Boō 騖 To gallop about in confusion: to go swiftly. Tit p'hèng wat tê, lwān tê wat boō 直騁曰馳.亂馳曰騖, *tit kë^nâ kóng tê, lâm sâm p'hàou kóng boō,* to ride straight is called tê, to gallop about in disorder is called boō.

Boō 鶩 A domestic duck; a wild duck is called 鳧 hoô, and a common duck 鶩 boō.
K'hek gok put sêng sëăng lūy boō 刻鵠不成.尙類鶩, *k'hek haê gô ām chë^nâ sëăng luy ăh,* trying to engrave a wild goose, if you do not succeed, you will only produce a tame duck;—said of those who try to imitate great men, and fail.

Boō 婺 Boō lé 婺女, the name of a star: Boō-chew 婺州, the name of a place.

上聲

Bún 刎 To cut, to cut off; choō bún 自刎 *ka tē kwăh aôu*, to cut one's own throat.

Tëang-jé, Tin-ê, lëáng jin sëang é, hō. wūy bún kēng kaou 張耳.陳餘.两人相與.號謂刎頸交, *Tēōng-jé kap Tân-ê, nō láng sëo é, hō kóng kwăh nâ aôu ây kaou*, Tēong-jé and Tân-ê both formed an intimacy, which they called "cut-throat friendship;"—which means that they would remain faithful to each other till death. See the 史記 Soó kè.

Bún 吻 The sides of the mouth, the dimples.

Bún 蚊 Vulg. *báng*: a musquito, a small gnat. Bún bêng chwan hoo, chek yēā put bē 蚊蝱嚌膚.則夜不寐, *báng kā. láng ây băh, maing kan bēy k'hwùn*, when the musquitoes bite our flesh, we cannot sleep by night. See 莊子 Chong-choó.

Bún 瞞 Dark.

Bún 伆 Separated to a distance, divided.

Bûn 葝 Ch'hëâng bún 藞葝, the name of a flower.

Bún 脗 United; bún hap 脗合, joined together.

Bún 抆 To wipe, to rub, to handle. Koe choó gīm, jê bún lūy 孤子唫而抆淚, *koe kēⁿá gīm haôu, jê ch'hit bak ch'haê*, an orphan child moans and wipes his eyes. Ke kwan kéw, bē sëâng bún sek k'hè yūng ke hok 居官久未嘗抆飾器用車服, *k'hëâ kwan koó, boēy woō bong ch'hōng k'hè yūng ch'hëa hok*, dwelling long in office, without handling or adorning the furniture, carriages, or apparel.

Bún 𢚇 The sides of the face: also, bad, improper.

Bún 捫 To hold: tê bún 持捫, to grasp, to lay hold of. Bok bún tīm seet 莫捫朕舌, *bô láng taīng gwá ây chëĕh*, there is no one to hold my tongue. See the 大雅 Tāe gnáy.

平聲

Bûn 文 Literary, literature: also, ornamental, ornament, surface. A surname. Bûn lé 文理, polished, civilized: bûn chëang 文章, *bûn chëōng*, literary composition. Hoo-choó soò kaòu, bûn, hêng, tëung, sin, 夫子四教.文行忠信, *Hoo-choó woō sè hāng ây kà hwùn, bûn chëōng, sëy kēⁿâ, chīn tëung, kap sin sit*, Confucius had four subjects of instruction, regarding literature, conduct, fidelity, and sincerity. See the 上論 Sëāng lūn.

Hêng yéw ê lek, chek é hak bûn 行有餘力.則以學文, *kēⁿâ chëy lëy yëâ woō ch'hun ây k'hwùy lat, chek yūng e ê hak bûn*, having done these, if a man has any remaining strength, let him employ it in learning. See the 上論 Sëāng lūn.

Bûn 旻 An autumnal sky, a clear sky. Sùn ho khip ê bûn thëen 舜號泣於旻天, *Sùn haôu t'hê tē bûn t'heeng*, Sùn cried and lamented under the clear heavens. See 孟子 Bēng choó.

Bûn 雯 The variegated appearance of the clouds.

Bûn 紋 The stripes in checked and embroidered cloth.

Bûn 捫 To hold, to lift, to move. Hàn ông sëang hëung, naé bûn chëuk 漢王傷胸乃捫足, *Hàn ông sëang tëŏh heng k'hám, chëw k'hè k'ha jê chaóu,* when the king of the Hàn dynasty was wounded in his breast, he took to his heels and fled. See the 史記 Soò kè.

Bûn 門 Bûn hoè 門戶 *mooi^ng hoē,* a door: ch'hut bûn 出門, *ch'hut mooi^ng,* to go out of doors, to go abroad; bûn k'hoé 門口, *mooi^ng k'haóu,* before the door: k'hae bûn 開門, *k'hwuy mooi^ng,* to open the door. Gē loē yëá, léy bûn yëá 義路也.禮門也, *gē chò loē, lèy chò mooi^ng,* righteousness is the road, and propriety the door (by which we must enter). See 孟子 Bēng-choó.
T'hëen choó kéw bûn 天子九門, *hóng tèy kaóu ây mooi^ng,* the Emperor has nine gates to his palace.
Bûn jîn put kèng Chóó-loē 門人不敬子路, *hak seng ūm kèng tëüng Chóó-loē,* the rest of the disciples did not respect Chóó-loē.

Bûn 聞 Vulg. *t'hë^na:* to hear; t'hàm bûn 探聞, *t'hàm t'hë^na,* to listen. Ch'hëep bûn 竊聞, *t'haou t'hë^na,* to hear by stealth, a humble expression, used at the beginning of essays, meaning, "I have heard," &c.
Bûn chëá bok put hin k'hé yëen 聞者莫不興起焉, *t'hë^na ây lâng bô ū^m hin k'hè yëen,* those who heard, universally arose to action. See the 下孟 Hāy bēng.
A surname; and 聞人 Bûn-jîn, a double surname.

Bûn 穈 A kind of grain.

Bûn 亹 An opening in a ravine, where the water runs out, and the two banks project, like a gate way; hoô e chaē bûn 鳧鷖在亹, the wild ducks stood in the mouth of the ravine. See the 大雅 Taē gnáy.

Bûn 頣 Bûn t'hoê 頣頭, *chëĕh t'haóu,* to hang down the head.

Bûn 們 The sign of the plural number; jé bûn 你們, *lín, ye,* you people; gnó bûn 我們, *lán,* we, us. This character is common in novels.

Bún 饅 Read bân: a cake; bân t'hoê péng 饅頭餅, *bân t'haóu pē^nd,* a flat cake made of meal, a biscuit: bân t'hoê 饅頭, *bân t'haôn,* bread.

Būn 問 (丟) Vulg. *mooi^ng:* to enquire, to ask; seng būn 聲問, *së^na būn,* a report, a sound.
Kwùy-loē būn soō kwúy sín, Chóó wat, hē lêng soō jîn, yëen lêng soō kwúy, 季路問事鬼神.子曰.未能事人.焉能事鬼, *Kwùy-loē mooi^ng hok saē kwúy sin ây soō; Hoo-chóó kóng, bōëy ēy hok saē lâng, bōëyh an chwⁿá ēy hok saē kwúy,* Kwùy-loē asked about worshipping ghosts and spirits: Confucius said, we cannot yet serve men properly, how then can we worship ghosts. See the 上論 Sëāng lūn.
Būn jîn 問仁, *mooi^ng jîn,* "He asked about benevolence:"—būn tē 問知, *mooi^ng tē,* "He asked about knowledge."

Būn 們 A fat and plump appearance.

Būn 聞 Report, fame anything that is heard. Lêng būn kóng ê, se ê sin 令聞廣譽施於身, *hó ây së^na būn kóng k'hwăh ây o ló, se ê hîn sin,* an honorable fame, and extensive praise bestowed upon a person. See the 下孟 Hāy bēng.

Būn 悶 Sorrow, trouble: yew būn 憂悶, *hwân lô*, to grieve. Hwân būn 煩悶, grief: wut būn 鬱悶, vexation. Tūn sè boô būn, 遯世無悶, *chaôu sèèm sè kan, jê bô wut chut*, to retire from the busy world without regret. See the 易經 *Yeăh keng.*

Būn 紊 To be in confusion, disordered. Kong kè būn lwān 綱紀紊亂, the affairs of government in confusion.

Būn 汶 The name of a stream: chek goê pit chaē Būn sëāng è 則吾必在汶上矣, *chek gwâ pit twā tē Bun têng è*, at that time I shall be dwelling upon the river Būn. See the 上論 Sëāng lūn.

入 But 魩 The name of a small fish: the tail of a fish.

But 沕 *But but á*, any thing small.

入 Bŭt 勿 Do not, an expression of prohibition. bŭt toê lô jê hóng kong 勿徒勞而罔功, *ūm t'hang k'hang k'hang bwâ jê bô kong lô*, do not put yourself vainly to trouble, without getting the merit of it. See the 尙書 *Sëōng se.*

Bŭt k'he yëá 勿欺也, *ūm t'hang p'hëèn*, do not deceive.

Bŭt 坳 To bury, to inter, to put under ground. T'hoe hăp ch'hê yûng, é tè bŭt sin 偷合取容以致坳身, *t'haou hăp t'hăyh yûng, è tè baê bŭt hîn sîn*, to contract clandestine intimacies, and to take everything easy, till we bury ourselves in ruin. See the 史記 Soó kè.

Bŭt 岉 K'hwut bŭt 崛岉, a lofty appearance; hilly.

Bŭt 扨 To beat, to strike, to whip with a stick or bamboo. E' má pëën bŭt 以馬鞭扨, *t'hó bây peeⁿᵍ bŭt*, to lash with a whip.

Bŭt 沒 To end, to finish, to die; not, not to be. Kwun choó put è bé bŭt léy 君子不以美沒禮, *kwun choó ây lâng bô è hó k'hwⁿà, bŭt bô léy soè*, the good man does not do away with propriety, for the sake of elegance. See the 禮記 Léy kè.

Kwun choó chĭt bŭt sè, jê bêng put ch'heng yëen 君子疾沒世.而名不稱焉, *kwun choó ây lâng chĭt paiⁿᵍ, yin wûy bŭt bô tē sè, jê mēⁿà ūᵐ ch'heng hoe yëen*, the honorable man is pained at being nothing in the world, and because his name is not celebrated.

Bŭt 物 Vulg: *meēⁿh*: a thing, an existence, a person, another person. Bān bŭt yëūk yëen 萬物育焉, *bān meēⁿh saiⁿᵍ yëuk*, all things nourished and growing. See the 中庸 Tëung yûng.

Bŭt gnó che kan 物我之間, *meēⁿh gwa ây tëung kan*, between one's self and others.

Bŭt kek jê hoē te chè 物格而後知至, *meēⁿh chè kek, jëën aōu te kaòu t'haôu*, when an acquaintance with things is carried to the utmost, then is knowledge at its height.

Bŭt 菱 Bŭt yëák 菱藥, myrrh.

Bŭt 芴 A kind of vegetable.

Bŭt 歿 To die, to decease: Sëuk-chëem wat Ch'hoé ông kê put bŭt hoē 叔詹曰.楚王其不歿乎, *Sëuk-chëem kóng, Ch'hoé ông kê ūᵐ sè hoē*, Sëuk-chëem said, why will not the King of Ch'hoé expire? See the 左傳 Chó twān.

声 Bwá 梚 Ka bwá 菱梚, a kind of wood: the spreading branches of a tree.

平 Bwâ 磨 Read mô: to grind: mô to 磨刀, bwâ to, to grind a knife. Jê tok jê mô 如琢如磨, ch'hin chëōng tok ch'hin chëōng bwâ, like chiselling and grinding. See the 上論 Sëang lŭn.

Mô lëy é se 磨礪以須, bwâ lëy è yūng, to grind anything for use. See the 左傳 Chó twān.

夫 Bwăh 抹 Read bwat: to paste, to besmear, to anoint. E' hwŭn bwat bëēn 以粉抹面, t'hô hwŭn bwăh bĭn, to smear the face with white paint.

入 Bwăh 末 Read bwat: the small end, the extreme point of any thing.

Bwăh 蓬 Read tat; as, kwun tat 莙蓬, kwun bwăh, the beta vulgaris; and hoë tat ch'haè 厚蓬菜, kaōu bwăh ch'haè, a kind of turnip.

Hong chín chëaou tat lëet 風振蕉蓬裂, hong chin tōng chëo bwăh kàou leĕh, the wind agitated the plantains and turnip tops, till their leaves were split.

声 Bwán 滿 Vulg. mwⁿá: to fill, to replenish, to complete; full. A surname. Ch'hó bwán tê tông, súy bwán gaê 草滿池塘.水滿涯, ch'haōu mwⁿá tê tông, chúy mwⁿá gaê, the grass overspread the pond, and the water filled it up to the brink.

Chè tek è bwán 志得意滿, sim chè tit tëŏh è soō mwⁿá, obtaining one's wish, and fulfilling one's intention.

Bwán 懣 Troubled: hwŭn bwán 憤懣, vexed. Soó jîn hwân bwán, sit put hāy 使人煩懣食不下, saē lâng hwân bwán, chëăh bēy lŏh, to make people so vexed, that they cannot stomach it. See the 史記 Soó kè.

Bwán 晚 Evening, dusk; late. Vulg. maiⁿᵍ hwuiⁿᵍ, evening; mooiⁿᵍ, late. Kwun hô këen che bwán 君何見之晚, lé sëo kcèⁿᵍ kaōu hëăh mooiⁿᵍ, how came you to see me so late? See the 史記 Soó kè.

Sëang këen hwŭn bwán 相見恨晚, sëo keèⁿᵍ hwŭn mooiⁿᵍ, it is a pity we have seen each other so late.

Bwán 挽 To pull, to drag: yín bwán 引挽, to lead. Bwán hôëy t'hëen è 挽回天意, bwán tô tooiⁿᵍ t'heeⁿᵍ ây è, to reverse the decree of heaven.

Bwán 輓 To pull a carriage.

Bwán 娩 Hwun bwán 分娩, to be in labour, to be delivered.

Bwán 䆆 To restrain, to hold back.

平 Bwân 㒼 To forget, to let slip out of the mind.

Bwân 蹣 Bwân ch'hëâng 蹣牆, pwⁿâ ch'hëōⁿᵍ, to climb over a wall. Bwân ch'hut k'hè 蹣出去, pwⁿâ ch'hut k'hè, to run over, as liquor.

Bwân 䊡 Rice water boiled to a consistency, and congealed.

Bwân 顢 Bwân ē 顢頇, a large face.

Bwân 瞞 Not clear-sighted, to conceal from view, to deceive. Taē jîn put bwân, goê sit yéw chöēy 大人不瞞.吾實有罪, *twā lâng bēy mwⁿâ, gwá sit oō chöēy*, your honour cannot be deceived, I am really in fault.

Chô-ch'hò seáou, joō á-hwân 曹操小字阿嚇, *Chô-ch'hò sèy, jē á-mwⁿâ*, when Chô-ch'hò was young his designation was "the little cheat."

大

Bwat 抹 Vulg. *bwăh*: to spread over, to rub, to smear; to anoint. San bwat bê yîn 山抹微雲, *swⁿa bwăh bê hwûn*, the hills were overspread with small clouds.

Bwat 秣 To feed a horse with corn.

Bwat 袜 Vulg. *mŏh*: the pellicle, thin skin.

兲

Bwat 末 The end, the extreme, a minor point; not, do not. But yéw pún bwat 物有本末, *meēⁿh woō pún bwăh*, things have beginning and end, (i. e. weightier and minor points).

Bwat 沫 The name of a water: yēēn bwat 涎沫, spittle. Sēang se é bwat 相濡以沫, *sëo bak è nwⁿā*, befouled with spittle.

Bwat 妺 Bwat hê 妺嬉, to rejoice.

Bwat 韈 Vulg. *böēyh*: a pair of stockings: bwat jê teng tông 韈而登堂, *ch'hêng böēyh jê chëōⁿᵍ tëⁿᵍ*, wearing stockings, he ascended the hall.

Bwat 襪 The same as the foregoing: lêng p'ho bê poē, lô bwat seng tîn 淩波微步.羅襪生塵, *köèy chúy sèy sèy ay poē, lô böēyh saiⁿᵍ tîn*, going over the water with small paces, our silk stockings get covered with dirt.

卒

Bwuy 溦 Small rain.

Bwuy 眛 Dark, the eyes not seeing well.

C

卒

Cha 查 *Cha boê lâng* 查厶人, a woman,—(a provincial expression). Hoō jîn sit sim mŏh tō lé 婦人識甚麼道理, *cha boê lâng bat sⁿa meēⁿh tō lé*, as to women, what do they know about reason!

去

Chá 早 Read chó: early, soon, quickly, formerly. Chó sîn 早晨, *chá k'hê sê*, in the morning, early.

Chó teâou 早朝, *chá k'hê ay teâou*, an early audience, at Court.

Chó yéw ê ê t'hëen hāy 早有譽於天下, *chá woō o ló tē t'heeⁿᵍ āy*, he would soon obtain celebrity throughout the Empire. See the 中庸 Tëung yûng.

Chó hêng put këèn ch'heng san bëēn 早行不見青山面, *chá k'hê sê kēⁿâ, bô k'hwⁿà ch'haiⁿᵍ swⁿa āy bīn*, travelling early in the morning, we cannot see the face of the blue mountains.

木
Chae 栽 To plant; a plant: chae laōu haōu 栽老莩, to plant nutmegs. Chae cheā pōēy che 栽者培之, *chae ây meē^{n}h pōēy yâng e*, fostering that which is planted. See the 中庸 Tēung yūng.
Te wat chae, tēāng wat sē 稺曰栽.長曰樹, *sèy châng kóng chae, twā châng kóng ch'hèw*, those of smaller growth are called plants, and those of larger growth trees.

Chae 哉 An expression of wonder, or exclation; a note of admiration. Hēēn chae Hōēy yeá 賢哉回也, *gâou chae Hōēy â*, how clever was Hōēy. See the 上論 Sēāng lūn.
Taē chae, Geâou che wūy kwun yeá 大哉堯之爲君也, *twā chae, Geâou ây chò jîn kwun*, how great was Geâou as a prince! See the same.
Thēen hô gân chae 天何言哉, *t'hee^{ng} t'hae t'hó woō kóng wā chae*, how can Heaven hold discourse! See the 下論 Hāy lūn.

Chae 災 Calamity, affliction: chae lān 災難, trouble. Kèw chae, sut lin, tō yeá 救災恤鄰道也, *kèw chae lān, sut kâyh pēāh lâng, sē tō yeá*, to deliver people from trouble, and pity one's neighbours, is the way of virtue. See the 左傳 Chó twān.
Boô chae boô haē 無災無害, *bô chae bô haē*, without trouble or danger.

Chae 菑 Distress and trouble: chae haē pēng chè, suy yéw sēēn cheā, ek boô jê che hô é, 菑害並至.雖有善者.亦無如之何矣, *chae haē chò poô kaòu suy oō hó ây lâng, yeá bô hwat e taē wā*, when calamity and affliction come all at once, although a good man were at the head of affairs, he could not help it. See the 大學 Taē hak.

Chae 齋 Pure, respectful; to fast, and purify one's-self; also, a quiet, retired place, a school.
Chae kaè bok yeuk, chek k'hó é soō sēāng tèy 齋戒沐浴.則可以祀上帝, *cheāh ch'haè châng ek, chēw t'hang hok saē sēāng tèy*, having fasted and bathed, then one may worship the highest Emperor (i. e. the Supreme). See 孟子 Bēng-choó.
Se chae chek cheng 書齋寂靜, *so ūh chek cheng*, a place of learning, quiet and retired.

Chae 亝 The ancient form of the above character; Put chae 勃亝, the name of a hill.

Chae 賳 Goods, wealth, treasure.

Chae 知 Read te: to know, to be acquainted with. Te che, wūy te che,—put te, wūy put te, sē te yeá 知之爲知之.不知爲不知.是知也, *chae e lēāh chò chae, u^{m} chae lēāh chò u^{m} chae, chēy chēw sē chae yeá*, when you know anything, account that you know it, and when you do not know anything, account that you do not know it; this is knowledge. See the 上論 Sēāng lūn.

宀
Chaé 宰 To rule, to regulate, to arrange: a surname. Choó chaé 主宰, a ruler.
T'haè chaé chēāng kēēn pang che lēuk tēēn, é chò ông pēng pang kok, 太宰掌建邦之六典.以佐王平邦國, *t'haè chaè chēâng kwàn pang ây lak tēēn, é hoô chò ông pai^{ng} tē pang kok*, the prime minister controls the six boards, in order to assist the sovereign in pacifying the country. See the 周禮 Chew léy.
Chaé sēàng 宰相, a prime minister. Choó-loē wūy Kwùy-sē chaé 子路爲季氏宰, *Choó-loē chò Kwùy-sē ây chaè*, Choó-loē was a steward over the household of Kwùy-sē. See the 上論 Sēāng lūn.
Chaé chè bān but 宰制萬物, *chaè kwàn bān meē^{n}h*, to govern all things.

Soó pêng tek chaé t'hëen hāy, ek jê ch'hoò jëuk 使平得宰天下.亦如此肉, *saé hoē gwā, ëy, tit, chaé tē t'heeng, āy, yeá, ch'hin cheōng chèy lëy bāh*, let me succeed in managing the Empire, just as I do this piece of flesh; — this was a wish expressed by 陳平 *Tân-pêng*, when he was offering a sacrifice, and cutting up the flesh for the same. See the 陳平傳 *Tân-pêng twān*.

Chaé 寀 P'heng chaé 烹寀, to boil, to cook.

Chaé 滓 The grounds or sediments of liquor: chey chaé 渣滓, sediment.

Chaé 儰 Bold, courageous, daring.

Chaé 崽 A child; the people of 江南 Kang-lâm province, formerly called their children chaé.

去

Chaè 載 A year; the beginning; an affair: then; also, an expletive. Jê sip yëw pat chaè, Hóng-hwun naé ckoé lok 二十有八載.放勳乃殂落, *jê chap kwà pāyh neeng, Hóng-hwun naè sè lōh*, after twenty eight years Hóng-hwun i. e. (Gêâou 堯) departed this life.

T'hong sé cheng, choō Kat chaè 湯始征.自葛載, *T'hong k'hé ch'hay cheng hwat, choō Kat k'hé t'hâou*, when T'hong began his military operations, he commenced from the Kat district. See 孟子 Bêng-choó.

Chaè 再 Again, to repeat; chaè sam 再三, *chaè sna*, again and again. Yit che wûy sïm, k'hé k'hò chaè hoē 一之爲甚.豈可再乎, *chit kwùy seōng chēy, k'hám ēy t'hang kōh hoē*, once is too often, how can it be repeated.

Chaè soo k'hó è 再斯可矣, *kōh chit hāy chëw t'hang*, once more repeated, and it will be sufficient. See the 上論 Seāng lūn.

Chaè 債 A debt: hoō chaè 負債, *hoō chày*, to be in debt. Maē tëên t'hek, yëuk choó sun, é ch'hëâng chaè 賣田宅鬻子孫.以償債, *bëy ch'hân ch'hoò, bëy kënà sun, é ch'heâng chày*, to dispose of fields and houses, and to sell children and grandchildren, in order to pay one's debts. See the 前漢書 Chëên Hàn se.

Sïm sëâng chéw chaé, hêng ch'hè yéw 尋常酒債.行處有, *sìm seâng āy chéw chày, chin chaē wūy woō*, common tavern scores for liquor, may be met with in every place.

平

Chaê 才 Talent; chaê lêng 才能, *chaê teâou*, ability. Chun hëën yëuk chaê, é chëang yéw tek 尊賢育才.以彰有德, *chùn keng gaôu lâng, yëuk ch'hë woō chaê teâou āy, é chëang bêng woō tek*, we should honour the good, and foster the clever, in order to bring to light those who have virtue. See the 下孟 Hāy bêng.

Chaê 材 Chaê leâou 材料, materials: kwan chaê 棺材, *k'wna ch'hâ*, a coffin. Chaê bok put k'hó sin yūng yëâ 材木不可勝用也, *ch'hâ bak bô T'hang leâou e āy yūng*, then the timber will be more than can be exhausted by use. See the 上孟 Seāng bêng.

Chaê 財 Money, wealth, cash: chëên chaê 錢財, *cheeng chaê*, money. Hwat chaê 發財, to get wealthy: chaê k'hè 財氣, a wealthy influence.

Chaê hoō 財阜, a cashier, a book-keeper, a clerk.

Lâm hong che sê hêy, k'hó é hoō goê bîn che chaê hêy 南風之時兮.可以阜吾

民之財兮, *lâm hong ây sè, t'hang ch'hòng chēy gwá pūyh sai^ng ây chaê*, the timely influence of the southern wind can increase the wealth of my people. Part of an ode made by 舜 Sùn.

Chaê 裁 To cut as with a scissors; to regulate, to measure. Chaê hông 裁縫, a tailor, one who cuts out, and stitches together.

Hoē é chaê sêng t'hēen tēy che tō 后以裁成天地之道, *lé t'hang chaê chē^n â t'hee^ng tēy ây tō*, your majesty can clip and contrive (act according to) the way of Heaven and Earth. See the 易經 *Yēāh keng*.

Chaê 臍 Read chêy: the navel; chêy taè 臍帶, *chaê twà*, the navel string. Jēak put chó toê, hoē chēang sē chêy 若不早圖, 後將嗜臍, *nā u^m chá chá toê e, aōu laê chēang chēāh toê chaê*, if you do not speedily lay a plan to circumvent him, he will eventually prevail so far as to eat your very navel.

至

Chaē 載 To load, to burden, to bear as a burden, to sustain, to hold. T'hēen hok tēy chaē 天覆地載, *t'hee^ng p'hak tēy chaē*, the heaven overspreads, and the earth under-props (all things).

Súy k'hó chaē chew, ek k'hó hok chew 水可載舟, 亦可覆舟, *chúy t'hang chaē chûn, yēá t'hang p'hak chûn*, water can float vessels, and the same element can also overwhelm them. The words of 楊子 Yâng-chóó.

Chaē 在 Vulg. *tē*: at, in, to consist in, to remain at, to be in existence, to be present. Chaē 在, *tē tit*, to be present; put chaē 不在, *bó tē tit*, to be absent.

Taē hak che tō, chaē bêng bêng tek, chaē sin bîn, chaē ché ē chè sēēn 大學之道, 在明明德, 在新民, 在止於至善, *Taē hak ây tō lé, tē bêng bêng ây tek, tē ch'hòng sin pūyh sai^ng, tē hày^nh twā tē chè hó*, the doctrine of the great school, consists in illustrating resplendent virtue, in renovating the people, and in stopping at the point of extreme virtue. See the 大學 Taē hak.

Chaē 廌 Haē chaē 獬廌, name of an animal.

Chaē 豸 Haē chaē 獬豸, an animal, found in the north-east, with one horn, which attacks only vicious persons.

夫

Chǎh 扗 To beat, to strike.

夾

Chǎh 閘 A portcullis; sêng bûn chǎh 城門閘, *sê^nâ moo^ng chǎh*, the portcullis of a city gate. Súy chǎh 水閘, *chúy chǎh*, a water-gate, a flood-gate.

Chǎh 牐 The same as the preceding.

Chǎh 截 Chēet twān 截斷, *chǎh tooi^ng*, to cut off, to cut short. Kim Têng chēet tēāng poé twán, chēang gnoé sip lé 今滕截長補短, 將五十里, *t^na Têng kok, chǎh tê^ng poè tèy, chēang bōēyh goē chap lé*, now if you cut off the longer parts of the Têng country, and take them to supply the shorter, you will find it to be about 50 square Lé in extent.

爭

Chai^ng 爭 Read cheng: To wrangle, to strive, to contend. Kwun chóó boô séy cheng 君子無所爭, *kwun chóó ây lâng bó sèy chai^ng*, a good man never wrangles. See the 上論 Sēāng lūn.

上聲

Chaiⁿᵍ 井 Read chéng: a well; a surname. Chéng yéw jîn yëen 井有人焉, chaiⁿᵍ uè woō lâng, there is a person in the well.

Chéng téy koè t'hëen 井底顧天, chaiⁿᵍ téy koè t'heeⁿᵍ, to be looking at the heavens, from the bottom of a well (by which means the heavens would look very small); — intimating that a person who does so has narrow views.

平聲

Chaîⁿᵍ 睛 Read chêng: clear weather, fine weather: é chêng 雨睛, hoē chaîⁿᵍ, the rain is cleared up.

去聲

Chaīⁿᵍ 靜 Read chēng: quiet, still; àm chēng 暗靜, àm chaīⁿᵍ, clandestine.

上入

Chak 促 Ak chak 偓促, narrow, confined.

下入

Chak 擉 A weight tied to a net, to sink it down in the water.

上平

Cham 臢 Am cham 腌臢, la sám, dirty, filthy, anything not clean.

Cham 䐶 The same as the preceding; also, to boil; sore lips.

Cham 戳 To peck at any thing, as a bird does.

Cham 喒 I, me; also, to vomit.

Cham 尖 Pointed, sharp.

Cham 簪 Vulg. chom: a bodkin, a hair-pin. Hwa cham 花簪, a flowered bodkin. Kim cham 金簪, a golden bodkin. Köëy cham 髻簪, a hair-pin.

Lúy taē cham eng 累代簪纓, kwúy nà tèy lè cham kwà eng, "for several generations, wearing hair pins and tassels;" — an allusion to families which, for successive ages, have been in office.

上聲

Chám 斬 To cut off, to behead; chám söey 斬衰, the edges of a garment, cut off, and left unhemmed, as is customary when mourning for a father.

Chám hwat soè kok 斬伐四國, chám hwat sì wūy ây kok, to cut off the nations all around. See the 小雅 Séaou gnáy.

Chám ch'hó tê kin 斬草除根, chám ch'háou tëŏh tê kin, when cutting off weeds, you should extract the roots; — intimating that the evil must be completely eradicated.

Chám séw bān kip 斬首萬級, chám t'háou chëⁿá bān kip, he cut off heads, to the amount of several myriads.

Chám 昝 A surname.

Chám 魙 The name of a devil.

去聲

Chàm 蘸 Anything steeped or soaked in water.

平聲

Châm 讒 To break; to slander; to speak evil of any one. Gnó yéw kèng è, châm gân kē hin 我友敬矣，讒言其興, gwá ây yéw, lè tëŏh sèy jē, saê p'hwà ây wā tit hin k'hé, my friend you must be careful, for slanderous accusations are about to arise. See the 小雅 Séaou gnáy.

丟

Chām 站 To stand alone, to stand long.

Chām 塹 K'heng chām 坑塹, *k'hai^ng chăm*, a ditch or moat round a city wall.

Chām 鏨 A chisel, to chizel and cut stones.

Chām 劖 To cut off, to file away.

Chām 蔪 Bushy, overgrown with thorns and briers.

奉

Chan 繒 A cord, a string: a general term for silk.

Chan 罾 A net for catching fish.

Chan 曾 Read cheng: a surname: Cheng-chóo yáng Cheng-sek pit yéw chéw jëuk 曾子養曾晳必有酒肉, *Chan-chóo yëó^ng ch'hē Chan-sek pit tëŏh wōo chéw kwà bāh*, Chan-chóó, in supporting Chan-sek, would always have wine and flesh for him. See 孟子 Bēng-chóo.

声

Chán 琖 A cup: chéw chán 酒琖, *chéw chw^n á*, a wine cup. Also written 盞 chán.

Chán 喒 I, myself. Vulg. *lán.*

Chán 儹 To collect, and assemble together.

Chán 趲 To run away: to be driven away.

圭

Chàn 贊 To help, to assist: chek k'hó é chàn t'hëen tēy che hwà yëuk 則可以贊天地之化育, *chëw t'hang chàn t'hee^ng tēy ây hwà yëuk,* then they (the sages) could assist the regenerating and fostering efforts of heaven and earth.

Chàn 瓚 A sacrificial implement used in the ancestorial temple.

Chàn 讚 Vulg. *o lö:* to praise, to applaud, to commend.

Chàn 纘 To connect, to continue, to succeed. Boó-ông chàn T'haè-ông, Ông-kwùy, Bûn-ông che sē 武王纘大王.王季.文王之緒, *Boá-ông kèy swà T'haè-ông, Ông-kwùy, Bûn-ông ây sw^n à,* Boó-ông connected the thread of succession from T'haè-ông, Ông-kwùy, and Bûn-ông. See the 中庸 Tëung yûng.

Chàn 酇 The name of a place: four lé make a chàn.

Chàn 層 A story, an upper chamber: yëuk këûng ch'hëen lé bok, keng sëang yit chàn loê 欲窮千里目.更上一層樓, *aè bōëyh këûng chīn chë^n á ch'heng lé ây bak, tëŏh kŏh chëo^ng chit chàn ây lâou,* if you want to see to the utmost of a thousand lé, you should still ascend another story of the gallery.

丟

Chân 殘 Superfluous; to add; also, oppressive, cruel, injurious. Chek gē chëá, wūy che chân 賊義者謂之殘, *chek haē gē, sē kóng këò chân,* to injure what is right, is called Chân, injurious.

Chân jîm 殘忍, cruel: chân paē 殘敗, to ruin.

Chân 飱 To injure another from covetous motives.

Chân 前 Read chëên: Before. Chëên hoē 前後, *chân aōu*, before and behind. Kwun chëên sîn bêng, hoō chëên choó bêng, put ėk che lé yëá 君前臣名. 父前子名. 不易之理也, *jîn kwun chân, jîn sîn lëŏh këò mē^n^â, nëó^ng^ pāy chân, haōu sai^ng^ lëŏh këò më^n^â, bŏ ê ėk ây tō lé*, in a prince's presence, a minister should use his own name (instead of the personal pronoun I); and in a father's presence, a son should use his own name; this is an invariable doctrine. See the 禮記 Léy kè.

去

Chān 助 Read choē: to help, to asisst, Pang choē 㨢助, *pang chān*, to help and aid. Höêy yëá, hwuy choē gnō chëá yëá, ê goê gân boô séy put wat 回也. 非助我者也. 於吾言無所不悅, *Höêy â, e bŏ chān gwá ây lâng, nā sē lē gwá ây wā, e bŏ sèy ū^m^ hw^n^a hè*, Höêy does not assist me in anything, but with respect to my words, he is invariably pleased with them. See the 下論 Hāy lūn.

Chān 棧 Chān pang 棧房, a warehouse, a store-house.

上平

Chang 椶 Read chong: the name of a tree,—p'hê k'hó chok chong söey 皮可作椶蓑, *p'hōëy t'hang chò chang söey*,—the hairy bark of which can be made up into rain mantles. It is also used for making brushes, trunks, and other things.

Chang 搶 To pull, to drag, to lead.

Chang 艐 Read chong: to run on a sand-bank, to run aground. Chûn chong chëak 船艐着, *chûn chang tëŏh*, the ship is aground.

Chang 騌 Read chong: a mane: má chong 馬騌, *báy chang*, a horse's mane. Chîn chew chin yit má, chong jê gêw hāng hāy sûy 秦州進一馬. 騌如牛項下垂, *Chîn ây chew chìn chit chëäh báy, chang ch'hin chëō^ng^ goô àm kwún hāy*, the Chîn country sent in a horse, as a present, whose mane was like the hanging dewlap of a bull's neck.

Chang 鯼 Read chong: a fish of the southern sea, which has a stone in its head, and is called, sėk séw gê 石首魚, *chëŏh t'haôu hê*, stone-headed fish. Also called, ch'hek chong gê 赤鯼魚, *ch'hëäh chang hê*, red fish.

Chang 鬃 Read chong: a tail; t'hoê chong 頭鬃, *t'haôu chang*, a tail of hair. T'hoê chong bé p'heàou 頭鬃尾票, *t'haôu chang bóëy p'hëò*, ticket for a tax on Chinamen's tails, levied in Batavia.

Chang 椶 Read chong: a lofty tree, with large leaves and no branches; a kind of palm, bushy at the head, like a cocoa nut tree.

上声

Cháng 鬃 Read chóng: a queue or tail, made of twisted hair.

Cháng 總 Read chóng: generally, entirely, altogether.

去

Chàng 粽 Read chòng: a kind of confectionary made of millet, folded up with sharp corners, and used on the feast of the 5th day of the 5th moon: it is also called kak sé 角黍, cornered millet.

Chàng 綜 Read chông: hëën chông 紘綜, heè^ng chàng, a part of a loom by which the threads are separated, to admit of the shuttle passing to and fro.

平

Châng 叢 Read chông: a bush; a numeral of trees and flowers; sē chông 樹叢 ch'hēw châng, a bush of a tree. K'heng loē sey chông këuk 輕露棲叢菊, k'hin ây loē chùy hai^nh tē chit châng këuk hwa, the light dew rested upon the bush of the chrysanthemun flower.

Châng 掙 To stab, to pierce; also, to hack.

上

Chaou 㩰 Wood half burnt; ch'haê chaou 柴㩰, ch'hâ chaou, a fire brand but half consumed, and put by for lighting again.

Chaou 糟 Read cho: the grains, or refuse, after brewing: chéw cho 酒糟, chéw chaou, the refuse of rice after fermentation. Gwân-hëën put yëèm cho k'hong 原憲不厭糟糠, Gwân-hëèn bô hëëm chéw chaou bê k'hèng, Gwân-hëèn did not refuse to cut grains and chaff. See the 史記 Soó kè.

Chaou 笊 Chaou lê, a sieve made of bamboo, for straining liquor. When birds dwell in caverns their retreats are called 笊 chaou, and when in trees they are called 巢 châou, nests.

去

Chaóu 僺 Long, anything that looks long. Yûng cháou é jê ch'hè yëen 傭僺宇而處焉, k'hè tè^ng tè^ng ây ch'hoò jê k'hëā, to erect a long building and dwell therein.

Chaóu 走 Read choé: To run, to run away, to run quickly. K'hè kap ē peng jê choé 棄甲曳兵而走, t'hek kak chëèn kūh, t'hwa lwa peng to, jê chaóu, they threw away their armour, reversed their weapons, and fled. See the 上孟 Sëāng bēng.

Chaóu 蚤 Read chó: a flea; kaóu chó 狡蚤, ka chaóu, a flea. Kaóu chó chò soō lüy sat bó 狡蚤做事累虱母, ka chaóu chò soō lüy sat bó, the flea makes a disturbance, and involves the louse in trouble. For the flea bites sharp, and immediately jumps away; while the lazier louse, lingering about the place, is caught and killed. Said of sharp, cunning fellows, who do all the mischief, and leave the duller ones to bear the brunt of it.

Chaóu 姐 Chaóu á, a daughter; this is an expression of inferiority, intimating the light esteem in which the Chinese hold their daughters; when asked if they have got a son, they say, chaóu á tē^nā tē^nā, only a daughter!

去

Chaòu 竈 Read chò: a furnace, a fire place, a cook-house. Chò këak 竈脚, chaòu k'ha, a cooking place. E' kê mē ê ò, lêng mē ê chò 以其媚於奧,寧媚於竈, pè ê ây sëep sē ê ò, lêng k'hó sëep sē ê chaòu, instead of flattering the god of the south-west corner of the house, (who, though he is commonly honoured, is yet held in but little esteem), is it not better to flatter the god of the kitchen, (who, though not entitled to a constant sacrifice, yet on certain occasions is served with the highest honours). Said to Confucius, by one who wanted him, instead of seeking the fovour of the acknowledged princes of his day, to get into the good graces of their ministers, who, at times, might be eabled to do him more service. See the 上論 Sëāng lūn.

Chaòu 奏 Read choè: to report to the Emperor; also, to play music. Choè kê gak 奏其樂; *chaòu e ây gak*, to play the music (of the ancient kings).

Tông-gwūy-tin hëèn sip soō soè, choè têng T'haè-chong 唐魏徵獻十思疏奏呈太宗, *Tông-gwūy-tin hëèn chap hūng sëō^ng ây soè pún, chaòu të^n â T'haè-chong*, Tông-gwūy-tin presented a document, recommending the consideration of ten things, which he reported to T'haè-chong.

平

Chaôu 巢 A nest, a bird's nest: a surname. Neaóu chaôu 鳥巢, *cheaóu sëw*, a bird's nest. Sëāng chëá wūy chaôu, hāy chëá wûy k'hwut 上者爲巢下者爲窟, *k'hăh kwân ây wūy chò chaôu, k'hăh kūy ây wūy chò k'hwut*, in the higher parts of the land they form nests, and in the lower, caverns. See the 上孟 *Chëō^ng bëng*.

Chaôu 漅 The name of a lake which produces gold.

Chaôu 勦 To exterminate, to kill: yéw chöēy chaôu sam chok 有罪勦三族, *woō chöēy chaôu s^na chok*, being criminal, the family must be exterminated to the third generation.

An yūng chaôu bin 安用勦民, *s^na soō tëŏh chaôu chwat păyh sai^ng*, what is the use of exterminating the people?

Chaôu 窲 A deep succession of chambers in a dwelling.

丟

Chaōu 找 Chaōu sim 找尋, *chaōu ch'hoèy*, to seek after, to search. Chaōu hwân 找還, to pay what is deficient, to liquidate all demands: when an account is squared, the Chinese write in their account books 找 Chaōu, settled.

Chaōu 櫂 A long oar, used for guiding and impelling a boat. K'hey ch'him sëâng këèn chaōu, sē wán hán bûn chëung 溪深常見櫂寺遠罕聞鐘, *k'hey chúy ch'him sëâng sëâng k'hw^nà kèe^ng chaōu, ëe^ng hwui^ng hán tit t'hē^na cheng*, when the river is deep we frequently observe the oar; when the temple is distant we seldom hear the bell. Also written 棹 chaōu.

Chaōu 淖 Mud; muddy and sloppy ground; also, amicable.

Chaōu 嘷 The noise of a multitude

Chaōu 巢 A gallery, a railing.

去

Chaŏuh 担 Read t'hán: to take, to hold.

去

Chap 帀 Complete; chew chap yit söey 周帀一歲, *chew chap chit höèy*, one whole year.

Chap 匝 The same as the foregoing; bwân chap 滿匝, *mw^nâ chap*, fully complete.

Chap 劄 Chap choò 劄子, a document: chap kè lëuk 劄記錄, a record. Lūn bé jîn Tëang sē, yin t'hëúng chap chóo 論美人張氏恩寵劄子, *lūn kip ch'hin ch'hai^ng ây lâng Tëō^ng sē, sëw yin t'hëúng ây chap â*, a document respecting Mrs. Tëō^ng, a fair lady, who enjoyed extraordinary favour.

o

Chap 浹 To soak through, to imbibe; also, full, complete. Kaòu hwà chap hëep 敎化浹洽, instruction diffused throughout the mind.
Chap sîn che kan, Ch'hoé k'hek sam toe 浹辰之間.楚克三都, *chap jê jit ây kan, Ch'hoé k'hăh yëⁿâ sⁿa ây toe yip*, in the course of twelve days, the Ch'hoe country conquered three capital cities. See the 左傳 Chó twān.

Chap 札 A small slip of bamboo, on which the ancients used to write notes and memorandums. Also, an early death. Se chap 書札, the modern term for a letter. Bîn put yaou chap 民不夭札, *pâyh 'saiⁿᵍ bô chá sè*, the people did not come to an early death. See the 左傳 Chó twān.

Chap 呫 When a fish opens its mouth to swallow anything, it is called chap: anything entering the mouth. Chap ch'hùy 呫嘴 to smack the lips.

入

Chap 襍 The five colours mixed together.

Chap 雜 To mix, to blend together; ch'ham chap 參雜, to mix together. Hoo hëen hông chëá, t'hëen tëy che chap yëá 夫玄黃者.天地之雜也, *hoo, oe kwà wutⁿᵍ sè t'heeⁿᵍ tëy ây sëo chap*, the mixture of black and yellow, intimates the blending of heaven and earth together. See the 易經 *Yëăh keng.*

Chap 譶 A chattering noise: ch'hùy chap chap káng 嘴譶譶講, *ch'hùy chap chap kóng*, the mouth constantly chattering.
Chô chô chap chap che seng, sëang bûn soò kéng che lōey 嘈嘈譶譶之聲.相聞四境之內, *chap chap jëáng jëáng ây sëⁿa, sëo t'hëⁿa tô sè kèng ây laē*, a chattering and busy sound is heard, uninterruptedly, within the four borders of the land.

Chap 什 Read sip; ten men are called one *chap*; ten of anything. Sip hⁿò 什貨, *chap hòèy*, a mixed assortment of goods; pedlar's ware.

Chap 十 Read sip: ten; sip chëá, soè che chëung 十者數之終, *chap chëw sè soè bak ây swăh bòèy*, ten is the termination of numbers: a decimal is a perfect number. See the 上論註 Sëāng lūn choò. Goê sip yëw gnòe jê chè ê hak 吾十有五而志于學, *gwá chap goē hòèy, jê sim chè twā tê t'hak*, at fifteen years of age, my mind was bent on learning. See the 上論 Sëāng lūn.

入

Chat 節 Read chëet: a knot in bamboo; a verse in a chapter: a section. *Chún chat* 準節, economical. Chëet yūng, jê aè jîn 節用而愛人, *chún chat hwùy yūng jê sëŏh làng*, economical in expenditure, and affectionate towards others. See the 上論 Sëāng lūn.

入

Chat 趧 To urge any one extremely.

Chat 鰂 Bok chek 目鰂, *bak chat*, the cuttle-fish; a certain fish found in the eastern seas, without bones or scales, having eight arms, and a ball of black matter in the inside, of which ink is made.

去

Chay 查 A wooden railing: yëak chay 藥查 *yëŏh chay*, the grounds or sediment of medicine. Also, to examine; the name of a place: a surname.

Chay 奓 To stretch out, to spread.

Chay 楂 Drift wood, floating down a river, upon which they fable that genii ride, in order to float into the milky way, or heavenly river, and thus get among the stars. Sëen chay hwān gnêw toé 仙楂犯牛斗, *sëen chāy chay, hwān tëŏh goô-taôu*, a genius sailing on a float, came across the *goô-taôu* star.

Chay 咱 Vulg. *lán*: I, myself.

Chay 渣 The name of a river.

Chay 樝 The name of a fruit, like a pear, but rather sour.

Chay 槎 To cut down; also, a float of drift wood. San bók put chay 山木不槎, *swⁿa. ch'hâ bô chëŏh*, not to cut down the wood on the mountains. See the 公羊傳 Kong yâng twān.
Gê jîn sêng chay tò t'hëen hô 漁人乘槎到天河, *t'hó hê ây lâng chây chay kaôu t'hee^{ng} hô*, a fisherman riding on a float arrived at the celestial river, (i. e. the milky way).

Chay 齋 Read chae: to fast; *chay. ch'hëem.* 齋懺, to fast and pray.

Chay 滓 Read chae: sediment; but chae 物滓, *mëëⁿh chay*, the sediment of anything. Sêng jê chëep chae seäng chëang 成而汁滓相將, *chëⁿâ jê chëep chay sëo chap*, when it (the wine) was made, the grounds and the liquor were mixed together. See the 周禮 Chew léy.

Chay 遮 Read chëa: to induce, to persuade; to hinder, to screen; to talk much. Sam-lô Tâng-kong chëa swat Hàn ông 三老董公遮說漢王, *Sⁿa-lo Tâng-kong chay sŏëyh Hàn ông*, the Sⁿa-lô officer named Tâng-kong prevented and persuaded the king of Hàn. See the 高帝紀 Ko-tèy kè.

声

Cháy 傗 The appearance of walking.

Cháy 鮺 A preparation of salted fish and sour rice, which, when cured, is put by for food.

Cháy 姐 Read chëá: a sister; used in addressing females generally.

Cháy 這 This: cháy kò joō 這個字, *chèy lèy jē*, this character. Cháy kò jîn 這個人, *chèy lèy lâng*, this man

去

Chày 詐 False, deceitful; to deceive, to tell lies. Put gek chày 不逆詐, *ū^m gek chày*, do not contend with deceit.
Gnô boô jé chày, jé boô gnô gê 我無爾詐爾無我虞, *gwá bô lè pàyh ch'hat, lè bô gwá sëet*, I will not deceive you, and do not you betray me. See the 左傳 Chó twān.

Chày 笮 A vessel for holding wine; a wine-cup. Keng-këung lē soō k'hat hwat, chày má hwùn chëep yím che 耿恭吏士渴乏笮馬糞汁飲之, *Keng-këung lē soō ch'hùy k'hwăh k'hëem k'hŏëyh, t'hó chëw chày yëō^{ng} bây pùn ây chëep, laé lim e*, Keng-këung, an inferior officer, being thirsty and in want, took a wine cup and gathered up the juices of horse dung, to drink it.

Chày 醡 A press for making wine; also written, 榨 chày.

Chày 債 Read chaè, a debt: hoō chaè 負債 *hoō chày*, to be in debt. Pêog-lwàn wŭy. Bêng-sëăng-kwnn sew chaè ε

Sëet 馮煖爲孟嘗君收債於薛, *Pâng-lwán wûy Bēng-sëâng-kwun sew chày tē Seĕh kok*, Pâng-lwán went to collect debts for Bēng-sëâng-kwun, in the Seĕh country.

Chày 炸 To burst: ch'hëüng chày k'hè 銃炸去, *ch'hèng chày k'hè*, the gun is burst.

Chày 嗻 To talk much.

Chāy 乍 Suddenly, unexpectedly. Kim jîn chāy këën jê choó chëang jip ê chéng, kae yéw t'hut t'hek ch'hek yîn che sim 今人乍見孺子將入於井,皆有怵惕惻隱之心, *t'na ây lâng chāy jëën k'hwⁿà sèy kèⁿá chëang bëëyh jip tē chaiⁿᵍ, chò poé wōo t'hut t'hek ch'hek yîn ây sim*, now if people were suddenly to see a little child about to fall into a well, they would all experience a feeling of anxiety and commiseration. See 孟子 Bēng-choó.

Chāy 砦 A pile of stones, put up against a wooden fence.

Chāy 寨 A camp, an encampment; hāy chāy 下寨, to encamp. Yîn hong san téng chāy 雲封山頂寨, *hwûn hong swⁿa téng ây chāy*, the clouds covered the camp on the mountain top.

Chāy 禮 A sacrifice offered at the end of the year.

Chāy 蛇 Vulg. *t'hāy*, a kind of fish, called also súy bó 水母, *chúy bó*, a water-mother. This fish is found in the eastern sea, in shape like a lump of clotted blood, sometimes square, and sometimes round; it has no head nor eyes, and is guided and assisted by prawns; hence the proverb, — súy bóe bok hây 水母目蝦, *chúy boé ê hây chò bak chew*, the water-mother makes use of lobsters as its eyes. Also written, 鮓 chāy.

Chāy 渣 The name of a river.

Chāy 坐 Read chō: to sit down; ch'héng chō 請坐, *ch'hëⁿá chāy*, pray sit down. Sek put chéng put chō 席不正不坐, *ch'hëöh ūᵐ chëⁿà ūᵐ chāy*, if the mat was not straight, he would not sit down; — said of Confucius.

Chăyh 仄 Read chek: oblique: chek yim 仄音, *chăyh yim*, an oblique sound; any sound that is not even.

The Chinese divide the tones into pêng 平, *paiⁿᵍ*, even; and chek 仄, *chăyh*, oblique; and are very particular in making their verses to arrange the even and oblique tones properly. Thus, in a verse of five words in each line, beginning with an oblique tone, the prosody would run in the following manner:

chek chek pêng pêng chek 仄仄平平仄,
chăyh chăyh paiⁿᵍ paiⁿᵍ chăyh.

pêng pêng chek chek pêng 平平仄仄平
paiⁿᵍ paiⁿᵍ chăyh chăyh paiⁿᵍ.

pêng pêng pêng chek chek 平平平仄仄
paiⁿᵍ paiⁿᵍ paiⁿᵍ chăyh chăyh.

chek chek chek pêng pêng 仄仄仄平平
chăyh chăyh chăyh paiⁿᵍ paiⁿᵍ.

If the verse begins with an even tone, the couplets must be reversed, the two last lines being put first.

Chăyh 雀 Read ch'hëak: a sparrow, a small bird. Wūy chông k'he ch'hëak chëá, chëen yëá 爲叢敺雀者鸇也, *yīn wūy ch'hëw châng kwⁿá chăyh á ây mëēⁿh, chëw sò laē hëŏh*, that which drives the sparrow into the woods is the hawk. See the 上孟 Sëang bēng.

Hé ch'këak hoe chêng 喜雀呼晴, *hó ây chăyh á këò t'heeng chaing*, the lucky sparrow calls for fair weather.

Chăyh 績 Read chek: to spin: hóng chek 紡績, *p'hâng chăyh*, to spin thread. E' ch'hëuk che kay jê ché, yêw chek, kê kan Kwùy-sê che noê yëá 以歜之家而主.猶績.懼干季氏之怨也, *è gwá ây kny chò choó lâng, yêw böëyh p'hâng chăyh, këna nê kan hwān Kwùy-sê ây sêw k'hè*, being the head of my now ennobled family, if you still persist in spinning thread, it is to be feared you will stir up the anger of Kwùy-sê (our chief). See the Kok gé 國語; — said by a man to his mother.

Chăyh 節 Read cheet: a division of time, a season: lëën chëet 年節, *neeng chăyh*, times and seasons. Yit lëën yêw soò sê pat chëet 一年有四時八節, *chit neeng woō sè sè păyh chăyh*, each year has four seasons and eight divisions of time.

Chăyh 揤 To take in the fingers.

夾

Chăyh 沠 Not very dry: the appearance of flowing water.

Chăyh 淁 The name of a river; also, the sound of running water.

Chăyh 饆 Rice turned sour; the water which drips from fermenting rice.

Chăyh 截 Read chëet: to cut off; chëet twān 截斷, *chăyh tooing*, to cut asunder.

Chăyh 絕 Read chwat: to exterminate; chwat chëúng 絶種, *chăyh chêng*, to cut off one's posterity.

卒

Che 之 Of, belonging to, with respect to; to go to, to proceed; also, he, she, it. Hoo choó che kêw che yëá, kê choo ê hoê jin che kêw che e 夫子之求之也.其諸異乎人之求之與, *Hoo choó ây kêw e, k'hăh kŏh yëong pat lâng ây kêw e*, our master's seeking (information) is perhaps different from the way in which others seek it. See the 上論 Sëang lūn.
E chëûng lëâng jin che séy che 施從良人之所之, *t'haou bâ á tùy k'hwnà ta po lâng sèy kaòu ây wūy*, they secretly followed to see where their husbands went. See 孟子 Bēng-choó.
Bek jê chè che 默而識之, *tëèm tëèm jê bat e*, silently meditating till one comprehends anything.
Ch'hëang ch'hëang hoê hô che 倀倀乎何之, *gông gông hoê ... ta lŏh k'hè*, where are you going so stupidly

Che 諸 All, every one; a surname; also, to go: ... hoê 諸侯, a prince of the Empire.
Che jin 諸人, *chëung lâng*, all people; che kong 諸公, sirs, gentlemen.
Put kê jê höëy chëá, pat pek che hoê 不期而會者.八百諸侯, *bô kê yëak, jê sëo höëy chëá, păyh păyh che hoê*, without previous contract there met together, eight hundred princes of the Empire. Also read, choo.

Che 芝 Che lân 芝蘭, a certain flower, very fragrant. Këën yit sëën jê ... che lân che sit, kêw jê put bûn k... heng 見一善如入芝蘭之室.久 ... 不聞其馨, *k'hwnà këeng chit lêy hŏ lâ ... ch'hin chëong jip che lân ây ch'hoò, koó jê ūm ... e ây p'hang*, an interview with a good ... like entering a house full of the *che-lân* flower, after a time we perceive not the fragrance. See the 家語 Kay gé.

Che 卮 A wine vessel; hŏng gëuk che, k'hé wūy T'haè-sëāng-hông sēw 奉玉卮.起爲太上皇壽, *hŏng gëuk ây chêw pōey, k'hé wūy T'haè-sëāng-hông ây tē^{ng} hōēy sēw*, he took the pearly wine-cup, and rising, drank to the long life of (his father) T'haè-sëāng-hông. Said of 漢高祖 Hân-Ko-choé.

Che 枝 Vulg. *ke*: a branch; lēy che 荔枝, the fruit called Litchi. Che yëep bē haē, pún sit sëen pwat 枝葉未害.本實先撥, *ke hëŏh bōēy haē, kin pún sit taē seng pwat*, the branches and leaves are yet uninjured, but the root is already destroyed. Said of those who in appearance are doing well, while they are really ruined.

Che 肢 A limb, a member; soò che pek kwut 四肢百骨, *sè ke păyh kwut*, the four limbs and hundred bones.

Che 支 An order, a number; also, to divide. A surname. Che lé 支理, to regulate.
Che p'haè 支派, a distinct family, a tribe.

Che 脂 Yëen che 胭脂, rouge, used by Chinese ladies for reddening the lips. Che ko 脂膏, ointment, salve; che yêw 脂油, oil.
Séw jê jêw ê, hoo jê géng che 手如柔荑.膚如凝脂, *ch'hêw ch'hin chëō^{ng} nooi^{ng} nooi^{ng} ây ch'haóu, băh ch'hin chëō^{ng} këen tàng ây yëw*, her hands were like soft yielding grass, and her flesh like congealed ointment. See the 國風 Kok hong.

Che 䳅 The name of a bird.

Che 潴 Standing water; tanks for holding water, in order to provide against a drought.

Che 戠 To plough.

Che 梔 Hông che 黃梔, *wui^{ng} kee^{ng}*, the name of a yellow wood, used as a dye; the yellow preparation of pulse, called toē kan 荳干, *taōu kw^{n}a*, much used among the Chinese, is died with this wood.

声

Ché 止 To stop, to halt, to rest, to dwell; only, alone. Wân jê ché che, jê ché 援而止之而止, *k'han jê lâôu e, e chëw hai^{n}h*, if any one pulled him to detain him, he would stop. Said of Lêw-hāy-hwūy.
Hông neaôu ché ê k'hew gê 黃鳥止於丘隅, *wui^{ng} chëâou hai^{n}h tē sw^{n}a kak*, the yellow bird rested on the corner of the hill.
Pang ke ch'hëen lé, wūy bîn sêy ché 邦畿千里.爲民所止, *pang kok chë^{n}â ch'heng lé, wuy păyh sai^{ng} sèy twā*, a district of a thousand lé in extent, for the people to dwell in.

Ché 址 Ke ché 基址, a foundation. T'haè pêng, ke ché ch'hëen lëën éng, hwūn yit, ke se bān koé chûn 太平.基址千年永.混一.車書萬古存, *t'haè pai^{ng}, ke ché ch'heng nee^{ng} êng,—hwūn yit, ch'hëa ch'hăyh bān koé chûn*, in the midst of tranquillity, the foundations of the state last for a thousand years; when contending interests are united, the chariots and books of a dynasty are preserved for a myriad of ages.

Ché 沚 A small island.

Ché 芷 Pek ché 白芷, the name of a fragrant medicinal herb.

Ché 旨 A sweet taste: sit ché put kam 食旨不甘, *chëăh tee^ng ū^m chae e ây hó*, to eat anything sweet, and not to know its excellence; said of those who are so affected by the death of their parents, that they do not know the taste of what they eat.
The intention, will; a decree, an order; ché è 旨意, will and pleasure; sèng ché 聖旨, an imperial decree; ch'héng ché 請旨, to request an order.

Ché 指 A finger; séw ché 手指, *ch'hêw châe*, a finger of the hand, a ring. Ché sè 指示, *ké sè*, to point out anything; ché tëém 指點, to beckon.
K'hwut ché k'hó swàn 屈指可算, *k'hwut ché t'hang swui^ng*, bending the fingers you can enumerate them.
Boô bêng che ché 無名之指, *bô mē^nâ ây châe*, the nameless finger; that is, the ring finger.

Ché 祉 Happiness, delight; also, to stop.

Ché 趾 A toe; chëuk ché 足趾, *k'ha chaê^ng*, the toes of the feet. Lin che ché, chin chin kong choó 麟之趾振振公子, *lin ây chaê^ng chāy chāy kong choó*, the toes of the griffin have produced very many children;—alluding to 文王 Bûn ông, who had ninety-nine children. See the 國風 Kok hong.

Ché 茝 The same as 芷 ché; ché lân 茝蘭, the name of a fragrant herb.

Ché 枳 A kind of a lemon-tree, full of thorns; a lime-tree.

Ché 褚 Cotton wadding, for clothes; to conceal; a surname.

Ché 扺 Ché chëâng 扺掌, to hold in the hand.

Ché 只 Only, alone; ché ch'hoò lëâng soō jê é è 只此兩事而已矣, *ché chêy nō hāng soō tē^nā tē^nā*, only these two things, and no more.
Lok ché kwun choó, bín che hoō boé 樂只君子.民之父母, *ch'hêng ch'hêng köèy è kwun choó ây lâng, sē pâyh saî^ng ây pāy boé*, a prince that is pleased with no other than good men, is the father of his people. See the 小雅 Seaóu gnây.

Ché 紫 A nankeen colour: ché hwa poè 紫花布, nankeen cloth. Hông ché put é wûy sëet hok 紅紫不以爲褻服, *âng kwà ché bô bōëyh chò soo ke ây s^na*, red and nankeen colours he would not use for common wear. Said of Confucius, in the 上論 Sëâng lûn.

Ché 軹 The spokes of a wheel; used for a carriage generally. Chîn ông choó, Eng, kàng ché tō pông 秦王子嬰降軹道旁, *Chîn ông ây kē^nâ, Eng, lōh ch'hëa tē loê pe^ng*, Eng, the son of the king of Chin, descended from his carriage by the side of the road. See the 史記 Soó kè.

Ché 咫 A measure of eight inches; ché ch'hek 咫尺, in a small degree.

Ché 紙 Vulg. *chwá* paper; kim ché 金紙 *kim chwá*, gilt paper. Ch'haè-lûn yūng sē p'hê, kip pē poé, gê bóng, wûy ché 蔡倫用樹皮.及敝布.魚網.爲紙, *Ch'hwà-lûn yūng ch'hēw p'höëy, kap p'hwà poè, hê bāng, chò chwá*, Ch'hwà-lûn, made use of the bark of trees, and old rags, with fishing nets, to manufacture paper. See the 漢紀 Hàn ké, record of the Hân dynasty, about the time of the Christian era. Also written 㕤 Ché.

Ché 㡳 To stop, to stay, to detain.

Ché 姊 A sister; taē ché 大姊, *twā chè*, a sister's husband; ché moōēy 姊妹, sisters.

Ché 笫 A mat: ch'hông ché che tēy, lân é jîn gân 牀笫之地.難與人言, *ch'hê^ng ch'hēōh ây tēy, ōh kap lâng kóng*, what is done in the land of beds and mats (behind the curtain), is difficult to talk about. See the 左傳 Chó twān.

Ché 楮 The name of a tree, of the bark of which paper is made.

Ché 夂 To follow behind, to come up from behind. One of the radicals.

Ché 煮 To boil, to seethe; ché hwān 煮飯 *chè pooi^ng*, to cook rice. Ché toē jēēn toē kin 煮荳燃荳根, *chè taōu hê^nâ taōu kin*, in boiling pulse, to burn the pulse roots: alluding to brethren of the same family, who injure one another. Said by 曹植 Chô-sit.

P'heng keng ché soó 烹經煮史, to seethe the classics and boil histories;—meaning, to get perfectly acquainted with them.

Ché 渚 A small island, the same as 沚 ché. È é ch'baé hwân, ê chaou ê ché 于以采蘩.于沼于渚, *gwá k'hè bân hwân, tē chaou tē chè*, I go to pick herbs, about the ponds and islands. See the 國風 Kok hong.

Ché 麈 A kind of stag.

Ché 䵂 H^nó ch'hēem ché 好針䵂, a needle finger, a good sempstress; the same as 指 ché.

Ché 䛗 To promise, to assent to.

Chè 志 (𡴓) The will, intention, aim, design, purpose, object; an historical account. Chè ê tō 志於道, *sim chè twā tē tō*, the mind bent on virtue.

Àp. kok gân jé chè 盍各言爾志, *s^na soō ū^m-suy lâng kóng lè ây sim chè*, why do you not each tell us of your purpose. See the 上論 Sēāng lūn.

Chè 忠 The same as the preceding.

Chè 忮 To injure, to hurt; put chè put kêw, hô yūng put chong 不忮不求.何用不臧, *bô haē lâng, yēâ bô k'hè kêw lâng, woō ta tōh k'hè ū^m hó*, when a person does not injure people nor seek their favour, where is the place where he would not be well off. See the 上論 Sēāng lūn.

Chè 誌 To remember, to recollect; se soó yit keng bok, tēēt chè ê sim 書史一經目輙誌于心, *ch'hāyh kap soó chit keng kōēy bak, chò poō kè tē sim*, books and histories having once passed before his eyes, be thoroughly remembered them in his mind.

Chè 輊 The covering of a carriage, let down in front.

Chè 痣 Vulg. *kè*: a black spot, a freckle, a mark in the skin. Chó koē ch'hit sip jē hek choó chè 左股七十二黑子痣, *tó ch'hēw pêng ây twā t'hōēy, woō ch'hit chap jē oe tēēm ây kè*, on his left thigh he had seventy-two black coloured spots. Said of the founder of the 漢 Hân dynasty.

Chè 至 To arrive at; to go to the utmost; the extreme. Chè chek hêng è 至則行矣, *kaòu tëy e tòe kōⁿà teâou*, when he arrived (the old man) was gone. See the 上論 Sëāng lūn.

Bùt kek jê hoē te chè 物格而後知至, *meēⁿh bat kaòu kek, jêên aōu tè hwūy chè*, when we obtain an universal acquaintance with things, knowledge may be carried to the utmost extent. See the 大學 Taē hak.

Seáou jin hân ke, wûy put sëēn, boô séy put chè 小人閒居,爲不善,無所不至, *seâou jin êng k'hëa, chò ūᵐ hó, bô sèy ūᵐ kaòu*, when worthless people are unemployed, and begin to do that which is evil, there are no lengths to which they will not go.

Chè 抧 To open; also, to strike.

Chè 質 A pledge, a hostage; Chew Tēng kaou chè 周鄭交質, the Chew and Tēng countries exchanged hostages. See the 左傳 Chó twān.

Chè 躓 A stumbling-block; to stumble.

Chè 製 To make, to make up a garment. Hwat chè 法製, regulations. Suy-yéw bé kím, put soò jîn hak chè yëen 雖有美錦,不使人學製焉, *suy woō hó ây kìm twān, k'hàm ūᵐ tëôh saè lâng ŏh chò*, although you have ever so fine a piece of embroidery, is it not necessary to set people to learn to make it up. See the 左傳 Chó twān.

Chè 摯 To hold in the hand: used for chè 贄.

Chè 幟 A flag, a standard. Hân-sin pwat Teaōu chè, sē Hàn ch'hek chè 韓信拔趙幟,樹漢赤幟, *Hân-sin pâyh Teō ây kè, chàh Hàn ây ch'hëăh kè*, Hân-sin plucked up the standard of Tëō, and planted the red standard of Hàn. See the 史記 Soò kè.

Chè 織 The same as the preceding.

Chè 贄 A present offered on the first introduction to a superior;—the most considerable presents offered by men, consisted of gems and silk stuffs; the inferior ones, of rare birds and beasts: women brought only chesnuts and other fruits. Chip chè 執贄, to hold a present in the hand.

Chè 鷙 The more ferocious among the birds and beasts. Chè neáou che put kwûn hêy, chōo chëēn sè jê koè jëēn 鷙鳥之不群兮,自前世而固然, *bêng ây cheâou bô chëⁿà kwûn, choō chêng sè koè jëēn*, ferocious birds not congregating together, has been usual from former ages.

Chè 制 To regulate, to adjust, to circumscribe, to form, to make. E' gē chè soō, lèy chè sim 以義制事,以禮制心, to regulate one's affairs by righteousness, and one's mind by propriety. See the 尚書 Sëāng se.

Hwat chè kìm lēng 法制禁令, orders and restrictions.

Chè 沮 Wet, damp; to make anything moist

平

Chê 薯 A potatoe, a yam; hwan chê 番薯, a foreign or sweet potatoe,—a term of reproach, as much as to say, "you foreign clod-hopper."

Chê 糍 *Kōëy chê* 粿糍, cakes and confectionary.

Chê 蠩 Chëang chuô 蟼蠩, *chëo^ng^ chê*, a toad.

Chē 住 To dwell; ke chē 居住, *k'hëä twā*, to reside, to stop, to stay. Têng ke chē má 停車住馬, *têng ch'hëa käy^n^h bóy*, to delay the carriage and stop the horses. Hwut Ló che hak, sim hoô sëy chē, jê lêng eng pëèn, chut tek chöëy ê sèng jîn 佛老之學.心無所住.而能應變.卒得罪於聖人, *Hwut-choê kwä Ló-choô äy hak hwut, sim kw^n^a bô sëy chē, jê ëy êng pëèn, swäh böëy tek chöëy ê sèng jîn*, the doctrines of Buddha and Ló-choô do not settle the mind, and by enabling their votaries to effect changes, they at length give offence to the sages. Said by 朱子 Choo-choó.

Chē 傶 Chē ch'hëuk 傶促, rapid, hurried.

Chē 柱 Ok chē 屋柱, *ch'hoò t'heaōu*, a pillar of a house. Tëung lêw tê chē 中流砥柱, *tëung laôu häy chëōh chò t'hëaōu*, in the middle of the stream, he placed a stone as a pillar.

Chē 炷 The wick of a lamp. Jëēn teng put chok chē, yêw yêw ná tek bêng 燃灯不作炷.有油那得明, *lëëm teng bô chò lëëm sim, woô yëw böëyh, an chw^n^ä ëy kwui^ng^*, when lighting a lamp, if you do not put a wick to it, although you have oil, how can it shine brightly.

Chē 跓 To stop, to stay one's steps.

Chē 駐 The standing of a horse; chē pit 駐蹕, any place where the Emperor stops in travelling.

Chē 巳 One of the horary characters.

Chē 舐 To lick anything with the tongue. P'he hoo sëaóu, chek wûn yung chē te; taē, chek sê hoo ê kwun 鄙夫小.則吮癰舐痔.大.則弑父與君, *p'hê loê êy lâng, sëy, chēw chwui^ng^ yung chē ch'he^ng^; twā, chēw t'haê pây kap kwun*, those who are vulgar fellows in a smaller degree, will suck sores and lick ulcers (for gain); and those who are such in a greater degree, will murder their parents and sovereigns. Said by 朱夫子 Choo-hoo-choó.

Chē 聚 To collect; chē chip 聚集, to gather together; chē lëëm che sîn 聚斂之臣, *chē lëëm äy jîn sîn*, a rapacious minister; a scrape-all.

Chaê chē chek bîn sàn, chaê sàn chek bîn chē 財聚則民散.財散則民聚, *chee^ng^ k'hëôh chò höëy, pâyh sai^ng^ chēw sw^n^à,—chee^ng^ sw^n^à, pâyh sai^ng^ chēw k'hëôh chò höëy*, when a prince scrapes money together, his people will disperse; but when he disperses his money, the people will collect around him. See the 大學 Taē hak.

Chëa 遮 Vulg. *jëa*: to cover over, to conceal, to hinder, to obstruct, to shelter, to screen.

Pän-t'heaou hok peng chëa kek 班超伏兵遮擊, *Pän-t'hëo hok peng jëa kek*, Pän-t'hëo laid an ambuscade to stop and assault the enemy.

Chëa 㒈 Chëa lâ 㒈儸, firm, but not virtuous.

Chëa 嗟 To sigh, to exclaim; an exclamation: he chëa 吁嗟, alas! alas!

Chëa 罝 A net for catching rabbits; t'hoè chëa 兎罝, a rabbit's net.

上聲

Chëá 者 That which, the person, who, what. Jê yéw ông chëá, pit sé jê hoê jin 如有王者.必世而後仁, *chëw woō ēy âng t'hee^ng āy ây; lâng, pit tëŏh chit sè, jëên aōu ēy jîn*, even if there were a person fit to reign, it would certainly be an age before the people were rendered virtuous. See 孟子 Bēng-chóo.

Wûy jîn chëá, lêng h^nò jîn, lêng oè jîn 惟仁者.能好人.能惡人, *tok jîn tek ây lâng, ēy sëŏh lâng, kwà ēy wàn lâng*, a benevolent man alone can properly shew his predilections for, and antipathies against, others. See the 上論 Sëāng lūn.

Chëá 㜺 The people of Këáng 羌 called a mother chëá;—a wet nurse. Sip chëá 拾㜺 *k'hëŏh chëá*, a midwife.

Chëá 赭 Red. Chëá e 赭衣, red clothes, the dress of criminals. Sat chëá e jê put chûn 殺赭衣而不準, *t'haê âng s^na ây chöēy lâng jê bô chún chat*, he killed the red apparelled criminals, without discrimination.

Chëá 姐 Sister, mother; also, to slight, to despise; sëáou chëá 小姐, *sëó chëá*, little sister; chëá chëá 姐姐, sisters; a title of respect, applied to young ladies. The people of 蜀 Sëuk called a mother 姐 chëá.

去聲

Chëà 借 Vulg. *chëŏh*: to lend, to borrow. Kày chëà lâp yūng 假借納用, *kây chëŏh laê yūng*, to borrow for use.

Yëw má chëá chëà jîn sêng che 有馬者借人乘之, *woō bây ây lâng chëŏh lâng k'hëâ*, those who had horses used to lend them to people to ride.

Ch'hó lé put chëà 草履不借, *ch'haôu ây ā^m saê chëŏh*, straw shoes need not be borrowed.

Chëà 柘 Song chëà 桑柘, the mulberry-tree also written 樜 chëà.

Chëà 蔗 Kam chëà 甘蔗, sugar-cane; kam chëà chëep k'hó gô t'hông 甘蔗汁可熬糖, *kam chëà ây chëep ēy gô tit t'hê^ng*, the juice of the sugar-cane may be manufactured into sugar.

Chëà 鷓 Chëà koe 鷓鴣, *chäyh koe*, a partridge.

Chëà 漈 The bank of a stream, the edge of water. On the west of 琉球 Lêw-kêw, there is an island, called P'hêng-hoê tó 彭湖島, where the water gradually descends, and is called lók chëà 落漈, 'descending to the water's edge:' when vessels enter by mistake, they never return. See the 吾學編 Goê hak p'hëen.

Chëà 炙 To roast, to heat by the fire; chëà jëuk 炙肉, *chëà bäh*, roasted flesh. Köēy chëà é yâng chó, sëuk bé? Bēng-chóo wat, köēy chëà chae 膾炙與羊棗孰美.孟子曰.膾炙哉, *sëó ây bäh kap yëô^ng chó, têy chit ây k'häh hó? Bēng-chóe kóng, köēy chëà chae*, Of roasted flesh and sheep's dates, which is the nicest? Bēng-chóo said, roasted flesh!

去

Chëā 藉 To offer up, to depend on, to help, to assist, to borrow, to lend; elegant, polished.

Hong lêw wûn chëā 風流醞藉, elegant and accomplished manners.

Chëā 謝 Read sëā: a surname.

上平
Chëⁿa **正** Read cheng: the first. Cheng gwat 正月, *chëⁿa göëyh*, the first month.

Chëⁿa **精** Read cheng: a fairy, an elf: yaou cheng 夭精, *yaou chëⁿa*, evil genii. Hé-hàn-bûn gē hek pek sëá cheng, é che wûy hoo hoō 許漢文遇黑白蛇精.與之爲夫婦, *K'hoé-hàn-bûn toó tëöh oe päyh chwâ chëⁿa, kap e chò ang pó*, K'hoé-hàn-bûn met an elf, which was really a black and white snake; and they became man and wife together. These elfs are supposed by the Chinese to be beasts, which transform themselves into human shape, for the purposes of mischief.

上聲
Chëⁿá **飷** Tasteless; ch'hoó bùt chëⁿá chëⁿá 此物飷飷, *chéy lëy meëⁿh chëⁿá chëⁿá*, this thing has no taste in it.

上去
Chëⁿà **正** Read chèng: right, square, correct, proper; soò chèng 四正, *sè chëⁿà* four square, in proper order. Pêng chèng 平正, *paiⁿᵍ chëⁿà*, just. Yéw taē jîn cheá chèng ké, jê bùt chèng cheá yëá 有大人者正己.而物正者也, *woō twā lâng ây lâng taè seng chëⁿà ka tē, jê pat lâng chëw chëⁿà*, wherever there is a great man, he first corrects himself, and then others will be corrected by him. See 下孟 Hāy-bēng.

下平
Chëⁿâ **成** Read sêng: to perfect, to complete, to adjust, to finish. Sêng bùt 成物, *chëⁿâ meëⁿh*, to perfect anything, to complete a thing.
Sêng jîn 成人, *chëⁿâ lâng*, to become a man; to be fit for something.
Boê soō chaē jîn, sêng soō chaē t'heen 謀事在人.成事在天, *soō nëöⁿᵍ soō chaē lâng, chëⁿâ soō chaē t'heeⁿᵍ*, to plan affairs rests with men, but to complete them rests with heaven.

Chëⁿâ **情** Read chêng: feelings, passions; jîn chêng 人情, *lâng chëⁿâ*, kindness.

下去
Cheⁿā **爭** Read chēng: a character in a play. Hè chēng 戲爭, *hè chëⁿā*, a part in a play. Hông chēng 紅爭, *âng chëⁿā*, a red-faced character. Oe chēng 烏爭, *oe chëⁿā*, a black-faced character.

上入
Cheăh **脊** Read chit: K'haou chit 尻脊, *k'ha cheăh*, the back, the back-bone. Lê k'hè chèng chit 狸去正脊, *hoê lë ūm teëⁿᵍh chëⁿà cheăh*, never eat the middle of the back of a fox.

Cheăh **隻** Read chek: single, only one, one; a numeral; yit chek gnêw 一隻牛 *chit cheăh gôo*, a cow. Yit chek ch'hwân 一隻船, *chit cheăh chûn*, one ship.

Cheăh **迹** Read chek: a trace; cheuk chek 足迹, *k'ha cheăh*, a foot-step. Leük keng sëen ông che tîn chek yëá 六經先王之陳迹也, *lak keng sē sëen ông ây koō cheăh*, the six classics contain the ancient traces of the former kings. See 莊子 Chong-choó.

下入
Cheăh **食** Read sit: to eat; sit hwān 食飯, *cheăh pooiⁿᵍ*, to eat rice. Chìn-Bûn-kong k'hit sit ê gnoê lòk che yëá, yëá jîn é che k'hwaé 晉文公乞食於五鹿之野.野人與之塊, *Chìn-Bûn-kong k'hit cheăh tē goê lôk ây yëá, yëá ây lâng hoē e chit tëy t'hoê*, Bûn the duke of Chìn, begged for something to eat in the five-stag desert, when the wild people gave him a lump of earth. See the 左傳 Cho-twān.

Sit put gé 食不語, *chëăh bô kóng wā*, he never spoke while eating.—Said of Confucius, in the 論語 Lūn-gé.

夫

Chëak 灼 To burn, to roast.

Chëak 妁 Böëy chëak 媒妁, *hŭ^m lâng*, a match-maker, a go-between, in order to make up marriages.

Put t'haē böëy chëak che gân 不待媒妁之言, *ū^m têng t'haē hŭ^m lâng ây wā*, without waiting for the mediation of the match-maker.

Chëak 勺 A handful, a ladle-full. Yit chëak súy che to 一勺水之多, *chit chëak chúy ây chēy*, a handful of water.

Chëak 杓 Pöey chëak 杯杓, a wooden cup or bowl, for holding wine.

Chëak 芍 Chëak yak 芍藥, the name of a flower, used in medicine.

Chëak 酌 Chëak chéw 酌酒, *tîn chéw*, to pour out wine. Chim chëak 斟酌, to consider, to weigh a matter.

Chëak chek sûy sëen 酌則誰先, *chëak chéw têöh chē chûy ā taē seng*, in pouring out wine, for whom should we pour out first?

Chëak 斫 To cut asunder with a knife, to hew down.

Chëak 爵 Chéw chëak 酒爵, a wine-cup; kwan chëak 官爵, *kw^na chëak*, rank, office.

Yéw t'hëen chëak chëá; yéw jîn chëak chëá 有天爵者.有人爵者, *wōo t'hee^ng chëak ây lâng, wōo lâng chëak ây lâng*, there are men of celestial rank, and men of human rank.

Chëak 嚼 To bite, to gnaw, to eat; choe chëak choo bē 咀嚼滋味, to try the taste of anything.

Chëak 爝 A light, a fire, a lighted torch.

Chëak 櫡 To cut, to hack.

Chëak 繳 The string of a bow; to fasten the string on a bow.

灭

Chëak 着 Vulg: *têöh*: to clothe, to put on; also added to verbs, to signify their taking effect; also,—ought, should, right, yes.

Chëak e sok taé 着衣束帶, *ch'hêng s^na hâh twà*, to put on clothes, and bind on a girdle.

K'hàn chëak 看着, *k'hw^nà têöh*, to get a sight of.

Chëak kip 着急, hurried, off one's guard.

Chëak soó loē chaē 着死奴才, *têöh sé loē chaē*, you slave, you ought to die!

卆

Chëang 章 Chëang ch'haé 章采, variegated colours; bûn chëang 文章; *bûn chëo^ng*, literary composition; chëang koò 章句, chapters and sections. A surname.

Hwàn hoē kê yéw bûn chëang 煥乎其有文章, *bêng kwui^ng hoē, e ây woō bûn chëang*, how splendid were his literary accomplishments! Said of 堯 Geâou, in the 上論 *Chëō^ng lūn*.

Kwun choó che chè ê tō yëá, put sêng chëang put tat 君子之志於道也.不成章不達, *kwun choó ây sim chè twā tē tō, ū^m chë^nâ chëo^ng ū^m swăh*, the good man, in bending his attention towards sound doctrine, does not stop till he has finished the chapter. See the 下孟 Hāy bēng.

Chëang 嫜 Koe cheung 姑嫜, *twā kay kwⁿa*, a husband's parents. Ch'hëep sin bē hwun bêng, hô ē paè koe chëang 妾身未分明何以拜姑嫜, *gwá ây sin yëá böëy hwun bêng, böëyh an chwⁿá ëy paè twā kay kwⁿa*, before my person is exhibited, how can I pay my respects to my husband's parents?—Said by a young bride (when veiled), on entering her husband's dwelling.

Chëang 傽 Chëang hông 傽惶, fear, alarm trepidation.

Chëang 彰 To display, to illustrate; chëang bêng 彰明, to shew clearly. Chëang k'hwat yëw sëâng 彰厥有常, *chëang bêng e ây woō keng sëâng*, to illustrate his possession of constancy. See the 尚書 *Sëōⁿg se.*

Chëang 漳 The name of a river; Chëang-chew 漳州, the name of a district in the province of 福建 Hok-këen, where the dialect is spoken which this Dictionary is intended to illustrate.

Chëang 將 Shall, will, about to be; to take, to undertake. Chëang jip bûn, ch'hek kê má wat, hwuy kám hoē yëá, má put chìn yëá 將入門策其馬曰非敢後也馬不進也, *chëang böëyh jip mooiⁿg p'hăh e ây báy, kóng, ūᵐ sē gwá kⁿá tùy aōu, sē bāy ūᵐ chìn këⁿá*, when about to enter the gate (after a defeat), Confucius whipped his horse saying, it is not that I dare to be behind-hand, it is because my horse will not go. See the 上論 Sëāng lūn. T'hëen chëang ê hoo-chóo wûy bok tok 天將以夫子爲木鐸, *t'heeⁿg chëang böëyh lëăh lán ây hoo-chóo chò bok tok*, heaven is about to take our master and make him an alarm (to the world). See the same.

Chëang 漿 Vulg. *chëōⁿg*: thick water, congee, syrup; bëën chëang 麵漿, *mëēⁿg chëōⁿg*, leaven, yeast; yëá chëang 椰漿, *yëâ chëōⁿg*, cocoa-nut milk. Bé chëang 米漿, *bé chëōⁿg*, rice water.

Chëang 璋 A precious stone, a kind of half gem. Lōng chëang 弄璋, a son.

Chëang 樟 E chëang 豫樟, the camphor tree.

Chëang 獐 A small kind of stag, without horns.

Chëang 鱆 Chëang gê 鱆魚, *chëōⁿg á hê*, a pomfret fish.

Chëang 蟼 A small kind of locust, of a green colour; chëang chê 蟼蠩, *chëōⁿg chê*, a toad.

Chëang 麞 Vulg. *këōⁿg*: a small kind of deer, very handsome; an antelope.

Chëang 諹 Chew chëang 譸諹, deceitful; insane, mad.

声

Chëáng 掌 Vulg. *chëóⁿg*: the palm of the hand; to hold in the hand; chëáng kwán 掌管, to manage, to rule; chëáng lé 掌理, to regulate: séw chëáng 手掌, *ch'hëw chëóⁿg*, the palm of the hand. Kê jê sê choo soo hoē, ché kê chëáng 其如示諸斯乎指其掌, *e ây ch'hìn chëóⁿg k'hwⁿà chëy lëy, kë e ây ch'hëw chëóⁿg*, it would be as easy as looking at this (said Confucius), pointing to his hand.

Chëáng 仉 A surname. 孟子 Bēng-choó's mother's family name was Chëáng 仉.

Chëáng 蔣 Vulg. *chëō^ng*: a surname.

Chëáng 奬 Chëáng k'hwàn 奬勸, to exhort, to induce, to persuade. Pó chëáng 褒奬, *pó. chëō^ng*, to praise, to applaud.

Chëáng 槳 Vulg. *chëō^ng*, an oar: kò chëáng 過槳, *kò chëō^ng*, to pull an oar, or rather to push over the oar, according to the Chinese manner.

Këën choò tōng sòng chëáng, ch'huy sòng bók ch'hew laê 縺子蕩雙槳. 催送莫愁來, *chūn á saè. nō̤ ây chëō^ng*, *ch'huy sàng ūm. saê hwân. lò bō laê*, if the boat is provided with a pair of oars, when pushing it along you need not be anxious about it's not coming.

Chëáng 長 Chëáng chìn 長進, to advance, to get forward in the world.

去

Chëàng 醬 Toē chëàng 荳醬, *taōu chëō^ng*, ketchup made of pulse. Seē^ng chëàng 豉醬, *seē^ng chëō^ng*, all kinds of pickles and sauces.

Put tek kê chëàng put sit 不得其醬不食, *ūm tit tëŏh e ây chëō^ng ūm chëăh*, if he did not get the proper sauce to anything, he would not eat it.—Said of Confucius, in the 上論 Sëăng lūn.

Chëàng 將 Chëàng söèy 將帥, a Generalissimo; taē chëàng kwun 大將軍, a great General; the middle finger is also called 將指 chëàng ché.

Hàn Ko-chóe tëuk tân, paè Hân-sìn wûy tāe chëàng 漢高祖築壇. 拜韓信爲大將, the first Emperor of the Hàn dynasty built a terrace, upon which he installed Hân-sìn into the office of great General. See the 史記 Soó kè.

Chëàng 嶂 A lofty and precipitous mountain.

Chëàng 障 To limit, to separate, to divide by a partition. Pêng chëàng 屏障, *pîn chëàng*, a screen, a partition.

Chìn Sé-hông tëuk têng chëàng, é tëuk jëûng jîn 秦始皇築亭障. 以逐戎人, *Chîn Sé-hông k'hê têng chëàng, è kw^nà jëûng hwan ây lâng*, the first Emperor of the Chin dynasty, built a defence, to keep out the western barbarians.

Chëàng 瘴 A kind of epidemic disease, called also 瘴癘 chëàng lëy.

平

Chëâng 爿 One of the radicals.

去

Chëāng 負 Read hoō: to carry on the back, to carry pick-a-back. Këàng hoō kê choó chëă yëá 襁負其子者也, *Chò kin chëāng e ây kē^nà*, to carry a child in a cloth over the back.

平

Chëaou 焦 Anything burnt black in the fire. A surname.

Chëaou 蕉 Kèng chëaou 芎蕉, *keng chëo*, a plantain, a banana. Pa chëaou lëw p'hëèn lëuk 芭蕉留片綠, *pa chëo laôu chit p'hee^ng lek*, the plantain leaf spreads a broad patch of green.

Chew Bok ông hok che è chëaou 周穆王覆之以蕉, *Chew Bok ông p'hak e è keng chëo hëŏh*, Bok, the king of Chew, covered it with a plantain leaf.

Chëaou 椒 Hoê chëaou 胡椒, *hoê chëo*, pepper. Hông hoê é chëaou toê pek, ch'hé kê wun yëá 皇后以椒塗壁.取其溫也, *hông hoê t'hó hoê chëo bwăh pëăh, ch'hé e ây sëo*, the empress rubbed the walls with pepper, in order to avail herself of the warmth;—(from the idea that pepper warms the outside as well as the inside of the body.)

Chëaou 膲 Sam chëaou 三膲, three divisions of the body; viz. from the head to the heart, from the heart to the navel, and from the navel to the feet. According to others, the chëaou 膲 is the œsophagus, the upper part being reckoned from the heart to the stomach, the second from the stomach to the navel, and the third from the navel to the bladder.

Chëaou 招 Vulg. *chëo*: to call with the hand, to beckon, to assemble. Chëaou hëên lap soō 招賢納士, *chëo gaôu lâng, kwà sëw t'hak ch'hăyh lâng*, to assemble clever people, and to receive learned men,—(in order to form a party and strengthen one's interests.)

Chëaou 僬 To examine clearly; intelligence; chëaou gëâou 僬僥, a dwarf.

Chëaou 昭 Bright, clear, to display, to illustrate. Chëaou bok 昭穆, the order of generation, the father's contemporaries being called Chëaou, and the son's Bok. The second word is otherwise written 繆 bok.

Bûn-ông chaē sëāng, oe chëaou ê t'hëen 文王在上.於昭于天, *Bûn-ông tē têng bīn, lwā chëô tē t'heeng*, Bûn-ông is highly exalted,—how brilliant even to the skies. See the 大雅 Tāe gnây.

Chëaou 釗 Distant; also, to urge.

Chëaou 嶕 Chëaou gëâou 嶕嶢, lofty, hilly; also, the peak of a hill.

Chëaou 炤 Clear, evident; chëêm suy hok ê, ek k'hóng che chëaou 潛雖伏矣.亦孔之炤, *têêm lok chúy suy jëên bat, yëá chin chaē chëaou bêng*, although they dive down (into the water) ever so deep, yet they are very visible. Said of fishes in a clear pond. See the 大雅 Tāe gnây.

Chëaou 瞧 To steal a glance with the eyes, to look askance.

上聲

Chëáou 沼 A pond: a round pool is called 池 tê, one not straight, 沼 chëáou. Ông lip ê chëáou sëāng 王立於沼上, *ông k'hëā lip 'tē chëáou peeng*, the king was standing by the side of the pond. See the 上孟 Sëāng bēng.

Chëáou 姊 Read ché: an elder sister; *chëáou hoo* 姊夫, an elder sister's husband.

Bûn gnó choo koe, sūy kip pek ché 問我諸姑.遂及伯姊, *mooi gwá ây koe, sūy kip kaôu twā ché*, he asked after my aunts, and then enquired about my elder sister. See the 衛風 Wōēy hong.

Chëáou 鳥 Read neáou: a bird; neáou che chëang soó, kê bêng yëá ae, jin che chëang soó, kê gân yëá sëēn 鳥之將死其鳴也哀.人之將死其言也善, *chëáou kâou bōëyh sé, e ây háou ae ch'hăm,—lâng kâou bōëyh sé, e ây kóng wā, hó*; when a bird is about to die it's voice is lamentable, and when men are about to die their words are good. See the 論語 Lŭn-gé.

去 Chëàou 照 Vulg. *chëò:* to display, to illustrate, to reflect, to illumine; according to. Bêng gwat sëŭng kan chëàou, ch'heng chwân sek sëăng lêw 明月松間照.清泉石上流, *bêng ây gōëyh tē ch'hëng kan chëò, ch'heng ây chwⁿâ tē chëŏh têng lâou,* the clear moon shining among the firs, and the limpid stream flowing over the stones. Taē jîn kèy bêng é chëàou 大人繼明以照, *twā lâng swà jīt gōëyh ây bêng, ê chëò kwuiⁿᵍ,* the great man (that is the sage) connects the brilliancy of the sun and moon, in order to illumine the world.

Chëàou 僬 To walk quickly, and in a hurried manner.

Chëàou 詔 To inform; a decree, an order from the Emperor. Kwun tëung bŭn chëàng kwun che bēng, put bŭn t'hëen choó chëàou 軍中聞將軍之命.不聞天子詔, *kwun tëung woō t'hēⁿa chëàng kwun ây bēng, bô t'hēⁿa hōng tèy ây chëàou,* in the army we attend to the orders of the general, and not to the decrees of the Emperor. See the 古文 Kóe bŭn.

平 Chëâou 樵 Chëâou hoo 樵夫, a wood-cutter. Cheâou hoo ch'hëàou soō 樵夫笑士, *chëŏh ch'hâ ây lâng ch'hëò t'hak ch'hāyh ây lâng,* the wood-man smiles at the scholar. Choo-maé-sîn chëâou ch'haé wûy hwat 朱買臣樵采爲活, *Choo-maé-sîn chëŏh ch'hâ t'hàn chëăh,* "Choo-maé-sîn used to cut and collect wood, for a livelihood;"—but afterwards he attained to high rank.

Chëâou 瞧 To steal a glance.

Chëâou 顦 Chëâou chûy 顦顇, grieved, wearied out, tired of; lean, emaciated. Bîn che cheâou chūy é gëak chèng, bē yéw sīm ê ch'hoó sê chëá yëá 民之顦顇於虐政.未有甚於此時者也, *pāyh saⁿᵍ ây hwân lô tē pò gëak ây chèng soō, bōēy woō k'hăh ch'hám ê chèy lèy sé,* the people have never been more wearied out with oppressive government, than at this present time. See the 上諭 Sëăng bēng.

Chëâou 憔 Chëâou chūy 憔悴, grieved to the heart, vexed.

Chëâou 譙 A chamber on the top of a city wall. Koé hëăng chëâou loê sëăng, kim bêng sek sit tëung 鼓響譙樓上.金鳴石室中, *koe tân tē chëâou lâôu chëōⁿᵍ, kim haôu tē chëŭh ch'hoò laē,* the drum sounds upon the chamber of the citadel, and the metal rings in th[e] midst of the stone-built dwelling.

Chëâou 鷦 The name of a small bird.

Chëâou 劁 To cut grass.

去 Chëāou 噍 To gnaw, to bite, to chew.

Chëāou 醮 Chò chëāou 做醮, *chò chëō,* to perform a sacrifice, and to have a religious procession.

大 Chëaoŭh 㖩 The chirping of birds.

大

Cheĕh 摺 Read lëep: to fold: lëep ché 摺紙, *cheĕh chwá*, to fold paper.

Cheĕh 接 Read chëep: to receive: gêng chëep 迎接, *gēⁿá cheĕh*, to meet, to welcome.
T'haē jîn chëep k'hek 待人接客, *k'hwán t'haē lâng, cheĕh lâng k'hāyh*, to treat people and receive visitors.
Ch'hoê kông chëep ê 楚狂接輿, *ch'hoê ây gōng lâng cheĕh ch'hēa*, a madman of the Ch'hoê country met the carriage (of Confucius).

Cheĕh 嚱 The chirping of insects; the squeaking of mice.

Cheĕh 瘤 Lwân chëet 瘢瘤, *nootⁿᵍ cheĕh*, a boil on the neck, or head.

入

Cheĕh 舌 Read sëet: the tongue: sëet keng 舌耕, *yūng cheĕh chŏh ch'hân*, to plough with the tongue, i. e. to follow the occupation of a school-master.
Soò put kip sëet 駟不及舌, *sè chĕāh bây jëuk bēy kaòu ch'hùy cheĕh*, four horses cannot overtake the tongue. See the 下論 Hāy lūn.

Cheĕh 櫼 Read chëet: to break; chëet chëet 折櫼, *at cheĕh*, to break in two.

去

Chëem 占 To divine, to find out by divination, to prognosticate. Put chëem jê é è 不占而已矣, *ūᵐ pok kwà tēⁿā tēⁿā*, you have not divined, that is all. See the 下論 Hāy lūn.

Chëem 佔 To look on.

Chëem 㦗 To stand in waiting; to stand awry.

Chëem 瞻 To look up at, to contemplate. Chëem che chaē chëên, hwut jëên chaē hoē 瞻之在前.忽然在後, *k'hwⁿà chun á tē t'haōu chêng, hwut jëên tē aōu*, (the doctrine of Confucius) appears, when looking at it, to be before us, and then suddenly seems behind us again; (meaning that it embraces a variety of objects).

Chëem 詹 To speak much, verbose. A surname. Gé gân chëem chëem, hô kê to yëá 語言詹詹何其多也, *kóng wā chēem chēem, sⁿa soā kaòu hēāh chāy*, your talk is quite verbose—why so much of it?

Chëem 尖 Pointed, sharp, of a conical shape; coming to a point. San chëem 山尖, *swⁿa chēem*, the sharp peak of a hill.

Chëem 針 A needle; sew chëem 修針, to work with a needle. Boô chëem put yin sëèn 無針不引線, *bô chēem bēy yin tit swⁿà*, without a needle we cannot draw the thread;—(meaning, that without an introduction, we cannot get into the acquaintance of people.

Chëem 苫 To cover, a thatched covering for a cottage; a straw bed used when mourning.

Chëem 鮎 The name of a large fish, with bands under the belly.

去

Chëém 颭 The blowing of the wind; to blow. Lōng tōng yêw hong chëém, seng he këèn gwat bêng 浪動由風颭.星稀見月明, *êng ûn tāng yêw hong* *ch'höey, ch'hai^{ng} chëö toc së k'hw^{n}à keè^{ng} göëyh kwui^{ng},* the waves are agitated, because the wind blows, and the stars appear few, because the moon shines bright.

去

Chëëm 占 To possess alone, to excel competitors, to top the whole, to be the first. Böëy chëëm pek hwa k'höey 梅占百花魁, *âm à chëëm chë^{n}à pâyh hwa ây t'haôu,* the plum blossom stands out as the head of a hundred flowers.

Gô t'hoê tok chëëm 鰲頭獨占, *gô t'haôu tok chëèm,* to ride on the head of the sea monster, alone distinguished; that is, tëùng chòng gwân 中狀元, *tëùng chëùng gwân,* to attain the highest literary rank.

平

Chëëm 潛 Vulg. tëëm: to hide under water, to conceal. Yâng k'hè chëëm chông 陽氣潛藏, *jit t'haôu ây k'hè tëëm k'hè^{ng},* the influences of the sun are hidden; i. e. the sun is set. See the 易經 *Yëàh keng.*

Gê chëëm chaē cho 魚潛在藻, *hê tëëm twā tē chúy ch'haôu,* the fishes dive down among the weeds. See the 詩經 Se keng.

Chëêm 燖 To steep anything in hot water, in order to get off the hair; to warm anything; to boil water. Gnóc jit, chek chëëm t'hong ch'héng yëùk 五日則燖湯請浴, *goè jit aôu, chëw kë^{n}à sëo chúy, ch'hë^{n}à châng ek,* after five days, (the new married wife) must warm some water, and invite (her husband's parents) to bathe.

去

Chëëm 暫 A short time, not long: chëëm sê 暫時, prô tempore. Sê hwun kéw chëëm, soō yêw lân ē 時分久暫.事有難易, *sê hwun koô kwà chëëm, soō woō ōh kwà k'hwaè,* times and seasons are divided into long and short,—affairs are some difficult, and some easy.

Chëëm 漸 Gradual, gradually, by degrees, step by step. Chìn gê jîn tò tô gwân tōng, chëëm jip kay kéng 晉漁人到桃源洞.漸入佳景, *Chìn teâou ây t'hó hê ây lâng, kaôu tô gwân tāng, chëëm jip kaôu hó kèng,* a fisherman of the Chìn dynasty, arriving at the "Peach fountain" cavern, gradually entered the fairy land.

Chëëm 賺 To sell, to sell again.

平

Chëen 亶 Tun chëen 屯亶, difficulty, inability to proceed.

Chëen 僐 To enter, to advance.

Chëen 邅 Tun chëen 迍邅, difficulty of getting forward, hampered, harrassed.

Chëen 鸇 A bird of prey, a hawk: wūy chông k'he ch'hëak chëá, chëen yëá, 爲叢敺爵者鸇也, *wūy ch'hëw châng kw^{n}à châyh à, së chëen yëá,* what drives little birds into the woods, is the hawk.

Chëen 氈 Soft hair or wool, worked up into cloth: chëen tëâou 氈條, *chee^{ng} tëâou,* a carpet, a blanket; chëen bō 氈帽, *chee^{ng} bō,* a felt hat or cap.

Chëen 氊 The same as the preceding: é t^{n}á yâng mô p'hëèn p'hëèn chëen 雨打羊毛片片氊, *hoē p'hâh yëō^{ng} mô, kaôu chë^{n}à p'hee^{ng} chë^{n}à p'hee^{ng} ây chee^{ng},* the rain beats the sheep's wool, till it forms into flakes of felt.

Chëen 鱣 A large kind of fish.

Chëen 饘 Thick rice-water, congee; the thick is called chëen 饘, and the thin chëuk 粥, *moöěy*.

Chëen 栴 A certain fragrant wood; also called t'hân hëang bok 檀香木, *t'hwⁿâ hëoⁿᵍ ch'hâ*, a kind of sandal-wood.

Chëen 旃 A flag with a crooked staff, used in summoning the common people. Sē jîn ê chëen 庶人以旃, *chëùng lâng tëöh tëâou e è chëen*, people in general must be summoned by a flag, with a crooked staff. See 孟子 Bēng-choó.

Chëen 煎 To boil, to cook, to fry: chëen tây 煎茶, *chwⁿa tây*, to boil tea; chëen gê 煎魚, *chëen hê*, to fry fish. Löēy yung chëáng chëen hô che soō 內饔掌煎和之事, *löēy yung ây kwⁿa chëáng kwân chwⁿa kap tëaou hô ây soō*, the Löēy-yung officer superintended the business of boiling and preparing the food.

Chëen 箋 Chëen pëâou 箋表, a public document; bamboo slips, which were anciently used for books.

Chëen 欑 Fragrant, scented wood.

Chëen 戔 To see clearly; also, small and shallow.

Chëen 羶 The smell of mutton; also, mutton fat.

Chëen 綫 A thread to sew with: put chwat jê chëen 不絕如綫, *bô tooïⁿᵍ ch'hìn chëöⁿᵍ swⁿâ*, unbroken, like a continued thread.

上声

Chëén 剪 To cut with a scissors; kaou chëén 交剪, *ka chëén*, a pair of scissors. Yéw ae lē pēng chëén che beâou 有哀鑢并剪之妙, *woō ae kay ây lēy kap pēng kay ây chëén ây hó*, it has all the excellent qualities of Ae files, and Pēng scissors.—Ae and Pēng were the most celebrated makers of scissors and files, and this expression is used to intimate the sharp, cutting nature of good literary compositions.

Chëén 俴 Shallow, not deep, applied to carriages.

Chëén 僎 Prepared, anything prepared, a plan or view: to number, to adjust. Ē hoē sam choó chëá che chëén 異乎三子者之僎, *köh yëöⁿᵍ hwut êⁿa lâng ây chëén*, how different from the views of those three gentlemen! See the 下論 Hāy lūn.

Chëén 棧 A scaffold, a temporary erection: chëén tō 棧道, temporary roads. Tëang-lëâng swat Hàn ông sëaou chwat chëén tō 張良說漢王燒絕棧道, *Tëoⁿᵍ-lëâng k'hwuiⁿᵍ Hàn ông sëo tooïⁿᵍ chân tō*, Tëoⁿᵍ-lëâng advised the king of Hàn to burn and destroy the temporary roads.

Chëén 踐 To tread upon, to walk over: chëén gân 踐言, *tàh wā*, to tread one's words, (i. e. to fulfil one's engagements).

Chëén kê wūy, hêng kê léy, choè kê gak 踐其位.行其禮.奏其樂, *tàh e ây wūy, kêⁿâ e ây lêy, châou e ây gak*, "to walk in their ways, to practise their ceremonies, and to play their music."—This when done by posterity towards their ancestors, is the height of filial piety. See the 中庸 Tëung yūng.

Chëén t'hëen choó wūy yëen 踐天子位焉, *tëh hóng tèy ây wūy*, to take upon one's-self the rank of an Emperor.

Chëén 餞 A glass drank at parting: a parting feast.

Chëén 戩 Happy, lucky; to exhaust.

Chëén 揃 To cut off: ê koe chëén bëet ch'hoó, jê tëâou sit 余姑揃滅此而朝食, *gwá ch'hēⁿâ chëén bëet chèy lëy, jê chëâh chá k'hé pooiⁿᵍ*, I will just cut off and exterminate this country, and then go to breakfast.

Chëén 膞 Broth made of flesh.

Chëén 譾 Shallow: shallow words.

Chëén 蟫 Worms found in books and clothes: they are yellow at first, but when old become covered with a white powder like silver; hence they are called pek gê 白魚, *pēyh hê*, white fish.

去

Chëèn 戰 To fight, to go to war; also, to fear and tremble. Choó che sëy sīn, chae, chëèn, chit 子之所愼.齊戰疾, *Hoo-choó ây sëy kīn sīn, chëâh ch'hae, chëèn t'hae, chit paiⁿᵍ*, the things about which Confucius was particularly careful, were feasting, war, and sickness.

Chëèn chëèn keng keng 戰戰兢兢, trembling and shaking.

Chëèn 濺 To splash with water; the rapid flowing of water. Ch'héng tek ê kéng bëet chëèn taē ông 請得以頸血濺大王, *ch'hēⁿâ tit ê kèng hëeyh chwⁿâ twā ông*, "I beg leave to take the blood of my neck and splash it over your majesty." A desperate expression of 藺相如 Līn-sëang-jê.

Chëèn 洊 Again, as before: súy chëèn chè 水洊至, *chúy chëâou koó kŏh kàou*, water flowing against the same place. See the 易經 *Yëăh-keng*.

Chëèn 箭 Vulg: *chèeⁿᵍ*; an arrow: sëà chëèn 射箭, *chŏh chèeⁿᵍ*, to shoot an arrow. Sëet-jîn-kwùy yit chëèn têng Kwun-san 薛仁貴一箭定軍山, *Sëĕh-jîn-kwùy chit ke chèeⁿᵍ an tēⁿâ Kwun-swⁿa*, Sëĕh-jîn-kwùy with one arrow pacified the region of Kwun-swⁿa. See the 史記 Soó kè.

Chëèn 荐 Again, over again; also, grass; a straw mat. Chin chëèn ke 晉荐饑, *Chìn kok kŏh ke hwuiⁿᵍ*, there was again a famine in the Chin country.

Chëèn 顫 A shaking of the head; a trembling of the limbs.

Chëèn 薦 To present, to send in, to introduce to notice, to bring forward, to offer up as a sacrifice.

Kwun soó seng, pit sëuk jê chëèn che 君賜生必熟而薦之, *jîn kwun soó hoē ch'haiⁿᵍ ây mëⁿh, pit tëŏh chë sek jê chëèn e*, when the prince bestows any thing raw, we must cook it, before we offer it up. See the 上論 Sëāng lūn.

Chëèn 蕺 The name of a herb, or grass.

平

Chëên 前 Vulg. *chêng*: Before, in time or place; t'hoê chëên 頭前, *t'hâou chêng*, in front. Bëēn chëên 面

前, *bīn chân*, before one's face; chëên jit 前日, *chêng jit*, a former day.
Séy oè ê chëên, boô é sëên hoē, séy oè ê hoē, boô é chëūng chëên 所惡於前.無以先後.所惡於後.無以從前, *sèy wàn tē t'haōu chêng, ū^m t'hang chò e tē aōu, sèy ēy wàn tē aōu laê, ū^m t'hang t'hàn e tē t'haōu chêng*, that which we have formerly disapproved, we must not subsequently prefer,—and that which we should in future dislike, we must not do previously. See the 大學 Taē hak.

Chëên 錢 Vulg. *chee^ng*: money, cash: Chwân chëên 賺錢, *t'hàn chee^ng*, to get money: tông chëên 銅錢, *tâng chee^ng*, copper cash, pice. Also, a surname. Tē tëung hô yëep, tëep ch'heng chëên 池中荷葉疊青錢, *tê k'hwuī â tëūng hô lëên â hëŏh, tëep ch'hai^ng chee^ng*, the leaves of the water lily in the midst of the pool, look like so much green money.

Chëên 媊 The name of a star: chëên chëuk 媊祝, a wish for longevity, addressed to females.

去 Chëên 賤 Base, mean, lowly: hāy chëên 下賤, vulgar. Pin é chëên sē jîn che séy oè yëá 貧與賤是人之所惡也, *sông hëung kap hāy chëên sē lâng lâng ây sèy wàn*, poverty and a mean condition are what all men dislike. See the 上論 Sëāng lūn.

Chëên 鏇 To turn round, to revolve.

平 Chee^ng 湔 *Chee^ng sey*, 湔洗, to wash.

Chee^ng 氈 Read chëên: a sort of woollen cloth, or felt: chëên teâou 氈條, *chee^ng teâou*, a carpet, a rug: chëên bō 氈帽, *chee^ng bō*, a felt hat.

Chee^ng 鬈 The hair collected together.

声 Chee^ng 少 Young in years, green, not come to age or maturity. Seâou che sê, hëet k'hè bē têng, kaè che chaē sek 少之時.血氣未定.戒之在色, *chee^ng ây sê, höëyh k'hè böëy tē^n â tëŏh këng kaè tē aè sek*, in the time of youth, before the animal spirits are settled, people should guard against the love of beauty. See the 下論 Hāy' lūn.

Chee^ng 茈 Ch'hoó këang 茈薑, *chee^ng këo^ng*, young, green ginger.

去 Chee^ng 搢 Read chìn: to stick in, to cram, to wedge; a wedge.

Chee^ng 箭 Read chëèn: an arrow: h^nó chëèn 火箭, *höèy chee^ng*, a fire arrow. Kong yim soō chëèn 光陰似箭, *kong yim chăn â chee^ng*, time flies like an arrow.

平 Chee^ng 錢 Read chëên: money, cash: boô chëên 無錢, *bô chee^ng*, no money. Yëá tông wûy chëên, chè choô Chew sé 冶銅爲錢.制自周始, *yëo^ng tâng chò chee^ng, chè choō Chew tëâou k'hé*, the regulation for melting copper in order to make money, began with the Chew dynasty.

Chee^ng 揃 To draw anything out, as wire: *chee^ng yìn* 揃引, to lead, to draw.

六

Chëep 接 Vulg. *cheĕh*: to receive, to connect. Kê kaou yëá é tō, kê chëep yëá é léy, 其交也以道,其接也以禮, *e ây sëo kaou chëàou tō lé, e ây sëo chëep chëàou léy soè*, intimacies according to virtue, and associations consistent with propriety. See the 下孟 Hāy bēng.
Chëep séw yim súy 接手飲水, *sëo chëep ch'héw lim chúy*, to descend by holding each other's hands, in order to drink water.

Chëep 汁 Gravy, juice, liquid: Thëen sê è chëep 天時雨汁, *t'hee^ng chëàou sê lŏh chëep*, heaven at proper seasons sends down its juice, (that is rain). Këung tëung pè k'hwùn, súy chëep put t'hong 宮中袝困水汁不通, *këung tëung pè k'hwùn kip kaòu chúy chëep bëy t'hong*, they were so straightened in the palace, that the least drop of liquid could not find a thoroughfare.

Chëep 睫 The eye lashes: bê chëep che kan 眉睫之間, between the eye lashes.

又

Chëep 倢 Going out aslant; also, sharp, profitable, convenient..

大

Chëet 折 Vulg. *chëĕh*: to break, to break off: aóu chëet 拗折, to twist off. Wûy tëáng chëá chëet che 爲長者折枝, *wûy sê twā at ch'hëw kè*, to pluck off the branch of a tree for a superior. See the 上孟 Sëāng bēng.

Chëet 㣶 To cut, to carve: chëet hông 㣶縫, to join a seam.

Chëet 晢 Star-light, the light of the stars.

Chëet 蜇 The sting of an insect; a kind of blubber.

Chëet 踅 To turn topsy-turvy; to leap to jump, to hop.

Chëet 櫛 A comb, to comb: kw^nâ kwun soo pē choô sē kin chëet 寡君使婢子侍巾櫛, *gwân ây kw^nâ kwun woō saé gwâ lé ây cha bóe gin â sē kin chëet*, my prince has sent me thine handmaid, to wait upon your towel and comb. Said by 懷嬴 Hwaê-eng, to her husband, when she went to be married. See the 左傳 Chó twān.

Chëet 儩 Chún chëet 㑒儩, *chún chat*, to be careful and economical.

Chëet 晣 Bright, clear

Chëet 浙 A river in the south-east of China, from which the name of the province of Chëet-kang 浙江 derived.

Chëet 卩 An insignia or seal of office, given by the sovereign, to ensure the confidence of the people in the officer appointed.

Chëet 節 A section, a verse: tëuk chëet 竹節, *tek chat*, a knot, or joint in a bamboo; hoô chëet 符節, a cheque cut through the middle, to establish confidence between two parties.
Tek chè, hêng hoê Tëung-kok, jëak hap hoô chëet 得志行乎中國,若合符節, *tit tëŏh sim chè, kë^nâ tè Tëung-kok, ch'hin chëō^ng hap hoô chëet*, obtaining one's aim, we may travel through the whole of China (and find all agreeing with us), like the correspondence of the two sides of a cheque.

Chún chëet 準節, *chún chat,* economical, keeping within bounds.

天 Chëet 捷 To overcome, to obtain a victory, to send news of a victory; also diligent, quick, accomplished. Chêy hoê laê hëen chëet 齊侯來獻捷, the prince of the Chêy country came and offered up the news of his victory. See the 左傳 Chó twān. Yit gwat sam chëet 一月三捷, *chit goëyh jit sⁿa kwùy tit yëⁿá,* to obtain three victories in one month. See the 小雅 Seáou gnáy. Cheng hoo chëet chëet 征夫捷捷, to carry on the war with vigour.

Chëet 倢 Chëet choó 倢伃, *chëet á,* a female office, first introduced in the time of the Hân dynasty: also written 婕 chëet.

[C]hëet 睫 The hair of the eye-lashes.

[Ch]ëet 疌 Rapid, quick.

Chëet 箑 A fan; in the east it is called chëet, and in the west sëen 扇, *seèⁿᵍ.* Boó-ông sé chok chëet 武王始作箑, *Boó-ông k'hè t'haôu chò seèⁿᵍ,* Boóông was the first who made fans.

Chëet 截 Chëet twān 截斷, *at tooïⁿᵍ,* to break off. Chëet ché 截止, to stop. Chëet léw 截柳, *at lêw teáou,* to break off willow branches.

Chëet 蠘 A kind of crab.

Chëet 巀 A lofty hill, a high mountain.

Chëet 諜 Verbose, talkative; many words.

Chëet 捷 To obtain in succession, to make progress from one to another. Lëen chëet sam gwân 聯捷三元, *sëo swà lëùng sⁿa gwân,* to obtain in succession the three highest literary prizes.

大 Chek 責 To reprove, to blame; to seek, to expect; to sustain an office, or burden. Bêng kē t'hëen t'hó, yew lek kwúy chek 明惧天討.幽慓鬼責, openly (in the upper world) afraid of Heaven's judgments, and secretly (in the lower world) apprehensive of the devil's torments. Chek hwat yéw chöëy 責罰有罪, *chek hwat woō chöëy,* to punish the guilty. Yéw gân chek chëá, put tek kē gân chek k'hè 有言責者.不得其言則去, *woō kóng wā chek jîn áy lâng, ūᵐ tit t'hëⁿa e áy wā chëw k'hè,* those who are entrusted with the office of admonishers, when their advice is not attended to, should quit their situations.

Chek 勣 Merit; meritorious work.

Chek 借 Vulg. *chëöh:* to borrow; also, if, supposing. Chek wat bē te, ek kè p'haôu choó 借曰未知.亦旣抱子, *ch'hin chëöⁿᵍ kóng yëá böëy chae, yëá woō p'hō sèy këⁿá,* if you say that you know nothing about the family, how is it that you are nursing their children? See the 詩經 Se keng.

Chek 乇 The blade of grass.

Chek 僁 Small.

Chek 績 To spin: hóng chek 紡績, *p'háng chăyh*, to spin thread; also, merit. Kong-hoō-bûn-pek che boé chek 公父文伯之母績, *Kong-hōo-bûn-păyh ây nëōng lëy p'háng chăyh*, Kong-hōo-bûn-păyh's mother was spinning thread.

Chek 積 To accumulate, to collect, to heap up together, to hoard up. Chek seēōu é ko tāe 積小以高大, *chek sèy è chēnâ kwân twā*, to accumulate little things till they become lofty and large. Chek tek lúy kong 積德累功, to accumulate virtue, and pile up merit.

Chek 畟 To advance; the appearance of sharpness.

Chek 簀 A sleeping mat; hwa jê wán, taē hoo che chek e 華而睆大夫之簀與, *hwa lëy kwà sáy kⁿâ, sē taē hoo ây ch'hëŏh*, so flowered and elegant! this is surely the mat of a great officer. See the 禮記 Léy kè.

Chek 嘖 The noise of crying aloud.

Chek 幘 The kerchief with which the hair is tied, to keep it in its place.

Chek 磧 Large stones in the middle of a pond; also, a name for the desert of Swa-bok 沙漠, Sha-mŏh. Kim kwun toē say chek, lúy gwat twān jîn yëen 今君渡沙磧, 累月斷人烟, *tⁿa lë kōēy say chek, kwúy gōēyh jít tooiⁿg lâng hwun*, now you have undertaken to cross the desert, for months together you will find no smoke of human habitations.

Chek 賾 Deep and confused; sèng jîn yew é këēn t'hëen hāy che chè chek 聖人有以見天下之至賾, *sèng jîn woō ēy k'hwⁿà këeⁿg t'heeⁿg hāy ây chè ch'hìm*, a sage can look into the most deep and confused things in the world. See the 易經 Yëăh keng.

Chek 蹟 A trace, a foot-step; koé chek 古蹟 antiquities.

Chek 迹 Chëuk chek 足迹, *k'ha chëăh*, foot-steps; T'haè-óng tëāou ke óng chek 太王肇基王迹, *T'haè-óng k'hé t'háou ch'hòng ke óng ây chëăh*, Thaè-ông first laid the foundation of the traces of royalty (in his family.)

Chek 跡 A foot-step, a track; ke tîn má chek sëy put keng che tëy 車塵馬迹所不經之地, *ch'hëa tîn bây chëăh sëy bô keng ây tëy*, lands where the dust of carriages and the foot-steps of horses have never been known.

Chek 蹠 To tread, to jump; also, the sole of the foot.

Chek 卽 To come to, to arrive at; then; chek kim 卽今, now; chek sê 卽時, lëem peeⁿg, immediately; chek sē 卽是, that is.—Also written 即 chek. Sëēn jîn kàou bîn, ch'hit lëēn ek k'hó é chek jëūng é 善人敎民七年亦可以卽戎矣, *hó lâng kà păyh saiⁿg, ch'hit neeⁿg yëā t'hang kaòu sëo t'haê*, when a clever man teaches the people, in seven years they can be fit for war. See the 下論 Hāy lūn.

Chek 喞 The noise of many voices, the humming of insects.

Chek 堲 To dislike, to be pained with; the snuff of a candle. Tìm chek ch'hâm swat t'hëén hêng 朕堲讒說殄行, gwá ch'hàyh saé p'hwà ày wā t'hëén chwat ây sëy kēⁿâ, I dislike slanderous words and ruinous actions;—said by the the Emperor 舜 Sùn.

Chek 鯽 Vulg. chat: the name of a fish: sëén chek gîn se k'hòëy 鮮鯽銀絲膾, ch'hee^{ng} ây chat hê ch'hìn chëō^{ng} gîn swnⁿà pàyh ây bāh, the raw flesh of the chat fish is white like silver thread.

Chek 鰿 The same as the preceding; vulg. chit hê.

Chek 稷 A kind of grain, like millet, but smaller; hoē chek 后稷, the name of an officer who presided over the grain.
Sëà chek 社稷, the gods of the land and grain.

Chek 仄 Oblique: chek yim 仄音, chàyh yim, an oblique sound; the Chinese have four tones, viz. pêng, sëāng, k'hè, jip 平上去入, pa^{ng}, chëō^{ng}, k'hè, jip, the even, ascending, departing, and contracted or entering tones; these are again multiplied, by dividing each of them into upper and lower, thus making seven or eight. But the general division of them is into pêng 平, pa^{ng}, and chek 仄, chàyh, even and oblique, according to which their verses are regulated. Hence they say, Chò se pit te pêng chek yim 做詩必知平仄音, chò se pit tëōh chae pa^{ng} chàyh yim, in making verses it is necessary to be acquainted with the even and oblique sounds.

Chek 昃 The sun declining toward the west. Jit chek jê ch'hē 日昃而市, jit t'haôuⁿâ sae chëw chēⁿâ ch'hē, when the sun declined to the west, the market was held. See the 周禮 Chew lêy.

Chek 迮 To urge, to incite, to bring into straits.

Chek 窄 Narrow, contracted: loē chek 路窄, loē ày̆h, the road is narrow.

Chek 隻 Single, alone: yit chek 一隻, chit chëăh, one, one of anything. Hêng tan êng chek 形單影隻, hêng twⁿa yëⁿá chëăh, a single form and a lonely shadow. Said of an only son, without brethren.

Chek 䰈 A dead ghost.

Chek 糘 White rice.

Chek 蹐 A small step; to walk with a short step; to sit with the legs crossed one over the other.

Chek 則 A rule, a law, an example; then, after that. Gân jê sè wûy t'hëen hāy chek 言而世爲天下則, kóng jê tëy tëy chò t'hee^{ng} hāy hwat chek, if he speaks (as a sage) a man becomes for ages an example to the Empire. See the 中庸 Tëung yûng.
Wán che chek yëw bōng, kin che chek put yëèm 遠之則有望.近之則不厭, hwui^{ng} ây lâng chëw wōō bāng-lân, kīn ây lâng yëàbô yëèm lân, (when we act properly) those who are at a distance will look towards us, and those who are near will not dislike us.

Chek 叔 Read sëuk: an uncle, a father's brother. Chew-kong naé Sêng-ông che sëuk hoō yëà 周公乃成

王之叔父也, *Chew-kong sē Sêng-ông ây chek pāy*, Chew-kong was the uncle of Sêng-ông.

Chek 燭 Read cheŏk: a candle: lap cheŭk kong hwuy, boô bē put cheāou 蠟燭光輝.無微不照, *lăh chek kwuiⁿᵍ hwuy, bô chit lêy sèy sèy ūᵐ chēŏ bêng*, by the brightness of a candle, there is nothing so minute but what it may be illumined.

灭

Chek 寂 Still, quiet, tranquil, retired, inactive, motionless. Chek jēēn put tōng 寂然不動, *tēèm tēèm bē tin tāng* still and unmoved.

Chek 宋 Far from the noise of men.

Chek 崱 The appearance of lofty hills; k'hae hēēn bōng ch'hâm chek 開軒望嶄崱, *k'hwuy ŏh bāng k'hwⁿà swⁿa kwân kwân*, on opening the school, we see the lofty hills afar off.

Chek 鰂 Oe chek 烏鰂, *oe chat*, the name of a fish, called also, bek chek 墨賊, *bak ch'hat*, the cuttle fish.

Chek 藉 Lông chek 狼藉, all in confusion.

Chek 籍 A book, a register, a record; tēēn chek 典籍, an historical record. A surname.

Choo hoê oē kê haē ké yēā, jê kae k'hè kê chek 諸侯惡其害己也.而皆去其籍, *choo hoê wàn e ây haē ka tē, jê chò poê t'hek kak e ây ch'hāyh*, the princes of the Empire were displeased that the history reflected on themselves, and therefore did away with the records. See the 下孟 Hāy bēng.

Chek 賊 Vulg. *ch'hat*, a thief, a robber, an injurious person; to injure. Chek jê hong k'hé 賊如蜂起, *ch'hat ch'hin cheōⁿᵍ p'hang k'hè*, thieves sprung up as thick as bees.

Chek jîn cheā wūy che chek 賊仁者謂之賊, *chek haē jîn ây lâng, kóng kēò ch'hat*, he who injures benevolence is called an injurious person.

𡿨

Cheng 曾 Then, how; the sign of the past tense; a surname: cheng sun 曾孫, a great-grandson.

Cheng sē é wūy hàou hoē 曾是以爲孝乎, *cheng an nēy chēw kóng kēò woō hàou*, how can this alone be considered filial piety? See the 上論 Sēāng lūn.

Goē é choó wūy ē che būn, cheng Yêw é Kêw che būn 吾以子爲異之問.曾由與求之問, *gwá lēāh chò lê woō kŏh yēōⁿᵍ ây mooîⁿᵍ, cheng sē Yêw kap Kêw ây mooîⁿᵍ*, I thought you would propose some rare question, how is it that you have only asked about Yêw and Kêw.

Cheng kēēn kê jîn, bē sit kê bêng 曾見其人.未識其名, *bat k'hwⁿà e ây lâng, bōēy bat e ây mēⁿā*, I have seen the man but do not know his name.

Cheng 僧 A priest of Budha, a monk, a recluse. Sē wân cheng laê seàou, keàou gwûy k'hek kò he 寺遠僧來少.橋危客過稀, *sēⁿᵍ hwuiⁿᵍ hōēy sēōⁿᵍ laê cheō, kēō gwûy lâng k'hāyh hân kōèy*, when the temple is afar off, few priests come to it; and when the bridge is dangerous, travellers seldom go over it.

Cheng 增 To increase, to add to: kay cheng 加增, to increase more and more. Hoē k'hoé sòèy cheng 戶口歲增, *mooîⁿᵍ ây tāou ch'hùy tak neēⁿᵍ k'hăh chēy*, the inhabitants of each dwelling increase year by year.

Cheng 憎 To hate, to abhor; cheng oè 憎惡, to abominate. Gé jîn é k'hoé kip, lúy cheng ê jîn, 禦人以口給屢憎於人, *k'hap lëŏh lâng ê ch'hùy ây wā, tak paè, hoē lâng, cheng hwūn*, attacking people in conversation, we frequently become hated by them. See the 上論 Sëāng lūn.

Cheng 繒 The general name of silk and cloth. Ch'he-yâng hwàn cheng chëá yëá 睢陽販綌者也, *tē Ch'he-yâng woō lâng báy bāy cheng*, at Ch'he-yâng people trade in cloth.

Cheng 矰 To tie a string on a bow.

Chëng 罾 A fishing net, a cast net.

Cheng 正 A target, or bull's eye, used as a mark for shooting at. Kwun choó sit choo cheng gok, hwán kêw choo kê sin 君子失諸正鵠反求諸其身, *kwun choó ây lâng sit e ây cheng gok, chēw hwán tŏh tooi^{ng} kêw tē e pún sin*, the good man, when he misses the centre of the target, turns and reflects upon himself. See the 中庸 Tëung yûng.

Cheng gwat 正月, *chē^{n}a göĕyh*, the first month of the year.

Cheng 佂 Hasty walking; afraid.

Cheng 征 To travel towards, to punish, to set to rights, to take. Cheng chëá sëāng hwat hāy yëá, tek kok put sëāng cheng yëá 征者上伐下也.敵國不相征也, *cheng sē sè twā hwat sè sèy, tek kok bô sëo cheng yëá*, "correction" is when a superior state corrects an inferior; equal states contending together, are not said to correct one another. See the 中庸 Tëung yûng. Kwan ke jê put cheng 關譏而不征, *tē kwan aè ke ch'hat hêng jîn, jê bô t'hăyh meĕ^{n}h*, at the passes of a country, examine (travellers), but do not take duties from them. See 孟子 Bēng-choó.

Cheng 延 The same as the above.

Cheng 鉦 A kind of gong, or copper instrument of music. Sē t'hoê ch'hay jit k'hwà tông cheng 樹頭初日掛銅鉦, *ch'hēw t'haôu tē k'hé ch'hay ch'hut jit ch'hin chëō^{ng} tâng lô*, the rising sun looks like a brass gong hung up on the top of the trees.

Cheng 眐 To view alone, to contemplate.

Cheng 貞 Correct, modest, chaste, firm: cheng lé 貞女, *chin chëet ây cha boè kē^{n}á*, a virgin, a modest young woman.

Kwun choó cheng jê put lëāng 君子貞而不諒, *kwun choó cheng tit, jê bô sèy sìn*, the good man is generally upright, without attending to the smaller points of sincerity.

Cheng 偵 To ask, to make enquiry, to spy: yêw cheng 游偵, a spy.

Cheng 楨 The name of a tree: lé cheng 女楨, an evergreen; planks used in building mud walls, which are bound together, and the earth is then beaten in between them.

Cheng 禎 Cheng sëâng 禎祥, lucky omens, fortunate emblems. Kok kay chëang hin, pit yéw cheng sëâng 國家

將興.必有禎祥, *kok kay chĕang bŏĕyh hin k'hé, pit woō cheng sĕăng*, when a country is about to rise into celebrity, there will certainly be favourable omens. See the 中庸 Tĕung yûng.

Cheng 爭 To wrangle, to strive, to contend; sëang cheng 相爭, *sëo chai^ng*, to quarrel.
Soō cheng bêng ê tëâou, sëang cheng lē ê ch'hē 士爭名於朝.商爭利於市, *t'hak ch'hăyh lâng chai^ng mē^n â sē^n a lē tëâou, chò seng lē lâng chai^ng lē te ch'hē*, the scholar strives for fame at court, and the merchant struggles after gain in the market. See the 史記 Soó kè.

Cheng 崢 Steep, lofty, difficult of ascent.

Cheng 箏 A kind of guitar, with twelve or thirteen strings.

Cheng 睛 The pupil of the eye; hong cheng cheá to sëw 方睛者多壽, *bak cheng sè kak ây lâng tē^ng hŏëy sëw*, those who have square pupils in their eyes will live long. Said by 管輅 Kwán-lŏk.

Cheng 蜻 Cheng têng 蜻蜓, the dragon-fly, an insect with four wings and six feet. Cheng têng tëém súy, hwún tëep sim hong 蜻蜓點水.粉蝶尋芳, *ch'hân ai^ng lëëm lē chúy, bŏëy yëăh ch'hoey hwa p'hang*, the dragon-fly dips in the water, and the painted butterfly seeks the flowers.

Cheng 菁 The appearance of fulness.

Cheng 鶄 *Ka cheng* 鵁鶄, the name of a bird that can keep down the calamity of fire.

Cheng 揨 To beat, to thump, to pound. Cheng kim koé, ch'höey bêng naē 揨金鼓吹鳴籟, *p'hăh kim kap koé, ch'höey bêng ây naē*, to beat the gongs and drums and blow the sounding pipe.

Cheng 晶 Clear brightness: súy cheng 水晶, *chúy chee^ng*, a crystal.

Cheng 旌 A flag, with feathers stuck in at the top of the staff. Chëaou tāe hoo é cheng 招大夫以旌, *chëo tāe hoo ê cheng*, a great officer must be summoned by a *cheng* flag. See 孟子 Bēng-choò

Cheng 精 Correct, good, pure, small, minute, subtle, fine. Gē cheng, jîn sëuk, jê bôo yit hô soo è 義精.仁熟.而無一毫私意, *gē cheng, jîn sek, jê bô chit hô ây sae k'hea ây è*, correct in righteousness and accustomed to benevolence without a single atom of sinister intention.

Cheng 舂 Read chëung: to pound in a mortar. Chëung bé 舂米, *cheng bé*, to pound rice. Chëung kēw 舂臼 *cheng koō*, a mortar.

Cheng 鍾 A cup: chéw cheng 酒鍾, a wine cup or glass.

Cheng 鐘 Read chëung: a bell: chëung bêng 鐘鳴, *cheng tân*, the bell rings. Gak yîn, gak yîn, chëung koé yin hoē chae 樂云.樂云.鍾鼓云乎哉, *lâng kóng chok gak, chok gak, k'ham sē cheng koé an nēy kóng chae*, people talk of music, and of music; as if bells and drums constituted music. See the 下論 Hāy lūn.

声

Chéng 井 Vulg. *chai^ng*: a well: a surname. Chéng sëang yéw lé 井上有李, *chai^ng lëng woō lé á*, there was a plum tree over the well.

P'hè jëák kwut chéng, kwut chéng kéw jīm, jê put kip chwân, yêw wûy k'hè chéng yëá 譬若掘井.掘井九仞.而不及泉.猶爲棄井也, p'hè jëák kwut chaiⁿᵍ kwut chaiⁿᵍ kaóu jīm, nā bô kip chwⁿâ, yêw wûy l'hek kak chaiⁿᵍ, like as in digging a well, if having dug nine rods deep, without coming to the spring, you cease your labour, you must give up the well. See the 下孟 Hāy bēng.

Chéng 整 To adjust, to regulate, to adorn, to put any thing to rights. Sew chéng 修整, to repair and beautify: chêy chéng 齊整, to adjust.

Kwa tëên put lap lé, lé hāy put chéng kwan 瓜田不納履.李下不整冠, kwa ch'hân bô păyh āy, lê āy bô chéng kin, in a field of melons, do not pull up your shoes; and when going under a plum tree, do not adjust your head dress:—(lest you should be suspected of stealing the melons or plums).

Chéng 灯 A convulsive motion of the skin and muscles.

Chéng 晸 The appearance of the rising sun.

Chéng 腫 Read chëúng: to swell: këak chëúng 脚腫, k'ha chèng, a swelling of the legs; tëàng chëúng 脹腫, tëòⁿᵍ chèng, swollen.

Chéng 種 Read chëúng: a seed; chëúng choó 種子, chèng chê, a single seed. Sip chëúng choó 十種子, chap chèng á, a term of abuse.

去

Chèng 正 Correct, straight, right: chèng keng 正經, honest, upright. Chèng tit 正直, tëàou tit, straight-forward, blunt; pêng chèng 平正, paiⁿᵍ chëⁿà, just.

Choó sut é chèng, sëuk kám put chèng 子帥以正.孰敢不正, lè ch'hwà lâng è chëⁿà tō, chē chwūy kⁿá ûᵐ chëⁿà, if you lead people on by correct principles, who will dare to be incorrect. See the 下論 Hāy lūn.

Chèng 政 To regulate, to rectify, to govern: chèng soō 政事, government, politics. Chèng chëá, chèng yëá, séy é chèng jîn che put chèng yëá 政者正也.所以正人之不正也, chèng chëw sê chëⁿà, sèy è chëⁿà lâng āy ûᵐ chëⁿà, to regulate means to put to rights,—that by which we set right people's wrongs. Said by 朱子 Choo-choó.

Chèng 種 Read chëùng: to plant, to sow. Chëùng hoê chëaou 種胡椒, chèng hoê chëo, to plant pepper; chëùng tek 種德, chèng tek, to plant virtue.

Chèng 薦 Read chëèn: a mat: kaou chëèn 茭薦, ka chèng, a thick mat or mattress, made of straw bound fast together, and used for sleeping on.

平

Chêng 情 The feelings, the passions: ch'hit chêng 七情, the seven passions; jîn chêng 人情, kindness; chêng lé 情理, reason, reasonable.

Hé, noè, ae, lok, bē hwat, wūy sèng,—hwat, chek wūy che chêng 喜怒哀樂未發.謂性.發.則謂之情, hwⁿa hè, sëw k'hè, ae ch'hám, t'hëùng lok, yëá bōêy hwat, kóng këà saiⁿᵍ,—hwat leaóu, chëw kóng këà chêng, joy, anger, grief, and pleasure, before they are displayed, are called nature; when displayed, they are denominated passions.

Chêng 晴 Vulg. chaiⁿᵍ: fair weather; a clear sky; calm, serene; é chêng 雨晴 hoē chaiⁿᵍ, the rain is cleared up. Also written 暒 chêng.

福建方言字典

T'hëen chĕng kéng seng hëèn 天晴景星見, *t'hee^ng chai^ng kwui^ng ch'hai^ng hëèn*, when the sky is clear, the bright stars appear. See the 史記 Soó kè.

Chêng 層 Vulg. *chàn*: a story of a house, a first or second floor, an additional chamber. Chêng këung 層宮, a palace, with a succession of chambers and courts.

Chêng 嶒 Chun chêng 崚嶒, the lofty appearance of hills.

去

Chĕng 靖 Tranquil, peaceful: also, to think; to regulate. An chĕng 安靖, rest and tranquillity;—answering in Chinese to "good night."

Lêng chĕng é tè wán, tām pok k'hó bêng sim 寧靖以致遠.淡泊可明心, *lêng chĕng é tè kaòu hwui^ng, tām pŏh t'hang bêng lâng ây sim*, peace and tranquillity will enable a man to extend his thoughts to distant objects, and a tasteless indifference to the world will enlighten the mind. Said by 諸葛武侯, Choo-kat-buó-hoê.

Chĕng 靜 Rest, the opposite of motion, stillness, quietness, inactivity. Te chëá tōng, jin chëá chĕng 知者動.仁者靜, *woō te ây lâng tin tāng, woō jin ây lâng chĕng chĕng*, men of knowledge are active, but men of benevolence still. See the 上論 Sëāng lūn.

Chek chĕng che ch'hè 寂靜之處, *seuk chĕng ây wūy*, a still, quiet place.

Chĕng 甑 An earthen pot to boil rice in: é hoó chĕng ch'hwàn 以釜甑爨, *t'hó të^nà bok kaōu chè pooi^ng*, to use pans and pots in cooking. See 孟子 Bēng-choó.

Chēng 贈 To present, to give as a present: hōng chēng 奉贈, to offer up.

Chēng 淨 Clean: këet chēng 潔淨, *ch'heng k'hè sëō^ng*, pure and clean. Lëuk chēng put k'hó söëy 淥淨不可唾, *Lëuk ây chûy ch'heng k'hè, ū^m t'hang p'hōëy nw^nā*, the waters of the Lëuk are clear, and must not be defiled by spittle.

Chēng 靚 To adorn; clear.

Chēng 諍 To reprove; koé chëá, kwun yéw chēng sin, hoō yéw chēng choó 古者.君有諍臣.父有諍子, *koé chá, jin kwun woō t'hang t^nà ây jin sin, nëō^ng pāy woō t'hang t^nà ây haōu sai^ng*, in former times, princes had ministers that could reprove them, and fathers, children that could advise them. See the 禮記 Léy kè.

Chēng 睜 To look displeased.

Chēng 穽 A pit, a hole. Jin kae wat, ê te,—k'he jê lap choo koé hwā hām chēng che tëung, jê bok che te pē jëá 人皆曰.予知.驅而納諸罟擭陷穽之中.而莫之知避也, *lâng chò poô. kóng, gwá woō tè,—nā böëyh kw^nà jê lap e koè hwā hām chēng ây tëung, chëw bó lâng ëy chae sëëm pee^ng*, people all say, "I am knowing,"—but if you were to drive and catch them, in a net or a trap, or in the midst of a pit-fall, they would none of them know how to escape. See the 中庸 Tëung yûng.

平

Che^ng 莊 Read chong: thus, chong gëëp 莊業, *che^ng gëëp*, a farm: chong kay 莊家, *che^ng kay*, a farmer. Also, a surname.

Chē^{ng} **妝** Read chong: an ornament, a head-dress; to adorn. Chong sek 妝飾, *chē^{ng} sèk*, to adorn; sey chong 梳妝, *sey chē^{ng}*, a toilette.
Put t'hāe chong chéng, choō jĕēn yáou t'hĕáou 不待妝整.自然窈窕, *ūm sat têng t'haē chē^{ng} chèng, choō jĕēn yaóu t'hĕáou*, without waiting for the aid of the toilette, she is naturally handsome.

Chē^{ng} **贓** Read chong: bribes received by inferior officers; stolen goods. Tuy chong 追贓, *tuy chē^{ng}*, to search for stolen goods.

Chē^{ng} **裝** Read chong: goods; chong h^{n}ó 裝貨, *chē^{ng} hòèy*, baggage, stores. O'ng laê che jîn, sok chong chēw tō 往來之人.束裝就道, *óng laê ây lâng pak chē^{ng} chēw kē^{n}â loē*, passengers travelling to and fro, pack up their luggage, and set out in the way.

Chē^{ng} **庄** Read chong: a farm; tēēn chong 田庄, *ch'hân chē^{ng}*, a farming estate.
Haê chong 鞋庄, *ây chē^{ng}*, a shoe warehouse.
Gwān hoē sè seng chaē tēēn chong 願後世生在田庄, *gwān aōu sè saì^{ng} twā tē ch'hân chē^{ng}*, I desire in the next birth to be born in some farm-house:—Said by a sovereign, when about to be killed.

去

Chē^{ng} **狀** Kò chōng 告狀, *kò chē^{ng}*, an indictment, an accusation. T'heen hāy bôo tō, jîn bîn bôo k'hó kò chōng 天下無道.人民無可告狀, *t'hee^{ng} ây bô tō ây sè, lâng pāyh saì^{ng} bô ta tōh t'hang kò chē^{ng}*, when the Empire is without the right way, the people have no where to go and prefer their indictments.

Chē^{ng} **藏** Read chōng: a warehouse; hoó chōng k'hong he 府藏空虛, *hoó chē^{ng} k'hang k'hang*, the treasury and store-house empty.

Chē^{ng} **臟** Read chōng: the viscera, the bowels: jîn yéw gnóe chōng 人有五臟, *lâng woō goē chē^{ng}*, people have five viscera.

上平

Chĕō **招** Read cheaou: to call, to beckon by the hand, to assemble. Bē kám chek chĕáou, sēen se hōng būn 未敢即招.先書奉聞, *bōēy k^{n}á lēem pee^{ng} chĕō, taē seng scá p'hay t'hàm t'hē^{n}a*, I do not dare directly to call you, but first write a letter to make enquiry.

Chĕo **蕉** Read chĕaou: a plantain; chĕaou choó kay 蕉仔街, *chĕo á kay*, the plantain street.

上聲

Chĕó **少** Read sĕáou: few, not many, scarce. Koé jîn bōéy chĕúng, kok ch'hut sĕáou hé é chèy 古人每種.各出少許以祭, *koē chá ây lâng bōēy chêng, kok ch'hut chĕó chĕó ē chèy*, the ancients, from every kind of grain, used to take a little of each, to sacrifice it (to the manes of those who first invented food).

去

Chĕò **照** Read chĕàou: to reflect, to illumine. Jit chĕàou bān hong 日照萬方, *jit t'haōu chĕò chē^{n}â bān he^{ng}*, the sun illumines myriads of places.

Chĕò **醮** Read chĕàou: a sacrifice, a religious procession. Chò chĕàou kê hok 做醮祈福, *chò chĕò kêw hok k'hè*, to perform a sacrifice in order to seek happiness.

下去

Chĕō **噍** Read chĕāou: to eat, to gnaw.

福建方言字典

大

Chëŏh 借 Read chëà: to borrow: ná lé chëà tck ch'hóo bùt 那理借得此物, *ta lŏh ëy chëŏh tit chèy lëy meëⁿh*, where can we borrow such a thing as this?

Chëŏh 焟 Sek hⁿó 焟火, *chëŏh höëy*, to warm one's-self at the fire. Hân laê boô e, tong sek hⁿó 寒來無衣.當焟火, *kwⁿâ laê nā bô sⁿa, tëŏh chëŏh höëy*, when the cold weather comes, if you have no clothes, you must warm yourself at the fire.

Chëŏh 斫 Read sek: to cut down. Sek sē 斫樹, *chëŏh ch'hëw*, to fell trees.

Chëŏh 墌 A foundation. Wûy kē sit, pit-sëen lip ke chëŏh 爲巨室.必先立基墌, *chò tŭā ch'hoò, pit tëŏh taē seng k'hëă ke chëŏh*, in making a great house, we must first lay a good foundation.

Chëŏh 稷 *Lëy chëŏh* 犂稷, the handle of a plough.

天

Chëŏh 石 Read sek: a stone; a measure of ten pecks; a surname. Kim hoo san, yit kwân sek che to 今夫山.一卷石之多, *tⁿa chèy lëy swⁿa, chit kwân chëŏh ây chëy*, now a hill is nothing more than a heap of stones. See the 中庸 Tëung yûng.

卒

Chëoⁿᵍ 章 Read chëang: a chapter, a section; a surname. Bûn chëang 文章, *bûn chëoⁿᵍ*, literary composition. Sóng, Ông-an-sek, tēng chok bûn chëang, é pat pé wûy lùt; chè Bêng naê é bûn chëang sè t'hëen hāy soō 宋王安石定作文章.以八比爲律.至明乃以文章試天下士, *Sòng tëâou, Ông-ân-chëŏh tëⁿā chò bûn chëoⁿᵍ, ê păyh koè chò lùt; chè kaôu Bêng tëâou, ch'hëⁿá ê bûn chëoⁿᵍ ch'hè k'hwⁿà t'heeⁿᵍ āy ây t'hak ch'hayh lâng*, Ông-an-sek of the Sóng dynasty settled the form of literary compositions, and confined them to eight sections; till in the Bêng dynasty, literary compositions were used for trying and examining scholars, throughout the Empire. See the 史畧 Soó lëak.

Chëoⁿᵍ 樟 Read chëang: the camphor tree.

Chëoⁿᵍ 漳 Read chëang: the name of a river, in the province of 福建 Hok-këën, which gave rise to the name of Chëang-chew 漳州, *Chëoⁿᵍ-chew*, the department where the dialect of this dictionary is spoken. There is, also, Chëang-p'hoé-hëën 漳浦縣, *Chëoⁿᵍ-p'hoé-kwān*, the district of Cheoⁿᵍ-p'hoé.

Chëoⁿᵍ 鱆 Read chëang: the name of a fish.

Chëoⁿᵍ 漿 Read chëang: starch, for stiffening clothes; âm chëang 涪漿, *âm chëoⁿᵍ*, starch.

去

Chëóⁿᵍ 蔣 Read chëáng: a surname.

Chëóⁿᵍ 掌 Read chëáng: the palm. Séw chëáng 手掌, *ch'hëw chëóⁿᵍ*, the palm of the hand. Gê gnó séy yëuk yëá, him chëáng ek gnó séy yëuk yëá 魚我所欲也.熊掌亦我所欲也, *hê gwá sëy aè yëá, him chëóⁿᵍ yëá gwá sëy aè yëá*, fish is a thing that I like,—a bear's palm is also what I like. See 孟子 Bêng-chóo.

Chëóⁿᵍ 槳 Read chëáng: an oar. Kò chëáng 過槳, *kò chëóⁿᵍ*, to pull or push over, the oar

w

去 Chëŏ^{ng} 障 Pó chëàng 保障, *pó chëŏ^{ng}*, a mound, a fence. Tāe sîn kok che pó chëàng yëâ 大臣國之保障也, *twā jîn sin kok ây pó chëŏ^{ng}*, a great minister is the defence of a country.

Chëŏ^{ng} 醬 Read chëàng: sauce or gravy. Toē chëàng 豆醬, *taōu chëŏ^{ng}*, a kind of ketchup made of pulse. Sëēn hoo chëàng yūng pek yéw sip jē yùng 膳夫醬用百有十二甕, *chè chëăh ây lâng yūng chëŏ^{ng} chē^{n}â pâyh kwà chàp jē àng*, the cook used one hundred and twelve jars of sauces. See the 周禮 Chew léy.

平 Chëŏ^{ng} 蠀 Chëâng chê 蠀蝫, *chëŏng ché*, a toad.

去 Chëō^{ng} 上 Read sëàng: to ascend; up, at the top, upon, above, on. Sëāng tong kae, chek sëen chó chëuk, sëāng sey kae chek sëen yēw chëuk 上東階則先左足.上西階則先右足, *chëō^{ng} tang kay, chēw taē seng tó ch'hēw ây k'ha, chëō^{ng} sae kay chēw taē seng chē^{n}à ch'hēw ây k'ha*, when ascending the eastern stairs first set down the left foot; and when ascending the western stairs, first set down the right foot. See the 禮記 Léy kè.

Chëō^{ng} 癢 Read yāng: to itch. Chwân sin chīn yāng 全身盡癢, *chwuî^{ng} hîn sin chëō^{ng} lëáou lëáou*, the body itches all over.

入 Chëuk 足 Sufficient, enough; the feet. Te chëuk 知足, to be content. Chëuk sit chëuk peng, bîn sìn che è 足食.足兵.民信之矣, *kaōu chëăh, kaōu peng, kwà pâyh sai^{ng} sìn lân*, "a sufficiency of food, a sufficiency of weapons, and the confidence of the people;"—three things which a good governor will seek to obtain. See the 下論 Hāy lūn.

Heng tēy jê séw chëuk, ch'hey choó soō e hok 兄弟如手足.妻子似衣服, *hē^{n}a tē ch'hin chëō^{ng} k'ha ch'hêw, boè kē^{n}á ch'hin chëō^{ng} s^{n}a k'hoè*, elder and younger brethren are like one's legs and arms, but wives and children are only like one's apparel.

Chëuk 屬 To confide to, to entrust with; also, to assemble, to connect. Hàn ông che chëàng, tók Hân-sìn k'hó chëuk taē soō 漢王之將.獨韓信可屬大事, *Hàn ông ây chëàng, tók Hân-sìn t'hang chëuk t'hok twā soō*, of all the generals of the king of Hàn, Hân-sìn alone could be entrusted with the great affairs of state. See the 史記 Soó kè.

Naé chëuk kê kê ló, jê kò che 乃屬其耆老而告之, *naè chîp hōēy e ây laōu lâng, jê kap e kóng*, he then assembled his elders, and informed them, &c. See the 上孟 Sëāng bēng.

Chëuk 柷 An instrument used for stopping music.

Chëuk 祀 The name of an officer, presiding over the ancestorial temple.

Chëuk 囑 To entrust to the care of. Hàn Chëàou-lëet tèy chëuk koe ê Choo-kat-boó-hôe 漢昭烈帝囑孤於諸葛武侯, *Hàn Chëàou-lëet tèy t'hok koe kē^{n}á hoē Choo-kat-boó-hoē*, the Emperor Chëàou-lëet of the Hàn dynasty entrusted his orphan child to Choo-kat-boó-hoē.

Chëuk 燭 A candle. Làp chëuk 蠟燭, *làh chek*, a wax candle. Chëuk chëàou bôo këang 燭照無疆, *chek chëò bô këang*, a candle illumines all around.

Chëuk 粥 Möëy chëuk 糜粥, *ăm möëy*, congee, rice water. Ch'hwat chëuk, bëën ch'him hek, chek wüy jê k'hok 啜粥.面深墨.卽位而哭, *ch'höëyh ăm möëy, bīn ch'him oe, chek wüy jê k'haòu*, "drinking watery gruel, and with a face as black as ink, he approached the throne and wept." This was the conduct of a filial son, on the death of his royal father. See the 上孟 Sëāng bēng.

Chëuk 粥 The noise made in calling fowls: chëuk key 粥鷄, *koē key*, to chuck like fowls.

Chëuk 瘃 Boils and blains, on the hands and feet.

Chëuk 祝 To bless, to felicitate, to wish well to, to pray for blessings on. A surname. Chëuk sëw 祝壽, to wish one long life. Chëuk sëà 祝謝, to thank.

Chëuk 韣 The belt, tied on the outside of a garment; a girdle.

Chëuk 叔 Read sëuk: an uncle, a father's younger brother.

卆

Chëung 鍾 To collect; a cup, a certain measure; a surname. Chéw chëung 酒鍾, *chéw cheng á*, a wine cup. Bān chëung ê gnó hô kay yëen 萬鍾於我何加焉, *bān chëung ây ch'hek tē gwá woō s^{n}a meē^{n}h kay*, what would ten thousand measures of grain add to me? See 孟子 Bēng-choó.

Chëung 鐘 Vulg. *cheng*: a bell. Yâou chëung 搖鐘, *yëô cheng*, to ring a bell. Chëung lê 鍾離, a double surname.

Sîn chëung, boē koé, lēng jîn beng seng 晨鐘.暮鼓.令人猛省, *chá k'hè ây cheng, maî^{ng} hwuî^{ng} ây koé, lêng lâng beng sêng*, the morning bell, and the evening drum, are to make people alert and watchful.

Chëung 舂 Chëung kēw 舂臼, *cheng koī* a pestle and mortar.

Chëung 㨂 Vulg. *cheng*: to pound, to beat; chëung bé 㨂米, *cheng bé*, to beat out rice.

Chëung 惷 Stupid, foolish: Ae-kong wat, kw^{n}á jîn chëung gê 哀公曰.寡人惷愚, *Ae-kong kóng, gwá woō chëung gaê*, Ae-kong said, I am stupid and foolish.

Chëung 螽 A kind of insect.

Chëung 終 The end, the issue, the termination final. A surname. Bût yéw pún bwat, soō yéw chëung sé 物有本末.事有終始, *meē^{n}h woō pún bwat, soō woō k'hè t'haóu swăh böëy*, things have their origin and termination; affairs have a beginning and an end.

Chëung 刣 To scrape anything.

声

Chëúng 種 Vulg. *chêng*: the seed of anything offspring. Chëúng chëúng 種種 short hair. Gnoé kok chëá, chëúng che bé chëá yeá 五穀者.種之美者也, *goé kok chëw sè chêng ây súy*, the five kinds of grain are the best of all seeds.

Chëúng 踵 The heel of the foot; to tread with the heel; to cut off. Chëúng bûn jê kò Bûn-kong 踵門而

告文公, *k'ha tàh mooi^ng jê kap Bûn-kong kòng*, treading on the threshold, they informed Bûn-kong, &c. See 孟子 Bêng-chóo.

Cheúng **腫** Tëàng cheúng 脹腫, *tëò^ng chèng*, to be swollen.

Cheúng **瘇** Këak cheúng 脚瘇, *k'ha chèng*, a swelling of the legs.

去

Cheùng **衆** All, the whole, many: cheùng jîn 衆人, *cheùng lâng*, all people. Kw^ná koè put k'hó é tek cheùng 寡固不可以敵衆, *chëó koè bëy tày tek chëy*, the few certainly cannot contend with the many.

Hwàn aè cheùng jê ch'hin jîn 汎愛衆而親仁, *hwàn aè cheùng lâng, jê ch'hin kîn woō jîn ây lâng*, generally kind to all, but intimate with the virtuous. See the 上論 Sëāng lūn. Also written 㐺 cheùng.

Cheùng **偅** Lëûng cheùng 儱偅, to seek and not meet with.

Cheùng **種** To plant, to sow; cheùng ch'haè 種菜, *chèng ch'haè*, to plant vegetables.

Sîn-lông kaòu bîn cheùng gnóe kok 神農教民種五穀, *Sîn-lông kà bîn chèng gnóe kok*, Sîn-lông taught the people to plant the five kinds of grain.

平

Cheûng **從** To follow, to comply with; from, out of. A surname. Also written 从 cheûng.

Yîn cheûng lëûng, hong cheûng hoé 雲從龍風從虎, *hwûn t'hàn lëûng, hong t'hàn hoé*, clouds follow the dragon, and wind the tiger. See the 易經 Yëàh keng.

去

Cheūng **從** To follow behind, to accompany; Cheūng gnó chëá, kê Yêw e 從我者其由歟, *tùy gwá ây lâng, e k^ná së Yêw e*, he that accompanies me, will it not be Yêw? See the 上論 Sëāng lūn.

平

Chew **舟** A boat, a vessel: chew ke séy chè 舟車所至, *chûn kwà ch'hëa sèy kaòu ây wūy*, wherever boats or carriages have travelled. See the 中庸 Tëung yûng.

P'hit má yaôu tê ch'hëen lé tëy, k'heng chew é kò bān tëūng san 匹馬遙馳千里地輕舟以過萬重山, *chit chëāh bây p'haòu chaóu ch'heng lé ây tëy, k'hin k'hin ây chûn è köëy bān tëûng ây sw^na*, with one horse we have galloped over a thousand miles of country, and with a light boat we have sailed past ten thousand ranges of hills.

Chew **侜** To cover over, to conceal, to hide: sûy chew ê bé 誰侜予美, *chë chūy pèy gwá ây hó*, who will conceal my excellencies. See the 國風 Kok hong.

Chew **譸** Garrulous, many words; to speak much.

Chew **輈** The axle or cross-bar, in front of a carriage; sometimes put for a carriage.

Êng-k'hó sëuk hëep chew, é choé 潁考叔挾輈以走, *Êng-k'hó-sëuk gnäyh ch'hëa, é kë^ná*, Êng-k'hó-sëuk took the carriage under his arm, and walked away with it. See the 左傳 Chó twān.

Chew **啁** A flock of little birds, chirping together; a cry of distress.

福建方言字典

Chew 週 To circulate, to perambulate, to revolve.

Chew 周 Round, all round, complete, universal, liberal; a surname. Kwun choó chew jê put pè 君子周而不比, *kwun choó ây lâng chew jê bô pè*, the good man is liberal and not narrow minded. See the 上論 Sëang. lūn.

K'hóng-choō chew lêw soò hong 孔子周流四方, *K'hóng-choó chew lêw sè he^{ng}*, Confucius rambled round about all parts.

Chew pē 周備, completely prepared; chew chêy 周濟, completely provided.

Chew 賙 Chew chêy 賙濟, to supply the wants of the poor. Soò che sëang chew 使之相賙, *saé e sëo chew chêy*, make them provide for one another.

Chew 州 A district, a department. Chew, hëën 州縣, *chew, kwān*, larger and smaller districts. Chew hoó 州府, a capital of a district, a colony.

Gân put tëung sìn, hêng put tok kèng, suy chew lé, hêng hoē chae 言不忠信.行不篤敬.雖州里.行乎哉, *kóng wā bô tëung sìn, sèy kë^{n}â bô tok kèng, suy chew lē, k'ham ēy kë^{n}â tit chae*, — when a man's words are not faithful and sincere, nor his actions true and respectful, although in his native district and village, how can he get forward!

Chew 盩 The turnings and windings of a stream.

Chew 啾 Chew chek 啾唧, the noise made by infants and children.

Chew 洲 High land in the midst of water, an island in a river. Chaē hô che chew 在河之洲, *twā tē kâng ây chew*, in the island of the river.

Chew 譸 Deceitful; to cheat.

声

Chéw 酒 Wine, fermented liquor. Sit chéw 食酒, *chëăh chéw*, to drink wine.

Gê tek chok chéw 儀狄作酒, *gê tek ây hwan chò chéw*, the north-western foreigners first invented wine.

E' oè ché chéw, jê h^{n}ò sëën gân 禹惡旨酒.而好善言, *E' wàn chè chéw, jê aè hó ây wā*, E' disliked the best wine, but loved virtuous words.

Yéw chéw soō sëen seng chwān 有酒食先生饌, *woō chéw pooi^{ng} hoē pāy hë^{n}a chëăh*, if when we have wine and food, we give it to our parents and elders to eat,—(how can this alone be considered filial piety!) See the 上論 Sëang lūn.

Chéw 帚 Sàou chéw 掃帚, a besom, a broom. Seáou-k'hong ch'hey chok ke chéw 少康初作箕帚, *Seáou-k'hong k'hè ch'hey chò saòu chéw*, Seáou-k'hong first invented besoms. See the 說文 Swat bûn.

Chéw 𧳜 The name of a beast, found in the west,—about the size of an ass, in shape like a monkey, and expert in climbing trees.

Chéw 守 Read séw; to keep, to guard, to take care of. Séw keng 守更, *chéw ka^{ng}*, to keep watch. Séw but 守物, *chéw mëe^{n}h*, to take care of any thing.

Séw, sëùk wûy taē? séw sin wûy taē 守孰爲大.守身爲大, *chèw, tēy chìt hāng k'hăh twā? chèw lân pùn sin k'hăh twā*, of all cares, which is the most important?—The care of one's own personal conduct is the most important. See the 下孟 Hāy bēng.

去 Chèw 呪 To swear; an oath. Chèw sē 呪誓, *chèw chwā*, to take an oath. Bîn hoé, chek k'hwat k'hoé choè chèw 民否.則厥口阻呪, *pāyh sai*^{ng} *ū*^{m} *hó, chèw k'hwat ch'hùy chèw chwà*, when the people have any disputes, they open their months with an oath. See the 尙書 *Sëō*^{ng} *sè*.

Chèw 㤼 Ch'han chèw 㑶㤼, scolding; railing words.

Chèw 蛀 Read choò: a kind of insect that eats wood.

去 Chēw 就 Then; to go to, to approach to; complete. Chēw yéw tō, jê chèng yëen 就有道·而正焉, *chēw wăh woō tō ây lâng, jê chē*^{n}*à ka tē*, to approach the virtuous, and adjust one's-self by them.

Jìt chëang gwàt chēw 日將月就, to make daily advances, and monthly improvements.

Chēw 僦 To load, to burden; to contemplate.

Chēw 鷲 A great bird, found in the south, with a yellow head, red eyes, and of a variegated colour. *Qu.* the eagle?

平 Chey 儕 Even; a sort, a class. Goê chey 吾儕, *gwán ây lâng*, we, us. Chìn Tēng tông chey 晉鄭同儕, *Chìn kok kap Tēng kok tâng chey*, the Chìn and Tēng countries were equal and alike.

Béng hoé suy yîn ok, ėk kok yéw p'hit chey 猛虎雖云惡.亦各有匹儕, *béng ây hoé suy kóng sē p'ha*^{n}*è, yëá kok wōo p'hìt chēy*, fierce tigers, although they may be called savage, yet have each their equals and companions.

Chey 隮 To ascend, to go up. Chey pé kong tông 隮彼公堂, *chëō*^{ng} *e ây kong tông*, to ascend up to the public hall. See the 國風 Kok hong.

Chey 擠 To involve, to be pushed in, or let fall. Seáou jîn ló jê bôo choó, te chey ê koe hok ê 小人老而無子.知擠於溝壑矣, *sèy ây lâng laōu jê bô kē*^{n}*á, chae ēy chey sak tē kaou hok è*, the little one (i. e. I) being old, and having no children, know that I shall be shoved into some ditch or another,—(when I die). See the 左傳 Chò twān.

Chey 穧 A sheaf of corn; to bind corn into a bundle.

Chey 躋 To ascend, to go up. Chey ê kéw lêng 躋于九陵, *chëō*^{ng} *kaòu kèw lêng*, to ascend up to the nine cemeteries.

Chey 齎 To present, to send as a gift. Sëáou-chong Pek sēw kê chëang pē che chey 小宗伯受其將幣之齎, *Sëáou-chong Pāyh, sēw e ây chëang pē ây chey*, the Seaóu-chong Păyh officer received the presents of silk and cloth.

Chey 薺 A certain sweet vegetable,—capsella pursa pastoris. Ké kam jê chey 其甘如薺, *e ây tee*^{ng} *ch'hìn chëō*^{ng} *chey*, as sweet as the *chey* vegetable. See the 國風 Kok hong.

Chey 劑 Yĕak chey 藥劑, *yŏh chaé*, medicinal drugs.

Chey 齏 To cut to pieces, to cut up into mince meat.

Chey 嚌 The noise of many voices.

Chey 臍 Toé chey 肚臍, *toé chaé*, the navel.

Chey 賫 To present, to send. Chey se 賫書, to send a letter. Má-wān-wŭy Gwŭy-gô chey se 馬援爲隗囂賫書, *Má-wān t'hēy Gwŭy-gô chey p'hay*, Má-wān carried a letter for Gwŭy-gô.

Chey 郟 Read choe. A surname. Choe é Loé hăng 郟與魯閧, *Chey kap Loé sëa p'hăh*, the Chey country went to war with the Loé country. See the 上孟 Sëăng bēng.

上声

Chéy 濟 The name of a stream; also, full and abundant. Chéy chéy to soō 濟濟多士, *chèy sĕng ây chèy t'hak ch'hăyh lâng*, abundant indeed was the multitude of scholars. See the 小雅 Seáou gnáy.

Chéy 姐 Elder sister: chéy chéy 姐姐, a respectful mode of addressing females. Seáou chéy 小姐, *sëó chĕá*, little miss; my young mistress.

Chéy 這 This, these. Chéy jîn put sē jîn, naé sē sey ông bóe, laê hwà sin 這人不是人.乃是西王母來化身, *chèy lêy lâng ū^m sē lâng, naé sē sae ông ay nēō^ng lèy, laê hwà sin*, this person is not a human being, but is the mother of the western king, metamorphosed into this form.

去声

Chèy 祭 To sacrifice, a sacrifice. Chèy but 祭物, *chèy meē^nh*, an offering. Chèy jê chaē, chèy sîn jê sîn chaē. Choò wat, goé put é chèy, jê put chèy 祭如在.祭神如神在.子曰.吾不與祭.如不祭, *chèy ch'hin chëō^ng tē tit, chèy sîn bĕng ch'hin chëō^ng sîn bĕng tē tit. Hoo-choó kóng, gwá bô chò poé chèy, ch'hin chëō^ng bô chèy*, sacrifice (to your ancestors) as though they were present, and sacrifice to the gods as though the gods were present. Confucius said, if I am not personally engaged in the sacrifice, it is to me as if there was no sacrifice. See the 上論 Sëăng lūn.

Chèy 穄 The name of a kind of grain.

Chèy 際 A meeting together; an opportunity, a season. Tông Gê che chèy 唐虞之際, in the time of Tông and Gê.

Chèy 瘵 To be pained, to be troubled. Boô choō chèy yëen 無自瘵焉, *bô ka tē hwăn lô*, do not distress yourself about it.

Chèy 霽 The cessation of rain; fair weather.

Chèy 濟 To supply, to assist, to regulate, to settle, to cross the water. Kew ch'hé che lē, bān bîn è chèy 臼杵之利.萬民以濟, *cheng kōo ây lē, chē^nâ bān lâng è chèy*, by the profits of the pestle and mortar, the wants of myriads of people are supplied. See the 易經 Yĕăh keng.

Chèy **嗻** Useless words, garrulity.

Chèy **漈** The name of a stream of water.

Chèy **縩** A kind of grass, of which cloth is made.

平

Chêy **蠐** The name of an insect.

Chêy **臍** The navel. Sē chêy hō kip 噬臍何及, *chēăh ka tē āy toē chaē, bōēyh an chw^{n}à ey kip kàou*, if wanting to eat one's own navel, how could it be got at!—(used to express an impossibility.)

Chêy **齊** To regulate, to set right, to put in order. A surname. Pit chēang sew léy é chêy tēâou, chèng hwat é chêy kwan, pēng tē é chêy bîn 必將修禮以齊朝.正法以齊官.平治以齊民, *tek k'hak tēōh sew lēy soè ê chêy tēâou têng, chē^{n}à hwat toē ê chêy chò kw^{n}a, paî^{ng} tē ê chêy pāyh saî^{ng}*, we must certainly cultivate propriety in order to regulate the court, adjust the laws in order to regulate the officers, and equalize the government in order to regulate the people. Said by 荀子 Sûn choó.

去

Chēy **嚌** To taste, to eat.

Chēy **多** Read to: many, not few, much. Sīm to 甚多, *sīm chēy*, very many. To bûn kēèn chēá, hak che p'hok 多聞見者.學之博, *chēy t'hē^{n}a k'hw^{n}à āy lâng, swui^{ng} chò p'hok hak*, those who have heard and seen much may be considered as extensively learned.

Chēy **坐** Read chō: to sit down. Ch'héng chō 請坐, *ch'hē^{n}à chēy*, pray sit down. Sek put chèng put chō 席不正不坐, *ch'hēōh bé sè chē^{n}à, bô bōēyh chēy*, if the mat was not put square, he would not sit down upon it;—said of Confucius, in the 上論 Sēāng lūn. Chō, gnô bêng gé choó 坐我明語子, *chēy, gwá bêng bêng kap lē kóng*, sit down, Sir, and I will clearly explain it to you. See 孟子 Bēng-choé.

平

Ch'ha **嗏** An auxiliary word, seldom used.

Ch'ha **叉** The hands entwined together. Jip kwūn, yaou sēāng chēet, hông jîn, séw chîn ch'ha 入郡腰常折.逢人手盡叉, *jip chew kwūn, yēo sēāng chēet,—toó tēōh lâng, ch'hew chîn ch'ha*, when entering a district, the loins are constantly bent; and when meeting with people, the hands are always joined—(in making compliments).

声

Ch'há **炒** To boil, or fry any thing.

Ch'há **侘** Ch'há chēy 侘傺, missing one's aim.

Ch'há **吒** To be angry, to be enraged.

去

Ch'hà **詫** To boast, to brag; to deceive. Kam gân ch'hà gé 甘言詫語, flattering words and boasting expressions.

Ch'hà 鈔 Chëên ch'hà 錢鈔, *cheē^ng ch'hà*, paper money; — to take.

平

Ch'hâ 查 Ch'hâ k'hó 查考, to examine, as at the public examinations.

Ch'hâ 材 Kwan ch'hâe 棺材, *kw^na ch'hâ*, a coffin.

Ch'hâ 柴 Read ch'hâe: fire-wood. Taē chëá k'hó sek wūy che sin, sëáou chëá hap sok wūy che ch'hâe 大者可析謂之薪.小者合束謂之柴, *twā ây t'hang p'hwà kóng këò sin, sèy ây hap sok kóng këò ch'hâ*, the great pieces of fire-wood, which can be split, are called logs; and the small pieces that are bound up in bundles, are called faggots.

平

Ch'hae 猜 To guess, to suppose. Ch'hae ch'hoè 猜錯, to conjecture wrong. Goè choó ek yëw ch'hae yëen 吾子亦有猜焉, *gwá ây choó yëā woō ch'hae*, you, my good sir, have your suspicions.

Ch'hae 釵 A hair-pin, a bodkin. Kim tè pó ch'hae yit song, k'hó yaou sëw, 今致寳釵一双.可糚首, *t^na tè sàng pó ch'hae chit tùy, t'hang yaou t'hâou*, now I send you a pair of precious bodkins, that may adorn your head.

Ch'hae 啋 An auxiliary word; not at rest.

Ch'hae 偲 Violent, strong; highly gifted; long bearded. Kê jin bé ch'hë^ná ch'hae 其人美且偲, *e ây lâng ch'hin ch'hai^ng kwà hó ch'hùy ch'hew*, the man is handsome, and has a fine beard.

上

Ch'haé 綵 Bûn ch'haé 文綵, variegated, ornamented.

Ch'haé 採 To pluck, to pick, to gather. Ch'haé tây 採茶, to gather tea. San yëw béng sèw, lêy-hok wūy che put ch'haé 山有猛獸.藜藿爲之不採, *sw^na woō bêng sèw, lêy-hok wūy e bô bân*, when the hills are infested by wild animals, the lêy-hok herbs are not gathered.

Ch'haé 睬 Ch'hew ch'haé 倸睬, to hold in estimation. K'hàn jîn boô ch'hew ch'haé 看人無倸睬, *k'hw^nà lâng bô ch'hew ch'haé*, to look down upon a man.

Ch'haé 寀 Leâou ch'haé 寮寀, a fellow student, a brother officer.

Ch'haé 采 To pluck, to gather; also, variegated colours. Gnoē ch'haé 五采, the five colours. Ch'haé ch'haé hoô-é, puk gân ch'haé che 采采芣苢.薄言采之, *laê bân ke chëên ch'habu, taē kay laê bân e*, let us go and gather the hoô-é plant; I say let us go and gather it. See the 國風 Kok hong.

Ch'haé 彩 Variegated colours; bright and shining. Hwa ch'haé 華彩, ornamented.

去

Ch'haè 蔡 A large tortoise; a rule. Vulg. *ch'hwà*: a surname. Chong-bûn-tëûng kê ch'haè 臧文仲居蔡, *Chong-bûn-tëûng ch'hòng só chaē hoē twā koo k'hëā*, Chong-bûn-tëûng made a house for a large tortoise to dwell in. See the 上論 Sëâng lūn.

Ch'haè 蠆 The name of an insect, whose venom lies in its tail; a scorpion. Ch'haè bé yëw tok, hông kwun che t'hëûng tēy hoē 蠆尾有毒.況君之家弟乎, *ch'haè ây boēy woō tok, hòng kwun lê ây twā seó tē hoē*, in the tail of the scorpion there is poison, how much more in your honorable younger brother.

Ch'haè 埰 The portion of territory allotted to nobles, and chief officers. Sëëm ê tong Chew-kong che ch'haè tēy 陝以東周公之埰地, *Sëëm ê tang Chew-kong ây ch'haè tēy*, to the eastward of Sëëm was the territory of Chew-kong. See the 國語 Kok gé.

Ch'haè 菜 Vegetables. Sit ch'haè 食菜, *chëăh ch'haè*, to eat vegetables only, to fast. Ch'haè kwa 菜瓜, cucumis Japonicus.

Suy soe soō, ch'haè keng, kwa, chèy pit chae jê yeá 雖疏食.菜羹.瓜.祭必齊如也, *suy ch'hoe ây chëăh, ch'haè t'he^ng, kap kwa, kaòu chèy tek k'hak tëŏh chae kaè*, although we have nothing but coarse provisions,—and vegetable soup, with melons, yet when we come to sacrifice we must do it with reverence. See the 上論 Sëāng lūn.

Ch'haè 瘥 A sickness.

平

Ch'haê 柴 Vulg. *ch'hâ*: fire-wood. Sew tëet sin ch'hâe 收秩薪柴, *sew k'he^ng sin ch'hâ*, collect and store up the fire-wood. A surname.

Ch'haê 祡 A burnt sacrifice, offered up to heaven, by the Emperor.

Ch'haê 纔 Just now, just then, then, thereupon; near, immediately: also written 才 ch'haê.

Gân-choô ch'haê yéw put sëën, pëën te che; ch'haê te che, pëën keng, put bêng chok 顏子纔有不善.便知之.纔知之.便更.不萌作, *Gân-choô toō toō â ū^m hó, pëën chae e; toō toō â chae e, pëën kây, bô kŏh chò*, Gân-choô no sooner had a fault, than he immediately knew it; and as soon as he knew it, he instantly amended it, and did not practise it again.

Ch'haê 豺 A wolf. Sò lek put wān, sē ch'haê lông yeá 嫂溺不援.是豺狼也, *he^n a sò tëëm lek ū^m kèw e, sē ch'haê lông*, a man, who, when a sister-in-law is drowning, will not help her, must be a wolf. See the 下孟 Hāy bêng.

Toê pe ch'haê hoé, ch'haê hoé put sit 投畀豺虎.豺虎不食, *hëet hoē ch'haê hoé, ch'haê hoé ū^m chëăh*, if you threw them to the wolves and tigers, the wolves and tigers would not eat them. See the 小雅 Sëáou gnáy.

去

Ch'haē 祀 Read soō: to sacrifice. Soō ong 祀尪, *ch'haē ang*, to sacrifice to an idol.

Ch'haē 睵 The eyes fixed, and not revolving or, wandering about.

入

Ch'hăh 唽 Chattering, garrulity.

Ch'hăh 插 Read ch'hap: to stick into, to pierce. Ch'hap hwa 插花, *ch'hăh hwa*, to stick flowers in the hair.

平

Ch'hai^ng 青 Read ch'heng: azure, blue. Ch'heng bêng 青盲, *ch'hai^ng ma^ng*, blind.

Ch'heng san put lô, swat pek t'hoê; lëuk sûy boô yew, hong jeàou hëën 青山不

福建方言字典

老.雪白頭.綠水無憂.風皺面, *ch'hai^{ng} sw^{n}a bô laôu, lŏh săyh chēw woō păyh t'haôu; lek chúy bô hwân lô, hong ch'hōey chēw woō jĕàou bīn*, the azure mountains grow not old, and yet when the snow falls they have hoary heads; the green waters are not troubled, and yet when the wind blows they have a wrinkled face.

Ch'hai^{ng} 菁 Read ch'heng: the flowers of leeks; full and luxuriant. Hwan ch'heng 番菁, *hwan ch'hai^{ng}*, indigo, the indigo plant.

Ch'hai^{ng} 星 Read seng: a star. H^{n}ò kim seng 火金星, *hōēy kim ch'hai^{ng}*, a fire-fly.

Jit, gwat, seng sin, hèy yëen 日月星辰繫焉, *jit, gōëyh, ch'hai^{ng} sin, tit tëàou*, the sun, moon, and stars are hung up therein (*viz.* in the heavens).

P'hè jê pok sin ke kê séy, jê chëùng seng këúng che 譬如北辰居其所.而衆星拱之, *ch'hin chëō^{ng} pak sin k'hëē e ây sò chaē, jê chëùng ch'hai^{ng} këúng e*, like the northern star, which rests in its place, and all the stars move round it. See the 上論 Sëāng lūn.

Ch'hai^{ng} 腥 Read seng: raw, uncooked. Kwun soò seng, pit sëuk jê chëèn che 君賜腥必熟而薦之, *kwun soò hoē ch'hai^{ng} ây meè^{n}h, pit tëŏh chè sek jê chëèn e*, when a prince bestows on us raw food, we should cook and then offer it. See the 上論 Sëāng lūn.

声

Ch'hai^{ng} 醒 Read sêng: to awake, to arouse, to be awake. Pè sè kae chùy, jê gnó tok séng 彼世皆醉而我獨醒, *hwŭh lēy sè chò poō chuy, tok gwá chit lâng ch'hai^{ng}*, this age is altogether intoxicated, and I alone am awake.

Ch'hai^{ng} 靘 Read ch'héng: cold, chilly. Ch'hin ch'héng 櫬靘, *ch'hin ch'hai^{ng}*, beautiful.

去

Ch'hai^{ng} 錚 The sound of metal, the ringing of metal, the beating of a gong.

入

Ch'hak 察 Read ch'hat: to examine. Ch'hat keng 察更, *ch'hak kai^{ng}*, to inspect the watch.

入

Ch'hak 鑿 Read ch'hok: a chisel; to cut with a chisel. Ch'hok san t'hong taē haé, lëēn sek poé lâm t'hëen 鑿山通大海.煉石補南天, *ch'hak sw^{n}a t'hong twā haè, nëô^{ng} chêŏh poè lam t'hee^{ng}*, chiselling through a hill, to afford a passage for the sea; and melting stones, to repair the southern heavens; — (all this, as the Chinese pretend, having been done, what then is difficult?)

平

Ch'ham 參 To mix, to blend; to be equal to; to wait upon, to visit. Kong ch'ham t'hëen tēy 功參天地, *kong lô ēy ch'ham tit t'hee^{ng} tēy*, merit which equals that of heaven and earth; — an expression foolishly applied by the Chinese to their sages.

Ch'ham 驂 A carriage horse, two horses appended to a carriage. Sëang t'hwat ch'ham é cheng che 嘗脫驂以贈之, *chap chap t'hâou bây ē hoē e*, he frequently took a horse from his carriage, and gave it to him; — said of Confucius, when he met an old friend.

Ch'ham 叅 The same as 參 ch'ham. To visit. Ch'ham këèn 叅見, *ch'ham kee^{ng}*, to wait upon.

Ch'ham 滲 Ch'ham loē 滲漏, *ch'ham laōu*, to leak out, to drip through.

Ch'ham 傪 A fine appearance, a man's name.

Ch'ham 欃 The name of a tree.

Ch'ham 鑱 A sharp instrument, a plough-share. Tēang ch'ham, tēang ch'ham, pek bok pèng, gnó seng t'hok choó é wûy bēng 長鑱長鑱白木柄. 我生托子以爲命, *tēng ch'ham, tēng ch'ham, pāyh ch'hā paing, gwá saing t'hok lè è, chò mēnā*, the long plough-share! the long plough-share! with the white wooden handle; as long as we live, we depend on this, for the support of life.

Ch'ham 劖 A small kind of chisel.

Ch'ham 攙 To assist; to pierce; sharp. T'hēen ch'ham 天攙, the name of a star.

去

Ch'hám 慘 Grieved, pained; painful, miserable, wretched. Yew sim ch'hám ch'hám lēem kok che gēak 憂心慘慘. 念國之虐, *hwān lô ây sìm kwna ch'hám ch'hám, lēem kok ay pò gēak*, with a sorrowful mind, miserable and wretched, pondering over the oppressions of the country. See the 小雅 Seáou gnáy.

Ch'hám 朁 To meet with; past and done.

Ch'hám 磣 Sand mixed in food.

去

Ch'hàm 懺 Ch'hàm hwùy 懺悔, to repent, to regret exceedingly.

Ch'hàm 讖 Ch'hàm gé 讖語, a prophecy, a divination. Hoô ch'hàm 符讖, a charm.

平

Ch'hâm 慙 To be ashamed. Ch'hâm k'hwùy 慙愧, *sēāou-lēy*, to be ashamed of. Goê sīm ch'hâm ê Bēng-choó 吾甚慙於孟子, *gwá chin chaē seāou lēy ê Bēng-choó*, I feel very much ashamed before Bēng-choó.

Ch'hâm 慚 The same as the preceding.

Ch'hâm 嶄 Ch'hâm gâm 嶄嵒, a lofty and precipitous hill.

Ch'hâm 饞 To be greedy; to eat without being satisfied. Suy sit pat kéw, boô ch'hâm bêng 雖食八九無饞名, *suy chēāh pāyh kaôu hwān, yēá bô ch'ham chēāh ây mēnâ sēna*, although he eats eight or nine tenths, yet he has not the name of a glutton;—said of the sun, when the moon is eclipsed.

Ch'hâm 毚 A cunning rabbit. Yēak ch'hâm ch'hâm t'hoè, gē k'hēen hok che 躍躍毚兎. 遇犬獲之, *yēak ch'hâm ch'hâm ây t'hoè, toô tēōh kaóu, hoē e lēāh*, the cunning rabbit, frisking about, when he meets with a dog, is taken. See the 小雅 Séaou gnáy.

Ch'hâm 讒 To revile, to slander, to backbite. Gnó yéw kèng che, ch'hâm gân kê hin 我友敬之讒言其興, *gwà ây yèw tēōh sèy jē, saè p'hwà ây wā tit k'hè*, my friend you had better take care, slanderous accusations are about to arise. See the 小雅 Seáou gnáy.

Ch'han 孱 Weak, cowardly: goê ông ch'han ông yëá 吾王孱王也, gwán ây ông nootng ông, our king is a weak prince;—said of the king of the 趙 Tëō country.

Ch'han 僝 To rail at, to scold.

Ch'han 潺 The noise of water gently rippling along; the appearance of weeping. Sêng gwăt lōng ch'han wān 乘月弄潺湲, sêng göĕyh kwuing t'hit t'hó t'hēna chúy ây k'hwna k'hwna laôu, availing ourselves of the moon-shine, let us go and amuse ourselves with the slowly rippling water.

Ch'han 飡 To eat, to swallow. Wûy choó che koè, soó gnó put lêng ch'han hêy 爲子之故.使我不能飡兮, wûy lé ây yëĕn koè, saé gwá bēy chëăh, on your account, I am so-affected, that I cannot eat.

Ch'han 餐 A meal. Yit ch'han hwān 一餐飯, chit tooing pooing, a meal of rice. Bwán ch'han 晚餐, matng hwuing tooing, the evening meal; the Lord's supper.

Ch'hán 羼 A red colour; also, damp, moist.

Ch'hán 筅 Ch'hán chéw 筅帚, a duster. Ch'hán tok 筅棹, ch'hêng tŏh, to dust the table.

Ch'hàn 燦 Bright, clear. Ch'hàn lān 燦爛, handsome, elegant.

Ch'hàn 粲 Rice, food, victuals; elegant; clear.

Ch'hàn 璨 The brilliancy of a gem.

Ch'hàn 綻 The seam of a garment; to unloose.

Ch'hân 蠶 Vulg. ch'hâm: a silk worm. Gnoé boé che t'hek, sē che é song, p'hit hoō ch'hân che, chek ló chëá chëuk é è pek è 五畝之宅.樹之以桑.匹婦蠶之.則老者足以衣帛矣, goē boé ây t'hàyh, chèng e è seng, p'hit hoō ch'hē ch'hâm e, chëw laōu ây chëuk kaōu ch'hèng twān è, a tenement of five acres, if planted with the mulberry tree, and silk worms fed on it by a single woman, will enable the old people of a family to wear silk. See the 上孟 Sëang bēng.

Ch'hân 田 Read tëên: a field. Keng tëên 耕田, chŏh ch'hân, to cultivate the ground. 'E gnó kong tëên, sūy kip gnó soo 雨我公田.遂及我私, lŏh hoē tē gwá ây kong ch'hân, suy kip gwá ây sac k'hëa ch'hân, rain first upon our public field, and then let it come upon our private fields. See the 小雅 Seáou gnáy.

Ch'hang 葱 Read ch'hong: an onion. Kóey ch'hun yūng ch'hung 膾春用葱, chëăh bák ch'hun t'heeng yūng ch'hang, eating flesh in the spring season we should use onions with it. See the 禮記 Léy kè.

Ch'hang 聰 Read ch'hong: clear, intelligent Ch'hong bêng 聰明, ch'hang mêna, clever, intelligent.

Ch'háng 鬆 The hair dishevelled.

上去

Ch'hàng 鬈 Not straight, all in confusion.

下平

Ch'hâng 饞 Read ch'hông: fond of eating. Ch'hâm ch'hông 饞饞, *ch'hâm ch'hâng*, to be greedy.

上上

Ch'haou 鈔 To take; to copy, to transcribe; also written 抄 ch'haou.

Ch'haou 橾 To catch fish, with fishing stakes.

Ch'haou 繅 Filaments, thin threads. Hoo jîn ch'hân ch'haou, é wûy e hok 夫人蠶繅.以爲衣服, *hoo jîn yûng ch'hâm ây swⁿà, è chò sⁿa yîn chëóⁿᵍ*, women use the filaments spun by the silk worm, in order to make clothes.

Ch'haou 譟 To speak for, or on behalf of any one.

Ch'haou 勦 Ch'haou swat 勦說, to borrow expressions, to commit plagiarism. Boô ch'haou swat, boô lûy tông 毋勦說.毋雷同, *ûᵐ t'hang ch'haou söëyh, ûᵐ t'hang lûy tâng*, do not commit plagiarism, do not use tautology. See the 禮記 Léy kè.

Ch'haou 操 Read ch'ho: to hold in the hand; to exercise. Ch'ho lëën 操練, *ch'haou lëën*, to drill soldiers. Bē lêng ch'ho to, jê soó kat, sëën put paē è, 未能操刀而使割.鮮不敗矣, *böëy ēy ch'haou to, jê saé kwăh meëⁿh, chëó ûᵐ paē*, if though unable to handle a knife, a person be set to cut any thing, it is seldom that he will not spoil the work.

上去

Ch'háou 炒 Vulg. *ch'há*: to fry, to cook any thing without water.

Ch'háou 謅 To joke with pleasing words; to whisper; to disturb.

Ch'háou 䫨 A wry face, a crooked mouth.

Ch'háou 草 Read ch'hó: grass. Sit ch'hó 食草, *chëăh ch'háou*, to eat grass. Sòng tëy chè Chëang-chew sé soō, pek ch'hó kae hwa 宋帝至漳州試士.百草皆花, *Sòng ây tèy kaòu Chëang-chew ch'hē thak ch'häyh ây lâng, chēⁿâ päyh ch'háou chò poô k'hwuy hwa*, when the emperor of the Sòng dynasty came to Chëang-chew, to examine the scholars, hundreds of plants all put forth their flowers.

去去

Ch'hàou 笊 Ch'hàou lê 笊篱, a strainer for rice, made of wicker work.

Ch'hàou 臭 Read hèw: stinking, rotten, ill-flavoured. Hèw ok put sit 臭惡不食, *ch'hàou p'haⁿē bô böëyh chëăh*, the stinking and bad he would not eat;—said of Confucius.

Ch'hàou 湊 To square accounts, to pay up all differences.

上入

Ch'hap 插 To stick in, to pierce. Ch'hē ch'hap 刺插, to stick in, to thrust.

Ch'hap 偛 Ch'hap tëep 偛僁, a little person, a dwarf.

Ch'hap 剒 The noise of slicing any thing.

Ch'hap 賐 Ch'hap paê 賐牌, to shuffle cards.

Ch'hap 鍤 A needle, a pick-axe, a crow-bar.

Ch'hap 歃 Ch'hap hëet 歃血, *ch'hap hoĕyh,* to draw blood, in order to confirm an oath. Kwûy-k'hew che höëy, choo hoê sok seng chaê se, jê put ch'hap hëet 葵丘之會.諸侯束牲載書.而不歃血, *Kwûy-k'hew ây höëy, choo hoê pak t'haôu sai^ng, chaè bĕng se, jê bô ch'hap höëyh,* at the assembly of Kwûy-k'hew, the princes of the empire tied up the victim, and brought the sworn contract, without drawing their blood in confirmation. See the 下孟 Hāy bēng.

Ch'hap 扱 To receive, to obtain, to lead, to commence.

Ch'hap 唼 Many words, garrulity, chattering. Ch'hap ch'hap káng 唼唼講, *ch'hap ch'hap kóng,* to chatter.

夭

Ch'hat 察 To examine, to search, to inquire into. Kong taē, chöëy sëaôu, put bông bêng ch'hat 功大罪小.不蒙明察, *kong lô twā, chöëy k'hăh sèy, böëy woô bông bêng ch'hat,* my merit has been great, and my fault trivial, only I have not had the advantage of a clear examination;—said by 李陵 Lé-lêng.

Ch'hat gân jê kwan sek 察言而觀色, *sêng ch'hat lâng ây wā, jê k'hw^nà e ây bīn sek,* examine a man's words, and survey his countenance.

Ch'hat 刹 A pillar, a flag-staff; also, a pagoda. Lëet ch'hat sëang bông 列刹相望, *chē^nà lëet ke t'hëāou, sëo bōng,* a row of pillars opposite to each other.

Ch'hat 橴 The name of a tree; the sound of waving trees and grass.

Ch'hat 詧 To speak slowly, and personally examine any thing.

Ch'hat 擦 To rub, to rub out, to blot out.

Ch'hat 漆 Read ch'hip: the name of a stream; also, a kind of varnish, paint. Soò ch'hip 使漆 *saè ch'hat,* to paint, to varnish.

天

Ch'hat 賊 Read chek: a thief. Chò chek 做賊, *chò ch'hat,* to turn thief. Haē chek 海賊, *haē ch'hat,* a pirate. Hoē chek 厚賊, *kaōu ch'hat,* full of thieves. Yèw jê put sūn tēy, tëáng jê hoô sut yëen, ló jê put soó, sē wûy chek 幼而不孫弟.長而無述焉.老而不死.是爲賊, *sedou lëén jê bô sūn tēy, twā hàn jê bô hwat sut, laoū jê bēy sè, sē kóng këò ch'hat,* in youth not to act the part of a grandson or younger brother; in riper years, not to have any settled employment; and in old age not to be (fit for) death; he who is such is no better than a thief.

幸

Ch'hay 差 Wrong, erroneous, uneven; to send on a message. Ch'hay che hô lê, bëw é ch'heen lé 差之毫釐.謬以千里, *ch'hay chit hô chit lê, bëw kàou chit ch'heng lê,* varying (at first) but the down of a feather, it may differ (at length) a thousand lé.

Ch'hay soó 差使, *ch'hay saè,* to send on an errand.

Ch'hay 叉 The hands folded together, and intertwined; also, to take.

Ch'hay 恅 Ch'hay chèy 恅憏, unfixed, unsettled in mind.

Ch'hay 杈 The outer branches of a tree.

Ch'hay 傑 Uneven.

Ch'hay 扠 To take under the arm.

声

Ch'háy 侘 Young, proud, at ease.

去

Ch'hày 吒 To be angry, to speak in anger; also written 咤 Ch'háy.

Ch'hày 詫 To boast, to deceive. Chëet jîu, böéy gāy teâou soó, pit lëet poē k'hê, é choō k'hwa ch'hày 浙人每迓朝使.必列步騎.以自誇詫, *Chëet-kang ây lâng, tak pâe gāy cheĕh teâou têng ây soó chĕá, pit paê lëet poē kĕ^{n}â kap k'hëâ bây ây peng, è ka tē k'hwa ch'hày*, the people of Chëet-kang, whenever they go to meet a messenger from the court, insist on drawing out their horse and foot soldiers, in order to boast and make a shew.

Ch'hày 厠 A privy; mixed, impure. Lȯk ch'hày 落厠, *lŏh ch'hày*, to go to stool.

Ch'hày 瘥 A sickness; also, recovery from sickness.

Ch'hày 嗄 A brokenness of voice; the voice broken and lost.

Ch'hày 脆 Brittle, easily broken, infirm.

平

Ch'hây 查 To examine minutely. Ch'hây k'hó 查考, to search and enquire. Chāy kwan kê jîu, chek sûn jê yëá; sèy ch'hây kê sim, chek kaón jê yëá 乍覩其人.則恂如也.細查其心.則狡如也, *tut jëên k'hw^{n}à e ây lâng, chek ch'hin chëō^{ng} sûn sit; sëâng sèy ch'hây e ây sim, chek ch'hin chëō^{ng} kaóu kwat*, on just seeing the man, he appeared honest and sincere; but on narrowly examining his heart, he appeared cunning and deceitful.

去

Ch'hāy 嚌 The noise of a multitude.

Ch'hāy 坐 Read chō. Chō h^{n}ò 坐貨, *ch'hāy hōèy*, to forestall goods, to buy up a quantity, in order to raise the price.

入

Ch'hăyh 冊 Read ch'hek: a book, a record. Se ch'hek séy ch'haè, kae sèng hëên che bêng gân yëá 書冊所載.皆聖賢之名言也, *se ch'hăyh sèy chaè, chò poó sē sèng jîn gâou lâng ây bêng wā*, the things contained in the books and records, are altogether famous sayings of philosophers and clever men.

Ch'hăyh 慼 Read ch'hek: sorrowful. Song léy ché yaòu ae t'hòng ch'hám ch'hek 喪禮只要哀痛慘慼, *se^{ng} hà ây lèy soè, chè lëŏh ae t'hë^{n}à ch'hám ch'hăyh*, in funeral obsequies, it is only requisite to feel anguish and sorrow of heart.

Ch'hăyh 撮 Read ch'hwat: a handful. Kim hoo tēy, yit ch'hwat t'hoé che to 今夫地一撮土之多, *t^{n}a* *chēy lēy lēy, chit ch'hăyh t'hoê ây chēy*, now the whole earth is merely a handful of ground. See the 中庸 Tëung yûng.

岽

Ch'he 睢 To lift up the eyes, to look full at any thing; to look angry. Ch'he-yâng 睢陽, the name of a district. T'hëen ch'he 天睢, the name of a star. Sometimes confounded with 雎 Ch'he.

Ch'he 雎 The name of a water bird, reputed for its fidelity to its mate. Kwan kwan ch'he k'hew, chaē hô che chew 關關雎鳩.在河之洲, *kwan kwan haôu ây, ch'he k'hew, twā tē hô ây chew*, the cooing turtle doves, dwelling in an island of the river. See the 詩經 Se keng.

Ch'he 且 To introduce; to walk slowly, without advancing; also, an expletive.

Ch'he 疽 Yung ch'he 癰疽, a sore, an ulcer. Chut yéw pēng ch'he cheă, K'hé wûy wún che 卒有病疽者.起爲吮之, *peng chut woō paing ch'heng ây lâng, K'hé taē kap e chwuīng*, when any of his soldiers had a sore or an ulcer, K'hé would suck it for them;—said of Goê-k'hé 吳起, who had such a love for his soldiers, that he would do any thing for them.

Ch'he 狙 A kind of monkey; to wait in order to find an advantage against any. Lëâng é K'hek ch'he kek Sé-hông 良與客狙擊始皇, *Lëâng kap K'hek têng haôu bōēyh p'hăh Sé-hông*, Lëâng and K'hek waited for an opportunity of attacking Sé-hông. See the 史記 Soó kè.

Ch'he 沮 The name of a river. Ch'he-tëong 沮中, the name of a place.

Ch'he 蛆 Chek ch'he 蝍蛆, a centipede; also called, goê kong 蜈蚣, *gëâ kang*. Chek ch'he sit sëâ, sëâ sit wâ, wâ sit chek ch'he, hoē sëang sit yëâ 蝍蛆食蛇.蛇食蛙.蛙食蝍蛆.互相食也, *gëâ kang chëăh chwâ, chwâ chëăh kap, á, kap á chëăh gëâ kang*, the centipede kills the snake, the snake eats the toad, and the toad poisons the centipede; thus they devour one another.

Ch'he 苴 A kind of hemp, without seeds: also, the name of a grass.

Ch'he 砠 A clay mound covered with stones; difficult of ascent.

Ch'he 䏣 The neck.

Ch'he 菹 Marshy ground, overgrown with grass. K'he sëâ lëûng jê hóng che ch'he 驅蛇龍而放之菹. *kwnă chwâ lëûng jê hây lē chúy lek*, he drove away the snakes and dragons, and sent them into the marshes. See 孟子 Bēng-choó.

Ch'he 胆 A fly-blow; the eggs of flies laid in raw meat.

Ch'he 伬 The same with the following.

Ch'he 癡 Foolish, unwise, simple; also, sick

Ch'he 雌 The female of birds. Tông kwat ch'he hëûng 同决雌雄, *kap lâng kwat ch'he hëûng*, to try one's strength with any one;—literally, to see which is the man and which the woman.
Sûy te oe che ch'he hëûng 誰知烏之雌雄, *chē chûy chae oe á ây kang boé*, who knows the male and female of the crow? See the 小雅 Seáou gnáy.

2 A

Ch'he 鴟 Ch'he heaou 鴟鴞, a bird of prey.

Ch'he 雛 A chicken; an animal that can eat as soon as it is born.

Ch'he 趨 To walk fast, to go quickly. Këèn lē pit ch'he, këèn haē pit pē 見利必趨.見害必避, *k'hw^{n}à woō lē pit tëŏh kin kē^{n}â, k'hw^{n}à woō haē pit tëŏh sëèm pee^{ng}*, seeing an advantage, you should hasten towards it, and seeing a danger, you should avoid it.

Ch'he 嗤 To laugh.

Ch'he 媸 Ugly. Gëên ch'he 妍媸, handsome, and ugly. Jê kàm che chëāou but, gëên ch'he chaē pé 如鑑之照物.妍媸在彼, *ch'hin chëō^{ng} kē^{n}à ây chëò meē^{n}h, ch'hin ch'hai^{ng} k'hëep sē tē hé taou*, like as when a mirror reflects things, the handsome and the ugly are there (faithfully represented).

Ch'he 差 An order, a series. Ch'ham ch'he put chêy 参差不齊, mixed, uneven.

Kok yéw téng ch'he 各有等差, *kok woō têng ch'he*, each one according to order.

Ch'he 觿 A vessel for holding wine.

Ch'he 嵯 Ch'ham ch'he 嵾嵯, the uneven appearance of hills.

Ch'he 髭 To collect.

Ch'he 蚩 An insect; also, stupid, foolish. Ch'he-yêw 蚩尤, the name of a country. Bîn che ch'he ch'he 氓之蚩蚩, *păyh sai^{ng} ây gaē gaē*, the stupid mob.

Ch'he 趄 Walking slowly, without being able to get forward.

Ch'he 瘀 Sickly; not thriving.

声

Ch'hé 取 To take, to lay hold on, to require, to receive. Vulg. *t'hăyh.* Loé-tëūng-lëên wūy jîn paê lân, kaé hwun, jê boô ch'hé 魯仲連爲人排難解紛.而無取, *Loé-tëūng-lëên kăh lâng paê k'hwuy kan lân, t'hâou ch'hut hwân lwān ây soō, jê bô bōĕyh t'hăyh ch'hee^{ng}*, Loé-tëūng-lëên used to dissolve difficulties, and disentangle confused matters, for people, without taking any money. See the 史記 Soó kè.

Ch'hé 侈 Extravagant; great, large. Hòng p'hek sëâ ch'hé, boô put wûy é 放僻邪侈無不爲已, *lâm sâm chò, kwà ch'hëa ch'hè, bô sèy ū^{m} k^{n}â*, dissolute and extravagant, and sticking at nothing. See the 上孟 Sëāng bēng.

Ch'hé 傑 Ch'hé te 傑傂, uneven.

Ch'hé 杵 A pestle. Kēw ch'hé 臼杵, *koō ch'hè*, a pestle and mortar. Chim ch'he 砧杵, *tëem ch'hè*, a stick with which washer-men beat clothes.

Ch'hé 處 To dwell, to rest in, to take up an abode. Tek put ch'hé jîn, yëen tek tè 擇不處仁.焉得知, *kân tŏh sò chaē, bô twā tē jîn ây wūy, bōĕyh an chw^{n}á ēy tit chò tè*, if in selecting a residence, a man does not fix upon a virtuous neighbourhood, how can he be considered wise? See the 上論 Sëāng lūn.

Put é kê tō tek che, put ch'hé yëá 不以其道得之.不處也, *bô chëàou e ây*

福建方言字典

tō tit tëöh, bô böëyh ch'hè twā tē e, anything not obtained according to the right way, (the good man) does not rest in.

Ch'hé 齒 Vulg. k'hé: the teeth. K'hoé ch'hé 口齒, *ch'hùy k'hé*, the teeth of the mouth; also, age. Tûn bông ch'hé hân 唇亡齒寒, *tûn bô, ch'hùy k'hè kwⁿâ*, when the lips are gone, the teeth will get cold,—(meaning, that without good neighbours, men are likely to fail).
T'hëen hāy yéw tat chun sam, chëak yit, ch'hé yit, tek yit 天下有達尊三. 爵一. 齒一. 德一, *t'heeⁿᵍ āy oō tat chun sⁿa hāng, chëak wūy chit hāng, ch'hùy k'hé chit hāng, tek hêng chit hāng*, there are three things much honoured and preferred under Heaven; one of which is office,—another, age,—and another, virtue. See 孟子 Bēng-choó.

Ch'hé 鼠 A mouse. Lô ch'hé 老鼠, *neaou ch'hé*, a rat. Ch'hé pōëy 鼠輩, you rats! Gé kwuy hëën tê súy, ch'hé tō teng kày yëw 蟻窺硯池水. 鼠盜燈架油, *hëā k'hwⁿā hëeⁿᵍ k'hwut â āy chúy, nëaou ch'hè t'haou teng kày āy yëw*, the ant peeps at the water in the hollow of the ink-stone, and the rat steals the oil in the stand of the lamp.

Ch'hè 癙 Sick and sad; also, a sick mouse.

去

Ch'hè 娶 To marry. Ch'hè ch'hey 娶妻, *ch'hwà boé*, to marry a wife. Ch'hè ch'hey jê hô, hwuy böëy put tek 娶妻如何. 匪媒不得, *ch'hwà boé an chwⁿá, bô hâᵐ lâng bēy chò tit*, how must we act in marrying a wife? without a mediator it will not do. See the 國風 Kok hong.

Ch'hè 佁 Congealed; not flowing; a hindrance in the way, preventing progress.

Ch'hè 傺 To stop, to cease from.

Ch'hè 切 Many. Yit ch'hè 一切, altogether, in general. Also read Ch'hëet.

Ch'hè 砌 The stones by the side of steps. Also written 磜 Ch'hè. Lëûk ch'hó bwân kae ch'hè 綠草滿階砌, *lëk ch'hâou mwⁿâ gīm kay āy ch'hè*, the green grass covers the stones of the steps.

Ch'hè 朿 The thorns of a tree.

Ch'hè 刺 To pierce, to stab,—either with a weapon or by words; to ridicule. Ko sëang ch'hé é ch'hè ke, hoô sè k'hew é sëûng bé 歌相鼠以刺譏. 賦鳲鳩以頌美, *ch'hëāⁿᵍ sëang ch'hè āy se, ē ch'hè ke lâng,—lëëm se k'hew āy hoô, ē o lô lâng*, recite "the mouse" ode in order to ridicule men; and repeat "the dove" ditty, in order to praise people.

Ch'hè 莿 A thorn, a prickle; as sharp as a needle.

Ch'hè 鰶 The name of a fish.

Ch'hè 趣 To go towards; the mind tending towards any thing. 'E ch'hè 意趣, intention.
Pleasant. Gân yéw ch'hè bē 言有趣味, *kóng wā woō ch'hè bē*, pleasant discourse.
Ch'hè hëàng put tông, séy wûy ek ē 趣向不同. 所爲亦異, *ch'hè hëàng bô sëo tâng, sëy chò yëá kòh yëōⁿᵍ*, when the tendency

of people's minds are dissimilar, their conduct will also differ.

Ch'hè 熾 The flaming up of fire. Hⁿó che ch'hè, put k'hó p'hok bëet 火之熾不可撲滅, *höëy ây ông ch'hè, bô t'hang p'hăh hwa*, a fire, when blazing up, cannot easily be quenched.

Ch'hè 饎 Wine and food.

Ch'hè 處 A place. Hô ch'hè 何處, *sⁿa meëⁿh wăy*, what place? where? Also written 処 ch'hè.

K'hëuk kèng t'hong yew ch'hè, sëên pông sëūng ch'hàm sê 曲徑通幽處.禪房誦讖時, *wan k'hëuk ây loē t'hong kaòu yew àm ây wăy, höëy sëōⁿᵍ pâng tit lëëm ch'hàm ây sé*, a crooked path leads to dark places, and when in a monk's chamber we should recite prayers.

Ch'hè 翅 A wing, a pinion. Tëang lëáng ch'hè yeá 張兩翅也, *tëoⁿᵍ nō ây sit*, spreading both its wings.

Ch'hè 試 Read sè: to try, to prove. Sè k'hàn 試看, *ch'hè k'hwⁿà*, to make a trial.

Gnó suy put bín, ch'héng sëâng sè che 我雖不敏.請嘗試之, *gwá súy bô chaē teāou, ch'hëⁿà ch'hè k'hwⁿà e*, although I am not clever, yet I beg you to try me.

平

Ch'hê 徐 Slow, gentle; to walk slowly; a surname. Ch'heng hong ch'hê laê 清風徐來, *ch'heng ây hong k'hwⁿa k'hwⁿa â laê*, the pure wind gently approaching.

Ch'hê 伹 Dull, stupid.

去

Ch'hē 市 A market. Kay ch'hē 街市, in the streets and markets. Koe chéw ch'hē hoó, put sit 沽酒市脯不食, *báy ây chéw, kay ch'hē ây băh, ūᵐ chëăh*, vintner's wine and market flesh, Confucius would not eat; (lest it should be unclean or injurious). See the 論語 Lūn gé.

Ch'hē 飼 Read soō: to feed, to give food, to bring up. Soō ch'hân t'hew se 飼蠶抽絲, *ch'hē ch'hâm t'hew swⁿà* to feed silk worms and spin the silk. Soō te 飼猪, *ch'hē te*, to keep pigs.

上

Ch'hëa 車 Read ke: a carriage. Mā ke 馬車, *báy ch'hëa*, a carriage drawn by horses. A surname.

Hông-tèy chok ke, yin tēūng tè wán, Sëáou-hō kay gnêw, chè Hêy-tëūng sê kay mā 黃帝作車.引重致遠.少昊加牛.至奚仲時加馬, *Wuīⁿᵍ-tèy chò ch'hëa, yin lāng tè hwuīⁿᵍ ây meēⁿh, Seáou-hō kay goô, chè kàou Hêy-tëāng ây sè kay báy*, Wuīⁿᵍ-tèy (B. C. 2622) first invented carriages, to carry heavy things, and convey them to a distance; Seáou-hō (B. C. 2538) added buffaloes; and in the time of Hêy-tëūng (B. C. 2142) they used horses. See the 古史 Koé soó.

Ch'hëa 硨 Ch'hëa kê 硨磲, a kind of stone, nearly resembling a gem.

Ch'hëa 奢 Extravagant, wasteful; stretched out, immense. Ch'hëa chek put sùn, k'hëëm chek koè 奢則不孫.儉則固, *ch'hëa ch'hè chēw ūᵐ sùn, sëoⁿᵍ k'hëëm chēw koè loē*, from being too extravagant, a man becomes careless; and from being too parsimonious, he becomes vulgar;—said by Confucius, who added, nevertheless vulgarity is better than carelessness.

声

Ch'hēá 偖 To tear open.

Ch'hēá 哆 To open the mouth wide.

Ch'hēá 灺 The snuff of a candle, the ashes of incense; also written 炨 Ch'hēá.

去

Ch'hēà 痄 To be purged; a dysentery; the same as 瀉 sēà.

去

Ch'hēna 磋 A stone.

Ch'hēna 笪 *Bēeh ch'hēna* 篾笪, a splinter of wood or bamboo; to run against.

声

Ch'hēná 且 Also, moreover; just, merely. Koé ch'hēná 苟且, disordely, careless. Koe ch'hēná 姑且, merely, just then, for a time.

Ch'hēná t'hëen che seng but yëá, soó che yit pún 且天之生物也.使之一本, *ch'hēná t'heeng ây saing mëënh, saé hoë e chit ây kin pún*, moreover heaven in its producing all things, gave them but one origin. See 孟子 Bēng-choó.

Ch'hēná 請 Read ch'héng: to invite, to beg, to request, to greet. Boē tēy put ch'héng 墓地不請, *bōng têy bó ch'hēná lâng chëăh*, at cemeteries, do not invite people to eat.

Kim sēng ê é kày ê, yéw soo bē te séy che, kám ch'héng 今乘輿已駕矣.有司未知所之.敢請, *tna bây ch'hëa ê kwà bây, yëw soo ây kwna bōëy chae sëy k'he ây wūy, kna ch'hēnà*, now the carriage is got ready, but the officer in attendance does not know where he is to go; I beg therefore to enquire. See 孟子 Bēng-choó.

去

Ch'hēnà 趄 Read k'hin: to stand awry; to walk lame.

Ch'hēnà 倩 Read ch'hèng: to hire, to employ, as a labourer. Boô chëên kọè ch'hēnà 無錢僱倩, *k'nám sē bó cheeng ch'hēnà*, just as if we had no money to hire them with;—said of work-people, when they are lazy, and neglect their duty.

平

Ch'hēnâ 成 Sêng but 成物, *ch'hēnâ mëënh*, to adjust anything that is awry.

入

Ch'hëăh 赤 Read ch'hek: red, a reddish brown colour; also, sincere. Ch'hek sim pò kok 赤心報國, *ch'hëăh sim pò kok*, to serve one's country with a sincere heart.

Ch'hëăh 刺 Read ch'hè: to prick, to pierce through. Ch'hè sèw, t'hëem gnoé bûn 刺繡添五文, *ch'hëăh sèw, t'heeng gōe têâou twnà*, "in working the embroidery, five threads were added." The ancient ladies added one thread to their embroidery, each day after the winter solstice; so that when five were added, it was of course five days after mid-winter; hence the poets used this expression; as an elegant way of designating time. See the 唐詩 Tông se.

入

Ch'hëăh 柰 *Yëw ch'hëăh* 油柰, oil cake,—something used in the manufacture of oil.

2 B

六

Ch'hëak 鵲 A felicitous bird. Hé ch'hëak 喜鵲, a bird of joy; also called, kan ch'hëak 乾鵲, the dry bird, from its abhorrence of damp.

Ch'hëak 雀 Vulg. *chäyh á*: a sparrow; said to be the most lascivious of birds. Süy wüy ch'hëak boô kak, hô é ch'hwàn gnó ok 誰謂雀無角,何以穿我屋, *chē chūy á kàng chäyh bô kak, an chw^n á ëy ch'hui^ng gwá äy. ch'hoó*, who says that the sparrow has no horns, — see how it has bored through my house. See the 國風 Kok hong.

Ch'hëak 碏 To respect; a stumbling-stone; also, the variegated colour of stones.

Ch'hëak 綽 Slowly, leisurely, easily. K'hwan ch'hëak 寬綽, gentle and easy. Chek gôe chìn t'höey, k'hé put ch'hëak ch'hëak jëên 則吾進退豈不綽綽然, *chek gwá chìn kap t'hëy, k'hé ū^m ch'hëak ch'hëak jëên*, thus my entering on, or retiring from office, how is it not free and unrestrained. See the 下孟 Häy bëng.

Ch'hëak 皵 Vulg. *lëëh*: a little rising of the skin; a wrinkling of the skin.

Ch'hëak 趞 To walk and stop, by fits and starts; to walk quickly.

韋

Ch'hëang 昌 Full, flourishing; also, good words. A surname. E' paé ch'heang gân 禹拜昌言, *E' paè hó äy wā*, E' bowed when he heard good words. See the 尙書 Sëō^ng se.

Ch'hëang 鯧 Ch'heang gê 鯧魚, *ch'hëo^ng á hé*, the pomfret fish.

Ch'hëang 鏘 The sound of metal and gems.

Ch'hëang 槍 A stick, sharpened at both ends, and used in repelling thieves.

Ch'hëang 倡 Ch'hëang yew 倡優, a female musician, a dancing girl.

Ch'hëang 猖 Ch'hëang kông 猖狂, extravagant and mad; rude and boisterous. Hô Këet Tëw che ch'hëang k'höëy 何桀紂之猖獗, *an chw^n á Këet Tëw äy ch'hëang k'höëy*, how wild and wicked were Këet and Tëw!

Ch'hëang 娼 A prostitute. *Ch'hëang bú*, 娼媌, a whore. Ch'hëang choó 娼子, *ch'hëang kë^n á*, a whoreson.

Ch'hëang 菖 Ch'hëang poê 菖蒲, a water plant.

Ch'hëang 閶 Ch'hëang k'hap 閶闔, the door of heaven.

Ch'hëang 鎗 The sound of a bell; a spear, a lance. Ch'hé ch'hëang 取鎗, *k'hëäh ch'hëo^ng*, to grasp a spear. Tëâng ch'hëang twán këëm, chëën chîn t'hëen häy béng chëäng 長鎗短劒,戰盡天下猛將, *të^ng ch'hëo^ng téy këëm, chëën swäh t'hee^ng äy äy bëng chëäng*, with a long spear and a short sword, we may contend to the utmost with all the fiercest generals in the empire. See the 兵書 Peng se.

Ch'hëang 倀 Ch'hëang kông 倀狂, to wander crazily about, without knowing whither.

Koê chëá boô sëäng, ch'hëang ch'hëang hoë, kë hô che 瞽者無相、倀倀乎其

何之, *ch'hai^{ng} mai^{ng} ây lâng, bó lâng tëo^{ng} e, chëw ch'hëang ch'hëang hoê, böëyh tăh lŏh k'hè,* a blind man, without a leader, wandering wildly about, where will he go? See the 禮記 Lêy kè.

Ch'hëang kwúy 倀鬼, an evil spirit; the soul of a person devoured by a tiger, which does not dare to quit the tiger, till it has led him to devour another person.

Ch'hëang 將 The noise of tinkling ornaments, hanging about a person.

上

Ch'hëáng 倘 To stop suddenly. Yin chëang hëen che, ch'hëáng jëen chê 雲將見之.倘然止, *hwûn chëang böëyh hëen e, ch'hëáng jëen hây^{n}h,* the clouds were about to appear, when suddenly they staid.

Ch'hëáng 儆 Liberal, gentle.

Ch'hëáng 敞 High, lofty; also, to open out, to discover. Hân-sin hêng êng, ko ch'hëáng têy 韓信行營高敞地, *Hân-sin këng ëng, tē kwân ch'hëáng ây têy,* Hân-sin commenced building his residence, on high and lofty ground.

Ch'hëáng 惝 Wicked, evil.

Ch'hëáng 昶 A long day; also, clear,—clearly perceived.

Ch'hëáng 廠 Vulg. *ch'hëó^{ng}*: a shed without walls.

Ch'hëáng 搶 To snatch, to take by force, to plunder. Ch'hëáng jîn 搶人, *ch'hëó^{ng} lâng,* to plunder people.

Pek tëw ch'hëáng twat 白晝搶奪 *pâyh jit ch'hëó^{ng} t'hŭyh,* plunder in the open day.

Ch'hëáng 氅 Bird's feathers; feathers plucked from birds, to make garments, and ornament flags.

Ông-këung chëak hok ch'hëáng 王恭着鶴氅, *Ông-këung ch'hèng hŏh mô ây s^{n}a;* Ông-këung wore a garment made of stork's feathers.

去

Ch'hëàng 倡 To harmonize, to agree with. Ch'hëàng hô 倡和, harmonious.

Ch'hëàng 唱 To sing; also, to lead, to introduce. Ch'hëàng k'hëuk 唱曲, *ch'hëò^{ng} k'hek,* to sing songs.

Yit ch'hëàng jê sam t'hàn 一唱而三嘆, *chit ây ch'hëò^{ng}, jê s^{n}a kwùy t'hàou k'hwùy,* when once he sang, (the bystanders) thrice applauded. See the 禮記 Lêy kè.

Kwan sëâng ch'hëàng choō Hông-têy 冠裳唱自黄帝, *kin yîn chëó^{ng} k'hè t'haôu choō Wui^{ng}-têy,* caps and clothes were first introduced by Wui^{ng}-têy (B. C. 2622).

Ch'hëàng 昶 Clear, bright.

平

Ch'hëâng 場 A field where grain is gathered; a barn floor.

Ch'hëâng 償 To pay, to make good. Ch'hëâng bēng 償命, to forfeit one's life.

Chùn-put-gê wûy lông, hek goē tê tông sëà lông kim k'hè; tông sëà lông ê Put-gê, Put-gê maé kim ch'hëâng che 儁不疑爲郎.或誤持同舍郎金去.同舍郎意不疑.不疑買金償之, when Chùn-put-gê was in office, some person (intending to steal from him) took away the gold of his fellow-lodger by mistake; the fellow-lodger suspected Put-gê, wherefore Put-gê bought some gold, and made it good to him.

Ch'hëâng 場 An arena, or public field. Chëën ch'hëâng 戰場, *chëën t'hëô^ng*, a field of battle. K'hó ch'hëâng 考場, *k'hó t'hëô^ng*, a place of public examination. Toé ch'hëâng 賭場, *këáou t'hëô^ng*, a place for gambling.

Ch'hëâng 戕 To cut, to injure. Ch'hëâng chek 戕賊, to hack and injure.

Ch'hëâng 嬙 Pīn ch'hëâng 嬪嬙, the name of an office held by females.

Ch'hëâng 腸 The bowels, the entrails. Taē ch'hëâng 大腸, *twā tĕ^ng*, the great gut. Ch'hëâng yëük twān 腸欲斷, *tĕ^ng á bōëyh toōï^ng*, "the entrails about to snap asunder;" meaning that a person is greatly affected with grief or anger, or that his heart is ready to burst.

Ch'hëâng 牆 A wall. Pwân ch'hëâng 蹣牆, *pw^nâ ch'hëô^ng*, to climb over a wall. Hwùn t'hoé che ch'hëâng put k'hó woo yëá 糞土之牆不可杇也, *pùn t'hôe ây ch'hëô^ng bô t'hang bwăh pāyh*, a wall made of dung and mud cannot well be white washed.

Ch'hëâng 墻 The same as the preceding.

Ch'hëâng 薔 Ch'hëâng bê hwa 薔薇花, *ch'hëô^ng bê hwa*, a rose.

Ch'hëâng 檣 Chûn ch'hëâng 船檣, the mast of a ship or boat.

去

Ch'hëâng 匠 A mechanic. Bŏk ch'hëâng 木匠, *bak ch'hëô^ng*, a carpenter. Ch'hëâng jîn ch'hok jê sëáou che, chek ông noē, ó wûy put sin kê jīm è 匠人斲而小之則王怒以爲不勝其任矣, *kang ch'hëâng ây lâng ch'hak jê ch'hòng k'hah sèy e, chëw ông sëw k'hè, yin wûy bëy sin e ây jīm*, if the work-people were to chisel (the timber), and make it too small, your majesty would be angry, thinking it insufficient to bear its weight. See the 上孟 Sëâng bêng.

Ch'hëâng 趙 Ch'hëâng këak hêng 趙脚行, *ch'hëâng k'ha kë^nâ*, to hop, to limp.

平

Ch'hëaou 鍬 Hwa ch'heaou 花鍬, *hwa ch'hëo*, a spade.

Ch'hëaou 搜 Read soe: to search, to look for, to seek after. Hwat sam hoô k'hê soō, taē sóe san lîm 發三輔騎士大搜山林, *hwat s^na hoō k'hê soō, twā ch'hëaou sw^na lîm*, he sent out three sets of horsemen, who fully searched the hills and woods.

上

Ch'hëáou 愀 Sorrowful, discomposed, displeased; to change colour. Ch'hëáou jëên chok sek 愀然作色, *ch'hëáou jëên peē^ng sek*, being displeased, he changed countenance.

Ch'hëáou 眧 To signify any thing by the eyes; to cast sheep's eyes.

Ch'hëáou 僺 Ch'hëáou gëâou 僺僥, tall in person.

Ch'hëáou 悄 Sorrowful, hasty, still. Yew sim ch'hëáou ch'hëáou 憂心悄悄, *hwân lô ây sim kwⁿa ch'hëáou ch'hëáou*, a sorrowful mind, discomposed and sad.

去

Ch'hëàou 笑 Vulg. *ch'hëò*: to laugh, to be pleased, to shew the teeth. Hⁿó ch'hëàou 好笑, *hò ch'hëò*, laughable. Këèn ch'hëàou 見笑, *këèn sëàou*, contemptible.

Boô ch'hëáng taē ch'hëàou 撫掌大笑, *kwăh ch'hêw chëóⁿᵍ twā ch'hëò*, he clapped his hands and laughed aloud.—Also written 关 Ch'hëàou.

Ch'hëàou 俏 Handsome, good-looking.

Ch'hëàou 偢 Not benevolent, not well-disposed, malevolent.

Ch'hëàou 嘯 To pipe with the mouth, to whistle; also written 歗 Ch'hëàou.

Ch'hëàou 鞘 A scabbard. To ch'hëàou 刀鞘, *to sëò*, the sheath of a sword. Chô-ch'hò kaé ch'hëàou hoò Poè 曹操解鞘付布, *Chô-ch'hò t'háou sëò hoē Poè*, Chô-ch'hò loosened the scabbard and gave it to Poè. See the 三國 Sam-kok.

平

Ch'hëâou 勦 To cut.

Ch'hëâou 愀 The changing of the countenance.

Ch'hëâou 稍 To walk further apart.

2 c

Ch'hëâou 譙 Ch'hin ch'hëâou 親譙, to bargain, to come near to one another's prices.

Ch'hëâou keng ko 譙更高, *ch'hëâou k'hăh kwân*, to get up the price; to raise the value of any thing.

入

Ch'hëaŏuh 踥 To walk backwards and forwards. Ch'hëaŏuh ch'hëaŏuh tëŏ, to dandle up and down.

Ch'hëaŏuh 箣 Slips of bamboo, with which they beat time, whilst singing songs.

入

Ch'hëaŏuh 踿 To approach, to come near.

入

Ch'hëĕh 頧 Read bûn: to bow down the head, to stoop.

入

Ch'hëĕh 蠘 A kind of craw-fish.

平

Ch'hëem 僉 All, the whole; the universal voice, all speaking.

Ch'hëem 籤 Slips of bamboo, used in prognosticating. T'hew ch'hëem 抽籤, to draw lots, to prognosticate.

Ch'hëem 簽 Ch'hëem se 簽書, a letter, a writing. Ch'hëem bêng 簽名, *ch'hëem mëⁿâ*, to sign one's name.

Ch'hëem 襜 A lap, the front lap of a garment: also, even, regular. Chëung tëaou ch'haé lâm, puĭ êng yit ch'hëem 終朝采藍.不盈一襜, *chit măyⁿh chaē k'hëŏh lâm, bô mwⁿâ chit ch'hëem*, all the morning busy in gathering the indigo plant, without getting a single lap-full.

E chëên hoē ch'hëem jê yëá 衣前後襜如也, *s^{n}a chêng aōu pai^{ng} chèng*, his garment was of an even length before and behind.

Ch'hëem 殲 To exterminate. Ch'hëem k'hwat kê k'höey 殲厥渠魁, *ch'hëem bëet e ây twā t'haōu lâng*, he exterminated their great chief.

Ch'hëem 笘 Slips of bamboo.

Ch'hëem 幨 The curtain of a carriage: also, to exterminate.

声

Ch'hëém 槧 Square pieces of wood, used to engrave letters on; printing blocks. Kán ch'hëém 簡槧, a block of wood, on which there is writing.

Ch'hëém 憸 To try to get near.

Ch'hëém 鐕 Hwa ch'hëém 花鐕, a hair-pin, a bodkin.

去

Ch'hëèm 僭 False, deceitful, erroneous; also, to usurp, to intrude. T'hëen bêng hwut ch'hëèm 天命弗僭, *t'hee^{ng} bēng bô ch'hò*, the decree of heaven is never wrong.

平

Ch'hëêm 襂 The name of a fruit, like an orange, abounding in Canton.

Ch'hëêm 劖 To stab, to thrust through.

卆

Ch'hëen 千 Vulg. *ch'heng*: a thousand. Ch'hëen lëên 千年, *chit ch'heng nee^{ng}*, a thousand years. Këung ch'hëep êng hêy, soè pek; sit k'hek kò hêy, sam ch'hëen 宮妾盈兮數百.食客過兮三千, *këung laē ây sèy ê êng mw^{n}ù, kwúy nā pāyh,—chëāh ây lâng k'hāyh keng, köèy s^{n}a ch'heng*, a palace full of concubines, to the amount of several hundreds; and passing strangers entertained, to the number of three thousand.

Ch'hëen 仟 The head over a thousand men.

Ch'hëen 芊 Luxuriance; luxuriant herbage. Wán sē aè ch'hëen ch'hëen 遠樹暧芊芊, *hwui^{ng} ây ch'hēw k'hw^{n}à ch'hëen ch'hëen*, the distant trees look thick with leaves.

Ch'hëen 阡 Ch'hëen bek 阡陌, *ch'hán hw^{n}ā*, a path between the paddy-fields; a road.

Ch'hëen 櫏 To stick in.

Ch'hëen 蹮 P'hëen ch'hëen 蹁蹮, to walk round and round.

Ch'hëen 遷 To remove. Ch'hëen sé 遷徙, to remove one's habitation. Sùn seng ê Choo-pâng, ch'hëen ê Hoō-hāy 舜生於諸馮.遷於負夏, *Sùn sai^{ng} twā tē Choo-pâng, swá wūy kaōu Hoō-hāy*, Sùn was born in Choo-pâng, and he removed to Hoō-hāy. See the 下 孟 Hāy bēng.

Ch'hëen 櫏 Cheāou ch'hëen 招櫏, the name of a tree.

Ch'hëen 躚 To gambol, to frisk.

Ch'hëen 韆 Ch'hew ch'hëen 鞦韆, *p'hăh teng ch'hew*, a swing; to swing. Ch'hew ch'hëen yëen lȯk, yëā tîm tîm 鞦韆院落夜沉沉, *p'hăh teng ch'hew tē ëeng lȯh, kaōu maīng ch'him ch'him*, swinging the cradle at the side of the hall, till late at night.

Ch'hëen 燀 The blazing up of a fire. Ch'hëen che é sin 燀之以薪, *hōe e tŏh tëŏh yūng ch'hâ*, in order to make it blaze, you must put on firewood. See the 左傳 Chó twān.

Ch'hëen 迁 To disperse, to scatter; the same as 遷 ch'hëen.

去

Ch'heén 淺 Shallow, not deep. Súy ch'heén ch'heén 水淺淺, *chúy k'hin k'hin*, shallow water.

Chēw kê ch'heén è, ēng che, yêw che 就其淺矣.泳之.游之, *chēw e ây k'hin ây wūy, ēng e, séw e*, approaching the shallow parts of the stream, you may wade through, or swim across them. See the 國風 Kok hong.

Ch'heén 幝 A broken carriage; the lining of a carriage.

Ch'heén 闡 To open, to display, to enlarge.

Ch'heén 撻 A slow buffalo.

Ch'heén 箋 A vessel made of bamboo, for holding fruits and flowers.

Ch'heén 棧 A vessel, similar to the above, made of wood.

Ch'heén 殫 To exhaust, to complete. Këûng lëen bȯk ch'heén 窮年莫殫, *chwuīng nëeng lēy swăh*, for whole years it would not be completed.

去

Ch'hëèn 倩 Handsome; a pretty, smiling, appearance; to hire and employ people; a son-in-law.

K'háou ch'heàou ch'hëèn hêy 巧笑倩兮, *k'há ch'hëŏ ch'hëèn hêy*, a pleasing smile, with handsome dimples. See the 衛風 Wöëy hong.

Chëëm koē soó lëng wat ch'hëèn 暫雇使令曰倩, *chëëm sè koē, kap saé yūng lâng, kóng kĕŏ ch'hēnā*, to hire people for a short time, and to order and employ them, is called ch'hëèn.

Ch'hëèn 傔 A tall person.

Ch'hëèn 蒨 The luxuriant appearance of grass and herbs; also, new and bright.

Ch'hëèn 茜 The name of a plant, used as a red dye.

Ch'hëèn 刋 To cut, to slice.

Ch'hëèn 綫 Slow, obstructed.

平

Ch'hëèn 讓 Read jëāng: to yield, to give preference to, to disclaim one's right to.

Lêng é léy jëāng, wûy kok hoē hô yéw, 能以禮讓.爲國乎何有, *ēy chëàou lèy soè sëo ch'hëèn, lëāou lè kok woō* *s^{n}a meè^{n}h ŏh*, he that knows how to yield according to propriety, what difficulty would he find in managing the country. See the 上論 Sëāng lūn.

Ch'hëên 諓 Good words, flattery, artful discourse.

Ch'hee^{ng} 鮮 Read sëen: new, — fresh, as meat, not stale or stinking. Sëen gê 鮮魚, *ch'hee^{ng} hê*, fresh fish. Wûy kwun yūng sëen 惟君用鮮, *lók jîn kwun yūng ch'hee^{ng} ây meè^{n}h*, the prince especially must have fresh food. See the 左傳 Chó twān.

Ch'hee^{ng} 攓 Read ch'hëen: to stick in.

Ch'hée^{ng} 淺 Read ch'hëén: a light blue colour, approaching to a grey. Song lêy yūng soe poè choo ch'hëén 喪禮用疏布緇淺, *se^{ng} hà ây lêy yūng ch'hoe poè oe ch'hee^{ng}*, in funeral rites use coarse cloth, of a dark grey colour. See the 儀禮 Gê lêy.

Ch'heè^{ng} 刺 Read ch'hè: to pierce, to perforate, to draw thread through a needle.

Ch'hee^{ng} 栻 Read sek: a carpenter's pencil. Bók sek 木栻, *bak ch'hee^{ng}*, an instrument used by carpenters, for marking the length of any thing.

Ch'hee^{ng}h 瞸 *Ch'hee^{ng}h ch'hee^{ng}h tê*, 瞸瞸啼, to sob and weep.

Ch'hëep 妾 Vulg. *sèy ê*: a concubine. Yit ch'hey yit ch'hëep 一妻一妾, *chit ây boè chit ây sèy ê*, one wife and one concubine.

Maé ch'hëep, put te kê sèng, chek pok che 買妾.不知其姓.則卜之, *bèy sèy ê, ū^{m} chae e ây sai^{ng}, chek pok e*, in buying a concubine, if you do not know her family name, then cast lots for it.

Ch'hëep 竊 To steal, to pilfer. Ch'hëep bûn 竊聞, *t'haou t'hē^{n}a*, to hear by stealth.

Yâng-h^{n}ò ch'hëep pó gëük taē këung 陽貨竊寶玉大弓, *Yâng-hò t'haou t'hâyh pó gëuk twā kèung*, Yâng-hò stole away the precious gem, and the large bow.

Ch'hëep 倠 A little man, a dwarf.

Ch'hëet 切 To cut, to slice; to urge, to be urgent with; earnest, true, real.

Put kám pek ch'hëet yēá 不敢偪切也, *ū^{m} k^{n}á pek ch'hëet*, not daring to urge or constrain.

Bêng kwun put oè ch'hëet k'hak che gân 明君不惡切愨之言, *bêng ây jîn kwun bô wàn ch'hëet k'hak ây wā*, an intelligent prince does not dislike true and faithful words.

Ch'hëet bûn jê kīn soō 切問而近思, *kin ch'hëet mooi^{ng} jê kīn sëō^{ng}*, earnestly enquiring, and narrowly considering.

Ch'hëet yaòu 切要, important. Ch'hëet ch'hëet 切切, earnest.

Ch'hëet 跕 Read lëem: to walk slip-shod.

Ch'hek 側 At the side, sidelong; to overturn; rebellious. Bîn-choó sē ch'hek, gîn gîn jê yēá 閔子侍側誾誾如也, *Bîn-choó k'hëā tē sin*

福建方言字典

peeng, hó wat ây yeōng, Bin-choô waited at his side, harmonious and delighted.

Soó hwán ch'hek choó choō an 使反側子自安, saé hwán lwān ây kēnà ka tē an, make the rebellious people become tranquil.

Ch'hek 拆 To open, to burst, as seeds and flowers, when vegetating. Lûy é chok, jê pek kó ch'hó bòk, kae kap ch'hek 雷雨作.而百菓草木.皆甲拆, lûy kwà hoē chŏh, jê pâyh hāng kôèy chê ch'haóu bak, chò pôo p'hwà k'hak, when the thunder and rain prevail, then the various fruits, plants, and trees, burst from their seeds.

Ch'hek 捌 To beat, to knock.

Ch'hek 測 To search, to examine. Ch'hek toē 測度, to fathom, to comprehend.

Yim yâng put ch'hek che wûy sîn 陰陽不測之謂神, yim yâng ây bēy ch'hek ây, wāy kóng kèó sîn, that which is unsearchable in the operations of nature is called 'divine.' See the 易經 Yēāh keng.

Ch'hek 惻 Grieved, affected. Ch'hek yín che sim, jîn che twan yēá 惻隱之心.仁之端也, ch'hek yín ây sim kwna, jîn ây twan yēá, the feeling of compassion is the principle of benevolence. See the 上孟 Sēāng bēng.

Ch'hek 尺 A foot measure. Ch'hùn ch'hek 寸尺, ch'hùn ch'hēŏh, inches and feet.

Yit sé wûy hwun, sìp hwun wûy ch'hùn, sìp ch'hùn wûy ch'hek 一黍爲分.十分爲寸.十寸爲尺, chit lēep sâyh á chò hwun, chàp hwun chò ch'hùn, chàp ch'hùn chò ch'hēŏh, a grain of corn is a division, ten divisions are an inch, ten inches are a foot.

2 o

Ch'hek tēy bòk hwuy kê yéw yēá 尺地莫非其有也, chìt ch'hēŏh tēy bô ūm sē e ây, there is not a foot of ground, but what belongs to him. See 孟子 Bēng-chôo.

Ch'hek 㡿 Few, great; to fill, to drive away; distant; to roof a house.

Ch'hek 慼 Grieved, pained, sorrowful; an excess of feeling. Ke song ae ch'hek 居喪哀慼, k'hēā sēng hà ae ch'hàm t'hòng ch'hek, being in mourning, a person should be sorrowful and affected.

Ch'hek 刺 To pierce, to perforate.

Ch'hek 册 A book. T'hòk ch'hek 讀册, t'hak ch'hāyh, to read books. A plank or board for writing, used before the invention of paper.

Chwân soo pó sìn che ch'hek 全師保勝之册, chwân peng soa pó sìn yēá ây ch'hāyh, the record of an undiminished army, and complete victory.

Ch'hek 侵 The appearance of little children walking.

Ch'hek 赤 Red: also, empty, waste, naked. Ch'hek bēēn 赤面, ch'hēăh bīn, a red face.

Ch'hek tēy ch'hēen lé 赤地千里, ch'hēăh tēy chēⁿá ch'heng lé, waste ground to the distance of a thousand lé. Ch'hek kēak 赤脚, ch'hēăh k'ha, bare-foot.

Ch'hek 戚 A hatchet; also, near, nearly related; sorrowful. A surname.

Pîn kēûng, chek hoō boé put choó, hoò kwùy, chek ch'hin ch'hek wûy kē 貧窮.則父母不子.富貴.則親戚畏懼, sông hēung, chek pāy boé ūm lēăh lán chò kēⁿá, poò kwùy, chek ch'hin ch'hek kēⁿn lán, when poor, our very parents will not acknowledge us for their children; and when rich, our nearest relatives will be afraid of us.

Ch'hek **策** A plan, a scheme; a book, a record; a whip, to whip. Boô kèy ch'hek k'hó se 無計策可施, *bô kèy ch'hek t'hang se*, having no plan to adopt; unable to suggest a scheme.
Bûn Boó che chèng, poè chaē hong ch'hek 文武之政.布在方策, *Bún-ông Bóo-ông ây chèng soō, poè tē hong ch'hek*, the government of Bûn-ông and Boô-ông is contained in the historical records. See the 中庸 Tëung yeûng.
Ch'hek ke má 策其馬, *bút e ây bêy*, he whipped his horse. See the 上論 Sëāng lūn.

Ch'hek **剌** The same as the preceding.

Ch'hek **彳** A small step; to walk slowly.

Ch'hek **坼** To break, to burst. Koe bêng kap ch'hek 勾萌甲坼, *kaôu bêng gây k'hak p'hwà*, when vegetation commences, the seeds burst.

Ch'hek **畟** An agricultural instrument.

Ch'hek **鴀** The noise made by birds.

Ch'hek **粸** Bad rice.

Ch'hek **趩** Not advancing; to make no progress.

Ch'hek **摵** A rub, to sift; also, to fall as a leaf.

Ch'heng **清** Pure, clear, clean. Gwat ch'heng t'hè té 月清徹底, *gōëyh ch'heng kaôu têy*, the moon is clear, through and through.
Hông hô sam ch'hëen lëên, yit têng ch'heng 黃河三千年.一澄清, *Wuîng hô sⁿa ch'heng nëen, chít ây têng ch'heng*, the Yellow river becomes still and clear once in three thousand years.

Ch'heng **僜** Lēng ch'heng 倰僜, to walk lame, to walk as if one were drunk.

Ch'heng **稱** To call, to name, to praise. Ch'heng hoe 稱呼, to praise. Kè put ch'heng kê lek, ch'heng kê tek yëá 驥不稱其力.稱其德也, *hó bây ūᵐ saē ch'heng hoe e ây lat, ch'heng hoe e ây tek*, a good horse must be praised, not according to its strength, but according to its good qualities. See the 下論 Hāy lūn.

Ch'heng **青** Vulg. *ch'haiⁿᵍ*; azure; light blue. Ch'heng sek 青色, *ch'haing sek*, an azure colour. Ch'heng t'hae 青苔, *ch'haiⁿᵍ t'hê*, green moss. Also written 靑 Ch'heng.

Ch'heng **圊** A privy, a necessary.

Ch'heng **檉** A kind of willow, growing by the side of rivers, of a reddish colour.

Ch'heng **鯖** The name of a fish, of a light green colour.

Ch'heng **蟶** Vulg. t'han; a kind of cockle. Bân jîn é têên chëông che, wūy ch'heng têên 閩人以田種

之.謂蟶田, *Bân saiⁿᵍ ây lâng tē ch'han ch'hē e, kóng kĕò t'han tēⁿâ*, the people of Hok-këèn province feed them in fields, which they call cockle pits. See the 正字通 Chèⁿà jē t'hong.

Ch'heng 赬 A reddish colour.

Ch'heng 餳 To give, to present.

Ch'heng 菁 The name of a creeping plant. Hwan ch'heng 番菁, *hwan ch'haiⁿᵍ*, indigo.

声

Ch'héng 請 To invite, to ask, to beg, to greet. Ch'héng jîn sit chéw 請人食酒, *ch'heⁿá lâng chëăh chéw*, to invite people to drink wine.

Ch'héng chō 請坐, *ch'hëⁿá chēy*, pray sit down.

Gê hong jîn ch'héng hëèn 儀封人請見, *Gê hong jîn ch'hëⁿá böëyh keèⁿᵍ*, the inspector of Gê begged to see (Confucius.)

Kwun ch'héng tek ê soo jē chëá 君請擇於斯二者, *kwun lê ch'hëⁿá kán tŏh tē chèy nō hāng*, I beseech your highness to choose between these two. See the 上孟 Sëāng bēng.

Ch'héng 箐 A duster. Ch'héng tok 箐棹, *ch'heng tŏh*, to dust the table.

去

Ch'hèng 倀 Bêng ch'hèng 萠倀, to miss the way.

Ch'hèng 揹 To rub: used for 倩 Ch'hëèn, to hire.

Ch'hèng 秤 To weigh, to regulate the weight of any thing; a pair of scales. Gnó sim jê ch'hèng, put lêng wūy jîn tey gōng 我心如秤.不能爲人低昂, *gwá ây sim ch'hin chëöⁿᵍ ch'hìn, bēy yin wūy lâng ch'hòng kay kwân*, my mind is like a pair of scales, which are not to be elevated or depressed for any man.

Ch'hèng 襯 Clothes worn underneath, an inner dress; to assist. Ch'hèng gê 襯儀, to accord with propriety.

Ch'hèng 𧡊 A sacrifice; also, money.

Ch'hèng 稱 Vulg. *ch'hìn*: to weigh, to find out the weight of any thing. Séy ê ch'hèng bùt, jê te kê k'heng tëūng cheá yëá 所以稱物.而知其輕重者也, *séy ê ch'hìn mëèⁿh, jê chae e ây k'hin tāng yëá*, that by which we weigh things, in order to ascertain whether they are light or heavy.

Ch'hèng 擤 Ch'hèng pít 擤鼻, *ch'hèng p'hēèⁿᵍ*, to blow the nose.

Ch'hèng 偵 Ch'hèng ch'hèng 偵偵, to run away, to run incessantly. Ch'hèng ch'hèng jê ch'hoó 偵偵如此, *ch'hèng ch'hèng an nēy*, merely thus; always so, invariably the same.

Ch'hèng 賵 Unsaleable, that cannot be disposed of.

Ch'hèng 凊 Ch'hèng lëâng 凊凉, *chew ch'hìn*, cool. Hwân wūy jîn choó che léy, tong wun jê hāy ch'hèng 凡爲人子之禮.冬溫而夏凊, *hwân chò lâng kēⁿá ây lëy, tëŏh tang t'heeⁿᵍ hoē pāy boē sëo, jê hāy t'heeⁿᵍ hoē e ch'hìn*, the duty of all children is, in the winter (to keep their parents) warm, and in the summer, cool.

Ch'hèng 倩 Vulg. *ch'hēⁿà*: to hire, to employ as a labourer. Ch'hèng jîn chò kong 倩人做工, *ch'hēⁿà lâng chò kang kwùy*, to hire people to work.

Ch'hèng 銃 Read ch'hëùng: a cannon, a great gun. K'hae ch'hèng tⁿá jîn 開銃打人, *k'hwuy ch'hèng p'hăh lâng*, to fire a gun and shoot people.

平

Ch'hêng 榕 Read yûng: the name of a tree, which first shoots up as a creeper, and afterwards becomes a very large tree; the Indian fig tree, or banyan tree,—very common in the provinces of Hok-këèn and Kóng-tong, but is never found north of the river 浙 Chëet, in the province of Chëet-kang.

Ch'hêng 松 Sëûng pek 松栢, *ch'hêng păyh*, a cedar or fir tree. Jê sëûng pek che yéw sim, kwàn soò sê, jê put kaé k'ho ek yëep 如松栢之有心,貫四時而不改柯易葉, *ch'hin chëōⁿᵍ ch'hêng păyh ây woō sim, Chaòu sè sê jê bô káy ke wⁿà hëŏh*, with a mind like the evergreen fir, which passes through the four seasons, without altering its branches or changing its leaves. See the 禮記 Léy kè.

Ch'hêng 傖 Ch'hêng hoó 傖父, an expression of respect.

Ch'hêng 剿 To pierce, to stick in; any thing with which to pierce a hole.

去

Ch'hēng 塩 A vessel for holding salt.

Ch'hēng 簾 An implement used in breeding silk-worms.

Ch'hĕng 穿 Read ch'hwàn: to put on, to wear. Ch'hwàn sam 穿衫, *ch'hĕng sⁿa*, to put on clothes. Ch'hwàn bëet 穿襪, *ch'hĕng bŏëyh*, to wear stockings.

平

Ch'heⁿᵍ 倉 Read ch'hong: to collect, to store up; a place for gathering, a granary.

Naé chek naé ch'hong 乃責乃倉, *woō ây chek, woō ây ch'heⁿᵍ*, some was collected, and some was stored by.

Ch'hong lîm hoó k'hoè 倉廪府庫, *ch'heⁿᵍ lîm hoó k'hoè*, a granary and treasury.

Ch'hong chut 倉卒, not hurried.

Ch'heⁿᵍ 艙 Read ch'hong: the hold of a ship. K'hae ch'hong 開艙, *k'wuy ch'heⁿᵍ*, to open the hold. Ch'hwân ch'hong 船艙, *ch'hûn ch'heⁿᵍ*, a ship's hold.

Ch'heⁿᵍ 瘡 Pán ch'hong 板瘡, *pán ch'heⁿᵍ*, an ulcer, a sore.

去

Ch'hèⁿᵍ 蹌 Ch'hòng choé 蹌走, *ch'hèⁿᵍ chaóu*, to run away.

平

Ch'hêⁿᵍ 床 Read ch'hông: a bed stead. Bëên ch'hông 眠床, *bîn ch'hêⁿᵍ*, a sleeping place.

Sùn chaē ch'hông k'hîm 舜在床琴, *Sùn twā tē ch'hêⁿᵍ twⁿá k'hîm*, Sùn was sitting on the bed-stead, playing the guitar. See the 下孟 Hāy bēng.

Ch'hëo 哨 Seaòu k'hoé 哨口, *ch'hëo ch'hùy*, a sharp mouth, clever at speaking.

Ch'hëo 鵃 Ch'hëo key, 鵃鷄, a game cock.

Ch'hëo 霄 Yîn-seäou 雲霄, *Wûn-ch'hëo*, the name of a district, in the province of Hok-këèn 福建, in the department of 漳州 Chëang-chew, and near the borders of 漳浦 *Chëo^{ng}-p'hoê*. Also, up in the clouds.

去

Ch'hëò 笑 Read ch'heàou: to laugh. H^{n}ò ch'hëàou 好笑, *hò ch'hëò*, laughable.

Yit k'héy ch'hé, jê lēng jîn ch'hëàou — 啟齒而令人笑, *chit ây k'hwuy ch'hùy k'hé, jê kà lâng ch'hëò*, when once you show your teeth, you give occasion to others to laugh.

平

Ch'hëô 蟯 Read jëâou. Kang jeâou 江蟯, *ka ch'hëô*, a small insect; a small shell fish.

入

Ch'hëŏh 尺 Read ch'hek: a foot measure. Yit ch'hek 一尺, *chit ch'hëŏh*, one foot.

Ch'hùn yéw séy twán, ch'hek yéw séy tëâng 寸有所短.尺有所長, *chit ch'hùn woō séy. k'hăh lèy, chit ch'hëŏh woō séy k'hăh tê^{ng}*, an inch is too short, and a foot is too long.

Ch'hëŏh 哧 The eating of a duck or goose.

Ch'hëŏh 蛈 A reddish kind of insect: a hairy caterpillar.

入

Ch'hëŏh 席 Read sek: a mat, for sitting or sleeping on; used also for a table, because the ancients ate their meals off mats spread upon the ground.

Guó sim hwuy sek, put k'hó kwán yëá 我心匪席.不可捲也, *gwán ây sim kw^{u}a u^{m} sē ch'hëŏh, bēy t'hang hoê lâng kwui^{ng}*, our hearts are not like mats, they cannot be rolled up at pleasure.

Sek kwán t'hëen hāy 席捲天下, *ch'hëŏh kwui^{ng} t'hee^{ng} āy*, he got possession of the empire, like the rolling up of a mat; i. e. rapidly.

平

Ch'hëo^{ng} 菖 Read ch'hëang: a water plant, a kind of sedge. Ch'hëang poê 菖蒲, *ch'hëo^{ng} poê*, the hanging sword plant.

Ch'hëo^{ng} 猖 *Ch'hëo^{ng} mô sin* 猖摩神, a furious kind of madness. Ch'hëang kông 猖狂, *ch'hëo^{ng} kông*, rude, boisterous.

Ch'hëo^{ng} 鯧 Read ch'hëang: a pomfret fish.

Ch'hëo^{ng} 鎗 Read ch'hëang: a spear. Put yūng tëâng ch'hëang chô t'hëen choò, ché se hwat lut tè t'haè pêng 不用長鎗佐天子.只施法律致太平, *u^{m} yūng tê^{ng} ch'hëo^{ng} hoō chăn hông tèy, chè se hwat lut tè kaòu t'haè pêng*, there is no need of using a long spear to assist the emperor; but it is only necessary to publish good laws, in order to promote universal tranquillity.

上

Ch'hëó^{ng} 搶 Read ch'hëáng: to snatch, to take by force, to plunder. Ch'hëáng twat chaê but 搶奪財物, *ch'hëó^{ng} t'hăyh ch'hee^{ng} mee^{n}h*, to plunder and take money and goods.

Ch'hëó^{ng} 廠 Read ch'hëáng: an open shed, without walls.

去

Ch'hëò^{ng} 唱 Read ch'hëàng: to sing. Ch'hëàng k'hëuk 唱曲, *ch'hëò^{ng} k'hek*, to sing songs.

Boô twan jê ch'hēàng 無端而唱, *bô s^n^a soō jê ch'hēō^ng^ khek,* to sing without any reason.

平

Ch'hēō^ng^ 薔 Ch'hēàng bê hwa 薔薇花, *ch'hēō^ng^ bê hwa,* a rose.

Ch'hēō^ng^ 牆 Read ch'hēâng: a wall. Ch'hēâng p'hek 牆壁, *chēō^ng^ pēăh,* a wall of a house.

Chùn ê tēaou ch'hēâng 峻宇雕牆, *kwân kwân ây ch'hoò, tēaou k'hek ây ch'hēō^ng^,* a high house, and sculptured walls. See the 尚書 *Sēō^ng^ se.*

Ch'hēō^ng^ 颺 Read yâng: to winnow. Yâng ch'heuk 颺粟, *ch'hēō^ng^ ch'hek,* to winnow corn.

Pò che yâng che, k'hong pê chaē chēên 簸之颺之,糠秕在前, *pwà e, ch'hēō^ng^ e, k'hc^ng^ pê tē t'haôu chêng,* sifting it and winnowing it, the husks and chaff will all fly before you.

去

Ch'hēō^ng^ 匠 Read ch'hēāng: a mechanic. Boô ch'hēāng ek jēēn 巫匠亦然, *sae kong bak ch'hēō^ng^ yēā sè an nêy,* "conjurers and carpenters are also thus;"—the former profiting by people's living, and the latter living by people's dying, in having to make coffins for them.

Ch'hēō^ng^ 傭 Read yûng: to hire, to let one's services, to engage in service. Tóng-koè soō k'hé, Hāy-hok pēēn sèng, wûy yēā kay yûng 黨錮事起,夏馥變姓,爲冶家傭, *Tóng-koè ây soō k'hé, Hāy-hok w^n^à sai^ng^, k'hè chò p'hăh t'hēēh kay ây ch'hēō^ng^,* when the troubles of Tóng-koè commenced, Hay-hok changed his surname, and hired himself into the family of a blacksmith.

Ch'hēō^ng^ 象 Read sēāng: an elephant. K'he hoê pà soo sēāng, jê wàn che, t'hēen hāy taē wat 驅虎豹犀象,而遠之,天下大悅, *kw^n^a hoê pà sae chēō^ng^, jê hoê e hwui^ng^, t'hee^ng^ ây chēw twā hw^n^a hê,* driving away tigers and leopards, lions and elephants, and removing them to a distance, the whole empire was greatly delighted. See the 上孟 Sēāng-bēng.

Ch'hēō^ng^ 汲 Read k'hip: to draw up. K'hip súy 汲水, *ch'hēō^ng^ chúy,* to draw water.

Kēng twán chēā, put k'hó é k'hip ch'him 綆短者不可以汲深, *sŏh tēy, bô t'hang ch'hēō^ng^ ch'him chúy,* when the rope is short, we cannot draw water from a deep place. Said by 莊子 Chong-choò.

入

Ch'hëuk 浞 Hân-ch'hëuk 寒浞, a man's name, who lived under the Hây dynasty.

Ch'hëuk 促 Near, close, short. Pek ch'hëuk 廹促, to urge, to hasten.

Ch'hëuk 齪 The teeth too near together. Ak ch'hëuk 齷齪, urgent; also, an instrument for marking a hole in a door.

Ch'hëuk 莡 Grass growing in luxuriance; a bushy appearance.

Ch'hëuk 俄 Grieved, sorrowful.

Ch'hëuk 僑 Ch'hëuk pöëy 僑佩, *jēŏh pöēy,* not straightened, not stretched out.

Ch'hëuk 亍 A small step. The two characters Ch'hek 彳 and Ch'hëuk 亍, both signifying a small step, when put together form the character 行 Hêng, to walk.

Ch'hëuk 矗 Stretching up, high, elevated, rising straight up. Ch'heng san têûng têep, put te ch'hëuk têy yéw ké to 青山重叠.不知矗地有幾多, *ch'heng sw^{n}a lêng lëep, ū^{m} chae ch'hëuk têy woō hwā chēy*, the green hills piled one upon another, I do not know how much elevated from the earth.

Ch'hëuk 蹴 To tread on, to trample under foot. Ch'heuk jé jê é che, k'hit jîn put sëak yëá 蹴爾而與之.乞人不屑也, *t'hat meë^{n}h jê hoē lâng, lëên k'hit chëûh ū^{m} k'hw^{n}à ch'heng k'hè sëō^{ng}*, if you trample on a thing, and then give it to any one, even a beggar will not consider it clean. See 孟子 Bēng-choó.

Ch'hëuk 斶 Gân-ch'hëuk 顏斶, the name of a man, who lived in the time of the 戰國 Chëèn kok, B. C. 250.

Ch'hëuk 蹵 To kick, to touch with the foot, to step over.

Ch'hëuk 捉 Vulg. *lëàh* : to seize, to apprehend, to catch, to take in the hand. Tok sūy lēng pëèn hêng bûn se, hwā éng toë hêng, ch'hëuk ná Chô-ch'hò. 卓遂令徧行文書.畫影圖形.捉拿曹操, *Tŏh sūy ch'hut lāng pëèn kë^{n}á bûn se, wā yë^{n}á toë yëō^{ng}, k'hè lëàh Chô-ch'hò*, Tŏh immediately gave orders for circulating hand-bills in all directions, describing the form and appearance of the man, in order to apprehend Chô-ch'hò. See the 三國 Sam kok.

Ch'hëuk 觸 To run against, to offend, to gore (as a bull). Seng sîn put sëang ch'hëuk 星辰不相觸, *ch'hai^{ng} sîn bô sëo hwān lëŏh*, the stars do not run against one another.

Ch'hëuk sèng sëāng noē 觸聖上怒, *hwān lëŏh sèng sëāng ây noē*, to excite his majesty's displeasure.

Gnêw ch'hëuk jîn 牛觸人, *goô tak lëŏh lâng*, an ox gores people.

Ch'hëuk 顣 To knit the brows, to draw up the forehead into wrinkles. Kê chit séw, ch'hëuk at, jê sëāng kò 舉疾首蹙頞.而相告, *chò pôa t'haôu kak t'hë^{n}à, p'heè^{ng} t'haôu gnëāou gnëāou, jê taē kay sëo kòng*, they all began to feel their heads ache, and knitting their brows, they addressed each other. See the 上孟 Sëāng bēng.

Ch'hëuk 數 Narrow, small, applied to the meshes of a net. Ch'hēuk koé put jip woo tê, gê pëet put k'hó sìn sit yëá 數罟不入污池.魚鼈不可勝食也, *bùt bat ây bāng bô jip lê-wan lê, chêw hê peëh bô t'hang lëaôu chëàh*, if you do not allow a net with close meshes to enter the pools, the fish and tortoises for consumption will be inexhaustible. See the 上孟 Sëāng bēng.

Ch'hëuk 臅 The fat part of a wolf's breast.

Ch'hëuk 蹙 To urge, to constrain, to distress, to hasten; near.

Ch'hëuk 閦 Many. O'ch'hēuk 阿閦, a name of Budha.

Ch'hëuk 踀 Careful, a careful appearance.

Ch'hëuk 諔 To speak quickly.

Ch'hëuk 娖 To seek for by flattery, to seek for by adulation.

Ch'hëuk 頎 Gak-ch'hëuk 樂頎, the name of a man, who lived in the time of Confucius.

Ch'hëuk 齱 The teeth meeting each other, wry teeth.

Ch'hëuk 尺 Vulg. ch'hëŏh: a foot measure; also read Ch'hek, which see.

Ch'hëuk 攊 To rub, to rub out; to brush, to dust.

Ch'hëung 充 To extend, to fill up, to carry out to the utmost, to stop up: a surname. Also written 克 Ch'hëung.
Ch'hëng kwun che paôu 充君之庖, ch'hëung mwⁿà jîn kwun ây paôu, to fill the prince's cook-house. See the 禮記 Léy kè.
Yew jê ch'hëung jê 褎如充耳, t'hó ch'hëw wuiⁿᵍ t'hat hē k'hang, to take one's sleeve and stop one's ears. See the 國風 Kok hong.
K'hok jê ch'hëung che 擴而充之, kóng k'hwăh jê ch'hëung mwⁿà e, to extend and carry it out to the utmost. See the 上孟 Sëäng bëng.

Ch'hëung 忼 The heart moved, the mind affected.

Ch'hëung 琉 A gem worn as an ear-ring.

Ch'hëung 沖 To move, to agitate; to fly up; also, deep and empty. Sat k'hè ch'hëung t'hëen 殺氣沖天, t'haè lâng ây k'hè ch'hëung kaôu t'heeⁿᵍ, the murderous spirit mounted up to the very heavens.

Ch'hëung 冲 Young, small; the noise made in perforating ice. Soo ê ch'heung jîn 肆予冲人, soo gwà seaôu lëën lâng, to me a young man.

Ch'hëung 种 Small, young: also, a surname.

Ch'hëung 傭 Even, equal, just. Hō t'hëen put ch'hëung, kàng ch'hoé k'hëuk hëung 昊天不傭降此鞠訩, twā t'heeⁿᵍ ūᵐ paiⁿᵍ, kàng chéy léy ūᵐ hó, "the great heavens are unjust, in sending down these calamities:"— an impatient complaint of the dealings of providence.

Ch'hëung 偅 The same as 憧 Ch'hëung; an unsettled state of mind.

Ch'hëung 從 Unconstrained, easy, unforced. Put bëen jê tëung, put soo jê tek, ch'hëung yûng tëung tō, sèng jîn yëá, 不勉而中不思而得從容中道聖人也, bô bëen këàng jê tëùng, ūᵐ saé sëòⁿᵍ jê tit tëŏh, ch'hëung yûng tê tang eⁿᵍ ây tō lé, chéy chëw sè sèng jîn yëá, without effort to hit upon the centre, without much thought to obtain any thing, and spontaneously to follow the due medium, is what a sage alone can attain to. See the 中庸 Tëung yûng.

Ch'hëung 衝 To withstand, to oppose, to come across, to rush abruptly. Ch'hëung hêng bān lé 衝横

萬里, *ch'hëung hwⁿâ bān lé*, spread across to the extent of ten thousand lé.

Ch'hëung tut 衝突, to rush abruptly.

Ch'hëung 蓯 The name of a plant.

Ch'hëung 忡 To be sad and sorrowful.

去

Ch'hëüng 縱 Slowly, leisurely; to allow; to give loose to, to give way to; although, even, if.

Ch'hëüng paē lêy, yëuk paē toē 縱敗禮.欲敗度, loose conduct injures propriety, lustful desires tend to the breach of the laws.

Kám yéw jē sim hoē! ch'hëüng yéw, këüng kê löëy, bok këüng kê göëy 敢有二心乎.縱有.共其內.莫共其外, *chae kⁿá woō nō ây sim kwⁿa! ch'hëng woō, êng kap laē bīn ây lâng, bô kap gwā bīn ây lâng*, how dare we encourage a double heart! and even if we did, it should be with those at home, and never with those abroad.

Ch'hëüng 銃 Vulg. *ch'hèng*: a cannon, a great gun.

Ch'hëüng 䝐 To come without being invited.

Ch'hëüng 儱 Awry, not straight, incorrect.

去

Ch'hëüng 穿 Vulg. *ch'hèng*: to put on, to wear. Ch'hëüng sam 穿衫, *ch'hèng sⁿa*, to put on clothes.

Yéw e put ch'hëüng, yéw sëäng put chëak, ch'hoó che wūy lân jin 有衣不穿.有裳不着.此之謂赧人, *woō sⁿa ūm ch'hèng, woō ŷin chëōⁿᵍ ūm chëak yung, chèy sê kōng sëáou lêy ây lâng*, one who has clothes and does not wear them, who has apparel and does not make use of it,—this is what is called a shameful follow.

上平

Ch'hew 秋 The autumn, harvest, ripe. A surname. Ch'hun, hāy, ch'hew, tong 春夏秋冬; *ch'hun, hāy, ch'hew, tang*, spring, summer, autumn, winter. Ch'hew hô che bwat 秋毫之末, *ch'hew hô ây bōëy*, "the end of an autumn's down;" i. e. a very insignificant thing.

Ch'hew 楸 The name of a tree, whose leaf falls in the early part of autumn.

Ch'hew 湫 The name of a river.

Ch'hew 鞦 Ch'hew ch'hëen 鞦韆, a swing, a cradle.

Ch'hew 鶖 The name of a bird.

Ch'hew 鰌 The name of a mud fish.

Ch'hew 鰍 The name of a fish, several thousand lê in length which is said to dwell in caverns at the bottom of the sea; when it enters these caverns, the tide rises, and when it comes out, the tide falls again:—this is the way in which the Chinese account for the tides.

Ch'hew 揫 To turn round with the hand, to twist any thing and make it small.

Ch'hew 鬚 Read se: a beard. K'hoé se 口鬚, ch'hùy ch'hew, the beard about the mouth.
Gō ch'hân bê, bé jēém se 卧蠶眉.美髯鬚, gō ch'hân ây bak baē, bé jēém ây ch'hùy ch'hew, eye-brows like sleeping silk-worms, and a beautiful flowing beard. See the 三國 Sam kok.

Ch'hew 鑐 Só ch'hew 鎖鑐, the spring of a lock.

去

Ch'hěw 俞 A surname.

Ch'hěw 醜 Vulg. k'hëep sē: ugly, ill-favoured. Ch'héw loē 醜陋, ugliness.
Ch'héw hoō put bëén këén kong koe 醜婦不免見公姑, k'hüh k'hëep sè ây cha boè bēy bëén tit keēng twā kay kwna, though a woman be ever so ugly, she cannot avoid seeing her father and mother-in-law.

Ch'héw 手 Read séw: a hand. Séw këak 手脚, k'ha ch'héw, hands and feet.
Chó sēw chip yëak, yēw séw pēng tek 左手執籥.右手秉翟, tè ch'hēw këäh yëak, chëⁿà ch'hēw gīm p'hin, in the left hand he held a pipe, and in the right hand, a flute. Yêw séw hⁿò hân che jîn 游手好閒之人, yéw ch'hēw aè êng ây lâng, a wandering hand, and a fellow fond of leisure;—said of those who have no certain employment.

Ch'héw 首 Read sěw: the head. Séw sek 首飾, ch'hèw sek, ornaments for the head, such as hair-pins, bodkins, &c.

Ch'héw 贖 Read sëuk: to redeem a pledge, to redeem any thing out of pawn.
E' kong sëuk chöey 以功贖罪, t'hó kong ch'hēw chöēy, to practise meritorious things in order to make up for one's faults.

去

Ch'hèw 儔 To bear a burden, to sustain any thing.

Ch'hèw 臭 Vulg. ch'haòu: stinking, putrid; also read hèw. Jê oè ok ch'èw 如惡惡臭, ch'hin chëōng wán p'haⁿè ch'haòu, like the being disgusted with a bad smell. See the 大學 Taē hak.

Ch'hèw 甃 To build up a wall, to raise a parapet. Chéng ch'hèw bôo kèw 井甃無咎, chaiⁿᵍ k'heēh k'hàh kwân, bô ūm hó, if the well were built higher, it would be no harm.

Ch'hèw 僽 Ch'hèw ch'haè 僽倸, to receive any one in a polite manner. Put yaòu é che ch'hèw ch'haé 不要以之僽倸, bô böëyh kap e ch'hèw ch'háe, to refuse proper attention to any one.

平

Ch'hêw 詶 Read sêw: to answer politely, to return a compliment. Pé sëäng jîn chëá, lân wūy sêw tùy 彼上人者.難爲詶對, hwut lêy sè twā lâng, ôh kap e ch'hêw tùy, with those great people, it is difficult to converse and pay compliments.

去

Ch'hēw 樹 Read sē: a tree. Sē bok 樹木, ch'hēw bak, timber. Wūy pok ch'hun t'hëen sē, Kang tong jit boè yîn 渭北春天樹.江東日暮雲, tē Wūy pak lê chò ch'hun t'heēⁿᵍ ây ch'hēw, tē Kang tang gwá chò jit âm ây hwûn, on the north of the river Wūy you are as a tree in the spring season, whilst I on the east of the Kang stream am as the clouds around the setting sun. Said by one poet, of another.

Ch'hēw 楊 Yâng bŏēy 楊梅, *ch'hēw ŭ^m*, a kind of plum.

𡕹 Ch'hey 妻 Vulg. *boé*: a wife. Hoo ch'hey 夫妻, *ang boé*, husband and wife.

Soō jê kwuy ch'hey, taē peng bē p'hwàn 士如歸妻迨冰未泮, *t'hak ch'hāyh lâng ch'hwà tooi^ng laê boé, t'hân seng bōēy yēō^ng*, the scholar taking home his wife, does it before the ice is melted. See the 國風 Kok hong.

Ch'hé ch'hey jê hô, pit kò hoō boé 娶妻如何必告父母, *ch'hwà boé tēŏh an chw^n â, pit tēŏh kap pāy boé kóng*, in marrying a wife how must we act? we ought certainly first to inform our parents. See the 小雅 Seaóu gnáy.

Ch'hey 萋 Grass growing luxuriantly; exuberant herbage.

Ch'hey 悽 Sorrowful, grieved.

Ch'hey 初 The first; former, early. K'hé ch'hey 起初, the beginning. Thaè ch'hey che sê, bîn kae tûn but 太初之時民皆沌物, *t'haè ch'hey ây sê chek, pāyh sai^ng chò poō tūn but*, at the time of the beginning, the people were generally all blunt and plain. See the 史記 Soó kè.

Ch'hey bēng wat, te put hàou 初命曰誅不孝, *k'hé t'haôu ây bēng lēng kóng, t'haê put hàou ây lâng*, the very first decree was—"put the unfilial to death."

Ch'hey 淒 The wind and rain rising up into a squall.

声 Ch'héy 批 To thump with the fist.

Ch'héy 紕 The different coloured threads in silk or cloth.

Ch'héy 眦 Gaê ch'héy 睚眦, to look angrily.

Ch'héy 泚 Perspiration; also, clear water. Kê sóng yéw ch'héy 其顙有泚, *e ây t'haôu hēāh woō kw^n â*, on his forehead stood the perspiration. See the 上孟 Sēāng bēng.

去 Ch'hèy 妻 To marry a person, to give a person in marriage to any one. K'hóng-choó é kê heng che choó ch'hèy che 孔子以其兄之子妻之, *K'hóng-choó t'hò e ây hē^n a ây kē^n â hoē e chò boé*, Confucius took his brother's daughter, and gave her to him in marriage. See the 上論 Sēāng lūn.

Ch'hèy 糏 Bé ch'hèy 米糏, rice flour.

Ch'hèy 刷 To scrub clean. Téng ch'hey 㽾刷, *tē^n â ch'hèy*, the scrapings of the pot.

Ch'hèy 脆 Read ch'ùy: brittle, easily broken.

平 Ch'hêy 躧 Unable to walk; to drag the feet in walking.

卆

Ch'him 深 Deep. Ch'him boô téy 深無底, a bottomless depth. Jip san wûy k'hëúng put ch'him, jip lim wûy k'hëúng put bit 入山惟恐不深.入林惟恐不密, *jip sw^{n}a wûy kë^{n}a ū^{m} ch'him, jip nâ wûy kë^{n}a ū^{m} bat*, entering the hills it is only to be feared we cannot go deep enough; and retreating into the woods we are only apprchensive lest we be not sufficiently concealed; — said by those who forsake the world and adopt a hermit's life. Kò jîn ch'him wân è 過人深遠矣, *k'hăh yē^{n}â lâng ch'him hwuī^{ng}*, surpassing others to a great depth and distance.

Ch'him 祲 A supernatural influence, producing both good and bad effects.

Ch'him 僭 Confused, in disorder.

Ch'him 㑴 To advance gradually.

Ch'him 侵 To enter by degrees, to invade, to pare off; calamitous. Gnoé kok put teng, wūy che tāe ch'him 五穀不登.謂之大侵, *goē kok bô k'hè laê, kóng këò twā ch'hím*, when the five kinds of grain do not come up, this is called a great calamity.
Tek jîn ch'him che 狄人侵之, *tek ây hwan ch'him hwat e*, the northern barbarians invaded him.

声

Ch'hím 寢 To sleep, to rest. Ch'him sit 寢室, *k'hwùn keng*, a sleeping chamber.
Chaé-ê tèw ch'hìm 宰予晝寢, *Chaé-ê, jit tāou sè k'hwùn*, Chaé-ê slept in the day time, (for which Confucius severely reproved him.) See the 上論 Sëāng lūn.
Ch'hím put se 寢不尸, *k'hwùn bô ch'hin chëō^{ng} sin se*, (Confucius) in his sleep, did not lie stretched out like a corpse. See the 上論 Sëāng lūn.

Ch'hím 㑴 Small of stature; not inclined to grow tall.

Ch'hím 鋟 To engrave wooden blocks for printing.

Ch'hím 賝 To game, to play at games of chance.

Ch'hím 梫 A kind of cinnamon tree.

Ch'hím 踸 Ch'him këak hêng 踸脚行, *ch'him k'ha kë^{n}â*, to walk on tip toe.

去

Ch'hìm 沁 The name of a river; to fathom the depth of water with any thing; to lade.
Gē chwân suy chè kīn, tō sek put kám ch'him 義泉雖至近.盜索不敢沁, *gē ây chw^{n}â chùy suy chè kīn, ch'hat ây sŏk u^{m} k^{n}á khè t'hàm*, the fountain of righteousness may be ever so near, yet we must not presume to draw from it with a thief's rope.

Ch'hìm 㾛 Yìm ch'hìm, a large house, with deep sets of chambers and courts.

卆

Ch'hin 親 Near, to draw near; near relatives; to hold near and dear. Ch'hin aè 親愛, to love intimately. Ch'hin kīn 親近, to approach. Lëáng ch'hin 两親, parents. Ch'hin choō 親自, *ch'hin ka tō*, one's self.

Hîn chaē loe pēen boô chê ch'hek, boô ke ch'hio san yéw wán ch'hin 貧在路邊無至戚.富居深山有遠親 *sòng hëung twā toē pēe^ng, bô che kîn ây ch'hek poò kwùy twā ch'him sw^n a woō hwuîng laê ây ch'hin*, the poor, though dwelling at the road side, have no near relatives to own them; while the rich, though retreating to the deep mountains, have distant relatives coming to seek them.

Ch'hin 皴 A little rising of the skin, a small blister. Chip pit ch'hëuk han, séw wûy ch'hin lëet 執筆觸寒.手爲皴裂, *kēāh pit ch'hëuk kwnâ ch'hêw cëh^n a ch'hin leëh*, holding the pencil in the cold weather, the hand becomes blistered and chapped.

声

Ch'hín 哂 To laugh. Teēn ch'hēen ch'hew yit gân tè sëáng, hëung noê ch'hin che 田千秋一言致相.匈奴哂之, *lëēn ch'hëon ch'hew chit koò wā, tè kaòu chè chaē sëàng hoē hënng noê ây hwan ch'hëò e*, Tëen-ch'heen-ch'hew, on account of one word was promoted to the officer of prime minister, at which the Hëung noê tartars laughed.

去

Ch'hìn 櫬 An inner coffin, a shell.

Ch'hìn 儭 The lining of a garment; also used for ch'hin 親 parents.

Ch'hìn 襯 Clothes worn near the body.

Ch'hìn 瀙 Read ch'hèng: cold; *ch'hew ch'hìn*, cool and pleasant.

2 Q

Ch'hìn 稱 Read ch'hèng: to weigh, to ascertain the weight of any thing; see ch'hèng.

夨

Ch'hip 偮 A multitude of people.

Ch'hip 㑏 Persons collected together.

Ch'hip 咠 A sound made by the mouth and tongue.

Ch'hip 咠 The same as the above; also, many mouths.

Ch'hip 湒 The descent of rain, water bubbling up.

Ch'hip 葺 Sew ch'hip 修葺, to repair, and put in order; also to cover a house.

Ch'hip 楫 A small oar, a paddle. Jëak chêy tāe ch'hwan, jé chok chew ch'hip 若濟大川.爾作舟楫, *nā lëāou twā ch'hwui^ng, lè chang chò chûn gëō*, when I want to cross a great river, you will serve for a paddle.

Ch'hip 緝 Connected, joined together, and handed down, without interruption.

Ch'hip 輯 United together, harmonious. Hô ch'hip 和輯, agreeing.

Ch'hip 戢 To store up, to lay aside; also, to stop, to put a stop to. Chaê ch'hip kan ko 載戢干戈, *chaê k'hè^ng kan ko*, to lay aside warlike instruments. Peng yëw h^nó yëá, hwut ch'hip, chëang choō hwûn yëá 兵猶火也.弗戢將自焚

也, *peng lo ch'hin chëō^ng hòèy, bô hoē e hāy^n h, chëang ka tē sëo,* military weapons are like fire, if we do not put a stop to them, they will burn our own fingers.

Ch'hip 桼 A tree out of which oozes a certain liquid, of which they make varnish; the varnish tree.

Ch'hip 漆 Vulg. *ch'hat:* varnish, paint; also the name of a river.

Ch'hip 膝 Vulg. *k'ha t'haôu woo:* the knee. Lëâng mâ tê t'hoê, k'hoé chè ch'hip yëá 良馬低頭口至膝也, *hò bày kây t'haôu, ch'hùy kaòu k'ha t'hôu woo,* a good horse keeps his head low, till his mouth reaches his knees.
Lëâng séw kò kê ch'hip 两手過其膝, *nō āy ch'hèw, kòèy e āy k'ha t'hâou woo,* both his hands reached over his knees (as he stood upright) said of Lêw pē 劉備, in the 三國 Sam kok.

Ch'hip 濈 United, harmonious.

Ch'hip 蝍 A kind of insect, found adhering to oyster-shells; also found on the bottom of uncoppered vessels at sea: shingles.

Ch'hip 諿 Harmonious; an appellation indicative of talent and wisdom.

Ch'hip 蕺 The name of a plant; grass growing thick together.

Ch'hip 膝 Gnêw ch'hip 牛膝, *gôo ch'hip,* the name of a vegetable medicine; very common in the Chinese apothecary's shops.

Ch'hit 七 Seven. Sip ch'hit 十七, *chap ch'hit,* seventeen. Ch'hit sip 七十, *ch'hit chap,* seventy.
Ch'hit sip jê chëûng sim séy yëuk, put jê ké 七十而從心所欲不踰矩, *ch'hit chap hòèy jê t'hàn sim kw^n a sèy aè bô kòèy hwat toē,* at seventy I followed whateuer my heart desirid, without overstepping the right rule. Said by Confucius, in the 上論 Sëâng lūn.

Ch'hit 柒 The same as the preceding.

Ch'ho 瑳 The colour of a gem; purely white. Ch'ho hêy ch'ho hêy kê che tëên yëá 瑳兮瑳兮其之展也, how white! and how pure! does it display itself! See the 國風 Kok hong.

Ch'ho 嵯 Ch'ho gô 嵯峨, hills covered with stones.

Ch'ho 磋 To grind and rub. Jê ch'hëet jê ch'ho 如切如磋, *ch'hin chëō^ng ch'hëet ch'hin chëō^ng ch'ho,* like splitting and filing (bones.) See the 上論 Sëâng lūn.

Ch'ho 蹉 Ch'ho tô 蹉跎, to miss an opportunity, to miss one's aim.

Ch'ho 操 To hold, to grasp; resolution, firm adherence to. Chëên hàn tëang t'hong k'hek, tëên këen yéw hëên ch'ho 前漢張湯客田見有賢操, *chëên hàn tëō^ng t'hong āy lâng k'hāyh tëên këèn, woō gaôu ch'ho gīm meē^n h,* in the former part of the Hàn dynasty-Tëō^ng t'hong had a guest called Tëên-këèng who was celebrated for his firm grasp. Ch'ho peng 操兵, *ch'haou peng,* to drill soldiers.

Ch'ho 臊 A raw smell; the smell of raw meat. Tong kay sat gnêw, woō hèw seng ch'ho 東家殺牛汙臭腥臊, *lang pee^{ng} ây ch'hoò t'haê goô lā sâm ch'haòu kwà ch'hai^{ng} ch'ho*, the next door neighbours on the eastern side were in the habit of killing oxen, which occasioned dirt and stink, connected with a raw smell.

Ch'ho 鯹 Gê ch'ho 魚鯹, *hê ch'ho*, the smell of raw fish.

声

Ch'hó 草 Vulg. *ch'haóu*, grass. Hô kó ch'hó 禾稿草, *têw kó ch'háou*, straw. Ch'heng ch'ho tê tông, ch'hè ch'hè wâ 青草池塘處處蛙, *ch'hai^{ng} ch'háou tê tê lông, lak wūy woō kap â*, when green grass grows about the pools, in every part there will be frogs.

Pē sim ch'hó ch'hòng che 諀諶草創之, *pē sim ch'haóu kó ch'hòng e*, Pē-sim made a rough sketch of it.

Ch'hó se 草書, *ch'hó jō sēá*, to write the running hand.

Ch'hó kó 草稿, a rough sketch, a hastily written thing.

Ch'hó ch'hó 草草, short and hasty.

Ch'hó 艸 The same as the preceding.

Ch'hó 懆 Grieved, sorrowful. Lô sim ch'hó hêy 勞心懆兮, *lēòh bwâ ây sim ch'hó hêy*, a troubled mind, how sorrowful! See the 國風 Kok hong.

Ch'hó 騲 The female of quadrupeds.

去

Ch'hò 操 Chëet ch'hò 節操, to hold to one's purpose: to adhere to self-prescribed rules.

K'hëuk ch'hò 曲操, the notes or rules for singing a song.

Ch'hò 挫 To push, to hurt. Soo é yit hô ch'hò ê jin, jëak tat che ê ch'hè têâou 思以一毫挫於人,若撻之於市朝, *sëō^{ng} nā woō chit hô ch'ho kap lâng, ch'hin chëō^{ng} tit p'hăh tô kay ch'hē têâou têng*, he thought that when he was in the least pushed by people, it was the same as though he had been struck in the market or the palace. See the 上孟 Sëāng bēng.

Ch'hò 脞 Small. Ch'hëet jëuk wûy ch'hò 切肉爲脞, *ch'hëet băh chò ch'hò*, to chop up meat till it becomes small.

Ch'hò 莝 To cut off grass; to mow down grass.

Ch'hò 睉 Small, minute. Chông ch'hò 叢脞, broken into small pieces.

Ch'hò 造 To go to, to enter, to wait upon. Ch'hò ch'hoò 造次, hurried. Ch'héng pit boô kwuy, jê ch'hò ê têâou 請必無歸,而造於朝, *ch'hēⁿá pit bô tooi^{ng} laê, jê ch'hò kaòu têâou*, we beseech you do not return home, but go to the court. See the 上孟 Sëāng bēng.

Ch'hò 剉 To break off, to maim; to cut to pieces, to dissect.

Ch'hò 慥 In actions to regard our words, and in words to regard our actions, is called ch'hò.

Ch'hò 糙 Rice mixed with the husk. Ch'hò bé 米糙, unbeaten rice.

Ch'hò 噪 The noise made by birds; to chirp, to whistle. Nëáou ch'hò ch'hëen lîm güēy 鳥噪千林外, *chëáou háou kaòu ch'heng lim gwā*, the birds whistled beyond the thousand groves.

Ch'hò 蹉 To miss an opportunity; to lose time; also to pass over. Jit gwat ch'hò tô, söèy put gnó é 日月蹉跎.歲不我與, *jit göëyh ch'hò tô, neë^ng höèy bô hoē gwá*, days and months are passed by, and years of long life are not afforded me.

平

Ch'hoe 粗 Coarse, large, gross, not fine. Cheng ch'hoe 精粗, fine and coarse. Noē sim kám chëá, kē seng ch'hoe é lēy 怒心感者.其聲粗以厲, *sëw k'hè ây sim kw^na kán tōng e ây së^na ch'hoe kwà lēy*, when a person is moved by an angry feeling, the sound of his music is coarse and shrill.

Ch'hoe 麤 Vulgar, coarse. Pé kê sëáou tāe, é kê ch'hoe lëāng, jê sëáng hwat che 比其小大.與其麤良.而賞罰之, *pé e ây sèy twā, kap e ây ch'hoe lëâng, jê sëö^ng hwat e*, compare the small and great, the coarse and refined together in order to reward or punish them.

Ch'hoe 屭 Ch'hoe hwún 屭糞, *ch'hoe pùn*, dirt and dung.

上聲

Ch'hóe 楚 A bushy tree; a clump of trees: name of a district. Chéng ch'hoē 整楚, properly arranged. Sin ch'hoé 辛楚, miserable, wretched.

Ch'hoé 濋 The name of a river.

Ch'hoé 礎 The stones at the bottom of pillars; a pedestal.

去聲

Ch'hoè 錯 To reject, to set aside. Kē tit, ch'hoè choo óng chek bin hok 舉直錯諸枉.則民服, *kê yûng tëâou tit ây lâng, k'hê t'hek kok óng k'hwut ây lâng chek pâyh sai^ng hok*, when we elevate the upright to places of trust, and set aside all crooked fellows, the people will then submit to us. See the 上論 Sëāng lūn.

Ch'hoè 醋 Vinegar. Swan jê ch'hoe 酸如醋, *swui^ng ch'hin chëö^ng ch'hoè*, as sour as vinegar. Lêng yim sam seng ch'hoè, put këèn ch'huy hông toē 寧飲三升醋.不見崔弘度, *lêng k'hè lim s^na seng ch'hoè. â^m t'hang k'hè keè^ng ch'huy hông toē*, it is better to drink three pints of vinegar, than to go and see Ch'huy-hong-toē, (who was a very bad tempered man.)

Ch'hoè 阼 The eastern step. Tëâou hok jê lip ê ch'hoè kae 朝服而立於阼階, *ch'hëng tëâou lâe ây hok, jê k'hëä lip tē tang peē^ng ây gîm kay*, dressed in his court apparel, (Confucius) stood on the eastern steps. See the 上論 Sëāng lūn.

Ch'hoè 祚 Happiness, emolument, rank. Lëên ch'hoè 年祚, long life. T'hëen ch'hoè bêng tek 天祚明德, *t'hee^ng soò hok k'hè hoē bêng tek ây lâng*, heaven bestows blessings on men of illustrious virtue.

Ch'hoè 䄍 The sacrifice offered at the close of the year.

Ch'hoè 措 To take, to manage, to arrange.

Ch'hoè 厝 To place, to lay: vulg. *ch'hoò*, a house. P'hāou h^nô, ch'hoè che chek sin che hāy 抱火厝之積薪之下, *p'hō hoèy, hây e tē chek ch'hâ ây hây tēy*, this would be to collect fire, and place it under a stack of fire-wood.

幸

Ch'höey 吹 Read ch'huy: blow, to blow a wind instrument. Ch'huy sëaou yin hông 吹簫引鳳, *ch'höey sëaou ch'hwā, hông*, to play on the pipe, and draw the fabulous bird hông out of it retreat.

Ch'höey 炊 Read ch'huy: to boil by steam. Ch'huy kó 炊粿, *ch'höey köey*, to boil dumplings. Ëk choó jê sit che, chëet haê jê ch'huy che 易子而食之. 折骸而炊之, *wⁿà kěⁿá jê chěăh e chěěh kwut jê ch'höey e*, the people exchanged their children and ate them (not bearing to devour their own offspring); and broke up the bones for firewood to cook them with (speaking of a famine.)

Yen tông 烟筒, *hwun ch'höey*, a tobacco pipe.

肃

Ch'höey 髓 Read ch'húy: marrow. T'hoê ló 頭腦, *t'haoû kak ch'höey*, the brains. T'hông jip kwut ch'húy 痛入骨髓, *t'hëⁿà jip kwut ch'höëy*, a pain that penetrates the bones and marrow.

Ch'höey 膸 Te ch'höëy 猪膸, pig's marrow.

平

Ch'höëy 箠 A Club or stick to beat people with.

去

Ch'höëy 尋 Read sin: to seek, to search. Jit sîm kan ko, é sëang cheng t'hó 日尋干戈.以相征討, *tak jit ch'höey kwâe á, ê kaou á, sëo çheng p'hăh*, every day looking for clubs and pikes, to fight and contend with. See the 左傳, Chó twān.

夫

Ch'höëyh 歠 Read ch'hwat: to quaff, to drink largely, to small. Poē kê cho jê ch'hwat kê lê 餔其糟而歠其醨, *poē e ây chëw chaou, jê ch'h höëyh e ây põh chëw*, to eat the grains, and drink the sweet wort of the liquor.

夫

Ch'hok 錯 To rub, to grind; to fill; also, to be in error. T'hna san che sek, k'hó é wûy ch'hok 他山之石可以爲錯, *pat swⁿa ây chëëk t'hang laê chò lëy á*, the stones of another hill, may be used for grinding stones.

Ch'hwân ch'hok 舛錯, an error. Ch'hok goē 錯悞, a mistake.

Ch'hok 簇 Shap. Chëen ch'hok 箭簇, *chëëⁿᵍ t'haôu*, the head of an arrows.

Ch'hok 躖 Ak ch'hak 齷齪, to urge, to distress.

Ch'hok 觕 A rhinoceros horn, not yet shaped into a cup.

Ch'hok 傶 A surname.

天

Ch'hok 鑿 Vulg. *ch'hak*: a chizel. Ch'hwan ch'hok 舛鑿, not successful.

幸

Ch'hong 倉 Vulg. *ch'heⁿᵍ*: a granary. Ch'hong chut 倉卒, unmoved, intrepid. Kwan che ch'hong lim sit, hoó k'hoê ch'hëung 君之倉廩實府庫充, *kwan tê ây ch'heⁿᵍ lim' teëⁿᵍ, hoó k'hoè mwⁿá*, your highness' granaries are full, and your treasuries overflowing. See the 孟子 Bêng-choó.

Ch'hong 滄 Expansive, wide; the name of a river. Ch'hong haé 滄海, the wide sea.

Ch'hong lông che súy ch'heng hêy, k'hó e chok gnó eng 滄浪之水清兮可以濯我纓, *ch'hong lông ây chúy ch'heng, t'hang laê sêy gwà ay kin twà*, the clear waters of the Ch'hong-lông, will serve to rinse the tassels of my cap.

Ch'hong 蒼 Green the colour of grass; a surname. Ch'hong t'hëen 蒼天, the azure heavens.
Ch'hong seng 蒼生, the people.

Ch'hong 葱 Vulg. *ch'hang*: an onions; also written 蔥 ch'hong. Köëy ch'hun yūng ch'hong 膾春用葱, *băh tē ch'hun t'heeng yūng ch'hang*, meat in the spring season must be cooked with onions.

Ch'hong 瑲 The sound tinkling gems.

Ch'hong 鶬 Ch'hong keng 鶬鶊, the name of a bird.

Ch'hong 瘡 Vulg. *ch'heng*: an ulcer. Seng ch'hong 生瘡, *saing ch'heng*, to have an ulcer.

Ch'hong 創 To injure; also written 刅 ch'hong, an injury done with a knife.

Ch'hong 聰 To hear clearly. Ch'hong bêng 聰明, *ch'hang mënâ*, intelligents, clever.
Soo k'hòng che ch'hong, put é lëuk lut, put lêng chèng gnoé yim 師曠之聰不以六律不能正五音, *soo k'hòng ây gaôu t'hëna, bô è lak ây lut, chëw bēy chënà goë yim*, even soo-k'hòng with all his clever hearing, if he had not the six ruler of music, could not correct the fine sounds. See the 下孟 Hāy bēng.

Ch'hong 怱 Hasty, in a hurry. Boô koè ch'hong ch'hong 無故怱怱, *bô sna soō kaôu hëăh ch'hong ch'hong*, without any cause, to be in a hurry also written 刅 ch'hong.

Ch'hong 悤 The same as the preceding.

Ch'hong 牕 Read *t'hang*: a window; also writting 窗, 牎, and 窻. Chaē ch'hëăng wat yéw, chaē ok wat ch'hong 在墻曰牖在屋曰牕, *tē ch'hëông kong yéw, tē ch'hoô kóng t'hang*, a hole in the wall is called Yéw, and an oppening in a house, is called *t'hang*.

Ch'hong 楤 A pole for carrying burdens, sharpened at both ends; also the name of a tree.

Ch'hong 驄 A horse of a white colour; others say, of a grey colour.

Ch'hong 䆫 A hilly, appearance.

去 Ch'hóng 愴 Ch'hey ch'hóng 悽愴, sarrowful, sad, affected. Söëy hwut hwut hêy wûy boē, ē kám sē hêy ch'hey ch'hóng 歲忽忽兮爲暮余感時悽愴, *neeng hōëy hwut hwut lëy lëeng peeng mooing, gwá kám e ây sē hëy, ch'hey ch'hóng*, the years go away so suddenly till the evening ot life; I feel affected with the lapse of time, till I am sad and sorrowful.

Ch'hóng 倉 Bông ch'hóng 莽倉, rude, uncultivated, like a wilderness.

去 Ch'hòng 創 To creat, to commence, to lay a foundation; also to adjust. Ch'hòng chò t'hëen tēy 創造

天地, *ch'hòng chò Chèe^ng tēy*, "to create the heavens and the earth." A Christian phrase.

Kwun choó ch'hòng gëèp, sûy t'hóng wûy k'hó kèy yëá 君子創業垂統爲可繼也, *kwun choó ây lâng ch'hòng sōo gëèp, ch'hë^ná sûy hây ây t'hòng t'hang sëo swa*, the good man commences an undertaking, and the clue of his scheme can be connected to succeeding ages. See the 上孟 Sëāng bëng.

Têng ch'hòng 懲創, to correct and adjust.

Ch'hòng 刱 To commence, to form; also written 刅, ch'hòng the same as the above.

Ch'hòng 賶 To store up goods.

平

Ch'hông 牀 Vulg. *ch'hê^ng*: a bed place. Bëên ch'hông 眠牀, *bîn ch'hê^ng*, a couch.

Ch'hông 饑 Vulg. *ch'hâng*: greedy, gluttonous.

声

Ch'hoó 此 This, the opposite of that; also to stop. Ló choó k'hè pó ch'hé ch'hoó 老子去彼取此, *ló choó k'hè hwut lëy, t'hăyh chëy lëy*, Ló-choó rejected that and selected this.

Ch'hoó 呰 Short; Confusedly; also written 跐 ch'hoō.

Ch'hoó 訾 To measure, to mete out. A surname.

Ch'hoó 泚 Clear water; the name of a river.

Ch'hoó 茈 Ch'hoó këang 茈薑, *ch'hè^ng ke^ng*, young ginger, green ginger.

Ch'hoó 玼 The colour of a gem; purely white.

Ch'hoó 佌 Small diminutive.

Ch'hoó 抯 To hold in the hand; the palm of the hand; a branch.

Ch'hoó 訿 Vulg. *t'hoŏh*: to prop up, to poke with a stick; to blame, to ridicule, to revile.

去

Ch'hoò 次 In order, second, next in order. Ch'hoò sē 次序, according to order.

Yit ch'hoò 一次, *chit paé*, the first. Ch'hoò jit 次日, the next day. Seng jê te che cheâ sëāng yëá, hak jê te che cheá ch'hoò yëá 生而知之者上也. 學而知之者次也, *sai^ng jê chae e ây lâng, sē sëāng têng yëá ŏh jê chae è ây lâng, sē lëy jê yëá*, to be born with the knowledge of any thing, is the highest order of talent; to acquire the knowledge of it by study is the next in order. See the 下論 Hāy lūn.

Ch'hoò 佽 A man's name; advantageous; also written 佽 ch'hoò.

Ch'hoò 佽 Advantageous; to help and assist, to substitute, to attain to. Jin boô heng tēy, hoê put ch'hoò yëen 人無兄弟胡不佽焉, *lâng bô hë^n tē, s^ná soō ū^m chāne*, those people have no brethren, why do you not assist them? See the 國風 Kok hong.

Ch'hoò 厝 Read ch'hoò: a house, to place; a place where we may put a person to dwell in. Ch'hoè t'hek 厝宇, *ch'hoò t'hah*, a dwelling.

平

Ch'hoô 玼 A flowin a gem; a stone in the midst of a gem.

Ch'hoô 疵 A sickness a fault, to find fault with. Ê ch'hé ê kêw, put jé hây ch'hoô 予取予求不女瑕疵, *gwá thäyh, gwá kêw, bô hoē lê hêêm ū^m hô*, whether I take it or ask, it I am not found with by you. See the 左傳 Chó twān.

Ch'hoô 茈 The name of a grass, rised as a dye; also edible.

入

Ch'hoŏh 焠 Read ch'hùy: the hissing of hot iron, when put into the water; also to harden steel, and temper the blade of a sharp instrument. Ch'heng súy ch'hùy kê hong 清水粹其鋒, *ch'hèng chùy ch'hoŏh e ây hong*, to temper the point, by putting it into pure water.

平

Ch'hui^{ng} 川 Read ch'hwan: a stream; also the anus. San ch'hwan 山川, *sw^{n}a ch'hui^{ng}*, mountains and river. Kew ch'hwan 尻川, *k'ha ch'hui^{ng}*, the anus.

Ch'hui^{ng} 村 Read ch'hun: a village. Hëang ch'hun 鄉村, *hëo^{ng} ch'hui^{ng}*, a contry village. Chëă būn chéw kay hô ch'hé yéw, bok tông yaôu ché hêng hwa ch'hun 借問酒家何處有,牧童遥指杏花村, *chëŏh mooi^{ng} chëw kay tá wûy woô, bok tông hwui^{ng} ké hêng hwa ch'hi^{ng}*, I begged to ask where the vintuer dwels, when the sheperd's boy pointed to the distant village of the almond blossom."

Ch'hui^{ng} 栓 *ch'ëa ch'hui^{ng}* 車栓, the axletree of a carreage.

Ch'hui^{ng} 穿 Read ch'hwan: to string through to run on a string. Kwàn ch'hwan keng twān 貫穿經傳, *kwni^{ng} ch'hui^{ng} keng, twān*, to run through the classics and records; i. e. to agree with them.

上

Ch'hui^{ng} 嗋 Read ch'hún: to pierce, to sting.

去

Ch'huì^{ng} 串 Read ch'hwùn: a string of any thing; to run any thing on a string. Lûh lûy hoē, jê choo che ch'hwàn 纍纍乎如珠之串, *sëo swà hoē ch'hin chëo^{ng} choo ây ch'hui^{ng}*, connected, together just like a string of beads.

Ch'huì^{ng} 穿 Read ch'hwàn: to perforate, to pass through. Gé ch'hwàn kéw k'hëuk choo 蟻穿九曲珠, *hëā ch'hui^{ng} kaôu āy wan āy choo*, an ant passes through the hole of a bead which has nine bends in it.

Ch'huì^{ng} 釧 Read ch'hwàn: an armlet, a bracelet. Hwa ch'hwàng 花釧, *hwa ch'hui^{ng}*, an ornamented bracelet; some say, a hair pin.

Ch'huì^{ng} 篅 Read ch'hún: to string any thing on a piece of bamboo.

平

Ch'hun 春 The spring season, the spring Ch'hun wûy yît söey séw höey chëem pek hwa k'höey 春爲

福建方言字典

一歲首.梅占百花魁, *ch'hun chò ka nooi^{ng} neē^{ng} ây t'haôu, â^{m} chëem chë^{n}â pâyh hwa ây twâ,* the spring is the head of a whole year, and the plum blossom is the chief of a hundred flowers.

Ch'hun 村 Vulg. *ch'hui^{ng}*: a village. Ch'hun tëung bûn yéw ch'hoó jîn, hâm laê bûn sìn 村中聞有此人.咸來問訊, *ch'hun tëung t'he^{n}a woō chèy lëy lâng, chè pöo laê mooi^{ng} seâou sit,* when they heard in the village that this man arrived, they all came to hear the news.

Ch'hun 邨 The ancient form of 村 ch'hun; also written 𦿏 ch'hun and 墫 ch'hun.

Ch'hun 伸 Read sin: to stretch out, to extend; to straighten anything that is bent.

声

Ch'hún 忖 To think, to conjecture, to measure, to estimate. T'ha jîn yéw sim, ê ch'hún tok che 他人有心.予忖度之, *pat lâng woō sim, gwâ ch'hún tok e,* another man has an idea, and I pass a judgement upon it.

Ch'hún 偆 Rich, affluent; thick, kind; also written 賰 ch'hún.

Ch'hún 僢 To turn back, to back; also used for the following.

Ch'hún 舛 Wrong, erroneous. Ch'hún ch'hok 舛錯, an error, a mistake. Kê se gnôe ke, kê tō ch'hún pak 其書五車.其道舛駁, *e ây ch'hâyh woō goē ây ch'hëa, e ây tō ch'hún ch'hok pak chap,* his books amounted to five waggon-loads, but his doctrines were erroneous and confused.

Ch'hún 荈 A kind of tea, which is gathered late in the season.

Ch'hún 瞬 The moving of the eyes; to blink. Ch'hún sit 瞬息, the twinkling of an eye.
Bok ch'hún jê tëen 目瞬如電, *bak chew nâyh ch'hin chëō^{ng} seěh nâ,* the eyes move like lighting.
Sëen hak put ch'hún, jê hoē k'hó gân seà ê 先學不瞬.而後可言射矣, *taē seng ŏh bak chew û^{m} tin tâng, jê âou t'hang laē kóng chöh cheè^{ng},* first learn to keep the eyes from blinking, and te then you can talk of archery.

Ch'hún 喘 Vulg. *ch'hwán*: to pant, to breathe hard; to speak in a whisper.

Ch'hún 蠢 The motion of insects; also stupid, dull. Ch'hún pún 蠢笨, stupid. Ch'hún jé bân keng 蠢爾蠻荆, *gōng lê chèy lëy bân keng,* you stupid savage.

Ch'hún 噋 To blow.

Ch'hún 鏱 Vulg. *ch'hui^{ng}*: to string any thing on a piece of bamboo.

去

Ch'hùn 寸 An inch. Yit ch'hùn k'hè 一寸氣, *chit ch'hùn k'hè,* an inch of breath.
Ch'hùn sim ch'hëen koé gëep 寸心千古業, *chit ch'hùng ây sim kw^{n}a sëō^{ng} kaoù chit ch'heng koé ây gëep,* an inch-square heart speculates for a patrimony of a thousand ages.

平

Ch'hûn 僔 To respect, to honour.

去

Ch'hūn 捘 To push, to beckon, to touch the elbow.

夫

Ch'hut 出 To go out. Ch'hut gōēy 出外, *ch'hut gwā*, to go abroad. Tēy choō jip chek haòu, ch'hut chek tēy 弟子入則孝.出則弟, *tēy choó jip tēŏh wŏo haòu, ch'hut tēŏh gâou chò sēóh tē*, young people at home should be filial to their parents, and abroad respectful to superiors. See the 上論 Sēāng lūn.

Ch'hut 齣 A stanza in a song; a scene in a play. Yit ch'hut 一齣, one scene.

隹

Ch'huy 崔 A surname.

Ch'huy 催 To urge, to constrain. Ch'huy ch'hëuk 催促, to urge, to hasten.

Ch'huy 推 To push forward, to extend and carry out. Ch'huy káng 推講, *ch'huy kòng*, to enlarge upon, and extend in speech; to expatiate.

Ch'huy hëên jëang lêng; sè kwan naé hô 推賢讓能.庶官乃和, *ch'huy gâou lâng jé nëō*^{ng} *ëy ây, choo kwⁿa chëw hô*, when clever people are pushed forward, and men of ability yielded to, then all the different officers will be harmonious. See the 尙書 Sëāng se.

Ch'huy 炊 Vulg. *ch'höey:* to boil, to steam, to cook.

Ch'huy 吹 Vulg. *ch'höey:* to blow, to play on a pipe; also written 龡 ch'huy.

Ch'huy 蓷 A vegetable; also called, ek boē ch'hó 益毋草, "profit mother grass."

耑

Ch'húy 惴 To be afraid of, and concerned about. Goê put ch'húy yëen 吾不惴焉, *gwá ūm kēⁿa e*, I should not be afraid of him. See the 上孟 Sëāng bēng.

Ch'húy 灈 Deep water.

Ch'húy 髓 Vulg. *ch'hëëy:* marrow. Hân jip kwut ch'húy 寒入骨髓, *kwⁿá jip kwut ch'höëy*, cold penetrating to the bones and marrow.

Ch'húy 璀 The brightness of a gem.

Ch'húy 揣 To measure; to rub, to wipe. Put ch'húy kê pún, jê chêy kê bwat, hong ch'hùn che bȯk, k'hó soó ko ê gim loê 不揣其本.而齊其末.方寸之木.可使高於岑樓, *ūm ch'húy tok e ây pún, jê ch'hëng chêy e ây böëy, chēw chit ch'hùn ây ch'hâ, t'hang saé k'hàh kwân ê gîm laôu*, if you do not measure from the root and put the ends together then a piece of wood an inch-square, may be raised higher than a lofty tower.

Ch'húy 遄 To go backwards and forwards.

卒

Ch'hùy 翠 The name of a bird about the size of a sparrow, whose feathers are of a deep green colour.
Ch'hùy yit 翠鳦, a bird like a swallow.

Ch'hùy 倅 Secondary, assisting. Ch'hùy ch'hëa 倅車, a spare carriage.

Ch'hùy 啐 To taste. Tut ch'hùy 咄啐, to scold, to vociferate.

福建方言字典

Ch'hùy 焠 Vulg. *ch'hoŏh:* to thrust hot iron into water, in order to harden it.

Ch'hùy 碎 Broken, broken to pieces. Ch'hùy ch'hùy 碎碎, all broken to shivers. Lêng ch'hùy 零碎, *lân san*, miscellaneous, few, odd. Sîn t'hoê é p'hek kē ch'hùy ê chē 臣頭與璧俱碎於柱, *gwá ây t'hâou kap hwut lêy p'hek, chò poô böĕyh p'hăh ch'hùy tē t'hēâou*, both my own head and this gem, will I break to pieces against the pillar.

Ch'hùy 脆 Vulg. *ch'hèy:* brittle, easily broken.

Ch'hùy 毳 The fine hair of animals; fine furs used for a carpet.

Ch'hùy 口 Read k'hoé: the mouth; an orifice. K'hoé ch'hé 口齒, *ch'hùy k'hé*, the teeth. Neáou k'hoé 鳥口, *chëáou ch'hùy*, a bird's beak, a tattler, a chatterer. K'hoé che ê bē yëá, bok che ê sek yëá, jé che ê seng yëá, sèng yëá 口之於味也.目之於色也.耳之於聲也性也, *ch'hùy ây tē bē, bak chew ây tē sek, hē k'hang ây tē sēⁿa, chèy sē sèng yëá*, the mouth in judging of tastes, the eye of colours, and the ear of sounds, are each according to nature. See the 孟子 Bēng choó.

Ch'hùy 崒 High and imminent.

Ch'hùy 脺 The countenance soft and obliging.

去

Ch'hwa 撾 To beat. Jit boē ch'hwa hwun koé 日暮撾昏鼓, *jit àm p'hăh maîⁿᵍ hwuiⁿᵍ ây koè*, when the day declines, we beat the evening drum.

Ch'hwa 髽 Ch'hwa köëy 髽髻, a piece of hempen cord, tied to the head-dress of women, to indicate that they are in mourning.

去

Ch'hwá 繟 Not tight; a rope not twisted tight.

去

Ch'hwà 蔡 Read ch'haè: a surname.

平

Ch'hwâ 檛 Ch'hwâ pwà 檛簸, to sift and winnow, as corn.

Ch'hwâ 蛇 Read sêâ: a snake. Tok sêâ 毒蛇, *tok ch'hwâ*, a poisonous snake; also pronounced *chwâ*. Gnêw é pit t'hèng, sêâ é gán t'hèng 牛以鼻聽.蛇以眼聽, *goô t'hò p'hēèⁿᵍ k'hang t'hēⁿa, ch'hwâ t'hò bak chew t'hēⁿa*, oxen hear with their noses, and snakes hear with their eyes.

去

Ch'hwā 悉 To abduct, to lead away. Tin sam hông gnoé lëâng, sëang ch'hwā choé 陳三黃五娘相悉走, *tân sⁿa kap wuiⁿᵍ goē nëôⁿᵍ sëo ch'hwā chaôu*, Mr. Tân-sⁿa and Miss Wuiⁿᵍ-goē absconded together.

Ch'hwā 娶 Read ch'hé: to marry, to take in marriage. Ch'hé ch'hey hwuy wūy yáng yëá, jê yéw sê hoē wūy yáng 娶妻非爲餋也.而有時乎爲餋, *ch'hwā boê ūᵐ sē yîn wūy aè e ch'hē lân, jê woō sē yëá aè e ch'hē lân*, when a man marries a wife, it is not merely because he wants her to support him, and yet sometimes he is glad of her assistance. See the 下孟 Hāy bēng.

Ch'hwā 導 Read tō: to lead. Tō loē 導路, *ch'hwā loē*, tó lead the way. Tō guó sëen loē è 導我先路矣, *ch'hwā gwá ây seng loē*, first lead the way for me.

Ch'hwⁿa 櫶 To bolt. Ch'hwan bûn 櫶門, *ch'hwⁿa mooiⁿᵍ*, to bolt the door.

Ch'hwⁿá 杶 Koé sûn 狗杶, *ká ch'hwⁿá*, the name of a wood, used for making handles.

Ch'hwⁿà 閂 A bolt. *Mooiⁿᵍ ch'hwⁿà* 門閂, the bolt of a door.

Ch'hwⁿà 穿 *Ch'hwⁿà tō*, 穿道, to get out of the way, to go by another route.

Ch'hwⁿā 鱇 A very small kind of fish.

Ch'hwăh 睻 The eyes moved away. Bok ch'hwăh 目睻, *bȧk chew ch'hwăh*, squinting eyes.

Ch'hwăh 敓 To take any thing by force, to snatch by violence.

Ch'hwăh 㩇 Read ch'hat: a grater; to grate any thing. Ch'haè t'hoê ch'hat 菜頭㩇, *ch'haè t'haŏu ch'hwăh*, a grater, for scraping turnip radishes.

Ch'hwăh 瘥 To be purged, to be griped.

Ch'hwan 川 Vulg. *ch'huiⁿᵍ*; a stream, a river. San ch'hwan 山川, hills and rivers. Wûy hāy pit yin ch'hwan tek 爲下必因川澤, *chò kāy pit t'hàn ch'hwan tek*, for a low situation, we must avail ourselves of the rivers and marshes. See the 下孟 Hāy bēng.

Ch'hwan 巛 The same as the preceding; also one of the radicals.

Ch'hwan 穿 Read *ch'huiⁿᵍ*: to perforate, to string through.

Ch'hwan 拴 To select, to choose.

Ch'hwan 詮 To explain, to confer with, to reason with. Bûn tèy sok é ch'hwan 文帝數與詮, *bûn tèy chap chap kap lâng ch'hwan lūn*, the Emperor Bûn frequently held people in argument.

Ch'hwan 銓 A scale; to weigh, to judge of, to put in order. Ch'hwan lëāng k'heng tëūng 銓量輕重, *ch'hwan nëōⁿᵍ k'hin tāng*, to weigh and discriminate the light from the heavy.

Ch'hwan 筌 Fishing stakes made of bamboo. Tek è bōng gân, tek gê bōng ch'hwan 得意忘言·得魚忘筌, *tit è bēy kè lân ây wā, tit hê bēy kè hwut lēy ch'hwan*, obtaining our wish, we forget our engagements, and when we have caught the fish we forget the fishing stakes. See the 莊子 Chong chóo.

Ch'hwan 痊 Whole, recovered from sickness; to heal. Sē é chëà ch'hè ch'hám t'hòng chëá, é ch'hwan pēng yëá 是灸以刺慘痛者以痊病也, *sē è chëà ch'hè ch'hám t'hēⁿà, chëá, ò ch'hwa hâ paiⁿᵍ*, thus we use caustics, probes, pain, and suffering, in order to remedy diseases.

Ch'hwan 悛 To change, to alter, to reform. Kēw ok put ch'hwan 舊惡不悛, *koō ay p'haⁿg bô kây*, not reformed from old vices. See the 尙書 Sëāng se.

Ch'hwan 湍 The fluidity of water; fluid and moveable like water. Sêng yêw ch'hwan súy yëá 性猶湍水也, *lâng ây saiⁿg ch'hin chëōⁿg ch'hwan chây*, human nature is like the fluid and flexible water.

声

Ch'hwán 歂 To pant, to breathe hard. Ch'hwán k'hè 歂氣, *ch'hwán k'hwùy*, to draw breath. Ch'hwán sit 歂息, to breathe; also writhen 喘 ch'hwán.

去

Ch'hwàn 串 Vulg. *ch'huiⁿg*: to string anything on a file or string.

Ch'hwàn 簒 To usurp, to take what does not lawfully belong to one. Jê ke gëâou che këung, pek gëâou che choó, sē ch'hwàn yëá 而居堯之宮.逼堯之子.是簒也, *ch'hin chëōⁿg k'hëā tē gëâou ây këung ch'hoò, kaⁿg gëâou ây hâou saiⁿg sē ch'hwàn yëá*, but if he had dwelt in Geâou's palace, and driven out Geâou's son, that would have been usurpation. See the 下孟 Hāy bēng.
Ch'hwàn wāy 簒位, to usurp the throne.

Ch'hwàn 纂 To collect together; to arrange in order; to compile a book. K'hóng choô san se se, têng léy gak, ch'hwàn chew ek, sew ch'hun ch'hew, kae sút jê put chok yëá 孔子刪詩書.定礼樂.纂周易.修春秋.皆述而不作也, *k'hóng chóp kéng se se, tëⁿā lêy gak, ch'hwàn chew ek, sew ch'hun ch'hew, chè poô sut kóng jê bô sin chò*, Confucius made selections from the odes, and classics, fixed the rules of ceremony and music, arranged the diagrams of the Chew dynasty, and compiled the spring and autumn records; in all of which he merely republished, and did not compose anything new. See 朱子 choo choó.

Ch'hwàn 穿 Vulg. *ch'hwiⁿg*: to perforate, to go through.

Ch'hwàn 僢 To separate; back to back, foot to foot: to go in opposite directions. Hwun lêw ch'hwàn tê 分流僢馳, *hwun laôu sëo pöëy cháou*, to flow in different directions, and gallop away from one another.

Ch'hwàn 竄 To run away, to abscond. Ch'hé ch'hwàn 鼠竄, to scamper off like mice.
Chin pek é tëy tëūng yung; tông ch'hwàn keng bân 泰伯與弟仲雍.同竄荆蠻, *chin pek kap e óy sëó tē tëūng yung, chò poô chaóu tē keng bân*, Chin-pek, and his younger brother Tëūng-yung, absconded together to the territory of the Barbarians.

Ch'hwàn 釧 Pè ch'hwàn 臂釧, *ch'hëw sóh*, a bracelet; an arm-ring.

Ch'hwàn 爨 To put wood on the fire, to cook food, to dress victuals. E' hoó chēng ch'hwàn 以釜甑爨, *t'hó tëⁿā kap öey laê chè meēⁿh*, to cook anything in a pot or a pan.

Ch'hwàn 錞 The ore of metals.

Ch'hwàn 瑏 A stone ring, a gem bracelet: an armlet made of a single gem.

平

Ch'hwân 船 Vulg. *chûn:* a ship, a boat. Chëèn ch'hwân 戰船, *chëèn chûn,* a ship of war. Hông têy sin Këung koé, Hⁿò-tek, chok ch'hwân 黃帝臣共鼓貨狄作船, *wuiⁿᵍ têy ây jîn sîn, Këung-koé kap Hⁿò-tek chò chûn,* the yellow Emperor's servants called Këung-koé and Hⁿò-tek first built vessels. (A. C. 2622).

入

Ch'hwat 歠 Vulg. *ch'höëyh:* to quaff, to drink largely. Also written 啜 ch'hwat. Seaóu gō taē ch'hwat, jê t'hong ak swat 小飦大歠如湯沃雪, *sèy chëăh twā lim ch'hin chëōⁿᵍ t'heⁿᵍ ak tëŏh säyh,* to eat little and drink much, is like throwing hot water on snow: It would soon melt a man away.

Ch'hwat 啜 To eat, to taste. Toê poē ch'hwat 徒餔啜, *ch'hêng ch'hêng sëōⁿᵍ chëăh lim ây soō,* to think of nothing but eating and drinking.

Ch'hwat 皴 The skin broken, or split.

Ch'hwat 撮 To collect, to take up with the fingers; to make a collection. Sam ché ch'hwat che yëá 三指撮之也, *sⁿa ây ch'hêw cháeⁿᵍ nüyⁿh e,* to take up anything with three fingers. Soò se ch'hwat gân 四書撮言, a compilation of sentences extracted from the four Books.

Ch'hwat 繓 A superfluity; anything over; the ends of threads in sowing.

Ch'hwat 襊 Black cloth, used in making caps, and head kerchiefs.

Ch'hwat 蕞 Small, insignificant.

平

Chim 斟 To pour out, to increase. Chim chéw 斟酒, *t'hîn chéw,* to pour out wine. Chim chëak 斟酌, to deliberate on, to consider. Jê hoē ông chim chëak 而後王斟酌, *jëên aōu ông t'hang chim chëak,* afterwards your majesty can consider of it.

Chim 椹 An instrument made of wood and iron, used in killing people. Sin che hëung put chëuk é tòng chim chit 臣之胸不足以當椹櫍, *gwá ây heng bô kaòu é tèⁿᵍ chim chit,* my breast is not equal to bear the iron club. See the 戰國策, Chëën kok ch'hek.

Chim 碪 A kind of chalk used in drawings, found in ravines and hills and to be met with after a thunder storm.

Chim 瑊 A stone resembling a gem; an inferior kind of gem.

Chim 鍼 Vulg. chëem: a needle, used in sewing. Chëem-hô e tok kâu se wûy lûn, bông chim wûy koe 詹何以獨繭絲爲綸.芒鍼爲鉤, *chëem hô, t'hò tok këng ây se chò swⁿà, t'hò maiⁿᵍ chëem chò kaou,* Chëem-hô took a single filamint of the silk worm's coocoon for thread and a sharp needle for a hook.

Chim 針 Vulg. *chëëm:* a needle. Tông tek jîn këet sëën chim sut 唐狄仁傑善針術, *tông tëâou ây Tek-jîn-këet gaôu chò sew chëem ây hwat sut,* Tek-jîn-këet, of the Tong dynasty, was well versed in the art of sewing.

Chim 唚 *Chim ch'ùy* 唚嘴, to kiss.

上

Chím 枕 A pillow. Chím t'hoê 枕頭, *chim t'haôu*, a pillow for sleeping on. Sûy put an chim 睡不安枕, *k'hwùn bĕy an chim*, unable to sleep easy on one's pillow.

Chím 頗 The back of the neck, the bone at the back of the neck.

Chím 顲 To hang the head down.

Chím 嬸 Read sim, an aunt, an uncle's wife.

去

Chìm 浸 To steep and soak, as in the water, to sink, to enter; gradually. Chìm jūn che chom 浸潤之譖, slander, soaking and spreading, like water.

Chìm 濅 The name of a river; also gradual, by degrees. Chìm bêng chìm ch'hëang 濅明濅昌, gradually becoming brights and clear.

平

Chîm 覃 Read t'hâm a surname; also written tâm 譚, *cham*, a surname.

Chîm 蟳 Read sim; a crab. Hông sim 紅蟳, *âng chîm*, a red crab.

上

Chin 眞 True, sincere. Chin sîn 眞神, the true god. Chin sit boô gwūy 眞實無僞, *chin sit bô pŭyh ch'hat*, true and real wthout dissimulation. Chin hⁿò 眞貨, *chin höèy*, the real article; something very good.

Chin 瞋 To stretch open the eyes. Hâng ông chin bok t'hey che 項王瞋目叱之, *hāng ông taiⁿᵍ k'hwuy bak chew t'hèy e*, the king of Hāng stretched open his eyes, and menaced him.

Chin 臻 Even to, until; to arrive at, to come to. Kwun hëung sēw te kek, pek lok hâm laê chin 群凶受誅殛百祿咸來臻, *chit tin ây hëung sēw thaê sè, chēⁿá pāyh ây lok chè poô laê kaòu* the multitude of evil things being killed out of the way, a hundred emoluments will arrive together and come.

Chin 蓁 Exuberant herbage. T'hô che yaou yaou, kê yëep chin chin 桃之夭夭其葉蓁蓁, *tô ch'hĕk ây ây ây, e ây hëŏh bōe sêng*, the Peach-tree is but a small plant, but its leaves are exuberant.

Chin 榛 A tree yielding a fruit, a little smaller than a chesunt. Lé chê put kò chin lek 女贄不過榛栗 *cha boê ây chip këen, put kò chin kwà läh á*, women offer as the introductory present, nothing but large and small chesunts.

Chin 溱 The name of a river. Choô sán è kê sêng ê chèy jîn e, chin wûy 子產與其乘輿濟人於溱洧, *chòo sán tē e chēy ēy ch'hea hôe lâng köèy te chin kap wūy ây chúy*, Choo-sán took the carriage he rode in to help people across the chin and wing rivers.

Chin 烝 To boil, to distil, to make warm; some say, to dry in the sun.

Chin 蒸 The name of a sacrifice, offered in the autumn. Yëak soē chin sëâng, ê kong sëen ông 禴祀蒸嘗以公先王, *yëak soē chin sëâng ây* chèy, laè hëèn sëen ông, the spring, summer, autumn and winter sacrifices, are offered to the manes of the ancient kings.

Chin 瘮 A pain in the bones.

Chin 珍 A pearl, a precious things. Chin choo 珍珠, a pearl. Chin kê 珍奇, precious and rare. Jê yéw sek sëäng che chin 儒有席上之珍, t'hak ch'häyh sō tŏh têng ây chin, learning is a pearl on the table; (a very valuable thing.) Choō wūy bēng sè chin 自爲命世珍, ka tē chà bēng sè ây chin, to consider one's self as the most valuable pearl of the age.

Chin 璡 A stone nearly resembling a gem.

Chin 甄 A potter, one who makes earthen vessels; a surname; read yëen, to cast, to mould; also bright, clear. Hoo sëäng che hwà hāy, hāy che chëūng sëäng, yêw nê che chaē kin, wūy chin chëä che sèy wūy 夫上之化下．下之從上．猶泥之在鈞．惟甄者之所爲, sè twā ây hwà sè sèy, sè sèy ây t'hàng sè twā ch'hin chëō^{ng} t'hoê ây tē kin, ch'hut chaē sëo hwūy ây lâng sèy chò, superiors reform their inferiors, and inferiors obey their superiors, just like clay in the pottery; it rests solely with the potter how he will work it.

Chin 津 A ford, a landing-place, a place where boats touch, a ferry. Soó chóo loē būn chin yëen 使子路問津焉, saè choó loē moo^{ng} chin, he ordered Choó loē to enquire after the ferry. See the 下論 Hāy lūn.

Chin 升 Read seng: a measure, the hundredth part of a peck. Sip hap wūy seng, sip seng wūy toé, sip toé wūy hak 十合爲升．十升爲斗．十斗爲斛, chap kap chò chit chin, chap chin chò chit taóu, chap taóu chò chit chëŏh, ten kaps make a chin, ten chins, make a peck, and ten pecks make a picul, or hundred weight.

虚

Chín 軫 The square piece of wood at the back of a carriages. Kaè wān sëäng t'hëen, chin hong sëäng tēy 蓋圓象天．軫方象地, koà ëe^{ng} chin chëō^{ng} t'hee^{ng}, chin sè kak ch'hin chëō^{ng} tey, the top of the carriage must be round like the Heavens, and the back square like the earth. See the 周禮 Chew léy.

Chín 畛 The paths between the paddy fields.

Chín 疹 A little rising of the skin.

Chín 袗 A single garment, without a lining. Tong sé chin t'he k'hek, pit pëaóu jê ch'hut che 當暑袗絺綌．必表而出之, tong jëet ây sè ch'hëūng two^{n}a s^{n}a, sē kwäh poè chè ây, pit tëŏh pëáou bêng jê hoē e ch'hut, in the warm weather, when you wear a single garment of grass cloth, (you should have another garment underneath) and let this be outside; (that your body be not exposed, through the thin cloth). See the 上論 Sëäng lūn.

Chín 紾 Bent, turned, twisted as a cord; a rope. Sē yêw hek chin kê heng che pè 是猶或紾其兄之臂, sè ch'hin chëō^{ng} at chin u^{n} hë^{n}a ây ch'hëw pè, that is like twisting round one's elder brother's arm. See the 下孟 Hāy bēng.

Chín 診 To look at, to examine. Chin ch'heet kê hek 診切其脉, chin ch'hëet e ây mây^{n}h, to examine the pulse.

Chín 鬒 Black hair, all in confusion; also written 㐱 chín.

Chín 縝 To tie, to bind.

Chín 拯 To save, to deliver. Chín kew 拯救, to help and save. E' wūy chín kĕ ê súy hⁿô che tëung yëà 以爲拯已於水火之中也, *lëàh chò sē bōēyh chín kèw ka tē ê chúy hóëy ây tëung*, they look upon it as delivering them from the midst of fire and water. See the 上孟 Sëāng bēng.

Chín 儘 All; the whole; altogether. Chew léy chín chaē loé ê 周禮儘在魯矣, *chew tcâou ây léy soè, chò poô twā tē loé kok*, the ceremonies of the Chew dynasty, are all existing in the Loé country.

Chín 賮 To give a present to any one on commencing a journey; also written 賰 chín. Hêng chëá pit ê chín 行者必以賮, *kēⁿâ loé ây láng pit tëŏh wuō mēēⁿh sàng e*, people setting out on a journey are accustomed to receive presents. See the 上孟 Sëāng bēng.

Chín 賑 To save, to help. Chín chèy 賑濟, to assist by charity, to supply wants. Hàn bûn tèy hwat ch'hong lim ê, chín bin 漢文帝發倉廩以賑民, *hàn bûn tèy k'hwuy hwat ch'heⁿᵍ lim, ê chín kèw pīyh saiⁿᵍ*, Bûn, the Emperor of the Hàn dynasty opened out his granaries, to supply the wants of the people.

Chín 胗 Sore lips; the same as 疹, chín; also written 脈, chin.

Chín 振 To act, to commence, to receive. Chín hô haé jê put sëet 振河海而不洩, *chín sëw hô haé jê bô hoé e laoū*, (the Earth) contains the rivers and seas, without letting them leak through. See the 中庸 Tëung yûng.

去

Chìn 進 To enter, to advance, to go forward. Chëên chìn 前進, to advance. Kwun choô sam yip jê chìn 君子三揖而進, *kwun choô ây láng sⁿa hāy chok yip jê aōu chìn*, the good man makes three bows and then advances; (speaking of the ceremonies usual in archery.) See the 上孟 Sëāng bēng. Chô sëen seng ê tō, ch'he jê chìn 遭先生於道趨而進, *loó tëŏh sin saiⁿᵍ tē loē, tëŏh māyⁿh kēⁿà jê chìn*, meeting our elders in the way, we should walk quickly and advance towards them.

Chìn 晉 The same as the above, the name of a state. Chìn kok t'hëen hāy bok këâng yëen 晉國天下莫強焉, *chìn kok, t'heeⁿᵍ āy bô k'hàh këâng bēng*, with respect to the Chìn country it may be said that there is not a more powerful state in the Empire.

Chìn 侲 A boy. Chìn choó bān tōng 侲子萬童, *sèy kēⁿà chèⁿà bān tông*, about a myriad of young men.

Chìn 晋 The same as 晉 Chìn; also written 晉 chìn.

Chìn 瑨 A beautiful gem.

Chìn 搢 To thrust in, to cram in; to wedge; a wedge. Chìn hwat 搢笏, to stick the sign-board, or insignia of office into one's girdle.

Chìn 縉 Chìn sin 縉紳, to wrap silk round a girdle, to be in office. Chìn sin sëen seng lân gân che 縉紳先生難言之, *chìn sin ây sin saiⁿᵍ ŏh kape kóng*, a gentleman in office is hard to be conversed with.

Chìn 証 To reprove, to bear witness to. Chò kan chìn 做干証, to bear witness. Soō wùy, é chìn chēng-kok-kwun, chēng-kok-kwun put t'hèng 士尉以証靖郭君.靖郭君不聽, soō wùy k'hè t'nà chēng kok kwun, chēng-kok-kwun āᵐ t'hēⁿa, Soō-wùy reproved Chēng-kok-kwun, but Chēng-kok-kwun would not listen to him. See the 戰國策 chēēn kok ch'hek.

Chìn 證 To prove, to testify. Chit chìn 質證 to verify, to substantiate. Kê hoō jēāng yâng jê choò chìn che 其父攘羊而子證之, e ây pāy t'haou yēōⁿᵍ jê haōu saiⁿᵍ chà kan chìn, the father stole a sheep and the son testified against him

Chìn 震 To be moved, to be moved with fear; to agitate. Lûy chìn pek lé, jit chēàou bān hong 雷震百里日照萬方, lûy tân kaòu chit pāyh lé, jit cheò kaoù chit bān heⁿᵍ, the thunder rolls to a hundred lé, and the sun illumines to a myriad climes.

平

Chîn 秦 The name of a country; also a surname, and the name of a dynasty. Chîn sé hông 秦始皇, the first Emperor of the Chîn dynasty, who burnt the books and imprisoned learned men; who also constructed the great wall of China (B. C. 204).

Chîn 螓 A small insect, a kind of snail, a periwinkle. Chîn sēw gô bê 螓首蛾眉, chîn ây t'haôu kak, ch'hêng ây bak baê, with a head like a periwinkle, and eyebrows like silk-worms. A Chinese beauty.

Chîn 澠 The name of a river.

Chîn 繩 A string, a line, a cord; also straight, a straight line. Sēāng koé kēet chîn jê tē 上古結繩而治, sēāng koè kat sŏh jê tē kok, in early antiquity, they tied knots in a string, as memorandums in managing affairs.

上

Chīn 盡 To exhaust, to carry to the utmost; very, extremely; Also written 尽 chīn.

Chīn t'hoê 盡頭, chīn t'hâôu, to the utmost; choō chīn 自盡, to commit suicide.

Se put chīn gân, gân put chīn è 書不盡言言不盡意, sēá bēy chīn gwâ ây wā, wā bēy chīn gwâ ây è, I cannot by writing exhaust all I have to say, nor by words express all my meaning. See the 易經, Ek keng.

Chīn 賮 Presents given to any one, on commencing a journey.

Chīn 藎 A kind of grass, used for a yellow dye; also to advance.

入

Chip 執 To hold, to keep, to seize, to imprison. Chip yêw 執友, one's father's friend.

Soō choo ch'hē tēāou, jê ch'hey ch'hēep chip 肆諸市朝.而妻妾執, t'haê twā tē ch'hē tēaôu, jê boê sèy ê hoē lâng lēăh, to be put to death in the market or public court, and to have one's wives and concubines seized. See the 禮記 léy kè.

Chip sēw 執手, gîm ch'hēw, to grasp one's hand. Chip bêy 執迷, to retain one's error.

Chip 𠍮 Chip soō chēā 𠍮事者, perons holding office.

Chip 縶 Ropes for tying a horse's feet.

Chip 嘬 The sound of crying.

Chip 蕺 Grass growing luxuriantly; a kind of coarse grass.

灭 Chip 集 To settle, to collect, to intermingle, to assemble, to meet together. Chē chip 聚集, to collect together. Chip hōēy 集會, *k'hĕŏh chò hōēy*, to assemble. Tông yêw choó soó keng chek, bûn chip soò k'hoè 唐有子史經籍文集四庫, *tông teâou woō choò soó keng chek, chĕā ay bûn chip, sè ây k'hoè*, the Tông dynasty had Philosophical and historical works, classics and records, with such kind of literary collections, enough to fill four store houses.

Chip 亼 Three people assembled together.

Chip 潗 The issning out of a fountain: a small opening for water.

火 Chit 隲 To arise, to ascend. Chit ma 隲馬, *pây̆h chĕāng báy*, to mount a horse. Yim chit 陰隲, secret influence, operating in one's favour: protection.

Chit 瘠 Thin, meagre.

Chit 鰿 The name of a fish.

Chit 鶺 Chit lēng 鶺鴒, *pit lĕ*, the name of a bird.

Chit 脊 Pōēy chit 背脊, *ka chĕăh*, the back; the brow of a hill. Lê k'hè chèng chit 狸去正脊, *hô lê k'hè chèⁿà chit*, never eat the middle of the back of a fox.

Chit 塉 Thin ground.

Chit 侄 Firm stubborn; also foolish.

Chit 厔 A crooked bend in a hill; also foolish.

Chit 挃 The sound of reaping corn.

Chit 桎 Fetters on the legs; stocks. Some read this character lit. Chit k'hok soó chĕá, hwuy chèng bēng yĕá 桎梏死者非正命也, *chit k'hok sè ây lâng, ūm sē chèⁿà bēng*, to die in fetters and manacles, is not a proper death. See the 下孟 Hnāy bēng.

Chit 窒 Stopped up, closed up, obstructed.

Chit 銍 A short reap hook, for reaping corn.

Chit 郅 To arrive at, to go to.

Chit 職 Office, employment. Chit hwūn 職分, a charge or duty. Kwan chit 官職, *kwⁿà chit*, an office under government.

Yéw gân chek chĕá, put tek kê chit chek k'hè 有言責者不得其職則去, *woō kóng wā ây chek chĕá, bēy lit chīn e ây chit hwūn chĕw k'hè*, sustaining the office of adviser, if we cannot fulfil the duties of our office, we should depart. See the 上孟 Sēāng bēng.

Chit 摭 To gather up, to take, to collect.

Chit 嗟 Chit t'hut 嗟咄, to speak disorderly and irregularly.

Chit 織 To weave. Chit poè 織布, to weave cloth. T'hëen sùn k'haôu chit yîn lé kim 天孫巧織雲裡錦, *t'heeng sun k'há chit hwûn laê ay kim*, the heavenly youths skilfully weave the variegated colours in the clouds.

Chit 諥 To talk without ending.

Chit 質 Plain, plainness, substance, form; to demonstrate. Kwun choó chit jê ê ê, hô ê bûn wûy 君子質而已矣何以文爲, *kwun chóo chit pok tēnā tēnā, bôêyh lêàh bûn chò s'â meēnh*, the good man is plain and nothing more, what has he to do with ornament! See the 下論 Hāy lûn.

疒

Chit 疾 Pain, sickness; sick, to be sick of, to dislike; hasty, speedy. Choó che sèy sîn, chae, chëèn, chit, 子之所愼齊戰疾, *k'hòng chao ây sèy kin sîn chëâh ch'haè, sëa chëèu, chit paīng*, the things which Confusius was particularly careful about were fasting, war, and sickness.
Chit hêng sëen tëâng cheā, wûy che put tèy, 疾行先長者. 謂之不弟, *maīnh kēnā taē seng sè twā ây lâng, kóng këò ūm gaôu chò sëò tē*, to walk quickly before a superior, is to fail in our duty as a younger brother. See the 下論, Hāy bêng.

Chit 㾜 Sick; poisonous.

Chit 嫉 Chit toē 嫉妒, envy, jealousy. Hoē hwuy lêng t'haē hāy, jê boô chit toē che sim, koè chëùng ch'hëep lok che 后妃能待下而無嫉妒之心. 故衆妾樂之, *koē hwuy ây kwûn t'haē sè sèy, jê bô chit toē ây sim kwnā, koè chëùng sèy ê kôêy e*, when the empress and princesses, can treat their inferiors well, without harbouring jealousy in their minds then all the concubines will be pleased with them.

Chit 蒺 Chit lêy 蒺藜, the name of a medicinal plant.

Chit 一 Read yit, one. Yit jîn 一人, *chit ây lâng*, one person. Höêy yëá, bûn yit jê te sip, soò yëá bûn yit jê te jē 回也聞一而知十. 賜也聞一而知二, *hôêy yëá t'hēnā chit hāng, chëw chae chap hāng, soò yëá t'hēnā chit hang, chëw chae ne hāng*, Höêy on hearing one thing knows ten; Soò on hearing one thing, knows only two. See the 上論 Sëāng lûn.

卒

Cho 倅 Quiet, at rest, peaceful. Kwan choó put jîp ch'hē, wûy kê cho lëëm 君子不入市爲其倅廉, *kwun choó ūm jîp ch'hē, yin wûy aè bôêyh k'hàh cho lëëm*, the good man does not enter markets, because he wishes to be quiet and pure.

Cho 傮 The end, the conclusion.

Cho 遭 To meet with, to fall in with. E sëaou yëā yêw, ê kwun sëang cho 依霄夜遊. 與君相遭, *t'hàn wōo hwûn maīng t'hit t'hô, kap kwun lê sëo toô tëôh*, taking advantage, of a cloudy sky, to wander out in the evening in order to obtain a meeting with you.

Cho 糟 Chëw cho 酒糟, *chëw chaou*, grains obtained from distilling liquor. Gwân hëën put yëèn cho k'hong che sit 原憲不厭糟糠之食, *gwân hëën bô hëën chëw chaou bè k'hēng ây chëâh*, Gwan-hëën (one of Confucius' disciples) did not refuse grains and chaff for his food.

Cho 齺 Lô cho 䱡齺, anything not yet purified or refined.

声

Chó 左 The left. Chó sëw 左手, *tó chëw*, the left hand. Chó yëw 左右, attendants. Chó yëw kae wat hëën, bē k'hó yëâ 左右皆曰賢未可也, *chó yëw ây lâng, chò poô kóng e gâou, yëâ böëy t'hang*, when your attendants all say that a man is clever, still you must not think of employing him.

Chó 𠂇 The same as the above; also to bend.

Chó 早 Vulg. *cha*: early. Chó k'hé 早起, *chá k'hè*, early in the morning. Ch'heng chó yit pöey tây 清早一杯茶, *ch'heng chá chìt aou tây*, early in the morning a cup of tea.

Chò chok yëâ bē 早作夜寐, *chá k'hè chò soō, mây^ng kan k'hwùn*, early to work and late to rest.

Chó 蚤 The same as the above early. Chó àn boô sit, pit sùn t'hëen tō 蚤晏無失.必順天道, *chá mooi^ng bô sit, pit sùn t'hëeng ây tō*, early and late being exempt from fault, we may be obedient to the celestial way.

Chó 蝨 Vulg. *ka chaóu u*, a flea.

Chó 澡 To wash, to cleanse, to purify. Chò sin yëuk tek, é këw hâp ê sëen ông che tō 澡身浴德.以求合於先王之道, *sèy hún sin, ch'heng ch'heng k'hè lân ây tek, ê kêw hap sëen ong ây tō*, we should cleanse our personal conduct and purify our virtue, in order to seek conformity with the doctrines of the ancient kings.

Chó 棗 A date. Bëën jê hông chó 面如紅棗, *bin ch'hìn chöō^ng âng chó*, having a face like a red date. Said of 關羽, Kwân é.

Cheng sek sē yâng chó 曾皙嗜羊棗, *cheng sek aè chëäh yëông chó*, Cheng-sek was fond of a certain kind of dates.

去

Chò 做 To make, to do, to perform. Chò kong hoo 做工夫, *chò kang kwùy*, to work.

Chò seng lê 做生理, to trade. Chò joō 做字, *chò jē*, to make an agreement, to make a written contract.

Chò 佐 To help, to assist, to second, to uphold. T'hëúng chaé é chò ông pêng pang kok 冢宰以佐王平邦國, *t'hëúng chaé ê boō chò ông, pêng tê pang kok*, the general superintendent is to assist the king in regulating the country.

Chò 做 To have; peaceful, quiet.

Chò 竈 Vulg. *chaóu k'ha*: a cook-house, a kitchen; also written 灶 chò. E' kē mē ê ò lêng mē ê chò 與其媚於奧.寧媚於竈, *káp e áy sëep sèy ch'hoò kak, lêng k'hó sëep sèy tē chaóu k'ha*, compared with flattering the God of the corner of the house, is it not better to flatter the God of the kitchen See the 上諭 Sëâng lūn.

平

Chô 曹 To arrange in order; an order, a class; the name of country; a surname. Hwun chô pêng chin 分曹並進, *hwun chë^nâ pöëy, chò poô chìn*, divided into classes they advance together.

Chô ch'hò kan hëông 曹操奸雄, Chô-ch'hò was a corrupt villain.

Chô 漕 The name of a city.

Chô 槽 A manger. Má chô 馬槽, *báy chô*, a horse's manger.

Chô 螬 The name of an insect. Chéng sēang yēw lé, chô sit sit chēá kò pwàn è 井上有李.螬食實者過半矣, *chai^ng têng oō lé, à, chô chēăh e ây sit, k'hŭh kay chit pw^nà*, over the well there hung a pear, more than the half of which had been eaten by insects. See the 上孟 Sēang bēng.

Chô 艚 A boat.

Chô 嘈 To make a noise, to talk incoherently.

Chô 篕 A kind of basket.

Chô 瘥 Sick, diseased.

Chô 䵽 Lô chô 𪎘䵽, anything not yet refined, or purified.

Chô 𤺐 A sickness.

去 Chō 坐 Vulg. *chāy*: to sit. Ch'héng chō 請坐, *ch'hc^nà chēy*, pray sit down. Choó loē, cheng sek, jēēm yéw, kong sey hwa, sē chō 子路曾晳.冉有.公西華侍坐, Choó-loē, Cheng-sek, Jēēm-yēw and Kong sey-hwa sat by the side (of Confucius.) See the 下論 Hāy lūn.
Chō é t'haē t'hàn 坐以待旦, *chey é têng haōu chá k'hé*, to sit and wait for the morning.

Chō 座 A seat, a settle, a throne. Chō sēang pin k'hek bwán 座上賓客滿, *chō têng lâng k'hèyh mw^nà*, the seats were full of visitors.

Chō 皁 A black colour. Chō lēy 皁隸, low people; also written 皂 chō. Chō pek put hwun 皁白不分, *oe pāyh bô hwun pēet*, not to distinguish between black and white.

Chō 譟 Swan chō 喧譟, to make a disturbance to talk at random.

Chō 漕 The mountain streams winding round and finding a passage out.

Chō 造 To make, to form, to create. Chō hwà 造化, creation; a lucky hit. Kwúy sîn chēá, t'hēen tēy che kong yūng, jê chō hwà che chek yēá 鬼神者天地之功用而造化之迹也, *kwúy sin ây sē t'hee^ng tēy ây kong yūng, chō hwà, ây chēăh*, Ghosts and spirits are the meritorious efforts of Heaven and Earth, and the traces of creation. See 朱子 Choo choō.

幸 Choe 鄹 The name of a city, the native town of Confucius. Sēuk wūy choe jîn che choó te léy hoē 孰謂鄹人之子知禮乎, *chē chūy à kóng choe lâng ây kē^nà bat lêy hoē*, who ever said that the son of the man of Chae understood propriety? See the 上論 Sēang lūn.

Choe 鄒 The name of a country; vulg. *chey*: a surname. Choe jîn é ch'hoé jîn chēen 鄒人與楚人戰, *choe ây lâng kap ch'hoé ay lâng sëo t'hae*, the people of Chae contended with those of Ch'hoé.

Choe 諏 To consult with any one. Choo choe 咨諏, to take counsel of any.

Choe **租** Choe söëy 租稅, taxes, rent. Tēy choe 地租, ground rent. Haoù bûn kè soò t'hëen hāy bîn tëën choe che pwàn 孝文給賜天下民田租之半, *haoù bûn ây sè soò t'hee^ng āy pâyh saī^ng ch'hân choe chit pw^nā*, in the time of Haoù-bûn, half of the taxes on rice fields were remitted to the people.

Choe **緅** A mixture of green and red.

Choe **陬** Choe gê 陬隅, a corner, a point. The 1st month of the year is also called choe gwat 陬月, the corner month.

Choe **菆** Grass growing luxuriantly.

Choe **趄** Choo choe 趦趄, not getting forward, unable to advance. Chëuk yëuk chìn jê choo choe 足欲進而趦趄, *k'ha böëyh chìn jê bēy kē^nā*, the feet desiring to proceed, but unable to advance.

Choe **騶** Choe gê 騶虞, a benevolent kind of animal.

Choe **徂** To go, to advance; to depart; also written 且 choe.

Choe **鉏** To hoe, to weed; also a hoe, a weeder. Hwuy kê chëúng cheá, choe jê k'hè che 其非種者.鉏而去之, *ā^m sē e ây chéng ây lâng tëöh t'hw^nā jê k'hè e*, those who do not belong to that race, must be weeded and rooted out.

Choe **聚** The name of a tree; also a surname.

Choe **芻** Grass. Seng choe yit sok 生芻一束, *saī^ng ch'hâou chit pây*, there grew a bundle of grass. See the 小雅 Seáou gnáy.

Choe **蒭** Pè choe 苾芻, fragrant grass: offered in sacrifice.

Choe **艄** A ship for going out to sea.

Choe **鯫** A small kind of fish.

唐

Choé **走** Vulg. *châou*: to run a way, to flee, to escape. Lêng choé 能走, *gaôu châou*, a good runner. Pāe choé 敗走, *pāe chaôu*, to be defeated. K'hè kap ē peng jê choé 棄甲曳兵而走, *t'hek kak chëèn kāh, t'hwa peng to, jê châou*, they threw away their armour, drew their weapons after them, and fled. See 孟子 bēng choó.

Choé **阻** To stop. Choé chè 阻止, to hinder. Lân choé 攔阻, *nw^nā choé*, to obstruct. Pè jîn yëw chong ch'hong cheá choé kwun 嬖人有臧倉者阻君, *tit hêng ây lâng woō chong ch'hong nw^nā choé jîn kwun*, a worthless favourite one Chong-ch'hong, hindered the prince. See the 上孟 Sëäng bēng.

Choé **爼** A vessel used in sacrifice. Choé toē che soō, chek seäng bûn che é 爼豆之事.則嘗聞之矣, *choé toē ây soō, chëw bat t'hē^na e*, the business of sacrificial vessels, I have heard something about.

Choé **俎** The same as the above.

Choé 祖 An ancestor. Sëen choé 先祖, a former ancestor. A surname. Choé chong 祖宗, ancestors. Choé tek 祖德, the virtue of progenitors. Sëen choé hoō boé, chek put gnó ch'huy 先祖父母.則不我摧, *seng choè pāy boè, chëw bô t'hek kak gwá*, my first ancestors and immediate parents will not reject me.

Choé 咀 To hold in the mouth. Choé chëak 咀嚼, to chew. Hâm eng choé hwa 含英咀華, "to chew blossoms and ruminate flowers" meaning to meditate on literary subjects.

Choé 殂 To die. Hong hwun naé choé lok, pek sèng jê song k'hó pé 放勳乃殂落.百姓如喪考妣, *hong hwun kaòu sè, pöyh saing ch'hín chëōng seng pāy boè*, when Hong-hwun (i. e. Geâou 堯) died: the people felt as if they had lost their father and mother. See the 下孟 bāy bēng.

Choé 組 The threads with which the seal of office is tied. Choé sëw 組綬, a fringe or border.

Choé 沮 To stop: to put a stop to. Hô jit soo choé 何日斯沮, *tëy chit jit chëy lëy swäh*, on what day will this stop.

Choé 琙 Choé chong 琙琮, a gem on which the seal of office is engraved; that for a prince of the Empire was five inches square, and that for an Emperor seven inches and a half.

Choé 䃚 Tëën choé 田䃚, a god presiding over rice-fields.

Choé 詛 Chëw choé 咒詛, *chèw chwā*, to curse, to swear. Hoê choé hoê chëw 胡詛胡咒, *lâm sâm chèw chwā*, swearing irregularly and cursing disorderly.

去

Choè 奏 Vulg. *chaòu*, to report, to send in a report. Choè gak 奏樂, *chaòu gak*, to play up music. Choè se këng sëäng, sèng tek put ch'hong 奏管競上.聖德不聰, *chaòu pùn t'heâu t'hâou chëōng, sèng sëäng bô böëyh t'hëna*, reports are perpetually sent in, but his majesty will not listen to them.

Choè 做 To do, to act, to perform. Choè kwan 做官, *choè kwna*, to become a mandarine. Choo soō k'hé ch'hay lân 做事起初難, *choè soā k'hè t'hâou ôh*, in performing anything, the commencement is difficult.

Choè 湊 Waters meeting in one stream, and rushing forwards.

Choè 輳 To assemble. Ke mâ hok choè 車馬輻輳, *ch'hëa bây chà poô kaòu*, the carriages and horses all arrived together.

Choè 祚 Happines. E'ng sek choè yīn 永錫祚胤, *èng koè soō hok koè kōnā sun*, (may Heaven) ever bestow happines on your posterity. See the 小雅 Sëáou gnáy.

Choè 咀 To swear; to take an oath regarding anything gone by. K'hwat k'hoé choè chëw 厥口咀咒, *e dy ch'hày chèw chwā*, his mouth vociferated oaths.

Choè 簇 A sort of music played in the first month of the year.

平

Choê 齟 Choê goê 齟齬 The teeth uneven and irregular; also used metaphorically for not agreeing together.

Choê 咀 To scold, to rail at.

上去

Choē 胙 The flesh of a sacrifice; also written 祚 choē.

Choē 驟 The galloping of a horse; to go swiftly, to gallop. Choē k'hé 驟起 to rise up quickly.

Choē 助 Vulg. *chān*: to help, to aid, to assist. Sēang choē 相助, *sëo chān*, to help one another. Hōēy yëá, hwuy choē gnó chëá yëá 回也非助我者也, *hōēy yëá, ū^m sē chān gwá ây lâng*, Hōēy does not afford me any help.

去

Chöēy 最 Very, extremely; the chief. Chöēy oé 最惡, *chin chāe wàn*, to take very much. E chëàng chut che tëung kong wûy chöēy 於將卒之中功爲最, *tē chëàng kwun peng chut ây tëung, kong lō tèy yit*, among generals and soldiers, merit is the principal thing.
Chek tek tong sëen, wûy sëen chöēy lok 積德當先爲善最樂, *chek tek tē^ng chò tuè seng, chò hó chin chae t'hëung lok*, the accumulation of virtue is of first importance: and the doing of good affords the greatest pleasure.

Chöēy 嘬 To bite, to eat, to gnaw. Sin jöēy koe chöēy che 蠅蚋姑嘬之, *hō sin t'hang á koe chëăh e*, the flies and grubs had gnawed and eaten it.

Chöēy 贅 Chöēy sēy 贅婿, *chin chöēy ây kē^n á saè*, a bridegroom who attaches himself to his father in law's family. Hoō chöēy 附贅, a fleshy excrescence, a wart.

Chöēy 蕝 Mâou chöēy 茅蕝, a whisp of coarse grass, stuck up as a sign for people to meet, and drink together.

Chöēy 癥 A fleshy excrescence, a swelling; the same as 贅 chöēy.

2 .N

Chöēy 綴 United, joined, connected; to connect.

平

Chöêy 摧 To break, to break in pieces. Chöêy kong wûy jêw 摧剛爲柔, *p'hăh ch'hày gnāy ây chò nooi^ng*, to break up hard things and make them soft.

Chöêy 漼 A collection of frost and snow; drifted snow.

上

Chöēy 皋 A crime, a fault. Boô chöēy boô koe 無皋無辜, faultless and sinless.

Chöēy 罪 A crime; a sin. Yéw chöēy 有罪, *woō chöēy*, sinful. Hek chöēy ē t'hëen boô séy tó yëá 獲罪於天無所禱也, *hek chöēy ē t'hē^ng bô sèy t'hang tó*, when a man sins against heaven, there is none that can intercede for him. See the 上論 Sëang lūn.
Chöēy jîn put noē 罪人不孥, *woō chöēy ây lâng bô lây kē^n á sun*, let not criminals involve their families in trouble.

Chöēy 睡 Read sûy, to sleep. Bwat to kok yéw gnóe bē ch'hó, sit che soó jîn put k'hap sûy 末多國有五味草食之使人不瞌睡, *bwat to kok woō chit lēy goē bē ch'haóu, chëăh e saè lâng bô kà chöēy*, in the Bwat-to country there is a plant of fine tastes, which when eaten will keep people from sleeping.

上入

Chŏh 作 Read chok: to make, to commence. Chok ch'hëâng 作墻, *chŏh ch'hëō^ng*, to build a wall. Sèy chok 細作, *sèy chŏh*, a spy.

下入

Chŏh 擲 Read tek; to throw. Tek sek 擲石, *chŏh chŏh*, to throw stones.

Chŏh 射 Read sek: to shoot with an arrow. Sek chëen 射箭, chŏh cheeng, to let fly an arrow. Ek put sek sëuk 弋不射宿, chŏh cheeng bŏ chŏh tëŏh haing, ây chedou, in archery he did not shoot a settled bird. See 上論, Sëang lūn.

Chok 作 To make, to commence operations, to do. Chok soō 作事, to make trouble.
Chok chëá che wūy sèng, sut chëá che wūy bêng 作者之謂聖.述者之謂明, chŏh ây lâng kóng këè sèng, t'hàn ây lâng kóng këè bêng, he that first invents a thing may be called a philosopher, and he who imitates it may be called, an intelligent man. See the 禮記 Léy kè.

Chok 昨 Chok jit 昨日, chá hwuing, yesterday.

Chok 怍 To be ashamed.

Chok 酢 When a guest pours out wine to a host, it is called chok 酢 and when a host answers the libation it is called sêw 酬.
Sêw chok 酬酢, mutually to pledge one another.

Chok 柞 The name of a tree; also to cut down wood.

Chok 濯 To wash, to rinse, to cleanse. Ch'heng soo chok eng, chok soo chok chëuk 清斯濯纓.濁斯濯足, ch'heng ay sèy kìn twà lŏ ây sèy k'ha, the clear water may serve to wash the tassel of one's cap and the muddy to wash one's feet.

Chok 濁 Vulg. lŏ: and tak, muddy dirty. Keng é wūy chok 涇以渭濁, keng chúy bak wūy chúy lŏ, the waters of the Heng, render the waters of the Wūy muddy. See the 國風 Kok hong.

Chok 擢 To elevate, to promote, to raise to office. Chok che hoē pin k'hek che tëung, jê lip che ê kwūn sîn che sëang 擢之乎賓客之中.而立之群臣之上, kè chok e tē lâng k'hâyh ây tëong, jê lip e tē kwun sîn ây têng, to elevate one in the midst of the guests, and to establish one over the host of ministers.

Chok 族 The barb of an arrow; a relative. Kéw chok 九族, the nine series of relatives.

Chok 瘯 A scorbutic disease.

Chok 鷟 An eagle. Boó tông têng che laê gê, bêng ke yâng che gak chok 舞唐庭之來儀.鳴岐陽之鸑鷟, boó tē tông lêng ây laê gê, haôu tē ke yâng ây gak chok, the Phoenix sporting on the hall of Tông (referring to Geaôu 堯), and the eagle screaming at the hill of ke yâng (referring to Bûn ông 文王), both betoken the appearance of a sage.

Chom 箴 Chom kwuy 箴規, a good rule. Chom kaè 箴戒, good counsel. Têng-bêng-tō, chok soò bùt che chom é kwuy kaè 程明道作四勿之箴以規戒, têng bêng tō chò sè bŭh ây chom, ê chò kwuy kaè, Têng-bêng-tō made a list of the four prohibitions, in order to form a rule and a caution.

Chom 簪 A bodkin, a hair-pin. Kim chom 金簪, a golden hair-pin. Lúy taē chom eng 累代簪纓, kwuy nā têy chăh chom kwà eng, for several generations they have worn hair-pins and tassels (i. e. they have been in office, and worn its insignia).

Chóm 怎 How. Chóm mŏh yang 怎麽様, an chwnâ yëong, in what manner. Chóm tek ch'hew p'ho yit chwân 怎

得愁波一轉, *an chw^{n}á ây tit tëŏh ch'hew p'ho chit ây toot^{ng}*, how shall we get the autumn waves to turn?

丢

Chòm 譖 Vulg. *saè p'hwà*, to defame, to slander, to blast a man's reputation. Pé chòm jîn chëá, sûy tek é boĕ, 彼譖人者誰得與謀, *hwăh lêy saè phwà ây lâng, chē chūy à tit è soō nëŏ^{ng}*, those slanderous fellows, who can join in counsel with them. See the 小雅, Séaou gnáy.

夫

Chŏmh 噆 To bite,, to chew; the noise made by eating.

卆

Chong 宗 An ancestor, a forefather; to honour; to respect as a master; a surname. Chong chèng 宗政, a double surname.

Choé chong 祖宗, forefathers. Chong bēaou, 宗廟, an ancestorial temple.

Chong bëăng che lêy, sêy é soō hoē kē sëen yëá 宗廟之禮所以祀乎其先也, *chong bōō ây lêy sêy ê ch'haē cây sëen lâng*, the ceremonies of the ancestorial temple, are in order to sacrifice to forefathers. See the 中庸 Tëung yûng.

Yin put sit kē ch'hin, ek k'hó chong yëá 因不失其親亦可宗也, *t'hàn lâng ū^{m} sit e ây t'hang ch'hin wá ây lâng, yëă t'hang lëăh e chò choó*, in following teachers, if we do not miss a person that can be nearly approached, we may also take him for a master. See 上諭 Sëăng lūn.

Chong 倧 A divine person of antiquity.

Chong 悰 To be pleased and delighted; also to consider, to reflect. Ch'hek ch'hek jëak boō chong 慼慼若無宗, *ch'hek ch'hâm, ch'hin chëŏ^{ng} bô koey* ... sad and sorrowful, as it were displeased.—

Chong 庄 Vulg. *che^{ng}*: a farm. Chong sëà 庄社, *che^{ng} sëà*, a farm house. Boē wûy tëĕn chong k'hek, tëaou chok t'hëen choó sîn 暮爲田庄客.朝作天子臣, *ma^{ng} hwui^{ng} chò ch'hân che^{ng} ây lâng k'hăyh, mîn a chaē chò hóng tèy ây jîn sîn*, in the evening he was a stranger at a country farm, and the next morning became a minister of the Emperor.

Chong 琮 A square gem; a precious stone, of an octagon shape, like the earth. P'hek chong 璧琮, a gem nine inches square, used in inviting the Emperor.

Chong 鬉 A high bunch of hair. T'hoê chong 頭鬉, *t'hâou chang*, a tail of hair.

Chong 騌 Má chong 馬騌, *bày chang*, a horse's mane.

Chong 妝 Vulg. che^{ng}: to ornament, to adorn. Hwa sek chong bé 華色妝美, *wâ sek che^{ng} kaôu sùy*, to paint and adorn, till it is very fine.

Chong 粧 A lady's toilette, apparatus for dressing. Teng loê k'hae chong kèng, é kok chëak sëen e 登樓開粧鏡.倚閣着鮮衣, *păyh laôu k'hwuy che^{ng} kë^{n}à, wá kŏh ch'hëng sin s^{n}a*, at one time she ascends the chamber to open her toilette and looking-glass, and at another she leans against the gallery dressed in new apparel.

Chong 糚 An adorning, a setting off; to ornament, to dress. Put chëak yit hwún chong, chin tek hong lêw t'haé 不着一粉糚.儘得風流態, *ū^{m} saè yūng chit ây hwún che^{ng}, chin tit tëŏh hong lêw ây yëŏ^{ng}*, without needing a single painting or adorning, she has altogether an elegant appearance. See the 古詩 Koé se, old poëms.

Chong 㽵 To be established, to stand firm.

Chong 蹤 A trace, a footstep. Hô ch'hè hek hong chong 何處覔芳蹤, *böëyh tá lōh k'hè ch'höey, e ây p'hang chëāh*, where shall we seek for his fragrant footsteps.

Chong 縱 Straight, upright; lengthways.

Chong 莊 Stern, sedate; correct; adorned; a farm; also a surname. Lim che ê chong, chek kèng 臨之以莊則敬, *laê kaôu e è chong gëēm lâng chëw kèng lán*, coming before the people with sedateness, they will respect us. See the 上論 Sëāng lūn.

Chong 牂 An ewe, a female sheep.

Chong 緵 A fishing net; also written 罭 chong.

Chong 淙 The noise of waters; the appearance of flowing water.

Chong 樁 A stick for beating anything; a post stuck in the ground.

Chong 裝 The inside, or contents of anything; to put in, to adorn. Chong hwún 裝粉, to dress. Chong chaè 裝載, *che^ng tëy*, to put anything in.

Chong 臧 Good, excellent, thick, kind. A surname. Choó wat, sē tō yëá hô chëuk ê chong 子曰是道也何足以臧; *hoo choó kóng, chëy lëy tō yeá böëyh chaè ëy kaôu ê kèng hó*, Confucius said how can such a way as this be sufficient to be called good. See the 上論 Sëāng lūn.

Chong 贓 A bribe. Sēw chong 受贓, *sëw cho^ng*, to receive bribes. Kê sew jëuk sìm ê t'ham woo chò chong 其羞辱甚於貪汙坐贓, *e ây sëw jëuk k'hūh sìm ê t'ham woo chëy che^ng*, the disgrace and shame of it would be greater, than coveting dirty advantages and sitting on bribes.

Chong 椶 Vulg. *chang*: the name of a tree; which has leaves without branches, of the bark of which rain cloaks may be made. A kind of palm tree, in appearance like the cocoanut tree.

Chong 艐 Vulg. *chang*: to run aground. Ch'hwân chong chëak say 船艐着沙, *chûn chang tëŏh swa*, the ship ran aground on the sand.

Chong 嵏 Wâ chong 嵅嵏 the name of a hill.

Chong 粧 To dress the head; when females come of age, and adorn their head dress, a congratulatory wish, is expressed by hō chong 賀粧.

去

Chóng 總 To collect and bind together; the whole; altogether, generally; also written 緫 偬 緦 and 捴.
Chóng sē 總是, after all, but if only. Chóng kae 總皆, *lóng chóng*, the whole.
Chóng bêng 總名, *chóng mëⁿâ*, a general term, an universal appellation.
Chóng tok 總督, a general superintendant; a Governor General of a Province.
Chóng pēng sē kwân 總秉勢權, to have a general hold of the reins of power.

Chóng 傯 K'hóng chóng 倥傯 poor and distressed; also not at leisure. Also written 偬, chóng.

Chóng 稯 A sheaf of corn.

Chóng 鬉 Chóng kak 鬉角 a horse's mane.

去

Chòng 壯 Strong, hale flourishing, robust. Chòng këèn 壯健 *chèⁿg kēⁿā*, robust. Kip kê chǒng yëá, hëet k'hè hong kong, kaè che chaē toè 及其壯也.血氣方剛,戒之在鬬, *kip kaǒu e ûy chìⁿᵍ yëá, höëyh k'hè toō toō á kong gnāy tëǒh kèng kaè tō sëò p'hǎh*, but when people are grown strong, and their blood and spirits are firm, they should be guarded against quarrelling and fighting.

Má-hòk-p'ho ló tòng ek chòng 馬伏波老當益壯, *má hòk p'ho, kaǒu laǒu tòng nā këēn chòng*, má-hòk-p'ho, when old became much stronger then formerly.

Chòng 塟 To bury, to inter, to put under ground; also written 葬 chòng. Seng soō che é léy, soó chòng che e léy 生事之以禮.死塟之以禮, *saiⁿᵍ hòk saē e chàou lèy soè, sè taē e chëàou lèy soè*, when our parents are alive we must serve them according to propriety, and when dead, we must bury them in proper manner. See the 上論 Sëāng lūn.

Chòng 髒 K'hòng chóng 骯髒, straight, stiff, unbending.

Chòng 綜 Transverse threads, in weaving.

Chòng 糉 Vulg. *chàng*: a kind of confectionary tied up in leaves, with sharp corners, and used on the 5th day of the 5th moon. Also written 粽 chòng.

2 o

Chòng 傯 Distressed, reduced to difficulties

Chòng 偆 The appearance of standing.

Chòng 豵 A male pig; a boar; a pig 6th months old.

平

Chông 崇 To exalt, to honour, to respect. Chun chông 尊崇, to honour, and obey. Chông ko bòk taē è hoò kwùy 崇高莫大於富貴, *chông kwân bô k'hǎh twā ê poò kwùy*, there are none more elevated than the rich and great. See the 易經 Yëǎh keng.

K'him chông t'hëen to 欽崇天道, *këung kèng t'hàn t'heeⁿᵍ ây to*, respectfully to follow the dictates of heaven. See the 尙書 Sëoⁿᵍ se.

Chông 賨 Taxes levied by barbarous states; among whom the wealthy were required to pay annually a piece of cloth, and the poorer sort about twenty feet of cloth; which was called 賨布 chông poè.

Chông 藏 Vulg. *k'hèⁿᵍ*: to hide, to conceal, to store up. San chông hoé pà, súy yín kaou lëûng 山藏虎豹水隱蛟龍, *suⁿa k'hèⁿᵍ hoè pà, chùy tëêm kaou lëûng*, in the hills are secreted tygers and leopards, and in the waters lie concealed serpents and dragons.

Yūng che chek hêng, sëá che chek chông 用之則行.舍之則藏, *yūng e chew kēⁿâ, pàng kak e chēw k'hèⁿᵍ*, if they employ us, then we commence operations, but if they reject us, then we lay ourselves by. See the 上論 Sëāng lūn.

Chông 叢 To collect in a bunch; to grow in a bush; a bush. Yit chông sē 一叢樹, *chit châng ch'hēw* a bush tree. Bê é sip chông lân 微雨濕叢蘭, *sêy hoē wun lâm ka nooī^ng châng ây lân hwa*, the small rain moistens the bushy lân flower.

Chông 藂 Plants growing bushy and luxuriantly.

Chông 巃 Gâng chông 岇巃, the lofty and grand appearance of hills.

Chông 瀧 To be annihilated. to die; not to be.

Chông 瀿 The name of a river.

Chōng 狀 A form, appearance; a sort; a document. Kò chōng 告狀, an indictment. Tëáng-choó-pông-chōng māou jē hoò jîn lé choó 張子房狀貌如婦人女子, *tëo^ng choó pông ây chē^ng māou ch'hin chëō^ng che boè lâng 'ìé choó*, Tëo^ng-choó-pông's appearance was like that of a woman or girl.

Bêng yâng kèy-sêng, ch'hey, sëà chōng choê, sëāng, ch'héng taē hoo soó 明楊繼盛妻寫狀奏上請代夫死, *bêng tëaou yëō^ng kèy sêng ây boó sëà chē^ng chaòu hông têy ch'hē^n á t'hèy e ây ang sé*, in the Bêng dynasty Yëō^ng-kèy-sêng's wife wrote out a document, and presented it to the Emperor begging to die in the stead of her husband.

Chōng 臟 The bowels. Gnoê chōng 五臟, *goē chē^ng*, the five viscera.

Chōng 奘 Strong, vigorous, great and flourishing.

Chōng 藏 To lay up goods in store; a storehouse, a treasury.

Choo 朱 Red, vermilion; a surname. Oè ché che twat choo yëá 惡紫之奪朱也, *wûn ché sek ây twat choo sek*, (Confucius) disliked a red colour because it took away from the beauty of the vermilion. See the 下論 Hāy lūn.

Choo 珠 A pearl. Chin choo 珍珠, a precious pearl. Soō che ē choo gëuk put tek bëēn yëen 事之以珠玉不得免焉, *hōk saē e 'ē choo gëuk bēy tit bëēn yëen*, if I serve them with pearls and gems, I shall not be able to avoid their aggressions. See the 上孟 Sëāng bēng.

Put chin choo gëuk, séy chin wûy sëēn jîn 不珍珠玉.所珍爲善人, *ūm chin choo gëuk, séy chin sē hó láng*, they did not value pearls and gems, but they valued good men.

Choo 硃 A vermilion coloured powder. Choo bek 硃墨, *gîn choo bak*, red ink. Gëēn choo tëēm ek, pá pit têy se, 研硃點易.把筆題詩, *gîn choo tëem yëăh keng, gîm pit taè têy se*, with vermilion ink he put stops to the book of diagrams; and then took up the pencil and composed odes. Choo sey 硃砂, cinnabar.

Choo 茱 Goê choo 茰茱, the name of a medicine.

Choo 洙 The name of a river.

Choo 資 To rely on, to borrow, to help; also to bestow. Choo p'hin 資品, natural abilities. Söèy ke chek hwat ch'hong lim, é choo t'hëen hāy bin 歲饑則發倉廩.以資天下

民, *baē neēng tang, chek k'hwuy ch'heng lim, ē choo t'heeng hāy pʰhy saīng*, in seasons of scarcity he opened the public granaries, in order to supply the people of the Empire.

Choo 玆 Black; also, this, here, now. Bûn ông kè bút, bûn put chaē choo hoē 文王旣沒文不在玆乎, *bûn ông kaòu sé, e ây bûn k'ham ūm sē wā chè taōu hoē*, since bûn-ông is dead, does not his literature still remain with me? Said by Confucius, in the 上論 Sēāng lūn.

Choo 滋 Juicy; also abundant. E' loē choo jūn 雨露滋潤, *hoē kwà loē chûy wun tâm*, moistoned with the dews and rain. Choo bē 滋味, taste, flaver.

Choo 孳 To produce, to be born, to increase.

Choo 鎡 An agricultural implement; a hoe. Suy yéw choo ke, put jê t'hāe sê 雖有鎡基.不如待時, *suy woō choo ke, ūm tat tëŏh têng t'hāe e ây sê*, although we have agricultural implements, there is nothing like obtaining the right season. See the 上孟 Sēāng bêng.

Choo 侏 Choo jê 侏儒, a dwarf, one of small stature. Choo jê choo jê, paē gnó ê te 侏儒侏儒.敗我於邾, *choo jê choo jê paē gwá twā tē te*, this diminutive dwarf defeated us at Te. See the 左傳 Chó twān.

Choo 茲 Abundance of grass and vegetables; this, here, now.

Choo 孜 Diligently, earnestly. Key bêng jê k'hé, choo choo wûy sëēn cheá, sùn che tôe yëá 鷄鳴而起.孜孜爲善者.舜之徒也, *key t'hê jê k'hè, choo choo chò hó ây lâng, sē sùn ây hak seng*, he who rises at cock-crowing, and diligently practices virtue, is a disciple of Sùn. See the 下孟 Hāy bêng.

Choo 姿 Form, appearance, talent, ability. T'hëen choo é hak lek pèng chin, sùy jëēn sēng tek che seō 天姿與學力並臻粹然成德之士, *t'heeng choo kap hak lek chò poô kaòu, chëw sùy jëēn chēnā tek ây lâng*, when heaven-bestowed talents, and powers devoted to learning, are both united together, then may one succeed in completing a virtuous character.

Choo 菑 A new rice field, that has only been cultivated for one year.

Choo 趑 Choo choe 趑趄, not able to advance, unable to make any progress.

Choo 粢 The six kinds of grain are called 粢 choo, when placed in vessels they are called 盛 sēng. Choo hoē keng choé, é këúng choo sēng 諸侯耕助.以供粢盛, *choo hoē sëo chān chŏh.ch'hân, ē këúng kip chôo sēng*, the princes of the Empire assist in ploughing, in order to provide the grain used in sacrifice.

Choo 咨 Choo boē 咨謀, to consult together. Choo chëa 咨嗟, an exclamation.

Choo 緇 Black. Choo e 緇衣, *oe sna*, black clothes.

Choo 輜 Waggons for carrying baggage. Choo tëūng 輜重, baggage waggons.

Choo 貲 Money, wealth. Hnó choo 貨貲, treasure. Choó k'hông hnó hwùy ké, é sê chwán hnó choo 子貢好廢舉.與時轉貨貲, *choo k'hông aè hwùy yūng chêe^ng, toé lëŏh e ây sè chwân hŏey choo,* choó-k'hòng was fond of spending money, yet when it came to the time, he got wealthy again. See the 史記, Soó kè.

Choo 齋 The lower hem of a garment, the border of a dress. Lëep choo seng tông 攝齋升堂, *nëe^nh s^na hāy pee^ng, pāyh chëō^ng tē^ng,* "he gathered up the border of his garment, when ascending the hall." Lest he should trip and fall. See the 上論 Sëāng lūn.
Choo e chëā 齋衣者, *twà hà ây lâng,* a person in mourning.

Choo 椔 A dead tree, still standing erect, a dry post.

Choo 淄 The name of a river, whose waters are as black as varnish.

Choo 鼒 A small kind of iron pan. Naē téng kìp choo 鼐鼎及鼒, *twā tē^nâ kap sèy tē^nâ,* great pans and small ones. See the 周頌 Chew sëūng.

Choo 髭 Hair on the upper lip; mustachios.

Choo 積 Corn collected together

Choo 鼅 Te choo 鼅鼄, *Lâ gëâ,* a spider.

Choo 䐢 Hard skin on the hands and feet.

Choo 澬 Gîm choo 淫澬, a long incessant rain; also the name of a river.

Choo 茨 Mâou choo 茅茨, a kind of coarse grass or rush; to thatch a house with coarse grass; also to collect.

Choo 錙 a weight of about eight ounces.

Choo 銖 A weight of about 14 ounces. Choo choo 錙銖, small weights.

Choo 諮 Choo chëā 諮嗟, an exclamation, a sigh. Choo jé sùn, t'hëen che lèk soè chāe jé këung 諮爾舜天之曆數在爾躬, *choo chëā lè chèy lèy sùn, t'hee^ng ây lek soè chāē lé ây sin,* O thou Sùn! Heaven's calculations centre in your person. See the 下論 Hāy lūn.

Choo 穧 Dead grain.

Choo 諸 An expletive, an auxiliary word all every one; a surname. Choo hoe 諸侯, a prince of the Empire. Ke jê sè choo soo hoē, ché kê chëáng 其如示諸斯乎.指其掌, *e ây ch'hin chëō^ng k'hw^nà choo chèy lèy, kè e ây ch'hèw chëō^ng,* it would be as easy as looking at this (said Confucius,) pointing to his hand. See the 下論 Sëāng lūn.
Choo hoê lêng chéèn jîn ê t'hëen chóó 諸侯能薦人于天子, *choo hoē ěy kè chëèn lang hoē hōng tèy,* the princes of the Empire may introduce a person to the Emperor. See the 下孟 Hāy bēng. Also 諸葛 a double surname.

Choó 子 Vulg. kē^nâ: a son, a child; a title of respect, a philosopher. Sè bîn choó laê 庶民子來, *pāyh sai^ng ch'hin chëō^ng kē^nâ laê,* the people came forward just like children. See the 上孟 Sëāng beng.
Choó sun suy gê, keng se put k'hó put t'hok

子孫雖愚.經書不可不讀, *kéⁿá sun, suy gaê, keng ch'hăyh ûm t'hang bô t'hak*, though children and grand children are dull, they must not neglect reading the classics.

Choó put gé kwaè, lëk, lwān, sîn 子不語怪.力.亂.神, *hoo chòo bô kóng, koo kwaè, k'hwùy lat, hwán lwān, sîn bêng*, Confucius never spoke of strange things, violent deeds, disorderly matters, and spiritual subjects. See the 論語 Lūn gé.

Choó 仔 To bear, to sustain, to overcome. Choó sèy 仔細, carefully.

Choó 㸚 Vulg. á: anything diminutive as, Guêw choó 牛仔, *goo á*, a young cow, a calf. To stop: also read ché.

Choó 学 The ancient from of the choó 子, character.

Choó 耔 To throw up earth on the root of the corn; also written 秄 choó.

Choó 梓 The name of a tree, said to be the king of the trees. Choó t'hân 梓檀, sandal wood.

Këâou choó 喬梓, an appellation signifying father and son.

Choó 丶 A mark, to know when we are to stop; a dot, a spot. Teng tëung hⁿó choó 燈中火丶, *teng tang ēng höèy tëèm*, a spark of fire in the lamp.

Choó 主 A master, a lord: also to rest in, to consider as most important. Chûn choó 船主 a ship-captain. Loê choó 爐主, a superintendant of a religious feast. Pin choó 賓主, a guest, and host.

Aè bin jê hⁿó soō, k'hó wūy bêng choó è 愛民而好士可謂明主矣, *sëăh păyh saiⁿg jê hwⁿa hè t'hak ch'hăyh lâng, t'hang kóng se bêng choó è*, he who loves the people and is found of literary men, may be called an intelligent prince.

Choó tëung sìn 主忠信, *lcăh tëung sìn chò yaôu kìn*, consider fidelity and sincerity as of the highest importance. See the 上論 Sëāng lūn.

Sîn choó paê 神主牌, the ancestorial tablet, near which it is supposed the spirit of the deceased settles.

去 Choò 注 Water flowing to one part, to settle, to fix. Choò è 注意, settled intention. Choò k'hàn 注看, a fixed look.

Cheng sîn kwàn choó, put tê göèy boō ch'hoò naé t'hok se che hwat 精神貫注.不馳外務.此乃讀書之法, *cheng sîn kwàn choò, hô tê chaôu tê gwā bīn ây soō boō, chèy lêy chëw sê t'hak ch'hăyh ây hwat*, to keep the spirits settled and the mind intent, not galloping after outward engagéments; this is the rule to be observed in study.

Choò 傳 To stick to stab, to thrust in; also written 剸 choò. Bok kám choò jīm kong che hok tëung 莫敢剸刃公之腹中, *ūⁿ kⁿá, chăt to tê kong tè ây pak toé*, I do not dare to thrust a weapon into your belly.

Choò 恣 Disordely unrestrained loose, wanton Sèng ông put chok, choo hoê hông choò 聖王不作.諸侯放恣, *sëⁿà ông bô k'hé, choo hoê lâm sâm*, when holy sovereigns do not arise, the princes of the Empire become disorderly.

Choò 漬 To soak; to steep in water. Chëëm choò 漸漬, to soak gradually through.

Choò 胾 Sliced flesh, minced meat.

2 P

Choò 註 To interpret, to comment on; a commentary. Soò se choò he chip choò yëá 四書朱熹集註也, *soò se, choo bûn kong chip choò yëá*, on the four books, choo-he compiled a commentary.

Choò 蛀 A worm that eats wood.

Choò 翥 To fly upwards, to mount up in flying.

Choò 澍 Timely rain, fertilizing showers.

Choò 鑄 To melt, to cast metal. Choò ch'hèng 鑄銃, to cast cannon. Jê kim chaē yëá yûng choò, bān sëāng kae k'hó jip hwân 如金在冶鎔鑄.萬象皆可入範, *ch'hin chëōng kim twā tē yëá yëōng choò, chēⁿá bān yëōng lóng t'hang jip hwân*, just like the metal melting in the foundry, in ten thousand forms it can be introduced in to the mould.

Choò 馵 A horse with his feet entangled; to tie up a horse.

Choò 足 Excessive, extreme, over and above. K'haóu gân, lēng sek, choò këung, chó k'hew bêng t'hé che 巧言令色足恭.左丘明恥之, *k'há ây kóng wā, hó ây bīn sek, köèy t'hadu ây këung, chó k'hew bêng sëáou lèy e*, artful words, a smooth countenance, and excessive respect, were what Chó-k'hew-bêng was ashamed of.

Choò 垜 To collect, to a accumulate.

Choò 貯 Chaê choò 財貯, money, wealth.

Choò 胔 Rotten flesh. Yëém lók baê choò 掩骼埋胔, *yëém koō kwut taê ch'hāou bàh*, to bury old bones and put under ground rotten flesh.

平

Choô 慈 Kind, affectionate, soft and mild. Wûy jîn hoô, chóu ê choô 爲人父主於慈, *chò lâng ây nëōⁿᵍ pōy, yaôu kin twā tē choô*, for one who is a father, the most important thing is kindness. See the 大學 Taē hak.

Choô 鷀 Loê choô neáou 鸕鷀鳥, *loî sê cheáou*, a kind of cormorant.

Choô 磁 Choô sek 磁石, *hëep chëōh*, a loadstone, a magnet. Choô sek yìn chëem 磁石引鍼, *hëep chëōh yón t'hëēh* the loadstone draws the steel.

Choô 瓷 A hard sort of earthenware.

Choô 餈 Rice cakes; a kind of confectionary. also written 粢 choô.

Choô 茨 Thatching, a thatched cottage. Gëâou wûy t'hëen choó sê, mâou choô t'hoé kae 堯爲天子時.茅茨土階, *geâou chò hông tèy ây sê, woō hûᵐ á ch'hoô t'hoé ây kay*, when Gëâou was Emperor, they had thatched cottages, and earthen steps.

Choô 喌 The noise made in calling fowls.

去

Choō 自 Self, one's-self; from. Choō ké 自己, *kā tē*, one's-self, a near relation. T'haè kap choō wàn choō gnaē, ê tông ch'hé jin ch'hëén gê 太甲自怨自艾.於桐處仁遷義, *t'haè kap ka tē wàn ka tē gnaē, twā te tông ch'hè jîn pwⁿa kaôu gē*, T'haè-kap vexed himself and reformed himself at Tông, where he dwelt in benevolence, and removed to righteousness. See the 尙書 Sëōng se.

Hwân soō choō gnó jô chok, ék choō gnó jê sew 凡事自我而作.亦自我而收, *hwân soō chëúng gwá jê chò yëá chëúng gwá jê sew jíp*, every thing rests with one's self to commence and with one's-self to complete.

Choō 吞 A small mouth.

卆

Chui^{ng} 磚 Read chwan: a brick, a tile. Oe chô chok chwan 烏曹作磚, *oe chô k'hè t'hâou chò chui^{ng}*, Oe-chô was the first who made bricks.

Chui^{ng} 鑽 Read chwàn: to perforate anything with an awl; to penetrate into. Chwàn che bé kēen 鑽之彌堅, *chui^{ng} e nā kēen koè*, the more we penetrate into the doctrine the more impenetrable it appears. An awl, a gimlet. Lëúk chwàn 六鑽, *lák chui^{ng}*, a bore.

Chui^{ng} 鱒 A kind of mud fish; with red eyes. To creep into the mud.

平

Chuî^{ng} 全 Read chwân: the whole. Chêy chwân 齊全, *cheabu chuî^{ng}*, complete, entire.

Ch'hoô hwuy bān chwân, che boê 此非萬全之謀, *chêy lêy ū^{m} sē bān chwuî^{ng} ây boê*, this is not a perfectly secure plan.

去

Chuī^{ng} 饌 Read chwān: to suck. Chwān jê 饌乳, *chuī^{ng} leng*, to suck milk.

Chuī^{ng} 鬊 A place where the hair turns or curls on the head; long hair.

卆

Chun. 僎 Ceremonies observed when drinking wine in a village.

Chun 尊 Lofty honourable, noble. Chun kèng 尊敬, to honour, to respect. T'hëen chun tēy pe, k'hëên k'hwun tēng è 天尊地卑.乾坤定矣, *t'hee^{ng} kwân tēy kāy, k'hëên k'hwun tē^{n}ā tëōh*, the heaven is lofty and the earth low, and thus the two great principles of nature are fixed.

Soó bîn yéw hoō che chun, yéw boé che ch'hin, jêên hoē k'hó é wûy bîn hoō boé 使民有父之尊.有母之親.然後可以爲民父母, *saé pāyh sai^{ng} wōo nëō^{ng} pāy ây chun, woō nëō^{ng} lèy ây ch'hin, jëên aōu t'hang chò pāyh sai^{ng} ây pāy boé*, in employing the people, if one maintain the dignity of a father and the affection of a mother, then may he be considered the parent of the people.

Chun 樽 A wooden vessel; a bottle made of wood.

Chun 罇 An earthen vessel, in the shape of a bottle. Hô é wùy kwun, tëung lé yit chun 何以慰君巾里一罇, *an chw^{n}á ēy wùy kwun, hāy tëung lê chit ây chun*, how shall I comfort you, Sir! But by setting down a bottle in the midst of the village.

Chun 遵 To follow, to obey, to learn. Chun sëen ông che hwat jê kò chëá, bē che yéw yëá 遵先王之法.而過者.未之有也, *t'hàn sëen ông ây hwat, jê wōo kùèy sit ây, bōēy woō chèy lêy soō yëá*, to follow the rules of the ancient kings and still to be in an error, is impossible. See 下孟 Hāy bēng.

Chun 嶟 The lofty appearance of hills.

Chun 蹲 Chun ke 蹲踞, to sit cross legged; to sit in a reclining, posture. To sit in an unceremonious manner.

Chun 惇 Sincerity of mind. Chun tek 惇德, sincere virtue.

Chun 屯 Anything beginning to grow; thick; difficult.

Chun 肫 Earnest and sincere.

Chun 窀 Chun sek 窀穸, laid up in a coffin; dark like a long night.

Chun 諄 To instruct repeatedly. Chun chun jëên bēng che hoē 諄諄然命之乎, *tëúng hok kóng, jè bēng lēng e*, how repeatedly was it inculcated and enjoined.

Chun 啍 To instruct any one personally; to repeat a caution.

Chun 噂 To collect words together; an accumulation of expressions; also read chŭn.

Chun 鱒 The name of a fish; also read chŭn.

Chun 濱 Cold and shivering, to tremble with cold. Hân tò gëet ch'hé chit 寒到齧齒濱, *kwⁿa kaoù kā ch'hùy k'hè chun*, to be cold till the teeth chatter.

声 Chún 准 To allow, to grant. Wún chún 允准, to permit. T'hëen choó chún choé 天子准奏, *kóng tèy chún chaòu*, the Emperor granted the request.

Chún 劕 To diminish, to cut off.

Chún 撙 To hold to, Chún chat 撙節, to hold to economical rules. Kwun choó küung kèng chún chat, t'hùy jëäng é bêng léy 君子恭敬撙節.退讓以明禮, *kwun choó këung kèng, chún chat, t'hèy nëōⁿᵍ lâng, è bêng lêy soè*, the good man is raspectful, economical and yielding in order to illustrate the rules of propriety.

Chún 準 Even; a rule, a pattern; to adjust. Chún sŏh 準索, a carpenter's line. Kè këet bok lek yëen, kèy che kwuy ké chún sin, é wûy hong wân pêng tit 既竭目力焉.繼之規矩準繩.以爲方員平直, *kè këet chīn bak chew ây k'hwùy lat sëo swà kwuy kè chún sŏh, è chò sè kak, eeⁿᵍ, paiⁿᵍ kwà tit*, having carried to the utensil the powers of vision the ancients added the compass and rule, and carpenter's line in order to make things square, and round, level and straight. See 孟子 Bēng choó.

Chún 僔 Respectful; to respect, numerous, collect together. Këung kêng jê chún 恭敬而僔, to honor and respect.

Chún 隼 The name of a bird of prey.

Chún 鶽 A very swift bird, the name of a bird that is rapid in its flight. Tëūng nê chaē tîn, yéw chún chip ê tîn hoê che têng 仲尼在陳.有鶽集于陳侯之庭, *tëūng nê twā tē tîn kok, woō chún chëaòu chip tē tîn hoê ây lëⁿâ*, when Confucius was in the tîn country, there was a flock of swift birds collected on the Hall of the prince of Tîn,

Chún 繜 A kind of petticoat; also to honour.

去

Chùn 俊 A man of superior wisdom and talent; one eminent for wisdom. Chùn këet 俊傑, a man of extraordinary talent; a hero.

Chùn këet chaĕ wūy, chek t'hëen hāy che soō kae wat, jê gwân lip ê kê tëâou 俊傑在位.則天下之士皆悅.而願立于其朝, *chùn këet ây lâng chaĕ wuy, chek t'hee^{ng} āy ây t'hak ch'hăyh lâng chò poĕ hw^{n}a hê jê gwân lip tē ê ây lëâou*, when a man of superior talent is on the throne, then all the learned men in the Empire will be pleased, and will desire to stand in his court.

Chùn 儁 Superior; to overcome; strange; wonderful; the same as the above. Tek chùn wat k'hek 得儁曰克, *tit tëŏh yē^{n}â, kòng këò k'hek*, to obtain a victory is called overcoming.

Chùn 雋 The same as 俊 chùn.

Chùn 峻 Lofty, high; also stern, urgent. Chùn kek ê t'hëen 峻極于天, *kwân chê kaoù t'hee^{ng}*, high as the heavens. Lē boō wūy gëêm chùn 吏務爲嚴峻, *chó kw^{n}a boō chò gëêm chùn*, an officer should study to be stern and urgent.

Chùn 嶲 Lofty, long, impending, dangerous. San gâm ko chùn 山巖高嶲, *sw^{n}a gâm, kwân chùn*, the hills and caverns, are lofty and dangerous.

Chùn 儶 Wise, prudent.

Chùn 狻 A cunning rabbit; also an animal that eats tygers and leopards.

2 Q

Chùn 竣 To be finished, to be concluded. Soō ê wân chùn 事已完竣, *soō ê wân lëâou,* the business is brought to a conclusion.

Chùn 浚 Deep; to deepen; to dig a well deeper. Soó chùn chéng, ch'hut, chëûng jê yëêm che 使浚井出.從而揜之, *saĕ e k'hwut chai^{ng}, kaòu ch'hut, chëûng aōu jê yëem e*, they ordered him (Sim) to dig a well deeper, and when he had made his escape sideways, they proceeded to cover him with earth; (thinking that he was still in the well). See the 下孟 Hāy bēng.

Chùn 逡 To retire, to hesitate, to be undecided; also read chūn. Chùn sûn wūy sëuk 逡巡畏縮, *chùn sûn, kē^{n}a lao kē^{n}â k'hè, wùy t'hèy*, to hesitate, going backwards and forwards, fearing and retiring.

Chùn 濬 To dig anything deeper: to deepen a ditch, in order to let the water flow. Chùn k'hëén köèy kē ch'hwan 濬畎澮距川, *k'hwut ch'him ch'hân kaou, ch'hòng twā chúy ch'hui^{ng}*, to deepen the ditches in the fields and enlarge the streams.

Chùn 畯 An officer whose business it was to encourage husbandry. Tëên chùn chè hé 田畯至喜, *k'hwui^{ng} chò ch'hân ây chùn kw^{n}a hw^{n}a hé*, the officer for encouraging agriculture was greatly pleased.

Chùn 餕 The remains after eating; the surplus of food, what is left. Soō k'hëúng hek chùn ê, koè put ê chëēn 食恐或餕餘.故不以薦, *chëăh ây meē^{n}h k'hëûng kē^{n}a hek chëă, sē chëăh sîn ây, chëa ūm k^{n}â laē haòu*, when food (is presented), fearing lest it much be the leavings (of the prince) it should therefore not be offered to the gods.—

Chùn 駿 A large fine horse. Bȯk ông sêng pat chùn má yêw pëèn t'hëen hāy 穆王乘八駿馬.遊遍天下, *bȯk ông k'hëâ päyh chùn bây, t'hit t'hô pëèn mwⁿâ t'heeⁿᵍ āy*, Bȯk-ông mounted on the eighth excellent horse travelled throughout the whole Empire.

Chùn 鱒 Vulg. chuiⁿᵍ: to wind through the mud. Gê chùn jip nê 魚鱒入泥, *hê chuiⁿᵍ jip nwⁿâ t'hoê*, the fish glided into the mud.

Chùn 睃 To look and stare at.

Chùn 圳 A ditch of water; a dyke. Súy chùn 水圳, *chúy chùn*, an aqueduct.

Chùn 鋑 To cut, to engrave. Also written 鐫, chùn.

平

Chûn 存 To preserve, to remain in existence, to retain. Kò chûn 告存, to enquire after one's health and preservation.

Sūn t'hëen chëá chûn, gek t'hëen chëá bông 順天者存.逆天者亡, *sūn t'heeⁿᵍ āy lâng chûn, gek t'heeⁿᵍ āy lâng bông*, he who complies with the dictates of heaven will be preserved, but he who disobeges heaven will perish.

Chûn 拵 The hands held, restricted, embarrassed.

Chûn 船 Read ch'hwân: a ship, a boat, a vessel. Tëong kok ché ch'hwân t'hëet jîn, hô lan t'hëet ch'hwan ché jîn 中國紙船鐵人和蘭鐵船紙人, *tëⁿᵍ suⁿa chwâ chûn t'heëh lâng, hô lan t'heëh chûn chwá lâng*, in China they have paper ships and iron men, but in Europe they have iron ships and paper men; meaning that the ships of the one country are weak and the men robust, while in the other country it is just the reverse.

丟

Chūn 銌 To bore through, to perforate.

仧

Chut 卒 A soldier, a private soldier; done, finished, at the end: suddenly. Goê k'hé wûy chëàng, é peng chut tông ch'hím sit 吳起爲將.與兵卒同寢食, *goê k'hé chò chëàng, kap peng chut tâng k'hwùn chëăh*, Goê-k'hé was a general who slept and ate with his soldiers.

Ch'hong chut 倉卒, busy, having no leisure.

Chut 倅 A body of a hundred men.

Chut 卆 The ancient form of 卒 chut, also written 卒 chut.

Chut 捽 To hold, to seize by the hair of the head.

Chut 窋 Anything in a cave; about to rush out of a cave.

入

Chut 崒 A lofty and dangerous hill. Chut peng 崒崩, to precipitate.

Chut 茮 Pek chut 白朮, a kind of medicine.

Chut 誶 To laugh at, to ridicule; to inform, to announce. Goê ông hwân choō hwat chêy chut sim se 吳王還自伐齊誶申胥, *goê ông hwân choō hwat chêy kok ch'hëò sin se*, when the king of the Gaê country returned from fighting against the Chêy country, he laughed at Sin-se (because he had dissuaded him from going).

Chŭt 秫 Chŭt bé 秫米, a glutinous kind of rice.

Chŭt 椊 The capital of a pillar; to insert in a hollow space. Chŭt gwŭt 椊杌, a blunt piece of timber without branches, to insert in any hollow space.

Chŭt 扨 To rub to grind. Chŭt k'hè 扨去, to rub out.

上平

Chuy 錐 An awl, anything pointed. Chuy to che bwăt, chëang chĭn ch'hĕ che 錐刀之末.將盡取之, *chëem to ây bŏëy, chëang chĭn t'hŭyh e*, even to the point of a knife or an awl (i. e. the minutest thing) all will be taken from them. Sùn boô lip chuy che tëy, è yëw t'hëen hây 舜無立錐之地.以有天下, *sùn bô k'hëä chëem ây tëy è woō t'hee^ng hây*, Sùn had not so much ground as to set up a bodkin on, and yet he obtained the Empire.

Chuy 椎 An iron bar, a crow bar; also to beat. Choo haē sëw soò sip kin t'hëet chuy, chuy sat chin p'hè 朱亥袖四十斤鐵椎.椎殺晉鄙, *choo haē k'hë^ng tē ch'hëw-wui^ng sè chăp kin tăng ây t'hëĕh chuy, bŏëyh chuy t'hoè chin p'hè*, choo-haē kept in his sleeve an iron bar of forty pounds weight, in order to beat to death chin-p'hé, See the 史記 Soó-kĕ.

Chuy ⿱契大 Great, large.

Chuy 臎 The fleshy part of a bird's tail; also fat; and a bare bone.

Chuy 榛 A small kind of chesnut; also read chin. San yëw chuy, sip yëw lêng 山有榛.濕有苓, *sw^na woō tat á, sip tëy woō lêng*, in the hilly parts are chesnut and in the damp grounds are rushes.

Chuy 鵻 Kaou chuy 交鵻, *ka chuy*, a dove.

上聲

Chúy 觜 a fowl's beak; to suck, to peck; also to know.

Chủy 嘴 Vulg. *ch'hày*: the mouth, a beak.

Chúy 水 Read sùy: water; a surname. Chwân sùy 水泉, *chw^nâ chúy*, a fountain of water.
Wûy yëw gwân t'hoê hwăt sùy laê 惟有源頭活水來, *wûy woō gwân t'haôu wăh chúy laê*, only from the fountain head, does the living water come.

上去

Chùy 醉 To be drunk. Chëw chùy 酒醉, drunk with wine. Yëem yëém yëä yim, put chùy hoô kwuy 厭厭夜飲不醉無歸, *yëem cheuk mai^ng yim, bô chëăh kaoù chùy, bô bŏëyh tooi^ng*, getting enough to drink of an evening, men will not return before they are intoxicated.

下平

Chûy 𠜾 Read sut: to cut up, to cut off.

下去

Chūy 萃 To collect together.

Chūy 悴 To be sorrowful, to be distressed. Gân sek chëâou chūy 顏色憔悴, the countenance cast down with sorrow.

Lew hëàng kéw t'hàn koè pók hoo che chëâou chūy 劉向九歎顧僕夫之憔悴, *laoû hëâng kaôu ây t'hò. k'hwùy k'hw^{n}à ch'hëa hoo ây cheaôu chūy,* Laôu-hëâng sighed nine times, on observing the distress of the charioteer.

Chūy 瘁 Distressed, pained. Chëâou chūy ê gëak chèng 焦瘁於虐政, *chëâou chūy ê pò gëàk ây chèng,* distressed by an oppressive government.

Chūy 崒 Collected together; the dangerous appearance of hills.

Chūy 顇 Distressed, grieved; the same as 悴, chūy and 瘁, chūy.

Chūy 蕞 Chūy jé 蕞爾, very small. Chūy jé kok 蕞爾國, a small country.

Chūy 誰 Read sûy: who, what, which, whose. Sē sûy 是誰, *chē chūy,* who is it? Choó wûy sûy, wat, wûy tëūng yêw 子爲誰曰爲仲由, *choó sē chē chūy, kóng, sē tëōng yêw,* who are you Sir? He answered, I am Tëūng-yêw.

Sē sûy che kò e 是誰之過與, *chē chūy ây köèy sit,* whose fault is it?

上聲
Chwá 紙 Read ché: paper. Sìn ché 信紙, *sìn chwá,* letter paper; also written 帋 ché.

Hoē hàn, ch'haé lûn ch'hò poè to ch'haou chok ché 後漢蔡倫挫布擣抄作紙, *hoē hàn tëaôu tëy. ch'hwà lûn ch'hò poè p'hàh ch'haou chò chwá,* in the latter Hàn dynasty (A. D. 250) ch'hwà-lûn, tore cloth and beat it small, in order to make paper.

上去
Chwà 漈 Water falling from a high place; a cataract.

上平
Chwa 蛇 Read sêa: a snake.

下去
Chwā 畷 A path between the paddy fields. Sêng chwā 成畷, *chë^{n}â chwā,* all in a row.

Chwā 誓 Read sè: to swear. Chèw sè 咒誓, *chèw chwā,* to take an oath. Lâm lé soo yëak ëk wät sè 男女私約亦曰誓, *lâ po cha boé sae k'hëa sëa yëak, yëā kóng chwā,* men and women making private engagements together, may also be called swearing.

上平
Chw^{n}a 煎 Read chëen: to boil. Chëen tây 煎茶, *chw^{n}a tây,* to boil tea. K'hip súy chëen tây jëên lêy chëâou se 汲水煎茶燃藜炤書, *chëō^{ng} chúy chw^{n}a tây, sëo lêy ch'hâ chëò kwui^{ng} ch'hāyh,* draw some water in order to boil the tea, and set fire to the lôg, in order to throw light on the book.

上聲
Chw^{n}á 盞 Read chán: a cup, a drinking vessel; also written chán 琖 *chw^{n}á.* Yit chán ch'heng tây 一盞清茶, *chít chw^{n}á ch'heng tây,* a cup of good tea.

上去
Chw^{n}à 讚 Read chàn: to praise. Chok chàn 作讚, *chò chw^{n}à,* to make an oration, in one's praise.

下平
Chw^{n}â 泉 Read chwân: a fountain. Súy chwân 水泉, *chúy chw^{n}â,* a fountain of water.

Jîn chaē ch'heng chwân sek sëāng, tō t'hong t'hëen kin gwat k'hwut 人在清泉石上, 通留天根月窟, *lâng tè ch'heng chw^{n}â chëöh tëng, e ây tō ëy t'hong kaôu t'hea^{ng} kin göëyh k'hwut,* the man is humbly seated on a stone by the side of the pure fountain, but his system of doctrine is lofty enough to penetrate

福建方言字典

to the root of Heaven, and to the cavern of the moon.

Chwⁿâ 𤆬 Embers. Hⁿô lêw chan 火留𤆬, hŏey laôu chwⁿâ, there are still in embers the fire. Hnó kaou chân 炙熮𤆬, hŏey ka chwⁿâ, a small fire or chimney.

Chwⁿâ 殘 Read chân: an overplus, a remmant of food. Chân pŏey é léng cheă 殘杯與冷炙, chwⁿâ pŏey kap léng băh, an odd cup of drink, and some cold roasted meat.

Chwⁿâ 濺 Read chēēn: to sprinkle. E' kĕng hēet chēēn jîn 以頸血濺人, t'hó âm kwán á hōēyh chwⁿâ lâng, to sprinkle one's life's blood on a person.

Chwⁿā 賤 Read chēēn: cheap, easily procurable. Bé chēēn 米賤, bé chwⁿā, the rice is cheap.

Chēēn chek maé che, kwùy chek put k'hó 賤則買之.貴則不可, chwⁿā chēw bēy e, kwùy chēw āⁿ t'hang, if it is cheap, buy it, if dear, refrain.

卒 Chwae 㩐 Chwae tú 㩐倒, to slip down. T'hap t'hoê chwae 塌頭㩐, tăh t'haôu chwae, to fall on one's head.

犬 Chwǎh 䆐 The mouth full of food.

Chwǎh 泏 To spout out. Súy chwǎh chut 水泏出, water spilling or running over.

天 Chwǎh 䗾 Ka chwǎh 蟉䗾, a cockroach.

Chwǎh 差 Read ch'hae: to differ, to fall short. Cheng ch'hae bôo kè to 爭差無幾多, cheng chwǎh bô jwā chāy, it does not come far short.

Choé ch'hae 走差, chaou chwǎh, to sprain, to slip aside.

卒 Chwan 專 To be given up to one thing; to be bent on anything; to engross wholly. Chwan sim tè chè 專心致志, a mind bent on, and the will given up to anything. See 下孟 Hāy bēng.

Hàn bwat tóng tok chwan kwân sēēn pèng 漢末董卓專權擅柄, hàn teâou āy bōēy, tâng tŏh chwan kwân gīm paiⁿᵍ, in the latter part of the Hàn dynasty. Táng-tŏh engrossed the authority, and seized on the reins of government.

Gê jê hⁿò choō yūng, chēēn jê hⁿò choō chwan 愚而好自用.賤而好自專, gaê jê aè ka tē yūng, hāy chēēn jê aè choō chwan, the stupid like to get themselves into employment, and the mean like to have every thing their own way. See the 中庸 Tēung yûng.

Chwan 蓴 The name of a water plant.

Chwan 鱄 The name of a large fish.

Chwan 甎 Vulg. chuiⁿᵍ, a brick; also written 磚 chwan. Wá chwan 瓦甎 hēā chuiⁿᵍ, bricks and tiles.

Chwan 耑 To display, to commence, to set forth. This character is used in modern letter writing, where at the close of an epistle, it is said, kin ch'hoó chwan bûn 謹此耑聞 This is respectfully set forth for the information of such a one, &c.

声 Chwán 囀 The whistling of birds; the screaming of a parrot; to turn; a sound.

Chwán 轉 Vulg. tooiⁿᵍ: to turn round, to return. Wūn chwán 運轉, to transports. Kew che bē tek, tēēn

2 R

chwán hwán ch'hek 求之未得.輾轉反側, *kéw e bōēy tit, pwⁿà tooiⁿᵍ, chwán tooiⁿᵍ, yēw hwán tò tooiⁿᵍ*, seeking her, without success, he turns and turns, and turns again. See the 國風 Kok hong.

Hân-an-kok, chwân ch'hëuk é wûy che pē 韓定國轉粟以爲之備, *hân-an-kok wān chwán ch'hek é chò tēoⁿᵍ tē*, Hân-an-kok transported grain, in order to make preparations.

去 Chwàn 鑽 Vulg. *chuìⁿᵍ*: to bore through, to perforate; an awl, a bore.

平 Chwân 全 Vulg. *chuîⁿᵍ*: the whole complete, fully prepared, to secure against all accidents. Wân chân 完全, *wân chuîⁿᵍ*, to complete; a surname.

Sèng ông ké soō, boē ch'hut bān chwan 聖王舉事.謀出萬全, *sèng òng ke yūng soō, e ây boē ch'hut bān chuiⁿᵍ*, a philosophic king in commencing an undertaking, will produce plans proof against all accidents. Also written 仝 chwân.

Chwân kwun hok but 全軍覆没, *chwnîⁿᵍ kwun pak lak sé*, the whole army was overthrown and annihilated.

Chwân 佺 Ak chwân 偓佺, the name of an ancient genius, in the time of 堯 geâou.

Chwân 牷 A sacrificial animal, perfect and without blemish.

Chwân 泉 Vulg. *chwⁿâ*: a fountain. Súy chwân 水泉, *chúy chwⁿâ*, a fountain of water.

Gwân chwân hwūn, put sëà tèw yëà 源泉混混.不舍晝夜, *gwân chwⁿâ hwun hwūn bô hāyⁿh jit maiⁿᵍ*, a fountain of water bubbling up, without cessation day or night. See the 下孟 Hāy bēng.

去 Chwān 撰 To inform, to announce; to publish; also a work, a business. Ē hoē sam choó chëä che chwān 異乎三子者之撰, *kōh yëōⁿᵍ chèy sⁿa lâng ây sèy kè ây soō*, my views are very differents from what those three gentlemen have stated.

Sēw chwān 修撰, to write a history.

Jīm kwun ke t'haè gwân, pek sēw k'hìn tè chwān 任君居大源.白首勤著撰, *jīm kwun twā tē t'haè gwân, pāyh t'haôu mô k'hin kang tè chwān*, Mr. Jīm dwells at T'haè gwân, and though his head is grey, he is still busilly employed publishing works.

Chwān 譔 The same as the above.

Chwān 饌 To eat and drink. Yéw chéw soō sëen seng chwān 有酒食先生饌, *woō chéw pooⁱⁿᵍ hoē sin saⁱⁿᵍ chëāh*, having wine and food, to give it to one's elders, to eat and drink. See the 上論 Sëāng lūn.

Chwān 詮 To tranquillize a business, to manage a matter to select words: to explain anything; to converse with any one.

Chwān 鏇 To turn on an axis.

入 Chwat 梲 The small posts an the tops of beams. Chong bûn tëūng ke ch'haè, san chëet cho chwat 臧文仲居蔡.山節藻梲, *chong bûn tëūng ch'hòng sò chaē hoē twā koo k'hëā, woō wā swⁿa te chat á, wā chúy ch'haòu tē t'heăou á*, Chong-bûn-tëūng made a place for a tortoise to dwell in, and painted hills on the joists, and water plants on the posts. See the 上論 Sëăng lūn.

Chwat 拙 Dull, not clever, unskilful. Soō yéw lân ē, jîn hwún k'haòu chwat 事有難易.人分巧拙, *soō woō ŏh k'hwaè lâng hwun k'há tūn*, things are both difficult and easy, men are sometimes clever, and sometimes unskilful.

Chwat 茁 The grass beginning to grow. Lân chwat kê gây 蘭茁其芽, *lân hwa toō á ch'hut e ây gây*, the lân flower just budding forth its leaves.

天

Chwat 絕 To cut off; To exterminate; strange; supereminent. Chwat tëâng poé twán 絕長補短, *chwat tĕ^ng poé tēy*, to cut off the long, in order to make up for the short.

Bëĕt chwat 滅絕, to exterminate, to annihilate.

E

E 伊 He, she, it; an expletive; a surname. Also written ⁖ e. E yin keng ê yéw sin che yëá 伊尹耕於有莘之野, *e yin chŏh ch'hân, tē yéw sin ây sw^na yëá*, E-yin ploughed in the wilderness of yéw-sin.

E 衣 Clothes; that which is worn on the body. E hok 衣服, *s^na k'hoèy* apparel. E sëăng chaē soo 衣裳在笥, *yin chëō^ng tē sëō^ng*, the clothes are in the box.

E 依 To rest and rely on; to follow, to comply. E he 依稀, a few. E ê jin 依於仁, *t'hàn ê jin*, to comply with the dictates of benevolence.

E 悠 An expression of sorrow, and pain. Sūn chêng chek he ê seng aè, wûy ê chek e choo hwaê chin 順情則嬉怡生愛.違意則悠懷憤嗔, *sūn lâng ây chêng chek hw^na hé sai^ng aè, gek lâng ây è chek e choo k'hè^ng chin*, complying with men's feelings, they are pleased and bear good-will towards one; but crossing their views, they are pained, and conceive displeasure.

E 戾 To return.

E 於 In, upon, at; from; to dwell in; an expletive. Also read ê: a surname. Chè ê tō, kè ê tek, e ê jîn, yêw ê gāy 志於道.據於德.依於仁.游於藝, *sim chē tē tō, chip sëw tē tek, t'hàn ê jîn, t'hit t'hó t'hó ch'hèw gāy*, have the will bent on learning, keep a firm grasp of virtue, follow the dictates of benevolence, and amuse yourself with the fine arts. See the 上論 Sëăng lūn.

Sam lëĕn boô kaé ê hoō chè tō, k'hó wūy haòu è 三年無改於父之道.可謂孝矣, *s^na nee^ng bô kày ê nëō^ng pāy ây tō, t'hang kóng haòu è*, for three years not to swerve from one's father's way, may be called, filial piety. See the 上論 Sëăng lūn.

E 扵 The same as the above.

E 淤 E nê 淤泥, mud. Ch'hut e nê jê put chok 出淤泥.而不濁, *ch'hut tē nw^nā t'hoè jê bô lō*, coming out of the slime and yet not muddy. Said of the water-lily, which grows in marshy ground, and yet looks so clean.

E 洢 The name of a river.

E 咿 To groan.

E 咿 Ak e 喔咿, a forced laugh; a strong laugh.

E 椅 The name of a wood.

E 漪 The streaks on rippling water; also synonimous with 兮 hêy.

E 旖 The waving appearance of a flag; also the appearance of fleeting clouds.

E 猗 An exclamotion of admiration or regret. E he 欹歔, alas! alas!

E 醫 A healer; to heal. E seng 醫生, a doctor; also written 毉 e. Jîn jê boô hêng, put k'hó é chok boô e 人而無恒.不可以作巫醫, *lâng kaoù bô hêng sim, ūm t'hang hoē e chò sae kong sin saing*, if a man has not a settled mind, he cannot become a conjuror or a doctor.

E 鷖 A kind of water fowl.

E 繄 An expletive; a particle; also to be, to do.

E 譩 An exclamation of one wounded or grieved.

E 于 A particle; in, at, upón; more frequently read ê; a surname.

去聲

E' 以 By, with; to use, to do; in order to. Te hô jê hô, put é léy cheět che. ek put k'hó hêng yëá 知和而和.不以禮節之.亦不可行也, *chae woō hó, jê ch'hêng ch'hêng hó, bô t'hó lèy soè chún chat e, yëá bēy kē^n^á*, to study harmony and nothing else, without regulating it by propriety; this will not do. See the 上諭 Sëang lūn.

Kwun soó sîn é léy, sîn soō kwun é tëung 君使臣以禮.臣事君以忠, *jîn kwun saé jîn sîn é lèy, jîn sin hok saē jîn kwun é tëung*, a prince should employ his minister according to propriety, and a minister should serve his prince with fidelity. See the 上諭 Sëang lūn.

Sè kê séy é 視其所以, *k'hw^n^à é sèy chò*, observe what he does.

Sëy é 所以, therefore. E' chè 以至, until, even to. E' hoē 以後, *è aoū*, afterwards.

E' 苡 E' jîn 苡仁, the seeds of the è plant, in shape like pearls.

E' 偊 The appearance of walking alone; the body bent.

E' 楀 The name of a wood; also a surname.

E' 瑀 Ke é 琚瑀, the name of a stone, like a gem.

E' 禹 The name of the first sovereign of the 夏 hāy dynasty; A surname. E' sēw sùn jëäng, yéw t'hëen hāy 禹授舜讓有天下, *è sēw sùn, ây nëō^ng^ woō t'hee^ng^ āy*, E' received what was yielded to him by sim and obtained the Empire.

E' 寓 The same as 宇 é.

E′ 倚 To rely on, to iucline to one side, to lean againt. E′ wá, to confide upon. Chaē ê, chek këèn ke é ê hêng yëá 在輿則見其倚於衡也, *twā tē ch'hëa, chek k'hwⁿà e wá te hwⁿâ ch'hô*, when he was in the carriage, he might be seen leaning on the cross bar. See the 下論 Häy lūn.

Boô p'hëen, boô é, ông tō chêng tit 無偏無倚王道正直, *bô p'hceⁿᵍ bô wá, ông ây tō chēⁿâ tit*, without partiality and without inclination, the royal way is correct and straight. See the 尙書 Sëäng se.

E′ 椅 Kaou é 交椅, a chair. *E′ t'haôu*, 椅頭, a stool. E′ tëaôu 椅條, a bench.

E′ 掎 To drag along on oue side. Chîn sit kê lok, lêw kwùy tëuk jê é che 秦失其鹿.劉季逐而掎之, *chîn ūᵐ kcèⁿᵍ e ây lok, laôu kwùy kwⁿâ jê k'han e*, the Chîn country lost their deer, when Lêw-kwùy over took and dragged them along.

E′ 予 To give, to bestow; the same as 與 é. Boó ông taē laē soò haé séy sek é chëá, wûy sëen jîn sō hoò 武王大賚四海所錫予者.惟善人是富, *boó ông twā se laē sè haé, séy soò haē chëá, tok tok hó ây lâng sè k'hàh poò*, Boó-ông bestowed great gifts on all within the four seas, but amongst the largesses he conferred, those to good people only were the richest. See the 周書 Chew se.

E′ 迆 To walk awry; to walk in succession.

E′ 苢 Hoô é 芣苢 the name of a plant; the plantago; now called ke chüên ch'hó 車前草, *ch'hëa chêng ch'haôu*, the grass before the carriage.

E′ 依 Hoô é 斧依, a kind of screen, placed before a door or window, to prevent persons looking into an appartment.

E′ 雨 Vulg. hoē: rain. Lok é 落雨, *lôk hoē*, to rain. T'hëen yêw jëên chok yîn, p'haé jëên häy é, chek bëaôu put jëên hin che è 天油然作雲.沛然下雨.則苗㶿然興之矣, *t'heeⁿᵍ yêw jëêu chò hwûn, p'haè jëên lôh hoē, chek têw put jëên hin k'hê è*, when the Heavens become overspread with clouds, and send down plentiful showers, then the corn suddenly springs up. See the 上孟 Sëäng bēng.

E′ 㑌 The excess of weeping.

E′ 傴 E′ loē 傴僂, not straightened, crooked. E′ chëá soò che toē 傴者使之塗, *ūᵐ tit ây tang, saê e saoù gāy*, crooked people were set to sweep the ground.

E′ 已 To stop, to finish, to end; extreme. Jê é 而已, *tëⁿâ tëⁿâ*, that and nothing else. Boô é, chek ông hoē 無已.則王乎, *boô swàh chek ông ây tō hoē*, if you will not desist from your enquiries, then I shall refer you to the royal way. See the 上孟 Sëäng bēng.

T'hëäng nê put wûy é sîn chëá 仲尼不爲已甚者, *tëüng nê bô böëyh chò k'hàh sîm ây soō*, Confucius did not do anything that was to the extreme. See the 下孟 Häy bēng.

Jê ch'hoó jê é è 如此而已矣, *an néy tëⁿâ tëⁿâ*, thus and thus only.

E′ 與 Vulg. hoē: to give, to bestow, to promise; also with, together with. K'hó é é, k'hó é boô é, é sëang hwûy 可以與.可以無與.與傷惠, *woō sé â sëōⁿᵍ t'hang hoē lâng, woō sé â sëōⁿᵍ ūᵐ t'hang hoē lâng hoō lâng, sëang yin hwûy*, sometimes we think we may give a thing, and sometimes we think we may not, when to give would be excessive generosity. See the 下孟 Häy bēng. Also written 与 é.

Wûy gnó é jé yéw sē hoo 惟我與爾有是夫, *tok tok gwá kap lé woō an néy saiⁿᵍ hoô*, you only and I are thus. See the 上論 Sëäng lūn.

E´ **宇** A covering a canopy; to spread over. E´ tēw 宇宙, the universe. E´ lōēy 宇內, in the world. E´ bûn 宇文, a double surname.

E´ **偊** Careful; to rely on.

E´ **羽** Feathers. E´ ek 羽翼, wings. E´ mô put hong bwán chëá put lêng ko hwuy 羽毛不豐滿者.不能高飛, *sit mô bô hong mwⁿá chëá, chëw bēy kwân pōey*, when wings and feathers are not rich and full, it is impossible to fly high.

E´ **庡** Hesitating, doubtful.

E´ **鄅** The name of a country.

E´ **扆** Hoó é 斧扆, a kind of screen.

E´ **噢** E´ hew 噢咻, the groaning of a sick person; internal sorrow.

去

`E **意** An intention. `E soō 意思, thought. Chè è 志意, design. Choó è 主意, purpose. Sëen sêng kê è 先誠其意, *taè seng ch'hòng sêng sit e ây è*, first purify the intention. See the 大學 Taē hak.

`E **鷾** A kind of swallow. Bok te kê è jê 莫知其鷾鴯, *ūᵐ chae e sē è jê*, not knowing that it was such a kind of swallow.

`E **噫** An exclamation intimating dissatisfaction and discontent: a cry of pain.

`E **薏** A certain plant. `E jîn 薏仁, the seeds of the water lily.

`E **⿺乚壴** `E pè ⿺乚壴費, few, scarce.

`E **曀** A dark and windy appearance of the weather.

`E **殪** To kill, to die, to put to death. Tēng pek gé jëûng, chëên hoē kek che, chīn è 鄭伯禦戎.前後擊之.盡殪, *tēng pek gè jëûng hwan, chêng aōu phăh e, chīn sè*, the prince of the Tēng country attacked the Jëûng foreigners, and beat them before and behind, till they were all dead. See the 左傳 Chó twān.

`E **饐** Rice heated and in a state of fermentation. Soò è jê aé, put sit 食饐而餲不食, *pooīⁿᵍ jwăh tâm, jê k'hëep, bô böëyh chëăh*, when the rice was heated by fermentation and sour he would not eat it. See the 上論 Sëāng lūn.

`E **懿** Constant and fine, permanent, good, amiable, and virtuous. Gnó kêw è tek 我求懿德, *gwá aè hó ây tek*, I love amiable virtue.

`E **豷** The offspring of a pig: a young pig.

`E **伿** Lazy, indolent; vulg, *yëà*, tired, fatigued, wearied.

`E **瘀** Clotted blood; blood coagulated into one mass.

`E **痤** A small swelling; a boil, a pustule. Tân è chëá t'hòng, yím yëak chëá k'hoé 彈痤者痛.飲藥者苦, *twⁿâ è ây t'hëⁿà chëăh yŏh ây k'hoé*, to fillip a boil is painful, and to drink medicine is bitter.

'E 医 A quiver and case for holding a bow and arrows. Peng put kaé è 兵不解医, *peng ū^{m} t'hang t'haóu e ây è*, a soldier must never take off his quiver and bow case.

'E 矣 A final particle, used at the close of a sentence; an expletive. Kē soo che wūy è 其斯之謂矣, *e sē an nēy kóng*, this is the meaning of it.

Tëaou bûn tō, sek soó k'hó è 朝聞道夕死可矣, *mūy^{n}h chaē t'hē^{n}a tō, mâi^{ng} hwui^{ng} sè yëá t'hang*, in the morning having heard the right doctrine, in the evening we may by content to die. See the 上論 Sëāng lūn.

'E 飫 To be satisfied, to be full, to be content; content. Boó ông k'hek yin chok è ko 武王克殷作飫歌, *boô ông k'hek yē^{n}â yin tëâou, chò è ây ko*, when Boó-ông conquered the Yin dynasty, he composed the song of content. See the 周語 Chew gé.

E 餱 To eat to the full, to feast.

'E 瞖 Sore eyes: a cataract in the eye; the name of a medicine good for the eyes. Hoē seng jê è yit bok 后生而瞖一目, *hông hoē sai^{ng}, jê pai^{ng} chit bak*, when the queen was born, she was blind of one eye.

'E 衣 To clothe, to put on clothes. Ló chëá è pek sit jëuk 老者衣帛食肉, *laōu lâng ch'hèng poè pek chëāh bāh*, the old people would then be able to wear silks, and eat flesh.

'E 雨 To rain, to rain upon. 'E gnó kong tëên, sūy kip gnó soo 雨我公田遂及我私, *lōh hoē gwá ây kong ch'hân, suy kip kaòu gwá ây sae k'hëa ây*, let it rain first upon our public field, and then let it come upon our private field. See the 小雅 Seáou gnáy.

'E 贀 Profitable; advantage.

平

Ê 于 In, at, upon; to go towards. Also written 亐, ê. Ê é ch'haé pin, lâm kan che pin, ê é ch'haé chó, ê pé hêng ló 于以采蘋南澗之濱于以采藻于彼行潦, *laê k'hè bân pîn, lâm kan ây pin, laê k'hè ch'haê chây ch'haâu, tē hwūh lêy hêng lō*, come and let us gather the Pin vegetable, on the borders of the southern shore; come and let us gather the water plants, in the running streames. See 國風 Kōk hong.

Ê 予 I, myself. T'hëen seng tek ê ê, hwân töêy kē jê ê hô 天生德於予,桓魋其如予何, *t'hee^{ng} sai^{ng} chêy lêy tek hoē gwá, hwân töêy e hwat gwá s^{n}a meē^{n}h taē wá*, Heaven has bestowed this degree of virtue upon me, and what can Hwân-töêy do to me. See 上論 Sëāng lūn.

Ê 侇 Even, equal.

Ê 徳 Plain, and even. Taē tō sîm ê 大道甚徳, *twā tō lê, chin chaē pâi^{ng} kap k'hwàe*, the great doctrine is very plain and even.

Ê 蛦 Tông ê 螗蛦, a kind of insect.

Ê 姨 Boé ê 毋姨, a mother's sister. Sèy ê 細姨, a wife's sister; also a concubine.

Ê 峓 Gê ê 嵎峓, the name of a hill, towards the rising sun.

Ê 咦 To call aloud; also to laugh.

Ê 踦 To sit cross legged, to squat on the ground. Gwân jëäng ê soō 原壤踦俟, *gwân jëäng p'hăh k'wùn k'ha téng haōu*, Gwân jëäng sat cross legged waiting (for Confucius). See the 下論 Hāy lūn.

Ê 余 I myself; loose; also a surname. Wūy ê put sìn yéw jê këäou jit 謂余不信. 有如皦日, *kóng gwá ūm sìn sit woō ch'hin chëōng béng jit*, if you say that I am not true, I appeal to the bright sun. See the 國風 Kok hong.

Ê 畬 When a field to is cultivated for one year, it is called 菑 choo; and when it is cultivated for two years, it is called 畬 ê.

Ê 餘 Superabundance, superfluity, excess, that which is over and above. Yéw sëy put chëuk, put kám put bëën, yéw ê put kám chīn 有所不足不敢不勉. 有餘不敢盡, *woō sëy bô kaōu, ūm kⁿá ūm bëën lëy, woō th'hun ūm kⁿá chīn*, having a deficiency in any-thing, we dare not neglect exertions; having a super-abundance we dare not exhaust it all. See the 中庸 Tëūng yūng.
Būn yéw ê, pit wat yéw, 問有餘必曰有, *moongⁿ woō ch'hun, pit kóng woō*, when he asked, if there was anything over, he would always say, there was. See the 孟子 Bēng chóo.

Ê 輿 A carriage, the bottom of a chariot, hand-some. Ê jîn 輿人 a wheelwright. K'ham ê 堪輿, a complimentary title for a determiner of the sites of buildings and graves, called a 地理先生, tēy lé sëen seng.
Choó sān é kë sëng ê, chëy jîn ê chîn wûy, 子產以其乘輿濟人於溱洧, *choó sán t'hô e sëy chëy ây ch'hëa, chëy lâng köëy ê chîn wûy ây chúy*, Choó-sán used the chariot in which he rode for helping people a cross the Chîn and Wûy waters. See the 下孟 Hāy bēng.

Ê 譽 To praise, to applaud, to give one a good name. Goê che ê jîn yëá sûy hwûy sûy ê, jê yéw sëy ê chëá, kë yéw sëy sè ê, 吾之於人也. 誰毀誰譽. 如有所譽者. 其有所試矣, *gwá ây kap lâng, yëá, chë chûy maīngⁿ chë chûy o ló, ch'hin chëōngⁿ woō sëy o ló, e woō sëy ch'hè*, in my intercourse with people, I do not know whom I should blame and whom I should praise, but if I praise any, it is because they have been tried. Said by confucius, in the 下論 Hāy lūn.

Ê 旟 An ornament for a flag, in the shape of a bird.

Ê 璵 A precious gem. Loé yâng hⁿò ch'hëep taē këung, hwan ê che gëuk, ê p'hùn, 魯陽貨竊大弓璠璵之玉以奔, *loé kok ây yëōngⁿ höëy t'haou twā këung, kap hwan ê ây gëuk ê chaôu*, Yëōngⁿ-böëy of the Loé county stole the great bow, with the Hwân ê gem, and then made his escape. See the 左傳 Chó twān.

Ê 轝 A sedan chair is called këen ê 肩轝, *keng t'haôu ch'hëa*, a shoulder waggon.

Ê 玗 A stone resembling a gem.

Ê 竽 A pipe, a flute. Chëy ông hⁿò ê, 齊王好竽, *chëy ông aè ê*, the king of the Chëy country was fond of the flute.

Ê 芋 Great. Kwun choó yew ê, 君子攸芋, the good man is truly great.

Ê 杅 A bathing vessel, a tub. Yëuk sê jip ê, yëuk kéng ch'hut ê, 浴時入杅. 浴竟出杅, *châng ek ây sê jip ê, châng swăh ch'hut ê*, when a person bathes he enters the tub, and when he has done he comes out of it.

Ê 好 Chëet ê 婕好, a female office, established under the Hàn dynasty.

Ê 詒 To leave, to hand down, to send, to present, to send word. Sëuk hëàng soó ê Choó-sán se, 叔向使詒子產書, *sëuk hëàng saé lâng k'hëà Choó-sán p'hay*, Sëuk-hëàng, ordered them to send a letter to Choó-sán.

Ê 台 I, myself: a character common in epistolary correspondence.

Ê 怡 Joyful, delighted. San tëung hô sëy yéw, léng sëäng to pek böëy, ché k'hó choō ê wat, put k'ham tê cheng kwun, 山中何所有.嶺上多白梅.只可自怡悅.不堪持贈君, *swⁿa tëung woō sⁿa meëⁿh, nëⁿà chëōⁿᵍ chëy pa'h ûᵐ, chè t'hang ka tē hwⁿa hè, ûᵐ k'ham t'hëyh lâe sàng kwun*, what is there on the hill? upon the mountain there are many white plum blossoms; but I can only enjoy them alone, and am not worthy to present them to your honour.

Ê 飴 Sugar.

Ê 移 To remove, to transplant, to change a place or thing. Ê hong ek sëuk bok sëen ê gak 移風易俗莫善於樂, *pwⁿa hong wⁿà sëuk, hó k'hëh hó ê gak*, in order to remove customs and change habits, there is nothing so good as music. See the 禮記 Léy kè.

Ê 貽 To present, to give; to hand down. Ê k'hwat choó sun, 詒厥子孫, *sàng e ây këⁿà sun*, Bestowed on his posterity.

Ê 匜 A bathing vessel, with a handle, used in pouring out water.

Ê 酏 A kind of spirituous liquor; made of rice; also water gruel, made of rice or millet; congee; thin rice water.

2 T

Ê 蛇 Wûy ê, 委蛇, respectful and diligent.

Ê 虵 The same as the foregoing.

Ê 痍 An ulcer, a wound; wounded. Bēng kwun lē ch'hat ê sëang 命軍吏察痍傷, *bēng leng kwun lëung ây kwⁿa lē ch'hat woō ê sëang ây lâng*, he ordered an officer of the army to inspect the wounded. See the 左傳 Cho twān.

Ê 扅 Yëëm ê 扊扅, the bar of a door. P'heng hok ch'he him yëëm ê, jé put kè tong sê 烹伏雌炊扊扅.汝不記當時, *p'heng key hoë hëⁿà moōⁿᵍ ch'hwⁿà, lé, bëy kè tong sè*, "when I boiled my last hen, and burned the bar of my door for fire wood (to give you a treat) do you forget the time." Said by the wife of 百里奚, pek-lé-hêy, when her husband was risen high in office, and had forgotten his former poverty.

Ê 彝 The vessels constantly employed in the ancestorial temple constant. Ê lûn 彝倫, the constant relations of life.

Ê 宧 The north-east corner of a house.

Ê 圯 A bridge. Ê sëäng ló jìn sëw tëang-lëäng se 圯上老人授張良書, *këö têng lau lâng hoë tëoⁿᵍ-lëâng ch'hëyh*, when upon the bridge an old man gave a book to Tëong-lëaⁿᵍ. See the 史記 Soó kè.

Ê 瓵 Aou ê 甌瓵, a brick or tile.

Ê 亏 The ancient from of the ê 于 character.

È 伃 The same as 好, ê, a female officer.

Ê 㰻 Ê ê 㰻㰻, the noise made by a fox.

Ê 雩 Boo ê 舞雩, a place for sacrificing to Heaven, and praying for rain.

Ê 佗 Wúy ê 委佗, diligent and earnest; the same as 蛇 ê.

Ê 頤 The chin, the side of the mouth. Kwan gnó tó ê, choō kêw k'hoé sit 觀我朶頤.自求口食, *k'hwⁿà gwá ây ch'hùy peeⁿᵍ, choō kêw ch'hùy chēăh*, look at the sides of my mouth (so fallen in) which for themselves beg for something to eat. See the 易經 Yēăh keng.

Ê 賹 To present, to give; the same as 貽 ê.

Ê 怡 Placid and agreeable.

Ê 歟 An exclamation implying doubt, used as a note of interrogation. Kê soo che wūy ê 其斯之謂歟, *ê sē an nêy kóng ê*, is not this the meaning of it?

Ê 與 Also an intimation of doubt and uncertainty as the above. Kwun choó jîn, ê, kwun choó jîn yēá 君子人與.君子人也, *chêy sē kwun choó ây lâng ê, chēw sē kwun choó ây lâng yēá*, is he a good man? In deed he is a good man! See the 上論 Sēāng lūn.

Ê 夷 Wounded, cut, cut off; also smooth and easy; a foreigner. Soò ê 四夷, all foreigners, barbarians from every quarter. Ê tek che yéw kwun, put jê choo hāy che boô yēá 夷狄之.有君.不如.諸夏之亡也, *ê tek ây woō jîn kwun, ūᵐ ch'hin chéōⁿᵍ choo hāy ây bô*, even the foreign barbarians have their princes; how unlike to China, which is without them! See the 上論 Sēāng lūn.

Ē 異 Strange uncommon, unusual, different. Goé ê choó wūy ē che būn, cheng yêw ê kêw che būn 吾以子爲異之問.曾由與求之問, *gwá lēăh chò lê woō sⁿa meēⁿh kŏh yēōⁿᵍ ây mooīⁿᵍ, cheng sē yêw kap kêw ây mooīⁿᵍ*, I thought that you would ask about some strange thing how come you to ask merely about yêw and kêw. See the 上論 Sēāng lūn.

Ē 𠂆 To draw towards one; also clear.

Ē 傷 Light, to look lightly upon, to disrespect.

Ē 易 Vulg. *k'hwaè*: easy, not difficult. Sēáou jîn hak tō, chek ê soó yēá 小人學道則易使也, *sèy ây lâng hak sip tō lê, chek k'hwaè saè yūng*, when the common people are acquainted with virtue, they are easily governed. See the 下論 Hāy lūn.

Ē 㐌 Ē ē 㐌移, to remove.

Ē 預 To arrive at, to reach to, to influence. Ch'ham ē 参預, mixed; also used for 豫 ē, easy and pleased; and sometimes put for 與 ê.

Ē 澦 The name of a river.

Ē 豫 To be pleased, to be at ease, and contented; also early. Ē pē 豫備, to prepare, to provide. Yêw ê 猶豫, undecided, hesitating. Thaè kap boô sê ê taē 大甲無時豫怠, *t'haè kah bô chit sê êng kwà twⁿā*, T'haè-kăh was never for a moment unemployed and idle.

福建方言字典

Yit yêw yit ê, wūy choo hoê toē 一遊一豫.為諸侯度, chìt ây t'hit chò chìt ây hwⁿa hè, chò choo hoê ây kwat, toē, [the Emperors] by this one jaunt, and by this one excursion became a pattern for the princes of the Emperor. See the 上孟 Sëāng bēng.

Kwun choó soo hwān, jê ē hông che 君子思患而豫防之, kwun choó sëōⁿᵍ woō hwān lò, chēw chá chá tëōⁿᵍ tê e, when the good man suspects that trouble is coming, he early provides against it. See the 易經 Ék keng.

Ē 泄 Many people. Song cheá ē ē hêy 桑者泄泄兮, bān seⁿᵍ ây lâng chēy chēy lâng, those who picked the mulberry leaves were numerous. See the 國風 Kok hong.

Ē 异 The ancient form of 異 ē.

Ē 勩 Trouble, labour. Bôk te gnó ē 莫知我勩, bô lâng chae gwá ay tëŏh, bwá, nobody knows my trouble. See the 小雅 Seáou gnáy.

Ē 忬 The same as 豫 ē, pleased, satisfied.

Ē 芋 Vulg. oē a yam, a bulbous rooted vegetable; the arum aquaticum. Soō chut sit ē sëuk 士卒食芋菽, soō chut chëăh oē kwà taōu, the common soldiers ate yams and pulse. See the 史記 Soá kè.

Ē 旟 A flag staff, a standard; used for 旟 ē. K'hëet k'hëet kan ē, chaē chûn che toe 孑孑干旟.在浚之都, twⁿa twⁿa chìt ây kê kwⁿo, twā tē chûn ây toe yìp, only one single standard, at the capital city of Chûn. See the 國風 Kok hong.

Ē 洩 Pleased, at ease; expanded, spread out.

Ē 譽 Praise, fame, a good name; also pleased, the same as 豫 ē. Lêng būn lêng ē 令聞令譽, hó ây mēnâ sëⁿa, hó ây o ló, a good report, and a good name.

Ē 曳 Slowly, to lead, to drag. K'hè kap ē peng jê choé 棄甲曳兵而走, t'hè kak chëen kăh, t'hwa lwa peng to jê chaóu, they throw away their armour, drew their weapons after them, and took refuge in flight. See the 上孟 Sëāng bēng.

Ē 肄 To study, to labour over. Ē gëep 肄業, to study in a college. Sëaóu gnáy ē sam 小雅肄三, seáou gnáy t'hák sⁿa kwùy, to read the Seaóu-gnáy (the book of odes) three times through.

Ē 㑊 The joining of a seam.

Ē 裔 The hinder part of a garment; posterity future generations. Tek sûy hoē ē 德垂後裔, tek hîng sây tŏh kaōu aōu laē ây kēⁿá sun, virtue handed down to succeeding generations.

Choó sun yîn ē 子孫雲裔, kēⁿá sun hoē ē, sons and grandsons to the latest posterity.

平

Eeng 𪫢 The noise made in order to get children to sleep.

去

Eēⁿᵍ 燕 Read yëèn: a swallow. Nê lâm yëèn choó, gé lëāng kan 呢喃燕子.語樑間, nê lâm haōu ây eēⁿᵍ á, tit kóng wā tē ch'hoò nëóⁿᵍ ây kan, the chattering swallows are talking between the beams of the house.

平

Eêⁿᵍ 丸 Read yëên: a pill, a bolus. Yëák yëên 藥丸, yŏh eêⁿᵍ, a medicinal pill.

Eē^ng 圓 Read wân: round. Sip gnóe yĕä, gwat twân wân 十五夜.月團圓, *chap goĕ maing göĕyh eēng teēng*, in the night of the fifteenth, the moon is round and full.

Eē^ng 員 Read wân: round, globular. Kwuy ké hong wân ehe chè yĕä 規矩方員之至也, *kwuy kè ch'hòng sè kak eēng eēng ây chè hó*, the compass and rule, have brought rounds and squares to perfection. See the 下孟 Hāy bĕng.

去

Eē^ng 異 Different, strange, uncommon, unusual, also read ē. Kwaè eē^ng yúng lek, pöèy lwān che soō, kae hoo choó séy put gé 怪異勇力背亂之事.皆夫子不語, *kwaè eēng yúng bèng, k'hwùy lat, pöèy lwān ây soō, chò poō hoo choō sèy ūm kóng*, strange, uncommon, ferocious and violent things, together with rebellions and confusions, Confucius would never speak of.

Eē^ng 寺 Read sē: a monastery, a temple. Kwān sē 觀寺, *kwn'ā eēng*, a monastery. Sē koé yīn hong t'hap, têng he gwat t'hoè lēēm 寺古雲封塔.庭虛月透簾; *oēng laōu hwán hong t'hăh, têng k'hang göĕyh t'haōu moong lē*, though the temple is old, the clouds cap the towers; and though the hall is empty, the moon shines through the door blinds.—

Eē^ng 院 Read yēēn: a hall. Se yēēn 書院, *se eēng*, a hall of learning, a college. Hān lim yēēn 翰林院, *hān lim eēng*, the Imperial College at Pekin. Koe kw^ná yēēn 孤寡院, *koe kwnā eēng*, an asylum for widows and orphans.

去

Eĕh 臆 Read ek: tripe. Te ek 猪臆, *te eĕh*, pig's tripes.

去

Ek 億 A lac; a hundred thousand. Sĕang che sun choó, kē léy put ek 商之孫子.其麗不億, *sĕang ây kĕnā sun e ây soè put chè chit ek*, the descendants of Sĕang, are not to be reckoned by lacs.

Ek 益 To increase, to add, to profit; a surname. Lē ek 利益, *lē yĕăh*, gain profit. Yīn yīn ê hāy léy, séy sún ek k'hó te yĕä 殷因於夏禮.所損益可知也, *yin tĕaōu t'hàn ê hāy tĕāou ây léy, séy sún séy ek t'hang chae*, the Yin dynasty imitated the ceremonies of the Hāy dynasty, and that which they added or diminished can be known. See the 上論 Sĕang lūn.

Ek 蕣 The ancient form of 益, ek.

Ek 嗌 A stoppage in the throat.

Ek 啞 The noise of laughing.

Ek 搤 To hold, to grasp, to seize upon.

Ek 抑 To rest on, to exceed; also, or, either. Kêw che ê, ek é che ê 求之與.抑與之與, *e woō kêw e, yĕä woō lâng hoē e*, Does he seek for it, or does any one afford it him? See the 上論 Sĕāng lūn. K'hwut ek 屈抑, to oppress.

Ek 厄 Trouble, difficulty; to be in straits. Kwun choó che ek ê tīn ch'haè che kan 君子之厄於陳蔡之間, *kwun choō ây chae ăyh, tē tin kok ch'haè kok ây tĕung kan*, the good man (Confucius) was brought into straights, between the countries of Tīn and Ch'haè. See the 下孟 Hāy bĕng.

Ek 阨 To be in straights. Ek këûng je put bîn 阨窮而不憫, *woō ăyh kwà sŏng hēung, jê bô hwan lô*, in distress and poverty, without being grieved.

Ek 憶 To remember, to think of. Kè ek 記憶, to remember. O'ng soō-e he, yew kè ek 往事依稀,猶記憶, *kŏey ŏng ây soō chëŏ chëŏ, yêw ēy kè tit*, past events are few and scattered, and yet they are as it were remembered.

Ek 臆 The flesh about the breast. Ch'héng é ek tùy 請以臆封, *ch'hē^{n}á e sim kw^{n}a tòèy*, I beg to reply with my bare breast; an expression intimating uprightness and sincerity.

Ek 繶 A cord, a rope.

Ek 戹 The same as 厄, ek, calamity; also a small door.

Ek 豟 A Strong pig.

Ek 軛 A yoke. Pok ek é kāy gnêw chëá 䋞軛以駕牛者, *pak ăyh é kāy goô ây*, (a piece of wood) on which they tie on the yoke, to yoke in the oxen. See the commentary on the 上論 Sëāng lūn.

亦

Ēk 亦 Vulg. yëä: also, and; an auxiliary expletive. Lôk ek chaē kê tëung é 樂亦在其中矣, *chëûng lok yëä tē e ây tang e^{ng}*, pleasure is also in the midst thereof. See the 上論 Sëāng lūn.

Put ek wat hoê 不亦悅乎, *ā^m yëä hw^{n}a hè hoē*, is it not also pleasing?

Ēk 㑊 A low state of the pulse; also a disease; to have a good appetite, and yet to continue thin, is called sit ek 食㑊.

Ēk 奕 Great, accumulated. ek ek lëâng san 奕奕梁山, *twā twā lëâng sw^{n}a*, how great is the Lëâng hill?

Ēk 弈 To play at chess. Ēk ch'hew t'hong kok che sëën ek chëá yëá 弈秋通國之善弈者也, *ek ch'hew t'hong kok ây gaôu wây kê ây lâng*, Ek-ch'hew was the best chess-player in the whole country. Phok ek 博弈 to play at chess.

Ēk 帟 A small curtain. Wûy ek 帷帟, behind the curtains.

Ēk 洂 The same the following.

Ēk 液 Sweat, perspiration. Hwàn hoê kê jëak súy cho ek 渙乎其若水之液, *lòng kòng laôu, ch'hin chëō^{ng} chúy ây laôu kw^{n}ā*, bursting out, just like water was the perspiration.

Ēk 腋 The arm-pits. Ch'hëen yâng che p'hê, put jê yit hoê che ek 千羊之皮不如一狐之腋, *chë^{n}á ch'heng yëō^{ng} ây p'hōèy ā^m tat tëôh chit ây hoê lê ây ek*, a thousand sheep-skins are not so good as one dress made of the fur under the arm-pits of foxes.

Ēk 掖 To hold to grasp to seize; a small building by the side of the principal house is called 掖庭 ek têng, and a wall on the side of a court, is called 掖垣 ek hwân.

Ēk 剨 The noise of any thing splitting.

Ēk 䂶 The splitting of any thing with a knife.

Ēk 劃 To split with a knife, to cut out, work.

2 U

Ĕk 畫 To describe, to draw, to delineate, to plant; also to define a limit. Paôu-he-sē sé ĕk pat kwà 庖犧氏始畫八卦 *paôu he-sē-k'hè t'haôu wā pat kwa*, Paôu-se-sē (or Hok-he) was the first, who described the eight diagrams. Yit ĕk 一畫 *chit wăh*, one stroke. Lêw-bûn-chēng wūy tông ch'hek ĕk 劉文靜爲唐策畫, *laou-bûn-chēng kap tông ch'hek ĕk*, Laôu-bûn-chēng described plans for the Tông dynasty.

Ĕk 譯 To translate, to explain any thing out of one language into another. T'hwân ê hāy che gân wat ĕk 傳夷夏之言曰譯, *t'hoot^ng hwan kap têng āy wā kông kĕô ek*, to turn foreign expressions into Chinese is called ĕk, to translate.

Ĕk 懌 To rejoice in, to be delighted. Ké kêèn kwun choó, sè ke wat ĕk 既見君子.庶幾.悅懌, *kaôu k'hw^nà kwun choó, sè ke hw^na hè*, when we see a good man, we may perhaps be delighted. See the 小雅, seáou gnáy.

Ĕk 斁 To be displeased, and disgusted with. Chaē pê boô oè, chaē ch'hoó hoô ĕk 在彼無惡.在此無斁, *tē ché tâou bô lâng wàn, tē hē taôu bô lâng yèèm*, in that place there will be none hating us, and in this place, none disgusted with us. See the 周頌 Chew sëâng.

Ĕk 繹 To spread out, to trace. Sîm ĕk 尋繹, to search. Soō ĕk 思繹, to think of. Wat jê put ĕk, chēûng jê put kaé, goê bwat jê che hô yēá ê ê 悅而不繹.從而不改.吾末如之何也已矣, *hw^na hé lân ây tō, jē bô soō ĕk e, bīn chēng t'hàn lân, jē k'ha chĕăh aōu bô bôëyh, káy, gwá bô hwat e taē wā*, to appear delighted with one's doctrine, and yet not to investigate it; to comply outwardly with one's requisitions and yet secretly not to reform:—I do not know what to do with such fellows. See the 上論 Sëāng lūn.

Ĕk 易 Ĕk keng 易經, *yĕăh keng*, the book of diagrams, so called from the sixty-four changes of the diagrams. A surname. To change, to alter, to exchange. Koé che wûy ch'hē chëá, é kê sêy yéw ĕk kê sêy beô 古之爲市者.以其所有易其所無, *koé chá āy chò ch'hè, t'hó e āy sêy woō, w^nà e āy sêy bô*, the ancients established markets, in order to take that which they had, and exchange it for what they had not. See 孟子 Bĕng choó.

Ĕk 瘍 A disease of the pulse; an epidemic.

Ĕk 蜴 A kind of insect.

Ĕk 疫 A pestilence. Wun ĕk 瘟疫, *wun yĕăh*, an epidemic. Bîn boô yaou ĕk 民無天疫, *paĭh sai^ng bô yaou sē wun yĕăh*, among the people there were neither early deaths nor epidemic disorders.

Ĕk 役 To serve, a servant. Ch'hae ĕk 差役, *ch'hay yĕăh*, a messenger. Gây ĕk 衙役, *gây yĕăh*, a police runner. Ĕk soó 役使, to employ. Kê pin k'hek soo ĕk kae t'hëen hāy chùn këet 其賓客厮役皆天下俊傑, *e āy lâng k'hăyh, saé yĕăh āy lâng, chò poô sē t'hee^ng hāy āy chûn kēet*, his guests and servants all consisted of the most clever men in the Empire. See the 陳餘傳, Tân ê twān.

Ĕk 伇 The same as the above; also to guard the borders of a country.

Ĕk 翼 A wing; to fly. E' ĕk 羽翼, wings, feathers. Ch'hap ĕk ĕk hwuy put ch'hut 插翼亦飛不出, *ch'hăh sit yĕá pōey bĕy ch'hut*, if you were to stick on wings, you would not be able to fly out.

Ch'he chìn, ĕk jê yeá 趨進翼如也, *kin kin kĕnâ jip ch'hin chēōng pōey*, he entered hastily, as it were flying. See the 上論 Sēāng lūn.

Ĕk 射 To shoot with a bow and arrows. Ĕk hoô é gān 射鳧與雁, *chŏh chùy cheâou kap gān*, to shoot the water fowl and the wild geese.

Ĕk 弋 To shoot. Ĕk put sek sēuk 弋不射宿, *chŏh cheèng bô bōēyh chŏh bāynh ây cheâou*, in shooting he would never let fly at a resting bird. See the 上論 Sēāng lūn.

Ĕk 翌 To morrow. Ĕk jit 翌日, the following day, also written 翊, ek.

Ĕk 杙 A post in the ground, for fastening a cow to.

Ĕk 豛 Another name for a pig. Also writhen 豟, ĕk.

Ĕk 昜 To change, to alter; the same as 易 ĕk.

Ĕk 黓 Black.

Ĕk 睪 To lead hastily along.

Ĕk 膌 The name of a bone, without a socket.

Ĕk 驛 A post house. Ĕk tō 驛道, *yĕăh loē*, a post road. Ĕk má 驛馬, *yĕăh bāy* a post horse; to go backwards and forwards without cessation, is called 絡驛, lŏk ĕk.

Ĕk 睪 The brightness of fire.

Ĕk 鳦 The name of a bird.

Ĕk 嶧 The name of a hill, near which Confucius was born.

Ĕk 浴 Read yēuk: to bathe. Sēĕn yēuk 洗浴, *sēy ĕk*, to bathe and wash one's self. K'hóng choó bŏk yēuk jê teâou 孔子沐浴而朝, *k'hóng choó sēy ĕk jê teâou ông*, Confucius washed and bathed before he waited on the king.

卆

Eng 英 A flower, a blossom; an heroic clever man. Eng hēûng 英雄, a hero. Sek ch'han ch'hew kēuk che lok eng 夕餐秋菊之落英, *maīng hwuīng chēăh ch'hew kēuk ây lŏh hwa*, in the evening he swallowed some of the falling blossoms of the autumnal chrysanthimums.

Tek t'hēen hāy eng chaê jê kaôu yēuk che 得天下英才而教育之, *tit tēŏh t'heeng āy ây eng chaê, jê kà sè jēōng ch'hē e*, to obtain all the talented men in the Empire in order to teach and bring them up. See 孟子 Bēng choó.

Eng 偀 Eng kēet 偀傑, a hero, a clever person: the same as the foregoing.

Eng 媖 A complimentary designation for elegant females.

Eng 瑛 A bright gem. Eng ke 瑛琚, a precious stone.

Eng 楧 The name of a fruit, said by some to be like the plum, and by others like the almond.

Eng 櫻 Eng t'hô: a kind of peach.

Eng **嚶** The harmonious singing of birds. Hwat bok teng teng, neâou hêng eng eng 伐木丁丁.鳥鳴嚶嚶, *chëŏh ch'hâ ây sëⁿa teng teng chëâou haôu ây sëⁿa eng eng*, the noise of chopping wood sounded like Teng teng, and the harmonious singing of the birds resembled the sound Eng eng.

Eng **瓔** Eng lông 瓔琅, a stone resembling a gem.

Eng **孆** Eng haê 孆孩, a little child.

Eng **攖** To run against, to encounter, to raise up. Hoé hoô gê, bok che kám eng 虎負嵎莫之敢攖, *hoé tëèm tē swⁿa nēⁿâ, bô lâng k'ⁿá hwàn tëŏh*, when a tiger is crouching on the hill, no one dares to encounter him.

Eng **癭** A wen or other disorder on the neck.

Eng **罌** A general term for jar. Eng hoé 罌缶, a jar with a large belly and a small mouth.

Eng **纓** The tassel of a cap. Hëên kwan choo choé eng, t'hëen choó chê kwan yëá 玄冠朱組纓天子之冠也, *oe kîn âng choé eng, sē hông tèy ây kîn*, a black cap with vermillion strings and tassels, is the cap of an Emperor.

Eng **賏** Ornaments for the neck; a string of beads round the neck.

Eng **鸚** A parrot. Eng boó lêng gân 鸚鵡能言, *eng boó ây kóng wā*, a parrot can talk.

Eng **鶯** A large beautiful bird; also called hông lêy 黃鸝. Ch'hek gê yëak p'hêng kan, eng só ch'hwàn léw té 尺魚躍萍間.鶯梭穿柳底, *chëⁿâ ch'hëŏh têng ây hê tëō tē p'hëŏ ây kan, ch'hin chëōⁿg só ây eng ch'hwuiⁿg kaôu lëw ây tëy*, the fishes of a foot long leap in the midst of the water plants, and the beautiful birds like shuttles dart to the deepest shade of the willow trees.

Eng **鷪** The same as the above.

Eng **鷹** Birds of courage, such as the hawk and falcon, a ravenous bird.

Eng **薨** To die, to demise; used to denote the demise of princes and nobles. Kwun eng pek kwan chóng ké, e t'hêng e t'hëûng chaê sam lëên 君薨百官總己.以聽於冢宰三年, *kîn kwun eng chëⁿâ pâyh kwⁿa tëŏh chóng kē hëá ây soō, ê t'hëⁿa ê t'hëûng chaê sⁿa neêⁿg*, when a prince dies, all the officers should bring every affair, and listen to the orders of the prime minister, for three years; (while the young prince is mourning for his father).

Eng **轟** The noise of many carriages.

Eng **⿱賏火** Clear, bright.

Eng **應** Eng kae 應該, ought, should. Eng tong 應當, suitable, right.

Eng **膺** The breast; also to come again, to beat; also written 蘡 eng. Tek yit sëên, chek k'hwân k'hwân hok eng, jê hwut sit che è 得一善則拳拳服膺而弗失之矣, *tit tëŏh chit ây hó, chek k'hwân k'hwân hok eng, jê bô ūᵐ keêⁿg ê*, when he obtained any thing good, he would firmly clasp it to his breast, and not loss it. Said of 顏回 Gân hôey.

Eng 癰 Read yung: an ulcer, a sore. Hōēy yung suy t'hông, sin yáng tok 潰癰雖痛勝養毒, *ch'hè eng suy t'hēⁿà k'hăh yēⁿá yēōⁿᵍ tok*, to pierce the ulcer though painful, is better than feeding the poison.

Eng 嬰 Eng haê 嬰孩 a little child, an infant; also to increase, to encounter.

声 Eng 永 Always, constant, lengthened, lasting. E'ng wán 永遠, eternal. E'ng gân p'hōēy bēng 永言配命, *èng kóng p'hōēy bēng*, always speaking of complying with destiny.

E'ng 栐 The Name of a wood, of which flutes can be made.

E'ng 穎 The sharp-pointed beards of grain; any thing sharp-pointed; an awl.

E'ng 頴 The same as the preceding.

E'ng 潁 The name of a wood.

E'ng 潁 The name of a river; also the name of a district.

E'ng 巊 The name of a hill.

E'ng 影 Vulg. *yēⁿá*: a shadow. Jê éng sûy hêng 如影隨形, *ch'hin chēōⁿᵍ yēⁿá sûy hêng*, like the shadow following the substance.

Gwat ê hwa éng sēăng lân kan 月移花影上欄杆, *gōēyh ê hwa yēⁿá chēōⁿᵍ lân kan*, the moon throws the shadow of the flowers upon the balustrade.

E'ng 景 The same as the above. Jē choó sêng chew, hwàn hwàn kê èng 二子乘舟汎汎其景, *nō āy kēⁿá chēy chûn, p'hoô p'hoô e āy yēⁿá*, the two children sat in the boat, while their shadows floated on the water.

去 'Eng 應 To answer, to reply; to correspond to: a surname. E'ng tap jê lêw 應答如流, *yin tap ch'hin chēōⁿᵍ chúy laôu*, to answer like the flowing of water.

Soō é lūy sëang chëûng, seng é yim sëang èng 事以類相從,聲以音相應, *soō é lūy sëo t'hân, sēⁿa é yim sëo yìn*, affairs should be classed according to their sorts; and sounds should correspond to their tones.

'Eng 譍 Vulg. yìn: to reply to a question by words.

'Eng 噟 The sound of hallooing.

'Eng 甕 Read yùng: a jar. Yùng ch'haé 甕菜, *èng ch'haè*, a kind of vegetable, the seeds of which were first brought from Cochin-China in jars.

'Eng 壅 Read yùng: to manure the ground. Yùng têen 壅田, *èng ch'hân*, to manure the rice fields; To put earth to the roots of plants.

平 Êng 榮 Glorious, resplendent; flowery; luxuriant. Êng kong 榮光, *êng kwuiⁿᵍ*, bright and glorious; a surname.

Te kê êng, sèw kê jëuk 知其榮守其辱, *chae woō êng kwuiⁿᵍ, tëóh chëw e āy jëuh*, if you would know what is glory, guard against disgrace.

Êng 熒 The shining of a lamp or candle; also doubt and suspicion.

Êng 塋 A grave, a tomb. Êng hek 塋域, a burial place.

Êng 瑩 A stone like a gem. Sèw êng 琇瑩, a gem worn behind the ear.

Êng 螢 A fire fly. Hoo ch'hó hwà wûy eng 腐草化爲螢, nwⁿá ch'hóu hwà chò hôey kim ch'haⁿᵍ, decayed vegetables are converted into fire-flies.

Êng 營 To build, to erect, to pile up. Êng chây 營寨, yëⁿá chây, a camp.

Êng 縈 To roll anything up; to suspend.

Êng 滎 To name of a water.

Êng 濴 The eddying of water.

Êng 瀯 Water flowing back, the turning of a stream. Also written 濙 êng, and 瀠 êng.

Êng 嵤 Lêng êng 岭嵤, the deep recesses of hilly places; also written 巆 êng. Cheng êng 崢嵤, the stupendous height of mountains.

Êng 巊 The loftiness of a hill.

Êng 瀛 The great sea, the ocean. Êng chew 瀛洲, the name of a place.

Egn 嬴 A surname.

Êng 贏 Vulg. yëⁿá; to win, to conquer, to get the advantage; also superabundant. Se êng bē hwūn 輸贏未分, soo yëⁿá bōēy chàe, the victory or defeat is not yet determined.

Êng 盈 Full, replete. Êng bwán 盈滿, êng mwⁿá, completely full. Cheng tēy è chëën, sat jîn êng yéá 爭地以戰殺人盈野, chaiⁿᵍ tēy è chëën t'hâe lâng mwⁿá yëá, when contending for territory in battle, the slain fill the country. See the 下孟 Hāy bēng. Sūy k'hé êng hê 瑞氣盈楣, hó ây k'hé mwⁿá mootⁿᵍ bâe, may lucky influences replete the lintel of your door.

Êng 楹 Vulg. aîⁿᵍ; a beam, a rafter. Ok êng 屋楹, ch'hoò aîⁿᵍ, the rafter of a house.

Tëēn è lëâng êng che kan 奠於两楹之間, tè chèy te nō ây ch'hoò aîⁿᵍ ây kan, to offer a sacrifice between the two beams of the house.

Êng 贏 Dung, ordure.

Eng 閒 Read hân, leisure. Boô hân 無閒, bô êng, no leisure. Yit jit ch'heng hân, yit jit sëën 一日淸閒一日仙, chit jit ch'heng êng chit jit sëën, one day's clear leisure, is one day's heaven.

去 Eng 詠 To chaunt, to sing. Eng sè 詠詩, ch'hëông se, to recite an ode. Eng jê kwny 詠而歸, ch'hôⁿᵍ se jê tooiⁿᵍ, they chaunted odes as they returned.

Ēng 咏 The same as the above. Eng t'hàn 咏嘆, to sigh and lament.

Ēng 泳 To dive under water. Chēw kê ch'him è, hong che chew che, chēw che, chēw kê ch'hëën è, ēng che yêw che 就其深矣方之舟之就其淺矣泳之游之, chēw kaôu e ây ch'him, yūng hwat yūng chún, chēw kaòu e ây k'hìn, ēng e, yêw e, coming to the deep parts (of the river) we raft it and boat it; and coming to the Shallow parts, we may dive and swim through them. See the 國風 Kok hong.

Ēng 瀅 T'heng ēng 汀瀅, water still and clear.

Ēng 禜 The name of a sacrifice, by which they deprecate wind and supplicate rain.

Ēng 鎣 To grind and rub sharp instruments, in order to make them bright; Also to adorn.

平 Eng 央 Read yang: the centre. Tëung yang 中央, tang eng, the middle. The five cardinal points correspond to the five elements, thus, Tëung yang t'hoé, tong hong, bòk, sey hong kim, lâm hong hⁿó pok hong súy 中央土.東方木.西方金.南方火.北方水, tang eng t'hoé, tang heng ch'hâ, sae heng kim, lâm heng höëy pak heng chúy, the centre corresponds to earth, the east to wood, the west to metal, the south to fire, and the north to water.

Eng 秧 Read yang: the tender shoots of corn.

去 Éng 影 Read E'ng: shadow, shade. Jîn êng e he 人影依稀, lâng éng chëó ch'hëó, the shadows of men are scarce, (i. e.) the population is thin.

Sē ëng ch'ham ch'hay. 樹影參差, ch'hēw éng ch'ham ch'hay, the shadows of the trees were mixed together.

平 Ey 挨 Read ae: to put off. Ae yëen kò jit 挨延過日, ey yëen köëy jit, to put off and procrastinate day by day.

上 E'y 矮 Read aé: short. Aé tek 矮的, éy ây, a short men, a dwarf.

平 Êy 鞋 Read haê: shoes. Ch'hwân haê 穿鞋, ch'hèng êy, to wear shoes.

Êy 譪 To speak stoutly.

下去 Ey 能 Read lêng: to be able; may, or can. Lêng hêng gnóe cheā ê t'heen hāy, wûy jîn ê: 能行五者於天下爲仁矣, ēy kèⁿâ chëy goē hâng tē t'heeng āy, sē jîn ê, he that can practice these five things throughout the Empire may be esteemed virtuous. Hwuy wat lêng che, gwān hâk yëen 非曰能之.願學焉, ūm chëng kóng gwā ēy, gwān böëyh ōh yëen, I do not say that I am capable but I wish to learn.

Ey 會 Read hwūy: to be able. Hwān k'hàn lūn gé se, se yaóu tek hwūy hëáou bûn gē put k'hó hwut lëak kò 凡看論語書.須要得會曉文義.不可忽畧過, hwán k'hwⁿà lūn gē ây ch'hāyh sae tëöh ēy hëdou bûn gē, ūm t'hang hwut lëak köëy, whosoever would look over the book lūn gē, must be able to understanding the words and meaning, and not pass over it slightly.

G

平 Ga 髼 The hair dishevelled and in confusion.

去 Gaé 豥 Gaê hây 豥猳, a pig.

Gaé 騃 Simple, ignorant.

平

Gaê 涯 The water's edge, a brink, a shore, a border. Jēak sēep taē súy, kô boô chin gaê 若涉大水其無津涯, ch'hin chēō^ng kōēy twā chúy, e ây bō chin gwê, like crossing the great waters where there is neither ford nor shore.

Gaê 厓 The side or border of anything.

Gaê 崖 San gaê 山崖, sw^na gaê, the side of a hill.

Gaê 捱 To oppose, to put off. Yēēn gaê 延捱, to procrastinate.

Gaê 痽 Silliness; bereft of one's senses.

Gaê 呆 Stupid foolish, silly; also written 敳 gaê.

Gaê 啀 The fighting of dogs. Pok kok yew koé, gaê gaê, tàn hoē yeuk gēet gnó hây 北郭有狗啀啀旦暮欲嚙我豭, pak kok woō kaóu gaê gaê chá k'hé mai^ng hwui^ng bōēyh kā gwá ây te, on the northern part of the suburbs there are dogs fighting, and quarrelling; every day wanting to bite my pigs. Said by 管子 Kwán choó.

Gaê 啀 The appearance of dogs wanting to bite.

Gaê 睚 Gaê ch'hey 睚眦, to lift the eyes, and look angrily at one another.

去

Gaē 礙 To stop, to oppose, to hinder, to prevent, to limit. Soó put lêng gaē 死不能礙, sé bēy gāe lēōh, death cannot be prevented.

Gaē 碍 The same as the above. Lit gaē 窒碍, a hindrance, an abstraction.

入

Gák 岳 A hill, a mountain. Gnóe gák 五岳, the five mountains, a surname. Gák hoō gák boé 岳父岳母, tēō^ng lâng tēō^ng á^m, a father and mother-in-law.

Gák 嶽 A mountain. Chaê hwa gák jê put tēūng 載華嶽而不重, chaè hwa gák sw^na jê bēy tāng, (the earth) bears up the large mountain without feeling the weight.

Gák 鸑 Gák chók 鸑鷟, an eagle.

Gák 樂 Music. Gák yim 樂音, the sounds of music. Chok gák 作樂, to play music; a surname.

Choó wat, goé choō wōēy hwán loé jēēn hoē gák chêng 子曰吾自衛反魯然後樂正, hoe choé kóng, gwá choō wōēy kok, tooi^ng laé loé, jēēn aōu gák chē^nà, Confucius said, from the time that I returned from the Wōēy country to the Loé country, the music was well regulated.—Jin jê put jin, jê gák hô 人而不仁如樂何, lâng nā bō jin iek, bōēyh hwat e ây gák s^na meē^nh taē wā, If men are destitute of benevolence what will become of their music! See the 上論 Sēāng lūn.

Gák 雝 The centre piece in a certain game of chess.

上

Gam 儑 Unwise; uneasy.

平

Gâm 巗 Lofty, high, dangerous; a recess in a mountain, a cavern. K'him gâm 嶔巗, precipitous, impending. Ch'hâm gâm 嶄巗, lofty.

San gâm tëep ch'hùy, yin sëaou göey 山巗叠翠.雲霄外, swⁿa gâm tëep ch'hùy tē hwán sëäou ây gwā, the lofty mountains piled up in green elevations beyond the highest tier of clouds.

Gâm 岩 The same as the preceding: also written 嵒 gâm, 喦 gâm, and 嵓 gâm.

Gâm 唫 To talk in one's sleep; to mutter and groan in dreams.

去

Gām 戇 Stupid, foolish. Ông lêng seàou gām, tîn pêng k'hó é choē che 王陵少戇.陳平可以助之, óng-lêng sëó k'hwá gām, tân paiⁿᵍ t'hang laē chān e, Ông-lêng is a little stupid and Tân-paiⁿᵍ can help him. (Said by the founder of a dynasty respecting his prime ministers).

声

Gán 眼 Vulg. bak chew: the eye. Gwán chek lêng wûy ch'heng pek gán 阮籍能為青白眼, wuiⁿᵍ chek ëy chò ch'haiⁿᵍ pëyh ây bak chew, wûiⁿᵍ-chek could make his eyes look both green and white.

Gán k'hong soò haé 眼空四海, bak chew k'hwⁿà k'hang sè haé, to have eyes that look empty the four seas; i. e. that is, to be so proud, as to see nothing valuable in all the world except one's-self.

Gán 俺 I myself: also great.

Gán 研 Read gëén: a muller. Gán sek 研石, géng chëöh, a grinding stone, a stone for grinding or polishing; also to exhaust.

2 w

平

Gân 顏 Yûng gân 容顏, the countenance, a surname. Gân sek 顏色, the appearance: a surname.

Chèng gân sek, soo kīn sin è 正顏色.斯近信矣, chěⁿà làn ây gân sek, chèy sē këö kīn sin sit ây lâng, Let us adjust our own outward appearance, and that will induce sincere people to approach us.

Gân 言 A word, to speak, to say. Gân gé 言語, words and expressions. Gân chëä sim che seng yëä 言者心之聲也, kóng wā sē sim kwⁿa ây sëⁿa, words are the expression of the feelings of the heart.

Gân put k'hó put sīn yëä 言不可不慎也, kóng wā, ūᵐ t'hang bô sèy jē, in conversation we must not neglect caution.

去

Gān 彥 An elegant scholar. Pé kê che choó, pang che gān hey 彼其之子.邦之彥兮, hwut lëy e ây këⁿà, pang ây hó t'hak ch'hëyh lâng, that son of his, is the most elegant scholar in the country. See the 國風 Kok hong.

Gān 偐 A false thing, a counterfeit.

Gān 諺 Gān gé 諺語, a proverb. Koé gān yëw che 故諺有之, koè cha ây gān gé woō e, it is in the ancient proverb, &c.

Gān 犴 A wild dog found in the northern regions, like a fox, but smaller.

Gān 厈 A high bank.

Gān 鴈 A wild goose: also written 雁 Gān. Hông gān ê hwuy, ae bêng gô gô 鴻雁于飛.哀鳴嗷嗷, twā *chĕăh gân tit pwuy, ae ch'hám ây sē^{n}a gô gô*, the large wild geese are flying, and make a melancholy noise altogether. See the 小雅 Seáou gnây.

Gān 岸 Vulg. *w^{n}ā*: a brink or side of a river. Sëen teng ê gān 先登于岸, *taē seng pâyh chëō^{ng} w^{n}ā*, he first arrived at the shore.

Gān 唁 To condole with the prince of a neighbouring country under bereavements.

Gān 贗 A false thing, a counterfeit.

平
Gâng 仰 Wuy gâng 威仰, the appellation of the azure Emperor, who is said to preside over the spring. See the 周禮 Chew léy.

Gâng 昂 High, lofty; also bright. Gâng hêng 昂行, *gâng kë^{n}â*, to walk proudly.

平
Gaôu 嶤 Chëaou gaôu 嶕嶤, a high hill, the loftiness of a mountain.

***Gaôu* 賢** Read hëên: clever, skilful, intelligent. Hëên jîn 賢人, *gaôu lâng*, a clever man. Hëên choé 賢走, *gaôu chaoú*, to run swiftly.

Soo má hwuy tân k'hîm, k'hîm yim hëàng lëăng, wat, ch'hóo kan pit yéw hëên jîn ch'hëep t'hèng 司馬徽彈琴.琴音响喨曰.此間必有賢人竊聽, *soo má hwuy tw^{n}â k'hîm, k'hîm ây sē^{n}a hëàng lëăng, chëw kóng, chëy lëy wōy pit woō gâou lâng t'haou t'hē^{n}a*, when Soo-má-hwuy was playing on his guitar, the guitar sounded loud and clear; upon which he said, there must be hereabouts some clever person, who is listening to the music.

入
Gap 㬎 Abstruse and minute; the ancient form of 顯 hëén, manifest.

入
Gat 屵 A high bank; the appearance of a high hill.

Gat 歹 Superfluous bones.

平
Gây 牙 A tooth, a grinder. Sûy wūy ch'hé boô gây, hô é ch'hwân gnó yûng 誰謂鼠無牙.何以穿我墉, *chê chûy â kóng nëáou ch'hé bô ch'hùy k'hè an chw^{n}â e ēy ch'hwui^{ng} gwá ây pëăh*, who says that mice have no teeth, how is it then that they have bored through my wall. See the 國風 Kok hong. Gây chëang 牙璋, a general's standard. Chok gây 作牙, to assist in making bargains.

Gây 芽 A bud, a young shoot. Bêng gây 萌芽, *paoûh eē^{ng}*, to shoot out buds.

Gây 衙 Gây bûn 衙門, *gây moot^{ng}*, a court of justice, a mandarine's court. Gây ek 衙役, *gây yĕăh*, a police officer.

Gây 疨 Bad teeth; the tooth ache.

去
Gāy 訝 Ch'hëa gāy 嗟訝, an exclamation of doubt and wonder; to meet.

Gāy 迓 Gêng gāy 迎迓, *gē^{n}â chëĕh*, to meet, to go forth to meet.

Gāy 御 To meet. Pek lëáng gāy che 百两御之, *chē^{n}â pâyh tëo^{ng} ch'hëa k'hè gāy c*, a hundred chariots went out to meet him. See the 召南 Sëâou lâm.

Gāy 訝 To ridicule and laugh at any one.

Ge 㖸 To smile. Ge ge ch'heäou 㖸㖸笑, *ge ge ch'hëò*, to laugh, to titter.

Gé 圉 Gé jîn 圉人, the name of an office, something similar to our master of the horse.

Gé 俁 Great, magnanimous.

Gé 偊 The same as the above; also a wounded appearance.

Gé 語 To converse; discourse, talk. Sëuk gé 俗語, a proverb. Sit put gé, ch'hím put gân 食不語.寢不言, *chëāh bô gē lân, k'hwùn bô kóng wā*, he would neither converse at meals nor talk in his sleep. Said of Confucius, in the 上論 Sëāng lūn.

Gé 麌 Gé gé 麌麌, flocking together, getting together into a herd.

Gé 擬 To deliberate, to judge; also to compare, alike. Gé che, jê hoē gân 擬之而後言, *sim gê e, jëén aōu kong*, deliberate and then speak. See the 易經 Yĕăh keng. Kwán tëūng sëàng chêy, ch'hé gé ê kwun 管仲相齊.侈擬於君, *kwán tëūng sëàng chêy kok, ch'hëa ch'hé gé pê e ây jîn kwun*, when Kwán tëūng was prime minister of the Chêy country, he equalled the prince in extravagance.

Gé 儗 To compare, to assort; also to usurp. Gé jîn pit ê kê lûn 儗人必於其倫, *pê gé lâng, pit tëŏh chëâou e ây lûn*, in assorting men, you must arrange them according to their relations.

Gé 薿 Luxuriant, abundant.

Gé 圄 Lêng gé 囹圄, a prison, a place of confinement.

Gé 敔 An instrument of music.

Gé 艤 A boat at anchor, or tied to the bank. Oe kang têng tëáng, gé chew, t'haē hāng é 烏江亭長.艤舟待項羽, *oe kang ây têng tëō^ng, pat chûn têng t'haē hāng ē*, the head of the station at the black river had prepared a boat at anchor, to wait for Hang-é. She the 項羽紀 Hāng é ké.

Gé 蟻 Vulg. *hëā*: an ant. Pek gé 白蟻, *pëyh hëā*, a white ant. Baē sëá hëáng chaé sëàng che hok, kèw gé tëūng chōng gwân che swàn 埋蛇享宰相之福.救蟻中狀元之選, *taê chwâ ēy hëáng chaé sëàng ây hok, kèw hëā ēy tëūng chëūng gwân ây kéng*, he who buries a snake will enjoy the happiness of a prime minister, and he who saves an ant, will be selected to fill the highest literary rank.

Gé 䑙 To fasten a boat to the shore, to bring a boat to shore.

Gé 禦 To stop, to hinder, to restrain, to oppose. Sûy lêng gé che 誰能禦之, *chê chûy ēy gé chê e*, who could stop them? Tëng bûn kong soé ko k'hek gé tek ê hô sëang 鄭文公使高克禦狄於河上, *tai^ng bûn kong saê ko k'hek gé chê tek hwan tē hô sëang*, Tai^ng-bûn-hong sent Ko-k'hek to stop the progress of the barbarians upon the banks of the river. See the 左傳 Chó twān.

Gé 籞 The Imperial gardens, from which the people are restricted; also a railing made of split bamboos, for inclosing and feeding fish.

平

Gê 儀 That which is right, and correct; usages, observances, ceremonies. Yéw wuy k'hó wùy, yéw gê k'hó sëāng 有威可畏有儀可象, *woō wuy hong t'hang hoē lăng kē^{n}a, woō gê lèy t'hang chò yëō^{ng}*, he has dignity sufficient to inspire terror, and manners that may be set up for a pattern.

Gê 驥 Choe gê 騶驥, an animal celebrated for its virtue.

Gê 娛 Pleasure, delight. Këûng hwan kek gê 窮歡極娛, *këûng hw^{n}a hê, kek gê lok*, to exhaust pleasure, and carry delight to the utmost.

Gê 宜 Suitable, proper; ought, should; also written 宜 gê. Ch'hé soō hap gê, wūy che gē 處事合宜謂之義, *ch'hé soō hap gê, kông këò gê*, to settle affairs according to that which is suitable is called righteousness.

Yin sê chè gê 因時制宜, *yin sê ch'hòng sèy èng kae*, to do that which is suitable, according to the time.

Gê 魚 Vulg. *hê*, a fish a surname. Gê gnó séy yëuk yëá 魚我所欲也, *hê gwá sèy aè*, Fish is what I am fond of. See the 孟子, Bēng choó.

Sek chëá yéw kwùy seng gê ê tēng choó sán 昔者有饋生魚.於鄭子.產, *chêng jit woō lăng sàng wâh hê hoē tai^{ng} choó sán*, on a former day, one presented a living fish to Tai^{ng}-choó-sán. See the 孟子, Bēng choó.

Gê 漁 To fish, to catch fish. Gê jin, 漁人, a fisherman. E' tëên é gê, 以佃以漁, *k'hè p'hàh lâh kwá t'hò hê*, to go a hunting and fishing.

Gê 愚 Vulg. *gōng*: stupid, foolish; also used for the first personal pronoun, in polite writing.

Koé che gê yëá tit, kim che gê yëá chày 故之愚也直.今之愚也詐, *koè chá ây gaê lâng lëâoú tit, tong kim ây gâe lang pâyh ch'hat*, formerly stupid people were honest, but now they are deceitful. See the 下論 Hāy lūn.

Gê 隅 A corner, an angle; a part. Kê yit gê, 舉一隅, to allude to a part. Kong t'hëen che hāy, chè ê haé gê, 光天之下.至於海隅, *t'hong t'hee^{ng} ây hāy, chè kaoù haè kak*, throughout the whole Empire, even to the corners of the sea. See the 尙書 Sëō^{ng} se.

Gê 腢 The shoulders. Tòng gê yūng kit k'hè, 當腢用吉器, *tè^{ng} heng t'haôu, tëōh yāng hō ây ke k'hè*, for the shoulders we should use something handsome. (Speaking of dress). See the 儀禮 Gê lèy.

Gê 嵎 Gê ê 嵎峓, the name of a place where the sun rises.

Gê 疑 Vulg. *ge gnaê*: to doubt, to hesitate, to suspect, to be in suspense. Gê soō būn 疑思問, *woō gê gnaê chëw sëō^{ng} mooī^{ng}*, having doubts, think of making enquiry.

To būn, k'hwat gê, 多聞闕疑, *chëy t'hē^{n}a k'hwat, twān gê gnaê*, in hearing much, decide those things which are doubtful. See the 上論 Sëāng lūn.

Gê 嶷 Kéw gê, 九嶷, the name of a hill in the 湖廣, hoê kòng, province.

Gê 虞 To be pleased, to rest, satisfied; to think of, to examine; a surname. Pà chëá che bîn, hwan gê jê yëá, 覇者之民歡虞如也, *pà chëá ây pâyh sai^{ng} ch'hin chëō^{ng} hw^{n}a hê*, the subjects of a despot are as it were pleased and satisfied, (for a time). See the 下孟 Hāy bēng.

Tông gê 唐虞, the appellations of 堯 geâou and 舜 sùn, two ancient Chinese Emperors, who flourished about the time of noah.

Gê 枇 Gê pây 枇杷, the name of a fruit. Read pê.

寓 Gē 寓 To lodge, to dwell; to entrust to. Gē séy 寓所, a lodging place. Boē gē jîn ê gnó sit, 無寓人於我室, *ām chang hoē lâng hāynh tē gwá ây. ch'hoò*, don't let any one lodge in my house.

Lêy hoê sit kok, gē ke ê wöēy 黎侯失國.寓居於衛, *lêy hoê sit kok, chēw hāyⁿh. k'hēā tē wöēy*, when the Prince of Lêy, lost his kingdom, he dwelt for a time in the wöēy country. See the 國風 Kok hong.

Gē 喁 To laugh. Gē gē ch'hëàou, 喁喁笑, *gē gē ch'hëòu*, to titter.

Gē 庽 The same as 寓 gē to lodge, to dwell.

Gē 語 To speak to, to converse, to discourse with any one. Choó gē loē t'haē soo gak wat, 子語魯大師樂曰, *hoo choó kòng kap loē t'haē soo gak kóng*, Confucius discoursed with the great music Master of the Loē country about music, saying &c. See 上論, Sëāng lūn.

Gē 馭 To harness horses, and put them to a carriage. Lím hoê, jëak héw sek che gē lëùk má 懍乎若朽索之馭六馬, *kèng kin, ch'hin chëōⁿᵍ woō yūng nwⁿā sŏh saē lak chëāh bāy*, be as careful and fearful, as if you were driving six horses harnessed with a rotten rope. See the 尙書, Sëāng se.

Gē 誼 Righteousness, equity; the same as 義 gē; also written 誼 gē. Jîn jîn chëá, chèng kê gē, put boē kê lē 仁人者.正其誼.不謀其利, *jîn tek ây lâng, ch'hòng chēⁿā e ây gē, bô böēyh boē e ây lē*, a truly benevolent, man will exactly conform to righteousness, without speculating for gain.

Gē 議 To deliberate with, to take counsel with, to discourse with. Gē lūn 議論, *soō nëōⁿᵍ*, to consult with.

Soō chê ê tō, jê t'hé ok e ok gît chëā, bē chëuk ê gē yëā 士志於道.而耻惡衣惡食者.未足與議也, *t'hak ch'hāyh lâng sim chè tē tō, jê seâou lêy p'haⁿê yin chëōⁿᵍ p'haⁿê chëāh ây lâng, chēw āᵐ chëūk kap e gē lūn*, when a scholar pretends to have his mind bent on the right way and yet is ashamed of bad clothing and bad food; he is not fit to be deliberated with. See the 上論 Sëāng lūn.

Gē 義 Righteousness, equity. Jîn, gē, lêy, tè, sìn 仁義禮智信, benevolence righteousness, propriety, wisdom, and truth; (the fine cardinal virtues.)

Ông hô pit wat lē, ek yéw jîn gē jê é è, 王何必日利.亦有仁義而已矣, *ông saē saē tëōh kòng lē, yëā woō jîn gē tëⁿā tēⁿā*, why must your majesty talk about gain; let us treat of benevolence and righteousness alone. See 孟子 Bēng choó.

Gē 毅 Kong gē 剛毅, bold and daring, courageous.

Gē 御 To wait upon, to enter, to lead, to rule, to regulate, to encourage; also to drive a carriage, any thing belonging to the Emperor.

Yim gē choo yéw 飲御諸友, *lim ây sē tëōh gē sē pêng yéw*, in drinking we should wait upon our friends.

T'hóng gē é löēy 統御宇內, *t'hóng kwán ê laē*, to regulate and manage every thing in the universe.

Hwân tê gē 樊遲御, *hwân tê tit saē ch'hëa*, Hwân-tê was driving the carriage.

2 x

Gē 遇 To meet with. Gē chëak 遇着, *toó tëŏh*, to fall in with. Gē choo tôe 遇諸塗, *toó tëŏh tē loē*, he met him in the road.

Gē 劓 A punishment, consisting in cutting off the nose. Boô hek gē jîn 無或劓人, *bô K'hè kwăh lâng ây p'hceⁿᵍ*, do not punish men by cutting off their noses. See the 尚書 Sëōⁿᵍ se.

平 Gëâ 呀 To open the mouth wide. Jê k'hoé k'hae gëâ gëâ 如口開呀呀, *ch'hin chëōⁿᵍ ch'hùy k'hwuy gëâ gëâ*, like the mouth opened wide.

Gëâ 蜈 Goê kong 蜈蚣, *gëâ kang*, a centipede. The Chinese say that it comes out in the spring, and disappears in the winter; at every joint it has feet, with a double beard, and a pointed tail;—and it is by nature afraid of spiders.

Gëâ 蝺 The name of an insect. *La gëâ* 蟼蝺, a spider. *La gëâ se* 蟼蝺絲, a spiders web.

Gëâ 抬 Read tâe: to carry between two. Taê bùt 抬物, *gëâ meēⁿᵍh*, to carry any thing.

平 Geⁿâ 迎 Read gêng: to meet, to meet with. Gêng chëep 迎接, *geⁿâ chēĕh*, to greet.

Sòng ông gêng laê, kay sëēn jê keng put lêng, séy é jêw wân jîn yëá 送往迎來.嘉善而矜不能.所以柔遠人也, *sàng óng geⁿâ laê, o ló hó jê keng lîn bêy ây lâng, séy é jêw hwüîⁿᵍ ây lâng*, to accompany those who are departing, and to meet those who are arriving, to encourage the good, and pity the incapable, is the way to conciliate people at a distance.

去 Gëăh 撠 To open, to part asunder. *Gëăh k'hwuy* 撠開, to spread open.

Gëăh 蹠 To open out the legs. *K'ha gëăh k'hwuy* 脚蹠開, to spread out the legs.

入 Gëăh 夆 That by which we frighten people.

入 Geak 虐 To oppress, to tyrannise; oppression. Geak chèng 虐政, an oppressive government. Pò geak 暴虐, to oppress violently.

Put kaoù jê sat, wūy che geak 不教而殺謂之虐, *ūᵐ kà jê t'haê kóng këò geak*, to put people to death for crime, without first instructing them is called oppression. See the 下論 Hāy lūn.

Geak 瘧 A fever; a disease in which there is a hot and cold stage.

上平 Gëang 鈃 A small kind of bell, with a long neck.

上声 Gëáng 仰 To hold up the head; a surname. Gëáng séw 仰首, *tⁿa k'hè t'haôu*, to hold up the head. Gëáng k'hàn 仰看, *gëáng k'hwⁿà*, to look up. Gëáng bōng 仰望, to hope.

Gëáng chëuk é soō hoō boé, boó chëuk é hëuk ch'hey choó 仰足以事父母.俯足以畜妻子, *tⁿa k'he t'haôu k'hwⁿà ēy kaōu é hok saē pāy boē k'hwⁿà lōh laê, ēy kaōu é ch'hē boé këⁿâ*, in looking upwards to have sufficient to serve one's parents with, and in looking downwards to have enough wherewith to feed one's wife and children. See the 上孟 Sëāng bēng.

平 Gêang 峣 K'hong gêang 崆峣, the lofty appearance of hills and mountains.

上去

Gëâng 仰 To rely upon, to help, to supply.

下去

Gëàou 嘄 To call.

下平

Gëâou 堯 The name of an ancient Emperor. Geâou é put tek sùn wûy ké yew 堯以不得舜爲已憂, *geâou yin wûy bēy tit tëŏh sùn chò ka tē ây hwân lò*, Geâou because he could not obtain such a man as Sùn, made this the subject of his grief.

Gëâou 僥 Chëaou gëâou 僬僥, a nation of dwarfs, said to be only three feet high.

Gëâou 嶢 Chëaou gëâou 嶕嶢, the lofty appearance of hills.

Gëâou 蕘 Fire wood, to collect fire wood, a wood cutter. Sûn ê choe gëâou 詢於芻蕘, *mooīng kap kwăh ch'haóu chëŏh ch'hâ ây lâng*, to enquire of the grass and wood cutters. See the 小雅 Seâou gnáy.

上去

Gëāou 㓞 To scrape.

上聲

Gëém 儼 To hold the head high; also to respect. Gëém jëak soo 儼若思, respectful and thoughtful.

Sek taē ch'hēⁿá gëém 碩大且儼, *sek twā kwà kwân*, great and tall.

下去

Gëèm 驗 To examine, to verify, to fulfil, to accomplish; also written 騐, Gëèm. Haòu gëèm 效驗, the fulfilment, or accomplishment of a thing.

K'hó bũn chó gëèm bêng pek 考問左驗明白, *k'hó mooīng tùy gëèm bêng pāyh*, to examine and scrutinize, and ascertain a thing clearly.

下平

Gëêm 嚴 Rigid, severe, strict; to give strict orders; a surname. Chong gëêm 莊嚴, severe.

Wuy gëêm 威嚴, dignified and stern. Gëêm kín 嚴謹, rigidly careful.

Gëêm, gê put kám ch'héng 嚴虞不敢請, *gëêm ây sè, gwá ām kⁿá ch'hēⁿá mooīng*, while you were thus rigidly strict (in your mourning) I did not dare to make enquiry. See 孟子 Bēng choó.

Gëêm 釅 Wine of great strength; very strong liquor.

Gëêm 巖 San gëêm 山巖, *swⁿa gâm*, the recess of a hill, or cavern. Sòng choo he sēen seng chaē tōng choó gëêm choò se 宋朱熹先生在洞仔巖註書, *sòng tëâou choo he sin saiⁿᵍ tē tāng á gëêm choò ch'hăyh*, in the Sòng dynasty the teacher Choo-he wrote a commentary on the four Books; in the recess of a cavern.

上聲

Gëén 研 A burnisher, or polisher. Gëén poè sek 研布石, *gêng poè chëŏh*, a smooth stone, for glazing cloth.

Lëuk t'hae ch'ham say hoē gëén sëāng 綠苔毿毿乎研上, *ch'haiⁿᵍ lek ây t'hê ch'ham say tē gêng chëŏh têng*, the green moss grows thick upon the polishing stone (owing to disuse).

Gëén 齴 The teeth bare, and sticking out of the mouth.

Gëén 詽 To litigate, to strive; to contend at law.

Gëên 礏 To grind, to break.

去 Gëèn 髒 Thin, meagre, shewing nothing but the bones. Also written 骯 gëèn. A' p'hëèn gëèn 亞片髒, meagre through being adicted to opium.

平 Gëên 妍 To flatter, to admire, to applaud; also wise, and contented. Gëên ch'héw 妍醜, ch'hin ch'hat^ng kwà k'hëep sē, beautiful and ugly.

Gëên 岍 The name of a hill.

Gëên 汧 The name of a river.

Gëên 研 To examine, to exhaust; also to grind.

去 Gëèn 醠 Drunk with wine; to be overcome with liquor. Tim gëën tim hong, put k'hó kaòu é tō, put k'hó jē é tek 沈醠酖茺.不可敎以道.不可喻以德., tîm gëën tîm hwui^ng, bô t'hang kà ê tō, bô t'hang jē ê tek, when a man is immersed in wine, and dissolute in his conduct, it is impossible to teach him the right way, or to make him understand virtue.

入 Gëep 業 Ke gëep 基業, a foundation. Soō gëep 事業, a business, an employment. Sán gëep 產業, a patrimony. Tëên gëep 田業, ch'hân gëep, a farm. Kay gëep 家業, an estate, family property. Soō lông kong sëang, bîn che soè gëep 士農工商民之四業, t'hak ch'hâyh chôh ch'hân chò kang, seng lë, pàyh sai^ng ây sè gëep, learning, agriculture, manual labour, and trade, are the four common employments of the people.

Kwun choó ch'hòng gëep, sûy t'hóng wûy k'hó kèy yëá 君子創業.垂統爲可繼也, kwun choó ch'hòng gëep, sûy t'hóng ëy t'hang söo swā, the good man lays the foundation of an interest, the clue of which may be handed down to posterity. See the 上孟 Sëang bēng.

Gëep 䕜 To lead.

Gëep 鄴 The name of a place.

Gëep 緤 The joining of a seam, in the repairing of a garment.

入 Gëet 齧 To bite, to gnaw. Boô gëet kwut 毋齧骨, ū^m t'hang kā kwut, do not gnaw the bones, (in eating). See the 禮記 Léy kè.

入 Gëet 孽 The son of a concubine, the fresh buds of a tree, trouble and calamity; also luxuriant and full. Tok koe sîn gëet choó, kè ch'ho sim yëá gwûy kè lē hwân yëá ch'him 獨孤臣孽子.其操心也危.其慮患也深, tok koe ây jîn sîn, sèy ê ây kë^nâ, e ây ch'ho sim kw^na gwûy hëêm, e ây lē hwân lô ch'him tim, only forlorn Ministers and illegitimate children, maintain their purpose with peril, and concern themselves about trouble deeply. See the 下孟 Hāy bēng. Hwuy boô bêng gëet che seng yëá 非無萌孽之生焉, ū^m sē bô paòuh ch^ng ây sai^ng, there is no want of the production of buds and blossoms.

T'hëen chok gëet, yêw k'hö wûy, choō chok gëet, put k'hó hwat 天作孽猶可違.自作孽不可活, t'hee^ng chò soō yëá t'hang cwûy, ka tē chô soō, bô t'hang wàh, when Heaven sends down a calamity, it may still be borne up against, but when we bring the calamity on ourselves, there is no escape.

Gëet 臬 The rules of archery; a law, a rule.

Gëet 闑 The posts of a door. Gëet é löëy kwⁿá jin chè che 闑以內寀人制之, mooⁿᵍ laë ây soö, gwà, ka tē, leâou lē, all the business within doors, I myself will attend to.

Gëet 糵 K'hëuk gëet 麴糵, pâyh k'hak, a substance used in fermenting liquor.

Gëet 蠥 Sëäng gëet 象蠥, ch'hëōⁿᵍ gëet, a scorpion, also any thing strange and uncommon among birds and beasts, is called 蠥 gëet.

Gëet 蘖 The buds sprouting out of a tree, after it is cut down. Bêng gëet 萌蘖, paoûh eëⁿᵍ, young buds shooting up.

Gëet 鯢 Gëet gwut 鯢䚳, uneasy, hazardous.

Gëet 鶂 A water bird; also the cackling of geese. Oe yūng sē gëet gëet chëä wûy chae 烏用是鶂鶂者爲哉, chò sⁿa meëⁿh yūng chèy lèy gëet gëet ây meëⁿh chae, of what use it this cackling thing? See the 上孟 Sëäng bēng.

夫

Gek 哘 To proclaim; great; to move; uneasy.

天

Gek 嶺 The rugged uneven appearance of hills; also high, lofty.

Gek 額 The forehead; the part below the hair, and above the eyebrows, is called 額 gek.

2 Y

Gek 頟 The same as the above. Sêng tëung hⁿó kóng bê, soò hong ch'hëⁿá pwàn gek 城中好廣眉.四方且半額, sëⁿá tang eⁿᵍ hò k'hwāh ây bâk baë, sè kak kwà kaöu pwⁿà hëâh, in the city there is one with fine broad eyebrows; square, and also half way up the forehead.

Gek 幝 A seam.

Gek 鷁 A bird with fine feathers; also called chin choo key 眞珠鷄, a pearl spotted bird; so called from its colour.

Gek 逆 Vulg. kâyh: to oppose, to resist, to strive against, also to meet. Gwân gek 頑逆, stubborn. Pöëy gek 背逆, pöëy kâyh, rebellious. Put sūn hoō boé, wát gnoé gek 不順父母曰忤逆, ūᵐ sūn pây boè kóng gnoè gek, to be disobedient to parents is called rebellion.

Get 噦 To vomit.

去

Géng 殀 Short, dwarfish. Géng chô 殀槽, a trough for grinding medicines.

平

Gêng 迎 To meet, to go out to meet. Put chëang put gêng 不將不迎, ūᵐ sàng ūᵐ gⁿëau cheëh, neither to accompany, nor to go out to meet one.

Gêng 凝 To freeze, to congeal. Soò koé gêng song 四股凝霜, k'ha ch'hëw gêng chëⁿá seⁿᵍ, the limbs all frozen to ice.

去

Gēng 硬 Vulg. gnāy: hard stiff, unbending. Se kwùy soè gēng, hong t'hong sin 書貴瘦硬方通神, sëá jē kwùy chaë sàn gnāy, ch'hëⁿá t'hong sin, good writing should be meagre and stiff, and then it will display the spirit of the character.

Gēng 迎 To go out to meet. Ch'hin gēng chek tek ch'hey, put ch'hin gēng chek put tek ch'hey, pit ch'hin gēng hoē 親迎則得妻.不親迎則不得妻.必親迎乎, *ch'hin gēⁿā, chēw ēy tit tëŏh boē, ū^m ch'hin gēⁿā chēw hēy tit tëŏh boē, pit tëŭh ch'hin gēⁿā hoē*, if only when we go ourselves to meet her, we can get a wife, and if we cannot obtain one without going in person to receive her, then ought we not to go in person?

平

Gëô 蟯 Read jeaôu: a cockle.

入

Gëuk 玉 A gem; a precious stone. Pó gëuk 寶玉, a precious gem. Yêw bé gëuk ê soo 有美玉於斯, *woā hó ây gëuk tē chêy lêy wūy*, There is a beautifull gem here.

Súy hwaê choo jê ch'hwan mē, sek wūn gëuk chek san hwuy 水懷珠而川媚石蘊玉則山輝, *chúy k'hè^{ng} choo jê ch'hwan kwui^{ng}, chëŏk têy gëuk chek swⁿa hwuy*, when the water contains pearls, the stream will be bright and when the stones conceal gems, the mountain will be resplendent.

Gëuk 鈺 Hard metal; precious.

Gëuk 獄 A prison, a place of confinement, those confined therein; cases of litigation. Hāy gëuk 下獄, *lŏh kⁿa k'hoo*, to put in prison.

Ok lōk tēy gëuk 惡落地獄, *p'haⁿé lŏh tēy gëuk*, the wicked go down into hell.

P'hëèn gan k'hó ê chëet gëuk chëá, kê yêw yëá e 片言可以折獄者其由也與, *chit koò wā t'hang laê p'hwⁿà twān gëuk sëūng ây lâng e sē yêw tēⁿā, tēⁿā*, with one word to be able to decide cases of litigation; it is only Yêw that can do this. See the 下論 Hāy lūn.

平

Gëūng 邛 Laborious, wearied; the name of a hill.

Gëūng 筇 A kind of jointed bamboo, of which walking-sticks are made.

Gëūng 顒 Great and manifest; magnanimous, virtuous. Gëūng gëūng gáng gāng, jê kwuy jê chëang 顒顒昂昂.如圭如璋, *twā twā kwui^{ng} kwui^{ng} ch'hin chëō^{ng} kwuy kap chëang*, bright and brilliant like pearls and gems. See the 小雅 Sëaôu gnáy.

去

Gëūng 岬 The name of a hill.

声

Géy 鬩 To wrangle, to strive, to contend. Géy sëūng 鬩訟, to quarrel. Heng tēy géy ê ch'hëāng, göëy gé kê boò 兄弟鬩於墻外.禦其侮, *hēⁿa tē wān kay tē lāe bīn, gwā bīn hoē lâng boô hān*, when brethren quarrel at home, the people abroad will despise them. See 小雅 Seáou gnáy.

Géy 盻 To look angrily at any one; to behold with displeasure. Soó bîn géy géy jëên 使民盻盻然, *saé pāyh sai^{ng} sim hòëy tŏh k'hwⁿà*, to make the people look at one with rage. See the 上孟 Sëāng bēng.

Géy 睨 To look askance, to look slantingly at anything. Géy jê sè che 睨而視之, to look askance at it.

Géy 詣 To go to, to proceed towards, to visit a place, to proceed far in learning, is called 造詣, ch'hò géy.

Taē ông gèy tëâng an 代王詣長安, *taē ông k'hè kaòu tëâng an*, Taē-ông paid a visit to Tëâng-an.

Géy 俔 Not to look straight at anything. The same as 睨 géy.

平

Gêy 倪 Twan gêy 端倪, exact, grave, decorous. Mô gêy 旄倪, old and young, a surname.

Hwán kê mô gêy 反其旄倪, *hwáu tŏh tooi*ng *e ây lâou lâng seàou lëên*, to send back their old men and youths. See the 上孟 Sëāng bêng.

Gêy 猊 Chùn gêy 狻猊, a kind of lion.

Gêy 霓 A rainbow. Jëak taē hān che bōng yîn gêw yëá 若大旱之望雲霓也, *ch'hin chëō*ng *twā w*n*ā ây bāng hwûn k'hêng*, like as when a great dearth expects the clouds and rainbow.

Gêy 麑 A fawn, a young stag. Soè e gêy kêw 素衣麑裘, *kăp pàyh s*n*a tëŏh ch'hèng lŏk kë*n*á ây hêw*, with white clothes, we should wear fawn furs.

Gêy 輗 A transverse beam in front of a carriage. Taē ke boô gêy, seáou ke boô gwat, kê hô é hêng che chae 大車無輗小車無軏其何以行之哉, *twā ch'hëa bô gêy, gòy ch'hëa bô gwăt, e ēy an chw*n*á. kë*n*á*; a large carriage without a pole, and a small carriage without a yoke—how can they travel! See the 上論 Sëang lūn.

Gêy 伢 An ignorant appearance.

丟

Gêy 乂 To cut grass: also to regulate.

Gēy 藝 An art, an employment. Séw gēy 手藝, *ch'héw gēy*, a handicraft. Lëŭk gēy 六藝, the six arts. Chaê gēy 才藝, talent.

Kêw yëá gēy, é chëūng chèng hoē hô yéw 求也藝於從政乎何有, *kêw woō chaê gēy, tē chëūng chèng soō, wōo s*n*a meē*n*h ŏh*, Kêw is skilled in the arts, what difficulty will he then have in following up the business of government. See the 上論 Sëang lūn.

Gēy 埶 To plant, to sow. Hoē chek kaou bin kày sek, sē gēy gnóe kok 后稷教民稼穡樹蓺五穀, *hoē chek kà pàyh sai*ng *kày sek, sē chèng gnoē kok*, Hoē-chek taught the people agriculture and the planting of the five kinds of grain.

Gēy 羿 An ancient prince, who was famed for his skill in archery. A surname. Gēy sëēn sëā 羿善射, *gēy gaóu chëŏ chee*ng, Gēy was skilled in archery.

声

Gîm 趛 To hold down the head and walk quickly.

平

Gîm 吟 To sing, to hum. Gîm se 吟詩, to recite odes. E' sē jê gîm 倚樹而吟, *wá ch'hēw jê gîm*, to lean against a tree, and hum a song.

Gîm 唫 The same as the preceding.

Gîm 岑 A hill that is high and conical; a surname.

Gîm 涔 The lees or sediment of any thing; also written 唫 gîm.

Gîm 㐺 All standing together; also written 㐺 gîm; the same as 眾 chëùng, all.

Gîm 硷 High, lofty.

Gîm 矜 Gîm kay 矜堦, stone steps.

去

Gîm 噤 The head shaking.

Gîm 扲 To hold firmly, to grasp. Gîm chaē sêw 扲在手, *gîm tē ch'hêw,* to grasp in the hand.

声

Gîn 听 To open the mouth wide, and laugh.

Gîn 䫀 Large thick lips.

平

Gîn 銀 Silver. Pek kim wūy che gîn 白金謂之銀, *pāyh kim kóng kēò gîn,* white gold is called silver. See the 爾雅 Jé gnáy.

Gîn 垠 A precious stone like a gem, a gem with a flaw in it.

Gîn 垠 A bank, a shore, a border, a limit. Kê taē boô gîn, kê sëaóu boô lōëy 其大無垠其小無內, *e āy twā bô kaè, e āy sèy bô laē,* it is so great as to have no limits around it, and so small, as to contain nothing within it (speaking of Doctrine).

Gîn 狺 The noise of much wrangling. Bêng k'hëën gîn gîn 猛犬狺狺, *bêng kaôu ch'hêng ch'hêng jëáng,* fierce dogs, making a great noise.

Gîn 誾 Harmonious and pleasing; placid and agreeable. Bîn choó sē ch'hek, gîn gîn jê yëá 閔子侍側誾誾如也, *bin choó k'hëā tē peeng á, hô wát āy yëōng,* Bîn-choó stood by the side of Confucius, as it were pleasing and agreeable. See the 下論 Hāy lūn.

Gîn 听 To laugh out loud.

Gîn 齗 The noise of wrangling and contention.

Gîn 沂 Gîn lûn 沂淪, the eddying of water.

Gîn 嚚 A servant with four mouths, to speak falsely, to deceive. Sùn hoō gwân, boé gîn, têy gō 舜父頑.母嚚.弟傲, *sùn āy neōng pāy gwân gek, neōng lêy ūm laōu sit, sëó tē këaou gō,* sûn's father was stubborn his mother false, and his brother proud. See the 尚書 Sëōng se.

去

Gîn 憖 To enquire; to be respectful and cautious; also, moreover.

入

Gîp 偮 Gîp gîp 偮偮, a multitude of people.

Gîp 岌 High, hazardous, uneasy; a small hill is called 岌 gîp, and a great one is called 峘 hwân. K'hóng choé wat, ê soo sê yëá, t'hëen hāy taē chae, gîp gîp hoē 孔子曰.於斯時也.天下殆哉岌岌乎, *k'hông choó kóng, tē chêy lêy sê, t'heeng āy gwāy hëëm, ūm an āy yëōng,* Confucius said, at this time the Empire is in danger, and as it were unsettled. See the 下孟 Hāy bēng.

夫

Git 仡 Bold and vigorous. Git git yúng hoo, gnó sëāng yêw che 仡仡勇夫.我尚有之, *chông bêng āy yúng*

福建方言字典

hoo, gwá sëăng woō e, Of bold and vigorous yeomen, I still have a few. See the 尙書 *Sëŏng se*.

Git 吃 Difficulty of utterance. K'hoé git put lêng tō swat, jê sëĕn tè se 口吃不能道說.而善著書, *ch'hùy git, bēy sⁿa kóng wā, jê gâou chò ch'hăyh*, the mouth stammering and not able to speak, but clever at making books. See the 史記 Soó kè.

Git 汔 Water dried up; also the name of a river.

Git 屹 A hill standing by itself.

Git 矻 Git lō 矻勞, troubled, and wearied.

Git 迄 To arrive at, even, until, to. E' git ê kim 以迄於今, *è kip kaau tong kim*, even to the present time.
Chaê soe ê kóng, git boô sêng kong 才疏意廣.迄無成功, *chaê teaôu sey ê soō k'hwăh, kaôu bô chëⁿâ kong*, his talents are too diversified and his ideas too widely diffused, so that no meritorious undertaking is completed. See the 孔融傳 K'hóng yûng twān.

Git 紇 The lower part of a thread. Also a man's name. K'hóng choó hoō, sëuk lëâng git 孔子父叔梁紇, *k'hóng choó ây pāy, mëⁿâ kèò sëuk lëâng git*, Confucius's father was called Sëuk-lëâng-git.

Git 訖 To stop, to exhaust, to finish, to conclude. K'hóng choó sē se, choō tông gê é hāy, git ê chew 孔子序書.自唐虞以下.訖于周, *k'hóng choó sē se keng, chëûng tông gê ê lōh, git kaôu chew*, Confucius arranged the historical classics, from the time of Tông-gê (i. e. Geaôu and Sùn) downwards, and concluded with the Chew dynasty.
Boô git tek 毋訖糴, *bô swat tëăh*, do not stop the buying of rice.

2 z

声 Gnaé 齩 To gnaw, to gnaw a bone, read gnaou. Ék choó jê gnaóu kê kwut 易子而齩其骨, *wⁿâ këⁿâ jê gnaé ây kwut*, they exchanged children and gnawed their bones: Speaking of a famine.

去 Gnaē 艾 Vulg. *hëⁿā*: a kind of grass used in cauterizing; the moxa, or mugwort; a period of 50 days is called 艾 gnaē. Sëaôu gnaē 少艾, a young person; also rest, at ease; a surname.
Kim che yëuk ông cheā, yêw ch'hit lëên che pēng, kêw sam lëên che gnāe 今之欲王者.猶七年之病.求三年之艾, *tⁿa ây böëyh chò ông ây lâng, ch'hin chëōⁿᵍ ch'hit neēⁿᵍ ây paīⁿᵍ kêw sⁿa neēⁿᵍ ây gnāe e*, those in the present day who want to become rulers are like those afflicted with a seven years sickness, seeking for cauterizing grass that has been three year's dried (Intimating that without previous preparation they will never succeed in their object. See the 下孟 Hāy bēng.

Gnaē 乂 To cut grass. Chùn gnaē 俊乂, a man of talent.

Gnaē 忞 Têng gnaē 懲忞, to regulate, to put in order.

Gnaē 刈 To cut grass is called 刈 gnaē; to reap corn is called 穫 hoē.

声 Gnaóu 齩 Vulg. *gnaé*: to gnaw, to bite.

平 Gnaôu 爻 To interchange, to lay across, to blend, to compare; one of the diagrams.
Leûk gnaôu pat kwà 六爻八卦, *lák gnaôu pǎyh kwà*, the six interchanges and eight diagrams.

Gnaôu 肴 Savoury food, spiced eatables; also written 餚 gnaôu. Chaè chew gnaôu ê tëên kan, hāou k'hin chëá jê lō che 載酒肴於田間.候勤者而勞之, *chaè chèw meë^{n}h p'höèy tē ch'hân kan, tèng haōu k'hìn ây lâng jē lō e*, to carry out wine and savoury food into the fields, in order to wait for the diligent, and reward them.

Gnaôu 崤 Gnaôu hâm 崤凾, the name of a hill.

Gnaôu ⿱艹殽 The roots of vegetables; also written 茭 gnaôu.

Gnaôu 虓 The roar of a tiger, when about to bite any one; the barking of a dog; the name of a country, and of a place.

Gnaôu 殽 The same as 肴 gnaôu; also a piece of meat with the bones in it.

Gnaôu 淆 To disturb water, to stir up the bottom, and make the water muddy. Gnaôu che put chok 淆之不濁, *keaou gnaôu, yēw bēy lò*, although you should stir it up, it would not be muddy. Spoken in reference to persons.

Gnaôu 嘐 A sound.

Gnaôu 樇 Gnaôu t'hô 樇桃, a kind of peach.

丟 Gnaōu 樂 To desire, to delight in, to like, to prefer; a friend; also read lok. Tè chëá gnāou súy, jîn chëá gnaōu san 知者樂水.仁者樂山, *tè ây lâng aè chúy, jîn ây lâng aè sw^{n}a*, men of knowledge prefer water, but men of benevolence prefer dry land. Intimating that the disposition of the one is more sedate than the other. See the 上論 Sëang lūn.

Gnāou 藕 Lëên gnāou 蓮藕, the fibres of the water lily. Gnaōu se lân chok sëèn 藕絲難作線, *gnāou ây se ŏh chò sw^{n}à*, the fibres of the water lily plant, can hardly be manufactured into thread.

卒 Gnay 訝 Words not widely proclaimed.

声 Gnáy 雅 Elegant, splendid, uncommon. Chéng gnáy 整雅, elegant and proper. Bûn gnáy 文雅, literary and accomplished. Jê gnáy 儒雅, an accomplished scholar. Gnáy gân 雅言, elegant discourse.

丟 *Gnāy* 硬 Read kēng: hard, stiff. Put jêw put kēng, naé këèn jê gnáy 不柔不硬.乃見儒雅, *ūm nooi^{ng} ūm gnāy, naé k'hw^{n}à gaôu ây t'hāk ch'hăyh lăng*, neither too yielding nor too stiff, shews the accomplished scholar.

夫 *Gnăyh* 筴 Read këep: to take up any thing with pincers, tongs, or chopsticks Këep choó 筴子, *gnăyh á*, a pair of pincers.

灭 *Gnăyh* 夾 Read këep: to hold under the arm, to hold right and left, to uphold. Chew kong këep hoò sêng ông 周公夾輔成王, *chew kong gnăyh hoò sêng ông*, Chew-kong upheld and assisted Seng-ông.

Gnăyh 挾 Read hëep: to hold under the arm, to squeeze. Hëep t'haè san é t'hëaou pok haé, wūy put lêng, sē chin put lêng yëá 挾大山以超北海謂不能是眞不能也, *gnăyh t'haè sw^{n}a jê t'hëaou kōèy pak haè, kóng bēy ēy, sē chin chē^{n}à bēy ēy*, as to grasping the great mountain under the arm, and jumping across the northern sea with it, to say that you can not do it, is truly a *can not*, (and not a *will not*.) See 孟子 Bēng choó.

去

Gneàou 㗖 The noise of a multitude.

入

Gnëaouh 岋 To move, to be agitated. T'hëen tōng tëy gnëaouh 天動地岋, *t'heeng tāng tëy gneaouh*, when the heaven is moved, the earth is agitated.

Gneaouh 蚜 To creep, as a worm.

平

Gnêw 牛 Vulg. *goô*: the cow kind. Hông gnêw 黃牛, *wuīng goô*, a common cow. Súy gnêw 水牛, *chúy goô*, a buffaloe. Gnêw toé 牛斗, *goô taóu*, the name of a star. Hwat peng che kay, put hëuk gnêw yâng 伐冰之家不畜牛羊, *hwat peng ây kay, bô ch'hê goô yëôⁿᵍ*, a break-ice family (i. e. the family of a great officer) should not keep oxen and sheep.—A surname.

Gnêw 苹 Gnêw ch'hip 苹膝, the name of a medicinal plant.

上

Gnó 我 Vulg. *gwá*: I myself. Gnó put te 我不知, *gwá ūm chac*, I do not know. Jé aè kê yâng, gnó aè kê léy 爾愛其羊我愛其禮, *lé sëôh e ây yëôⁿᵍ, gwá sëôh e ây léy*, you pity the sheep, but I pity the ceremony. See the 上論 Sëâng lūn.

Gnó 戈 A spear, a lance.

Gnó 硪 The loftiness of a hill; height.

上

Gnoé 五 Vulg. *goē*: five. Gnoé sip 五十, *goē châp*, fifty; a surname, also written 乂 gnoé.

Goê sip yéw gnoé, jê chè è hak 吾十有五而志於學, *gwá châp goē hòèy, jê sim chè tē t'hak*, when I was fifteen years of age my mind was bent on learning. See the 上論 Sëâng lūn.

Gnoé 伍 A file of five men. Hâng gnoé 行伍, rank and file; a surname. Sam gnoé sêng kwûn 三伍成群, *sⁿa goē chëⁿâ kwûn*, three or five forming a company. See the 左傳 Chó twān.

Gnoé 午 One of the horary characters. Jit gnoé 日午, *jit taōu*, mid-day.

Gnoé 仵 Inimical, hostile. E' put gnóe che soô sëang èng 以不仵之詞相應, *t'hó ūᵐ gnoé ây wā sëo yìn*, he answered in expressions by no means hostile.

Gnoé 忤 Obstinate, opposed. Gnoé gek 忤逆, perverse and rebellious.

Gnoé 迕 To meet with, to come against, to oppose. Ch'hoé gnoé 錯迕, Confused.

Ông hoó sê ch'hut é hwan sëang gnoé 王甫時出與萑相迕, *ông hoó hwüh sê ch'hut kap ông hwan sëo loó tëôh*, when Ông-hoó went out, he just met with Ông-hwan.

Gnoé 耦 Double, together. Tëâng choé këet lek, gnoé jê keng 長沮桀溺耦而耕, *tëâng-choé këet-lek sëo tùy chöh ch'hân*, Tëâng-choé and Këet-lek ploughed the ground together. See the 下論 Hāy lūn.

Gnoé 偶 United together, opposite, double; also suddenly, unexpectedly. Soè song wat gnoé, chek wat kê 數雙曰偶隻曰奇, *soè ây seⁿᵍ kóng gnoé, chit chëâh kóng k'hëa*, in numbers, double are called Gnoé, and Single k'hea.

Gnoé jëên 偶然, suddenly.

声

Gó 戹 A knot in wood; a bone without any meat.

Gó 娓 Kó gó 娿娓, the appearance of a waiting maid.

平

Gô 峨 Ch'he gô 嵯峨, the lofty appearance of a hill. Gô bê san 峨眉山, the name of a hill.

Gô 俄 A moment, a short space of time, a little while. Neáou sèw gô sûn sûn, gô tô tô 鳥獸俄旬旬.俄逃逃, *chēâou kap sèw tëep à koó sîm sîm, yëw tëep à koó chaôu laê chaôu k'hè*, birds and beasts are for a moment still, and another moment full of gambols.

Gô 訛 To change one's speech, to talk falsely or foolishly. Bîn che gô gân 民之訛言, *păyh saing ây păyh ch'hat wā*, the foolish stories of the people. See the 小雅 Seáou gnáy.

Gô 吪 The same as the above: also to speak, and chatter; also written 僞 gô. Sëang mē boô gô 尙寐無吪, *laê k'hè k'hwùn bŏh kàng wā*, let us go to sleep and not prattle.

Gô 蛾 The silk worm, the moth into which the silk worm turns; also a flying insect. Ch'hâm gô 蠶蛾, the silk worm generally.

Gô 鼇 A large sea tortoise. Yéw sîn gô, pöèy hoē hông laê che san, chaē haê têung 有神鼇背負蓬萊之山.在海中, *woā sîn gô, k'ha chëăh gēā hông laê ây swna tē haê têung*, there is a divine tortoise in the middle of the sea, who carries on his back the Hông-laê hill. The Chinese fable that 女媧, lê wâ cut off a leg of this tortoise to prop up one corner of the heavens, which was in danger of falling.

Gô 哦 To chaunt to hymn, to sing; also written 誐 gô.

Gô 娥 Good, beautiful. Sëâng gô 嫦娥, the name of a beautiful lady, said to be caught up into the moor.

Gô 珴 The appearance of offering up a gem or present.

Gô 莪 A fine kind of vegetable.

Gô 誐 Good words; also to chaunt, to sing. Gô se 誐詩, to recite verses.

Gô 鼉 An animal found in the waters, the skin of which is used for making the heads of drums.

Gô 敖 To wander, to ramble, to stroll about for pleasure. Má wān gô yêw jê tèy kan 馬援敖遊二帝間, *báy wān ch'hit t'hô tē jê tèy ây kan*, Má-wān strolled backwards and forwards between the two Emperors. A surname.

Gô 嗷 The noise of a multitude, the sound of many voices, lamenting. Hông gān ê hwuy, ae bêng gô gô 鴻雁于飛.哀鳴嗷嗷, *twā chëăh gā tit pwuy, ae ây haôu gô gô*, the wild geese are flying about, and their melancholy scream sounds like the voice of a multitude.

Gô 厫 Ch'hong gô 倉厫, not fearful.

Gô 遨 Gô yêw 遨遊, to ramble for pleasure. Gô he 遨嬉, to stroll about in sport.

Gô 嚻 The sound of sighing, and lamentation; the bustle of a market. Gô gô 嚻嚻, self-satisfaction and complacency.

Gô 螯 A large tortoise; the same as 鼇 gô.

Gô 鰲 The name of a fish.

Gô 驁 A fine horse, a horse not yet broken in.

Gô 謷 To deceive. Gô gân 謷言, deceitful words.

Gô 䳘 A goose. Thⁿa jit kê hoê sat sō gô yëá, é che sit che 他日其母殺是鵝也與之食之, pat jit e ây nëôⁿᵍ lêy t'hâe chêy lêy gô, hoê e chëâh e, the next day his mother killed this goose, and gave it him to eat. See the 上孟 Sëâng bēng.

Gô 熬 To boil, to cook without oil; to brew, to distil. Gô chéw 熬酒, to distil liquor or wine.

去

Gō 餓 To be hungry, to starve. Gō soó 餓死, gō sé, to be starved to death. Pek ê sëuk chêy gō ê séw yâng che hāy 伯夷叔齊餓于首陽之下, pek ê sëuk-chêy gō tē séw yâng ây k'ha, Pek-ê and Sëuk-chêy, starved themselves to death at the foot of the Sêw-yâng hill. See the 下論 Hāy lūn.

Gō 奡 To be proud, to treat contemptuously.

Gō 卧 To sleep. Gō pâng 卧房, a bed-chamber. Also written 臥 gō. Yin ké jê gō 隱几而卧, pak tōh jê k'hwùn, he leaned over the table and slept. See the 上孟 Sëâng bēng.

Gō 鏊 A pan for making cakes.

Gō 傲 To treat proudly. Gō bān 傲慢, to treat with scorn. Gō put k'hó tëâng 傲不可長, kēaou ây sim kwⁿa ūᵐ t'hang hoē e tëⁿᵍ, do not allow proud dispositions to grow. See the 禮記 Léy kè.

平

Goê 吾 I myself. Goê jit sam séng goê siu 吾日三省吾身, gwá tak jit sⁿa hāng séng ch'hat gwá, ây sin, I examine myself every day as to three things. See the 上論 Sëâng lūn.

Goê 浯 The name of a river.

Goê 梧 Goê tông 梧桐, the name of a tree, which at mid-autumn lets fall one leaf by which people know that the autumn season is arrived.

Goê 珸 A stone like a gem.

Goê 鯃 K'he goê 鮈鯃, the name of a fish.

Goê 吳 A surname; the name of a country.

Goê 蜈 Goê kong 蜈蚣, gëâ kang, a centipede.

Goê 鯸 The name of a fish; the same as 鯃 goê; also used for the following.

Goê 鼯 A kind of flying squirrel, like a small fox; also called 夷由, ê yêw.

Goê 菩 The name of a plant.

去

Goē 悟 To understand. Leaóu goē 了悟, to comprehend. Séng goē 醒悟, to awaken; to be in a mistake is called 迷 bêy, to find out one's error, is called 悟 goē.

3 A

Goē 晤 Bêng goē 明晤, clear; perception; the understanding. Goē tùy 晤對, opposite, face to face.

Goē 寤 To awake. Goē bē kēw che 寤寐求之, *ch'hai^ng k'hwùn kêw e*, waking and sleeping he seeks for her. See the 國風 Kok hong.

Goē 俉 To meet.

Goē 悮 To deceive, to cheat.

Goē 誤 To be in a mistake; to throw into confusion. Kwun hô gân che goē yëá 君何言之誤也, *kwun an-chw^n á kóng, kaôu hëá goē*, how is it that you make such a mistake in what you say. See the 張耳傳, *Tëo^ng jê twān.*
Yit goē, k'hé yûng chaē goē 一誤豈容再誤, *chit ây goē, k'hám ēy yúng, tit chaē goē*, having once made a mistake, how will it do to repeat the error.

Goē 五 Read gnoé: five. Gnoé sip jê te t'hëen bêng 五十而知天命, *goē cháp jê chae t'hee^ng ây bêng*, at fifty I knew the decrees of Heaven. See the 上論 Sëang lûn.

丟
Göēy 外 Vulg. *gwā*: without, on the outside; beside, except. Lëok hap che göēy sêng jîn chûn jê put lûn 六合之外聖人存而不論, *lák hap ây gwā sèng jîn chûn jê bô gē lūn*, whatsoever is beyond the six cardinal points (or on the outside of the visible creation) the philosopher meditates on, but does not discourse about.
Göēy gân put jip ê k'hwûn 外言不入於閫, *gwā bīn ây wā, ū^m t'hang jip ê pûng keng*, out-of-door talk should not be brought in doors.

Göēy 甥 Göēy seng 甥甥, cousins, and nephews, by the sister's side, a sister's son or daughter.

兲
Göëyh 月 Read gwat: a month, the moon. Yit gwat 一月, *chit göëyh*, one month. Jit gwat seng sîn 日月星晨, *jit göëyh, kap ch'hai^ng*, sun, moon, and stars. E jûn gwat, têng soô sê, sêng söëy 以閏月定四時成歲, *è lūn göëyh tē^n á sè sè chē^n á neē^ng*, by the aid of the intercalary month he fixed the four seasons, and completed the year. See the 堯典 Geâou tëën.

兲
Gok 偔 Numerous, many.

Gok 咢 To be always beating a drum; also the sound of a drum.

Gok 愕 Ch'hok gok 錯愕, fearful, alarmed, apprehensive. Gok jëên 愕然, suddenly alarmed.

Gok 萼 The bud of a flower; also written 蕚 gok. Ch'hun hwa hwat gok, hāy këet kê sit 春華發萼夏結其實, *ch'hun t'hee^ng hwa hwat gok hāy t'hee^ng këet köëy chê*, in the spring season flowers open their buds, and in the summer form their fruit.

Gok 鵠 The name of a bird, used as a bull's-eye in a target. Sit choo chëng gok, hwân kêw choo kê sin 失諸正鵠反求諸其身, *sit choo chèng gok, tëôh hwán kêw tē ka tē ây hin sin*, missing the mark in the centre of the target, we should turn inwards, and blame our own persons. See the 中庸 Tëung yûng.

Gok 諤 Këén gok 謇諤, honest words, upright discourse. Ch'hëen jîn che lok lok, put jê yit soô che gok gok 千人之諾諾不如一士之諤諤, *chē^n á ch'heng lâng ây yìn hô, ūm pé chìt ây t'hak ch'hâyh lâng ây tit wā*, the mere assent of a thousand men, is not so good as the plain declaration of one scholar.

Gok 崿 The side of a hill, a precipice; also written 㠋 gok and 㖾 gok.

Gok 碍 Chim gok 礁碍, stones piled up in a dangerous way.

Gok 鄂 The name of a country, spoken of in ancient history. A surname.

Gok 噩 Stern, rigid, severe. Chew se gok gok jé 周書噩噩爾, *chew ây ch'hâyh gok gok ây yëōng*, the writings of the Chew dynasty have an appearance of severity.

Gok 巕 The peak of a hill; the ridge of a hill.

Gok 剻 The point or edge of a sword.

Gok 鱷 Gok gê 鱷魚, *gok hê*, an alligator, a crocodile. Hân jé chok chèy gok gê bûn 韓愈作祭鱷魚文, *hân bûn kong chò chèy gok hê ây bûn*, Hân-bûn-kong composed an essay announcing his sacrifice to the alligators: (in consequence of which sacrifice, the Chinese fable, that the alligators all left the coast of China). See the 古文 Kóe bûn.

声

Góng 骯 A horse with a high head.

平

Gông 卬 I myself; high, to mount a high place, in order to look to a distance. Gông se gnó yéw 卬須我友, *gwá sae tëōh gwá ây pêng yéw*, I have need of my friends. See the 國風 Kok hong.

Sëāng chëuk gông 上足卬, *pâyh chëōng k'ha bāng k'hwⁿà*, to lift up the feet and look to a distance.

Gông 昂 The rising of the sun; to raise, to elevate; bright, clear. Gông gông kwun che tek 昂昂君之德, *bêng bêng kwun ây tek*, bright and clear is the prince's virtue.

Gông 駉 A startled horse, a furious steed; also a horse with a white belly.

Gông 茚 A kind of water plant, growing by the side of pools.

去

Gōng 䩕 K'hōng gōng 㰠䩕, uneasy, unsettled.

Gōng 岇 The name of a hill.

Gōng 鴚 The name of a bird.

Gōng 戇 Vulg. *gām*: stupid, foolish, silly. Gōng jîn 戇人, *gām lâng*, a stupid fellow. Sîm é, k'hip âm che gām yëâ 甚矣汲黯之戇也, *chin chëⁿà chèy k'hip âm ây gōng*, how excessive is K'hip-âm's stupidity; also written 戅 gōng.

声

Goó 語 Read gé: a saying. Sëuk gé 俗語, *sëuk goó*, a proverb, an adage. The people of 勒畢, lek pit, are said to be about three inches high, having wings, and because of their skill in talking and joking they are called the Sëen goó kok 善語國, the eloquent nation. This does not differ much, either in sound or sense, from the fabled account of *Lilliput*.

平 Goô **牛** Read gnêw: an ox, or cow. Gnêw yâng 牛羊, *goô yëô^ng*, cows and sheep; A surname.

Yôw k'hëen gnêw jê kô e tông hāy chëá 有牽牛而過堂於下者, *woō lâng k'han goô köëy e tông hāy*, there was a person leading an ox and passing by at the foot of the hall. See the 上孟 Sëāng bēng.

去 Goō **遇** Read gē: to meet, to meet with, to befal. Haē hoē sëang gē 邂逅相遇, *bô tëo^ng tê, sëo toó tëôh*, to meet one another unexpectedly.

上 Gwá **我** Read gnó: I, myself. Gnó yëuk jîn, soo jîn chë e 我欲仁.斯仁至矣, *gwá aē böëyh jîn soo jîn kaoù è*, when I desire benevolence, benevolence comes.

去 Gwà **宼** Nê gwà 泥宼, a house, a mud cottage.

去 Gwā **嚄** An exclamation of wonder or surprise; a calling out loud. Boó tēy hāy ke k'hip wat, gwā, taē ché hô chông che ch'him hoē 武帝下車泣曰.嚄大姊何藏之深乎, *boô tèy lôh ch'hëa k'haòu kóng, gwā, twā ché an chw^n è taē kaoù hëäh ch'him*, Boó-tëy descended from his carriage and weeping said alas, my sister, how is it they have buried you so deep! See the 史記 Soó kè.

Gwā **外** Read göēy: without, on the outside; beside, and beyond. Tek chëá pún yëá, chaē chëá bwat yëá, göēy pún löēy bwat, cheng bîn se twat 德者本也.財者末也.外本內末.爭民施奪, *tek hêng chô kin pún, chee^ng chaē böēy böēy, nā böëyh gwā e āy pún, jê laē e āy bwat, chek sëo chai^ng āy pāyh sai^ng laē ch'hëô^ng*, virtue is the principal thing and money is of less importance, now if we exclude the principal thing, and engross the less important, the wrangling people will begin to plunder us.

平 Gwaê **詭** Këet gwaê 㜸詭, lazy, indolent; also read k'hwúy, deceitful.

去 Gwaē **顡** Unskilful, not clever; dull, stupid.

上 Gwán **玩** To delight in, to play, to sport, to study, to meditate on. Gwán swá 玩耍, *t'hit t'hô*, to play to sport, to gambol, to ramble.

Gwán lōng koē chëáng che sëāng 玩弄股掌之上, *t'hit t'hô hê lâng tē twā kaē ch'hēw chëô^ng āy têng*, to play with and daudle upon one's knees and hands.

Soō wûy te kê soó, lê wûy wat ké gwán 士為知己死女為悅己玩, *t'hak ch'hāyh lâng wûy chae kê āy lâng sé, cha boē wûy aē kê āy lâng gwán*, a scholar will die for a dear friend, and a woman will sport with one she loves.

Gwán sim soō but 玩心事物, *gwán sim sëô^ng sëō mee^nh*, with a studious mind to meditate on affairs and things.

Gwán **翫** To study, to bend the mind to any thing; to dislike; to ramble, to desire.

Gwán sip 翫習, to study, to exercise one's-self in.

Gwán yêw 翫遊, to stroll about for pleasure.

Gwán **阮** Vulg. wûi^ng: a surname. Gwán chek 阮籍, and Gwán hâm 阮咸, were reckoned among the seven wise men of the bamboo grove.

Gwán **朊** To see, to behold.

Gwán 䀨 Good, fine lovely, valuable; when written with a 貝 by the side it refers to things, and when with a 女, to women.

平

Gwân. 元 Great; the origin, the principal, the chief; a surname. Gwân söèy 元帥, a generalissimo.

Taē chae k'heen gwân, bān but cho sé 大哉乾元. 萬物資始, *twā chae, t'hee^{ng}, chò t'haôu, bān meē^{n}h k'hè t'haôu*, how great are the supreme Heavens, from which all things originate. See the 易經 *Yēàh keng*.

Gwân séw bêng chae, koé keng lëâng chae 元首明哉. 股肱良哉, *gwân t'haôu nā bêng, k'hà ch'hèw sūn lëâng*, when the principal head (the Emperor) is intelligent, the members (his ministers) will be honest. See the 尙書, *Sëō^{ng} se*.

Chōng gwân 狀元, *chëāng gwân*, the highest literary rank.

Gwân 刓 To rub off the edges, till a thing becomes round. Hāng é 項羽, having employed people in his service, upon their acting meritoriously, and deserving a reward, would k'hek yìn gwân 刻印刓, rub the edges of the seal round before he could find in his heart, to promote them to office.

Gwân 頑 Stupid, dull. Gwân gek 頑逆, stupid and stubborn. Sim put chek tek gē che keng, wûy gwân 心不則德義之經爲頑, *sim ūm chek hwat tek gē ây keng, chò gwân*, when the mind is not regulated by the laws of virtue and righteousness, a man becomes stupid. See the 左傳 Chò twān.

Gwân 黿 A large tortoise. Gwân gô kaou lëûng 黿鼉蛟龍, tortoises, large fishes and dragons. See the 中庸, Tëûng yûng.

Gwân 原 An origin, a fountain, a head. Pêng gwân 平原, a wide waste. Gwân chwân hwūn hwūn, put sëà têw yëā 原泉混混不舍晝夜, *gwân chwân hwūn hwūn, bô hǎy^{n}h jit maî^{ng}*, the fountain bubbles without ceasing day or night. See the 下孟 Hāy bēng.

Këang pek yëak kéw hwat tëung gwân 羌伯約九伐中原, *këang pek yëak kaôu hāy hwat tëung gwân*, Këang-pek-yëak, nine times attacked the centre of China.

Gwân 源 The same as the above; a fountain of water. Chêng kê pún, ch'heng kê gwân 正其本. 清其源, *chë^{n}à e ây kin pûn, ch'heng e ây gwân t'haôu*, correct the root, and purify the fountain.

Gwân 嫄 Këang gwân 羌嫄, the name of a woman, the mother of the sovereigns of the chew 周 dynasty.

Gwân. 邧 The name of a city.

Gwân 騵 A black horse with a white belly; a white horse wounded.

Gwân 螈 A kind of insect.

去

Gwān 愿 Careful and kind; respectful.

Gwān 傆 Talents employed in a bad cause.

Gwān 願 To desire, to wish, to long for, to desire anxiously. Kam gwām 甘願, willing.

Gwān bûn choó che chè 願聞子之志, *aè bōëyh t'he^{n}a hoo choó ây chè*, I desire to hear what is your great aim. See the 論語 Lūn gé.

Hô súy yim yim, chêng séy gwān hêy 河水淫淫，情所願兮, *kang chúy teêng teêng chêng sêy gwān*, when the waters of the river are full, it is just what we desire.

Gwān 䕺 A kind of vegetable.

兲

Gwat 月 Vulg. *göëyh*: a moon, a month. Yit söèy sip jē gwat, gwat sam sip jit 一歲十二月，月三十日, *chit neēng chap jē göëyh; chit göëyh sⁿa chap jit*, one year contains twelve months and every month thirty days.

Gwat 伄 The name of a place.

Gwat 刖 To cut off; a punishment consisting in cutting off the legs.

Gwat 軏 A yoke. Taē ke boô gêy, sëáou ke boô gwat, kê hô é hêng che chae 大車無輗，小車無軏，其何以行之哉, *twā ch'hëa bô gêy sèy ch'hëa bô gwat é böëyh an chŏⁿá ëy hëⁿé*, a large carriage without a cross-bar, and a small one without a yoke,—how can they travel? See 上論 Sëāng lūn.

Gwat 鈅 A military weapon.

Gwat 岄 The name of a hill.

夫

Gwut 㟊 Rapid, swift, hasty.

Gwut 矻 To be troubled in the extreme. Sëāng gwut gwut é keāng lëēn, 常矻矻以窮年, *sëāng tëōh bwâ é këāng neēng*, always troubled throughout the year.

Gwut 猖 Këet gwut 狤猖, the name of a beast, found in the west, which eats incense, and has no hair.

兲

Gwut 兀 High, and level at the top; also to amputate the legs.

Gwut 仡 The motion of a boat.

Gwut 杌 Gëet gwut 臲杌, uneasy, hazardous; agitated, disturbed.

Gwut 屼 K'hwut gwut 崫屼, the bare appearance of a hill.

Gwut 扤 To move, to agitate, to act upon. T'hëen che gwut gnó, jê put gnó k'hek 天之扤我，如不我克, *t'heeⁿᵍ ây tín tāng gwá, ch'hin chëōⁿᵍ gwá bēy yëⁿá*, heaven acts upon us, so that we cannot resist.

Gwut 杌 A piece of wood, without branches; a post, a pole.

Gwut 㧾 Hazardous, uneasy. The same as 杌 Gwut.

壴

Gwúy 隗 Ch'huy gwúy 嶊隗, lofty, high. A surname.

Gwúy 頠 To study manners and polite appearances.

Gwúy 媿 A good woman, still and quiet in her family.

平

Gwûy 隗 Lofty, high.

Gwûy 嵬 Ch'huy gwûy 崔嵬, a rocky hill, mixed with earth.

Gwûy 巍 Lofty, elevated, noble. Gwûy gwûy hoē, wûy t'hëēn wûy taē 巍巍乎.惟天爲大, *kwân twā hoē, tok tok t'hee^{ng} k'hăh twā*, how lofty and noble (is Geâou)!—Heaven alone is greater! See the 上諭 Sëāng lūn.

Gwûy 危 High, dangerous, hazardous, uneasy; difficult; a surname. Gwûy kip 危急, in difficulties, in straits. Gwûy jëên boē an 危然後安, *gwûy jëēn aōu ēy an*, after having been in danger we may enjoy tranquillity.

Këèn gwûy sēw bēng 見危授命, *k'hw^{n}à keè^{ng} gwûy hëēm tëŏh sēw sai^{ng} më^{n}ā*, seeing a danger, we ought to venture our lives.

去

Gwūy 僞 False, hypocritical. Chok gwūy sim lô 作僞心劳, *chò pāyh ch'hat, sim kw^{n}a tëŏh bwā*, to practice deceit, troubles the mind.

Seaóu choó boô gwūy 小子無僞, *sèy kë^{n}à bó păyh ch'hat*, infants are no hypocrites.

Gwūy 魏 Chëāng gwūy 象魏, a book of orders; a surname, the name of a state. Goê sëuk, gwūy 吳蜀魏, constituted the three kingdoms of the 三國, Sam kok, on which that celebrated novel is formed.

Gwūy 䰎 O gwūy, 阿䰎, assafœtida.

H

平

Ha 㰫 To open the mouth wide, and blow out the breath. Read hay.

Ha 嘘 The warm breath blown out of the mouth.

上

Há 㗿 To laugh out loud. K'hoé há há 口㗿㗿, *ch'hùy há há*, to laugh há há.

去

Hà 嚇 To laugh, the sound of laughing.

Hà 罅 A split, a crack, a crevice. Hà k'hek 罅隙, a crevice, a cranny.

Hà 嘑 To halloo at any one, to bawl out aloud. K'hoé hà 口嘑, *ch'húy hà*, to bawl out with the mouth.

Hà jé jê é che, hêng tō che jîn hwut sēw 嘑爾而與之.行道之人弗受, *hwăh lâng jê hoē lâng, kë^{n}â loē ây lâng ū^{m} sēw*, whenever you bawl and scold people in giving them any thing, even a passing strangers on the road side, would not take it. See the 下孟 Hāy bēng.

Hà 襾 To cover any thing; to cover what is underneath, with anything from above; hence the form of the character.

Hà 孝 Read haòu: mourning for parents. Taè haòu 帶孝, *twà hà*, to wear mourning. Ke song wat, yéw haòu hok 居喪日有孝服, *k'hëā se^{ng} hà, kóng twà* *hà ây yîn chëö^ng*, when people are in mourning, they are said to put on mourning clothes.

平 Hâ 縖 Read hăh: to bind any thing together.

上 Hā 嚇 Hā hā ch'heaòu 嚇嚇笑, *hā hā ch'hëò*, to laugh heartily.

去 Hae 奓 Vulg. *t'hà*: great, immense, of wide dimensions. Sim hae t'héy t'haè 心奓體泰, *sim kw^na hae, sin t'hèy twā*, great in mind and body.

Hae 咍 To laugh, the appearance and sound of laughing.

去 Haé 駭 To be afraid, to be alarmed. Keng haé 驚駭, *kē^na haé*, to be frightened. Choo taē hoo këën che, kae sek jëën jê haé 諸大夫見之.皆色然而駭, *choo taè hoo k'hw^nà e, chò pod pëën sek jê kē^na haé*, all the great officers, on seeing him, universally changed countenance, and were afraid. See the 左傳 Chó twān.

Haé 醢 Minced meat preserved with some liquor. Hey haé 醯醢, all kinds of pickle. K'hóng choó k'hok choó loē ê tëng têng, chìn soó chëá jê būn koé, wat, haé che è, sūy bēng hok haé 孔子哭子路於中庭.進使者而問故.曰.醢之矣.遂命覆醢, *k'hóng choó tit k'haòu choó loē tē tëung têng, chēw chìn soó chëá jê mooi^ng yëën koè, kóng leàh e chò băh chëö^ng, sūy kā lâng tò hëet băh chëö^ng*, when confucius was weeping for Choó-loē, in the middle hall, he ordered the messenger to be brought in and enquired the circumstances of his death; who said, They made mince meat of him; upon which he ordered them to throw away the mince meat, (prepared for his dinner) not being able to eat of it.

Haé 海 The sea. Haé wûy pek kok che ông 海爲百谷之王, *haé sè chē^nà păyh k'hai^ng ây ông*, the sea is king over the hundred vallies.

Haé put yâng p'ho, è tëung kok yéw sêng jîn hoê 海不揚波.意中國有聖人乎, *haé bô k'hè p'ho nē^ng, lán sëö^ng tëung kok k^nà wōo sêng jîn*, the sea did not raise her waves, hence we thought that perhaps China had produced a sage. Said by a foreign nation, who came from far to seek a sage in China.

Haé 唉 Read ae: an exclamation of surprise and regret. Ae yëâ 唉唧, *haé yëá*, an expression of astonishment, very common among the Chinese.

A, hoó 亞父, finding that 項羽, hāng ê would not listen to his advice threw the pearly vessel (which had been sent as a present) on the ground, and drawing his sword, dashed it in pieces, saying. Ae, sē choó put chëuk é boê 唉豎子不足與謀, *haé, chèy lëy gin á, bô kaoù t'hang kap è soō nëö^ng*, pshaw! this boy is not fit to be consulted with.

去 Haè 欬 To draw the breath short and quick; also, the breath.

平 Haê 孩 A child. Haê jê 孩兒, *sèy kē^ná*, a youth, a little child. Haê têy che tông, boô put te aè kê ch'hin 孩提之童.無不知愛其親, *haê têy ây sèy kē^ná bô ū^m chac sëöh c ây pāy boé*, every infant and child in the arms, knows how to love its parents. See the 下孟 Hāy bēng.

Haê 諧 United, harmonious, paired. K'him sek haê hô 琴瑟諧和, *k'hîm sek tëöh haê hô*, harps and guitars should be harmonious.

Haê 骸 Kwut haê 骨骸, a bone, a knuckle, a joint. Chëet haê é ch'hwàn 折骸以爨, *at chëĕh kwut haê é hēⁿâ höëy*, to break up the bones in order to make a fire.

Haê 鞋 Vulg. ây: a shoe, a straw shoe. Yit song haê 一雙鞋, *chit sang ây*, a pair of shoes.

Haê 鞵 The same as the above, leather shoes.

Haê 鮭 Vulg. kêy: a small kind of fish, used in pickles.

去

Haē 亥 One of the horary characters.

Haē 丯 Danger; the same as the following.

Haē 害 To injure, to hurt; danger, loss, injury. Sëang haē 傷害, to wound. Lē haē 利害, dangerous.

Hwuy toê boô ek, jê yēw haē che 非徒無益而又害之, *āᵐ chêng twⁿā twⁿā bô lē yëāh, jê yēw sún haē e*, not only is it of no use, but still more, it is injurious. See 孟子 Bēng chóó.

Haē 解 To disperse, to scatter. A surname. Read kaé, to loose, to solve.

Haē 邂 To meet suddenly. Haē hoē put kê jê höēy 邂逅不期而會, *haē hoē bô kê yëak jê sëo höēy*, to meet accidentally and without previous agreement.

Haē 懈 Lazy, idle, indolent. Haē taē 懈怠, slothful, negligent. Sëuk yëā hwuy haē 夙夜匪懈, *jit maiⁿᵍ bô twⁿā*, not idle day nor night.

Haē 獬 Haē chaē 獬豸, a wild animal, said to have but one horn. Ch'hoé bûn ông hⁿò hòk haē kwan 楚文王好服獬冠, *ch'hoé bûn ông aè tè haē p'höëy ây kin*, "Ch'hoé-bûn-ông loved to wear a cap made of the skin of this animal."—Called by some an executioner's cap.

Haē 械 Manacles. Ke haē 機械, artful contrivances, tricks. K'hè haē 器械, implements; weapons.

Te bîn k'hè haē che soè 知民器械之數, *tëöh chae pâyh saiⁿᵍ ke k'hè ây jwā chēy*, you should know the number of weapons in the hands of the people.

Haē 薤 A kind of vegetable; a sort of leek.

Haē 譮 The face flushed with anger, and the voice raised.

Haē 蟹 Pông haē 螃蟹, pâng hēy, a crab. Mô haē 毛蟹, *mô hēy*, a hairy crab. Pông haē hwûn sin kae kap tēw 螃蟹渾身皆甲冑, *pâng hēy chwuiⁿᵍ sin ťhong sē kăh tēw*, the crab, over the whole of his body is defended by armour.

去

Haⁿê 欸 The sound of shortness of breath, or hard breathing; a sigh.

平

Haⁿê 偕 A cry of pain, a sigh.

入

Hăh 唊 Hăh hăh ch'heàou 唊唊笑, *hăh hăh ch'hëò*, to laugh heartily.

入

Hăh 繕 Vulg. há: to tie up anything, to bind anything together. Hăh taè 繕帶, *hăh twà*, to bind on one's girdle.

入

Hak 豿 The grunting of a pig.

入

Ha̍k 學 Vulg. ŏh: to learn, to receive instruction. Ha̍k tông 學堂, a school. Ha̍k ê koé hwùn, naé yéw he̍k 學於古訓.乃有獲, ŏh koè chá ây kà hwùn, naé woō sèy tit tëŏh, by studying the instructions of the ancients we may get something. See the 尙書 Sëōⁿᵍ se.

Ha̍k chek sam taē këūng che 學則三代共之, twā ŏh chek sⁿa tēy kāng chit yëōⁿᵍ, with respect to the name of the great school, then all the three dynasties were the same.

Ha̍k 斛 Yit ha̍k 一斛, chit chëŏh, a measure of ten pecks.

Ha̍k 礐 Sé ha̍k 屎礐, saè ha̍k, a necessary, a privy. Lo̍k ha̍k 落礐, lŏh ha̍k, to go to stool.

上平

Ham 蚶 A cockle.

Ham 邯 Ham tan 邯鄲, the name of a place.

Ham 憨 Stupid, foolish.

Ham 崰 A great valley; a wide ravine.

Ham 酣 Merry with wine, tipsy. Ham t'hëāng 酣暢, cheerful with wine. Ham ko ê sit 酣歌于室, chëăh chéw kaòu ham, ch'hëōⁿᵍ kwa tē ch'hoò, to be merry with wine, and sing songs in the house. Chéw si̍t pwàn ham 酒食半酣, chéw chëăh kaòu pwⁿà hom, to drink wine till a person is half tipsy. Also written 甘 ham.

上聲

Hám 喊 To call out aloud, to bawl with a lond voice. Hám seng jê lûy 喊聲如雷, seⁿa, ch'hin chëōⁿᵍ lûy, a shout like thunder.

Hám 撼 To move, to agitate. Hám t'haè san ē, hám ga̍k kay kwun lân 撼泰山易撼岳家軍難, hám tāng t'haè swⁿa k'hwaè hám tāng ga̍k kay ây kwun ŏh, to move the great mountain would be easy, but to move the army of the Ga̍k family is dificult. See the history of the 宋 sòng dynasty.

Hám 噞 The noise of a multitude eating and drinking. To eat much, to stuff.

Hám 闞 The clamour of one angry; to be angry.

Hám 醓 The gravy of meat. Hám haé é chëen 醢醓以薦, băh chëep băh chëōⁿᵍ ê laê haòu, to take the gravy of meat and minced meat with its liquor, in order to sacrifice. See the 大雅 Taē gnáy.

Hám 噉 To eat. Hám si̍t 噉食, hám chëăh, to eat and devour.

Hám 橄 Hám lám 橄欖, kán ná, an olive.

Hám 饕 To eat without appetite.

去聲

Hàm 譀 To call in anger.

Hám 儑 High and hazardous.

Hàm 膁 A dropsical swelling of the lower extremities. Këak hàm 脚膁 k'ha hàm, a swelling of the legs.

Hàm 賗 Covetous, greedy of gain.

平

Hâm 含 To contain, to include, to inclose, to hold in the mouth. Paou hâm chaē löēy 包含在內, *paou hâm chaē laē*, included within any thing.

Hâm noē 含怒, *hâm sēw k'hè*, to harbour resentment.

Hâm eng choé hwa 含英組華, *chēăh eng ch'hèng hwa*, to eat flowers and wear blossoms; applied figuratively to learning and literary pursuits.

Hâm 咸 All, every one, the whole; a surname. Sè chek hâm he 庶績咸熙, *e ây kong lô chò paô sē kwuiⁿᵍ*, their merits were altogether illustrious. See 尙書 Sëāng se.

Hâm 誠 United, harmonious. Hâm hô bān bin 諴和萬民, *hâm hô chēⁿâ bān ây pāyh saiⁿᵍ*, united harmony prevailing among myriads of people. See the 尙書 *Sëōⁿᵍ se.*

Hám 鹹 Vulg. *kēēm*: saltish, briny. Hâm súy 鹹水, *kēēm chúy*, salt water.

Hâm 函 To include, to contain; also armour and an armourer. Hâm yûng 函容, to include, to contain within itself.

Hâm jîn wûy k'hëúng sëang jin 函人惟恐傷人, *chò 'chēèn lâh ây lâng wûy kēⁿa sëang tëōh lâng*, an armourer's only fear is lest people should be wounded; (which induces him to make his armour strong and therefore he is better than an arrow maker whose only anxiety is to make his arrows sharp, that they may wound people). See the 上孟 Sëāng bēng. Also written 凾 hâm.

Hâm 涵 To moisten, to soak, as water when plentifully collected together. Hák chëá tòng yew yêw hâm ēng, put k'hó láp téng jê chin 學者當優游涵泳不可躐等而進, *'hak ây lâng tëōh yew yew hâm ēng ūᵐ t'hang láp têng jê chin*, the learner should follow out his subject and get his mind imbued with it, without jumping over the forms and advancing irregularly. Also writtin 涵 hâm.

Hâm 鋡 Armour: the same as 函 hâm.

Hâm 啣 To hold anything in the mouth and chew it.

Hâm 蜬 An insect that devours melons, or feeds on the mulberry.

Hâm 銜 To hold in the mouth. Hⁿó k'hoé hâm 好口銜, *hó k'haôu hâm*, a good appetite. Kwan hâm 官銜, *kwⁿa hâm*, a degree in office.

Má k'hè kim, jin hâm höēy 馬去金人銜枚, *bēy k'hè kim, lâng hâm bōēy*, the horses were deprived of their metal ornaments and the men were ordered to hold the wooden gag in their mouths (in order to proceed without noise). See the 三國 Sam kok.

Hâm 㖤 Hām hoê 㖤㗅, to talk incoherently; also to be enraged.

Hâm 椷 A box, a casket; some say, a cup.

Hâm 𦛜 The mouth not opened.

Hâm 菡 A flower about to bud, and not yet budded.

去

Hām 憾 Displeased, to be angry. Hām hwūn 憾恨, to be displeased, to be angry. Choó loē wat, gwān ke má, e k'heng kêw, é pêng yéw kēūng, pē che jê boô hām 子路曰.願車馬.衣輕裘.與朋友共.敝之而無憾 *choó loē kóng, gwān būĕyh ch'hea bêy, yin chêō^{ng}, k'hin kêw, kap pêng yéw kāng, pē p'hwà, jê bô hām hwân*, Choó-loē said, I wish to have carriage, horses clothes and light fur-dresses, and enjoy them in common with my friends, when if they are broken and torn I shall not be displeased. See 上論 Sēang lūn.

Hām 陷 Vulg. *lăp, lŏh k'hè:* to fall in, to sink down, to involve, to entrap. Ham chēng 陷阱, *hām k'hai^{ng}*, a trap, a pit fall.

Hām ê choēy 陷於罪, to involve in crime.

Hām [月+監] The mince meat of a pie, or tart.

Hām 銜 Hām sēēn 銜擅, an implement used on board of ship.

上

Han 頇 Bwân han 顢頇, a large face.

去

Hán 僩 Stern, dignified, severe.

Hán 瞯 To look at, to spy, to see. Tē choó wat, ông soó jîn hán hoo choó 儲子曰王使人瞯夫子, *tē-choó kóng, ông saé lâng lué k'hw^{n}à hoo choó*, Tē-choó said, the king has sent some one to look at you, Sir! See the 下孟 Hāy bēng.

Hán 覵 The same as the above. Sêng hán 成覵, a man's name.

Hán 罕 Few, seldom, scarce, rare; also a rabbit net. Choó hán gân lē 子罕言利, *hoo choó hán tit kóng lē*, Confucius seldom spoke of gain.

Hán 悍 Brave, courageous, bold, violent. Chîn sēuk kēâng hán, lòk ê chēēn toè 秦俗強悍.樂於戰鬬, *chîn ây hong sēuk k'hăh kēâng hán, kūēy è sēo p'hăh*, the manners of the Chîn country are violent and bold, and they take pleasure in fighting.

Hán 鼾 Vulg. *hw^{n}ā bīn:* to snore in sleep.

去

Hàn 漢 The milky way. Hàn teâou 漢朝, the Hàn dynasty. Hàn jîn 漢人, a man of Hàn, a Chinese, in distinction from a Tartar, who is called bwân jîn 滿人, a man of Man-chow Tartary.

H^{n}ó hàn 好漢, *hó hàn*, a good son of Hàn, a brave fellow.

Kēng hàn 硬漢, *gnāy hàn*, a sturdy fellow.

Hàn [亻+𦰩] A surname.

Hàn 暵 Dry, dried at the fire or in the sun. Hàn kē kan ê 暵其乾矣, *hàn, e kaoù ta*, expose it till it is dry.

平

Hân 閒 Vulg. *êng:* leisure, ease, freedom from employment. Séâou jîn hân ke, wûy put sēēn 小人閒居爲不善, *sēâou jîn êng k'hēā, bô būēyh chò hó*, the worthless man, when dwelling at his ease, will not practice that which is good. See the 大學 Taē hăk.

Kok kay hân hāy 國家閒暇, a country at leisure.

Hân 嫺 Still, quiet, retired; also to study, to learn, to practice. Hoē hwuy yéw yew hân cheng chēng 后妃有幽嫺貞靜, *hoē hwuy woō yew hân cheng chēng*, the Empress Hwuy, (the wife Bûn-ông) was retired and still, chaste and tranquil.

K'hwut gwân hân ê soô lēng 屈原嫺于辭令, *k'hwut gwân hân sip ê kong wā*, K'hwut-gwân was practiced in rhetoric.

Hân 鷳 A white sort of bird, in shape like a wild fowl, with a long tail.

Hân 閑 To hinder, to obstruct; a boundary, a limit. Taē tek put jê hân, seáou tek ch'hut jip k'hó yēá 大德不踰閑.小德出入可也, *twā tek hēng bô kōèy hwⁿā, sèy tek ch'hut jip ēy chò tit*, with respect to the great points of virtue, we must not overstep the boundaries, but in minor points, we may go in and out at pleasure. See the 下論 Hāy lūn.

Hân 寒 Vulg. *kwⁿā:* cold, chilly, frigid. Hân jëet 寒熱, *kwⁿā jwăh*, cold and hot, a fever and ague. Sëang hân 傷寒, a cold, to take cold. Hân kay 寒家, a cold family,—a polite expression, when speaking of one's own family.

Jı̆t gwat wun hēng yit hân yit sé 日月運行.一寒一暑, *jı̆t göĕyh wun kēⁿá chı̆t āy kwⁿá chı̆t āy jwăh*, the sun and moon pursue their revolving motion, and thus produce a season of heat, and a season of cold. See the 易繫詞 Ēk hēy soô.

Hân yēā k'hek laê, tây tông chëw 寒夜客來.茶當酒, *kwⁿā maiⁿᵍ lâng k'hăyh laê tēŏh tây tông chëw*, on a cold night when a guest arrives, tea must be substituted for wine.

Hân 韓 The low wall round the top of a wall: also, the name of a country, and a surname. Hân-bûn-kong 韓文公, a famous literary character.

丟

Hān 旱 Vulg. *wⁿā:* drought, dearth, want of rain. Jê taē hān che bōng sê é 如大旱之望時雨, *ch'hin chëōⁿᵍ twā wⁿā ây bāng sê hoē*, just as a great drought expects the timely rain.

Hān kè t'haè sīm 旱既太甚, *wⁿā kaôu t'haè sīm*, the drought has become excessive in the extreme. See the 大雅 Taē gnáy.

Hān 汗 Vulg. *kwⁿā:* sweat, perspiration. Lêw hān 流汗, *laôu kwⁿā*, to perspire. Hwuy hān sêng é 揮汗成雨, *ch'hut kwⁿā chëⁿá hoē*, the perspiration started out like rain. See the 史記 Soó kè.

Hān 旰 The evening, the close of the day. Jı̆t hān t'hëen choó bōng sı̆t 日旰天子忘食, *jı̆t kaôu àm hōng tèy bēy kè tit chëăh*, even till the close of the day the Emperor forgot his food.

Hān 捍 To shield, to guard, to ward off a blow. Also written 仠 hān, and 扞 hān. Choó tēy che wŏēy hoō heng, jê séw chëuk che hān t'hoê bok 子弟之衞父兄.如手足之捍頭目, *haôu saiⁿᵍ sëò tē āy hoo wŏēy pāy hēⁿa, ch'hin chëōⁿᵍ ch'hëw k'ha āy hān t'hâou bak*, sons and nephews should protect their parents and elders, as the hands and feet, guard the eyes and head.

Hān 閈 A village gate; also, a wall.

Hān 銲 Armour for defending the arms; a gauntlet. Sê këung t'hwat hān 弛弓脫銲, *pàng k'hwⁿa kēung t'hooiⁿᵍ hān*, to unstring the bow, and take off the gauntlet.

Hān 骭 The bones of the legs, the shin bone. Twán poè tan e, sek chè hān 短布單衣.適至骭, *tèy poè twⁿa sⁿa, chè kaôu k'ha kwut*, a short cloth and a single dress, reaching only to the shin bone.

Hān 皯 A black colour of the face.

Hān 瀚 The northern sea, the great desert of Tartary. Teng lîm hān haé 登臨瀚海, *pāyh chëōⁿᵍ pak haé*, to ascend to the northern sea.

Hān 翰 The feathers of a bird; to guard, to protect, in which sense it is employed only in books. Hān lim yēēn 翰林院, *hān lim eēng*, the imperial college, or literary institute, in Peking. Hān yim 翰音, a fowl.

Hān 晘 Hān sùy 晘睡, to sleep.

Hān 澣 Water flowing swiftly; also dry.

平 Hang 烘 Read hong: to dry anything at the fire. Hong lô 烘爐, *hang lô*, a furnace, a fire-place, a portable stove. Gông hong ê sim 卬烘于煁, *gwá hang tē hōèy*, I warmed myself at the fire. See the 小雅 Seáou gnáy.

Hang 魧 Read hông: the skate. Hông gê 魧魚, *hang hê*, the skate fish.

Hang 峐 Read hong: the name of a hill, now belonging to Cochinchina.

去 Hàng 胮 To swell; a swelling.

平 Hâng 杭 Hâng-chew 杭州, the name of the capital district, of the province of Chēēt-kang.

Hâng 降 To submit, to surrender, to come over to the opposite party. Tëang-ek-tek k'hìm Gëëm-gân, t'hèy che wat, jé k'héng hâng hoê? Gëëm-gan wat, gnó chew yéw twān t'hoê cheàng kwun, boô hâng cheàng kwun 張翼德擒嚴顏.叱之曰.汝肯降乎.嚴顏曰.我州有斷頭將軍.無降將軍, *Tēong-ek-tek lëäh Gëëm-gân, t'hèy e kóng, lê k'hêng hâng yëá bô? Gëëm-gân kóng, gwán ây chew woō tooing t'hâou chëàng kwun, bô hâng ây chëàng kwun*, Tëong-ek-tek seized Gëëm-gan, and roared at him, saying, will you surrender? when Gëëm-gân replied, in our country we have "lose-head" generals, but no "surrender" generals.

Hâng 桁 An instrument of punishment.

Hâng 㤚 Yùng hâng 㒚㤚, to appear openly, not to lie in ambush.

Hâng 行 A row, a rank. Hâng lëët 行列, arranged in a row. Hâng gnó 行伍, rank and file. Hâng soō 行肆, a warehouse, a store. Sip sam hâng 十三行, *châp sna hâng*, the thirteen factories or foreign hongs, at Canton.

Hâng 㳴 A fence in the water, made of stones or bamboos, in order to catch fish.

去 Hāng 項 The back part of the neck; also, great; and a surname. Ch'hoé pà ông Hāng-é 楚霸王項羽, Hāng-é was the despotic king of the Ch'hoé country,—very famous in Chinese story.

Hāng 巷 A lane, a narrow street in a city, an alley. Yit tan soō, yit p'hëāou yím, chaē loé hāng 一簞食.一瓢飲.在陋巷, *chit nâ â pooing, chit pôo â k'hak ây lim, twā tē loē hāng*, with only a basket of rice, and a calabash full of drink, to dwell in a narrow lane. See the 上論 Sëāng lún.

Hāng 鬨 The noise of fighting, and wrangling; to contend. Choe é Loé hāng 鄒與魯鬨, *Chey kok kap Loē kok sëo p'hàh*, the Chey country contended with the Loé country. See the 上孟 Sëāng bēng.

Hāng 行 Valiant and bold. Choó-loē hāng hāng jê yëá 子路行行如也, *Choó-loē kong këāng āy yëong*, Choó-loē appeared valiant and bold. See the 下論 Hāy lūn.

Hāng 衖 A road in a village.

Hāng 鍂 An earthen vessel, with a long neck, in which records or money may be inserted; it being easy to put things in, but difficult to get them out.

上

Haou 僥 Haou laou 僥佬, great, large.

Haou 㾁 A sore throat; the breath unsettled, and a palpitation of the heart.

Haou 寥 Lofty. Yew kok hat é haou lēāou 幽谷豁以寥寥, àm k'ha^{ing} hat è haou lēāou, the dark vallies became suddenly elevated to a lofty height.

Haou 虓 An enraged tiger. Hám jê haou hoé 闞如虓虎, kēò twā sē^{n}a, ch'hin chēō^{ng} sēw k'hè ây hoé, to roar out aloud, like an enraged tiger. See the 太雅 Taē gnáy.

Haou 哮 The noise of a frightened pig. Haou hek 哮赫, greatly enraged.

Haou 烋 To boast one's-self strong and firm. Jé paou haou ê tēung kok 女包烋于中國, you alone are boasting of your strength in the middle country. See the 太雅 Taē gnáy.

Haou 嘐 To boast, to brag. Kē chè haou haou jēēn wat, koé che jin, koé che jin 其志嘐嘐然曰古之人古之人, e ây sim chè ka tē choō k'hwa, kóng, koé chá ây lâng, koé chá ây lâng, their dispositions are only bent on boasting, saying, we are as good as the ancients, as good as the ancients. See the 下孟 Hāy bēng.

去

Haóu 吼 Read hoé: to roar, to bellow, to make a loud noise. Soo choó pek sèw che ông, wūy sēāou t'hēūng hoé, chek wūy chēūng ch'heàou 獅子百獸之王爲小虫吼則爲衆笑, sae á chò chē^{n}á păyh sèw ây ông, yin wūy sèy t'hâng à haóu, chek hoē chēàng lâng ch'hèò, when the lion, which is the king of beasts, roars on account of a small insect, he becomes the laughing stock of all.

Haóu 犼 An animal found in the north, which is in shape like a dog, and devours people.

去

Haòu 孝 Filial piety; to be filial. Yéw haòu 有孝, woō haòu, to possess filial piety.

Sēēn soō hoō boé wat haòu 善事父母曰孝, gaôu hok saē pāy boé kóng haòu, to serve one's parents well is called filial piety.

Tēy choó jip chek haòu, ch'hut chek tēy, 弟子入則孝出則悌, sēó tē haòu sai^{ng} jip tēōk woō haòu, ch'hut tēóh gaôu chò sēó tē young people at home should be filial, and abroad fraternal. See the 上論 Sēang lūn.

平

Haôu 嫯 Alluring, engaging, pretty.

上

Haōu 傚 To imitate; a pattern, an example. Haōu bwat 傚法, to follow a rule. Kwun choó sē chek sē haōu 君子是則是傚, the good man is a rule and a pattern. See the 少雅 Seáou gnáy. Also written 俲 haōu.

Haōu 恔 Pleased, delighted, pleasant, happy. Ê ê sim tok boō hāou hoē 於予心獨無恔乎, tē gwá ây sim kw^{n}a, k'ham tok bô k'hw^{n}a uāh hoē, is it my mind alone, that is destitute of delight? See 上孟 Sēāng bēng.

Haōu **候** Read hoē: to wait for, to wait upon, to enquire. Téng hāou 等候, to wait, to stay. Būn hāou 問候, to make enquiries after a person's welfare. Soō hoē ê kong k'heng che bûn 伺候於公卿之門, *soō haōu tē kong k'heng ây mooⁿᵍ*, to wait at the gates of nobles and great men.

Haōu **校** A school, an academy, a college. Haōu wûy 校尉, the name of a military office, in ancient times. Sëet wûy sëâng sē hak haōu é kaòu che 設爲庠序學校以教之, *sëet chò sëâng sē hak haōu é kà e*, they then appointed the minor schools and larger colleges, for the instruction of the people). See 孟子 Bēng choó.

Haōu **効** Haōu gēēm 効驗, the fulfilment or accomplishment of anything. Kong haōu 功効, the meritorious results of endeavors. Sëen kê soō che séy lân, jê hoē kê haōu che séy tek 先其事之所難而後其効之所得, *taē seng chò e ây soō ây sèy ŏh, jê aùy āou k'hwⁿà e ây haōu gēēm ây sèy tit tëŏh*, first attend to the difficult part of a business, and afterwards look for the results that are to be obtained from it.

Haōu **斅** To instruct, to teach.

Haōu **效** To imitate; meritorious result; accomplishment. Tuy soō kê kong haōu 追思其功效, *tuy sëōⁿᵍ e ây kong haōu*, to meditate on the meritorious results of one's endeavours.

Haōu **鱟** A curious shell fish, found in the sea. Haōu hëā, a scoop made of the shell of the same.

Hap **呷** Hông hap 喤呷, the noise of a multitude.

Hap **合** To unite, to join, to meet together, to agree. Sëang hap 相合, *sëo hap*, joined together. Hap kae 合該, suitable, agreable to what is right. Hap sim këet lek 合心竭力, to unite all hearts and exhaust all energies. Ch'hey choó hô hap 妻子和合, *boé këⁿá hô hap*, wife and children harmonious and united. See the 小雅 Seaóu gnáy.

Hat **曷** Why, how. Hat che yūng 曷之用, *woō sⁿa mëeⁿh yūng*, of what use was it? See the 易經 Yëăh keng.

Hat **喝** Vulg. *hwăh*: to speak loud and angrily. Tōng gê he hat 恫疑虛喝, when alarmed and suspicious, to bawl out in vain.

Hat **褐** Hairy cloth, coarse clothing, sackcloth of hair. Kae ê hat, k'hwún kè, chit sek, é wûy sit 皆衣褐捆屨織席以爲食, *chò poē ch'hèng mō poè, p'hăh, ëy chit ch'hëŏh ê chò chëăh*, they all of them wore hairy sackcloth, and made straw shoes and mats in order to get a livelihood. See the 上孟 Sëāng bēng.

Hat **鶡** The name of a bird, like a wild fowl.

Hat **舝** The iron at the head of an axletree.

Hat **轄** The rumbling of a carriage. T'hêy hat 提轄, to regulate;—an office in the Sōng dynasty.

Hat **瞎** Blind of one eye; blind, not able to see. Goê bûn hat jê yit lūy, sin hoē 吾聞瞎兒一淚信乎, *gwá woō t'hëⁿa ch'haiⁿᵍ maiⁿᵍ lâng laōu chit bak saé, k'ham woō yëⁿá hoē*, I have heard that blind people shed tears from only one eye; is it true?

Hat 豁 To understand ... perceive, to unr ... lek che kéw, jê yit tân hat jëen, kwàn t'hong yëen 至於用力之久.而一旦豁然貫通焉, *chê kaôu yūng lat ây koó, jê chit mai chāe bêng jëên kwàn t'hong e*, when a man exerts his strength for a long time, he one day or another comprehends the subject, and thoroughly understands it. See the 大學 Taē hak.

Hat 𩜱 A prisoner suddenly making his escape.

Hat 偦 Bit hat 傛偦, firm, strong, robust; not fearful.

Hat 黠 Cunning, artful, clever. Sëuk ch'he sëuk hat 孰癡孰黠, *chê chūy á gaê, chê chūy á chêng sìn*, who is stupid, and who is clever?

灭

Hat 觳 Hat sok 觳觫, a frightened, terrified appearance. Ong wat, goê put jîm kê hat sok 王曰吾不忍其觳觫, *ông kóng, gwá bēy lán e ây kēⁿa hēⁿá*, the king said, I cannot bear to see the fear and trepidation (of the animal). See the 上孟 Sëāng bēng.

奉

Hay 颬 The appearance of wind; to open the mouth and blow out the breath.

Hay 痚 Read haou: a sore throat. Haôu sok 痚瘶 *Hay sâou.*

Hay 咳 The noise of coughing: an infant's laugh. Put kám wöëy è tè hay 不敢噦噫嚔咳, *ūᵐ kⁿá wöèy è tè hay*, not daring to breathe hard, sneeze, or cough. See the 禮內則 Léy löëy chek.

3 E

平

Hây 瑕 A flaw or red spot in a ... ki ... lek hây 瑾瑜匿瑕, *bê gëuk k'hèⁿᵍ hây*, the most precious gem has its flaws. See the 左傳 Chó twān.

Hây 蝦 Hây boē 蝦蟇, a toad. Wâ hây boē toè 鼃蝦蟆鬬, *kap á cheōⁿᵍ chê sëo p'hăh*, the toads and tadpoles fought together.

Hây 遐 To ascend; distant, afar off. Teng hây 登遐, the death of an Emperor. Sim hoē aè è, hây put wūy è 心乎愛矣遐不謂矣, *sim kwⁿa kaôu sëöh e, chēw hwuīⁿᵍ, bô kóng*, when the heart loves a person, distance is never thought of. See the 小雅 Sëaôu gnáy.

Hây 假 The same as the above.

Hây 豭 A male pig, a boar.

Hây 鰕 A shrimp, a prawn; the cancer species.

Hây 霞 Fog, mist. Hông hây 紅霞, *âng hây*, a redness in the sky. Lok hây é kee boō chêy hwuy 落霞與孤霧齊飛, *lóh hây kap koe boō chò poōⁿ tit pwuy*, the falling mists and the solitary fogs were flying about together.

Hây 蕸 The leaves of the hoô yūng 芙蓉 plant, used as medicine.

去

Hāy 下 Vulg. ay: below, down; under, underneath; to go down, to descend. Also written 二 Hāy. Sey oe é sëang, boô é soó hāy, sey oe é hay boô é soó sëang 所惡於上.毋以使下.所惡於下毋以事上, *sey wⁿn é lân ay* sè twā, lŏh sá-c hoē sè sèy séy, wăn ê lán ây sè sèy, bŏh hok saē sè twā, that which we dislike in our superiors, we must not manifest to our inferiors, and that which we dislike in our inferiors, we must not serve our superiors with. See the 大學 Taē hak.

Hëung tē ê hwuy, hāy sëang ke yim 雄雉于飛.下上其音, kang ây t'hé key tit pwuy kwăn kāy ay sëⁿa yim, the male of the wild fowl is flying about and its cry is sometimes loud and sometimes low. See the 衛風 Wŏēy hong.

Hāy 夏 The summer season; also great. A surname; and 夏侯, hāy hoê, a double surname. Hwa hāy 華夏, "the flowery summer," and choo hāy 諸夏, "constant summer," are both names for China.

Hāy, sëang chew 夏商周, the names of the three early dynasties.

Hāy sëang lëuk hô tê 夏賞綠荷池, hāy t'heeⁿᵍ k'hè sëōⁿᵍ lëuk lëuk hô lëên hwa ây t'hâm á, in the summer we may admire the ponds of the green water lily.

Hāy 厦 A great house. Taē hāy, hwuy yit bok sëy che 大厦非一木所支, twā ch'hoò ūᵐ sē chit ke ch'hâ sèy ēy ch'hòng, a large house is not to be made with a single stick of timber.

Hāy 暇 Leisure, opportunity. Hân hāy 閒暇, êng êng, at leisure, at ease.

Hāy 係 To connect. Kwan hāy 關係, consequences.

犬 Hăyh 哧 The noise of laughing, the sound of anger.

灭 Hăyh 歇 Read hëet: to stop, to rest. Hëet sūy 歇睡, hăyh k'hwùn, to stop, to take rest; sometimes pronounced hăyⁿh.

Lîm ch'hâm boê chîn, kàn k'hwùy put hëet 林慙無盡.澗愧不歇, ch'hëw nâ ch'hâm sew bēy chīn, swⁿa key sëaou lēy ūᵐ hăyh, the grove is ashamed of not having grown to perfection, and the torrent blushes that it cannot stop. Referring to persons who are ever learning, but never arrive at knowledge.

幸 He 禧 Happiness, good luck, prosperity. Sin he 新禧, the new year. He soō kò sêng 禧事告成, hó soō kò chëⁿâ, to give notice of the accomplishment of anything good.

He 俙 E he 依俙, unsettled, uncertain.

He 僖 Delighted, pleased.

He 嘻 'E he 噫嘻, an exclamation of surprise. He kê sīm yëâ 嘻其甚也, he kaòu hëá sīm, indeed! Is it so excessive!

He 嬉 He bê 嬉戲, to play, to sport, to gambol. K'hóng choó sëàou he hê, sëâng tîn chóe toē 孔子少嬉戲.常陳俎豆, k'hóng choó sèy ây, sê t'hit t'hô, sëâng sëâng pâe tîn choé toē when Confucius was young he used to play at spreading out sacrifices and offerings. See the 史記 Soó kè.

He 熹 To burn, to roast, to toast at the fire; a little light of the sun; also written 熺 he.

He 譆 To cry out when in pain.

He 希 Few; dispersed; to hope, to look forward to. Ké he 幾希, scarce, a little. He put sit è 希不失矣, chëë bô lōng pŏēy, there are few that are not lost.

Soō he hëên, hëên he sêng, sêng he t'hëen 士希賢.賢希聖.聖希天, t'hak ch'hăyh lâng bāng

福建方言字典

ēy gaôu, gâou lâng bāng ēy chò seng jîn, seng jîn bāng ēy ch'hin cheōng t'heeng, the scholar looks forward to become a philosopher, the philosopher looks forward to become a sage, and the sage looks forward to be like Heaven.

He 欷 He he 歔欷, a sigh of sadness; the appearance of fear; to sob.

He 晞 Dry, dried in the sun.

He 稀 Scarce, rare, few.

He 郗 The places between the joints of the limbs. A surname.

He 嘘 Ch'huy he 吹嘘, to breathe; to draw the breath fast, is called 吹 ch'huy; and to do it slowly, is called 嘘 he.

He 巇 Hills standing opposite one another, in a dangerous position are called 嶮巇 heém he.

He 𡾊 Kê he 崎𡾊, a road over the hills; lofty.

He 墟 A great hill; an old city; a market. 'Hoò he 赴墟, to go to market.

He 歔 To laugh together. He he 歔欷, the sound of sobbing when overcome with grief.

He 虛 Empty, vain, hollow, useless. Put sìn jîn heên, chek kok k'hong he 不信仁賢則國空虛, *ūm sìn jîn tek kwà gaôu ây lâng, chek kok k'hang k'hang*, when benevolent and clever men are not confided in, the country will soon become empty and deserted See the 下孟 Hāy bēng.

He 于 An exclamation of surprise and regret; also written 吁 he. He ch'hea 'hoè choe ge 于嗟乎騶虞, *he ch'hea, toe sé choe gê*, alas! alas! it is the benevolent animal (that is shot). See the 召南 Seāou lâm.

He 忓 To be sorrowful; to be grieved.

He 旴 The rising sun.

He 盱 To open the eyes wide, and look as far as possible; to stare.

He 訏 Great; also to boast.

He 羲 Hok he 伏羲, the name of an ancient Emperor, who is said to have flourished about the time of Noah.

He 犧 He seng 犧牲, a sacrificial animal. Boô é kēung he seng yeâ 無以供犧牲, *bô sèy t'hang kēung kip t'hâou saing*, we have nothing wherewith to supply the animals for sacrifice. See the 上孟 Seāng bēng.

He 曦 The light of the sun.

He 熙 Bright, large, extensive, elevated.

He 昫 The sun coming out, and affording a genial warmth.

He 欸 A covetous person, desiring to eat.

He 屎 A groaning from sorrow and pain. Also read sé 屎 excrement.

He 噫 An exclamation of regret. Choó wat, he, toé soe che jîn, hô cheuk swàn yëá 子曰噫斗筲之人何足算也, *koo choó kóng, he, toé soe ây lâng hô cheuk swuing yëá,* Confucius (speaking of the princes of his time) said, alas! men of such contracted views, how can they be sufficient to be reckoned on. See the 下論 Häy lūn.

圭 Hé 喜 To be delighted, to be pleased. Hwan hé 歡喜, *hwna hé,* to be glad. Ké him him jëën, yéw hé sek 衆欣欣然有喜色, *chò poë him jëën wōo hwna hé ây bîn sek,* they were all delighted, and pleasure beamed from their countenances. See 孟子 Bēng choó. Goē bûn che hé, jê put bē 吾聞之喜而不寐, *gwá kaôu t'hëna e hwna hé, jê bēy k'hwùn,* when I heard of it, I was so delighted, that I could not sleep.

Hé 蟢 The name of an insect.

Hé 許 To promise, to engage, to bestow, to assent to, to allow of; also, vulg. *k'hoé:* a surname.

Lē wun noé lē kong, bóng é lé hé lêw kwúy 呂媼怒呂公妄與女許劉季, *lē wun sëw k'hè lē-kong, lam sàm t'hāyh chāou'iá yîn, hoé laôu kwùy,* old mother Lē, was very angry with her husband Lē-kong, for carelessly promising their daughter to Laôu-kwùy in marriage; and Laôu-kwùy afterwards became an Emperor.

Chek ông hé che hoē 則王許之乎, *chek ông lê k'ham böëyh yin e,* would your majesty then allow and assent to it?

Hé 訏 Great.

Hé 栩 The name of a tree.

Hé 詡 Great words; to enlarge.

Hé 煦 Harmonious, gentle; to afford a genial warmth.

Hé 踽 Hé hé 踽踽, to walk alone, to be without intimates.

去 Hè 肺 Vulg. *hwùy:* the lungs. Hé hoó chè gân 肺腑之言, *pak laē ây wā,* anything very secret; very intimate discourse.

Hè 呬 Still, quiet, tranquil.

Hè 愾 Angry; to be displeased with. Choo hoē tek ông sëy hè, jê hëën kê kong 諸侯敵王所愾而獻其功, *choo hoē tùy tek ông ây sëy sëw k'hè, jê hëën e ây kong lô,* the princes opposed those with whom the king Wân, was displeased, and then reported their deeds. See the 左傳 Chó twān.

Hè 咥 To laugh. Heng tëy put te, hè ke ch'hëaôu è 兄弟不知咥其笑矣, *hëna tē âm chae, hè hè, e ây ch'hëô,* his brethren being ignorant of it, how heartily he laughed! See the 衛風 Wöëy hong.

Hè 㤩 To be foolish; some say, to rest, and be still.

Hè 戲 To play, to sport, to gambol. Hè lōng 戲弄, *hè lāng,* to sport with. Chò hè 做戲, to act plays.

Hwân hè boô ek 凡戲無益, all play is unprofitable.

Kwuy bûn che lōëy, hè jê put t'hàn 閨門之內戲而不歎, *kwuy moîng ây laē, gaôu chëën jê bô t'hó k'hwùy,* within the female apartments, we can sport without sighing. See the 禮記 Léy kè.

Hè 覷 To spy, to look at. Pok k'hoè hè pëen 北寇覷邊, *pak hong ày ch'hat tit k'hw^{n}à lán peë^{ng}*, the northern robbers are overlooking our borders.

Hè 酗 Roaring drunk, furiously drunk, to be enraged when in liquor. Hè êng 酗醟, mad drunk; also written 酡 hè and 酗 hè.

Hè 餼 To make a present of food. Soo gê tè yung hè 司儀致饔餼, *soo gê tè sàng yung hè*, the master of the ceremonies presented the food, cooked and prepared. See the 周禮 Chew léy.

Hè 屭 To exert strength; also firm and strong.

Hè 呴 To breathe, to blow on anything, to make it warm.

平

Hê 魚 Read gê, fish. Poē gê 捕魚, *lëàh hê*, to catch fish. Yëen hwûy lèy t'hëen, gê yëak ê yëen 鳶飛戾天.魚躍于淵, *chëáou pwuy kaòu t'hee^{ng}, hê tëŏ tē yëen*, the birds fly up to Heaven, and the fishes sport in the deep.

丟

Hē 耳 Read jé, the ear. Jé k'hóng 耳孔, *hē k'hang*, the hole of the ear. Jé bûn put jê bok këèn 耳聞不如目見, *hē k'hang t'hë^{n}a ä^{m} tat tëŏh bak chew k'hw^{n}à*, hearing with the ear, is not so good as seeing with the eye.

卆

Hëa 鞾 Boots, high leathern shoes; also written 靴 hëa. P'hê hëa 皮鞾, *p'hŏëy hëa*, leathern boots.

Hëa 檝 A spoon, or ladle. Haou hëa 蠔檝, a ladle made of the shell of a fish.

丟

Hëā 瓦 Read wá, a tile. Wá chwan 瓦磚, *hëā chu^{ng}*, tiles and bricks. Hāy k'hwun goê sê chok wá 夏昆吾氏作瓦, *hāy tëăou k'hwun goê sê chò hëā*, K'hwun-goê, of the Hāy dynasty, invented tiles; (B. C. 2100.)

Këet wûy wá sit 桀爲瓦室, *këet chò hëā ch'hoò*, Këet was the first who built tiled houses. (B. C. 1756).

Hëā 蟻 Read gé, an ant a pismire. Ch'hé tō teng yêw, gé kwuy hëen súy 鼠盜燈油蟻窺硯水, *nëaou ch'hè t'haou teng yêw, kaōu hëā k'hw^{n}à heë^{ng} chúy*, the rats steal the oil of the lamp, and the ants peep at the water of the ink stone.

卆

Hë^{n}a 兄 Read heng: an elder brother. Heng têy 兄弟, *hë^{n}a tē*, brethren. E' kê heng che choó ch'hèy che 以其兄之子妻之, *t'hó e ày hë^{n}a ày kë^{n}á, hoē e chò boē*, he took his elder brother's daughter and married her to him. See the 上論 Sëang lûn.

Hë^{n}a 馨 A fragrance that may be perceived afar off; a distant smell. Sé chek hwuy hëang, bêng tek wûy hëang 黍稷非馨.明維德馨, *sè chek u^{m} sē hë^{n}a, bêng tek tok tok hë^{n}a*, corn and grain are not fragrant, resplendent virtue alone is fragrant. See the 尙書 Sëō^{ng} se.

Hë^{n}a 癢 Read hëang, a disease of the nose.

去

Hë^{n}à 向 Read hëàng, to open out, to go to a distance from, to give a wide birth. Hëàng k'hao 向開, *hë^{n}à k'hwuy*, to desert, to reject.

T'hëen hāy hëàng êng, sè hoē chóo tek che sûn ch'hoô 天下向應.視乎主德之純

3 F

疵, *t'hee^ng ây ây hē^n à èng, k'hw^n à hoē choó sëāng ây tek k'hāh sûn sèng yëá k'hāh p'hwà pa^ng*, the people's deserting from or reverting to a standard, may be observed to be according to the purity or faultiness of the ruling monarch.

平 Hē^n â 惶 Read hông, to fear, to be alarmed, to be in trepidation. Keng hông 驚惶, *kē^n a hē^n â*, to be affrighted, to tremble.

Hông k'hëúng hoô é 惶恐無已, *kē^n a hē^n â bô swâh*, to be incessantly afraid.

去 Hē^n ā 艾 Read gnaē: a kind of grass or moss used in cauterizing; tinder. H^n ó gnaē 火艾, *höéy hē^n ā*, tinder; a vegetable production, used for tinder.

Pé ch'haé gnaē hêy 彼采艾兮, *e k'hè bán hē^n ā*, he is gone to gather tinder. See the 詩王風 Se ông hong.

入 Hëäh 額 Read gek, the forehead. Lëûng gek hoê 龍額侯, *lëûng hëäh hoê*, the dragon forehead lord; a title of rank.

去 Hëäk 謔 Hè hëak 戲謔, to joke, and play tricks with any one. Sëēn hè hëak hêy, put wûy geak hêy 善戲謔兮不爲虐兮, *gâou gâou chëèn ây lâng, ū^m t'hang hoē e chò chin chē^n à*, those who are fond of sport, must not let it come to serious reality. See the 衛風 Wöëy hong.

入 Hëak 仢 Hëak yëak 仢約 a falling star.

平 Hëang 香 Vulg. *p'hang*: fragrant, scented, aromatic; vulg. *hëo^ng*, incense. Chè tē hêng hëang, kám ē sîn bêng, 至治馨香,感於神明, *chè tē p'hang p'hang, kâm tông sîn bêng*, a well arranged government is so fragrant that it even influences the gods in its favour. See the 尙書 Sëō^ng se.

Seaou hëang tëém chëuk 燒香點燭, *sëo hëo^ng tëém chek*, to burn incense and light candles (in worship).

Sëā hëang 麝香 *sëā hëo^ng*, musk. Teng hëng 丁香 *teng hëo^ng*, cloves.

Hëang 鄉 Heang lé 鄉里 *hëo^ng lé*, a village, a country place. Hëang tông bok jé ch'hé, 鄉黨莫如齒, *hëo^ng lé bô ch'hin chëō^ng woō höëy*, in the villages nothing is so much respected as age. See the 上孟 Sëäng bëng.

Hëang jîn yim chéw, tëäng chëá ch'hut, soo ch'hut è 鄉人飲酒.杖者出斯出矣, *hëo^ng lé ây lâng tit lim chéw, kaôu këāh kwäē ây lâng ch'hut, lân ch'hëá ëy ch'hut*, when drinking wine among villagers, upon seeing the old people walking with sticks, go out, then we may also depart. See the 上論 Sëäng lûn.

Hëang 膷 Fine fat cattle; the fat of fed beasts; fat; suet.

Hëang 瘖 Vulg. *hē^n a*: a disease of the nose; foul breath.

Hëang 享 Haōu hëang 孝享, materials used in a sacrifice; to offer a sacrifice.

声 Hëang 響 To sound, to resound, to echo. Ch'hëûng hëáng 銃響, *ch'hèng tân*, the cannon's roar. Lûy hëáng 雷響, *lûy tân*, the thunder rolls.

Hëáng che hoô seng, jê éng che tē hêng 響之附聲,如影之著形, *tân ay hoō së^n a, ch'hin chëō^ng yē^n á ây tē bêng hêng*, the echo depends on the sound, as the shadow displays the substance.

福建方言字典

Hëàng 饗 To drink wine. Yit tëaou hëàng che 一朝饗之, *chit ây mäyⁿh chaê cheăh e*, to drink it out in one morning. See the 小雅 Sëaóu gnây.

Hëáng 享 To enjoy, to receive, to sacrifice; to feast. Hëáng hok 享福, to enjoy happiness.

Soó che choó chěy, pek sin hëáng che 使之主祭,百神享之, *saĕ ĕ choó chěy soō pāyh sín chëw hëáng e*, if you set him to preside, at a sacrifice, all the gods will enjoy it. See 孟子 Bēng choó.

去

Hëàng 向 Vulg. *hèⁿᵍ*; towards, opposite; aforetime. Hëàng laê 向來, hitherto; a surname.

Sey hëàng soō chîn 西向事秦, *hèⁿᵍ sae, hok saē chîn*, to go towards the west and serve the Chin country. See the 戰國策 Chëèn kok ch'hek.

Hëàng 嚮 The same as the preceding.

Hëàng 鄉 Formerly, aforetime, some time ago, just now. The same as 向 hëàng. Hëàng yëñ, goé hëèn ê hoo choó jê bûn tè 鄉也,吾見於夫子而問知, *pê tong sê gwá keèⁿᵍ hoo choó, jê mooiⁿᵍ tè ây soō*, some time ago, I waited upon Confucius, and enquired respecting knowledge. See the 下論 Hāy lūn.

Hëàng 曏 Past time, not long ago, the period of youth; also, clear.

Hëàng 亯 To offer, to offer up in sacrifice; to present up to a superior.

Hëàng 餉 To present, to offer up. Taxes. Hëàng kwan 餉官, *heàng kwⁿᵃ*, a taxgatherer. Kò hëàng 過餉, *köèy bây â*, to be subject to duties.

Yéw tông choó ê sé jëuk hëàng 有童子以黍肉餉, *woō sèy kēⁿâ t'hó sǎyh â kwà bǎh laê sàng*, there was a young lad, who brought millet and flesh to present it. See the 上孟 Sëāng bēng.

丟

Hëàng 痐 Pained and grieved.

幸

Hëaou 僥 Heaou hēng 僥倖 lucky, accidental; by mere chance. Kwun choó ke ē ê soō bēng, seaóu jîn hêng hëëm, ê heaou hēng, 君子居易以俟命,小人行險以徼倖, *kwun choó k'hëă tē ê paiⁿᵍ ây wûy ê tèng haôu mēⁿā, seäóu jîn kēⁿâ te hëëm haē ây sò chaē ê tit tëôh hëaou hēng*, the good man rests contented with plain and easy things, waiting for his fate; but the worthless character ventures into dangerous places, in order to seek his luck. See the 中庸 Tëung yûng.

Hëaou 邀 To invite, to incite, to call, to request; to detain. Ké pöey heäou bêng gwat 舉杯邀明月, *kēăh k'hè chëw pöey, ch'hēⁿâ bêng göëyh*, to elevate the wine cup and toast the clear moon. Soó soè jîn hëaou che ê loē 使數人邀之於路, *saĕ kwǎy lâng hëaou chăh e tē loē*, he sent some people to stop him on the road. See the 上孟 Sëāng bēng.

Hëaou 嗃 Hëaou jëên 嗃然, void and immense, the wide expanse, of boundless space.

Hëaou 徼 To pillage, to borrow other's ideas and make them our own, to practice plagiarism. Oè hëaou ê wûy tè chëa 惡徼以智者爲, *wàn hëaou ây làng këò e ka tē woō tè hwûy*,

I abhor plagiarists calling themselves wise. See 下論 Hāy lūn.

Hëaou 嘵 Afraid, and recounting one's misfortunes.

Hëaou 枵 Empty, emptiness, space. Gwân hëaou 元枵, the name of a star.

Hëaou 鴞 Ch'he hëaou 鴟鴞, a bird of prey, a kite or hawk. Ch'he hëaou ch'he hëaou, kè ch'hé gnó chuó, boô hwûy gnó sit 鴟鴞鴟鴞旣取我子.無毀我室, *ch'he hëaou ch'he hëaou, kè jëên wōo t'hûyh gwá ây kë"à ām t'hang t'hëâh gwá ây ch'hoò*, oh thou ravenous bird! thou ravenous bird! since you have taken my young one, do not destroy my dwelling. See the 邠風 Pin hong.

Hëaou 𠑊 Proud, arrogant.

Hëaou 𠾂 An unlucky bird, with four wings and a dog's tail; also to cut off the head, and expose it in order to terrify others. The same as 梟 hëaou. Hëaou séw 𠾂首, to expose any one's head on a pole.

Hëaou 県 The same as the above. Also written 𠯸 hëaou.

Hëaou 驍 A good horse; also military and courageous. Hëaou má 驍馬, *hëaou báy*, a good horse.

Hëaou 憿 The same as 儌 hëaou.

Hëaou 㬵 To declare aloud, to vociferate; also contented, self satisfied, well pleased. Jîn te che ëk hëaou hëaou, jîn put te ëk hëaou hëaou 人知之亦県県.人不知亦県県, if people know us, we must be satisfied, and if men do not know us, we must still be content. See the 下孟 Hāy bēng.

Hëaou 嬝 Hëaou nó 嬝娜, waving in the wind; pliant and lissom.

Hëaou 獥 A young wolf.

Hëaou 梟 A fabulous evil bird; an unfilial bird; also to expose any one's head on a pole; courageous. Hëaou séw sè chëùng 梟首示衆, *hëaou t'haôu kak, hoē chëùng lâng k'hw"à*, to expose the head on a pole, in the sight of every body.

声

Hëáou 曉 To understand; to perceive clearly, to comprehend, to know; bright, clear. Gnó put hëáou tek 我不曉得, *gwá bēy heáou tit*, I cannot understand it. Hëáou gwat chëàou ko loê 曉月照高樓, *bêng göëyh chëò kwân ây laôu*, the clear moon illumines the high gallery. Bêng hëáou 明曉; to understand clearly; also tomorrow morning.

Hëáou 嫐 Indecent, abandoned, whorish.

去

Heĕh 哯 Heĕh heĕh ch'hëaôu 哯哯笑, *heĕh heĕh ch'hëò*, to laugh heartily.

平

Hëem 杴 A kind of spade.

Hëem 忺 That which the mind approves of and delights in, to desire.

Hëem 甉 Sweet, both in taste and smell.

Hëem ⿰木芡 The grain hurt by too much manure.

Hëem 鍁 A shovel. Hⁿó hëem 火鍁, *höëy hëem*, a fire-shovel.

声

Hëém 險 Hazardous, dangerous, impenetrable. Hëém haē 險害, dangerous. Ông kong sëet hëém, é séw kê kok 王公設險以守其國, *ông kong sëet hëèm haē ây wūy, é chéw e ây kok*, the kings and rulers established dangerous passes, in order the better to defend their country. See the 易經 *Yëàh keng*.

Hëém 獫 A long nosed dog.

Hëém 玁 Hëém wún 玁狁, another name for the northern Tartars.

去

Hëèm ⿺走劦 To run away, to drive anything away.

Hëèm 喊 Read hám: to bawl. Hat hám 喝喊, *hwăh hëèm*, to bawl out aloud. Hám gnâw 喊牛, *hëèm: goô*, to drive cattle.

Hëêm 嫌 To have doubts of; to dislike, to disapprove, to be disgusted with. Léy chëá, séy é tēng ch'hin soe, kwat hëêm gê yëá 禮者所以定親踈.决嫌疑也, *lëy soè sē sëy è tëⁿā tëöh ch'hin sey, kwat tooiⁿᵍ hëêm gê*, proper ceremonies are the means by which we fix the distinctions between near and distant relatives, and decide on what is doubtful and disgusting. See the 曲禮 K'hëuk léy.

Hëēm ⿱殳女 Beautiful, fine.

丟

Hëen 軒 A carriage used by a great officer: a carriage box, a curtain of a carriage. To lift up the low roof of a house, in order to admit light.
Se hëen 書軒, a school, a place of learning.
Hëen wân 軒轅, a double surname.

Hëen 掀 To lift up with the hands; to raise up.

Hëen 仚 To elevate gently; to raise up lightly. Nëáou hëen gê yëàk 鳥仚魚躍, *chëáou hëen k'hé, hê tit tëó*, the birds gently rise, and the fishes leap.

Hëen 蓒 A kind of vegetable, that grows in the water.

声

Hëén. 顯 To display, to manifest, to shew clearly. Hëén tè 顯著, to illustrate.
Hëén choé êng chong 顯祖榮宗, to set forth one's ancestors, and glorify one's forefathers.
P'he hëén chae bûn ông boê, p'he sîn chae boó ông lëet 丕顯哉文王謨.丕承哉武王烈, *twā t'hang hëèn bêng chae bûn ông ây kwuy boê, twā ēy sëo swà chae boó ông ây cheng lëet*, how greatly illustrious were the plans of Bûn-ông, and how eminently were they carried on by the zeal of Boó-ông! See the 尙書 *Sëōⁿᵍ se*.

Hëén 咺 To lament incessantly; also to proclaim.

Hëén 晛 To look at anything distinctly; to see clearly: to stare.

Hëén 蜆 A small kind of cockle. Lêw chin hⁿò tám hëén 劉臻好啖蜆, *laôu chin aè chëäh hëèn*, Lêw-chin was fond of cockles.

Hëén 俔 A spy.

Hëén 峴 The name of a hill, in 襄陽, sëang yâng. There was in the 晉 chin dynasty, a man of the name of 羊祜, yâng hoë, who on ascending this hill, and witnessing the picturesque scenery around him, shed tears, saying. Choō yéw é têw, pëēn yéw ch'hoó hëën san 自有宇宙便有此峴山, *choō woō t'heeⁿᵍ tëy, pëēn woō chëy lëy hëén swⁿa*, as long as the universe has stood, this hill has been here; he therefore set up a tablet, which has been called, the Tūy lūy paê 墮淚碑, "shed tear tablet."

Hëén 粯 The coarser parts of grain after it has been pounded into meal.

Hëén 臔 Fat; also an involuntary motion of the muscles.

Hëén 譞 To reprove, to contend with.

去 Hëèn 獻 To offer up, to present, to send in; also wise and clever men. Hëèn sêw kaou ch'hok 獻酬交錯, *hëèn chêw kŏh tap sëo kaou p'hoëy*, to present wine and answer the compliment, in mutual exchange one with another. See the 小雅 Seaôu gnáy. Hëèn chèy 獻祭 to offer up a sacrifice. Bûn hëèn put chëuk koè yëá 文獻不足故也, *ch'hŏyh kwà gaôu lâng bô kaôu äy yëën koè*, it is because the books and clever men of that period were not sufficient. See the 上諭 Sëāng lūn.

Hëèn 巘 The peak of a hill. Sek chek chaē hëèn, hēw kàng chaē gwân 陟則在巘復降在原, *pâyh chëōⁿᵍ k'hè chek tē swⁿa chëem, kŏh lŏh laê, chek tē paiⁿᵍ gwân*, (in our rambles) when we ascend, we get upon the peak of the hill, and when we descend again, we come into the plains. See the 大雅 Taē gnáy.

Hëèn 甗 An iron pan, smoothly finished at the bottom, without the broken knob or protuberance, usually found at the bottom of all cast metal pans. Ké hëèn 紀甗, a valuable pan, formerly sent as a present from one state to another. See the 左傳 Chó twān.

Hëèn 楥 A last for stretching shoes upon; also written 楦 hëèn.

Hëèn 絢 Variegated colours, the ornamental colouring of pictures. Soè ē wûy hëèn hêy 素以爲絢兮, *pâyh lëy ē chò bûn ch'haê*, the white ground is intended for laying the colouring on. See the 上諭 Sëāng lūn.

Hëèn 憲 A rule, a pattern, a magistrate. Hëèn taê 憲臺 an open chair, in which high officers are accustomed to ride. Bûn boô sê hëèn 文武是憲, *bûn ông boô ông sē chò hwat toē*, Bûn-ông and Boô-ông are patterns (for after ages). See the 大雅 Taē gnáy.

Hëèn 讞 To deliberate on doubtful judicial cases.

平 Hëên 伭 Anger, wrath, not to be pacified.

Hëên 玄 Black, with a tinge of red; also deep, abstruse, and distant. Thëên jê tëy hông, 天玄而地黄, *t'heeⁿᵍ oe jé tëy wuíng*, the heavens are black and the earth is yellow. See the 易經 *Yëáh keng.* T'hàm tō hⁿò yëen hëên 探道好淵玄, *t'hàm t'hëⁿa tō lé, sē aè k'hāh ch'him bê*, in fathoming doctrines, we should prefer the deep and abstruse.

Hëên 泫 The name of a river.

Hëên 炫 Bright refulgent, brilliant.

Hëên 弦 Këung hëên 弓弦, the string of a bow. Yéw soo yëw chip hëên, chó chip hoó, jê sëw këung 有司右執弦.左執弣.而授弓, *yëw soo kwⁿa chëⁿà ch'hëw gīm hëên, tó ch'hëw gīm pân chê, jê sëw hoē lán këung*, the proper officer, in his right hand holding the bowstring, and the thimble in his left, delivers us the bow. See the 儀禮 Gê léy.

Hëên 蚿 Má hëen 馬蚿, the name of an insect.

Hëên 舷 Chûn hëên 船舷, the side of a ship or vessel; the bulwarks.

Hëên 眩 The eyes not constantly fixed on one object; the eyes wandering.

Hëên 絃 The string of a musical instrument; a stringed instrument of music. Choó che bóo sêng, bûn hëen ko che seng 子之武城.聞絃歌之聲, *hoo choó kaòu boó sèⁿâ, t'hëⁿa këèng hëên ko ây sëⁿa*, when Confucius arrived at the city of Buó, he heard the sound of a stringed instrument, accompanied with singing. See the 下論 Hā lūn.

Hëên 鉉 The ear of an iron pan, the handle by which to lift it up.

Hëên 衒 To boast of one's self, to vaunt one's own praises. Choō hëên 自衒, to brag. Hëên lé put cheng, hëên soō put sìn 衒女不貞.衒士不信, a bragging woman is never modest, and a boasting scholar is not to be believed.

Hëên 懸 To hang, to suspend. Hëên k'hwà 懸掛, to hang up. Yëw kaé tó hëên 猶解倒懸, *ch'hin chëōng t'haóu tó tëaòu ây lâng*, (it would be a deliverance) like loosing one hanged up by the heels with his head downwards. See the 上孟 Sëāng bēng.

Hëên 縣 To connect, to draw, to lead, to suspend. The same as the above.

Hëên 賢 Vulg. *gaôu*: virtuous and clever, intelligent; skilful. Hëên jîn 賢人, *gâou lâng*, a philosopher. Sèng hëên 聖賢, sages and wise men. Hëên chae hoëy yëá 賢哉回也, *gaôu chae chèy lëy hoëy*, how clever is this Hoëy. See the 論語 Lūn gé. Jīm kwan wûy hëên chaê 任官惟賢才, *jīm kwⁿa tok tok gaôu lâng ây chaê tëâou*, the talents of clever men alone are equal to sustain the weight of office. See the 尙書 Sëōng se.

Hëên 𡄾 Difficult.

Hëên 現 (mark: 丟) To display, to manifest, to appear, to be present. Hëēn kim 現今, the present time. Hëēn chaē 現在, at present.

Hëēn 莧 Hëēn ch'haé 莧菜, *hēng ch'haè*, a kind of vegetable, the amaranthus oleraceus.

Hëēn 見 To appear in the presence of, to wait upon, to have an audience. Cheūng chēā hëēn che 從者見之, *tây ây lâng hoē e keè^ng*, the followers (of Confucius) admitted him into the sage's presence. See the 上論 Sëāng lūn.
Hëēn kē jê choó yëen 見其二子焉, *ch'hwā e nō ây kē^n á hoē e'keè^ng*, he then brought out his two sons, and introduced them to him. See the 下論 Hāy lūn.

Hëēn 硯 Vulg. *heē^ng*: an ink stone, used by the Chinese for rubbing the ink upon. Koé hëēn bē t'hap chē bek to 古硯微凹聚墨多, *koé châ ây heē^ng, sèy sèy ây k'hwut á k'hëŏh bak chēy*, an old ink stone with only a small hollow place in it, collects much ink.

Hëēn 縣 Vulg. kwān: a district, a country, a department. Chîn sé hông pēng t'hëen hāy, hwùy hong këèn, sé ché kwûn hëēn 秦始皇幷天下.廢封建始制郡縣, *chîn sé hông pēng t'hee^ng hāy, hwùy bô hong këèn ây wūy, k'hé t'haôu ch'hòng, kwûn kwān*, the first Emperor of the Chîn dynasty united the Empire under one head, and did away with the independant possessions; from which time departments and districts began to be formed. See the 史記 Soó, kè.

Hëēn 晛 The sun shining out clear; fair weather. 'E swat p'hëaou p'hëaou, këèn hëēn wat sëaou 雨雪瀌瀌見晛曰消, *lŏho sâyh p'hëaou p'hëaou, keè^ng jit ch'hut chēw kông sëaou*, when the snow has fallen and drifted along, on the appearance of the sun it melts.

平

Hee^ng 哼 The sound of groaning; or crying.

Heeng 誒 An exclamation of disapprobation, and abhorrence.

平

Heē^ng 弦 Këung hëēn 弓弦, *këung heè^ng*, a bow-string.

Heē^ng 絃 K'hîm hëēn 琹絃, *k'hîm heē^ng*, the string of a harp or guitar. Sùn chok gnóe hëēn, é ko lâm hong 舜作五絃以歌南風, *sùn chò goē heē^ng ây k'hîm, é ch'hëŏng kwa lâm hong*, Sùn made a five-stringed harp, in order the sing of the southern wind. See the 禮記 Lêy kè.
Hëēn chong 絃粽, *heē^ng chang*, a kind of confectionary.

去

Heē^ng 齂 A whizzing through the nose.

Hee^ng 硯 Read hëēn: an ink-stone. Ché, pit, bek, hëēn, bûn pông soò pó 紙筆墨硯文房四寶, *chwá, pit, bak, heē^ng bûn pâng sè pò*, paper, pencils, ink, and ink stone, are the four precious things of the literary chamber.

入

Hëep 偞 Low, mean; beautiful; also written 偞 hëep.

Hëep 熁 Fire advancing near, and blazing upwards.

Hĕep 磁 Read choô: a magnet. Choô sek 磁石, *hëep chëŏh*, a loadstone. Choô sek yin t'hëet, ê kim put lëēn 磁石引鐵.於今不連, *hëep chëŏh yin t'heĕh, tong kim bô sëo swà*, the loadstone draws the iron, but now they are not near together! Said by choô sit 曹植, when separated from his brethren.

夾

Hëep 俠 Jîm hëep 任俠, to form a party, and collect partizans by favours shewn. Hô hëep 豪俠, undaunted, and disinterested.

Hëep 挾 Hwaê hëep 懷挾, to hold to in one's mind, to adhere to. Hëep tê 挾持, to hold under the arm, to squeeze, to grasp.

Kè hëep soò hoê 旣挾四鏃, *knòu gnâyh sè ây chèè^ng*, having grasped the four arrows. See the 大雅 Taē gnáy.

Put hëep tëáng, put hëep kwùy 不挾長.不挾貴, *ū^m hëep lân ây sè twā, ū^m hëep lân ây hoè kwùy*, not to adhere to one's superiority, nor to stick pertinaciously to one's own nobility. See 孟子 Bēng choò.

Hëep 狹 Vulg. *āyh*: narrow, contracted, not wide. Boô choō kóng é hëep jîn 無自廣以狹人, *bô ka tē k'hwāh twā, é ch'hèng āyh lâng*, do not extend yourself, in order to straighten others. See the 尙書 Sëō^ng se.

Sîn këèn kê séy tê chéá hëep, jê séy yëuk chëá ch'hëa 臣見其所持者狹.而所欲者奢, *gwá k'hw^nā e séy gîm tê ây āyh, jê séy aè böëyh ây ch'hëa*, I perceive that, that which he adheres to is contracted, and that which he desires extravagant.

Hëep 劦 Strong, violent. The same as 力 lëk.

Hëep 恊 Hëep hô 恊和, harmonious, united. Tông yîn hëep keung 同寅恊恭, *tâng chò kw^na hëep hô këung kèng*, to be harmonious and respectful with one's brother officers.

Hëep 協 The same as the above; also written 叶, hëep and 勰 hëep.

Hëep 愶 Fearful, alarmed; to terrify one by violence.

Hëep 脅 The ribs. Chó yëw lëáng hëep 左右兩脅, *tó ch'hëw chë^nà ch'hëw nō ây hëep kwut*, the two rows of ribs, on the right and left.

Tëûng jé kò chô, bûn kê pëën hëep, yëuk kwan kê chōng 重耳過曹.聞其駢脅.欲觀其狀, *tëûng jé köëy chô kok, lâng t'hë^na o'woō sëo swá hëep, chëw böëyh k'hw^nà e ây yëō^ng*, when Tëûng-jé passed through the Chô country they heard that his ribs were connected and wished to look at his appearance. Also written 脇 hëep.

Hëep 洽 United, harmonious; also to soak in, to imbibe, to diffuse. Hëep pé kê lîn 洽比其隣, *sëo hâp e ây kāyh pëāh lâmg*, to be harmonious, with one's neighbours.

Hông yin këep hëep 皇恩浹洽, *hông tèy ây yin këep hëep tē sîm*, to have a sense of the Imperial kindness imbued in the mind.

犬

Hëet 血 Vulg. *höëyh*: blood. Hëet k'hè 血氣, the animal spirits. Hwân yéw hëet k'hè chëá, bok put chun ch'hin 凡有血氣者.莫不尊親, *hwân woō höëyh k'hè ây lâng bô ū^m chun e ây pāy boé*, whoever has blood and spirits, will never neglect to honour his parents. See the 中庸 Tëung yûng.

Sat jîn pëèn yëá, hëet lôw sêng hô 殺人遍野血流成河, *t'haê lâng mw^nā yëá, höëyh laôu chë^nā kâng*, the slaughtered people filled the waste, and the blood flowed like a river.

Hëet 乢 Hëet tok 乢毒, the name of a country.

Hëet 猲 A dog with a short nose.

Hëet 繳 To draw, to pull, to drag; also anything broken asunder.

Hëet 歇 Vulg. *hăyh*, and *hăyⁿh*: to stop, to rest, to cease. Hëet tëèm 歇店, *hăyⁿh tëèm*, an inn, a resting place, Yit sit sëăng chûn, ch'hoó t'hok se che chè, put yûng sëáou hëet 一息尙存.此讀書之志.不容少歇, *chit ây ch'hwán k'hwùy sëăng tē tit, chèy lèy t'hak ch'hăyh ây chè, am yûng sëo k'hwá hăyⁿh*, as long as a breath remains, this design of studying books should not be permitted for a moment to cease. Said by 劉靜修 lêw cheng sew.

Hëet 穴 A cave, a cavern, a den. Hëet k'hong 穴空, *hëet k'hang*, a hole in the earth. Sëăng koé hëet ke, jê yeá ch'hé 上古穴居而野處, *sëăng koē ây lâng, k'hëă tē hëet k'hang, jê twā tē yëá, gwā*, the earlier ancients resided in caves and dwelt in the wilderness.

Hëet 泬 Water issuing out of a cavern, also deflective, partial, erroneous.

Hëet 絜 To measure, to ascertain the size of anything. Hëet ké 絜矩, to measure by a rule.

Hek 赫 Hek hek 赫赫, lofty and illustrious; fully displayed. Bêng bêng chaē sëăng, hek hek chaē hāy 明明在上.赫赫在下, *bêng bêng tē têng bīn, hek hek tē hāy tèy*, bright and clear above, and fully displayed below. See the 大雅 Taē gnáy. Also 赫連, hek lëĕu, a double surname.

Hek 嚇 Vulg. hwăh: to be angry, to be enraged at, to threaten, to bawl out. Ông hek soo noē, wān chêng kē lé 王嚇斯怒爰整其旅, *ông hwăh e ây sëw k'hē, chĕw chèng e ây peng*, the king gave vent to his anger, and immediately drew out his army. See the 小雅 Sëáou gnáy.

Hek 郝 A surname.

Hek 黑 Vulg. oe: black. Hek jîn 黑人, *oe lâng*, a black man. Pok hong sëuk súy, hek sek 北方屬水黑色, *pak heng sëuk chúy, oe ây sek*, the north belongs to the element of water, and claims black for its colour.

Hek 虩 To be afraid, to be alarmed. Lé hoé bó hek hek k'hëúng kē 履虎尾虩虩恐懼, *tăh tëŏh hoó bóey, hek kek kēⁿa hēⁿā*, treading on a tiger's tail, we become alarmed and terrified. See the 易經 Ēk keng.

Hek 或 Or, if, either, perhaps; to deceive, to doubt, to hesitate. Hek chëá 或者, *t'hëem chaé*, perhaps. Hek jîn 或人, a certain person. Hek wat, kwán tëŭng k'hëèm hoē 或曰管仲儉乎, *woō lâng kóng, kwán tëŭng k'hëèm á bô*, a certain person said, is Kwán-tëŭng, parsimonious? See the 上論 Sëăng lūn.

Hek 㽣 Territory a tract of country. The same with 域 hek.

Hek 域 A region, a border. Sey hek ch'hut sêng jîn 西域出聖人, *sae t'heeng ēy ch'hut chit ây sèng jîn*, the western region will produce a sage.

Hek 㖪 The same as the above; a boundary. Boô sey chin hek 無所畛㖪, *bô sèy kaou kaé*, without bounds or limits.

Hek 罭 The ancient form of 域 hek; some say, a net.

Hek 䮚 The whistling of the wind, the sound of wind.

Hek 惑 To be deceived, to be led astray, to be confused, to doubt. Yéw hek 誘惑, to be tempted. Bêy hek 迷惑, to be deceived. Gê hek 疑惑, to doubt, to be suspicious. Hek lwān 惑亂, to be confused.

Tè cheá put, hek 知者不惑, *woō lè sit ây lâng bô hek*, a man of knowledge is not to be deceived. See the 上諭 Sëāng lūn.

Hek 蜮 A short kind of fox.

Hek 緎 The seam of a garment: a row of stitching.

Hek 聝 To cut off the ears of prisoners taken in war. Sêng kong sain lëên, é wûy hoo hek 成公三年以為俘聝, *sêng kong sna seeng, lëăh sêw ây lâng kwăh hē á*, in the third year of Sêng-kong, they took, the prisoners and cut off their ears.

Hek 馘 To decapitate prisoners taken in war.

Hek 閾 The threshold of the door. Lip put teung bûn, hêng put lé hek 立不中門.行不履閾, *k'hëă bô lē moo*ng *tang e*ng, *kē*n*â bô tāh tëŏh moo*ng *têng*, in standing he would not stop in the middle of the door way; and in walking, he would not tread on the threshold. Said of confucius, in the 上論 Sëāng lūn.

Hek 檄 Hek bûn 檄文, a proclamation, a paper announcing anything to the people. Hàn ko choé é é hek tin t'hëen hāy peng 漢高祖以羽檄徵天下兵, *hàn ko choé t'hô chëáou mô ây hek bŭn, tin teaòu t'hee*ng *āy ây peng*, Hàn-ko-choó made use of a proclamation with a feather in it (to denote speed) in order to summon all the soldiers in the Empire.

Hek 棫 The name of a tree.

Hek 核 To take a general survey, to inspect, to examine. Chòng hek bêng sit 綜核名實, *k'hó k'hàm e ây mē*n*â sē*n*a, kap e ây chëak sit*, to examine whether a thing is merely nominal, or real.

Hek 劾 To examine the rights of a judicial case. 'An hek 按劾, to enquire into the merits of a case.
Hek chong 劾狀, an indictment, a brief.

Hek 覈 To examine an affair, in order to know the rights of it. Hô é hek choo 何以覈諸, *an chw*n*â ēy k'hó k'hàm e*, how shall we enquire into the business. Hek sit 覈實, to investigate the truth.

Hek 榝 A club, or pole; an implement used in husbandry.

Hek 獲 To obtain, to get. Hek yin 獲恩, to obtain favour. Hek chöēy ê t'hëen, bôo séy tô yëá 獲罪於天.無所禱也, *hek chöēy ê t'hee*ng *bô sêy ēy kē tó tit*, when one offends against Heaven, there is no pleading for him. See the 上論 Sëāng lūn.
A scolding epithet for a female slave; is 獲 hek.

Hek 覡 A conjurer, a wizard; a witch is called 巫 boô, and a wizard 覡 hek.

Hek 碻 Stony ground; good soil spoiled by the multitude of stones in it.

Hek 齕 To bite, to gnaw; also a man's name.

Hek 㩇 The noise of tearing cloth.

Hek 淢 A city ditch; a moat round the walls of a city.

Hek 蒮 Chông hek 虈蒮, the name of a bushy plant.

夲

Heng 亨 Pervious, thoroughly pervading; a lucky meeting; success.

Heng 兄 Vulg. hēⁿa: an elder brother; a superior, an elder in years. Soò haé che lōey, kae heng tēy yēá 四海之內皆兄弟也, *sè haé ây laē, chò poō sē hēⁿa tē*, all within the four seas are our brethren. Ch'hut chek soō kong k'heng, jip chek soō hoō heng 出則事公卿.入則事父兄, *ch'hut chek hòk saē kong k'heng, jip chek hòk saē pāy hēⁿa*, abroad we must be obedient to officers and nobles, and at home to fathers and elder brethren. See the 上論 Sēāng lūn.

Heng 馨 Vulg. hāⁿa: fragrant, aromatic sending forth a fragrance to a distance. Soo wûy loé sit, wûy goê tek heng 斯爲陋室.惟吾德馨, *chéy lêy sē p'hwà ch'hoò, tok tok gwá ây tek p'hang*, this is indeed a vulgar dwelling, but my virtue is fragrant enough.

Heng 胷 Read hëung: the breast. Hëung tëung chèng, chek boê choó lëáou yëen, hëung tëung put chèng chek boê choó mō yëen 胷中正.則眸子瞭焉.胷中不正.則眸子眊焉, *heng tang e^{ng} chēⁿà chek bak ang á kwuī^{ng}; heng tang e^{ng} ū^m chēⁿà chek bak ang á àm*, when a man's breast is honest and upright, the pupil of his eye will be clear; but if he is not honest at heart, the pupil of his eye will be dim. See the 下孟 Hāy bēng.

𠁥

Héng 悻 To be enraged, to be displeased. Kàn ê kê kwun jê put t'hèng, chek noē héng héng jëën hëèn ê kê bëën 諫於其君而不聽.則怒悻悻然見於其面, *tⁿà e ây jîn kwun, jê ū^m t'hēⁿa chek sëw k'hè héng héng ây yëō^{ng} hëèn tē e ây bīn sek*, when these people reprove their princes and are not listened to, then wrath is strongly depicted in their countenances. See the 上孟 Sëāng bēng.

Héng 緈 Straight.

𡗗

Hèng 啈 The sound of danger; to speak with an angry tone.

Hèng 興 Pleased, delighted, elevated with joy. Tòk yéw ch'heng ch'hew jit, lêng soó ko hèng chīn 獨有清秋日.能使高興盡, *tok wōo ch'heng ch'hew ây jit, ëy saē ko hìn chīn*, there is nothing better than a pure autumn's day, in which we can carry to the utmost our elevated enjoyments.

Hèng 釁 A swelling and pain; an inflammation.

平

Hêng 形 Form, substance, appearance. Hêng t'héy 形體, form and substance. Ch'hoó wûy sêng ê tëung hêng ê göëy 此謂誠於中.形於外, *chéy sē kóng këò chìn chēⁿà tē tàng e^{ng}, chëw hêng hëèn tē gwā bīn*, this is what is called, really existing within, and exhibiting its form without. See the 大學 Taē hak.

Hêng 刑 To punish, to inflict punishment; an example, a pattern, a rule. Hêng hwat 刑罰, punishment. Hêng lëuk 刑戮, capital punishment.
Kwun choó é chëet gëuk tè hêng 君子以折獄致刑, *kwun choó é p'hwⁿà. tùän gëuk än tè. ch'hòng, hêng hwat*, the good man after deciding on criminal cases, inflicts punishment. See the 易經 *Yëäh keng*.
Hêng ke ê boô hêng 刑期於無刑, *hêng hwat lâng, yëá tit kè bäng bô hêng hwat*, by punishing, we still hope to render punishment unnecessary. See the 尙書 *Sëōⁿᵍ se.*
Hêng poē 刑部, the board of punishments.

Hêng 侀 A rule, a pattern; also, to complete.

Hêng 佷 Hêng san 佷山, the name of a district.

Hêng 刲 To punish crime; also a pattern; and, to complete; the same as 刑 hêng.

Hêng 行 Vulg. *këⁿá*: to walk, to go, to travel; to practice, to do. Hêng loē 行路, *këⁿá loē*, to travel. Séy hêng 所行, *séy këⁿá*, actions, conduct.
Choó loē hêng é koè 子路行以告, *choó loē këⁿá k'hè kap é kóng*, Choó-loē went to inform him of it. See the 下論 Hāy lūn.
Yūng che chek hêng 用之則行, *böëyh yūng e chek këⁿá*, if any will employ us, then we go to them. See the 上論 Sëāng lūn.

Hêng 巠 The same as 恒 hêng.

Hêng 型 A mould for casting metal, all moulds made of earth, are called 型 hêng, those of wood are called 模 boē, and those of metal are called 範 hwān. Tëen hêng 典型, an example.

Hêng 硎 A grinding stone. To jīn jëak sin hwat é hêng 刀刃若新發於硎, *to laē ch'hin chëōⁿᵍ sin bwá tē chëöh*, the knife is as sharp as if it had been newly set on the grind-stone.

Hêng 鉶 A pot for soup or broth.

Hêng 衡 Kwân hêng 權衡, scales, steel-yards, a balance; also, even. A surname.
Kwân hêng k'heng tëūng 權衡輕重, *kwán hêng ch'hin k'hin tāng*, the balances shew the lightness and heaviness of things.

Hêng 珩 Gems worn on the back.

Hêng 蘅 A fragrant kind of grass.

Hêng 恆 Constant, perpetual. Hêng sim 恆心, a constant mind. Put hêng kè tek, hek sîn kê sew 不恆其德或承之羞, *nā ūᵐ hêng sëáng e ây tek hêng, hek chëá sîn é ây sëáou léy*, if a man is not constant in his virtue, he may find it succeeded by disgrace.

Hêng 姮 Hêng gô 姮娥, a beautiful lady, supposed to be caught up into the moon.

Hêng 横 Vulg. *hwⁿá*: across, athwart. Ch'hëung hêng 縱横, *ch'hàn hwⁿá*, things laid across at right angles.

Hêng 桁 The cross beam of a house.

Hêng **臟** Cooked meat.

Hêng **雄** Read hëûng: male, the male of birds. Heroic, brave. The appellation of a military officer.

Hêng **還** Read hwân: to pay, to refund, to give back. Hwân chaè 還債, *hêng chēy*, to pay debts. Kim sè put hwân, hoē sè pit hwân 今世不還.後世必還, *kìm sè ū^{m} hêng, aōu sè tëŏh hêng*, if you don't pay your debts in this life, you must pay them in the next.

Hêng **㣙** The appearance of walking.

Hêng **恒** The Moon increasing, and approaching the full, is called hêng. Jê jit che seng, jê gwat che hêng 如日之升如月之恒, *ch'hin chëō^{ng} jit ây k'hè, ch'hin chëō^{ng} göëyh ây twā*, like the rising sun, and the waxing moon. See the 小雅 Seáou gnáy.

Hêng **邢** The name of a country; also a surname.

丟

Hēng **幸** To hope, to expect, gracious, favourable, fortunate, happy. A surname. T'hëen hāy hēng sīm, kok kay hēng sīm 天下幸甚.國家幸甚, *t'hee^{ng} āy yēâ hó kok kay yëâ hó*, the whole Empire would then be happy, and the country fortunate. Put hēng tëung che yit hēng yëá 不幸中之一幸也, *ū^{m} hó tang eng ây chit ây hó*, one lucky circumstance in the midst of misfortune.

Hēng **倖** Heaou hēng 儌倖, lucky, accidental by mere chance. Sëaóu jîn hêng hëém é hëaou hēng 小人行險以儌倖, *seáou jin kë^{n}â hëem haē ây wāy è heaou hēng*, the worthless character ventures into danger, with the hope of accidental advantage. See the 中庸 Tëung yûng.

Hēng **併** To accompany, to go in company with any one. Koé chëá choo hoê ch'hê hoo jîn, chek tông sèng jê jîn hēng che 古者諸侯取夫人.則同姓二人併之, *koè chá ây choo hoè ch'hwā hoo jîn, chek lâng sai^{ng} nō lâng sëo p'hw^{n}ā e*, when the princes among the ancients, went to bring home their newly married ladies, two persons of the same family name accompanied them.

Hēng **㚔** To meet with an early death, is called 不㚔, put hēng, unlucky.

Hēng **杏** An almond-tree. Hēng jîn 杏仁, almonds. Yit che hông hēng ch'hut ch'hëâng laê 一枝紅杏出墻來, *chit ke âng hēng ch'hut ch'hëō^{ng} laê*, a branch of red almond blossoms topping over the wall.

Hēng **行** P'hín hēng 品行, actions, conduct, behaviour. Gân tëung sìn, heng tok kèng, suy bân bek che pang, hêng è 言忠信.行篤敬.雖蠻貊之邦行矣, *kông wā tëûng sìn, sêy kë^{n}â tok kèng, suy jëên bân bek ây só chaē yëá ēy kënâ*, when a man's conversation is faithful and sincere and his actions truly respectful, he may safely travel even to barbarons countries. See the 下論 Hāy lūn.

Hēng **荇** Hēng ch'àe 荇菜, a kind of vegetable, commonly used in cooking.

Hēng **誶** To speak angrily. Hēng tit 誶直, to speak bluntly.

Hēng **莧** Read hëēn: a culinary vegetable. Hëēn ch'haē 莧菜, *hēng ch'haè*, the amaranthus oleraceus, *L.*

上平 Hĕ^{ng} **方** Read hong: a place, a district. Yëak hong 藥方, *yŏh he^{ng}*, a medicament.
Hoō boé chaē, put wán yêw, yêw pit yéw hong 父毋在.不遠遊.遊必有方, *pāy boē tē tit ū^{m} t'hang hwuī^{ng} t'hit t'ho nā t'hit t'ho pit wōo he^{ng}*, while our parents are still living, we should not wander far, and if we wander, we must always, have a settled place. See the 上諭 Sëāng lūn.

Hĕ^{ng} **坊** Read hong: a village, a hamlet.

Hĕ^{ng} **荒** Read hong: uncultivated, waste, unfruitful, barren, sterile. when grain is unproductive, or fruit trees do not bear, it is called hong 荒 *he^{ng}*. Ke hong 饑荒, *ko he^{ng}*, dearth and famine.

上去 Hé^{ng} **呟** The sound of displeasure; out upon it! fie.

下平 Hĕ^{ng} **防** Kwan hông 關防, *kwan hê^{ng}*, a pass, a barrier.

下平 Hëô **呺** The whistling of the wind; the sound of wrath; a cry by which birds and beasts are called.

下入 Hëŏh **葉** Read yëep: a leaf, the leaves of trees. Lô yëep 荖葉, *laōu hëŏh*, the siri leaf used by the asiatics, in chewing with their betel nut.
Che koë yëep boē 枝葉茂固, *ke këen koë, hëŏh boē sëong*, the branches were firm and the leaves luxuriant.

上平 Hëo^{ng} **香** Read hëang: fragrant; incense. Hwûn hëang 焚香, *sëo hëo^{ng}*, to burn incense.
Yit che hëang t'hoë kéw t'hëen 一枝香透九天, *chit ke hëo^{ng} t'haòu kaóu āy t'hee^{ng}*, one stick of incense will diffuse its fragrance through the nine Heavens.

Hëo^{ng} **鄉** Read hëang: a country district. Hëang lé 鄉里, *hëo^{ng} lé*, a village. Five families constitute a 鄰 lîn, neighbourhood; five neighbourhoods constitute a 里 lé, hamlet; four hamlets constitute a 族 chok, clan; five clans constitute a 黨 tóng, village; five villages constitute a 州 chew, a large village; and five larger villages constitute a heang 鄉 *hëo^{ng}*, a district; Thus 12,500 families comprise one country district. See the 漢志 Hàn chè.

上去 Hëò^{ng} **向** Jê ch'hoó 如此, *an hëò^{ng} sai^{ng}*, is it thus?

下去 Hëō^{ng} **稆** The husk of corn, chaff.

下入 Hëuk **畜** Vulg. *ch'he*: to feed, to nourish, to bring up. Hëuk seng 畜生, *t'haou sai^{ng}*, a brute, a domestic animal.
Yáng hoō boé, hëuk ch'hey. choó 養父毋畜妻子, *yëô^{ng} pāy boé, ch'hē boé kë^{n}á*, to nourish one's parents, and feed one's wife and children.

Hëuk **蓄** To collect, to hoard up. Chek hëuk 積蓄, to accumulate. Hëuk chek jëâou to 蓄積饒多, *k'hëŏh lëŏh chīn chēy*, to accumulate in great abundance.

Hëuk **慉** To nourish, to feed; the same as 畜 hëuk. Put guó lêng hëuk, hwân é gnó wûy sêw 不我能慉.反以我爲讎, *bēy ēy ch'hē gwá, hwán ê gwá chò kêw sêw*, you can not support me, but, on the contrary you hold me for an enemy. See the 邶風 Pöëy hong.

Hëuk 奥 A gulf, a hollow receptacle for water.

Hëuk 旭 The appearance of the rising sun, hëuk jit sé tàn 旭日始旦, *jit k'hè toō toō à kwui^ng*, at the rising of the sun, it then begins to shine.

Hëuk 勖 To urge on to exertion, to encourage.

Hëuk 馥 Fragrant breath, an aromatic flavour.

Hëuk 郁 Literary, elegant. Chew kàm ê jê taē hëuk hëuk hoē bûn chae, 周監於二代.郁郁乎文哉, *chew k'hw^n à ê nō tëàou tēy, chin chaē súy e ây bûn ch'haē*, the Chew dynasty observed the two former dynasties, and thus rendered elegant the literature of those times.' See the 上論 Sëāng lūn. A surname.

Hëuk 彧 Literary, ornamented. Hëuk hëuk 彧彧 luxuriant and full.

Hëuk 頊 Respectful, and careful. Ch'hwán hëuk 顓頊 the name of an ancient. Emperor, who flourished, B. C. 2400.

Hëuk 薁 Eng hëuk 蘡薁 the name of a fruit.

Hëuk 燠 Warm, internally hot.

凶

Hëung 凶 Unlucky, unfortunate. Hëung tëàou 凶兆 an unlucky, omen. Kit hëung hò hok 吉凶禍福, *hò baē, hò hwān hok k'hè*, good and bad luck, misery and happiness.

Hëung 兇 Hëung ok 兇惡, *hëung p'ha^n ê*, vicious in the extreme. Hëung sin 兇身 a murderer: also called. Hëung sêw 兇手 a murderous hand. Tê hëung pò ch'hëen koé 除兇報千古, *tê k'hè hëung p'ha^n ê ê pò ch'heng koē*, to exterminate the vicious in order to testify our gratitude to all antiquity.

Hëung 匈 Hëung noê 匈奴, the name of a Tartar race, on the north-west of China.

Hëung 胷 Vulg. *heng*: the breast. Hëung hwaê 胷懷, the bosom; also written 胸 hëung.

Hëung lô jê sip pat sèw 胷羅二十八宿, *heng k'ham k'hè^ng jē chap pàyh sèw*, "in his breast is included the whole twenty-eight constellations." Intimating an extensive acquaintance with astronomy.

Hëung 胸 The same as the preceding.

Hëung 恟 To be alarmed. Tek bōng è yêw hëung 謫夢意猶恟, *kw^n a lut aōu tit bāng è soō yëë kë^nà, kë^nà*, since dismissal from office, my thoughts in my dreams have been troubled. Said by 韓愈 Hân jé.

Hëung 詾 To accuse; the voice of a multitude. T'hëen hāy hëung hëung, bē te sëuk sē 天下詾詾未知孰是, *t'hee^ng āy hëung hëung, bōēy chae chē chūy à k'hàh tëöh*, the Empire is all in confusion, so that we do not know which is right.

Hëung 洶 The bursting forth of water; the violence of a stream.

声

Hëung 哅 The noise of a multitude.

上平

Hëùng 趬 To go, to make haste.

下平

Hëûng 雄 The male of birds; also brave, heroic. Eng hëûng 英雄, a hero. T'hëen hāy che heûng kok, yëá 天下之雄國也, *t'hee^ng āy k'hăh bêng ây kok*, the most valiant state in the Empire.

Hëung tē ê hwuy 雄雉于飛, *kang ây t'hê key tit pœuy*, the cock of the wild fowl was flying about.

上平

Hew 休 Elegant, beautiful; also, to stop, to cease. Hew ch'hey 休妻, *hëet boé*, to divorce a wife. Hew gân 休言, *ū^m saé kóng*, don't mention it!

Sit bān sè boô këang che hew 實萬世無疆之休, *sit bān, sè bô t'hang swăh ây hó*, it is truly an excellence not to be limited by myriads of ages. Pek kong hew 百工休, a cessation of all labour.

E' t'hëen tēy tông hew 與天地同休, *kàp t'hee^ng tēy chò pôo swăh*, to last as long as Heaven and Earth.

Hew 庥 Secret protection, an invisible influence in one's favour.

Hew 不 Hoo hew 夫不, the name of a bird; also written 夫鴀, hoo hew, the negative particle 不 put, is also read hew, in poetry as.

Bē te chëûng kim k'hè, tong hèw jê ch'hoó hew 未知從今去當復如此不, *bōëy chae chëûng tong kim k'hè, tëŏh kŏh an nêy sai^ng yëá bô*, we cannot tell whether, from our present departure, we shall ever be again thus, or not.

Hew 咻 To bother, to dun. Yit chêy jin hoō che, chëùng ch'hoé jin hew che 一齊人傅之.衆楚人咻之, *chit ây chêy kok ây lâng kà e, jê chëùng ch'hoé kok ây lâng hew e*, "if only one man of Chêy were to be teaching him (the language of that country,) and all the men of Ch'hoé, were to be bothering him (with another tongue,") then though you should beat the lad every day to make him speak the language of Chêy, he would not be able to do it. See 孟子 Bēng choó.

Hew 貅 Pê hew 貔貅, a ferocious wild beast, like a leopard.

Hew 鵂 Hew lêw 鵂鶹, the name of a bird.

Hew 烋 Hew bé 烋美, elegant, beautiful; emolument; happiness; harmony.

上聲

Héw 朽 Vulg. *nw^nā*: rotten, decayed. Héw hȯk 朽木, *nw^nā ch'hâ*, rotten wood. Chaé ê tèw ch'hím, choó wȧt, héw bȯk put k'hó teäou yëá, 宰予晝寢.子曰.朽木不可雕也, *chaé ê jit taōu tit k'hwùn, hoo choò kóng, nw^nā ch'hâ bô t'hang teaou k'hek*, Chaé-ê was sleeping at mid-day, when Confucius said, rotten wood! that cannot be engraved on. See the 論語 Lūn gé.

Héw 殑 Anything rotten, and falling into decay: on the south of the Ch'hoé country there is a 炎人, yëêm jîn, nation, whose parents and relations when dead are left, héw kê jëȯk 殑其肉, *nw^nā e ây băh*, till their flesh rots, when it is thrown away, and the bones are buried.

上去

Hèw 仆 Fallen down. Hin hèw 興仆, to raise that which is fallen down.

Hèw 齅 To smell anything with the nose.

去 Hèw 嗅 To inhale an effluvia. Sam hèw jê chok 三嗅而作, *sⁿa kwùy hèw e ây bē, chēw k'hé*, he (Confucius) thrice inhaled the effluvia, and then rose up to go away. See the 上論 Sëāng lūn. Also vulg. *ch'haòu*, stinking.

Hèw 糗 Roasted rice or wheat. Hèw lëāng 糗糧, dry provisions for a journey.

去 Hēw 復 Again. Hēw hwat 復活, *köh wăh*, to live again; the resurrection. Ch'héng hēw che, këáng jê hoē k'hó 請復之强而後可, *ch'hēⁿà köh e, këóⁿᵍ pāyh naīⁿᵍ, jëēn āou t'hang*, he begged that he would try it again; when, after some urging he consented. See the 上孟 Sëāng bēng.

平 Hey 瞖 The rolling of the eyes; the eyes moving.

Hey 醯 Vinegar. Hey ch'hoè 醯醋, vinegar, pickle. Sëuk wūy bê seng ko tit, hek k'hit hey yëen, k'hit choo kê lîn jê é che, 孰謂微生高直.或乞醯焉.乞諸其隣而與之, *chē chūy à kóng bê seng ko tëaou tit, wōo lâng k'hit ch'hae, e k'he k'hit kap e ây ch'hoò peeⁿᵍ lâng, jé hoē e*, who will say that Bê-seng-ko is an honest man? — When one came begging for vinegar, he begged some of his neighbour, and gave it to him (in his own name). See the 上論 Sëāng lūn.

去 Héy 眭 Deep eyes, wicked eyes; also, the eyes deeply sunk in the head. E' hòk héy jîn 以目眭人, *t'hó bák chew hêy lâng*, to look savagely at any one.

Héy jëēn lêng sè 眭然能視, *bák ch'hìm yëâ ēy k'hwⁿà*, to be able to see notwithstanding the eyes being deeply sunk the in head.

Héy 匸 To hold or contain any thing. One of the radicals.

平 Hêy 傒 The name of a harbarous country, on the north-east of China. Sē hô hêy hoé 是何傒狗, *chēy sē sⁿa meēⁿh hêy kàou*, what dog of a barbarian is this?

Hêy 徯 To expect, to wait for, to be in expectation of. Hêy gnó hoē, hoē laê ké soe, 徯我后后來其蘇, *teng haōu gwán ây jîn kwun, jîn kwun laê chēw köh chaē wăh*, let us wait for our prince; when our prince comes, there will be a revival. See the 書經, Se keng.

Hêy 蹊 A small by-path, a cross-way. San kèng che hêy 山徑之蹊, *suⁿa kèng ây sèy loē* cross-ways about hill roads. See 孟子 Bēng choó.

Hêy 攜 Vulg kwⁿā, to carry in the hand, to hold in the hand; also to separate. Hêy séw tông kwuy 攜手同歸, *k'han ch'hêw chò poō tooiⁿᵍ*, to hold one another's hands and return. See the 國風 Kok hong. Chëaou hêy é léy 招攜以禮, *chëo lê swⁿà ây lâng è lëy soè*, to collect those who are dispersed, by propriety. See the 左傳 Chó twān.

Hêy 携 The same as the above. Hêy lâm 携籃, *kwⁿā nâ*, to carry a hand-basket; Also written 蠵 hêy.

Hêy 畦 A piece of land, fifty acres in extent. Hêy tëēn 畦田, a large tract of land.

Hëep këen t'hëëm ch'hëaòu, pēng ê hay hêy 脅肩諂笑病於夏畦, *pāyh k'hê keng t'haōu, sëep sëy jê ch'hëò, chēy lëy k'hàh ch'hàm ê hāy t'heeⁿᵍ ây ch'hān*, to see people shrug up the shoulders, and to come with a flattering smile, 'is more insupportable to me, than the open fields in a hot summer's day. See the 上孟 Sëāng bēng.

Hêy 奚 Why? where fore? Also, a slave, a servant. A surname. Chooó hêy put wûy chèng 子奚不爲政, *hoo. chooó lé sⁿa soō ûm chò chèng soō*, why do not you (speaking to Confucius) undertake to manage the affairs of government. See the 上論 Sëāng lūn.

Lé hō sëāou hêy noē pöey koé kim lông, gē séy tek se, toē lông tëung 李賀小奚奴.背古錦囊.遇所得詩.投囊中, *lé. hō sèy ây sê chò gîm á, k'hn chëăh aōu gēā chit ây koō ây kim lóng, toò tëŏh sèy tit ây se, chĕw hëct tē lông tëung*, Le-hō, in his youth was a servant, when he carried on his back an old embroidered bag, and whatever verses he met with, that he could get at, he used to throw them into his bag.

Hêy 兮 An expletive, used at the end of sentences in poetry. Lâm hong che hwun hêy, k'hó é kaé goē bin che wùn hêy 南風之薰兮.可以解吾民之慍兮, *lâm hong ây p'hang, t'hang laé kèw gwán pêyh saiⁿᵍ ây hwân ló*, the southern wind which is so aromatic, will serve to dissipate the anxiety of my people. See 舜歌 Sùn ko, the ode of Sùn.

Hēy 系 A line, a thread; a genealogical line. To connect together.

Hēy 繫 To connect together, to hand down in continuance. Hēy lëēm 繫念, to think of incessantly.

Sè hēy 世繫, sucessive generations; a line of genealogy.

Hēy 係 To connect, to continue; to bind; also to be; to belong to. Kwan hēy 關係, consequences, results, that which belongs to an affair.

Hēy 禊 Pwat hēy 祓禊, a sacrifice offered with the view of averting calamities.

Hēy 蠏 Mô hēy 毛蠏, a kind of hairy crab, read baē.

Hēy 毅 Bold, firm, undaunted; also written 毅 hāy, and pronounced gē. Cheng chooó wat, soō put k'hó é put hông hāy 曾子曰.士不可以不弘毅, *cheng chooó kóng, t'hak ch'hăyh lâng aᵐ t'hang bô hông hēy*, Cheng-chooó said, a scholar should not be otherwise than magnanimous and bold.

掉

Him 欣 To rejoice, to be glad. Him hé 欣喜, pleased, delighted. Ké him him jëën yéw hé sek 皆欣欣然有喜色, *lué kay him him jëën woo hwⁿa hé ay bîn sek*, they would all appear delighted, and joy would beam from their countenances. See 孟子 Bēng chooó.

Him 僛 Rejoiced, delighted; the name of a district; also written 忻 him. Keang gwân këën kē jin chek, sim him jëën wat, yëuk chëën che 姜嫄見巨人跡.心忻然悅.欲踐之, *këang gwân k'hwⁿà keēⁿᵍ twā lâng ây chëăh, chĕw sim kwⁿa him jëën hwⁿa hé, aè böĕyh tàh e*, Këang-gwân on seeing the footsteps of a large sized man, was pleased and delighted to her very heart, and desired to set her foot on it (which doing, she conceived, and bare 后稷 hoē chek.)

Him 昕 Very early in the morning, when the sun is about to rise.

Him 歆 The enjoyment which the gods derive from sacrifices; also to desire. Him swān 歆羡, to delight in, to enjoy.

Him 訢 To be pleased, to be delighted; the same as 欣 Him. Chëung sin him jëën, lok jé bông t'hëen hāy 終身訢然.樂而忘天下, *chit sè lâng hwⁿa hé, t'hëung lok jé bēy kè t'heeⁿᵍ hāy ây soō*, to be all one's life delighted, and in one's joy to forget the whole world. See the 下孟 Hāy bēng.

去
Hìm 𤒹 To roast, the violence of fire; heat.

Hìm 廞 To be earnestly desirous of; seeing a thing, new and splendid, and longing after it; ardour of mind.

Hìm 歆 A man's name. Lêw hìm 劉歆, a man of the 漢 hàn dynasty.

平
Hîm 熊 A bear. Jîn hîm 人熊, lâng hîm, a baboon; a surname. Gê gnó séy yeúk yēá, hîm chēáng ek gnó séy yeúk yēá 魚我所欲也熊掌亦我所欲也, hêgwâ séy aè, hîm chēóng yēá gwá sèy aè, fish is what I am fond of; and bear's palm is also what I am fond of. See 孟子 Bēng choó.

上
Hīm 噤 To shut the mouth, to be mute, unwilling to speak. Hīm k'hoe put kám 'hēw gân 噤口不敢復言, hap ch'hùy ūm kⁿá kóh kóng, to shut the mouth, and not dare to speak again.

去
Hìn 興 To do, perform; to begin, to commence operations; to succeed, to prosper.
Hìn ōng 興旺, to prosper. Hìn soo 興師, to raise troops. Hìn k'hé 興起, to commence, to arise.
T'hong boó é jîn, hìn yēá put yēen, kēét tēw é pō bōng yēá hwut yēen 湯武以仁興也勃焉.桀紂以暴亡也忽焉, t'hong boó kēⁿá jîn, chēw e ây hìn put yēen, kēét tēw kēⁿá pō chēw e ây bô yēá hwut yēen; T'hong and Boó practised benevolence, thus their prosperity was rapid; Kēét and Tēw practised oppression, thus their ruin was also sudden.

去
Hín 痛 A burn or scald on the skin; a swelling.

去
Hìn 釁 To besmear, to rub with blood; a cause of quarrel; a crime. Sat ch'he yêw jê hìn koé 殺蚩尤而釁鼓, t'hat ch'he yêw jê bwâh kóe, he killed Ch'he-yêw, and smeared the drum with his blood.

Hìn 興 To be pleased. Hìn wat 興悅, pleased, delighted with. Sêng hìn jê yêw hìn chīn chek hwán 勝興而遊.興盡則返, sêng hìn wat chēw k'hè t'hìt t'hô hìn chīn chēw tooⁿg, we should take advantage of a merry humour, to go on pleasure rambles, and when our merry humour is exhausted, we can return home.

平
Hîn 眩 Read hēên: a dizziness of the head; to be giddy. T'hoê hēên 頭眩, t'haôu kak hîn, a swimming in the head.
Hēên ch'hwân 眩船, hîn chûn, sea-sickness. Kám hēên chit, put yeúk ch'hut hong 感眩疾.不欲出風, kám hîn ây paīⁿg ūm kⁿá ch'hut hong, having got a dizziness of the head. I do not dare to go out in the wind.

上
Hīn 恨 Read hwūn: to be enraged at, to hate. Hwūn oè 恨惡, hīn oè, to abhor. Hwūn sēang kēèn che bwán è 恨相見之晚矣, hīn sēo kēèⁿg kaôu hēāh mooⁿg, it is a pity that we got acquainted with each other so late
Ông ch'hìm é wūy hwūn 王深以爲恨, ông ch'hîm é wūy hīn, the king was greatly displeased about it.

入
Hip 翕 United, harmonious; obedient, compliant. Heng tēy kè hip, hô lok ch'hēⁿá tam 兄弟旣翕.和樂且湛, hēⁿa tē káôu sëo hap, chēw hô lok ch'hēⁿá tam, when brethren are united, harmony and delight mingled with pleasure, prevail.

Hip 傄 To collect, to take up.

Hip 噏 To draw in the breath, to inhale, to suck in. Hip ch'heng yîn che lêw hây 噏清雲之流瑕, *k'hip ch'heng hwûn ây laôu hây*, to suck in the flowing pearls of the pure clouds.

Hip 潝 The appearance of water flowing rapidly.

Hip 謪 To talk fast. Hip hip ch'hoó ch'hoó 謪謪訿訿, to chatter and scold.

Hip 歙 Hip pit 歙鼻, *hip p'hëe^{ng}*, to contract the skin of the nose, to snuff up the nose; also to draw in the breath, to shrivel up.

夨

Hit 肸 To take up, to perform. Pit bit 佛肸, a man's name.

Hit 盻 To look at, to observe.

Hit 肐 The breast bone.

Hit 矞 To look alarmed, to look on with fear.

平

H^{n}aôu 偦 To stab; the cry of pain.

卆

Ho 饕 Ho sit 饕食, *t'ham chëāh*, to be gluttonous, to eat to excess; also, covetous.

Ho 嗀 The sound of blowing out the breath; a whizzing, whistling sound.

3 L

Ho 薅 To pluck up weeds; to eradicate the rank grass of the fields.

Ho 訶 To talk loud and angrily. Bê hêng gân put sùn sūn, hông choé ch'ham náe ho che 禰衡言不遜順.黃祖慙乃訶之, *bé hêng kóng wā ū^{m} sèy jē, hô sūn, wuî^{ng} choé ch'hë^{n}á sëaou lèy twā së^{n}a hwăh e*, Bé-hêng spoke without humility and submission, hence Wuî^{ng}-choé was vexed with shame, and scolded him. See the 後漢書 Hoē hàn se.

Ho 蒿 Tall grass; long, rank grass. Sit yëá che ho 食野之蒿, *chëăh yëá gwā ây tê^{ng} ch'haôu*, (the deer) eat the long grass in the wilderness. See the 小雅 Seaôu gnáy.

Ho 呵 To blow out the breath. Ho ho 阿阿, the sound of laughing.

卢

Hó 好 Read h^{n}ó: good, fine, excellent. H^{n}ó jîn 好人, *hó lâng*, a good man. Chëā sëen kwun che bēng, këet jū kok che h^{n}ó 藉先君之命.結二國之好, *k'hò lán sëen kwun ây bēng, lāng këet hap nō kok ây hó*, relying on the injunctions of our former princes, we would connect the good understanding of both countries. See the 左傳 Chó twān.

Hó 傐 The name of a country, on the north of China.

平

Hô 何 Why? what? how? wherefore? A surname. Hô koè 何故, *s^{n}a soō*, for what reason? When confucius complained that no one knew him, one of his disciples asked, saying, hô wūy kó bok te choó yëá, 何共爲莫知子也, *s^{n}a soō e ū^{m} chae choó lè*, why is it that they do not know you? See the 下論 Hāy lūn.

Hô **荷** Hô lëen 荷蓮, the water lily. Sip yéw hô hwa 濕有荷花, *tâm ây wāy wōo hô lëên hwa*, in damp places we find the water lily.

Hô **河** A river. Hông hô 黃河, *wui^ng hô*, the yellow river. Jit gwat kong t'heen tek, san hô chòng tèy ke 日月光天德. 山河壯帝居, *jit gŏëyh kwui^ng t'hee^ng ây tek, sw^na hô chòng hông tèy k'hëä ây wāy*, the sun and moon illumine the glories of Heaven, while hills and rivers stengthen the residence of the Emperor.

Hô **訶** To be enraged, to scold with anger; also read ho.

Hô **壕** A ditch round a city wall; a moat round a fort. E' hāy k'hong hô 雨下空壕, *hoē lŏh tē k'hang tê*, the rain descended into the empty moat.

Hô **豪** A hero, a man distinguished for talents and wisdom. Hô hëep 豪俠, a brave man, a distinguished hero. Swán hô chùn, káng bûn hak 選豪俊講文學, *swán kéng hô chùn, káng kèw bûn hak*, to select wise and brave men, in order to discourse over literature and learning.

Hô **毫** The down of a feather, anything very small; ten atoms make one down of a feather. Ch'hay che hô lê, bëw é ch'heen lé 差之毫釐. 繆已千里, *ch'hay chit t'haôu mô se, chēw ēy bēw kaòu chit ch'heng lé*, a variation of a hair's-breadth, will lead to an error of a thousand le in extent.

Hô **嚎** The name of a hill.

Hô **濠** The name of a river.

Hô **蠔** Vulg. *ô*: an oyster; a shell-fish.

Hô **禾** Vulg. *tëw*: grain, corn, paddy. Kat hô 割禾, *kwăh tëw*, to reap the corn. Sip gwat lap hô kày 十月納禾稼, *chap göëyh lap sëw hô kày*, in the tenth month we gather in the harvest. See the 邠風 Pin hong.

Hô **和** Harmonious, soothing, agreeable; not stiff, nor stubborn. A surname. Hô sūn 和順, obedient. Hô sëäng 和尙, *hôëy sëö^ng*, a priest of Buddha.
Hëep hô ban pang 協和萬邦, to unite all nations in harmony.
Tè tëung hô, t'hëen tëy wūy yëen, bān bút yëuk yëen 致中和天地位焉萬物育焉, *tè kek tëung kwà hô, chew t'hee^ng tëy tit tëŏh e ây wāy, bān mee^nh yëá tit ch'hē*, when we carry to the utmost the happy medium, and the principles of harmony, heaven and earth will keep their proper stations, and the myriads of things will obtain nourishment. See the 中庸 Tëung yûng.

Hô **嘷** The name of a beast, the roaring of a wild beast.

Hô **龢** The same as 和 hô, harmonious.

Hô **號** To call out aloud, to cry, to lament. Sùn hô k'hip ê bûn t'hëen 舜號泣于旻天, *sùn hô haôu tē ch'hew t'hee^ng*, Sùn lamented and cried towards the autumnal Heavens.

去

Hō **賀** K'héng hō 慶賀, to congratulate, to felicitate. A surname. Soò hong laê hō, 四方來賀, *sè he^ng laê hō 'hè*, the people from all quarters came to offer their congratulations.

Hō 荷 To carry a burden, to bear, to sustain a weight. Yéw hō kwūy jê kò k'hóng sē che bûn chēā 有荷蕢而過孔氏之門者, *woō lâng t^na ch'haóu lâng á, jê köèy k'hóng sē ây moot^ng*, there was a man carrying a wicker basket, who passed by the door of Confucius. See the 下論 Hāy lūn.

Hō 灝 The distant expanse of water.

Hō 顥 A white luminous appearance; also great; also written 皓 hō.

Hō 號 A mark, a signal, a denomination, to call, to designate. Hō lēng 號令, an order, a signal. Joō hō 字號, *jē hō*, a mark.
Ông chēā sēw bēng ê t'hëen, pit tek hé hō é wūy hō 王者受命于天.必擇美號以爲號, *ông ây lâng sēw bēng ê t'hee^ng, pit kán tŏh hó ây hō è chò hō*, when the royal ones receive the decree from Heaven (to found a dynasty), they should select an elegant designation, in order to become their distinctive mark. See the 春秋傳 Ch'hun ch'hew twān.

Hō 皞 White, a bright white appearance.

Hō 和 To respond to any one; to sing a second part in music. Ch'hëàng ê hō jé 唱予和汝, *gwá ch'hëò^ng, lé hō*, I will sing, and you respond.

Hō 昊 The vernal Heavens, the appearance of the sky in spring; also, expansive Hō t'hëen 昊天, the wide expansive Heavens.

Hō 禍 Calamity, affliction, misery. Hō hwān 禍患, trouble, sorrow. Hō hwān lîm sin 禍患臨身, *hō hwān lîm kaòu lân hîn sin*, calamity coming upon one's own person.

Hō 囮 The noise made when a boat advances; the boatman's song.

Hō 浩 Expansive, wide, as the ocean; great, magnanimous. Gnó sëen yáng goê hō jëen che k'hè 我善養吾浩然之氣, *gwá gaôu yëô^ng ch'hē gwá ây hō jëen ây k'hè*, I am skilful in nourishing up my great and expansive spirit. See 孟子 Bēng choó.

Hō 譹 To deceive and cheat one another. To scold.

Hō 謴 To contend, to wrangle.

Hō 譋 Hàm hō 譀譋, the sound of anger wrathful clamour.

Hō 嗬 To answer slowly.

Hō 何 To bear a burthen; the same as 荷 hō.

Hō 俰 Harmonious; the same as 和 hô.

Hō 号 A mark, a designation; the contracted form of 號 hō. Hëên se sëàng gwūy ê hō lēng bān sèng 懸書象魏.以号令萬姓, *tëaôu bûn se tē sē^nà moot^ng, ê hō lēng bān sai^ng*, to hang up a proclamation at the city gate, in order to give a signal to all the people. See the 周禮 Chew léy.

奉

H^no 訶 To talk hastily, and scoldingly.

Hno 薅 To pull up weeds.

Hnó 蒿 Long grass; also, ch'heng hno 青蒿, Pek hno, 白蒿, and hëang hno 香蒿, all names of medicinal herbs.

上聲

Hnó 好 Vulg. *hó:* good, excellent, well. Pēng hnó 病好, *paīng hó*, recovery from sickness; returning health.
E'ng é wūy hnó yëá 永以爲好也, *éng koó é chò sëo hó*, to promote constant friendship and good will. See the 衞風 Wöëy hang.

Hnó 火 Vulg. *höëy:* fire. Kèw hnó 救火, *kèw höëy*, to help to put out fire. Jëák hnó che sé jëën 若火之始然, *ch'hin chëōng höëy ây k'hè t'hâou tŏh*, like fire beginning to burn.

Hnó 夥 A number of people together; a company. Hnó kè 夥記, *höëy kè*, a partner, an associate, a messmate.
Chò hnó 做夥, *chò höëy*, to be together, to be in company.

去聲

Hnò 好 Vulg. *aè:* to love, to delight in, to approve of, to consider good. Jin chëá lêng hnò jin, ek lêng put twat jin séy hnò 仁者能好人.亦能不奪人所好, *jin ây lâng ëy aè lâng, yëá ëy bô ch'hëōng pat lâng ây sèy aè*, benevolent men can love their fellow men, and can also refrain from seizing that which others love.
Chëûng goê séy hnò 從吾所好, *t'hàn gwá sèy aè*, to follow that which I myself approve. See the 上論 Sëāng lūn.

Hnò 貨 Vulg. *höëy:* goods, merchandize, wealth, property. Hnò hnò chaê 好貨財, *aè höëy kap cheēng*, to be fond of property and wealth.

Lē put wûy këën chin kwùy jin wat, kê hnó k'hó koé 呂不韋見秦貴人.日.奇財可買, *lē put wûy k'hwnà keēng chin kwùy jin, chëw kóng, chêy sē hó höëy t'hang bêy*. Lē-put-wûy, seeing the noble prince of the Chin country (in bonds) said, This is a good article; I can buy it: (meaning that what money he might expend in assisting the prince would be amply repaid; he accordingly expended his whole fortune in the prince's behalf, and afterwards saw him rise to supreme power.) Hence this has become a proverb.

Hnò 耗 To decrease, to diminish; empty, vain, unproductive. Sè lëën che hong hnò 視年之豐耗, *k'hwnà neēng ây hó yëá baè neēng tang*, we should observe whether the season of the year has been fruitful or unproductive, (when we levy the taxes). See the 王制 Ông chè, royal regulations.

Hnò 秏 The finest of the grain; also fine rice.

Hnò 薃 Pô hnò 蔢薃, peppermint; now called 薄荷, pok hô.

平聲

Hoe 呼 To call; to breathe out. Ch'heng hoe 稱呼, to name, to applaud. To breathe out the breath is called 呼 hoe, and to draw it in 吸 k'hip. An exclamation. Oe hoe hat kwuy 嗚呼曷歸, alas! why not return.
Yit hoe pek lók 一呼百喏, *chit ây këò chēnà pàyh lâng yìn e*, at one call, a hundred voices answered.

Hoe 虍 The stripes of a tiger; also one of the radicals.

Hoe 戲 An exclamation of admiration. Oe hoe chëën ông put bōng 於戲前王不忘, *oe hoe chêng ây ông bô bēy* kè til, behold! the example of the former kings is not forgotten. See the 大學 Taē hak.

Hoe 滹 The name of a river.

Hoe 戲 To call; the same as 呼 hoe.

Hoe 嘑 To be enraged; to vociferate; a surname.

Hoe 苸 The name of a plant

去

Hoé 虎 A tiger; the prince of wild beasts. Hoé soō ch'hut ē ap 虎兕出於柙, hoē kap swⁿa goô ch'hut ē ap, the tigers and wild oxen broke out of their cages.

Hoé 蜣 Hoé sîn 蜣蝇, a fly. Hoé sîn hoé 蜣蝇虎, a lizard.

Hoé 否 If not; no, not. Bēng-choó wat, hoé, put jëēn, hⁿò soō cheă wûy che yēă 孟子曰.否.不然.好事者爲之也, Bēng-choó kóng, bô, ū^m sē, aè chò soō ây lâng ch'hòng e, Bēng-choó said, no, it's not so: people who like to create trouble, have invented the story.

Hoé 岵 A hill without any vegetation on it, a bare mountain.

Hoé 滸 The water's edge; the brink of a river, or lake. Sut sey sûy hoē 率西水滸, khè àn sae, t'hàn chúy gaê, he travelled towards the west, along the water's edge.

Hoé 缶 An earthern pot or pan, for holding wine, pickles, &c.

Hoé 吼 Vulg. haôu: to bawl out aloud, to roar, to cry aloud. Hoé bêng hoé yûng yēak 虎鳴吼踊躍, hoé twā sēⁿa haôu, yûng yēak t'hëō, the tiger roared aloud, and jumped about.

Hoé 冔 The name of a cap, in the Sëang dynasty.

去

Hoè 戽 Hoè toe 戽斗, hoè taóu, a bucket for lading out water, or baling a boat.

Hoè 滬 Hoè sûy 滬水, hoè chúy, to bale out water.

平

Hoê 侯 Beautiful, excellent; a title of rank, about equal to earl. Choo hoê 諸侯, the nobles of the Empire. Vulg. kaôu, a surname.

Kong hoê pek choó lâm 公侯伯子男 five degrees of titular rank.

Hoê 矦 The same as the preceding.

Hoê 篌 An instrument of music.

Hoê 猴 Vulg. kaôu: a monkey, an ape Jin gan, Ch'hoé jîn bok hoê jê kwan jé, kó jöên 人言楚人沐猴而冠耳.果然, lâng tit kóng, Ch'hoé kok ây lâng sē sêy t'haôu ây kaôu, kwà tè kin, kó jëên chin chēⁿà, people say, that the men of the Ch'hoé country are a parcel of washed monkeys with caps on, — and truly it is so. — Said by 漢高祖 Hàn-ko-choé, in ridicule of his rival the king of Ch'hoé.

Hoê 喉 Vulg. nâ aôu: the throat. Ch'hut lap ông bēng, ông chē hoê sëet 出納王命.王之喉舌, ch'hut lap ông ây bēng lēng, se ông ây nâ aôu ch'hùy cheĕh, they who go abroad bearing the royal commands, are the throat and tougue of the king

3 M

Hoê 壺 A wine vessel, a pot. Toê hoê 投壺, a kind of game of chance. Ch'heng chéw pek hoê 清酒百壺, *hó chéw chēⁿâ pāyh hoê*, a hundred pots of pure wine.

Hoê 瓠 Bladders or air-bags, used to assist in floating on the water. To take up anything out of the water.

Hoê 胡 Vulg. *oê*: a surname.

Hoê 湖 Vulg. *oê*: a lake, a large sheet of water. Gooé hoê 五湖, the five lakes. Yêw hêng kang hoê 遊行江湖, *yêw kēⁿâ kaug hoê*, wandering about the rivers and lakes.

Hoê 瑚 San hoê 珊瑚, coral. San hoê chông seng 珊瑚叢生, *san hoê ka.nooiⁿᵍ chăng saiⁿᵍ*, the coral grows in bushes.

Hoê 猢 The name of a beast of the ape species.

Hoê 蝴 Hoê teep 蝴蝶, *bōêy yēăh*, a butterfly. Chong-chew bōng wûy hoê teep 莊周夢爲蝴蝶, *Chong-chew bāng chò bōêy yēăh*, Chong-chew dreamed that he was a butterfly.

Hoê 餬 Hoê k'hoé 餬口, to depend on other's for one's food. Also, vulg. *koê*, to paste; paste for sticking anything up.

Hoê 鶘 T'hêy hoê 鵜鶘, a cormorant, a water fowl. Gê put wûy bóng, jê wûy t'hêy hoê 魚不畏網而畏鵜鶘, *hê ūᵐ kēⁿa bāng, jê kēⁿa t'hêy hoê*, fishes are not so much afraid of nets, as of cormorants.

Hoê 狐 Hoê lê 狐狸, a fox. Hoê gê 狐疑, to doubt, to suspect. Hoê lê yéw hëet 狐狸有穴, *hoê lê woō k'hang*, the foxes have holes.

Hoê 弧 A wooden bow.

Hoê 瓠 Hoê lô 瓠顱, *poô á*, a calabash. Hwan hwan hoê yëep, ch'haé che p'heng che 幡幡瓠葉采之亨之, *hoê sēng ây poô á hĕŏh, laê bân laê chè e*, look at the luxuriant calabash leaves; let us pluck them and boil them. See the 小雅 Sëáou gnáy.

Hoê 餱 Dry provisions; that which cannot easily be swallowed.

Hoê 糇 Dried rice, prepared for a journey. Naé kó hoê lëâng 迺裹糇糧, bundle up the dried provisions.

Hoê 鍭 The head of an arrow.

去

Hoē 后 A prince, a princess or queen. Hông hoē 皇后, an empress. Hông t'hëen hoē t'hoé 皇天后土, imperial heaven and royal earth.
T'hán ch'hong bêng, chok gwân hoē 亶聰明作元后, *twā ch'hang mēⁿâ, chēw ây chò gwân hoē*, when a man is greatly intelligent, he may become a supreme ruler.

Hoē 乎 A character used at the end of a sentence, as a mark of interrogation. Hak jê sê sip che, put ek wat hoē 學而時習之不亦說乎, *t'hak, jê sëâng sê wūn sip e, āᵐ yēá hwⁿa hê hoē*, to learn and constantly to exercise one's self in it, — is it not delightful? See the 上諭 Sëâng lūn.

Hoē 互 Mutual, connected; differing. Hoē sëang hwan hé 互相歡喜, *taē kay sëo hwⁿa hé*, all mutually delighted.

Hoē 冱 Cold, frozen, congealed. Song swat kaou hāy, ch'hwan tê p'hok hoē 霜雪交下川池暴冱, *sⁿᵍ sāyh kaou lŏh, ch'hui^ng tê p'hŏk hoē*, when the frost and snow come down together, the rivers and ponds become frozen.

Hoē 楛 The name of a tree.

Hoē 戶 A door, an inner door. Bûn hoē 門戶, *mooi^ng hoē*, doors and entrances. Sûy lêng ch'hut put yêw hoē 誰能出不由戶, *chē chūy ēy ch'hut, bŏ an mooi^ng*, who can go out, except by the door? See the 上論 Seāng lūn.

Hoē 逅 Haē hoē 邂逅, to meet unexpectedly.

Hoē 護 To guard, to protect. Kèw hoē 救護, to guard from danger. Pó hoē 保護, to protect. Hoē wōēy chëàng-kwun 護衛將軍, a general of the guards. T'hëen sin hoē wōēy 天神護衛, *t'hee^ng sin pó pē*, may the gods defend and protect you.

Hoē 扈 The tail; behind. Hoē chëūng 扈從 to follow after. A surname.

Hoē 槴 An instrument for catching fish; a book case.

Hoē 濩 Taē hoē 大濩, the name of the music adopted by the Emperor 湯 T'hong.

Hoē 矱 A measure, a rule.

Hoē 蠖 Ch'hek hoē 尺蠖, a worm that draws itself up, and stretches itself out again.

Hoē 後 Vulg. *aōu*: behind, after, late, the last, to be behind. A surname. Hoē laê 後來, *aōu laê*, afterwards. Tùy hoē 對後, *tùy aōu*, behind. Soó sëen te kak hoē te 使先知覺後知, *saè taê seng chae áy lâng, kak tùy āou chae áy lâng*, set those who have come early to the knowledge of a thing, to awaken those who come later to the knowledge of it. Choó-loē chëūng jê hoē 子路從而後, *Choó-loē t'hàn jê laê k'ha chëāh aōu*, Choó-loē followed, and came after. Hoē seng chëá 後生者, *tùy aōu sai^ng áy lâng*, young people.

Hoē 穫 To cut down the corn, to reap the grain.

Hoē 鑊 An iron; a caldron; an iron spoon used to stir up a caldron. Maôu-chëaou put wùy téng hoē, jê kàn 茅焦不畏鼎鑊而諫, *Maôu-chëaou ū^m kë^na tē^nà hoē, jê t^nà*, Maôu-chëaou did not dread being boiled in the caldron, but faithfully reproved his prince.

Hoē 候 The same as 候 hoē, to wait.

Hoē 厚 Vulg. *kaōu*: thick, not thin, kind, liberal. Hoē bëen p'hê 厚面皮, *kaōu bīn p'hōēy*, having a thick skin to the face, i. e. being unable to blush. P'hok hoē p'hōëy tēy 博厚配地, *k'hwăh kaōu p'hōèy tēy*, expansive and thick, like the earth. See the 中庸 Tëung yûng. Hoē yin 厚恩, *kaōu yin*, thick, substantial kindness.

Hoē 睺 Covetous, greedy of gain.

Hoē 候 Téng hoē 等候, *téng haōu*, to wait. Sê hoē 時候, *sê haōu*, time. Bün hoē 問候, *bün haōu*, to wait upon, to enquire after.

Hoē 祜 Pé hoē 庇祜, protection, favour; to protect. Sêw t'hëen che hoē 受天之祜, *sêw t'he^ng áy hok*, to obtain the favour of Heaven. See the 小雅 Sëaóu gnáy.

Hoē 雨 Read ē: rain. Lok é 落雨, *lŏh hoē,* to rain. Yîn hêng é se, p'hín but lêw hêng 雲行雨施.品物流行, *hwân kë^n^â hoē lŏh, p'hín meë^n^h lêw kë^n^â,* when the clouds travel the rain is dispersed, and all sorts of things are put in motion. See the 易經 Ek keng.

平 Höey 灰 Vulg. *höey hoo*: ashes; also, vulg. *chëŏh höey,* lime. Bwat höey 抹灰, to whitewash, to besmear with line. Ché höey hwuy chok pek hoê têep 紙灰飛作白蝴蝶, *chwá ây höey hoo tit-pwuy chò pëyh ây böey yëăh,* the ashes of the burnt paper are flying about, like so many white butterflies.

Höey 虺 Höey töey 虺隤, tired, fagged, knocked up. T'hek pé ch'huy gwûy, gnó má höey töey 陟彼崔嵬我馬虺隤, *pëyh chëō^ng^ e kwân ây wûy, gwá ây báy toe yëà,* by mounting up those high places, my horse is fagged out. See the 周南 Chew lâm.

Höey 隳 Hwaē höey 壞隳, to be dilapidated, to be broken down.

去 Höéy 火 Read h^n^ó: fire. K'he h^n^ó 起火, *k'hè höéy,* to kindle a fire. Sam keng teng h^n^ó, gnóe keng key 三更燈火五更雞, *s^n^a kai^ng^ teng höëy yëá tŏh, goē kai^ng^ t'hë^n^a key t'hé,* at the third watch my study lamp was still burning, and at the fifth watch I heard the cock-crow.

Höéy 夥 Read h^n^ó: assembled together, associated. H^n^ó kéy 夥計, *höëy kè,* an associate, a partner, a mate.

去 Höèy 悔 To repent, to be sorry for, to regret. Gân kw^n^á yêw, hêng kw^n^á höèy, lok chaē kê tëung è 言寡尤.行寡悔.祿在其中矣, *kóng wā chëo kò yêw, sêy kë^n^â chëŏ hwân höëy, lok tē e ây tang e^ng^,* when with respect to our words, we have few faults, and with respect to our actions, few regrets; then emolument will be found to centre in this. See the 上論 Sëāng lūn.

Höèy 晦 Dark, not clear, dim, dull. Hong é jê höèy, key bêng put é 風雨如晦.鷄鳴不已, *hong hoē ch'hin chëō^ng^ àm, key t'hê bô swăh,* when the wind and rain prevail and it is as it were dark, then the cocks crow without ceasing. See the 鄭風 Tēng hong.

Höèy 誨 To teach, to instruct. Höèy jîn put kwān 誨人不倦, *kà lâng bô sëō^ng^ yëà,* to teach people, without feeling tired. See the 上論 Sëāng lūn. Yêw, höèy jé te che hoē 由.誨女知之乎, *Yêw, gwá kà lé chae ây tō lé,* Yew, I will teach you what is knowledge. See the same.

Höèy 靧 To wash the face. Ch'héng höèy 請靧, *ch'hë^n^á sèy bīn,* to request (a superior) to wash his face, which was to be done by inferior relatives, when they had prepared water for their elders.

Höèy 燬 To boil anything to rags.

Höèy 痗 A sickness, pain; diseased. Suó gnó sim höèy 使我心痗, *saè gwá ây sim kw^n^a paī^ng^,* to make my heart pained.

Höèy 貨 Read h^n^ò: goods, property, wealth. Kay h^n^ò 家貨, *kay höèy,* goods and chattels. Chaè h^n^ò 載貨, *chaè höèy,* to transport goods. H^n^ò chin kày sit 貨眞價實, *höèy chīn kày chëw sit,* when goods are of the right sort, the price will be of the proper kind.

平 Hôey 徊 Paê hôey 徘徊, hesitating, undecided, without advancing.

Höêy **回** To turn round, to revolve, to return; also, depraved. T'hēen chew tēy göēy, yim yâng gnóe hêng, höêy chwán kê tëung 天周地外.陰陽五行.回轉其中, *t'heeng chew tē tēy ây gwā, yĕà yim yâng goē hêng, hwat lîn tooing tē e ây tang eng*, the Heavens encircle the earth around, while the male and female principle, with the five elements, revolve in their centre.
Höēy kay 回家, *tooing k'hè ch'hoò*, to return home. Also written 囘 höēy.

Höêy **廻** To return; the same as the above.

Höêy **痐** Long worms in the stomach; the tape worm.

Höêy **洄** The name of a river; to go against the stream; clear water. Soé höēy chëûng che 溯洄從之, *kâyh laôu t'hàn e*, to follow up against the stream. See the 詩經 Se keng.

Höêy **茴** Höêy hëang 茴香, *höēy hëong*, a fragrant herb.

Höēy **和** Hô sëāng 和尙, *höēy sëōng*, a priest of the sect of Buddha. Sëēm ông soō sëāng, sëēm lé soō hô sëāng 暹王飼象.暹女飼和尙, *sëēm ây ông ch'hē ch'hëōng, sëēm cha boé ch'hē höēy sëōng*, the king of Siam feeds elephants, and the women of Siam feed the priests.

丢

Höēy **會** To meet, to assemble, to unite; an assembly, a society. Boó-ông taē höēy choo hoê ê Bēng-chin 武王大會諸侯于孟津, *Boó-ông twā höēy choo hoê tē Bēng-chin*, Boó-ông convened a great assembly of the princes of the Empire at Bēng-chin. See the 史記 Soó kè.

T'hēen tēy höēy 天地會, *t'heeng tēy hoēy*, heaven and earth society, a kind of secret masonic club.

Höēy **岁** The ancient form of the preceding character.

Höēy **繪** The ornamental colouring of a picture, also written 繢 höēy. Höēy soō hoē soé 繪事後素, *höēy ây soō tùy aōu pāyh tēy*, the business of colouring comes after the white ground of a picture. See the 上論 Sëāng lūn.

Höēy **憒** Confusion of mind, mental perturbation. Soō put tòng lé, chek höēy höēy è 事不當理則憒憒矣, *soō nā ūm tòng tō lé, chek sim kwna lwān*, when affairs are not consistent with reason, the mind becomes confused.

Höēy **潰** Dispersed, scattered, in confusion; angry. Höēy lwān 潰亂, confused and in disorder.

Höēy **聵** Deaf, hard of hearing.

Höēy **瞶** Blind, unable to see; the eyes dim: sore eyes.

Höēy **滙** Water turning round and uniting.

Höēy **僯** To bargain fairly for a thing.

六

Höēyh **血** Read hëet: blood. Lông hëet 膿血, *lông höēyh*, blood and matter. Hëet chëēn tek t'hwat 血戰得脫, *höēyh chëēn tit t'hàou*, after a bloody fight he got away.

3 x

犬

Hŏh 熇 Read, hok: thoroughly dried, burnt up.

天

Hŏh 鶴 Read hok: a stork. Hok bêng ê kéw ko, seng bûn ê t'hëen 鶴鳴于九皐.聲聞于天, *hŏh haôu tē kéw ko, sëⁿa t'hēⁿa kaòu t'heeⁿᵍ*, the stork screams over the nine marshes, and his voice is heard up to Heaven. See the 小雅 Seäou gnây.

犬

Hok 福 Happiness. E'ng hok 永福, *éng koó ây hok k'hè*, everlasting happiness. Hō hok boô put choō ké kêw che chēá 禍福無不自已求之者, *hō hwān hok k'hè bô ūᵐ sē ka tē kéw e*, misery and happiness are invariably the results of men's own seeking. See 孟子 Bēng choō.

Hok 侐 Still, quiet, retired.

Hok 洫 A ditch, a channel for water, a drain for irrigation. Pe kēung sit, jē chīn lek hoē koe hok 卑宮室而盡力乎溝洫, *sèy e ây kēung ch'hoò, jē chīn k'hwùy lat tē kaou hok*, he had but small palaces and houses, while he exhausted his strength upon ditches and drains (for the purpose of irrigating the rice fields). See the 論語 Lūn gé.

Hok 畐 The ancient form of 福 hok, happiness.

Hok 幅 Vulg. *pak*: a broad piece of cloth. Hok kin 幅巾, a scarf made of silk.

Hok 輻 The axle of a carriage.

Hok 蝠 Pëén hok 蝙蝠, *bit pŏ*, a bat. Hông hwûn tò sē, pëén hok hwuy 黃昏到寺蝙蝠飛, *maîⁿᵍ hwuiⁿᵍ kaoù ēeⁿᵍ, bit pŏ tit pwuy*, in the evening time, arriving at the temple, we may see the bats flying about.

Hok 腹 The entrails. Hok toē 腹肚, *pak toē*, the belly. Kéw kéw boô hoo, kong hoê hok sim 赳赳武夫公侯腹心, *yúng bêng ây boô hoo, sē kong hoê ây pak sim*, bold and courageous warriors are the heart and entrails of princes. See the 周南 Chew lâm.

Hok 復 Vulg. *kŏh*: to repeat; again. Hwân hok 反復, over and over again. Teng lêng hwân hok 叮嚀反復, *kŏh chaē teng lêng*, to enjoin again and again.

Hok 複 To repeat, double. Hok tō 複道, a place where two ways meet.

Hok 覆 To turn upside down, to overturn; to repeat; to examine. Hok tó 覆倒, *pak tó*, to turn upside down. Hok paē 覆敗, to defeat an enemy.

Hok 霍 A surname.

Hok 籗 An implement for catching fish, made of bamboo.

Hok 癨 A disordered state of the body. Hok lwān t'hoè sëà 癨亂吐瀉, to vomit and purge in a disorderly manner.

Hok 壑 A valley, a ravine, a pit, a gulf. Taē hok che wûy hut yëá, choô yëen put bwán, chëak yëen put hëet 大壑之爲物也.注焉不滿.酌焉不竭, *twā hok ây chô meēⁿh, choò kwān e bēy mwⁿá, yëóⁿᵍ ch'hut e bēy ta*, a large gulf is a sort of thing that cannot be filled up by pouring in, nor exhausted by lading out.

Hok 嗃 Stern rigid, severe.

Hok 㺉 The noise made by an angry pig.

Hok 熇 Vulg. *hŏh:* hot, burnt, dried up.

Hok 涸 Dry. Tēung ch'hew che gwat, súy sé hok 仲秋之月水始涸, *tēung ch'hew ây göĕyh, chúy k'hé t'haŏa ta,* in the middle month of autumn the waters begin to be dry.

Hok 佫 A surname.

Hòk 伏 To secrete, to conceal; to lie down, to prostrate: a surname. Kay gân bóng yew hok 嘉言罔攸伏, *hó ây uā nm t'hang baē hok,* good words must not be concealed.

Lēăng pông baē hok 两旁埋伏, *nun péng peeng woō baē hok,* there was an ambuscade on both sides of the way.

Hòk 茯 Hok lêng 茯苓, amber. Fable says that the gum of the cedar tree after having been a thousand years in the ground, is converted into amber.

Hòk 袱 Paou hok 包袱, a bundle, a bag for containing clothes.

Hòk 蕧 A hill overturned; the ravine of a hill.

Hòk 澓 Water eddying, and flowing rapidly.

Hòk 復 To return, to repeat, to go backwards and forwards on the same road; to answer, to speak.

Gân kwuy soo hok 言歸思復, *kóng böĕyh kwuy, sëōng tooing k'hè,* to talk of returning, and to think of going back. See the 小雅 Seăou gnây.

Yew hok ê ông chëá wat, goê lek chëuk é ké pek kin 有復於王者曰吾力足以舉百鈞, *nā woō lâng kap ông kóng, gwá ây lat ēy kăou gēă k'hè chin à pâyh kin,* "if any one were to tell your majesty, that his strength was sufficient to lift a hundred Kin, (or three thousand pounds) [would you believe him]." See 孟子 Bēng-chóo.

Hòk 緮 A kind of silk.

Hòk 鶴 Vulg. *hŏh:* a stork, a crane. Hok seēn 鶴扇, *hŏh seèng,* a fan made of stork's feathers. Also written 隺 hok.

Bēng hok chaē yim, kê chóo hō che 鳴鶴在陰其子和之, *haóu ây hŏh tē ch'hĕw yim, e ây kĕnà kap e hō,* the stork is screaming in the shade, and his young one is answering him.

Hòk 虙 The ancient form of 伏 hok, in the name of 伏羲, Hok-he.

Hòk 宓 A surname.

Hòk 服 E hok 衣服, clothes, apparel. Pöēy hok 佩服, to wear. Hâng hok 降服, to submit, to surrender. Hok soō 服事, *hok saē,* to serve.

E hok put pō, put kám é chêy 衣服不備不敢以祭, *sna k'hoè ūm chêy pē, ūm kná chèy,* not having suitable clothes prepared, we do not dare to sacrifice. See 孟子 Bēng choo.

Yew soō têy chóo hok kê lō 有事弟子服其勞, *woō sna soō têy chóo tëŏh hok e ây tëŏh bwâ,* when there is anything to do, children and nephews should subject themselves to the trouble. See the 論語 Lŭn gè.

Hong 風 The wind; spirit; influence; instruction. Hong sëuk 風俗 custom. Beasts at heat, or persons viciously inclined, are said to be 風 hong. Hong hwà 風化, renovating instruction.

Yéw hân chit, put k'hó é hong 有寒疾不可以風, *woō kwⁿâ ây paiⁿᵍ ṅᵐ t'hang lëóh hong*, I have a cold, I cannot go out in the wind. See the 上孟 Sëang bēng.

Hong 颯 The name of a country.

Hong 丰 The face full and good looking; also, luxuriant.

Hong 伴 The name of a sage.

Hong 凬 The ancient form of 風 hong.

Hong 楓 Hong sē 楓樹, *pooiⁿᵍ ch'hēw*, the sycamore tree. Fable says, that when the gum of the sycamore tree has been in the ground a thousand years, it becomes 琥珀 hoó pek, amber.

Hong 瘋 Head ache, a pain in the head; the medical books say, that when this pain is on the left side, it originates in phlegm and heat; and when on the right, it must be referred to inflammation and the state of the blood.

Hong 渢 The noise of water rushing along.

Hong 匚 A vessel for containing anything; one of the radicals.

Hong 方 A part, a place; a rule, a law. Vulg. *pooiⁿᵍ*, a surname. Sùè hong 四方, *sè neⁿᵍ*, all parts. Tēē hong 地方, *têy heⁿᵍ*, a place. Hong hwat 方法 a plan, a method. Yëák hong 藥方, *yóh heⁿᵍ*, a medicinal receipt.

Yéw pêng choō wán hong laê 有朋自遠方來, *woō pêng yéw thoā hwuiⁿᵍ heⁿᵍ laê*, having a friend coming from a distance (is it not delightful?). See the 上論 Sëang lūn.

Kaoù choó é gē hong 教子以義方, *kà sèy kèⁿà é jîn gē ây heⁿᵍ*, we must teach children by the rules of righteousness.

Hong 仿 To dislike, to injure.

Hong 枋 The name of a tree, of which carriages can be made.

Hong 坊 The name of a city or village. Jūn gwat chae tëông yâng, sëen é lëk pó hong 閏月再重陽.仙輿歷寶坊, *lūn göëyh kōh tëung yâng, sëen ây ch'hëa lëk köèy po heⁿᵍ*, the intercalary month falls again in the middle of summer, when the angel's chariot passes by the precious district.

Hong 祊 The name of a sacrifice within doors. Also, a sacrifice repeated on the following day; and a sacrifice to the four quarters.

Hong 汸 The expanse of water.

Hong 芳 Fragrant herbs, a sweet smell. Hwun hong 芬芳, fragrant odour.

Hong 峯 The peak of a hill. San hong 山峯, *swⁿa chēem*, the summit of a hill. Ko hong bān tëāng 高峯萬丈, *kwân ây swⁿa t'haôu chēⁿâ bān teⁿg*, a lofty peak, ten thousand fathoms high. Also written 峰 hong.

Hong 蜂 Vulg. *p'hang*: a bee. Bit hong 蜜蜂, a honey bee. Hông hong 黄蜂, *wuiⁿg p'hang*, a wasp. Hoé t'hoê hong 虎頭蜂, *hoé t'haôu p'hang*, a hornet. Hong bân yéw tok 蜂蠆有毒, *p'hang bân wōo tôk*, the sting of a bee is poisonous. See the 左傳 Chò-twān.

Hong 蠭 The same as the above. Chek yëw hong k'hé 賊猶蜂起, *ch'hat ch'hin chēōⁿg p'hang k'hé*, thieves spring up as thick as bees.

Hong 鋒 The point of a weapon, a sharp point. To hong 刀鋒, the point of a sword. Hong tek che jīm 鋒鏑之刄, the point and edge of a weapon.

Hong 灃 The name of a river.

Hong 酆 The name of a city, where 周文王 Chew-bûn-ông removed to. A surname.

Hong 豐 Full, replete, great, arrived at maturity. A surname. E' mô put hong bwân chëâ, put lêng ko hwuy 羽毛不豐滿者.不能高飛, *sit mô bô hong mwⁿâ, chēw bēy pwuy kaôu kwân*, when the feathers and wings are not replete and full, it is impossible to fly high. Hong sēng 豐盛, exuberant and full. Hong lëēn 豐年, *hô nceⁿg tang*, a fruitful year.

Hong 㒥 The name of an ancient man. Also written 倗 hong.

3 0

Hong 烽 A signal fire lighted on the borders, to give notice of the approach of an enemy. Hong yëen 烽烟, *yēen tun*, signal smoke.

Hong 烘 Vulg. *hang*: to warm at the fire, to toast, to roast. Hong lô 烘爐, *hang lô*, a furnace, a stove.

Hong 葑 The name of a vegetable, the leaves of which are sweet, but the root bitter. Ch'haé hong ch'haé bwuy, boô é hāy t'héy 采葑采菲.無以下體; *bân hong bân hwuy aᵐ t'hang e' ây hāy t'hèy*, in gathering the Hong and Hwuy vegetables, you must not take the bottom part. See the 衛風, Wöēy hong.

Hong 駹 A gallopping horse; the footsteps of a horse.

Hong 封 Great; added to, to promote to office. A surname. Hong wūy 封位, to bestow a rank. Hong sin 封信, *hong p'hey*, to close a letter. Hong këang che kaè 封疆之界, the borders of a territorial district.

Hong 搈 To beckon; to strike.

Hong 䀶 The eyes dim.

Hong 䳜 A bright colour.

Hong 荒 Overgrown with weeds, uncultivated, barren, unproductive; broad. Tëēn têw hong boô 田疇荒蕪, *ch'hân têw hwuiⁿg boô*, the fields growing wild and covered with underwood. Ke hong 饑荒, *yaou hwuiⁿg*, a famine.

Hong 㠦 The name of a hill.

声

Hóng 仿 Hóng hông 仿徨, agitated, undecided. Hóng hông put lêng k'hè 仿徨不能去, so agitated as to be unable to proceed. Also written 彷 hông.

Hóng 俸 Hóng lók 俸祿, emolument, pay of office. Cheng pek kwan hóng 增百官俸, kay cheng chēⁿâ păyh kwⁿa ây hông lók, to increase the salaries of all the officers.

Hóng 倣 To imitate, to learn. Ék sëang hâou hóng 亦相傚倣, yëá sëo ŏh t'hàn to learn of and imitate one another.

Hóng 澒 The quicksilver that is manufactured out of cinnabar. Bông hóng 濛澒, a great water, a wide expanse of water.

Hóng 放 To imitate, to follow; to rely on; to go to; inclined to, set upon. Hóng e lē jê hêng, to wàn 放於利而行多怨, t'hàn ê lē jê kēⁿâ, chēy wàn, to follow after gain in all our actions is a source of great bickering. See the 上論 Sëāng lūn.

Hóng 彷 Hóng hwut 彷彿, undecided; to see a thing indistinctly.

Hóng 髣 Hóng hwut 髣髴, the same as the above; not to acertain exactly.

Hóng 昉 The day beginning to be bright.

Hóng 恍 Hóng hwut 恍惚, undecided, hesitating.

Hóng 紡 The threads of a net. Hóng chek 紡績, p'háng chăyh, to spin thread.

Hóng 訪 To enquire, to ask, to visit. Hóng būn 訪問, hóng mooīⁿᵍ, to make enquiries.

Hóng 諷 To recite odes and music; to hint at; to ridicule. Jêng sëuk chok se, é hóng che 仍叔作詩以諷之, jêng chek chò se ê hóng ch'hè e, Jêng-sëuk made poetry to ridicule him.

Hóng 唪 To laugh out loud; also, a high mouth.

Hóng 謊 Hóng gân 謊言, păyh ch'hat wā, lies, deceitful words. Swat hóng 說謊, kóng păyh ch'hat, to tell a lie.

Hóng 捧 Vulg. p'hâng: to hold up in both hands, in order to present a thing.

Hóng 貺 To present, to give. Hóng soò 貺賜, to confer.

Hóng 況 Cold, ice.

Hóng 況 A form, a substance, appearance.

Hóng 珠 A valuable stone, like a gem.

Hóng 晃 Bright, luminous; broad, expansive. Kong hóng 光晃, resplendent.

Hóng 幌 A curtain, a screen.

Hóng 旰 The name of a place, in the 魯 Loé country.

Hóng 榥 A screen, or curtain; also, a reading couch.

Hóng 風 The same as 諷 hóng, to recite; also, to ridicule.

Hóng 舫 Two boats sailing abreast. Two boats tied together. Sêng hóng hāy kang kwan 乘舫下江關, *chēy sang chûn, lŏh káng kwan,* to sail in a double boat down to the pass on the river's side.

去

Hòng 放 Vulg. *pàng*: to let go, to set loose; to give way to; to allow; to set aside. Hòng soō 放肆, to be disorderly. Hòng sëà 放舍, to do away with. Hòng hoē tëung lêw 放乎中流, *pàng tē tëung laôu,* to let go down the middle of the stream.

Hòng lōng hêng haê 放浪形骸, *pàng êng lán ây hîn soo,* to give one's bodily powers up to sloth and self-indulgence.

Hòng 况 To compare. To make a visit of enquiry is called 來况, laê hòng.

Hòng 況 Moreover. Hô hòng 何況, how much rather: Sèng jîn ëk yew kò, hô hòng hwân sëâng che pöèy hoē 聖人亦有過.何况凡常之輩乎, *sèng jîn yëá wōo köèy sit, hô hòng hwân sëâng ây lâng,* even sages have their errors, how much more common people.

Hòng 眖 To look at; also a man's name.

Hòng 吽 A charm, an incantation, a prayer. Séw lōēy hwan cheng jit lëēm hòng 守內番僧日念吽, *twā hà ây laē, hwan á hoêy sëō^ng tàk jit laê lëēm keng* during the time of mourning the foreign priests came every day to recite their incantations.

Hòng 琩 To make presents for the service of the dead, even to one's carriage and horses.

Hòng 賵 To present anything for the service of the dead.

Hòng 貺 To give, to present. Lé sîn k'hong ëk boô hòng yëá 女承筐亦無貺也, *cha boē kw^nā nâ á, yëá bô sàng meē^nh,* a woman bringing a basket, but without any present.

平

Hông 皇 Elegant, great; a prince. Hông tèy 皇帝, an Emperor Sam hông 三皇, three fabulous Emperors, said to have existed before the time of Noah. Chîn-sé-hông hwûn se k'heng jê 泰始皇焚書坑儒, *Chîn-sé-hông sëo ch'hăyh, k'hai^ng Chàk ch'hăyh lâng,* the first Emperor of the Chîn dynasty burned the books and shut up the learned men in a pit (B. C. 200). Also, 皇甫 Hông-hoó, a double surname.

Hông 㣚 A great belly, a large stomach.

Hông 偟 Hông hông 彷偟, agitated, in confusion.

Hông 凰 A fabulous bird. Hōng-hông bêng è, è pé ko kong 鳳凰鳴矣于彼高岡, *hōng-hông lit haôu, twā tē hwùh lëy kwân sw^na,* the (fabulous birds) Hōng-hông are singing, on yonder lofty ridge. See the 小雅 Sëáou gnáy.

Hông 徨 Hông hông 彷徨, Hesitating, uncertain. Pông hông 徬徨, deliberating.

Boē-boé sek choo, jê keng k'hwa, Sey-choó hông hông jê boô kay 嫫母飾姿而矜夸.西子彷徨而無家, *Boē-boē che^ng t^na jê tëō^ng ka lē twā, Sey-choó hông hông, jê ch'hin chëō^ng bô kay,* the ugly Boē-boé when ornamented would boast of her greatness; but the handsome Sey-choó appeared in confusion as though belonging to no great family.

Hông 媓 A mother, according to the dialect of the southern 楚 Ch'hoé, state.

Hông 喤 The cry of a little child.

Hông 湟 The name of a river.

Hông 璜 The sound of gems.

Hông 蝗 A locust, an insect that devours the grain. T'hëûng hông wûy chae 蟲蝗爲災, *t'hâng hông chò chae haē*, insects and locusts are very injurious.

Hông 潢 A pool in which water collects. Gîn hông 銀潢, the milky way.

Hông 惶 To be deceived, to be alarmed. Hông k'hëúng 惶恐, to be afraid. Keng hông 驚惶, *kë^{n}a hë^{n}â*, to tremble with fear.

Sëaou-kóng ch'hëûng pô, pek sêng hông jëaóu 蕭廣縱暴百姓惶擾, *Sëaou-kóng lam sàm pò gëak, pàyh sai^{ng} kë^{n}a hë^{n}â jëaou lwân*, Sëaou-kóng was outrageously oppressive, till the people were alarmed and thrown into confusion.

Hông 煌 K'hwun hông 焜煌, bright and luminous; clear. Tong bûn che yâng bêng seng hông hông 東門之楊明星煌煌, *tang mooi^{ng} ây yâng lêw, bêng ch'hai^{ng} kwui^{ng} kwui^{ng}*, through the willow-tree at the eastern gate, the bright stars shine very clear.

Hông 篁 The name of a bamboo very hard, and with short joints.

Hông 遑 Leisure; haste. Put hông hây sit 不遑暇食, *bô êng t'hang chëăh*, no leisure even to eat.

Hông 崲 The name of a place. Hew hông hoê 休崲湖, the name of a lake.

Hông 艎 A boat, a vessel. Hwuy hông 飛艎, a flying boat, i. e. swift.

Hông 黃 Vulg. *wui^{ng}*: yellow, a yellow colour. A surname. Hông këang 黃薑, *wui^{ng} këo^{ng}*, turmeric. Hong sëâng gwân kit 黃裳元吉, *wui^{ng} yîn, chëô^{ng} twā hó*, a yellow robe is in the highest degree lucky. See the 易經 Ek-keng.

Hông 簧 A pipe; a lute; the tongue of a flute. Ch'huy seng koé hông 吹笙鼓簧, *ch'höey p'hin p'hun hông*, to blow the flute, and play upon the pipe.

Hông 隍 The moat under a city wall; a city ditch.

Hông 鐄 A great bell.

Hông 鍠 The sound of bells and drums. Chëung koé hông hông 鍾鼓鍠鍠, *cheng koé hông hông*, the bells and drums gave a rumbling sound.

Hông 航 A boat, a vessel. P'hè lîm hô jê boô hông 譬臨河而無航, *ch'hin chëô^{ng} laē kaôu kâng, jê bô chûn*, it is like coming to a river, and not finding a boat.

Hông 䲳 To fly down; to dart down from a height.

Hông 鴻 A large king of wild goose. Hông gân 鴻雁, wild geese.

Hông 黌 A place of learning.

Hông 癀 Hông chëúng 癀腫, *wui^{ng} chéng*, the jaundice.

Hông 妨 A hindrance; to injure; to impede. Sûy t'haè choò yúng, soe pē ch'hâm hwûy, t'hàn wat, gnó taē kak sin hông 隨太子勇.數被讒毀.歎曰.我大覺身妨, *sûy t'haè choò kĕò yúng tak paē hōē lâng saē p'hwà hwûy pòng, chēw t'hò k'hwùy kóng, gwá twā kak hìn sin woō hông gaē*, the heir apparent to the state of Sûy, named Yúng, was frequently slandered and reviled; when he, sighing, exclaimed, I am fully aware that I am personally impeded.

Boô hông 無妨, *bô gaē tēŏh*, no impediment, no hindrance.

Hông 魴 Hông gê 魴魚, *hâng á hê*, the skate fish.

Hông 防 To obstruct, to oppose, to forbid, to provide against. Tey hông 隄防, to obstruct. Hông pē 防備, *tëo^{ng} tē*, to provide against. Kwun choò soo hwân, jê ē hông che 君子思患.而豫防之, *kwun chóo sëö^{ng} kan lân jê taē seng tëo^{ng} tē*, the good man anticipates evil, and provides against it. See the 易經 Ek keng.

Hông kim 防禁, to forbid.

Hông 縫 Vulg. *pâng*: to sew, to stitch; a seam.

Hông 逢 To meet with, to befal, to come in contact with. Soō hoē kong k'heng, hong gêng è ché 伺候公卿逢迎意旨, *têng haōu kong k'heng, böëyh g^{n}ëă cheĕh e ây è chè*, to wait for the princes and nobles, in order to meet their wishes and pleasure. See the 戰國策 Chëèn kok ch'hek.

S. 2

Hông 洚 The name of a river.

Hông 弘 Great, large, immense. To enlarge. A surname. Jîn lêng hông tō 人能弘道, *lâng ëy hông twā e ây tō*, people have it in their power to enlarge their way. See the 論語 Lūn gé.

Hông 芃 Luxuriant herbage. Hông hông kê bek 芃芃其麥, *boē sëng e ây bäyh bow*, luxuriantly that wheat grows. See the 衛風 Wöēy hong.

Hông 蓬 Tall grass, long grass, not kept in order. A surname.

Hông 髼 Hông song 髼鬆, dishevelled hair.

Hông 宏 Great, immense. Chông lūn hông gē 崇論宏議, *kwân twā ây gē lun*, lofty and magnanimous discourse and reasonings.

Hông 紘 A thread, a string; the belt in which a cross bow is worn.

Hông 泓 Water deep and clear.

Hông 閎 The gate at the head of a lane. Ko kê hān hông 高其閈閎, *ch'hòng kwân e ây hëo^{ng} lē mooi^{ng}*, to raise higher the gate of the village.

Hông 葒 A kind of water plant; grass and rushes growing in the water.

Hông 葓 The same as the above.

Hông 洪 Great. Hông sûy 洪水, *twā chúy*, great water, a flood; Vulg. *âng*: a surname.

Seang sëang hông súy hong kat 湯湯洪水方割, *sëang sëang ây twā chúy toō toō ch'hòng haē*, when the overwhelming floods bagan first to cut off and destroy, (alluding to the great flood about the time of *Noah.*) See the 堯典 Geâou tëên.

Hông 帪 A kind of flag.

Hông 紅 Vulg. *âng*: red. Hông bëen 紅面, *âng bīn*, a red face. A surface. Hông ché put é wûy sëet hok 紅紫不以爲褻服, *âng chèe^ng bô lëăh e chò sae k'hëā ây yîn chëō^ng*, he would not use red and vermilion colours for his private dress. Said of Confucius, in the 論語 Lūn gé.

Hông 虹 Vulg. *k'hēng*: a rainbow. Kwùy ch'hun hông sé hëen, bēng tong hông chông put hëen 季春虹始見孟冬虹藏不見, *ch'hun bōëy k'hēng k'hè t'haôu hëen tang t'haôu k'hēng k'hè^ng ū^m hëen*, in the latter month of spring the rainbow appears, and in the first month of winter it retires and is not seen.

Hông 璜 A half gem; a kind of gem. T'haē kong tëàou é wûy, tek gëuk hông 太公釣於渭得玉璜, *t'haē kong tëò hê tē wûy chúy, chēw tit tëŏh gëuk hông*, T'haê-kong was angling in the waters of the Wûy, and fished up a gem. See the 史記 Soó kè.

Hông 紘 The tassels of a cap or crown.

Hōng 奉 To receive from a superior; to offer up; to present, to nourish. Lïn sëang jê hōng p'hek jip chin 藺相如奉璧入秦, *līn sëang jê sàng p'hek jip chîn kok*, Lin-sëang-je carried the gem as a present into the Chin country. See the 史記 Soó kè.

Hok lô hōng yáng, bē chëuk wûy haôu yëa 服勞奉養.未足爲孝也, *hok e ây tëŏh bwâ hōng yáng pāy boē, bô kaōu swui^ng chò woō haôu*, to labour for, and support our parents, is not enough to constitute filial piety. See the commentary of the 上諭 Sëang lūn. Hōng soō 奉事, to serve. Hōng kaòu 奉敎, to receive instruction.
Hōng hëen 奉獻, to offer up, to present.

Hōng 鳳 A fabulous bird, said to appear when sages spring up. A surname. Sùn sê hōng hông laê gê 舜時鳳凰來儀, *sùn ây sê hōng hōng ây chëâou laê kë^nā lêy gê*, in the time of Sūn the lucky birds appeared to pay their compliments to him.

Hōng 汞 Quicksilver, mercury; The same as 澒 hóng.

Hōng 䎫 A sound or drumming in the ears.

Hōng 哄 The sound of singing; singing in a chorus. Hōng p'hëen 哄騙, to deceive.

Hōng 俸 Hōng lok 俸祿, emolument, salary; also read hóng. Kong sun hông, hōng lok sīm to 公孫弘俸祿甚多, *kong sun hông ây hōng lok chîn chaē chēy*, Kong-sun-hông's emoluments were very great.

Hoo 夫 Tëāng hoo 丈夫, a yeoman, a full-grown man; a husband. Taē hoo 大夫, a great officer. Hoo ch'hey 夫妻, *ang chëa*, husband and wife. Pok hoo 僕夫, a servant. Tam hoo 擔夫, a carrier. Má hoo 馬夫, *bēy hoo*, an ostler. Hoo choo 夫子, the designation of a philososopher, generally applied to Confucius; a particle used at the beginning of a sentence.

Ch'hoó che wūy taē tëāng hoo 此之謂大丈夫, *chëy sē kóng këò twā tëāng hoo,* this is what is called a truly great man. See 孟子 Bēng choō.

Tëāng hoo seng, jê gwān wūy che yéw sit 丈夫生而願爲之有室, *ta po kēⁿá saiⁿᵍ jê aè kap e woō ch'hoō,* when a man is grown up, it is desirable that he should have a family. See 孟子 Bēng choō.

E t'hwat hok, hoo ch'hey hwán bok 輿脫輻夫妻反目, *ch'hëa t'hwat e ây hok, ang poè hwán bák,* when the carriage is deprived of its axletree, husband and wife begin to turn their eyes from each other, (i. e. when poverty comes in at the door, love flies out at the window.) See the 易經 Ék keng.

Hoo 玞 Boó hoo 珷玞, a stone like a gem; also written 砆 hoo.

Hoo 趺 Kay hoo 跏趺, to sit cross legged; to sit large and full.

Hoo 鈇 A kind of hatchet. Put noē jê t'in wuy ê hoo wat 不怒而民威於鈇鉞, *ūᵐ saè sim böëy tŏh, jê pāyh saiⁿᵍ kēⁿa lán ây wuy hong, k'hăh ch'hám e hoo wat,* without being angry, the people will respect our dignity more than they will dread axes and hatchets.

Hoo 桴 A raft made of split bamboos; also, a drum-stick. Tō put hêng sêng hoo hoō ê haé 道不行乘桴浮於海, *to bëy kēⁿá, taè payh chëōⁿᵍ hoo, p'hoō köëy haé,* our doctrines do not spread, let us then mount a raft, and float over the sea. See the 上論 Sëāng lūn.

Kwūy hoo jê t'hoé, kóe 蕢桴而土鼓, *ch'haou hoo, jê t'hoé koé,* a straw drum stick and an earthenware drum. See the 禮記 Léy kè.

Hoo 稃 The husk of grain; coarse chaff.

Hoo 麩 The husk of wheat.

Hoo 孚 Tō believe. Gê hêng Bûn Ông bān pang chok hoo 儀刑文王萬邦作孚, *gê lëy hêng hwat t'han bûn ông bān pāng ây lāng chëw sin lán,* when in polite ceremonies and penal laws we imitate Bûn-ong, all nations will believe us.

Hoo 琈 Oo hoo 瑀琈, a beautiful gem.

Hoo 敷 To spread, to diffuse, to spread out to arrange. Hoo poè 敷布, to diffuse. Kèng hoo gnoé kaòu 敬敷五教, *kèng hoo poè gnoé lūn ây kaoù,* respectfully to diffuse the five rules of instruction.

Hoo 不 The central part of a flower, the calyx also written 柎 hoo.

Hoo 痡 Sick, diseased. Gnó pok hoo ê 我僕痡矣, *gwá ây gīn á paiⁿᵍ,* my servant is sick. See the 南周 Chew lâm.

Hoo 柎 The calyx or foot of a flower. The same as 不 hoo.

Hoo 膚 The skin. P'hê hoo 皮膚, skin and flesh; also, elegant, and great. Hoo jê gêng che 膚如凝脂, *hoo p'höëy ch'hin chëōⁿᵍ këen làng ây yëw,* with a skin as smooth as congealed ointment. See the 衛風 Wöëy hong.

Hoo 罦 Hoo bóng 罦網, a net. Yéw t'hoé, wān wān, lê lê ê hoo 有兔爰爰雉離于罦, *woō t'hoè wān wān, t'hê key ló tê bāng,* there was a rabbit thereabouts.

and lo! a wild fowl was caught in the net. See the 詩經 Se keng.

Hoo 罘 The same as the above; a net that turns on a wheel for catching birds and small beasts.

Hoo 俘 A prisoner of war; one taken in battle. Hoo hek 俘獲, to take prisoner. Chêy jin laê kwuy wöëy hoo 齊人來歸衛俘, *chêy kok ây láng laê sàng tó tooi^{ng} wöëy kok ây hoo*, the people of the Chêy country came to return the prisoners of the Wöëy country.

Hoo 傅 A teacher; the name of an office. T'hëen choó yéw t'haè soo, t'haè hoo, t'haè pó, wûy sam kong 天子有大師.大傅.大保.爲三公, *hông tèy wöo t'haè soo, t'haè hoo, t'haè pó, chò s^{n}a kong*, the Emperor has a great teacher, a great instructor, and a great preserver, who are called the three nobles.

Soo hoo 師傅, an instructor; a title of respect for a Buddhist priest.

Hoo 休 Hoo jin lé 休仁李, a kind of fruit.

虛

Hoó 甫 An elegant appellation for a man; also, great; beginning; all. Confucius was called 孔甫 k'hóng hóo.

Hoó 俌 To assist; the same as 輔 hoō.

Hoó 俯 To look down at, to bend downwards to behold those beneath us. Gëäng chĕuk ê soō hoō boĕ, hoó, chĕuk é hëuk ch'hey choó 仰　以事父母.俯足以畜妻子, *t^{n}a k'hè k'hw^{n}à, ëy kaōu hok saē pāy boĕ, p'hak lŏh laê keē^{ng} ëy kaōu yëō^{ng} ch'hē boĕ kē^{n}á*, on looking upwards we shall have sufficient where-with to serve our parents, and on looking down, we shall have enough where-with to feed one's wife and children. See 孟子 Bēng choó.

Hoó 頫 Like, resembling, accordant with. Léy gak hoó t'hëen tēy che chêng 禮樂俌天地之情, *lèy gak ēy ch'hin chëō^{ng} t'hee^{ng} tēy ây chêng*, suitable ceremony and music are accordant to the feelings of Heaven and earth, (i. e. of nature).

Hoó 府 Hoó k'hoè 府庫, a treasury. Chew hoó 州府, a district, a colony. Ong hoó 王府, a palace. Kwan hoó 官府, *kw^{n}a hoó*, a magistrate or mandarin.

Bē yéw hoó k'hoè chaê hwuy kê chaê chöá yëá 未有府庫財非其財者也, *böëy woō hoó k'hoè ây chee^{ng}, a^{m} sē e ây chee^{ng}*, there is no such thing as the money in a man's treasury, not being his own money. See 大學 Bēng choó.

Hoó 俛 To look down-wards; the same as 俯 hoó. Also used for 勉 bëën, to encourage, to exert.

Hoó 黼 Hoó hwut 黼黻, a cap of dignity; hatchets and other weapons embroidered on a ruler's cap, to inspire terror into his subjects.

Hoó 釜 A caldron without feet. E' hoó chëng ch'hwàn 以釜甑爨, *t'hó tē^{n}á à bók k'haōu á chè*, to use pans and earthen pots in cooking.

Hoó 莆 Chëet hoó 萐莆, a fortunate plant, spoken of in the time of 堯 geāou.

Hoó 脯 Dried meat. Koe chéw ch'hē hoó put sit 沽酒市脯不食, *bëy ây chèw, kay ch'hē ây bŭh kw^{n}a, ū^{m} chëăh*, wine bought in the shops, and dried meat brought in from the market, Confucius would not eat: (because he feared they might be unclean). See the 論語 Lūn gê.

Hoó 簠 Hoó k'hwúy 簠簋, a sacrificial implement; a vessel for holding the fruits offered in sacrifice; used in the 周 chew dynasty.

Hoó 撫 To cherish, to soothe, to encourage, to stroke; also read Boó. Hoō hêy seng gnó, hoé hêy këuk gnó, hoó gnó, hëuk gnó 父兮生我.母兮鞠我.撫我畜我, *nëō^{ng} pāy sai^{ng} gwá, nëō^{ng} lêy këuk gwá, hoó gwá, ch'hē gwá*, my father begat me, my mother sustained me, cherished me, and nourished me. See the 小雅 Sëāou gnáy.

Hoó joō tān bîn 撫字萬民, to cherish and soothe all the people.

Hoó 斧 A hatchet. Hoó jip lîm 斧入林, *poó t'hâou jip eh'hēw nâ*, the hatchet enters the woods.

K'hóng choó chok ch'hun ch'hew, yit joō che pëén gëêm ê hoó wat 孔子作春秋.一字之貶嚴於斧鉞, *k'hóng choó chò ch'hun ch'hew, chit jē ây pëén t'hek lâng, k'hăh gëêm ê hoó wat*, when Confucius composed the Ch'hun-ch'hew (a history of his own life and times) every character implying blame, was felt more severely than a hatchet. See the 史記 Soó kè.

Hoó 父 A title of respect.

Hoǒ 拊 To beat, to strike; also the same as 撫 hoó, to stroke, to soothe.

Hoó 腑 Chōng hoó 臟腑, the viscera, the intestines. Choo hoê choó tēy, jëak he hoǒ 諸侯子弟若肺腑, *choo hoê ây choó tēy, ch'hin chëō^{ng} pak sim*, the children and nephews of the princes should be like our lungs and viscera. See the 史記 Soó kè.

Hoó 腐 Vulg. *nw^{n}ā*: rotten, decayed. Hoó ch'hó hwà wûy êng 腐草化爲燃, *nw^{n}ā ch'haòu hwà chò hüêy kîm ch'hai^{ng}*, decayed vegetables produce fire flies.

Hoó jê 腐儒, *nw^{n}ā t'hak ch'hăyh lâng*, a rotten scholar.

Hoó 簠 The same as 簠 hoó, a sacrificial implement.

去

Hoò 富 Vulg. *poò*. rich, affluent, abundant, wealthy. A surname; also written 冨 hoò.

Kwùy sē hoò ê chew kong 季氏富於周公 *kwùy sē k'hăh poò ê chew kong*, Kwùy-sē was richer than Chew-kong. See the 論語 Lūn gé.

Hoò yéw t'hëen hāy, jê put chëuk ê kaé yew 富有天下.而不足以解憂, *poò woē t'hee^{ng} āy jê bô kaòu ê kày hwân lô*, he was so wealthy as to possess the whole Empire, and yet this was not sufficient to dissipate his sorrow. See 孟子 Bēng choó.

Hoò 付 To give, to give over, to deliver into any one's hands. Hoò t'hok 付托 to give in charge. Maē hoō 賣付 to betray.

Jëak k'hó hoò chek kè put lô, jê hëên chaê put sit ê 若可付則己不勞而賢才不失矣, *ch'hin chëō^{ng} ēy hoò t'hok, chek ko tē ū^{m} lëŏh bwá, jê gaôu ây chaê lëaōu bey ū^{m} kee^{ng}*, if we can entrust any one with the charge, then we ourselves shall not be troubled, and clever talent will not be lost. Said by Confucius.

Hoò 賦 To exact; to require, to diffuse. Kòng hoò 貢賦, taxes, revenue. Peng hoò 兵賦, military levies. Se hoò 詩賦, a diffuse, loose poem; a ditty. Pín hoò 稟賦, to receive.

Sèng chëá, jîn séy pín hoò ê t'hëen yëá 性者人所稟賦於天也, *sai^{ng} sē lâng sëy pín hoò ê t'hee^{ng}*, nature is that which men have received from Heaven.

Hoò 仅 The same as 付 hoò, to give over.—

Hoò **仆** To lie down, to throw down, to throw down flat; also written 踣 hoò. Yëuk chëang hoò che, pit ko ké che 欲將仆之必高舉之, *aè böëyh hëet mëⁿh lăh k'hè, pit tëŏh këăh kè k'hăh kwân*, if you want to throw anything down flat, you must lift it up high.

Hoò **赴** To go to, to visit. Hoò he 赴墟, to go to market. Hoò tek sëang toè 赴敵相鬪, *hoò tek sëo p'hăh*, to go and fight with the enemy.

Hoò **訃** To inform; to inform of the decease of any one. Hwân choo hoê tŏng, bêng eng, chek hoò é kò 凡諸侯同盟薨則訃以告, *hwân choo hoê tâng bêng kadu sè, chek tëŏh k'hè kap e kòng*, all the princes of the Empire that were of the same confederacy, on the demise of any one, informed one another of it. See the 左傳 Chó twān.

Hoò **覆** Vulg. *k'hèng*: to cover, to overspread. T'hëen che séy hoò, tēy che séy chaé 天之所覆地之所載, *t'heeⁿᵍ ây sèy k'hèng, tēy ây sèy chaè*, whatever the Heaven overspreads, or the earth sustains. See the 中庸 Tëung yûng.

Hoò **副** To assist, to second, to help, to abet. Hoò jē 副貳, an assistant.

Hoò **咐** Hwûn hoò 吩咐, *hwân hoò*, to order, to enjoin, to insist upon, to give any one charge.

平 Hoô **扶** To hold, to sustain, to hold up, to assist. A surname. Hoô k'hé 扶起, to lift up.

Gwûy jê put tê, tëén jê put hoô, chek chëang yëen yūng pé sëàng è 危而不持顛而不扶則將焉用彼相矣, *gwûy hëëm jê bô tê gīm, lëën tó jê bô hoô k'hè, chek chëang an chwⁿa yūng e chò sëàng*, if a man does not sustain his prince, when in danger, nor in his overthrow uphold him; of what use will he be as his minister. See the 論語 Lūn gé.

Hoô **夫** A particle, implying wonder or enquiry. Choó chaē ch'hwan sëāng wat, se chëā jê soo hoô 子在川上曰逝者如斯夫, *hoo choó lē chúy têng kóng, e köèy k'hè kadu an nêy saiⁿᵍ hoô*, when Confucius was upon (the banks of) a stream, he exclaimed, how incessantly does it flow! See the 論語 Lūn gé.

Hoô **芙** Hoô yûng 芙蓉, the name of a plant, the marsh mallow.

Hoô **符** A cheque. Hoô hap 符合, the two parts of a cheque put together. Hoô sē 符誓, a charm. Hwā hoô 畫符, to write charms. A surname.

Tek chè hêng hoē tëung kok, jëak hap hoô chëet 得志行乎中國若合符節, *tit lëŏh gwûn ây sim chè, chēw èy këⁿâ t'hong tëung kok, ch'hin chëōⁿᵍ hap hoô chëet*, obtaining my wish, I should be able to travel through the whole of China, (and find correspondent feelings,) like uniting the two parts of a cheque. See 孟子 Bēng choó.

Hoô **蚨** Hoô sëên 蚨蟬, a certain water insect which never separates from its off-spring; so that if you take the one, you are sure to get the other; hence foolish people rub some of the blood of this insect on various pieces of money, one of which being kept in the till, and others put into circulation, the one is sure to bring all the others back to it.

Hoô **浮** Vulg. *poô*: to float on the surface of the water. Hoô haé jê yêw 浮海而遊, *poô tē haè jê t'hit t'hô*, to float and sport on the bosom of the deep.

Hoô **鳧** A wild duck, a water fowl. Hoô e chaè keng 鳧鷖在涇, *ăh kwà chúy chëaóu twā tē keng chúy*, ducks

福建方言字典

and wild fowl upon the Keng waters. See the 大雅 Taē gnáy.

Hoô 蜉 Hoô yêw 蜉蝣, an insect, a kind of grasshopper.

Hoô 芣 Hoô é 芣苢, a kind of medicinal plant.

Hoô 枹 A drum-stick; a stick for beating any-thing. Chó chip pè, yēw chip hoô jê koé, má yit put lêng ché 左執轡右援枹而鼓馬逸不能止, *tó ch'hèw gīm pè, chēⁿà ch'hèw gīm hoô, jê p'hăh koé, bèy chēw chaóu bēy hăyh,* holding the bridle in the left hand, and the drum-stick in the right, if we beat the drum, the horse will gallop off without stopping. See the 左傳 Chó twān.

Hoô 咐 To blow out the breath; to order, to enjoin; also read hoó.

Hoô 颫 A great wind, a wind coming down from a height.

Hoô 苻 The name of a plant; also called 鬼目草, kwúy bòk ch'ho, devils eye grass.

Hoô 涪 The name of a river, and of a district.

Hoô 紑 White clothes, clean and new.

Hoô 榑 Hoô song 榑桑, a kind of super-natural mulberry tree that grows on the east of the 崑崙, K'hwun Lûn hill towards the sun rising; hence the common expression, that the sun rises at 榑桑 Hoô Song.

去 Hoō 輔 To help, to assist, to aid, to second; also, the checks. Chew kong këep hoô sêng ông 周公夾輔成王, *chew kong hoô chăn sêng ông,* Chew-kong sustained and assisted Sêng-ông. See the 史記 Soó kè.

E' yéw hoō jîn 以友輔仁, *é pêng yéw hoō choē jîn tek,* we should have friends that will assist us in virtue. See the 論語 Lūn gé.

Hoō 父 Vulg. *neōⁿᵍ pāy:* a father. Hoō boé 父母, *pāy boé,* father and mother. Hoō boé wûy kê chit che yew 父母唯其疾之憂, *pāy boé tok kēⁿa haōu satⁿᵍ woō paiⁿᵍ. ây hwān ló,* parent's only anxiety is lest their children should be sick. See the 論語 Seāng lūn.

Hoō 伏 Vulg. *poō:* to sit on eggs, as a bird. Hêung key hoō choó 雄雞伏子, *key kak poō kēⁿá,* a cock is said to have once sat on fowl's eggs.

Hoō 傅 Soo hoō 師傅, a teacher, the name of an office. Vulg. *poè:* a sorname. Hoō hōey 傅會, a constrained com-pliance.

Hoō 媍 The same as 婦 hoō, a woman. Ló hoō 老媍, a common appellation for mother.

Hoō 負 To carry on the back or shoulders; to bear; to sustain; to turn the back upon. Vulg. *yang:* to carry pick-a-back. Pan pek chëá put hoō taē ô tō loē è 頒白者不負戴於道路矣, *mó pwⁿà pàyh ây lâng, bô gîâ keⁿᵍ meēⁿh tē tō loē,* men half grey would not then have to carry burthens in the roads. See 孟子 Bēng choó.

Hoō choó 負主, to turn the back on one's master.

Hoō 駙 Assisting aiding. Hoō má 駙馬, the name of an office, given to one who marries a princess.

Hoō 附 To rely on, to lean upon; elegant; to add, to increase. San hoō ê tēy 山附于地, *swⁿa wá tē tēy,* the hills rest upon the ground.

Hoō yûng 附庸, an inferior state depending on a superior one.

Kēw yëá wûy che chē lëëm jè hoō ek che 求也爲之聚斂而附益之, *kēw yëá t'hēy e k'hëöh sëèy, jê, t'hëem e k'hăh chêy,* Kēw gathered the taxes for him, and thus increased his wealth. See the 論語 Lūn gé.

Hoō 祔 To asociate in sacrificing i. e. to place the memorial tablet of one's immediate parent with these of remote ancestors, and to sacrifice to them alike; also, to bury together, to put in the same grave.

Hoō 阜 A wide grassy plain; full, luxuriant. Soo hoō 師阜, *sae hoō,* a master workman, one who is clever at his business.

Hoō 婦 Vulg. *cha hoé:* a woman, a female, a married woman. Sit hoō 媳婦, *sim poō,* a daughter-in-law; a son's wife.

E sūn wûy chèng chëá, ch'hëep hoō che tō yëá 以順爲正者妾婦之道也, *é sūn lëâng chò chèng keng sē sèy ê cha boé ây tō lé,* to consider obedience as the point of perfection, is the highest duty of concubines and women. See 孟子 Bēng choó.

Hoō 賻 To assist people on funeral occasions; to contribute money towards burying the dead.

K'hóng choó gē kēw kwán jīn che song, sëàng t'hwat ch'ham è hoō che 孔子遇舊舘人之喪嘗脫驂以賻之, *k'hóng choó toó tëŏh keō kwán sëà ây lâng woō se^{ng} hà, bat t'haöu bèy è hoō e,* Confucius meeting with an old host of his, in mourning, took one of the horses out of his carriage, and sold it to assist him in burying his dead.

Hoō 鮒 A small fresh water fish.

Hoō 腐 Toē hoō 豆腐, *taou hoō,* a jelly-like preparation from pulse, very much eaten by the Chinese.

平

Hûm 媒 Read böēy, a match-maker; a go-between to make up matrimonial connections. Böēy jîn 媒人, *hû^{m} lâng,* a mediator in marriages.

Kim sek che hô sek hêy, gnó tok boô ch'hoo lëâng böēy 今夕之何夕兮我獨無此良媒, *t$_{n}$a mai^{ng} hwui^{ng} sē hô mai^{ng} gwá lok bô chèy lëy hó hû^{m} lâng,* this evening is a lucky evening, but alas! I have not got a good match-maker; (in order to get married).

Hûm 茅 Read maoû: long grass used in thatching. Maôu ok 茅屋, *hû^{m} á ch'hoò,* a thatched cottage.

声

Hwa 㓦 To cut, to split.

Hwa 花 A flower; also read hwà, which see.

上

Hwá 觟 A she goat with horns.

Hwá 踝 The bones on the sides of the legs, are called 踝足 hwá chëuk.

Hwá 倮 The naked body.

去

Hwà 化 Chò hwà 造化, to create. Chó boô wûy yéw, hwà yéw wûy boô, wûy che chò hwà 造無爲有化有爲無謂之造化, *chò bô chë^{n}á woō hwà woō ây chë^{n}á bô kóng keò chó hwà,* to make something out of nothing and to connect something into nothing, is called to create and annihilate; also written 七 hwà.

Pëén hwà 變化, to change, to convert, to reform. Kaòu hwà 教化, to instruct, to teach; instruction, philosophy.

平 Hwâ 花 A flower, the blossoms of trees and plants. A surname. Hwâ yéw ch'heng hëang, gwat yéw yim 花有清香.月有陰, *hwâ woō ch'heng p'hang göëyh woō yim*, flowers have a pure fragrance, and the moon shews a pleasing shade.

Hwâ 蕚 Hwâ eng 蕚英, flowers and blossoms The same as the above.

Hwâ 譁 Swan hwâ 諠譁, to make a noise, to make an uproar; the noise of many people talking together.

Hwâ 華 The same as 花 hwâ, a flower, flowery. Hwâ hāy 華夏, the flowery summer, another name for China; also called, tëung hwâ 中華, the middle flower. A surname.

Hwâ 驊 Hwâ lêw má 驊騮馬, a very fine horse.

Hwâ 鏵 A kind of spade.

去 Hwā 畫 Vulg. *wā*: to paint, to describe, to draw, to draw a line, a stroke; also written 畫 hwa.

Höēy hwā che suō hoē soé kong 繪畫之事後素功, *höēy wā ây soō tùy āou soé pàyh ây kang*, the business of painting comes after the trouble of forming the ground.

Hwā 話 Vulg. *wā*: discourse, language, talk. Kàng hwā 講話, *kóng wā*, to talk, to discourse. Tông hwā 唐話, *tĕⁿᵍ wā*, the chinese language.

Boē t'hok yit kwàn se, hōēy è jê kay hwā 暮讀一卷書,會意如嘉話, *maîⁿᵍ hwuiⁿᵍ t'hak chit gún ch'háyh, kaòu hōēy e ây è ch'hin chëōⁿᵍ kóng hó wā*, in the evening when we peruse a book, as soon as we understand its meaning, it is like holding an elegant conversation.

Hwā 喀 Hwā hwā hoé 喀喀吼, *hwā hwā haóu*, to call and bawl out aloud.

Hwā 擭 A cage or trap for confining wild beasts. K'he jê lap choo koé hwā, hām chēng che tëung 驅而納諸罟擭陷阱之中, *kwⁿá jê lap tē koé wā, hām chaîⁿᵍ ây tang eⁿᵍ*, to drive on and entrap in some net or cage, or in the middle of some pit-fall. See the 中庸 Tëung yûng.

平 Hwⁿa 歡 Read hwan: to be pleased. Hwan hé 歡喜, *hwⁿa hé*, to be delighted. Ch'hwat sëuk yim súy, chīn kê hwan 啜菽飲水盡其歡, *ch'höëyh sëyh á lim chúy, chīn e ây hwⁿa hé*, even when quaffing preparations of pulse and drinking water, he experiences the utmost delight. See the 禮記 Léy kè.

上 Hwⁿá 擱 Read jwàn: to rub anything between the hands, in order to wash it clean. Jwàn sëén 擱洗, *hwⁿá sèy*, to wash by the hand.

去 Hwⁿà 旦 Read tàn: the clear day, late in the morning. Bêng tàn 明旦, *bîn hwⁿà jit*, tomorrow. *Bîn hwⁿà*, by and bye.

平 Hwⁿâ 横 Read hêng: across, athwart, lying crossways, transverse. Chêûng hêng 從横, *ch'hân hwⁿâ*, athwart, transverse.

Kê hêng gek yêw sē yëá, kwun choó pit choō hwán yëá 其横逆猶是也.君子必自反也, *e ây hwⁿâ kàyh yëâ an nëy saîⁿᵍ, kwun choó pit ka tē hwán yëâ*, when these cross and perverse things still continue the same, the good man will turn in and reflect upon himself. See 孟子 Bēng-choó.

3 R

Hwⁿâ **蔽** Read kêng: a stalk or stem. Ē kêng 芋莖, oē hwⁿâ, the stalk of the *arum*, a plant with a large leaf and edible root, growing in marshy places.

Hwⁿâ **桁** Read hêng: a cross-beam. Ok hêng 屋桁, ch'hoò hwⁿâ, the cross-beam of a house.

Hwân sē hêng sëâng boû hëên e 還視桁上無懸衣, *tŏh toŋiⁿᵍ k'hwⁿà hwⁿâ chëōⁿᵍ bô teaòu ây sⁿa*, turning round he saw that there were no clothes hanging upon the cross-beam to dry.

去 Hwⁿā **岸** Read gān: a bank, an embankment. Kang gān 江岸, *kâng hwⁿā*, the bank of a river. Tëên gān 田岸, *ch'hân hwⁿā*, a raised bank between the paddy fields, used both for retaining the water, and as a path way.

Hwⁿā **按** Read àn: to stop, to hold back, to lay the hand on, to lean. An kè 按據, *hwⁿā chăh*, to stop, to prevent incursions.

Mô-sûy àn këèm lek kae jê sëāng 毛遂按劍歷階而上, *Mô-sûy hwⁿā këèm kèy gîm kay jê chëōⁿᵍ*, Mô-sûy, leaning on his sword, crossed the steps and ascended (the hall).

上 Hwae **竵** Slanting, devious; incorrect.

去 Hwaè **瀤** The noise of water dashing about.

Hwaè **櫰** The name of a tree, the bark of which is used for making tow-ropes.

平 Hwaê **褱** To hide, to conceal under the arm. Kê yéw hek chëá, hwaê kê hek 其有核者褱其核, *ē nā woō hwut, tëŏh k'hèⁿᵍ e ây hwut*, when there are any stones (in the fruit), we must hide the stones. See the 曲禮 K'hëuk léy.

Hwaê **懷** To think, to imagine, to conceive in the mind, to hide in the bosom. A surname.

Sim hwaê 心懷, the bosom. Hwaê lēēm 懷念, to reflect upon.

Kwun choó hwaê tek, seaóu jîn hwaê t'hoé 君子懷德小人懷土, *kwun choó sëōⁿᵍ tek, sèy ây lâng sëōⁿᵍ t'hoé*, the good man thinks on virtue, the worthless man thinks of the earth. See the 論語 Lūn gé.

Hwaê **淮** The name of a river. Hwaê kang 淮江, one of the principal rivers of China.

Hwaê **槐** The name of a tree, having a large black leaf, and bearing an edible fruit.

Gwân-hêng-paou sē hwaê, t'hèng sëūng kê hāy 元明包樹槐。聽訟其下, *Gwân-bêng-paou chèng hwaê ch'hëw, t'hëⁿa sëùng tē ây k'ha*, Gwân-hêng-paou planted a *hwaê* tree, and heard law-suits under its shade.

去 Hwaē **壞** Vulg. k'hëep: to be destroyed, to be corrupted, to spoil; degenerated, corrupt.

Paē hwaē 敗壞, *p'hăh k'hëep*, to destroy. Hwaē hêng 壞行, corrupt conduct.

K'hóng-choó ko wat, t'haè san kê tùey hoē, lëâng bok kê hwaē hoē 孔子歌曰。泰山其頹乎。梁木其壞乎, *K'hóng-choó ch'hëōⁿᵍ kwa kóng, t'haè swⁿa e ëy pang hoē, nëōⁿᵍ ch'hâ e ëy k'hëep hoē*, Confucius chanting a ditty said, the great hill will fall, the principal beam will break:—(alluding to his own expected decease).

去 Hwăh **喝** Read hat: to bawl. Hat taē seng 喝大聲, *hwăh twā sëⁿa*, to bawl out loud.

K'hëúng hat choo hoê, e kêw kat têy 恐喝諸侯，以求割地，*k'hëúng hwăh choo hoê, ê kêw kwăh têy,* they terrified and scolded the princes of the Empire, in order to get them to surrender part of their territory. See the 戰國策 Chëèn kok ch'hek.

天 *Hwăh* **跬** Read k'hwúy: a step, a stride. Kwun choó k'hwúy poè, jê put bông ê haòu yëá 君子跬步而不忘於孝也，*kwun choó chit hwăh poè, jê ūm bēy kè tit wōo haòu,* the good man at every single step, never forgets the duties of filial piety.

Hwáh **跨** Read k'hwa: to stride, to straddle. K'hwa kò k'hè 跨過去，*kwăh kōey k'hè,* to stride across, to step over. Ch'hóo hwuy séy k'hwa haé löëy, chè choo hoê che sut yëá 此非所跨海內制諸侯之術也，*chéy lêy ūm sê sëy hwăh haè laē, chè choo hoê ây hwat sut,* this is not what may be called a proper plan for straddling over all within the four seas, and managing the princes of the Empire.

夲 Hwan **歡** Vulg. *hwⁿa*: to delight in, to be pleased. Hwan hé 歡喜，*hwⁿa hè,* to be glad. Him hé hwan aè, gak che kwan yëá 欣喜歡愛，樂之官也，*him hè hwⁿa aè, sē chok gak ay kwan yëá,* delight, pleasure, joy, and love, are the principles of music. See the 禮樂記 Léy gak kè. Also written, 懽 hwan. Hap hwan 合歡，united joy, the name of a plant.

Hwan **驩** The name of a horse; a gentle, well-tamed horse; also, to delight in. The people under the government of a despot, are said to be—hwan gê jê yëá 驩虞如也，*hwⁿa hè ây yëōⁿᵍ,* as it were well pleased, for the moment. See 孟子 Bēng-choó.

Hwan **讙** To make a noise and bother. Hwan hoe 讙呼，to make a clamour.

Hwan **番** The next in order, and quality; a time, a turn; to change; foreign, outlandish. Yit hwan 一番，*chit poè,* once, one time, for once.
Hwan jîn 番人，*hwan lâng,* or *hwan á,* a foreigner, one of another country.
Hwan put jê tông 番不如唐，*hwan bēy ch'hin cheōⁿᵍ tēⁿᵍ,* foreign things are not so good as Chinese.

Hwan **幡** A cloth for wiping anything; also, a kind of flag. When 鮑宣 Paòu-swan was in prison, his disciple, 王成 Ông-sêng,—ké hwan yëuk kèw Swan 舉幡欲救宣，*këăh k'hè hwan kê, aè bōëyh kèw Swan,* raised a flag (as a signal), desiring to save his master.

Hwan **旛** The same as 番 hwan; a turn, a time; also, to collect.

Hwan **潘** Vulg. *p'hun*: the water in which rice is washed, and which is used for feeding pigs.—Vulg. *p'hwⁿa,* a surname.

Hwan **旙** A flag, a standard. Hwan kê 旙旗，a signal flag. Lip ch'heng hwan 立青旙，to set up an azure standard.

Hwan **瀿** Great waves, billows.

Hwan **翻** To fly, to arrive at, to reach; also, to return. Chëûng nëáou p'hëen hwan 衆鳥翩翻，*chëùng chëaòu tit pwuy,* all the birds were flying about.

Hwan **墦** A cemetery, a burial place. Chut che tong kok, hwan kan che chèy chēá 卒之東郭墦間之祭者, *swăh bōēy kaòu tang kok, hwan kan ây chèy ây lâng*, he finally proceeded to the eastern suburbs, to where the people were sacrificing among the tombs.

Hwan **璠** Hwan ê 璠璵, a beautiful gem. Confucius said, Bé chae hwan ê 美哉璠璵, *súy chaę hwan ê ây gēuk*, how beautiful is the *hwan ê* gem.

Hwan **磻** Hwan k'hey 磻溪, the name of a stream, where 太公 T'haè-kong used to angle.

Hwan **燔** Anything burnt in the fire; the fire burning anything.

Hwan **膰** Sacrificial flesh. Hwan jēuk put chê, put t'hwat bēēn jê hêng 膰肉不至.不稅冕而行, *chèy băh ūm kaòu chēw, ūm t'hèy bō jê kēⁿá*, when the sacrificial flesh was not duly provided, Confucius departed without even taking off his cap of office. See the 下孟 Hāy bēng.

Hwan **𥻗** White rice.

Hwan **嚾** To make a clamour and noise; the same as 讙 hwan. Sè sēuk che koe, yêw hoō jê, hwan hwan jēēn, put te kê wûy hwuy yēá 世俗之溝.猶瞽儒.嚾嚾然.不知其爲非也, *sè sēuk ây kaou, ch'hin chēōng chh'aing maⁿg ây t'hâk ch'hâyh lâng, ch'hùy chap chap kòng, jê ūm chae e chò ūm tēŏh*, the current of this world's manners, is like a blind scholar, who babbles away and does not know that he is in the wrong.

Hwan **爟** To kindle a fire; also, the name of an office.

上聲

Hwán **反** To return; again; to rebel, rebellious. Hwán hok 反復, again and again. Hwán lwān 反亂, to rebel, and create confusion.

Tīn-sìn soó jīn óng kēèn Tēang-jé, soó chēá gnoé hwán 陳勝使人往見張耳.使者五反, *Tân-sìn saè lâng óng keèng Tēōng-jé, saè ây lâng goē ây tooing*, Tīn-sìn, sent some persons to get an interview with Tēang-jé, when the messengers had to go and come five times.

Hwán **仮** Disobedient, refractory; the same as the foregoing.

Hwán **阪** An uneven field.

Hwán **坂** P'ho-hwán 坡坂, the name of a place.

Hwán **飯** To eat, to eat rice. Hwán soe soō yim súy 飯疏食飲水, *chēăh ch'hoe pooing lim chúy*, to eat coarse rice, and drink water. See the 論語 Lūn gé.

Hwán **返** Vulg. *tooing*: to return, to come back. O'ng chēá put hwán 往者不返, *k'hè ây lâng bô tooing*, those who went did not return.

去聲

Hwàn **煥** Bright, shining. Hwàn hoē kê yêw bûn chēang 煥乎其有文章, *hwuing hoē e ây woō bûn chēong*, how brilliant was their literature. See the 論語 Lūn gé.

Hwàn **奐** Great, beautiful, illustrious. Bé chaē hwàn yēen 美哉奐焉, how beautiful and illustrious!

Hwàn **喚** To call. Hoe hwàn 呼喚, to call aloud. Kê hwàn put laê 其喚不來, *e kēò ūm laê*, he called him, but he would not come.

Hwàn 泛 To float, to flow, to overflow. Hông sûy hông lêw, hwàn lām ê t'hëen hāy 洪水横流泛濫於天下, *twā chúy hwⁿā laôu, hwàn lām tē t'heeⁿᵍ āy*, the great flood flowed out of its course, and overwhelmed the Empire.

Hwàn 氾 To overflow, to inundate; to float about; the same as the preceding. Hwàn lām ê tëung kok 氾濫於中國, *hwàn lām tē tëung kok*, inundating the middle country. See 孟子 Bēng-choó. Hwàn hoē jëak put hēy che chew 氾乎若不繫之舟, *p'hoô p'hoô ch'hin chëōⁿᵍ bô pak āy chûn*, floating about like a boat that is not fastened.

Hwàn 汎 To float, to flow, to overflow; the same as the preceding; also written 氾 hwàn, to flow over. Also, a surname.

Hwàn 換 Vulg. *wⁿā*: to change, to exchange, to barter. Hwān kwut hô sê hwàn 凡骨何時換, *chēy lēy hwān kwut te sê ēy wⁿā*, when will these vulgar bones of mine be changed?—(alluding to the transmigration of souls from vulgar to ethereal bodies.)

Hwàn 瑍 The sparkling of a gem. The same as 煥 hwàn, bright.

Hwàn 伬 To treat lightly, to disesteem.

Hwàn 渢 The sound of the happy medium.

Hwàn 渙 Dispersed, loose, scattered.

Hwàn 販 To buy; to deal, to trade. O'ng pok hwàn má 往北販馬, *k'hè pak sè bēy bây*, to go to the north, in order to buy horses.

Hwàn 幻 To change; to trick. Pëēn hwàn 變幻, artful changes, deceptions. Bōng hwàn 夢幻, dreams and visions of the night.

平

Hwân 環 To surround, to encircle, to environ; also, a gem, a ring. Hwân jê kong che jê put sìn 環而攻之而不勝, *hwân jëâou kong p'hăh e, jê bēy yëⁿā*, to surround and besiege a place without mastering it. See 孟子 Bēng-choó.

Hwân 儇 Intelligent, clever, cunning; advantageous. Yip gnó, wûy gnó hwân hêy 揖我謂我儇兮, *kap gwá chok yip, kēò gwá gaôu*, they bow to me, considering me clever. See the 詩經 Se keng.

Hwân 鐶 A ring, a circle. Kim hwân 金鐶, a golden ring. Séw hwân 手鐶, *ch'hèw chè*, a finger-ring. Jè hwân 耳鐶, *hē kaou á*, an ear-ring.

Hwân 圜 Round; a circle; to encircle, to environ. Hwân jëâou 圜繞, to enclose. Ê jîn wûy ke, hwân cheā tëūng kwuy, hong cheā tëūng kē 輿人爲車,圜者中規,方者中矩, *ch'hēa āy lâng chò ch'hēa, eⁿᵍ āy tëūng kwuy, sè kak āy tëūng kē*, the wheel-wrights in making carts, form the circles by a compass, and the squares by a rule.

Hwân 闤 A wall round a market.

Hwân 寰 The territory assigned to an Emperor, as his peculiar domain. Hwân é 寰宇, the universe.

Hwân 還 Vulg. *tooi^ng:* to retire, to return. Vulg. *hêng:* to pay, to repay; besides. Hwân chaè 還債, *hêng cheê^ng*, to pay debts. Jé hwân jê jip, gnó sim ē yēá 爾還而入我心易也, *lé tooi^ng jê jip, gwá ây sim chēw k'hw^na wăh*, if you return and come home, my mind will be easy. See the 小雅 Sēáou gnáy.

Hwân 墦 A cemetery, a burial place; also read hwan, which see.

Hwân 璠 Hwân ê 璠璵, a beautiful gem. Lēâng gēuk se ch'hēet ch'ho, ê hwân chōw kê hêng 良玉須切磋璵璠就其形, *hó ây gēuk sae tēōh ch'hēet ch'ho, ê hwân chēw e ây hêng yēō^ng*, every fine gem needs to be cut and rubbed, but the *ê hwân* may retain its shape.

Hwân 燔 Hot, warm; to roast, to burn. Hek hwân hek chēà 或燔或炙, *woō ây sē sēo, woō ây sē chēà*, some of it was roasted, and some burnt. See the 小雅 Seaóu gnáy.

Hwân 蟠 Crooked, bent, coiled up. Lēûng hwân ê nê 龍蟠於泥, *lēûng hwân tee^ng tē nw^nâ t'hoê*, a dragon coiled up in the mud.

Hwân 蹯 To grow; to water, to irrigate; luxuriant vegetation.

Hwân 磻 The name of a stream.

Hwân 膰 Sacrificial flesh; flesh left over after a sacrifice. T'hēen choó yéw soō hwân yēen, é kwûy tông sêng choo hoê 天子有事膰焉,以饋同姓諸侯, *hêng tèy woō soō kap hwân băh, chēw t'hó e sàng tâng sai^ng ây choo hoê*, when the Emperor has a sacrifice and sacrificial flesh, he takes and presents it to the princes of the same family name. See the 春秋傳 Ch'hun ch'hew twān.

Hwân 蹯 The foot of an animal. Him hwân 熊蹯, a bear's paw.

Hwân 煩 Vulg. *tēōh bwâ:* to trouble. Soō hwân 事煩, busy. Lōēy sin hwân taē chè Pa sêng 内信煩帶至巴城, *laē p'hay tēōh bwâ twà kàou Pa sē^nâ*, the inclosed letter, I will trouble you to take to the city of Pa (Batavia).

Hwân 蕃 A screen, a fence, a railing. Taē hong tông sêng, é hwân pin Chew sit, 大封同姓,以蕃屏周室, *twā hong tâng sai^ng, é chò hwân pín tē Chew ây sit*, he greatly apportioned those of the same family name, in order to render them a fence to the house of Chew. See the 史記 Soó kè.

Hwân 藩 A fence, a railing; the same as the former; also, the whole, general, common. Taē hwân 大藩, upon the whole.

Hwân 澴 Water; water bubbling up.

Hwân 鬟 The hair generally; the hair tied up in a knot.

Hwân 擷 To rub in the hand, to wash clothes by the hand. Numerous.

Hwân 繁 Numerous, many. Chēûng chēá sit hwân 從者寔繁, *tây ây lâng sit chēy*, the followers were numerous.

Hwân 蘩 A sort of vegetable; a fragrant and edible plant.

Hwân 凡 Anything round.

Hwân 帆 Sek hwân ch'hó 石帆草, *chëòh hwân ch'haóu*, a kind of sub-marine vegetable, which grows upon rocks, said to be like the fir-tree.

Hwân 樊 A surname. Hwân-tê 樊遲, the name of a disciple of Confucius.

Hwân 礬 Hwân sek 礬石, *hwân chëòh*, alum; also called, pek hwân 白礬, *päyh hwân*, white alum.

Hwân 垣 A wall. Hwân ch'hëâng 垣牆, *hwân ch'hëô^ng*, a wall. Tān-kan-bok jê hwân jê pē che 段干木踰垣而避之, *Tān-kan-bok kòëy ch'hëô^ng jê sëèm peç^ng e*, Tān-kan-bok climbed over the wall, to get out of his way. See 孟子 Bēng-choó.

Hwân 繙 The liquor of rice.

Hwân 藩 A large sieve or basket, for collecting dirt.

Hwân 瀿 The name of a river; water overflowing and running over.

Hwân 鳺 Hwân têy 鳺鵜, the name a bird, which pecks the tails of snakes.

Hwân 糫 Ko hwân 膏糫, a kind of cake or confectionary.

Hwân 環 A round gem, without any corner or projecting part.

Hwân 擐 To string; to perforate.

Hwân 儇 Sharp; gainful, advantageous.

Hwân 䙴 Unskilled, dull, not clever; also written 䙴 hwân.

Hwân 礬 Alum; the same as 礬 hwân.

Hwân 驔 A horse hesitating, and unable to proceed.

Hwân 桓 To display; martial. Pwan hwân 盤桓, hesitating, unable to advance. Chëy-hwân-kong 齊桓公, the name of an ancient despot. A surname.

Hwân 吩 Read hwún: to order. Hwún hoó 吩咐, *hwân hoò*, to enjoin.

去

Hwān 范 A surname.

Hwān 侸 Hwān sîn 侸臣, a servant, a minister.

Hwān 宦 A person in office, a minister. Hwān kwan 宦官, a eunuch of the palace. A surname. Hwān hak soō soo, bwuy lêy put ch'hin 宦學事師非禮不親, *chò kwⁿa ây lâng t'hak hok saē sin saiⁿg, nā ūᵐ chëòdu lêy soē, chëw ūᵐ ch'hin*, when persons in office study and follow a teacher, if they do not observe politeness, there will be no intimacy between them. See the 禮記 Lêy kè.

Hwān 犯 To come in contact with; to offend; to attack; to reprove. Kwun choó hwān gē, sëaóu jîn hwān hêng 君子犯義小人犯刑, *kwun choó hwān lëòh gē lê, sëaóu jîn hwān lëòh hêng hwat*, when the prince offends against the rules of righteousness, and the common people come in contact with punishment, (the country is then in a sad condition.)

Hwān hwat 犯法, to transgress the laws. Hwān chōey 犯罪, to commit sin. Kan hwān 干犯, to offend, to provoke.

Hwān 範 A law, a rule, a pattern. Boē hwān 模範, a rule, a plan. Hwān wûy t'hëen tēy, jê put kô 範圍天地而不過, to imitate the revolutions of heaven and earth without transgressing the rule.

Hwān 帆 Vulg. *p'hâng*: a sail; to sail. Soó hwān 使帆, *saé p'hâng*, to set sail. T'hey san hwān haé 梯山帆海, *t'huy sw^{n}a p'hâng haé*, to climb the hills with ladders, and cross the seas with sails.

Hwān 棉 Boô hwān 無棉, the name of a tree.

Hwān 飯 Vulg. *pooī^{ng}*: rice. Sit hwān 食飯, *chëăh pooī^{ng}*, to eat rice. Hwān sé boô é tē 飯黍毋以箸, *chëăh pooī^{ng} kap sëy á, ū^{m} t'hang yūng tē*, in eating rice and millet, do not use chopsticks.

Hông tê 黃帝 was the first who boiled rice out of paddy (B. C. 2622.)

Hwān 凡 All, every one, the whole. Tān hwān 但凡, whosoever, whensoever. Hwān soō 凡事, whatsoever. Taē hwān 大凡, on the whole.

Hwān sëâng 凡常, common, usual, ordinary. Sêng hwan put yit 聖凡不一, *sèng jîn hwān sëâng ây lâng, ū^{m} chit yëō^{ng}*, sages and common people are by no means the same.

Hwān 患 To be concerned, to be grieved, to be anxious; evil; difficult. Put hwān jîn che put ké te 不患人之不已知, *ū^{m} saé hwān lô lâng ū^{m} chae lâu*, do not be concerned that people do not know you.

Soê hwān lān, hêng hoê hwān lān 素患難行乎患難, *toô tëŏh hwān lān, tëŏh kë^{n}á hoē hwān lān*, when we come into trouble, we should act consistently with one in trouble. See the 中庸 Tëung yûng.

Hwān 豢 To feed with corn; to eat corn. Yêw choe hwān che wat gnó k'hoé 猶芻豢之悅我口, *ch'hin chëō^{ng} ch'haôu ch'hek ëy hw^{n}a hé gwá áy ch'hùy*, just as vegetable and grain please one's palate. See 孟子 Bēng-choó.

Hwān 軓 The front of a carriage.

Hwān 幻 Deceitful tricks, airy visions. He hwān 虛幻, vain dreams. Yaou hwān 妖幻, artful contrivances; also read, hwàn.

Hwān 芄 The name of a plant.

Hwān 梵 A region of the west, said to be the native country of Buddha. Hwān hwā 梵話, the original language of Buddha.

Hwān këung 梵宮, a royal palace.

声 *Hwâng* 鈁 Money, cash. Yit hwâng 一鈁, *chit hwâng*, one fanam. Boô hwâng 無鈁, *bô hwâng*, no money.

夫 Hwat 法 A law; a rule, a pattern; to imitate; to punish according to law. Hwat toē 法度, a law, a rule. Hong hwat 方法, means, a plan, contrivance.

Hêng hwat 刑法, to punish.

Hwat gé che gân, lêng boô chëûng hoē 法語之言能無從乎, *ëy chò hwat toē ây wā k'ham ëy ū^{m} t'hàn hoē*, words worthy of imitation; how can we do otherwise than obey them? See the 論語 Lūn gé.

Hwat 灋 The ancient form of 法 hwat: a law. Also written, 佱 hwat. T'haè c'aé é pat hwat tē pang kok 太宰以八灋治邦國, *t'haè chaè t'hò payh hāng ây hwat toē tē pang kok*, the great minister of state regulated the country according to eight rules. See the 周禮 Chew lêy.

Hwat 發 To display, to manifest; to spring forth, to rise up; to send abroad. Hwat k'hé 發起, to spring up. Hwat hēèn 發現, to display, to manifest. Hwat yēuk ban bu̇t, chūn kek e t'hēen 發育萬物峻極于天, *hwat k'hè hâm yēuk bān mcē^{n}h, sèng jîn kwân chè kaòu t'hee^{ng}*, in producing and bringing up the various kinds (of grain), — (the merit of the sages) is exalted, up to the heavens. See the 中庸 Tēung yûng.

Hwat 髮 The hair of the head. T'hèy hwat 剃髮, *thè mô*, to shave off the hair. Hwat twán jê sim tēâng 髮短而心長, *mô tèy jê sim tē^{ng}*, your hair is short but your heart is long (meaning that though the man was nearly bald through age, yet his views were long and deep).

犬

Hwȧt 乏 To be wanting, to be destitute of; to be without. Hwȧt k'hong kê sin 乏空其身, to impoverish his person.

Hwȧt 伐 To cut; to strike, to chastise; to invade; also, to boast. Hwȧt k'ho jê hô, hwuy hoó put k'hek 伐柯如何, 匪斧不克, *p'hăh ch'hâ an chu^{n}á, bô poó t'hâou bēy yē^{n}â*, in cutting wood for handles, how shall we manage? without an axe we cannot succeed.

Cheng chēá, sēāng hwȧt hāy yēá 征者上伐下也, *cheng hwȧt, sē sè twā hwȧt sè sèy*, the meaning of *cheng* is that of superiors chastising their inferiors. See 孟子 Bēng-choó.

Gwān boô hwȧt sēēn 願無伐善, *gwân bô tēèn gua ây hó*, I wish not to brag of my goodness. See the 論語 Lūn gé.

Hwȧt 佸 To meet, to assemble. Hwȧt hwȧt 佸佸, strong.

Hwȧt 活 Vulg. *wăh*; alive, not dead. Chaē hwȧt 再活, *k'h wăh*, to revive, to live again.

Wûy yéw gwân t'hoe hwȧt suy laê 惟有源頭活水來, *tok woō gwân t'haôu ây uah chúy laî*, only from a fountain head do living waters come.

Hwȧt 筏 A raft, made of wood or bamboos, for crossing the water.

Hwȧt 閥 Hwȧt wȧt 閥閱, doors on each side of an officer's dwelling, the former, on the left, and the latter on the right; hence taken figuratively for office, or for the merit which entitles to office.

Beô hwȧt wȧt kong lô 無閥閱功勞, *bô chò ku^{n}a ây kong lô*, having no merit that entitles to office.

Hwȧt 罰 To punish. Chek hwȧt 責罰, to reprove, to chastise. Sēáng hwȧt chēá, ông che taē kwân yēá 賞罰者王之大權也, *siô^{ng} chek hwȧt ây sê, sē ông ây twā kwân sè*, rewarding and punishing people, is a royal prerogative.

Hwȧt 佸 To assemble; strong; the same as 佸 hwȧt.

Hwȧt 橃 A float made of timber, in distinction from 筏 hwȧt, a bamboo float. Also, to cross the water on a raft.

Hwȧt 舌 A vessel under weigh; a boat sailing.

3 2

卆 Hwui^ng 荒 Read hong: wild, waste, overgrown with weeds; unfruitful, barren. Têên têw hong boô 田疇荒蕪, ch'hân hwui^ng p'hăh hwui^ng, the fields and plantations were all overgrown with weeds. Ke hong 飢荒, ke hwui^ng, a famine.

Hwui^ng 昏 Read hwun: the evening. Bêng hwun 冥昏, mai^ng hwui^ng, in the evening. Hwun bōe k'hoe jîn che bûn hoē 昏暮扣人之門戶, mai^ng hwui^ng sê p'hăh lâng ây mooi^ng hoē, late in the evening to go and knock at people's doors.

Hwui^ng 蟒 Read hong: a snake. Oe hong 烏蟒, oe hwui^ng, a black snake, very venemous.

Hwui^ng 𩜾 Ke heng 飢𩜾, yaou hwui^ng, a famine, hunger.

平 Hwui^ng 園 Read wân: a garden. Ch'hae wân 菜園, ch'haè hwui^ng, a vegetable garden.

Kwuy k'hè laê hêy, têên wân chëang boô 歸去來兮.田園將蕪, taē kay laê tooi^ng, ch'hân hwui^ng bōëyh boô, come and let us return home, for our fields and gardens are getting wild and overgrown.

Hwui^ng 磺 Read hông: sulphur. Lêw hông 硫磺, nëô^ng hwui^ng, brimstone.

去 Hwui^ng 圂 Read hwūn: a railing, a frame. Paôu hwūn 匏圂, paô hwui^ng, a frame for calabashes to grow upon.

Hwui^ng 捆 Read hwūn: to encircle, to encompass; to embrace; to put the arms round anything, in order to lift it up.

Hwūn pūn 捆笨, hwui^ng pūn, a round frame of bamboos, made for holding grain.

Hwui^ng 遠 Read wán: far, distant, not near. Hoō bóe chaē, put wán yêw 父母在.不遠遊, pāy boē tē tit, ū^m t'hang hwui^ng t'hit t'hô, when our parents are alive, we must not wander far. See the 上論 Sëang lūn.

卆 Hwun 分 Vulg. pun: to divide, to share, to distribute, to distinguish; a small particle.

Hwun pëet 分別, to distinguish. Hwun lëet 分裂, pun lëëh, to tear asunder. Hwun k'hae 分開, pun k'hwuy, to open, to set apart. Yit hwun 一分, chit hwun, a part, a portion; a very small particle.

Hwun jîn é chaê wūy che hwūy 分人以財謂之惠, pun lâng ê chëê^ng, kóng kèò sëó hwūy, to distribute money among people is called (a trifling) kindness. See the 上孟 Sëang bēng.

Bûn-ông sam hwun t'hëen hāy yëw kê jē 文王三分天下有其二, Bûn-ông ^ng^a hwun t'hee^ng āy woō e ây nō hwun, Bûn-ông out of three parts of the empire had two parts.

Hwun 昬 Vulg. hwui^ng: the evening, dark. Hong hwun sê hwun 黃昬時分, 'toō toō mai^ng hwui^ng ây sê, just about the time of dusk.

Hwun 昏 The common form of the preceding; also used for the next, 婚 hwun, marriage, because marriages were celebrated in the evening.

Hwun 婚 Hwun yin 婚姻, marriage, a wedding. Also written 昏 hwun. Yëèn jé sin hwun, jê heng jê têy 宴爾新婚如兄如弟, chëăh chêw tē lé ây sin hwun, ch'hin chëô^ng hē^n a kap tē, to feast at your newly celebrated wedding, like elder and younger brethren.

Hwun 惛 The mind not clear, not fully convinced, not clearly understood.

Hwun 惽 Not to understand, to be dull; confused. Goê hwun put lêng chìn ê sē 吾惽不能進於是, *gwá hwun, bēy chìn ê chèy lěy tō*, I am dull, and can make no progress in this study. See 孟子 Bēng-choó.

Hwun 閽 A door-keeper; a common porter at the door. Hwun jîn 閽人, a porter.

Hwun 熏 Smoke issuing forth, to smoke anything. K'hëung sit hwun ch'hé 穹窒熏鼠, *an K'hang hwun nēaou ch'hé*, to smoke mice out of their holes. See the 詩經 Se keng.

Hwun 薰 A fragrant kind of grass.

Hwun 燻 Fire burning with violence. Hwun lëet yëen sëāng 燻烈烟上, *hōěy töh hwun chëōⁿᵍ*, when the fire burns violently the smoke ascends.

Hwun 曛 The remnant of light, after the sun has gone down; twilight.

Hwun 矄 The eyes dim and dark.

Hwun 醺 To be inebriated.

Hwun 獯 Hwun yëuk 獯鬻, the name of a foreign nation on the west of China. T'haè-ông soō Hwun yëuk 太王事獯鬻, *T'haè-ông hok sae Hwun yëuk dy hwan*, T'haè-ông served the western foreigners. See 孟子 Bēng-choó.

Hwun 臐 A sheep; sheep's flesh, or fat; mutton.

Hwun 塤 An instrument of music, made of earthenware. Pek sē ch'huy hwun, tëūng sē ch'huy tê 伯氏吹塤仲氏吹篪, the elder persons played on the hwun, and the younger on the tê. See the 小雅 Seàou gnáy.

Hwun 壎 The same as the preceding.

Hwun 勳 Merit, meritorious desert. Hwun lô 勳勞, merit. Also written, 勛 hwun. Kê k'hek yéw hwun 其克有勳, *e ây chò yēⁿâ woō kong lô*, his succeeding had some merit in it. See the 尚書 Sëāng se.

Hwun 葷 Strong, pungent, and fragrant vegetables, such as leeks, onions, &c. Put jê hwun 不茹葷, he did not eat fragrant vegetables.

Hwun 煇 Bright. Hwun kong 煇光, brilliant, effulgent.

Hwun 焄 A fragrant scent.

Hwun 芬 Fragrant plants.

Hwun 氛 A felicitous influence, some say, an infelicitous influence.

Hwun 棼 Confused, disordered; to ravel, to rumple. Yêw tē se, jê hwun che yëā 猶治絲而棼之也, *ch'hin chëōⁿᵍ bōěyh ch'hòng se, jê hwun hwān e*, like one who wants to manage thread, and lets it ravel into confusion. See the 左傳 Chô twān.

Hwun 雰 The appearance of falling snow. 'E swat hwun hwun 雨雪雰雰, *töh süyh hwun hwun*, the snow fell in flakes. See the 小雅 Sëäou gnáy.

Hwun 紛 Confused, mixed together. T'hëen hāy hwun hwun 天下紛紛, *t'hee^ng āy hwun hwun*, the empire was all in confusion.

Hwun 棻 The name of a fragrant wood.

Hwun 殙 To be sick; to die while an infant —before receiving a name. Also written, 殙 hwun.

Hwun 馚 Hwun wun 馚馧, a fragrant breeze, an aromatic smell.

Hwun 緡 A thread or skein of silk. Kê tëäou wûy hô, wûy se e hwun 其釣維何維絲伊緡, *e tëò hê yāng s^nà meë^nh, tok tok se e āy hwun*, in angling what did he use? nothing but a skein of silk. See the 召南 Sëàou lâm.

Hwun 痻 A sickness; sick, ill. To gnô koe hwun 多我覯痻, *chëy gwá k'hw^nà pai^ng*, I have been witness to many evils. See the 大雅 Taē gnáy.

Hwun 烟 Read yëen; tobacco—useful for keeping out cold; smoke. Sit yëen 食烟, *chëàh hwun*, to eat (i. e. smoke) tobacco. Hông yëen 紅烟, *âng hwun*, common tobacco. Oe yëen 烏烟, *oe hwun*, black tobacco, i. e. opium.

Hwun 纁 A light grey colour.

Hwun 惛 Dark. Ch'hëen choo yew hwun 闡諸幽惛, *hëèn choo yew àm*, to display all that is abstruse and dark.

Hwun 汾 The name of a river.

声

Hwûn 粉 Rice flour, any kind of powder. Hwûn sek 粉飾, to adorn. Hoê hwûn 胡粉, and Bé hwûn 米粉, a kind of cosmetic, made of a preparation of bismuth and lead, used also for white lead. Hwûn p'hek 粉壁, *hwún pëäh*, to plaster or whitewash a wall.

Hwûn 佷 Overbearing, arbitrary, self-willed; the same as the following. Tóng-tok choō hwûn yūng 董卓自佷用, *Táng-tŏh ka tē hwún yūng*, Táng-tŏh was an arbitrary overbearing man.

Hwún 很 Hwún lēy 很戾, oppressive, overbearing. H^nò yúng toē hwún, é gwûy hoō loé 好勇鬪很以危父母, *aè yúng toè hwun, é gwûy hëèm pāy boè*, to be fond of displaying one's bravery, and contending for one's own way, till we endanger our parents. See the 下孟 Hāy bēng.

Hwûn 坋 Dust or dirt; an atom, dust.

Hwûn 坌 The same as the preceding; also, to collect. Hwûn chip kēng soo 坌集京師, *k'hëŏh chò höèy tē kë^na së^nâ*, to assemble at the capital.

Hwún 忿 To be enraged, to be angry with. Hwún noē 忿怒, anger, wrath. Jé hoē hwún chit ê gwân 爾無忿疾于頑, *lé ū^m t'hang sëw k'hè gām lâng*, you should not be angry and vexed with the dull and stupid.

Hwún 倱 Hwun tūn 倱伅, impervious, unintelligible, deficient in apprehension.

Hwún 黺 Variegated, ornamented.

Hwún 黗 Black, of a dark colour.

Hwún 僨 To overturn, to overthrow. Ch'hóo che wūy yit gân hwūn sōo 此謂一言僨事俫, chèy sē kóng chit koō wā hwún lwān soō, this is what is called one word's throwing an affair into disorder. See the 大學 Taē hák.

Hwún 吩 To blow out the breath; also, to issue orders. Hwún hoò 吩附, hwún hoò, to enjoin, to bid, to tell, to order.

Hwún 惲 Thick and heavy, substantial and liberal; also, to reason with.

Hwún 憤 To be enraged, to be stirred up, to rouse one's-self. Put hwún put k'héy 不憤不啟, na $\bar{u}^m$ hwat hwún, e $\bar{u}^m$ k'hèy kaòu lán, if any did not rouse themselves up, he (Confucius) would not open out the subject to them. See the 上論 Sëāng lūn. Hwat hwún bông sit 發憤忘食, hwat hwún bēy kè tit chëāh, when he (Confucius) was roused by anything, he forgot his food.

去

Hwùn 訓 To instruct, to explain; instruction explanation, meaning. Kaòu hwùn 教訓, kà hwùn, instruction. Hwùn bông 訓蒙, to teach youth. Hak ê koé hwùn naé yéw hek 學於古訓乃有獲, l'hak ê koé chá ây kà hwùn naé woō sêy tit lëŏh, by studying the instruction of the ancients, something may be obtained.

Hwùn 僨 To overturn, to upset, to throw down. Guêw suy chit, hwùn ê tûn sëāng, kê wūy put soō 牛雖瘠僨于豚上其畏不 ... án, k'hè pak hāy ê te lêng, e ki' ... though ever so meagre, yet if th ... r a little pig, is there not reason t ... be the death of him. See the 左 ... n.

3 v

Hwùn 肕 Mutton broth.

Hwùn 馴 The ancient form of 訓 hwùn, to instruct. Lëet hoê ek bwō yêw kaou hwùn kê bin 列侯亦無由教馴其民, lëet hoê yëā bô an chwⁿá kà hwùn e ây pāyh saiⁿᵍ, the various princes also had no method of instructing their people. See the 史記 Soó kè.

Hwùn 奮 To display, to unfold, to spread abroad, as a bird opens its wings. Hwùn chê tek che kong 奮至德之光, hwùn yâng che tek ây kwuiⁿᵍ, to display abroad the glory of super-excellent virtue. Put lêng hwùn hwuy 不能奮飛, bēy k'hwuy sit laê pwuy, unable to spread out its wings and fly. See the 詩經 Se keng.

Hwùn 糞 Vulg. pùn: dung, manure. Pek boé che hwùn 百畝之糞, chēⁿ... pāyh boe ây pùn, the manure for a hundred acres of land. See the 上孟 Sëāng bēng.

Hwùn 燻 Anything dried by the fire; to toast at the fire.

Hwùn 楥 A shoemaker's last. Haê hwùn 鞋楥, ây hwùn, a last for shoes.

平

Hwûn 僤 A surname.

Hwûn 墳 A grave. Hwûn boê 墳墓, hwûn bōng, a tomb, a burial place. Ch'hoé Lêng-ông che sè, Hêng san peng, jê Chëuk-yûng che hwûn hwaē 楚靈王之世衡山崩而祝融之墳壞, Ch'hoé Lêng-ông ây sè, Hêng swⁿa pang lōh k'hè, jê Chëuk-yûng ây bōng k'hëep, in the time of Lêng-ông, of the Ch'hoé country, the Hêng hill fell in, and destroyed the grave of Chëuk-yûng.

Hwûn 幩 The ornaments under the neck of a horse.

Hwûn 汾 The name of a river.

Hwûn 渾 Muddy. Hwûn hêy, kê jëak chok 渾兮其若濁, *hwûn hêy, ch'hin chëō^ng lō*, how thick is it? just like mud.

Hwûn 濆 The banks of a river, the water's edge. Chûn pê jé hwûn 遵彼汝濆, *t'hûn e jé ây kee^ng*, to follow along the banks of the Jé river. See 周南 Chew lâm.

Hwûn 枌 The name of a tree.

Hwûn 蕡 Trees and plants yielding much fruit. Yéw hwûn kê sit 有蕡其實, *woō chēy e ây kwúy chê*, it has plenty of fruit. See the 周南 Chew lâm.

Hwûn 痕 A wrinkle; a scar, a mark of a wound, or of the small pox. T'hòng hwûn 痛痕, *t'hē^nà hwûn*, the scar of a wound.

Hwûn 癉 Foolish, silly.

Hwûn 羵 A sheep or goat with a large head.

Hwûn 朌 To have a large head. Gê chaē chaē chó, yéw hwûn kê sew 魚在在藻有朌其首, *hê twā'tē chúy ch'haou, woō twā e ây t'haôu*, there is a fish among the rushes having a large head. See the 小雅 Seäóu gnây.

Hwûn 焚 To burn, to set on fire, to consume by fire. Hwûn hëang 焚香, *sëo hëo^ng*, to burn incense.

H^nó yëên K'hwun keng, gëuk sek kē hwûn 火炎崑崗玉石俱焚, *hóey tŏh K'hwun swa^na, gek chëŏh chò poō sëo*, when the fire burst out on the brow of the K'hwun hill, both gems and stones were consumed.

Hwûn 緄 To stitch, a seam.

Hwûn 餛 Hwûn t'hûn 餛飩, a kind of cake, or confectionery.

Hwûn 魂 A spirit. Lêng hwûn 靈魂, the soul. Jin yéw sam hwûn ch'hit p'hek 人有三魂七魄, *lâng woō s^na ây hwûn ch'hit ây p'hek*, people have three souls and seven spirits. Hwûn seng ê thëen, p'hek kàng ê tēy 魂升於天. 魄降於地, *hwûn chëō^ng kaôu t'hee^ng, p'hek lŏh kaôu tēy*, the soul ascends to heaven and the spirit descends to the earth.

Hwûn 棞 A whole piece of timber that is not broken.

Hwûn 雲 Read yîn: a cloud, the clouds. T'hëen yîn 天雲, *t'hee^ng hwûn*, the clouds of heaven.

Put gē jê hoò ch'hë^nà kwùy, ê guó jê hoô yîn 不義而富且貴.於我如浮雲, *a^m gē jê poō kwà kwùy, tē gwà ch'hin chëō^ng p'hoô p'hoô ây hwûn*, wealth and honours gotten by unrighteousness, are to me like the floating clouds. Said by Confucius, in the 論語 Lūn-gé.

去 Hwūn 混 A muddy stream; mixed, jumbled [illegible]ether, in confusion; also, flowing. [illegible] chap 混雜, mixed together. Yêw but [illegible] [illegible]n t'hëen tēy seng 有物混成[illegible]地生, *woō mee^nh hwûn chë^n[illegible]* [illegible] *tēy sai^ng*, there was a mixed ch[illegible] [illegible]ch was produced before heav[illegible] [illegible] See the 道德經 Tō tek ke[illegible]

Gwân chwân hwūn hwūn, put sëá tëw yëā 原泉混混不舍晝夜, *gwân chwân hwūn hwūn laôu, bô häyⁿh jit maiⁿᵍ*, the fountain bubbles up, without ceasing night or day. See 孟子 Bēng chóó.

Hwūn 院 Finished; to finish, to bring to an end; to disgrace.

Hwūn 分 A portion. Bēng hwūn 名分, *meⁿâ hwūn*, a name, a station. Chit hwūn 職分, a duty, an office. Pún hwūn 本分, obligation, duty. Hwūn lëāng 分量, a small weight, or measure. Chīn kê pún hwūn 盡其本分, to do one's duty to the utmost. Léy tat jê hwūn tēng 禮達而分定, *léy soè t'hong tat, jé mēⁿâ hwūn tēⁿā tëŏh*, when politeness is fully attended to, then people's stations will be fixed.

Hwūn 渾 Blended together, amalgamated; one mass; the whole. Sèng jin che sim, hwūn jëên t'hëen lé 聖人之心渾然天理, *sèng jîn ây sim kwⁿa, hwūn jëên t'heoⁿᵍ lé*, the mind of a sage is blended together with the celestial principle. Hwūn jëên 渾然, one undistinguished mass.

Hwūn 溷 Confused, in disorder; muddy. Se hwūn hwūn jê put hwūn 世溷溷而不分, *sè kan hwūn hwān, jî bô hwun pëet*, the world is confused without distinction.

Hwūn 慁 Grieved, sorrowful, troubled. Chóó put hwūn pin 主不慁賓, *chóó lâng bô hwūn lò lâng k'häyh*, the host did not trouble himself about his guest. See the 左傳 Chô twān.

大 Hwut 弗 Not, no, do not. Hwuy léy che ley hwuy gē che gē, taē jîn hwut wûy 非禮之禮非義之義.大人弗爲, *ûᵐ hap lèy ây léy, ûᵐ hap gē ây gē, twā lâng ûᵐ chò*, improper ceremonies, and unjust performances, the magnanimous man will not practise.

Hwut 乀 To lean to the left.

Hwut 彿 Hong hwut 彷彿, an uncertain appearance, undecided.

Hwut 佛 The same as the preceding. Hong hwut kê jëak bong 仿佛其若夢, *hong hwut ch'hin chëōⁿᵍ bānᵍ* indistinct, like a dream. Also, *hwut lëy* 佛戾, that, that thing.

Hwut 拂 To brush, to dust, to wipe away dirt; also, to abolish. Chin ké tëāng chëá, hwut che 進几杖者拂之, *chin jip tŏh á kwaê á tëŏh ch'hit e*, bringing in a table or a staff (to our superiors) we should first wipe them. See the 曲禮 K'hëuk léy.

Hwut 帗 A napkin used for tying up the hair.

Hwut 怫 To oppose, to resist, stubborn, rebellious. Gnoe kay che gân hwut ē 五家之言怫異, *goē lâng ây wā hwat gëk kwaè ē*, those five gentlemen's words are rebellious and strange.

Hwut 咈 To resist, to act contrary to. Bông hwut pek sèng, ê chëŏng kê che yëuk 罔咈百姓.以從巳之欲, *ûᵐ t'hang käyh päyh saiⁿᵍ ē t'hàn ka tī sèy aè*, do not oppose the people, in order to follow out your own desires. See the 書經 Se keng.

Hwut 㤇 To be sorrowful.

Hwut 紼 A rope. Ông gân jê se, kê ch'hut jê hwut 王言如絲.其出如綍, *ông kòng wā ch'hin chëōⁿᵍ se, e chò ch'hut ch'hin cheōng sòh*, the king's words are like threads, his practicing of them like ropes.

Hwut 紼 A rope, the rope with which a coffin is tied. Choē chòng pit chip hwut 助葬必執紼, *chān lāng sàng seng pit lëŏh gīm sòh á*, in assisting at a funeral, you must lay hold of the rope. See the 禮札 K'hëuk léy.

Hwut 紱 The string with which a seal of office is tied. Choo hwut 朱紱, a red string; used also for the following.

Hwut 袚 A string; a knee-cap, a part of the dress which comes over the knee.

Hwut 韍 A knee-cap. Tè bé hoē hwut bëēn 致美乎韍冕, *ch'hòng súy e ây hwut bëēn*, to make the knee-cap and crown as fine as possible. See the 論語 Lūn gē.

Hwut 黻 Hoo hwut 黼黻, a cap, adorned with hatchets, and various figures. Hwut bëēn 黻冕, an embroidered.

Hwut 祓 To deprecate calamities, and invoke blessings; a sacrifice for the same. Hwut tê woo wöey 祓除汚穢, *hwut tê la sâm*, to abolish all defilements.

Hwut 髴 Hông hwut 髣髴, undecided, indistinct; not clearly perceived.

Hwut 惚 Hông hwut 恍惚, to miss one's aim, to be disconcerted.

Hwut 忽 Suddenly, for a short time; to exhaust, to exterminate. Sē chwat, sē hwut 是絕是忽, it is exterminated and done. Hwut jëēn 忽然, suddenly. Hwut lëak 忽畧, to despise, to disesteem. Yit ch'hân wûy hwut, sip hwut wûy se 一蠶爲忽十忽爲絲, *chit ây ch'hân chò hwut, chap hwut chò se*, one filament spun by the silk worm is a line, and ten lines make a thread.

Hwut 囫 Hwut lûn 囫圇, anything round, whole, and unbroken.

Hwut 笏 Geük hwut 玉笏, a long flat piece of stone, or gem, held by king's and officers when they go to court.

Hwut 曶 To utter, and express one's self.

Hwut 甶 A devil's head.

Hwut 㤈 A name of Buddha.

Hwut 㴲 High, lofty.

Hwut 豽 A kind of pig; also written 㣊 hwut.

Hwut 颵 A light breeze, same say; a pierce wind; also written 颰 hwut.

Hwut 敹 Broken.

Hwut 颮 A fierce wind arising.

Hwut 歘 The wind arising; to arise.

仸 Hwut 佛 The name of Buddha, the sage of the west. Hàn Bêng-tèy k'hëén jin soò T'hëen-tëuk, kêw che, tek Hwut keng jē sip soò chëang 漢明帝遣人使

福建方言字典

天竺求之.得佛經二十四章, *Hàn Bêng-têy saé lâng chok soò k'hè T'hëen-tëuk kok këw e, tit tëŏh hwut keng jē chap sè chëang,* Hàn-Bêng-têy sent some people as messengers to the country of India, to look for this sage, and obtained 24 sections of the books of Budha.

Hwut 僵 The common form of the preceding.

Hwut 茀 Hwut wut 茀嵂 a hilly appearance.

Hwut 核 Read hek: the stone, or seed of a fruit. Sit chô t'hô lé, hwut tè ê hwut 食棗桃李.弗致于核 *chëăh chô t'hô lè, ūm t'hang lâm sàm hëet e ây hwut,* in eating dates, peaches, and plums, do not throw about the seeds.

Hwut 紱 A thread, the end of a thread; also, to bind.

Hwut 艴 A large ship or vessel.

Hwut 唿 Hwut lé 唿哩, the name of a foreign state.

Hwut 坲 Hwut put 坲埣, the rising of dust, a cloud of dust.

柰 Hwuy 飛 Vulg. *pwuy:* to fly. P'hëen p'hëen chëâ chuy, chaé hwuy chaé ché 翩翩者騅.載飛載止, *tit pwuy ây ka chuy, woō sè à pwuy woō sè à hàyⁿh,* the fluttering doves, are sometimes flying and sometimes resting. See the 小雅 Seaóu guày.

Hwuy 扉 The leaf of a door.

3 Y

Hwuy 霏 To snow, the appearance of falling snow. 'E swat kê hwuy 雨雪其霏, *lŏh sëyh e ây hwuy,* the snow falls in flakes.

Hwuy 倠 Pé hwuy 仳倠, ugly, ill-favoured. Boê hoé pé hwuy 嫫母仳倠, a woman who has had many children looks ugly.

Hwuy 菲 Fragrant; luxuriant.

Hwuy 緋 A deep red, a crimson colour.

Hwuy 騑 Horses galloping on without stopping.

Hwuy 非 To oppose; not; not right, wrong; an error; to reproach, to blame. Hwuy kê kwúy jê chèy che, t'hëém yëá 非其鬼而祭之.諂也, *ūm sè e ây kwúy jê chèy e, sè t'hëém mē,* to sacrifice to the ghost of a person with whom we were not related is flattery.

Boô t'hé kò chok hwuy 無恥過作非, *ūm t'hang seaou lëy jîn kòëy, sit tè kaòu chò ūm tëŏh,* do not be ashamed of acknowledging your errors, lest you be confirmed in that which is wrong.

Hwuy sèng jîn cheá boô hwat, hwuy haòu chëá boô ch'hin 非聖人者無法.非孝者無親, *hwuy maī^{ng} sèng jîn ây lâng pit bô hwat toé, hwuy maī^{ng} woō haòu ây lâng pit bô pāy boè,* he who reviles the sages, must be without law; and he who ridicules filial piety, must be without parents. See the 孝經 Haòu keng.

Hwuy 翬 To fly abroad; a large wild fowl with various colours.

Hwuy 輝 Kong hwuy 光輝, bright and brilliant.

Hwuy 暉 Bright, luminous, like the brightness of the sun.

Hwuy 煇 The brightness of fire, as bright as fire.

Hwuy 徽 Elegant, beautiful; a certain musical instrument.

Hwuy 蜚 The name of an insect; the ancient method of writing 飛 hwuy.

Hwuy 撝 To tear asunder; to point with the hand.

Hwuy 麾 A sort of standard or banner. Ché hwuy 指麾, to point with the hand.

Hwuy 鰴 The name of a fish.

Hwuy 妃 The next in rank to the Empress, among an Emperor's concubines, is called 妃 hwuy. Also the wife of the heir apparent.

Hwuy 揮 To brandish; to wield; to disperse; to point. Hwuy to 揮刀, to brandish a sword. Ché hwuy soò 指揮使, the name of an office. Yim gëuk chëak hwut hwuy 飲玉爵弗揮, *lim gëuk ây chëw chëak bŏh hwuy e*, when drinking out of a pearly cup, do not brandish it (lest you should break it). See the 曲禮 K'hëuk léy.

Hwuy 犤 An animal, like an ox, with a white head and one eye.

声

Hwúy 匪 No, not. Hwúy lûy 匪類, banditti.

Hwúy 俷 To ruin, to destroy; to turn the back upon. Boô hwúy tek 無俷德, *bŏh pöèy tek hĕng*, do not turn the back on virtue.

Hwúy 倄 Pé hwúy 仳倄, ugly, deformed.

Hwúy 篚 A round basket.

Hwúy 誹 Hwúy pòng 誹謗, to revile, to slander. Sûy hwúy sûy ê 誰誹誰譽, *chē chûy â maī^ng, chē chûy â o lŏ*, who will blame and who will praise?

Hwúy 菲 Thin, meager. Hwúy yím sit 菲飲食, *pŏh ây lim chëăh*, poor eating and drinking. See the 論語 Lūn gé.

Hwúy 斐 Elegant, literary. Yéw hwúy kwun choó 有斐君子, *woō hwúy ây kwun choó*, here is a literary accomplished person.

Hwúy 悱 To stammer, to wish to speak without being able. Put hwúy put hwat 不悱不發, *e nā ū^m hwúy kóng, chëw bŏ hwat bĕng hoē e*, if he does not attempt to stammer out something himself, it will not be explained to him. See the 論語 Lūn gé.

Hwúy 棐 To assist, to help; the name of a fruit tree. Hwúy ké kwut chēng 棐几滑淨, *hwúy ch'hâ ây tŏh kwut kwà ch'heng k'hè*, a table made of the *hwúy* wood, polished and clean.

Hwúy 翡 A red-feathered sparrow; a bird about the size of a swallow, the male of which is red, and is called hwúy 翡,—while the female is azure, and called 翠 ch'hùy.

Hwúy 蜚 A destructive insect, that injures people's clothes; also, the name of an animal, in shape like an ox, with a white head, one eye, and a serpent's tail.

Hwúy 蜰 Loê hwúy 蠦蜰, an excrementitious insect.

Hwúy 虺 Ê hwúy 蛇虺, the name of a serpent. Wûy hwúy wûy ê, lé choó che sëâng 維虺維蛇.女子之祥, *tok tok hwúy kap ê ây chwâ, sē cha boë ây sëâng*, but the *hwúy* and *ê* snakes are prognostics of getting daughters. See the 小雅 Seaóu gnáy.

Hwúy 虫 The ancient form of the preceding; the generic term for all the scaly tribe.

Hwúy 毀 To destroy, to break down; to injure; to revile, to blame. Kay pit choō hwúy, jê hoē jîn hwúy che 家必自毀.而後人毀之, *kay pit ka tē p'hăh k'hëep, jëên aōu lâng p'hăh k'hëep e*, a family must first ruin itself, before people think of ruining it.

Tëŏng-nê put k'hó hwúy yëá 仲尼不可毀也, *Tëong-nê bēy hoē lê hwúy pòng*, Tëŏng-nê (Confucius) is not to be reviled by you.

Hwúy 燬 Fire burning fiercely; anything burnt and destroyed by fire.

Hwúy 烜 To kindle a fire; an officer whose business it was to draw fire from the sun. Soo-hwúy-sē chëăng é hoo sûy ch'hé bêng hⁿó ê jit 司烜氏掌以夫遂取明火于日, *Soo-hwúy-sē chëăng kwăn l'hó hoo sûy ch'hé bêng höëy tē jit*, the Soo-hwúy-sē (officer's) business was to take the burning-glass and draw fire from the sun. See the 周禮 Chew léy. This shews that the Chinese understood the nature of the burning-glass very early (about 2000 years before Christ); — but they also talk of a mirror by which they could extract water from the moon.

Hwúy 喟 To sigh, the sound of sighing. Gân-yëen hwúy jëên t'hàn wat 顏淵喟然嘆曰, Gân-yëen, fetching a long sigh, exclaimed, &c. See the 論語 Lûn gé.

Hwúy 諱 Hwúy pòng 諱謗, to revile, to slander, to blame.

圭

Hwùy 費 To waste, to expend, to spend money. A surname. Séy hwùy 所費, *sé hwùy*, expence.

Kwun choó hwŭy jê put hwùy 君子惠而不費, *kwun choó woō yin hwŭy, jê bô p'hwà hwùy*, the good man is kind without being extravagant. See the 論語 Lûn gé.

Hwùy yūng sīm to 費用甚多, *hwùy yūng sīm chēy*, the expences are very great.

Hwùy 狒 Hwùy hwùy 狒狒, the name of an animal, in the shape of a man, with shaggy hair, has a swift pace, and devours people.

Hwùy 芾 Exuberant herbage, thick foliage.

Hwùy 廢 To set aside, to abolish, to render nugatory, not to adopt. Hwān chèy yéw kê hwùy che, bok kám ké yëá, yéw kê ké che, bok kám hwùy yëá 凡祭.有其廢之莫敢舉也.有其舉之莫敢廢也, *hwān chèy lêy, wōo ây hwùy bô, lâng kⁿâ kê yūng, wōo ây kê yūng, bô lâng kⁿâ hwùy bô*, with respect to sacrifices, whatever has been abolished no man dares to re-establish, and whatever is established, no man dares to abolish. See the 曲禮 K'hëuk léy.

Hwùy 諱 To conceal, to avoid; the name of a parent or prince, which should be concealed or avoided, in common conversation.

Hwùy bêng put hwùy sèng 諱名不諱姓, *ēy hwùy til mēⁿâ, bēy hwùy lil saiⁿᵍ*, we may conceal the name (of our parents), but not their surname. See 孟子 Bēng choó.

Hwùy 翽 The noise of flying, the clapping of wings. Hōng hông ê hway, hwùy hwùy kê é 鳳凰于飛翽翽其羽, *hōng hông til pwuy, hwùy hwùy e ây sit*, the felicitous birds are flying, and clapping their wings. See the 大雅 Taē gnây.

Hwùy 𤻈 Extreme, very; the same as 𤸃 hwūy. Ê pēng hwùy è 余病𤻈矣, *gwá ây paiⁿᵍ sīm*, my sickness is extreme.

丟 Hwûy 肥 Vulg. *pwûy*: fat, corpulent. Paôu yéw hwûy jëuk, kêw yéw hwûy má 庖有肥肉廐有肥馬, *toó pâng woō pwûy bāh, bây tëâou woō pwûy bây*, in the larder there is fat meat, and fat horses in the stable. See 孟子 Bēng choó.

Hwûy 腓 The calf of the leg.

Hwûy 淝 Hap-hwûy 合淝, the name of a river.

Hwûy 磁 Read choô: earthenware. Choô k'hè 磁器, *hwûy k'hè*, crockery-ware.

丟 Hwūy 惠 Favour, kindness, to be obedient; to bestow. A surname. Also written 僡 hwūy.

Wûy hwūy che hwaê 惟惠之懷, *wûy yin hwūy ây sim hwaê*, only to have thoughts of kindness.

An bîn chek hwūy 安民則惠, *an pâyh saiⁿᵍ chek choô hwūy*, to tranquillize the people is a kindness.

Hwūy 橞 The name of a tree.

Hwūy 蟪 Hwūy koe 蟪蛄, an insect that exists only for a short time. Hwūy koe put te ch'hun ch'hew 蟪蛄不知春秋, *hwūy koe ūᵐ chae ch'hun ch'hew*. the *hwuy koe* knows nothing about spring and autumn, (owing to its short existence, for if born in spring it dies in summer, and if produced in summer it dies in autumn.)

Hwūy 彗 An infelicitous star. Hwūy seng 彗星, a comet.

Hwūy 蕙 A fragrant plant, which grows in low marshy places; if it yields but one flower on each stalk, and is very fragrant, it is called 蘭 lân, but if it yields several flowers, and is deficient in fragrance, it is called 蕙 hwūy.

Hwūy 慧 A pliant disposition, susceptible of instruction; intelligent, wise. Tè hwūy 智慧, wisdom.

Gwūy Boó-tèy tè hwūy, put lêng k'hè kē ok 魏武帝智慧不能去其惡, *Gwūy Boó-tèy woō tè hwūy, bēy k'hè t'hek kak e ây phaⁿè*, the Emperor Boó of the Gwūy dynasty was wise, but he could not throw away his wickedness.

Hwūy 篲 A besom made of bamboo. Hàn Ko-choé tëâou T'haè-kong yung hwūy 漢高祖朝太公擁篲, *Hàn Ko-choé teaôu keēⁿᵍ T'haè-kong ch'hêw gnâyh saôu chèw*, Ko-choé of the Hàn dynasty waited on Thaè-kong, (his father,) with a bamboo besom under his arm; — (ready to sweep for him, if necessary). See the 史記 Soó kè.

Hwūy 嘒 Clear, bright; also, a small voice, a whisper. Hwūy pé seaóu seng 嘒彼小星, *bêng hwut lēy sèy lēep ch'hai^ng*, how bright is that little star. See the 召南 Sëaòu lâm.

Hwūy 吠 Vulg. *pwūy:* to bark like a dog. Key bêng koé hwūy sëang bûn, jê tat hoē soò kéng 雞鳴狗吠相聞.而達乎四境, *key t'hê kaôu pwūy sëo t'hē^n a, jê tat hoē sè kéng*, the crowing of cocks and barking of dogs may be distinctly heard, throughout the four quarters of the kingdom. See 孟子 Bēng-choó.

Hwūy 卉 The generic term for plants and vegetables. San yēw kay hwūy 山有嘉卉, *sw^n a woō hó ch'haôu*, in the hills there are fine plants. See the 小雅 Sëaóu gnây. Also written 芔 hwūy.

Hwūy 喙 To stop; a fowl's beak; a white horse with a black nose. Jîn che ke, sêy é put sit nëáou hwūy chëá, é soó tông hwān yëá 人之飢.所以不食鳥喙者.與死同患也, *lâng ây ke yaou, sêy é ū^m chëāh chëáou ch'húy, sē kap e chò poó sè tâng hwān ló*, the reason why people ever so hungry will not eat a fowl's beak, is because they are concerned lest they should be brought to the same untimely end. See the 戰國策 Chëèn kok ch'hek.

Hwūy 緯 The cross threads in weaving; the woof is called 經 keng, and the warp is called 緯 hwūy. Roads from north to south, are also called 經 keng, and those from east to west 緯 hwūy.

Hwūy 恚 Angry, enraged.

Hwūy 譓 To examine various devices.

I

For words beginning with i, such as in, im, ip, and it, look under the letter y, as yim, yin, &c.

J

上聲

Jé 乳 Vulg. *leng:* the nipples; milk. Jé boé 乳母, *leng boé*, the teats, the dugs; a wet nurse.

Bûn-ông soò jé, sē wûy chè jin 文王四乳.是謂至仁, *Bûn-ông woō sè ây leng, ch'hē^n á kóng chè jîn*, Bûn-ông had four nipples, hence he is called the most benevolent.

Boé yëuk choó é jé 母育子以乳, *nëō^ng lêy ch'hē haōu sai^ng ê leng*, a mother feeds her offspring with milk.

3 w

Jé 汝 The name of a river. Also, vulg. *loó or lé*, you. Kwat Jé Hàn, paê Hwaê Soò, jê choò che Kang 決汝漢.排淮泗.而注之江, *kwat tooī^ng Jè Hàn, paê Hwaê Soò, jê ch'hwà jip Kang*, he cut off the Jé and Hàn rivers, and led on the Hwaê and Soò, till he brought them to fall into the Kang. See 孟子 Bēng-choó.

Jîn lêng ch'hëung boô sēw jé jé che sit, boô sêy óng jê put wûy gē yëá 人能充無受爾汝之實.無所往而不爲義也; *lâng nā ēy ch'hēung mwⁿá bô sēw jé jé ây chëak sit, chek bô ta tŏh k'hè jé ūm chò gē,* when people fulfil the honest part of not receiving what is given them with a "you! you!"—then wherever they go they will practise nothing but uprightness;—hence the Chinese do not like to be addressed with a plain "*you*," when anything is given to them. See 孟子 Bēng-choó.

Jé 女 The same as the preceding.

Jé 尒 You; also, a particle.

Jé 爾 You; also an euphonic particle; near. Soò ê é jé chēùng soō, hong soô hwat chŏey 肆予以爾衆士.奉辭伐罪, *ch'hēⁿa gwá kap lē chēà ây lâng, hong t'heeⁿᵍ ây bēng cheng hwat woō chŏey,* thus I and all of you, have received the decree, to punish the guilty. Said by 成湯 Sêng-t'hong.
Put te ló che chëang chè yîn jé 不知老之將至云爾, *ūm chae laōu ây bōēyh kaòu,* without knowing that old age is approaching. See the 論語 Lūn gé.

Jé 璽 Geük jé 玉璽, the great seal of the Empire, the royal signet; it was first formed by 秦始皇 Chîn-sé-hông, and constituted a part of the regalia of China.

Jé 耳 Vulg. *hē:* the ear, the organ of hearing; also, a euphonic particle. Jé che ê seng yëá 耳之於聲也, *hē k'hang ây tē sēⁿa,* the ear, with respect to sounds, (performs its natural office). See 孟子 Bēng-choó.
Jé tek jîn yëen jé hoê 汝得人焉耳乎, *lé woō tit tëŏh gaôu lâng á bô,* did you meet with any clever men there? See the 論語 Lūn gé.

Jé 邇 Near, easy. P'hè jê hêng wán pit choō jé 譬如行遠必自邇, *p'hè jé kēⁿá hwuiⁿᵍ, pit àn kīn,* like as when we want to travel far, we must begin with what is ne[ar]. See the 中庸 Tëung yûng.

Jé 禰 A temple erected to the honour of on[e's] parents. Kê chaē kwun, chek sëw kong jé 其在軍則守於公禰 *bōēyh hêng kwun, tëŏh taē seng chëw tē kong jé,* wh[en] about to go out with the army, it is necessary fi[rst] to visit the parental shrine.

Jé 濱 To present wine; also, full, replenish[ed].

Jé 珥 Gems worn dangling at the ears.

Jé 庾 The name of a measure, containing [up]wards of six pecks. A surname. ... che jé 與之庾, *hoē e chit ây jé,* g[ave] her six pecks. See the 論語 Lūn gé.

Jé 緝 Jé jé 緝緝, full reins,—leaving [the] bridle loose and full.

Jé 駬 Lëuk jé 騄駬, the name of a ho[rse] belonging to 周穆王 Chew Bok-ô[ng].

Jé 醑 Good wine.

Jé 茹 To cut; to devour; to quaff. Ch'haé 菜茹, dried vegetables. Jé mô y[ëet] hëet 茹毛飲血, *chëäh hâm mô, [ē]hâm hōēyh,* (the early ancients) ate flesh with [the] hair on, and drank together with it the bloo[d] (this is spoken of as a sign of their uncivili[zed] state).

Jé 瘉 To heal; to get well, to recover fr[om] sickness. Hàn ông chit·jé 漢王[疾]瘉, *Hàn ông pūyⁿᵍ hó,* the king of H[an] recovered from his sickness.

Jé 窳 A crack in an earthern vessel. Sùn tô pin, k'hè put k'hoé jé 舜陶河[濱]器不苦窳, *sùn sëo hwûy lē hô* ...

ây wûy, ke k'hè bô hëëm woō k'heĕh, when Sùn burnt pottery at the banks of the river, there was no complaint of cracks in the vessels. See the 史記 Soó kè.

Jé 窳 Idle, lazy, indolent. Séw chëuk tō jé 手足惰窳, *k'ha ch'hèw p'hán twⁿā*, the arms and legs lazy and indolent.

Jé 愈 To exceed, to surpass; also, to recover from sickness. Jé é Höëy yëá sëuk jé 女與回也孰愈, *lè kap Höëy yëá chē chúy k'hăh gaôu*, which is the cleverest you or Höëy? See the 論語 Lūn gé.

Kim peng sëäou jé, ch'he ch'hò ê tëäou 今病小愈趨造於朝, *tⁿa paīⁿᵍ lëŏh lëŏh á k'hăh hó, woō kin kin kēⁿâ jip tëâou*, now his sickness is a little better, and he has hastened to the court. See 孟子 Bēng-choó.

Jé 瘐 To die of cold and hunger, to be starved to death; also, disappointed. Jé soó gëuk tëung 瘐死獄中, *yaou kwⁿâ sè tē kⁿa k'hoo laē*, to be starved to death in prison.

平

Jê 如 Alike, like, if, as; if it is thus: jê ch'hoó 如此, *an ney saiⁿᵍ*, thus: jê jëak 如若, *ch'hin chëōⁿᵍ*, if, in that case.

Te che chëá put jê hⁿò che chëá, hⁿò che chëá put jê lok che chëá 知之者不如好之者.好之者不如樂之者, *chae e ây lâng bēy ch'hin chëōⁿᵍ yit lëŏh e ây lâng, yit lëŏh e ây lâng bēy ch'hin chëōⁿᵍ t'hëàng lok e ây lâng*, those who know (virtue) are not to be compared with those who love it, and those who love it are not so good as those who are delighted with it. See the 論語 Lūn gé.

Jê put k'hó kêw, chëûng goê séy hⁿò 如不可求.從吾所好, *nā bēy kêw lit, t'hàn gwá sèy aè*, if these (riches and honours) cannot be sought after indiscriminately, then let me follow that which I love. See the 論語 Lūn gé.

Jê 侞 Even, plain, level. Yëük an wán hong, tong sëen sūn jê kē kīn 欲安遠方.當先順侞共近, *nā bōëyh an hwuīⁿᵍ pang, tëŏh taē seng sūn jê e ây kīn*, if you wish to tranquillize distant countries, you must first render those near obedient and tranquil.

Jê 侞 Numerous, abundant.

Jê 俞 To answer, to reply to; the sound of assent; a boat made of a hollow tree. A surname.

Lâm wûy lé jê 男唯女俞, *ta po yìn lâng wûy, cha boê yìn lâng jê*, males should answer with a 'wûy,' and females with a 'jê.' See the 禮記 Léy kè.

Jê 嚅 Verbose, talkative.

Jê 儒 A learned man, a scholar. Jê kaôu 儒教, the sect of the learned. Jé wûy kwun choó jê, boô wûy sëäou jîn jê 女爲君子儒.無爲小人儒, *lè chò kwun choó ây t'hak ch'hăyh lâng, ūⁿ t'hang chò sëâou jîn ây t'hak ch'hăyh lâng*, do you become a good sort of a learned man, and not a worthless sort of a learned man. See the 論語 Lūn gé.

Jê 濡 To moisten; to be wet with dew or rain. Jê tē 濡滯, to go about anything slowly, like the slow dripping of water.

Jê 襦 A short jacket. Put pek jê k'hwà 不帛襦袴, *ūⁿ t'hang ch'hòng twān, tëy sⁿa kap kwún*, do not make short jackets and petticoats of silk.

Jê 孺 A child, an infant. Jê choó k'hó kaôu 孺子可教, *sèy kēⁿâ yëá ēy kà lit*, (I see) my lad that you are teachable. Said by an old man to 張良 Tëōⁿᵍ lëang, when he had complied with his request to pick up his shoe from under a bridge, and afterwards was willing to assist him in putting it on.

Jê 洏 Lëên jê 漣洏, trickling down, as tears. T'hèy lêw lëên jê 涕流漣洏, *laôu bàk chaē lëên jê*, the tears flowed trickling down.

Jê 而 A connective particle; and, but, also; you. Hak, jê sê sip che 學而時習之, *t'hak jê. ĕăngs sê wun sip e*, to learn, and constantly to exercise one's-self in it. See the 上論 Sëăng lŭn.
Chó-loē 子路 asked Confucius about firmness; when Confucius replied, do you mean the firmness of the north country, or the firmness of the south country,—ek jê këăng e 抑而強與, *á sē lê ây këăng*, or your own firmness. See the 中庸 Tëung yûng.

Jê 袻 The hem of a garment.

Jê 醹 Strong wine.

Jê 胹 To boil thoroughly. Swan-kong jē lëên, chaē hoo jê hîm hwan put sëuk 宣公二年.宰夫胹熊蹯不熟, *Swan-kong nō neē^ng, chaē hoo chê hîm chëō^ng bēy sek*, in the second year of Swan-kong, the royal cook boiled a bear's palm, and did not boil it thoroughly.—See the 左傳 Chó twān.

Jê 臾 Se jê 須臾, a moment. Tō yëá chëá, put k'hó se jê lê yëá 道也者.不可須臾離也, *tō lê ây soō, ū^m t'hang chit bak nāy^n h lê k'hwuy*, the right way must not be quitted for a moment. See the 中庸 Tëung yûng.

Jê 萸 Choo jê 茱萸, the name of a plant, which if plucked on the 9th day of the 9th moon, and stuck in the hair, will banish all noxious influences. See the 風土記 Hong t'hoé kè.

Jê 腴 The part under the belly. Hwûy jê 肥腴, fat, corpulent.

Jê 諛 To flatter. T'hëëm jê 諂諛, *sëep sëy*, to cringe to any one. Chek ch'hàm t'hëëm bëën jê che jîn chè è 則讒諂面諛之人至矣, *chek saè p'hwà t'hëëm mē, bīn chëng sëep sëy lân ây lâng kaôu*, then slandering, flattering, and sycophantic persons would come (around the prince). See 孟子 Bēng choó.

Jê 兒 Vulg. *sëy kë^nā*: a child, a boy, an infant. Jê sun pit yēw jê sun hok 兒孫必有兒孫福, *kë^nā sun pit woō kë^nā sun ây hok*, posterity will certainly obtain the measure of happiness that belongs to posterity.

Jê 瑜 Kin jê 瑾瑜, a beautiful gem, a precious stone. Hây put jëëm jê 瑕不掩瑜, *hây tëëm bô jëëm jê gëuk*, a slight flaw does not spoil the gem.

Jê 瘉 Sick, a sickness. Hoō bóe seng gnó, hoê pe gnó jê 父毋生我.胡俾我瘉, *pāy boē sai^ng gwá, s^nā soō hoê gwá an nëy ch'hâm*, my parents have brought me forth, but why have they inflicted on me such pain.

Jê 榆 The name of a tree; whose blossoms fall like pieces of money. Tám jê chek bëën put yëuk kak 啖榆則眠不欲覺, *chëăh jê chek k'hwùn ū^m aè ch'hai^ng*, on eating of the *jê* tree; a person sleeps without desiring to awake.

Jê 逾 To step over, to transgress, to overstep, to go over. Jê ê Lok 逾于洛, *köëy tê Lok cháy*, he crossed the river Lok. Jit gwat jê maē 日月逾邁, *jit göëyh tit köëy*, the days and months are passing away.

Jê 踰 The same as the preceding.

Jê 渝 To change, to alter.

Jê 艅 A boat made out of a hollow tree.

Jê 褕 Clothes ornamented with feathers.

Jê 揄 To lead, to draw; also, to spread abroad a fame or report.

Jê 袽 Old rotten clothes, used as oakum, for caulking boats, and stopping leaks.

Jê 洳 The name of a river. Ch'he jê 沮洳 damp and low.

Jê 儒 A learned man, a scholar; the same as 儒 jê. Choo jê 侏儒, a dwarf.

Jê 穤 A dwarf, a diminutive person; also, the same as 孺 jê, a child.

Jê 覦 K'haé jê, to desire to obtain anything, to peep at, to spy with a wish to obtain. Boô k'haé jê é kêw hêng 無覬覦以求幸, *bôh t'hâôu k'huⁿâ bāng seōng, ê kêw hēāou hēng*, do not peep and long, in order to obtain some lucky chance.

Jê 歈 Pa jê 巴歈 the name of a song. T'hé jê 歋歈, to clap the hands and laugh.

Jê 窬 To bore a hole through a plank for a door way; to perforate anything, in order to get through by stealth. Jê ch'hēâng 窬牆, *nooiⁿᵍ kōèy ch'hēōⁿᵍ*, to creep through a hole in the wall.
He who is outwardly and inwardly foul is said to be — yêw ch'hwàn jê che tō yêâ 猶穿窬之盜也與, *ch'hìn chēōⁿᵍ t'haou nooiⁿᵍ kōèy ây ch'hat*, like a thief who bores his way through a fence and creeps in. See the 論語 Lūn gé.

Jê 毹 A mattrass formed of horse hair. K'hēak jê 氍毹, a hair mattrass.

Jê 茹 Roots entwined together; to pull up together with the roots. A surname. Pwat maôu lêên jê 拔茅連茹, *pūyh k'hê hâᵐ â tēōh hâm kin*, in pulling up the long grass, you should pull up the roots with it.

3 X

Jê 桋 The name of a tree.

弍

Jē 二 Vulg. *nō*; two. Jē sip 二十, *jē chap* twenty. Sip jē 十二, *chap jē*, twelve. Jē chēâ yit che tùy 二者一之對, *jē sē chit ây tōèy*, two is the opposite of one. Jē goê yêw put chēuk 二吾猶不足, *nō ây gwâ yéâ ūᵐ kaôu*, two-tenths are not sufficient for me, (how much less one-tenth?) See the 下論 Hāy lūn.

Jē 佴 To be next to, to second, to help, to assist; to be involved in. Soo-ma-ch'hēen 司馬遷 blamed Lé-lêng 李陵 for submitting to the barbarians, and thereby disgracing his family, adding, — jē pōk yēw jē ch. ch'hân sit 而僕又佴之蠶室, *jē gwâ yā tēy jē e lōh kⁿa k'hoo*, I, also, in consequence, am involved in the silk-worm's house, (i. e. the prison.)

Jē 貳 The large form of 二 jē two; also, to have a double mind; to suspect. Jin hēen bût jē 任賢勿貳, *jīm yāng gaôu lâng ūᵐ t'hang jē sim e*, in employing clever men, do not treat them with a double heart (i. e. do not entertain suspicions of them.)

Jē 樲 Jē kek 樲棘, a sour date tree. Sēâ kē goê káy, jê yâng kē jē kek 舍其梧檟而養其樲棘, *pàng t'hek kak e ây goê kây, jē ch'hi e ây jē kek*, to give up the fine timber of the goê-káy, and to keep merely a sour date tree. See 孟子 Bēng-choó.

Jē 僨 To assist, and benefit; to stand by.

Jē 膩 Hwûy jē 肥膩, fat, lusty, corpulent; glossy, shining.

Jē 蛆 A bait for angling; the same as 餌 jē.

Jē 珥 Jē tong 珥瑺, a gem worn dangling before the ear. Naé hāy tēēn k'hè chom-jē 迺下殿去簪珥, *e chēw lŏh tēēn k'hè e ày chom jē*, and then descending the hall, he laid aside his hair-pin and ear-gems.

Jē 餌 A bait for angling.

Jē 諭 To inform, to announce, to make known. Sēw kaòu bēng jē kok tō yëā 受敎明諭國道也, *sēw kà bēng hēāou jē, sē kok ày tō*, to receive instruction well, and to give clear orders is the way of ruling a nation.

Jē 裕 K'hwan jē 寬裕, slowly, leisurely, at ease. Chek goê chìn t'hōey k'hè put ch'hēak oh'hēak jēen, yēw ê jē chae 則吾進退豈不綽綽然.有餘裕哉, *chek gwà chìn t'hèy, K'ham-ūm k'hwⁿa k'hwⁿa ày yēōⁿᵍ, kwà woō ch'hun ày jēaōu jē chae*, thus with respect to my entering on or retiring from office, how can I not be free, unrestrained, and abundantly at my ease? See 孟子 Bēng-choò.

Jē 喩 To inform, to announce, to instruct. A surname. Sēng jîn sēet kaòu, hwuy pit kay jē, jē hoè hēaòu yëá 聖人設敎.非必家喻而戶曉也, *sēng jîn sēet kà hwā, ūm saè tak keng ch'hoò k'hè kóng, jē tak mooiⁿᵍ, k'hè hēdou bēng*, the sages, having appointed the methods of instruction, do not need to inform every family of them, and to make them known at every door.

Jē 裋 Short garments. Jē hat 裋褐, hairy garments. Hân chēā lē twán jē 寒者利短裋, *kwⁿá ày lâng lē yēāh tèy sⁿa*, when people are cold, they will be glad even of a coarse short jacket.

Jē 字 Read joō: a character, a letter. Sëāng koé hē yew bûn joō 上古未有文字 *sēāng koè ày lâng bōēy woō bûn jē*, the early ancients had no characters — till in the time of 黃帝 Hông tèy, B. C. 2622, 倉頡 Ch'hong-k'hēet first invented them.

Sit joo 識字, *bat jē*, to know how to read.

卋

Jëa 遮 Read chëa: to screen, to hide, to shelter.

声

Jëá 唏 The sound of answering, a reply, an affirmative.

Jëá 嗻 To answer respectfully. Ch'hëāng jëá 唱嗻, *ch'hëōⁿᵍ jëá*, to bow without kneeling down; also written 喏 jëá.

Jëā 惹 Deceitful, disordered; also, to excite, to bring on, to stir up, to enkindle. Jëā noē 惹怒, *jëá lâng ày sēw k'hè*, to stir up one's wrath.

Hⁿò jëá soō 好惹事, *aè jëá soō*, fond of making trouble.

Jëā 諾 To assent, to reply to: also read jëá.

丟

Jëa 偌 A surname.

天

Jëak 若 Vulg. *nā*: if, like as, suppose; a fragrant herb; obedient. Jëak boô chöēy jē chēw soó tēy 若無罪而就死地, *ch'hin chëōⁿᵍ bô chōēy, jē chēw kàou sè ày tēy*, like one who has committed no fault, and yet proceeds to the place of slaughter. See the 上孟 Sëāng bēng.

Jëak sêng é jîn, chek goê k'hé kám 若聖與仁.則吾豈敢, *ch'hin chëōⁿᵍ sêng kwà jîn, chek gwà k'hè kⁿá*, but if you speak of being a sage, or benevolent, then how dare I presume to that; — said by Confucius.

Jëak **箬** Tëuk jëak 竹箬, the outer surface of bamboo. Jëak lip 箬笠, *tek läyh*, a bamboo hat.

Jëak **弱** Lwân jëak 軟弱, *nooi^ng chē^nā*, weak, feeble. Jëak koè put k'hó é tek keâng 弱固不可以敵強, *nooi^ng chē^nā koè jëën bēy tùy tek keâng bêng*, the weak certainly cannot oppose the strong. See 孟子 Bêng-choó.

Jëak **蒻** Poê jëak 蒲蒻, a kind of reed or rush.

Jëak **溺** The name of a river; also read lek, to drown.

声

Jëâng **壤** A clod of earth; a plot of ground; the loose earth on the surface of the ground. Hoo yin, sëâng sit kō jëâng, hây yim hông chwân 夫蚓上食槁壤下飲黃泉, *hoo t'hoē kin, têng bîn chëâh tà ây t'hoē, hây tëy lîm wui^ng chwⁿd*, now the earth worm, above eats the light clods, and below drinks the yellow fountains, (and is thus independent of every one.) See 孟子 Bêng-choó.

Jëâng **攘** To disturb, to throw into confusion. Jëâng ê tek 攘夷狄, to confound the barbarians.

Jëâng **嚷** To make a noise, to bawl out incessantly with a loud voice.

Jëâng **宂** Read jëûng: chap jëûng 雜宂, *chap jëâng*, intermixed and in confusion.

平

Jëâng **攘** To steal, to pilfer. Goê tóng yew tit kēung chëá, kê hoō jëâng yâng, jê choó chìn che 吾党有直躬者.其父攘羊而子證之, *gwân ây tóng woō chit ây tcâou tit ây lâng, e ây nëō^ng pây t'haou tâng ây yëō^ng, jê haōu sai^ng chò kan chìn e*, in our village there was a straight forward sort of a man, whose father having stolen a sheep, (the son) appeared against him as a witness. See the 論語 Lūn-gé.

Jëâng **瀼** Much dew, a heavy dew; to be much wet with the dew.

Jëâng **穰** Rich, full, abundant, plentiful. Hong lëên jëâng jëâng 豐年穰穰, *hó neē^ng tang jëâng jëâng*, a fruitful season, what abundance does it yield!

Jëâng **禳** A sacrifice offered for the purpose of averting calamity.

Jëâng **釀** To distil spirituous liquors; good strong liquor or wine. Bêng-sëâng-kwun naē to jëâng chëw, maé hwûy gnëw 孟嘗君乃多釀酒買肥牛, *Bêng-sëâng-kwun naē chēy jëâng chëw, bēy pwûy ây goô*, Bêng-sëâng-kwun distilled great quantities of liquor and bought fat oxen, (in order to treat his numerous guests.)

Jëâng **瓤** Tong jëâng 瓠瓤, the seeds of the melon.

去

Jëâng **讓** Vulg. *nëō^ng* to yield, to give place, to give way to, to relinquish, to recede. Sëâng jëâng 相讓, *nëō^ng*, to give way to each other. Chëung sin jëâng loē, put sit pek poē 終身讓路.不失百步, *chit sè lâng nëō^ng loē, bēy a^m k... chit pâyh poē*, if all your life long you give way to people in walking, you will not lose a hundred paces in the end.

声

Jeáou **爪** Claws talons, nails. Kê-hoō-ê ông ... jeáou gây 祈父予王之爪牙, *Kê-hoō-ê sè ông ây jeáou gây*, Kê-hoō-ê was the king's talons and teeth. See the 小雅 Seáou gnáy.

Jeáou 抓 To claw, to scratch, to tear with the nails. Chŏng-choŏ yew yit ch'he yĕen, wûy ê k'hĕak jĕaôu, kĕĕn k'haóu hoē ông 莊子有一狙爲.委蛇攫抓見巧乎王, *Chŏng-choŏ woō chit chĕăh kaôu, wûy ê k'hĕak jĕaôu, lĕăng k'hà hoē ông*, Chong-choŏ had an ape, who by his easy antics and constant scratching, shewed his agility to the king.

Jeáou 擾 To disturb, to throw into confusion. Kan ko jeáou jeâng 干戈擾攘, military weapons tumultuously brandished about.

Jeáou 繞 To surround, to twine round. Thĕĕn jĕaou 纏繞, to entwine and entangle. Chĕùng seng-soò bĕĕn swân jeáou pok kek 衆星四面旋繞北極, *chĕùng ch'haing sè bīn swân jeáou pak kek*, all the stars on every side revolve round the north star.

去 Jeàou 抓 To scratch, to claw, to tear with the nails.

Jeàou 皺 Wrinkled, furrowed. Bĕēn jĕàou 面皺, *bīn jeàou*, a wrinkled face. Hong ch'huy lĕuk súy, súy jĕàou bĕĕn 風吹緑水.水皺面, *hong tit ch'hoèy lek chúy, chúy chĕw woō jeàou ây bīn*, when the wind blows over the green waters, they get a wrinkled face.

Jeàou 縐 Jeaou sey 縐紗, crape.

平 Jeâou 橈 Vulg. *jĕŏ*: a short paddle, for rowing a boat.

Jeâou 嬈 Keaou jeâou 嬌嬈, winning, handsome, agreeable.

Jeâou 澆 To sprinkle, to rinse; also, thin.

Jeâou 蟯 Short worms in the intestines. Gnó chè yit sin loëy pēĕn jĕâou hoêy 我之一身內變蟯蛔, *gwá ây chit sin laē peēng lây chăng*, the inside of my whole body is turned into short worms.

Jeâou 鱙 Jeâou gê 鱙魚, a small kind of fish.

Jeâou 饒 Full, abundant, rich, sufficient. A surname. Taē hëang, put bŭn pok, put jeâou hoô 大饗.不問卜.不饒富, *twā ch'hēnā lâng k'hâyk, ūm mooīng pok kwà, yĕá ūm hwun pĕet jeâou poò*, at a great feast, do not enquire about oracles, nor distinguish the rich and full. See the 曲禮 K'hëuk lëy.

Jeâou 皺 To furrow, to wrinkle. Lëuk súy hoô yew, hong jĕâou bēĕn 綠水無憂.風皺面, *lek chúy bô hwân lô, hong jeâou bīn*, the green waters are not troubled, but it is the wind which wrinkles their face.

Jeâou 縐 To rumple up anything, or to wrinkle it; crape.

去 Jeàou 溺 Vulg. *jĕŏ*: urine.

入 Jeĕh 廿 A union of two characters, — jē chap 二十, *jeĕh*, signifying twenty.

上 Jëém 染 Vulg. *neeng*: to dye. Jëém sek 染色, *neeng sek*, to dye of some colour. Vulg. bak, to soil, to dirty. Jĕëm woo 染污, *bak lā sâm*, to be soiled with dirt. Kēw jĕëm woo sëuk, hâm ê wûy sin 舊染污俗.咸與維新, *koō bak lā sâm ây hong sëuk, ī a chò poō sè sin*, before he was befouled with filthy habits, but now he is altogether renovated. See the 尚書 Sëō^ng se.

Jëém 染 The same as the preceding.

Jëém 冉 Weak, feeble; also, a surname;—Confucius had two disciples of this clan. Jëém-choó t'höēy teâou 冉子退朝, *Jëém-choó t'hèy teâou*, Jëém-choó retired from the audience. Also written 冄 jëém.

Jëém 髯 A beard.

Jëém 苒 Jim jëém 荏苒, weak, lither, pliant; exuberant herbage.

Jëēm 㚩 The people of 淮南 Hwaê-lâm call their mothers jëēm, mother!

Jëén 橪 A small sour date tree; also, to defile; to dye various colours.

Jëén 蹨 Jéw jëén 蹂蹨, to trample on, to tread under foot.

Jëên 然 To burn, to inflame; also, a disjunctive particle,—but, if, if it is thus, thus; right, yes, it is so. Kó jëên 果然, indeed! Suy jëên 雖然, although. Jëák h^nó che sé jëên, chwân che sé tat 若火之始然.泉之始達, *ch'hin chëō^ng höēy ây khê t'hâou tŏh, chw^nâ ay k'hê t'haôu tat*, like fire when it begins to burn, or water when it begins to flow. See 孟子 Bēng-choó. Jëên chek Kwán-tëūng te léy hoē 然則管仲知禮乎, *nā sē, chek Kwán-tëūng bat lèy hoē*, but then does Kwán-tëūng understand propriety?

Ké jëên,—k'hé kê jëên hoē 其然.豈其然乎, *e sē an nèy, e k'ham sē an nèy*, is he thus? how can he be thus? See the 論語 Lūn gé.

Jëên 燃 To burn, to inflame.

Jëên 肰 Dog's flesh; commonly, but improperly used for 然 jëên.

Jëên 蹨 To tread under feet.

Jeé^ng 爾 Vulg. *lé*, and *loó*: you; also read jé, which see. Jeé^ng wûy jeé^ng, gnó wûy gnó, suy tān t'hek kó têng, è gnó ch'hek, jeé^ng yëên lêng büéy gnó chae 爾爲爾.我爲我.雖袒裼裸裎.於我側.爾焉能浼我哉, *lé chò lé, gwá chò gwá, suy lé peĕh ch'hèw wui^ng loē sin t'hèy, k'hëā tē gwá sin pee^ng, lé böēyh an chw^nâ ēy bak la sâm gwá chaē*, you are you, and I am I,—and though you were a poor person with sleeves turned up, or entirely naked, standing at my side, yet how could you defile me. See 孟子 Bēng-choó.

Jeé^ng 禰 A parental shrine, a temple in which a father is worshipped. Seng ch'heng hoō, soó ch'heng k'hó, jip beaōu ch'heng jeé^ng 生稱父.死稱考.入廟稱禰, *sai^ng chew ch'heng hoe pāy, sé chēw ch'heng hoē k'hó, kâou jip beō chēw ch'heng hoe jeé^ng*, when alive a parent is called father, when dead k'hó, and when brought into a temple to be worshipped, jeé^ng.

Jeé^ng 乳 Taōu jeé^ng 豆乳, a preparation of pulse mixed up with pickle. Gnéw jeé^ng 牛乳, *goô lêng*, cow's milk.

Jëep 顳 The cheek bones, the bones on the side of the face.

3, Y

灭 Jëet 熱 Vulg. *jwăh*: hot. Jëet t'hëen 熱天, *jwăh t'hee^ng*, hot weather. Sûy lêng chip jëet, sē put é chok 誰能執熱逝不以濯, *chē chŭy ëy gīm jwăh ây meē^nh, nā bó sëy ch'hĕw*, who can take hold of hot things without first wetting his hands?

夫 Jek 揉 To work anything up with the hands; to knead (as dough); to squeeze.

Jek 趘 To pursue, to follow, to chase.

平 Jêng 仍 Because, then, as, as before. Jêng kéw 仍久, *jêng koó*, as formerly. Ke kīn jêng chin 飢饉仍臻, *kê yeaou lêng koò kaòu*, hunger and famine came as before. Also read jëûng which see.

平 Jëô 橈 Read jeâou: a small paddle for rowing or steering a boat.

去 Jëō 尿 Read jeâou: urine; also written 溺 jeâou.

灭 Jëŏh 傗 Read ch'hëuk; crooked, contracted, not stretched out.

夫 Jëuk 揉 To work up anything with the hands; to knead (as dough); also read jek.

Jëuk 趘 To chase, to pursue, to follow after. Choé sëang jëuk 走相趘, *chaôu sëô jëuk*, to run after one another, in play.

灭 Jëuk 辱 To disgrace, to put to shame. Lêng jëuk 淩辱, to degrade. Pek-ê Sëuk-chêy put kàng kê chè, put jëuk kê sin 伯夷叔齊不降其志.不辱其身, *Pek-ê Sëuk-chêy bó boĕyh kàng e ây sim chè, bó boĕyh jëuk e ây hin sin*, Pek-ê and Sëuk-chêy would not lower their views, nor degrade their persons. See the 論語 Lūn gé.

Jëuk 蓐 Grass springing up again; also, a straw mat.

Jëuk 溽 Damp and hot; moist. Lîm boô put jëuk 林無不溽, *ch'hëw nā bó ū^m tâm*, a forest is always damp.

Jëuk 縟 Ornamented with various colours.

Jëuk 鄏 Këep-jëuk 郟鄏, the name of a place.

Jëuk 肉 Vulg. *băh*: flesh. Kwut jëuk 骨肉, bone and flesh, anything near and dear. Gnoé chōng é kē, jê hoē seng jëuk 五臟已具而後生肉, *goē chōng é kè pē, jëën aōu sai^ng băh*, when the five viscera are in good order, then the flesh will begin to grow. Said by 管子 Kwán-choó.

Jëuk 月 A contracted form of the preceding.

Jëuk 衄 To cut with a knife; a sabre wound.

Jëuk 塲 Damp and hot; the same as 溽 jëuk.

Jëuk 褥 A mattrass, a bed.

声 Jëúng 偖 Many, numerous; also, the same as 茸 jëûng.

Jëúng 宂 Vulg. *jëáng:* intermixed, in confusion; dispersed; supernumerary; ruinous. Jëúng wân 宂員, a supernumerary officer, one who has received his title, but is waiting for an appointment.
Wûy chèng chaē k'hè sam jëûng 爲政在去三宂, *chò chèng soō chaē k'hè t'hek kak: sⁿa āy jëáng,* the practice of government consists in excluding the three ruinous measures, (i. e. having too many officers of government, too great a standing army, and too many public works.)

Jëúng 茸 Low, vulgar, mean.

平

Jëûng 娀 A surname; the surname of the rulers of the 商 Sëang dynasty.

Jëûng 仍 Because, according to, as before; repeated. Also read jêng. Jëûng kēw kwàn jê che hô 仍舊貫如之何, *jëûng koō āy soō, chò nê,* if it is done as before, how will that do? See the 論語 Lûn gé.
Kit suy lûy jëûng 吉瑞累仍, *hó āy teāou chap chap tëûng hok,* lucky omens constantly redoubled.

Jëûng 俄 A race of people with three horns.

Jëûng 戎 Soldiers, troops; you; also, a foreign nation on the west. A surname. Sëēn jîn kaòu bîn ch'hit lëên, ek k'hó é chek jëûng è 善人教民七年亦可以卽戎矣, *hó lâng kà pǎyh saiⁿᵍ kaòu ch'hit neeⁿᵍ, yëâ t'hang è chek jëûng,* when a clever man instructs the people for seven years, they can then be employed as soldiers. See the 論語 Lûn gé.

Jëûng 絨 Fine silk threads; also, fine cloth, woollen cloth.

Jëûng 䋪 Happiness.

Jëûng 茸 Grass growing luxuriantly; in confusion; rough; rumpled together. Hoe kêw bông jëûng 狐裘蒙茸, *hoê tê āy hêw bông jëûng,* a fox-skin dress, with the fur rough and in confusion.

Jëûng 陾 The noise of building a wall; the Chinese in Hok-këèn generally build their walls of mud, which is pounded and beaten between two boards fastened together, and jëûng is supposed to be the [illegible]ord of the thumping and pounding. Also, numerous.

Jëûng 械 The name of a tree.

Jëûng 氄 The small feathers of birds, or soft hair of beasts; down. Neaou sew jëûng mô 鳥獸氄毛, *che[illegible] kap sëw āy jëûng mô,* birds' and beasts' do[illegible] and soft hair. See the 堯典 Gêâou tëèn.

Jëûng 茙 Thick, solid, substantial.

Jëûng 狨 The name of an animal, lik[illegible] with shaggy hair, and of a yellow red colour, the skin [illegible] which is used for making saddles.

去

Jëùng 毧 Adorned with feathers.

声

Jéw 蹂 To tread on, to trample; also, to rub out the grain from the husk. Ê k'hê sëang jéw chëén 餘騎相蹂踐, *ch'hun āy k'hëâ bêy sëo jéw tăh,* the

rest of the horsemen trampled on one another. See the 史記 Soó kè.
Hek pò hek jéw 或簸或蹂, *woō ây tit pwà ch'hek, woō ây tit jéw*, some were winnowing the grain, and some rubbing it out of the husk. See the 大雅 Taē gnáy.

Jéw 揉 To bend anything with the hand; to curve, to warp. Jéw bok wûy jöēy 揉木爲耒, *aóu ch'hâ chò jöēy*, to curve a piece of wood in order to make a plough handle. See the 易經 *Yeăh keng*.

Jéw 糅 To mix, to intermingle; mixed and in disorder.

Jéw 煣 To bend a piece of timber by means of fire. The same as 揉 jéw.

Jéw 厹 The trace of a wild beast's paw on the ground; a three cornered spear; a lofty spirit. Also written 内 jéw.

平

Jêw 柔 Soft, pliable. Jêw jëak 柔弱, weak, pliant. Jêw sūn 柔順, obedient. Tīm chēêm kong k'hek, ko bêng jêw k'hek 沉潛剛克.高明柔克, *tim chēêm ây lâng tēŏh kong gnây k'hek yēⁿâ e, ko bêng ây lâng tēŏh jêw nooiⁿᵍ k'hek yēⁿâ e*, people whose minds are sunk and immersed must be attacked with harshness, but lofty and intelligent people with softness.

Jêw 渘 The name of a river.

Jêw 鰇 Jêw gê 鰇魚, *jêw hê*, the cuttle-fish; a fish without bones.

Jêw 蝚 The name of an insect; or, some say, a sort of ape.

Jêw 揉 Obedient, pliable; easily bent; bent or curved with the hand. Jêw ch'hoó bān pang 揉此萬邦, *ch'hóng jêw sūn chēⁿâ bān pang*, to render obedient these myriads of nations. See the 大雅 Taē gnáy.

Jêw 腬 The countenance harmonious and smooth.

去

Jēw 迫 To run. Jēw jēw choé 迫迫走, *jēw jēw chaóu*, to run without stopping.

声

Jím 忍 Chân jím 殘忍, cruel. Jím naē 忍耐, *t'hun lún*, patient, to bear patiently. Kwán-tëūng bông kwun soō sêw, jím sim haē lé, put k'hó wûy jîn 管仲忘君事讎.忍心害理.不可謂仁, *Kwán-tëūng bēy kè jîn kwun, hók saē kêw sêw, chân jîm ây sim haē lō lé, aᵐ t'hang kóng sē jîn*, Kwán-tëūng forgot his prince and served his enemies, with a cruel mind outraging reason itself, and therefore cannot be called benevolent.
Jím che se jê, naé chwân jé k'he 忍之須臾乃全汝軀, *lún é tëep â koó, naē ēy chwân lê ây hîn sin*, bear it patiently but a little while, and then you will come off with a whole skin.

Jím 恁 Humility of mind; thus, in this way.

Jím 稔 Ripe corn; the harvest, which comes but once a year. Put kip gnóe jím 不及五稔, *hó kip kaôu tēw sek goē kwùy*, it did not extend to five harvests. See the 左傳 Chó twān.

Jím 飪 Dressed food; food thoroughly cooked. Sit jím put sit 失飪不食, *nā bô ché loō hó e aᵐ chëăh*, if the food was not well dressed, he (Confucius) would not eat it. See the 論語 Lūn gé.

Jím 衽 The lappet of a coat, the breast of a coat which laps over. Bê Kwán-tëũng, goê kê pē hwat chó jím è 微管仲. 吾其被髮左衽矣, *nā bô Kwán-tëũng, gwân ây láng chëw pē t'haou'mô, tó ch'hëw pêng kat jîm è*, if it had not been for Kwán-tëũng (beating off the barbarians), we should have been obliged to twist our hair, and button the lappets of our coats on the left side;—(said by Confucius in the 論語 Lūn gé. The ancient Chinese used to allow all their hair to grow, and fastened their dresses in front; but since their subjection by the Tartars they have been obliged to adopt the customs which Confucius so much deprecated). Also written 袵 jím.

Jím 荏 Soft, lissome, pliable. Jím jëém 荏苒, soft and yielding.

Jím 荵 Jim tong 荵冬, a medicinal plant.

平

Jîm 壬 One of the horary characters. Also, great, full.

Jîm 任 To bear, to sustain, to bear as a burden, to undertake. Jin é wûy ké jîm, put ek tëũng hoē 仁以爲己任不亦重乎, *jîn tek è cho ka lē ây jîm tⁿà, āᵐ yëā lāng hoē*, to take the task of benevolence upon ourselves for our burthen, would it not be heavy? See the 論語 Lūn gé.
Chëũng noē lân jîm 衆怒難任, *chëàng láng ây sëw k'hè ŏh tⁿa*, the anger of the multitude is hard to be borne. See the 左傳 Chó twān.

Jîm 妊 To be pregnant, to conceive in the womb.

去

Jīm 仞 A measure of eight feet; a fathom. Hoo choó che chëâng soé jīm 夫子之墻數仞, *lán hoo choó ây ch'hëõⁿᵍ kwûy nā jīm*, our master's wall is several fathoms high: (and therefore he is not to be overlooked by little people). See the 論語 Lūn gé.

Jīm 任 A burden, a weight, that which is sustained; an office. A surname. E t'hëen hāy wûy ké jīm 以天下爲己任, *lëāh t'heeⁿᵍ ây chò ka lē ây jīm*, he took the whole weight of the Empire upon him as his burthen.
Tëōng jīm 重任, *tāng jīm*, a heavy burthen.
Kwuy jīm 歸任, *tooiⁿᵍ laê jīm*, he returned to his office.

Jīm 妊 That which is conceived, the foetus in the womb. Also written 姙 jīm.

Jīm 刃 A sharp weapon. Hong jīm 鋒刃, a sharp-pointed weapon. Peng jīm ké chëep 兵刃既接, *peng to kaé sëo kaou chëep*, when the swords and weapons crossed each other (in battle). See the 上孟 Sëāng bēng.

Jīm 牣 Full, replete. Oe jīm gê yëak 於牣魚躍, *an chuⁿà muⁿà hē tit ...*, how full is it of jumping fishes! See the 大雅 Taē guáy.

Jīm 賃 To borrow, to hire, to employ any one for money. Sin wûy jīn yūng jīm 臣爲人庸賃, *gwá sē hoē lang yūng ch'hēⁿà*, I am a person hired by others. Said by 范睢 Hwān-ch'he.

Jīm 軔 Anything hindering the progress of a chariot; a stop on the wheels, which when taken away allows the chariot to proceed.

Jīm 紉 A thread; anything that may be put through a needle, in order to sew with. E sëāng tëng lëet jīm chom ch'hēng poé twat 衣裳綻裂紉箴請補綴. *yîn chëõⁿᵍ tëng lëëh, t'hëyh swⁿà chëem ch'hēⁿà la*

3 z

poè twat, the apparel being ragged and torn, pray let us take a needle and thread, and mend it. See the 禮記 Léy kè.

Jīm 訒 To speak slowly and cautiously, to be guarded in conversation. Jîn chëá kê gân yëá jīm, 仁者其言也訒, *jîn ây lâng, e ây kóng wā yëá jīm*, a virtuous man speaks with caution and reserve. See the 論語 Lūn gé.

Jīm 眒 To see, to look at.

上 Jín 恁 *Jín mŏh* 恁麽, what? —Also, to think, to reflect.

平 Jîn 人 Vulg. *lâng*: a man. Lâm jîn 男人, *ta po lâng*, a male person. Lé jîn 女人, *cha boé lâng*, a female person.
Jîn wûy bān bùt che lêng 人爲萬物之靈, *lâng sē bān meēⁿh ây lêng*, man is the soul of all things, (or the most intelligent of creatures.)
Jîn che séy é ē ê k'him sèw chëá, kè he 人之所以異於禽獸者幾希, *lâng ây séy ê kŏh yëāⁿᵍ ê k'him sèw ây, sē bô jwā chēy*, that by which man is distinguished from the brutes is very trifling. See 孟子 Bēng-choó.

Jîn 仁 Benevolence, virtue; affection; to love; the seed of fruits. Jîn chëá sim che tek, aè che lé yëá 仁者心之德愛之理也, *jîn sē sim kwⁿa ây tek hêng, aè lâng ây tō lé*, benevolence is the virtue of the mind, and the principle of love. Said by 程子 Têng-choó.
Hēng jîn 杏仁, almonds. T'hô jîn 桃仁, the kernel of the peach.

去 Jīn 認 To acertain, to recognize, to acknowledge, to confess. Put jīn 不認, *a^{m} jīn*, to deny.
Lim soū put jīn chin, k'hé chīn tëung che tō hoē 臨事不認眞.豈盡忠之道乎, *lim soū nā ū^{m} jīn chin; k'ham sē chīn tëung ây tō hoē*, when anything happens, not to ascertain the truth, how is this the way to fulfil the duty of fidelity?
Jīn tek gnó mŏh 認得我麽, *jīn tit gwá ā bēy*, do you recognize me?
Jīn chöēy 認罪, to confess one's faults.

入 Jip 趿 To run, to follow after.

入 Jip 入 To enter, to go in; to receive. Séy jip 所入, income. Jip chek haòu, ch'hut chek tēy 入則孝出則弟, *jip chek tëŏh woā haòu, ch'hut chek tëŏh gaòu chò sëó tē*, on entering be filial, and on going out fraternal. See the 上論 Sëāng lūn.

Jip 亼 To receive, to take in.

入 Jit 日 The sun; a day. Jit t'hoê 日頭, *jit t'haôu*, the sun. Jit gnoé 日午, *jit taòu*, noon day. Jit kan 日間, by day. Jit jit 日日, every day.
Chèy jëūk put ch'hut sam jit, ch'hut sam jit put sit che è 祭肉不出三日.出三日不食之矣, *chèy ây bàh ū^{m} ch'hut s^{n}a jit, ch'hut s^{n}a jit chëw ū^{m} chëăh e*, the sacrificial meat was not to be kept over three days, and when it was kept over that time, (Confucius) would not eat of it. See the 論語 Lūn gé.

Jit 衵 Every day clothes, common dress; the inner dress of females.

Jit 馹 A post horse. Yêw jit 郵馹, a courier's horse.

亟

Jöēy 蘂 Fruits and flowers displaying their blossoms; a note in music.

Jöēy 緌 The strings of a bonnet hanging down. Kwan jöēy 冠緌, the tassel of a cap.

Jöēy 捼 To rub anything in the hands; to rumple anything up.

去

Jöēy 叡 Deep and distant; clear and intelligent. Jöēy tè 睿智, wise and clever.

Jöēy 汭 The name of a river, which flows to the north.

Jöēy 枘 A pointed piece of wood, used for the handle of a chizel. Jöēy ch'hok 枘鑿, a handle and chizel, which when apart are both useless; thus used figuratively for a useless person.

Jöēy 蚋 A small kind of insect, found about putrid and sour things. Hey swan jê jöēy chē yëen 醯酸而蚋聚焉, ch'hoè swui^ng jê jöēy chē chip, when the vinegar is sour the little flies collect about it.

Jöēy 芮 The appearance of growing grass. A surname.

Jöēy 耒 A crooked piece of wood, used as the handle of a plough. Hoō jöēy soō jê choō Sòng che Têng 負耒耜而自宋之滕, gēā e ây jöēy sóō, jê choō Sòng kok che kàou Têng, bearing his plough and ploughshare, he went from the Sòng country to the Têng country. See 孟子 Bēng-choō.

Jöēy 銳 Sharp-pointed; a sharp-pointed weapon. Jöēy k'hè 銳氣, courage. Yit jîn bëen chip jöēy 一人冕執銳, chit lâng tè bëen gîm jöēy, a man wearing a crown and holding a sharp instrument. See the 尚書 Sēāng se.

Jöēy 埘 Deep and still.

声

Joō 乳 Vulg. leng, milk; also, to sit on eggs as a bird, read jé, which see.

去

Joō 字 Vulg. jē, a character, a letter. Bun joō 文字, bûn jē, letters, literary writings. Boó joō 撫字, to soothe; also, to promise in marriage. Ch'hong-k'hëet sé lip bûn joō che hêng 倉頡始立文字之形, Ch'hong-k'hëet k'hé t'hâu lip bûn-jē ây yëō^ng, Ch'hong-k'hëet was the first who fixed the forms of characters. (B. C. 2622.) Hoō put lêng joō k'hwat choo 父不能字厥子, pāy bey joō e ây kë^n á, a father not able to soothe his child. See the 尚書 Sēāng se. Sip lëen put joō 十年不字, chāp hoey ya bëēy yin lâng kày, she is ten years of age, and not yet promised in marriage. See the 易經 Yëāh keng.

Joō 牸 A cow; the female of the ox.

去

Jūn 潤 Jūn tek 潤澤, to moisten, to enrich, to improve. Choo jūn 滋潤, to mollify, to fatten, to cherish, to moisten. Jëak hoo jūn tek che, chek chaē kwun ú choo e 若夫潤澤之,則在君與子矣, ch'hin cheō^ng jūn tek e, chek tē jîn kwun kap lí, but as to the enriching and improving of these points, it rests entirely with the prince and with yourself. See 孟子 Bēng-chóó.

Jūn 㠇 Pek-jūn 白㠇, the name of a place.

Jūn 閏 Vulg. *lun*: intercalary. Jūn gwat 閏月, *lūn göëyh*, an intercalary month. The Chinese have only about 360 days in the common year; consisting of twelve moons, hence they need an intercalary month, to make up the deficiency.

Jūn 嫩 Weak, soft, pliable, tender; also, young and handsome.

Jūn 嫩 The same as the preceding. Wun jūn 溫嫩, soft and agreeable, gentle and harmonious.

Jwā 若 Read jëak: how. Jëak kan 若干, *jwā chēy*, how much. Jëak kēw 若久, *jwā kwó*, how long.

Jwăh 熱 Read jëet: hot, fervid. Hân jëet pēng 寒熱病, *kwⁿā jwăh paⁱⁿᵍ*, fever and ague. Sam ch'hun che ch'hey, yim yâng kaou chèy, hân k'hè kè tê, wun put chè jëet 三春之初.陰陽交際.寒氣既除.溫不至熱, *sⁿa ch'hun ây k'hè t'hâon, yim yâng kaou chèy, kwⁿā k'hè kaôu tê, wun bô kaôu jwăh*, in the beginning of the three months of spring, when the male and female principles unite, then the cold air has just been excluded, and the gentle warmth is not yet excessively hot.

Jwán 軟 Vulg. *nooiⁿᵍ*: weak, soft, pliable. Ch'hey choó jwán jëak 妻子軟弱, *bóe kēⁿá nooiⁿᵍ chēⁿá*, my wife and children are weak and feeble.

Jwán 輭 Weak, soft,—the original form of the preceding. An ke jwán lûn 安車輭輪, *an ây ch'hëa nooiⁿᵍ ây lûn*, an easy carriage upon soft wheels.

Jwán 餪 Weak. Jwán lé 餪女, to send a present to a daughter, three days after her marriage.

Jwán 孾 Weak, soft, effeminate; young and handsome.

Jwân 撋 Vulg. *hwⁿâ*: to rub anything between the hands; to wash by the hand.

Jwān 鍈 Soft silver.

Jwûy 蕤 Këang jwûy 薑蕤, the root of ginger, when old and dry,—as distinguished from the ch'hoó këang 茈薑, *cheēⁿᵍ këoⁿᵍ*, which is the young tender ginger plant.

K

Ka 膠 Read kaou: glue. Gûew kaou 牛膠, *goô ka*, glue made of cow's hide. Gê kaou 魚膠, *hê ka*, fish glue. Sē kaou 樹膠, *ch'hēw ka*, vegetable gum.

Ka 交 Read kaou: to come in contact, together or across one another. Kaou chëen 交剪, *ka chëen*, a pair of scissors. Kaou to 交刀, *ka to*, shears. Kaou twān 交斷, *ka tooiⁿᵍ*, to cut off with a pair of scissors.

Ka 吉 Read kit: kit pöey 吉貝, *ka pöey*, cotton, the cotton of which cloth is made.

Kà 尻 Read k'haou: the back. K'haou chit 尻脊, *ka chëăh*, the back. K'haou chit kwat 尻脊骨, *ka chëăh kwut*, the back bone. K'haou chit hoē 尻脊後, *ka chĕăh aōu*, behind one's back.

Ka 江 Read kang: — Kang jeaôu 江鐃, *ka ch'hēō*, a small shell-fish.

Ka 狡 Read kaôu: cunning, artful. Kaóu chò 狡蚤, *ka chaôu*, a flea.

Ka 甘 Read kam: — kam tông sē 甘棠樹, *ka tang ch'hēw*, the name of a tree.

Ka 茭 Read kaou: the name of a grass. Kaou chëèn 茭薦, *ka chèng*, a kind of mattrass, made of straw bound together, both soft, and warm to sleep on.

Kaou pek 茭白, *ka păyh*, the bandage which is tied round the Chinese women's feet, in order to prevent their growing large.

Ka 筊 Read kaòu: — kaòu lėk 筊篨, *ka lăyh*, a large sieve, or bamboo frame, for exposing corn or fruits to dry in the sun.

Ka 箬 Read k'hŏ: — k'hó lŏ 箬笼, *ka lò*, a vessel for holding corn, in shape like a pig's loins, with a mouth to it, in order to shoot the corn.

Ka 袈 Read këa: — këa say 袈裟, *ka say*, a surplice, a priest's robe, a long gown worn by the priests of Buddha.

Ka 鉸 Ka e 鉸衣, to cut out clothes: the same as kaou 交 *ka*.

Ka 鵁 Read kaou: — as kaou lēng neáou 鵁鴒鳥, *ka lēng cheáou*, a magpie. Kaou chuy 鵁鵻, *ka chuy*, a dove.

Ka 鮫 Read kaou: — má kaou 馬鮫, *báy ka*, a fish with a large head; a species of squalus or dog-fish.

Ka 咬 Read kaou: — Kaou-lêw-pa 咬噹吧, *Ka-lā-pa*, the Chinese name for the town of Batavia, island of Java.

4 A

Ka 瞌 Read k'hap: — k'hap sùy 瞌睡, *ka choēy*, to slumber, to dose, to go to sleep.

声 *Ká* 絞 Read kaóu: to tie a string fast round anything, to strangle. Kaóu soó 絞死, *ká sè*, to kill by strangling.

Ká 痰 Read kaôu: kéw kaóu 疝痰, *kéw ká*, a severe pain in the stomach; a cholic.

去 *Kà* 教 Read kaòu: to instruct; instruction, teaching. Kaòu hwùn 教訓, *kà hwùn*, to teach.

Sîn bûn kaòu choó, kaòu é gē hong 臣聞教子. 教以義方, *gwá t'hē^{n}a keè^{ng} kà kaōu sai^{ng} tëŏh kà è gē āy hong hwat*, I have heard that in teaching children, we should teach them by the rules of righteousness. See the 左傳 Chó twān.

Kà 窖 Read kaòu: Tëâng-kaòu 長窖, *Tè^{ng}-kà*, the name of a place, in the province of 福建 Hok-këèn, in the county of 漳州 Chëang-chew, and in the district of 南靖 Lâm-chēng. Also written Tëâng-kaòu 長竂 *Tè^{ng}-kà*.

丟 *Kā* 齩 Read gnaôu: to bite, to fasten on anything with the teeth. Gnaóu jin 齩人, *kā lâng*, to bite people.

卆 *K^{n}a* 監 Read kam: to confine, to shut up in prison. Kam lô 監牢, *k^{n}a k'hoo*, a prison. Kam séw 監守, *k^{n}a séw*, to imprison.

Chew-kong soò Kwán-sëuk kam Yin 周公使管叔監殷, *Chew-kong saè Kwán-sëuk k^{n}a Yin*, Chew-kong ordered Kwán-sëuk to imprison Yin. See 孟子 Bēng choó.

K^{n}a 橄 Read kám: Kám lám 橄欖, *k^{n}a ná*, an olive.

声 Kⁿá **敢** Read kám: to dare, to presume, to venture. Kám chò kám wûy 敢作敢爲, kⁿá chò kⁿá wûy, to dare to do anything.

Kám būn hoo choó che put tōng sim 敢問夫子之不動心; kⁿá mooiⁿᵍ hoo choó ây ūᵐ tōng sim, I would presume to enquire respecting your stability of mind. See 孟子 Bēng-choó.

去 Kⁿà **酵** Read haòu: leaven. Haòu boé 酵母, kⁿà boé, leaven.

平 Kⁿā **擓** Read kâm: to run before and stop a person who is attempting to escape.

上 Kae **皆** Vulg. chò poé: all, every one, every; and lóng chóng, the whole. Jîn kae wat ê te 人皆曰予知, lâng chò poé kóng gwá chae, every body says, I know, I know. See the 中庸 Tëung yûng.

Kae séy é bêng jîn lûn yëá 皆所以明人倫也, lóng chóng séy é bêng tè hëá ây jîn lûn, all is with a view of illustrating the relations of life.

Kae **偕** The whole; together with, in company; violence, force, united strength. Kae kae soō choó, teaou sek chëūng soō 偕偕士子朝夕從事, chò poé sē t'hak ch'hāyh lâng, chá khè maiⁿᵍ hwuiⁿᵍ chëūng soō, they are altogether scholars and philosophers, who morning and evening attend to the business. See the 小雅 Seaóu gnáy.

Kae **侅** Kê kae 奇侅, singular, uncommon, unusual.

Kae **喈** Harmony of sounds, the harmonious singing of birds. Hong é ch'hey ch'hey, key bêng kae kae 風雨淒淒.鷄鳴喈喈, hong kap hoē ch'hey ch'hey, key t'hê kae kae, the wind and rain getting up uncomfortably, while the cocks crow harmoniously. See the 詩經 Se keng.

Kae **堦** Gîm kae 砛堦, gîm kay, steps, by which to ascend, stone steps. Geâou sê maôu chuo t'hoé kae, put sëāng bûn ch'haé 堯時茅茨土堦不尙文采, Geaôu ây sê hâᵐ á ch'hoò, t'hoé ây gîm kay, ūᵐ tè tëūng bûn ch'haé, in the time of Geâou they had thatched cottages, and earthen steps, without studying ornament or elegance.

Kae **湝** The flowing of water, to flow. Hwaê súy kae kae 淮水湝湝, Hwaê ây chúy káe kae, the waters of the Hwaê flow gently by.

Kae **該** To prepare, to get ready; fully prepared, united, got together. Bān but këem kae 萬物兼該, bān meēⁿh chò poé chún pè, every thing fully prepared.

This character is commonly used in conversation, to designate that which is suitable or proper; as èng kae 應該, ought, should, it should be so; kae jëên 該然, that which is proper and right.

Kae **階** A step, a stair, a ladder, that by which we ascend. Hoo choó che put k'hó kip yëá, yêw t'hëen che put k'hó kae jê seng yëá 夫子之不可及也.猶天之不可階而升也, hoo choó ây bēy kip kaôu, ch'hin chëōⁿᵍ t'heeⁿᵍ ây bēy ch'hong t'huy jê chëōⁿᵍ, our master's exalted qualities are unattainable, just as heaven cannot be ascended by a common ladder. Said of Confucius, in the 論語 Lūn gé.

声 Kaé **改** Vulg. káy: to change, to alter, to reform. Kaé pëèn 改變, káy peèⁿᵍ, to alter. Kò chek but tān kaé 過則勿憚改, woō köèy sit chek ūᵐ t'hang wùy kan lân káy, having a fault, do not dread difficulties in seeking to amend it. See the 上論 Sëāng lūn.

Kaé **解** Vulg. t'haôu and t'hooiⁿᵍ: to loosen, to disperse, to scatter; to release; to explain, to unfold; to divide. Kaé k'hae 解開, t'haôu k'hwuy, to loosen. Kaé sàn 解

散, *kaè sw^n à*, to disperse. Kaè swat 解說, *kây söëyh*, to explain. Kaè e 解衣; *t'hooi^ng s^n a*, to take off one's clothes.

K'hëúng t'hëen hāy kaè yëá 恐天下解也, *këⁿa ne t'hee^ng āy āy lâng kaè sw^n à*, it is to be feared that the people of the empire will disperse.

Paôu-teng kaè gnêw 庖丁解牛, *Paôu-teng gaôu t'haè k'hwuy goô*, Paôu-teng was very clever in dividing and cutting up an ox.

Kaé 儝 Chëen kaé 儦儝, bold and strong.

Kaè 介 Great, immense; to help; armour; small, insignificant; a numeral. Chëet kaè 節介, to hold to one's sentiments and opinions.

Kaè jé hok 介爾福, *twā lé āy hok k'hè*, how great is your happiness.

Wûy ch'hoó ch'hun chew, é kaè bē sêw 爲此春酒.以介眉壽, *wûy chéy lëy ch'hun chëw, é chān lé āy baè sêw*, the reason of presenting this spring cup of wine, is to assist your mutual longevity. See the 詩經 Se keng.

Kaè tëw chek yêw put k'hó hwān che sek 介冑則有不可犯之色, *ch'hëng kāh tëw chek woō sëy bëy hwān tëöh āy bîn sek*, a man wearing armour and a helmet, presents an appearance not to be trifled with. See the 曲禮 K'heuk léy.

Yit kaè put é é jîn 一介不以予人, *chit āy sëö k'hwà āy meeⁿh c a^m hoë lâng*, he would not give a person a single thing (more than what was proper) speaking of 伊尹 E yin.

Kaè 丐 To beg to request; to take; to give. Kaè k'hit chëá 丐乞者, *k'hit chëáh āy lâng*, a beggar.

Kaè 价 Good, virtuous, great, large. Kaè jîn wûy hwān 价人維藩, *hoë lâng chō lé pa*, good people are our fence. See the 大雅 Taē gnây.

Kaè 玠 A large gem. Sek jé kaè kwuy, e chok jé pó 錫爾玠圭.以作爾寶, *soù hoë lé twā kwuy gëuk, è chō lé āy pó pöëy*, I present you with a large gem in order to constitute your treasure. See the 大雅 Taē gnây.

Kaè 界 A border, a limit, a boundary. Kaou kaè 郊界, a border of a country. Sè kaè 世界, the world.

Hek bîn put é hong këang che kaè 域民不以封疆之界, *àn pāyh sai^ng bëy t'hó s^n a meeⁿh hong këang āy kaou kaè*, in settling the people we cannot do it according to any authorized limits or borders.

Kaè 尬 Këem kaè 尲尬, to walk uneven.

Kaè 芥 Kaè lat 芥辣, *kaè lwāh*, mustard. Kaè ch'haè 芥菜, *kwà ch'haè*, the mustard plant. Ch'hó kaè 草芥, *ch'haôu kaè*, a stick or a straw, a trifle.

Sëem kaè 纖芥, anything small and insignificant. Kaè taè 芥蔕, a trifling cause, a thing of no moment.

Kaè 疥 Small scabs or sores. Seng kaè 生疥, *sai^ng kày*, to break out in small sores, to have the itch.

Kaè 尬 Lâm kaè 尷尬, *lâm kwà*, irregular, out of order.

Kaè 庎 A vessel for holding eatables, only, alone.

Kaè 儭 A false master.

Kaè 戒 To warn, to be aware of, to caution, to guard against; to restrict one's self, to restrain from. Chaè kaè 齋戒, *ch'hëāh ch'haè*, to fast, and restrict one's self.

Suy yéw ok jin, chae kaè bok yëuk, chek k'hó é soō sëäng tèy 雖有惡人，齋戒沐浴，則可以祀上帝, *suy woō k'hëep sè ây lang, nä chëäh ch'haè këng kaè chek t'hang laè ch'haè sëäng tèy*, although a man be ever so ugly, yet having fasted and bathed himself, he can even do service to the highest emperor (i. e. the supreme being.) See 孟子 Bēng-choó.

Kaè put gē 戒不虞, *këng kaè ū^m ch'hek ây soō*, beware of unforeseen events. See the 易經 Ek keng.

Kwun choó yéw sam kaè 君子有三戒, *kwun choó woō s^na hāng soō këng kaè*, the good man has three things which he guards against, (i. e. beauty, quarrelling, and avarice.)

Kaè 誡 To announce, to command, to enjoin; an injunction, a commandment. Hwat kaè poè lēng, jê tek t'höèy, sē choō wuy yëä 發誡布令而敵退是主威也, *hwat kò kaè poè bëng lēng, jê tùy tek ây lâng t'hèy, sē choō kong ây wuy hong*, to issue orders, and give directions, whereupon the enemy instantly retires, shews the dignity of the chief.

Kaè 解 To send under arrest; to conduct to the presence of a superior. Kaè sëà 解舍, the residence of an officer. T'hëen hāy che soō, péng ch'hé san lim, lēng kam soo sëw sin, kaè sòng sëäng bûn 天下之士屏處山林，令監司守臣解送上聞, *t'hee^ng ây t'hak ch'hëyh lâng pêng k'hëà tē swⁿa lim, bēng lēng k^na soo kap sëw ây jîn sin, kày sàng kaòu sè twā lâng t'hē^na*, the clever scholars of the empire are gone aside to dwell in hills and forests, and this is to order the restricting officers and great keepers to send them under arrest, into the presence of the sovereign; (an order issued in the 宋 Sòng dynasty.)

Kaè 蓋 Vulg. *k'hàm*, and *k'hèng*: to cover, to cover over; — vulg. *k'hwà*: a cover. A surname. A conjunctive particle,— for, because; an expletive; also written 盖 kaè. Kè ko boê kaè 其高無蓋, *c ây kwân, bô k'hwà*, it is so high, that it is without a covering. Kaè bûn 蓋聞, "for we have heard; — &c." an expression generally used at the beginning of literary composition.

Kaè 盖 The same as the preceding. Also written 葢 kaè.

Kaè 屆 To arrive at, to come unto; also written 屆 kaè. Wûy tek tōng t'hëen, boê wán hwut kaè 惟德動天，無遠弗屆, *wûy tek hēng kâm tōng t'hee^ng, bô chit ây lâng tē hwui^ng ây wûy ū^m kaòu*, when our virtue is so great as to move the heavens, there is not a distant individual but what will be induced to come to us.

Kaè 匃 To beg. K'hit kaè boê sëy tek 乞匃無所得, *k'hit ây lâng bô sëy tit tëöh*, beggars get little or nothing. Also written 匄 kaè.

Kaè 緳 Torn clothes, ragged apparel; also, to wash dirty clothes. Ch'hè chëem tê kaè 挫鍼治緳, *këäh chëem ch'hòng p'hwà s^na*, to take a needle and mend old clothes.

Kaè 犗 A strong ox; a stout strong animal.

Kaè 誺 To warn, to caution.

Kaè 廨 Kaè sëà 廨舍, the residence of an officer of Government.

Kaè 槩 Toè kaè 斗槩, *taòu kaè*, a piece of wood for striking off the top of a measure, in measuring corn; a strike; to strike.

福建方言字典

Kae^ng 間 A corruption of kan, in the hāy bûn 厦門, *hāy moot^ng*, dialect. Yit kan ok 一間屋, *chit kae^ng ch'hoè*, a house.

Kaé^ng 醐 The face wrinkled or furrowed with age.

Kăh 鉀 Armour, a coat of mail. K'hōey kăh 盔鉀, a panoply of armour. Kwàn kăh sëang mā 貫鉀上馬, *ch'hèng kăh cheō^ng bāy*, he put on his armour, and mounted his horse.

Kăh 胛 Read këep: the place between the ribs. Këen këep 肩胛 *keng kăh*, between the shoulders. Tëūng maôu kwàn këep 中矛貫胛, *tëūng ch'hëo^ng t'haòu kăh*, he was hit by a spear, which pierced him through between the shoulders.

Kăh 裥 A waistcoat, a jacket without sleeves.

Kăh 教 Read kaòu: to tell, to order to do anything. Kaòu kē chò 教其做, *kăh e chò*, he ordered him to do it.

Kăh 甲 Read kap: one of the horary characters. Kap choó 甲子, *kăh chè*, the primary characters of the cycle of sixty years.
K'ho kap 科甲, *k'ho kăh*, the order of the literary examinations.

Kai^ng 更 Read keng: a watch of the night. Sěw keng 守更, *chéw kai^ng*, to keep watch. Sam keng 三更, *s^na kai^ng*, the third watch. Keng leâou 更寮, *kai^ng leâou*, a watch house.
Sam keng chok hwān, gnoē keng k'hè hêng 三更作飯.五更起行, *s^na kai^ng chè pooi^ng, goē kai^ng k'hè kē^nâ*, at the third watch they were to cook their rice, and at the fifth watch to commence their march.

Kai^ng 庚 Read keng: one of the horary characters.

Kai^ng 耕 Read keng: to plough. Keng tëên 耕田, *kai^ng ch'hân*, to plough the fields.
Gnó këet lëk keng tëên, këùng wûy choó chit jê é è 我竭力耕田.供爲子職而已矣, *gwá këet chin k'hwùy lat kai^ng ch'hân, këùng chò haòu sai^ng ây chit hwûn tē^nā tē^nā*, I exhaust my strength in ploughing the fields, and fulfilling the duties of a son, without minding anything else. See 孟子 Bēng-choó.

Kai^ng 羹 Read keng: broth, soup. Ch'haè keng 菜羹, *ch'haè kai^ng*, vegetable soup. T'hëaou keng 挑羹, *t'hëaou kai^ng*, a soup spoon.
Soe soō ch'haè keng 蔬食菜羹, *ch'hoe pooi^ng ch'haè kai^ng*, coarse food and vegetable broth. See the 論語 Lūn gè.

Kai^ng 經 Read keng: a thread. Mō keng 帽經, *bō kai^ng*, the red tassel or fringe on the top of a cap.
Hëên keng 絃經 a kind of cloth composed of a mixture of silk and flax, the warp being wove with silken and the woof with flaxen threads. Chit keng 織經, *chit kai^ng*, to weave silk.

Kai^ng 耞 Lëên kai^ng 連耞, *lëên kai^ng*, a flail for threshing out corn.

Kai^ng 骾 Read kéng: to be choked by a bone sticking in the throat.

Kai^ng 徑 Read kèng: a way, a path, a hill path. San kèng che hēy kan, kaı jëên yūng che, jê sêng loē 山徑之蹊間.介然用之而成路, *swa kai^ng ây sèy loē á kan, nā twā jëên yūng e, jê chēw chē^nâ loē*, the small bye-paths among the mountain ways, if greatly used, will be converted into roads. See 孟子 Bĕng-choó.

Kaing 楹 Read kĕng: the space between the beams of a house. Kĕng êng 楹楹, *kaing aing*, the joices and rafters.

夫 Kak 角 The horn of a beast, a horn, a corner of anything, an angle. Soò kak 四角, *sè kak*, four-square. Tĕūng hāy lók kak kaé, tĕūng tong bô kak kaé 仲夏鹿角解.仲多麋角解, *tĕūng hāy lok ây kak t'hooing, tĕūng tang bê ây kak t'hooing*, in the middle of summer the bucks shed their horns, and in the middle of winter the does shed their's.

Kak 桷 The rafters of a house. Êng kak 楹桷, *aing kak*, beams and rafters.

Kak 覺 To understand, to perceive, to know, to be aware of, to feel, to apprehend. Kak goē 覺悟, to comprehend. T'heen che seng soo bîn yĕâ, soò sĕen kak kak hoē kak 天之生斯民也.使先覺覺後覺, *t'heeng ây saing chêy lêy pâyh saing, saè taē seng kak kak goē lùy aōu kak ây lâng*, when heaven produced this people, it was ordered that those who were earlier awakened should awaken those who were later in coming to a sense of things. See 孟子 Bĕng-choó.

Kak 珏 A double gem, two gems united in one.

Kak 掎 E' kak 掎掎, to beset anything, before and behind, in hunting. P'hè jê poē lók, Chìn jîn kak che, choo jĕūng é che 譬如捕鹿.晉人掎之.諸戎掎之, *chek sē ch'hin chĕōng lĕāh lók, lin Chìn ây lâng kak e, yĕâ lán jĕūng ây lâng è e*, just like when we were catching the deer, you people of Chìn beset them before, and we foreigners beset them behind; (intimating that the men of Chìn had once been assisted by the foreigners, and why should they now attack them.) See the 左傳 Chó twăn.

Kak 榷 A piece of timber laid across water, for a bridge.

Kak 屩 Straw shoes. Bȯk kak 木屩, *bak kĕak*, wooden shoes, clogs. Lê soe sek kak 離疏釋屩, *lê ch'hoe t'hooing kĕah* to leave coarse food and get rid of clogs; (i. e. to better one's circumstances and get into office.)

Kak 鵅 *Key kak* 鷄鵅, a cock.

天 *Kak* 磔 Read kĕet: to tear asunder, to rip open, to tear people asunder by horses. Choo soó hêng kae kĕet ê ch'hē 諸死刑皆磔於市, *choo sè ay hêng hwat chò poê kak kĕh tē hay ch'hē*, all the capital convicts were torn asunder in the market place.

幸 Kam 甘 Vulg. *teeng*: sweet, of a sweet taste, pleasing. A surname. Kam gwān 甘願, to be well pleased, to be content with. Kam sim 甘心, to be willing. Kam ch'hó 甘草, liquorice. Kam chĕâ 甘蔗, sugar-cane.

Kam 柑 An orange. Swan kam 酸柑, *swuing kam*, a lemon.

Kam 泔 Rice water.

Kam 疳 Kam chek pēng 疳積病, *kam chek paing*, a disease in children originating in eating too many sweet things.

Kam 監 To receive, to review, to examine. Vulg. *kna*, to imprison, to guard. T'hĕen choó soó kê taē hoo wûy sam kam,

kam ê hong pek che kok 天子使其大夫爲三監監於方伯之國, *hōng tèy saè e ây taē hoo chò sⁿa ây kam, kⁿa tē hong pek ây kok,* the Emperor ordered his great officers to constitute three inspectors, in order to inspect the states of the different princes. See the 王制 Ông chè.

Kam 獭 To hold firmly and retain obstinately; some say, to shut the mouth.

上
Kám 感 To move, to influence, to work upon. Kám yin 感恩, to be moved by and to be grateful for favours. Kám èng 感應, to be influenced by and to respond to. Kám kek 感激, to move, to arouse. Kám tōng 感動, to move and work upon. Kám hwà 感化, to convert.

T'hëen tēy kám, jê bān bu̍t hwà seng 天地感而萬物化生, *t'heeⁿᵍ tēy kám tōng, jê bān meēⁿh hwà saiⁿᵍ,* heaven and earth is moved, and then the myriads of things are metamorphosed and produced.

Kám 敢 Vulg. *kⁿá*: to dare, to presume. Kó kám 果敢, daring, bold. K'hé kám 豈敢, how dare I? how can I presume? a complimentary expression.

Kám put chûn bēng 敢不遵命, *kⁿá ūᵐ chûn lè ây bēng lēng,* how dare I refuse to obey your commands?

Sûy kám put jēang 誰敢不讓, *chê chûy kⁿá ūᵐ nēōⁿᵍ,* who dares refuse to yield? See the 易經 Ék keng.

Kám 橄 Kám lám 橄欖, *kⁿa nâ,* an olive.

Kám 艦 The two sides of a ship or vessel.

Kám 𩰪 The cover of a pot or vessel; also, turned upside down.

Kám 篕 A tool with a pointed end; a vessel of a conical shape.

Kám 籃 A covering made of bamboo. Tëuk kám 竹籃, a bamboo lid.

去
Kàm 監 To inspect, to observe, to behold. T'haé kàm 太監, a eunuch officer. Chew kàm ê jê taē 周監於二代, *Chew teâou kàm ê nō teaôu tēy,* the Chew dynasty could observe the two former dynasties. See the 上諭 Sēāng lūn.

Kàm 灩 The name of a river; and the name of a district.

Kàm 鑑 A large basin; also, a mirror, a looking-glass; to reflect. Bêng sim pó kàm 明心寶鑑, the precious mirror for enlightening the mind;—(the title of a celebrated moral work.)

Kong kàm ē te 綱鑑易知, an historical mirror, easily known, (the title of one of the histories of China.)

平
Kâm 菡 Read hâm: the name of a plant; a flower about to bud.

Kâm 銜 Read hâm: to hold in the mouth. But soō hâm böëy 勿士銜枚, *bòh hoē hēā ây peng kâm tē,* don't make the troops hold the wooden gag in their mouths.

上
Kām 鰔 Koe kām 鮎鰔 the name of a fish.

平
Kan 干 To seek for, to aim at; to offend. A surname. Jëak kan 若干, *jwā chēy,* how much?

Choó-tëang hak kan lok 子張學干祿, *Choó-tëang t'hak ch'hāyh kan kēw hong lok,* Choó-teang in his studies aimed at emolument. See the 上諭 Sëāng lūn.

Kê kám kan taē léy, é choō ch'hé lēy 其敢干大禮.以自取戾, *e kⁿá kan hwān twā lēy, è ka tē ch'hè lēy*, he dares to offend against the great rules of propriety, and thus bring himself into trouble. See the 左傳 Chó twān.

Put sëang kan 不相干, it is no matter. Kan ko 干戈, blunt and sharp weapons.

E' jé hô kan 與爾何干, what is it to you?

Kan 乾 Dry, arid. Tëong kok yëw ch'huy, hàn kē kan è 中谷有蓷暵其乾矣, *k'haiⁿᵍ tang eⁿᵍ wōo ch'huy ch'haòu, kaòu p'hak e chëw ta*, in the middle of the valley grows the Ch'huy vegetable, but when it is exposed to the sun, it becomes dry. See the 詩.王風 Se, ông hong.

Kan 竿 Vulg. *kwⁿa*: a pole. Tëuk kan 竹竿, *tek kwⁿa*, a bamboo pole. Tek tek tëuk kan, ē tëàou ê kê 籊籊竹竿.以釣于淇, *teⁿᵍ teⁿᵍ ây tek kwⁿa, è tëò hè twā tē kê chúy*, he took a long bamboo pole, to go and angle in the river Kê. See the 衛風 Wöëy hong.

Kan 玕 Lông kan 琅玕, the name of a gem.

Kan 奸 To offend against modesty and propriety. Kan yîm 奸淫, lascivious, wanton. Kan sîn 奸臣, an abandoned minister. Of the usurper 曹操 Chō-ch'hò, it was said that he would be,—tē sè che lêng sîn, lwān sè che kan hëûng 治世之能臣亂世之奸雄, *tē sè ây gaôu ây jîn sîn, lwān sè ây kan hëûng*, in peaceful times an able minister, and in troublous times a fraudulent scoundrel.

Kan 杆 Lân kan 欄杆, a railing, a gallery. Kê kan 旗杆, *kê kwⁿa*, a flag-staff. Gwat ê hwa éng sëang lân kan 月移花影.上闌杆, *gōëyh ê hwa yëⁿá chëōⁿᵍ lân kan*, the moon threw the shadow of the flowers up into the gallery.

Kan 間 Between, amongst, whilst. Tëung kan 中間, the middle, the midst. Sè kan 世間, in the world.

Kwun choó boô chëung sit che kan wûy jîn 君子無終食之間違仁, *hwun choó bô chëăh chit tooiⁿᵍ pooiⁿᵍ ây kan wûy kâyh jîn*, the good man does not oppose virtue for the small space of time requisite for a single meal. See the 上論 Sëang lūn.

Kan 矸 Sek kan 石矸, *chëŏh lân kan*, a stone railing.

Kan 肝 Vulg. *kwⁿa*: the liver. Sim kan 心肝, *sim kwⁿa*, the heart, the mind. Jîn che sè ké, jê këèn kē hè kan jëên 人之視己如見其肺肝然, *lâng ây k'hwⁿà lán, ch'hìn chëōⁿᵍ k'hwⁿà e ây hè kwⁿa chit yëōⁿᵍ*, men will be able to observe one as intimately as though they scrutinized into the liver and lungs. See the 大學 Taē hak.

Kan 蕑 A species of the 蘭花 lan hwa, epidendrum. Soō é lé hong péng kan hêy 士與女方秉蕑兮, *ta po kap cha boè toō toō ú gîm kan hwa*, a lady and gentleman just holding the kan flower. See the 鄭風 Tēng hong.

Kan 艱 Kan lân 艱難, trouble, difficulty. Kan k'hoé 艱苦, distressing, sad. K'haè kē t'hàn è, gē jîn che kan lân è 慨其嘆矣.遇人之艱難矣, *k'haè e ây t'hó k'hwùy toó tëŏh lâng ây kan lân*, disconcerted he sighed, upon meeting with people in trouble. See the 詩.王風 Se,—ông hong.

Kan 姦 Wanton, lascivious, clandestine, false. Kan yîm 姦淫, fornication. Kan hoo 姦夫, an adulterer.

Kan jîn hoō lé, jîn pit kan kē hoō lé 姦人婦女人必姦其婦女, *kan lâng ây boè kēⁿá, lâng pit kan è ây boè kēⁿá*, he who defiles

福建方言字典

people's wives and daughters, will have his wife and daughters defiled by people.

去
Kán 柬 To distinguish, to select, to choose. Kán tek 柬擇, *kéng tŏh*, to choose;

Kán 簡 Important; contracted. Kán yaòu 簡要, the most important part of a subject. Kán lëak 簡略, a summary, a contraction, to contract, and abbreviate, to do things in a short abrupt manner.
Kán swán 簡選, to select, to choose.
Kán pán 簡板, slips of bamboo, on which the ancients used to write before the invention of paper; hence books and records are called 簡 kán; and 錯簡, ch'hok kán, intimates an error in the record.
Khŏ yëá kán 可也簡, he can be admired, for his short abrupt method,—but—ke kán, jê hêng kán, boô naé taē kán hoē 居簡.而行簡.無乃大簡乎, to be constantly abrupt and to do everything in a short abrupt manner, would not this be an excess of abruptness? See the 上論 Sëāng lūn. A surname.

Kán 襇 The plaits or folds in a petticoat.

Kán 稈 The stalk of corn.

Kán 赶 Vulg. *kwⁿà*: to chase, to pursue, to drive away. Also written 趕 kán. K'hàn k'hàn kán sëāng 看看赶上, *k'hwⁿà k'hwⁿà kwⁿá chëōⁿᵍ*, he seemed just about to overtake him. See the 三國 Sam kok.

Kán 繭 Ch'hán kán 蠶繭, the ball of silk formed by the silk worm, the cocoon.

去
Kàn 澗 A mountain torrent.

4 c

Kàn 旰 The inferior degree of light afforded when the sun is just rising.

Kàn 幹 Lêng kàn 能幹, ability, strength; also, the stalk of corn, the stem of a flower, or the stump of a tree.

Kàn 榦 The boards and mallet, used in building mud walls.

Kàn 諫 Vulg. *tⁿà*: to reprove, to speak bluntly and honestly; to ridicule. Hoē chëūng kàn chek sèng 后從諫則聖, *jin kwun t'hân lâng tⁿà chēw ēy sëⁿà*, when a prince listens to reproof he will become as wise as a sage. See the 書說命 Se wat bēng. Soō hoō boé ke kàn 事父母幾諫, *hok saē pāy boē tëŭh cheó tⁿà*, in serving our parents we should seldom reprove them. See the 論語 Lūn gé.

Kàn 間 Kàn kek 間隔, to separate, to divide people one from the other. Soō hwàn kàn kèy 使反間計, *saé hwán kàn kèy*, to make use of trickery for setting people at variance. See the 三國 Sam kok. Pēng kàn 病間, *paīⁿᵍ k'hŭh hō*, an alleviation of sickness; an interval.

Kàn 蠲 Kàn kèy 蠲鮭, a small kind of shell fish.

平
Kang 江 A river, a large stream. Yâng choó kang 洋子江, one of the principal rivers of China. A surname.

Kang 杠 A small bridge, for foot passengers. Söey sip yit gwat toê kàng sêng 歲十一月徒杠成, *neēⁿᵍ kaòu chàp yit göëyh sèy ây këō chēw chēⁿà*, in the eleventh month of the year, the foot bridges should be finished. See 孟子 Bēng choó.

Kang 矼 To take stones, and put them in a stream, in order to enable people to cross it; stone steps across a stream.

Kang 畕 Fields compared together.

Kang 工 Read kong: work. Kong hoo 工夫, *kang hoo*, work, labour. Chò kong 做工, *chò kang*, to work, to labour.
Pek kong ke soō, é sêng kê soō 百工居肆以成其事, *pāyh kang k'hēā tē têèm è chēⁿā e āy soō*, the hundred kinds of labourers dwell in the shop in order to complete their labours. See the 論語 Lūn gé.

Kang 公 Read kong: the male of animals. Kong boé 公母, *kang boē*, male and female.
Gnêw kong 牛公, *goô kang*, a bull.

Kang 蚣 Read kóng: Goê kóng 蜈蚣, *gēā kang*, a centipede.

去

Káng 講 Vulg. *kóng*: to speak, to say. Káng hwā 講話, *kóng wā*, to converse. Káng lūn 講論, to reason. Káng kèw 講究, research, to reason.
Hak jê put káng sē goê yew yëá 學而不講是吾憂也, *t'hak jê bô káng kèw sē gwá āy hwān lô*, to learn without research is a grief to me. Said by Confucius, in the 論語 Lūn gé.

Káng 港 A river, a canal, an arm of the sea. Kò káng 過港, *kōèy káng*, to go over the water. Káng pëen 港邊, *káng kēⁿᵍ*, the river's side.

Káng 犺 The male of the ox. Gnêw káng 牛犺, *goô káng*, a bull.

Káng 傋 Káng bâng 傋佹, blunt, simple, plain; incapable of flattery.

去

Kàng 絳 A deep crimson colour.

Kàng 降 To descend, to go down, to put down, to degrade. Kàng hwān 降凡, to descend among common people, to come down into the world. E' kàng 雨降, *lōh hoē*, to descend as rain. Kàng yit kip 降一級, to degrade a step in rank.
Hân-jé kàn gêng hwut kwut, sëāng noē kàng wûy Teâou-chew ch'hè soó 韓愈諫迎佛骨.上怒降爲潮州刺史, *Hân jé tⁿā sè twā gēⁿā chēēh hwut kwut, hoē sè twā sëw k'hè, kàng chò Tëô-chew ch'hè soó*, Hân-jé remonstrated against the Emperor's going to meet the bone of Buddha, upon which the Emperor was enraged, and degraded him to be the governor of Tëô-chew, (a very remote district in the province of 福建 Hok këèn.)—Also written 夅 kàng.

Kàng 洚 Water flowing out of its course. Kàng súy hêng lêw 洚水横流, *kàng chúy hwⁿā laôu*, the overwhelming waters flowing across the country.

Kàng 蜣 Read tòng: Sek tòng 石蝀, *chēōh kàng*, a kind of frog or toad found in deep vallies between high hills.

丟

Kāng 共 Read kēūng: together, alike, in common. Sëang kēūng 相共, *sëo kāng*, associated together, and assisting one another.
Kēūng yūng 共用, *kāng yūng*, to use in common.

Kaou 交 To associate with, to blend, to mix. Kaou chăp 交雜, mixed together. Kaou p'hōèy 交配, to accompany, to associate with.

E' pêng yéw kaou, gân jê yéw sìn 與朋友交言而有信, *kap pêng yéw haou p'höèy, kòng wā tëöh woō sìn sìt*, when associating with friends, we should be sincere in our conversation. See the 上論 Sëāng lūn.

Kaou 郊 The suburbs of a city. Kaou göēy 郊外, *kaou gwā*, beyond the suburbs.

Sîn bûn kaou kwan che löēy yéw yēw hong ch'hit sìp lé 臣聞郊關之內有囿方七十里, *gwà t'hēⁿa keèⁿᵍ kaou kwan ây laē wōo chìt ây yēw hwuiⁿᵍ k'hwāh ch'hit chàp lé*, I have heard that within the compass of the suburbs, there is a park 70 le in extent. See 孟子 Bēng choó.

Kaou 咬 The chirping of birds. Kaou kaou hông neaóu 咬咬黃鳥, *kaou kaou ây wuiⁿᵍ cheaóu*, the chirping yellow birds.

Kaou-lêw-pa 咬嗰吧 *Ka-lâ-pa*, the Chinese name for Batavia.

Kaou 蛟 A large kind of fish, a crocodile. Kaou lëûng 蛟龍, leviathans and dragons.

Kaou 鮫 Má kaou 馬鮫, *bây ka*, a species of squalus, or dog-fish.

Kaou 膠 Vulg. *ka*: glue, lime. Lûn jin kaou pit hoē se 輪人膠必厚施, *chò ch'hëa lûn ay lâng tëöh yūng ka k'hūh kaoū*, wheelwrights should use their glue very thick.

Kaou 鵁 Vulg. *ka*: the name of a bird. Kaou lēng 鵁鴒, *ka lēng*, a magpie. Kaou chuy 鵁鵻, *ka chuy*, a dove. Kaou ch'heng 鵁青, *ka ch'haiⁿᵍ*, the name of a bird, like a duck, with long legs, and a crested head.

Kaou 嘐 The cackling of fowls. Key bêng kaou kaou 雞鳴嘐嘐, *key t'hê kaou kaou*, the fowl's cackle with the sound of kaou kaou. See the 鄭風 Tēng hong.

Kaou 粄 Kaou teaôu 粄糶, cakes made of vermacelli.

Kaou 茭 The name of a plant; a kind of grass.

Kaou 溝 Read koe: a ditch, a dyke, a channel for conveying the water for irrigation. Pe këung sit, jê chīn lèk hoē koè hok 卑宮室而盡力乎溝洫, *ch'hông kāy e ây këung ch'hoò, jê chīn k'hwùy lat tē kaou hok*, he suffered his dwelling to remain low and mean, while he exhausted his strength upon the dykes and channels for irrigation. Said of 禹 E', in the 論語 Lūn gé.

Kaou 鉤 Read koe: a hook. T'hëet koe 鐵鉤, *t'heĕh kaou*, an iron hook. Teàou koe 釣鉤, *tèò kaou*, a fish hook.

Kaóu 狡 Vulg. *ka*: artful, deceitful, cunning, mad, outrageous. Put këèn choó ch'hëung, naé këèn kaóu tông 不見子充乃見狡童, *bô k'hwⁿá keèⁿᵍ choó ch'hëung, naê k'hwⁿà keèⁿᵍ ka ây sèy hēⁿá*, I did not see Mr. Choó-ch'hëung but I saw a parcel of wild children.

Kaóu 佼 Beautiful, fair, handsome; also written 姣 kaóu.

Kaóu 絞 Vulg. *ká*: to tie round, to strangle; also, urgent, pressing. Tit jê boô léy chek kaóu 直而無禮則絞, *teaôu tit jê bô lèy soè, chek kaóu*, to be blunt without politeness, is drawing the cord too tight. See the 論語 Lūn-gé.

Kaóu **瘕** Vulg. *ká:* a cholic. Kèw kaóu pēng 疚瘕病, *kèw ká pa*^{ng}, a violent pain in the stomach.

Kaóu **口** Read k'hoé: the mouth. Ây k'hoé 瘂口, *ây kaóu*, dumb, unable to speak.

Kaóu **九** Read kéw: nine. Kéw sip 九十, *kaóu chap*, ninety. Sip kéw 十九, *chap kaóu*, nineteen. Kwun choó yéw kéw soo 君子有九思, *kwun choó woō kaóu ây sëō*^{ng}, the good man has nine subjects of reflection. See the 論語 Lūn-gé.

Kaóu **狗** Read koé: a dog. Koé gëet 狗齧, *kaóu kā*, the dog bites. Chêy sëuk toè key choé koé 齊俗鬬雞走狗, *Chêy kok ây hong sëuk hoē key sëo p'hăh, hoē kaóu sëo jëuk chaóu*, the customs of the Chêy country consisted in fighting cocks and racing dogs. See the 戰國策 Chëèn kok ch'hek.

Kaóu **垢** Read koé: dirt and filth grimed into the skin. Yêw koé 油垢, *yêw kaóu*, the scruff of the head, the grease and grime collected about the face. Put sëén koé, jê ch'hat, lân te 不洗垢而察難知, *bô sêy kaóu, jê ch'hat k'hw*^{n}*à sëāng. ŏh chae*, in examining (the lines of the countenance), without washing away the filth, it will be difficult to ascertain (a man's fortune.) Said by those who practise palmistry.

去

Kaòu **教** Vulg. *kà:* to intruct, to teach. Kaòu hwùn 教訓, *kà hwùn*, instruction. Yit hak, yéw jê kaòu kwan 一學有二教官, *chit ây ŏh woō nō ây kà kw*^{n}*a*, each college has two doctors. (a principal and an assistant.)

Kaòu **較** To compare. Pé kaòu 比較, to compare together.

Kaòu **校** To compare, to liken; the same as the preceding. Hwān jê put kaòu 犯而不校, *e hwān lân, chëw bô kap e kèy kaòu*, when any offend us, we should not lower ourselves to a comparison with them. See the 論語 Lūn gé.

Kaòu **珓** Pöey kaòu 柸珓, a couple of gems, flat on one side and round on the other, used in divination.

Kaòu **窖** A hoarding-place; to hoard, or store up. Tëâng kaòu 長窖, *tê*^{ng} *kà*, the name of a place, in 福建 Hok këèn.

Kaòu **挍** To compare, to bring into a comparison; to quibble about. Kwun hoō che bēng put kaòu 君父之命不挍, *jîn kwun nëō*^{ng} *pāy ây bēng lēng bô kèy kaòu*, the commands of princes and parents most not be quibbled about. See the 左傳 Chó twān.

Kaòu **到** Read tò: to arrive at, to reach, to come to one. Chek chëùng bŭt che peáou lé cheng ch'hoe boô put tò 則衆物之表裏精粗無不到, *chek chëùng meè*^{nh} *ây laē gwā cheng ch'hoe bô a*^{m} *kaòu lân*, then both the externals and internals, the fine and coarse of all things, would universally come to us: (i. e. we should comprehend them.) See the 大學 Tāe hak.

Kaòu **夠** Read koè: enough, sufficient; also written 穀 koè.

Kaòu **筊** Pöey kaòu 柸筊, a couple of pieces of the roots of hamboo, round on one side, and flat, an the other, used in divining; these are thrown up by persons consulting the oracle, and if they fall with the flat sides uppermost they denote good luck, but if with the round sides above they denote

福建方言字典

ill-luck; they were formerly made of some precious stone.

平 Kaôu 候 Read hoē: a surname.

Kaôu 猴 Read hoē: a monkey, an ape.

去 Kaōu 厚 Read hoē: thick, solid, substantial; liberal, kind; to pay attention to. Kē séy hoē chēâ pok, jê kē séy pok chēâ hoē, bē che yéw yēá 其所厚者薄而其所薄者厚.未之有也, *e ây séy tēŏh kaōu ch'hông pŏh e, jê e ây séy tēŏh pŏh ch'hông kaōu e, bōēy woō chēy lêy chêng lê*, to pay more solid regard to that in which we may be indifferent, and to be indifferent in that to which we ought to pay more solid regard, would never do. See the 大學 Taē hak.

入 Kaoùh 餄 To mix things together in eating. Kaoùh jwán péng 餄軟餅, *kaoùh lún pēⁿá*, a kind of mince pie, or mixed meat pie.

Kaoùh 硧 A measure for liquids. Yêw kaoùh 油硧, an oil measure.

入 Kap 蛤 A sort of cockle. Kap choó 蛤仔, *kap á*, a kind of toad, or frog.

Kap 佮 To collect together; also, a surname.

Kap 船 A vessel moving; a ship under sail. Kap pán chûn 船板船, a square rigged vessel; derived from the Malay word *kapal*, a ship.

Kap 鴿 A pigeon. Tông-bêng-hông hoe kap wûy hwuy noê 唐明皇呼鴿爲飛奴, *Tông-êng-hông têy kēŏ kap sē hwuy noê*, the Emperor Bêng of the Tông dynasty called pigeons flying slaves.

Kap 合 A very small measure; also, and, together with; read hap. Lëáng yëak wûy kap, sip kap wûy seng 两龠爲合十合爲升, *nō ây yëŏh á chò chit kap, chàp kap chò chit chin*, two finger-fulls make a kap, and ten kap make a chin, (which is the tenth part of a peck.)

Kap 扴 To take anything up between the fingers; to move.

Kap 岬 A cape, a promontory; the side of a hill. Paē hwaē ê san kap che pông 徘徊於山岬之旁, *kēⁿá laē kēⁿá k'hè tē swⁿá kap ây pông*, to walk backwards and forwards on the side of the hill.

Kap 甲 Vulg. *kăh*: one of the horary characters. Hoo kap 莩甲, the budding of plants and herbs, when beginning to grow. Kap têw 甲胄, *kăh têw*, armour. Lîn kap 鱗甲, *lân kăh*, scales and shells. K'ho kap 科甲, *k'ho kăh*, the order of literary examinations. Pó kap 保甲, *pó kăh*, the arrangement of the people into tens, and hundreds. Kap têáng 甲長, *kăh têóⁿᵍ*, the head of a hundred, a constable. Ché kap 指甲, *chaéⁿᵍ kăh*, the nails of the fingers.

Bēng taē soo má kaôu bîn é kap têw 命大司馬敎民以甲胄, *bēng taē soo má kà pàyh saìⁿᵍ é ch'hèng kăh têw*, he ordered the master of the horse to instruct the people in the use of armour. See the 王制 Ông chè.

Hàn yêw kap, yit, péng, k'ho, é ch'hé soo 漢有甲.乙.丙.科.以取士, *Hàn teaôu wōo kăh, yit, pēⁿá, têng k'ho, é ch'hé t'hak ch'hāyh lâng*, the Hàn dynasty used the horary characters *kăh, yit*, and *pēⁿá*, to arrange and select clever scholars.

入 Kat 葛 Vulg. *kwăh*: a kind of grass, of which cloth is made; a sort of flax. A surname.

Lâm kat che t'hâm hēy, se ê tēung kok 南葛之覃兮施於中谷, *lâm kwăh ây poe k'hwuy se tē k'haiⁿᵍ â tang eⁿᵍ*, the southern flax plant is spread abroad, till it has filled the middle of the valley. See the 周南 Chew lâm.

Kat 割 Vulg. kwăh: to cut, to injure. Kat twān 割斷, *kwăh tooiⁿᵍ*, to cut asunder. Kat put chêng put sit 割不正不食, *kwăh bô sè chēⁿâ ūᵐ chēăh*, if the meat was not cut square, he (Confucius) would not eat of it. See the 論語 Lūn gé.

Kat tēy ch'hêng hô 割地請和, *kwăh tēy ch'hēⁿâ bōēyh hô*, they cut off some of their territory, to beg for peace.

Kat 結 Read këet: to tie. Tⁿa këet 打結, *p'hăh kat*, to tie a knot. Sëang koē këet sîn jê tē 上古結繩而治, *sëăng koē ây lâng kat sŏh jê tē kok soā*, the early ancients tied knots in cords, and thus carried on the affairs of government. See the 易經 Ek keng.

Kat 墼 T'hoē kat: 土墼, unburnt bricks.

平 Kay 嘉 Good, excellent, admirable; to praise, to admire; the meeting and uniting of the male and female principle.

Kay gân sëen hêng 嘉言善行, *kay ây wā, hó ây sèy kēⁿâ*, good words and virtuous deeds.

Kay 佳 Fine, good, excellent. Yēw k'hek hwut k'hoē bûn, gé gân ek hô kay 有客忽叩門, 語言亦何佳, *woō lâng k'hàyh hwut jëên k'hâou mooiⁿᵍ, kóng wā yēâ an chwⁿâ hó*, to have a friend suddenly knock at our door, and then to enter into conversation, how pleasant is it!

Kay 家 A house, a dwelling, a family, a household. A surname. Kay kwàn 家眷, *kay aōu*, a private family. Ch'hin kay 親家, a family related by marriage.

Yit kay jîn, yit kok hin jîn 一家仁一國興仁, *chit kay jîn, chit kok hin k'hè bōēyh jîn*, when one family is virtuous, the whole country will begin to be virtuous.

Kay 假 Excellent, good, admirable. Kay lok kwun choó 假樂君子, *Chang o 'lò Chang kòëy ê ây kwun choó*, an admirable and pleasing good man. See the 大雅 Taē gnây.

Kay 葭 A reed, a rush.

Kay 加 To add, to increase; more; to give, to display; to give an insult. Yēw hô kay yëen 又何加焉, *yēâ woō sⁿa meēⁿh Chang kay*, is there anything that can be added to this?

Ch'hêng kay 請加, *ch'hēⁿâ k'hăh kay*, be requested an addition.

Gnó put yëuk jîn che kay choo gnó yëâ, goé ek yëuk boô kay choo jîn 我不欲人之加諸我也, 吾亦欲無加諸人, *gwá ūᵐ aè pat lâng lêng jëuk hoē gwá, gwá yēâ aè bô lêng jëuk hoē lâng*, in that in which I do not wish another to give an insult to me, I also wish not to give such an insult to others. See the 上論 Sëang lūn.

Kay 珈 The ornaments of a woman's head-dress.

Kay 笳 Hoē kay 胡笳, a pipe made of a bamboo leaf rolled up together, which, when blown, produces a sound; much used by the Tartars.

Kay 跏 Kay têet 跏趺, a kind of stocks, in which a person is made to sit with his legs bent up under him.

Kay 茄 The name of a plant; vulg. këô: the brinjal, or egg-plant.

Kay 𨖸 Unable to proceed.

Kay 迦 Sek kay 釋迦, sek këa, a name of Buddha.

𡉕

Káy 賈 A surname.

Káy 椵 The name of a wood, used for making tables and bedsteads.

Káy 檟 The name of a small shrub. Bok-këang soò tek bé káy 穆姜使擇美檟, Bok-këang saè lâng kéng tóh hó ây káy, Bok-këang ordered them to select a good stalk of the káy plant. See the 左傳 Chó twān.

Káy 斝 A cup or vase; also written 斚 káy.

Káy 假 False, not true; to borrow; great. Káy gân 假言, pay ch'hat wā, a lie. Káy tō ê Gê, ê hwat K'hek 假道於虞以伐虢, chëŏh loē 'ê Gê, böëyh hwat K'hek, they borrowed a road through the Gê country, in order open to a track to the K'hek country. Also written 叚 káy.
Káy chaé t'hëen bēng 假哉天命, twā chae t'heeⁿᵍ ây bēng lēng, how great is the will of heaven! See the 大雅 Tuē gnáy.

Káy 嘏 Happiness; great; distant.

𡊁

Kày 嫁 To give in marriage, to marry out a daughter. Kày lé choé 嫁女子, kày chaôu á, to give a daughter in marriage.
Lé choó che kày yëá, boé hêng che 女子之嫁也,母命之, cha boé këⁿá ây kày ch'hut k'hè, něóⁿᵍ lèy bēng lēng e, when a young woman is married out, the mother must give directions. See 孟子 Bēng choó.

Kày 稼 To sow grain. Kày sek 稼穡, agriculture, husbandry. Hwân-tê ch'héng hak kày, Choó wat, goé put jê lō lông 樊遲請學稼,子曰吾不如老農, Hwân-tê ch'hëⁿá böëyh òh chò ch'hân, Hoo choó kóng, gwá bēy ch'hin chëóⁿᵍ laōu ây lóng hoe, Hwân-tê wanted to learn agriculture; when Confucius replied, I am in that not so good as an old farmer. See the 論語 Lūn gé.

Kày 假 Kò kày 告假, to request leave of absence; to be absent on furlough.

Kày 價 The price of anything, that at which a thing is valued. K'hóng-choó wûy chèng sam gwat, yëuk ko tûn chëá put sek kày 孔子爲政三月,鬻羔豚者不飾價, K'hóng-choó hwⁿà chèng soà sⁿa göëyh, chëw bēy yëóⁿᵍ bàh le bàh ây lâng, bô hōng kày, Confucius managed the affairs of government for three months, when the people were so improved that the sellers of mutton and pork did not garnish their prices, (or ask more than they intended to take). See the 家語 Kay gé.
Kày chëên 價錢, kày cheeⁿᵍ, the price. K'hé kày 起價, to rise in price.
Put jē kày 不二價, "no two prices!" written up by some shopkeepers who resolve to make no abatement in their prices.

Kày 賈 The same as the foregoing. Ch'hē kay 市賈, the market price.

Kày 架 A stand, a frame, a scaffolding, a shelf. Ok kà y 屋架, ch'hoò kày, a scaffolding. E kày 衣架, a clothes-horse. Sip joō kày 十字架, *chap jē kày*, a frame in the form of the character 十, a cross.

Kày 駕 To harness horses, or other animals, to a carriage. Kwun ke chëang kày 君車將駕, *kwun ày ch'hëa böëyh kày bày*, the prince's carriage is about to be harnessed in.

平 Kây 枷 The cangue, or wooden collar, worn by criminals in China. T'hae kây 枱枷, *gëa kây*, to wear the wooden collar.

Kây 㑪 A pain in the limbs.

Kây 抲 To take.

Kāy 下 Read hāy: low, not high. Wûy hāy pit yin ch'hwan tek 爲下必因川澤, *chò kāy pit tëŏh t'hàn ch'huiⁿᵍ tek*, in seeking to place anything low, we must avail ourselves of the rivers and marshes. See 孟子 Bēng choó.

Kāy 低 *Kāy gin* 低銀, low silver, adulterated silver.

去 Kăyh 骼 Kwut kăyh 骨骼, the joints of bones. Hⁿō kwut kăyh 好骨骼, *hó kwut kăyh*, well shaped, well proportioned limbs.

Kăyh 垎 The layers or strata of earth, under the earth's surface.

Kăyh 挌 To parry off a blow. Kăyh k'hae 挌開, *kăyh k'hwuy*, to parry off.

Kăyh 格 Read kek: a pattern. Joō kek 字格, *jē kăyh*, a copy for writing, a blank copy book for children.

Kăyh 膈 ... the region of the breast. ... 胸膈, *heng kăyh*, the ... part about the bosom.

Kăyh 篱 Tëuk kek 竹篱, *tek kăyh*, a bamboo screen, a partition, a wainscot.

Kăyh 隔 Read kek: to part asunder. Kek twān 隔斷, *kăyh tooiⁿᵍ*, to separate.

Kăyh 莢 Read këep; as Bêng këep 蓂莢, *bêng kăyh*, a felicitous plant spoken of in the time of Geâou. Toē këep 荳莢, *taōu kăyh*, a preparation of pulse.

Kăyh 鍥 Read këet: a reap-hook, a grass-knife; also, to cut off with a knife. Këet teaou sëep che kēng 鍥朝涉之脛, *kăyh măyⁿh chaē sè köëy chúy ày k'ha*, he cut off the legs of those who were crossing the water early in the morning; (done by a tyrant to see how their marrow looked on a cold frosty morning.) See the 戰國策 Chëen kok ch'hek.

Kăyh 裓 The flap of a coat, the lappet of a garment.

入 Kăyh 逆 Read gek: rebellious, disobedient, unruly. Pöëy gek 背逆, *pöëy kăyh*, to turn the back on, and oppose. Gek t'hëen 逆天, *kăyh t'heeⁿᵍ*, to oppose the will of heaven. Wûy gek 違逆, *wûy kăyh*, to oppose rebelliously.

平 Ke 居 To dwell, to stay, to remain, to reside, to rest, to sit down. A surname. Kwun choó sit boô kêw paóu, ke boô kêw an 君子食無求飽.居無求安, *kwun choó chëăh bô kêw pá, k'hëă bô kêw an*, the good man in his eating does not seek satiety, nor in his dwelling ease. See the 上論 Sëāng lūn. Ke, goê gé jé 居吾語女, *chāy, gwá kap lé kóng*, sit down, and I will tell you.

Ke **墼** A border, a boundary; also, a foundation. Kaou ke ch'hëen le 郊墼千里, *kaou ke chë^{n}á ch'heng lé*, a border extending to a thousand le, (or about 400 miles.)

Yêw gân k'heuk sit sëën lip ke ché 猶言築室先立墼址, *ch'hin cheō^{ng} kóng k'hé ch'hoō, teŏh taē seng k'hëā ke ché*, just as in building a house, it is necessary first to lay the foundation.

Ke **饑** Vulg. *yaou:* hungry. Ke hong 饑荒, *ke hwui^{ng}*, a famine; also written 飢 ke. Ke chëa ē wûy sit 饑者易爲食 *yaou ây lâng yûng ē chò chëăh*, a hungry man is not particular about what he eats. See 孟子 Bēng-choó.

Ke **磯** Stones in the middle of a stream; a stumbling block. Ch'haé sek ke 采石磯, the name of a place, near Cochin China, where a great battle was fought.

Ke **譏** To ridicule, to point at in one's discourse, to blame, to censure. Ke ch'hè 譏刺, to point at with piercing sarcasms.

Yin jîn jê ke 因人而譏, to stab one through the sides of another.

Ke **畿** The territory assigned as the peculiar domain of an Emperor. Pang ke ch'hëen lé wûy bîn séy ché 邦畿千里爲民所止, *pang ke chë^{n}á ch'heng lé, wûy pâyh sai^{ng} séy ēy hây^{n}h*, an Imperial domain extending to a thousand lé, is what the people can settle on. See the 詩經 Se-keng.

Ke **僟** Felicitous influences; also, near.

Ke **機** Ke pëèn 機變, crafty stratagems. Ke bit 機密, *ke bat*, secret springs. Ke k'hè 機器, an instrument, a machine.

Wûy ke pëèn che k'haóu chëá 爲機變之巧者, *chò ke pëèn ây k'há chëá*, those who are cunning at devising crafty stratagems. See 孟子 Bēng-choó.

Ke **幾** Little, minute, small; near; dangerous; to aim at. Jîn che séy é ē ê k'hîm sèw chëá, ke he 人之所以異於禽獸者幾希, *lâng ây séy è kŏh yëō^{ng} ê k'hîm sèw bô jwā chēy*, that in which man differs from the brutes is very insignificant. See 孟子 Bēng-choó.

Ke **璣** A pearl, a gem. Jöēy ke gëuk hêng 璿璣玉衡, instruments made of gems and precious stones, (by which Sùn studied astronomy).

Choo ke 珠璣, an imperfect pearl.

Ke **基** A foundation, a commencement, a patrimony, an estate. Ke tēy 基地, a foundation. Ke gëëp 基業, an inheritance.

T'haè-ông tcaou ke ông chek 太王肇基王迹, *T'haè ông k'he t'haóu ch'hòng tēy ke ông ây chëăh*, T'haè-ông first laid the foundation of the traces of royalty in his family.

Ke **朞** A whole year; a re-commencement of time after a given period. Chaé-gnó būn sam lëên che song, ke é kéw è 宰我問三年之喪非已久矣, *Chaè-gnó mooi^{ng} s^{n}a nee^{ng} ây se^{ng} hà, k'hw^{n}à kà nooi^{ng} nee^{ng} woō kaòu koó bô*, Chaè-gnó asked respecting the three years' period of mourning for parents, whether one whole year was not long enough. See the 論語 Lūn gé. Also written 期 ke.

Ke **箕** A basket for collecting dirt. Hwŭn ke 糞箕, *pùn ke*, a hod for dirt. Pò ke 簸箕, *pwà ke*, a close kind of sieve.

Ke **錤** Choo ke 鎡錤, agricultural implements; also written 基 ke. Suy yéw choo ke, put jê t'haē sê 雖有鎡錤不如待時, *suy woō chŏh ch'hân ây ke k'hè, ū^{m} tat tëŏh tëng haōu sê*, although we have agricultural implements ready, yet it is better to wait the proper time for husbandry. See 孟子 Bēng-choó.

Ke **乩** To divine, in order to ascertain doubtful things.

Ke 俱 All, altogether. Hoĉ boé ke chûn 父毋俱存, *pāy boĕ chò poŏ tĕ tĭt*, his parents were both alive. See 孟子 Bēng-choŏ.

Ke 奇 Strange, uncommon. Vulg. *k'hēa:* single, one alone, an odd one. Ke h^n^ò k'hó ke 奇貨可居, *ke hoèy t'hang k'hēā*, this is an extraordinary piece of merchandize, and should be secured.

Ke 倚 Ke k'höey che hēng 倚魁之行, strange and surpassing conduct.

Ke 姬 An elegant appellation for a lady; also, a lady. A surname.

Ke 𣂷 To lade out as with a ladle; to bale; a ladle; to take.

Ke 飢 To be hungry; the same as 饑 ke. Lêy bîn put ke put hân 黎民不飢不寒, *oe t'haŏu păyh sai^ng^ bēy. yaou bēy kwo^n^á*, the common people (the black-headed folks) are neithr hungry nor cold. See 孟子 Bēng-choé.

Ke 車 Vulg. *ch'hēa:* a carriage, a waggon, a vehicle of any kind. A surname. Hông-tèy kwan chwán hông, bēng Kēung-koé chok ke 黄帝覩轉蓬命共鼓作車, *Wui^ng^-têy k'hwo^n^á loĕ wúy lēĕn tooi^ng^, chek bēng lēng Kēung-koĕ chò ch'hēa*, Wui^ng^-têy seeing the reeds rolling along, ordered Këung-koĕ to make carriages; (he also conceived the idea of boats, from observing the fallen leaves floating down the stream; this was about B. C. 2000.)

Ke 羈 A horse's halter, a head-stall.

Ke 凥 The ancient form of the character 居 ke. to dwell.

Ke 琚 A gem or precious stone, carried on the back.

Ke 裾 The skirts of a coat, the hinder part of a garment. Tông pok hoê bûn, tē choó k'hēen ke 童僕候門稚子牵裾, *gîn á têng haŏu tē mooi^ng^, sèy kē^n^á k'hun s^n^a aŏu pee^ng^*, (on our return we find) the servants waiting at the door, and the children ready to pull the skirts of our coats.

Ke 椐 The name of a species of wood.

Ke 腒 To sell, to vend; also, to hoard up.

Ke 涺 The name of a river.

Ke 枝 Read che: a branch, a twig. Wūy tēáng chēà chēet che 爲長者折枝, *wuy sè twā at ch'hēw ke*, to pluck a twig for a superior.

声

Ké 己 Vulg. *ka tē:* self, one's self, one's own person. Kwun choó kêw choo ké 君子求諸已, *kwun choó kēw tak háng e ka tē*, the good man seeks for everything from himself. See the 論語 Lūn gē.

Ké 圮 To overturn, to destroy; destructive, ruinous, wicked. Hong bēng ké chok 方命圮族, *gek bēng ay lâng, k'hēep ây chok lūy*, he is a transgressor of commands, and belongs to a ruinous set. See the 堯典 Geaŏu tēĕn.

Ké 紀 A line, a part of a net. A surname. Kong ké 綱紀, the upper and lower parts of a net; to arrange, to set in order, to govern. Kong ké soò hong 綱紀四方, to arrange and regulate the people in all quarters. To record, to note down; a record, a history; a period of twelve years is called 紀 ké.

Ké 莒 The name of a plant; also, the name of a country.

Ké 筥 A vessel for containing rice; a sort of a basket; anything round.

Ké 机 The name of a tree. Ké lêw 机柳, a sort of willow.

Ké 几 A table, a bench, a stand to rest or lean upon. Yîn ké jê gō 隱几而臥, *p'hak tē tŏh jê k'hwùn*, he leaned upon the table, and slept.

Ké 麂 A fawn; others say, a large doe.

Ké 蟣 A louse. Hĕuk soè ké ê hëên tēw 畜素蟣于玄冑, *ch'hē pàyh ây sat boè tē oe ây t'haòu k'höey*, to feed a white louse upon a black helmet.

Ké 幾 A few; how. Kè hô 幾何, *jwā chēy*, how much. Ké to 幾多, *jwā chēy*, how many. Boô ké 無幾, *bô jwā chēy*, not many.

Hoô seng jëak bōng, wūy hwan ké hô 浮生若夢爲歡幾何, *p'hoô p'hoô ây saiⁿᵍ mēⁿā chò hwⁿa, hê woô jwā chēy*, this floating life is like a dream; the pleasures we enjoy, what are they?

Ké 舉 To bear, to carry, to raise, to lift up, to elevate; to praise; all. Goê lek chëuk é ké pek kin, jê put chëuk é ké yit ê 吾力足以舉百鈞.而不足以舉一羽, *gwā ây lat ēy chëuk kaòu gëá kè chit pàyh kin, jê bēy chëuk kaòu gëá kè chit ây cheaòu mô*, my strength is sufficient to lift up a hundred *kin*, (each 30 pounds weight,) and yet is not sufficient to lift a feather. (To say this, would shew a want of will and not a want of power.) See 孟子 Bēng-choó.

Ké 矩 A rule, a law, a constant law. Kwuy ke 規矩, custom, usage. Ch'hit sip, jê chëûng sim séy yëuk, put jê ké 七十.而從心所欲.不踰矩, *ch'hit chàp, jê t'hàn sim kwⁿá sèy aè, ūᵐ köèy hwat toē*, at seventy, I followed that which my heart desired, without overstepping the rule. Said by Confucius, in the 上論 Sëāng lūn.

Kè 記 (去) To remember, to recollect, to record, to note down. Kè tek 記得, *kè tit*, to bring to remembrance. Kè soè 記數, *kè sèaòu*, to note down in a memorandum-book. Chó yéw kè gân che soó, yēw yéw kè soō che kwan 左有記言之史.右有記事之官, *tó ch'hëw woō kè wā ây soò, chëⁿá ch'hëw woō kè soō ây kwⁿa*, on the left were the historians ready to record the words spoken, and on the right were the officers for commemorating the events that occurred.

Kè 倨 Proud, haughty, imperious. Kwùy wûy t'hëen choó, jê put keaou kè 貴爲天子而不驕倨, *kwùy chò hông tèy, jê ūᵐ keaou kè*, in nobility he was raised to the rank of Emperor, and yet was not proud.

Kè 鋸 A saw, to cut with a saw. Tëung hêng yūng to kè 中刑用刀鋸, *tëūng ây hêng hwat yūng to kwà kè*, for the middling order of punishments, they made use of the knife and the saw.

Kè 踞 Chun kè 蹲踞, to sit cross-legged. Ke kè 箕踞, to sit with the legs under one. Tok ch'hè jê kè 獨處而踞, *tok k'hëā jê p'hàh kòèy chëèn chāy*, to dwell alone, and sit down cross-legged.

Kè 瞿 To be afraid. A surname. Cheng-choo bûn che kè jëên 曾子聞之瞿然, *Cheng-choó t'hëⁿa e, chëw këⁿa ây yëāⁿᵍ*, Cheng-choó on hearing this was alarmed.

Kè 蘧 Self possession, to come to one's-self. Also, a surname. Chong-chew bōng wūy hoê têep, gô jê kak, chek kè kè jëen Chew yëá 莊周夢爲蝴蝶.俄而覺.則蘧蘧然周也, *Chong-chew bāng chò bōey yëāh têep, á koó ch'haing, chek choō tek ây yëōng k'hwnà sē Chew*, Chong-chew dreamt that he was a butterfly, but a moment after, awaking and coming to himself, he found that he was Chong-chew.

Kè 遽 Hasty, sudden, rapid, hurried, precipitate. Suy chaē ch'hong chut, bē sëāng chit gân kè sek 雖在倉卒未嘗疾言遽色, *suy jëēn twā tē ch'hong chut yëd bōey woō hin ây kóng wā, kè ây bīn sek*, although he was frequently in hurried circumstances, yet he never spoke precipitately, or manifested hurry in his countenance. Said of 劉寬 Lêw-k'hwan.

Kè 籧 Kè tê 籧篨, a bamboo mat, a vessel made of bamboo.

Kè 據 To hold, to grasp, to rest on, to comply with; according to. Kè ê tek 據於德, to grasp firmly at virtue. See the 論語 Lūn gé.

Kè 賮 Earnest money; money given as a pledge.

Kè 冀 To expect, to hope, to desire. Kè bōng 冀望, *kè bāng*, to hope for. Also written 兾 kè.
Bê-choô k'hè Yin, yêw kè sëuk che yit pëēn, kwun che yit goē yëá 微子去殷.猶冀俗之一變.君之一悟也, *Bê-choó lê k'hè Yin teaôu, yëá tit kè bāng hong sëuk ây chit kây peèng, jîn kwun ây chit sèng goē*, when Bê-choô departed from the court of Yin, he was still anxiously expecting the manners of the people to take one turn for the better, and the prince to be once awakened. See the 史記 Soô kè. A surname.

Kè 驥 The name of a good horse. Kè put ch'heng kè lek, ch'heng kè tek yëá 驥不稱其力.稱其德也, *hó báy bô o lô e ây lat, naê o lô e ây tek*, a good horse is not to be admired for its strength, but for its temper. See the 論語 Lūn gé.

Kè 寄 Vulg. *këà*: to confide in, to intrust to any one's care; to dwell, to reside. K'hó é kè pek lé che bēng 可以寄百里之命, *t'hang laê këà e chit pàyh lé ây bēng lēng*, he can be entrusted with a message to the distance of a hundred lé.
Kok boô kè gē 國無寄寓, *kok kwun bô t'hang hoē e këà hàynh*, (the prince of a fallen) country cannot be intrusted to reside among us.

Kè 穊 Close, secret, hidden.

Kè 羈 A halter, a leathern thong for tying a horse. Kè tek, séy é gē má yëá 羈靮所以馭馬, *p'hoêy sŏh sêy ê pak báy*, a leathern thong is that with which we tie up a horse.

Kè 羇 A stranger sojourning in a place. Kè lé 羇旅, to sojourn.

Kè 旣 To eat a little, a small meal; exhausted, finished, done; since, already. Sêng soō put swat, sūy soō put kàn, kè óng put kēw 成事不說.遂事不諫.旣往不咎, *chënā ây soō bô kóng, sùy ây soō bô tnà, kaou koèy óng chēw bô lëāh e woō koèy sit*, when a thing is done it is of no use to speak of it, nor when it is persisted in to reprove it, nor to blame what is already gone by. See the 上論 Sëāng lūn.
Kè wat chè chè yëen 旣曰志至焉, *kè jëēn kóng sim chè woō chè kek*, since you say, the intention is the principal thing, &c. See 孟子 Bēng-choó.

Kè 屨 Straw shoes. Kéw kéw kat kè, k'hó é lé song 糾糾葛屨可以履霜 *teèng neèng kwăh ây ch'haóu ây, t'hang laê lăh seng*, they set us to twist up a pair of straw shoes out of the hemp plant, that we might be enabled to walk on the snow. See the 詩魏風 Se gwūy hong.

Kè 薊 The name of a tree. Kè chew 薊州, the name of a district. A surname.

Kè 句 Vulg. koò: a sentence. Chëang kè 章句, chëo^ng koò, sections and sentences.

Kè 痣 Read chè: a black spot; a freckle. Hàn Ko-choé 漢高祖 had seventy two such black spots on his left thigh.

Kê 其 He, she, it, that, that which, his, her's, their's it's. Kê soo che wūy 其斯之謂與, e k^nà sè an nèy kóng, this is perhaps the meaning of it? See the 論語 Lūn gé.
Kê jëak sē, sëuk lêng gé che 其若是孰能禦之, e kaòu an nèy, clē chày ëy kàyh e, when the affair is come to this pass, who can stop it?
Kê yâng bin yöá hwūy 其養民也惠, e ch'hē pàyh soi^ng woō yin hwūy, in the cherishing of the people, he displayed kindness.

Kê 期 To fix a time, a fixed period; to limit; to hope. Kwuy mūèy k'hëen kê 歸妹愆期, sàng looi^ng laè sìò mōèy woō koèy kê, in sending home the younger sister (to her husband's dwelling), the appointed time was exceeded. See the 易經 Ék keng.
Kê ê ê tē 期于予治, k bāng gwa ày tē, they are anxiously waiting for the time of my government. See the 書禹謨 Se é-boê.

Kê 萁 The stalk of pulse, bean stalks.

Kê 祺 Happy, lucky, felicitous. Sèw k'hó wūy kê 壽考爲祺, woō hòèy ây laou lâng sē kit kê, the appearance of a venerable old man is lucky.

4 F.

Kê 淇 The name of a river.

Kê 蜝 A small kind of crab. Goê kê 蜈蜝, a leech.

Kê 騏 A horse of a variegated colour.

Kê 麒 Kê lin 麒麟, a fabulous beast, considered the most noble of the brute creation. Kê lin che ê choé sèw 麒麟之於走獸, kê lin twā tē chaóu sèw, the Kê-lin among four-footed animals. See 孟子 Bêng-choó.

Kê 琪 A gem, a precious stone found in the east.

Kê 綦 A green azure colour. Also written 綨 kê.

Kê 鵸 A small goose. Seaou sin che h^nò, sea kê gân 小臣之好射鵸雁, sèy sin ay aè, chūh kê gân, that which your humble servant is fond of, is to shoot the large and small wild geese. See the 史記 Soò kè.

Kê 旗 A flag, a standard, an ornament of a flag, consisting of two rampant dragons, crossing each other. Kê che 旗織, a standard.
Cheaou soō ê kê 招士以旗, cheo t'hak ch'hàyh lâng ê kê, a scholar must be summoned by a standard. See 孟子 Bêng-choó.

Kê 棋 Pok kê 博棋, the game of chess. Söang kê 象棋, ivory chess-men. Wūy kê 圍棋, to play at chess. Also written 碁 kê, and 棊 kê.
Geâou chò wūy kê, Tan-choo sëén che 堯造圍棋丹朱善之, Geâou chò wūy kê, Tan-choo o lò e, Geâou invented the game of chess (B. C. 2230.) and Tan-choo (his worthless son) admired it.

Kê 俟 Bok kê 万俟, a surname.

Kê 伎 An extra toe on the foot; talent, skill. Kê k'haóu 伎巧, clever.

Kê 歧 Kê loē 歧路, a double road; anything double; wheat come to perfection.

Kê 岐 Kê san 岐山, kê swⁿa, the name of a hill, where the 周 Chew dynasty laid the foundation of its future greatness.

Kê 技 Kê gāy 技藝, an ingenious contrivance. Kê k'haóu 技巧, kê k'há, clever. Twàn twàn hèy, boô t'ìⁿa kê 斷斷兮無他技, ch'hin chēⁿà bô pat meēⁿh kê k'há, there certainly is no other contrivance. See the 大學 Taē hak.

Kê 妓 Female musicians, dancing-girls; formerly there were no dancing girls, but 漢武帝 Hàn Boó-tèy first established the practice, in order to accommodate those of his soldiers who had no wives.

Kê 蚑 The appearance of an insect creeping, to creep. Also, the name of an insect with a small body, and long legs, hence called tēâng kê 長蚑, têⁿg k'há kê, long-shanks.

Kê 跂 A superabundant toe on the foot; the same as 伎 kê.

Kê 倛 Speaking of another person or thing; he, she, it.

Kê 蕖 Hoô kê 芙蕖, the name of the water lily when in flower. Ch'hut súy hoô kê 出水芙蕖, ch'hut chúy ây ... ê, the water lily peeping above the water.

Kê 渠 Water, a piece of water, a pond, ... a h great. Kê lông 渠儂, a common appellation for he, she, it.

Bûn kê ná ... k ... t neng ... hé 問渠那得清如許, mou... ...uy an chwⁿâ ēy tit ch'heng kaòu an nēy, ask h... t... water comes to be so clear.

Kê 磲 Ch'hea kê 硨磲, a precious stone, like a crystal, of which the button on inferior mandarins' caps is made.

Kê 畸 An odd field, anything odd or superabundant. The Chinese used to divide their fields into nine squares, called 井田, chéng tēên, well fields, but those which were too small or narrow for such a division were called 畸田 kê tēên, odd fields.
Kê lêng 畸零, kê lân, anything odd, over and above, miscellaneous.

Kê 碕 The head of a crooked bank; a jutting head-land.

Kê 崎 Vulg. kēâ: steep. K'he kê 嶇崎, steep of ascent, a hill road, very crooked, and with many turns in it.

Kê 奇 Wonderful, strange, extraordinary. Kê kwaè 奇怪, koô kwaè, strange. Kê bûn kēūng hîm sēāng 奇文共欣賞, kê āy bûn taē kay laē hwⁿa hê sēēⁿg e, extraordinary pieces of literary composition! let us delight in and admire them together.
Kê ē 奇異, strange and uncommon. Vulg. k'hēa, odd, not even.

Kê 琦 A gem, a precious stone. Also, great.

... 錡 A caldron with three feet, as distinguished from 釜 hoô, an iron pan without feet.

K... 剞 Kê k'hwat 剞劂, a crooked knife, a reap-hook.

Kê 踦 Lame of one leg; having only one leg.

Kê 祈 To pray, to beg for happiness. Kê tó 祈禱, to supplicate. E kê kam é 以祈甘雨, é kê kêw kam koē, in order to pray for sweet rain. See the 小雅 Sëáou gnáy.
Kê kêw yëw êng 祈求有應, kê kêw woō yin, those who present supplications are sure of receiving an answer. Vauntingly said of many idol shrines, in order to induce the people to offer sacrifices there.

Kê 圻 A border; a royal territory 1000 lê in extent, is called 圻 kê.

Kê 沂 The name of a river.

Kê 蘄 The name of a plant; also, the name of a district.

Kê 旂 A flag, or standard, with a pair of rampant dragons crossed upon it. The same as 旗 kê.

Kê 頎 Long, tall. Kê jê tëáng hëy 頎而長兮, ló kwà tëⁿᵍ, tall and long.

Kê 祇 Tëy kê 地祇, the terrestrial gods, in contradistinction from the t'hëen sîn 天神, t'heeⁿᵍ sîn, the celestial gods.
Tó jê ê sëáng hāy sîn kê 禱爾于上下神祇, kê tó tē têng bīn hāy tēy āy sîn kê, pray to the celestial and terrestrial gods above and below. See the 論語 Lūn gē.
Also, rest. Pe gnó kê yëá 俾我祇也, hoē gwá pêng an, give me rest. See the 小雅 Sëáou gnáy.
Also, great. Put wán hok bôo kê hüëy 不遠復無祇悔, bô hwuīⁿᵍ k'hè, chëw bô twā āy sëōⁿᵍ tōh kèy, do not go far and you will not have occasion for any great regret. See the 易經 Ek

Kê 茋 Hông kê 黄茋, the name of a medicinal plant.

Kê 疧 Sick, sad, pained, grieved. Che choo che wán, pe gnó kê hëy 之子之遠俾我疧兮, kaôu lé k'hè hëāh hwuīⁿᵍ, hoē gwá hwān lō, your having gone thus far away, has occasioned me much pain. See the 小雅 Sëáou gnáy.

Kê 祁 Great, numerous, loose and lingering; surname. Tong kê hân 冬祁寒, tang t'heeⁿᵍ twā kwⁿā, the winter very cold.
Ch'haé hwân kê kê 采蘩祁祁, bán hwân ... láng chëy, those who were busied in plucking the hwân plant were numerous.

Kê 劬 Troubled, distressed, wearied. Boé sē kê l... 母氏劬勞, nëóⁿᵍ lëy t'haè tëóh hwa, a mother is put to much trouble.

Kê 鴝 Kê yëuk 鴝鵒, the name of a bird, which has a comb on its head, and always flies in company; some say a parrot or a loory.

Kê 瞿 A surname.

Kê 衢 A wide street, a general thoroughfare. Kay kê 街衢, a public way.

Kê 鸜 Kê yëuk 鸜鵒, the name of a bird; the same as 鴝 kê.

Kê 氍 Kê jê 氍毹, a mattrass or carpet, made of hair.

Kê 癯 Lean, meagre. Lëet sëen che jê, ke sau tek kan, hêng yûng sîm kê 列仙之儒居山澤間形容甚癯, l... sëen āy t'hak ch'hāyh láng, k'hëá tē swⁿā tek kan, h... ng yûng chin chaē sán, the various literati among the genii, who dewell amongst the hills and marshes, are very meagre in their form and appearance.

Kê 臞 Poor in flesh; meagre; the same as the foregoing. Choo häy sim cheen jê kê, tek tō jê hwûy 子夏心戰而臞. 得道而肥. *Choó-häy sim kwⁿa cheen keng chēw sân, kaou tit leoh tō chēw pwûy.* Choó-häy, when his mind was agitated (with study), became thin; but when he obtained a knowledge of the doctrine, he grew fat.

Kê 蘧 Kê kê 蘧蘧, self-possession; to come to one's self. Also read ke.

Kê 璩 A kind of ring. A surname.

Kê 丌 The ancient form of the character 其 kê this; also, the game of chess.

Kê 鰭 The back bone of a fish.

Ké 耆 Kê ló 耆老, old people, elders. Naé chëuk kê kê ló jê kò che 乃屬其耆老而告之, *naé chëuk t'hok e ây laōu lâng, jê kap e kóng,* and then enjoined on his old people, and informed them, saying &c. See 孟子 Bēng-choó.

Kē 具 Prepared, ready; to discriminate; a tool. K'hè kē 器具, an implement, a vessel, utensils. All.

Kē 俱 All, together. Tō k'hó chaè jê é che kē 道可載而與之俱, *tō t'hang chaè jê kap e chò poō,* virtue may be borne and kept in company.

Kē 颶 A hoisterous wind at sea. Kē k'hé chöey k'hó wûy 颶起最可畏, *twā hong chit ây k'hé, chöey t'hang kēⁿa,* when a typhoon gets up, it is very formidable.

Kē 惧 To ... the same as 懼 kē. P... kè 不憂不惧, neither sad nor alarmed.

Kē 懼 To be afraid, to be apprehensive, the same as the foregoing. Yúng chëá put kē 勇者不懼, *yúng ây lâng bô kēⁿa,* brave men are not afraid. See the 論語 Lūn gè.

Kē 偈 Military, martial, courageous.

Kē 伎 To accompany, to have fellowship with. Kê lëäng 伎倆, artful, cunning.

Kē 彐 A pig's head; one of the radicals.

Kē 技 A plan, an art, a contrivance; an art or trade. Sëäng kē jê chëen ke chek bîn hin gäy 尚技而賤車則民興藝, *sëāng ch'hëw kē, jê chëen báy ch'hëa, chek pāyh sqⁿg hin h'hè k'hà gây,* to patronise the arts, and to discourage riding in carriages, will make the people increase in skill.

Kē 妓 Ki gak 妓樂, singing women. Ch'heang kē 娼妓, a prostitute.

Kē 芰 A water plant; yielding; an angular seed.

Kē 忌 To fear, to dread; to be envious, and malicious. Hoê soo wûy kē 胡斯畏忌, *sⁿā soō kaou heăh kēⁿa,* why so fearful and alarmed. See the 大雅 Taē gnây. Bîn te yéw p'hek, chek put kē é sëäng 民知有辟則不忌于上, *pāyh sqⁿg chae woō hwat toē, chek ūm wān kē é sè twā,* when people know the law, they will not be jealous of their superiors. See the 傳 Chó twān.

Kē 跽 To kneel down to prostrate one. Chin ông kē wat seen seng put heng kaòu kwⁿá jîn hoē, 秦王跽曰先生不幸教寡人乎, *Chîn ông twā kwùy kóng, sin saiⁿᵍ ūᵐ hēng kà gwá kuⁿá jîn,* the king of Chîn then prostrated himself, and said, Oh, Sir! will you not do me the favor of instructing me?' See the 戰國策 Chëèn kok ch'hek.

Kē 惎 To respect, to honor, to esteem, to reverence.

Kē 洎 To arrive at, to reach to, to attain.

Kē 巨 Great, large; wûy kē sit, 爲巨室 *keĕh twā ch'hoò,* to construct a large house. See 孟子 Bēng choó. Kē k'hoé sèy lîn, 巨口細鱗 *twā ch'hùy sèy lân,* a large mouth and small scales.

Kē 拒 To oppose, to withstand, to stop; kē gé 拒禦 to withstand. K'hó chëá é che, kē put k'hò chëá kē che 可者與之其不可者拒之, *t'hang ây lâng chëw kap e kaou, e ây ūᵐ t'hang ây lâng chëw kē ché e,* with those who can be associated, unite; but those who cannot be associated with, reject. See the 論語 Lūn gé.

Kē 距 Kim kē 金距 a metal spur for fighting cocks. Kwùy-sē kaè kē key, Hoē-sē wûy che kim kē, 季氏介其鷄郈氏爲之金距, *Kwùy-sē ch'hëng kăh key, Hoē-sē kap e ch'hëng chit ây kim kē,* Kwùy sē dressed his cock in armor, and Hoē-sē furnished his cock with metal spurs. See the 左傳 Chó twān.

Kē 炬 A flambeau made of a bundle of reeds bound together and ignited.

Kē 詎 How? in what way? Jëák tê yit kaè soò hong, kē put hëáng èng, 若馳一介四方詎不響應 *nā saé chit ây gîn á k'hè sè heⁿᵍ, k'hé ūᵐ hëáng yìn,* if you send a messenger into all parts, how would not your message be re-echoed and answered. The same as 豈 k'hé.

Kē 鉅 Steel, hard metal; wàn jê kē t'hëet, 怨如鉅鐵 *wàn ch'hin chëoⁿᵍ kèⁿᵍ t'heĕh,* hardened in malice, like steel and iron. Also, great.

去

Këa 迦 Sek këa, 釋迦, one of the names of Buddha.

Këa 跏 Këa t'hëet 跏趺, to sit cross-legged; to be confined in that position; to be fettered with the legs bent up under one.

Këa 袈 Këa sa, 袈裟, a surplice, a priest's robe.

去

Këà 寄 Read kè, to intrust, to lodge in any one's hands; kè t'hok, 寄托 *këà t'hok,* to confide anything to a person's care. Ch'héng kè, boô séy t'hèng, 請寄無所聽 *ch'hèⁿá këà, bô sëy t'hèⁿa,* he wished to lodge it with some one, but no one would listen to him. See the 史記 Soó kè. Kè sìn, 寄信 *këà p'hay,* to send a letter by any one.

平

Këá **伽** Këá lâm 伽藍, the name of a heathen deity.

Këá **岐** Read kê, the name of a place.

Këá **荷** Read ho, to bear, to carry anything on the shoulders.

上

Këā **崎** Read kê, steep, difficult of ascent, a dangerous hill-path.

Sëāng pêng yëén jê k'hòng tōng, hāy bōng lëūng jê kê k'he, 上平衍而曠蕩下崇巃而崎嶇 *chëōng k'hè pang pang jê k'hwăh k'hwăh, lôh laê ōng ōng jê këā këā,* going up, the road was even and wide, but coming down, it was overgrown and steep.

平

Këna **驚** Read keng, to be afraid, to fear, to alarm.

Keng t'hëen tōng tēy che jîn, 驚天動地之人 *këna t'heeng tāng tēy ây lâng,* a man that will alarm the heavens, and move the earth.

Këna **京** Read keng, a capital city; pok keng, 北京 *pak kënâ,* the northern capital, Peking; keng sêng 京城 *këna sënâ,* a metropolis.

Këna **椋** Read keng; as kim keng bôk, 金椋木 *kim këna ch'hâ,* the name of a tree.

上

Kënâ **子** Read choó, a child, a boy, a son; choó sun, 子孫 *kenâ sun,* sons and grandsons.

Choó sun suy gê, keng se put k'hó put t'hok, 子孫雖愚經書不可不讀 *kënâ sun suy jêên gaê, keng ch'hăyh ūm t'hang bô t'hâk,* although young people may be dull, they should not neglect reading the classics.

去

Kënà **鏡** Read kèng, a looking-glass, a mirror; bëën kèng, 面鏡 *bīn kënà,* a looking-glass; bôk kèng, 目鏡 *bàk kënà,* spectacles.

Lē to put twân kèng tëung jîn, 利刀不斷鏡中人 *laē to bēy tooīng kenà tang eng ây lâng,* if a sword is ever so sharp, it will not cut asunder the reflection of a man in a mirror.

平

Kënâ **行** Read hêng, to walk, to go, to travel; to act; këak hêng, 脚行 *k'ha kënâ* to go on foot; hêng loē 行路 *kënâ loē,* to travel on the road.

Séy hêng, 所行 *séy kënâ,* that which is done; an action, a deed.

Sam jîn hêng, pit yéw gnó soo yëen, 三人行必有我師焉 *sna lâng tit kënâ, pit woō gwán ây sin saing,* when three people are walking together, there will certainly be one among them, who can be our teacher; see the 論語 Lūn gé.

Kënâ **垳** Read hêng, the name of a place; the same as 衡 hêng.

Kënâ **筕** Sae toé hêng, 篩斗筕 *t'hae taóu kënâ,* the edges of a sieve.

去

Kënā **件** Read këēn, a thing, an article; bút këēn, 物件 *mcēnh kenā,* a thing, a piece of goods; yit këēn, 一件

chit keⁿā, one thing; ké këën, 幾件 *kwúy këⁿā*, how many things?

Këⁿā 健 Read këën, robust, strong, vigorous; sin këën, 身健 *sin keⁿā*, hale in body; gnêw këën, 牛健 *goô keⁿā*, a stout ox.

K'hong këën sin t'héy, 康健身體 *an keⁿā sin t'héy*, to compose and invigorate one's body.

Këⁿā 揵 Read këën, a threshold; to shut a door.

屐

Këäh 屐 Read kėk, clogs; bòk kėk 木屐 *bàk këäh*, wooden shoes.

Këäh 擽 Read ké, to lift up anything, to take up; séw ké, 手擽 *ch'héw keäh*, to take in the hand; ké k'hé, 擽起 *këäh k'hé*, to raise anything up.

夫

Këak 脚 Vulg. *k'ha*, the foot; këak t'hòng, 脚痛 *k'ha t'hëⁿà*, a sore foot. Këak lwán sin boô pēng, t'hoê hân bók pöëy bêng, 脚煖身無病頭寒目倍明 *k'ha sëo hín sin bô paiⁿᵍ, t'haôu kwⁿâ bàk chëw pöëy kwuiⁿᵍ*, when the feet are kept warm, the body will be free from disease; and when the head is kept cool, the eyes will be doubly bright.

屐

Këak 矍 Këak sëak 矍鑠 firm, strong, robust.

Këak sëak chae, ch'hoó ong yëá, 矍鑠哉此翁也 *chong këⁿā chae, chéy léy laoû lâng*, what a stout man this old fellow is! said of 馬援 Má wân.

Këak 臄 The flesh over the mouth.

Këak 劇 To increase; exceeding, very; to sport, to trifle.

Gwüy-tèy hông lông chin hè këák, 魏帝縫囊真戲劇 *Gwüy-tèy pâng hëoⁿᵍ tëy chin chëⁿà hè keàk*, Gwüy-tèy's stitching the incense bag, was truly a trifling and foolish thing.

卋

Këang 姜 A surname.

Këang 羗 The name of a tribe of foreigners to the west, who are chiefly shepherds; also a euphonic particle. Written 羌 këang.

Këang 僵 To throw down, to overturn, to turn upside down.

Ch'huy jê këang che, 推而僵之 *ch'huy hoē e tó*, push him down.

Këang 疆 Këang kaè, 疆界 a boundary, a border, a limit.

Jip kê këang, t'hoé tëy pit, tëên yëá tē, chek yéw k'hèng, 入其疆土地闢田野治則有慶 *jip e ây këang kaè, k'hwⁿâ t'hoé tëy k'hwuy pit, ch'hân yëá tē ch'hòng, chek woō kh'hèng hō*, (the emperor) on entering the boundaries (of his nobles), and seeing the ground opened out, and the fields and wastes cultivated, will offer them congratulations; see the 孟子 Bêng choó.

Këang 薑 Vulg. *këo^ng^*, ginger. Put t'höet këang sit, 不撤薑食 *ū^m^ lê k'hè këo^ng^ chĕăh*, he would never be without ginger at his meals; said of Confucius.

Këang 韁 Má këang, 馬韁 *báy këo^ng^*, a horse's bridle. Also written 繮 këang.

T'hòk se kwuy laê, má këang hëáng, 讀書歸來馬韁響 *t'hàk ch'hăyh tooí^ng^ laê, báy këo^ng^ tân*, returning home after study, the horse's bridle rings with a tinkling sound.

Këang 橿 An oar; the handle of a hoe; a durable kind of wood.

Këang 蜣 Këang lông, 蜣蜋, insects found in excrementitious matter.

上

Këáng 襁 A cloth for binding a child, in order to carry it on the back. Vulgar, *chëāng*, to carry pick-a-back.

Këáng 繦 A string of money or cash; chông këáng ch'hëen bān, 藏繦萬里 *k'hè^ng^ cheé^ng^ kwuì^ng^ kadu chë^n^â ch'heng bān*, to lay up strings of money by the thousands and myriads.

Këáng 強 Bëén këáng, 勉強 *këó^ng^ păyh naī^ng^*, to force, to constrain. Written 彊 këáng.

Këáng wûy sëēn jê é è, 強為善而已矣 *bëén këáng chò hó tē^n^ā tē^n^ā*, you should exert yourself to do good; see 孟子 Bēng choó.

平

Këâng 強 Robnst, strong, firm; a surname. Soò sip wát këâng jê soō, 四十曰強而仕 *sè chàp hòèy kóng këâng chēw tëŏh chò kw^n^a*, at forty a person is said to be robust, and should then enter on office. See the 曲禮 K'hëuk léy.

Këâng 彊 Këâng béng, 彊猛, violent, boisterous. Këâng hwut yéw kong k'hek, 彊弗友剛克 *këâng pò ây lâng, bó kap e chò pêng yéw, tëŏh é kong gnāy yë^n^â e*, with violent persons make no friendship, but overcome them with firmness.

去

Këāng 倞 Firm, violent, harsh.

Këāng 強 Not soft, unyielding, stiff. Chew-ch'hëang bók këāng jîn yëá 周昌木强人也 *Chew ch'hëang ch'hâ gnāy ây lâng*, Chew-ch'hëang was a man as stiff as wood.

Këāng 䞶 Unbending asseverations, firm declarations.

Këāng 殭 As stiff as a dead body.

平

Keaou 嬌 A form, an appearance; yaou keaou, 妖嬌, a beautiful woman.

Jëák tek yaou keaou, tong é kim ok t'hé che, 若得妖嬌當以金屋貯之 *nā ēy tit tëŏh yaou keaou, tëŏh t'hó kim ch'hoò k'hè^ng^ e*, if I obtain a beautiful woman, I will make a golden house to put her in.

Keaou 僥 False, hypocritical; greedy of gain, and seeking it in improper ways.

Keaou 嘄 Keaou yâng, 嘄陽, the name of an animal; san ch'hut keaou yâng, 山出嘄陽 *swⁿa ch'hut keaou yâng*, the hills produce the keaou yâng animal.

Keaou 簥 A musical instrument, a large pipe. This character is now used for a sedan-chair.

Keaou 獢 To boast, to pity, to commiserate.

Keaou 驕 Keaou gō, 驕傲 *keaou t'haôu*, proud, arrogant, haughty. Hoò jê boô keaou, pîn jê boô t'hëém, hô jê? 富而無驕貧而無諂何如 *poò jê bô keaou t'haôu, sông jê bô sëep gêy, an chwⁿá?* to be rich without pride, and to be poor without flattery, what do you think of that? See the 上論 Seāng lūn.

声

Keaóu 皎 Clean, bright, white, clear. Keaóu keaóu pék k'he, 皎皎白駒 *keaóu keaóu păyh bāy*, milk-white steeds. Gwát ch'hut keaóu hêy, 月出皎兮 *gôëyh ch'hut keaóu kwuiⁿᵍ*, the moon shines bright and clear. See the 詩經 Se keng.

Keaóu 矯 False; pretending to counterfeit orders from superiors; valiant. Chô-bwân hwat keaóu cheaôu, tin sip pat tîn choo hoê t'hó Tóng-tok, 曹瞞發矯詔徵十八鎮諸侯討董卓 *Chô-mwⁿâ hwat káy cheaôu bêng, tin teaôu chàp păyh tín choo hoê, k'hè t'hó Táng-tŏh*, Chô-mwⁿâ issued a counterfeit imperial order, and summoned eighteen princes of districts to attack Táng-tŏh; see the 三國 Sam kok. Këang chae keaóu, 強哉矯, how firm and unbending! See the 中庸 Tëung yûng.

Keaóu 蹻 Proud and stubborn; also, violent and martial. Seaóu choó keaóu keaóu, 小子蹻蹻 *sèy këⁿá keaóu*, that boy is very proud. Kê má keaóu keaóu, 其馬蹻蹻 *e ây bây keaóu keaóu*, his horse is very bold.

Keaóu 攪 Keaóu jeaóu, 攪擾, to confuse, to throw into disorder. Té keaóu gnó sim, 秖攪我心 *keaóu lwān gwá ây sim*, it disturbed my mind. See the 小雅 Seaóu gnáy.

Keaóu 灚 The noise of stirring about water.

Keaóu 繳 To round; to tie a thread around an arrow, when shooting at a bird.

Keaóu 曒 Clear, bright as the sun.

Keaóu 皦 Bright and clear like a gem. Yéw jê keaóu jit, 有如皦日 *woō ch'hin chëōⁿᵍ keaóu păyh ây jit*, as bright and clear as the noonday sun; see the 王風 Ông hong.

Keaôu jô yëá, 皦如也, (the music) must be clear and distinct; see the 上論 Sëāng lūn.

Keaóu 曒 Clear, bright; to call out aloud.

Keaóu 儌 To walk, to travel.

Keaóu 賭 Read toé: to gamble, to game; toé pók, 賭博 *pwāh keaóu*, to play games of chance. Sē sûy sëet ch'hóó toé ch'hëâng séy, lóng lók hoo kwun boē chok teaou? 是誰設此賭塲所籠絡夫君暮作朝 *chē chūy sëet chéy léy keaóu t'hëōng séy, láng lók gwá ây ang matng chò chá?* who could have established these gambling-houses to entrap my husband, so as to turn the night into day?

Keaóu 褾 Read peáou: to stick up with paste; peáou pöèy, 褾褙 *keaóu pöèy*, to paste paper.

声

Keaòu 呌 Vulg. *këò:* to call, to bawl, to cry out. Also written 叫 keàou. Hék put te keaòu hoe, 或不知呌呼 *woō ây ūm chae këò hoe*, there are some who do not know how to call; see the 小雅 Seaóu gnáy.

平

Keaôu 僑 High; a lodging-house for strangers.

Keaôu 喬 High, lofty: lâm yéw keaôu bók, 南有喬木 *lâm woō kwân ây ch'hâ*, on the south there are some tall trees; see the 周南 Chew lâm. A surname.

Keaôu 嶠 A high hill, with a conical top.

Keaôu 橋 Vulg. *këô:* a bridge; kò keaôu, 過橋 *kòèy këô*, to go over a bridge. Cheaôu ông ch'hey chok hô keaôu, 昭王初作河橋 *Cheaôu ông k'hé ch'hey chò hô këô*, Cheaôu ông first made bridges over the large rivers.

Keaôu 鷮 The name of a wild fowl.

Keaôu 翹 The long feathers in a bird's tail; keaôu sëw, 翹首, to lift up the head; to look forward with expectation; dangerous, hazardous. E sit keaôu keaôu, 予室翹翹 *gwá ây sēw gwūy hëëm*, my nest is in jeopardy; see the 詩經 Se keng.

Keaôu 荍 The name of a plant.

去

Këāou 轎 Vulgar, *këō:* a sedan-chair, a chair borne on mens' shoulders. San hêng chek këāou, 山行則轎 *swna loē kënâ chek tëŏh chëy këō*, when traveling in mountainous regions, it is necessary to use chairs. Chō këāou, 坐轎 *chëy këō*, to ride in a sedan-chair.

Këāou 撟 To raise anything by a lever; to wrench.

福建方言字典

夬
Keaoûh 㔍 To lift up the foot in walking.

夬
Keaoûh 噭 To halloo, to cry out loud, to answer roughly; vicious, corrupt. Boô keaoûh èng, 毋噭應 *bôh keaoûh yìn*, do not answer roughly.

夬
Keĕh 築 Read këuk and tëuk: to build, to erect; këuk ch'hëâng, 築墻 *keĕh ch'hëŏ^ng*, to build a wall; këuk ok, 築屋 *keĕh ch'hoo*, to build a house.

Keĕh 砌 *Keĕh gîm*, 砌砛 the stones round the steps of a front door.

Keĕh 嘩 The cry of the wild fowl.

兼
Këem 兼 To unite, to join, to associate together, to blend, to include. Chew-kong soô këem sam ông, ê se soò soô, 周公思兼三王以施四事 *Chew-kong sëŏ^ng këem chéy s^na óng, ê se hêng chéy sè hāng soō*, Chew-kong thought of uniting the qualities of these three sovereigns, to practice these four good things. See the 孟子 Bēng choó.

Këem 蒹 The name of a reed, a kind of rush; këem hây ch'hong ch'hong, 蒹葭蒼蒼 *këem hây ch'hai^ng ch'hai^ng*, how green are the reeds and rushes! See the 秦風 Chîn hong.

Këem 鶼 The name of a bird, that always flies in pairs, found in the south.

Këem 縑 Cloth wove with a double thread; twilled silk. Wun wûy ong se chok tan këem e, 媼為翁須作單縑衣 *boé wûy ang tëŏh chò two^na sw^ná s^na*, a wife should weave for her husband a garment of a single thread.

Këem 緘 To seal up; to paste anything over an orifice. K'hóng choó kwan Chew beâou yéw kim jîn, sam këem kê k'hoé, 孔子觀周廟有金人三緘其口 *K'hóng choó k'hw^ná Chew bëō woō kim ây lâng, s^na hây këem e ây ch'hùy*, Confucius saw in the Chew temple, a gilt statue with its mouth thrice sealed; see the 家語 Kay gé.

兼
Këém 減 To lessen, to diminish, to detract from; kay këém, 加減, more or less. Léy choo ê këém, 禮主于減 *léy ây yaôu kín tē këém cheé*, the most essential thing in ceremony is to have as little of it as possible.

Këém 檢 To arrange, to sort out; to take account of; këém téém, 檢點, to take a list of; sûn këém, 巡檢 to go round and inspect; an office. Këem téém jit séy wûy, 檢點日所爲 *këém téém tāk yit séy chò*, to examine one's daily conduct.

Këém 撿 See këém, 搜撿, to examine, to search; këém ch'hat, 撿察, to inspect. Këém kaôu, 撿校, the name of an officer.

Këëm 鋟 The ornaments used on a horse's head.

去 Këèm 劍 A sword; pwȧt këèm, 拔劍, to draw a sword. Also written 劒 këèm. Hⁿò tê má sè këèm, 好馳馬試劍 *aè k'hëá báy ch'hè këèm*, I love to ride on horseback, and make proof of my sword; See the 孟子 Bēng chóó.

平 *Kéëm* 鹹 Read hâm: saltish, briny, of a saltish taste.

Súy wȧt jūn hāy, jūn hāy chok hâm, 水曰潤下潤下作鹹 *chúy kóng teĕh lŏh k'hè, kaòu teĕh lŏh k'hè chēw chēⁿȧ këëm*, water is said to flow downwards, and when it descends (to the sea), it becomes saltish.

上 Këëm 鐱 To stick in, to insert.

平 Këen 堅 Firm, stable, hard; këen koë, 堅固, fixed, steady. K'hó soó chè t'héng é t'hat Chîn Ch'hoé che këen kap lē peng è, 可使制梃以撻秦楚之堅甲利兵矣 *t'hang saè ch'hòng t'hûy é p'hăh Chîn Ch'hoé ây këen kăh laē to è*, (if your government is good,) you can set (your people) to make clubs, and beat down the firm armor and sharp weapons of the Chîn and Ch'hoé countries; see the 孟子 Bēng chóó.

慳 Niggardly, stingy, parsimonious; këen lin, 慳吝, close, niggardly. Tó chîn se lông, bē hé këen, 倒盡詩囊未許慳 *tó chîn se têy, bòëy chun këen līn*, turn out the whole budget of your poetical effusions; you must not be stingy.

Këen 鞬 A case for a bow.

Këen 餰 Rice water, congee, gruel.

Këen 肩 Vulg. *keng:* the shoulder; këen t'hoê, 肩頭 *keng t'haôu*, the top of the shoulder; also, to bear on the shoulders, to sustain.

Soò che ch'hëâng yëá kip këen, kwuy këèn sit kay che hⁿó, 賜之牆也及肩窺見室家之好 *soò gwá ôy ch'hëēⁿᵍ kip kaòu keng t'haou, k'hwⁿȧ ây lâng téng keèⁿᵍ ch'hoò laê ây hó*, my wall is only up to the shoulders, so that inquisitive people can see all the good that is on the premises; (meaning, that his attainments were not of that high order that could not be overlooked.)

Këen 犍 A stout ox; some say, a wild animal like a leopard, with a man's face and one eye.

Këen 豜 A three year old pig.

上 Këén 搴 To pull up; difficult; lame, halt. Boê këén hwa chwȧt ē, 毋搴華絕芋 *bŏh păyh hwa hâm kin*, do not pull up the flowers together with the bulbous roots.

Këén 驏 Këén loê, 驏驢, a kind of mule.

Kéén 謇 To speak with difficulty, to stutter.

Këén 謇 The same as the above: also, blunt discourse, straight forward words. Kóng láp këén, é k'hac soò ch'hong, 廣納謇以開四聰 *kóng k'hwŭh láp sēw tit gnāy ây wā, ê k'hwuy sè bīn ây ch'hang më^{n}â*, extensively receive straight forward discourse, in order to open out the intelligence of all quarters.

Këén 倢 Difficult; to elevate.

Këén 梘 Vulg. *kéng:* a wooden spout to carry off the water.

Këén 筧 Vulg. *kéng:* a bamboo spout; súy këén, 水筧 *chúy kéng*, a water-spout.

Këén 罥 To look aslant at anything; a kind of net.

Këén 囝 Këén choó, 囝子 *kín á*, a boy, a varlet, a slave.

Këén 僊 Yëén këén, 偃僊, proud, haughty, insulting. Also written 僭 and 倦, këén.

Këén 褰 To hold up the clothes; to tuck up the skirts of a garment. Këén sëâng sëep Chin, 褰裳涉溱 *ch'haou yín chëó^{ng} köèy Chin chúy*, to tuck up the petticoats in order to cross the Chin waters.

Këén 襪 The same as the above.

去

Këèn 見 Vulg. *keè^{ng}:* to see, to behold, to visit, to appear before. Këèn hëên soo chêy yëen, 見賢思齊焉 *keè^{ng} gaôu láng sëō^{ng} kap e chêy*, seeing a clever man, think of equaling him; see the 論語 Lūn gé. Goê bē këèn h^{n}ò tek jê h^{n}ò sek chëá yëá, 吾未見好德如好色者也 *gwá böēy k'hw^{n}à chit ây aè tek ch'hin chëō^{ng} aè sek ây lâng*, I have never seen any love virtue as they love beauty; see the same.

Këèn 建 To build, to establish. Hok-këèn, 福建, the province of Hokkëèn. When 忽必烈 Hwut-pit-lëét, or Kublai, tho Tartar conqueror of China (A. D. 1296), came to 燕京 Yëèn keng, he (bēng këèn chè sèng sëen soo K'hóng choó che heāou é, 命建至聖先師孔子之廟宇 *bēng lēng këèn tè chè sèng sin sai^{ng} K'hóng choó ây bëō ē,*) commanded them to erect the temple of the most holy sage, and first teacher, Confucius.

去

Këēn 健 Firm, strong; vulg. *kë^{n}ā:* hale, robust. Tông-t'hëen-pó, 唐天寶, in his 14th year raised an army of 100,000 men, whom he called (T'hëen-pó këēn jê, 天寶健兒 *T'hëen-pó kë^{n}ā kë^{n}á,*) T'hëen-pó's stout boys.

Këēn 件 Vulgar, *kë^{n}ā:* a thing, an article; bút këēn, 物件 *meë^{n}h kë^{n}ā*, articles.

Këēn 鍵 A lock, a fastening to a door.

Këën 犟 A stubborn ox, a bullock unaccustomed to the yoke.

Këēn 揵 The threshold of a door; to close and fasten a door.

Këen 腱 A large tendon; a principal sinew.

上

Kee^{ng} 梔 Read che: as, hông che, 黃梔 *wuî^{ng} kee^{ng},* a kind of yellow fruit, used in dyeing.

Kee^{ng} 鹻 Read këem: potash, used in the preparation of certain confectionaries, and washing clothes; hwan këen, 番鹻 *hwan kee^{ng},* soap.

去

Keè^{ng} 見 Read këèn: to see, to wait upon, to have an interview with. Tông-t'haè-chong é Pông-hëên-lêng, yit këèn bëen, jê kēw sëang sit, 唐太宗與房玄齡一見面如舊相識 *Tông t'haè chong kap Pông-hëên-léng, chit keè^{ng} bīn, ch'hin chëō^{ng} koō sëō bat,* Tông-t'haè-chong, at the first interview with Pông-hëên-lêng appeared as if he had known him for a long time. Këèn sëen jê put kip, 見善如不及 *keè^{ng} hó ch'hin chëō^{ng} bēy kip kaoù,* seeing anything good he felt as though he could not attain it.

平

Keê^{ng} 墘 Read këên: the brink, or edge of anything: haé këên, 海墘 *haé keê^{ng},* the sea-shore; káng këên, 港墘 *káng keê^{ng},* the river's side.

入

Këep 俠 By the side, side by side, together with. Têng Sëet këep kok, 滕薛俠轂 *Têng kap Seĕh ây jîn kwun-sëo këep ch'hëa kë^{n}ā,* the princes of Têng and Seĕh rode in their chariots side by side; see the 公羊傳 Kong yâng twān.

Këep 夾 To hold up on both sides, to press or squeeze together; to unite with and support. Këep kong, 夾功, to attack on both sides. Chew-kong T'haè-kong këep hoō Sêng ông, 周公太公夾輔成王 *Chew-kong kap T'haè-kong sëang pêng hoō Sêng ông,* Chew-kong and T'haè-kong held up and sustained Sêng ông on both sides; see the 左傳 Chó twān.

Këep 頰 The sides of the face, the cheeks; bëēn këep, 面頰 *bīn këep,* the jaws of the face.

Këep 筴 A sinew, a tendon; an ox sinew, used as a thong, for tying on the barb of an arrow.

Këep 郟 Këep jëùk, 郟鄏, the name of a place, where 武王, Boó ông laid the foundation of his kingdom, which he prognosticated would last for 30 ages, and 700 years. A surname.

Këep 莢 Bêng këep, 蓂莢 the name of a felicitous plant in the time of Geaôu. Jê këep, 榆莢, the leaf or blossom of a certain tree resembling copper cash:—the rulers of the Hàn dynasty finding that the current coin of the former dynasty Chîn was heavy and difficult to use, ordered the people to strike a new kind of coin like the blossom of the above tree.

Këep 鋏 The handle of a sword; also a sword.

福建方言字典

Këep 蛺 Këep tëep, 蛺蝶, a kind of butterfly.

Këep 篋 A box, a casket; këep bān, 篋槾 *kap bān*, a trunk, a chest; also written 匧 këep. Jip hák koé këep 入學鼓篋 *jip ŏh koé tē kap á*, on entering the school, they drum upon the box (containing their books, &c).

Këep 愜 To have one's wishes fulfilled; to obtain one's desires. T'hëen hāy jîn bîn bē yéw këep chè, 天下人民未有愜志 *t'hee^ng āy ây lâng pāyh sai^ng bōëy woō këep mw^n á e ây sim chè*, the people and subjects of the empire have not fully got their desires; see the 漢文帝紀, Hàn bûn tèy ké.

Këep 峽 Waters confined among the hills.

Këep 梜 Chopsticks, used by the Chinese for taking up their food. Keng che yéw ch'haè chëá yūng këep, kê boô ch'haè chëá, put yūng këep, 羹之有菜者用梜其無菜者不用梜 *t'he^ng ây woō ch'haè ây chëw yūng tē, e ây bô ch'haè ây bô yūng tē*, when the broth has any vegetables in it, we may use chopsticks (to take it up); but when there are no vegetables, we must not use chopsticks; see the 曲禮 K'hëuk léy.

Këep 劫 To take by force, to snatch away, to seize forcibly. Also written 刧 and 刦 këep. Këep ch'hëáng 劫搶 *këep ch'hëō^ng*, to rob, to plunder. Chêy Hwân-kong këep ê Loé-chong, 齊桓公劫於魯莊 *Chêy Hwân-kong ch'hëóng këep é Loé-chong*, Hwân-kong of the Chêy country plundered Loé-chong.

Këep 㧻 To plunder, to take by force; the same as the foregoing.

Këep 袷 Clothes without cotton wadding; thin clothes; këep e, 袷衣 *kap e*, a loose, flowing dress.

Këep 胛 Vulg. *kăh*: armor for the back; the flesh between the shoulders.

夬

Këet 結 Vulgar, *kat*: to tie a knot, a knot; këet lëên, 結連, to connect, to join together. Sim jû këet hêy, 心如結兮 *sim kw^na ch'hin chëō^ng kat*, the mind is, as it were, tied and bound.

Këet 袺 To hold anything in the lap; këet e, 袺衣, to hold up the skirts of the garment in order to contain anything in the lap.

Këet 桔 Vulg. *kit á*: a lemon, a lime; also written 橘 këet. Bân tëung êng këet yëw, 閩中榮桔柚 *bân sai^ng ây tang e^ng, êng hwa kit á kap nooi^ng á*, in the provinces of Hok-këèn and Canton, the lemon and the pumelo flourish.

Këet 潔 Clean; këet ch'heng, 潔清 *ch'heng k'hé sëō^ng*, clean and pure. Jîn këet ké é chìn, é kê këet yëá, 人潔己以進與其潔也 *lâng ch'hêng këet ch'heng ka tē ê chìn, lán tëōh yín e ây këet ch'heng*, when people purify themselves and enter (on office), we should allow that they are pure; see the 論語 Lūn gé. Also written 絜 këet.

Këet 偈 To exert one's strength, martial; also, hasty, vehement. Kê jîn hwuy ch'hëⁿá këet, 其人暉且偈 *e ây lâng hwuy kwuiⁿᵍ kwà këet bêng*, that man is both illustrious and courageous.

Këet 揭 To raise anything on high; to hold up; këet t'hëep, 揭帖, to open the budget, to commence an affair. Këet kan wûy kê, 揭竿爲旗 *këâh k'hê tek kóng chò kê*, they raised up a bamboo pole for a standard. Ch'him chek lēy, ch'hëén chek këet, 深則厲淺則揭 *ch'him chëw lēy köèy k'hè, k'hín chëw pǎyh k'hé sⁿa*, in the deep parts (of a river), dash through, but in crossing the shallow parts, hold up (your garments); see the 衛風 Wöèy hong.

Këet 羯 A ram; an encampment of Tartars.

Këet 鍥 A hook, a reaping-hook a crooked knife.

Këet 擑 To bale out the water; a vessel for lading out water.

Këet 桀 The same as 磔 këet, a kind of stone: rough as a stone. Also, used for 傑 këet, a hero. Also, a henroost, a place where fowls roost.

Këet 傑 A hero; chūn këet, 俊傑, a superior and clever man. Tëang-lëâng, Seaou-hô, Hân-sìn, sam cheá kae jîn këet yëá, 張良蕭何韓信三者皆人傑也 *Tëoⁿᵍ-lëâng, Seaou-hô, Hân-sìn, chéy sⁿa lâng chò poô sē jîn këet yëá*, Tëoⁿᵍ-lëâng, Seaou-hô, and Hân-sìn, these three were all heroic fellows. Also written 杰 këet.

Këet 碣 Këet sek, 碣石, the name of a hill in the eastern seas.

Këet 磔 To split, to draw out, to pull, to open, to tear asunder. Choo soó hêng kae këet ch'hē, 諸死刑皆磔市 *choo sé ây hêng hwàt chò poô tëōh këet lëet tē kay ch'hē*, all capital offenders must be punished by being pulled to pieces in the market.

Këet 竭 To exhaust, to exert to the utmost; këet chīn, 竭盡, to exhaust utterly. Soō hoō boé lêng këet kê lék, 事父母能竭其力 *hòk saē pāy boé ēy këet chīn e ây k'hwùy làt*, in serving one's parents, to be able to exert one's strength to the utmost; see the 上論 Sëang lūn.

Kek 格 To extend to the extreme point; to know thoroughly; to influence, to regulate; kek sek, 格式, a rule, a pattern. Tè te chaē kek bût, 致知在格物 *tè te sit twā tē kek chīn meēⁿh*, the highest point of knowledge is to scrutinize all things thoroughly.

Kek 亟 Hasty, rapid, vehement; keng se bût kek, sè bîn choo laê, 經始勿亟庶民子來 *k'he t'haôu ch'hông kóng bŏh kín, pǎyh saiⁿᵍ ch'hín chëōⁿᵍ kēⁿá laê*, at the commencement of the work, (he told them) not to hasten, but the people came like children; see the 大雅 Taē gnây.

Kek 假 To arrive at. Also read káy: to borrow, false; ông kek Yéw-beaōu, 王假有廟 *ông kaòu Yéw-beaōu*, the king came to Yéw-beaōu; see the 易經 Ëk keng.

Kek 𠊳 The name of some foreign nation on the west of China.

Kek 棘 Keng kek, 荊棘, thorns and briers. Also, hasty, rapid. P'he keng chám kek, 披荊斬棘 *p'he höëy keng ch'haöu chám tooi^ng kek ch'hè*, to remove the weeds and cut down the briers; see the 左傳 Chó twān.

Kek 慼 Hasty, rapid. Also, fixed, determined.

Kek 激 To collect stones together in order to stop the course of water; to influence. Kek jê hêng che, k'hó soó chaē san, 激而行之可使在山 *kek jê hoē e tó kē^n â t'hang saè e köëy sw^na*, if you stop up (the stream) with stones, and lead it along, you may make it pass over a hill; see the 孟子 Bēng choó. Kám kek bông sin, 感激忘身 *kám kek kaôu bēy kè e ây hîn sin*, to be so moved as to forget one's self.

Kek 膈 Hëung kek, 胸膈 *heng kăyh*, the midriff, the diaphragm; that which divides the upper from the lower part of the inside of the body.

Kek 嗝 The cry of a wild fowl, the crowing of a cock.

Kek 隔 To stop up, to obstruct, to separate; kek pek, 隔壁 *kăyh pëăh*, a neighbor, one who is separated from us merely by a wall.
Hông kek lōëy gōëy 防隔內外 *hong kăyh laē gwā*, to cut off all intercourse between those without and those within.

4 K

Kek 翮 The middle part of a feather, a quill; a wing. Hông hwŭn kek jê hwuy, 鳳奮翮而飛 *hōng tëō^ng e ây sit jê pwuy*, the hōng bird stretched its wings, and flew away.

Kek 篇 A bamboo screen put before a door.

Kek 槅 The yoke of a large carriage: sëang lê lëên kek, 商旅連槅 *chò seng lê ây lâng k'hăyh sëo sëò ăyh*, the caravan of traders crowded each other so much in the roads, that the yokes of their carriages touched one another.

Kek 殛 To kill, to put to death; Sŭn kek Kwún ê é-san, 舜殛鯀于羽山 *Sŭn t'haê Kwún tē é-sw^na*, Sŭn put Kwún to death at E-san.

Kek 㠚 The name of a hill.

Kek 㚇 A man under the water; to be drowned.

Kek 戟 A spear, a lance, a military weapon; tê kek, 持戟, to grasp one's spear.

Kek 擊 To beat, to strike; é sèk kek jîn, 以石擊人 *t'hó chëōh kek sê lâng*, to stone people to death. Choó kek k'hèng ê Wöëy, 子擊磬于衛 *hoo chòò p'hăh h'hèng tē Wöëy*, Confucius played on the k'hèng (a musical instrument) at Wöëy; see the 論語 Lūn gé.

Kek 格 To arrive at, to go to the extreme.

Kek **狊** The appearance of a dog staring at any one.

Kek **耤** To plough, to till the ground.

Kek **嘩** Vulg. *keĕh:* the cry of a wild fowl.

Kek **革** To change, to drive away, to deprive of office; also, leather, skin. T'hëen tēy kek, jê soò sê sêng; 天地革而四時成 *t'hee^ng tēy wⁿà jê sè sê chëⁿâ hó,* when the heavens and the earth (i. e. the dynasty) are changed, then the four seasons become good; see the 易經 Ėk keng. Kek chit wûy bîn, 革職爲民 *lut kwⁿa chò păyh sai^ng,* to be deprived of office, and to be degraded to the level of the common people. Ko yâng che kek, 羔羊之革 *ko yëô^ng ây p'höêy,* a kid-skin.

Kek **菊** Read këuk: as këuk hwa, 菊花 *kek hwa,* a chrysanthemum flower. Ch'haé këuk tong lê hây, yew jëên këèn lâm san, 採菊東籬下悠然見南山 *bắn kek hwa tē tang lê pa hāy, hwui^ng jëên k'hwⁿà lâm pee^ng ây swⁿa,* while plucking the chrysanthemum flowers in the eastern garden, I looked thoughtfully towards the southern hills.

天

Kėk **極** The topmost beam in a house; anything high; extreme, the extremity. T'haè kėk, 大極, the great extremity, which the Chinese suppose existed before the production of heaven and earth; this was itself preceded by a boô kėk, 無極 *bô kėk,* no extremity, a boundless infinity. Kwun choó boô séy put yūng kê kėk, 君子無所不用其極, *kwun choó bô séy ūm yūng e ây kėk,* the good man invariably adapts things to their best use; see the 大學 Taē hák.

Kėk **倄** Weary.

Kėk **屐** Bók kėk, 木屐 *bák këák,* wooden shoes, clogs. Soo-má-ê soó kwun soō sam ch'hëen jîn, chëak jwán chaê pêng téy bók kėk chëên hêng, 司馬懿使軍士三千人著軟材平底木屐前行, *Soo-má-ê saê e ây kwun soō sⁿa ch'heng lâng ch'hèng nooi^ng ch'hâ paî^ng tēy ây bák këák taē seng kēⁿâ,* Soo-má-ê ordered three thousand of his troops to put on wooden clogs made of soft wood with flat soles, and then to march on in front; (after which he followed with the whole army.)

Kėk **局** Read këúk: an arsenal, an armory; chëuk këúk, 促局 *chek kėk,* to bend the body, in a flattering fawning manner. Kê këúk, 棊局 *kê kėk,* the game of chess, the chess-board.

冂

Keng **冂** The uttermost border; one of the radicals.

Keng **經** Keng lûn, 經綸, a thread, a string, a series; sëâng keng, 常經, the common series of human relations. Keng hwüy, 經緯, the woof and the warp in weaving cloth; keng êng, 經營, to build, to construct; keng se, 經書, books and classics; é keng, 已經, and cheng keng, 曾經, past, gone by, already done; chèng keng, 正經, honest, upright. A surname.

Wûy lêng keng lûn t'hëen hây che taē keng, 惟能經綸天下之大經 *tók tók ēy keng lûn t'hee^ng ây twā keng*, just capable of arranging the great relations of the empire; see the 中庸 Tëung yûng.

Chaē keng yéw che, 在經有之 *tē keng woō e*, it is contained in the classics.

Keng 涇 The name of a river; Keng é Wūy chok, 涇以渭濁, *Keng ây lô chúy ch'hông Wūy ây ch'heng chúy yëá lô*, the foul waters of the Keng render the clear waters of the Wūy muddy (by mixing with them); see the 衛風 Wōēy hong.

Keng 莖 The stalk of grass, or corn.

Keng 硜 The sound of stones rattling together.

Keng 京 Vulg. *kë^na:* great, a very high hill; keng soo, 京師 *kë^na së^ná*, a capital city, a metropolis. Jip keng, 入京 *jip kë^na*, to enter the capital.

Keng 京 A granary.

Keng 庚 Vulg. *kai^ng:* one of the ten horary characters.

Keng 鶊 Ch'hong keng, 倉鶊, the name of a bird.

Keng 冏 Bright.

Keng 矜 Keng lîn, 矜憐, to pity, to commiserate. Chek ae keng jê, bût hé, 則哀矜而勿喜 *chek ae keng e, jé bô hw^na hé*, you must then pity them, and not rejoice; see the 論語 Lūn gé.

Keaou keng, 驕矜, to be proud and vaunting, to brag.

Keng 賡 To connect, to continue in succession. Naé keng chaè ko, 乃賡載歌 *naé sëo swà ch'hëò^ng kwa*, he continued to sing.

Keng 扃 The place beyond the suburbs or borders; keng keng boé má, chaē keng che yëá, 駉駉牡馬在扃之野, *pwúy pwûy ây boé báy, twā tē keng ây yëá*, fine and fat mares, in the fields beyond the suburbs; see the 詩經 Se keng; also written 坰 keng.

Keng 駉 A mare; others say, a fine fat horse.

Keng 粳 Rice; edible rice, in distinction from the glutinous rice. Tê p'hèng keng tō che tëy, 馳騁粳稻之地 *p'haòu chaôu tē keng tō ây tëy*, to gallop about amongst the corn.

Keng 更 To change, to alter, to repeat; keng loē, 更漏 *kai^ng laōu*, an hour glass. Kwun choó che kò yëá, jê jit gwàt che sit yëen; kip kê keng yëá, jîn kae gëáng che, 君子之過也如日月之食焉及其更也人皆仰之 *kwun choó ây kòëy sit ch'hin chëö^ng jit göëyh ây sit; kaòu e keng w^nà lâng chò poê gëáng k'hw^nà e*, the errors of good men are like the eclipses of the sun and moon; when they alter, all men look up to them; see the 論語 Lūn gé. Séw keng, 守更 *chéw kai^ng*, to keep watch.

Keng 耕 To plough: keng têên, 耕田 *chŏh ch'hân*, to cultivate the ground.

Tëâng-ch'he Këêt-lêk gnoé jê keng, 長沮桀溺耦而耕 *Têâng-ch'he Këêt-lêk sëo tùy chŏh ch'hân*, Tëâng-ch'he and Këêt-lêk ploughed side by side; see the 論語 Lūn gé.

Keng 荆 The name of a tree; a surname; Keng chew, 荆州, the name of a district.

Keng 肱 The upper part of the arm: keng t'hoê, 肱頭 *keng t'haôu*, the shoulders.

Hwuy che é keng, 麾之以肱 *ké hwuy e é ch'hêw*, he beckoned to them with his arm; see the 小雅 Seaóu gnáy.

K'hëuk keng jê chim che, 曲肱而枕之 *k'hëuk wan keng ch'hêw jê ch'hông chìm t'haôu*, he bent his arm under him for a pillow.

Keng 羹 Soup; ch'haè keng, 菜羹 *ch'haè kai^ng*, vegetable soup; t'heaou keng, 挑羹 *t'heaou kai^ng*, a spoon, a soup-spoon.

Keng 驚 Vulg. *kë^na*: to frighten, to alarm, to fear, to be afraid. Chín keng pek lé, 震驚百里 *chín kë^na kaôu chit păyh lé*, (the thunder) agitates and alarms to the distance of a thousand lé. Keng soó, 驚死 *kë^na sé*, to be frightened to death.

Keng 兢 Not at one's ease, uneasy: extremely anxious and careful.

Chëên chëên keng keng, 戰戰兢兢, trembling and anxious.

Keng 供 Read këung: as këung chōng, 供狀 *keng chōng*, a document drawn up respecting a man's own life and conduct to be presented to a magistrate: a written defense.

声

Kéng 景 Great, extensive, bright; kong kéng, 光景, a landscape, view of a country; a surname.

Boô pëen kong kéng, yit sê sin, 無邊光景一時新 *bô pee^ng á ây kong kéng, chit sê á sin*, a boundless prospect, which all of a sudden appears new.

Kéng gëáng, 景仰 to look up to with expectation.

Kéng 憬 To awake out of sleep, to have the attention excited; also, far, distant.

Kéng 璟 The brightness of a gem.

Kéng 儆 Kéng kaè, 儆戒 to warn, to caution, to admonish.

Kéng kaè boô gê, 儆戒無虞 *kéng kaè lâng tëo^ng tê bô t'hang ch'hek ây soō*, to admonish people to beware of unforeseen circumstances.

Kéng 警 To admonish: sûn kéng, 巡警, to go round in order to caution with authority.

T'hëen choó sûn hêng choo hoê che kok yūng kéng hoê sim, 天子巡行諸侯之國用警侯心 *hông tèy sûn kë^nâ choo hoê ây kok, yūng kéng kaè choo hoê ây sim*, the emperor perambulates the countries of the princes, in order to impress caution on their minds.

Kéng 憼 Respectful, sedate.

Kéng 竟 To exhaust, to finish, to conclude; kèw kéng, 究竟, to examine thoroughly.

Chek taē hé, lëäk te kē è, yēw put k'héng kéng hák, 籍大喜略知其意又不肯竟學 *Chék twā hwⁿa hé, lëŏh á chae e ây è, yēw ūⁿ k'héng kéng chīn t'hàk*, Chék (i. e. 項羽 Hāng-é) was greatly pleased when he understood a little of his meaning, but after all he would not complete his studies; see the 史記 Soó kè.

Kéng 境 Kéng kaè, 境界, a border, the limits of a territory.

Jip kéng jê būn kìm, 入境而問禁 *jip kéng kaè chēw mooiⁿᵍ twā kìm*, on entering the borders, ask respecting the prohibitions (or laws of the country); see the 曲禮 K'hëuk léy. Háp kéng pêng an, 合境平安, peace be within thy borders!

Kéng 耿 Kéng kaè, 耿介, noble, high-minded; also, sorrowful, distressed; a surname.

Seaóu lëên hoō chōng k'hè kéng kaè, lip ch'hëung kwan, 少年負壯氣耿介立衝冠 *sèy hàn nā hoō chit ây chōng k'hè kwà kéng kaè, chek kaôu lip ēy ch'hëung kwan*, in his youth he had a firm spirit coupled with a noble mind, and when he stood he wore his cap awry (as though he would terrify one by his looks); said of 徐敬業, Ch'hê-kèng-gëëp. Kéng kéng put bē, jê yéw yïn yew, 耿耿不寐如有隱憂 *kéng kéng bēy k'hwùn, ch'hïn chëōⁿᵍ woō yïn k'hïⁿᵍ ây hwān ló*, he was distressed and unable to sleep, as though he had some internal grief; see the 衛風 Wōëy hong.

Kéng 褧 A single garment; è kím kéng é, 衣錦褧衣 *ch'hēng kím sèw ây sⁿa, tëŏh woō twⁿa nēⁿá tē laē bīn*, when wearing a dress of embroidered silk we should have a single garment underneath; see the 鄭風 Tēng hong.

Kéng 烱 Fire burning brightly.

Kéng 炯 Very bright, clear; to examine clearly.

Kéng 泂 Distant, far; also written 迥 kéng, and 泂 kéng.

Kéng chëak pé hêng ló, 泂酌彼行潦 *hwuiⁿᵍ k'hè yëōⁿᵍ hwut léy hêng ló*, to go far and lade water out of yonder running stream.

Kéng 絅 A single garment; kéng e, 絅衣, a thin robe.

Kéng 哽 Anything stopping in the throat; to be choked with grief.

Yüng chek kéng, kéng jê put ché, chek chín, 噎則哽哽而不止則跈 *yùng t'hat chēw aè kaiⁿᵍ, kaiⁿᵍ nā bēy swăh, chēw păyh k'hé laé kēⁿá*, if you cram yourself you will be choked; but if the choking does not stop, you had better get up and walk.

Kéng 鯁 Vulgar, *kaiⁿᵍ*: to be choked with a fish-bone.

Kéng 骾 To be choked with a bone in the throat.

Kéng 熲 The brightness of fire.

Kéng 剄 To cut off the head with a knife; to decapitate, to behead. Lēng chêûng chēá Gwūy-kèng kéng che, 令從者魏敬剄之 *bēng lēng tùy ây lâng lēăh Gwūy-kèng t'haê t'haoû*, he ordered his followers to take Gwūy-kèng and decapitate him; see the 史記 Soó kè.

Kéng 拱 Read kēúng: to put the hands together; kēúng séw, 拱手 *kéng ch'héw*, to fold the hands together before the breast, as is customary with the Chinese, when they bow to a friend. Sûy kēúng jê t'hëen hāy tē, 垂拱而天下治 *pàng lŏh laê kéng ch'héw jê t'hee^ng āy paî^ng*, he merely let fall his folded hands, and the empire was regulated; said of 武王 Boó ông.

Kéng 栱 Read kēúng: as toé kēúng, 斗栱 *taôu kéng*, the capital of a pillar, in the form of a measure of corn.

Kéng 梘 Read kēén: as súy kēén, 水梘 *chúy kéng*, a rain-gutter, a spout put along the eaves of a house to carry off the rainwater.

Kéng 裥 Read kán: a plait, or fold; kwûn kán, 裙裥 *kwún kéng*, the plaits or folds of a petticoat.

去 Kèng 徑 A small road, a pathway; straight; also written 俓 kèng. Hêng put yêw kèng, 行不由徑 *kē^nâ ū^m ân kèng loē*, to travel without going along the proper road; to go out of the right way.

Kèng 逕 A road, a thoroughfare; to approach near; to go along the road.

Kèng 桱 A kind of wood like deal, but harder; beech wood.

Kèng 亙 Extreme, at length, finally.

Kèng 更 To repeat, again; more, increasing; kèng to, 更多 *k'hăh chēy*, much more. Kèng ch'hëàng tëét hō, 更唱迭和 *kŏh ch'hëŏ^ng yēw kŏh kap e hō*, to sing again, and again to reply to it.

Kèng 敬 To respect, to esteem, to reverence, to honor. Ke ch'hè këung, chip soō kèng, 居處恭執事敬 *k'këā tē lán ây wūy tëŏh këung chip lán ây soō tëŏh kèng*, dwelling in our place we should maintain a feeling of reverence, and engaging in any affair we should manifest respect; see the 論語 Lūn gé.

Kèng 鏡 Vulg. *kë^nà*: a mirror, a glass; bëën kèng, 面鏡 *bīn kë^nà*, a looking-glass. Bêng seng êng êng, k'hae chong kèng yēá, 明星熒熒開粧鏡也 *bêng ch'hai^ng yēá kwui^ng, tëŏh k'hwuy che^ng kë^nà*, when the bright stars are still twinkling, females ought to open their toilets and mirrors.

Kèng 曔 Bright, clear.

Kèng 供 Read kēùng: to afford, to offer; kēùng chae, 供齋 *kèng chae*, to offer sacrifices with respect and fasting.

Kèng 粠 Read kēùng: as ch'haè kēùng, 菜粠 *ch'haè kèng*, fruits and vegetables offered in sacrifice.

平

Kêng 睘 Standing alone, without any support; tók hêng kêng kêng, 獨行睘睘 *tók kĕⁿá bô e 'wá*, to walk alone without support.

Kêng 儝 Good; also sorrowful.

Kêng 煢 Sorrowful, distressed: sëuk yëā kêng kêng, 夙夜煢煢 *jit maiⁿᵍ hwân ló*, night and day distressed.

Kêng 惸 Sorrowful; also alone, solitary, friendless.
Yew sim kêng kêng, 憂心惸惸 *hwân ló ây sim kwⁿa kêng kêng*, a sorrowful mind, very much distressed; see the 小雅 Seaóu gnáy. Boô gëák kêng tók, 無虐惸獨 *bôh pô gëák kêng tók ây lâng*, do not oppress the solitary and friendless; see the 詩經 Se keng.

Kêng 檠 Teng kêng, 燈檠, a lamp-stand, a candlestick.

Kêng 瓊 A red gem, a precious stone of a red color.
Toê gnoê é bók lé, pò che é kêng kéw, 投我以木李報之以瓊玖 *taôu gwá ê bók lé, pò e ê kêng kéw*, they handed over to me the fruit of a tree, and I rewarded them with gems and precious stones; see the 衛風 Wōēy hong.

Kêng 擎 To beat out, to manufacture; se chëûng chuy choó kêng, 背從椎子擎 *ch'hâyh chëûng pit bōéy ch'hông*, books are manufactured by the point (of the pencil).

Kêng 黥 Bék kêng, 墨黥 to mark any one's flesh by means of puncturing it so that the figures cannot be obliterated; a punishment formerly in use in China, in order to mark and degrade criminals.

Kèng 䝩 Goods, merchandise.

Kêng 窮 Read këûng: poor, poverty; kwung choó ék yéw këûng hoê? 君子亦有窮乎 *kwun choó yëá woō kêng hoê?* may a good man also be poor? see the 論語 Lūn gé.

去

Kēng 勁 Firm, strong, hard; Teng-kong, 鄭公, drew up the "fish-net" line of battle, which was (tëung kwân hoē kēng, 中權後勁 *tang eⁿᵍ kwân sē, aōu bīn kēng kĕⁿ ā*), powerful in the centre, and firm in the rear.

Kēng 頸 The neck; t'hoê kēng pit tëung, 頭頸必中 *t'haôu kak âm kwun á, pit tëōh tek kê téung*, the head and the neck must be kept in a perpendicular line; (not bent forwards;) see the 禮記 Léy kè.

Kēng 脛 The bone of the leg; keak kēng, 脚脛 *k'ha kēng*, the shin bone. E tëāng k'hoè kê kēng, 以杖叩其脛 *t'hó kwaè á k'haôu e ây k'ha kwut*, he then took his staff and hit him over the shin; see the 論語 Lūn gé.

Kēng 烴 Warm.

Kēng 涇 The name of a river; kēng ché, 涇紙 *kēng chwá*, a kind of drawing paper.

Kēng 綆 A well-rope, a rope with which to draw water. Kēng twán chëá, put k'hó é k'hip ch'him, 綆短者不可以汲深 chaí^ng sŏh têy bô t'hang é ch'hëō^ng chúy ch'him, when the well-rope is short, we cannot take it to draw water out of a deep place.

Kēng 梗 The name of a wood; straight, correct; also, to stop up, the surface. Goê séy hák chëá, tit t'hoé kēng jé, 吾所學者直土梗耳 gwá séy ŏh ây, ch'hëng ch'hëng t'hoê kēng, that which I have studied, amounts only to the surface (or the superficial part of a doctrine). Kit kēng, 桔梗, the name of a medicinal drug.

Kēng 哽 To stop up, to be hindered, to be stiff.

Kēng 競 Forcible, violent, striving, to wrangle; cheng kēng, 爭競, to dispute.

卒

Ke^ng 鋼 Read kong: a jar, a large earthen jar; also written 㼚 kong.

Ke^ng 岡 Read kong: the name of a place, the brow of a hill. Choo kat-lëāng ke gō lëûng kong, 諸葛亮居卧龍岡 Choo-kat-lëāng k'hëà te gō lëûng ke^ng, Choo-kat-lëāng dwelt on the brow of the sleeping dragon hill.

Ke^ng 扛 Read kong, to carry on a pole between two or more people. Kong bút, 扛物 ke^ng meē^nh, to carry anything.

Ke^ng 擡 Read tae: to lift or carry anything; tae keaōu, 擡轎 ke^ng këō, to carry a sedan-chair.

去

Kè^ng 槓 Read kòng: a burden; lóng kòng, 籠槓 láng kè^ng, a burden, a load.

Kè^ng 焵 Read kòng: to harden or temper steel.

Kè^ng 鋼 Read kòng: steel; chèng kòng, 正鋼 chè^nà kè^ng, pure steel. Lëēn kòng ch'hek to, yūng che ch'hëet gëük jê ch'hëet nê yëen, 鍊鋼赤刀用之切玉如切泥焉 lëēn kè^ng ch'hëăh to, yūng e ch'hëet gëük, ch'hin chëō^ng ch'hëet t'hoé, a bare knife of molten steel may be made use of to split gems, just like splitting mud.

卒

Këo 茄 The egg-plant, called brinjal.

去

Këò 叫 Read keaòu: to call, to cry out; hék put te keaòu hō, 或不知叫號 woō ây ūm chae këò hō, there are some who do not understand the call and signal; see the 小雅 Seaóu gnáy.

平

Këô 茄 The egg-plant, called brinjal; called këo, by the people on the sea-coast.

Këô 橋 Read keaôu: a bridge; gnoé këak keaôu, 五脚橋 goé k'ha këô, the five bridges.

去

Këō 蕎 Loē keaōu, 藠蕎 loē këō, a kind of garlic. Keaōu bék, 蕎麥 këō bâyh, Polygonum fagopyrum.

Këō 轎 Read keaōu: a chair, a sedan-chair; chō keaōu, 坐轎 chēy këō, to ride in a sedan-chair.

去

Këŏh 脚 Read këak: a foot, a leg.

上

Këo^ng 薑 Read këang: ginger; ch'hae tëüng kaè këang, 菜重芥薑 *ch'haè séy tē tëüng sē kwà ch'haè kap këo^ng*, the most important among vegetables are the mustard and ginger plants; see the 千字文 Ch'hëen joō bûn.

Këo^ng 荊 Poe këang, 補荊 *poe këo^ng*, the name of a wood; also written poe këang, 補姜 *poe këo^ng*.

Këo^ng 蝠 Ch'hek këang, 赤蝠 *ch'hëăh këo^ng*, another name for a cricket; some say the appearance of a dead silkworm.

Këo^ng 韁 Read këang: a bridle; má këang, 馬韁 *báy këo^ng*, a horse's bridle.

Këo^ng 麠 Read chëang: a kind of deer without horns; the Chinese speak of a gîn chëang, 銀麠 *gîn këo^ng*, a silver antelope, of a white color, which only appears when kings inflict punishments in reason.

平

Këō^ng 強 Read këâng: strong, violent, superior; é ch'hoó kaòu pé, ch'hoó chek këâng ô pé yëá, 以此較彼則強於彼也 *t'hó chéy lëy kap hwut lëy pé kaòu, chéy lëy chëw k'hăh këō^ng ê hwut lëy*, taking this to compare with that, this then is superior to that; see the 正雅 Chèng gnáy.

平

Këō^ng 彊 Read këâng: to speak perversely, to answer harshly. Gêk këâng, 逆彊 *kăyh këō^ng*, to dispute obstinately.

Këō^ng 彊 Read këăng: awry, slanting, on one side; këăng toē, 彊脰 *këō^ng taōu*, to hold the head on one side, to keep the neck awry.

入

Këuk 匊 A handful, as much as the hands can hold; the hand bent. Chëung tëâou ch'haé lëuk, put êng yit këuk, 終朝采綠不盈一匊 *chit māy^nh chaè bán lèk ch'haôu, bô mw^ná chit ch'hëw ak*, to be gathering greens all the morning long, without filling a single handful; see the 小雅 Seaóu gnáy.

Këuk 菊 Vulg. *kek*: a chrysanthemum, an autumnal flower. Hông këuk yéw kay sek, 黃菊有佳色 *wui^ng kek hwa woo hó ày sek*, the yellow chrysanthemum has a very pretty appearance.

Këuk 掬 To take in the hand, to hold a handful. Lōng hwa hëang bwán e, këuk súy gwàt chaē séw, 弄花香滿衣掬水月在手 *lāng hwa p'hang mw^ná s^na, këuk chit ch'hëw chëō^ng āy chúy, göëyh chëw twā tē ch'hëw*, when we play with flowers the scent will fill our clothes, and if we take up a handful of water, (the reflection of) the moon will be in our hand.

Këuk 踘 To kick; táp këuk, 蹹踘, a football: now called p'hô kêw, 皮球 *p'höëy këw*, a leathern football.

Këuk 畮 A field of scallions and leeks.

Këuk 椈 Pek këuk, 柏椈 a pestle made of cedar wood.

Këuk 鞠 To nourish, to feed, to bring up; also to bend, to stoop; glorious. Boé hêy këuk gnó, 母兮掬我 *nëŏng lêy ch'hē gwá*, my mother nourished me; see the 小雅 Seaóu gnáy. A surname. Jip kong bûn, këuk këung jê yëá, 入公門鞠躬如也 *jip kong áy moot^ng chēw këuk sin áy yëōng*, (Confucius,) on entering the prince's gate, would exhibit an appearance of bending his body; see the 論語 Lŭn gé.

Këuk 鞫 To examine criminals; to inquire into, to exhaust, the utmost. Sìn këuk lûn pò, 訊鞠論報, to inquire to the utmost into criminal accusations, and to deliberate on the proper retribution.

Këuk 檋 A straight pole to a carriage; also, a short piece of iron fastened to the carriage to prevent its going backwards, used in ascending steep places. San hêng sêng këuk, 山行乘檋 *sw^na kën^á sêng këuk*, traveling over hills, we must make use of the këuk.

Këuk 臼 The hands crossed or clasped together; the same as 匊 keuk.

Këuk 暴 A vessel for bringing up food.

夾

Këuk 局 To divide, a separate portion, a division of labor; the hair twisted. Kok soo kê këuk, 各司其局 *kok lăng kwán e ây hwŭn*, let each one attend to his particular charge; see the 曲禮 K'hëuk léy. E hwat k'hëuk këuk, 予髮曲局 *gwá ây mô k'hëuk këuk*, my hair is all twisted together; see the 小雅 Seaóu gnáy. Këuk chëuk, 局促, deformed, dwarfish. Kê këuk, 棊局, the game of chess.

Këuk 跼 Bent, crooked; wŭy t'hëen kaè ko, put kám put këuk, 謂天蓋高不敢不跼 *kóng këò t'hee^ng kaè kwán, ŭ^m k^ná ŭ^m këuk*, we may say of heaven that it is high, and therefore we dare not refuse to stoop under it; see the 小雅 Seaóu gnáy.

Këuk 侷 Këuk chëuk, 侷促, small and dwarfish.

共

Këung 恭 To respect, to have a reverence for, to esteem, to venerate. Kê hêng ké yeá këung, kê soō sëang yëá kèng, 其行已也恭其事上也敬 *e kën^á tē ka tē ây soō yëá këung, e hòk saē sè twā yëá kèng*, he was respectful in his private conversation, and reverential in serving his superiors; see the 論語 Lŭn gé.

Këung 共 The same as the preceding.

Këung 恭 Careful, thoughtful; also, respectful.

Këung 龔 A surname.

Këung 供 To offer up, to provide, to prepare; to nourish, to present with. Gnó këët lêk keng tëên, këung wûy choó chit jê é è, 我竭力耕田供爲子職而已矣 *gwá chīn k'hwùy lát chŏh ch'hân, këung chò haōu sai^ng ây chit hwūn tē^n ā tē^n ā,* I exert my strength in cultivating the fields in order to provide what is necessary to fulfill the duties of a son, and nothing else; see 孟子 Bēng choó. Kám put këung kip, 敢不共給 *k^n á u^m këung kip,* how dare we not afford and present it!

Këung 弓 A bow; a surname; këung sé soo tëang, 弓矢斯張 *këung chee^ng tëŏh tëo^ng,* the bow and arrow drawn out and ready; see the 大雅 Taē gnáy.

Këung 躬 The body, one's own person; the body bent, as a bow; also written 船 këung.
Koé chëá gân che put ch'hut, t'hé këung che put taē yëá, 古者言之不出耻躬之不逮也 *koé chá ây lâng kóng wā ū^m ch'hut, sē seaōu léy hîn sin ây kë^n â bēy kaōu,* the ancients were unwilling to speak out, because they were ashamed when not in person (i. e. in reality,) equal to their professions.

Këung 宮 A palace; këung sit, 宮室, a house, a dwelling, a surname.
Pe këung sit, jê chīn lĕk hoē koe hok, 卑宮室而盡力乎溝洫 *pe sèy ch'hoò t'hâyh, jê chīn k'hwùy làt tē kaou hok,* he left his residence small and mean, while he exhausted his strength on the channels and water-courses; see the 語論 Lūn gé.

Këung 蠪 A kind of insect; séw këung, 守蠪, the name of an insect which is said to guard the house.

Këung 膣 Gwàt këung, 月膣, *göëyh keng,* the menses.

上聲

Këúng 拱 To hold anything in both hands; këúng pá che tōng choó, 拱把之桐梓 *këúng páy ây tōng choó,* a tōng choó tree that may be spanned with both hands; see 孟子 Bēng choó.

Këúng 栱 A large wooden ladle; toé këúng, 枓栱 *taōu kéng,* the capital of a pillar; also small rafters sticking out in the front of a pillar in order to support the extended roof.

Këúng 珙 A large gem; suy yéw këúng p'hek boô ek yëá, 雖有珙璧無益也 *suy woō twā ây p'hek yëá bô lē yëăh,* although one may have a large gem, it is of no use; said by 老子 Ló choó.

Këúng 共 To verge towards, to move towards, to be opposite to.
P'hè jê pok sîn, ke kê séy, jê chëùng seng këúng che, 譬如北辰居其所而衆星共之 *ch'hin chëō^ng pak ch'hai^ng, k'hëā tē e ây só chaē, jê chëùng ch'hai^ng ^nâ e,* just like the north star, which rests in its position, and all the rest of the stars verge towards it; see the 上論 Sëāng lūn.

Këúng 鞏 Firm, stable; to strengthen, to establish.
E këúng ông sit, 以鞏王室 *é këúng koē ông kong ây ch'hoò,* in order to establish the royal house; see the 左傳 Chó twān.

Këúng 廾 One of the 214 radicals.

去聲

Këùng 供 To appoint; also to afford, to bring in, to offer.

平

Këûng 窮 Poor, destitute, exhausted, to exhaust; pîn këûng, 貧窮 sông hëung, poor and exhausted; këûng chīn, 窮盡, to carry to the utmost.

Soò haé k'hwùn këûng, t'heen lók éng chëung, 四海困窮天祿永終 sè haé kaôu k'hwùn kéng, t'hee^ng ây hông lòk éng chëung, when all within the four seas are poor and distressed, the emoluments of the ruling power will surely come to an end; see the 論語 Lūn gé.

Këûng gwân kéng wûy, 窮源竟委 këûng e ây gwân t'haôu, kéng e ây wûy k'hëuk, to exhaust the springs, and search to the utmost the windings of an affair.

Këûng 藭 Ch'hwan këûng, 川藭, the name of a medicine.

Këûng 竆 K'heung këûng, 嶗竆, a hilly appearance.

Këûng 窮 The name of a country, to which 羿 Gēy was appointed ruler, who afterwards usurped the chief sway in China.

Këûng 倸 To scold, to rail; këûng sëûng, 倸倯, to ridicule a person as dwarfish and contemptible.

Këûng 粱 Fine rice.

去

Këûng 共 Together with, all alike, to share equally with any one. E pông yéw këûng, pē che jê boô hâm, 與朋友共敝之而無憾 hap pêng yéw këûng yûng, pē p'hwà jê bô hâm hwûn, to allow one's friends the common use of anything, and not to be grieved when our things are spoiled; see the 論語 Lūn gé.

上

Kew 丩 Anything twisted and tied together.

Kew 疝 Kew kaôu, 疝絞 kew ká, a griping pain in the intestines; the colic.

Kew 繆 Kew kaôu, 繆絞, to strangle, to hang; Teaōu hông hoē choō kew soó, 趙皇后自繆死 Tëō hông hoē ka tē kew sé, the empress of Tëō strangled herself.

去

Kéw 久 Vulg. koó: long, a long time; kéw è, goê put hëw bōng këèn Chew kong, 久矣吾不復夢見周公 koó è, gwá bô bô kŏh bāng kee^ng Chew kong, it is now a long time since I dreamed of Chew kong; see the 論語 Lūn gé.

Kéw 九 Vulg. kaôu: nine; kéw sip, 九十 kaôu chàp, ninety; sip kéw, 十九 chàp kaôu, nineteen. Kéw tëûng, 九重, the nine times doubled apartments, alluding to the emperor's palace, and sometimes to the emperor himself. Kéw tëûng ch'hun sek chùy sëen t'hô, 九重春色醉仙桃 kaôu tëûng ây ch'hun sek ch'hin chëō^ng woō chùy sëen ây t'hô, the vernal countenance of his majesty looks as if he were intoxicated with angels' peaches.

Kéw 咎 To destroy, to demolish, to injure.

福建方言字典

Kéw 玖 A black stone, resembling a gem; kêng kéw, 瓊玖, precious stones.

Kéw 韭 An aromatic vegetable; kéw ch'haĕ, 韭菜 koó ch'haĕ, scallions; a kind of leeks. Tûn ch'hun chek yūng kéw, 豚春則用韭 te băh ch'hun t'hee^ng chek yūng koó ch'haĕ, eating pork in the spring, we must use scallions with it; see the 內則 Lōēy chek. One of the radicals.

Kéw 糾 A rope twisted together; Hwân-kong kéw háp choo hoĕ, 桓公糾合諸侯 Hwân-kong kéw háp choo hoĕ, Hwân-kong collected and united the princes together; see the 左傳 Chó twān.

Kéw 赳 Military, martial; kéw kéw boó hoo kong hoĕ kan sêng, 赳赳武夫公侯干城 kéw kéw ây boó hoo sē kong hoĕ ây kan ko sĕ^n â tē, martial and fierce brave fellows are the shields and fortresses of a prince; see the 周南 Chew lâm.

Kéw 殧 A surname.

Kéw 糺 Three ropes twisted together; a threefold cord.

去

Kèw 救 To save, to deliver; kèw sè, 救世, to save the world. Chēw T'hong jê söēy che, é hwát Hāy kèw bîn, 就湯而說之以伐夏救民 chēw kaôu T'hong jê söēy e, tĕŏh hwát Hāy teaôu kèw păyh sai^ng, he went to T'hong, and advised him to attack the Hāy dynasty, and save the people; see 孟子 Bēng choo.

Kèw 究 To search, to examine thoroughly; káng kèw, 講究, to inquire into. Sēng tek put kip. kèw ê t'hëen hāy, 盛德不及究於天下 hó ây tek bēy kip kèw tē t'hee^ng hāy, your complete virtue has not yet extended to all in the empire.

Kèw 灸 To cauterize, to apply fire to the body for medicinal purposes.

Kèw 疚 A chronic disease; a long sickness. Yew sim k'hóng kèw, 憂心孔疚 hwân ló ây sim kwⁿa chin chaē koó pai^ng, a sorrowful mind, long distressed; see the 小雅 Seaóu gnáy.

Kèw 廐 A stable; má kèw, 馬廐 báy teaôu, a stable for horses. Kèw hwún, choó t'hùy teaôu wát, sëang jîn hoĕ, put būn má, 廐焚子退朝曰傷人乎不問馬 báy teaôu sīo, hoo choó t'hèy teaôu kóng woō sëang lâng hoĕ, bô mooi^ng báy, when the stable was burnt, Confucius, on returning from court said, 'is any man hurt?' not inquiring after the horses; see the 論語 Lūn gé.

平

Kêw 求 To ask, to seek for, to pray; kêw sîn, 求神 to pray to God. Kwun choó kêw choo ké, seaóu jîn kêw choo jîn, 君子求諸己小人求諸人 kwun choó kêw choo ka tē, seaóu jîn kêw choo pat lâng, the man of worth seeks everything from himself, but the worthless character seeks everything from others; see 程子 Têng choó.

Kêw 俅 The ornament of a cap.

Kêw 捄 Long, lengthened out; also, bent; yéw kêw kê kak! 有捄其角 woō tê^ng e ây kak! how very long was his horn! see the 周頌 Chew sëüng.

Kêw 九 The name of a country.

Kêw 仇 An enemy, an antagonist, an opponent; also a surname. E choó tông kêw, 與子同仇 kap lé chò tâng kêw, he and you are mutual foes; see the 秦風 Chîn hong.

Kêw 逑 A partner, a fellow, a mate; yaóu t'heaóu sëuk lé kwun choó h^n ó kêw, 窈窕淑女君子好逑 yaôu t'heaôu ây hó cha boé kap kwun choó hó chò sëo kêw, a modest and retired woman is an excellent partner for a man of worth; see the 周南 Chew lâm.

Kêw 球 A beautiful gem; a globe; t'hëen kêw, 天球, a celestial globe; tēy kêw, 地球, a terrestrial globe. Also, the sound of a gem.

Kêw 絿 Hasty, rapid; some say, slow.

Kêw 毬 A ball; hè kêw, 戲毬, a play ball; p'hê kêw, 皮毬 p'höéy kêw, a football.

Kêw 裘 A fur dress, a dress of skins with the hair on. A surname. Sêng hwûy má, è k'heng kêw, 乘肥馬衣輕裘 k'hëâ pwûy báy, ch'hèng k'hin kêw, to ride on fat horses, and to wear light fur dresses; see the 論語 Lūn gé.

Kêw 賕 To employ wealth in order to pervert the laws; to use bribes.

Kêw 觩 Bent, crooked; soō kong kê kêw! 兕觥其觩 sae kak ây chêw pöey, e ây wan k'hëuk! a wine-cup made of a rhinoceros' horn, how crooked it is! see the 小雅 Seaóu gnáy.

Kêw 厹 Three cornered, triangular, a triangular spear.

Kêw 紌 Hasty, rapid; to seek.

Kêw 虯 A horned dragon; some say, a dragon without horns; also written 虬 kêw.
Yëen yéw kêw lëūng, hoō hîm é yêw? 焉有虯龍負熊以遊 t'hae t'hó woō kêw lëûng gëâ chit hîm ê t'hit t'hó? when was there ever seen a horned dragon carrying a bear in his rambles? see the 楚詞 Ch'hoé soô.

Kêw 鼽 A stoppage of the nose through cold, a catarrh.
Kwùy ch'hew hêng hāy lêng bîn to kêw t'hè, 季秋行夏令民多鼽嚏 ch'hew böëy kë^n â ch'hin chëö^ng hāy t'hee^ug lêng pâyh sai^ng chëy sât p'hee^ng, kwâ p'hâh ch'hêw, in the end of autumn to act as we do in summer will occasion frequent colds and sneezings.

Kêw 銶 A kind of chisel; kè p'hô gnó hoó, yêw k'hwat gnó kêw, 既破我斧又缺我銶 kè jëên p'hwâ gwá ây poó t'haôu, yëw k'hè k'heëh gwá ây ch'hàk á, having broken my hatchet, they have also notched my chisel; see the 詩經 Se keng.

丟

Kēw **舊** Vulg. *koō:* old, original, former; kêw lëên, 舊年 *koō neë^ng^*, last year.

Koe kēw put wûy, 故舊不遺 *koè koō ây jîn sîn, ū^m^ t'hang wûy k'hè*, do not neglect old servants. Kê sin k'hóng kay, kê kēw jê hô? 其新孔嘉其舊如何 *e ây sin sìm hó, e ây koō an chw^n^á?* if (our wives) when new were so very good, how much better must they be now they are old? see the 詩經 Se keng.

Kēw **臼** Vulg. *koō:* a mortar; chëung kēw, 舂臼 *cheng koō*, a pestle and mortar.

Twān bók wûy ch'hé, kwut tēy wûy kēw, kēw ch'hé che lē, bān bîn é chèy, 斷木爲杵掘地爲臼臼杵之利萬民以濟 *tooì^ng^ ch'hâ chò cheng, kwut tēy chò koō, cheng koō ây lē yëäh, chë^n^â bān bín e chèy kîw*, cut off a piece of wood for a pestle, and dig a hole in the ground for a mortar; for the profit of the pestle and mortar tends to supply myriads of people; see the 易經 Ėk keng.

Kēw **咎** A fault, a crime; to find fault with. Kè óng put kēw, 旣往不咎 *kè jëën ông kö'y, bô lëäh ê chò kēw*, when a thing is past, do not find fault with it; see the 上諭 Sëāng lūn.

Kēw **柩** Kwan kēw, 棺柩 *kw^n^a ch'hâ*, a coffin.

Kēw **舅** Bó kēw, 母舅 *bó koō*, a mother's brother: ch'hey kēw, 妻舅, a wife's brother.

Gnó sòng kēw sē, wát chê Wûy yâng, 我送舅氏曰至謂陽 *gwá sàng gwá ây koō ó, kóng böëyh kaòu Wûy ây lám*, I accompanied my maternal uncle, saying, that I would go as far as the south of the river Wûy; see the 秦風 Chîn hong.

卆

Key **稽** To examine; key k'hó, 稽考, to investigate at the public examinations; also written 稽 key, to detain, to keep. A surname.

Key k'hó ch'hut sin, 稽考出身, to come forward in the world by means of the literary examinations.

Key **嵇** A surname; Key-k'hong 嵇康, was one of the seven wise men of the bamboo grove.

Key **鷄** A domestic fowl; key boé, 鷄母, a hen. Also written 雞 key.

Lé wát key bêng, soō wát möëy tàn, 女曰鷄鳴士曰昧旦 *cha boé kóng key tit t'hé, ta po kóng âm böëy kwui^ng^*, the wife said, 'the cocks are crowing' (it is time to rise); but the husband replied, 'it is not yet light;' see the 鄭風 Tēng hong.

Key **鸂** Key laē, 鸂鶒 *key lwā*, a water fowl.

Key **街** A street, a way; key loē, 街路, a street, a road. Kap tèy bëën tëàng key, 甲第面長街 *ch'hoò t'hâyh bīn^n^â t^ng^ key*, a range of buildings facing the long street.

Key **乩** To divine, in order to discover things which are doubtful. In the western countries they divine by goat's blood, which they call 厮乩 soo key.

Key **笄** A hair-pin, the knot in which the hair is tied.

Sip yéw gnoé lëën jê key, 十有五年而笄 *chàp goē höëy jê key*, (females) at fifteen years of age tie up their hair and use a hair-pin.

Key 階 Read kae: a step; gîm kae, 砛階 *gîm key*, a flight of steps. Bût kae ch'he, ėk jê yĕá, 沒階趨翼如也 *bût chīn gîm key, chēw máy^nh kē^nâ ch'hin chēō^ng pwuy ây yĕō^ng*, when he had descended all the steps (from the throne), he walked quickly, as though he were flying; (said of Confucius, when he had an audience with the prince;) see the 論語 Lūn gé.

上聲

Kéy 改 Read kaé: to change, to alter, to reform. Kò jê put kaé, sē wūy kò è, 過而不改是謂過矣 *woō kōèy sit jê ū^m kéy, sē kóng kēò woō kōèy sit*, having a fault and not reforming, this is what may be called having a fault indeed; see the 論語 Lūn gé.

Kéy 解 Read kaé: to dissolve, to disperse, to loosen, to untie. Kaé swat, 解說 *kéy söĕyh*, to explain; kaé k'hae, 解開 *kéy k'hwuy*, to unravel, to unfold; kaé këet, 解結 *t'haóu kat*, to untie a knot. Wûy sūn ê hoō boé, k'hó é kaé yew, 惟順於父母可以解憂 *tòk tòk sūn tē pāy boé t'hang é kéy hwân ló*, but to render his parents obedient to virtue, this alone could dissipate his sorrow; see 孟子 Bēng choó.

去聲

Kèy 計 A plan, a scheme; to plan, to calculate; to reckon; a surname. Sip lëên ch'hut chēw göèy hoō hák se kèy, 十年出就外傳學書計 *châp hōèy tëōh ch'hut kee^ng gwā bīn ây sin sai^ng ŏh sĕá jē kap swui^ng sĕdou*, at ten years of age, boys should go abroad to a teacher out of doors, and learn writing and arithmetic. Hāng-lëâng tëâou choo chëâng kèy soō, 項梁召諸將計事 *Hāng-lëâng tëâou e ây chëâng soō nëō^ng soō*, Hāng-lëâng called all his generals to consult over the business; see the 史記 Soó kè. Kèy boê, 計謀 a plan, a contrivance; kwúy kèy, 詭計 artful schemes.

Kèy 繼 To connect; kèy sëùk, 繼續 *sëo swà*, to hand down in connection. Kèy chwàt sè, ké hwùy kok, 繼絕世舉廢國 *sëo swà chwàt tooi^ng ây sè, ch'hòng k'hé hwùy bŏ ây kok*, to keep up the succession of a declining family, and to raise a ruined nation.

Kèy 檵 Koé kèy, 枸檵, the name of a wood.

Kèy 髻 A lady's cap; a small kerchief, used for tying up the hair.

Kèy 疥 Read kaè: a small sore, a breaking out; hāy sê yéw yāng kaè che chit, 夏時有痒疥之疾 *hāy t'hee^ng ây sê, woō chëō^ng sai^ng kèy ây pai^ng*, in the summer time people get the itch and cutaneous disorders.

平聲

Kēy 鮭 Read haê: pickled fish, or salted shrimps; kèy chëep, 鮭汁, catchup or soy.

去聲

Kēy 易 Read ē: easy, not difficult; ē soō, 易事 *kēy soō*, an easy matter.

入聲

K'ha 脚 Read këak: the leg, the foot; këak t'hong, 脚痛 *k'ha t'hē^nâ*, a sore foot.

福建方言字典

聲

K'há **巧** Read k'haóu: clever, artful; kê k'haóu, 奇巧 *kê k'há*, strange, wonderful. Kong-se-choó che k'haóu, put é kwuy ké, put lêng séng hong wân, 公輸子之巧不以規矩不能成方圓 *Kong-se-choó áy k'há, nā bô yūng kwuy ké, chêw bēy chēⁿâ sè kak eé^{ng} cé^{ng}*, with all Kong-se-choó's cleverness, if he had not rule and compass, he could neither make squares nor circles; see 孟子 Bēng choó.

聲

K'hà **扣** Read k'hoè: to beat, to strike; k'hoè bûn, 扣門 *k'hà mooi^{ng}*, to rap at the door. Tëang-hwa wát, k'hò ch'hó tông chaê, k'hek wûy gê hêng, k'hoè che chek bêng, 張華日可取桐材刻爲魚形扣之則鳴 *Tëo^{ng}-hwa kóng, t'hang t'hăyh tâng ch'há, k'hek chô hê áy yëō^{ng}, k'hà e chēw tân*, Tëo^{ng}-hwa said, 'you can take a piece of the tông wood, and carve it into the shape of a fish, and when struck, it will sound.'

聲

K'hⁿa **坩** Hwān kam, 飯坩 *pooi^{ng} k'hⁿa*, a rice-dish.

K'hae **開** Vulg. *k'hwuy*: to open, to unfold, to open out. Kwun choó che kaôu jê yëá, k'hae jê bút tát, 君子之教喻也開而勿達 *kwun choó áy kâ hwün k'hwuy jê bô tát bêng*, the good man in communicating instruction, expounds the subject, without fully explaining it; see the 禮學記 Léy hák kè.

K'hae **揩** To rub, to wipe; to wave the hand.

40

聲

K'haé **愷** To rejoice, to be glad; also written 豈 k'haé. K'haé lók yím chéw, 愷樂飲酒 *k'haé lók lim chéw*, to rejoice and drink wine.

K'haé **塏** Sóng k'haé, 爽塏, swept and cleansed.

K'haé **鎧** K'haé kap, 鎧甲, armor, a coat of mail. Ch'he-yêw sé chok k'haé 蚩尤始作鎧 *Ch'he-yêw k'hé t'haôu chò k'haé kăh*, Ch'he-yêw was the first that invented armor (in order to fight with); 黄帝, Hông tèy (B. C. 2622).

K'haé **覬** K'haé jê, 覬覦, to hope for; to desire. Hāy boô k'haé jê, 下無覬覦 *hāy téy áy pāyh suì^{ng} bô t'hang bāng*, the lower classes have nothing to look forward to; see the 左傳 Chó twān.

K'haé **凱** Good, excellent; a triumph after victory; harmonious, soothing. Choè k'haé jê kwuy, 奏凱而歸 *chaòu k'haé jê tooi^{ng} laê*, they sang a triumph on their return. K'haé hong choō lâm, 凱風自南 *hô áy hong choō lâm*, the genial breezes blow from the south; see the 詩經 Se keng.

K'haé **楷** A form, a pattern; a mould, a plan; the correct form of writing. T'hëen hāy boē k'haé, 天下楷模 *t'hee^{ng} āy áy boē yëō^{ng}*, a pattern for the whole empire; k'haé se, 楷書, the correct form of writing, without contractions or alterations.

圭

K'haè 嘅 The sound of sighing.

K'haè 漑 To pour, to inundate, to bring under water. Sey-bûn-pà yín Chëang súy k'haè Gëëp, 西門豹引漳水漑䲜 *Sey-bûn-pà yín Chëang chúy k'haè Gëëp sëⁿâ*, Sey-bûn-pà led the waters of the Chëang and inundated Gëëp; see the 史記 Soó kè.

K'haè 槩 A striker for leveling the top of a measure; taē k'haè, 大槩, generally. Tëūng ch'hun che gwåt, chèng kwân k'haè, 仲春之月正權槩 *tëūng ch'hun ây gōëyh tëōh chëⁿâ ch'hìn kap k'haè*, in the middle month of spring, rectify the steelyards and strikers; see the 禮月令 Léy gwåt lēng. Also written 概 k'haè.

K'haè 慨 K'hóng k'haè, 慷慨, a noble mind under disappointment, to be ready at promising. K'hóng k'haè tâm sim ē, chëûng yûng chēw gē lân, 慷慨談心易從容就義難 *k'hóng k'haè tâm sim k'hwaè, chëûng yûng chēw gē ŏh*, to be ready at promising, and to speak out all one's mind is easy, but to go cheerfully where duty calls is difficult.

K'haè 墍 K'haè ok, 墍屋 *bwåt ch'hoò*, to plaster a house.

K'haè 暨 To arrive at, to reach to. A surname.

K'haè 愾 To fetch a long sigh, to breathe hard; to arrive at. Kwun hêng ch'hoó gnoé chëá, chek k'haè hoē t'hëen hāy è, 君行此五者則愾乎天下矣 *lé kèⁿâ chéy goē hāng, chek kaòu hoē t'heeⁿᵍ āy è*, prince, if you do these five things, you will influence the whole empire.

K'haè 𡠩 Very firm; anything solid and substantial.

K'haè 欬 The wind rising in the throat; to cough.

K'haè 咳 To cough; k'haè sok 咳嗽 *k'hám saòu*, to have a cough. Hēng bûn k'haè sok che seng, 幸聞咳嗽之聲 *hēng t'hëⁿa k'hám saòu ây sëⁿa*, I luckily heard the sound of coughing.

K'haè 揩 To rub or wipe anything.

夲

K'haeⁿᵍ 唛 The sound of joy.

夬

K'hăh 籗 Kead k'hap: a wicker-basket with a small mouth, used by fishermen to put the fish in when they are caught; tëuk k'hap choó, 竹籗子 *tek k'hăh á*, a wicker fish-basket.

K'hăh 袷 A single thin garment; chèy k'hăh, 縩袷, a kind of cloth.

夾

K'hăh 𤸪 Hoē k'hăh, 瘕𤸪, anything sticking in the throat.

夲

K'haiⁿᵍ 坑 Read k'heng: a valley, a ravine.

大

K'haiⁿᵍʰ 喀 The noise of vomiting, or the sound of coughing.

丆

K'haiⁿᵍʰ 嗄 Read ch'hày: the noise of coughing, or sobbing.

大

K'hak 確 Certain, sure; tek k'hak, 的確, true, real; truly.

K'hak hoē kē put k'hó pwát, 確乎共不可拔 *k'hak sit, kadu bēy pwát*, so sure that it cannot be altered.

K'hak 佸 The name of an ancient emperor; also written 嚳 k'hak.

K'hak 傕 A man's name; Lé-k'hak, 李傕, a famous general in the 三國, Sam kok.

K'hak 殼 The shell of anything. Also written 壳 k'hak, the outer skin.

K'hak 愨 Sincere, careful; yéw k'hak soō chëá, 有愨士者 *woō sêng k'hak ây t'hàk ch'hǎyh lâng*, here is a sincere scholar.

K'hak 恪 To respect, to esteem; chip soō yéw k'hak, 執事有恪 *chip soō woō kèng k'hak*, to attend to business seriously.

K'hak 麴 Read k'heuk: leaven; pèk k'hëuk 白麴 *pây̆h k'hak*, a preparation of grain, used in fermenting liquor; also written 粬 k'hëuk.

丆

K'hàk 㱿 The appearance of a tent; also, to vomit; also written 声 k'hàk.

求

K'ham 堪 Worthy; k'ham tek, 堪得, worthy to obtain; put k'ham, 不堪, unworthy, insupportable.

Sîn yéw hô kong, k'hó é k'ham che? 臣有何功可以堪之 *lé woō sⁿa meëⁿh kong lô, t'hang k'ham kadu hwut lêy soō?* what merit have you, to render you worthy of such an office?

K'ham 嵁 K'ham gâm, 嵁巖, ground that is uneven, a hilly appearance.

K'ham 𢇓 To press down.

K'ham 嵌 A deep part of the hills.

K'ham 戡 To kill, to put to death; also written 㦸 k'ham.

K'ham 龕 A shrine for inclosing an idol; sîn k'ham, 神龕, an idol's shrine. Sèng jîn k'ham, 聖人龕, the shrine of a sage.

声

K'hám 坎 Dangerous, hazardous; k'ham k'hó, 坎坷, unfortunate, full of difficulties.

K'hám 凵 To open the mouth wide; one of the radicals.

K'hám 砍 To cut with a knife; to cut down, to lop off.

K'hám 轗 K'hám k'hó, 轗 軻, difficulties, troubles; also written 埳 k'hám.

K'hám 歁 Insufficient, sorrowful, sad, dissatisfied. Hoō che é Hân Gwūy che kay, jê kē choō sè k'hám jëên, 附之以韓魏之家而其自視欿然 *t'hëep e é Hân Gwūy ây kay soō, jê c ka tē k'hwⁿà ch'hin chëōⁿᵍ bó kadu*, if you were to give him all the riches of the houses of Hân and Gwūy, he himself would look dissatisfied; see 孟子 Bēng choó.

去

K'hàm 勘 To compare, to examine, to investigate an affair. Sím k'hàm soō lé, 審勘事理, to judge and examine into things.

K'hàm 瞰 To look upon; to look downwards from a height.

K'hàm 矙 To look at, to espy; Yâng-hⁿò k'hàm K'hóng choó che bông yëá, jê kwūy K'hóng choó tûn, 陽貨矙孔子之亡也而饋孔子豚 *Yâng-hⁿò k'hwⁿà K'hóng choó ây bó tē tit, jê sàng K'hóng choó te*, Yâng-hⁿò watched till Confucius was from home, and then presented him with a pig; see 孟子 Bēng choó.

K'hàm 闞 To look at, to spy; the same as the above. A surname.

K'hàm 墈 A high shore or bank.

K'hàm 磡 A precipitous bank.

K'hàm 嵌 Lofty; a high dangerous bank.

K'hàm 紺 A deep azure, a kind of purple color. Kwun choó put é k'hàm choe sek, 君子不以紺緅飾 *kwun choó bó lëâh k'hàm choe ây sek chò nëⁿá*, the good man does not use a purple or a crimson color to make the collar of his coat; see the 論語 Lūn gé.

K'hàm 戡 To take.

平

K'hâm 痷 K'hâm k'hoé, 痷 痁, a disease not easily cured.

去

K'hām 硆 Sëang k'hām 相硆 *sëo k'hām*, to push against one another, to dodge one another's elbows.

去

K'han 刊 To cut, to carve, to scrape, to eradicate, to erase. Pit se wûy pe bûn, jëên hoē k'han sék yëen, 必須爲碑文然後刊石焉 *pit tëôh chò chit ây pe bûn, jëên aōu k'han chëôh*, you must draw up an inscription, and then we will have it engraven on stone. K'han pán, 刊板, to cut wooden blocks for printing.

K'han 看 To behold, to look, to see; also pronounced k'hàn.

Ch'héng k'han che hék tëung, kéng sē sûy kay che t'hëen hāy, 請看之域中竟是誰家之天下 *ch'hëⁿá k'hwⁿa e hék tëy tang eⁿᵍ, kéng sē chē chūy kay ây t'heeⁿᵍ āy*, pray look abroad into the country, and see after all to whose family the empire will belong.

K'han 牽 To draw, to drag, to pull, to lead; k'han bwán, 牽挽, to pull and haul. Yéw k'han gnêw, jê kò tông hāy cheá, 有牽牛而過堂下者 *woō k'han goó, jê kŏèy tē tông āy ây lâng*, there was one leading an ox, and passing by at the foot of the hall; see the 上孟 Sëāng bēng.

声

K'hán 侃 Stiff and straight; rigid and upright; also, harmonious and agreeable. E hāy taē hoo gân, k'hán k'hán jê-sëá, 與下大夫言侃侃如也 *kap hāy taē hoo kóng wā, ch'hin chëō^ng gnāy tit ây yëō^ng*, when he conversed with any of the inferior officers, he was friendly and upright; see the 論語 Lūn gé.

K'hán 衎 Pleased, harmonious and agreeable; sincere.

K'hán 肯 Read k'héng: to be willing.

去

K'hàn 看 Vulg. *k'hwⁿà*: to look, to see, to behold. Ch'hëen lé soo san bōng tëung këèn, yaòu se pà kwūn kwuy laê k'hàn, 千里思山夢中見要須罷郡歸來看 *ch'heng lé sëō^ng swⁿa, bāng tang e^ng k'hwⁿà, tek k'hak tëōh pà kwūn toot^ng laê k'hwⁿà*, when a thousand miles from our native hills, we think and dream of them, and feel obliged to give up our government and return to visit them.

声

K'hang 空 Read k'hong: empty, exhausted, void; k'hong hwát kê sin, 空乏其身 *k'hang hwát e ây hin sin*, empty and exhausted is his person; see 孟子 Bēng choó.

4 P

K'hang 孔 Read k'hóng: a hole; p'hek k'hong, 壁孔 *pëăh k'hang*, a hole in the wall.

K'hang 眶 Read k'hong: a socket; bók k'hong, 目眶 *bàk k'hang*, the socket of the eye.

声

K'háng 孔 Read k'hóng: a hole; bëēn k'hóng, 面孔 *bīn k'háng*, the face, the countenance. Boô bëēn k'hóng, 無面孔 *bô bīn k'háng*, ashamed to look at any one.

去

K'hàng 掐 To take up anything with the nails.

K'hàng 曠 Read k'hòng: wide, waste; k'hòng tēy, 曠地 *k'hàng tēy*, a wilderness; k'hòng poe, 曠埔 *k'hàng poe*, a wide field.

K'hàng 炕 K'hòng ch'hông, 炕床 *k'hàng ch'hêng*, a wide place for a bed, having neither posts nor curtains.

声

K'haou 敲 To knock, to strike; also, to shave, to plane. Seng k'haou gwát hāy bûn, 僧敲月下門 *hŏèy sëō^ng k'haou goĕyh ây moot^ng*, the priest knocks at the door by moonlight.
K'haou to, 敲刀, a plane; k'haou pang, 敲梆, to plane boards.

K'haou 鬮 To draw out, to draw lots; a lot, a share. Lëem k'haou ch'hé hwun, 拈鬮取分 *k'hëŏh k'haou t'hăyh hwun*, to divide by lot.

K'haou 墝 An unevenness of ground; a poor, barren soil.

K'haou 磽 Stony ground; poor, barren soil: niggardly, parsimonious. Chek tēy yéw hwûy k'haou, 則地有肥磽 *chek tēy woō pwûy woō sán*, some parts of the soil are fertile and some sterile; see 孟子 Bēng chóo.

K'haou 尻 The back; k'haou chit, 尻脊 *ka chëăh*, the back, the spine. T'hoè k'hè k'haou, 兔去尻 *t'hoè tëŏh k'hè ka chëăh*, the back-bone of a rabbit should be taken out; see the 禮內則 Léy lōëy chek.

上聲

K'haóu 巧 Vulg. *k'há:* clever, artful, expert; intriguing, specious. K'haóu gân lêng sek, sëén è jîn, 巧言令色鮮矣仁 *hó kaōu e ây wā, hó e ây bīn sek, chëó woō jîn*, when persons are fair in their words, and smooth in their appearance, they are seldom virtuous; see the 上論 Sëāng lūn.

K'haóu 口 Read k'hoé: the mouth; swá k'hoé, 洒口 *swá k'haóu*, to rinse the mouth.

去

K'haòu 噭 An uneven stony place; also, real; and to carve.

K'haòu 哭 Read k'hok: to weep, to cry, to howl. K'hok k'hip che ae, 哭泣之哀 *k'haòu k'hip ây ae*, the lamentations of weeping and howling.

K'haòu 扣 Read k'hoè: to cut off; k'hoè tê, 扣除 *k'haòu tê*, to deduct.

K'haòu 釦 Read k'hoè: a loophole; léw k'hoè, 鈕釦 *léw k'haòu*, a button-hole.

K'haòu 簆 Read k'hoè: as k'hoe k'hong, 簆框 *k'haòu k'hong*, an instrument used in weaving.

去入

K'haŏuh 餗 K'haŏuh pók péng, 餗薄餅 *k'haŏuh pŏh pēⁿá*, a mince-pie, a sort of confectionary made of mince meat.

K'haŏuh 确 Stony ground; yêw k'haŏuh, 油确, an oil measure.

下入

K'haŏuh 礉 K'hòng k'haŏuh, 硡礉, stony, uneven ground; rough traveling.

去

K'hap 閤 An inner door; the door of an inner apartment. Gō kwuy k'hap lōëy put ch'hut, 臥閨閤內不出 *k'hwùn tē kwuy k'hap laē ūᵐ ch'hut*, sleeping within the inner apartments, and not coming out; see the 史記 Soó kè.

K'hap 郃 The name of a river. Peaceful, harmonious.

K'hap 跲 To stumble; gân chëên têng, chek put k'hap, 言前定則不跲 *kóng wā taē seng tëⁿā tëŏh, chek bēy k'hap tëŏh*, when words are previously settled, there will be no misunderstanding; see the 中庸 Tëung yûng.

K'hap 祫 A general united sacrifice to ancestors; k'hap chèy, 祫祭, a general sacrifice.

K'hap 恰 Union of heart, attention; just then; k'hap hⁿó, 恰好, apropos.

K'hap 鞈 Leather coverings for the knees.

福建方言字典

K'hap 闔 The leaf of a door; to shut a door. The whole, generally.

K'hap 蓋 The name of a city; also read kaè: for, to cover. Ong soó K'hap taē hoo, Ong-hwan, wûy hoō hêng, 王使蓋大夫王驩爲輔行 *ông saé K'hap ây taē hoo, Ong-hwan, chò hoō hêng*, the king sent a great officer of the city of K'hap, named Ong-hwan, to be his assistant in the expedition; see 孟子 Bēng choó.

K'hap 榼 A wine vessel; hêng jîn chip k'hap sîn yím, 行人執榼承飲 *hêng jîn gim chêw k'hè nēⁿá lim*, the attendants held the wine vessels, and received the liquor; see the 左傳 Cho twan.

K'hap 磕 The sound of stones striking against one another.

K'hap 瞌 To sleep; k'hap sùy, 瞌睡 *ka chŏēy*, to slumber, to doze. Bók k'hap, 目瞌 *bák k'hăyh*, the eyes closed.

K'hap 搕 To take; k'hap sap, 搕𢶍, dirty, filthy.

入

K'hat 戞 A long spear, a lance; also, to strike. K'hat súy, 戞水, to lade water. Also written 戛, k'hat.

K'hat 㓤 To take off the skin, to flay; k'hat bëēn, 㓤面, to tattoo; to brand as a punishment.

K'hat 渴 Vulg. *kwăh:* thirsty; k'hoé k'hat, 口渴 *ch'hùy kwăh*, to be thirsty. K'hat chëá ē wûy yím, 渴者易爲飲 *kwăh ây lâng k'hwaè chò lim*, thirsty people are not particular about what they drink; see 孟子 Bēng choó.

K'hat 尅 Read k'hek: to fix, to appoint; k'hek sê tēng jit, 尅時定日 *k'hat sê tëⁿā tëŏh jit*, to appoint a time, and fix a day.

上平

K'hay 伽 Cheng k'hay, 僧伽, the appellation of a priest.

K'hay 茄 Vulg. *kêô:* the egg-plant, brinjal; the Solanum melongena.

K'hay 骩 A pain in the limbs; a contraction of the hands and feet.

K'hay 呿 The mouth wide open.

K'hay 佉 The name of a god.

K'hay 恪 To be afraid, to be alarmed; to have many underhand schemes. Also read 佫, k'hày: as k'hày gây, 恪伢, to abound in secret plans; hidden, concealed.

下平

K'hây 㧙 To be jammed between anything; not straight, distorted.

上入

K'hăyh 搿 To lay hold of anything; to hold anything in the hand.

K'hăyh 客 Read k'hek: a guest; jîn k'hek, 人客 *lâng k'hăyh*, a stranger, a guest. Sin k'hek, 新客 *sin k'hăyh*, a new-comer; k'hek jîn, 客人 *k'hăyh lâng*, a native of the mountainous districts in the province adjoining to Canton.

K'hek laê choó put koè, choō sē boô lëâng pin, 客來主不顧自是無良賓 *k'hăyh laê choó lâng ūm chëâou koè, choō jëên sē bô sⁿa hó ây lâng k'hăyh*, when a stranger comes, and the master does not pay proper attention to him, it is certainly because he is not a respectable guest.

K'hăyh 鵲 Read ch'hëak: a felicitous bird; ch'hëak nëáou, 鵲鳥 *k'hăyh chëáou*, a certain bird, which by its cry is said to indicate the approach of strangers. Wûy ch'hëak yéw chaôu, 維鵲有巢 *tòk tòk k'hăyh chëáou woō chò sëw*, the felicitous bird makes its nest, &c.; see the 召南 Seaôu lâm.

K'hăyh 䁟 Bòk k'hăyh, 目䁟 *bàk cheo k'hăyh*, the eyes closed.

K'hăyh 篋 Read keëp: a box, or satchel, for carrying books to school.

幸

K'he 欺 To deceive, to betray; to disgrace, to despise; k'he kwun, 欺君, to betray the confidence of one's prince; k'he hoō, 欺負, to despise. Boô choō k'he yëá, 毋自欺也 *ūm t'hang ka tē p'hëèn*, do not deceive yourself; see the 大學 Taē hák.

K'he 駒 A colt, a young horse; a steed above five feet high is called 駒, k'he, a colt; and one above six feet high is called 馬, má, a horse. Ló má hwán wûy k'he, 老馬反爲駒 *laōu báy hwán chò báy á*, an old horse turned colt; see the 小雅 Seaóu gnáy.

K'he 倛 Bông k'he, 蒙倛, an ugly mask for frightening away evil spirits.

K'he 袪 A kind of sacrifice, for imploring blessings and averting evils; to refuse; to send; also written 佉 k'he. Also signifies a sleeve, the cuff of a sleeve; to lift up the clothes.

K'he 拘 To stop, to hold, to take hold of, to seize. Chīn chip k'he, é kwuy ë Chew, 盡執拘以歸于周 *chò poê lëăh lëăh, é kwuy kaôu Chew*, they were all apprehended and taken back to Chew; see the 書經 Se keng.

K'he 痀 The back bent; a humpback, a curved spine.

Tëūng-nê sek Ch'hoé, ch'hut ê lîm tëung, këèn k'he loê chëá, 仲尼適楚出于林中見痀僂者 *Tëūng-nê k'hè kaôu Ch'hoé, ch'hut ê ch'hëw nâ tang eⁿg, k'hwⁿà keèⁿg wun koo ây lâng*, Tëūng-nê (Confucius) went to the Ch'hoé country, and when he came out of the forest, he saw some humpbacked people.

K'he 劬 K'he lô, 劬勞, labor, fatigue; wearied, tired. Boé sē k'he lô, 母氏劬勞 *nëóⁿg léy tëŏh bwâ*, our mothers undergo much labor and fatigue; see the 衛風 Wöēy hong.

K'he 區 A class, a sort, a share, a portion; k'he lūy, 區類, a class; k'he hwun, 區分, to separate; yit k'he, 一區 *chit k'hoo*, a small portion.

P'hè choo ch'hó bòk, k'he é pëet è, 譬諸草木區以別矣 *ch'hìn chëōⁿg ch'haôu bàk, k'he lūy é hwun pëet*, like as vegetables and trees, which may be classed, in order to distinguish them; see the 論語 Lūn gé.

K'he 軀 K'he t'héy, 軀體, the body; sin k'he, 身軀, one's own body. Hat chëuk é bé ch'hit ch'hek che k'he chae? 曷足以美七尺之軀哉 *an chwⁿá ēy o ló ch'hit ch'hëŏh ây hîn sin chae?* how can you admire a mere body seven spans long? (The mind is the standard of the man.)

K'he 樞 The name of a spinous tree; an outer garment; also, deep.

K'he 敺 To drive, to urge on by force. Wûy chông k'he ch'hëak chëá chëen yëá, 爲叢敺爵者鸇也 *wûy ch'hēw châng kwⁿá chäyh á sē lae hëŏh chëáou,* that which drives the sparrows into the bush, is the hawk; see 孟子 Bēng choó.

K'he 驅 To ride on horseback, to beat a horse; to drive away. Chaè tê chaè k'he, 載馳載驅 *woō ây tê chaóu woō ây tit k'he,* some were galloping, and some were ambling; see the 衛風 Wōëy hong.

K'he 軀 The same as 軀 k'he, the body.

K'he 犄 The name of an ox.

K'he 攲 To take up anything with chopsticks, or pincers. Uneven.

K'he 蹊 K'heaou k'he, 蹺蹊, to lift up the feet in walking; also, a road. T'hô lé put gân, hāy choō sêng k'he, 桃李不言下自成蹊 *t'hô lé bô kóng wā, āy téy ka tē chēⁿá loē,* the peach and plum trees do not speak (to call people to them), and yet underneath a track is soon formed (by those who come for the fruit).

4 Q

K'he 僛 To sport and gambol, when merry with wine.

K'he 摳 To lift up with the hand; k'he e, 摳衣, to lift up one's clothes. K'he e ch'he gê, 摳衣趨隅 *päyh k'hé sⁿa á, jê chaóu k'hè kak,* hold up your clothes, and get into a corner (on seeing a superior); see the 曲禮 K'hëuk léy.

K'he 嶇 Kê k'he, 崎嶇, uneven ground, a steep rough ascent; a hill-path.

声

K'hé 起 To arise, to elevate, to raise up, to get up; k'hé laê, 起來, to rise up; hin k'hé 興起, to elevate; k'hé chok, 起作, to commence; k'hé ch'hey, 起初, the commencement, in the beginning; k'hé sin, 起身, to set out on a journey. K'hé è chëá, Sëang yëá, 起予者商也 *ēy hwat k'hé gwá ây lâng, sē Sëang,* he who will be able to display my doctrines, is Sëang; said by Confucius in the 論語 Lūn gé. Chó k'hé ē chëûng lëâng jîn che séy che, 蚤起施從良人之所之 *chá k'hé laê k'hwⁿa k'hwⁿa á t'hàn ta po lâng ây séy kaōu,* she arose secretly and followed to see where her husband went; see 孟子 Bēng choó.

K'hé 豈 How? An exclamation indicating doubt. Jëák sèng é jîn, chek goê k'hé kám? 若聖與仁則吾豈敢 *ch'hin chëōⁿᵍ sèng kap jîn, chek gwá chae kⁿá?* how can I presume to be considered as a sage or a virtuous man? said by Confucius in the 論語 Lūn gé.

K'hé 企 Vulg. *naiⁿᵍ:* to stand on tiptoe, and look forward with expectation.

Jit yeā k'hè, jê bōng kwuy, 日夜企而望歸 *jit maing naing k'hé, jê bāng tooing,* day and night on the tiptoe of expectation, and hoping to return (to one's native village); see the 高祖紀 Ko choé ké. By some this character is read t'hé.

K'hé 豈 The name of a vegetable.

K'hé 芑 A fine kind of grain like millet; also, the name of a garden vegetable.

K'hé 綺 A kind of silk; thin sarsnet.

K'hé 齒 Read ch'hé: a tooth; k'hoé ch'hé, 口齒 *ch'hùy k'hé,* the teeth. One of the radicals.

去

K'hè 去 To go, to depart; ch'hut k'hè, 出去, to go out. K'hè che jit, sūy sew kê tëēn lé, 去之日遂收其田里 *k'hè ây jit, lëem peeng sew e ây ch'hân lé,* on the very day of (a minister's) departure, immediately withdraw his emoluments from the land; see 孟子 Bēng choó.

Bê-choó k'hè che, 微子去之 *Bê-choó k'hè e,* Bê-choó departed from him; see the 論語 Lūn gé.

K'hè 厺 The ancient form of the above.

K'hè 亟 Hastily, frequently, often, repeatedly. Hnò chëûng soō jê k'hè sit sê, k'hó wūy tè hoē? 好從事而亟失時可謂知乎 *aè chëûng soō, jê tàk puè sit sê, t'hang kóng woō tè hwùy hoē?* to be fond of engaging in public affairs, and repeatedly to miss the proper time; can such a man be considered wise? see the 論語 Lūn gé.

K'hè 企 Vulg. *naing:* to stand on the tiptoe of expectation. Also written 𠈌 k'hè.

K'hè 跂 The same as the above; k'hè ê bōng che, 跂予望之 *naing k'hé laè gwá tit bāng e,* standing on tiptoe, I look forward with expectation; see the 衛風 Wöēy hong.

K'hè 契 To unite, to join together; sorrowful, miserable. K'hè háp, 契合, united; k'hè se, 契書, a bond, an agreement.

K'hè 氣 Spirit, breath, influence; ch'hwán k'hè, 喘氣 *ch'hwán k'hwùy,* to draw the breath, to breathe, to pant; also written, 炁 k'hè.

Gnó sëēn yáng goê hō jëên che k'hè, 我善養吾浩然之氣 *gwá gaōu yëōng ch'hē gwá hō jëên ây k'hè,* I am skillful in maintaining my buoyant spirits; see the 孟子 Bēng choó.

Pîn k'hè soō put sit chëá, 屏氣似不息者 *pîn chăh e ây k'hwùy ch'hin chëōng bēy ch'hwán,* he held in his breath, as though he could not breathe; said of Confucius, when he waited on his sovereign; see the 論語 Lūn gé.

K'hè 气 Yîn k'hè, 雲气, the influence of the clouds. One of the radicals.

K'hè 棄 To reject, to cast away; to desert, to turn the back upon.

K'hè jê wûy che, 棄而違之 *t'hek kak jê wûy k'hè e,* he rejected it and departed from thence; see the 上論 Sëāng lūn.

Jé chwán k'hè ê, 爾轉棄予 *lé hwat lìn tooing*

福建方言字典

t'hck kak gwá, you have changed and discarded me; see the 小雅 Seaóu gnáy.

K'hè 揭 To lift up the clothes, in crossing the water.

K'hè 憩 K'hè sit, 憩息, to stop, to desist; also written 憇 k'hè.

K'hè 愒 To stop, to stay; put sëāng k'hè yëen, 不尙愒焉 *ūm sëāng hāyⁿh twā*, he did not judge it right to stop; see the 小雅 Seaóu gnáy.

K'hè 器 An implement, an instrument, a tool, a vessel, an utensil.
Kwun choó put k'hè, 君子不器 *kwun choó āy lāng bēy ch'hin chëóng ke k'hè*, a good man is no tool (that can be applied merely to one use, and not to another); see the 論語 Lūn gé.
Seng sat k'hè béng e hók put pē, put kám é chèy, 牲殺器皿衣服不備不敢以祭 *t'haou saiⁿᵍ k'hè béng yin chëóng bô chëdou pē, chëw ūm kⁿá laê chèy*, the sacrificial animals, implements, vessels, and suitable apparel, not being fully prepared, we do not presume to sacrifice; see 孟子 Bēng choó.

K'hè 弃 The ancient form of 棄, k'hè.

平

K'hê 騎 Vulg. *k'hëâ*: to ride astride; k'hê má, 騎馬 *k'hëâ báy*, to ride on horseback.
Pék má k'hwà kim an, k'hê ch'hut bān jîn k'hàn, 白馬掛金鞍騎出萬人看 *pāyh báy k'hwà kim wⁿa, k'hëâ ch'hut bān lâng k'hwⁿà*, a white horse, furnished with a golden saddle; to ride out on such, amongst myriads of spectators.

K'hê 蜞 P'hêng k'hê, 蟛蜞, a kind of crab, or crawfish, not eatable.
Goê k'hê, 蜈蜞, a leech.

去

K'hē 柹 Hông k'hē, 紅柹, a kind of China fig or date; the Diospyrus kaki. Also written 柿 k'hē.
K'hē kó, 柹菓, dried figs, for exportation.

上

K'hëa 奇 Read kê: odd, an odd number.
Yâng kê jê yim gnoé, 陽奇而陰偶 *yâng soè k'hëa, jê yim soè gnoé*, the male numbers are odd, and the female are even.

K'hëa 單 Read tan: only, single, the opposite of double. Söèy boē e sëâng tan, 歲莫衣裳單 *neëⁿᵍ matⁿᵍ jê yin chëóⁿᵍ k'hëa*, the year is approaching to a close, and I have only a single garment.

平

K'hëâ 騎 Read k'hê: to ride on horseback; chëên yéw ke k'hê, 前有車騎 *chêng tëōh woō báy ch'hëa kap lâng k'hëâ*, in front let there be carriages and people on horseback; see the 曲禮 K'hëuk léy.

去

K'hëā 伽 *K'hëā lâm sîn*, 伽藍神, the name of a god of the Budhists.

K'hëā 豎 Read sē: to place erect, to raise up, to establish, to set upright. Sē chē, 豎柱 *k'hëā t'heaōu*, to erect a pillar; sē kê, 豎旗 *k'hëā kê*, to hoist a flag.
K'hwà pëên sē kê, 掛匾豎旗 *k'hwà peëⁿᵍ k'hëā kê*, to hang up a board and hoist a flag; (done for those who have attained literary honors.)

去

K'hēⁿà 慶 Read k'hèng: to congratulate; k'hèng hō, 慶賀 *k'hēⁿà hō*, to felicitate.

Haôu sun yéw k'hèng, 孝孫有慶 *woō haôu ây sun woō k'hēⁿà hō*, a filial grandchild will congratulate (his ancestors); see the 大雅 Taē gnáy.

入

K'hĕăh 隙 Read k'hek: fluted, an interstice; k'hòng k'hek, 壙隙 *k'hàng k'hĕăh*, waste ground.

Ong-bóng lwān, sé k'hae k'hek tēy, 王莽亂始開隙地 *Ong-bóng chok lwān, chēw k'hé t'haôu k'hwuy k'hĕăh tēy*, when Ong-bong stirred up rebellion, the people began to clear waste ground for cultivation.

入

K'hëak 却 To refuse, to reject, not to receive. Lo! behold! also written 郤 k'hëak. K'hëak che! k'hëak che! 却之却之 *ūᵐ t'heēⁿᵍh e! ūᵐ t'heēⁿᵍh e!* refuse it! refuse it! see 孟子 Bēng choó. A surname.

K'hëak 怯 To be afraid, to be alarmed at, to be apprehensive.

Kēèn seaôu tèk k'hëak, kēèn taē tèk chek put k'hëak, 見小敵怯見大敵則不怯 *k'hwⁿà keèⁿᵍ sèy ây tèk chēw kēⁿa, k'hwⁿà keèⁿᵍ twā ây tèk chēw ūᵐ kēⁿa*, on seeing a small enemy he used to be alarmed, but on seeing a great enemy, he was never afraid; said of 光武 Kong-boó.

K'hëak 埆 Uneven ground; some say, barren ground, sterile soil.

K'hëak 皵 Dry skin, the skin dried up.

K'hëak 㲉 To strike the head.

K'hëak 躩 To kick the heels about; to keep walking backwards and forwards. When Confucius was employed in the business of his prince, he (chëuk k'hëak jê yëá, 足躩如也 *k'ha tin tāng ây yëōⁿᵍ,*) kept his feet always in motion; see the 論語 Lūn gé.

入

K'hëák 壆 A hard lump of earth.

去

K'hëang 腔 K'hëang tcaôu, 腔調, hollow vain ostentation; also a note in music. Vulg. *k'hëoⁿᵍ*: a dialect.

K'hëang 鏗 Read k'hëen: the noise of metal or gems tinkling together.

Koé sek he, k'hëen jé, 鼓瑟希鏗爾 *p'hăh koé sek swăh, yëá woō k'hëang ây sēⁿa*, when the playing on the drum or guitar has ceased, there is still a tinkling noise; see the 論語 Lūn gé.

去

K'hëáng 嬈 The appearance of disorder and confusion; disordered.

去

K'hëàng 哓 The incessant crying of children.

去

K'heaou 橇 A kind of carriage or vehicle for traveling through the mud.

Nê hêng sêng k'heaou, 泥行乘橇 *kēⁿà tē nwⁿā t'hoê, chēw chēy k'heaou*, in traveling across the mud he used a sledge; said of 禹 E, when he regulated and drained off the waters.

K'heaou 敲 To strike, to beat.

K'heaou 蹺 To raise the foot in walking; to stand on one leg; also written 蹻 k'heaou. K'hó k'heaou chëuk t'haē yëá, 可蹻足待也 *t'hang k'heaou k'hé k'ha têng haōu*, we can stand on one leg and wait for it; (intimating that it will not be long;) see the 高祖紀 Ko choó ké.

K'heaou 蹺 To stand on tiptoe, to raise the leg; k'heaou k'he, 蹺蹊, to lift up the leg in walking.

K'heaou 撬 To raise anything up by means of a lever, to wrench.

去

K'heáou 翹 High; k'heaóu sin, 翹身, to raise up one's body; finely dressed, elegant.

去

K'heàou 竅 A hole, a hollow place, a cavity, a cave, an opening.
Ch'hit k'heàou lêw hëet, 七竅流血 *ch'hit k'hang laôu höëyh*, blood flowed from the seven orifices; (i. e. the ears, eyes, nostrils, and mouth.)
Goê bûn sèng jîn sim yéw ch'hit k'heàou, 吾聞聖人心有七竅 *gwá woō t'hëⁿa sèng jîn ây sim kwⁿa woō ch'hit ây k'hang*, I have heard that there are seven apertures in the heart of a sage. (Said by a tyrant, who under pretense of looking for them put a wise man to death.)

K'heàou 徼 To follow out, to perambulate; to go around the borders; a small road, or pathway.
K'heàou beāou, 徼妙, abstruse and profound.
K'heàou sûn keng soo, 徼循京師 *k'heàou sûn këⁿa seⁿâ*, to perambulate the capital; k'heàou tō, 徼道, a pathway. Ló-choó sëâng yéw é kwan kê k'heàou, 老子常有以觀其徼 *Ló-choó sëâng woō ê k'hwⁿà e ây k'heàou*, Ló-choó was constantly occupied in investigating abstruse subjects.

K'heàou 敿 K'hòng k'heàou, 硑敿, high and low; uneven.

去

K'heaŏuh 嘐 *K'heaŏuh k'heaŏuh*, 嘐嘐, an unintelligible jargon.

入

K'heaŏuh 碻 Read köëy: the name of a place.

去

K'heĕh 缺 Read k'hwat: cracked, split, having a flaw, not perfect, incomplete.

入

K'heĕh 臞 Read kê: thin, meagre; hêng yûng sim kê, 形容甚臞 *e ây yëōⁿᵍ chin chaē sán*, his appearance was very meagre.

平

K'hëem 謙 Humble, diffident; k'hëem sûn, 謙遜, humble, lowly, meek.
K'hëem k'hëem kwun choó, 謙謙君子 *sèy jē ây kwun choó*, a meek and unassuming good man; see the 易經 Ék keng.

上

K'hëém 慊 Not easy, dissatisfied; a discontented mind; unsettled purpose.

K'hëém 歉 Grain blasted in its growth; corn not coming to perfection.
Lëên yéw hong k'hëém, 年有豐歉 *neêⁿᵍ woō hó kap baē neêⁿᵍ tang*,

4 R

the years are sometimes fertile, and sometimes unproductive.

K'hëém 慊 Dissatisfied, indignant. Also read k'hëet: contented, happy. Hêng yéw put k'hëém ê sim, chek lŏéy è, 行有不慊於心則餒矣 *këⁿâ nā woō ūᵐ k'hwⁿa wăh tē sim kwⁿa, chek lŏĕy è*, when there is anything in our conduct that our minds are dissatisfied about, then the spirit of magnanimity is extinguished; see 孟子 Bēng choó.

K'hëém 嗛 The pouch on the side of the mouth, where monkeys store their food; to hold or contain anything; the crop or craw of a bird. The same as the above.

K'hëém 謙 Quiet and still; contented, satisfied, pleased. Ch'hoó che wūy choō k'hëém, 此之謂自謙 *chéy sē kóng kĕò ka tē k'hëĕm chëuk*, this is what is called being self-satisfied; see the 大學 Taē hák.

K'hëém 槏 The posts on the side of a window.

去

K'hëèm 欠 To owe, to come short, to be indebted; k'hëèm chëèn, 欠錢 *k'hëèm cheéⁿᵍ*, to owe money; k'hëèm k'hwat, 欠闕 *k'hëèm k'hŏëyh*, to be deficient.

Kim chëá sông choō hêng, séy hwaê boĕ yit k'hëèm, 今者誠自幸所懷無一欠 *tⁿa ây sé chin chëⁿâ ka tē heâou hĕng, séy sëōⁿᵍ ây soō bŏ chit hăng k'hëèm*, at this time I am truly fortunate; for I have everything that I desire.

K'hëèm 芡 K'hëèm sit, 芡實, a medicinal herb.

K'hëèm 傔 To wait upon; k'hëèm jîn, 傔人, an attendant, a follower.

平

K'hëêm 伶 K'hëêm choo, 伶侏, a musician, a performer.

K'hëêm 拑 To hold fast, to hold under one's arm; k'hëêm k'hoé, 拑口 to shut the mouth, to be silent.

T'hëen hāy che soō k'hëêm k'hoé put kám hĕw gân è, 天下之士拑口不敢復言矣 *t'heeⁿᵍ āy ây t'hàk ch'hāyh lâng chò poĕ háp ch'hùy ūᵐ kⁿá kŏh kóng*, all the scholars in the empire are obliged to shut their mouths, and they dare not speak any more.

K'hëêm 笘 The name of a bamboo; also, k'hëêm k'hoé, 笘口, to close the mouth.

K'hëêm 鉆 To take hold of anything with pincers; to bind anything round with iron.

K'hëêm 鈐 K'hëêm sûy, 鈐鏞, a large kind of ploughshare.

K'hëêm 鉗 The same as 鉆, k'hëêm. Vulg. *k'heĕⁿᵍ á:* a pair of pincers.

K'hëêm 黚 A dark yellow color.

K'hëêm 黔 Black; k'hëêm séw, 黔首, the black-headed people. A designation of the Chinese.

福建方言字典

K'hëëm 喊 Read hám: to shut the mouth.

妻

K'hëëm 儉 Saving, thrifty, parsimonious; t'haè k'hëëm, 太儉, over-stingy, niggardly.

K'hëëm goê chëûng chëûng, 儉吾從衆 *k'hëëm soō gwá t'hàn chëùng lâng*, in that which is saving, I follow the generality; see the 論語 Lūn gé.

Hoo choó wun lëâng këung k'hëëm jëâng, 夫子温良恭儉讓 *hoo choó wun jêw, lëâng tit, këung kèng, k'hëëm chat, sëo nëóng*, our master (Confucius) is affable, kind, respectful, parsimonious, and yielding; see the 論語 Lūn gé.

牵

K'hëen 愆 A fault, an error, a crime; chöëy k'hëen, 罪愆, a sin.

Kwun choó yéw sam k'hëen, 君子有三愆 *kwun choó woō sna hâng k'hëen sit*, the good man is apt to fall into three mistakes.

K'hëen 幵 Even, level, flat; a surname; also written 开, k'hëen.

K'hëen 僁 The common way of writing 愆, k'hëen, a fault.

K'hëen 搴 To take up; k'hëen kê, 搴旗, to seize a standard.

Kwŭy-poè lé kwun k'hëen kê chëá sok è, 季布履軍搴旗者数矣 *Kwŭy-poè tŭy kwun ch'hëóng kê kwúy nā paé*, Kwŭy-poè, when following the army, succeeded in seizing the enemy's standard several times.

K'hëen 褰 To lift up; k'hëen e, 褰衣, to lift up the clothes.

K'hëen sëâng sëëp Chin, 褰裳涉溱 *tëóng k'hé yin chëóng, leâou köëy Chin chúy*, he lifted up his garments, to wade through the Chin river.

K'hëen 騫 A horse's belly-band; a girth; also, to injure, to fail.

Lâm san che sëw, put k'hëen put peng, 南山之壽不騫不崩 *lâm sna ây têng höëy sëw, bëy k'hëep bëy pang*, the southern mountains are longlived, neither decaying nor falling; see the 小雅 Seáou gnáy.

K'hëen 牽 Vulg. *k'han*: to lead, to pull, to drag; to stick to.

Khëen ke gnëw, 牽車牛 *k'han ch'hëa kap goô*, to lead along wagons and oxen.

Hák chëá k'hëen ê séy bûn, 學者牽於所聞 *t'hák ây lâng k'he k'hëen tē e séy woō t'hëna ây soō*, learners are led by what they have heard (without giving heed to others' opinions); see the 史記 Soó kè.

A tow-rope is called pek tëäng k'hëen, 百丈牽 *păyh têng k'han*, a hundred fathoms' puller.

K'hëen 鏗 Vulg. *k'hëang*: the sound of metal, a chiming.

Chëung seng k'hëen, 鍾聲鏗 *cheng ây sëna k'hëang*, the sound of a bell is tinkling; see the 禮樂記 Léy gák ké.

K'hëen 僁 The old form of 愆, k'hëen, a fault.

声

K'hëén 犬 Vulg. *kaóu*: a dog; k'hëen choó, 犬子, a puppy: a polite expression used by the Chinese, when speaking of their own children.

Chè ê k'hëén má, kae lêng yéw yáng, 至於犬馬皆能有養 *chè kaòu kaóu báy, chò poó ëy woō lâng ch'hē*, with respect to dogs and horses, they can all be fed and nourished; (and if we do nothing more than this for our parents, where lies the difference?) see the 上論 Sëäng lūn.

K'hëén 畎 A ditch or furrow in a field, six of which constitute an acre. Gnó ch'hè k'hëén boé che tëung, 我處畎畝之中 *gwá twā tē k'hëén boé ây tang e^ng*, I dwell amongst the furrows and acres; see 孟子 Bēng choó.

K'hëén 遣 To present, to send, to send away; ch'hay k'hëén, 差遣, to send on an errand. Kè sék se k'hëén ê ch'hek, 既夕書遣于策 *kaòu àm chëw kè k'hëén sàng ây meē^nh tē ch'hăyk*, when it is evening, set down the number of presents in a book; see the 儀禮 Gê léy. Këang-sē é Choó-hwān boê chùy jê k'hëén che, 姜氏與子犯謀醉而遣之 *Këang-sē kap Choó-hwān soō nëó^ng ch'hòng e chëw chùy, jê ch'hay k'hëén e*, Këang-sē and Choó-hwān planned to make him drunk, and then to send him away; see the 左傳 Chó twān.

K'hëén 掔 A stubborn ox, that will not be led.

K'hëén 繾 K'hëén k'hwán, 繾綣, attached, indissolubly attached to any one.

去

K'hëèn 俔 To compare, to bring a comparison, to speak a parable; like as. K'hëèn t'hëen che möëy, 俔天之妹 *ch'hin chëō^ng t'hee^ng ây sëo möëy*, just like heaven's younger sister; see the 大雅 Taē gnáy.

K'hëèn 僆 K'hëèn lëên, 僆鏈, to march in a row, close together.

K'hëèn 牽 To pull, to pluck; also read k'hëen.

K'hëèn 譴 To inquire into; k'hëèn chek, 譴責, to scold, to blame. Lëâng-sè-choé, 梁世祖, the first prince of the Lëâng dynasty was very friendly with Sông-hông-kéng, 宋弘景, and used (sê sê soó jîn k'hëèn būn, 時時使人譴問 *sê sê saé lâng k'hëèn mooi^ng*,) constantly to send people to inquire after him.

K'hëèn 摼 To knock the head; to hit against, to come in contact with.

平

K'hëên 乾 Heaven; the male principle of nature; k'hëên k'hwun, 乾坤, heaven and earth. The visible heavens are called t'heen, 天, and the superintending principle k'hëên, 乾.

K'hëên 虔 Respectful, reverential, religious; k'hëên sêng, 虔誠, pious and sincere. K'hëên sîn, 虔神, to fear God.

平

K'heē^ng 拑 Read k'hëêm: to take up anything with princers or tweezers.

K'heē^ng 鉗 Read k'hëêm: a pair of pincers, nippers, or pliers.

入

K'hëep 怯 To be very much afraid, to be full of fears; cowardly.

K'hëep 𤝞 To fear, to dread difficulty.

K'hëep 壞 Read hwaē : to destroy, to deface; destroyed, ruined; vicious, corrupt. Bút hwaē k'hè, 物壞去 *meē^nh k'hëep k'hè*, anything spoiled.

Hwaē hēng, 壞行 *k'hëep sëy kë^nā*, corrupt conduct.

大

K'hëet 拮 To do anything with the mouth and hands; ê séw k'hëet k'he, 予手拮据 *gwá ây ch'hëw k'hëet k'he*, my hands are at work; see the 詩經 Se keng.

K'hëe^t 丩 Motion, the appearance of motion.

K'hëet 詰 To regulate; to inquire; to blame; also, the next day.

K'hëet te pō bān, 詰爾暴慢 *mooi^ng chek pō bān*, to inquire into and reprove oppressions and insults; see the 禮月令 Léy gwát lēng.

K'hëet teaou sëang këèn, 詰朝相見 *bín a chaē sëo keè^ng*, to-morrow we can see each other; see the 左傳 Chó twān.

K'hëet 刲 To flay, to skin the face; to tattoo the skin.

K'hëet 契 Sorrowful, mournful; k'hëet k'hwat, 契闊, separated to a distance.

K'hëet k'hëet goē t'hàn, 契契寤歎 *hwân ló kaôu ch'hat^ng t'hó k'hwùy*, mournful and distressed, on awaking we sigh; see the 小雅 Seáou gnáy.

K'hëet 鴶 A bird which gives the signal for sowing the seed.

K'hëet 頡 A straight neck, like a swallow's neck. Ch'hong-k'hëet, 倉頡, the man who first invented letters (B. C. 2622).

K'hëet 襭 To hold anything in the lap; pók gân k'hëet che, 薄言襭之 *ch'hë^ná kóng p'hày e tē s^na*, they were saying, 'hold it in your lap;' see the 周南 Chew lâm.

K'hëet 纈 To bind with a thread.

K'hëet 擷 To pick, to pluck, to strip off.

K'hëet 挈 To take in the hand, to carry in the hand; to take hold of, to support. Pan pék put t'hèy k'hëet, 斑白不提挈 *t'haôu mô pan pâyh ây lâng, ū^m hoē e kw^nā meē^nh*, people with gray hairs were not allowed to carry things; see the 王制 Ong chè.

K'hëet 恝 Not grieved, free from grief.

Hoo Kong-bêng-ko é haôu choó che sim, wûy put jëák sè k'hëet, 夫公明高以孝子之心爲不若是恝 *hoo Kong-bêng-ko ê haôu kë^ná ây sim, chô nā bô an nëy, chëw bëy swăh hwân ló*, now Kong-bêng-ko maintained the feelings of a filial child, and if he did not so, he was grieved; see 孟子 Bēng choó.

K'hëet 孑 One, only, alone, single; over and above. A surname.

Chew ê lëy bîn, bê yéw k'hëet wûy, 周餘黎民靡有孑遺 *Chew laôu ây oē t'haôu payh sai^ng bōëy woō tw^na chit lâng wûy tē*, of the remnant of the black-haired people of Chew, there is not a single one left; see the 太雅 Taē gnáy.

K'hëet 訐 To attack and expose people's secret vices; to find out secrets.
Oè k'hëet é wûy tit chëá, 惡訐以爲直者 *gwá wàn hwut lêy k'hëet ây lâng, yin wūy e lëăh e sē tcáou tit ây*, 'I detest those exposers of mens' secret faults, because they do it under the pretense of honesty;' said by Confucius in the 語論 Lūn gé.

K'hëet 朅 Martial, military, bold, courageous.
Sè soō yéw k'hëet, 庶士有朅 *chëūng e ây t'hák ch'hăyh lâng woō bob ây yëōng*, all his learned men had a martial appearance; see the 衛風 Wōey hong.

K'hëet 砝 Hard, a hard stone, an uneven road.

K'hek 克 To be able; to be superior to; to overcome, to repress.
K'hek ké, 克已, to overcome one's-self.
K'hek bêng tek, 克明德 *ēy k'hek bêng tek*, to be able clearly to understand virtue; see the 康誥 K'hong k'hò.
Gnó chëèn pit k'hek, 我戰必克 *gwá nā sëo t'haé pit yëⁿā*, 'when I fight, I am sure to win;' said by Confucius.

K'hek 㑶 Weary, tired.

K'hek 劾 To constrain one's-self; to exert one's-self; to boast one's-self.

K'hek 尅 To conquer; to kill; k'hek kê, 剋期, to appoint a time. Also written 尅, k'hek.

K'hek 客 Vulg. *k'hăyh*: a guest, a stranger, a visitor.
K'hó soó é pin k'hek gân yëá, 可使與賓客言也 *t'hang saé e kap lâng k'hăyh kóng wā*, he can be employed to speak with guests and visitors; see the 論語 Lūn gé.

K'hek 刻 Teaou k'hek, 雕刻, to cut, to engrave. K'hek joō, 刻字 *k'hek jē*, to cut letters. Sê k'hek, 時刻, times, constantly; yit k'hek, 一刻 *chit k'hek*, a moment.

K'hek 綌 The coarse kind of hempen or grass-cloth; coarse linen; sackcloth.
Chín t'he k'hek, pit peáou jê ch'hut che, 袗絺綌必表而出之 *ch'hēng twⁿā nëⁿā kwăh poē, tëōh peáou jê ch'hut e*, wearing a single garment of coarse or fine linen, it is necessary (to have something next the skin); and let this be on the outside; see the 論語 Lūn gé.

K'hek 虢 The name of a country; káy tō ê Gê, é hwát K'hek, 假道於虞以伐虢 *chëōh loē tē Gê, é hwát K'hek*, they availed themselves of the road through the country of Gê, in order to attack that of K'hek; see 孟子 Bēng choó.

K'hek 闃 Still, quiet, tranquil; k'hek kê boô jîn, 闃其無人 *k'hek chēng bô lâng*, still and solitary, without any one near; see the 易經 Ék keng.

K'hek 喫 To eat; k'hek hwān, 喫飯 *chëăh pooīⁿg*, to eat rice.
Bôey sëùk hé tông Choo ló k'hek, 梅熟許同朱老喫 *hūⁿ á sèk yín tâng Choo ló chëăh*, when the plumbs are ripe, I have promised to eat them in company with old Mr. Choo.

K'hek 嘝 To laugh.

K'hek 磍 A hard stone.

K'hek 隙 A chink, a cranny, a hole; k'hong k'hek, 孔隙 a crevice; hāy k'hek, 暇隙 leisure, freedom from labor.

Chwàn hëét k'hek sëang kwuy, 鑽穴隙相窺 *chwuiⁿᵍ k'hang k'hek sëo k'hwⁿà*, to bore a hole and peep at one another; see 孟子 Bēng choó.

Lông k'hek káng boó, 農隙講武 *chŏh ch'hân êng laê kóng boó*, when there is leisure from agriculture, then is the time for talking about military affairs.

K'hek 曲 Read k'hëuk: a song; ch'hëàng k'hëuk, 唱曲 *ch'hëòng k'hek*, to sing songs.

去

K'heng 傾 On one side, inclined, lateral, partial; injured, falling.

T'hëen k'heng sey pok, tēy k'hwat tong lâm, 天傾西北地闕東南 *t'hceⁿᵍ k'heng tē sae pak, tēy k'hwat tē tang lâm*, the heavens are partially inclined on the northwest, and the earth is hollow towards the southeast; (hence the Chinese say, that their emperors always come from the northwest, as coming down from heaven; and the rivers of China generally flow to the southeast, that being the lowest part of the world;) see the 天文訓 T'hëen bûn hwùn.

K'heng tó, 傾倒, overturned; k'heng hók, 傾伏, prostrate.

K'heng 卿 A noble, a high officer; a subject.

Ch'hut chek soō kong k'heng, jip chek soō hoō heng, 出則事公卿入則事父兄 *ch'hut chëw hòk saē kong k'heng, jip chëw hòk saē pāy hëⁿa*, on going abroad serve the chiefs and nobles, and coming home, serve your parents and elder brethren; see the 論語 Lūn gé.

K'heng 輕 Vulg. *k'hin*: light, not heavy; kwân jëēn hoē te k'heng tëūng, 權然後知輕重 *ch'hìn, jëēn aōu ēy chae k'hin tāng*, weigh a thing and then you may know whether it is light or heavy; see 孟子 Bēng choó.

K'heng 坑 Vulg. *k'haiⁿᵍ*: a dell, a ravine, a hollow place; to let into a hole or pit.

E chày k'heng Chîn hâng chut sam sip bān, 羽詐坑秦降卒三十萬 *é chày hām Chîn ây hâng peng sⁿa chàp bān*, (Hâng-é) deceitfully decoyed into a pit, (and destroyed) 300,000 of the surrendered troops of Chîn; see the 史記 Soó kè.

K'heng 硎 A stony cavern; a rocky dell.

K'heng 筐 Read k'hong: a basket; ch'haé ch'haé kwân-jé put éng k'heng k'hong, 采采卷耳不盈傾筐 *bán bán kwân-jé ây ch'hai, bô mwⁿá chit k'heng*, picking and gathering the kwân-jé vegetable, and after all not getting enough to fill one basket; see the 周南 Chew lâm.

K'heng 銎 Read k'heung: the hole of an axe or chisel, in which the handle is fixed.

去

K'héng 頃 A piece of land, containing one hundred acres. Gô k'héng, 俄頃, a moment. Bûn chëên soè k'héng tëên, 門前數頃田 *mooiⁿᵍ chéng kwúy pāyh boé ây ch'hân*, before the door are several hundred acres of land.

K'héng k'hek, 頃刻, a small space of time, immediately.

K'héng **傾** Gô k'héng, 俄 傾, a moment of time.

K'héng **肎** Any part of the body, where the bones and sinews unite.

K'héng **肯** To be willing, to assent to; k'héng put k'héng? 肯不肯, are you willing or not? Hwũy jëên k'héng laê, 惠然肯來 *hwũy jëên kaôu k'héng laê*, to be so kind, as to be willing to come; see the 衛風 Wöëy hong.

K'héng **檾** K'héng mâ, 檾麻, a kind of flax or hemp; also written 蘔 k'héng.

去

K'hèng **慶** To congratulate; k'hèng hō, 慶賀, to felicitate; also, happiness. Chong-pek é hō k'hèng che léy, ch'hin ē sèng che kok, 宗伯以賀慶之禮親異姓之國 *chong-pek ây kwⁿa lëâh hō k'hèng ây léy soè, chò ch'hin pat saiⁿᵍ ây kok*, the chong-pek officer, with ceremonies of congratulation, contracted matrimonial alliances with countries of a different surname; see the 周禮 Chew léy.

K'hèng **磬** A musical instrument formed out of a gem or precious stone. Choó kek k'hèng ē Wöëy, 子擊磬于衛 *hoō choó p'hah k'hèng tē Wöëy*, Confucius played on the k'hèng at Wöëy; see the 論語 Lūn gé.

K'hèng **声** The ancient form of the above.

K'hèng **罄** Empty, void; an empty vessel, exhausted. Pîn che k'hèng è, wûy lûy che t'hé, 瓶之罄矣維罍之恥 *chêw pân ây k'hang sē chêw ûng ây seáou léy*, when the wine-cup is empty, it is a disgrace to the wine-jar; see the 小雅 Seáou gnáy.

平

K'hêng **傾** K'hêng gîn, 傾銀, to melt silver.

丟

K'hēng **桓** The name of a tree; also written 栯 k'hēng.

K'hēng **虹** Read hông: a rainbow. Kwùy ch'hun hông sé këèn beng tong, hông put këèn, 季春虹始見孟冬虹不見 *ch'hun böëy k'hēng k'hé t'haôu hëèn, kaôu tang t'haôu k'hēng chêw ūᵐ keèⁿᵍ*, in the latter month of spring the rainbow begins to appear, and in the first month of winter it ceases to be seen; see the 禮月令 Léy gwàt lēng.

夲

K'heⁿᵍ **康** Read k'hong: a surname.

K'heⁿᵍ **糠** Read k'hong: chaff; bé k'hong, 米糠 *bé k'heⁿᵍ*, the husk of rice.

去

K'hèⁿᵍ **藏** Read chông: to secrete, to conceal, to hide, to stow away, to store, to hoard; chōng bút, 藏物, *k'hèⁿᵍ meēⁿh*, to conceal anything.

夲

K'hëò **儌** Read k'hëàou: as chò k'hëàou, 做儌 *chò k'hëò*, to make a bargain, to go between in making a bargain, as a broker.

夫

K'hëŏh **拾** Read sip: to take up, to pick up, to gather up. Loē put sip wûy, 路不拾遺

toe bó k'hëöh ka laöuh ây meë^n^h, they did not pick up anything that was dropped in the roads (speaking of a highly improved state of society).

[kiang]

K'hëo^ng^ 腔 Read k'hëang: a dialect; Teâou-chew k'hëang, 潮州腔, *Tëô-chew k'hëo^ng^*, the dialect of Tëô-chew.

[kiam]

K'hëo^ng^ 儉 Read k'hëem: sparing; k'hëem sit, 儉食 *k'hëo^ng^ chëâh,* to be sparing at meals.

K'hëuk 曲 Bent, crooked, not straight; wúy k'hëuk, 委曲, bent and curved.

Ko k'hëuk, 歌曲 *kwa k'hek,* songs and ballads; sim k'hëuk, 心曲, ideas.

K'hëuk è sûn jîn, 曲意徇人 *k'hëuk lán è ây è, laê t'hùn pat lâng,* to accommodate one's own ideas, in order to comply with others.

Lwān gnó sim k'hëuk, 亂我心曲 *p'hăh lwān gwá ây sim k'hëuk,* to disturb one's thoughts and wishes.

K'hëuk 麴 Vulg. *k'hak:* leaven, a preparation of rice to cause a fermentation in liquor; a surname.

Chím k'hëuk chék chô, 枕麴藉糟 *ìeăh k'hak chò chîm t'haöu, lëăh chô chò ch'hëôh,* to take leaven for one's pillow, and grains for one's bed (speaking of a confirmed drunkard, who is buried in liquor).

K'hëuk 粬 The same as the above; pék k'hëuk, 白粬 *păyh k'hak,* a kind of fermenting substance.

[kiong]

K'hëung 芎 Ch'hwan k'hëung, 川芎, a medicinal plant, used as an antidote to poisons.

K'hëung 蛩 The name of an animal, like a horse, found in the northern sea.

K'hëung 穹 K'hëung ch'hong, 穹蒼, the azure heavens; vast as the blue expanse.

Bê yéw lé lèk, é lëem k'hëung ch'hong, 靡有旅力以念穹蒼 *böëy woō twā lât, é lëem k'hëung ch'hong,* there is no great strength in us, but we are apt to call upon the azure heavens for help; see the 大雅 Taē gnáy.

K'hëung 跫 The sound of people walking; the noise of a footstep.

Bûn jîn chëuk yim k'hëung jëên, jê hé è, 聞人足音跫然而喜矣 *t'hë^n^a keë^ng^ lâng ây k'ha yim, k'hëung jëên chëw hw^n^a hé,* hearing the sound of people's noisy steps coming along, I am delighted; see the 莊子 Chông choó.

K'hëung 銎 Vulg. *k'heng:* the hole of an axe or chisel in which the handle is fixed.

K'hëung 蛲 K'hëung lông, 蛲蜋, insects found in excrementitious matter.

K'hëung 鞏 A leathern thong, to tie anything with a leathern thong; a surname.

K'hëung yūng hông gnêw che kek, 鞏用黃牛之革 *chò k'hëung tëöh yūng wui^ng^ goô ây p'höëy,* for a thong, you must make use of a cow's hide; see the 易經 Ëk keng.

K'hëung 崆 K'hëung këûng, 崆㟅, the appearance of the sky; a hilly appearance.

K'hëung 㤟 Sorrowful, grieved.

上聲

K'hëúng 恐 To fear, to be alarmed, to be apprehensive; k'hëúng p'hⁿà, 恐怕, to be afraid. Choó-loē yéw bûn, bē che lêng hêng, wûy k'hëúng yéw bûn, 子路有聞未之能行惟恐有聞 *Choó-loē woō t'hëⁿa, yëá böëy ëy këⁿâ, wûy këⁿa woō kŏh t'hëⁿa*, when Choó-loē heard anything, before he could put it in practice he was afraid lest he should hear something else (necessary to be done); see the 論語 Lūn gé.

去聲

K'hëùng 㑋 Small, diminutive; some say, bent and crooked; cold.

K'hëùng 㬧 To dry anything in the sun.

上平

K'hew 丘 A hillock, a mound, a little hill; a sacrificial area; a surname. Wûy ko pit yin k'hew lêng, 爲高必因丘陵 *chò kwân pit wá k'hew lêng*, in making anything high, we must take advantage of hillocks and mounds; see 孟子 Bēng choó.

K'hew 邱 Vulg. *k'hoo*: a surname.

K'hew 蚯 K'hew yín, 蚯蚓, *t'hoê kín*, a worm, the common earthworm. Sē gwàt k'hew yín ch'hut, 是月蚯蚓出 *chëy chit göëyh goô wûn ch'hut*, in this month, the worms come out; see the 禮月令 Léy gwàt lêng.

K'hew 坵 Great, large; to collect, to assemble together; the same as 丘, k'hew.

K'hew 㤹 Malice and enmity; also to assemble together.

K'hew 鳩 To assemble together; the name of a bird of the genus Columba; k'hew chuy, 鳩鵻 *ka chuy*, a dove. Wûy ch'hëak yéw chaōu, wûy k'hew ke che, 維鵲有巢維鳩居之 *wûy chăyh á wōo sëw, wûy ka chuy k'hëâ e*, the magpie builds its nest, and the pigeon comes and dwells in it; see the 召南 Seàou lâm.

K'hew 樛 The name of a tree; the branches of a tree bending downwards.

K'hew 虯 A young dragon; k'hew, 虯, is a young dragon with horns, and kêw, 虬, is a young dragon, without horns.

上聲

K'héw 㧓 To take or raise up with the hand.

K'héw 醜 An ugly face.

去聲

K'hèw 趉 Lame, to walk lame.

K'hèw 跔 The appearance of walking.

平聲

K'hêw 球 Read kêw: an instrument of music made of a precious stone. T'hëen kêw, 天球, *t'hecⁿg k'hêw*, a celestial globe. Lêw Kêw, 琉球, *Lêw K'hêw*, the Lêw Kêw, or Lew Chew islands. T'hëen kêw hô toē chaē tong sē, 天球河

圖在東序 *t'heeng k'hew hô toè twā tē tang peeng ây ch'hoò*, the celestial globe and the map of the river were kept in the eastern range of the building; see the 書經 Se keng.

K'hêw 趣 The legs bent, not straightened out; shriveled up, shrunk.

幸

K'hey 溪 A rivulet, a stream, a mountain torrent; also written 嵠, 磎, and 谿, k'hey.

Koè kok put é san k'hey che hëém, 固國不以山溪之險 *këen koè ây kok, bô twā tē swna k'hey ây hëém*, a firm state does not consist in the precipitous nature of its mountains and torrents; see 孟子 Bēng choó.

K'héy 啓 To open out, to unfold, to inform, to explain, to communicate instruction. Put hwún, put k'héy, 不憤不啓 *nā bô hwat hwún, e bô bëñyh k'héy kà*, if any would not arouse themselves to exertion, he would not explain anything for their information; see the 論語 Lūn gé.

K'héy é séw, k'héy é cheuk, 啓予手啓予足 *k'héy k'hwuy gwá ây ch'héw, k'héy k'hwuy gwá ây k'ha*, 'stretch out my arms, and stretch out my legs;' (said by a person when he was going to die;) see the 論語 Lūn gé.

K'héy 褄 To open, or take off, the collar of a garment.

K'héy 綮 To believe; the barb of a spear. K'héng k'héy, 肯綮, those parts of the body where the bones and sinews meet, a joint.

去

K'hèy 契 To unite, to join together, to agree; a bond, a check, a covenant. Chaé hoo chëáng kwan k'hèy, é tē chông, 宰夫掌官契以治藏 *chaé hoo ây kwna chëáng kwna k'hèy, é tē k'hèng*, the proper officer holds the public bonds, in order to take care of them; see the 周禮 Chew léy.

K'hèy 喫 K'hek kwa choó, 喫瓜子 *k'hèy kwa ché*, to crack the seeds of a melon.

幸

K'him 欽 Respectful, majestic, to command respect. K'him ch'hay, 欽差, an imperial envoy, an embassador. K'him bēng, 欽命, an imperial order. K'him bêng bûn soō, 欽明文思, (Geâou was) respectful, intelligent, elegant, and thoughtful; see the 書堯典 Se geâou tëén.

K'him 衾 A large coverlid, a quilt.

K'him 衿 The collar of a garment; ch'heng ch'heng choó k'him, 青青子衿 *ch'haing ch'haing á nëná*, a light blue collar; see the 鄭風 Tēng hong.

K'him 紟 A single coverlid; also, a girdle; to bind up one's garment.

K'him 襟 The part of a garment which lays over, in order to fasten it. Tông k'him heng tēy, 同襟兄弟 *tâng k'him hëna tē*, brethren by marriage (as the husbands of the sisters of one's wife).

去

K'hím 埁 A cave, a pit, a dell.

K'hím 㲉 A thickness or induration of the skin.

K'hím 昑 Clear, light, intelligent.

K'hím 澿 Cold, chilly, refrigerant, an intense cold; k'hím saòu, 澿嗽, a very bad cough.

K'hím 噤 K'hím k'hoé, 噤口, to stop the mouth, to observe silence.

去

K'hìm 搇 To place the hand on, to rest.

平

K'hîm 琴 A harp; k'hîm sek, 琴瑟, a harp & guitar. Ch'hey choó hⁿó háp, jê koé sek k'hîm, 妻子好合如鼓瑟琴 *boê kēⁿá hó hó sëo hàp, ch'hin chëōⁿᵍ twⁿâ sek k'hîm*, wives and children living in concord and harmony, like the playing on the harp and guitar; see the 小雅 Seáou gnáy.

K'hîm 芩 Hông k'hîm, 黄芩, a medicinal plant.

K'hîm 檎 Lîm k'hîm, 林檎, the name of a fruit tree, like the wild plum.

K'hîm 擒 To take, to seize, to apprehend, to to take prisoner; hwát k'hîm, 活擒 *wâh k'hîm*, to take alive. Choo-kat-lëāng k'hîm Bēng-hék, ch'hit k'hîm ch'hit hòng, 諸葛亮擒孟獲七擒七放 *Choo-kat-lëāng lëâh Bēng-hék, ch'hit āy lëâh ch'hit āy pàng*, Choo-kat-lëāng in taking Bēng-hék, caught him seven times, and seven times let him go; see the 三國 San kek.

K'hîm 禽 A bird, one of the feathered tribe, a fowl; k'hîm sèw, 禽獸, birds and beasts, the brute creation. Chëung jit jê put hêk yit k'hîm, 終日而不獲一禽 *chit jit koó, jê bô lëâh chit chëáh cheáou*, they were all the day without catching one bird; see 孟子 Bēng choó.

去

K'hìn 欦 Small, few; to sneeze, to cough.

K'hin 輕 Read k'heng: light, not heavy, unimportant. K'heng, tëūng tông, chek kày sëang jëák, 輕重同則價相若 *k'hin tāng sëo tāng, chek kày cheéⁿᵍ sëo ch'hin chëōⁿᵍ*, when things are equally light and heavy, the prices would be the same; see 孟子 Bēng choó.

上

K'hín 蠸 An earthworm, a worm of the genus Lumbricus.

K'hín 赾 Vulg. *ch'hëⁿà*: to walk with difficulty, to walk carefully, to walk lame.

K'hín 淺 Read ch'hëén: shallow, not deep. Jê kê ch'hëén ch'him hoē pók che put yit chëá, yēw yéw léy é yit che, 而其淺深厚薄之不一者又有禮以一之 *jê e āy k'hín ch'him kaōu pōh, āy ūᵐ paīⁿᵍ chēy yëá woō léy é ch'hòng chēy*, and as for the difference of things which are shallow and deep, thick and thin, we have the principles of propriety to equalize them.

平

K'hîn 勤 Diligent; k'hîn kong, 勤工, *k'hîn kang*, diligent in business. Ong-kwùy kê k'hîn ông kay 王季其勤王家 *ông-kwùy e ēy k'hîn kang ông āy ch'hoô*, Ong-kwùy was diligent in the palace

K'hin 懃 Sorrowful, anxious; yin k'hîn, 慇懃, earnest and exact in the fulfillment of duties, studious to please. Yin k'hîn sòng k'hek, 慇懃送客, *yin k'hîn sàng lâng k'hăyh*, assiduous and obliging in attentions to guests.

K'hîn 芹 K'hîn ch'haè, 芹菜, celery. Soō lók P'hwàn súy, gân ch'haé kê k'hîn, 思樂泮水言採其芹 *sëō^ng tek kaé P'hwⁿà chúy, kóng böëyh bán e ây k'hîn ch'haè*, thinking about taking our pleasure upon the P'hwàn waters and talking of picking the celery there; see the 魯頌 Loé sëūng.

K'hip 吸 To inspire, to draw in the breath; hoe k'hip, 呼吸, to respire and inspire. Also, to drink. K'hip tam loē chē hoô lëāng, 吸湛露之浮涼 *lim tam loē ây p'hoô léng*, to drink the light and cool drops of the pleasant dew.

K'hip 汲 Vulg. *ch'hëō^ng:* to draw water; k'hip k'hip, 汲汲, incessant; a surname. Twán kēng put k'hó k'hip ch'him, 短綆不可汲深 *téy ây sŏh bô t'hang ch'hëō^ng ch'him chúy*, a short well-rope will not serve to draw up water from a great depth.

K'hip 芨 Vulg. *k'hit:* as pêk k'hip, 白芨 *păyh k'hit*, a medicinal plant.

K'hip 笈 A sachel, or box, for containing school books. Hoō k'hip chëūng soo yëw, 負笈從師遊 *gëā k'hăyh t'hàn sin sai^ng yéw*, to shoulder one's sachel and follow one's teacher.

K'hip 泣 To cry, to bewail, to lament, to shed tears. K'hip t'hèy lëën lëën, 泣涕漣漣 *laôu bàk saé sëo sWà*, the tears flowed rapidly.

K'hip 掐 Vulg. *k'hàng:* to tear with the nails, to scratch.

K'hit 乞 To beg, to supplicate, to implore; to take, to give; k'hit sit, 乞食 *k'hit chëăh*, a beggar; k'hit soo, 乞士, a begging priest. K'hit kē ê put chëuk, yëw koè jê che t'hⁿa, 乞其餘不足又顧而之他 *k'hit e ây sîn bô kaôu, yëw k'hwⁿà jê k'hè kaôu pat wūy*, he begged what was left (of the sacrifices), and not finding it sufficient, looked around, and went to another place (of sacrifice); see 孟子 Bēng choó.

K'ho 柯 A branch, a twig; the handle of an ax. Vulg. *kwa:* a surname. Kwun choó put kaé k'ho jê ék yëëp, 君子不改柯而易葉 *kwun choó bô káy ke jê wⁿà hëŏh*, the good man (like an evergreen plant,) does not change his branches nor cast his leaves. Hwát k'ho, hwát k'ho, kê chek put wán, 伐柯伐柯其則不遠 *p'hăh poô t'haôu pai^ng, p'hăh poô t'haôu pai^ng, e ây kwat chek bēy hwui^ng*, in cutting an ax-handle, in cutting an ax-handle, the pattern is not far from us (for that is the pattern in our hand, while we are cutting).

K'ho 珂 A stone resembling a gem; sòng é ché gëūk k'ho, 送以紫玉珂 *sàng é âng gëūk ây k'ho*, to make a present of a vermilion colored gem.

K'ho 軻 The axles of carriages joined together; a man's name; 孟子, Bēng-choó's name was 孟軻, Bēng-k'ho.

K'ho 䈖 A particular sort of bamboo.

K'ho 科 An order, a class, a measure, a rule; lōey k'ho, 內科 *laē k'ho*, a physician; gōey k'ho, 外科 *gwā k'ho*, a surgeon.

Sėk put choó p'hê, wūy lėk put tông k'ho, 射不主皮爲力不同科 *chŏh chëo^{ng} bô choó tē t'haôu p'hŏëy, yin wūy k'hwùy làt ū^{m} tâng têng*, archery does not consist in shooting through the leather because men's strength is not of an equal power; see the 上論 Sëäng lūn.

Eng k'ho jê hoē chìn, 盈科而後進 *êng mwⁿá k'ho jëên aōu chìn*, (the waters) fill up their measure, and then flow onwards; see 孟子 Bēng choó.

K'ho 蝌 K'ho hây, 蝌蝦, a kind of toad; k'ho toé, 蝌蚪 *k'ho taôu*, the common toad.

K'ho 窠 Empty, void, a hole. A hole in the earth is called 窠, k'ho, and a nest in a tree is called 巢, chaōu.

K'ho 䶗 Handsome, beautiful.

声

K'hó 可 Vulg. *t'hang*: can, may; to be able; put k'hó, 不可 *ū^{m} t'hang*, it may not be.

Gnó chek ē ê sē, boô k'hó, boô put k'hó, 我則異於是無可無不可 *gwá chēw kŏh yëō^{ng} ê chéy lêy, bô t'hang, bô ū^{m} t'hang*, I am different from these people, not having any particular thing that I may, or may not do, (but acting in all respects according to circumstances;) said by Confucius in the 論語 Lūn gé.

K'hó 坷 K'hám k'hó, 坎坷, to be crossed, to meet with constant difficulties.

K'hó 舸 A large boat, or ship.

K'hó 丂 To desire, to breathe freely.

K'hó 哿 Can, may, to be able; excellent, commendable.

K'hó è hoô jîn, ae ch'hoó keng tók, 哿矣富人哀此煢獨 *t'hang è poō lâng, ae chéy sòng hëung kwⁿá tók*, rich people can do it, but alas! for the wretched and solitary; see 孟子 Bēng choó.

K'hó 笴 K'hó ló, 笴笭, crooked wood or bamboo of which utensils are made.

K'hó 考 To examine; key k'hó, 稽考, a literary examination; sēw k'hó, 壽考, age; k'hó pé, 考妣, deceased parents; k'hó kaôu, 考較, to examine.

Soó kwun sēw k'hó, 使君壽考 *saé hoē kwun lé, chëăh tê^{ng} hōëy sēw*, may you, Sir, enjoy a good old age; see the 小雅 Seáou gnáy.

Pek sèng jê sòng k'hó pé, 百姓如喪考妣 *păyh saì^{ng} ch'hin chëō^{ng} sé pāy boé*, the people felt as though they had lost their parents; see 孟子 Bēng choó.

K'hó 栲 A certain wood, resembling that of the varnish tree.

K'hó 拷 To beat, to strike.

K'hó 洘 Water become dry; anything wet dried up; k'hó gê, 洘魚 *k'hó hê*, to dry up the water in a pond, in order to catch the fish.

K'hó 攷 To examine, to inspect.

去

K'hò 課 K'hò k'hwàn, 課勸, to exhort; k'hò têng, 課程, rules, regulations, to arrange; to exact duties, to levy taxes. K'hwàn k'hò lông song, 勸課農桑 *k'hwuì^ng k'hò lâng chòh ch'hân chaè se^ng*, to exhort the people to attend to agriculture and the cultivation of the mulberry tree; kong k'hò, 工課 *kang k'höèy*, an exercise, a task.

Sêng k'hè put k'hò, 成器不課 *kadu chē^nâ höèy bô làp e söèy*, when a person becomes a complete article (i. e. a learned man), he is not to be taxed. Söèy k'hò, 稅課 *söèy k'höèy*, taxes, duties.

K'hò 顆 A small head; vulg. *k'höèy*: a bead or pearl. The numeral of small globular things.

K'hò 騍 A stallion.

K'hò 靠 To rely on; é k'hò, 倚靠, to confide in, to trust to.

K'hò 捁 To beat, to strike.

K'hò 焀 Dry, and burnt up

K'hò 渮 Vulg. *k'hwà*: to run on a sand-bank, to run a ship aground.

K'hò 誥 To inform. The name of several sections in the 尙書 Sëäng se.

平

K'hoe 箍 A hoop, a hoop or ring around a barrel; t'hëet k'hoe, 鐵箍 *t'hëh k'hoe*, an iron hoop; k'hoe cho 箍子 *k'hoe á*, a circle, a cypher.

K'hoe 篐 A wooden hoop.

K'hoe 粿 Tây k'hoe, 茶粿, the refuse of the tea nut, which is used for washing clothes.

Yêw k'hoe, 油粿, an oil cake.

K'hoe 員 Read wân: a dollar; yit wân, 一員 *chit k'hoe*, a dollar.

上

K'hoé 口 Vulg. *ch'hùy*: the mouth; hàp k'hoé, 合口, *hàp ch'hùy*, to shut the mouth; bûn k'hoé, 門口 *mûi k'haóu*, the entrance of the door; aè k'hoé, 隘口 *aè k'haóu*, a narrow pass, a defile.

K'hoé che ê bē yëá, 口之於味也 *ch'hùy, áy tē bē*, the mouth with respect to tastes.

K'hoé 苦 Misery, difficulty, calamity; bitter, acrid; kan k'hoé, 艱苦, wretched. K'hoé ê bān soó, 苦於萬死 *k'hăh kan k'hoé kùy chē^nâ bān sé*, more miserable than ten thousand deaths.

K'hoé ch'hoé, 苦楚, painful, wretched; sin k'hoé 辛苦, bitter, distressing.

K'hoé 笘 A certain kind of bamboo.

K'hoé 䵺 Lô k'hoé, 勞䵺, troubled, distressed.

K'hoé 許 Read hé: a surname; Hé-yêw put sêw Geâou sëēn, 許由不受堯禪 *K'hoé-yêw, ūm sêw Geâou sëēn*, K'hoé-yêw would not receive Geâou's empire, (but went and washed his ears after hearing the proposition, as though he had heard something very bad.)

去

K'hoè 叩 To inquire, to ask; k'hoè sêw, 叩首 *k'hok t'haōu*, to knock the head against the ground, in obeisance; k'hoè bûn, 叩門 *k'haōu mooi^ng*, to rap at the door.

Gnó k'hoè kê lëáng twan jê köët yëen, 我叩其兩端而竭焉 *gwá mooi^ng e ây nō t'haōu jê köët chīn yëen*, I inquired on two points, and exhausted the subject; see the 論語 Lūn gé.

K'hoè 扣 K'hoè kek, 扣擊, to beat, to strike; k'hoè tê, 扣除 *k'haōu tê*, to cut off, to deduct; k'hoè chëēn, 扣錢 *k'haōu cheē^ng*, to deduct from one's wages.

Taē k'hoè chek taē bêng, seáou k'hoè chek seáou bêng, 大扣則大鳴小扣則小鳴 *twā p'hăh chek twā tân, sëó p'hăh chek sëó tân*, when we strike (the musical instruments) forcibly, they emit a loud sound, but when we strike them gently, they make but little noise; see the 禮樂記 Léy gák kè.

K'hoè 寇 A robber, a plunderer, a bandit; jip k'hoè, 入寇, to invade; a surname. Yéw Wât k'hoè, hék wât k'hoè chè, áp k'hè choo? 有越寇或曰寇至盍去諸 *woō Wât kok ây ch'hât, woō lóng kóng, ch'hât kaōu, s^na soō ūm k'hè?* there were some robbers from the Wat country, when some one said, 'the robbers are coming, why do you not get out of the way?' see 孟子 Bēng choó.

K'hoè 蔻 Toē k'hoè, 荳蔻 *laōu haōu*, nutmegs; toē k'hoè hwa, 荳蔻花 *laōu haōu hwa*, mace, the second coat of the nutmeg.

K'hoè 簆 Vulg. *k'haōu:* a bamboo implement used in weaving.

K'hoè 佝 Dwarfish and ugly.

K'hoè 庫 Hoó k'hoè, 府庫, a treasury, a treasure-house; gîn k'hoè, 銀庫 a mint. Jê kwun che ch'hong lîm sit, hoó k'hoè ch'hëung, 而君之倉廩實府庫充 *jê kwun lé ây ch'he^ng lîm teē^ng, hoó k'hoè mwⁿá*, and your majesty's granaries are full, and your treasuries replenished, (while your people are starving;) see 孟子 Bēng choó.

K'hoè 褲 Breeches, pantaloons; sam k'hoè, 衫褲 *s^na k'hoè*, a jacket and trowsers.

K'hoè 袴 The breech, the space between the legs; the clothing for the thighs.

K'hoè 釦 To gild; lêw k'hoè, 鈕釦 *léw k'haōu*, a button-hole.

K'hoè 絝 The clothing for the thighs; the same as 袴, k'hoè.

平

K'hoê 痞 K'hâm k'hoê, 瘄痞, an inveterate, incurable, disease.

K'hoê 瘸 K'hoê hoē, 瘸瘻, anything stopping in the throat.

K'hoê 荰 Overgrown grass, and reeds.

卑

K'höey 盔 A helmet; k'köey kap, 盔甲, armor. Tëúng kê t'hoê k'höey, 中其頭盔 *tëung e ây t'haôu k'höey*, it just hit his helmet.

K'höey 詼 To laugh, to sport; k'höey ch'heàou, 詼笑, to play the fool.

K'höey 恢 Magnanimous, great, noble minded.

K'höey 魁 K'höey seng, 魁星 *k'höey ch'haing* the head star in Ursa Major; the head, the principal, the chief; taē k'höey t'hëen hāy, 大魁天下 *twā chò k'höey t'haôu tē t'hëeng ây*, to become a great chief in the empire.

K'höey 悝 To sport; a sickness; a man's name.

K'höey 蒘 A sort of rattan.

K'höey 科 Read k'ho: the transplanting of grain.

卥

K'höey 踝 A curtesy, a woman's salutation.

去

K'höèy 課 Read k'hò: to tax; to instruct, to exhort; kong k'hò, 功課 *kang k'höèy*, labor, a task. A piece of literary composition is also called *k'höèy*.

4 V

K'höèy 踝 The bone of the leg.

K'höèy 蹶 To stumble, to fall down. Kim hoo ch'he cheá k'höèy cheá, sē k'hè yeá, jê hwán tōng kê sim, 今夫趨者蹶者是氣也而反動其心 *t'na chéy lêy kín chaôu ây láng pwăh tó ây lâng, sē k'hè tëⁿā tëⁿā, jê ëy hwán tin tāng c ây sim*, now when people walk quick or stumble, it merely concerns the animal powers, and yet it agitates the mind; see 孟子 Bēng choó.

平

K'höey 瘽 Read k'hwân: a cramp in the arms or legs.

夫

K'höĕyh 缺 Read k'hwat: short, deficient, vacant, scarce, rare, few. Chêy chwân boô k'hwat, 齊全無缺 *cheôu chuîng bô k'höĕyh*, perfectly complete without a single defect.

天

K'höĕyh 爜 To cook anything at the fire; k'hwat hⁿo, 爜火 *k'höĕyh höĕy*, to strike fire.

犬

K'hok 牿 A stable or shed for cattle and horses; to take care of cattle.

K'hok 梏 Manacles, handcuffs; chit k'hok, 桎梏, fetters and manacles. Chit k'hok soó cheá, hwuy chèng bēng yeá, 桎梏死者非正命也 *kⁿa k'hoo laē sé, ūᵐ sē chëⁿà bēng*, to die in fetters and manacles, is an ignominious fate; see 孟子 Bēng choó.

K'hok 告 To inform, to make known, to command. Tëung k'hok, jê sëen tō che, 忠

告而善道之 *chīn tëung kap e kóng, jê cheàou hó yîn ch'hwā e*, faithfully instruct (your friends), and lead them on to virtue; see the 論語 Lūn gé.

K'hok 酷 To oppress, to injure; këûng bīn hwān hwat, k'hok lē kek twān, 窮民犯法酷吏擊斷 *sòng hëung păyh saing hwān hwat, sē pò gëák āy kwna lē kek toong*, when the poor people transgress the laws, it is because oppressive officers beat and goad them to it.

K'hok 哭 Vulg. *k'haòu*: to weep, to bewail, to lament.
Ch'hím ê soo, k'hok ê soo, 寢於斯哭於斯 *k'hwùn tē chéy lêy wūy, k'haòu tē chéy lêy wūy*, here will we sleep, and here will we weep.

K'hok 廓 To open, wide, large, empty; Chew-jê sèng toē k'hae k'hok, 周瑜性度開廓 *Chew-jê áy sèng t'héy k'hwuy k'hok*, Chew-jê's disposition was generous and expansive.

K'hok 鄭 Leaou k'hok, 廖鄭, a deep ravine, a high precipice.

K'hok 擴 To widen out, to extend, to amplify; large, expansive.
K'hok jê ch'hëung che, 擴而充之 *tëŏh k'hok jê ch'hëung mwná e*, we must expand and consolidate (those good dispositions); see 孟子 Bēng choó.

K'hok 欔 To tear with the nails, to seize with the talons.

K'hok 钁 A large hoe, an implement of husbandry.

K'hok 礖 The sound of stones rattling.

K'hok 㯓 A kind of rattle, on which they beat the rounds at night.
Sêng bûn kek keng k'hok, 城門擊更㯓 *sëná moong p'hăh kaing k'hok*, at the city gate they sound the watchman's rattle.

K'hok 郜 A surname.

K'hok 硞 The noise of stones.

K'hom 嗛 K'hom saòu 嗽嗛 *k'ham saòu*, the sound of coughing; to cough.

K'hong 亢 To oppose, to contend with; wuy boê bê k'hong, 威謀靡亢 *wuy boê bēy tèk*, terrific plans, which cannot be opposed.

K'hong 空 Vulg. *k'hang*: empty, vacant; exhausted; k'hong sim, 空心 *k'hang sim*, an empty, vacant mind.
Höêy yëá, kê sè hoē, lé k'hong, 回也其庶乎屢空 *Höêy yëá, e sē ch'ha put to ūm hàp tàk paē k'hang*, Höêy is very near (attaining to perfection), but he is frequently empty (i. e. poor); see the 論語 Lūn gé.

K'hong 倥 Inadequate, incapable; k'hong tông, 倥侗, ignorant, rude.
K'hong k'hong jê put sìn, 倥倥而不信 *k'hong k'hong jê bēy ēy sìn*, incapable not trustworthy; see the 論語 Lūn gé.

K'hong 悾 Simple, plain, undesigning; k'hong k'hong, 悾悾, ignorant, rustic.

K'hong 崆 K'hong tông, 崆峒, the name of a hill.

K'hong 硿 Earthen ware; hwān k'hong, 飯硿 pooi^ng k'hong, a rice vessel.

K'hong 箜 K'hong hoê, 箜篌, a musical instrument; the name of a tune which was said to have a very wanton and pernicious influence on those who heard it.

K'hong 康 Harmonious, peaceful, tranquil. Vulg. k'he^ng: a surname. K'hong lêng t'hëen hāy, 康寧天下 k'hong lêng t'hee^ng āy, to tranquilize the empire.

K'hong 糠 Vulg. k'he^ng: chaff; the husk of corn. Pîn chëá sit cho k'hong, 貧者食糟糠 sòng hëung lâng chëăh p'höh kwà k'he^ng, poor people are obliged to eat bran and chaff.

K'hong 㟿 K'hong lông, 㟿㟿, the name of a hill in the west.

K'hong 㝩 K'hong lông, 㝩㝗, a high house, a dwelling; a house shut up.

K'hong 匡 Correct, exact, regular; to correct, to adjust, to assist, to help; a surname.

Kwán-tëūng sëàng Hwân-kong, pà choo hoê, yit k'hong t'hëen hāy, 管仲相桓公霸諸侯一匡天下 Kwán-tëūng sëàng choê Hwân-kong, pà choó hoê, jê chit ây k'hong t'hee^ng hāy, Kwán-tëūng was prime minister to Hwân-kong, and ruled the tributary princes despotically, bringing the whole empire under one regulation; see the 論語 Lūn gé.

K'hong 眶 Vulg. k'hang: a socket; bòk k'hong, 目眶 bàk k'hang, the socket of the eye.

Gê bòk ko k'hong, 隅目高眶 chë^nâ kak ây bàk chew, kwân kwân ây bàk k'hang, sharp cornered eyes, and high eye-sockets.

K'hong 筐 A basket for containing rice, a basket generally.

K'hong 框 The lid of a coffin; a threshold.

上聲

K'hóng 孔 Thorough, pervious, porous; a hole; extreme; a surname. K'hóng hëet, 孔穴 k'hang hëet, a hole or cave. K'hóng-choó, 孔子, Confucius. Ėk k'hóng che cheaou, 亦孔之炤 yëá sim cheaou beng, it is also extremely clear and bright; see the 小雅 Seáou gnáy.

K'hóng 空 A hole, a cavity; a surname; Sùn chëūng lêk k'hóng pông ch'hut, 舜從匿空旁出 Sùn ân chit lêy âm k'háng tê-pee^ng á ch'hut, Sùn got out through the side of a secret passage (which he had made in the well); see the 史記 Soó kè.

K'hóng 倥 K'hóng chóng, 倥偬, hurried, busy.

K'hóng 忼 K'hóng k'haè, 忼慨, dissatisfied, displeased, sorrowful.

Hâng-é pe ko k'hóng k'haè, 項羽悲歌忼慨 Hâng-é ch'hëò^ng pe ae ây kwa, kèk kè k'hóng k'haè, Hâng-é sung a melancholy ditty, to show his dissatisfaction.

K'hóng 慷 K'hóng k'haè, 慷慨, stiff, haughty, truly sincere.

K'hóng 㟅 K'hóng lông, 㟅 㟖, a hollow in a mountain, a ravine.

K'hóng 㑌 K'hóng lëâng, 㑌 㑝, uneven.

去

K'hòng 亢 To pass over, to transgress; high; to oppose; k'hòng yâng, 亢 陽, a drought. K'hòng lëûng yéw höèy, 亢 龍 有 悔 *k'hòng köèy ây lëûng woō hwán höèy,* an erring dragon is penitent; see the 易 經 Ek keng.

To strengthen, to support; gân put lêng k'hòng sin, yëen lêng k'hòng chong? 言 不 能 亢 身 焉 能 亢 宗 *kóng wā bēy k'hòng këâng pún sin, böëyh an chwⁿá ëy k'hòng këâng chong chok?* words are not sufficient to give stability to myself, how then could I thereby establish my family?

K'hòng 伉 To pair, to match; to oppose, to contend; upright, honest.

Soō sìn soō chek k'hòng, 事 勝 辭 則 伉 *chò soō k'hăh yëⁿâ kóng wā, chek tehou tit,* when our deeds surpass our professions we may be considered honest and upright.

K'hòng 抗 To lift up, to raise with the hand, to elevate, to shake.

Chew-kong k'hòng sè chóó, hwat ê Pek-k'hîm, 周 公 抗 世 子 法 于 伯 禽 *Chew-kong k'hòng ké sè chóó k'wⁿâ hwat tē Pek-k'hîm,* Chew-kong roused the young prince, (his pupil,) by pointing to the example of (his own son) Pek-k'hîm; (for Chew-kong having the heir-apparent for his pupil did not dare to punish him for his faults, but used to beat his own son, by which means the prince was led to reflection.)

K'hòng 砊 K'hòng lông, 砊 硠, the sound of stones rattling.

K'hòng 吭 To swallow, to swallow down the throat.

K'hòng 骯 K'hòng chòng, 骯 髒, fat, corpulent, lusty.

K'hòng 頏 To fly, as a bird; to fly upwards is called 頡, k'hëet, and to fly downwards 頏 k'hòng.

K'hòng 壙 A wilderness; a waste place; a pit; k'hòng yëá, 壙 野, a desert.

Sèw che choé k'hòng yëá, 獸 之 走 壙 也 *sèw ây chaóu tē k'hòng yëá,* the beasts flee into the desert; see 孟 子 Bēng chóó.

K'hòng 曠 Empty, void, to make void, to vacate, clear, wide, distant.

Löēy boô wàn lé, göēy boô k'hòng hoo, 內 無 怨 女 外 無 曠 夫 *laē bīn bô wàn hwŭn ây cha boé, gwā bīn bô k'hang k'hang ây ang,* within there are no spiteful wives, and without no solitary husbands; see 孟 子 Bēng chóó.

K'hòng 㬃 The name of a hill

K'hòng 纊 Fine silken threads, the raw silk; cotton for wadding.

Sam kwun che soō kae jê hëep k'hòng, 三 軍 之 士 皆 如 挾 纊 *sⁿa kwun ây soō chò poé ch'hin chëōⁿᵍ woō gnâyh meēⁿᵍ,* the troops of the three divisions are all (as hot for fighting) as if they were stuffed with cotton; see the 左 傳 Chó twān.

K'hòng 貢 Chóó-k'hòng, 子 貢, the name of one of the disciples of Confucius.

福建方言字典

K'hòng 贑 A man's name; the name of a district.

K'hòng 鞚 To bridle in a horse.

K'hòng 控 To lead, to inform; to exceed. K'hòng ê taē pang, 控于大邦 *k'hòng kò tē twā pang*, to inform a great nation of anything; see the 衛風 Wōēy hong.

K'hòng 空 To empty, to render destitute, to impoverish. K'hòng hwàt kê sin, 空乏其身 *k'hòng hwàt e ây hîn sin*, to impoverish and render destitute his person.

K'hòng 誆 To deceive; k'hòng p'hëèn, 誆騙, to cheat, to deceive. Chìn soó Kaé-yâng k'hòng Ch'hoé, 晉使解揚誆楚 *Chìn kok saé Kaé-yâng k'hè k'hòng p'hëèn Ch'hoé*, the government of Chin sent Kaé-yâng to deceive the people of the Ch'hoé country; see the 史記 Soó kè.

去

K'hōng 崆 Uneven, high and low, not even.

平

K'hoo 丘 Read k'hew: a surname; also written 邱, *k'hoo*.

K'hoo 坵 Read k'hew: a parcel; yit k'hew tëên 一坵田 *chit k'hoo ch'hân*, a piece of ground. Chew chè, yit lé wûy yit chéng, wûy tëên kéw k'hew, tëung yit k'hew kong tëên, gōēy pat k'hew soo tëên, 周制一里爲一井爲田九坵中一坵公田外八坵私田 *Chew ây chè, chit lé chò chit ây chatⁿᵍ, chò ch'hân kaóu k'hoo, tang eⁿᵍ chit k'hoo chò kong ch'hân, gwā bīn păyh k'hoo chò sae k'hëa ây ch'hân*, according to the regulations of the Chew dynasty, every square furlong of land was made into a 井 chéng, or well, which formed nine parcels of land; the middle parcel was the public field, and the eight outer parcels were private lots.

K'hoo 祛 K'he sëâ, 祛邪 *k'hoo sëâ*, to expel noxious influences.

去

K'hoò 去 Read k'hè: to go, to depart, to go far away.

平

K'hoô 跍 *K'hoô lòk k'hè*, 跍落去, to squat down.

去

K'hoō 臼 Read kēw: a mortar, in which to pound anything. Kēw ch'hé che lē, é chëy bān bîn, 臼杵之利以濟萬民 *cheng k'hoō ây lē, é chëy bān bîn*, the advantageous use of the pestle and mortar supply the wants of myriads of people; see the 易經 Ek keng.

平

K'hwa 呱 K'hwa sëâ, 呱邪, distorted, perverse.

K'hwa 誇 To boast, to brag; choō k'hwa, 自誇, to brag of one's-self; also written 侉, k'hwa. Keaou, yîm, keng, k'hwa, 驕淫矜誇 *keaou t'haôu, yîm hwān, keng tëên, choō k'hwa*, proud, wanton, bragging, and boastful; see the 書經 Se keng.

K'hwa 夸 The same as the above; to talk extravagantly.

K'hwa 跨 Vulg. *hwǎh*: to stride over, to step across; a stride.

K'hwa 胯 To cut open, to rip open; also written, 刳, k'hwa.
Tèw-ông k'hwa yīn hoō che hok, 紂王胯孕婦之腹 *Tèw-ông p'hwà k'hwuy woō yīn ây cha boé ây pak*, Tèw-ông ripped open the bellies of pregnant women.

上

K'hwá 㐄 A step, a stride. Also read k'hwà.

K'hwá 銙 An implement used in carrying burdens.

去

K'hwà 罣 K'hwà gaē, 罣碍, to hinder, to obstruct.

K'hwà 掛 To hang, to suspend; k'hwà bòk kèng, 掛目鏡 *k'hwà bàk kēⁿà*, to wear spectacles; also written 挂, k'hwà.
Gwát ê hwa éng k'hwà ko hwân, 月移花影掛高垣 *göëyh ê hwa yēⁿá k'hwà tē kwân ch'hëôⁿᵍ*, the moon removed the shadow of the flower, and suspended it on the high wall.

K'hwà 跨 To step over, to stride across; k'hwà yëá má, 跨野馬 *k'hwà yëá gwā ây báy*, to bestride a wild horse.

K'hwà 漥 Read k'hò: to run aground; k'hò say san, 漥沙山 *k'hwà swa swⁿa*, to run upon a sand-bank.

K'hwà 秙 Empty grain, husks without any fruit in them.

K'hwà 絓 To bind anything about; to intertwine grass ropes about a fence, in order to strengthen it.

平

K'hwâ 桍 The name of a certain tree.

上

K'hwⁿa 寬 Read k'hwan: easy, forgiving; leisurely, indulgent, gentle.
K'hwan hêng, 寬行 *k'hwⁿa kēⁿâ*, to walk leisurely and slowly.

去

K'hwⁿà 看 Read k'hàn: to see; k'hàn keèn, 看見 *k'hwⁿa keèⁿᵍ*, to behold.
Ch'hó sek yaôu k'hàn, kīn k'hëak boô, 草色遙看近却無 *ch'haóu sek kwuīⁿᵍ ëy k'hwⁿà kaôu kīn k'hëak bô*, the color of the newly springing grass may be seen from a distance, but when near it disappears.

K'hwⁿà 寬 Read k'hwan: loose, easy; sok bút k'hwan, 束物寬 *pák meēⁿh k'hwⁿà k'hwⁿà*, to tie anything gently.

上

K'hwae 㔞 A strong man; athletic, muscular strength.

去

K'hwaè 快 Quick, hasty, speedy; pleasant, grateful, agreeable; easy.
K'hwaè laê, 快來, come quickly; k'hwaè chò, 快做, easily done.
Sóng k'hwaè, 爽快, healthy, hearty; k'hwaè lók, 快樂, cheerful.
Ong wát goê hô k'hwaè ê sē? 王曰吾何快于是 *ông kóng gwá k'ham sē k'hwⁿa wǎh tē chéy*

福建方言字典

lêy? the king said, 'how can I be pleased and gratified with such things as these?' see 孟子 Bēng choó.

K'hwaè jîn k'hwaè gé, 快人快語 *k'hwaè lâng k'hwaè wā*, a hearty man is sure to say something hearty and agreeable.

K'hwaè 駃 K'hwaè má, 駃馬, *k'hwaè báy*, a swift horse.

K'hwaè 噲 To swallow anything, the throat; the same as 快 k'hwaè.

K'hwaè 塊 A lump of anything; yit k'hwaè tēy, 一塊地 *chit tēy t'hoè*, a clod of earth; taē k'hwaè, 大塊, the great lump, heaven and earth, creative power. Chìn kong choó Tëūng-jé ke, k'hit sit ê Gnoé-lòk yëá jîn, é che k'hwaè, 晉公子重耳飢乞食于五鹿野人與之塊 *Chìn ây kong choó Tëūng-jé kaòu yaou, k'hit chëăh kap Goē-lòk ây yëá lâng, é hoē e chit tēy t'hoè*, the prince of the Chin country, named Tëūng-jé, when hungry, begged food of some savages in the Five-stag desert; upon which they gave him a clod of earth; (he was disposed to be angry at it, but his consellors advised him to receive the clod thankfully, for it was a prognostic of his getting the country, which he afterwards did really obtain.)

Taē k'hwaè káy gnó é bûn chëang, 大塊假我以文章 *twā tēy chëŏh gwá ê bûn chëo^ng*, the great lump (heaven and earth) has lent me the talent for making literary compositions; said by 李白文 Lé pėk bûn.

六

K'hwăh 闊 Read k'hwat: wide, expansive, broad, ample.

Haé k'hwat yêw gê yëák, 海闊由魚躍 *haé k'hwăh keè^ng chaē hê yūng yëák*, the sea is wide, therefore let the fishes jump about in it.

平

K'hwan 寬 Vulg. *k'hwⁿa*: gentle, easy, soft, leisurely, liberal, kind.

K'hwan chek tek chëùng, 寬則得衆 *k'hwⁿa ch'hòng chek tit chëùng lâng*, be gentle, and you will win the hearts of all; see the 語論 Lūn gé.

上

K'hwán 款 Truly; to knock, to beat; k'hwán t'haē, 款待, to intreat, to entertain. K'hwán kwan ch'héng këèn, 款關請見 *k'haòu kwan ch'hëⁿá keè^ng*, he knocked at the gate of the pass and begged an interview; see the 史記 Soó kè.

K'hwán 欵 The same as the above; congenial, pure, unmixed.

K'hwán 欵 K'hwán tong hwa, 欵冬花, the name of a medicinal plant.

K'hwán 窾 Emptied, hollow.

K'hwán 欵 The noise of a number of pestles working in the same mortar.

K'hwán 綣 K'hëén k'hwán, 綣綣, kindness of intention, to treat one kindly.

去

K'hwàn 勸 Vulg. *k'hwui^ng*: to advise, to exhort, to counsel. K'hwàn sè bûn, 勸世文, religious tracts.

Ké sëēn jê kaòu put lêng, chek k'hwàn, 舉善而教不能則勸 *ké yūng hó ây jê kà bēy ây, chek păyh sai^ng sëo k'hwui^ng*, if you promote the good, and instruct the incapable, then the people will begin to exhort one another; see the 論語 Lūn gé.

K'hwan 券 An agreement, a check, the two parts of which are held by the different parties; to labor, to be troubled.

平

K'hwân 拳 The hand bent, the arms folded; diligent, earnest, anxious. K'hwân t'hoê, 拳頭 *k'hwân t'haôu*, the fist. Tek yit sëen, chek k'hwân k'hwân hòk eng, jê bút sit che è, 得一善則拳拳服膺而勿失之矣 *tit tëòh chit ây hó, chek k'hwân k'hwân hòk tē sim kwⁿa t'hâon, jê bŏh sit e*, having attained to one virtue, then fold it in your arms and clasp it to your breast, without allowing it to escape; see the 中庸 Tëung yûng.

K'hwân 惓 K'hwân k'hwân, 惓惓, diligent application, anxious desire.

K'hwân 圈 A fold for cattle, an inclosure for keeping cattle.

K'hwân 瘓 Vulg. *k'höëy*: a cramp in the arms and legs.

夬

K'hwat 闕 The leaves of a door, to lose, to miss, empty, void, defective; a surname. Kwun chóó ê kê séy put te, kaè k'hwat jê yëá, 君子於其所不知蓋闕如也 *kwun choó tē e séy ūᵐ chae kaè k'hwat jê yëá*, the good man, in those things which he does not know, acknowledges his deficiencies.

K'hwat 厥 An euphonic particle; also used for the pronouns he, she, it, his, her's, &c. K'hwat ch'hó wûy yaou, k'hwat bók wûy keâou, 厥草爲夭厥木爲喬 *e ây ch'haôu sē cheēⁿᵍ, e ây ch'hâ sē kwân*, this plant is tender, and that tree is high; see the 書經 Se keng.

K'hwat 蕨 K'hwat ch'haè, 蕨菜, the name of a plant, a sort of pot-herb; k'hwat hwŭn, 蕨粉, the powdered root of the k'hwat plant.

K'hwat 劂 Kê k'hwat, 剞劂, a crooked knife.

K'hwat 撅 To hold anything in the hand; to plunder, to take by force.

K'hwat 瘚 A rising of the wind in the stomach.

K'hwat 蹶 To slip with the foot; to jump, to walk fast. Këêt k'hwat jê ch'he che, 竭蹶而趨之, to walk as fast as possible, and get forward.

K'hwat 礮 To throw stones, out of a sling or engine.

K'hwat 橛 Yit k'hwat, 杙橛, a post stuck in the ground, for fastening cattle to. Bûn k'hwat, 門橛, a door-post at the side of a door.

K'hwat 劈 Force, main strength.

K'hwat 闋 The end, to finish, to be concluded. Yéw soo kò é gák k'hwat, 有司告以樂闋 *yêw soo ây kwⁿa kò é chok gák swăh*, the proper officer announced that the music was finished.

K'hwat 闊 Vulg. *k'hwăh*: broad, ample, expansive, wide; also written 濶, k'hwat. Seng sûy pêng yëá k'hwat gwát yúng taē kang lêw, 星隨平野闊月湧大江流 *ch'haiⁿᵍ tit tûy tē paⁿᵍ yëá ây k'hwăh göëyh tit*

福建方言字典

yúng tē twā kang ây laôu, the stars appear to fall on the breadth of the expansive plain, and the moon to bubble up in the stream of the mighty river.

K'hwat 缺 Vulg. *k'höĕyh:* short, deficient, few, scarce, wanting.
Vulg. *k'heĕh:* having a flaw, or crack; broken, injured.
Boô seáou k'hëèm k'hwat, 無少欠缺 *bô sëó k'hwá k'hëèm k'höĕyh,* not in the least wanting or deficient.

K'hwat 觖 K'hwat bōng, 觖望, to give up hope, to despair; to look at with malice.

K'hwat 缺 Empty, deficient, injured.

K'hwat 觼 A ring with a tongue in it, a lock.

K'hwat 乚 A hook.

去 K'hwuìng 勸 Read k'hwàn: to advise, to exhort, to counsel.
Lîm che é chong, chek k'hwàn, 臨之以莊則勸 *lîm kaôu pāyh saìng é chong gëĕm, c chēw sëo k'hwuìng,* when you appear before the people with stern rigor, they will begin to exhort one another; see the 語論 Lūn gé.

平 K'hwun 坤 The female or inferior principle of nature; k'hëên k'hwun, 乾坤, heaven and earth, the male and female principle, which the Chinese suppose produced all things.
K'hëên k'hwun tēng è, 乾坤定矣 *k'hëên k'hwun tēⁿā tëŏh,* the male and female principle became fixed; see the 易經 Ēk keng.

4 X

K'hwun 昆 An elder brother; brethren; k'hwun tēy yëá, 昆弟也 *hëⁿa tē yëá,* elder and younger brethren; see the 中庸 Tëung yûng.
Wūy t'hⁿa jîn k'hwun, ék bók gnó bûn, 謂他人昆亦莫我聞 *kóng pat lâng sē hëⁿa, yëá bô gwá t'hëⁿa,* to call another man elder brother is what I have never heard of; see the 詩王風 Se ông hong.

K'hwun 崑 K'hwun lûn san, 崑崙山 *k'hwun lûn swⁿa,* the name of a famous hill on the N.W. of China, supposed to be the source of the 黄河 Hông hô.

K'hwun 蜫 A general name for insects.

K'hwun 鯤 The name of a large fish, found in the northern sea; the spawn of fish.

K'hwun 鵾 The name of a bird, resembling a domestic fowl, but larger.

K'hwun 琨 Yaôu k'hwun, 瑶琨, the name of a precious stone.

K'hwun 焜 Bright, clear; to illumine.
K'hwun yaōu kwⁿá jîn che bōng, 焜燿寡人之望 *kwuìng yaōu kwⁿá jîn ây bāng,* to illumine and brighten my hopes; see the 左傳 Chó twān.

K'hwun 髡 To cut off the hair. Sûn ô k'hwun, 淳于髡, a man's name.

K'hwun 囷 A granary, a sheaf of corn, a bundle of anything.
Put kày put sek, hoê ch'hé hô

sam pek k'hwun hêy? 不稼不穡胡取禾三百囷兮 ūm chò kày sek, böëyh an chwⁿá ëy k'hëŏh tëŏh hô kaòu sⁿa pāyh k'hwun hêy? without cultivation and agriculture, how could we collect three hundred granaries full of corn? see the 魏風 Gwūy hong.

K'hwun 菌 A mushroom; k'hwun kwuy, 菌桂, a sort of cinnamon bark, brought from Cochinchina, of which mats can be made.

K'hwun 麕 The general name for deer. Yëá yéw soó k'hwun, pék maôu paou che, 野有死麕白茅包之 yëá gwā woō sé ây lòk, pāyh hûᵐ á ch'háou paou e, in the desert there is a dead stag, with coarse white grass wrapped around it; see the 召南 Seàou lâm.

K'hwun 峮 Lîn k'hwun, 嶙峮, the connected appearance of hills.

声

K'hwún 捆 To twist, to plait; to beat and bind firmly together. Kae è hat k'hwún kè chit poè é wûy sit, 皆衣褐捆屨織布以爲食 chò poê ch'hēng ch'hoe poè, p'hăh ây, chit poè, ê t'hàn chëăh, they all wore coarse apparel, plaited straw sandals, and wove cloth, in order to get their livelihood; see 孟子 Bēng choó.

K'hwún 悃 Sincere, pure, disinterested.

K'hwún 綑 To weave, to bind and twist together; k'hwún sék, 綑席, k'hwún ch'hëŏh, to weave mats.

K'hwún 裍 To weave cloth; the same as the above.

K'hwún 稛 Anything become ripe; full; to bind up; a sheaf of corn.

K'hwún 梱 A door-post, the side posts of a door; also written 閫, k'hwún. Göēy gân put jip ê k'hwún, löēy gân put ch'hut ê k'hwún, 外言不入于梱內言不出于梱 gwā bīn ây wā bô jip tē k'hwún, laē bīn ây wā bô ch'hut tē k'hwún, let not out of door scandal enter within the door-posts, nor domestic concerns be talked of abroad; see the 曲禮 K'hëuk léy.

K'hwún 綑 A sheaf of corn; the same as 稛, k'hwún.

K'hwún 丨 Connected above and below, from the top to the bottom. One of the radicals.

K'hwún 窘 Poor, exhausted, pressed by poverty, urged by want. Yēw k'hwún yim é, 又窘陰雨 yēw woō k'hwún këâng lân chêy lêy yim àm ây hoē, we are still pressed by this threatening rain.

K'hwún 捃 To collect, to gather; k'hwún chëá, 捃摭, to pick or take up.

K'hwún 僒 To exhaust.

K'hwún 懇 Earnest, sincere, pressing; k'hwún kêw, 懇求, to beg earnestly; also written 墾, k'hwún.

K'hwún 豤 To bite, to bite anything deeply.

K'hwún 墾 To exert one's-self in setting anything to rights; to clear the ground.

K'hwún 壼 A passage in the ladies' apartment, an entry in a dwelling.

去 K'hwùn 困 Pressed by want, poor, wretched, miserable, fatigued.

Hwān-ch'he Ch'haè-tek, jē choó put k'hwùn ek, oe lêng jê sē? 范雎蔡澤二子不困阨惡能如是 *Hwān-ch'he Ch'hwà-tèk nō lâng, nā bŏ k'hwùn yĕăh, bōĕyh an chwⁿá ēy an nēy saiⁿᵍ?* if those two great scholars Hwān-ch'he and Ch'hwà-tèk had not been reduced to great straits and distresses, how would they have consented to be thus (employed by 秦 Chîn)? see the 史記 Soó kè.

K'hwùn 睏 The name of a tune in music.

K'hwùn 嶇 The appearance of hills.

K'hwùn 睔 The light of the sun.

K'hwùn 睡 Read sūy: to sleep; sūy pông, 睡房 *k'hwùn pâng*, a bedchamber.

Yâng gé soō lëăng kéw, Haòu-kong sūy jê hwut t'hèng, 楊語事良久孝公睡而弗聽 *Yâng kóng soō kaòu sëōⁿᵍ koó, Haòu-kong k'hwùn jê ūᵐ t'hēⁿa*, while Yang was talking over affairs for a long time, Haòu-kong went to sleep, and did not hear him; see the 史記 Soó kè.

平 K'hwûn 梱 Short and collected together.

K'hwûn 蜠 Wūn k'hwûn, 蝹蜠, to coil up, as a snake.

K'hwûn 緄 K'hwûn sek, 緄索 *k'hwûn sŏh á*, to coil up a rope; an ornamented girdle. Pōēy to k'hwûn taè, 佩刀緄帶, to gird on a sword, and bind around a girdle.

去 K'hwut 窟 A hole, a pit; súy k'hwut, 水窟 *chúy k'hwut*, a pond, a pool.

Koé chëá sëen ông, bē yéw këung sit, tong chek ke êng k'hwut, 古者先王未有宮室冬則居營窟 *koé chá ăy sëen ông, bōēy woō këung ch'hoò, kaòu tang t'heeⁿᵍ chek k'hëă êng k'hwut á*, the first kings of remote antiquity had neither palaces nor houses, but in the winter they dwelt in holes and caverns; see the 禮記 Léy kè.

K'hwut 滵 Deep water, a deep pit.

Boô yûng k'hwut jê chwân ch'hut, 無溶滵而泉出 *bó yûng k'hwut jê chúy chwⁿâ yëá ch'hut*, there is here no depth of water, yet the fountain springs up; see the 王充論 Ong ch'hëung lūn.

K'hwut 堀 The same as 窟 k'hwut: a hole, a pit; hók soó k'hwut hëét, 伏死堀穴 *hók sé tē k'hwut hëét*, to die secreted in some hole or cavern.

K'hwut 崛 K'hwut gwút, 崛屼, a bluff part of a mountain, a cave.

K'hwut 屈 To bend, to make crooked, to stoop; a surname; k'hwut ch'hip, 屈膝, to bend the knee.

Wuy boó put lêng k'hwut, 威武不能屈 *wūy boó bēy hoē lâng k'hwut*, grandeur and martial display cannot make (the good man) stoop; see 孟子 Bēng choó.

Kong chek put k'hwut e bút yëúk, 剛則不屈於物慾 *kong chek bēy k'hwut tē pat meēⁿh soo yëúk*, when a man is firm, he will not be overcome by visible objects and carnal lusts.

K'hwut 緆 The garments of barbarians; to tie, to bend and straighten.

K'hwut 胐 The arm.

K'hwut 胐 The leg.

入

K'hwút 淈 Exhausted, water all run out; a scarcity of water.

K'hwút 榾 Broken wood.

上

K'hwuy 虧 To injure; a deficiency, a defect, scarce, to be in arrears. Sin t'héy sēw ê hoō boé, put k'hó hwúy sëang, hòng k'hwuy kê hēng; é jëúk kê ch'hin hoē! 身體受於父母不可毀傷况虧其行以辱其親乎 *sin t'hēy sē sēw tē pāy boé, ūᵐ t'hang p'hăh sëang, hô hòng p'hăh k'hēep e ây sēy kēⁿâ; é lêng jëúk e ây ch'hin hoē!* man has received his body from his father and mother, and therefore he ought not to injure it; how much less should he by corrupt practices bring disgrace on his parents!

K'hwuy 睽 K'hwuy wûy, 睽違, to be separated.

K'hwuy 開 Read k'hae: to open, to spread out; k'hae bûn, 開門 *k'hwuy mootⁿᵍ*, to open a door; p'hò k'hae, 破開 *p'hwà k'hwuy*, to burst open.

Jê chok bûn, yëúk hàp che, pit sëen ch'huy k'hae, é hêuk kê sè, 如作文欲合之必先推開以蓄其勢, *ch'hin chëōⁿᵍ chò bún chëōⁿᵍ nā aè böëyh hàp e, pit tëöh taē seng ch'huy k'hwuy, é k'hëök lëöh e ây sè*, just as in making literary compositions, if you intend them to be solid and concise, you must first write them out diffusely, that you may afterwards be able to concentrate their force.

上

K'hwúy 軌 The track of a carriage wheel, the rut of a wheel; the rule or plan of chariot driving; ke tông k'hwuy, 車同軌 *ch'hëa tâng chit ây k'hwuy*, carriages should be driven in the same rut; see the 中庸 Tëung yûng.

K'hwúy 匭 A box, a casket, a case; to put into a box.

K'hwúy 垝 A broken wall; to demolish, to throw down. Sêng pé k'hwúy hwân, 乘彼垝垣 *păyh chëōⁿᵍ hwut lêy k'hëep ch'hëōⁿᵍ*, to get upon that broken wall; see the 衛風 Wöëy hong.

K'hwúy 詭 Deceitful; k'hwúy ē, 詭異, strange and wonderful; k'hwúy chāy, 詭詐, false and deceitful; k'hwúy kè, 詭計, cunning tricks. K'hwúy soê jê ch'hut, 詭詞而出 *k'hwúy wā toe ch'hut*, deceitful expressions come into vogue.

K'hwúy 磈 K'hwúy lúy, 磈碨, stones heaped up together.

K'hwúy 跬 A step; k'hwúy poè, 跬步 *hwăh poè*, a pace; to step quickly.

K'hwúy 趌 The same as the above; one lifting up of the foot, a step, a pace.

福建方言字典

K'hwúy 頍 The appearance of a cap; to wear a cap.

K'hwúy 晷 The shadow of the sun, a gnomon; jit k'hwúy, 日晷, a sun-dial.

K'hwúy 簋 Hoó k'hwúy, 簠簋, a square vessel made of bamboo, for containing the offerings of the first fruits, in sacrifices.

K'hwúy 傀 K'hwúy lúy, 傀儡 *kā léy*, puppets, a puppet-show.

去

K'hwùy 愧 To be ashamed; ch'hâm k'hwùy, 慙愧 *seáou léy*, to be filled with shame. Put k'hwùy ê ok loē, 不愧於屋漏 *bô seáou léy ê ch'hoò laōu*, not to be ashamed of a leaky house; (poverty's no sin;) see the 大雅 Taē gnáy.

K'hwùy 媿 The same as the above; to be ashamed; to be modest. Boô k'hwùy ê k'hoé, put jëák boô k'hwùy ê sim 無媿於口不若無媿於心 *bô seáou léy tē ch'hùy, ūm tāh tëŏh bô seáou léy tē sim*, not to be ashamed in the mouth, is not so good as not to be ashamed in the heart; (i. e. it is better to *feel* than to *express* modesty.)

K'hwùy 季 Read kwùy: a season; soò kwùy, 四季 *sè k'hwùy*, the 4 seasons. The last of anything is called *k'hwùy*; as kwùy gwát, 季月 *k'hwùy göĕyh*, the last month of a season; kwùy sè, 季世 *k'hwùy sè*, the last age.

K'hwùy 氣 Read k'hè: the breath, wind, force; ch'hwán k'hè, 喘氣 *ch'hwán k'hwùy*, to breathe, to pant; k'hè lék, 氣力 *k'hwùy lát*, the strength, stout.

4 Y

Jîn che k'hè lék, pín che ê t'hëen, 人之氣力稟之於天 *láng ây k'hwùy lát pín sëw ê t'hee*^{ng}, mens' strength is derived from heaven.

K'hwùy 悸 The heart moved; agitation of mind.

K'hwùy 瘁 Sick through fear and perturbation.

平

Kim 金 Metal, gold; hông kim, 黃金, yellow gold. A surname. Kim tëūng ê é chëá, 金重於羽者 *kim k'hāh tāng ê cheáou mô*, metal is heavier than feathers; see 孟子 Bēng choò. Kim, bók, súy, h^{n}ó, t'hoé, 金木水火土 *kim, bàk, chúy, höéy, t'hoé*, metal, wood, water, fire, and earth, (are the five elements according to the Chinese.)

Kim 今 Vulg. *t*^{n}*a*: now, at present; hëēn kim, 現今, at this time. Tong kim che sè, [illegible] gnó kê sûy yëá? 當今之世舍我其誰也 *tong kim ây sè, pàng t'hek kak gwá, yëá woō chē chûy?* if they reject me at the present crisis, whom else will they obtain? see 孟子 Bēng choò. Kim yëá put jëên, 今也不然 *t*^{n}*a chëw bô an néy*, at present it is not so.

Kim 禁 That which may be restrained by force; a restraint.

Kim 惍 Gain, profit, advantage.

上

Kím 錦 Embroidery, variegated silk; kím sèw, 錦繡 ornamented silk. E kím sëāng kéng, 衣錦尙

絅 *ch'hēng kim sèw ây sⁿa, teŏh laê bīn yūng chit twⁿa nēⁿá*, when you wear an embroidered dress, you should have a single garment underneath; see the 詩經 Se keng.

去 Kìm **禁** To forbid, to restrain, to interdict; an interdiction, a restraint.

Kìm tēy, 禁地, the forbidden ground; i. e. the precincts of the palace.

Sîn sé chè ê kéng, būn kok che taē kìm, 臣始至於境問國之大禁 *gwá k'hé t'haôu kaôu kēng kaè, chēw mooiⁿᵍ kok ây twā kìm*, when I first came to the borders, I inquired into the great prohibitory laws of the country; see 孟子 Bēng choó.

Kìm **㒇** The name of a kind of music, played by the northern foreigners; according to the ceremonies of the Chew 周 dynasty, the officer who presided over the northern part of the empire was called kìm.

Kìm **噤** To shut the mouth; kìm k'hoé put kēng gân, 噤口不能言 *kìm ch'hùy bēy kóng wā*, to shut the mouth without being able to speak.

Kìm **勬** To exert one's strength.

丟 Kīm **懔** Earnest, resolved, determined.

Kīm **妗** An aunt by marriage, a mother's brother's wife.

平 Kin **巾** A napkin, a kerchief; t'hoê kin, 頭巾 *t'haôu kin*, a head kerchief, a turban; séw kin, 手巾 *ch'héw kin*, a handkerchief. One of the radicals.

Jê lé keúng teem kin, 兒女共沾巾 *ta po cha boé sëo kāng wūn tâm ch'hêw kin*, a young man and woman bedewing their handkerchief together (with their tears).

Kin **斤** A catty, a Chinese pound, about 1⅓lb. English; also, a hatchet.

Sip lëúk lëáng wûy yit kin, 十六两爲一斤 *chàp làk nëóⁿᵍ chò chit kin*, sixteen ounces make one catty.

Hoó kin é sê jip san lîm, 斧斤以時入山林 *poó t'haôu to a chdou sé jip swⁿa lîm*, the hatchet and ax should be employed in the forest at the proper time; see 孟子 Bēng choó.

Kin **均** Even, plain, upon a level, alike; all together; kin sē jîn yëá, 均是人也 *paîⁿᵍ paîⁿᵍ sē lâng*, we are all alike men; see 孟子 Bēng choó.

Kin **筋** The epidermis or skin of bamboo.

Kin **根** A root; kin pún, 根本, the root, the fundamental thing; the principle. Kat lûy yêw pè kê pún kin, 葛藟猶庇其本根 *kwăh lûy yëá teŏh pè yēw e ây kin pún*, even hemp and flax must have some care bestowed on their roots; (how much more men!) see the 左傳 Chó twān.

Kin **跟** The heel, the back part of the foot; kin sûy, 跟隨, to follow.

Kin **觔** The common character for 斤, kin, a catty.

Yit lŏk ch'hëen kin tëūng, 一落千觔重 *chit lŏh ch'heng kin tāng*, at once a thousand catties' weight.

Kin **皸** The hands or feet chapped with the cold.

Kin **筋** A tendon, a sinew, a nerve; këen kin, 堅筋, to brace the nerves; hëet kin, 血筋 *höëyh kin*, a vein, or artery.

Jîn sin yéw sam sip lëük chëet kin kwut, 人身有三十六節筋骨 *lâng ây sin woō s^{n}a châp lâk chat kin kwut*, the human body contains thirty-six joints of sinews and bones.

声

Kín **謹** To be careful; kín sīn, 謹愼 *sèy jē*, to take care; sedate, careful, cautious; veneration, respect.

Kín jê sìn, 謹而信 *sèy jē kwà sìn sit*, be careful and sincere; see the 上論 Sëang lūn.

Kín **瑾** A handsome gem, a precious stone. Kín jê lëk hây, 瑾瑜匿瑕 *kín jê ây gëuk woō tëëm lëk hây tëëm*, the most beautiful pearl contains a flaw; see the 左傳 Chó twān. Also read kīn.

Kín **堇** A certain plant, called also oe t'hoê ch'hó, 烏頭草 *oe t'haôu ch'haôu*, the black-headed plant.

Kín **縸** A kind of cloth, wove with a very fine and close texture.

Kín **緊** Fast, urgent, pressing, hasty; kín yaôu, 緊要, very urgent.
Jé choé jé kín, 愈走愈緊 *nā chaôu nā kín*, the more he ran, the faster he went.

Kín **卺** A gourd cut in halves for wine cups, used on marriage occasions. Also written 巹, kín.

Kín **蚓** Read yín: a worm; t'hoé yín, 土蚓 *t'hoê kín*, an earth-worm.
Hoo yín sëāng sit ko jëáng, hāy yím hông chwân, 夫蚓上食槁壤下飲黃泉 *hoo t'hoê kín têng bīn chëăh tā ây t'hoê, hāy têy lim wui^{ng} ây chw^{n}â*, now the worm above eats nothing but the dry clods, and below it drinks only the yellow fountains; see 孟子 Bēng choó.

去

Kìn **艮** Fast, urgent, pressing; also, to stop. One of the radicals.

Kìn **絹** Sarsnet, a kind of thin silk.

丟

Kin **僅** Almost, nearly, just enough; kīn k'hó, 僅可 *toō toō hó*, just suitable, just adequate.
Kīn yéw chûn chëá, 僅有存者 *toō toō woō chûn tē*, it is just preserved.

Kīn **墐** To besmear, to plaster.

Kīn **槿** The name of a tree.

Kīn **饉** Famine, a dearth of vegetables.
Kay che é soo lé, yin che é ke kīn, 加之以師旅因之以饑饉 *kay e ê peng pë^{n}a, yin e ê yaou kīn*, add to this an invading army, and join to it the calamities of dearth and famine; see the 論語 Lūn gé.

Kīn **覲** To have an audience with an emperor; to have an audience in spring is called, 朝, teâou, and in autumn, it is called 覲, kīn.

Kīn 靳 Firm, stable; niggardly, sparing; also, a surname.

Kīn 近 Near, not distant; to approach, to draw near.
Kim hoo Ch'hwán-jê koē jê kīn ê Pè, 今夫顓臾固而近於費 *t'n^a chéy léy Ch'hwán-jê kēen koē jê kīn wá tē Pè yip*, now the country of Ch'hwan-jê is well defended and near to our city of Pè; see the 論語 Lūn gé.
Sìn kīn ê gē, gān k'hó hòk yēá, 信近於義言可復也 *sìn kīn ê gē lé, kóng wā t'hang hòk*, when our promises approximate to justice, our engagements may be fulfilled; see the 上論 Sëāng lūn.

Kīn 腱 Read këēn: a gizzard; key këēn, 雞腱 *key kīn*, the gizzard of a fowl.

夫

Kip 急 Hasty, urgent, vehement, pressing, quick; straitened.
Kwun chóó chew kip, put kèy hoō, 君子周急不繼富 *kwun chóó chew chèy gwūy kip, bô bōēyh kèy swà poō ây lâng*, the good man supplies the wants of the necessitous, bnt does not add to the stores of the rich; see the 論語 Lūn gé.

Kip 伋 The same as the above; also a man's name; K'hóng-kip, 孔伋 the grandson of Confucius.

Kip 級 An order, a rank; a step, or degree of rank; a numeral of heads.
Kay kip, 階級, steps, stairs; téng kip, 等級, a step; seng kip, 升級, to raise a step in office; kàng kip, 降級, to degrade a step.
Séw kip, 首級, a head; chám séw bān kip, 斬首萬級 *chám t'haôu chĕ^nâ bān kip*, to cut off a myriad of heads.

Kip 給 To give, to afford; këūng kip, 供給, to afford, to furnish, to give.
Ch'hew séng lëém, jê choē put kip, 秋省斂而助不給 *ch'hew sat^ng sew lëém jê choē bô kip*, in harvest time exact moderately, and assist those who cannot furnish anything; see 孟子 Bēng chóó.
K'hoé kip, 口給, conversation, discourse, the talent for conversing.

又

Kip 及 To arrive at, to reach; and, together with.
Hoo chóó che put k'hó kip yēá, yêw t'hëen che put k'hó kae jê seng yēá, 夫子之不可及也猶天之不可階而升也 *hoo chóó ây bēy kip kaôu, ch'hin chëō^ng t'hee^ng ây bēy ch'hòng gîm kay jê chëō^ng*, our master (Confucius,) cannot be equaled, the same as heaven cannot be scaled with a ladder; see the 論語 Lūn gé.
Kip kê sêng kong yit yēá, 及其成功一也 *kip kaôu e chĕ^nâ kong lô chit yëō^ng*, (mens' natural talents vary,) but when they arrive at perfection, they are the same; see the 中庸 Tëung yûng.

Kip 芨 Pêk kip, 白芨 *pāyh kip*, a medicinal herb. Also read k'hip.

Kip 𨒪 The ancient form of 及, kip, to arrive at.

去

Kit 吉 Lucky, fortunate, happy; kit hëung, 吉凶, lucky and unlucky, good and evil; kit jit, 吉日 *hó jit*, a lucky day. A surname.
Jē gwát ch'hay kit, 二月初吉 *jē gōēyh ch'hay sē kit*, the beginning of the second month contains lucky days.

Kit 姞 A surname.

Kit 桔 A lime, a small lemon, a sour orange; also written 橘, kit. Kim kit, 金桔, the golden orange, a small variety of the mandarin orange; kit kēng, 桔梗, lime stalks, a medicine.

Kit 蛣 Kit këang, 蛣蜣, insects found in excrementitious matter.

Kit 佶 Correct, exact; firm, robust.

Kit 拮 To hold fast, to grasp.

Kit 橘 A small lemon; Bân tëung êng kit yēw, 閩中榮橘柚 *Bân sat^{ng} êng kit kap noot^{ng} á*, in the region of Bân (Canton and Hok-këèn), the lemons and shaddocks flourish.

天 *Kit* 糷 Thick, glutinous, as rice-water, or congee.

夲 Ko 高 Vulg. *kwân:* high, lofty; above, upon; distant. A surname. P'hè jê teng ko, pit choō pe, 譬如登高必自卑 *ch'hin chëō^{ng} pǎyh chëō^{ng} kwân, pit choō kāy*, just as in ascending a high place, we must commence from a low one; see the 中庸 Tëung yûng. Chông ko, bòk taē hoē hoà kwùy, 崇高莫大乎富貴 *chun chông kap kwân, bô k'hǎh twā ē poâ kwùy*, among the honored and elevated, there are none more so than the rich and great; see the 易經 Ék keng.

4 Z

Ko 篙 Tëuk ko, 竹篙 *tek ko*, a bamboo pole, for pushing forward a boat.

Ko 膏 Fat, ointment, grease; ko tèk, 膏澤, smooth favors, genial blessings; ko yêw, 膏油, grease, oily substances. Hwûn ko é kèy k'hwöy, 焚膏以繼晷 *sëo yêw è swà jit yë^{n}á*, to burn oil in order to connect the light of the sun (i. e. to study incessantly).

Ko 戈 A spear, a barbed spear; a hook, a pointed weapon. A surname. Tōng kan ko ê pang löēy, 動干戈於邦內 *tin tāng kan ko tē pang kok laē*, to set in motion the clubs and spears in a nation; see the 論語 Lūn gé.

Ko 哥 An elder brother; à ko, 亞哥 *ä^{n} ko*, my elder brother. Ko ko hô soō lūy chëèm chëèm? sat sin sêng jîn chaē ch'hoò kan, 哥哥何事淚潸潸殺身成仁在此間 *ä^{n} ko s^{n}a soō laôu bàk saē tâm tâm? t'haî hîn sin chë^{n}â jîn tek chë^{n}à tē chêy kan*, Oh, my brother! why are you so dissolved in tears? now is the time for sacrificing our lives in the cause of virtue.

Ko 鴰 Eng ko, 鸚鴰, a general name for parrot.

Ko 歌 Vulg. *kwa:* a song, a ditty; ch'hëàng ko, 唱歌 *ch'hëō^{ng} kwa*, to sing songs. Choó é jîn ko jê sëèn, pit soó hwân che, jê hoē hô che, 子與人歌而善必使反之而後和之 *hoo choō kap lâng ch'hëō^{ng} kwa jê hó, pit saē hwân hôk e, jëèn aôu hō e*, Confucius used to sing songs with people, and if they were well sung, he would order them to be repeated, and afterwards he would harmonize with them; see the 論語 Lūn gé.

Ko 羔 A young sheep, a lamb; yâng ko, 羊羔 *yëóng ko*, fur clothing, woolen hose.
Ko yâng che p'hê, 羔羊之皮 *ko yëóng ây p'höéy*, the skin of a young sheep, (with the wool on); see the 召南 Seàou lâm.

Ko 糕 Ko choó, 糕子 *köey á*, a kind of confectionary.
Lëük toē ko, 綠荳糕 *lèk taōu köey*, green grain pies.

Ko 皐 A marsh; ko ték, 皐澤, a marshy place; also, a bank.
Hók bêng ê kéw ko, 鶴鳴于九皐 *höh tit haóu tē kaóu ko*, the stork is screaming in the nine marshes; see the 小雅 Seáou gnáy.

Ko 槹 Kit ko, 桔槹, a machine for drawing water, a well-bucket.
Kit ko chëá yín che chek hoó, sëá che chek gëáng, 桔槹者引之則俯舍之則仰 *prä taóu kaóu k'han e, e chëw p'hak lŏh k'hè, kaóu hëet e, e chëw tⁿa k'hé laê*, if the well-bucket is drawn along, it will turn with the top downwards (and fill); but if it is thrown forwards it will remain with the top upwards, (without sinking in the water.)

Ko 翺 Ko sëâng, 翺翔, to fly backwards and forwards.
Chëang ko chëang sëâng, ék hoô é gān, 將翺將翔弋鳧與雁 *tit pwuy köëy laê pwuy köëy k'hè, laê chŏh ăh kwä gô*, they are flying backwards and forwards, let us go and shoot the wild ducks and geese; see the 鄭風 Tēng hong.

Ko 皋 To advance, to enter, to bring in.

Ko 過 To pass by; E pat lëên ê gwūy, sam ko kê bûn jê put jip, 禹八年於外三過其門而不入 *E păyh neêⁿᵍ tē gwā, sⁿa āy köëy e óy moonᵍ jé bô jip*, E was eight years from home, and during that time thrice passed his own door without entering, (so intent was he on the public business;) see 孟子 Bēng choó.

Ko 櫜 A sheath or case for a bow.
Chaè ch'hip kan ko, chaè ko këung só, 載戢干戈載櫜弓矢 *chaè k'hèⁿᵍ kan ko, chaè sew këung cheèⁿᵍ*, let us lay down our arms, and put our bows and arrows into the case; see the 周頌 Chew sëūng.

Ko 鼛 A large drum; ko koé, 鼛鼓, to beat a drum.

声

Kó 果 The fruit of a tree; determined, resolute; kó kwat, 果决, decided, fixed; kó kâm, 果敢 *kó kⁿá*, brave, bold; kó jëên, 果然, truly, really.
Yêw yëá kó, ê chëûng chèng hoē hô yéw! 由也果於從政乎何有, *Yêw yëá sē kó kwat, tē chëûng chèng soō woō sⁿa meēⁿh ŏh!* Yêw is decided and resolute; and if set to manage the affairs of government, what difficulty would he find! see the 論語 Lūn gé.
Kó yéw sē chêng hoē? 果有是情乎 *kó jëên woō chéy lêy chêng lê hoē?* is that really the case?

Kó 倮 Narrow and contracted.

Kó 菓 Kó choó, 菓子 *köěy ché*, fruit; këet kó, 結菓 *këet köěy ché*, to bring forth fruit, to produce good results; ch'heng kó, 青菓 *ch'hai^{ng} köěy*, the green fruit, an olive.

Kó 粿 Vulg. *köěy:* confectionary, pastry; kó choó, 粿仔 *köěy á*, a tart.

Kó 餜 Vulg. *köěy:* a cake, a pie.

Kó 裸 Vulg. *pak t'hăyh:* naked, without clothes, stripped to the skin. Suy t'hān t'hek kó têng ê gnó ch'hek, jé yëen lêng böéy gnó chae? 雖袒裼裸裎於我側爾焉能浼我哉 *suy peĕh ch'héw wui^{ng} pak t'hăyh, tē gwá ây sin pee^{ng}, lé böëyh an chw^{n} á ēy bàk la sâm gwá chae?* although with your sleeves up or stripped to the skin, you should stand by my side, yet how could you defile me? see 孟子 Bēng choó.

Kó 躶 Naked; the same as the preceding.

Kó 蜾 Kó ló, 蜾蠃 *wan yëo^{ng}*, an insect resembling the dragon fly, with a slender waist. Bêng lêng yéw choó kó ló hoō che, 螟蛉有子蜾蠃負之 *lâ gëâ woō kë^{n}á wan yëo^{ng} gëâ chaóu e*, the spider gets a young one, and the dragon fly carries it away (to its nest, where after certain days, it becomes a young dragon fly;) see the 小雅 Seáou gnáy.

Kó 裹 To bundle up anything, to tie around, to wrap up. Naé kó hoê lëâng, 乃裹餱糧 *naé paou ta ây bé nëō^{ng}*, they packed up their dry provisions; see the 大雅 Taē gnáy.

T'hoê kó hông kin, 頭裹黃巾 *t'haôu paou wui^{ng} kin*, their heads were bound up with yellow turbans; see the 三國 Sam kok.

Kó 杲 The appearance of the sun peeping out from under the clouds. Kê é kê é, kó kó ch'hut jit! 其雨其雨杲杲出日 *lŏh hoē yëw lŏh hoē, lëem pee^{ng} yëw ch'hut jit!* it has rained and rained again, and now, the bright sun appears! see the 衛風 Wöey hong.

Kó 稿 The stalk of grain, the straw; hô kó ch'hó, 禾稿草 *tëw kó ch'haóu*, straw; ch'haou kó, 抄稿, a rough copy of a piece of writing. E hông kok choe, yēw ch'hut kó söèy, 已奉穀租又出稿稅 *é keng hōng jip gnoé kok ây choe, yēw tëŏh ch'hut tēw kó ây söèy*, having already sent up the portion of revenue in grain, we must also pay a tax of straw. Also written 槁, kó.

Kó 槀 Dry, rotten; koe kó, 枯槀, dry, rotten wood. Ch'hit pat gwàt che kan hān, chek beâou kó è, 七八月之間旱則苗槀矣 *ch'hit păyh gŏëyh ây kan woō hw^{n}ā, chek tëw ta è*, if there is a drought within the period of the seventh or eighth months, then the corn is dried up; see 孟子 Bēng choó. Also written 槁, kó.

Kó 鎬 A vessel for warming anything; also, the name of a place.

Kó 皜 Purely white; kó kó hoê, put k'hó sëāng é, 皜皜乎不可尚已 *chin păyh hoē, bēy sëāng ch'hin chëō^{ng} e*, be they ever so pure and white, they can never emulate him (Confucius); see 孟子 Bēng choó.

Kó 縞 White, a light color.

Kó 暠 The lips hanging down.

Kó 薧 Dried fish; anything spread out and dried.

Kò 告 To inform, to announce, to instruct, to command, to go to law. Kò sè, 告示, a proclamation; sëang kò, 相告 *sëo kò*, to go to law together. Lâm put chwan ch'ìè, pit kò hoō boé, 男不專娶必告父母 *ta po bēy choō chwan ch'hwà boé, pit tëōh kò pāy boé*, a young man may not marry according to his own pleasure, but must inform his parents.

Kò 箇 A numeral; yit kò, 一箇 *chit ây*, one. Hoō sè gnoé sìp kò, 負矢五十箇 *gëā cheèng tëōh goē châp lâng*, tho bearers of arrows must be fifty in number, (to follow after an army.)

Kò 個 The same as the above; numeral for mankind; also written 个, kò, one. Jëák yéw yit kò sîn, 若有一個臣 *nā woō chit ây jîn sîn*, if there were but one faithful servant, &c.

Kò 過 To pass by, to pass over; to transgress; kò sit, 過失 *köèy sit*, a transgression; kò k'hè, 過去 *köèy k'hè*, to pass by; kò t'hoê, 過頭 *köèy t'haôu*, to exceed. Kwan kò soo, te jîn è, 觀過斯知人矣 *k'hwⁿà lâng ây köèy sit, an nëy chëá ēy chae e ây lâng*, look at a man's errors; thus you may know what sort of a man he is. Kò kéw kang, 過九江 *köèy kaôu ây kang*, ... the nine rivers; see the 書禹貢 Se é kòng.

Kô 翱 To fly.

Kō 膏 To anoint anything with oil or ointment; to grease anything.

Koe 沽 To sell, to vend, to dispose of. Kêw sëēn kày jê koe choo, 求善賈而沽諸 *këw hó kày jê bēy*, to seek for a good price and sell a thing; see the 論語 Lūn gé.

Koe 酤 Koe chéw, 酤酒, to sell wine; some say, to buy.

Koe 枯 Dry wood; koe kó, 枯槁 rotten wood; putrid. Koe káw chëá ē wûy lèk, 枯朽者易爲力 *ta kwà nwⁿâ ây ch'hâ k'hwaè yung lât*, anything dry and rotten docs not require much strength (to push it down); see the 史記 Soó kè.

Koe 蛄 Hwûy koe, 螅蛄, a kind of insect.

Koe 骷 The bones of the loins, ribs, or knees.

Koe 姑 An aunt, a father's sister; *koé ch'hēⁿá*, 姑且, leisurely, gently, for the time being. Koe sëá sē, 姑舍是 *koe ch'hēⁿá pàng k'hwuy chēy lēy*, let us just set this aside (to speak of something else.)

Koe 鴣 Chëa koe, 鷓鴣, a partridge.

福建方言字典

Koe 鮬 The name of a fish.

Koe 觚 Anything with corners, or angles; angular; the same as 觚, koe.

Koe 菰 A kind of mushroom; hëang koe, 香菰 *hëo^ng koe*, a fragrant mushroom; ch'hó koe, 草菰 *ch'haóu koe*, an edible mushroom.

Koe 孤 Alone, destitute; an orphan; used for the first personal pronoun, by princes, when speaking politely. Yèw jê boô hoō wàt koe, 幼而無父曰孤 *seáou lëên jê bô nëô^ng pāy kóng koe*, one left without parents when young, is called an orphan; see 孟子 Bēng choó.

Koe 罛 A fish-net; also written 𦊂, koe.

Koe 觚 A wine vessel, a cup for drinking.

Koe 辜 A crime, a fault; boô koe, 無辜, without crime, innocent. Hêng yit put gē, sat yit put koe, kae put wûy yëá, 行一不義殺一不辜皆不爲也 *k^na chit hāng ū^m gē, t'haé chit lâng bô chöēy, lóng ū^m k^ná chò*, to practice one unrighteous action, or to put to death one innocent person, was what he would not do; see 孟子 Bēng choó.

Koe 嫴 To stand security for a female criminal whose offense is slight. Koé chëá hoō jîn chöēy k'heng put jip gëúk, pó jîm é t'haō chöēy, 古者婦人罪輕不入獄保任以待罪 *koé chá ây cha boé lâng chöēy k'hăh k'hin bô jip k^na k'hoo, chēw pó jîm é têng t'haē sím chöēy*, among the ancients, when females were guilty of any light crimes, they were not put in prison, but were bailed out to wait for their sentence.

Koe 勾 Anything crooked; also written 句 koe. A surname.

Koe 鉤 Vulg. *kaou*: a hook; gê koe, 魚鉤 *hê kaou*, a fishhook. Gwàt hwûn k'hëuk soō koe, 月痕曲似鉤 *göëyh hwûn k'heuk ch'hin chëô^ng kaou*, the new moon is bent like a hook.

Koe 溝 Vulg. *kaou*: a ditch; ch'him koe, 深溝 *ch'him kaou*, a deep ditch. Ló jëák chwán hoē koe hok, 老弱轉乎溝洫 *laōu ây noo^ng chí^ná hwat lin too^ng tē kaou hok*, the old and weak would die weltering in the ditches; see 孟子 Bēng choó.

Koe 媾 The consummation of a marriage, the union of the sexes.

Koe 構 To build a house, to construct a building; to join together. Also read koè.

Koe 購 To seek, to obtain anything by money; to purchase, to bribe. Chëang sey koe ê Chîn, 將西購於秦 *chëang sae pêng k'hì koe bây tē Chîn*, to go to the west and bribe the Chîn country; see the 史記 Soó kè.

Koe 覯 To have an interview with; to see a person accidentally. Also read koè.

Koe 遘 To meet with, to occur, to happen; gō koe, 遇遘, to fall in with.

声

Koé 古 Ancient, distant, of old, koé sê, 古時, antiquity. A surname. Koé che tō yëá, 古之道也 *koé chá ây tō lé*, the custom of the ancients. P'hok koé t'hong kim, 博古通今 *p'hok koé chá chac tòng kim*, to be extensively acquainted with ancient writings, and to be thoroughly versed in modern ones.

Koé 估 Market duties, or prices; to debate about a price; to buy.

Koé 牯 The male of a species; gnêw koé, 牛牯 *goô kang*, a bull.

Koé 羖 Yâng koé, 羊羖 *yëôⁿᵍ kang*, a ram.

Koé 詁 Hwùn koé, 訓詁, to instruct, to teach; the instructions of ancient books. Jê Jé-gnáy naé hwùn koé che se yëá, 如爾雅乃訓詁之書也 *ch'hin chëōⁿᵍ Jé-gnáy naé sē hwùn koé ây ch'hăyh*, such as the Jé-gnáy, which is a very instructive book.

Koé 罟 A fishing net; bóng koé, 網罟, a net. Ch'hëuk koé put jip woo tê, 数罟不入洿池 *bát bát ây bāng ūm t'hang jip tē chúy k'hwut á*, a close meshed net ought not to be thrown into the pools; see 孟子 Bēng choó.

Koé 笱 A crooked bamboo basket or snare, for catching fish.

Koé 苟 Truly, if, but; koé ch'hëⁿá, 苟且 remiss, careless, disorderly. Koé chè ê jîn è, boô ok yëá, 苟志於仁矣無惡也 *chin cheⁿa nā sim chè tē jîn tek, chēw bô p'haⁿé*, if a man's mind is truly bent on virtue, he will practice no wickedness; see the 論語 Lūn gé.

Koè 狗 Vulg. *kaóu*: a dog; koē hwūy, 狗吠 *kaóu pwūy*, the dog barks. Koé tē sit jîn sit, jê put te këém, 狗彘食人食而不知檢 *kaóu te chëăh lâng chëăh, jê ūm chae kēém téém*, your dogs and pigs eat men's food, and you do not know how to take account of it; see 孟子 Bēng choo.

Koé 枸 The name of a wood; koé ké choó, 枸杞子, the seeds of the medlar used as a medicine.

Koé [犭苟] The barking of a dog.

Koé 盬 Salt; a salt-cellar or pan; also, not firm, insecure.

Koé 蠱 The name of one of the diagrams; worms in the stomach.

Koé 鼓 A drum; lūy koé, 擂鼓, to roll the drum; also written 皷 koé. Kek koé kê tong tong, 擊鼓其鏜鏜 *phăh koé e ây sëⁿa tong tong*, beating the drum with the sound of tong tong; see the 衛風 Wōēy hong. One of the radicals.

Koé 瞽 Blind, unable to see; koé bông, 瞽盲, totally blind. Këèn bëén chëá é koé chëá, këèn che söey seáou pit chok, 見冕者與瞽者見之雖少必作 *k'hwⁿà keēⁿᵍ tè bëén bō ây lâng kap ch'haiⁿᵍ maiⁿᵍ ây lâng; k'hwⁿà keēⁿᵍ e söey k'hăh sèy lán, yëá tëōh k'hé laé*, when we see any persons wearing a crown, or blind,

福建方言字典

although they are younger than ourselves, we should rise up; see the 論語 Lūn gé.

Koé 耇 A very old man, with a face as though it were grimed with filth. Hông koé tae pöèy, 黄耇駘背 *wuíng mô koé bīn ka chĕăh wun koo ây laôu lâng*, a yellow haired, grime faced, and humpbacked, old man; see the 大雅 Taē gnáy.

Koé 股 The thigh; koé keng, 股肱, a limb; séw koé, 手股 *ch'héw koé*, an arm; p'hè koé, 屁股 *ka ch'huíng*, the posteriors.

Gwân séw bêng chae, koé keng lëâng chae, 元首明哉股肱良哉 *gwân t'haôu nâ bêng, k'ha ch'héw chĕw lëâng*, when the head (of a state) is intelligent, the members will be good; see the 詩經 Se keng.

Koé 羖 A ram, a goat; the same as 羖, koé.

Koé 冓 The most secret and retired part of a dwelling. Tëung koé che gân, put k'hó tō yëá, 中冓之言不可道也 *koé tang eng ây wā, ūm t'hang kóng*, what is said in the secret chambers, must not be published; see the 鄭風 Tēng hong.

Koé 垢 Dirt, filth; tîn koé, 塵垢, dust, dirt. Hóng hông hoē, tîn koé che tëung, 彷徨乎塵垢之中 *hóng hông hoē tē, tîn koé ây tang eng*, hurried and bustled, in the midst of dust and dirt; see 莊子 Chong choó.

Koé 賈 To sell, to keep goods for sale. Yëük yúng chëá? koé ô ô yúng, 欲勇者賈余餘勇 *aē bōëyh yúng bêng ây lâng? gwá laê bēy gwá ây yúng bêng*, who wants courage and bravery? I will dispose of the excess of my bravery; see the 左傳 Chó twān.

Koè 固 Firm, stable; këen koè, 堅固, firm, unmoved; koè loē, 固陋, niggardly, mean; koè è, 固意, on purpose, with a fixed intention, determined.

Kwun choó put tëüng chek put wuy, hâk chek put koè, 君子不重則不威學則不固 *kwun choó bô tëüng hoē chëw bô wuy gëëm, t'hàk bēy këen koè*, if the good man is not grave, he will lose his dignity, and that which he learns will be unstable; see the 下論 Sëäng lūn.

Koè chae, Ko-soé che wûy se yëá! 固哉高叟之爲詩也 *koè loē chae, Ko-soé ây chò se!* how mean is the poetry of Ko-soé! see 孟子 Bēng choó.

Koè 痼 A chronic disease, an inveterate malady of long standing.

Koè 雇 To hire any one for money.

Koè 僱 Koè ch'hèng, 僱倩 *koè ch'hèng*, to hire a laborer.

Koè 顧 To look at, to contemplate, to turn around and look at any one; a surname. Cheàou koè, 照顧, to regard with favor and compassion. Koè wân, 顧園 *koè hwuíng*, to look after a garden.

Ke tëung put lōëy koè, 車中不內顧 *ch'hëa tang eng bōh laē bīn koè*, when you are in a carriage, do not turn around to look at it; see the 論語 Lūn gé.

Koè 句 Koè tòng, 句當 *koè tàng*, business, engagement. Jé chok sīm mōh koè tòng? 你作甚麽

句當 *lé tit chò s^{n}a meĕ^{n}h koè tàng?* what are you doing?

Koè 雊 The crowing of the cock of the wild fowl.

Koè 够 Vulg. *kaðu:* enough, sufficient.

Koè 搆 To lead, to drag, to pull; to scheme.

Koè 媾 A second marriage, love or affection for.

Koè 購 To procure with money; to buy, to bribe. Koè é ch'hëen kim, 購以千金 *bëy é ch'heng kim,* to purchase for a thousand pieces of gold; see the 史記 Soó kè.

Koè 遘 To meet with, to fall in with.

Koè 姤 To meet together; junction of the two elements of nature.

Koè 詬 To be ashamed, to rail at, to abuse; to disgrace.

Sëang é jê sëang koè pēng, 常以儒相詬病 *sëāng woō t'hàk ch'hăyh lâng sëo mai^{ng} pai^{ng},* constantly do we see learned men railing at and finding fault with each other.

Koe 彀 To draw a bow to its full stretch; vulg. *kaðu:* enough.

Gāy che kaðu jîn sëà, pit chè ê koè, 羿之教人射必志於彀 *Gāy ây kà lâng chŏh she^{ng}, pit töŏh sim chè twā tē töŏh këung mw^{n}á,* when Gāy taught people archery, he would have them pay great attention to drawing the bow out to the full; see 孟子 Bēng choó.

Koè 故 Old; a business, a reason, a cause; for, because, therefore; yëên koè, 緣故, a cause, a reason; taē koè, 大故, a great affair, a great mourning; sin koè, 身故, to die; koè yéw, 故友, an old friend; sē koè, 是故, because of this, for this reason.

Wun koè jê te sin, 温故而知新 *wun sip chá ây, jé chae sin ây,* to study old lessons, and acquire new ones; see the 上諭 Sëāng lūn.

Yéw koè jê k'hè, 有故而去 *woō s^{n}a soō jé k'hè,* having some cause of dislike, and departing on that account, &c.; see 孟子 Bēng choó.

Koè chëang taē yéw wûy che kwun, 故將大有爲之君 *koè chëang twā woo chò ây jin kwun,* therefore, when we meet with a prince with whom we can undertake great things, &c.; see 孟子 Bēng choó.

Koè 錮 To melt copper or iron, in order to stop a crack or crevice in a pan; to forbid, to restrict.

平 Koê 糊 To stick, to paste up; a kind of paste made from rice; koê yëák, 糊藥 *koê yëŏh,* sticking plaster, for wounds and ulcers.

Koê 麫 A kind of paste made of wheaten flour.

去 Koē 怙 To rely upon, to depend on any one; also written 㤽, koē.

Boô hoō hô koē, boô boé hô sē? 無父何怙無母何恃 *kaðu bô pāy woō s^{n}a meĕ^{n}h koē, kaðu bô boé woō s^{n}a meĕ^{n}h sē?* having no father, what shall we rely on, and when we have no mother, on what shall we depend? see the 小雅 Seáou gnáy.

Koē 詁 To explain the meaning of expressions in ancient and modern books.

Yâng-hëûng 楊雄, when young was fond of learning, and in studying did not so much regard sections and sentences, but (hwŭn koē t'hong jê é, 訓詁通而已,) he was very particular in explaining the meaning of the words.

上平

Köey 檜 Kōey hëang bók, 檜香木 *köey hëo^ng ch'hâ*, the name of a fragrant wood.

Köey 傀 Gigantic, great, extraordinary, excellent; monstrous.

Köey jëên tók lip t'hëen tēy che kan, jê put wùy, 傀然獨立天地之間而不畏 *köey twā ây yëō^ng tók k'hëā tē t'hee^ng tēy ây tëung kan, jé ū^m kë^na lâng*, great of stature, he stood peerless between heaven and earth, without being afraid of any; see 荀子 Sûn choó.

上声

Köéy 粿 Read kó: pastry, confectionary; kó choó, 粿仔 *köëy á*, tarts, pies, &c.

Köéy 餜 Read kó: cakes, made of flour.

Köéy 碻 To raise anything from the ground by putting stones under it, in order to prevent its being injured by the damp.

上去

Köèy 噲 To swallow, to drink.

Köèy 檜 The name of a tree, whose wood is used for making boxes and coffins; a kind of pine.

Köèy 薈 Luxuriant, abundant, foliage.

Köèy 儈 Gây köèy, 牙儈, a person who goes around the market, inducing people to combine in raising the price of commodities in special cases.

Köèy 會 Köèy kè, 會計, to reckon, to count up; an account, a reckoning. A surname. K'hóng-choó sëâng wûy wúy lē è, wát, köèy kè tòng jê éè, 孔子常爲委吏矣曰會計當而已矣 *K'hóng-choó bat chò sèy kw^na, chēw kóng, swui^ng seàou tëŏh chēw hó*, when Confucius was in an inferior office, he used to say, "see that the accounts be correct, and that is enough;" see 孟子 Bēng choó.

Köèy 澮 Koe köèy 溝澮 *kaou k'hwut á*, a ditch, a puddle, a gutter.

Ch'hit pat gwát che kan, é chip, koe köèy kae êng, 七八月之間雨集溝澮皆盈 *ch'hit pǎyh göëyh ây kan, hoē chip chò höëy, chēw kaou á k'hwut á chò poó tee^ng tee^ng*, in the seventh or eighth months, when the rains collect, the ditches and pools all become full; see 孟子 Bēng choó.

Köèy 獪 Kaóu köèy, 狡獪, artful, crafty, fraudulent.

Köèy 穭 The husk of grain; chaff.

Köèy 劊 To cut asunder.

Köèy 膾 Minced meat; as beef, mutton, or fish, sliced together, and chopped small.

5 B

Koèy put yëèm sèy, 膾不厭細 *köèy bŏ wàn e sèy*, minced meat can never be chopped too small; see the 論語 Lūn gé.

Köèy 鱠 Fish chopped up very small.

Köèy 鄶 The name of a country.

Köèy 懀 Sorrowful; a vicious mind.

Köèy 冠 Read kwan: a cap; key kwan, 鷄冠 *key köèy*, a cock's comb; key kwan hwa, 鷄冠花 *key köèy hwa*, the cockscomb flower, Celosia coccinea.

Köèy 過 Read kò: to pass over, to transgress; kò k'hè, 過去 *köèy k'hè*, to pass by; kò t'hoê, 過頭 *köèy t'haôu*, to exceed, to go beyond; kò sit, 過失 *köèy sit*, a fault; kò hwān, 過犯 *köèy hwān*, a transgression.

K'hóng-choó kò che, 孔子過之 *K'hóng-choó köèy e*, Confucius passed by that way; see the 論語 Lūn gé.

Köèy 髻 Lé köèy, 女髻 *cha boé köèy*, a woman's headdress; kim köèy, 金髻, a golden headdress, worn only on particular occasions.

平

Köēy 㚘 Köēy kēen, 㚘肩 *köēy keng t'haôu*, to put the arms around any one's neck. To remove a burden from one shoulder to another.

去

Köēy 跒 Köēy këak, 跒脚 *köēy k'ha*, lame, halt; köēy këak chō, 跒脚坐 *köēy k'ha chēy*, to sit cross-legged.

夫

Köëyh 刮 Read kwat: to scrape anything with a knife.

Köëyh 郭 A surname. Read kok: the suburbs of a city.

Köëyh 蕨 Read k'hwat: a plant with a bulbous root; k'hwat hwún, 蕨粉 *köëyh hwún*, the root of the same reduced to powder.

入

Köëyh 饋 Thick, muddy; thick liquor.

夫

Kŏh 閣 Read kok: a water pavilion, a gallery over the water. Têng ông ko kok lîm kang ché, 滕王高閣臨江渚 *Têng ông ây kwân kŏh lîm kaôu kang keê^ng*, Têng ông's lofty gallery overshadowed the river's brink.

Kŏh 各 Read kok: different; kok yāng, 各樣 *kŏh yëō^ng*, in a different mode.

Kŏh 胳 Read kok: the armpits; kok k'hong hāy, 胳空下 *kŏh k'hang āy*, under the armpits.

Kŏh 袼 Read kok: the clothes under the armpits.

Kŏh 復 Read hok: again, over again, to repeat; hok chaè, 復再 *kŏh chaè*, over again; hok hwàt, 復活 *kŏh wăh*, to live again, to rise again to life.

Hék é kò ông Lëâng, Lëâng wát, ch'héng hok che, 或以告王良良曰請復之 *woō lâng kò ông Lëâng, Leâng kóng, ch'hë^ná kŏh e*, some one told king Lëâng, when he said, "I pray you let us try again;" see 孟子 Bēng choó.

犬

Kok 國 A country, a state; a surname; pang kok, 邦國, a kingdom; kok kay, 國家, the state; kok kwun, 國君, a prince, a sovereign; kok boé, 國母, the queen mother; kok tē jê hoē t'hëen hāy pêng, 國治而后天下平 *kok kaðu tē jëên aōu t'hee*ng *ây pai*ng, when every state is well regulated, the whole empire will be tranquil; see the 大學 Taē hák.

Koh 幗 Kin kok, 巾幗, a cap worn by females at funerals. Choo-kat-lëāng, 諸葛亮, had several times challenged Soo-má-ê, 司馬懿, out to fight, and when Soo-má-ê would not come out, he (wûy ê kin kok, 遺懿巾幗 *sàng ê chit ây cha boé kin,*) sent a woman's cap to him.

Kok 郭 The suburbs of a city; kok göēy, 郭外 *kok gwā*, the environs of a city. Vulg. *köēyh:* a surname. Sam lé che sêng, ch'hit lé che kok, 三里之城七里之郭 *s*n*a lé ây së*n*â, ch'hit lé ây kok,* a city three miles in extent, and suburbs of seven miles; see 孟子 Bēng choó.

Kok 崞 The name of a hill.

Kok 椁 The outer envelop of a coffin: also written 槨, kok. Ch'hêng choó che ke, ê wûy che kok, 請子之車以爲之椁 *ch'hë*n*á hoo choó ây ch'hëa, ê chò e ây kok,* he requested the carriage of Confucius, (to buy it,) in order to make an outer coffin (for his son); see the 論語 Lūn gé.

Kok 鞹 A skin free from the hair; dressed leather. Hoé pà che kok, yêw k'hëên yâng che kok, 虎豹之鞹猶犬羊之鞹 *hoé pà ây p'hòey kaðu bô mô, ch'hin chëō*ng *kaðu yëō*ng *ây p'höëy,* a dressed tiger or leopard's skin is just like a dressed sheep or dog's skin, (for without the hair, it is hard to tell the difference;) see the 論語 Lūn gé.

Kok 𨛫 The name of a market.

Kok 谷 A valley; san kok, 山谷 *sw*n*a k'hai*ng, a vale, a ravine; one of the radicals; a surname. Ch'heng san hêng kok k'hoé, lëûk súy jeâou wân tëung, 青山橫谷口綠水繞園中 *ch'hai*ng *sw*n*a t'hàn hw*n*â tē kok ây k'haðu, lêk chúy jeâou teê*ng *tē kwui*ng *ây tëung,* an azure hill lying across the mouth of the valley, and green waters winding around the midst of the garden.

Kok 各 Each, every one; kok yāng, 各樣 *kŏh yëō*ng, different. Ap kok gân jé chê? 盍各言爾志 *s*n*a soō bô tàk ây kóng lé ây sim chè?* why does not each of you state your own views? see the 論語 Lūn gé.

Kok 胳 Vulg. *kŏh:* the armpits; kok k'hong hāy, 胳空下 *kŏh k'hang āy,* under the armpits.

Kok 袼 The clothes under the armpits; a seam.

Kok 閣 Vul. *kŏh:* a gallery, a water pavilion. Kok hāy gê jê hè, loē chëên yëèn choó sey, 閣下魚兒戲樓前燕子栖 *kŏh āy hê á gaðu chëên, laðu chêng eê*ng *á chò sëw,* under the pavilion the little fishes play, while before the gallery the swallows make their nests.

Kok 穀 The name of a tree, from whose bark paper is made.

Kok 穀 Grain; gnoé kok, 五穀, the five kinds of grain; emolument, good; also written 糓, kok. Sē gēy gnoé kok, 樹藝五穀 *chaè chèng goē kok*, to plant and cultivate the five kinds of grain; see 孟子 Bēng choó.

Emolument, revenue, salary; as, sam lëên hȧk, put chè ê kok, 三年學不至於穀 *sⁿa neéⁿᵍ t'hȧk, bô sëōⁿᵍ kaôu kok lòh*, to study for three years, without thinking of emolument; see the 論語 Lūn gé.

Kok 轂 Ke kok, 車轂, the axle of a carriage; a carriage. To introduce any one into notice, is called ch'huy kok, 推轂, to push along his carriage.

Kok 縠 Crape, a sort of cloth.

Kok 䅵 The name of a kind of pulse.

Kok 𦧲 To stop the mouth.

天 Kók 咯 The crowing of the wild fowl; the crowing of cocks.

幸 Kong 公 Public, general; a surname; and kong yâng, 公羊, and also kong yëá, 公冶, a double surname; kong tō, 公道, just, equitable; kong sim, 公心, a public spirit; kong soo, 公司 *kong se*, a public company; used also for the place or superintendent of that company; kong wūy, 公位 a rank of nobility. Kong sun, 公孫, a double surname.

Taē tō che hêng t'hëen hāy wûy kong, 大道之行天下為公 *twā tō ây këⁿâ t'heeⁿᵍ hāy, chò kong*, a magnanimous way of acting, that will extend through the whole empire, is called equity.

Kong hoê pek choó lâm, 公侯伯子南, the five ranks of nobility.

Kong 玜 The name of a gem.

Kong 蚣 Goê kong, 蜈蚣 *gëâ kang*, a centipede.

Kong 工 Vulg. *kang:* an officer; work, a workman; kong hoo, 工夫 *kang hoo*, labor; kong jîn, 工人 *chò kang ây lâng*, a laborer.

Kong yëuk sëên kê soō, pit sëen lē kê k'hè, 工欲善其事必先利其器 *chò kang ây lâng böëyh ch'hòng hó e ây soō, tëŏh taē seng ch'hòng laē e ây ke k'hè*, when a workman wishes to execute his work in a proper manner, he must first sharpen his tools.

Kong 攻 To attack, to oppose, to engage; to give the whole attention to anything.

Seáou choó bêng koé jê kong che, k'hó yëá, 小子鳴鼓而攻之可也 *sèy këⁿá p'hăh koé jê kong kek e, ēy chò tit*, Oh, my children! if you like to beat the drum, and oppose him, you may do it; see the 論語 Lūn gé.

Kong hoē ē twan, soo haē yëá é, 攻乎異端斯害也已 *chwan ch'hòng chéy kŏh yëōⁿᵍ ây tō lé, chéy sē haē lâng*, to give the whole attention to foreign opinions, is extremely dangerous; see the 上諭 Sëâng lūn.

Kong 功 Merit; kong lô, 功勞, meritorious desert; mourning.
Bín chek yéw kong, 敏則有功 *kip kēy chek woō kong lô*, diligence will insure merit; see the 論語 Lūn gé.
Taē kong, 大功, a great period of mourning, extending to nine months.
Seáou kong, 小功 a small period extending to five months.

Kong 扛 Vulg. *keng*: to carry between two or more persons.
Lėk k'hó kong téng, 力可扛鼎 *làt t'hang keng tēná*, strength sufficient to carry the caldron; (signifying that such a one may become emperor.)

Kong 硿 The noise of striking against the stones.

Kong 幊 A napkin for tying up clothes in; kong twān, 幊緞, a kind of satin.

Kong 伉 Honest, blunt, harsh, upright; soō sìn soō chek kong, 事勝辭則伉 *chò soō k'hăh yēná kóng wā chēw teáou tit*, when greater attention is paid to the subject than to the phraseology, the style becomes harsh.

Kong 甿 A border, a division; a raised path between the rice fields.

Kong 光 Vulg. *kwuing*: bright, light; kong bêng, 光明 *kwuing bêng*, refulgent; gwát kong, 月光 *göèyh kwuing*, moonlight.
Kong pē ê soò peáou, 光被於四表 *kwuing kip kaòu sè heng*, light spreading to all the four quarters; see the 堯典 Geâou töén.

5 C

Kong 侊 Great, large, enlarged.

Kong 洸 A martial appearance; boô boo kong kong, 武夫洸洸, military men with a very martial appearance; see the 大雅 Taē gnáy.

Kong 胱 Pông kong, 膀胱, the region of the groin, the bladder.

Kong 觥 A wine cup, made from the horn of a rhinoceros.
Kong têw kaou ch'hok, 觥籌交錯 the cups and glasses interchanged backwards and forwards (as at a feast).

Kong 罡 A broken net.

Kong 僙 A martial appearance.

Kong 岡 The ridge of a hill; also written 崗 kong.
Sëëp pé ko kong, 涉彼高岡 *kōèy hwut lêy kwân ây swna nēná*, to cross over yonder high ridge; see the 周南 Chew lâm.

Kong 豈 The ancient form of the preceding.

Kong 鋼 Vulg. *keng*, and *kèng*: steel.

Kong 甌 Vulg. *keng*: a large jar; hâm kong, 皕甌 *âm keng*, a water jar; also written 㼚, and 瓨, kong.

Kong 剛 Hard, firm, stiff; kong ch'haē, 剛纔 toō toō á, just now. Kong këâng put k'hwut, 剛強不屈, firm and unbending.

Goê bē këèn kong chëá, 吾未見剛者 gwá böëy woō k'hwⁿà kong gnāy ây lâng, "I have not yet seen a firm and resolute person;" said by Confucius in the 論語 Lūn gé.

Kong 綱 To tie around with a rope; to draw in a net with a large rope; to include, to superintend, to generalize; general, connected together.

Choó teàou jê put kong, 子釣而不綱 k'hóng choó tëò hê jê boó tëŏh bāng, Confucius used to angle for fish, but would not draw in a net; see the 論語 Lūn gé.

Sam kong gnoé sëâng, 三綱五常, the three superintending (of prince, father, and husband), and the five constant, relations (i. e. benevolence, justice, decorum, knowledge, and truth) of life. Kong kàm, 綱鑑, the general mirror, a general view of history.

Kong 罡 T'hëen kong, 天罡, the name of a star in Ursa major.

Kong 罰 The same as 岡, kong, the ridge of a hill.

Kong 剛 The ancient form of 剛, kong, firm.

去

Kóng 廣 Vulg. *k'hwăh:* great, wide, extensive, expansive, broad, ample; a surname. Tè kóng taē, jê chīn cheng bê, 致廣大而盡精微 *tè kèk k'hwăh twā, jê chīn t'haôu cheng yèw,* to extend to the greatest and most expansive, and to exhaust the most minute and subtle things; see the 中庸 Tëung yûng. Kóng-tong 廣東 *Kwetⁿᵍ-tang,* Canton.

Hàn che kóng è put k'hó êng soo, 漢之廣矣不可詠思 *Hàn chúy ây k'hwăh bô t'hang bē köèy,* the literature of the Hàn dynasty is so extensive, that it cannot even be conned over in one's thoughts; see the 周南 Chew lâm.

Kóng 礦 Metallic ore; kê hāy chek kim kóng tan sëak, 其下則金礦丹礫 *e ây āy téy chek kim kóng âng chëŏh,* underneath (those hills) there is nothing but metallic ore and bare stones.

Kóng 鉚 The same as the above.

去

Kòng 貢 To offer up, to present as tribute; tribute, taxes, dues; a surname. Chìn kòng, 進貢, to pay tribute, as a sign of homage.

Jé kòng paou maôu put jip, 爾貢包茅不入 *lé kòng hëèn paou maôu ūᵐ jip,* your tributary offering of a bundle of rushes has not been sent in; see the 左傳 Chó twān.

T'hëen choó soó lē tē kê kok, jê làp kê kòng söèy yëen, 天子使吏治其國而納其貢稅焉 *hóng tèy saé chit ây kwⁿa leâou lé e ây kok, jê làp e kòng söèy,* the emperor sent an officer to govern his country, and to receive the tribute and taxes from him; see 孟子 Bēng choó.

Kòng 誆 To deceive, to cheat, to impose upon; also written 誑, kòng. Kòng che é lé che sóy yéw, 誆之以理之所有 *p'hëèn e é tō lé ây sóy woō,* to impose upon a person by that which appears reasonable.

Kòng 焵 A hardened knife, a tempered blade; to harden steel.

Kòng 鋼 Vulg. *kèng* and *keng*: steel.

Kòng � To go backwards and forwards; to go to a distance.

平 Kông 狂 Ambitious, highminded, wild, mad; to appear mad. Tëen kông, 癲狂, mad, silly, out of one's wits. Goê tóng che seáou choó kông kán, 吾黨之小子狂簡 *gwá ây tóng áy sèy këⁿá k'hăh sëōng kông kán*, "the young people of my clan are too ambitious and sincere;" said by Confucius of his disciples.

Ch'hoé kông chëep û, 楚狂接輿 *Ch'koé ây tëen kông ây lâng cheĕh ch'hëa*, a madman of the Ch'hoé country met the carriage (of Confucius); see the 論語 Lūn gé.

Kông 瘋 A hot disease, a fever.

Kông 徨 Kông kông, 徨徨, fearful, and agitated.

去 Kōng 狂 To do anything on the spur of the moment; to be deceived.

平 Koo 艍 The name of a boat or vessel.

Koo 龜 Read kwuy: a tortoise; kwuy choó, 龜仔 *koo á*, a beetle, a marigold. One of the radicals.

Koo 亀 The same as the above.

上 *Koó* 久 Read kéw: long; a long time, a long while ago. Put jîn chëá, put k'hó é kéw ch'hé yëak, 不仁者不可以久處約 *ūm jîn ây lâng, bô t'hang koó twā tē kan k'koé*, people destitute of virtue cannot long endure afflictions; see the 論語 Lūn gé.

Koó 韭 Read kéw: a kind of leek; kéw ch'haè, 韭菜 *koó ch'haè*, scallions.

去 Koò 句 A sentence; yit koò, 一句 *chit koò*, a single sentence. Chëang koò, 章句 *chëong koò*, sections and sentences.

Koò 灸 Read kèw: to cauterize, to burn the flesh for medicinal purposes.

平 Koô 帕 Koô là, 帕㡎, a child's cap; *cheeng koô là*, 氈帕㡎, a woolen cap.

Koô 鏁 To present up; to do away with.

Koô 毬 Read kêw: a ball; mô kêw, 毛毬 *mô koô*, a hairy ball.

去 *Koō* 舊 Read kēw: old, not new; kēw lëên, 舊年 *koō neeⁿg*, last year. Kēw kok kè bút, 舊穀既没 *koō ch'hek kaðu bô*, the old corn is all consumed; see the 論語 Lūn gé.

Koō 舅 Read kēw: an uncle; bó kēw, 母舅 *bó koō*, a mother's brother. Ch'hey kēw, 妻舅 *ch'hey koō*, a wife's brother.

Koō 哈 Read kok: the singing of birds.

夬
Koŏh 欱 The gurgling noise made in drinking.

Kwa 瓜 A melon; se kwa, 西瓜, a water melon; kim kwa, 金瓜, a pumpkin; tong kwa, 冬瓜, *tang kwa*, a calabash; ch'hè kwa, 莿瓜, a cucumber; k'hoé kwa, 苦瓜, a bitter cucumber; ch'haè kwa, 菜瓜, a species of Momordica. Ch'hit gwát sit kwa, 七月食瓜 *ch'hit göěyh chëăh kwa*, in the seventh month we may eat melons; see the 詩經 Se keng.

Kwa 柯 Read k'ho: a surname.

Kwa 歌 Read ko: a song, a ballad; ch'hëàng ko, 唱歌 *ch'hëŏ^ng kwa*, to sing songs. Ko jê kò K'hóng-choó, 歌而過孔子 *ch'hëŏ^ng kwa jê köěy K'hóng-choó*, he chanted a ditty as he passed by Confucius; see the 論語 Lūn gé.

Kwa 過 Read ko: to pass by; ko këak, 過脚 *kwa k'ha*, to stop in passing by. Ko yit sëuk, 過一宿 *kwa chit ma^ng*, to lodge for a night in a place, when passing by.

圭
Kwà 卦 To divine; a divination; pok kwà, 卜卦, to find out by divination; pat kwà, 八卦, the eight diagrams.

Hòk-he sé chok pat kwà, 伏羲始作八卦 *Hòk-he h'hé t'haŏu ch'hòng pat kwà*, Hòk-he first invented the eight diagrams.

Kwà 諜 To deceive, to impose upon.

Kwà 怪 Read kwaè: to find fault with any one; to take offense.

Kwà 蓋 Read kaè: to cover; the cover of a vessel, a lid; téng kaè, 鼎蓋 *tē^n á kwà*, the cover of an iron pan or caldron.

Kwà 襤 Read kaè: an outer coat, a great coat; má kaè, 馬襤 *báy kwà*, a horse cloak, to wear when riding on horseback.

Kwà 芥 Read kaè: mustard; kaè ch'haè, 芥菜 *kwà ch'haè*, the mustard plant, Sinapis Chinensis.

平
Kwâ 檬 The name of a tree.

圭
Kw^n a 官 Read kwan: an officer of government, a civil officer, a mandarin; chò kwan, 做官 *chò kw^n a*, to be in office; kwan hoó, 官府 *kw^n a hoó*, an officer, a magistrate; kwan loē, 官路 *kw^n a loē*, a highway.

Hoō chok ko kwan, choó ch'hòng gwân, yit ch'hey yit ch'hëep bé ch'hë^n á hëen, 父作高官子狀元一妻一妾美且賢 *pāy chò twā kw^n a, haōu sai^ng tëùng ch'hëùng gwân, chit ây boé chit ây sèy é ch'hin ch'hai^ng kwà gaōu*, to have one's father holding a high office, and one's son attaining to the highest literary honors; with one wife and one concubine, both handsome and clever; (this, according to Chinese ideas, is the summit of human bliss.)

Kwⁿa 棺 Read kwan: a coffin; kwan chaê, 棺材 *kwⁿa ch'hâ*, a wooden coffin. Tëung koé kwan ch'hit ch'hùn, kok ch'hèng che, 中古棺七寸槨稱之 *tëung koé ây sè kwⁿa ch'hâ ch'hit ch'hùn, gwā kok t'hàn e*, in the middle ages of antiquity, the coffins were made seven inches in thickness, and the outer envelop in proportion; see 孟子 Bēng choó.

Kwⁿa 肝 Read kan: the liver; sim kan, 心肝 *sim kwⁿa*, the heart, the mind. Kan ló toê tëy jê put koè, 肝腦塗地而不顧 *kwⁿa ló bwāh tē tëy jê ūᵐ k'hwⁿà*, although our liver and brains should be smeared on the ground (in your service), we would not mind it; see the 史記 Soó kè.

Kwⁿa 冠 Read kwan: a cap; kim kwan, 金冠 *kim kwⁿa*, a lady's headdress: hōng kwan, 鳳冠 *hōng kwⁿa*, a headdress ornamented with embroidered birds.

Kwⁿa 關 Read kwan: to shut; kwan bûn, 關門 *kwⁿa mooiⁿᵍ*, to shut the door. Bûn suy sëet jê sëang kwan, 門雖設而常關 *mooiⁿᵍ suy sëet jê sëâng kwⁿa*, although a door is put there, yet it is always shut.

上聲

Kwⁿá 寡 Few, solitary, alone; kwⁿá hoō, 寡婦 *kwⁿá boē*, a widowed woman. Kwⁿá jîn 寡人, the solitary one, or the man of few virtues; (a polite expression, used by princes in designating themselves.)

Kwⁿá 鉲 Metallic ore; the substance of all metals.

Kwⁿá 礦 Read kóng: ore; the same as the above.

Kwⁿá 擀 Read kán: to spread anything out with the hands; kán bëēn, 擀麵 *kwⁿá mcēⁿᵍ*, to knead dough.

Kwⁿá 倜 *Tek kwⁿá*, 倜倜, the appearance of walking.

Kwⁿá 趕 Read kán; to pursue, to chase, to follow. Tuy kán, 追趕 *tuy kwⁿá*, to follow in pursuit. Kán sëāng, 趕上 *kwⁿá chëōⁿᵍ*, to overtake.

去聲

Kwⁿà 觀 Read kwàn: a temple; kwàn sē, 觀寺 *kwⁿà eēⁿᵍ*, a monastery.

Kwⁿà 灌 Read kwàn: to pour out; kwàn chéw, 灌酒 *kwⁿà chéw*, to pour out wine; kwàn tëy, 灌地 *kwⁿà tëy*, to pour out a libation on the ground.

Kwⁿà 鑵 Read kwàn: an agricultural implement; kwàn ch'hùy, 鑵嘴 *kwⁿà ch'hùy*, a kind of pickaxe.

Kwⁿà 鸛 Read kwàn: the name of a water bird, a kind of heron; kwàn bêng ê tëét, 鸛鳴于垤 *kwⁿà tit kaóu tē swⁿa á*, the water bird is screaming on the hillock; see the 詩經 Se keng.

平聲

Kwⁿâ 寒 Read hân: cold; sëang hân, 傷寒 *sëang kwⁿâ*, to take cold. Hân yëā k'hek laê tây tòng chéw, 寒夜客來茶當酒 *kwⁿâ maiⁿᵍ lâng k'hăyh laê tây tòng chò chéw*, when a visitor comes on a cold night, tea will serve instead of wine.

去聲

Kwⁿā 汗 Read hān: sweat, perspiration; lêw hān, 流汗 *laôu kwⁿā*, to perspire.

Hān má ch'hut sin, 汗馬出身 kw^{n}ā báy ch'hut sin, to enter on life like a sweating horse; (i. e. to attain everything by personal labor.)

Kw^{n}ā 捾 Read kwān: to carry anything in the hand.

Kw^{n}ā 携 Read hêy: to carry in the hand, as a basket.
Hêy song kam toé chéw, é t'hèng êng seng, 携雙柑斗酒以聽鶯聲 kw^{n}ā chit tùy kam chit taóu chéw, é t'hë^{n}a eng ây së^{n}a, to take in the hand a pair of oranges and a measure of wine, in order to go and listen to the singing of the birds.

Kw^{n}ā 綰 Read kwān: to tie anything.

Kwae 乖 Perverse, wicked, strange; also, gentle, tame, cunning.
Kay tō këûng, pit kwae, 家道窮必乖 kay laē ây tō lé këûng chîn, pit kwae lèy, a family without sufficient means of subsistence is ready for revolt; see the 易經 Ek keng.

Kwae 鱥 A kind of fish, the oil of which is poisonous.

Kwaé 拐 Kwaé p'hëèn, 拐騙, to deceive; kwaé choó, 拐子 laóu á, a cheat, a rogue.

Kwaé 枴 Kwaé choó, 枴仔 kwaé á, a walking-stick, an old man's staff.

Kwaé 夬 The name of one of the eight diagrams; to determine.

Kwaé 蒯 The name of a herb or rush used to make cords; a surname.

圭
Kwaè 怪 Strange, extraordinary; kê kwaè, 奇怪 koô kwaè, unaccountable; cheng kwaè, 曾怪 kăh kwaè, how strange! Also written 恠, kwaè.
Choó put gé kwaè lèk lwān sîn, 子不語怪力亂神 hoo choó bô kóng kwaè làt lwān, kap sîn ây soō, Confucius never conversed about strange, or violent, or turbulent, or spiritual, things; see the 上論 Sëāng lūn..

Kwaè 圣 To exert one's strength in cultivating the ground.

Kwae^{ng} 閂 To bolt; kwae^{ng} bûn, 閂門 kwae^{ng} mooi^{ng}, to bolt the door.

夫
Kwăh 啯 Kwăh kwăh, 啯啯, troublesome discourse; a clamorous noise.

Kwăh 摑 To beat, to strike: kwăh chùy, 摑嘴 kwăh ch'hùy páy, to give a slap on the mouth.

Kwăh 摅 Kwăh jé, 摅耳 kwăh hē k'háng, to box the ear.

Kwăh 割 Read kat: to cut, to cut off, to slice; kat lëûng hoē, 割嚨喉 kwăh nâ aôu, to cut one's own throat.
Kat put chèng put sit, 割不正不食 kwăh ūm chë^{n}à bô chëăh, if the meat was not cut square, he (Confucius,) would not eat of it; see the 論語 Lūn gé.

Kwăh 葛 Read kat: a kind of creeping plant, of whose tendrils linen is made; the Dolichos hirsutus, Thunb.

福建方言字典

Kat poè, 葛布 *kwăh poè*, grass cloth; also, a surname.

Kwăh 渴 Read k'hat: thirsty; k'hoé k'hat, 口渴 *ch'hùy kwăh*, the mouth dry. K'hat cheă ē wûy yím, 渴者易爲飲 *kwăh ây lâng k'hoaè chò lim*, thirsty people are not particular about what they drink.

Kwan 觀 To look at, to observe; kwan kê séy yêw, 觀其所由 *k'hwⁿà e séy yêw*, observe the motives of a man's actions; see the 上論 Sēāng lūn.

Kwan 官 Vulg. *kwⁿa*: an officer of government; kwan chit, 官職 *kwⁿa chit*, an office; kwan to, 官刀, a broad-sword; tⁿá kwan soo, 打官司 *p'hăh kwⁿa se*, to go to law.
Pek kwan chóng ké, é t'hèng ê t'höûng chaé, 百官總已以聽於冢宰 *păyh kwⁿa chóng suō é ka tē, é t'hēⁿa tē chaé sĕāng*, all the officers must attend to their respective duties, and obey the orders of the prime minister, (while the young prince mourns for his deceased father;) see the 論語 Lūn gé.

Kwan 倌 One who has charge of the prince's chariots. Bēng pé kwan jìn, 命彼倌人 *bēng lēng kwán ch'hĕa ây lâng*, give orders to the master of the chariot.

Kwan 棺 Vulg. *kwⁿa*: a coffin; kwan bók, 棺木 *kwⁿa ch'hâ*, a wooden coffin. Soó ték bé káy é wûy kwan, 使擇美檟以爲棺 *saé lâng kán tŏh hó káy ch'hâ é chò kwⁿa ch'hâ*, send people to pick out a good piece of timber in order to make a coffin; see the 左傳 Chó twān.

Kwan 涓 A small stream, a dripping; pure, to select. Kwan kwan put yūng, chēung wûy kang hô, 涓涓不壅終爲江河 *k'hwⁿa k'hwⁿa laōu bó t'hat, kaōu swăh böëy chēⁿâ kang hô*, a perpetual dripping without stopping, will in time become a large river.

Kwan 捐 To take away, to remove; kwan tê, 捐除, to take out of the way; kwan têy, 捐題, to levy contributions.
Hoō boé soó Sùn wân lím, kwan kae, 父母使舜完廩捐階 *pāy boé saé Sùn ch'hóng hó ch'heⁿg lím, yĕá chēw kwan köëy laōu t'huy*, his father and mother sent Sùn to finish the repairs of the granary, and when he was upon it, they took the ladder away; see 孟子 Bēng chóo.

Kwan 娟 Handsome, beautiful, lovely.

Kwan 鵑 Toē kwan, 杜鵑 the name of a kind of cuckoo; also of a flower; called also choó kwuy, 子規.
Toē kwan che t'hoê choó kwuy t'hêy, 杜鵑枝頭子規啼 *toē kwan ây ke t'haōu choó kwuy t'hê*, on the topmost branch of the toē kwan, the choó kwuy sits and sings.

Kwan 悁 Sorrowful, sad; tëung sim kwan kwan 中心悁悁 *sim kwⁿa tang eⁿg kwān ló*, the middle of the heart filled with distress; see the 陳風 Tîn hong.

Kwan 痯 A weariness in the bones.

Kwan 瘝 A sickness; also written 瘰, kwan.

Kwan 鰥 The name of a fish, the eyes of which always seem to be sparkling. To be old, and without a wife; an old bachelor, a widower.

Kwan kwⁿá koe tók, 鰥寡孤獨, widowers, widows, orphans, and childless people; see 孟子 Bēng choó.

Kwan 蠲 Pure, clean; clear, bright; to do away with, to avoid. Kwan tê, 蠲除, to remit.

Hwūy-kong kwan kê taē tek, 惠公蠲其大德 *Hwūy-kong kwan bêng e ây twā tek*, Hwūy-kong clearly displayed his great virtue; see the 左傳 Chó twān.

Kwan 冠 Vulg. *kwⁿa:* a cap, a bonnet, a hat. Bān kok e kwan paè bēén lêw, 萬國衣冠拜冕旒 *bān kok ây sⁿa kin tëŏh paè bēén léw*, the caps and clothes of all nations must pay obeisance to the emperor's crown.

Kwan 棬 A basin or vessel made of crooked wood; a round wooden basin. Choó lêng sūn ké léw che sèng, jê é pöey kwan hoē? 子能順杞柳之性而以桮棬乎 *lé ëy sūn tit ké léw ây saiⁿᵍ, jé ch'hông pöey kwan hoē?* can you subdue the nature of the willow wood, and make bowls and basins of it? see 孟子 Bēng choó.

Kwan 關 Vulg. *kwⁿa:* to shut, to close; kwan aè, 關隘, a narrow pass, a defile; kwan hēy, 關係, consequences, results; a surname.

Kwan ke jê put cheng, 關譏而不征 *kwⁿa aè ke ch'hat, jê bô t'hó lâng söëy*, institute examinations at the passes (respecting all travelers), but do not exact duties from them; see 孟子 Bēng choó.

Kwan-yîn-tëáng, 關雲長, the great hero of the Sam kok, 三國, now worshiped by the Chinese, as the representative of fidelity.

Kwán 琯 (声) A gem; a precious stone. When 舜, Sùn succeeded 堯, Geâou in the government, (the 西王母, sey ông boé,) the mother of the western king came and presented him with (pêk kwán, 白琯 *pāyh kwán,*) a white gem.

Kwán 綰 Vulg. *kwⁿā:* to bind, to tie, to run on a string.

Kwán 館 A hotel, a resting place, a lodging house, an inn; a school. Yëá kwán lông hwa hwat, 野館濃花發 *yëá gwā ây kwán sëà woō lông hwa tit hwat*, near the inn on the moor the flowers spring up abundantly.

Káy kwán gwān lêw, jê sēw gëëp ê bûn, 假館願留而受業於門 *chëŏh kwán gwān böëyh laôu lé, jê sēw gëëp tē mooⁿᵍ*, having rented a school-house, we wish to detain you, and receive instruction at your gate; see 孟子 Bēng choó.

K'hae kwân, 開館 *k'hwuy ôh*, to open school.

Kwán 舘 The same as the preceding. Hák kwán, 學舘, a school.

Kwán 痯 Sick, wearied; finished, concluded.

Kwán 管 A pipe, a flute, an instrument of music; a tube of any kind; a surname. Kwân yëák che yim, 管籥之音 *kwán yëák ây sëⁿa yim*, the sound of the pipe and lute; see 孟子 Bēng choó.

Kwán lé, 管理, to rule, to regulate; kwán hāy, 管下, subject to; a surname; Kwán-tëüng, 管仲, a prime minister of the 齊 C'hêy country.

Kwán 逭 To run away, to escape; choō chok gëĕt put k'hó kwán, 自作孽不可逭 *ka tē chok gëĕt chēw bō t'hang chaóu*, when a man brings calamity on himself, there is no escaping; see the 書太甲 Se t'haè kap.

Kwán 錧 An implement of husbandry. The name for a plough, or ploughshare in the region to the south of the 江, kang.

Kwán 輨 An iron spike in a wheel.

Kwán 卷 Vulg. *kwui^{ng}:* to roll up, as a scroll; to take in, to fold up.
Kwán che, chek t'hoèy chông ê bit, 卷之則退藏於密 *kwui^{ng} e chek t'hèy k'hè^{ng} tē bàt bàt*, when you roll it up, then it retires and shuts itself up in secrecy; see 程子 Têng choó.

Kwán 捲 To roll up; kwán lëĕm heaou bêng gwát, 捲簾邀明月 *kwui^{ng} mooí^{ng} lê ch'hè^{n}á bêng göĕyh*, to roll up the door screen, and invite the clear moon (to shine into the house).

Kwán 筦 Kwán hëĕn, 筦絃, the strings of an instrument of music; also, a mat.

Kwán 盥 To wash the hands.

去 Kwàn 貫 Vulg. *kwui^{ng}:* a string of anything; chëĕn kwàn, 錢貫 *chee^{ng} kwui^{ng}*, a string of cash; choo kwàn, 珠貫, a string of beads. To string anything, to run anything on a string; kwàn t'hong, 貫通, to pass through the whole.

4 E

Cheĕn pek bān kwàn, 錢百萬貫 *chee^{ng} păyh bān kwui^{ng}*, a hundred myriad strings of cash. Gê kwàn jê chìn, 魚貫而進 *hê kwui^{ng} kŏèy jê chìn*, the fish bores through the water and gets forward.

Kwàn 慣 To be accustomed to; kwàn sip, 慣習 *kwàn sè*, used to anything.

Kwàn 鏆 To bore through; to put bracelets on the arms.

Kwàn 串 To be accustomed to, to be familiar with.

Kwàn 丱 The hair twisted up into two knots, one on each side of the head, like a pair of horns, commonly done with the hair of young children.
Chong kak kwàn hêy, 總角丱兮, like a pair of horns is the hair twisted up; see the 齊風 Chêy hong.

Kwàn 瓘 The name of a gem, or a precious stone.

Kwàn 鑵 A vessel used for drawing water; kwàn. k'hoé, 鑵口 *kw^{n}à ch'hùy*, a kind of pickaxe.

Kwàn 觀 Vulg. *kw^{n}à:* a convent; Tō kwàn, 道觀 *Tō kw^{n}à*, a monastery belonging to the sect of 道, Tō.

Kwàn 鸛 Vulg. *kw^{n}à:* the name of a water bird; a species of heron.

Kwàn 灌 To pour out; kwàn chéw, 灌酒 *kw^{n}à chéw*, to pour out a libation to the gods; also, to irrigate, to spread water over the land.

Choō kè kwàn jê óng chëá, goê put yé... kwàn che è, 自既灌而往者吾不欲觀之矣 *choō è kwⁿà têy jê köëy k'hè, gwá ū' aè k'hwⁿà e*, from the time of pouring out the libation, I had no desire to look at (their sacrifice); see the 上論 Söăng lūn.

E súy kwàn kaè tëên wân, 以水灌漑田園 *t'hó chúy kwàn kaè ch'hân hwuiⁿᵍ*, to irrigate the gardens and fields with water.

Kwàn 礶 Tây kwàn, 茶礶, a teapot.

Kwàn 桊 Vulg. *kwuiⁿᵍ*: the ring which is put through the nose of an ox or buffaloe.

Kwàn 眷 To regard with favor, to behold; to be near, intimate. Hông t'hëen kwàn bēng, 皇天眷命 *hông t'heeⁿᵍ k'hwⁿà bēng*, may the imperial heavens look down on this decree; see the 禹謨 E boè. Ch'hin kwàn, 親眷, near relatives; to be intimately allied to.

Kwàn 睠 To look around upon; to look towards with longing anxiety.

Kwàn 卷 So kwàn, 書卷, a section of a book; a volume. K'hae kwàn pëēn yéw ek, 開卷便有益 *k'hwuy kwàn pëēn woō lē yëăh*, in opening the volume there is profit; see the 史記 Soó kè.

Kwàn 絭 Vulg. *kwuiⁿᵍ*: a cord; the string of a crossbow; bent; an incense bag tied around the neck.

Kwàn 絹 A snare for catching birds; a gin. Eatables are placed within the noose of a string, and when the birds come down to eat them, the string is pulled, and they are caught.

Kwàn 弓 The leaf of a book; also written 弓, kwàn, the same as 卷, kwàn, a volume.

Kwàn 狷 To be strenuous on one point; to have moderate talents, and yet to be exceedingly particular in attending to one's duty.

Pit yëá kông kwàn hoē, 必也狂狷乎 *pit tëŏh kông kap kwàn hoē*, (in the absence af honest people,) we must put up with ambitious persons, and those who have only a mediocrity of talent; see the 論語 Lūn gé.

Kwàn 券 K'hèy kwàn, 契券, an account, a reckoning.

Kwàn 睊 To look askance, to look at with an angry eye. Kwàn kwàn se ch'hâm, 睊睊胥讒 *sëā bàk k'hwⁿà jê chò poê ch'hâm lēng*, they will look askance, and universally complain; see 孟子 Bēng choó.

Kwàn 獧 The same as 狷, kwàn; also, light; the swift running of a dog.

Kwàn 祼 The same as 灌, kwàn, to pour out a libation.

Kwàn chëang ê keng, 祼將于京 *laê k'hè kwàn chëŏ tē kiⁿa sëⁿà*, let us go and pour out libations at the capital; see the 大雅 Taē gnáy.

Kwàn 盥 To wash the hands in a wash basin. Also read kwán.

Kwàn 冠 To put a cap on the head; a ceremony performed in China, when a young man comes of age at 16.

Tëāng hoo che kwàn yëá hoē bēng che, 丈夫之冠也父命之 *ta po lâng ây tè kin,*

福建方言字典

néŏng pāy bĕng lĕng e, at the ceremony of capping a young man, the father gives him directions; see 孟子 Bēng choó.

平

Kwân 權 A weight; to weigh; to weigh circumstances, and act accordingly; kwân sè, 權勢, power, authority; lōng kwân, 弄權, to get the power into one's own hands; chĕûng kwân, 從權, to act according to circumstances.

Kwân jĕĕn hoē te k'heng tĕūng, 權然後知輕重 *kwân tùy ch'hìn jĕĕn aōu ēy chae k'hin tāng,* weigh a thing, and then you may know its evity and gravity; see 孟子 Bēng choó.

Séw keng, hêng kwân, 守經行權 *chĕw keng sēâng, kĕnâ kwân sè,* to adhere to the constant rule, or to act according to circumstances. Kwân pèng, 權柄, the handle of power, power. A surname.

Kwân 鬈 The fine glossy appearance of the hair; kwân hwat jê jîn, 鬈髮如雲 *kwân hó āy mô ch'hìn chĕŏng hwûn,* fine black hair, like the dark clouds; see the 衛風 Wōēy hong.

Kwân 婘 Handsome, good looking.

Kwân 高 Read ko: high, lofty, eminent. Ko san gëáng ché, 高山仰止 *kwân āy swâ, tĕŏh gĕâng k'hé laē k'hwnà,* a high hill must be looked up to; see the 小雅 Seáou gnáy.

去

Kwān 縣 Read hëen: a district, a small county or township; a city of the third order.

Kwān 倦 Vulg. yĕd: weary, tired, fatigued. Hwŭy jîn put kwān, 誨人不倦 *kà lâng bēy yĕd,* I teach people without being tired; see the 論語 Lūn gé.

Kwān 惓 Fagged out, heartily tired.

Kwān 券 To labor; to be wearied through labor, fatigue.

平

Kwang 光 *Kwang kwang,* 光光, only.

入

Kwat 适 Hasty, fleet; a man's name.

Kwat 佸 To reckon, to sum up an account; also, to arrive at. Hat kê y... kwat? 曷其有佸 *e ti woō kaòu?* when will he arrive? see the 王風 Ong hong.

Kwat 活 The flowing of water; read hwt: alive, moving, cheerful. Pok lê kwat kwat, 北流活活 *pak chúy tit laòu kwat kwat,* the northern stream flowing and rippling along; see the 衛風 Wōēy hong.

Kwat 刮 To grind or rub a knife; kwat sëak, 刮削, to scrape. Kwat koé mô kong, 刮垢磨光 *kwat k'hè la sâm bwâ kaòu kwuīng,* to scrape off the dirt, and polish anything.

Kwat 括 To include, to encompass, to bundle up, to take account of. Lông kwat soò haé, 囊括四海 *poè tĕy á laē, paōu kwat sè haé,* to inclose all within the four seas in a bag.

Kwat 聒 To look angrily; the eyes dark.

Kwat 趏 To run, to go quickly.

Kwat 乢 The appearance of motion, as if hooked and pulled different ways.

Kwat 决 The same as 決, kwat, to decide; kwat twān, 决斷, to determine, to sentence.

Kwat 決 The appearance of water flowing; to decide, to fix, to cut short. Kwat choo tong hong, chek tong lêw, 決諸東方則東流 *kwat choo tang heng, chēw tang laŏu*, if you lead water eastward, it will flow to the east; see 孟子 Bēng choó. Kwat è, 決意, fixed determination.

Kwat 玦 Gems worn upon a dress of ceremony.

Kwat 抉 A cross line in a bow; to pull a bow-string, to let go the string.

Kwat 弽 An ivory thimble, used to protect the thumb when pulling a bow.

Kwat 鴂 The name of a singing bird of the tropics; also written 鴃, kwat. Kim yëá lâm bân kwat sëët che jîn, 今也南蠻鴂舌之人 *tⁿa woō chit lêy lâm bân cheáou cheĕh ây lâng*, now here comes a fellow from among the southern barbarians, with his bird's tongue, (and you believe him); see 孟子 Bēng choó.

Kwat 訣 Parting words, a farewell; to distinguish, to divide, to exterminate; conjuring arts. Seng soó éng kwat, 生死永訣 *saiⁿᵍ sé éng kwat pëet*, life and death make an eternal separation. Taē E bûn tëâng seng che kwat, 大禹聞長生之訣 *twā E t'hēⁿa tëⁿᵍ koó wāh ây kwat toē*, the great E asked concerning the method of insuring constant life; see the 魏書 Gwūy se.

Kwat 駃 A good horse.

Kwat 刔 To rub, to scrape.

Kwat 昳 The color of an eclipse.

Kwat 趹 To go fast, to walk quickly.

Kwat 湙 Kwat bêng hwa, 湙明花, the name of a flower. Kae hāy kwat bêng gân sek sëen, 階下湙明顏色鮮 *gîm kay āy ây kwat bêng gân sek yëá cheēⁿᵍ*, the appearance of the kwat bêng flower under the steps, is still fresh and gay.

Kwat 鵙 The name of a bird; called also pek lô neáou, 伯勞鳥 *pit lô cheáou*. Tëūng hāy che gwăt kwat sé bêng 仲夏之月鵙始鳴 *tëūng hāy ây göëyh kwat cheáou k'hé t'haŏu haŏu*, in the middle month of summer, the kwat bird begins to sing; see the 禮月令 Léy gwăt lēng.

Kwat 譎 Artful, deceitful; kwúy kwat, 詭譎, false, intriguing. Chìn-bûn-kong kwat jê put chèng Chêy-hwân-kong chèng jê put kwat, 晋文公譎而不正齊桓公正而不譎 *Chìn-bûn-kong kwúy kwat jê bēy chèng keng, Chêy-hwân-kong chèng keng jê bēy kwúy kwat*, Chìn-bûn-kong was artful and not honest, Chêy-hwân-kong was honest and not artful; see the 論語 Lūn gé.

夾 Kwát 橜 A post stuck in the ground; a door-post. Also written 橛, kwát.

Kwát 亅 A hook turned up at the end, a barbed weapon; one of the radicals.

卒 *Kwuìng* 褌 Read kwun: a small pair of drawers; a kind of petticoat.

Kwuìng 光 Read kong: light, clear, bright, shining, resplendent.
Chëak hnó che kong put lêng wán cheàou, 灼火之光不能遠照 *chit chëak höëy ây kwuìng bëy hwuìng chëò bêng*, the light of a small fire will not reflect far; see the 晉語 Chìn gé.

声 *Kwuíng* 捲 Read kwán: to roll anything up; kwán ch'hòk, 捲鑿 *kwuíng ch'hák á*, a round chisel, a gouge.

Kwuíng 管 Read kwán: a tube, or pipe; bé kwán, 米管 *bé kwuíng*, a hollow bamboo, used for measuring rice.

去 *Kwuìng* 卷 Read kwàn: a book, a volume, a roll; séw kwàn, 手卷 *ch'héw kwuìng*, a manuscript, an autograph, written by one's own hand.
K'hò kwàn, 考卷 *k'hó kwuìng*, an exercise written out by the candidates at public examinations.

Kwuìng 絭 Read kwàn: a small bag, containing incense ashes from the altar of an idol, which is hung round the neck of a child, in order to insure its good luck.
Kwān kwàn, 揹絭 *kwnā kwuìng*, to wear such a bag around the neck.

5 F.

Kwuìng 貫 Read kwàn: to perforate, to connect; kwàn jé, 貫耳 *kwuìng hē á*, to bore the ears, in order to insert ear-rings; kwàn pit, 貫鼻 *kwuìng p'heèng*, to bore a hole through the nose of a pig or buffaloe.

Kwuìng 桊 Read kwàn: to insert a string through the nose of a buffaloe.
Kwàn pit, 桊鼻 *kwuìng p'heèng*, to bore a hole through the nose.

Kwuìng 串 Read kwàn: a string of anything, to run anything on a string.
Chëên kwàn, 錢串 *cheeng kwuìng*, a string of cash.

卒 Kwun 君 A prince, a sovereign, an honorable person; kwun choó, 君子, a good man; kwun ông, 君王, a king.
Taē chae Geâou che wûy kwun yëá! 大哉堯之爲君也 *twā chae Geâou ây chò jîn kwun!* how great was Geâou as a prince!

Kwun 褌 Vulg. *kwuìng*: a pair of drawers, a kind of petticoat.
Kwûn sat che ch'hé kwun tëung, Wán-chék é wûy kit teàou yëá, 群蝨之處褌中阮籍以爲吉兆也 *chënā tìn ây sat boé twā tē kwuìng tang cng, Wuíng-chék k'ăh chò sē hó teàou*, when a brood of lice took up their residence in his breeches, Wuíng-chék used to think it was a good omen.

Kwun 軍 Numerous, many; an army or legion of 12,500 men; an emperor had 6 legions, and a powerful state three.
Choó hêng sam kwun, chek sûy é? 子行三軍則誰與 *hoo choó lé nā kënā sna kwun, chek yîn chē chûy á?* if you, sir, had to lead on the three legions of the army, to whom would you intrust them? see the 論語 Lūn gè.

Chëàng kwun, 將軍, a general; ch'hëung kwun, 從軍, to be transported.

声

Kwún 滚 The appearance of a wide sheet of water; bubbling, foaming up. Kwún súy, 滚水 *kwún chúy*, boiling water.

Kwún 袞 The robes of an emperor, ornamented with five embroidered dragons.

Kwún 撌 To turn around, to revolve; Hông-tèy kwan kwún hông jê chok ke, 黃帝觀撌蓬而作車 *Wuîng-tèy kh'wⁿà kwuîng hông ch'haôu jê chò ch'hëa*, Wuîng-tèy saw the reeds rolling along, and thought of making wheeled carriages. (B. C. 2622.)

Kwún 謴 To speak indistinctly; to sport and jest with people. Hëên kwún, 賢謴 *gaôu kwún*, to play tricks.

Kwún 輥 The rushing of carriages.

Kwún 緄 A cord or string. Also read k'hwûn: an ornamented girdle.

Kwún 䃂 To plough and cultivate the ground.

Kwún 呁 To vomit, to belch forth words.

Kwún 鯀 A great fish; a man's name, the father of 禹, E, who being unsuccessful in regulating the waters, after the great flood, was put to death by 舜, Sùn. Tèy wát oe Kwún chae! 帝曰於鯀哉 *tèy kóng há yëá chéy léy Kwún!* the emperor said, "alas! that Kwún!" see the 堯典 Geâou tëèn.

Kwún 䘾 Bending and fawning; an emperor's robes. Also written 倱, kwún.

去

Kwùn 棍 A staff, a stick; bòk kwùn, 木棍 *ch'ha kwùn*, a wooden club; kong kwùn, 光棍, a bare stick, a pettifogging lawyer, a roguish fellow, a swindler.

Kwùn 諢 To soothe people by one's conversation.

Kwùn 䵪 A jet black color.

平

Kwûn 群 A flock, a herd, a troop, a multitude; also written 羣, kwûn. Kwûn yâng, 群羊 *chit tîn yëôⁿᵍ*, a flock of sheep. Goê lê kwûn sek ke, 吾離群索居 *gwá lê kwûn tîn ka tē k'hëā*, I have left the multitude, and dwell alone; see the 禮記 Léy kè.

Kwûn 宭 Kwûn ke, 宭居, to dwell in company. The same as the above.

Kwûn 裙 A petticoat; lé kwûn, 女裙 *cha boê kwûn*, a woman's petticoat.

Kwûn 帬 The same as the above; also written 峮, kwûn.

去

Kwūn 郡 A district, an inhabited place, a place where many people assemble together. The state of 秦 Chîn, engrossed possession of the whole empire, and divided the land into 36 郡, kwūn, which division was still maintained under the 漢, Hàn dynasty.

Kwŭn 咽 The appearance of vomiting.

夭
Kwut 骨 A bone; chëet kwut, 折骨 *cheĕh kwut*, to break a bone. Chêng sîn chëá t'hëen che hwun, kwut haê chëá tëy che hwun, 精神者天之分骨骸者地之分 *chêng sîn ây sē t'heeng ây hwun, kwut t'haôu ây sē tëy ây hwun*, the animal spirits are the gift of heaven, the bones and joints are from the earth.

Kwut 榾 Koé kwut, 枸榾 *kaôu kwut*, the name of a wood, used in making the shafts of arrows.

Kwut 穭 The stalk of grain.

兀
Kwút 滑 Confused, disordered; smooth, slippery; loē kwút, 路滑, a slippery path. Kam kwút, 甘滑, sweet and greasy. A surname.
Kwút k'hey, 滑稽, fawning and flattering.

Kwút 愲 The mind confused.

Kwút 猾 Confused, to disorder; kaóu kwút, 狡猾, cunning, artful, corrupt. Bân ê kwút hāy, 蠻夷猾夏 *bân ê kwút hwân choo hāy*, the barbarians disturb the rest of China; see the 舜典 Sùn tëén.

Kwút 磆 Kwút sék, 磆石, the name of a medicine.

Kwút 鶻 A kind of dove.

Kwút 汩 Confused, disordered; also, annihilated.

Kwút 崛 Kwút k'hé, 崛起, to rouse up one's intellect; to rise alone, as a man of eminent talents.
Bêng t'haè choé kwút k'hé ê Kim-lêng, sëak pêng kwŭn k'hoè, 明太祖崛起於金陵剷平羣寇 *Bêng t'haè choé, kwút k'hé te Kim-léng, sëak pai^ng chëⁿâ tîn ây ch'hat*, the first emperor of the Bêng dynasty rose up into notice at Kim-lêng, where he scraped smooth all the robbers; (i. e. exterminated the rebels.)

Kwút 倔 Obstinate and hardened in vice; kwút këâng, 倔強, perverse.
Teāou-teng, 趙鼎 *Tëō-tëⁿá* would not listen to terms of adjustment, when 檜, Köèy said, (ch'hoó ló kwút këâng yëw sek, 此老倔強猶昔 *chéy lëy laōu kwút këâng ch'hin chëōng chá*,) "this perverse old fellow is as unbending as ever."

Kwút 掘 To dig, to delve; kwút chéng, 掘井 *kwút chai^ng*, to dig a well.
Yéw wûy chëá p'hè jëák kwút chéng, 有爲者譬若掘井 *woō chò ây lâng p'hè jê kwút chai^ng*, those who will engage in any great undertaking, are like those who dig a well; see 孟子 Bēng choó.

Kwút 僪 Highminded, ambitious.

赤
Kwuy 規 A rule, a compass; kwuy ké, 規矩, the compass and rule; a rule to walk by, according to rule, suitable, proper, orderly, a usage, a custom.
Kwuy ké hong wân cho chè yëá, 規矩方員之至也 *kwuy ké sē hak ee^ng ây chīn t'haôu*, the

compass and rule bring squares and circles to the utmost perfection; see 孟子 Bēng choó.

Kwuy 窺 To peep at, to look at by stealth. Kwuy këèn sit kay che hⁿó, 窺見室家之好 *t'haou k'hwⁿà ch'hoò laē ày hó höèy*, people can peep at all the good things in one's dwelling; see the 論語 Lūn gé.

Kwuy 闚 To look out at a door; to have an eye to, to spy, to observe. Chîn put kám kwuy peng hô lōëy, 秦不敢闚兵河內 *Chîn ūm kⁿá t'hó peng t'haou k'hwⁿà lân hô laē*, the Chîn government will not dare with their troops to have an eye to the district within the river.

Kwuy 鸃 Choó kwuy, 子鸃, the name of a bird.

Kwuy 佹 Nearly alike; almost.

Kwuy 傀 Great, gigantic, large of stature. Kwuy wûy ték lip, 傀偉特立 *twā hàn ây lâng ka tē k'hëā*, men of great stature can stand alone; see the 史記 Soó kè.

Kwuy 瑰 The name of a bead, or a pearl.

Kwuy 圭 A precious stone of an oblong form, held by civil officers, when they wait upon their sovereign; gëùk kwuy, 玉圭, the badge of office. Chip kwuy këuk këung jê yëá, 執圭鞠躬如也 *gîm gëùk kwuy ây sê e ch'hin chëōng këuk sin ây yëōng*, when (Confucius) held before him the badge of office, he appeared as it were to bend his body; see the 論語 Lūn gé.

Kwuy 珪 The same as the above.

Kwuy 閨 The door of an inner apartment; the pearly door; generally taken to intimate the female apartments of a dwelling.

Kwuy 奎 The name of a constellation. Sòng t'haè choé gnoé lëên, gnoé seng chē kwuy, 宋太祖五年五星聚奎 *Sòng t'haè choé goē neēng, goē lëëp ch'haiⁿg chò hōëy tē kwuy*, in the 5th year of the first emperor of the Sòng dynasty, five stars collected together in the region of the kwuy constellation; see the 史記 Soó kè.

Kwuy 邽 The name of a district. A sruname.

Kwuy 雉 Choó kwuy, 子雉, the name of a bird.

Kwuy 皈 Kwuy e, 皈依, a cant term in use among the priests of Buddha.

Kwuy 龜 Vulg. *koo:* a tortoise; also written 龜, kwuy. Hëèn hoē se kwuy, 見乎蓍龜 *keèⁿg tē se koo*, destinies may be discovered by the reeds and the tortoise-shell.

Kwuy 溈 The name of a river.

Kwuy 歸 To return, to revert, to go back; kwuy sūn, 歸順, to return to obedience. Choó chaē Tîn wát, kwuy ê! kwuy ê! 子在陳曰歸與歸與 *choó twā tē Tîn kóng, tooⁿg laê! tooⁿg laê!* when Confucius was in the Tîn country he said, "let us return! let us return!" see the 語論 Lūn gé.

声

Kwúy 鬼 A ghost, a spirit, a demon, an imp; mô kwúy, 魔鬼, the devil. Hwuy kê kwúy jê chèy che, t'hëém yëá, 非其鬼而祭之諂也 *ūm sē lán ây kwúy jê chèy che, sē sëep sèy yëá*, to sacrifice to a departed spirit, with whom we have no business, is flattery; see the 論語 Lūn gé. Kwúy sîn, 鬼神, demons and spirits; k'hàn kwúy, 看鬼 *k'hwⁿâ kwúy*, to see a ghost, considered an unlucky omen.

Kwúy 宄 Traitorous, villainous, roguish. K'hoè chék kan kwúy, 寇賊姦宄 *chò ch'hàt kan kwúy*, thieves are roguish and traitorous fellows; see the 舜典 Sùn tëén.

Kwúy 佹 Repeated; also, wicked, corrupt. Also read kwuy.

去

Kwùy 季 Few, young, inferior, the last; a surname; soò kwùy, 四季 *sè kwùy*, the four seasons.

Kwùy 悸 The mind moved and affected.

Kwùy 筀 The name of a particular sort of bamboo.

Kwùy 桂 The Laurus cassia; a surname; kwùy hwa, 桂花, the Olea fragrans. Gwát tëung tan kwùy tèy yit che, 月中丹桂第一枝 *gōëyh tang eⁿᵍ ây tan kwùy tèy chit ke*, the red cassia is the finest flower in the moon; see the 古詩 Koé se.

5 G

Kwùy 癸 The last of the ten horary characters.

Kwùy 貴 Dear, not cheap.

Kwùy 貴 Noble, honorable, dear, valuable; bùt kwùy, 物貴 *meēⁿh kwùy*, dear things. Kwùy yéw t'hëen hāy, jê put chëuk é kaé yew, 貴有天下而不足以解憂 *kwùy woō t'heeⁿᵍ hāy, jê bô kaòu é káy hwân ló*, in point of rank, he was in possession of the empire, and yet he found all that insufficient to dissipate his sorrow; see 孟子 Bēng choó.

平

Kwûy 葵 The name of a vegetable; the sunflower; the genus Helianthus. Wûy yéw kwûy hwa hëàng jit k'heng, 惟有葵花向日傾 *tók tók kwûy hwa ⁿâ jit k'heng*, the sunflower is the only flower that turns towards the sun.

Kwûy 揆 A rule, a measure. Sëāng boô tō kwûy yëá, 上無道揆也 *sè twā bô tō lé hwat toē*, those in the higher circles have neither reason nor principle; see 孟子 Bēng choó.

Kwûy 騤 A horse walking stately along.

Kwûy 逵 A road with nine branches; also written 馗, kwûy, a man's name.

Kwûy 頄 The cheek bones.

Kwûy 夔 A man's name, one of the servants of 舜, Sùn. A surname.

丟

Kwūy 蕢 A basket of earth; a basket for carrying earth. Wûy san kéw jím, kong k'hwuy yit kwūy, 爲山九仞功虧一簣 chò swⁿa kaóu sëëm kwán, kang ché këëm chit láng á t'hoé, in making a hillock of nine fathoms height, to leave the work when there was only a basket of earth needed to finish it, &c.

Kwūy 蕢 A grass basket; a hamper made of rushes. Yéw hō kwūy jê ko K'hóng sē che bûn, 有荷蕢而過孔氏之門 woō lâng gëâ ch'haóu láng á jê köëy K'hóng sē ây mootⁿᵍ, there was a man carrying a straw basket, who passed by before the door of Confucius; see the 論語 Lūn gé.

Kwūy 遺 To present, to offer, to send as a present; also written 餽, kwūy. Ch'héng é kwūy che, 請以遺之 ch'hēⁿá t'hó laê sàng e, we beg to present it.

Kwūy 饋 To present food to any one; food, victuals. Ló jëâk kwūy soō, 老弱饋食 laōu ây seáou lëën ây sàng chëâh, the old and weak men were engaged in bringing food (to the laborers); see 孟子 Bēng choó.

Kwūy 匱 A casket, a chest for containing anything; to want, to be destitute. Sêk sit kim kwūy, 石室金匱 chëōh ch'hoò kim ap á, the stone house and golden casket. The name of a book.

Kwūy 櫃 A chest, a trunk; tok kwūy, 棹櫃 tŏh kwūy, a counter, a table with drawers. Lâp chek ê kim kwūy che tëung, 納册于金櫃之中 làp ch'hàyh tē kim kwūy ây tang eⁿᵍ, to keep the records in a golden casket.

Kwūy 簣 A basket of earth; the same as 蕢, kwūy.

Kwūy 傒 To look on both sides.

Kwūy 跪 To kneel down, to make obeisance. Sēw lip put kwūy, 授立不跪 woō meëⁿh sēw hoē lán, tëōh k'hëā ūᵐ t'hang kwūy, when anything is given, stand up to receive it, and do not kneel; see the 典禮 K'hëuk léy.

国家出版基金项目
NATIONAL PUBLICATION FOUNDATION

海上絲綢之路文獻集成

總主編　陳支平　陳春聲

科技與文化編 86

主編　王揚宗　葉　農

海峽出版發行集團
THE STRAITS PUBLISHING & DISTRIBUTING GROUP
福建人民出版社

本册目次

福建方言字典［二］

(*A Dictionary of the Hok-këèn Dialect of the Chinese Language, According to the Reading and Colloquial Idioms*)

〔英〕麥都思（Walter Henry Medhurst）編

L

上平

La 拉 Read lëëp: to draw, to pull; lëëp këung, 拉弓 *la këung*, to draw a bow. Sëang-kong soó P'hêng-seng lëëp sat Loé-hwân-kong, 襄公使彭生拉殺魯桓公 *Sëang-kong saé P'hêng-seng la t'haé Loé-kwân-kong*, Sëang-kong sent P'hêng-seng to put Loé-hwân-kong to death; see the 史記 Soó kè.

上去

Là 縿 *Kaóu là*, [illegible]縿, a child's cap. Là sè, 縿絮, cotton wadding for clothes.

下平

Lá 嚨 Read lëûng: the throat; lëûng hoê, 嚨喉 *lâ aóu*, the gullet.

Lâ 攏 Read lëûng: to push aside; lëûng yūng, 攏壅 *lâ yūng*, to remove a stoppage. Lëûng k'hae, 攏開 *lâ k'hwuy*, to push open a passage.

Lâ 熮 Read lô: to burn, to roast at the fire.

Lâ 磟 Read lô: a rake; lô tók, 磟碡 *lâ tàk*, a harrow, a roller, for leveling and smoothing the ground.

Lâ 蜊 Read lê: a kind of cockle. Ch'hë^{n}á sit kap lê, 且食蛤蜊 *ch'hë^{n}á chëâh geó lâ*, let us just eat these cockles.

Lâ 蟧 Read lêw: a poisonous insect; lêw gê, 蟧蝺 *lâ gëâ*, a spider; lêw gê se, 蟧蝺絲 *lá gëâ se*, a spider's web.

Lâ 膋 Read leâou: the fat of the inwards; te leâou yêw, 猪膋油 *te lâ yéw*, the fat of a pig's kidnies. Ch'hé kê hëet leâou, 取其血膋 *ch'hé e ây höëyh lâ*, take the blood and the fat of the entrails; see the 小雅 Seáou gnáy.

Lâ 鯪 Lêng lé, 鯪鯉 *lâ lé*, a kind of scaly otter, found in the mountains, but something resembling a fish; the scales of which are used for medicinal purposes; (the pangolin.)

下去

Lā [illegible] Disturbed in mind; the mind confused.

Lā 朖 P'hók lōng, 曝朖 *p'hàk lā*, to spread about in the sun to dry.

Lā 撈 Read lô: to dive the hand into a liquid in order to take hold of anything.

Lā [illegible] Read lō: the name for beating anything.

上声
Laé 柰 A small boat; the name of a wild plum. Kó tin lé laé, 菓珍李柰 *köëy ché tëùng lé laé*, of fruits, the most precious are the plum and the laé.

Laé 㡾 Laé saé, 㡾㢝, ragged clothes.

下平
Laê 來 To come, to induce to come; óng laê, 往來, to come and go. Yéw pêng choō wán hong laê, put ėk lȯk hoē? 有朋自遠方來不亦樂乎 *woō pêng choō hwuī^{ng} pang laê, ū^{m} yëá tek kaê hoē?* to have a friend who comes from a distance, is it not delightful? see the 論語 Lūn gé.

Laê 倈 To come; the same as the above; also written 徠, laê. T'hëen má laê chëûng sey kėk, 天馬徠從西極 *t'hee^{ng} báy laê chëûng sae kėk*, when the celestial horse (the dragon,) comes, it is always from the utmost west; (this is an expression used by the pretended judges of the sites of dwellings and graves, who consider that the dragon, the emblem of fortune, lies always towards the west.)

Laê 崍 The name of a hill.

Laê 唻 Lô laê, 囉唻, the sounds used in humming a tune; also read laé.

Laê 睞 Tëên laê, 田睞, the ground outside of a cultivated field.

Laê 騋 A horse seven feet high; laê pīn sam ch'hëen, 騋牝三千 *báy boé s^{n}a ch'heng*, three, thousand large mares; see the 衞風 Wöëy hong.

Laê 萊 The name of a kind of grass, or weed; thistles. Pit ch'hó laê, jīm t'hoé tēy, ch'hoò che, 闢草萊任土地次之 *k'hwuy pit ch'haóu laê, jīm chŏh t'hoê tēy, tèy jē e*, to clear away the grass and weeds, and to cultivate the earth, is the next in the degree of merit; see 孟子 Bēng choó.

Laê 庲 A shed, a dwelling; tëâng laê, 長庲, the name of a terrace.

Laê 郲 The name of a city; Sê laê, 時郲, a city in the 鄭, Tēng country.

Laê 棃 A pear; laê sèng léng lē, to sit sún jīn, 棃性冷利多食損人 *laê ây sai^{ng} léng kwà laē chēy chëăh e haē lâng*, the nature of the pear is cold and acid; to eat much of this fruit is injurious.

Laê 梨 The same as the above.

下去
Laē 來 To induce to come; wán jîn put hȯk, chek sew bûn tek é laē che, 遠人不服則受文德以來之 *hwuī^{ng} ây lâng ū^{m} hȯk lán, chek sēw bún tek é hoē e laê*, when people from a distance will not submit to us, we should by literature and virtue induce them to come.

Laē 徠 To encourage any to come; lō che laē che, 勞之徠之 *o ló e ây tëŏh bwâ këò e laê*, praise their exertions, and encourage them to come; see 孟子 Bēng choó.

Laē 睞 The pupil of the eye not even; wry looks; p'hàn laē, 盼睞, to squint, to ogle.

Laē 賚 To present, to confer, to bestow, to give to an inferior.
Chew yéw taē laē, sëēn jîn sē hoò, 周有大賚善人是富 *Chew teâou woō twā laē, hó lâng chëⁿâ poò*, when the king of the Chew dynasty gave his large gifts, the good people were enriched; see the 論語 Lūn gé.

Laē 內 Read lōēy: within, inner, on the inside.
Hàp gòēy lōēy che tō yëá, 合外內之道也 *hàp gwa laē ây tō lé*, thus joining the inward and outward principles; see the 中庸 Tëung yûng.

Laē 利 Read lē: sharp, gainful; to lē, 刀利 *to laē*, a sharp knife; lē chëēn, 利錢 *laē cheeⁿᵍ*, the interest of money.
Lē to put twān kèng tëung jîn, 利刀不斷鏡中人 *laē to bēy chám tooiⁿᵍ kēⁿâ tëung ây lâng*, the sharpest knife will never cut asunder the (reflection of a) man in the mirror.

大
Lăh 踏 Lăh k'hak, 踏碓, a small kind of mortar; to jump, to leap.

灭
Lăh 蠟 Read lâp: wax, the wax of bees; lâp chëuk, 蠟燭 *lăh chek*, a wax candle.
Bit hong ch'haé hwa chok hông lâp, 蜜蜂採花作黄蠟 *bit p'hang k'hëŏh hwa chò wuiⁿᵍ lăh*, the honey bee seeks the flowers, in order to make yellow wax.

Lăh 爉 Read lâp: the appearance of fire; lâp jéuk, 爉肉 *lăh băh*, to roast flesh lâp chëuk, 爉燭 *lăh chek*, a candle.

Lăh 獵 Read lâp: hunting; tⁿá lâp, 打獵 *p'hăh lăh*, to hunt.
Kim ông tëēn lâp ê ch'hoó, 今王田獵於此 *tⁿa ông p'hăh lăh tē chéy léy wūy*, now suppose your majesty were hunting here; see 孟子 Bēng choó.

大
Lak 橐 Lak taē, 橐袋 *lak tēy*, a bundle, or bag.

灭
Làk 六 Read lëuk: six; lëuk sip, 六十 *làk chàp*, sixty; sip lëuk, 十六 *chàp làk*, sixteen.
Lëuk sip jê jé sūn, 六十而耳順 *làk chàp hòēy jé hē kang sūn*, at sixty years of age, my ear was obedient; see the 上論 Sëāng lūn.

Làk 搙 To scrape up, or scramble together with the hand.

Làk 𤸁 To scrape up anything with the nails.

Làk 搦 To take hold of anything; to rest the hand on anything.

幸
Lam 婪 Covetous, greedy; also written 惏, lam.
T'ham lam boô yëèm, 貪婪無厭 *t'ham lam bó yëà*, to covet and desire without being satisfied; see the 左傳 Chó twān.

Lam 喃 The chirping of a swallow.
Yëèn choó nê lam gé lëâng kan, 燕子呢喃語樑間 *cèⁿᵍ á nê lam haôu kóng wā tē nëóⁿᵍ kan*, the little swallows are chirping and chattering together among the rafters

上聲
Lám 覽 To look at, to observe, to inspect, to look over.
Yëên lám eng hô, 廷覽英豪 *yëën k'hwⁿà eng hëûng hô këët*, to survey extensively all the heroes and brave men; see the 光武記 Kong boó kè.

Lám 欖 Kám lám, 橄欖 *kán ná*, an olive.

Lám 擥 The same as the above.

Lám 擥 To take up in the hand.

Lám 攬 To take hold of.

Lám 揇 To take hold of, and keep fast.

Lám 𦢊 Weak, without strength; inferior, bad, cowardly.

去聲
Làm 坔 Làm tëên, 坔田 *làm ch'hân*, moist ground, a marshy, sloppy place.

平聲
Lâm 男 A male person; lâm jîn, 男人 *ta po lâng*, a man; lâm lé, 男女 *ta po kap cha boé*, men and women; also written 侽, lâm.
Chëàng sëâng pún boô chëúng, lâm jê tong choō këâng, 將相本無種男兒當自強 *chëàng kwun chaé sëâng pún téy bô chéng, ta po këⁿá tëôh ka tē choō këâng bêng*, generals and prime ministers have originally no hereditary succession, (their offices are not hereditary,) but every young man must depend on his own exertions.

Lâm 萳 Gê lâm, 宜萳, the name of a plant.

Lâm 南 The south; lâm haé, 南海, the southern sea. Yūng yëá, k'hó soò lâm bëēn, 雍也可使南面 *Yūng yëá, t'hang saé chëy lâm bīn*, Yūng can be set to face the south; (i. e. can be put in office, as all magistrates sit in their courts with their faces towards the south;) see the 論語 Lūn gé.

Lâm 喃 Nê lâm, 呢喃, the chirping noise made by swallows.

Lâm 楠 The name of a wood; lâm hëang bók, 楠香木 *lâm hëoⁿg ch'hâ*, a fragrant kind of wood.

Lâm 諵 Lâm lâm, 諵諵, the appearance of much talking, loquacity.

Lâm 藍 Blue; a plant, Polygonum Chinense; oe lâm, 烏藍, purple; kay lâm sîn, 伽藍神, the name of an idol; the name of a plant, used for dyeing an azure color.

Lâm 襤 Lâm lúy, 襤褸, torn and ragged clothes; tattered garments. Pit loē lâm lúy é k'héy këang, 篳路襤褸以啟疆 *pit loē ch'hëa lâm lúy sⁿa é k'héy k'hwuy këang kaè*, with only a bamboo carriage, and tattered garments, he opened out the borders of his territory; see the 左傳 Chó twān.

Lâm 儖 Lâm sàm, 儖㒎, disorderly, corrupt, vicious.

Lâm 尶 Lâm kaè, 尶尬, *lâm kwà*, anything incorrect, out of order.

Lâm 籃 Vulg. nâ: a basket; a surname.

Lâm 嵐 A hilly appearance; a mountain breeze.

Lâm 郴 The name of a country; also written 枏, lâm.

Lâm 啉 To drink off; to covet.

Lâm 枏 The name of a fruit, like an almond, but sour; some say, that it is like a plum; the leaves are like those of the mulberry.

去

Lām 濫 Inundated, overflowing; hwàn lām ê tëung kok; 汎濫於中國 hwàn lām tē tëung kok, overflowing the middle country; see 孟子 Bēng choó.

Lām 檻 A railing; lām ke 檻車 lān ch'hëa, a prison cart, or cage, for the conveyance of prisoners from one place to another.
Chëet lām seng tit sîn, 折檻旌直臣 cheĕh lān kan seng peáou teâou tit ây jîn sîn, the broken railing will remain as a signal for faithful ministers; (this was said by a prince who sentenced one of his ministers to death, for faithfully reproving him, and afterwards, when his minister broke the railing rather than be taken away, ordered him to be reprieved, and the broken railing to be left as an encouragement to others;) see the 史記 Soó kè.

Lām 艦 The bulwarks of a ship of war, intended as a defense against stones and arrows.

Lām 轞 The sound of carriages, the rumbling of carriage wheels.

Lām 濫 The bubbling up of a fountain.

Lām 纜 A tow-rope for pulling a boat along.

Lām 賺 Lām kam, 賺䝨, covetous of wealth.

Lām 䩑 Soft leather.

去

Lan 趼 A corn, or induration of the skin on the hands or feet.

去

Lán 懶 Lán tō, 懶惰 p'hûn twⁿā, lazy, idle; also written 嬾, lán.

Lán 赧 A face covered with shame, and red with blushes. Kwan kê sek lán lán jëên, 觀其色赧赧然 k'hwⁿà e ây sek âng âng ây yëōⁿᵍ, look how his countenance is suffused with blushes; see 孟子 Bēng choó.

Lán 戁 To respect, to reverence, to fear.

Lán 咱 Read choō: we, us; choō tông jîn, 咱唐人 lán tĕⁿᵍ lâng, we Chinese.

平

Lân 闌 To screen, to interpose between; bûn lân, 門闌 mootⁿᵍ lân, a screen before a door.

Chìn k'hè Lëâng ch'hëen ê lé, yéw hô san é lân che, 晉去梁千餘里有河山以闌之 *Chìn kok k'hè Lëâng kok chëⁿâ ch'heng gwā lé, woō kâng hô swⁿa nëⁿá é jëa lân e*, Chìn is distant from the Lëâng country upwards of a thousand furlongs, and rivers and mountains divide them from one another; see the 戰國策 Chëèn kok ch'hek.

Lân 蘭 Lân hwa, 蘭花, the name of a flower; the general name for the class Gynandria. *Morrison.* When there is only one flower on each stalk, and the fragance is abundant, it is called 蘭, lân; but when there are many flowers on one stalk, and the fragrance is diminished, the flower is called 蕙, hwŭy.

Lân 攔 Lân chap, 攔閘 *nwⁿâ chăh*, to hinder, to stop; chëa lân, 遮攔 *jëa nwⁿâ*, to obstruct; lân ché, 攔止 *nwⁿâ ché*, to stop, to intercept.

Lân 瀾 Waves, a flowing expanse of water.

Lân 斕 P'hëen lân, 斒斕, mixed colors.

Lân 難 Vulg. *ŏh*: difficult; kan lân, 艱難, troubled, distressed. Chek lân ê kwun, wŭy che këung, 責難於君謂之恭 *tⁿà ŏh ây soō kap jîn kwun, kóng këò këung*, to reprove one's prince in difficult matters is a tóken of respect; see 孟子 Bēng choó.

Lân 欄 Lân kan, 欄杆, a railing, a balustrade, a balcony; gnêw lân, 牛欄 *goô lân*, a fold for cattle.

Lân 尠 Few, scarce.

Lân 零 Read lêng: superabundant, superfluous; lêng ch'hùy, 零碎 *lân sán*, odd, miscellaneous; over and above.

Lân 鱗 Read lîn: scales; gê lîn, 魚鱗 *hê lân*, the scales of a fish. Hwān lîn chëá seng e sè gê, 凡鱗者生於庶魚 *hwān woō lân ây meēⁿh saiⁿᵍ twā tē chëùng hê*, all scales are produced on what are generally considered fish (fishes have scales).

去

Lān 爛 Vulg. *nwⁿā*: rotten, boiled to rags, decayed, and decomposed; ch'han lān, 燦爛, bright, clear, refulgent. Bêng seng yéw lān, 明星有爛 *bêng ch'haiⁿᵍ woō lān*, the bright stars are clear; see the 鄭風 Tēng hong.

Lān 瀾 Lān bān, 瀾漫, dripping, constantly wet.

Lān 難 Chae lān, 災難, misfortune, affliction; to compare. Lîm lān boô koé bëēn, 臨難無苟免 *lîm kan lān ây sê bô koé ch'hëⁿá bëēn*, on coming into trouble, do not improperly seek deliverance; see the 曲禮 K'hëuk léy. E k'hîm sèw yēw hô lān yëen? 於禽獸有何難焉 *kap k'hîm sèw pé woō sⁿa meēⁿh ŏh?* why should we compare ourselves with birds and beasts? see 孟子 Bēng choó.

卆

Lang 硠 Sék leng, 石硠 *chëŏh lang*, a hole in a rock.

Lang 儜 Ch'hong lêng, 傖儜 *ch'hang lang*, the noise of calling to one another. The sound of a drum beating the retreat.

Lang 壟 K'hong lóng, 坑壟 *k'haing lang*, a level place in a valley, fitted for cultivation; also written 巃, lóng.

声 Láng 籠 Read lóng: a basket; sëang lóng, 箱籠 *sëong láng*, a basket or trunk; neáou lóng, 鳥籠 *cheáou láng*, a bird's cage; teng lóng, 燈籠 *teng láng*, a lantern.

Láng 朗 Read lóng: clear; bêng lóng, 明朗 *bêng láng*, distinct and clear.

平 Lâng 人 Read jîn: a man; hnó jîn, 好人 *hó lâng*, a good man. Jîn jê put jîn, jê léy hô? 人而不仁如禮何 *lâng nā ūm jîn tek, e hwat léy sna meēnh taē wâ?* if people have no benevolence, what can they do towards fulfilling propriety? see the 上論 Sëāng lūn.

Lâng 韸 To beat, to strike.

Lâng 礱 To rub, to grind, to polish.

Lâng 聾 Read lông: deaf; jé lông, 耳聾 *ch'haou hē lâng*, deaf, unable to hear. Jé put t'hèng gnoé seng che hô, wát lông, 耳不聽五聲之和曰聾 *hē k'hang bô t'hēna goē sëna ây hô, kóng kēò lâng*, when the ear cannot distinguish the harmony of the five sounds, it is called deafness.

Lâng 籠 Read lông: a cage; neáou lông, 鳥籠 *cheáou lâng*, a bird's cage; teng lông, 燈籠 *teng láng*, a lantern. Jit gwát lông tëung neáou, 日月籠中鳥 *jit göèyh lâng teung ây cheáou*, the sun and moon (in the heavens) are like a bird in the cage.

Lâng 膿 Lông hëet, 膿血 *lâng hŏëyh*, matter and blood. Hoē pat jit oé lông, 後八日嘔膿 *aōu pāyh jit chëw aóu lâng*, after eight days (the patient) will vomit matter.

去 Lāng 䍀 To amuse children by soothing words.

Lāng 拵 Pëèn hoê lōng, 變猴拵 *peèng kaôu lāng*, to play apish tricks; to juggle, to perform sleight of hand tricks.

Lāng 弄 Read lōng: to sport with, to trifle; hè lōng, 戲弄 *hè lāng*, to play. E-goê jëák jê put hnò lōng, 夷吾弱而不好弄 *E-goê nooing chēná jê ūm aè gaôu chëèn*, E-goê was weak (in his childhood), and was not fond of play; see the 左傳 Chó twān.

Lāng 笭 An instrument for catching fish; a hand-net.

上 Laou 佬 Laou haou, 佬㑆, great of stature, gigantic.

声 Laóu 荖 Laóu yëèp, 荖葉 *laóu hëŏh*, the siri leaf or leaf of the betel pepper, chewed with the areca nut.

Laóu 咾 A sound, a noise.

Laóu 撓 To bend, to flinch, to draw back. Put hoo laóu, put bók tô, 不膚撓不目逃 *ūm nëw bāh, ūm shaóu bàk*, not to allow one's flesh to flinch, or eyes to blink; see 孟子 Bēng choó.

Laóu **拐** Read kwaé: a rogue; kwaé choó, 拐子 *laóu á*, a cheat.

Laóu **𣀳** Taóu laóu, 𣀳𣀳, soldiers plundering people's goods.

去

Laòu **落** Read lòk: to fall; lòk yëèp, 落葉 *laòu hëŏh*, the fall of the leaf. Goê tông lòk yëèp, t'hëen hāy ch'hew, 梧桐落葉天下秋 *goê tông laòu hëŏh t'hee^{ng} āy ch'hew*, when the goê tông casts its leaves, all the world knows that it is autumn.

平

Laôu **樓** Read loê: a gallery, an upper room, a chamber. Heáou gwàt cheàou kang loê, 曉月照江樓 *heáou göëyh chëò kang laôu*, the clear moon shines upon the gallery by the river's brink.

Laôu **流** Read lêw: to flow, to run down like water. Lêw súy che wûy bùt yëá, put êng k'ho put hêng, 流水之爲物也不盈科不行 *laôu chúy ây chò meë^{n}h, bô mw^{n}á k'ho chēw bô kë^{n}â*, flowing water is of such a nature that if it does not first fill up its measure, it does not flow on; see 孟子 Bēng choó.

Laôu **留** Read lêw: to detain; sëang lêw, 相留 *sëo laôu*, to entertain one. Yéw yëuk wûy ông lêw hêng chëá, 有欲爲王留行者 *woō ây aè t'hēy ông laôu e kë^{n}â*, there was one who wished on behalf of the king, to detain him from his journey; see 孟子 Bēng choó.

Laôu **劉** Read lêw: a surname; Lêw-pang, 劉邦 *Laôu-pang*, the founder of the 漢, Hàn dynasty.

Laôu **鐃** A small gong, or a bell without a tongue which is held by the captain of a troop, in order to arouse the attention of his soldiers.

Laôu **嚠** Read lêw: as Kaou-lêw-pa, 咬嚠吧 *Ka-laôu-pa*, Batavia.

去

Laōu **鬧** Busy, not tranquil; laōu jëèt, 鬧熱 *laōu jwăh*, bustling, all alive. Laōu tōng, 鬧動, to disturb one; also written 丙, laōu.

Laōu **𣀳** Laōu taōu, 𣀳𣀳, an ugly deformed child.

Laōu **瘺** Laōu ch'hong, 瘺瘡 *laôu ch'he^{ng}*, a running sore.

Laōu **扇** A leaky house.

Laōu **漏** Read loē: to leak; loē sëet, 漏泄 *laŏu sëet*, to leak out, as a secret; ch'hwân loē, 船漏 *chûn laōu*, a leaky ship; ok loē, 屋漏 *ch'hoò laōu*, a leaky house; loē choó, 漏仔 *laōu á*, a funnel, a tundish; loē ch'hut, 漏出 *laōu ch'hut*, to leak out; keng loē, 更漏 *kai^{ng} laōu*, an hourglass, formed of water instead of sand; a clepsydra. Loē chīn gëuk hoê kan, 漏盡玉壺乾 *laōu chīn gëuk hoê ta*, when the hourglass is run out, the pearly cup is dry.

Laōu **老** Read ló: old; ló jîn, 老人 *laōu lâng*, an old man. Kip kê ló yëá, kaè che chaē tek, 及其老也戒之在得 *kip kaòu e laōu, tëŏh kéng kaè tē aè tit tëŏh*, when people are old, they should be careful of the desire to obtain everything, (i e. of covetousness;) see the 論語 Lūn gé.

福建方言字典

大
Lap 仴 Ch'hap lap, 偛仴, a dwarfish person.

Lap 剳 To sink down, as in the mud; *loē lap*, 路剳, a muddy road.

Lap 㕊 Loose skin; the skin loose and shriveled.

兲
Lăp 納 To receive, to obtain; lăp hok, 納福, to obtain happiness; lăp hëàng, 納餉 *lăp báy á*, to pay tribute.

Ch'hut lăp che lĭn, wuy che yéw soo, 出納之吝謂之有司 *ch'hut lăp ây lĭn, sek kóng kĕò woō soo kwⁿa*, to display niggardliness in bringing out presents is what may be called a man in office; (because Chinese officers are generally backward in making presents;) see 孟子 Bēng chóó.

Lăp 内 To receive, to allow to enter; also read lōēy: within. Pē bŭn jê put lăp, 閉門而不內 *kwⁿa mootⁿᵍ jê ūᵐ lăp sēw*, to shut the door, and refuse to admit one; see 孟子 Bēng chóó.

Lăp 衲 Lăp e, 衲衣, the garments of the priests of Buddha; bwăt lăp, 末衲, a priest's cap.

Lăp 臘 The end of winter; lăp gwăt, 臘月, the twelfth month, when sacrifices are offered to all the gods together; also written 臈, lăp.

Lăp 獵 Vulg. *lăh:* to hunt; tⁿá lăp, 打獵 *p'hăh lăh*, to hunt. Lăp chëá kaou ch'hok ê tō loē, 獵者交錯於道路, *p'hăh lăh ây lâng sëo kaou ch'hok tē tō loē*, the hunters meet and cross one another in the roads.

Lăp 躐 To step over, to jump across; lăp téng, 躐等, to step over to another class; to jump over the regular series, aiming to be wise all at once.

Put k'hŏ lăp téng jê chìn, 不可躐等而進 *ūᵐ t'hang lăp kŏēy téng kay jê jip*, do not seek to get forward by stepping over the classes; see 朱文公 Choo bŭn kong.

Lăp 擸 Lăp chăp, 擸搔, to be mixed and jumbled together.

Lăp 儠 Lăp chăp, 儠偛, disorderly, wicked.

Lăp 䈤 A party-colored rope for towing a boat.

Lăp 爉 Vulg. *lăh:* the appearance of fire; to roast at the fire; lăp jëük, 爉肉 *lăh băh*, to roast flesh.

Lăp 蠟 Vulg. *lăh:* wax; lăp chëuk, 蠟燭 *lăh chek*, a wax candle.

大
Lat 漯 The name of a river; yëăk Chèy Lat jê choò choo haé, 瀹濟漯而注諸海 *k'hwuy teăou Chèy kap Lat ây chúy, jê ch'hwā jip haé*, he opened out the Chèy and Lat rivers, and led them into the sea; see 孟子 Bēng chóó.

兲
Lăt 辣 Vulg. *lwăh:* acrid, pungent, hot to the taste.

Lăt 辢 The same as the above.

Làt 剌 Wicked, perverse, warped by prejudice and error.
Boô kwae làt che sim, 無乖剌之心 *bôh woō kwae làt ây sim kwⁿa*, do not harbor a perverse and wicked mind.

Làt 揦 Pwat làt, 撥揦, the hand stretched out, the arm made bare.

Làt 鯻 The name of a fish; also written 鰳, làt.

Làt 捺 To press anything heavily with the hand.

Làt 諫 Lô làt, 謱諫, an exclamation, intimating thankfulness, and obligation:—"I put you to a great deal of trouble."

Làt 力 Read lék: strength, energy; k'hè lék, 氣力 *k'hoùy làt*, animal strength; yéw lék, 有力 *woō làt*, to be strong.
Hwuy këâng yéw lék chëá, put lêng hêng yëá, 非強有力者不能行也 *nā ūᵐ këâng bêng, woō làt ây lâng, bēy këⁿâ chêy lëy soō*, except a man be powerful and strong, he cannot do this.

Làt 栗 Read lék: a chestnut-tree; lék choó, 栗子 *làt ché*, chestnuts.

Làt 瀝 Lô làt, 瘰瀝, a kind of sore.

平

Lây 敓 A sound.

Lây 嗹 Lé lé lây lây, 哩哩嗹嗹, ambiguous and unintelligible.

去

Lăyh 靂 Read lek: loud thunder; p'hek lek, 霹靂 *p'hek lăyh*, a violent clap of thunder.

Lăyh 噫 Read yim: the violent crying of a child, till its voice is gone.

入

Lăyh 鱺 Read lék: the name of a fish.

Lăyh 剟 To split open; to strike.

Lăyh 闢 To open a door.

Lăyh 笠 Read lip: a hat; tëuk lip, 竹笠 *tek lăyh*, a bamboo hat.

上

Le 飃 A light breeze; le hong, 飃風, a gentle wind; *le le á*, a little.

声

Lé 里 Hëang lé, 鄉里 *hëoⁿᵍ lé*, a village; lîn lé, 鄰里, a neighborhood; also, a Chinese mile or furlong, a little less than the third of an English mile.
Lé jîn wûy bé, 里仁爲美 *hëoⁿᵍ lé laê woō jîn k'hăh hó*, in a village benevolence is amiable; see the 上論 Sëâng lūn.
Tëy che chëang k'hè yëá ch'hëen yéw ê lé, 地之相去也千有餘里 *tëy ây sëo k'hè yëá, woō chit ch'heng gwā lé*, the countries are distant from one another more than a thousand lé; see 孟子 Bēng choó.

Lé 俚 P'hé lé, 鄙俚, vulgar, low; any how. Chit jê put lé, 質而不俚, plain without being vulgar,

Lé 裡 Th.. inside, ...un · sa... ..., 裡 s^{n}a le, the lining of a ... ..
Chek chëùng bút che peáou lé cheng ch'hoe boô put tò, 則衆物之表裡精粗無不到 *chek chëüng meē^{n}h ây gwā laē cheng ch'hoe bô ū^{m} kaòu*, then the external and internal parts, the coarse and subtle matter of all things, will be altogether known; see the 大學 Taē hák.

Lé 鯉 Lé gê, 鯉魚 *lé hê*, a kind of carp, the chief of fresh water fish.
Hô lé teng lëûng bûn, 河鯉登龍門 *hô laē bīn ây lé hê päyh chëō^{ng} lëûng ây moot^{ng}*, the river carp has ascended the dragon's gate; (alluding to the successes of literary students.)

Lé 娌 Brother's wives call one another, 妯娌, yêw lé.

Lé 旅 Many, a multitude; an army; a stranger, a guest.
Yin-sëang che lé, kê höèy jê lîm, 殷商之旅其會如林 *Yin-sëang ây chëûng lâng, e ây chò höèy ch'hin chëō^{ng} ch'hëw nâ*, the multitude of the Yin-sëang dynasty, when assembled together, resembles a forest; see the 書經 Se keng.
Ong-sun-káy tê kwun lé, 王孫賈治軍旅 *Ong-sun-káy tê kwán kwun lé*, Ong-sun-káy managed the army; see the 論語 Lūn gé.
Boô bông pin lé, 無忘賓旅 *ū^{m} t'hang bēy kè tit lâng k'hăyh*, don't forget strangers and guests; see 孟子 Bēng choó.

Lé 祣 The name of a sacrifice, offered to the hills and rivers.
Kwùy-sē lé ê T'haē-san, 季氏祣於泰山 *Kwùy-sē hëèn lé chèy tē T'haē sw^{n}a*, Kwùy-sē offered the lé sacrifice at T'haē-sw^{n}a; see the 論語 Lūn gé.

5 J

Lé 膂 The backbone; lé lek hong kong. 膂力方剛 *k'ha chëăh kwut ây lát toō toō á kong gnāy*, the strength of the backbone was just then firm; see the 小雅 Seáou gnáy.

Lé 屢 Various, many, several; lé ch'hoò 屢次 *tàk paé*, several times, often.
Lé cheng ê jîn, 屢憎於人 *tàk paé hoē lâng sēw k'hè*, often hated by people; see the 論語 Lūn gé.

Lé 褸 Lâm lé, 襤褸, ragged torn clothes, tattered garments.

Lé 縷 Jé lé, 覶縷 crooked, intertwined; lâm lé, 襤縷, ragged.

Lé 李 A small kind of plum; hêng lé, 行李, traveling baggage; a surname.
Kwa tëên put láp lé, lé hāy put tân kwan, 瓜田不納履李下不彈冠 *kwa ch'hân bòh päyh k'hé ây, lé k'ha bòh tu... kìn*, in a melon field don't pull up the heels of your shoes, and under a plum tree don't fillip the dust of your cap; (lest you should be suspected of stealing the melons or plums.)

Lé 女 A female, a young woman, an unmarried woman.
Lông yéw ê ch'hëuk, lé yéw ê po, 農有餘粟女有餘布 *chŏh ch'hân wo... ch'hun ây ch'hek, cha boé woō sin ây poè*, thus husbandmen would have a superabundance of corn, and females would have plenty of cloth; see 孟子 Bēng choó.

Lé 汝 Read jé: you, thou.

Lé **履** That which the foot treads upon, a shoe; to tread; also, happiness. Lók ché kwun choó, hok lé sēw che, 樂只君子福履綏之 *t'hëùng lòk kwun choó, hok lé teē^{ng} neē^{ng} e*, how happy is the good man! prosperity and good fortune cleave to him; see the 小雅 Seáou gnáy.

Lé **理** To regulate, to adjust, to manage; reason, principle, meaning; tō lé, 道理, doctrine; yéw lé, 有理, reasonable; t'hëen lé, 天理, the celestial principle, Providence; leāou lé, 料理 to manage. Sëet lé yim yâng, 燮理陰陽 *bô leāou lé yim yâng*, to regulate the yin and yang (dual principles); see the 書經 Se keng. T'hëen lé cheàou jëên, 天理昭然 *t'hee^{ng} lé chëò kaòu tëöh*, the celestial principle reflects all things plainly.

Lé **邐** E lé, 迤邐, to walk aside, to follow secretly; connected.

去

Lè **剺** To flay; lè p'hê, 剺皮 *lè p'höëy*, to flay off the skin.

平

Lê **离** Clear, bright, elegant; also, a wild beast. Jê jit gwát che lê bêng, 如日月之离明 *ch'hin chëō^{ng} jit göëyh ây lê bêng*, like the brightness of the sun and moon.

Lê **離** To leave, to separate; to be separated to a small distance is called 離, lê, and to a great one 別, pëet. Hoō choó lê sàn, 父子離散 *pāy kë^{n}á lé swa^{n}à*, parents and children separated one from another; see 孟子 Bēng choó.

Lê **漓** Lîm lê, 淋漓, a perpetual dropping, a constant rain, thoroughly wet. Taē é lîm lê, 大雨淋漓 *twā hoē lîm lé*, a heavy shower drenching down.

Lê **[illegible]** Happiness, and prosperity; happy omens.

Lê **蘺** The name of a plant, a sort of grass like foxtail.

Lê **褵** A woman's petticoat, or apron; also, a girdle.

Lê **縭** The same as the above; ch'hin këet kê lê, 親結其縭 *ch'hin kat e ây lé*, she tied her own girdle; see the 詩經 Se keng.

Lê **䍦** Chëep lê, 接䍦, a white hat.

Lê **籬** Lê pa, 籬笆, a fence, a bamboo railing. Ch'haé këuk tong lê hāy, 採菊東籬下 *bán kek hwa tē tang lê ây k'ha*, to pluck a chrysanthemum flower from under the eastern fence.

Lê **篱** Ch'haòu lê, 笊篱, a bamboo strainer, used in taking rice out of the pot.

Lê **璃** Lêw lê, 琉璃, the name of a pearl; p'ho lê, 玻璃 *p'ho lêy*, glass, anything transparent, and vitreous.

Lê **魑** The name of an evil spirit.

Lê 螭 A kind of dragon; kaou lêûng ch'hek lê, 蛟龍赤螭, all sorts of dragons, and red serpents.

Lê 醨 Thin, weak wine; poē cho yím lê, 餔糟歠醨 chëăh chaou lim lê, to chew the grains and quaff the thin wine.

Lê ⿰忄离 Che lê, 忮⿰忄离, an affair in which there is much trouble.

Lê 莉 Bwát lê, 茉莉, the name of a flower, the Jasminum grandiflorum.

Lê 蜊 Kap lê, 蛤蜊, a sort of oyster.

Lê 麗 Ko lê, 高麗, the country of Corea.

Lê 鸝 Hông lê, 黃鸝, a yellow kind of bird. Lîm bòk chwán hông lê, 林木囀黃鸝 *ch'hëw nâ ây ch'hâ tit haóu hông lê*, in the trees of the wood the yellow finches are screaming.

Le 酈 A surname.

Lê 驪 A horse of a beautiful jet black.

Lê 蘆 Jê lê, 茹蘆, the name of a plant, used for dyeing red, a kind of reed.

Lê 廬 A shed; ch'hó lê, 草廬 *ch'haóu lê*, a straw shed; sëà lê, 舍廬, a cottage. Lâm Yâng Choo-kat lê, 南陽諸葛廬 *lâm Yâng woō Choo-kat ây lê*, on the southern Yâng is the hut of Choo-kat-lëäng.

Lê 驢 An ass; yëá lê, 野驢, a wild ass.

Lê 漦 Spittle, saliva; lëûng lê, 龍漦 *lëûng nw^{n}ā*, dragon's spittle.

Lê 釐 To regulate, to manage; hô lê, 毫釐, a down and an atom, the smallest particle of anything. K'hóng-choó lê têng choo se, 孔子釐定諸書 *K'hóng-choó leâou lê tē^{n}ā tëöh choo ch'hăyh*, Confucius regulated and fixed all the books; see the 史記 Soó kè.

Lê 嫠 A widow, a woman, who has lost her husband. Lê yëá, hô haē? 嫠也何害 *kw^{n}á boé, woō s^{n}a meē^{n}h haē?* widows, what harm can they do? see the 左傳 Chó twān.

Lê 蔞 A kind of straw; coarse grass; gân gnaē kê lê, 言刈其蔞 *kong kwăh e ây ko ch'haóu*, talking about cutting the coarse grass; see the 周南 Chew lâm.

Lê 瘻 K'he le, 痀瘻, a hump back; a crooked spine.

Lê 厘 Hwun lê, 分厘, a very minute division; small weights.

Lê 梩 A wheelbarrow, anything for carrying earth in; a hod, a basket. Kaè kwuy hwán lûy lê jê yëém che, 蓋歸反虆梩而掩之 *kaè tŏh too^{ng} laê, yūng lúy kap lê k'hè yëém k'hàm e*, for he returned back again, and took a basket and a wheelbarrow to get earth with, in order to bury (his parents); see 孟子 Bēng choó.

Lê 貍 Hoê lê, 狐貍, a fox; t'hⁿa jit kò che hoê lê sit che, 他日過之狐貍食之 *pat jit keng kŏèy e, hoê lê chĕăh e,* another day passing by, he found that the foxes had been eating (the corpse); see 孟子 Bêng choó.

Lê 狸 The same as the preceding.

Lê 俚 Lê gé, 俚語, coarse, vulgar expressions.

Lê 閭 The gate of a village; a hamlet consisting of 25 families.
Tek chŏēy ê hëang tóng chew lê, 得罪於鄉黨州閭 *tek chŏēy kap hëoⁿᵍ tóng chew lê ây lâng,* to offend against the people of one's district or circuit, village or hamlet; see the 禮內則 Léy lŏēy chek.

Lê 罹 To be sorrowful, to be grieved; hông ch'hoó pek lê, 逢此百罹 *toó tëŏh chéy lêy chëⁿâ păyh hāng ây hwâⁿ ló,* meeting with these hundred troubles; see the 王風 Ong hong.

Lê 黎 Read lêy: a kind of black wood; lê bîn, 黎民, the black-headed people, the Chinese.

Lê 簾 Read lëêm: a blind, a screen; bûn lëêm, 門簾 *mooⁿᵍ lê,* a door blind.

去 Lē 利 Vulg. *laē:* gain, advantage, interest; sharp, cutting; a surname.
Seáou jîn jē ê lē, 小人喻於利 *sèy ây lâng bat chéy lêy lē,* little minded people think of nothing but gain; see the 上論 Sëāng lūn.
Chaê lē, 財利, profit, gain; lē chëên, 利錢 *laē chêⁿᵍ,* interest of money.

Lē 俐 Lēng lē, 伶俐 *lêng laē,* cunning, artful, clever.

Lē 痢 Seáou lē, 小痢 *sëó lē,* a diarrhea, or looseness of the bowels.

Lē 浰 To flow rapidly; the same as the above.

Lē 例 A law, a rule, a regulation; to compare, to adjust; lùt lē, 律例, laws and regulations.

Lē 栵 A tree growing crosswise.

Lē 㽞 To sink in, as in the mud.

Lē 吕 A follower, a friend, a companion, a fellow.
Lîn pût lē hêng, 麟不侶行 *lîn bô sëo pwⁿâ kēⁿâ,* the fabulous animal lîn does not go about in herds.

Lē 侶 Lùt lē, 律吕, laws and regulations; the spine; also, long; a surname. Lē sông, 吕宋, Manila.

Lē 㾖 A long standing sickness.

Lē 梠 The lintel of a door.

Lē 莅 To come to, to come before, to descend toward; also written 涖, lē.
Chong é lē che, 莊以莅之 *gëêm chong é laē kaōu e,* to come before the people with severity and rigor; see the 論語 Lūn gé.

Lē 離 To be separated from, to a small distance, or for a short time. E kwun lē chēá, 與君離者 *kap lé sëo lē*, when separated from you, &c.

Lē 儢 Indifferent, indisposed for exertion.

Lē 詈 To rail at; lē mā, 詈罵 *lē maīⁿᵍ*, to scold. Seáou jîn wàn jé lē jé, 小人怨汝詈汝 *seáou jîn wàn hwūn lé lē maīⁿᵍ lé*, worthless people dislike you and rail at you; see the 詩經 Se keng.

Lē 慮 To consider; soō lē, 思慮, to ponder over, to be anxious about. An jê hoē lêng lē, 安而后能慮 *an jê aōu ēy soō lē*, when people are at rest, then they may consider; see the 大學 Taē hák.

Lē 濾 To strain any liquid; lē choó, 濾仔 *lē á*, a strainer.

Lē 鑢 Vulg. *lēy:* a file; to file anything.

Lē 哩 An euphonic particle, used at the end of colloquial sentences.

Lē 棣 The name of a tree, of the bark of which paper is made.

Lē 吏 Kwan lē, 官吏 *kwⁿa lē*, an officer of government. T'hëen choó soó lē tê kê kok, 天子使吏治其國 *thóng tèy saé chit ây kwⁿa lē tê e ây kok*, the emperor employed an officer to manage the affairs of his province; see 孟子 Bēng choó."

5 K

Lëa [illegible] Soup made of bones.

Lëa 伌 Loose skin.

Lëăh 剩 To cut off, to break short; to stick.

Lëăh [illegible] Read lëák: to take by force.

Lëăh 拏 Read ná: to take hold of; ná jîn, 拏人 *lëăh lâng*, to apprehend people.

Lëăh 拿 The same as the above; to seize, to take.

Lëăh 捕 Read poē: to catch; lē boō tuy poē che k'hoé, 吏無追捕之苦 *kwⁿa lē bô tuy lëăh lân ây kan k'hoé*, we are not harassed with officers coming to take us up.

Lëák 略 A little, trifling; hwut lëák, 忽略, to treat lightly; kán lëák, 簡略, to cut short, to abbreviate; yaōu lëák, 要略, the most important part. Tëang-lëâng sēw sam lëák che swat, 張良受三略之說 *Tëoⁿᵍ-lëâng sēw sⁿa ây boē lëák ây söëyh*, Tëoⁿᵍ-lëâng received the explanation of three important plans. Also written 畧, lëák.

Lëák 掠 To plunder, to take as a prey; lëák ê kaou yëá, 掠於郊野 *lëák meēⁿh tē kaou yëá*, to plunder on the borders and in the wilderness; see the 戰國策 Chëèn kok ch'hek.

Lëák 㑥 The name of a god.

上聲

Lëáng 兩 Vulg. *nō:* two in number; also vulg. *nëó^ng^:* a tael in weight; sìp lëúk lëáng wûy yit kin, 十六兩爲一斤 *chàp lák nëó^ng^ chò chit kin,* sixteen taels make one catty; (a tael is 1⅓ oz. troy.)

Lëáng 倆 Kê lëáng, 伎倆, clever, ingenious, artful.

Lëáng 魎 Bōng lëáng, 魍魎, the spirits infesting marshy ground.

下平

Lëâng 良 Good, virtuous; sëēn lëâng, 善良, good and gentle. Yit jîn gwân lëâng, bān pang é cheng, 一人元良萬邦以貞 *chit lâng sëēn lëâng, bān pang é cheng keng,* when one man is eminently excellent, all countries will be purified by him; see the 書太甲 Se t'haè kap.

Lëâng 娘 Vulg. *nëô^ng^:* a young lady; sin lëâng, 新娘 *sin nëô^ng^,* a bride. When the daughter of the first emperor of the 唐, Tông dynasty raised a troop in defense of her father's cause, the regiment she raised was called (lëâng choó kwun, 娘子軍 *nëô^ng^ á ây kwun,*) 'the young lady's troop;' see the 唐書 Tông se.

Lëâng 俍 The same as 良, lëâng: good.

Lëâng 粮 The same as 糧, lëâng: provisions; lëâng ch'hó, 粮草 *nëô^ng^ ch'haóu,* provender. Sëen hêng lëâng, hoē hêng peng, 先行粮後行兵 *taē seng kë^n^â nëô^ng^, tūy aōu kë^n^â peng,* first send the provisions and afterwards the troops.

Lëâng 糧 Vulg. *nëô^ng^:* provisions, necessaries; chëên lëâng, 錢糧 *chê^ng^ nëô^ng^,* taxes, revenue; bé lëâng, 米糧 *bé nëô^ng^,* rice and provender. Naé kó hoē lëâng, 乃裹餱糧 *naē paou pàk ta ây bé nëô^ng^,* and then bundle up the dry provisions (ready for a march); see the 大雅 Taē gnáy.

Lëâng 量 To measure; sëang lëâng, 商量 *soo nëô^ng^,* to consult, to deliberate. Lëâng kê lèk, chò kê soō, 量其力做其事 *nëô^ng^ e ây làt, chò e ây soō,* to measure one's strength, before engaging in anything. Sòng-t'haè-choé, 宋太祖, the first emperor of the Sòng dynasty, with Teō-p'hoé, 趙普, (sëang lëâng tēng T'haè-gwân, 商量定太原 *soo nëô^ng^ të^n^ā tëōh T'haè-gwân,*) consulted about settling the region of T'haè-gwân.

Lëâng 凉 Ch'heng lëâng, 清凉, cool and agreeable. A slight degree of cold is called 凉, lëâng, coolness.

Lëâng 涼 Thin, slender; K'hek to lëâng tek, 虢多涼德 *K'hek kok ây lâng chēy woō pōh ây tek hēng,* the people of the K'hek country are generally possessed of a very moderate share of virtue; see the 左傳 Chó twān.

Lëâng 孃 Vulg. *nëô^ng^ léy:* a mother; put bûn yëâ lëâng k'hok choó seng, 不聞耶孃哭子聲 *bô t'hë^n^a yëâ nëô^ng^ tit k'haòu kë^n^á ây së^n^a,* we do not hear the sound of a mother's voice weeping for her children.

Lëâng 粱 A kind of grain, Barbadoes millet; the Holcus sorghum. Vulg. *nëô^ng^:* a surname. Sin ch'huy bûn hông lëâng, 新炊聞黃粱 *sin ch'höey t'hë^n^a böëyh wut^ng^ lëâng,* for a new boiling of the pot, we have heard that the yellow grain is requisite.

福建方言字典

Lëâng 輬 A ditty, a kind of ode.

Lëâng 樑 Ok lëâng, 屋樑 ch'hoò nëóng, the beam of a house.

Lëâng 梁 A bridge; choè chew wûy lëâng, 造舟爲梁 ch'hōng chûn chò lëâng, to construct a bridge of boats; also, a beam.

丟 Lëāng 亮 To believe, to act sincerely; a distant light; clear; a man's name. Kwun choó put lëāng, oe hoē chip? 君子不亮惡乎執 kwun choó ūm lëāng sìn böĕyh t'hó sna meēnh laĕ chip? when the good man is without sincerity, how can he feel attachment? see 孟子 Bēng choó.

Bêng lëāng, 明亮, clear and distinct.

Lëāng 諒 To believe in a partial degree; to suppose a thing probable; lëāng pit, 諒必, it is likely, one should suppose; also, to examine, to assist.

Lëāng put gnó te, 諒不我知 lëāng bô lâng chae gwá, surely no one knows me; see the 小雅 Seáou gnáy.

Lëāng 兩 The numeral of carriages; yit lëāng ke, 一兩車 chit tëong ch'hëa, one carriage; pek lëāng chëang che, 百兩將之 păyh tëong ch'hëa tùy e, a hundred chariots accompanied him.

Lëāng 輛 Ke lëāng, 車輛, a carriage wheel. Yit ke lëáng lëāng, yit lëāng lëáng má, 一車兩輛一輛兩馬 chit tëong ch'hëa nō āy lûn, chit āy lûn nō chëăh báy, each carriage has two wheels, and each wheel two horses.

Lëāng 倞 Far, distant.

Lëāng 量 A measure; toē lëāng, 度量, a measure, a capacity. Chëàng kwun tám tè taē, chaé sëāng toē lëāng hông, 將軍膽智大宰相度量宏 chëàng kwun āy tná tè twā, chaé sëāng āy toē lëāng hae, a general's courage and skill should be great, and a prime minister's capacity should be comprehensive.

幸 Leaou 瘷 Straight, upright.

古 Leáou 了 Finished, done; determined; fully comprehended. Seáou jê leáou leáou, taē bē pit kê, 小而了了大未必奇 sèy jê leáou leáou, twā bē pit ēy kê, although a person in youth is very intelligent, it is not certain that he will be anything wonderful in riper years.

Leáou 撩 To take, to take away; to take hold of with the hand; a good appearance. Wân neáou bók sëang leáou, 猿鳥莫相撩 kaôu kap cheáou bô sëo t'haou t'hăyh, apes and birds do not steal from each other.

Leáou 瞭 Clearness of the eyes; clear vision; hëung tëung chèng, chek boé choo leáou yëen, 胸中正則眸子瞭焉 heng tang eng chëⁿà, bák ang á chëⁿ kwuing, when the feelings of a man's breast are correct, the pupil of his eye will be clear; see 孟子 Bēng choó.

Leáou 繚 To entwine, and twist about, to wrap around, to bind.

Leáou 嫋 Long and slender, like the twigs of a willow.

Leáou 蓼 A very acrid kind of vegetable; Polygonum barbatum.

Leáou 嫽 A polite designation for a female; also, to sport.

Leáou 憭 Leáou lek, 憭慄, feelings of compassion, to be grieved about anything.

平

Leâou 僚 A friend, an associate, a colleague in office. A surname.

Leâou yéw, 僚友, friends and associates.

Leâou 嘹 To cry out, to scream; leâou lëàng, 嘹喨, a distant noise.

Leâou 寮 A small window; ch'hó leâou, 草寮, a straw shed.

Leâou 撩 To manage; to stir up, to provoke, to challenge.

Tān tê tëâng maôu leâou chëèn, 但持長矛撩戰 *twⁿā gim têⁿᵍ maôu leâou chëèn*, only holding a long spear, and provoking to battle.

Leâou 燎 Têng leâou, 庭燎, signal fires, lighted candles.

Têng leâou yéw kong, 庭燎有光 *têng leâou woō kwuiⁿᵍ*, the signal fires are bright; see the 小雅 Seáou gnáy.

Leâou 遼 Far, distant, remote; kê leâou leâou hêy! 其遼遼兮 *e ây hwuiⁿᵍ hwuiⁿᵍ!* how distant and remote! see the 楚辭 Ch'hoé soô.

Leâou 嶛 A high and precipitous mountain.

Leâou 䠐 Long legs.

Leâou 繚 Twisted and entwined around.

Leâou 獠 To hunt by night; naé sëang é leâou ê hwŭy poé, 乃相與獠於蕙圃 *naé sëang kap e p'hăh matⁿᵍ kan ây lăh tē hwūy hwa ây hwuiⁿᵍ*, come and let us have an evening hunt together in the hwuy flower garden.

Leâou 蟟 The name of an insect, a kind of cricket.

Leâou 譑 To speak artfully, and ambiguously.

Leâou 佬 Haou leâou, 㤊佬, great in stature.

Leâou 寥 Empty, void; still, retired.

Leâou 蹘 To run away; to cross the legs.

Leâou 鷯 Cheâou leâou, 鷦鷯, a small kind of bird.

Leâou 聊 Moreover; carelessly; anyhow; to depend on, to rely upon.

Soó t'hëen hāy hoō choô put sëang leâou, 使天下父子不相聊 *saé t'heeⁿᵍ āy ây pāy kēⁿá bô sëo e wá*, thus you will cause the parents and children throughout the empire, not to depend on each other; see the 陳餘傳 Tîn ê twān.

Leâou 嵺 A lofty appearance of hills; distant, and wide. Also written 嵺, leâou.

Leâou 憀 Sorrowful, displeased.

Leâou 膋 Vulg. *lâ*: the fat of the inwards; te leâou yêw, 豬膋油 *te lâ yêw*, the fat around pig's kidnies.

丟
Leāou 料 To measure, to calculate, to number; leāou lé, 料理, to manage.
Chaê leāou, 材料, materials for constructing anything.
Leāou bîn ê T'haè-gwân, 料民於太原 *leāou swuîng pâyh saîng twā tē T'haè-gwân*, to number the people in T'haè-gwân.
Tong seang leāou lé, 當相料理 *tëŏh sëo leāou lé*, we should manage it together.

Leāou 炓 The brightness of fire.

Leāou 廖 A surname.

Leāou 療 To be sick; to stop a disease; leāou ke, 療饑, to stop one's hunger.

Leāou 燎 A fire burning, a flame; to let the fire burn.
Leāou che hong yâng, put k'hó p'hok bëët, 燎之方揚不可撲滅 *leāou hōë ây toō toō á tŏh, chëw bô t'hang p'hăh hwa*, when the flame is just spreading, it cannot be extinguished.

5 L

天
Leaŏuh 撟 To lift up the hands; a person weary.

夫
Leĕh 皵 *Leĕh p'höëy*, 皵皮, the skin coming off.

天
Leĕh 裂 Read lëĕt: to tear, to rip; lëĕt k'hae, 裂開 *leĕh k'hwuy*, to tear open.

卒
Lëem 拈 Vulg. *neeng*: to take anything up between the fingers.
Song yëëp k'hó lëem, 桑葉可拈 *seng hëŏh t'hang neeng*, the leaves of the mulberry tree can be plucked with the fingers.

Lëem 跕 Lëom këak hêng, 跕脚行 *lëem k'ha kënâ*, to walk slowly along.

声
Lëém 斂 To receive, to collect, to gather.
Lëém chaê yêw, 斂財賄 *k'hëŏh lëém cheeng kwà sàng ây meenh*, to collect together money and presents; see the 風禮 Chew léy.

Lëém 瀲 Full up to the brim.

Lëém 蘞 Pêk lëém, 白蘞, a medicinal plant of a creeping habit.

Lëém 臉 The cheeks, the countenance; t'há lëém, 打臉 *kwăh ch'hùy p'háy*, to give any one a slap in the face.

Lëém 臁 The thin part of the loins, the flank.

去
Lëêm 捻 To pick up any one with the fingers.

平
Lëêm 廉 Pure, uncorrupted by avarice, moderate; a surname; ch'heng lëêm kwan hoó, 清廉官府 *ch'heng lëêm ây kwⁿa hoó*, pure and uncorrupted magistrates.

Tïn-tëüng-choó k'hé put sêng lëêm soō chae? 陳仲子豈不誠廉士哉 *Tân-tëüng-choó k'ham ūm sē chin chēⁿ â ch'heng lëêm ây t'hàk ch'hayh lâng chae?* is not Tân-tëüng-choó truly an uncorrupted scholar? see 孟子 Bêng choó.

Lëêm 簾 Vulg. *lê:* a screen, a blind; bûn lëêm, 門簾 *mooîⁿᵍ lê*, a door-blind.

Lëêm 濂 The name of a river, near which dwelt a very learned man.

Lëêm 臁 Këak lëêm, 脚臁 *k'ha lëêm*, the shin bone.

Lëêm 鐮 Koe lëêm, 鉤鐮 *kaou lëêm*, a bill hook, a crooked knife.

Lëêm 幨 Poè lëêm, 巾幨, a curtain.

Lëêm 奩 A box containing a looking-glass; chong lëêm, 粧奩 *cheⁿᵍ lëêm*, a lady's toilet.

Lëêm 拈 Vulg. *neeⁿᵍ:* to pick up anything with the fingers. Also read lëem.

Lëêm 簷 Lëêm chëên, 簷前 *neêⁿᵍ cheêⁿᵍ*, the eaves of a house.

Lëêm 粘 To stick, to paste up anything; clammy, sticky; also written 黏, lëêm. Kaou lëêm, 膠粘 *ka lëêm*, glue.

Lëêm 蘞 The name of a plant.

Lëêm 帘 A flag stuck out as the sign of an alehouse.

Lëêm 臨 Read lîm: to come; lîm sê, 臨時 *lëêm sê*, the time arrived; when the appointed time comes; lîm chëet, 臨節 *lëêm peeⁿᵍ*, immediately.

去
Lëêm 念 To think of continually; to meditate on; to recite, to rehearse. Soō lëêm, 思念, to ponder; lëêm se, 念書 *lëêm ch'hăyh*, to recite books. Lëêm keng, 念經, to say prayers. Pek-ê Sëuk-chêy put lëêm kēw ok, 伯夷叔齊不念舊惡 *Pek-ê Sëuk-chêy ūᵐ lëêm koō p'haⁿê*, Pek-ê and Sëuk-chêy did not think of old evils; see the 論語 Lūn gé.

Lëêm 殮 Pìn lëêm, 殯殮, to prepare a body for interment; sêw lëêm, 收殮, to manage a funeral; also written 殓, lëêm. There is a seáou lëêm, 小殮, 'a small preparation,' which consists in winding of the body in six or seven bandages; and a taē lëêm, 大殮, 'a great preparation,' when a corpse is wound up in ten or more bandages.

平
Lëen 嗹 Loe lëen, 嘍嗹, wordy, talkative; sounds used in singing similar to "fa, sol, la," &c. Also read lëên.

声
Lëén 璉 A sacrificial vessel; hoê lëén yëá, 瑚璉也, a vessel used in sacrifices to contain grain.

Lëén 健 Lëén choó, 健仔 *lëén á*, twin children.

Lëén 摙 To carry things backwards and forwards. Hô-wán é chëên maé chéng súy, put sëw chëên chëá, chek lëén súy hwân che, 何遠以錢買井水不受錢者則摙水還之 *Hô-wán t'hó cheéng béy chaing chúy, ūm sëw cheéng chëá, chek lëén chúy hwân e*, Hô-wán took some money to buy well water, and when they would not receive his money, he conveyed the water back to them.

Lëén 輦 A carriage, a cart pushed along by people; lëén kày, 輦駕, the emperor's chariot; lëén hāy, 輦下, under the wheels; i. e. near the imperial residence; pwan lëén, 搬輦, to transport goods.

Lëén 撚 To rub or roll up anything in the hands; ché lëén, 紙撚 *chwá lëén*, a roll of twisted paper, used as a match.

Lëén 蹨 Read jëén: to roll anything under the feet.

Lëén 輾 To turn round, to revolve, as a wheel on its centre.

Lëén 碾 A round stone roller used in grinding anything, or in breaking husks.

去

Lëèn 圝 Round; lëèn bút, 圝物 *lëèn meénh*, to roll a thing up round.

Lëèn 攊 To roll anything up in the hand, till it becomes round. To bowl along as a ball; to be run over by a carriage.

平

Lëên 年 Vulg. *neéng*: a year; bêng lëen, 明年 *maíng neéng*, next year. Sam lëên boô kaé ê hoō che tō, k'hò wūy haòu è, 三年無改於父之道可謂孝矣 *sªa neéng bô káy ê nëöng pāy ây tō lé, t'hang kóng woō haòu è*, for three years not to change from one's father's way may be called filial piety; see the 上論 Sëāng lūn.

Lëên 聯 Read bëên: an opposite; tùy bëên, 對聯 *tòëy lëên*, a pair of antithetical sentences.

Lëên 季 The ancient form of the preceding.

Lëên 連 Connected, united, carried on in a continuous succession. Vulgarly, *neéng*: a surname. Sëang lëên, 相連 *sëo lëên*, connected, joined together. Lëên choo hoê chëá ch'hoò che, 連諸侯者次之 *sëo lëen choo hoê ây tëy jē e*, those who can connect the princes of the different states together, are next in the order of merit; see 孟子 Bēng choó.

Lëên 蓮 Lëên hwa, 蓮花, the water lily; and hô lëên, 荷蓮, the lotus. Lëêm k'hey sëen seng sèng hªò lëên, 濂溪先生性好蓮 *Lëêm k'hey sin saing sèng t'héy aè lëên hwa*, the teacher who dwelt on the brook Lëêm was naturally fond of the water lily.

Lëên 鰱 The name of a fish; haé lëên, 海鰱, a salt water fish about the size of a perch, much used in making offerings to the gods.

Lëên 漣 The rippling on the water, occasioned by the action of the wind. Hô súy ch'heng ch'hëªá lëên,

河水清且漣 *kang chúy ch'heng kwà lëên,* the waters of the river are clear and rippling; see the 魏風 Gwūy hong.

Also, the flowing of tears; k'hip t'hèy lëên lëên, 泣涕漣漣 *laŏu bàk saé lëên lëên,* he shed tears most profusely; see the 衛風 Wōēy hong.

玉

Lëēn **練** To boil any thing thoroughly; to become experienced; to exercise. Ch'ho lëēn, 操練, to exercise or train soldiers. Kân lëēn, 簡練, to essay, to prove.

Lëēn **健** A young fowl, a chicken.

Lëēn **揀** To choose, to select; also read kán.

Lëēn **楝** A species of cherry, which grows to the height of ten feet and upwards, with a very exuberant foliage.

Lëēn **鍊** To smelt metals; to refine and purify by repeated trials; lëēn gëúk, 鍊獄, the Catholic term for purgatory; t'hëet lëēn, 鐵鍊 *t'heĕh lëēn á,* an iron chain.

Kim pek lëēn, jëên hoē cheng, jîn ék jê ch'hoó, 金百鍊然後精人亦如此 *kim chit păyh kwùy lëēn, jëēn aōu ēy cheng, lâng yëá an nëy sai*^{ng}, metals after having been refined a hundred times become pure; so it is also with men.

Lëēn **煉** To try and refine in the fire; to melt metals, and separate the dross. Lé-wâ-sē lëēn gnoé sek sėk, é poé ch'hong t'hëen, 女媧氏煉五色石以補蒼天 *Lé-wâ-sē lëēn goē sek ây chëŏh, é poé ch'hong t'hee*^{ng}, Lé-wâ-sē smelted the five colored stones in order to repair the azure heavens. Lëēn jîn sim, 煉人心, to try men's hearts.

犬

Lëep **聶** To bend down the ear, in order to listen to a whisper; a whisper in the ear. Also, a surname.

Naé haōu jê lé choó, tëem lëep jé gé, 乃效兒女子呫聶耳語 *naé t'hàn sèy cha boé kë*^{n}*á, tëem lëep hē k'hang ây wā,* following the example of little girls, whispering in each other's ears.

Lëep **囁** The mind affected; to scold privately, to rail at in secret. Lëep jê, 囁嚅, verbose, talkative.

Lëep **懾** To miss one's aim; also, to be afraid.

Lëep **攝** To join together, to connect, to unite. Kwan soō boô lëep, 官事無攝 *kw*^{n}*a soō bó këem lëep,* the duties of the various offices were not united; see the 上論 Sëāng lūn.

Lëep **躡** To ascend, to tread on, to walk; to step over, to jump out of order. Lëep chëuk hâng gnoé che kan, 躡足行伍之間 *lëep k'ha tē hâng gnoé ây tëung kan,* to lift up the feet while marching in rank and file; see the 史記 Soó kè.

Lëep **鬣** The mane on a horse's neck; the whiskers about the mouths of some fish; kong lëep, 剛鬣, a pig.

Lëep **儠** Lëep tëáng, 儠長, a strong, robust appearance; hale.

Lëep **慴** To be afraid, to fear, to be alarmed. Yit hoó tëung kae lëep hòk, 一府中皆慴伏 *chit hoó tëung ây lâng chò poō kë*^{n}*a,* all the people in the whole district were afraid of him; see the 項羽紀 Hāng é ké.

Lëep 摺 To fold, to double up, to break, to ruin, to overthrow.

Lëep 涅 To dye black; lëep jê put choo, 涅而不緇 *neĕ^ng jê bēy oe*, to dye without its becoming black; see the 論語 Lūn gé. Also written 湼, lëep.

Lëep 揑 To take up with the fingers, to collect, to grasp in the hand.

Lëep 拉 To break, to ruin, to overthrow. Vulg. *la:* to draw, to pull. Hwān-ch'he lëep hëëp chëet ch'hé ê Gwūy, 范雎拉脇折齒於魏 *Hwān-ch'he cheĕh hëëp kwut, at ch'hùy k'hé tē Gwūy*, Hwān-ch'he had his ribs broken, and his teeth knocked out at Gwūy.

Sëang lëep, 相拉 *sëo la*, to pull one another about, in play.

Lëep këung, 拉弓 *la këung*, to draw a bow.

Lëep 粒 A grain, a bead; yit lëep bé, 一粒米 *chit lëep bé*, a kernel of rice.

Lók söèy lëep bé lông lēy, to ch'hé che jê put wûy gëák, 樂歲粒米狼戾多取之而不爲虐 *hó neĕ^ng tang lëep bé chīn chēy, k'hăh chēy t'hăyh e, jê bēy chò pò gëák*, in a good season, when rice is abundant, to take a little more from the people would not be considered oppression; see 孟子 Bēng choó. Ké lëep, 幾粒 *kwúy lëep*, a few.

Lëep 㘝 To steal anything and stow it away secretly.

Lëĕt 列 A rank, a row, an order; to arrange in order; to draw up in a row; several; a surname.

Paê lëĕt, 排列, to arrange in order.

K'hae lëĕt, 開列, *k'hwuy lëĕt*, to spread out, to separate and arrange.

Put koé put sêng lëĕt, 不鼓不成列 *ū^m p'hăh koé ū^m chëⁿâ lëĕt*, without beating the drum, it is impossible to form the rank and file; see the 左傳 Chó twān.

Lëĕt wūy sëang kong! 列位相公, gentlemen, all!

Lëĕt 冽 A cold air; the extreme of cold.

Lëĕt 洌 Clear water; clear, transparent. Chwân hëang jê chéw lëĕt, 泉香而酒洌 *chwⁿâ p'hang jê chéw ch'heng*, when the spring is fragrant, the wine will be clear.

Lëĕt 烈 The fierce violence of fire; fierce, raging, ardent, zealous, chaste. Lëĕt ê béng hⁿó, 烈于猛火 *k'hăh lëĕt ê béng höëy*, fiercer than lurid flames. Lëĕt lé put hēw kày, 烈女不復嫁 *chin chëet ây cha boé bô kŏh kày*, truly chaste females do not marry a second time.

Lëĕt 裂 Vulg. *leĕh:* to tear, to rip; lëĕt k'hae, 裂開 *leĕh k'hwuy*, to tear open. Lëĕt kê e, jê twān kê taè, 裂其衣而斷其帶 *leĕh e ây sⁿa, jê tooi^ng e ây twā*, he tore his clothes, and burst asunder his girdle.

Lëĕt 捩 To break, to oppose; to twist, to turn. Tong sey lëĕt tō, bān chew hwûy, 東西捩柁萬舟回 *tang sae aóu twā, bān chûn tooi^ng*, twisting the rudder to the east and west, a myriad of vessels would turn.

5 M

夫

Lek **栗** The chestnut-tree; lek choó, 栗子 *lat á*, a chestnut; to fear, to tremble; chëèn lek, 戰栗, to tremble with fear. Also written 㮚, lek. Chew jîn é lek, 周人以栗 *Chew ây lâng chae lat á*, the people of the Chew dynasty planted the chestnut tree (at the place of sacrificing to the gods of the land); see the 上論 Sëāng lūn.

Lek **傈** The presiding shrine in a temple.

Lek **剽** To cut off, to scrape. Also written 剌, lek.

Lek **慄** To be afraid; to feel alarm and apprehension. E ke jîn sëāng, lek lek jê put bwán jit, 禹居人上慄慄如不滿日 *E k'hëä tē lâng ây têng bīn, lek lek kë^{n}a ch'hin chëō^{ng} bēy mw^{n}á jit*, when E presided over the people he was perpetually apprehensive, as though he could not enjoy a whole day's comfort.

Lek **篥** Pit lek, 觱篥, a kind of pipe like a rude clarinet made of bamboo, with the mouthpiece made of reed; used by the Tartars.

Lek **慗** Hungry, famishing.

Lek **膣** Flesh; the part of the flesh where the muscles are bent.

Lek **襵** To stitch up a rent in a garment.

灭

Lėk **力** Vulg. *làt*: strength; k'hè lėk, 氣力 *k'hwùy làt*, bodily strength. E lėk hȯk jîn chëá, hwuy sim hȯk yëá, 以力服人者非心服也 *è k'hwùy làt hȯk lâng, ū^{m} sē sim kw^{n}a hȯk yëá*, when we employ main force to subjugate people, their minds will not be subdued; ('a man convinced against his will, is of the same opinion still.') Jëȧk lông hȯk tëên lėk sek, naé ėk yéw ch'hew, 若農服田力穡乃亦有秋 *ch'hin chëō^{ng} lông hoo chò ch'hân, yūng làt tē kay sek, naé yëá woō ch'hew*, just as the husbandman labors in the field, and employs his strength in agriculture, he will be sure after some time to get a harvest; see the 書經 Se keng.

Lėk **仂** The overplus of anything; the residue, what is left over, an odd number.

Lėk **屴** The connected appearance of hills.

Lėk **扐** To place a number of straws between the fingers, in order to reckon and prognosticate. Kwuy ke ê lėk é sëāng jūn, 歸奇于扐以象閏 *kwuy k'hëa ây tē ch'hëw chae^{ng} kan, é chëāng lūn göëyh*, to put the odd straw between the fingers, in order to denote the intercalary month; see the 易繫詞 Ėk hêy soê.

Lėk **朸** The noise of water; also written 泐, lėk.

Lėk **勒** The bit in a horse's mouth; to restrain, to oppress; to engrave. Lėk sek, 勒索, to oppress, to extort money by oppression. Lėk má, 勒馬, to rein in a horse.

Lĕk 鴗 A bird like a duck, but smaller; a teal; some say, that it is another name for a dove.

Lĕk 鰳 Lĕk gê, 鰳魚 *lăt hê*, the name of a fish, (a shad?) which in the 4th month appears on the face of the water, and the fishermen on hearing the noise, go and catch them. They are in appearance like the 鰣魚, sê gê, with smaller heads.

Lĕk 僫 A man's name.

Lĕk 㔏 To cut; also written 劦, lĕk.

Lĕk 瀝 The dripping of water; to pour out by drops.

Lĕk 櫪 The post to which a horse is tied. Ló kè hók lĕk, chè chaē ch'hëen lé, 老驥伏櫪志在千里 *laöu báy hòk tē lĕk sim chè twā tē ch'heng lé hwuīng*, "I am like an old steed submitting to be tied to a stake, but my designs stretch to the distance of a thousand lé;" (said by 桓温, Hwân-wun, when he had designs of aiming at supreme power.)

Lĕk 瘳 Loê lĕk, 瘰癧 *loê lăt*, a kind of ulcer.

Lĕk 鬲 A kind of iron pan; lĕk ch'hëang, 鬲鎗, a kind of spear.

Lĕk 轣 The rut of a wheel.

Lĕk 歷 To pass over, to pass by, to carry, to carry to the utmost; an order, a series. Put lĕk wūy jê sëang é gân, 不歷位而相與言 *ūm köëy wūy jê sëo kap lâng kóng wā*, do not cross over from your place (at court), to go and speak with people; see 孟子 Bēng choó.
Lĕk lëên che kéw, 歷年之久 *lĕk neêng ây koó*, after a long succession of years.

Lĕk 曆 The arrangement of the times and seasons throughout the year.
T'hëen che lĕk soè chaē jé këung 天之曆數在爾躬 *t'heeng ây lĕk sedou twā tē lé ây hîn sin*, the numerical arrangements of fate centre in your person; see the 論語 Lūn gé.

Lĕk 鱱 The name of a fish.

Lĕk 靂 P'hek lĕk, 霹靂, a peal of thunder, a loud thunder clap.

Lĕk 溺 To drown; tîm lĕk, 沉溺 *teêm lŏh chúy*, to be immersed in water.
Só lĕk put wān, sē ch'haê lông yëá, 嫂溺不援是豺狼也 *hëna só tëêm lŏh chúy jê ūm kêw, sē ch'haê lông*, if a man's sister-in-law should be sinking in the water, and he did not go to help her, he would be a wolf; see 孟子 Bēng choó.

Lĕk 酈 A surname. Name of a place.

Lĕk 搦 To lay the hand on; to provoke, to challenge; lĕk chëèn, 搦戰, to challenge out to fight.

Lĕk 匿 To secrete, to conceal, to hide.
Lĕk wàn jê yéw kê jîn, Chó-k'hew-bêng t'hé che, 匿怨而

友其人左丘明恥之 *k'hèng wàn hwûn, jê kap e ây lâng chó hó pêng, Chó-k'hew-bêng seáou léy e,* Chó-k'hew-bêng was ashamed to harbor malice, and at the same time manifest friendship to a person; see the 論語 Lūn gé.

Lèk 暠 Clear, bright.

Lèk 櫟 The name of a kind of oak; Quercus serrata.

Lèk 陸 Read lëùk: high and even; song lëùk, 雙陸 *song lèk,* the game of dominoes.

Lèk 蛙 Read lëùk: a kind of sea cockle, round, thick, and of a variegated color.

Lèk 綠 Read lëùk: green; a green color; lëùk e hông sëâng, 綠衣黃裳 *lèk sⁿa wuiⁿᵍ kwûn,* a green coat and yellow trowsers.

平

Leng 乳 Read jé: milk; gnêw jé, 牛乳 *goô leng,* cow's milk; gnêw jé yêw, 牛乳油 *goô leng yêw,* butter; jê chóó 乳子 *leng á,* the nipples.

Bûn-ông soò jé, sē wūy chè jîn, 文王四乳是謂至仁 *Bûn ông sè ây leng, chëä kóng këò chè jîn,* Bûn ông had four nipples, and therefore was called the most benevolent.

Leng 嬭 Read naéⁿᵍ: a woman's breasts; naéⁿᵍ chóó, 嬭子 *leng á,* the nipples.

Leng 湩 Milk, the milk of animals.

Kē-soe che jîn, kē gnêw má che leng, é sëén t'hëen chóó che chëuk, 巨蒐之人其牛馬之湩以洗天子之足 *Kē-soe ây lâng, ch'hòng goô bây ây leng, é sêy hông tèy ây k'ha,* the men of Kē-soe prepared the milk of horses and cows to wash the feet of the emperor; see the 穆天子傳 Bòk t'hëen chóó twān.

上

Léng 冷 Cold, frigid; extreme cold. A surname.

Léng 罜 Léng teng, 罜罣, a small kind of net.

Léng 嶺 Vulg. nëⁿá: the neck; san léng, 山嶺 *swⁿa nëⁿá,* the ridge of a hill, a range of mountains.

Tê léng pèk yîn kan, 置嶺白雲間 *tè nëⁿá tē pâyh hwûn ây kan,* (traveling along,) he left the hill-tops far among the white clouds.

Léng 領 Vulg. nëⁿá: the neck; sam léng, 衫領 *sⁿa nëⁿá,* the collar or neck of a coat.

Léng bēng, 領命 *nëⁿá bēng,* to receive any one's order; literally, to take them on one's neck. Léng chëên, 領錢 *nëⁿá cheèⁿᵍ,* to receive money; pó léng, 保領 *pó nëⁿá,* to secure, to engage.

Léng 濘 Mud, mud and water, slippery; nê léng, 泥濘, muddy.

T'heng léng, 汀濘, a small stream of water.

去

Lèng 踜 To kick at anything.

平

Lêng 令 To order, to command; to cause, to influence.

Pëën pè put chëuk soó lêng ê chëên gé, 便嬖不足使令于前與 *pëën pè bó k'ha saé lêng tē bīn chêng,* favorites and minions cannot be employed and ordered about in your presence; see 孟子 Bēng chóó.

福建方言字典

Lêng 陵 A large mound of earth is called lêng. Also, to scorn, to despise. Chaē sëāng wūy put lêng hāy, 在上位不陵下 *tē sëāng wūy ūm lêng jëùk tē hāy ây lâng*, when those in superior stations do not despise those beneath them; see the 中庸 Tëung yûng. Hông lêng, 皇陵, the imperial tombs. San lêng, 山陵, royal cemeteries.

Lêng 淩 An ice-house; lêng sit, 凌室, a place for keeping ice, which is used in various sacrifices, and needs therefore to be always at hand. A surname.

Lêng 倰 To pity, to commiserate.

Lêng 菱 A kind of plant; lêng kak, 菱角, a vegetable, called water caltrops; the Trapa bicornis.

Lêng 薐 Po lêng, 菠薐, a kind of vegetable; spinach.

Lêng 綾 Vulg. *lîn:* a thin kind of silk, sarsnet.

Lêng 稜 Divine awe, majesty; veneration. Husbandmen, in reckoning the distance and quantity of land, say, ké lêng? 幾稜, how far?

Lêng 鯪 Lêng lé, 鯪鯉, the name of a fish, said to have feet, and to eat boats.

Lêng 棱 Square wood; anything pointed and angular.

Lêng 夌 Slanting, sloping.

5 N

Lêng 淩 The name of a river.

Lêng 伶 Alone; to play and sport; lêng jîn, 伶人 a buffoon; lêng kwan, 伶官, the leader of a band of music. Lêng lē, 伶俐 *lêng laē*, artful, cunning, clever, ingenious.

Lêng 怜 The mind exhausted, at one's wits' end.

Lêng 囹 Lêng gé, 囹圄, a prison, a place of confinement. Tëūng ch'hun bēng yéw soo séng lêng gé, 仲春命有司省囹圄 *tëūng ch'hun ây sê kăh yéw soo kwⁿa séng ch'hat kⁿa k'hoo*, in the middle month of spring officers were ordered to examine the prisons; see the 禮月令 Léy gwăt lēng.

Lêng 苓 Hók lêng, 茯苓, the name of a medicine; the root of the Smilax China, called China root.

Lêng 拎 To hold in the hand.

Lêng 玲 Lêng lóng, 玲瓏, the sound of gems; a stone curiously cut; applied to persons in a good sense, when speaking of their talents or dispositions.

Lêng 蛉 An insect that infests the mulberry tree; ch'heng lêng, 蜻蛉, a locust. Bêng lêng yéw choó, kó ló hoō che, 螟蛉有子蜾蠃負之 *bêng lêng woō kⁿá, wân nëoⁿᵍ gëâ e*, the bêng lêng insect gets a young one, and the dragon fly carries it away, (to adopt it for its own); see the 小雅 Seáou gnáy.

Lêng 岭 Lêng êng, 岭嶝, the deep appearance of hills; far among the hills.

Lêng 聆 To hear, to listen.

Lêng 泠 The name of a river. Lêng lêng, 泠泠, the noise of water.

Lêng 鈴 A small bell; small bells attached to horses and banners.

Lêng 羚 Lêng yâng, 羚羊, a wild goat.

Lêng 零 Superfluous rain, anything remaining over. Lêng seng, 零星 *lân sán*, a remnant. Lêng ch'hùy, 零碎 *lân sán*, odd. A cypher or 0.

Lêng 澪 The name of a river.

Lêng 舲 A small cabin in a boat.

Lêng 齡 A year, age. Bōng tèy sek jé kéw lêng, 夢帝錫爾九齡 *bāng sëāng tèy soò hoē lé kaôu neēng*, I dreamed that the highest emperor bestowed upon you nine years more of life; see the 禮記 Léy kè.

Lêng 鴒 Chit lêng, 脊鴒, the name of a bird, a lark; pék lêng neáou, 白鴒鳥 *păyh lêng cheáou*, a paddy bird. Also written 鴒, lêng, bird's feathers.

Lêug 曚 The same as 曨, lêng; the rising sun.

Lêng 儜 Weak and distressed; hô yūng k'hoê k'he lêng? 何用苦拘儜 *saê saê kaôu héá k'hoê chip lêng?* "why should you thus miserably cling to your troubles?" said by 韓愈, Hân-jé.

Lêng 嚀 Teng lêng, 叮嚀, to insist upon, to enjoin, to bid again and again. Teng lêng chaè sam, lêw sîn ê ch'hoó, 叮嚀再三流神於此 *teng lêng chaè sⁿa, laôu chêng sîn tē chéy léy wūy*, to enjoin repeatedly, that the attention may be kept to this subject.

Lêng 寧 Peaceful, tranquil; rest, tranquillity; lêng k'hó, 寧可, better, rather. Lēng-chēng tè wán, tām pók bêng sim, 寧靜致遠淡薄明心 *an lêng chēng chēng ēy tè kaôu hwuiⁿg, chēⁿá chēⁿá pŏh pŏh ēy bêng lán ây sim*, "in peace and tranquillity, we can extend our thoughts to distant objects; and a complete indifference to the world will illumine and brighten the mind;" said by 諸葛武候, Choó-kat Boó-hoê.

Lêng 寍 Peaceful, tranquil; same as the preceding.

Lêng 楞 Lêng gëêm, 楞嚴, the name of a book belonging to the sect of Buddha.

Lêng 靈 A spirit, a soul; spiritual; excellent; lêng hwûn, 靈魂 *sîn hwûn*, the soul. Wûy jîn bān bút che lêng, 惟人萬物之靈 *tók lâng chò bān meēⁿh ây lêng*, man alone is the soul of all things; see the 書泰誓 Se t'haè sè. Keng sé lêng taê, 經始靈臺 *k'hé t'haôu chò hó ây taê*, they began to make the excellent terrace; see the 上孟 Sëāng bēng.

福建方言字典

Lêng 櫺 The bars of a window frame.

Lêng 靈 The same as 靈, lêng: a spirit.

Lêng 𩃬 Lêng lē, 𩃬利, sharp, cunning, clever.

Lêng 曨 Lêng lóng, 曨曨, the light of the sun.

Lêng 能 Vulg. *ëy:* to be able, may, can; chaê lêng, 才能 *chaê teăou,* power, ability. A surname.
Hô kê to lêng yëá? 何其多能也 *an chwⁿá e kaðu hëá chëy ëy?* how is it that he possesses such a multiplicity of talent? said of Confucius in the 論語 Lūn gé.
Wûy sèng chëá lêng che, 唯聖者能之 *tòk sèng jîn ây lâng ëy e,* only a sage can accomplish this; see the 中庸 Tëung yûng.

Lêng 灵 The same as 靈, lêng: the soul; also, a little warm.

Lêng 龍 A dragon; the chief of the scaly tribe; also read lëûng. Hëèn lëûng chaē tëên, t'hëen hāy bûn bêng, 見龍在田天下文明 *hëèn lêng tē ch'hân, t'heeⁿᵍ āy bûn bêng,* when a dragon appears in the field, the whole empire will become literary and illustrious; see the 易經 Ek keng.

玉 Lēng 令 Good, fine, honorable; a command, an order. Lēng hoê, 令狐, a double surname. K'haóu gân lēng sek, sëén è jîn, 巧言令色鮮矣仁 *k'há āy wā, hó āy bīn sek, chëó k'höëyh woō jîn,* artful words and a smooth countenance are seldom found connected with virtue; see the 上論 Sëāng lūn.
Lēng chun, 令尊, 'your honorable father;' a term of respect, when speaking of another's parent.
Hwat lēng, 法令, the rules of an order.
Hëēn lēng, 縣令 *kwān lēng,* the magistrate of a district.

Lēng 㓏 To cut off.

Lēng 佞 Talkative, verbose, eloquent, skilled in discourse; also written 侫, lēng. Yung yëá, jîn jê put lēng, 雍也仁而不佞 *Yung yëá, jîn âe, jê bëy gaðu kóng wā,* Yung is benevolent but not eloquent; see the 論語 Lūn gé.

Lēng 倰 Lēng lēng, 倰蹬, weary, tired.

Lēng 鴒 Kaou lēng neáou, 鵁鴒鳥 *ka lēng cheáou,* a magpie.

Lēng 𢔧 Lēng lēng, 𢔧𢔧, the appearance of walking.

Lēng 濘 Mud, muddy; ch'ham yit ê lēng, 驂溢於濘 *báy lap tē nwⁿā t'hoê,* the horses were covered with the mud; see the 左傳 Chó twān.

Lēng 另 To dwell apart, to cut asunder; besides, another.

肅 Lëó 𥄵 The eyes just getting a glimpse of anything.

平
Lëô 蜊 Read lê: a kind of cockle or oyster.

入
Lëŏh 略 Read lëåk: a little; *lëŏh lëŏh á*, in a small degree.
Lëåk tek, 略得 *lëŏh lëŏh á tit tëŏh*, to obtain anything in some measure.

去
Lëŭk 忸 Lëŭk nê, 忸怩, ashamed, to blush for shame.
Sëäng wåt, wut tô soo kwun jé; lëuk nê, 象曰鬱陶思君爾忸怩 *Sëăng kóng wut chut sëŏ^ng kwun lé; yëá chëw seâou léy*, Sëäng said, "I have been anxiously thinking about your majesty;" saying which, he blushed for shame; see 孟子 Bĕng choó.

Lëŭk 脛 Read kĕng: bent, to stoop; kĕng lòk k'hè, 脛落去 *lëuk lŏh k'hè*, to stoop down.

Lëŭk 襵 To fold in the hem of a garment. To fold anything.

入
Lëŭk 陸 Anything high and flat; dry ground; a surname; lëŭk tō, 陸道, a journey by land; lëŭk sëŭk, 陸續, connected, in succession.
Chok ke é hêng lëŭk, 作車以行陸 *chŏ ch'hëa é kë^nâ sw^na loē*, they made carriages for traveling by land.

Lëŭk 蛙 Vulg. *lĕk:* a kind of sea cockle, round, thick, and party-colored.

Lëŭk 僇 To disgrace; wûy t'hëen hāy taē lëŭk, 爲天下大僇 *hoē t'hee^ng āy twā jëŭk*, to be despised by the whole world.

Lëŭk 蓼 Grass long and high; luxuriant herbage.

Lëŭk 戮 To kill, to put to death; to disgrace; to unite strength.
T'hëen jîn këŭng lëŭk, 天人共戮 *t'hee^ng lâng chŏ poē laê t'haê*, the gods and men both conspiring to destroy.
Pang boē tō, bëén ê hêng lëŭk, 邦無道免於刑戮 *pang bô tō lé, bëén ê hêng lëŭk*, when a country has not the right way, to be able to avoid being put to death; see the 論語 Lūn gé.
Lëŭk kip sëen jîn, 戮及先人 *lëng jëŭk taē seng āy lâng*, to disgrace one's predecessors.

Lëŭk 磟 Lëŭk tòk, 磟碡 *lăk tàk*, a rake, a harrow.

Lëŭk 穋 A sort of corn that is later sown, but sooner ripe.

Lëŭk 菉 Green; lëŭk tëuk, 菉竹 *lĕk tek*, green bamboo; lëŭk toē, 菉荳 *lĕk taōu*, a kind of green pulse.

Lëŭk 錄 To copy a writing, to record; a record, a writing; to collect.
Sèng lëŭk, 聖錄, sacred writings.

Lëŭk 籙 Toê lëŭk, 圖籙, to scheme, to plan.

Lëŭk 逯 Lëŭk lëŭk, 逯逯, to walk carefully; a surname. Hwŭn jëên jê laê, lëŭk jëên jê óng, 渾然而來逯然而往 *hwŭn lwăn jê laê, kîn sīn jê óng*, they came in confusion, but returned with caution; see the 淮南子 Hwaê lâm choó.

福建方言字典

Lëúk 醁 Good wine; lêng lëúk, 醽醁, a kind of wine.

Lëúk 綠 Vulg. *lėk:* green; lëúk e hông lé, 綠衣黄裏 *lėk sⁿa wuîⁿᵍ lé,* a green garment with a yellow lining.

Lëúk 六 Vulg. *làk:* six; sip lëúk, 十六 *chàp làk,* sixteen.
Lëúk sip tëāng ê hëang, 六十杖於鄉 *làk chàp hōèy këāh kwaè á tē hëoⁿᵍ lé,* those who are sixty years of age may carry a staff in the village; see 朱註 Choo choò.

声

Lëûng 寵 To show favor to, to distinguish by favors; to love.
Hô t'hëen che lëûng! 何天之寵 *hô t'heeⁿᵍ ây lëûng aè!* what distinguishing favor from heaven! see the 詩經 Se keng.

Lëûng 壟 A mound of earth.

去

Lëûng 踜 To kick with the foot.

平

Lëûng 隆 Full, abundant; high, as a mountain, great, eminent. A surname.
Tō lëûng chek chëûng jê lëûng, tō woo chek chëûng jê woo, 道隆則從而隆道汚則從而汚 *tō lé lëûng sēng, chek t'hàn e lëûng sēng, tō lé la sâm, chek t'hàn e la sâm,* when the principles are exalted, those who practice them will be exalted; and when the principles are corrupt, those who follow them will be corrupt also; see the 禮檀弓 Léy t'hân këung.

5 O

Lëûng 癃 Wearied, tired, fatigued.
Lëûng pēng bùt k'hëén, 癃病勿遣 *yëà ây paiⁿᵍ ây bô ch'hay saè,* the weary and the aged must not be sent on an errand.

Lëûng 窿 K'hëung lëûng, 穹窿, the high expansive appearance of the heavens; the vaulted firmament.

Lëûng 鼕 The sound of a drum.

Lëûng 龍 A dragon, the chief of the lizard tribe; a surname; lëûng wûy, 龍位, the imperial throne.
Sêng lëúk lëûng ê gē t'hëen, 乘六龍以御天 *k'hëà làk lëûng ê gē t'heeⁿᵍ,* to ride on six dragons, and ascend to heaven; see the 易經 Ėk keng.

Lëûng 竜 The ancient character for 龍, lëûng, a dragon.

Lëûng 襱 The breech; the covering for the same, trowsers.

Lëûng 朧 Tông lëûng, 朣朧, the rising moon; the moon not clear.

Lëûng 櫳 A cage for birds; an aviary; a cage for animals.

Lëûng 礱 A mill for grinding corn; to rub, to grind; to sharpen tools.

Lëûng 蘢 The name of an herb.

本 Lew 鰍 The name of a fish, found in the rice fields; nê lew, 泥鰍 *t'hoê lew*, a mud fish.

声 Léw 柳 The willow tree; also, a surname. Léw teâou, chëûng seáou wut, tëâng taē wut put k'hwut, 柳條從小彎長大彎不屈 *léw teâou, tëŏh chëûng sèy wut, kaôu tē^ng twā wut bēy k'hwut*, a willow twig must be bent when it is green, for as soon as it is grown large, it can no longer be bent. Alluding to children, who should be trained up in the way they should go, for when they once become old, they are past management.

Léw 抑 To rub anything, to feel, to handle.

Léw 㶭 A kind of firework, a squib or a cracker.

Léw 飀 A sudden gust of wind.

Léw 紐 Anything bound and tied; to knot and bind together. E Sùn che séy léw yëá, 禹舜之所紐也 *E sē Sùn ây séy kat léw*, E was bound and engaged by Sùn; see 狂子 Chông choó.

Léw 扭 To turn or twist the hand; séw léw, 手扭, to twist anything with the hand, to wring.

Léw 杻 Wooden stocks for confining the legs.

Léw 鈕 Anything fastened, or secured; léw choó, 鈕仔 *léw á*, a button. Léw k'hoè, 鈕扣 *léw k'haôu*, a button-hole. A surname.

Léw 狃 Léw sip, 狃習, familiar with, free, disrespectful. Léw ê kan kèw, 狃于姦宄 *léw sip kap kan kèw ây lâng*, familiar with vicious and worthless people.

Léw 罶 An instrument for catching fish, made of bamboo.

Léw 霤 The god supposed to preside over the centre of a dwelling. Kê soō tëung léw, 其祀中霤 *e ch'haē tang e^ng ây léw*, he sacrificed to the divinity of the middle of the house; see the 禮月令 Léy gwàt lēng.

Léw 澑 A place where the water descends low; a cataract, or whirlpool. Sam ch'hëen chew hêng, gē hong yit sit, jip léw chek súy jëák jê bút lék, 三千舟行遇風一失入澑則水弱而没溺 *s^na ch'heng chún kē^nâ toó tëŏh hong chit ây sit, jip léw chek chúy ēy noo^ng, jê tëëm lèk*, three thousand boats sailing along, and meeting with a foul wind enter the whirlpool, where the water is slack, and being ingulphed therein, are lost.

去 Lèw 溜 The water flowing down; water rushing downwards, as in a whirlpool.

平 Lêw 流 Vulg. *laôu*: to flow, as water; lêw hêng, 流行, *laôu kē^nâ*, to flow along; lêw t'hwân, 流傳 *laôu t'hwut^ng*, to hand down by tradition.
Súy lêw jê put sit, bút seng jê put këûng, kae é tō wûy t'héy, 水流而不息物生而不窮皆以道爲體 *chúy laôu jê bô hāy^nh, meē^nh sai^ng jê bô këûng, kae yin wûy tō lê chô t'héy*, "the waters flowing without intermission, and things being produced without exhaustion,

are all because of a certain principle which is embodied in them all;" said by 朱子 Choo choó.

Lêw 硫 Lêw hông, 硫磺 nëŏ^ng wut^ng, sulphur, brimstone. Also written 磂, lêw.

Lêw 鎏 Fine gold; pendent ornaments.

Lêw 旒 Bëĕn lêw, 冕旒, an emperor's crown; the crown of the emperor of China used to be square on the top with (chëĕn hoē sip jē lêw, 前後十二旒 cheng aōu chàp jē laôu,) twelve strings of pearls hanging down both before and behind; this form of the imperial diadem has been in use (according to the Chinese) from the time of Hông tèy, 黃帝 Wut^ng tèy, (B. C. 2622,) but the present Tartar dynasty seems to have adopted another form.

Lêw 琉 Lêw lê, 琉璃, a kind of pearl, or transparent gem; a vitreous substance. Also written 瑠, lêw. E gnó lêw lê t'hap, ch'hut tê chëĕn ch'hong hāy, 移我琉璃榻出置前牕下 pwⁿa gwá ây lêw lê t'hap, ch'hut laê hāy tē chêng t'hang āy, remove my pearly bedstead, and place it under the front window; see a 古詩, Koé se, an ancient ode.

Lêw 瀏 Clear water; Chin é Wúy, lêw kê ch'heng è! 溱與洧瀏其清矣 Chin chúy kap Wúy chúy, lêw e ây ch'heng! the waters of the Chin and Wúy, how clear are their streams! see the 鄭風 Tēng hong.

Lêw 榴 Sék lêw, 石榴 sāyh lêw, a pomegranate; introduced into China by Tëăng-k'hëen, 張騫, when he went on an embassy to the west.

Lêw 橊 The same as the preceding.

Lêw 鎏 Hanging pearls, or gems, suspended as ornaments from the top of a crown.

Lêw 遛 Pek lêw, 逼遛, not to be able to get forward.

Lêw 留 Vulg. laôu: to detain, to entertain.

Lêw 瘤 A wen on the neck; seng lêw, 生瘤 sai^ng lêw, to have a wen.

Lêw 鶹 Lêw lê, 鶹離, the name of a bird of a cruel disposition.

Lêw 騮 A red horse, with a black tail.

Lêw 劉 To kill; vulg. laôu: a surname.

Lêw 駵 A red horse, with a black mane.

Lêw 懰 Sorrowful, distressed.

去 Lēw 膢 Doubly damp.

Lēw 鰡 The name of a fish.

上聲 Léy 禮 Ceremony, politeness, propriety; bûn léy, 文禮, polite. Léy che yūng, hô wûy kwùy, sëen ông che tō, soo wûy bé, seáou taē yêw che, 禮之用和爲貴先王之道斯爲美小大由之 *léy ây yūng, hô chò kwùy, seng ông ây tō chéy lêy k'hăh súy, sèy twā t'hàn e*, in the use of ceremonies, harmony is important; according to the doctrine of the former kings this was considered excellent; great and small affairs were all made to conform to this; see the 上論 Sëāng lūn. Also written 礼, léy.

Léy 豊 The ancient form of 禮, léy: some say, ceremonial implements.

Léy 澧 The name of a river.

Lèy 醴 Sweet wine; ch'hëⁿá é chëak léy, 且以酌醴 *ch'hëⁿá laê t'hìn teeⁿᵍ ây chéw*, let us pour out the sweet wine; see the 小雅 Seáou gnáy.

Léy 𧯛 To oppose; to bend.

Léy 纚 To twist, to entwine.

Léy 蠡 A kind of spheroidal cockle; an insect that eats wood.

平 Lêy 黎 All, every one; also, a surname. Lêy bîn put ke put hân, 黎民不飢不寒 *chëùng păyh saiⁿᵍ bēy yaou bēy kwⁿá*, when all the people can escape hunger and cold, &c.; see 孟子 Bēng choó.

Lêy 瓈 P'ho lêy, 玻瓈, glass, any vitreous substance; the gems of western countries.

Lêy 藜 The name of a plant or tree of which walking sticks may be made; a surname; T'haè-yit jëên lêy cheàou t'hòk, 太乙燃藜照讀 *T'haè-yit ây ch'haiⁿᵍ hëⁿâ lêy chëò e t'hàk*, the spirit of the T'haè-yit star set fire to a brand of the lêy wood, in order to give him a light to read by; see the 史記 Soó kè. Chit lêy, 蒺藜, the name of a plant, armed with thorns; a kind of furze or land caltrops.

Lêy 犂 A plough; lêy tëên, 犂田 *lêy ch'hân*, to plough the fields.

Lêy 螺 A snail; tëên lêy, 田螺 *ch'hân lêy*, field snails, eaten by the Chinese. A general name for spiral univalve shells.

去 Lēy 麗 To lean against, to adhere to; elegant, fair, graceful; a number. Jit gwàt lēy hoē t'hëen, 日月麗乎天 *jit göëyh hoē twā tē t'heeⁿᵍ*, the sun and moon are placed in the heavens; see the 易經 Ek keng. Bé lēy, 美麗, elegant and beautiful. Sëang che sun choó, kê lēy put ek, 商之孫子其麗不億 *Sëang teâou ây këⁿá sun, e ây lēy soè, ūᵐ chē chit păyh bān*, the descendants of the Sëang dynasty, are not less than a million; see the 大雅 Tāe gnáy.

Lēy 儷 K'hòng lēy, 伉儷, a mate, a fellow; a couple, a pair; a competitor. Also written 㑦, lēy.

Lēy 蘺 A creeper, a parasite; commonly called kè seng, 寄生 *këà saiⁿᵍ*, a plant that lives on another.

Lēy 灑 The wind moving anything; anything scattered by the wind.

Lēy 荔 Lēy che, 荔枝, the lēy che, the fruit of the Dimocarpus litchi.

Lēy 厲 Stern, severe; shrill, loud; tyrannical, wicked; to grind.
Choó wun jê lēy, 子溫而厲 *hoo choó wun jūn jê lēy gêém*, Confucius was benign but stern; see the 論語 Lūn gé.
Lēy seng, 厲聲 *lēy sēⁿa*, a shrill voice.
Mô lēy, 磨厲, to rub, to grind. A surname.

Lēy 禲 Calamities occasioned by evil spirits.

Lēy 礪 A grinding stone; a whetstone; also to grind.

Lēy 癘 A sickness, a pestilence, a violent disease or sore.
Lēy chit put kàng, 癘疾不降 *lēy paīⁿᵍ bô kàng lôh*, let not pestilences and diseases come down upon us; see the 左傳 Chó twān.

Lēy 糲 Unclean rice, coarse rice.

Lēy 勵 Bēén lēy, 勉勵, to exert one's strength, to urge, to encourage.
Lēy chè tông jê kwan póng jit, 勵志當如覩榜日 *bēén lēy ây sim chè tĕŏh ch'hin chēōⁿᵍ k'hwⁿà pēⁿᵍ ây jit*, the spirit of energy should continue the same as it was in the day when we first saw the schedule (of literary graduates.)

5 P

Lēy 鱱 The name of a fish.

Lēy 隸 To lean against, to rely on; attendants, dependants.
Lēy se, 隸書, a certain form of writing the Chinese characters.

Lēy 悷 Angry; hwún lēy, 很悷, enraged.

Lēy 戾 Strange, perverse, rebellious, tumultuous, wicked; a crime.
Kwae lēy, 乖戾, froward; hwún lēy, 忿戾, wrathful.
Kê kám kan taē tëén, é choō ch'hé lēy, 其敢干大典以自取戾 *e kⁿá kan hwān twā tëén, é ka tē ch'hé chōēy*, he dares to disobey the great command, and thus bring guilt upon himself; see the 左傳 Chó twān.

Lēy 篱 Cho lê, 糟篱 *chaou lēy*, a strainer, for straining the grains from the liquor; a perforated ladle for taking rice out of the water; a skimmer.

去

Lím 凜 Cold, stiff; frigid; wuy hong lím lím, 威風凜凜, a dignified and austere manner.

Lím 懍 To be alarmed; terrified, affrighted; to respect, to fear; hazardous.
Pek sèng lím lím, 百姓懍懍 *pâyh sⁿīⁿᵍ kēⁿa hīⁿà*, the people were fearful and alarmed.

Lím 廩 Ch'hong lím, 倉廩, a granary, a storehouse for grain.
Jê kwun che ch'hong lím sit, hoó k'hoè ch'hëung, 而君之倉廩實府庫充 *jê kwun lé ây ch'heⁿᵍ lím tcēⁿᵍ, hoó k'hoè mwⁿá*, and all the while your majesty's granaries are

full, and your treasuries overflowing; see 孟子 Bēng choó.

Lím 禀 Lím sit, 禀食, food, wages. Also written 亩, lím.

Lím 澟 Distressed in the extreme.

Lím 檁 A cross beam on the top of a house.

去

Lìm 盷 To look; some say, a dizziness of the head.

Lìm 顲 To lean forward the head, and doze.

平

Lîm 林 Sē lîm, 樹林 *ch'hēw nâ*, a forest, a grove; san lîm, 山林, hills and woods; a surname. Lîm ch'him put këèn jit, 林深不見日 *nâ ch'him bēy k'hwⁿà keèⁿᵍ jit*, when the forest is deep, we cannot see the sun.

Lîm 琳 A fair gem. Name of a state.

Lîm 淋 To rinse anything with water; water descending from the hills. Lîm lê é, 淋漓雨 *lîm lê hoē*, a drenching rain.

Lîm 霖 Timely rain, seasonable showers. Jëák söèy taē hān, yūng jé chok lîm é, 若歲大旱用汝作霖雨 *neēⁿᵍ tang twā wⁿā, yūng lé chò lîm hoē*, if the season is very dry, we will make use of you as an opportune shower; see the 書經 Se keng.

Lîm 痳 A disease consisting in a stoppage of urine.

Lîm 臨 To come to, to visit, to arrive at; lîm soó, 臨死 *lîm sé*, to be about to die. Cheàou lîm hāy t'hoé, 照臨下土 *chëò lîm āy bīn āy t'hoé*, to pay a gracious visit to this lower world.

丟

Līm 䔽 Fire beginning to burn.

平

Lin 鼕 Lin lông koé, 轔鼕鼓, a small drum, or rattle, used by pedlars to give notice of their arrival, in order to sell their wares.

去

Lín 僯 To feel ashamed. Also read lîn: a neighborhood.

Lín 您 You, ye; you people!

Lín 橉 The threshold of a door, according to the dialect of the 楚, Ch'hoé country.

平

Lîn 璘 The color of a gem; the veins in a gem.

Lîn 鄰 To compare with; to be near to; a near neighbor; near to, adjoining. T'hëen gaê jëák pé lîn, 天涯若比鄰 *t'heeⁿᵍ peeⁿᵍ āy lâng ch'hin chëōⁿᵍ pé lîn*, the inhabitants of heaven's utmost borders should be treated like our near neighbors; see the 杜甫詩 Toē hoó se.

Lîn 潾 Clear water; spring water.

Lîn 燐 Lîn hⁿó, 燐火 *lîn hŏèy*, devil's fire; supernatural fire.

Lîn 驎 A piebald horse.

Lîn 麟 Kê lîn, 麒麟, a fabulous beast, said to be the most princely of animals. Kê lîn che ê choé sèw, lūy yëá, 麒麟之於走獸類也 *kê lîn ây twā tē chaóu sèw lūy yëá*, though the noblest among four footed beasts, the kê lîn is still of the same class; see 孟子 Bēng choó.

Lîn 轔 The sound of carriages; yéw ke lîn lîn, 有車轔轔 *woō ch'hëa ây sëⁿa lîn lîn*, the carriages rolled along to the sound of lîn lîn; see the 秦風 Chîn hong.

Lîn 鱗 Vulg. *lân*: the scales of a fish.

Lîn 憐 To pity, to commiserate; k'hó lîn! 可憐, what a pity! Tông pēng sëang lîn, 同病相憐 *tâng paiⁿg sëo lîn bîn*, those who are alike indisposed can feel for each other; see the 春秋 Ch'hun ch'hew. Sim sêng lîn pék hwat, 心誠憐白髮 *sim kwⁿa chin chëⁿà lîn sëŏh pâyh t'haôu mô ây lâng*, the mind truly commiserates gray-haired people; see a 古諺, koé gān, old proverb.

Lîn 嶙 Deep recesses in the hills; successive ridges of hills, deep and distant.

Lîn 磷 Stones appearing at the bottom of a clear stream. Yâng che súy pék sék lîn lîn, 揚之水白石磷磷 *Yâng ây chúy pâyh chëŏh lîn lîn*, in the waters of the Yâng, the white stones appear; see the 唐風 Tông hong.

Lîn 粼 A limpid stream; the same as the above.

Lîn 僯 Lîn ke, 僯居, a neighborhood.

Lîn 粦 Lîn hⁿó, 粦火 *lîn hŏèy*, devil's fire.

Lîn 麐 The female of the 麒麟, kê lîn, a fabulous animal; ông chëá chè jîn, chek lîn ch'hut, 王者至仁則麐出 *ông ây lâng chè jîn, chek lîn ēy ch'hut*, when kings are eminently benevolent, this animal appears.

Lîn 綾 Read lêng: a kind of silk, or sarsnet; lêng twān, 綾緞 *lîn twān*, a kind of satin.

丟 Lîn 吝 Mean, niggardly, sparing, stingy; to be sorry for, to be ashamed. Hŏèy lîn, 悔吝, to regret; lîn sek, 吝惜, to be sparing of. Soó keaou ch'hëⁿá lîn, kê ê put chëuk kwan yëá é, 使驕且吝其餘不足觀也已 *saé woō keaou t'haôu kwà lîn sek, e ây sîn bó kaôu t'hang hoē gwán k'hwⁿà*, if such a person becomes proud and stingy, all the other traits of his character are not worth looking at; see the 論語 Lūn gé.

Lîn 恡 Këen lîn, 慳恡, stingy, sparing. Sëang sîm lîn ê chaê, 商甚恡於財 *chò seng lé ây lâng chin chëⁿà gaôu sëŏh cheéⁿg*, trading people are very sparing of their money; see the 家語 Kay gé.

Līn 粦 Supernatural fire, Will-o'-the-wisp, ignis fatuus; wherever a battle has been fought, and human carcases mixed with those of horses and cattle, this fire is said to burst out. Fire-flies are also called 粦, lîn.

Līn 磷 A thin stone; mô jê put lîn, 磨而不磷 *bwâ jê bēy pŏh*, with all the grinding, the stone does not become thin.

Līn 遴 To walk with difficulty; to select; lîn swán, 遴選, to choose.

Līn ⿰亻臨 Līn gīm, ⿰亻臨仱, the head bending forwards.

Līn 藺 A surname. Līn-sëang-jê, 藺相如, a famous man in the 趙, Tëō country.

Lip 立 Vulg. *k'hëă:* to stand, to establish. Sam sip jê lip, 三十而立 *s^na chàp hŏ̀y jê lip*, "at thirty years of age, I was established;" said by Confucius, in the 上論 Sëang lūn.

Lip 苙 To hinder, to stop, to catch in a trap. Kê jip kê lip, yēw chëûng jê cheaou che? 既入其苙又從而招之 *kaòu jip e ây te teâou, saé saé jëuk jê pàk e?* since (the pig) has entered the sty, what is the use of proceeding to tie it up? see 孟子 Bēng choó.

Lip 笠 A defense against the rain; tëuk lip, 竹笠 *tek lăyh*, a wide bamboo hat, used as an umbrella.

Lip 粒 Read lëëp: a grain, a kernel of rice. Lëëp sit kae bîn ko, 粒食皆民膏 *chit lip chëăh chò poē sē pāyh sai^ng ây yëw*, every grain of food is procured by the sweat of the people; see the 史記 Soó kè.

Lit 尼 To stop, to hinder. Hêng bèk soó che, ché hèk lit che, 行或使之止或尼之 *kë^nâ hèk woō lâng saé e, hăy^nh hèk woō lâng chăh e*, if I enter on office, there will perhaps be some one to urge me to it; and when I refrain, there will perhaps be some one to hinder me; see 孟子 Bēng choó.

Lit 窒 Stopped up, closed up, not pervious, not thoroughly clear. Oè kó kán, jê lit cheá, 惡果敢而窒者 *wàn hwut lêy kó k^ná, jê bēy t'hong ây lâng*, "I detest bold and forward people, particularly when they do not thoroughly understand the subject;" said by Confucius, in the 論語 Lūn gé.

Lo 覶 Good looking, to look well; lo lé, 覶縷, cunning, artful.

Ló 老 Old; ló jîn, 老人 *laōu lâng*, an old man. Ch'hit sip wát ló, 七十曰老 *ch'hit chăp hŏ̀y kóng laōu*, a person seventy years of age is called old. Ló goê ló, é kip jîn che ló, 老吾老以及人之老 *kèng gwá ây laōu lâng, é kip kaòu pat lâng ây laōu lâng*, let us respect our own aged people, in order to benefit the aged people of others.

Ló ⿱竹老 K'hó ló, ⿱竹考⿱竹老 *ka ló*, a basket made of crooked bamboos.

Ló 栳 A vessel made of bent wood.

Ló 㑼 A surname.

Ló 惱 Sorrowful, distressed, grieved; hwân ló, 煩惱, to be sorry.

Ló 瑙 Má ló sék, 瑪瑙石 báy ló chëŏh, a cornelian stone.

Ló 腦 Chëang ló, 樟腦 chëo^ng ló, Chinese camphor; t'hoê ló, 頭腦 t'haôu ló, the brains.

Ló 䗪 Kó ló, 蜾䗪, an insect like a dragon fly, that feeds on mulberry leaves.

Ló 嫐 Disturbed, troubled.

Ló 蓏 Fruits of the earth, ground fruits; fruits growing on trees are called 菓, ko, and earth fruits or those on bushes are called 蓏, ló.

Ló 潦 A gutter in a road; ló súy, 潦水, a puddle.
Hô haé che ê hêng ló, lüy yëá, 河海之於行潦類也 hô haé ây kap chúy k'hwut á, lüy yëá, the rivers and seas, though expansive compared with running ditches, are still of the same kind; see 孟子 Bêng choó.

去

Lò 𩡧 Long and great.

Lô 𨂿 Long, tall; a long shanks; ch'hoó jîn sîm lô, 此人甚𨂿 chéy lêy lâng chin chaē lô, this man is very tall.

平

Lô 勞 To labor; to be diligent; kong lô, 功勞, labor, merit; lô sim, 勞心, to exert the mind; lô lêk, 勞力, to exert one's strength. Vulg. *lô lâi:* a common expression of gratitude, intimating, "I put you to a great deal of trouble." Sin lô, 辛勞, wages. Vulg. *bwâ:* to labor, to drudge, to toil. A surname. Boô se lô, 無施勞 *bô tëen ka tē ây kong lô*, boast not of your own merits; see the 論語 Lūn gé.
Lô ê ông soō, 勞於王事 *bwâ tē ông ây soō*, laboring in the service of the king; see the 小雅 Seáou gnáy.

Lô 僗 Hwun lô, 勳僗, merit. The same as the above.

Lô 撈 Vulg. *lâ:* to stir anything about in the water; to feel after anything, and seek to take it out of the water.

Lô 澇 The name of a river; also, great waves, and violent rain.
E yéw ch'hit lô che chae, 而有七澇之災 *E woō ch'hit lô ây chae haé*, E met with the seven calamities of overwhelming rains.

Lô 𠢴 Lô so, 𠢴𠢽, anything coarse.

Lô 嘮 A voice, a sound; sonorous.

Lô 羅 A sort of silk; a surname; lîn lô say kin, 綾羅紗絹, satin, silk, crape, and sarsnet.

Lô 籮 Bëet lô, 篾籮 *beĕh lwâ*, a vessel made of basket work.

Ló **蘿** Têng lô, 藤蘿, a kind of creeping plant, a sort of bindweed; lô pók, 蘿蔔, Raphanus sativus, turnip; hoê lô pók, 胡蘿蔔, Daucus carota, the common carrot.

Lô **灑** The name of a river.

Lô **儸** Chëa lô, 僬儸, firm, but not virtuous.

Lô **囉** Lé lô, 嘍囉, a humming sound, to assist in making out a tune.

Lô **鑼** A gong, a martial instrument of music. Tông lô, 銅鑼 *tâng lô*, a brazen gong.

Lô **㦬** The mind grieved, and sorrowful; also, a net. Hông ch'hoó pek lô, 逢此百㦬 *toó tëöh chéy chë^{n}â päyh tëöh bwâ*, meeting with these hundred troubles.

Lô **侔** Great; kà lô, 儚侔, large and coarse.

Lô **牢** An inclosure for cattle; also, firm; kam lô, 監牢, a prison. Lô put k'hó p'hò, 牢不可破 *këen lô haðu bëy p'hwà*, he is too firm to be broken in upon.

Lô **驘** A mule, the progeny of a she ass and a stallion.

Lô **騾** The same as the above; seáou kwun k'hê haé, jîn këèn sē ch'heng lô, 少君騎海人見是青騾 *sèy hwun k'hëâ te haé, lâng k'hw^{n}â sē ch'hai^{ng} lô*, the young prince was riding on horseback over the sea, and people saw that he was mounted on a green mule.

Lô **嫪** To love, to be enamored with. Lô tók, 嫪毒, a man's name; lewd.

Lô **醪** The sediment of liquor.

Lô **醪** A kind of wine.

Lô **螺** Also read lêy: a kind of sea-shell; also written 蠃, lô. Lô se, 螺絲 *ch'han lêy*, a field snail.

Lô **猱** A kind of ape; boô kaðu lô seng bók, 無教猱升木 *bôh kà lô chëö^{ng} ch'hâ*, don't teach an ape to climb the trees; (i. e. don't teach your grandmother to suck eggs.)

Lô **濁** Read chók: muddy, not clear.

Lô **哪** Lô ch'hëa, 哪吒, the name of a god.

去

Lō **澇** A drenching rain.

Lō **僗** P'hwān lô, 伴僗, a companion, a mate, a fellow.

Lō **撈** To rake about in the water in order to find anything.

Lō **憥** To repent, to regret.

福建方言字典

Lō 勞 To reward labors, to applaud exertions. Tēng pek soó jîn lō ông, 鄭伯使人勞王 *Taīng păyh saé lâng kĕò ông lô làt*, the ruler of the Tēng country sent some one to extol the labors of the king; see the 左傳 Chó twān.

Lō 嫪 Wanton, lascivious.

Lō 䜌 A drumming in the ear.

Lō 攎 To strike anything.

Lō 哪 An auxiliary particle, at the end of a sentence, sometimes used as a note of interrogation.

Lō 栳 A measure of 5 pecks.

Lō 邏 To perambulate; migratory troops.

上聲

Loé 魯 The name of a country, the native state of Confucius. A surname.

Loé 櫓 An oar, a long oar used both to steer and row with; a scull.

Loé 瘖 Toō loé, 痘瘖, a kind of small pox.

Loé 虜 Loé lëák, 虜掠, to take prisoner in war; to capture; to take alive is called 虜, loé, and to obtain dead is called 獲, hék.

Loé 擄 To take, to seize; the same as the above.

Loé 譖 To converse.

Loé 艣 An oar; the same as 櫓, loé.

Loé 鹵 A saltish soil in the west; loé bóng, 鹵莽 *bóng chóng*, coarse, vulgar, unmannerly.

Loé 掵 Loé tōng, 掵動, to shake, to move, to agitate.

Loé 樐 An oar; the same as 櫓, loé.

Loè 慮 The mind deceived.

Loé 塿 Pöêy loé, 培塿, a small mound, a hillock.

Loé 努 Loé lêk, 努力, to exert the strength; a strenuous exertion. Loé lek chông bêng tek, 努力崇明德 *chīn làt chun chông bêng ây tek*, to exert the strength in honoring illustrious virtue.

平

Loê 樓 Vulg. *laôu:* a gallery, an upper chamber, a loft. Ko kwán loê taê seng sèy sèy, 歌管樓臺聲細細 *ch'hëòng kwa p'hun kóng tē laôu taê chëōng, sëⁿa sèy sèy*, when chanting and piping up in the gallery, or on the terrace, the sound appears very faint.

Loê 僂 A hunchback, a crooked-backed person.

Loê 摟 To pull, to hawl, to drag. Jê tong kay ch'hëâng, jê loê kê ch'hé ch'hoó, chek tek ch'hey? 踰東家墻而摟其處子則得妻 *pwⁿâ köëy tang kay ây ch'hëôⁿᵍ, jê k'han 'e ây chaē sit lé, chek ēy tit tëŏh boê?* if you could climb over your neighbor's wall, and lead off an unmarried female, in order to get a wife, (I suppose you would do it?) see 孟子 Bēng choó.

Loê 婁 One of the 28 constellations. A surname.

Loê 縷 A kind of thread or silk.

Loê 螻 Loê gé, 螻蟻, a sort of ant; tëen loê, 天螻, a bat.

Loê 髏 The skull, the bone of the head.

Loê 鏤 The name of a sword.

Loê 瘻 An inveterate ulcer; k'he loê, 痀瘻, a crooked back.

Loê 瞜 Hoē loê, 睺瞜, covetous, fond of money.

Loê 貗 A little pig.

Loê 蔞 Kwa loê, 瓜蔞, the name of a medicinal plant. The betel leaf.

Loê 瓟 Paou loê, 瓟瓟, a sort of calabash, but round. Hoê loê, 葫瓟, a calabash; the name of a river.

Loê 瀘 The name of a river; called also "the bitter waters."

Loê 爐 Hëang loê, 香爐 *heoⁿᵍ loê*, an incense pot, a censer; hⁿó loê, 火爐 *höëy loê*, a furnace; loê choó, 爐主, one who presides at a sacrifice. Kim loê hëang chīn, loē seng chân, 金爐香盡漏聲殘 *kim loê ây hëoⁿᵍ chīn, laōu ây sëⁿa böëyh leáou*, the incense in the golden censer is burnt out, and the dripping of the clepsydra is almost done; (intimating that it is towards morning.) Also written 炉, loê.

Loê 壚 An earthen vessel for containing wine.

Loê 鑪 A fire bedstead; sêw loê, 袖鑪, a kind of hand warming pan, carried about in the sleeve of a garment to keep a person warm.

Loê 纑 Flaxen threads; ch'hey p'hek loê, 妻辟纑, the wife prepares the flax; see 孟子 Bēng choó.

Loê 蘆 Loê wûy, 蘆葦, long grass, or rushes, a reed growing in the water, Zizania palustris. Hoo chèng yëá chëá, poê loê yëá, 夫政也者蒲盧也 *hoo chèng soō, ēy ch'hin chëoⁿᵍ poê loê*, (the results of) good government will be as rapid as the growth of rushes; see the 中庸 Tëung yûng.

Loê 鱸 The name of a fish belonging to the salmon class.

Loê 顱 T'hoê loê, 頭顱 *t'haôu loê*, the skull.

Loê 鸕 Loê choê, 鸕鶿 *loê se cheâou*, a cormorant; Carbo cormoranus.

Loê 盧 A surname; a vessel for containing rice.

Loê 臚 The flesh on the front of the belly. Hông loê, 鴻臚, the name of an office in the 漢, Hàn dynasty.

Loê 轤 Lók loê, 轆轤, a well-sweep or other machine for drawing water.

Loê 奴 A slave, a man servant; loê chaê, 奴才, a slave, a varlet; an affected title of humility.

圡

Loê 路 A road; kay loē, 街路, a street; hêng loē, 行路 *kē^n^â loē*, to travel along the road; loē pêng, 路旁 *loē pee^ng^*, by the roadside. A surname. Hoo gē loē yēá, léy bûn yēá, 夫義路也禮門也 *hoo gē sē loē yēá, léy sē moot^ng^ yēá*, now righteousness is the road, and propriety is the door (by which we are to enter;) see 孟子 Bēng choó.

Loê 鷺 Loê choê, 鷺鷥 *loē se*, a kind of crane or paddy bird; an egret. Yit hâng pėk loē sēâng ch'heng t'hēen, 一行白鷺上青天 *chit hāng păyh lēng se, chēō^ng^ ch'hai^ng^ t'hee^ng^*, a flock of white cranes ascended up towards the azure heavens.

5 R

Loē 潞 The name of a river.

Loē 璐 A beautiful gem.

Loē 蕗 A kind of fragrant grass; loē keu, 蕗蕎, a sort of leeks.

Loē 露 Dew; loē súy, 露水 *loē chúy*, the dew; to discover, to appear. Pék loē bē he, 白露未晞 *păyh loē yēá bōēy ta*, the hoary dew was not yet dry; see the 秦風 Chîn hong. Loē hēèn, 露現, to appear, to show itself, to be discovered.

Loē 賂 To present anything; to bribe; yēw loē, 賄賂, bribes. Chìn Boó kong chĭn é kê pó k'hè loē Chew Lê ông, 晋武公盡以其寶器賂周釐王 *Chìn Boó kong chò pó t'hó e ây pó k'hè saé yēw loē kap Chew Lê óng*, Boó, the ruler of the Chìn country took all his precious things and used them as bribes to Lê, the king of Chew; see the 詩序 Se sē.

Loē 輅 A carriage; sêng Yin che loē, 乘殷之輅 *păyh chēō^ng^ Yin teâou ây ch'hēa*, to ride in the carriages of the Yin dynasty; (i. e. to imitate their manners) see the 論語 Lûn gé.

Loē 漏 Vulg. *laōu:* to leak, to drip through; a leak; ch'ham loē, 滲漏 *ch'ham laōu*, to leak out; loē keng, 漏更 *laōu kai^ng^*, a kind of hourglass, composed of dripping water, instead of falling sand; loē sëet, 漏洩 *laōu sëet*, to let out a secret.

Loē 瘺 A kind of sore; kan loē chit, 乾瘺疾 *kan laōu paing*, a disease, like dry ulcers on the skin.

Loē 陋 Narrow; p'hé loē, 鄙陋, niggardly, mean; loē hëep, 陋狹, narrow, contracted.

Chaē loē hāng, 在陋巷 *twā tē loē hāng*, dwelling in a narrow lane.

Soo wûy loē sit, wûy goê tek heng, 斯爲陋室惟吾德馨 *chéy sē loē äyh ây ch'hoò, tòk tòk gwá ây tek heng p'hang*, "this is a narrow house, but my virtue is fragrant;" said by 劉禹錫文 Lêw-é Sek-bûn.

Loê 弩 Këung loē 弓弩, a crossbow. K'hó kê këung loē, 考其弓弩 *k'hó ch'hat e ây këung loē*, examine the bows and crossbows; see the 周禮 Chew léy.

Loē 滷 A salt ground in the west.

Loē 僂 Loē k'he, 僂佝, a dwarf.

去

Löéy 餒 Hungry, to starve with hunger. If a person about to go on a journey were to intrust his family to the care of a friend, and on his return were to find that he had (tòng löéy kê ch'hey choó, 凍餒其妻子 *gō sé e ây boé kë**n**á*,) starved his wife and children to death, what would he think of him? see 孟子 Bēng choô.

Löéy 鮾 Stinking fish; gê löéy jê jeúk paē, put sit, 魚鮾而肉敗不食 *hé ch'haòu jé bäh paē ūm chëäh*, if the fish was tainted, and the meat turned, he would not eat of it; said of Confucius in the 論語 Lūn gé.

Löéy 矮 Wöey löéy, 猥矮, weak.

平

Löêy 羸 Thin; a meagre sheep; poor, lean, emaciated, old.

Löêy 儽 Fallen down, prostrate.

去

Löēy 内 Vulg. *laē*: inner, within, inside, in. Hàp löēy göēy che tō yëá, 合內外之道也 *hàp laē gwā ây tō lé*, uniting the internal and external principles; see the 中庸 Tëung yûng.

入

Lŏh 剳 To cut open; to cut the bones out of meat.

Lŏh 落 Read lòk: to descend, to fall down; Sëāng lòk, 上落 *chëōng lŏh*, to go up and down; *bô häy lŏh*, is an expression intimating contempt. Lòk laê, 落來 *lŏh laê*, to come down. Song che lòk è, 桑之落矣 *seng hëŏh ây lŏh*, the fall of the mulberry leaf; see the 衛風 Wöēy hong.

Lŏh 絡 Read lòk: a thread, a fibre; keng lòk, 經絡 *keng lŏh*, threads and fibres; the veins and arteries.

大

Lok 角 The name of an animal; a surname.

Lok 衂 To be cut with a knife; a sabre wound.

Lok 衄 A bleeding at the nose.

Lok 橐 Read t'hok: e sàn t'hok, 雨傘橐 *hoē swⁿa lok*, a case for an umbrella.

仄 Lók 洛 The name of a river; Lok-yâng, 洛陽, an ancient city.

Lók 烙 Paôu lók, 炮烙, an instrument of punishment, made in the form of a brazen pillar, to which criminals were bound; after which it was gradually heated, till the unfortunate beings were roasted to death. Tēw chè paôu lók che hêng, 紂制炮烙之刑 *Tēw ông ch'hòng paôu lók ây hêng hwàt* Tēw ông invented the paou lók instrument of torture; see the 史記 Soó kè.

Lók 珞 Eng lók, 瓔珞, ornaments for the neck.

Lók 絡 Joined, connected together. Vulg. *lŏh:* a thread, or fibre. Lóng san lók yëá, 籠山絡野 *láng swⁿa lŏh yëá*, the Lóng hills and deserts are conterminous. Bĕk lók, 脉絡 *măyⁿh lŏh*, the veins and arteries.

Lók 駱 A white horse with a black mane. Also, a surname.

Lók 酪 The unctious part of milk, cream.

Lók 落 Vulg. *lŏh:* to fall down, to descend, a place where people collect together to dwell in, is called 村落 ch'hun lók, a village. When a house is finished, and people meet to sacrifice in it, it is called 成落, sêng lók.
Bé lók kày, 米落價, the rice has fallen in price. Hwán sin lók má, 反身落馬 *hwán sin lŏh báy*, he turned round and tumbled off his horse.

Lók 雒 The name of a bird; also, the name of a horse.

Lók 馲 Lók tô, 馲駝, a camel.

Lók 祿 Hóng lók, 俸祿, emolument, salary. Good things, advantages. Choó-tëang hák kan lók, 子張學干祿 *Choó-tëang t'hàk ch'hăyh kan kéw hóng lók*, Choó-tëang studied for the sake of the emoluments of office; see the 上論 Sëāng lūn. A surname.
Sēw t'hëen pek lók, 受天百祿 *sēw t'heeⁿᵍ chëⁿá păyh ây hó*, we have received a hundred benefits from heaven; see the 小雅 Seáou gnáy.

Lók 碌 A place where there are many stones. Lók lók chëá lân háp, 碌碌者難合 *chëy chëŏh ŏh sëo háp*, men's minds are obdurate, and with difficulty made to agree.

Lók 粶 Rice roasting at the fire.

Lók 僇 K'hoè-lók-kwan, 庫僇官, a triple surname.

Lók 鹿 A stag, a deer; lók kak, 鹿角, stag's horns, and lŏk kin, 鹿肋 stag's tendons; both used as aphrodisiacal medicines.
Koè hông gān bê lók, 頋鴻雁麋鹿

k'hwⁿà twā chëăh gô kap lòk boĕ, the king was observing the large wild geese, and the full grown stags; see the 上孟 Sëāng bēng.

Lòk 漉 To drip through, to leak; to exhaust. Lòk chëep swá tëy, 漉汁灑地, the dripping gravy besprinkled the ground; see the 戰國策 Chëèn kok ch'hek.

Lòk 轆 Lòk loê, 轆轤, a windlass over a well.

Lòk 麓 The foot of a hill; chëem pé hān lòk, 瞻彼旱麓, look at the arid foot of yonder hill; see 大雅 Taē gnáy.

Lòk 鏕 Kē lòk, 鉅鏕, the name of a place.

Lòk 簏 A basket made of wicker work.

Lòk 剹 To scrape, to rub.

Lòk 犖 Tok lòk, 卓犖, to excel, to surpass, to exceed.

Lòk 諾 Eng lòk, 應諾, to answer; hé lòk, 許諾, to assent. Choó-k'hòng wát lòk, goê chëang būn yëá, 子貢曰諾吾將問也 *Choó-k'hòng kóng hó, gwá laê k'hè mooiⁿᵍ*, Choó-k'hòng said, "very well; I will ask (Confucius);" see the 論語 Lūn gé.

Lòk 樂 To be pleased, to be delighted with; yúng lòk, 踊樂, joy; rejoiced. Hé lòk, 喜樂, happiness. Gák che sit, lòk soo jē chëá, hwut k'hè sē yëá, 樂之實樂斯二者弗去是也 *gàk ây chëak sit, sē yúng lòk chéy nō hāng ūᵐ hoē e k'hè*, real music consists in enjoying these two things, which are indispensable; see 孟子 Bēng choó.

Lòk 櫟 The name of a tree.

卆

Long 鼕 Lin long koé, 鼕鼕鼓, a small drum or rattle with a handle, used by pedlars.

声

Lóng 朗 Bright, clear; ko lóng, 高朗, high and clear.

Lóng 晄 The bright appearance of the rising sun. Also written 晃, lóng.

Lóng 烺 The appearance of fire.

Lóng 曩 Yesterday, before, previously, formerly. Lóng jê gân hè hoē? 曩而言戲乎 *cha hwuiⁿᵍ séy kóng, k'ham gaōu chëèn hoē?* what was said yesterday, was it in joke? see the 晋語 Chìn gé.

Lóng 籠 Neáou lóng, 鳥籠 *cheáou láng*, a bird-cage. E t'hëen hāy wûy che lóng, chek neáou ch'hëak boô séy tô, 以天下爲之籠則鳥雀無所逃 *lëăh t'heeⁿᵍ hāy jê chò chit ây láng, chek cheáou á chäyh á bô ta lŏh t'hang chaôu*, "if we were to make a bird-cage of the empire, then even the birds and sparrows would not be able to escape;" said by 莊子 Chong choó.

Lóng 壠 A high place in a field; twat keng jê che lóng sëăng, 輟耕而之壠上 swăh chŏh jê k'hè kaòu láng téng, they stopped ploughing, and got upon the mound. (*Lang*, 壟, on the 249th page should be this.)

Lóng 壟 A tomb, a little mound over a tomb. Sek boē put teng lóng, 適墓不登壟 keng köèy hwûn bōng, ūm t'hang păyh chëōng lóng téng, when passing by a grave, do not get upon the tumulus; see the 曲禮 K'hëuk léy.

Lóng 儱 Tông lóng, 侗儱, anything incomplete.

平 Lông 郎 The name of an office established by the 秦, Chîn dynasty, but altered by the 隋, Sûy dynasty to se lông, 侍郎 sē nêng, gentlemen in waiting. A surname. A young person, the epithet of a young man. Pók wát jîn to è, boô jê ch'hoó lông chëá, 僕閱人多矣無如此郎者 pók gwá woō k'hwoⁿà lâng chēy, bô ch'hin chëōng chéy léy lông chëá, I your servant has seen many individuals, but never one like this young gentleman; said of the founder of the 唐, Tông dynasty.

Lông 峎 Chûn lông, 峻峎, the name of a hill, where the sun goes down in the winter solstice.

Lông 稂 Long grass, like the blade of corn, very injurious to the grain; tare, darnel.

Lông 榔 Pin lông, 檳榔 pin nêng, the areca nut, the betel nut. Tó tam pin lông lòk Kóng-tong, 倒擔檳榔落廣東 tó tⁿa pin nêng lŏh Kwuïng-tang, to be carrying betel nuts back to Canton; (to carry coals to Newcastle.)

5 S

Lông 㝗 High, lofty.

Lông 狼 Ch'haê lông, 豺狼, a wolf. Só lèk put wān, sē ch'haê lông yëá, 嫂溺不援是豺狼也 hëⁿa só tëëm lèk kaòu ūm kèw, sē ch'haê lông, when a sister-in-law is drowning, a man must be a wolf not to help her; see 孟子 Bēng choo.

Lông 螂 Tông lông, 螳螂 am koe cháy, a kind of cricket, or grasshopper.

Lông 琅 Lông kan, 琅玕, a precious stone, like a pearl.

Lông 瑯 Lông yëá, 瑯琊, the name of a place.

Lông 廊 An apartment on the side of the principal dwelling; a chamber, a porch.

Lông 鋃 Lông tông, 鋃鐺, a kind of lock.

Lông 閬 A high door; empty, vain.

Lông 㝗 High; empty.

Lông 筤 Ch'hong lông, 蒼筤, the tender shoots of bamboos eaten as salad.

Lông 勆 Strong.

Lóng 浪 Ch'hong-lông, 滄浪, the name of a river.
Ch'hong-lông che súy ch'heng hêy, k'hó é chók gnó eng, 滄浪之水清兮可以濯我纓 *Ch'hong-lông ây chúy k'hăh ch'heng, t'hang laé sêy gwá ây kin twâ*, the clear waters of the Ch'hong-lông will serve to rinse the tassel of my cap; see 孟子 Bēng choó.

Lóng 農 Lông soō, 農事, husbandry; lông hoo, 農夫, a husbandman.
A surname.
Seăng lông hoo soō kéw jîn, 上農夫食九人 *sēāng téng ây lóng hoō ēy ch'hē tit kaóu lâng*, the first class of husbandmen can support nine persons by their labors; see 孟子 Bēng choó.

Lông 儂 I, myself.

Lóng 濃 Thick, rich, applied to liquids.
Lêng loē lông lông, 零露濃濃 *lân loē kit kit*, the superabundant dews were rich and thick; see the 小雅 Seáou gnáy.

Lóng 穠 Luxuriant herbage, overgrown grass and jungle.
Hô pé lông è? 何彼穠矣 *an chwⁿá kaóu hĕăh lông?* how comes it to be thus thick and overgrown? see the 召南 Seáou lâm.

Lông 膿 Matter, pus; lông hëet, 膿血 *lâng höëyh*, blood and matter.

Lông 醲 Thick wine.

Lông 攏 To pierce; yūng to lông jîn, 用刀攏人 *yūng to lâng tëŏh lâng*, to stab people with a knife.

Lông 籠 Neáou lông, 鳥籠 *cheáou lâng*, a bird-cage.
Tëuk lông, 竹籠 *tek lâng*, a quiver for containing arrows.
Sëang lông, 箱籠 *sëoⁿᵍ lâng*, a wooden trunk.

Lông 瓏 Lêng lông, 玲瓏, the noise of tinkling gems.

Lông 聾 Vulg. *ch'haou hē lâng*, deaf; jé lông, 耳聾 *hē lâng*, hard of hearing.

Lông 囊 A bag, a sack. Also written 嚢, lông. E t'hok ê lông, 于槖于囊 *twā tē t'hok kap lông*, (the provision was contained) in cases and bags; see the 大雅 Taē gnáy.

Lōng 弄 (also 挊) Vulg. *lāng*: to sport, to play, to manage; to work up; to dandle.
Hàn ko choé tê gē soó taē hoo yìn, lōng che, 漢高祖持御史大夫印弄之 *Hàn ko choé gîm gē soó taē hoo ây yìn lāng e*, the first emperor of the Hàn dynasty used to hold in his hand the seal of an imperial adviser or other great officer, and play with it.
E-goê jëák put hⁿò lōng, 夷吾弱不好弄 *E-goê nooⁱⁿᵍ chëⁿá ây sé ŭᵐ aè t'hit t'hô*, Kwán E-goê, when young and feeble, was not fond of sport; see the 左傳 Chó twān.

Lōng 挵 Stupid, dull, foolish.

Lōng 哢 The humming of birds.

Lōng 峅 A cave in a hill.

Lōng 儱 Slow, gentle.

Lōng 巄 The corner of a hill.

Lōng 浪 Vulg. *nēng*: a wave; p'ho lōng, 波浪 *p'hō nēng*, the waves of the sea. Bēng lōng, 孟浪, inappropriate discourse, not to the purpose. Lōng chēng chew hêng wún, 浪靜舟行穩 *nēng chēng chûn kēnâ wún*, when the waves are still the vessel rides securely.

Lōng 眼 Vulg. *lā*: to dry in the sun.

Lōng 閬 Lōng hong, 閬風, the name of a hill; an angel's garden.

Lōng 烺 A kind of fire works; hòng lōng, 放烺 *pàng lōng*, to let off a sky-rocket.

声 Loó 汝 You; read jé: and communly pronounced *lé*, in daily conversation; but *loó*, in the districts bordering on the seacoast.

夫 Loŏh 踛 To limp, to walk lame.

本 Lun 縮 T'hoê sëuk, 頭縮 *t'haôu lun*, to hang down the head.

声 Lún 愢 To think; to walk disorderly.

Lún 稐 A sheaf of corn.

Lún 綸 A sheaf of corn; some say, to plough.

Lún 碖 A stone mill, for grinding wheat into flour; sêk lún, 石碖 *chëöh lún*, a millstone.

Lún 忍 Read jím: to bear with, to bear patiently; jím naē, 忍耐 *t'hun lún*, to be patient, to forbear. Seáou put jím chek lwān taē boê, 小不忍則亂大謀 *sëó k'hwá bēy lún chek lwān twā boê*, a little impatience will confound great undertakings; see the 論語 Lûn gé.
When 高宗, Ko-chong of the 唐, Tông dynasty visited 張公藝, Tëang-kong-gāy, he asked him, how his family managed to live together for nine generations, when 藝, Gāy wrote out a (pek jím toê, 百忍圖 *päyh lún toê*,) 'hundred forbear chart,' (or a sheet of paper with the word *patience* repeated 100 times,) and presented it to him.

Lún 輑 The axletree of a carriage.

去 Lùn 愢 Tough, difficult to break asunder.

Lùn 淪 To drag anything through the water.

平 Lûn 輪 The wheel of a carriage. Also, great. Ke lûn, 車輪 *ch'hëa lûn*, a carriage wheel; lûn hôey, 輪廻, the doctrine of the transmigration of souls. Ch'hat ke choō lûn sé, 察車自輪始 *k'hwnâ ch'hëa choō lûn k'hé t'haôu*, in examining a carriage, we should begin with the wheels.

Lûn 侖 To think, to arrange; k'hwun lûn, 昆侖, the appearance of the heavens; anything round and circular.

Lûn 倫 An order, a series, a sort; constant; gnoe lûn, 五倫, the five constant relations of life. Jîn lûn, 人倫, the human relations.
Lâm lé ke sit, jîn che taē lûn yĕá, 男女居室人之大倫也 *ta po cha boé k'hēā ch'hoò, sē lâng ây twā lûn yēá*, for men and women to form themselves into families, is one of the great human relations.
Gé jîn pit ê kê lûn, 儗人必于其倫 *pé lâng pit cheàou e ây lûn*, in judging of people, you must compare them with their kind.

Lûn 圇 Bún lûn, 囫圇, to hesitate in speaking, to swallow one's words.

Lûn 掄 To choose, to select. Lûn hëēn jîn che chaê, 掄賢人之才 *kéng tŏh gaôu lâng ây chaê teâou*, to select the talents of clever men.

Lûn 腀 The skin.

Lûn 綸 To arrange; se lûn, 絲綸, threads, to arrange according to the threads. Wûy lêng keng lûn t'hëen hāy che taē keng, 惟能經綸天下之大經 *tòk tòk ēy keng lûn t'hee^{ng} āy ây twā keng*, to be able to arrange the great concerns of the empire; see the 中庸 Tëung yûng.

Lûn 論 To discourse, to deliberate on, to think over; concerning. E sèy lûn bûn, 與細論文 *kap lé sëâng sèy lûn bûn chëo^{ng}*, to discourse with you minutely on literary subjects.

Lûn 淪 To sink down into perdition; lûn bút, 淪沒, to be annihilated. Tîm lûn, 沉淪, to fall into utter ruin. Kin Yin kê lûn song! 今殷其淪喪 *t^{n}a Yin teâou e lûn se^{ng}!* "how the Yin dynasty is sunk into ruin!" said by 微子 Bê-choó.

Lûn 喻 To turn the tongue, and call out. Also written 嚕, lûn.

Lûn 崙 K'hwun lûn, 崑崙, the name of a hill. Also read lūn: as san lūn, 山崙, the ridge of a hill. Also written 崘, lûn.

去
Lūn 論 A discourse; pëēn lūn, 辯論, to argue; gē lūn, 議論, to reason. Lūn kong hêng sëáng, 論功行賞 *lūn kong lô kë^{n}â sëó^{ng}*, to administer rewards according to merit; see the 史記 Soó ké.

Lūn 閏 Jūn gwát, 閏月 *lūn göĕyh*, an intercalary month, occurring once every four or five years, in order to make up the difference between the solar and the lunar years.
E jūn gwát tēng soò sê sêng söèy, 以閏月定四時成歲 *t'hó lūn göĕyh tëⁿā tëŏh sè sê chëⁿâ neé^{ng}*, he made use of the intercalary month to fix the four seasons and complete the year; see the 堯典 Geâou tëĕn.

Lūn 軟 Read lwán: soft; lwán péng, 軟餅 *lūn pëⁿá*, a soft thin cake.

去
Lut 甪 Read lok: to draw out; lok jé, 甪乳 *lut leng*, to express milk out of the dugs.

Lut 厘 A man's name.

Lut 角 Not to retain, to be deprived of; lut kwan, 角官 *lut kwⁿa*, to be deprived of one's office.

又

Lu̇t 律 The principal and head of anything.

Lu̇t 律 A law, a rule; hwat lu̇t, 法律, laws and regulations. Taē Ch'heng lu̇t lē, 大清律例, the laws of the present dynasty of China. Put é lëúk lu̇t, put lêng chèng gnoé yim, 不以六律不能正五音 *bŏ t'hó chéy lêy làk teâou ây lu̇t, chêw bēy chēⁿâ chéy lêy gnoé yim*, if we do not make use of the six rules of music, we shall not be able to regulate the five sounds; see 孟子 Bēng choó.

Lu̇t 捸 To rub the stains out of anything. To hold in the hand.

Lu̇t 㨯 To strain off the dregs of anything.

Lu̇t 嵂 Ch'hu̇y lu̇t, 崒嵂, the high and lofty appearance of hills.

Lu̇t 膟 The fat about the intestines.

Lu̇t 糨 Coarse rice.

Lu̇t 繂 A bamboo hawser or cable, used for securing ships and vessels.

Lu̇t 訥 To feel a difficulty in speaking; a backwardness to speak; dull. Kwun choó yëúk lu̇t ê gân, jê bín ê hēng, 君子欲訥於言而敏於行 *kwun choó aè bōëyh ŏh kóng tē e ây woā, jê bín ch'hëet tē e ây séy kēⁿâ*, the good man desires to be backward in speaking, and diligent in action; see the 論語 Lūn gé.

卒

Luy 腄 Marked with the small pox.

Luy 鐳 Pice, coppers, farthings; small coin.

声

Lúy 壘 A mound, a trench, a mud fort. Soò kaou to lúy, k'heng taē hoo che jëúk yëá, 四郊多壘卿大夫之辱也 *sè kaou chēy lúy, sè k'heng taē hoo ây lêng jëúk*, to have many fortifications around the four borders, is a disgrace to the nobles and great officers; see the 曲禮 K'hëuk léy.

Lúy 藟 Kat lúy, 葛藟, the tendrils of a certain creeping plant.

Lúy 儡 K'hwúy lúy, 傀儡 *kā léy*, puppets, a dumb show. Also written 㑍, lúy. In the time of 周穆王, Chew-bók ông, a clever fellow of the name of 偃師, Yëén-soo made wooden images which could dance and sing, and this was the origin of the puppets.

Lúy 礧 Lúy lók, 礧硌, large stones. Lúy sék sëang kek, 礧石相擊 *lúy chëōh sëo p'hăh*, they beat each other with large stones.

Lúy 讄 An ode in praise of accumulated virtue. An elegy in which the meritorious deeds of the deceased are summed up, in order to express our lamentations over him.

Lúy 籯 A bamboo vessel, for containing grain.

Lúy 儽 Lazy, indolent; also, sickly. Also written 㑍, lúy.

Lúy 累 To increase, to add to; lúy ch'hoǒ, 累次 *tàk paé*, several times. Kwân k'heng tëūng chëá, put sit sé lúy, 權輕重者不失黍累 *ch'hìn k'hin tāng ây meēⁿh, chëā bēy ūᵐ keèⁿᵍ chit sé lúy*, by ascertaining the heaviness or lightness of things, you will not miss an additional grain of millet.

Lúy 瘰 Lúy lèk, 瘰癧, a disease consisting in a contraction of the tendons.

Lúy 蕾 The opening of a flower; a bud expanding.

Lúy 傫 Second in order.

Lúy 誄 Lúy bûn, 誄文, an elegy; an elegiac composition in praise of any one that is deceased. Lúy wát, tó jé ê sëāng hāy sîn kê, 誄曰禱爾于上下神祇 *lúy woō kóng, kè tó kap lé ây sëāng hāy ây sîn kê*, the elegy says, "pray to the celestial and terrestrial gods above and below;" see the 論語 Lūn gé.

Lúy 蘂 The body of a flower. An expanded flower. Also written 蕊, lúy. The bud is called 蕚, gòk, and the expanded flower 蘂, lúy.

Lúy 蘃 The same as the above.

Lúy 磊 A number of stones, heaped up together. Jê lúy lwán che gwûy, 如磊卵之危 *ch'hin chëōⁿᵍ lúy key nooiⁿᵍ ây gwûy*, in as dangerous a condition as eggs piled upon one another.

Lúy 絫 A very small weight; sip sé wûy lúy, 十黍爲絫 *châp lëep säyh á chò chit ây lúy*, ten grains of millet make one lúy.

平

Lûy 雷 Thunder; a surname; lûy kong, 雷公, the god of thunder; lûy tëēn, 雷電, thunder and lightning; lûy hëáng, 雷響 *lûy tân*, the thunder rolls. Sín lûy hong lëèt, pit pëèn, 迅雷風烈必變 *kín ây lûy kwà hong lëèt, pit pëèn sek*, when the thunder roared, and the wind blew furiously, (Confucius) would change color; see the 論語 Lūn gé.

Lûy 癗 Hwut lûy, 疿癗, a pimple; a small blister caused by the heat.

Lûy 擂 To triturate anything in a mortar.

Lûy 櫑 The name of a tree.

Lûy 樏 The fruit of a tree.

Lûy 縲 A black rope; bonds. Suy chaē lûy sëet che tëung, hwuy kê chöēy yëá, 雖在縲紲之中非其罪也 *suy tē lûy sëet ây tang eⁿᵍ, ūᵐ sē e ây chöēy sit*, although he was in bonds and imprisonment, it was not his fault; see the 上論 Sëāng lūn.

福建方言字典

Lùy 纍 To bind, to tie together.

Lûy 虆 A basket for carrying earth. Kaè kwuy hwán, lûy lê jê yëém che, 蓋歸反虆梩而掩之 *kaè tooⁿᵍ k'hè, t'hó lûy lê jê yëém baè e,* for he returned and got baskets and hods to carry the earth in, and covered the body over; see 孟子 Bēng choó.

Lùy 罍 A pitcher for wine.

去 Lūy 淚 Tears; lêw lūy, 流淚 *laôu bàk chaè,* to shed tears. Lūy jê é hāy, 淚如雨下 *bàk saè ch'hin chëōⁿᵍ hoē lôh,* his tears flowed like rain. When 方孝孺, Hong-haòu-jê was about to be put to death, (lîm hêng gán lūy, 臨刑眼淚 *lîm hêng hwàt bàk chew laôu saè,*) on approaching the place of punishment, his eyes were full of tears.

Lūy 泪 Tears; the same as the preceding.

Lūy 唳 The screaming of a stork.

Lūy 擂 To beat a drum rapidly; lūy koé, 擂鼓, to roll the drum.

Lūy 礧 To roll over a stone; to roll a stone down from a height.

Lūy 儡 Poor and distressed; to injure.

Lūy 彙 A sort, a kind, a class, a genus; joô lūy, 字彙 *jê lūy,* a dictionary.

Lūy 累 To involve in; lëên lūy chëùng jîn, 連累衆人 *lëên lūy chëùng lâng,* to involve the whole in trouble. Söāng sê jê tōng, boô lūy hoē jîn, 相時而動無累後人 *tëöh söāng sê jê tīn tāng, bô lūy tëöh aōu laê ây lâng,* we should calculate the time before we commence operations, and not involve future generations in trouble; see the 左傳 Chó twān.

Lūy 類 A sort, a class; téng lūy, 等類, a sort; chëúng lūy, 種類, a genus, a kind. Ch'hut ê kê lūy pwàt hoē kê chûy, 出於其類拔乎其萃 *ch'hut ê e ây lūy pwăh hoē e ây téng,* to excel one's kind, and to surpass all one's compeers; see 孟子 Bēng choó.

Lūy 酹 To pour out a libation of wine upon the ground.

Lūy 錸 To pierce, to bore through, to perforate.

声 Lwá 磊 *Lwá twá,* 磊磋, not to hit the centre; clay not properly worked up.

去 Lwà 瀨 Read naē: water flowing over the stones; a shallow in a river, where the water is broken by stones. A rapid in a river. Sêk naē hêy, ch'hëén ch'hëén, 石瀨兮淺淺 *chëöh lwà hêy, k'hín k'hín,* where there are stones in a stream, the water is shallow; see the 楚詞 Ch'hoé soô.

平 Lwâ 籮 Read lo: a bamboo vessel for containing rice, a basket, a hamper.

去 Lwā 賴 Read naē: to depend on; é naē, 倚賴 *wá lwā*, to rely on. A surname.

入 Lwăh 揦 Read lát: to stroke down with the hand; to rub down.

入 Lwăh 捋 Read lwát: to twist off, to pluck by handfuls.

Lwăh 埒 Read lwát: to mark out a boundary, and to divide a district; *hwăh kaè*, 埒蓋, to strike a bushel.

Lwăh 捺 Read lát: to press heavily on anything with the hand.

Lwăh 畤 To turn up the earth, in ploughing the ground.

Lwăh 辣 Read lwát: and lát: acrid, pungent.

上 Lwán 煖 Vulg. *sëo:* hot, warm, comfortable, genial. Ch'hit sip hwuy pék put lwán, 七十非帛不煖 *ch'hit châp höëy bó ch'hèng pék bēy sëo*, at seventy, except a person be clothed in silks, he cannot keep himself warm; see the 禮王制 Léy ông chè.

Lwán 暖 The warm genial influences of the sun. The same as the above.

Lwán 餪 A present made to a daughter, three days after her marriage.

Lwán 㬉 Warm, genial; sit teaou hoê che lwán, 褻貂狐之㬉 *ch'hèng teaou ch'hê hoê lê ây sëo hëw*, to wear the warm furs of the ermine and fox.

Lwán 㬉 Warm, through the influence of the sun; the same as the above.

Lwán 卵 Vulg. *nooi^ng:* an egg; key lwán, 雞卵 *key nooi^ng*, a fowl's egg.

Lwán 輐 Round, deprived of the corners; rounded off.

Lwán 軟 Vulg. *nooi^ng:* weak, lissom, pliable, lwán jëák, 軟弱 *nooi^ng chë^ná*.

平 Lwân 鑾 A bell, the sound of a tinkling bell; lwân kày, 鑾駕, the imperial equipage, so called from certain bells hanging from the ornaments of it, peculiar to the emperor.

Lwân 巒 A hill small and conical at the top; the summit of a hill; san lwân, 山巒, the peak of a hill.

Lwân 欒 The name of a wood of a yellow hue. Also, a surname.

Lwân 鸞 Lwân hông, 鸞凰, the female of the fabulous hong bird, represented as part eagle, part pheasant, and of a blue color. The harmonious singing of the same.

Lwân 灤 To leak, to run out.

Lwân 攣 To confine, to bind criminals with a black rope; to attach as by ligatures.

Lwân 戀 Warm affection, ardent attachment. Heng tēy sëang lwân, 兄弟相戀 hëⁿa tē sëo sëŏh, brethren tenderly attached to each other.

Lwân 孌 Wán lwân, 婉孌, handsome, elegant in form.

Lwân 劆 To scrape anything.

Lwân 䜌 The time of evening.

䜌
Lwān 亂 To regulate disturbances; to make disturbances; to throw into confusion, confused, disturbed; chok lwān, 作亂, to rebel; to cause disorder.
Boó ông wát, ē yéw lwān sîn sip jîn, 武王曰予有亂臣十人 Boó ông kóng, gwá woō ēy tē lwān ây jîn sîn chàp lâng, Boó ông said, "I have ten ministers able to quell disturbances;" see the 論語 Lūn gé.
Lwān pang put ke, 亂邦不居 lwān pang bô böëyh k'hëā, he would not dwell in a disturbed district; see the 論語 Lūn gé.

Lwān 乱 The contracted form of the preceding character.

Lwān 薍 Lwān ch'hó, 薍草, overgrown grass and weeds.

Lwān 㝈 Weak, not strong.

Lwān 戀 Kwàn lwān, 眷戀, to be ardently attached to.

犬
Lwat 劣 Weak, no strength; vulgar, small; lwat pȯk, 劣薄, weak, insufficient, just adequate.

㕦
Lwȧt 捋 Vulg. lwȧh: to pluck, to pick, to take; to feel with the fingers.
Ch'haé ch'haé hoô é, pȯk gân lwȧt che, 采采芣苢薄言捋之 laê bán hoo é ây ch'haè, pȯk kóng lwȧh e, "let us pluck the hoô é plant;" I say, "let us pluck it;" see the 周南 Chew lâm.

Lwȧt 埒 Vulg. lwȧh: a low wall, a division, a partition between fields.

Lwȧt 頪 An ugly face.

Lwȧt 辣 Vulg. lwȧh: acrid, pungent.

M

上声 Má 馬 Vulg. *báy:* a horse; k'hê má, 騎馬 *k'hëâ báy,* to ride on horseback. A surname.
Hëuk má sēng, put ch'hat ê key tûn, 畜馬乘不察於雞豚 *ch'hē báy kwà báy ch'hëa, ūⁿ t'hang ch'hat k'hwⁿà lâng ây key kap te,* when a person keeps carriages and horses he should not examine people's fowls and pigs; see the 大學 Taē hák.

Má 碼 Má ló sèk, 碼硓石 *báy ló chëöh,* a cornelian stone.

Má 媽 A grandmother; ló má, 老媽 *laōu má,* old granny.

下平 Mâ 痳 Mâ hong, 痳瘋 *bâ hong,* a kind of leprosy.

Mâ 麻 Bëēn mâ, 面麻 *bīn mâ,* marked with the small pox. A surname.

去 Mā 傌 To disgrace, to degrade.

Mā 禡 The place where an army halts, and where they offer a sacrifice.

Mā 罵 Vulg. *maīⁿᵍ:* to rail at, to scold, to vituperate.
Mā put chwát k'hoé, 罵不絶口 *maīⁿᵍ bô tooīⁿᵍ tē ch'hùy,* his mouth did not cease from railing; see the 史記 Soó kè.

Mā 伯 Read pek: the name of a goddess of the four quarters; also called 馬祖, *má choé.*

上声 Maé 買 Vulg. *bëy:* to buy, to purchase.
Seáou chaé t'hèng maē maé, é chit chey, 小宰聽賣買以質劑 *sèy kwⁿa t'hëⁿa bēy béy, ê chit paīⁿᵍ chëⁿâ,* an inferior officer attends to the selling and buying, in order to promote equity; see the 周禮 Chew léy.

平 Maê 䁼 To peep at, to spy.

去 Maē 賣 Vulg. *bēy:* to sell, to dispose of, to vend.

Maē 休 The name of a medicine; the name of a foreign nation to the east.

Maē 邁 To travel to a distance; old, decrepid; to pass by; to exceed.
Jit gwát jê maē, 日月逾邁

jit göĕyh keng köĕy, days and months are passing by; see the 秦誓 Chin sē.

幸 *Mai^ng* 搣 To take up with the hand.

声 *Mai^ng* 猛 Read béng: fierce, bold, daring; béng chëĕt, 猛捷 *mai^ng chëĕt*, rapid.

平 *Mai^ng* 夜 Read yëā: the night; kim yëā, 今夜 *kim mai^ng*, to-night. Po tèw chok yëā, 俾晝作夜 *hoĕ jit chò mai^ng*, to turn the day into night; see the 小雅 Seáou gnáy.

Mai^ng 冥 Read bêng: dark; bêng hwun, 冥昏 *mai^ng hwui^ng*, the evening, dusk.

Mai^ng 明 Read bêng: the next; bêng lëên, 明年 *mai^ng neĕ^ng*, the next year.

Mai^ng 盲 Read bông: blind; ch'heng bông, 青盲 *ch'hai^ng mai^ng*, totally blind.

Mai^ng 芒 Read bông: the beard of wheat; any sharp point.

Mai^ng 鋩 Read bông: sharp pointed; to bông, 刀鋩 *to mai^ng*, a sharp pointed knife.

Mai^ng 籃 Kek lâm ch'haè, 隔籃菜 *kăyh mai^ng ch'haè*, a kind of vegetable, greens; young cabbages.

去 *Mai^ng* 罵 Read mā: to scold, to rail; sëang mā, 相罵 *sëo mai^ng*, to rail at one another.

去 *Mai^ng h* 咩 The bleating of sheep.

Mai^ng h 蛘 Ch'hó mai^ng h, 草蛘 *ch'haóu mai^ng h*, a grasshopper.

Mai^ng h 急 Read kip: hasty, quick.

入 *Mai^ng h* 脉 Read bêk: the pulse; boĕ bêk, 摸脉 *bong mai^ng h*, to feel the pulse.

平 Maôu 矛 A spear; tëâng maôu, 長矛 *të^ng maôu*, a long spear. E choó tông maôu, 與子同矛 *kap lé tâng maôu*, to use the same spear with you; see the 秦風 Chin hong.

Maôu 茅 Maôu ch'hó, 茅草 *û^m á ch'haóu*, a coarse kind of grass, used in thatching; Erianthus Japonicus. Maôu ok, 茅屋 *û^m á ch'hoò*, a thatched cottage. A surname. Pèk maôu tun sok, 白茅純束 *păyh û^m á hâ lâ chë^n á pàk*, white grass bound up into bundles.

Maôu 蝥 Pwân maôu, 盤蝥 *pân bâ*, a poisonous insect, cantharides.

Maôu 蟊 An insect which eats the inside of grain. Maôu chêk, 蟊賊, the insect injurious to the roots.

Maôu 鍪 A helmet.

去 Maōu 貌 An appearance. Yûng maōu, 容貌, the face, the countenance; also written 皃, maōu. Tōng yûng maōu, soo wàn pò bān è, 動容貌

斯遠暴慢矣 *hó tin tāng yŭng maōu, chěy lěy chēw hwuiⁿᵍ k'hè pò bān è*, by enlarging our views, we shall be enabled to remove oppression and insult; see the 論語 Lūn gé.

Maōu 貌 The same as the above; appearance, manner, aspect, air.

Maōu 偕 A good look, a fair appearance.

上 Me 彌 For words written me, see under meeⁿᵍ.

平 *Mēⁿâ* 名 Read bêng: a name; bêng seng, 名聲 *mēⁿâ sēⁿa*, fame, report; sèng bêng, 姓名 *saiⁿᵍ mēⁿâ*, the name and surname.

Sē é seng bêng yâng yit hoē tëung kok, 是以聲名洋溢乎中國 *sē é sēⁿa mēⁿâ ëy yâng yit tē tëung kok*, thus a man's fame would spread throughout the whole middle country (China); see the 中庸 Tëung yûng.

Mēⁿâ 榵 Ch'haê mēⁿâ, 柴榵 *ch'hâ mēⁿâ*, touchwood; some say, the gum of a tree which easily ignites.

去 *Mēⁿā* 命 Read bēng: an order, the decree of heaven, fate; hⁿó bēng, 好命 *hó mēⁿā*, good fortune; swàn bēng, 算命 *swuiⁿᵍ mēⁿā*, to calculate destinies. Choó hán gân lē, é bēng, é jîn, 子罕言利與命與仁 *hoo choó hán tit kóng lē, kap mēⁿā, kap jîn*, Confucius seldom spoke of gain, or fate, or benevolence; see the 論語 Lūn gé.

上 Meeⁿᵍ 彌 O meeⁿᵍ tô Hwŭt, 阿彌陀佛, Amida Buddha, commonly used by the Chinese as an oath. Sa meeⁿᵍ, 沙彌, a priest of Buddha.

平 *Meêⁿᵍ* 綿 Read bëên: wool, cotton; bëên yâng, 綿羊 *meêⁿᵍ yëôⁿᵍ*, a sheep; bëên hwa, 綿花 *meêⁿᵍ hwa*, raw cotton for making cloth.

Meêⁿᵍ 彌 An incantation.

去 Meēⁿᵍ 謎 A riddle; chok meēⁿᵍ, 作謎, to make a riddle.

Meēⁿᵍ 媚 To please, to flatter; t'hëém meēⁿᵍ, 諂媚 *sëèp sèy*, to adulate; also, to love.

Pëēn p'hek chek meēⁿᵍ, 便辟側媚 *sëōⁿᵍ pëēn p'hek ây soō, chēw aē meēⁿᵍ lâng*, being depraved, we shall begin to flatter people.

Meēⁿᵍ choo yit jîn, 媚茲一人 *sëŏh chěy chit ây lâng*, they all love the one man; (i. e. the emperor;) see the 大雅 Taē gnáy.

Meēⁿᵍ 麵 Read bëēn: flour, wheaten flour; also written 麪, meēⁿᵍ. Bëēn paou, 麵包 *meēⁿᵍ paou*, a cake, a bun.

入 *Meĕⁿᵍh* 咩 The bleating of sheep.

Meĕⁿᵍh 乜 A foreign surname; commonly used for 'yes,' 'right!'

Meĕⁿᵍh 麽 Read mŏh: as sîm mŏh? 甚麽 *sⁿa meĕⁿᵍh?* what? Jé chò sîm mŏh? 你作甚麽 *lé chò sⁿa meĕⁿᵍh?* what are you doing?

入 *Meĕⁿᵍh* 物 Read bŭt: a thing; bān bŭt, 萬物 *bān meĕⁿᵍh*, all things. Bān bŭt pèng yëŭk, jê put

福建方言字典

sëang haē, 萬物並育而不相害 *bān meĕngh sëo yáng yëúk, jê bó sëo haē,* all things would then be nourished, without injuring one another; see the 中庸 Tëung yûng.

去声

Mo 蕳 The name of a plant, like a kind of wheat, the grains of which are eatable.

去声

Mó 捫 To hold anything in the hand.

Mó 冃 Repeated, redoubled.

Mó 䔘 A poisonous plant.

Mó 㒵 Small, minute, diminutive.

Mó 㦳 Mó lô, 㦳㦬, ashamed.

平

Mô 毛 Hair; the hair of the head, and eyebrows; hông mô, 紅毛 *âng mô,* red haired, generally applied to the English people. A surname.
Tek yêw jê mô, mô yêw yéw lûn, 德輶如毛毛猶有倫 *tek hêng k'hin sèy ch'hin chëŏng mô, mô yĕá woō lûn lüy,* though my virtue is as light as a hair, yet even a hair may be classified.

Mô 芼 Overgrown with weeds. Mô ch'haè, 芼菜, herbage, vegetable food. Mô keng, 芼羹 *ch'haè t'heng,* vegetable broth.

Mô 髦 Hair; the hair on the side of the head, tied and twisted up into little tails, as is commonly done with children. Mô soō, 髦士, a clever scholar.

Mô 旄 A cow's tail, held by those who brandish it about to give signs and orders.

Mô 酕 Mô tô, 酕酡, drunk.

Mô 摩 To rub, to rub up, to stir up; to persuade one another to that which is good, is called 摩, mô.

Mô 磨 To grind, to sharpen on a stone. Mô lëy é se, 磨礪以須 *bwâ lwâ laê saê,* to grind anything for use; see the 左傳 Chó twān.

Mô 魔 Mô kwùy, 魔鬼, the devil, a spirit which misleads people.

上去

Mō 耄 An old man, 80 or 90 years of age. Also, wandering and forgetful. Mō kê kwān ê k'hîn, 耄期倦於勤 *pâyh kaóu châp hāèy ây laôu lâng, sëŏng twnā tē k'hìn ây soō,* old people of 80 and 90 years of age are loth to exert themselves; see the 尚書 Sëāng se.

Mō 眊 Old, superannuated; the eyes dim. Hëung tëung put chèng, chek boê choó mō yëen, 胸中不正則眸子眊焉 *heng tang eng ūm chèna, chek bàk ang á bó kwuing,* when a man is not upright in his own breast, then the pupil of his eye will be dim; see 孟子 Bēng choó.

Mō 冒 To cover over, to overturn; to transgress; káy mō, 假冒, to pretend to make a bargain.
Also written 冐, mō: to rush headlong.
Mō yëen tut hnó, 冒烟突火 *mō hwun tùt höéy,* to rush through the smoke, and to dash through the fire.

Mō **娼** To envy; jîn che yéw kê, mō chit é oè che, 人之有技娼嫉以惡之 *lâng ây woō kē, mō chit é wàn e*, when men are possessed of talents, you immediately envy and dislike them; see the 大學 Taē hȧk.

Mō **悁** Poor, indigent; covetous.

Mō **芼** Vegetable food thoroughly cooked and offered up.

上去 Möèy **妹** A sister; seáou möèy, 小妹 *séó möèy*, a younger sister; möèy hoo, 妹夫, a younger sister's husband.

Möèy **沬** The name of a river; rather dark.

Möèy **昧** Am möèy, 暗昧, dark, and dusk.

下平 *Möêy* **糜** Read bê: rice water; ám bê, 涾糜 *ám möêy*, congee, gruel.

上入 Mŏh **麽** Anything very small; sīm mŏh? 甚麽 *s^{n}a meē^{n}h?* what?

Mŏh **枂** To take away.

下入 Mŏh **披** Pellicle, thin skin.

上平 *Mooi^{ng}* **麽** Anything extremely small; *mooi^{ng} mooi^{ng}*, 麽麽, very little indeed.

上聲 *Mooi^{ng}* **晚** Read bwán: late, the evening, sunset; sit bwán hwān, 食晚飯 *chëăh mooi^{ng} pooi^{ng}*, to eat the evening meal.

Hoē höèy pit bwán, 後悔必晚 *aōu höèy pit mooi^{ng}*, a future repentance will be too late.

Mooi^{ng} **葋** Koé bún ch'hó, 茍葋草 *k^{n}á mooi^{ng} ch'haóu*, a very poisonous plant, which when eaten, causes the entrails to burst asunder.

下平 *Mooi^{ng}* **門** Read bûn: a door, an entrance, a gate; k'hae bûn, 開門 *k'hwuy mooi^{ng}*, to open the door.

Bûn hoē, 門戶 *mooi^{ng} hoē*, doors and gateways.
Lip put tëung bûn, 立不中門 *k'hëā bô tè mooi^{ng} tang e^{ng}*, he would not stand in the middle of the doorway; said of Confucius, in the 論語 Lūn gé.

下去 *Mooi^{ng}* **問** Read būn: to ask, to inquire; put t'hé hāy būn, 不恥下問 *ū^{m} lëăh chò seáou lêy hāy têy mooi^{ng} lâng*, he was not ashamed to consult his inferiors.

Goê chëang būn che, 吾將問之 *gwá chëang laē mooi^{ng} e*, I will ask him; see the 論語 Lūn gé.

上平 *Mw^{n}a* **縵** A garment without sleeves or fastenings, like the sarongs, and round frocks, worn by the eastern islanders.

Mw^{n}a **庢** *Sëâ mw^{n}a*, 家庢, a room built in a verandah, or under the eaves of a house.

Mw^{n}a **帽** A garment without buttons or fastenings.

Mwⁿa 䘑 To wear a garment without buttons or loops.

聲
Mwⁿá 滿 Read bwán: full, replete; ch'hëung bwán, 充滿 *ch'hëung mwⁿá*, filled up full.

Bwán teâou hoè kwùy chëá, chīn sē t'hók se jīn, 滿朝富貴者盡是讀書人 *mwⁿá teâou poè kwùy ây chīn sē t'hàk ch'hăyh lâng*, all the rich and great people who fill the court are every one of them scholars; (said to young people, to encourage them to perseverance in study.)

平
Mwⁿâ 麻 Hemp; hông mâ, 黃麻 *wutⁿᵍ mwⁿâ*, yellow hemp; hoê mwⁿá, 胡麻, Sesamum orientale. A surname.

Mwⁿâ 瞞 Read bwân: to deceive, to cheat, to smother anything.

T'hëen put k'hó bwân, 天不可瞞 *t'heeⁿᵍ bēy mwⁿâ tit*, heaven cannot be deceived.

Mwⁿâ 鰻 Read bân: an eel; haé bân, 海鰻 *haé mwⁿâ*, a conger eel.

N

聲
Ná 拏 Vulg. *lëâh:* to take, to seize, to apprehend, to catch. Also written 拿, ná. K'he ná chöëy jīn, 拘拏罪人 *k'he lëâh chöëy lâng*, to apprehend criminals.

Ná 那 Ná kò, 那個 *hwut lêy*, that, those. A surname. How? ná lêng sêng jīn? 那能成人 *an chwⁿá ēy chëⁿá lâng?* how can such a one ever become a man?

Ná 欖 Kám lám, 橄欖 *kán ná*, an olive.

平
Nâ 藍 Read lâm: a surname.

Nâ 林 Read lîm: a wood, a grove; sō lîm, 樹林 *ch'hēw nâ*, a forest of trees. Kwuy má ê hwa san che yâng, hòng gnêw ê t'hô lîm che yëá, 歸馬於華山之陽放牛於桃林之野 *hoē báy tó tootⁿᵍ tē hwa swⁿa ây lâm, pàng goô twā tē t'hô nâ ây yëá*, let us send back our horses to the south of the flowery hill, and allow our oxen to graze on the moor of the peach forest. (Speaking of returning to a period of tranquillity.)

Nâ 籃 Read lâm: a basket; a surname; ch'haè lâm, 菜籃 *ch'haè nâ*, a basket for carrying vegetables.

Nâ 嚨 Read lëûng: as lëûng hoê, 嚨喉 *nâ aôu*, the throat.

Nâ 巖 Read gâm: as Lëûng gâm, 龍巖 *Lëûng nâ*, the name of a district in the province of 福建 Hok-këèn.

上去

Nā 那 An auxiliary word.

Nā 電 Read tëen: vulg. *seĕh nā:* lightning.

上入

Naé 乃 For, because; but, instead of; is, to be; you. Put këèn Choó-toe, naé këèn kaóu tông, 不見子都乃見狡童 *bô k'hwⁿà keèⁿᵍ Choó-toe, naé k'hwⁿà keèⁿᵍ ká ây gîn á*, we did not see Choó-toe, but we saw a hair brained youth. Boô naé jé sē kò e? 無乃爾是過與 *bô naé lé woō köèy sit?* is it not the case that you are in the wrong? see the 論語 Lūn gé.

Naé 迺 The same as the above; also written 廼, naé.

Naé 嬭 Naê choó, 嬭仔 *leng á*, the nipples, the breasts; also written 妳, naé.

Naé 奶 The same as the above; naé naé, 奶奶, an elegant female.

下平

Naê 腝 The breasts, the nipples.

Naê 䑋 A child begotten by an old man.

上去

Naē 佴 A surname.

Naē 奈 Naē hô? 奈何 *woō sⁿa meēⁿᵍh taē wâ?* how then? what resource is there? Boô naē hô, 無奈何 *bô taē wâ*, there is no resource, we cannot help it.

Naē 柰 The name of a fruit; kó tin lé naē, 果珍李柰 *köèy chê tin pó lé kap naē*, the most valuable among fruits are the pear and the plum.

Naē 耐 Jím naē, 忍耐 *t'hun lún*, to bear patiently, to exercise patience. Sëûng naē söèy hân, 松耐歲寒 *ch'hêng păyh ēy naē tit neēⁿᵍ tang kwⁿâ*, the fir trees can endure the cold patiently.

Naē 耏 P'hó naē, 叵耏, able to endure. Also, the same as the above.

Naē 賴 To depend on; é naē, 倚賴 *wá lwā*, to rely on. Also read laē. Boô naē, 誣賴, to trust in vain. Vulg. *lwā:* a surname.

Naē 蘱 The name of a certain water plant.

Naē 癩 Naē pēng, 癩病 *t'hae ko paīⁿᵍ*, a kind of leprosy; kaè naē, 疥癩 an inveterate malady.

Naē 籟 A pipe with three holes in it; a big pipe is called 笙, seng; a middling one 籟, naē; and a smaller one 箹, yëak.

Naē 瀨 Vulg. *lwā:* water flowing over the sand and stones; a shallow or rapid in a river.

Naē 糲 Naē bé, 糲米, coarse rice; the refuse of pounded rice; also written 糲, naē.

Naé 蠣 A kind of shell-fish; boó naē, 牡蠣, a kind of medicine.

Naē 鬲 A large iron pan, or caldron.

Naē 櫳 Naē taè, 櫳樧, not skillful in business; dull.

平 *Nai^ng* 嬣 Read lêng: as koe lêng, 姑嬣 *koe nai^ng*, an aunt. P'eng lêng, 姘嬣 *pai^ng nai^ng*, a weak and silly woman.

Nai^ng 薴 Mô lêng hwa, 芼薴花 *mô nai^ng hwa*, the name of a flower. Cheng lêng, 箏薴 *chai^ng nai^ng*, the name of a medicinal plant.

去 *Naì^ng* 企 Read k'hè: and t'hé: to stand on tiptoe, and look to a distance. T'hé këak, 企脚 *nai^ng k'ha*, to stand on tiptoe.

平 *Naî^ng* 擰 *Naî^ng poè*, 掭布, to hang out clothes to dry.

去 *Nai^ng* 儜 Read lêng: weak, exhausted; the noise made by foreigners in calling to one another.

Nai^ng 矃 *Tai^ng nai^ng*, 盯矃, to look staringly at any one.

5 W

去 Naóu 撓 To twist, to flinch. Put hoo naóu, put bók tô, 不膚撓不目逃 *p'höëy ū^m k'hëw k'hwut, bák ū^m tô chaóu*, his muscles did not flinch, nor his eyes blink; see 孟子 Bëng choó.

Naóu 惱 To disturb, to stir up to anger; naóu tōng, 惱動, to disturb any one's mind. Naóu jëet, 惱熱 *laóu jwăh*, all in a bustle.

平 Naôu 撓 To throw into confusion. Hëung noê che chëùng ē naóu lwān, 匈奴之衆易撓亂 *hëung noê ày chëùng lâng, yúng ē naóu lwān*, the hosts of Tartars are easily thrown into confusion.

Naôu 鐃 A small gong, a cymbal.

Naôu 怓 Hwun naôu, 惛怓, the mind confused. Boô ch'hëùng k'hwûy sûy é kín hwun naôu, 無縱詭隨以謹惛怓 *ū^m t'hang ch'hëùng hwut léy k'hwûy sûy, e sèy jē hwun naôu*, do not give way to deceitful and crafty people, in order to guard against confusion; see the 大雅 Taē gnáy.

Naôu 呶 Swan naôu, 喧呶, to make a noise, to create a disturbance. Pin kè chùy ché, chaè hô chaè naôu, 賓既醉止載號載呶 *lâng k'hāyh kaôu chëw chùy, woō ây tit hwăh woō ây tit jëáng*, when the guests become heated with liquor, some will be hallooing, and some will be bawling; see the 小雅 Seáou gnáy.

N. B. For words spelled ne, look under nee^ng.

去 Nē^ná 領 Read lëng: the neck; to receive, to secure; to govern. Yéw êng kê léng, 有鶯其

領 *woō hwa ch'haĕ e ây nĕⁿá*, how variegated were the necks (of the birds); see the 小雅 Seáou gnáy. Léng bĕng, 領命 *nĕⁿá bĕng*, to receive orders. Pó léng, 保領 *pó nĕⁿá*, to stand security for.

Nĕⁿá 嶺 Read léng: a mountain top; san léng, 山嶺 *swⁿa nĕⁿá*, the top of a hill.

Yîn hêng Chîn léng, kay hô chaē? swat yûng lâm kwan, má put chëên, 雲橫秦嶺家何在雪擁南關馬不前 *hwûn t'hàn hwⁿâ tē Chîn ây nĕⁿá, ch'hoò twā tē ta lôh wūy? sāyh t'hat lâm kwan, báy bēy kĕⁿâ ân t'haôu chêng*, the clouds are seen stretched across the brow of the Chîn mountain, and where now is our dwelling? the snow has filled up the southern pass, so that the horse cannot get forward; said by 韓愈, Hân-jé, when he was traveling to the southward.

去 Nĕⁿā 岭 Lêng êng, 岭巆 *nĕⁿā yĕⁿâ*, far and deep amongst the hills.

平 Neaou 猫 Read beâou: a cat; beâou kong put chaē, ló ch'hé chok kwaè, 猫公不在老鼠作怪 *neaou kang bô tē tit, neaou ch'hé chò koo kwaè*, when the cat is away, the mice begin to play.

上 Neáou 鳥 Vulg. *cheáou*: a bird; neáou bêng eng eng, 鳥鳴嚶嚶 *cheáou haôu eng eng*, the birds sing harmoniously; see the 小雅 Seáou gnáy.

Neáou 蔦 A parasite, a creeper. Neáou é lé lô, sè é sëûng pek, 蔦與女蘿施于松柏 *neáou kap lé lô, sē twā tē ch'hêng păyh*, the parasites and creepers entwine around the cedars; see the 小雅 Seáou gnáy.

Neáou 㒡 Yaôu neáou, 偠㒡, tumblers turning their bodies into the form of a ring; to perform feats of tumbling and agility.

去 Neàou 䤒 Bëēn neàou, 面䤒 *bīn neàou*, the face furrowed and wrinkled; old, decrepid.

平 Neeⁿᵍ 拈 Read lëem: to take up anything with the fingers.

上 Neéⁿᵍ 你 You, thou; neéⁿᵍ tek, 你的 *lé ây*, your's. Also written 伲, neéⁿᵍ.

Neéⁿᵍ 詎 To inform any one by word of mouth; to instruct orally; to call.

Neéⁿᵍ 染 Read jëém: to dye; jëém poè, 染布 *neéⁿᵍ poè*, to dye cloth.

平 Neêⁿᵍ 尼 Harmonious; neêⁿᵍ koe, 尼姑, a nun, a priestess.

Tëūng neêⁿᵍ, 仲尼, the name of Confucius.

Neêⁿᵍ 呢 Neêⁿᵍ lâm, 呢喃, talking incessantly, to chatter without end.

Neêⁿᵍ lâm yëèn choó gé lëâng kan, 呢喃燕子語樑間 *neéⁿᵍ lâm ây eèⁿᵍ á, kóng wā tē nëöⁿᵍ aiⁿᵍ kan*, the chattering swallows are twittering between the beams; see the 杜甫詩 Toē hoó se.

Neêⁿᵍ 怩 Lëuk neêⁿᵍ, 忸怩, to feel ashamed; to blush with confusion.

Sëâng wât, wut tô soo kwun jé, lëuk neêⁿᵍ, 象曰鬱陶思君爾忸怩 *Sëāng kóng, wut chut sëöⁿᵍ kwun lé, yëá chëw seâou léy ây yëöⁿᵍ*, Sëâng said, "I have been anxiously

福建方言字典

thinking of your highness;" (saying which) he looked ashamed and confused; see 孟子 Bēng choó.

Neê^{ng} 泥 Vulg. *nw^{n}â t'hoê:* mud, earth mixed with water. Hô wûy hoê neê^{ng} tëung? 何爲乎泥中 *s^{n}a soo twā tē nw^{n}â t'hoê tang e^{ng}?* what do you do in the midst of the mud? see the 詩經 Se keng.

Neê^{ng} 妮 The epithet of a female.

Neê^{ng} 訑 The noise of calling people.

Neê^{ng} 旎 E neê^{ng}, 旖旎, the appearance of a flag waving in the wind.

Neê^{ng} 年 Read lëên: a year; lëên lëên, 年年 *neê^{ng} neê^{ng}*, every year. Gnoé pek lëên, pit yéw ông chëá hin, 五百年必有王者興 *goê păyh neê^{ng} pit woō ông ây lâng hin k'hé*, in the course of five hundred years, there will certainly spring up some of a royal spirit; see 孟子 Bēng choó.

Neê^{ng} 哖 *Tô lô neê^{ng}*, 陀囉哖, woollen cloth. *Seáou neê^{ng}*, 小哖, a sort of kerseymere.

Neê^{ng} 連 Read lëên: as hông lëên, 黃連 *wui^{ng} neê^{ng}*, a refrigerant, a cooling medicine. A surname.

Neê^{ng} 黏 *Tó neê^{ng}*, 倒黏, a blackberry.

去

Neē^{ng} 女 To give one's daughter in marriage. T'hèy ch'hut jê neē^{ng} ê Goê, 涕出而女於吳 *laôu bàk saê ch'hut jê kày chaôu á tē Goê*, he wept as he went out, and gave his daughter in marriage to the prince of Goê; see 孟子 Bēng choó.

Neē^{ng} 泥 Impervious, obtuse, not thoroughly understood, dull. Suy seáou tō, pit yéw k'hó kwan chëá yëen; tè wán k'hëúng neē^{ng}, sē é kwun choó put wûy yëá, 雖小道必有可觀者焉致遠恐泥是以君子不爲也 *suy sèy ây tō, pit woō t'hang k'hw^{n}à keè^{ng}; nā sē tè kaôu hwui^{ng}, kē^{n}a ne ū^{m} t'hong, sē é kwun choó ū^{m} chò*, even an inferior degree of virtue may be worthy of one's observation; but when extended to a distance it is to be feared it will not be thoroughly intelligible, therefore the good man does not practice it; see the 論語 Lūn gé.

Neē^{ng} 莅 Read lē: to come to, to appear before, to arrive at. Also written 涖, and 沴, neē^{ng}. Chong é neē^{ng} che, 莊以莅之 *chong gëëm ê lîm kaôu pàyh sai^{ng}*, appear stern before the people; see the 論語 Lūn gé.

Neē^{ng} 䵑 An imprecation.

Neē^{ng} 莉 Bók neē^{ng}, 木莉, the name of a flower, white in color, and very fragrant.

入

Neē^{ng}h 躡 Read lëep: to wink; lëep bók, 躡目 *neē^{ng}h bàk*, to wink the eyes. Bók lëep kéw, 目躡久 *bàk neē^{ng}h koó*, in the twinkling of an eye.

去

Nëó^{ng} 兩 Read lëáng: an ounce; yit lëáng gîn, 一兩銀 *chit nëó^{ng} gîn*, an ounce of silver. Kat kè gnoé lëáng, 葛屨五兩 *ch'haôu ây goê nëó^{ng} tāng*, a pair of straw shoes five ounces weight; see the 齊風 Chêy hong.

平

Nëô^{ng} **娘** Read lëâng: a lady, a mother; a father is called 爺, yëâ, "Sir," and a mother, lëâng, 娘, *nëô^{ng}*, "lady." In common conversation, *nëô^{ng} pāy*, is used for father, and *nëô^{ng} léy*, for mother.

Nëô^{ng} **孃** Read lëâng: mother; Jîn-chong, 仁宗, called Lêw se, 劉氏 *Laôu sē* (his adopted mother), taē lëâng lëâng, 大孃孃 *twā nëô^{ng} nëô^{ng}*, 'the great lady;' while he called Yâng se, 楊氏 *Yëô^{ng} sē* (his real mother), seáou lëâng lëâng, 小孃孃 *sëó nëô^{ng} nëô^{ng}*, 'the little lady.'

Nëô^{ng} **糧** Read lëâng: provisions; bé lëâng, 米糧 *bé nëô^{ng}*, rice and provisions. Soo hêng jê lëâng sit, 師行而糧食 *peng kë^{n}â tëôh woō nëô^{ng} chëâh*, when troops commence their march, they should have suitable provisions; see 孟子 Bēng choó. Also written 粮, *nëô^{ng}*. Chëên lëâng, 錢糧 *cheê^{ng} nëô^{ng}*, taxes, soldiers' pay.

Nëô^{ng} **梁** Read lëâng: a beam, the principal beam of a house. A surname. Sëāng lëâng, 上梁 *chëô^{ng} nëô^{ng}*, to get up the principal beam of a house.

Nëô^{ng} **量** Read lëâng: to deliberate; sëang lëâng, 商量 *soo nëô^{ng}*, to deliberate, to consult. Sòng t'haè choé, 宋太祖, the first emperor of the Sòng dynasty, went one cold night to the house of Teâou-p'hoé, 趙普 *Tëō-p'hoé*, to (sëng lëâng têng t'haè gwân, 商量定太原 *soo nëô^{ng} tē^{n}ā tëôh T'haè gwân,*) consult with him about tranquilizing T'haè gwân, (the capital of Sanse.)

Nëô^{ng} **凉** Read lëâng: cool; lëâng sán, 凉傘 *nëô^{ng} sw^{n}á*, a state umbrella, carried before officers of government.

去

Nëō^{ng} **量** Read lëāng: as taē lëāng, 大量 *twā nëō^{ng}*, a large steelyards, for weighing heavy goods.

Nëō^{ng} **讓** Read jëāng: to yield; sëang jëāng, 相讓 *sëo nëō^{ng}*, to yield to one another.

Keng chëá jëāng pwān, hêng chëá jëāng loē, 耕者讓畔行者讓路 *chŏh ch'hân ây lâng nëō^{ng} pwān, kë^{n}â loē ây lâng nëō^{ng} loē*, the ploughmen yielded the furrow, and the travelers gave way to each other on the road; said to have taken place in the time of 周文王, Chew-bûn ông.

平

Nê^{ng} **郎** Read lông: a young gentleman; sē lông, 侍郎 *sē nê^{ng}*, a gentleman in waiting, a vice president of a trbunal, introduced in time of 文帝 Būn-tèy, of the 隋, Sûy dynasty.

Nê^{ng} **廊** Read lông: an antichamber; lëáng lông, 兩廊 *nō ây nê^{ng}*, the two apartments on each side of a hall or court.

Nê^{ng} **榔** Read lông: as pin lông, 檳榔 *pin nê^{ng}*, the areca nut; Pin lông sē, 榔檳嶼 *Pin nê^{ng} soō*, the island of Pinang, or Prince of Wales' island.

Nê^{ng} **莨** Chê lông, 薯莨 *chê nê^{ng}*, a kind of yam, used as a red dye.

Nê^{ng} **篖** Read lông: the inside of bamboos; bëêt lêng, 篾篖 *bëĕh nê^{ng}*, the soft inner part of bamboo, used in making basket work.

Nê^{ng} **䏊** Read lông: the flesh immediately under the skin; jëùk lông, 肉䏊 *bàh nê^{ng}*, the fat of meat, between the lean and the hide.

去 Nēng 浪 Read lōng: the waves of the sea; p'ho lōng, 波 浪 p'ho nēng, waves and billows. Haé súy k'hé taē p'ho lōng, 海水起大波浪 haé chúy k'hé twā p'ho nēng, the ocean rises into great waves.

去 Néw 肘 The wrist, the region of the pulse; sēw néw, 手肘 ch'héw néw, the wrist.

上 Nó 娜 O nó, 婀 娜, handsome, beautiful; also, easy, loose.

平 Nô 那 What? many; read ná: that; how? K'hè kap chek nô? 棄甲則那 t'hek kak chëën kūh chek chô nô? if we throw away our armor, what then? see the 左 傳 Chó twān.
Sēw hok put nô, 受 福 不 那 sēw hok bô jwā chēy, we have not received much happiness; see the 小 雅 Seáou gnáy.

Nô 郍 The same as the above; this character is very common in the books of Buddha.

Nô 哪 Nô nô, 哪 哪, the noise made in driving away noxious influences.

Nô 儺 To drive away noxious influences, to expel pestilential vapors. Hëang jîn nô, teâou hok jê lip ê ch'hoè kae, 鄉人儺朝服而立於阼階 hëōng lê ây láng kwōⁿá wun yëǎh, e chëw ch'hēng teâou ây yîn chëōng jê k'he tē tang peēng ây gîm kay, when the villagers were driving away noxious influences, Confucius would put on his court dress and stand on the eastern steps; see the 論語 Lūn gé.

Nô 猱 The name of a hill.

Nô 獶 A kind of monkey, with long soft hair.

Nô 臑 Bones chopped up, to make gravy. Also, fat and ugly.

Nô 懦 Weak, cowardly; nô jëák, 懦 弱, pusillanimous. Koè bûn Léw-hāy hwūy che hong chëá, gwân hoo lëëm, nô hoo yéw lip chè, 故聞柳下惠之風者頑夫廉懦夫有立志 chëâ woō t'hëⁿa Léw-hōy hwūy ây hong, gwân gaé ây lâng chëⁿá ch'heng lëëm nooⁿg chëⁿá ây lâng woō lip chè, therefore when any listen to the principles of Léw-hāy hwūy, the dull become pure, and the cowardly acquire resolution; see 孟子 Bēng choó.

Nô 獳 An enraged hound, an angry dog. A surname.

Nô 稬 Nô bé, 稬 米, a glutinous kind of upland rice, of which liquor can be made; called also 秫 米, chút bé. Also written 穤, nô, and 糯, nô.

去 Nō 那 An expletive, or an auxiliary word, used sometimes at the end of a period, as a note of interrogation. Also written 哪, nō. Same as 嗏, nō.

Nō 二 Read jē: two; yit hwân yit, jē hwân jē, 一 還 一 二 還 二 chit hwân chit, nō hwân nō, let your one be one, and your two, two; (similar to the scriptural phrase, "let your yea, be yea; and your nay, nay.")
Soô yëá, bûn yit é te jē, 賜也聞一以知

二 *gwá t'hëⁿa chit hāng, chëw chae nō hāng*, when I hear of one thing, I know two; see the 論語 Lūn gé.

去 Noé 努 Noé lék, 努力, to exert one's strength; to rouse one's energies.

平 Noê 伮 Noê lék, 伮力, to exert one's utmost strength. The same as the above.

Noê 奴 A slave; noê pē, 奴婢, male and female slaves.

Noê chaê, 奴才 *loê chaê*, a slave, often used as a term of reproach. Noê pók, 奴僕, a servant.

Noê 駑 Noê t'hae, 駑駘, an ugly horse, used as a term of self-reproach.

Ch'hò-hoó sëēn gē, put lêng gē noê t'hae, 造父善御不能御駑駘 *Ch'hò-hoó gaôu saê ch'hëa, bêy heáou saê lám báy*, Ch'hò-hoó was a good charioteer, but he could not drive bad horses.

去 Noē 怒 Anger, wrath, to be angry, to be in a passion; hwún noē, 憤怒 *sëw k'hè*, rage, to be in a rage.

Bûn ông yit noē, jê an t'hëen hāy che bîn, 文王一怒而安天下之民 *Bûn ông chit ây sëw k'hè, jê an t'heeⁿᵍ āy ây păyh saiⁿᵍ*, Bûn ông, once displaying anger, tranquilized the people of the empire; see 孟子 Bēng choó.

Noē 檽 Koe noē, 構檽, a kind of wood, the bark of which is used for dyeing a red color.

Noē 耨 To weed the ground, to clear away grass and weeds.

Ch'him keng ē noē, 深耕易耨 *ch'him chŏh ch'hân, kwà tê ch'haôu*, to plough deep, and to clear away the weeds; see 孟子 Bēng choó.

去 Nooiⁿᵍ 軁 *Nooiⁿᵍ kŏèy k'kè*, 軁過去, to squeeze one's-self through a hole.

上 Nooiⁿᵍ 軟 Read lwán: weak, feeble, flexible, pliable; weary.

Swan lwán, 痠軟 *sooiⁿᵍ nooiⁿᵍ*, weariness, lassitude. Këak sëw lwán, 脚手軟 *k'ha ch'hëw nooiⁿᵍ*, helplessness of the limbs. Lwán këak pēng, 軟脚病 *nooiⁿᵍ k'ha paiⁿᵍ*, loss of the use of the limbs.

去 Nooiⁿᵍ 趡 *Nooiⁿᵍ chaôu*, 趡走, to creep through, and get away.

平 Nooiⁿᵍ 柚 Read yëw: the shaddock, the pumelo fruit; Citrus decumana. Also written 柘, yêw.

去 Nooiⁿᵍ 卵 Read lwán: an egg; key lwán, 鷄卵 *key nooiⁿᵍ*, a fowl's egg. Also written 蛋, *nooiⁿᵍ*.

上 Nwⁿá 雫 To knead, or squeeze anything with the hand.

Nwⁿá bút, 雫物 *nwⁿá meēⁿᵍh*, to knead anything.

平 Nwⁿâ 攔 Read lân: to stop, to hinder; lân chăh, 攔閘 *nwⁿâ chăh*, to obstruct.

去 Nwⁿā 爛 Read lān: rotten, over ripe; boiled to rags, overdone; torn, ragged.

Bút hoó wát lān, 物腐曰爛 *meēⁿᵍh ch'haôu kóng nwⁿā*, when anything stinks, it is called rotten.

Nwⁿā 妹 Read mōèy: as key mōèy, 鷄妹 *key nwⁿā*, a pullet, a young hen that has not yet laid eggs.

Nwⁿā 涎 Read yëên: spittle; sûy yëên, 唾涎 *p'hŏèy nwⁿā*, to spit.

O

卒

O 窩 To secrete, to conceal; to dwell in a cave; a cavern. An lok o, 安樂窩, the cavern of peace and joy. O chông, 窩藏 *t'haou k'hèng*, to secrete stolen goods.
O kay, 窩家, a receptacle for stolen goods.
Yëèn o, 燕窩, the edible birdsnests, much prized by the Chinese.

O 鍋 Vulg. *wöey:* a pot or pan, for cooking victuals.

O 堝 The same as the above, when made of earth; an earthen pot.

O 斛 An earthen pot.

O 蝸 O gnêw, 蝸牛 *o goô*, a kind of snail, or worm; a slug.

O 萵 Tong o, 東萵 *tang o*, and o ch'haè, 萵菜 *wöey ch'haè*, salad.

O 訶 To speak loud and angrily, to scold. Hwuy kám té o koé jîn tek sit yëá, 非敢詆訶古人得失也 *ūm kná té o koé lâng ây tek sit*, we dare not scold and rail at the rights or wrongs of the ancients.

O 阿 A great mound of earth; part of a name.

O 屙 To go to stool.

O 痾 Sick; a fright into which children fall.

O 呵 O o ch'heàou, 呵呵笑 *o o ch'hëò*, to laugh out loud.

O 苛 Any small kind of plant; a troublesome and annoying sort of government; to oppress, and annoy; also, to examine.
Hoō ló k'hoé Chîn o hwat kéw è, 父老苦秦苛法久矣 *pāyh saing ây hoō ló woō chae kan k'hoé Chîn ây o hwat koó è*, the aged fathers of the people have been wearied and distressed by the oppressive government of Chîn for this long time; see the 高祖紀 Kó choé ké.
Soo kwan chëáng o ch'hat, kan jîn, 司關掌苛察姦人 *soo kwan ây kwna, chëáng o ch'hat kan haê ây lâng*, the officer who kept the pass attended to the examination of improper people.

O 倭 A foreign nation, from beyond the eastern sea; the Japanese. Some read this character wuy.

O 蒿 A kind of grass; the daffodil. Yew yew lòk bêng, sit yëá che o, 呦呦鹿鳴食野之蒿 *yew yew lòk haóu, chëăh yëá ây ch'haóu*, the stags cry with the sound of *yew yew*, and eat the grass of the wilderness; see the 小雅 Seáou gnáy.

O 滈 The eddying of water.

O 猗 Soft and pliable; also, the full and luxuriant appearance of bamboos.

O 鏖 To venture one's life in battle; to fight till death.

上聲 Ó 襖 A fur dress; twān ó, 緞襖 a satin dress; sin lëâng ó, 新娘襖 *sin nëó^ng ó*, a bridal dress.

Ó 婀 O nó, 婀娜, beautiful, handsome; slowly, leisurely.

Ó 娿 O nó, 娿娜, a soft and effeminate appearance.

Ó 婐 To attend on any one, as a female servant. The services rendered by ladies. Also written 果, ó.

Ó 捰 To pick or pluck anything.

去聲 Ò 澳 Deep, mysterious, unfathomable.

Ò 奧 The southwest corner of the house, to which the Chinese offer sacrifice. Ch'him ò, 深奧, deep and abstruse.

E kê meē^ng ê ò, lêng meē^ng ê chò? 與其媚於奧寧媚於竈 *pé ê ây sëëp sèy tē ch'hoò kak, lêng k'hó sëëp sèy tē chaóu k'ha?* rather than worship the southwest corner of the house, is it not better to flatter the god of the kitchen? see the 上論 Sëāng lūn.

Ò 隩 The brink of water, the water's edge; land near the water's side.

Ò 懊 To regret, to be vexed, to be enraged; ò hwûn, 懊恨, to repent.

Ò 侉 To cry out for pain.

Ò 啊 The sound of love or hatred.

Ò 欸 O naé, 欸乃, the boatman's song.

平聲 Ô 蠔 Read hô: an oyster; hô sëang lëêm wûy san, pek sip kok choō seng, 蠔相黏爲山百十各自生 *ô sëo lëêm chò sw^na, pâyh ây châp ây, kok ka tē sai^ng*, if oysters stick together like a hill, be they hundreds, or be they tens, each one grows by itself.

去聲 Ô 嗃 The sound of replying; the noise made in answering any one.

上平 Oe 烏 Black; oe a, 烏鴉, a crow; kim oe, 金烏, a three-legged bird, supposed to inhabit the sun.

A surname.

Chëem oe wān ché, e sûy che ok, 瞻烏爰止伊誰之屋 *k'hw^nâ oe tē ta lōh hây^nh, chê chŭy ây ch'hoò*, look where the crow settles, and on whose house he sits; see the 小雅 Seáou gnáy. The perching of a crow on any one's house is considered by the Chinese as an unlucky omen.

Oe 嗚 Oe hoe, 嗚呼, an exclamation of surprise. Alas! to lament, to sigh. Oe hoe! cheng wūy T'haè san put jê Lîm-hōng hoē? 嗚呼曾謂泰山不如林放乎 *oe hoe! bōēyh chae ēy kóng T'haè san ây sîn ŭm tàt Lîm-hōng hoē?* alas! who could have said that the spirit of the T'haè mountain was not so discriminating as Lîm-hōng? see the 上論 Sēāng lūn.

Oe 於 The same as the preceding.

Oe 槝 Oe yûng, 槝櫹, the name of a water plant, of whose stalks the shafts of arrows may be made.

Oe 鄔 A surname.

Oe 鷗 The name of a water bird.

Oe 謳 The chanting with a number of voices.
Oe ko chēá, put oe ko Geâou che choó, jê oe ko Sùn, 謳歌者不謳歌堯之子而謳歌舜 *ch'hëò^ng kwa ây lâng, bô ch'hëò^ng kwa Geâou ây haōu sai^ng, jé ch'hëò^ng kwa Sùn*, those who chanted ditties, did not chant to the honor of Geâou's son, but to the honor of Sùn; see 孟子 Bēng choò.

Oe 漚 To steep in the water, to soak in the water; to macerate.
Tong bûn che tê, k'hó é oe mwⁿâ, 東門之池可以漚麻 *tang mooi^ng ây chúy k'hwut á, t'hang laê chìm mwⁿâ*, the pond without the eastern gate will serve to soak the hemp in; see the 陳風 Tîn hong.

Oe 惡 How! what? an exclamation of surprise.
Oe! sē hô gân yēá? 惡是何言也 *oe! chēy sē sⁿa meē^ngh wā?* how! what words are these? see 孟子 Bēng choò.

Oe 籠 Oe lâm, 籠籃 *oe ná*, a cradle for rocking children to sleep.
Also read oē.

声

Oé 隝 A small encampment; a mud fort.
Also written 塢, oé.
Tóng-tok, 董卓 *Táng-tŏh*, made an encampment at 郿 Bê, which he called bān sòey oé, 萬歲隝, the ten thousand years' encampment.

Oé 鄔 The name of a district; read oe: a surname.

Oé 嶋 The name of a hill.

Oé 潟 The name of a river.

Oé 瑦 The name of a gem.

Oé 嫗 An old woman, a mother; ló 老嫗, an old dame.
Gēēm-yëên-lëên, 嚴延年 belonged to a family of five brothers, who all attained to high offices, and enjoyed salaries of two thousand measures of corn each; hence their mother was called (bān sék oé, 萬石嫗 *bān chēoh oé*, the old lady of a myriad measures of grain.

Oé 漚 To be soaked long in the water.

Oé 嘔 Vulg. *aóu:* to vomit; oé t'hoè, 嘔吐 *aóu t'hoè,* to vomit and spew.

Oé 歐 The same as the above; to belch, to spit; also written 㗈, oé. Vulg. *aou:* a surname.

Oé 堊 A small fort, a redoubt. The same as 隖, and 塢, oé.

去

Oè 惡 To hate, to dislike, to seem evil in one's eyes. Wûy jîn chĕá lêng hⁿò jîn, lêng oè jîn, 唯仁者能好人能惡人 *tòk tòk jîn tek ây lâng ēy aè lâng, ēy wàn lâng,* the benevolent man alone can love people, or dislike them, in a proper way; see the 上論 Sëäng lūn.

Oè 偲 The same as the above. Also written 亞, oè.

平

Oê 胡 Read hoê: a surname.

Oê 湖 Read hoê: a lake, a wide valley. Gnoé hoê, 五湖 *goē ây oê,* the five lakes. Pëèn yêw kang hoê, 徧遊江湖 *pëèn yêw kang oê,* he had traveled over all the rivers and lakes.

Oê 瓳 A water pot.

上

Oē 芋 Read ē: a water plant with a large leaf, and an edible root, taro; called the Arum aquaticum, in the Batavian Transactions.

N. B. For words spelled öey and oo, see also under wöey and woo.

上

Öey 隈 A point of land, a bend in a river, where the stream takes a turn; a point is called 隈, öey, and a bay is called 隩, ò.

Öey 偎 To love; in Corea, the expression öey jîn, 偎人, means to love people.

Öey 喂 To be afraid.

Öey 猥 Vulgar; pe öey, 卑猥, low and mean; öey p'hé, 猥鄙, niggardly.

Öey 碨 Öey lúy, 碨磊, stones piled up together; öey à, 碨砈, uneven.

Öey 煨 Anything cooked over the fire; öey chîn, 煨燼, ashes.

Öey 蒉 The name of a plant.

Öey 鍡 Öey luy, 鍡鑸, uneven; to cut and mince; öey jëùk, 鍡肉 *öey băk,* to mince meat; öey k'hae, 鍡開 *öey k'hwuy,* to cut open.

Öey 殨 Sick, diseased; dried up and decayed; withered away.

Öey 瘺 A disease arising from damp.

Öey 倭 Oey tê, 倭遲, the name of a foreign country; to return from a distance. The islands of Japan, said to contain upwards of 100 states. Oey jîn, 倭人, a Japanese.

Öey 鍋 A pot, or pan; an earthen pan.

Öey 剮 To cut up, to cut open.

Öey 鋼 Tông öey, 銅鋼, a brass pot, or kettle.

去
Öèy 穢 Bad, filthy, dirty, overgrown with weeds. Boê öèy put tê, 蕪穢不治, overgrown and uncultivated; oo öèy, 汙穢, dirty, unclean.

Öèy 薉 Overgrown with weeds; disordered, confused, unclean.

Öèy 濊 Waters deep, wide, expansive, and overflowing.

Öèy 劌 To cut, to injure.

Öèy 噦 The noise of carriage wheels.

Öèy 翽 The sound of flying; the fluttering and clapping of wings. Hŏng hông ê hwuy, öèy öèy kê é, 鳳凰于飛翽翽其羽 *hông hông ây cheáou tit pwuy, öèy öèy e ây sit,* when the phœnix is flying, the fluttering of its wings sounds like *öèy öèy;* see the 大雅 Taē gnáy.

Öèy 饖 Rice spoiled by being overheated.

Öèy 廆 A place of concealment.

平
Öey 禾 A kind of chestnut; *bŏk öey,* 木禾, the fruit of a certain tree, which is edible; *öey ch'haè,* 禾采, a sort of vegetable, salad?

去
Öēy 衛 Hoē öēy, 護衛, to guard, to protect; to fence, to ward off danger. Jê choó tēy che öēy hoō heng, 如子弟之衛父兄 *ch'hin chëōng choó tēy ây hoē öēy pāy hēⁿa,* just as sons and younger brethren protect their parents and elders. A surname.

入
Öĕyh 挃 To take; to pluck, to scoop out; séw öĕyh bùt, 手挃物 *ch'héw öĕyh meēngh,* to take hold of anything with the hand.

入
Öĕyh 唷 The noise made in vomiting, the sound of anything going out.

Öĕyh 穡 Read köèy: the husk of grain; k'hong köèy, 糠穡 *k'hēng öĕyh,* bran.

Öĕyh 割 Read ėk: to cut open; ėk bùt, 割物 *öĕyh meēngh,* to scoop out anything, to split anything open.

入
Ŏh 難 Read lân: difficult, hard, not easy. Kwun choó ē soō, jê lân wát yēá, 君子易事而難悅也 *kwun choó k'hwaē chò soō, jê ŏh kwⁿa hé,* the good man is easily engaged in business, but with difficulty pleased; see the 論語 Lūn gé.

夭 Ŏh **學** Read hák: to learn; a school; jip hák, 入學 *lŏh ŏh*, to go to school. Hák jê sê sip che, 學而時習之 *ŏh jê sëâng sê wun sip e*, to learn and constantly to study anything; see the 上論 Sëăng lūn.

夭 Ok **惡** Vulg. *p'haⁿé*: wicked, evil, bad, vicious, depraved, ugly. Koé chè ê jîn è, boô ok yëá, 苟志於仁矣無惡也 *chin chëⁿà nā ëy sim chè twā tē jîn, chëw bô p'haⁿé*, when a man's mind is truly set on virtue, he will be able to avoid vice; see the 語論 Lūn gé.

Ok **僫** Faulty, vicious, not good.

Ok **堊** To plaster a wall; also written 亞, ok.

Ok **屋** Vulg. *ch'hoó*: a house, a dwelling, a residence. Hoò jûn ok, 富潤屋 *poò chëw ch'hòng hó ch'hoó* when a man is rich, he beautifies his dwelling; see the 大學 Taē hák.

夲 Ong **翁** An old man; lò ong, 老翁, an old gentleman; ong sëuk, 翁叔 *ūⁿ chek*, a familiar epithet for uncle; applied also to strangers by courtesy. A surname. In the 明, Bêng dynasty, there was an old man who attained to the highest literary honors, whose name was 翁正春, Ong-chèng-ch'hun, 'old man just spring;' which circumstance tickled the emperor's fancy, who exclaimed, "that though he was an old man, he was just in his spring or the prime of life."

Ong **尢** Crook-shanked; also, one of the radicals.

Ong **蓊** Ong wut, 蓊鬱, luxuriant foliage, exuberant vegetation.

Ong **蝓** Wán ong, 蜿蝓 *wán nëō^{ng}*, a kind of wasp, a gadfly.

Ong **尩** Vulg. *ang*: an idol; an image; chëên che jê ong, 賤之如尩 *hây chëën e, ch'hin chëō^{ng} ang*, as base as an idol; see 荀子 Sûn choó.

Ong **尪** Vulg. *ang*: an idol; soō ong, 祠尪 *ch'haē ang*, to sacrifice to an idol.

Ong **尫** Humpbacked; the back bent through age and disease.

Ong **汪** The deep and expansive appearance of water; the ocean. Vulg. *ang*: a surname. Chëúng goê seng ê ong yâng, 終吾生於汪洋 *chëung swăh gwá ây sai^{ng} mëⁿā tē ang yâng*, to spend one's whole life on the expansive ocean.

声 Óng **往** To go, to depart; óng laê, 往來, to go and come; to have intercourse with. Kò óng, 過往 *köèy óng*, to depart this life, to die. Kong-san Hwut-jeáou é Pè pwān, teàou, choó yëúk óng, 公山弗擾以費畔召子欲往 *Kong-san Hwut-jeáou é Pè yip pwān hwán, kaòu teàou hoo choó, hoo choó böëyh k'hè*, Kong-san Hwut-jeáou rebelled with the city of Pè, when on summoning Confucius, the sage was about to go to him; see the 論語 Lūn gé.

Kè óng put kēw, 旣往不咎 *kaòu köèy ây soō, ūᵐ t'hang lëăh e chò ūᵐ tëŏh,* do not blame one for things already gone; see the 上論 Sëāng lūn.

Óng 枉 To bend, to stoop; to pervert; bent, crooked, perverse, wicked. Ong ch'hek jê tit sîm, 枉尺而直尋 *óng k'hwut chit ây ch'hëŏh, jê ch'hòng tit chit ây sëëm,* to bend a cubit, in order to rectify a fathom; see 孟子 Bēng choó.

Wan óng, 寃枉, to oppress, to treat unfairly.

Óng 嵡 A hilly appearance.

Óng 坱 Dust; kò ê óng bóng che yëá, 過於坱漭之野 *köèy ê tìn ae ây yëá,* to pass through the dusty wilderness.

Óng 蓊 A dark recess in a house.

Óng 暡 Ong bông, 暡曚, the sun obscured and not shining clear; an unlucky day.

去

Òng 坱 Dust, the rising of dust.

Òng 塕 The appearance of dust rising; the rushing sound of the wind.

Òng 瞈 Ong bông, 瞈矇, defect of vision; the eyes not clear.

Òng 瓮 Vulg. *àng:* a kind of jar.

5 Z

Òng 甕 Vulg. *àng:* a jar, a pitcher, a water pot.

平

Ông 任 To walk quickly.

Ông 王 A king, a sovereign prince, a royal personage. A surname.

Tāē chae ông gân! yit chae ông sim! 大哉王言一哉王心 *twā chae ông ây wā! chit yëōⁿᵍ ông ây sim!* how great are your majesty's words! how single your intentions! see the 尚書 Sëōⁿᵍ se.

去

Ōng 王 To elevate to royal dignity, to attain to supreme power; to rule.

Pó bîn jê ōng, bók che lêng gé yëá, 保民而王莫之能禦也 *pó pe páyh saiⁿᵍ jê chò ông, bô lâng ëy kâyh,* when we aim at universal empire by protecting the people, none can oppose us; see 孟子 Bēng choó.

Ōng 旺 Hin ōng, 興旺, to elevate, to prosper, to rise to affluence and power; bright, illuminated.

平

Oo 迂 Oo wán, 迂遠, distant, far removed, vague; crooked, to pervert.

Oo 紆 Bent, crooked; sè tëung jëák chek oo, 矢中弱則紆 *cheèⁿᵍ tang eⁿᵍ nootⁿᵍ chëw wan,* when an arrow is thin in the middle, it will bend.

Oo 杇 To plaster, to whitewash a wall; also written 圬, oo.

Hwùn t'hoê che ch'hëâng, put k'hó oo yëá, 糞土之墻不可杇也 *pùn t'hoê ây ch'hëôⁿᵍ bô t'hang bwăh pâyh,* a wall made of dung and mud cannot be well whitewashed; see the 上論 Sëāng lūn.

Oo **肟** Këak t'hoê oo, 脚頭肟 *k'ha t'hau oo*, the knee.

Oo **洿** A hollow place, where the water collects. A pond, a pool.
Ch'hëuk koé put jip oo tê, 数罟不入洿池 *bàt bàt ây bāng, bô jip tē chúy-k'hwut á*, a close meshed net should not be suffered to be spread in the pools; see 孟子 Bēng choó.

Oo **汚** Dirty, muddy, filthy; standing water; oo öèy, 汚穢, dirty, filthy.
Jit jëém oo söuk, 日染汚俗 *tàk jit bàk tëŏh la sâm ây hong sëuk*, to be daily defiled with filthy customs; also written 汙, oo.

Oo **跍** To stoop, or crouch down.

上声 *Oó* **鄔** Read oé: a surname.

上去 Oò **汚** To defile, to soil, to make dirty.

上平 Oô **盂** A drinking vessel; a cup.

下去 *Oō* **有** Read yéw: to have, to possess, to be, to exist; existence; more.
Būn yéw ê, pit wàt yéw, 問有餘必曰有 *mooⁿᵍ oō ch'hun, pit kóng oō*, when asked if there was anything over, he would always say there was; see 孟子 Bēng choó.

上入 Oŏh **噎** Tⁿá oŏh, 打噎 *p'hăh oŏh*, to belch.

P

卆
Pa 巴 A surname; Pa-chew, 巴州, the name of a district; pa sëâ, 巴蛇 *pa chwâ*, the name of a large snake, perhaps the boa constricta, which can devour an elephant, and does not discharge its bones for three years.

Pa 吧 *Ka-lâ-pa*, 咬𠺘吧, the Chinese name for Batavia; Pa sêng, 吧城 *Pa sëⁿâ*, the city of Batavia. Pa gây, 吧呀, children quarreling; to box and fight.

Pa 疤 The scar or seam of a wound.

Pa 鈀 A military weapon; a warlike instrument.

Pa 豝 A sow, the female of a pig.

Pa 齙 Crooked teeth.

Pa 笆 Lê pa, 籬笆, a railing, a thorny fence made of bamboo.

Pa 芭 Pa cheaou, 芭蕉, *pa chëo*, a plantain; Musa coccinea.

Pa 羓 Roasted meat; pa jeùk, 羓肉 *pa bă'h*, broiled flesh.

Pa 鱟 Pa lông, 鱟鯨, the name of a fish.

声
Pá 把 To hold, to grasp firm, to hold in the hand; pá pèng, 把柄 *pá pèng*, to hold by the handle; pá sëw, 把守 *páy chëw*, to watch, to guard. Numeral of things grasped by the hand, as knives, &c.

Pá 飽 Read paóu: full, satisfied, to eat to the full.
Kwun choó sit boô kêw paóu, 君子食無求飽 *kwun choó chëăh bô kêw pá*, the good man in eating, does not seek satiety; see the 上論 Sëāng lūn.

去
Pà 霸 The chief, to become chief; to act the usurper. Also written 伯, pà. Kwán-tëūng sëāng Hwân kong, pà choo hoê, 管仲相桓公霸諸侯 *Kwán-tëūng sëāng Hwân kong, pà choo hoê*, Kwán-tëūng was prime minister to Hwân-kong, and assisted him to become chief over the princes of the empire; see the 語論 Lūn gé.

Pà 覇 The same as the preceding.

Pà 壩 A bank, a dyke, a mound to keep in water. In the province of Canton, there is a bank called the sey hoê pà, 西湖壩, bank of the western lake.

Pà 擺 To hold, to take hold of.
The teachers of archery are particular in instructing their pupils to pà séw, 擺手 *pây ch'hêw*, hold the bow firm in the hand.

Pà 灞 The name of a river.

Pà 豹 A leopard; hoé pà, 虎豹, tigers and leopards.
K'he hoé pà soo sëăng, jê wàn che, 驅虎豹犀象而遠之 *kwⁿá hoé pà sae ch'hëōⁿᵍ, jê hoē e hwuiⁿᵍ*, to drive away the tigers and leopards, rhinoceroses and elephants, to a distance; see 孟子 Bëng choó.

Pà 弝 Këung pà, 弓弝, a thumb-ring, used in archery.

Pà 杷 An instrument for reaping corn; some say an implement for leveling and harrowing the ground; a harrow; a handle.
Pà pèng, 杷柄 *pà paiⁿᵍ*, a handle.

Pà 靶 To pà, 刀靶, the handle of a knife.

Pà 爸 Pà pà, 爸爸 *nëōⁿᵍ pây*, a familiar epithet for father.

Pà 垻 A bank, a mound, a dyke.

平
Pâ 爬 Vulg. *pây*: to scratch; pâ yăng, 爬癢 *pây chëōⁿᵍ*, to scratch any place that itches; pâ hêng, 爬行 *pây kèⁿá*, to crawl, to creep.

Pâ 杷 Pâ put, 杷朳, a wooden shovel or rake, for shifting about grain while exposed to the sun to dry.

Pâ 琶 Vulg. *pây*: a guitar; pê pâ, 琵琶 *pé pây*, a harp, or guitar.

Pâ 笆 Vulg. *pây*: a bamboo rake, a harrow; a rake with five teeth, for raking together straw and dung.

Pâ 鲃 Pâ ló, 鲃鱸, the name of a fish.

去
Pā 罷 To give over, to finish, to do away with; pā leáou, 罷了, enough of it. Yëuk pā put lêng, 欲罷不能 *aè böëyh swăh bēy ēy*, we may wish to desist, but shall not be able; see the 論語 Lūn gé.
Pā chit, 罷職, to retire from office; to put out of office.

上
Paé 擺 Paé k'hae, 擺開 *paé k'hwuy*, to spread out, to open out, to arrange.
Paé seng pan k'hîm, 擺牲班禽 *paé t'haou saiⁿᵍ pan lëët cheáou*, they spread out the animals, and arranged the birds, (for sacrifice.)

去
Paè 拜 To bow down, to worship, to make obeisance, to pay respect to.
Paè sîn, 拜神, to worship the gods. Paè hoē, 拜候 *paè aōu*, to wait upon.
Paè hāy, léy yëá, 拜下禮也 *kaðu paè lōh gîm kay hāy sē lêy soè*, when making a bow (to the prince), if we descend (to the bottom of the steps,) it is according to propriety; see the 論語 Lūn gé.

福建方言字典

平 Paê 庍 Arriving at a place, to part asunder.

平 Paê 排 To push, to push open; to spread out, to arrange. Hwân-köèy paê t'hat tit jip, 樊噲排闥直入 *Hwân-köèy paê k'hwuy moot^ng tit jip*, Hwân-köèy pushed open the palace gate, and entered straightways; see the 史記 Soó kè.

An paê poè tê, 安排布置, to spread out, and put in order.

Paê 徘 Paê hôëy, 徘徊, to hesitate, to walk backwards and forwards in doubt. Ch'heng säang sûy hong hwat, tëung tit chèng paê hôëy, 清商隨風發中直正徘徊 *ch'heng ây säang sē^n a t'hàn hong tit hwat, tëung tit ây chē^n â tit paê hôëy*, the clear musical notes are conveyed whichever way the wind blows, but the honest upright man hesitates which way he shall go; see the 古詩 Koé se.

Paê 俳 Paê yew, 俳優, mixed sport, dissipation. The same as the above.

Paê 棑 A raft, a float; also, a club, a stick.

Paê 簰 A large bamboo raft; the same as the above.

Paê 牌 A board, a tablet, a plank, a sign; paê pêng, 牌牓, a tablet; sék paê, 石牌 *chëŏh paê*, a stone tablet; hwûn boē paê, 墳墓牌 *hwûn bōng paê*, a tombstone.

6 A

去 Paē 敗 To ruin, to destroy, to decay; to defeat; to overthrow. Bông kok paē kay, 亡國敗家 a lost country and a ruined family.

Paē tīn jê choé, 敗陳而走 *paē tīn jê chaóu*, to lose the battle and run away. Anciently written 敳, paē.

Paē 憊 Wearied to the extreme; fagged, jaded; distressed.

Paē 粺 A fine kind of white rice.

Paē 稗 Vulg. *p'hêy*: a sort of grain, like rice, but smaller; a kind of grass like foxtail; paē kwan, 稗官, an inferior kind of office.

去 Pai^ng 拚 Peng k'hae, 拚開 *pai^ng k'hwuy*, to pull open. Also, to fillip with the finger.

平 Paî^ng 棚 Read pêng: a scaffolding, a stage, a terrace, a tent. Hè pêng, 戲棚 *hè paî^ng*, a stage for theatrical performances, a theatre.

Kwa pêng, 瓜棚 *kwa paî^ng*, a frame for melons to grow on.

Paî^ng 平 Read pêng: even, smooth, level, equal; a surname; pêng chèng, 平正 *paî^ng chè^n â*, just and equal; pêng tit, 平直 *paî^ng tit*, equitable and honest. Kok tē, jê hoē t'hëen hây pêng, 國治而後天下平 *kok tē, jëëu aōu t'hee^ng āy ēy paî^ng*, when the different states are well regulated, the whole empire will be tranquil.

Paî^ng 臺 Read taê: a stage; hè taê, 戲臺 *hè paî^ng*, a theatrical stage.

𡚁
Paiⁿᵍ 病 Read pēng: sick, unwell; sickness, disease. Choó chit pēng, 子疾病 *hoo choó woō paiⁿᵍ*, Confucius was sick; see the 論語 Lūn gé.

𡘤
Pak 剝 To fall down, to cut, to carve; to strip off the skin, to flay; pak p'hê, 剝皮 *pak p'hōēy*, to skin; pak t'hek, 剝裼 *pak t'hăyh*, naked.
Hék pak hék p'heng, 或剝或烹 *woō ây tit pak, woō ây tit p'heng*, some were carving, and some were boiling; see the 小雅 Seáou gnáy.

Pak 駁 Party-colored, mixed colored, variegated, piebald; pak sek má, 駁色馬 *pak sek báy*, a piebald horse; pak chàp, 駁雜, variegated.
To distinguish, to argue; pēen pak tō lé, 辨駁道理, to debate and argue on the reason of things.

Pak 駮 The same as the preceding; to argue, to distinguish.

Pak 北 Read pok: the north; Pok keng, 北京 *Pak kēⁿa*, Peking, the northern capital of China.
Choō sey, choō tong, choō lâm, choō pok, boô soo put hòk, 自西自東自南自北無思不服 *choō sae, choō tang, choō lâm, choō pak, bó chit ây sēōⁿᵍ ūᵐ hòk*, from the west, and east, from the south and north, there was not even one who meditated resistance; said of 文王 Bûn ông.

Pak 腹 Read hok: the belly; hok toé, 腹肚 *pak toé*, the belly; hok sim 腹心 *pak sim*, the bowels, as dear as one's own bowels; p'hò hok, 剖腹 *p'hwà pak*, to rip open the belly, to dissect.
Hok yéw se se, k'hè choō hwa, 腹有詩書氣自華 *pak laē woō se kwà ch'hăyh, k'hè chēw ka tē hwa gnáy*, when the belly is full of odes and classics, a man's spirit will become spontaneously elegant.

Pak 幅 Read hok: a broad piece of cloth; a roll or bundle of silk.
Ké hok? 幾幅 *kwúy pak?* how many rolls of silk?

𡗜
Pàk 縛 Read pòk: to bind, to tie; páng pòk, 綁縛 *páng pàk*, to tie up.
Pòk jê sat che? 縛而殺之 *tēōh pàk jê t'haé e?* "shall we tie him up, and kill him?" said by some domestics, when about to kill a pig; but 曹操, Chô-ch'hò hearing it, thought they were intending to kill him; whereupon he first commenced the work of slaughter, and murdered them all; see the 三國 Sam kok.

Pàk 贌 *Pàk sēā*, 贌社, to insure anything; an insurance.
Pàk kwⁿa, 贌官, a farmer of the public revenue.

𡘏
Pan 班 Pan lēét, 班列, to arrange, to put in order; to part, to divide; to confer rank; a surname.
Kwan yéw pan bēēn che wūy, 官有班聯之位 *kwⁿa woō pan lēēn ây wūy*, offices are arranged according to different stations.

Pan 斑 Variegated, party-colored; sêng pan, 成斑 *chēⁿâ pan*, pock-marked.

Pan 媥 Pan lân, 媥爛, a mixed color.

Pan 頒 Pan sùò, 頒賜, to give, to bestow; to distribute, to disperse.
Pan toē lēāng jê t'hēen hāy tae hók, 頒度量而天下大服 *pan hwat toē, kap nēōⁿᵍ ch'hìn, jê t'heeⁿᵍ āy twā hòk*, bestow

福建方言字典

on the people proper rules and measures, and the whole empire will become submissive.

Pan **便** Pan gê, 便宜, suitable, convenient, cheap.

上去
Pán **版** A board for keeping reckoning on; a tablet used as a register, in taking a census of the inhabitants.
Bók pán, 木版 *ch'hâ pán*, a plank, a board for writing or engraving upon.
Sek hoō pán chëá, 式負版者 *p'hak ch'hëa kadu toó tëŏh gëâ pán ây lâng*, (Confucius) leaned on the front of his carriage when he met any one carrying the population register, (out of respect;) see the 論語 Lūn gé.

Pán **板** A board or plank; the same as the above; also, to turn aside; to become cross-grained and morose.

Pán **昄** Great, extreme; jé t'hoé woó pán chëang, 爾土宇昄章 *lé ây t'hoé tëy twā kwuiⁿᵍ*, your territory is greatly illumined.

Pán **舨** Kap pán, 舺舨, a square rigged vessel, seemingly derived from the Malay word *kapal*, a ship.
Sam pán, 杉舨, a boat, a pinnace; also derived from the Malay word *sampan*, a small boat.

Pán **㿶** A pain at the heart, accompanied with vomiting.

下平
Pân **瓶** Read pîn: a pot; chéw pîn, 酒瓶 *chéw pân*, a wine pot; hwa pîn, 花瓶 *hwa pân*, a flower pot.
Also written 缾, *pân*.

下去
Pān **槾** *Kap pān*, 夾槾, a box, a trunk.

Pān **辦** Read pëēn: to manage; pëēn soō, 辦事 *pān soō*, to manage an affair; maé pān, 買辦 *báy pān*, a comprador, one who buys things for another; tⁿá pān, 打辦, to prepare, to provide.

Pān **瓣** Read pëēn: the divisions in a melon or orange.

Pān **扮** Chong pān, 裝扮 *cheⁿᵍ pān*, to adorn, to ornament one's person.
Tⁿá pān, 打扮, to dress fine, a manner of dress, a fashion.

上平
Pang **邦** A country, a state; pang kok, 邦國, a kingdom. A surname.
Pang yéw tō, pîn ch'hëⁿá chëēn yëen, t'hé yëá, 邦有道貧且賤焉恥也 *pang woō tō ây sé, sòng hëung kwà hāy chëēn, sē seâou léy yëá*, when a country possesses the right way, (i. e. is tranquil,) to continue poor and mean is disgraceful; see the 論語 Lūn gé.

Pang **梆** A plank, a board; k'haou pang, 敲梆, to plane boards.

Pang **幇** Pang choē, 幇助 *pang chān*, to help, to assist.

Pang **幫** To bind shoes, to finish the edges of shoes.

Pang **挷** To guard, to defend; sëang pang, 相挷 *sëo pang*, to assist one another; pang choē, 挷助 *pang chān*, to assist, to help.

Pang **鞤** To bind shoes. The same as 幫, pang.

Pang **崩** Read peng: to fall down, as a rock or hill; to precipitate; used also in speaking of the death of an emperor.
San peng tēy lëĕt, 山崩地裂 *swⁿa pang tēy leĕh*, the hills fall, and the earth opens.

Pang **枋** Sam bong, 杉枋 *sam pang*, a deal board.

去

Páng **綁** Páng pók, 綁縛 *páng pák*, to bind, to tie.

Páng **挷** *Páng pók*, 挷縛, to seize and tie up.

Páng **琫** The ornaments of a dress sword.

Páng **菶** Luxuriant herbage.

去

Páng **放** Read hòng: to let go, to let out, to let pass away; hòng hông, 放紅 *pàng âng*, to pass blood, diarrhea. Hòng gnêw ê t'hô lîm che yëá, 放牛於桃林之野 *pàng goô tē t'hô nâ ây swⁿa yëá*, to let the oxen go in the common of the peach grove; see the 尚書 Sëâng se.

平

Pâng **房** Read pông: a chamber; a surname; pông këen, 房間 *pâng keng*, an apartment.

Pâng **馮** Read pêng: a surname.

Pâng **縫** Read hông: to hem, to sew; hông e, 縫衣 *pâng sⁿa*, to hem a garment.

去

Pāng **捧** Read hóng: to receive; a staff; to beat with a staff.

Pāng **蚌** A cockle, a muscle; pāng kap choo t'hae, ó gwát k'hwuy chwân, 蚌蛤珠胎與月虧全 *pāng kap k'hĕⁿᵍ choo ây pak toé, kap gäĕyh k'hwuy chuîⁿᵍ*, the cockles and muscles, with their pearly wombs, correspond to the moon in her wax and wane.

去

Paou **包** To include, to inclose; paou hâm, 包含, to include; paou kó, 包裹, to bundle up; paou hók, 包袱, a bundle. A surname.
Sëen seng che lëāng paou huē t'hëen tēy, 先生之量包乎天地 *sin saiⁿᵍ ây lëāng paou hoē t'heeⁿᵍ tēy*, your capacity, Sir! is large enough to include both heaven and earth; see the 范仲淹文 Hwân tëūng yëem bûn.

Paou **苞** The name of a bamboo, which sends forth its shoots in the winter.

Paou **胞** An embrace; paou t'hae, 胞胎, the womb; tông paou heng tēy, 同胞兄弟 *tâng paou hëⁿa tē*, a brother by the same parents.

Paou **勹** To bundle up; paou bút, 勹物 *paou meëⁿᵍh*, to bundle up anything.

去

Paóu **飽** Vulg. *pá*: to be satisfied, to be full; to enjoy satiety; sit paóu, 食飽 *chëăh pá*, to eat to the full; paóu hák, 飽學, extensively learned, erudite.
Paóu sit chëung jit, boô séy yūng sim, lân è chae, 飽食終日無所用心難矣哉 *chëăh pá chëung jit, bô séy yūng sim, ŏh è chae*, when a man eats to the full all day long, without

ever exerting his mind, how difficult it is to do anything with him; see the 論語 Lūn gé.

Paóu 鮑 Fish preserved in brine; dried, offensive fish. A surname.

去 Paòu 餃 Paòu tëêm, 餃甜 *paòu teeng*, to suck sweetmeats; a sort of sweetmeat or pie.

Paòu 胞 Bók paòu, 目胞 *bák chew paòu*, the eyes flashing with rage.

平 Paôu 苞 The name of a grass, of which mats and shoes are made; to fold up in a mat.

Paôu 炰 Vulg. *poô:* to bake, to broil in the fire. Also written 炮, paôu.

Paôu 咆 Paôu haou, 咆哮, the roar of a tiger; to roar.

Paôu 袍 A long flowing garment, a gown; a dress of ceremony.

Lé-koè bông léw chëep jëém paôu, hoē tëùng chōng gwân, 李固夢柳汁染袍後中狀元 *Lé-koè bāng léw chëep ncēng tëŏh p'haôu, jëën aōu tëùng ch'hëūng gwân*, Lé-koè dreamed that the juice of a willow tree spotted his gown, and afterwards he rose to the highest literary honors.

Paôu 跑 To kick; paôu choé, 跑走 *paôu chaôu*, to gallop away; to run.

Paôu 匏 Vulg. *poô:* a calabash. Goē k'hé paôu kwa yëá chae? 吾豈匏瓜也哉 *gwá k'ham sē poô kap kwa?* how can I be like a calabash or a melon? (that is confined to one place, and unable to help itself;) said by Confucius, in the 論語 Lūn gé.

6 B

Paôu 刨 To scrape; paôu pang, 刨枋, to plane boards.

Paôu 庖 A slaughter-house; paôu toô, 庖廚, a kitchen. Paôu yéw hwûy jëùk, 庖有肥肉 *paôu woō pwûy ây băh*, in the killing house there is plenty of fat meat; see 孟子 Bēng choó.

Paôu 敲 Paôu hong, 敲風, to hold the wind in sailing.

去 Paōu 皰 To strike with the hand.

Paōu 鉋 A plane, for smoothing boards; paōu to, 鉋刀, a carpenter's plane.

去 Paoùh 皺 A rising of the skin, a pimple· to rise as a blister.

去 Pat 仈 A surname.

Pat 八 Vulg. *păyh:* eight; pat sip, 八十 *păyh chàp*, eighty. E yit hòk pat, hô é ē, ê Chuc tèk Ch'hoé chae, 以一服八何以異於鄒敵楚哉 *t'hó chit ây lué hòk păyh ây, woō sⁿa mëëngh kŏh yëōng kap Choe kok tŏèy tèk Ch'hoé kok chae*, for one to seek the reduction of eight, is not much unlike the Choe country (which is small) opposing the Ch'hoé (a much larger country); see 孟子 Bēng choó.

Pat 捌 To split asunder, to divide; also used as the large form of the preceding character.

Pàt 别 Read pëĕt: another; pëĕt jin, 别人 pàt lâng, another person; pëĕt soō, 别事 pàt soō, another affair.

Pay 䟫 Pay hwān, 䟫飯 pay pooi^ng, to eat rice with two chopsticks, in the Chinese way.

Páy 把 Read pá: to hold, to take hold of, to keep; pá séw, 把手 páy chéw, to guard; pá bûn, 把門 páy mooi^ng, to keep the door; ch'haè pá, 菜把 ch'haè páy, a bundle of vegetables.
Tèk-ch'heng pá séw sam kwan, 狄青把守三關 Tèk-ch'heng páy ch'héw s^na kwan, Tèk-ch'heng kept and guarded the three passes.

Pây 琶 Read pâ: as pê pâ, 琵琶 pê pây, a kind of guitar with three strings.

Pây 爬 Read pâ: to scratch, to rub, to crawl; pâ yāng, 爬癢 pây chëō^ng, to scratch a place that itches; pâ hêng, 爬行 pây kë^nâ, to crawl.

Pây 笆 Read pâ: a bamboo rake, with five teeth, for raking sticks and straws together.

Pây 鈀 Read pâ: a military weapon, like a prong, or fork.

Pây 杷 Read pâ: as pâ put, 杷杋 pây put, a wooden shovel or hoe, used in spreading out grain to dry.
Pê pâ, 枇杷 pê pây, the loquat, a sort of medlar, the Mespilus Japonicus.

Pāy 爸 Read pā: a father; nëō^ng pāy, father.

Pāy 耙 T'hëet pāy, 鐵耙 t'heĕh pāy, an iron rake, a harrow, for leveling the clods in a ploughed field.

Pāy 父 Read hoō: a father; hoō hêy seng gnó, 父兮生我 nëō^ng pāy sai^ng gwá, my father begat me.

Păyh 伯 Read pek: an uncle; pek hoō, 伯父 ü^n păyh, my uncle.

Păyh 叭 P'hwat k'hae k'hoé, 叭開口 păyh k'hwuy ch'hùy, to stretch open the mouth.

Păyh 柏 Sëûng pek, 松柏 ch'hêng păyh, a fir or cedar tree.
Söèy hân, jëên hoē te sëûng pek che hoē teaou yëá, 歲寒然後知松柏之後彫也 neé^ng ta^ng kw^nâ, jëén aōu chae ch'hêng păyh ây tùy aōu teaou lòh, when the season is cold, then we know that the fir tree is late in casting its leaves; see the 論語 Lūn gé.

Păyh 擘 Read pek: to stretch open anything with the hand.

Păyh 百 Read pek: a hundred; pek bān, 百萬 păyh ban, a million.
Sip sip wûy yit pek, 十十爲一百 chàp chàp chò chìt păyh, ten times ten make a hundred.

Păyh 八 Read pat: eight; sip pat, 十八 chàp păyh, eighteen.

Păyh 白 Read pèk: white. Yin jîn sëāng pèk, 殷人尚白 Yin teâou ây lâng sëāng păyh, the people of the Yin dynasty preferred a white color.
Bêng pèk, 明白 bêng păyh, clear, evident.

Păyh 帛 Read pék: silk, cloth; këak pék, 脚帛 *k'ha păyh*, the bandage for binding up womens' feet in China.

Păyh 箔 Read pók: a door blind; a bamboo instrument for catching fish.

Păyh 拔 Read pwăt: to pull up, to bring up; to introduce.
Pwăt k'hé, 拔起 *păyh k'hé*, to pull up.

幸

Pe 悲 Sorrowful, pitying. Choô pe, 慈悲, merciful, compassionate.
Pe ae, 悲哀, to lament, to commiserate. Lé sim pe ché, 女心悲止 *cha boê ây sim kwⁿa pe ché*, the hearts of females are compassionate.

Pe 卑 Low, mean, vulgar; chëang soó po jê chun, 將使卑踰尊 *chëang saê kāy ây lâng k'hăh yëⁿâ chun ây lâng*, to place the mean before the honorable; see 孟子 Bēng choó. Also written 畀 pe.
P'hè jê teng ko, pit choō pe, 譬如登高必自卑 *ch'hin chëōⁿᵍ păyh chëōⁿᵍ kwân, pit choō kāy*, like as in ascending a high place, we must begin from a low one; see the 中庸 Tëung yûng.

Pe 埤 A low damp place; sëûng pek put seng pe, 松柏不生埤 *ch'hêng păyh bô saiⁿᵍ tē kāy tâm ây wûy*, the fir tree does not grow in low marshy ground.

Pe 碑 Vulg. *paê*: a stone tablet, erected to record any meritorious event.
Toē-hëèn hwăt hëung noê, lip pe ké kong, 竇憲伐匈奴立碑紀功 *Toē-hëèn hwăt hëung noê ây hwan, k'hëā chit chëôh paê ké e ây kong lô*, when Toē-hëèn subdued the Huns, they set up a stone tablet to record his merits.

Pe 裨 To make up for, to aid, to assist, to help; to benefit, to give to; to supply a deficiency; to permit.
A surname.

Pe 陂 A pool, an aqueduct, a water gate.
Wûy këung sit, taê sëā, pe tê, é chân haē ê jé bān sèng, 爲宮室臺榭陂池以殘害於爾萬姓 *chô këung ch'hoô, taê sëā, chûy k'hwut á, ê chân haē lé bān păyh saiⁿᵍ*, to be building palaces and houses, terraces and arenas, ponds and aqueducts, to the ruin and injury of all your people; see the 周書 Chew se.

Pe 睥 A field.

𡿨

Pé 彼 That, the opposite of this; he, she, it.
Chaē pé boô oè, chaē ch'hoó boô toè, 在彼無惡在此無斁 *twā tē hê taōu bô wûn, twā tē ché taōu bô paē*, with those there will be no hatred, and with these no ruin; see the 周頌 Chew sëung.

Pé 佊 Awry; corrupt; incorrect.

Pé 比 To compare; pé pèng, 比並, to compare with another.
Pé këen jê chō, 比肩而坐 *pé keng t'haôu jê chēy*, to sit shoulder by shoulder (i. e. together).

Pé 仳 To separate, to take leave, to part asunder.
Yéw lé pé lê, 有女仳離 *woō cha boê pé lê*, having a female from whom we are separated; see the 王風 Ong hong.

Pé 秕 Empty unfruitful ears of corn.

Pé 粃 The same as the above; pé k'hong, 粃糠 *p'hⁿà k'hⁿᵍ*, empty grain and chaff.

Pé 狴 Pé gān, 狴犴, a prison.

Pé 妣 To die, anything dead; a deceased mother is called 妣, pé, and a father 考, k'hó. Pek sèng jê song k'hó pé, 百姓如喪考妣 *pāyh saiⁿᵍ ch'hin chëōⁿᵍ seⁿᵍ pāy boé*, the people felt as though they had lost both father and mother; see 孟子 Bēng choó.

Pé 匕 A spoon, a kind of wooden ladle; pé séw, 匕首, the name of a sword. Sëen choó hong sit, sit pé tē, 先主方食失匕箸 *sëèn choó toō toō á chëāh, p'hăh ka laŏuh sê kop tē á*, when the first prince (of the latter Hàn dynasty) was eating, he let fall his spoon and chopsticks, (on hearing himself extolled;) see the 三國 Sam kok.

Pè 疪 The shade of a house; to screen, to shelter; the same as 庇, pè. Kat lúy yêw lêng pè pún kin, 葛藟猶能疪本根 *kat lúy yëá ēy pè yīm e ây pún kin*, even the hemp and creeping plants can screen their own roots; (how much more ought men!) see the 左傳 Chó twān.

Pè 庇 To screen, to shelter; pó pè, 保庇, to protect.

Pè 芘 To shade, to cover over; the shade of plants and foliage.

Pè 芆 To open out the heads of hemp; pè jeàou, 芆皺, shriveled, shrunk.

Pè 泌 The appearance of a flowing fountain; the flowing of water. Pè che yâng yâng, k'hó é lòk ke, 泌之洋洋可以樂飢 *k'hwⁿà chúy laôu yëōⁿᵍ yëōⁿᵍ, chēw t'hang kōěy è haôu bēy kè tit yaou*, when we see the water flowing thus abundantly, we may be so delighted as to forget our hunger; see the 陳風 Tîn hong.

Pè 秘 Pé bit, 秘密, secret, hidden, mysterious; the same as the following.

Pè 祕 To secrete, to hide; secret, hidden. Gnoé keng pè se, 五經祕書, five volumes of books containing secrets.

Pè 毖 To labor; to be cautious of, to be careful.

Pè 苾 Fragrant; pè hwun haôu ké, 苾芬孝紀 *p'hang p'hang woō haôu ây ké*, how fragrant are the records of filial piety; see the 大雅 Taē gnáy.

Pè 閟 To shut up, to conceal without displaying. Sè jé put chong, gnó soo put pè, 視爾不臧我思不閟 *k'hwⁿà lé ây ūᵐ hó, gwá sëōⁿᵍ ūᵐ k'hèⁿᵍ*, looking at your want of goodness, I do not think of concealing it; see the 衛風 Wōēy hong.

Pè 怭 To treat disrespectfully, to act unmannerly, to despise. Pin kè chùy ché, wuy gê pè pè, 賓既醉止威儀怭怭 *lâng k'hăyh kaôu chùy, wuy gê pè bān*, when the guests become tipsy, manners are disregarded; see the 小雅 Seáou gnáy.

Pè 飶 Savory food; yéw pe kê heang, 有飶其香 *woō chëăh e ây p'hang*, having food that is savory; see the 周頌 Chew sëūng.

Pè 駜 A horse well fed, and fat.

Pè 費 The name of a city in the 魯, Loé country.

Pè 臂 The arm; séw pè, 手臂 *ch'héw pè*, an arm. Taē hong che tëung, yéw jîn hwán pè, bêng wát, t'hëen gê, 大荒之中有人反臂名曰天虞 *twā hong ây tang cng, woō lâng hwán ch'héw pè, mëná kóng t'heeng gê*, in the midst of the great wilderness, there is a set of people with their arms turned round who are called the *t'heeng gê*; see the 山海經 San haé keng.

Pè 畀 To give, to bestow; also written 畁 pè. Pé te chëá choó, hô é pè che? 彼姝者子何以畀之 *e ch'hin ch'hatng ây këná, böëyh t'hó sna meëngh hoë e?* that handsome person, what shall we give him? see the 衛風 Wöëy hong.

Pè 淠 The appearance of a boat moving; to move; the same as 渒, pè.

Pè 痺 A coldness of the extremities; a numbness of the legs, when the circulation of the blood is stopped. Wûy pè, 痿痺, a lame palsy.

Pè 賁 Adorned, ornamented; to come quickly; a surname. Pè jëên laê soo, 賁然來思 *kín kín chëw laê*, he came quickly; see the 小雅 Seáou gnây.

Pè 閉 To shut the door; to stop up, to close. Sëet-léw pè bûn jê put láp, 泄柳閉門而不內 *Sëet-léw kwna moo tng jê ūm sëw*, Sëet-léw shut the door, and would not receive the message; see 孟子 Bēng choó.

Pè 嬖 To favor; one who is favored; a minion, a favorite. Pè jîn yéw Chong-ch'hong chëá choé kwun, 嬖人有臧倉者沮君 *pè sëōh ây lâng woō Chong-ch'hong chëá choé ché jîn kwun*, a minion, one Chong-ch'hong, stopped the prince from coming; see 孟子 Bēng choó.

Pè 賆 To re-bestow; to give away a second time; to increase.

Pè 轡 A bridle, the reins of a horse. Chip pè jê choé, 執轡如組 *gîm pè ch'hin chëong yîn sōh*, he held the bridle like the tassels of a seal; see the 晋書 Chìn se.

Pè 贔 Distressed, miserable.

平

Pê 枇 Pê pây, 枇杷, the loquat fruit; the medlar; Mespilus Japonicus.

Pê 琵 Pê pây, 琵琶, a guitar, with 3 strings, used by the Tartars.

Pê 毗 Adjoining as fields; manifest; thick, substantial, solid; to help, to assist.

Pê 埤 To add to, to increase; abundant, to be attached.

6 Q

Pê 禆 Pê chëàng, 禆將, an adjutant general.

Pê 鼙 A drum beaten on horseback; a cavalry drum; to drum. Lé söèy chip pê, 旅帥執鼙 *lé söèy gîm pê ây koê*, the commander of a troop holds the equestrian drum.

Pê 脾 Pê wūy, 脾胃 *ch'hëuk á*, the stomach; bēng ch'hun che gwàt, chèy sëen pê, 孟春之月祭先脾 *bēng ch'hun ây göëyh, chèy sëen ch'hòng chëāh ây lâng ê pê*, in the first month of spring, sacrifice to the inventors of food, the stomach of an animal; see the 禮月令 Léy gwàt lēng.

Pê 陴 A small parapet, on the top of a fortification; pè bûn teng pê, 閉門登陴 *kwⁿa mootⁿᵍ pâyh chëōⁿᵍ sëⁿâ ch'hëōⁿᵍ*, he closed the gates, and ascended the parapet on the city wall; see the 左傳 Chó twān.

Pê 貔 A ravenous beast; jê hîm jê pê, 如熊如貔 *ch'hin chëōⁿᵍ hîm kap pê*, (the warriors of) 武王, Boó ông were like bears and ravenous beasts; see the 泰誓 T'haè sē.

丟 Pē 陛 The steps of the imperial throne; pē hāy, 陛下, your majesty! used in addressing the emperor. Kim haé löëy naē pē hāy sîn lêng yit t'hong, 今海內賴陛下神靈一統 *tⁿa haê laē e wá pē hāy ây sîn lêng chit t'hóng*, now all within the four seas rely on the spiritual energies of your majesty, and are brought under one head; see the 泰紀 Chîn ké.

Pē 比 To proceed towards, even to; to be attached to a party, equal. Pē kip sam lëên, 比及三年 *pē kip sⁿa neêⁿᵍ*, even to the period of three years; see the 論語 Lūn gé. Kwun choó chew jê put pē, 君子周而不比 *kwun choó chew pëên, jê bô pē pëên tē chit tóng*, the good man is public spirited, and not attached to the interests of a party; see the 論語 Lūn gé.

Pē 紕 To weave, to weave across; soè se pē che, 素絲紕之 *pâyh swⁿâ chit köëy laê chit köëy k'hè*, to cross it in weaving with white threads; see the 鄘風 Yûng hong.

Pē 俾 To stretch open the legs in walking.

Pē 婢 Lé pē, 奴婢 *cha boê kán*, a female slave; noê pē, 奴婢 *gín á*, male and female slaves.

Pē 庳 Yéw pē, 有庳, the name of a country, spoken of in 孟子 Bēng choó.

Pē 埤 A piece of land, containing a hundred Chinese acres.

Pē 俾 To send, to employ; to let; to follow. Pē ê chëûng yëùk, 俾予從欲 *hoē gwá t'hàn séy aē*, to let me follow my desires; see the 禹謨 E boē.

Pē 糒 Dry provisions; hèw pē, 糗糒, dried rice, for a journey.

Pē 備 To prepare; pē pān, 備辦, to get ready; chún pē, 準備 *tëōⁿᵍ té*, to be provided against. Also written 俻, pē.

福建方言字典

Boô kēw pē ê yit jîn, 無求備於一人 *bŏh kēw chedou pē tē chit lâng*, do not expect everything complete in one man; see the 論語 Lūn gé.

Pē 敝 To tear (clothes); to wear out; torn clothes; spoiled things.
Pē che jê boô hām, 敝之而無憾 *pē p'hwà jé bŏ hām hwŭn*, when one's things are spoiled, not to be vexed; see the 論語 Lūn gé.

Pē 幣 Cloth; pē pék, 幣帛, cloth and silk, usually sent in presents.
T'hong soó jîn, é pē p'hèng che, 湯使人以幣聘之 *T'hong saé lâng t'hó pē pek p'hèng c*, T'hong sent messengers to engage his services with presents of cloth; see 孟子 Bēng choó.

Pē 獘 Distressed, reduced to extremity; brought into straits.
T'haē kê pē jê kek che, 待其獘而擊之 *tĕng t'haē e ây pē k'hwŭn, jê p'hăh e*, wait till they are reduced to extremity, and then attack them; see the 史記 Soó kè.

Pē 斃 To die, to depart this life.
Goê tek chèng jê pē yëen, soo ó è, 吾得正而斃焉斯已矣 *gwá tit tĕŏh chë^n à tō jê sé, chêy chĕw swăh è*, "if I can obtain the right way and then die, that will be enough;" said by 曾子 Cheng choó.

Pē 弊 Ruined, bad, corrupt, vicious.

Pē 避 To avoid; pē hō, 避禍, to avoid evil. Also written 辟, pē.
Ch'hë^n á jê, é kê chëûng pē jîn che soō yëá, k'hé jëák chëûng pē sè che soō chae? 且而以其從避人之士也豈若從避世之士哉 *ch'hë^n á lé, kap e ây t'hàn pē lâng ây t'hàk ch'hăyh lâng, k'hé woō ch'hìn chëo^ng t'hàn pē sè ây t'hàk ch'hăyh lâng chae?* and for you, rather than follow a scholar who avoids a few people, would it not be better to follow a scholar who is retired from the world? (said by a retired philosopher to 子路, Choó loé, who followed Confucius in his wanderings from one state to another;) see the 論語 Lūn gé.

Pē 薜 Pē lēy, 薜荔, a kind of fragrant grass; celery, parsley.

Pē 被 To cover; pē tan, 被單 *p'höēy tw^na*, a coverlid, a bedquilt.
To reach to, to bear, to endure; the sign of the passive voice.

Pē 髲 An ornament for the head; a covering for [illegible]; a headdress.

Pē 濞 [illegible] coun[illegible] roaring a[illegible].

Pē 奰 To [illegible] kok, t'hâm kip k[illegible] ho[illegible] 於中國覃及鬼方 *laē bīn noē tē tëung kok, kip kadu kw'y hc^ng*, at home his anger overspreads the middle country (China); and extends even to the devil's regions (foreign parts); see the 商頌 Seang seúng.

Pē 贔 Pē hoō, 贔屓, using great energy and strength; angry.

Pē 痺 Sore legs; a weakness of the legs.

卑 Pë^n a 兵 Read peng: a soldier; a weapon of war.

声 Pë^n á 丙 Read péng: one of the horary characters.

Pĕ^n^á 餅 Read péng: a cake; sit péng, 食餅 chĕăh pĕ^n^á, to eat cakes.

去 Pĕ^n^à 併 Read pèng: to join, to inclose, to unite; sëang pèng, 相併 sëo pĕ^n^à, to push one another's shoulders. The same as 并, pĕng.

Këem pèng pat hong, lông kwat soò haé, 兼併八荒囊括四海 këem pĕ^n^à păyh heng, lông kwat sè haé, to unite together the eight deserts, and to inclose all within the four seas.

平 Pë^n^â 抄 Read ch'haou: to copy; ch'haou joō, 抄字 pë^n^â jē, to transcribe.

入 Pëăh 壁 Read p'hek: a wall; ok p'hek, 屋壁 ch'hoò pëăh, a partition wall; ... hek p'hek, 隔壁 kăyh pëăh, a next door neighbour.

When 秦始皇, Chîn-só hông, the first emperor of the Chin dynasty burnt the books, the ancestor of 孔安國, K'hông-an-kok, (chông kê kay se ê ok p'hek, 藏其家書於屋壁 k'hè^ng^ e ây kay laē ây ch'hăyh tē ch'hoò pëăh,) secreted the books of his family in a wall of the house; see the 尙書序 Sëang se sē.

入 Pëăk 擢 The sound of hitting anything in archery.

去 Pëàng 乒 Pìn pëàng, 乒乓, to stamp with the foot in walking

去 Pëàng 踭 To stamp with the foot.

上 Peaou 臕 Che peaou, 脂臕, very fat, corpulent.

Peaou 嘌 The peak of a hill; ch'haé yëak Lêng san peaou, 採藥靈山嘌 ch'haé yŏh tē Lêng swⁿa ây peaou, to pluck medical plants from the highest peak of the Lêng hill.

Peaou 標 The end of a tree, the utmost extremity of a plant; a flag; a signal; to elevate, to display on the outside; to write down, to record.

Taē pún seáou peaou, 大本小標 twā pún sèy peaou, a great root having a small extremity.

Bêng peaou ê kê ké, 名標於奇紀 mê^n^â peaou tē kê ây kè, to have one's name recorded in strange annals.

上 Peáou 表 The outside; clear, clearly displayed; a man's conduct excelling that of his fellows is called 表表, peáou peáou; also when an inferior addresses a superior it is called peáou; also peáou ch'hin, 表親, a relative by consanguinity; seng peáou, 旌表, a flag, a signal.

Peáou lé cheng ch'hoe, 表裏精粗 gwā laē cheng ch'hoe, the external and internal, with the fine and coarse parts of things.

Peáou chëang, 表章, a memorial presented to a superior. Peáou heng tëy, 表兄弟 peáou hĕ^n^a tē, a cousin by marriage.

Peáou 婊 Yew peáou, 優婊, a woman of pleasure, a prostitute.

Peáou 裱 Peáou pöey, 裱褙, a neck kerchief used by females.

Peáou 殍 Starved with hunger; toê yéw gō peáou, 塗有餓殍 loē woō lâng gō sé, in the roads are people starved to death; see 孟子 Bēng choó.

Peáou 莩 The same as the preceding.

Peáou 摽 To fall, as fruit or leaves from the trees. Also written 擲, peáou. Peáou yéw böêy, kê sit ch'hit hêy, 摽有梅其實七兮 *peáou lók woō hâm á e ây kwûy ché ch'hit lëëp*, the plums are fallen, and of the fruit only six are remaining; see the 召南 Seàou lâm.

Peáou 嘌 The peak of a hill.

去
Peàou 俵 Peàou sàn, 俵散, dispersed, scattered, to distribute.

Peàou 裱 A female neckerchief, a gorget; some say the cuff of a sleeve.

Peàou 䙳 To distribute pieces of cloth among the soldiers.

入
Pečh 擎 Read p'hëet: to divide, to strike, to pull up; p'hëet séw sëw, 擎手袖 *pcĕh ch'héw wuī^ng*, to pull up one's sleeve.

Pečh 鱉 Read pit: a kind of tortoise; a land tortoise. Lók kê yéw bô lók gê 謹爾 *pëen pëen ây kóng wā, tók tók tëŏh kín sīn*, in discoursing argumentatively, we should be cautious; see the 論語 Lūn gé.

Pëen 編 Kán pëen, 簡編 *kán pee^ng*, a book, a page or section of a book; also, to arrange. K'hóng choó t'hók ék, wûy pëen sam chwát, 孔子讀易韋編三絶 *K'hóng choó t'hàk yëăh keng, p'höēy tèng tē ch'hăyh s^na hāy tooi^ng*, when Confucius studied the book of diagrams, the leather binding of the volume burst thrice asunder; (implying that he studied the book very closely.)

Pëen 鞭 A whip; má pëen, 馬鞭 *báy pee^ng*, a horsewhip. Confucius said, "if riches and honors may be sought after, (suy chip pëen cho soō, goê ẽ wûy che, 雖執鞭之士吾亦爲之 *suy gīm báy pee^ng ây soō, goá yá chò e*,) although it be the office of a whipper-in, I will still engage in it; see the 上論 Sëāng lūn.

Pëen 邊 Vulg. *pee^ng*: the side, the edge, the border; pông pëen, 旁邊 *pông pee^ng*, on one side; sëém pëen, 閃邊 *sëēm pee^ng*, to get on one side, to avoid: Kê chaē pëen yip, 其在邊邑 *e twā tē pee^ng á ây yip*, he dwells in a city on the borders; see the [illegible] of providing sacrificial vessels, there are the proper officers ready; see the 論語 Lūn gé.

Pëen 㥦 The body not upright.

去
Pëén 扁 The leaves of doors opposite one another; vulg. *peéⁿᵍ:* flat, as a dollar, not round as a ball; oblong, oval.

Sam-hân seng jê, yëúk kê t'hoê pëén, ap che é sék, 三韓生兒欲其頭扁壓之以石 *Sam-hân saiⁿᵍ këⁿá, aè e ây t'haôu peéⁿᵍ, chëw t'hô chëŏh ap*, the people of Sam-hân, when they get children, wish to make their heads flat, and therefore press them between stones; see the 東夷傳 Tong ê twān, 'the record of the eastern foreigners.'

P… 匾 Vulg. *peéⁿᵍ:* flat, not round, thin as a wafer, or a shilling.

P'ee… 褊 A small garment; small, narrow; also, urgent.

Chêy kok suy pëén seáou, 齊國雖褊小 *Chéy koh suy sē pëén sèy*, although the Ch… country is small and narrow, &c.; see …子 B…ng choó.

Pëén 蝙 Pëén hok, 蝙蝠 *bit pŏ*, a bat; some say, an animal as white as silver.

Hông hwun tò sē, pëén hok hwuy, 黃昏到寺蝙蝠飛 *maiⁿᵍ hwuiⁿᵍ kaôu eēⁿᵍ bit pŏ tit pwuy*, arriving at the temple about eventide, we see the bats flying about; see the 韓愈詩 Hân jé se.

Pëén 騗 To jump upon a horse; also read p'hëèn: to deceive.

Pëén 稨 A kind of pulse, that grows on bamboo railings.

Pëén 藊 Pëén toē, 藊豆, the name of a sort of pulse, used medicinally.

Pëén 貶 To blame, to censure, to detract from, to deteriorate.

Ch'hun Ch'hew wûy é yit joō wûy po pëén, 春秋惟以一字爲襃貶 *Ch'hun Ch'hew tòk tòk ê chit jē chò o ló kap pëén tek*, the Spring and Autumn Record (Confucius' history of his own times,) conveys either praise or blame to people, in only one single word.

Pëén 砭 To puncture the flesh for medical purposes, by a needle passing through a stone.

去
Pëèn 徧 Chew pëèn, 周徧, to pervade every place; all over; universal.

Kwûn lêy pek sèng, pëèn wûy jé tek, 群黎百姓徧爲爾德 *chëⁿá tîn ây oe t'haôu pāyh saiⁿᵍ, chò poô sē lé ây tek*, the multitude of black-haired people everywhere partake of your virtue; see the 小雅 Seáou gnáy. Also written 遍, pëèn.

Pëèn 窆 To let down a coffin into the tomb.

Pëèn 變 Vulg. *peèⁿᵍ:* to change, to alter, to convert; pëèn hwà, 變化, to transform; kaè pëèn, 改變 *káy peèⁿᵍ*, to alter.

Kwun choó yéw sam pëèn, 君子有三變 *kwun choó woō sⁿa ây pëèn*, the good man has three changes; see the 論語 Lūn gé.

Pëèn sek, 變色 *peèⁿᵍ sek*, to change countenance.

平

Pëên 胼 To indurate, to grow hard; pëên tê, 胼胝, an induration of the skin of the hand, occasioned by hard labor.

K'hóng choó wát, yéw jîn ê séw chëuk pëên tê, ê yáng kê ch'hin, 孔子曰有人於手足胼胝以養其親 *K'hóng choó kóng, woō lâng tē ch'héw k'ha pëên tê, ê ch'hē e ây pāy boē,* Confucius said, "here is a man the skin of whose hands and feet is hardened by providing for his parents."

Pëên 駢 Connected, joined; Chìn kong choó, Tëûng-jé, yéw pëên kê hëép, 晉公子重耳有駢其脅 *Chìn ây kong choó, Tëûng-jé, woō sëo swâ e ây hëép kwut,* the prince of the Chìn country, Tëûng-jé, had his ribs connected and joined together. Also written 骿, pëên.

Pëên 緶 To hem a garment; the hem of a garment.

Pëên 平 To argue, and regulate. Also read pêng: even.

去

Pëên 便 Obedient, advantageous, ready, suitable; hong pëēn, 方便, convenient, charity, alms; pëēn gê, 便宜, *pān gé*, cheap, advantageous; sûy pëēn, 隨便, anyhow, no matter how, as it suits convenience; taē pëēn, 大便, to go stool; seáou pëēn, 小便, to void urine.

Jé séy wûy pëēn chëá, put pëēn che pëēn yëá; séy wûy jîn gē chëá, taē pëēn che pëēn yëá, 汝所謂便者不便之便也所謂仁義者大便之便也 *lé séy kóng hong pëēn chëá, sē ūm pëēn ây pëēn; séy kóng jîn gē chëá, sē twā pëēn ây pëēn,* "that which you call convenient, is an incovenient convenience; but that which is called benevolence and righteousness is a very convenient sort of convenience;" said by 荀子 Sûn choó. Also written 㑢, pëēn.

Pëēn 卞 The name of a place; also, a surname.

Pëēn 汴 The name of a river. Also written 汳, pëēn.

Pëēn 忭 Pleased, delighted.

Pëēn 釆 To divide, to distinguish, to tear asunder as with claws.

This character is to be distinguished from 采 ch'haé, to pluck.

Pëēn 辧 To divide, to separate.

Pëēn 辦 To exert one's strength.

Hāng-lëâng sëâng wûy choó pëēn, 項梁常爲主辦 *Hāng-lëâng sëâng wûy e ây choó kong tè làt,* Hāng-lëâng constantly exerted his strength for his lord; see the 史記 Soó kè.

Pëēn 辯 To distinguish; pëēn lūn, 辯論, to discuss, to argue; to discriminate clearly, to divide.

Bêng pëēn che, tok hêng che, 明辯之篤行之 *bêng bêng pëēn lūn e, tok sit k'hè kēⁿ â e,* clearly discuss it, and sedulously practice it; see the 中庸 Tëung yûng.

Pëēn 辨 Vulg. *pān*: the same as the above; to distinguish, to judge of.

Pëĕn 骿 The flesh between the thighs.

Pëĕn 辮 Mixed threads in weaving. Vulg. *peĕ^{ng}:* to plait, to twist, to twine.

Pëĕn 瓣 Vulg. *păn:* a section in a melon or orange; kam pëĕng, 柑瓣, *kam păn,* a section or division in an orange.

Pëĕn 緶 To twist hemp; to hem a garment.

卒 *Pee^{ng}* 邊 Read pëen: the side; *pee^{ng} á,* on one side; pông pëen che jîn, 旁邊之人 *pee^{ng} á ây lâng,* a by-stander.

声 *Peé^{ng}* 扁 Read pëén: flat, thin, oval, oblong, not round.

去 *Peè^{ng}* 變 Read pëèn: to change, to alter; kaé pëèn, 改變 *káy peè^{ng},* to alter, to convert.

Chêy yit pëèn chè ê Loé, Loé yit pëèn chè ê tō, 齊一變至於魯魯一變至於道 *Chêy kok chit ây peè^{ng} chè kaðu Loé, Loé kok chit ây peè^{ng} chè kaðu tō,* if the Chêy country should take a turn for the better, it would equal the Loé country, and if the Loé country should take a turn, it would attain to virtue; see the 上論 Sëāng lūn.

丢 *Peē^{ng}* 辮 Read pëen: to twist, to plait; pëen t'hoê chong bê, 辮頭鬃尾 *peē^{ng} t'haðu chang böêy,* to plait a tail of hair.

天 *Peĕ^{ng}h* 要 Read yaðu: to want; put yaðu, 不要 *ŭ^{m} peĕ^{ng}h,* not to want, to refuse. In some districts this is vulgarly pronounced *ŭ^{m} teĕ^{ng}h.*

夫 Pëet 別 To distinguish, to divide, to separate, to set apart. A surname.

Hwun pëet, 分別, to distinguish, to make a difference.

P'hè choo ch'hó bók, k'he é pëet è, 譬諸艸木區以別矣 *ch'hin chëō^{ng} ch'háou bàk, k'he ê hwun pëet,* like grass and trees, which may be divided, in order to be distinguished; see the 語論 Lūn gé.

Pëet 鼈 Vulg. *peĕh:* a tortoise, a terrapin.

Gwân gô kaou lëûng, gê pëet seng yëen, 黿鼉蛟龍魚鼈生焉 *gwân gô kaou lëûng, hê kap peĕh toe sai^{ng},* the large tortoises, leviathans and dragons, with the fishes and turtles would grow and flourish; see the 中庸 Tëung yûng.

Pëet 瞥 To pass before the eyes; just seen, suddenly observed.

Gnoé këĕn pëet hwan, 偶見瞥覩 *gnoé jëĕn h'hw^{n}à pëet jëĕn keè^{ng},* to look suddenly and see casually. Also written 覕, pëet.

天 Pëet 襒 Pëet sëak, 襒𧝎, elegant apparel, fine clothes.

Pëet 別 Vulg. *pàt:* different, another; to divide from, to separate from, to part, to take leave; pëet jîn, 別人 *pàt lâng,* another man.

夫 Pek 伯 A superior, an elder. Vulg. *ŭ^{n} păyh:* an uncle.

Pek sē, 伯氏, is used for an elder brother; and tëūng sē, 仲氏, for a younger. Taē pek kong, 大伯公 *twā păyh kong,* great uncle! the designation of an idol commonly worshiped by the Chinese; he is represented as a lusty old man, and is supposed to preside over the district where he is worshiped.

Pek 佰 A centurion; a hundred men.

Pek 百 Vulg. *păyh:* a hundred; pek ch'hëen, 百千 *păyh ch'heng*, a hundred thousand. Sē ch'hëep soè pek jîn, 待妾數百人 *téng haōu ây sèy ê kwóy păyh lâng*, attending concubines amounting to several hundreds; see 孟子 Bēng choó.

Pek 栢 The fir tree; sëûng pek, 松栢 *ch'hêng păyh*, a fir tree. A surname.

Pek 偪 To urge, to distress, to straiten. Kwun choó put ch'hëèm sëâng, put pek hāy, 君子不僭上不偪下 *kwun choó bô ch'hëèm sè twā, bô pek sè sèy*, the good man does not usurp from his superiors, nor distress his inferiors.

Pek 逼 To straiten; to drive; kip pek, 急逼, to hasten, to urge.

Pek 愊 To be extremely sincere.

Pek 煏 To roast anything at the fire; pek key, 煏鷄, a grilled fowl.

Pek 稫 To roast and dry at the fire; pek jëûk, 稫肉 *pek băh*, roasted meat.

Pek 檗 A kind of yellow wood, the bark of which is used in dyeing.

Pek 擘 Vulg. *păyh:* to pull open, to part asunder with the hand. Kè-lêng pek t'haè hwa, 巨靈擘太華 *Kè-lêng păyh k'hwuy t'haè hwa ây swⁿa*, a genius of the name of Kè-lêng, ('great soul') parted asunder the great flowery mountain.

Pek 迫 To urge, to straiten, to trouble; pek pek, 迫逼, to urge extremely. Gōëy pek kong soō, 外迫公事 *gwā bīn pek kong ây soō*, abroad to be hurried with public affairs. Pek soo k'hó é këèn è, 迫斯可以見矣 *kaòu pek ch'heet, soo t'hang hoē e keèⁿᵍ*, when urged extremely, we may grant an interview; see 孟子 Bēng choó.

Pek 壁 Vulg. *pëăh:* a wall; ok pek, 屋壁 *ch'hoò pëăh*, the wall of a house; a fortification. Tèy sîn tê jip Hân-sìn Tëang-jé pek, twât che kwun, 帝晨馳入韓信張耳壁奪之軍 *tèy chá k'hê sè té jip Hân-sìn Tëoⁿᵍ-jé ây pëăh, ch'hëóⁿᵍ e ây kwun sè*, the emperor early in the morning galloped within the encampment of Hân-sìn and Tëoⁿᵍ-jé, and deprived them of the command of the army; see the 高祖紀 Ko choé ké.

Pék 白 (下入) Vulg. *păyh.* white, pure, clean; a surname; kò pék, 告白, to inform, to announce. Pék maôu sûn sok, 白茅純束 *păyh hûᵐ á, chëⁿá pák*, long white grass tied up in bundles; see the 召南 Seàou lâm. Bêng pék, 明白 *bêng păyh*, to understand, clear, intelligible.

Pék 帛 Silk, cloth; chaê pék, 財帛, riches, wealth. Taē pék che kwan, 大帛之冠 *twā poè ây kin*, a cap made of a broad piece of cloth. Pē pék, 幣帛, presents of cloth.

6 E

Pék 舶 A great vessel used at sea.

夆
Peng 冰 Ice, congealed water; also written 氷, peng, and anciently 仌, peng.
Ch'hòk peng ch'hëung ch'hëung, 鑿冰冲冲 *ch'hàk se^ng ây së^n a ch'hëung ch'hëung*, the chiseling of the ice in winter sounds like *ch'hëung ch'hëung*.

Peng 冫 The same as the above; also one of the radicals.

Peng 伻 To order, to send; hasty; to follow.

Peng 兵 A weapon of war, a person who uses such a weapon, a soldier.
K'hè kap ē peng jê choé, 棄甲曳兵而走 *t'hek kak chëèn kăh, t'hwa hwa peng to jê chaóu*, to throw away one's armor, reverse one's weapons, and flee; see 孟子 Bēng choó.
Anciently written 倿, peng.

Peng 崩 Vulg. *pang:* to fall down, to be precipitated, as a part of a hill from its summit; also used to denote the demise of an emperor.
San t'hëúng ch'hùy peng, 山冢崒崩 *sw^na t'hëúng ch'hùy pang*, the hills and peaks were precipitated and fell; see the 小雅 Seáou gnáy.

Peng 絣 The name of a kind of cloth.

Peng 帲 A curtain of a tent.

Peng 栟 Peng lê, 栟櫚, a species of palm tree.

Peng 傍 Peng peng, 傍傍, unavoidable; see the 小雅 Seáou gnáy.

Peng 祊 An offering to former ancestors, at the side of the temple gate.

耈
Péng 炳 Clearly illustrated, well displayed; bright, luminous.

Péng 丙 Vulg. *pë^n á:* one of the ten horary characters.

Péng 眪 To look at, to observe; bòk péng pék, 目眪白 *bàk chew pêng pāyh*, the eyes clear.

Péng 併 Together with, at the same time; péng k'hé, 併起, to arise together.

Péng 屏 To screen, to shelter; also, to do away with, to lay aside.
Taē pang wûy péng, 大邦維屏 *twā pang kok chò péng*, great nations screen and shelter us; see the 大雅 Taē gnáy.
Gnó naé péng p'hek é kwuy, 我乃屏璧與珪 *gwá naé péng p'hek kap kwuy*, I laid aside all gems and jewels.

Péng 庰 To screen, a screen put in a doorway.

Péng 倂 To do away with, to set aside, to keep out of the way, to remove.
Këung k'hëëm cheá, péng gnoé peng yëá, 恭儉者倂五兵也 *këung kèng kap sai^ng k'hëëm, ēy péng k'hè goē hāng ây peng to*, "respect and economy will do away with the five kinds of weapons;" said by 荀子 Sûn choó.

Péng 屏 The common form of 屛, péng.

Péng 迸 To flee away, to disperse; to drive away.
Péng choo soò ê, put é tông tëung kok, 迸諸四夷不與同中國 *péng kaòu soò ê, ū^{m} hoē e kap lân tëung kok sëo tâng*, drive (the vicious) away among the foreigners, and let them not be associated with us in the middle country (China); see the 大學 Taē hâk.

Péng 𩴾 The lofty appearance of a hill.

Péng 餅 Vulg. *pē^{n}á:* a cake.
Sok-sek, 束皙, made a péng hoō, 餅賦, cake ode.

Péng 秉 To grasp in the hand, to hold; bòk péng, 木秉, the stem of a tree.

Péng 鞞 The sheath of a sword; the upper part is called 鞞, péng, and the lower part of a sheath is called 琫, páng.

去

Pèng 並 Together with, united, all together, equal to.
Koè ké suy choō hé sim ch'hek yêw bē pèng, 顧已雖自許心迹猶未幷 *koè lân ka tē-suy choō hé, sim chëăh yëá böëy hàp*, "in glancing at ourselves, we may find matter for applause, but our heart's core will not be in unison with it; said by 謝靈運 Sëà-lêng-wūn.

Pèng 併 The same as the above; to engross, to unite the whole.

Pèng 邴 A surname.

Pèng 柄 Vulg. *pai^{ng}:* a handle; to pèng, 刀柄, *to pai^{ng}*, the handle of a knife; kwân pèng, 權柄, the handle of power, authority.
Choō chip kwân pèng, 自執權柄 *ka tē gîm kwân pèng*, to seize the helm of affairs with one's own hand.

Pèng 窆 To let down a coffin into the grave.

Pèng 恲 To make inquiry.

平

Pêng 朋 Pêng yéw, 朋友, a friend; h^{n}ò pêng, 好朋 *hó péng*, a good friend.
E pêng yéw kaou, jê put sìn hoē? 與朋友交而不信乎 *kap pêng yëw kaou p'höèy jê ū^{m} sìn sit hoē?* in associating with my friends, am I insincere? see the 論語 Lūn gé.

Pêng 倗 To assist, to help; to assist those of like mind. A surname.

Pêng 傰 A surname. In the Hàn dynasty there were a number of thieves, who bore this surname.

Pêng 棚 Vulg. *pai^{ng}:* a stage, a platform, a scaffolding; pêng chān, 棚棧, a military road, across mountainous parts.

Pêng 枰 A chess-board; p'hok ék séy chè, put kò yit pêng che sëāng, 博奕所志不過一平之上 *pwăh keáou séy chè, put kò twā tē chit ây kē pw^{n}â ây têng bīn*, the mind of a gamester is set on nothing else but the chess-board.

Pêng 平 Vulg. *pat^ng*: even, plain, level, just, peaceful, to be at peace; to regulate, to pacify; pêng chèng, 平正 *pat^ng chë^nà*, just and equal; kin peng, 均平 *kin pat^ng*, even, level; t'hëen hāy t'haè pêng, 天下太平 *t'hee^ng āy t'haè pat^ng*, the whole world at peace. A surname.
Sông jîn kip Ch'hoé jîn pêng, 宋人及楚人平 *Sông āy lâng kap Ch'hoé āy lâng pat^ng*, the people of Sông were at peace with the men Ch'hoé; see the 春秋 Ch'hun ch'hew.

Pêng 胼 Peng chëet, 胼胝, the fat of oxen or sheep, suet.

Pêng 馮 According to; as; to cross a river on foot. Vulg. *pâng*: a surname.
Pō hoé pêng hô, 暴虎馮河 *lëăh hoé pâng hô*, to seize a tiger, and dart through a river with him; see the 論語 Lūn gé.

去 Pēng 病 Vulg. *pai^ng*: sick, very sick; disease; to feel sick, to be weary of; to be sick of, to be distressed with; yéw pēng 有病 *woō pai^ng*, to be sick.
Pēng put tek kê chëùng yëá, 病不得其衆也 *hoân lô bēy tit tëŏh chëùng lâng*, to be distressed at not being able to get the hearts of the multitude; see the 禮樂記 Léy gák kè.

Pēng 竝 To compare with, to be associated with; together, at the same time; also, moreover; pēng lék, 竝力, united strength; pēng kāy jê hêng, 竝駕而行 *pēng ch'hëa jê kë^nâ*, to ride out together.

Pēng 並 The same as the preceding; also, moreover.

Pēng 傡 All, altogether; arranged in a row.

Pēng 偋 Out of the way, on one side, removed to a distance.

Pēng 庰 A solitary place, a lonely spot; a privy.

上 *Pē^ng* 榜 Read pông: a wooden board; pông sè, 榜示 *pē^ng sē*, a proclamation; ch'hut póng, 出榜 *ch'hut pē^ng*, to issue a proclamation.

去 *Pē^ng* 傍 Read pōng: to approach near, to stand by, to rely on.
Sêng ông che seng, jîn chëá yáng che, haòu chëá këâng che, soò sèng pōng che, 成王之生仁者養之孝者强之四聖傍之 *Sêng ông āy sai^ng, jîn āy lâng ch'hē e, haòu āy lâng këâng bêng e, sè āy sèng jîn pē^ng e*, when Sêng ông was born, benevolent people brought him up, filial people strengthened him, and four sages stood by him.
Also vulg. *pē^ng*: the side, on one side; a surname.

平 *Pëo* 標 Read p'heaou: a prize, a goal; ch'hëáng p'heaou, 搶標 *ch'hëó^ng pëo*, to struggle for the prize, as is done in boatracing, &c.
Lëûng chew twăt kím p'heaou 龍舟奪錦標 *lëûng chûn ch'hëó^ng kím āy pëo*, the dragon boat seizes the embroidered prize.

Pëo 臕 Read peaou: fat; che peaou, 脂臕 *che pëo*, a fat appearance.
Má peaou, 馬臕 *báy pëo*, a horse in good condition, fat.

上 *Pëó* 表 Read peáou: a memorial; peáou chëang, 表章 *pëó chëang*, a public document; chìn peáou, 進表 *chìn pëó*, to present a memorial to government.

卒
Pëung 餘 Pëung ch'hâm, 餘饞, to be gluttonous; to be greedy of food.

Pew 彪 The stripes on a tiger; a young tiger; yit pew jîn má, 一彪人馬 *chit pew lâng báy*, a troop of men and horses.

Pew 滮 The appearance of flowing water.

Pew 髟 The hair long, and hanging down. Also, one of the radicals.

Pey 篦 Tëuk pey, 竹篦 *tek pey*, a bamboo comb; a ferula; a flat piece of wood for slapping the hands.

Pey 鎞 A knife like the barb of an arrow; pey ch'hók, 鎞鑿 *pey ch'hàk*, a broad chisel.

去
Pèy 蔽 To screen, to hide, to cover over; to overspread.
Se sam pek, yit gân é pèy che, wát soo boô sëâ, 詩三百一言以蔽之曰思無邪 *se woō sⁿa păyh, chit koō wā ê pèy e, kóng sëōⁿᵍ bô lâm sám*, the odes are three hundred, and one sentence is sufficient to comprise them all, namely, "thought not licentious;" see the 上論 Sëāng lūn.

平
P'ha 葩 A flower; the bud of a flower; a flower in bloom.
Pek hwa t'hoè p'ha, 百花吐葩 *chëⁿà păyh hwa t'hoè p'ha*, all the flowers will put forth their buds.

P'ha 吧 A bragging, blustering appearance.

P'ha 瞟 P'ha bók, 瞟目 *p'ha bàk*, weak, sore eyes.

上
P'há 䦉 Short, dwarfish.

去
P'hà 怕 To fear, to be afraid, to be terrified at; put p'hà, 不怕 *ūᵐ saé kēⁿa*, don't be afraid; k'hëúng p'hà, 恐怕, to be alarmed.

P'hà 帕 A veil, a covering for the head; t'hoê p'hà, 頭帕 *t'haôu p'hày*, a veil. E kím tëên koé, é hông p'hà sew, 以錦纏股以紅帕首 *t'hó kím teeⁿᵍ tê k'ha, t'hó âng p'hày t'haôu*, take embroidered work to wind round the legs, and cover the head with a red veil; see the 韓愈詩 Hân jé se.

P'hà 帊 Superfluous silk; three pieces of silk are called 帊, p'hà.

去
P'hā 皻 A rising of the skin; the skin broken.

去
P'hⁿà 粃 Read pé: hollow, empty grain.

P'hⁿà 冇 Anything hollow, and vain; good for nothing.

平
P'hae 巃 The noise of a mountain falling.

上
P'haé 擘 To divide, to open out.

6 F

去

P'haè 𠂢 Water flowing in different channels. The same as the following.

P'haè 派 Various channels of water; che p'haè 支派, a tribe, posterity.

Pek ch'hwan p'haè pëet, kwuy haé jê hōèy, 百川派别歸海而會 *chëⁿá pǎyh ch'hwuiⁿᵍ p'haè pëet, kwuy kaòu haé, chēw chò hōèy,* the hundred streams are divided into channels, but when they revert to the sea, they all meet together; see the 左思賦 Chó soo hoō.

P'haè 霈 The appearance of rain; the flowing of water.

P'haè 沛 The name of a river; weeds growing in the water; suddenly; tëen p'haè, 顛沛, ruined, in distress, overwhelmed with calamity.

P'haè jëên hây é, 沛然下雨 *p'haè jëên lōh hoē,* suddenly the rain descends; see 孟子 Bēng choó. Also written 㳈, p'haè.

P'haè 肺 Luxuriant foliage; superabundant vegetation.

Tong bûn che yâng, kê yëep p'haè p'haè, 東門之楊其葉肺肺 *tang mooiⁿᵍ ây yëōⁿᵍ ch'hēw, e ây hëōh p'haè p'haè,* the willow tree, at the eastern port, exhibits an abundant foliage; see the 陳風 Tîn hong.

P'haè 湃 Pông p'haè, 滂湃, the noise of rippling, rushing water.

去

P'haⁿé 歹 Read taé: wicked, vicious, bad; put te hⁿó taé, 不知好歹 *ūᵐ chae hó p'haⁿé,* not knowing good from bad.

入

P'hǎh 打 Read tⁿá: to beat, to strike, to thump, to invade.

E wá sék kek tⁿá kong bûn, 以瓦石擊打公門 *t'hó hëā chëōh kek p'hǎh kong mooiⁿᵍ,* they took tiles and stones and beat at the public gate; see the 張爨傳 Tëang ê twān.

平

P'haiⁿᵍ 摒 *P'haiⁿᵍ tê,* 摒除, to deduct, to take off.

去

P'haìⁿᵍ 柄 Read pèng: a handle of anything; a numeral.

Hân-hwuy choó, 韓非子 made (jē pèng p'hëen, 二柄篇 *nō p'haìⁿᵍ p'heeⁿᵍ,*) two sections of literary composition.

平

P'haîⁿᵍ 彭 Read p'hêng: a surname.

P'haîⁿᵍ 抨 Read pêng: to fillip with the fingers.

Kê è put lòk, tân pêng soō, 其意不樂彈抨事 *e ây è ūᵐ t'hëúng lòk, chēw tⁿoâ p'haîⁿᵍ ây soō,* when his mind was not pleased, he turned to filliping and fingering (the harp and guitar.)

入

P'hak 仆 Anything turned upside down.

Hin p'hok sit këang, 興仆植僵 *hin k'hé p'hak tó, chae sit yëên këang,* to elevate those who are overturned, and to raise up those who are fallen.

P'hak 覆 Read hok: prostrate; sin hok, 身覆 *sin p'hak,* to lie prostrate, with the face to the ground.

入

P'hàk 曝 Read p'hók: to dry in the sun; p'hók jit ak é, 曝日沃雨 *p'hàk jit ak hoē,* to be burnt by the sun, and drenched in the rain.

卆
P'han **扳** To lead, to draw, to pull; to handle; p'han wān, 扳援, to deliver, to assist.

Ch'heng yîn tek loē, séw p'han kwuy, 青雲得路手扳桂 *ch'hai^ng hwûn tit těŏh e ây loē, ch'héw chēw p'han kwùy*, when we make our way to the azure clouds, (i. e. attain to literary honors,) our hands may handle the cassia; see a 古詩 koé se, ancient ode.

P'han **攀** To climb up, from a low place to a higher one; p'han sē, 攀樹 *p'han ch'hēw*, to climb a tree.

P'han lëûng hoō hông, 攀龍附凤, to lead the dragon, and help the phœnix; (i. e. to assist a man in aiming to be emperor.)

声
P'hán **盼** A large proportion of white in the eye; p'hán cheng, 盼睛, to show the white of tho eyes.

P'hán **闆** To stand in the doorway and look.

去
P'hàn **盼** To look at any one; the black and white of the eyes distinctly marked.

Bé bók p'hàn hêy, 美目盼兮 *ch'hin ch'hai^ng ây bàk chew oe păyh p'hun hó hó*, beautiful eyes, with the black and white clearly divided; see the 上論 Sëăng lūn.

P'hán **襻** Léw p'hàn, 鈕襻, a button-hole.

卆
P'hang **香** Read hëang: fragrant, scented, sweet smelling, as flowers.

Hwún tëëp sîm hëang, 粉蝶尋香 *păyh ây böéy yëâh ch'höey p'hang*, the white butterfly seeks for fragrance.

P'hang **蜂** Read hong:—a bee; bit hong, 蜜蜂 *bit p'hang*, a honey bee.

Chék jê hong k'hé, 賊如蜂起 *ch'hàt ch'hin chëö^ng p'hang k'hé*, the thieves got up as thick as bees.

声
P'háng **紡** Read hóng: to spin; hóng chek, 紡績 *p'háng chăyh*, to spin thread.

去
P'hàng **胖** Read pwân: fat, corpulent, lusty; hwûy pwân, 肥胖 *pwûy p'hàng* fat.

平
P'hâng **篷** Read hông: a sail; ch'hwân hông, 船篷 *chûn p'hâng*, a ship's sail.

P'hâng **捧** Read hóng: to bring, or carry in both hands.

P'hâng **蓬** Read hông: a surname.

丟
P'hāng **縫** Read hông: a seam; hwûn hông, 痕縫 *hwûn p'hāng*, the scar of a wound.

Lê hông, 離縫 *lê p'hāng*, the opening of a seam.

P'hāng **梼** P'hāng koé, 梼鼓, a small drum, made of a long bamboo, with a bladder stretched over it, and beat about the streets by ballad singers.

卆
P'haou **拋** To throw away, to cast away; to throw, or spread around.

P'haou se jê sùy, 拋書而睡 *tek k'hak ch'hăyh jê k'hwùn*, he threw aside the book and went to sleep.

P'haou **泡** To pour boiling water on anything; p'haou tây, 泡茶, to make an infusion of tea, to pour boiling water on tea; a bubble.

P'haou 櫙 Sëen p'haou, 櫛櫙, the name of a wild and edible fruit.

声

P'haóu 翎 To fly.

去

P'haòu 砲 A machine for throwing out stones, when attacking fortified towns.

P'haòu 礮 The same as the above; a catapult.

P'haòu 炮 A cannon, a great gun; formerly stones were thrown out by a machine; now they make use of gunpowder.

Hòng p'haòu, 放炮 pàng p'haòu, to let off crackers.

P'haòu 皰 Vulg. p'hà: a sore or boil on the face.

P'haòu 疱 A swelling; t'hëen p'haòu, 天疱 t'hee^ng p'hà, a kind of sore.

丟

P'haōu 抱 Vulg. p'hō: to embrace, to hug; hwaê p'haōu, 懷抱 hwaê p'hō, an embrace.

Kwun choó p'haōu tō chaē këung, 君子抱道在躬 kwun choó p'hō tō tē kin sin, the good man clasps virtue to his bosom, and embraces it.

犬

P'haŏuh 博 Read p'hok: large, great.

入

P'haŏuh 皺 A rising of the skin; a blister.

P'haŏuh 雹 Hail, frozen rain; lók p'haŏuh, 落雹 lŏh p'haŏuh, to hail.

Sèng jîn chaē sëang boô p'haŏuh, suy yéw, put wûy haē, 聖人在上無雹雖有不爲害 sèng jîn tē téng bîn bô lŏh p'haŏuh, suy woō bô chò sëang haē, when a sage is at the head of affairs there will be no hail; and if there should be some, it would not be injurious; see the 左傳 Chó twān.

P'haŏuh 鑤 The neck of a pestle; or the narrow part of a large pestle, which is held in the hand.

犬

P'hat 汃 The waters in the extreme west; the western ocean; the 爾雅 Jé gnáy says, "that at the extreme east is 泰遠, t'haè wán, 'the great distance,' and at the extreme west is the 汃國, P'hat kok, 'the country of P'hat;'" some say, this character means the appearance of water; and others, the sound of waves striking against other.

P'hat 軎 The sound of a carriage breaking.

去

P'hày 帕 Read p'hà: a veil; séw p'hà, 首帕 t'haôu p'hày, a veil for the head; hwa p'hà, 花帕 hwa p'hày, a flowered veil.

卆

P'he 丕 Great, large.

P'he hëén chae, Bûn ông boè! p'he sîn chae, Boó ông lëét! 丕顯哉文王謨丕承哉武王烈 twā hëên bêng chae, Bûn ông ây boè! twā sëo swà chae, Boó ông ây lëét! how greatly illustrious were Bûn ông's plans! how well connected was Boó ông's zeal! see the 尙書 Sëāng se.

P'he 坯 Unburnt bricks and tiles.

P'he yëá yit tô, kwûn seng tek lé, 坯冶一陶群生得

理 *bōēy sëo ây hwūy k'hè chit ây ch'hòng, kwān saiⁿᵍ ây lâng tit tëŏh leāou lé,* the unburnt earthen ware when once burnt in the pottery, all the people can obtain the use of it; see the 崔駰傳 Ch'huy yëen twān.

P'he 伾 Strong; also, numerous; é ke p'he p'he, 以車伾伾 *e ch'hëa chēy chēy,* with an abundance of chariots; see the 魯頌 Loé sëūng.

P'he 秠 A black kind of millet; a species of wheat.

P'he 呸 The noise of wrangling.

P'he 邳 The name of a place; P'hêng-wát chëèn ê Hāy-p'he, 彭越戰於下邳 *P'haiⁿᵍ-wát sëo t'haĕ tē Hāy-p'he,* P'haiⁿᵍ-wát fought a battle at Hāy-p'he; see the 史記 Soó kè.

P'he 蚽 The name of an insect.

P'he 豾 A young fox, a cub; some call a fox 豾狸, p'he lé.

P'he 駓 A horse, with yellow and white hairs mixed.

P'he 披 To open; p'he k'hae, 披開 *p'he k'hwuy,* to open out. Also, to put on clothes or armor. Séw put têng p'ho ê pek kay che p'hëen, 手不停披於百家之編 *ch'hĕw bô têng p'he k'hwuy tē pāyh kay ch'hāyh,* "the hands should not cease turning over the pages of the hundred philosophers;" said by 韓愈 Hân jé.

P'he k'hwà sëāng má, 披掛上馬 *p'he k'hwà chëōⁿᵍ báy,* he dressed himself, and mounted his horse.

P'he 帔 A petticoat, a woman's under garment.

P'he 鈹 Hair.

P'he 批 To strike with the hand; to push, to turn round; to inform. Sòng-bān gē kĕw, p'he jê sat che, 宋萬遇仇批而殺之 *Sòng-bān toó tëŏh kêw sêw, p'he jê t'haĕ e,* Sòng-bān met his enemy, when he struck and killed him; see the 左傳 Chó twān.

P'he 砒 P'he song, 砒霜 *p'heeⁿᵍ scⁿᵍ,* arsenic.

P'he 坏 A hill incomplete; unburnt pottery; the same as 坯, p'he.

声

P'hé 嚭 Great; a man's name. Also written 噽, p'hé.

P'hé 否 To stop up; also, bad, not good. Bē te chong p'hé, 未知臧否 *bōēy chae hó baĕ,* not knowing whether it is good or bad; see the 大雅 Taē gnáy.

P'hé 痞 An induration of the spleen; when not painful is called 痞, p'hé, but when painful it is called 結胸, keet hëung.

P'hé 鄙 Vulgar; p'hé loē, 鄙陋 low, vulgar; pëen p'hé, 邊鄙, aside, out of the way; toe p'hé, 都鄙, a capital city, and its suburbs.

P'hé hoo k'hó é soō kwun yëá é chae? 鄙夫可與事君也與哉 *p'hé hoo t'hang kap e hòk saē jîn kwun e chae?* how can a vulgar fellow be employed with us in the service of the prince? see the 論語 Lūn gé.

P'hé 啚 The same as the preceding.

P'hé 庀 To regulate, to prepare.

P'hé 疕 A pain in the head; the bursting of an ulcer; sores on the head.

P'hé 㼰 A vessel cracked, but not yet broken to pieces.

去

P'hè 俾 P'hè gêy, 俾倪, to look askance.

P'hè 睥 P'hè gêy, 睥睨, to look on one side, to squint.

P'hè 譬 To speak of anything by way of comparison; p'hè jê, 譬如, for example, for instance, like as.

P'hè jê wûy san, bē sêng yit kwŭy, ché goē ché yëá, 譬如爲山未成一簣止吾止也 *p'hè jê chò swⁿa, böëy chëⁿâ chit pùn ke á t'hoê nā swăh, sē gwá swăh yëá,* as when making an artificial hill, if we leave it incomplete, only wanting a single basket of earth, our relinquishing the undertaking will be our own fault; see the 論語 Lūn gé.

P'hè 屁 Vulg. *p'hòèy:* a foul wind; hòng p'hè, 放屁 *pàng p'höèy,* to break wind. P'hè koé, 屁股 *k'ha ch'huiⁿᵍ,* the posteriors. Also written 氣 p'hè.

平

P'hê 皮 Vulg. *p'höêy:* the skin, the surface of anything. A surname.

Hoē bëën p'hê, 厚面皮 *kaōu bīn p'höêy,* a thick-skinned face; said of a person who cannot blush; an impudent, shameless one.

Sit kê p'hê, put sit kê kwut, 識其皮不識其骨 *bat e ây p'höêy, ūᵐ bat e ây kwut,* to know the skin, without knowing the bones of a thing; (to have a superficial knowledge of anything.)

P'hê 疲 Wearied with labor; exhausted; p'hê kwān, 疲倦, wearied, tired.

P'hê noē, boê é hoō tē, 疲駑無以輔治 *yëà yëà, bô t'hang hoō chān tē soō,* wearied and unable to assist in the government.

P'hê 詖 Hëëm p'hê, 險詖, unfair reasoning; artful debates.

P'hê soê, te kê séy pèy, 詖辭知其所蔽 *hëëm p'hê ây wā, chae e séy pèy,* with respect to unfair reasoning, we should know in how far it obscures a subject; see 孟子 Bēng choó.

P'hê 罷 The same as 疲, p'hê, weary.

P'hê 羆 Hîm p'hê, 熊羆, the name of a wild beast, a sort of bear.

P'hê 槐 Small pillars or supporters under the eaves of a house.

去

P'hē 被 P'hē tan, 被單 *p'höēy twⁿa,* a coverlid, a palampore for protecting one from cold, at night.

卒

P'hëⁿa 簰 Read p'heng: the name of a carriage; a sort of bamboo cart; or a bamboo mat hung up behind a carriage to keep out the dust; pöëy p'heng, 背 箳 *pöëy p'hēⁿa*, the spine.

P'hēⁿa 骿 Read p'heng: the ribs joined one to another.
K'héw chit p'heng, 尻 脊 骿 *k'ha chëăh p'hēⁿa*, the spine of the back.

声
P'hēⁿá 腁 Read p'hëèn: a slice, a piece; but yit p'hëèn, 物 一 腁 *meēⁿᵍh chit p'hēⁿá*, a slice of anything.

平
P'hēⁿâ 堋 San pêng, 山 堋 *swⁿa p'hēⁿâ*, the ridge, or range of a hill.

P'hēⁿâ 硑 Kēng p'hêng, 硬 硑 *gnāy p'hēⁿâ*, as stiff as a stone.
To strike with a stone.

入
P'hëăh 僻 Read p'hek: lateral, aside, out of the way; wán p'hek, 遠 僻 *hwuiⁿᵍ p'hëăh*, far out of the way, removed to a distance.
P'hëen p'hek, 偏 僻 *p'hëen p'hëăh*, strange, out of the way.

P'hëăh 癖 Read p'hek: a sickness common to children; a disposition, a propensity; hⁿó p'hek, 好 癖 *hó p'hëăh*, a good disposition; ok p'hek, 惡 癖 *p'haⁿé p'hëăh*, a bad temper.
Jîn kae yéw yit p'hek, gnó p'hek chaē chëang kè, 人 皆 有 一 癖 我 癖 在 章 句 *lâng chò poō woō chit ây p'hëăh, gwá ây p'hëăh tē chëoⁿᵍ kòò*, every one has his peculiar bent of mind, but my hobby is to be devoted to chapters and sections.

入
P'hëăh 甓 P'hek chwan, 甓 磚 *p'hëăh chuiⁿᵍ*, tiles and rubbish.

上
P'hëang 剻 To cut down.

P'hëang 脝 P'hêng p'hëang, 膨 脝, a swelling of the stomach.

上
P'heaou 麃 The appearance of frisking and prancing; also, to weed the ground.

P'heaou 儦 To be in motion; also, many, numerous.
Hêng jîn p'heaou, 行 人 儦 儦 *kēⁿâ ây lâng p'heaou p'heaou*, the people walked ploddingly along; see the 齊 風 Chêy hong.

P'heaou 瀌 Incessant rain and snow.

P'heaou 鑣 The iron on the outside of a horse's bit.

P'heaou 穮 To weed the ground, to clear away the grass from the fields.

P'heaou 猋 A dog running very swiftly; p'heaou hong, 猋 風, a fierce wind.

P'heaou 摽 To strike, to point, to make signals, to wave backwards and forwards.
Tëâng bók che pē, boô put p'heaou yëá, 長 木 之 斃 無 不 摽 也 *tëⁿᵍ ch'hâ ây ka laōuh, bô ūᵐ p'hăh tëŏk*, when a large tree falls, nothing near can escape being struck by it; see the 左 傳 Chó twān.
Chô-choó p'heaou këèm, jê k'hè che, 曹 子 摽 劍 而 去 之 *Chô-choó p'heaou këèm jê k'hè e*, Chô-choó waved his sword, and departed; see the 公 羊 傳 Kong yâng twān.

P'heaou 漂 To float; also, to move, to flow down; to be agitated. Hëet lêw p'heaou ch'hé, 血流漂杵 *höëyh laôu kaôu ēy p'hoô cheng ch'hé*, the blood flowed sufficient to float a wooden pestle.

P'heaou 熛 The appearance of fire flying about.

P'heaou 縹 Light, buoyant, elegant; to rise up lightly and gently; as a bird beginning to fly.

P'heaou 飄 The sound of wind, a whirlwind, a violent gust of wind. Hong p'heaou p'heaou, kê ch'huy e, 風飄飄其吹衣 *hong p'heaou p'heaou e ây ch'höey sⁿa*, a sudden gust of wind blew aside his clothes.

P'heaou 飃 The same as the preceding; an easy flowing gait. P'heaou jëên jê k'hè, 飃然而去, he went off in an easy graceful manner.

P'heaou 飈 A fierce wind blowing down from above; to roll up.

P'heaou 魒 The name of a star in Ursa Major.

P'heaou 翲 To fly high.

P'heaou 瞟 P'heaou beáou, 瞟眇, to see indistinctly.

P'heaou 勡 To take anything by force, to plunder.

P'heaou 慓 Hasty, sudden.

P'heaou 杓 The first star in the handle of the Dipper or Charles's-wain.

去

P'heáou 剽 The end, the extremity of anything.

P'heáou 皫 A bird's feathers changing color.

去

P'heàou 僄 To make light of one's own person; light, trifling, volatile, active. P'heàou k'hè, chek cheaou che é hō chae, 僄棄則招之以禍災 *p'heàou t'hek kak pún sin, chek chëo é hō hoān chae haē*, to make light of, and to disregard one's-self, is the way to bring down calamity and trouble.

P'heàou 嫖 P'heàou yaôu, 嫖姚, the name of an office, in the Hàn dynasty.

P'heàou 票 To shake, to move, to agitate; also vulg. *p'hëò*: a ticket, a passport. Tⁿa p'heàou, 打票 *p'hàh p'hëò*, to take out a passport. T'hoê chong bó p'heàou, 頭鬃尾票 *t'haôu chang böëy p'hëò*, a tax on the cues of the Chinese, levied in Batavia.

P'heàou 僄 To make light of one's-self.

P'heàou 瞟 To put anything in the wind or sun, to dry.

P'heàou 驃 K'hê p'heàou, 騎驃, the name of an office.

P'heàou 嘌 A carriage driving furiously; p'heàou yaôu, 嘌搖, uneasy.

P'heàou 勡 To oppose, and plunder; to seize.

P'heàou 漂 Vulg *p'hëò:* to bleach; p'heàou poè, 漂布 *p'hëò poè,* to bleach clothes.

Kéng p'heàou soè sip jit, 竟漂數十日 *kéng p'hëò kwóuy chàp jit,* bleached for several tens of days.

P'heàou 剽 To perforate, to stab; to flay; also to take by violence.

平.

P'heâou 嫖 A place where prostitutes dwell, a brothel; p'heâou ch'hëang, 嫖娼, a prostitute, a courtezan; p'heâou, toé, yîm, 嫖賭飲, the three vices of horedom, gambling, and drunkenness.

P'heâou 瓢 Vulg. *poô:* a calabash; yit p'heâou yîm, 一瓢飲 *chit poô á ây t'he^ng,* a calabash full of liquor; see the 論語 Lūn gé.

P'heâou 薸 Vulg. *p'hëô:* a kind of duck-weed or lemna like floating moss found on the surface of the water; also written p'hêng, 苹 *p'hëô.*

上

P'hëen 偏 Partial, lateral, inclined to one side. Boô p'hëen boô p'hó, ông tō tōng tōng, 無偏無頗王道蕩蕩 *bô p'hëen p'hëăh bô p'hó p'hó, ông ây tō lé tōng twā,* neither partial nor confined, the royal way is immense and grand; see the 書經 Se keng.

P'hëen 扁 A small boat.

P'hëen 篇 Vulg. *p'hee^ng:* the section or leaf of a book, a piece of composition. Loé lūn jē sip p'hëen, Chêy lūn kay būn-ông, te-tō, këūng jē sip jē p'hëen, 魯論二十篇齊論加問王知道共三十二篇 *Loé kok ây lūn gé woō jē chàp p'hee^ng, Chêy kok ây lūn gé kay chit ây būn-ông, te-tō, këūng jē chàp jē p'hee^ng,* the collection of the 'sayings of Confucius,' belonging to the Loé country, contained 20 sections; but that belonging to the Chêy country, with the addition of the chapters beginning 'būn-ông' and 'te-tō,' amounted to 22 sections.

P'hëen 艑 The name of a ship or vessel.

P'hëen 蹁 P'hëen ch'hëen, 蹁躚, to parade, to walk up and down.

P'hëen 翩 To fly swiftly; lëên p'hëen, 聯翩, incessant.

P'hëen 編 To arrange, to put in order.

去

P'hëén 惼 Yëén, p'hëén, 匽惼, a narrow mind.

去

P'hëèn 片 Vulg. *p'hee^ng:* a slice, a part, a half. P'hëèn gân k'hó é chëet gëúk chëá, ké Yêw yëá e! 片言可以折獄者其由也與 *chit p'hee^ng ây wā, t'hang laé chëet twān p'hwàn gëuk ây soō e sē Yêw yëá e!* with half a word to be able to decide cases of litigation, is not this Yêw alone! see the 論語 Lūn gé.

P'hëèn 騙 To jump on a horse at one spring; now used to intimate deceit. Hōng p'hëèn, 哄騙, to deceive, to cheat, to take advantage of.

幸
P'hee^{ng} **篇** Read p'hëen: a section of a book. Kim sè soō, yit yit che lèk chok bún sam p'hëen, 今試士一日之力作文三篇 *t^{n}a ch'hè k'hw^{n}à t'hàk ch'hăyh lâng, chit jit ây k'hwùy lât, chò bûn chëo^{ng} s^{n}a p'hee^{ng}*, now in examining scholars, one day's labor is employed in making three sections of literary composition.

P'hee^{ng} **便** Read pëen: cheap, reasonable.

去
P'heè^{ng} **片** Read p'hëèn: a chip of wood; wá p'hëèn, 瓦片 *hëā p'heè^{ng}*, a piece of tile.

去
P'heē^{ng} **欪** The sound of wind going out.

P'heē^{ng} **砒** P'he song, 砒霜 *p'heē^{ng} se^{ng}*, arsenic.

P'heē^{ng} **鼻** Read pit: the nose; pit k'hong, 鼻孔 *p'heē^{ng} k'hang*, the nostrils.
Pit che ô hèw yëá, 鼻之於臭也 *p'heē^{ng} ây tē hèw lē*, the nose with respect to smells, &c; see 孟子 Bēng choó.

去
P'hëet **丿** A leaning to the right, as if inclining to the left; a slanting stroke in writing. One of the radicals.

P'hëet **撆** To strike gently; a little; to lead, to pull up; also written 撇, p'hëet. P'hëet séw sèw, 撆手袖 *peëh ch'héw wuí^{ng}*, to strip up the sleeves.

P'hëet **瞥** To pass before the eyes; to get a sight of. Yêw tîn göëy, jê p'hëet t'hëen, 遊塵外而瞥天 *t'hit t'hô âng tîn gwā, jê k'hw^{n}à t'hee^{ng}*, "to wander beyond the dusty world, and get a sight of the heavens;" said by 張衡思 Tëang hëên soo.

P'hëet **蹩** P'hëet p'hó, 蹩跛, lame, halt.

P'hëet **騙** To jump on a horse; to deceive; also read p'hëèn.

入
P'hëet **獙** To fly; the appearance of flying.

去
P'hek **珀** Hoé p'hek, 琥珀, amber.

P'hek **拍** To prop up; to strike; p'hek pán, 拍板, to strike the board, in order to keep time, while playing music.

P'hek **岶** Boē p'hek, 嶑岶, secret, a secret appearance, clandestine.

P'hek **碧** A fine azure stone; a deep azure color.

P'hek **魄** A spirit; the Chinese suppose that each individual has (sam hwûn ch'hit p'hek, 三魂七魄 *s^{n}a ây hwûn, ch'hit ây p'hek*,) three souls and seven spirits; of which they say, (hwûn chek sëāng seng, p'hek chek hāy kāng, 魂則上升魄則下降 *hwún chëw chëō^{ng} têng bîn, p'hek chëw lôh hāy téy*,) the soul ascends, and the spirit goes downwards.

P'hek **辟** A prince, a ruler, a law; to do away with, to set aside; aside.

Sëăng wûy p'hek kong, t'hëen choó bók bók, 相維辟公天子穆穆 *sëăng hoō woō p'hek kong, hóng tèy bòk bók*, the princes of the empire assisted at the sacrifice, while the emperor stood musing; see the 上論 Sëang lün.

P'hëen p'hek, 偏辟, inclined to one side, partial.

P'hek **璧** A round and valuable gem; kwuy p'hek, 圭璧, a precious stone.

P'hek **壁** Ok p'hek, 屋壁 *ch'hoò pëăh*, the wall of a house; kek p'hek, 隔壁 *kăyh p'hëăh*, a next door neighbor, separated only by a party wall.

T'hëûng seng bêng soò p'hek, 蟲聲鳴四壁 *t'hâng ây sëⁿa tit bêng haóu tē sè āy pëăh*, the noise of the insects was heard on every wall; see a 古詩 koé se.

P'hek **擗** To beat one's breast; to open out, to spread open, to break.

P'hek yúng k'hok k'hip, 擗踊哭泣 *p'hăh heng k'hám, yúng tëŏ, k'haòu, kwà t'hè*, to beat the breast, to stamp with the foot, to cry and weep, (at the death of a parent;) see the 孝經 Haòu keng.

P'hek **僻** P'hek loē, 僻陋, vulgar, mean; sëâ p'hek, 邪僻, corrupt, perverse; yew p'hek, 幽僻, secret, dark; hòng p'hek, 放僻, dissolute.

Hòng p'hek sëâ ch'hé, boô put wûy é, 放僻邪侈無不爲已 *hòng p'hek sëâ ch'hé, bô sêy ūm chò*, a dissolute, vulgar, corrupt and extravagant man would go to any lengths; see 孟子 Bēng choó.

P'hek **憵** Hasty, sudden, speedy.

P'hek **劈** To cut open, to split, to tear asunder.

P'hek **緝** To weave; pé sin chit kò, ch'hey p'hek loê, é ék che yëâ, 彼身織屨妻辟纑以易之也 *e pún sin p'hăh ch'haóu ây, e ây boê chit ch'hoe mwⁿâ poè, ê wⁿâ ch'hek*, he himself made straw shoes, and his wife wove hempen cloth, to barter for corn; see 孟子 Bēng choó.

P'hek **霹** P'hek lék, 霹靂 *p'hek lăyh*, the rattling of thunder.

Jê p'hek lék che seng, 如霹靂之聲 *ch'hin chëōⁿᵍ p'hek lăyh ây sëⁿa*, like a clap of thunder.

P'hek **癖** Vulg. *p'hëăh:* a sort of disease, a peculiar propensity, temper, disposition.

Ch'hut p'hek, 出癖 *ch'hut p'hëăh*, to have the measles.

Ok p'hek, 惡癖 *p'haⁿê p'hëăh*, a bad temper. Also written 腁, p'hek.

P'hek **澼** To bleach anything, till it becomes white.

P'hek **躃** Lame of both legs.

幸

P'heng **烹** To boil, to cook, to dress food. Also written 亨, p'heng.

Haòu jîn p'heng che, 校人烹之 *haòu jîn p'heng e*, the man who took care of the pools, boiled (it...h); see [illegible]

P'heng 俜 To order, to command, to give in charge of.

P'heng 僒 To order, to send; to make up for.

P'heng 娉 P'heng têng, 娉婷, a beautiful appearance; an elegant carriage.

P'heng 甹 To intrust to, to give in charge of; also, to draw out.

P'heng 砰 The sound of stones.

P'heng 脉 A swelling of the abdomen.

P'heng 磞 To strike with a stone; to beat on a stone.

P'heng 淜 The noise of striking water.

上

P'héng 俜 A hypocrite, a pretender.

P'héng 崩 The name of a village, or district.

去

P'hèng 聘 To inquire, to ask; to betroth; p'hèng léy, 聘禮, a betrothing present; p'hèng bũn, 聘問, to pay a visit of inquiry.

P'hèng 騁 To drive, to gallop along, to run away. K'he p'hèng teên làp, hoō ke ch'heen sëng, gnó te' chè hwut wûy yëá, 馳騁田獵後車千乘我得志弗爲也 *sëo jëuk p'hadu chaou kwà p'hãh làh, aõu ch'hëa chëⁿà ch'heng tëoⁿᵍ, gwá nā tit chè è, ūᵐ chò yëá,* to drive and gallop about, and go a hunting, followed by a thousand chariots; if I were to get my will I would not prefer such things; see 孟子 Bēng choó.

平

P'hêng 彭 A way; full, complete; also vulg. *p'hatⁿᵍ:* a surname.

P'hêng 蟚 A kind of lobster or crawfish, found on the seashore, in the mud.

P'hêng 評 To discourse on, to give an opinion upon. P'he p'hêng bûn chëang, 批評文章 *p'he p'hêng bûn chëoⁿᵍ*, to examine and criticise a piece of literary composition.

P'hêng 苹 A kind of grass; straw.

P'hêng 萍 Vulg. *p'hëô:* a kind of duck-weed, usually found floating on standing water. P'hêng chong, 萍踪, to meet suddenly.
Jit gwát lóng tëung neáou, k'hëên k'hwun súy sëâng p'hêng, 日月籠中鳥乾坤水上萍 *jit göĕyh sē láng tang eⁿᵍ ây cheáou, t'heeⁿᵍ tëy sē chúy têng ây p'hëô,* the sun and moon are like birds in a cage, and heaven and earth resemble the duck-weed floating on the surface of the water; see 杜甫詩 Toē hoó se.

P'hêng 鵬 Yîn p'hêng, 雲鵬, the name of a great bird.

去

P'hëò 票 Read p'heàou: a ticket; paê p'heàou, 牌票 *paê p'hëò,* a direction on a board; tëèm p'heàou, 店票

福建方言字典

tëèm p'hëò, a sign-board set up in front of a shop. T'hoê chong bé p'heàou, 頭鬃尾票 *t'haôu chang böëy p'hëò*, a ticket held by those who have paid the poll-tax in Batavia; persons found without such a ticket are taken up and imprisoned.

P'hëò 剽 K'heng p'heàou, 輕剽 *k'hin p'hëò*, to make light of one's-self; to turn one's hand lightly to anything. Also written 僄 p'heàou.

P'hëò 漂 Read p'heàou: to bleach; p'heàou poè, 漂布 *p'hëò poè*, to bleach cloth.

卑
P'hew 夢 To speak in one's sleep. Also read bōng.

卑
P'hey 批 To strike with the hand; also, to inform, to announce, to give an opinion on anything; p'hey p'hêng, 批評, to criticise literary productions; to compare, to discuss, to decide.

P'hey 破 To cut up flesh.

P'hey 紕 P'hey bēw, 紕繆, to be in an error, to be wrong.

声
P'héy 䪁 The face; *ch'hùy p'héy*, 嘴䪁, the cheeks; *kwăh ch'hùy p'héy*, 摅嘴䪁, to give any one a slap in the face.

P'héy 睥 *P'héy géy*, 睥睨, to look slantwise; to look askance.

去
P'hèy 𣎴 To open out and divide the fibres of a certain flax plant.

P'hèy 紕 To card hemp or flax; a bundle of flax.

下
P'hēy 稗 Read paē: a kind of grain, like rice, but yielding a smaller seed; some say tares, empty grain; Eleusine coracana.

卑
P'hin 繽 P'hin hwŭn, 繽紛, confused, crowded.

P'hin 翸 To fly.

声
P'hín 品 An order, a sort, a class, a series; p'hín hêng, 品行, conduct, actions. Kwan yéw kéw p'hín, 官有九品, *kwⁿa woō kaôu p'hín*, there are nine ranks or degrees in office.

去
P'hìn 覕 To see gradually.

入
P'hit 匹 A fellow; a mate, an equal, a partner; also, a numeral for horses. Wûy kwun choó lêng hⁿò kè p'hit, 惟君子能好其匹 *tòk tòk kwun choó ây lâng ëy sëŏh e ây p'hit p'höèy*, the good man alone can truly love his associates; see the 禮記 Léy kè.
Soò p'hit wûy sēng, 四匹爲乘 *sè chëăh báy chò chit ây sēng*, four horses make one stud.

P'hit 疋 A piece; yit p'hit poè, 一疋布 *chit p'hit poè*, a piece of cloth. Ké p'hit? 幾疋 *kwúy p'hit?* how many pieces?

卑
P'ho 波 A wave; p'ho lōng, 波浪 *p'ho nëⁿg*, the waves of the sea. Haé put yâng p'ho, è tëung kok

yéw sèng jîn hoē, 海不揚波意中國有聖人乎 *haé ŭm yâng p'ho nēng, è tëung kok woō sèng jîn á bô*, the sea has not lately risen into waves, hence we conceive that China has produced a sage; see the 史記 Soó kè.

P'ho 坡 A bank, a ridge; san p'ho, 山坡 *swna p'ho*, the declivity or side of a hill.

P'ho 玻 P'ho lêy, 玻璃, glass, any vitreous substance.

P'ho 頗 P'hëen p'ho, 偏頗, partial, lateral, inclined to one side, awry.

P'ho 皤 Hoary hairs; p'ho p'ho lëâng soō, gnó sëâng yéw che, 皤皤良士我尙有之 *pâyh t'haôu mô ây hó t'hàk ch'hâyh lâng, gwá sëâng woō e*, of hoary-headed and virtuous scholars, I have still a few; see the 書秦誓 Se chîn sē.

声

P'hó 叵 Do not, cannot, may not; when 呂布, Lē-poè was not befriended by 劉備, Lêw-pē, and was about to be put to death, he exclaimed, (taē jé jê! chöèy p'hò sìn, 大耳兒最叵信 *twā hē k'hang ây kënâ! chöèy ŭm t'hang sìn,*) "you great eared churl! you are by no means to be believed."

P'hó 叵 P'hó naē, 叵耐, unbearable, that which cannot be borne.

P'hó 跛 Lame; p'hò këak, 跛脚 *köëy k'ha*, lame of the feet.
P'hó lêng lé, 跛能履 *köëy k'ha ēy kënâ*, the lame can walk; see the 易經 Ēk keng.

P'hó 頗 A little, to be able in a small degree; p'hó p'hó sit joō, 頗頗識字 *p'hó p'hó bat jē*, to be in some measure acquainted with letters.

去

P'hò 破 Vulg. *p'hwà*: broken, to break, to tear open; tná p'hò 打破 *p'hăh p'hwà*, to burst open; p'hò sam, 破衫 *p'hwà sna*, torn clothes.
Hwà kay wûy kok chëá ch'hoó choó, p'hò kok bông kay chëá ék ch'hoó choó, 化家爲國者此子破國亡家者亦此子 *hwà kay chënâ kok ây, sē chêy lêy kënâ, p'hwà kay bông kok ây yëá sē chêy lêy kënâ*, "he who would be likely to convert his family into a nation, is this child; and he who would be likely to ruin his country and annihilate his family, is also such a child as this;" said of the founder of the 唐, Têng dynasty, by his father, who early perceived the rising genius of his son.

去

P'hō 抱 Read p'haōu: to embrace, to clasp to one's bosom.
Hwaê jîn p'haōu gē, 懷仁抱義 *k'hêng jîn p'hō gē*, to embosom benevolence and embrace righteouness.

平

P'hoe 菩 P'hoe sat, 菩薩, an idol, an image of the Budhists. Also read p'hoê.

P'hoe 鋪 To spread out; p'hoe tëang, 鋪張 *p'hoe tëong*, to spread out; p'hoe tîn, 鋪陳, to arrange.

P'hoe 麱 Meal, bran; bêk p'hoe, 麥麱 *bâyh p'hoe*, the coarse meal of wheat.

P'hoe 䴸 A large kind of pulse; coarse flour.

P'hoe 稀 The husk of wheat, bran.

声

P'hoé 浦 The banks of a stream, the edge of the water. A surname.
Sut pé Hwaê p'hoé, 率彼淮浦 t'hàn e Hwaê chúy ây peeng, to follow the banks of the Hwaê; see the 大雅 Taē gnáy.

P'hoé 圃 A gardener; one who cultivates flowers and vegetables.
Ch'héng hák wûy p'hoé, choó wát, goê put jê ló p'hoé, 請學爲圃子曰吾不如老圃 ch'hëⁿá ôh chŏh hwutng, hoo choó kóng, gwá ǔm tàt tëŏh chit ây laōu chò hwutng ây lâng, one asked to learn gardening, when Confucius replied, "I am not so good (for that) as an old gardener;" see the 論語 Lūn gé.

P'hoé 溥 Great, large, extensive, wide.
P'hoé t'hëen che hây, bók hwuy ông t'hoé, 溥天之下莫非王土 p'hoé t'heeng ây hāy, bô ūm sē ông ây t'hoé tēy, under the wide heavens, there is no place which is not the royal territory; see the 小雅 Seáou gnáy.

P'hoé 譜 A register; chók p'hoé, 族譜, a family register; a genealogical table; also, a biography, a list.

P'hoé 普 All, altogether, the whole; p'hoé t'hëen hây, 普天下 p'hoé t'heeng āy, under the whole heavens; p'hoé se, 普施, to distribute widely.

P'hoé 剖 To cut open, to cut through the middle; p'hó hok, 剖腹 p'hwà pak, to rip open the belly.

去

P'hoè 鋪 A shop; p'hoè tëèm, 鋪店, a stall for exposing goods to sell.

P'hoè 舖 P'hòe tông, 舖堂, a watch-house, a guard house.

平

P'hoê 捗 A bill for collecting taxes.

P'hoê 蜅 P'hoê é, 蜅蝣, the name of an insect.

上

P'hoē 簿 A register, a record; tëang p'hoē, 張簿 seáou p'hoē, an account book; also, to receive; and a flat piece of wood held in the hand.
Këen këen sëāng p'hoē, 件件上簿 kēⁿā kēⁿā chëōng p'hoē, everything is entered into the account.

P'hoē 蔀 A small mat.

P'hoē 廍 Chëà p'hoē, 糖廍, a sugar mill, a place for making sugar.
K'hae p'hoē, 開廍 k'hwuy p'hoē, to open a sugar-mill.

平

P'höey 坏 Unburnt bricks, or tiles. Also written 坯, p'höey, and 𤬪, p'höey.

声

P'höéy 㕷 Do not, it cannot be.

P'höéy 琲 A string of 500 beads.

P'höéy 唔 The noise of wrangling.

去
P'höèy **配** To couple with, to associate with, to unite; p'hit p'höèy, 匹配, a fellow, a mate; bút p'höèy, 物配 *meē^ngh p'höèy*, savory relishes, used with rice; sëang p'höèy, 相配, to couple together. Also written 妃, p'höèy.

P'höèy **朸** A chip of wood, a shaving; bók p'höèy, 木朸 *ch'há p'höèy*, chips of wood.

P'höèy **唾** Read sûy: to spit; sûy yëën, 唾涎 *p'höèy nw^nā*, to void spittle.
Sûy bëēn choō kan, 唾面自乾 *p'höèy bīn tëŏh hoē e ka tē ta*, when any one spits in our face, we should let it dry of itself; (lest by wiping it off, we should provoke our antagonist to anger.)

平
P'höêy **皮** Read p'hê: the skin; yâng p'hê, 羊皮 *yëô^ng p'höêy*, a sheep's skin.

去
P'höēy **被** Read p'hē: a covering; p'hē tan, 被單 *p'höēy tw^na*, a coverlid, a blanket, a sheet.

入
P'höëyh **沫** Read bwàt: foam; súy bwàt, 水沫 *chúy p'höëyh*, the foam of water.

P'höëyh **坺** *T'hoê p'höëyh*, a clod of earth.

去
P'hŏh **朴** Read p'hok: the refuse of anything; chëà p'hok, 樜朴 *chëà p'hŏh*, the husk of sugar-cane, after the juice is expressed.

P'hŏh **粕** Read p'hok: grains; cho p'hok, 糟粕 *chaou p'hŏh*, the grains of liquor, the refuse left after a brewing.

Koé jîn che cho p'hok, 古人之糟粕 *koé chá ây lâng ây chaou p'hŏh*, the dregs and grains of the ancients; (said of those who make compositions by borrowing from old books.)

入
P'hŏh **泊** Read pòk: a vessel moored to the water's edge; to moor a vessel, to come to an anchor; an anchorage.

去
P'hok **搏** To strike with the hand; vulg. *p'hăh*: to beat, to strike.
Chìn hoê bōng é Ch'hoé choó p'hok, 晉侯夢與楚子搏 *Chìn hoê bāng kap Ch'hoé choó sëo p'hăh*, the prince of the Chìn country dreamed that he was fighting with the ruler of the Ch'hoé country; see the 左傳 Chó twān.

P'hok **博** A game of chance; to play; extensive, very, exceedingly.
Put yéw p'hok ék chëá hoê? 不有博奕者乎 *ū^m yëá woō toé p'hok wûy kê chëá hoê?* is it not better to play at drafts or chess then to sit still and do nothing? see the 論語 Lūn gé.
P'hok hák, 博學, extensively learned.

P'hok **膊** Këen p'hok, 肩膊, the flesh on the shoulders, the shoulders.

P'hok **鎛** An implement of husbandry, a kind of hoe; a musical instrument, a sort of bell.

P'hok **撲** To pat, to beat with the hand, to cuff, to brush off dust.
H^nó leâou ê gwân, put k'hó p'hok bëĕt, 火燎于原不可撲滅 *höéy tŏh tē gwân, bô t'hang p'hăh hwa*, when the fire is blazing in the plain, it cannot be extinguished.

P'hok **樸** White, unvarnished close grained wood, the substance as distinguish- from the ornaments; honest, true.

P'hok 朴 Vulg. *p'hŏh:* the substance of anything; simple, plain, sincere.
T'haè sëăng k'hè hwa, sëăng soè p'hok hêy, séy kwùy chaē jîn bwuy kim gëùk hêy, 太上去華尙素朴兮所貴在人匪金玉兮 *t'haè sëăng k'hè t'hek hwa lêy, sëăng aè soè p'hok hêy, séy kwùy twā tē lâng, bô twā tē kim gëùk hêy*, the great supreme rejects ornament, and prefers what is simple and substantial; thus what we ought to esteem in men is not gold or gems.

P'hok 髆 The shoulders.

P'hok 墣 A lump of earth; Ch'hoé Lêng ông ch'hut bông, chím che e p'hok, 楚靈王出亡枕之以墣 *Ch'hoé Lêng ông ch'hut bông ây sí, lëăh chit têy t'hoé chò chím t'haôu*, Lêng, the king of the Ch'hoé country, when banished from his country, took a lump of earth for his pillow; see the 楚語 Ch'hoè gé.

P'hok 璞 An unpolished gem; a diamond in the rough.
Kim yew p'hok gëùk ê ch'hoó, 今有璞玉於此 *tⁿa woō p'hok gëùk tē chê taôu*, now there is an unpolished gem here; see 孟子 Bêng choó.

P'hok 濮 The name of a river.

P'hok 䉤 Bé p'hok, 米䉤, coarse rice.

P'hok 鏷 Unwrought iron; iron ore.

6 K

P'hok 攴 To strike gently; one of the radicals.

P'hok 矸 P'hok seaou, 矸硝, saltpetre.

P'hok 扑 A club, a staff; to beat with a stick.
P'hok chok kaòu hêng, 扑作敎刑 *p'hăh chò kà ây hêng hwat*, the stick forms the instrument of punishment in schools.

P'hok 貝卜 Full of treasure; abundance of wealth.

P'hok 臠 P'hok lô, 臠卒, mixed, confused; sacrificial flesh.

P'hŏk 暴 Vulg. *p'hàk:* to dry in the sun; to bask in the sun; to expose to view; to promulge, to publish; p'hók jit, 暴日, to dry in the sun.
Yit jit p'hók che, sip jit hân che, 一日暴之十日寒之 *chit jit p'hàk e, chàp jit kwⁿà e*, to warm it in the sun for one day, and to let it freeze for ten days; see 孟子 Bêng choó.
P'hók che ê bîn, jê bîn sêw che, 暴之於民而民受之 *p'hók e kaòu păyh saiⁿᵍ, jê păyh saiⁿᵍ sëw e*, he exhibited him before the people and the people accepted of him; see 孟子 Bêng choó.

P'hŏk 曝 The same as the preceding.

P'hŏk 爆 A blazing up of fire; an ardent flame.

P'hŏk 瀑 A fountain or cataract, which sends out its waters far, and with noise.

P'hók 襮 The collar of a coat; soè e choo p'hók, 素衣朱襮 *păyh s^n a ăng nē^n á*, a white garment with a red collar; see the 唐風 Tông hong.

𠀁
P'hong 磅 P'heng p'hong, 砰磅, the noise of stones falling, (as in a well.)

P'hong 䡐 The flesh ris'ng up in blisters.

P'hong 胮 The belly swelled up.

𠀃
P'hóng 覫 The appearance of looking at anything.

P'hóng 捧 To hold up anything in both hands; to take both hands full.

𠀄
P'hòng 烽 The noise of fire.

P'hòng 膨 To swell, to puff up; hollow, swelled out.

P'hòng 胖 Vulg. *p'hàng:* fat, corpulent, swelled; some say, stinking.

𠀂
P'hông 篷 Bamboos matted together, in order to form a covering for boats or carriages; also, a bamboo carriage.

𠀅
P'hōng 膨 *P'hōng p'hëang,* 膨脝, a swelling of the abdomen.

𠀁
P'hoo 呼 The sound of blowing.

𠀃
P'hoó 蛹 *T'hoé p'hoó,* 土蛹, a kind of insect found on the ground; a sort of crab.

P'hoó 瞢 The eyes dim; p'hoó p'hoó kong, 瞢瞢光 *p'hoó p'hoó kwui^ng*, a dim light, scarcely visible; the dawn of day.

𠀂
P'hoô 浮 Read hoô: to float; hoô chaē súy sëāng, 浮在水上 *p'hoô tē chúy tēng,* to float on the surface of the water.

E sè hoô tîm, 與世浮沉 *kap sè chò poô p'hoô á tëēm,* to sink or swim with the world.

𠀅
P'hoō 䎀 The noise of birds flying away.

𠀆
P'hoŏh 謏 Cunning, artful; to deceive, to rail.

P'hoŏh 吹 Read ch'huy: to blow anything in, as at the nose.

𠀁
P'hooi^ng 鐇 Read hwan: an adze, a round axe for felling trees.

𠀄
P'hooi^ng 湿 The ebbing of the tide; low water.

𠀁
P'hun 賁 Hoé p'hun, 虎賁, brave, tiger-like soldiers.

Hoé p'hun sam ch'hëen jîn, 虎賁三千人 *hoé p'hun s^n a ch'heng lâng,* three thousand tiger-like soldiers; see 孟子 Bēng choó.

P'hun 噴 To snort, to spurt out; p'hun hong, 噴風, to whistle.

P'hun 奔 To run away; p'hun choé, 奔走 *p'hun chaóu*, to flee away after a defeat.

P'hun 犇 The same as the above.

P'hun 歕 To blow out the breath; to spurt anything out of the mouth.

P'hun 糙 Bé p'hun, 米糙, the water in which rice has been boiled.

声

P'hún 㨤 The arched covering or hood of a carriage; fine, grand.

P'hún 翸 To fly upwards.

P'hún 翉 To fly away.

P'hún 呠 To spurt water out of the mouth; also written 啈, p'hún.

去

P'hùn 吩 To blow out the breath; also written 噴, p'hún.

P'hùn 喯 To spurt out water, from the mouth.

P'hùn 逩 To flee away, to run away.

P'hùn 噴 P'hùn t'hè, 噴嚏 *p'hăh k'ha ch'héw*, to blow the nose; to sneeze. P'hùn súy, 噴水 *p'hùn chúy*, to spurt out water.

P'hùn 湓 Water flowing rapidly; a fountain bubbling up.

平

P'hûn 盆 A wash hand-basin: a dish, a pot; a general name for jars, pots, &c.; hwa p'hûn, 花盆, a flower pot.

P'hûn 葐 Hok p'hûn choó, 覆葐子, the name of a medicinal herb.

P'hûn 噴 To vomit; to blow out the breath.

P'hûn 湓 Water overflowing, and bubbling up; rain collected together.

大

P'hut 昢 The sun just risen, and not yet shining out with its full splendor.

P'hut 朏 The moon in the first quarter, not yet come to the full.

P'hut 竴 The sound of laying anything down.

P'hut 馞 Pit p'hut, 馝馞, fragrant.

P'hut 媄 Jé p'hut, 乳媄, a fat woman, a milk nurse.

下

P'hu̍t 粹 Rice cleansed.

P'hu̍t 餑 Rice flour.

P'hut 荸 P'hút chey, 荸薺, the name of a vegetable, the water chestnut; the Scirpus tuberosus.

P'hwa 鰟 Pa lông, 鰟䱎 *p'hwa lang*, the name a fish.

P'hwà 破 Read p'hò: to break, to break in pieces; but p'hò, 物破 *mĕe^ngh p'hwa*, anything broken to pieces.

P'hwâ 鮀 *P'hwâ lô*, 鮀老, the name of a fish.

P'hw^na 潘 Read p'hwan: a surname.

P'hw^nà 判 Read p'hwàn: to judge; p'hwàn twān, 判斷 *p'hw^nà twān*, to decide on a case; sím p'hwàn, 審判 *sím p'hw^nà*, to examine and judge, judgment.

P'hw^nâ 枰 Kê pêng, 棋枰 *kê p'hw^nâ*, a chess-board.

P'hw^nā 伴 Read p'hwān: to accompany; p'hwān hêng, 伴行 *p'hw^nā kē^nâ*, to go in company, to go together.

P'hwăh 潑 P'hwat súy, 潑水 *p'hwăh chúy*, to throw out water with a scoop.

P'hwăh 鏺 Read p'hwat: a knife for cutting grass; p'hwát ch'hŏ, 鏺草 *p'hwăh ch'háou*, to cut down grass.

P'hwăh 拔 Read pwát: to lade; pwát t'hong, 拔桶 *p'hwăh t'háng*, a bucket, for lading water out of a well.

P'hwan 潘 Vulg. *p'hw^na*: a surname.

P'hwan 拌 To throw away anything; to reject; also written 拚, p'hwan.

P'hwán 坢 An even plain; also written 坪, p'hwán.

P'hwán 趕 The appearance of running away; to flee.

P'hwàn 泮 P'hwàn kĕng, 泮宮, the name of a school of learning; to dissolve.

Soō lók p'hwàn súy, 思樂泮水 *sëō^ng kŏēy è tē p'hwàn këung ây chúy*, let us think about delighting in the waters of the academy; see the 魯頌 Loé sëŭng.

Taē peng bē p'hwàn, 迨冰未泮 *kip kaòu se^ng böēy yëō^ng*, before the ice is dissolved; see the 詩經 Se keng.

P'hwàn 泮 The melting of ice; to dissolve; ē ê peng p'hwàn, 易於冰泮 *k'hăh k'hwaè ê se^ng yëō^ng*, easier than the melting of ice.

P'hwàn 袢 Clothes of no color.

P'hwàn 伴 P'hwàn hwàn, 伴奐, loose, easy, leisurely.

P'hwàn 判 Vulg. *p'hwⁿà:* to judge, to decide, to distinguish, to divide.
T'hëen tēy p'hwàn hȧp, 天地判合 *t'heeⁿᵍ tëy p'hwⁿà hȧp,* heaven and earth divide and unite.
P'hwàn twān, 判斷 *p'hwⁿà twān,* to judge and decide.

去

P'hwān 伴 To accompany; sëang p'hwān, 相伴 *sëo p'hwⁿā,* to go in company.

入

P'hwat 叭 Vulg. *payh:* to open the mouth wide.

P'hwat 嘙 To speak disorderly.

P'hwat 發 To tread down the grass with one's feet.

P'hwat 潑 Vulg. *p'hwăh:* to throw out water with a scoop; to dash about the water.

P'hwat 鏺 Vulg. *p'hwăh:* a knife for cutting grass.

去

P'hwùy 屁 Read p'hè: a foul wind; hòng p'hè, 放屁 *pàng p'hwùy,* to break wind.

平

Pin 賓 A guest, a visitor, a stranger; pin k'hek, 賓客 *pin k'hăyh,* a guest; pin choó, 賓主, guest and host.
Ch'hek yëá, sok taè lip ê teâou, k'hó soó é pin k'hek gân yëá, 赤也束帶立於朝可使與賓客言也 *Ch'hek yëá, hăh twà k'hëā tē teâou têng, t'hang saè kap pin k'hăyh kóng wā,* Ch'hek, having belted on his girdle and standing in the court, may be permitted to converse with strangers and guests; see the 論語 Lūn gé.

Pin 濱 The water's edge; haé pin, 海濱, the seashore.

Pin 獱 A small kind of otter.

Pin 鑌 A good kind of iron, of which sharp knives may be made.

Pin 檳 Pin lông, 檳榔 *pin nêⁿᵍ,* the betel nut, the areca nut; a tree without branches, with the fruit coming out of the heart.

Pin 邠 The name of a district, on the north-west of China.

Pin 豳 The name of a country; sek chëá T'haè ông ke Pin, 昔者太王居豳 *chá T'haè ông k'hëā tē Pin,* formerly T'haè ông dwelt at Pin; see 孟子 Bēng choó.

Pin 彬 Ornament and plainness equally displayed, moderate, natural. Also written 斌, pin.
Bûn chit pin pin, jëên hoē kwun choó, 文質彬彬然後君子 *bûn chit pin pin, jëên aōu chò kwun choó,* when ornament and plainness are equally displayed, it shows a man of worth; see the 論語 Lūn gé.

Pin 份 The ancient form of the preceding character.

Pin 𠛒 To divide, to distinguish.

去
Pín 稟 To announce, to inform, to receive orders, to send up a petition. Sín hāy bêng yew pín lēng, 臣下罔攸稟令 *hāy têy ây sín bô séy pín bēng*, the inferior officers would not have any one from whom they could receive orders; see the 書說命 Se wât bēng.

Pín 禀 The same as the preceding.

Pín 篺 Tëuk pín, 竹篺 *tek pín*, a wainscot or partition made of split bamboos twisted together; a bamboo screen.

Pín 臏 The knee-pan; the punishment of cutting off the legs.

去
Pìn 儐 To lead, to assist, to help, to accompany.

Pìn 擯 To blame, to reject; pìn ch'hek, 擯斥, to cast out, to condemn.

Pìn 殯 Pìn lëëm, 殯殮, to prepare a corpse for burial; during the 夏 Hāy dynasty this was done on the eastern steps of the house; during the 殷 Yin dynasty, between the two beams; and during the 周 Chew dynasty, on the western steps.

Pìn 鬢 The hair on the temples; pìn pëen, 鬢邊 *pìn pee^ng*, the sides of the head.

Pìn 篦 A comb, for cleaning and smoothing the hair; sàt pìn, 虱篦, a fine toothed comb.

平
Pîn 貧 Vulg. *sòng hëung*: poor, indigent, having no money. Pîn é chëën sē jîn che séy oè yëá, 貧與賤是人之所惡也 *sòng hëung kwà hāy chëën sē lâng ây séy wàn yëá*, a poor and mean condition is what people very much dislike; see the 論語 Lūn gé.

Pîn 頻 Several; hasty, urgent; pîn soè, 頻數, continually.

Pîn 嚬 Pîn ch'heàou, 嚬笑 to smile.

Pîn 顰 To draw up the eyebrows into wrinkles; to contract the brow; haōu pîn, 效顰, to imitate badly, to counterfeit.

Pîn 瀕 The water's edge; a bank, a shore.

Pîn 蘋 A kind of large water plant; pîn hwân, 蘋蘩, a water plant.

Pîn 缾 Vulg. *pân*: a pot, a jar, a vessel; hwa pîn, 花缾, a flower pot; chéw pîn, 酒缾 *chéw pân*, a wine vessel. Also written 瓶, pîn. Gîn pîn tê chéw jé boô hwun, 銀缾置酒汝無分 *gîn pân têy chéw lé bô hwun*, of the silver pot filled with wine you shall have no share; (said to a dwarfish person, in contempt;) when he replied, (kim póng têy bêng gnó ke tëung, 金榜題名我居中 *kim pé^ng têy më^nâ gwá k'hëā tē tang e^ng*,) "I shall stand in the centre of the names in the golden list of graduates;" (meaning that he should attain to the highest literary honors.)

Pîn 凭 To lean upon a table; pîn ó, 凭倚, to lean on anything.

Pîn 憑 To rest or rely on; pîn gëùk ké, 憑玉几, to lean on the pearly table; according to; pîn jé swat, 憑爾說, according to what you say, &c.

Pîn 凴 Bûn pîn, 文凴, a ticket, a pass; pîn kè, 凴據, a proof, evidence. Also written 凭, pîn, a surname.

Pîn 屏 Wûy pîn, 圍屏, a screen, a fence. T'hëen choó göëy pîn, choo hoê lōëy pîn, 天子外屏諸侯內屏 *hông tèy sëet gwā bîn ây pîn, choo hoê sëet laē bîn ây pîn,* the emperor placed his screen without the door, but the princes within.

去 Pîn 牝 The female of birds and beasts. Pîn key boô sîn, 牝鷄無晨 *key boê bô chêw mây^n h chaē,* the hen does not give notice of the morning; see the 書泰誓 Se t'haè sē.

Pîn 臏 The knee-pan, the cap of the knee.

Pîn 嬪 A female office.

Pîn 蹁 Pîn p'hong, 蹁蹔, the noise made by stamping on the ground.

去 Pit 蹕 To stop passengers on the road, when the sovereign is about to pass by; pit jê put kéng, 蹕而不警 *pit chăh lâng, jê bô kêng kaè e,* to stop the passengers without alarming them; see the 周禮 Chew léy.

Pit 僤 The same as the preceding.

Pit 畢 To finish, to conclude; the end; a surname; pit kéng, 畢竟, after all. Vulg. *kwùy kè:* finished, done, completed.
Jit chè jê pit, 日至而畢 *tang chăyh kaôu, kang kwùy swăh,* when the winter solstice arrives, all work is at an end; see the 左傳 Chó twān.

Pit 滭 A cold wind.

Pit 熚 The sound of fire burning.

Pit 篳 Pit bûn, 篳門, a bamboo gate.

Pit 嗶 A sound going out.

Pit 韠 A leathern cap for the knees, a pad for the knees, used when kneeling at sacrifices.

Pit 必 Must, certain, absolute; bē pit, 未必, it is not yet certain; hô pit? 何必, why must you do so? pit jëên, 必然, it must be so; pit tēng, 必定, determined on, fixed.
Ch'hò ch'hoò pit ê sē, tëen p'haè pit ê sē, 造次必於是顛沛必於是 *kín kip tek k'hak tëôh tē chêy lêy, lōng pöëy tek k'hak tëôh tē chêy lêy,* when in seasons of hurry, we must still adhere (to benevolence); and when overwhelmed with trouble, we must nevertheless abide by the same; see the 論語 Lūn gé.

Pit 珌 The ornaments of a sword; also written 琿, pit.

Pit 筆 A pencil, a hair pencil, with which the Chinese write; to write with a pencil; ké pit, 擳筆 *këăh pit*, to take up the pencil.
Sëá tò pit t'hoê kan, 寫到筆頭乾 *sëá kaðu pit t'haðu ta*, to write till the end of the pencil is dry.
Choó-soo, 子思, was afraid lest the doctrines of the 中庸, Tëung yûng should be forgotten through the lapse of time, (koè pit che e se, 故筆之於書 *chëá sëá e tē ch'hăyh,*) he therefore wrote them in a book, and delivered them to 孟子, Bēng-choó.

Pit 畋 A vessel cracked but not broken.

Pit 觱 A kind of pipe, played upon by the Tartars.

Pit 皴 Read ch'hin: a little rising of the skin.

天 Pit 弼 An assistant, a helper; hoō pit, 輔弼, to assist, to help.
Bōng tèy laē ê lëâng pit, 夢帝賚予良弼 *bāng sëang tèy hoē gwá hó ây sëăng pit*, I dreamed that the supreme bestowed on me a good assistant; see the 書說命 Se wát bēng.

Pit 佛 High, lofty, eminent; the same as the above.
Jip chek boô hwat kay, pit soō, 入則無法家佛士 *jip tē laē bīn, chek bô t'hang chò hwat ây kay, pit kwân ây t'hâk ch'hăyh lâng*, when at home we have no exemplary families, nor eminent scholars; (this is a bad thing for a country;) see 孟子 Bēng choó.

Pit 佖 Dignified, and properly behaved.

Pit 邲 The name of a country.

Pit 褾 A kind of short petticoat.

Pit 鼻 Vulg. *p'heeng*: the nose; pit k'hóng, 鼻孔 *p'heeng k'hang*, the nostrils.

Pit 闢 To open; k'hae pit, 開闢 *k'hwuy pit*, to open out, to commence.
Pit ch'hó laê, 闢草萊 to clear away the grass and weeds; see 孟子 Bēng choó.

Pit 辟 The same as the above.

Pit 擗 To beat one's breast; pit yúng k'hok k'hip, 擗踊哭泣 *p'hăh k'hám tëó k'ha, k'haðu kwà t'hé*, to beat on one's breast, to stamp with the foot, to cry and weep; see the 孝經 Haðu keng.

Pit 愎 Stubborn, perverse.

卆 Po 褒 To praise, to applaud; K'hóng-choó che chok Ch'hun Ch'hew, yit joō che po êng ê hwa kwûn, 孔子作春秋一字之褒榮於華袞 *K'hóng-choó ây chò Ch'hun Ch'hew, chít jē ây o ló, k'hăh êng ê hwa ch'haé ây kwûn bëên*, when Confucius composed the Spring and Autumn Record, each word of approbation therein contained was more glorious than a flowery crown.

'Po 皤 The same as the preceding.

Po 嶓 Po t'hëúng, 嶓冢, the name of a hill.

Po 艕 A boat, short and deep.

Po 菠 Po lêng ch'haè, 菠薐菜, the name of a vegetable; spinach.

Pó 保 To protect, to favor, to preserve; pó pē, 保庇, to protect; pó léng, 保領 *pó nëⁿá*, to secure; pó chwân, 保全, to keep safely; also, to nourish, to keep, to guard.

T'hëen pó têng jé, ėk k'hóng che koē, 天保定爾亦孔之固 *t'heeⁿᵍ pó tëⁿā lé yeá sīm këen koè*, if heaven keeps you safely, you will be very secure; see the 小雅 Seáou gnáy.

Pó 褓 A cloth in which children are carried; swaddling-clothes.

Sêng ông seàou, chaē këáng po che tëung, 成王少在襁褓之中 *Sêng ông yëá sèy twā tē këáng pó áy tang eⁿᵍ*, when Sêng ông was young, and yet in his swaddling clothes, &c.

Pó 葆 Grass and trees, growing luxuriantly, thick foliage.

Pó 堡 A small fort.

Pó 寶 Precious, anything precious, and valuable; pó tin, 寶珍, a pearl; pó pöèy, 寶貝, precious, valuable.

6 L

Hwaê kê pó, jê bêy kê pang, k'hó wūy jîn hoē? 懷其寶而迷其邦可謂仁乎 *k'hèⁿᵍ e áy pó pöèy, jê t'haou köèy láng áy pang kok, t'hang kóng sē jîn tek á bô?* to conceal one's valuable talents, and steal through a country, can such an one be considered benevolent? see the 論語 Lūn gé.

Pó 寳 The same as the above; also written 寚, pó.

Pó 鴇 The name of a solitary water bird.

Pó 賲 To have, to possess.

Pò 報 To answer, to recompense, to reward, to return a compliment; to repay; to inform, to announce. Sëen yéw seēn pò, ok yéw ok pò, jëák bē yéw pò, sê jit bē tò, 善有善報惡有惡報若未有報時日未到 *hó woō hó áy pò, p'haⁿê woō p'haⁿê áy pò, nā böèy woō pò, sê jit yëá böèy kaòu*, virtue has a good reward, and vice a bad reward, but if yet no reward, it is because the time has not yet come. T'hong pò, 通報, to announce one's name.

Pò 簸 To winnow corn, in order to clear it from the chaff.

Pò kè, 簸箕 *pwà kè*, a sieve.

Pò 播 To sow, to spread the seed, to scatter; to reject.

Kê sé pò pek kok, 其始播百穀 *e áy k'hé t'haóu yëá pùyh hāng áy kok*, when they begin to sow the various kinds of grain; see the 豳風 Pin hong.

平 Pô 婆 The epithet of an old woman; lo pô, 老婆, an old woman.

去 Pō 暴 To beat with the hand; violent, oppressive, perverse; a surname.
Pō hoé pâng hô, 暴虎馮河 *p'hăh hoé sêw kŏèy kâng hô*, to be able to beat a tiger with the hand, and to dash through a river without a boat; see the 論語 Lūn gé.
Kông hong ch'hē^{ng}á pō, 狂風且暴, a fierce and strong wind; pō gëăk, 暴虐, oppression, tyranny.

Pō 㬥 Upright conduct of officers.

平 Poe 晡 The time of half a day; noonday; sëāng poe, 上晡 *chëō^{ng} poe*, the forenoon; hāy poe, 下晡 *āy poe*, the afternoon.

Poe 埔 A plain; ch'hó poe, 草埔 *ch'haóu poe*, a grassy plain.

Poe 楠 Poe këang, 楠姜, the name of a tree.

Poe 蒲 A bamboo vessel.

上 Poé 補 To mend, to repair, to make up a deficiency; to fill up.
Ch'hun séng keng, jê poé put chëuk, 春省耕而補不足 *ch'hun t'hee^{ng} seng ch'hat chŏh ch'hân, jê poé bô kaôu*, in the season of spring, the prince should inspect the ploughing, and make up deficiences to the cultivators; see 孟子 Bēng choó.

Poé 綁 To mend clothes. The same as the preceding. Also written 緥 poé.

去 Poè 布 Cloth; to spread, to scatter; to disperse.
Poè pék, 布帛, cloth and silk; poè sàn, 布散 *poè sw^{n}à*, to scatter. A surname.
Poè pék tëâng twān tông, chek kày sëang jëăk? 布帛長短同則價相若 *poè pèk tê^{ng} têy sëo tâng, chek kày chee^{ng} sëo ch'hin chëō^{ng}?* when cloths and silks are equally long, would you have the prices equal? see 孟子 Bēng choó.

Poè 佈 Universally diffused; extensive, general.

Poè 抪 To disperse, to scatter; to beat.

Poè 怖 To be afraid, to be alarmed; to make afraid, to alarm.
Kê boô chëuk yéw e t'hok kwúy sîn chāy poé gê bîn, 其巫祝有依托鬼神詐怖愚民 *e ây saē kong á woō wá t'hok kwúy sin p'hëèn păyh sai^{ng} hoè e kë^{n}a*, those cojuring fellows, relying on ghosts and spirits, deceive and alarm the people.

Poè 傅 A surname.

Poè 誧 To reprove; also, a man's name.

平 Poê 匍 To lie prostrate on the ground; poê pôk, 匍匐, to creep on the ground.
Poê pók, chëang jip chéng, 匍匐將入井 *poê pòk chëang bŏëyh jip chai^{ng}*, creeping along

the ground and about to fall into a well; (speaking of an infant;) see 孟子 Bēng choó.

Poê 蒲 Ch'hëang poê, 菖蒲, the name of a water plant, a sort of mat rush; the Acorus calamus. A surname.

Poê 莆 Poê-têên hëēn, 莆田縣 *Poê-ch'hân kwān*, the name of a district in Hok-këèn.

Poê 酺 To drink wine and play music.

Poê 餔 An afternoon meal; poê ch'hwat, 餔啜, to eat and drink.

Poê 逋 To run away, to escape; to bear, to sustain.

Poê 葡 Poê tô, 葡萄, a grape, the grape vine.

Poê 裒 To collect, to assemble; to lessen, to decrease.

Poê to ek kwⁿá, 裒多益寡 *kēém e ây chēy t'heeⁿᵍ e ây chëó*, to lessen that which is excessive, and to add to that which is defective.

Poê 襮 The front of a garment; a form, appearance.

Poê 誧 The name of a man.

Poê 抔 To take anything up in the hollow of the hand, as water.

Koé chëá poê yím, 古者抔飲 *koé ây lâng poê chúy tē ch'hëw ch'hēⁿá lim*, the ancients used to take up water in the hollow of the hand, and drink.

Poê 捕 To apprehend, to seize; poê haē, 捕害, to persecute.

Lē boê tuy poê che k'hoé, 吏無追捕之苦 *sëó kwⁿa bô tuy lëāh ây kan k'hoé*, we shall not be troubled with inferior officers seizing and apprehending us; see the 韓延傳 Hân yëên twān.

Poê 苞 Tĕnk paôu, 竹苞 *tek poê*, a cluster of bamboos.

Poē 歨 步 A step, a pace, to walk, to walk on foot. A surname.

Hék pek poē jê hoē ché, hék gnoé sip poē jê hoē ché, 或百步而後止或五十步而後止 *woō ây chaóu chit păyh poē jëén aōu hâyⁿᵍh, woō ây chaóu gcē châp poē jëén aōu hâyⁿᵍh*, some would run a hundred paces, and then stop, and some only fifty paces, and then stop; see 孟子 Bēng choó.

Poē 蜅 Poē é, 蜅蛦, the name of an insect.

Poē 捕 To seize, to apprehend; poē haē, 捕害, to persecute.

K'hëén lē hwun chô tëùk poē, 遣吏分曹逐捕 *saé sèy kwⁿa hwun lūy kwⁿá lëāh*, he sent officers in different parties to pursue and take him; see the 灌夫傳 Kwân hoo twān.

Poē 哺 To chew in the mouth, to masticate; a chew.

Chew-kong yit hwān sam t'hoè poē, 周公一飯三吐哺 *Chew-kong chit tooīⁿᵍ pooīⁿᵍ sⁿa āy t'hoè poē*, Chew-kong at one meal, thrice spit out what he was chewing, (in order to get up and speak with clever people, who called upon him;) see the 史記 Soó kè.

Poē 餔 The same as the preceding; to eat, to devour.

Gnó put è, choó hák koó che tō,

jê é poē ch'hwat yĕá, 我不意子學古之道而以餔啜 *gwá bô sëōng choó woō t'hăk koĕ lâng ây tō lé, jé sëōng tē chëăh lim ây soō,* I never should have thought, that you who had studied the doctrines of the ancients, would have been taken up with eating and drinking; see 孟子 Bēng choó.

Poē 勊 Poē hoē, 勊劻, to exert one's strength.

Poē 部 Altogether, the whole; an order, a general class, a series, a radical; poē hwūn, 部分, a sort; lĕuk poē, 六部, the six courts, or boards of control; joō poē, 字部 *jē poē,* the radical of a character.

Poē 篰 A bamboo vessel, a flat piece of bamboo.

Poē 埠 Poē t'hoê, 埠頭, an anchorage, a harbor, a town on the seacoast, a mart; a place of merchandize.

土 Pöey 杯 A wine cup; chéw pöey, 酒杯, a wine glass; also written 坯, pöey.

Pöey chéw sëak peng kwân, 杯酒削兵權 *pöey chéw ây kan e sëak k'hè peng kwăn,* over a cup of wine, he deprived his generals of their military authority; said of the first emperor of the 宋 Sòng dynasty.

Pöey 桮 Pöey kwan, 桮棬, a drinking vessel, made of bent wood.

Choó, lêng sūn ké lĕw che sèng, jê é wûy pöey kwan hoē, 子能順杞柳之性而以爲桮棬乎 *lê, ēy sūn ké lĕw ây saing, jé lëăh e chò pöey kwan,* sir, I suppose you are able, by following the grain of the willow tree, to make round drinking vessels out of it; see 孟子 Bēng choó.

声 Pöéy 倍 To double; hék sëang pöéy sé, 或相倍蓰 *woō ây sëo pöéy woō ây goē têng pöéy,* some will be doubled, and some fivefold; see 孟子 Bēng choó.

Pöéy 裱 Read peáou: a neckerchief; *pöéy k'hwuy,* 裱開, to open out.

Pöéy 摰 Séw p'haé k'hae, 手擘開 *ch'héw pöéy k'hwuy,* to open out with the hand.

去 Pöèy 貝 A pearl; pó pöèy, 寶貝, precious, valuable; a surname.

Kē naé pöèy gëuk, 具乃貝玉 *pē pëēn woō pöèy gëuk,* there were prepared both pearls and gems; see the 書盤庚 Se pwan keng.

Pöèy 唄 An expression of the Budhists, signifying to praise.

Pöèy 背 The back; pöèy hoē, 背後 *k'ha chëăh aōu,* behind the back.

Pöèy 褙 Clothes for the back.

Pöèy 輩 A sort, a class, an order, many; the sign of the plural number.

Hāy chëēn che pöèy, 下賤之輩 a low, vulgar set of fellows.

Léy k'hé wûy gnó pöèy sëet? 禮豈爲我輩設 *léy soè k'ham sē gwán ây lâng sëet?* "were the ceremonies appointed by us?" said by 老子 Ló choó.

Pöèy 昁 The sun not clear.

Pöëy 蓓 Pöëy boé, 蓓毋, the name of a medicine; a species of Althea.

Pöëy 眛 The eyes dim.

平 Pöëy 陪 To help, to assist, to associate; a domestic, an officer of the palace.
Jé tek put bêng, é boô pöêy boô k'heng, 爾德不明以無陪無鄉 *lé ây tek ūm bêng chè kaòu bô lâng t'hang chān, bô lâng chò kwⁿa*, if your virtue is not clear, you will have none to assist, and none to become your officers; see the 大雅 Taē gnáy.
Pöêy sîn chip kok bêng, sam sè he put sit è, 陪臣執國命三世希不失矣 *kay sîn gîm kok ây bêng lêng, sⁿa sè têy chëó ūm sit lôh*, when domestic officers hold the reins of government, it seldom happens that a dynasty lasts longer than three generations; see the 論語 Lūn gé.

Pöêy 倍 Pöêy o, 倍阿 the name of a devil, who takes possession of the eastern part of a dwelling.

Pöêy 培 To nourish, to foster, to increase, to cause to grow.
Chae chëá pöêy che, 栽者培之 *chèng ây meêⁿgh tëŏh pöêy yâng e*, what things are planted should be nourished; see the 中庸 Tëung yûng.

Pöêy 醅 Unstrained wine.

Pöêy 掊 To collect, to gather together.

Pöêy 賠 Pöêy poé, 賠補, to make anything good that is lost or deficient, to compensate.

6 M

Pöëy 俳 Pöêy yew, 俳優, a mixed kind of play; pöêy höêy, 俳佪, a sort of game.

Pöëy 裴 Long flowing robes; a surname.

Pöëy 菠 Pöêy lêng ch'haè, 菠蔆菜, the name of a vegetable.

去 Pöëy 珮 Gems and precious stones; pöëy gëük, 珮玉, gems worn by those in office.

Pöëy 佩 A large girdle; to wear a girdle, or to wear anything as a girdle.
K'hè song, boô séy put pöëy, 去喪無所不佩 *k'hè seⁿg hâ, chëw bô séy ūm pöēy*, when we are out of mourning, there is no kind of ornament that we may not wear attached to our girdle; see the 論語 Lūn gé.

Pöēy 粑 Mixed rice.

Pöēy 倍 Two fold, double; vulgar, mean; kay têng pöëy, 叻重倍 as much again.
Jê koé sam pöëy, 如賈三倍 *ch'hin chëóⁿg t'hân sⁿa têng pöēy*, like making a gain of three hundred per cent; see the 大雅 Taē gnáy.
Be careful in your expressions, soo wàn p'hé pöëy é, 斯遠鄙倍矣 *chëy ch'hēⁿá ēy hwuiⁿg k'hè p'hé loē ēy lâng*, thus you will be enabled to keep vulgar people at a distance; see the 論語 Lūn gé.

Pöēy 悖 Stubborn, rebellious, disobedient; pöēy gék, 悖逆, rebellious.
Hêng soō put pöēy, 行事不悖 *chò soō bô pöēy gék*, to do things without disobedience; see the 周語 Chew gé.

Pöēy 焙 To roast; pöēy jŏúk, 焙肉 *pöēy băh*, roasted meat.

Pöēy 誖 To speak disorderly; soò tát jê put pöēy, 四達而不誖 *soō wŭy bô lâm sám kóng*, in every place to avoid improper discourse.

Pöēy 偝 To stand uneven, not to face a thing properly.
Toê hoê boê pöēy lip, 投壺毋偝立 *taôu cheèng tē hoê, ūm t'hang k'hëā bô sè chĕnd*, in throwing (the arrows) at the pot, do not stand awry.

Pöēy 焅 The same as 焙, pöēy, to roast.

Pöēy 背 To turn the back upon; to desert, to betray; to reject.
Kè óng, pöēy soo pó che hwŭn, 既往背師保之訓 *kaôu köēy k'hè, chĕw pöēy bông sin saing ây kà hwùn*, when he departed, he turned his back on the instructions of his teachers; said of 太甲, T'haè-kap, in the 書經 Se keng.

Pöēy 邶 The name of a country.

Pöēy 旆 The small extremity of a tree.

Pöēy 晡 The sun not clear.

Pöēy 筏 The appearance of flying about.

Pöēy 瑁 Taē pöēy, 玳瑁, a valuable kind of tortoise-shell.

Pöēy 狽 Lông pöēy, 狼狽, two species of wolf, one with short fore, and the other with short hindor feet; the one well adapted for ascending a hill, and the other for descending, but when they walk in the plain country, the one is obliged to put his paws on the rump of the other; hence the expressions, lông pöēy sëang e, 狼狽相依, the *lông* and *pöēy* depend on one another; lông pöēy, 狼狽, is now commonly used to denote a state of ruin and misery.

Pöēy 棑 Trees giving out branches and leaves. The branches of trees growing straight up.

叐
Pŏh 薄 Read pók: thin, slender; sparing, niggardly.
Jê lé pók peng, 如履薄冰 *ch'hin chëōng tăh pŏh seng*, like treading on thin ice; see the 小雅 Seáou gnáy.

夫
Pok 卜 To divine; that by which people divine; to give; a surname.
Pok sē, 卜筮, instruments of divination; pok kwà, 卜卦, to divine.
Kwuy wûy pok, këep wûy sē, 龜爲卜筴爲筮 *koo kap chò pok, këep ch'haôu chò sē*, the *pok* mode of divination is made by the tortoise-shell, and the *sē* divination by certain pieces of grass.

Pok 北 Vulg. *pak:* the north; pok seng, 北星 *pak ch'haing*, the north star.
Choō sey, choō tong, choō lâm, choō pok, boô soo put hók, 自西自東自南自北無思不服 *choō sae, choō tang, choō lâm, choō pah, bô chit ây sëōng ūm hók*, from the west, and east, from the south, and north, every thought will be subjected; see the 大雅 Taē gnáy.
Chëèn paē choé ék wát pok, 戰敗走亦曰北 *chëèn paē chaôu yëá kóng këò pok*, to be defeat-

ed in an engagement, and to flee away is called 北, pok, 'to north it.'

Pok 焤 Pit pok, 熚焤, the noise of fire burning bamboos; pit pok keàou, 熚焤叫 *pit pok haóu*, the bursting bamboos make a noise like '*pit pok*.'

Pok 鳪 A jungle fowl, a wild pheasant, the cry of which sounds like *pok*.

Pók 僕 A servant, a slave, a dependant; also used for the first personal pronoun; choó pók, 主僕, master and servant; noê pók, 奴僕, a slave. Choō ch'heng wûy pók 自稱爲僕 *ka te ch'heng hoe chô pók*, people when speaking of themselves say *pók*, 'your servant.'

Pók 僕 The same as the preceding.

Pók 濮 A surname; and pók yâng, 濮陽 a double surname.

Pók 幞 A veil, a covering for the head, a head-kerchief; also written 襆, pók.
Pók t'hoê, 幞頭 *pák t'haóu*, to tie a kerchief round the head.

Pók 匐 Poê pók, 匍匐, to creep along the ground, to crawl.
Poê pók óng chëang sit che, 匍匐往將食之 *pây lây tē t'hoê óng k'hè chëáh e*, he crept along the ground, and went to eat it; see 孟子 Bēng choó.

Pók 簙 A bamboo frame, for feeding silkworms; a door-blind.

Pók 薄 Vulg. *pŏh:* thin, slender, meagre, mean, niggardly; a door-blind.
Goê t'haē jé put pók, hô koè hwán yëá? 吾待爾不薄何故反也 *gwá kwán t'haē lé bēy pŏh, sⁿa soō lé hwán yëá?* I have never treated you ill, why do you then rebel? A surname.

Pók 縛 Vulg. *pák:* to bind, to tie.
Choō pók laê hâng, 自縛來降 *ka tē pák laê hâng*, he bound himself and came to tender his submission.

Pók 伏 The same as 匐, pók, to crawl.

Pók 亳 The name of a place, where 湯, T'hong held his capital.

Pók 䡬 To urge, to drive.

Pók 泊 To stop, to come to an anchor; to moor a vessel to the shore. Vulg. *p'hŏh:* an anchorage.
Tam pók, 淡泊, thin, vacant, insipid,

Pók 箔 Vulg. *pāyh:* a door-blind.

Póng 榜 A board, a plank of wood, a placard; a proclamation.
Peaou póng, 標榜, to speak of, to make remarks on.
Ch'hut póng cheaou soō, 出榜招士 *ch'hut pêⁿg chëo t'hák ch'hāyh lâng*, he issued a proclamation to collect recruits. Also written 牓, póng.

Póng 菶 Luxuriant herbage.

Póng 琫 The ornaments of a dress sword. Also written 鞛, póng.

去 Pòng 謗 To revile, to reproach; hwúy pòng, 毀謗, to slander. Kè lé che sîn, kám jëük ko wūy, é sok kwan pòng? 覊旅之臣敢辱高位以速官謗 *chò lâng k'hàyh ây jîn sîn, kⁿá jëük kwân ây wūy, é maīⁿgh chëo chò kwⁿa lâng ây hwúy pòng?* a stranger and a foreigner, how dare I disgrace an elevated office, and thus speedily draw down upon me the animadversions of my brother officers? see the 左傳 Chó twān.

平 Pông 旁 The side, on one side; jê pông boô jîn, 如旁無人 *ch'hin chëōⁿg pông peeⁿg bô lâng*, just as if there was no one near.

Pông pëen, 旁邊 *pông peeⁿg*, on one side.

Pông 傍 The same as the above; a surname.

Pông 逄 A surname.

Pông 徬 Pông hông, 徬彷, unsettled, undetermined; to pace backwards and forwards.

Pông hông put jím k'hè, 徬彷不忍去 *kēⁿâ laê kēⁿâ k'hè, bēy lún k'hè*, he paced backwards and forwards, without venturing to go; see the 詩序 Se sē.

Pông 螃 Pông hây, 螃蟹, a crab, an animal that goes on one side. Pông hây wun sin kae kap tēw, 螃蟹渾身皆甲冑 *pông hây chit hín sin chò poô sē kà'h tēw*, the crab is all over armed with a coat of mail; see a 古詩 koé se.

Pông 膀 Pông kong, 膀胱, the groin, the region of the bladder.

Pông 房 Vulg. *pâng*: a room; pông këen, 房間 *pâng keng*, a chamber; pông ok, 房屋 *pâng ch'hoò*, a house, a dwelling. A surname.

Pông 馮 A surname; also read pâng. Bōng këèn Pông-hoō, ch'he jê gêng che, 望見馮婦趨而迎之 *bāng kcèⁿg Pông-hoō, kín kēⁿâ jê gēⁿâ chcĕh e*, when they saw Pông-hoō at a distance they hastened to meet him; see 孟子 Bēng choó.

Pông 滂 Pông tô, 滂沱, great rain.

去 Pōng 傍 Near, by the side, adjoining; vulg. *pēⁿg*: to rely on, to live near. Pōng hwa sûy léw, kò chëên ch'hun, 傍花隨柳過前村 *pēⁿg hwa sûy léw köèy chêng ch'huiⁿg*, going near to the flowers, and following the row of willows, let us pass over to the opposite village.

上 *Poó* 斧 Read hoó: a hatchet; hoó t'hoê, 斧頭 *poó t'haôu*, an ax. Hwât k'ho jê hô? hwuy hoó put k'hek, 伐柯如何匪斧不克 *p'hăh poó t'haôu paīⁿg an chwⁿá? bô poó t'haôu bēy chò tit*, in cutting an ax-handle, how must we manage? if we do not use an ax, we shall never succeed; see the 詩經 Se keng.

去 *Poò* 富 Read hoò: rich, affluent, wealthy. Hoò é kwùy sē jîn che séy yëük yëá, 富與貴是人之所欲也 *poò kap kwùy sē lâng ây séy aē*, riches and honors are what men desire; see the 論語 Lūn gé.

平 *Poô* 匏 Read paôu: a calabash; goê k'hé paôu kwa yëá chae? 吾豈匏瓜也哉 *gwá k'ham sē poô á kwa á chae?* do you think I am a calabash or a melon? see the 論語 Lūn gé.

Poô 炰 Read paôu: to roast anything in the fire.

去 Poō 毰 Poō lwán, 毰卵 *poō nooi^ng*, to hatch eggs.

Poō 婦 Read hoō: a woman, a wife; sit hoō, 媳婦 *sim poō*, a daughter-in-law.

入 *Poŏh* 窋 Read chut: anything in a cavern or hole.

平 *Pooi^ng* 方 Read hong: a surname.

Pooi^ng 楓 Read hong: the name of tree; hong sē, 楓樹 *pooi^ng ch'hew*, the maple, the sycamore; the Acer genus.

Pooi^ng 風 Read hong: as hong sê é, 風時雨 *pooi^ng sé hoē*, a slight shower.

去 *Pooi^ng* 飯 Read hwān: rice; sit hwān, 食飯 *chëăh pooi^ng*, to eat rice.

平 Pun 黺 A black spot.

Pun 分 Read hwun: to divide; hwun k'háe, 分開 *pun k'hwuy*, to separate. Hwun tëên chè lòk, 分田制祿 *pun ch'hân chè hóng lòk*, to divide the fields, and regulate the emoluments; see 孟子 Bēng choó.

上 Pún 本 A root; an essential, fundamental thing; kin pún, 根本, the origin; gwân pún, 原本, originally; pún chëên, 本錢 *pún chëê^ng*, a capital in trade; pún bwát, 本末, the head and tail, the first and last in importance; sëāng pún, 上本 *chëō^ng pún*, to send up a document to the emperor; se pún, 書本, a volume of a book.
Kwun choó boō pún, pún lip jê tō seng, 君子務本本立而道生 *kwun choó chwan boō kin pún, kin pún nā k'hëă tō lê chëw sai^ng*, the good man attends to the principal thing; for when the principal thing is established virtue springs up; see the 上論 Sëāng lūn.

Pún 畚 A vessel in which seed is kept.

Pún 畚 A basket or hod for holding earth; pún ke, 畚箕, a hod for dirt.

Pún 匾 Read pëén: flat; pëén tam, 匾擔 *pún t^na*, a flat piece of wood, with which burdens are carried across the shoulders.

去 *Pùn* 糞 Read hwùn: dung, excrement; lók hwùn, 落糞 *lôh pùn*, to manure the ground.
K'hó é hwùn tëên tëw, 可以糞田疇 *t'hang laé pùn ch'hân tëw*, this can be employed in manuring the fields; see the 月令 Gwàt lēng.

平 Pûn 歕 To hold anything in the mouth, and spurt it out, as water; pûn h^nô, 歕火, to blow the fire.

去 Pūn 笨 A dull, stupid mind.

6 N

Pūn 笨 The inside of bamboo; ch'hoe pūn, 粗笨, to go to stool; ch'hún pūn, 蠢笨, stupid, dull, foolish; tëuk pūn, 竹笨 *tek pūn*, a bamboo frame, for stowing away grain.

Pūn 体 Weak, coarse; the same as the preceding.

Pūn 笆 A frame made of split bamboo, and rolled up, in order to contain grain; also written 笹, pūn.

夫 Put 不 Vulg. *ūm*: not, no, do not, not yet; put k'hó, 不可 *ūm t'hang*, do not, should or ought not.

Kwun choò put tëūng, chek put wuy, hák chek put koè, 君子不重則不威學則不固 *kwun choó ây lâng bô tē tëūng, chēw bēy wuy hong, t'hàk yëá bēy këen koè*, if the good man is not sedate, he will not be dignified, and his learning will not be solid; see the 上論 Sëāng lūn.

Put 扒 To scrape together; to scratch.

Put 朳 Pây put, 杷朳, a rake without teeth, a board rake, for raking up corn into a heap, or spreading it out to dry.

㔾 Pu̍t 勃 To terminate; finally; to change countenance; suddenly.

Ong pu̍t jëên pëèn hoē sek, 王勃然變乎色 *ông pu̍t jëên peē^ng sek*, the king changing countenance looked angrily; see 孟子 Bēng choó.

Pu̍t 倖 Violent, strong.

Pu̍t 渤 Pu̍t haé, 渤海, the northern sea. Pok yéw pu̍t haé che lē, 北有渤海之利 *pak pee^ng woō pu̍t haé ây lē*, on the north we have the advantage of the northern sea.

Pu̍t 浡 To arise, or to rise up suddenly, as a spring gushing out.

Pu̍t 孛 An unlucky star; a comet.

Pu̍t 郣 The name of a district, which is said to have risen out of the sea, hence it is called pu̍t-haé kwūn, 郣海郡, rise-out-of-sea district.

Pu̍t 鵓 The name of a bird; a kind of speckled pigeon.

Pu̍t 艴 An angry look; Cheng-sey pu̍t jëên put wát, 曾西艴然不悅 *Cheng-sey pu̍t jëên ūm hwⁿa hé*, Cheng-sey looked angry, and displeased; see 孟子 Bēng choó.

Pu̍t 颰 The sound of wind; a violent wind.

Pu̍t 鋍 A pot boiling over.

Pu̍t 馞 Pit put, 馝馞, fragrant.

Pu̍t 埻 Dust; the rising of dust.

Pu̍t 拷 To pluck up.

上去 *Pwà* 簸 Read pò: to sift; pò ke, 簸箕 *pwà ke*, a seive.

下平 *Pwâ* 抛 Read p'haou: to throw; p'haou bóng, 抛網 *pwâ bāng*, to cast a net.

Pwâ 拚 Read pwân: to throw away; pwân bēng, 拚命 *pwâ mē^{n}ā*, to venture one's life; pwân chêên, 拚錢 *pwâ cheê^{ng}*, to expend money.

上平 *Pw^{n}a* 搬 Read pwan: to remove; to shift anything; pwan sé, 搬徙 *pw^{n}a swá*, to remove to another place.

Pw^{n}a 般 Read pwan: a kind; yit pwan, 一般 *chit pw^{n}a*, the same, alike.

上聲 *Pw^{n}á* 坂 Read pwán: the bank of a morass; the name of a place.

上去 *Pw^{n}à* 半 Read pwàn: the half; pwàn seng pwàn soó, 半生半死 *pw^{n}à sai^{ng} pw^{n}à sé*, half alive and half dead; yit pwàn, 一半 *chit pw^{n}à*, one half; Confucius' sleeping dress was (tëâng yit sin yéw pwàn, 長一身有半 *t^{ng} chit sin kwā chit pw^{n}à*,) as long as his body, and half as long again; see the 論語 Lūn gé.

Pw^{n}à 絆 Read pwàn: ropes for tying or entangling horses' feet.

下平 *Pw^{n}â* 磐 Sék pwân, 石磐 *chëŏh pw^{n}â*, a flat stone, used as a pedestal for a wooden pillar.

Pw^{n}â [般+足] Read pwân: the instep; këak pwan, 跤盤 *k'ha pw^{n}â*, the flat part of the top of the foot.

Pw^{n}â 盤 Read pwân: a plate; pwan wán, 盤碗 *pw^{n}â w^{n}á*, plates and basins. Pwân tëëp, 盤碟 *pw^{n}â tëëh*, plates and dishes.

Pw^{n}â 蹣 Read pwân: to climb over; pwân ch'hëâng, 蹣牆 *pw^{n}â ch'hëô^{ng}*, to climb over a wall; pwân san kò léng, 蹣山過嶺 *pw^{n}â sw^{n}â köèy nē^{n}á*, to climb over hills and surmount precipices.

上去 Pwaè 扒 To pluck up.

上入 *Pwăh* 鉢 Read pwat: a vessel containing food; e pwat, 衣鉢 *e pwăh*, a trunk.

Pwăh 撥 Read pwat: to turn anything round; pwat kong, 撥工 *pwăh kang*, to lend a hand; pwat chëën, 撥錢 *pwăh cheê^{ng}*, to spend money.

Pwăh 盋 Oô pwat, 盂盋 *oô pwăh*, a kind of dish.

下入 *Pwăh* 跌 Read tëét: to fall, to stumble; tëét tó, 跌倒 *pwăh tó*, to fall down. Tëét tó seáou se seng, hoô k'hé taē hák soō, 跌倒小書生扶起大學士 *pwăh tó sèy hák seng, hoô k'hé twā hák soō*, when he fell down, he looked like a little schoolboy, but when he was helped up he appeared as a great doctor; said of 林竹溪 Lim Teuk-k'hey, who was very small in stature, but great in mind.

Pwăh 鈸 Jeâou pwát, 鐃鈸 *lâ pwăh*, a pair of cymbals. Yit pwát, 一鈸 *chit pwăh*, a piece of money, a quarter of a dollar, or a quarter of a real.

平 Pwan 般 Vulg. *pwⁿa:* to remove, to convey, to transport; pwan wūn chaê bŭt, 般運財物 *pwⁿa wūn cheēⁿᵍ meēⁿᵍh*, to transport goods or money.
Yit pwan yāng, 一般樣 *chit pwⁿa yëōⁿᵍ*, of the same kind.

Pwan 搬 Vulg. *pwⁿa:* to remove; to exercise; pwan yëén boó gāy, 搬演武藝 *pwⁿa yëén boó āy soō*, to perform military tactics, to drill.

上 Pwán 坂 Vulg. *pwⁿá:* the name of a place; a a bank to a marsh.

Pwán 阪 The brow of a hill.

Pwán 舨 Tông pwán, 艟舨, a kind of a boat.

Pwán 般 A large slice; the name of a district.

去 Pwàn 半 Vulg. *pwⁿà:* the half; yit kò pwàn, 一個半 *gây pwⁿà*, one and a half.
Boô tò yit pwàn, 無倒一半 *bô kaòu chit pwⁿà*, not amounting to one half.

Pwàn 絆 Pwàn má sek, 絆馬索 *pwⁿà báy sŏh*, ropes used for entangling horses' feet, in order to throw their riders.

去 Pwān 叛 Pöëy pwān, 背叛, to rebel against, to turn the back on any one.
P'hok hàk ê bûn, yëak che é léy, èk k'hó é hwut pwān è hoo, 博學於文約之以禮亦可以弗叛矣夫 *p'hok hàk tē bûn, yëak sok e é léy soè, yëá t'hang é bô pwān è hoo*, when men are generally acquainted with literature, and governed by propriety, they may be restrained from rebellion; see the 論語 Lūn gé.

Pwān 畔 Tëên pwān, 田畔 *ch'hân pwⁿā*, the furrow of a field, a landmark.
Keng chëá jëāng pwān, hêng chëá jëāng loē, 耕者讓畔行者讓路 *chŏh ch'hân āy lāng nëōⁿᵍ pwⁿā, kēⁿā loē āy lāng nëōⁿᵍ loē*, "the ploughmen yielded the furrow, and travelers yielded the road;" said of an improved state of society in the time of 周文王 Chew Bûn-ông.

平 Pwân 弁 A cap, a hat, used in the 周, Chew dynasty.

Pwân 槃 Pwân hwân, 槃桓, self-possession, to obtain one's wish.

Pwân 鎜 Tông pwân, 銅鎜 *tâng pwⁿâ*, a large brazen dish, for holding presents.

Pwân 鞶 A large girdle.

Pwân 瘢 Pwân hwûn, 瘢痕, the cicatrice of a wound.

Pwân 胖 Great, fat, lusty; hwûy pwân, 肥胖 *pwûy p'hàng*, corpulent, fat.
Sim kóng t'héy pwân, 心廣體胖 *sim k'hwàh t'héy p'hàng*, a gross mind and a fat habit of body; see the 大學 Taē hàk.

Pwân 媻 An old woman; some say, a young wife.

Pwân 弄 Ch'hëak pwân, 雀弄, the name of a plant.

Pwân 拚 To fly; the appearance of flying.

Pwân 般 Pwân lók, 般樂, pleasure, voluptuousness.
Pwân lók taē gō, sē choō kēw hō yëá, 般樂怠敖是自求禍也 *pwân lók p'hun twⁿā gō bān, sē ka tē kēw hō hwān*, voluptuousness and contemptuous negligence is the way to bring misery on one's-self; see 孟子 Bēng choó.

Pwân 蹬 Këak pwân, 脚蹬 *k'ha pwⁿâ*, the instep.

Pwân 磐 Vulg. *pwⁿâ:* a great stone; sék pwân, 石磐 *chëŏh pwⁿâ*, a flat stone.
Tëēn jê pwân sék, 奠如磐石 *tëⁿā tëŏh ch'hin chëōⁿᵍ pwⁿâ chëŏh*, as firm as a flat stone.

Pwân 盤 Vulg. *pwⁿâ:* a plate, a vessel for containing anything; taē seáou pwân, 大小盤 *twā sèy pwⁿâ*, great and small plates; also, at rest.

Pwân 蹣 Vulg. *pwⁿâ:* to climb over; pwân ch'hëâng t'hoê hëét, 蹣牆透穴 *pwⁿâ ch'hëōⁿᵍ t'haòu k'hang*, to climb over walls and to creep through holes; pwân san, 蹣跚, to walk lame, to go round.

上入

Pwat 撥 Vulg. *pwăh:* to spread out, to turn around; to direct, to arrange.
Pwat k'hae, 撥開 *pwăh k'hwuy*, to open out, to spread abroad.

Pwat 癶 One of the radicals; intended to represent two legs striding.

Pwat 鉢 Vulg. *pwăh:* a vessel for containing food; e pwat, 衣鉢, *e pwăh*, the dress and begging dish of a Budhist priest.

Pwat 砵 This character should be pronounced *at*, and is read pwat, by mistake.

Pwat 般 Pwat jëák, 般若, a foreign expression, introduced with the Budhistic religion, and meaning wisdom.

下入

Pwát 犮 To run away; the appearance of a dog running away.

Pwát 拔 Vulg. *păyh:* to select, to pick, to pull up; to pluck up.
Pwát maôu jê, é kê lūy cheng kit, 拔茅茹以其彙征吉 *păyh hⁿm a ch'haôu, chedou e ây lūy t'hăyh e woō kit*, in plucking up the long coarse grass, it is lucky to pick it according to its sort; see the 易經 Ėk keng.
Pwát këèm, 拔劍 *păyh këèm*, to draw out a sword.

Pwát 跋 Pwát sëëp, 跋涉, to cross hills and rivers; to be wearied with rough traveling.

Pwát 鈸 Jeâou pwát, 鐃鈸 *lâ pwăh*, a pair of cymbals; a piece of money.

Pwát 軷 To sacrifice to the gods of the road, on undertaking a journey.

Pwát 袚 The dress of the western foreigners.

Pwåt **茇** A straw shed, a thatched cottage. Seàou-pek séy pwåt, 召伯所茇 *Seàou-pek twā tē ch'haôu ch'hoò*, Seàou-pek dwelt in a thatched cottage; see the 召南 Seàou lâm.

Pwåt **魃** Hān pwåt, 旱魃, the demon of drought: also written 越, pwåt. Hān pwåt wûy gëåk, 旱魃爲虐 *twā wⁿā chò gëåk haē*, the demon of drought is very destructive; see the 大雅 Taē gnáy.

Pwåt **跋** To tread upon, to step over; lông pwåt kê bé, 狼跋其尾 *ch'haê lông tăh tëŏh e ây böëy*, the wolf trod on his tail; see the 邠風 Pin hong.

Pwuy **悲** Choo pwuy, 慈悲, merciful: applied to the instructions of Budha.

Pwúy **悟** To rely on.

Pwùy **沸** To bubble up, to boil up; at the Hông-laê, 蓬萊, hill, there is said to be pwùy súy, 沸水, a hot spring, a boiling fountain.

Jê pwùy jê keng, 如沸如羹 *ch'hin chëōⁿᵍ pwùy kwûn, ch'hin chëōⁿᵍ kaiⁿᵍ t'heⁿᵍ*, like boiling water, or broth; see the 大雅 Taē gnáy.

Pwùy **疿** Pwùy choó, 疿子 *pwùy á*, small pustules produced by the heat.

Pwûy **肥** Read hwûy: fat, corpulent, lusty. Paôu yéw hwûy jëûk, kèw yéw hwûy má, 庖有肥肉廐有肥馬 *paôu toô woō pwûy băh, báy teâou woō pwûy báy*, in the larder there is fat meat, and in the stable fat horses; see 孟子 Bēng choó.

Pwûy **吠** Read hwūy: to bark; koé hwūy, 狗吠 *kaôu pwūy*, the dog barks.

Key bêng koé hwūy sëang bun, jê tát hoē soò kéng, 鷄鳴狗吠相聞而達乎四境 *key t'hê kaôu pwūy sëo t'hēⁿa, jê tát hoē sè kêng*, the crowing of cocks and the barking of dogs could be heard from one place to another, and spread throughout the four quarters of the country; see 孟子 Bēng choó.

Pwūy **蟦** Sék hwūy, 石蟦 *chëŏh pwūy*, a kind of stinking insect, which appears about the time when the 'cat's eyes' begin to ripen.

S

卓

Sa 些 A little, a few; vulg. *kwúy lëëp:* a small quantity.

Sa 尖 The same as the above; also written 尠, sa.

Sa 栅 Bȯk sa, 木栅, a wooden fence, a palisade.

Lëên êng lip sa, 連營立栅 *sëo swa yë^{n}â k'hëā bȯk sa,* a connected encampment, with upright palisades.

卓

S^{n}a 衫 Read sam: a jacket, a coat; hān sam, 汗衫 *kw^{n}ā s^{n}a,* a shirt.

Hëëp hān sam é tòng jëët, 脅汗衫以當熱 *gnăyh kw^{n}ā s^{n}a ê tè^{ng} jwăh,* he took his shirt under his arm, to enable him to bear the heat.

Sam k'hoè, 衫褲 *s^{n}a k'hoè,* jacket and trowsers.

S^{n}a 三 Read sam: three; sip sam, 十三 *chăp s^{n}a,* thirteen.

虛

S^{n}á 甚 Read sīm: what; sīm soō? 甚事 *s^{n}á soō?* what's the matter?

卓

Sae 顋 The cheeks; këep sae, 頰顋, the sides of the face.

Sae 鰓 The bones about the gills of a fish.

Sae 腮 The flesh under the throat; gnêw hâm sae, 牛頷腮, *goô âm sey,* the dewlap of an ox.

Sae 鬛 Bushy whiskers, a long beard.

Sae 篩 Vulg. *t'hae:* a sieve; bé sae, 米篩 *bé t'hae,* a sieve for rice.

Sae 獅 A lion; yit tùy sėk soo, 一對石獅 *chit tùy chëŏh sae,* a pair of stone lions; generally placed in the front of houses or temples.

Sae 簏 A bamboo sieve for separating the coarse from the fine.

Sae 犀 Sae gnew, 犀牛, a rhinoceros; the skin of which may be used as medicine.

Sae 西 Read sey: the west; sey t'hëen, 西天 *sae t'hee^{ng},* the western heavens.

Sey hong bé jîn, 西方美人 *sae he^{ng} ây hó lâng,* the excellent person from the west; see the 衛風 Wöëy hong.

卤

Saé 𢿛 Laé saé, 𧝓𢿛, ragged clothes.

Saé 使 Read soó: to send, to employ, to cause, to order; soó yūng, 使用 *saé yūng*, to employ; ch'hay soó, 差使 *ch'hay saé*, to send on an errand. Soó bîn é sê, 使民以時 *saé pāyh sai^ng cheāou sé*, to employ the people in the proper season; see the 論語 Lūn gé.

Saé 史 Read soó: a surname.

Saé 屎 Read sé: dung, ordure; hòng soó, 放屎 *pàng saé*, to go to stool.

去

Saè 塞 To separate; a partition; a border, a side, a boundary. Saè pok t'hëen k'hè hân, 塞北天氣寒 *keē^ng pak ây tēy t'hee^ng k'hè jwâh*, in the countries bordering on the north, the climate is very cold.

Saè 賽 To reward, to remunerate; to pay, to repay; saè gwān, 賽願, to pay one's vows.

Saè 曬 Vulg. *p'hàk*: to dry or be scorched in the sun; saè jit ak é, 曬日沃雨 *p'hàk jit ak hoē*, to be scorched in the sun, and drenched in the rain. Also written 晒, saè.

Saè 殺 To descend, to lessen, to diminish. Also read sat: to kill. Hwuy wûy sëâng, pit saè che, 非帷裳必殺之 *ū^m sē twā yîn chëô^ng, chēw pit saè e*, if it was not a public or court dress, he (Confucius) would always be for diminishing it; see the 論語 Lūn gé.

Saè 婿 Lé sèy, 女婿 *kë^ná saè*, a son-in-law.

Saè 使 Read soò: a messenger; kok soō, 國使 *kok saè*, an envoy, an ambassador. Taē soò yëâ, 大使爺 *twā saè yëâ*, a commissioner.

丟

Saē 祀 Read soō: an offering; gnoé soō, 吾祀 *goē saē*, the altars to the gods of the five parts of a dwelling house.

Saē 事 Read soō: to serve; hòk soō, 服事 *hòk saē*, to render service to any one. E hòk soō Yin, 以服事殷 *é hòk saē Yin*, and still he served the Yin dynasty; see the 論語 Lūn gé.

Saē 姒 Tông soō, 同姒 *tâng saē*, the wives of one's elder or younger brethren; a sister-in-law.

Saē 似 Read soō: alike; sëùk soō, 熟似 *sèk saē*, well acquainted, familiar.

入

Săh 煠 To boil or simmer anything; *săh ch'haè*, 煠菜, to boil vegetables.

Sⁿăh 唽 To speak much; garrulous.

卆

Sai^ng 生 Read seng: to be born, to produce; alive; living; to live; seng choó, 生子 *sai^ng kë^ná*, to bring forth a child; sëen seng, 先生 *sin sai^ng*, an elder born, a teacher. Kwun soò seng, pit hëuk che, 君賜生必畜之 *jîn kwun soò hoē sai^ng wăh ây mee^ngh, pit tëŏh ch'hē e*, when a prince presents anything alive, we should bring it up; see the 論語 Lūn gé.

Saiⁿᵍ 牲 Read seng: a brute animal; hëuk seng, 畜牲 *t'haou saiⁿᵍ*, a domestic animal; sometimes used as a term of reproach.

Boô é këüng he seng yëá, 無以供犧牲也 *bô t'hang këüng kip t'haou saiⁿᵍ*, we have nothing wherewith to procure sacrificial animals; see 孟子 Bēng choó.

声 *Saiⁿᵍ* 省 Read séng: sparing, frugal; to examine; a province; séng k'hëèm, 省儉 *saiⁿᵍ k'hëèm*, to spare, to be economical; séng sêng, 省城 *saiⁿᵍ sëⁿâ*, a capital city of a province.

T'hëen hāy sip pat séng, 天下十八省 *t'heeⁿᵍ āy chàp păyh saiⁿᵍ*, in the whole empire there are 18 provinces.

Séng chëên, 省錢 *saiⁿᵍ cheeⁿᵍ*, to save money.

去 *Saìⁿᵍ* 姓 Read sèng: a surname; pek kay sèng, 百家姓 *păyh kay saiⁿᵍ* the hundred family names, or clans, into which the people are divided.

Pek sèng, 百姓 *păyh saiⁿᵍ*, the people.

Sèng bêng, 姓名 *saiⁿᵍ mëⁿâ*, the name and surname.

Saìⁿᵍ 性 Read sèng: nature, disposition; sim sèng, 心性 *sim saiⁿᵍ*, natural disposition; hⁿó kè sèng, 好記性 *hó kè saiⁿᵍ*, a good memory.

入 *Sak* 摉 To push; ae sak, 挨摉 *ay sak*, to push and drive; some say, to respect; to ascend, to move; to take.

平 *Sam* 三 Vulg. *sⁿa*: three; sam sip, 三十 *sⁿa chàp*, thirty.

Sam lëên yéw sêng, 三年有成 *sⁿa neeⁿᵍ pit woō chëⁿâ kang*, "in three years I should be enabled to complete the work;" said by Confucius, in the 論語 Lūn gé.

Sam 弎 The large form of the preceding character; also written 叁, sam.

Sam 杉 A kind of fir-tree; sam pán, 杉舨 a small boat.

Sam 彡 The coloring of hair; also, a foreign surname. One of the radicals.

声 Sám 摻 To look on, to take; lâm sám, 覽摻, disorderly, in confusion.

Sám 糝 Broken rice; mixed.

去 Sàm 三 Three times, thrice repeated; sàm hók, 三復, to repeat thrice.

Kwùy-bûn choó sàm soō jê hoē hêng, 季文子三思而後行 *Kwùy-bûn choó sⁿà ây sëōⁿᵍ, jëên aōu këⁿâ*, Kwùy-bûn choó reflected thrice before he did anything; see the 論語 Lūn gé.

Sàm 罧 Gê sàm, 魚罧 *hê sàm*, stakes driven into the water in order to catch fish.

Sàm 槮 The same as the above.

Sàm 毿 The appearance of long hair.

Sàm 彡 Things connected together, and hanging down.

6 P

Sàm 釤 A large reaping-hook; a scythe.

Sàm 傪 T'ham sàm, 僋傪, foolish, stupid.

Sàm 鬖 Lâm sàm, 鬛鬖, long hair hanging down; sàm mô, 鬖毛 disheveled hair, the hair all in confusion.

平
Sâm 儳 Mixed, not in order, confused; lâm sâm, 儖儳, confused, bad, light, mean; trifling discourse.

去
San 山 Vulg. *swⁿa*: a hill; a surname; tông san, 唐山 *tēng swⁿa*, China. K'hóng-chóo teng tong san, jê seáou Loé, teng t'haè san, jê seáou t'hëen hāy, 孔子登東山而小魯登泰山而小天下 *K'hóng-chóo păyh chëōng tang swⁿa, je k'hwⁿà sèy Loé, păyh chëōng t'haè swⁿa, jê k'hwⁿà sèy t'heeng āy*, Confucius ascended the eastern hill, and the Loé country looked small; but when he ascended the great mountain, the whole empire looked diminutive; see 孟子 Bēng chóo.

San 珊 San hoê, 珊瑚, coral that grows at the bottom of the ocean, and by the side of the rocks, of a red color.

San 跚 Pwân san, 蹣跚, to walk lame.

San 刪 To exclude, to throw out; to fix, to determine.
K'hóng-chóo san se se, 孔子刪詩書 *K'hóng-chóo san tëⁿa se se*, Confucius corrected and arranged the odes and classics; see the 史記 Soó kè.

San 姍 Good, elegant; to revile, to ridicule. Chîn choò jīm soo tè, san ch'heàou san taē, 秦自任私智姍笑三代 *Chîn ka tē jīm ka tē woō tè hwūy, san ch'hëò sⁿa tēy*, the Chîn dynasty took to themselves the sole credit of being wise, and ridiculed the three former dynasties.

San 衫 Vulg. *sⁿa*: a jacket, a small coat.

San 潸 To shed tears, to weep; san jëên k'hip hāy, 潸然泣下 *san jëên laōu bàk chaé*, shedding tears, he wept abundantly; see the 史記 Soó ké.

San 芟 To cut grass; to eradicate.

San 邖 The name of a place.

上
Sán 產 That which is produced; seng sán, 生產, productions; t'hoê sán, 土產, the productions of the soil; sán gëëp, 產業, a patrimony, an estate.
Boô hêng sán, jê yéw hêng sim chëá, wûy soō wûy lêng, 無恒產而有恒心者惟士爲能 *bô hêng sëāng ây sán gëëp, jê wōo hêng sëāng ây sim kwⁿa, tòk tòk t'hàk ch'hāyh lâng ch'hëⁿá ēy*, to be without a means of constant support, and yet to retain an equable mind, only a true scholar can attain to this; see 孟子 Bēng chóo.

Sán 弗 Skewers, or a spit, used in roasting meat.

Sán 傘 Vulg. *swⁿà*: an umbrella; é sán, 雨傘 *hoē swⁿà*, a rain umbrella.

Sán 鏟 An iron tool for smoothing wood.

Sán 散 Dispersed and scattered abroad.
Chaê chē chek bîn sán, chaê sán chek bîn chē, 財聚則民散財散則民聚 *cheêng k'hëŏh chò hŏëy chek păyh saing swnà, cheêng swnà chek păyh saing chò hŏëy*, when a prince is given to hoarding up money, his people will disperse, but when he disperses his money, the people will gather around him; see the 大學 Taē hák.

Sán 瘦 Read soé: thin, meagre, lean not fat, emaciated.

去 Sàn 散 Vulg. *swnà*: to disperse, to scatter, to spread abroad.
Sëāng sit kê tō, bîn sàn kéw è, 上失其道民散久矣 *sè twā sit e ây tō, păyh saing sè swnà koó è*, superiors have erred from the right way, and the people have been scattered for a long time; see the 論語 Lūn gé.

Sàn 㪚 Mixed meat.

Sàn 霰 Flakes of snow.

Sàn 疝 A pain in the heart.

Sàn 訕 To rail at, to revile, to reproach.
Oè ke hāy lew, jê sàn sëāng cheá, 惡居下流而訕上者 *wàn k'hëā tē hāy lêw ây lâng, jê maing e ây sè twā*, he detested those who, dwelling in a mean station, reviled their superiors; see the 論語 Lūn gé.

Sàn 汕 The appearance of ease and freedom, like fishes sporting in the water.

Sàn 線 Vulg. *swnà*: a thread; chim sàn, 針線 *chëem swnà*, a needle and thread.
Boô chim put yín sàn, 無針不引線 *bô chit ke chëem bēy yín tit swnà*, there is never a needle, but what will draw its thread.

平 *Sang* 鬆 Read song: loose, not tight; pók song, 縛鬆 *pàk k'hăh sang*, to tie it looser.

Sang 雙 Read song: double; yit song, 一雙 *chit sang*, a pair; yit song haê, 一雙鞋 *chit song ây*, a pair of shoes; song seng, 雙生 *kăh sang saing*, twins, two at a birth.

上 *Sáng* 搡 Read sóng: to throw anything, to pitch, to fling.

去 *Sàng* 送 Read sòng: to present, to make a present; to accompany.
Sòng se, 送書 *sàng ch'hăyh*, to give away books; sòng song, 送喪 *sàng seng*, to accompany a funeral.
Chaè paè jê sòng che, 再拜而送之 *chaè paè jê sàng e*, he again made an obeisance, and accompanied him; see the 論語 Lūn gé.

Sàng 宋 Read sòng: a surname.

平 Saou 捎 To cut off, to cut grass; to rob, to plunder.

Saou 梢 The branches of a tree; the handle of a rudder.

Saou 弰 The case for a bow; to let fly an arrow from a bow.

Saou 鞘 A whip, a whip case; to saou, 刀鞘, the sheath of a sword.

Saou 嘲 To ridicule; to make game of; also written 誚, saou.

Saou 蛸 A small spider.

声
Saóu 敹 To beat, to strike; to move, to affect.

Saóu 擻 Toé soé, 抖擻 *taóu saóu*, to rouse one's-self.

去
Saòu 哨 Sûn saòu, 廵哨, to keep up a patrole, in order to guard against thieves.
Saòu kak, 哨角, a great trumpet, a bugle horn.

Saòu 掃 Read sò: to sweep; sò chéw, 掃帚 *saòu chéw*, broom; sò ch'hè, 掃處 *saòu gāy*, to sweep the ground.
Sò tēy sē lêw éng, 掃地樹留影 *saòu tēy ch'hēw laòu yēⁿá*, if you sweep the ground ever so clean, the tree still leaves its shadow there.

Saòu 嗽 Read soè: hoarse, with a cold; to cough; haé soè, 咳嗽 *k'hám saòu*, to take cold, to be taken with a hoarseness.

入
Sap 㒔 Not to arrive at, insufficient; to speak hastily, without caution.

Sap 㒔 T'hap sap, 傝㒔, incautious.

Sap 搔 Lap sap, 攋搔 mixed, jumbled together.

Sap 颯 A fierce wind, the whistling of the wind.

Sap 靸 To lift up lightly; straw shoes, children's shoes.

Sap 霅 The appearance of rain; an opening; the voice of a multitude.
E sap sap, 雨霅霅 *lôh hoē sap sap*, a drizzling rain.

入
Sàp 卅 A contraction of sam sip, 三十 *sⁿa chàp*, thirty.

入
Sat 殺 Vulg. *t'haé*: to kill, to put to death, to slay.
Sat sam Beâou ê sam Gwûy, 殺三苗于三危 *t'haé sⁿa ây Beâou, tē sⁿa Gwûy*, he slew the three Beâou, at the three Gwûy.

Sat 鎩 A long spear.

Sat 撒 Sat pwat, 撒潑, to disperse, to scatter.

Sat 薩 P'hoē sat, 菩薩, an idol; a god of the Budhist sect.

Sat 虱 Read sek: a louse; t'heàou sek, 跳虱 *t'heàou sat*, a flea; bòk sek, 木虱 *bàk sat*, a bug; t'hoê sek, 塗虱 *t'hoê sat*, a mud fish.

Ong-béng bûn sek jê tâm sê boō, 王猛捫虱而談時務 *Ong-béng bún sat jê tâm lūn sê boō*, Ong-béng held a louse in his fingers while he discoursed about the operations of the times; see the 晉記 Chìn ké.

Sat 煞 To injure; to exterminate; vulg. *swăh:* to finish, to make an end of.

平

Say 沙 Vulg. *swa:* sand; a surname; say sék k'hé hwuy, 沙石起飛 *swa chĕŏh k'hé pwuy*, the sand and stones began to fly. Also written 砂, say.

Say 紗 Jeàou say, 縐紗, crape.

Say 裟 Këa say, 袈裟, a priest's robe; a surplice.

Say 鯊 Say gê, 鯊魚 *swa hê*, the white shark; the genus Caracharias.

Say 鈔 Say lô, 鈔鑼, a brazen gong, which may be used as a wash hand-basin.

上

Sáy 傻 A slight degree of wisdom; sáy seàou, 傻俏, not benevolent.

去

Sày 灑 Vulg. *swà:* to sprinkle; sày súy, 灑水 *swà chúy*, to sprinkle water.

Sày 洒 The same as the above. Also written 㶕, sày. Sày saòu, 洒掃, to sprinkle and sweep.

Sày 刿 To stab, to pierce.

平

Sây 儕 A sort, a class; Chìn Tēng tông sây, 晉鄭同儕 *Chìn kok kap Tai^ng kok tâng chit ây têng*, the Chìn and Tai^ng countries are of the same class. Goê sây, 吾儕, we, us.

平

Sāy 癠 Sick, diseased; ch'hin sāy sek yûng put sêng, 親癠色容不盛 *pāy boê pai^ng, tëŏh bīn sek yûng maôu ü^m hw^na hé*, when parents are sick, the countenances (of children) should not look cheerful.

入

Săyh 霎 A small drizzling rain; *săyh săyh*, 霎霎, the sound of rain.

Săyh 湅 To wash the hands; also, the sound of a gentle rain.

Săyh 雪 Read swat: snow; song swat, 霜雪 *se^ng săyh*, frost and snow; lók swat, 落雪 *lŏh săyh*, to snow.

Săyh 攝 Read lëep: as lëep hông, 攝縫 *săyh p'hăng*, to stop up a seam.

平

Se 施 To give, to bestow; to use, to appoint; to add; se yin, 施恩, to dispense favors. A surname. E gnoé ch'haé chëang se ê gnoé sek, 以五采彰施于五色 *é goê ây ch'haé chëang se tē goê ây sek*, to take the five ornaments, and add them upon the five colors.

Se 胥 Mutual; all, altogether; to assist. A surname. Bîn hwuy hoē, bông k'hek se k'hong é seng, 民非后罔克胥匡以生 *păyh sai^ng nâ bô jîn kwun, chëw bēy sëo an ê sai^ng wăh*, when the people have no ruler, they cannot live together in mutual peace; see the 書太甲 Se t'haè kap.

Se 傦 Se soe, 傦疏, far apart.

Se 湑 The appearance of dew; lêng loē se se, 零露湑湑 *lân sán loē chúy lŏh se se*, the drops of dew fell thickly around; see the 小雅 Seáou gnáy.

Se 糈 Provisions; also the rice used in sacrificing to the gods.

Se 諝 The appellation of a wise and talented person.
Boê boô wûy se ké put sit ch'hek, 謀無遺諝舉不失策 *sëo boé nā bô pàng t'hek kak gaôu lâng, séy ké ây soō chēw bēy sit ch'hek*, when forming our plans, if we do not neglect clever men, then whatever we undertake will be sure not to fail.

Se 揟 A vessel for taking up water. Also written 捉, se.

Se 楈 A kind of wood, of which plough handles can be made.

Se 尸 A corpse; to be stretched out like a corpse; to stand, to set up, to establish; to set up as a master.
Ch'hím put se, 寢不尸 *k'hwùn bô ch'hin chëō^ng se*, when (Confucius) slept, he did not stretch himself out like a corpse; see the 論語 Lūn gé.
Koé jîn chèy soō, pit lip se, é sëāng choé k'hó, 古人祭祀必立尸以象祖考 *koé chá ây lâng chèy soō, tek k'hak tëŏh k'hëā lip sin se, é chò ch'hin chëō^ng choé k'hó*, "when the ancients sacrificed, they would always set up a figure, to resemble their ancestors and forefathers;" said by 朱子 Choo choó.

Se 屍 A corpse; sin se, 身屍, a dead body; the same as the preceding.

Se 鳲 Se k'hew, 鳲鳩, a kind of dove.

Se 蓍 Se ch'hó, 蓍草 *se ch'haôu*, a kind of grass or reed used in divination.
Hëèn hoê se kwuy, 見乎蓍龜 *hëèn twā tē se ch'haôu kwā koo k'hak*, it will appear from the divining straws and the tortoise-shell; see the 中庸 Tëung yung.

Se 需 The name of one of the diagrams; to require, to demand; put se, 不需 *ū^m saé*, unnecessary.

Se 濡 To moisten, to wet, to stain.

Se 須 The hair of the face; to wait for; that which we desire, what is requisite and necessary; se yūng, 須用, useful. A surname.
Gëûng se gnoé yéw, 卬須我友 *gwá téng haōu gwá ây pêng yéw*, I will wait for my friends; see the 詩經 Se keng.

Se 湏 Spittle; improperly used for the preceding character.

Se 鬚 Vulg. *ch'hew*: a beard, whiskers, or the fringes of garments.
K'hoé se, 口鬚 *ch'hùy ch'hew*, the beard around the mouth, especially on the chin.

Se 鬚 The same as the above.

Se 蕬 T'hoè se, 菟蕬, the name of an aquatic medicinal plant.

Se 絲 Silk, raw silk, as it is spun by the silkworm; silken threads.

Se 鷥 Loē se, 鷺鷥, a white crane; pėk lêng se, 白鴒鷥, a paddy-bird, a kind of stork.

Se 詩 An ode, a verse, poetry; chò se, 做詩, to make verses; se ong 詩翁, a poet; se keng, 詩經, the classic ode.

Se sam pek, yit gân é pèy che, wát soō boô sëâ, 詩三百一言以蔽之曰思無邪 *se woō sⁿa păyh p'heeⁿᵍ, chit koò wā kaôu é jëa pèy e, kóng söōⁿᵍ bô lâm sám,* the odes amount to three hundred, and one sentence is sufficient to express the whole, viz: "do not indulge in licentious thoughts;" see the 上論 Sëâng lūn.

Se 紓 Loose, easy, slow, gentle.

Se 舒 The same as the above; also, to spread out, to disperse; a surname. Se wān, 舒緩, slow, remiss, negligent.

Se 書 Vulg. *ch'hăyh:* a book, a record; a letter; to write, to record. T'hȯk se, 讀書 *t'hȧk ch'hăyh,* to read a book.

Soô se gnoé keng, 四書五經, the four books, and five classics.

Kè se, 寄書 *këâ p'hay,* to send a letter.

Se 輸 To receive, to take and give; vulg. *soo:* to lose, not to gain. Chîn se ch'hëuk ê Chîn, 秦輸粟於晉 *Chîn kȯk lȧp ch'hek hoē Chîn kok,* the people of Chîn gave corn as a tribute to the Chîn country; see the 左傳 Chó twān.

Se êng bē hwun, 輸贏未分 *soo yëⁿâ böēy hwun,* victory or defeat still undecided.

Se 渝 The name of a river.

声

Sé 始 The beginning, to begin, to commence; sé chëung, 始終 *k'hé t'haôu swăh böēy,* the beginning and ending.

Yéw sé yéw chut chëá, kê wûy sèng jîn hoē, 有始有卒者其惟聖人乎 *woô k'hé t'haôu, woô swăh böēy ây lâng, e sē sèng jîn ây lâng hoē,* he who endures from the beginning to the end, is no doubt a sage; see the 論語 Lūn gé.

Se 乿 The beginning; the same as the preceding.

Se 枲 The female plant of hemp which yields seeds.

Sé 暑 Hot, heat, hot weather; sé t'hëen, 暑天 *jwăh t'heeⁿᵍ,* the summer. Tòng sé chîn k'hek t'he pit peáou jê ch'hut che, 當暑袗絺綌必表而出之 *tòng jwăh t'heeⁿᵍ ch'hèng twⁿa nëⁿá kwăh poè, tëŏh peáou jê hoē e ch'hut,* in the summer season, when wearing a single garment of grass cloth, it is necessary to wear something underneath, and to let it appear on the outside; see the 論語 Lūn gé.

Sé 偦 The appellation of wise and clever person.

Sé 偦 A surname.

Sé 佡 Small, diminutive.

Sé 徙 Vulg. *swá:* to remove, to go to another place.
Soó jîn jit sé sëën, wàn chöëy jê put choō te yëá, 使人日徙善遠罪而不自知也 *saé lâng tàk jit sé swá kaôu hó, hwuīng k'hè woō chöëy, jê bēy ka tē chae,* to cause the people daily to advance in the practice of that which is good, and to discard crime, without themselves being aware of it.

Sé 蹝 A shoe; straw sandals; also written 屣, sé.
Sùn sè k'hè t'hëēn hây, yêw k'hè pē sé yëá, 舜視棄天下猶棄敝蹝也, Sùn looked upon rejecting the empire just like throwing away an old shoe.

Sé 鞑 A leathern shoe.

Sé 蓰 Fivefold, five times as much.
Hèk sëang pōëy sé, 或相倍蓰 *woō ây sëo têng pōëy, woō ây goē têng pōëy k'hăh kay,* some were double, and some were fivefold; see 孟子 Bēng choó.

Sé 䌛 Small.

Sé 屎 Vulg. *saé:* dung, ordure: hòng sé, 放屎 *pàng saé,* to go to stool.

Sé 葸 To be afraid, frightened; terror; timidity, bashfulness.
Kö jê boô léy chek sé, 愼而無禮則葸 *kēnajê bô léy, chek sé,* to be alarmed so as to forget propriety, may be called terror; see the 論語 Lūn gé.

Sé 枲 Vulg. *séy á:* the common species of Barbados millet.

Sé 豕 The generic name for swine.
Má gnêw yâng, key k'hëēn sé, naé lëúk hëuk, jîn séy soō, 馬牛羊鷄犬豕乃六畜人所飼 *báy goô yëōng, key kaôu te, naé làk hâng ây t'haôu saing, lâng séy ch'hē,* the horse, cow, and sheep; the cock, dog, and pig are the six kinds of domestic animals which men bring up; see the 三字經 Sam joō keng.

Sé 矢 An arrow; as straight as an arrow; also, to swear.
Sé jîn k'hé put jîn ê hâm jîn chae? 矢人豈不仁於函人哉 *chò cheēng ây lâng, k'hám ūm k'hăh woō jîn köëy chò chëēn kăh ây lâng chae?* is not the maker of arrows more wanting in benevolence than the manufacturer of armor? (because the former is only anxious to make his arrows sharp, that they may wound people, while the latter seeks to make the armor as strong as possible, to keep them from being wounded;) see 孟子 Bēng choó.

Sé 弛 To unstring a bow, to let a bow go back; vulg. *lēng:* loose, not tight; hòng sé, 放弛 *pàng k'hăh lēng,* to loosen anything.
Kwun choó che tō, yit tëang yit sé, 君子之道一張一弛 *kwun choó ây tō lé, chit ây tëong chit ây pàng,* the way of a good man is to keep his bow sometimes strung and sometimes loose.

Sé 死 Read soó: to die, to depart this life; anything dead, extinct.
Soó chòng che é léy, 死葬之以禮 *sé taé e cheâou léy soè,* when parents are dead, inter them according to propriety; see the 上論 Sëāng lūn.

去

Sè 貰 To borrow, to lend, to sell on credit, also, to be angry.

Sè 世 An age, a generation, the world; sè jîn, 世人 *sè kan ây lâng*, the men of the world; sè sè taē taē, 世世代代 *sè sè tēy tēy*, for ages and generations; kak sè, 覺世, to arouse the age.
Choó-tëang būn sip sè k'hó te yëá, 子張問十世可知也 *Choó-tëoⁿᵍ mooiⁿᵍ châp sè t'hang chae yëá*, Choó-tëang asked if the affairs of ten generations could be previously known; see the 上諭 Sëāng lūn.

Sè 勢 Power, influence, authority; kwân sè, 權勢, authority.
Hⁿò sëēn jê bōng sè, 好善而忘勢 *aè böëyh hó lâng, tëöh bēy kè lán ây sè*, when a ruler wants to get good men in his service, he must forget his own power, (and stoop to them;) see 孟子 Bēng choó.

Sè 摭 To take anything in the hand; a handful.

Sè 施 To disperse, to scatter, to confer favors on people.
Jê yéw p'hok sè ê bîn, jê lêng chèy chëùng hô jê? k'hó wūy jîn hoē? 如有博施於民而能濟衆何如可謂仁乎 *ch'hin chëoⁿᵍ woō p'hok sè hoē pāyh saiⁿᵍ, jê ēy chew chēy chëùng lâng, chēy sē an chwⁿá? t'hang kóng woō jîn tek á bô?* when a prince confers extensive benefits on the people, and is able to assist men in general, what sort of a man must he be? Can he be considered benevolent? see the 論語 Lūn gé.

Sè 弑 To murder a superior; to kill a parent or a prince.
Sîn sè kê kwun chëá yéw che; choó sè kê hoō chëá yéw che, 臣弑其君者有之子弑其父者有之 *jîn sîn t'haê e ây jîn kwun ây woō e; haōu saiⁿᵍ t'haê e ây neⁿᵍ pāy ây woō e*, for a minister to murder his prince, there are instances of this; and for a son to commit parricide, such things have occurred; see 孟子 Bēng choó.

Sè 恕 To excuse, to deal gently with; to do to another as we would wish another to do to us.
Hoo choó che tō, tëung sè jê é è, 夫子之道忠恕而已矣 *hoo choó ây tō lé, chîn têung kwà sèo sè tëⁿā tëⁿā*, the whole system of Confucius' doctrine consists in fidelity and lenity alone; see the 論語 Lūn gé.

Sè 絮 Cloth; cotton, anything made of cotton; silken threads.

Sè 庶 All, numerous, many; almost; sè choó, 庶子, a child by a concubine.
Sè bîn, 庶民, all the people; sè ke, 庶幾, almost, nearly.
Choó wat, sè è chae? 子曰庶矣哉 *hoo choó kóng, chēy è chae?* Confucius said, "how numerous are they?" (meaning the people of a certain state, which he visited;) see the 論語 Lūn gé.
Tek choó, 嫡子, a legitimate son; sè choó, 庶子, illegitimate offspring.

Sè 四 Read soò: four; soò hong, 四方 *sè heⁿᵍ*, in all quarters; soò kak, 四角 *sè kak*, foursquare; soò bîn, 四民 *sè bîn*, the four orders of the people.

Sè 試 Vulg. *ch'hè*: to try, to make trial of, to prove.
Ch'héng sëâng sè che, 請嘗試之 *ch'hëⁿá laê ch'hè k'hwⁿà e*, pray let us try it; see 孟子 Bēng choó.

6 R

平

Sê 時 A time, a season, a period, an hour; a surname; soò sê, 四時 sè sé, the four seasons; sîm sê? 甚時 sⁿá meēⁿᵍh sé? at what time; ké sê? 幾時 té sé? when? sê sê, 時時, constantly.

T'hëen hô gân chae, soò sê hêng yëen, 天何言哉四時行焉 t'heeⁿᵍ woō sⁿá meēⁿᵍh kóng wā, sè sé tit kēⁿâ, what orders does heaven issue, and yet the four seasons revolve; see the 論語 Lūn gé.

Se 蒔 To plant; sê sē yit kin, é seng chëèn kong, 蒔樹一根以旌戰功 chaè ch'hēw chit châng, é seng chëèn ây kong lô, he planted a tree, in order to be a signal of his military exploits.

Sé 殳 Read soô: a surname.

Sê 鰣 The name of a fish; the mackerel.

Sé 塒 Key sê, 鷄塒, a hen-roost.

Sé 匙 A spoon; tây sê, 茶匙, a tea-spoon; hwān sê, 飯匙 pooīⁿᵍ sé, a rice spoon; t'hong sê, 湯匙 t'heⁿᵍ sé, a soup spoon.

Sé 提 Choo sê, 朱提, the name of a district, said to produce silver.

Se 蜍 Sëèm sê, 蟾蜍, a kind of toad; said to have 8 red characters under its belly.

Se 蠩 Sëang sê, 蟚蠩 chëoⁿᵍ ché, a toad.

Sē 辭 Read soô: to refuse, not to accept, to take leave of.

Gwân-soō wûy che chaé, é che ch'heuk kéw pek soô, 原思爲之宰與之粟九百辭 Gwân-soō kap e chò kay chaé, hoē e ch'hek kaôu pàyh sé, Gwân-soō was the steward of Confucius' household, when he gave him nine hundred measures of corn; but the other refused it; see the 論語 Lūn gé.

去

Sē 是 To be, it is, it is this, this; right, not wrong; yes; sē put sē? 是不是 sē ūᵐ sē? is it so or not? sē, 是, it is so.

Sē sē hwuy hwuy tēy, bêng bêng pék pék t'hëen, 是是非非地明明白白天 tëŏh kap ūᵐ tëŏh ây tēy, bêng bêng pāyh pāyh ây t'heeⁿᵍ, on this earth there are many rights and wrongs, but in heaven all is clear and plain.

Sē 昰 The same as the preceding.

Sē 諟 This; to look at, to observe, to judge of, to reason.

Sē 侍 To wait on, to attend, to be in attendance.

Bîn-choó sē ch'hek, 閔子侍側 Bîn-choó k'hëā tē sin peeⁿᵍ, Bîn-choó was waiting at his side; see the 論語 Lūn gé.

Sē 㑥 The same as the preceding; to stand, to wait; also written 偫, sē.

Sē 鯷 K'ham sē, 堪鯷, a kind of fish.

Sē 寺 Vulg. eēⁿᵍ: a temple, a monastery, an abbey; sē jîn, 寺人, an eunuch.

福建方言字典

Hong san koé sē cheng laê seáou, 荒山古寺僧來少 *hwuing swna koé cēng höéy sëōng laê chëó*, among desolate hills and old temples, the priests seldom come; see a 古詩 koé se.

Sē 峙 A hill standing alone; a promontory, a peak; to stand alone.

Sē 恃 To rely on, to depend upon, to place confidence in.

Boô hoō hô koē? boô boé hô sē? 無父何怙無母何恃 *bô nëōng pāy woō snā meëngh t'hang kōe? bô nëōng léy woō snā meëngh t'hang sē?* having no father what shall we rely on? And being motherless, on whom shall we depend? see the 小雅 Seáou gnáy.

Sē 庤 To stand upright, under a house; to prepare, to get ready.

Sē 畤 The place of sacrifice, in making an offering to the five emperors of heaven and earth.

Sē 蒔 To plant; to transplant; to plant in another place.

Sē 序 The wall on the eastern and western sides of a house; to arrange in order; a preface to a book; the name of a school.

Cheàou ch'hoò sē, 照次序, according to order.

Sē pin ê hëën, 序賓以賢 *sē lëët lâng k'hăyh chedou e ây gaôu*, arrange the guests according to their talents; see the 大雅 Taē gnáy.

Sëâng sē, 庠序, a place of instruction.

Sē 示 To teach, to instruct, to inform, to show; kaòu sē, 教示 *kà sē*, to communicate instruction.

Kê jê sē choo soo hoē, 其如示諸斯乎 *e ây ch'hin chëōng ké sē chéy léy*, it would be as easy as showing this, (pointing to his hand;) see the 論語 Lūn gé.

Sē 視 To look at, to behold, to observe; to imitate, to compare.

Bók put sē hwuy léy che sek, 目不視非禮之色 *bàk chew bŏh k'hwnà ūm hàp léy ây sek*, let not the eyes look upon improper beauty.

T'hëen sē choō gnó bîn sē, 天視自我民視 *t'heeng. k'hwnà t'han lán păyh saing k'hwnà*, heaven looks on a thing, as we people view it; (vox populi vox Dei;) see the 書經 Se keng.

Sē 敘 To spread out, to discourse on, to use; to arrange in order.

Pek kwûy sê sē, 百揆時敘 *chënà păyh hwat tōe sëâng sê chedou ch'hoò sē*, the hundred plans were constantly arranged in order; see the 舜典 Sūn tëén.

Sē 墅 A shed in a field; a garden; an extra lodging place; a village.

Sëā-an, 謝安, with his nephew Hëên, 玄, played at chess, and (toé pëét sē, 賭別墅 *pwăh soo yēnà pát ây hwuing,*) gambled for an extra garden; see the 晉書 Chìn se.

Sē 緒 A line, a thread of communication, a rule, a connecting thread.

Boó ông chàn T'haè ông che sē, 武王纘太王之緒 *Boó ông sëo swà T'haè ông ây swnà*, Boó ông connected the line of communication from T'haè ông; see the 魯頌 Loé sëūng.

Sē 逝 To pass by, to flow by, to pass away; to go, to depart; when Confucius was standing on the river's brink, he said of the waters, (sē chëá jê soo hoo yëá, 逝者如斯夫也 *köéy k'hè ch'hin chëōng an néy,*) "how the waters flow by, and pass away;" see the 論語 Lūn gé.

Sē **謚** Ardent, glowing; the traces of conduct; a name given to persons of eminence after their decease, indicative of their previous conduct; a posthumous title.

Sē **誓** An oath, a swearing; to swear; chèw sē, 呪誓 *chèw chwā*, to take an oath, in order to insure belief.

Sē **豎** To stand, to stand erect, to set up on end; also written 竪, sē.
Sē lip, 豎立 *k'hëā lip*, to stand upright; sē kê, 豎旗 *k'hëā kê*, to erect a standard.
Sē choó, 豎子, a boy, an insignificant person.

Sē **嶼** Vulg. *soō:* an island, a hill in the midst of the sea. Also written 嶨 sō.
Pin-lông sē, 梹榔嶼 *Pin-nêng soō*, the island of Pinang or Prince of Wales.
Sē sêng, 嶼城 *soō sêⁿâ*, a fortified island; applied to the island of Onrust, in front of Batavia roads, which was once fortified.

Sē **鱮** The name of a fish.

Sē **藇** Fine, elegant, agreeable.

Sē **氏** A family name; sèng sē, 姓氏 *saìⁿᵍ sē*, the surname of any one.
Loé yéw Bēng-sun sē, Sëuk-sun sē, Kwùy-sun sē, 魯有孟孫氏叔孫氏季孫氏 *Loé kok woō Bēng-sun sē, Sëuk-sun sē, Kwùy-sun sē*, in the Loé country there were the families and clans of Bēng-sun, Sëuk-sun, and Kwùy-sun.

Sē **筮** Pok sē, 卜筮, to divine, to use divination; the former character alludes to the use of the tortoise-shell, and the latter to that of a certain kind of grass, employed in divination.

Sē **噬** To gnaw, to eat, to chew.
Hwūn put lêng hwát sē jé jëuk, 恨不能活噬爾肉 *hwūn bēy wăh kā lé ây băh*, I am vexed that I cannot devour your flesh alive; see the 三國 Sam kok.

Sē **嗜** To relish, to like, to be fond of, to taste.
Sîn sē yím sît, soó kwun sēw k'hó, 神嗜飲食使君壽考 *sîn bèng sē aè lé ây lim chëăh, hōe kwun lé chëăh têⁿᵍ hōèy sēw*, may the gods enjoy your offerings of food and drink, and cause you to attain to great longevity; see the 小雅 Seáou gnáy.

Sē **署** A book; an official lodge.

Sē **樹** Vulg. *ch'hēw:* a tree; sē lîm, 樹林 *ch'hēw nâ*, a forest.
Taē sē p'hò yéw ch'haê, seáou yâng ch'hè boô hëet, 大樹破有柴小羊刺無血 *twā châng ch'hēw p'hwà woō ch'hâ, sèy chëăh yëôⁿᵍ t'haê bô hōëyh*, a great tree when cut up will produce plenty of firewood, but a small kid when killed, will scarcely afford any blood.

Sē **曙** Morning, daybreak.

Sē **儓** The same as 豎, sē, the name of a god; also, a surname.

卓 Sëa **賒** Distant, far removed; to sell on credit, to give on trust.
Sêng k'hwat suy kīn, hong yîn sëāng sëa, 城闕雖近風雲尙賒 *sêⁿâ kak suy jëēn kīn, hong hoê sëāng hwuiⁿᵍ*, al-

福建方言字典

though the corner of the city may be near, the winds and clouds are distant.

Sëa 賒 Not to associate with.

上聲 Sëá 舍 To reject, to give up, to cease. Confucius, speaking of a flowing stream, said, (put sëá tèw yëā, 不舍晝夜 *bô hat^{ng}h jit mai^{ng},)* "it does not cease day or night;" see the 論語 Lûn gé.

Sëá 捨 To reject, to give up, to cast off. Aè hⁿó bûn gē bē sëâng wûy sëá, 愛好文義未甞達捨 *yit tëŏh hó ây bûn gē, bōëy cheng pàng t'hek kak,* he who is fond of good writings will never cast them away.

Sëá 寫 To overturn, to exclude, to exhaust, to drive away; to write, to copy. Kày gân ch'hut yêw, é sëá gnó yew, 駕言出遊以寫我憂 *kày báy ch'hëa kóng bōëyh ch'hut k'hè t'hit t'hô, é sëá k'hè gwá ây hwân ló,* put to the carriage and talk about going out to ramble, in order to drive away my sorrow; see the 詩經 Se keng. Sëá joō, 寫字 *sëá jē,* to write or copy anything.

去聲 Sëà 舍 A shed, a cottage, a dwelling; to halt for a night. Sëà kwán bē tēng, 舍舘未定 *hat^{ng}h ây wûy bōëy tēⁿā tëŏh,* I have not yet fixed upon my lodgings; see 孟子 Bēng choó.

Sëà 赦 To forgive, to pardon, to remit an offense; sëà chöēy, 赦罪, to forgive sins; sëà seáou kò, 赦小過 *sëà sëó k'hwá ây köēy sit,* to pass over slight offenses; see the 論語 Lûn gé.

6 S

Sëà 卸 To put off, to lay aside; sëà kap, 卸甲 *t'hoot^{ng} kăh,* to throw off one's armor.

Sëà 厙 A surname.

Sëà 瀉 To purge; sëà yëák, 瀉藥 *sëà yëŏh,* a purgative medicine.

平聲 Sëâ 佘 A surname.

Sëâ 畬 The name of a hill.

Sëâ 斜 Slanting, oblique, not straight; irregular, incorrect.

Sëâ 邪 Incorrect, corrupt, vicious; kan sëâ, 奸邪, vicious people. Sëâ sút, 邪術, corrupt arts; sëâ kaòu, 邪教, erroneous doctrines.

Sëâ 衺 Incorrect, vicious; a left handed course, that must not be followed.

Sëâ 蛇 Vulg. *chwâ:* a snake, a poisonous reptile. K'hc sëâ lëûng, jê hông che ch'he, 驅蛇龍而放之菹 *kwⁿá chwâ lëûng jê pàng hāy tē chúy k'hwut ó,* he drove away the snakes and dragons, and confined them to the marshes; see 孟子 Bēng choó.

上去 Sëā 社 A god of the land, or soil; also, a village, a hamlet. Yéw bîn jîn yëen, yéw sëā chek yëen, 有民人焉有社稷焉 *woō pāyh sai^{ng} lâng tē tit, yëá woō sëā chek tē tit,* where there are people and inhabitants, there are also gods of the land and grain; see the 論語 Lūn gé.

Sëā 射 To shoot; sëā chëèn, 射箭 *chŏh chee^{ng}*, to shoot with an arrow. Kwun chóó boê séy cheng, pit yëá sëā hoē, 君子無所爭必也射乎 *kwun chóó bô séy chai^{ng}, nā tek k'hak bōĕyh, tëŏh chaē chŏh chee^{ng} hoē,* the good man wrangles about nothing, but if he must strive, let it be in archery; see the 上論 Sëāng lūn.

Sëā 榭 Taê sëā, 臺榭, a terrace and a parterre. Wūy këung sit taê sëā, é chân haē ê jé bān sèng, 爲宮室臺榭以殘害于爾萬姓 *chò këung ch'hoō taê sëā, é chân haē tē lé chë^{n}â bān pāyh sai^{ng},* making houses and palaces, terraces and parterres, to the injury of your myriads of people; see the 書經 Se keng.

Sëā 謝 To decline, to refuse, to take leave of, to thank, to express an obligation on the reception of a present; kám sëā, 感謝, to thank, to be grateful; to sëā, 多謝, much obliged to you. Vulg. *chëā*: a surname.

Sëā 麝 Sëā hëang, 麝麞 *sëā hëo^{ng}*, the musk deer.

Sëā 埜 The same as 社, sëā, a village.

Së^{n}a 聲 Read seng: a voice, a sound; bêng seng, 名聲 *më^{n}â së^{n}a*, fame, report; seng yim, 聲音 *së^{n}a yim*, a tone of voice.

Sē é seng bêng yâng yit hoē tëung kok, 是以聲名洋溢乎中國 *sē é së^{n}a më^{n}â yâng yit tē tëung kok,* thus your fame would overspread the middle country (China); see the 中庸 Tëung yûng.

Së^{n}à 聖 Read sèng: holy, sacred, powerful and efficacious; applied in common conversation to temples and shrines, which are said to be sacred and efficacious in affording answers to the prayers of those who pay homage to them. Sèng jîn, 聖人 *së^{n}à lâng*, a holy man, a sage.

Së^{n}â 城 Read sêng; a city; sêng kok, 城郭 *së^{n}â kok*, a city and suburbs. Ch'hok soo tê yëá, k'hëuk soo sêng yëá, 鑿斯池也築斯城也 *ch'hok chëy lëy chúy kaou k'heĕh chëy lëy së^{n}â ch'hëo^{ng},* dig this ditch deeper, and build this wall higher; (to provide a defense against your enemies;) see 孟子 Bēng chóó.

Së^{n}â 成 Read sêng: to complete; sêng chēw, 成就 *së^{n}â chēw*, to attain one's object.

Së^{n}a 櫼 Read sēng: a large basket or hamper, for containing grain.

Së^{n}ā 堿 Read sēng: a vessel for containing salt.

Së^{n}ā 簸 Read sēng: a bamboo vessel, for holding anything.

Sëăh 削 Read sëak: to scrape anything with a knife; to shave off.

Sëăh 錫 Read sëak: tin; sëak kwān, 錫礶 *sëăh kwān*, a tin pot.

叐 *Sëăh* 席 Read sėk: a mat, a table, a feast; yëĕn sėk, 筵席 *yëĕn seăh*, a feast, an entertainment.

Sëăh 魰 The name of a fish.

夫 Sëak 削 Kwat sëak, 刮削 *kwăh sëăh*, to scrape with a knife; sëak tëy, 削地, to cut off territory.

Also, weak.

When the princes of the empire neglected waiting on the sovereign, for the first offense, they were degraded in rank, and (chaè put teâou, sëak t'hoé tëy yëá, 再不朝削土地也 *koh ūm teâou keèng chēw kwăh sëak t'hoĕ tëy yëá*,) when they neglected it a second time, they were deprived of a part of their territory.

Sëak 屑 To consider clean, to account pure. Put gnó sëak é, 不我屑以 *bŏ lëăh gwá chò ch'heng k'he sëōng*, not considering me pure and clean; see the 詩經 Se keng.

Sëak 鑠 To melt metals; used also metaphorically. Sëak kim pek yit, 鑠金百鎰 *yëŏng kim chit păyh yit tāng*, they melted gold to the amount of 100 yit's in weight; see the 史記 Soó kè.

Sëak 爍 To burn brightly; a bright light.

卒 Sëang 相 Mutual, together with; sëang cheng, 相爭 *sëo chaing*, to strive together.

Sëang k'hip ê tëung têng, 相泣於中庭 *sëo k'haòu tē tëung têng*, they wept together in the midst of the house; see 孟子 Bēng choó.

Sëang 廂 A chamber on the side of a dwelling; an antechamber.

T'haē gwàt sey sëang hāy, gêng hong hoē pwàn k'hae, 待月西廂下迎風戶半開 *têng t'haē gŏëyh tē sae sëong āy, gëná cheĕh hong woō mooíng pwná k'hwuy*, wait for the moon under the western antechamber; welcome the wind with the door half open.

Sëang 湘 The name of a river.

Sëang 箱 Vulg. *sëong*: a box, a trunk, a coffer; a granary.

Sëang 緗 Cloth of a light yellow color.

Sëang 傷 To wound, to injure; to wound the feelings, to grieve.

Ae jê put sëang, 哀而不傷 *ae jê bëy sëang*, grieved without being wounded; see the 論語 Lūn gé. Sëang haē, 傷害, to injure.

Sëang 湯 A superabundance of water; inundating, overflowing.

Hông súy sëang sëang, 洪水湯湯 *twā chúy sëang sëang*, the inundation was overwhelming; see the 堯典 Geâou tëén.

Sëang 殤 To die at an early age; to die before the age of puberty.

Sëang 觴 A wine cup, a vessel for drinking wine out of.

Sëang 商 A merchant; sëang lëâng, 商量 *soo nëóng*, to deliberate, to consult. Soō, lông, kong, sëang, 士農工商 *t'hàk ch'häyh, chöh ch'hân, chò kang, seng lé*, the scholar, the husbandman, the mechanic, and merchant; (the four classes of people among the Chinese.)

Sëang 賔 The ancient form of the above.

Sëang 襄 To assist, to help.

Sëang 驤 A horse going swiftly.

Sëang 鑲 A hook, a military weapon.

Sëang 勷 Hasty, quick.

去

Sëáng 賞 Vulg. *sëóng*: to reward, to admire, to express admiration. Kàm sëáng, 鑒賞, to look at, and admire; gwán sëáng, 玩賞, to stay the mind on in wonder and admiration; sëáng soò, 賞賜, to confer, as a reward. Sëáng sëēn hwàt ok, 賞善罰惡 *sëóng hó hwàt p'hané*, to reward the good, and punish the bad.

Sëáng 上 Vulg. *chëóng*: to ascend, to go up; to exalt. Lëên poē é sëáng, 連步以上 *sëo swà poē é chëóng*, to ascend with successive steps; see the 禮曲禮 Léy k'hëuk léy.

Sëáng 鯗 Gê sëáng, 魚鯗, *hê sëóng*, dried fish.

Sëáng 想 Vulg. *sëóng*: to think, to reflect. Bōng sëáng hëên soō, 夢想賢士 *bāng sëóng gaôu ây t'hàk ch'häyh láng*, to think and dream of clever scholars.

去

Sëàng 相 To look at, to survey; to assist, to help; an assistant. K'hàn sëàng, 看相 *kwⁿà sëàng* to look at a person's countenance, and to judge by the lines and marks in it of his future destiny. Chaé sëàng, 宰相, a prime minister. Sëàng chaē jé sit, 相在爾室 *k'hwⁿà tē lé ây ch'hoò*, to take a survey of your house. A surname.

平

Sëâng 庠 To enter school; a school, a seminary. Kín sëâng sē che kaòu, 謹庠序之教 *kín sīn sëâng sē ây kà*, be careful of the instructions in the schools; see 孟子 Bēng choó.

Sëâng 祥 Kit sëâng, 吉祥, a lucky omen, a favorable prognostic. Kok kay chëang hin pit yéw cheng sëâng, 國家將興必有禎祥 *kok kay chëang böëyh hin k'hé, pit tëöh woō hó ây sëâng*, when a country is about to flourish there will certainly be some good omens; see the 中庸 Tëung yûng.

Sëâng 詳 Sëâng sèy, 詳細, minute, the particular minutiæ of anything. E put kè kê sëâng, 已不記其詳 *é keng bēy kè e ây sëâng sèy*, we have already forgotten the particulars.

Sëâng 翔 To fly round about, to fly backwards and forwards. Sek soo ké è, sëâng jê hoē chip, 色斯舉矣翔而後集 *keéng láng ây sek, e chëw k'hé, kaòu pwuy laê pwuy k'hè, jëên aōu kŏh chip*, birds, on seeing the faces of men, get up; but when they have flown about a little, they afterwards collect again; see the 論語 Lūn gé.

Sëāng 甞 To taste, to try the taste of anything. Sëēn hoo p'hín sëāng sit, ông naé sit, 膳夫品甞食王乃食 *ché pooi^ng ây lâng chedou p'hín lûy ch'he cheăh, ông chēw chĕăh*, the cook must first taste of every sort of food, after which the king eats; see the 周禮 Chew léy.

Sëāng 嘗 To try, to taste; the same as the preceding.

Sëâng 常 Constant, perpetual, constantly, always; a surname; sëâng kéw, 常久 *sëâng koó*, everlasting.
Tōng chĕng yéw sëâng, 動靜有常 *tāng chĕng woō sëâng*, to be constant and regular in one's business and recreations.
Gnoé sëâng, 五常 *goē sëâng*, the five constant virtues; (which are, according to the Chinese, benevolence, righteousness, propriety, wisdom and truth.)

Sëâng 裳 A garment; e sëâng, 衣裳 *yin chëô^ng*, clothes, apparel.

丟

Sëāng 上 Up, upon, above, that which is above; high; vulg. *chëō^ng*: to ascend.
Chaē sëāng wūy put lêng hāy, 在上位不陵下 *tē têng lūn ây lâng bô k'he lêng tē hāy téy ây lâng*, let not those in superior stations despise those who are beneath them; see the 中庸 Tëung yûng.
Sëāng kwān, 上官, a double surname.

Sëāng 二 The same as the above.

Sëāng 象 An appearance, a form; alike. Vulg. *ch'hëō^ng*: an elephant.
K'hè sëāng, 氣象, manner, constitution; hêng sëāng, 形象, form, substance.
K'hé hoe pà sae sëāng jê wàn che, 驅虎豹犀象而遠之 *kw^ná hoé pà sac ch'hëō^ng, jê hoē e hwui^ng*, to drive away the tigers, leopards, rhinoceroses, and elephants, in order to remove them to a distance; see 孟子 Bēng choó.

Sëāng 豫 Alike; chèng sëāng, 正豫 *ch'hìn chëō^ng*, just like, like as.

Sëāng 像 The same as the above.

Sëāng 尚 To emulate, to esteem highly; to add to, to come over; still, yet, even, if; hô sëāng, 和尚 *hôéy sëō^ng*, a priest of the sect of Budha.
Sëāng se, 尚書 *sëō^ng se*, a president of one of the principal boards.
Kwun choó gē, è wûy sëāng, 君子義以爲尚 *kwun choó lëāh gē chò t'hang sëāng*, the good man considers righteousness worthy of his imitation; see the 論語 Lūn gé.
Ch'hó sëāng che hong pit yëén, 草尚之風必偃 *ch'haóu kay hong tē téng lūn tek k'hak tó*, when grass is acted upon by the wind, it bends down; see the 論語 Lūn gé. A surname.

卓

Seaou 消 To exhaust, to finish, to diminish; to melt away; seaou sit, 消息, news, intelligence.
Peng tòng seaou sék, 冰凍消釋 *se^ng këen tàng ēy seaou yëô^ng*, ice and frost can dissolve and melt away.

Seaou 俏 Seaou jëên, 俏然, the sound of the harp.

Seaou 綃 A kind of silk or satin.

Seaou 宵 The night, evening, obscure; gwân seaou, 元宵, the evening of the 15th day of the 1st moon, commonly called the feast of lanterns.

Seaou 痟 Swan seaou, 酸痟, a headache; seaou k'hat, 痟渴, a kind of sickness.

Seaou 痟 A pain in the head, and languor in the limbs.
Hāy seaou, 下痟, an involuntary emission of semen.

Seaou 霄 Yîn seaou, 雲霄, the upper region of the clouds; the name of a place.

Seaou 蹜 A cramp in the legs; keak kin seaou, 脚筋蹜 *k'ha kin seaou*, the cramp.

Seaou 逍 Seaou yaôu, 逍遙, easy, at leisure, satisfied, contented.
Hô sëāng hoē seaou yaôu, 河上乎逍遥 *tē kāng chúy têng seaou yaôu*, taking an excursion of pleasure on the river; see the 鄭風 Tēng hong.

Seaou 蛸 Song seaou, 桑蛸, an insect found on the mulberry tree.
Haé p'heaou seaou, 海螵蛸, the bone of the cuttle fish, which is used as medicine.

Seaou 銷 To fuse metals, to melt any metal.
Chîn sew t'hëen hāy peng, seaou é wûy chëung kè, 秦收天下兵銷以爲鍾鐻 *Chîn sew t'hee^ng āy ây peng to yëō^ng chò cheng kè*, the Chîn dynasty collected all the military weapons throughout the empire and melted them down into implements of music and husbandry.

Seaou 焇 To dry anything at the fire; dry.

Seaou 硝 Yëèm seaou, 焰硝, saltpetre; seaou yëák, 硝藥 *seaou.yëŏh*, gunpowder.

Seaou 魈 San seaou, 山魈, a ghost with one leg, which is said to haunt the district of 汀州, T'heng-chew.

Seaou 瀟 Seaou sëang, 瀟湘, the name of a river; a storm of wind and rain.

Seaou 簫 A musical instrument; a pipe; ch'huy seaou, 吹簫 *ch'höey seaou*, to play on the pipe.

Seaou 彇 The small end of a bow.

Seaou 蕭 A kind of reed. A surname.

Seaou 翛 The sound of fluttering wings.

Seaou 燒 Vulg. *sëo:* to burn; h^nó seaou, 火燒 *höey sëo*, the fire burns.
Tëüng hāy boô seaou höey, 仲夏毋燒灰 *tëüng hāy ū^m t'hang sëo höey*, in the middle month of summer do not burn lime; see the 禮月令 Léy gwât lëng.

Seaou 焦 Read cheaou: the fire burning anything black; also, to roast.
Sam cheaou h^nó, 三焦火 *s^na seaou höey*, three flames of fire.

声

Seáou 小 Vulg. *sèy:* small, minute, diminutive; *sëo kwá*, a little.
Seáou jîn, 小人, a worthless man, a little minded fellow.

Seáou taē yêw che, 小大由之 *sèy soō twā soō-t'hàn ē*, both small and great affairs are arranged according to this (viz. harmony); see the 上論 Sëāng lūn.

Seáou 少 Little, not much; few, scarce, not many.
Bút yéw é seáou wûy kwùy chëá, 物有以少爲貴者 *meēngh woō é chëó chò kwùy chëá*, there are some things the more valuable for being scarce; see the 禮記 Léy kè.

Seáou 篠 A small kind of bamboo, a sort of arrow.

Seáou 嬲 To sport with wantonly.

去

Seàou 少 Youthful, small, few in years; seàou lëên, 少年, a young person. Seàou che sê, hëet k'hè bē tēng, kaè che chaē sek, 少之時血氣未定戒之在色 *sèy ây sé, hōëyh k'hè bōëy tëⁿā tëōh, kéng kaè chaē sek*, in the time of youth, before one's blood and spirits are settled, we should guard against vice; see the 論語 Lūn gé.

Seàou 肖 Alike, similar, of the same sort; put seàou, 不肖, unlike; when applied to children, means that they are unfilial, i. e. unlike their parents.

Seàou 哨 Not to be able to restrain one's mouth; to rail; also, to blow a pipe, in order to sound an alarm. Sûn seàou, 巡哨, to go about and examine, to patrole. Hâm seàou, 菡哨, the name of a flower.

Seàou 俏 Like, alike, similar; the same as 肖 seàou.

Seàou 峭 A hill extremely lofty.

Seàou 誚 To scold, to rail; seàou jîn, 誚人, to reproach any one.

Seàou 糈 A sort of congee or rice water.

Seàou 數 Read soè: an account, a reckoning; swàn soè, 算數 *swuⁿg seàou*, to cast up a reckoning; soè bók, 數目 *seàou bàk*, an account.

Seàou 帳 Read tëàng: an account; tëàng p'hoē, 帳簿 *seàou p'hoē*, an account book.

平

Seâou 韶 To connect; a name given to the music of 舜, Sûn, because he connected the good government of 堯, Geâou. A surname.

Seâou 佋 Seâou bók, 佋穆, the names given in the ancestorial temple, to the successive generations of those offered to; the line of fathers being called seâou, and that of the sons, bók.
Also read seāou: to walk in company.

Seâou 精 The male semen.

去

Seāou 邵 To exhort to energy, to urge; also, the name of a country; a surname.

Seāou 劭 To urge; to exert one's-self.

Seăou 紹 To connect, to carry on in succession. Seăou hòk sëen ông che taē gēēp, 紹復先王之大業 seăou hòk seng ông ây twā gēēp, to carry on and restore the great establishment made by former kings; see the 庚盤書 Se pwăn keng.

大

Seĕh 噝 A sound, a noise; seĕh seĕh sut sut, 噝噝哎哎, a little.

Seĕh 顫 Read chëen: to shake the head, as in the palsy; to tremble. Soò che hân chëen, 四支寒顫 sè ke kwⁿâ seĕh, the four limbs shaking with cold.

Seĕh 洩 Sëet lëêm, 洩炶 seĕh nâ, lightning.

Seĕh 媟 Sëet chùn, 媟嫚 seĕh chwⁿà, a wanton, a lewd woman, a slut.

Seĕh 祴 The name of a sacrifice.

Seĕh 蟋 Sit sut, 蟋蟀 seĕh sut, a cricket. Sit sut chaē tông, söëy yit kê boē, 蟋蟀在堂歲聿其暮 seĕh sut twā tē tέⁿᵍ neēⁿᵍ kaòu neēⁿᵍ maiⁿᵍ, when the crickets are upon the hearth, the year is about to close.

Seĕh 薛 Read söet: the name of a country; a surname.

入

Seĕh 蝕 Read sit: to eat as a worm doth, to consume, to injure, to break in upon.
Sit pún, 蝕本 seĕh pún, to lose money, to break in upon one's capital, to suffer loss.
Sit jit, 蝕日 seĕhjit, an eclipse of the sun.

上平

Sëem 摻 A clever hand, a skillful hand. Sëem sëem lé séw, k'hó é hông sëâng 摻摻女手可以縫裳 gaôu chò ây cha boē ây ch'hêw, t'hang laē pâng jîn chëôⁿᵍ, a clever seamstress can be employed in stitching the clothes; see the 魏風 Göēy hong.

Sëem 纖 Small, minute; finely-wove silk; sëem bê, 纖微, minute.

Sëem 韱 Mountain leeks, of a small kind; small minute.

Sëem 痁 A fever; Chêy hoê kaè sûy sëem, 齊侯疥遂痁 Chêy hoē saiⁿᵍ kày, sûy kwⁿâ jwăh, the prince of the Chêy country had a scrofulous disorder, which afterwards turned into a fever; see the 左傳 Chó twān.

Sëem 銛 A sharp instrument; sharp.

Sëem 憸 Skillful in debate, wrangling; cutting in one's conversation. Boô nê ê sëem jîn, 無昵于憸人, don't be intimate with wranglers.

上聲

Sëém 閃 Tó sëém, 躲閃, to avoid, to get out of the way. Sëém pëen, 閃邊 sëêm peeⁿᵍ, to start on one side.

Sëém 陝 The name of a state; sëém sey, 陝西, one of the provinces of China.

Sëém 剡 Sharp, sharp pointed; to scrape; also, luminous.

Sëém 掞 To loose, to dissolve; to scrape.

Sëém 广 The roof of a house; the head of a beam; one of the radicals.

下去
Sëèm 潓 Read sìm: water about to flow out.

下平
Sëêm 蟾 Sëêm ê, 蟾蜍, a kind of toad, which is said to have eight red spots on its belly.
Sëêm keung, 蟾宮, one of the palaces of the moon. Yit sëêm tëâng, 一蟾長 *chit sëêm téng*, a fathom long.

下上
Sëēm 贍 To give charitably; to supply wants, to lend; hasty, sufficient.
Ch'hoó wûy kèw soó, jê k'heúng put sëēm, 此惟救死而恐不贍 *chéy léy tòk tòh kèw soó, jê kēⁿa ne bô kaòu*, this merely to prevent death, would perhaps not be sufficient; see 孟子 Bēng choó.

Sëēm 暹 The light of the sun rising up; sëēm lô, 暹羅, Siam.
Sëēm ông soō sëāng, Sëēm lé soō hô sëāng, 暹王飼象暹女飼和尚 *Sëēm ây ông ch'hē ch'hëōng, Sëēm ây cha boé ch'hē höèy sëōng*, the king of Siam feeds elephants, but the women of Siam feed priests.

下入
Sëen 仙 A fairy, a sylvan deity, an elf, a genius; sîn sëen, 神仙, an angel; chò sëen, 做仙, to become a fairy. Also, a surname.
Sèng jîn put soo sëen, 聖人不師仙 *sèng jîn bô ǒh chò sëen*, "philosophers do not aim to become fairies;" said by 揚雄 Yâng-hëûng.

Sëen 茌 The name of a grass.

Sëen 僊 The same as 仙, sëen, a fairy; also to frisk and gambol about, when tipsy; also written 僲, sëen.

Sëen 先 Before, first, previously; to precede; to go before. Sëen seng, 先生 *sin saiⁿg*, a teacher, an elder born.
Tān sëen teng ê gān, 誕先登于岸 *kóng taē seng chëōⁿg tē hwⁿā*, it is said that he (Bûn ông) first ascended the bank; (i. e. made the greatest progress in virtue;) see the 大雅 Taē gnáy.
Jîn chëá sëen lān, jê hoē hèk, 仁者先難而後獲 *jîn ây lâng taē seng sëōⁿg tē kan lân, jëên aōu tē séy tit tëŏh*, the benevolent man thinks first of the difficulties, and then of the advantages; see the 論語 Lūn gé.

Sëen 鮮 Vulg. *ch'heⁿg*: fresh, of a good color, new; good, excellent.
Sek pit yūng sëen, 腊必用鮮 *ta ây băh pit tëŏh yūng ch'heeⁿg ây*, dried meat should be used in sacrifice when it is fresh.

Sëen 鱻 The same as the above; sëen gê, 鱻魚 *ch'heeⁿg hê*, fresh fish.

Sëen 羴 The smell of mutton; also written 羶, sëen.

Sëen 鏽 Read sèw: rust, the rust of iron; seng sèw, 生鏽 *saiⁿg sëen*, to become rusty; t'hëet sèw, 鐵鏽 *t'heĕh sëen*, the rust of iron.

上上
Sëén 洗 Vulg. séy: to wash, to cleanse, to rinse.
Sèng jîn ê ch'hoó sëén sim, 聖人以此洗心 *sèng jîn t'hó chéy léy séy*

sim kwⁿa, the sages make use of this wherewith to cleanse their minds; see the 易繫辭 Ĕk hêy soô.

Sëén 筅 Vulg. *ch'hêng*: a duster, to dust anything; key mô sëén, 鷄毛筅 *key mô ch'hêng*, a duster made of fowl's feathers.

Sëén 跣 Barefoot; sëén chëuk, 跣足 *ch'hëăh k'ha*, naked feet.
Jëák sëén, hwut sè têy, k'hwat chëuk yūng sëang, 若跣弗視地厥足用傷 *nā ch'hëăh k'ha bô k'hwⁿà tē têy, e ây k'ha ēy tëŏh sëang*, if we walk barefoot without looking at the ground, our feet may be wounded; see the 書說命 Se wát bêng.

Sëén 毨 The hair or feathers of birds and beasts growing again.

Sëén 癬 A scrofulous complaint; the same as 癬, sëén.

Sëén 銑 Bright, and highly polished metal; a small chisel.

Sëén 㦏 Hastiness of mind, accompanied with fear.

Sëén 僊 Wán sëén, 婉僊, the appearance of moving; elegant motion.

Sëén 尟 Scarce, few, seldom; the same as 鮮, sëén.

Sëén 洒 To wash out, to wash away a stain, to wipe off a reproach.
Gwân pé soó chëá yit sëén che, 願此死者一洒之 *gwān bōëyh t'hēy sè ây lâng chit ây sēy ch'heng k'he*, I wish for the sake of those who are dead, to wipe off this reproach; see 孟子 Bēng choó.

Sëén 癬 Scurf, a scrofulous disorder; seng sëén, 生癬 *saiⁿg sëén*, to get the scurvy, to have a breaking out.

Sëén 蘚 T'hae sëén, 苔蘚, a sort of moss, moss on walls.

Sëén 鮮 Seldom, few, scarce.
K'haóu gân lēng sek, sëén è jîn, 巧言令色鮮矣仁 *ch'hòng hó e ây wā, jê súy e ây bīn sek, chëŏ woō jîn*, those who render their countenance and conversation smooth and agreeable have seldom any share of virtue; see the 論語 Lūn gé.

Sëén 燹 A fire in the wilderness.

Sëén 尠 Few, scarce; the same as 尟, sëén.

Sëén 獮 To kill; the autumnal hunt.

去

Sëèn 扇 Vulg. *seèⁿg*: a fan; bûn sëèn, 門扇 *mootⁿg seèⁿg*, the leaf of a door.
Sùn chok gnóé bêng sëèn, 舜作五明扇 *Sùn chò goē bêng āy seèⁿg*, Sùn invented the five clearness fan.

Sëèn 煽 To fan the flame, to make the fire blaze; a blazing appearance.

Sëèn 搧 To move, to waive, as a fan; to fan.

Sëèn **騸** To geld, to castrate; sëèn mà, 騸馬 *yëem báy*, to geld a horse.

Sëèn **煽** The blazing of fire; the same as 煽 sëèn.

Sëèn **先** To precede, to go before, to walk in front.
Chit hêng sëèn tëáng chëá, wūy che put tēy, 疾行先長者謂之不弟 *mai^{ng}h kë^{n}â taē seng sè twā chëá, kóng ū^{m} hó chò séó tē*, to walk quickly in front of a superior is not to act the part of a good younger brother; see 孟子 Bēng choó.

Sëèn **綫** A thread, a line, a connecting line.

Sëèn **線** Vulg. *sw^{n}â:* a thread; chim sëèn, 針線 *chëem sw^{n}â*, a needle and thread.

Sëèn **信** Read sìn: to believe; gnó put sìn, 我不信 *gwá ū^{m} sëèn*, I will not believe.

平

Sëên **禪** Still, retired, private meditation; to be absorbed in thought; chō sëên, 坐禪 *chēy sëên*, to sit in a meditating posture, as is customary with the priests of Budha.

Sëên **單** Sëên ê, 單于, a name given to the northern Tartars; a double surname.

Sëên **嬋** Sëên kwan, 嬋娟 elegant, beautiful.

Sëên **蟬** Vulg. *àm koe chêy:* a kind of beetle, the dorr beetle; a cockchaffer; a kind of cricket.

Chêy ông hoē hwún soó, se pëèn wûy sëên, 齊王后忿死尸變爲蟬 *Chêy ông ây böē sim hoêy tŏh kaòu sé, sin se peè^{ng} chò àm koe chêy*, the queen of the ruler of the Chêy country died from vexation, when her corpse was metamorphosed into a cockchaffer.

Sëên **儃** A form, a manner; sëên hôêy, 儃佪, to walk backwards and forwards, without being able to advance.

去

Sëēn **善** Good, virtoous, excellent, mild, gentle, moral; virtue, goodness. Much.
T'hëen tō hok sëēn hō yîm, 天道福善禍淫 *t'hee^{ng} ây tō lê kàng hok k'hè tē hó ây, jē hō hwān tē yím lwān ây*, the way of Providence is to send down happiness on the good, and misery on the wanton; see the 書湯誥 Se t'hong hō.

Sëēn **僐** An elegant form, a fine manner.

Sëēn **墡** Pék sëēn t'hoê, 白墡土, a kind of white clay. Also written 磰, sëēn.

Sëēn **膳** Prepared food; chìn sëēn, 進膳, to present food to a superior.
Kê lēng taē kwan, kwan sëēn sêng chaé, 其令大官損膳省宰 *e kăh twā kw^{n}a, kwan k'hè sëēn băh yêw sai^{ng} t'haê meē^{ng}h*, he ordered the great officers to retrench the quantity of prepared food, and to spare the slaughtering of animals; see the 漢宣帝記 Hàn swan tèy kè.

Sëēn **繕** To make up for, to repair; to mend; sëēn lêng gé, 繕囹圄 *poé k^{n}a k'hoo*, to repair the prisons; see the 禮月令 Léy gwàt lēng.

Sëēn 鱔 The name of a fish, or eel, like a snake, without scales, and always covered with slime. Also written 鱓, sëēn.

Sëēn 墠 A flat level place before an altar, where people sacrifice.

Sëēn 禪 The same as the above; when a place is built up of earth, it is called 封, hong, but when the soil is cleared away to form a level, it is called 禪, sëēn. To change, to transfer from one to another.

Sëēn 單 Sëēn hoó, 單父, the name of a city in the 魯, Loé country.

Sëēn 燀 The burning of fire.

Sëēn 嬗 To have one's own way; to act according to one's own inclinations; to obtain sole rule and authority. The same as 禪, sëēn.

Sëēn 擅 The same as the preceding; sëēn kok che wūy ông, 擅國之謂王 *choō chwan tē kok kóng këò ông*, to have one's own way in a country is called being a king.

Sëēn 熯 Dry; fire burning strongly; to respect.

平 *Seeng* 兹 Read choo: as ch'hó choo, 草兹 *ch'haôu seeng*, a straw matrass.

去 *Seèng* 扇 Read sëèn: a fan; bûn sëèn, 門扇 *moot^ng seèng*, the leaf of a door. Jëët t'hëen yūng sëèn, 熱天用扇 *jwâh t'heeng yūng seèng*, in warm weather people use fans.

平 *Seeng* 𧿶 A pickle; kám lám seêng, 橄欖𧿶 *kán ná seeng*, a preparation of pickled olives.

去 *Seèng* 豉 Toē seèng, 豆豉 *taōu seèng*, a preparation of pickled pulse. To pickle anything, to put it in pickle.

入 Sëep 澀 Rough, not smooth; also, a rough, sour, kind of taste.

Sëep 㴊 Hard, firm.

Sëep 澁 Sew sëep, 羞澁, ashamed; difficult, hard to turn.

Sëep 霎 Sëep é, 霎雨 *sëep sé hoē*, a slight shower; sëep sê kan, 霎時間, the time of a shower of rain.

Sëep 攝 To join together, to unite several offices in one. Also read lëep: to receive, to assist.

Sëep 啑 To speak much; sëep sē, 啑嗜, to flatter any one.

入 Sëëp 涉 To wade across the water. K'hëen sëâng sëëp Chin, 褰裳涉溱 *k'hëen jîn chèông leâou köèy Chin chúy*, to pull up one's clothes to wade across the Chin waters; see the 鄭風 Têng hong.

Sëëp 揲 Sëëp sē, 揲蓍, to draw out the reeds or stalks of grass, used in divination.

Sëëp 攝 To be bewitched; kwúy kwaè sëëp bêy, 鬼怪攝迷, to be cozened and bewitched by ghosts and hobgoblins.

大

Sëet 佌 To be extravagant; to remove.

Sëet 泄 To let out; hwat sëet, 發泄, to display; sëet sëà, 泄瀉, to act as a purge.
Kwùy ch'hun che gwàt, yâng k'hè hwat sëet, 季春之月陽氣發泄 *kwùy ch'hun ây göëyh, yâng ây k'hè chëw hwat sëet*, in the latter month of spring, the procreative principle of nature begins to be displayed; see the 禮月令 Léy gwàt lēng.

Sëet 紲 A horse's bridle, anything by which a horse or a cow is tied; a long rope.

Sëet 疶 The same as 痩, sëet, a dysentery; sëet sëà, 疶瀉, to purge.

Sëet 偰 A surname. Also, the same as the following.

Sëet 契 The name of a man, who was an officer in the court of 堯, Geâou, and the ancestor of 商湯, Sëang t'hong.

Sëet 僁 A small voice, a whisper, a groan, a hum. Also written 㑵, sëet.

Sëet 絏 To bind; bonds.
Suy chaē lûy sëet che tëung, hwuy kê chöëy yëá, 雖在縲絏之中非其罪也 *suy twā tē lûy sëet ây tang e^ng, ū^m sē e ây chöëy*, although he was in the midst of bonds and imprisonments, it was not his fault; see the 論語 Lūn gé.

Sëet 卨 A man's name; also a surname.

Sëet 洩 Loē sëet, 漏洩 *laōu sëet*, to leak out, to let out a secret.
Chín hô haé, jê put sëet, 振河海而不洩 *chín sëw hô haé ây chúy, jê bēy hoē e sëet laōu*, (the earth) holds the rivers and seas, without allowing them to leak out; see the 中庸 Tëung yûng.

Sëet 痩 To purge; sëet sëà che chit, 痩瀉之疾 *laōu sëà ây pai^ng*, a dysentery; a looseness of the bowels.

Sëet 燮 Harmonious; to harmonize; also written 燮, sëet.

Sëet 噯 The sound of anything breaking.

Sëet 媟 To be familiar with, to despise, to defile.
Taē sîn put sëet, 大臣不媟 *twā jîn sîn ū^m t'hang sëet bān*, do not despise great ministers.

Sëet 屧 The felt worn in shoes.

Sëet 爇 To burn, to set fire to, to consume; also written 焫, sëet.

Sëet 褻 Private, a private dress, common apparel; familiar, free; sëet tók, 褻瀆, to despise, to revile, to blaspheme.
Hông choo put é wûy sëet hók, 紅紫不以

爲褻服 *ăng choo bŏ bŏëyh ch'hèng chò sae k'hëă ây yîn chëŏng*, he would not wear a red or crimson color for his private dress; said of Confucius in the 論語 Lūn-gé.

Sëet 薛 A kind of sedge grass, the Cyperus genus. Vulg. *seĕh:* a surname.

Sëet 設 To appoint, to arrange, to establish, to set up.
Sëet wûy sëâng sē hák hadu-é kadu che, 設爲庠序學校以教之 *sëet chò sëâng sē ŏh hadu ĕ kâ e*, and then appointed schools and seminaries of instruction to teach the people; see 孟子 Bēng choó.

Sëet 蔎 A kind of fragrant grass.

灭
Sëet 舌 The tongue; k'hoé sëet, 口舌 *ch'hùy cheĕh*, the tongue of the mouth.
Bók bûn tîm sëet, gân put k'hó sè è, 莫捫朕舌言不可逝矣 *bŏ lăng tai^ng gwá ây cheĕh, nā sē kóng wā ū^m t'hang-lâm sám ch'hut*, nobody holds our tongue, and yet our words should not disorderly escape us; see the 大雅 Taē gnáy.

Sëet 磼 To tan leather, to curry leather; sëet lé, 磼里, the name of a country.

Sëet 㓶 The same as the above.

夫
Sek 昔 Formerly, before, previously; sek jit, 昔日, on a former day.
Sek chëá, yêw yëá bûn choo hoo choó, 昔者由也聞諸夫子 *chá sê, guá woō t'hë^na kap hoo choó*, formerly I heard it from our master; see the 論語 Lūn gé.

Sek 惜 To pity, to feel for, to commiserate; k'hó sek, 可惜, alas! alas!
Sek hoē! hoo choó che gé kwun choó yëá, 惜乎夫子之語君子也 *k'hó sek hoē! hoo choó lé ây kóng sē ch'hin chëŏng kwun choó*, alas! what you say is like the speech of a good man, (but you err in altogether rejecting elegance;) see the 論語 Lūn gé.

Sek 腊 Dried flesh.

Sek 熣 Vulg. *chëŏh:* dry, anything dried; the same as the above.

Sek 斮 To cut off, to amputate.

Sek 色 The countenance, color, beauty, lust; ch'haé sek, 采色, variegated colors; h^nò sek, 好色, to be addicted to venery.
Chèng gân sek, soo kīn sìn è, 正顏色斯近信矣 *chë^nà lán ây gân sek, chéy lêy chëw kīn sìn è*, adjust the countenance properly, and then you will induce faithful men to draw near; see the 論語 Lūn gé.

Sek 傺 Tek sek, 倜傺, vicious, wicked.

Sek 摖 Boē sek, 摸摖, to feel.

Sek 索 To seek, to search for, to require, to take; lêk sek, 勒索, to extort money. Vulg. *sŏh:* a cord, a rope. A surname.
Sek sit k'he ék, 索室毆疫 *ch'hŏey ch'hoō*

福建方言字典

kwⁿá wun yĕăh, to search the house and drive out noxious influences; see the 周禮 Chew léy.

Sek 糁 To boil rice with plenty of water.

Sek 嗇 Sek hoo, 嗇夫, a field laborer, a husbandman; hard, to covet.

Sek 儥 The same as the above; also, a surname.

Sek 穡 Kày sek, 稼穡, husbandry, tillage, farming; a barn floor. Anciently written 嗇, sek.

Put kày put sek, hoê ch'hé hô sam pek ek hêy, 不稼不穡胡取禾三百億兮 *ūᵐ kày ūᵐ sek, bŏĕyh an chwⁿá ēy k'hĕŏh tĕw sⁿa păyh ek,* without tillage and husbandry, how could we obtain three hundred million bundles of corn; see the 魏風 Göēy hong.

Sek 劏 To pierce, to stab.

Sek 歗 Lamentation, grief.

Sek 懎 To be enraged, to hate; to be vexed.

Sek 析 To split wood, to divide; a surname; also written 枂, sek.

Sek sin jê che hô? hwuy hoó put k'hek, 析薪如之何匪斧不克 *p'hwà ch'hâ an chwⁿá? bô poó t'haŏu bēy yēⁿâ,* in splitting firewood how shall we manage? without an ax we shall never succeed; see the 齊風 Chêy hong.

Sek 晳 A white color.

Sek 晳 To distinguish clearly.

Sek 淅 Sek bé, 淅米, to wash rice before boiling, to rinse rice.

K'hóng-choó che k'hè Chêy, chëep sek jê hêng, 孔子之去齊接淅而行 *K'hóng-choó ây k'hè Chêy kok, chëep sek bé jé kēⁿâ,* when Confucius left the Chêy country, he (was in such a hurry, that his disciples) took up the rice with the water in which it was washed, and went away (without waiting to boil it); see 孟子 Bēng choó.

Sek 晰 Sek sek, 晰晰, the chirping of birds.

Sek 瑟 A kind of guitar; k'hîm sek, 琴瑟, a harp and guitar.

Koé sek he, k'hëen jé, 鼓瑟希鏗爾 *p'hăh koé twⁿā sek kaŏu he, sëⁿa yēá tit k'hëen jé,* when the drum and guitar have ceased to be played upon, there still remains a humming sound; see the 論語 Lūn gé.

Sek 濇 The remains of a slight shower; also written 涑, sek.

Sek 餙 Séw sek, 首餙, the ornaments of the head. Chong sek, 裝餙 *cheⁿᵍ tⁿâ,* to ornament, and adorn.

Sek 飾 Sew sek, 修飾, to adorn, to decorate.

Hêng jîn Choó-é sew sek che, 行人子羽修飾之 *hêng jîn ây kwⁿa,*

Choó-ê sew sek e ây bûn, the traveling officer Choó-é polished and improved (the style of the documents); see the 論語 Lūn gé.

Sek 錫 Vulg. *sĕăh:* tin; sek kwān, 錫礶 *sĕăh kwān,* a tin pot; also, to bestow.

T'hĕen naé sek ông tè yúng, 天乃錫王智勇 *t'heeⁿᵍ naé soò hoē ông tè hwà yúng,* heaven has bestowed upon the king wisdom and courage; see the 商書 Sēang se.

Sek 緆 Fine cloth.

Sek 暘 The sun not shining.

Sek 唈 Sek sek, 唈唈, the chirping of birds.

Sek 倏 Sek hwut, 倏忽, suddenly; the appearance of a dog running swiftly.

Sek 倐 The same as the above.

Sek 螫 The sting of a bee; the pain produced by a sting.

Choō kêw sin sek, 自求辛螫 *ka tē kĕw sin k'hoé kwà p'hang têng,* to draw on one's self stings and reproaches; see the 周頌 Chew sĕūng.

Sek 塞 Vulg. *t'hat:* to stop up, to dam, to obstruct; to fill.

Kim maôu sek choó che sim è, 今茅塞子之心矣 *tⁿa hūᵐ á ch'haôu woō t'hat tĕŏh lé ây sim kwⁿa,* now grass and weeds have stopped up the entrance to your mind; see 孟子 Bēng choó.

Ch'hĕung sek jîn gē, 充塞仁義 *ch'hĕung mwⁿá jîn gē,* filled and replenished with benevolence and righteousness.

Sek 舄 A shoe, a slipper; a double soled shoe.

Sek 嬕 A woman's name.

Sek 釋 To wash rice.

Sek 釋 To loose, to let go, to release, to dissolve, to explain.

Sek Kê-choó sêw, 釋箕子囚 *pàng Kê-choó ây sêw,* he released Kê-choó from his confinement; see the 周書 Chew se.

Hwàn jĕĕn peng sek, 渙然氷釋 *hwàn jĕĕn seⁿᵍ yĕŏⁿᵍ,* melting away the ice dissolved; said by 程子 Têng choó.

Sek 適 To go to, to proceed towards, to meet with; self-satisfied.

Choó sek Wŏēy, 子適衛 *hoo choó k'hè kaôu Wŏēy kok,* Confucius went to the Wŏēy country; see the 論語 Lūn gé.

Sek gnó gwān hêy! 適我願兮 *sek mwⁿá gwá ây gwān!* how fully satisfied are my desires! see the 鄭風 Tēng hong.

Sek 栻 Vulg. *ch'heēⁿᵍ:* a wooden instrument, by which to divine; a mould.

Sek 蝨 Vulg. *sat:* a louse; bòk sek, 木蝨 *bàk sat,* a bug.

Kap tēw seng ké sek, 甲胄生蟣蝨 *kăh tēw saiⁿᵍ ké sat,* his helmet and armor (from long wear) bred vermin.

Sek 虱 The common form of the preceding.

Sek 奭 Full, complete; a red color.

Sek 襫 P'hwat sek, 襏襫, a coarse rough garment, to keep out the rain.

汉

Sek 石 Vulg. *chëŏh:* a stone; sek t'hoê, 石頭 *chëŏh t'haôu*, a large stone; also, a measure of about 10 pecks, or 133 pounds weight.
Kim hoo san, yit kwán sek che to, 今夫山一卷石之多 *t^na chêy lêy swo^na chit kwut^ng chëŏh ây chēy*, now a hill consists of but a lump of stones; see the 中庸 Tëung yung. A surname.
Ké sek? 幾石 *kwûy chëŏh?* how many bushels?

Sek 妬 A barren woman; sek t'hae, 妬胎, a barren womb.

Sek 碩 Great, large; bók te kê beâou che sek, 莫知其苗之碩 *bô lâng chae e ka tē ây tëw ây sai^ng twā*, no one perceives how tall his own corn grows; (i. e. no one is aware of his own mercies;) see the 大學 Taē hák.

Sek 夕 The evening, dusk, the close of the day. Teaou sek sîn hwan, 朝夕承歡 *cha k'hê mat^ng hwui^ng sëo swä pāy boê ây hwo^na hê*, morning and evening keep up your parents' joy, (by waiting on them incessantly;) see the 禮内則 Léy löëy chek.

Sek 汐 The tide of the sea; the morning tide is called 潮, teâou, and the evening one 汐, sek.

Sek 席 Vulg. *ch'hëŏh:* a mat; a table, a feast; a surname.
Sek put chèng put chō, 席不正不坐 *ch'hëŏh ūm sè chē^nâ bô böëyh chēy*, if the mat was not spread square and even, (Confucius) would not sit down upon it.
Hoô sek, 赴席, to come to table; sek yëên, 席筵, a feast.

Sek 蓆 Great, large.

Sek 射 Vulg. *chŏh:* to shoot with an arrow, to practice archery.
Ek put sek sëuk, 弋不射宿 *chŏh chee^ng bô böëyh chŏh tëŏh hai^ngh chaôu*, in archery, (Confucius) would not shoot at a resting bird; see the 論語 Lūn gé.

Sek 穸 The hollow part of a grave.

Sek 熟 Read sëuk: ripe, thoroughly boiled; accustomed to, acquainted with.
Kwun soô seng, pit sëuk jê chëên che, 君賜腥必熟而薦之 *jîn kwun sâng ch'hai^ng ây mē^ngh, pit tëŏh chê sek, jê haôu e*, when a prince presents us with anything raw, we should boil it thoroughly before we offer it in sacrifice; see the 論語 Lūn gé.

卋

Seng 生 Vulg. *sai^ng:* to be born, to bear, to bring forth; alive, living.
Jîn sip gwát jê seng, 人十月而生 *lâng kaôu chàp göëyh jit chëw sai^ng*, men are born after a gestation of ten (lunar) months; sëen seng, 先生 *sin sai^ng*, elder born, a teacher.

Seng 胜 The smell of dog's fat; anything uncooked and raw.

Seng **牲** He seng, 犧牲, a sacrificial animal; hëuk seng, 畜牲 *t'hëuk sai^{ng}*, a domestic animal, a brute. Boô é këung he seng yëá, 無以共犧牲也 *boô t'hang këung kip he seng*, we have nothing wherewith to furnish animals for sacrifice; see 孟子 Bēng choó.

Seng **笙** A pipe, an instrument of music; vessels used in sacrifice.

Seng **泩** A rising and overflowing of the waters; water deep and wide.

Seng **鼪** A kind of flying rat, a bat.

Seng **甥** Sister's children are called göëy seng, 外甥, cousins; a son-in-law is also called 甥, seng. Tèy kwán seng ê jē sit, 帝館甥於貳室 *tèy sëw kë^{n}á saè tē e ây sëang pêng ch'hoò*, the emperor lodged his son-in-law (Sùn) in his two side apartments; see the 下孟 Hāy bēng.

Seng **星** Vulg. *ch'hai^{ng}:* a star, a planet, stars in general. Yit gwát seng sîn hëy yëen, 日月星辰繫焉 *jit göëyh ch'hai^{ng} sîn hëy tcàou yëen*, the sun, moon, and stars are suspended (in the firmament); see the 中庸 Tëung yûng.

Seng **惺** Intelligent, clever, wise.

Seng **猩** Seng seng, 猩猩, an orang outang, a beast which is said to be able to speak; a baboon; an ape. Seng seng lêng gân, put lê ê k'hîm sèw, 猩猩能言不離於禽獸 *seng seng ēy kóng wā, yëá sè bēy lê ê k'hîm sèw*, even if the orang outang could talk, it would still be nothing better than a brute; see the 曲禮 K'hëuk léy.

Seng **醒** Vulg. *ch'hai^{ng}:* to awake, to recover from the effects of liquor. Jîn chùy gnó seng, 人醉我醒 *lâng chò poô chùy, gwá tòk tòk ch'hai^{ng}*, all men are drunk, and I alone am sober.

Seng **腥** Vulg. *ch'hai^{ng}:* raw, undressed, uncooked, unripe, inexperienced. Seng hwūn, 腥分 *ch'hai^{ng} hwūn*, unacquainted with, not familiar.

Seng **鮏** Raw fish.

Seng **湦** The name of a river.

Seng **曐** The ancient form of 星, seng, a star.

Seng **陞** To ascend; like the rising of the sun; to exalt, to elevate.

Seng **升** To ascend, to advance. Vulg. *chin:* a measure, the tenth part of a peck. Hoo choó che put k'hò kip yëá, yêw t'hëen che put k'hò kae jê seng yëá, 夫子之不可及也猶天之不可階而升也 *hoo choó ây bô t'hang kip yëá, ch'hin chëö^{ng} t'hee^{ng} ây bô t'hang ch'hòng gîm kay jê chëö^{ng} yëá*, our master (Confucius) is not to be equaled, just as heaven is not to be scaled by ladders; see the 論語 Lūn gé.
Seng kàng, 升降, to ascend and descend.

Seng 昇 The rising of the sun; to arise, to ascend; tranquil, peaceful.
Jê jit che seng, 如日之昇 *ch'hin chëōng jit t'haôu ây k'hé*, like the rising of the sun.

Seng 聲 Vulg. *sëⁿa:* a voice, a noise; seng yim, 聲音 *sëⁿa yim*, a sound; bêng seng, 名聲 *mëⁿá sëⁿa*, fame, report. Also written 声, seng.
Tông seng sëang èng, 同聲相應 *tâng sëⁿa sëo yìn*, those who are of a similar speech can answer one another.

Seng 榺 Luxuriant herbage, abundant foliage.

Seng 旌 Seng kê, 旌旗, a flag, a standard; seng peáou, 旌表, to denote anything by signals.

Séng 省 (省) Séng ch'hat, 省察, to examine, to inspect; séng k'hëém, 省儉 *saiⁿᵍ k'hëēm*, to spare, to be parsimonious; séng sêng, 省城 *saiⁿᵍ sëⁿá*, the capital city of a province.
Goê jit sam séng goê sin, 吾日三省吾身 *gwá tàk jit sⁿa hāng séng ch'hat gwá ây hìn sin*, I daily examine myself in three particulars; see the 上論 Sëāng lūn.

Séng 偗 Straight; also, long.

Séng 瘠 Thin, meagre.

Séng 醒 Vulg. *ch'haiⁿᵍ:* to awake from liquor, to awake from sleep.
Séng é ko tëük Choó-hwān, 醒以戈逐子犯 *kaôu ch'haiⁿᵍ chëw t'hó kaou á k'hè jëuk Choó-hwān*, when he awoke he took a hooked spear and pursued after Choó-hwān; see the 左傳 Chó twān.

Séng 眚 (眚) A disease of the eyes; also, a fault, to transgress; also, a strange and supernatural sickness.

Sèng 姓 Vulg. *saiⁿᵍ:* a surname, a family name; pek sèng, 百姓 *päyh saiⁿᵍ*, the hundred clans, i. e. the Chinese people.
Sèng séy tông yëá, bêng séy tók yëá, 姓所同也名所獨也 *saiⁿᵍ séy sëo tâng yëá, mëⁿá séy twⁿa tók yëá*, there may be an uniformity of family names, and a singularity of individual epithets; see 孟子 Bēng choó.

Sèng 性 Vulg. *saiⁿᵍ:* nature, natural parts and dispositions; sèng t'héy, 性體 a disposition; kè sèng, 記性 *kè saiⁿᵍ*, the memory; sèng bēng, 性命 *saiⁿᵍ mëⁿā*, the life.
T'hëen bēng che wūy sèng, 天命之謂性 *t'heeⁿᵍ bēng lēng hoē lán, sē kóng kèò saiⁿᵍ*, that which heaven decrees to bestow on us is called nature; see the 中庸 Tëung yûng.

Sèng 賸 Riches, wealth; affluent, opulent.

Sèng 聖 Holy, sacred; sèng jîn, 聖人, a sage, a holy man, a philosopher.
Lêng sèng, 靈聖 *lêng sëⁿá*, sacred, and sure in its answers, like an oracle; applied to the shrines of particular deities.
Sèng jîn che ê t'hëen tō yëá, sèng yëá, 聖人之於天道也性也 *sèng jîn ây bat t'heeⁿᵍ ây tō lé, sē saiⁿᵍ yëá*, the acquaintance of a sage with the way of heaven is entirely natural; see 孟子 Bēng choó.

平
Sêng **成** Vulg. *chë^n â:* complete, finished; to perfect, to accomplish; good, even; a surname.

Hwān kong chut gëëp chëw wūy che sêng, 凡功卒業就謂之成 *hwān kong swăh gëëp chëw, hóng këò chë^n â,* whenever work is finished, and a business accomplished, it is said to be completed.

Sêng **誠** Sincere, pure, without any mixture of falsehood, upright.

Kò chè sêng jê sîn, 故至誠如神 *ch'ië^n á chè sêng ch'hin chëö^ng sîn,* therefore the highest point of sincerity is as it were divine; see the 中庸 Tëung yûng.

Sêng **城** Vulg. *së^n â:* a city, a citadel; hoó sêng, 府城 *hoó së^n â,* the capital city of a district; Pa sêng, 吧城 *Pa së^n â,* the city of Batavia.

Ch'hok soo tê yëá, tëuk soo sêng yëá, 鑿斯池也築斯城也 *ch'âk chê lêy chúy k'hcut á, këh chéy lêy së^n â,* dig this moat deeper, and build this city wall higher; see 孟子 Bēng choó.

Sêng **盛** Sacrificial fruits in their vessels, ready for offering.

Choo sêng put këet, put kám ê chèy, 粢盛不潔不敢以祭 *choo sêng ūm ch'heng k'hē, ūm k^n á laê chèy,* the sacrificial fruits and vessels not being clean, we do not dare to sacrifice; see 孟子 Bēng choó.

Sêng **筬** Hëê sêng, 絃筬 *hëé^ng sey,* the comb used in weaving, to keep the threads separate.

Sêng **乘** To mount, to ascend a carriage; to ride in a carriage, or on horseback, to take advantage of; sêng sê, 乘時, to embrace an opportunity.

Sêng lëûk lëûng ê gē t'hëen, 乘六龍以御天 *k'hëâ lák chëäh lëûng, ê gē t'hee^ng,* to mount six dragons, in order to ride to heaven; (an expression intimating the elevation to imperial dignity.)

Sêng **傖** A term of reproach, used by the people of one district against another.

去
Sēng **盛** Great, full, abundant, flourishing; a surname; boē sēng, 茂盛, luxuriant.

Jit sin che wūy sēng tek, 日新之謂盛德 *tàk jit sin sē kóng këò sēng tek,* to be daily renewed is called abundant virtue.

Sēng söey, 盛衰, to flourish and decay.

Sēng **晟** Clear, bright; to burn.

Sēng **乘** The numeral of a chariot; yit sēng ke, 一乘車 *chit tëo^ng ch'hëa,* one chariot; ch'hëen sēng che kok, 千乘之國 *chit ch'heng tëo^ng ch'hëa ây kok,* a country capable of producing a thousand chariots.

Sēng **椉** The ancient form of the preceding character; also written 乗, sēng.

Sēng **賸** Superabundant, overflowing.

去
Se^ng **喪** Read song: to lose by death; song haòu, 喪孝 *se^ng hà,* a funeral, mourning at a funeral, mourning at the death of relatives.

Sam lëên che song, t'hëen hāy che t'hong song yëá, 三年之喪天下之通喪也 *s^na neë^ng ây se^ng hà, t'hee^ng ây t'hong tàt ây se^ng hà,* the three years' mourning (for parents) is a mourning universally adopted throughout the whole empire; see the 論語 Lūn gé.

Se^ng 桑 Read song: the mulberry tree. Gnoé boé che t'hék, sē che é song, 五畝之宅樹之以桑 *goē boĕ áy t'hăyh, chèng e é se^ng*, a tenement of five acres should be planted with the mulberry tree; see 孟子 Bēng choó.

Se^ng 霜 Read song: hoar-frost; song swat, 霜雪 *se^ng săyh*, frost and snow; t'hông song, 糖霜 *t'he^ng se^ng*, sugar-candy; p'he song, 砒霜 *p'he^ng se^ng*, arsenic.

声 Sé^ng 傸 Read ch'hëáng: to play pranks; ch'hëáng chëên, 傸錢 *séng cheé^ng*, to squander money.

平 Sê^ng 牀 Read ch'hông: a bed; lóng ch'hông, 籠牀 *láng sé^ng*, a kind of frame used in steaming dumplings.

声 Sëo 燒 Read seaou: to burn; h^nó seaou, 火燒 *höéy sëo*, the fire burns.

Sëo 煖 Read lwán: warm, lukewarm, comfortably warm; well clothed. Gnoé sip hwuy pék put lwán, 五十非帛不煖 *goē chàp höëy nā bô ch'hèng twān bēy sëo*, at fifty years of age, without wearing silk, people cannot keep themselves warm; see 孟子 Bēng choó.

Sëo 爇 Read jëët: warm, lukewarm, as applied to food.

Sëo 暖 Read lwán: warm, as applied to the weather.

Sëo 相 Read seang: mutual; seang haē, 相害 *sëo haē*, to injure one another; seang aè, 相愛 *'sëo sëŏh*, to love one another.

声 Sëó 小 Read seáou: small, minute, little; seáou tēy, 小弟 *sëó tē*, a younger brother; gwát seáou, 月小 *göëyh sëó*, a short month.

去 Sëò 杪 Read beáou: the tender branch of a tree.

Sëò 鞘 Read seàou: a scabbard; to seàou, 刀鞘 *to sëò*, the sheath of a sword.

大 Sëŏh 惜 Read sek: to pity, to commiserate, to love.

入 Sëŏh 膌 Read sék: the dirt on the soles of the feet; hèw këak sék, 臭脚膌 *ch'haòu k'ha sëŏh*, stinking feet.

Sëŏh 鯗 Hèw sëáng, 臭鯗 *ch'haòu sëŏh*, stinking, fetid.

卒 Sëo^ng 相 Read sëang: mutual; sëang soo, 相思 *sëo^ng se*, to think of one another; also, the name of a plant.

Sëo^ng 廂 Read sëang: the corner of a house. T'haē gwát sey sëang hāy, 待月西廂下 *tëng t'haē göëyh tē sae sëo^ng āy*, waiting for the moon under the western corner of the house.

Sëo^ng 箱 Read sëang: a box, a trunk; lóng sëang, 籠箱 *láng sëo^ng*, a box or trunk for keeping clothes in.

Sëo^ng 傷 Read sëang: to wound; chëák sëang, 着傷 *tëŏh sëo^ng*, to be wounded.

Bûn ông sē bîn jê sëang, 文王視民如傷 *Bûn ông k'hw^nà păyh sai^ng ch'hin chëo^ng tëŏh sëo^ng*, Bûn ông looked upon his people as though they had been wounded (by his bad government); see 孟子 Bēng choó.

*Sëo^ng^* 鑲 Read sëang: to inlay with gold or silver, or any other metal. Sëang kim, 鑲金 *sëo^ng^ kim*, to inlay or garnish with gold.

上声 *Sëó^ng^* 賞 Read sëáng: to reward, to remunerate, to bestow, to admire; sëáng hwa, 賞花 *sëó^ng^ hwa*, to admire fine flowers. Yéw kong kae sëáng, 有功該賞 *woō kong teōh sëó^ng^*, those who have any merit should be rewarded.

*Sëó^ng^* 想 Read sëáng: to think, to consider.

*Sëó^ng^* 鮝 Gê sëáng 魚鮝 *hê sëó^ng^*, dried salt fish; ăh sëáng, 鴨鮝 *ăh sëó^ng^*, dried smoked ducks, a delicacy among the Chinese.

去 *Sëò^ng^* 相 Read sëàng: to look at a person's physiognomy, in order to tell his fortune; sëàng bēng, 相命 *sëò^ng^ mē^n^ā*, to practice palmistry.

平 *Sëô^ng^* 常 Read sëâng: common; pêng sëâng, 平常 *pêng sëô^ng^*, usual.

*Sëô^ng^* 湷 Read sëâng: pus, matter; lêw sëâng, 流湷 *laôu sëô^ng^*, running matter; lông sëâng, 膿湷 *lâng sëô^ng^*, thick matter.

去 *Sëō^ng^* 尙 Read sëāng: to emulate; hô sëāng, 和尙 *hôëy sëō^ng^*, a priest of the sect of Budha; sëāng taē, 尙大 *sëō^ng^ twā*, too large.

*Sëó^ng^* 想 Read sëáng: to think, to reflect; put heáou sëáng, 不曉想 *bēy heáou sëó^ng^*, unable to think or reflect.

入 Sëuk 叔 Vulg. *chek:* an uncle, a father's younger brother; *ū^n^ chek*, 'uncle,' is a common mode of address, on meeting a stranger. Also written 俶 sëuk.

Sëuk 俶 To begin; also, good; to move, to do; excellent; liberal, thick.

Sëuk 菽 Pulse, any kind of beans or peas. Sëuk ch'hëuk jê súy h^n^ó, jê bîn yëen yéw put jîn cheá hoē? 菽粟如水火而民焉有不仁者乎 *săyh sëuk ch'hin chëō^ng^ chúy hōëy, jê păyh sai^ng^ t'haē t'hó woō ū^m^ jîn tek hoē?* when pulse and corn are as plentiful as fire and water, how can the people help being virtuous? see 孟子 Bēng choó.

Sëuk 淑 Good, amiable, harmonious; sëuk lé, 淑女, a virtuous woman. Sëuk jîn kwun choó, 淑人君子, a good and virtuous man.

Sëuk 踧 Cautious, respectful; uneasy; sëuk sek, 踧踖, hesitating.

Sëuk 㑛 The ancient form of 夙 sëuk, early; also written 俶, sëuk.

Sëuk 倲 Sëuk sëuk, 傝倲, a motion of the head.

Sëuk 嗽 To suck, to inhale.

Sëuk 遬 Hasty, speedy, quick, rapid.

Sëuk 儵 Sëuk hwut, 儵忽, suddenly; the appearance of a dog running swiftly.

Sëuk 倏 The same as the preceding.

Sëuk 宿 To stay, to rest, to lodge, to remain; to retain; to rest; read sèw: a constellation; toĕ sëuk, 投宿 *taŏu haïngh*, to seek a lodging.

Yéw k'hek sëuk sëuk, 有客宿宿 *woō k'häyh laĕ haïngh*, strangers come to lodge; see the 周頌 Chew sëüng.

Sëuk 蓿 Bók sëuk, 苜蓿, the name of a plant or root which cattle eat.

Sëuk 蹜 To urge, to stir up, to press on.

Sëuk 縮 Straight, upright; to cultivate, to retire; short; to bind.

Choō hwán jê sëuk, 自反而縮 *ka te hwán jĕ tit*, turning in upon one's-self, and finding one's conduct upright; see 孟子 Bēng choó.

Sëuk 肅 To respect, respectful; to advance; dread, fear, awe; especial.

Säuk 翻 The flying of a bird.

Sëuk 鷫 The name of a fabulous bird.

Sëuk 驌 A good horse.

Sëuk 粟 Read ch'hëuk: and ch'hek: corn, grain; bé ch'hëuk, 米粟 *bé sëuk*, paddy, growing rice.

Bé ch'hëuk hwuy put to yëá, 米粟非不多也 *bé sëuk ūm chêng ūm chēy*, the paddy is not otherwise than abundant; see 孟子 Bēng choó.

Sëuk 夙 Chó sëuk, 早夙, early, early in the morning.

Sëuk hin yëā bē, 夙興夜寐 *chá k'hé laĕ, maīng kan k'hwùn*, to rise early in the morning and to go to bed late at night.

Sëuk 孰 (also 㷊) Who, what, which.

Sē k'hó jím yëá, sëuk put k'hó jím yëá? 是可忍也孰不可忍也 *chêy lêy nā ēy lún tit, sē sⁿá meēngh bēy lún tit?* if this can be endured, what cannot then be borne? see the 上論 Sëāng lūn.

Sëuk 熟 Vulg. *sêk:* ripe, mature, well done, thoroughly boiled; acquainted.

P'heng sëuk chëen hëang, 烹熟羶薌 *k'ho sêk haŏu ây meēngh*, boil the sacrificial meat thoroughly; see the 祭義 Chèy gē.

Söèy chek taē sëuk, 歲則大熟 *neēng tang chëw twā sêk*, the year was very fruitful.

Sëuk 塾 An antechamber or kind of lodge on the side of the door.

Kē chwān ê sey sëuk, 具饌于西塾 *ch'hông meēngh chëāh tē sae sëuk*, prepare the food in the western antechamber; see the 儀禮 Gê léy.

Sëuk 俗 Hong sëuk, 風俗, manners, customs; vulgar, common; sëuk gé, 俗語, a common saying, a proverb, the provincial dialect.

K'hó wūy te cheá tō, lân é sëuk jîn gân, 可謂知者道難與俗人言 *t'hang kóng te ây lâng tō lé, ŏh kap sëuk ây lâng kóng wā*, we can speak with men of understanding on various doctrines, but it is difficult to converse with common fellows.

Sëùk 僞 Sëùk sëuk, 僞倲, the head moving

Sëùk 蜀 Sey-sëùk, 西蜀, the name of a district in the west of China, now the province of 四川, Soò-ch'hwan.

Sëùk 屬 To belong to; of the same sort or kind; sëùk kok, 屬國, a tributary kingdom; sëùk hāy jîn sîn, 屬下人臣, a dependant officer.

Sëùk 属 The contracted form of the preceding.

Sëùk 續 Vulg. *swà:* connected, joined; to link together; to hand down in succession; continuously.
Lëùk sëùk, 陸續, in succession, in a row, one after the other.
Soō sëùk pé choé, 似續妣祖 *ch'hin chëōⁿᵍ sëo swà pāy boé,* as it were maintaining the line of succession from our parents.

Sëùk 贖 To ransom, to repurchase anything; sëùk chöëy, 贖罪, to atone for sins, to redeem from sin.
Kim chok sëùk hêng, 金作贖刑 *kim ēy chò sëùk hêng hwàt,* money can be used to redeem from punishment; see the 舜典 Sùn tëén.

Sëùk 焇 Read seaou: dry; seaou che, 焇支 *sëùk ke,* a dry twig.

平

Sëung 嵩 High, lofty; sëung ko wûy gàk, 嵩高維嶽 *sëung kwân tòk tòk swⁿa gàk,* for height and loftiness, we look to the mountains; see the 大雅 Taē gnáy.

Sëung 㣝 K'hëûng sëung, 倮㣝, small of stature, and despicable. Idle, according to the dialect of some districts.

去

Sëúng 從 Quick, rapid; sëúng hong, 從風, a violent gust of wind.

Sëúng 嵷 The point of a hill; a conical mountain top.

Sëúng 悚 To be afraid, alarmed.

Sëúng 竦 To respect; sëúng tōng, 竦動, to move carefully.

Sëúng 聳 Sëúng ch'hùy, 聳翠, a deep green color.

平

Sëûng 松 A fir tree; sëûng pek, 松柏 *ch'hêng păyh,* a cedar-tree. A surname.
Hāy hoē sē é sëûng, 夏后氏以松 *Hāy teâou tēy é chèng sëung,* the Hāy dynasty was distinguished by the planting of the fir tree; see the 論語 Lūn gé.

Sëûng 淞 The name of a river.

Sëûng 菘 Kam sëûng, 甘菘, the name of a medicine.

Sëûng 崧 A mountain high and large, is called 崧, sëûng.

Sëûng 嫦 Sëûng gô, 嫦娥, name of a female, supposed to be in the moon. Sëûng-gô Gēy ch'hëep, ch'hëep

Gēy put soo yëăk, p'hun gwàt, kip che wûy sëôm sô, 嫦娥羿妾竊羿不死藥奔月及之爲蟾蜍 *Sëâng-gô sē Gēy ây sèy é, t'haou Gēy ây bēy sé yčŏh, p'hun kaou göēyh, kaôu jĕuk tëŏh, peēng chò sëēm sé,* when Seûng-gô was Gēy's concubine, she stole Gēy's medicine of immortality, and ran away to the moon; upon being overtaken she turned into a toad.

Sëûng 倯 Idle, according to the dialect of a certain district.

丟
Sëūng 訟 To contend, to wrangle, to litigate, to engage in lawsuits.

T'hèng sëūng goē yĕw jîn yeá, pit yeá soó boô sëūng hoē, 聽訟吾猶人也必也使無訟乎 *t'hēna p'hwàn sëūng gëùk gwá ēy ch'hin chëōng lâng, nā sē tëŏh saé bó sëūng gëùk,* "in hearing litigious cases, I am as good as other people, but the principal thing is to cause litigations to cease;" said by Confucius in the 論語 Lūn gé.

Sëūng 誦 To read, or chant over a book, in a singing tone.

Sëūng se sam pek, 誦詩三百 *ch'hëōng se sna pāyh,* to chant over the three hundred odes; see the 論語 Lūn gé.

Sëūng 頌 To sing, to chant, to praise, to sing praises; sëūng chān, 頌讚 *o ló,* to praise, to laud; sëūng bé, 頌美, to admire.

Sëūng kê se, t'hók kê se, 頌其詩讀其書 *sëūng e ây se, t'hăk e ây ch'hāyh,* to chant their odes, and read their books.

幸
Sew 修 To cultivate, to adorn, to repair, to mend; sew lé, 修理, to regulate; ch'hòng keâou sew loē, 創橋修路, to make bridges, and repair roads.

Leúk hoo k'hòng sew, 六府孔修 *làk ây ong hoó chin chaē sew chëng,* the six palaces were very much adorned.

Sew sin, 修身, to cultivate personal virtues.

Sew 脩 Dried flesh; sok sew, 束脩, a piece of dried flesh, anciently presented by a scholar to his teacher, on commencing his studies; hence employed to signify a teacher's salary; but now, since the teachers are paid in money, a salary is called 束金 sok kim.

Choō hêng sok sew é sëăng, goē bē sëâng boô hōëy yëen, 自行束脩以上吾未常無誨焉 *choō kēnâ sok sew ây léy é sëăng, gwá bōëy sëăng bó kà,* "from those who brought the first common present, and upwards, I have refused instruction to none;" said by Confucius in the 論語 Lūn gé.

Sew 收 To receive, to collect; sew sip, 收拾, to gather together; also, to take account of; sew lëém, 收斂, to gather in the harvest; sew chëên, 收錢 *sew cheēng,* to collect money; sew tan, 收單 *sew twna,* a receipt.

Choō gnó hwat che, ék choō gnó sew che, 自我發之亦自我收之 *ch'hut chaē gwá hwat e, yëá ch'hut chaē gwá sew e,* it depends upon me to open out, and upon me to draw in again.

Sew 攸 The name of a district.

Sew 羞 To send in, or present food; sew t'hé, 羞恥 *seaou léy,* to be ashamed.

Sëēn huo sew yūng pek yéw jē sip p'hín, 膳夫羞用百有二十品 *ché chëâh áy lâng sew yūng chit pāyh wcō jē chàp p'hín,* the cook must send in for use a hundred and twenty kinds of food; see the 禮周 Chew léy.

6 Z

Wûy k'hoé k'hé sew, 惟口起羞 *tók tók ch'hùy k'hé seaou léy*, the mouth alone is the cause of bringing shame upon us; see the 書說命 Se wát bēng.

Sew 饈 Food, articles prepared for food.

声 Séw 守 Vulg. *chéw:* to keep, to guard, to maintain; pá séw, 把守 *páy chéw*, to keep guard over; séw kaè, 守誡, to keep the commandments; séw keng, 守更 *chéw kai^ng*, to keep watch.

E bîn séw che, 與民守之 *kap pāyh sai^ng chéw e*, to guard (the city) in unison with the people; see 孟子 Bēng choó.

Séw 首 The head, the principal, the first. Gwân séw bêng chae, koé keng lëâng chae, 元首明哉股肱良哉 *gwân t'haôu nā bêng, k'ha ch'héw chēw lëâng*, when the head of a state is intelligent, the members will be virtuous; see the 尙書 Sëāng se.

Ch'hun wûy yit söèy séw, 春爲一歲首 *ch'hun chò chit neé^ng ây t'haôu*, the spring is the head of the whole year.

Séw 手 Vulg. *ch'héw:* a hand; séw chëuk, 手足 *k'ha ch'héw*, hands and feet; yêw séw, 游手 *yêw ch'héw* a wandering hand, an idle fellow.

Kwun sē sîn jê séw chëuk, chek sîn sē kwun jê hok sim, 君視臣如手足則臣視君如腹心 *jîn kwun nā k'hw^n à jîn sîn ch'hin chëō^ng k'he ch'héw, chek jîn sîn k'hw^n à jîn kwun ch'hin chëō^ng pak sim*, when a prince looks on his ministers as his arms and legs, then the ministers will hold their prince as dear as their stomach and heart; see 孟子 Bēng choó.

Séw 糔 To wash the meal of corn, in order to make a preparation of food.

去 Sèw 秀 Elegant, adorned, accomplished; sèw chaê, 秀才, a man of accomplished talents, a literary graduate. Sèw boē, 秀茂, luxuriant.

Sèw 琇 Sèw êng, 琇瑩, a beautiful gem; pendant pearls used as ornaments on the ears.

Sèw 綉 Ch'hè sèw, 刺綉, to embroider, to work embroidery.

Ch'hè sèw, t'hëem gnoé bûn, 刺綉添五紋 *ch'hè sèw t'hee^ng goē teâou bûn*, to add five threads to the embroidery; (which was done five days after the winter solstice, in order to denote the time;) see the 杜甫詩 Toē hoó se.

Sèw 宿 A constellation; seng sèw, 星宿 *ch'hai^ng sèw*, the fixed stars and constellations. A surname.

Jē sip pat sèw lô sim hëung, 二十八宿羅心胸 *jē chàp pǎyh sèw lô k'hè^ng tē sim heng*, the 28 constellations are all inclosed as in a net within my breast; (intimating a great degree of learning;) see the 天官書 T'hëen kwan se.

Sèw 鏽 Vulg. *sëen:* rust; t'hëet sèw, 鉄鏽 *t'heěh sëen*, iron rust.

Sèw 守 Sûn sèw, 巡守, to perambulate and guard; t'haè sèw, 太守, the head of a province or district; a great keeper.

T'hëen choó sek choo hoê, wát, sûn sèw, 天子適諸侯曰巡守 *hông tèy k'hè k'hw^n à choo hoê, kóng, sûn sèw*, when an emperor goes round to see the princes of the empire, it is called a visit of inspection; see 孟子 Bēng choó.

Sèw 狩 The winter hunt.

Sèw 獸 A beast, a four footed animal; k'him sèw, 禽獸, birds and beasts. E k'hîm sèw hô ē chae? 與禽獸何異哉 *kap k'hîm sèw woō sⁿá meēⁿgh kŏh yëōⁿg?* in what is such a fellow different from a brute?

Sèw 繡 To embroider; the same as 綉, sèw.

Sèw 首 Ch'hut sèw, 出首, to turn king's evidence; to turn the head towards any place. Tong sèw, kay teâou hók, t'ho sin, 東首加朝服拖紳 *tang peeⁿg hèⁿg t'haôu, kay teâou têng ây yîn chëōⁿg, yëw t'hwa chëōⁿg chit teâou twā,* (when Confucius was visited by his prince in his illness,) he turned his face to the east, had a court robe thrown over himself, and a girdle drawn across it; see the 論語 Lūn gé.

平

Sêw 醻 To pledge a guest in wine; hëèn sêw, 献醻, to offer up the cup to another. Also written 酬, sêw, and 酧, sêw.

Sêw 訓 To answer any one; also, the same as 呪, sêw, to curse.

Sêw 犨 The breathing of an ox; also, the name of an ox.

Sêw 讎 Enmity; kêw sêw, 仇讎, an enemy. Kwun hoō che sêw, put këung taè t'hëen, 君父之讎不共戴天 *jîn kwun kap nëēⁿg pāy ây kêw sêw sē bô kang tèy t'heeⁿg,* a prince or a parent's enemy should not be suffered to live under the same heaven; see the 禮記 Léy kè.

Sêw 售 To sell anything, to dispose of an article.

Sêw 囚 To incarcerate any one, a prisoner. Chaē p'hwàn hëèn sêw, 在泮献囚 *tē p'hwⁿà këung chêng, hëèn sêw ây láng,* before the royal college, they presented the prisoners; see the 魯頌 Loé sëūng.

Sêw 泅 To swim, to float on the surface of the water. Súy ló sêw, 水裡泅 *tē chúy lé sêw,* to swim in the water.

Sêw 汓 To swim; the same as the preceding.

Sêw 酋 The chief butler; mellow wine. Tëūng tong che gwát, naé bēng taē sêw, 仲冬之月乃命大酋 *tëūng tang ây göëyh, tëöh bēng lēng twā sêw,* in the middle of the winter months, the chief butler gets his orders; see the 禮月令 Léy gwát lēng.

Sêw 醜 To reject; bad, ugly, disgusting. Sêw hoō lân bëén këèn kong koe, 醜婦難免見公姑 *k'hëep sē ây cha boé ŏh bëén keèⁿg twā kay kwⁿa twā kay boé,* the ugly woman will find it difficult to avoid seeing her husband's parents. (Chinese brides, being sent home screened and veiled, can for a time conceal their ugliness, but eventually they must be seen.)

Sêw 鯈 The name of a man in former times; a kind of fish.

Sêw 遒 To urge, to press; to collect together; strong, robust.
Pek lók sē sêw, 百祿是遒 chē^n à păyh ây hóng lòk sē k'hēŏh chò bōēy, the hundred emoluments collected together; see the 商頌 Sēang sēung.

Sēw 壽 Long life; tēâng sēw, 長壽 tē^ng hōēy sēw, longevity. A surname.
Soó kwun sēw k'hó, 使君壽考 saé jîn kwun chēăh tē^ng hōēy sēw, may your honor enjoy long life; see the 小雅 Seáou gnáy.

Sēw 綬 The string and tassels with which a seal is tied.
Yìn sēw, 印綬, a seal or emblem of office.

Sēw 授 To give, to impart; sēw se, 授書 sēw ch'hăyh, to give a lesson.
Lâm lé sēw sēw put ch'hin léy yēá 男女授受不親禮也 ta po cha boé sēw sēw bô ch'hin sē léy yēá, for males and females when they give and take, not to come into immediate contact is a rule of propriety; see 孟子 Bēng choó.

Sēw 受 To receive, to take; to allow, to admit to.
Kim yéw sēw jîn che gnêw yâng, jê wûy che bók che chēá, 今有受人之牛羊而爲之牧之者 i^na woō lâng sēw lâng ây goé yēō^ng, jê kap e ē^ng e ây lâng, now if any one were to receive a person's cows and sheep, and undertake to look after them, &c.; see 孟子 Bēng choó.

Sēw 袖 Séw sēw, 手袖 ch'héw wuī^ng, the sleeve of a garment.
Séw lé pó, 袖裡寶, ch'héw wuī^ng laē ây pó, a sleeve gem; the title of a small book.

Sēw 岫 San sēw, 山岫, the peak of a hill.

Sey 西 Vulg. sae: the west; tong sey, 東西 tang sae, east and west, sometimes taken to mean different things.
Sey hong bé jîn, 西方美人 sae he^ng ch'hin ch'hai^ng ây lâng, the elegant person of the west; (referring to 文王 Bûn ông.)

Sey 恓 Sey hông, 恓惶, troubled, grieved, afraid.

Sey 栖 To remain, to lodge, to rest.
Key sey ê sê, 鷄栖于塒 key hai^ngh tē sê, the fowls roost in the fowl-house.

Sey 犀 Vulg. sae: a rhinoceros.
K'he hoé pà sey sëāng jê wàn che, 驅虎豹犀象而遠之 kw^n á hoé pà sae ch'hēō^ng jê hoē e hwui^ng, to expel the tigers and leopards, rhinoceroses and elephants, and make them retire to a distance; see 孟子 Bēng choó.

Sey 樨 Bók sey, 木樨, another name for cassia buds.

Sey 棲 To rest, to stop, to abide, to roost.
Neáou sey sē sëāng, 鳥棲樹上 cheáou hai^ngh tē ch'hēw téng, the birds nestle in the trees.

Sey 捿 To dwell in secret, to live in solitude.

Sey 萋 Luxuriant herbage.
Wûy yëēp sey sey! 維葉萋萋 wûy hēŏh sey sey! how exuberant is the foliage! see the 周南 Chew lâm.

Sey 嘶 To snort, to neigh, as a horse. Taē seng jê sey, 大聲而嘶 *twā sëⁿa jê haðu*, and then neighed with a loud noise; see the 漢書 Hàn se.

Sey 梳 Soe hwat, 梳髮 *sey t'haðu mô*, to comb the hair. Bé lé k'haóu soe chong, 美女巧梳粧 *ch'hin ch'hatⁿᵍ ây cha boé, k'há sey t'haôu chang*, pretty women are skilled in combing and adorning themselves.

Sey 筬 Hëên sêng, 絃筬 *heēⁿᵍ sey*, the toothed reed used in weaving, to keep the threads separate.

Sey 疏 Read soe: distant, distantly related, not a near relative. Chëang soó pe jê chun, soe jê ch'hek; k'hó put sīn chae? 將使卑踰尊疏踰戚可不愼哉 *chëang nā saê kay ây lâng k'hăh yëⁿâ chun ây lâng, jê sey ây k'hăh yëⁿâ ch'hin ây; t'hang ūᵐ sèy jē chae?* if men put mean people above the honorable, and confide in strangers more than in near relatives; should we not be careful in such cases? see 孟子 Bēng choó.

Sey 踈 Read soe; distant, far apart, not close or near together.

Sey 所 That which, which; vulg. *só chaē:* a place. Choó séy gnáy gân se se chip léy, kae gnáy gân yëá, 子所雅言詩書執禮皆雅言也 *hoo chοό séy gnáy kóng, se, kap ch'hăyh, kap chip lēy soè, chò poê gnáy kóng*, that which Confucius talked elegantly about, consisted in odes, compositions, and attention to propriety; upon all these be talked elegantly; see the 論語 Lūn gé.

Séy ke hô ch'hè? 所居何處 *séy k'hëā sē sⁿá meëⁿgh só chaē?* where do you reside?

Séy 洗 Read sëēn: to wash; sëēn sim, 洗心 *séy sim*, to purify the mind. Séy léy, 洗禮 *séy léy*, baptism.

Séy 黍 Read sé: the common kind of cultivated millet; the generic term for panic grasses.

Sèy 壻 Lé sèy, 女壻 *kēⁿá saè*, a son-in-law. Hwun léy, sèy óng hoō kay ch'hin gêng, 婚禮壻往婦家親迎 *chedou hwun yin ây léy, kēⁿá saè tëöh k'hè cha boé ây ch'hoð jê ch'hin gnëⁿâ*, according to the ceremonies of marriage, the bridegroom should go to the house of the bride and meet her in person; see the 詩序 Se sē.

Sèy 些 A little; also, this; and an expletive.

Sèy 細 Minute, small; sëâng sèy, 詳細, minute, particular; choó sèy, 仔細 *sèy jē*, careful, attentive; sèy hàn, 細漢, a diminutive person, a dwarf; a young man; vulg. *yèw:* fine, smooth. Put keng sèy hêng, chëung lûy taē tek, 不矜細行終累大德 *ūᵐ tëën ka tē ây sëô k'hwá ây séy kēⁿâ, kēⁿa ne lûy tëöh twā tek*, do not boast of your own trifling actions, lest in the end you mar your greater virtues.

Sim 心 The heart, the mind; sim kan, 心肝 *sim kwⁿa*, the heart; ok sim, 惡心 *p'haⁿé sim*, a bad heart. Geâou Sùn che bîn, kae é Geâou Sùn che sim wûy sim, 堯舜之民皆以堯舜之心爲心 *Geâou Sùn ây păyh saiⁿᵍ chò poê e Geâou Sùn ây sim kwⁿa chò sim kwⁿa*, Geâou and Sùn's people all embodied the feelings of their rulers, and made them their own feelings.

Sim 芯 The name of a plant, of the pith of which lamp-wicks are made; hence called teng sim ch'hó, 灯芯草 *teng sim ch'haôu*, the candle-wick plant.

声

Sím 沈 A surname.

Sím 伈 An appearance of alarm, to be terrified.
Sím sím hëén hëén, 伈伈俔俔, terrifying and alarming.

Sím 審 To judge of, to examine, to inquire into; sím p'hwàn, 審判 *sím p'hwⁿà*, to judge; sím soo, 審司, a judge.
Sím būn che, tok hêng che, 審問之篤行之 *sím mooīⁿᵍ e, tok kēⁿâ e*, examine and inquire into a thing, and zealously practice it; see the 中庸 Tëung yûng.

Sím 嬸 Vulg. *chím:* an uncle's wife; an aunt; a father's younger brother's wife.

Sím 哂 To smile with contempt.
Hoo choó sím che, 夫子哂之, Confucius smiled at him; see the 論語 Lūn gé.

Sím 諗 To reflect on anything, to consider.

去

Sìm 趛 To hold down the head and walk quickly; yaou kwut sìm, 腰骨趛 *yëo kwut sìm*, the loins giving with a spring, as when carrying loads; also applied to the elasticity of wood, or bamboo.

平

Sîm 尋 Vulg. *ch'hôey:* to seek, to search, to inquire into the grounds of anything; to connect; also, suddenly; sîm sëâng, 尋常, common, usual.
Gé ch'hoò sîm êk, 語次尋繹 *wā ây ch'hoò sē ch'hôey sëōⁿᵍ*, search into and consider the order of the expressions.

Sîm 潯 Deep water by the side of a river; a shore, a river's brink.

Sîm 燖 To cook anything at the fire; vulg. *tîm:* to stew.

Sîm 蟳 Vulg. *chîm:* a crab; hông sîm, 紅蟳 *âng chîm*, a red crab.

Sîm 忱 To believe, to credit; sincere, true, upright.

Sîm 諶 To believe; true, sincere. The same as the above.

Sîm 葚 Vulg. *sāy:* the fruit of the mulberry tree.

Sîm 煁 A three cornered furnace.

Sîm 鬵 A pan or pot for cooking; also written 鬻, sîm.

Sîm 覃 Vulg. *chîm:* a surname.

去

Sīm 倴 Lîm sīm, 䫐倴, to hold the head forward when walking.

Sim 甚 Very, extremely, excessive, deep; sīm to, 甚多 sim chēy, very much.
Pé chòm jîn cheá, ėk ó t'haè sīm, 彼譖人者亦已太甚 e saé p'hwà lâng ây lâng, yĕá woō t'haè sīm, those who slander people, have ever gone too far; see the 大雅 Taē gnáy.

Sin 身 The body; sin t'héy, 身體, a substance, a body; pún sin, 本身, one's-self; ch'hut sin, 出身, to enter life, to begin business.
Hoò jūn ok, tek jūn sin, 富潤屋德潤身 poò jūn tėk ch'hoò, tek jūn tėk sin, riches improve the appearance of one's buildings, but virtue benefits one's person; see the 大學 Taē hák.

Sin 㑗 The name of a god; a surname.

Sin 申 A horary character; to stretch out, double. A surname.
Sin toê, 申屠, a double surname.

Sin 呻 To hum; sin se, 呻詩, to hum an ode.

Sin 紳 A large girdle; Choó-tëang se choo sin, 子張書諸紳 Choó-tëang sëá tē twà, Choó-tëang recorded it on his girdle; see the 論語 Lūn gé.

Sin 伸 To stretch out, to spread abroad, to unravel, to set to rights; sin tit, 伸直 ch'hun tit, to stretch out straight.
Sin jîn wan óng, 伸人寃枉 ch'hun ch'hut lâng ây wan óng, to remedy people's grievances.

Sin 侁 The appearance of walking.

Sin 信 Straight; k'hwut jê put sin, 屈而不信 k'hwut jê bēy tit, crooked and not straight; see 孟子 Bēng choó.

Sin 駪 The appearance of a troop of horses going swiftly.

Sin 先 Read sëen: before; sëen seng, 先生 sin sai^{ng}, one elder born, a teacher, an instructor.

Sin 詵 A placid, harmonious appearance.

Sin 辛 Bitter, of a bitter taste; sin k'hoé, 辛苦, wretched and miserable, bitter toil. A surname. One of the radicals; a horary character.

Sin 莘 Sèy sin, 細莘, a medicinal plant, wild spikenard. A surname.

Sin 騂 A red dun color, a brindled color.
Lêy gnêw che choó, sin ch'hēⁿá kak, 犁牛之子騂且角 lêy goô óy kēⁿá woō ch'hëăh sek kwà sai^{ng} kak, the calf of a brindled cow may be of a red dun color, and have regular horns. (By the laws of the Chew dynasty, a brindled cow was not to be offered in sacrifice, but if such a cow got a red calf, there was no reason for rejecting it; Confucius quoted this in the 上論 Sëāng lūn, to intimate that a clever son was not to be rejected, though he sprang from a worthless father.)

Sin 新 New, fresh; sin kēw, 新舊 sin koō, new and old.
Wun koè jê te sin, k'hó é wûy soo è, 温故而知新可以爲師矣 wun sip koō ây jê ēy chae sin ây, chēw ēy chò lâng

ây sin saing, he who is versed in ancient lore, and is daily acquiring a fresh store of knowledge, can become a teacher; see the 上論 Söăng lūn.

Sin 薪 Firewood; ch'haê sin, 柴薪, logs and faggots of firewood. Yéw ch'haé sin che yew, 有採薪之憂 *woō k'hëŏh ch'hâ ây hoân ló*, being too sick to go and collect firewood; see 孟子 Bēng chóo.

Sin 娠 To conceive in the womb; a conception; yéw sin yīn, 有娠孕 *woō sin yīn*, to be with child.

Sin 甡 To stand together.

Sin 勝 To bear, to sustain; to exhaust, to surpass. Sit che é sê, yūng che é léy, chaê put k'hó sin yūng yëá, 食之以時用之以禮財不可勝用也 *chëăh e cheàou sê, yūng e cheàou léy soè chēw cheeng bô t'hang lcáou e ây yūng*, if we eat things in their proper seasons, and use property with propriety, then our resources will be inexhaustible; see 孟子 Bēng chóo.

声

Sín 矧 Still, moreover.

Sín 蜃 A kind of large muscle; tē jip taē súy wûy sín, 雉入大水爲蜃 *t'hê key jip twā chúy chò twā kap*, when the wild fowl enters the great waters it becomes a large cockle; see the 禮月令 Léy gwát lēng.

This name is also applied to a certain fabulous sea monster, like a snake or dragon.

去

Sìn 勝 To conquer, to overcome; vulg. *k'hăh yëⁿâ*: to exceed. Pek chëèn pek sìn, 百戰百勝 *chit păyh ây chëèn chit păyh ây yëⁿá*, in a hundred battles, to gain a hundred victories; see the 史記 Soó kè.

Sìt sìn sëēn yëá; bêng sìn t'hé yëá, 實勝善也名勝恥也 *chëăk sit nā yëⁿâ, chēw hó; ch'hēng ch'hēng mëⁿâ yëⁿâ, chēw seâou léy*, when the reality exceeds it is good; but when men surpass only in name, it is shameful.

Sìn 訊 To inquire, to ask; to inform, to announce. Teàou pé koè ló, sìn che chëem bōng, 召彼故老訊之占夢 *këò hwut léy koō laōu, mooīng e chëem bāng*, call those old ancient people, and ask them about the divinations and dreams; see the 小雅 Seáou gnáy.

Sìn 汛 To sprinkle; sìn sò, 汛掃 *swà saòu*, to sprinkle and sweep.

Sìn 迅 Quick, swift; rapid, fierce. Sìn lûy hong lëĕt pit pëèn, 迅雷風烈必變 *kin ây lûy hong kaòu lëĕt hoo choé pit pëèn sek*, when the thunder rolled rapidly, and the wind blew fiercely, Confucius would change countenance; see the 論語 Lūn gé.

Sìn 囟 The covering for the brain, the skull; sìn bûn, 囟門 *sìn mooīng*, the top of the head.

Sìn 顖 The same as the above.

Sìn 卂 The ancient form of the following.

福建方言字典

Sìn 信 To believe, to confide; sincere, true, unsuspicious; sincerity.
E pêng yéw kaou, jê put sìn hoê? 與朋友交而不信乎 *kap pêng yéw kaou p'hòèy, jé ūm sìn sit hoê?* in my intercourse with my friends, am I insincere? see the 論語 Lūn gé.
Se sìn, 書信 *p'hay sìn*, a letter.

平

Sîn 辰 A horary character; jit sîn, 日辰, a day, a time.

Sîn 晨 Early; chó sîn, 早晨 *chá k'hé*, early in the morning.
Sîn chëung, boē koé, lēng jîn béng séng, 晨鍾暮鼓令人猛省 *chá k'hé yëó cheng, mat^ng hwui^ng p'hăh koé, lēng lâng béng ch'hat^ng*, the bell in the morning, and the gong in the evening, are to make people rouse up and awaken; see a 古詩 koé se.

Sîn 宸 A deep retired apartment in a dwelling; an emperor's residence.
Sîn këung, 宸宮, a palace.

Sîn 鷐 Sîn hong, 鷐風, a kind of hawk.

Sîn 丞 To assist, to help, to second any one; a second in office; sîn sëāng, 丞上, a prime minister.
Hëēn sîn, 縣丞 *kwān sîn*, the second ruler of a district.

Sîn 承 To enter upon, to go into; to present, to offer up; to receive.
Put hêng kê tek, hék sîn che sew, 不恒其德或承之羞 *bô héng sëâng e ây tek, hék jip kaôu seāou léy*, if you are not constant in your virtue, you may be brought into disgrace; see the 易經 Ék keng.

Sīn 臣 Jîn sîn, 人臣, a servant, a minister, a statesman.
Kwun soó sîn é léy, sîn soō kwun é tëung, 君使臣以禮臣事君以忠 *jîn kwun saé jîn sîn é léy soê, jîn sîn hók saē jîn kwun é tëung*, when a ruler employs his ministers according to propriety, the statesmen will serve their prince with fidelity; see the 論語 Lūn gé.

Sîn 神 A god, a spirit; sîn bêng, 神明, the gods; chin sîn, 眞神, the true God; sîn hwûn, 神魂, the human spirit and soul.
Ch'heng bêng chaē këung, chè k'hè jê sîn, 清明在躬志氣如神 *ch'heng bêng tē hîn sin, chè k'hè ëy ch'hin chëō^ng sîn*, when purity and intelligence rest on our persons, our minds and spirits will be like the gods; see the 禮記 Léy kè.

去

Sīn 愼 To be careful, to be cautious; kín sīn, 謹愼 *sèy jē*, attentive, careful. A surname.
Choó che séy sīn, chae, chëèn, chît, 子之所愼齊戰疾 *hoo choó ëy séy kín sīn, chëäh ch'haê, sëo t'hat, woō pai^ng*, the things which Confucius was careful about were fasting, war, and sickness; see the 論語 Lūn gé.

Sīn 昚 The ancient form of the preceding character.

Sīn 剩 The residue, the surplus, that which is left over; yéw sīn, 有剩 *woō ch'hun*, over and above.

Sīn 賸 The increase of anything, a superfluity.

Sīn 腎 The kidneys. Göēy sīn, 外腎, the testicles.

Sin 燼 Embers, the remains of a fire; ashes. Kim che léy se, kae twat sip ê wöey sin che ê, 今之禮書皆掇拾於煨燼之餘 tⁿa ây léy kè se keng, chò poé sē k'hëöh lëöh tē höëy chín ây sin, the books of ceremonies and odes now in use are all picked out of the remnant of the embers and ashes; see the 朱註 Choo choò.

夫

Sip 㒧 Not to attain to.

Sip 濕 Vulg. *tâm:* moist, damp; sip k'hè, 濕氣, a damp air.

Sip 隰 Low, marshy ground; gwân sip, 原隰, high and low ground. San yéw chin, sip yéw lêng, 山有榛隰有苓 *swⁿa ây wūy woō chin ch'hēw, sip ây wūy woō hòk lèng ch'haóu*, in hilly places the chestnut is found, and water plants in marshy ground; see the 衛風 Wöey hong.

Sip 溼 Low, marshy ground.

Sip 霫 Lip sip, 雴霫, a heavy rain.

夭

Sip 十 Vulg. *chàp:* ten; choō sip chè pek, 自十至百 *choō chàp chè kaòu päyh*, from ten to a hundred. Höëy yëá, bûn yit ó te sip, 回也聞一以知十 *Höëy yëá, t'hëⁿa chìt hāng, chëw chae chàp hāng*, Höëy on hearing of one thing knew ten things; see the 論語 Lūn gé.

Sip 什 Ten men, a company of ten people; sip hⁿò, 什貨 *chàp höèy*, pedler's wares, a mixed assortment of goods.

Sip 拾 Vulg. *k'hëöh:* to collect, to gather, to pick up. Poé sip wûy, sin che gwān yëá, 補拾遺臣之願也 *poé k'hëöh ka laòuh ây meëⁿgh, sē gwá ây séy gwān*, to collect and repair what is neglected and forgotten is all my desire.

Sip 習 To study, to exercise one's-self in, to con over a task; hàk sip, 學習 to learn and get perfect in; àp sip, 狎習, to be intimate with, to be familiar; ch'hwàn sip, 串習, thoroughly versed in; a surname. Hàk jê sê sip che, put èk wàt hoē? 學而時習之不亦悅乎 *t'hàk, jê sëâng sê wun sip c, ūᵐ yëá hwⁿa hé hoē?* to learn and constantly practice one's-self in it, is it not delightful? see the 上論 Sëāng lūn.

Sip 㴱 The noise made by people when they try to shake off the cold; a shivering sound.

夫

Sit 式 A rule, a plan, a law, a model; sometimes read sek. Koé hwùn sē sit, 古訓是式 *koé chá ây kà hwùn ëy chò lán ây hwat toē*, the instructions of the ancients are our rule and pattern; see the 大雅 Taē gnây.

Sit 拭 Vulg. *ch'hit:* to wipe, to rub; clean; sometimes read sek. Pok bëën chō sit kwuy, 北而坐拭圭 *pak bīn chēy ch'hit gëuk*, he sat with his face towards the north, and rubbed the gem clean.

Sit 息 To breathe; ch'hwán sit, 喘息 *ch'hwán k'hwùy*, the breath; ché sit, 止息, to stop; t'hàn sit, 嘆息 *t'hó k'hwùy*, to sigh; seaou sit, 消息, news; chóó sit, 子息, posterity; lō sit, 利息, interest, gain; an sit, 安息, rest.

Yit sit sëāng chûn, ch'hoó chè put yûng seáou haē, 一息尚存此志不容少懈 *chit ây ch'hwán k'hwùy sëāng chûn tē, chéy lêy sim chè ūm yûng tit sëó k'hwá haē taē*, as long as a breath remains, this inclination (for study) should not be allowed for a moment to decline; see the 朱註 Choo choò.

Sit 瘜 A fleshy excrescence growing in the nose; a nasal polypus.

Sit 媳 Sit hoō, 媳婦 *sím poō*, a daughter-in-law.

Sit 箑 Seaou sit, 消箑, an instrument for cleansing the ear when it itches.

Sit 失 To lose; sit goē, 失誤, to make a mistake; kò sit, 過失 *kòèy sit*, a fault, an error; sit lók, 失落 *sit lŏh*, to lose, to miss.
E yëak sit che chëá, sëén è, 以約失之者鮮矣 *é kán yëak sit e ây lâng chëó è*, when a man is precise, he seldom errs; see the 論語 Lūn gé.

Sit 識 Vulg. *bat*: to know, to understand, to have an acquaintance; këèn sit, 見識, knowledge, acquaintance with things; sëang sit chëá, 相識者 *sëo bat ây lâng*, an acquaintance.
Put sit put te, sûn tèy che chek, 不識不知順帝之則 *ūm bat ūm chae, t'hàn tèy ây hwat chek*, we neither know nor understand, but follow the rules of the emperor; see the 古歌 Koé ko.

Sit 悉 Altogether, entirely; also read sek.

Sit 蟋 Vulg. *seĕh*: sit sut, 蟋蟀 *seĕh sut*, a cricket.
Sit sut chaē tông, 蟋蟀在堂 *seĕh sut twā tē tĕng*, the cricket in the hall; see the 唐風 Tông hong.

Sit 室 A house, a dwelling, a residence, a chamber, an apartment.
Yêw yëá sêng tông è, bē jip ê sit yëá, 由也升堂矣未入於室也 *Yêw yëá woō chëōng tĕng böëy jip kaòu ch'hoò*, Yêw (as it respects his acquirements in learning,) has ascended the hall, but not yet entered into the house; see the 論語 Lūn gé.

Sit 食 Vulg. *chëăh*: to eat; sit hwan, 食飯 *chëăh pooīng*, to eat rice.
Kwun choó sit boô kêw paóu, 君子食無求飽 *kwun choó chëăh bô kêw pá*, the good man in eating does not look for satiety; see the 論語 Lūn gé.

Sit 蝕 Vulg. *seĕh*: to be injured, to be broken in upon, to be eaten.
Jit sit, 日蝕 *seĕh jit*, an eclipse of the sun.
Gwát sit, 月蝕 *seĕh goĕyh*, an eclipse of the moon.
Sit pún, 蝕本 *seĕh pún*, to break in on one's capital; to lose money.

Sit 實 True, real; ló sit, 老實 *laōu sit*, sincere, true; chëák sit, 着實, really, truly; kó sit, 菓實 *köéy ché*, fruit; sit bwán, 實滿 *sit mwⁿá*, full, replete.
T'hut hwa boō sit, 黜華務實 *t'hek kak he hwa ây, chwan boō chëák sit ây*, reject the flowery and vain, while you attend to what is real and solid.

Sit 寔 The same as the above.

Sit 湜 Clear, limpid water, the bottom of which may be seen.

Sit 植 To stand upright, to place erect; to plant, to cause to grow.
Sit kê tëāng jê yîn, 植其杖而芸 *k'hëā e ây kwaê á, jê t'hwⁿá ch'haôu*, (the old man) then stuck his staff in the ground and began to weed the field; see the 論語 Lūn gé.
Seng sit, 生植, to plant and grow.

Sit 殖 To grow, to increase.
Hⁿò chaê sit yëen, 貨財殖焉 *hòëy cheêⁿᵍ saiⁿᵍ k'hăh kay*, property and wealth increasing; see the 中庸 Tëung yûng.

Sit 襲 To wear a double suit of clothes; because, on account of; to succeed to; to invade; sit wūy, 襲位, to succeed to the throne.
Chêy soo sit Ch'hoé, 齊師襲楚 *Chêy ây peng sit Ch'hoé kok*, the troops of the Chêy country invaded that of the Ch'hoé.

Sit 翅 Read ék: the wings of a bird; neáou tëâng kê ék, 鳥張其翅 *cheáou tëoⁿᵍ e ây sit*, the bird stretches its wings.

卆 So 搔 Séw so, 手搔 *ch'héw so*, to rub with the hand; to rub the hands together.
So séw tê toô, 搔首踟躕 *so t'haôu kak tê toô sëōⁿᵍ*, he scratched his head, and walked up and down in suspense; see the 衛風 Wöëy hong.

So 傜 Proud, haughty.

So 騷 Sorrowful; lê so, 離騷, a poem, made by 屈原, K'hwut-gwân. Troublesome; so jîn, 騷人, to trouble people.
So jeâou, 騷擾, to annoy people, by playing pranks.

So 慅 Agitated, moved, troubled.

So 瘙 Pây so, 爬瘙, to scratch.
Kek hëa so yāng, 格靴瘙癢 *kăyh hëa pây chëōⁿᵍ*, to scratch one's itching legs through a boot; (i. e. making ineffectual efforts to remove an evil.)

So 颾 The whistling of the wind.

So 嫂 An appellation for a female.

So 膰 The smell of pig's fat; the same as 臊, so.

So 溞 So so, 溞溞, the sound of washing rice.

So 些 The sound used at the end of certain carols.

So 傞 So so, 傞傞, to frisk and gambol about, as when in liquor.

So 唆 So soó, 唆使, to blast a man's reputation; teâou so, 條唆, to instigate a person to comply with one's wishes.

So 梭 A weaver's shuttle.

So 鯪 The name of a fish.

So 糉 A kind of confectionary.

So 傞 To walk, to frisk about incessantly.

So 娑 Po so, 婆娑, to dance, to gambol.

So 莎 The name of a plant; a water grass, a species of Cyperus.

So 挱 To rub anything; mô so, 摩挱, to rub with the hand.

So 臊 The smell of pig or dog's fat.

So 趖 To run about; to frisk about as a child.

So 簑 So e, 簑衣 *söey e*, a rain mantle, made of bamboo leaves or rushes; a rough coat to keep out the rain.

去

Só 瑣 The filings of gems; very small, minute. Só só yin à, 瑣瑣姻婭, inferior relations.

Só 鎖 Só yëák, 鎖鑰, a lock; só sê, 鎖匙, a key.

Só 鏁 A lock, a fastening for a door; also written 鎖, só.

Só 璅 A fastening for a door.

Só 嫂 A sister-in-law; heng so, 兄嫂 *hëⁿa só*, an elder brother's wife. Só lėk put wān sē ch'haê lông yëá, 嫂溺不援是豺狼也 *hëⁿa só kadu tëèm lôh chúy, ūᵐ kèw sē ch'haê lông yëá*, when a sister-in-law is drowning, not to go and save her a man must be a wolf; see 孟子 Bēng choó.

Só 篗 A sort of bamboo.

去

Sò 燥 Dry, to dry anything, to parch. Sò bān bút chëá, bók hàn hoē hⁿó, 燥萬物者莫熯乎火 *sò ta bān mcⁱⁿᵍh ây, bô k'hăh kín ê hööy*, of the things which dry all substances, there is not one so fierce as fire; see the 易說卦 Ėk wát kwà.

So 躁 Sò kip, 躁急, hasty, headstrong.

So 掃 Vulg. *sadu:* to sweep; sò chéw, 掃帚 *sadu chéw*, a broom. Swá sò têng löëy, 洒掃廷內 *hew chúy sadu gāy tē téng á laē*, to sprinkle and sweep in the hall; see the 大雅 Taē gnáy.

Sò 埽 The same as the above.

Sò 臊 The gravy of bones.

丟 Sō 卒

Soe **唆** Soó sō, 使唆, to instigate any one to comply with one's views.

Soe **穌** To revive as from the dead, to rise again; Yëà-soe, 耶穌, JESUS. Hëy gnó hoē, hoē laê kê soe, 徯我后后來其穌 *têng haōu gwán ây jîn kwun, jîn kwun nā laê gwán chëw kŏh wăh*, let us wait for our prince, for when our prince comes, we shall revive; see the 尙書 Sëāng se.

Soe **甦** To revive; to resuscitate; to recover, as from a fit, or as insects do; the same as the preceding.

Soe **蘇** The name of a plant; soe bòk, 蘇木, sapan wood. A surname.

Soe **櫯** Soe bòk, 櫯木, sapan wood, a kind of wood, used in dyeing red.

Soe **酥** A sort of curd, made from a cow or goat's milk; soe yêw, 酥油, a kind of butter or cheese; called in the north 馬思哥, má soo ko.

Soe **踈** Few, thinly scattered; open, coarse. Tām-gwăt soe song jeáou köèn chëang, 淡月踈星繞建章 *tām göëyh soe ch'hai^ng jeáou teê^ng twā tē këèn chëang ây këung*, the solitary moon and a few thinly scattered stars turned and entwined around the palace; see the 杜甫詩 Toē hoó se.

Soe **梳** Vulg. *sey:* a comb; kak soe, 角梳 *kak sey*, a horn comb.

Soe **蔬** Soe ch'haè, 蔬菜, culinary vegetables of any sort; common food.

Soe **疏** Vulg. *sey:* distantly related; open, far apart, wide asunder. Tēng ch'hin soe, 定親疏 *tëⁿā tëŏh ch'hin kap sey*, to fix the distinctions between near and distant relations.

Soe **蹠** Kwat soe, 佸蹠, distantly related.

Soe **蒐** To seek for, to inquire after; to regulate troops; a medicinal plant. Taē soe sam jit, 大蒐三日 *twā ch'höey kaôu sⁿa jit*, a great search for three days; see the 史記 Soó kè.

Soe **筲** A kettle shaped bamboo vessel without handles, in which rice is washed; a small measure.

Soe **溲** To make water; to steep in water.

Soe **搜** Vulg. *ch'heaou:* to search, to seek for, to search out; to shake. Hwat Sam-hoō kê soō, taē soe sëāng lîm, 發三輔騎士大搜上林 *hwat Sam-hoō ây kê soō, twā ch'heaou têng bîn ây ch'hëw nâ*, he ordered out the cavalry of Sam-hoō, to search all throughout the upper forest; see 漢武帝紀 Hàn boó tèy kè.

Soe **艘** The general name for a ship or vessel. Also read soé.

Soe **颼** The sound of the wind.

Soe **棷** The same as 搜, soe, to search.

Soe 㮄 To conceal one's-self, to hide one's character.

Jîn yëen soe chae? 人焉廋哉 *lâng böëyh an chwⁿā ēy soe lëk?* how can men conceal themselves? see the 論語 Lūn gé.

去

Soé 叟 A title for an elderly person; venerable sir.

Ong wát, soé put wàn ch'hëen lé jê laê, 王曰叟不遠千里而來 *óng kóng soé, ūm k'hwⁿà chò hwuiⁿᵍ chit ch'heng lé jê laê,* the king said, "Venerable sir! you have not considered it too far to come a thousand miles (to visit me);" see 孟子 Bēng choó.

Soé 瞍 Blind, having eyes without pupils.

Soé 瘦 Vulg. *sán:* thin, lean, meagre, emaciated.

San sat soé, 山殺瘦 *swⁿa kaôu t'haê, k'hwⁿà keèⁿᵍ sán,* when a hill is cleared it looks barren.

Soé 傁 A venerable old man; also written 傻 soó.

Soé 瀴 The name of a large marsh.

Soé 漱 To wash, to rinse; soé k'hoé, 漱口 *swá k'haóu,* to rinse the mouth.

Soé 摟 To drag, to draw; toé soé, 抖摟 *taôu saôu,* to rouse up, to brush up.

Soé 溯 Soé höëy, 溯洄, to go up against the stream; soé yêw, 溯游, to go with the stream; also written 遡, soé; and 泝, soè.

去

Soè 素 White, the ground of a picture, plain, unornamented; pèng soè, 並素 formerly, hitherto; kim soè, 今素, at present, now.

Soè e gêy kêw, 素衣麑裘 *pāyh sⁿa lòk kēⁿá ây hêw,* a white garment and a fawn colored fur-dress; see the 論語 Lūn gé.

Soè hoò kwùy, hêng hoē hoò kwùy, 素富貴行乎富貴 *hëèn chaē poò kwùy, chēw kēⁿà tē poò kwùy,* if at present in wealthy circumstances let us act according to wealthy circumstances; see the 中庸 Tëung yûng.

Soè 傃 To act according to the usual course; towards.

Soè 愫 Feelings, the affections of the mind. P'he sim hok, këèn chêng soè, 披心腹見情愫 *p'he k'hwuy sim pak & k'hwⁿà chêng soè,* to open the heart and bowels, and exhibit one's real feelings and affections.

Soè 餗 Plain food without any mixture of aromatic vegetables.

Soè 訴 To inform, to anounce, to appeal to. Boô k'hó kò soè, 無可告訴 *bô t'hang kò soè,* having no one to complain to, or inform of one's condition.

Soè 疏 To reprove; to record.

Soè 數 Vulg. *sedou:* an account, a reckoning; a number; several; boô soè, 無數 *bô t'hang swuiⁿᵍ,* numberless; swàn soè, 算數 *swuiⁿᵍ sedou,* to cast up an account.

K'hè yéw tēng soè, 器有定數 *ke k'hè woō*

të^{n}a tëŏh ây soè, utensils amounting to a certain number.

Soè **嗽** Hay soè, 咳嗽 *hay sadu,* to have a cough, to be hoarse; an asthma. Tông sê yéw soè, 冬時有嗽 *tang t'hee^{ng} woō hay sadu,* in the winter season people get colds.

Soè **瘶** To cough; a cold; the same as the above.

Soè **漱** Soè k'hoé, 漱口 *swá k'háou,* to rinse the mouth. Soè e hók, 漱衣服 *séy s^{n}a k'hoè,* to rinse one's clothes.

Soè **塑** To form an image of clay; soè gnoé, 塑偶, a clay image. Jê nê soè jîn, 如泥塑人 *ch'hin chëō^{ng} nw^{n}ā t'hoè ch'hông ây lâng,* just like the clay image of a man.

Soè **愬** To announce, to accuse, to plead; the same as 訴, soè.

上平 Söey **衰** To fade, to dwindle away, to fail; weak, decayed; hin söey, 興衰, to flourish and decay. Also written 衰 söey.

Sīm è goê söey è, 甚矣吾衰矣 *sīm è gwá t^{n}a söey yëá,* "what a sad pass things are come to; I shall now fail and fade away;" said by Confucius, in the 論語 Lūn gé.

Söey **榱** A beam or post.

Söey **縗** Mourning apparel; chám söey, 斬縗, a mourning dress, with the borders unhemmed.

Söey **夊** To walk slowly; one of the radicals.

上聲 *Söéy* **嫂** *Seĕh söéy,* 婰嫂, an unchaste woman.

上去 Söèy **歲** Vulg. *höèy:* a year; kē söèy? 幾歲 *kwúy höèy?* how old are you? Bān söèy yêâ, 萬歲爺, the lord of ten thousand years; a title given exclusively to the emperor.

Jit gwàt sē è, söèy put gnó é! 日月逝矣歲不我與 *jit göëyh köèy k'hè neê^{ng} höèy bô kaōu hoē gwá!* days and months pass swiftly by, and years are not left me! see the 論語 Lūn gé.

Söèy **嵗** The same as the preceding.

Söèy **稅** Rent, hire, taxes, revenue; ok söèy, 屋稅 *ch'hoò söèy,* house rent; làp söèy, 納稅, to pay taxes.

Söèy **帨** A napkin, a towel.

Söèy **說** To persuade, to advise, to endeavor to bring any one over to one's own party or persuasion.

Söèy taē jîn chek beáou che, bùt sē kê gwûy gwûy jëên, 說大人則藐之勿視其巍巍然 *k'hè söèy sè twā lâng chëw k'hw^{n}à sèy e, bô k'hw^{n}à e ây gwûy twā ây yëō^{ng},* in trying to persuade great men, we should think little of them, and not look at their lofty and elevated appearance; see 孟子 Bēng choó.

Söèy **睟** A whole year; when a child is one year old, it is called söèy sê, 睟時, a year's time.

Söèy 帥 A commander in chief; gwân söèy, 元帥, a generalissimo. Sam kwun k'hó twát söèy yëá, p'hit hoo put k'hó twát chè yëá, 三軍可奪帥也匹夫不可奪志也 *sⁿa chëw ây peng ëy t'hang ch'hëó^{ng} e ây gwân söèy, chit ây p'hit hoo bô t'hang hoë lâng ch'hëó^{ng} e ây sim chè*, the three bands of an army may deprive a general of his command, but a common man cannot be turned from his purpose and aim; see the 論語 Lūn gé.

平 *Söèy* 垂 Read sûy: the branches of a tree hanging down; nearly, near to.

去 Söèy 涶 To flow down; gán lūy söèy lêw, 眼淚涶流 *bák saé söèy laôu*, the tears flowed abundantly.

大 *Söëyh* 說 Read swat: to explain, to comment upon, to unfold the meaning. Koè swat se chëá, put é bûn haē soô, 故說詩者不以文害辭 *chëá söëyh se ây lâng, ū^m t'hang t'hó e ây jē haē e ây wā*, therefore those who explain the odes should not by adhering to the letter injure the sense; see 孟子 Bēng choó.

大 *Söh* 嗽 Read sok: to suck, to draw in the breath, to draw as by a poultice. Seáou jê sok jé, 小兒嗽乳 *sèy këⁿá söh leng*, children draw in the milk.

Söh 索 Read sek: a rope, a cord; sîn sek, 繩索 *sîn söh*, twine.

天 *Söh* 釧 Read ch'hwàn: a bracelet; séw ch'hwàn, 手釧 *ch'hëw söh*, armlets for the wrist. Also written 鋉, sok, a ring.

夫 Sok 束 A bundle; to bind, to tie. A surname. Seng choe yit sok, 生芻一束 *ch'hai^{ng} ch'haôu chit pák*, a bundle of green grass; see the 小雅 Seáou gnáy.

Sok 速 Hasty, quick, hurried, speedily, swift, rapid, to call, to invite. Ong sok ch'hut lēng, 王速出令 *ông lé k'häh kín ch'hut lēng*, may it please your majesty immediately to issue your orders; see 孟子 Bēng choó. Yéw put sok che k'hek sam jîn laê, 有不速之客三人來 *woō bô këò ây k'häyh sⁿa lâng laê*, there were three strangers who came uninvited.

Sok 遬 Chae sok, 齋遬, to respect and venerate.

Sok 蔌 The general term for culinary vegetables.

Sok 樕 P'hok sok, 樸樕, small twigs.

Sok 螋 The name of an insect.

Sok 嗽 Vulg. *söh*: to suck, to draw.

Sok 觫 Hát sok, 觳觫, a frightened appearance; terrified. Goê put jím kê hát sok, jëák boô chöëy jê chēw soó tēy, 吾不忍其觳觫若無罪而就死地 *gwá bēy lún e ây këⁿa hëⁿâ ây yëó^{ng}, ch'hin chëó^{ng} bô chöëy jé chëw kaôu sé ây tēy*, "I cannot bear its frightened and terrified appearance, as if for no fault it was led away to the place of slaughter;" said by a king when he saw an animal going away to be sacrificed; see 孟子 Bēng choó.

Sok 錸 Metal; kim sok, 金錸 *kim sŏh*, a gold ring; séw sok, 手錸 *ch'héw sŏh*, a bracelet.

Sok 餗 The contents of a pot or pan; the meat in the caldron.
Téng chëet chëuk, hok kong sok, 鼎折足覆公餗 *tiⁿá kadu cheĕh k'ha chëw pak tó kong ây meëⁿgh chëăh*, the foot of the caldron being broke, the ruler's food was upset; see the 易經 Ék keng.

Sok 槊 A kind of lance or spear, 18 feet long; also written 矟, sok.

Sok 朔 The first day of the moon; gwát sok, 月朔 *göëyh sok*, the new moon. Sok hong, 朔方, the northern region.

Sok 剟 Anything sliced very small.

Sok 數 Frequently, many times, repeatedly, hurried; read soò: several.
Soō kwun sok, soo jëúk è, 事君數斯辱矣 *hók saē jîn kwun nā chap chap tⁿà, chéy lëy chëw ch'hé lëng jëúk*, in serving a ruler, (if we repeatedly reprove him,) we shall get into disgrace; see the 論語 Lūn gé.

卒

Som 森 The thick foliage of trees, a thick grove.

Som 宗 To conceal; deep, hidden.

Som 參 Jîn som, 人參, ginseng, the Panax quinquefolium, a plant in much esteem among the Chinese; yâng som, 洋參 *yëôⁿg som*, foreign ginseng; haé som, 海參, tripang, biche de mer.

卒

Song 霜 Vulg. *seⁿg*: frost, frozen dew; p'he song, 砒霜 *p'heëⁿg seⁿg*, arsenic.
Loē këet wûy song, 露結爲霜 *loē chúy këet chô seⁿg*, frozen dew becomes hoarfrost; see the 千字文 Ch'hëen joō bûn.

Song 孀 A widow.

Song 鬆 Hông song, 髼鬆, disheveled hair. Vulg. *sang*: loose, not tight.

Song 雙 Double; a surname. Vulg. *sang*: a pair, a couple; song seng, 雙生 *sang saiⁿg*, twins; yit song bëét, 一雙韈 *chit sang böëyh*, a pair of stockings.
Kok soō boô song, 國士無雙 *kok soō bô sang tûy*, among all the scholars in the country, he has no equal; see the 蕭何傳 Seaou hô twān.

Song 艭 The name of a boat or vessel.

Song 桑 Vulg. *seⁿg*: the mulberry tree, Morus multicaulis. A surname.
Ch'hân gwát teâou song, 蠶月條桑 *ch'hē ch'hêng ây göëyh, woō hwat chëⁿâ teâou seⁿg ch'hëw*, in the month for breeding silkworms, the mulberry tree puts forth its branches.

Song 喪 Song haòu, 喪孝 *seⁿg hà*, mourning clothes; sòng song, 送喪 *sàng seⁿg*, to attend a funeral.

福建方言字典

Ke che song tát hoē taē hoo, sam lëēn che song tát hoē t'hëen choó, 期之喪達乎大夫三年之喪達乎天子 *chew neēng ây seng hà tát kadu taē hoo, sna neēng ây seng hà tát kadu hóng tèy,* the period of one year's mourning for parents extends to the great officers, but the time of three years reaches to the emperor; see the 中庸 Tëung yûng.

上聲

Sóng 搡 To throw, to pitch; sóng ch'haê, 搡柴, to pitch firewood into the grate, to feed the fire in a furnace.

Sóng 磉 The stone under a pillar.

Sóng 顙 The forehead; kim hoo súy, p'hok jê yëák che, k'hó soó kò sóng, 今夫水搏而躍之可使過顙 *tna hoo chúy, p'hàh jê hoē e tëô, t'hang saê e köey t'haôu hëàh,* now with respect to water, if we beat and splash it, we can make it go over our foreheads; see 孟子 Bëng choó.

Sóng 鎟 A piece of wood like a drum.

Sóng 䉀 A case for holding chopsticks.

Sóng 爽 Clear, pleasant; hearty, cheerful; grand, fine; sóng k'hwaè, 爽快, good health and spirits, well.

去聲

Sòng 喪 To lose one's office; vulg. *seng:* to lose, to bury, to be ruined, to be lost; forgotten, destroyed.

Jē sam choó hô hwān ê sòng hoē! 二三子何患於喪乎 *nō sna ây kēnâ, saê saê hwān lô ê sit wûy hoē!* my two or three children, what need have you to be troubled about losing office! see the 論語 Lūn gé.

Sòng bông, 喪亡, to be lost, and undone; sòng sit, 喪失, to lose anything.

Sòng 宋 The name of a country; also, of a dynasty; and vulg. *sàng:* a surname.

Sòng teâou, 宋朝, the famous dynasty of Sòng, which commenced A. D. 950.

Sòng 送 To accompany out of respect; to present, to give; sòng hêng, 送行, to accompany any one a part of his journey; sòng se, 送書 *sàng ch'hăyh,* to present a book.

Chaè paè jê sòng che, 再拜而送之 *kòh paè jê sàng e,* he made a second obeisance, and accompanied him out; see the 論語 Lūn gé.

Sòng 送 The same as the preceding.

平

Sông 傗 Sông lê, 傗偉, a corresponding sound.

Soo 思 To think, to consider, to reflect; soo lē, 思慮, to consider; soo lëēm, 思念, to reflect; soo sëáng, 思想, to think.

Kwùy-bûn-choó sam soo jê hoē hêng, 季文子三思而後行 *Kwùy-bûn-choó sna hāy sëōng, jëên aôu kēnâ,* Kwùy-bûn-choó used to consider thrice before he did anything; see the 論語 Lūn gé.

Soo 緦 A three month's mourning, worn for distant relatives.

Soo 鬛 Pöey soo, 髤鬛, a full beard.

Soo 偲 To urge one another to do anything. Pêng yéw ch'hëet ch'hëet soo soo, 朋友切切偲偲 *pêng yéw ch'hëet ch'hëet sëo k'hwui^ng*, friends should be earnest and serious in stirring one another up (to virtue); see the 論語 Lūn gé.

Soo 颸 A cool wind.

Soo 罳 A kind of wooden screen, to put in the doorway.

Soo 顋 Vulg. *sae:* the cheeks, the sides of the face.

Soo 腮 The same as the preceding.

Soo 斯 This, these; then, forthwith. Kê soo che wūy è, 其斯之謂矣 *e sē chéy ne sai^ng kóng*, this is the meaning of it; see the 論語 Lūn gé. Chaè soo k'hó è, 再斯可矣 *kŏh an néy, chēw t'hang*, once more thus, and it will do; see the 論語 Lūn gé.

Soo 厮 A boy, a servant, a menial; a wood or grass cutter. Yéw soo yáng chut, 有厮養卒 *woō kwăh ch'habu ch'hē bāy ây peng chut*, there are some grass cutting and housekeeping menials.

Soo 㒋 The same as the above.

Soo 嘶 To neigh; má soo, 馬嘶 *báy habu*, the horse neighs. To belch. Má soo hong, 馬嘶風 *báy habu hong*, the horse snorts to the wind.

Soo 澌 The water exhausted, and dry; to exhaust, to diminish, as from the melting of ice.

Soo 司 To superintend anything; yéw soo, 有司, a presiding officer. An ch'hat soo, 按察司 *an ch'hat se*, a civil judge; poè chèng soo, 布政司, a treasurer; kong soo, 公司 *kong se*, a company, the place where the company meets. Pëen toē che soō, chek yéw soo chŭn, 籩豆之事則有司存 *pëen taōu ây soō, chek yéw soo chŭn*, with respect to the vessels and materials for sacrifice, there are the proper officers to attend to these things; see the 論語 Lūn gé. A surname. Soo má, 司馬, a double surname; also, soo toê, 司徒, and 司空, soo k'hong.

Soo 伺 Soo hoē, 伺候 *soo haōu*, to wait, to tarry.

Soo 笥 A square bamboo trunk for containing clothes or other things. Wûy e sëâng chaē soo, 惟衣裳在笥 *wûy yin chëō^ng tē sëo^ng*, the clothes are in the case; see the 書說命 Se wát bêng.

Soo 師 A teacher, an instructor; a multitude, a host, an army. A surname. Kè būn che hák, put k'hó é wûy jîn soo, 記問之學不可以爲人師 *kè mooi^ng ây t'hàk ch'háyh, bô t'hang chò lâng ây sin sai^ng*, the man whose learning consists partly of recollections and partly of inquiries, cannot become any one's instructor; see the 禮記 Lêy kè. Hin soo, 興師, to begin a march, to commence a campaign.

Soo 螄 Lêy soo, 螺螄 *lô soo*, a kind of sea slug; a snail; a spiral univalve molluscous animal.

福建方言字典

Soo 獅 Soo choó, 獅子 *sae á*, a young lion, a lion.

Soe-lék ông laê hëèn soo choó, 疎勒王來献獅子 *Soe-lék ông laê hëèn sae á*, the king of Soe-lék came bringing the present of a lion.

Soo 私 Vulg. *sae k'hëa:* private, not public; soo sim, 私心, private views, sinister ends; soo yëúk, 私慾, selfish propensities or lusts.

E gnó kong tëên, süy kip gnó soo, 雨我公田遂及我私 *lŏh hoē tē gwán ây kong ch'hân, jëên aōu kip kaòu gwán ây sae k'hëa ây*, rain first on our public fields, and afterwards let it come to our private fields; see the 大雅 Taē gnáy.

Soo 釃 Fine wine strained from the dregs; to divide.

Soo 輸 Read se: to lose, to lose a battle, or a wager.

Se êng bē hwun, 輸贏未分 *soo yëⁿâ böëy woō hwun pëët*, the gaining or losing of the contest is not yet decided.

去

Soó 史 A record, a history; soó kwan, 史官 *soó kwⁿa*, a historian, a recorder; soó kè, 史記, a historical record. Vulg. *saé:* a surname.

Sëëp láp se soó, 涉獵書史 *sëëp láp köëy se kap soó*, to pass through and hunt amongst the classics and historians.

Soó 駛 A horse going swiftly; to hasten, as a courier does.

Soó 使 Vulg. *saé:* to order, to send, to cause, to occasion; ék soó, 役使, a servant.

Pëën pè put chëuk soó lëng ê chëên é? 便嬖不足使令于前與 *pëën yüng kap pè ây láng k'hám bó kaòu saé lëng tē lé ây bīn chêng?* is it because menials and sycophants are not sufficient to be ordered about in your presence? see 孟子 Bēng choó.

Soó 死 Vulg. *sé:* to die, to decease. Also written 歺, soó.

Kwun choó soó wát chëung, seáou jîn soó wát soó, 君子死曰終小人死曰死 *kwun choó ây sé kóng këò chëung, seáou jîn ây sé kóng këò sé*, when a good man dies, it is called finishing his course; but when a bad man dies, it is called death.

去

Soò 四 Vulg. *sè:* four; also written 亖, soò, twice two. Soò sip jé put hék, 四十而不惑 *sè chap höëy jé bó gë hék*, "at forty I was without doubts;" said by Confucius in the 論語 Lūn gé.

Soò 駟 Four horses, a team of four horses. Soò put kip sëët, 駟不及舌 *sè chëâh báy bëy jëuk kaòu ch'huy chëeh*, four horses cannot overtake the tongue; see the 論語 Lūn gé.

Soò 使 A messenger; kok soò, 國使, an ambassador, an envoy.

Choó-hwâ soò ê Chêy, 子華使於齊 *Choó-hwâ chò kok soò tē Chêy*, Choó-hwâ became an ambassador to the Chêy country; see the 論語 Lūn gé.

Soò 泗 The name of a river and of a place

Soò 賜 To bestow anything on an inferior; to give, to confer.

Kwun soò sít, pit chèng sék sëen sëâng che, 君賜食必正席先嘗之

jin kwun nā soò hoē chëăh ây meē^ngh, pit tëŏh ch'hòng chë^nà ch'hëŏh, taē seng ch'hè k'hw^nà e, when a prince conferred a gift of food, he would put his mat square and first taste of it; said of Confucius in the 論語 Lūn gé.

Soò 肆 Ch'hē soò, 市肆, a market; hòng soò, 放肆, disorderly, to give way to one's evil passions.
Pek kong ke soò, 百工居肆 *chë^nà pâyh ây kang k'hëā tē tëèm,* all the handicraft trades can be found in the shops; see the 論語 Lūn gé.

Soò 思 E soò, 意思, thought, intention, idea; the will.
Bōng ch'heng ch'hó tê tông, se soò pùt jëên, 夢青艸池塘詩思勃然 *bāng ch'hai^ng ch'haôu tē chúy tê, se ây soò chēw pùt jëěn k'hé,* "when dreaming of green grass by the side of the ponds, poetical thoughts immediately arise;" said by 謝靈運 Sëā-lêng-wūn.

Soò 笥 A square basket, made of wicker work; a trunk.

平 Soò 辭 Vulg. *sê:* to refuse, to take leave of any one; an expression, a sentence.
Gwân-soo wûy che chaé, é che ch'hëuk kéw pek, soô, 原思爲之宰與之粟九百辭 *Gwân-soo kap e chò kay chaé, hoē e ch'hek kaôu pāyh, sê,* Gwân-soo was steward of the household of Confucius who offered him nine hundred measures of corn, but he refused to accept of them; see the 論語 Lūn gé.
Bûn soô, 文辭, a style; gân soô, 言辭, an expression.

Soô 詞 A word, a phrase, an expression, a style.

Soô 祠 Vulg. *ch'haē:* to sacrifice to, to worship; chèy soô, 祭祠, to sacrifice.
Kwun choó chëang êng këung sit, sëen lip soô tông, 君子將營宮室先立祠堂 *kwun choó chëang k'hé këung ch'hoò, tëŏh taē seng k'hëā ch'haē sín ây tê^ng,* when a good man is about to build a house or palace, he first sets up a temple for sacrificing (to the gods).

Soô 柌 The handle of a sickle.

Soô 嗣 To inherit, to succeed to an inheritance; posterity; hereafter.
Choó soô hoō gëëp, 子嗣父業 *haôu sai^ng soô nëô^ng pây ây kay gëēp,* the son inherits the father's patrimony.

Soô 殊 Different, diverse, various.
Soô soô ē gē, 殊詞異義 *kŏh yëô^ng wā, yēw kŏh yëô^ng ây è,* different expressions and bearing various significations.

Soô 殳 A stick, a staff, a military weapon. A surname. One of the radicals.

Soô 銖 Choo soô, 錙銖, very small weights; ten grains of millet make one 絫, lúy; ten 絫, lúy make one 銖, soô; and ten 銖, soô, make one 錙, choo.

去 Soō 事 A business, an affair, trouble; to soō, 多事, troublesome.
Soō boô soō jê sit put k'hó yëá, 士無事而食不可也 *t'hàk ch'hâyh lâng kaôu bô soō, jê chëăh lâng ây hóng lòk sē ū^m t'hang,* when a learned men is without employment, to enjoy a salary is improper; see 孟子 Bēng choó.

Soō 士 Jê soō, 儒士, a learned man; soō chut, 士卒, a soldier, a private. Confucius said, "if riches may be sought after, (suy chip pëen che soō, goê èk wûy che, 雖執鞭之士吾亦爲之 *suy këăh báy pee^{ng} ây soō chut, gwá yëá chò c,)* although it should be the mean condition of a whipper-in I would fill it; but if they are not to be sought after, let me follow that which I prefer;" see the 上論 Sëang lūn.

Soō 仕 An officer, one in office, one employed under government. Soō sip wát këăng jê soō, 四十曰強而仕 *sè chàp höèy kóng këăng bêng jê chò kwⁿa,* at forty a man may be said to be in his prime, and should enter on office; see the 曲禮 K'bëuk léy.

Soō 似 To inherit; sëang soó, 相似 *sëo ch'hin chëōⁿᵍ,* alike. Bûn suy put tông, jê gē chek sëang soō, 文雖不同而義則相似 *bûn hwat suy bô sëo tâng jê è soō sëo ch'hin chëōⁿᵍ,* although the expressions vary, the idea is the same.

Soō 姒 Têy soō, 娣姒, sisters-in-law.

Soō 涘 The banks of a stream; the water's edge. Chaē hô che soō, 在河之涘 *twā tē káng keēⁿᵍ,* on the banks of the river; see the 王風 Ong hong.

Soō 竢 To wait for, to tarry. Soō chöēy Tëâng-say, 竢罪長沙 *t'haē chöēy tē Tëâng-say ây wūy,* I wait for the punishment of my offense at Tëâng-say; see the 賈誼傳 Káy gē twān.

Soō 俟 To wait, to tarry for; soō soō, 俟俟, a multitude walking slowly. Kwun bēng teàou, chaē kwan put soō kè, chaē göēy put soō ke, 君命召在官不俟屨在外不俟車 *jîn kwun bēng lēng këò, nā twā tē teâou têng ūᵐ saé têng haōu ây, nā twā tē gwā bîn ūᵐ saé têng haōu ch'hëa,* when a prince issues an order to summon you into his presence, if at court do not wait for your shoes, or if abroad do not tarry for your carriage, (but go immediately;) see the 禮玉藻 Léy gëúk ch'ho.

Soō 飤 To feed any one; soō jîn, 飤人 *ch'hē láng,* to feed people.

Soō 飼 Vulg. *ch'hē:* to feed, to nourish, to supply with food. Pëĕt jîn tok lé ch'hé jëük, soō taē koe, 別人桌裡取肉飼大姑 *pát lâng ây tŏh lé t'hâyh băh, ch'hē twā kay,* you can take meat from another person's table to feed your own mother-in-law; (said of those who are inclined to be filial at the expense of others.)

Soō 食 Food, eatables; also read sit: to eat. Hwán soe soō yím súy, 飯疏食飲水 *chëăh ch'hoe pooiⁿᵍ lim chúy,* to eat coarse rice and drink water; see the 論語 Lūn gé.

Soō 佀 The same as 似, soō, alike.

Soō 祀 Chèy soō, 祭祀 *chèy ch'haē,* to sacrifice to, to worship. Chèy soō choé sëen, 祭祀祖先 *chèy ch'haē choé chong,* to sacrifice to one's ancestors; also written 禩, soō.

Soō 耜 A ploughshare; the colter at the end of a plough.

Hoō jöēy soō, jê choō Sông che Têng, 負耒耜而自宋至滕 gēā jöēy soō, jê chēāng Sông kok che kaòu Têng, they shouldered their colters and ploughshares, and from the Sông country come to that of the Têng; see 孟子 Bēng choó.

Soō 兕 A wild ox; hoé soō ch'hut ê àp, 虎兕出於柙 hoé kap yēá goē ch'hut ê àp, the tigers and wild oxen got out of their cages.

Soō 嗣 An inheritance; kèy soō, 繼嗣, to inherit.

平 Sun 孫 A grandson; choó sun, 子孫 kēⁿá sun, posterity.

Vulg. swuiⁿᵍ: a surname.

Haòu sun yéw k'hèng, 孝孫有慶 woō haòu ây sun á woō hok k'hè, a filial grandson will possess happiness; see the 大雅 Seáou gnáy.

Sun 蓀 A fragrant herb.

Sun 猻 A kind of ape, or monkey.

Sun 櫞 The name of a tree.

Sun 飧 Dressed food.

Sun 飱 An evening meal, a supper; teaou yung sék sun, 朝饔夕飱 chá k'hé chēāh yung maīⁿᵍ hwuiⁿᵍ chēāh sun, in the morning we eat our breakfast, and in the evening our supper.

上 Sún 損 To injure, to diminish, to detract from; sún haē, 損害, to corrupt. Lē kè sún jîn, 利己損人 lē yēāh ka tē, sún haē pat làng, to benefit one's-self and injure others.

Sún 榫 A pointed piece of wood, used as the fastening of a door.

Sún 筍 Tēuk sun, 竹筍 tek sún, the young shoots of bamboo.

Sún 笋 The same as the above.

Sún 簨 Sún gê, 簨簴, a cross bar from which a bell or drum is suspended.

去 Sùn 舜 The name of an ancient emperor.

Yéw kwan chaē hāy wát Gê-sùn, 有鰥在下曰虞舜 woō twⁿa sin ây làng chaē hāy wūy, mēⁿâ kēò Gê-sùn, there is an individual in an inferior stiuation called Gê-sùn; see the 堯典 Geâou tēèn.

Sùn 蕣 The stalk of a flower, or plant.

A pretty ephemeral flower which fades the day it blossoms.

Sùn 瞬 Sùn sit, 瞬息 bàk naīⁿᵍh, the twinkling of an eye.

Sùn 橓 The trunk of a tree; the name of a tree.

Sùn 巽 The name of one of the diagrams; to enter in, to be obedient.

Also, a young man with gray hairs is called 巽髮, sùn hwat. Also written 巺, sùn.

Sùn 僎 To follow; to follow to the other world, by dying at the same time; distant; hasty, speedy.
Sé hông taē sîn sip jē jîn, kae ke lëét é sùn, 始皇大臣十二人皆車裂以僎 *sé hông ây twā sín chàp jē lâng, chò poè t'hó ch'hëa leēh é töèy e*, the first emperor's great ministers, to the number of twelve persons, were all torn in pieces by chariots in order to follow him into the other world.

Sùn 潠 To spurt out water.

Sùn 噀 The same as the above.

Sùn 遜 To yield respectfully; k'hëem sùn, 謙遜, humility; lowliness.
Gnoé p'hín put sùn, 五品不遜 *goē lún ây tō lé ūm sùn chëúng*, the five classes of virtues are not complied with; see the 書舜典 Se sùn tëén.

Sùn 孫 To be humble, to be submissive; the same as the above.

Sùn 瞚 The movement of the eyes.
Chëung jit sē, jê bòk put sùn, 終日視而目不瞚 *chwut^{ng} jit tit k'hw^{n}à, jê bàk chew ūm tin tāng*, to be looking all day without moving the eyes.

平
Sûn 巡 To inspect, to go about and survey; sûn sèw, 巡守, the visits of inspection paid by an emperor; chûn sûn, 逡巡, to retire, to be rejected.
Gnoé chaè yit sûn sèw, 五載一巡守 *goē neē^{ng} chit ây sún sèw*, every five years there should be a visit of inspection; see the 舜典 Sùn tëén.

Sûn 旬 A period of ten days; sam sûn, 三旬, three decades, a month.
Ke sam pek yéw lëúk sûn, yēw lëúk jit, 朞三百有六旬有六日 *chit neē^{ng} woō s^{n}a pāyh kap làk chàp jit, yēw làk jit*, a whole year consists of three hundred and sixty days, and six days besides; see the 堯典 Geâou tëén.

Sûn 侚 Swift, rapid; also written 僎, sùn.

Sûn 徇 To soothe, to pacify; to be obedient to, to comply with.
Tîn-sìn soò Chew-ch'hē sûn Gwūy tëy, 陳勝使周市徇魏地 *Tân-sìn saé Chew-ch'hē k'hè boè sûn Gwūy ây tēy*, Tân-sìn sent Chew-ch'hē to soothe and pacify the Gwūy country.

Sûn 狥 The same as the preceding.

Sûn 洵 To believe; sincere, true, real.

Sûn 恂 To believe; also, stern and cautious.
Tek hêng sûn sûn, 德行恂恂, his virtue was strict and careful.

Sûn 詢 To ask, to inquire; ch'hoò sûn, 咨詢, to make inquiry.

Sûn 殉 To bury persons along with a deceased sovereign, in order to accompany him into the other world; to pursue anything immoderately, even to death.
Sûn chông hwuy léy yëá, 殉葬非禮也

tùy lâng taē ūm hàp lêy, to be buried with the dead is not consistent with propriety.

T'ham hoo sûn chaê, lëët soō sûn bêng, 貪夫殉財烈士殉名 *t'ham ây lâng sûn tē cheêng, lëët ây t'hàk ch'hăyh lâng sûn tē mēⁿâ sëⁿa*, the covetous man follows immoderately after wealth, and the zealous scholar after fame.

Sûn 珣 The name of a gem.

Sûn 峋 An uneven appearance of hills; a steep and rugged hill.

Sûn 帕 A neckerchief.

Sûn 荀 The name of a plant; a surname.

Sûn 郇 The name of a country; a surname.

Sûn 栒 The name of a tree.

Sûn 徇 To declare, to make known; to transmit to others.

Sûn 循 To comply with, to follow, to be obedient; sûn chëûng, 循從, to obey; sûn hwân, 循環, to revolve; sûn lëâng, 循良, docile.

K'heng taē hoo é sûn hwat wûy chëet, 卿大夫以循法爲節 *k'heng kap taē hoo é sûn hwat toē chò chëet*, nobles and great officers should make a point of obeying the laws.

Sûn ch'hëâng jê choé, 循墻而走 *t'hàn ch'hëêng jê chaóu*, he went along under the wall, and ran away; see the 左傳 Chó twān.

Sûn 緍 Jeâou sûn, 繞緍, the seam on the back of a garment.

Sûn 淳 Plain, honest, upright, unadorned, great; sûn he, 淳于, a double surname.

Sûn 惇 Thick, liberal, real, sincere, faithful.

Sûn 犉 A yellow cow with black lips.

Sûn 醇 Thick, strong wine; liberal, kind.

Sûn 鶉 Yëem sûn, 鵪鶉 *yëen ch'hun*, a quail.

Sûn 焞 Full, replete.

Sûn 馴 To follow, to comply with; to approach gradually.

E bùt boô haē, koè bùt sûn yëen, 與物無害故物馴焉 *kap meëngh bô sëo haē, koe meëngh sûn sûn yëen*, "when we do not injure animals, they will be submissive to us;" said by 莊子 Chong-choó.

Sûn 杶 Koe sûn, 狗杶 *ká ch'hunâ*, a kind of wood, used for making the handles of hoes.

Sûn 純 Pure, unadulterated, unmixed.

Sûn ék put é, 純亦不已, pure without intermixture, spot or blemish.

丟
Sūn 順 To be obedient, to comply with. Haòu chóo sūn sun, 孝子順孫 *woō haòu ây kē^n á sëo sūn ây sun*, filial children and obedient grandchildren. Sūn soō, 順事, to comply with circumstances, to serve faithfully.

犬
Sut 率 To lead, to receive orders, to obey; sut soo é laê, 率師以來 *ch'hwā peng ê laê*, he led on the troops and came; see the 左傳 Chó twān. Tae sut, 大率, generally speaking, an average.

Sut 倅 To walk.

Sut 逹 To obey, to render obedient.

Sut 蟀 Sit sut, 蟋蟀, *sêeh sut*, a cricket.

Sut 颵 The sound of wind.

Sut 剶 Vulg. *chûy*: to cut off, to amputate.

Sut 恤 To pity, to compassionate; sut lîn, 恤憐, to commiserate. E sut hëung hong, 以恤凶荒 *ê sut lîn hëung hwui^ng*, in order to pity those distressed with famine; see the 周禮 Chew léy.

Sut 卹 Chín sut, 賑卹, to relieve distresses. Also written 賉, sut. Kèw chae sut lîn, 救災卹鄰 *kèw chae lân, sut kăyh pëùh kok*, to save those in misfortune, and to relieve neighbors; see the 左傳 Chó twān.

Sut 戌 One of the horary characters.

Sut 哦 To whistle with the mouth; k'hoé bêng sut sut, 口鳴哦哦 *ch'hùy haôu sut sut*, the mouth makes a whistling sound.

Sut 窣 To come last out of a hole.

Sut 帥 To guide, to lead on; a leader. Choó sut é chèng, sëùk kám put chèng, 子帥以正孰敢不正 *choó lé ch'hwā ê chë^n á 'chē chûy k^n á ū^m chë^n á*, it you lead them on in a correct way, who dares to be incorrect; see the 論語 Lūn gé.

天
Sút 述 To connect, to cultivate; to state, to declare; to record. Sëen sút jîn che soō, 善述人之事 *gaôu swà lâng ây soō*, to be skillful in connecting and handing down people's affairs; see the 中庸 Teung yûng.

Sút 術 An art, a contrivance; ke sút, 技術, skill; sim sút, 心術, the workings of the mind; hwat sút, 法術, an art, a plan; sëâ sút, 邪術, superstitious errors, corrupt opinions. Kaòu ók to sút è, 教亦多術矣 *kà lâng yëá chēy hāng hwat sút*, there are various methods of instruction; see 孟子 Bēng choó.

Sút 遾 The same as 述, sút, to state.

幸
Suy 雖 Although; suy jëên, 雖然, although it may be so. Suy wát bē hák, goē pit wūy che hák è, 雖曰未學吾必謂之學矣

suy jëĕn kóng yëá böëy t'hàk, gwá pit kóng e bat t'hàk köëy, although any should say such a one is not learned, I would certainly affirm that he had learned; see the 上論 Sëäng lūn.

Suy 倠 Lateral, inclined, partial.

Suy 荽 Hoê suy, 胡荽, a fragrant kind of vegetable.

Wán suy, 莞荽, the genus Carum, coriander.

Suy 綏 Peaceful, at rest; to retire.

Suy 浽 Suy bê, 浽溦, a gentle shower of small rain.

Suy 鑵 The name of a vessel or utensil.

Suy 蓑 Chong suy, 棕蓑 *chang suy*, a coarse kind of rain mantle.

Suy e, 蓑衣, garments to defend from the rain.

上聲 Súy 水 Vulg. *chúy*: water; sit súy, 食水 *chëăh chúy*, to drink water. A surname.

Súy chae! súy chae! 水哉水哉 *chúy chae! chúy chae!* O water! O water!

Súy 鬌 Pìn súy, 鬢鬌, the hair on the sides of the head.

Súy 美 Read bé: handsome, fine, elegant, beautiful; when 華父督, Hwa-hoó-sëuk saw 孔嘉父 K'hóng-kay-hoó's wife, he stared at her, and accompanying her said, (bé jê yëĕm, 美而艷 *súy kwà ch'hin ch'hang*,) "how beautiful and enchanting!"

去聲 Sùy 睡 Vulg. *k'hwùn*: to sleep. Also vulg. *kā chùy*: to slumber.

Sëang-kwun lūn soō, Chîn ông böëy sùy jê put t'hèng, 商君論事秦王每睡而不聽 *Sëang-kwun gē lūn soō Chîn ông tàk paē k'hwùn jê bô t'hëⁿa*, when Sëang-kwun was discoursing on business, Chîn ông frequently went to sleep, and did not hear; see the 史記 Soó kè.

Sùy 粹 Unmixed, pure; sûn sùy, 純粹, pure and unadulterated.

Sùy 睟 The eyes looking harmonious and agreeable.

Sùy jëĕn këèn ê bëēn, 睟然見於面 *ch'heng hô hëèn tē bīn*, harmony and delight beamed from his countenance; see 孟子 Bēng choó.

Sùy 誶 To ridicule, to blame, to inform; verbose; to reprimand.

Goê ông hwân choō hwàt Chêy, sùy Sin-se, 吳王還自伐齊誶申胥 *Goê ông tooiⁿg choō hwàt Chêy kok, ch'hëò Sin-se* when the king of the Goê country returned from attacking the Chêy, he ridiculed Sin-se.

Sùy 淬 To harden steel, by means of water.

Sùy 祟 Calamities produced by evil spirits.

Sùy 邃 Deep and distant.

Sùy 帥 A commander-in-chief; gwân sùy, 元帥, a generalissimo.

Sùy 戍 To guard the borders of a country. Put é gnó sùy Sin, 不與我戍申 *bô kap gwá chéw Sin kok*, they will not guard the borders of the Sin country for me; see the 王風 Ong hong.

平

Sûy 誰 Vulg. *chē chūy:* who, what, which? Choó wûy, sûy? 子爲誰 *lé sē chē chūy?* who are you, Sir?

Sûy 脽 The back; the body.

Sûy 𠂸 Trees and plants hanging down.

Sûy 倕 Heavy; also written 俀, sûy. The name of a man famous for his ingenuity.

Sûy 箠 A staff, a club, a switch for a horse. Hàn Kéng-tèy tēng sûy pëen taō chöey jîn, 漢景帝定箠鞭笞罪人 *Hàn Kéng-tèy tëⁿā töoh sûy kwaé á báy peeⁿᵍ, p'hāh wōō chöey ây lâng*, Kéng-tèy, of the Hàn dynasty, appointed the club and whip for the punishment of offenders.

Sûy 陲 The borders of a country; distant borders. The edge of a precipice.

Sûy 錘 The weight which is attached to a pair of steelyards.

Sûy 垂 To let fall, to hang down; to spread abroad; near, nearly. Hông tèy sûy e sëâng, jê t'hëen hāy tē, 黃帝垂衣裳而天下治 *wuīⁿᵍ tèy pàng lòh k'hè yîn chëöⁿᵍ, jê t'heeⁿᵍ āy ka tē tē*, the yellow emperor merely let his garments hang down, and the whole empire was regulated.

Sûy 棰 An instrument of torture.

Sûy 隨 To follow; sûy tùy, 隨對, to follow in procession; forthwith. Chëên hoē sëang sûy, 前後相隨 *chéng aōu sëo sûy*, before and behind joining in procession; see the 道德經 Tō tek keng.

Sûy 瓍 A pearl; choo sûy, 珠瓍, a kind of pearl.

Sûy 葚 Read sîm: the fruit of the mulberry tree. Song sîm, 桑葚 *seⁿᵍ sûy*, mulberries.

去

Sūy 遂 To complete, to occasion, to extend to, to advance; then; sūy chek, 遂即, forthwith. Sêng soō put swat, sūy soō put kàn, 成事不說遂事不諫 *chëⁿā āy soō bô kóng, sūy āy soō bô tⁿà*, when a thing is done it is useless to speak about it, and when it is completed, it is unnecessary to reprove it; see the 論語 Lūn gé. Būn gnó choo koe, sūy kip pek ché, 問我諸姑遂及伯姊 *moeiⁿᵍ gwán choo koe, sūy kip kaōu ūⁿ pāyh twā ché*, let us ask all our aunts, and then let us go to our uncles and elder sisters; see the 衛風 Wöey hong. Also written 㒸, sūy.

Sūy 繸 The strings and tassels with which a gem is tied.

Sūy 璲 A gem worn by persons in office; a gem attached to girdles.

Sŭy 隧 A pathway in a vault, or a subterranean passage in a grave; a way. K'hwat tēy kip chwân, sŭy jê sëang këèn, 闕地及泉隧而相見 *k'hwuy tēy kip kaðu chwⁿâ chúy, sūy t'hàn bōng loē, jé sëo keèⁿᵍ*, dig deep into the ground till you come to the fountains, and then by a subterranean passage meet each other; this expedient was recommended to a prince, who had vowed never to see his mother again, till he met her under the yellow fountains (i. e. in the grave); see the 左傳 Chó twān.

Sŭy 燧 The embers of fire; also, a kind of wood which is used for producing fire, by friction.

Sŭy 檖 The name of a wod, like the mountain pear. Sip yéw sē sŭy, 隰有樹檖 *wūn sip ây wūy woō chè sūy ch'hâ*, in marshy places they plant the wild pear; see the 秦風 Chîn hong.

Sŭy 𤻖 A kind of rheumatic complaint.

Sŭy 穟 An ear of corn, the fruitful appearance of corn.

Sŭy 憢 The mind deeply exercised with thought.

Sŭy 穗 An ear of corn.

Sŭy 瑞 A gem used as an insignia of office; also, a lucky omen.

去

Swa 搓 Swa k'hae, 搓開, to open out, to spread out.

声

Swá 耍 To sport; hè swá, 戲耍, to play; gwân swá, 玩耍 *t'hit t'hô*, to play, to sport, to take one's pleasure.

Swá 灑 To sprinkle the ground with water. Tòng swá sò, 當灑掃 *ēy tèⁿᵍ tit hèw chúy saðu tēy*, lie is fit for sprinkling and sweeping the ground; see the 語論 Lūn gé.
Seaou swá, 瀟灑, solitary.

Swá 洒 To wash out, to obliterate, the same as tho preceding. Gwān pé soó chëá yit swá che, 願比死者一洒之 *gwān t'hēy sé ây lâng chit ây swá e*, I wish to wipe out this stain for the sake of the dead; see 孟子 Bēng choó.

Swá 譈 To discourse violently, to show violence in discourse.

Swá 徙 Read sé: to remove; pwan sé pëet ch'hè, 搬徙別處 *pwⁿa swá pàt wūy*, to remove to another part.

Swá 漱 Read soé: to wash, to rinse; soé k'hoé, 漱口 *swá k'haðu*, to rinse or gargle the mouth.

去

Swà 續 Read sëuk: unbroken, incessant, continued without intermission. Sëang sëuk, 相續 *sëo swà*, connected, joined together.

平

Swâ 沙 Read say: sand; a surname; say sëèn, 沙線 *swâ swⁿà*, a sand bank.

Swâ 鯊 Read say: a fish; say gê, 鯊魚 *swâ hê*, the shark fish.

福建方言字典

坴 Sw^n^a 山 Read san: a hill; tông san, 唐山 *tĕ^ng^ sw^n^a*, China. A surname. Wûy san kéw jīm, kong k'hwuy yit kwūy, 爲山九仞功虧一簣 *chò sw^n^a kaòu jīm kwân, kang hoo k'hwuy chit lâng á t'hoé*, in making a hillock 72 feet high, to leave the work unfinished from the lack of only a basket of earth; (referring to those who make some progress in learning, but leave their education unaccomplished by only a very little;) see the 尙書 Sëăng sē.

声 Sw^n^á 產 Read sán: to bear, to bring forth; when a woman is pregnant and has not fulfilled her months, she is said to be (sán lōëy, 產內 *sw^n^á laē*,) in her pregnancy.

去 Sw^n^à 傘 Read sàn: an umbrella; é sàn, 雨傘 *hoē sw^n^à*, a rain umbrella. Lëâng sàn, 凉傘 *nëô^ng^ sw^n^à*, a parasol, a round umbrella of state.

Sw^n^à 散 Read sàn: to disperse, to scatter; hwun sàn, 分散 *hwun sw^n^à*, divided and dispersed.

Sw^n^à 線 Read sëèn: a thread; chim sëèn, 針線 *chëem sw^n^à*, needle and thread.

Boô chim put yín sëèn, 無針不引線 *bô chëem bēy yín tit sw^n^à*, without a needle we cannot draw the thread; (i. e. without the introduction of one friend we cannot get acquainted with another.)

丢 Swaē^ng^ 檨 The mango fruit; swaē^ng^ choó, 檨仔 *swaē^ng^ á*, a bubo, a venereal ulcer.

夬 Swaē^ng^h 㗹 A change of the voice.

夬 Swăh 䢪 Swăh swăh hêng, 䢪䢪行 *swăh swăh kē^n^â*, the appearance of walking.

Swăh 杀 To spoil; ch'hit swăh pat paē, 七杀八敗 *ch'hit swăh păyh paē*, seven spoilings and eight ruinings; (alluding to persons who spoil everything which they put their hands to.)

Swăh 煞 Read sat: to injure, to strike with noxious influences; to finish; the same as sat, 殺, to kill.

Swăh 殺 Read sat: to kill; sëang sat, 相殺 *sëo swăh*, to kill and injure one another.

坴 Swan 宣 To proclaim, to spread abroad, to publish; to summon. A surname. Jit swan sam tek, 日宣三德 *tâk jit swan bêng s^n^a hāng ây tek hêng*, every day proclaiming the three virtues.

Swan 亘 To seek for; to proclaim abroad.

Swan 喧 To proclaim, to publish.

Swan 暄 The warm and genial influences of the sun.

Swan 煊 To dry in the sun; the brightness of fire; dry.

Swan 萱 The name of a plant.

Swan 揎 To draw, to pull, to lead.

Swan 暄 The warm and genial influence of the sun.
Hân kok sêng swan, 寒谷成暄 *kwⁿâ k'haiⁿᵍ chěⁿâ sëo*, the cool vallies become warm.

Swan 瑄 A gem six inches square; yéw soo hông swan gëuk, 有司奉瑄玉 *yěw soo ây kwⁿa hông hëèn swan gëuk*, the proper officer presents the gem of office.

Swan 諠 Swan hwa, 諠譁, to make a noise and disturbance.
Chooˇ hoê swan hwa, 諸候諠譁, the princes made a clamorous noise.

Swan 喧 The same as the above.

Swan 酸 Vulg. *swuiⁿᵍ*: sour; swan kam, 酸柑 *swuiⁿᵍ kam*, a lemon.
Bêng ch'hun che gwàt, kê bē swan, 孟春之月其味酸 *bēng ch'hun ây göëyh, e ây bē tëöh swuiⁿᵍ*, in the first month of spring, the taste of what we eat should be sour; see the 禮月令 Léy gwàt lēng.

Swan 痠 Vulg. *swuiⁿᵍ*: a weariness and lassitude of the limbs.
Sin t'héy swan t'hòng, 身體痠痛 *sin t'héy swuiⁿᵍ t'hëⁿᵃ*, the whole body listless and weary. Swan lwán, 痠軟 *swuiⁿᵍ nooiⁿᵍ*, weak and listless.

Swan 蕿 The name of a plant, and of a vegetable.

Swan 齹 Ch'hé swan, 齒齹, *ch'hùy k'hé swuiⁿᵍ*, the teeth set on edge.

Swan 諼 Deceitful, treacherous; also, to forget.
He chò chày swan che ch'hek, 虛造詐諼之策 *k'hang k'hang sëet pâyh ch'hàt ây kèy ch'hek*, he vainly adopted a few deceitful plans; see the 漢息夫傳 Hàn sit hoô twān.

Swan 扆 The bolt of a door.

Swan 楥 A bolt; bòk swan, 木楥, *ch'hâ swan*, a wooden bolt.

声

Swán 選 To select, to choose; swán ték, 選擇 *kán tŏh*, to pick and choose.
Sûn yéw t'hëen hāy, swán ê chëùng, ké Ko-yaôu, 舜有天下選於衆舉皐陶 *Sûn woō t'heeⁿᵍ āy, swán kèng tē chëùng lâng, kê yūng Ko-yaôu*, when Sûn obtained the empire, he made a selection from amongst the whole, and elevated to office Ko-yaôu; see the 論語 Lūn gé.

Swán 潠 To hold water in the mouth, and spurt it out.

Swán 梭 A piece of wood used in weaving.

Swán 㮨 An instrument of torture; thumb screws.

Swán 撈 To urge, to press.

去

Swàn 算 Vulg. *swuiⁿᵍ*: to reckon, to count; swàn pwàn, 算盤 *swuiⁿᵍ pwⁿô*, an abacus, a reckoning board.
Also written 筭, swàn.

Hông tèy sê, Lēy-séw chok swàn soè, 黄帝時隸首作筭數 *wui^ng tèy ây sê, Lēy-séw chò swui^ng sedou,* in the time of the yellow emperor (B. C. 2622,) Lēy-séw invented accounts.

Swàn 蒜 Swàn t'hoê, 蒜頭 *swàn t'haôu,* garlic.

Swàn 祘 To look at, and make a calculation of anything.

平

Swân 旋 Chew swân, 周旋, to turn round, to revolve; to circulate.

Pwân swân, 盤旋, to turn round and round.

Swân 漩 Water turning around in an eddy. Also written 淀, swân.

Swân 璇 A precious gem, used for astronomical purposes.

Swân 璿 The same as the above.

Swân 掟 To turn round, to revolve.

去

Swān 掟 To turn round, to revolve.

Swān 銓 Also read ch'hwan: a diamond; kim gîn swān, 金銀銓, gold, silver, and diamonds.

Swān sék, 銓石 *swān chëôh,* a diamond stone.

Swān 羨 To desire, to rejoice in; to covet, to long after.

Boô jëên him swān, 無然欣羨 *bô jëên hw^na hê him swān,* having no delight or pleasure.

7 H

入

Swat 雪 Vulg. *săyh:* snow; frozen rain; swat pék, 雪白 *swat pŭyh,* as white as snow.

Kim gnó laê soo, é swat hwuy hwuy, 今我來思雨雪霏霏 *t^nagwá laê sôo, hoē săyh hwuy hwuy,* now that I come, the rain and snow is drifting about; see the 小雅 Seáou gnáy.

Swat 䨮 The ancient form of the preceding character.

Swat 㓤 To scrape, to pare off, to cut.

Swat 說 Vulg. *kóng:* to speak, to discourse; vulg. *söĕyh:* to explain; explanation.

Chaé-gnó Choó-k'hòng sëēn wûy swat soô, 宰我子貢善為說辭 *Chaé-gnó Choó-k'hòng gaôu chò söĕyh soô,* Chaé-gnó and Choó-k'hòng were skillful in conversation and discourse; see 孟子 Bēng choó.

Swat tek yēw lé, 說得有理, it is reasonably said.

Swat 刷 Vulg. *loò:* to brush, to rub; to sweep, to cleanse.

Swat t'hé kaé hêng, 刷恥改行 *loò k'hè seaou lēy káy séy kë^nâ,* to rub out the disgrace, and reform one's actions.

入

Swàt 㲉 Withered, shriveled; to gather up the skin.

平

Swui^ng 孫 Read sun; a surname.

*Swuì^ng^* **酸** Read swan: sour, acid; hâm tëêm swan, 鹹甜酸 *këêm tee^ng^ swuì^ng^*, salt, sweet, and sour; the name of a confectionary which unites all these tastes.

*Swuì^ng^* **痠** Read swan: weary, listless; weakness, lassitude.
Këak séw swan, 脚手痠 *k'ha ch'héw swuì^ng^*, a weariness of the limbs.

声
*Swuì^ng^* **水** Súy gnêw, 水牛 *swuì^ng^ goô*, a buffalo, a water cow.

*Swuì^ng^* **損** Read sún: to injure; sún sit, 損失 *swuì^ng^ sit*, to injure and loso; sún hwaē, 損壞 *swuì^ng^ k'hëep*, injured, destroyed.

去
*Swuì^ng^* **算** Read swàn: reckon, to count; swàn hwáng, 算鈁 *swuì^ng^ hwáng*, to count money.
Swàn kèy, 算計 *swuì^ng^ kèy*, to scheme, to plan.

*Swuì^ng^* **纉** Read swàn: to tie; swàn kín, 纉緊 *swuì^ng^ kín*, to tie very tight.

T

卒
Ta **乾** Read kan: dry, arid, not moist; bŭt kan, 物乾 *meë^ng^h ta*, anything very dry.

Ta **礁** Stones in a stream, to serve for steps; the name of a place.
Choó-kat-ta-sē, 硃葛礁氏, the Chinese method of pronouncing the word 'secretary.'

去
Tà **罩** To catch; a basket for catching fish; to cover, to overspread; to spring on like a tiger.

Tà **跼** To jump and frisk about; seáou jê tà laê, 小兒跼來 *sèy kë^n^á tà laê*, the child came frisking along.

Tà **帳** Read tëàng: a curtain; bún tëàng, 蚊帳 *báng tà*, musquito curtains.

平
Tâ **焦** Read cheaou: to be burned in the fire; chëen tò cheaou, 煎到焦 *chëen kaòu tâ*, to broil to a cinder.

上平
T^{n}a **今** Read kim: now, at present; kim che jîn, put pé tek koé che jîn, 今之人不比得古之人 *t^{n}a ây lâng bēy pê tit koê chá ây lâng*, the people of the present day are not to be compared with those of former times.

T^{n}a **擔** Read tam: to bear, to carry; tam bùt, 擔物 *t^{n}a meē^{ng}h*, to carry a weight by means of a stick across the shoulders; something in the way in which milk is carried in London, only the yoke is straight and flat, and not made to fit the shulders.

T^{n}a **檐** Read tam: pëén tam, 匾檐 *pún t^{n}a*, the flat stick or pole with which burdens are carried across the shoulders.

T^{n}a **中** Read tëung: the middle; tëung yang, 中央 *t^{n}a e^{ng}*, the centre.

T^{n}a **瞠** T'heng bòk, 瞠目 *t^{n}a bàk chew*, to lift up the eyes.

上上
T^{n}á **打** Vulg. *p'hăh*: to beat, to strike; sëang t^{n}á, 相打 *sëo p'hăh*, to fight with one another; t^{n}á t'hèng, 打聽 *t'hàm t'hë^{n}a*, to listen; t^{n}á pān, 打辦, to prepare, to provide.

上去
T^{n}à **擔** Read tàm: a burden; that which can be carried by one man; a hundred weight; a pecul.

T^{n}à **說** Read swat: to speak to, to reprove, to discourse.
H^{n}ó swat, 好說 *hó t^{n}à*, you speak well, you are very polite.

下平
T^{n}â **爡** To sport about the fire.

下去
T^{n}ā **掟** Read tēng: to throw; tēng lòk, 掟落 *t^{n}ā lŏh*, to throw down, to open and spread out.

上平
Tae **懛** Tae gaê, 懛獃, to miss one's aim through haste; stupid.

Tae **秪** Corn just ripe; a kind of large grain.

Tae **鯳** The name of a fish.

上上
Taé **歹** Vulg. *p'ha^{n}ê*: wicked; taé jîn, 歹人 *p'ha^{n}ê lâng*, a bad man.
Put te h^{n}ó taé, 不知好歹 *ū^{m} chae hó p'ha^{n}ê*, not knowing how to distinguish between good and bad.

上去
Taè **帶** Vulg. *twà*: a girdle; këet taè, 結帶 *kat twà*, to bind on a girdle; kaé taè, 解帶 *t'haóu twà*, to unbind a girdlo; taè laê, 帶來 *twà laê*, to bring. Sok taè lip ê teâou, 束帶立於朝 *hăh twà k'hëā tē teâou laē*, to bind on a girdle, and stand in the court; see the 論語 Lūn gé.

Taè **戴** Vulg. *tèy*: to put on anything, to wear anything on the head; taè bō, 戴帽 *tèy bō*, to wear a hat or cap. A surname.
Put këūng taè t'hëen che kêw, 不共戴天之仇 *bó kāng tèy t'hee^{ng} ây kêw sêw*, a deadly enmity which will not allow the parties to live under the samo heavens.

Taè **襶** T'haè taè, 褦襶, ignorant of affairs, unacquainted with business.

Taè 蔕 The roots of plants.

平

Taê 臺 A terrace, a high platform, hustings; an altar; exalted.

Keng sé lêng taê, 經始靈臺 *k'hé t'haôu chò hó ây taê*, they began to make the fine terrace; see the 大雅 Taē gnáy.

Heng taê, 兄臺, or 兄台, exalted brother; an expression commonly used in letter writing.

Taê 籉 Taê lip, 籉笠, a bamboo hat, in the form of an umbrella, to keep out the rain.

Taê 儓 Pōēy taê, 倍儓, a servant, a minister, a menial.

Taê 檯 Vulg. *paⁿᵍ*: a terrace, a stage; hè taê, 戲檯 *hè paⁿᵍ*, a stage; kèng taê, 鏡檯 *kēⁿà paⁿᵍ*, a frame for a looking-glass.

Taê 蛤 A sea animal with a black shell, and said to contain pearls. An insect resembling the locust.

Taê 埋 Read baê: to bury; baê bùt, 埋物 *taê meēⁿᵍh*, to bury anything; baê sin se, 埋身屍 *taê sin se*, to bury a dead body.

去

Taē 大 Vulg. *twā*: great, large; k'hwat taē, 闊大 *k'hwăh twā*, ample.

Taē chae! Geâou che wûy kwun yeá, 大哉堯之爲君也 *twā chae! Geâou ây chò jîn kwun*, how great was Geâou as a prince! see the 論語 Lūn gé.

Taē sëuk, 大叔, a double surname.

Taē 伏 The name of a country.

Taē 代 To change, to come instead of, to substitute; sè taē, 世代 *sè tēy*, a generation; teâou taē, 朝代 *teâou tēy*, a dynasty.

Taē jîn sëuk chōēy, 代人贖罪 *t'hēy lâng sëuk chōēy*, to become a substitute for men in order to redeem them from their sins.

Koé che ông cheá, ėk taē kaé hō, 古之王者易代改號 *koé chá ây ông wⁿà teâou tēy káy kok hō*, the kings of ancient times, on the change of a dynasty, altered the designation of the country; see the 家語 Kay gé.

Taē 岱 Taē chong, 岱宗, a name of the great eastern mountain.

Taē 袋 Vulg. *tēy*: a sack; poè taē, 布袋 *poè tēy*, a bag.

Taē 貸 To borrow, to give; yēw ch'heng taē jê ėk che, 又稱貸而益之 *yēw ch'heng chëŏh jê t'heeⁿᵍ e*, also borrowing and adding to it; see 孟子 Bēng choó.

Taē 玳 A kind of tortoise shell.

Taē 黛 Black eyebrows; ch'heng taē, 青黛, the name of a plant.

Taē 殆 Dangerous, in danger, hazardous; near, about to be.

K'hóng-choó wát, ê soo sê yeá, t'hëen hāy taē chae, 孔子曰於斯時也天下殆哉 *K'hóng-choó kóng, tē chēy lêy sê, t'heeⁿᵍ āy gwūy hëém*, Confucius said, "at that time the country was in danger;" see 孟子 Bēng choó.

Gân sē che choō, kō taē sē ke hoē? 顔氏之子其殆庶幾乎 *Gân sē ây kēⁿá, c chëang ch'ha put to hoē?* is not the son of the house of Gân almost about to attain to perfection? see the 易繋詞 Ek hēy soō.

Taē 迨 To attain, to reach; till, until. Taē peng bē p'hwàn, 迨氷未泮 *taē seng böēy yëōng*, when the ice is yet unthawed; see the 衛風 Wōēy hong.

Taē 怠 Haē taē, 懈怠, lazy, idle, indolent; taē tō, 怠惰, slothful. Jé wûy put taē, 汝惟不怠 *lé tòk tòk ūm p'hún twⁿā*, only be not you slothful; see the 大禹謨 Taē ó boé.

Taē 靆 Aó taē, 靉靆, cloudy, the sun overspread with clouds.

Taē 逮 To reach, to attain; even to, until. Koé chëá gân che put ch'hut, t'hé këung che put taē yëá, 古者言之不出恥躬之不逮也 *koé chá ây lâng kóng wā bēy ch'hut, kēⁿa hìn sin bēy kip kaōu hwut lëy soō*, the ancients were backward in making any protestations, being ashamed lest they should not be equal to the performance of them; see the 論語 Lūn gé.

Taē 瑇 The same as 玳, taē, tortoise-shell.

夫

Tăh 搭 Read tap: to feel; to join to anything.

Tăh 舴 Tăh chûn, 舴船, to embark on board of a ship.

7 I

平

Tăh 搨 To strike with the hand; tăh tok, 搨棹, to strike the table.

入

Tăh 踏 Read tâp: to tread on anything; këak tâp, 脚踏 *k'ha tăh*, to tread with the feet.

上

Taīng, 撐 Read teng: to push; teng k'hae, 撐開 *taīng k'hwuy*, to force open.

Taīng 瞪 Tông bók, 瞪目 *taīng bák chew*, to stretch open the eyes; to stare.

Taīng 骨 Read teng: a heel; keak hoē teng, 脚後骨 *k'ha aōu taīng*, the heel.

去

Taīng 打 Read tⁿá: to beat, to strike.

去

Taīng 盯 Taīng naīng, 盯瞕, to stare, to look staringly.

Taīng 侹 Taīng sè, 侹試, to pretend to do anything. Taīng boô lèk, 侹無力 *taīng bô làt*, to pretend to have no strength.

平

Taīng 揨 Taīng lŏh k'he, 揨落去, to throw down; to knock down, as the hoops of a barrel, to repair a barrel.

Taīng 桯 T'hóng têng, 桶桯 *t'háng taīng*, the wedge or chisel used by the coopers for knocking down the hoops of a barrel.

去

Taīng 鄭 Read tēng: a surname.

Taiⁿᵍ 柄 Read têng: to hold, to grasp; sêv têng bůt, 手柄物 *ch'hew taiⁿᵍ meeⁿᵍh*, to hold anything in the hand.

夫

Tak 觸 Read ch'hëuk: to gore, to push with the horns.
Gnêw sëang ch'hëuk, 牛相觸 *goô sëo tak*, oxen goring one another.

Tak 喌 Chëuk chëuk, 喌喌 *tak tak*, the noise made in calling fowls; chëuk key, 喌鷄 *tak key*, to chuck fowls.

灭

Tàk 濁 Read chŏk: muddy; súy chŏk, 水濁 *chúy tàk*, muddy water.
Ch'heng soo chŏk eng, chŏk soo chŏk chëuk, 清斯濯纓濁斯濯足 *ch'heng ây chëw sêy eng twà, tàk ây chëw sêy k'ha*, the clear waters will serve for washing my tassel, and the muddy for washing my feet; see 孟子 Bēng choó.

Tàk 毒 Read tŏk: poison, poisonous; ch'hoó bůt yéw tŏk, 此物有毒 *chéy lêy meeⁿᵍh woō tàk*, this thing is poisonous.

Tàk 逐 Read tëŭk: every; tëŭk këën, 逐件 *tàk kĕⁿā*, every one; tëŭk jit, 逐日 *tàk jit*, every day.

Tàk 碡 Leâou tŏk, 磟碡 *lâ tàk*, a harrow, a field rake.

𡗗

Tam 耽 Large ears, hanging down; tam lŏk, 耽樂, the excess of pleasure.
K'hwa-hoó tam jé, 夸父耽耳 *K'hwa-hoó têⁿᵍ hē á*, K'hwa-hoó had long flabby ears; see the 淮南子 Hwaê lâm choó.

Tam 眈 To look at something near, but to have the mind set on something distant.

Tam 躭 The same as 耽, tam, long eared; but now commonly used for tam jin, 躭認, to act as a security.

Tam 酖 To be fond of wine; hong tam ê chéw, 荒酖於酒, to be given to much wine; see the 尚書 Sëāng se.

Tam 擔 Vulg. *tⁿa*: to carry by means of a stick across the shoulders.
Tam tŏng, 擔當 *tⁿa tèⁿᵍ*, to bear the responsibility of anything.
Tam hoo, 擔夫 *tⁿa ây lâng*, a bearer, a carrier.
Also written 儋, tam.

Tam 繵 Slow, leisurely.

Tam 湛 Tam lŏk, 湛樂, rejoiced, pleased.
A surname.
Choó sun kê tam, 子孫其湛 *kēⁿá sun hwⁿa hé*, posterity will be pleased and happy; see the 小雅 Seáou gnáy.

Tam 聃 Dull of hearing; also written 聸 tam.

声

Tám 膽 Vulg. *tⁿá*: the gall bladder, put by the Chinese metaphorically for courage; boô tám, 無膽 *bô tⁿá*, no courage.
Sim yëŭk kê sèy, tám yëŭk kê taē, 心欲其細膽欲其大 *sim aè e ēy sèy, tⁿá aè e ēy twā*, we should desire to keep our hearts small, but our galls large; (i. e. our minds humble, but our courage great.)

Tám 蘑 Tám poĕ, ... a flower.

Tám 啖 To eat, to ... also written 啗, tám; and 噉, tám. Kit hoō ch'hé chó é tám kit, 吉婦取棗以啖吉 *Kit ây boĕ t'hăyh chó hoē kit chĕăh,* Kit's wife took dates and gave him to eat; see the 王吉傳 Ong kit twān.

Tám 丼 A surname; the sound of anything falling into a well.

Tám 菡 Marsh mallows before they are opened, are called 菡萏, hâm tám.

Tám 窞 A pit, the bottom of a pit; k'hám tám, 坎窞, a pit or hole.

Tám 倓 To stop.

Tám 紞 The strings of pearls hanging round an official cap.

Tám 髧 The hair hanging down.

Tám 偡 Tám jêên, 偡然, an exact and regular appearance.

去

Tàm 儋 A kind of jar; chëang ch'hëen tàm, 漿千儋 *chëw ch'heng àng,* a thousand jars of wine.

Tàm 擔 Vulg. $t^{n}\grave{a}$: that which is carried, a burden, as much as a man can carry; a hundred weight, a pecul, equal to 133⅓ lbs. avoirdupois.

Tàm 丼 The sound of anything falling into a well.

平

Tâm 談 To discourse, to converse, to prate; a surname; hëang tâm, 鄉談, country talk, brogue; also written 譚, tâm: a surname. Ong laê boĕ pék teng, tâm ch'heàou yéw hông jê, 往來無白丁談笑有鴻儒 *óng laê bŏ ch'hut sin ây lâng, tâm ch'hëò lóng sē hông jê,* of those who come and go, there is not one private obscure person, but all those who talk and laugh here are phœnix-like learned men; see the 劉禹錫傳 Lêw é sek twān.

Tâm 餤 To advance, to enter; to serve up food.

Tâm 郯 The name of a country; also, a surname.

Tâm 惔 To burn; yow sim jê tâm, 憂心如惔 *hwân ló ây sim $kw^{n}a$ ch'hin $ch\ddot{e}\ddot{o}^{ng}$ hŏëy sëo,* grief of mind burning like a fire; see the 小雅 Seáou gnáy.

Tâm 倓 Still, peaceful, ...; ... written 倒, tâm.

Tâm 澹 Damp, wet, m... 氣, moisture ...

去

Tām 賧 When foreigners ... the payment ... 賧, tām; al...

Tām 錟 The name of a ...

Tām 淡 Thin, weak, insipid; tasteless. Lē hoē é pē hāy, kong k'hoé sit tām, 呂后與陛下攻苦食淡 *Lē hoē kap pē hāy, kong kan k'hoé chēăh chēⁿá, chēⁿá*, the empress Lē has with your majesty borne afflictions and eaten insipid things; see the 史記 Soó kè.

Tām 惔 Still, quiet, retired.

Tām 醈 Thin wine.

Tām 菼 Tām lwān, 菼亂, a kind of reed or bullrush.

Tām 鹹 A poor, thin, insipid taste.

Tām 琰 A kind of gem.

Tām 澹 Tām pók, 澹泊, still, quiet, retired, unemployed; tām taê, 澹臺, a double surname. Tām pók bêng chè, lêng chēng tè wán, 澹泊明志寧靜致遠 *tām pók ēy bêng lán ây chè, ... chēng ēy tè kaōu hwuiⁿᵍ soō*, "stillness and quietness enlighten the views, tranquillity and rest enable a man to contemplate distant things;" said 諸葛武侯 Choo-kat boó hoê.

Tām 禫 A long period of mourning; tām hók, 禫服, an extra mourning dress for a period of three months beyond the usual time.

Tām 憺 Still, quiet.

幸

Tan 丹 A red color; tan sim, 丹心, a red heart, a sincere mind. Kwan-yîn-tēáng ch'hek bēēn tan sim, 關雲長赤面丹心 *Kwan-yîn-tēáng ch'hēăh bīn âng sim*, Kwan-yîn-tēáng had a red face and a crimson heart; (i. e. a sincere mind.) Tan sey, 丹砂, cinnabar.

Tan 單 Alone, only; vulg. *twⁿa:* single, unaided; a note; a surname; sēw tan, 受單 *sēw twⁿa*, a receipt; t'hó chēēn tan, 討錢單 *t'hó cheēⁿᵍ twⁿa*, a bill, an account for goods delivered. Hêng tan éng chek, 形單影隻 *hêng twⁿa yēⁿá chit chēăh*, a solitary body, and a single shadow; tan ê, 單于, a double surname.

Tan 簞 A small round bamboo vessel, for containing food. Yit tan soō, yit p'heâou yím, 一簞食一瓢飲 *chit láng á pooīⁿᵍ, chit p'hoô á chúy*, one basket of food, and one calabash full of drink; see the 論語 Lūn gé.

Tan 癉 Hⁿó tan, 火癉 *höéy tan*, a kind of eruption, to which children are liable; the chicken pox.

Tan 襌 Clothes without lining, a single garment.

Tan 殫 Exhausted, to the utmost, very much.

Tan 鄲 Kam tan, 邯鄲, the name of a place.

声

Tán 刪 To cut, to hack.

去

Tàn **旦** Early, the morning; bêng tàn, 明旦, to-morrow morning. Chō é t'haē tàn, 坐以待旦 *chēy é têng t'haē chá k'hé,* to sit still and wait for the morning; see 孟子 Bēng choó.

Tàn **⿸广旦** A small shed, a cottage.

Tàn **僤** Real, sincere, true.

平

Tân **陳** Read tîn: a surname. Tông Tîn-gwân kong, k'hae Bân Chëang, sè sit lîm Chëang hoê, 唐陳元公開閩漳世襲臨漳候 *Tông teâou Tân-gwân kông, k'hwuy Bân saiⁿᵍ Chëang chew, sè têy sit lîm Chëang hoī,* Tân-gwân kong of the Tông dynasty was the first who settled the district of Chëang chew, in the province of Bân (i. e. Hok-këèn), and for successive generations his posterity inherited the title of lîm Chëang hoê, (i. e. the earl who first came to Chëang.)

上

Tān **憚** To fear, to dread difficulties. Kò chek bút tān kaé, 過則勿憚改 *woō kòey sit, chek bŏh wùy kan lán káy,* when you have any faults, do not dread difficulties in seeking to amend them; see 上論 Sëāng lūn.

Tān **彈** Vulg. *twⁿā:* to fillip anything, to strike a round ball, to shoot with round shot from a crossbow. Filial young persons among the ancients could not bear to see their parents' corpses devoured by wild beasts, (koè chok tān é séw che, 故作彈以守之 *chëà chò twⁿā é séw e,*) they therefore made crossbows with balls to guard them.

Tān **⿰亻延** Great, large.

Tān **但** Only, but; tān hwân, 但凡, whosoever, whenever. Wûy soō kò ch'hëa, tān hwùy cheng sîn jê é, 為事過奢但費精神而已 *chò soō k'hăh ch'hëa hwâ, tān hwùy cheng sîn têⁿā têⁿā,* when we are too prodigal in affairs, we only waste our spirits and nothing else; see 史記 Soó kè.

Tān **袒** Tān t'hek, 袒裼, the arms bare, the sleeves turned up. Suy tān t'hek ké têng ê gnó ch'hek, jé yëen lêng bōéy gnó chae? 雖袒裼裸裎於我側爾焉能浼我哉 *suy peěh ch'hëw wuiⁿᵍ t'huiⁿᵍ pak t'hàyh lé bōéyh an chwⁿá ēy bàk la sâm gwá chae?* although a bare-armed naked-bodied fellow should stand at my side, yet how could he defile me? see 孟子 Bēng choó.

Tān **靛** To dye anything with indigo; ch'heng tān, 青靛, a purple color.

Tān **蛋** Vulg. *nooīⁿᵍ:* an egg; key tān, 雞蛋 *key nooīⁿᵍ,* a fowl's egg. Tān kay, 蛋家, an egg house, the small boats in which the Chinese live.

Tān **段** Vulg. *twⁿā:* a piece, a slice; a surname.

Tān **襢** The same as 袒, tān, bare-armed.

Tān **誕** Dissolute, loose, disorderly, to talk at random; to believe; to bring up also, great.

7 K

平 *Tang* 東 Read tong: the east; tong sey lâm pok, 東西南北 *tang sae lâm pak*, east, west, south, north. Tong hong bêng è, 東方明矣 *tang heng bêng kwuing*, the east is clear and bright; see the 齊風 Chêy hong.

Tang 菄 Read tong: the name of a vegetable; tong hong ch'haè, 菄風菜 *tang pooing ch'haè*, a certain plant.

Tang 冬 Read tong: the winter; tong t'hëen, 冬天 *tang t'heeng*, the winter season. Tong gîm pék swat se, 冬吟白雪時 *tang t'heeng gîm păyh săyh se*, in the winter we sing the white snow ode.

Tang 棠 Read tong: as kaou tong, 膠棠 *ka tang*, a certain wood.

Tang 瑠 Teng tong, 玎瑠 *tin tang*, the sound of tinkling gems.

Tang 蹚 Tang chëak, 蹚着 *tang tëŏk*, to strike the foot against anything, to kick.

上 *Táng* 党 Táng som, 党參, a kind of ginseng.

Táng 董 Read tóng: a surname.

Táng 陡 Read toé: a bar, a dam; toé bûn, 陡門 *táng mooing*, a water gate.

去 *Tàng* 凍 Read tòng: ice; këen tòng, 堅凍 *këen tàng*, to freeze. Bêng tong têy sé tòng, 孟冬地始凍 *bêng tang têy k'hé t'haôu këen tàng*, in the first month of winter, the ground begins to be frozen; see the 禮月令 Léy gwàt lēng.

Tàng 儅 P'hwān tòng, 伴儅 *p'hwnā tàng*, a lad, a companion.

Tàng 檔 Read tòng: a cross piece of wood; bûn tòng, 門檔 *mooing tàng*, the threshold of a door.

平 *Tâng* 同 Read tông: the same; alike; sëang tông, 相同 *sëo tâng*, together with, at the same time; to unite. Tông sim hëëp lèk, 同心協力 *tâng sim hëëp làt*, with united hearts, and collected strength.

Tâng 筒 Read tông: the name of a bamboo; tëuk tông, 竹筒 *tek tâng*, a bamboo tube or pipe.

Tâng 童 Read tông: a boy; tông choó, 童子 *tâng kënά*, a servant boy.

Tâng 銅 Read tông: brass; pèk tông, 白銅 *pàyh tâng*, white copper.

Tâng 髖 Read tông: a bone; këak tông kwut, 脚髖骨 *k'ha tâng kwut*, the shin bone.

去 *Tāng* 動 Read tōng: to move; motion; *tin tāng*, to set in motion. Tè chëá tōng, jîn chëá chēng, 知者動仁者靜 *woō tè, ây lāng tin tāng woō jîn ây lāng chēng chēng*, men of knowledge are always in motion, but men of benevolence remain at rest; see the 論語 Lūn gé.

Tāng 重 Read tëūng: heavy, not light, weighty. Bút sìm tëūng, 物甚重 *mcëngh sìm tāng*, the article is very heavy.

福建方言字典

Tāng 甋 *Yùng tāng*, 甕甋, a kind of jar.

Tāng 洞 Read tōng: a cave; koé tōng, 古洞 *koé tāng*, an ancient cave; sèk tōng, 石洞 *chëŏh tāng*, a rocky cavern.

卒 Taou 兜 Taou maôu, 兜鍪, a helmet.

Taou 撧 To rub, to take in the hand.

声 *Taóu* 斗 Read toé: a measure of a peck, a gomtang. One of the radicals. Toé soe chc jîn, hô chëuk swàn yëá? 斗筲之人何足筭也 *taóu soe ây lâng, an chwⁿá kaōu swuiⁿᵍ?* fellows whose understandings are equal only to a peck or a pint, what is the use of thinking of them? see the 論語 Lūn gé.

Taóu 抖 Read toé: to stir up, to rouse up; toé soé, 抖擻 *taóu saóu*, to rouse one's self up.

去 *Taòu* 午 Read gnoé: noon; jit gnoé, 日午 *jit taòu*, noontide; sëāng gnoé, 上午 *tëng taòu*, forenoon; hāy gnoé, 下午 *āy taòu*, afternoon.

Taòu 鬬 Read toè: to fight; sëang toè, 相鬬 *sëo taòu*, to wrangle together, to quarrel one with another.

平 *Taôu* 投 Read toê: to throw, to cast, to cast one's self on another's protection. P'hun toê, 奔投 *p'hun taôu*, to flee away, to escape: toê kwun, 投軍 *taôu kwun*, to enter the army; toê hëet, 投歇 *taôu haiⁿᵍh*, to seek a lodging; toê soê, 投詞 *taôu lâng ây wā*, to make a complaint to any one.

Taôu 骰 Read toê: dice, used in gambling; pwàt toê, 拔骰 *pwăh taôu á*, to play with dice.

丟 *Taōu* 荳 Read toē: pulse, beans; oe toē, 烏荳 *oe taōu*, black beans: lëûk toē, 綠荳 *lèk taōu*, green grain; pèk toē, 白荳 *pāyh taōu*, white beans; t'hoé toē, 土荳 *t'hoé taōu*, earth nuts, Manila gram.

Taōu 脰 Read toē: the neck; léng toē, 頜脰 *nëⁿá taōu*, the nape of the neck.

Taōu 讀 Read toē: a sentence; hⁿó kè toē, 好句讀 *hó koò taōu*, a good style.

夫 Tap 答 A wicker basket for weighing articles in; to reply, to answer; to correspond to; to remunerate. Also written 荅, tap. Hoo choó put tap, 夫子不答 *hoo choó bô yìn*, Confucius did not answer; see the 論語 Lūn gé. Tap sëà, 答謝, to repay with gratitude; pò tap, 報答, to remunerate.

Tap 褡 Torn clothes, ragged garments.

Tap 搭 To lean against, to hang upon; vulg. *tăh:* to intrust to.

Tap 嗒 To talk together, to converse with any one. Chun tap pöëy cheng, 噂嗒背憎 *kap lâng kóng wā, yēw k'ha chëăh aôu wân e*, to converse familiarly with people, and yet to abhor them behind their backs.

Tap 傛 To run suddenly against any one.

夊 Tȧp 偺 Sip tȧp, 偡偺, not to undertake any business.

Tȧp 沓 To repeat, to reiterate; to debase, to degrade.

Tȧp 踏 Valg. *tăh:* to tread; këak tȧp tēy, 脚踏地 *k'ha tăh tëŏh tēy,* to tread on the ground with one's feet; to stamp on the ground.

Tȧp 蹋 To tread, to kick; tȧp këuk, 蹋踘 *tăh k'ha hḗw,* to kick a football.

Tȧp 讋 To speak fast; to talk incessantly.

Tȧp 遝 To walk and stand.

Tȧp 譅 To speak disorderly.

犬 Tat 妲 Tat ké, 妲己, the name of an infamous woman, the concubine of 紂王, Tēw ông.

Tat 噠 Ap tat, 啞噠, the name of a foreign country to the west.

夊 Tȧt 達 T'hong tȧt, 通達, to understand, thoroughly intelligent.

Yêw yëá tȧt, ê chëûng chèng hoē hô yéw! 由也達於從政乎何有 *Yêw yëá t'hong tȧt, tē chëûng chèng soō woō sⁿá meēⁿᵍh ŏh!* Yêw is intelligent, but in attending to the business of government what difficulty would he find! see the 論語 Lūn gé.

Tȧt 蓬 The name of a plant.

Tȧt 值 Read tē: to be worth; tē chëên, 值錢 *tȧt cheēⁿᵍ,* worth money. Ch'hoó bůt tē ké to chëên? 此物值幾多錢 *chéy lēy meēⁿᵍh tȧt jwā chēy cheēⁿᵍ?* how much is this thing worth?

Tȧt 鰣 The name of a fish.

卓 Tay 臭 A kind of confectionary; bėk tay, 麥臭 *băyh tay,* a preparation of burnt wheat and treacle.

虛 Táy 奓 To exalt one's self; to look big.

Táy 短 Read twán: short; twán bēng, 短命 *táy mēⁿā,* shortlived.

Táy 鮓 The name of a fish.

去 *Tày* 笮 Tek chéw, 笮酒 *tày chéw,* a press for making wine.

Tày 退 Read t'hòëy: to retire; t'hòëy hoē, 退後 *tày aōu,* to retire backwards.

平 *Tây* 茶 Tea; sit tây, 食茶 *chëăh tây,* to drink tea.

Hân yëā k'hek laê tây tong chéw, 寒夜客來茶當酒 *kwⁿâ maiⁿᵍ lâng k'hăyh laê, tây teⁿᵍ chò chéw,* when a stranger arrives on a cold night, tea may be served for wine.

福建方言字典

Tây 炱 A kind of confectionary; mwⁿâ tây, 麻炱, hemp seeds and treacle mixed up together; toē tây, 豆炱 *taōu tây*, a like preparation, made of pulse and treacle.

Tāy 袋 Read taē: a sack; poè taē, 布袋 *poè tāy á*, a bag.

Tāy 代 Read taē: a generation; sè taē, 世代 *sè tāy*, an age; teâou taē, 朝代 *teâou tāy*, a dynasty.

Tǎyh 壓 Read ap: to press down, to crush, to squeeze by falling down upon. E kō yéw hok ap che sëang, 予懼有覆壓之傷 *gwá kēⁿa woō tǎyh lǎyh ây sëang*, I am afraid lest there should be some evil arise from being too heavily pressed upon; see the 左傳 Chó twān.

Tǎyh 簀 Read chek: a bamboo frame work, put upon a bedstead to sustain the matress; ch'hông chek, 床簀 *ch'hêⁿᵍ tǎyh*, the bottom of a bedstead.

Tǎyh 啄 Read tok: to peck at anything, like a fowl.

Tǎyh 汐 Read sëk: low water; súy sék, 水汐 *chúy tǎyh*, the ebb of the tide. The morning tide is called teâou, 潮 *teô*, and the evening one sék, 汐 *tǎyh*.

Tǎyh 汮 The same as the above.

Tǎyh 艀 Tǎyh béng, 艀艋, a small boat or vessel; also written 舠, tǎyh.

Tǎyh 奪 Read twát: to take anything, to snatch, to take away.

Te 邾 The name of a country.

Te 姝 Handsome, beautiful.

Te 株 The roots of trees, which appear above the ground.

Te 誅 To reprove, to blame; to kill, to slay.

E ê é hô te? 於予與何誅, "with respect to E, what is the use of reproving him?" said by Confucius of 宰予, Chaé-ê, one of his disciples whom he found sleeping in the day-time; see the 上論 Sëāng lūn.

Sùn te soò hëung, 舜誅四凶 *Sùn t'haê sè ây hëung p'haⁿé*, Sùn put to death the four miscreants; see the 史記 Soó kè.

Te 知 Vulg. *chae*: to know, to be acquainted with; put te, 不知 *ūⁱⁿ chae*, I don't know.

Soò sëen te kak hoē te, 使先知覺後知 *saé taē seng chae ây lâng kak goē tùy aōu chae ây lâng*, it was ordered that those who became first acquainted with things, should awaken those who came latest to the knowledge of them; see 孟子 Bēng choó.

Te che chin, hêng che lék, 知之眞行之力, knowing the truth, practice it strenuously.

Te hoó, 知府, the magistrate of a hoó district.

Te 蜘 Te too, 蜘蛛 *la gëâ*, a spider; te too se, 蜘蛛絲 *la gëâ se*, a spider's web.

7 L

Te 猪 A pig; te jëúk, 猪肉 *te bàh*, pork; sat te, 殺猪 *t'haé te*, to kill pigs.

Te 豬 The same as the preceding.

Té 氐 To arrive at, to attain to; the root, the original.

Té 抵 To push, to come in contact with, to proceed towards, to bear.
Té tong put chē, 抵當不住 *té te^{ng} bēy twā*, unable to withstand.
Sëang jin kip tō té chöëy, 傷人及盜抵罪 *sëang haē lâng kap chò ch'hat te^{ng} e ây chöëy*, those who injure people and steal must bear their sin; see the 高祖記 Ko choé kè.

Té 底 Vulg. *téy:* the bottom of anything; hāy té, 下底 *āy téy*, below.
San téng haé té, 山頂海底 *sw^{n}a téng haé téy*, the tops of the hills, and the bottom of the sea.

Té 厎 A grinding stone; the same as 砥 té.

Té 呧 To rail at; o té, 呵呧, to scold, to blame.

Té 弤 The name of a bow, belonging to the emperor 舜, Sùn.
K'hîm tìm, té tìm, 琴朕弤朕 *k'hîm chò gwá ây, këung chò gwá ây*, his harp shall be mine, and his bow mine; see 孟子 Bēng choó.

Té 軧 The back part of a large carriage.

Té 邸 A shed, a cottage, a lodge; chè té jê gē, 至邸而議 *kaòu té sëà chëā laé soō nëô^{ng}*, when we come to the lodge, we will consult about it; see the 漢文帝紀 Hàn bûn tèy ké.

Té 詆 To rail at, to revile; té hwúy sèng hëên, 詆誹聖賢 *té hwúy sèng jîn gaôu lâng*, to rail at and abuse sages and wise men.
Ch'héw té, 醜詆, malicious slanders.

Té 砥 A grinding stone; even, plain.
Chew tō jê té, 周道如砥 *Chew tō ây loē pai^{ng} ch'hin chëô^{ng} to chëŏh*, the roads of Chew were as level as a grinding stone; see the 小雅 Seáou gnáy.
Té lēy, 砥礪, a stone on which to grind tools, metaphorically, to correct vicious conduct.

Té 觝 To come in contact, to contend with, to oppose.
Té paê ē twan, 觝排異端 *té paê kŏh yëô^{ng} ây tō lé*, to contend against and expose strange doctrines.

Té 祇 Even, unto, only.

Té 搋 The same as 抵, té.

Té 傂 Ch'haê té, 偨傂, uneven, unequal.

Té 豸 The name of an insect; one of the radicals; insects with feet are called 虫, t'hëûng, and without feet, 豸, té.

Té 黹 An embroidered garment; one of the radicals.

去

Tè **致** To extend to; to cause, to occasion; the uttermost, superlative.

Tè te chaē kek bu̍t, 致知在格物 *tè lán ây te sit chaē kek t'hong ta̍k hāng ây meēngh*, the utmost extent of knowledge consists in fully comprehending things; see the 大學 Taē ha̍k.

Tè **緻** Secret, close; closely woven cloth.

Tè **智** Wisdom; tè hwūy, 智慧, wisdom and intelligence.

Jîn gē léy tè sìn, 仁義禮智信, benevolence, righteousness, propriety, wisdom, and truth; the five cardinal virtues, according to the Chinese.

Tè **知** Wise, knowing; tè cheá lo̍k, jîn cheá sēw, 知者樂仁者壽 *woō tè hwūy ây lâng t'hëúng lo̍k, woō jîn ây lâng têng hōëy sēw*, wise men are joyful, but benevolent men longlived; see the 論語 Lūn gé.

Tè **貿** To deposit money as a pledge.

Tè **置** To place, to establish, to set up, to set aside.

Ong tè choo kê chó yēw, 王置諸共左右 *ông hāy tè e ây chó yēw*, the king places them on his left and right.

Hwùy tè, 廢置, to set aside; an tè, 安置, to place securely; këèn tè, 建置, to establish, to build.

Tè **寘** To set aside; sūy tè Këang-sē ê Sêng-éng, 遂寘姜氏於城潁 *sūy tè hwùy Këang-sē tè Sêng-éng*, he therefore set aside Këang-sē and removed her to Sêng-éng; see the 左傳 Chó twān.

Tè **觶** A wine cup, made of a rhinoceros' horn.

Chun cheá ké tè, 尊者舉觶 *chun ây lâng këàh k'hé chëw poey*, the honorable people raise the cup of wine; see the 禮記 Léy kè.

Tè **著** To set forth, to display, to make clear.

Hêng chek tè, 形則著 *hêng yëōng chëw tè hëèn*, the substance of a thing is displayed; see the 中庸 Tëung yûng.

Tè bêng, 著明, to illustrate clearly; tè chok, 著作 to manifest.

平

Tê **池** A pool, a pond; súy tê, 水池, a sheet of water. A surname.

Choó-sán soò haōu jîn hëuk che tê, 子產使校人畜之池 *Choó-sán saē haōu jîn ch'hē e tē chúy tê*, Choó-sán ordered an inferior officer to keep the live fish in the pool; see 孟子 Bēng choó.

Tê **馳** To gallop; tê má, 馳馬 *chaôu báy*, to gallop on horseback.

Hⁿò tê má sè këèm, 好馳馬試劍 *aè chaôu báy ch'hè këèm*, I love to gallop on horseback, and brandish my sword; see 孟子 Bēng choó.

Tê **訑** The appearance of one rejecting and discarding people; to oppose, to withstand.

Tê **傂** A wheel, to revolve; a bustling martial appearance.

Tê **篪** A musical instrument.

Pek sē ch'huy hwun, tëūng sē ch'huy tê, 伯氏吹塤仲氏吹篪 *twā hēⁿa ch'hōey hwun, sëo tē ch'hōey tê*, the elder brethren blew an instrument made of earthen ware, and the younger brethren one of bamboo; see the 小雅 Seáou gnáy.

Tê **虒** A tiger with horns.

Tê **僁** Lêng tê, 夌僁, to kill gradually by cutting into small pieces.

Tê **墀** A step; stairs; tan tê, 丹墀, the vermilion steps, used with regard to the steps of the imperial throne.

Tê **遲** Slow, leisurely, long; late; t'haè tê, 太遲, too late.

K'hóng-choô che k'hè Loé, wát, tê tê goê hêng yëá; 孔子之去魯曰遲遲吾行也 *K'hóng-choó ây k'hè Loé kok, kóng, k'hwⁿa k'hwⁿa á gwá kēⁿâ*, when Confucius left the Loé country, he said, "let us go as slowly as possible;" see 孟子 Bēng choó.

Tê **儲** To assist, to second; the heir apparent to a princedom is called 儲君, tê kwun. Also, to store up, to stow away.

Tê chek gnoé kok, 儲積五穀 *k'hëöh lëöh gnoé kok*, to collect the various kinds of grain.

A surname.

Tê **徲** To walk, to travel.

Tê **踟** Tê toô, 踟蹰, to walk backwards and forwards, in a hesitating way.

So séw tê toô, 搔首踟蹰 *so t'haôu kak tè toô*, he scratched his head, and paced up and down; see the 衛風 Wöëy hong.

Tê **滁** The name of a district.

Tê **除** Steps, stairs; to exclude, to abolish; to deduct, to except.

Gëúk tê tan têng, 玉除丹庭 *gëúk ây gîm kay êng ây tēⁿâ*, pearly steps and a vermilion hall; see the 西都賦 Sey toe hoō.

Tê ok boō pún, 除惡務本 *tê k'hè p'haⁿé boō kin pún*, to exclude that which is evil, and to attend to the most essential thing; see the 書泰誓 Se t'haè sē.

Tê **篨** Kè tê, 籧篨, a bamboo mat; an ugly appearance.

Tê **泜** To stop, to stay.

Tê **坻** A small island, or rising ground in the middle of a sheet of water.

Tê **胝** A fleshy excrescence; an induration of the skin.

Tê **蚳** Ant's eggs; small ants.

Tê **治** Regulated, well arranged, peaceful.

Tê **乿** The same as the above.

Tê **持** Vulg. *gîm*: to hold, to grasp; to attend to; tê këung, 持弓, to hold the bow.

Tê séw taē gëëm, 持守大嚴, to hold fast with too great severity.

Tê **躇** Têw tê, 躊躇, to hesitate, to walk backwards and forwards.

Tē 劕 Lêng tê, 㚘劕, to kill by cutting into small pieces.

丟
Tē 治 To regulate, to govern, to bring into order.
Kay chêy jê hoē tē kok, 家齊而後治國 kay chéy jëên aōu ēy tē kok, when a man's family is well managed, then he may regulate a country; see the 大學 Taē hak.

Tē 乿 The same as the preceding.

Tē 値 To meet with, to come in contact with, to hold.
Vulg. tàt: to be worth; tē chêên, 値錢 tàt cheeng, to be worth money.

Tē 待 To wait for; to hoard; to prepare.

Tē 偫 To prepare, to provide for.

Tē 賘 To hoard up, to store up; also written 畤, tē.

Tē 痔 Tē ch'hong, 痔瘡 tē ch'heng, an ulcer.
P'hé hoo, seáou chek wún yung chè tē; taō chek sè hoō sé kwun, 鄙夫小則吮癰舐痔大則弑父弑君 p'heeng hoo ây lâng sèy chek sŏh yung, chē ch'heng; twā chek t'haê pūy t'haê kwun, low vulgar fellows who are such only in a small degree will suck ulcers and lick sores (for gain); and those who are such in a greater degree, will kill their parents or princes (for profit); see the 朱註 Choo choō.

Tē 畤 A rising ground; also, to store up.

Tē 傲 To understand or comprehend things.

Tē 雉 A wild fowl; tē key, 雉鷄 t'hê key, a jungle fowl.
San lëâng ch'hê tē, 山梁雌雉 swⁿa nëëng t'hê key boê, a mountain bridge, and a jungle hen; see the 論語 Lūn gé.
Sêng tē, 城雉, the fortifications of a city.

Tē 薙 To clear away grass and weeds; to falling off of the hair.
Kwùy hāy seaou tē hêng súy, 季夏燒薙行水 kwùy hāy tëŏh sëo ch'haou, këⁿá chúy, in the latter month of summer burn the weeds and clear away the grass, in order to open passages for the water.

Tē 稚 Small, young, lately born; also written 稺, tē; and 穉, tē.
Tē choó k'hëen e, 稚子牽衣 sèy kiⁿá k'han sⁿa, the children come pulling one's clothes; see the 陶潛文 Tō chëem bûn.

Tē 滯 To congeal; to freeze; to proceed slowly.

Tē 𤸊 A long standing dysentery.

Tē 箸 Chopsticks; the two small pieces of wood or bamboo, with which the Chinese take up their food.
Ch'héng chëā tē jê tîn, 請借箸而陳 ch'hëⁿá chëŏh tē jê tìn bêng, "just lend me your chopsticks, and I will point it out to you;" said by

a general to his prince, when discoursing on the drawing up of an army: see the 史記 Soò kè.

Tē 觔 The same as the preceding.

Tē 豩 A pig; key tun koé tē, 雞豚狗豩 *key te kaóu kap te á*, fowls, pigs, dogs, and little pigs; (articles of food among the Chinese;) see 孟子 Bēng choò.

Tëa 爹 Father; vulg. *ūⁿ tëa*: a familiar epithet for a father, something like our 'papa.'

Ló tëa, 老爹, a respectful term for the governor of a district.

Tëá 阤 A term used in incantation; also written 虵, tëá.

Tëà 瓞 A foreign word used in charms.

Tëā 吔 The same as the preceding.

Tëⁿa 敱 To run against, to run foul of; lwān tëⁿa, 亂敱, to run disorderly against any one.

Tëⁿa 朾 *Ka tëⁿa*, 筊朾, a certain wood, used for a dye.

Tëⁿá 鼎 Read téng: a pan for cooking or boiling anything, a caldron.

Lok yêw téng, 落油鼎 *lŏh yêw tëⁿá*, to make people descend into a caldron of boiling oil; an experiment sometimes employed to try the courage of daring fellows.

Tong téng, 當鼎 *teng tëⁿá*, properly established.

Tëⁿà 椗 Read tèng: an anchor; pā tèng, 罷椗 *p'hā tëⁿà*, to cast anchor.

Tëⁿâ 呈 Read têng: to represent anything to a superior.

Têng kò, 呈告 *tëⁿâ kò*, to inform, to announce.

Tëⁿâ 埕 Read têng: an arena, or paved yard, in front of a house, for the purpose of drying grain upon.

Tëⁿâ 程 Read têng: a road, a journey; k'hé têng, 起程 *k'hé tëⁿâ*, to commence a journey.

Ch'heng têng bān lé, 青程萬里 *ch'haiⁿᵍ tëⁿâ bān lé*, to pass over green roads to the distance of a myriad of miles; (speaking of the flight of a bird, and alluding to the rapid strides which some scholars make to the highest literary honors.)

Tëⁿâ 庭 Read têng: a hall, a court; a passage. Lé ch'he jê kò têng, 鯉趨而過庭 *Lé maiⁿᵍh këⁿâ jê kòey tëⁿâ*, Lé walked quickly and passed across the hall; see the 論語 Lūn gé.

Tëⁿā 定 Read tēng: fixed, settled, quiet, tranquil, composed.

T'hëen hāy pêng tēng, 天下平定 *t'heeⁿᵍ āy patⁿᵍ tëⁿā*, the empire is quiet and settled.

Tēng chëak, 定着 *tëⁿā tëŏh*, fixed, decided.

Chò tēng, 做定 *chò tëⁿā*, to give an earnest, or pledge.

Tëⁿā 錠 Read tēng: a block, a log; kim tēng gîn tēng, 金錠銀錠 *kim tëⁿā gîn tëⁿā*, blocks of gold or silver.

Ch'hwân tēng, 船錠 *chûn tëⁿā*, an anchor.

大
Teăh 摘 Rea... t... pluck, pick, or gather. T..k h... 摘花 *teăh hwa,* to ...ach... ...ers.

Tek ok, 摘屋 ..., to pull down a house.

天
Teăh 糴 R... ...uy rice or grain; tek bé, 糴米 *teăh bé,* to buy rice; t'heaou bé, 糶米 *t'hèò bé,* to sell rice.

Boô at tek, 無遏糴 *bô at chwăt teăh bé,* do not restrain the buying of rice (by neighboring states); see 孟子 Bēng choó.

卒
Teang 張 K'hwa teang, 夸張 *k'hwa teōng,* to boast; k'hae teang, 開張 *k'hwuy teōng,* to open, to spread out; choó teang, 主張 to superintend. A surname; a numeral of things flat and extended.

Sûy teang pit k'hè seáou kok, 隨張必棄小國 *Sûy kok choō teōng, pit k'hè sèy kok,* the Sûy country is vain and boasting, and will certainly despise inferior countries; see the 左傳 Chó twān.

He teang seng sè, 虛張聲勢 *he teōng sèna sè,* vainly to exhibit one's fame and influence; to make a vain show.

声
Teáng 仗 A military weapon, warlike instruments in general.

Teáng 長 Superior to another, in rank, influence, or age.

Teáng yèw po chun, 長幼卑尊 *laōu, seáou lëën, pe hāy, chun kwùy,* old and young, base and honorable; see 孟子 Bēng choó.

Seng teáng, 生長 *saing twā,* to grow up to maturity.

去
Teàng 脹 Vulg. *tèòng:* to swell; hok teàng, 腹脹 *pak toé tèòng,* a swelling of the belly.

Teàng 帳 Vulg. *tèòng:* a tent, a curtain; vulg. *seàou:* an account, a reckoning. Wûy teàng, 帷帳 *wûy tèòng,* the curtain of a tent.

Swàn teàng, 算帳 *swuing seàou,* to cast up accounts.

Teàng 瘬 Full, swollen; teàng bwán pēng, 瘬滿病 *tèòng mwŏá paing,* a swollen, bloated state of body.

Teàng 漲 Vulg. *tèòng:* to rise as the tide; súy teàng, 水漲 *chúy tèòng,* the rising of the waters an inundation.

Teàng 韔 The case for a bow.

Teàng 悵 Teaou teàng, 惆悵, disappointed, vexed.

平
Teâng 長 Vulg. *têng:* long, not short; teâng kéw, 長久 *têng koô,* a long time.

Tòk jëên hoē te teâng twán, 度然後知長短 *nèòng tòk, jëën aōu ëy chaę e ây têng tëy,* measure, and then you may know the long and short of a thing; see 孟子 Bēng choó.

Teâng 萇 The name of a certain fruit.

玉
Teāng 丈 Vulg. *têng:* a measure of ten feet; ló teāng, 老丈, an old man; teāng hoo, 丈夫, a husband; taē teāng hoo, 大丈夫, a great man.

Teāng 杖 A staff, a walking stick.

E teāng k'hoè kë kēng, 以杖叩其脛 *t'hó kwaë á k'haôu e ây k'hà kwut,* he smote him across the shins with his staff; see the 論語 Lūn gé.

Tëāng **長** To measure the length of anything; to exceed, to surpass.

Pit yéw ch'hím e, tëâng yit sin yéw pwàn, 必有寢衣長一身有半 *pit woō k'hùn ây s^{n}a, k'hăh tê^{ng} chit sin woō pw^{n}à*, he would have a sleeping dress half as long again as his body; said of Confucius in the 論語 Lūn gé.

Tëāng sun, 長孫, a double surname.

Tëāng **仗** To rely upon; é teāng, 倚仗, to confide in.

Kīn sîn é put chëuk tëāng è, 近臣已不足仗矣 *kīn ây jîn sîn, é keng bô kadu e wá*, my near attendants are not to be depended upon; see the 李尋傳 Lé sîm twān.

𡗗

Teaou **朝** The morning, the early part of the day; teaou sék, 朝夕 *chá k'hé mat^{ng} hwui^{ng}*, morning and evening.

Ong-hwan teaou boē hëèn, 王驩朝暮見 *Ong-hwan chá k'hé mat^{ng} hwui^{ng} sëo kê^{ng}*, Ong-hwan came into his presence morning and evening, (but Bēng-choo would not speak to him;) see 孟子 Bēng choó.

Teaou **彫** To cut, to engrave; also to drop the leaves, as a tree in autumn.

Teaou k'hek chëùng hêng, jê put wûy k'haòu, 彫刻衆形而不爲巧 *teaou k'hek chëùng yëō^{ng}, jê bô swui^{ng} chò k'há*, "to engrave and carve all sorts of shapes is not to be considered a proof of skill;" said by 莊子 Chong-choó.

Söèy hân, jëên hoē te sëûng pek che hoē teaou yëá, 歲寒然後知松柏之後彫也 *nee^{ng} höèy kw^{n}â, jëên aōu chae ch'hêng păyh ây tùy aōu teaou lôh*, when the cold season of the year comes on, then we perceive the cedar and fir trees casting their leaves; see the 論語 Lūn gé.

Teaou **凋** To be partly injured; teaou lók, 凋落, to drop the leaves.

Teaou **鵰** A ferocious bird, of whose feathers the wings of arrows may be made.

Teaou **琱** To work gems, to cut and polish precious stones.

Teaou **雕** To cut, to carve, to engrave.

Héw bók put k'hó teaou yëá, 朽木不可雕也 *nw^{n}â ch'hâ bô t'hang teaou k'hek*, porous wood cannot be engraved upon.

Teaou **貂** A species of squirrel or martin; teaou ch'hé, 貂鼠, the martin.

The skin of this animal is said to be such a defense against the dew, that a person wearing a dress made of them may safely sleep in the open air, and the dew will not fall within a yard of him.

The animal itself is said to be of a nature so kindly, that on seeing persons without clothes in the winter, it will creep into their bosoms to warm them; in this way it is sometimes caught, and such a bad return for kindness is considered so abominable, that ungrateful people are sometimes called "martin catchers." Also written 鼦, teaou.

Teaou **刁** Utensils for holding rice used in the army.

Teaou **鳭** Teaou leâou, 鳭鷯, a small kind of bird.

Teaou **鳥** An unfilial bird, which eats its mother.

上

Teáou 儋 Teáou t'heáou, 儋佻, light and vain.

Teáou 科 The ears of corn hanging down.

Teáou 帗 Teáou se, 帗纚, an ornamental kerchief for the head.

Teáou 㑩 To stand alone.

去

Teàou 弔 To condole with persons on the decease of a relative; teàou song, 弔喪, to mourn for the dead; to be grieved, to lament.

Te seng cheá teàou, te soó cheá sëang, 知生者弔知死者傷 *chae hwut lëy wăh ây lâng tëŏh teàou maē, chae sé ây lâng tëŏh sëang sim*, if we are acquainted with the survivors, we should condole with them; and if with the dead, we should be grieved for them; see the 曲禮 K'hëuk léy.

Also written 吊, teàou.

Teàou 佣 Teàou tòng, 佣儻, uncommon, unusual.

Teàou 綿 To hang up, to suspend; teàou soó, 綿死 *teàou sé*, to put to death by hanging; *jēĕh teàou*, to strangle.

Teàou 釣 Vulg.. *tëò*: to angle; teàou gê, 釣魚 *tëò hê*, to angle for fish.

Choó teàou jê put kong, 子釣而不綱 *hoo choó tëò hê jê bô böëyh t'hó bāng lëăh*, Confucius used to angle for fish, but would not employ a net for capturing them; see the 論語 Lūn gé.

Teàóu 窵 Teâou beâou, 窵窅, deep, abstruse; also, the name of a bird.

Teàou 瘹 Madness; also, a sickness incident to children.

平

Teâou 條 A small twig, a branch; a line, a string; teâou bók, 條目 *teâou bák*, a list; teâou këēn, 條件 *teâou këⁿā*, an item.

Hwát kê teâou böêy, 伐其條枚 *hwát c ây ke kwⁿa*, cut down the branches and stem; see the 周南 Chew lâm.

Teâou 鰷 The name of a fish.

Teâou 鞗 A leathern bridle.

Teâou 苕 The name of a flower.

Teâou 岧 A high hill; a lofty appearance.

Teâou 笤 Teâou chéw, 笤箒, a broom.

Teâou 迢 Distant and unattainable; teâou teâou, 迢迢, lofty.

Teâou 髫 The hair of children hanging down.

Teâou hwát lëy chè, 髫髮厲志 *teâou suy t'haôu mô ây woō bëēn lëy sim chè*, from the time that the hair hangs down (in youth), to have the mind roused to action.

Teâou 齠 The shedding of the teeth.
'Lâm choó pat gwăt seng ch'hé, pat söèy teâou ch'hé, 男子八月生齒八歲齠齒 *ta po kĕⁿá păyh göĕyh saiⁿᵍ ch'hùy k'hé, păyh hōèy laōu ch'hùy k'hé*, a boy at eight months gets his teeth, and at eight years loses them.

Teâou 潮 Vulg. *tĕŏ*: the tide; haé teâou, 海潮 *haé tĕŏ*, the tide of the sea, which the Chinese ascribe to the breathing and panting of the earth.

Teâou 朝 A court, a hall of audience, a court of justice.
Teâou é hāy taē hoo gân, k'hán k'hán jê yĕá, 朝與下大夫言侃侃如也 *tē teâou têng laē, kap hāy taē hoo kóng wā, chēw kong tit ây yĕōⁿᵍ*, Confucius, when at court, in speaking with the inferior officers, observed a stiff and straight forward manner; see the 論語 Lūn gé. Teâou ông, 朝王, to have an audience with the king.

Teâou 蜩 A kind of insect, which begins to make a noise in the 5th month.

Teâou 調 To unite, to amalgamate, to accord, to harmonize.

Teâou 椆 The name of a tree.

Teâou 佻 The appearance of walking alone.

玊
Teâou 召 To call, to summon, to send for by authority.
Kwun bēng teâou, put soō kāy hêng è, 君命召不俟駕行矣 *jîn kwun bēng lēng kĕò lán, ūᵐ saē têng haōu báy ch'hĕa jê kĕⁿá*, when a prince's order comes to call us, we must not wait for our carriage to be harnessed, but go immediately; see the 論語 Lūn gé.

Teāou 兆 A prognostic, an omen, a presage; also, a hundred thousand.
T'haè pok chëáng sam teāou che hwat, 太卜掌三兆之法 *t'haè pok ây kwⁿa tëŏh chëáng kwán sⁿa hō teāou soō ây hwat toē*, the great augurer should attend to the laws of the three methods of prognostication; see the 周禮 Chew lĕy.

Teāou 銚 A cooking vessel; a small pan with a handle.

Teāou 趙 Vulg. *tēŏ*: a surname.

Teāou 旐 A flag ornamented with tortoises and serpents.

Teāou 晁 A surname.

Teāou 鼂 A surname; the same as the above.

Teāou 駣 A horse nearly three year's old.

Teāou 肇 A commencement, to commence, to begin.
T'haè ông teāou ke ông chek, 太王肇基王迹 *T'haè ông k'hé t'haōu ch'hông ông ây chĕăh*, T'haè ông first laid the foundation of the traces of royalty in his family.

Teāou 肈 The same as the above; also a kind of spear.

夬 Teĕh 滴 Read tek: to drop, to drip; a drop. E tek kae hāy, 雨滴階下 *hoē teĕh gîm kay āy*, the rain falls in drops on the steps.

Yit tek súy, 一滴水 *chit teĕh chúy*, a drop of water; tek lók, 滴落 *teĕh lŏh*, to drop down.

夾 Teĕh 碟 Read tëëp: a plate; pwân tëëp, 盤碟 *pwⁿâ teĕh*, plates and dishes.

卓 Tëem 沾 To moisten, to tinge, to receive a tinge; tëem tëem, 沾沾, light and thin, trifling. Tëem yin, 沾恩, to receive favors.

Hān ch'hut tëem pōèy, 汗出沾背 *kwⁿā ch'hut bàk tëŏh k'ha chëăh*, the perspiration issued out till it moistened his back.

Tëem 佔 Tëem taōu, 佔佤, light and trifling.

Tëem 霑 To be wet in the rain; é tëem hòk, 雨霑服 *hoē ak tëŏh yìn chëōⁿᵍ*, the rain wet his clothes.

声 Tëém 點 A dot, a spot, a speck, to point anything; yéw tëém, 有點 *woō tëém*, dotted, speckled.

Këém tëém jit séy wûy, 檢點日所爲 *këém tëém tàk jit séy chò*, to make a memorandum of every day's proceedings.

Tëém se, 點書 *tëém ch'hăyh*, to dot a book, to punctuate it.

圭 Tëèm 店 A shop, a place for depositing and disposing of goods.

K'hae tëèm, 開店 *k'hwuy tëèm*, to open a shop. Also written 佔, tëèm.

Chéw tëèm, 酒店, a tavern, where spirits and provisions are sold.

Tëèm 覘 To spy, to peep; kong soò jîn tëèm che, 公使人覘之 *kong saé lâng tëèm k'hwⁿà e*, the chief sent some emissaries to spy and observe him; see the 左傳 Chó twān.

Tëèm 玷 A flaw in a gem. Pék kwuy che tëèm, sëāng k'hó mô yëá, 白圭之玷尚可磨也 *păyh kwuy ây tëèm, sëāng t'hang bwâ*, the flaw in a white gem may yet be rubbed down, (but flaws in discourse cannot be remedied;) see the 大雅 T'haè gnáy.

Tëèm 坫 A screen, an earthen stand between two pillars.

Pang kwun wûy lëáng kwun che hⁿó yéw hwán tëèm, 邦君爲两君之好有反坫 *pang kwun wûy nō ây jîn kwun sëo hó woō hwán tëèm*, the prince of a country, on occasion of the friendly meeting of two princes, inverts the wine cup on the earthen stand; see the 上論 Sëāng lūn.

Tëèm 墊 To sink, to drown; é tëèm, 椅墊, a chair cushion.

Tëèm 㡇 A house overturned.

平 Tëêm 恬 Peaceful, at rest, quiet.

E tëêm yáng chè, 以恬養志 *é an tëêm yáng sim chè*, "to feed one's mind by quiet retirement;" said by 莊子 Chong choó.

Tëêm 甜 Vulg. *teeⁿᵍ*: sweet, of a sweet taste; also written 恬, tëêm.

Swan tëêm choo bē, pek chëúng ch'heen bêng, 酸甜滋味百種千名 *swuiⁿᵍ teeⁿᵍ ây choo bē, woō chit păyh chëúng chit ch'heng mē^n ā*, sour and sweet tastes are of a hundred sorts and of a thousand names; see the 張衡賦 Tëang hêng hoè.

Tëëm 沉 Read tîm: to sink in the water. Hwàn hwàn yâng chew, chaè tîm chaè hoô, 汎汎楊舟載沉載浮 *hwàn hwàn ây yâng chûn, woō sê á tëëm woō sê á p'hoô*, the boat adrift upon the wide waters sometimes sinks and sometimes floats again; see the 小雅 Seáou gnây.

Tëëm 簟 A bamboo mat.

Tëëm 椰 The threshold of a door.

Tëëm 啖 To eat, to devour.

Tëen 顛 The top, a head; also to overturn, to upset; tëen tó, 顛倒, to be turned topsy-turvy.

Gwûy jê put tê, tëen jê put hoô, 危而不持顛而不扶 *gwûy hëëm jê bō tê gîm, tëen tó jê bō hoô k'hé*, in circumstances of danger, not to uphold any one, nor when overturned to raise them up; see the 論語 Lūn gé.

Tëen 傎 Tëen tó, 傎倒, turned upside down.

Tëen 巔 The summit of a hill.

Tëen 癲 Tëen kong, 癲狂, mad, out of one's senses, foolish.

To hé wûy tëen, to noē wûy kông, 多喜爲癲多怒爲狂 *sëō^ng chëy lwo^n a hé chë^n ā tëen, sëō^ng chëy sëw k'hè chë^n ā kông*, too much joy throws men into ecstasies, and excessive anger drives them mad.

Tëén 展 To turn round, to revolve; to open out, to spread abroad.

Tëén chwán hwán ch'hek, 展轉反側 *tëén chwán hwán pee^ng*, he turned round and round from side to side; see the 周南 Chew lâm.

Yéw soo tëén pē é kò, 有司展幣以告 *yéw soo ây kwo^n a tëén k'hwuy pē pek é kò*, the proper officer must display the offering of silk, in order to announce it; see the 儀禮 Gê léy.

Tëén 輾 To turn round; the same as the preceding.

Tëén 典 A lord, a master; to preside over anything; a record, a book.

Ch'hut keng jip tëén, 出經入典, out of one book into another; (i. e. to speak according to the classics.)

Joō tëén, 字典 *jē tëén*, a dictionary.

Tëên 田 Vulg. *ch'hân*: a field, a paddy field, arable land; a surname; also, to hunt.

Gno këet lek keng tëên, këûng wûy chóo chit jé é è, 我竭力耕田供爲子職而已矣 *gwá këet chīn k'hwùy làt chŏh ch'hân këung chò haōu sai^ng ây chit hwun të^n ā të^n ā*, I will exhaust my strength in ploughing the ground, and thus fulfill the duties of a child, without looking for anything further; see 孟子 Bēng chóo.

Tëên 佃 To cultivate the ground.

Tëên 鈿 Gold and flowery ornaments, for a lady's headdress.

福建方言字典

Tëen 畋 To take birds and beasts in hunting.

Tëen 廛 A place for selling goods; a shop, a stall in a market.
Tëĕn boŏ hoó lé che poè, 廛無夫里之布 *tëèm bŏ hoo lé ây poè*, shops should not pay the tax of a piece of cloth for every lé; see 孟子 Bēng choó.

Tëen 壥 The same as the preceding. Also written 廛, tëen.

Tëen 躔 To tread upon, to pass over.

Tëen 纏 To entwine, to wind round, to bind; tëĕn haĕ, 纏鞋 *teĕ^ng ây*, to stitch shoes.

Tëen 𢋈 Even, level, plain.

去
Tëen 殿 A hall; keung tëen, 宮殿, a palace; tëen hāy, 殿下 a crown-prince.
Tëûng tëen, 重殿, a palace with front and back suites of apartments.

Tëen 田 To plough, to cultivate the ground.
Tëĕn tĕw, 田疇, a cultivated field.

Tëen 佃 To hunt; tëĕn lâp, 佃獵, to go a hunting.
E tëĕn é gê, 以佃以漁 *é p'hăh lăh é lëăh hê*, to go a hunting and fishing; see the 易繫詞 Ek hēy soó.

Tëen 鈿 Gold and flowery ornaments, for a lady's headdress.

Tëen 甸 A district of a hundred lé, 里, is called 甸服, tëen hŏk.

Tëen 電 Vulg. *seĕh nā*: lightning; lûy tëen, 雷電, thunder and lightning.

Tëen 靛 A kind of plant that floats on the top of the water.

Tëen 奠 To sacrifice; tëen seen seng, 奠先聖 *chèy taĕ sèng jin*, to sacrifice to the former sages.
Tëen chéw, 奠酒, to pour out a libation.

上平
Tee^ng 甜 Read tëèm: sweet, of a sweet taste.

下平
Tee^ng 纏 Read tëĕn: to twist, to entwine.
Tëĕn sam, 纏衫 *teĕ^ng s^na*, to stitch a garment, to make raiment.

去
Tee^ng 淀 Full, to the brim.

上入
Tëep 輒 Suddenly; to turn round; also written 輙, tëep.

Tëep 尐 Small, very small, very little; tëep taē, 尐大 *tëep á twa*, very small, not very large; tëep kéw, 尐久 *tëep á koó*, a short space of time, not very long.

下入
Tëep 疊 Repeated, piled up; heaped one on another; to be alarmed.
Tëûng tëûng teep tëep, 重重疊疊, repeated again and again.
Lúy yëep pek tëep, 累葉百疊 *lúy hŏh păyh tëep*, a heap of leaves piled up by hundreds.

Tëëp 疊 The same as the preceding.

Tëëp 牒 A board for writing; the leaf of a book, a book, a document; an official order from an officer of government is called tëëp; a genealogical register; boards belonging to a bed.

Tëëp 蝶 Hoê tëëp, 蝴蝶 *höëy yëăh*, a butterfly.

Tëëp 諜 Kàn tëëp, 間諜, a spy.

Tëëp 渫 The connected appearance of waves; to abolish.

Tëëp 堞 A small parapet on a city wall; to fortify with a parapet.

Tëëp 蹀 To tread, to stamp; to walk.

Tëëp 喋 Verbose, to speak much.

Tëëp 氎 Cloth made of fine hair.

Tëëp 韘 A thumb ring used in archery.

Tëëp 惵 Peaceful, quiet.

大

Tëet 嚞 A man's name.

Tëet 哲 Clear, intelligent, wise; te che wat, bêng tëet, 知之曰明哲 *chae e kóng bêng tëet*, to know a thing is called intelligence.

Tëet 喆 Same as the preceding.

天

Tëet 佚 Tëet tëet, 佚佚, slowly.

Tëet 秩 Orderly, according to order, well arranged; an office. Also, to collect, an assemblage; a period of ten years in called 秩, tëet.

Tëet 跌 Vulg. *pwăh:* to stumble, to fall down; tëet tó, 跌倒 *pwăh tó*, to tumble down.

Tëet jê put chín, 跌而不振 *pwăh jê bó kèw*, to stumble without having any one to help.

Tëet këak, 跌脚 *pwăh k'ha*, to stumble with the feet.

T^{n}a tëet, 打跌, to slip, to fall.

Tëet 迭 To change, to substitute, to repeat, to change alternately.

Soò kok tëet hin, 四國迭興 *sè kok sëo t'hëy hin k'hé*, four states rising up in succession.

Tëet yûng, 迭用, the alternate use of.

Tëet 鉄 To stitch, to sow, to join a seam.

Tëet 紩 Vulg. *t'hee^{ng}:* the same as the preceding.

Tëet 軼 To assault, to attack, to invade; to rush forward as war chariots do in all directions against an enemy.

福建方言字典

Tëet 瓞 A small melon; kwa tëet, 瓜瓞, a large and small melon; metaphorically, children and grandchildren descending from the same parent.

Tëet 袠 The wrapper of a book, a book cover; a period of ten years is called a 袠, tëet.

Tëet 胅 A bony excrescence; an unevenness of the bones.

Tëet 趃 To run very fast.

Tëet 蛈 The name of a insect; called also 蛈母, tëet boé.

Tëet 祑 Orderly, according to order; an orderly sacrifice.

Tëet 垤 An ant hill, a rising ground. T'haè san cho ê k'hew tëet, 泰山之於邱垤 *t'haè swⁿa ây twā tē k'hew tëet*, the great mountain among hillocks and ant hills, (is a thing of one and the same kind;) see the 孟子 Bêng choó.

Tëet 耋 A person eighty years of age. Also written 耊, tëet. Sē chëá kê tëet, 逝者其耋 *köëy k'hè sē păyh chàp höëy ây lâng*, the departed are only old men of fourscore; see the 秦風 Chîn hong.

Tëet 絰 A piece of coarse white cloth worn on the head and around the waist by persons in mourning; the traces of a carriage wheel.

Tëet 峌 High as a hill, the appearance of a high hill.

Tëet 徹 To exclude, to take out of the way, to remove; also oven. Sam kay chëá é yung tëet, 三家者以雍徹 *sⁿa kay ây lâng ê yung ây se tëet chèy ây meēⁿgh*, the three families sang the yung ode when they removed the sacrifices; see the 上論 Sëang lūn.

Tëet 屮 Vegetation just springing up; one of the radicals.

Tëet 轍 The traces of a carriage wheel; the track of a carriage. Bûn göëy to tëáng chëá ko tëet, 門外多長者車轍 *mooⁿᵍ gwā chëy sè twā lâng ây ch'hëa tëet*, before the door are many tracks of the carriages of great men; see the 陳平傳 Tîn pêng twān.

大

Tek 德 Virtue, kindness, favor; happiness; or whatever is attained in one's own person. E tek pò tek, 以德報德, to recompense good with good. Wûy chèng é tek, 爲政以德 *chò chèng soō ê tek hēng*, to conduct the affairs of government according to the principles of virtue; see the 論語 Lūn gé. Tek hēng, 德行, virtue; yéw tek, 有德 *woō tek*, virtuous.

Tek 悳 The same as the preceding; also written 㤫, tek.

Tek 得 To obtain; tek chëak, 得着 *tit tëŏh*, to get, or acquire, to procure. Chaê boô koé tek, 財毋苟得 *chêⁿᵍ bŏ lâm sám tit tëŏh*, do not desire to get money in an improper way; see the 曲禮 K'hëuk léy.

Tek 滆 The appearance of water.

Tek 啇 The root, the origin; that part on which the others rest, as the bottom, the stem, the sole, &c.

Tek 僪 To dread difficulties; tek sek, 僪傢, bad, ugly.

Tek 滴 Vulg. *tëĕh:* a drop, to drop, to fall drop by drop.
Hëang loē tek lek, 香露滴瀝 *hëang ây loē chúy tëĕh lëĕh,* the fragrant dews descend in drops.

Tek 嫡 A principal wife is called 嫡室, tek sit, and the son of a lawful wife is called 嫡子, tek choó.
Tek boé, 嫡母, the queen.

Tek 適 To arrive at, extreme; near, intimate; kind, liberal.

Tek 鏑 The point of an arrow.

Tek 蹢 A hoof, a foot; yéw sé pek tek, 有豕白蹢 *woō te pâyh k'ha,* there is a pig with white feet; see the 小雅 Seáou gnáy.

Tek 讁 To blame, to reprove, to find fault with.
Kok choo tek gnó, 國子讁我 *kok kwun tek maing lán,* the ruler of the country will blame us.

Tek 摘 To pluck; vulg. *tëăh:* to pick, to gather; to twitch.
Yit tek soó kwa hnó, chaè tek lêng kwa he, sam tek sëāng yîn k'hó, soò tek p'haōu bān kwuy, 一摘使瓜好再摘令瓜稀三摘尚云可四摘抱蔓歸 *chit ây bán saè woō kwa hó, nō ây bán lêng kwa k'hăh chëó, sna ây bán yëá kóng ēy chò tit, sè ây bán p'hō tìn á tooing,* on the first gathering if the melons are good, on the second they will be found fewer; on the third gathering they will still be tolerable, and on the fourth, people will return bringing the vines with them.

Tek 讁 The same as 謫, tek, to blame.

Tek 的 Bright; shining; real, true; tek k'hak, 的確, really, truly; vulg. *ây:* of, belonging to; the sign of the genitive case.
Seáou jîn che tō tek jëēn jê jit bông, 小人之道的然而日亡 *seáou jîn ây tō, kwuing jëĕn jê chit jit bŏ k'hè,* the way of a worthless man is glittering, but in a single day he is forgotten; see the 中庸 Tëung yung.
Tek tek yéw poáou chìn, 的的有表證 *tek tek woō peáou chìn,* it is certainly true, and there are witnesses of it.
Tek pit, 的筆, written with one's own hand.

Tek 菂 The root, or origin of anything; the fruit of the water lily.

Tek 扚 To lead, to take anything in the hand.

Tek 罒 To bind, to tie.

Tek 笮 Narrow, straight, urgent, speedy.

Tek 罘 A rabbit net.

Tek 弔 To arrive at, to reach to.

Tek 竹 Read tëuk: bamboo; tëuk lîm, 竹林 *tek nâ*, a bamboo grove.

又 Tèk 澤 Water collected together in one place; a marsh; also, to moisten, and foster by genial influences; virtue, favor, kindness.

Jëák hoô jûn tèk che, chek chae kwun é choó ë, 若夫潤澤之則在君與子矣 *ch'hin chëōⁿᵍ böëyh jûn tèk e, chek tē jîn kwun kap choó lé*, but with respect to fostering the people by kindness, it depends on the prince in conjunction with yourself; see 孟子 Bēng choó.

Tèk 擇 To choose, to select; vulg. *tŏh:* to pick and choose.

Tèk put ch'hé jîn, yëen tek tè? 擇不處仁焉得知 *kăn tŏh wūy, bŏ twā tē jîn ây só chaē, böëyh an chwⁿá ëy kóng woō tè?* in selecting a residence, not to pitch upon a virtuous neighborhood, how can a person be considered wise? see the 論語 Lûn gé.

Tèk 擲 To throw; vulg. *tèk kak:* to throw away, to throw down.

Tèk këèm ô tēy, 擲劍於地 *tèk kak këèm tē tēy*, he threw the sword on the ground.

Tèk 狄 The name of a race of foreigners on the north of China; a surname.

Lâm bëen jê cheng, pok tèk wàn, 南面而征北狄怨 *lâm bīn jê chēng, pak peeⁿᵍ ây hwan wân*, when he went to adjust

affairs in the south, the northern foreigners were displeased (because he did not commence with them); see 孟子 Bēng choó.

Tèk 躑 To stand still.

Tèk 荻 A sort of reed.

Tèk 翟 The tail of a wild jungle fowl; a surname.

Tèk 籊 Anything originally long and made shorter.

Tèk 糴 Vulg. *tëàh:* to buy corn, or grain; tèk bé, 糴米 *tëàh bé*, to buy rice.

Tèk 滌 To wash any vessel; sëén tèk, 洗滌 to wash, to rinse; also a cage in which sacrificial animals are kept and fed. To exclude; still.

Tèk 敵 To oppose, to withstand, an enemy, an opponent.

Jîn chëá boô tèk, 仁者無敵 *jîn ây lâng bô tùy tèk*, a benevolent man has no enemies; see 孟子 Bēng choó.

Tèk 歒 Tèk sëà 歒[illegible], the smiles of children.

Tèk 特 Only, especial, particular; tèk bēng, 特命, an especial order.

Tèk swán, 特選, especially selected.

Tèk 廸 To advance, to enter; to open out the way.

Tēk 椇 A post, a pole stuck in the ground.

Teng 丁 One of the horary characters; to sustain; also a person arrived at 20 years of age is said to be 成丁 sêng teng, come of age.
Peng teng, 兵丁, a soldier. A surname.

Teng 行 To walk alone; lêng teng, 伶行 the appearance of walking alone; same as 仃, teng.

Teng 叮 Teng lêng, 叮嚀, to enjoin, to urge again, and again.
Kê hwán hok teng lêng, sē jîn che è, chè ch'him ch'hëet è, 其反復叮嚀示人之意至深切矣 e hwán hok teng lêng kā lâng ây è soō chè ch'him ch'hëet, his repeated injunctions and his frequent exhortations show that his intention in teaching mankind was earnest and sincere; see 朱子 Choo choó.

Teng 罕 Teng lēng, 罕罘, a small net.

Teng 疔 A kind of sore or blister.

Teng 釘 A nail; t'hëet teng, 鐵釘 t'hëĕh teng, an iron nail.

Teng 灯 A lamp; teng hⁿó, 灯火 teng höëy, a lamp; teng sim, 灯心, the wick of a lamp; teng lóng, 灯籠 teng lâng, a lantern.
Sam keng teng hⁿó, gnoé keng key, 三更灯火五更鷄 sⁿa kaiⁿg teng höëy, goē kaiⁿg key, (sitting up at study) till the lamp burns to the third watch, (and rising again in the morning,) while the cock crows the fifth watch; (speaking of those who study hard.)

Teng 燈 The same as the preceding.

Teng 登 To ascend; to grow up, to ripen; teng ko, 登高, to ascend up on high; teng wūy, 登位, to ascend the throne.
Gnoé kok put teng, 五穀不登 gnoé kok bô teng kwân, the five kinds of grain do not grow; see 孟子 Bēng choó.

Teng 簦 A bamboo hat, with a handle.

Téng 頂 The top, the crown; t'hoê téng, 頭頂 t'haôu kak têng, the crown of the head; san téng, 山頂 swⁿa têng, the top of a hill.

Téng 嵿 The name of a hill.

Téng 町 The divisions of the rice fields.

Téng 酊 Béng téng, 酩酊, very drunk.

Téng 虰 A small insect.

Téng 鼎 Vulg. tēⁿá: a pan for cooking, a frying pan; also new.

Téng 鼑 The same as the preceding.

Téng 等 A step, a grade, a degree; a class, a sort, the sign of the plural number; gnó téng, 我等 *lán*, we.

Kàng yit téng, 降一等 *kàng chit téng*, to degrade a person one step.

Téng t'haē, 等待 *téng haōu*, to wait, to tarry.

Téng 戥 Téng choó, 戥仔 *téng á*, scales for weighing silver.

去

Tèng 訂 Tèng gē, 訂誐, to deliberate on, to consult; to criticise.

Tèng 釘 o nail anything with nails.

Tèng 鐙 A stirrup; má tàp tèng, 馬踏鐙 *báy tăh tëⁿà*, a stirrup iron.

Hô kwûn ch'hwàn gëùk tèng, 和裙穿玉鐙 *ch'hòng hô e ây kwún, yëá chëw ch'hwuiⁿᵍ gëùk tèng*, having arranged his riding dress he put his foot in the pearly stirrup; see the 韓致堯傳 Hân tè geâou twān.

Tèng 磴 A small plank, or slab of stone; a stone bridge.

Tèng 嶝 The same as the preceding; a small mound of earth.

平

Têng 亭 A pavilion, a shed by the roadside; upright, straight.

Têng 婷 P'hèng têng, 娉婷, beautiful, elegant.

Têng 棖 Sin-têng, 申棖, the name of one of the disciples of Confucius.

Têng 渟 To stop the flowing of water, a dam, a mound.

Kwat têng súy, tè che haé, 決渟水致之海 *kwat tuiⁿᵍ têng chúy, tè e kaòu haé*, he cut off the water dam, and led the water into the sea; see the 李斯傳 Ló soo twān.

Têng 諪 Teaou têng, 調諪, to manage, to regulate.

Têng 廷 Teâou têng, 朝廷, the court, the palace, the hall of audience; sometimes used for the government, the ruling power.

Kē chaē chong beâou teâou têng, pëên pëên gân wûy kín, 其在宗廟朝廷便便言唯謹 *e twā tē chong bëō teâou téng, pëên pëên kóng woā wûy sèy jē*, when he was in the ancestorial temple, or at court, he would speak sedately and with caution; said of Confucius in the 論語 Lūn gé.

Têng 庭 The hall just within the front door; kay têng, 家庭, a hall.

Têng 霆 Lûy têng, 雷霆, a clap of thunder.

Têng 籐 Rattan; têng teâou, 籐條 *tîn á*, a rattan cane; also a bamboo vessel.

Têng 滕 The name of a country; a surname; also to open the mouth, and utter anything.

Têng 縢 A rope, a string, a cord; to bind.

Têng 藤 A creeping plant; the rattan.

Têng 幐 A bag, a sack; also written 縢, têng.

Têng 澄 Waters still and clear. Hông hô sam ch'hëen lëen yit têng ch'heng, 黄河三千年一澄清 *Hông hô s^na ch'heng nee^ng chit ây têng ch'heng*, the Yellow river settles and becomes clear once in 3000 years.

Têng 橙 A kind of orange. Chëng sē têng hông kit lŏuk sê, 正是橙黄桔綠時 *chē^nâ sē têng â wui^ng, kit â lèk ây sê*, it was just at the time when oranges became yellow, and citrons green.

Têng 呈 Even, plain, level; for an inferior to address a superior is called têng; also, to discover, to come to light. Vulg. *tē^nâ*: to announce, to inform, to present up a document.

Têng 裎 To wear anything; kó têng, 裸裎 naked and bare.

Têng 程 An order, a series; a limit; chëang têng, 章程, laws and regulations; loē têng, 路程 a journey, traveling; k'hé têng, 起程 *k'hé tē^nâ*, to commence a journey; vulg. *t'hē^nâ*: a surname. Tëang-ch'hong têng chëang têng, 張蒼定章程 *Tëo^ng-ch'hong tē^nâ tëŏh hwat toē*, Tëo^ng-ch'hong fixed the laws and regulations; see the 高祖記 Ko choé kè.

Têng 酲 Drunk, and not yet awake from wine. Yew sim jê têng, 憂心如酲 *hwân ló ây sim kw^na ch'hin chëo^ng chëw chùy*, sad at heart as though intoxicated with grief; see the 小雅 Seáou gnáy.

Têng 懲 To warn, to be aware of; têng ch'hông, 懲創, to form, to make; têng chèng, 懲正, to reform, to correct.

Têng 重 Read tëûng: double, repeated, over again; kay tëûng pöey, 加重倍 *kay têng pöey*, as much again, double.

丟

Tēng 鄧 The name of a country, a surname.

Tēng 僜 Lēng têng, 倰僜, not fit for business.

Tēng 鄭 Vulg. *tai^ng*: the name of a country; a surname.

Tēng 定 Vulg. *tē^nâ*: fixed, settled, at rest, still; determined. Te ché jê hoē yéw têng, têng jê hoē lông chēng, 知止而後有定定而後能靜 *chae t'hang soăh jëën aōu ēy tē^nā, tē^nā jëën aōu ēy chēng*, when we know how to stop, then we may be settled; being settled, then we may become still; see the 大學 Taē hak.
Tēng chëak, 定着 *tē^nā tëŏh*, fixed, certain.

Tēng 掟 Vulg. *t^nā*: to spread, to open out; to throw away.

Tēng 錠 A kind of white copper; gîn têng, 銀錠 *gîn t^nâ*, a bar of silver. Chûn têng, 船錠 *chûn tē^nā*, an anchor.

幸

Te^ng 當 Read tong: as ché tong, 紙當 *chwá te^ng*, a bundle of gilt paper used in sacrifice containing 5000 sheets.

Sèk-kám-tong, 石敢當 *Chëŏh-kám-tê^ng*, the name of a very strong man, supposed to be able to prevail against noxious influences; hence his name is frequently written on a board, and placed at the corners of streets to keep away evil genii.

去 *Tê^ng* 漲 Read tëàng: the rising of the tide; súy tëàng, 水漲 *chúy tê^ng*, the tide is risen.

去 *Tê^ng* 當 Read tòng: to bear, to sustain, to pawn, to put in pledge. K'hae tòng tëèm, 開當店 *k'hwuy tê^ng tëèm*, to open a pawn shop.

平 *Tê^ng* 唐 Read tông: a surname; the name of a dynasty; Tông teâou, 唐朝 *Tê^ng teâou*, the Tông dynasty; applied also to the whole empire generally, as Tông san, 唐山 *Tê^ng swⁿa*, China; Tông jîn, 唐人 *Tê^ng lâng*, a Chinese.

Tê^ng 塘 Read tông: a pond; gô tông, 魚塘 *hê tê^ng*, a fish pond.

Tê^ng 長 Read tëâng: long, not short; tëâng kéw, 長久 *tê^ng koó*, a long time.

Kim Tông chwát tëâng poé twán, 今滕絶長補短 *tⁿa Têng kok chwát k'hè tê^ng ây poé tây ây*, now with respect to the Têng country, if the longer parts are cut off to make up for the shorter, (it will only be 50 lé in extent;) see 孟子 Bêng choó.

Tê^ng 堂 Read tông: a temple, a hall; t'hêng tông, 廳堂 *t'hëⁿa tê^ng*, a hall. Yêw yëá seng tông è, bê jip è sit yëá, 由也升堂矣未入於室也 *Yêw yëá, woō păyh chëō^ng tê^ng, bōēy jip è ch'hoò téy*, Yêw has ascended the hall, but has not yet entered the dwelling; (intimating that he had made a certain progress in learning, but had not penetrated into the recesses of wisdom;) see the 論語 Lūn gé.

Tê^ng 腸 Read ch'hëâng: the entrails, the bowels; kat jîn sim ch'hëâng, 割人心腸 *kwăh lâng ây sim tê^ng*, to wound a person's feelings very severely like cutting the bowels asunder.

上 *Tê^ng* 丈 Read tëāng: a measure of ten feet; yit tëāng tëâng, 一丈長 *chit tê^ng tê^ng*, ten feet long.

Tê^ng 撞 Read tōng: to run against, to strike, to push against. Sëēn būn chëá jê tōng chëung, 善問者如撞鍾 *gaôu mooī^ng ây lâng ch'hin chëō^ng tê^ng cheng*, a skillful inquirer is like one who strikes a bell; (i. e. he is sure to get an answer;) see the 學記 Hák kè.

Tê^ng 盪 Read tōng: to wash, to bathe in warm water; sëén tōng, 洗盪 *séy tê^ng*, to take a warm bath.

去 *Tëò* 釣 Read teàou: to fish, to angle; teàou gê, 釣魚 *tëò hê*, to catch fish. T'haè kong teàou ê Hwan key, 太公釣於磻溪 *T'haè kong tëò hê tè Hwan key*, T'hae kong angled in the *Hwan* rivulet; see the 史記 Soó kè.

平 *Tëô* 長 Read tëâng: long; this character forms a part of the names of several places, as Tëâng-t'haè, 長泰 *Tëô-t'hwà*, a district in 漳州, Cheang chew; and Tëâng-lók, 長樂 *Tëô-lóh*, a district in 福州, Hok chew, both in the province of 福建 Hok-këēn.

Tëô 潮 Read teâou: the tide; haé teâou, 海潮 *haé tëô*, the tide of the sea. Teâou chew, 潮州 *Tëô chew*, a district in the province of Canton.

𠀃 Tëō **趙** Read teāou: a surname.

Tëō **嘲** To ridicule people.

Tëŏh **拕** Read t'ho: to draw out; t'ho bŭt ch'hut laê, 拕物出來 *tëŏh meēngh ch'hut laê*, to pull anything out.

Tëŏh **着** Read chëak: to engage in anything; as chëak kê, 着棋 *tëŏh kê*, to play at chess.
Also an affix to certain verbs, as gē chëak, 遇着 *toó tëŏh*, to meet with; k'hàn chëak, 看着 *k'hwnà tëŏh*, to see.

Tëŏh **着** Read chëäk: right, yes, it is so.

Tëōng **張** Read tëang: to spread out, to stretch; tëang yāng, 張様 *tëōng yëōng*, to make a show; a surname.

Tëōng **長** Read tëáng: a superior; kay tëáng, 家長 *kay tëōng*, the master of a family; lé tëáng, 里長 *lé tëōng*, the head of a village.

Tëōng **帳** Read tëàng: an account; hòng tëàng, 放帳 *pàng tëōng*, to let an account run on, to give credit.

Tëōng **漲** Read tëàng: to swell, to rise as water, to inundate.

Tëōng **脹** Read tëàng: to swell, to puff up; toé tëàng, 肚脹 *toé tëōng*, a swelling of the abdomen.

Tëōng **瘬** Read tëàng: a dropsical swelling.

Tëōng **場** Read ch'hëâng; a stage, an arena, a place of resort; k'hó ch'hëâng, 考場 *k'hó tëōng*, the place of literary examination; chëèn ch'hëâng, 戰場 *chëèn tëōng*, a field of battle; toé ch'hëâng; 賭場 *keáou tëōng*, a gaming house.

Tëōng **丈** Read tëāng: as tëāng jîn, 丈人 *tëōng lâng*, a father-in-law; tëāng boé, 丈姆 *tëōng ú^m*, a mother-in-law; koe tëāng, 姑丈 *koe tëōng*, an aunt's (mother's sister's) husband; ê tëāng, 姨丈 *ê tëōng*, a wife's sister's husband.

Tëuk **竹** Vulg. *tek:* bamboo; tëuk lūy lëúk sìp yēw jē, 竹類六十有二 *tek lūy làk châp woō jē*, there are sixty-two species of the bamboo.

Tëuk **竺** T'hëen tëuk kok, 天竺國, the name given by the Chinese to the native country of Budha.
A surname.

Tëuk **筑** A musical instrument of the 秦, Chîn dynasty.

Tëuk **築** To beat, to thump, to pound; to build, to erect; also read këuk. Kéw gwăt tëuk Ch'hëâng-poé, 九月築場圃 *kaóu gŏëyh k'hé Ch'hëâng-poé*, in the ninth month, they built Ch'hëâng-poé.

Tëuk **斸** To cut and hack; a kind of hoe.

Tëu̍k **軸** The nave of wheel; kwán tëúk, 卷軸, a roll of writing, a volume of a book, a scroll.

Tëúk 柚 An instrument used in weaving.

Tëúk 廸 To advance, to enter; also read tèk. Wún tëúk k'hwat tek, 允廸厥德 *chin chëⁿà tëúk chìn e ây tek hëng*, truly it advanced his virtue; see the 皐陶謨 Ko yaôu boē.

Tëúk 妯 Sisters-in-law are called 妯娌, tëúk lé.

Tëúk 逐 To drive, to drive out, to expel; tëúk yit, 逐一 *tàk ây*, every one.

Kwán-tëüng sam soō sam këèn tëúk, 管仲三仕三見逐 *Kwán-tëüng sⁿa ây chò kwⁿa, sⁿa ây hoē làng kwⁿá*, Kwán-tëüng was thrice in office, and thrice turned out.

Tëúk 蓫 A kind of vegetable, called also 羊蹄菜, yâng têy ch'haè, sheep's foot vegetable.

Tëúk 篴 The name of a certain sort of bamboo

𡗗

Tëung 中 The middle. Vulg. *tang eⁿᵍ:* the centre; tëung kan, 中間, between.

Llp put tëung bûn, 立不中門 *k'hëä bô tē mooiⁿᵍ tang eⁿᵍ*, (Confucius) would not stand in the middle of the doorway; see the 論語 Lūn gé.

Put p'hëen che wūy tëung, 不偏之謂中 *bô p'heeⁿᵍ kóng këò tang eⁿᵍ*, not to be inclined to one side is called hitting the centre.

Tëung 忠 Faithful; fidelity; chīn ké che wūy tëung, 盡己之謂忠 *chīn lán ka tē kóng këò tëung*, to exert one's self to the utmost is called fidelity.

Choó tëung sìn, 主忠信 lay the greatest stress on fidelity and sincerity; see the 論語 Lūn gé.

𡗗

Tëùng 中 To hit the centre, to hit the mark; tëùng kèy, 中計, to be taken in a stratagem.

Hoo jîn put gân, gân pit yéw tëùng, 夫人不言言必有中 *hoo chëy lëy lâng ūⁿ kóng, nā kóng pit woō tëùng*, now this man does not speak but if he did, he would certainly speak to the purpose; see the 論語 Lūn gé.

𡗗

Tëūng 重 Repeated, reiterated; vulg. *tëng:* double; tëūng tëëp, 重疊, to repeat again and again.

𡗗

Tëūng 仲 The eldest son of a concubine is called 仲, tëūng; also, a surname. Pek tëūng, 伯仲, elder and younger brethren; tëūng sun, 仲孫, a double surname.

Tëūng 重 Vulg. *tāng:* heavy, weighty, important; chun tëūng, 尊重, to treat with seriousness; pó tëūng, 保重 to take care of the main chance.

Kwun choó put tëūng, chek put wuy, 君子不重則不威 *kwun choó bô chun tëūng, chek bô wuy gëëm*, if the good man is not sedate, he will not be dignified; see the 上論 Sëāng lūn.

𡗗

Tew 丟 To throw away, to cast down, to reject; tew hāy, 丟下, to throw down. This character should be written 丢, being composed of two characters, 一去, yit k'hé, once gone, never to return.

𡗗

Tèw 晝 Day, daytime; Chaé-é tèw ch'hím, 宰予晝寢 *Chaé-é jit kan k'hwùn*, Chaé-é slept by day, (for which Confucius severely reproved him;) see the 論語 Lūn gé.

Tèw 咮 A bird's beak.

Tèw 洲 To walk.

平

Têw 紬 A large thread; têw twān, 紬緞, silks and satins.

Têw 綢 Têw bêw, 綢繆, intertwined, and interwoven; to wrap about, to bind round and round.

Têw 稠 Close, near, not distant.
Bîn ke têw bit, 民居稠密 *pāyh sai^ng k'hēā têw bàt*, the people dwell closely together.

Têw 裯 A covering, a single coverlid.

Têw 惆 Têw tëāng, 惆悵, sorrowful, sad, disappointed.

Têw 疇 Cultivated ground, arable land.
E kê tëên têw, 易其田疇 *chŏh e ây ch'hân têw*, to cultivate the fields; see 孟子 Bēng choó.

Têw 儔 A sort, a fellow, a companion; têw lē, 儔侶, a mate.

Têw 躊 Têw tê, 躊躇, to be in doubt, to hesitate, to be undecided, to walk backwards and forwards in suspense.

Têw 籌 To reckon, to calculate; small bamboo arrows to be thrown at a pot, a game very common in China; têw ch'hek, 籌策, a plan.

Ko choé wūn têw wûy ak che tëung, 高祖運籌帷幄之中 *ko choé wūn têw tê wûy ak ây tang e^ng*, the first emperor of the Hàn dynasty used to turn over his plans beneath the curtains of the tent; see the 高祖記 Ko choé kè.

去

Tēw 胄 Posterity, heirs, descendants; also written 伷, tēw.
Sè tēw chom eng, 世胄簪纓 *sè tēy tè chom kat twā*, for ages and generations to wear bodkins and tassels; (i. e. for a family to hold offices for successive generations.)

Tēw 冑 A helmet; kap tēw, 甲冑, *kăh tēw*, armor.
This and the preceding are often confounded in Chinese books.

Tēw 穧 Ripe grain; kat tēw, 割穧, to reap the corn.

Tēw 宙 E tēw, 宇宙, the universe.
Tuy kwaè bút ch'hut ê tēw, 追怪物出宇宙 *kw^ná kwaè meē^ngh ch'hut é tēw*, to drive all strange things out of the universe; see the 上林賦 Sëāng lîm hoó.

Tēw 酎 Double distilled wine.
Bēng hāy che gwát, t'hëen choó yím tēw, 孟夏之月天子飲酎 *bēng hāy ây göēyh hōng tèy lim tēūng jëāng ây chêw*, in the first month of summer the emperor should drink double distilled wine; see the 禮月令 Léy gwát lēng.

Tēw 紂 A rope for a horse, a trace; the name of an ancient tyrannical emperor, who flourished B. C. 1100.

Tēw 籀 The seal character, or the name of the person who invented the seal character.

Tēw 膭 A pain in the small gut; the colic.

Tēw 繇 An oracle; the result of a divination; the words used in an incantation.

𡈼

Tey 低 Low, to stoop down; also written 仾, tey.

Tey 羝 A ram, a buck, a he-goat. Tey ch'hëuk, 羝觸, to push with the horns, to gore.

Tey 隄 To guard against; tey hông, 隄防, to take care of; a bank, or dyke, to prevent water overflowing. Sew lē tey hông, 修利隄防, to repair the banks and dykes.

Tey 堤 A bank or a dam constructed across a stream; to stop up, to dam. Tey gān, 堤岸, the bank of a stream.

𡈼

Téy 𠾁 To put anything in a bag or vessel; téy bŭt, 𠾁物 *téy meengh*, to stow anything away.

Téy 底 Read té: the bottom of anything; hāy té, 下底 *āy téy*, down at the bottom. Boô té wàt t'hok, yéw té wàt lông, 無底曰橐有底曰囊 *bô téy kóng t'hok, woô téy kóng lông*, a sack without a bottom is called t'hok, but one with a bottom is called lông, a bag; see 朱子 Choo choó. Haê té, 鞋底 *êy téy*, the sole of a shoe.

Téy 抵 Read té: to withstand, to resist, to oppose; to arrive at. Té tòng put chē, 抵當不住 *téy tòng bēy twā*, not able to resist.

Téy 短 Read twán: short, not long; teàng twán, 長短 *tèng téy*, long and short. Sëet kêw tëâng, twán yēw bēy, 褻裘長短右袂 *sac k'hëā ây hêw tèng, téy chëⁿà ch'hêw ây ch'hêw wuíng*, (Confucius) would have his common fur dress long (to keep him warm); but he made the right hand sleeve short, (to enable him readily to attend to any business;) see the 論語 Lūn gé.

𡈼

Tèy 帝 An emperor, a ruler, a sovereign; hông tèy, 皇帝, the emperor; tèy wūy, 帝位, the emperor's throne. Sam hông gnoé tèy, 三皇五帝, the three sovereigns and five emperors; (a very early period of Chinese history.)

Tèy 偙 To raise up; noble, clever, talented.

Tèy 諦 To judge, to examine, and decide.

Tèy 蝳 A kind of insect; a sort of cricket.

Tèy 褅 A coverlid, a quilt.

Tèy 締 To tie, without being able to loose.

Tèy 琋 The name of a gem.

Tèy 禘 The name of the great imperial sacrifice.

Tèy 渧 The dripping of water; a drop.

Tèy 揥 To arrange the hair in order.

Tèy 僀 Clever, possessed of talents.

Tèy 蔕 Small roots and fibres.

Tèy 蝃 A rainbow; tèy tông chaē tong, 蝃蝀在東 *tèy k'hēng twā tē tang*, the rainbow is in the east.

Tèy 戴 Read taè: a surname.

平

Têy 題 An order, a series; to record; têy bêng, 題名 *têy mëⁿâ*, to record one's name; têy bòk, 題目 *têy bàk*, a theme, a thesis; têy yëên, 題緣, to make a subscription; têy se, 題詩, to compose an ode.

Têy 蹄 A foot, a hoof; këak têy, 脚蹄 *k'ha têy*, the foot of an animal. Yâng têy, 羊蹄 *yëô^ng têy*, a sheep's foot; te têy, 猪蹄, a pig's foot.

Têy 偍 To advance with difficulty.

去

Tēy 地 The earth; t'hëen tēy, 天地 *t'hee^ng tēy*, the heavens and the earth; t'hoé tēy, 土地, land, territory.

T'hëen tēy wūy yëen, 天地位焉 *t'hee^ng tēy k'hëā e ây wūy*, (if men carried to the utmost the principles of fidelity and harmony,) heaven and earth would then retain their proper places; see the 中庸 Tëung yûng.

Choo hoê che pó sam, t'hoé tēy, jîn bîn, chèng soō, 諸侯之寶三土地人民政事 *choo hoê ây séy pó pöēy woō sⁿa hāng, t'hoé tēy, pâyh saiⁿg, chèng soō*, there are three things which the princes of the empire should consider valuable; viz., territory, population, and good government; see 孟子 Bēng choó.

Tēy hong, 地方, a place, a country, territory.

Tēy 遞 To change, to alter, to transpose; also written 遆, tēy.

Jit gwát tēy keng, 日月遞更 *jit göëyh sëo tēy wⁿâ*, the sun and moon change alternately.

Tēy 第 Ch'hoò tēy, 次第, an order, a series; tēy yit, 第一, the first.

Koé jîn wûy hák ch'hoò tēy, 古人為學次第 *koé chá ây lâng wûy hák cheàou ch'hoò tēy*, the ancients used to study in due order; see 程子 Têng choó.

Tēy 苐 The name of a certain kind of grass.

Tēy 悌 K'haé tēy, 愷悌, to rejoice.

To have the affection of a younger brother.

Tēy 娣 Tēy hoō, 娣婦, a younger brother's wife.

Tēy 弟 A younger brother; heng tēy, 兄弟 *hëⁿa tē*, brethren.

Heng kip tēy è, sek sëang hⁿó è, 兄及弟矣式相好矣 *hëⁿa kap sëó tē cheàou hoat tëôh sëo hó*, elder and younger brethren according to the rule should be agreed; see the 小雅 Seáou gnáy.

Tēy 禘 The great imperial sacrifice. Hék bān tēy che swat, choó wát, put te yēá, 或問禘之說子曰不知也 *woō chit ây lâng mooi^ng tēy ây söēyh, hoo choó kóng, ū^m chae*, a certain person asked the meaning of the great imperial sacrifice; when Confucius replied, "I don't know;" (adding that if a person knew the hidden meaning of it, he could manage the empire as easily as looking at his hand;) see tho 論語 Lūn gé.

Tēy 杕 A single stump of a tree without branches.

Tēy 棣 The name of a flower and wood.

Tēy 埭 To dam up water, and make it flow back again.

Tēy 髢 The growth of hair; an increase of hair.

Tēy 代 Read taē: an age, a generation; sè taē, 世代 *sè tēy*, a generation; teâou taē, 朝代 *teâou tēy*, a dynasty; hoō taē, 後代 *aōu tēy*, future generations, posterity.

Lék taē, 歷代 *lék tēy*, successive generations.

Tēy 袋 Read taē: a sack; poè taē, 布袋 *poè tēy*, a bag.

Tēy 紵 Read t'hé: a kind of flax, the fibres of which may be spun into cloth. Tong bûn che tê, k'hó é oé t'hé, 東門之池可以漚紵 *tang moo^ng ây tê, t'hang laê chìm tēy*, the pond without the eastern gate will serve to soak our flax in; see the 陳風 Tîn hong.

去 *T'hà* 奓 Read hae: to open out, to spread abroad, to bluster, to brag; wide, expansive.

Pâng-he kong choó, sim hae t'héy t'haè, 馮虛公子心奓體泰 *Pâng-he kong choó, sim k'hwuy k'hwăh sin t'héy twā*, the young squire Pâng-he has an inflated mind and an unwieldy body; see the 西京賦 Sey keng hoò.

平 T'h^na 他 He, she, it; another, others. Jîn te kê yit, bók te kê t'h^na, 人知其一莫知其他 *lâng-chae e ây chit hāng, ū^m chae woō pàt hāng*, men attend to one thing, and do not care about anything else; see the 小雅 Seáou gnáy.

T'h^na jit, 他日 *pàt jit*, another day; t'h^na óng, 他往 *k'hè pàt wūy*, to go to another place.

去 T'h^nā 靘 Chong t'h^nā, 粧靘 *che^ng t'h^nā*, to ornament, to adorn.

平 T'hae 台 Sam t'hae, 三台, the name of a star; t'hae téng, 台鼎, a title of respect.

In letter writing, this character is used as a title of respect; as lō t'hae, 老台, venerable sir! heng t'hae, 兄台, respected elder brother!

T'hae 苔 Green fuci floating on the surface of the water; also the green lichens growing on walls; ch'heng t'hae, 青苔 *ch'hai^ng t'hé*, green moss.

T'hae 胎 A womb, a conception in the womb. Boé t'hae, 毋胎, a mother's womb. Put sat t'hae, 不殺胎, not kill pregnant (animals).

T'hae 駘 Noē t'hae, 駑駘, a bad horse, a sorry steed.

T'hae 鮐 The name of a fish.

T'hae 邰 Yéw-t'hae, 有邰, the name of a country. A surname.

T'hae 擡 Vulg. ke^ng: to carry between two, as a sedan is carried.
T'hae keäou, 擡轎 ke^ng kēō, to carry a sedan chair.
T'hae k'hé, 擡起, to raise up anything.

T'hae 篩 Read sae: to sift; bé sae, 米篩, *bé t'hae*, a rice sieve.

声

T'haé 嚀 T'haé laé, 嚀喨, to talk incessantly, to talk incoherently.

去

T'haè 太 Great, large, immense; t'haè kek, 太極, the great extremity, a certain imaginary point, at the extremity of all things, which is however exceeded by a boô kek, 無極, boundless something, of which they have no distinct idea.
T'haè choó, 太子, the eldest son of the emperor, the heir apparent.
T'haè chó, 太早 *t'haè chá*, too early; t'haè tê, 太遲, too late.
T'haè to, 太多, too much, excessive. T'haè yâng, 太陽, the sun; t'haè yim, 太陰, the moon.

T'haè 泰 To have intercourse with; broad, great, extensive; extravagant, extreme; kok t'haè bîn an, 國泰民安, the country flourishing and the people tranquil.
Sëang hāy kaou t'haè, 上下交泰 *sè twā sè sèy sëo kaou chëep*, superiors and inferiors associating together; see the 易經 Ek keng.

T'haè 汰 Tô t'haè, 淘汰, to wash and rinse.

T'haè 態 A form, manner, appearance; an idea; chêng t'haè, 情態, feelings; keaou t'haè, 嬌態, beauty. Also written 能, t'haè.
E put jím wūy ch'hoó t'haè yëá, 余不忍爲此態也 *gwá bēy lún chò kaòu hwut lêy yëō^ng*, "I could not bear to act in such a way;" said by 屈原 K'hwut-gwân.
Ch'he t'haè, 癡態, a foolish manner.

平

T'haê 殺 Read sat: to kill, to slaughter, to cut in pieces.
Sat key wūy sé, jê soō che, 殺鷄爲黍而食之 *t'haê key ch'hong köëy jê hoē e chëāh*, he killed a fowl, and made dumplings for him to eat; see the 論語 Lūn gé.
Sat jîn, 殺人 *t'haê lâng*, to kill people.

去

T'haē 待 To meet with, to intreat; to entertain; k'hwán t'haē, 欵待, to treat; téng t'haē, 等待, to wait, to tarry for.

T'haē 駘 T'haē tōng, 駘蕩, great, and extensive; the fresh appearance of spring.

夫

T'hăh 塔 Read t'hap: a tower, a pagoda; built by the Budhists.

入

T'hăh 沓 One thing laid upon another; to pile one thing on another.

卓

T'hai^ng 撐 Read t'heng: to push; t'heng ch'hwân, 撐船 *t'hai^ng chûn*, to push a boat along with a pole, in shallow water.

去 T'haiⁿᵍ 撑 Read t'hèng: a prop to keep anything from falling.

平 T'haîⁿᵍ 程 Read têng: a surname.

T'haîⁿᵍ 瞪 Read t'heng: to stare, to look full at any one.

T'haîⁿᵍ 騰 Read t'hêng: to ascend high, to fly, to leap. Yîn t'hêng tè é, 雲騰致雨 *hwûn chëöⁿᵍ kwûn tè hoē*, the clouds fly high and occasion rain.

入 T'hak 剔 Read t'hek: to patch; t'hek poé, 剔補 *t'hak poè*, to patch a garment by putting a piece under.

入 T'hàk 讀 Read t'hòk: to read; t'hòk se, 讀書 *t'hàk ch'hăyh*, to read a book. Sëēn t'hòk cheá gwán sek jê yéw tek yëen, 善讀者玩索而有得焉 *gaôu t'hàk ây lâng gwán sek hwut lêy ch'hăyh, jê woō tit tëŏh*, the good reader studies and searches into what he reads, and thus makes it his own; see 程子 Têng choó.

平 T'ham 貪 To covet, to desire anything; t'ham sim, 貪心, a covetous mind. T'ham tek cheá boô yëèm, 貪得者無厭 *t'ham tit tëŏh ây lâng bô sëōⁿᵍ yëd*, covetous people are never satisfied.

T'ham 探 To dive into, to fathom; to try, to seek to discover, to peep into. T'ham t'hèng, 探聽 *t'ham t'hëⁿa*, to listen. Këèn put sëēn jê t'ham t'hong, 見不善如探湯 *k'hwⁿà keèⁿᵍ ūᵐ hó ây soō tëŏh ch'hin chëōⁿᵍ t'ham t'heⁿᵍ*, on seeing anything bad, we should be like those who dip their hands into hot water; (and who are anxious to get them out as soon as possible;) see the 論語 Lūn gé.

上 T'hám 忐 T'hám t'hek, 忐忑, empty; alarmed, frightened; the mind discomposed.

T'hám 菼 A kind of plant, like a reed, but smaller.

T'hám 毯 Vulg. *t'hán*: hairy cloth; a hairy mat; a carpet.

T'hám 糫 A preparation of rice.

去 T'hàm 探 To dive into, to fathom; ch'hè t'hàm, 刺探, to penetrate; t'hàm choó, 探子, a spy.

T'hàm 闖 The appearance of a horse going out of a gate; kwuy t'hàm, 窺闖 to peep at, to spy. Jê bûn suy taē k'héy, kan séw put kám t'hàm, 儒門雖大啟姦首不敢闖 *t'hàk ch'hăyh ây mooⁿᵍ suy twā k'hwuy, kan séw ūᵐ kⁿá t'hàm k'hwⁿà*, although the portico of the learned be opened wide, wicked heads do not dare peep therein.

T'hàm 儑 T'hàm sòng, 儑倯, a foolish appearance.

平 T'hâm 覃 To reach to, even to, unto; also distant and deep. T'hâm kip kwûy hong, 覃及鬼方 *kip kaôu kwûy heⁿᵍ*, even to the regions of ghosts and genii; see the 大雅 Taē gnáy.

T'hâm 潭 Deep waters; waters in general; a sheet of water.
Ch'hëen t'hâm yit gwát yìn, 千潭一月印 *ch'heng chúy chit göëyh ēy yìn*, one moon impresses its image on a thousand sheets of water.

T'hâm 曇 The appearance of the clouds overspreading the heavens.

T'hâm 墰 Chéw t'hâm, 酒墰, a liquor jar.

T'hâm 甔 A kind of jar.

T'hâm 痰 Phlegm, slime; put lêng hwà hëet, naé hwà t'hâm, 不能化血乃化痰 *bēy hwà hōëyh naé hwà t'hâm*, (when our food) cannot be converted into blood, it is converted into phlegm.

上
T'hām 隮 To involve, to be involved in.

平
T'han 嘽 Full, replete, abundant.
Ong lé t'han t'han, 王旅嘽嘽 *ông ây peng chēy chēy*, the royal troops were numerous; see the 大雅 Taē gnáy.

T'han 灘 Vulg. *t'hwⁿa:* a rapid in a river, a part of a stream over which the water rushes violently.

T'han 攤 To open, to spread out with the hand; t'han k'hae, 攤開 *t'hwⁿa k'hwuy* to open out.

T'han 蟶 Read sèng: a kind of cockle; the Chinese feed them in beds of salt water, constructed near the sea for that purpose, which beds are called sèng tëên, 蟶田 *t'han t'hëⁿâ*, cockle beds.

去
T'hán 亶 Truly, really; also, greatly, very, extremely.
T'hán kê jëên hoē? 亶其然乎 *chin chëⁿâ sē an ñêy saiⁿᵍ hoē?* is it really thus? see the 小雅 Seáou gnáy.
T'hán ch'hong bêng, chok gwân hoē, 亶聰明作元后 *twā ch'hang mëⁿâ ēy chò twā jîn kwun*, he who is most intelligent, may become the greatest prince; see the 書泰誓 Se t'haē sē.

T'hán 坦 Plain, even, level; broad, extensive.
Kwun choó t'hán tōng tōng, 君子坦蕩蕩 *kwun choó k'hwăh twā hwuiⁿᵍ hwuiⁿᵍ ây yëōⁿᵍ*, the good man is liberal, noble, and exalted in his views; see the 論語 Lūn gé.

T'hán 担 To brush, to sweep away dust; t'hán tîn, 担塵, to brush away dust.

T'hán 疸 Hông t'hán, 黄疸 *wuiⁿᵍ t'hán*, the jaundice.

T'hán 綫 Cloth of a yellowish green color.

T'hán 毯 Read t'hám: a hairy carpet: mô t'hám 毛毯 *mô t'hán*, a rug.

T'hán 趆 T'hán chó, 趆早 *t'hán chá*, very early, as soon as possible.

去
T'hàn 歎 To sigh; vulg. *t'hó k'hwùy:* to fetch a long breath.
Gân-yëen hwúy jëên t'hàn wát, 顔淵喟然歎曰 *Gân-yëen t'hó k'hwùy*

福建方言字典

t'hàn kóng, Gân-yëen fetched a long breath, and sighing, said, &c.; see the 論語 Lūn gé.

T'hàn 嘆 To sigh; the same as the preceding.

T'hàn 炭 Vulg. *t'hwⁿà*: coals; hⁿó t'hàn, 火炭 *höëy t'hwⁿà*, charcoal.
Jê ó teâou o teâou kwan, chō ê toê t'hàn, 如以朝衣朝冠坐於塗炭 *ch'hin chëöⁿᵍ ch'hëng teâou sⁿa tè teâou kin, chëy tē t'hoê t'hwⁿà*, (he felt, when sitting by the side of vicious persons,) as though with a court dress and wearing a court cap, he should sit down in mud and charcoal; see 孟子 Bēng choó.

T'hàn 趁 Read t'hìn: to follow, imitate; t'hìn yāng, 趁樣 *t'hàn yëöⁿᵍ*, to follow an example.

平 T'hân 檀 T'hân hëang bók, 檀香木 *t'hân hëöⁿᵍ ch'hâ*, sandal wood.

T'hân 壇 A level space, or arena, prepared for offering a sacrifice on.

T'hân 彈 Vulg. *t'hwⁿâ*: to fillip with the fingers; to shoot with pellets.
Lêng kong chëûng taê sëăng t'hân jîn, jê kwan kê pē wân yëá, 靈公從臺上彈人而觀其避丸也 *Lêng kong tē taê têng t'hwⁿâ lâng jê k'hwⁿà c sëëm peeⁿᵍ wân yëá*, Lêng kong used to shoot at people from his terrace, and amuse himself with seeing how they tried to avoid the pellets; see the 左傳 Chó twān.

去 T'hang 牕 Read ch'hong: a window; also written 窗, and 窓, ch'hong.
Bêng gwát sëăng sey ch'hong, 明月上紗牕 *bêng göëyh chëöⁿᵍ tē sey t'hang*, the clear moon shone into the crape window.

上 T'háng 桶 Read t'hóng: a barrel, a bucket, a tub

去 T'hàng 疼 Read tông: to feel for; t'hòng tông, 痛疼 *t'hèⁿà t'hàng*, to have a great affection and concern for any one.

平 T'hâng 蟲 Read t'hëûng: a worm, an insect.

T'hâng 瓶 Read tông: as wá tông, 瓦瓶 *hëā t'hâng*, a kind of pantile.

T'hâng 桐 Read tông: as tông yêw, 桐油 *t'hâng yêw*, paint oil, varnish.

去 T'hāng 弄 Read lōng: as t'hew lōng, 抽弄 *t'hew t'hāng*, to be moved about, as puppets in a show.

上 T'haou 偷 Read t'hoo: to steal, to thieve; t'hoo ch'hé, 偷取 *t'haou t'hăyh*, to take anything by fraud.

上 T'haóu 解 Read kaé: to open, to loosen, to dissolve, to untie.
Kaé këet, 解結 *t'haóu kat*, to untie a knot.

去 T'haòu 透 Read t'hoè: thorough, throughout, through; to understand thoroughly, to have a thorough acquaintance with.
Hok ló t'hong t'hoè, 腹裡通透 *pak laē t'hong t'haòu*, a mind thoroughly intelligent.
Tông hwā sit t'hoè, 唐話識透 *Têⁿᵍ wā bat t'haòu*, he thoroughly understands the Chinese language.

平 *T'haôu* 頭 Read t'hoê: the head; t'hoê bók, 頭目 *t'haôu bàk*, the principal, a chief.

Ké t'hoê bōng bêng gwàt, 舉頭望明月 *këäh k'hé t'haôu bāng k'hwⁿà bêng göëyh*, to lift up the head, and look at the clear moon.

T'hoê bé, 頭尾 *t'haôu böëy*, head and tail.

入 T'hap 榻 A bedstead; gō t'hap, 臥榻 a sleeping place; t'hap chëên, 榻前 *t'hap chêng*, the bedside.

T'hap yin ko soō hāy, yung wūy koè jîn k'hae, 榻因高士下甕爲故人開 *t'hap yin kwân ây t'hàk ch'hàyh lâng hāy, yung wūy koō ây pêng yëw k'hwuy*, the bedstead is placed ready for the eminent scholar, and the jar of wine is opened for an old friend; see a 古詩 koé se, old song.

T'hap 塌 A low spot of ground; a low place, below the surface of the ground. To fall down, or to cause to be thrown down.

T'hap 傝 A man of inferior talents.

T'hap 遢 To walk securely; the appearance of walking.

T'hap 塔 Vulg. *t'hăh:* a tower, a pagoda, a Budhist temple; t'hap yëën, 塔院 *t'hăh eeⁿg*, a monastery belonging to the Budhists.

T'hap 墖 The same as the preceding.

T'hap 凹 A hollow place, in the ground, an indent, a niche; this character is also read *aou*.

入 T'hat 撻 To beat, to strike; also written 韃 t'hat.

Jëák t'hat che ê ch'hē teâou, 若撻之於市朝 *ch'hin chëōⁿg p'háh e tē ch'hē teâou*, he looked upon it in the light of a blow given in the market place or in a public court; see 孟子 Bēng choó.

T'hat 羍 A small goat, or kid; also written 㚘, t'hat.

T'hat 闥 A forbidden door, the door of the inner apartments of a house, which is always barred against strangers.

Hwan-köëy paê t'hat jê jip, 樊噲排闥而入 *Hwan-köëy paê k'hwuy t'hat mooⁿg jê jip*, Hwan-köëy burst open the forbidden door and entered; see the 高祖記 Ko choé kè.

T'hat 蹚 To kick; chëuk t'hat, 足蹚 *k'ha t'hat*, to kick with the feet.

T'hat 㒓 To run away, to abscond; to rebel.

T'hat 汏 To wash or rinse anything; to dash the water over it.

T'hat 怛 T'heaou t'hat, 怮怛, alarmed, grieved, sorrowful, affected.

T'hat 獺 Vulg. *t'hwăh:* an otter, an animal which lives on fish.

Wūy yëen k'he gê chëá t'hat yëá, 爲淵毆魚者獺也 *yin ch'him yëen kwⁿá hê ây sē t'hwăh yëá*, that which drives the fish into deep waters is the otter; see 孟子 Bēng choó.

The beaver is also called t'hat according to some authors.

T'hat 塞 Read sek: to stop up a hole, to dam; sek k'hoé, 塞口 *t'hat ch'hùy*, to stop one's mouth.

T'hat 踢 Read t'hek: to kick, to strike with the foot.

T'hát 浡 Water issuing forth.

T'hay 㮇 A beautiful appearance.

T'hay 推 Read ch'huy: to push, to push out, to push off.
Ch'huy t'hok soō koè, 推托事故 *t'hay t'hok soō koè*, to put off by any kind of excuse.

T'hay 胎 Read t'hae: the womb; hwaê t'hae, 懷胎 *hwaê t'hay*, to conceive in the womb.

T'hāy 蛇 Read chāy: the blubber, a kind of fish, called also súy boé, 水母 *chúy boé*, the water mother; it is said to be without eyes, and to be led about by lobsters or prawns.

T'hāy 蚱 The same as the preceding.

T'hāy 鮓 The name of a fish; also used for the preceding.

T'hăyh 裼 Read t'hek: naked; pak t'hek, 剝裼 *pak t'hăyh*, stark naked.

T'hăyh 貼 Read t'heep: as t'heep say, 貼鯊 *t'hăyh say*, a kind of plaice or skate.

T'hăyh 宅 Read t'hek: a house, a dwelling; ch'hoè t'hek, 厝宅 *ch'hoè t'hăyh*, a dwelling house, a residence.

T'hăyh 提 Read t'hêy: to take anything in the hand; t'hêy bùt, 提物 *t'hăyh meè^ng^h*, to carry anything in the hand.

T'he 絺 The finest kind of grass cloth or linen.

T'he 郗 A surname.

T'he 笞 To beat, to bastinado.

T'he 樞 A pivot, or hinge of a door; also read k'he.

T'he 樗 The name of a tree.

T'he 攄 To expand, to extend.

T'he 黐 K'hoe t'he, 杋黐, a sort of birdlime.

T'he 銖 Read choo: a small weight, equal to a hundred grains of millet; the name of an ancient coin; a very small piece of silver.

T'he 摴 T'he poê, 摴蒱, a certain game, in which something is thrown.

7 T

声

T'hé 佇 Long, a long time; to stand long. Cheem bōng put kip, t'hé lip é k'hip, 瞻望不及佇立以泣 *chēem bāng bŏ kip, koŏ k'kēä ĕ k'haŏu*, he looked towards it without being able to reach it, and stood so long that he began to weep; see the 詩經 Se keng.

T'hé 佇 An improper form of the preceding character.

T'hé 宁 To distinguish, in accumulating things; also, the front hall of a house.

Thé 羜 A kid or lamb, five months old.

T'hé 苧 Grass of which ropes can be made.

T'hé 紵 A kind of flax plant, of the fibres of which cloth can be made, called t'hé poè, 紵布, grass cloth.

T'hé 貯 Vulg. *téy:* to store up, to accumulate, to place anything in a vessel or bag, in order to preserve it.

T'hé 竚 To stand long.

T'hé 抒 To take hold of, to take out of the way.

T'hé 杼 A shuttle used in weaving cloth.

T'hé 褫 To plunder; to loosen; to take off a person's clothes.

T'hé 恥 To be ashamed; shame, disgrace; sew t'hé, 羞恥 *seăou léy*, filled with shame.

Kwun choó t'hé kê gân jê kò kê hêng, 君子恥其言而過其行 *kwun choŏ ây lăng seăou léy e ây wā ēy köēy e ây séy kēⁿā*, the good man is ashamed lest his words should exceed his actions; (i.e. lest his profession should surpass his practice;) see the 論語 Lūn gé.

T'hé sim, 恥心, an inward feeling of shame.

去

T'hè 翅 The wings of a bird; put t'hè, 不翅, is the same as put t'hèy, 不啻, not only, it is thus.

T'hè 疐 To stamp with the foot; to doubt. Hindered, impeded, wishing to advance, but prevented by embarrassments.

T'hè 懥 Enraged, roused up to anger. Sim yéw séy hwūn t'hè, chek put tek kê chèng, 心有所忿懥則不得其正 *sim kwⁿa woō séy hwŭn t'hè, chēw bēy tit tčŏh e ây chēⁿā*, when the mind is agitated by passion, it cannot obtain equanimity; see the 大學 Tūē hak.

T'hè 鼸 Hwŭn t'hè, 噴鼸 *p'hăh k'ha ch'héw*, to sneeze, to blow the nose.

T'hè 滯 Unharmonious sounds, discordance.

T'hè 剃 Read t'hèy: to shave; t'hèy t'hoê, 剃頭 *t'hè t'haŏu*, to shave the head after the Tartar fashion.

平

T'hê 鋤 To weed the ground, to root up grass and weeds; to eradicate; t'hê t'hoê, 鋤頭 *t'hê t'haŏu*, a hoe.

T'hê kong kwŭy choō hong, 鋤耕桂自芳

t'hé ch'haóu chŏh tēy, kwùy hwa ka tē p'hang, weed the grass and dig the ground, and then the cassia flowers will yield a spontaneous fragrance.

T'hé 苔 Read t'hae: moss; ch'heng t'hae, 青苔 ch'haiⁿᵍ t'hé, green moss or lichens.

T'hê 啼 Read t'hêy: to crow; to cry; key t'hêy, 鷄啼 key t'hê, the cock crows.

T'hê 雉 Read tē: a wild fowl; tē key, 雉鷄 t'hê key, a jungle fowl. Hëung tē ê hwuy, 雄雉于飛 kang ây t'hê key tit pwuy, a male jungle fowl is flying about.

平

T'hëⁿa 聽 Read t'hèng: to hear, to listen, to attend to. T'hèng kê gân jê kwan kê hēng, 聽其言而觀其行 t'hëⁿa e ây wā, jê k'hwⁿâ e ây sêy këⁿâ, "I listen to men's words, and at the same time observe their actions;" said by Confucius, in the 論語 Lûn gé.

T'hëⁿa 堂 Read t'heng: a hall; t'heng tông, 廳堂 t'hëⁿa têⁿᵍ, the front hall of a house; a front room.

上

T'hëⁿá 奵 Bâ t'hëⁿá, 媌奵, a term of reproach for a lewd woman, a slut.

T'hëⁿá 苧 Mwⁿá t'hëⁿá, 蔴奵, a kind of hemp.

去

T'hëⁿà 痛 Read t'hòng: painful, pained; to love, to have an affection for; t'hòng tông, 痛疼 t'hëⁿà tàng, to be moved with compassion; pēng t'hòng 病痛 paiⁿᵍ t'hëⁿà, sickness; seng t'hòng, 生痛 saiⁿᵍ t'hëⁿà, to get sick, to have an inflammation. T'hòng höèy, 痛悔 t'hëⁿà höèy, bitter contrition.

平

T'hëⁿâ 程 Read têng: a surname; loē têng, 路程 loē t'hëⁿâ, a journey; a stage, k'hé têng, 起程 k'hé t'hëⁿâ, to commence a journey.

T'hëⁿâ 綪 A kind of rope or cord; the sound of a stringed instrument.

入

T'hëăh 拆 Read t'hek: to open; t'hek k'hae, 拆開 t'hëăh k'hwuy, to pull open, to tear asunder; when thunder and rain prevail, plants and vegetables are said (kap t'hek, 甲拆 kăh t'hëăh,) to burst asunder their seeds, and vegetate.

T'hëăh 折 Read chëet: to break in pieces, to break asunder; aou chëet, 拗折 aou t'hëăh, to break in two, to pluck asunder: chëet ok, 折屋 t'hëăh ch'hoò, to break down old buildings. Chëet hok, 折福 t'hëăh hok, to ruin one's happiness, by vice.

T'hëăh 絎 To bind anything with a cord.

去

T'hëàng 暢 T'hòng t'hëàng, 通暢, thoroughly joyful; k'hwaè t'hëàng, 快暢, cheerful; ham t'hëàng, 酣暢, merry with wine. Ch'hó bók t'hëàng boē, 草木暢茂 ch'haóu bák t'hëàng boē, plants and trees thriving and luxuriant; see 孟子 Bēng choó.

T'hëàng 鬯 A kind of wine made of black millet, and rendered palatable by fragrant herbs; wut t'hëàng, 鬱鬯, wine mixed with aromatic herbs. One of the radicals.

T'hëàng 畼 Long, growing long; thorough; distant, full.

T'hëàng 畼 The same as the preceding; also, to cultivate the ground without obtaining any return.

卓

T'heaou 佻 A light and trifling person. Also written 恌, t'heaou.

T'heaou 祧 To remove a person's shrine out of the ancestorial temple, and place it in a separate building; this is done after five generations have passed away.

T'heaou 挑 To take up, to pick up; to carry a burden by means of a pole across the shoulder; t'heaou tàm, 挑担 *t'na t'nà*, to carry a burthen; t'heaou hoo, 挑夫 *t'na ây lâng*, a carrier; t'heaou ch'hé, 挑取 to select, to choose.

T'heaou 弨 A bow turned the wrong way; a bow unstrung.

T'heaou 超 To pass over, to leap over, to jump across. T'heaou jîn yit téng, 超人一等 *t'heaou köëy lâng chit téng*, to leap from one rank or degree of people to another.

T'heaou 招 A man's name; a surname.

T'heaou 刁 Difficult; read teaou: a rice vessel used in the army; a surname.

T'heaou 怊 The appearance of melancholy; distress of mind.

T'heáou 窕 Virtuous, good; yaóu t'heáou, 窈窕, good, excellent; deep and still, tranquil. Yaóu t'heáou söuk lé, kwun choó hⁿó kôw, 窈窕淑女君子好逑 *gaôu kwà hó ây cha boê, kwun choó hó chò p'hit kew*, a clever and virtuous female is a good helpmate to a worthy man.

T'heáou 挑 To stir up, to excite; t'heáou lōng, 挑弄 *t'heáou lāng*, to play the fool with; t'heáou hè, 挑戲, to excite to sport; t'heáou chëèn, 挑戰, to stir up to battle, to excite to a contest.

T'heáou 誂 To call and induce one another to do anything; to allure.

T'heáou 嚎 The same as the preceding.

T'heáou 掉 To shake, to move; to move backwards and forwards.

T'heáou 嶭 A hilly appearance.

去

T'heàou 跳 To jump, to leap, to bound across anything. Tê p'ho t'heàou mòëy, 馳波跳沫 *tê chaôu tē p'ho têng t'heàou yëàk köëy chúy möëy*, to gallop over the waves, and leap across the surf.

T'heàou 糶 Vulg. *t'hëò*: to sell corn or grain; t'heàou bé, 糶米 *t'hëò bé*, to sell rice.

T'heàou 頫 To hold down the head; a large assemblage of great officers at an imperial audience is called *t'heàou*.

T'heàou 眺 The eyes irregular; to look awry; to look to a distance. K'hó é wán t'heàou bōng, 可以遠眺望 *t'hang é hwuiⁿᵍ t'heàou bāng*, to be able to look to a distance; see the 禮月令 Léy gwàt lêng.

平
T'heâou 鮡 The name of a fish.

T'heâou 痳 A freckle or spot on the face; a pimple.

下去
T'heāou 柱 Read choō: a pillar, a post; sėk choō, 石柱 *chëŏh t'heāou*, a stone pillar; êng choō, 楹柱 *atng t'heāou*, the posts and rafters of a house.

上入
T'heĕh 鐵 Read t'hëet: iron, called by the Chinese, the black metal; t'hëet k'hè, 鐵器 *t'heĕh k'hè*, instruments of iron.

下入
T'heĕh 怢 Not to be separated from; inseparable.

上平
T'hëem 添 Vulg. *t'heeng*: to increase, to add, to replenish.
T'hëem teng chìn chaê, 添丁進財 *t'heeng lâng hwat chaê*, to add to one's family and increase one's wealth.
T'hëëm, këëm, 添減, to add and to diminish.

上上
T'hëëm 忝 To involve, to disgrace; t'hëëm jëük, 忝辱, to disgrace.
T'hëëm chaē hāy wūy, 忝在下位 *t'hëëm twā tē kāy ây wūy*, shame and disgrace exist in low stations.

T'hëëm 諂 To flatter; t'hëëm mē, 諂媚 *sëep sē*, to fawn, to flatter.
Hwuy kê kwúy jê chèy che, t'hëëm yëá, 非其鬼而祭之諂也 *ūm sē lân ây hwúy jê k'hè chèy e, sē sëep sē yëá*, to sacrifice to the shrine of a deceased person with whom we had no family relation is flattery; see the 論語 Lūn gé.

7 U

T'hëëm 餂 To taste with the tongue; to lick; sweet, excellent of its kind; to try one with discourse.

T'hëëm 畭 Fields from which a revenue is derived.

上去
T'hëèm 桼 Wood used in the cook house; firewood.
Bók t'hëèm chò k'hóng, 木桼竈孔 *ch'hâ t'hëèm tē chaòu k'hang*, firewood put into the hole of the fireplace.

T'hëèm 栝 The same as the preceding; a certain kind of wood.

T'hëèm 丙 To lick anything with the tongue.

T'hëèm 圅 The ancient form of the preceding; also the outward part of the bamboo.

下去
T'hëēm 沉 To throw anything into the water.

T'hëēm 隵 To sink down, to fall in; tëy t'hëēm, 地隵 *tēy hām*, the ground giving way from underneath.

上平
T'hëen 天 Vulg. *t'heeng*: heaven; reason; providence; the presiding principle of nature; t'hëen tēy, 天地 *t'heeng tēy*, heaven and earth, frequently used by the Chinese to designate the Supreme Being.
Hëk chöēy ê t'hëen boô sëy tó yëá, 獲罪于天無所禱也 *hék chöēy ê t'heeng, bô sëy t'hang kê tó yëá*, he who offends against heaven has no one to intercede for him; see the 論語 Lūn gé.
T'hëen hāy, 天下, under the heaven, the world.
T'hëen ch'heng, 天清, a serene sky.

T'hëen 芙 The name of a plant.

声

T'hëén 倎 Thick, liberal, bountiful.

T'hëén 腆 The same as the preceding; large, many, much, abundant, plentiful, good; also, to arrive at.

T'hëén 琠 The name of a gem.

T'hëén 覥 Shame covering the face; to blush.

T'hëén 靦 The same as the above; also, the countenance.

T'hëén 殄 To exhaust, to carry to the utmost; to destroy, to exterminate.
Soò put t'hëén k'hwat wūn, ėk put wún k'hwat būn, 肆不殄厥愠亦不隕厥聞 *soò ūm chĭn e ây sim höéy tŏh, yëá bēy tūy lŏh e ây hó mēnâ sēna*, because he did not carry his anger to the uttermost, he preserved his fame from decline; said of 文王 Bûn ông in 孟子 Bēng choó.
Bē t'hëén, 未殄, interminable.

T'hëén 蚕 A cold kind of worm; also written 蠶, t'hëén.

去

T'hëèn 瑱 To wear gems in the ear.

平

T'hëên 嗔 A full influence; a full appearance.

T'hëên 闐 Full, replete; same as the preceding.

T'hëên 塡 To stop up, to fill up, to increase; also, the sound of a drum.
T'hëên jëên koé che, 塡然鼓之 *t'hëên ây sēna, p'hăh koé e*, with a rolling sound, he beat the drum; see 孟子 Bēng choó.

T'hëên 謄 To transcribe; t'hëên sëá, 謄寫, to copy a writing.
T'hëên lëuk kwan, 謄錄官 *t'hëên lëuk kwna*, a transcribing officer, a copyist.

T'hëên 瘨 A sickness; a disease.

平

T'heeng 天 Read t'hëen: heaven; t'hëen sîn, 天神 *t'heeng sîn*, celestial spirits.
T'hëen têy che taē yëá, yêw yéw séy hām, 天地之大也猶有所憾 *t'heeng têy ây twā yëá, woō láng hām hwūn*, although heaven and earth are so great, yet there are those who find fault with them (i. e. with Providence); see the 中庸 Tëung yûng.

T'heeng 添 Read t'hëem: to add, to increase.

去

T'heēng 紩 Read têêt: to stitch, to sew; têêt haê, 紩鞋 *t'heēng ây*, to mend shoes.

T'heēng 縴 To sew; têên sam, 縴衫 *t'heēng sna*, to mend a garment.

入

T'hëep 貼 To lean against, to rely upon; pang t'hëep, 幇貼, to confide in; t'hëep jëên, 貼然, suddenly, immediately.

福建方言字典

T'hëep 帖 A writing board; kán t'hëep, 簡帖, a plank or flat piece of bamboo, used for writing on before the invention of paper; the same characters are now employed to denote a piece of writing, a card of invitation, &c.; kwán t'hëep, 卷帖, a scroll of writing; pín t'hëep, 禀帖, a petition; paè t'hëep, 拜帖, a visiting card; t'hó t'hëep, 妥帖, firm, secure.

T'hëep 㩞 To hang upon, to suspend; to pile one on another.

T'hëet 鐵 Vulg. *t'heĕh*: iron, the black metal; also written 銕, t'hëet, and 鉄, t'hëet.

T^{n}á t'hëet chëá, 打鐵者 *p'háh t'heĕh ây lâng*, a blacksmith.

T'hëet sim, 鐵心, iron-hearted, unfeeling.

T'hëet 驖 A black horse.

T'hëet 㑇 Cunning, artful. T'hëet t'hwat, 㑇侻, cunning.

T'hëet 撤 To take away, to remove, to exclude. Put t'hëet këang sit, 不撤薑食 *ūm t'hëăh këo^{ng} chëăh*, (Confucius) never eat a meal without ginger; see the 論語 Lūn gé.

T'hëet 徹 To go through; thorough, pervious, permeable; clear; even, equal; to take away.

Sé t'hëet ch'hit chap, 矢徹七札 *cheè^{ng} t'haòu ch'hit têng ây pang*, he could send an arrow through seven planks; see the 左傳 Chó twān.

T'hëet 餮 To covet; to be greedy; gluttonous.

T'hëet 澈 Clear water; transparent; súy t'hëet té ch'heng, 水澈底清 *chúy t'haòu têy ch'heng*, water clear to the bottom.

T'hek 惕 To respect, to venerate, to fear; to be alarmed.

Kim jîn chāy këèn jê choó chëang jip ê chéng, kae yéw t'hut t'hek ch'hek yîn che sim, 今人乍見孺子將入於井皆有怵惕惻隱之心 *t^{n}a woō lâng hwut jëèn k'hw^{n}à keè^{ng} sèy kë^{n}á chëang jip tē cha^{ng}, chò poē woō kë^{n}a hë^{n}â ch'hek yîn ây sim*, now if people were suddenly to see a child about to fall into a well, they would all have a feeling of alarm and commiseration; see 孟子 Bēng choó.

T'hek 剔 To dissect bones; to remove the flesh from the bones by scraping; to pick from; to reject entirely; to scrape off.

T'hek 揚 To stir up, to excite.

T'hek 踢 Vulg. *t'hat*: to kick with the foot.

T'hek 逷 Distant, afar off; k'hé kám lê t'hek? 豈敢離逷 *k'hé k^{n}á lê hwui^{ng}?* how can I dare to leave you at a distance? see the 左傳 Chó twān.

T'hek 逖 The same as the preceding; t'hek è sey t'hoé, 逖矣西土 *hwui^{ng} è sae t'hoé*, how distant are the western regions.

T'hek 裼 T'hek kêw, 裼裘 *tō^{n}a s^{n}a*, a single fur garment; tān t'hek, 袒裼, bare to the shoulders, naked arms.

T'hek 斥 To exclude, to drive away, to put out of office.

T'hek 拆 To open, to burst open, as seeds when vegetating.
Lûy é chọk, jê pek kó ch'hó bòk kae kap t'hek, 雷雨作而百菓草木皆甲拆 *lûy kwà hoē chŏh, jê păyh hāng kwúy ché ch'haŏu bàk chò poŏ t'hĕāh kăh*, when thunder and rain prevail, then the various kinds of fruits, plants, and trees, all begin to burst their seeds.

T'hek 㤁 To be alarmed, to be apprehensive.
E kê sim t'hek jêên, 於其心㤁然 *twā tē e ây sim woō kēⁿa ây yĕōⁿᵍ*, apprehension prevailed in his mind; see the 齊語 Chêy gé.

T'hek 㑨 T'hàm t'hek, 僋㑨 a silly appearance.

T'hek 忒 Uneven, unequal, erroneous; in an error; ch'hay t'hek, 差忒 mistaken.

T'hek 俶 To begin, to commence; t'hek chaō lâm boé, 俶載南畝 *k'hé t'haŏu k'hè lâm bóé*, let us first go to the southern acres; see the 小雅 Seáou gnáy.

T'hek 倜 T'hek t'hóng, 倜儻, strange; unusual; sudden, unexpected.

T'hek 㸿 To butcher; to slaughter; to cut up meat.

T'hek 慝 Vicious, bad, corrupt, wicked.
Kám būn chông tek sew t'hek, 敢問崇德修慝 *kⁿá mooiⁿᵍ chŭn chông tek hĕng, sew k'hè p'haⁿé t'hek*, I beg to inquire how men are to honor virtue, and get free from vice; see the 論語 Lūn gé.

Kan t'hek, 姦慝, villainous, profligate, seditious, traitorous.

T'hek 忑 T'ham t'hek, 忐忑, the mind uneasy, palpitation of the heart.

T'hek 叱 Vulg. *t'hây*: to vociferate, to bawl out, to drive away.
Chun k'hek che chêên put t'hek koé, 尊客之前不叱狗 *chun k'hăyh ây bîn chêng bŏh hwăh kaŏu*, in the presence of respectable guests, do not bawl at the dogs to drive them away; see the 禮曲禮 Léy k'hëuk léy.

T'hek 陟 To promote, to raise higher in office; t'hut t'hek, 黜陟, degradation and promotion.

T'hek 𥻘 To stick, to adhere.

T'hek 畜 Read hëuk: as hëuk seng, 畜生 *t'hek saiⁿᵍ*, you brute! you beast!

T'hėk 宅 Vulg. *t'hăyh*: a house, a dwelling, a tenement.
Gnoé boé che t'hėk, sē che é song, 五畝之宅樹之以桑 *goē boé ây t'hăyh chaè e é seⁿᵍ*, a tenement of five acres should be planted with the mulberry tree; see 孟子 Bēng choó.

T'hėk 𡼖 The name of a hill.

T'hėk 𡾊 The same as the above.

T'hėk 賾 Deep, concealed; exact, correct.

T'hék 岾 A hilly appearance; also written 岞, t'hék.

岦

T'heng 汀 The level ground on the banks of a stream.

T'heng 廳 Vulg. *t'hëⁿa:* a hall, a front room; t'heng tông, 廳堂 *t'hëⁿa tëng*, a principal hall.

K'hek t'heng, 客廳, a hall for receiving visitors.

T'heng 聽 Vulg. *t'hëⁿa:* to hear, to listen to; t'heng soō, 聽事 *t'hëⁿa soō*, to hear a cause; t'heng chëûng, 聽從, to yield obedience to.

T'heng 橕 A slanting pillar, a prop.

T'heng 橕 Vulg. *t'haiⁿᵍ:* a prop, to keep any-thing from falling.

T'heng 撐 Vulg. *t'haiⁿᵍ:* to push with a long pole; t'heng ch'hwân, 撐船 *t'haiⁿᵍ chûn*, to push a boat forward with a pole.

T'heng 瞠 To look straight at any one; t'heng bók, 瞠目 *t'haiⁿᵍ bàk chew*, to stare.

T'heng 鐺 A kind of pan, or copper kettle.

声

T'héng 逞 To boast and exalt one's self; to be pleased with, to delight in.

Kwûy sîn sit put t'héng û Hé kwun, 鬼神實不逞於許君 *kwûy sîn sit bô böëyh hwⁿa hé kap Hé kwun*, the gods are really displeased with the prince of the Hé country; see the 左傳 Chó.twân.

T'héng 郢 The name of a country.

T'héng 侱 To serve; a road, a way.

T'héng 徎 A road, to travel on the road; a hill path.

T'héng 鞓 A leathern girdle.

T'héng 侹 A long extended appearance; to strike against the ground; instead of.

T'héng 梃 A club, a cudgel, a bludgeon.

Sat jîn é t'héng é jīm; yéw é è hoē? 殺人以梃與刃有以異乎 *t'haé lâng û t'héng á û to á; woō kŏh yëōⁿᵍ bô?* to kill people with a cudgel or with a sword; is there any difference? see 孟子 Bēng choó.

T'héng 王 Good, virtuous, complete, perfect.

T'héng 頲 A narrow head; straight.

T'héng 挺 Straight; to grow straight; to pass over, to exceed; to brandish, or poise a weapon.

Lēy t'héng seng, 荔挺生 *lēy che á tit saiⁿᵍ*, the lēy che fruit tree shoots straight up.

T'héng 艇 A small long boat; a boat generally; k'hwae t'héng, 快艇, a fast boat, such as are common about Canton; hwa t'héng, 花艇, a flower boat, an ornamental boat used by pleasure parties.

T'héng 儻 Bold and courageous.

去
T'hèng 聽 Vulg. *t'hëⁿa*, to hear, to listen; also written 听, t'hèng.
T'hèng kê gân yëá, kwan kê boê choó, jîn yëen soe chae? 聽其言也觀其眸子人焉廋哉 *t'hëⁿa e ây wā, k'hwⁿà e ây bàk ang á, láng böëyh an chwⁿá ëy tëëm k'hëⁿg?* listen to a man's words, and look at the pupil of his eye, how can he then disguise himself? see 孟子 Bēng choó.
T'hèng bēng, 聽命, to receive and obey orders.

T'hèng 僜 Immoveable, unwavering.

T'hèng 撐 Vulg. *t'haiⁿg*: to prop anything, or push anything along with a pole.

T'hèng 濎 T'hèng èng, 濎濙, a small stream of water.

T'hèng 澄 Small streams of water, contributing one to another, and overflowing.

平
T'hêng 停 To stop in the middle of a journey.
Tēng-é t'hêng ke lō laê, 鄧禹停車勞來 *Taiⁿg-é haiⁿgh ch'hëa kóng tëöh bwâ laê ây lâng*, Taiⁿg-é stopped his chariot, and applauded those who came to him; see the 光武記 Kong boó kè.

T'hêng 儯 Lēng t'hêng, 倰儯, a long extended appearance.

T'hêng 騰 To jump, to prance, to leap, to fly.

T'hêng 謄 To transcribe, to copy.

去
T'hëⁿg 湯 Read t'hong: hot water; broth; any warm liquid; a surname.

去
T'hëⁿg 湯 Read t'hòng: to scald with hot water.

T'hëⁿg 𦋺 A hand net or instrument for catching fish.

平
T'hëⁿg 糖 Read t'hông: sugar; chëà t'hông, 蔗糖 *chëà t'hëⁿg*, sugar made of the sugar-cane; pék t'hông, 白糖 *päyh t'hëⁿg*, white sugar; oe t'hông, 烏糖 *oe t'hëⁿg*, black sugar.

去
T'hëⁿg 碭 Read tōng; to glaze pottery; tōng kong, 碭光, *t'hëⁿg kwuiⁿg*, to glaze anything bright.

T'hëⁿg 䏴 Séw t'hëⁿg, 手䏴 *ch'héw t'hëⁿg*, the lower part of the arm.
Këak t'hëⁿg, 腳䏴 *k'ha t'hëⁿg*, the lower part of the leg.

去
T'hëo 挑 Read t'heaou: to stir up; t'heaou hⁿó, 挑火 *t'hëo höëy*, to stir up the fire.

去
T'hëò 糶 Read t'heàou: to sell corn; t'heàou bé, 糶米 *t'hëò bé*, to sell rice.

入
T'hëuk 斥 To rail at, to scold; koè hoo choó t'hëuk che, 故夫子斥之 *chëà hoo choó maiⁿg e*, therefore Confucius scolded him; see 朱註 Choo choò.
T'hëuk mā, 斥罵, to find fault with in an abrupt and scolding manner.

T'hëuk 畜 Read hëuk: as hëuk seng, 畜生 *t'hëuk 'saing*, you brute! you beast!

𠂭

T'hëung 衷 Good, goodness; sincere; correct; within, internally.

Wûy hông sëäng tèy kàng t'hëung ê hây bîn, 惟皇上帝降衷于下民 *tòk tòk hông sëäng tèy kàng t'hëung tē hây tèy ây păyh saing*, only the imperial supreme Ruler causes his goodness to descend on the inferior people; see the 書經 Se keng.

T'hëung cheng, 衷正, internal rectitude of mind.

Hwat bēng che put tëung, 發命之不衷 *hwat bēng lēng ây ūm chèng keng*, issuing out orders which are not just and correct; see the 左傳 Chó twān.

𠂭

T'hëúng 冢 Great; the top of a hill; a grave, a cemetery.

Pek kwan t'hèng ê t'hëúng chaé, 百官聽於冢宰 *pàyh kwna t'hèna ê t'hëúng chaé*, the hundred officers should listen to the chief minister of state; see the 論語 Lūn gé.

San t'hëúng ch'hûy peng, 山冢崒崩 *swna t'haôu hëëm pang*, the top of the hill is in danger of falling; see the 小雅 Seáou gnáy.

The firstborn son is called 冢子, t'hëúng chóo.

T'hëúng 塚 A grave; a cemetery; a flat grave is called 墓, boē; a tumulus is called 塚, t'hëúng; and a high one 墳, hwûn.

T'hëúng 嵸 The name of a hill.

T'hëúng 寵 Grace, favor; t'hëúng aè, 寵愛 to love, and favor any one.

Tek t'hëúng, 得寵, to get into fa---.

𠂭

T'hëùng 暢 Cheerful, pleased; hâm t'hëùng, 酣暢, delighted, intoxicated with pleasure; t'hëùng lók, 暢樂, joy and pleasure.

Be t'hëùng, 美暢, excellent, pleasing, agreeable.

T'hëùng sûy, 暢遂, according to one's wishes.

𠂭

T'hëûng 蟲 Vulg. *t'hâng*: a general term for worms, or insects.

Insects with feet are called 蟲, t'hëûng, and without feet 豸, chaē.

T'hëûng 虫 Vulg. *t'hâng*: the same as the preceding; one of the radicals.

T'hëûng 爞 Dry and hot; drought.

𠂭

T'hew 抽 To lead, to pull or draw out; to pump.

T'hew 妯 To move; not to be at rest, to be in motion.

T'hew 瘳 Convalescent, to recover of a disease.

T'hew 紬 A thread, a line; to draw the end of a thread.

𠂭

T'héw 丑 One of the horary characters.

𠂭

T'hey 梯 Vulg. *t'huy*: a ladder; loê t'hey, 樓梯 *laôu t'huy*, a pair of stairs.

Poē yîn t'hey, 步雲梯 *poē hwûn t'huy*, to tread the cloudy ladder; (i. e. to ascend to the highest literary honors.)

T'hey 釵 Kim t'hey, 金釵, a golden hair pin.

T'hey 胎 Read t'hae: the womb; boé t'hae, 母胎 boé t'hey, a mother's womb.

T'hey 推 Read t'huy: to put off; t'huy t'hok, 推托, to put off with an excuse; sëang t'huy, 相推 sëo t'hey, to put a thing off from one to another.

上

T'héy 體 A body; a substance; sin t'héy, 身體, the body.
Sim kóng t'héy p'hwàn, 心廣體胖 sim kwⁿa k'hwăh sin t'héy pwûy, when the heart is liberally enlarged, the body will grow fat; see the 大學 Taē hák.

去

T'hèy 啻 Put t'hèy, 不啻, not only, not merely.

T'hèy 替 For, instead of, in the place of; to dissolve, to exclude.

T'hèy 涕 Tears; lêw t'hèy, 流涕 laŏu bàk saé, to shed tears.

T'hèy 剃 To shave; t'hèy t'hoê, 剃頭 t'hè t'haôu, to shave the head.

T'hèy 鬄 Hwat t'hèy, 髮鬄, a headdress of hair.

T'hèy 退 Read t'höèy: to retire, to draw back; t'höèy hoē, 退後 t'hèy aōu, to retire, to withdraw; to decline, to refuse.
Jé boô bëēn chëûng, t'höèy yéw hoē gân, 爾無面從退有後言 lé ūᵐ t'hang bīn chêng t'hàn, jê t'hèy aōu woō aōu laē ây wā, do not you comply before one's face, and on retiring invent some after stories; see the 尙書 Sëāng se.

平

T'hêy 瑅 T'hêy tông, 瑅瑭, the name of a gem.

T'hêy 禔 Happiness, peace, tranquillity; sëāng hāy t'hêy hok, 上下禔福 téng bīn hāy têy chò poô sē hok k'hè, above and below all is peace and happiness; see the 史記 Soò kè.

T'hêy 鵜 The name of a bird; the same with the following.

T'hêy 鶙 The name of a bird; t'hêy koe, 鶙鴣, a kind of partridge.
Wûy t'hêy chaē lëâng, put se kê ék, 維鶙在梁不濡其翼 wûy t'hêy cheáou twā tē këô, bô wun tâm e ây sit, the t'hêy bird perches on the bridge, and does not wet its wings; see the 曹風 Chô hong.

T'hêy 啼 Vulg. t'hê: to cry, to weep, to howl; to crow as a cock.
Key t'hêy hoê t'hêy, 雞啼猴啼 key t'hê kaôu haôu, the cock crows, and the monkey screams.
T'hêy k'hok, 啼哭, to bewail, to weep.

T'hêy 提 To take anything in the hand; to take up; haê t'hêy, 孩提 sèy këⁿá, a little child; t'hêy hông, 提防 téoⁿᵍ tê, to take care of; t'hêy tok, 提督, a general in chief.

上

T'him 琛 Precious, precious things, laê hëèn kê t'him, 來獻其琛 laê hëèn e ây pó pöèy, they came presenting their precious things; see the 魯頌 Loé sëūng.

福建方言字典

上聲
T'hìm 戡 To strike deep.

去聲
T'hìm 鴆 A poisonous bird, whose feathers dipped in wine render it poisonous; a deadly poison.

Tê t'hìm ê chéw, 寘鴆於酒 *häy t'hìm ây tók tē chéw*, to put the poison of the t'hìm bird in wine; see the 晉論 Chìn gé.

T'hìm 疢 A hot sickness, a fever; a voracious, craving appetite.

T'hìm 傪 Lîm t'hìm, 䫐傪, the head stooping forwards; t'hìm t'hoê, 傪頭 *t'hìm t'haôu kak*, to bend the head forwards.

平聲
T'hîm 痽 A pain in the stomach, the colic.

T'hîm 痝 The same as the preceding.

去聲
T'hìn 趁 To tread upon; to drive out; to drive away.

T'hìn 趂 Vulg. *t'hàn*: to follow; t'hìn yëōng, 趂樣 *t'hàn yëōng*, to follow a pattern.

去聲
T'hīn 伔 Even, equal; t'hīn taē, 伔大, equally great.

入聲
T'hit 勅 An especial order from the emperor is called 勅命, t'hit bēng.

T'hit hong taē chëàng kwun, 勅封大將君, especially appointed to be a commander in chief.

T'hit 敕 To guard against, to caution.

T'hit 勑 Kín thit, 謹勑, careful, cautious, wary.

Haōu Pek-ko put tek, yêw wûy kín t'hit che soō, 交伯高不得猶爲謹勅之士 *t'hàn Pek-ko bēy tëōh, yêw chò sèy jē āy t'hàk ch'häyh làng*, if you canot imitate Pek-ko, still you may become steady scholars; see the 馬援傳 Má wān twān.

T'hit 遫 To stretch out, to open.

T'hit 飭 To get in order; to repair; sew t'hit, 修飭, to adorn, to put in order.

T'hit 鷘 K'hey t'hit, 谿鷘, a water bird.

平聲
T'ho 縚 To secrete, to conceal; broad, extensive; the sheath of a sword; also to twist silk and thread.

T'ho 韜 The sheath of a sword; the case for a bow.

T'ho 慆 To be pleased; to treat disrespectfully.

T'ho 滔 To treat disrespectfully; waters flowing abundantly without returning.

T'ho t'ho chëá, t'hëen hāy kae sē yëá, 滔滔者天下皆是也 *t'ho t'ho laôu, t'hee^ng āy chò poô sē an nëy*, overwhelming in its influence, the whole empire follows in the same way; see the 論語 Lūn gé.

T'ho 幍 A napkin; a middle cap, part of the dress of a scholar.

T'ho 拖 Vulg. *t'hwa:* to draw, to pull, to lead. Kay teâou hók, t'ho sin, 加朝服拖紳 *kay chit nē^n^á teâou hók, t'hwa twà tē téng bīn,* Confucius threw a court mantle over himself, and drew a girdle across it, (when visited by his prince in his sickness;) see the 語論 Lūn gé.

T'ho 絛 To twist or plait thread or silk.

T'ho 叨 To disgrace; to overwhelm; to covet.

T'ho 弢 The case for a bow.

T'ho 佗 He, she, it; the same as 他, t'h^n^a.

声

T'hó 妥 Secure, certain; t'hó t'hëep, 妥貼, sure, and certain. T'hó ch'hwân, 妥船 *t'hó chûn,* a safe vessel, a secure conveyance.

T'hó 討 To require, to demand, to seek; to regulate, to set to rights. T'hó chëên, 討錢 *t'hó cheê^ng^,* to demand the payment of money. T'hëen choó t'hó jê put hwát, 天子討而不伐 *hông tèy t'hó jê bô hwát,* the emperor regulates the states of the empire but does not attack them; see 孟子 Bēng choó.

去

T'hò 唾 Vulg. *söëy:* to let fall, as spittle; t'hò yëên, 唾涎 *söëy nw^n^ā,* to let fall spittle.

T'hò 套 Long; an outer garment; gōe, t'hò, 外套 *gwā t'hò,* a great coat; se t'hò, 書套 *ch'hăyh t'hò,* the outer covering of a book.

平

T'hô 桃 A peach, the peach tree; t'hô wân, 桃園 *t'hô hwui^ng^,* a peach garden.

上

T'hoe 偷 Vulg. *t'haou:* to steal, to pilfer; to treat lightly and unkindly; any how, no matter how. Koè kēw put wûy, chek bîn put t'hoe, 故舊不遺則民不偷 *koò pēng ū^m^ wûy k'hè chek păyh sai^ng^ bô pŏh t'haē lán,* when we do not neglect our old friends and servants, then the people will not treat us lightly; see the 論語 Lūn gé.

T'hoe 媮 T'hoe yûng, 媮容, to soften one's countenance, in order to get into the good graces of people.

T'hoe 暮 The sun obscured.

声

T'hoé 土 Vulg. *t'hoé:* the earth; t'hoé tēy, 土地, earth, ground, territory. Jip kê këang t'hoé tēy pit, 入其疆土地闢 *jip e ây këang kaè t'hoé tēy k'hwuy pit,* on entering the borders of the various states, (the emperor sees) the territories of each enlarged; see 孟子 Bēng choó.

T'hoé 斛 A surname.

T'hoé 歕 Dumb; also a naughty child.

T'hoé 黈 A yellow color; t'hoé k'hòng, 黈纊, to stop the ears, in order to prevent hearing.

去
T'hoè. **兔** A rabbit; san t'hoè, 山兔 *swⁿa t'hoè*, a hare. Also written 兎, thoè.

Yéw t'hoè wān wān, 有兔爰爰 *woō t'hoè bān á kēⁿá*, a rabbit walking slowly along; see the 王風 Ong hong.

T'hoè **菟** T'hoè se, 菟絲, the name of a medicine.

T'hoè **吐** To vomit, to spit out, to void.
Chew kong yit hwán sam t'hoè poē, 周公一飯三吐餔 *Chew kong chit tooiⁿᵍ pooiⁿᵍ sⁿa hāy t'hoè chĕăh*, Chew kong at one meal thrice spat out his mouthful, (in order to go and speak to some clever men who waited on him.)
Oé t'hoè, 嘔吐, to vomit.

T'hoè **透** Vulg. *t'haôu:* through, to pass through, to pass over; thorough; to understand thoroughly; permeable, pervious.
K'hàn t'hoè, 看透 *k'hwⁿà t'haôu*, to see through and through.

平
T'hoê **亠** One of the radicals; the meaning unknown.

T'hoê **頭** Vulg. *t'haôu:* the head; t'hoê bòk, 頭目 *t'haôu bàk*, a headman.
Ké t'hoê bōng bêng gwát, 舉頭望明月 *kĕăh k'hé t'haôu bāng bêng gōĕyh*, to lift up the head, and look at the clear moon.

T'hoé **土** Read t'hoé: earth, ground, land.

T'hoê **泥** Read nê: mud, soft ground, clay.

T'hoê **涂** Read toê: a surname.

去
T'hŏey **焞** Full, abundant.

T'hŏey **煺** To scald off hair or feathers with hot water.
T'hŏey sîm mô, 煺燖毛, to scald off hairs or feathers.

去
T'hŏèy **退** Vulg. *t'hèy:* to retire, to retreat, to recede, to go backwards.
Kêw yĕá t'hŏèy, koè chìn che, 求也退故進之 *Kêw yĕá aè t'hèy chĕá chìn e*, Kêw is of a retiring disposition, we must therefore urge him forward; see the 論語 Lûn gé.
T'hŏèy jēăng, 退讓, to yield and give way to.

T'hŏèy **蛻** The skin or shell which is cast by some insects and reptiles.
Sêâ t'hŏèy k'hak, 蛇蛻殼 *chwâ t'hŏèy k'hak*, the snake casts its skin.
Sêen t'hŏèy, 蟬蛻, the shell of a certain insect used as a medicine. Also written 蜕, t'hŏèy.

平
T'hŏêy **瘣** A small boil, or sore; seng t'hŏêy, 生瘣 *saiⁿᵍ t'hŏêy á*, to get a boil, to have a sore.

去
T'hŏēy **儽** Ló t'hŏēy, 老儽, a dull, lazy fellow.

入
T'hŏh **拓** Read t'hok: to push anything open with the hand; to burst open; to break; to receive.
T'hok lók, 拓落 *t'hŏh lŏh*, unsocial, disagreeable.

入
T'hŏh **鱑** Nê t'hok, 泥鱑 *t'hoê t'hŏh*, a kind of mud fish, short and thick, hence applied to a dwarf.

夭

T'hok 託 To confide to one's care, to intrust with, to give in charge of; hoō t'hok, 付託, to commit to any one's charge.

Paè t'hok, 拜託, to request courteously.

T'hok 托 The same as the preceding; to intrust with.

K'hó é t'hok lëuk ch'hek che koe, 可以托六尺之孤 *t'hang laê t'hok làk ch'hëŏh ây koe kë^n^á,* (a person) to whom we can confide the care of a young orphan; see the 論語 Lūn gé.

T'hok 仛 The same as the preceding; to confide in; also, to destroy.

T'hok 侂 The same as the preceding.

T'hok 㑂 The same as the preceding; to fix a reliance on any one.

T'hok 乇 The roots of trees or plants, appearing above ground, and hanging down.

T'hok 杔 T'hok loê, 杔櫨, the name of a tree.

T'hok 㯉 A hollow piece of wood, which is beaten by watchmen to give an alarm; a watchman's rattle.

Gnoé keng wōēy soō, chew lê kek t'hok, 五更衛士周廬擊㯉 *goē-kai^ng^ ây wōēy soō, chew wûy lê seā tit p'hăh t'hok,* the guards of the fifth watch go round about the pavilion beating the alarm; see the 漢書 Hàn se.

T'hok 籜 The young shoots of bamboo; also, the outer bark of bamboo.

T'hok 蘀 The leaves and bark of plants and trees falling to the ground.

T'hok 拓 Vulg. *t'hŏh:* to push open, to burst out; to receive anything in the hand.

T'hok 魄 Lók t'hok, 落魄 *lŏh t'hok,* the mind dejected and depressed with poverty and want. Also read p'hek: a spirit.

Kay pîn lok t'hok, 家貧落魄 *ch'hoō lé sòng chēw lŏh t'hok,* when one's family is poor we become depressed in mind.

T'hok 橐 A bag open at both ends.

E t'hok ê lông, 于橐于囊 *twā tē t'hok twā tē lông,* some of the provision was put in open bags and some in closed ones; see the 大雅 Taē gnáy.

T'hok 柝 A hollow piece of wood, struck upon at nights, as an alarm.

P'haōu kwan kek t'hok, 抱關擊柝 *chēw kwan mooi^ng^, p'hăh ch'hā t'hok,* to guard a pass, and beat the alarm; see 孟子 Bēng choó.

亥

T'hók 讀 Vulg. *t'hàk:* to read, to peruse; t'hók kê se, 讀其書 *t'hàk e ây ch'hāyh,* to read their books; see 孟子 Bēng choó.

T'hók 殰 To die in the womb, through hurt or injury; an abortion.

Mô t'hae cheá put t'hók, 毛胎者不殰 *mô t'hey ây meē^ng^h bô t'hók,* in the wombs of hairy animals, the fetus does not die.

T'hók. 黷 Dirt, filth.

福建方言字典

去

T'hong 通 To pass through, to go through; to make a thoroughfare; to communicate between one another; pervious, clear, intelligible.
Choó put t'hong kong ék soō, é yëën poé put chëuk, 子不通功易事以羨補不足 lé ūm saé t'hong kang wnā soō, é yëën é poé bô kadu, why do you not have a mutual communication of talent, and an interchange of employments, in order to make up for what is deficient in one place by what is superfluous in another? see 孟子 Bēng choó.
A surname.

T'hong 㡏 T'hong kwûn, 㡏裙, a foreign article of apparel.

T'hong 恫 The same as the preceding.

T'hong 涌 The noise of water.

T'hong 湯 Vulg. *t'heng*: hot water, broth, any warm liquid, soup; a surname.
Tong jit chek yím t'hong, 冬日則飲湯 *tang t'heeng ây jit chek lim t'heng*, on a winter's day we should drink warm liquids; see 孟子 Bēng choó.

T'hong 鏜 The sound of bells and drums.
Kek koé kê t'hong, 擊鼓其鏜 *p'hăh koé t'hong e ây sēna*, the sound of a drum beating is like t'hong.

声

T'hóng 倘 To stop suddenly; if, perhaps; t'hóng yëën, 倘然, suddenly.
Yîn chëang hëèn che t'hóng jëên ché, 雲將見之倘然止 *hwûn chëang k'hwnâ e t'hóng jëên haīngh*, the clouds appear, and suddenly vanish away; see 莊子 Chong choó.

7 X

T'hóng 侗 Lóng t'hóng, 儱侗, straight, long, great.

T'hóng 偒 Long and large; tall and robust. The same as the above.

T'hóng 㑝 Stupid, dull.

T'hóng 儻 Strange, uncommon; if, should, perhaps; a conditional particle.

T'hóng 戃 Disappointed, to miss one's aim.

T'hóng 矘 Eyes deprived of the pupil; stone blind.

T'hóng 曭 The sun darkened.

T'hóng 桶 Vulg. *t'háng*: a bucket, a tub; súy t'hóng, 水桶 *chúy t'háng*, a water barrel; chéw t'hóng, 酒桶 *chéw t'háng*, a wine barrel.

T'hóng 統 A thread, a line, a connecting skein; to manage, to arrange; t'hóng lé, 統理, to have the general superintendence of; t'hóng sē, 統緒, a clue to the whole; yit t'hóng, 一統, the entire quantity.
Kwun choó ch'hòng gëëp, sûy t'hóng wûy k'hó kèy yëâ, 君子創業隨統爲可繼也 *kwun choó ch'hòng ke gëëp, sûy chit ây t'hóng, chò kadu ēy sëo swâ*, the good man lays the foundation of a family, and hands down a clue to his posterity, which can be successively perpetuated; see 孟子 Bēng choó.

T'hong 綂 The same as the preceding.

去

T'hòng 盪 To move a boat along on dry ground Gō t'hòng chew, 奡盪舟 *Gō ēy sw^{n}a tēng saē chún,* Gō could push a boat along on dry ground; see the 論語 Lūn gé.

T'hòng 痛 Vulg. *t'hē^{n}à:* grieved, wounded, pained; pain, painful; to be in pain, to love tenderly. Aè t'hòng ch'hek t'hat, 愛痛慼怛 *aè t'hē^{n}à ch'hek t'hat,* to love tenderly and be moved with affection.

平

T'hông 糖 Vulg. *t'hê^{ng}:* sugar; t'hông song, 糖霜 *t'hê^{ng} se^{ng},* sugar candy.

去

T'hoō 筯 Read tē: chopsticks.

去

T'hooì^{ng} 毻 To cast the hair; *t'hooì^{ng} mō,* 毻毛, to have the hair fall off.

T'hooì^{ng} 褪 Read t'hùn: to cast off; t'hùn sam, 褪衫 *t'hooì^{ng} s^{n}a,* to throw off one's clothes.

平

T'hooî^{ng} 傳 Read t'hwân: to hand down; t'hwân tō, 傳道 *t'hooî^{ng} tō lé,* to hand down doctrines. Heō choó sëang t'hwân, 父子相傳 *pāy kē^{n}á sëo t'hooî^{ng},* to hand down from father to son.

T'hooì^{ng} 塊 *T'hoè t'hooì^{ng},* 土塊, a lump of earth.

去

T'hooī^{ng} 閭 Read t'hūn: a bar; bûn t'hūn, 門閭 *mooî^{ng} t'hooī^{ng},* the bar of a door.

上

T'hun 吞 To swallow, to gulp down; t'hun jím, 吞忍 *t'hun lún,* to bear patiently. Yéw pēng t'hun t'hëen hāy che sim, 有併吞天下之心 *woō pēng t'hun t'hee^{ng} āy ây sim kw^{n}a,* having an intention of swallowing up and engrossing the whole empire; see the 戰國策 Chëèn kok ch'hek.

T'hun 焞 A spark of fire; bright, clear.

T'hun 暾 The appearance of the rising sun; a genial warmth.

T'hun 椿 The name of a tree, which puts forth its leaves once in 8000 years, and in 8000 years more bears fruit. A father is called 椿, t'hun; and a mother 萱, swan.

T'hun 涒 T'hun lān, 涒潾, water flowing in a winding, serpentine course.

T'hun 軘 A carriage for conveying a coffin.

T'hun 黗 T'hun wun, 黗黷, unclean; a yellow color.

声

T'hún 氽 The water bearing anything along; to float on the top of the water is called 氽, t'hún, to sink to the bottom is called 溺, lék.

T'hún 惛 Stupid and foolish.

T'hún 黗 Black; also a dark yellow.

T'hún 腯 Fat, corpulent, lusty; also written 腞, t'hún.
Goê seng chwân hwûy t'hún, 吾牲牷肥腯 *gwá ây t'haou saiᵑᵍ pwúy t'hún*, my sacrificial animals are fat and perfect; see the 左傳 Chó twān.

去

T'hùn 㾯 A diseased and over greedy appetite.

T'hùn 褪 Vulg. *t'hooiᵑᵍ*: to cast off, to put off; to fall off as blossoms.
T'hùn sam, 褪衫 *t'hooiᵑᵍ sⁿa*, to throw off one's clothes; t'hùn mô, 褪毛 *t'hooiᵑᵍ mô*, to cast feathers.

T'hùn 飩 A strong, savory taste.

T'hùn 黗 T'hùn kwùn, 黗䵪, not to concern; some say, to be lost.

平

T'hûn 坌 Dust, dirt; t'hûn koé ae, 坌垢埃, dirt, filth.

T'hûn 豚 Read tûn: a pig.

T'hûn 黗 Dirty, defiled, filthy, unclean.

T'hûn 貚 A wild hog.

上

T'hūn 塡 Read t'hëên: to fill up with earth, to raise by adding more earth.
Yëêm tèy, 炎帝, the emperor Yëêm's daughter being drowned in the sea, is said to have been metamorphosed into a bird which busied itself in (hâm bòk sèk é t'hëên haé, 啣朩石以塡海 *hâm ch'hâ chëŏh e t'hūn haé*,) collecting wood and stones to fill up the sea.

T'hūn 坉 Water confined, without any outlet; stagnant water; also, to mix mud with straw and build forts; a bank to restrain water, made of reeds and mud.

入

T'hut 怵 To be afraid; t'hut t'hek, 怵惕 afraid, alarmed, concerned.
Kae yéw t'hut t'hek ch'hek yín che sim, 皆有怵惕惻隱之心 *chò poô woō keng kēⁿa sëo t'hēⁿà ây sim kwⁿa*, all men cherish a feeling of concern and compassion for their fellows; see 孟子 Bēng choó.

T'hut 拀 The ferrule of a walking stick.

T'hut 禿 Bald; t'hut t'hoê, 禿頭 *ch'haôu t'haôu*, a bald head.

T'hut 頹 A bald head; t'hut ch'hew, 頹鶖, the name of a bird.

T'hut 踈 Weak in the legs, unable to get forward.

T'hut 黜 To degrade from rank; t'hut chit, 黜職, to put out of office.
T'hut t'hek, 黜陟, to degrade and promote.

T'hut 瘯 A sore head.

平

T'huy 推 To push forward, to carry out, to extend to the utmost.
T'huy hëên jëāng lêng, 推賢讓能 *ch'huy gaôu lâng, nëōᵑᵍ ēy ây*, to put for-

ward clever people, and to give place to men of ability; see the 周書 Chew se. Also read ch'huy.

T'huy 熥 To scald the hair off anything.

T'huy 梯 Read t'hey: a ladder, a pair of steps; loê t'hey, 数梯 *laôu t'huy*, a pair of stairs; a flight of steps.

Këūng teng ch'heng yîn t'hey, 共登青雲梯 *kāng teng chëōⁿᵍ ch'haiⁿᵍ hwûn ây t'huy*, to ascend the ladder of the azure clouds together; (alluding to the united efforts of scholars to advance in learning.)

去

T'húy 腿 The thigh; taē t'húy, 大腿 *twā t'húy*, the large part of the thigh; hⁿó t'húy, 火腿 *höéy t'húy*, a ham. Paôu t'húy, 跑腿 *p'haôu t'húy*, to walk about, as if hurried by business. Also written 骽, t'húy.

T'húy 倭 Weak, feeble.

平

T'hûy 槌 To beat, to strike, an instrument with which to beat, a hammer; bòk t'hûy, 木槌 *ch'hâ t'hûy*, a wooden mallet.

Jit boē t'hûy hwun koé, 日暮槌昏鼓 *jit àm p'háh maîⁿᵍ hwuiⁿᵍ ây koé*, when the day declines, they beat the evening drum.

T'hûy 鎚 To melt, to smelt, to forge; t'hëet t'hûy, 鐵鎚 *t'heĕh t'hûy*, a sledge hammer, an iron hammer.

T'hûy 錘 A weight; ch'hèng t'hûy, 秤錘 *ch'hìn t'hûy*, the weight attached to a pair of steelyards.

T'hûy 癨 A swelling of the legs; a disease of the extremities.

T'hûy 汆 Blunt, not pointed; bùt t'hûy, 物汆 *meēⁿᵍh t'hûy*, anything not sharp pointed.

上

T'hūy 倕 Read sûy: heavy; sûy tëūng, 倕重 *t'hūy tāng*, heavy and weighty.

T'hūy 膇 A swelling of the lower extremities; a chronic disease.

去

T'hwà 泰 Read t'haè: as Tëâng-t'haè, 長泰 *Têô-t'hwà*, the name of a district in the province of 福建 Hok-këèn.

平

T'hwâ 汰 Read t'haè: to wash; tô t'haè, 淘汰 *tô t'hwâ*, to wash and rinse.

上

T'hwā 涚 Lukewarm water; to cleanse by repeated washings.

T'hwā 豸 Read chaē: an insect; haē chaē, 獬豸 *haē t'hwā*, the name of an animal.

入

T'hwⁿa 灘 Read t'han: the rushing of water; súy t'han, 水灘 *chúy t'hwⁿa*, a narrow part of a river, through which the water rushes rapidly; a rapid. The same as t'han, 灘 *t'hwⁿa*.

T'hwⁿa 攤 To open out, to spread out with the hands, to spread abroad.

Ong-jëûng bwán ch'hông t'han se, 王戎滿牀攤書 *Ong-jëûng mwⁿá bîn ch'hêⁿᵍ t'hwⁿa ch'hâyh*, Ong-jëûng used to have his books spread all over his bed place.

去

T'hwⁿá 担 Read t'hán: to brush or wipe away anything; to strike, to elevate,

丰
T'hwà 炭 Read t'hàn: charcoal; h^n^ô t'hàn, 火炭 h^n^ó t'hw^n^à, charcoal for a fire.

Jê ê teâou e teâou kwan [illegible] oê t'hàn, 而以朝衣朝冠坐於塗炭 *ch'hin chëo^ng^ kap teâou têng ây s^n^a, teâou têng ây bō chëy tē t'hoê t'hw^n^à*, it would be just like a person dressed in court apparel and an official cap, sitting down in the midst of mud and charcoal; (speaking of a good man's aversion to associate with bad people;) see 孟子 Bēng choó.

T'hw^n^à 湠 An overflowing of water; an inundation.

夫
T'hwăh 獺 Read t'hat: an otter; the beaver is also called t'hat.

T'hat chèy gê, jëên hoē gê jîn jip tèk lëâng, 獺祭魚然後虞人入澤梁 *t'hwăh chĕăh hê, jëên aōu lĕăh hê ây lâng jip cháy tèk kap lëâng*, when the otter begins to devour the fish, then the fishermen should enter the marshes and stakes; see the 王制 Ong chè.

T'hwăh 汰 To dash water over a place; to wash.

丰
T'hwan 湍 To flow rapidly; water flowing very rapidly.

声
T'hwán 疃 A pathway in the woods, formed by wild beasts; a place trodden by wild beasts; also written 畽, t'hwán.

T'hwán 踹 The heel of the foot, to stamp with the heel.

T'hwán chëuk jê noē, 踹足而怒, to stamp with the heel in anger.

T'hwán 貒 A wild hog.

圭
T'hwàn 鍛 To smelt metal, to forge iron; to grind; t'hwàn naé ko maôu, 鍛乃戈矛 *ch'hòng hwut ây kaou á ch'hëo^ng^ á*, to manufacture spears and lances.

T'hwàn 煅 The same as the above; t'hwàn lëēn 煅鍊, to fuse metals.

T'hwàn 彖 Ek t'hwàn, 易彖, the name of one class of the diagrams, formed by Confucius.

T'hwàn 撥 To thump, to beat.

T'hwàn 碫 T'hwàn sèk, 碫石, a grindstone.

平
T'hwân 傳 Vulg. *t'hooi^ng^*: to hand down, to perpetuate; to promulge.

Sim t'hwân sip lëùk joō, 心傳十六字 *sim t'hooi^ng^ tsoō châp lák jē*, there was a mental tradition consisting of sixteen characters.

T'hwân tō, 傳道, to promulge doctrines; t'hwân sin, 傳信, to proclaim news.

T'hwân 椽 A rafter; chaê taē soō t'hwân, 才大似椽 *chaî teāou tsēă ch'hin chëo^ng^ at^ng^ á*, talents as big as rafters.

夫
T'hwat 脫 Light, easy; to get rid of, to get out of; to escape, to avoid, to put off; t'hwat bëén, 脫免, to avoid, to get free from.

Lân é t'hwat bëén, 難以脫免, difficult to escape.

T'hwat 侻 Cunning, artful; light, trifling. Lêw-peáou é Ong-ch'han t'héy jëák t'hong t'hwat, put sīm tëüng yëá, 劉表以王粲禮弱通侻不甚重也 *Lâou-peáou lëăh Ong-ch'han chò sin t'héy mooi^ng chë^n á chò poô k'hin ū^m sīm tëüng e,* Laôu-peáou considered that Ong-ch'han was weak in body and altogether light and trifling, wherefore he not did much esteem him.

T'hwat 稅 T'hwat bëén, 稅冕 *t'hèy bō,* to take off one's cap. Also, to put aside, to exclude; to rub off dust.
Hwan jëük put chè put t'hwat bëén jê hêng, 膰肉不至不稅冕而行 *chèy bâh bô kadu ū^m saé t'hèy bō chëw kë^n â,* when the sacrificial meat was not sent (to Confucius), he departed without taking off his cap of office; see 孟子 Bêng choó.

T'hwat 說 The same as the preceding.

T'hwat 皗 To strip off the skin; the skin broken, the skin rubbed off.

𡨥
Tim 魫 Anything strange and monstrous; a ghost, an apparition.

𡨥
Tím 戡 To pierce, to stab, to kill; to conquer, to overcome.
Sey pek tím Lêy, 西伯戡黎 *sey pek k'hăh yë^n â Lêy kok,* the western lord conquered the Lêy country; see the 商書 Sëang se.

Tím 丼 Vulg. *tŏm:* to throw a stone into a well.
Also read tám: the sound of things falling into a well.

𡨥
Tìm 抌 To beat severely, to strike [illegible].

Tìm 紞 To dig a hole in the ground, to [illegible] anything into the gr[illegible]; [illegible], dark red color.

Tìm 瓭 A melon of an az[illegible] color.

平
Tîm 沉 To sink, to be drowned; tîm lûn, 沉淪, destruction.
Sëăng jîn lék ê sip sëük, hák chëá tîm ê séy bûn, 常人溺於習俗學者沉於所聞, people in general are addicted to custom, but scholars are taken up with what they hear.

Tîm 疣 The colic; a severe pain in the stomach.

𡨥
Tīm 朕 The first personal pronoun, I; now used solely by the emperor, as monarchs in the west are accustomed to say 'we;' also, a sign; and the place of a seam.

Tīm 㶴 To stew or boil by steam; tīm ăh, 㶴鴨, a stewed duck. Also written 燖, tīm.

𡨥
Tin 徵 To testify, to bear witness to; tin teâou, 徵召, to call, to summon.
Hāy léy goê lêng gân che, Ké put chëuk tin yëá, 夏禮吾能言之杞不足徵也 *Hāy teâou ây léy soè gwá ē y kóng e, nā sē Ké kok bô kadu t'hang tin chìn e,* the ceremonies of the Hāy dynasty I might speak of, but (their descendants) in the Ké country are not sufficient to prove them; see the 上論 Sëāng lūn.

福建方言字典

Tin 珍 A pearl; tin pó, 珍寶, anything precious.
Jê yéw sek seăng tin, 儒有席上珍 t'hàk ch'háyh lâng sē tŏh téng ây tin, a learned man is like a treasure on the table.

Tin 玎 Teng tông, 玎璫 tin tàng, the tinkling of gems.

去 Tìn 鎮 To brandish, to flourish; to keep, to guard; tìn ap, 鎮壓, to keep under authority, to control.
Sun-kwân tók tìn yit hong, 孫權獨鎮一方 Sàng-kw'n tàk tìn sêw chit heng, Swuing-kwân kept sole charge of one region.

平 Tîn 塵 Dust, dirt; tîn ae, 塵埃, small dust.
Put sĕw tîn ae pwàn tēém ch'him, 不受塵埃半點侵 ūm sĕw tîn ae pwnd tēém ây ch'him, not to be soiled by half a grain of the smallest dust.

Tîn 藤 Read têng: rattan, any kind of tendril or creeping plant.
Têng paê, 藤牌 tîn paê, a shield, a buckler.

Tîn 陳 To arrange, to spread out, to draw up in a row; vulg. *tân*: a surname.
Tîn kê chong k'hè, 陳其宗器 tîn lëét chèy chol chong ây ke k'hè, to spread out the sacrificial vessels for ancestors; see the 中庸 Tëung yûng.

去 Tìn 陳 A row, a series, a rank, a line of battle.
Wōēy-lêng kong būn tìn ê K'hóng choó, 衛靈公問陳於孔子 Wōēy-lêng kong mooīng paē tīn kap K'hóng choó, Wōēy-lêng kong inquired of Confucius respecting a line of battle; see the 論語 Lūn gé.

Tìn 陣 The same as the above.

失 Tip 囚 To move.

Tip 釟 An instrument of iron; a pair of pincers.

失 *Tit* 得 Read tek: to obtain, to get, to acquire.
Kêw chek tek che, seá chek sit che, 求則得之舍則失之 kêw chēw tit tĕŏh pàng k'hè chēw sit lók, (virtue) if sought for may be obtained, but if rejected will be lost; see 孟子 Bēng choó.

入 Tit 直 Straight, not crooked, upright, correct; morally upright.
Ké tit ch'hoè choo óng, chek bîn hòk, 舉直錯諸枉則民服 kēăh k'hé téh tit ây lâng, ch'hoè k'he choo wan óng ây lâng, chek pàyh saing hòk lé, when we elevate the upright and remove the corrupt, the people will be rendered obedient to us; see the 論語 Lūn gé.

Tit 囟 The same as the preceding.

Tit 蟄 An insect in its hole; a sting.

Tit 姪 A nephew, a cousin.

平 To 偖 A surname.

To 多 Vulg. *chēy:* many, numerous, plentiful, much.
Hô kê to lêng yēá! 何其多能也 *an chwⁿá e ây chēy hâng ēy!* how capable is he of many things! see the 論語 Lūn gé.

To 刀 A knife, a sword, a military weapon; to lē, 刀利 *to laē,* the knife is sharp.
Bē lêng ch'ho to, jê soó kat yēá, 未能操刀而使割也 *bōēy ēy gîm to, jê saé kwat meēⁿᵍʰ,* when not yet able to hold a knife, he is set to cut things; see the 左傳 Chó twān.

To 忉 Sorrowful, grieved.
Sim yēen to to! 心焉忉忉, how sad is my heart!

To 舠 A small boat, in the shape of a knife.

To 釖 To cut with a knife.

To 魛 The name of a fish.

去 Tó 倒 Upset, turned upside down; to overturn, to invert; still, yet.
Tëet tó, 跌倒 *pwăh tó,* to fall down; tó chaē ch'hông, 倒在床 *tó tē ch'hèⁿᵍ,* to lie down on the bed; tëen tó, 顚倒, turned upside down.

Tó 禱 To pray, to intercede, to intreat; kê tó, 祈禱, to pray.
Hëk chōëy ê t'hëen boô sóy tó yēá, 獲罪於天無所禱也 *hèk chōëy kap t'heeⁿᵍ bô t'hang kē tó,* he who offends against heaven has no one to intercede for him; see the 上論 Sëāng lūn.

Tó 擣 To beat with the hand; to strike, to pummel.
Gwăt hāy tó e, 月下擣衣 *gōëyh āy p'hăh sⁿa,* to be beating the clothes by moonlight; (the Chinese method of washing them.)

Tó 搗 The same as the preceding.

Tó 幬 To overspread, to overshadow, as with a canopy; also, a single curtain, or canopy, an awning.

Tó 島 A mountain in the sea; an island; haé tó, 海島, an island of the sea.

Tó 朶 A tree hanging downward; hwa tó, 花朶, a flower; yit tó hwa, 一朶花, one stalk of flower.

Tó 躱 To avoid, to get out of the way; tó pē, 躱避, to shrink from.
Sëém tó, 閃躱, to jump aside, to run out of the way.

Tó 剁 To cut and hack.

Tó 埵 Hard earth is called tó; also the appearance of fruits hanging downwards.

去 Tò 到 To arrive at, to come to; to attain; vulg. *kaòu:* to reach to, unto.
Chek chëùng bût che peáou lé cheng ch'hoe boô put tò, 則衆物之表裡精粗無不到 *chek chëùng meēⁿᵍʰ ây gwā laē cheng ch'hoe bô ūm kaòu,* then the external and internal, subtle and gross nature of things would be universally attained to; see the 太學 Taē hák.

平 Tô 陶 To convert, to change; to metamorphose; also, pottery ware, earthen ware; to delight in. A surname.

Tô choô bān bŭt, 陶鑄萬物 hwà ch'hòng bān meē^ngh, to metamorphose and manufacture all sorts of things.

Bān sit che kok, yit jîn tô, k'hó hoē? 萬室之國一人陶可乎 chē^nâ bān keng ch'hoô ây kok, chit lâng sëo hwŭy k'hè, t'hang kaôu hoē? in a country containing ten thousand houses, would one man alone be sufficient to burn pottery? see 孟子 Bēng choó.

Tô 匋 To manufacture pottery ware.

Tô 淘 To wash with water, to rinse; to to scour; to stir about.
Tô swa tek kim, 淘沙得金 sëy swa ēy tit tëŏh kim, by washing sand we obtain gold.

Tô 綯 To tie, to strangle.

Tô 萄 Poê tô, 葡萄, grapes; poê tô kàn, 葡萄幹 poê tô kw^nâ, raisins.

Tô 他 Yin kong che tô, 尹公之他, a man's name; see 孟子 Bēng choó.

Tô 佗 He, that, another; who? wŭy tô, 委佗, handsome, beautiful.
Also a surname.

Tô 拕 To draw, to draw over; sŭy tô, 水拕 chŭy tô, a sounding lead.

Tô 駝 Lók tô, 駱駝, a camel; also written 馲駝, lòk tô, a dromedary.
Sëēn-sëēn kok to lòk tô, 鄯善國多馲駝 Sëēn-sëēn kok chēy lòk tô, in the Sëēn-sëēn country there are many camels.

7 Z

Tô 沱 Water flowing in a different channel; pông tô, 滂沱, a hard shower of rain.

Tô 跎 Chay tô, 蹉跎, to slip the foot, and to miss one's aim; to be disappointed, unfortunate, unlucky.

Tô 陀 P'ho tô, 波陀, uneven; p'hoé tô, 背陀, the name of a hill.
O mê tô hwut, 阿彌陀佛, the name of Amida Budhá; used in the form of an oath or profane exclamation by the Chinese.

Tô 酡 A countenance flushed with wine.
Bé jîn kè chùy, choo gân tô sa, 美人既醉朱顏酡些 ch'hin ch'hai^ng ây lâng kaôu chùy, âng bīn le le á tô, the handsome man being tipsy, his red countenance is a little flushed with liquor; see the 楚詞 Ch'hoé soô.

Tô 鮀 Swa tô, 鯊鮀, the name of a fish; a small kind of shark.

Tô 逃 To avoid, to escape; tô pè, 逃避, to get out of the way.
Kwùy-chap jëàng tô k'hè, 季札讓逃去 Kwùy-chap sëo neō^ng jë tô k'hè, Kwùy-chap yielded (the crown), and escaped out of the way; see the 吳語 Goê gé. Tô jîn, 逃人 a runaway, a fugitive.

Tô 迯 The same as the preceding; also written 迯, tô.

Tô 鼗 A small drum, or rattle, with a handle to it; used by pedlers.
Pò tô Boó jip ê Hàn, 播鼗武入於漢 yëô koé mē^nâ këò Boó jip tē Hàn, Boó, who sounded the small hand drum, entered into the district of Hàn; see the 論語 Lūn gé.

Tô 檮 Hard wood; bad wood; tô gwút, 檮杌, the name of a book containing a record of the 楚, Ch'hoé country.

Tô 濤 Great waves, billows, raging waves.

Tô 馱 Burdens carried on the backs of horses, mules or camels are called 負馱, hoō tô.

丢

Tō 道 Doctrine, the true doctrine, the truth; also a way, the right way, virtue; to speak, to say; tō lé, 道理, reason; tō tek, 道德, virtue; tō loē, 道路, a road, a way; swat tō, 說道, to speak; Tō kaōu, 道教, the sect of Tō; Tō soō, 道士 *sae kong á*, a priest of the sect of Tō; tō chew, 道周, a winding road.

Tō t'hóng t'hwân choō tông gê, 道統傳自唐虞 *tō lé ây t'hóng se t'hwuíng choō Geâou Sùn*, the thread of the right doctrine has been handed down from Geâou and Sùn.

Tō 導 To lead; yín tō, 引導 *yín ch'hwā*, to guide, to direct; to comfort.

Tō che é tek, chêy che é léy, 導之以德齊之以禮 *ch'hwā e é tek, chêy yit e é léy*, lead them on by virtue, and reduce them to a certain uniformity by propriety; see the 論語 Lūn gé.

Tō 蹈 To tread, to walk in, to stand on.

Bē këèn tō jîn, jê soó chēá yēá, 未見蹈仁而死者也 *bōēy woō k'hwⁿà tăh tēŏh jîn, jê sé ây lâng*, I have never yet heard of any walking in conformity with virtue, and meeting with their death in this way; see the 論語 Lūn gé.

Tō 稻 One of the five kinds of grain; rice.

Tō 炧 The remains of a candle.

Tō 舵 Vulg. *twā*: a rudder, a helm; tō kong, 舵公, the man who steers; also written 柁, tō.

Tō 惰 Lán tō, 懶惰 *pún twⁿā*, lazy, idle.

Gē che jê put tō chēá, kê hōêy yēá e, 語之而不惰者其回也歟 *kap e kóng jê bô sēōⁿg twⁿā, e sē hōēy yēá e*, "(among my disciples) he who displays no listlessness when spoken to, is Gân-hoêy alone;" said by Confucius in the 論語 Lūn gé.

Tō 悼 To be wounded, to be grieved, to lament.

Tëung sim sē tō, 中心是悼 *sim kwⁿa tang eⁿg sē tō sëang*, grieved to the centre of the heart; see the 邶風 Pöēy hong.

Tō 盜 A thief, a robber: tō chék, 盜賊 *tō ch'hàt*, banditti.

Kwùy-k'hong-choó hwân tō, 季康子患盜 *Kwùy-k'hong-choó woō hwân lân tō ch'hàt*, Kwùy-k'hong-choó was assaulted by banditti; see the 論語 Lūn gé.

丵

Toe 都 Toe yip, 都邑, a capital city; all, general, universal; sêng toe, 城都 *sēⁿâ toe*, the metropolis of a country; toe tok, 都督, a general superintendant. A surname.

Toe 闍 A terrace without a city gate; an outer fortification; outworks; a battlement or terrace on a wall, from which observations are madé.

去

Toé 斗 Vulg. *taóu*: a measure, containing about a peck.

Toé soe che jîn, hô chëuk swàn yëá? 斗筲之人何足算也 *taóu saou ây lâng an chwⁿá kaóu t'hang swuiⁿᵍ?* people of capacities equal only to a peck or a pint, how can they be sufficient to be taken into the account? see the 論語 Lūn gé.

Toé 抖 To stir up, to lift up; toé soé cheng sîn, 抖擻精神 *taóu saóu cheng sîn*, to rouse up one's spirits.

Toé 枓 A small rafter jutting out at the top of a pillar, to support the eaves of the house.

Toé 蚪 K'ho toé, 蝌蚪, a young frog, or toad.

Toé 豋 A vessel used on ceremonial occasions, like the modern tray or waiter.

Toé 覩 To see, observe, look, or behold.

Toé 睹 The same as the above.

Sē koè kwun choó kaè sîn hoē kê séy put toé, 是故君子戒愼乎其所不睹 *yin wūy an ney, kwun choó sèy jê tē e séy bēy k'hwⁿà*, on this account the good man is particularly careful about those things which he cannot behold; see the 中庸 Tëung yûng.

Toé 堵 A wall, the part of a wall which is beaten hard together between two boards. A surname.

Toé 陡 To stand on high, to be elevated; high; lofty.

Toé 賭 To game; toé pók, 賭博 *pwăh keáou*, to play at games of chance. P'heàou toé yím, 嫖賭飲, whoring, gaming, and drinking.

Toé 賥 The same as 賭, toé, to game; toé k'hè sëang cheng, 賥氣相爭 *keáou k'hè sëo chaiⁿᵍ*, with a spirit of gambling they contended together.

Toé 蠹 Toé tëàng, 蠹痮, a pain in the stomach, occasioned by worms.

去

Toè 鬭 To wrangle, to quarrel, to fight; cheng toè, 爭鬭 *chaiⁿᵍ toè*, to contend, to wrangle.

Kim yëw tông sit che jîn toè chëá, kèw che suy p'hē hwat eng kwan jê óng kèw che, k'hó yëá, 今有同室之人鬭者救之雖被髮纓冠而往救之可也 *tⁿa oō tâng chit keng ch'hoò ây lâng sëo chaiⁿᵍ toè, lân k'hè kèw e, suy p'hē sam t'haóu mô, tè pâyh ây kin k'hè kèw e, yëá t'hang*, now if there were people in the same house, quarreling and fighting, and we wished to part them; although we went with disheveled hair, or a white napkin on the head to do so, it would be allowable; see 孟子 Bēng choó.

Toè 鬥 Two warriors standing opposite one another; one of the radicals.

Toè 鬪 The same as 鬭 toè; also written 鬧, toè.

Toè 妒 Envious, jealous; chit toè, 嫉妒, jealousy. Also written 妬, toè.

Hoē hwuy put toè kè, jê choó sun chëùng to, 后妃不妒忌而子孫衆多 *hoē hwuy ūᵐ chit toè wân kè, jê kēⁿá sun ëy chëùng chēy*, (Bûn ông's) queen was not jealous or evil-eyed, (allowing her husband to have as many concubines as he pleased,) and in consequence his sons and grandsons were very numerous; (for Bûn ông had 99 children.)

Toê 蠹 The name of an insect which eats books; a bookworm; called also 白魚, pek gô, white fish.

Toè 斁 To be injured, to be ruined.

Toê 梌 The name of a wood.

Toê 黗 A very deep black color; a black muddy color.

平 Toê 圖 To scheme, to plan, to circumvent; tēy toê, 地圖, a chart, a map; àm sim toê boê, 暗心圖謀 to plan anything in secret; hoê toê, 浮圖, a pagoda.

Toê 梌 The name of a wood.

Toê 酴 A certain kind of wine.

Toê 荼 A bitter kind of vegetable.

Toê 途 A road, a way; toê loē, 途路, a way. Gē choo toê, 遇諸途 toé tëŏh tē loē, he met him in the road.

Toê 涂 Vulg. t'hoê: a surname.

Toê 塗 Mud; dirt; a road, a way; vulg. koê: to besmear, to plaster.

Toê 余 Tó toê, 檮余, the name of a hill in Tartary.

Toê 屠 Chaé toê, 宰屠, a butcher. A surname.

Toê 瘏 Distressed and diseased; sick from fatigue.

Toê 骰 Vulg. taôu: dice; pwat toê, 拔骰 pwăh taôu á, to play at dice.

Toê 投 Vulg. taôu: to cast, to throw one's self upon; to confide in; to throw. Sëang toê, 相投 sëo taôu, to cast one's self on any one's protection; toê kwun, 投軍 taôu kwun, to enter the army.

Toê 捊 To state one's grievances.

Toê 徒 Bûn toê, 門徒, a disciple; toê tēy, 徒弟, a follower; toê hêng, 徒行, k'ha kēⁿâ, to go on foot.

E goê chëûng taē hoo che hoē, put k'hó toê hêng yëá, 以吾從大夫之後不可徒行也 ê gwá t'hàn taē hoo, ây aōu, ūᵐ t'hang k'ha kēⁿâ, ever since I have followed in the rank of great officers, I cannot think of going on foot; see the 論語 Lūn gé.

去 Toē 豆 Choé toē, 俎豆, sacrificial implements; also pulse, peas. Choé toē che soō, chek sëang bûn *che è*, 俎豆之事則嘗聞之矣 *choé toē ây soō, chek bât t'hë"a e*, "the ceremonies of arranging sacrificial implements, I have heard something about, (but not about drawing up a line of battle;") said by Confucius in the 論語 Lūn gé.

Toē 荳 Vulg. *taōu:* pulse, legumes, beans, or pease; leúk toē, 綠荳 *lêk taōu*, green gram; t'hoé toē, 土荳 *t'hoé taōu*, earth nuts (Arachis), also called Manila gram; toē hoo, 荳腐 *taōu hoo*, a kind of jelly, made of pulse; toē kan, 荳干 *taōu kw"a*, a preparation of pulse salted and pickled; toē chëem, 荳針 *taōu chëem*, 'pulse needles,' a kind of vermicelli.

Toē 痘 Toē chín, 痘疹, the small-pox; also called 出朱, ch'hut choo, a production of pearls.

Toē 逗 To stop, to detain, to remain, to stay.

Toē 脰 The neck; hāng toē, 項脰 *hāng taōu*, the back part of the neck.

Toē 度 Hwat toē, 法度, a rule, a law; toē lëāng, 度量, a measure. Sím hwat toē, 審法度, examine the regulations; see the 論語 Lūn gé.

Toē 渡 To cross a river, to ford a stream. Kò kang toē súy, 過江渡水 *köëy káng toē chúy*, to cross rivers and ford streams.

Toē 鍍 Toē kim, 鍍金, to gild.

Toē 塿 To fill up, to stop up.

Toē 土 The bark of the roots of trees t'hëet pé song toē, 徹彼桑土 *t'hëăh e ây se"g á ch'hëw kin p'höëy*, take away the bark from the roots of the mulberry tree; see the 邠風 Pin hong.

Toē 肚 The belly; hok toē, 腹肚 *pak toē*, the belly, the abdomen.

Toē 莊 The name of a fragrant plant.

Toē 杜 The name of a tree; a surname.

Toē 讀 Vulg. *taōu:* a sentence; h"ó kò toē 好句讀 *hó koò taōu*, a good style.

Toē 塢 A den, a cavern; a hamlet.

Toē 竇 A hole in the wall, a den, a cavern; a surname.

去 *Töèy* 對 Read tùy: to be opposed to, an opposite, an antithesis; chò tùy, 做對 *chò töèy*, to make antithetic, or corresponding sentences, a practice very common among the Chinese; bëên tùy, 聯對 *lëên töèy*, a pair of corresponding sentences written on scrolls of paper, and hung opposite on the walls in Chinese houses.

Töêy 從 Read chëûng: to follow; sëang chëûng, 相從 *sëo töêy*, to follow any person, to imitate one.

平 Töêy 兌 To barter or dispose of anything; the name of one of the diagrams. Also written 兊, töêy.

Töêy **隤** To fall, to be cast down, to decay. Soō chëùng bëët hêy, bêng é töêy, 士象滅兮名已隤 *soō chēy bëët hêy, mënà sëna é töêy lòk kāy*, when a great number of warriors are slain, a great name is ruined; see the 蘇武傳 Soe boó twăn.

Töêy **僓** Obedient, compliant, submissive.

Töêy **䭪** Höey töêy, 虺䭪, a sick horse.

Töêy **墤** To fall down, to be cast down.

Töêy **䫭** A boisterous wind.

Töêy **頹** To be cast down, to be destroyed; to fall, to precipitate; to blow a gale.

T'haè san kê töêy hoē, 泰山其頹乎 *t'haè swna e woō pang hoē*, "the great mountain is about to be precipitated;" said by Confucius, when he was about to die; see the 禮記 Léy kè.

Töêy **蘈** A kind of grass.

Töêy **魋** An animal, like a bear, but smaller; hwân töêy, 桓魋, a man's name; see 孟子 Bēng choó.

入

Tŏh **卓** Read tok: a surname; to stand alone, high, lofty.

Tŏh **桌** Read tok: a table; é tok, 椅桌 *é tŏh*, chairs and tables.

入

Tŏh **擇** Read têk: to select, to pick and choose.

Têk sëēn jê koē chip che, 擇善而固執之 *tŏh hó jê gim e këen koè*, to select that which is good, and to hold it fast; see the 中庸 Tëung yûng.

Tŏh **擿** To draw up, to lift up.

入

Tok **篤** Sincere, real, thick, substantial, firm, strong, important, pure, unmixed; tok sit, 篤實, real, in sincerity.

Kwun choó tok ê ch'hin, chek bîn hin ê jîn, 君子篤於親則民興於仁 *kwun choó tok sit tē aè ch'hin, chek pāyh saing hin k'hé é jîn tek*, when a prince is sincere in loving his parents, the people will be elevated in benevolence; see the 論語 Lūn gé.

Tok **卓** Vulg. *tŏh:* to stand alone, to be elevated; a surname.

Gân-k'hoé K'hóng che tok, 顏苦孔之卓 *Gân-höêy k'hwnà kan k'hoè K'hóng choó ây kwân*, Gân-höêy used to consider difficult the exalted doctrines of Confucius.

Tok **倬** Great; to enlarge.

Tok **桌** Vulg. *tŏh:* a table; tok sëāng sëen seng, 桌上先生 *tŏh téng sin saing*, a teacher on the table, i. e. a dictionary.

Tok **棹** The same as the above; also, the name of a wood.

Tok **啅** The same as the following.

Tok 啄 To peck, as a bird at that which it eats.
Boô tok gnó lëâng, 無啄我粱 *bô tok gwá ây ch'hek*, don't peck at my corn; see the 小雅 Seáou gnáy.

Tok 涿 To beat, to pound, to thump. Also written 㧻, tok.

Tok 涿 Tok lók, 涿鹿, the name of a place.

Tok 琢 To work up gems; to prepare precious stones.
Jê tok jê mô, 如琢如磨 *ch'hin chëō^ng tok ch'hin chëō^ng mô*, like hammering and grinding (jewels); see the 衛風 Wöëy hong.

Tok 豝 The dragon tail star.

Tok 豝 The name of a star; the same as the preceding.

Tok 豛 To grind anything, by rolling a weight over it; a pig.

Tok 督 To rule, to lead, to instruct, to warn; chóng tok, 總督, a viceroy, or governor of a province.
Gê yéw é kaòu tok, 宜有以敎督 *èng kae woō é kà tok*, there should be some method of instruction and warning.

Tok 斲 To scrape, to shave off, to pare, to cut and hack.
Ch'hëâng jîn tok jê seáou che, chek ông noē, 匠人斲而小之則王怒 *bàk ch'hëō^ng tok jê ch'hòng e k'hŭh sèy, chek ông sëw k'hè*, should the carpenters cut and hack the timber, and make it smaller, your majesty would be displeased; see 孟子 Bēng choó.
Also written 斵, tok.

Tỏk 毒 To injure, to afflict; poisonous, poison; tók haē jîn, 毒害人 *tók haē lâng*, to poison any one.
E toê tók ê jê bān sèng, 以荼毒于爾萬姓 *é toê tók kap lé bān sai^ng ây lâng*, to injure and embitter all your people; see the 尚書 Sëāng se.

Tỏk 𠍿 To move.

Tỏk 碡 Leâou tók, 磟碡 *lâ tàk*, a harrow, a rake.

Tỏk 纛 A great flag, a standard, which is sacrificed to, on commencing a campaign.

Tỏk 獨 Only, alone; sole; koe tók, 孤獨, orphanlike and solitary.

Tỏk 髑 Tók loê, 髑髏, the crown of the head, the top of the skull.

Tỏk 鐲 A kind of gong.

Tỏk 躅 Tek tók, 蹢躅, the appearance of walking.
Ték tók, 躑躅, unable to proceed.

Tỏk 匵 A chest, a coffer.
Wûn tók jê chông choo, 韞匵而藏諸 *hāy tē tók jê k'hè^ng choo*, would you put it in a coffer and conceal it, (when you had found a gem, or would you try and get a good price for it?) see the 論語 Lūn gé.

Tók 黷 Black, dirty, filthy, muddy.

Tók 櫝 A coffer, a chest; tók kwùy, 櫝匱 a chest of drawers.
Kwuy gëùk hwúy ê tók tëung, sē sûy che kò e? 龜玉毀於櫝中是誰之過歟 *koo kap gëùk p'hăh k'hëep tē tók kwùy tang e^ng, sē chē chŭy ây köèy sit?* when tortoise-shells or gems are spoiled in the casket, whose fault is it? see the 論語 Lūn gé.

Tók 牘 A board for writing, an indictment, a public document.
Tók àn, 牘案, documents relative to judicial proceedings.

Tók 瀆 Koe tók, 溝瀆, a ditch, a gutter; sëet tók, 褻瀆, to treat with disrespect; mō tók, 冒瀆, to annoy, to offend.
Choō keng ê koe tók, jê bók che te yëá, 自經於溝瀆而莫之知也 *ka tē choo aē tē kaou á tók á, jê bô lâng ēy chae,* a poor man may hang himself in a ditch, and no one would know anything about it; see the 論語 Lūn gé.

Tók 犢 A steer, a young heifer; an animal for sacrifice.
Bók tông k'hê tók hwán, 牧童騎犢返 *è^ng goô ây sèy kë^ná k'hëă chìh chëak goô á tit toot^ng,* the cow boy riding on a heifer returns home; see the 杜牧詩 Toē bók se.

Tók 覿 To see, to look at, to visit.
Soo tók jê jê jê yëá, 私覿愉愉如也 *sae k'hëă k'hè k'hw^nà lâng, hoo choô woō hô sūn ây yëō^ng,* when he went to pay a private visit, Confucius wore an appearance of harmony; see the 論語 Lūn gé.

Tók 嬻 Tëep tók, 媟嬻, wanton, lascivious, debauched.

Tók 讟 Wàn tók, 怨讟, displeased and complaining; murmuring; to murmur, to complain of.

Tók 度 To reckon, to measure, to calculate.
T'ha jîn yéw sim, ê ch'hùn tók che, 他人有心予忖度之 *pàt lâng woō sim, gwá ch'hùn tók e,* another man gets an idea, and I calculate and consider on it; see the 小雅 Seáou gnáy.

Tók 罜 A fishing net.

Tók 鐸 Bók tók, 木鐸, a wooden bell, an alarum, a rattle.
T'hëen chëang é hoo choó wûy bók tók, 天將以夫子爲木鐸 *t'hee^ng chëang lëăh hoo choô chò bók tók,* heaven is about to take Confucius, and make a wooden clapper of him; see the 小雅 Seáou gnáy.

平 Tôm 丼 Read tìm: the noise of throwing a stone into a well.

去 Tŏmh 嚄 The vulgar noise made by the mouth in eating.

上 Tong 東 Vulg. *tang:* the east; tong sey, 東西 *tang sae,* east and west; also used to denote here and there, one thing and another.
Tong hong bêng è, 東方明矣 *tang he^ng toe kwui^ng,* the eastern region is enlightened; (i. e. the day is breaking;) see the 齊風 Chêy hong.
A surname; and 東方 tong hong, a double surname.

Tong 倲 Lóng tong, 儱倲, weak, feeble.

Tong [illegible] Stupid, foolish.

Tong 冬 Vulg. *tang:* the winter; tong t'hëen, 冬天 *tang t'hee^ng^*, the winter season.

Tong gîm pék swat se, 冬吟白雪詩 *tang t'hee^ng^ gîm păyh sáyh ây se,* in the winter we may chant the white snow ode.

Tong 佟 A surname.

Tong 當 That which is suitable; ought, should; to sustain, to bear; to meet with, to befal; kae tong, 該當, ought, should; té tong, 抵當, to bear up against; tong k'hé, 當起, to bear up, to sustain; tong kim, 當今, now, just at this time; tong jëên, 當然, suitable, proper, it should be so. Tong jîn, put jëäng che soo, 當仁不讓之師 *é jîn chò tong jîm ūm saé nëō^ng^ e ây sin sai^ng^,* he who takes up virtue for his burden, needs not yield even to his teacher; see the 論語 Lūn gé. Tong sē sê yëá, 當是時也 *tong chêy lêy sē,* just at this time; see 孟子 Bēng choó.

Tong 襠 A sort of garment; sèw tong, 綉襠, an embroidered robe.

Tong 艡 Té tong, [illegible]艡, a sort of boat or vessel.

Tong 鐺 The sound of a drum.

Tong 璫 A gem worn in the ears; teng tong, 玎璫 *tin tang,* the sound of tinkling gems.

Jé chëak bêng gwàt tong, 耳着明月璫 *hē k'hang tè bêng göëyh ây tong,* the ear furnished with a gem like the bright moon; see a 古詩 koé se, ancient ode.

Tong 澢 Water.

声

Tóng 董 To govern, to regulate, to arrange. Vulg. *táng:* a surname.

Tóng [illegible] The noise of anything falling into the water.

Tóng 懂 The mind confused and disturbed.

Tóng [illegible] Fat, lusty, corpulent.

Tóng 党 Tóng som, 党参 *táng som,* a kind of ginseng; a surname.

Tóng 黨 Hëang tóng, 鄉黨, a village, a district of country; ok tóng, 惡黨, bad associates, the bands of the wicked.

K'hóng-choó ê hëang tóng, sûn sûn jê yëá, 孔子於鄉黨恂恂如也 *K'hóng-choó twā tē hëang tóng, chëw sin sit ây yëō^ng^,* when Confucius was in the villages, he wore an honest, unsuspecting appearance; see the 論語 Lūn gé.

Tóng 讜 Tóng gân, 讜言, to speak bluntly.

8 B

去

Tòng 棟 A beam, a rafter; tòng êng, 棟楹 *tòng at^ng*, beams and rafters. Used also metaphorically to denote eminent statesmen, and other public servants.

Tòng 凍 Vulg. *tàng:* to freeze, to congeal. Bēng tong tēy sé tòng, 孟冬地始凍 *toō toō tang t'hee^ng, tēy k'hé t'haôu kēen tàng*, in the first month of winter the ground begins to be frozen; see the 禮月令 Léy gwàt lēng.

Tòng 倲 Lōng tòng, 儱倲, a dull, a stupid appearance.

Tòng 蝀 A rainbow; tèy tòng chaē tong, 蝃蝀在東 *k'hēng tòng twā tē tang*, there is rainbow in the east; see the 鄘風 Yûng hong.

Tòng 當 To hit upon, to centre in; safe, secure; wún tòng, 穩當, sure; vulg. *tè^ng:* to pawn, to put out money on pledge; tòng tèèm, 當店 *tè^ng tèèm*, a pawnbroker's shop; chè tòng, 質當, a pledge. Gân put bōng hwat, hwat pit tòng lé, 言不妄發發必當理 *wā bô lâm sám hwat, hwat pit tòng tō lé*, his words were not lightly expressed, and when he uttered anything, it was always consistent with reason; see the 朱註 Choo choó.

Tòng 譡 To speak according to reason.

Tòng 檔 A wooden sleeping place, a bedstead.

Tòng 儅 To stop, to centre in the middle.

Tòng 闓 A person who hides within the door.

平

Tông 同 Vulg. *tâng:* the same, alike; with, together with; united, of the same class, agreeing. E jé chëûng soō, tông sim lëûk lèk, 與汝衆士同心勠力 *kap lé chëa ây peng soō tâng sim lëûk làt*, together with all your warriors, I will unite my heart, and exert my strength in murdering; see the 泰誓 T'haè sē.

Tông 仝 The same as the preceding.

Tông 侗 An appearance of ignorance; uninformed, unwise; rude. Tông jê put gwân, 侗而不愿 *ū^m chae ây lâng, yëá bēy teâou tit*, when ignorant people are destitute of honest bluntness, (it is difficult to know what to do with them;) see the 論語 Lūn gé.

Tông 峒 K'hong tông, 崆峒, the name of a hill.

Tông 桐 Goê tông, 梧桐, the name of a tree; the Dryandra; the Jatropha. Goê tông lòk yëèp, t'hëen hāy te ch'hew, 梧桐落葉天下知秋 *goê tông lòh hëŏh, t'hee^ng hāy chae woō ch'hew*, when the goê tông tree lets fall a leaf, all the world knows that autumn is come.

Tông 舸 The name of a boat.

Tông 局 The echo in a house; the sound of hollow ground.

福建方言字典

Tông 筒 The name of a bamboo; a bamboo tube; a pipe; yëen tông, 烟筒 *hwun tâng*, a chimney.

Tông 衕 A street, a thoroughfare, a lane.

Tông 銅 Copper; also brass; pėk tông, 白銅 *păyh tâng*, white copper, tutenague.

Tông luy, 銅鐳 *tâng luy*, copper farthings.

Choō jëên tông, 自然銅 *choō jëên tâng*, a kind of medicine.

Tông 鮦 The name of a fish.

Tông 瓹 A small kind of tile.

Tông 唐 Vulg. *tê^ng*: the name of a country; a surname; Tông teâou, 唐朝, the Tông dynasty; Tông jîn, 唐人 *Tê^ng lâng*, a Chinese; Tông san, 唐山 *Tê^ng swⁿa*, China.

Tông 傏 Tông tût, 傏傑, unhumbled, disobedient, wayward, rash.

Tông 塘 Tê tông, 池塘, a pool of water, a pond; a fish-pond, an artificial reservoir, common in the pleasure grounds of the Chinese. Pwàn boé tê tông, yit kàm k'hae, 半畝池塘一鑑開 *pwⁿà boé chûy k'hu t á, chit ây kēⁿà k'hwuy*, a pond of half an acre in extent looks like an open looking-glass; see the 朱子詩 Choo choó se.

Tông 螗 A kind of insect, like a cricket.

Tông 磄 Stones on the bank of a river; a wharf.

Tông 堂 Vulg. *tê^ng*: a temple, a pavilion; t'heng tông, 廳堂 *t'hēⁿa tê^ng*, a hall; t'hëen tông, 天堂 *t'hee^ng tê^ng*, the celestial palace, heaven.

Yêw yëá, seng tông ê, bē jip ê sit yëá, 由也升堂矣未入於室也 *Yêw yëá, păyh chëo^ng tê^ng, böëy jip ê ch'hoò*, Yêw has ascended the hall, but not yet entered into the dwelling (of virtue); see the 論語 Lūn gé.

Tông 坣 The ancient form of the preceding character.

Tông 偒 The same as 侗, tông, ignorant.

Tông 棠 Kam tông, 甘棠 *ka tang*, the name of a certain tree.

Tông 螳 Tông lông, 螳螂, the name of an insect, like a dragon fly.

Chêy Chong kong ch'hut láp, yéw tông lông ké chëuk p'hok lûn, 齊莊公出獵有螳螂舉足搏輪 *Chêy Chong kong böëyh ch'hut p'hăh lăh, woō chit ây tông lông t'hâng këăh k'hê k'ha p'hăh ch'hëà lûn*, when Chong kong of the Chêy country was about to go out a hunting, there was a dragon fly which lifted up its foot and struck the wheel of his chariot; (this was considered an omen for him to stop, but not regarding it, he went to the chase, and was killed.)

Tông 童 Tông choó, 童子, a youth, a young person under 10 years of age; a surname; sîn tông, 神童 a divine youth; tông gân, 童顏, a youthful countenance.

Suy soó gnoé ch'hek che tông sek ch'hē, bŏk che hĕk k'he, 雖使五尺之童適市莫之或欺 suy jëĕn saé goē ch'hëŏh kwân ây sêy këⁿá hoò ch'hē, bŏ lâng kⁿá hĕk p'hëèn e, (when good government prevails,) although you should send a boy five spans long to the market, no one would cheat or deceive him; see 孟子 Bēng choó.

Tông 瞳 Tông choó, 瞳子 bàk ang á, the pupil of the eye. Sùn tëûng tông, 舜重瞳 Sùn woō nō ây bàk ang á, Sùn had a double pupil in his eye.

Tông 潼 The name of a river; tông kwan, 潼關, the name of a pass.

Tông 犝 A young cow without horns, a calf.

Tông 羶 A goat without horns.

Tông 艟 Bông tông, 艨艟, a vessel of war.

Tông 曈 Tông bông, 曈曚, the sun about to shine.

Tông 朣 The moon just appearing.

Tông 僮 A general name for minions and servants.

Tông 罿 A curtain thrown over a carriage.

Tông 幢 Tông bông, 幢幪, a hilly appearance.

Tông 疼 Painful; tông aè, 疼愛, to love tenderly; tông t'hòng, 疼痛 t'hëⁿà tâng, to pity, to compassionate.

Tông 庝 The same as 痌, tông, the echo of a room.

Tông 鼕 The sound of a drum.

Tông 胗 Painful; the same as 疼, tông.

Tông 甋 A small tile; the same as 瓹, tông.

Tông 筩 A pipe made of a bamboo cut short.

Tông 彤 Red; tông këung, 彤弓, a red bow.

去

Tōng 洞 A cave, a hole, a dark recess; deep; sèk tōng, 石洞 chëŏh tāng, a rocky cavern.

Tōng 恫 Grieved; chóng tōng, 憁恫, disappointed and grieved.

Tōng 動 Vulg, tin tāng: to move, to be moved, to be agitated. Tè chëá tōng, 知者動 woō tè ây lâng k'hàh woō tin tāng, men of knowledge are active; see the 論語 Lūn gé.

Tōng 慟 To be immoderately grieved, to be deeply agitated with grief; ae tōng, 哀慟, deeply grieved, the feelings distressed.

Choó k'hok che tōng, 子哭之慟 *hoo choó k'haòu e kaòu tōng*, Confucius wept for him till he was excessively agitated; see the 論語 Lūn gé.

Tōng 愓 Water moved and agitated.

Tōng 燙 To bathe in warm water. Tōng toé, 燙斗, a smoothing iron.

Tōng 碭 A variegated stone, a stone with veins and various colors.

Bông tōng, 芒碭, the name of a hill.

Tōng 踼 Tëĕt tōng, 跌踼, to stumble, to halt, to be unable to proceed.

Tōng 湯 Hot water; to sprinkle with hot water.

Tōng 蕩 Wide and expansive, distant; hòng tōng, 放蕩, dissolute, loose.

Tōng tōng hoē! bîn boô lêng bêng yëen, 蕩蕩乎民無能名焉 *kóng kwuiⁿᵍ hoē! pǎyh saiⁿᵍ bô t'hang kèò e mēⁿâ*, how wide and expansive (were the virtues of Geâou!) the people were not able to designate them suitably; see the 論語 Lūn gé.

Tōng 宕 A cavern; also, the same as the preceding; loose, dissolute.

Tōng 盪 Ch'huy tōng, 推盪, to extend, to carry out; great, extensive.

8 C

Tōng 崵 Tōng san, 崵山, the name of a hill; also written 嵣, tōng.

Tōng 撞 Vulg. *teⁿᵍ*: to strike against, to run against anything.

Sëēn būn chëá, jê tōng chëung, 善問者如撞鐘 *hó mooiⁿᵍ áy lâng ch'hin, chëōⁿᵍ teⁿᵍ tëŏh chëung*, he who is able to propose a question well is like one who strikes a bell; (i. e. he is sure to get an answer;) see the 禮樂記 Léy gak kè.

𡗗

Too 鼄 Te too, 鼅鼄 *lā gëâ*, a spider.

Too 蛛 Te too, 蜘蛛 *lā gëâ*, the same as the above.

𡗗

Toó 抵 Read té: to resist, to withstand; té tong, 抵擋 *toó teⁿᵍ*, to stand against; té chëak, 抵着 *toó tëŏh*, to meet with, to fall in with.

Loē sëāng sëang té, 路上相抵 *loē ne sëo toó tëŏh*, to meet with a person on the road.

Toó 柢 Toó t'huy, 柢槌, a kind of prop, or pole.

𡗗

Toò 注 Read choò: a heap; chëên choò, 錢注 *cheeⁿᵍ toò*, a heap of money; a cant phrase, used to denote the stakes in gaming.

𡗗

Toô 廚 Paôu toô, 庖廚, a cook-house, a slaughter-house. Also written 厨, toô.

Kwun choó wân paôu toô, 君子遠庖廚 *kwun choó ch'hông hwuiⁿᵍ paôu toô*, the good man removes slaughter-houses and kitchens to a distance; see 孟子 Bēng choó.

Toô 𨇮 To toô, 踟𨇮, to be in doubt, and unable to proceed.

Toô 躕 The same as the above.

Tŏŏh 拄 Read ché: to push, to prop up; a prop; to thrust in.

Tooiⁿᵍ 返 Read hwán: to return; ch'hut göëy hwán laê, 出外返來 ch'hut gwā tooiⁿᵍ laê, to go abroad and return.

Tooiⁿᵍ 轉 Read chwán: to turn round; hwat lëén chwán, 發輾轉 hwat lín tooiⁿᵍ, to turn right round.

Chwán sin sëāng má, 轉身上馬 hwat lín tooiⁿᵍ sin chëōⁿᵍ báy, to turn around and mount a horse.

Tooìⁿᵍ 頓 Read tùn: a meal; yit tùn hwān, 一頓飯 chit tooìⁿᵍ pooīⁿᵍ, a meal of rice; yit tùn súy, 一頓水 chit tooìⁿᵍ chúy, one turn of the tide.

Tooīⁿᵍ 斷 Read twān: a piece, an end; chëĕt chok lëáng twān, 截作两斷 chăyh chò nō tooīⁿᵍ, to be cut into two pieces.

Tooīⁿᵍ 斷 Read twān: to discontinue, to cut short, to cease, to break in on a regular succession; twān jîn, 斷人 tooīⁿᵍ lâng, the population have all dwindled away.

Tun 敦 Thick, substantial, large, big; kind; to impel, to animate, to rouse, to urge; to give importance to; to press upon; affluent.

Tun hoē, 敦厚, affluent, substantial.

Tun 墩 A heap of earth, in the middle of a plain; a barrow.

Yëá sêng wûy chek, yêw yéw Sëā kong tun, 冶城遺跡猶有謝公墩 Yëá sëⁿâ ây wûy chëăh, yëá woō Chëā kong ây hwûn tun, among the antiquities of the city of Yëá, there still exists the tomb of Chëā kong; see the 白李詩 Lé pék se.

Tun 憞 To murmur at, to complain of, to be grieved with.

Tun 嶜 A hilly appearance.

Tun 燉 A great fire, a raging fire.

Tun 噋 K'hoé tun, 口噋, discourse, verbal professions. An unhealthy state of body or mind.

Tun 諄 Minute, particular; tun sëâng, 諄詳, minute, express.

Tun 迍 Tun chëen, 迍邅, unable to proceed, difficult to decide.

Tun 芚 The appearance of plants just shooting forth, sprouts; also an ignorant state and appearance.

Sèng jîn gê tun, 聖人忽芚 sèng jîn k'hê t'haôu gōng tun, even sages are at first stupid and unlearned.

Tun 窀 Tun sék, 窀穸, a carriage or truck for conveying a coffin down into a tomb; a hearse; a tomb.

Tun 鈍 Blunt, as a knife; not sharp.

福建方言字典

上 Tún 盾 A club or cudgel; all kinds of blunt weapons. Soo peng' sē chëáng gnoé tún, 司兵氏掌五盾 *kwán peng to ây lâng yëá kwán goē hāng ây tún*, the person who takes care of the military weapons, should also have charge of the five kinds of blunt instruments; see the 周禮 Chew léy. This character is also used to denote a rupee.

Tún 楯 The same as the preceding; also, a railing, a gallery; lengthwise a railing is called 欄, lan, and crosswise 楯, tún.

Tún 伅 Hwún tún, 倱伅, the name of one of the four wicked persons in ancient times; thick, dense, muddy, impervious.

Tún 笹 A receptacle for grain, made of matted reeds; a grain vessel.

Tún 磬 A stone broad and flat enough to sit upon.

去 Tùn 頓 To bow the head; tùn séw paè, 頓首拜, to bow the head, and make obeisance; also, to devour, to destroy; to lay up, to store away.

Tùn 扽 To lead, to draw; to rub, to grind.

Tùn 蒈 Gnêw tùn, 牛蒈, the name of a plant.

平 Tûn 脣 The lips; k'hoé tûn, 口脣 *ch'hùy tûn*, the lips of the mouth. Tûn bông ch'hé hân, 脣亡齒寒 *ch'hùy tún bô ch'hùy k'hé kwⁿâ*, when the lips are gone, the teeth will be cold; (intimating the necessity of preserving good neighbors, for the sake of one's own comfort.) Also written 唇, tûn.

Tûn 漘 The banks of a stream; chaē hô che tûn, 在河之漘 *twā tē káng keéⁿᵍ*, on the banks of the river; see the 王風 Ong hong.

Tûn 豚 A small pig, a young swine. Böéy tek yit tûn, é wûy tin sëên, 每得一豚以爲珍膳 *tàk paé tit tëòh chìh sèy chëăh te, chēw lëăh chò tin hó ây băh*, whenever he got a small pig, he considered it a precious piece of meat; see the 晋謝琨傳 Chìn sëā k'hwun twān.

Tûn 豘 The same as the preceding.

Tûn 屯 To guard a place with soldiers; to be quartered in a place, and cultivate the land, as is customary with Chinese soldiery. Këang-pek-yëak tûn tëên Hàn tëung, 姜伯約屯田漢中, Këang-pek-yëak stationed his troops and cultivated the fields in the centre of the Hàn region.

Tûn 魨 The name of a fish.

Tûn 吨 Tûn tûn, 吨吨, incessant, indistinct language.

Tûn 軘 A war chariot.

Tûn 臀 The thigh; also, the bottom of anything.

丟
Tŭn 遁 To run away, to escape, to avoid; to abolish; to avoid.
E ch'haĕ jê tŭn, 曳柴而遁 *t'hwa eh'hâ jê chaŏu*, they dragged branches of trees after them and retreated; (this is a common expedient in Chinese warfare, to make the enemy believe from the dust made, that their numbers are greater than they really are.

Tŭn 腯 Fat, corpulent, lusty.
Goê seng chwân hwûy tŭn, 吾牲牷肥腯 *gwá ây t'haŏu saing kap chèy ây goŏ woō pwúy tŭn*, my animals and sacrificial oxen are fat and in good condition; see the 左傳 Chó twăn.

Tŭn 循 To depart.

Tŭn 屯 To collect; to station troops in any place for its defense.

Tŭn 沌 Hwŭn tŭn, 混沌, the chaotic mass which existed before the organization of matter.
Hwŭn tŭn ch'hay k'hae, 混沌初開 *hwŭn tŭn k'hê t'haŏu k'hwuy*, at the first opening out of chaos.

Tŭn 鈍 Blunt, not sharp; dull, stupid, not clever.

Tŭn 伅 Hwún tŭn, 倱伅, impervious, unintelligible.

Tŭn 遯 To retire, to conceal, to hide.

犬
Tut 咄 Short.

Tut 咄 To vociferate, to bawl at any one; to make a frightful noise, so as to alarm people.

Tut 怏 A disconsolate mind; grieved.

Tut 柮 Kwut tut, 榾柮, a log of wood, a stump of a tree.

Tut 餶 Kwut tut jê, 餶飿兒, a kind of confectionary.

犬
Tŭt 突 To see any one suddenly; to offend against any one; to deceive.
Bē ké këĕn hêy, tŭt jê pwân hêy, 未幾見兮突而弁兮 *bōëy lwā koŏ k'hwnà keèng, tŭt jëĕn k'hwnà twà hân*, not having seen a youth for a short time, on meeting him suddenly we find him grown up to be a man; see the 齊風 Chêy hong. Ch'hëung tŭt, 衝突, to rush against, in word or action.

Tŭt 揬 Tông tŭt, 搪揬, to offend by rude manners.

Tŭt 傑 Tông tŭt, 儻傑, a rude insolent, behavior.

Tŭt 湥 The appearance of water flowing.

Tŭt 崫 Tŭt gwŭt, 崫屼, hills, mountains.

Tŭt 朮 Pĕk tŭt, 白朮 the name of a medicine.

Tút 秫 Tút bé, 秫米, a glutinous kind of rice.

Tút 凸 A projecting appearance; a rising up, or jutting out.

Tút 祋 A military weapon.

Tút 嘞 The same as the following.

Tút 咄 To converse together.

卒 Tuy 追 To follow, to pursue after any one; tuy kán, 追趕, *tuy kwⁿá*, to follow in pursuit; tuy che put kip, 追之不及 *tuy e bëy kip*, to follow without overtaking.

The people of 鄭, Tēng sent a person to attack the 衛, Wöēy country, and (Wöēy soó Jé-kong-che-soo tuy che, 衛使庾公之斯追之 *Wöēy kok saé Jé-kong-che-soo k'hè tuy e,*) the people of the Wöēy country sent Jé-kong-che-soo to pursue after him; see 孟子 Beng choó.

Tuy 自 Earth collected together; a heap.

Tuy 磓 Stones collected together; a heap of stones.

Tuy 堆 A heap of earth; hwǔn tuy, 糞堆 *pùn tuy*, a dunghill; ch'hó tuy, 草堆 *ch'haóu tuy*, a heap of grass. Tuy kim chek gëük, 堆金積玉 *tuy kim k'hëŏh gěk*, to heap up gold, and collect gems.

Tuy 䯔 A projection of the bone.

Tuy 隹 A general name for birds with short feathers.

Tuy 鵻 Kaou tuy, 交鵻 *ka chuy*, a dove.

Tuy 騅 The color of a horse.

声 Túy 劯 To pull with all one's might.

去 Tùy 對 To reply, to answer, to correspond to; tùy tap, 對答, to reply; tùy ték, 對敵, an enemy, an opponent; chò tùy, 做對, to make antithetical sentences, corresponding to one another; yit tuy, 一對 *chit tùy*, a pair; tùy bëēn, 對面, face to face, opposite.

Kwun choó bŭn, keng twan, chek k'hé jê tùy, 君子問更端則起而對 *kwun choó ây lâng woō mooīⁿᵍ lán, nā wⁿā teâou twan, tëŏh k'hé jê yîn*, when respectable people ask us questions, on varying the subject, we ought to rise in giving our reply; see the 曲禮 K'hëuk léy.

Tùy 碓 A pestle; cheng tùy, 舂碓, a pestle to pound with in a mortar.

平 Tûy 搥 To beat, to strike.

Chok gák koé hwân tûy, 作樂鼓還搥 *chok gák ây sí koé yëá tit tûy*, whilst playing the music, the drum is still beaten.

Tûy 瞳 Jé tûy, 耳 瞳, earrings.

丟

Tūy 墜 To fall down, to descend, to sink down.
Bûn boó che tō, bē tūy ê tēy, 文武之道未墜於地 *bûn boô ây tō lê, böëy woō tūy tē tēy*, the sciences of civil and military pursuits are not yet fallen to the ground; see the 論語 Lūn gé.

Tūy 隊 A group, a troop, a company.
Ch'hoé soo hwun wûy jê tūy, 楚師分爲二隊 *Ch'hoé ây peng hwun chò nō tūy*, the troops of the Ch'hoé country were divided into two bands; see the 左傳 Chó twān.

Tūy 隧 A road, an underground passage; a dangerous pass amongst mountains.
Also read sūy: which see.

Tūy 縋 To let down by cords.
Yëā tūy jê ch'hut, 夜縋而出 *mai^{ng} kan tūy jé ch'hut*, he was let down with cords by night, and got out; see the 左傳 Chó twān.

Tūy 懟 To be displeased, to murmur, to complain.

Tūy 憝 To complain, to murmur.
Hwān bîn bông put tūy, 凡民罔不憝 *hwān păyh sai^{ng} bô $ū^{m}$ wān e*, of all the people there were none who did not complain; see the 書經 Se keng.

Tūy 駾 Suddenly, unexpectedly.

卢

Twá 磋 *Lwá twá*, 蕠蕿, not to hit the due medium, to act strangely.

去

Twà 帶 Read taè: a girdle, a band.
Ch'hek yëá, sok taè lip ê teâou, 赤也束帶立於朝 *Ch'hek yëá, t'hang hăh twà k'hëā tē teâou têng*, Ch'hek can put on his girdle, and stand in the court; see the 論語 Lūn gé.

平

Twâ 拖 Read tô: to drag, to draw, to pull.

丟

Twā 大 Read taē: great, large; sè taē, 世大 *sè twā*, superiors.
K'hó é boô taē kò è, 可以無大過矣 *t'hang é bô twā köèy sit*, he can be without any great faults; see the 論語 Lūn gé.

Twā 舵 Read tō: a rudder, a helm.

卒

$Tw^{n}a$ 單 Read tan: only, alone, a single one; a receipt; koe tan, 孤單 *koe $tw^{n}a$*, solitary.
Hêng tan éng chek, 形單影隻 *$tw^{n}a$ chit ây hîn sin $yë^{n}á$ chit chëăh*, a single figure, and a solitary shadow.

$Tw^{n}a$ 癉 Read tan: a sickness incident to children.

$Tw^{n}a$ 簞 Read tan: a bamboo vessel, for containing rice.

卢

$Tw^{n}á$ 訑 Repeated talking.

去
Twⁿà 旦 Read tàn: as hè tàn, 戲旦 *hè twⁿà*, a female character in a play.

平
Twⁿâ 壇 Read t'hân: a terrace; chèy t'hân, 祭壇 *chèy twⁿâ*, a terrace for offering sacrifices on.

Twⁿâ 檀 Read t'hân: as t'hân hëang, 檀香 *twⁿâ hëoⁿᵍ*, a fragrant kind of wood.

Twⁿâ 彈 Read t'hân: to play on the harp or guitar; t'hân k'hîm, 彈琴 *twⁿâ k'hîm*, to play on the harp.
K'hîm gō te yim t'hân, 琴遇知音彈 *k'hîm toó tëŏh chae yim ây lâng chëw twⁿâ*, with respect to a harp, we should find a person who understands music before we play upon it.

Twⁿâ 團 Read twân: round; twân wân, 團圓 *twⁿâ cëⁿᵍ*, round and globular.

丟
Twⁿā 段 Read tān: an end, a slice, or piece of anything.

Twⁿā 彈 Read tān: as tān choó, 彈子 *twⁿā á*, pellets for shooting at birds; also, bullets, balls for guns, any small and round thing.

Twⁿā 撣 Read tān: to fillip with the finger.

Twⁿā 惰 Read tō: lazy; lán tō, 懶惰 *pún twⁿā*, idle.

夬
Twăh 剟 To cut off, to cut to pieces.

卒
Twan 端 Correct, exact; the end of a clue; the head of anything.
Hoo Yin kong twan jîn yëá, 夫尹公端人也 *hoo Yin kong sē chèng keng lâng*, now Yin kong is a correct man; see 孟子 Bēng choó.

Twan 偳 Small, little.

声
Twán 短 Vulg. *téy*: short, not long.
Sëet kêw tëâng, twán yēw bēy, 褻裘長短右袂 *sac k'hëā ây hêw tëⁿᵍ, téy chéⁿa ch'hêw ây ch'hêw wuīⁿᵍ*, Confucius had his private dress long, with the right hand sleeve short; see the 論語 Lūn gé.

去
Twàn 斷 Kwat twàn, 決斷, to determine.
E twàn t'hëen hāy che gê, 以斷天下之疑 *é twàn t'heeⁿᵍ āy ây gê gnaé*, to settle the doubts of the whole empire; see the 易繫詞 Ék hēy soô.

平
Twân 團 Wân twân, 圓團 *cëⁿᵍ teëⁿᵍ*, round and globular; conglomerated; forming a roundness; dwelling together as one body.
Twân wân soō bêng gwát, 團圓似明月 *cëⁿᵍ teëⁿᵍ ch'hin chëōⁿᵍ bêng ây göëyh*, as round as the full moon; see the 班婕詩 Pān chëét se.

Twân 漙 The appearance of much dew.

Twân 慱 To be grieved, and distressed.

Twân 糰 A kind of confectionary.

Twân 摶 To roll anything up in the hand. Boŏ twân bwān, 毋摶飯 *boŏ twân pooing*, don't roll your rice up into round pellets, (when you eat it;) see the 曲禮 K'hëuk léy.

彖
Twān 篆 Twān joō, 篆字 *twān jē*, the seal character.

Twān 緞 T'hew twān, 紬緞, silk and satin.

Twān 斷 Vulg. *tooing*: to be cut short, to be cut off. Se sìn twān chwàt, 書信斷絶 *p'hay sìn tooing chwàt*, the cutting off of all correspondence.

Twān 傳 A book of instruction, an historical record. E twān yéw che, 於傳有之 *tē twān woō e*, it is in the record.

犬
Twat 掇 To pluck, to gather, to pick, to receive.

Twat 惙 Sorrowful, grieved.

Twat 綴 To stop, to put a stop to. Léy chëá séy é twat yîm yëá, 禮者所以綴淫也 *léy chëá, sē séy é ch'hòng swàh kan yîm*, politeness is designed to put a stop to lasciviousness; see the 禮樂記 Léy gak kè.

Twat 輟 To stop, to cease; twat kong, 輟工, to stop work. Yew jê put twat, 耰而不輟 *yew pây jê bŏ haïnh*, he continued to harrow the ground, without stopping; see the 論語 Lûn gé.

Twat 裰 To mend and repair clothes.

Twat 剟 To cut, to cut off, to scrape away, to engrave.

Twat 啜 The appearance of standing; to talk much, without ceasing.

Twat 逿 To run away, to run quickly; to go far.

Twat 蹳 To hop and skip; also written 趨, twat.

Twat 錣 A walking stick with a sharp point.

Twat 涰 To weep; the noise of water.

夊
Twȧt 奪 To plunder, to take by force, to snatch. Cheng bîn se twȧt, 爭民施奪 *chaing ây pâyh saing sëo ch'hëóng*, the contentious among the people will begin to plunder one another; see the 大學 Taē hȧk.

U

聲 上
Úm 姆 Read boe: an uncle's wife; tëăng boé, 丈 姆 tëo^{ng} úm, a mother-in-law; ch'hin boé, 親 姆 ch'hai^{ng} úm, the mother of a son's wife.

平 上
Ûm 梅 Read böëy: a prune, a plum; ch'heng böëy, 青 梅 ch'hai^{ng} ûm, a green plum.

去 上
Ūm 不 Read put: not, will not, a token of refusal.
Gnó put, 我 不 gwá ūm, I will not, cannot, or may not.

去 上
Un 亞 Read à: as à sëuk, 亞 叔 u^{n} chek, uncle! a term of salutation among equals for one who is older.

W

上 聲
Wá 瓦 Vulg. hëā: a tile; wá ok, 瓦 屋 hëā ch'hoò, a tiled house.
Song song wá ch'hëak hêng se àn, 雙 雙 瓦 雀 行 書 案 chit sang hëā têng ây chăyh á kë^{n}â tē ch'hăyh tŏh têng, a pair of sparrows from the tiles walked over the writing table; see the 杜 甫 詩 Toē hoó se.

Wá 倚 Read é: to rely on, to confide in, to lean against, to place trust in; inclined to one side.
Chaē ê chek këèn kê é ê hêng yëá, 在 輿 則 見 其 倚 於 衡 也 twā tē ch'hëa, chek k'hw^{n}à e wá tē ch'hëa hêng, when in the carriage, we can see them leaning on the cross-bar of it; see the 論 語 Lūn gé.

8 E

Wá 掗 To take, to take away by violence.

Wá 蚙 Read é: as poē é, 蛂蚙 *poē wá*, a kind of insect.

去

Wà 㳿 To lead water into the rice fields, in order to irrigate them.

Wà 攨 To draw, to pull, to drag.

平

Wâ 娃 A handsome woman.

Wâ 哇 Wanton sounds; to vomit, to spit out. Ch'hut jê wâ che, 出而哇之, he went out and vomited it up; see 孟子 Bēng choó.

Wâ 蛙 A frog; the croaking of frogs. Tê tông wâ choè koé, 池塘蛙奏鼓 *tê tê tông kap á tit p'hăh koé*, the frogs in the pools are making a noise like the beating of drums.

Wâ 鼃 A kind of frog or toad.

Wâ 窪 Deep, abstruse; a ditch.

Wâ 漥 Clear water; the water collected in the footsteps of an ox.

Wâ 窊 The hole made by the hoof of an animal; a dirty puddle; soiled, dirty.

Wâ 呱 The sound of children crying; sobbing.

Wâ 媧 Lé-wâ sē, 女媧氏, the name of an ancient empress, who is said to have melted down stones, in order to repair the southern heavens.

Wâ 騧 A white horse, with a black nose.

Wâ 洼 The name of a river; a deep ditch.

Wâ 椏 Sē wâ, 樞椏 *ch'hēw wá*, the main branches of a tree.

去

Wā 画 Read hwā: to paint, to draw, to delineate; hwā kong, 画工 *wā kang*, a painter, or his work. Also written 畵, hwā. Ong-mô-kēet hwa tëung yéw se, 王摩結画中有詩 *Ong-mô-kēet tē wā tang eng woō chò se*, Ong-mô-kēet in the midst of his drawings would insert a piece of poetry.

Wā 話 Read hwā: words, discourse, conversation, speech; to tell; káng hwā, 講話 *kóng wā*, to talk, to converse.

上

Wna 安 Read an: peaceful; an wún, 安穩 *wna wún*, safe, secure.

Wna 鞍 Read an: a saddle; má an, 馬鞍 *báy wna*, a horse's saddle.

Wna 垵 Read an: a haven; an ò, 垵澳 *wna ò*, a harbor, an anchorage.

福建方言字典

上聲
Wⁿá 埦 Read wán: a cup, a basin, a dish; yit wán hwăn, 一埦飯 *chit wⁿá pooⁱⁿᵍ*, a cup of rice. Also written 碗, wán.

上去
Wⁿà 案 Read àn: a table; an official bench, that which is placed on it; a law case; àn tok, 案桌 *wⁿà tŏh*, a table, a magisterial bench.

Wⁿà 晏 Read àn: late, not early. Choó wát, hô àn yëá, 子曰何晏也 *hoo choó kóng, sⁿa soō kadu hëá wⁿà*, Confucius said, "how is it that you are so late?" see the 論語 Lūn gé.

下去
Wⁿā 旱 Read hān: a drought, a want of rain. Jëák taē hān che bōng yîn gêy yëá, 若大旱之望雲霓也 *ch'hin chëōⁿᵍ twā wⁿā ây bāng hwⁿn kap k'hēng*, (to expect any one) just as a great drought looks for the clouds and rainbow; see 孟子 Bēng choó.

Wⁿā 換 Read hwàn: to change, to exchange; kaou hwàn, 交換 *kaou wⁿā*, to barter.

Hwân kwut hô sê hwàn? 凡骨何時換 *hwân sëâng ây kwut te sê ēy wⁿā?* when shall I be enabled to exchange these common bones? (alluding to the metempsychosis, in which the Chinese suppose that common bodies will be exchanged for more ethereal ones.)

上平
Wae 歪 Awry, uneven, not straight; wae këak, 歪脚 *wae k'ha*, a wry leg. Sim wae, 心歪 *sim kwⁿa wae*, a perverse mind.

上聲
Waé 踈 Këak waé, 脚踈 *k'ha waé*, to sprain one's foot.

上去
Waè 黯 A dark color, nearly black.

Waè 鼿 To snuff through the nose.

上平
Waeⁿᵍ 閂 The bar of a door; the sound of a door creaking on its hinges.

上入
Waĕh 孬 Vulg. *baé:* bad, not good.

上入
Waiⁿᵍh 輵 The noise of a carriage.

下入
Waiⁿᵍh 閣 The creaking of a door on its hinges.

上入
Wăh 頞 Pit hëăh, 鼻頞 *p'heēⁿᵍ wăh*, the bridge of the nose.

下入
Wăh 活 Read hwát: life, alive, to live; k'hwaè hwát, 快活 *k'hwⁿa wăh*, comfortable.

Bîn hwuy súy hⁿó put seng hwát, 民非水火不生活 *păyh saiⁿᵍ bô chúy höěy bēy saiⁿᵍ wăh*, if the people possess not fire and water, they cannot live; see 孟子 Bēng choó.

上平
Wan 冤 Bent, crooked; to injure, to ill use; to force; wan óng, 冤枉, oppression, injustice; wan k'hwut, 冤屈, to treat wrongfully.

Wan 剜 Wan sëak, 剜削, to cut and carve.

Wan 彎 Crooked, bent, not straight. Yit wan Sey-choó pè, 一彎西子臂 *chit ây wan Sey-choó ây ch'hêw pè*, one turn of the beautiful Sey-choó's arm.

Wan 灣 A winding stream; a crooked shore. Yit wan k'hey súy p'haōu san laê, 一灣溪水抱山來 *chit wan ây k'hey chúy p'hō swⁿa laê*, the brook in its serpentine course embraced the hill.

Wan 鴛 Wan yang, 鴛鴦 *wan yëoⁿᵍ*, the name of a bird; the species of duck called the 'mandarin duck,' peculiar to China; they are considered as emblems of conjugal fidelity; also the name of an insect.

上聲

Wán 俒 Pleased, delighted; to exhort.

Wán 宛 Wán jëên, 宛然, as if, according to. Wán chaē súy tëung yang, 宛在水中央 *ch'hin chëōⁿᵍ tē chúy tang eⁿᵍ*, just as if it were in the middle of the water.

Wán 碗 Vulg. *wⁿá:* a cup, a basin; pwan wán, 盤碗 *pwⁿa wⁿá*, cups and saucers.

Wán 埦 The same as the above.

Wán 菀 Wán yéw, 菀囿 a park, a place for deer; a game walk, a garden.

Wán 盌 A small bowl; also written 椀, wán.

Wán 琬 The name of a gem.

Wán 腕 The wrist, the joint near the hand; séw wán, 手腕 *ch'hêw wán*, the elbow.

Wán 畹 A piece of ground, 20 acres in extent; also written 畱, wán.

Wán 婉 Obedient, submissive; handsome, beautiful; accommodating. Wán jê pëen, 婉而辨 *wán sùn jê ēy pëēn lūn*, obedient and yet disposed to argue matters; see the 春秋 Ch'hun ch'hew. Ch'heng yâng wán hêy, 清揚婉兮 *bàk baê ch'hin ch'haiⁿᵍ*, handsome about the eyebrows; see the 齊風 Chêy hong.

Wán 浣 To wash away filth; wán e hók, 浣衣服 *séy sⁿá*, to wash clothes.

Wán 莞 A smile; to smile; hoo choó wán jé jê ch'heàou, 夫子莞爾而笑 *hoo choó wán jëên jê ch'hëô*, Confucius smiled and laughed; see the 論語 Lūn gé.

Wán 遠 Vulg. *hwuiⁿᵍ:* far, distant, far off; a long time ago. Tō che yîn wán, 道之云遠 *loē ây kóng kēò hwuiⁿᵍ*, the way may be called distant and far. Sè wán lëên yëen, 世遠年湮 *sè hwuiⁿᵍ neëⁿᵍ bô k'hè*, in ages far removed, and in years that are gone by.

Wán 阮 Vulg. *wuiⁿᵍ:* a surname, the name of a country.

去聲

Wàn 怨 Inimical, displeased; to murmur, to complain; wàn hwūn, 怨恨, to hate, to dislike; wàn t'hëen, 怨天, to repine at heaven.

Kêw jîn jê tek jîn, yēw hô wàn? 求仁而得仁又何怨 *kêw jin jê tit tĕŏh jin, yĕá woō sⁿá mèⁿgh wàn?* having sought after virtue they obtained it; where then was the reason of complaint? see the 論語 Lūn gé.

平

Wân 丸 Anything round and small; yëák wân, 藥丸 *yĕŏh wân*, a pill. Tân wân, 彈丸, a pellet, anything very small.

Wân 紈 White; also, to tie; a white cord.

Wân 芄 The name of a plant.

Wân 袁 A surname.

Wân 猿 A monkey, an ape; kó sëùk wân sim tōng, 菓熟猿心動 *köéy chë sèk, kaôu ây sim kwⁿa tin tăng*, when fruits become ripe the minds of monkeys are moved.

Wân 轅 A crooked piece of wood in front of a carriage. The eastern and western gates of a magistrate's hall are also called wân bûn, 轅門 *wân mooⁿg*.

Wân 園 Vulg. *hwuiⁿg*: a garden; chok wân, 作園 *chŏh hwuiⁿg*, to cultivate a garden; ch'haè wân, 菜園 *ch'haè hwuiⁿg*, a kitchen garden; hwa wân, 花園 *hwa hwuiⁿg*, a flower garden.

Wân 袁 Long garments.

Wân 員 The numeral of valuable things, and of magistrates. Kwan wân, 官員 *kwⁿa wân*, an officer of government; wûy wân, 委員, an official messenger. Vulg. *k'hoe*: a dollar.

Wân 圓 Vulg. *ⁿg*: round, circular. Kwuy kó hong wân che chè yëá, 規矩方圓之至也 *kwuy kê sē sè kak kap ēⁿg ây chè kèk*, the compass and square have brought squares and circles to perfection; see 孟子 Lêng chuó.

Wân 嵈 An indented part of a hill.

Wân 幁 Hok wân, 幅幁, broad and extensive.

Wân 萑 A small reed or rush; pat gwat wân wûy, 八月萑葦 *pāyh gĕ yh woō wân wûy*, in the 8th month is the time for reeds and rushes.

Wân 完 To finish, to complete; wân chwân, 完全, complete, perfect. Seáou yéw wát, koé wân è! 少有曰苟完矣 *sió k'hwá woō, chēw kóng, chin chīⁿà wân chwân è!* when he had a little, he would exclaim "truly I have a completion!" see the 論語 Lūn gé.

Wân 莞 The name of a plant; wân suy, 莞荽, coriander seed.

Wân 烷 Fire; wân lân, 烷蘭, the name of a flower.

去

Wān 爰 In, at; this, to lead, to change.

Wān 媛 A handsome woman.

Wān 瑗 A gem with a large hole in it.

Wān 緩 Slowly, leisurely, gently; wān tê, 緩 遲, late, behindhand.

Wān 援 To help, to save; to receive, to take, to pull, to drag; wān kèw, 援 救, to rescue, to save, to reform. Só lèk chek wān che é séw hoē? 嫂溺則援之以手乎 *hëⁿa só tëëm lèk chek kèw wān e é ch'hëw hoē?* when a sister-in-law is drowning (in a well), will you help her out with your hand? see 孟子 Bēng choó.

Wān 褑 A kind of cloak, thrown over the back.

Wān 湲 The name of a stream.

Wān 遠 Vulg. *hwuiⁿᵍ:* to remove to a distance; to keep at a distance. Tōng yûng maōu, soo wān pō bān è, 動容貌斯遠暴慢矣 *gaōu tin tāng yúng maōu, chéy lēy chēw ch'hòng hwuiⁿᵍ pō bān è,* if we keep up a respectable appearance, it will remove to a distance insult and reproach; see the 論語 Lūn gé.

夫

Wat 穵 Great and extended; to feel with the hand in a hole or cavity.

Wat 屼 A crooked part of a hill.

Wat 軏 The wheel of a carriage, the turning of a wheel; to strive, or contend together.

Wat 搰 To take, to deliver, to save.

Wat 欸 The breathing in the throat not free and easy.

Wat 斡 To turn round, to revolve; the handle of anything; the knob in the middle of a gong.

天

Wȧt 曰 Vulg. *kóng:* to speak, to say, to assert. Choó wȧt, hȧk jê sê sip che, 子曰學而時習之 *hoo choó kóng, t'hȧk jê sëâng sé wun sip e,* Confucius said, "learn, and constantly exercise yourself in it;" see the 上論 Sëāng lūn.

Wȧt 悅 To be pleased, to be delighted; pleasant, delightful. Put ék wȧt hoē? 不亦悅乎 *ūᵐ yëá hwⁿa hé hoē?* is it not delightful? see the 上輪 Sëāng lūn.

Wȧt 說 The same as the preceding; also read swat: to speak.

Wȧt 閱 To look at, to observe; to pass over; hwȧt wȧt, 閥閱, accumulated merit, merit accumulated in a family from one generation to another.

Wȧt 粤 At, in; to examine, to inspect; wȧt séng, 粤省, a classical name for the province of Canton. Wȧt key koé sèng, 粤稽古聖 *wȧt k'hwⁿȧ key k'hó koé chá ây sèng jîn,* to examine and inspect the ancient sages.

福建方言字典

Wàt 戉 A great hatchet.

Wàt 越 To display; to pass over, to exceed, more and more; a surname. Wàt kéw wàt ko, 越攵越高 *nā I kwân*, the longer the higher.

Wàt 樾 The shady place between two trees.

Wàt 鉞 Hoó wàt, 斧鉞, a hatchet or ax. When Confucius wrote the history of his own times, every word of praise was said to be (êng ê hwa kwún, 榮於華袞 *k'hăh êng kwuiⁿᵍ ê hwa kwún,*) more glorious than a flowery crown; and every word of censure was (gëêm ê hoó wàt, 嚴於斧鉞 *k'hăh gëêm ê poó t'habu,*) more severe than an ax or hatchet.

去

Wöey 隈 A winding stream, a crooked bank.

Wöey 偎 To love; wöey jîn, 偎人 *t'hëⁿà lâng*, to love people.

Wöey 喂 To be afraid; wöey má, 喂馬 *ch'hē báy*, to feed a horse.

Wöey 猥 Vulgar, low, mean.

Wöey 煨 The fire in a chaffing-dish. Hwān pèk jīm, tō wöey höey, 犯白刃蹈煨灰 *hwān tëōh pâyh to, tăh tëōh wöey laē ây höey*, to come in contact with naked swords, and to tread on the ashes of the chaffing-dish.

Wöey 碨 Wöey lúy, 碨磊, a heap of stones; wöey laê, 碨硋, uneven.

Wöey 葨 Grass; the name of a plant.

Wöey 鍡 To cut, to chop meat; wöey k'hae, 鍡開 *wöey k'hwuy*, to cut open.

Wöey 倭 Wöey jîn, 倭人, a Japanese; Wöey tê, 倭遲, Japan.

Wöey 矮 Sick, dried to death, withered.

Wöey 痿 A sickness arising from damp.

Wöey 鍋 An earthen vessel, a pot.

Wöey 剮 To chop up meat.

Wöey 鈳 Tông o, 銅鈳 *tâng wöey*, a brazen pot.

去

Wöèy 穢 Filthy, dirty, defiled, overgrown with weeds and jungle. Boô wöèy put tē, 蕪穢不治, not to clear away the weeds and rubbish; see 荀子 Sûn choó.

Wöèy 薉 Dirty, filthy, overgrown with jungle. Toê wöèy chek hân, 塗薉則寒 *loē kabu sëōⁿᵍ lâ sâm chëw këⁿa*, when the road is much overgrown with jungle, people are afraid.

Wöèy 濊 Ong wöèy, 汪濊, deep and expansive, immense and overwhelming. Tam yin ong wöèy, 湛恩汪濊 *hó ây yin hwūy ong wöèy*, your pleasing kindness is vast and overwhelming; see the 史記 Soó kè.

Wöèy 劌 To cut, to wound.

Wöèy 噦 The sound of chariot wheels.

Wöèy 翽 The sound of birds flying high. Hông hông ê hwuy, wöèy wöèy kê é, 鳳凰于飛翽翽其羽 *hông hông tit pwuy, woō wöèy wöèy c ây sit*, the phœnixes are flying about, and the sound of their wings is like "*wöèy, wöèy;*" see the 大雅 Taē gnáy.

Wöèy 餯 Rice heated and turned sour.

Wöèy 廆 A secret place, a hiding place.

平 Wöêy 禾 A kind of chestnut; the name of a place; wöêy ch'haè, 禾菜, the salad vegetable.

去 Wöēy 衛 To guard, to defend, to ward off a blow; the name of a country. A surname. Wöēy seng, 衛生, to take care of one's health.
Hoè wöēy, 護衛, to protect, to escort, to defend.
Jê choó tëy che wöēy hoō heng, 如子弟之衛父兄 *ch'hin chëōng haōu saing sëó tē ây hoè wöēy pāy hëⁿa*, just as sons and younger brethren defend their fathers and elder brethren.

入 Wöĕyh 挖 To take anything in the hand, to pluck anything out. Wöĕyh bók, 挖目 *wöĕyh bák chew*, to pluck out the eyes.

入 *Wöĕyh* 噦 To make a noise; to belch.

Wöĕyh 穭 K'heng *wöĕyh*, 穅穭, the bran or husk of grain.

Wöĕyh 剨 Read ék: to scoop anything out; to break.

平 Woo 迂 Woo wán, 迂遠 *woo hwuīng*, distant, far off; woo k'hwat, 迂濶, wide, far apart.
Jê sût woo soe kwⁿá haōu, 儒術迂踈寡效 *t'hàk ch'háyh lâng ây hwat sût hwuīng sey, chëó woō haōu gëèm*, the precepts of the learned respect distant things, of which the accomplishment is seldom seen; see the 戰國策 Chëèn kok ch'hek.

Woo 汙 Muddy, dirty, stagnant, water; foul, impure, unclean, low, both physically and morally; woo wöèy, 汙穢, filthy, defiled; overgrown with weeds.
Woo súy, 汙水 *la sâm chúy*, muddy, dirty water.
Tëên chut woo laê, 田卒汙萊 *ch'hân kaōu swăh böēy woo laê*, the fields were finally overgrown with weeds; see the 小雅 Seáou gnáy.

Woo 圬 An implement used in plastering a wall, a trowel; to plaster.
Hwùn t'hoé che ch'hëâng put k'hó woo yëá, 糞土之墻不可圬也 *pùn t'hoè ây ch'hëōng hëy hoē lé bwăh*, a wall built of mud and dung cannot be plastered; see the 論語 Lūn gé.

Woo 杇 The same as the preceding.

Woo 跒 To squat down, to sit down on the ground.

Woo 紆 Bent, crooked; a rope.

Woo 骬 Këak t'hoê woo, 脚頭骬 *k'ha t'haôu woo*, the knee.

Woo 洿 A hole in which water collects; a puddle.

上聲
Woó 鄔 A surname.

上去
Woò 污 To dirty, to defile.

下平
Woô 盂 A vessel for drinking from; a bowl; also written 盂, woô.

下去
Woō 有 Read yéw: to have, to possess, to exist, to be.

Būn yéw ê, pit wát yéw, 問有餘必曰有 *mooi^{ng} woō ch'hun, pit kóng woō*, (Cheng-choó's father) always asked, if there was anything left (of the food), when he would always reply that there was; see 孟子 Bēng choó.

上平
Wui^{ng} 揖 To throw, to cast, to throw away; wui^{ng} k'hoé, 揖口 *wui^{ng} ch'hùy*, to stop the mouth with the hand; wui^{ng} soó, 揖死 *wui^{ng} sé*, to stifle, to smother.

上聲
Wuí^{ng} 抚 To hold in the arms, to embrace.

Wuí^{ng} 阮 Read wán: a surname.

Wuí^{ng} 笎 Read wún: a basket; wún choó, 笎仔 *wuí^{ng} á*, a small basket, in which things are put in order to be weighed.

下平
Wuî^{ng} 黃 Read hông: yellow; a surname; hông gnêw, 黄牛 *wuî^{ng} goô*, a dun cow, a cow.

Hông e hoê hêw, 黄衣狐裘 *wuî^{ng} s^{n}a hoê ây hêw*, a yellow garment should be worn with a fox skin fur; see the 論語 Lūn gé.

Wuî^{ng} 癀 Read hông: hông chëúng, 癀疸, the jaundice; gnêw hông, 牛癀 *goô wuî^{ng}*, a kind of medicine.

Wuî^{ng} 禳 Chok wuî^{ng}, 作禳, to perform incantations, for the purpose of laying evil spirits; this is said to be effected by (tëang t'hëen soo, 張天師 *tëo^{ng} t'hee^{ng} soo*,) the lama of China.

Wuî^{ng} 彎 *Lèy wuî^{ng}*, 犁彎, the crooked handle of a plough.

下去
Wuī^{ng} 暈 Read wūn: a halo round the sun or moon; the eyes dim.

上平
Wun 溫 Amicable, harmonious; a surname; wun jêw, 溫柔, soft and gentle; wun lwán, 溫煖, genial and warm; wun hô, 溫和, mild and benign; wun hong, 溫風, a gentle breeze.

Choó wun jô lēy, 子溫而厲 *hoo choó wun jūn*

8 G

jé gëëm lēy, Confucius was benignant and yet stern; see the 論語 Lūn gé.

Wun 氤 Wun yin, 氤氳, the original influence of heaven and earth, germinating in secret.

Wun 熅 Curling smoke.

Wun 瘟 Wun ėk, 瘟疫 *wun yëăh*, a pestilence, an epidemical disorder.

Wun 薀 A kind of water vegetable.

Wun 馧 Wun pút, 馧馞, very fragrant.

Wun 豱 The name of a pig; a pig running off.

Wun 鰮 The name of a certain kind of fish.

Wun 蒀 P'hûn wun, 蒶蒀, luxuriant; also the name of a plant.

Wun 昷 The warmth produced by the rising sun.

Wun 縕 Yin wun, 絪縕, the original influence of heaven and earth, secretly producing all things.

T'hëen tēy yin wun, bān bút hwà sûn, 天地絪縕萬物化醇 *t'heeng tēy yin wun ây k'hè, bān mëengh hwà sún*, by the germinating influence of heaven and earth all things are produced and nourished; see the 易繫詞 Ék hēy soô.

上聲

Wún 允 Truly, faithfully, really; sincere, upright; also written 㐾, wún. Kong wát, kò jé tīm wún, 公曰告汝朕允 *Kong kóng, kap lé kóng gwá sìn sit*, Chew-kong said, "I tell you that I am sincere;" see the 書經 Se keng.

Wún 狁 Hëém wún, 玁狁, the name of one of the northern hordes of Tartars.

Wún 吮 To suck, to draw in, to inhale; also written 吮, wún. Chut yéw pēng ch'he chëá, Goê-k'hé wūy wún che, 卒有病疽者吳起爲吮之 *peng chut woō paīng ch'heng ây lâng, Goê-k'hé t'hëy e wún so e*, when any of his soldiers had a sore or an ulcer, the general Goê-k'hé would lick it for them; (so anxious was he to please them.)

Wún 隕 To fall; wún tūy, 隕墜, to fall down from a high place. Lek lek gwûy kē, jëák chëang wún ê ch'him yëen, 慄慄危懼若將隕于深淵 *lek lek gwûy këna, ch'hin chëōng chëang wún tūy tē ch'him yëen*, trembling and apprehensive of danger, like one about to fall into a deep pit; see the 書湯誥 Se t'hang kò.

Wún 殞 To die, to decease; to fade.

Wún 傊 To be sorrowful, to grieve.

Wún 穩 Grain collected together; to moisten grain before distilling; quiet, composed, easy, secure; an wún, 安穩 *wna wún*, safe, secure; wún tòng, 穩當, safe, without apprehension of danger.

海上絲綢之路文獻集成 科技與文化编

Wún 愪 To be grieved, to be agitated with grief.

Wún 碩 To fall, to fall down.

Wún 賱 Wún ch'hún, 賱賰, rich, affluent.

Wún 頵 A wry face, a distorted countenance.

去

Wùn 慍 To be displeased, to be vexed; inward displeasure, murmuring; jîn put te, jê put wùn, 人不知而不慍 lâng ūm chae lán, jê lán bô sim hŏey tŏh, when people do not know us, not to be vexed; (this is the sign of a good man;) see the 上論 Sēăng lūn.

Wùn 蘊 To collect, to accumulate, to store up.

Wùn 搵 To press the finger on anything; to take anything out of the water.

Wùn 縕 Wadded with cotton; silk-cotton wadding; anything warm, genial, and soothing.

E pē wùn p'haôu, 衣敝縕袍 ch'hèng koō ây sëō p'haôu, he wore an old wadded garment; see the 論語 Lūn gé.

Wùn 醞 Ripe, mellow, as wine; wùn chëā, 醞藉, decided, settled, repressed feeling.

Wùn 温 Wùn chëā, 温藉, settled, decided repressed feeling; wùn súy, 温水, to steep in water.

Wùn 韞 To store up, to stow away, to lay aside, to conceal.

Wùn tòk jê chông choo, 韞匱而藏諸 hāy tē tòk kwùy jê k'hèng choo, (having found a valuable gem,) will a man store it away in a locker, (or will he seek to get a good price for it?) see the 論語 Lūn gé.

平

Wûn 沄 Water flowing back; water turning round.

Wûn 澐 Great waves in a river.

Wûn 緷 A rope, a cord, a string with which a net is tied.

去

Wūn 運 To travel, to convey, to move, to remove; wūn chwán, 運轉, to circulate; wūn lëâng, 運糧 wūn nëô^ng, to transport grain.

Jit gwát wūn hêng, 日月運行 jit gŏëyh wūn kë^nâ, the sun and moon moving in their orbits; see the 易繫詞 Ék hēy soô.

Wūn 暈 Vulg. wui^ng: the halo around the sun or moon; two armies drawn up opposite one another.

Wūn 緷 All sorts of feathers; to entwine around; a large girdle.

Wūn 鄆 The name of a place in the 魯 Loē country.

Wūn 韻 To harmonize, to chime, to come in rhyme; a rhyme, a symphony, a correspondence of tone; yim wūn, 音韻, a sound, an accent, a cadence; lók wūn, 落韻 lôh wūn, to come in rhyme.

Sew pek sè che k'hwat bûn, ch'haé ch'hëen chaè che wûy wūn, 收百世之闕文采千載之遺韻 *sew chit pǎyh sè ây k'hwat bûn, k'hëŏk chit ch'heng neêng ây wûy wūn*, to gather the deficient compositions of a hundred ages, and to collect the neglected rhymes of a thousand years.

Wūn 韵 The same as the above.

犬

Wut 熨 An iron for smoothing clothes, &c. Also written 尉, wut. Wut toé, 熨斗 *wut taóu*, a smoothing iron.

Wut 尉 The same as the above. A surname.

Wut 菀 Luxuriant, exuberant.

Wut 鬱 A feeling, an emotion, not expressed in words; ek wut, 抑鬱 *wut chut*, to be uneasy, to be vexed, to be worried. A surname. Wut tô, 鬱陶, high wrought, anxious feeling.

Wut tô soo kwun jeéng, 鬱陶思君爾 *wut chut sëōng jïn kwun lé*, I have been uneasy while thinking of your highness; see 孟子 Bēng choó.

Wut 欝 The same as the above.

Wut 欎 Aóu wut, 拗欎, to twist anything and break it off. Wut ch'haê, 欎柴, to break off a piece of firewood.

Wut 鬱 A kind of a fragrant plant; wut t'hëàng, 鬱鬯, fragrant herbs infused into wine.

Wut 殟 The mind distressed; an injury of the womb.

Wut 頞 To put the head under water.

Wut 窢 A spark of fire.

𡗗

Wuy 威 Dignity, awe, majesty, pomp; wuy gëêm, 威嚴, gravity, sternness; wuy hong, 威風, a dignified, majestic manner; wuy pek, 威逼, despotic, tyrannical, harshly imperious.

Wuy jê put béng, 威而不猛 *wuy gëêm jê bô béng*, be dignified without being ferocious; see the 論語 Lūn gé.

Wuy 葳 Luxuriant herbage.

Wuy 逶 Wuy tê, 逶迤, leisurely walking about, sauntering.

𠁼

Wúy 洧 The name of a river. Choó-sán é kê sêng ê chèy jîn ê Chin Wúy, 子產以其乘輿濟人於溱洧 *Choó-sán t'hô e chēy ây ch'hëa, chèy lâng köèy Chin Wúy ây chúy*, Choó-sán employed the chariot in which he rode, to help people across the Chin and Wúy rivers; see 孟子 Bēng choó.

Wúy 鮪 The name of a fish.

Wúy 唯 An affirmative, yes; the way in which inferiors answer their superiors, when called by them.

Cheng-choó wát, wúy, 曾子曰唯 *Cheng-choó kóng, wúy,* Cheng-choó said, 'yes!' see the 論語 Lūn gé.

Wúy 韋 Soft leather; that which has been dressed. A surname; one of the radicals.

Wúy pwân, 韋弁, a sort of leathern cap worn by soldiers.

Wúy 偉 Great, extraordinary; chùn wúy, 俊偉, a hero, an extraordinary man.

Wúy 瑋 A precious gem, a valuable stone.

Wúy 煒 A very red appearance; bright and luminous; a raging fire.

Wúy 葦 Loê wúy, 蘆葦, a reed.

Wúy 韙 Right, it is so; to approve of; to defend what is right, and oppose the wrong.

Wúy 韡 Full, luxuriant, exuberant herbage.

Wúy 褘 Elegant, excellent; a queen's robe, embroidered with feathers.

Wúy 咼 The noise made in calling ducks.

Wúy 蔿 Grass; also a surname.

Wúy 薳 The same as the above.

Wúy 諉 To confide, to intrust; to involve, to implicate; to put off, to decline, to make an excuse.

Kê tëung sëāng yéw k'hó wúy chëá, 其中尚有可諉者 *e ây tang e^ng sëāng woō ây t'hang wúy t'hok,* amongst them there are still some who may be confided in; see the 賈誼傳 Káy gê twān.

Wúy 委 To bend, to bow; to commit to, to follow; wúy jīm, 委任, to sustain; wúy tè, 委致, to reject; wúy t'hok, 委托, to confide to any one's care; göēy wúy, 外委 *gwā wúy,* a serjeant; wúy kêw, 委求, to solicit of another something troublesome. Wúy jê k'hè che, 委而去之 *wúy t'hek kak jê k'hè e,* to reject and throw anything away; see 孟子 Bēng choó.

The origin of anything is called 原, gwân, and the termination of it is called 委, wúy.

Wúy 虺 The name of a snake; a man's name. Wûy wúy wûy ê, lé choó che sëâng, 維虺維蛇女子之祥 *tôk tôk wúy kap chwâ, sē cha boé ây kit sëâng,* only snakes and serpents are prognostics of women; see the 小雅 Seáou gnáy.

去

Wùy 尉 To wait; haōu wùy, 校尉, the name of an office.

Bûn sîn hoē wùy, 門神戶尉, door gods and gate officers; (referring to the figures which the Chinese paint on their doors.)

Wùy tè, 尉遲, a double surname.

Wùy 蔚 Luxuriant, exuberant.

Wùy 慰 The same as the following.

Wùy 慰 To console, to comfort, to condole with, to soothe. E wùy gnoé sim, 以慰我心 *é an wùy gwá ây sim kwⁿa*, to comfort my heart; see the 小雅 Seáou gnáy.

Wùy 畏 To fear, to dread, to venerate. Kwun choō yéw sam wùy, 君子有三畏 *kwun choó woō sⁿa hāng kēⁿa ây soō*, the good man has three things which he venerates; see the 論語 Lūn gé.

平 Wûy 帷 A curtain, a tent. Chè sìn ch'hëen lé göēy, wūn têw wûy ak tëung, 制勝千里外運籌帷幄中 *chè yëⁿâ kaòu chit ch'heng lé gwā, chaē wūn têw tē wûy ak ây tang cⁿg*, to be able to accomplish victories to the distance of a thousand lé, depends upon the plans formed within the curtained tent; see the 高祖紀 Ko choé kè.

Wûy 惟 To scheme, to plan, to think, to deliberate; only, alone. Chaè boē chaè wûy, 載謀載惟 *twā tē boē, twā tē wûy*, sometimes employed in consulting, and sometimes in deliberating; see the 詩經 Se keng.
Sè wán wûy bêng, 視遠惟明 *k'hwⁿà hwuiⁿg wûy bêng*, to be able to see far, is alone to be considered intelligence.

Wûy 唯 Only, alone; kê wûy sèng jîn hoē, 其唯聖人乎 *e tók tók sē sèng jîn hoē*, he alone may be considered a sage; see the 易經 Ĕk keng.

Wûy 維 The same as the preceding; to bind, to tie, to connect, to circumvent, to plan.
This and the two preceding are all used as auxiliary particles, denoting but, only, alone, only that, &c.

Wûy 濰 The name of a river.

Wûy 幃 An incense bag; a single curtain; wûy tëàng, 幃帳, a tent.

Wûy 褘 The same as the preceding.

Wûy 闈 A small door in a palace; a private door. Hoo jîn chè, jip choō wûy bûn, 夫人至入自闈門 *cha boē lâng kaòu, jip choō sèy mootⁿg*, when ladies come, they should enter by the private door; see the 禮雜記 Léy chàp kè.

Wûy 圍 To surround, to circumvent; chew wûy, 周圍, all around, on all sides; wûy choō, 圍住, to beseige. Also written 囗, wûy.

Wûy 違 To resist, to oppose, to leave, to forsake; wûy gĕk, 違逆 *wûy kāyk*, to resist; wûy léy, 違禮, opposed to the rules of propriety.
Choō wát, boô wûy, 子曰無違 *hoo choó kóng, bô kāyh*, Confucius said, 'do not oppose;' see the 論語 Lūn gé.

Wûy 遺 To lose, to cast away; to leave by will, to hand down; wûy se, 遺書, a will, a testament.
Tō put sip wûy, 道不拾遺 *loē bô k'hëŏh ka laòuh ây meēⁿgh*, in the roads no one picked up what was dropped.

Wûy 桅 The oar, or rudder of a small boat; chûn wûy, 船桅, a ship's mast; sam che wûy, 三枝桅 *sⁿa ke wûy*, three masts.

Wûy 爲 To do, to act, to perform, to manage. Wûy kē sit, 爲巨室 *chò twā keng ch'hoò*, to make a great house; see 孟子 Bēng choó.
Sē put wûy yëá, hwuy put lêng yëá, 是不爲也非不能也 *chéy sē ūm k'héng chò, ūm chêng këò bēy ēy*, this is because men will not do it, not that they cannot; see 孟子 Bēng choó.

Wūy 位 (also 𡍲) A station, a post, an office, a dignity; a place, a seat; ông wūy, 王位, a throne; sëāng wûy, 上位, to ascend the throne, yit wūy, 一位 *chit wūy*, a person; lëët wūy, 列位, gentlemen! Kwun choó soō put ch'hut kê wūy, 君子思不出其位 *kwun choó sëōng ūm ch'hut e āy wūy*, a good man contrives not to leave his station; see the 易經 Ék keng.

Wūy 胃 The stomach; pê wūy, 脾胃, the receptacle for food; wūy jëák, 胃弱, a weak stomach.

Wūy 渭 The name of a river; Chew-lē-sëāng teàou ê Wūy súy, 周呂尙釣於渭水 *Chew-lē-sëāng tëò hê tē Wūy chúy*, Chew-lē-sëāng used to angle in the Wūy waters.

Wūy 謂 To speak to, to address. Hék wūy K'hóng-choó, wát, 或謂孔子曰 *woō lâng kap K'hóng-choó kóng*, a certain person addressed Confucius, saying, &c.; see the 論語 Lūn gé.

Wūy 蝟 The name of an animal, like a pig, but smaller, and armed with strong bristles; a hedgehog, or porcupine. Hwán chëá jê wūy mô jê k'hé, 反者如蝟毛而起 *hwán āy lâng ch'hin chëōng wūy mô jê k'hé*, the rebels rose like porcupine's quills.

Wūy 爲 For, on account of; to be for, to aid, to abet; yin wūy, 因爲, because. Hoo choó wūy Wöēy kwun hoê? 夫子爲衛君乎 *hoo choó woō chān wöēy kwun á bô?* will Confucius assist the prince of the Wöēy country or not? see the 論語 Lūn gé.

Wūy 磑 A broken vessel, a potsherd; to grind.

Wūy 壝 A lump of earth, a piece of ground.

Wūy 諉 To involve, to draw into trouble. Chip soō put wūy sëāng, 執事不諉上 *chip soō āy lâng bēy lûy tëōh e āy sè twā*, the inferior officers cannot involve their superiors.

Wūy 鄬 The name of a country.

Y

平
Yang 央 The centre; tëung yang, 中央 *tang e^ng*, the middle.

Yang 泱 Deep and expansive.

Yang 秧 Vulg. *e^ng*: the ear of corn; the young shoots of paddy, fit for transplanting.

Yang 殃 Calamity, affliction, trouble, misfortune. Chok sëĕn kàng che pek sëâng, chok put sëĕn kàng che pek yang, 作善降之百祥作不善降之百殃 *chò hó kàng e chit păyh ây hok sëâng, chò ŭ^m hó kàng e chit páyh ây hò yang*, upon those who do good, will descend a hundred felicities, but upon those who do evil will come down a hundred calamities.

Yang 鴦 Wan yang, 鴛鴦 *wan yëo^ng*, the name of a bird, the mandarin duck (*Anas galericulata*), noted for always going in pairs; considered by the Chinese as emblems of fidelity and conjugal love; also, the name of an insect.

Yang 㑆 Yang hâng, 㑆佭, unsubdued, unsubmitting. A surname.

上
Yáng 養 Vulg. *yeó^ng*: to nourish, to feed, to bring up; a surname; yáng yëuk, 養育, to breed; seng yáng, 生養, to nourish; hâm yáng, 涵養, to cherish. Yáng kê taē t'héy wûy taē jîn, yáng kê seáou t'héy wûy seáou jîn, 養其大體爲大人養其小體爲小人 *yëó^ng ch'hē e ây twā t'héy chò twā lâng, yëó^ng ch'hē e ây sëó t'héy chò scáou jîn*, he who cultivates the most important part is a great man, but he who nourishes the inferior part is a worthless man; see 孟子 Bēng choó.

Yáng 瀁 Yáng bóng, 瀁漭, the appearance of water flowing all abroad.

Yáng 㕒 An inclination to vomit.

去
Yàng 映 Vulg. *yë^nà*: to reflect, to illumine. Jit yàng lê kan, key lëĕn seng jê hoĕ ch'hëàng, 日映籬間雞連聲而互唱 *jit chëò tē lê pa kan, key lëĕn së^na jê sëo ch'hëò^ng*, when the sun peeps through the railing, the cocks one after another begin to crow together.

Yàng 怏 An unsatisfied feeling; a discontented mind.

Yàng 泱 Yàng bóng, 泱漭, wide, expanded water.

Yàng 盎 A bowl, a dish; a jar.

Yàng 鞅 A saddle girth.

Yàng 怏 Yëén yàng, 偃怏, unable to stoop and take up anything.

平

Yâng 楊 Yâng léw, 楊柳, the willow tree; yâng sē, 楊樹 *yëóng ch'hēw*, the banian or Indian fig; yâng t'hô, 楊桃, the Averrhoa carambola.

A surname.

Sek gnó óng è, yâng léw o e, 昔我往矣楊柳依依 *chá gwá k'hè è, yëóng léw toō toō á saing*, the other day when I went away, the willows were just budding; see the 小雅 Seáou gnáy.

Yâng 瑒 A gem used for pouring out libations.

Yâng 揚 To emblazon abroad, to spread far and wide; yâng bêng, 揚名, to spread one's praise; ch'heng yâng, 稱揚, to praise, to applaud.

Yâng 颺 Yâng gân, 颺言, great swelling words. Vulg. *ch'hëóng:* to winnow the grain.

Yâng 昜 To open; long; bright.

Yâng 煬 Vulg. *yëóng:* to melt, to fuse metals.

Yâng 陽 The male principle of nature; yim yâng, 陰陽, the male and female principles of nature; t'haè yâng, 太陽, the sun; yâng kan, 陽間, the visible world.

Yâng 諹 To praise, to please.

Yâng 暘 The sun coming out; clear.

Yâng 羊 Vulg. *yëóng:* a goat; bëên yâng, 綿羊 *meéng yëóng*, a sheep.

Hwât peng che kay, put hëuk gnêw yâng, 伐冰之家不畜牛羊 *taē hoo ây kay bô ch'hē goô yëóng*, the family of a great officer should not breed cows and sheep; see the 大學 Taē hák.

Yâng 烊 Vulg. *yëóng:* to melt, to fuse metals; to dissolve; rotten.

Yâng 佯 To pretend, to feign, to dissemble. Ch'hoé Lëúk-t'hong yâng kông pè sè, 楚陸通佯狂避世 *Ch'hoé Lëúk-t'hong káy gōng pè sè*, Lëúk-t'hong of the Ch'hoé country pretended to be mad, and withdrew from the busy world.

Yâng 洋 Full, replete, overwhelming, broad, extensive; yâng haé, 洋海 *yëóng haé*, the ocean; yâng ch'hwân, 洋船 *yëóng chûn*, a foreign ship; sey yâng, 西洋 *sae yëóng*, the western ocean; formerly applied to Europe, now limited to Portugal.

Yâng yâng hoē, êng jé chae! 洋洋乎盈耳哉 *yâng yâng hoē, êng mwná hē k'hang!* how replete is such music! how it fills the ears! see the 論語 Lūn gé.

Yâng 痒 Sick, pained; distressed.

丟

Yāng 樣 Vulg. *yĕō^{ng}:* a manner, a form; sīm mŏh yāng? 甚麼樣 *s^{n}a-mcĕ^{ng}h yĕō^{ng}?* in what way? K'hàn yāng chĕûng yāng, 看樣從樣 *k'hwo^{n}à yĕō^{ng} t'hàn yĕō^{ng}*, to look at a pattern, and to follow an example.

Yāng 儫 The appearance of standing and moving.

Yāng 攁 A rule, a manner.

Yāng 漾 The waters moved and agitated.

Yāng 恙 Sorrow, trouble, calamity, sickness. Pēĕt laê boô yāng hoē? 別來無恙乎 *sĕo pēĕt é laé k'hám bó pai^{ng} hoē?* since we parted, have you been free from sickness?

Yāng 養 Nourishment, feeding; to afford nourishment. Chè ê k'hëén má kae lêng yéw yāng; put kèng hô é pēĕt hoē? 至於犬馬皆能有養不敬何以別乎 *chè é kaóu báy chò poô ēy woō yĕō^{ng} ch'hē; nā ū^{m} kèng, woō s^{n}a mcĕ^{ng}h kwun pēĕt hoē?* now even with respect to dogs and horses, they can all obtain nourishment; but if we (merely nourish) and do not respect (our parents), where lies the difference? see the 上論 Sĕāng ūn.

Yāng 癢 Vulg. *chĕō^{ng}:* to itch, to smart. Pây put chĕak yāng, 爬不着癢 *páy ū^{m} tĕŏh chĕō^{ng} ây wūy,* to scratch where it does not itch.

夭

Yaou 夭 An amicable, easy appearance; agreeable; anything pretty and elegant, though young and tender. T'hô che yaou yaou, 桃之夭夭 *t'hô ây sèy chăng hó k'hwo^{n}à*, the peach tree when young looks very pretty.

Yaou 妖 A cunning and wanton person is called yaou; strange, supernatural, ominous; yaou kwaè, 妖怪, strange and monstrous. Kok kay chĕang bông, pit yéw yaou gĕèt, 國家將亡必有妖孽 *kok kay chĕang lōng pōēy, pit woō yaou gĕèt*, when a nation or a family is about to be ruined, there will surely be some monstrous omens; see the 中庸 Tĕung yûng.

Yaou 祅 When any calamity arises out of the earth it is called 祅, yaou, and when it descends from heaven, it is called 災, chae.

Yaou 幺 Vulg. *yĕo:* small, minute, diminutive; also written 么, yaou.

Yaou 要 To persuade, to induce, to influence by mean motives, to seek; to screen, to cover; to rob, and plunder. Suy wát put yaou kwun, goê put sìn yĕá, 雖日不要君吾不信也 *suy jĕĕn kóng, e ū^{m} yaou kèw e ây jīn kwun, gwá ū^{m} sìn*, although such a one should say, he had not meanly influenced his prince, I would not believe him; see the 論語 Lūn gé.

Yaou 飢 Read ke: to be hungry; toé ke, 肚飢 *pak toé yaou*, a hungry belly; put lêng ke, 不能飢 *bēy yaou*, no appetite.

Yaou 腰 Vulg. *yëo:* the loins, the waist.

Yaou 喓 To emit a sound, to hum as insects.

Yaou 葽 The name of a plant.

Yaou 褄 Yaou sëâng, 褄裳, a garment.

去 Yaóu 夭 Short, broken off short, short-lived; an untimely death.

Yaóu 殀 Short-lived, an early death.
Yaóu sēw put jē, sew sin e soō che, 殀壽不貳修身以俟之 *téy kap tēng hōèy sèw bō tēnā tëŏh, sew kīn sin é téng haōu e,* an early death and a long life are both uncertain; our duty is therefore to cultivate personal virtues, and wait the result; see 孟子 Bēng choó.

Yaóu 窔 Deep, abstruse.

Yaóu 仸 Yaóu keâou, 仸僑, bent, not straightened out.

Yaóu 舀 Expanded; yaóu súy, 舀水 *yëóng chúy,* to bale out water.

Yaóu 窈 Deep and still, profound, recondite, hidden, tranquil; a commendatory appellation for females.
Yaóu t'heáou sëuk lé, 窈窕淑女 *yaóu t'heáou hó ây cha boé láng,* retired and quiet, like a virtuous woman.

Yaóu 偠 Small, insignificant, small waisted.

Yaóu 鷕 The cry of a wild fowl, the noise made by a jungle fowl.

Yaóu 䶧 Yaóu k'heáou, 䶧齩, a crooked face.

去 Yaòu 要 Vulg. *bōëyh:* to want, to require; to desire, to wish; necessary, urgent, important.
Seng ông yéw chè tek yaòu tō, 生王有至德要道 *seng ông woō chè ch'hëet ây tek yaòu kín ây tō,* the former kings had a most essential virtue, and a most important doctrine (i.e. filial piety, which they inculcated); see the 孝經 Haòu keng.

Yaòu 窔 A secret place; the southeast corner of a house.

Yaòu 獟 The leaping and frisking of horses and cows. Also, the name of an animal.

平 Yaôu 姚 Vulg. *yëô:* a surname.

Yaôu 佻 Slowly, leisurely.

Yaôu 徭 To serve, to do service, to employ on any service.

Yaôu 謠 Children's ballads.

Yaôu 搖 Vulg. *yëô:* to shake, to wave, to move backwards and forwards.
Yaôu lâm, 搖籃 *yëô nâ,* a cradle.

Hong é séy p'heaou yaôu, 風雨所飄搖 *hong hoē séy p'heaou yëô*, moved and agitated by the wind and rain.

Yaôu 遙 Far, distant; yaôu k'hàn, 遙看 *hwuiⁿᵍ k'hwⁿà*, to see at a distance; yaôu wán, 遙遠, remote, far off.

Yaôu 瑤 A precious gem.

Yaôu 颻 P'heaou yaôu, 飄颻, anything agitated by the wind.

Yaôu 傜 To employ, to engage in any service; to serve.

Yaôu 儓 To be pleased; things differing in size.

Yaôu 窰 A jar; also a vessel for holding meat.

Yaôu 窯 Vulg. *yëô*: a kiln; wá yaôu, 瓦窯 *hëā yëô*, a tile kiln; höey yaôu, 灰窯 *höey yëô*, a lime kiln.

Yaôu 窑 A place for burning bricks or tiles.

Yaôu 陶 The same as the preceding, a pottery; also read tô.

Yaôu 僥 Cheaou yaôu, 僬僥, a nation of dwarfs on the southwest.

Yaôu 嶢 High, lofty; cheaou yaôu, 嶕嶢, a high mountain.

丟

Yaōu 曜 The light of the sun; light, brilliant. Jit gwát gnoé seng, wûy ch'hit yaōu, 日月五星爲七曜 *jit göëyh goē ây ch'haiⁿᵍ chò ch'hit ây yaōu*, the sun, and moon, and five planets constitute the seven lights.

Yaōu 燿 Bright and illuminated; kong yaōu, 光燿 *kwuiⁿᵍ yaōu*, luminous, splendid.

Yaōu 耀 The same as the preceding.

Yaōu 臛 The back.

Yaōu 鷂 A ferocious bird of prey, like an osprey or fish hawk.

声

Yëá 也 A final particle, used at the end of a sentence. Suy pek sè k'hó te yëá, 雖百世可知也 *suy chit păyh ây sè yëá t'hang chae*, the events of even a hundred ages may be known; see the 上論 Sëāng lūn.

Yëá 野 A wilderness, a desert, a wild uncultivated place; clownish, vulgar; yëá göēy, 野外 *yëá gwā*, without in the desert; yëá jîn, 野人 *yëá ây lâng*, a clownish person.
Chit sìn bûn chek yëá, 質勝文則野 *chit k'hăh yëⁿá bun chek yëá*, when plainness exceeds elegance, a man is clownish; see the 論語 Lūn gé.

Yëá 仔 Read choó: anything small or young; as téng choó, 鼎仔 *tëⁿá yëá*, or *tëⁿá á*, a small iron pan.

Yeá 冶 To melt or fuse, to cast anything in melted metal; yaou yeá, 妖冶, strange, uncouth, wicked.

Ch'heá Hé-choó bô put wûy tô yeá? 且許子何不爲陶冶 *ch'heá Hé-choó sⁿa soō ŭᵐ chò sëo höëy choò mcëⁿᵍh?* and now why does not Hé-choó become a potter or a founder? see 孟子 Bēng choó.

Yeá yûng höëy yîm, 冶容誨淫 *yeá áy yûng maôu kà lâng yîm lwân*, a vicious countenance induces men to be lascivious; see the 易繫詞 Ēk hēy soô.

去

Yëà 伿 Read è: wearied, fatigued, sick of anything, indisposed. Jîn è, 人伿 *lâng yëà*, the man is sick.

Chò tò è, 做到伿 *chò kaòu yëà*, to do a thing till one is tired.

平

Yëâ 爺 A father, an elder, a title of respect; ló yëâ, 老爺, a magistrate; applied by courtesy to nobles, gentlemen, and their sons, whether old or young.

Yëâ 耶 A final particle, indicative of doubt and inquiry.

Yëâ-soe, 耶穌, the name of Jesus, mentioned in the imperial dictionary.

Yëâ 椰 Yëâ choó, 椰子 *yëâ ché*, a cocoa nut; yëâ yêw, 椰油, cocoa nut oil; also written 梛, yëâ.

Yëâ 琊 Lông yëâ, 琅琊, the name of a place.

Yëâ 鋣 The name of a sword.

Yëâ 邪 The same as 耶, yëâ.

平

Yëā 夜 Vulg. *maîⁿᵍ*: night, the night; yëā kan, 夜間 *maîⁿᵍ kan*, by night; pwàn yëā, 半夜 *pwⁿà maîⁿᵍ*, by midnight.

Put sëá tèw yëā, 不舍晝夜 *bô haîⁿᵍh jit maîⁿᵍ*, not to stop by day or by night.

Yëā 揲 To scatter, to strew abroad with the hand; yëā chëúng, 揲種 *yëā ché*, to sow seed, by scattering it abroad.

Yëá 也 A final particle, denoting decision.

Kwun choó jîn e? kwun choó jîn yëá, 君子人與君子人也 *chëy lëy lâng sē kwun choó á bô? chëy lëy lâng sē chin chëⁿà kwun choó*, is this a good man? truly this is a good man; see the 論語 Lūn gé.

平

Yëⁿa 纓 Read eng: a tassel; bō eng, 帽纓 *bo yëⁿa*, the tassel of a cap.

上

Yëⁿá 影 Read éng: a shadow; yéw éng, 有影 *woō yëⁿá*, anything that has the shadow of truth; boô éng, 無影 *bô yëⁿá*, there is not the least shadow of truth in it.

Gwàt ê hwa éng sëāng lân kan, 月移花影上欄杆 *göëyh ê hwa yëⁿá chëöⁿᵍ lân kan*, the moon throws the shadow of the flowers on the railing of the gallery.

去

Yëⁿà 映 Read yàng: to illumine, to shine; yàng cheàou, 映照 *yëⁿà chëò*, to reflect, to illuminate.

平

Yëⁿâ 營 Read êng: a camp; êng chēy, 營寨 *yëⁿâ chēy*, an encampment; kwun êng, 軍營 *kwun yëⁿâ*, a military encampment.

Yëⁿâ 贏 Read êng: to win, to conquer, to surpass, to overcome. Toé chaê se êng, 賭財輸贏 *toé cheêⁿᵍ soo yëⁿâ*, to play for money and win or lose.

Yëⁿâ 捷 Read chëêt: to conquer, to overcome in battle.

去
Yëⁿā 颺 Read yâng: agitated by the wind; yâng hong, 颺風 *yëⁿā hong*, waving in the wind.

犬
Yëáh 益 Read ek: gain, profit, advantage; lē ek, 利益 *lē yëáh*, advantage. Hák yéw chìn ek, 學有進益 *ŏh woō chìn yëăh*, learning has its advantages.

入
Yëăh 帙 A leaf; *ch'hăyh yëăh*, 冊帙, the leaf of a book.

Yëăh 頁 Read yëëp: the same as the above. One of the radicals.

Yëăh 易 Read ék: a diagram, a change; Ek keng, 易經 *Yëăh keng*, the book of diagrams, one of the five classics of the Chinese.

Yëăh 蜴 Read ék: a flying insect.

Yëăh 役 Read ék: to serve, a servant; ch'hay ék, 差役 *ch'hay yëăh*, a messenger; gây ék, 衙役 *gây yëăh*, a police runner.

Yëăh 驛 Read ék: a post; a governmental dispatch; ék má, 驛馬 *yëăh báy*, a post horse; ék loē, 驛路 *yëăh loē*, a post road.

Yëăh 蝶 Read tëëp: a butterfly, hoê teëp, 蝴蝶 *böêy yëăh*, a butterfly. Këep tëëp ch'hwàn hwa k'hwán k'hwán hwuy, 蛺蝶穿花欵欵飛 *böêy yëăh ch'hwuiⁿᵍ hwa êng êng tit pwuy*, the butterflies occupied in piercing the flowers are leisurely flying about.

犬
Yëak 約 To bind, to agree, to covenant, to engage; yëak sìn, 約信, a covenant, an agreement; k'hëëm yëak, 儉約, to spare, to economize; këûng yëak, 窮約, distress, poverty. Put jîn cheâ put k'hó é kéw ch'hé yëak, 不仁者不可以久處約 *ŭᵐ jîn ây lâng, bó t'hang koó twā tē këûng yëak*, people without benevolence cannot long bear to be in circumstances of poverty and distress; see the 論語 Lūn gé.

入
Yëák 藥 Vulg. *yëŏh*: medicine, physic; sit yëák, 食藥 *chëăh yëŏh*, to take physic. Lëâng yëák k'hoé k'hoé, lō ê sin, 良藥苦口利於身 *hó áy yëŏh k'hoé tē ch'hùy, hó tē hìn sin*, good medicine is bitter in the mouth, but profitable to the body.

Yëák 躍 To leap, to jump; t'heàou yëák, 跳躍, to frisk about. Oe jîm gê yëák! 於牣魚躍 *an chwⁿá mwⁿá hê tit t'hëŏ!* how joyfully do the fishes sport about! see 孟子 Bēng choó.

Yëák 龠 A small measure, a handfull; the 200th part of a peck, estimated as being equal to 1200 grains of millet.

Yëák 鑰 Só yëák, 鎖鑰, a lock, a fastening, a bolt. Ko choé ch'hut cheng, Seaou-hô ke séw kwán yëák, 高祖出征蕭何居

福建方言字典

守管鑰 *ko choé ch'hut k'hè cheng p'hăh, Seaou-hô k'hëā chéw kwăn yëăk,* when the first emperor of the Han dynasty went out on his wars, his minister Seaou-hô remained at home, and guarded the fastnesses.

Yëák 籥 A small pipe with three holes in it, a pipilo.

Yëák 瀹 To lead off, and drain water.
Yëák Chëy Lat, jê choō che haé, 瀹濟漯而注之海 *yëák k'hwuy Chëy Lat äy chúy jê choō e kaòu haé,* he drained the Chëy and Lat rivers, and led them off into the sea; see 孟子 Bēng choó.

Yëák 禴 A sacrifice offered in spring. Also written 礿, yëák.

Yëem 奄 To look long at anything, to stare, to gaze.

Yëem 淹 To collect as water, to settle; a long time.
Goô choó yëem kéw ê pē yip, 吾子淹久於敝邑 *gwá äy choó woō yëem koó tē pē sëy äy yip,* my lord, you have been a long time in that mean city; see the 左傳 Chó twān.

Yëem 醃 Anything pickled, or salted.

Yëem 閹 Yëem jîn, 閹人, an eunuch; yëem key, 閹鷄, a capon; to castrate; yëem te, 閹猪, to geld a pig.

Yëem 俺 To cleanse, to purify.

Yëem 厭 Satisfied, to have sufficient, to be content.
Chëûng sëw boô yëem wûy che hong, 從獸無厭謂之荒 *tuý k'hìm sëw bēy yëem 'chëuk, kóng 'këò hong,* to hunt after wild beasts without being satisfied is called wildness; see 孟子 Bēng choó.

Yëem 懕 Peaceful, at rest.

Yëem 饜 To eat to the full, to be satisfied, to have enough.
Chek pit yëem chéw jëúk, jê hoē hwán, 則必饜酒肉而後反 *chek pit chëăh pá chéw băh, jëên aōu toońg,* on such occasions he would always eat flesh and wine to the full before he returned; see 孟子 Bēng choó.

Yëem 猒 The same as 厭, yëem.

Yëém 掩 To screen, to hide, to conceal, to soothe with the hand, to take and put under shelter, to shut up.
Also written 揜, yëém.
Yëém kê put sëën, jê tè kê sëën, 掩其不善而著其善 *yëém jëa e äy ūm hó, jê tè bêng e äy hó,* to conceal that which is bad, and to display the good; see the 大學 Taē hăk.
Tók sëuk, bûn put yëém, 獨宿門不掩 *tók k'hëā, mooińg yëá bô kwńa,* to dwell alone without being obliged to close the doors.

Yëém 奄 Suddenly, unexpectedly.

Yëém 罨 A fishing net.

Yëém 弇 To cover, to screen; anything in the shape of a bell.

Yëém jit wûy pèy yîn, 弇日爲蔽雲 *yëém jëá jit sē pèy hwûn*, that which covers the sun is the overspreading cloud; see the 爾雅 Jé gnáy.

Yëém 渰 Clouds rising up.

Yëém 黶 A black spot on the face or body.

Yëém 靨 The projecting part of the cheek bone.

Yëém 魘 Bōng yëém, 夢魘 *bāng yëém*, the nightmare; also, an uncomfortable sleep, disturbed repose.

Yëém 扊 Yëém ê, 扊扅, the bar of a door. P'heng hòk ch'he, ch'höey yëém ê, 烹伏雌炊扊扅 *sâh key boé, hēⁿā mooiⁿᵍ ch'hwⁿā*, she boiled her last pullet, and burned the bar of her door for firewood; (said of the wife of a learned man, who was thus reduced to the last extremity before her husband embarked in life, but was afterwards raised to a high station.)

Yëém 琰 A sharp cut, bright, luminous, gem.

平

Yëêm 炎 A fire blazing up, to flame, to blaze; yëêm jëét, 炎熱 *yëêm jwăh*, blazing hot, very warm.

Hⁿó yëêm ch'hëung t'hëen, 火炎冲天 *höéy yëêm tŏh kaôu t'heeⁿᵍ*, the flame of the fire blazed up to heaven.

Yëêm 鹽 Salt; sit hwān p'höèy yëêm, 食飯配鹽 *chëăh pooiⁿᵍ p'höèy yëêm*, to eat rice and salt. Yëêm wūn soó, 鹽運使, a superintendent of salt.

Yëêm 壛 The same as the above; also contracted to 塩, yëêm.

Yëêm 櫩 The name of a foreign kind of wood, of which rudders are made.

Yëêm 閻 The gate of a village; a surname.

Yëêm 閆 The same as the above; a surname.

Yëêm 檐 Yëêm chëên, 檐前 *neéⁿᵍ cheéⁿᵍ*, the eaves of a house.

Bŏk gân sîn put këèn, bŏk chaē yëêm chëên t'hoê, 莫言神不見目在檐前頭 *bŏh kóng sîn bŏ k'hwⁿà, bàk chew tē neéⁿᵍ cheéⁿᵍ t'haôu*, don't say that spirits cannot see, their eyes are on the eaves of the house.

去

Yëêm 豓 Handsome, enchanting, captivating; lascivious.

Bé jê yëêm, 美而豓 *súy jê ch'hin ch'haiⁿᵍ*, lovely and enchanting; see the 左傳 Chó twān.

Yëêm 豔 The same as the preceding; erroneously written 艷, yëêm; and 艶, yëêm.

Yëêm 灧 Water full and overflowing.

Yëêm 爓 Hⁿó yëêm, 火爓, a blazing fire.

Yëĕm 焰 The brightness of fire; also written 燄, yëĕm.

去

Yëèm 厭 To be satisfied, to have sufficient, to have enough; to loathe.

Ek wûy che put yëèm, hōèy jîn put kwān, 抑爲之不厭誨人不倦 yëá chò e bēy yëà, kà lâng bēy kwān, "I strive to practice (virtue) without tiring, and instruct men without weariness;" said by Confucius, in the 論語 Lūn gé.

Yëèm 檿 The name of a tree.

Yëèm 饜 To be full, to be satisfied; surfeited, disgusted; yëèm è, 饜饫, filled, satisfied.

Ch'hoó kê wûy yëèm chëuk che tō yëá, 此其爲饜足之道也 chéy sē e chò yëèm kaòu ây tō lé, this is the way in which he obtains such an abundance and sufficiency; see 孟子 Bēng choó.

Yëèm 俺 Great, large.

Yëèm 淹 To sink, to be overwhelmed, to be annihilated.

Yëèm but súy tëung, 淹没水中 yëèm bô tē chúy tang e^ng^, to sink and be overwhelmed in the water.

Yëèm 揜 Bright, clear.

平

Yëen 煙 Vulg. *hwun:* smoke; tobacco; sit yëen, 食煙 *chëāh hwun*, to smoke tobacco; yëen tông, 煙筒 *hwun ch'hûy*, a tobacco-pipe.

Yëen 烟 The same as the above; hông yeen, 紅烟 *âng hwun*, common Chinese tobacco; oe yëen, 烏烟 *oe hwun*, black tobacco (opium).

Yëen 湮 To sink in the water, to be lost and gone; to stop up.

Sè wán lëên yëen, 世遠年湮 *sè hwui^ng^ neê^ng^ koò*, after distant ages, and a lapse of years.

Yëen 咽 Yëen hoê, 咽喉 *nâ aôu*, the throat, the gullet.

Hân t'hëen hāy che yëen hoê yëá, 韓天下之咽喉也 *Hân kok sē t'hee^ng^ āy ây nâ aôu*, the district of Hân is the throat, (i. e. the most important part,) of the empire; see the 戰國策 Chëèn kok ch'hek.

Yëen 胭 Yëen che, 胭脂, rouge, a vermilion cosmetic used by Chinese ladies, for reddening their lips.

Also written 臙, yëen.

Yëen 姻 Hwun yëen, 婚姻, a marriage, a wedding; also written 婣, yëen.

Hoō jîn yin jîn jê sêng, koè wát yëen, 婦人因人而成故曰姻 *hoō jîn lâng yin wûy ta po lâng jê chë^n^â, chëà kóng yëen*, ladies are made by the fortune of their husbands, hence marriage is called 姻, yëen.

Yëen 燕 The name of a country.

A surname.

Yëen 焉 A final particle; also, how? whence? Jîn yëen soo chae! 人焉廋哉 *lâng böëyh an chw^n^á ëy k'hè^ng^ chae!* how can men hide themselves! see the 上論 Sëāng lūn.

Yëen 漹 The name of a river.

Yëen 嫣 A smiling appearance; handsome, beautiful.

Yëen jëën yit ch'heàou! 嫣然一笑 *yëen jëên chit ây ch'hëò*, with a pleasing countenance she laughed.

Yëen 鄢 The name of a city.

Yëen 蔫 The name of an insect.

Yëen 淵 A place where water collects, a pit, a gulf, a ravine.

Jê lîm ch'him yëen, 如臨深淵 *ch'hin chëō^ng lîm kaòu ch'him ây yëen*, like approaching an abyss; see the 小雅 Seáou gnáy.

Yëen 㴞 An ancient mode of writing the preceding.

Yëen 鳶 The name of a bird, resembling a sparrow-hawk or falcon.

Yëen hwuy lëy t'hëen, 鳶飛戾天 *ee^ng á pwuy kaòu t'hee^ng*, the falcon flies up towards heaven.

Yëen 闉 The gate of a city.

Yëen 甄 To cast, to mould; a surname; yëen pëet, 甄别, to distinguish; yëen ch'hat, 甄察, to examine, to search; also read chin.

上聲 Yëén 偃 To fall down, to lie down, to be prostrate; to recline, to lie at ease.

Ch'hó sëāng che hong pit yëén, 草上之風必偃 *ch'haóu kay woō hong tē têng bîn pit tó*, when grass is acted on by the wind it will lie down flat; see the 論語 Lūn gé.

Hék sit yëén chaë ch'hông, 或息偃在牀 *woō ây hai^ngh k'hwùn tē bîn ch'hê^ng*, some are lying down and resting on their beds; see the 小雅 Seáou gnáy.

Yëén 堰 To dam up water, to collect water into a pond.

Yëén 鰋 The name of a fish.

Yëén 鶠 The name of a bird, said to be the chief of the feathered tribe.

Yëén 衍 Water overflowing, abundant; broad, extensive, exuberant.

Ak yëén, 沃衍, to irrigate.

Yëén 演 Water flowing to a great distance; to extend, to lengthen.

Yëén hè, 演戲, to perform plays; pwan yëén, 搬演 *pw^na yëén*, to go through any exercise.

Yëén 嚝 To laugh out aloud.

Yëén 兗 The name of a district.

Yëén 琰 A gem in which there is a brilliant color.

去聲 Yëèn 燕 To rest, to be tranquil; to be at ease; to be pleased, and delighted; yëèn chnó, 燕子 *ee^ng á*, the swallow or martin family; yëèn o, 燕窩, the edible birds-nests.

Chóo che yëèn ke, 子之燕居 *hoo choó ēng ēng k'hëā*, when Confucius dwelt at his ease, &c.; see the 論語 Lūn gé.

Yëèn jé sin hwun, 燕爾新婚 *hwⁿa hé lé ây sin hwun yëèn*, rejoice in your newly contracted marriage; see the 衛風 Wōey hong.

Yëèn 嬿 Elegant, lovely, beautiful; yëèn wán, 嬿婉, yielding, complying.

Yëèn 嚥 To swallow; also written 咽, yëèn.

Yëèn 讌 To eat and drink together.

Yëèn 傿 To agree to the price of anything; yëèn lëük, 傿緣, the name of a spirit or genius.

Yëèn 宴 To rest, to be at ease; to delight in, to be pleased with; also to enjoy; sit yëèn, 食宴, a feast; chéw yëèn, 酒宴, an entertainment; sëet yëèn, 設宴, to appoint a feast; yím yëèn, 飲宴, to partake of a feast.

Yëèn 䁙 Things compared one with another.

平 Yëên 延 To advance, to go forward; long, distant; to receive, to reach to; ch'hëen yëên, 遷延, to procrastinate, to delay, to protract.

K'hóng-choó soó Chóo-loē, chip këung sé ch'hut yëên sëà, 孔子使子路執弓矢出延射 *K'hóng-choó saé Choó-loē gīm këung cheèⁿᵍ, ch'hut k'hè yëên sëd*, Confucius ordered Chóo-loē to take his bow and arrows and sally forth to shoot (birds); see the 禮射義 Léy sëà gē.

Kong-sun-hông k'hae tong kwán, é yëên hëën, 公孫弘開東館以延賢 *Kóng-sun-hông k'hwuy tang kwán, é yëên lap gaôu lâng*, Kóng-sun-hông opened the eastern lodge for the reception of clever people.

Yëên 筵 A bamboo mat, on which the ancients used to sit and eat their meals; chéw yëên, 酒筵, an entertainment; yëèn yëên, 宴筵, a feast.

Yëên 涎 Vulg. *nwⁿā*: spittle, saliva, phlegm, scum; sōey yëên, 唾涎 *p'hōey nwⁿā*, to spit.

Yëên 梴 A wooden lever, attached to a stone mortar, for beating out the husks of rice.

Yëên 唌 To sigh, to utter an exclamation.

Yëên 沿 To follow a stream, to sail with the stream; to comply with.

Yëên ë kang haé, 沿於江海 *t'hàn ē kang haé*, to follow the streams and currents of rivers and seas.

Yëên 鉛 Lead, called by the Chinese black tin.

Yëên 緣 On account of, because; to follow, to comply; yëên koè, 緣故, a cause, a reason.

Yêw yëên bók, jê kêw gê yëá, 猶緣木而求魚也 *ch'hin chëōⁿᵍ yin hwut lêy ch'hâ jê kêw hé*, it would be like climbing a tree to catch fish; see 孟子 Bēng choó.

Yëên 椽 Ok yëên, 屋椽 *ch'hoò atⁿᵍ*, the rafters of a house.

Sòng é taē këung che yëên, kwuy wûy Loē bûn che yëên, 宋以大宮之椽

歸爲盧門之榱 *Sông kok t'hó twā këung ây aing, tooing laê chò Loê mooing ây aing,* the Sông people took the rafters of the great palace, and brought them back to make the rafters of the Loê port; see the 左傳 Chó twān.

Yëēn 臅 To steep flesh in hot water; meat soaked in broth.

盂
Yëēn 衍 A broad marsh, an extensive morass, overflowing; yêw yëēn, 游衍, at ease, luxuriant; bān yëēn, 曼衍, endless, without termination.

Yëēn 掾 An inferior officer, under one's command.

Yëēn 緣 The bordering of a garment.

Yëēn 羨 Superabundant, superfluous, a superfluity.

E yëēn poé put chëuk, 以羨補不足 *é ch'hun ây poé bô kaòu,* to make up for deficiencies in one thing by what is superfluous in another; see 孟子 Bēng choó.

Yëēn 院 Vulg. *eēng:* a college, a receptacle for learned men; cheng yëēn, 僧院 *höêy sëōng eēng,* a priest's monastery; se yëēn, 書院 *ch'hăyh eēng,* a literary college.

犬
Yëep 曄 Bright, clear, shining.

Yëep 燁 Bright, glistening.

Yëep 饁 To carry presents of food to workmen in the fields.

Yëep 㢢 A narrow confined dwelling.

Yëep 奄 To cover, to screen, to shelter.

夾
Yëëp 葉 Vulg. *hëôh:* a leaf; che yëëp, 枝葉 *ke hëôh,* branches and leaves; ló yëëp, 荖葉 *laōu hëôh,* the betel leaf, chewed by Asiatics with their areca nut; ék yëëp, 奕葉, successive generations. A surname.

Che yëëp bē yéw haē, pún sit sëen pwat, 枝葉未有害本實先撥 *ke hëôh böëy woō haē pún sit taē seng pwat,* while the branches and leaves are yet uninjured, the root and stump are destroyed; see the 小雅 Seáou gnáy.

Yëëp 偞 Light and coarse.

Yëëp 楪 A window.

Yëëp 頁 Vulg. *yëăh:* the leaf of a book; the same as 帙, yëëp.

犬
Yëet 蠮 E ong, 蠮螉 *yëet yëōng,* an insect remarkable for its small loins.

Yëet 謁 To declare, to inform, to inquire; yëet këèn, 謁見, to have an interview with any one.

Jê kēw hwun koe che laê ch'héng yëet, 如舊婚媾之來請謁 *ch'hin chëōng koō ây hwun koe laē ch'hën á yëet keëng*, like as when an old relation by marriage comes to request an interview; see the 左傳 Chó twăn.

Yëet 蠍 A poisonous reptile; the gecko.(?)

Yëet 咽 A stoppage in the throat; a melancholy sound; a loss of the voice.

Yëet 噎 Vulg. *oŏh:* to bring up wind from the stomach; tⁿá yëet, 打噎 *p'hăh oŏh*, to eruct.

入 Yëet 搧 Sëèn hong, 搧風 *yëet hong*, to fan, to agitate the wind with a fan.

上平 Yëo 腰 Read yaou: the loins, the waist.

Yëo 幺 Read yaou: small; yaou tëém, 幺點 *yëo tëém*, the ace at dice.

Yëo 邀 Read heaou: to invite, to induce, to urge.
Sëang heaou yêw gwán, 相邀遊玩 *sëo yëo t'hit t'hô*, to invite one another out to parties of pleasure.

上聲 Yëó 抶 To beat, to strike.

下平 Yëô 搖 Read yaôu: to shake, to jumble together, to swing backwards and forwards; yaôu lâm, 搖籃 *yëô nâ*, a cradle.

Yëô 窰 Read yaôu: a kiln; chwan choó yaôu, 磚仔窰 *chwuing á yëô*, a brick kiln; höey yaôu, 灰窰 *höey yëô*, a lime kiln.

姚 Yëô 姚 Read yaôu: a surname.

下入 Yëŏh 勺 Ten beards of corn make a 勺 yëŏh; a very small measure.

Yëŏh 蚐 A kind of green frog.

Yëŏh 億 Read ek: to guess, to hit at, to form an idea of.
Ek chek lé tëüng, 億則屢中 *yëŏh chek tàk paē tëùng*, in forming an idea of anything, he always hit the mark; see the 論語 Lūn gé.

Yëŏh 約 Read yëak: to agree with, to covenant; twān yëak, 斷約 *tooiⁿg yëŏh*, to determine an agreement.

入 Yëŏh 藥 Read yëak: medicine, physic.
K'hong-choó kwuy yëak, 康子饋藥 *K'hong-choó sàng yëŏh*, K'hong-choó presented some medicine (to Confucius); see the 論語 Lūn gé.

Yëŏh 鑰 Read yëak: the lock, or bar of a door.

上平 Yëoⁿg 鴦 Wan yang, 鴛鴦 *wan yëoⁿg*, a bird (the Chinese duck,) noted for being faithful to its mate; also the name of an insect.

Yëoⁿg 蝓 Read ong: as è ong, 蠮蝓 *yëet yëoⁿg*, the name of an insect, a species of ichneumon fly or wasp.

上聲 Yëóⁿg 舀 Read yaóu: to lade; yaóu súy, 舀水 *yëóⁿg chúy*, to bale out water.

Yëŏ^ng^ 養 Read yáng: to nourish; yáng soō, 養飼 *yëŏ^ng^ ch'hē*, to feed.

Yëŏ^ng^ 礬 Read yáng: flat bricks used beneath the tiles in Chinese houses.

平

Yëô^ng^ 羊 Read yàng: a goat; bëên yàng, 綿羊 *meê^ng^ yëô^ng^*, a sheep.
Kim yéw sēw jîn che gnêw yàng, jê wūy che bȯk che chëá, 今有受人之牛羊而爲之牧之者 *t^n^a woō sēw lâng ây goô yëô^ng^, jê wūy e è^ng^ c ây lâng*, now if a person should receive people's cows and sheep, and undertake to feed them, (he ought to seek for good pasturage for them;) see 孟子 Bēng choó.

Yëô^ng^ 洋 Read yàng: the ocean; yàng haé, 洋海 *yëô^ng^ haé*, seas and oceans; yàng ch'hwân, 洋船 *yëô^ng^ chûn*, foreign ships.

Yëô^ng^ 楊 Read yâng: a surname.

Yëô^ng^ 瘍 Broken to pieces, torn to rags.

Yëô^ng^ 鎔 Read yûng: to melt, to fuse.

去

Yëō^ng^ 樣 Read yāng: a manner, a form, an appearance.

Yëō^ng^ 樣 Read yāng: the young branches of a tree just shooting up.

大

Yëuk 益 Read ek: abundant; chêên chaê ek, 錢財益 *chee^ng^ chaê yëuk*, money abundantly, plenty of cash.

入

Yëu̇k 育 To feed, to nourish, to bring up.
Sëāng yáng hoō boē, hāy yëu̇k ch'hey choó, 上養父母下育妻子 *têng bīn yëŏ^ng^ pāy boē, hāy tèy ch'hē boē kë^n^á*, above (with respect to our superior relations,) to support our parents; and below (with respect to the inferior,) to nourish one's wife and children.

Yëu̇k 毓 The same as the preceding.

Yëu̇k 儥 To sell, to dispose of.

Yëu̇k 浴 To bathe; sëén yëu̇k, 洗浴 *séy ék*, to wash and bathe.
Yëu̇k hoē Kê, 浴乎沂 *châng ék twā lē Kê chúy*, to bathe in the Kê river; see the 下論 Hāy lūn.

Yëu̇k 鵒 The name of a bird.

Yëu̇k 欲 To desire, to wish, to prefer, to long for.
Hoô é kwùy sē jîn che séy yëu̇k yëá, 富與貴是人之所慾也 *poò kap kwùy sē lâng ây séy aē yëá*, riches and honors are what all men desire; see the 論語 Lūn gé.

Yëu̇k 慾 Lust, carnal desires; soo yëu̇k, 私慾, corrupt dispositions; yëu̇k sëáng, 慾想, lewd and lascivious thoughts. Yáng sim bȯk sëēn ê kw^n^á yëu̇k, 養心莫善於寡慾 *böëyh yáng sim, bô k'hàh hó é chëô soo yëu̇k*, in order to strengthen the mind, there is nothing so good as restraining the carnal desires; see 孟子 Bēng choó.

Yëuk 昱 To-morrow; yëuk jit, 昱日, the following day; jit yëuk, 日昱, the light of the sun.

Yëuk 喅 A sound, a voice.

Yëuk 煜 Bright, clear, the brightness of fire.

Yëuk 鬻 To sell, to dispose of; also to nourish and bring up.
Maē choó yëuk lé, 賣子鬻女 *bēy haōu sai^{ng} bēy chaóu á,* to sell one's sons and dispose of one's daughters.

Yëuk 儥 The same as the preceding.

幸
Yew 憂 Vulg. *hwân ló:* to be sorry; yew būn, 憂悶, sorrowful, sad.
Jëên hoō te, seng û yew hwân, jê soó û an lók yëá, 然後知生於憂患而死於安樂也 *jëên aōu chae, lâng sai^{ng} tē hwân ló, jê sé tē an lók yëá,* then we may know, that people may thrive in circumstances of trouble and sorrow, and die by giving way to ease and pleasure; see 孟子 Bōng choó.
Yew sim, 憂心, an anxious, grieved state of mind.

Yew 優 Superfluous, superabundant, over and above, luxurious ease; affluent; yew yêw, 優游, to saunter about, ease and leisure.
Soō jê yew chek hák, 仕而優則學 *chò kw^{n}a ây lâng êng chek t'hák ch'háyh,* an officer when at leisure should attend to learning; see the 論語 Lūn gé.
Ch'hëang yew, 娼優, a prostitute.

Yew 耰 To sow seed, to cast abroad seed; yew jê put twat, 耰而不輟 *yëà chê jê bô hai^{ng}h,* he continued sowing and would not stop; see the 論語 Lūn gé.

Yew 攸 That which, which; a place.

Yew 悠 Distant, far; yew wán, 悠遠 *yew hwui^{ng},* afar off.

Yew 滺 The appearance of water flowing.

Yew 幽 Deep, dark, umbrageous, hidden; abstruse, recondite; yew ke, 幽居, to dwell in retirement.
Ch'hut choō yew kok, 出自幽谷 *ch'hut tē yew âm ây k'hai^{ng},* to come out of the dark ravine; see the 小雅 Soáou gnây.
Bêng yéw léy gák, yew yéw kwúy sîn, 明有禮樂幽有鬼神 *bêng kwui^{ng} woō léy gák, yew âm woō kwúy sîn,* in the light we have ceremonies and music (by which to regulate our conduct); and in the dark, we have demons and spirits (of whom we should be afraid.)

Yew 呦 The cry of a deer, the noise made by a stag.

Yew 麀 A female deer, a doe; yew lók chók chók, 麀鹿濯濯 *boê kap kang ây lók kwút kwui^{ng} ây yëō^{ng},* the does and bucks looked sleek and fat; see the 大雅 Taē gnáy.

声
Yéw 友 A friend; pêng yéw, 朋友, an intimate friend.
E pêng yéw kaou jê put sìn hoē?

與朋友交而不信乎 *kap pêng yéw kaou p'höèy jê ŭm sìn sìt hoê?* in associating with my friends am I wanting in sincerity? see the 上論 Sëäng lūn.

Yéw 叒 The same as the preceding.

Yéw 酉 One of the horary characters. Yéw sê, 酉時, the hours from five to seven in the evening.

Yéw 有 Vulg. *woō:* to have, to possess, to be, to exist; a surname.
Put hṇ̄ò hwān sëäng, jê hṇ̄ò chok lwān chëá, bē che yéw yëá, 不好犯上而好作亂者未之有也 *ŭm aè kan hwān sè twā, jê aè chok lwān ây lâng, böëy woō chëy lëy soō,* not to be disposed to offend one's superiors, and still to be fond of creating rebellion, there is no such thing in existence; see the 上論 Sëäng lūn.

Yéw 丣 To shut the door; the time of the setting sun.

Yéw 佑 To help, to assist, to aid, to protect. Sëäng t'hëen hoo yéw hāy bîn, 上天孚佑下民 *t'heeng têng chin chëⁿà woō pó pē hāy bîn ây päyh saⁱⁿᵍ,* the high heavens will surely protect the common people; see the 書湯誥 Se t'hóng kò.

Yéw 莠 Something like grain, but not really grain; tares and not wheat.
Oè yéw k'hëúng kê lwān beâou yëá, 惡莠恐其亂苗也 *wàn p'hëy, këⁿá nò e ëy hwān poè ch'hè á,* he disliked tares lest they should injure the wheat; see 孟子 Bēng choó.

Yéw 羑 Yéw lé, 羑里, the name of a place.

Yéw 誘 To lead, to allure; yín yéw, 引誘, to lead on; yéw hèk, 誘惑, to tempt, to draw into vice.
Hoo choó sûn sûn jëên, sëēn yéw jîn, 夫子循循然善誘人 *hoo choó sûn sûn ây yëōⁿᵍ, gaôu yín yéw lâng,* Confucius with his compliant manner, was very skillful in leading men forward; see the 論語 Lūn gé.

Yéw 卣 A vessel for containing the aromatic wine.

Yéw 槱 A collection of wood, to burn as a sacrifice to heaven.

Yéw 懮 Grieved, distressed, sad thoughts.

Yéw 牖 To lead, to guide, to urge on; the same as 誘, yéw.

Yéw 牖 A window; also towards; to open out clearly.
Choó yéw chip kê séw, 自牖執其手 *choó t'hang á gîm e ây ch'héw,* he took hold of his hand through the window; see the 論語 Lūn gé.

去

Yèw 幼 Young, small, tender, weak; yéw lëên, 幼年 *seáou lëên,* young.
Hoo jîn yèw jê hák che, 夫人幼而學之 *hoo lâng seáou lëên chëw ôh e,* now when a man is young, he learns these things; see 孟子 Bēng choó.

平

Yêw 遊 To wander, to ramble. Vulg. *t'hit t'hô:* to go on an excursion of pleasure.
K'heng gô yêw jē tèy, 卿遨遊二帝 *k'heng t'hit t'hô kap nō ây hông tèy,* you, sir! have been

playing between the two emperors; see the 光武紀 Kong boó ké.

Yêw 攸 A surname.

Yêw 滺 To follow the stream, and float downwards; to glide down; also written 游, yêw, a surname.

Yêw 斿 The fringe at the end of a flagstaff, turning over and hanging down.

Yêw 蝣 Hoô yêw, 蜉蝣, the name of an insect.

Yêw 篰 The name of a certain sort of bamboo.

Yêw 偤 To rely on.

Yêw 猶 As, like as, as if; to plan, to scheme; yêw ê, 猶豫, undecided.
T'hèng sëüng, goê yêw jîn yëá, 聽訟吾猶人也 *t'hëⁿa sëüng gwá ëy ch'hin chëöⁿᵍ pat lâng*, in hearing cases of litigation, I am equal to others; see the 論語 Lūn gé.

Yêw 蕕 Fetid, stinking herbs; yit hwun yit yêw, 一薰一蕕 *chit ây p'hang ch'haôu, chit ây ch'haôu ch'haôu*, the one is a fragrant plant, and the other a stinking herb; see the 左傳 Chó twān.

Yêw 輶 Light; not heavy; tek yêw jê mô, 德輶如毛 *tek hëng k'hin yêw ch'hin chëöⁿᵍ t'haôu mô*, virtue is a small and light thing like a fine hair; see the 大雅 Taē gnáy.

Yêw 蝤 Yêw boê, 蝤蛑, a kind of shell fish, like a crab, but larger, and found on the seacoast.

Yêw 尤 To murmur, to complain, to find fault with; a fault; to exceed; a surname.
Sëāng put wàn t'hëen, hāy put yêw jîn, 上不怨天下不尤人 *tëng bīn bô wàn t'hceⁿᵍ, hāy têy bô yêw lâng*, above, not to murmur against heaven, and below not to find fault with men; see the 論語 Lūn gé.
Also written 尢, yêw.
Boê k'hëen yêw, 無愆尤, without fault; faultless.

Yêw 訧 A fault, a crime, a sin.
Pe boê yêw hêy, 俾無訧兮 *saé e bô köëy sit*, cause them to avoid crime; see the 國風 Kok hong.

Yêw 肬 A fleshy excrescence.

Yêw 由 From, out of, by, through; the means by or through which; yin yêw, 因由, a leading cause, an inducement; to let, to allow; yêw kê wûy, 由其爲, let him do it.
Kwan kê séy yêw, 觀其所由 *k'hwⁿa e séy yêw laê*, observe the motives from which his actions spring; see the 上論 Sëāng lūn.
Gwān këën, boê yêw tát, 願見無由達 *aē böëyh këëⁿᵍ, bô yin yêw ëy t'hong tát*, I wish to get an interview, but I have no means of introduction; see the 儀禮 Gê léy.

Yêw 油 Oil, fat, grease, any oily substance.
Chek yêw bwān bān sèk, choō jëën seng hⁿó, 積油滿萬石自然生火 *k'hëⁿᵍ yêw kaôu mwⁿá chëⁿᵍ*

bān chëoh, choō jëēn saing hōëy, when we collect oil to the amount of a myriad of peculs, it will of itself produce fire.

Yêw 甹 A tree shooting out its branches.

Yêw 卣 A vessel for containing aromatic wine.

Yêw 逌 To laugh; choó jîn yêw jé jê ch'heàou, 主人逌爾而笑 *choó jîn yêw jëēn jê ch'hëò,* the host smiling, laughed out aloud.

Yêw 郵 A post; yêw ėk, 郵驛 *yêw yëăh,* a post house.
Sok ê tê yêw jê t'hwān bēng, 速於置郵而傳命 *k'hăh kín ê yëăh báy jê t'hoong bēng lēng,* to convey orders swifter than a post; see 孟子 Bēng choó.

丟
Yēw 右 The right; yēw séw, 右手 *chëⁿà ch'hêw,* the right hand; chó yēw, 左右, right and left, attendants.
Séy oè ê chó, boô é kaou ê yēw, 所惡於左毋以交於右 *séy wān tē tó ch'hêw, bŏh é kaou tē chëⁿà ch'hêw,* that which you dislike on the left, do not associate with on the right; see the 大學 Taē hák.

Yēw 佑 To assist, to help, to aid, to abet.

Yēw 祐 To protect; pé yēw, 庇祐 *pó pē,* to protect with divine favor.

Yēw 又 Also, again, and, moreover; besides, still, yet.
Këèn chè put chëûng, yēw kèng put wûy, 見志不從又敬不違 *k'hwⁿà heèng e ây sim chè ūm t'hàn lán, yēw teŏh kèng, ūm t'hang wûy kăyh,* seeing our parents' intention is not to comply with our advice, we must still respect, and not oppose them; see the 論語 Lūn gé.

Yēw 囿 A park, a pleasure garden; wán yēw, 苑囿, a garden of pleasure.
Bûn ông che yēw, hong ch'hit sip lé, 文王之囿方七十里 *Bûn ông ây yēw woō sè kak ch'hit chàp lé,* Bûn ông's park was 70 square lé in extent; see 孟子 Bēng choó.

Yēw 宥 To spare, to treat liberally, to be indulgent, to forgive.
Kwun choó é sëà kò yēw chöēy, 君子以赦過宥罪 *kwun choó woō sëà köèy sit, yēw k'hwⁿa lāng ây chöēy,* the good man makes a point of forgiving faults, and being indulgent towards crimes; see the 易解卦 Ėk kaé kwà.

Yēw 栯 Yēw lé, 栯李, a kind of fruit, which if eaten expels jealousy.

Yēw 有 Also, again; the same as 又, yēw.

Yēw 賄 Wealth, money; to give, to present; yēw loē, 賄賂, a bribe.
E gnó yēw ch'hëen, 以我賄遷 *t'hó gwá ây cheeng ch'hëen swá k'hè pàt wūy,* to take my wealth, and remove it elsewhere; see the 衛風 Wöēy hong.

Yēw 侑 To assist, to help, to urge and incite one to eat; to couple, to pair.
E gák yēw sit, 以樂侑食 *é chok gák k'hwuiⁿg chëăh,* they played up the music, to incite the emperor to eat; see the 周禮 Chew léy.

Yēw 鼬 A kind of field mouse.

Yēw 柚 Vulg. nooi^ng á: a pumelo, a shaddock.
Bân tëung êng kit yēw, 閩中榮桔柚 *Bân sai^ng êng hwa kit kap nooi^ng á,* in the province of Hok-këèn lemons and pumelos flourish luxuriantly.

Yēw 狖 A black monkey.

Yēw 褎 The sleeve of a coat; also the appearance of much laughing.

去
Yim 陰 The female principle of nature; yim yâng, 陰陽, the male and female principle, which the Chinese suppose to have produced all things; t'haè yim, 太陰, the moon; yim kan, 陰間, the invisible world, the dark regions; kong yim, 光陰, time. A surname.
T'haè E sek ch'hùn yim, goê pöèy tong sek hwun yim, 太禹惜寸陰吾輩當惜分陰 *t'haè E woō sëöh chit ch'hùn ây yim, gwán ây lâng yëá tëöh sëöh chit hwun ây yim,* the great E used to spare every inch of time, and we ought to spare every tenth of an inch.

Yim 侌 The ancient form of the preceding; also written 陰, yim.

Yim 音 A sound, a tone; seng yim, 聲音 *sëⁿa yim,* a sound, a noise, a voice; hân yim, 翰音, a fowl.
Pat yim k'hek haê, 八音克諧 *páyh ây yim kèk kë haê hô,* the eight sounds excessively harmonious; see the 書舜典 Se sùn tëén.

Sip gnoé yim, 十五音, the fifteen initial sounds; the name of a Chinese dictionary of the Hok-këèn dialect on which this work is founded.

Yim 愔 Peaceful and harmonious; tranquil, still, retired.

Yim 喑 The incessant crying of children; to lose one's voice from grief.

Yim 瘖 Dumb, unable to speak.
Gîm jê put gân, put jê yim lông che chó hwuy, 吟而不言不如瘖聾之指麾 *gîm jê ū^m kóng wā, ū^m tat tëöh ây kaóu ch'haou hë lang ây kë chò yëō^ng,* to mumble and not speak out is worse than a deaf and dumb person pointing and beckoning; see the 淮陰候傳 Hwaê yim hoê twān.

Yim 漲 Read tëàng: to overflow, to be brimful, overflowing.

上
Yím 飲 Vulg. *lim:* to drink; yím chéw, 飲酒 *lim chéw,* to drink wine.
Yit p'heâou yím, 一瓢飲 *chit poô á ây lim,* a calabash full of drink; see the 論語 Lūn gé.

去
Yìm 廕 To screen; pè yìm, 庇廕, protection, shelter.
Choé chong pè yìm, 祖宗庇廕, the overshadowing protection of one's ancestors, (which the Chinese believe is advantageous to posterity.)

Yìm 蔭 To screen, to overshadow; umbrageous, that which can cover; a shade, a shelter.
Sē sêng yìm, jê chëûng neáou sit, 樹成蔭而衆鳥息 *ch'hēw chëⁿâ yìm jê chëûng*

cheáou hai^ngh, the trees form a covert, and all the birds of the air rest underneath; see 荀子 Sûn choó.

Yîm 婬 Private leisure, luxurious self-indulgence; lascivious.

Yîm 淫 Lascivious, lewd, lustful; kan yîm, 姦淫, fornication; yîm lwān, 淫亂, wantonness, voluptuousness, disorderly conduct. Yîm se, 淫書, obscene books.

Kwan ch'he lòk jê put yîm, 關雎樂而不淫 *Kwan ch'he t'hëung lòk, jé bēy yîm lwān*, the Kwan ch'he ode is pleasant without being obscene; see the 論語 Lūn gé.

Yîm 冘 The appearance of walking. Also written 冗, yîm.

Yîm 霪 A long continued rain. Bòk yëuk yîm é, 沐浴霪雨 *chāng ėk koó tê^ng ây hoē*, to be drenched in the long continued rain; see the 淮南子 Hwaê lâm choó.

Yîm 蟫 A book-worm.

丟 Yîm 訡 Hām yîm, 譀訡, angry words.

夲 Yin 因 To follow, to comply with; for, because; yin wûy, 因爲, on account of; yin yêw, 因由, a reason, a cause.

Yin yin ê Hāy léy, 殷因於夏禮 *Yin teáou t'hàn ê Hāy teáou ây léy*, the Yin dynasty followed the ceremonies of the Hāy dynasty; see the 上論 Sëāng lūn.

Yin 囙 The same as the preceding.

Yin 姻 A marriage; hwun yin, 婚姻, a wedding.

Yin 婣 The same as the preceding.

Yin 茵 A matress for sleeping or sitting on. Lūy yin jê chō, lëêt téng jê sit, 累茵而坐列鼎而食 *t'hëëp jëùk á jê chēy, lëêt tē^ná jê chëăh*, they sleep on a number of matresses piled one upon another; and eat of food prepared in a whole row of cooking-pans; (speaking of rich people.)

Yin 恩 Grace, favor, kindness; yin tëén, 恩典, gracious regards; yin aè, 恩愛, love, affection; yin hwūy, 恩惠, kindness.

Yin tek kip bān bîn, 恩澤及萬民 *yin tek kip kaòu chē^nâ bān ây păyh sai^ng*, gracious favor extending to myriads of people.

Yin 氤 Yin wun, 氤氳, the original germinating principle of heaven and earth, operating in secret.

Yin 駰 A horse with white hairs here and there intermingled.

Yin 禋 To sacrifice with a pure intention.

Yin 闉 A short low wall at the gate of a city.

Yin 殷 Numerous, many, all, plentiful, abundant, luxuriant; a surname.

Yín 慇 Yin k'hîn, 慇懃, to be very earnest and attentive; anxious and diligent.

声 Yín 隱 Secret, abstruse, minute; to secrete; yín ke, 隱居, to retire from the world, to dwell secretly.

To feel acutely, to compassionate, painful, grieved, mourning.

Bók hëèn hoê yín, 莫見乎隱 *bó k'hăh hëèn bêng hoē yín k'hèng*, there is nothing more evident than what is abstruse; see the 中庸 Tëung yûng.

Ch'hek yín che sim, jîn che twan yëá, 惻隱之心仁之端也 *ch'hek yín ây sim kwⁿa sē jîn ây twan yëá*, the feeling of pity and commiseration is the principle of benevolence; see 孟子 Bēng choó.

Yín 㥯 The same as the preceding. Also written 隱, yín.

Yín 阭 The common method of writing 隱, yín.

Yín 乚 To secrete, to conceal; the same as 隱, yín.

Yín 檼 To rely on, to comply with.

Yín 引 To lead, to guide, to induce, to influence, to seduce, to introduce.

Yín tō, 引導 *yín ch'hwā*, to guide in, or clear, the way; seáou yín, 小引, a short or inferior preface to a book.

Yín yéw, 引誘, to allure, to tempt.

Yín 紖 A cow rope, a rope for tying a cow.

Yín 蚓 Vulg. *kín:* a worm; k'hew yın, 蚯蚓 *t'hoê kín*, an earthworm. Hoo yín sëāng sit ko jëáng, hāy yím hông chwân, 夫蚓上食槁壤下飲黃泉 *hoo t'hoê kín têng bīn chëăh ta ây t'hoê, āy têy lim wutⁿᵍ ây chwⁿâ*, now the worm feasts above on the dry clods, and beneath it drinks the yellow fountains; see 孟子 Bēng choó.

Yín 靷 A rope for fastening an ox or a horse to a carriage.

Yín 尹 To advance, to enter; a surname; lēng yín, 令尹, the name of an office.

Yín 蚓 To tie a rope through the nose of an ox.

Yín 殷 The sound of thunder.

Yín 許 Read hé: to promise, to engage, to undertake.

去 Yìn 印 A seal, a stamp; an impression, to print, to press; a surname.

Jē ch'hëen sék kae gîn yìn, 二千石皆銀印 *nō ch'heng chëŏh chò poô woⁿ gîn ây yìn*, those officers who enjoyed an income of 2000 peculs of grain all held silver seals of office; see the 漢制 Hàn chè.

Yìn se, 印書 *yìn ch'hăyh*, to print books; yìn pán, 印板, the wooden blocks used for printing.

Yìn 檼 To rely on any one, to comply with.

Yìn 應 Read èng: to answer, to reply.

平
Yîn 云 To speak, to say, to declare. Se yîn, haòu hoē, 書云孝乎 *se kóng, tĕŏh woō haòu hoē*, does not the classic say, "be filial;" see the 論語 Lūn gé.

Yîn 沄 Water flowing back again.

Yîn 芸 A fragrant herb.

Yîn 紜 Raveled; in confusion, as threads; hwun yîn, 紛紜, in confusion.

Yîn 耘 To clear away the grass and weeds, in the cornfields; to weed; to remove whatever does harm.

Yîn 雲 Vulg. *hwûn*: a cloud; atmospheric fog, vapor; cloudy; a surname; san ch'hwan ch'hut yîn, 山川出雲 *swⁿa ch'hui^{ng} ch'hut hwûn*, the hills and rivers produce clouds.

Yîn 澐 Great waves raised up in a river.

Yîn 橒 Wood in which the grain is very strongly marked.

Yîn 寅 One of the horary characters; also to respect.

Yîn 夤 Yîn yêên, 夤緣, to give occasion to.

Yîn 匀 Even, plain, equal, alike.

Yîn 畇 Rice fields.

去
Yīn 胤 Posterity, successive generations. Eng sek choè yīn, 永錫祚胤 *éng koó soò hoē woō hok k'hè ây kēⁿá sun*, ever bestow upon us happy posterity; see the 大雅 Taē gnáy. Also written 亻胤, yīn, and, 胤, yīn.

Yīn 𦙍 The ancient form of the preceding.

Yīn 媵 To escort a daughter when going to be married.

Yīn 賸 To give a present.

Yīn 孕 A fœtus in the womb; hwaê yīn, 懷孕 *woō sin yīn*, to conceive in the womb. Seng yīn hwut slt, 牲孕弗食 *t'haou sai^{ng} woō sin yīn, bô chēăh*, when animals were pregnant, they did not eat of them.

入
Yip 邑 A city; toe yip, 都邑, a capital city. Sùn sóy ke yit lëên sêng chē, jê lëên sêng yip, 舜所居一年成聚二年成邑 *Sùn sóy k'hëā chit neē^{ng} chēⁿâ chē, nō neē^{ng} chēⁿâ yip*, wherever Sùn dwelt for a year, it became a neighborhood, and in two years a city.

Yip 俋 A bold, robust appearance.

Yip 唈 Oe yip, 嗚唈, shortness of breath, palpitation.

Yip 悒 The mind uneasy, the mind disturbed; disquietude.
Boó Hwat sat Yin hô séy yip? 武發殺殷何所悒 *Boó êng mēⁿá Hwat t'haê Yin, woō sⁿá meēⁿgh an sim?* Boó êng, whose name was Hwat, and who killed the prince of the Yin dynasty, how could he set his mind at ease? see the 楚詞 Ch'hoé soô.

Yip 筥 A bamboo instrument for catching fish.

Yip 裛 A satchel, a bag for books. Also to wind and entwine.

Yip 浥 To soak, to wet.

Yip 挹 To scoop out, to bale out water, to lade water, to take hold of with the hand, to pour out, to remove.

Yip 揖 Chok yip, 作揖 *ch'hcōⁿg jēá*, to make a bow or salutation.
Yip jēāng jē seng, 揖讓而升 *chok yip sēo nēōⁿg jē chēoⁿg*, they bowed to each other, mutually gave way, and ascended; see the 上論 Sēāng lūn.

Yip 熠 Full, abundant, bright.

犬

Yit 一 True, sincere, even; the beginning of numbers; one.
Yit kò, 一個 *chit ây*, one thing; yit jîn, 一人 *chit lâng*, one man.
Kip kê seng kong yit yēá, 及其成功一也 *kip kaôu e chēⁿa kang chit yēōⁿg*, but when they complete their work, it is one and the same thing; see the 中庸 Tēung yûng.

Yit 弌 The ancient form of the preceding character.

Yit 壹 The same as 一, yit, one; being a kind of capital letter or form of it; also, uniform, unmixed.

Yit 乙 One of the horary characters; one of the radicals.

Yit 乚 A black kind of bird.

Yit 鳦 A kind of swallow.
Lé-sew t'hun yit choo jê seng Taē-gēep; 女修吞鳦子而生太業 *Lé-sew t'hun eēⁿg á, jê saiⁿg Taē-gēep*, Lé-sew devoured a young swallow and brought forth Taē-gēep; see the 史記 Soó kè.

Yit 憶 Read ek: to think of, to remember; tēāng kéw sēang ek, 長久相憶 *tēⁿg koô sēo sēōⁿg*, to think of each other for a long time.
Ek chēak, 憶着 *yit tēōh*, to set the mind upon, to like, to be fond of.

天

Yit 佚 An yit, 安佚, at ease, at leisure; rest, tranquillity.
Soò che che ê an yit yēá, 四肢之於安佚也 *sè ke ây tē êng êng*, the four limbs are disposed to ease and rest; see 孟子 Bēng choò.

Yit 泆 Water overflowing; yîm yit, 淫泆, wanton, disorderly.

Yit 軼 To surpass, to exceed; the same as 佚, yit, at ease.

Yit 佾 A row of musicians; a choir of singers.
Pat yit boō ê têng, 八佾舞於庭 *pǎyh yit ây chok gàk ây lâng ko boó tē têng*, eight bands of musicians performing in the hall; see the 上論 Sëāng lūn.

Yit 遹 To follow, to obey.

Yit 驈 A black horse with white trappings.

Yit 鷸 A bird that knows when it is about to rain.

Yit 逸 To secrete; to flee, to run, to give up restraint; to follow; retirement, luxurious ease, leisure; yit soō, 逸士, a retired, unambitious scholar.
Má yit put lêng ché, 馬逸不能止 *báy chaôu bēy haiⁿgh*, the horses ran away, and there was no stopping them; see the 左傳 Chó twān.

Yit 溢 Full, overflowing; running over; yâng yit, 洋溢, to inundate.
Bwán jê put yit, 滿而不溢 *mwⁿá jê put bēy pwⁿâ ch'hut*, full without running over; see the 孝經 Haòu keng.

Yit 鎰 A weight of 24 ounces.
Suy bān yit pit soó gëúk jîn teaou tok che, 雖萬鎰必使玉人雕琢之 *suy bān yit tàt ây gëúk pit saé gëúk lâng teaou tok e*, although the gem may be of the value of a myriad of yit, yet he would employ a jeweler to work it up; see 孟子 Bēng choó.

Yit 聿 Then, following, only.

卋

Yung 邕 Harmonious, peaceable.

Yung 嗈 The singing of birds; also written 雝, yung.

Yung 癰 A sore, a boil, an ulcer; seng yung, 生癰 *saiⁿg eng á*, to have a boil.

Yung 雝 Harmonious, peaceable; genial, kind.

Yung 灉 The waters of a river overflowing; or bursting out of the banks and then flowing in again.

Yung 廱 P'hek yung, 辟廱, an imperial academy.

Yung 罋 A vessel made out of a gem.

Yung 饔 Dressed food; the dishes for the morning meal are called 饔, yung and those for the evening 飧, sun.

Yung 雍 Harmonious; p'hek yung, 辟雍, an imperial academy.

声

Yúng 俑 Wooden images of men, made to be burned at funerals.
Sé chok yúng chëá, kê boô hoē hoē, 始作俑者其無後乎 *k'hé t'haôu chò yúng ây lâng, e bô aôu tēy hoē*, he who first made those wooden images would doubtless be deprived of posterity; (because they were like living men, and might lead to the employment of real human beings for the same purpose;) see 孟子 Bēng choó.

Yúng 踊 To leap, and jump; also a kind of round shoe worn by those who have had their feet chopped off; a wooden leg.

Yúng yëák yūng peng, 踊躍用兵, they leaped and danced while using their swords; see the 邶風 Pöëy hong.

Yúng kwùy kè chëën, 踊貴屨賤 *yúng kwùy ây chwⁿā*, (so many persons had their feet chopped off,) that wooden legs became dear, and shoes cheap; see the 左傳 Chó twān.

Yúng 涌 A fountain bubbling up; to spring up as a well, to issue forth as a fountain; also written 湧, yúng.

Gwát yúng taē kang lôw, 月涌大江流 *göëyh yúng tē twā kang laôu*, the moon seemed to issue forth, and flow down with the waters of the great river; see the 杜甫詩 Toē hoó se.

Yúng 筩 A case for arrows, a quiver.

Yúng 衕 The middle way in front of a magistrate's hall.

Yúng 勇 Bold, courageous, daring.

Yúng chëá put kē, 勇者不懼 *yúng ây lâng bô kïⁿa*, bold men have no fear; see the 論語 Lūn gé.

Yúng 甬 A certain road; a sort of measure.

去 Yùng 壅 To stop up, to dam up; to manure, to fatten.

Hô kwat put k'hó hëw yùng, 河決不可復壅 *kâng p'hwà bô t'hang kŏh yùng*, the river has burst its bounds, and cannot be dammed up again; see the 史記 Soó kè.

Yùng 擁 To hold, to grasp in the hand; to escort, to accompany.

T'haè kong yùng hwŭy, 太公擁彗 *T'haè kong gīm saôu chëw*, T'haè kong held the broom, (when his son became emperor;) see the 高祖記 Ko choó ké.

Yùng 甕 A jar, a pitcher; yùng ch'haè, 甕菜 *èng ch'haè*, a kind of pickled vegetable kept in jars.

平 Yûng 庸 Common, usual, not out of the way; unchangeable; to use.

Tëung yûng, 中庸, the universal medium; the name of a Chinese classic.

Yûng 傭 Vulg. *ch'hëōⁿᵍ*: to hire people to work; to engage.

Yûng 墉 A city, a wall, a citadel.

E hwat chông yûng, 以伐崇墉 *é p'hăh kwân ây sëⁿâ*, to attack high-walled cities; see the 大雅 Taē gnáy.

Yûng 慵 Lazy, idle.

Yûng 鏞 A large bell.

Yûng 傛 Accustomed, used to; uneasy.

Yûng 容 A countenance, a visage; to allow, to admit of, to bear with; yûng maōu, 容貌, the appearance, air, demeanor; hâm yûng, 涵容, to include, to inclose, to receive. A surname.

T'hëen lé séy put yûng, 天理所不容 *t'heeⁿᵍ lé séy ūᵐ yúng*, that which Providence did not permit.

Yûng 蓉 Hoŏ yûng, 芙蓉, marsh mallows, the Hibiscus mutabilis; applied also to some other kinds of Malvaceous plants.

Yûng 溶 Water flowing peacefully along.

Yûng 榕 The name of a tree; yûng sē, 榕樹 chĕng ch'hēw, the banian tree.

Yûng 瑢 Chëûng yûng, 瑽瑢, to walk along adorned with gems.

Yûng 融 Steam or vapor rising up and blending; harmonious, peaceful. A surname.

Kê lòk yëá yûng yûng, 其樂也融融 e ày kŏèy è yûng yûng, their joy was harmonious and agreeable; see the 左傳 Chó twān.

Yûng 鎔 Vulg. yëŏng: to melt, to fuse; the mould used in melting metals.

Yûng hwà, 鎔化, to transform into another shape.

Yûng 㝐 The ancient form of 容, yûng.

Yūng 用 𤰃 To use, to employ; with, by; yéw yūng, 有用 woō yūng, useful.

Suy yëùk bút yūng, san ch'hwan kê sëá choo, 雖欲勿用山川其舍諸 suy aè bŏ yūng, swna ch'huing e woō pùng t'hek kak hoē, although we should be disposed not to use such an animal in sacrifice, would the spirits of the hills and rivers reject it; see the 論語 Lūn gé.

Chëet yūng jê aè jîn, 節用而愛人 chûn chat sěy yūng, jê sëŏh lâng, to be economical in the use of things, and kind to people; see the 論語 Lūn gé.

A

TABLE OF THE RADICALS;

Showing their order and meaning, together with the sound given them in reading.

N. B. In the following Table, the forms which accompany several of the radicals are contractions or modifications which they take when entering into composition.

Characters formed by one stroke of the pencil.

1 Yit 一 one.
2 K'hwŭn 丨 to descend.
3 Choó 丶 a point.
4 P'hëet 丿 bent out.
5 Yit 乙 one.
6 Kwăt 亅 hooked.

Formed by two strokes.

7 Jē 二 two.
8 T'hoô 亠 (undefined.)
9 Jîn 人 亻 a man.
10 Jîn 儿 a man.
11 Jip 入 to enter.
12 Pat 八 eight.
13 Keng 冂 a wilderness.
14 Bék 冖 to cover.
15 Peng 冫 an icicle.
16 Ké 几 a niche, a bench.
17 K'hám 凵 gaping.
18 To 刀 刂 a knife.
19 Lék 力 strength.
20 Paou 勹 to fold.
21 Pé 匕 a spoon.
22 [illegible] 匚 a receptacle.
[illegible] Hong 匸 a re[illegible] place.
24 Sip 十 ten.
25 Pok 卜 to divine.
26 Chëet 卩 㔾 a seal.
27 Hán 厂 a shelter.
28 Boé 厶 crooked.
29 Yēw 又 the hand, again, more.

Formed by three strokes.

30 K'hoé 口 the mouth.
31 Wûy 囗 an inclosure.
32 T'hoé 土 the ground.
33 Soō 士 a scholar.
34 Ché 夂 to follow.
35 Söey 夊 to walk slowly.
36 Sek 夕 the evening.
37 Taē 大 large, great.
38 Lé 女 a woman.
39 Choó 子 a son, a child
40 Bëên 宀 to collect.
41 Ch'hùn 寸 a punto, the tenth of a cubit.
42 Seáou 小 little, small.
43 {Ong Yêw} 尢 尣 兀 允 an irregular edge.
44 Se 尸 a corpse.
45 T[illegible] 屮 a bud
[illegible] 山 [illegible]
47 Ch'hwan 巛 巜 川 a channel for water.
48 Kong 工 work, a workman.
49 Ké 己 one's self.
50 Kin 巾 a napkin.
51 Kan 干 a shield.
52 Yaou 幺 slender.
53 Sëém 广 to protect.
54 Yín 廴 a long journey
55 Kéúng 廾 to join hands.
56 Ék 弋 to dart, a dart.
57 Këung 弓 a bow.
58 Ke 彐 彑 彑 a hog's head.
59 S[illegible] 彡 hair.
60 Ch'hek 彳 to pace.

Formed by four strokes.

61 Sim 心 小 忄 heart.
62 Ko 戈 a lance.
63 Hoē 戶 an inner door.
64 Sêw 手 扌 the hand.
65 Che 支 a branch.
66 P'hok 攴 攵 a slight stroke.
67 Bû 文 攵 letters, fair.
68 [illegible]
[illegible]
[illegible] 斤 a pound, a catty.
70 Hong 方 square, then.
71 Boô 无 旡 not, wanting.
72 Jit 日 the sun, day.
73 Wăt 曰 to say.
74 Gwăt 月 the moon.
75 Bók 木 wood.
76 K'hëèm 欠 to owe.
77 Ché 止 to stop.
78 Taé 歹 歺 evil, bad.
79 Soô 殳 to kill by striking.
80 Boô 毋 not, do not.
81 Pe 比 to compare.
82 M[illegible] 毛 hairs.
83 Sè 氏 a family name
84 K'h[illegible] 气 living principle
85 Súy 水 氵 氺 water
86 Hnó 火 灬 fire.
87 Jeáou 爪 爫 nails of the hand.
88 Hoó 父 a father.
89 Gnaôu 爻 to imitate.
90 Chëâng 爿 (undefined.)
91 P'hëèn 片 a splinter.
92 Gây 牙 the teeth.
93 G[illegible] 牛 牜 a cow.
94 K'hëen 犬 犭 dog.

Formed by five strokes.

95 Hëên 玄 blackish.
96 { Gëük 玉 a gem, / Ong 王 a king.
97 Kwa 瓜 a melon.
98 Wá 瓦 tiles.
99 Kam 甘 sweet.
100 Seng 生 to produce.
101 Yūng 用 to use.
102 Tëên 田 a field,
103 P'hit 疋 正 a measure of length.
104 Lek 疒 sickness,
105 Pwat 癶 a mound.
106 Pék 白 white,
107 P'hê 皮 skin.
108 Béng 皿 dishes.
109 Bók 目 the eye.
110 Maôu 矛 a spear.
111 Sé 矢 an arrow.
112 Sék 石 a stone. [ish.
113 Sē 示 礻 to admon-
114 Jéw 内 to creep.
115 Hô 禾 grain.
116 Hëet 穴 a den, a cave.
117 Lip 立 to erect.

Formed by six strokes.

118 Tëuk 竹 ⺮ bamboo.
119 Bé 米 paddy, rice.
120 Bék 糸 糹 silk, thread.
121 Hoé 缶 crockery.
122 Bōng 网 罒 罓 冈 net.
123 Yâng 羊 a sheep.
124 E 羽 feathers, wing.
125 Ló 老 old, aged.
126 Jê 而 a whisker, and.
127 Jōey 耒 handle of a
128 Jé 耳 the ear. (plow.
129 Yit 聿 a pencil.
130 Jëük 肉 月 flesh.
131 Sîn 臣 a statesman.
132 Choō 自 self, himself.
133 Chè 至 reaching to, at.
134 Kēw 臼 a mortar.
135 Sëét 舌 the tongue.
136 Ch'hún 舛 to disturb, error.
137 Chew 舟 a boat.
138 Kîn 艮 disobedient.
139 Sek 色 color.
140 Ch'hó 艸 艹 herbs.
141 Hoe 虍 a tiger.
142 T'hëûng 虫 an insect.
143 Hëet 血 blood.
144 Hêng 行 to go, to walk.
145 E 衣 clothes.
146 { Hà 襾 to cover; / Sey 西 west.

Formed by seven strokes.

147 Këèn 見 to see.
148 Kak 角 a horn.
149 Gân 言 words, to express.
150 Kok 谷 an aqueduct, a valley.
151 Toē 豆 pulse.
152 Sé 豕 a hog.
153 Chaē 豸 a reptile.
154 Pöèy 貝 pearls.
155 Ch'hek 赤 a carnation color.
156 Choé 走 to walk.
157 Chëuk 足 ⻊ the foot.
158 Sin 身 the body.
159 Ke 車 a carriage, a wheel.
160 Sin 辛 bitter. (hour.
161 Sîn 辰 to tremble, an
162 Ch'hëak 辵 辶 to walk swiftly.
163 Yip 邑 阝 a city.
164 Yéw 酉 new wine.
165 Pëen 釆 to pluck.
166 Lé 里 Chinese mile.

Formed by eight strokes.

167 Kim 金 metal, gold.
168 Tëâng 镸 長 long.
169 Bûn 門 a door. (earth
170 Hoō 阜 阝 a mound of
171 Taē 隶 at a certain point.
172 Tuy 隹 short tailed birds.
173 E 雨 rain.
174 Ch'heng 靑 azure.
175 Hwuy 非 false, not.

Formed by nine strokes.

176 Bëen 面 the face. (ther
177 Kek 革 untanned lea-
178 Wûy 韋 back to back.
179 Kéw 韭 leeks.
180 Yim 音 a sound.
181 Yëep 頁 the head.
182 Hong 風 the wind.
183 Hwuy 飛 to fly.
184 Sit 食 to eat.
185 Séw 首 the head.
186 Hëang 香 smell, fragrance.

Formed by ten strokes.

187 Má 馬 a horse.
188 Kwut 骨 a bone.
189 Ko 高 high.
190 Pew 髟 long hair.
191 Toè 鬥 to fight.
192 T'hëàng 鬯 wine used in sacrifice.
193 Kek 鬲 a perfume pot.
194 Kwúy 鬼 an evil spirit.

Formed by eleven strokes.

195 Gô 魚 a fish.
196 Neáou 鳥 a bird.
197 Loé 鹵 insipid.
198 Lók 鹿 a stag.
199 Bék 麥 wheat.
200 Mâ 麻 hemp.

Formed by twelve strokes.

201 Hông 黃 yellow.
202 Só 黍 millet.
203 Hek 黑 black.
204 Té 黹 to embroider.

Formed by thirteen strokes.

205 Bín 黽 a toad.
206 Téng 鼎 a tripod.
207 Koé 鼓 a drum.
208 Ch'hé 鼠 a mouse.

Formed by fourteen strokes.

209 Pit 鼻 the nose.
210 Chêy 齊 even.

Formed by fifteen strokes.

211 Ch'hé 齒 the teeth.

Formed by sixteen strokes.

212 Lëûng 龍 a dragon.
213 Kwuy 龜 a tortoise.

Formed by seventeen strokes.

214 Yëak 龠 a wind instrument of music.

AN

INDEX OF THE CHARACTERS

WHICH OCCUR IN THIS DICTIONARY

ARRANGED ACCORDING TO THE RADICALS.

The figures found in the following pages denote the number of strokes in the character independent of the radical.

一 Yit / *Chit*

丁 Teng

丂 K'hó

七 Ch'hit

2

万 Bék

丈 Teâng / *Tëōⁿg* / *Tēⁿg*

三 Sam / *Sᵃa* / Sàm

上 Seāng / *Chëⁿg* / Seáng

下 Hāy / *Āy* / *Kāy*

丌 Kô

不 Put / *Ūm* / Hew / Hoo

与 É

4

丏 Büén

丐 Kaè

丑 T'héw

且 Ch'hëⁿá / Ch'ho

丕 P'ho

世 Se

丘 K'hew / *K'hoo*

丙 Péng / *Pëⁿá*

丙 T'hëèm

丞 Sîn

丟 Tew

6

丣 Yéw

並 Pēng

丙 T'hëèm

兕 Toé

丨 K'hwún

丩 Kew / K'hëet

个 Kò

丫 A

丮 K'hwá

3

中 Tëung / Tëùng / *Tⁿa*

丯 Haō

丰 Hong

丱 Kwàn

6

串 Ch'hwàn / *Ch'huiⁿg* / Kwàn / *Kwuiⁿg*

弗 Sán

丶 Choó

丷 E

丸 Wân / *Eēⁿg*

丸 Hwân

丹 Tan

4

主 Choo

丼 *Tôm* / Tám / Tím / Tàm

乒 Peāng

一 1

丨 2

丶 3

8 Q

丿 4
乙 5
亅 6
二 7
亠 8
人 亻 9

丿 P'hëet
乀 Hwŭt
厂 Ē
乂 Gēy / Gnaē
ナ Chó
乃 Naé
2
久 / 乆 Kéw / *Koó*
么 Yaou
乇 Chek / T'hok
之 Che
4
乍 Chāy
乎 Hoē
乐 Ché / Choó
乏 Hwát
乑 P'haè
乑 Gîm
乕 E
乑 Tuy
6
乖 / 乖 Kwae
乘 Sêng / Sēng
乑 Sûy

乙 Yit
乙 Yit / At
乚 Yín
乜 *Bëá* / *Mcē^ngh*
九 Kéw / *Kaóu* / Kêw
2
乞 K'hit
也 Yëá / Yëā
乩 Sé
乩 Ke / Key
6
乱 Lwān
乱 Hëet
乳 Jé / Jeé^ng / Joó / *Leng*
乿 Tëá
10
乾 K'hëên / Kan / *Ta*
乿 Tê / Tē
12
亂 Lwān
乿 È
乿 Gëép

亅 Kwát
亅 K'hwat
了 Leáou
乿 Kwat
3
予 Ê̂ / E'
乿 Tëá
乿 Sē
事 Soō / *Saē*
乿 Tëà

二 Jē / *Nō*
二 Sëāng
二 Hāy
亍 Ch'hëuk
于 Ê̂ / E / He
亏 Ê̂
云 Yîn
互 Hoē
五 Gnoé / *Goē*
井 Chéng / *Chai^ng*
亖 Soò
亗 Gnoé
亘 Swan
亙 Kèng
亚 Hòng
些 Sa / So / Sèy
亟 Hêng
亝 Chae
亞 À / Oè / A / *U^n* / Ok
亟 Kek / K'hè

亠 T'hoê
亡 Bông / Boê
亢 K'hong / K'hòng
4
交 Kaou / *Ka*
亥 Haē
亦 Ėk
亨 Heng / P'heng
6
享 Héang / Hëáng / Hëàng
京 Keng / *Kë^na*
亩 Lím
亭 Têng
亮 Lëāng
亩 Tit
8
亳 Pȯk
亹 Sēng
亶 Chëen / T'hán
亹 Bé / Bûn

亼 Jîn / *Lâng*
亼 Chip
2
什 Sip / *Chảp*
仁 Jîn
仂 Lėk
仃 Teng
仄 Chek / *Chăyh*
仅 Hoò
仆 Hoò / Hèw / *P'hak*
仇 Kêw
仈 Pat
仉 Chëáng
今 Kim / *T^na*
介 Kaè
仌 Peng
仍 Jêng / Jëûng
从 Chëûng
3
仔 Choó / *Yëá*
仕 Soō
仙 Sìn
他 T'h^na / Tô

人 亻 } 9

仗 Tëāng / Tëáng
参 Chín
付 Hoò
仙 Sëen
仚 Hëen
仛 Ch'háy / T'hok
仜 Hông
仝 Tông
仞 Jīm
仟 Ch'hëen
仠 Hān
仡 Gwŭt / Git
㐲 Taē
仉 Hwàn
仢 Hëák
代 Taē / *Tāy* / *Tēy*
令 Lêng / Lēng
以 É
𠆶 Gwŭt
仮 Hwán
仯 Beáou

仰 Gëáng / Gëāng / Gâng
仱 K'hëêm
伙 Ch'hoò
仲 Tëūng
仳 Pé
臾 Laou
伢 Gêy
仴 Gwát
仵 Gnoé
件 Këēn / *Kë^{n}ā*
伔 Tám
价 Kaè
仸 Yaóu
仹 Hong
伄 T'hīn
任 Jîm / Jīm
任 Ŏng
伌 Tey
仿 Hóng
企 K'hé / K'hè / *Naîng*
伢 Ê

份 Pin
伂 P'hoè
伄 Teàou
伅 Tún / Tūn
伈 Sím
伆 Bún
伇 Ėk
伉 Kong / K'hòng
伊 E
伋 Kip
伌 Aè
伍 Gnoé
伎 Kê / Kē
伀 Chëùng / Gîm
伏 Pok / Hók / Hoō
伐 Hwát
休 Hew / Hoo
伭 Hëên
伮 Noê
伷 Tut
伱 K'hwa

伯 Pà / Pek / *Pāyh* / *Mā*
估 Koé
伒 Hong
你 Jé / Neé^{ng}
伲 Neé^{ng}
伳 Sëet / Ē
伴 P'hwàn / P'hwān / *P'hw^{n}ā*
伵 Ch'hëuk
伵 Hè
伶 Lêng
伷 Tēw
伸 Sin / *Ch'hun*
伹 Ch'hê
伺 Soo
伻 Peng
似 Soō / *Saē*
伨 Soō
伽 Këâ / *K'hëā* / *K'hay*
伾 P'he

佁 Ch'hè
佀 È / *Yëā*
佂 Cheng
佃 Tëên / Tëēn
佄 Ham
佅 Mae
但 Tān
佇 T'hé
佈 Poè
佉 Boó
佉 K'hay / K'he
佊 Pé
佋 Seâou
佌 Ch'hoó
位 Wūy
低 Tey / *Kāy*
住 Chē
佐 Chò
佑 Yēw / Yéw
佒 Yàng
体 Pūn

佔 Tëèm / Chëem
何 Hô / Hō
佖 Pit
佗 Ê / T'ho / Tô
佘 Sëâ
余 Ê
佚 Tëėt / Yit
佛 Pit / Hwut / Hwŭt
作 Chok / *Chŏh*
佝 K'hoè
佞 Lēng
佟 Tong
佩 Pöëy
佢 Hwān
佫 Hok
佬 Laou / Leâou
佭 Hâng
佮 Kap
佯 Yâng
佰 Pek

八 亻 } 9

金 Hwat
佪 Hwúy
佲 Béng
佳 Kay
価 Sëuk
㑊 Ëk
佴 Jē / Naē
併 Péng / Pèng / Pē^{n}g
佶 Kit
佷 Kwún / Hêng
佸 Kwat / Hwát
㑋 K'hëùng
佹 Kwuy / Kwúy
㐰 Sé
佺 Chwân
佻 T'heaou / Teàou / Yaôu
佼 Kaôu
佽 Ch'hoò
佾 Yit
侀 Hêng

使 Soó / *Saé* / Sòò / *Saè*
侁 Sin
侂 T'hok / *Tai^{ng}*
侃 K'hán
侄 Chit
侅 Kae
來 Laê / Laē
侇 Ê
侈 Ch'hé
俇 Ong
侉 Ò
侊 Kong
例 Lē
侌 Yim
侍 Sē
佗 Lëa
侏 Choo
侐 Hok
侑 Yëw
侒 An

律 Lut
侔 Boê
侕 Jê
侖 Lûn
俫 Lúy
侗 T'hóng / Têng
侘 Ch'há
侙 T'hek
侚 Sûn
供 Këung / *Keng* / Këùng / *Kèng*
侜 Chew
依 É / E
侶 Ló
伐 Jëûng
伽 Jê
侍 T'hé
侮 Boó
身 Sin
侓 Lô
侹 Tān
企 K'hè

侯 Hoê / *Kaôu*
㑂 Peng
侱 T'héng
侲 Chìn
仯 Sò
侳 Cho
侴 Ch'héw
侵 Ch'him / Ch'hím
侶 Lē
侷 Këuk
侸 Sō
侹 T'héng
㑗 *Lap* / Ch'hëep
侺 Sīm / T'hìm
侻 T'hwat
侼 Put
侽 Lâm
㑚 Nô
倄 Hwát
便 Pëen / Pëen / Pan / *P'hee^{ng}*

侾 Haou
俀 T'húy
俁 Gé
係 Hây / Hëy
促 Ch'hëuk / *Chak*
俄 Gô
㑌 Ch'he
倗 Bóng
俅 Kêw
㑝 Kông
俶 Sëuk
俈 K'hak
俉 Goē
俊 Chùn
俋 Yip
伋 Gip
俌 Hoó
俍 Lëâng
俎 Choé
俏 Ch'heàou / Seàou / Seaou
俐 Lē

俑 Yúng
俒 Hwûn
俓 Kèng
俔 Hëén / K'hëèn
㑣 Chëet / Ē
㑵 T'hek
俢 Yêw
俾 Pē
㑩 Sàm
倰 Lōng
𠈑 Hēng
俖 P'hōéy
俗 Sëuk
俗 Kêk
俘 Hoo
俙 He
俚 Ló / Lê
俛 Hoó
俜 P'heng
保 Pō
信 Sín / Sin / *Sëèn*

俢 Sew
俜 P'héng
俟 Soō / Kê
俠 Hëëp / Këëp
[illegible] Kwún
修 Sew 8
俯 Hoó
[illegible] Hō
俱 Ke / Kē
傚 Haōu
俳 Pöêy / Paê
俴 Chëën
[illegible] Hwun
俵 Peàou
偽 Ē
俶 T'hek / Sëuk
[illegible] Hwúy
俸 Hóng / Hōng
俹 À
俺 Yëèm / Gán
俻 Pē

[illegible] Yëuk
[illegible] Him
俾 P'hè / Pē
俿 Tê
倀 Ch'hëang / Ch'hèng
[illegible] Tê
[illegible] Táp
[illegible] Yīn
倂 Pèng
倃 Kéw
[illegible] Sëuk
倄 Hⁿaôu / Hnⁿê
倅 Chut / Ch'hùy
倆 Lëáng
[illegible] Chē
[illegible] Këep
倇 Wán
倈 Laê
倉 Ch'hong / Ch'hóng / *Ch'heⁿg*
倊 Chòng
個 Kò

倌 Kwan
倍 Pöéy / Pöêy / Pöēy
倎 T'hëén
倏 Sëuk / Sek
倐 Sëuk / Sek
[illegible] Lêy
[illegible] Tók
們 Bûn / Būn
倒 Tó
倓 Tâm / Tām
倔 Kwút
倕 Sûy / *T'hūy*
倖 Hēng
倗 Pêng
[illegible] Hëëp
倘 Ch'hëáng / T'hóng
候 Hoē / *Haōu*
倚 É / Ke / *N'á*
倛 K'he
倜 T'hek

倝 Kàn
借 Chek / *Chëŏh* / Chëà
倞 Këāng / Lëāng
倠 Hwuy
倡 Ch'hëang / Ch'hëàng
倢 Chëëp / Chëët
倣 Hóng
值 Tē / *Tàt*
倥 K'hong / K'hóng
倦 Kwān
倧 Chong
倨 Kè
倩 Ch'hëèn / Ch'hèng / *Ch'hëⁿà*
倪 Géy / Gêy
倫 Lûn
倬 Tok
[illegible] Kòng
倭 Öey / Wöey / O
倮 Kó / Hwá

倰 Lēng
倯 Sëung / Sëûng
倱 Hwún
倲 Tong / Tòng
倳 Choò
[illegible] Ch'hek
9
[illegible] Pēng
偀 Eng
偂 Chëen
偃 Yëén
偄 Lwān
偅 Chëûng / Ch'hëung
偆 Ch'hún
假 Kay / Káy / Kày / Hây / Kek
偈 Këet / Kē
偉 Wúy
偊 É
偋 Péng / Pēng
偌 Jëā
偍 Têy

[illegible] Hwûn
偎 Öey / Wöey
[illegible] Sē
[illegible] Sùn / Sûn
[illegible] K'hek
偏 P'hëen
[illegible] K'hëém
偐 Gān
[illegible] Hong
偒 T'hóng
偓 Ak
偔 Gók
偕 Kae
偖 Ch'hëá
偗 Séng
[illegible] Boē
偙 Tèy
做 Chò / Choè
[illegible] Soé
偛 Ch'hap
停 T'hêng
偝 Pöēy

9 八 亻

傑 Hëep
倘 Kw^{n}á
偟 Hông
偠 Yaóu
偡 Tám
偢 Ch'hèw / Ch'heàou
偣 Yëem
偤 Yêw
健 Këén / Këēn / Kë^{n}ā
偨 Tựt
偩 Sé
偪 Pëēn
偦 Sc / Sé
像 Hwùy
偧 Chay
偫 T'hok
偞 Ch'hay / Ch'hé
偬 To
偭 Hoó
偪 Pek
偫 Tē

傯 Chóng
偭 Bëēn
偮 Ch'hip
偯 É
偰 Sëet
偱 Sûn / Tūn
偲 Soo / Ch'hae
偳 Twan
側 Ch'hek
偵 Cheng
偶 Gnoé
偷 T'hoe / T'háou
偹 Hoē
偺 Maōu
傀 Kwuy / K'hwúy / Köey 10
傚 Tē
傁 Soé
傂 Ch'hèw
傃 Té
傅 Ch'him
傃 Soè

傄 Hat
傆 Sëet
傈 Sek
傒 Kwūy
傔 Tâm
傅 Hoo / Hoō / Poè
傆 Gwān
傇 Jëúng
傈 Lek
傉 Lok
傊 K'hëèn
傋 Káng
傌 Mā
傍 Peng / Pông / Pōng / Pé^{ng} / Pē^{ng}
傏 Chit
傎 Tëen
傐 T'haè
傏 Tông
傐 Hó
傑 Këet

傖 Ch'hëèn
傗 Këûng
傒 Hêy
傓 Wún
傓 Sëèn
傔 K'hëèm
傕 K'hak
傖 Ch'hêng / Sêng / Sông
傗 Ch'hëuk / Jëŏh
傘 Sán / Sw^{n}à
備 Pē
傜 So
傚 Haōu
傛 Yûng
傜 Yaôu
傝 T'hap
傞 So
傟 Áng
傠 Chek
傡 Ch'ham 11
傫 Lúy / T'höēy

俾 Pit
傕 Ch'huy
傀 Tê
傭 Yûng / Ch'hëung / Ch'hëō^{ng}
傮 Cho
傛 Sut
傯 Chóng
傰 Pêng
傱 Süúng
傲 Chëa
傲 Gō
傫 Lēy
傿 Lëak
傾 Kaè
傳 T'hwân / T'hooi^{ng} / Twān
傴 É
傶 Sùy
債 Chaè / Chày
傷 Tông
傶 Ch'hok

傜 Yaôu
傓 Chëem
傘 Kây
傝 Chòng
傷 Sëang / Sëo^{ng}
傹 Teáou
傸 Ch'hëáng / Sé^{ng}
傺 Ch'hè
傻 Sáy
傼 Hàn
傽 Hwâ
傽 Chëang
傾 K'heng / K'héng / K'hêng
傿 Yëèn
僂 Chaòu
僁 Chip
僄 Tèy
僅 Tek / Cháy
僁 Sëet
僂 Loê / Loē

備 Pē
僄 P'heàou / *P'hĕ̤ò*
僅 Kīn
僆 Lëén / Lëēn
僫 Gé
僇 Lëúk
僈 Bān
僻 Péng / Pēng
僉 Ch'hëe̤m
僊 Sëen
僋 T'hàm
僌 Söey
僜 Sûy
僘 Pëët
僎 Chun / Chëén
像 Sëāng
僟 Jē
僐 Sëēn
僑 Keâou
僒 Kwún / K'hwún
僓 Töêy

僔 Ch'hip
僖 Kê
僝 Ch'hûn / Chún
僕 Pók
僙 He
僗 Lô / Lō
僦 Ch'hëáng
僭 Kong
僲 Sëén
僚 Leâou
僛 K'he
僜 Ch'heng / Tēng
僝 Ch'han
僞 Ek
僞 Gwūy / Gô
僟 Ke
僠 Hwan / Po
僡 Hwūy
僢 K'héy
僣 Ch'hún / Ch'hwàn
僤 T'hëet

僤 Tan / Sëén
僥 Keaoú / Yaôu / Geâou
僦 Hip
僦 Chēw
僧 Boó
僧 Cheng
僩 Hàm
僨 Hwún / Hwùn
僫 K'hëen
僬 Yāng
僩 Hán
僪 Kwút
僮 Jê
僮 T'hóng / T'héng
僰 Ok / Oè
僬 Cheaou / Cheàou
僭 Sip / Sap
僭 Ch'him / Ch'hëèm
僰 Kek
僯 Lín / Lîn

僱 Soo
僮 Tông
僰 Pók
僱 Koè
僒 Tap

13

僵 Këang
僶 Bín
僷 Yëép
僸 Kìm
價 Sap
價 Kày
僾 Höēy
僿 K'ho
儀 Ch'heáou
儂 P'hek / *P'hëăk*
儃 Sek
億 Hong
儈 Chèw
儉 Aè
儀 Gê
儌 Pók
儁 Chùn

儂 Lông
儃 Sëên
億 Ek / *Yëŏh*
儃 T'hat
儅 Tòng / *Tàng*
儆 P'heàou
儇 Kêng
儈 Sëúk
儉 Këén
儆 Kéng
儇 Hwân
儉 K'hëēm / *K'hëōng*
儊 Yang
儋 Kaó
儋 Tam / Tàm
儌 Keáou / Heaou
儍 Tē
儈 Köèy
儑 K'hëen

14

儐 Pìn
儑 Gam

儒 Ê
儒 Jê
儓 T'héng
儔 Yín / Yìn
儓 Taê
儔 Têw
儘 Teáou
儙 P'heng
儕 Chey / Sây
儖 Lâm
儗 Këén
儙 É
儗 Gó
儘 Chín
儚 Pâng
儛 Boó
儜 *Lang* / Lêng / *Nai*ng
儝 Chaé

15

償 Ch'hëâng
儠 Lap / Lëép
儦 Pëen

9 人 亻
10 儿
11 入
12 八

儡 Lúy
儨 Chëet
儢 Lē
儣 K'hóng
儤 Pō
儥 Yëuk
儩 Sē
儦 P'heaou
儧 Chán
優 Yew
16
[illegible] Neáou
儯 T'hêng
儭 Ch'hìn
儮 Lék
儱 Lóng
儚 Bêng
儲 Tê
17
[illegible] Këén
[illegible] Lĩn
儳 Sâm
儇 Hwân
[illegible] Hwut

18
[illegible] Lŏêy
儶 Hēy
[illegible] Hong
[illegible] Lúy / Lŭy
19
儷 Lēy
儸 Lô
[illegible] Sëen
儹 Chán
儺 Nô
[illegible] Ch'hëùng
20
儻 T'hóng
儼 Gëém
[illegible] Heaou
儽 Lúy
[illegible] Lōng

儿 Jîn
兀 Gwút
2
允 / 允 } Wún
元 Gwân
兄 { Heng / Hë^{n}a
4
充 / 充 } Ch'hëung
兆 Teāou
兇 Hëung
先 { Sëen / *Sin* / Sëèn
光 { *Kwang* / Kong / *Kwui^{ng}*
兊 Töëy
5
克 K'hek
兌 Töëy
免 Bëén
兎 / 兔 } T'hoè
兒 Jê
兕 Soō
7
羌 Kēang

兖 Yëén
党 Tòng / *Táng*
兜 Taou
兟 Sin
兢 Keng

入 Jip
亼 Jip
兦 Bông
內 { Löēy / *Laē* / Láp
仝 / 全 } Chwân / *Chui^{ng}*
兩 / 两 / 両 } Lëáng / Lëāng / *Nëó^{ng}*
兪 Jê

八 { Pat / *Păyh*
公 { Kong / *Kang*
六 { Lëúk / *Làk*
兮 Hêy
4
共 { Këung / Këúng / Këūng / *Kāng*
关 Ch'heàou
兵 { Peng / *Pē^{n}a*
6
其 Kê
具 Kē
典 Tëén
7
㒸 Sūy
兼 Këem
兾 / 冀 } Kè

冂 Keng
冃 Mó
冇 P'h^{n}à
3
冉 Jëém
册 { Ch'hek / *Ch'hăyh*
再 Chaè
冋 Keng
6
冐 Mō
冒 Mō
冑 Tēw
冓 Koé
冔 Hoé
9
冕 Bëén
冪 Lê

冖 Bék
冗 } 冘 } Yîm
7
冠 { Kwan / *Kw^{n}a* / Kwàn / *Köèy*
冡 Bông
冢 T'hëúng
冥 { Bêng / *Maī^{ng}*
9
冨 Hoò
冩 Tìm

冫 Peng
冬 { Tong / *Tang*
4
冰 Peng
冲 Ch'hëung
决 Kwat
5
况 Hòng
冶 Yëá
冷 Léng
9
泮 P'hwàn
洞 Kéng
冽 Lëėt
8
准 Chún
凾 Hâm
凉 { Lëâng / *Nëó^{ng}*
凊 Ch'hèng
凋 Teaou
凌 Lêng
凍 { Tòng / *Tàng*
9
減 Këém
滭 Pîn
滭 Pit
凚 Kăet

13
凚 K'hím
凛 Lím
凝 Gêng
凟 Chun
艴 { *Ch'hìn* / *Ch'haī^{ng}*

几 Ké
凡 } 凢 } Hwān
処 Ch'hè
6
凭 Pîn
凰 Hông
9
凱 K'haé
凴 Pîn

凵 K'hám
凶 Hëung
3
凸 Tút
凹 { Aou / T'hap
出 Ch'hut
4
函 Hâm
凾 Hâm

冂 13
冖 14
冫 15
几 16
凵 17

8 S

18 刀 刂

刀 Tó
刁 T'heaou / Teaou
刃 Jīm

2

刅 Ch'hong
分 Hwun / Hwŭn / *Pun*
切 Ch'hëet / Ch'hè
刈 Gnaē

3

刊 K'han
刋 Ch'hëèn

4

刓 Gwân
刎 Bún
刿 Sày
刑 Hêng
刐 Tán
𠛅 Pin
刔 Kwat
刖 Gwát
列 Lëėt

5

初 Ch'hey
删 San
刡 Bín
𠛛 Hwa
创 Chëung
判 P'hwàn / *P'hwⁿà*
别 Pëet / Pëėt / *Pàt*
刦 / 刧 Këep
刨 Paôu
利 Lē / *Laē*

6

刮 Kwat / *Köĕyh*
到 Tò / *Kaðu*
刱 Ch'hòng
刳 K'hwa
刴 Tó
𠛸 *Lŏh*
制 Chè
刷 Swat / Ch'hèy
券 Kwàn
刹 Ch'hat
刺 Ch'hè / *Ch'heèng* / Ch'hek / *Ch'hëăh*
刻 K'hek

7

㓤 K'hëet / K'hat
剃 T'hèy / *T'hè*
剄 Kéng
則 Chek
剉 Ch'hò
削 Sëak / *Sëăh*
𠜾 Lek
剹 Lók
剋 K'hek
剌 Làt
前 Chëên / *Chân*
𠝏 Hêng
㓾 T'hek
剛 Kong

8

剒 Ch'hok
剺 Lè
剔 T'hek / *T'hak*
𠠵 P'hëang
剏 Ch'hòng
剖 P'hoé
剚 Choð
𠜶 Kong
剜 Wan
剝 Pak
𠝹 Ėk
𠝔 Sëėt
剳 *Lap*
剞 Kê
剟 Twat / *Twăh*
剡 Sëém

9

剨 Ėk / *Wöĕyh* / *Öĕyh*
𠝤 Ch'hap
剩 Sīn
剪 Chëén
㓻 Öey / Wöey
副 Hoð

10

割 Kat / *Kwăh*
𠞌 Kong
創 Ch'hong / Ch'hòng
𠞰 Lek / *Lëăh*
劋 Sut / *Chûy*
𠟃 Ch'hêng
剷 Tê
剻 P'héng
剽 P'heáou / P'heàou / *P'hëð*
劀 Swat

12

𠟱 Sok
剿 Ch'heâou
劁 Cheâou
𠠗 Lėk
劄 Chap
𠠎 Ch'hëêm
劕 Chún
劂 K'hwat
劃 Ėk
𠢀 Geãou
劅 Gók

13

𠠸 Lēng
𠠼 Sek
劇 Këák
劈 P'hek
劊 Köèy
劉 Lêw / *Laðu*
劌 Wöèy / Öèy
劍 Këèm
劒 Këèm

14

劑 Chey
劓 Gē
𠢐 *Lăyh*
𠢓 Lėk
𠢕 Lêng
劖 Chām
劘 Bê
𠢩 Lwân

力 { Lėk / *Lăt*
3
功 { Kong / *Kang*
[illegible] Hō
加 Kay
劣 Lwat
劦 Hëėp
5
助 { Choē / *Chān*
努 { Noé / Loé
劫 Këep
[illegible] { K'he / Kê
劭 Seāou
6
券 { K'hwàn / Kwān
効 Haōu
[illegible] Túy
劾 Hėk
7
勀 K'hek
勁 Kēng
勃 Pŭt
勅 T'hit
[illegible] Bók
勇 Yúng
[illegible] L r

勉 Bëén
[illegible] Poē
[illegible] K'hwae
勑 T'hit
9
勒 Lėk
動 { Tōng / *Tāng*
勗 Hëuk
勘 K'hàm
務 Boō
10
勝 { Sin / Sìn
勞 { Lô / Lō
募 Boē
勡 { P'heaou / P'heàou
勢 Sè
勣 Chek
勤 K'hîn
勦 { Chaôu / Ch'haou
12
[illegible] *Aôu*
[illegible] K'hwat
勩 Ē
[illegible] Keǎouh

[illegible] Hëet.
勠 Lô
勰 Hëėp
13
[illegible] Kìm
勳 Hwun
勵 Lēy
勷 Sëāng
勸 { K'hwàn / *K'hwunᵍ*

勹 Paou
勺 Chëak
勺 Yëŏh
2
匀 Yîn
勾 Koe
勿 Bŭt
匃 / 匄 } Kaè
包 Paou
匈 Hëung
6
匊 Këuk
匋 Tô
匍 Poô
8
[illegible] Yëep
匏 { Paôu / *Poô*
匐 Pók
匒 *T'hăh*

匕 Pé
𠤎 Hwà
化 Hwà
北 { Pok / *Pak*
匙 Sê

匚 Hông
匜 Ê
匝 Chap
4
匠 { Ch'hëāng / *Ch'hëōⁿg*
匡 K'hong
匣 Āh
匧 Këep
8
匪 Hwúy
匭 K'hwúy
匯 Höëy
12
匱 Kwŭy
匵 Tók
[illegible] Kám

力 19
勹 20
匕 21
匚 22

23 匸
24 十
25 卜
26 卩
㔾
27 厂
28 厶

匸 Héy
匹 P'hit
医 È
9
匾 { Pëén / *Pún*
匿 Lék
區 K'he

十 { Sip / *Cháp*
千 { Ch'hëen / *Ch'heng*
2
卄 *Sȧp*
卆 Chut
升 { Seng / *Chin*
午 { Gnoé / *Taȯu*
3
卉 Hwūy
半 { Pwàn / *Pw^{n}à*
6
卑 Pe
卒 Chut
卓 { Tok / *Tŏh*
協 Hëėp
南 Lâm
博 { P'hok / *P'haŏuh*

卜 Pok
卞 Pëēn
占 { Chëem / Chëèm
卣 { Yéw / Yêw
6
卦 Kwà
卨 Sëet

卩 Chëet
卬 Gêng
卯 B[illegible]óu
印 Yìn
4
危 Gwûy
却 K'hëak
卵 { Lwán / *Nooī^{ng}*
6
卷 { Kwán / Kwàn / *Kwuī^{ng}*
卸 Sëà
卹 Sut
卻 K'hëak
卼 Gwut
卽 Chek
即 Chek
卿 K'heng

厂 Gān
2
厄 { Ek / *Ăyh*
厈 Gān
厎 Té
6
厓 Gaê
厔 Chit
厖 Bâng
厘 { Lê / Lut
厙 Sëà
厚 { Hoē / *Kaōu*
8
厝 { Ch'hoè / *Ch'hoȯ*
原 Gwân
厠 Ch'hày
10
厥 K'hwat
厦 Hāy
厫 Gô
12
厭 { Ap / Yëem / Yëèm
厮 Soo
厲 Lēy

厶 Boé
厹 { Kêw / Jéw
风 Jéw
3
厺 K'hè
去 { K'hè / *K'hoȯ*
叁 Sam
9
參 { Ch'ham / Som
叅 Ch'ham

又 Yēw
叉 Ch'hay, Ch'ha
2 及 Kip
友 Yéw
叐 Yéw
反 Hwán
犮 Pwát
6 叔 Söuk, *Chëuk*, *Chek*
取 Ch'hé
受 Sēw
7 叙 Sē
叚 Káy
叛 Pwān
叟 Soé
16 叢 Chông, *Chăng*

口 K'hoé, *K'haó*, *Kaóu*, *Ch'hoé*
2 古 Koé
句 Koé, Koè, Kè, Ko
另 Lēng
叨 T'ho
叩 K'hoè
只 Ché
叫 Keàou
召 Teāou
叭 P'hwat, *Pāy*
叮 Teng
可 K'hó
台 Ê, T'hae
叱 T'hek
史 Soó, *Saé*
右 Yōw
叵 P'hó
叶 Hëëp
号 Hō
司 Soo
3 吮 Wún

[illegible]
吃 Kit
各 Kok, *Kŏh*
合 Háp, Kap
吉 Kit, *Ka*
吊 Teàou
同 Tông, *Tăng*
名 Bêng, *Mē^n â*
后 Hoē
吏 Lē
吐 T'hoè
向 Hëàng, *Hëò^ng*, *Hë^n â*
吒 Ch'há, Ch'hày
吽 Keàou, *Kèò*
君 Kwun
吚 E
吝 Lin
吞 T'hun
吠 Hwūy, *Pwūy*

吟 [illegible]
[illegible]
吧 [illegible] ha
吨 Tûn
[illegible] Kok
吩 Hwun, *Hwân*, P'hùn
吪 Gô
含 Hâm
听 Gín, Gîn, T'hèng
吭 K'hòng
吮 Wún
呈 Têng, *Tē^n â*
吲 Ch'hìn
吳 Goê
吸 K'hip
吹 Ch'huy, *Ch'höey*, *P'hoŏh*
吻 Bún
吼 Hoé, *Haôu*
吽 Hòng

唔 Goê
告 Kò, K'hok
呭 Chap
呀 Gëâ
呁 Kwún
呂 Lē
呆 Gaê
5 呟 *Hé^ng*
呠 P'hún
呢 Neê^ng
呦 Yew
呧 Té
周 Chew
呪 呪 Chèw
咐 Hoò, Hoê
呰 Ch'hoó
呱 Wâ
味 Bē
呴 Hè
呵 Ho, O

呶 Naôu
呷 Hap
呸 P'he
呺 Heaóu, *Hëó*
号 Heaou
呻 Sin
呼 Hoe
命 Bēng, Bān, *Mē^n â*
呿 K'hay
咀 Choé, Choè, Choê
咊 Jëá
咄 Tut, Tút
咆 Paôu
咈 Hwut
和 Hô, Hō, *Hôëy*
咎 Kēw
咏 Ēng
咛 Neê^ng
6 咠 Ch'hip
咢 Gók

又 29
口 30

8 T

30 口

咤 Ch'hày
哬 Hò
㖡 Ê
咨 Choo
咫 Ché
咬 { Kaou / *Ka*
咮 Tèw
咯 Kók
咱 { Chay / *Lán*
咳 { Hay / K'haè
㖠 Hâm
咺 { Swan / Höén
咻 Hew
咽 { Yëen / Yëèn / Yëet
咾 Laóu
咿 E
㖦 Ae
品 P'hín
哂 Sím
哎 Sut
响 Hëúng

㖀 *Swaĕ^{ng}h*
哄 Hōng
哆 Ch'hëá
哇 Wâ
哈 Ap
哉 Chae
哘 P'hún
哋 Tëā
員 { *K'hoe* / Wân / *Eĕ^{ng}* 7
哢 Lōng
哣 { Bê / Wúy
哤 Bâng
哥 Ko´
哦 Gô
哧 { *Ch'hëŏh* / Hăyh
哨 { Sadu / Seàou / *Ch'hëo*
哩 Lē
哪 { Lô / Lō / Nô / Nō
哫 Ch'hëuk

[illegible] { K'ɔk / *Ch'heou*
哮 Hoou
哯 Gneàou
哲 Tëet
哳 Cheăouh
哶 { Bé / *Maĭ^{ng}h* / *Meĕ^{ng}h*
哷 *P'hoo*
哺 Poē
哻 Hān
哽 Kéng
哿 K'hó
唀 Sëuk
唁 Gān
唂 *Koō*
唄 Pōèy
唆 { So / Sō
唇 Tûn
唈 { Yip / Ap
唉 Haé
唐 { Tông / *Tĕ^{ng}*

唌 Y
唔 [illegible]
唚 Chim
唬 Hăh
唭 { Ge / Ģē 8
唪 Hóng
唫 Gîm
唻 Nō
售 Sêw
唯 { Wûy / Wûy
唱 { Ch'hëàng / *Ch'hëŏ^{ng}*
唲 Heĕh
唴 K'hëàng
啂 Lūy
唵 Àn
唶 { Äyh / Öĕyh / *Wöĕyh*
唻 Laê
啺 Sek
唽 Sek
啃 P'hún
啗 Hâm

啅 { T'hò / *P'höèy*
啀 Gaê
啁 { Cham / Oé
啑 Sëep
啄 Chew
啒 Kwūn
啓 Tap
啛 Gnaôu
啄 { Tok / *Tăyh*
啅 Tok
啇 Sëang
啇 Tek
啈 Hèng
啉 Lâm
啊 Ò
啋 { Gek / Ch'hae
啍 { Chun / *Hee^{ng}*
問 { Būn / *Mooĭ^{ng}*
啕 *K'hcăouh*
啐 Ch'hùy

啓 / 啓 } K'héy
啖 { Tám / Tëēm
啗 Tám
啙 Ch'hóó
啚 P'hé
啜 { Ch'hwat / Twat
啞 { Áy / A / Ek
啷 Lāng
啽 Lûn
啻 T'hèy 9
啼 { T'hêy / *T'hé*
唫 Gâm
啣 K'hek
啾 Chew
喀 *K'haĭ^{ng}h*
喍 Hwút
喂 { Öey / Wöey
喯 P'hûn
喘 { Ch'hún / *Ch'huĭ^{ng}*

喃 Lam, Làm
善 Sëēn
喥 Yëuk
喆 Tëet
喈 Kae
喉 Hoê, Aôu
喏 Hō, Ō
喊 Hám, *Hëèm*, *K'hëēm*
喋 Tëëp
喌 喌 Chëuk, Choô, *Tak*
喏 Jëá
喑 Yim, *Lăyh*
喒 Chán
喓 Yaou
喔 Ak
喘 Ch'hwán, Ch'hún
喙 Hwūy
喚 Hwàn
喜 Hó

喝 Hat, *Hwăh*
喞 Chek
喟 Hwúy
喢 Ch'hăh, Ch'hap, *Sⁿăh*
喫 Kek, *Keĕh*
喤 Hông
喛 *Tŏmh*
喧 Swan
喩 Jē
喪 Song, Sòng, *Seⁿᵍ*
喫 K'hek, *K'hèy*
喦 Ch'hip
喬 Keâou
單 *K'hëa*, Sëēn, Sëēo, Tan, *Twⁿa*
喯 P'hùn
10
喰 K'haeⁿᵍ
嗂 Gèk
嗃 Hok

嗄 Ch'hày, *K'hatⁿᵍh*
嗅 Hèw
嗇 Sek
嗈 Yung
嗌 Ek
嗎 Má
嗏 Ch'ha
嗑 Áp
嗔 T'hëēn
嗥 Geâou
嗐 Hwā
嗚 Oe
嗛 K'hëém
嗜 Sē
嗝 Kek
嗟 Chëa
嗣 Soô, Soō
嗤 Ch'he
嗦 Lêw, *Laôu*
11
嗶 Pit
嗷 Gô

嗹 Lëen, Lây
嗻 Chày, Chèy
嗽 Soè, *Saôu*, Sok, *Sŏh*
嗿 Hám
嗛 K'hom
嘄 Keaou
嘅 K'haè
嘆 T'hàn
嘓 Kok
嘏 Kó
嘈 Chô
嘉 Kay
嘐 Hoe
嘊 Gaê
嘋 Chit
嘌 P'heàou
嘕 Yëén
嘈 Chaōu
嘒 Hae
嘏 Káy
嘒 Sip

嘐 Kaou, Haou
嘑 Hà
嘓 Kwăh
嘒 Hwūy
嘔 Oó, Aóu
嘋 T'heáou
嘖 Chek
嘗 Sëâng
嘘 He, Ha
嘿 *Seĕh*
12
嘬 Chōèy
嘯 Ch'heàou
嘱 Chëuk
嘲 Saou
嘴 Chúy, Ch'hùy
嘵 Heaou
嘶 Soo, Sey
嘷 Hô
嘹 Leâou
嘻 He
嘽 T'han

噎 *Oŏh*, Yëet
噀 Sùn
噂 Chun
噆 Chŏmh
噉 Hám, Tám
噋 Tun
發 P'hwat
噍 Cheāou, *Chëō*
噏 Hip
12
[illegible]
[illegible]
噤 K'hím, Kìm, Hìm
噦 Wöèy, Öèy
器 K'hè
噩 Gòk
噪 Ch'hò
噫 È, He, Aē, *Ăyh*
噬 Sē
嚆 Ho

30 口
31 囗
32 土

噭 Keäôuh
喝 Há
䆟 Chwǎh
唅 Köèy / K'hwaè
噴 P'hun / P'hùn
噓 Jëá
14
𡁏 P'hé
嚀 Lêng
嗡 / 㗳 Ham
9
[illegible] Gwè
嚉 T'haé
嚅 Jê
嚇 Hek / Hà / Hā
嘾 Chîn
對 Tùt / Tëō
嗅 Hēeng
嚌 Che / Chëy / Ch'hāy
15
嚽 Hëên
嚿 Chëëh
嚚 Gîn
嚽 Ch'hwat
嚞 Tëet
嚕 Lûn
16
嚥 Yëèn
嚙 Nâ / Lá
嚬 Pîn
嚮 Hëàng
嚭 P'hé
嚩 Meê^ng
嚶 Sëet
嚳 K'hak
嚫 Yîn
嚴 Gëêm
嚶 Eng
嚷 Jëáng
嚳 K'hoé
18
嚼 Chëak
嚾 Hwan
囀 Chwán
囁 Lëep
囂 Gô / Heaou
囃 Yung
囉 Lô
囊 Lông
囑 Chëuk

囗 Wûy
2
囘 Höêy
囙 Yin
囜 Lëëp
囚 Sêw
四 Tip
四 Soò / Sè
3
团 Këén
回 Höêy
囟 Sìn
因 Yin
4
囫 Hwut
囮 Böûy
困 K'hwùn
囷 K'hwun
囹 Lêng
固 Koè
6
囿 Yëw
圂 Hwui^ng
圃 P'hoé
圄 Gé
8
圇 Lûn
圈 K'hwân
圉 Gé
圊 Ch'heng
國 Kok
圍 Wûy
10
園 Wân / Hwui^ng
圓 Wân / Eéng
圖 / 圗 Toè
團 Twán / Tw^n á
圜 Hwân
圝 Lëên

土 T'hoé / T'hoé / Toē
圠 At
壬 T'héng
圣 Kwaè
3
在 Chaē
圩 Oo / Woo
圭 Kwuy
圯 E
圮 Ké
地 Tēy
圳 Chùn
4
圻 Kê / Ch'hek
圽 Bút
址 Ché
坂 Hwán / Pwán / Pw^n á
坅 K'hím
均 Kin
坈 Jöëy
坉 T'hûn
坊 Hong / He^ng
坋 Hwún

土 32

坌 Hwún / T'hûn
坎 K'hám
坏 P'he / P'höey
坐 Chō / *Chāy* / *Chēy* / *Ch'hāy*
坑 K'heng / *K'hai^{ng}*
坔 Làm
5
坡 P'ho
坢 P'hwán
坣 Tông
坤 K'hwun
坦 T'hán
坩 *K'h^{n}a*
坪 P'hwán
坫 Tëèm
坯 P'he / P'höey
坰 Keng
坱 Óng / Òng
坲 Hwút
坳 Aou

坵 K'hew / *K'hoo*
坷 K'hó
坻 Tê
垂 Sûy / *Söêy*
6
型 Hêng
垎 *Kăyh*
垝 K'hwúy
垠 Gîn
垢 Koé / *Kaóu*
垣 Hwân
垵 *W^{n}a*
垤 Tëét
7
垺 Pút
垻 Pà
垾 Hān
埀 Sûy
埃 Ae
埔 Poe
埆 K'hëak
埋 Baê / *Taê*
城 Sêng / *Së^{n}á*

埒 Lwát / *Lwăh*
埕 *Tē^{n}á*
8
埜 Sëā
域 Hék
埠 Poē
埡 Oé
埤 Pe / Pê / Pē
埦 Wán / *W^{n}á*
埭 Tēy
埰 Ch'haè
埵 Tó
埶 Chip
培 Pöêy
基 Ke
埽 Sò
堀 K'hwut
堂 Tông / *Tē^{ng}* / *T'hē^{n}a*
堅 Këen
堆 Tuy
堊 Ok

堋 *P'hē^{n}á*
9
堛 *P'höēyh*
[illegible] Toē
堞 Tëëp
堡 Pó
堤 Tey
堦 Kae
堪 K'ham
堯 Geâou
堰 Yëén
報 Pò
堲 Chek
場 Ch'hëâng
堳 Bê
堵 Toé
10
[illegible] Chit
塊 K'hwaè
塋 Êng
塌 T'hap
塏 K'haé
塒 Sê
塓 Bék

塔 T'hap / *T'hăh*
塑 Soè
塕 Òng / *Àng*
塗 Toê
塘 Tông / *Tē^{ng}*
塚 T'hëúng
塞 Sek / *T'hat* / *Saè*
[illegible] Chòng
[illegible] *T'hoot^{ng}*
塡 T'hëên / *T'hūn*
塢 Oé / Ch'hek / Toē
塤 Hwun
[illegible] Jeúk
11
塲 Ch'heâng / *Tëó^{ng}*
塵 Tîn
塹 Châm
塾 Sëúk
[illegible] Loé
墀 Tê

墁 Bân
境 Kéng
墅 Sō
墈 K'hàm
墉 Yûng
墊 Tëèm
墌 *Chëŏh*
墍 K'haè
墐 Kîn
墓 Boē / *Bōng*
墘 *Kee^{ng}*
墖 T'hap
12
墜 Tūy
墝 K'haou
墼 Ke
增 Cheng
墟 He
墠 Sëēn
墡 Sëēn
墣 P'hok
墤 Tōêy
墩 Tun

32 土
33 士
34 夂
35 夊
36 夕

播 { Hwan, Hwân
墨 { Bĕk, *Băk*
墳 Hwûn
13
牆 { Ch'hëâng, *Ch'hëōng*
墼 *Kat*
墾 K'hwún
壁 { P'hek, Pek, *Pëáh*
壅 { Èng, Yùng
墈 K'hám
壆 K'hëak
壇 { T'hân, *Tŭⁿā*
14
壎 Hwun
壑 Hok
壓 { Ap, ~~[illegible]~~
壕 Hô
壥 Tëên
壘 Lúy
壙 K'hòng
16
壚 Loê
壜 T'hâm

壝 Wûy
壞 { Hwaē, *K'hëep*
壟 { Lóng, Lëúng
壠 { Lóng, *Lang*
壤 Jëáng
20
壩 Pà

士 Soō
壬 Jîm
壳 K'hák
4
壯 Chòng
壳 K'hàk
声 Seng
声 K'hèng
9
壹 Yit
壺 Hoê
壼 K'hwún
壽 Sēw

夂 Ché
夅 Kàng

夊 Söey
夌 Lêng
7
夏 Hāy
夔 Kwûy

夕 Sĕk
外 { Göēy, *Gwa*
3
夙 Sëuk
多 { To, *Chēy*
夜 { Yëā, *Maiⁿᵍ*
8
够 { Koè, *Kadu*
夠 Göēy
夢 { Bōng, *Bāng*, P'hew
夣 Bōng
夤 Yîn
夥 { Hⁿó, *Höēy*

夳 Taē / *Twā*
天 T'hëen / *T'hee^{ng}*
太 T'haè
夫 Hoo / Hoô
夬 Kwaé
夭 Yaou / Yaóu
2
央 Yang / *E^{ng}*
失 Sit
夷 Ê
夸 K'hwa
夾 Këep / *Gnăyh*
5
夵 T'hûy
奃 Táy
奄 Yëem / Yëém
卒 *Gëăh*
奇 Ke / Kê / *K'hëa*
奈 Naē
奉 Hōng
6
奎 Kwuy
奏 Choè / *Chaòu*
奐 Hwàn

契 K'hëet / K'hèy / K'hè / Sëet
奔 P'hun
奓 Hae / *T'hà*
奕 Ėk
7
套 T'hò
奘 Chōng
奚 Hêy
9
奠 Tëēn
奡 Gō
奯 K'hwat
奢 Ch'hëa
10
奧 Ò / Hëuk
奩 Lëêm
契 Chuy
奪 Twát / *Tăyh*
奬 Chëáng
12
奭 Sek
奰 Pō
奮 Hwùn
奰 Pō

女 Lé / Neē^{ng} / Jé
奴 Noê / Loê
奵 *T'hè^{n}á*
3
奸 Kan
好 H^{n}ó / H^{n}ò / *Hó*
妁 Chëak
奶 Naé
如 Jô
妃 Hwuy
妄 Bōng
4
妊 Jîm / Jīm
妍 Gëên
妒 Toè
妓 Kê / Kē
妖 Yaou
妗 Kīm
妙 Beāou
妝 Chong / *Che^{ng}*
妤 Ê
妣 Pé
妥 T'hó

妨 Hông
5
妬 Toè / Sèk
妮 Neê^{ng}
妯 T'hew / Tëuk
妲 Tat
妳 Naé
妸 ó
妹 Mōèy / *Nw^{n}ā*
妺 Bwát
妻 Ch'hey / Ch'hèy
妾 Ch'hëep
姆 *Úm* / Boó
㚼 *Saē*
姊 Chó / *Cheáou*
始 Sé
姍 San
姐 Chëá / *Cháy* / Chéy / *Chaóu*
姑 Koo
姒 Soō
委 Wúy

姓 Sèng / *Sai^{ng}*
姕 Ch'hoó
6
姙 Jīm
姚 Yaôu / *Yëô*
姜 Këang
姝 Te
姞 Kit
姖 Gó
姣 Kaóu
姤 Koè
姥 Boó
姦 Kan
姨 Ê
姪 Tìt
媳 *Seĕh*
姬 Ke
姭 Hëēm
姮 Hêng
姶 Ap
姌 Jëēm
姸 Gëên

姻 Yin / Yëen
姽 Gwúy
姿 Choo
娀 Jëûng
威 Wuy
娃 Wâ
7
娉 P'heng
娌 Lé
娑 So
娘 Lëâng / *Nëó^{ng}*
娛 Gê
娜 Nô
娞 *Söēy*
娝 P'hut
娟 Kwan
娠 Sin
娣 Tōy
娥 Gô
娩 Bwán / Bëén
娬 Boó
娭 Haôu

大 37
女 38

38 女

39 子

娶 Ch'hè / *Ch'hwā* 8
娼 Ch'hëang
娿 ŏ
婁 Loê
婆 Pô
娆 K'hëáng
婉 Wán
婐 ó
婕 Chëet
婘 Kwân
婚 Hwun
婢 Pē
婣 Yin / Yëen
婦 Hoō / *Poō*
婪 Lam
婬 Yîm
婭 À
婷 Têng 9
婺 Boō
婚 Hwun
婿 Sèy / *Saè*

婾 T'hoe
媆 Jūn
媥 Chëên
媌 *Bá*
媍 Hoō
媎 Chëá
媒 Böêy / *Hâ*^{m}
媓 Hông
媖 Eng
媚 Meō^{ng}
媛 Wān
媟 Sëet
媢 Mō
媧 Wâ
媳 Sit 10
媵 Yīn
媸 Ch'he
媻 Pwân
媼 Aóu
媽 Má
媾 Koe / Koè

媿 K'hwùy
嫁 Kày
嫂 Só
嫄 Gwân
嫉 Chit
嫋 Leáou
嫌 Hëêm
嫐 Ló
嫑 Heáou
婊 Peáou
嫍 So
嫖 P'heàou / P'heâou
嫗 Oé
嫚 Bān
嫜 Chëang
嫠 Lê
嫡 Tek
嫣 Yēen
嫦 Sëûng
嫩 Jūn
嫶 Heaou
嫫 Boê

嫪 Lô / Lō 12
嫴 Koo
嫵 Boó
嫺 Hân
嫽 Leáou
嬈 Jeâou
嬉 He
嬋 Sëên
嬌 Keaou
嬕 Sek
嬖 Pè
嬗 Sëēn
嬙 Ch'hëâng 14
嬣 *Na*^{ng}
嬤 Bó
嬪 Pīn
嬭 Naé / *Leng*
嬰 Eng
嬲 Seáou
嬴 Êng
嬸 Sím / *Chím*

嬻 Tók
嬾 Lán
嬿 Yëèn
嬽 Jwán
孀 Song
孃 Lëâng / Nëo^{ng}
孌 Lwân

子 Choó / *Kë*^{n}*á*
孑 K'hëet
孔 K'hóng / *K'hùng* / *K'hang* 3
孕 Yīn
字 Joō / *Jē*
孖 Choó
存 Chûn 4
孚 Hoo
孛 Pút
孜 Choo
孝 Haòu / *Hà* 5
孟 Bēng
季 Kwùy / *K'hwùy*
孤 Koe 6
孩 Haê
孫 Sun / Sùn / *Swui*^{ng}
孬 Waěh
孰 Seuk 9
孱 Ch'han
孳 Choo

[illegible] Jê
13
學 Hȧk / Öh
孺 Jê
孻 Naê
孽 Gëét
孾 Eng

宀 Bëên
宁 T'hé
宂 Jëúng / *Jëáng*
宄 Kwúy
3
宅 T'hėk / *T'hăyh*
宇 É
守 Séw / Sēw / *Chéw*
安 An / *Wⁿa*
4
宋 Sòng / *Sàng*
完 Wân
宊 Yûng
宏 Hông
宎 Gô
5
宓 Bit / Hȯk
宗 Som
[illegible] Gwà
宕 Tōng
宗 Chong
官 Kwan / *Kwⁿa*
宙 Tēw
定 Tēng / *Tëⁿā*

宛 Wán
宜 Gê
客 K'hek / *K'háyh*
6
宣 Swan
宋 Chėk
室 Sit
宥 Yew
宦 Hwān
7
宧 Ê
宲 T'hay
㝗 Lông
宮 Këung
宰 Chaé
害 Haē
宴 Yëèn
宵 Seaou
家 Kay
宸 Sîn
容 Yûng
8
宿 Sëuk / Sèw
寁 Chëét
寀 Ch'haé

寂 Chėk
寃 Wan
寄 Kè / *Këà*
寅 Yîn
密 Bit / *Bȧt*
[illegible] Ay
寇 / 寇 K'hoè
9
[illegible] Wut
富 Hoò / *Poò*
寍 Lêng
寐 Bē
寒 Hân / *Kwⁿà*
[illegible] Bwán
[illegible] É
寓 Gē
寔 Sit
10
寗 Bēng
寘 Tè
[illegible] Jé
[illegible] Óng

[illegible] Pó
康 K'hong
[illegible] Tëèm
寞 Bȯk
察 Ch'hat / *Ch'hak*
寡 Kwⁿá
寢 Ch'hím
寤 Goē
寥 Leâou
實 Sit
寧 / 寧 Lêng
12
寨 Chāy
審 Sím
寫 Sëá
[illegible] K'hwán
寬 K'hwan / *K'hwⁿa* / *K'hwⁿà*
寮 Leâou
寰 Hwân
寶 Pó
寵 T'hëúng

寶 Pó
[illegible] *Eeⁿᵍ*

子 39
宀 40

41 寸
42 小
43 尢
兀
尣
44 尸
45 屮

寸 Ch'hùn
峙 { Sē / Eĕng }
5
尀 P'hó
封 Hong
7
射 { Ėk / Sëä / Sėk / *Chŏh* }
尅 { K'hek / *K'hat* }
將 { Chëang / Chëàng / Ch'hëang }
9
專 Chwan
尉 { Wùy / Wut }
尊 Chun
尋 { Sîm / *Ch'hŏëy* }
對 { Tùy / *Töèy* }
導 { Tō / *Ch'hwā* }

小 { Seáou / *Sëó* }
少 { Seáou / Seàou / *Chëó* }
尐 { Tëep / *Cheĕng* }
尔 Jé
3
尖 Chëem
[illegible] Kwùy
尛 { Mó / *But* }
[illegible] Cham
[illegible] Sa
5
尙 { Sëāng / *Sëōng* }
[illegible] Sa
尟 Sëén
[illegible] { Cho / Chô }
[illegible] Lân
[illegible] Ch'ham

尢 { Yêw / Ong }
尤 Yêw
4
尨 Bāng
尩 Ong
尪 { Ong / *Ang* }
尬 Kaè
就 Chēw
12
尵 Töēy
[illegible] K'heàou
尷 Lâm

尸 Se
尹 Yín
尺 { Ch'hek / Ch'hëuk / *Ch'hëŏh* }
尼 { Neêng / Lit }
尻 { K'haou / *Ka* }
尽 Chīn
4
尾 { Bé / *Böëy* }
尿 *Jëō*
局 { Këuk / *Kėk* }
屁 { P'hè / *P'hwùy* }
5
居 Ke
屃 Ke
屆 / 届 Kaè
屈 K'hwut
6
屋 Ok
屍 Se
屎 { Sé / *Saé* / He }
屏 { Péng / Pîn }
屐 { Kėk / *Këăh* }

屑 Sëak
展 Tëén
8
屙 O
[illegible] Hwut
屛 Péng
[illegible] Ėk
9
[illegible] Sëuk
屠 Toô
屢 Lé
屣 Sé
屜 Ch'hoe
層 { Chàn / Chêng }
履 Lé
12
屧 Sëet
屩 Kè
[illegible] Kak
屬 { Sëuk / Chëuk }
屭 Hè

屮 Tëét
屯 { Chun / Tûn / Tūn }
[illegible] Hēng

山 46

山 San / *Sw^{n}a*
屲 Wat
2
屴 Lėk
屶 Hōēy
屵 Gȧt
屹 Git
屼 Gwṳ̇t
4
岄 Gwȧt
岟 Gëūng
岇 Gông
岉 Bṳ̇t
岋 Gneȧouh
岌 Gip
岐 Kê / *Kĕâ*
岑 Gîm
5
岝 T'hėk
岞 T'hėk
岡 Kong / *Ke^{n}g*
岧 Teȧou
岩 Gâm
岪 Hwṳ̇t
岫 Sēw

岬 Kap
岭 Lêng / *Nĕ^{n}ā*
岱 Taē
岳 Gȧk
岵 Hoé
岶 P'hek
岷 Bîn
岸 Gān / *Hw^{n}ā*
6
峇 Bā
峋 Sûn
峌 Tëėt
峗 Gëâng
峒 Tông
峓 Ê
岍 Gëên
峙 Sē
峵 *Kĕ^{n}â*
7
峨 Gô
峮 K'hwun
峭 Seȧou
峼 Lōng

峯 Hong / *Hang*
峰 Hong
峵 Bông
崀 Lông
峴 Hëén
島 Tó
峺 Kēng
峻 Chùn
峆 Ham
峽 Këep
峾 Gîn
8
崆 K'hong
崇 Chông
㟅 K'hëung
峼 T'hėk
崍 Laê
崎 Kê / *Këā*
崑 K'hwun
崒 Ch'hùy / Chūy / Chṳ̇t
崔 Ch'huy
崖 Gaê

崗 Kong
崘 Lûn
崙 Lûn
崛 Kwṳ̇t
崞 Kok
崢 Cheng
崤 Gnaôu
崧 Sëûng
崩 Peng / *Pang*
9
嵑 Kek
嵴 Chėk
崲 Hông
崵 Tōng
崽 Chaé
崿 Gȯk
嵃 Gȯk
嵁 K'ham
嵂 Lṳ̇t
嵆 Key
嵋 Bê
嵌 K'ham / K'hàm

嵎 Gê
嵏 Chong
嵸 Ch'hong
嵐 Lâm
嵒 Gâm
嵓 Gâm
10
嵢 Wân
嵷 T'hëûng
嵠 K'hey
嵡 Óng
嵤 Êng
嶋 Oé
嵩 Sëung
嵬 Gwûy
嵱 Këûng
嵯 Ch'ho / Ch'he
嵲 Kong
11
嶅 K'hok
嶀 Sëúng
嵺 Leȧou
嵻 K'hong
嵻 K'hóng

嵨 Bėk
嵿 Téng
嶂 Chëàng
㟼 Peaou / Peáou
嶀 K'hwùn
嵺 Leȧou
嶊 Bóng
嶇 K'ho
12
嶨 Hȯk
嶏 P'hae
嶍 Tōng
嶟 Jūn
嶝 Tông
嶒 Chêng
嶬 He
嶓 Po
嶕 Cheaou
嶲 Chùn
嶜 Tun
嶙 Lîn
嶚 Leȧou
嶝 Tèng

46 山
47 巛 〈 巜 川
48 己
49 工
50 巾

崛 Gwut
嚻 Heaou
嶟 Chun
嶠 Keâou
嶢 { Geâou / Yaôu }
嶤 Gaôu
嶧 Ėk
崫 { K'hwut / Tút }
14
㠓 Bông
嶷 Gê
嶨 Hô
嶸 Êng
嵺 Leâou
嶺 { Léng / *Nëⁿá* }
巀 Chëêt
嶼 Sē
嶼 Sē
嶽 Gák
15
齰 T'hėk
巊 Gėk
㠺 K'hòng

嶽 Gók
嵭 Péng
巇 He
17
巆 Êng
巊 Éng
巑 Chông
巍 Gwûy
巐 T'heáou
巏 Hong
巒 Lwân
巔 Tëen
20
巖 { Gëêm / *Nâ* }
巗 Gâm
巘 Hëèn
巄 Lōng

巛 Ch'hwan
川 { Ch'hwan / *Ch'huiⁿᵍ* }
3
州 Chew
巟 Hong
巡 / 廵 } Sûn
8
巢 { Chaôu / Chaōu }
粼 Lîn

工 { Kong / *Kang* }
2
左 Chó
巧 { K'haóu / *K'há* }
巨 Kē
巫 Boô
7
差 { Ch'hay / Ch'he / *Chwŭh* }
𢀖 P'hong

己 Ké
已 É
巳 Chē
巴 Pa
2
厄 Gó
巵 Che
6
巷 Hāng
巽 Sùn

巾 Kin
帀 Chap
市 Ch'hē
布 Poè
帄 Teáou
帆 { Hwân / Hwān }
4
帊 P'hà
帋 Ché
希 He
5
帗 Hwut
帔 P'he
帇 Koô
帕 { P'hà / *P'hày* }
帖 T'hëep̄
帘 Lëêm
帙 { Yëėp / *Yëăh* }
帚 Chéw
帛 { Pėk / *Păyh* }
6
帝 Tèy
帟 Ėk
𢃇 Sûn
帲 Pęng

巾50 干51 幺52 广53

𢃇 T'hong
𢃈 Hông
帥 Sōèy / Sùy / Sut
7
帨 Sōèy
師 Soo
帬 Kwûn
𢃳 Kwûn
席 Sėk / *Sŏăh* / *Ch'hëŏh*
8
帳 Tëàng / *Tëòⁿᵍ* / *Sedou* / *Tà*
帶 Taè / *Twà*
帷 Wûy
常 Sëâng / *Sëôⁿᵍ*
帽 Bō / *Mwⁿa*
9
𢄂 Gėk
幃 Wûy
幄 Ak
幅 Hok / *Pak*
幇 Pang
幐 Têng

10
㡜 Saé
㡘 Lëêm
幏 Bông
幌 Hóng
幍 T'ho
幊 Kong
幁 Wân
幎 Bėk
𢄙 Tⁿng
11
𢄂 T'hong
幔 Bān
幕 Boē
幗 Kok
幘 Chek
12
㡔 Hėk
幝 Ch'hëén
幞 Pók
幟 Chè
幡 Hwan
幣 Pē
㡞 Lak
幦 Bėk

幨 Ch'hëem
幩 Hwûn
14
幪 Bông
幫 Pang
幬 Tó
㡣 Laé

干 Kan
平 Pêng / Pêên / *Patⁿᵍ*
年 Lëên / *Neêⁿᵍ*
开 幵 𢆉 K'hëen
4
罕 Hán
并 幷 Pèng / *Pëⁿà*
幸 Hêng
幹 Kàn

幺 Yaou / *Yëo*
幻 Hwàn / Hwān
幼 Yèw
幽 Yew
6
幾 Ke / Ké
㡭 Sé

广 Sëém
3
庀 P'hé
庅 *Mwⁿa*
庄 Chong / *Cheⁿᵍ*
4
庇 Pè
床 *Ch'hêⁿᵍ*
庍 Paè
庎 Kaè
序 Sē
5
底 Té / *Tëy*
庖 Paôu
店 Tëèm
㡧 Tëên
庙 Beāou
庚 Keng / *Kaiⁿᵍ*
𢇁 Tàn
府 Hoó
庝 Tông
6
㢆 K'ham
庠 Sëâng
㡷 Ān
𢇼 Tŏng

53 广
54 廴
55 廾
56 弋

庍 Ch'hek
庡 É
庤 Sē
庥 Hew
度 Toē / Tók
庲 Hàng
7
座 Chō
庝 Lông
庄 Chong
庫 K'hoè
[illegible] ...ng / *Tēⁿâ*
庨 Seaou
8
庰 Péng
庼 Keng
庲 Laê
庳 Pē
庮 Laōu
庶 Sè
康 K'hong / *K'heⁿg*
庸 Yûng
庵 Am

9
廅 Gē
庾 Jé
廆 Öèy / Wöèy
廊 Pēng
廅 Yëep
廂 Sëang / *Sëoⁿg*
10
廌 Chaē
廉 Lëêm
廊 Lông / *Néⁿg*
廋 Soe
廍 P'hoē
廞 Ch'hìm
廏 / 廐 Kèw
廓 K'hok
廕 Yìm
廖 Leāou
12
廚 Toê
廛 Tëên
廟 Beāou / *Bëō*
廡 Boó

9
廠 Ch'hëáng / *Ch'hëóⁿg*
廢 Hwùy
廣 Kóng
廨 Kaè
13
廞 Hìm
廩 Lím
10
廥 Keng
廬 Lê
廱 Yung
廳 T'heng / *T'hëⁿg*

廴 Yín
4
廷 Têng
延 Yëên / Cheng
廹 Pek
廸 Tek / Tëuk
6
建 Këēn
廻 Höêy
廼 Naé

廾 / 廿 Këúng
廿 Jeĕh
弁 Pwân
3
异 Ē
弃 K'hè
弄 Lōng / *Lāng* / *T'hāng*
6
弆 Sùn
弇 Yëém
7
弈 Ék
弊 Pē

弋 Ék
弌 Yit
弍 Jē
3
弎 Sam
式 Sit
弑 Ék
9
弒 Sè

弓 Këung
弔 { Teàou / Tek }
引 Yín
弖 Kwān
2
弗 Hwut
弘 Hông
弛 Sé
4
弝 Pà
[illegible] Kwat
弟 Tēy
5
弢 T'ho
弤 Té
弦 { Hëên / *Heé^{ng}* }
弧 Hoê
弨 T'heaou
弯 Loē
[illegible] Yêw
6
弭 Bé
弰 Saou
弱 Jëȧk
張 { Tëang / *Té^{ng}* }
9
弼 Pit

強 { Këáng / Këâng / Këāng / *Këó^{ng}* }
彀 { Koè / *Kaòu* }
12
彇 Seaou
彈 { T'hân / *Tw^{n}â* / Tān / *Tw^{n}ā* }
彊 { Këáng / Këâng / Këāng / *Këō^{ng}* }
彌 { Me / Bé / Bê / Mee^{ng} }
彎 Wan

彐 Kē
彖 T'hwàn
8
彗 Hwūy
10
彘 Tē
12
彙 Lūy
彝 Ê

彡 Sam
4
形 Hêng
彤 Tông
彣 Sàm
6
彦 Gān
彧 Hëuk
8
彩 Ch'haé
彪 Pew
彫 Teaou
彬 Pin
9
彭 { P'hêng / *P'hai^{ng}* }
彰 Chëang
影 { Éng / *É^{ng}* / *Yë^{n}á* }

彳 Ch'hek
行 Teng
4
彷 Hóng
役 { Ėk / *Yëăh* }
5
彴 Gōng
彼 Pé
彽 Swăh
彿 Hwut
往 Óng
征 Cheng
徂 Choe
6
很 Kek
待 T'haē
徊 Hêng
徇 Tèw
徇 Sûn
很 Hwún
徊 Hōêy
徛 Ê
律 Lu̇t
後 { Hoē / *Aōu* }
7
徎 T'héng

徐 Ch'hê
徜 Ch'heâou
徑 { Kèng / *Kai^{ng}* }
徒 Toê
8
得 { Tek / *Tit* }
徘 Paê
徙 { Sé / *Swá* }
從 { Chëûng / Chëūng / Ch'hëung / *Töèz* }
徠 { Laê / Laē }
御 { Gē / Gāy }
9
徧 Pëèn
徨 Hông
徝 Ch'hèng
復 { Hok / Hȯk / *Kȯh* / Hēw }
循 Sûn
10
徬 Pông
徭 Yaôu
微 Bê

弓 57
彐 58
彑
彡 59
彳 60

徯 Hêy
微 Bê
12
徵 Tin
德 Tek
徹 { Tëét / T'hëet }
徼 { Heaou / K'heàou / *K'hëò* }
儜 Lēng
徽 Hwuy

心 Sim
必 Pit
2
忥 Gnaē
忉 To
忛 T'heaou
3
忌 Kē
忍 { Jím / *Lún* }
忐 T'hám
忑 T'hek
忒 T'hek
忓 He
忖 Ch'hún
志 Chè
忚 K'hëung
忘 Bông
忙 Bông
忝 T'hëém
忞 Bîn
忠 Tëung
忡 Ch'hëung
忤 Gnoé
忣 Hòng
忥 Hè

忩 Ch'hong
快 K'hwaè
忬 Ē
忭 Pëēn
忮 Chè
忯 Chè
忱 Sîm
念 Lëēm
忸 Lëuk
忺 Hëem
忻 Him
忼 K'hóng
忽 Hwut
5
忿 Hwún
怍 Chók
怎 Chóm
怏 Yàng
怒 Noē
怓 Naôu
怕 P'hà
怖 Poè
怙 Koē

怛 T'hat
怜 Lông
思 { Soo / Soò }
体 Pūn
怠 Taē
怡 Ê
怢 *T'heĕh*
急 { Kip / *Maĭ^{ng}h* }
怞 Tut
性 { Sèng / *Saĭ^{ng}* }
怨 Wàn
怩 Neê^{ng}
怪 { Kwaè / *Kwò* }
怫 Hwut
怭 Pè
怯 { K'hëep / K'hëak }
怱 Ch'hong
怵 T'hut
6
恕 { Lún / Lùn }
恁 { Jím / Jīm }

恂 Sûn
恃 Sē
恆 Hêng
恇 Ch'hëung
恊 Hëep
恑 Ch'hay
恌 T'heaou
恍 Hóng
恐 K'hëúng
恒 Hêng
恓 Sey
恔 Haōu
恕 Sè
恙 Yāng
恚 Hwūy
恛 Bék
恝 K'hëet
恟 Hëung
恑 Kwaè
恢 K'höey
恣 Choò
恤 Sut

恥 T'hé
恨 *Hīn*
恩 Yin
恫 Tōng
恬 Tëêm
恪 K'hak
恭 Këung
息 Sit
恰 K'hap
恲 Pèng
7
悁 Kwan
悃 K'hwún
悄 Ch'heáou
悅 Wát
悉 Sit
悋 Līn
悌 Tēy
悍 Hán
悔 Höèy
悒 Yip
悟 Pwúy
悖 Pöēy

心 61 忄 ⺗

- 悚 Sëúng
- 惾 Ch'hwan
- [illegible] Kē
- 悝 K'hōey
- 悞 Goē
- 悟 Goē
- 悠 Yew
- [illegible] Hwut
- 患 Hwān
- 悤 Ch'hong
- 悋 Lín
- [illegible] T'hún
- 悰 Chong 8
- 悔 Hwúy
- 悖 { Pe / Pwuy }
- 悳 Tek
- 悳 Tek
- 悴 Chūy
- 悵 Tëàng
- 悶 Būn
- 們 Bún
- 悻 Héng

- 悸 { K'hwùy / Kwùy }
- 悼 Tō
- [illegible] K'hew
- 㥄 Lêng
- 惃 Koē
- 悽 Ch'hey
- 悾 K'hong
- 情 { Chêng / *Chē^{n}â* }
- 惄 Lek
- 惆 Têw
- 惇 { Sûn / Chun }
- 惵 Tëëp
- [illegible] É
- 惧 Kē
- 惍 Kim
- 惏 Lam
- 㥂 Tong
- 惑 Hék
- 惓 { K'hwân / Kwān }
- 惔 { [illegible] / Tâm }
- 惕 T'hek

- [illegible] Bèng
- 惘 Bóng
- 惙 Twat
- 惚 Hwut
- 惚 Hwut
- 惛 Hwun
- 惜 { Sek / *Sëŏh* }
- 惟 Wûy
- 惠 Hwūy
- 惡 { Oc / Ok / *Baè* }
- 悪 Oò 9
- 惰 { Tō / *Tw^{n}ā* }
- 惱 { Naóu / Ló }
- 惲 Hwún
- 想 { Sëáng / *Sëó^{ng}* / *Sëō^{ng}* }
- 惴 Ch'húy
- 惶 { Hông / *Hē^{n}â* }
- 惸 Kêng
- 惹 Jëá

- 惺 Seng
- 惻 Ch'hek
- 惼 P'hëén
- 惽 Hwun
- [illegible] *Lā*
- 愀 { Ch'heáou / Ch'heâou }
- 愆 K'hëen
- 愈 Jú
- 愉 Ê
- 愊 Pek
- 愍 { Bín / Bëén }
- 愎 Pit
- 意 È
- 愒 K'hò
- 愔 Yim
- 愕 Gòk
- [illegible] Mō
- 愘 { K'hay / K'hày }
- 愚 Gû
- 愜 Këep
- 愛 Aè

- 感 Kám
- 愧 K'hwùy 10
- 愪 Wún
- 愫 Soè
- 愬 Soè
- [illegible] Yín
- 愲 Wut
- 愴 Ch'hóng
- 愶 Hëëp
- 愷 K'haé
- 慎 Sīn
- 愾 { Hè / K'haè }
- 愿 Gwān
- 慁 Hwūn
- 慄 Lek
- 慅 So
- 慆 T'ho
- 慇 Yin
- 慈 Choê
- 慉 Hëuk
- 慊 K'hëém
- 態 T'haè

- 慐 Këung
- 慍 Wùn
- 慓 P'heaou 11
- 慕 Boē
- [illegible] Lê
- 慘 Ch'hám
- 慙 Ch'hâm
- 慚 Ch'hâm
- 慝 T'hek
- 慟 Tōng
- 慢 Bān
- 慣 Kwàn
- 慤 K'hak
- 慥 Ch'hò
- 慧 Hwūy
- [illegible] Bòng
- 慨 K'haè
- 慮 Lē
- 慰 Wùy
- 慰 Wùy
- 慱 Twân
- 慲 Bwân

8 X

61 心 小 小
62 戈

慳 Këen
慴 Lëep
慵 Yûng
慶 { K'hèng / *K'hëⁿà* }
慷 K'hóng
憇 K'hè
慼 Ch'hek
慾 Yëuk
凴 Pîn
憀 Leâou
憂 Yew
憃 Chëung
12
憊 Paē
憎 Cheng
憐 Lîn
憑 Pîn
憒 Höëy
憔 Cheâou
憖 Gīn
憚 Tān
憝 Tun
憞 Tūy

憤 Hwún
憦 Lō
憧 Ch'hëung
憨 Ham
憩 K'hè
憫 Bín
憅 Tōng
憬 Kéng
憭 Leáou
憮 Boó
憲 Hëèn
懾 Sëep
13
憵 P'hek
憶 Ek / *Yit*
憸 Sëem
憺 Tām
憼 Kéng
㦗 Kīm
憾 Hām
憹 Loé
憿 Heaou
㦸 Kek

懀 Köèy
懂 Tóng
懃 K'hîn
㥞 Sūy
懆 Ch'hó
懇 K'hwún
懈 Haē
應 { Èng / Eng }
懊 { Ò / Aòu }
懋 Boē
懌 Ek
懍 Lím
懎 Sek
懏 Chùn
14
懕 Yëem
懘 T'hè
懛 Tae
懜 Bōng
懟 Tūy
懡 Mó
懣 Bwán
懥 T'hè

懦 Nô
15
懮 Yéw
懰 Lêw
懲 Têng
16
懶 Lán
懷 Hwaê
懸 Hëên
18
懺 Ch'hàm
懻 Kē
懽 Hwan
懾 Lëep
懿 È
19
戀 { Lwân / Lwān }
戁 Lán
㦬 Lô
20
戃 T'hóng
戅 { Gōng / Gām }
戇 Gōng

戈 Ko
戉 Wát
2
戊 Boē
戌 Sut
戍 Sùy
戎 Jëûng
我 Gnó
3
成 { Sêng / *Chëⁿâ* / *Sëⁿâ* / *Ch'hëⁿâ* }
我 { Gnó / *Gwá* }
4
戒 Kaè
戔 Chëen
或 Hék
戓 K'ham
戕 Ch'hëông
6
咸 Hék
戚 { Ch'hek / *Ch'hăyh* }
8
戛 K'hat
戞 K'hat
戟 Kek
戡 { K'ham / K'hàm / Tím }
戢 Ch'hip

戥 Téng
10
戧 Paôu
戩 Chëén
截 { Chëét / *Chăh* / *Chăyh* }
戲 Hoe
戮 Lëuk
12
戰 Chëèn
戱 Hè
戯 Hoe
戴 { Taè / *Tèy* }

戶 63 手 64 才

戶 Hoē
戹 Ek
4
戽 Hoè
戾 Lēy
房 Pông / *Pâng*
所 Séy / *Só*
扁 P'hëen / Pëén / *Peé^{ng}*
扃 Keng
6
扅 Ê
扆 É
扇 Sëèn / *Seè^{ng}*
扈 Hoē
8
扉 Hwuy
扊 Yëém
[illegible] Swan

手 Séw / *Ch'héw*
才 Ch'haê / Chaê
扎 Kit
2
扐 Lék
扑 P'hok
扒 Put / *Pwaè*
打 T^{n}á / *P'hăh* / *Tai^{ng}*
3
托 T'hok
⿰扌冃 Mó
扚 Tek
扛 Kong / *Ke^{ng}*
扞 Hān
扠 Ch'hay
扣 K'hoè / *K'haou* / *K'hà*
扤 Gwut
4
抇 Chút
扴 Kap
扭 Léw
扮 Pān
扲 Gīm / *K'heé^{ng}*

扱 Ch'hap
扳 P'han
扵 E
扶 Hoô
扷 Yëó
批 P'hey / P'ho
扽 Tùn
找 Chaōu
承 Sîn
技 Kê / Kē
抙 P'hóng
抏 *Wut^{ng}*
抄 Ch'haou / *Pë^{n}â*
抆 Bún
抉 Kwat
把 Pá / *Páy*
抌 Tìm
⿰扌牙 K'hây
扼 Ek
抒 T'hé
抓 Jeáou / Jeàou

抖 Toé / *Taou*
投 Toê / *Taou*
抗 K'hòng
折 Chëet / *T'hëăh* / *Bán*
⿰扌勿 Bút
5
抦 *Tai^{ng}*
抧 Chè
抨 *P'hai^{ng}*
⿰扌疋 Se
抪 Poè
披 P'ho / Mōh
抬 *Gëâ*
扭 *Chaouh*
抱 P'haou / *P'hō*
抵 Té / *Téy* / *Toó*
抸 Chăh
抹 Bwat / *Bwăh*
押 Ăh
抽 T'hew
⿰扌加 Kây

拂 Hwut
⿰扌卯 Léw
拄 Ché / *Toŏh* / Ch'hoó
担 T'hán / *T'hw^{n}á*
拆 Ch'hek / T'hek / *T'hëăh*
拇 Bó
拈 Lëem / Lëêm / *Nee^{ng}*
拉 Lëep / *La*
拊 Hoó
拋 P'haou / *Pâ*
拃 [illegible]wan
拍 P'hek
批 Ch'héy
⿱此手 Ch'he / Choo
拎 Lêng
拏 Ná / *Lëăh*
拐 Kwaó / *Laou*
拑 K'hëêm
拒 Kē

拓 T'hok / *T'hŏh*
拔 Pwăt / *P'hwăh* / *Păyh*
拕 Tô / *Tëŏh*
拖 T'ho / *Twâ*
拗 Aóu / Aòu
拘 K'he
拙 Chwat
拚 P'hwan
招 Cheaou / *Chëo*
拜 Paè
投 Toê
6
括 Kwat
拭 Sit
拮 K'hëet
拯 Chín
拱 Këúng / *Kéng*
拳 K'hwân
拴 Ch'hwan
拵 Chûn
拶 Swán

64 手 扌

挎 K'hó
拼 Pai^{ng}
拾 Sip / *K'hëŏh*
拿 Ná / *Lëăh*
持 Tê
挂 K'hwà
捋 Lůt
挃 Chit
指 Ché
挈 K'hëet
按 Àn / *Hw^{n}ā*
挍 Kadu
拏 Ná
挑 T'heaou / T'heáou / *T'hëa*
7
挨 *Ey*
挫 Ch'hò
捊 Pụt
捀 P'haé / *Pöëy*
振 Chín
挰 Tai^{ng}

抄 So
拼 *Lāng*
挷 *Páng*
挹 Yip
挺 T'héng
挽 Bwán / *Bán*
挩 T'hut
拵 Pwân / *Pwâ*
挾 Hëep / *Gnăyh*
捁 K'hò
捄 Kêw
捃 K'hwûn
捆 [illegible]
捉 Ch'hëuk
捋 Lwát / *Lwăh*
捌 Pat / *Păyh*
捓 Haē
捘 Swân / Swân
捏 Lëep
捎 Saou
捐 Kwan

捒 Sak
捔 Kak
捕 Poê / Poē / *Lëăh*
捗 P'hoê
捘 Ch'hūn
8
捔 Tok
捧 Hóng / *P'hâng* / *Pāng*
捨 Sëá
捩 Lëet
捫 Bún / Bûn
捬 Chong
捰 Ó
捱 Gaê
捲 Kwán / *Kwu^{ng}*
捷 Chëet / *Yē^{n}ā*
捺 Lát / *Lwăh*
捻 Lëèm
捼 Jōêy
捽 Chut
捾 Wat / *Kw^{n}ā*

捿 Sey
掀 Hëen
掂 Kwăh
掽 Pai^{ng}
掃 Sò / *Sadu*
掄 Lûn
掅 Ch'hèng
掇 Twat
授 Sēw
掉 T'heáou
掊 Pöêy
掋 Té
掐 *Chang*
掌 Chëáng / *Chëo^{ng}*
掎 É
掐 K'hip / *K'hâng*
排 Paê
掖 Ėk
掗 Wá / Wöëyh / *Öëyh*
掘 Kwut

掙 Châng
掛 K'hwà
掞 Sëém
掟 Tēng / *T^{n}ā*
掠 Lëák
採 Ch'haé
探 T'ham / T'hàm
接 Chëep / *Cheĕh*
掦 T'hek
控 K'hòng
推 T'huy / Ch'huy / *T'hay* / *T'hey*
掩 Yëém / Yëèm
措 Ch'hoè
掬 Këuk
9
掾 Yëēn
揀 Lëēn
揁 *Chee^{ng}*
揃 Chëén
揄 Jê

揤 Ch'hek
揬 T'hwàn
揆 Kwûy
揇 Lám
揈 Hong
揉 Jéw / Jêw
揋 Wui^{ng}
揎 Swan
描 Beâou / *Bëó*
揊 Pang
揘 Lůt
提 Sê / T'hêy / *T'hăyh*
插 Ch'hap / *Ch'hăh*
揓 Sè
揖 Yip
揚 Yâng
換 Hwàn / *W^{n}ā*
揜 Yëém
揟 Se
揠 At

手 才

握 Ak
掿 K'hăyh
揣 Ch'húy
揤 *Chăyh*
揥 Tèy
揦 Lát / *Lwăh*
揩 K'hae / K'haè
揪 Ch'hew
揬 Tút
揭 Këet / K'hè
揮 Hwuy
揲 Sëëp
援 Wān
揵 Këēn / *Kēⁿā*
揽 Lám
揞 *Ân*
10
搆 Koè
捦 K'hìm
揕 Ch'hëén
損 Sún / *Swui^{ng}*
搎 Sek
搏 P'hok
搁 *Hwui^{ng}*
搓 Swa
搔 So
搕 K'hap
搖 Yaôu / *Yëŏ*
搗 To
搙 *Lák*
搜 Soe / *Ch'heaou*
搝 K'héw
搡 Sóng
搢 Chìn / *Chcè^{ng}*
搣 *Mai^{ng}*
搤 Ek
搥 Tûy
搧 Sëèn / *Yëét*
搦 Lék
搬 Pwan / *Pwⁿa*
搭 Tap / *Tăh*
搮 Jëuk / *Jek*
搨 Tăh
搴 K'hëen
搵 Wùn
携 Hêy / *Kwⁿā*
搶 Ch'hëáng / *Ch'hëō^{ng}*
搞 *Kăyh*
搩 Këet
11
摏 Chëung
摇 Taou
摑 Kwăh
摖 Kwún
摒 *P'hai^{ng}*
摘 Tek / *Tëăh*
摙 Lëén
摛 Loé
摟 Loê / Soé
摤 *Sáng*
摧 Chöêy
摩 Mô
摭 Chit
摯 Chè
摳 K'he
摴 T'he
摵 Ch'hëuk
摶 Twân
摸 Boê / Bong
摹 Boê
摻 Yāng / *Yëō^{ng}*
摺 Lëep / *Chëĕh*
摼 *Lëăh*
摻 Sëem / Sâm
摼 K'hëèn
摽 P'heaou / Peáou
撁 *Ch'hee^{ng}*
12
撅 K'hwat
撆 P'hëet / *Pëĕh*
撇 P'hëet
撈 Lô / Lō / *Lâ*
撋 Jwân / *Hwⁿá*
撐 T'heng / *T'hai^{ng}* / *T'hai^{ng}*
撑 T'hèng
撒 Sat
撓 Laóu / Naóu / Naôu
撙 Chún
撚 Lcén
撝 [illegible]
撞 [illegible]
撟 *Leăouh*
撠 Keāou / *Gëăh*
撡 *Twⁿā*
撤 T'hëet
撥 Pwat / *Pwăh*
撨 Ch'heâou
撩 Leáou / Leâou
撪 P'hún
撫 Boó / Hoo
撬 K'heaou
播 Pò
撮 Ch'hwat / *Ch'hüyh*
撰 Chwān
撲 P'hok
13
撻 T'hat
撼 Hám
撾 Ch'hwa
撿 Këém
擀 *Kwⁿá*
擁 Yùng
[illegible]
[illegible]
[illegible]
擄 Loê
擅 Sëēn
擐 Hwân
擇 Ték / *Tŏh*
擉 Chák
擊 Kek
操 Ch'ho / Ch'hò / *Ch'haou*
擎 Kêng
擘 Pëak
擐 Hwân
擒 K'hîm

8 Y

64 手
扌
65 支
66 攴
攵

揷 Sap
㨢 *Nai^ng*
擔 Tam / Tàm / *T^na* / *T^nà*
擕 Hêy
擗 Pit / P'hek
擘 Pek / *P'eyh*
[illegible] Kè
14
擇 Ch[illegible]
[illegible] Peáou
擡 T'hae / *Ke^ng*
擢 Chók
擣 Tó
擤 Ch'hèng
擥 Lám
擝 *K^nà*
擦 Ch'hat
擧 Ké
擬 Gé
擭 Hwā
擮 *Cheĕh*

擯 Pìn
15
擲 Tek / *Chŏh*
擴 K'hok
擸 Láp
擷 K'heet
[illegible] Pae
[illegible] Lëèn
[illegible] *T'hw^na*
擿 Tŏh
擻 *Saóu*
擾 Jeáou
攄 Ch'hek
攀 P'han
攂 Lûy
攄 T'he
16
攏 Lâng
攏 *Lá*
攔 Lân / *Nw^nâ*
攑 *Keăh*
攖 *Tai^ng*
攖 Eng

攘 Jëáng / Jëâng
18
攙 Ch'ham
攛 Ch'hëuk
攜 Hêy
攎 Lō / *Lā*
攝 Sëep / Sëëp / Lëep / *Săyh*
攫 Chaou
攤 T'han
攣 Lwân
20
攨 Wà
攪 Keáou
攬 Lám
攭 Pà
22
攮 T'hëëp
攬 Wut

支 Che
跂 Pit
散 Sàn

攴 P'hok
收 Sew
攷 K'hó
3
攸 Yew
改 Kaé / *Kéy*
攻 Kong
4
攽 Pay
攼 Pit
放 Hóng / Hòng / *Pàng*
5
政 Chèng
敄 Hwut
敀 Paōu
故 Koè
6
效 Haōu
敉 Bé
7
敝 Poē
教 Kaòu / *Kà* / *Kăh*
敏 Bín
救 Kèw
敔 Gé
敕 T'hit

敖 Gô
敗 Paē
8
敝 Pē
敞 Ch'hëáng
敜 Cham
敢 Kám / *K^ná*
散 Sán / Sàn / *Sw^nà*
敪 Yëā
敧 Ch'hwăh
敦 Tun
9
敧 K'he
敨 T'hím
敬 Kèng
10
敱 Saóu
敹 *Lák*
敲 K'haou
敵 Ték
敷 Hoo
數 Soò / Sok / *Sedou* / Ch'hëuk / *Laōu*

敺 K'he / Aòu

12

敲 K'heaou

敦 Tëⁿa

散 Sàn

整 Chéng

斄 Léy

斁 Ek / Toè

𣀔 Ch'hëùng

斃 Pē

敗 Paē

斆 Haōu

文 Bûn

8

斌 Pin

斐 Hwúy

斑 Pan

9

斒 Pan

斕 Lân

斗 Toé / *Taóu*

料 Leāou

斚 Káy

7

斛 Hák

斜 Sëâ

斝 Káy

9

斟 Chim

斡 Wat

斢 Laóu

斣 Ke

斤 Kin

斥 T'hek / T'hëuk

4

斧 Hoó / *Poó*

斫 Sek / Chëak / *Chëöh*

斬 Chám

8

斮 Sek

斯 Soo

新 Sin

斲 Tok

斳 Kīn

斵 Tok

13

斶 Ch'hëuk

斷 Twàn / Twān / *Tooiⁿᵍ* / *Tootⁿᵍ*

斸 Tëuk

方 Hong / *Heⁿᵍ* / *Póoiⁿᵍ*

於 E / Oe

施 Se / Sà

斿 Yêw

6

旁 Pông

旂 Kê

旃 Chëen

旄 Mô

旅 Lé

旆 Pöēy

7

旋 Swân

旌 Seng / Cheng

旎 Neêⁿᵍ

族 Chók

8

旐 Teāou

旒 Lêw

旖 E

旗 Kê

旘 Chè

旛 Hwan

旟 Ê

无 Boô

旡 Kè

𣄼 Choō

7

旣 Kè

既 Kè

攴66

攵

文67

斗68

斤69

方70

无71

72) 日

日 Jit
旦 { Tàn / Tw^{n}à / Hw^{n}à
旨 Ghé
早 { Chó / *Chá*
旪 Hëëp
旬 Sûn
旭 Hëuk
3
旰 Hān
旱 { Hān / *W^{n}ā*
旴 He
4
旺 Ōng
旻 Bûn
旽 Pōëy
昂 { Gâng / Gông
昃 Chek
昄 Pán
昆 K'hwun
昇 Seng
昉 Hóng
昊 Hō
昌 Ch'hëang

明 { Bêng / *Maí^{ng}*
昏 { Hwun / *Hwui^{ng}*
昑 K'hím
昒 Hwut
易 { Ē / *Kēy* / Ėk / *Yëāh*
昳 Kwat
昔 Sek
昕 Him
5
昜 Yâng
昝 Chám
星 { Seng / *Ch'hai^{ng}*
映 { Yàng / *Yë^{n}à*
昢 P'hut
春 Ch'hun
昧 Möëy
昨 Chók
昬 Hwun
昫 He
昭 Cheaou

是 Sō
昰 Sō
昱 Yëuk
昴 Baóu
昶 { Ch'hëáng / Ch'hëàng
6
晁 Teāou
時 Sê
晃 { Hóng / Lóng
晄 Lóng
晅 Swan
晉 Chìn
晋 Chìn
晏 { Àn / *W^{n}à*
晟 Sēng
晒 Saè
7
晱 { Lōng / *Lā*
晚 { Bwán / *Moot^{ng}*
晛 Hëēn
晝 Tèw
晞 He
晡 Poe

晢 Chëet
晣 Chëet
晤 Goē
晦 Hōèy
晨 Sîn
晭 K'hwùn
8
晬 Sōèy
普 P'hoé
景 { Éng / Kéng
晳 Sek
晴 Cheng
晶 Cheng
晷 K'hwúy
晇 K'hëùng
最 Chéng
晹 Sek
智 Tè
睔 K'hwùn
9
暄 Swan
暇 Hāy
暉 Hwuy
暙 Ch'hún

暈 { Wūn / *Wui^{ng}*
暆 T'hoe
暌 K'hwuy
暑 Sé
暒 Chêng
暴 Ch'hán
暍 Wun
暖 Lwán
暖 { Lwán / *Sëó*
暗 Àm
暘 Yâng
10
暝 Bêng
暡 Óng
暢 { T'hëàng / T'hëùng
暦 Lėk
暡 Bóng
暩 P'heàou
暪 Bún
暫 Chëēm
暮 Boē
暴 { Pō / P'hók

暵 Hàn
12
暹 Sëēm
暾 T'hun
曀 È
曆 Chìn
曁 K'haè
曄 Yëep
曆 Lėk
曇 T'hâm
曷 Gáp
曈 Tông
曉 Heáou
曎 Ėk
曏 Hëàng
曐 Seng
曒 Keáou
曔 Kèng
曖 Lêng
14
曙 Sē
曚 Bông
曛 Hwun
曜 Yaōu

曝 { P'hòk / *P'hàk*
曠 K'hòng
16
曦 He
曨 Lóng
曫 Lwân
曬 Saè
20
曭 T'hóng
[illegible] Lêng

曰 Wát
曲 { K'hëuk / *K'hek*
曳 Ē
更 { Keng / Kèng / *Kai^ng*
曷 Hat
6
書 Se
曹 Chô
曼 { Bân / Băn
8
曾 { Cheng / *Chan*
替 T'hèy
最 Chòèy
朁 Ch'hám
9
會 { Hōëy / Kōèy / *Ēy*
朅 K'hëet

月 { Gwàt / *Gōĕyh*
有 { Yéw / Yēw / *Woō* / *Oō*
4
朋 Pêng
服 Hòk
朏 P'hut
6
朔 Sok
朕 Tīm
朗 { Lóng / *Láng*
望 { Bōng / Bōng / *Bāng*
8
朝 { Teaou / Teâou
朞 Ke
期 { Ke / Kê
朢 Bōng
12
朣 Tông
朦 Bông
朧 Lëûng

木 { Bòk / *Bàk*
未 { Bē / *Bōēy*
末 { Bwát / *Bwăh*
本 Pún
札 Chap
朮 Tút
2
朱 Choo
朳 Put
朴 { P'hok / *P'hŏh*
朶 Tó
机 Ké
朽 Héw
朾 *Tē^n a*
朿 Ch'hè
3
杅 Ê
杆 Kan
杇 { Oo / Woo
杈 Ch'hay
杉 Sam
栦 { Sûn / *Ch'hw^n á*
杌 Gwút
李 Lé

杏 Hēng
材 { Chaê / *Ch'hâ*
村 { Ch'hun / *Ch'hui^ng*
杓 { Chëak / P'heaou
杔 T'hok
杕 Tēy
杖 Tëāng
杀 Swăh
杙 Ėk
杜 Toē
束 Sok
杠 Kang
枂 Mŏh
4
杪 { Beáou / *Bōĕy* / *Sëò*
杭 Hâng
杮 P'hōèy
柿 K'hē
杯 { Pōey / Poê
東 { Tong / *Tang*
果 Kó

杳 Beáou
杴 Hëem
杵 Ch'hé
杷 { Pà / Pâ / *Pây*
杻 Léw
杼 T'hé
松 { Sëûng / *Ch'hêng*
板 Pán
枇 { Pê / Gô
枉 Óng
枋 { Hong / *Pang*
枌 Hwûn
枏 Lâm
析 { Sek / T'hok
枕 Chím
枓 Toé
林 { Lîm / *Nâ*
枘 Jōēy
枚 Bōêy
柝 Sek

8 Z

75 木

枝 Che / *Ke*
果 Ó / Kó
枯 Koe
枰 Pêng / *P'hw*^{n}*â*
枲 Se
枳 Ché
枴 Kwaé
枵 Heaou
架 Kày
枷 Kây
枸 Koé
枹 Hoê
柿 K'hē
柂 Tō
柄 Pèng / *P'hai*^{ng}
栂 Boé
某 Boé
柎 Hoo
柏 *Păyh*
染 Jëém / *Neé*^{ng} / *Bàk*

柑 Kam
柒 Ch'hit
5
柔 Jêw
柘 Toè / Chëà
柘 *Nooi*^{ng}
柙 Ap
柚 Tëuk / Yēw / *Nooi*^{ng}
柞 Chȯk
柡 Éng
查 Chay / Ch'hây / *Cha* / Ch'hâ
柢 Toó
柌 Soê
柩 Kēw
柬 Kán
柭 Pōēy
柮 Tut
柯 K'ho / *Kwa*
柰 Naē / Laé
柱 Chē / *T'heāou*

枏 Lâm
柳 Léw
柴 Ch'haê / *Ch'hâ*
柵 Sa
柷 Chëuk
6
栖 Sey
栓 *Ch'hui*^{ng}
栗 Lek / *Lȧt*
栝 T'hëèm
校 Kaòu / Haōu
栢 Pek
栨 Jëûng
栩 Hé
株 Te
栯 Yēw
栰 Hwȧt
栱 Këúng / *Kéng*
栲 K'hó
栳 Ló / Lō
栵 Lē
核 Hėk / *Hwùt*

栫 Chëen
根 Kin
栻 Sek / *Ch'heē*^{ng}
格 Kek / *Kàyh*
栽 Chae
桀 Këėt
桁 Hêng / Hâng / *Hw*^{n}*â*
桂 Kwùy
桃 T'hô
桅 Wûy
案 Àn / *W*^{n}*à*
桊 Kwàn / *Kwui*^{ng}
框 K'hong
桎 Chit
桌 Tok / *Tŏh*
桍 K'hwâ
桐 Tông / *T'hâng*
桑 Song / *Se*^{ng}
桔 Këet / *Kit*

桓 Hwân
桁 K'hēng
桬 Jëém / *Neé*^{ng}
桫 Swán
7
栢 Pōey
梃 *Tai*^{ng}
梛 Yëâ
桱 Kèng / *Kai*^{ng}
桴 Hoo
桶 T'hóng / *T'háng*
梢 Poe
桷 Kak
桼 Ch'hip
梁 Leâng / *Nëô*^{ng}
梃 T'héng
梅 Böêy / *Ùm*
梆 Pang
梌 Toê
梏 K'hok
梔 Che / *Kee*^{ng}

梓 Choó
梗 Kēng
梭 Swán
梘 Këén / *Kéng*
梙 Hwān
梚 *Bwá*
梜 Këep
梊 Chuy
條 Teâou
梟 Heaou
梠 Lē
梱 Tëēm
梣 Hėk
梢 Saou
梤 Hwun
梧 Goê
梨 Laê
梩 Lê
梭 So
械 Haē
梱 K'hwún
梵 Hwān

梲 Chwat
梯 T'hey / *T'huy*
梳 Soe / *Sey*
梴 Yëên
棃 Laê
棄 K'hè
梥 Ch'hong
棉 Bëên
棊 Kê
棋 Kê
棍 Kwùn
棐 Hwúy
棑 Paê
棒 *P'hāng*
棕 *Chang*
棖 Têng
棗 Chó
棘 Kek
棚 Pêng / *Paî^ng*
梱 K'hwûn
棠 Tông / *Tang*

棣 Tëy
梢 Gnaôu
棫 Hėk
棬 Kwan
8 森 Som
棰 Sûy
棱 Lêng
棲 Sey
棸 Choe
棹 Tok / Chaōu
棺 Kwan / *Kwⁿa*
棼 Hwun
椀 Wán
椐 K'hwut
椁 Kok
椅 É / E
椕 Pėng
椆 Teâou
椷 Hàm
椋 *Këⁿa*
椈 Këuk
棟 Tòng

𣝗 Këuk
棄 Sēng
棧 Chëén / Ch'hëén / *Chān*
椊 Chut
植 Sit
椎 Chuy
椏 Wâ
椐 Ke
椖 Póng
椒 Cheaou
椔 Choo
椗 *Tëⁿà*
9 椰 Yëâ
椓 T'hok / *K'hok*
椵 Káy
椶 Chong / *Chang*
椹 Chim
楂 Chay
椿 T'hun
椸 É
椽 Yëên / T'hwân

楈 Se
楊 Yâng / *Yëóⁿg* / *Ch'hēw*
楖 K'hēng
楓 Hong / *Pooiⁿg*
楚 Ch'hoé
楛 Hoē
楝 Lëēn
楞 Lêng
楠 Lâm
楡 Jê
楰 Jê
楥 Hëèn / Hwùn
楦 Hëèn
楧 Eng
楨 Cheng
楽 Lek
楪 Yëėp
楫 Ch'hip
業 Gëėp
楷 Ché
楯 Tún

楣 Bê / *Baê*
㮇 T'hëèm
極 Kėk
楷 K'haé
楸 Ch'hew
楹 Êng
10 榑 Hoê
榼 *Kèⁿg*
榔 Lông / *Nêⁿg*
榕 Yûng / *Ch'hêng*
榖 Kok
榛 Chin / Chuy
榜 *Pêⁿg*
榅 Oe
榥 Hóng
榦 Kàn
榨 Chày
榫 Sún
榭 Sëā
榮 Êng
榱 Söey

榴 Lêw
榷 Kak
榲 Hwûn
榿 P'hê
槎 Seng
榻 T'hap
榼 K'hap
榾 Kwut
槀 Kó
槁 Kó
槂 Sun
槃 Pwân
槆 Sûn
槅 Kek
槧 Ch'hím
槓 Tėk
槊 Sok
構 Koe
槌 T'hûy / Tûy
槍 Ch'hëang
槎 Chay
槏 K'hëém

75 木

槐 Hwaê
11
樨 Seÿ
槧 Ch'hëém
槩 K'haè / *Kaè*
概 K'haè
槨 Kok
槮 Sàm
槱 Yéw
槳 Chëáng / *Chëó^{ng}*
槴 Hoō
槹 Ko
槽 Chô
槾 *Pān*
槿 Kīn
樁 Chong
樂 Lók / Gák / Gnaōu
樫 Ch'hëen
樊 Hwân
樏 Ch'hat
樑 Lëâng
樒 Bit

樓 Loô / *Laôu*
樔 Ch'haou
樕 Sok
樗 T'he
標 Peaou / *Pëo*
樛 K'hew
樜 Chëà
樝 Chay
樟 Chëang / *Chëo^{ng}*
樞 K'he / T'he
樠 *Më^{n}â*
模 Boê
樣 Yāng / *Yëō^{ng}*
樰 *Së^{n}ā*
穎 Éng
樲 Jē
12
樵 Cheâou
樸 P'hok
樹 Sē / *Ch'hēw*
橄 Hám / Kám / *K^{n}a*

樽 Chun
橘 Wát
橇 K'heaou
橈 Jeâou / *Jëô*
橉 Lîn
橊 Lêw
橋 Keâou / *Këô*
橐 T'hok / *Lok*
橛 K'hwán
橒 Yîn
橓 Sùn
橕 T'heng
橗 Bêng
橘 Kit / Këet
橙 Têng
橜 K'hwat
橛 Kwát
橡 Lûy
橞 Hwüy
機 Ke
橫 Hêng / *Hw^{n}â*

橪 Jëén
橤 *Swaē^{ng}*
13
橿 Këang
檀 T'han / *Tw^{n}â*
檁 Lím
檄 Hèk
檑 Loé
檉 Ch'heng
橶 Këuk
檎 K'hîm
檐 Yëêm / *T^{n}a*
檑 Lûy
檔 Tòng / *Tàng*
檖 Süy
檗 Pek
檛 Ch'hwâ
檜 Köey / Köèy
檟 Káy
檠 Kêng
檢 Këém
檣 Ch'hëâng

檥 Gé
檫 *Ch'hwŭh*
14
檮 Tô
檯 Taô
檳 Pin
檵 Kèy
檴 *Kwâ*
檻 Lām
檽 Noē
檾 K'héng
檿 Yëèm
櫼 Chëen
櫂 Chaōu
櫃 Kwūy
櫇 P'haou
15
櫏 Ch'hëen
櫋 Bëên
櫓 Loé
櫛 Chëet
櫜 Ko
櫝 Tȯk
櫟 Lȯk / Lėk

櫡 Chëak
16
櫪 Lėk
櫬 Ch'hìn
櫰 Hwaè
櫯 Soe
櫨 Lē
欖 Lám / *Ná*
櫳 Lëûng / Naē
17
櫺 Lêng
櫻 Eng
欃 Swan / *Ch'hw^{n}a*
櫼 Hëa
欃 Ch'ham
欄 Lân
18
權 Kwân
欒 Lwân
20
欔 K'hok
欖 Lám
欝 Wut
欞 Yëêm

欠 K'hëèm
次 Ch'hoò
4
𣢁 *P'hee^{ng}*
欣 Him
欦 K'hin
欱 Haè
6
欯 *Koŏh*
欬 K'haè
欲 Yëúk
欶 T'hoé
欵 K'hwán
欸 Ò
欷 He
8
欹 E
弞 ^{N}à
欺 K'he
欽 K'him
款 K'hwán
欿 K'hám
9
歂 Ch'hwán
歃 Ch'hap
歆 Him
歇 { Heet / *Hàyh*

歈 Jê
10
歋 Ha^{n}é
歉 K'hëém
歌 { Ko / *Kwa*
歎 T'hàn
歐 { Oé / Aou
歒 Ték
12
歔 He
歊 Ch'heàou
歘 Hwut
歙 Hip
13
歕 { P'hun / Pûn
歛 Lëém
𣤷 Sek
𣦁 Hìm
歖 Ê
15
歠 { Ch'hwat / *Ch'höĕyh*
歡 { Hwan / *Hw^{n}a*

止 Ché
正 { Cheng / Chèng / *Chë^{n}a* / *Chë^{n}à*
此 Ch'hoó
步 Poē
4
武 Boó
歧 Kê
歪 Wae
8
歯 Téy
歲 歳 } Söèy
𣦗 T'hék
12
歷 Lék
𣦍 K'heaou
歸 Kwuy

歹 { Taé / Gát / *P'ha^{n}é*
𣦵 Héw
死 { Soó / *Sé*
4
𣦼 Soó
歿 Bút
殀 Yaóu
5
殂 Choé
殃 Yang
殄 T'hëén
𣧑 { Oè / Aòu
𣦿 P'hey
殆 Taē
6
殉 Sûn
殊 Soô
殍 Peáou
𣨌 Lōéy
8
殓 Lëēm
𣩂 { Öey / Wöey
殖 Sit
殘 { Chân / *Chw^{n}â*
殙 Hwun

9
殙 Hwun
殛 Kek
殨 Hwùy
殞 Wún
10
殟 Wut
殤 Sëang
12
殪 È
殫 { Tan / Ch'hëén
殮 Lëēm
殯 Pìn
殲 Ch'hëem

殳 { Soô / *Sé*
段 { Tān / *Tw^{n}ā*
6
殷 { Yin / Yín
殺 { Sat / Saè / *T'haé* / *Swăh*
8
殼 K'hak
殽 Gnaou
9
殿 Tëēn
毀 Hwúy
㱿 K'hak
10
毃 K'hëak
毅 { Hēy / Gē

欠76
止77
歹78
殳79

80 毋
81 比
82 毛
83 氏
84 气
85 水

毋 Boô
母 { Boé / Bó
每 Böéy
毒 { Tók / *Tăk* 4
毓 Yëúk

比 { Pé / Pē
毖 Pè 5
毗 Pê
毚 Ch'hâm

毛 Mô
毴 P'he 5
毞 Poō
毤 *T'hoot^{ng}*
毨 Sëén
毫 Hô 7
毬 { Kêw / *Koŏ*
毯 { T'hám / *T'hán* 8
毳 Ch'hùy
毦 Jê
毿 Sàm
氄 Jëûng 12
氅 Ch'hëáng
氈 { Chëen / *Chee^{ng}*
氊 Chëen
氍 Kê 18
氎 Tëëp

氏 Sē
氐 Té
民 Bîn
氓 Bîn

气 K'hè
氛 Hwun
氣 { K'hè / *K'hwùy* 6
氤 Yin
氳 Wun

水 { Súy / *Chúy* / *Swuíng*
冰 Peng
永 Éng 2
氻 Lék
氼 Kek
氽 T'hun
氾 Hwàn
汀 T'heng
汁 Chëep
求 Kêw
汃 P'hat 3
汍 Hwàn
汎 Hwàn
汏 T'hwăh
汐 { Sék / *Tăyh*
汓 Sêw
汖 *P'hèy*
汔 Git
汕 Sàn
汗 { Kăn / *Kw^{n}ā*
汛 Sìn
汙 { Oo / Woo

污 Oo / Oò / Woò
汝 Jé / *Lé* / *Loó*
汞 Hōng
江 Kang / *Ka*
池 Tê
汩 Kwút
汪 Ong / *Ang*
汭 Jōēy
汰 T'hat / T'haè / *T'hwâ*
汲 K'hip / *Chēō^{n}g*
汳 Pēēn
汴 Pēēn
汶 Būn
沠 Chāyh
決 Kwat
汾 Hwun / Hwûn
沁 Ch'hìm
沂 Kê
沄 Yîn / Wûn

沃 Ak
汐 *Tāyh*
沈 Sím
沉 Tîm / *Tēēm* / T'hēēm
沌 Tūn
沍 Hoē
沐 Bók
没 Bút
沓 Tāp
沔 Bēén
沕 Bit
沖 Ch'hëung
沙 Say / *Swâ*
沚 Ché
沛 P'haè
沫 Bwát / *P'hōēyh*
沬 Mōēy
沮 Choó / Chè / Ch'ho
沱 Tô
河 Hô

沸 Pwùy
油 Yêw
治 Tê / Tē
沼 Cheáou
沽 Koe
沾 Tēem
沿 Yēên
況 Hóng / Hòng
泂 Kéng
泄 Sēet / Ē
泗 Sêw
泆 Yit
泉 Chwân / *Chw^{n}â*
泊 Pók / *P'hŏh*
泌 Pè
泍 P'hùn
泏 Chwăh
泓 Hông
泔 Kam
法 Hwat
泗 Soò

泚 Ch'hoó / Ch'héy
泛 Hwàn
泜 Tê
泝 Soé
泠 Lêng
泡 P'haou
波 P'ho
泣 K'hip
泥 Neê^{n}g / Neē^{n}g / *T'hoê*
注 Choò / *Toò*
泩 Seng
泪 Lūy
泫 Hēēn
泬 Hēet
泮 P'hwàn
泯 Bîn
泰 T'haè / *T'hwâ*
泱 Yang / Yàng
泳 Ēng
泎 Ēk

洄 Hōêy
洊 Chēèn
洋 Yâng / *Yēô^{n}g*
洌 Lēet
洎 Kē
洏 Jê
洒 Sày / *Swá* / Sēén
洓 Sek
洗 Sēén / *Séy*
洘 K'hó
洙 Choo
洚 Kàng
洛 Lók
洞 Tōng / *Tāng*
洟 E
津 Chin
洧 Wúy
汧 Gēēn
洩 Ē / Sēet / *Seĕh*
洫 Hok

洪 Hông / *Âng*
洲 Chew
洳 Jê
洵 Sûn
洶 Hëung
洸 Kong
活 Kwat / Hwát
[illegible]
洽 Hēép
派 P'haè
洿 Oo / Woo
流 Lêw / *Laôu*
浙 Chēet
浞 Ch'hëuk
浡 Pút
浣 Wán
浥 Yip
浦 P'hoé
浩 Hō
浪 Lông / Lōng / *Nē^{n}g*

85 水 氵

浮 { Hoô / *P'hoô*
浯 Goô
浰 Lē
浲 Hông
浴 { *Ek* / Yëuk
海 Haé
浸 Chìm
浹 Chap
浼 Bœ́y
浽 Suy
涂 { Toô / *T'hoê*
涅 Lëep
浫 Hān
涇 { Keng / Kōng
浿 Pè
消 Seaou
涉 Sëép
漩 Swân
涌 Yúng
涎 { Yëên / *Nwⁿā*
涑 *Săyh*

涒 T'hun
涓 Kwan
涔 Gîm
涕 T'hèy
涖 { Lē / *Neē^{ng}*
涗 T'hwā
涘 Soō
浚 Chùn
涪 Hoô
涼 Lëâng
涿 Tok
淀 *Teē^{ng}*
淂 Tek
淄 Choo
淅 Sek
淆 Gnaôu
淇 Kê
淈 K'hwut
淊 Ám
淋 Lîm
淑 Sëuk
淒 Ch'hey

淖 Chaōu
淘 Tô
淙 Chong
淚 Lūy
淝 Hwûy
淞 Sëûng
游 Yêw
灑 Sày
淠 Pò
淏 Hoò
淡 Tām
淢 Hék
淤 E
淨 Chēng
淩 Lêng
淪 Lûn
淁 { Chăyh / *Sëèm*
淫 Yîm
淬 Sùy
淮 Hwaê
深 Ch'him
涯 Gaê

涬 T'hát
涰 Twat
涱 *Té^{ng}*
液 Ėk
涵 Hâm
涶 Söēy
[illegible] Ay
涸 Hok
涺 Ke
淳 Sûn
淵 Yëen
混 Hwūn
清 Ch'heng
淹 { Yëem / Yëèm
淺 { Ch'hëén / *Ch'hëē^{ng}* / *K'hín*
添 { T'hëem / *T'hee^{ng}*
淼 Beáou
渘 Jôw
渙 Hwàn
渚 Ché
減 Këém

渝 { Se / Jê
渟 Têng
渠 Kê
渡 Toē
渢 { Hong / Hwàn
渣 { Chay / Chāy
渤 Put
渥 Ak
渧 Tèy
温 { Wun / Wùn
渫 Tëèp
測 Ch'hek
渭 Wūy
港 Káng
渰 Yëém
渴 { K'hat / *Kwŭh*
游 Yêw
渺 Beáou
渼 Būóy
渾 { Hwûn / Hwūn
湃 P'haè

湄 Bê
涾 Tâm
湊 { Choè / Ch'haòu
湍 { Ch'hwan / T'hwan
湎 { Bëén / Bëēn
湏 Se
湑 { Jé / Se
湒 Ch'hip
湓 P'hûn
湔 *Chee^{ng}*
湖 { Hoê / *Oê*
湘 Sëang
湛 Tam
湜 Sit
湝 Kae
湟 Hông
湠 *T'hwⁿà*
湣 Bín
湥 Tút
渏 { K'hò / *K'hwò*
湦 Seng

水 85 氵

湧 Yúng
湩 *Leng*
湫 Ch'hew
湱 Hwaè
湮 Yëen
湯 { T'hong / Tọ̄ng / *T'he^{ng}* / *T'hè^{ng}* / Sëang
湲 Wān
10
源 Gwân
準 凖 } Chún
溛 Wà
溜 Lèw
溝 { Koe / *Kaou*
溞 So
溟 Bêng
溢 Yit
溣 Lùn
溥 P'hoé
溦 Bwuy
溩 Oé

溪 K'hey
溫 Wun
濅 Chìm
溯 Soé
溱 Chin
溲 Soe
溶 Yûng
溷 Hwūn
溍 Beáou
溺 { Lék / Jëák / Jëāou / *Jëō*
溼 Sip
溽 Jëúk
滁 Tê
滂 Pông
滄 Ch'hong
滅 Bëét
滈 O
滋 Choo
滌 Tėk
滎 Êng

滑 Kwút
滓 { Chaé / *Chay*
滔 T'ho
滕 Têng
11
滖 *P'hoo^{ng}*
滮 Pew
滯 Tē
滴 { Tek / *Teĕh*
滷 Loē
滸 Hoé
滹 Hoe
滺 Yew
滾 Kwún
滿 { Bwán / *Mw^{n}á*
漁 Gê
漂 { P'heaou / P'heàou / *P'hëò*
漅 Chaôu
漆 { Ch'hip / *Ch'hat*
漈 { Chèy / Chëà / Chwà

漉 Lȯk
漏 { Loē / *Laōu*
漑 K'haè
漓 Lê
演 Yëén
漕 { Chô / Chō
漘 Tûn
漙 Twân
漚 { Oe / Oé
漠 { Bȯk / Boê
漢 Hàn
漣 Lëên
漥 Wa
漟 T'hong
漦 Lê
漩 Swân
漪 E
漫 { Bân / Bān
漬 Choò
漭 Bóng
漯 Lat

漰 P'heng
漱 { Soé / Soè / *Swá*
漲 { Tëàng / *Tëò^{ng}* / *Yim*
漳 { Chëang / *Chëo^{ng}*
漸 Chëēm
漼 { Chöêy / Ch'húy
漹 Yëen
漾 Yāng
漿 { Chëang / *Chëo^{ng}*
潁 Éng
漡 *Sëó^{ng}*
12
潑 { P'hwat / *P'hwàh*
潔 Këet
潗 Chip
潘 { Hwan / P'hwan / *P'hw^{n}a*
潙 Kwuy
潛 Chëêm
潜 Chëêm

潝 Hip
潠 Sùn
潢 Hông
澗 Kàn
潤 Jūn
潦 Ló
潭 T'hâm
潮 { Teâou / *Têô*
潯 Sîm
潰 Höëy
潴 Che
潸 San
潺 Ch'han
潼 Tông
潹 Ch'ham
潾 Lîn
澀 Sëep
澁 Sëep
澄 Têng
澆 Jeâou
澈 T'hëet
澍 Choò

9 B

85 水 氵

澇 Lâ / Lō
澌 Soo
澐 Yîn / Wûn
澑 Léw
澒 Hòng
澓 Hók
潟 Sek
濮 P'hok
13
澱 Tōng
澟 Lím
澠 Chîn
澡 Chó
澢 Tong
澤 Ték
澦 Ē
澧 Léy
濶 K'hwut
澪 Lêng
澬 Choo
濁 Chók / *Tàk* / *Lô*
潞 Loē

澮 Kōèy
激 Kek
澳 Ò
澹 Tām
澼 P'hek
濂 Lëêm
濃 Lông
濆 Hwûn
濈 Ch'hip
濊 Öèy / Wöèy
濋 Ch'hoé
濎 T'hèng
14
濕 Sip
濗 Bék
濘 Léng / Lēng
濙 Èng
濛 Bông
濞 Pē
濟 Chéy / Chèy
濠 Hô
濡 Se / Jê

濔 Boò
濤 Tô
濩 Hoē
濫 Lām
濬 Chùn
濮 Pók
濯 Chók
濰 Wûy
濱 Pin
濴 Èng
15
瀒 Soé
濺 Chëen / *Chwⁿā*
濾 Lē
㵃 *T'hwⁿa*
瀅 Ēng
瀆 Tók
瀉 Sëà
瀌 P'heaou
瀑 P'hók
16
瀏 Lêw
瀕 Pîn
瀘 Loê

灠 Lām
瀚 Hàn
瀛 Êng
瀝 Lék
瀟 Seaou
瀠 Êng
潠 Swán
瀧 *Lang*
瀨 Naē / *Lwā*
17
瀯 Êng
瀰 Bê
瀲 Lëém
瀿 Hwân
瀹 Yëák
瀵 Hwan
瀼 Jëâng
瀓 T'hèng
瀾 Lân / Lān
瀁 Yáng
澴 Hwân
灃 Hong

灂 Chông
灉 Yung
灇 Chông
瀗 Hwat
灌 Kwàn / *Kwⁿà*
灑 Sày / Swá / Lêy
灓 Lwân
灩 Yëēm
灑 Lô
灘 T'han / *T'hwⁿa*
20
灚 Keáou
灝 Hō
灞 Pà
22
灣 Wan
灨 Kàm

86 火

火 Hⁿó / *Höéy*
灯 Teng
灰 Hōey
2
灵 Lêng
灶 Chò
灸 Kèw / *Koò*
灺 Ch'hëá
灼 Chëak
災 Chae
4
𤆍 Ch'hwā
炁 K'hè
炉 Loê
炊 Ch'huy / *Ch'höey*
炎 Yëêm
炐 P'hòng
炒 Ch'haóu / *Ch'há*
炓 Leāou
炕 *K'hàng*
炙 Chëà
5
炤 Cheaou
炑 Baé
炨 Tō / Ch'hëá

火 86 畑

炫 Hëên
炬 Kē
炭 T'hàn / *T'hw^{n}à*
炱 Tay / Tây
炮 P'haôu / *Paôu*
烔 Kéng
炰 Paôu / *Poô*
炳 Péng
烼 Léw
炸 Chày
炷 Chē
6
烈 Lëét
烊 Yâng
烋 Hew / Haou
烏 Oe
烕 Bëét
烘 Hong / *Hang*
烙 Lók
烝 Chin
烜 Hwúy / Swan

烞 Pok
烟 Yëên / *Hwun*
烱 Kéng
烴 Kēng
烷 Wân
烹 P'heng
烺 Lóng / Lōng
烽 Hong
焁 He
焄 Hwun
焈 Wut
焇 Seaou / *Sëuk*
焉 Yëen
8
焙 Pöēy
焚 Hwûn
焜 K'hwun
焞 T'hun / T'höey / Sûn
焟 Sek / *Chëôh*
焠 Ch'hùy / *Ch'hoôh*
無 Boô / *Bô*

焎 Sëet
7
焦 Cheaou / *Seaou* / *Tâ*
焮 Hìm
焱 Yëēm
焰 Yëēm
焵 Kòng / *Kè^{n}g*
然 Jëên
9
煁 Sîm
煆 T'hwàn
煇 Hwuy / Hwun
煉 Lëēn
煌 Hông
煎 Chëen / *Chw^{n}a*
煏 Pek
煑 Ché
煒 Wúy
煕 He
煟 Pöēy
煖 Lwán / *Sëo*
煩 Lwán

煙 Yëen / *Hwun*
煜 Yëuk
煞 Sat / *Swăh*
煠 *Săh*
煚 Kêng
煣 Jéw
煤 Böēy
煥 Hwàn
煦 Hé
照 Cheàou / *Chëô*
煨 Öey / Wöey
煩 Hwân
煬 Yâng
煽 K'hò
10
熄 T'huy / T'höey
熌 Lîn
熑 Sëèn
熏 Chaé
熁 Hëep
熅 Wun
熇 Hok / *Hŏh*

熊 Hîm
熏 Hwun
熑 *T^{n}â*
熒 Êng
熑 Tîm
熚 Pit
熛 P'heaou
熟 Sëuk / *Sèk*
熠 Yip
熨 Wut
熬 Gô
熮 *Lâ*
熯 Sëēn
熱 Jëét / *Jwăh* / *Sëo*
熲 Kéng
12
熹 He
熇 Ho
熾 Ch'hè
燀 Sëēn / Ch'hëen
燁 Yëep
燃 Jëên

燄 Yëēm
燈 Têng
燩 *K'höēyh*
燉 Tun
燎 Leâou / Leāou
燐 Lîn
燒 Seaou / *Sëo*
燜 Höēy
燓 Lîm
燙 Tōng / *Tē^{n}g*
燔 Hwan / Hwân
燕 Yëen / Yëèn / *Eè^{n}g*
燖 Sîm / Chëêm / Tîm
13
營 Êng / *Yē^{n}â*
燠 Hëuk
燥 Sò
燦 Ch'hàn
燧 Sūy
燬 Hwúy

86 火
87 爪
爫
88 父
89 爻
90 爿
91 片

燮 Sëet
燭 { Chëuk / *Chek* }
燹 Sëén
燻 Hwun
燼 Sin
燿 Yaōu
爂 Eng
爆 P'hòk
爇 Sëet
爉 { Làp / *Lăh* }
爍 Sëak
爋 Hwùn
爐 Loê
爕 Sëet
爛 { Lān / *Nwⁿā* }
爝 Chëak
爞 T'hëûng
爟 Hwan
爨 Ch'hwàn

爪 Jeáou
4
爬 { Pâ / *Pây* }
爭 { Cheng / *Chaiⁿᵍ* / *Chëⁿā* }
爰 Wān
8
爲 { Wûy / Wūy }
[illegible] So
[illegible] Lák
爵 Chëak

父 { Hoó / Hoō / *Pāy* }
爸 { Pà / *Pāy* }
6
爹 *Tëa*
爺 Yëâ

爻 Gnaôu
爼 Choé
7
爽 Sóng
爾 { Jé / Jeéⁿᵍ }

爿 Chüâng
牀 { Ch'hông / *Sêⁿᵍ* }
6
牂 Chong
牆 { Ch'hëâng / *Ch'hëōⁿᵍ* }

片 { P'hëèn / *P'hèⁿᵍ* }
版 Pán
8
[illegible] Yüen
牌 Paê
牕 Ch'hong
牐 Chăh
9
牒 Tëëp
牎 { Ch'hong / *T'hang* }
牖 Yéw
牘 Tók

福建方言字典

牙 Gây
牚 T'heng

牛 { Gnêw / *Goô* }
牝 Pīn
牟 Boê
3
牡 Boé
牢 Lô
牣 Jīm
4
犺 Káng
牧 Bôk
物 { Bŭt / *Meĕngh* }
牯 Koé
牲 { Seng / *Saing* }
6
牷 Chwân
牸 Joō
特 Tèk
7
牽 { K'hëen / K'hëèn / K'han / Hat }
牿 K'hok
犀 { Sey / *Sae* }
8
犂 Lêy
犄 K'he
[illegible] { Këēn / K'hëén }

犇 P'hun
犉 Sûn
9
犍 Këen
犖 Lôk
犗 Kaè
12
犝 Tông
[illegible] Yaôu
[illegible] Hwân
犢 Tôk
16
犧 He
犨 Sêw

犬 K'hëén
犯 Hwān
犴 Gān
4
狀 { Chōng / *Chēng* }
犼 Haôu
狁 Wún
狂 { Kông / Kŏug }
狃 Lĕw
狄 Tèk
5
狊 Kek
狤 K'hëep
狎 Àp
狐 Hoê
狒 Hwùy
狖 Yēw
狗 { Koé / *Kaóu* }
狙 Ch'he
6
狡 { Kaóu / *Ká* }
狥 Sûn
狨 Jëûng
豻 Këen
狩 Sèw

狴 Pé
狷 Kwàn
狸 Lê
狹 { Hëëp / *Àyh* }
狺 Gîn
狻 Chùn
[illegible] Nô
狼 Lông
狽 Pōēy
8
猇 Gnaôu
猊 Gêy
猋 P'heaou
猒 Yëem
猖 { Ch'hëang / *Ch'hëong* }
[illegible] Gwut
猗 O
猛 { Béng / *Maing* }
9
猜 Ch'hae
猢 Hoê
猪 Te
猩 Seng

7
猫 *Neaou*
猥 { Öey / Wöey }
猱 { Lô / Nô }
[illegible] Koé
猲 Hëet
猴 { Hoê / *Kaôu* }
猶 Yêw
10
猻 Sun
猾 Kwŭt
猿 Wân
獃 Gaê
獄 Gëûk
獅 { Soo / *Sae* }
獐 Chëang
12
[illegible] Sëāng
獠 Leaou
獢 Keaou
獥 Heaou
獧 Kwàn
獨 Tôk
獪 Köèy

牙 92
牛 93
牜
犬 94
犭

9 C

94 犬
95 玄
96 玉

	玄 Hëên	玉 Gëuk			
獫 Hëém	玅 Beāou	王 { Ông / Ōng	玼 { Ch'hoó / Ch'hoê	琅 Lông	琲 P'höéy
獬 Haē	玆 Choo	5			
14		玎 Tin	珊 San	理 Lé	琳 Lîm
獮 { Sëén / Bê	率 Sut	玕 Kan	珌 Pit	琇 Sèw	琴 K'hîm
獯 Hwun		玖 Kéw	珍 { Tin / Chin	琈 Hoo	琵 Pê
獱 Pin		玗 Ê	6	琉 Lêw	琶 { Pâ / Pây
獲 Hek		4	珓 Kaòu	琊 Yëâ	9
獳 Nô		玜 Kong	珙 Këúng	8	瑀 É
15		玞 Hoo	珞 Lòk	琖 Chán	瑁 { Hòng / Pöēy
獵 { Lap / Lăh		玟 Bîn	珠 Choo	琚 Ke	瑄 Swan
獸 Sèw		玠 Kaè	珢 Gîn	琛 T'him	瑅 T'hêy
獻 Hëèn		玒 Hông	珣 Sûn	琠 T'hëén	瑇 Taē
獺 { T'hat / T'hwăh		玦 Kwat	珥 { Jé / Jē	琢 Tok	瑊 Chim
玁 Hëém		玨 Kak	珩 Hêng	琥 Hoé	瑋 Wúy
		玩 Gwán	珪 Kwuy	琦 Kê	瑍 Hwàn
		5	珫 Ch'hëung	琨 K'hwun	瑒 Yâng
		玲 Lêng	班 Pan	琪 Kê	瑕 Hây
		玳 Taē	珮 Pöēy	琫 { Pòng / Páng	瑗 Wān
		玷 Tëèm	7	琬 Wán	瑙 Ló
		玻 P'ho	珴 Gô	琰 { Yëém / Yëén / Tām	瑚 Hoê
		珀 P'hek	珸 Goê	琮 Chong	瑛 Eng
		珂 K'ho	琡 Ch'hwàn	琯 Kwán	瑜 Jê
		珇 Choé	現 Hëēn	琱 Teaou	瑝 Hông
		珈 Kay	球 { Kêw / K'hêw		
		珉 Bîn			

瑅 Tèy
瑞 Sūy
瑟 Sek
10
瑢 Yûng
瑣 Só
瑣 Só
瑤 Yaôu
瑦 Oé
瑨 Chìn
瑩 Êng
瑪 *Báy*
瑬 Lêw
瑰 Kwuy
瑯 Lông
瑱 T'hëèn
瑲 Ch'hong
瑳 Ch'ho
㻫 Pit
瑾 Kín
璀 Ch'húy
璃 Lê
璇 Swân

璉 Lüén
璋 Chëang
12
璘 Lîn
璜 Hông
璞 P'hok
璟 Kéng
璠 { Hwan / Hwân
璡 Chin
璢 Lêw
璣 Ke
13
璫 { Tong / *Tang*
[illegible] Yung
璧 P'hek
璨 Ch'hàn
璐 Loê
璩 Ke
環 Hwân
璲 Sūy
14
璵 Ê
璽 Jé
璿 Swân

瓃 Lêy
瓊 Kêng
16
瓍 Sûy
瓏 Lông
瓔 Eng
瓛 Hwân
瓘 Kwàn
瓚 Chàn

瓜 Kwa
2
𤬪 Tìm
瓞 Tëet
瓠 Hoê
6
𤬯 Hoê
瓢 P'heâou
瓣 { Pëēn / *Pān*
瓥 Loê
瓤 Jëâng

瓦 { Wá / *Hëá*
4
瓪 P'höey
瓮 Òng
瓨 Oê
瓵 Ê
6
瓽 { Tông / *T'hâng*
瓷 Choê
7
瓭 Tông
瓿 Âm
瓻 Ch'he
甈 Kong
甁 { Pîn / *Pân*
9
甃 Ch'hèw
甄 { Chin / Yëen
甌 Aou
甍 Bêng
甎 Chwan
12
甏 *Tāng*
甑 Chēng
甓 *P'hëāh*
甕 { Òng / *Àng* / Yùng / *Èng*

甔 T'hâm
甗 Hëèn

玉96
瓜97
瓦98

99 甘
100 生
101 用
102 田

甘 Kam / *Ka*
甚 Sīm / *Sⁿá*
甛 Tëêm / *Tee^{ng}* 6
甜 Tëêm
甞 Sëâng 8
嗛 Hëem
甝 Chay

生 Seng / *Sai^{ng}*
甡 Sin
產 Sán / *Swⁿá* 7
甤 Jöêy
甥 Seng
甦 Soe

用 Yūng
甪 Lok / *Lut*
甫 Hoó 2
甬 Yúng
甯 Bēng

田 Tëên / Tëēn / *Ch'hân*
由 Yêw 2
甲 Kap / *Káh*
申 Sin
甴 Hwut
男 Lâm 2
甸 Tëēn
甹 P'heng
町 Tèng
画 Hwā
甿 Hóng 3
畀 Ch'hek
畁 Pè
画 Hwā / *Wā*
畂 Kong 4
畆 Boé
畇 Yîn
畈 Che
畋 Tëên
界 Kaè
畎 K'hëén
畏 Wùy

畑 Choe 5
畔 Pwān
畕 Kang
畗 Hok
留 Lêw / *Laòu*
畚 Pún
畛 Chín
畜 Wán
畜 Hëuk / *T'hëuk* / *T'hek*
畝 Boé
畟 Chek
畢 Pit 6
畤 Sē / Tē
略 Lē
畧 Lëák / *Lëŏh*
畧 Lëák
畦 Hêy
畩 *Lwăh* 7
番 Hwan
畬 Ê / Sëâ

畯 Chùn
畫 Ék
異 Ē / Eē^{ng}
畱 Lêw 8
畫 Hwā / *Wā*
畭 Laê
睥 Pe
畷 T'hëén
畹 Hek
畼 T'hëang
畽 Këuk
當 Tong / Tòng / *Te^{ng}* / *Tè^{ng}*
畚 Pún
畷 Chwā
畸 Kê
畹 Wán 9
畼 T'hëàng
疃 T'hwān
疆 Sek
畿 Ke

疃 T'hwán
14
疆 Këang
疇 Têw
疊 Tëëp
疊 Tëëp

疋 P'hit
7
疎 Soe
疏 Soè / *Sey*
9
疐 T'hè
疑 Gê

疒 Lek
2
疔 Teng
疛 Kew
疕 P'hé
3
疚 Kèw
疝 Sàn
4
疢 T'hìm
疣 T'hîm / Tîm
疤 Pa / *Ba*
疲 Pán
疥 Kaè / *Kèy*
疨 Gây
疪 Pè
疫 Ék
5
疱 P'haôu
疲 P'hô
疳 Kam
疴 O
疵 Ch'hoô
疶 Sëet / Ch'hwăh
疷 Kô
疸 T'hán

疹 Chín
疼 Tông / *T'kàng*
疽 Ch'he
疾 Chit
疿 Pwùy
痀 K'he
痁 Sëem
病 Pēng / *Paiⁿg*
6
痊 Chwân / Ch'hwan
痍 Ê
痸 Sëet
痃 Sëén
痐 Hëâng
痏 Hōêy
痎 Kaôu / *Kú*
痓 Gaô
㽗 T'hcâou
痒 Yâng
痔 Tō
痕 H...
痯 Kwan

痗 Hōèy
痘 Toū
痦 Lē
痚 T'hùn
痚 Haou / *Hay*
痛 T'hòng / *T'hëⁿà*
痜 T'hut
痛 Hín
痞 P'hé
痟 Seaou
痡 Hoo
痠 Swan / *Swuiⁿg*
痢 Lē
痺 Ch'hëà
痣 Chè / *Kè*
痤 È
痥 T'hōêy
痙 Kông
8
瘍 Ek
痲 MA / *Bâ*

痮 *Tëòⁿg*
痯 Kwán
痰 T'hâm
痳 Lîm
痴 Ch'he
痵 K'hwùy
痽 K'hwân / *K'hōëy*
痷 K'hâm
痺 Pè
痹 Pè
痻 Hwun / Bìn
瘃 *Cheĕh*
痼 Koè
痿 Öey / Wöey
瘀 È
瘁 Chūy
瘂 Áy
瘃 Chëuk
9
瘇 Chëúng
瘖 Séng
瘉 Jé / Jô

田 102
疋 103
正
疒 104

9 D

104 疒
105 癶
106 白

瘋 Hong
瘍 *Yëō^ng*
瘄 { Hëang / *Hëⁿa* }
瘎 T'hîm
瘏 Toê
瘝 Kwan
瘈 Jé
瘷 Leaou
瘒 Hwûn
瘔 K'hoê
瘑 K'hoê
瘖 Yim
10
瘚 K'hwat
瘝 Kwan
瘟 Wun
癄 Chin
瘠 Chit
瘡 { Ch'hong / *Ch'he^ng* }
瘢 Pwân
瘤 Lêw
瘦 { Soé / *Sán* }

瘥 { Chê / Ch'haè / Ch'hày }
㾽 T'hûy
瘧 Gëak
瘨 T'hëên
痺 Pē
瘬 Tëàng
瘄 Chê
瘯 Chók
瘛 Tē
瘳 T'hew
瘰 Lúy
瘴 Chëàng
瘵 Chèy
瘶 Soè
瘹 Teàou
瘺 { Loē / *Laōu* }
瘻 { Loê / Lê }
瘞 Èng
瘼 Bók
12
癀 { Hông / *Wu[illegible]* }

癥 Chöèy
療 Leāou
癃 Lëûng
瘤 Lêw
癉 { Tan / *Twⁿa* }
13
癖 { P'hek / *P'hëăh* }
癗 Lûy
癘 Lēy
瘨 Ch'hé
㿗 Sûy
癨 *K'hăh*
癠 Sāy
癡 Ch'he
癢 { Yāng / *Chëō^ng* }
16
癧 { Lėk / *Lȧt* }
癐 Loé
癨 Hok
癩 Naē
癬 Sëén
癭 Eng
癰 Kê

癰 { Eng / Yung }
癲 Tëen

癶 Pwat
4
癸 Kwùy
癹 P'hwat
7
登 Teng
發 Hwat

白 { Pėk / *Păyh* }
百 { Pek / *Păyh* }
2
皁 Chō
皂 Chō
的 Tek
4
皅 Bā
皆 Kae
皇 Hông
皈 Kwuy
皋 Ko
6
皎 Keáou
皓 Hō
皙 Sek
10
皛 Beáou
皜 Kó
皤 P'ho
皞 Hō
皦 Keáou
皫 P'heáou

皮107 皿108 目109

皮 P'hê / *P'höéy*
𤿍 Chéng
皱 P'hā / P'haǒuh
4
皯 P'hé
𤿎 Pè
𤿏 Lām
皰 P'haǒu
𤿐 Bwat / *Mwⁿa*
6
𤿑 Lap
𤿒 Swát
𤿓 K'hëak
皴 Ch'hin / *Pit*
𤿔 T'hwat
8
皵 Ch'hëak / *Leĕh*
𤿕 K'hím
𤿖 Ch'hwat
皷 Koé
皸 Kin
10
𤿗 Pang
皺 Jeàou / Jeâou
皻 Choo
皾 Paǒuh

皿 Béng
盂 Oô / Woô
盂 Woô
4
盆 P'hûn
盈 Êng
5
益 Ek / *Yëuk* / *Yëăh*
盋 *Pwăh*
盌 Wán
盍 Ăp
盎 Yàng
6
盒 Ăp
盔 K'höey
盖 Kaè
盛 Sêng / Sēng
盙 Hoó
盜 Tō
8
盐 Yëêm
葢 Kaè
盞 Chán / *Chwⁿá*
盟 Bêng
盝 Ch'hōng / *Sëⁿā*

盡 Chīn
監 Kam / Kàm / *Kⁿa*
10
盤 Pwân / *Pwⁿâ*
盥 Kwán / Kwàn
盧 Loê
盩 Chew
盪 Tōng / T'hòng
盬 Koé

目 Bók / *Bàk*
盯 *Taiⁿᵍ*
盱 He
盷 Jīm / *Lìm*
盲 Bêng / *Maiⁿᵍ*
直 Tit
4
盶 Gwán
相 Sëang / Sëàng / *Sëoⁿᵍ* / *Sëòⁿᵍ* / *Sëo*
県 Heaou
盻 Géy
盼 P'hàn
盽 Hong
盾 Tún
眀 Bêng
省 Séng / *Saiⁿᵍ*
眅 P'hán
眣 Hit
眂 Pöèy
眇 Beáou
眈 Tam

眉 Bê / *Baê*
眊 Mō
看 K'han / K'hàn / *K'hwⁿà*
5
看 K'han
𥄳 P'hoó
眐 Cheng
眖 Hòng
眘 Sīn
眚 Séng
眛 *Bwuy*
眞 Chin
眠 Bëên
眗 Paǒu
眦 Ch'héy
眧 Ch'heáou
眩 Hëên / *Hìn*
眪 Péng
6
眭 Héy
䀨 Kwat
眶 K'hong / *K'hang*

眯 Bé
眷 Kwàn
眫 Boê
眺 T'heàou
眼 Gán
眽 *Lëó*
眾 Chëùng
7
着 Bê
睃 Chùn
睉 Ch'hò
睊 Kwàn
睍 Hëén
8
睘 Kêng
睚 Gaê
睛 Cheng / *Chaiⁿᵍ*
睜 Chēng
睞 Laē
睟 Sùy
睠 Kwàn
睡 Sùy / *Chöēy* / *K'hwùn*
睢 Ch'he

109 目
110 矛
111 矢
112 石

瞉 *K'háyh*
督 Tok
睥 { P'hè / *P'hēy* }
睦 Bók
睨 Géy
睪 Ek
睫 { Chëët / Chëep }
睬 Ch'haé
9
睸 Ch'hwăh
睹 Toé
睐 Ch'haē
睿 Jöēy
瞀 Boō
10
瞈 Òng
瞋 Chin
瞌 K'hap
瞍 Soé
瞎 Hat
瞖 Hey
瞑 { Bêng / Bēng }
瞖 È

瞚 Sùn
瞞 { Bwân / *Mwⁿá* }
瞟 { P'heaou / P'ha }
瞠 { T'heng / *Taiⁿᵍ* / *Tⁿa* }
瞢 Bēng
12
瞧 *Ch'heēⁿᵍh*
瞥 { Pëet / P'hëet }
瞧 { Cheaou / Cheâou }
瞪 *T'haiⁿᵍ*
瞬 { Sùn / Ch'hún }
瞭 Aou
瞭 Leáou
瞯 Hán
瞰 K'hàm
瞲 Hit
瞳 Tông
瞶 Höēy
13
瞰 Keáou
瞻 Chëem
瞽 Koé

瞿 { Kè / Kê }
瞕 *Naiⁿᵍ*
矄 Hwun
矇 Bông
矌 *K'hàng*
矍 Këak
矐 *Neēⁿᵍh*
矗 Ch'hëuk
20
矓 T'hóng
矙 K'hàm

矛 Maôu
矜 Keng
矟 Sok

矢 Sé
矣 È
知 { Te / Tè / *Chae* }
4
矦 Hoê
矧 Sín
矨 Géng
矩 Ké
7
短 { Twán / *Táy* / *Tēy* }
矮 { Wúy / Aé / *Áy* / *Êy* }
12
矯 Keáou
矰 Cheng
矱 Hoē

石 { Sèk / *Chëŏh* }
3
矴 P'hok
矸 Kan
矻 { Git / Gwut }
矼 Kang
4
砂 Say
砆 Hoo
砊 { K'hòng / K'heng }
砌 { Ch'hè / *Keĕh* }
砍 K'hám
砒 { P'he / *P'heēⁿᵍ* }
砛 Gîm
5
砠 Ch'he
砥 Té
砦 Chāy
砭 Pëén
砵 Pwat
砰 P'heng
砱 *Lang*
砲 P'haôu
砌 Aôu
破 { P'hò / *P'hwà* }

6

硃 Choo
硆 K'hám
硈 K'hëét
硎 Hêng
研 { Gëén / Gëên / *Gán*

7

硜 Keng
硝 Seaou
硞 K'hok
硡 K'hông
硨 Ch'hëa
硪 Gnó
硫 Léw
硬 { Gēng / *Gnāy*
硼 Bông
确 { Kaŏuh / K'haŏuh
硯 { Heēn / *Heē*^{ng}

8

硺 Tok
硿 K'hong
碁 Kê
碌 Lók
碍 Gaē
碎 Ch'hùy
碏 Ch'hëak
碑 Pe
碒 Gîm
碗 { Wán / *W*^{n}*á*
碓 Tùy
碔 Boo
碕 Kê
碖 Lún
碄 Hwân
碞 Gâm

9

碟 { Sëét / Tëét / *Tëëh*
碡 { Tók / *Ták*
碢 O
碣 Këet
碦 K'hek
碧 P'hek
碨 { Öey / Wöey
礘 Gók
碩 Sèk
碪 Chim
碫 T'hwàn
碭 { Tōng / *T'hë*^{ng}

10

確 K'hak
碻 { Köéy / *K'heăouh*
碼 { Má / *Báy*
碽 Kong
磏 Lëén
䃒 Hék
磁 { Choô / *Héep* / *Hwûy*
磄 Tông
磅 P'hong
磆 Kwút
磈 K'hwúy
磉 Sóng
磭 Gëén
磊 Lúy
磋 Ch'ho
磎 K'hey
磐 { Pwân / *Pw*^{n}*â*
磑 Wûy
磒 Wún
磓 Tuy
磔 { Këét / *Kák*
磕 K'hap
磚 { Chwan / *Chui*^{ng}
磛 Ch'hâm
磜 Ch'hè
磞 P'heng
磟 { Leúk / *Lá*
碅 K'hok
䃗 Ch'hë^{n}a
磡 K'hàm
磣 Ch'hám
磧 Chek
磨 { Mô / Bō / *Bwā*
磬 K'hèng
磤 Gîn

12

[石彭] P'hë^{n}a
磯 Ke
磰 Sëēn
𥗃 K'hwat
磲 Kê
磴 Tèng
磷 { Lîn / Lin
磻 { Hwan / Hwân
磺 *Hwut*^{ng}
礅 Tun
磽 K'haou
礁 Ta

13

礉 { K'haòu / K'haouh
礎 Ch'hoé
礐 Hák
礙 Gaē
礚 K'hap

15

礦 { Kong / *Kw*^{n}*á*
礧 { Lúy / Lüy
礪 Lëy
礬 Hwân
礢 Yëó^{ng}
礱 { Lëûng / Lâng
礮 P'haòu
礶 Kwàn

D E

113 示
礻
114 内
115 禾

示 Sē
礼 Léy
礽 Jëûng
3
社 Sëā
礿 Yëák
祀 { Soō / *Ch'haē* / *Saē* / Chëuk
祁 Kê
4
祆 Yaou
祇 Kê
祈 Kê
祉 Ché
祊 { Hong / Peng
祋 Tút
5
祐 Yēw
祑 Tëét
祔 *Sëēh*
祓 / 祓 } Hwut
祜 Hoō
祕 Pè
祖 Choé

祘 Swàn
祗 Té
祚 { Choè / Ch'hoè
祛 { K'he / *K'hoo*
祜 Hoē
祝 Chëuk
神 Sîn
祟 Sùy
祠 Soô
祡 Ch'haê
6
祣 Lé
祥 Sëâng
祧 T'heaou
票 { P'heàou / *P'hëò*
祫 K'hap
祭 Chèy
祲 Ch'him
8
禂 { Ch'hoè / Chāy
祺 Kê
祼 Kwàn
祿 Lók

禀 Pín
禁 { Kim / Kìm
9
禈 *Wut*^{ng}
禊 Hēy
禋 Yin
禍 Hō
禎 Cheng
福 Hok
禔 T'hêy
禖 Böêy
禘 { Tèy / Tēy
10
禜 Ēng
禡 Mā
禠 Lê
禦 Gé
禧 { He / Hé
禩 Soō
禪 { Sëên / Sëēn
禮 Léy
14
禰 { Jé / Jeé^{ng}
禱 Tó

禷 Lēy
禳 Jëâng
禴 Yëák

内 Jéw
禹 É
离 Lê
禽 K'hîm

禾 Hô
朮 { *Öëy* / Wöêy
秃 T'hut
秀 Sèw
私 Soo
3
秄 Choó
杓 Teáou
秉 Peng
秊 Lëên
4
秋 Ch'hew
种 Ch'hëung
秏 H^{n}ò
科 { K'ho / *K'höey*
秒 Beáou
秕 Pé
5
秘 Pè
秙 K'hwà
租 Choe
秠 P'he
秣 Bwat
秤 Ch'hèng
秧 { Yang / *E*^{ng}

禾115 穴116

黍 Chîa
秩 Tëët
秖 Tae
秫 Tůt / Chůt
移 É
7
秿 P'hoe
稀 He
稂 Lông
稃 Hoo
稅 Söèy / T'hwat
稇 K'hwún
稈 Kan
稉 Keng
程 Têng / *Teⁿá* / *T'hëⁿâ* / *T'hatⁿg*
8
稲 Choo
稐 Lún
稔 Jím
稗 Paē / *P'hēy*
稆 *Hëöⁿg*
稚 Tō

稘 Key
稜 Lêng
稟 Lím / Pín
稠 Têw
稴 Hëem
9
稨 Pëén
稍 Têw
稬 Nô
種 Chëûng / *Chéng* / Chëûng / *Chèng*
稱 Ch'heng / Ch'hèng / *Ch'hìn*
10
稭 Kwut
稷 Chek
稺 Tō
稻 Tō
稼 Kày
稿 Kó
稾 Kó
穀 Kok
稽 Key

穄 Chèy
稯 Chóng
穆 Bók
穈 Bûn
穉 Tē
穊 Kè
穋 Lëük
穌 Soe
積 Chek
穎 Éng
穗 Sūy
13
穟 Sūy
穢 Köèy / *Öĕyh* / *Wŏĕyh*
穠 Lông
穡 Sek
穧 Choo
穢 Öèy / Woèy
14
穤 Nô
穧 Chey
穩 Wún
穫 Hoe

穮 P'beaou
穰 Jëâng

穴 Hëet
穵 Wat
究 Kèw
3
穸 Sèk
穹 K'hëung
空 K'hong / *K'hang* / K'hóng / K'hòng
4
穽 Chēng
穾 Yaóu / Yaòu
穿 Ch'hwan / Ch'hwàn / *Ch'huiⁿg* / *Ch'huiⁿg* / Ch'hëûng / *Ch'hĕng* / *Ch'hwⁿā*
窀 Tun / Chun
突 Tůt
5
窄 Chek
窅 Beáou
窆 Pëèn
窈 Yaóu
窊 Wâ
窋 Chut / *Poŏh*
6
窑 Yaôu

窒 Chit / Lit
窓 Ch'hong / *T'hang*
窔 Beáou
窕 T'heaou
7
窖 Kaòu / Kà
窗 Ch'hong / *T'hang*
窘 Kwûn / K'hwún
窙 Haou
8
窉 Pèng
窞 Tám
窟 K'hwut
窠 K'ho
窢 Hék
窣 Sut
9
窿 Hong
窩 O
窪 Wâ
窬 Jê
窮 Këûng / *Kêng*
窯 窰 Yaôu / *Yëô*

116 穴

窲 Chaôu
窳 Jé
窾 P'hè
窵 Teàou
窺 Kwuy
窻 Ch'hong
13
窿 Lëûng
竄 Ch'hwàn
竅 K'heàou
竆 Këûng
竇 Toē
竈 Chò / *Chaðu*
竉 *Ïng*
竊 Ch'hëep

117 立

立 Lip
妑 P'há
5
站 Chām
竨 T'hé
竝 Pēng
竟 Kéng
章 Chëang / *Chëo^{ng}*
7
𥪯 P'hut
竣 Chùn
竢 Soō
童 Tông / *Tâng*
竦 Sëúng
竪 Sē
9
竭 Këet
端 Twan
竵 Hwae
競 Kēng

118 竹

竹 Tëuk / *Tek*
竺 Tëuk
竽 Ê
竿 Kan
4
笐 *Wui^{ng}*
笆 Pa
笈 K'hip
笊 Chaou / Ch'haðu
笋 Sún
笢 Pūn
笏 Hwut
笑 Ch'heàou / *Ch'hëð*
5
笒 K'hëêm
笘 Ch'hëem
笙 Seng
笝 Lâp
笞 T'he
笠 Lip / *Lǎyh*
笡 *Ch'hë^{n}a*
笣 Paou
笴 K'hoé
笤 Teâou
笥 Soo / Soò
符 Hoô
笨 Pūn
笩 Pöëy
笫 Ché
第 Tëy
笭 Lāng
笮 Tek / *Tày* / Chày
笱 Koé
笳 Kay
6
筀 Kwùy
䈞 Ch'hún / *Ch'hui^{ng}*
筆 Pit
笷 Ló
筅 Ch'hán / Sëén / *Ch'héng*
箒 *Ch'hcäouh*
筇 Gëûng
等 Téng
筊 Kaðu / *Ka*
筋 Kin
筌 Ch'hwan
筹 K'hó / *Ka*
筍 Sún
筏 Hwàt
筑 Tëuk
筐 K'hong / *K'hcng*
筒 Tông / *Tâng*
筓 Key
筬 Seng / *Sey*
答 Tap
筕 *Kë^{n}â*
策 Ch'hek
7
筠 Kin
筢 Pâ / *Pây*
筤 Lông
筥 Ké
筪 Yip
筦 Kwán
筧 Këén
筩 Yúng / Tông
筭 Swàn
筮 Sē
筯 Tē / *T'hoō*
筲 Soe
筴 Keep / *Gnàyh*
筵 Yëen
筃 Pin
筞 *Ch'hē…*
箄 Pín
箆 Pìn
箇 Kò
箋 Chëen / Ch'hëén
箍 K'hoe
箎 Tê
箏 Chêng
箑 Chëet
箔 Pók / *Pǎyh*
箕 Ke
算 Swàn / *Swui^{ng}*
箜 K'hong
箠 Ch'höêy / Sûy

竹118 ⺮ 米119

管 { Kw… / *Kwu*
[illegible] Tām
9
箬 Jëák
箭 { Chëèn / *Chee^{ng}*
箱 { Sëang / *Sëo^{ng}*
箴 Chom
箸 Tē
箍 K'ho
[illegible] Só
[illegible] Yêw
篾 *Beĕh*
節 { Chëet / *Chat* / *Chăyh*
篁 Hông
範 Hwān
篆 Twān
篇 { P'hëen / *P'hee^{ng}*
築 { Tëuk / *Keĕh*
[illegible] Hâng
篋 { Këep / *K'hăyh*

[illegible] Hoê
10
[illegible] Sit
篗 Ak
篙 Ko
篚 Hwúy
[illegible] Poe
篠 Seáou
篡 Ch'hwàn
[illegible] Kám
篤 Tok
[illegible] Chô
篥 Lek
篦 Pey
篨 Tê
篩 { Sae / *T'hae*
簑 So
篰 Poē
篲 Hwūy
篳 Pit
篴 Tëúk
簰 Paê
篾 Bëét

篱 { Lê / *Lēy*
篷 { P'hông / *P'hâng*
簀 { Chek / *Tăyh*
簆 { K'hoè / *K'haòu*
簇 { Choè / Ch'hok
[illegible] *P'hë^{n}a*
簋 K'hwúy
[illegible] *Nê^{ng}*
[illegible] *Së^{n}ā*
簏 Lók
[illegible] K'hoe
12
簞 { Tan / *Two^{n}a*
簟 Tëem
簠 Hoó
簡 Kán
簣 Kwūy
簥 Keaou
簦 Teng
簧 Hông
[illegible] Kám
簨 Sún

簪 { Cham / *Chom*
簫 Seaou
簷 Lëêm
簸 { Pò / *Pwà*
簽 Ch'hëem
簾 { Lëêm / *Lê*
[illegible] { Kek / *Kăyh*
簿 { Pók / P'hoē
14
籃 { Lâm / *Nâ* / *Maî^{ng}*
籄 Kwūy
[illegible] Sóng
籉 Taê
[illegible] Ch'hēng
籊 Tók
籌 Têw
籍 Chék
籐 Têng
[illegible] Oe
籀 Tēw
[illegible] Lúy

籓 Hwân
籗 Hok
籙 Lĕúk
籜 T'hok
籞 Gé
籟 Naē
籠 { Lóng / *Láng* / Lông / *Lâng*
17
籤 Ch'hëem
籥 Yëák
籧 Kè
籩 Pëen
籬 Lê
籭 Sac
籮 { Lô / *Lwā*
籱 *K'hăh*

米 Bé
[illegible] K'hoe
敉 Chong
粃 { Pé / *P'h^{u}à*
粉 Hwún
5
粒 { Lëép / *Lip*
粕 *P'hŏh*
粗 Ch'hoe
粘 Lëêm
6
[illegible] T'he
粟 Sëuk
粠 *Kèng*
[illegible] Ch'hek
[illegible] Hwan
[illegible] Pōēy
粱 Këûng
[illegible] Bêng
粢 Choo
[illegible] Kaou
粤 Wát
粥 Chëuk
粦 Lĩn

119 米

120 糸

糹

糾 K'hëuk / *K'hak*
粧 Chong
7
粮 Lëâng
粯 Hëén
梭 So
粱 Lëâng
粰 P'hút
粲 Ch'hàn
8
粺 Paē
粹 Sùy
粽 Chòng / *Chàng*
精 Cheng / *Chë^{n}a* / Seâou
粿 Kó / *Köëy*
9
糵 *Kit*
糅 Jéw
稫 Pek
糇 Hoê
糈 Se
糉 Chòng
糊 Koê

糑 Neē^{ng}
糌 Choê
10
糏 Ch'hèy
糐 P'hoe
糒 Pē
糓 Kok
糗 Sek
糔 Séw
糕 Ko
糍 *Ché*
糖 T'hông / *T'hē^{ng}*
糗 Hèw
糙 Ch'hò
糚 Chong
糫 Hwân / P'hun
糰 Twân
糖 T'hek
糠 Lút
糜 Bê. / *Möëy*
糒 Bwân
積 Chek

糝 Sám
糞 Hwùn / *Pùn*
糟 Cho / *Chaou*
糠 K'hong / *K'he^{ng}*
12
糠 Lȯk
糧 T'hám
糖 Seàou
糢 P'hok
糧 Lëâng / *Nëô^{ng}*
釋 Sek
糯 Naē
糫 Hwân
14
糯 Nô
糲 Lēy / Naē
糴 Tėk / *Tëăh*
蘗 Gëėt
糶 T'heàou / *T'hëò*

糸 Bėk
糺 Kéw
係 Hēy
紈 Kêw
糾 Kéw
3
紀 Ké
紂 Tēw
約 Yëak / *Yëŏh*
紅 *Âng* / Hông
紆 Oo / Woo
紇 Hwút / Git
紈 Wân
紉 Jīm
4
紊 Bûn
紋 Bûn
納 Láp
紐 Léw
紑 Hoê
紓 Se
純 Sûn
紕 Pē / P'hey / *P'hèy*

紗 Say
紖 Yín
紘 Hông
紙 Ché / *Chwá*
紛 Hwun
級 Kip
紜 Yîn
紞 Tám
紟 K'him
素 Soè
紡 Hong / *P'hang*
索 Sek / *Sŏh*
5
紹 Teàou
紤 *T'hëăh*
紩 Tëėt / *T'heē^{ng}*
紫 Ché
紪 Ch'héy
紬 Têw / T'hew
紲 Sëet
細 Sèy
紳 Sin

累 Lúy / Lūy
紱 } Hwut
紼 }
紵 T'hé / *Tēy*
紹 Seăou
紺 K'hàm
紼 Hwut
紾 Chín
終 Chëung
絃 Hëên / *Heē^{ng}*
組 Choé
絅 Kéng
6
絆 Pwàn / *Pw^{n}à*
絏 Sëet
結 Këet / *Kat*
絔 Bék
絕 Chwát / *Chăyh*
緝 Jé
絡 Lȯk / *Lŏh*
絞 Kaóu / *Ká*

糸 120 糹

絜 Hëet
絛 T'ho
絢 Hëèn
給 Kip
絨 Jëûng
絫 Lúy
絭 Kwàn / *Kwui*^{ng}
絮 Sè
絰 Tëét
統 T'hong
絲 So
絳 Kàng
7 絹 Kwàn / *Kìn*
絺 T'he
絿 Këw
䋠 Poé
綁 Páng
綂 T'hong
綃 Seaou
綆 Kēng
綉 Sèw

紘 Hông
綌 K'hek
綍 Hwut
綏 Suy
綑 K'hwún
經 Keng / *Kai*^{ng}
8 綜 Chòng / *Chàng*
綠 Lëúk / *Lèk*
綢 Têw
綣 K'hwán
綦 Kê
綨 Kê
綪 *T'hè*^{n}*ā*
綫 Chëen / Sëèn
綬 Sēw
維 Wûy
綮 K'héy
絣 Peng
綯 Tô
綴 Twat / Chöèy
綱 Kong

綰 Kwán / *Kw*^{n}*ā*
網 Bóng / *Báng* / *Bāng*
綵 Ch'haé
綶 K'hwà
綸 Lûn
綺 K'hé
綻 Ch'hàn
綽 Ch'hëak
綾 Lêng / *Lîn*
綿 Bëên / *Meé*^{ng}
緂 T'hán
緄 K'hwún / Kwún / Kwûn
緅 Choe
緆 Sek
緇 Choo
緈 Héng
緊 Kín
緋 Hwuy
緌 Jōëy

[illegible] K'hwut
緍 Bîn / Hwun
緎 Hèk
9 緒 Sē
緗 Sëang
緘 Këem
線 Sëèn / Sàn / *Sw*^{n}*à*
緥 Poé
緝 Ch'hip
緞 Twān
締 Tèy
緡 Bëên / Bîn
縇 Sûn
緣 Yëên / Yëēn
緦 Soo
編 Pëen / P'hëen
緩 Wān
總 Chóng
緬 Bëên
緮 Hók

緯 Hwūy
緲 Beáou
練 Lëēn
縿 *Là*
緵 Chong
緶 Pëên / Pëēn
緷 Wūn
10 緻 Tè
緼 Wun / Wùn
縈 Êng
縉 Chìn
縊 Aè
縋 Tūy
縐 Jeàou / Jeâou
縑 Këem
縖 Hăh / *Hâ*
縗 Söey
縚 T'ho
縛 Pók / *Pák*
縜 Wûn
縝 Chín

縡 *T'hee*^{ng}
縞 Kó
縟 Jëúk
縠 Kok
縢 Têng
縣 Hëên / Hëēn / *Kwān*
縩 Chèy
縫 Hông / *Pâng* / *P'hāng*
[illegible] Kín
縭 Lê
縮 Sëuk / *Lun*
縱 Ch'hëûng / Chong
縲 Lûy
縵 Bān
縶 Chip
縷 Lé / Loê
縹 P'heaou
總 Chóng / *Cháng*
績 Chek / *Chăyh*

120 糸
121 缶
122 网 罒 罓

縻 Bê
緐 Hwân
繂 Lut
緊 E
繅 Ch'haóu
繆 { Kew / Bêw / Bĕw / Bòk
繈 Këáng
繐 Sŭi^{ng} 12
縿 { Cheng / Chan
綴 Ch'hwat
織 Chit
繕 Sëēn
繚 { Lèáou / Leâou
繜 Chún
繞 Jeáou
繟 Ch'hwá
繡 Sèw
繢 Höēy
繩 Chîn
繪 Höēy

繫 Hĕy
繭 Kán
繇 Tēw
緤 Gëep
繮 Kéang
繵 Tam
繲 Kaè
繳 { Keáou / Chëak
繴 P'hek
繾 Ch'hëèn
繿 Kam
繶 Ek
繵 Ley
繸 Sūy
繹 Ek
辮 { Pëēn / Pee^{ng} 14
繼 Kèy
繽 P'hin
纏 K'hëén
纁 Hwun
纂 Ch'hwàn

纈 K'hëet
纊 K'hòng
續 { Sëuk / Sŵa
纍 Lûy
纏 { Tëên / Teē^{ng}
纜 Lám 16
纑 Loê
纓 { Eng / Yē^{n}a
纔 Ch'haê
纖 Sëem
纘 Chàn
纛 Tòk
欘 Chëuk

缶 Hoé
缸 Yaôu 4
缺 { K'hwat / K'höèyh / K'heĕh
缻 Kong
缾 { Pîn / Pân
缿 Hāng 8
鋼 { Kong / Ke^{ng}
罄 K'hèng
罐 Suy
罅 Hà
罇 Chun
罌 Eng
罍 Lûy

网 Bóng
罕 Teng
罔 Bóng
罡 Tòk
罕 Hán
罘 Tek 4
罘 Tek
罛 Hoo
罜 Léng
罛 Koe
罝 Chëa
罞 Bōng
罟 Koé
罡 Kong 6
罠 Kong
罣 K'hwà
罦 Bōng
罥 Këén
罦 Hoo
罧 Sàm
罛 Kòe 8
罨 Yëém
罩 Tà

罪 Chöēy
罭 Hek
置 Tè
罰 Hwàt
罿 Chong
署 Sē
罳 Soo
罵 { Mā / Maī^{ng} 10
罽 Ke
罶 Léw
罷 { P'hê / Pā
罹 Lê
羀 T'hè^{ng}
羃 Boê
罾 { Cheng / Chan
罿 Tông
羃 Bék
羆 P'hê
羅 Lô
羈 Kè
羇 Kè

羊 { Yâng / *Yëŏ*^{ng} }
羌 Këang
幸 T'hat
羍 T'hat
美 { Bé / *Súy* }
羙 Yéw
4
羓 Pa
羔 Ko
羖 Koé
羗 Këang
5
羚 Lêng
羜 T'hé
羖 Koé
羝 Tey
羞 Sew
着 { Chëák / *Tëŏh* / *Tëŏh* }
7
羣 Kwûn
群 Kwûn
羡 { Swàn / Yëēn }
義 Gē
羹 { Keng / *Kai*^{ng} }

羯 Küet
羲 He
12
羴 Sëen
羶 Tông
羷 Hwân
羵 Hwûn
羶 { Chëen / Sëen }
羸 Lôëy

羽 É
羿 Gêy
4
翁 { Ong / *Ang* }
翅 { Ch'hè / T'hè }
翂 P'hún
翊 Ėk
翌 Ėk
習 Sip
6
翔 Sëâng
翕 Hip
翗 Kô
翑 P'haóu
翛 Seaou
8
翟 Ték
翎 *P'hoō*
翠 Ch'hùy
翡 Hwúy
9
翥 Choò
翩 P'hëen
翫 Gwán
翬 Hwuy
10
翮 Kek

翰 Hān
翲 P'heaou
12
翹 Keâou
翱 Ko
翷 P'hëet
翻 Hwan
翿 Sëuk
翼 Ėk
翸 P'hún
翽 { Hwùy / Öèy / Wöèy }
耀 Yaōu

老 { Ló / *Laōu* }
考 K'hó
4
耄 Mō
者 Chëá
耆 Kê
耈 Koé
6
耋 Tëét
耋 Tëét

而 Jê
耐 Naē
3
耍 Swá
耏 Naē
耑 Chwan

羊 123
羽 124
老 125
而 126

127 耒
128 耳
129 聿
130 肉 月

耒 Jōey
耔 Choó
耕 {Keng / *Kaiⁿᵍ* 4
耗 Hⁿò
耘 Yîn
耙 Pāy
耜 Soō
耞 *Kaíⁿᵍ* 6
⿰耒各 Kek
耣 Lún
⿰耒昆 Kwún
⿰耒困 K'hwún
⿰耒兒 Gnoé 10
⿰耒畟 *Chëŏh*
耨 Noē
耰 Yew

耳 {Jé / *Hē* 4
耶 Yëâ
耼 Tam
耽 Tam
耿 Kéng
聃 Tam
聊 Leâou
聆 Lêng 7
聕 Hōng
聖 {Sèng / *Sëⁿà*
聘 P'hèng 8
聚 Chē
⿰耳垂 Tûy
聝 Hèk
聞 {Bûn / Būn
聦 *Ch'hang* 10
聯 {Bëên / *Lëên*
聰 {Ch'hong / *Ch'hang*
⿰耳翏 Lô
聲 {Seng / *Sëⁿa*
聳 Sëúng 12
聵 Hōëy
聶 Lëep
職 Chit
聽 {T'heng / T'hèng / *T'hëⁿa*
聾 {Lông / *Lâng*

聿 Yit
畫 Hwā
肄 Ē 8
肅 Sëuk
肆 Soò
肇 Teāou
肈 Teāou

肉 {Jëúk / *Băh*
肋 Lék
肎 K'héng 3
肐 Hit
肖 Seàou
⿰月川 Hwùn
肘 Néw
肚 Toē
肝 {Kan / *Kwⁿa* 4
育 Yëúk
肟 Oo
肼 *P'hëⁿá*
股 Koé
肢 Che
肥 {Hwûy / *Pwûy*
肦 Hwûn
肩 Këen
肨 P'hòng
肫 Chun
肬 Yêw
肯 {K'héng / *K'hán*
肰 Jëên
肱 Keng
肴 Gnaôu
肸 Hit
肺 {P'haè / Hè / *Hwùy* 5
胃 Wūy
胄 Tēw
胅 Tëėt
胨 Tông
背 {Pōèy / Pōēy
胎 {T'hae / *T'hey* / *T'hay*
胐 K'hwut
胓 Pêng
胔 Choò
胖 {Pwân / *P'hàng*
胗 Chín
⿰月尓 Chín
胙 Choē
⿰月且 Ch'he
胛 {Këep / *Kăh*
胝 Tê

胜 Seng
胞 Paou
胡 Hoê / *Oê*
胤 Yĭn
胥 Se
6
脉 P'heng
胭 Yëen
胮 P'hong
胯 K'hwa
胱 Kong
胳 Kok / *Kŏh*
胷 Hëung / *Heng*
胸 Hëung
胹 Jê
胖 Boê
胒 Ay
胼 Pëên
能 Lêng / *Êy*
胾 Choŏ
脅 / 脇 Hëép

脂 Che
脃 Ch'hùy / *Ch'hày* / *Ch'hèy*
脈 Bék / *Mai^{ng}h*
脉 Bék
脊 Chit / *Chëŭh*
7
脗 Bún
脚 Këak / *K'ha*
脛 Kēng / *Lëuk*
脝 P'hëang
脞 Ch'hŏ
脢 Böêy
脣 Tûn
脩 Sew
脫 T'hwat
脯 Hoó
脰 Toē / *Taōu*
脙 Hàm
脪 Yĭn
8
脑 Hàm
脮 K'hwut

脹 Tëàng / *Tëŏ^{ng}*
脺 Ch'hùy
脽 Sûy
脾 Pê
腀 Lûn
腁 Pëên
腄 Luy
腅 P'hòng
腆 T'hëén
腉 Naê
腊 Sek
腋 Ėk
腌 Am
腎 Sīn
腐 Hoó / Hoō
腑 Hoó
腓 Hwûy
腔 K'hëang / *K'hëo^{ng}*
腕 Wán
9
腜 Ba
腢 Gê

腤 Am
腥 Seng / *Ch'hai^{ng}*
腦 Ló
腬 Jêw
腫 Chëúng / *Chéng*
腮 Soo / Sae
腯 T'hún / Tūn
腰 Yaou / *Yëo*
腱 Këēn / *Kīn*
腳 *Këŏh*
腴 Jê
腸 Ch'hëâng / *Té^{ng}*
腹 Hok / *Pak*
10
腿 T'húy
膀 Pông
膁 Lëém
膂 Lé
膆 Sit
膇 T'hūy
膈 Kek / *Kĕyh*

膉 *Ka*
膊 P'hok
膄 So
膈 Lek
膋 Lēw
膛 Këung
膐 Yĭn
膋 Leâou / *Lâ*
膏 Ko / Kō
膎 Hëëp
膝 *Sëŏh*
膚 Hoo
膜 Boê
膝 Ch'hip
膟 Lŭt
膠 Kaou / *Ka*
12
膦 Lám
膨 *P'hōng*
膩 Jē
膳 Cham
膰 Hwan / Hwân

膲 Cheaou
膳 Sëēn
膴 Boó
13
膷 Hëang
膸 Ch'höéy
膺 Eng
膽 Tám
膾 Köèy
膿 Lông / *Lâng*
臀 Tûn
臁 Lëêm
臃 Tóng
臄 Nô / Lëa
臂 Pè
臂 P'hek
臄 Këák
臅 Ch'hëuk
臆 Ek / *Eĕh*
臇 Chëén
臈 Láp
臉 Lëém

130 肉 月
131 臣
132 自
133 至
134 臼

臊 { Ch'ho / So
14
臍 { Chey / Chêy / *Chaê*
𦢊 Yaōu
臎 Chuy
𦡾 Tēw
臏 { Pín / Pīn
臐 Hwun
𦣁 Hām
15
𦢸 Hêng
𧸘 T'hȯk
𦢊 Yáng
臔 Hëén
臕 { Peaou / *Pëo*
舋 Hèng
𦢊 P'hok
16
臘 Lȧp
臙 Yëen
𦣃 Êng
𦣄 Yëên
臚 Loê

臝 Ló
臞 { Kê / *K'heĕh*
臟 { Chōng / *Chĕng*
臢 Cham

臣 Sîn
臥 Gō
8
臧 Chong
𦣞 Lëûng
臨 { Lîm / *Lëëm*

自 Choō
4
臬 Gëët
臭 { Ch'hèw / *Ch'haðu*
臯 Ko
臲 Gëët

至 Chè
致 Tè
7
䑓 Taê
臺 { Taê / *Paîng*
臻 Chîn

臼 { Kēw / *Koō* / *K'hoō* / Këuk
臾 Jê
4
舀
舀 { Yaôu / *Yëóng*
舂 { Chëung / *Cheng*
舄 Sek
舅 { Kēw / *Koō*
8
與 { É / Ê / Ē
興 { Hin / Hìn / Hèng
擧 Ké
舊 { Kēw / *Koō*

舌 Sëét / *Cheĕh*
舍 Sëá / Sëà
4
舐 Chē
舒 Se
舖 P'hoè
舘 Kwán

舛 Ch'hún
舜 Sùn
舝 Hat
舞 Boó

舟 Chew
舠 To
舡 Tăh
舦 Tăyh
4
舨 Pán / Pwán
航 Hông
舫 Hóng
般 Pwan / Pwán / Pwân / *Pw^{n}a* / Pwat
5
舲 Lêng
⿰舟弗 Hwut
舴 Tăyh
舵 Tō / *Twā*
舶 Pék
舷 Hëên
舸 K'hó
船 Ch'hwân / *Chûn*
6
⿰舟舌 Hwát
⿰舟合 Kap
⿰舟同 Tông
艇 T'héng

艀 Po
8
艋 Béng
艍 Koo
艎 Hông
艅 Jê
艐 Chong / *Chang*
艑 P'hëen
10
⿰舟芻 Choe
艘 Soe
艙 *Ch'he^{ng}*
艚 Chô
12
⿰舟敢 Kám
艟 Tông
艠 Tong
艤 Gé
14
艦 Lâm
艨 Bông
艪 Loé
艭 Song

艮 Kìn
良 Lëâng
艱 Kan

色 Sek
艴 Put
艷 Yëēm
艶 Yëēm

舌135
舛136
舟137
艮138
色139

140 艸 廾

艸 Ch'hó
芊 T'hĕ^{n}á
艾 { Gnaē / Hĕ^{n}ā
芄 Wân 3
芃 Hông
芉 Ch'hëen
芋 { Ê / Ē / Oē / Bé
芍 Chëak
芎 K'hëung
芑 K'hé
芒 } Bông
茫 } Mat^{ng}
芔 Hwūy 4
芘 Pè
芙 Hoô
芚 Tun
芝 Che
芟 San
芶 Hwān
芉 Gnêw
芡 K'hëèm

芣 Hoô
芤 K'hoê
芥 { Kaè / Kwà
芨 { Kip / K'hip / K'hit
芩 K'hîm
芪 Kê
芬 Hwun
芭 Pa
芮 Jōēy
芯 Sim
芰 Kē
花 { Hwa / Hwâ
芳 Hong
芴 Bút
芷 Ché
芸 Yîn
芹 K'hîn
芻 Choe
芽 Gây
芺 T'hëen
芃 Gông

芾 Hwúy
芼 { Mô / Mō 5
茀 Tēy
苑 Wán
苒 Jëém
苓 Lêng
苔 { T'hae / T'hê
苕 Teâou
苗 Beâou
苙 Lip
苛 O
苜 Bók
苞 { Paôu / Poê
苟 Koé
苡 É
苢 É
若 { Jëák / Jwā
苦 K'hoé
苧 T'hô
苫 Chëem
茅 { Maôu / Hû^{m}

茝 Sëen
英 Eng
茮 Chút
苴 Ch'he
苹 Hoe
苹 P'hêng
苻 Hoô
苾 { Bit / Pè
茁 Chwat
茂 Boē
范 Hwān
茄 { Kay / K'hay / Këo / Këô
茆 Baóu
茇 Pwát
茈 { Ch'hoó / Ch'hoô / Cheē^{ng}
茉 Bàk
茻 Pwân 6
茗 Béng
茘 Lēy
茙 Jëûng

茜 Ch'hëèn
茱 { Choo / Choô
茫 Bông
茭 { Kaou / Ka
茯 Hók
茰 Jê
茶 Choo
茲 { Choo / See^{ng}
茴 Hōêy
茵 Yin
茶 Tây
茸 { Jëúng / Jëûng
茹 { Jé / Jê
荀 Sûn
荅 Tap
荊 { Keng / Këo^{ng}
荇 Hēng
荈 Ch'hún
草 { Ch'hó / Ch'haôu
荍 Keâou

荏 Jím
荐 Chëèn
荒 { Hong / He^{ng} / Hwui^{ng}
荖 Laóu 7
荰 Toē
荎 Ché
莔 { Bún / Mooi^{ng}
荁 Pōèy
荳 { Toē / Taōu
荵 Jím
荷 { Hô / Hō / Këâ
荸 P'hút
荻 Ték
荼 Toê
荽 Suy
菌 Tún
莅 { Lē / Neē^{ng}
莆 { Poê / Hoó
莉 { Lê / Neē^{ng}

艸 140
廿

菝 Bút
莊 Chong / *Che^{ng}*
莎 So
莕 Goê
莒 Kó
莓 Bōêy
莖 Keng
莘 Sin / *Ch'hëuk*
莝 Ch'hò
莞 Wán / Wân
莟 Hâm / *Kâm*
莠 Yéw
莢 Kwat
莢 Këep / *Kăyh*
莧 Hëēn / *Hēng*
莩 Peáou
莪 Gô
莫 Bók / *Bôh*
莮 Lâm
莽 Bóng
8

菶 Bóng
莿 Ch'hek
莿 Ch'hè
菀 Wut
菁 Ch'heng / *Ch'hai^{ng}* / Cheng
菂 Tek
菄 *Tang*
菆 Choe
菉 Lëúk
菊 Këuk / *Kek*
菌 K'hwun
菑 Choo
菓 Kó
菖 Ch'hëang / *Ch'hëo^{ng}*
菘 Sëûng
菜 Ch'haè
菟 T'hoè
菠 Po / Pöêy
菩 P'hoe
堇 Kín

菮 Hėk
華 Hwâ
菰 Koe
菱 Lêng
菲 Hwuy / Hwúy
菵 Mo
菶 Póng / *Páng*
菹 Ch'he
菼 T'hám / Tâm
菽 Sëuk
萁 Kê
萃 Chūy
萄 Tô
萅 Ch'hún
萇 Tëâng
萋 Sey / Ch'hey
萌 Bêng
萊 Laê
萍 P'hêng / P'heâou
萏 Tám
萑 Wân

萊 Chae
9
萕 K'höey
萬 Bān
萱 Swan
萵 O
萼 Gók
落 Lók / *Lôh* / *Laôu*
葆 Pó
葉 Yëėp / *Hëôh*
葐 P'hûn
葑 Hong
葒 Hông
葓 Hông
葙 Tè
葚 Sîm / *Súy*
葛 Kat / *Kwăh*
葡 Poê
董 Tóng / *Táng*
葦 Wúy
葨 Öey / Wöey

葩 P'ha
葬 Chòng
葭 Kay
葱 Ch'hong / *Ch'hang*
葳 Wuy
葵 Kwûy / Köêy
葷 Hwun
葸 Sé
葺 Ch'hip
葽 Yaou
蒀 Wun
10
蒐 Soo
蒔 Sê / Sē
蒙 Bông
蒞 Neē^{ng}
蕤 Jwûy
蒜 Swàn
蒁 *Hw^{n}â*
蒨 Ch'hëèn
蒩 Choe
蒯 Kwaé

蒲 Poê
蒸 Chìn
蒹 Këem
蒺 Chit
蒻 Jëák
蒼 Ch'hong
蒉 K'hé
蒿 O / Ho / H^{n}o
蓀 Sun
蓁 Chin
蓂 Bêng
蓄 Hëuk
蓆 Sėk
蓈 *Nê^{ng}*
蓉 Yûng
蓊 Ong
蓋 Kaè / *Kwâ* / K'hap
蓍 Se
蓏 Ló
蓐 Jëúk

140 艸 卄

蓑 Suy
萱 Hëen
蓩 Mó
11
蓫 Tëuk
蓬 Hông / *P'hâng*
蓮 Lëên
蓯 Ch'hëung
蓰 Só
蓴 Chwạn
蓷 Ch'huy
蔻 K'hoè
蓺 Gēy
蓻 Chip
蔚 Wụy
蓿 Sëụk
蔀 P'ḥoē
蔌 Sọk
蔎 Sëẹt
蔑 Bëét
蔓 Bạ̄n
蔗 Chëà
[illegible] Tùn

蔕 Taè / Tèy
蓼 Leáou / Lëúk
蔞 Lê / Loê
蔡 Ch'haè / *Ch'hwà*
蔣 Chëáng / *Chëóⁿᵍ*
蔥 Ch'hong
蔦 Neáou
蔬 Soè
蔭 Yìm
12
蔽 Pèy
蔿 Wúy
葺 Ch'hip
蕃 Hwận
蔜 Gnâou
蕊 Lúy
蕋 Lúy
蕎 *Këō*
蕑 Kạn
蕕 Yêw
蕖 Kê
蕘 Geâou

蕉 Cheaou / *Chëo*
蕙 Hwūy
蕚 Gók
蕞 Ch'hwat / Chūy
蕢 Kwúy
蕣 Sùn
蕤 Jōêy
蕨 K'hwat / *Köëyh*
蕩 Tọng
蕪 Boô
[illegible] K'hwáṇ
蕬 Se
蕭 Sẹaou
薟 Lëêm
13
蕝 Chöèy
蕸 Hây
蕗 Loē
蕾 Lúy
蕡 Hwûn
薀 Wun
薁 Hëuk

薅 Ho / Hⁿo
薄 Pók / *Pŏh*
薇 Bê
薈 Köèy
薉 Öèy / Wöèy
薊 Kè
薍 Lwān / Gwān
薐 Lêng
薏 È
薑 Këang / *Këoⁿᵍ*
薔 Ch'hëâng / *Ch'hëōⁿᵍ*
薘 Tạt / *Bwăh*
薙 Tē
薛 Sëẹt / *Seĕh*
[illegible] Hⁿò
薜 Pē
薝 Tám
薤 Haē
薧 Kó
薨 Eng

薦 Chëèn / *Chèng*
薩 Sat
薪 Sin
14
藷 Chê
薰 Hwun
薳 Wúy
薴 *Naiⁿᵍ*
薸 P'heâou
薺 Chey
薾 Chẹ́
薿 Gẹ́
藂 Chạ̄m
藇 Sẹ̄
[illegible] Swan
藉 Chék / Chëā
藊 Pëén
藍 Lâm / *Nâ*
藎 Chīn
藏 Chông / Chōng / *Chēⁿᵍ* / *K'hàⁿᵍ*
藐 Beáou

15
藕 Gnaōu
[illegible] Ch'hip
藜 Lêy
藝 Gēy
蓏 *Lwá*
藟 Lúy
[illegible] Twá
藤 Têng / *Tîn*
藥 Yëák / *Yëŏh*
藩 Hwân
藭 Këûng
16
蘸 Chëèn
藹 Aé
藺 Līn
藾 Naē
蘀 T'hok
蘂 Lúy
蘄 Kê
蘅 Hêng
蘆 Loê / Lô
蘇 Soe

藬 Töêy
蘢 Lëûng
蘊 Wùn
蘋 Pìn
17
蘖 Gëet
蘚 Sëén
蘞 Lëém
蘡 Eng
蘧 { Kè / Kô }
蘩 Hwân
蘪 Bô
蘭 Lân
蘱 Chông
19
蘸 Chàm
蘼 Lêy
蘺 Lê
蘿 Hwân
虀 Bê
蘿 Lô
虆 Lûy

虍 Hoe
虎 Hoé
4
虐 Gëák
虒 Tô
虓 Haou
虔 K'hëên
處 { Ch'hé / Ch'hè }
虖 Hók
7
虗 He
虜 Loé
虞 Gê
虙 Bék
號 { Hô / Hō }
9
虢 K'hek
虧 K'hwuy
虩 } Hek
虪 }

虫 { T'hëûng / Hwúy }
4
蚪 Kêw
虰 Téng
虱 { Sek / *Sat* }
虳 Yëŏh
虵 Ê
虹 { Hêng / *K'heng* }
虺 { Hwúy / Wúy / Hòey }
蚊 { Bún / *Búng* }
蚋 Jöêy
蚌 Pāng
蚑 Kê
蚓 { Yín / *Kín* }
蚕 T'hëén
蚣 { Kong / *Kang* }
蚼 *Gneŏouh*
蚤 Cho
蚨 Hoô
蚩 Ch'he
蚪 Toé
5
蚯 K'hew

蚱 *T'hāy*
蚳 Tê
蚶 Ham
蚸 Taê
蚽 P'he
蚿 Hëên
蛀 { Choò / *Chèw* }
蛄 Koe
4
蛆 Ch'he
蛇 { Ê / Séâ / *Ch'hwâ* / *Chwâ* / Chāy / *T'hāy* }
蛈 Tëét
蛉 Lêng
蛋 { Tan / *Nooi*ng }
6
蛙 Wâ
蛤 [illegible]
蛟 [illegible]
蛦 Jē
蛣 Kit
蛾 Ê

蛤 Kap
蛩 K'hëung
7
蛸 { Seaou / Saou }
蛺 Këep
蛻 T'höèy
蛾 Gô
蜢 *Maī*ngh
蜀 Sëûk
蜂 { Hong / *P'hang* }
蜃 { Sín / Yin }
蜅 *P'hoó*
蜆 Hëén
蜇 Chëet
蜈 { Goê / *Géâ* }
蛷 Ch'hëŏh
蜉 Hoê
[illegible] { Lo[illegible] / [illegible] / *l·ō* }
蜍 Sê
8
蜘 Te
蜚 { Hwuy / Hwúy }

蜝 Kê
蜜 } Bit
蜜 }
蜞 K'hê
蜠 K'hwûn
蜦 { Lëûk / *Lék* }
蜣 { Këang / K'hëung }
蜻 Wá
蜾 Hoé
蜩 Teâou
蜫 K'hwun
蜮 Hék
蜼 Hwúy
蜴 { Ek / *Yëăh* }
蜻 Cheng
蜾 Ke
[illegible] { T[illegible] / K[illegible] }
蝃 Tèy
蜉 { P'hoê / Poe }
9
蝌 K'ho
蝗 Hông

艸 140
艹
虍 141
虫 142

9 I

142 虫

143 血

蝙 Pëén
蝚 Jêw
螮 Tèy
蝟 Wŭy
蝠 Hok
蝣 Yêw
蝤 Yêw
蝥 { Maôu / *Bâ* }
蝦 Hây
螫 Sek
蝱 Bêng
蝸 *Gëâ*
蝍 Ch'hip
蝴 Hoê
蝶 { Tëëp / *Yëăh* }
[illegible] O
10
螂 Lông
螃 Pông
螄 Soo
蛩 Këung
螉 { Ong / *Yëo^{ng}* }

螈 Gwân
融 Yûng
蚤 { Chó / *Chaóu* }
螓 Chîn
螗 Tông
螟 Bêng
[illegible] T'hëén
螢 Êng
螁 T'höèy
蟥 *Hwui^{ng}*
[illegible] *Lâ*
[illegible] Yëen
螫 Sek
螬 Chô
螭 Lê
螯 Gô
[illegible] Hâm
螣 Têng
蟔 Bék
螻 Loê
螼 K'hín
螽 Chëung

螺 { Lô / Lêy }
螿 { Chëang / *Chëo^{ng}* }
蟀 Sut
蟄 Tit
[illegible] Sok
蟋 { Sit / *Scëh* }
蟊 { Maôu / Boê }
12
蟒 Bóng
蟛 P'hêng
蟦 Pwŭy
蟟 Leâou
蟢 Hé
蟣 Ké
蟪 Hwŭy
蟫 { Chëén / Yîm }
蟬 Seên
蟯 { Jeâou / *Ch'heô* / *Giô* }
蟲 { T'hëûng / *T'hâng* }
蟳 { Sîm / *Chim* }

蟠 Hwân
[illegible] Kàn
蟶 { Ch'heng / *T'han* }
[illegible] *Keo^{ng}*
蟹 { Haē / *Hēy* }
蟻 { Gé / *Hëā* }
蟾 Sëêm
蠃 { Ló / Lô }
蠆 { Ch'haè / Bān }
蠍 Yëet
14
蠐 Chêy
蠓 Bông
蠔 { Ô / Hô }
蠖 Hoē
蠘 { Chëët / *Ch'heëh* }
[illegible] *Chwăn*
蠟 { Lăp / *Lăh* }
蠠 Bit
蠡 Léy
蠢 Ch'hún

[illegible] Naē
16
蠹 Toè
蠨 { Se / *Chè* }
蠭 Hong
蠮 Yëet
蠱 { Koé / Toé }
蠲 Kwan
蠥 Gëét
蠶 Ch'hân
蠻 Bân

血 { Hëet / *Höëyh* }
卹 Sut
衄 { Jëúk / Lok }
6
衆 Chëùng
衊 Bëét
[illegible] Lok

行 { Hêng / Hĕng / Hâng / Hăng / *Kĕⁿâ* }
衍 { Yēén / Yĕēn }
衎 K'hán
5
衒 Hēēn
術 Sút
衕 Tông
衖 Hāng
街 Key
7
衕 Yŭng
衙 Gây
9
衛 / 衞 } Öēy / Wōēy
衝 Ch'hēung
衡 { Heng / *Kĕⁿâ* }
衢 Kê

衣 { È / E }
卒 Chut
表 { Peáou / *Pĕó* }
衫 { San / *Sⁿa* }
4
衰 Sŏey
衲 Lăp
衵 Jit
衷 T'hēung
袁 Wân
衺 Sēâ
衽 Jím
衿 K'him
衾 K'him
袁 Wân
袂 Bēy
5
袈 { Kēa / *Ka* }
袋 { Taē / *Tāy* / *Tēy* }
袍 Paôu
袑 T'heaou
袒 Tān
袖 { Sēw / *Wuiⁿg* }

𧘿 Kăh
袗 Chín
袚 { Pwát / Hwut }
衮 Kwún
袠 Tēét
袢 P'hwàn
被 { Pē / P'hē / *P'hōēy* }
6
袱 Hók
袴 K'hoè
袵 Jím
袷 { Kēēp / *K'hăh* }
袺 Kēēt
袽 Jê
袼 { Kok / *Kŏh* }
袻 Jê
裁 Chaê
裂 { Lēét / *Lēĕh* }
7
𧙣 Jē
裌 *Kăyh*
裍 K'hwún

裎 Têng
裡 Lé
裒 Poê
裔 Ē
裕 Jē
裘 Kêw
裙 Kwûn
裛 Yip
補 Poé
裝 / 装 } Chong / *Cheⁿg*
裟 Say
8
裨 { Pe / Pê }
裧 Ch'hēêm
裯 Têw
裰 Twat
裱 { Peàou / Peáou / *Pōēy* / *Keáou* }
裳 Sēâng
裴 Pōēy
裼 { T'hek / *T'hăyh* }

裸 Ko
裹 Kó
製 Chè
裾 Ke
9
褅 Tèy
複 Hok
褊 Pēén
𧛅 Yaou
褌 { Kwun / *Kwuiⁿg* }
褎 Yēw
褐 Hat
褑 Wān
褒 Po
褓 Pó
褕 Jê
褘 { Wúy / Wûy }
褙 Pōèy
褚 Chó
10
褡 Tap
褥 Jēúk
褪 { T'hùn / *T'hooiⁿg* }

褧 Kéng
褫 T'hé
褰 { Kēén / K'hēen }
褱 Hwaê
褵 Lê
褲 K'hoè
褸 Lé
襔 *Mwⁿa*
褻 Sēet
襁 Kēáng
襄 Sēang
12
襇 { Kán / *Kéng* }
襊 Ch'hwat
襌 Tan
襍 Cháp
襑 Tām
襏 Poê
襖 Ó
襜 Ch'hēem
襛 *Àng*
襟 K'him

145 衣
146 襾
147 見
148 角
149 言

襠 Tong
襢 Tān
14
襡 Choo
襣 Pit
襤 Lâm
襘 Kwà
襦 Jê
襪 { Bwåt / *Böëyh*
襫 Sek
襭 K'hëet
襮 P'hòk
16
襯 { Ch'hìn / *Ch'hèng*
襱 Lëûng
襲 Sit
襺 Këén
襹 { Lek / *Lëuk*
襶 Taè
襻 P'hàn

襾 Hà
西 { Sey / *Sae*
要 { Yaou / Yaòu / *Böëyh* / *Peëngh*
6
覃 { T'hâm / Sîm / *Chîm*
覆 { Hok / Hoò / *P'hak*
覇 Pà
覈 Hèk

見 { Këèn / Hëēn / *Keèng*
4
規 Kwuy
覓 覔 } Bėk
覗 Sē
覘 Tëèm
覡 Hėk
8
覢 T'hëén
覦 Jê
覧 Lám
覩 Toé
親 Ch'hin
覫 P'hóng
覬 K'haé
覯 Koe
覰 Hò
覲 Kīn
12
覵 Hán
𧢈 Maé
覕 Pëet
覼 Lo
覺 Kak

𧢋 P'hìn
覿 Tòk
觀 { Kwan / Kwàn / *Kwⁿà*

角 { Kak / Lut
觔 Kin
觖 K'hwat
2
觚 Koe
觡 Koe
觝 Té
觟 Hwá
解 { Kaé / Kaè / Haē / *Kēy* / *T'haóu*
觥 Kong
7
觩 Kêw
觫 Sok
觱 Pit
觳 Hàt
觴 Sëang
12
觶 Tè
觸 { Ch'hëuk / *Tak*
觼 K'hwat

言 Gân
訂 Tèng
訃 Hoò
計 Kèy
3
訊 Sìn
討 T'hó
訏 { He / Hé
訐 K'hëet
訑 Tê
訒 Jīm
訓 Hwùn
訕 Sàn
訖 Git
託 T'hok
記 Kè
4
訛 Gô
訝 Gāy
訟 Sëûng
訢 Hîm
訣 Kwat
訥 Lut
訰 *Twⁿá*
訧 Yêw

訪 Hóng
設 Sëet
許 Hé; *K'hoé*; *Yín*
訏 Yīm
5
訴 Soè
訶 Hô; O; Ho; H^{n}o
診 Chín
註 Choò
証 Chìn
訾 Ch'hoó
訿 Ch'hoó
詁 Koé; Koē
詠 Poè
詆 Té
詈 Lē
詉 Lây
詎 Kē
詐 Chày
詑 Neé^{ng}; Neê^{ng}

詒 Ê
詔 Cheàou
評 P'hêng
詖 P'hê
詛 Choé
詞 Soô
詠 Ēng
6
詡 Hé
詢 Sûn
詣 Géy
試 Sè; *Ch'hè*
詧 Ch'hat
詩 Se
詫 Ch'hà; Ch'hày
詬 Koè
詭 K'hwúy; Gwaê
詮 Ch'hwan; Chwān
詰 K'hëet
話 Hwā; *Wā*
該 Kae
詳 Sëâng

詵 Sin
詹 Jëá
詶 Sêw; *Ch'héw*
詷 Chew
詹 Chëem
詼 K'höey
詽 Gëén
詾 Hëung
誠 Sêng
誂 T'heáou
誄 Lúy
誅 Tc
誆 Kòng; K'hòng
誇 K'hwa
7
誌 Chè
認 Jīn
誐 Gô
誑 Kòng
誒 *Hee^{ng}*
誓 Sē; *Chwā*
誕 Tān

誖 Pöēy
誘 *P'hoŏh*
誘 Yéw
誋 Gē
誚 Seàou; Saou
語 Gé; Gē; *Goó*
誡 Kaè
誢 Hëén
誣 Boô
誤 Chó
誩 Ch'hëuk
誤 Goē
誥 K'hò
誦 Sëūng
誨 Höèy
說 Swat; Söèy; *Söĕyh*; Wát; T'hwat; *T^{n}à*
8
誳 Chëang
誰 Sûy; *Chûy*

諜 Chëét
課 K'hò; *K'hôèy*
誶 Chút; Sùy
誸 Hēng
誹 Hwúy
誼 Gē
誾 Gîn
調 Teâou
諄 Chun; Tun
談 Tâm
諉 Wúy; Wūy
請 Ch'héng; *Ch'hë^{n}á*
諍 Chēng
諏 Choe
諒 Lëāng
諓 Ch'hëên
論 Lûn; Lūn
諗 Sím
諦 Pòng
諛 Jê
9
諜 Tëep

諝 Se
諟 Sē
諠 Swan
諤 Gòk
諦 Tèy
諧 Haê
諫 Kaè
諪 Têng
諫 Kàn
諫 Lát
諭 Jē
諮 Choo
諯 Yéw
諰 Gnay
諻 Hwúy
諱 Hwùy
諳 Am
諴 Hâm
諵 Lâm
諶 Sîm
諷 Hóng
諸 Choò; Che

149 言

150 谷

諹 Yâng
諺 Gān
諼 Swan
諾 Lók / *Ā* / *Aōu*
諿 Ch'hip
謀 Boê
謁 Yëet
謂 Wūy

10

謄 T'hëên / T'hêng
謅 Ch'haóu
謇 Këén
謊 Hóng
謎 Bē / Meē^{ng}
謐 Bit
謔 Hëak
謙 K'hëem / K'hëém
謚 Sē
講 Káng
謝 Sëā / *Chëā*
謟 T'hëém

謠 Yaôu
謨 Boê
謫 Tek
謬 Bēw
謭 Chëén
謏 Swá
謳 Oe
謴 Kwún
譟 Ch'haou
謶 Chit
譜 Chō
謹 Kín
謽 Këāng / *Këō^{ng}*
謾 Bān

12

譀 Hàm
譁 Hwâ
譹 Hō
諱 Hō
譆 He
證 Chìn
譧 Leâou
譌 Gô

謵 Hip
譎 Kwat
譊 Lô
譏 Ke
譓 Hwūy
譔 Chwān
譕 Boê
譖 Chòm
識 Sit / *Bat*
譙 Cheâou
譚 Tâm / *Chîm*

13

譜 P'hoé
譍 Èng
譡 Tòng
警 Kéng
譗 Chảp
譩 E
諢 Kwùn
譬 P'hè
譮 Haē
譯 Ėk

課 Kwà
謼 Hō
議 Gē

14

譴 K'hëèn
譶 Tảp
護 Hoē
譸 Chew
譅 Tảp
譽 Ê / Ē
讀 T'hỏk / *T'hảk* / Toē / *Taōu*
讁 Tek
讇 Loé
讆 *Wui^{ng}*
讃 *Chw^{n}à*
讄 Lúy

16

變 Pëèn / *Peè^{ng}*
讌 Yëèn
讎 Sêw
讒 Châm / Ch'hâm
讂 Këén

讓 Jëāng / *Nëō^{ng}* / *Ch'hëên*
讖 Ch'hàm
讗 Êy
讙 Hwan
讚 Chàn

20

讜 Tóng
讞 Hëèn
讟 Tỏk

谷 Kok
谿 K'hey
谽 / 豁 Hat

豆 Toē
豈 K'hé / K'haé
4
豉 *Seē^{ng}*
登 Kín
豊 Léy
8
豎 Sē / *K'hëā*
豍 Seē^{ng}
豋 Bȯk
䜺 Kín
豰 Kok
豐 Hong
12
豏 Sóng
豓 Yëēm
豔 Yëēm

豕 Sé
4
豙 Hwut
豖 Hwut
豘 Tûn
豛 Tok
豝 Pa
豞 Tok
豚 Tûn / *T'hûn*
豞 Hok
豟 Ek
豤 Gaē
象 Sëāng / *Ch'hëō^{ng}*
6
豢 Hwān
豣 Këen
豤 K'hwún
豥 Tok
豛 Ėk
豪 Hô
8
豵 Chòng
豷 Ėk
豫 Ē
豬 T'hûn

豬 Te
豭 Hây
10
豱 Wun
豳 Pin
豰 Loē
豷 È

豸 Chaē / Té / *T'hwā*
豹 Pà
豺 Ch'haē
4
豾 P'he
豿 Hak
貂 Teaou
6
貅 Hew
貊 Bek
貌 Maôu
貍 Lê
8
貎 Chéw
貒 T'hwán
貓 Beâou / *Bâ* / *Neaou*
貔 Pê

貝 Pōèy
貞 P'hók
貞 Cheng
負 Hoō / *Chëāng*
3
財 Chaê
貢 Kòng / K'hòng
4
貦 Gwán
貧 Pîn
貨 H^{n}ò / *Höèy*
販 Hwàn
貪 T'ham
5
貫 Kwàn / *Kwui^{ng}*
責 Chek
貯 T'hé
貰 Sè
貱 Pè
貲 Choo
貳 Jē
貴 Kwùy
貶 Hàm
買 Maé / *Báy* / *Béy*

貶 Pëén
貸 Taē
貹 Sèng
貯 Choò
貺 Hóng
費 Hwùy / Pè
貼 T'hëep / *T'hăyh*
貽 Ê
貿 Boē / *Baôuh*
賀 Hō
6
賁 Pè / P'hun
賂 Loē
賆 Hòng
賃 Jīm
賄 Yēw
資 Choo
賋 Tē
賈 Káy / Kày / Koé
賉 Sut
賊 Chék / *Ch'hȧt*

豆 151
豕 152
豸 153
貝 154

154 貝
155 赤
156 走

賑 Chín 7
賒 Sëa
賛 Chân
賫 K'haè
賏 Eng
賙 Sò
賔 / 賓 Pin
賕 Kêw
賙 Chew 8
賖 Lëâng
賚 Laē
賜 Sòò
賀 Tè
賞 Sëáng / *Sëó^{ng}*
賠 Pöêy
賥 Ke
賢 Hëên / *Gaôu*
賣 Maē / *Bāy* / *Bēy*
賤 Chëēn / *Chw^{n}ā*

賖 Sëa
賦 Hoò
賧 Tām
賨 Chông
質 Chit / Chè
賭 Tē 9
賭 Toé / *Keáou*
賰 Toé
賵 Ch'hap
賮 Chín
賯 Hoē
賱 Kêng
賰 Ch'hún
賳 Yëèn
賱 Wún
賲 Pó
賳 Chae
賴 Naē / *Lwā*
賵 Ch'hèng
賶 Hòng
賷 Peàou

賸 Ch'hòng 10
賹 Chey
贊 Pè
賾 Hat
贈 Sēng / Sīn / Yīn
賺 Chëēm
賻 Hoō
賽 Ê
購 Koe / Koè
賽 Saè
賾 Chek
贅 Sëang
贀 È
贇 P'hin
贂 Ch'hím
贄 Loê
贄 Chè
贅 Chöèy
贈 Chēng 12
贊 Chàn
贌 *Pak*

贍 Sëēm
贏 Êng / *Yë^{n}â*
贐 Chín 14
贔 Kè
贓 Lām
贓 Chong / *Che^{ng}*
贔 Pē
贖 Sëuk / *Ch'héw*
贗 Gān
贘 Ch'hèng
贛 K'hòng

赤 Ch'hek / *Ch'hëăh*
赦 Sëà
赧 Lán 5
赫 Hek
赬 Ch'héng
赭 Chëá

走 Choé / *Chaôu*
赳 Kéw
赴 Hoò
赶 Kán / *Kw^{n}á* 3
起 K'hé
趵 K'hêw
趹 Kwat
赾 K'hín / *Ch'hë^{n}à*
趁 T'hìn. 5
趂 T'hìn / *T'hán* / *T'hàn*
趃 Tëét
趄 Ch'he / Choe
超 T'heaou
趈 P'hwán
趇 Jip
趉 K'hèw
越 Wát
趍 Hëèm 6
趌 K'hwúy
趏 Kwat
趐 *Sit*

趕 Kán
趖 So
趘 { Jek / Jëuk
趙 { Teāou / *Tëō*
8
趛 { Sìm / Gím
趟 Ch'hëāng
趨 Twat
趡 *$Nooi^{ng}$*
趣 Ch'hè
趦 Choo
10
趨 Ch'he
趜 Hëùng
趯 Ch'hék
趬 Leâou
趲 Chán

足 { Chëuk / Choò
趶 { Köëy / Oo / Woo
4
趺 Hoo
趼 Lan
趾 Ché
跂 { Kê / K'hè
5
跋 Pwát
跌 { Tëët / *Pwăh*
跎 Tô
跏 { Këa / Kay
跑 Paôu
踇 Bó
跓 Chē
跕 { Lëem / *Ch'hëët*
跒 K'hèw
跚 San
跛 P'hó
距 Kē
6
跟 Kin
跠 È
跡 Chek

跣 Sëén
跨 { K'hwa / K'hwà
跭 *Hwăh*
跢 Tà
𨀈 *Loŏh*
跪 Kwūy
跫 K'hëung
跬 { K'hwúy / *Hwăh*
路 Loē
跊 Waé
跲 K'hap
跳 T'heàou
7
跼 Këuk
跽 Kē
踀 Ch'hëuk
踃 Seaou
踅 Chëet
踍 *K'ho̤ô*
䟽 } Soo
踈 }
踊 Yúng

壴 Lò
8
踏 { Táp / *Tăh*
䟾 Twat
踐 Cheén
踘 Këuk
踢 { T'hek / *T'hat*
踣 Hoò
踥 *Ch'heăouh*
踜 { Lëùng / Lèng
踤 T'hut
踝 { Hwá / K'höéy / K'höèy
踞 Kè
踋 Tê
踧 Sëuk
踦 Kê
9
踰 Jê
䟿 *Chát*
踵 Chëúng
踸 Ch'hím
踹 T'hwán
踼 Tōng

踽 Hé
踾 *Peĕh*
踿 *Ch'heăouh*
蹀 Tëëp
蹁 P'hëen
蹂 Jéw
蹄 Têy
10
蹆 T'húy
蹇 Këén
𨂿 Lăh
蹈 Tō
蹉 { Ch'ho / Ch'hò
蹊 { Hêy / K'he
蹋 Táp
𨃊 { Pwân / *$Pw^{n}â$*
蹐 Chek
蹕 Pit
蹘 Leâou
蹙 Ch'hëuk
𨄸 Ch'hêy
蹜 Sëuk

蹝 Sé
蹟 Chek
蹠 Chek
蹢 Tek
蹣 { Bwân / Pwân / *$Pw^{n}â$*
蹤 Chong
12
蹨 { Jëén / Jëên / Lëén
蹩 P'hëet
𨆻 Toô
躚 Ch'hëen
蹯 Hwân
躕 Toô
𨆊 Pëăng
蹲 Chun
蹵 Ch'hëuk
蹴 Ch'hëuk
蹶 { K'hwat / K'höèy
蹺 K'heaou
蹻 { K'heaou / Keáou
𨇨 *Gëăh*

走 156
足 157
𧾷

9 L

157 足

158 身

159 車

踈 Sò
躂 T'hat
躃 P'hek
躅 Tók
蹚 *Tang*
躇 Tê
14
躊 Têw
躋 Chey
蹁 Pīn
躍 Yëák
躐 Láp
躑 Ték
躓 Chè
躔 Tëên
16
躅 Ch'hok
躚 Ch'hëen
躡 Lëëp
躩 K'hëak

身 Sin
躬 Këung
躭 Tam
6
躲 Tó
躳 Këung
躶 Kó
軀 K'he
軁 *Nooi^ng*

車 { Ke / *Ch'hëa* }
軋 Wat
軌 K'hwúy
軍 Kwun
3
軏 Gwát
軒 Hëen
軕 T'hun
軓 Hwān
軔 Jīm
4
軘 T'hn
軛 *Ăyh*
軟 { Jwán / Lwán / *Lŭn* / *Nooi^ng* }
5
軧 Té
軫 Chín
軎 P'hat
軶 Ek
軷 Pwát
軸 Tëúk
軹 Ché
軻 K'ho
軼 { Tëët / Yit }

6
較 Kaðu
輅 Loē
輈 Chew
載 { Chaè / Chaē }
輊 Chè
7
輐 Lwán
輥 Lún
輒 Tëep
輓 Bwán
輔 Hoō
輕 { K'heng / *K'hin* }
8
輗 Gêy
輙 Tëep
輛 Lëāng
輜 Choo
輝 Hwuy
輞 Bóng
輟 Twat
輦 Lëén
輨 Kwán
輪 Lûn

輩 / 軰 } Pöèy
9
輭 Jwán
輯 Ch'hip
輳 Choè
輵 *Waĕ^ng h*
輶 Yêw
輸 { Se / *Soo* }
輻 Hok
10
輾 { Tëén / Lëén }
輿 Ê
轂 Kok
轄 Hat
轅 Wân
轘 Kwún
轆 Lòk
轉 { Chwán / *Tooi^ng* }
12
轍 Tëët
轎 { Keāou / *Kēō* }
轔 Lîn
轗 K'hám

轝 Ê
轞 Lām
轟 Eng
轡 Pè
轣 Lék
轤 Loê

辛160 辰161 辵162 辶

辛 Sin
𨐨 Koe
6
辟 Pē / Pit / P'hek
辠 Chöëy
辣 Låt
辢 Låt / Lwåt / *Lwăh*
9
辦 Pëën
辨 Pëën
辧 Pëën / *Pān*
辩 Pëën
辭 Soô / *Sê*
辯 Pëën

辰 Sîn
辱 Jëük
農 Lông

辵 Ch'hëak
辻 Ch'hëen
迂 迃 Oo / Woo
迄 Git
迅 Sîn
迆 É
4
迌 Jēw
迍 Tun
迎 Gêng / Gêng / *Gëⁿa*
近 Kîn
迓 Gäy
返 Hwán / *Tooiⁿᵍ*
迕 Gnoé
5
迢 Teåou
迥 Kéng
迦 Kay / Këa
迨 Taē
迪 Tëuk / Tėk
迫 Pek
迭 Tëët

迮 Chek
迯 Tô
述 Sút
6
迷 Bêy / *Bê*
迸 Péng
迹 Chek / *Chëăh*
迺 Naé
追 Tuy
退 T'höèy / *T'hèy* / *Tày*
送 Sòng / *Sàng*
适 Kwat
逃 Tô
逄 Pông
逅 Hoē
逆 Gėk / *Kăyh*
7
逋 Poê
逌 Yêw
逍 Seaou
透 T'hoè / *T'hadu*
逐 Tëük / *Ták*

逑 Kêw
逓 Têy
途 Toê
逕 Kèng
逖 T'hek
逗 Toē
這 Chéy / Cháy
通 T'hong
逝 Sē
逞 T'héng
速 Sok
造 Chō / Ch'hò
逡 Chùn
逢 Hông
連 Lëên / *Neēⁿᵍ*
8
逩 P'hùn
逯 Lëük
逫 Twat
逭 Kwán
逮 Taē
週 Chew

迌 Tô
進 Chìn
送 Sòng
逵 Kwûy
逶 Wuy
逷 T'hek
逸 Yit
9
遊 遊 Yêw
逼 Pek
逾 Jê
遁 Tūn
遂 Sūy
遄 Kay
遄 Ch'húy
遇 Gō / *Goō*
遉 Wūn
遍 Pëèn
過 Ko / Kò / *Köèy* / *Kwa*
遏 At

162 辵 辶

163 邑 阝

遐 Hây
遑 Hông
遒 Sêw
道 Tō
達 Tát
違 Wûy
10
遘 { Koe / Koè }
遀 Ch'hè^{ng}
遙 Yaôu
遛 Lêw
遜 Sùn
遝 Táp
遞 Tēy
遠 { Wán / Wàn / *Hwui*^{ng} }
遡 Soé
遤 Sút
遢 T'hap
遣 Kip
遣 K'hëén
遫 Sut
適 { Sek / Tøk }

遨 Gô
遬 { T'hit / Sëuk / Sok }
遭 Cho
遮 { Chëa / *Jëa* / *Chay* }
遯 Tūn
12
遲 Tê
遴 Lîn
遵 Chun
遷 Ch'hëen
選 Swán
遹 Yit
遺 { Wûy / Kwūy }
遼 Leâou
遽 Kè
避 Pē
邀 Ch'hëém
邀 { Heaou / *Yëò* }
邁 Maē
邂 Haē
邃 Sùy

邅 Chëen
還 { Hwân / *Hêng* }
14
邇 Jé
邈 Beáou
邊 { Pëen / *Pee*^{ng} }
邏 Lō
邐 Lé

邑 Yip
邕 Yung
邖 San
邙 Bông
邛 Gëûng
4
邠 Pin
邢 Hâng
那 { Ná / *Nā* }
郍 { Nô / Nō }
邦 Pang
邧 Gwân
邨 Ch'hun
邪 { Sëâ / Yëâ }
5
邯 Ham
邰 T'hae
邶 Lâm
邱 { K'hew / *K'hoo* }
邲 Pít
邳 P'he
邴 Pèng
邵 Seāou
邶 Pöēy

邸 Té
6
邽 Kwuy
郱 Te
郁 Hëuk
郃 K'hap
郅 Chit
郇 Sûn
郊 Kaou
7
郗 { He / T'he }
郜 K'hok
郝 Hek
郎 { Lông / *Nê*^{ng} }
郟 Këep
郡 Kwūn
郢 T'héng
郣 Pút
郤 K'hëak
8
部 Poē
郭 { Kok / *Köēyh* }
郯 Tâm
郲 Laê

郵 Yêw
9
都 Toe
郿 Bê
鄂 Gók
鄍 É
鄆 Wūn
10
鄏 Jëuk
鄒 { Choe / *Chey* }
鄔 { Oe / Oé / Oó / Woó }
鄉 { Hëang / Hëàng / *Hëo*^{ng} }
鄙 P'hé
鄢 Yëen
12
鄧 Tēng
鄬 Wūy
鄭 { Tēng / *Tai*^{ng} }
鄰 Lîn
鄲 Tan
鄴 Gëép
鄶 Köèy

鄹 Choe
酆 Hong
酇 Chàn
酈 { Lê / Lėk }

酉 Yéw
酊 Téng
酋 Sêw
3
酌 Chëak
配 P'höèy
酎 Tēw
酏 Ê
酒 Chéw
4
酕 Mô
酖 Tam
酗 Hà
5
酮 Hò
酡 Tô
酢 Chók
酣 Ham
酤 Koe
酥 Soe
6
䣯 Hò
酧 Sêw
酩 Béng
酪 Lók
酬 Sêw
7
酲 Têng

酴 Toê
酵 K^{n}à
酶 Böêy
酷 K'hok
酸 { Swan / *Swui*^{ng} }
酹 Lūy
酺 Poê
8
醁 Lëuk
醃 Yëem
醅 Pöêy
醇 Sûn
醓 Tām
醉 Chùy
醋 Ch'hoè
9
䤄 Gëên
醑 Jé
醒 { Seng / Séng / *Ch'ha*^{ng} }
醶 Hám
10
醜 Ch'héw
醞 Wùn

醡 Chày
醢 Haé
醨 Lê
醪 Lô
醫 / 毉 } E
醬 { Chëàng / *Chëô*^{ng} }
12
醮 { Cheāou / *Chëō* }
醪 Lô
醯 Hey
醲 Lông
醴 Léy
醹 Jô
醺 Hwun
醻 Sêw
釀 Jëâng
釁 Hìn
釃 Soo
釅 Gëêm

釆 Pëên
采 Ch'haé
釋 Sek

里 Lé
重 { Tëūng / *Têng* / Tëūng / *Tāng* }
野 Yëá
4
量 { Lëâng / *Nëō*^{ng} / Lëāng / *Nëō*^{ng} }
釐 Lê

邑163
阝
酉164
釆165
里166

9 M

167 金

金 Kim
釖 To
釗 Cheaou
釘 Teng / Tèng
針 Chëem / Chim
釜 Hoó
釞 Tip
3
釣 Teàou / *Tëò*
釤 Sàm
釦 K'hoè / *K'haòu*
釧 Ch'hwàn / *Ch'hui*ⁿᵍ / *Sŏh*
釵 Ch'haé / T'hey
4
釾 Yëâ
鈀 Pa / *Pây*
鈁 *Hwang*
鈄 T'hoé
鈅 Gwàt
鈇 Hoo
鈍 Tun / Tūn
鈎 Koe
鈐 K'hëêm

鈔 Say / Ch'hà / Ch'haou
鈕 Léw
鈡 Kóng
5
鈴 Lêng
鈸 Pwàt / *Pwăh*
鈺 Gëúk
鈿 Tëên / Tëēn
鉀 Kăh
鉄 Tëėt / T'hëet
鉅 Kē
鉆 K'hëêm / Sëem
鉉 Hëên
鉋 Paōu
鉏 Choe
鉗 K'hëêm / *K'heê*ⁿᵍ
鉛 Yëên
鉞 Wàt
鉢 Pwat / *Pwăh*
鉤 *Kaou*
鉦 Cheng

鉧 Bóng
6
鉶 Hêng
鉸 *Ka*
銀 Gîn
銃 Ch'hëùng / *Ch'hèng*
銅 Tông / *Tâng*
銇 Lūy
銌 Chūn
銍 Chit
銎 K'hëung / *K'heng*
銑 Sëén
銒 Gëang
銓 Ch'hwan / Swān
銕 T'hëet
銖 Choo / Soô / *T'he*
銙 K'hwá
銘 Béng
銚 Teāou
銜 Hâm / Hām / *Kâm*

銲 Hān
7
鋭 Jöēy
銶 Kêw
銷 Seaou / Sô
鋂 Böêy
鋃 Lông
鋄 Këém
鋈 Ak
鋉 Sok / *Sŏh*
鋍 Pút
鋏 Këep
鋑 Chùn
鋒 Hong
鋛 Ch'hwàn / *Kwⁿá*
鋟 Ch'hím
鋤 T'hê
鋩 Bông / *Mat*ⁿᵍ
鋪 P'hoe / P'hoò
8
鋼 Kong / *Ke*ⁿᵍ / Kòng / *Kè*ⁿᵍ

鋸 Kè
錄 Lëúk
錎 Hâm
錐 Chuy
錗 Öey / Wöey
錘 Sûy / T'hûy
錙 Choo
錚 *Ch'hai*ⁿᵍ
錠 Tēng / *Tèⁿā*
錡 Kê
錢 Chëên / *Cheê*ⁿᵍ
錣 Twat
錤 Ke
錦 Kím
錧 Kwán
錫 Sek / *Sëăh*
錁 Koè
錯 Ch'hoè / Ch'hok
鍁 Hëem
9
鍊 Lëēn
鍋 O

鍈 Jwān
鍍 Toē
鍛 T'hwàn
鍠 Hông
鍡 Öey / Wöey
鍤 Ch'hap
鍥 Këet / *Kăyh*
鍪 Maôu
鍬 Ch'heaou
鍭 Hoê
鍵 Këēn
鍼 Chim
鍾 Chëung / *Cheng*
10
鎏 Lêw
鎔 Yûng / *Yëô*ⁿᵍ
鎖 Só
鎗 Ch'heang / *Ch'hëo*ⁿᵍ
鎚 T'hûy
鎛 P'hok
鎜 Pwân
鎞 Pey

鎡 Choo
鎣 Ēng
鎧 K'haé
鎩 Sat
鎬 Kò
鎮 Tìn
鎰 Yit
鏁 Só
鐰 Koê
鏆 Kwàn
鏇 { Chëēn / Chwān }
鏊 Gō
鏌 Bòk
鏑 Tek
鏕 Lók
鏗 { K'hëen / *K'hëang* }
鏘 Ch'hëang
鏓 T'hong
鏞 Yûng
鏟 Sán
鏡 { Kèng / *Kē^{n}à* }

鏤 Loê
鏥 { *Sèw* / *Sëen* }
鏨 Châm
鏵 Hwâ
鏷 P'hok
12
鏺 { P'hwat / *P'hwăh* }
鐃 { Laôu / Naôu }
鐄 Hông
鐇 *P'hooi^{ng}*
鐕 Ch'heém
鐘 { C'hëung / *Cheng* }
鐙 Tèng
鐮 Lëêm
鐫 Chùn
鐱 Këêm
鐲 Tók
鐳 Luy
鐵 { T'hëet / *T'heĕh* }
鐶 Hwân
鐺 { Tong / T'heng }

鐸 Tók
鑤 P'haôuh
14
鑄 Choò
鑊 Hoē
鑌 Pin
鑐 Ch'hew
鑑 Kàm
鑩 Bêng
鑠 Sëak
鑢 Lē
鑣 P'heaou
16
鑗 Lék
鑪 Loê
鑰 { Yëák / *Yëŏh* }
鑱 Ch'ham
鑲 { Séang / *Sëo^{ng}* }
18
鑵 { Kwàn / *Kw^{n}à* }
鑼 Lê
鑾 Lwân
鑿 { Ch'hók / *Ch'hàk* }
钁 K'hok

鑽 { Chwàn / *Chui^{ng}* }

長 { Tëáng / Tëâng / Tëāng / Chëáng / *Tëó^{ng}* / *Tē^{ng}* / *Tëô* }
𨲠 Lò

門 { Bûn / *Mooi^{ng}* }
門 { *Ch'hw^{n}à* / *Kwae^{ng}* / *Wae^{ng}* }
閃 Sëém
3
閆 Yëêm
閈 Hân
閉 Pè
4
閪 *T'hooi^{ng}*
開 { K'hae / *K'hwuy* }
閎 Hông
閏 { Jūn / *Lūn* }
閑 Hân
閒 { Hân / *Êng* / Ân }
間 { Kan / Kàn / *Kae^{ng}* }
閔 Bín
5
閘 Chăh
閟 Pò
6
閣 { Kok / *Kŏh* }
閤 K'hap
閥 Hwàt

金 167
長 168
門 169

閦 Ch'hëuk
閨 Kwoy
閩 Bân
7
閫 K'hwún
閬 { Lông / Lōng
閭 Lê
閱 Wȧt
8
閶 Ch'hëang
閹 Yëom
閻 Yëêm
閽 Hwun
閾 Hėk
闀 Wa^{ngh}
闃 K'hek
闇 { Àm / Am / Ám
闆 P'hán
闈 Wûy
闉 { Yëen / Yin
闊 K'hwat / *K'hwăh*
闋 K'hwat

闌 Lân
闍 Toe
闐 T'hëên
10
闑 Gëėt
闔 K'hap
闕 K'hwat
闒 T'hàm
闚 Kwuy
12
關 { Kwan / *$Kw^{n}a$*
闓 K'haou
闞 { Hám / K'hàm
闡 Ch'hëén
闢 Pit
闛 Tòng
闤 Hwân
闥 T'hat
闠 *Lăyh*

阜 自 } Hoō
阡 Ch'hëen
阨 { *Ăyh* / Ek
阪 { Hwán / Pwán
4
阭 阢 } Yín
阮 { Gwán / Wán / *Wu^{tng}*
防 { Hông / *$H\hat{e}^{ng}$*
5
阻 Choé
阼 Ch'hoè
阿 { Á / O
陀 T
陂 Pe
附 Hoō
陋 Loē
陌 Bėk
降 { Kàng / Hâng
限 Ān
7
陛 Pē
陜 Sëém

陞 Seng
陟 T'hek
陡 { Toé / *Táng*
院 { Yëēn / *$E\bar{e}^{ng}$*
陣 Tīn
除 Tê
8
陪 { Pöêy / Pöēy
陬 Choe
陰 Yim
陲 Sûy
陳 { Tîn / Tīn / *Tân*
陴 Pê
陵 Lêng
陶 { Yaôu / Tô
陷 Hām
陸 { Lëúk / *Lėk*
9
陽 Yâng
陾 Jëûng
隂 Yim
隄 Tey

隅 Gô
隆 Löûng
隈 { Öey / Wöey
隊 Tūy
隍 Hông
階 { Kae / *Key*
10
隔 { Kek / *Kăyh*
隕 Wún
隖 Oé
隗 { Gwúy / Gwûy
隘 Aè
隙 隟 } K'hek / *K'hëăh*
際 Chèy
隠 Yín
障 { Chëàng / *$Ch\ddot{e}\hat{o}^{ng}$*
12
隤 Töêy
隌 T'hām
隒 T'hëēm
隧 { Sūy / Tūy
隨 Sûy

險 Hëém
隩 Ò
14
隮 Chey
隰 Sip
隱 Yín
隳 Höey
隲 Chit

隶 Taē

隸 } Lēy
隷 }

隹 Tuy

隻 { Chek / *Chëăh*

隼 Chún

雀 { Ch'hëak / *Chăyh*

2

雁 Gān

推 Kwuy

雄 { Hëûng / *Hêng*

雅 Gnáy

集 Chip

雇 Koò

5

雉 { Tē / *T'hê*

雊 Koè

雋 Chùn

雌 Ch'he

雍 Yung

雎 Ch'he

6

雒 Lók

雘 Gák

雕 Teaou

雖 Săy

雖 Suy

10

雙 { Song / *Sang*

雛 Ch'he

雜 Cháp

雝 Yung

雞 Key

離 { Lê / Lō

難 { Lân / Lān / *Ŏh*

雨 { É / È / *Hoē*

雩 Ê

雪 { Swat / *Sŭyh*

雫 *Nw^{n}á*

4

雪 *Sŭyh*

雯 Bûn

雰 Hwun

雲 { Yîn / *Hwún*

5

零 { Lêng / *Lân*

雷 Lûy

雹 P'haòuh

雺 Bông

電 { Tëēn / *Nā*

需 Se

7

霂 Bók

霄 { Seaou / *Ch'hëo*

霅 Sap

霆 Têng

震 Chìn

霈 P'haè

霉 Bôëy

8

霍 Hok

霎 Sëep

霏 Hwuy

霑 Tëem

霓 Gêy

霖 Lîm

9

霝 Lêng

霜 { Song / *Se^{n}g*

霞 Hây

霢 Bék

10

霡 Bék

霤 Léw

霧 Boō

[illegible] Swat

霪 Yîm

霫 Sip

12

霰 Sàn

露 Loō

霸 Pà

霹 P'hek

霽 Chèy

霾 Baê

16

靂 { Lék / *Lăyh*

靄 Aé

靆 Taē

靈 Lêng

靉 Aé

隶 171
隹 172
雨 173

174 青
175 非
176 面
177 革
178 韋

靑 } Ch'heng
青 } *Ch'haing*
靖 Chēng
靘 T'hnā 7
靚 Chēng
靛 { Tëēn / Tān
靜 { Chēng / *Chaing*

非 Hwuy
靠 K'hò
靡 Bé

面 { Bëēn / *Bīn*
酐 Hān
䩉 *P'hēy* 5
靤 Ch'haóu
䩕 Yaóu
䩖 Neàou
靦 T'hëén
[illegible] *Kaêng* 9
[illegible] K'héw
靧 Höèy
靨 Yëém

革 Kek 4
靴 Hëa
靭 Yín
[illegible] Jëūng
靸 Sap
鞅 Yàng 6
[illegible] K'hoè
鞋 { *Êy* / Haê
鞍 { An / *Wna*
鞏 { K'hëung / Këúng
鞓 T'héng
鞗 Teâou
鞘 { Saou / *Sëò* / Ch'heàou 8
鞚 K'hòng
鞟 Kok
鞛 Póng
鞞 Péng
鞠 Këuk
鞦 Ch'hew
鞫 Këuk
鞬 Këen

鞭 Pëen 10
鞵 Haê
鞶 Pwân
[illegible] Sé
鞾 Hëa 13
[illegible] *Àng*
韁 { Këang / *Këong*
韃 T'hat
韆 Ch'hëen
韈 { Bëét / Bwát

韋 Wúy
韍 Hwut 6
韐 K'hap
韓 Hân
韔 Tëàng
韘 Tëép
韙 Wúy 10
韜 T'ho
韞 Wùn
韠 Pit
韡 Wúy

非 { Kéw / *Koó*
𩇯 Kéw
𩇷 Sëem

音 Yim
韵 Wūn
5
韶 Seâou
韻 Wūn
響 Hëáng

頁 { Yëëp / *Yëăh*
頂 Téng
頃 K'héng
3
項 Hāng
順 Sūn
頄 Kwûy
頇 Han
須 Se
4
頊 Hëuk
頌 Sëūng
頍 K'hwúy
頎 { Kê / Ch'hëuk
頏 K'hòng
預 Wún
頉 Ē
頑 Gwân
頔 Chím
頒 Pan
頓 { Bûn / *Ch'heĕh*
頞 Wut
頓 { Tùn / *Tooīng*
5
頕 Ch'he

頗 { P'ho / P'hó
領 { Léng / *Nēⁿá*
6
頞 { At / *Wăh*
頟 Gék
頠 Gwúy
頡 K'hëet
頤 / 頥 } Ê
頫 T'heàou
7
頭 { T'hoê / *T'haôu*
頰 Këep
頱 Lwát
頷 Gīm
頲 T'héng
頴 Éng
頷 Ām
頸 Kēng
頹 Maōu
頺 { T'hut / *Töëy*
8
頻 Pîn
頼 Lìm

顆 K'hò
顀 Chūy
9
顋 { Soo / Sae
題 Têy
額 { Gėk / *Hëăh*
顏 Gân
顒 Gėûng
10
願 Gwān
顙 Sóng
顛 Tëen
類 Lūy
顖 Sìn
顡 Gwaē
顢 Bwân
12
顣 Ch'hëuk
顩 Chím
顥 Hō
顦 Cheâou
顧 Koè
顫 { Chëèn / *Seĕh*
14
顯 { Hëén / Gáp

顰 Pîn
顱 Loê
顳 Jëėp

非 179
音 180
頁 181

182 風
183 飛
184 食

風 Hong / Hóng / *Pooi*^{ng}
凬 Hong
2
颫 Hoô
颬 Hay / *Ha*
颮 Léw
颭 Chëem
颯 Sap
颵 Hwut
颰 Hwut
颲 Pút
3
颶 Kē
颸 Hwut
颼 Soo
颺 Yâng / *Ch'hëô*^{ng} / *Yē*^{n}*ā*
10
颻 Yaôu
颾 Soe
飋 So
飍 Sut
飀 Le
飃 P'heaou
飄 P'heaou

飌 Töêy
飇 P'heaou

飛 Hwuy
飜 Hwuy

食 Sït / *Chëăh* / Soō
2
飡 Ch'han
飢 Ke / *Yaou*
飤 Soō
飧 Sun
4
飩 Tûn / T'hùn / *Tooi*^{ng}
飪 Jím
飫 È
飭 T'hit
飲 Yím
飯 Hwán / Hwān / *Pooi*^{ng}
飱 Sun
5
飴 Ê
飶 Pē
飷 *Chë*^{n}*á*
飸 *Hwui*^{ng}
飼 Soō / *Ch'hē*
飽 Paôu / *Pá*
飾 Sek

飿 Tut
6
餂 T'hëém
蝕 Sït / *Seĕh*
餃 Paôu
餅 *Pë*^{n}*á*
餈 Choô
餉 Hëàng
餡 Bám
養 Yáng / Yāng / *Yëô*^{ng}
餌 Jō
7
餐 Ch'han
餑 P'hùt
餒 Löéy
餓 Gō
餔 Poô / Poē
餕 Chùn
餗 Sok
餖 K'haŏuh / *Kaŏuh*
餘 E
餝 Sek

8
餚 Gnaôu
餛 Hwûn
餳 Ch'heng
餜 Kó / *Köéy*
餞 Chëén
餠 Péng / *Pë*^{n}*á*
餧 È
餡 Nā
餤 Tâm
館 Kwán
餴 Pëung
9
餪 Jwán / Lwán
餬 Hoô
餰 Këen
餮 T'hëet
餱 Hoô
餲 Aé
10
餼 Hè
餿 Soè
餽 Kwūy
饁 Yëep

饅 Bân / *Bûn*
饛 Ch'hông / *Ch'hâng*
饈 Sew
饉 Kîn
12
饋 Kwūy
饌 Chwān / *Chuīng*
饐 Ch'hè
饕 Hâm
饐 È
饑 Ke
饒 Jeâou
13
饘 *Köëyh*
饔 Yung
饆 Chăyh
饇 Ho
饖 Öèy / Wöèy
饗 Heáng
饘 Chëen
饞 Ch'hâm
饜 Yëem / Yëèm

首 Séw / Sèw / *Ch'héw*
馗 Kwûy
馘 Hék

香 Hëang / *Hëong* / *P'hang*
馚 Hwun
5
馛 P'hut
馞 Put
馥 Hëuk
10
馧 Wun
馨 Heng / *Hëna*
馫 Gwûy

馬 Má / *Báy*
馭 Gē
馮 Pêng / *Pâng* / Pông
3
馱 Tô
馲 Lók
馳 Tê
馴 Hwûn / Sûn
馵 Choò
馹 Jit
駁 Pak
駉 Gông
駍 Góng
駃 Kwat / K'hwaè
5
駉 Keng
駐 Chō
駑 Noê
駒 K'he
駓 P'he
駕 Kày
駘 T'hae / T'haē
駙 Hoō

駛 Soó
駜 Pè
駝 Tô
駟 Soò
6
駣 Teâou
駪 Sin
駬 Jé
駭 Haé
駮 Pak
[illegible]
[illegible]
7
駵 Lêw
駾 Tûy
駿 Chùn
騁 P'hèng
騂 Sin
騃 Gaé
8
騅 Tuy
騈 Lëên
騋 Laê
騌 Chong / *Chang*
騍 K'hò

騏 Kê
騎 K'hê / *K'hëâ*
騐 Gëèm
騑 Hwuy
9
騖 Boō
騗 P'hëèn / P'hëet / Peén
騤 Kwûy
騧 Wâ
10
[illegible] K'heen
騮 Lêw
騰 T'hâng / [illegible]
騭 Ch'h
騵 Gwân
騶 Choo
騷 So
騯 Hong
騸 Sëèn
騾 Lô
驁 Bék
驁 Gô

食184
首185
香186
馬187

187 馬
188 骨
189 高
190 髟

驂 Ch'ham
驃 P'heàou
驄 Ch'hong
驅 K'he
12
驈 Yit
驊 Hwâ
驌 Sëuk
驍 Heaou
驎 Lîn
驕 K[illegible]
[illegible] Gê
驖 T'hëet
驗 Gëèm
驢 Lô
驚 { Keng / *Kèⁿà* }
驛 { Ėk / *Yëàh* }
驟 Choē
17
驪 Lê
驤 Sëang
驥 Kè
[illegible] Këén

驩 Hwan
驪 Lê
[illegible] Hwàn

骨 Kwut
[illegible] *Taiⁿᵍ*
骭 Hãn
骬 Woo
[illegible] Pà
骯 K'hòng
[illegible] Wat
[illegible] Sëén
骰 { Toê / *Taðu* }
[illegible] K'hay
[illegible] Koe
6
骸 Haê
[illegible] Tuy
骼 *K'ayh*
[illegible] { *Nêⁿᵍ* / *T'hēⁿᵍ* }
骾 { Kéng / *Kàiⁿᵍ* }
8
骿 { Pëên / *P'hëⁿa* }
髆 P'hok
[illegible] Gëèn
[illegible] K'he
髏 Loê
12
[illegible] *Tàng*

髑 Tók
髒 Chòng
髓 { Ch'húy / *Ch'höey* }
體 T'héy

高 { Ko / *Kwân* }
敲 K'heáou

髟 Pew
髡 K'hwun
髢 { T'hèy / Têy }
4
髣 Hóng
髦 Mô
髧 Tám
髫 Teâou
髭 Choo
髮 Hwat
[illegible] K'hëe
髲 Pē
髴 Hwut
6
髻 { Kèy / *Köèy* / K'hok }
[illegible] [illegible]ew
髽 C[illegible]wâ
8
鬃 { Chong / *Chàng* / *Cháng* }
鬆 { Song / *Sang* }
鬈 Kwân
[illegible] *Ch'háng*
鬚 { Soo / *Sae* }

鬀 Se
鬇 Cheeng
鬡 Ga
鬌 Súy
鬒 Chín
鬆 Chóng
鬖 Sàm
12
鬛 { Se / Ch'heu
[illegible] p
[illegible] au
鬢 Pìn
鬤 Ch'hàng
鬟 Chuing

鬥 Toè
鬦 Toe
鬧 Laôu
鬨 Hāng
鬩 Géy
鬪 鬬 } Toè
鬭 { Toè / Taòu

鬯 T'hëàng
鬰 Wut
鬱 Wut

鬲 Kek
鬹 { Öey / Wöey
鬵 Sîm
鬺 Sîm
鬻 Yëak

[illegible] ty
4
魁 K'höey
魂 䰟 } Hwûn
魃 Pwat
魄 { P'hek / T'hok
魈 Seaou
8
魋 Töêy
魍 Bóng
魎 Lëáng
魏 Gwûy
魑 Lê
魒 P'heaou
魔 Mô
14
䰠 Sêw
[illegible] { Chéin / Chek
魘 Yeém

魚 { Gê / Hê
魛 To
魜 Sëāh
4
魩 But
魯 Loé
魨 Tûn
䰾 { Pâ / P'hwâ
魴 { Hông / Hang
5
鮀 Tô
鮇 Tac
鮎 Chëem
鮐 T'hae
鮓 { Táy / T'hāy
鮑 Paóu
鮒 Hoō
6
鮝 { Sëáng / Sëóng / Sëôh
鮡 T'heaou
鮦 Tông
鮪 Wûy
鮫 { Kaou / Ka
鮕 Koe

髟 190
鬥 191
鬯 192
鬲 193
鬼 194
魚 195

195 魚
196 鳥

鮭 { Haê / Kêy
鮮 { Sëen / Sëén / Ch'hee^{ng}
7
鯇 Bëén
鮻 So
鯃 Goê
鯘 Lōëy
鯀 Kwún
鯁 Kéng
鯃 Goê
鯈 Sêw
鯉 Lé
鯊 { Say / Swâ
8
鯤 K'hwun
鯖 Ch'heng
鮆 { Pa / P'hwa
鯧 { Ch'heang / Ch'hëo^{ng}
鯪 { Lêng / Lâ
鯫 Choo
鯹 { Ch'ho / Seng
9
鯽 Chek

鯯 { Ci
鯨 Chang
鰇 Jêw
鰂 { Chék / Chàt
鰋 Yeén
鰌 Ch'hew
鰍 { Ch'hew / Lew
鰓 Sae
鰕 Hây
鰨 Tàt
10
鰡 Lêw
鰣 Sô
鰥 Kwan
鰿 { Chit / Chek
鰭 Kê
鰮 Wun
鰱 Lëen
鰲 Gô
鰳 { Lék / Làt
鰴 Hwuy
鱟 Haōu

鰷 Teâou
鰻 { Bân / Mw^{n}â
鱁 Ch'hw^{n}ā
鱄 Chwan
鱖 Kwae
鱆 { Chëang / Chëo^{ng}
12
鱒 { Chun / Chùn / Chu^{ng}
鱓 Sëēn
鱔 Sëēn
鱗 { Lîn / Lân
鱙 Jeâou
鱠 Köëy
鱣 Chëen
14
鱮 Sē
鱤 Kām
鱧 Lēy
鱯 T'hôh
鱭 Cháy
鱷 Gók
鱸 Loê

鱳 { Lék / Lāyh
鱻 Sëen

鳥 { Neáou / Cheáou
鳦 Yit
2
鳭 Teaou
鳧 Hoê
鳨 Lék
鳩 K'hew
鳭 Teaou
鳪 Pok
3
鳱 Hwân
鳲 Se
鳳 Hōng
鳴 Bêng
鳶 Yëen
鳦 Ek
4
鴄 Gōng
鳷 Che
鴆 T'hìm
鴃 Kwat
鴂 Kwat
鴻 Hông
鴇 Pó
鴈 Gān
鴉 A

5
鴒 Lêng
鴛 Wan
鴝 Kê
鴞 Heaou
鴟 Ch'he
鴣 Koe
鴦 { Yang / Yëo^{ng}
鴨 Ah
鴰 [illegible]
鴻 [illegible]
鴥 T'hit
鴿 Kap
鴳 { Kaou / Ka
鴸 U
鴴 Ch'hio
鴰 Kwan
鴪 Yëuk
鵓 Pút
鵙 Kwat
鵜 T'hêy
鵝 Gô

鵠 Gok
鵡 Boó
鵅 Kak
鵪 An
鵬 P'hêng
鵰 Teaou
鵲 { Ch'hëak / *K'hăyh*
鴒 Lêng
鵻 { Chuy / Tuy
鵾 K'hwun
鵋 Kê
鶄 Cheng
鶃 Gëét
鶉 Sûn
鶊 Keng
9
鶖 Ch'hew
鶗 T'hêy
鶘 Hoê
鶠 Yëén
鶡 Hat
鶥 Böëy
鶩 Loô
10
鶢 Cu hong
[illegible] Eng
[illegible] Ko
[illegible] { Hók / *Hŏh*
鶹 Lêw
鶺 Chit
鶻 Kwut
鶼 Këem
鶽 Chûn
鷀 Choô
鷥 Se
鷕 Yaôu
鷄 Key
鷁 Gek
11
鷐 Sîn
鷢 Kwuy
鷓 Chöà
鷂 Yaôu
鷖 E
鷗 Oe
鷙 Chè
鷟 Chók
12
鷦 Cheâou
鷫 Sëuk
鷮 Keâou
鷯 Leâou
鷲 Chēw
鷳 Hân
鷸 Yit
13
鷹 Eng
鷺 Loē
鷧 È
鸂 Key
鸇 Chëen
14
鸎 Eng
鸑 Gak
鸓 Loê
鸚 Eng
18
鸛 { Kwàn / *Kwⁿà*
鸐 Kê
鸝 Lê
鸞 Lwân

鹵 Loé
[illegible] Tām
[illegible] Yëêm
鹹 { Hâm / *Këêm*
鹼 *Keeⁿg*
鹽 Yëêm

鹿 Lók
麀 Yew
麂 Ké
麃 P'heaou
麈 Ché
6
麋 Bê
麑 Gé
麐 Lîn
8
麑 Gêy
麒 Kê
麓 Lók
麕 K'hwun
麌 O
{ 麗 Lê / Lêy
9
麝 Sëā
麞 { Chëang / *Këoⁿg*
麟 Lîn
麤 Ch'hoe

麥 { Bĕk / *Băyh*
麩 Hoo
麪 *Meēⁿg*
麰 Boê
麬 P'hoe
麯 { K'hëuk / *K'hak*
麵 { Bëēn / *Meēⁿg*
[illegible] Koê

鳥 196
鹵 197
鹿 198
麥 199

200 麻
201 黃
202 黍
203 黑
204 黹
205 黽

麻 { Má / *Moâ*	黃 { Hông / *Wông*	黍 { Sé / *Séy*	黑 Hek	黹 Té	黽 Bá
麽 { Mŏh / *Mooing* / *Meengh*	黈 T'hun	黎 { Lê / Lêy	黓 Tọẹ	黺 Hwún	黿 Gwân
麾 Hwuy	黊 T'hoé	黏 { Lëêm / *Neeng*	默 Ek	黻 Hwut	鼀 K'ew
	黌 Hông		黔 K'hëêm	黼 Hoó	鼂 Te ou
			黕 { T'hún / T'hûn		鼃 Wá
			黙 Bėk		鼄 { Choo / Too
			黚 K'hëêm		鼇 Gô
			黛 Taē		鼈 { Pëet / *Peĕh*
			黜 T'hut		鼉 Gô
			點 Tëém		
			黠 Hat		
			黗 T'hùn		
			黫 Kwùn		
			黂 Hwún		
			黺 Pun		
			黥 Kêng		
			黨 Tóng		
			黯 Ám		
			黴 Bōęy		
			黵 Wąė		
			黶 Yëém		
			黷 { Tók / T'hók		

鼎 Téng / *Tēⁿá*
鼏 Téng
鼐 Naē
鼒 Choo

鼓 Koé
鼕 Tông
6
鼗 Tô
鼙 Pê
[illegible] Long
鼛 Ko
12
[illegible] Lin
[illegible] Lëûng

鼠 Ch'hé
鼦 Teaou
鼪 Seng
鼬 Yêw
鼯 Goê

鼻 Pit. / *P'heēng*
鼽 Kêw
鼾 Há[illegible]
齁 Hèw
齆 *Àng*
[illegible] Waè
[illegible] T'hè

[illegible] [illegible]y
[illegible] Chey
[illegible] Chey

齒 Ch'hé / *K'hé*
齕 Hék
4
[illegible] Pa
齗 Gín
齣 Ch'hut
齟 Choê
齠 Teâou
齡 Lêng
6
齧 Gëet
齩 Gnaóu / Gnaé / *Kā*
齪 齰 Ch'hëuk / Ch'hok
齭 Swan
8
齱 Ch'hëuk
齴 Gëén
齷 Ak

鼎206
鼓207
鼠208
鼻209
齊210
齒211

212龍	龍 {Lëúng / Lëûng / Lêng}	[illegible] {Kwuy / [illegible]}	龠 Yëak			
213龜	龐 Bâng	龜 {[illegible] / [illegible]}	龡 Ch'huy			
214龠	龔 Këung		龢 Ho			
	龕 K'ham					
	龘 Beáou					

国家出版基金项目
NATIONAL PUBLICATION FOUNDATION

海上絲綢之路文獻集成

總主編 陳支平 陳春聲

科技與文化編 87

主編 王揚宗 葉 農

海峽出版發行集團
THE STRAITS PUBLISHING & DISTRIBUTING GROUP
福建人民出版社

本册目次

厦英大辭典

（*Chinese-English Dictionary of the Vernacular or Spoken Language of Amoy, with the Principal Variations of the Chang-chew and Chin-chew Dialects*）

〔英〕杜嘉德（Carstairs Douglas）編

《厦英大辭典》，英國杜嘉德編。杜嘉德（Carstairs Douglas，一八三〇—一八七七），蘇格蘭長老會傳教士。一八五五年來華，抵厦門，居閩南地區二十餘年，後逝世於此。此書係首部厦門腔白話華英辭典，一八七三年於英國倫敦出版。書前有引言，詳述厦門話聲韻調系統。全書收録閩南方言四萬餘條，先列單字，字後録詞，皆不書漢字，徑以羅馬字母注音，英語釋義，其讀音以厦門腔爲主，亦兼及漳州、泉州、永春、惠安、安溪等地腔音。據一八七三年倫敦版影印。

DICTIONARY

OF THE

VERNACULAR OR SPOKEN LANGUAGE

OF

AMOY.

厦英大辭典

CHINESE-ENGLISH

DICTIONARY

OF THE

VERNACULAR OR SPOKEN LANGUAGE

OF

AMOY,

WITH THE PRINCIPAL VARIATIONS
OF THE CHANG-CHEW AND CHIN-CHEW DIALECTS.

BY

REV. CARSTAIRS DOUGLAS, M.A., LL.D. Glasg.,
MISSIONARY OF THE PRESBYTERIAN CHURCH IN ENGLAND.

LONDON:
TRÜBNER & CO., 57 & 59 LUDGATE HILL.
1873.

GLASGOW:
W. G. BLACKIE AND CO., PRINTERS,
VILLAFIELD.

TO

REV. JAMES LEGGE, D.D.,

AS AN ACKNOWLEDGMENT FOR MUCH KINDNESS,

AND A TRIBUTE

TO HIS UNWEARIED LABOURS

AS A CHRISTIAN MISSIONARY,

AND HIS PRE-EMINENT POSITION

AS A CHINESE SCHOLAR.

PREFACE.

THE vernacular or spoken language of Amoy, which this Dictionary attempts to make more accessible than formerly, has been also termed by some "The Amoy Dialect" or "The Amoy Colloquial;" and it partially coincides with the so-called "Hok-kien Dialect," illustrated by the Rev. Dr. Medhurst in his quarto Dictionary under that title. But such words as "Dialect" or "Colloquial" give an erroneous conception of its nature. It is not a mere colloquial dialect or patois; it is spoken by the highest ranks just as by the common people, by the most learned just as by the ignorant; learned men indeed add a few polite or pedantic phrases, but these are mere excrescences (and even they are pronounced according to the Amoy sounds), while the main body and staple of the spoken language of the most refined and learned classes is the same as that of coolies, labourers, and boatmen.

Nor does the term "dialect" convey anything like a correct idea of its distinctive character; it is no mere dialectic variety of some other language; it is a distinct language, one of the many and widely differing languages which divide among them the soil of China.

The so-called "written language" of China is indeed uniform throughout the whole country; but it is rather a *notation* than a language; for this universal written language is pronounced differently when read aloud in the different parts of China, so that while as written it is *one*, as soon as it is pronounced it splits into several languages. And still further, this written language, as it is read aloud from books, is not *spoken* in any place whatever under any form of pronunciation. The most learned men never employ it as a means of ordinary oral communication even among themselves. It is in fact a *dead language*, related to the various spoken languages of China somewhat as Latin is to the languages of South-western Europe.

A very considerable number of the spoken languages of China have been already more or less studied by European and American residents in the country, such as the Mandarin, the Hakka, the vernaculars of Canton and Amoy, and several others. These are not dialects of one language; they are cognate languages, bearing to each other a relation similar to that which subsists between the Arabic, the Hebrew, the Syriac, the Ethiopic, and the other members of the Semitic family; or again between English, German, Dutch, Danish, Swedish, &c.

There is another serious objection to the use of the term "dialect" as applied to these languages, namely, that within each of them there exist *real dialects*. For instance, the Mandarin, the greatest of all, contains within itself at least three very marked "dialects," the Northern, spoken at Pekin; the Southern, spoken at Nanking and Soo-chow; and the Western, spoken in the provinces of Sze-chuen, Hoo-peh, &c.

In like manner the language which for want of a better name we may call the Amoy Vernacular or spoken language, contains within itself several real dialects, especially those of Chang-chew, Chin-chew, Tung-an, and of Amoy itself. In this Dictionary the form of the language spoken at Amoy itself is taken as the standard, and the principal variations of the Chang-chew and Chin-chew dialects are marked, as also a considerable number of the variations occurring in Tung-an, Chang-poo, and some other regions.

The language of Amoy, including these subordinate dialects, is believed to be spoken by about eight or ten millions. This is the first dictionary of the spoken language. There are numerous dictionaries of the universal written language of China. One of these, by the

Rev. Dr. Medhurst, called "Dictionary of the Hok-kien Dialect," gives the Chang-chew sound (or more accurately the sound of Chang-poo, *i.e.* **Chiuⁿ-phó**) of the written characters. Some colloquial words are also given in Dr. Medhurst's Dictionary, but they are few, and entirely in the Chang-chew or Chang-poo dialect, and unhappily the colloquial forms given are often far from accurate. The only other publications that have anything of the form of a dictionary are the very brief vocabularies in the Manuals of Doty and Macgowan.

The basis of this Dictionary is the manuscript vocabulary prepared by the late Rev. J. Lloyd, Missionary of the American Presbyterian Church. When I arrived at Amoy in 1855 I copied it for my own use, adding the additional words in Doty's Manual, and have been constantly enlarging and re-arranging the collection of words and phrases ever since. A few years after copying Lloyd's Vocabulary I collated the manuscript dictionary written by the Rev. Alexander Stronach of the London Missionary Society. I also at a later date went over all the words in the native dictionaries of the Chang-chew and Chin-chew dialects, and in a native vocabulary which attempts to give the Mandarin words and phrases for the Amoy ones. Of these native works the only really good one is the Chang-chew or rather Chang-poo Dictionary, named the **Sip-ngó-im**, which is the basis of Medhurst's Dictionary. Having thus the original source to refer to, I have made but little use of Medhurst's work; for such colloquial phrases in it as are not drawn from the **Sip-ngó-im** are very questionable, while its valuable book-phrases do not serve my purpose. Macgowan's Manual, though very useful for a beginner, was of course published too late for my use. In looking over it I found very few words which I had not already in my manuscript.

No one can be more sensible of the defects of the work than I am myself. It was at first prepared for my own use alone; as it grew larger I hoped that it might be used in manuscript by beginners, or copied, abridged, or expanded by successive missionaries; and it was only after repeated solicitations, culminating in a formal request by all the members of the three Protestant missions at Amoy, that I consented to prepare it for the press. This is my apology for all its faults and imperfections. It attempts to fill a real blank and to supply an urgent want; and I shall only be too glad when it shall be superseded and forgotten, or remembered only as the foundation on which a far more complete and accurate work shall have been reared.

When the Amoy missionaries asked me to prepare for the press the manuscript which I had compiled, the Rev. John Stronach of the London Missionary Society, and the Rev. John Van Nest Talmage, D.D., of the American Reformed Mission, were at the same time appointed to assist me in the revision of it. Mr. Stronach went over the whole from beginning to end, but Dr. Talmage was prevented by other duties from revising more than a few dozen pages. After their revision it was necessary for me to harmonize and recast the whole (with large additions and alterations which never came under their eyes), when writing out the copy for the printer. So that while a large share of what is good in the book should be put to the credit of my coadjutors, I must myself be held responsible for all its faults.

The most serious defect is the want of the Chinese character. This is due to two causes: (1) There are a very large number of the words for which we have not been able to find the corresponding character at all, perhaps a quarter or a third of the whole; and the time when it was necessary for me to take my furlough made it impossible to make the search for the missing characters, many of them rare, and many difficult to recognize from the great variations that take place between the written and spoken forms of the language. (2) Even if the characters had been found, it would have been very difficult or impossible for me to use the Chinese character in printing at home. But it was necessary to print it during my furlough at home, because we have not the means of printing such a work at Amoy; and on my return to China I could not have been spared from the mission long enough to go to some other port to carry it through the press. I cherish the hope of publishing a Key or

Sequel in two or three years, giving the characters so far as they can be found. Meantime, while I greatly regret that the Chinese character does not appear in the book, I am in one sense glad that it is absent. For it may serve to make manifest the fact that the Vernacular of Amoy is an independent language, which is able to stand alone without the help of the written character. And I should hope that many persons may thus be encouraged to study this language who would have been repelled by the sight of the complicated and fantastic characters. Of course every missionary, and every one who would be counted a scholar, must study the written character too, for the Vernacular or Colloquial cannot for a very long time to come possess any literature worthy of the name.

Another defect, which I greatly regret, is the very scanty identification of plants, animals, medicines, &c. Want of time is here also the excuse, which I trust my readers will count sufficient. Many such names have been put in with a query, being taken from such works as The Fuh-chau Recorder, Notes and Queries on China and Japan, The Phœnix, Dr. Porter Smith's Book on Medicines, the various dictionaries of the written language, &c., while I had not the means of verifying them.

To some it seems also a great want that there is no English-Chinese part. But that must really be a separate work. The whole style and character of Chinese thought and expression is so different from the nearest English equivalents, that the work of reversing a dictionary, which at first sight seems very easy, would really be enormous, falling not very far short of the original composition.

With all its imperfections I trust that this book shall prove helpful to those who study the language of Amoy. My chief object has been to assist those who are engaged in the work of Christian missions; but for this purpose I have endeavoured to give a full view of the language so far as I have been able to learn it; and the book is fitted to be equally useful to merchants, travellers, mariners, interpreters, and students. It is most desirable that foreigners residing among the Chinese should learn their language, so as to hold direct intercourse with them, instead of using the miserable jargon called Canton-English or "pigeon English," or being left at the mercy of interpreters. Few things would so much tend to remove causes of dispute or bad feeling, and to make the intercourse between these nations both pleasant and beneficial.

The explanations in the Introduction and Appendix have been much condensed from want of time at the last; I have therefore not been able to give the several subjects a scientific treatment, but have contented myself with such practical directions as will facilitate the use of the book and the acquisition of the language.

In conclusion I would express my thanks to Hugh M. Matheson, Esq., Convener of the Foreign Mission Committee of the Presbyterian Church in England; to Robert Barbour, Esq., of Bolesworth; and to C. E. Lewis, Esq., M.P., for the kind liberality which has enabled me to publish the work.

Ayr, *4th April, 1873.*

INTRODUCTION;

WITH

REMARKS ON PRONUNCIATION

AND

INSTRUCTIONS FOR USE.

ORTHOGRAPHY AND PRONUNCIATION.

VOWELS.

The vowels **a, e, i, o, u,** are pronounced much as in Italian and German.

a as in *far*. It must never be pronounced with the peculiarly English sound of *a* in *man*.

e as in *grey*. But in the syllables **ien, iet,** it is nearly the same as in *men, yet,* and sometimes approaches to the English *a* in *man*.

i as in *machine*, not with the short English *i* in *swift*. Thus the Amoy word **sin** is almost the same as the English *seen*, but quite different from the English *sin*. Almost the only words which I have observed where it comes near the short English sound are **chit,** "this," and **hit,** "that," which often come very near the English words spelled alike.

O, when final, is pronounced as in *no, go*. It is also thus pronounced when followed by **h**; for, as is explained below, the final **h** is silent, and merely indicates that the vowel is short and abrupt, so that final **oh** is just short final **o.**

But when **o** is followed by **m, ng, p,** or **k,** it is pronounced as in the English *hop, sock, long*.

When followed by another vowel it has the first of the above sounds, as in *go, no,* but in some cases very short, almost like **w,** as is fully explained below under the head of the diphthongs.

u as in *put, rude*.

ɵ has the sound of *aw* in *law, saw*. This sound is really the same as the second sound of **o,** as explained above, so that strictly speaking this letter **ɵ** should have been used in place of **o** before **m, ng, p,** and **k**; but I have followed the spelling now universal at Amoy by using the letter **o** before these consonants for the sound more accurately written **ɵ.**

ɛ is the French *è*, or like the English *e* in *there*. It scarcely ever occurs except in the Changchew dialect, so that persons who cannot catch the sound may use *e* as the nearest approximation.

In vowels with double dots, the double dot always indicates a change of the vowel sound, and is never used for the diæresis.

ö is the same as the German *ö*. It occurs only in the dialects of Chin-chew and Tung-an, where it is often used instead of the Amoy and Changchew **e.** Thus any one who cannot catch the sound of **ö** will be most safe to use **e** instead. It must by no means be confounded with **o**; only Cn. **öe** corresponds with A. **oe.**

ü is nearly the German *ü* or French *u*, but not quite the same, having often a slight variation from that sound in the direction of *ö*.

It occurs only in the dialects of Chin-chew and Tung-an, in which it frequently takes the place of the Amoy **u.** It almost invariably does so when the Amoy **u** corresponds to the Changchew **i,** but it often occurs also when the Amoy and Changchew agree in **u.** Persons who cannot get hold of the sound may therefore use **u** as an approximation.

ĭ is a sound very rarely heard. It is exactly the short English *i* in *sit, swift*. I have used it in **chĭh, chĭt, hĭh, hĭt, tĭh,** where they occur as leading words in alphabetical order; but where they occur in the phrases and examples under other leading words, I have written such words **chit, hit,** and **tih** or **teh,** as their pronunciation is very indefinite. When slowly and carefully pronounced, **chit, hit,** are the sounds given. But **tĭh, tih,** or **teh,** is never pronounced slowly or carefully, it is always unaccented and rapid, so that its sound is much disputed. I refer in these remarks to one word only under each of these syllables, for the other words under each syllable always retain the clear sound of **i.**

DIPHTHONGS.

In all the diphthongs each vowel is heard distinctly with its own proper sound.

In **ai, au,** and **oe,** the first vowel is accented, the second unaccented. **ai** like the English *ie* in *tie;* **au** like the English *ow* in *now;* **oe** very nearly as in the English *Noel*.

In **oa,** on the other hand, the **a** is accented; the **o** is unaccented and generally extremely short, almost like **w,** indeed in many words it might be written **w** when pronounced at the usual rate; but when pronounced long, the sound of the **o** is clearly heard, *e.g.* sometimes in the "**chiū^{n}-piâ^{n}**" and "**ē-khì**" tones; and in the nasal form **oa^{n}**, the **o** is distinctly heard; but in all cases great care must be taken not to exaggerate the **o** sound, but to make the **a** the principal vowel.

The same remarks apply to **oai,** where the accent is on the **a,** the whole coming very near the English *Wye*, but with rather more of the **o** sound.

In diphthongs beginning with **i** the accent is usually on the second vowel, while the **i** is sounded very nearly like **y**. Thus, in **ia, iau,** the accent is on **a**; in **io** it is on **o**.

But in the nasal form **ia**^{n}, the accent falls nearly equally on the two vowels, and the vowel sound of **i** is distinctly heard, though **a** is still more prominent.

In **iu** the accent is nearly equal on the two vowels, and sometimes seems even to fall on the **i**, especially when the word is the last word of a clause.

When the two vowels of a diphthong are almost equally accented, it may often be observed that if the whole word lose the accent it is the first vowel which loses it most thoroughly; *e.g.* in the word "**kiù**" a considerable portion of accent falls on the **i**, but in the phrase **kiù-sè**, where the chief accent falls on **sè**, the unaccented **kiù** is pronounced almost like the English *Kew*.

NASALS.

A small ^{n} suspended or written above the line at the end of a syllable indicates that the whole syllable becomes nasal. If the syllable contain a diphthong, the nasal mark, though placed at the end, qualifies the preceding vowel or vowels as well as the last.

In words beginning with **m, n,** and **ng**, I have not preserved absolute uniformity. It has been usual with many, especially in the American Reformed Mission, to write no nasal mark (small ^{n}) at such words, but to lay down the rule that all words beginning with **m, n,** and **ng**, are to be pronounced nasally. It seems to me that in some such words the vowel has not any distinctly nasal sound, and I have therefore endeavoured to write it where the sound is really nasal. But through the force of habit I have often omitted to write it where it should be. Initial **j** is also somewhat irregular.

CONSONANTS.

The great majority of the consonants are pronounced as in English, or very nearly so.

ch always as in *church;* only in the aspirated form **chh** it sometimes approaches to the aspirated sound of **ts**, as is explained below in the remarks on the aspirated consonants.

g is always hard.

h is always really pronounced, and must never be left silent as in many English words.

j always as in *judge*.

l is often pronounced in a very thick indistinct manner, approaching to the sound of **d**, so much so that as the language of Amoy has no proper **d**, the Amoy people usually employ a syllable beginning with **l** when trying to imitate a foreign word beginning with **d**.

ng as in *sing, hang;* so even at the beginning of a syllable. Care must be taken never to bring in the sound of *g*, as in *anger*, but to preserve the sound of **ng** simple and pure. To a beginner it is often difficult to pronounce **ng** as an initial; it is somewhat as if in the word *singer* or *longing* the *si-* or *lo-* were cut off.

s has always the sharp sound, as in *so, sing;* never sounded like *z*, as in *lose*.

Final consonants are pronounced much more gently and softly than in English. In English there is usually a slight emission of vocal breath at the end of a final consonant, but in Chinese there is not the slightest emission of breath at the end of the final consonant, which is thus *final* in the strictest sense, the organs of speech remaining at the end of the word in the position for pronouncing the final consonant; *e.g.* at the end of the Chinese word **sam** the lips are still shut, at the end of **kat** the tip of the tongue remains touching the palate near the teeth, and immediately afterwards the lips are opened or the tongue removed without the faintest sound. This is the cause of the great softness and gentleness of the final consonants in Chinese.

The finals, **k, p, t,** are pronounced so gently that it is sometimes very difficult to distinguish them from each other.

Final **m, n,** and **ng**, do not break off abruptly as in English, but are somewhat prolonged, being sounded with a sort of vowel or vocal murmur in the consonant itself. In some tones these finals are much prolonged; in the second tone (chiū^{n}-sia^{n}) they are briefer, but even in it not so short as in English. This prolonged murmur is specially remarkable in final **eng**, which sounds almost as if there were an indistinct half pronounced vowel between the **e** and the **ng**.

m and **ng**, having a half pronounced vowel within the liquid consonant, sometimes make words of themselves, standing quite alone without any vowel attached, *e.g.* **ng, n̂g, m̄, ḿ**. They are also often found with a consonant prefixed, but without any vowel, *e.g.* **sng, hn̄g, hḿ**. The nature of these syllables without a distinct vowel becomes at once unmistakable in singing, as at such a word all clear vocal sound at once ceases, and nothing is heard but a dull nasal murmur.

The ASPIRATED CONSONANTS are a very remarkable feature in all the languages of China, and require very special attention. They are **kh, ph, th,** and **chh**. The sounds are the same as those indicated by the same notation in the languages of India, being formed by a real distinct aspiration pronounced after the respective consonants. In the other languages of China it has been usual to indicate them by a small inverted or suspended comma, thus **k', p', t', ch', ts'**, but **h** has been commonly used at Amoy, and is much more distinct. The sounds are almost the same as those often used by Irishmen when pronouncing with a strong brogue such words as *come, pig,* &c.; they are also often heard in the mouths of the Scottish Highlanders.

kh may be thus described:—Pronounce *block-house* with a clear distinct *h;* remove the letters *blo-* from the beginning and the *-se* from the end, and you have almost exactly the Chinese "khau." Or pronounce *look here!* rapidly and clearly, cut off *loo-* and *-re*, and you have the Chinese "khi."

ph must by no means be confounded with the English *ph*, which is just *f*; for the Chinese **ph** preserves the clear sound of **p** followed by an aspiration; *e.g.* say *loophole* very rapidly and sharply, cut off *loo-* and *-le* from the two ends, and there remains the Chinese "pho." So, by removing *ha-* and *-zard* from *haphazard*, you get the Chinese "pha."

th must not be confounded with the English *th*, which is really a simple sound. The Chinese **th** is a clear distinct **t** followed by the aspirate. Thus the Chinese "thau" may be carved out of *out-house* or *hot-house*.

chh is formed in a similar way from the *ch* of *church*. Take such a word as *watch-house* or *coach-house*, remove the *wa-* or *coa-* from the beginning and the *-se* from the end, and something very near the Chinese "chhau" remains.

Sometimes **chh** has a sound more nearly approaching to an aspirated **ts**. This occurs occasionally when **chh** is followed by **a, o, ɵ, u,** or **ng**. Generally even before these letters the sound remains the same, or very nearly the same, as the usual **chh**, but sometimes it might have been written **tsh** or **ts'h**, especially in the dialects of Chin-chew and Tung-an, and in other cases it seems about half-way between **chh** and **ts'h**. But as these sounds are not very common, and as they shade gradually into the normal **chh**, I have thought it best not to make any change in the spelling usual at Amoy.

ch itself is *not* one of these aspirated consonants, for, as explained above, it is just the English *ch* of *church*, which is really **t-sh**, not containing the real sound of **h** at all.

TONES.

The tones are commonly supposed to be a great obstacle in the way of learning Chinese, but they really present no very great difficulty if studied carefully from the first. They can be properly learned only by the ear, and it is much better to get them directly from the lips of a native. The following remarks are intended merely as a help to direct the student in catching the intonations of the natives, but they may also be of some slight use in giving a general idea of the nature of the tones to those who have no opportunity of hearing them spoken.

It is not the tones themselves, *but the use made of the tones*, which is the peculiar characteristic of the Chinese group of languages. Similar tones exist in all languages, only differently used. In English, for instance, we pronounce the word *go* very differently when we give a hasty and angry command, "*Go!*" and when we ask the question with a mixture of astonishment and horror, "Can you dare to *go?*" The difference of tone is as great in English as in Chinese, but in English it indicates merely the different feelings of the mind or the different grammatical or rhetorical relations of the same word, while in Chinese the same syllable with two different tones makes two thoroughly distinct words.

The Chinese divide the tones into four great classes, named at Amoy—1st, **piâ^n** (C. pê^n); 2d, **chiū^n**; 3d, **khì** (Cn. khù); 4th, **jip**, or according to the Mandarin sounds, Ping (or more accurately p'ing), Shang, K'ü (or Ch'ü), and Juh.

Each of these four classes is or may be divided into two subdivisions, called the "upper" and "lower." Doubtless when these four classes with their subdivisions first received their names, all these names described with tolerable accuracy the inflexion and pitch of the several tones, but now there is no part of China where the names of the tones correctly describe their character. It is therefore best in speaking of the tones not to translate the Chinese words, but either to transfer the Chinese terms or to speak of them by their numbers.

In some parts of China all the eight tones are used; in one place they have even been increased to *nine;* in two of the great dialects of Mandarin there are four tones and five tones in use respectively. In Amoy, though nominally there are eight, yet really there are only *seven*, as the second tone class, the "chiū^n-siá^n," is not divided into two. I shall describe these seven tones used at Amoy, not according to the Chinese order, but according to their actual nature.

The two **jip** tones, or the upper and lower fourth tone, stand quite by themselves. They are distinguished by being pronounced with an abrupt or clipped ending, almost with a jerk. Originally they all ended in **k**, **p**, or **t**, but now the final consonant has in many cases been dropped, leaving, however, its trace in a sharp abrupt ending which makes something like a hiatus: this abrupt vowel-ending is indicated by the final **h**, which is absolutely silent. The two **jip** tones therefore can always be recognized by the final letters **h**, **k**, **p**, and **t**. All words ending in these letters belong to the **jip** tones, and no others do.

Any such word, if it have no accent mark, belongs to the **chiū^n-jip** or upper fourth tone. It begins moderately high, rises very slightly at first, and then comes down with a short, sharp, rapid movement, somewhat like the English *not* when spoken in a very emphatic or imperative manner, as in the sentence, "*You shall* NOT."

The **ē-jip** or lower fourth tone is indicated by a perpendicular accent, *e.g.* **jip**, **ha̍k**, **lo̍h**. It begins rather lower than the other, and is pronounced with a curious upward jerk, which the form of the perpendicular accent is intended to suggest, somewhat like *not* in the sentence "*Will you* NOT?" pronounced simply as an interrogation with a mere upward movement, without the previous fall of the voice that would be given if it indicated strong surprise.

The other five tones are distributed among the words which do *not* end in **h**, **k**, **p**, or **t**.

Two of these five tones are perfectly level, just like musical notes, at an interval of about a musical fifth from each other. The exact distance of the interval is quite immaterial, and in fact it often varies from about a musical third to about an octave in the mouth of the same speaker, with the nature of the emphasis or emotion with which he speaks; all that is necessary for the distinction of the tones, and for being well understood, is that there be a marked difference of the pitch.

The higher level tone is called the **chiū^n-piâ^n** (C. téng-pê^n), or the upper first tone. It is indicated by the absence of any tonal mark, just as the "**chiū^n-jip**" has no tonal mark; but these two tones can always be at once distinguished at a glance, as the "**chiū^n-piâ^n**" never ends in **h**, **k**, **p**, or **t**, while the "**chiū^n-jip**" always has one of these finals.

The tone with a low level intonation is called the **ē-khì** or lower third tone. It is indicated by a horizontal accent, *e.g.* **ē**, **hū**. It must not be confounded with the "**ē-piâ^n**" tone, the *name* of which means "low level," but the *intonation* of which is very far from level, as will be seen from the explanation given three paragraphs lower down. But the lower third or "**ē-khì**" is *really* low and level in its tone, though the *name* does not indicate the fact.

The three tones which remain are more or less inflected, and cannot be represented by any musical notes.

The **chiū^n-khì** or upper third tone is a low, slow, downward slide; it begins low, about as low as the low level (**ē-khì**) tone, and from that low level it gradually slides lower till it quite dies away; great care must be taken at the end not to allow the voice to turn up again at all; it is represented by the downward slope of the grave accent, *e.g.* **pù**, **khì**. It is heard in English when one lets the voice fall into a low key, sinking down lower and lower till it quite dies away, as when sadly musing in simple grief and sorrow (without any anger or excitement) on some mournful and depressing news; *e.g.* saying "*Gone!*" or "*Dead!*"

The **ē-piâ^n** (C. ē-pê^n) or lower first tone first falls and then rises. It is the intonation used in English to express great astonishment or a strongly marked interrogation, *e.g.* "*You?*" "*How?*" Its mark is the circumflex, *e.g.* **kî**, **sô**.

The **chiū^n-siá^n** or second tone, called in Mandarin the "Shang" tone, begins somewhat high, rises slightly and rapidly, and then comes down with a rapid swing, much like a decided imperative in English; *e.g. gone*, in the phrase "*Be gone!*" This tone is indicated by an acute accent, *e.g.* **lí, sú, kóng**, &c.

The above explanations may be summarized as follows:

ABRUPT AND SHORT. All ending in **h, k, p, t.**			**chiū^{n}-jip**, rising slightly and then falling rapidly; **toh.** **ē-jip**, rising abruptly; **tȯh.**
NOT ABRUPT. Never ending in **h, k, p, t.**	LEVEL MUSICAL NOTES.		**chiū^{n}-piâ^{n}**, high and level; **to.** **ē-khì**, low and level; **tō.**
	SINGLE INFLECTION.		**chiū^{n}-khì**, low, slow, downward slide; **tò.**
	DOUBLE INFLECTION.		**ē-piâ^{n}**, slow circumflex, first falling and then rising, as in astonishment or interrogation; **tô.** **chiū^{n}-sia^{n}**, slightly upward and rapidly downwards, like a strong imperative; **tó.**

The Chinese at Amoy, &c., usually arrange the tones in the following order:—

chiū^{n}-piâ^{n}.
chiū^{n}-sia^{n}.
chiū^{n}-khì.
chiū^{n}-jip.
ē-piâ^{n}.
chiū^{n}-sia^{n}.
ē-khì.
ē-jip.

In this arrangement the "**chiū^{n}-sia^{n}**" appears twice, because it is not divided into an upper and a lower subclass. This has caused great confusion in the nomenclature of the tones (by Europeans and Americans) according to numbers, for while it has been usual to number the first five—

1. **chiū^{n}-piâ^{n}.**
2. **chiū^{n}-sia^{n}.**
3. **chiū^{n}-khì.**
4. **chiū^{n}-jip.**
5. **ē-piâ^{n}.**

from that point there has been a divergence, some numbering on according to the exact form of Chinese usage.

6. **chiū^{n}-sia^{n}.**
7. **ē-khì.**
8. **ē-jip.**

Others have counted them as follows:—

6. **ē-khì.**
7. **ē-jip.**

To avoid this ambiguity in naming the sixth and seventh tones, I have arranged them as follows:—

FIRST TONE. piâ^{n}. { **chiū^{n}-piâ^{n}**, upper first; **to.**
{ **ē-piâ^{n}**, lower first; **tô.**

SECOND TONE.—**chiū^{n}-sia^{n}**; **tó.**

THIRD TONE. { **chiū^{n}-khì**, upper third; **tò**
{ **ē-khì**, lower third; **tō.**

FOURTH TONE. { **chiū^{n}-jip**, upper fourth; **toh.**
{ **ē-jip**, lower fourth; **tȯh.**

In the alphabetical arrangement of the words in this Dictionary the order is therefore "**to, tô, tó, tò, tō.**" This does not include the two subdivisions of the fourth tone, as the difference of spelling places them in a different position in the alphabetical arrangement, namely "**toh, tȯh.**"

TONES IN COMBINATION.

The description of the tones given above applies strictly only to a word pronounced separately, or to a word ending a clause, and pronounced with the primary accent (as is usual at the end of a clause or group of two or more words); or to a word which, though not last, yet has the primary accent, being followed by an enclitic or unaccented word.

But in many cases a word loses the form of tonal inflection described above.

Sometimes a word becomes *enclitic* (see Appendix V.), in which case the tone dies away somewhat like the "chiū^{n}-khì" or the "chiū^{n}-jip," or rather like something intermediate between them pronounced very short and gentle. No matter what the original tone of a word be, this is the one form assumed when enclitic; and so it happens that if an enclitic word be not common in its accented form, or if it be not recognized and identified, the learner is apt to be misled even by well-educated Chinese saying that the word belongs to the "chiū^{n}-khì" or to the "chiū^{n}-jip" tone. The mark which I use to indicate an enclitic word is a double hyphen placed before the enclitic: this mark has at the same time the effect of catching the eye readily, so as to show that the word preceding the double hyphen has the strong primary accent; *e.g.* **jit--sî**, day-time; **bô--khì**, to disappear or vanish.

Sometimes in a group of three words two words follow the double hyphen. In that case the primary accent is on the first of the three, and the last two are enclitic; a slight trace of a secondary accent is sometimes heard on the last of the three, but yet it does not recover its own proper tonal inflection; *e.g.* **sak--lȯh-khì**, to push down to a lower level; **poah--lȯh-lâi**, to fall down from a higher level.

When a word stands *first in a group of two*, of which the second has the strong accent, then the first word experiences a very marked change in its tonal inflection.

The **chiū^{n}-piâ^{n}** or upper first tone becomes somewhat lower in key, coming down about half-way towards the "ē-khì," but remaining quite level and equable.

The **ē-piâ^{n}** or lower first loses its inflection, becoming

厦英大辭典

very nearly or quite level. In some places it becomes extremely like the unaccented "chiū^{n}-piâ^{n}," as described in the preceding paragraph; in other places, especially in Tâng-oa^{n}, it becomes undistinguishable from the unaccented "ē-khì" tone.

The **chiū^{n}-sia^{n}** or second tone in such a position entirely loses its second half, namely, the falling inflection, and retains only its first half, namely, a slight upward motion. Great care must be taken not to give its usual downward intonation, because (as will be seen from the next paragraph) it would in that case be confounded with the altered or unaccented form of the "chiū^{n}-khì" tone.

The **chiū^{n}-khì** or upper third tone is lifted up so as to become a high, rapid, falling tone, almost the same as the original inflection of the "chiū^{n}-sia^{n}." It is also pronounced with great energy, so that the two syllables sound more like a spondee than an iambus.

The **ē-khì** or lower third tone sinks a very little lower than its original form, with perhaps a very slight downward motion. In most cases the alteration of this tone is scarcely perceptible, but when the two words are both of the "ē-khì" tone, then the first is distinctly lower than the second; *e.g.* **chīn-tsāi, chēng-chēng, siū-tsōe.**

The two **jip** tones (the upper and lower fourth) simply change places with each other, the **chiū^{n}-jip** being pronounced with the original intonation of the "ē-jip," and the **ē-jip** taking the original intonation of the "chiū^{n}-jip." It should also be observed that in this connection the "chiū^{n}-jip" is pronounced with much more energy than the "ē-jip;" *e.g.* **hok-khì** being almost like a spondee, or the "hok" being given with a sort of staccato effect; while **hòk-sāi** is an ordinary iambus, with the "hòk" thoroughly unaccented.

ACCENT.

As all the words in the language are monosyllables, they are usually grouped together in groups of regular form and regular accentuation. These *groups*, of two, three, or four words (and sometimes of more), are often so absolutely fixed in the usage of the language as to become very similar to the polysyllabic *words* of other languages; and within such groups the laws of accent in relation to the several words are quite as strict as the accentual laws for the several syllables of the words in polysyllabic languages.

The general rule is that the primary accent falls on the last word of a group, whether it be a group of two, three, or more words. When the accent falls on the second last or penult, I have indicated the fact by placing a *double hyphen* after the accented word. This has also the effect (as explained in the previous section and in Appendix No. V.) of indicating that the word which follows the double hyphen is enclitic. When two words making a group have no hyphen between them, the meaning is that the first word has a sort of secondary accent, and retains its own tone unchanged or but slightly changed; *e.g.* **hong chhe**, the wind blows; but in **hong-chhe**, a paper-kite, the "hong" is quite unaccented, as is shown by the presence of the hyphen. Such are the more important rules for groups of two words.

GROUPS OF THREE.

In a group of three words the general rule is that the *primary* accent falls on the last word, a *secondary* accent on the first, and that the second word is quite unaccented; *e.g.* **kóng**^{2}-**bô**^{0}-**iá**^{n}^{1} has the primary accent on "iá^{n}," the secondary on "kóng," and no accent on "bô."

But sometimes, while the primary accent is on the last word, the secondary accent is on the second word, and it is then the first word that becomes quite unaccented. Such cases may generally be reduced to one or other of the following rules, (1) when the second is a much *more important word* than the first, or (2) when the *tone* of the second is a much stronger tone than that of the first.

If the first be a mere auxiliary or a comparatively unimportant word, while the second is a word of much importance, then the first is apt to lose the tone. Among the words which often thus lose the tone at the beginning of a group of three, the following may be noted:— **ū**, to have; **bô**, not to have; **ēng**, "to use," when in the sense of "by" or "with;" **lâi**, "to come," when used as a mere connective; **khì**, "to go," as a mere connective; **teh, tiòh, thang**, as auxiliaries to verbs, &c.; **beh**, will; **tī, kàu, kah**, and such prepositions; **ná^{n}, nā^{n}, kap, chiah, chiū**, and some adverbs and conjunctions; **tsáp**, ten; **chit**, "one," often used somewhat like the indefinite article. Such words often do take the secondary accent; but it is very common for them to lose the accent, allowing it to pass on to the second word; *e.g.* **bô**^{0}-**kàu**^{2}-**hùn**^{1}, "no instruction," has the secondary accent on "kàu," and none on "bô." So with **tiòh-koâ^{n}-jiét**, to have fever and ague; **teh-kóng-ōe**, in the act of speaking; **beh-poa^{n}-chhù**, will remove one's residence; **tsáp-goā-lâng**, more than ten men; **chit-sì-lâng**, one's whole life.

Another principle which sometimes may explain the secondary accent falling on the second word, is when it has a very strong tone, such as the "chiū^{n}-khì" or the "chiū^{n}-jip," while the first word is not in either of these two tones; or as when the second word is of the "chiū^{n}-sia^{n}" tone, while the first is not in any of these three tones. But on the other hand, if the first word be specially important in meaning, it keeps the secondary accent, though the second word may have a tone that is naturally stronger; *e.g.* **chīn**^{2}-**khùi-lát**^{1}, "to exert one's strength to the utmost," where the secondary accent is on "chīn."

When the principal accent in a group of three falls on the *second* word, I place a double hyphen after it; in this case the first word has a secondary accent, or loses or changes its tone, and the last word becomes enclitic.

When the principal accent falls on the *first*, this is indicated by the double hyphen after it; then the second and third words become enclitic, the second being quite unaccented, and the third either unaccented or else having a faint secondary accent.

GROUPS OF FOUR.

The most usual arrangement is that a group of four words consists of two groups of two, each having an accent on its second word; the first of these subordinate groups is usually pronounced somewhat less strongly than the second; thus in **bô-lâng**^{2} **beh-khì**^{1}, "there is no one who will go," the primary accent is on "khì," the secondary on "lâng;" but this secondary accent is often almost as strong as the primary.

When the first two words in a group of four are such as **kap--i, kap--lâng, kā--i, hō--i, khit--i,**

chit--ē, that half is pronounced very much more gently than the second; *e.g.* **khit--i thâi--sí**, to be killed by him; **kap--i kóng-ōe**, to converse with him.

When **tsáp**, "ten," stands in the second place, it is unaccented, and throws the secondary accent usually forward on the third word, while a still weaker or tertiary accent is heard on the first word; *e.g.* **jī-tsáp-sì-lâng**, twenty-four men; **saⁿ-tsáp-gō͘-tø**, the thirty-fifth division of a Hien district.

A similar effect is produced if any other word weak in tone or sense (see above on Groups of Three) stands in the second place; *e.g.* **kàu-beh-sit-sîn**, "to the very point of going to faint."

Sometimes a specially important word in the first place draws the secondary accent to itself; *e.g.* **nn̄g-ki-poàⁿ-ûi** (where a sort of tertiary accent is heard on "poàⁿ," but "nn̄g" is the important word), *two* and a half masts, *i.e.* a barque. In the latter part of the Dictionary I have sometimes written such phrases thus, "**nn̄g--ki-poàⁿ-ûi**."

Groups of five or more are compounded of shorter groups in a similar way.

USE OF HYPHENS.

I am painfully conscious that my system of using hyphens is not wholly consistent in the several parts of the Dictionary; this is especially the case in groups of three words, which I have sometimes joined all together, and sometimes left one and two, or two and one. But my apology is, that too sparing a use of hyphens, as it seems to me, has hitherto been made by others; and it has been necessary for me to write out the copy for the press at home without the opportunity of consulting others.

My leading idea in the use of hyphens has been to connect together those words which are pronounced together without pausing, like the syllables of a polysyllabic word, and where consequently the tone of one word is more or less affected by its being joined to another; but in some cases where I have not used the hyphen, the tone of one word is also somewhat affected by the relation to another; for the attempt to string together *all* the words that are mutually affected would have made combinations of an unwieldy length.

VARIOUS AMBIGUITIES AND ERRORS WHICH STILL REMAIN.

There are many ambiguities which, though occasionally noted, are in many or most places left without remark.

Such is very specially the case with the ambiguities produced by the want of moods, tenses, numbers, persons, cases, gender, articles, &c., in Chinese grammar. So also with the frequent interchange of the parts of speech, *e.g.* adjective with adverb, adjective with substantive, verb with preposition, substantive with postposition, conjunction with preposition, &c., or sometimes three or four parts of speech.

Names of relationships partake very largely of such ambiguity, *e.g.* **peh** and **chek**, meaning not only senior and junior uncle, but also senior and junior cousins (even any distant cousins) of father when of the same surname. Still more extensive is the use of **hiaⁿ-tī** and **chí-bē**, meaning not only brothers and sisters, but also male and female cousins in great variety.

Titles of office but rarely correspond to the English words, partly from the different number of steps in the various gradations, and partly because the number of troops supposed to be commanded by military and naval officers is often widely different from the reality. So also when we speak of the emperor Kang-hi or the emperor Kien-lung, we cannot always stop to explain that such a name as Kang-hi, Kien-lung, Hien-fung, is not a name or title of a person at all, but only the title of the period of the reign of the sovereign, whose personal name is far too sacred to be either spoken or written, and who is properly spoken of, *e.g.* as Hâm-hong-kun, *i.e.* the sovereign who reigned in the period or reign called in Amoy "Hâm-hong," and in Mandarin "Hien-fung."

The whole system of the so-called civil and military degrees is quite different from what we call degrees, and comes much nearer to our examinations for the civil and military services, though differing from them also in many important respects, especially in this—that the man who has passed his examination and gained his degree has by that very fact had his political position quite changed, having many special privileges denied to the common people in regard to the action of courts of justice and intercourse with the magistrates.

Of other words a very few examples must suffice; *e.g.* **chiú**, often translated "wine," but which really means any spirituous liquor, and rarely if ever means "wine" in our sense; **be̍h**, either wheat or barley; **bú**, usually translated "military," but really including military and naval; **siáh**, marble or soap-stone; **iûⁿ**, used for "sheep," but properly "goat;" **tha̍k**, commonly rendered "to read," but really only to read aloud; **kong-chhin**, "an arbiter," but very far from our idea of arbitration, meaning simply a person or persons put forward by one or both of the parties to use their good offices, and endeavour to reconcile the parties (usually by a compromise), who are at perfect liberty either to accept the solution or not.

In many other cases too the meanings given are merely approximations. It must often have happened that, instead of grasping the full meaning of a phrase, I have only caught one of its particular applications, while at other times a particular use may have been too hastily generalized. It is in order to avoid these dangers that I have so largely used particular examples instead of attempting to combine them in a general expression.

The student need not be at all surprised if his Chinese teacher, or even several of them, object to certain phrases or meanings. In such a case let him use those words and phrases about which there is no question; but let him not too hastily conclude that the book is wrong. Many many times I have erased passages which I afterwards found quite correct and restored to their places. For there is no absolute standard of the spoken language; and the usage of various towns, villages, and regions varies so much, that phrases in constant use in one part are unknown in another.

At the same time the student must not lean too much on the Dictionary. The sounds, and especially the tones, must be carefully learned from the lips of a native; and when some words and phrases have been learned, it is only by constant intercourse with the people that one can master the art of combining them into sentences in a correct and natural manner.

The teachers themselves are the source of one sort of

error which is doubtless still represented to some extent in these pages. They are accustomed to adorn their own language with a variety of polite and literary phrases, and they are very apt to teach us such phrases as if they were really colloquial, while to the great mass of the people they are as unintelligible as Latin or French to an average Englishman. I have inserted many such phrases with the note "(R.)" to show that they belong to the Literary or Reading form of the language; but doubtless not a few have escaped my notice.

There are also a considerable number of phrases which have somehow come to be used by those Chinese who have much intercourse with foreigners, and which they continue to use because foreigners are supposed to understand them. Against such expressions the student must be very much on his guard.

I observe on looking over the pages some inconsistencies of spelling; *e.g.* **má=mah**, the interrogative particle; **ah=á**, the final indicative or vocative particle; **cheh=chit-ē**, &c. I fear also that some mistakes which I made in my early scrolls have not been fully eliminated, *e.g.* **chīn** sometimes written where it should be "chin," in such phrases as **chin-hó**, very good.

In noting the variations of the dialects of Chang-chew, Chin-chew, &c., there is a peculiar sort of error which has sometimes crept in, viz. changing one part of a phrase into the dialect in question without making the corresponding change in the other part, as if in illustrating the change of **mn̂g** into **mûi**^{n} in Chang-chew, one should write **ē-mûi**^{n}, as the Chang-chew name of Amoy, while it is really **ɛ̄-mûi**^{n}; or as if in a sentence of the Chin-chew dialect one had failed to change **kóng** into **söh**, or **kè** into **kö̀**.

Some more remarks on these dialects will be found in the Appendix Nos. II. and III.; but neither there nor in the body of the Dictionary is there anything like a full treatment of their variations. The Chang-chew dialect is the one most copiously treated, so that it is believed that in the leading words most of its variations are noted. The next in copiousness is the Chin-chew dialect, but it is not nearly so fully treated. Of the other dialects very little is noted except those of Tung-an and Chang-poo. Therefore the student must not conclude that a given word or phrase remains unchanged in one of these dialects merely because no variation is noted.

EXPLANATION OF ABBREVIATIONS,

AND OF

PECULIAR MARKS, &c.

A. Amoy dialect.
An. or Ank. Ankoi or An-khoe dialect.
Bud. Buddhist.
C. Chang-chew dialect.
cf. compare.
Cn. Chin-chew dialect.
col. colloquial or vernacular, as opposed to the literary or reading form.
dist. distinguish from.
E. dialect of Eńg-chhun or Yung-chun.
esp. especially.
F. phrases especially used in Formosa.
f. foreign phrases, viz. names or phrases invented to describe foreign things or ideas, or phrases used only or chiefly by those Chinese who have intercourse with foreigners.
fig. figurative.
gen. generally.
H. dialect of Hūi-an or Hūi-oaⁿ.
K. or Kk. dialect of Kwan-kow or Koàn-kháu.
L. dialect of Nan-an or Lâm-oaⁿ.
lit. literally.
Mand. Mandarin dialect, or Vernacular of Northern, Central, and Western China.
opp. opposed to.
P. dialect of Chang-poo or Chiuⁿ-phó͘.
R. reading or literary style, as to sound or meaning.
When written in parentheses after a Chinese word or phrase, means that it is a literary or polite word or phrase, not used in the colloquial.
When written before a Chinese word, both being in brackets or parentheses, means that it is the reading sound of the character of which the colloquial form is given in the context.
When followed by an English word or phrase, means that the rendering given is used only in the reading or literary style, or transferred to the colloquial only in a few set phrases.
r. rare.
s. see; this abbreviation is used only when there are two phrases having exactly the same sound and tone, *e.g.* **tsâi-tsú**, either "a man of wealth" or "a talented man;" where it occurs under "wealth" it has the note "(s. talent);" and where it occurs under "talent" it has the note "(s. wealth)." I refer merely to the *English* meaning, because the Chinese word referred to is, and must be *always*, the very same sound and tone with the leading word (in this case "tsâi"), under which the phrase occurs.
T. dialect of Tung-an or Tâng-oaⁿ.
Tt. dialect of Chang-tai or Tiô-thoà.
v. see; referring to a *Chinese* word where more full information is given, or where additional examples are collected.
vulg. vulgar or coarse expression.
X. phrase used by the missionaries or native Christians; either not used at all by others, or used rarely or in a different sense.

I have not loaded this table with such well-known abbreviations as id., do., &c.

The abbreviations for the varieties of the dialects are used thus:—Within parentheses *immediately* after the leading word, and with nothing else in the parentheses, they mean that *all the words and phrases* under that leading word belong to the dialect referred to, unless otherwise noted; *e.g.* "**boeh** (C.), = A. beh," implies that any phrase given under that leading word "boeh" belongs to the Chang-chew dialect. So also "**tāⁿ**(Cn.)," implies that all the phrases under that leading word "tāⁿ" belong to the Chin-chew dialect; but in this latter example some of the phrases have the note "(A.)," meaning that they are used in Amoy.

When the abbreviation for a dialect is used within parentheses followed by a Chinese word or phrase, it means that this is the form in the said dialect for the Amoy word or phrase that precedes the parenthesis.

When preceded by the word "also" it means that while the word in some other sense or usage belongs, for instance, to the Amoy dialect, yet in the cases specified it belongs to that one of the dialects which is specified; but in such case the examples of phrases given afterwards belong to the Amoy.

When "R." stands at the beginning of a sentence within brackets or parentheses, and before the end of the parenthetic part the abbreviation "=col." occurs, the "=" is used merely in an *etymological* sense, denoting that the subjoined colloquial words belong to the same reading form, or spring from the *same root*, and does not mean that they have the same *meaning*.

A double hyphen "--" is used to indicate that the succeeding word is enclitic.

A small cross "(+)" is used as the mark of addition, to indicate that other examples of the phrase, or another phrase of the same sound and tone, will be found in another part of the collection of phrases under the same leading word. Thus under the word **thâu**, "head," the phrase **koaⁿ-thâu** occurs twice in very different senses, each time with this mark. In the earlier part of the Dictionary this mark is not used.

3.3, 1.15, and such like combinations, *i.e.* a numeral in large type followed by a dot at the bottom and a numeral in smaller type, are used for the Chinese month and day, *e.g.* 1.15 is the 15th day of the first month.

A full explanation of the orthography and tonal marks will be found in the Introduction. Some of the more important rules may be briefly stated as follows:—

The vowels are all pronounced according to the sounds usual in Germany, Italy, &c., and not according to the English usage when it differs from the continental.

ɵ expresses the sound of **o** in the English *lord, long, lot;* **o** has sometimes this sound, sometimes the sound of **o** in the English *no* (see the rule in the Introduction).

ɛ is the sound of the French "è," or of the English "e" in *there.*

Double dots are *never* used as marks of diaeresis, but always indicate a vowel of a really different *sound.* The mark of diaeresis is never required, because in all diphthongs each vowel retains its own original sound.

ö and **ü** as in German.

The consonants are for the most part used much as in English. **g** always hard; **ch** always as in *church.*

th and **ph** must *not* be sounded as in English. They are pronounced by appending a real aspirate sound to the usual sounds of **t** and **p** respectively.

kh and **chh** are in like manner formed from **k** and **ch** by adding a clearly-pronounced aspirate.

The accent marks have nothing to do with the *sounds* of the vowels or consonants: they indicate the modulations of *tone,* as is partially explained in the Introduction. In a diphthong they do not refer to one vowel only, but to the whole syllable.

ORDER OF ALPHABETIC ARRANGEMENT IN THIS DICTIONARY.

chh, kh, ng, ph, th, and **ts** are used in the alphabetic arrangement like single consonants; thus, for instance, all the words beginning with the unaspirated **k** are given to the end, as far as **kut** and **kwat**, before **kha** and the others which have **kh** as their initial.

ɛ is mixed up with **e**, and **ü** with **u**, for convenience of reference, as they are respectively mere dialectic variations of these vowels.

ɵ and **ö** are placed just after the corresponding *syllables* which are formed with **o**; *e.g.* **tɵ** and **tö** follow **to**; **töh** follows **toh**; and **töng** follows **tong**. I am not sure whether this be the best plan to follow, but it is the arrangement which I at present use.

Words that have a nasal, indicated by a small suspended "ⁿ" at the end, follow immediately the same syllables without the nasal. But when the initial is **m, n, ng,** or **j,** the nasal and non-nasal forms are mixed up, as this makes reference easier, because many words are written both ways.

The tones of any one syllable are arranged thus:— **chiūⁿ-piâⁿ, ē-piâⁿ; chiūⁿ-siaⁿ; chiūⁿ-khì, ē-khì;** *e.g.* "seng, sêng; séng; sèng, sēng." This does not include the two **jip** tones, which, being differently spelled, *i.e.* always ending in **h, k, p,** or **t,** are found usually at a little distance off: their order is—**chiūⁿ-jip, ē-jip;** *e.g.* "sek, se̍k."

ERRATA.

p. 14, col. 2, line 6 from bottom, for **bé-chiòng-kun** read **bé-chiong-kun.**
p. 89, col. 2, line 37, for **ôe-phāng** read **ōe-phāng.**
p. 94, col. 1, line 20, after "blue flowers" insert a query.
p. 94, col. 2, line 4 from bottom, for "v. hông" read "v. hōng."
p. 119, col. 1, line 19, for **sek** read **sėk.**
p. 138, col. 2, line 10 from bottom, for **sah** read **sah**^{n}.
p. 150, col. 1, line 18, for **hui** read **kui.**
p. 181, col. 2, line 23, for **tsám-jien** read **tsám-jiên.**
p. 188, col. 1, line 11, for **kúi-nà** read **kúi-nā.**
p. 256, col. 2, line 17, for **sek** read **sėk.**
p. 315, col. 1, line 30, for "v. ióng" read "v. jī."
p. 338, col. 2, line 29, for "thoân" read "toân."
p. 474, col. 2, line 15 from bottom, for **tong-tong** read **tang-tang.**

Doubtless there must be many more errors which have not been observed.

DICTIONARY

OF THE

AMOY COLLOQUIAL LANGUAGE.

a

a (R. id.), a prefix in some nouns and in names of Cantonese. **a-pan,** a sailor who climbs masts; obstinate (v. pan). **a-gûi,** asafœtida. **a-ko,** son of a first-class mandarin. **a-hoat,** name of a Cantonese, = A. hoat--á.

a— **a-ka,** medicine made from turtle-bones.

a (R. id.) **a-phièn,** opium (v. phièn).

a— **a-put-tó,** = àh-put-tó, a sort of doll.

a (R. id.) **i-i a-a,** sound of a flute. **a-a-kiò,** sound of a child just beginning to make the sound "a-a."

a— **a-tsa,** = am-tsam, dirty, unclean (lit. or fig.)

a— **a-thâu** (imit. of mand.), a female slave.

a— **jiáu-a,** a large sort of gong.

a [R. a crow]. **o͘-a,** a crow. **o͘-a-lêng,** an artificial feather, worn by some officers (v. lêng). **o͘-a kiò pái-sûi** (the crow has called the lame man Sûi), said of a man who formerly had a good character, being suddenly led away into vice and ruin.

â, exclamation of surprise.

â (C.), = A. lâ, —. **â-sâm,** = A. lâ-sâm, dirty.

á [R. tsú, a son], (Cn. ngá, ngiá ká^{n}), (T. sometimes á or ah enclitic), suffix of nouns, often diminutive. **kù-á,** a saw. **kū-á,** wife's younger brother. **î-á,** wife's younger sister. **káu-á,** a dog; a little dog. **kha-á,** inferior assistants.

á (R. tsú ?), enclitic suffix in names of common people, acquaintances, or persons about same rank (Cn. only said of young boys, while it is a *prefix* for adults) —. **hoat--á,** the man named "hoat," more politely called "hoat-ló."

á (T.) **á-î,** = A. am-po͘-chê, the cicada.

á (Cn.), prefix to names of persons. **á-sóng** = A. "sóng--á" or "sóng-ló."

á = án, prefix to titles of relations superior to us. **á-tia,** papa. **á-peh,** uncle! sometimes papa!

á [R. pek, a hundred, = col. pah]. **poeh-á-chî^{n},** eight hundred cash. **káu-á-làk,** nine hundred and six.

á (sometimes ná), syllable used in forming some phrases: *e.g.* **bîn-á-tsài,** to-morrow; **m̄-á,** but indeed (v. m̄).

á = ka. **phah-á-chhiù^{n},** to sneeze.

á (R. ek = col. iá), or. **á-bô,** or not. **á-sī,** or it is; or.

à^{n}

á = iáu. **á-bē,** not yet.

à = iàh (R. èk). **à-ná^{n}-beh, à-ná^{n}-m̄,** having half a mind to it.

à [R. secondary]. **à-sèng,** a sage of secondary rank, as Mencius or as Yen-hwuy (Gân-hôe). **à-goân,** a Keujin near the head of the list for the year.

à (R. àu). **à-pà,** very cross and bad-tempered, as a child.

ā = iàh (R. èk), also.

a^{n}, imitative sound. **a^{n}-a^{n}-háu,** sound of children crying. **a^{n}-a^{n}-jióng,** incessant noise. **i-i a^{n}-a^{n},** sound as of several men rowing a boat, or of many children. **i^{n}-i^{n} a^{n}-a^{n},** sound as of musical instruments.

â^{n}— **pûn â^{n}-m-chhê^{n}** (C.), sound of wind instruments.

â^{n}, an exclamation of great surprise.

â^{n} (R. lân = col. noā^{n}), to guard or protect, as by arm or wing (*e.g.* a hen guarding her brood); to put the arm or arms round a person loosely, so as gently to keep from falling or going away, or to ward off a stroke, or screen from an enemy. **â^{n}-tsàh,** to defend one party in a quarrel. **khah-â^{n} hit-pêng,** throws his influence rather on that side. **â^{n}-chiàh,** to keep things for oneself to eat, as by arm put round them. **â^{n} toā-hūn,** to take the lion's share.

á^{n}, to embrace tightly with one or both arms; to fold to one's breast; to hold or carry between arm and breast, but not so tightly as "ngóeh;" to shelter by arm tightly pressed. **á^{n}--teh,** to cover or shelter below or behind one's arm, &c. **á^{n}--ê,** an adopted child. **á^{n}-ná^{n} tsōe-chit-ē,** to hold several things at once under the arm, or between the arm and the breast.

á^{n}, to lean against. **chhùi á^{n}-chhùi,** to put mouth to mouth.

á^{n}— **kong-á^{n}-tāu,** a long dark red legume.

á^{n} (Cn.), sometimes = A. ká^{n} —. **m̄-á^{n},** = A. m̄-ká^{n}, not dare.

à^{n} (R. hiòng = col. ǹg, hià^{n}), to stoop or bend down; to face towards. **à^{n}-thâu,** to bend down the head. **à^{n}-io,** to bend forwards, bending the loins as in making a bow. **à^{n}-teh-chiàh,** bending down to eat. **à^{n}-teh-khoà^{n},** bending down to look. **à^{n}--lóh-lâi thia^{n},** bend down to hear, as superior. **à^{n}-teh-thia^{n},** to bend the ear to listen. **à^{n}-à^{n} teh-thia^{n},** several persons listening thus. **à^{n} hī-khang,** to bring the ear near another's mouth. **phí-phak-à^n**, appearance of falling forward with arms extended. **sa^n-chiȧh-à^n**, fitting well together, as parts of a piece of furniture; friendly; of one mind. **bīn à^n-lâm**, facing south, as house. **à^n-hái**, facing the sea.

ā^n (R. hām), stuffing or contents of pies, tarts, cakes, &c. **ā^n-piá^n**, cakes with stuffing of pease-meal, &c. **bô-ā^n**, solid and uniform, as cake with no stuffing. **ké-ā^n**, stuffing of steamed cakes. **ti^n-ā^n**, sweet stuffing. **kiâm-ā^n**, salt do. **ti^n-phê kiâm-ā^n** (a sweet cake with salt stuffing), a man who seems friendly, but is really hostile. **cheng-sîn-phê gōng-ā^n**, appearance of intelligence while really stupid.

ā^n, sound of a cow bellowing.

ah (R. ek). **ah-lȧh**, to compel. **ah-jih**, to force an unwilling man to do something. **ah-lȯh**, to repress or curb, as temper or desires, or as other man. **ah iáu-bē-lȯh**, not yet subdued, as temper, &c.

ah (R. ap), to guard, escort, restrain; to write the regular words or dates with red ink on an official document; to make a stroke with the stern larboard oar, worked by the right hand, so as to turn the boat's head to the right.

ah-ūn, to rhyme.

ah-kng, a ship's carpenter.

ah-tang, to pass the season (especially the winter) abroad, as vessel. **tê ah-tang**, the tea is stored up for next year's market.

ah-âu, to follow, as guard or escort. **ah-hiòng**, to send government money, under escort, to superior mandarins. **ah-tsûn**, to convoy a ship. **ah-sàng**, to escort. **ah-hoān**, to guard or escort a criminal. **ah-soah**, to restrain. **ah-hè**, to take charge of cargo. **ah-hu**, overseer of numerous coolies carrying burdens, or of chair-coolies. **khu-ah**, to keep in ward, as a criminal, or as parties in a lawsuit. **ah-koán**, to be confined in the less miserable prison.

ah-chiú^n, to row hard with the stern oar, so as to turn the boat's head round, almost like a helm. **hē-lí-ah**, you take the stern oar (position of honour in a boat). **khah-sit-ah**, strike very gently with the oar in your right hand. **ah bé-chiú^n**, give a stroke with the larboard oar, so as to turn boat's head to right. **ah thâu-chiú^n**, strike with port oar (held in left hand), so as to turn boat's head to left. **ah thâu-tit** (C.), id.

ah jit-chí, to mark the date with red ink on an official document. **ah-jit**, id. **chhiam-ah**, to write the date and make the regular marks in red ink on an official document; the official who writes them. **chhiam-ah toā-iâ**, this official. **hoe-ah**, the mark on a document below the name, serving as signature.

ah, enclitic particle at end of exclamations and of indicative sentences. **chhám--ah**, alas!

ah (T.), = A. á, enclitic particle at end of names of things.

ah [R. ek, to benefit, = col. iah]. **ah-bú-chháu**, a medical plant used for the menses of females.

ah (R. ap), a duck. **ah-hêng**, a young drake (v. hêng, male). **ah-hêng**, embryo in duck's egg (v. hêng, form). **ah-kak**, a drake. **ah-bú**, a duck (female). **ah-bú tsng-kim-sin, iā-sī pí^n-chhùi** (a duck, though adorned with gold on its body, yet has a flat bill), said of a dandy appearing ludicrous with all his finery. **ah-bú-chhùi**, a duck's bill; a hook worn on one's dress for carrying small things. **ah-bú-chhùi bóng-lu** (duck's bill dabbling about at random), to make an attempt or ask a favour with very small hope of success, but may just as well make the attempt. **ah-bú-tôe** (having a sole like a duck), said of a man whose foot is very broad and flat at the instep instead of the usual hollow; also of a peculiar vulgar waddling gait, shaking from side to side.

ah-chiú^n, duck's web-foot. **ah-nn̂g**, duck's eggs (v. nn̂g). **ah-hièn**, small feathers at duck's tail; two small balls near its tail. **ah-pa**, dried duck. **ah-siú^n**, id. **thâi koe-ah**, to kill fowls and ducks.

ah-kha-sóe, a grain like small millet. **ah-kha-sek**, id.

chhài-ah, a sort of duck much in use. **thé-hoan-ah**, the common duck. **chià^n-hoan-ah**, a similar sort. **tsúi-ah**, wild duck; also said of the "chià^n-hoan-ah." **hái-ah**, a sort of wild sea-bird.

chhit-gėh-poà^n ah-á m̄-tsai-sí (a duck in the middle of the seventh month, when ducks are usually offered to the spirits of the dead, and yet not fearing death!), said in scolding a man for bad conduct without fear in spite of impending calamity.

ȧh— **ȧh-chhioh**, a square-shaped ruler for drawing lines or cutting paper straight.

ȧh (R. ȧp), a casket or small case. **ȧh-bá**, id. **siu^n-ȧh**, trunks and caskets. **hoe-ȧh**, a flowered casket; a case for flowers. **gėk-ȧh**, a casket made of jade. **siȧh-ȧh**, a marble casket. **chhâ-ȧh**, a wooden casket. **ìn-sek-ȧh**, box with red ink for stamping. **bȧk-ȧh**, a paper or wooden case for sticks of ink. **kià^n-ȧh**, a case for a mirror. **hún-ȧh**, a case for hair-powder. **hun-ȧh**, a tobacco-box. **bō-ȧh**, an hat-box. **thiap-ȧh**, case for invitation cards (v. thiap). **téng-ȧh**, case for small steelyard. **chiam-ȧh**, a small needle-case.

ȧh, to support, as a screen or partition in danger of being blown in, as by a cross-bar, or as by one's arm laid along it. **ȧh--teh**, id. **ȧh hit-sì**, turn it in that direction. **ȧh-kè-lâi, ȧh-kè-khì**, to turn a thing back and forwards. **ȧh-tó**, to bend or throw down. **khit-hong ȧh-tó**, to be blown down, as a screen; to be thrown on her beam-ends, as a ship. **ȧh-put-tó**, a doll made with a heavy round base, so that when pushed over it always rights itself. **hê-lâm ȧh-sai**, to turn to the south and west, as fair-weather wind in spring.

ai [R. dust]. **tîn-ai** (R.), dust floating in the air. **lâm-hong-ai**, mist caused by the south wind. **ai-bū**, id. **thûn-ai** (C.), soot.

ai— **tiô-chiu-ai**, plays in the Swatow dialect.

ai (R. id.), exclamation of grief, pain, or distress. **ai-chhám**, id. **ai-ai-kiò**, to call mournfully. **pi-ai** (R.), very sad and sorrowful. **ai-oàn**, to repine bitterly (v. oàn). **ai-ėh**, grieved, and murmuring inwardly. **khit-ai kiû-lîn**, to beseech earnestly for some favour when in distress.

ai [R. to pass time, &c., = col. oe]. **ū-lâi-ai** (T.), to have such connection with a man (as by relationship, friendship, or business), that we have some influence with him, or that we are involved in his troubles.

âi— **âi--iā**, exclamation on a sudden feeling of surprise, regret, or pain. **âi--ò**, id. **âi--ioh**, id. **âi-ioh-thià^n**, oh, how painful!

ài— **ài-â**, expression of wonder (somewhat deliberate).

ài [R. a pass, or gate at a pass]. **ài-mn̂g**, street gates. **ài-kháu**, a fortified gate or pass. **koan-ài**, a gate in a pass. **hiám-ài**, very important as a pass.

àì (R. id.), to wish, to desire, to like; apt to; to have a tendency to. **àì-beh**, to wish; to desire. **àì-chia**, to wish to be here. **m̄-àì**, not to wish; indisposed (of mind or body); I don't want it. **seng-khu m̄-àì**, unwell. **àì-thè̤**, having a tendency to vomit. **àì-thè̤**, to desire a rabbit. **àì-kè-lâng**, infectious. **àì kāu-pīⁿ**, unhealthy, as a place. **hit-só̤-tsāi, lâng àì-sí--khì**, that place is very unhealthy and deadly. **àì tek-tsōe lâng**, apt to give offence.

ì-àì, to desire very much; to desire and purpose. **àì-sioh**, to love; to compassionate. **kèng-àì**, to reverence and love. **thióng-àì** (R.), to love, to favour, as a concubine. **le̍k-àì**, to love too much, as son or nephew; to love blindly and with partiality, so as not to observe or punish his faults, and rather screen him. **le̍k-àì put-bêng**, id. **iú-àì** (r.), very affectionate (as brothers). **sit-àì**, to be less loved than others, as child when parents are partial. **lēng-jîn khó-àì**, lovable. **khó-àì** (r.), id. **siong-àì**, mutually loving (as man and woman). **un-àì**, to love greatly, as man and woman. **lēng-àì** (R.), your daughter.

sûn-àì, a short wide-mouthed trumpet (counted difficult to play). **àì-á**, a sort of wind-instrument.

àì — **un-àì**, mumps (v. un).

aiⁿ — **aiⁿ-aiⁿ-chhan**, to groan mournfully.

aîⁿ, interjection expressing surprise and pleasure.

aîⁿ (T.), = A. êng, leisure.

aīⁿ (P.), = iāng, to carry on the back, as a man or child.

aihⁿ, exclamation of regret at a loss or misfortune (cf. ėh and ùt). **ihⁿ-aihⁿ**, discontented, grumbling state of mind, as at a misfortune, or as in a dilemma, when either choice is very inconvenient. **m̄-sái ihⁿ-aihⁿ**, don't distress and worry yourself about it. **ihⁿ-ihⁿ aihⁿ-aihⁿ**, grumbling at something that has happened and cannot now be put right, *e.g.* when it would not be polite to find fault, or when the man who has done it is too powerful.

ak (R. id.), to water; to drench. **ak-tsúi**, to water. **ak-pûi**, to water with liquid manure. **ak-hō̤**, drenched with rain. **ak-hoa-hé**, to extinguish fire with water. **ak-sit-hé**, id. **ak-tâm**, to drench. **ak nn̄g-saⁿ seng-khu**, drenched to the skin several times. **ak kàu-saⁿ-thàu-thàu**, wet to the skin.

ak — **ak-tsak**, disorderly and inconveniently crowded with articles, as a lumber-room; sad or anxious.

ak (R. ok). **mn̂g-ak**, sort of outer gateway or porch.

ak — **ak-á-chhài**, sort of vegetable.

åk (R. ők), a reel or spool for winding thread. **åk-á**, id. **se-åk**, id. for cotton. **si-soàⁿ-åk**, id. for silk.

am (R. id.), a Buddhist monastery, nunnery, or temple. **am-īⁿ**, id. **am-tn̂g**, id. **hê-siūⁿ-am**, Bud. monastery. **lî-ko̤-am**, Bud. nunnery. **bōng-am** (C.), a grave with a sort of shrine or pinnacle at the back. **phó̤-am-hu̍t**, one of the Buddhas. **tō̤-tn̂g-am** (temple of stomach and bowels), said of a literary man absorbing funds collected on the pretext of building a temple.

am — **am-pê-chê**, the cicada. **am-kóng-tsûn** (C.), id. (v. tsûn).

am [R. to understand]. **put-am**, not understanding matters. **put-am sè-bū**, does not know how to manage matters. **put-am sè-sū** (r.), ignorant of the rules of politeness.

am — **am-am**, foolish; stupid. **am-gōng**, do. **am-khám**, do. **am-khám-gōng**, very very stupid. **am-tham**, foolishly greedy.

am — **am-am**, mixed together without distinction. **am-lam**, id. **am--teh**, id. **hó-am-pháiⁿ**, good and bad mixed. **am-lâi am-khì**, taking a whole lot on an average, good and bad together. **am-lâi kah-khì**, id. **am-lam-báuh**, count the price in one lot on an average.

am — **am-koe**, a long and slender kind of pumpkin, often used salted.

am — **koe-am**, a basket for fowls (C. ke-lam).

am — **am-tsam** (Cn.), filthy (v. tsam).

âm (R. hâm), a small covered drain or run for water. **tsúi-âm**, id.; also tubular tiles used for them. **táu-âm**, a sluice. **sò-âm**, a sink. **kau-âm**, a covered drain. **khiā-âm**, a perpendicular water-pipe or drain. **âm-thâu**, a funnel-shaped tube of stoneware or metal placed where the gutter of a roof runs off. **âm-khang**, a small covered drain. **âm-khang-ku** (a tortoise in a drain), a man who seldom goes out.

ám (probably = âm). **ám-péng-sui-khang**, holes for running off water from deck; scupper-holes. **ám-páiⁿ-sui-khang** (T.), id.

ám (R. hám). **ám-tām-hio̍h**, a leaf used for adulterating tea. **ám-lē** (P.), a tree (v. lɛ̄).

ám — **ám-pūi** (Cn.), a stinging insect, = A. chhiū-gūi.

ám, rice-water. **ám-ám**, thin and watery, like thin rice-water; also (T.), flabby, as man's skin and flesh. **ám-chiuⁿ**, rice-water. **ám-bê**, congee; rice boiled very soft and watery. **ám-sng**, soured rice-water (for bleaching). **ám-tàng**, coagulated rice-water. **ám-phe̍h**, scum of rice-water. **ám-pūi**, do. **ám-phí** (Cn.), do. **chhìn-ám**, cold rice-water. **ám-thng**, warm rice-water. **phun-ám**, rice-water mixed with the water in which rice had been washed. **chiuⁿ-ám**, to starch with rice-water.

àm (R. id.), dark; secret; surreptitious; dark and evil; late at night; to keep secret improperly—or make secret improper gains.

kōe-àm, getting soon dark, as short or cloudy day. **beh-àm**, almost dark. **àm-hō̤ tiâu-mîⁿ**, rain about dark lasts through the night. **ge̍h-àm-mîⁿ**, a dark moonless night. **hông-hun-àm**, twilight of the evening; dusk. **àm-iū** (Cn.), very late at night. **àm-hé**, giving a bad flame (as damp wood). **àm-hóe** (C.), at dark. **àm-thâu**, the dark night. **àm-hûn**, dark and cloudy, as night (v. hûn). **àm-chhiùⁿ**, dark as night. **àm-chhiûⁿ**, dark and dismal, as house.

o̤-àm, dark (v. o̤). **àm khám-gōng**, very foolish. **àm--tè**, a dark place; hades.

saⁿ-jit-àm, the third night after marriage, or after the ceremony of changing natal flowers (oāⁿ-hoe), &c. **tiám saⁿ-jit-àm**, to keep a lamp burning three whole days without ceasing, after certain rites. **chhoā bē-saⁿ-jit-àm**, not yet three days after marriage; said of an early quarrel.

àm-tām, indistinct, as a colour, or as cloudy weather; dull-coloured. **àm-sek**, dark-coloured. **sek-tsúi àm**, the colour is dull. **àm-lâm**, dark-blue.

àm-so-so, very dark. **àm-sō-sō**, id. **àm-sô-sô**, id. **àm-bók-bók**, id. **àm-bong-bong**, id. **àm-bong-sa**, to grope. **o̤-àm-bong**, id. **àm-tsut-tsut**, quite dark. **àm-hông**, very dark, as room; very dim, as lamp. **àm-phông**, id.

àm-hóng, *incognito*, in people's dress, or sending messengers to make secret inquiry; to investigate secretly, as mandarin. **àm-kùi**, a secret mark on the skin, as a wart. **àm-kúi**, a secret bolt, as of a door or drawer. **àm-iok**, to make a secret agreement. **àm-chīⁿ**, secret. **àm-chìⁿ**, a secret arrow (v. chìⁿ). **àm-siūⁿ**, to meditate silently on some purpose. **thau-lâi àm-khì**, to come and go secretly. **àm-kè**, a secret plot. **àm-hūn**, to hate secretly. **àm-bô**, to conspire. **sái àm-tók**, to conspire to injure a man. **àm-sim tê-bê**, id. **chhāi àm-tók**, id. **sái àm-pō**, id. **àm-tsông**, to secrete; to hide.

àm-sàm, dark and dirty, as room; improper and depraved (v. sàm). **kiàh-teng, m̄-tsai kha-ē àm** (carrying a lamp, does not know the dark place under his feet), said of a man not knowing his own faults. **kiâⁿ-àm-lō**, to practise gambling, licentiousness, &c. **àm-lō káⁿ-kiâⁿ; chíⁿ-gûn bô-thiàⁿ**, wasting money lavishly in licentious pleasures.

àm--khì, to keep secret improperly. **àm lâng-ê-chîⁿ**, to make secret unfair gains out of a man's money. **àm-nihⁿ tām-póh**, id. **àm-khàm**, to get secret gains at employer's expense (v. khàm). **su-àm**, secretly appropriate part of public funds.

àm-kong-chiáu, the owl. **àm-oàⁿ-chiáu** (T.), id. **àm-koà-chiáu** (T.), id.

àm — **àm-kiàm siong-hông**, = àn----, two persons watching each other (v. àn).

ām (R. hām, or hāng), the neck. **ām-á**, do. **ām-kún**, do. **ām-kún-kut**, vertebræ of neck. **ām-kún-khū**, the prominent part on back of neck, where the back-bone joins. **ām-kún-kū**, Adam's apple. **ām-kún-tsu**, id. **ām-kún-kun**, muscles of neck. **kek ām-kún-kun teh-kóng**, to talk in a very irritated way. **ām-kún chhāi-chhāi**, neck very short. **ām-kún siⁿ-liû tú--tióh**, it cannot be helped.

ām-kui, the front of the throat. **kóng-ōe tiùⁿ ām-kui**, almost choking with rage in speaking. **tiùⁿ ām-kún-kui**, id.

ām-á-kńg, the throat, the gullet. **ām-ē**, the throat below the chin. **ē-ām**, id. **teńg-ām**, the upper part of the neck.

ām-sê, dewlap of cow; babies' napkin or bib. **ām-séh** (C.), id. **ām-koāⁿ**, a child's napkin; also (Cn.), a string of various things hung round a child's neck. **péh-ām-tsoā**, a very venomous serpent with white breast. **péh-ām-koāⁿ** (C.), id. **péh-ām--ê**, a worm with white breast, used in medicine.

niàuⁿ-ām, neck having a scar from a sore. **jiàuⁿ-ām**, id. **chhàu-ām**, neck having a large sore on it. **toā-ām-liû**, large tumour or goitre on neck. **oai-ām**, having a wry neck, and head bent down on one side. **oai-ām-á**, id. **oan-ām**, said of an affair difficult to manage, in which many blunders are made; also, of suddenly meeting a man whom we wish to avoid. **tiàu-ām**, to hang oneself. **thìⁿ-ām**, to stretch out its neck and look up, as a beast (not said of man).

tsúi im-ām (water up to neck), said of very great and imminent danger. **lun-thâu bih-ām**, attitude of looking or listening intently with head drawn back. **náuⁿ-thâu tsūn-ām** (C.), to shake about head and neck improperly.

âm (R. hâ). **ām-bôɛ**, a young frog. **ām-mûiⁿ**, id.; some say (esp. T.) a tadpole.

âm (R. iām), dense and luxuriant, as grass or shrubs, or foliage.

an (T.), = hoan. **an-tsû**, = A. han-tsû, sweet potatoes.

an [R. peace; to set at rest, = col. oaⁿ], to put on, as gilding, turf, &c. (to make orderly arrangement); to consecrate, *i.e.* to perform rites when anything is first made or used, so that it may be fortunate. **an-ún**, safe. **an-jiân**, in quiet ease and comfort. **an-jiân tsū-tsāi**, id. **an-hân tsū-tsāi**, id. **an-chēng**, at peace and quiet without any trouble. **an-lòk** (R.), happy, peaceful, and comfortable (v. lòk). **an-sek-jit**, Sabbath. **an-hioh-jit**, id. **pêng-an**, peace and quiet. **pêng-an-bô-sū**, id. **pêng-an-chhì**, the cactus. **pêng-an tāi-kiet**, peace and great prosperity. **pêng-an-chiò**, Tauist rites to procure blessings. **pêng-an-soáⁿ**, a medicine for colic. **chhéng-an**, to salute, as by letter or by messenger.

an-sim, cheer up, keep your mind at rest; a peaceful mind. **an-ùi**, to comfort. **an-bîn**, to quiet the minds of the people. **an-bîn**, may you sleep quietly, good-night. **an-sin**, to dwell in quietness. **bô-tè thang an-sin**, having no place to rest or live at peace. **an-hūn**, contented with our state or our business. **an-ka**, to put one's household matters pretty straight by some money given or advanced by employer (or borrowed), before going abroad. **an-ka-gûn**, money thus given or lent. **an-iúⁿ** (Cn.), to bring up as an adopted child or slave. **an-tì**, to prepare, as place; or set in order, as room for guests. **an-tùn**, to put in order, as a room; to set an affair in a somewhat safer state. **an-pâi**, to tidy up, to put in nice order, as furniture, &c. (v. pâi). **an-chhah**, to arrange, as troops in garrisons or quarters (v. chhah). **an-tah**, id.; also, to make arrangements for an affair going on well, *e.g.* by getting a party to delay a little, or by talking over influential persons; to make arrangements for persons getting a livelihood. **an-tah hó-sè**, id. **an-tsòng**, to bury with all due rites. **an-iâⁿ**, to encamp. **an-chē**, id. **an iàh-tsām**, to set regular relays of couriers or horses. **an kî-chí**, to set out the chess-men ready for a game.

an-chìⁿ, to place the arrow on the string. **an-keng tah-chìⁿ**, id. **an chek-bâng**, to attach the reed in making candles. **an chháu-phiáⁿ**, to lay turf. **an-kim**, to gild with gold-leaf. **an-joán**, to glue on the bright-coloured feathers called "chhùi-joán."

an-hû, to affix a charm. **an-mn̂g**, to consecrate a new door. **an-ūi**, to consecrate an idol's seat; to invite a specially-honoured guest to take his seat at a feast, by special rites (v. ūi). **an-chhiám**, to lay the keel of a vessel with superstitious rites. **an-thai**, to perform Tauist rites to remove pain in the womb. **an-thé**, to set down a coffin for burial; to perform rites to ease the pain of a child or pregnant woman (v. thé). **an-thèh**, consecrate a new house and its courtyard. **an-chhn̂g**, to consecrate the marriage-bed. **an-lêng**, to begin the worship of a person recently deceased, done by the relatives and priests.

an-kiⁿ, the first watch in the night. **an-kiⁿ-chhèng**, the signal-gun fired at the beginning of it.

an-hui, Ngan-hwuy province. **an-lâm**, Cochin China. **an-khoe**, Ankoi. **kang-an**, the provinces of Kiang-su and Ngan-hwuy (v. tō).

àn (R. àn: cf. col. hoāⁿ, hoā), to lay the finger or hand gently on. **an-khang**, to put the fingers on the holes of a flute, &c. **chhiú an--i**, lay hand on, as on his head (esp. Cn.)

ân (R. êng), tight; hard-up for cash. **pák-ân**, to tie tight. **kat-ân**, to make a knot tight. **pek-ân**, to press urgently, as for debt. **ân tong-tong**, very firm, as a knot. **ân-sò**, hard-up for cash. **ân-khang**, do. **chîⁿ ân**, do. **chîⁿ-chhà ân**, id. **ân-tan**, tightly tied, as parcel; stiff and tight, as drawer; strongly made, as furniture; tightly stretched, as the skin of a diseased swelling or of an over-fat man. **sia^n ân-tan,** voice distinct, clear, and ringing, as in reciting books or giving orders, or as man who has got a little liquor. **ân-thán** (C.), tightly drawn, as rope or cloth; fitting too tight, as dress; tightly roped, as box; firm and fat, as healthy flesh. **phê pi^n-khi-ân,** make your skin tight and ready for a beating.

ân (C.), = A. êng, leisure.

án, = á, ńg (Cn. ín), familiar prefix to titles of relations, &c. **án-né,** mamma! **án-koa^n,** said by a female slave to her master's father. **án-niû^n,** said by female slave to master's mother. **án-gū,** phrase used to babies.

àn [R. a table, = col. oà^n], a lawsuit; a legal case. **àn-toh,** a long high narrow table set at the wall, generally at middle of room, for idols, &c. **tiong-àn,** id. **tiong-àn-toh,** id. **tiong-àn pat-sien,** a set of two tables, one long, the other square.

àn-kiā^n, a lawsuit (classifier "khí"). **àn-chêng,** circumstances of a lawsuit. **sió-àn,** a small unimportant case. **tiōng-àn,** a serious case. **sí-àn,** a case fully settled or ended; a capital case. **tsōe-àn,** a case of a great crime. **kiap-àn,** case of robbery. **bēng-àn,** case of murder or homicide.

tsòe-àn, to make a false complaint in a legal case. **teh-tsòe-àn,** telling falsehoods.

hoān-àn, to be accused. **tsāi-àn,** to have a suit pending. **tó-àn,** to lose one's case. **kiet-àn,** to wind up a case finally, as the parties do by signing an agreement. **siau-àn,** to give up or end a case, either by a regular settlement or by letting it drop. **chhip-àn,** letting a case sleep for a time. **phoe-àn,** to write the official answer to the complaint. **phoe àn-kiā^n,** id. **chhâ-àn,** to examine the case legally. **mn̄g-àn,** to examine as judge. **sím-àn,** to judge in a case. **phoà-àn,** to come to a clear understanding of a case, so as to see through the lies and know the true state of it; said figuratively of dismissing a bad employé. **phoà^n-àn,** to decide a case, as of disputed property. **tēng-àn,** to give judgment. **tsûn-àn,** to lay up the papers of case. **thê-àn,** to call up a case from the lower court, as on appeal. **tiàu-àn,** id. **hoan-àn,** to reverse the decision of the lower court.

àn-tók-iâ, a prime minister of the Han dynasty, worshipped by the underlings in yamuns.

àn [R. an, peace]. **àn-sek-hiu^n,** gum-benzoin.

àn (R. ièn). **àn-chhài,** please eat! said to guests.

àn [R. to lay the hand on; according to; to examine, = col. an, hoā^n, hoâ], according to; to deposit an article as security for payment in a short time, only with an acquaintance, and on much better terms than a pawnshop gives.

àn-chhat-si, provincial judge (v. chhat). **àn-si,** id.

àn-sǹg, to make a rough estimate on fingers, or mentally. **àn-chí^n,** to borrow money from an acquaintance at a very easy rate, giving some article as security. **chhiá^n-àn-hā,** just leave that matter over till more pressing matters have been attended to. **àn-giàh,** to lay by a sum for some special purpose, or for a man not present when his share falls due. **àn-hē--teh** (T.), id. **àn-kiàm siong-hông** (each having his hand on his sword and on his guard), said of two men mutually watching each other.

àn-hoat (R.), according to law. **àn-sî,** according to the time. **àn-sî àn-tsūn,** id. **àn-jit,** according to the day; reckoning days; day by day. **àn-sî àn-jit,** according to the proper day and hour. **àn-chia,** this way. **àn-hia,** that way. **àn-ni^n,** thus, so. **àn-ni^n-si^n,** id. **àn-hi** (r.), id. **àn-hí** (T. C.), id. **àn-hiù^n-sì** (C. T.), in that way (v. hiù^n). **àn-ni^n-ngá** (Cn.), so. **àn-tsái^n-iū^n,** how?

ān [R. hān, a limit, to limit, = col. hiēn, hāt], to promise to pay a debt at a fixed time, or to have some work finished at a certain date, later than it ought to have been. **ān--chit-ē,** id. **ān-chè,** to promise to pay a debt at a fixed time. **hō-i-ān,** to allow him the delay to the date he asks. **khoan-ān,** to extend the time; to act with forbearance as to the date. **bōe-ān--tit,** no delay can be allowed; must pay or finish the work at date first agreed upon. **kè-ān,** to pass the time fixed. **thiap-kè-ān ê-gûn,** payment for lateness; demurrage. **ān-kî,** to appoint a date. **ān sî-khek,** to fix the time to a moment. **ān tī-sî,** what time is appointed? **ān sím-mih^n sé-tsāi,** what place is fixed, as for payment.

bô-kài-ān, boundless, unlimited. **iú-ān** (C.), = iú-hiēn, few; of limited number.

ang (R. ong), the surname Wang.

ang, a husband. **ang-sài** (r.), a husband. **kè-ang,** to marry a husband. **ang-bó,** man and wife; husband and wife. **ang-pô,** id. **ang-chiá** (C.), id. **ang-á-chiá** (P.), id. **kiet tsòe ang-bó,** to become man and wife. **bô ang-bó-chêng,** not according to the feelings that should exist between married persons, *e.g.* quarrelling or beating, or as widower marrying very soon after wife's death. **lō-thâu-ang,** man cohabiting with woman without marriage.

ang [R. ong, an old man], the surname Wung.

tiò-hí-ang, the kingfisher; also a picture of an old fisherman.

ang— **hái-ang,** the whale, = keng-hî.

ang [R. kong; a duke, a lord], an idol, an image (esp. C.)

ang-á, pictures of men; toy images. **ang-á-jîn,** the pupil of the eye. **ang-á-thâu,** a head (without a body), for children to play with; the reflection of the observer in another man's eye; a man's name written at the top corner of a page in ledger.

ang-î, a sorceress, a witch (not Cn.)

ang-sîn, an idol. **ang-hút** (C.), = A. sîn-pût, idols in general. **ang-kong-tsé,** an idol. **ang-kong** (C. T.), id. **mûi^n-ang-á** (C.), = A. mn̂g-sîn, figures painted on doors. **chiòh-ang** (C.), stone images at graves or temples. **ang hién, tē-tsú lók-lién** (C.), when the idol is powerful, his votaries lose their fortune (as they spend so much money on their idol).

âng (R. hông), red; red colour much used on joyful occasions, and by women, especially at marriages; also, a surname, but rarely, the usual surname being the following word. **put-chí-âng,** very red; said also of a man whose word is readily followed by mandarins, or by the head of a mercantile house.

tǹg-âng, to stamp with red ink, as a document. **âng-téng,** first-class mandarin. **káu-sái-âng** (colour of dog's excrement), opaque red button of lower rank. **âng-ia^n-bō,** cap of mandarin servants and runners. **âng-pâi,** a vessel's papers or register. **âng-tiâ^n,** a petition or complaint on red paper, used by gentry or literati or strangers.

âng-mn̂g, red-haired; vulgar word for British. **âng-mn̂g-lâng,** a British or English man. **âng-mn̂g-kok,** Britain. **âng-thâu,** large Cantonese junks. **âng-liāu**, bricks and tiles of all sorts. **âng-hê**, red clouds, as in evening. **âng-hê**, red shrimps.

âng-tsó, dried fruit of the jujube-tree (commonly called Chinese dates). **âng-khī**, the common persimmon. **âng-hoe**, a plant used in dyeing. **âng-iûⁿ** (Cn.) = khơ-koe, the bitter cucumber. **âng-thơ̂**, Turkey opium. **kim-hoe-âng**, id.

oāⁿ-âng, to put on ordinary dress at end of mourning. **tńg-âng**, id.; also, of colour, to change to red. **âng-pau**, a small cumshaw or reward to a literary man. **âng-ó**, red bridal dress. **âng-ôe**, bridal shoes. **âng-kiō**, bridal sedan. **kā i koà-âng**, to give him some red thing (especially a red scarf), or money wrapped in red paper, to a man who does some unlucky thing in our behalf, *e.g.* who assists at the funeral of our relative, or makes arrangements for the re-marriage of a widow.

âng-chiāⁿ, a red-faced actor in a play. **ơ-âng-bīn**, face painted, as in plays or incense processions.

pàng-âng, bloody dysentery. **phùi-âng**, to spit blood.

thih sio-âng, heat iron red-hot. **hé kek kàu-chin-âng**, make the furnace very hot. **âng-thiⁿ chhiah-jit-thâu**, cloudless hot sky.

âng-tiu-tiu, very red. **âng-phà-phà**, do. **âng hám-hám**, do. **âng-ki-ki**, do. **âng-kòng-kòng**, do. **toā-âng-sek**, rich crimson. **âng-khàm-sek**, dark brownish red. **âng-hoáⁿ**, dull indistinct red. **hún-âng**, whitish red. **âng-kháu**, reddish. **tsúi-âng**, light red. **chhiò-âng**, light red. **gûn-âng**, bright red, brighter than "tsúi-âng." **thô-âng**, rich red of peach blossoms and Chinese card-paper. **tsu-âng**, rich bright red; vermilion. **iûⁿ-âng**, a bright foreign red. **iû-âng**, do.; also to paint red.

âng (R. hông), a surname; mand. Hung, the surname of Tai-ping-wang.

âng (R. iam). **âng-lék-kôe**, sort of salted shell-fish from the north.

áng— **áng-láng**, obstinate; sour-tempered, and rather stupid, so as to be difficult to consort with. **áng-láng-siūⁿ**, planning or thinking foolishly, *e.g.* to get improper things, or forming impracticable plans, or afraid when there is no cause for fear. **áng-láng-pháiⁿ**, stupidly overbearing, angry, or threatening in manner; angry without sufficient cause, and generally stupidly angry; said of any one, but especially of a raw foolish lad. **áng-láng-ok**, id.

àng (R. òng), a large narrow-mouthed earthen jar. **àng-á**, small do. **tiong-àng**, medium-sized do. **kāu-phê-àng**, a jar made very thick and strong; impudent. **gû-phê-àng**, large jars made of cow-hide (from Straits). **bí-àng**, a rice-jar. **bit-àng**, a honey-jar. **ū-bit-àng**, said of a very sweet bit of sugar-cane, having a crack full of saccharine matter. **chiàh-bit-àng**, to suck the fingers (as children). **suh bit-àng**, id. **chiú-àng**, a wine-jar. **chiú-àng-thơ̂**, a cement for closing up wine-jars. **bóh--tit ló-kun-kong ê chiú-àng** (T.), don't behave in that swaggering way like a drunk fellow (jocular allusion to "thien-thóh"). **àng-tāng**, larger and smaller earthen pots (v. tāng).

àng (R. òng). **siâⁿ-àng**, the space between the outer and inner walls at a city gate. **àng-siâⁿ**, the additional wall inclosing that space. **thô-àng**, a nest or hole in the ground. **thô-sat-àng**, hole of mud-fish. **jip-àng-lāi**, to get into a cul-de-sac, or road that has no outlet; to keep in the house, not going out.

àng (R. òng). **bėh-àng**, the leg of a stocking. **hia-àng**, the leg of a boot.

àng— **hī-àng-á**, the cavity of the ear. **siⁿ hī àng-á**, the ear suppurating (v. hī). **phīⁿ-àng**, inner cavity of the nose. **phīⁿ-àng-á**, id.

àng— **phīⁿ àng**, the nose stuffed. **phīⁿ àng-àng**, id. **àng-phīⁿ**, id. **àng-phīⁿ--ê**, man who has the nostril naturally somewhat obstructed. **hī-khang àng-àng**, ear stuffed or obstructed internally, so that hearing is difficult. **kóng-ōe àng-àng**, to talk nasally and indistinctly. **siaⁿ àng**, voice indistinct from obstruction of nose. **siaⁿ àng-àng**, id. **siaⁿ àng--lâi**, sound re-echoed, as from a cave, &c.

ap (C.) = A. gap, to swallow water, as a fish.

ap (R. id.), to repress. **ap-kiaⁿ**, to repress fear, as by liquor, or as in children by medicine. **pān-chiú ap-kiaⁿ**, to keep down fear by liquor. **tìn-ap**, to keep down, as people (by troops), or as evil influences of demons. **tân-ap**, to prevent disturbance or rebellion, as by a display of force. **chè-ap**, to repress, as evil spirits (v. chè). **ap-chè**, id., or to oppress, as a powerful man (v. chè).

áp (R. id.) **áp-siet**, to treat with much rudeness and want of respect, as by rude talk.

áp (R. hȧp). **thiⁿ áp-áp**, sky cloudy and overcast, as when about to rain.

áp = àh (R. id.), a casket. **hoe-áp**, a case for artificial flowers; a flowered casket. **poâⁿ-áp**, a round wooden basket with several horizontal divisions. **chièn-áp**, a small wicker basket or paper parcel of a few sweetmeats offered to idols. **chièn-áp-khoeh**, small box for holding them. **saⁿ-keh chièn-áp**, do. with three compartments. **lák-keh chièn-áp**, do. with six. **chièn-áp-kè**, frame on which tâm-chièn is put when offered. **tâm-chièn-áp**, offerings of fruits preserved in honey stuck on the frame on bamboo slips. **tâng-chièn-áp**, do. on any sort of frame.

at [R. àn, according to]. **at liâu-phek**, according to proper rules and time (v. phek). **at-hē--teh** (T. àn-hē--teh), to lay by a sum of money, *e.g.* the share of a man not present when the division is made, or as a sum to be ready for some special purpose or emergency (s. bend).

at (R. id.), to break; to bend; to hinder; to split the difference. **at-khiau**, to bend crooked. **at-tit**, to bend straight. **at--lóh-lâi**, to bend down, as branch.

at-á, a small bit of wood nailed on to keep something in its place. **at-lá**, id. **kè-at** (Cn.), id.

at-chí, to restrain; to repress (v. chí). **at hơ̄-i-chí**, to staunch. **at-chè**, to prevent a man (by power) from doing what he intended. **at-chhih**, to prevail on a man (by strong pressure or powerful influence) to do what he was very unwilling to do. **at-jih**, do.; said also of an arbiter or friend urging a party to submit in a hopeless case. **at gê-mn̂g**, to prevail on yamun subordinates (by powerful influence or bribes) to delay issuing a warrant, or let a case sleep. **at-hē--teh**, to get people to suspend further action in a quarrel or law-suit, till means be taken for having it finally and fully settled (s. according).

at-chih, to break, as a limb, &c. **at-tn̄g**, to break off. **at-hoe**, to pluck a flower. **at tsòe-n̄ng-tn̂g**, to break (as a stick, &c.) into two pieces. **at ko-á**, to divide profits (lit. break cake). **at chià-khōng**, to gamble by breaking sugar-cane. **at moâⁿ-liâu**, to gamble by breaking a confection.

海上絲綢之路文獻集成 科技與文化編

au (R. id.), a surname. **au-iông**, a double surname.

au (R. id.), a small cup. **au-á**, id. **tê-au**, a teacup. **hip-au**, a cup with a cover. **khàm-au**, id. **kim-au**, a golden cup. **kim-au gėk-tsoáⁿ**, cups of gold and of jade. **tâng-au**, a small brass cup, as for lamp. **chhâ-chek-au**, id. on top of a wooden imitation candle. **chiú-au**, a wine-cup. **mûiⁿ-au** (C.), small iron rings or ferules put on the "mn̂g-lûn," which serve instead of hinges for a Chinese door, to keep them from wearing away by use.

au — **au-tsau**, ugly, as face; filthy (v. tsau). **au-lâu**, having an ugly filthy face. **au-au lâu-lâu**, id.

au — **au-saⁿ**, to soak clothes in water before washing. **au lo̍h chhìⁿ-kng**, to steep in the dye-vat, as cloth.

au, to crumple. **au-lau**, to crumple up. **au tsòe-chit-tui**, to put things carelessly together in a heap. **chiàⁿ-au tò-au**, to lay things about in disorder; careless in managing a matter.

âu (R. hê), the throat; (a narrow pass). **âu-lāi**, within the throat. **âu tīⁿ**, choking feeling, as if about to weep. **âu tsa̍t**, id. **âu ta, chih khoah**, very very thirsty. **só-âu**, to seize by the throat, as dogs or men fighting. **koah-âu**, to cut the throat. **kè-âu**, to be swallowed. **ū âu-ūn**, pleasant feeling in mouth after good tea (v. ūn). **lo̍h-âu**, to swallow. **thun bōe-lo̍h-âu**, difficult to swallow, as unpleasant food. **ké-khek, chhiùⁿ-bōe-lo̍h-âu**, said of a man telling transparent lies that cannot be swallowed.

nâⁿ-âu, the throat. **nâⁿ-âu-kńg**, the gullet; the windpipe (v. kńg). **kéⁿ--tio̍h nâⁿ-âu**, choking in throat. **toā nâⁿ-âu-khang**, talking loud and angrily. **nâⁿ-âu tih-á**, the uvula. **nâⁿ-âu-ngê**, a deadly swelling of glands of throat (v. ngê).

nâⁿ-âu-tóe, lower part of throat. **âu-tóe**, id. **chīn âu-tóe ê-siaⁿ**, to sing or read as loud as possible. **toā-âu-khòng**, voice so strong that it can be heard at a great distance (v. khòng). **tit-âu**, monotony, or broken voice in singing, &c.; indistinct and almost inarticulate sound in throat of a man near death; a long inspiration, as in smoking tobacco through water. **kiò kàu tit-âu**, to shout out loud and long till hoarse, and losing the voice. **chhiùⁿ kàu tit-âu**, to sing till quite hoarse. **káu-siaⁿ**, **khit-chia̍h-âu**, said of a man talking in a clamorous way, or singing very unpleasantly.

ien-âu (r.), the throat; an important pass.

âu (R. hê), to call out loud, as hawkers or pedlars, &c. **âu-kiò**, to shout very loud; to yell; to cry out loud. **âu-kiù**, to call out loud for help. **toā-siaⁿ-âu**, to shout loud. **khòng-khòng-âu**, incessant loud calling. **siông-siông-âu**, constantly calling out loud, as pedlar.

áu (R. id.), to bend; to fold; to hem; to droop (as leaves); to oppress violently; (obstinate).

áu chit-thâu, to carry one load on a pole.

n̂ng-áu, drooping, as leaves in drought. **ê-áu**, black and withered, as leaves or decaying fruit; black and blue, as when beaten.

áu-pê, to fold a hem; to hem. **áu-phâng**, the sail suddenly bulged out, and blown half over the side by a squall. **khah-áu-pūn**, sail much too full, and bulging too much, as in tacking.

áu-khiau, to bend crooked. **áu-tit**, to bend straight. **áu-tsoá**, to fold paper, as for columns of writing. **áu-jiâu**, to wrinkle; to crease, as dress, or as dog's ears in books. **áu-chhiú**, to bend the arm. **áu chhiú-bé**, to try which of the two can pull the other's arm back (the arms being bent at right angle). **áu-chih**, to break by bending.

áu-ut, to insist violently and falsely that a man has done something bad, so as to oppress him. **áu-peh-jîn**, unjustly and perversely refusing to pay what is due. **áu-bān**, obstinately and injuriously in the wrong, *e.g.* unjustly defrauding, &c. **chip-áu**, obstinate. **áu-phiah**, id. **chip-sí-áu**, extremely dogged. **áu-hoāiⁿ**, very unfair, violent, and overbearing, or oppressive, as in demanding too much, or refusing to pay. **áu-hoāiⁿ-thėh**, extremely rapacious. **áu-khì--lâng**, to scold a man very violently and unfairly because of something wrong, which is not his fault, though it may have some slight colour of reason. **khit lâng áu-khì**, to be thus scolded unjustly. **áu-kióng**, violently, or very urgently press another to do what he is unwilling to do; very determined to make others take his way. **kiông-kiông-áu**, violently press to confess, as a mandarin, by repeated beatings.

áu [R. é, to strike, to beat]. **áu-jio̍k**, to beat and insult. **áu-táⁿ** (R.), to beat. **áu-chhe**, to beat a constable on duty.

áu — **gām-áu-á**, a sort of fish. **lêng-áu**, sort of fish.

áu (R. é), to vomit. **áu-thè**, to vomit. **áu-hông**, to vomit blood. **áu-huih**, id. **áu-tsúi**, to vomit water; unable to accomplish what one takes in hand. **khang-áu**, trying to vomit, but bringing up nothing. **chhiⁿ-áu**, do., or only a little sour water. **pėh-áu**, id. **chhiⁿ-áu pėh-áu**, id. **chí-áu**, to cure the tendency to vomit. **áu-làu** (C.), cholera.

àu (= áu). **chip-àu**, obstinate. **àu-chìⁿ**, doggedly dispute on wrong side.

àu, stinking, decaying. **àu-chhàu**, do., rotten and decaying. **àu-pak**, having a hollow decayed trunk, as tree. **àu-chiet**, tainted smell. **àu-khì**, rotten smell. **àu--khì**, spoiled and rotten. **àu-miâⁿ**, of bad reputation. **àu-lông**, very stinking, as a dead rat, &c., said also in scolding men or women.

àu (R. ò). **àu-náuⁿ**, vexed; displeased; feeling of impatient discontent. **àu-láu**, id. **àu-làu**, id. **àu-ėh**, grieved and discontented; murmuring inwardly (v. ėh).

àu — **bīn àu-àu**, angry face. **àu-bīn**, do. **àu-thâu àu-bīn**, do. **àu-tū-tū**, morose and displeased; sulky. **àu-pū-pū**, id.

āu (R. hē), after; behind. **āu-bīn**, behind. **āu-piah**, do. **āu-bé**, behind; the end. **bé-āu**, do. **āu-thâu**, do. **āu-thâu** (Cn.) = goā-ke, a wife's own relations. **chêng-thâu boé, āu-thâu im**, to lose heavily on goods by the price falling. **āu-lâi**, afterwards; generally some time after, when the work first spoken of has been completed. **āu-sin**, afterwards; farther back (as back premises). **sin-āu**, behind one's back; after death. **sin-āu-sū**, matters after death. **tī-lí-sin-āu**, behind your back. **jiân-āu**, afterwards, next, then. **liân-āu**, id. **chit-sî í-āu**, from this time onwards.

ka-chiah-āu, behind one's back. **ôe-āu**, the back part of a shoe. **to-āu** (T.), the corner of the edge of a square knife close to the handle. **āu-tsō-bah**, meat of hind-quarter. **āu-thúi-bah**, id.

chiūⁿ-āu, to go to stool. **thè-āu**, to walk backwards (v. thè). **sûi-āu**, to follow after. **sûi-āu**

chiū-lâi, will come immediately. **chhûn āu-pē̍**, to have some plan or some money in reserve for emergencies.

ke-āu, wife; wife and children. **kè-āu**, already past. **āu-pái**, next time. **āu-tso**, id. **āu-kè** (C. āu-kòe, T. āu-kō͘), next time. **āu-kè** (C. āu-kè), to marry a second husband after the death of the first. **āu-chhoā**, to marry a second wife after death of first. **āu-pē**, step-father (none of these phrases are polite). **āu-chek**, id. **āu-bú**, step-mother.

āu-chhin, the back part of a house; posterity (v. chhin). **āu-sûn**, descendants. **āu-tāi**, posterity, after generations. **āu-sì**, a future state of transmigration.

āu-sàng, elder brother accompanying the bride to her husband's house.

hù āu-chhiú, to assist a man, as in a quarrel, or by money. **hù i āu-chhiú**, id. **tsān i āu-chhiú**, id. **siap āu-chhiú**, to give a small bribe or douceur (v. siap).

chêng-āu, before and behind; before and after (of time or place). **bô-chêng-bô-āu**, neither head nor tail; neither before nor behind. **chêng-sì āu-jit**, former and later times. **chêng-khì āu-khang**, advancing, but leaving rear unguarded; to lose more than is gained by some action.

āu-kài, the vacant ground at back of a house within the inclosing wall. **tī-hí it-āu**, at the very furthest back part of the suite of buildings. **āu-lòh**, back part of a house. **āu-lâu**, back part up-stairs. **āu-iâⁿ**, rear division of army. **āu-chím**, the projecting part of the neck at the back; the nape of the neck.

āu-jit, a future day. **āu--jit**, the day after to-morrow. **lòh-āu--jit**, the second day after to-morrow. **āu-gėh**, next month. **āu-mî**ⁿ, next night. **āu-nî**ⁿ, in a following year, either the next or any following year. **āu--nî**ⁿ, the year after next.

auⁿ— **auⁿ-auⁿ-háu**, always crying as child, or barking as dog.

áuⁿ, to stutter or lisp, or articulate indistinctly; often put before the name of a man who speaks so. **ut-áuⁿ**, having a bad lisp or defect in articulation, as from a fault in palate or tongue. **kóng-ōe ut-aúⁿ**, to speak with more or less of that fault in articulation.

āuⁿ— **pûn-āuⁿ-u**, to blow a sort of trumpet (v. u).

B

b, often pronounced like M, or interchanged with it. If a word be not found here, look under M.

ba— **phah-ba-ba**, to beat the mouth (as child) in sport. **kap-lâng phah-ba-ba**, to refuse to pay what is due. **chhiò-ba-ba**, to smile pleasantly or laugh slightly (with or without a sound), as on receiving a guest. **ba-bún-chhiò**, to smite.

bâ (a harlot). **bâ-thâu**, mistress of brothel. **āu-bú-bâ**, stepmother harlot (vile scolding). **chhiong-bâ**, a harlot (in vile scolding).

bâ (R. mâ), numb. **kóng kàu-chhùi-bâ**, to talk till lips are quite wearied. **bâ-bīn**, shameless (s. pock-marked). **bōe-bâ-bīn**, shameless (said to one's face). **bâ-pì**, feeling of weariness or satiety, as after hard work, long sleep, or sexual intercourse (v. pì).

bâ-hong, leprosy in its early stage.

bâ— **bâ-iòh**, anaesthetic medicine.

bâ [R. mâ, hemp, = col. moâⁿ]. **bâ-bīn**, pock-marked (s. numb). **bâ-bīn, boán-thien-seng**, the pock-marked face became like the sky full of stars; said of a pock-marked man who became a Tain-sze. **seng-bâ**, a medicine (Thalictrum ?).

bâ-jî-tek, a fine sort of bamboo (v. tek).

bâ [R. biâu, an anchor]. **thih-bâ-jî**, a sort of iron anchor with three prongs.

bâ— **bâ-bui**, pleased and smiling (v. bui).

bâ— **bâ-bui** (C.), a fruit used as soap.

bâ— **bâ-lî**, a sort of small cabin in a junk.

bâ (R. bâu). **pan-bâ**, the blistering fly, or Spanish fly. **pi-bâ** (Cn.), id.

bâ (R. biâu), a wild cat. **soaⁿ-bâ**, id. **iá-bâ**, id.; also said in vile scolding (harlot). **ké-chí-bâ**, a large bat that eats fruit. **siáu-bâ**, restless and making a great noise, as cats in pairing time. **bâ-chhú tông-biên** (cat and rat sleep together), said of mandarins or servants, or watchmen, &c., becoming accomplices of wicked men. **ke-lâi bô-bâ, niáu-chhú khiau-kha**, when the cat's away the mice do play. **hó-bâ koán pah-ke** (a good cat guarding a hundred houses), a man able to take care of others' affairs.

lâi-bâ (C.), a sort of fox. **phah bâ-á** (C.), to hunt small animals. **chhiám-bâ** (C.), id. **bâ-káu** (C.), sort of dog used for hunting. **bâ-chhɛ-á** (C.), three-pronged weapon used in hunting.

bá, final particle (= á), sometimes heard, esp. after P. **kap-bá**, = kap-á, a frog. **áp-bá**, or **áh-bá**, a small casket.

bā [R. bit, = col. bàt], closely jointed, or joined so as hardly to show the joint. **tah-bā**, very well joined; very intimate and friendly. **ún-tàng tah-bā**, the affair will certainly succeed, esp. as the man who undertakes it is well able.

bā— **bā-bā**, half-caste Chinese (from the Straits).

bā (T. nāiⁿ, lāi). **bā-hiòh**, the kite (v. hiòh).

bā [R. bèk, = col. bāi] (T. bàh), to search or make inquiries for what is not known (but "chhē" is to search for a known thing or person that is lost). **bā thâu-lō̍**, to look out for a situation. **bā-chhù**, to look out for a house, as in order to rent or live in it. **bā-tsûn**, to search if there be any vessel, as for taking a passage or sending something.

bā (R. má), a yard.

bā, having mildew or rust spots, as paper or tin-foil, &c. **chhiūⁿ-bā**, to become thus spotted or mildewed. **bā-bū**, dim or spotted, as mirror, gem, or sky (v. bū).

bah = ba. **bah-bún-chhiò**, to smile.

bah, flesh; pig's flesh; pork (if not otherwise specified); the pulp or edible part of fruit; the blade of a knife; glass of mirror; paper of fan, &c.

ū-bah, there is flesh; there is some sense or something good in it. **kiàⁿ-bah**, a mirror as distinguished from its frame. **chìⁿ-bah**, an arrow-head. **to-bah**, the blade of a sword or knife. **sìⁿ-bah**, the paper of a fan. **thô-bah**, the good opium in a ball of opium, as distinguished from the skin.

koaⁿ-bah, dried dragon's eye (lung-yen), or li-chi, without stones or skin. **hok-oân-bah,** dried dragon's eye without stones or skin.

bah-soâiⁿ, an inferior yellow sort of mango. **bah-lê,** a sort of shell-fish.

koah-bah, to cut a criminal in pieces alive (v. koah). **bōe-bah-chîⁿ,** wages of a "tâng-chí," who cuts himself in idolatrous rites; wages of a substitute who hires himself to be beaten by mandarins. **chiáh-pûi, thang hō͘--lâng thâi-bah,** said of a man who only eats and sleeps, like a pig fattened for slaughter.

chhàu-bah, putrid flesh, as in a sore. **siⁿ iù-bah,** clean new flesh forming when the scab falls off. **pháiⁿ-phê-bah,** having a bad constitution, so that a wound or sore heals ill. **siau-bah,** to grow lean. **bah-liû,** a fleshy tumour, as on neck or head. **lân-san-bah,** excrescences on body, as extra finger or thumb. **chîm-kóng-bah,** the large prominent muscle between thumb and fore-finger, said to be wanting in men about to take leprosy. **kha-chhiú-bah-chhoah,** body all trembling with terror. **hoâiⁿ-bah-bīn,** repulsive, ugly, ill-formed face.

kut-bah, bones and flesh; said also of near relations. **kut-chih bah-lih,** flesh and bones broken, as by a heavy blow. **bah hō͘-lâng-chiáh, kut m̄-chiâⁿ hō͘-lâng-khòe** (let people eat the flesh but not gnaw the bones), to allow our friends to be somewhat injured or reviled, but will not let it go too far.

gû-bah, beef. **iûⁿ-bah,** mutton. **chiaⁿ-bah,** the lean of meat, esp. of pork. **chhiah-bah,** id. **tīm chhiah-bah,** to stew lean of meat, for medical preparation. **péh-bah,** the fat. **bah-nn̂g,** the fat among the lean (v. nn̂g). **bah-iû,** pork fat. **sam-tsân-bah,** pork having fat and lean in alternate layers. **kièn-chí-bah,** meat from the loin, esp. pork. **bah-phê,** pork skin. **bah-tàng,** coagulated pork, soup, or jelly. **bah-jiông,** meat (pork) minced small. **chhò-bah-sîⁿ,** to mince meat. **bah-mīⁿ,** vermicelli cooked with shrimps and some fat. **bah-oân,** pork balls. **bah-thn̂g,** sort of confection containing pork fat. **bah-hú,** pork boiled, dried, and reduced to fine fibres.

báh (C.), = boáh. **báh-á,** the crocodile.

báh (T.), = bā; to look out for, as situation or house.

bai (R. pi). **chi-bai,** the female organ, the vulva (vulgar).

bâi [R. id., = col. tâi], to bury; (to hide or lay ambush). **bâi-tsòng,** to bury. **siu-bâi,** id.

bâi-hók, to lie in ambush. **bâi-tsông** (R.), to hide a thing secretly. **bâi-thâu put-chhut,** to keep out of the way when sought for. **bâi-bêng tsà-sú,** pretend to be dead (v. tsà). **bâi-bút,** to conceal or make away with, to swindle. **bâi-bút sin-si,** to make away with and conceal a corpse. **bâi-bút sèng-bêng,** to conceal one's own real name and surname.

bâi-oàn, to cherish envy or constant hatred. **khioh-hūn bâi-oàn,** to cherish and increase hatred in one's heart.

bâi (R. bî). **mn̂g-bâi,** door-lintel, above the door-frame. **thang-á-bâi,** lintel of window. **kè-bâi,** cross-bar built into the wall above the top of the frame of door or window.

bâi (R. bî). **bák-bâi,** eyebrows. **bák-bâi oan,** eyebrows arched. **bák-bâi phah tsòe-chit-kat,** eyebrows drawn together from great sorrow or anxiety. **bák-bâi-mn̂g sa-m̄-khí** (you have not pulled up your eyelashes, and so don't see clearly), said in scolding a man who is raising a matter that must injure himself, or insulting a powerful man, or otherwise behaving very absurdly and only hurting himself. **bák-bâi-mn̂g sa-bô-khí,** id. **bák-bâi-mn̂g bô-chiuⁿ-ám,** do. (lit. your eyebrows are not starched!) **bák-bâi-bé jiâuⁿ-jiâuⁿ,** the outer corners of the eyebrows much wrinkled, as in an old man. **bák-bâi-bé ngeh hō͘-sin,** do. (wrinkles large enough to catch flies). **bák-bâi-thâu,** the space between the eyebrows. **bâi-thâu,** id. **bák-bâi-thâu jiâuⁿ-jiâuⁿ,** slight wrinkling on brow between the eyebrows, as when distressed or anxious. **bák-bâi-thâu khioh-kéng,** said of the wrinkled face of an old man.

bâi-bák hun-bêng, very correctly finished and all straight; said of any work or affair. **hiáh-bâi,** the part of the forehead just above the eyebrows; an ornament worn there by women (v. hiáh). **ūi-bâi,** to paint the eyebrows, as women. **it-jī-bâi,** eyebrows in a straight line (v. it).

géh-bâi, the crescent moon. **chit-bâi-á,** the crescent moon very small.

bái, = pháiⁿ, bad. **bái-jī,** an ill-formed word. **sí-bái,** having lost colour; wanting in vivacity, and having no appearance of intelligence; almost going out, as a light. (or next word?)

bái, dim, as light of a lamp. **teng-hé bái-bái,** the lamp burns dimly. **tiám--khì bái-bái,** light a lamp giving but little light.

bái — **bái-kúi,** a large sort of spider with eight legs and thin body (while "lâ-giâ" has seven legs and a large body); it is supposed to place itself right opposite the face of a man sleeping on his back, so as to produce a very oppressive feeling. **hō͘ bái-kúi teh,** to have this oppressive feeling, as if the breast were pressed down by a dark demon; it is removed by shaking one's self or turning on the side. **khit bái-kúi teh,** id. **náⁿ bái-kúi--nih** (like that large spider), said as of a thief coming silently and secretly so that no one knows, or of a man stealthily enticing to bad courses. **tú--tióh bái-kúi,** to be unexpectedly deceived or swindled; to meet accidentally a man who seduces into wicked courses, or deludes into keeping up a feud that would otherwise have been settled. **khit bái-kúi bái--teh,** to be suddenly seduced into vicious courses. **khit i bái--khì,** id. **bái--teh,** suddenly to appear and vanish, like a thief or a spy.

bāi [R. bėk, to search, = col. bā], to visit, to make polite inquiries. **saⁿ-bāi,** id. **bāi-bėh,** to feel the pulse. **bāi-pīⁿ,** to visit the sick, and ask about his health. **bāi-song,** to visit a house containing an unburied corpse, and worship it. **kià-bāi,** to send salutations.

tam-bāi (Cn.), = tam-khoàⁿ, to examine by tasting. **chhì-bāi** (Cn.), to examine and try. **chhâ-bāi** (Cn.), = chhâ-khoàⁿ, to make minute inquiries about a matter.

bak, to soil, to infect, to pollute (lit. or fig.) **bak-lak,** id. **bak-kiaⁿ-lâng,** to soil, to defile. **bak-lâ-sâm,** id. **bak-tâm,** to wet, to moisten. **bak-tang bak-sai,** to soil many things, or in many ways. **bak--tióh i-ê-sin** (T.), he got involved (as in lawsuit) through no fault of his.

bak chit-ê-miâⁿ, said of a man supposed to be doing work, but really idle or absent.

ài-bak-chhiú, to meddle, in order to make some money, where one has no business. **miⁿ-bak,** to make some money secretly on a transaction committed to him. **it--tióh miⁿ-bak,** wishing to have the man-

2

agement of the matter for the sake of the underhand gain on it.

bák (R. bók), the eye; a knot in wood, the swelling at a joint; meshes of a net, holes of sieve; measure for rows of bamboo leaves in a bamboo sail.

siàu-bák, an account. **tôe-bák**, a thesis or text. **tiâu-bák**, a list of articles or account. **jī-bák chhim**, very good at reading and writing. **jī-bák chhién**, not well educated.

thâu-bák, a leading man, &c. (v. thâu).

ka-tsui-bák, a staple. **chhâ-bák**, a knot in wood. **tek-bák**, a bamboo joint. **ū làu-bák**, have few knots far apart, as wood or bamboo. **tsōe-bák**, knots numerous, as in wood. **kut-bák**, the projection at a joint, especially small joint. **kha-bák**, the ankle. **chhiú-bák**, the protuberance at the wrist; also, the knuckles. **tsńg-thâu-á-bák**, the knuckles at middle of finger.

bák-kiàⁿ, spectacles (v. kiàⁿ). **hè lêng-bák**, to wash the eye of the dragon boat. **bīn-bák**, countenance (v. bīn).

khoàⁿ-chiūⁿ-bák, to think well of, to respect (v. chiūⁿ). **bák-lāi ū--i**, to think well of him. **bák-tē ū--i**, id. **bák-tē-bô**, to despise (v. tē).

bák-péh, to miss stays in tacking.

pè-bák, the interstices between the threads in cloth (v. pè). **khah-toā-bák**, having large holes, as a sieve, &c.

bák-chiu, the eye. **bák-chiu-jîn**, the eyeball. **bák-chiu péh-jîn**, the white of the eye. **bák-chiu ang-á-jîn**, the pupil. **bák-chiu-chí**, the eyeball. **bák-chiu-oáⁿ**, the socket of the eye. **bák-kháng-khū**, id. **bák-kháng**, id. **bák-khang**, id. **bák-chiu-phê**, eyelid. **bák-chiu-mn̂g**, eye-lashes. **bák-chiu-khe toā-lúi**, so proud as not to recognize or look at one. **bák-thâu**, inner corner of the eye. **bák-chiu-thâu iu-iu**, brows knitted between the eyebrows. **bák-thâu koâiⁿ**, proudly looking down on people, as on poor relatives. **bák-bé**, the outer corner of the eye. **bák-bé jiâuⁿ**, wrinkles at outer side of eyes, as in old man. **sái bák-bé**, to give a side glance of displeasure or lasciviousness (v. sái). **bák-thâu jiâuⁿ-jiâuⁿ**, wrinkles between the eyes, as when distressed or anxious. **bák-thâu khá**, skilful at recognizing or calculating at a glance. **bák-thâu tāng-tāng**, heavy feeling and slight headache about eyes.

bák-bâi, eyebrows (v. bâi). **bák-kîⁿ**, edges of eyelids (v. kîⁿ). **bák-sûn**, wrinkle on edge of upper eyelid (v. sûn). **bák-kun âng**, eyes red with liquor. **ū bák-kun**, to have good and rapid perception of the right course to be taken in any case. **bák-sek**, power of calculating or recognizing at a glance (v. sek, "to know").

bák-iû, tears drawn by cold or smoke, &c. **bák-sái**, tears; but (C.), = A. bák-sái-ko (v. sái). **bák-tsái** (C.), tears.

bák ham, swollen eyelids. **hong-bák**, inflamed eye. **siⁿ bák-chiam**, to have a stye on the eyelid. **bák hoe**, eyes dim. **kūn-sī-bák**, near-sighted. **thap-bák**, sunken eyes. **bák-sā-sī**, to doze.

hóe-bák, to look askance angrily. **péng péh-bák**, to turn up the white of the eyes, as in pride or anger. **khoeh-bák**, to close the eyes (as in sleep), said to children (v. khoeh). **sut-bák**, to wink, as a signal (v. sut). **nihⁿ-bák**, to wink (v. nihⁿ). **sái-bák-chîⁿ**, to cast an angry or amorous glance (v. sái). **tn̄g-bák**, to glance sidewise, to turn the eye (v. tn̄g). **té-bák**, to calculate roughly by sight. **tāⁿ-bák**, to make a mistake in looking. **hiáⁿ-bák**, to catch the eye, as gaudy goods. **kè-bák** (C. kòe-bák), to be looked at (v. kè, "to cross").

bák-kng ê-lâng, a man who can see (not blind). **thiⁿ bô-bák**, Heaven observes not, as when great crimes pass unpunished. **toā-sòe-bák**, eyes of different size, partial. **pàng-toā-sòe-bák**, to wink at the faults of a favourite person. **chhùi pá, bák m̄-pá**, the mouth may be satisfied, but the eye is insatiable.

koe-bák (eye like a fowl's), fond of sleep, going soon to bed. **iûⁿ-bák** (like a sheep's), eyes not fully closing in sleep. **iûⁿ-á-bák**, id. **chhát-bák**, a covetous thievish eye. **gōng-bák**, a stupid eye. **pùt-bák**, immovable eyes, like an idol's. **péh-bák-pùt**, the idol called Keh-sèng-ông (v. pùt).

bák-kim, at present (v. kim), at this time. **bák-ē**, id. (v. ē). **bák-chêng**, at present. **tī-bák-chêng**, before one's eyes.

sì-bák saⁿ-tùi, two persons (esp. man and wife, or partners) looking helplessly at one another, as when without money and having no resource; or as when in great danger, calamity coming on; said also of the four needle-holes in good embroidery, forming a perfect square. **chhài-ki, sì-bák saⁿ-tùi**, should be equitable in dealings (fig. from embroidery). **ang-bé, sì-bák saⁿ-tùi**, man and wife without money or means of getting it, looking vacantly at each other. **sì-bák bô-chhin**, having no relations.

bák (cf. bong, bók). **àm-bák-bák**, very dark.

bák [R. bit, close, = col. bát, bā], **bák-sit**, a great many, only of *things*, not of men or affairs.

bák [R. bók, wood, tree]. **bák-chhiūⁿ**, a carpenter. **tsòe-bák**, to do carpenter work. **toā-bák**, carpenter who makes the wood-work of houses. **sió-bák**, carpenter who makes furniture.

bák-hiuⁿ, a wood used as medicine for diarrhœa, &c., putchuk (*Costus amarus?*) **bák-hiuⁿ-chhâ**, id. **e-bák**, ebony (v. e), (s. ink). **so-bák**, sapan-wood, a red dye. **bák-tsát-chháu**, a plant used like sand-paper.

chhiū-bák, trees in general. **hoe-bák**, flowering bushes and shrubs. **lóng-sī hoe-bák**, it is full of flowers and shrubs.

bák-liāu, timber (materials), whether in rough form or cut and sawn up. **bák-sa**, a wooden railing. **bák-kiáh**, wooden clogs (v. kiáh). **bák-pê**, a weapon with three or more prongs (v. pê).

bák-sat, a bed-bug (v. sat).

bák (R. bók). **bák-nīⁿ**, white jessamine. **bák-nīⁿ-hoe**, id.

bák (R. bék), ink, solid or liquid. **boâ-bák**, to rub down ink. **ùn-bák**, to dip the pen in ink. **e-bák**, black ink (s. wood). **e-bák-bák**, very black. **bô-jī bô-bák**, without written proof, as a marriage or agreement without documents.

bák-tiâu, a stick of ink. **chit-tiâu-bák**, one stick of ink. **bák-thûi**, a large round stick of ink. **se-bák**, ink from Soo-chow. **kiaⁿ-bák**, ink from Pekin.

bák-hīⁿ, ink and ink-stone. **pit-bák-hīⁿ**, pen, ink, and ink-stone. **bák-poah**, sort of ink-stand like a bowl for writing large characters. **bák-hái**, a brass vessel filled with cotton saturated with ink, for examinations. **bák-tsúi**, liquid ink. **bák-tsúi-sek**, inky gray. **bák-tsúi-saⁿ**, clothes all spotted over with ink, worn in deep mourning. **pak-té, bô poàⁿ-tiám bák-tsúi** (not half a drop of ink in his belly), said of a pretender to learning who is quite unable to compose, and has no real learning. **bák-tsúi-koàn**, an ink-bottle. **bák-koàn**, id.

bák-thâu-chîn, an ink-line, used by stretching it tight over a plank and touching it with the nail so as to make a line. **bák-chîn**, id. **bák-táu**, box in which the ink-line, and the black powder for it, are kept.

bák-tsát, the cuttle-fish. **bák-hî**, id. **bák-hî-ien**, paint from it. **bák-koaⁿ**, dried cuttle-fish. **bák-tsát-koaⁿ**, id. **bák-tsát-tsûn**, the bone of the cuttle-fish. **bák-chiet** (T.), a marine animal like thê-poe.

bân (R. id.) **lâm-bân**, the southern barbarians.

bân (R. id.), ancient name of Fuh-kien; the river Min, on which Fuh-chau stands. **bân-chiet**, the two provinces of Fuh-kien and Cheh-kiang, ruled by one governor-general. **bân-koāiⁿ**, Min-hien, one of the districts of Fuh-chau city. **bân-chhiaⁿ**, Min-tsing Hien.

bân [R. boân, secret, = col. moâⁿ]. **thau-bân** (C.), secret, secretly. **àm-bân** (C.), crafty and designing.

bân, constantly delaying (through sheer idleness) to do the work or make the things promised. **tiáⁿ bân**, the pan is slow in cooking. **bân-bân ê-pīⁿ**, a chronic disease.

bân (R. goân), stubborn, obstinate, said of children only. **áu-bân**, perversely disobedient or unfair in dealings, *e.g.* refusing to pay what is due; to treat a man unjustly and injuriously in business, &c. **bōe áu-bân--tit**, no extra improper gains can be got out of him, &c. **bân-phê**, incorrigible. **thiau-bân**, refusing to do what is ordered, obstinate as in a quarrel or lawsuit, refusing or delaying to pay money, or causing much trouble in some such way. **tiau-bân**, id.

bân — **bân-khóng**, strongly made, or firmly fixed, as house, table, &c.

bân, to cover (as with cloth or leather), as a shoe or coverlet, or fire-screen; not so stiff as "piⁿ." **bân-moâⁿ**, to cover with sackcloth, as shoes in mourning. **koh-bân chit-têng**, put on another thickness of cloth, as on a shoe.

bán (R. bán, boán), to pull or draw out, as nail or tooth; to pluck, as fruit or flowers. **bán-bán**, impatient attitude, as of one unwilling to hear. **keng-thâu bán-bán**, shoulders naturally high. **bán-mn̂g**, to pluck out hair or feathers from animals. **bán-bīn**, to pluck out hair from woman's face. **bán-hoe**, to pluck a flower. **bán-béh**, to pluck up corn, instead of reaping. **bán-sit**, to pluck the wings of a fowl.

kiông-bán, obstinately to refuse to pay money due. **i beh-bán--goá**, he will not pay me the debt he is due me. **bán-tò-tn̂g**, to get back by much exertion, as a thing stolen or as money due, &c. **bán-tit-tióh**, can be pulled, as fruit not out of reach; to recover a debt from a debtor who will not pay, by getting it from a man who owes money to him, and pays it to us. **bán-tit-i-tióh**, to recover a debt in that way. **chîⁿ khit-i-bán--khì**, he owes me money and I cannot get it out of him. **hō-i bōe-khan-bán--tit**, to make it impossible for him longer to avoid paying the money. **i kàu-lí-khan-bán**, he is quite a match for you, as in a lawsuit. **kàu-lí-khan-bán**, id. **kàu-i-khan-bán**, quite a match for him, able to hold his own, and not afraid of him; able to get it out of him, proud and disobedient to superior, as young fellow. **ōe-kham--tit khan-bán**, able to hold his own, able to stand firm against temptation, as reformed opium-smoker, &c.

bán-koe chhiû-tîn, to get a clue and follow it up step by step, so as to learn the truth of a matter. **bán-hôe thiⁿ-ì**, to influence Heaven to favour us, as by virtuous conduct (v. hôe).

bán [R. boán, full, = col. moáⁿ]. **bán-thien-kong**, = **boán-thien-kong**, a hanging lamp with several wicks.

bān — **bān-jī**, a character like a cross with each limb bent at a right angle, all in the same direction; like the Scandinavian Thor's hammer and Sanskrit Svastica; considered auspicious, and therefore embroidered at the middle of the neck of a child's dress, at the back. **tiò bān-jī**, to embroider it so. **khûn bān-jī**, to work it in braid. **put-toān bān-jī**, this character worked as a border all round the edge of a dress, &c. **bān-jī-kha**, do., worked at the foot of a dress or curtain, or wood-work, &c. **bān-jī-hoe**, this character worked in large quantities all over the surface. **bān-jī-keh**, open work, as of a screen in this form. **bān-thien**, the open-work frame forming the top of a bedstead. **bān-thien-pang**, a boarding sometimes put on the top of it.

bān (R. id.), ten thousand, a myriad, all (in many phrases), a surname.

bān-sòe (myriad years), title of emperor (v. sòe). **bān-siū**, the emperor's birth-day (v. siū).

bān-kó (R.), from remotest ages. **bān-bān-nîⁿ**, innumerable years. **bān-liân hù-kùi**, prosperous for a myriad of years, said as a good wish. **bān-liân-chhun**, a sort of tree, *Ficus Afzelii.* **thien-tsú bô-bān-liân** (even an imperial family does not reign ten thousand years), said in exhorting a man not to be too anxious about the world's affairs. **bô-thang thien-tsú bān-liân**, id. **bān-tāi**, all generations. **bān-kok**, all nations. **bān-bu̍t**, all things. **bān-mihⁿ**, id. **bān-hāng-mihⁿ**, id. **bān-sîn-má** (Cn.), the collective female ghosts that have no descendants (v. sîn). **bān-kim**, vast quantities of gold. **bān-gûn bô-thang-bóe**, cannot be got for money. **bān-sū jû-ì**, everything just as one would wish. **bān-jîn-soàⁿ**, honorary umbrella presented by the people to a popular mandarin when he leaves a place; it has the names of the donors on it. **bān-jîn-i**, a robe (with the names on it) given in like manner; much more honourable than the umbrella. **bān-lē-chìⁿ tsôe-hoat**, many calamities coming all at once (lit. arrows from myriad cross-bows).

chhien-bān, I earnestly entreat you to — (v. chhien). **chheng-bān**, ten millions. **tsáp-bān**, a hundred thousand. **pah-bān**, a million. **bān-jī**, twelve thousand. **bān-it**, ten thousand to one; eleven thousand. **bān-hūn ê-chit-hūn**, one ten thousandth-part; ten thousand to one. **bān bû it-sit**, not one mistake; most certainly.

bān-lí tn̂g-siâⁿ, the great wall of China. **bān-lí tiông-sa**, the Prata shoals.

bān-sī-má (Cn.), a female idol of surname Bān. **bān-sī niûⁿ-niûⁿ** (Cn.), id.

bān (C. pān). **kap-bān**, a strong money-chest.

bān, slow. **bān-bān**, id.; do it slowly, or slower. **bān-bān-kiâⁿ**, to walk slowly; good-bye. **bān--chiah**, stop a little. **bān-chiah-sì**, id. **bān-chiah-kóng**, wait a little before speaking; don't speak just now. **bān-chiah-kiâⁿ**, don't walk for a little. **kín-bān**, quick and slow; rate of speed. **kín-bān-chiam**, regulator of watch. **kín-bān-poàⁿ**, id.

ham-bān, awkward; wanting in ability; stupid. **bān-tūn**, stupid at learning; slow at work (v. tūn).

bān (R. id.) **tāi-bān**, to slight; to treat disrespectfully. **kheng-bān**, id.; to treat lightly. **bú-bān**, to slight; to insult. **bú-bān-bān**, to treat very contemptuously. **siōng put-chèng, chek hā-bān**, when superiors are not correct in conduct, inferiors do not treat them with respect.

bān-pî-hong, a dangerous disease of children (v. hong).

bān— **jip-bān, chhut-bān**, certain throws in gambling with the "liên-pó."

bān, = pān (R. pān), a section or lobe of an orange, &c. **kam-bān**, a lobe of an orange. **iū-bān**, a lobe of pumelo. **kiet-á-bān**, a lobe of a lime. **soàn-bān**, sections of garlic root peeled off.

bān (R. id.) **bān-thô-hoe**, *Datura alba* (v. thô).

bang (R. bông, = col. mng, mɵ). **bang-bang**, very small, as rain, powder, &c. **chhùi bang-bang**, broken to shivers. **iù-bang-bang**, very fine, as silk or powder. **hɵ̄ bang-bang**, small drizzling rain. **hɵ̄-á bang-bang**, id.

bâng (R. bông), mist. **hái bâng-bâng**, dim misty appearance, or the sea at a distance, as when wind is coming. **tsúi bâng-bâng**, id.; also, the water not clear.

bâng (R. bông). **tsùi bâng-bâng**, so much intoxicated as to be quite confused in mind. **bák-chiu bâng-bâng**, unable to see clearly. **khoà^{n}-bâng-bâng**, seeing dimly, as through a mist. **khoà^{n}-kì^{n}-bâng**, id.

bâng (C.), a surname.

bâng (R. bông), (C. bông), mind confused, perplexed, and bewildered or bustled, as with many matters. **bâng-bâng**, id. **sim bâng**, id. **sim-koa^{n} bâng**, id. **bâng-bū**, id. **bâng-bâng loān-loān**, id. **chhiú bâng kha loān**, very much so, or hurried, with no leisure. **toā-bâng**, id. **bâng-soàh-soàh**, id. **bâng-iah-iah**, id. **lí teh-bâng**, your mind is bewildered. **kín-bâng-bâng**, in a great hurry.

bâng, a stalk of grass, or a reed with the flower or empty ear on it. **sàu-chiú-bâng**, a stalk of a reed, for a sort of broom or brush. **sóe-á-bâng**, stalk of millet with empty ear on, for a brush. **sóe-bâng**, id. **hoan-sóe-bâng**, id.

bâng (R. bông). **koa^{n}-bâng**, a sort of reed, very common by streams. **chek-bâng**, candle-stems made of it. **bâng-tang**, sort of reed (v. tang).

báng— **chhú-báng**, having small eyes, as a near-sighted man. **bāi-báng** (T.), id.

báng (R. bóng). **khi-báng**, to treat a superior with disrespect or slight his orders.

báng— **kòng-báng**, to conspire together to fleece a man.

báng [R. bóng, a net, = col. bāng]. **báng-kun**, a head-band used (in the Ming dynasty) for the head-dress of females; now only used in plays.

báng [R. bóng, a sort of dragon]. **toā-báng**, a flowing robe used in plays (by kings and princes), having these dragons on it.

báng (R. bún), a mosquito. **báng-tèng**, mosquito's bite. **báng-chhùi**, do., or its proboscis. **ɵ-tèng-báng**, a black mosquito with large proboscis. **ɵ-kha-báng**, sort with black feet. **ka-tsáu-báng**, a small water-insect used for feeding birds.

báng-hia, small hand-net for catching mosquitoes. **báng-sut**, flapper for driving them away. **báng-sak** (Cn.), id. **báng-tà**, mosquito-curtains. **báng-keng**, a semicircular mosquito-curtain on a folding frame. **báng-tà-keng**, id. **báng-tiù^{n}**, hanging mosquito-curtains. **báng-hiu^{n}**, sort of drug burned to drive away mosquitoes. **báng-hun**, a composition for this purpose made up in long rolls in paper. **báng-á-hun**, id. **tiám-báng-hun thiā^{n}-tá^{n}**, to keep up our spirits, as by getting a companion, or by some slight and insufficient precaution. **tiám-báng-hiu^{n} thiā^{n}-tá^{n}**, id. **tiám-báng-hun phoā^{n}-tá^{n}**, id. by a companion. **báng-á-si**, sentences of poetry pasted up on 5. 5, to drive away mosquitoes (a jocular superstition).

hun-báng, to smoke mosquitoes (as above). **iét-báng**, to fan away mosquitoes. **phah-báng**, to drive them away by striking. **poā^{n}-báng**, do. by shaking something. **pì^{n}-báng**, to become a mosquito, as a larva; said also of a boy growing idle, ill-behaved, and fond of low pleasures, esp. a lad coming of age, and running into gambling or licentiousness; also of an employé acting somewhat dishonestly towards employers. **teh-pì^{n} sím-mih^{n}-báng**, why do you begin these bad courses?

báng— **khin-báng-báng**, very light (not heavy).

bāng (R. bōng), to hope. **ǹg-bāng**, do. **tsáñg-bāng**, to place all one's hope on him. **sit-bāng**, to lose hope. **tsoát-bāng**, utter despair. **bāng kàu-bô--khì**, to hope on till all hope is lost. **liâu-bāng**, to watch and look earnestly for arrival (as of enemy or friend).

bāng-táu, a square box near top of flagstaff.

bāng-thâu (P.), = khoà^{n}-thâu, to watch against detection whilst some evil action is done (v. khoà^{n}).

bāng (R. bōng), a dream. **tsòe-bāng**, to dream. **bāng--kì^{n}**, to dream. **bāng-khoà^{n}--kì^{n}**, to see in a dream. **bîn-bāng**, to dream.

jû-sù-bāng, confused dreaming of all sorts of things (esp. in spring), often making one call out in sleep. **phái^{n}-bāng**, nightmare. **phái^{n}-bāng chhut-bōe** (nightmare to sell), phrase written up after having had an unlucky dream. **khoà-sim-bāng**, a dream about what one has been anxiously thinking upon. **chhoā-jiō-bāng** (vulg.), an empty baseless dream.

oân-bāng, to interpret a dream. **oân-sien-bāng**, to dream in the temple of the Genii or on their incense, so as to get an augury. **ûn-sien-bāng**, id. **khùn sien-kong-bāng**, id. **khùn-bāng**, to sleep at a grave or temple in order to get instruction from the spirits. **thok-bāng**, to give instruction by a dream, as a spirit does (v. thok).

bāng (R. bóng), a net; to catch in a net; to darn by cross-stitches.

bāng-tang-á, the tailor-bird (v. tang). **ti-tu-bāng**, a spider's web when round and entire.

bāng-tsûn, a fishing-boat. **bāng-tūi**, weights for a net. **bāng-so**, a large wooden bodkin or pin for weaving nets. **bāng-kì^{n}** (Cn.), id. **bāng-hia**, a small hand-net for scooping fish out of a large net. **bāng-se**, material of old nets, used for caulking, &c. **bāng-se-kè**, a frame covered with nets (in a junk) for protection in fighting.

bāng-hî, to catch fish in nets. **bāng-chiáu**, to catch birds in nets. **bāng chhek-chiáu-á**, to catch sparrows in nets. **bāng-kha-chiáu** (T.), sparrows caught in nets.

hē-bāng, to set a net. **koà-bāng**, id. **khan-bāng**, to pull along a net, as by two boats, or by one boat and men on shore. **sîn-bāng**, to take fish out of the mud and shallow water inclosed by a net at low water. **khoà^n-bāng**, to guard nets (at sea), taking a large percentage, like blackmail. **pha-bāng**, to cast a net. **phah-bāng**, to make a net. **chhiah-bāng**, id. **kiet-bāng**, id., especially for dress.

khiā-bāng, stake-nets. **hé-bāng**, a sort of net with a broad mouth, fastened between two boats. **tng hé-bāng**, to set this sort of net and wait for the tide.

bāng-sa^n, to darn a coat or shirt. **giâ-kang-bāng**, to darn (as a tear) by cross-stitches. **sì-kak-bāng**, to darn in both directions.

bat [R. pék, white, clear, = col. péh], (T. pat), to know; to be acquainted with; to have done a thing, as opposed to having never done it at any time. **m̄-bat-khì**, I have never gone there. **bat-chiàh**, to have tasted it (at some time); fond of good eating. **khah-bat-sek**, knowing well how to act in any circumstances. **bat-ê-lâng**, a man well acquainted with a matter. **bat-jī**, able to read. **bat-lō͘**, to know the road. **bat-gûn**, able to distinguish good and bad dollars. **bat-lâng**, to have skill in knowing men. **bat-kûn-thâu**, good at boxing. **bat-sóng**, knowing how to have things neat and comfortable, or how to make one's self comfortable; *e.g.* keeping from hard work. **bat sè-bīn**, to know how to act in special circumstances. **bat chhin-soe**, acting with propriety according to relative relationships. **bat toā-sòe**, knowing how to act properly, as to superiors and inferiors; *e.g.* to maintain one's dignity towards inferiors. **bat koāi^n-kē**, id.

bat jîn-chêng, to feel grateful.

sa^n-bat, acquainted with each other. **m̄-bat--i**, I am not acquainted with him.

bàt [R. bók, wood]. **bàt-sat**, a bed-bug (v. sat).

bàt [R. bèk, ink]. **bàt-tsàt**, = bàk-tsàt, the cuttle-fish. **bàt-koa^n**, dried cuttle-fish.

bàt (R. bit, = col. bā, bák), close; secret; to close up a corpse in the coffin. **bàt-pîn**, a close partition. **bàt-hûn**, thick clouds. **hûn tà-bàt-bàt**, clouds all over the sky, and very low. **tìn-bàt-bàt**, crowded. **khoeh-bàt bàt**, id.

bàt-chiet, closely shut up, as house, &c.; securely closed against danger. **iám-bàt**, to cover and conceal. **pì-bàt**, to keep close, as a secret (v. pì). **khǹg-bàt**, to hide a thing. **siap-bàt**, carefully shut and closed, as against danger; filled up closely, as a crevice; well arranged (as affairs), without any flaw, and without letting out any secret. **that-bàt**, to close up, as an opening. **that-bàt-bàt**, crowded (as things). **chhùi that-bàt**, hold your tongue!

bàt á-bē, is he coffined yet?

bàt-ê-lâng, a man who can keep a secret. **tsòe-tāi-chì m̄-bàt**, to manage a matter ill so that the secret leaks out. **chhùi bàt**, he speaks little and cautiously. **chhùi kàu-chiah-bàt**, why did you not speak of it? **koe-nn̄g bàt-bàt, to ū-phāng** (though an egg be very close yet it has holes), the closest secret may leak out. **kau-chiam tèng, bàt-liú thī^n**, very careful of money, and rather over-cautious. **kau-chiam tèng, bàt-liú poâ^n**, id. **kau-chiam tèng, koh bàt-pâng**, id.

bàt-liú-liú, very close. **bàt-siám-siám**, very dense, as foliage, or as a densely peopled district; safely stowed away or guarded. **bàt-tiu-tiu**, closely crowded, as men; safely hid and guarded so that no one knows; all very tight and no chink left. **bàt-chiuh-chiuh**, very crowded, as street at a play.

bàt-sit, = bàk-sit, very many, as things; very cheap and many for the money.

bau [R. pau, to inclose], to fold in a rounded edge or border. **bau-lau**, id. **bau--lâi**, folded or curved inwards. **bau-kì^n**, to fold the edge or border. **bau-oá**, fold it close. **bau-sûn**, to fold so as to make a border or rim (v. sûn). **chhùi bau-bau**, lips folded inwards and mouth shut; silent. **chhùi-tûn bau-bau**, lips naturally rather turned inwards. **bau-tûn**, to turn in the lips, as children; to cover an article with some other material (as pewter over stoneware) turning over the edges.

bâu (esp. T.), = mâu^n. **bâu-bâu**, taking it easy; not particular; not standing on our right (v. mâu^n).

bâu [R. id., sort of spear]. **bâu-tún** (lit. sword and shield), opposite uses; contradiction. **ka-kī bâu-tún**, to contradict one's self. **tsū-siong bâu-tún**, id.

bâu (T.), = A. mâu^n, a helmet.

báu (R. id.), the Pleiades, = ke-chhì^n, = báu-chhì^n.

báu (R. id.), a cyclical character, also 5–7 A.M. **báu-sî**, 5–7 A.M. **în-tsòng báu-hoat**, as soon as buried the good influence of the grave is manifested. **tsáp-jī-géh báu, put-kièn-chháu**, in winter, at the hour "báu," one cannot see (grass).

tiám-báu, to mark the roll, as of soldiers or of employés in yamun. **èng-báu**, to answer to one's name on roll. **báu-miâ^n**, name on the books of a yamun as if employed, but really only for protection. **phû chit-ê báu-miâ^n**, to have one's name thus entered. **ìm chit-ê báu-miâ^n**, id. **koà-báu**, id. **jip-báu**, id. **pài-báu**, id. **pài hú-báu**, have one's name on the books of the Foo. **hú-báu**, name on books of the Foo. **koāi^n-báu**, name on books of the Hien. **tō-báu**, on books of the Tau-tai.

báu (esp. T.), = mauh^n (q. v.), to embezzle; to cheat.

bāu — **bōe-bāu--tit**, cannot be frightened so as to be cheated or defrauded.

bāu, to mix up, as food; in some special phrases. **bāu-lāu**, id. **bāu-mī^n**, to mix vermicelli with other eatables. **bāu m̄-hó-chiàh**, not well compounded, so as not to taste well.

bāu (esp. T.), = māu^n, face, &c. (q. v.)

bàuh, to bargain or contract for in the lump, as work or goods. **té-bàuh**, calculating roughly by sight. **bàuh-tui**, bargain for in gross. **am-teh-bàuh**, id. **tsoân-bàuh**, contract for the whole at once. **tsòe-chit-ē-bàuh**, id. **bàuh-bōe-liáu**, cannot be all bargained for at once (too much). **bàuh thô-thâu**, bargain for removing rubbish. **bàuh-kang**, to contract for a work by the job, including all the various sorts of work. **bàuh siók-mih^n**, to buy things cheap in a lot.

bàuh — **bàuh-soah**, to dare a man to do his worst; to deride a man's attempts as contemptible, futile, and quite useless. **bàuh-siáh**, id. **bàuh-soah--i bô-tsâi-tiāu**, to deride him as quite unable. **goá-ká^n bàuh-soah--i**, I am not afraid to say that his attempts are utterly futile.

bê (R. mûi^n). **lóh-hē-bê**, gentle showers. **lóh-hē-bê**, long drizzling rains that make everything damp.

bê (R. bî), (T. bô͘, C. moâi^n, P. Cn. mâi^n), rice cooked soft and moist; some vegetable soups. **han-tsû-bê**, broth of rice and sweet potatoes, or of sweet potatoes alone. **lèk-tāu-bê**, broth of rice and small green peas. **bê-pn̄g**, cooked rice of all sorts. **bê-**

pn̄g bōe-chiáh, cannot eat rice cooked in any way. **ám-bê**, congee; rice boiled soft and swimming in much rice-water. **beh-ám m̄-tih-bê**, can take nothing but rice-gruel, said of a sick man; said also of a man so poor that but little money can be extracted from him. **hi-bê**, very thin-boiled rice. **khó-thâu-bê**, rice boiled quite soft, but almost dry and adhesive like paste. **khioh-liáp-bê**, congee with the rice-grains still whole. **poàⁿ-míⁿ-bê chiáh-kàu-ià**, spending long wearisome hours at night learning boxing, sometimes said of other things. **poàⁿ-míⁿ-bê chiáh-kàu-m̄**, id.

bê — **hé-thoàⁿ-bê**, broken-down charcoal (v. thoàⁿ).

bê (R. ní). **thô-bê**, mud. **thô-bê-chiuⁿ**, thin slushy mud. **chhàu-kau-bê**, dirty stinking mud of a drain.

bê (R. id.), to deceive; to seduce into evil or error. **bê-lê**, id. **bê--khì**, deluded; to vanish, as an apparition. **bê-hék**, to delude; to seduce into evil. **hun-bê**, deluded; bewildered; faint from sickness or wearied by long discussion, or by drink. **bê-loān**, deluded by vicious pleasure. **sim-sîn bê-loān**, mind led astray, as by lustful desires. **tham-bê**, enslaved by vicious desire. **tham-bê lú-sek**, enslaved by lust. **tham-bê chiú-sek**, do. by liquor and lust. **chiú put-tsùi-jîn, jîn tsū-tsùi; hoa put-bê-jîn, jîn tsū-bê**, it is men who make themselves drunk and depraved; it is not the liquor and women that do it.

chip-bê, doggedly; set on a bad or wrong course. **sit-bê** (R.), to lose one's way. **bê-lō**, id. **kiâⁿ bê-lō**, to go on in wicked ways, having been deluded into them. **kiâⁿ--liáu bê-lō**, walking by a wrong road.

bê-hûn-ió̍h, anæsthetic medicine. **bê-hûn-tîn**, a band of soldiers bewitching the enemy by spells; men deluding the simple and unwary and seducing them into vice and crime. **bê-bák**, to deceive the eyes.

chiáu-bê (better "bôe"), a decoy-bird. **tsòe-bê**, to be a decoy.

bé (R. má), (C. bé). **bé-ka**. mackerel (v. ka).

bé (C. bóe). **bé-chí**, a sort of root (v. chí).

bé (R. má), (C. bé). **bé-chí**, contracted characters for the numerals, used in calculations, and read exactly as the Arabic numerals, from left to right, according to the decimal notation; counters used in gambling (s. horse). **bé-á**, id., numerals (s. horse). **bé-jī**, id. (s. end). **phah bé-chí**, to calculate by these numeral characters; to use them.

phah bé-á, to farm the revenue of an article, as of opium. **bé-thâu**, a large busy trading port (s. horse).

chió̍h-bé, a pile of stones projecting into a stream; the town of Chioh-bey or Shimma below Chang-chew (s. horse).

bé (R. má), (C. bé). **bé-ló**, cornelian (v. ló).

bé (C. bóe). **bé-iáh**, a butterfly (v. iáh).

bé (C.), = A. bóe, to buy.

bé (R. má), (C. bé), a horse; a surname; a man who writes essays for others; used in many phrases for men.

bīn-bé, shape of the face. **bīn-bé tn̂g**, face long-shaped. **bīn-bé sì-pang**, face well formed and well proportioned, rather round and full. **bīn-bé sù-thīn**, id.

bé-á, a colt; a very low, mean sort of servant or person of bad character (s. numerals). **bé--ko**, servant in a bad house. **bé-chí**, servant in a bad house; a very mean sort of servant (s. numerals). **lâng-bé**, persons in general (numerous). **toaⁿ-sin phit-bé**, a solitary man, without relations. **lāu-bé tién-tsang** (the old horse erects his mane), said of an old man with youthful vigour. **hó-bé**, a good horse; a stout brave man; a good walker. **hó-bé-chhát**, a very bold robber. **chhát-bé**, thieves and robbers. **hiáng-bé**, highway-robbers (v. hiáng). **peng-bé**, soldiers. **bé-khoài**, underling of yamun, who has the oversight of thieves and stolen property. **chhien-lí-bé**, a very fast horse or courier. **pò-bé**, an express messenger with despatches. **thàm-tsú-bé**, a spy. **chhiàⁿ-bé**, to have a man to write an essay for examination.

bé-chiūⁿ, on horseback. **bé-téng**, id. **téng-bé**, boys on horseback in a procession with incense. **téng-bé-koaⁿ**, a small mandarin on horseback before a high mandarin. **chiūⁿ-bé**, to mount a horse. **chiūⁿ-bé-hong**, a mortal venereal disease (v. hong). **lo̍h-bé**, to dismount. **kā-i-lo̍h-bé**, to give a feast (or make presents of food) on occasion of a man returning from abroad, or from a long journey. **kā-i-khí-bé**, to give a feast when a man is starting for a long journey. **khí-bé-toh**, a feast given by the parents just before the marriage ceremony. **pē-bé**, to harness a horse. **sè-bé**, to hire a horse. **khiâ-bé**, to ride. **pháu-bé**, to ride fast.

sái kè-bé, to manage to pass a bad article or bad money (v. kè, to cross).

bé-peng, cavalry. **chièn-bé**, a war-horse. **bé-tūi**, a troop of cavalry. **bé-chìⁿ**, archers on horseback (v. chìⁿ). **bé-hu**, groom; a stable-boy. **bé-lô**, a slave who attends horses (said only in scolding or jesting).

bé-tôe, horse's hoof (v. tôe). **bé-iaⁿ**, mane. **bé-tsang**, id. **bé-oaⁿ**, saddle. **bé-táh-thèng**, stirrup. **bé-táh-tèng**, id. **bé-kā-kiuⁿ**, the bit. **bé-chhé-chhiú**, reins; bridle. **bé-soh**, a halter for leading a horse. **bé-piⁿ**, a switch; a whip. **bé-pâng**, a stable. **bé-tiâu**, id. **bé-noâⁿ**, a stall (v. noâⁿ). **bé-chhia**, a cart or carriage drawn by horses. **bé-long**, horses' bells. **bé-hâm-lêng**, id. **bé-lân** (T.), id.

bé-chhèng, a pistol. **bé-n̄g**, sort of confection.

bé-koà, a jacket or short outer Chinese coat (v. koà). **bé-tháng**, a close stool or chair for going to stool. **bé-í**, short narrow benches for supporting a tressel-bed or platform (gen. of bamboo). **tek-bé**, id. **tek-bé** (C.), id.; also, a sort of fixed hobby-horse.

thih-bé, a musical instrument made of bits of glass hung so as to rattle in the wind; three-cornered spikes, used against thieves. **saⁿ-kha-bé**, three-cornered spikes thrown on a place where thieves or enemies are expected; three-legged socket for lamp-wick, set in cup of oil.

bé-kháu-thih, tin-plate, probably originally "iron from Macao."

hái-bé, the seal. **tsúi-bé**, a sort of small water-insect.

bé-lō, a straight ditch in review ground for horse exercise; said also of foreign-made roads (s. end).

tsáu-bé-lâu, an upper verandah. **tsáu-bé-teng**, a revolving lantern with horses on it. **tsáu-bé khoàⁿ-chin-tsu**, to fail to observe a thing from haste.

chhiⁿ-bé, an unbroken horse; a very incautious, hasty, ungovernable man (v. chhiⁿ). **sek-bé**, a trained horse.

bé-chiòng-kun, a horse-headed idol, attendant of Giâm-lô-ông. **bé-sài-iâ**, an idol holding a horse, as at the tutelary temple of a city. **bé-kong-iâ**, an idol of the surname Ma, esp. at C. **hûn-bé**, small square bits of paper with pictures and words on them, burned on 12.24 and 1.4. **sià-bé**, to unsaddle a horse; also,

海上絲綢之路文獻集成　科技與文化編

paper horses burned for the dead. **chì^n sià-bé,** to stuff these paper horses before burning them.

kúi kap-bé háu, meddling when one has no business, and saying what has no connection with the matter. **kúi kap-bé háu; liáh-ti, káu chham-teh-pūi,** do. (lit. ghosts and horses making a noise, on catching the pig, the dog too barks). **bô-gû sái-bé,** take what you can get (v. gû). **chióh-bé,** a stone horse (s. numeral and port).

bé (R. bí), (C. bóe, T. Cn. bö́), tail, end, point, top (as of tree or mast); mouth-end of trumpet or pipe; the last; classifier of fish, worms, serpents, &c.

bé-bé (C. bóe-bóe), the very last. **bé-bé** (C. bé-bóe), a horse's tail. **soah-bé,** the end; the last (v. soah). **lō͘-bé,** do.; end of the road. **āu-bé,** behind. **bé-āu,** do.; end; afterwards. **bé-bīn,** afterwards; end. **bé-chhiú,** id. **kàu-bé-sin,** at last. **khah tè-bé** (C. tòe-bóe), at a later time (v. tè).

boát-bé, degenerate or ruinous state, as near the end of family or dynasty. **thi^n-tōe-bé,** end of heaven and earth, said of very great calamities. **chhiú-bé,** end of hand about the fingers; small articles of personal property left at death (v. chhiú). **toā-pha-bé,** a large tail (as of silver-fish); an affair becoming very serious; expenses heavy, so as to leave but small net gains. **bô-bé,** not to have numerous posterity or good fortune at the last, as a butcher. **kau--lâng bô-bé,** short and changeable in friendships. **hó-bé,** happy end, as of an affair (s. horse). **chit-ê-lâng kúi-nà ê-bé,** many ends are possible for one man, as great changes of fortune. **bé-kéng,** last years of a man's life (v. kéng). **bé-ūn,** do., as in fortune-telling. **bé-ūn,** the rhyming word in the last line of an ode.

khí chhú-bé, there is a waterspout. **tn̂g-bé-chhi^n,** a comet (v. chhi^n). **bé-ku,** a kite shaped like a turtle with a long tail.

mî^n-bé, raw cotton (for spinning) in long rolls (v. mî^n). **hè-bé,** remnant of a lot of goods. **chî^n-bé,** balance of money (esp. cash) on hand. **tsāu chî^n-bé,** to pay the balance. **lóh chî^n-bé,** a rich man losing all.

tsúi-bé, the part of a stream below us. **ì^n-bé,** back part of woman's hair. **thâu-mn̂g-bé,** end of a man's hair (v. mn̂g). **thâu-tsang-bé,** tassel at end of a man's queue, or end of it. **kha-bé,** the part of the foot about the toes. **tsûn-bé,** stern of boat or junk. **oân-keng-bé,** raised rounded stern of junk. **khui-bé,** having no boards at stern, leaving it quite open. **bák-bé,** outer corner of eye. **to-bé,** the corner of the edge of a square knife near the handle. **hun-chhe-bé,** mouth-end of pipe. **î^n-bé,** smaller end of beam. **ûi-bé,** top of mast. **chhiū-bé,** top of tree.

chhiâ^n-bé, to complete, to finish well. **chiâ^n-bé,** an entire animal of sort classified by "bé." **thoa-bé,** to lengthen out and procrastinate (v. thoa). **séh bé-lê,** to put off paying money over and over. **tò-bé-lun,** to push straight back, as boat aground. **tak-bé,** slightly blunted, as a needle.

chit-bé ná^n-hî--nih^n (as bare as a fish), very poor, or plundered by robbers.

bé-kháu, to dress gaudily, as a fast young fellow; walking with large turban, and with jacket half-open, in a swaggering or bullying manner, eating much betel-nut, and ready to quarrel with any one.

bé-pà-thâu, the small of the back. **bé-tsui-kut,** the coccyx bone (v. tsui). **bé-sàng,** the mizzen-mast. **bé-miâ^n,** the last name on a list. **bé-séng** (the last province), said of Fuh-kien. **bé-tsái^n,** the little finger. **bé-jī-tsái^n,** the second last finger, the ring-finger. **bé-jī-tsoā,** the second last line. **bé-jī-iáh,** second last page. **bé-jī--ê,** the second last (of any thing). **bé-jī,** the last character (s. numeral).

thâu-bé, beginning and end; first and last; from first to last; head and tail. **chhù-pi^n thâu-bé,** the neighbours on both sides. **thâu-bé bô-sa^n-kè̤,** beginning and end not agreeing, as of essay or evidence (v. kè̤). **lō͘-thâu lō͘-bé,** beginning and end of journey. **lō͘-thâu, ta^n teng-sim; lō͘-bé, ta^n thih-thûi,** easy at first, but very difficult at last. **hó-thâu hó-bé,** beginning and end good and fortunate. **hó-thâu put-jû hó-bé,** a good end is more important than a good beginning. **ū-thâu bô-bé,** begun indeed, but not well ended; not to the point, as talk. **bô-thâu bô-bé,** ill-composed, as document without order; worthless and bad, as a man; having no suitable clue, as a case, &c. **bô khí-thâu, bô soah-bé,** having neither beginning nor end. **tàu-thâu tàu-bé,** to give some assistance here and there, as in work. **thi^n-thâu thiap-bé,** to give a little occasional help (in money) so that a man is just able to get on. **kia^n-thâu kia^n-bé,** irresolute through fear of possible consequences. **hó͘-thâu niáu-chhú-bé** (tiger's head, rat's tail), beginning very boldly, but ending in nothing. **thâu kàu-bé,** from first to last. **thâu tióh, bé sī,** good fortune, or all right from beginning to end. **si^n-thâu hoat-bé,** to have boils, pimples, or eruptions all over. **kóe-thâu oā^n-bé,** to make a thorough repair, so as to make an old thing look new. **koe-thâu chhī-bé,** all the market and busy streets. **soa^n-thâu niá^n-bé,** mountains and hills. **phah-thâu, chiū-tsai tn̂g-bé,** on hearing a little about it he can tell it all, or can manage it all right. **chiam-thâu soà^n-bé,** needle and thread.

bé— **loān-bé-bé,** confused in mind, so as to do things in an insufficient way. **jû-bé-bé,** id.

bē (R. bī), (C. bōe, Cn. bȫ), not yet. **á-bē,** do., or not yet. **iá-bē,** id. **iáu-bē,** id. **bē-bat,** never yet —. **bē-thang,** do not yet; not yet allowable. **chiáh--bē,** have you eaten? good morning. **ū--bē,** have you or have you not yet (and so in such questions).

bē (R. mūi^n), (T. bȫ, C. moāi^n, mōɛ^n, P. māi^n). **sió-bē,** younger sister; younger female cousin. **tông-sió-bē,** younger female cousin of same surname. **piáu-sió-bē,** younger female cousin by mother's side. **khòe-bē,** daughter of a sort of adoptive mother (v. khòe).

chí-bē, sisters, elder and younger; female cousins. **hia^n-bē,** a man and his younger sister; *e.g.* as in saying that they only remain of the family. **bē-sài,** husband of younger sister. **bē-hu,** do (r).

bē (C.), = A. bōe, unable.

bē (C.), = A. bōe, to sell. **bē tn̂g-kang,** to bind one's self for a long time as labourer at fixed wages.

beh (C. boeh, Cn. böh, boh), to wish, to will; auxiliary verb of future, will or shall; almost, just about to —. **beh m̄,** will you or will you not? **teh-beh,** about to —. **tih-beh,** id. **ài-beh,** to wish or desire. **teh-ài teh-beh,** just (at the time) wishing to have or to do something. **ài-beh-sí, bōe-tit--thang khùi-tn̂g,** said of very great grief or pain. **tit-thàu-beh,** determined to have or to do at all risks and by whatever means.

beh-kàu, almost arrived; almost enough; almost up to. **beh-kàu-tn̂g,** almost long enough. **beh-àm,** almost dark.

beh-goá loā-tn̂g loā-toā, how much money do

you wish from me? **beh ē-mn̄g--mah,** do you want to go to Amoy?

beh, = mihⁿ (R. mihⁿ). **beh--tāi,** what now? what is the matter? what do you want? (slightly finding fault). **beh--lāi,** id. **beh-thài,** how! **beh-thái,** how? (v. thái). **beh-tsáiⁿ,** id. (v. tsáiⁿ). **beh-siáⁿ-táⁿ-kín,** of what consequence is it? (v. kín). **beh-siáⁿ-tsai,** how can any one know? who can tell? **lí beh-siáⁿ-tsai,** how can you possibly know? **beh-siáⁿ-hoat--i,** what possible resource can there be?

béh (R. biét), (C. bóeh), a stocking, a sock. **kha-béh,** warm leggings without feet worn by women. **béh-tsū,** cloth worn inside the stocking. **béh-pè̤,** id. **béh-toà,** a garter. **béh-tn̂g,** a sock. **béh-tsūn,** the quilted part of a stocking-foot, not including the sole. **béh-tóe,** the sole of a stocking, sewed on. **láp béh-tóe,** to make the padded soles of stockings. **kap-béh,** to sew the soles on the stockings. **chhiūⁿ-béh,** id. **béh-tháng,** the leg of a stocking. **béh-àng,** id. **béh-phìⁿ,** the halves which are sewed together to make a stocking-leg.

chhēng-béh, to put on or wear stockings. **thap-béh,** to put on stockings as well as shoes. **chhēng-ôe tioh-béh,** to wear shoes and stockings.

pau-á-béh, soft stockings (for children) like bags, without the usual stiff soles. **mô͘ tāi-siáu-béh,** elastic stockings (woollen). **poàn-chiét-béh,** stockings with legs and feet of different stuffs. **chhiu-béh,** thin stockings, often short. **chhiu-á-béh,** id. **toaⁿ-têng-béh,** stockings of one thickness of cloth. **siang-têng-béh,** stockings of double cloth.

béh (R. bék), = méhⁿ, the pulse (esp. T. and Cn., and sometimes A., while méhⁿ is A. and C.) **khùi-béh** (T.), = A. khì-méhⁿ, the pulse. **bāi-béh** (Cn.), = A. bong-méhⁿ, to feel the pulse.

béh (R. bék), (C. béh), bearded grain; barley; bearded wheat; wheat; corn. **béh-á,** wheat (bearded). **sió-béh,** id. **toā-béh,** barley. **toā-béh-bê,** barley boiled soft. **chiáh toā-béh-bê, kóng hông-tè-ōe,** a poor man boasting greatly. **giâ-kang-béh,** a sort of grain. **chhim-kun-béh,** another sort.

kiô-béh, buck-wheat; also used as medicine. **hoan-béh-sūi,** Indian corn.

béh-sūi, an ear of wheat or barley. **béh-chhiu,** its beard. **béh-kó,** a stalk of straw of wheat or barley (v. kó). **béh-gê,** dried sprouted barley. **béh-lê,** a sort of shell-fish. **béh-lê-ko,** a sort of glutinous inspissated syrup. **béh-te,** a fried cake made of meal. **béh-hún,** wheaten meal or coarse flour. **béh-thâu,** larger lumps riddled out of the flour. **béh-phe̍,** bran. **béh-hu,** parched grain pounded small.

béh-chhu, prickly heat (v. chhu).

béh-tang, wheat and barley harvest. **béh-kíⁿ,** a flail. **béh-soe,** an iron comb for separating the ear from the stalk. **béh-tui,** a heap of cut grain, or of grain. **béh-pū** (C.), a heap of cut wheat or barley. **lún-béh,** to send the wheel over wheat or barley.

béh [R. bit, close, = col. bát, bā, bàk]. **béh-béh-sī,** = bát-bát-sī, very numerous.

béh (Cn. bóh). **béh-sī,** slowly.

bék [R. bearded grain, = col. béh]. **tō liông siok, bék sú chek,** the six grains. **bék-būn,** the seed of a tree (medicinal). **bék-būn-tong,** a medicinal plant.

bék [R. silent, secret], to write from memory. **àm-bék,** id. **bék-jī,** to write out characters from memory. **bék-chheh,** to write out part of a book from memory, as a scholar. **bék-keng,** write from memory a part of the classics.

bék-bék put-gú (R.), silent; without one word. **bék-sī** (X.), to reveal or inspire; inspiration.

bék [R. the pulse, = col. béh, méhⁿ]. **hiet-bék--ê** (of one's own blood and pulse), said of one's real son. **chhin-hiet-bék,** id.

bék [R. ink, = col. bák]. **chí-bék,** to sketch pictures or write characters with nail of finger or thumb dipped in ink; sometimes with slip of bamboo. **chí-bék-ūi,** to sketch pictures in this way. **hó-pit-bék,** having a good hand (writing).

būn-bék, polite; learned; gentlemanly (as man or place).

bêng [R. to engrave]. **bōng-chì-bêng,** an engraved stone from which copies are printed for friends, and which is then buried with the coffin (only used by rich or learned men). **bē-chì-bêng,** id.

bêng [R. to make a solemn agreement]. **bêng-iok,** a solemn covenant (s. clear). **hōe-bêng,** to confederate, as allied princes. **tèng-bêng** (R.), to fix the bargain for marriage of son or daughter. **bêng-hiaⁿ-tī,** sworn covenanted brethren. **goán-bêng--ê,** one of our league; my sworn brother. **chhap-hiet tông-bêng,** to make a league by mixing and drinking blood (a great crime), (v. chhap). **bêng-pē-bú-hōe,** a club the members of which assist each other at the burial of parents.

bêng (R. id.), clear, bright, plain, just (as mandarin); Ming dynasty; ripe, as pine-apple.

sîn-bêng, objects of idolatrous worship.

bêng-tiâu, the Ming dynasty.

chheng-bêng = chhiⁿ-miâⁿ, the "feast of tombs," on or about 5th April. **chheng-bêng-hoe,** a mountain shrub with white linear petals. **chheng-chheng bêng-bêng,** correct and free from involved details, as affair; honest and straightforward, as man who does not meddle in improper matters.

bêng-pėk, plain; to understand; finished (v. pėk). **bêng-láng,** clear, perspicuous. **phín-bêng,** to specify distinctly in an agreement. **thiah-bêng,** to explain distinctly, in speaking. **thiàⁿ-bêng,** to repeat over (as instructions), that they may be fully understood. **tsù-bêng,** to explain by notes or commentary. **kóe-bêng,** to explain the meaning, as of a book. **kóe-bêng,** to correct and make clearer. **hun-bêng,** clear and distinct; clearly discriminated. **hién-bêng,** to manifest. **piáu-bêng,** to illustrate; to show forth. **chí-bêng** (R.), to point out clearly. **bêng-iok,** to make a distinct agreement (s. covenant). **bêng-phín,** id. (verbally). **bêng-toàn,** id. **bêng-he̍,** id. **bêng-bóe bêng-bōe,** fair open sale, with no fraud or mistake. **bêng-moāⁿ àm-phièn,** to deceive and cheat openly. **bêng-jîn put-tsok àm-sū,** an upright man does not practise secret wickedness. **bêng-lí,** clearly understanding the principles of a matter.

put-bêng, unjust, as a settlement or judgment, when the wrong is not redressed; having a flaw, as a sale, &c. **bêng-kèng,** you are very just (mandarin), (v. kèng, "a mirror"). **bêng-khì,** upright and honourable in dealings (s. name). **sí, khah-bêng-khì,** better die than this.

bêng-bók, credentials; clearness of case (v. bók, "eye"). **bêng-būn,** credentials, certificate.

bêng-kim, good large first-class cash (s. sound).

oân-bêng, settled, as account or affair.

bêng-liāng, bright, as lamp; clear, as glass (v.

海上絲綢之路文獻集成 科技與文化编

liāng); also (C.) clear, as voice. **bêng-kak**, thin transparent horn, as for lanterns. **khé-bêng-chhiⁿ**, the morning star. **bêng-hé̤ⁿ kiap-liòk**, housebreaking with lighted torches.

chhong-bêng (P.), = chhang-miâⁿ, intelligent, talented. **chhong-bêng tsāi-níⁿ-bòk**, talent is indicated by the appearance of the ears and eyes, in fortune-telling.

ông-lâi ū-bêng, the pine-apple is yellow and ripe. **ông-lâi put-chí-bêng**, id. **bêng-kiuⁿ**, preserved ginger. **bêng-thn̂g**, a sweet half-transparent confection with hemp-seeds on top.

bêng-īⁿ, sort of oil mixed with varnish, to make it dry quickly. **bêng-ī**, id. **koat-bêng**, cooling medicine for eyes and boils; one kind from a shell, another from a plant (Cassia tora?); the shell itself (Haliotis?). **koat-bêng-hún**, the medicine from the shell, in powder. **chióh-koat-bêng**, the shell itself.

khóng-bêng, a famous man of the "Three Kingdoms" (Sam-kok). **khóng-bêng-teng**, a fire-balloon.

bêng [R. sort of insect], to buy a child and adopt it. **bêng--ê**, a child thus bought and fully adopted (quite different from "khòe-kiáⁿ," which is a mere friendly alliance, not actual adoption). **bêng-lêng--ê**, id. **bêng-lêng-ê-kiáⁿ**, id.

bêng (R. id.) **bêng-kiap-chháu**, a sensitive plant (fabulous).

bêng [R. to make a loud noise, as trumpet or clock]. **bêng-kim siu-kun**, to sound a retreat. **tsū-bêng-cheng** (Cn.), a clock that strikes.

bêng [R. name, famous, reputation, = col. miâⁿ]. **bêng-hūn**, rank, station, office and duty. **bêng-bōng**, influential or honourable standing (v. bōng). **bêng-chiet**, character of person (v. chiet). **bêng-sek**, fame, reputation. **bêng-sek-chióng**, very fine Sou-chong tea. **bêng-chióng-tê**, id. **ū sím-mihⁿ bêng-sek**, whose name has he, as a proof, &c. **chià-lâng-bêng-sek**, falsely using another man's name and reputation. **bûn-bêng**, famous (v. bûn, "hear"). **bêng-lī**, fame and wealth (v. lī). **kong-bêng hién-tát** (R.), rapidly getting high literary honours. **sêng-bêng**, to become famous (as man). **it-kú sêng-bêng, thien-hā ti**, all the world knows his fame at once, said of a man becoming a Kujin. **bêng iông sù-hái**, everywhere famous. **sù-hái iông-bêng**, id. **bêng-kong kū-kheng**, illustrious mandarins, as in speaking of their native place.

bē-bêng, trying to get the acquaintance of a talented or important man. **bē i-ê-bêng**, id. **bē-bêng chiáh-khé-koe**, to follow the fashion, though it may be very expensive or inconvenient. **mēⁿ-bêng**, to use another's name falsely; to pretend to rank, power, or reputation, to which one has no claim. **ké-bêng-sū**, to put on a proud look, like a great scholar (v. sū). **iú-bêng bû-sit**, having the name without the reality. **bâi-bêng tsà-sú**, to conceal one's name, pretending to be dead. **jîn sú, liû-bêng; hó sú, liû-phî**, as a tiger leaves only his skin, so with a man's reputation after death.

hêng-bêng, the private secretary in a yamun who attends to legal cases. **tiâu-têng ê-bêng-khì**, insignia of rank worn by high mandarins.

bû-bêng-tsáiⁿ, the ring-finger. **bû-bêng siáu-tsut** (lit. nameless soldier), one of the nameless, worthless common people. **bêng-ka**, a distinguished family. **bêng-ka-ūi**, pictures by famous artists. **bêng-ka-jī**, large finely written characters on ancient scrolls. **bêng-jī**, id.

tāi-bêng (polite, as all the following), what is your name, sir? **ko-bêng**, id. **ko-sèng tsun-bêng**, what are your surname and name? (v. sèng). **chiēn-bêng**, my name is —. **siáu-bêng**, id.

béng [R. bēng, the surname]. **gê-béng**, the boy who allowed the mosquitoes to sting him that his parents might not be stung. **lí beh-tsòe gê-béng**, are you going to sleep without mosquito-curtains?

béng (R. id.), brave; fierce; powerful and influential, as having a powerful protector, or great prestige, or a numerous clan to back him. **toā-liáp-béng**, exceedingly powerful (in that sense). **béng-lám**, the strong and the weak, as families or clans; the principle of influence and prestige. **khò-lí-béng**, you are trusting in the powerful backing that you have. **it-bī béng**, only daring and nothing else (as if going to fight people). **béng bô-tóe**, braggardly; vain boasting without real power. **chhùi teh-béng**, brave and great only with the mouth. **kan-ta béng**, trying to frighten people, and effect the purpose by mere threats or boasting. **tàu-béng**, two men trying to overcome each other, as in fighting or gymnastics; or in simple threatening, or each saying "you must," while the other says "I won't." **té-béng**, id.

ióng-béng, brave. **béng-chiòng**, a brave military commander.

béng-siù, wild beasts. **béng-hó**, a fierce tiger (v. hó).

bēng [R. to command, fate, = col. miāⁿ], fate, life. **bēng-lēng**, a command; to command. **ûi-bēng** (R.), to disobey commands. **ûi-bēng** (R.), last will and testament. **hōng-bēng**, to receive a command. **léng-bēng**, I have received your commands (polite phrase).

thien-bēng, the will of Heaven, especially as to kings and kingdoms. **gék thien-bēng**, to transgress the commands of Heaven. **thèng-thien iû-bēng**, we can but submit to the decree of Heaven.

sú-seng iú-bēng, life and death are fated. **sat-seng hāi-bēng**, to kill living creatures. **m̄-sat-seng, m̄-hāi-bēng**, not to take life at all (Buddhist virtue).

sî-ūn-bēng, a man's fortune, as very good or bad (v. ūn). **san-i-bēng pok-siòng**, the arts of medicine and divination, &c. (v. siòng). **bēng-tē to-chhún**, my fate is very bad. **hông-gân to pók-bēng**, beautiful women are usually unfortunate. **bān-poan, tē sī-bēng: poàn-tiám, put-iû-jîn**, all is from fate, nothing from man's will.

tsâi-bēng siong-liên, wealth and life are most closely connected. **bê-tsâi hāi-bēng**, to take the life of another for gain. **ōe-siong-bēng**, deadly, as blow or poison. **ōe-tì-bēng**, deadly, as wound or disease. **jîn-bēng**, a man's life, as to the legal consequences of death. **jîn-bēng-àn**, a case of murder or homicide, &c. **bēng-àn**, id. **tng-jîn-bēng**, to bear the responsibility for a death. **chiáh-jîn-bēng**, to take money in compensation for a death. **chhiúⁿ-jîn-bēng**, to plunder a house where a death has taken place. **giâ-jîn-bēng**, to accuse falsely, and lay the responsibility of the death on him. **sat-jîn siông-bēng**, life for life.

bēng (R. id.), a surname. **bēng-tsú**, Mencius. **khóng-bēng**, Confucius and Mencius. **bēng-bú**, the mother of Mencius.

bi = boe, to dodge or skulk about. **thau-bi**, id. **bi-lâi bi-khì**, id. **bi--kè-khì**, to move stealthily

3

past. **bi tī-ka-chiah-āu**, to dodge behind one's back.

bî = bî. **hong bi-bi**, wind very gentle. **hong-á bi-bi**, id. **chhiò-bi-bi**, to smile or laugh slightly. **bi-bi-chhiò**, id.

bî — **bî-chhi**, lock gone wrong, so that it cannot be opened; food or drink causing a slight unpleasant obstruction in throat at the root of the nose, less than kéⁿ-tioh.

bî [R. small]. **hong bî-bî**, wind very gentle. **bî-bî-á-hong**, a very gentle breeze. **bî-bi ê-hō͘**, very slight rain. **bî-bi-á-chhiò**, to smile.

hi-bî, few and scanty. **jîn-teng hi-bî**, population scanty. **bí-chhek hi-bi**, rice-crop scanty. **soe-bî**, to diminish; to lose prosperity; to decline in fortune. **heng-ōng soe-bî**, to prosper and decline. **bî-boát**, very small and unimportant, as trade or gains. **pi-bî** (R.), very low in rank or station. **bî-hêng**, to go incognito (as mandarin).

bî-biáu, vague; without proof; undecided in purpose.

siūⁿ kàu-jìp-bî, to think very carefully or minutely.

chí-bî-chhiⁿ, a star near the Great Bear. **chí-bî tāi-tè**, the god of that star.

bî, to dose, as under influence of opium, or of a long weary talk. **bák-chiu bî-bî**, eyes hardly able to keep open.

bî (R. bí). **bî-lèk-hút**, name of an idol (v. lèk).

bî (R. id.) **bî-chiu**, an island near Hing-hwa (called on charts Mei-chen, for Mei-cheu), where Má-tsó͘-pô was born.

bî [R. a lintel, &c., = col. bâi]. **tiùⁿ-bî**, fixed top of a pair of curtains, across top of bed at front, generally embroidered or having a picture on it. **báng-tà-bî**, fixed top of mosquito-curtains at front. **bîn-chhn̂g-bî**, wooden screen-work across top of Chinese bed in front. **chhn̂g-bî**, id. **teng-bî**, top of the frame of a Chinese lantern. **bî-té-pang**, panelling over top of a Chinese door. **hián-iâu-bûn-bî** (R.), to be a mandarin (lit. have a magnificent door).

bî (R. id.) **chhiûⁿ-bî-hoe**, a rose. **tê-bî-hoe**, a sort of rose.

bî [R. eyebrows, = col. bâi]. **chê-bî**, a heavy club about a man's height. **chê-bî-thûi**, id. **hoe-bî**, a bird like a thrush, that can talk, and is fond of fighting. **hoa-bî** (C.), id. **siū-bî**, a sort of tea with long leaves from Lung-yen-chow.

bî — **bî-bî-bî**, sound used in calling ducks. **niauⁿ-bî**, sound used in calling cats. **khe niauⁿ-bî**, to call cats in this way.

bí [R. tail, end, = col. bé]. **sú-bí**, a flapper (like mosquito flapper) used by the genii. **ùi-siú ùi-bí** (afraid of beginning and end), afraid to meddle with a matter or see a man, for fear of the consequences.

bí (R. id.), rice in grain, already separated from the husk (in the husk it is "chhek"); said also of many small round things. **péh-bí**, rice beaten white in the mortar, and so cleaned from the bran. **chhò-bí**, rice separated from the husk, but not yet cleaned of the bran. **chhùi-bí**, rice broken in the process of cleaning. **chhùi-bí-niauⁿ**, pock-marked with small sort of pocks. **chhiah-bí**, a reddish sort of rice. **âng bí**, id. **chiam-á-bí**, the best sort of rice. **tsá-bí**, rice of the summer crop. **ún-bí**, rice of the winter crop. **tēng-bí**, hard rice. **tsùt-bí**, glutinous rice (v. tsùt). **chhng-bí**, rice (inferior), from the public granaries.

tai-á-bí, a small grain like millet. **siā-ko͘-bí**, sago. **sòe-á-bí**, a small sort of millet for feeding birds.

hê-bí, dried shrimps. **sòng-bí**, do. very small, from Luzon. **o͘-bí** (black rice), said of opium. **tê-bí** (Cn.), tea as sold. **giâ-lan-bí**, cochineal. **lân-hoe-bí**, the picked flowers of the "lân" plant. **soàn-thâu-bí**, roots of garlic. **chhài-pó-bí**, long turnips sliced and sun-dried. **thô-bí-soa**, fine gravel for mixing in mortar. **tek-bí** (C.), the flower of the bamboo.

chiam-bí-koà, to divine by rice grains. **ū-bí-bú**, to have some remnant of rice in the jar; to have something over for time of distress. **lâu--koá tsòe-bí-bú**, keep a little for emergencies.

bí-niûⁿ, provisions. **bí-chîⁿ**, money due for rice got on credit for daily use. **khiàm bí-chîⁿ**, to owe such an account. **bí-tāu**, a small dark legume. **bí-chiú**, liquor distilled from rice. **bí-chiuⁿ**, pulp made by grinding rice in water. **bí-hún**, rice flour; vermicelli (v. hún). **bí-chhòe**, rice dough ground from wet rice (v. chhòe). **bí-khng**, rice-bran, separated from the rice by the mortar. **bí-phun**, water in which rice has been washed (v. phun). **bí-phang**, a confection made from rice. **bí-láu**, another sort.

bí-tsûn, a large rice junk or ship. **bí-tsô**, a boat carrying rice. **bí-kau**, a wholesale rice store. **bí-tiàm**, a retail rice-shop. **bí-tùi**, a large mortar (gen. worked by foot) for cleaning rice. **bí-lāu**, a square box (with funnel) for cleaning rice. **bí-thai**, a rice-sieve. **bí-lô**, a large flat wicker tray for shaking rice, to separate the heavy from the light. **bí-loâ**, a large flat tray for holding rice. **bí-táu**, a rice measure for one "táu." **bí-kài**, a small stick for smoothing the top of the rice in the measure. **bí-chhiám**, an instrument for taking samples from bags without opening them (v. chhiám).

niûⁿ-bí, to buy rice; to measure rice. **tiáh-bí**, to buy rice. **thiò-bí**, to sell rice. **toâ-bí**, to stir rice in water (to separate sand) before boiling. **thoah-bí**, to rub rice between the hands in water so as to make it clean.

iâm-bí, salt and rice mixed, for superstitious use (v. iâm). **chhâ-bí**, fire-wood and rice. **chhâ khang, bí-niûⁿ chīn**, wood and food exhausted. **chit-iūⁿ-bí chhī pah-iūⁿ-lâng**, men having the same food vary much in character. **chheng-tsúi tsú-péh-bí** (white rice cooked in clear water), candid, open, and truthful.

bí (R. id.) **tsōe-bí-moáⁿ**, in vast abundance; very great quantity.

bí [R. beautiful, good]. **bí-biāu**, excellent. **bí-jîn**, a beautiful woman. **ūi-bí-jîn**, to paint a female figure. **bí-jîn-chio**, sort of red arum. **soán bí-lú**, to choose beautiful girls for imperial harem. **kun-tsú sêng jîn-chi-bí**, a good man assists others to be good.

bí (R. lúi). **bí-lát**, = lí-lát, a scrofulous sore on the neck.

bī (R. id.), taste, odour, flavour, smell. **bī-sò**, taste, flavour. **bô-bī bô-sò**, insipid. **tsu-bī**, taste, flavour. **khì-bī**, odour, flavour; disposition of a man. **khì-bī siong-tô**, dispositions harmonize.

chhù-bī, agreeable; pleasant.

ì-bī, deep meaning, as of a book.

it-bī, only; wholly. **it-bī-béng**, bold and nothing more. **tan-hong tók-bī**, medicine that produces its effect by itself without mixing other drugs.

kam-bī, various sorts of eatables used as condiments; *e.g.* dried flesh (but not sweetmeats or cakes), sold at shops like grocers'. **kan-bī**, id. **kam-bī-tiàm**, a grocery for such things. **hái-bī**, fish in general (as eatable). **san-tin hái-bī**, delicacies of land and sea.

iá-bī, a bad or coarse taste; also (R.), flesh of wild animals. **khá-bī**, a fine delicate flavour. **sin-bī**, fresh taste or flavour. **ù-bī**, rotten smell, as of something corrupting. **sng-bī**, having a sour smell. **tái-bī**, too strong smelling, though somewhat pleasant. **chiáⁿ-bī**, insipid taste. **sit-bī**, turned by keeping too long, as food; tainted. **tsoáh-bī**, slightly tainted; just beginning to spoil. **ū-chiú-bī**, to have the smell of liquor.

ngé-bī, the five tastes or flavours: pork, mutton, beef, fowl, duck; or "kiâm sng khó loàh tiⁿ;" also, a medicine. **ngé-bī-chí**, that medicine. **sam-chhoaⁿ ngé-bī**, very good eating.

kè-sî-láh-bī (taste of an old almanac); said of an old affair now out of date, that need not be again raised, or of a man coming far too late.

bī (Cn.), a particle used in beginning a sentence, prefixed to verbs and adjectives. **bī-ū**, there are, &c.

bī — **chhiò-bī-sī**, to smile, as on hearing something, but making no remark (v. chhiò). **hó-bī-sī**, easy and good-natured; *e.g.* letting things pass that are not quite rightly made or done, or letting small insults pass unnoticed.

bī (R. id.), a cyclical character; the time from 1 to 3 P.M.; also [R. not yet]. **bī-sî**, 1-3 P.M. **sîn sut, thiú bī; m̄ toā-sòe-bák,iáh koāiⁿ-kē-hī**, a man born in one of these hours has either eyes of different size or ears of different height.

bī-pit, I think it is not (v. pit). **bī-kièn kî-biēn** (R.), I have never seen him.

bī, to dive; to dabble in mud, as duck with its bill. **bī-tsúi**, do. do. **bī tsúi-tóe**; to dive. **tiàm-bī**, id. **bóng-bī**, to feel about, as duck's bill in mud.

bī (R. bē), a riddle; a puzzle; to solve or guess a riddle. **chhai-bī**, guesses and riddles, as for children; to solve a riddle. **ioh-bī**, to guess a riddle, as child.

biân, biàt (in the several tones), better; biên, biét, &c. (q.v.)

biâu [R. posterity]. **biâu-hoan**, the aborigines in centre of China; the Miau-tse.

biáu (R. id.) **biáu-sī** (r.), to despise; to slight one whom we should respect. **biáu-siáu**, very small; to treat with indignity.

biáu (R. id.) **bî-biáu**, vague; without proof; undecided in purpose, neither helping nor opposing.

biáu (R. id.) **bông-bông biáu-biáu**, uncertain; fabulous; misty.

biáu (R. id.), a second. **biáu-chiam**, the second-hand of watch or clock.

biāu (R. id.), excellent; in good health. **bí-biāu**, excellent. **bî-biāu** (R.), abstruse; mysterious. **ò-biāu**, mysterious; profound. **sîn-biāu**, wonderfully excellent and efficacious, as medicine. **kék-biāu**, most excellent. **biāu-î**, kind and friendly, as in receiving a guest or managing an affair. **chiah-kú, biāu--mah** (r.), have you been well of late? **ū-khiàu-biāu**, attractive and interesting to look at (as an article); very clever; very skilfully made.

biāu [R. a Confucian or Tauist temple, = col. biō]. **sèng-biāu** (r.), Confucian temple. **tsé-biāu**, ancestral temple. **sêng-hông-biāu**, temple of tutelary god of city.

biên [R. to sleep, = col. bîn]. **bâ-chhú tông-biên** (cat and rat sleep together), said of officials becoming accomplices with those whom they should punish or keep away. **cheng-chhe toát-tiên, kièn-sú jû-biên**, look on death as a sleep when contending for wife or lands.

biên [R. biên, = liên, connected]. **biên-hiong**, of the same villages; villages combined (v. hiong). **biên-lòk**, united under a head-man, as the people of some towns (v. lòk). **biên-tiông** (R.), lasting very long.

biên [R. cotton, = col. mîⁿ]. **biên-iông**, a sheep; a dressed sheep-skin. **biên-iâng**, id. **biên-iûⁿ**, id. **ko-tùt-biên**, a glossy foreign woollen stuff. **bòk-biên**, the cotton-tree.

bién (R. id.) **bién-hî**, a sort of fish, good to eat. **âng-koe ka-láh bién**, three very good sorts of fish; said in joke, alluding to "bién," no need.

bién — **bién-kī**, birth-day, as kept after death.

bién (R. id.), (C. boán). **hun-bién**, to be delivered of a child.

bién (R. id.), to avoid; to forgive, as a debt; no need; you need not; don't. **bién--tit**, in order to avoid —. **sià-bién**, to forgive. **kiû-bién**, to ask to be excused or forgiven. **sia-chioh bién-giên**, no use asking for credit; no credit given here. **î-chioh bién-giên**, id. **m̄, bién** (Cn.), no need of it; no, I thank you.

bién (R. id.) **bién-kióng**, to force; to compel. **bién-lē** (r.), to incite to zeal; to stir up to good actions.

bién (R. id.) **bién-liû**, a sort of crown (v. liû).

biēn [R. the face, = col. bīn], in many phrases has the idea of prestige, respectability, or influence.

chêng-biēn, character, as having influence or power with another. **toà--tióh i--ê chêng-biēn**, out of consideration for him, as doing a favour on his account to a third party. **khoàⁿ i--ê chêng-biēn**, id.

liám-biēn, prestige; reputation. **phái ⁿ-liám-biēn**, condition of having little or no influence, so as to be ashamed.

thé-biēn, respectability; power or influence; prestige; influential position. **kè-thé-biēn**, to take care of one's respectability or prestige. **sioh-thé-biēn**, id. **bô-sioh thé-biēn**, careless of one's own good name. **sit thé-biēn**, to lose prestige, reputation, influence, or good name. **sià-thé-biēn**, to make our superior lose respectability or good name through our misconduct. **thé-biēn-ōe**, exaggerated boastful talk about one's self or one's connections.

hong-biēn, acting in a liberal manner, as a wealthy man does; liberal in gifts or rewards. **toā-hong-biēn**, do.; also, having considerable influence or importance through wealth, rank, power, &c. **tāi-hong-biēn**, do. do. **ū-hong-biēn**, to be thus influential or of consequence. **sàng--khì hong-biēn**, making liberal presents.

kièn-tāi-sék-biēn, acquainted with men of influence or distinction. **kìⁿ-tāi sék-biēn**, id.

it-biēn, at the same time, and —, *e.g.* **it-biēn chiáh-pn̄g, it-biēn khoàⁿ-chheh**, eating and reading at once. **it-biēn chi-kau**, having met but once or seldom; slightly acquainted.

hōe-biēn, to meet face to face. **biēn-hōe**, to settle an account or a matter face to face. **biēn-hē**, id. **biēn-biēn siong-koan**, looking at each other in speechless astonishment, as unable to ward off some danger. **hoán-biēn bû-chêng**, inconstant, as in friendship (v. hoán). **jîn-biēn siù-sim**, having a human face but a brute's heart. **boán-biēn chhun-hong**, face looking fat and healthy, as if getting on well in the world. **thiet-biēn bû-su**, impartial (with an iron face).

biét (R. id.), to destroy utterly; to exterminate. **biét-bô**, id. **tsâu-biét**, id. **biét-tsoát**, id. **biét-tsók**, to exterminate a whole family. **tsoân-ke biét-bông**, may the whole family perish (cursing). **thiⁿ beh-biét**, Heaven will utterly destroy (him or them).

biét-si, to destroy (or put out of the way) a corpse to avoid inquiry. **biét-hâi**, to put old bones out of the way improperly (v. hâi). **chhat-biét** (r.), to blot out, as account.

bih — **kūn-bih-bih**, very near.

bih, to conceal one's self. **thau-bih**, id. **bih-khi-tiàm**, to keep out of the way to avoid being seen. **siám-bih**, id. **bih-chêng bih-āu**, to hide in any corner. **bih-chhih**, to keep out of the way, as afraid to see people. **liam-kha bih-chhiú**, to advance secretly so as not to be observed. **lun-thâu bih-ām**, attitude of looking or listening attentively and secretly. **bih-u**, to hide in a hole, or behind a wall, &c., as in order to catch or kill men.

bih (R. biét), thin slips of bamboo or wood, esp. used for wicker-work. **bih-ki-á**, id. **tek-bih**, a thin slip of bamboo. **tek-sàu-bih**, slip of bamboo from broken brush. **bih-phê**, bamboo slip from outside of bamboo (best). **bih-khak**, do. from the extreme inside (too soft, useless). **bih-nñg**, do. from middle.

koa-bih-bih, too hard and fibrous, as vegetables.

bih-hè, wicker-work goods. **bih-khì-tiàm**, shop for wicker-work. **bih-hiuⁿ**, an incense-stick, having a bit of bamboo as its backbone. **bih-khơ**, a bamboo hoop. **bih-lām**, a large bamboo cable. **bih-chhióh**, bamboo mat. **bih-siuⁿ**, wicker-work box. **bih-pín**, a stiff bamboo frame hung as screen at door. **bih-lî**, bamboo screen that rolls up. **bih-nâⁿ**, a wicker basket.

chhng-bih, to make bamboo wicker-work. **tsòe-bih sai-hū**, a man who makes baskets and other wicker articles of bamboo. **phoà-bih sai-hū**, man who splits bamboos in large quantities for sale, but does not make the goods. **phoà-bih--ê**, id.

bîn [R. pêng, level, = col. pîⁿ, piâⁿ], (Cn. T.), sloping gently, as an inclined plane, or as a road not level but not steep. **soaⁿ bîn-bîn**, the hill sloping gently. **tōe bîn-bîn**, ground sloping gently. **bîn-tōe**, parts of the sea-bottom that are nearly level.

bîn [R. bêng, clear, to-morrow], (C. mêⁿ, bûn). **bîn-á-jit**, to-morrow. **bîn-ná-jit**, id. **bîn-á-tsài**, id.

bîn-hng (T. Cn.), = ê-hng, the evening; this evening. **bîn-hoàⁿ** (Cn.), after this time, esp. after a short time. **bîn-toàⁿ** (Cn.), id.

bîn (R. bân), (C. bûn). **bîn-thâu**, = bîn-thâu, soft steamed round cakes, used in worshipping the dead. **bîn-thâu-kheh**, you are awfully dull and stupid (as if you were eating cakes for deceased relatives). **thô-bîn-thâu bōe-khí-kàⁿ** (leaven cannot raise earthen cakes), a man so dull that though you teach him ever so carefully (literary or manual work) he cannot learn. **ùi sí-pē, beh-chiáh bîn-thâu** (very desirous to eat the cakes, but afraid of father's death), very desirous to get money wrongfully, but afraid of the consequences.

bîn [R. biên, to sleep]. **bîn-bîn**, sleepy; drowsy. **tsau-bîn**, worn out by long want of sleep. **an-bîn**, good night; a pleasant sleep to you (s. people). **koe-bîn**, to talk in sleep (v. koe). **hâm-bîn**, to talk or walk in sleep; to tell lies (v. hâm). **bîn-bāng**, to dream. **toā-bîn sió-sí**, to sleep almost as if dead, said of a man not hearing thieves, &c. **tham-bîn**, to sleep very sound; hard to waken. **tāng-bîn**, deep sleep. **tāng-bîn-khùn**, id. **khín-bîn**, to sleep so as to be easily wakened. **khùn-bōe-lòh-bîn**, cannot sleep. **khùn bē-kàu-bîn**, not having got enough of sleep. **khùn bô-kàu-bîn**, id. **bô-chiok-bîn**, id. **khùn bô-chiok-bîn**, id. **khùn--khì chiok-bîn**, having had sufficient sleep.

tuh-bîn, to dose while sitting. **kiáu-lâng-bîn**, to startle a man out of his sleep (either intentional or unintentional). **phah-chhíⁿ-bîn**, unintentionally awake a man (v. chhíⁿ).

bîn-chhñg, a bed (v. chhñg); (C. bûn-chhñg), (T. also mñg-chhñg), both only in this phrase.

bîn (R. id.), the people. **gī-bîn**, volunteers or militia. **bîn-tsòng**, lictors of civil mandarin. **liông-bîn**, a good subject. **liû-bîn**, a vagabond (v. liû). **thó-bîn**, the vulgar; the rabble. **bîn-hong thó-siók**, manners and customs of a place. **bîn-phè**, a distance of ten li, according to the measure common among the people; about four miles. **bîn-ka**, the households of the people. **bîn-sim**, the affections of the people. **tek-bîn-sim**, to gain the hearts of people, as mandarin or master.

an-bîn, to quiet the minds of the people (s. sleep). **kok-thài bîn-an**, the nation prosperous and the people at peace. **i--ê tsú-bîn**, his people, looked on as his children. **sù-bîn** (C. sì-bîn), the people in general. **thien-tsú hoān-tsōe, ú sù-bîn tông**, if the emperor sin he is not different from the people. **kun-bîn**, sovereign and people. **kun-bîn jîn-téng**, soldiers and people. **koaⁿ-toàn put-jû bîn-goân**, the willing obedience of the people is better than the exercise of authority by mandarins.

bín (R. id.) **lîn-bín**, compassion; pity; to pity.

bín (R. id). **bín-chiét** (R.), skilful and energetic.

bín [R. be destroyed]. **bín-bùt** (R.), to be made away with (v. bùt).

bín (R. id), a brush; to brush. **bín-á**, a small brush. **ôe-bín**, a shoe-brush. **khí-bín**, a tooth-brush. **thâu-mñg-bín**, a hair-brush. **thâu-bín**, id. **bín-ôe**, to brush shoes.

bīn (R. biēn), the face; face, surface, side, or direction (esp. proper side); countenance; respectability. Classifier of shields, gongs, mirrors, verandahs, &c.

chiah-toā-bīn, so large, said of anything of which "bīn" is the classifier.

ū-bīn, to have a wind that can be used for the course; to be able to appear without shame, or to speak to a man to advantage, or to take up a matter with good hope of success. **bô-bīn**, feeling ashamed to see one or to speak to him, because of some awkward, inconvenient, or shameful state of matters; having a wind that is of no use for our course. **bô-bīn thang-kìⁿ--tióh i**, ashamed to go and see him. **lak-bīn**, to lose one's character, prestige, or respectability. **bīn-bák**, countenance. **bô-bīn-bák**, ashamed to look people in the face. **toà--tióh i-bīn-chiūⁿ**, in consideration for him (*e.g.* doing a favour to a third party).

jī-bīn, a book phrase. **sè-bīn**, influence; suitable state or position (v. sè). **sì-bīn** (C.), id. **ū-kiók-**

海上絲綢之路文獻集成 科技與文化编

bīn, now getting on better, as business or lawsuit. **sái ōe-kè-bīn**, can be passed, as bad money; can be used, as a plan more or less improper.

gûn-bīn, silver-plated. **kài-bīn**, to put on a surface finish, or a new surface, as on furniture or idol, &c. **khioh-bīn**, to make a smooth polished surface; to take a miniature likeness. **thì-bīn**, to make the surface smooth, as of a brass mirror. **phe-bīn**, to put the best articles on the top (v. phe).

thia^{n}-bīn, the central hall of a house. **chhù-bīn**, the front of a house. **toh-bīn**, the top of a table; presents of food made to bridegroom. **tò-bīn**, the wrong or reversed side of anything. **lí bīn**, the inside and outside of a dress. **sa^{n}-bīn**, the outside of a dress. **hiû-bīn**, the outside of a thick dress. **ôe-bīn**, the uppers of shoes. **í-bīn**, the seat of a chair, &c. **kià^{n}-bīn**, the face of a mirror. **sì^{n}-bīn**, the paper of a fan. **chhiú-bīn**, the palm of the hand (v. chhiú). **hái-bīn**, the surface of the sea; at sea. **thô-bīn**, the surface soil. **soa^{n}-bīn**, the surface of the ground, *e.g.* as let for cultivation.

kháu-bīn, at the port or mouth of river; outside. **tùi-bīn**, opposite; towards. **bīn-téng**, on the top; above; upstairs. **téng-bīn**, above. **chiū^{n}-bīn**, id. (v. chiū^{n}). **ē-bīn**, below. **bé-bīn** (C. bóe-bīn), at the end; the last. **āu-bīn**, behind. **sì-bīn**, the four sides; all round. **bīn-chiū^{n}**, on the surface. **bīn-chêng**, in front of. **tang-bīn**, on the east. **hong-bīn**, the direction of the wind. **bô-hong-bīn**, not a favourable wind; can't make a fair wind of it. **tang-pak, tang khah-toā-bīn**, wind between N.E. and E. **phâng-bīn**, the starboard (right) side of a junk. **lé-bīn**, the port (left) side of junk.

phî-bīn, having no regard for one's own character and respectability; unblushingly doing shameful acts, esp. greed or dishonesty. **phî-bīn, ké kong-gán**, of unblushing effrontery, *e.g.* caught in some shameful act, and just laughing at it. **toā-bīn-sîn**, wanting in modesty, as girl. **hoán-bīn**, to change countenance, as in anger (v. hoán). **pì^{n}-bīn**, to change countenance. **chhi^{n}-bīn**, readily taking offence (v. chhi^{n}).

tng-bīn, face to face. **hōe-bīn**, to meet face to face. **bán-bīn**, to pluck hairs out of woman's face. **kē kàu-chít-bīn-hún**, to smear one's face all over with face paint. **kâu-bīn**, having a face as ugly as a monkey's; a mask like a monkey's face. **siáu-kúi-bīn**, sort of mask; frame of the lock of door or drawer; face painted like a demon. **tì siáu-kúi-bīn** (to wear such a mask), said of a man doing something very bad, so that he is apprehended or becomes infamous.

bīn-tūi^{n} (Cn.), threshold.

bīn-sėk, known by face only.

bīn-sek, complexion (v. sek). **bīn-bé** (C. bīn-bé), shape of face. **bīn-bé tn̂g**, long-faced. **bīn-bé sì-pang**, face square and full; having a sedate look. **bé-bīn** (C. bé-bīn), having a long horse-like face. **bīn-bē toā**, having a broad face (v. bē). **bīn-kheng**, shape of the face. **bīn-māu**, countenance. **bīn-iông**, id. **bīn-kháng**, appearance of countenance (v. kháng). **phái^{n}-bīn-chhiu^{n}**, appearance of face that repels or frightens people. **bīn-tē**, appearance of face. **hó-bīn-tē**, a pretty face. **bô-bīn-tē**, ugly face (scolding). **phái^{n}-bīn-tē**, id. **bīn-phê**, skin of face (v. phê).

n̂g-sng-bīn, pallid face. **chhàu-bīn**, sour ill-natured look; face full of sores. **hoâi^{n}-bah-bīn**, ugly distorted face, as of thief or rowdy. **bīn-bah siau-sán**, face very lean.

bīn-pè, a small cloth used for washing the face. **bīn-kun**, do. **bīn-tháng**, a bason (v. tháng), gen. wooden. **bīn-phûn**, do. metal or stoneware. **bīn-to**, a razor for the face.

thâu-bīn-téng-lâng, man of very good position. **thâu-bīn**, head and face. **khàm-thâu khàm-bīn**, behaving in a foolish reckless way. **gōng-thâu gōng-bīn**, foolish or stupid. **chiū^{n}-thâu chiū^{n}-bīn**, shameless and impudent (v. chiū^{n}). **gû-thâu bé-bīn**, two images in the Gák temple, having heads of cow and horse. **iu-thâu khé-bīn**, sad countenance. **kâu-thâu chhú-bīn**, very ugly (like monkey and rat). **chhàu-thâu chhàu-bīn**, sour and ill-natured. **chhut-thâu lō-bīn**, to appear openly in public (as woman), at yamuns or at plays. **kóe-thâu oā^{n}-bīn**, to make an old thing new (v. kóe).

bīn [R. biēn, meal, = col. mī^{n}]. **bīn-pau**, bread; a loaf.

bīn (R. bân). **bīn-thâu**, round cakes used in worship of the dead; better "bín," *q.v.*

bīn — **bīn-thâng** (esp. C.), = bûn-thâng, intestinal worms.

biô (R. biâu), to trace a copy on transparent or thin paper. **biô jī-keh**, to trace copy-lines, as scholars.

biô, tapering and lightly made, as bow of boat or bamboo-pole. **biô-chhio**, id.

bīô (Cn.), = A. bô, to plan.

bīó (Cn.), = A. bó (R.), mother —.

bīó (Cn.), = A. bó, Mr. So-and-so, &c.

bīó (Cn.), = A. bó. **bīó-tan**, the tree peony, &c.

bīó (Cn.), = A. bó, a Chinese acre.

biō (R. biāu), a temple of the dead (Confucian or Tauist). **keng-biō**, temples in general. **am-biō**, id. **tsó-biō**, ancestral temple. **bûn-biō**, temple of Confucius. **bú-biō**, official temple of Kwanti. **tiong-liėt-biō**, temple to distinguished mandarins who met their death in the service of the state.

bīō (Cn.), (R.), = A. bō, to trade.

bīō (Cn.), = A. bō (R.), luxuriant.

bit [R. secret, quiet, close, = col. bát, bā]. **chhin-bit**, closely united, as friends. **jîn-ien tiû-bit**, population numerous. **jîn-ien chiu-bit**, id. **chiu-bit**, well arranged so as to leave no flaw; careful, as not to leave a flaw, or not to let out a secret. **pì-bit** (R.), secret. **ki-bit**, kept secret, as affair; managing a matter carefully, so as to keep secrets. **tsok-sū put-bit**, to manage carelessly, so as to let out a secret. **ki-sū put-bit, chek hāi-sêng** (R.), a secret coming out may make the matter impracticable.

bit-jit, phrase which stands in the Chinese (heathen) almanacs of Amoy and Chin-chew on every day that is our Sunday; said to have come down from ancient times.

bit (R. id.), honey. **phang-bit**, id. **bit-phang**, a bee. **bit-pô**, honey-comb. **bit-pâng**, id. **bit-àng**, a honey-jar, &c. (v. àng). **bit-tsúi**, honey syrup. **ti^{n}-bit-bit**, very sweet. **bit-n̂g**, bright light yellow. **pėh-bit chhiū-m̂**, white arbutus (myrica). **bit-iū**, a very sweet sort of pumelo. **bit-chièn**, fruits preserved in sugar, to be presented to idols. **bit-kam**, candied oranges. **kam-á-bit**, a substance chewed with areca and siri. **tsoh-bit**, to make honey. **pàng-bit** (v.), id.

bit-tô-cheng, litharge.

pho-lô-bit, the jack-fruit; this last word is sometimes written with bit, "secret."

bit (C.), = A. lit. **bit-á-soh**, the halyard rope.

bit (R. id.) **bit-pô**, a bat (the animal).

biū (R. id.) **chha-biū** (R.), a mistake; a fault. **chha chi hô-lí, biū í chhien-lí** (R.), an error of a hair's-breadth causes a difference of a thousand li. **pōe-biū**, to offend, as against doctrine.

bô (R. bû), there is not; there are not; not to have; no; not; denying existence or possession (but denial of *will* is "m̄," and denial of correctness or identity is "m̄-sī"). Often enclitic, in asking a question, *e.g.* **ū-lâng-lâi--bô**, has any one come? Often repeated in a divided phrase, though it makes no sense with one of the halves. Often at beginning of an answer has almost no meaning, suggesting surprise at being asked.

ū-bô, to have or not to have, &c. (v. ū). **goá-bô**, I have not. **iá-bô**, no more; all done; and no more; is that all? **iáh-bô**, id. **iáu-bô**, id. **éng-bô**, never. **lóng-bô**, not at all; not one; by no means. **tsóng-bô**, though antecedently improbable, yet one is shut up to believe that — (v. tsóng).

ké-bô, to pretend not to have. **the-bô**, falsely deny having. **bōe-bô**, it cannot but be (there or here, &c.); certainly it is not lost, &c. **bōe-bô**, to fail in selling, because a high enough price is not offered. **bóe-bô**, to fail in buying, because there is none of the article, or it is too dear. **tiáh-bô-bí**, there is no rice to be got in the place. **thák-bô-chheh**, to study, but make no progress. **hù-bô-tsûn**, to be too late for the boat. **phah-bô-mn̂g**, to knock at the door, but get no answer.

biét-bô, to destroy utterly. **sí bô-lâng**, to die off till no one is left. **bô--khì**, to vanish; to be lost; to perish, or waste away and disappear. **bô-lô--khì**, id. **phah-bô**, to let a thing be lost or spoiled in our hands. **lóng-bô--lah**, it is all gone; none of it remains.

bák-tē-bô, to despise (v. tē). **bô-pêng-iú**, has no friends; does not associate with friends as a friend ought. **bô-pē bô-bú**, an orphan; also (scolding), surely you have no parents to keep you in order. **bô-poà^{n}-lâng**, not a single person. **bô-hoat--i**, no resource (v. hoat). **bô-tā-oâ**, id. (v. oâ). **bô-lâu bô-tsúi**, not a good tide; slack water; not a suitable tide for the purpose.

bô-beh, will not. **bô-kàu**, insufficient (v. kàu), **bô-n̂g**, family dead or gone wrong; no hope of a man's return, or reform, or good fortune. **bô-siá^{n}-sū**, no trouble; no reason. **bô-iá^{n}**, untrue; not a shadow of reality.

bó (C.) **bó-kū**, = A. bú-kū, mother's brother.

bō (R. id.), a hat; a cap not broad-brimmed (that is "lòeh"). **âng-ia^{n}-bō**, red tasselled cap of mandarin's attendants; a mandarin's attendant. **ə-âng-bō**, the four lictors of a mandarin, two with red, and two with black caps. **toā-bō**, a ceremonial cap. **sió-bō**, an unceremonial cap, specially when a mandarin puts off his ceremonial cap, and puts on an unceremonial one. **oá^{n}-bō**, a skull-cap. **chhiu-bō**, a light cap worn in autumn. **se-oá^{n}-bō**, a light summer cap. **se-bō**, a cap of the Ming dynasty with two long ears. **seng-bō**, a cap worn in plays. **seh-bō**, a winter cap worn by children. **sìn-bō**, cap worn by young children (v. sìn). **hó-bō**, cap worn by children, made like a tiger's head. **hē-bō**, a rain-cap, of oiled cloth or paper, with flap for back. **hong-bō**, a hood worn by men. **n̂g-bō**, quilted cap, used in winter. **mn̂g-bō**, sort of fur cap, for mandarins and wealthy men. **téng-bō**, a cap with an official button. **tiâu-bō**, a court-cap. **koâ^{n}-bō**, a mandarin's warm cap, with button. **joáh-bō**, mandarin's summer-cap, with button. **chhí^{n}-bō**, a blue cap, half mourning. **sə̀-bō**, a cap of plain black cotton with no red. **háp-chióng-bō**, cap with a ridge in centre, worn by Bud. priests, also by children to keep off demons. **hê-siū^{n}-bō**, id. **kun-ki-bō**, a cap sometimes worn by mil. officers. **khoe-chhèng-bō**, sort of close-fitting cap for soldiers.

tì-bō, to wear a cap or hat. **ài-tì koâi^{n}-bō**, fond of praise and flattery; vain and conceited. **ài-tì toā-bō**, id. **ài-tì toā-téng se-bō**, id. **chhòng-chit-téng toā-bō hə̄-i-tì**, to make him by flattery to take the lead, as in an expensive subscription or troublesome matter, so that he may have to bear the expense or responsibility. **chhòng-chit-téng toā-téng-se-bō hə̄-i-tì**, id.

bō-the, the inner frame of a cap (made first) made of stiff paper or thin bamboo. **bō-khə**, a skull-cap without the crown, specially worn by boys. **bō-á-khə**, id. **bō-ia^{n}**, tassel of cap. **bō-á-toà**, string for tying on a cap, esp. child's cap. **bō-koà^{n}**, string for keeping on a hat or cap. **bō-á-kè**, frame for hanging a cap. **bō-áh**, a hat-box.

bō (R. id.), a millstone; a mill (only for grinding); to grind. **bō-á**, a millstone. **toā-chióh-bō**, a large millstone. **chit-tún-bō**, a pair of millstones. **bō-pâng**, a mill (building). **bō-keng**, id. **gû-bō**, a mill worked by a cow. **tsúi-bō**, a water-mill. **sái tsúi-bō**, to work a water-mill. **oe-bō**, to turn a mill, as by hand.

bō-kau, the hook by which a millstone is turned. **bō-á-chhiú**, the projection on the upper millstone, having the hole for that hook. **bō-sim**, the metal centre on which the millstone turns. **bóh--tit liáh-goá tsòe bō-á-sim**, do not set me to be used and abused by both parties in the dispute.

bō-hún, to grind flour. **bō-chhòe**, to grind rice and water into wet dough.

bə (Cn.), = A. bong, to touch.

bə̂ (R. biên). **phak-bə̂**, the 40th radical, written at top.

bə̂ (R. id.), (Cn. bîô), to plan; to plot. **kè-bə̂**, id.; a plot or plan. **tə̂-bə̂**, to plot (v. tə̂). **àm-bə̂**, to conspire secretly. **ēng-bə̂ siet-kè**, to plot deceitfully. **tông-bə̂**, to plan or plot together (gen. bad). **thong-bə̂**, to conspire or plot together. **thong-bə̂ tsō-kè**, id. **thò-bə̂**, secretly conspire to mislead or injure some one.

ké-bə̂, to start a joint trade or business.

chham-bə̂, an officer on general's staff, who assists in planning battles, &c.

bə̂-sū, to make a plan in any matter. **bə̂-sū tsāi-jîn: sêng-sū tsāi-thien**, man proposes, but Heaven disposes. **bə̂-hoán**, to make a rebellion. **bə̂-tsâi hāi-bēng**, to seek wealth at the expense of another's life. **bə̂-iâ^{n}**, to plan a surprise (by night) on a camp. **iú-ióng bû-bə̂**, boastful and overbearing, but without wisdom or skill.

bə̂ (R. bông), (C. bông), mist: thick haze. **tàu-bə̂**, mist or thick haze, as on the sea. **tà-bə̂**, id. **kàu-bə̂**, thick haze. **kauh-bə̂**, id.

bə̂ (R. id., = col. mûi^{n}, bôe). **hâ-bə̂**, dried toads for medicine.

bə̂ (R. id.), a mould; the swelling made by a blow or an insect's bite; a mass or lump, as of clay or dough.

bə̂-iū^{n}, a pattern; a model (v. iū^{n}). **phe-bə̂**, a pattern. **thə̂-kat-bə̂**, a mould for making sun-dried bricks; also used for pressing tobacco. **bîn-bə̂**, general shape of face. **bīn-bô͘ toā**, having a large broad face. **phah-chhiú-bô͘**, to make the impression of one's hand (with ink) on a deed of sale, esp. selling a wife. **pang-kok kui-bô͘** (R.), the rules and laws of a kingdom (v. kui, a rule).

kui-bô͘, to become one mass, as dough or clotted blood, &c.; a whole mass of such things. **ka-nn̂g-bô͘**, a whole mass of such sort. **jiók tsòe-chit-bô͘**, to work up into a lump, as clay or dough.

bó͘ (R. id.), (Cn. bió), such a man or thing; Mr. So-and-so. **bó͘-bó͘**, such-and-such surname and name. **bó͘-lâng**, Mr. So-and-so; what you call him; often said when for some reason it is undesirable to mention his name. **bó͘-mih-lâng**, id. **bó͘-siá^{n}-lâng**, id. **bó͘-sím-mih-lâng**, id. **bó͘-jit**, on such a day. **bó͘-sî**, such-and-such an hour or time. **bó͘-mih^{n}**, such a thing (not naming it).

bó͘ — **oat-bó͘**, the 28th radical; this word is often written as a contracted form of "bó͘," so-and-so.

bó͘ [R. hū, a woman], a wife; observe that in Chang-poo the sound of "bú," mother, comes very near this sound.

ang-bó͘, husband and wife (v. ang). **āu-bó͘**, wife married after death of first wife. **chhoā-bó͘**, to marry a wife. **khit-bó͘**, to buy a wife. **tsòe-bó͘**, to get a bride betrothed for one's self (v. tsòe) **bó͘-kiá^{n}**, wife and children. **lō͘-thâu-bó͘**, woman who cohabits with a man without marriage. **bó͘-thâu-chhin**, wife's relations. **bó͘-kīm**, wife of wife's brother. **ùi-bó͘, taī-tiōng-hu; phah-bó͘, ti káu gû**; he who fears his wife is a bold fellow indeed; but he who beats her is a pig, dog, or cow; the last clause is also given "chin sī-gû," is really a cow.

bó͘-kat, a loosely tied knot. **tsa-bó͘-kat**, id.

tsa-bó͘, a woman; (somewhat a vulgar or at least not polite phrase); this name is sometimes given to a male child to deceive the demons. **tsa-bó͘--ê**, name often given by a mother to a young daughter. **tsa-bó͘-lâng**, a woman. **tsa-bó͘ gín-ná**, a girl. **siá tsa-bó͘-gín-ná-jī**, to write a document for the sale of a girl, as slave or concubine; only done by low fellows who keep stalls in the streets. **tsa-bó͘-kán**, a female slave; a concubine. **tsa-bó͘-sun**, a granddaughter; a prostitute. **tsa-bó͘-sun-keng**, a brothel. **tsa-bó͘-keng**, id. **thó-tsa-bó͘**, to go after lewd women. **chhī-tsa-bó͘**, to keep a concubine.

bó͘ [R. mother, = col. bú], (Cn. bió). **hū-bó͘**, father and mother. **tông-bó͘ ī-hū**, having the same mother, but different fathers.

ti-bó͘, = ti-bú, a cooling medicine. **pòe-bó͘**, = pòe-bú, a medicine.

bó͘ [R. male], (Cn. bió). **bó͘-tan-hoe**, the tree peony. **bó͘-lē**, a medicine (v. lē).

bó͘ (R. id.), (Cn. bió), a Chinese acre; a mow; it is less than one-sixth part of an English acre. **chhân-bó͘**, fields in general.

bó͘ (R. id.) **kang-bó͘**, = kang-bú, a tree from which potash is made, also good for soles or heels of shoes. **kang-bó͘-chhâ**, its wood.

bō͘ (R. id.), a cyclical character.

bō͘ (R. id.) **chio-bō͘**, to enlist soldiers.

bō͘ (Cn.), = A. bōng, a grave.

bō͘ (Cn. boah), to smooth the point of a Chinese pen after it has been dipped in the ink, removing the superfluous ink. **bō͘-pit**, id.

bō͘ (R. id.) **him-bō͘**, to desire greatly; to long after. **loân-bō͘** (R.), id. **bō͘-bêng**, to try to get acquainted with an influential man (v. bêng).

bō͘ (R. id.) **bō͘-ek** (R.), to buy and sell.

bō͘ [R. hō͘, time, = col. pō͘, hāu]. **tsā-bō͘-jit**, yesterday. **tsā-bō͘ ê-hng**, yesterday evening. **tsá-bō͘** (C.), formerly; a long time ago.

bō͘ [R. a curtain]. **bō͘-pin** (R.), = su-iâ, a private secretary of a mandarin.

bō͘ (R. id.), (Cn. biō). **bō͘-sēng** (R.), luxuriant, as the abundant vegetation of many trees. **siù-bō͘**, elegant, luxuriant, and beautiful, as a plant; beautifully formed and free from rough features, as a smooth conical hill; also (R.), elegant, polite, and of graceful form, as a gentleman.

bŏ (T.), = A. bê, soft cooked rice.

bŏ (T.), = A. bôe. **chiáu-bŏ**, a decoy-bird.

bŏ (T.), = A. mûi^{n}. **koa^{n}-bŏ**, a sort of female jailer for women.

bŏ (T. Cn.), = A. bé, end; tail.

bŏ (T. Cn.), = A. bē, not yet.

bŏ (T.), = A. bē, younger sister.

boâ (R. mô or mô͘), to grind; to rub down, as ink; to polish smooth. **boâ-kim**, to polish smooth. **boâ-bàk**, to rub down ink. **boâ-to**, to sharpen a knife. **boâ-kià^{n}**, to polish a mirror. **boâ-chiòh**, a whetstone.

boâ, to toil; to labour hard. **boâ-làt**, laborious. **boâ lâng-ê-làt**, to make men toil hard. **boâ kàu-sí**, to toil all one's life. **boâ kàu-beh-sí**, to toil very very hard. **tiòh-boâ**, to toil hard. **siū-boâ**, id. **siū-boâ-thoah**, to have passed through many hard experiences (v. thoah). **thoa-boâ**, to toil very hard; to be ill, long and painful. **khang-boâ**, to labour and get no pay or thanks. **ùi-boâ**, unwilling to exert one's self. **boâ-chhùi boâ-chih**, to talk a great deal with no result, or not much. **boâ-sim-boâ-koa^{n}**, to exert one's self very much. **thoa-sim-boâ-miā^{n}**, to exert one's self very very much.

boâ (Cn. T.), = A. moâ^{n}, hemp.

boâ — **boâ-bui** (P.), = (C.) bâ-bui, a fruit used as soap.

boah — **it-jī-boah**, all laid along quite level, as books on a table.

boah (R. boat), to besmear; to anoint; to plaster (as wall). **boah-iû**, to anoint. **boah-hún**, to smear with powder (as face). **boah-kô͘**, to spread paste (in pasting). **boah-he**, to plaster with lime. **boah-piah**, to plaster a (partition) wall. **boah-pit** (Cn.), = A. bō͘-pit, to smooth the point of a pen before writing.

boah — **iù-boah-boah**, very smooth, as the skin of a young person or of a melon; in fine powder.

boàh [R. boát, end], articles powdered or broken down small. **iù-boàh-boàh**, finely powdered. **hiu^{n}-boàh**, powdered incense. **tê-boàh**, broken down tea leaves, cheaper than the whole leaves. **tê-kho͘-boàh**, broken down refuse from the manufacture of camellia oil (used in washing). **iû-kho͘-boàh**, id. **géng-boàh**, to grind to powder. **sio-hu géng-boàh**, to calcine and grind to powder. **liàh lâi sio-hu géng-boàh**, seize him, and deal with him severely, violently, or cruelly (sometimes said of a tremendous scolding).

boàh — **boàh--kè-khì**, to brush lightly over (as with one's sleeve) without hurting.

boàh (cf. bā). **boàh-hiòh**, the hawk.

boàh, to seize with claws, as a hawk; to seduce (as by fair speeches) into evil, danger, or calamity.

boàh (C. bàh). **boàh-á**, the crocodile (or alligator). **boàh-á-khí**, crocodiles' teeth, used as ornaments.

boàh —. **sù-lí-boàh**, Souribaya.

boàh (perhaps different characters). **kā-boàh-chhài**, a vegetable (lettuce?). **ka-boàh-chhài**, id. **kāu-boàh-chhài**, id. **kāu-boàh-hông** (C.), a medicinal plant (v. hông). **boàh-tîn** (C.), a shrub with white flowers that grows by water-courses.

boán [R. late, = col. mńg]. **boán-pòe**, polite phrase for "I," when speaking to a teacher or an old man. **boán-seng**, id. especially said to a mandarin. **boán-seng-tsái**^{n}, said in scolding a man for assuming airs or authority above his position. **boán-chhan** (X), the Communion.

boán (C.), = A. bién. **hun-boán**, to be delivered of a child.

boán [R. full; Manchu = col. moá^{n}]. **oân-boán**, finished, completed, as work or time fixed; fully paid, as money. **tsōe-ok koàn-boán**, measure of guilt full. **boán-khé èng-sêng**, mouth full of fair promises. **boán-biēn chhun-hong**, full ruddy face. **boán-tsāi**, full cargo. **boán-tsāi êng-kui**, to return prosperously with full cargo; said also of an emigrant coming home rich.

boán-thien-kong, a hanging lamp with several wicks. **boán-tông-hông**, hanging chandelier with many lamps.

boán-chiu, Manchuria. **boán-lâng**, a Manchu. **boán-á**, id. **boán-peng**, Manchu soldiers. **boán-á-ôe**, shoes for large-footed woman, with narrow sole and up-turned point. **boán-hàn**, Manchu and Chinese. **boán-hàn-toh**, a feast of mixed Manchu and Chinese style. **boán-hàn-sèk**, id. **boán-hàn-kah**, a vest edged with black velvet, and having many foreign buttons.

boán [R. koán, to roll up = col. kńg]. **boán-chien-ké**, a sort of long cake folded, twisted, and fried. **boán-chien-ko**, id.

boàt [R. end]. **bí-boàt**, small and unimportant, as trade, gains, or wages. **lí-boàt**, id. **boàt-bé**, in a decayed degenerate state, about to perish and come to ruin, as family. **boàt-kiap**, Buddhist phrase for the (future) last age of the world. **boàt-jit** (X), the last day.

boe = bi, to dodge about; to go along slyly, or peep secretly, as a spy or thief, or any one wishing to avoid observation. **thau-boe**, id. **boe-lâi boe-khì**, id. **toà-teh-boe**, id. **boe--jip-lâi**, to come in slyly or secretly. **boe--chhut-khì**, to go out slyly.

bôe [R. bî, soft-boiled rice, = col. bôe]. **tsú kàu bôe-bôe** (= mûi^{n}), to cook very soft, as meat or rice, &c.

bôe [R. mûi^{n}? bôe?]. **bôe-lâng** (C.), = A. hm̂-lâng, sort of go-between for marriages. **koa^{n}-bôe** (esp. T.), = koa^{n}-mûi^{n}, a sort of female jailer.

bôe (T. bô), a decoy, as in a trap. **chiáu-bôe**, a decoy bird. **chiáu-á-bôe**, id. **kiáu-bôe**, a man employed to entice men to gambling. **chhát-bôe**, a spy used by thieves for spying out things to be stolen, or for enticing a man into their gang. **kheh-bôe**, the passenger who first takes his seat in a small boat, and so leads others to take passage in it rather than in the other boats which are empty; he gets his passage rather cheaper.

bôe (T. C.), = A. mûi^{n}, name of a flower. **bôe-hoa** (C.), = A. mûi^{n}-hoe.

bôe (R. bô), (T. mûi^{n}). **ām-bôe**, a young frog; some say "tadpole."

bôe — **ôe-bôe** (T.), = A. ôe-phàn, the loops at the side of a woman's shoe for pulling it on.

bóe (R. mái), (C. bé), to buy. **chhái-bóe**, to select and buy, as goods. **bóe kui-hāng**, to buy wholesale. **bóe-m̄-tát**, to buy too dear. **bóe-bô**, to fail in buying, as because it is too dear, or none of it in market. **tham-sia kùi-bóe**, buying on credit is expensive. **bóe-tn̄g**, to buy for ever, without right of redemption. **bóe chīn-kun**, id.

bóe-pān, a steward in a vessel, or a servant who buys provisions (v. pān). **bóe-chhài**, to buy provisions. **bóe-kheh**, a customer.

bóe-tê-chî^{n}, a small reward or cumshaw. **bóe-tê**, to buy tea. **hē-lí bóe-tê**, take that small reward. **hē-lí bóe-hun**, do. (tobacco). **hē-lí bóe-chiú**, id. (liquor).

bóe-lō-chî^{n}, black-mail levied on a road by powerful villages. **bóe-hó**, to use means to get a judge, arbiter, or influential man to take our side, *e.g.* to get one of the owners of a property to use his influence (esp. in an underhand way) to let us have it cheap. **bóe-soà^{n}**, to give money so as to find out stolen articles, or the thief, &c. (v. soà^{n}). **bóe-miā^{n}**, to buy long life by burning idolatrous paper; to ransom a capital criminal (?).

bóe-bōe, to buy and sell; to trade. **bóe-bōe-chhùi**, fast and loose tongue, as of trader; said of two bowls overlapping when laid mouth to mouth; said of folding-doors laid to, but not closely shut, the one leaf slightly overlapping the other. **bóe-bōe chhát**, traders are thieves. **bóe-bōe sǹg-hun; sa^{n}-chhiá^{n} bô-lūn**, in trade people count to a fraction; in treatment of guests, don't count how much. **bêng-bóe bêng-bōe**, to buy and sell openly and fairly. **bóe--chiá put-bêng, bōe--chiá tí-tng**, if the buyer was not fully informed, the seller is responsible.

bóe (C.), = A. bé, end. **chiòh-bóe**, a town near Chiòh-bé; so pronounced also in A., to avoid confusion with Chiòh-bé.

bóe (C.), = A. bé. **bóe-iàh**, a butterfly.

bóe (C.), = A. bé. **bóe-chí**, a sort of root.

bóe (T.), to add an extra rope or cord to strengthen one that is not strong enough, so as to serve instead of a thicker rope. **ke-chit-tiâu lâi-bóe**, id.

bōe (C.), = A. bē, not yet.

bōe (R. māi), (C. bē), to sell; to betray. **bóe-bōe**, to buy and sell; to trade (v. bóe). **pièn-bōe**, to sell. **bōe-tn̄g** (C. bē-tūi^{n}), to sell without right of redemption. **bōe-chīn**, id. **bōe chīn-kun**, id. **bōe-bô**, to fail to sell, as from asking too much (s. unable).

bōe-lâng, to sell men, as slaves or coolies (commonly said of the coolie emigration). **bōe--lâng**, to sell to people. **bōe-sin**, to sell one's self.

bōe-chî^{n}, to sell for copper cash. **bōe-hiēn**, to sell for ready money. **bōe-hiēn-gûn**, do. paid in silver. **bōe-gûn**, to sell for silver. **gû bōe-gûn**, to sell a cow for silver.

bōe-peng, to sell the position of a soldier. **bōe-koa^{n}**, to sell official rank or place. **bōe-kòng**, to sell the rank of "kòng-seng."

bōe kui-hāng, to sell wholesale. **lân-san-bōe**, to sell by retail or piece-meal. **chhùi-chhùi-bōe**, id.

厦英大辭典

hó-bōe, saleable. **hoat-bōe**, for sale. **pháiⁿ-bāng chhut-bōe** (a nightmare for sale), written after an ill-omened dream. **bōe-bah-chiⁿ**, wages of a "tâng-chí," or of a man who sells himself to personate another, and be beaten by mandarins.

bōe chit-tiâu-lō͘, to throw away a good position or acquaintanceship for some improper gain or indulgence; *e.g.* by stealing from a kind patron, so that one dares not go back to him.

bōe (C. bē), unable; cannot; am not; is not (in some phrases); no, in answer to questions asked by "ōe." **bōe-ōe**, unable; cannot. **ōe-bōe**, able or unable; can you, or can you not? can it be so?

bōe-koâⁿ, I am not cold. **bōe-ià**, I am not tired. **bōe-iau**, I am not hungry. **bōe-joàh**, the weather is not hot. **bōe-hiáu--tit**, I do not understand; not to understand.

bōe-tit, cannot —. **bōe-tit--thang**, id. —. **bōe-sǹg--tit**, cannot be numbered. **bōe-kì--tit**, to forget. **bōe-tsòe--tit**, it won't do. **bōe-sái--tit**, id.; this last phrase must not be said in Cn.

hêng-bōe-khí, unable to pay. **hóng-bōe-khí**, cannot manage to make the copy like. **kóng-bōe-chhut**, unable to speak it out. **kóng-bōe-lâi**, unable to persuade or to accomplish by talking. **óh-bōe-lâi**, unable to learn though making the attempt. **óh-bōe**, id.

bōe-ê-lâng, a man of no ability. **bōe-bô**, it cannot but be there, &c.; it cannot be gone (s. sell).

boeh (C.), = A. beh, to wish; will.

boeh (C.), = A. beh or mih, what? in some special phrases. **boeh-níⁿ**, what are you about? what do you want?

bóeh (C.), = A. béh, stockings.

boh, said in An-khoe and Lâm-oaⁿ (some parts), = A. beh, to wish; will.

bóh (R. bók). **bóh--tit**, do not! **bóh--tit, khah-hó**, it is better not to do it, or not to meddle with him. **bóh, khah-hó**, id. **kah-i-bóh**, if he will have it so, let him please himself (I will not meddle; let him do it if he pleases, we don't care, and are not afraid of him). **bóh-kioh** (following such a word as "liân" or "siōng-chhiáⁿ" in the previous clause), how then can —, *e.g.* liân i-ê-kiáⁿ, to m̄-káⁿ; bóh-kioh lí-káⁿ, even his own son dares not do it, how then could you dare!

böh (Cn.), = A. beh, to wish, will.

böh (Cn.), = A. béh, stockings.

bók [R. the eye, = col. ba̍k]. **níⁿ-bók**, ears and eyes. **iám-jîn níⁿ-bók**, to delude people with false appearances while acting wickedly. **chiau-iâu níⁿ-bók**, to attract thieves, as a show of wealth (v. iâu).

bīn-bók chhiú-lok, a cloth put over the face and mits on the hands of a corpse.

bók-liók, a list of contents.

bók-tông, blind, said in scolding (s. tend). **siáu-chiet-bók**, unimportant, as a few cash or a small affair.

bók-liân, one of the eighteen Lohan, who delivered his mother from suffering in the other world.

bêng-bók, credentials, as of a small official. **bô-bêng-bók**, not clear, as a document or an affair about which there is not clear evidence. **chheng-sim bêng-bók**, heart comfortable and eyes clear, as after drinking good tea.

it-bók, having only one eye; blind of one eye. **it-bók liáu-jiân**, to perceive at one glance. **it-bók, koan thien-siōng**, the one-eyed man became a great astronomer (said in joke of a man blind of one eye).

bók — **bók-bû tsun-tióng**, contemptuous towards persons in authority or superiors.

bók — **jiók-bók**, to insult; to treat with contempt; to abuse, as a person.

bók [R. do not, = col. bóh]. **bók-koài kì-jiân**, don't be offended because of that; it is quite natural; there is no cause of offence in it. **iú-lō͘, bók teng-chiu**, if there be a road, don't enter a boat.

bók (= bong, bák). **àm-bók-bók**, very dark, as night or room.

bók [R. to tend, as cattle]. **bók-tông**, a shepherd boy (s. eye). **bók-su** (X.), a pastor, minister, or missionary. **bók-chiá** (R.), one who tends or feeds (lit. or fig.)

bók [R. to bathe by throwing water over one's self]. **tsai-kài bók-iók**, to fast and cleanse one's self ceremonially (v. tsai). **bók-ék-têng**, a paper figure of a bath-room, used in worshipping the recently deceased.

bók (R. id.) **bān-lí sa-bók**, the great desert of Shamo or Gobi.

bók [R. wood, = col. ba̍k]. **bók-pún**, having a woody or shrubby stem, as a plant; said also of a thing having an origin. **bók-pún súi-goân**, a tree has its root, water has its spring (v. goân, a fountain-head).

bók-á, a small coffin, as for a child. **si-siá koan-bók**, to give away coffins gratuitously (v. siá). **bók-tsú**, ancestral tablets. **bók-chí** (C.), id. **bók-kùn**, a club. **bók-gû**, a wooden drum shaped like a fish. **bók-hî** (C.), id. **bók-siâⁿ**, a temporary fort made for a review.

bók-seng, large-boned and awkward-looking in shape (as a man). **bók-chhiⁿ** (R.), the star Jupiter.

chhó-bók, plants of all sorts; herbs and trees. **chhó-bók-sîn**, an idol not regularly canonized, but which has recently become popular; an upstart, not likely to be permanent.

bók-koa, the quince. **bók-pit**, a flower like amaryllis (v. pit). **bók-níⁿ**, a fungus that grows on trees (v. níⁿ). **bók-pih-thiông**, an insect used medicinally.

bong (R. bô͘), (Cn. bo), to touch; to feel (actively); to feel about; to feel for; to catch, as shell-fish, by feeling in the sand; to handle; to set to work; to procrastinate; to put one's hand to this and that, making an appearance of diligence.

bong-bāi, to try by touching. **bong-khoàⁿ**, id. **bong-jiâu**, to crumple by touching.

chhun-chhiú, bong sim-koaⁿ (touch your heart with your hand); let your own conscience speak.

gâu-bong, always procrastinating. **put-sî teh-bong**, doing work by small bits at a time.

bong sím-mihⁿ hāng-tàng, what is your business or trade? **tióh-khì-bong**, you should set to work and not be idle. **bong-tang bong-sai**, always at work at various things, so as to have no leisure. **ū-sū thang-bong; bô-chîⁿ thang-thàn**, unprofitable affair.

bong-so-tīⁿ, to touch in a lascivious or indelicate manner, as man touching a woman. **bong-leng**, to touch a woman's breast (counted a pledge of illicit intercourse). **loān-tsú-bong**, to grope about; to touch the person improperly.

bong-bô-tsáng, to seek in vain for a clue. **bong-bô-lō͘**, unable to find the road; unable to find any way of doing it. **bong-bōe-lâi**, tried and found it could not be done. **bong bōe-tit-lâi**, id. **hái-tóe bong-chiam**, to feel for a needle at the bottom of the sea.

4

bong chhân-lê, to catch field-snails with the hand, for food.

àm-bong-sa, to grope. **e-àm-bong**, id.

àm-bong-bong, very dark; thick weather.

bong (cf. bông). **tsùi-bong-bong**, dead-drunk.

bong — **toā-bong**, flower making a large head, said of the cockscomb.

bông (R. hong). **pēng-jip-ko-bông**, disease incurable.

bông [R. to receive]. **bông-ké**, Mongol, Mongolia.

bông (R. id.) **bông-sék**, a medicine.

bông (R. id.) **bông-chéng**, the term that falls about June 6th or 7th (v. chéng).

bông [R. to perish]. **bông--lâng**, a dead man. **sin-bông**, a man newly dead. **kū-bông**, a man long dead. **tīn-bông**, to die in the ranks. **tsoân-ke biét-bông**, all the household dead; often said as a curse. **siàu-liên-bông**, may you die young! said also of an unlucky grave.

bông-hûn, the soul of a corpse. **khan-bông**, to bring up the spirits of the dead by incantations. **lí teh-khan-bông**, you are telling a great lie, esp. said to women or children.

bông — **bông-bông**, very dim, as eyes. **bông-bū**, id. (a. mist).

bông — **àm-bông-bông** (C.), = A. àm-bong bong, very dark.

bông (C.), = A. bē, thick mist.

bông-bū (A.), misty.

chhiū^n-bông (C.), thick mist coming on. **hái bông-bông** (C.), = A. hái bāng-bāng, dim misty appearance of sea, as at horizon. **chhun-bông phàk-sí kúi; hē-bông tsò-toā-tsúi** (C.), a mist in spring dries up even the ghosts; a mist in summer causes great rain.

bông (R. id.) **bông-bông**, obscure, as sky. **bông-bông biáu-biáu**, uncertain; fabulous; obscure.

bông [R. quick]. **hông-hông bông-bông**, carelessly; hurriedly.

siōng-hā-bông, the two stated yearly payments of house-tax or land-tax. **siōng-bông**, the first of them. **hā-bông**, the second of them.

bông-bông (C.), = A. bâng-bâng, perplexed.

bông [R. lông, sort of insect]. **tông-bông** (Cn.), = chháu-kâu, an insect like a large grasshopper.

bông — **tsùi-bông-bông**, dead-drunk.

bông [R. to forget]. **bông-un pōe-gī**, ungrateful. **liām-liām put-bông** (r.), to remember and not forget. **kám-un put-bông**, gratefully remembering favours.

bóng (R. id.), tolerable; not very good; not very well; just will do; so-so; never mind.

sui-bóng, although.

lé-bóng, hurried, reckless, or careless in action; rude in manner. **bóng-tóng**, id. **bóng-tóng-tóng**, id. **bóng-chhóng** (C.), id.

bóng-khì, tolerable; not very good, but may do. **bóng-bóng**, id. **tióh-bóng**, may let it pass; let it do. **bóng-kiâ^n**, barely willing to go, but without much heart. **bóng kiâ^n-kiâ^n**, merely taking a walk or stroll. **bóng-kóng**, to talk at random; chit-chat; sometimes slight jesting, half-joke half-earnest; well now, just speak. **bóng-chiáh**, never mind, just eat it. **bóng-kè**, can just get on; so-so; barely getting on. **bóng-oe bóng-kè**, id. **bóng-thoah bóng-kè**, just getting on, though with difficulty (v. thoah).

bóng-chhiá^n, just let —, please just —. **bóng-chhiá^n-chē**, please sit a little longer. **hó-sim bóng-bóng**, you benevolent man, just please give me anything you like (said by beggars).

bóng (R. id.) **khoah bóng-bóng**, very vast. **it-bóng bû-chè**, = it-bōng bû-chè, illimitably vast, as a great flood.

bóng (C.), = A. bú; only in the phrase, **toā-bóng**, = A. toā-bú, large, abundant, *e.g.* **bák-chiu tè^n toā-bóng-lúi**, to stare angrily. **toā-bóng sì-keng-kè**, everywhere.

bóng [R. = col. bāng, a net]. **lô-bóng** (R.), a net; net-work. **thien-lô tē-bóng**, heaven and earth are a net, which wicked men cannot escape; their wickedness will surely be punished; a sort of net-work to protect a vessel from pirates; a sort of rat-trap. **it-bóng tá^n-chīn**, to take the whole at one haul, *e.g.* one man taking the whole of what should have been shared with others. **ti-tu kiet-bóng** (spider makes a net); ornamental net-work, esp. on top of a mandarin's sedan.

bóng [R. not], (cf. báng). **sè-sip bóng-thè** (R.), hereditary (of rank or office). **khi-bóng** (R.), to treat a superior with disrespect or neglect his orders.

bóng [R. = col. báng, a large sort of snake or dragon]. **bóng-phàu**, a long ceremonial robe with dragons on it, worn by some mandarins. **bóng-ó**, dress of wives of high mandarins, embroidered with these dragons; worn also by rich lady at marriage. **bóng-kûn**, under-dress (or petticoat) thus embroidered. **chhēng-bóng**, to wear such a robe, esp. at plays.

bòng — **bòng-bòng**, careless, reckless; intentionally running a great risk (for a special purpose), as of pirates. **sim bòng-bòng**, reckless. **bòng-tá^n**, recklessly running into danger. **hîn-bòng-bòng**, head swimming; feeling giddy.

bòng — **kim-koe-bòng** (T.), = A. kim-kòng-thûi, a sort of mace before idols, mandarins, &c.

bōng (R. bē), (Cn. bē), a grave. **hûn-bōng**, id. **bōng-tui**, mound of grave. **bōng-ku**, do. **bōng-toh**, the flat stone or table in front of grave. **bōng-pâi**, tombstone. **bōng-chì-bêng**, engraved stone put inside the grave (v. bêng). **bōng-chhiú**, the long arms encircling a large grave. **bōng-tiâ^n**, the level place in front of a grave. **bōng-tō**, stone tablet at side of road directing to the adjoining grave of a distinguished person. **bōng-am** (C.), grave with a sort of pinnacle. **bōng-moa^n**, the circular back of a grave. **bōng-khòng**, the cavity or pit of a grave (v. khòng).

tsòng-bōng, to bury. **pài-bōng**, to worship at grave. **teh bōng-tsoá**, to scatter paper on graves. **chhiū^n-bōng**, to make offerings and worship solemnly at graves (on the "chhi^n-miâ^n" term). **chè-bōng**, id.

thô-bōng, a grave with a mound of earth or turf. **he-bōng**, a grave made with a mound of cement in shape of tortoise.

bōng (cf. bòng). **bōng-bōng**, giddy. **bōng-bōng-hîn**, id.

bōng [R. disorderly]. **bōng-tsōng**, careless, awkward, unmannerly (v. tsōng). **kông-bōng** (?) braggardly. **bōng tsū tsun-toā**, self-conceited; making one's self of importance.

bōng [R. = col. bāng, to look at]. **bōng-hiong-tâi**, an elevation in Hades, from which the dead see their old home and family.

bêng-bōng, distinction, fame, reputation. **ū-bêng-bōng**, to be of some importance, distinction, or consideration, as a man whom others respect. **bô-bêng-bōng**, of no consequence or position, or of bad reputation.

sok-bōng, the first and fifteenth of the Chinese month; new and full moon.

it-bōng bû-chè, very vast, as a flood.

bōng [R. = col. bāng, to dream]. **bōng-siet**, involuntary emission of semen. **bōng-û̂i**, id.

bu (cf. bû). **tsòe-chit-bu**, to meet together, as men; to make one lot, as things.

bu (cf. tu). **chit-bu-thô**, a small mound of earth.

bû (T.), = A. pû. **tsòe-chit-bû**, to meet together. **chháu ka-nn̂g-bû**, a dense luxuriant clump of grass or other plants.

bû [R. = col. bô, no, not, there is not]. **bòk-bû tsun-tióng**, contemptuous towards persons in authority. **liòk-bû**, to have no near relatives, said in reviling. **chéh-liòk-bû**, utterly exterminated. **liòk-bû-lâng**, man with no relations (esp. Cn.), said in reviling an unfriendly unneighbourly fellow who will not lend a hand to help. **bû-tėk**, superior to all others in power or excellence (v. tėk). **bû-sé put-û̂i**, addicted to every evil (v. sé). **bû-bêng-tsáiⁿ**, the ring finger (v. bêng, "name"). **bān bû it-sit**, without a single mistake or failure.

bû-tō, unjust, unprincipled, and wicked, as a ruler. **bû-lí**, to scold violently and unjustly (v. lí).

sù-bû khī-tān, recklessly wicked; fearing neither gods nor men. **sù-bû--lâng**, to insult people by violent language, so as to put to shame before others; generally improperly and unjustly. **khit--i sù-bû--khì**, to be so insulted and put to shame by some one.

lâm-bû o-bî-tô-hùt, a Buddhist phrase used in invoking Buddha (Sansk. "nama").

bû (R. id.) **bû-loā**, to accuse falsely. **ka-bû**, id. **bû-kò**, id. before mandarins.

bú — **kang-bú**, male and female, of animals. **bú--ê**, a female, of animals.

núiⁿ-bú (C.), walking like a woman (said in scolding). **thû̂n-bú**, a sterile woman.

bú (R. id.), (C. often sounded like bó or bé), mother; capital of money; used as the final in a great many miscellaneous phrases.

pē-bú, parents (v. pē). **chīn-bú-lát**, to exert all one's bodily strength. **î-bú**, mother's sister. **bú-î**, id. (s. military). **bú-kū**, maternal uncle (v. kū). **bú-kīm**, wife of maternal uncle.

lāu-bú, mother. **bú-chhin** (r.), id. **sien-bú**, your deceased mother (polite). **siⁿ-bú**, real mother. **kè-bú**, step-mother. **āu-bú**, id. **āu-bú-bīn**, sour look, as of a step-mother. **gák-bú**, mother-in-law. **khòe-bú**, a woman taken as a sort of adoptive mother, but not actual adoption. **ióng-bú**, wife of adoptive father, who treats the child quite as a son. **tek-bú**, principal wife of father, said in relation to the son of a secondary wife. **toā-bú**, id. **ché-bú**, title of a large-footed concubine (said about her, not to her) in relation to her child. **sù-bú**, similar title of secondary wife, but more respectful, usually small feet. **sòe-î bú**, id.

tsé-bú (R.), paternal grandmother. **lāi-tsé-bú** (R.), id. **goā-tsé-bú** (R.), maternal grandmother.

kok-bú, empress-dowager **lin-bú**, a wet-nurse. **jú-bú**, id. **io-kiáⁿ-bú**, id. **bú--á**, a nurse. **khioh-chiá-bú**, a midwife.

chhiú-bú-nn̄g, the first egg that a fowl lays (v. nn̄g). **koe-bú**, a fowl that has laid eggs. **ti-bú**, a sow that has or had a litter. **chhut-bú-thai**, newly born, as child. **bú-sin**, body of woman about to have a child, or within a month after delivery. **bú-sin-sí**, to die within a month after having a child, supposed to go to the "huih-tî" in the Buddhist hell.

hái-koe-bú, a broker (with no warehouse of his own) who inquires about cargoes not yet landed, and either buys small quantities on his own account, or negotiates the sale for merchants. **toā-keng hái-koe-bú-tiàm**, shop of a sort of broker who buys and sells all sorts of things wholesale.

lâng--ê hùi-bú, what a man is terribly ashamed to have talked of (v. hùi).

sat-bú, a louse (v. sat).

bú-chîⁿ, principal of money; capital lent. **bú-lāi**, principal and interest (v. lāi).

jī-bú, the radical of a word; a letter of alphabet.

kàⁿ-bú, leaven. **chiú-bú**, materials for making liquor all mixed ready for fermenting. **kiuⁿ-bú**, hard dry ginger root (v. kiuⁿ). **chhài-bú**, a very salt sort of sauce. **bí-bú**, small reserve for future use (v. bí).

soa-bú, small gravel or coarse sand, about the size of small peas. **soaⁿ-bú**, the peak from which auspicious influence takes its beginning.

liâu-bú, the large rope or sheet in which the small ropes of a sail meet. **hoe-bú**, the original plant from which smaller shoots or young plants are taken. **chhiū-bú**, main stem of a tree, as opposed to suckers and secondary stems. **tîn-bú**, crown of the root of a trailing plant, as of a potato. **kun-bú**, crown of the root; origin of a thing.

hùt-bú, the goddess with eighteen hands, Sansk. Maritchi. **tsún-thê hùt-bú**, do. **sèng-bú**, the goddess Má-tsé-pô; also the Virgin Mary, as named by the Romanists. **thien-siōng sèng-bú**, Má-tsé-pô. **chiá-bú**, a spirit that guards an infant. **chhn̂g-bú**, id. **hâu théh-bú**, to make offerings to the goddess of the court-yard. **se-ông-bú**, the queen of the fairies, who reigns at "iâu-tî." **tiēn-bú**, the goddess of lightning (v. tiēn). **pài táu-bú**, to worship the Great Bear (v. táu).

pòe-bú, a medicinal plant (= pòe-bé), Uvularia and some similar roots (?). **ti-bú**, a medicinal plant (= ti-bé) that allays fever and inflammation; Celandine or Anemarhena (?). **ti-bú n̂g-peh**, two medicines often given in one dose. **ek-bú-oân**, a sort of pill (v. ek). **chí-bú**, a fish like trout. **chí-bú-á**, id.

bú (R. bé). **kang-bú**, = kang-bé, a small tree with light wood (v. kang), (s. female).

bú (R. id.) **bú-bān**, to insult; to slight. **bú-lōng** (R. ?), to make a fool of; to play practical jokes upon; to take undue liberties with a superior (s. brandish). **bú-lōng tsun-tióng**, to make game of a superior.

bú — **bú-thán-chhoáh**, diagonal (v. chhoáh).

bú [R. to brandish, to dance]. **bú-kiàm**, to brandish a two-edged sword (so with other weapons). **bú-lōng** (R.), to brandish or gesticulate. **bú-lōng pit-bák**, to make pedantic display in composition. **bú-lāng**, to brandish, &c. **bú-bú lāng-lāng**, brandishing weapons or instruments. **bú toā-ki koan-to** (able to brandish the great sword of Kwanti), to have considerable influence or power, so as to be able to manage matters of importance. **bú-pè**, to manage a matter unfairly without the knowledge of superior, as subordinates in yamun or in a hong.

thiàu-bú, to gesticulate with hands and feet; leaping and dancing and moving arms.

bú [R. id.], military (including naval), as opposed to civil (so all through)—**bú--ê**, a military one, *e.g.* a military mandarin. **bú-biō**, the official temple of Kwanti. **bú-gōe**, military affairs (v. gōe).

pí-bú, to practise military exercises. **ȯh-bú**, to learn them. **khó-bú**, to have examination of military candidates.

bú-ȯh, a military Sew-tsae. **bú siù-tsâi**, id. **bú-tông**, military students or candidates. **bú kú-jîn**, a military kujin. **bú-kú**, id. **bú-khoe**, id. **bú-koaⁿ**, a military mandarin. **bú-iâⁿ**, id. **bú-hu**, said in disparagement of military mandarins on account of their want of learning. **bú--jī bô-chit-phiet** (the character "bú" has no down stroke), said with the meaning that military mandarins don't know the characters well. **bú-toàⁿ**, a man (actor) representing a female warrior.

ién-bú-têng, pavilion for mandarins at the review ground. **iâu-bú iông-ui**, a man showing himself of importance (v. ui).

bûn-bú, civil and military; Wen-wang and Wu-wang. **bûn-bú-tiâⁿ**, an accusation lodged at same time before the civil and military authorities. **bûn-bú koaⁿ-oân**, civil and military mandarins. **bûn-bú tsoân-tsâi**, having both civil and military ability. **kêng bûn, pù bú**, the poor study in order to get civil office, but military *students* are usually from the wealthier classes. **bûn-pan bú-pan**, ranks of civil and military mandarins at imperial audience.

bú-ông, Wu-wang, the founder of the Chow dynasty. **bú-î-soaⁿ**, the Bohea hills.

chin-bú tè-kun, = Hiên-thien Siōng-tè. **bú-tong-san**, his birthplace. **bú-tong-tiēn**, his temple.

hiên-bú, the Tauist spirit presiding over one quarter of the sky. **hiên-bú tāi-tè**, id. **goân-bú**, id.

bú — **bú-thún-bú-thún**, short and stout, as a man.

bú — **chhī-bú chhī-chhū**, to whisper. **chī-bú chī-tsū**, id. **lī-bú lī-lê**, talking on far too much.

bú (C. bóng), (Cn. sometimes ḿ). **toā-bú-liàp**, very large man. **toā-bú-hàn**, id. **toā-bú-lâng**, id. **toā-bú-siaⁿ**, loud noise or voice. **toā-bú-kóng**, large, long, and hollow, as a large bamboo, or as a crab's claw, or as a large suppurating sore. **chē toā-bú-ūi**, to sit so as to take up a great deal of room. **tìn toā-bú-ūi**, to take up a great deal of room. **sim-koaⁿ toā-bú-ê**, asking far too much.

toā-bú sì-kòe, everywhere; very abundant. **toā-bú sì-kong-kòe**, id. **toā-bóng sì-keng-kè** (C.), id.

bú (R. id.) **toā-pē-bú**, the thumb; the big toe. **kha toā-pē-bú**, the big toe. **tsńg-thâu-bú**, the thumb. **kha tsńg-thâu-bú**, the big toe.

kûn-thâu-bú, the closed fist.

bú (R. id.) **eng-bú**, a sort of parrot.

bú [R. hú, to stroke, to tranquillize]. **bú-īⁿ** (Cn. hú-īⁿ), the lieutenant-governor, *i.e.* the governor of *one* province. **bú-tâi**, do. **tok-bú**, the governor-general and the lieutenant-governor.

bú-ióng, to nourish and carefully bring up, as a child.

bū [R. affairs]. **sè-bū**, the affairs of the world. **put-am sè-bū**, ignorant of the way of managing matters. **put-sek sî-bū**, does not know how to regulate one's self by circumstances, *e.g.* making a quarrel with a very powerful adversary. **sè-bū-si**, commissioner of customs (foreigner in Chinese service). **tsúi-bū** (r.) marine matters. **m̄-bat tsúi-bū**, ignorant of navigation and seamanship.

bū, to blow water from the mouth. **bū-tsúi**, id.

bū, dim, as eyes. **bák-chiu bū**, eyes dim.

bū, mist, fog. **hûn-bū**, id. **bông-bū**, id. **ien-bū**, id. **ien-bū-hē**, thick dark rain. **ien-bū-sap**, drizzling mist, or very small drizzle; Scotch mist. **tà-bū**, misty or foggy all over. **tàu-bū**, id. **khí-bū**, misty weather; mist spreading. **chhiūⁿ-bū**, id. **ai-bū**, mist caused by the south wind. **lâm-hong-bū**, id.

bā-bū, dim and spotted; dim and indistinct, as mirror or window-glass not clear, or as water, or as sky. **thiⁿ bā-bū**, the clouds just beginning to get bright with the light of the yet unrisen sun.

búh — **sih-búh sih-sut**, talking secretly in whispers.

bui — **tsu-bui**, pleased with one's self, as at getting good profits in trade or any good fortune; pleased, as with pleasant food. **kek tsu-bui**, to put on a pleased self-satisfied look. **bâ-bui**, = tsu-bui, much pleased with one's self. **bâ-bui-chhiò**, to laugh heartily, without sound. **khùn kàu bâ-bui**, sleeping soundly and comfortably.

bui — **bák-chiu bui-bui**, eyes half closed, as in excessive laughter or weariness, or naturally so formed. **chhiò kàu bák-chiu bui-bui**, to laugh so that the eyes almost close. **sa-bui**, appearance of the eyes almost closed, as if ready to sleep, as from exhaustion or liquor. **kek-kàu sa-bui**, to put on this appearance; eyes small and almost closed, as man putting on a false appearance of being pleased, or as a bad woman trying to entice people. **soa-bui** (esp. C.), eyes almost closed, as from sleep, &c.

bui — **bâ-bui** (C.), a fruit that is used as soap (s. pleased). **boâ-bui** (P.), id.

būi (R. pūi, = col. gūi). **chhiū-būi**, a stinking insect.

bun — **chhùi-bun-bun**, mouth slightly opened in smiling. **chhiò-bun-bun**, to smile with mouth slightly opened.

bûn (C.), = A. bîn. **bûn-thâu**, cakes used in worship of the dead.

bûn (C.), = A. bîn. **bûn-chhn̂g**, a bed.

bûn (C.), = A. bîn. **bûn-á-jit**, to-morrow.

bûn (C.), = A. hm̂ (R. mûiⁿ). **bûn-lâng**, a sort of go-between for making marriages.

bûn (R. id.), literary; civil, as opposed to military; a writing, esp. an official document, or prayer; (polite). **bûn-lí**, polite. **bûn-ngá**, id.; elegantly accomplished; well composed, as essay or ode. **su-bûn**, learned and accomplished. **bûn-bėk**, do. of man or place. **bûn-hong**, character of a place, as to learning (s. hear). **bûn-hong sēng**, very literary, as a place. **bûn-hong soe**, not literary (as place). **chhiú ū-bûn-pit**, there is a line on his palm going straight to the interstice of the fingers; he will be a graduate. **bûn-chiuⁿ**, a literary essay. **moáⁿ-pak bûn-chiuⁿ**, he is very learned and literary, good at writing essays. **bûn-keh-tsoá**, ruled paper for essays.

bûn-bú, civil and military (v. bú). **bûn-koaⁿ**, a civil mandarin. **bûn-biō**, temple of Confucius. **bûn-ȯh**, = bûn siù-tsâi, a literary graduate of the Sew-tsae degree. **bûn-khoe**, a literary Kujin.

pē-bûn, a decree issued by one of the Six Supreme Boards by imperial order. **bûn-su**, an official document; a despatch (v. su). **bûn-tsu**, id. **kong-bûn**, id. **hok-bûn**, to reply to an official communication. **siông-bûn**, to send a despatch to a superior officer.

厦英大辭典

tâu-bûn, to give in an official letter, as the courier does. **bêng-bûn**, credentials. **bûn-pîn**, official proof of a mandarin's office, &c.

sè-bûn (R.), paper prayers, burned. **chiok-bûn**, written prayers recited and burned, as in worship of Confucius. **chè-bûn**, a paper informing the dead about the offerings; this also is burned.

thien-bûn, astronomy. **teng-chhai-bûn**, riddles on transparent paper, put on lamps at doors. **im-chek-bûn**, small tracts, pretended to be by Bûn-chhiong. **khoàn-sè-bûn**, do., sometimes larger, and of various reputed authors. **péh-bûn**, the text of a book, as dist. from commentary. **pún-bûn**, the original text. **pn̂g-bûn**, the text of an imperial proclamation. **ké-bûn**, a book consisting of a selection of ancient essays; elegant extracts. **liên-bûn**, ornamental written scrolls. **chhien-jī-bûn**, the thousand character classic (all different words), much used for naming a consecutive series.

bûn-chhiong, the god of literature, Wen-chang (v. chhiong). **tsu-bûn-kong**, the commentator Choo-hi, once magistrate of Changchew. **bûn-kong-sû**, his temple.

thien-bûn-tong, a medicinal plant. **bék-bûn-tong**, another sort. **soat-bûn**, soap. **sap-bûn**, do. **siap-bûn**, do.

hoán-bûn, the 66th or 67th radical written at the side. **páiⁿ-bûn** (T.), id.

bûn [R. wavy lines]. **bûn-gûn**, sycee silver. **bûn-gûn pīⁿ-tsòe bé-kháu-thih**, sycee changed to tinplate; a valuable thing changed to worthless.

ka-bûn-chhio̍h, a finely woven mat made of reeds. **lô-bûn-tsoá**, a sort of lined writing paper. **chhiâ-bûn-pè**, cotton drill; drill or twilled cloth. **chhiâ-bûn**, id. **siâ-bûn-pè**, id.

bûn [R. = col. mn̂g, a door]. **oân-bûn**, the side gates of the open space in front of main-gate of a yamun; often a street passes through them. **ngé-bûn**, do. in front of imperial palace. **hién-iâu bûn-lû**, to become a great mandarin or very illustrious graduate. **hién-iâu bûn-bî**, id.

kúi bûn-koan, the gate of Hades, Buddhist (v. koan). **thien-bûn khai**, heaven's gate open on 6.7: a mirror is put in water in a new wooden basin, and the splendours of heaven with the "thien-sin" are seen; this day "thiⁿ-kong" is specially worshipped, and it is ten times more use to burn mock paper this day than on other days.

sin-bûn, the soft place on a child's head.

hu̍t-bûn, the Buddhist sect or society (v. hu̍t). **bûn-seng** (R.), a pupil.

liông-bûn-soa, a sort of edible shark.

chhut-bûn kièn-hí, to see a good omen on leaving the door. **ngé-hok lîm-bûn**, may the five blessings descend on this house.

bûn [R. to hear]. **sin-bûn**, news. **sin-bûn-tsoá**, a newspaper. **thoân-bûn--lâi**, learned only by report. **bûn-hong** (r.), to hear a rumour (s. literary). **bûn-hong sòng-tám**, lost courage at the news. **bûn-bêng** (polite phrase), famous, as man or thing; I have heard that name. **bûn kì-bêng, bī-kièn kì-biēn**, I have heard of him but have never seen him.

bún (R. id.) **tsū-bún**, to cut one's own throat.

bún [R. corner of mouth]. **hó-kháu-bún**, good at talking in a winning pleasing manner. **ba-bún-chhiò**, to smile. **bún-bún-á-chhiò**, id.

bún (Cn.), = A. ún. **tē-bún**, a worm.

būn [R. sad]. **iu-būn**, sad. **būn-iu-iu**, id. **ut-būn**, grieved; vexed; dull; having a feeling of ennui. **ùn-būn**, do. **sim būn**, mind sad. **sim-koaⁿ būn-chiau-chiau**, very sad. **būn-tsau-tsau**, id. **kóe-būn**, to remove sorrow, as by amusement. **kóe sim-būn**, id. **siau-chhiû kái-būn**, id. **chhiùⁿ-khek, kóe sim-būn**, to sing songs to put away sorrow.

būn — **būn-būn**, dull throbbing pain. **būn-thiàⁿ**, id.

būn — **lién-būn**, the rose-apple, = hoan-ké-chí (foreign fruit): Sansk. Djamba.

būn (T. lūn; C. chhèng). **būn-pn̄g**, to boil rice dry with little water and moderate fire.

būn (C. bīn). **būn-thâng**, worms in the abdomen.

būn [R. = col. mn̄g, to ask]. **būn-pok**, to consult a diviner. **būn-song** (R.), to make a visit of condolence to a house where a corpse is lying and worship it.

būn-tsōe (R.), to condemn. **būn-tê** (R.), to condemn to be transported. **būn-liû** (R.), id. (different distance).

būn [R. reputation, by change of tone from "bûn," to hear]. **hák-būn**, learning; scholarship; literary knowledge. **ū-hák-būn**, to be a learned man. **hák-būn chhim**, id. **thàm lâng--ê hák-būn chhim-khín**, to try the depth of a man's scholarship.

būn [R. hūn, a division, a part]. **hê-lê-būn**, a paper with divisions and figures or characters on it, used in a sort of gambling. **lìn hê-lê-būn**, to throw the dice upon it.

but — **tiⁿ-but-but**, very sweet.

but — **iù-but-but**, very small, as infant; said also in general. **but-but-á**, very small, as fish, &c. **but-but-á-toā**, id.

but — **seng-taⁿ-but**, a small edible white sea-worm, sharp at both ends.

but (R. id.) **but-á-hî**, a small white fish. **sék-but-á-hî**, do. cooked ready, and so sold in streets.

bu̍t (R. id.), to strike with a thin stick, switch, or whip; to switch. **bu̍t-sut**, id.

bu̍t (R. id.) **bu̍t-io̍h**, myrrh.

bu̍t [R. to sink; to perish]. **bu̍t-koaⁿ**, to be confiscated. **bâi-bu̍t**, to bury or hide so that it may never be found (v. bâi). **bín-bu̍t** (R.), to be destroyed; to disappear, leaving no trace, as merit unacknowledged, or as a thing put out of the way.

bu̍t [R. do not!] **chhiet-chhiet bu̍t-gō**, be careful to make no mistake (phrase much used in letters).

bu̍t [R. = col. mihⁿ, a thing]. **put-sêng-bu̍t**, an ill-behaved worthless fellow. **giét-bu̍t**, you vile thing; you wretch (said to children). **koài-bu̍t**, a very malicious demon in shape of an animal (v. koài). **hè-bu̍t**, goods.

sù-bu̍t, four drugs counted of great use, viz. "kui, kiong, chiok, tē." **sù-bu̍t-thng**, an infusion of these four drugs mixed.

bān-bu̍t, all things in heaven and earth. **thien-tē bān-bu̍t**, heaven, earth, and all things. **jîn ûi bān-bu̍t chi-lêng**, man is the most excellent and intelligent of all beings.

jîn-bu̍t, distinguished men, in relation to their place of birth, &c. **toā-jîn-bu̍t**, a high mandarin or Tsin-sze, said in relation to the grave or village or family from which he comes. **chhut jîn-bu̍t**, to produce distinguished men. **bô sím-mih jîn-bu̍t,** no illustrious man belongs to the place. **hó-jîn-bu̍t,** a fine-looking man; a man above the common average. **it-piáu ê jîn-bu̍t,** a fine-looking and elegant man. **ūi jîn-bu̍t,** to draw or paint pictures of men. **jîn-chêng bu̍t-lí,** the proper way of action; the principles of what is right and proper in any affair.

iông-bu̍t, the male organs; the penis. **im-bu̍t** (R.), the female organs.

bwâ, better "boâ" (q.v.)

bwah, and **bwa̍h**; better "boah, boa̍h" (q.v.)

bwán, better "boán" (q.v.)

bwa̍t, better "boa̍t" (q.v.)

CH.

ch always has the sound in "church." By others it is used both for that sound and for **ts**; but never in this Dictionary except sometimes in the aspirated form **chh** (q.v).

cha, châ^{n} (in various tones); better tsa, tsâ^{n}, &c. (q.v.)

chah, cha̍h; better tsah, tsa̍h (q.v.)

chai, **chai^{n}, chak, cham, chan, chang, chap, chat, chau, chauh** (in various tones); better tsai, tsai^{n}, tsak, tsam, tsan, tsang, tsap, tsat, tsau, tsauh, &c. (q.v.)

che (R. id.), this; those. **che-lâng,** this man, &c. &c.

che (C.), = A. tsoe, dough.

che [R. tsai, to fast ceremonially], (C. chɛ). **che-chhàm,** Buddhist rites (generally for several days) for getting souls out of hell. **kong-tek che-chhàm,** id. **tsòe-che-chhàm,** to perform these rites shortly after death. **tsò-chɛ** (C.), id. **phoâ^{n}-chɛ** (C.), = tiàu-tsoá, to call and present offerings while these rites are going on.

che (R. tsa), (C. chɛ), dregs; sediment. **che-tái,** do. **chɛ-tsái** (C.), id. **kāu-che-tái,** full of dregs; said of a troublesome meddling man.

io̍h-che, second infusion of drugs. **tāu-che,** refuse from making bean-curd. **han-tsû-che,** refuse from making potato-starch. **iû-chɛ** (C.), = A. iû-tái, sediment of oil.

che-liû, a soft tumour, white within (v. liû).

chɛ (C.), = A. tsa. **san-chɛ,** small crab-apple.

chɛ (C.), = A. tsa, to investigate; a surname.

chê (R. siên), (C. chê, P. tê, Cn. also tsûn). **am-pê-chê,** the cicada. **am-pó-chê** (C.), id. **ka-chê** (Cn.), id.

chê— **lê-ién-chê** (T.), = A. lô-ién-sê, a band of boys with music in idolatrous processions.

chê [R. together, even, regulate]; "chê" and "tsôe" are sometimes interchanged in some phrases, esp. chê (C.) often = A. tsôe.

chê-kok, the state of Tsi in the Chow dynasty.

chê-ka (R.), to rule one's household well.

chê-pī, complete in number. **chê-chip,** to assemble in full number (v. chip). **ngé-lê chê-hoat,** affairs or persons coming all at once from various quarters. **ngé-koan put-chê,** having some ugly blemish in the features. **chê-tsûi^{n}** (C.), complete; perfect.

chê-bî, a heavy club about the height to a man's eyebrows (v. bî).

e-lé-bo̍k-chê, Urumutsi, a Chinese province in Central Asia; said also in reference to travellers' tales, "all bosh."

ché— **ché-á,** a short, dark-grayish edible sea-slug, = koe-lun.

ché— **pin-pin ché-ché,** clean and neat in dress and person; elegant and polite.

ché (R. chiá), affix to names of some women. **ché-bú,** a large-footed concubine, said of her when spoken of as a mother. **ché-á,** a secondary wife; a concubine. **ché-á-ôe,** shoes for large-footed women. **ché--á,** mother (large-footed concubine)! **á-ché,** do., said by her child; also, "elder sister!"

chè [R. to rule, to shape], to ward off evil influences. **chè-soah,** to ward off the evil influence of the demons called "soah-sin." **sai-thâu chè-soah,** lions' heads doing so. **chè-iám,** to ward off or expel demons.

at-chè, to keep down (by power) so as to prevent doing something. **chè-ap,** id. **ap-chè,** id.; to oppress, as a powerful man; to keep down or ward off danger. **ap-chè siâ-kúi,** to ward off the evil influence of demons. **ap-chè ōe-tit-kè,** able to keep off the danger or trouble. **hia̍p-chè,** to use improper pressure or strong influence to force a man to do what he does not wish.

chè-tâi, the governor-general. **chè-tō͘,** the rules (of a dynasty) as to dress, &c. (v. tō͘).

in-sî chè-gî, to accommodate one's actions to the circumstances. **bô-chiet-chè,** too free and lavish in the use of money. **sī-toā ê-chiet-chè,** rules and regulations of our superiors.

chè [R. pattern; to compound]. **chè-io̍h,** to compound or prepare medicines. **chién-chè,** do. both by cutting and by the use of fire. **chè-chhá,** to prepare by roasting, as medicines.

kó͘-chè, old-fashioned, as dress or other articles. **sî-chè,** fashionable form of dress. **khoán-chè,** pattern or form; character or behaviour. **pún-tiâu ho̍k-chè,** the form of dress prescribed by the present dynasty.

ū keng-chè, correct in style, as a composition (some assign this phrase to the next word): this word and the former are sometimes interchanged.

chè [R. to cross; to make successful; to assist]. **chín-chè,** to give alms to. **si-chè,** to give alms. **ióng-chè-ī^{n},** a sort of public poor's-house.

put-chè-sū, it will not do; will not effect the purpose. **bōe-chè,** id. **tòng-bōe-chè,** all efforts to prevent it are unsuccessful. **kóng--liáu put-chè,** utterly useless to raise the subject.

kong-jiû siong-chè, firmness and gentleness well united and balanced. **un-jiû siong-chè** (Cn.), two parties settling a quarrel by each yielding a little.

chè (R. tì; cf. piau-tì). **cheng-chè,** beautiful, as person or thing.

chɛ̀ (R. tsà). **chɛ̀-khui** (C.), to burst, as a gun.

chɛ̀ (C.), = A. tsà, false.

chɛ̀ (R. tsà). **chiú-chɛ̀** (C.), a sort of vat for making liquor (r.)

chè [R. a limit]. **it-bōng bû-chè**, vast; illimitable, as a great flood.

chè — **tə̄-chè**, just one year from birth. **mɛ̄^{n}-chè** (C.), id.

chè — **oan-ke niū^{n}-chè**, to have a feud or violent quarrel. **oan-ke niû^{n}-chè**, id.

chè — **koân-chè** (Cn.), = koân-sè. power.

chè (R. id.), (C. chɛ̀), a debt; a loan of money. **chioh-chè**, to borrow. **chioh liû-hoān-chè**, to borrow from northern exiles, the worst usurers in Amoy. **moā^{n}-teng-chè**, debts to be paid when father dies. **khiàm-chè**, to owe a debt. **khiàm-chè ê-lâng**, a debtor; the borrower. **khiàm-kha-chè**, to have a walk to no purpose. **khiàm-chè oàn-tsâi-tsú**; **put-hàu oàn-pē-bú**, the debtor hates the creditor; the unfilial son hates his parents.

chè-tsú, the lender; the creditor. **pàng-chè**, to lend on interest (v. pàng). **bô-kiá^{n}-chè**, usury so heavy that Heaven refuses posterity to the usurer. **thó-chè**, to demand payment. **pek-chè**, do. very urgently; to dun for payment.

chē-chè, to be responsible for payment of a debt. **ān-chè**, to promise to pay a debt at a fixed time. **hoân-chɛ̀** (C.), to pay a debt. **hiau-chè**, to refuse to pay a debt, or insist that it has been paid. **tsáu-chè**, to abscond in order to avoid paying a debt. **tô-chè**, id.

giáp-chè, very miserable condition because of wickedness in a former life, for which full satisfaction has not yet been made. **phái^{n}-miā^{n}-chè**, id. **lô-lók-chè**, id. **lô-lók-chè bē-moá^{n}**, id.; lit. the debt of misery not yet fully paid.

chè, better "cheh," or "chit-ē," an enclitic particle; v. cheh.

chè (R. id.), a sacrificial offering; to make a sacrificial offering to. **chè-mih^{n}**, things offered. **chè-sū**, a sacrificial offering. **chè-bûn**, a written or printed prayer, read and burned.

chè-sò, to make offerings and sweep the tombs. **chè-hièn**, to worship by offerings. **hièn-chè**, id. **tsú-chè**, to preside at a sacrifice. **hióng-chè**, to accept or receive an offering. **pâi-chè**, to make a visit to a family where a death has occurred, and worship the dead with a great quantity of offerings, much more than in the rite of "tiàu-tsoá."

chè-teng, to make offerings on those days that contain the cyclical character "teng," in the spring and autumn worship of Confucius. **chè-tang**, to make offerings to ancestors at the winter solstice. **chè-kî**, to sacrifice to the flag. **chè-tók**, do. to general's flag. **chè-bōng**, to make offerings at the tombs. **chè-kang**, to make offerings at an inlet or strait, as to call back the soul of a drowned person, or as to avert calamities when *e.g.* an army is about to cross. **chè-kə**, to make offerings to deceased persons who have no posterity; said also in scolding a man eating voraciously. **chè-thien**, to make offerings to Heaven. **kâu-chè-thien**, the monkey who sacrificed to Heaven, and became ancestor of the foreigners.

bōe-chè--tit, not pleasant to eat, as food ill cooked. **tsāi-si^{n}**, **m̄-chè nâ^{n}-âu**; **sí--liáu chiah-hàu koa^{n}-chhâ-thâu**; will not support parents while alive, but will make offerings to the coffin after death.

chē [R. sūi, to sleep], (C. tsōe, T. tsö). **ka-chē**, to nod in sleep; drowsy. **tuh-ka-chē**, id. **tok-ka-tsö** (T.), id.

chē [cf. chhē, to seek]. **gâu-phī^{n}-chē**, very knowing (v. phī^{n}).

chē [R. tsōe, guilt], (T. Cn. tsö), also in H. = A. tsōe, guilt.

chē-koà, guilt, crime as related to punishment. **sí-chē**, guilt involving punishment of death. **sí-chē**, **bô gō-chē-tāng**, the penalty of death is not so severe as that of starvation; a starving man does not fear to risk anything. **siū-chē**, to bear guilt, penalty, or responsibility for it. **sóe-chē**, to atone for guilt by burning paper, and making offerings, &c., esp. for killing cows. **tháu-chē**, do. as Tauist priests do.

chē (C.), = A. tsōe, many.

chɛ̄ (C.), = A. chià. **chɛ̄-kə**, a partridge; some say "chè."

chē — **tò-chē**, = "lun," to push a boat straight backwards. **chē-á**, id.

chē (R. tsō), (Cn. tsö), to sit; to be responsible for (C. chhē, in this sense only); to settle, as sediment or foundation; to abate, as pain; to have its back to a direction, as house.

āu-chē, the hind part of a carcass, as of a pig or goat, about one-third part of it. **bé-chē**, the upper support of a Chinese helm.

chē-the, to conceive; to have in the womb.

tāi-ke pī^{n}-chē-khiā, all about a similar position in life, *e.g.* all mandarins or graduates (v. khiā).

chē-soa^{n}--ê, the charterer or owner of a vessel, who lives on shore, as opposed to the supercargo (chhut-hái); either may be called "tsûn-tsú." **khui-hâng chē-tiàm**, to have a hong or shop, as merchant. **chē-tang hiòng-sai**, having its front to the west, as house, &c. **siāng-chē**, facing the same way, as two houses.

chē-chheng, to settle and become clear, as a fluid. **chē-tóe**, to settle down, as sediment. **khah-chē**, abated, as pain. **chē--lòh-khì**, to sink or settle down in one part, as a house on a soft foundation. **chē-khū**, a Chinese door become too low, by the gradual wearing away of the socket on which it turns like a hinge.

chē-kiō, to travel in a sedan. **chē-tsûn**, to go by boat. **chē-chhia**, to travel in a carriage or cart. **chē-lién**, to use the imperial sedan or idol's sedan.

chē-thi^{n}, to be emperor. **chē-tiâu**, to give audience, as emperor. **chē-tiēn**, id. **chē-ūi**, to sit on a throne; to take a seat, as guest or scholar. **chē-tn̂g**, to sit on the tribunal, as mandarin.

chē-siên, to sit in profound abstraction or meditation, as Buddhist priest. **chē-tsō**, to sit performing certain rites, as Tauist or Buddhist priests. **chē phə́-tə̄**, to sit performing special rites (called "phə́-tə") for getting souls out of hell.

chē-bōe-tiâu, cannot sit still; I cannot sit idle. **chhiá^{n}-chē**, please sit down; don't go away. **chē-chih**, to break by sitting upon. **chē-khi-chià^{n}**, sit straight, looking straight forward, not sidewise. **chē-khi-thêng**, sit straight up.

chē-tâu, to accept the responsibility, as for a man's conduct, or for payment (C. chhē, in this and all the following phrases). **chē-giàh**, to be responsible for payment. **chē-chî^{n}**, to be responsible for payment of money. **chē-siàu**, to accept the responsibility of payment of account. **chē-chè**, do. of a debt. **chē-tù**, to accept the responsibility for another person. **chē-toa^{n}**, to accept a bill. **m̄-chē** (C. m̄-chhē), refuse to pay, as a bill; protest a bill; also (C. m̄-chē), will not sit. **chē-tò-tn̂g**, to agree to take back a thing sold if the purchaser does not like it. **chē-tsōe**, to bear the responsibility of a fault or crime. **thòe--lâng chē-**

tsōe, do. in place of another. goá-chē--lí, I am responsible to you for it, as for the sum. goá kā-lí-chē, id. hē-lí-chē, you must be responsible for the payment. chē-î^{n}, bô-chē-pí^{n}, taking the praise of success, but not willing to bear responsibility in case of failure (lit. round, not flat).

chē (C. chɛ̄), a fort, a camp, esp. small. **chē-á**, id. **iâ^{n}-chē**, a military encampment. **soa^{n}-chē**, a hill fort. **chhát-chē**, a robber's den or fort. **an-chē**, to encamp. **an-iâ^{n} tsat-chē**, id. **jip-chē, bô-thâi-lâng**, even an enemy is not injured when he comes into our house.

chɛ^{n} (C.), in all the tones, = A. chi^{n}, when it comes from the reading form "cheng."

chɛ̄^{n} (C.), = A. chēng, chi^{n}. **chɛ̄^{n}-chɛ̄^{n}**, be quiet! (said to child). **àm-chɛ̄^{n}**, secret.

cheh (Cn. tsöh). **cheh-thoah**, to use wastefully, as money or things.

cheh (R. chek), (C. chɛh), oblique, as any tone except the piâ^{n} (ping) tone. **piâ^{n}-cheh**, the ping tone and the other tones; the two great divisions of tones; the arrangements of rhymes and sequences according to the tones. **bô-piâ^{n}-cheh**, not properly composed as regards the tones. **cheh-sia^{n}**, any tone except the ping.

cheh (=chit-ē), an enclitic particle after some verbs; originally "once," but the meaning is often very slight, *e.g.* once and again; now and then.

sih--cheh, sih--cheh, twinkling; glancing now and then. **lun--cheh, kiu--cheh**, unsettled state of mind, now afraid, now almost ready to do it.

cheh (T. Cn.), = A. chhèk. **chhiau-cheh**, appearance of great delight.

cheh (R. chek), (C. chɛh), to separate fibres (as of flax) with the hand, joining them into one continuous thread by twisting the ends together. **cheh-tōe**, to pick thus the fibres of flax, making them into one thread, done by women. **pháng-cheh**, to make thread (in general) of cotton, flax, &c. **cheh-kheng**, the basket for holding the flax thread when made.

cheh (C.), = A. tsoeh, a feast day; a term in the year. **tang-cheh**, the winter solstice. **tâng-cheh**, at the same time. **sî-cheh**, a time; a period or point of time. **cheh-khì**, = A. tsoeh-khùi, the 24 terms of the solar year.

cheh (Cn. tsöh), to dry by pressing gently with a cloth, without wiping or rubbing; also to dry by a gentle touch with the tip of finger, &c. **cheh-ta**, id. **cheh--khí-lâi**, id.

cheh — **bák-kiáh-cheh**, wooden heel taps of women's small shoes.

cheh (R. tsòe), (C. tsòe). **cheh-á**, a wart.

cheh [R. siok, =col. chek, a younger uncle, &c.] **á-cheh** (Cn.), papa! father! sometimes said, but considered not respectful.

chɛh (C.), = A. chiah. **chiáu-chɛh**, birds, in general. **chhù-thâu chɛh-á**, = chhek-chiáu-á, a house-sparrow.

chéh [R. tsoát, to cut off], (Cn. tsöh), all exterminated, as a family. **sí-chéh**, id. **sí-chéh-chéh**, id. **chiù sí-chéh-tsoā**, to imprecate death on one's self and one's whole family, if what is sworn be false. **sí-kiá^{n} chéh-sun**, may all your posterity be cut off! **chéh-chéng**, having no descendants, or all extirpated. **chéh-bô-lâng**, id. **chéh-āu-tāi**, id. **chéh-sam-tāi**, the three generations cut off. **chéh-liók-bû**, relatives utterly exterminated.

chéh (C.), = A. tsóeh, to slice vertically. **poà^{n}-chéh-bóeh**, stockings of two colours or stuffs at the foot and leg.

chɛ́h (C.), sound of walking on a wet road.

chek [R. form, traces, = col. jiah]. **pit-chek**, handwriting. **chhin-pit-chek**, one's own handwriting. **tsong-chek**, traces, as of a thief, or of things lost or stolen (v. tsong). **kó-chek**, ancient remains. **sèng-chek-mih^{n}**, things having some traditional connection with ancient sages. **ū-hêng-chek**, to have traces or clue, as to something stolen, &c. **hêng-chek khó-gî**, ground for suspicion.

hoat-chek, to rise to high station, wealth, or distinction from a low position, so as to "make one's mark."

chek (R. siok), (P. chiok, chioh), younger brother of father; any man of same surname or clan who is one degree nearer the common ancestor than we are, but younger than our father; polite title to a moderately old man, not so old as "peh." **án-chek**, do., esp. vocative; sometimes "father!" **á-chek**, id. **pau-chek**, father's younger brother. **chhin-chek**, id. **tông-chek**, a man of same clan who is one degree nearer common ancestor than we, and younger than our father, but not his brother; father's younger cousin of same surname, however distant the cousinship may be. **chiông-tông-chek**, father's younger second cousin, or more distant cousin, of same surname. **piáu-chek**, younger son of paternal grand-aunt, or of grandmother's brother, &c.

chek-peh, paternal uncles in general; and all cousins of father having the same surname. **chek-peh hia^{n}-tī**, cousins of same surname; relatives of the same surname. **chek-kong**, paternal grandfather's younger brother; any junior cousin of paternal grandfather (of same surname) however distant; also, polite address to old man. **chek-kong-tsó**, younger brother of paternal great-grandfather, or any junior cousin of his, however far removed, only of the same surname. **lāu-chek-kong**, venerable sir!

āu-chek, step-father. **chhin-ke-chek**, younger brother of man whose son or daughter is married to our daughter or son. **tiū^{n}-lâng-chek**, younger brother of wife's father. **chek-koa^{n}**, younger brother of husband's father. **sió-chek**, husband's younger brother. **sè-chek** (C.), id. **sōe-chek** (An.), id.; (T.), youngest uncle.

chek (R. chiok), (C. chek, chiok), a candle. **iû-chek**, a tallow candle. **láh-chek**, a wax candle. **chhâ-chek**, a wooden imitation candle with a lamp at the top. **chhâ-chek-kó**, id. **chek-kó** (Cn.), id. **chhâ-chek-au**, small cup on top of it, holding oil. **chhâ-chek-tih**, candlestick for imitation candle. **hoe-chek**, flowered candles for festive occasions. **thong-siau-chek**, long red candles.

tsúi-chek, a sort of reed with a head like a bulrush, used for stanching blood. **chióh-chek**, two pillars (shaped like candles) at graves of high mandarins. **tsûn chhah-chek**, the boat has sunk to the bottom, leaving only the mast visible.

chek-sim, wick of candle. **chek-bâng**, candle-stems, made of a sort of reed. **an chek-bâng**, to attach the stem to the candle. **chek-kè**, a frame used in making candles. **chek-tâi**, a candlestick, esp. large. **hóh-á chek-tâi**, a stork-shaped candlestick. **chek-tih**, a small candlestick. **chek-chhang**, socket of candlestick. **chek-lūi**, candle-droppings. **chek-sái**, candle-snuffings. **chek-hoe**, ornamental wax flowers stuck on large candles. **liâm chek-hoe,** to put them on. **chek-chiên**, snuffers.

chek — **chek--tio̍h**, to sprain.

chek, to squeeze out, as blood or matter from a sore; to strain through a cloth by squeezing.

chek (R. id.), to punish; to reprove; (to count responsible). **chek-pī**, to reprove; to punish. **chek-tok,** to instruct and educate into good conduct, often including idea of reproof or chastisement. **tok-chek,** id. **chek-hoa̍t,** to punish, as the gods. **khiàn-chek,** id.

lí--ê chek-jīm, it is your affair; the responsibility is upon you. **lí--ê chek-sêng**, id. **chek-tsōe**, to lay the blame on.

chek [R. chit, nature; to confront]. **tùi-chek,** the two parties stating their case face to face, as before a superior or arbiter.

chek (R.id.), to collect or gather together; to crowd together. **chek-oá**, to crowd close to, as to place or person. **saⁿ-chek**, crowded together. **chek-lek--teh,** id. **chek-hē**, to collect more and more. **chek-tsū**, to gather up; to amass; to collect. **chek-thiok,** id. gradually. **thiok-chek,** id. **tūn-chek,** to accumulate gradually quantities of goods. **chek-chek tsòe-chit-tui,** to gather into a heap. **tui-chek,** to gather in great abundance. **tui-soaⁿ chek-hái,** to gather in vast quantities, like mountains and oceans. **tui-kim chek-gio̍k,** to gather heaps of gold and jade. **lia̍p-chek,** to hoard up little by little; to save and store up carefully, as money. **sam-tāi lia̍p-chek; it-tàn khèng-khong,** to spend in one morning the accumulations of three generations. **sam-liân** &c., id. of three years.

chek-oàn, to harbour resentment or envy. **chek-tek,** to increase gradually in virtue or character (good or bad), (v. tek). **chek-ok bie̍t-sin,** accumulated guilt leading Heaven to punish by death. **ok-chek,** accumulated guilt calling down Heaven's judgments. **tsòe-ok-chek,** to act continually very wickedly, *e.g.* oppressing people, or causing feuds, or bringing false accusations. **ok-chek sé-tì,** the result of accumulated guilt.

chhut-jit, tio̍h-chek hō-lâi-niūⁿ, in sunny weather collect food for rainy seasons.

sit-chek, unwell (as child) from over-eating. **sit-chek siong-pî,** id. **kam-chek,** indigestion and illness (of children) from over-eating. **chek-siong,** illness from hard toil or over-exertion for many days. **sim-koaⁿ-thâu peh-peh chek-chek,** feeling of heaviness from indigestion or dyspepsia.

chek (R. id.), (C. chit). **im-chek,** works of supererogation; meritorious virtue deserving reward from Heaven. **sún im-chek,** to commit sins that draw down Heaven's anger. **bān-tāi im-chek,** very great meritorious virtue. **im-chek-bûn,** Buddhist tracts distributed to gain merit. **im-chek-hûn,** lines on the countenance showing benevolent acts, and portending prosperity. **im-chek-hûn chiūⁿ-bīn,** such lines appearing on the face.

chek [R. a rule; then]. **chek-lē**, a tariff.

chek [R. immediately; supposing]. **chek-sî,** immediately. **chek-koán-kóng** (T. chiok, &c.), speak on if you like; don't be afraid to speak. **chek-koán-lâi,** come if you like.

chek (R. sok). **chek-phò-si** (Cn.), = A. sok-pò-si, an attendant of Sêng-hông-iâ.

chek (R. id.) **chek-lêng** (R.), a sort of bird that is a model of fraternal affection.

chek [R. a sort of millet]. **hō-chek,** the author of agriculture; the god of agriculture. **siā-chek** (R.), the place for the Imperial worship of the gods of the land and grain. **siā-chek-toāⁿ**, the altar at that temple. **siā-chek-sîn,** the gods of grain and the guardian spirits of the mountains in the several regions; none but the emperor may worship them in person or by commission. **san-chhoan siā-chek** (R.), mountains, rivers, and this altar; said of the emperor's possessions. **tō-liông-siok, be̍k-sú-chek,** the six grains.

che̍k (R. id.) **che̍k-lê** (Cn.), = A. chit-lê, a medicinal plant.

che̍k (R. id.) **che̍k-tò** (Cn.), = A. chit-tò, envy.

che̍k [R. a thief, = col. chha̍t]. **lio̍k-che̍k,** idle scoundrels; rowdies or loafers. **ka-che̍k lân-hông,** it is difficult to guard against a thief in the house. **chhông-che̍k,** to destroy one's own health or life by wicked courses. **chhiông-che̍k,** id.

che̍k [R. chit, a disease]. **lī-che̍k,** dysentery. **kò-che̍k,** an old or inveterate disease that comes back after cure. **ài-khí kò-che̍k,** tendency to take the old disease again. **hòe-che̍k** (T.), = A. hòe-chit, useless (as man) because of some incurable disease or deformity.

che̍k (R. id.), (= chip), a census-roll according to the district to which our ancestors belong. **bīn-che̍k,** id. **ē-mn̂g-che̍k,** belonging to Amoy by descent, &c.

cheng (R. chiong). **chiú-cheng,** a small wine-cup. **khàm-cheng,** a large bowl-shaped cup with cover (often of fine ware), often used for infusing tea. **tê-cheng,** a small tea-cup, but not the smallest size. **chit-cheng-tê,** a cup of tea.

cheng (R. chiong), a bell; a gong with a boss in the middle (those without a boss are called "lô"); (a clock; o'clock).

tè-cheng, a small hand-bell used by priests. **tâng-cheng,** a gong with a boss in the middle; a brass or copper bell. **cheng-lui,** knob or boss of a gong. **cheng-lin,** id. **cheng-tsâi,** the hollow on the obverse of a gong. **cheng-thûi,** mallet for striking a gong or bell. **cheng-lâu,** a belfry or steeple.

khau-cheng, to strike a large bell, as in Buddhist temple. **phah-cheng,** to strike a bell. **kòng-cheng,** to strike a bell or gong.

sî-cheng, a clock. **tēng-sî-cheng** (Cn.), id. **kúi-tiám-cheng,** what o'clock? (v. tiám). **tsûi-bêng-cheng** (Cn.), a clock that strikes.

âu-cheng (C.), Adam's apple in the throat. **nâⁿ-âu-cheng** (C.), id.

cheng [R. id., = col. "tsan," a surname; also read "chêng," already; Cn. tsöng, chöng].

cheng-sun, great-grandson. **cheng-tsó,** great grandfather. **cheng-tsó-bú,** great-grandmother.

cheng-tsú, a famous disciple of Confucius.

cheng [R. = col. chiⁿ, to dispute; Cn. tsöng, chöng].

cheng-chha, to be different for the worse (v. chha). **tsáu-cheng,** id. **cheng-tsoa̍h,** difference. **bô-cheng-tsoa̍h,** no difference. **cheng-tsoa̍h iú-hiān,** differs but little.

cheng-chiàn, to fight, as in battle. **cheng-thien toa̍t-kok,** to aim at the throne, as in rebellion (v. toa̍t). **cheng-khì, put-cheng-tsâi,** the quarrel is for feeling or anger, and not for money.

cheng, = teng, to levy some sorts of taxes.

5

cheng (Cn.), = A. chiang. **cheng-chiu**, Chang-chew city.

cheng (R. id.), to go out to battle, as against rebels, banditti, or pirates. **chhut-cheng**, to go out to battle against inferiors, as rebels, &c. **gū-kà chhin-cheng**, the emperor going out to war in person. **cheng-chhát**, to go to attack pirates or bandits, as mandarins. **cheng-hoan**, to invade a foreign country; to bring foreigners to submission. **cheng-hoan** (Cn.), to eat sweet potatoes (said in joke).

cheng-lâm tsáu-pak, kiāⁿ-tang khì-sai, to travel in all directions.

cheng (R. seng). **lêng-cheng**, a banner with name and titles of the dead (used at funerals of the rich or of persons of distinction).

cheng (R. id.) **cheng-chiet**, chaste and pure, as a virgin keeping single, or as a widow who will not marry a second time. **cheng-chiet-hng**, memorial archway erected by imperial permission in memory of such a widow. **cheng-lú**, a woman who remains a virgin all her life.

cheng [R. to increase; Cn. chöng]. **cheng-tāng**, to adulterate with an inferior article so as to add to the weight; also, to make an article of *fixed* price (*e.g.* a cake) a little larger when the price of the said material falls, instead of changing the price of the article. **ke-cheng-tāng**, id. **ke-cheng hō͘--i**, give him a little more, *e.g.* when the amount is calculated in gross instead of reducing to net weight.

cheng (R. chiong), (P. chiong), to pound with a pestle or such instrument, not triturating, but only striking or pounding; to strike or pound a man with the fist; to clean rice by pounding; to make a wall of clay and cement, or a mud wall; to beat hard (as mortar on a floor).

cheng-piàng, housebreaking (v. piàng).

cheng-khū, a mortar for pounding, not for triturating (v. khū). **cheng-chhú**, a stick used for mixing mortar, &c. **cheng-chhí** (C.), a pestle for a pounding mortar.

cheng-tùi, to work the pestle of a rice-mortar with the foot. **cheng-bí**, to clean rice in such a mortar. **cheng-péh**, to beat (rice) till white.

cheng-chhòe, to beat and work soaked rice into dough. **cheng-ku**, to pound and work up rice for making the cakes called "ku;" and so with other cakes. **cheng-îⁿ**, do. so as to make balls. **cheng iòh-oân**, to work up mixed medicines for pills.

cheng-he, to beat mortar hard, as on a floor or drain. **cheng chháu-phiáⁿ**, to beat straw cut small so as to mix it in mortar. **cheng-chhiūⁿ**, to beat the mud or clay mixed with lime (in a frame) in making a wall without stones or bricks at all; to build a mud-wall, &c., by pounding it in this way.

cheng— **cheng--tiòh**, to run against, as person or thing. **thâu-khak saⁿ-cheng**, knocking against each other's heads. **sio-cheng-thâu** (C.), id.

cheng [R. minute, lively; also = col. chiⁿ, chiaⁿ, evil spirits], intelligent; acute (as hearing); animal semen.

cheng-sîn, animal spirits; animated, lively; skilful (v. sîn). **cheng-eng**, lively; intelligent (v. eng). **cheng-thong**, skilful at some special sort of work or business. **cheng-kong**, very finely made; very fine and accurate, as workmanship; very skilful, as at any work or at managing affairs. **cheng-chè**, beautiful, as man or thing; very skilfully made. **cheng-tì**, made with very minute but distinct and beautiful workmanship; small and finely made.

gán cheng, chhiú khoài, eye and hand very quick, as of thief or juggler. **khoàⁿ-cheng-cheng**, to see accurately. **khoàⁿ-m̄-cheng**, to see indistinctly. **hī-khang put-chí-cheng**, hearing very acute. **chhiⁿ-mîⁿ cheng; é-káu lêng**, blind people and dumb people are very skilful (said of people who cannot read, but who have a good memory for the money they pay out).

kut-cheng, animal semen. **cheng-tsúi**, id. **tūi-cheng**, spermatorrhea. **pó-cheng**, assisting men to act lasciviously without injury, as medicine. **hū-cheng bó-hiet**, male and female generative principles (v. hiet).

kok-cheng-chí, a medicine (v. kok).

cheng (R. id.), (C. chin). **kut-cheng-hé toā**, a severe form of seminal flux.

cheng [R. a Buddhist priest], (Cn. chöng). **ū-tsai-cheng**, to have the rule of giving lodging and food for some days to travelling priests who have certificates, as some temples do.

bit-tô-cheng, litharge.

cheng [R. seng, a domestic or sacrificial animal]. **cheng-siⁿ**, domestic animals. **ná ti-káu cheng-siⁿ**, as stupid as pigs, dogs, and cattle! (said in scolding.) **ti-káu cheng-siⁿ**, id.

chêng— **hiēn-chêng** (Cn.), at present.

chêng (C.), = A. chiông. **chêng-tông**, distant cousins (v. tông).

chêng [R. fair weather, = col. chîⁿ]. **hong chêng, ú lō͘**, four states of the weather and sky, as in paintings.

chêng (R. iông), (Cn.), = A. chhêng, the banyan-tree. **chêng-chhiū**, id. (v. chhêng); sometimes said also in Amoy. **kang-chêng**, a sort of banyan supposed to be male.

chêng (R. siông), better "chhêng." **chêng-peh**, the fir-tree.

chêng (R. id.), circumstances; affairs; affections, feelings, desires, &c.

sin-chêng, one's appearance or manner, as indicating what he means to do. **sim-chêng**, the desires and feelings. **sèng-chêng**, character and disposition. **chhit-chêng**, the seven affections and desires. **chin-chêng**, one's real thoughts and feelings. **thè-chhut chin-chêng**, to manifest one's real thoughts and feelings; to speak the truth.

chêng-goān, heartily willing (v. goān). **goân-chêng**, to forgive; having a forgiving disposition (v. goân). **liōng-chêng**, to forgive; to act with gentleness or forbearance. **léng-chêng chiū-sī**, no, I thank you (*e.g.* declining a present).

tsoát-chêng, quite alienated in feelings. **pók-chêng**, having grown cold or ungrateful towards a friend (v. pók). **bû-chêng**, unkind; ungrateful. **put-chêng**, id. **hoán-bīn bû-chêng**, suddenly ungrateful, or causelessly angry at a man who was our friend. **hoán-biēn bû-chêng**, id.

tsòe-chêng, to behave kindly; to do a favour. **tsòe-chêng hō͘-lâng**, id. **bô-sûn-chêng**, impartial (v. sûn). **liām--tiòh i-ê-chêng**, in consideration for him, as doing a favour to a third party. **hièn-chêng**, to do a favour to a third person at a friend's request. **kóng-chêng**, to ask a favour for another. **kiû-chêng**, to beg for a favour. **ti-chêng**, grateful (v. ti). **un-chêng**, kindness; grace (v. un).

jîn-chêng, favour; kindness. **bô-jîn-chêng**, want

海上絲綢之路文獻集成 科技與文化编

厦英大辭典

ing in kindness; unkind. **bat-jîn-chêng**, grateful. **goá ū-jîn-chêng tī-in-tau**, he owes me a favour. **kóng jîn-chêng**, to ask a favour for another. **thó-jîn-chêng**, id. **hē-jîn-chêng**, to claim the credit of having procured a favour to another (v. hē). **hōe-jîn-chêng** (C.), id. **hong-thó jîn-chêng**, character of people and customs of place.

chêng-biēn, influence with others (v. biēn). **ū-chêng-gī**, to be grateful, as to a friend (v. gī).

hó-kheh-chêng, polite and kind to visitors. **ū-kheh-chêng**, id. **bô-kheh-chêng**, wanting in politeness to visitors.

chêng-ì, temper; disposition. **hó-chêng-ì**, having a kind and friendly manner; kind and polite. **bô-chêng-ì**, cold, unpolite, or unfriendly. **phái**ⁿ**-chêng-ì**, id. **ū-chêng-ì**, habitually kind and friendly.

lē-chêng (Cn.), interjection finding fault for breaking a thing, or for utterly spoiling an affair by mismanagement, or by letting out a secret.

kièn-kéng siong-chêng, sympathy stirred by other's sorrows (v. kéng).

sū-chêng, a matter; an affair. **sit-chêng**, the real facts of the case. **chêng-iû**, causes; circumstances. **chêng-hêng**, state and circumstances of affair. **chêng-chiet** (r.), circumstances of affair. **chêng-kéng**, circumstances or condition, as of a place, person, or affair.

àn-chêng, the circumstances of a lawsuit. **chhàt-chêng bēng-àn**, legal cases of robbery or murder. **kang-chêng**, work, as to its amount (v. kang). **hâng-chêng**, market price of goods (v. hâng). **tsâi-chêng**, talent; ability. **kun-chêng**, affairs of an army; state and circumstances of an army. **thàm-kun-chêng**, to make secret inquiries about state of army, as a spy; fig. of other matters. **tá**ⁿ**-thàm kun-chêng**, id.

chīn-chêng, to exert one's self to the utmost for another. **chīn-chêng tì-ì**, id.

sè-chêng, the ways of the people of the world, esp. prevailing character and customs of the people of a place. **sè-chêng-tāi**, usual customs, *e.g.* as to polite intercourse among friends, or as to idolatrous celebrations. **khoà**ⁿ**-phoà sè-chêng**, to see through and despise the world's ways. **sè-chêng, khàn léng-loán**, the way of the world is to look whether a man is rich or poor, influential or not, and act accordingly. **sè-chêng léng-loán**, id.

chêng-lí, the correct principles for right action in a case (v. lí).

chêng (R. chiên), (Cn. tsûi**ⁿ**, T. tsâi**ⁿ**, C. tsân, but P. chêng), before, in time or place; former; front. **chêng-āu**, before and after, of time or place (v. āu).

chhùi-chêng-ōe, conventional polite phrases used when people meet.

tsoeh-chêng, before the term or festival. **sa**ⁿ**-nî**ⁿ**-chêng**, three years ago. **tsá-chêng**, formerly; long ago. **chêng-sî**, formerly. **chêng-ē**, on a former occasion. **chêng-pái**, id. **chêng-jit**, a previous day. **chêng-nî**ⁿ, a former year; the former year. **chêng-sì**, in a former life. **chêng-tāi**, former generations. **chêng-lâng-kiá**ⁿ, wife's son by former husband; husband's son by former wife.

bák-chêng, before the eyes; at present. **gién-chêng** (C.), at present.

bīn-chêng, in front of. **pâi bīn-chêng-khiā**, to put on the appearance of great diligence or obedience in master's presence, or before some one whom we wish to please, *e.g.* by talking obsequiously, or working hard at that time. **hiàh-chêng**, the forehead. **heng-chêng**, the breast; the bosom.

chêng-thâu, the front load on a pole; also (C.), formerly. **chêng-thâu bóe; āu-thâu im**, first to buy a great quantity of goods, and then lose heavily by a fall of price. **chêng-bīn**, front side; the front. **chêng-lòh**, front part of a house. **chêng-iâ**ⁿ, vanguard. **chêng-kun**, do. in march or action.

chìn-chêng, to advance; to go forward; also (C.), formerly. **chì**ⁿ**-chêng**, to strive hard to be first, as in a race. **tsòe-chêng**, please walk first. **kiâ**ⁿ **tsòe-chêng**, to walk first. **tsòe-chêng seng-lâi**, to arrive first. **tsòe-thâu-chêng**, to walk first. **kūn-chêng**, to approach. **hiòng-chêng**, facing forwards.

chéng [R. a well, = col. chí**ⁿ**]. **chéng-tí-oa** (frog at bottom of well), an inexperienced fellow.

chéng (R. id), to put in order; to adorn; to fit out or set up, as boat or school; to invest, as capital.

tsôe-chéng, neatly arranged, as furniture or dress, &c.; in good regular order, as teeth. **chê-chéng**, id. **chéng-tsôe**, to put in order. **chéng-chê**, id. **tūi-ngé chéng-tsôe**, the ranks in good order.

siu-chéng, to repair; to set in order; to beautify. **tá**ⁿ**-chéng**, to adorn one's self. **chéng-tùn**, to put in good order. **chéng-thek**, do. as one's person or house. **chéng-thit** (C.), id. **chéng-lí**, to arrange neatly.

chéng-kó, to beat drums just before a play. **chéng-hì**, to engage a company of actors to play. **sa**ⁿ**-kap-chéng**, to do so together, &c. **chéng-óh**, to set up a school, as the patron (tong-ka) does. **chéng tsu-pâng**, id. **chéng-tsûn**, to fit out a vessel with all its fittings, goods, &c., as owner or charterer does. **chéng chhàt-tsûn**, to fit out a pirate vessel. **chéng-pún**, to invest capital. **bô-chí**ⁿ **thang-chéng**, have no capital to invest. **goá kā-lí chéng-chí**ⁿ, I advance the money, paying expenses for you, as a favour, not expecting interest.

chéng (R. chióng), (P. chióng), to swell; a swelling. **chéng-chéng**, swollen; dropsical. **hàm-chéng**, very much swollen; dropsical. **kha chéng**, leg swollen. **ni**ⁿ **chéng**, the breast (of any one) swollen by disease. **chéng-ni**ⁿ, breasts of a girl grown to full size, when about come of age.

n̂g-chéng, jaundice.

chéng (C.), = A. tsńg. **chéng-kah**, finger nails.

chéng [R. thién, to destroy], (= chín). **pē-chéng thien-bût**, to misuse things by a wasteful or lavish use.

chéng [R. chióng, embers]. **hé-chéng**, live embers or coals for kindling a fire; the spark of a conflagration.

chéng (R. chióng), (C. chióng, esp. P.), seed, of any sort; posterity.

han-tsû-chéng, potato slips. **chhek-chéng**, seed rice. **chéng-chí**, seed of plants. **iā-chéng**, to sow seed, esp. broadcast (v. iā). **chìm-chéng**, to soak the seed before sowing.

tsu-chéng, scab of small-pox, for inoculation.

phah-chéng (vulg.), to copulate, as animals. **tsáp-chéng**, a bastard. **tsáp-chéng-kiá**ⁿ, id.

chéng-lūi, descendants. **i-ê chéng-tsák**, his own real posterity (v. tsák). **thoân-chéng**, to leave posterity. **chéh-chéng**, posterity all exterminated.

bông-chéng, one of the 24 terms of the solar year, a fortnight before midsummer; June 6th or 7th. **bông-chéng-hō**, rain on that day, supposed to cause drought. **bông-chéng, hō: lák-géh, hé-sio-po**, if it rain on that day, the grass will all be burned up in the sixth moon. **bông-chéng-iàh, thó-bô-chiàh,** insects that come out about this term are too late to get food.

chèng (R. chiòng), (C. chiòng), to sow, esp. by carefully dropping the seeds; to set, as potatoes or as shell-fish; (to inoculate or vaccinate).

chèng-tsoh, to cultivate the ground; to farm. **tsai-chèng,** to sow and plant out; to plant in general. **chèng-tāu,** to sow leguminous plants. **chèng-bėh-tāu,** to sow wheat, barley, pease, and beans.

chèng-tsu, to inoculate; to vaccinate. **chèng thê-kúi,** to set beds of the shell-fish called thê-kúi.

chèng (R. id.) **kàn-chèng,** to expostulate with a superior, and exhort him to reform, as son to father, or minister to sovereign.

chèng [R. testimony], (C. chìn). **kan-chèng,** testimony; evidence given by a witness. **tsòe-kan-chèng,** to give testimony. **tsòe-chèng,** id. **tsòe-chèng-kì^{n},** to give evidence of what we have seen. **chèng-kù,** evidence of what we have seen. **tùi-chèng,** to examine and compare the evidence on both sides (s. disease). **sa^{n}-tùi-chèng,** id.

chèng (R. id., = col. chià^{n}), correct; right. **chèng-tsong,** correct in conduct. **chèng-keng,** correct and right, as actions, person, or principles; honest, virtuous, moral. **m̄-chèng-keng-hong,** an unsteady troublesome wind. **chèng-tit,** upright; honest; straightforward; just. **chèng-khì,** virtuous; just. **put-chèng,** depraved. **sù-chèng,** correct, as in conduct. **toan-hong sù-chèng,** id. **chèng-thò,** safe to have to do with, as man or affair.

chèng-lí, correct doctrine or principles. **chèng-kàu,** do.; a moral and correct sect or school. **chèng-hoat,** to execute a criminal; right way or plan (v. hoat).

chèng-sîn, any idol regularly canonized or very widely worshipped; esp. thê-tī-kong (v. sîn), (s. all).

siâ-chèng, depraved and correct; false and true (as doctrine); bad and good in character or conduct. **siâ-chèng put-lióng-lip,** the good and the bad cannot live long together. **khì-siâ kui-chèng,** to reform one's self. **siâ put-tàu-chèng,** the evil or false cannot resist or overcome the true or good.

chèng (R. id.), a disease. **pī^{n}-chèng,** id. **chèng-thâu,** do. **toā-chèng-thâu,** a severe and dangerous chronic disease. **phái^{n}-chèng-thâu,** a very dangerous disease, almost certainly and speedily mortal. **phái^{n}-chèng,** id. **phái^{n}-kiá^{n}-chèng,** venereal disease. **kín-chèng,** a sudden dangerous disease, as cholera, &c. **kín-kip-chèng,** id. **sî-khì-chèng,** an epidemic. **phiah-chèng,** a disease to which a man is constitutionally liable. **sí-chèng,** a mortal disease. **lōe-chèng,** a deep internal disease. **jiét-chèng,** fever. **im-chèng,** a deep-seated pain causing a swelling that often lasts several months and does not come to a head, gen. inside of thigh. **si^{n} im-chèng,** to have such a swelling.

tùi-chèng, suited to the disease, as medicine (s. testimony). **khoà^{n}-chèng,** to examine the disease; to visit a patient. **tsàp-chèng tsôe-khí,** taking many diseases at once.

chèng (R. chiòng), (C. chiòng), all, esp. said of persons. **chèng-lâng,** all the people; everybody; very many people. **chèng-peh-sì^{n},** all the people.

chèng-sîn, all the spirits (s. correct). **chèng-sîn-bêng,** id. **chèng-kong-má,** a shrine containing numerous tablets of persons who have no posterity.

chèng-hāng, all sorts or kinds. **chèng-hāng-mih^{n},** all sorts of things.

kong-chèng, public, common; possessed or shared in common. **kong-chèng-lō,** a public road. **kéng-chèng,** common to a ward or division of a town, as idols or idolatrous ceremonies. **toā-ke kháu-chèng,** family very large.

ōe-kì^{n}-chèng--tit, fit for the view of all men, as person or matter all correct, not afraid of publicity. **ōe-kièn-chèng--tit,** id. **bōe-kì^{n}-chèng--tit,** not fit to be looked into, as a matter that is shameful or that has a serious flaw. **bōe-kièn-tit-chèng,** id. **bōe-kì^{n}-tit-chèng,** id. **bōe-kham--tit kì^{n}-chèng,** id. **liên-hôe sì-chèng,** utterly disgraced for ever in the sight of all men, as for some vile action (v. hôe).

chèng [R. government]. **chèng-sū,** government; government matters. **pān chèng-sū,** to manage government matters. **put-tsāi kî-ūi, put-bê kî-chèng,** not being in office, I do not meddle with government matters; that is not my affair.

pò-chèng-si, the provincial treasurer (v. pò). **tsûn-chèng,** superintendent of arsenal and naval docks, as at Fuh-chau. **tsûn-chèng-thia^{n},** id.

chèng (R. chièn), (T. tsài^{n}; Cn. tsūi^{n}; C. tsàn; but P. chèng). **ka-chèng,** a sort of straw mat. **chháu-chèng,** a very coarse sort of mat put under bedding to make it warm and soft. **tsang-chèng,** a mat made of palm fibre. **koa^{n}-chèng,** a coarse under-mat made of the reed called "koa^{n}," esp. put under the marriage-bed.

chēng [R. cheng, to add]. **chēng-tsúi,** to mix water, as with wine or milk, for adulteration. **chēng-tāng,** to adulterate (s. cleanse). **ke-chēng-tāng,** to charge a little more than the real weight (?).

chēng (R. id.), quiet; silent; still. **chēng-chēng,** very quiet; be quiet! **lí chēng-chē,** sit still now! **an-chēng,** enjoying peace and quiet. **pêng-chēng,** at peace and all tranquil, as a region or as the sea. **hong-pêng lōng-chēng,** winds and waves quiet. **pêng-hong chēng-lōng,** id. **hong-thiâm lōng-chēng,** id. **thiâm-chēng,** quiet in taste and habits; not fond of gaiety or much talking or company. **tiām-chēng,** id. **chēng-sim,** quiet steady mind; not fond of meddling.

tōng-chēng, to raise a subject; to start a question.

sok-chēng, quiet; still, as a place. **léng-chēng,** lonely; desolate; too quiet and dull, as a neighbourhood. **chēng-tsauh,** still, as a place. **chip-chēng,** (r.), id. **chēng kàu-tn̂g-sîn-pe tn̂g-báng-háu,** so quiet that not even a fly or mosquito is heard.

chēng [R. pure; to cleanse]; net, as weight; to cleanse or purify ceremonially by passing over burning incense (called "chēng-hiu^{n}"), &c., as hands after touching something defiling; or as clothes after a funeral, or before marriage or worship.

chheng-chēng, clean; pure. **put-tek kan-chēng,** can never get out of the trouble. **chēng-tsúi-koah,** white grass-cloth. **chēng-pháng,** finest white bleached grass-cloth.

chēng, joā-tsōe, how much net weight? **chēng-sit,** net, as calculated. **chēng-tāng,** net weight, as calculated; rather more is given (s. add).

sóe-chēng, to cleanse ceremonially, as after a burial, &c. **chēng-hiu^{n},** purifying incense used for this purpose. **chēng-tsûn,** to perform rites for the good-luck of a boat or junk. **chēng-iû,** to purify (as Tauist priests do) by oil and wood in a rice-boiler; also, lighting a lamp and cutting it off with a knife. **chēng-iû táh-hé,** to do this and walk over a fire.

chi [R. ki, muscular flesh]. **seng-chi-sán**, a powder for sprinkling on sores, to assist in the formation of healthy flesh.

chi [only R.], it, him, them, &c.; also "of," only used in book phrases become colloquial or half so.

chi (R. id.) **lêng-chi-chháu**, a fabulous plant of good omen. **liên-chi-chhó**, id. **tsu-chi**, gunpowder tea.

chi (R. name of several plants, *e.g.* = col. kiⁿ, *Gardenia*). **chi-tsú**, a cooling medicinal seed. **pien-chi**, the Bombax or cotton-tree, sometimes erroneously called a magnolia. **pien-chi-hoe**, id. **pan-chi-hoa** (C.), id.

chi [R. to separate; a clan; the 65th radical], some of the phrases are sometimes interchanged with the next word.

tē-chi, the twelve characters for the double hours of the day and night. **thien-kan tē-chi**, that cycle of twelve along with the cycle of ten, used in combination to make the cycle of sixty years.

chi-phài (R.), a division of a clan; a tribe.

chi-chhî, to help a little so as to keep matters from going wrong. **chi-lí**, to bear the responsibility, as for a debt or for the management of an affair (v. lí). **chi-lî**, troublesome to set right, as an affair; troublesome to deal with, as a man constantly insisting on trifles, or raising new objections. **chi-chi lî-lî**, id.

chi [R. = col. ki, a branch]. **to-chi-chiet**, troublesome to deal with, as a man or matter (v. chiet).

nāiⁿ-chi, the lichi or laichi fruit. **lē-chi** (C.), id. **nūiⁿ-chi** (Cn.), id.

chi (R. id.) **ien-chi**, rouge, used for painting the lips. **ien-chi-hoe**, a flower of bright-red colour. **kā ien-chi**, to moisten the rouge with the lips before painting with it. **tiám-ien-chi**, to paint with rouge.

chi (vulg.), the female organ; the vulva. **chi-bai**, id.

chi [R. a limb]. **sù-chi**, the four limbs: arms and legs. **sù-chi ngé-koan**, the members of the body. **sù-chi pek-hâi**, id.

chî (R. tsû), small round soft cakes, esp. of glutinous rice. **sóe-á-chî**, do. made with millet. **chhòe-hún-chî**, do. with rice-flour. **tāu-chî**, do. with pulse inside. **tsút-bí-chî**, such cakes of glutinous rice. **moâⁿ-chî**, do. of hemp-seed, sugar, and rice. **moâⁿ-chî-kê**, paste made of these cakes softened, used for shoes, &c.

khī-chî (Cn.), dried persimmons.

nńg-chî-chî, soft and tenacious, as a cake; weak, as a delicate child (v. nńg).

chî (C.), = A. tsû, potatoes, &c.

chî — **bé-chî**, a roundish black sweet root. **bóe-chî** (C.), id. **bé-chî-hún**, a cooling flour like starch made from it. **soaⁿ-bé-chî**, a trailing shrub with lance-shaped leaves: the root is used for poisoning dogs and birds; the juice is used for corroding brass.

chî (C.), = A. tsû. **chiuⁿ-chî**, sort of toad.

chî (R. tsû), (T. jî). **lô-chî**, the cormorant.

chí (R. id.), an imperial decree. **chí-ì**, id. **sèng-chí**, id. **sèng-chí-pâi**, a tablet worshipped by mandarins. **sèng-chí-chhùi**, said of a man who will not change the price he has named. **gék-chí**, treason. **gék-chí khi-kun**, id. **hok-chí**, to report to the emperor having fulfilled his commands. **kiáu-chí**, id.

hoat-chí, the (Tauist) commands of Lau-tsze. **hút-chí**, the commands of Buddha. **giók-chí**, commands of Yuh-hwang Shang-ti.

chí (R. id.) **chí-khak**, a medicine.

chí (R. id.) **péh-chí**, a medicinal root good for headache (Iris or orris root?).

chí — **chí-kiuⁿ**, = chíⁿ-kiuⁿ, young soft ginger-shoots with a purplish white tinge.

chí [R. tsú, purple]. **chí-sek**, dark purple colour. **chí-hoe**, nankeen cloth. **chí-hoe-pò**, id.

chí-keng, a tree with red flowers (v. keng). **chí-jû**, a yellow wood for furniture. **chí-so**, a cooling medicine. **chí-chhài**, a broad sea-weed (tangle?) used for food. **chí-kim-tiāⁿ**, a medicine made up in form of a gold ingot (v. tiāⁿ).

chí-bî tāi-tè, the god of a star (v. bî). **chí-iông**, the temple of Choo-he, the commentator (and school), in E-mn̂g-káng.

chí [R. tsú, a son, seed], a seed; fruit; a small ball or bullet; bars or rails in windows or stairs, &c.; affix in forming several names of trades and other nouns.

jit-chí, a day. **kiàn-chí-bah**, meat of the ham. **sió-liáp-chí**, a very little man. **kài-chí**, a square bit of wood used by Buddhist priests for striking on the table between the prayers (s. finger; s. land-mark). **hong-chí**, a small square bit of wood with which mandarins strike the table of the tribunal when scolding the people before them. **tìg-hong-chí**, to strike the table with it.

kah-chí, the cyclical characters (v. kah). **bé-chí**, the abbreviated numeral characters, used like the Arabic numerals; sort of counters used in gambling; very low sort of servants, especially in a bad house. **chhiàⁿ bé-chí** (in Tiô-thoâ), to hire labourers.

tô-chí, a man who prepares feasts to order; a keeper of a cook-shop. **kìm-chí**, a door-keeper in a prison (s. prevent). **tâng-chí**, an idolatrous juggler, or sorcerer, or fakeer, who cuts himself, &c.

kî-chí, chess-men. **o-péh-chí**, chess-men having 32 of each colour. **chhùn-chí**, the "cat" or small stick struck in the game of tipcat (v. chhùn).

chéng-chí, seed. **ké-chí**, fruit. **kóe-chí** (C.), id. **koe-chí**, melon seeds.

koe sòe, chí sek, the melon is small, but has good seeds; said of a man who looks small, but is older or has more in him than appears. **chhiū-chí**, wild nuts and fruits of trees. **chhêng-chí**, the fruit of the banyan. **chhiⁿ-chí**, the nut of the indigo plant. **chí-á-chhiū** (P.), the wax-tree.

hî-chí, fish roe. **hîm-chí**, bits of stone that stand for bear's cubs in a game (v. hîm).

io-chí, the kidneys. **bák-chiu-chí**, the ball of the eye. **siēn-chí**, the testes. **sǹg-poâⁿ-chí**, the balls of an abacus. **chhèng-chí**, a bullet or ball of a gun or cannon. **iân-chí**, a lead bullet. **toāⁿ-chí**, balls or pellets shot from toy bows. **tô-chí**, weights for scales, &c.

ká-chí, a rod used in twisting a rope tight (v. ká). **soán-chí**, the instrument for torturing women's fingers. **lâu-thui-chí**, the steps of a ladder. **siàⁿ-tó-chí**, battlements. **kè-á-chí**, upright bars of a frame, as in shop's counter. **bák-sa-chí**, rails of a high wooden railing. **than-kha-chí**, rails of a railing cut almost in two by long longitudinal slits. **thang-á-chí**, upright bars in a window. **soe-chí-thang**, window with upright built bars. **hoe-thang-chí**, ornamental trellis tiles. **gān-chí-tsng**, small fire-bricks for such work. **hang-lô-chí**, perforated face of a hand-furnace.

chí (C.), = A. tsú, to cook.

chí (C.), = A. tsú, a lord; only in some phrases, esp. those originally book phrases transferred to the colloquial, *e.g.* bók-chí, thien-chí-kàu, &c.

chí (Cn.), affix to an old man's name, = chek, in this sense only.

chí [R. only], a bundle of idolatrous paper. **chit-chí**, a small bundle of idolatrous paper fastened together; gen. about 20 sheets, counted as 50; but in the case of "khè-chí^{n}," each "chí" is counted as ten thousand!

chí-ū, there is only; there are only.

chí (R. id.) **chí-hî-á**, a small fish like trout. **chí-á-hî**, id. **chí-bú** (C.), id. **chí-hū** (Cn.), id.

chí (R. id.) **kài-chí**, a land-mark; a boundary stone (s. finger, s. son). **tsō-chí**, place of residence, as set down in a deed, or in an address given for a letter. **khui tsō-chí**, to put down one's address, as above.

chí [R. a finger], to point at; to point out; (a ring). **chí-bėk**, to write characters or draw sketches with one's nail dipped in ink (v. bėk).

chhiú-chí, a finger-ring. **chhiú-chí-sok**, rings worn as guards on each side of the principal ring. **pan-chí**, a thumb-ring, as for archery. **kài-chí** (R.), a finger-ring (s. landmark, s. son).

chhâ-chí, a very small bundle of firewood, costing about two cash.

tùi-chí, the two parties making statements face to face. **tng-bīn chí**, id.

chí-tiám, to instruct; to give information about some matter. **chí-sī**, to point out; to teach. **chí-bêng** (R.), to explain clearly, as a book or doctrine.

chí [R. embroidery]. **chiam-chí**, needlework; embroidery. **hó-chiam-chí**, good embroidery; a good sempstress; good needlework.

chí (R. che), this; these. **chí-kúi-ê**, these several (persons, &c.) **chí-tso**, this time or occasion. **tī-chí-tau** (T. Cn.), here. **chí-pē** (T.), now.

chí — **pâi-chí**, gaudy, as house or dress; proud self-satisfied bearing; wearing fine dress, and putting on proud airs, as being successful or powerful.

chí [R. to prevent, to stop], to allay; to stanch; (to terminate; to hinder).

put-chí, very. **put-chí-hó**, very good. **ū-tí-chí**, to have a limit, bound, or termination, as an affair of which we can say, this is the last of it. **bô-tí-chí**, without any limit, as inordinate covetousness or wickedness; or as a hopeless calamity, or endless borrowing of money, or any affair that never comes to an end. **chiėt-chí**, to terminate, as a payment at stated times. **ûi-chí**, to be the limit; only so far as this. **kàu-chia ûi-chí**, it comes so far, and no farther (as a piece of ground, &c.)

hêng-chí, behaviour (v. hêng). **hêng-tōng kú-chí**, id.

chí-pē, to stop in walking, as at a door or notice to stop (s. this). **tsé-chí**, to prevent; to hinder. **noâ^{n}-chí**, id. **kìm-chí**, (r.) to forbid, (s. son). **at-chí**, to repress; to keep from action; to restrain, as others, or as one's own feelings and desires. **chí-tién hāu-siók**, to close a pawn-shop, and wait a fixed time to let the goods be redeemed.

chí-ki, to alleviate hunger; to appease its cravings slightly. **chí-khoah**, to quench thirst. **chí-khat**, id. **chí-chhùi-ta**, id. **chí-thià^{n}**, to allay pain. **chí-sià**, to cure diarrhœa. **chí-áu**, to cure the tendency to vomit. **chí-huih**, to stanch blood. **huih chí**, the blood is stanched.

chí [R. the toes]. **tàng-chí**, a sort of frost-bite or chilblain; gen. on foot or ear. **si^{n} tàng-chí**, to have this frost-bite. **kha si^{n} tàng-chí**, foot frost-bitten, esp. on heel.

chí [R. tsúi, water]. **n̂g-chí-kiô**, a plant (v. kiô).

chí [R. elder sister], also (Cn.), = A. ché, suffix to names of women.

toā-chí, elder sister. **tông-toā-chí**, elder female cousin of the same surname. **chí-bē**, sisters, elder and younger; a sister, in general. **chí-māi^{n}** (P.), id. **chí-mōɛ^{n}** (C.), id. **piáu-chí-bē**, female cousins by their mother's side, she being sister of our father or mother. **î-piáu chí-bē**, daughter of mother's sister. **kɵ-piáu chí-bē**, daughter of father's sister.

chí-hu, elder sister's husband. **chí-pɵ** (Cn.), id. **chí-tiū^{n}** (Cn.), id. **sàng-kè-chí** (T.), an old woman who accompanies a bride to teach her what to do.

chì [R. purpose, will]. **ū-chì**, decided in purpose, to do what is right or noble, and avoid what is mean or shameful. **bô-chì**, idle and lazy; without proper spirit. **chì-khì**, purpose; will; intention. **ū-chì-khì**, having self-respect, or sense of honour, or proper spirit, so as not to do what is mean or dishonourable. **sim-chì**, purpose; intention; will. **kien-sim lip-chì**, with fixed determination. **bô-sim-chì**, undecided in purpose. **tsoan-sim tì-chì**, to apply one's mind earnestly.

lip-chì, with determination; stedfastly. **hùn-chì**, with energy and earnestness (v. hùn). **lok-chì**, faint-hearted; dispirited. **lóe-chì**, id. **sûi-thâu sòng-chì** (R.), dispirited and hanging one's head.

chì-liōng toā, aiming high, as a student who aims at high rank.

oán-chì, a medicinal plant (*Polygala tenuifolia?*). **oán-chì-jiók**, do. after its long fibres have been pulled out.

chì — **tāi-chì**, business; any affair or matter esp. troublesome. **bô-tāi-chì**, nothing wrong. **pān tāi-chì**, to manage an affair or dispute so as to arrange it, or try to do so.

chì [R. to record], historical and statistical works (in this sense interchanged with "purpose"). **chiang-chiu-chì**, statistical account of Chang-chew. **ē-mn̂g-chì**, statistical account of Amoy.

bōng-chì-bêng, an engraved stone put inside a grave.

chì [R. to reach to, to arrive], extremely —; sign of superlative; a beat of the pulse.

chiu-chì, all the arrangements quite correct (v. chiu). **bū-sé put-chì**, addicted to all sorts of wickedness. **hêng-hêng sù-chì**, perversely wicked.

chì-u, with regard to (v. u). **kip-chì kàu-hit-sî**, when that (past) time came. **sīm-chì kàu àn-ni^{n}**, even to that extent (R.), (v. sīm).

chì-tsun, most honourable. **chì-toā**, greatest. **kàu-chì-kėk**, to the very utmost.

hē-chì, midsummer day, June 20th or 21st. **tang-chì**, the shortest day.

kúi-chì-mėh^{n}, how many beats (of the pulse)? **hɵ-khip kúi-chì**, how many beats of the pulse for one expiration and inspiration? four or five counted healthy.

chì — **ì-chì**, dirty; filthy.

chì (R. id.) **chì-kiàn**, a present given to a teacher on engaging him, additional to salary; a fee to a doctor when first called, repeated after two or three visits. **chì-kièn-lé**, id.

chì (C.), = A. chè. **chì-tâi**, governor-general.

chì (C.), = A. tsù. **ka-chì**, a straw bag.

chī (C.), = A. tsū (to assemble).

chī, to lick. **tham-chiáh ê-lâng, liên-oáⁿ iáh-chī**, a greedy man licks even the bowl after eating. **káu chī chien-poâⁿ; phīⁿ ū, chiáh-bô**, the dog licks the frying-pan, getting the flavour but no food.

chī [R. sī, to be]. **chī-tsūi**, who? **chī-tsūi-á**, id.

chī (R. id.), (Cn. sü), a cyclical character. **chī-sî**, the double hour, 9–11 A.M. **kí-chī**, a year of the cycle, 1869 was one of them; these two characters are very similar.

chī — **chī-bú-chī-tsū**, to talk indistinctly; to whisper.

chiⁿ [R. cheng, rock-crystal]. **tê-chiⁿ**, tea-coloured rock-crystal, used for dark spectacles. **ə-chiⁿ**, a darker crystal. **tsúi-chiⁿ**, clear rock-crystal. **tsúi-chiⁿ-ku**, turtle-shaped cakes, made of rice, with white stuffing made of legumes. **tsúi-chiⁿ-āⁿ**, this stuffing. **tsúi-chiⁿ-piáⁿ**, another sort of cake, made from wheat.

chiⁿ [R. cheng, = col. tiⁿ, the heel]. **ēng-kha-chiⁿ tò-that**, to give a kick backward with the heel. **ēng kha-āu-chiⁿ tò-that**, id.

chiⁿ, a wedge; to wedge; to press out oil by use of wedges. **chiⁿ-khui**, to open by wedges. **chiⁿ-iû**, to press out oil from seeds by a machine worked by wedges.

chiⁿ, = chîⁿ, to pull the ears. **chiⁿ hī-á**, id.

chiⁿ (R. cheng), (C. cheⁿ), to quarrel; to dispute; to strive. **chiⁿ-chhân**, to quarrel or dispute about land. **chiⁿ ke-hé**, to quarrel about dividing family property. **hə̄--i chiⁿ--khì**, to have the place we expected taken from us by him. **saⁿ-chiⁿ**, to quarrel, dispute, or strive. **sio-cheⁿ** (C.), id. **tàu-saⁿ-chiⁿ**, to strive for victory or superiority. **saⁿ-chiⁿ tāi-seng**, to strive who shall be first. **saⁿ-chiⁿ-thàn**, great competition in trade, so that the profits are very small. **saⁿ-chiⁿ pun-toā-hūn**, to take the largest share.

chiⁿ — **mîⁿ-chiⁿ**, very persevering, urgent, and unremitting or importunate, esp. in asking. **mîⁿ-chiⁿ-thák**, very diligent at study. **mîⁿ-chiⁿ siūⁿ-chîⁿ**, determined on gain. **tióh khah-mîⁿ-chiⁿ**, should be more urgent and unremitting.

chiⁿ (R. chien), felt and such stuffs. **chiⁿ-bō**, a felt cap. **chiⁿ-tiâu**, a rug or mat like a carpet. **chhə-chiⁿ**, coarse woollen stuff like serge. **iù-chiⁿ**, a fine woollen stuff from the north. **chiâⁿ-chiⁿ**, to get into a clotted mass, as uncombed hair, &c. **kiet-chiâⁿ-chiⁿ**, id.

chiⁿ [R. cheng, minute, fine], (C. chiaⁿ), evil spirits that take any form; too sharp and cunning, as a man. **iau-chiⁿ**, malicious demons in Protean shapes. **tióh-chiⁿ**, bewitched. **tsoâ-chiⁿ**, a demon in form of snake. **chiáu-chiⁿ**, a demon in shape of a bird; said of a man who is too sharp. **chiâⁿ-chiⁿ**, to become such a demon; to be quite too sharp in dealings. **chiâⁿ-lâng-chiⁿ**, to be quite too sharp; fond of intrigue and deceit, most usually of a young fellow about twenty. **put-chí-chiⁿ**, id. **chiⁿ-kúi**, do. as a young person.

chîⁿ (R. chêng), (C. chêⁿ), fair weather; fine weather. **thiⁿ chîⁿ**, id. **hə̄ chîⁿ**, the rain has cleared off. **poàⁿ-im poàⁿ-chîⁿ**, dark clouds and sunshine mixed, with perhaps sometimes a little rain.

chîⁿ — **nîⁿ-chîⁿ**, the eaves of a house. **nîⁿ-chîⁿ-tsúi**, water from the eaves. **nîⁿ-chîⁿ-kéng**, bamboo gutter at the eaves. **nîⁿ-chîⁿ-khiò**, id. **nîⁿ-chîⁿ-kháu**, the space of ground covered by the eaves, and a little more. **chîⁿ-kháu**, id. **chîⁿ-kháu-kong**, the guardian spirit or god of the eaves. **chîⁿ-kháu hu-jîn**, the goddess of the eaves, worshipped at many terms.

chhut-chîⁿ, to have wide projecting eaves (a. cash).

chîⁿ — **chiū̂ⁿ-chîⁿ**, troublesome behaviour of children (esp. towards parents) pressing on people, wishing to be fondled or petted. **kek-chiū̂ⁿ-chîⁿ**, pretending to be ill, &c., so as to get fondled. **ké-chiū̂ⁿ-chîⁿ**, id.

chîⁿ, = chiⁿ, to pull the ears.

chîⁿ (R. chiên), a round coin; a copper or brass cash; a mace weight, = ten "hun;" one-tenth of a tael; money in general; a surname. **chiâⁿ-chîⁿ**, about one mace; a good deal of money. **thàn--khì chiâⁿ-chîⁿ**, to earn a good deal of money.

phû-chîⁿ, the round flat socket for a lamp-wick, either floating or fixed. **ham-khak-chîⁿ**, cockle-shells used by children in games of chance. **gûn-kǹg-chîⁿ**, silver medals worn as charms.

lién-chîⁿ, a solid wheel without spokes, esp. for grinding in a long trough-shaped mortar. **lién-chîⁿ**, to twirl a cash; to get money by intimidation or such means.

chîⁿ-chhú, a sort of rat (v. chhú). **chîⁿ-kə́**, a tambourine (v. kə́).

chit-chîⁿ, one mace weight. **chit-chîⁿ-tāng**, do. **chit-chîⁿ-gûn**, one mace of silver; one-tenth of a tael of silver. **saⁿ-chîⁿ-jī**, three mace and two candareens. **chîⁿ-hū** (Cn.), a receipt for a mace or more of land-tax.

gûn-chîⁿ, a dollar. **tēng-chîⁿ**, bad dollars (full of brass or copper). **tiong-chîⁿ**, half a dollar. **tiōng-chîⁿ**, brokerage commission for selling goods (v. tiōng).

tâng-chîⁿ, best copper or brass cash. **âng-chîⁿ**, good copper cash, but not so good as the above. **chîⁿ-phí**, small bad thin cash. **chîⁿ-phí-á**, id. **lák-jī-chîⁿ**, cash with six characters (current everywhere). **kong-tiong ê-chîⁿ**, cash with four characters (not current at Fuh-chau). **gâi-chîⁿ**, bad cash. **iên-chîⁿ**, lead counterfeit cash; also, small cash fastened in dress of bride and bridegroom. **iên-chîⁿ**, the cash collected by subscription. **hé-sio-chîⁿ**, bad cash burned to make them look good. **kim-pien-chîⁿ**, large good cash.

bú-chîⁿ, principal, capital lent. **pún-chîⁿ**, capital; also, the member's ticket of the Small Knife Society or Triads. **lāi-chîⁿ**, interest. **kang-chîⁿ**, wages. **kè-chîⁿ**, price. **tsāi-chîⁿ**, freight. **chiú-chîⁿ**, money paid for bringing a letter or small parcel, &c.; a small cumshaw. **bóe-tê-chîⁿ**, id. **lē-chîⁿ**, black-mail levied on a road. **bóe-lə̄-chîⁿ**, id. **khioh-lə̄-chîⁿ**, to levy blackmail. **chhiú-bé-chîⁿ**, a cash hung from the wrist by a white string; sign of mourning.

chîⁿ-pó, a sort of gambling (v. pó). **phak-chhiò-chîⁿ**, to toss odds and evens. **chiú-chîⁿ-lê**, a slave to money; a miser. **kiⁿ-chîⁿ-sí**, very covetous. **chîⁿ sì-kha; lâng nn̄g-kha**, money has four legs to your two, don't run after it.

chîⁿ-bé, balance in hand. **chîⁿ-niû̂ⁿ**, land-tax; soldiers' pay (v. niûⁿ). **lē-chîⁿ**, rates levied by mandarins or underlings for allowing forbidden things (v. lē). **chîⁿ-kék**, a government bank. **chîⁿ-phiò**, a bank note for cash. **chîⁿ-tiàm**, a money changer's shop. **chîⁿ-kūi**, a long money-chest. **chîⁿ-tâng**, a till, made of a bamboo. **chîⁿ-tsô**, a frame for counting cash. **chîⁿ-kǹg**, twine such as is used for stringing cash. **chîⁿ-chhēng**, a long bag for cash. **chîⁿ-chhēng-kah**, a vest with money pocket. **chit-kat-chîⁿ**, a string of a few cash. **chit-koāⁿ-chîⁿ**, a string of several hundred cash. **chit-tiàu-chîⁿ** (r. esp. mand.), a string of a thousand cash. **chit-tiâu-chîⁿ**, an item of money to be paid or collected.

chî^n-sia^n, the denomination of copper cash (v. sia^n). chî^n-tsâi, wealth. chî^n-gûn, money. chî^n-chhà, do. chî^n-tsúi, do. as to quantity (v. tsúi). chî^n-thâu, money in general, as to quantity; also, a sort of fish. chî^n-thâu khah-ân, in want of funds. ū-chî^n-lâng, a wealthy man.

tát-chî^n, valuable. tsù-chî^n, to cast cash in the mint. nn̂g-chî^n-khang, too sharp at making money. thàn-chî^n, to earn or make money. tsoán-chî^n, do.; may also be said of beggars. khit-chî^n, to ask or beg money. thó-chî^n, to demand money due us. siu-chî^n, to collect money, as debts or subscriptions. sa-chî^n, to sweep up cash with the hand, as on a table; to borrow money from many places. siàu-chî^n, to count cash. kéng-chî^n, to select good cash from bad. tùi-chî^n, to transfer money by a bill or draft, &c., either paying or receiving.

chhut-chî^n, to spend money; to pay expenses; to offer a price (s. eaves). seng-chhut-chî^n, to advance money. liáu-chî^n, to spend money. phoà-chî^n, to waste money lavishly, or spend it very freely. sái-chî^n, to spend money. ēng-chî^n, id. ēng-gōng-chî^n, to spend fool's pence. gâu-iû^n-chî^n, spendthrift. su-chî^n, to lose money in gambling. chiáh-sí-chî^n, to live on one's capital or property, so that it gradually wastes away. siú^n-chî^n, to give money as a reward. sioh-chî^n, to use money carefully. thè-chî^n, become less profitable than formerly, as a shop.

tsoá-chî^n, idolatrous paper money (v. tsoá). kim-chî^n, yellow do. for gold. péh-chî^n, white do. for worshipping "kúi." khè-chî^n, paper money, in short slips, with long incisions, for worship of the dead (v. khè). ke-tai-chî^n, bundles of long shreds of idolatrous paper (v. tai). tn̂g-chî^n (Cn.), id. chî^n-lô, a furnace for burning idolatrous paper (v. lô).

chí^n — chí^n-á, a pigeon.

chí^n — àn-chí^n (T.), thus, = àn-chì^n-sí.

chí^n (R. chéng), (C. ché^n), a well. tsúi-chí^n, a well. chí^n-tsúi, well water. chí^n-noā^n, a well curb. chí^n-sîn, presiding spirit of a well. tô-chí^n, to clean out a well. khui-chí^n, to sink a well. khui-chí^n pùih-tsoā^n, to draw off a neighbour's custom by an opposition shop, &c. (v. tsoā^n).

lit-chí^n, the upper end of the halyard where it is tied to the sail.

sò-chí^n, a cesspool for slops. hé-chí^n, a vault for safety from fire.

thi^n-chí^n, a skylight window. lâu-chí^n, an opening for a trap-door in an upper story. lêng-hé-chí^n, space at door of a temple. chhim-chí^n, the open area in the centre of a house. chhim-chí^n-tàu, framework of bamboo poles over this opening to guard against thieves. chhim-chí^n-tà, id.

chí^n, tender, young, delicate (of men, animals, shoots of plants, &c.) iù-chí^n, young, as person. chí^n-chhioh, id. lāu chí^n, old and young. sek chí^n, stiff or hard, and soft, as branches, &c. thn̂g chí^n, the sugar is boiled soft, not hard or stiff.

chí^n-kiu^n, = chí-kiu^n, young esculent shoots of ginger.

chì^n (C. chè^n), to contradict or dispute doggedly. sa^n-chì^n, to wrangle. chì^n-bô, doggedly deny what is really true. chì^n-jī, to dispute about the sound or meaning of a word. àu-chì^n, doggedly maintain the wrong side of a quarrel. kiông-kiông-chì^n, id. chì^n-chhùi, long and animated disputing and contradicting. chì^n-chhùi chì^n-chih, id. chì^n-sí, doggedly deny the truth. chì^n-sí chì^n-oáh, id. chì^n-iâ^n, to win in the debate. chì^n-su, to lose in the debate. chì^n-chêng, to strive hard to be first, as in a race. chì^n-tsòe-thâu, id.

chì^n (R. chièn), an arrow. keng-chì^n, bow and arrow. keng-chì^n-koán, a school for archery. keng-chì^n-tūi, the company of archers in an army; military mandarins are usually selected from them. liam-keng tah-chì^n, to take the bow and draw the arrow ready to shoot. tah-chì^n, id. an-keng tah-chì^n, id.

hī-chì^n, arrows stuck in the ears of criminals, esp. soldiers. chhah hī-chì^n, to put such arrows in their ears. chhèng-ki-chì^n, a sky-rocket. chhiú-chì^n, a dart; a javelin. hé-chì^n, a fiery arrow. àm-chì^n, a secret arrow; said of secretly injuring others. sái-àm-chì^n, to injure a man secretly. bān-lē-chì^n, a cloud of arrows from cross-bows (v. lē). hoān--tióh lē-chì^n, good luck (as of a house) injured by having a long straight road pointing directly at it. lēng-chì^n, an arrow given by a high mandarin to a messenger, to show that his orders are urgent. sái-bák-chì^n, to cast a piercing secret glance, as in half-dissembled displeasure, or as in making lewd advances.

pē-chì^n, archers on foot. bé-pē-chì^n, foot and cavalry archers. bé-chì^n, cavalry archers. khó bé-chì^n, trial of archery on horseback.

chì^n-bah, arrow-head; arrow-shod. chì^n-phi, id. chì^n-thâu, id. chì^n-pe (C.), id. chì^n-bé, hinder end of arrow. chì^n-khàu, notch of arrow, for the string. chì^n-lêng, feathers of arrow. chì^n-koái^n, shaft of arrow. chì^n-tē, quiver. chì^n-pé, target or mark for archery. khó chì^n-pé, to compete at archery. khó-chì^n, id. tsòe chì^n-pé (lit. to be a target), said of a soldier, made to be shot at, like "food for powder."

an-chì^n, to put the arrow on the string. tsóh-chì^n, to shoot an arrow. siā-chì^n, id. tióh-chì^n, to be struck by an arrow. tiòng-chì^n, id.

chì^n — àn-chì^n-sī (T.), this way.

chì^n (R. chien), to fry swimming in a large quantity of melted fat. chì^n-iû, id. chì^n-soán, sort of cakes fried in fat. chì^n-tsó, round fried balls of rice with stuffing of minced meat. chì^n-te, sort of cake fried in fat. hê-chì^n, shrimps covered with dough and fried. ô-te-chì^n, oysters, rice, and pulse fried together.

chì^n (R. chìn), to stuff into. chì^n-nì^n--teh, stuffed full and tight. chì^n-kui, to stuff a fowl's crop, to make it sell better. chì^n-khui, to press open as with a wedge.

chī^n [R. chēng, quiet, still], (C. chē^n), calm, as weather. soah-chī^n, fine, fair, calm weather. sah^n-chī^n, sudden lull in the wind. hong chī^n, wind fallen; calm. hong chī^n, éng pī^n, wind and waves quiet. sio-chī^n, warm and calm, as in spring. chhun-hē koā^n; tang-hē chī^n (Cn.), rain in spring is cold, when there is rain in winter the wind falls.

chī^n-chī^n (T.), = A. chēng-chēng, be quiet! (said to children).

àm-chī^n, secret; clandestine; secretly. àm-tsòe-chī^n (T.), id.

chia [R. = col. jia, to cover or screen]. moa^n-chia, an open shed with roof of only one slope.

chia — hia-chia, very cumbrous; greatly in the way, as a large piece of furniture.

chia (R. che), here. tī-chia, id. àn-chia, this way; by this road. tùi-chia, id. ōe-kè-tit-chia, bōe-kè-tit-hia, able to attend to one place, but not to the other.

chiá [R. red coloured]. chiá-sek, a medicine.

chiá [R. elder sister, mother, concubine, &c.] **chiá-hu**, = chí-hu, elder sister's husband. **goán-chiá--ê**, husband of my elder sister. **goán-chiá** (Cn.), my elder sister.

sió-chiá, daughter of a mandarin.

khioh-chiá, a midwife. **khioh-chiá-bú**, id. **pô-chiá**, inferior female spirits, supposed to have charge of infants (v. pô). **chiá-bú**, id. **hàu-chiá** (C.), = A. haù pô-chiá, to make offerings to these spirits. **sîn-chiá** (Cn.), a sorceress. **sià^{n}-chiá** (Cn.), id.

ang-chiá (C.), husband and wife. **ang-á-chiá** (C.), id. **toā-chiá** (C.), principal wife. **in-chiá** (C.), = A. in-ché-bú, his father's concubine, who is his own real mother.

chiá [R. a final relative particle, nearly "who," "which," "that which," often used to form an adjective; slightly colloquial in C., but still R.] **sūn-thien--chiá tsûn**; **gėk-thien--chiá bông**, they who obey Heaven are preserved; they who offend perish.

sù-chiá, a messenger sent by a sovereign. **bȯk-chiá** (X.), a pastor or (fig.) shepherd.

sū-chiá-kong, a large innocuous serpent that is worshipped. **sī-chiá-kong** (C.), id.

hóe--**chiá tī**, it is then too late to change one's mind. **hėk-chiá** (R.), perhaps.

chià (R. id.), sugar-cane. **kam-chià**, soft succulent sugar-cane, cultivated to be sold for sucking. **chhah-kam-chià**, to plant esculent sugar-cane. **tek-chià**, a harder sort (sweeter), grown for making sugar. **koa^{n}-chiá**, id. **khoeh-chià**, to press sugar-cane in the mill.

chià-chhia, a sugar-mill. **chià-phō͘**, the premises where there is a sugar-mill. **chià-phoh**, the cane when the juice has all been pressed out. **chià-tsai**, young plants of sugar-cane. **chià-ku**, an edible insect found in the cane-roots. **chià-háh**, the outer sheathing leaves of the cane. **pak chià-háh**, to pull off these leaves. **lân chià-háh**, id.

chià [R. to borrow, to use as a pretext]. **chià lâng--ê bêng-sek**, to make improper use of a man's name or influence for private ends. **chià-chhùi-gú**, pretending to have a verbal order, so as to get things and appropriate them. **ká-chià**, to pretend to have authority from another.

tsu-chià, to rely upon. **tsu-chià i--ê sè-thâu**, to rely on his influence or power. **tsu-chià i--ê hȧk-būn**, to get the benefit of his learning (as by friendly intercourse) for improving our own.

chià [R. tsā, suddenly]. **chià-phó**, the city Chapoo, near Ningpo, from which junks trade to Japan.

chià [R. to roast or toast]. **iû-chià-ké**, a sort of cake. **mī^{n}-chià**, a long lump of glutinous dough made of coarse wheat meal, sold uncooked. **kiâm-mī^{n}-chià**, salted do. **mī^{n}-chià chhá-bah**, do. cooked with pork.

chià-chhó, sliced, dried, and sugared liquorice. **chià-kî**, a sort of medicine.

chià (R. id.), (C. chē). **chià-ko͘**, a partridge.

chiā [R. siā, to thank], = siā, a surname.

chia^{n} (C.), = A. chi^{n}, a malignant demon.

chia^{n} [R. chhek, red], the lean of meat. **chia^{n}-bah**, id. **poà^{n}-chia^{n}-péh**, lean and fat mixed in one piece of meat.

chia^{n} [R. chèng, correct, = col. chià^{n}]. **chia^{n}-géh**, the first month. **chia^{n}-géh-chhoe**, the first ten days of the year. **chia^{n}-géh chia^{n}-thâu**, the first few days of the year (sometimes including to about 15th), in which time debts are not collected and ill-omened language is avoided. **sin-chia^{n}**, new-year's-day. **tsòe-chia^{n}**, to keep the new year. **hō-chia^{n}**, to pay new-year visits, esp. making presents. **pài-chia^{n}**, to pay visits in the first few days of the year, esp. first five days. **oàn-kúi pài-chia^{n}** (the ghost of the murdered man paid a new-year's visit to the murderer, got him in liquor so as to let out the secret of his guilt), said of a witness or proof of guilt suddenly coming to light. **koa-chia^{n}** (T.), the new-year's holidays past. **khah-koa-chia^{n}** (T.), id. **koa-chia^{n}, siōng-goân kè** (T.), after the middle of the first month. **chia^{n} koa** (Cn.), new-year's time past, about 15th or 20th of first month.

chiâ^{n} [R. chêng, desires, feelings; affairs]. **chhin-chiâ^{n}**, connections by marriage in any way; relatives of different surname. **chhin-chiâ^{n}-kan**, among such relatives. **tsòe-chhin-chiâ^{n}**, to betroth or espouse husband or wife (said either of self or son, &c.) **kap-goán ū-chhin-chiâ^{n}**, connected (by marriage in any way) with some relative of ours. **chhin-chiâ^{n} gō͘-géh**, relatives, neighbours, and friends (v. géh).

ū-sim-chiâ^{n}, to have heart for doing a thing.

ko͘-chiâ^{n}, to coax; to entreat, as a superior to inferior, or of equals. **kê-chiâ^{n}**, id.

kan-chiâ^{n}, adulterous or lascivious conduct, as matter of an accusation in court.

chiâ^{n} (R. sêng = col. chhiâ^{n}), to become; complete; almost or about; in round numbers or in rough quantity.

pún-chiâ^{n}, originally. **hiān-chiâ^{n}**, just now; at this time; at present.

si^{n}-chiâ^{n}, to produce and complete; natural; not artificial; naturally. **chiâ^{n}-tsòe**, to become. **tsòe-chiâ^{n}**, to complete; to be completed. **tsòe-tit-chiâ^{n}**, to accomplish. **tsòe kàu oân-chiâ^{n}**, to work at it till it is all right. **oân-chiâ^{n}**, completed; finished, as an affair. **pì^{n}-chiâ^{n}-hó**, to become good. **kè chhut-chiâ^{n}--lah**, the price is quite fixed.

hūn-chiâ^{n}, extremely like; undistinguishable, as an imitation or a counterfeit; as a tear or hole, &c., mended so that it cannot be observed; or as lies so well told as to appear quite true.

chiâ^{n}-thi^{n}, a clear sky; fine weather. **chiâ^{n}-kiâ^{n}**, determined to take a journey. **chiâ^{n}-tsoā**, making or becoming a row or line. **chiâ^{n}-khoán**, of good behaviour or pattern, &c. **chiâ^{n}-iū^{n}**, good or good-looking, &c.

chiâ^{n}-hāng, in considerable quantities. **chiâ^{n}-bé**, an entire animal of any sort of which "bé" is the classifier. **chiâ^{n}-tsàu-hé**, fuel enough for once using the cooking-place or fire-place. **chiâ^{n}-chhù-mih^{n}**, a houseful of things. **chiâ^{n}-siu^{n}**, a whole trunkful or so. **chiâ^{n}-soa^{n}**, in great quantities; whole mountains of —. **chiâ^{n}-soa^{n} chiâ^{n}-hái**, in vast quantities; mountains and oceans of (as of crops, &c.) **chiâ^{n}-mî^{n}**, a whole night or so. **chiâ^{n}-géh-jit**, about one month. **chiâ^{n}-bān-lâng**, about ten thousand men. **chiâ^{n}-pah**, about a hundred.

chiâ^{n}-lâng, to be married. **chiâ^{n}-lâng sêng-khì**, to get married and get on in business. **chiâ^{n}-lâng-tsâi**, fine-looking man. **iáu-bē chiâ^{n}-lâng**, not yet married. **m̄-chiâ^{n}-lâng**, poor or unfortunate; deformed or useless, as a man.

m̄-chiâ^{n}-mih^{n}, not very good; does not come to anything; of little or no use. **m̄-chiâ^{n}-khoán**, not of a good manner, model, or conduct. **tńg m̄-chiâ^{n}-chhiâ^{n}**, weak and sickly about the time of coming of age. **m̄-chiâ^{n}-thi^{n}**, uncertain weather, scarcely either rain or fair. **m̄-chiâ^{n}-hō͘**, very slight rain. **m̄-**

chiâ^{n} iau-pá, neither hungry nor full. **chhut-m̄-chiâ^{n}-kè**, to offer too low a price. **m̄-chiâ^{n} tông-seng, m̄-chiâ^{n} chhèng-peng**, not fit for any work, neither for literary work nor for labour (lit. soldier). **m̄-chiâ^{n}-chhe m̄-chiâ^{n}-iù**, id.

chiá^{n} (R. id.), insipid; tasteless; fresh, not salt; wanting in saltness or sweetness **pėh-chiá^{n} bô-bī**, quite tasteless. **chiá^{n}-pùh-pùh**, very insipid. **chiá^{n}-káuh-káuh**, id.

chiá^{n}-tsúi, fresh water. **kiâm-chiá^{n}**, salt and fresh. **tú-hó kiâm-chiá^{n}**, just sufficiently salt to be well tasted. **poà^{n}-kiâm-chiá^{n}**, half salt. **thàu-khah-chiá^{n}**, dilute it that it may not be so salt or so sweet.

chiá^{n} [R. jiȯk, C. jiȧk, weak]. **nńg-chiá^{n}**, weak; delicate (as in health); belonging to a weak clan or family, not having much influence or power; feeble. **núi^{n}-chiá^{n}** (C.), id.

chià^{n} (R. chèng), correct; real, true; right (hand); principal; (middle of Chinese hour).

chià^{n}-lē, well-behaved; of good conduct. **chià^{n}-hoat**, the fit way to accomplish an end. **chià^{n}-pān**, fair profit; goods of the right sort. **chià^{n}-kī**, anniversary of a person's death. **chià^{n}-pē**, one's real father **chià^{n}-miâ^{n}**, one's own proper name, as opp. to a nick-name. **chià^{n}-tsu**, real small-pox, opp. to "tsúi-tsu."

chià^{n}-jī, the mandarin dialect. **chià^{n}-im-hì**, plays in the mandarin dialect.

chià^{n}-thâu, at first; at the very beginning of the matter. **chià^{n}-thâu-lâi**, on first arrival. **hē chià^{n}-thâu**, to lay in the proper direction, opp. "tò-thâu." **chià^{n}-sėh**, to revolve in the direction of the hands of a watch. **chià^{n}-tńg**, id. **chià^{n}-oe**, to turn a hand-mill in that direction. **chià^{n}-kóng tò-kóng**, to say yea and nay at different times; to talk first on the one side and then on the other. **chià^{n}-tsòe tò-tsòe**, to do a thing in an irregular and rather improper way. **chià^{n}-chhák tò-phut**, piercing and cutting in all directions (v. phut). **tò-oai^{n} chià^{n}-oai^{n}**, to make overcharges right and left.

chià^{n}-hù, the principal and secondary, as the principal copy and the duplicate; officer and deputy; principal and assistant. **chià^{n}-kà**, the vessel carrying a very high mandarin. **chià^{n}-tn̂g**, the principal mandarin of a place, as opposed to his assistant (v. tn̂g). **chià^{n}-it-phín**, the very first rank of mandarins. **chià^{n}-keng**, the empress.

chià^{n}-chhiú, the right hand. **chià^{n}-chhiú-pêng**, the right-hand side; on the right hand. **chià^{n}-pêng**, the right face or side (as of a mirror or picture or other flat thing).

chià^{n}-sī, yes, it is so; quite true; that's so; yes. **chin-chià^{n}**, truly; true. **chià^{n}-chhin-chhiū^{n}**, exactly alike. **chià^{n}-chià^{n}**, quite square, even, or correct; certainly. **chià^{n}-chià^{n} tī-hia**, certainly is there. **sì-chià^{n}**, square, even, or straight; all correct and right. **toan-hong sì-chià^{n}**, set quite straight; correct in conduct (v. toan). **toan-chià^{n}**, correct in conduct. **kóe-chià^{n}**, to correct (as a document); to put right or make correct. **siá-chià^{n}**, to write out a fair clean copy (as from a scroll). **têng-chià^{n}**, id. **chiū^{n}-chià^{n}**, id.

pì^{n}-chià^{n}, ordinary middling quality; not very good (of men or things); fair; not partial. **pì^{n}-chià^{n}-lâng**, a person who is just middling in appearance. **tsòe-lâng pì^{n}-chià^{n}**, tolerably good man. **m̄-pì^{n}-chià^{n}**, partial; unfair (as man or affair). **m̄-chiàu-pì^{n}-chià^{n}**, id. **sim-koa^{n} pì^{n}-chià^{n}**, fair in dealings. **pì^{n}-chià^{n}-sim**, impartial towards inferiors (as teacher, father, or master). **pān--liáu pì^{n}-chià^{n}**, settled fairly (as by mandarin or arbiter).

chià^{n}-tng-sî, just at the best time; just in season. **báu-chià^{n}**, the middle of the double hour "báu," *i.e.* 6 A.M. **báu-sî-chià^{n}**, id. **sîn-chià^{n}**, = **sîn-sî-chià^{n}**, 8 A.M. **chī-sî-chià^{n}**, 10 A.M.; and so with the other hours.

chiā^{n} (Cn.), = A. iáng, to carry (a person) on the back. **sa^{n}-chiā^{n}**, standing back to back, as two houses near each other (= T. sa^{n}-chiāng).

chiā^{n}, a character in a play, esp. a bold fellow with a painted face. **o-chiā^{n}**, do. with face painted black. **âng-chiā^{n}**, do. with face red. **tsng-chiā^{n}**, to act such a character. **tsòe-chiā^{n}**, id.

chiā^{n} [R. kiông, strong]. **ngī^{n}-chiā^{n}**, stiff, as starched cloth, &c.; strong and ready for work; fond of work, as a man not afraid of weather, or as a woman who is fit for hard work.

chiah — **lín-chiah-ê**, you (plural). **lín chiah-ê-lâng**, id. **lán chiah-ê-lâng**, we.

chiah [R. chek], thus —; so —; (these); then, as connective particle either of time or of immediate effect or consequence.

chiah-ê, these. **chiah-hn̄g**, thus far; so far. **chiah-sòe**, so small. **chiah-kú**, so long; this long time. **chiah-kú hó**, have you been well of late? how do you do?

àn-ni^{n}, chiah hó-sè, it will be all right if done so. **khah-oà^{n}, chiah-lâi**, come later. **sa^{n}-tiám, chiah-lâi**, come at three o'clock. **ta^{n} chiah-lâi**, now come at last. **tú--chiah**, just now (past). **tú-á-chiah**, id. **tú-chiah-lâi**, just arrived. **chhím-chhím chiah-lâi**, has just this moment arrived. **gėh chiah-chhut**, the moon just risen.

chiah — **bān--chiah**, wait a little (v. bān).

chiah — **chiah-mî^{n}**, unable to see well at night.

chiah [R. chek, the backbone]. **ka-chiah**, the back. **pa-chiah** (Cn.), id. **ka-chiah-āu**, behind one's back; in his absence. **ka-chiah-sim**, middle of the back along the backbone. **ka-chiah-sien**, dirt in the hollow along the spine. **ka-chiah-kut**, the back-bone. **ka-chiah-chit**, id. **tái^{n}-ka-chiah**, to cut and hack a man's back, as a housebreaker when caught.

io-chiah-kut, the lower end of the backbone.

chiah (R. chiet). **bák-chiah-mn̂g**, the eye-lashes.

chiah (R. chek), classifier of beasts, birds, boats, ships, ingots of silver, &c.; also (C.) of tables and chairs; sometimes contemptuously of men.

tsûn-chiah, boats and ships in general. **chiáu-chiah**, birds in general. **hoan-chiah-á**, a small pretty cage-bird. **chiah-ngá** (Cn.), small birds.

chiah [R. chek, a footstep, a trace], (cf. jiah).

ū-iá^{n}-chiah, real. **bô-iá^{n}-chiah**, without a shadow of truth. **bô-iá^{n} bô-chiah**, id. **bô-iá^{n}-chiah ê-mih^{n}**, very unimportant things.

chiah — **thn̂g-chiah-kha**, barefooted (cf. chhiah).

chiah — **kha-chiah-té** (P.), = A. kha-chhioh-tóe, the sole of the foot. **kha-chiah-tóe** (T.), id.

chiàh [R. chià, to roast or toast]. **iû-chiàh-ké**, long twisted cakes fried in fat, = iû-chià-ké.

chiàh (R. sit), to eat; to live on; to get money out of; (to entertain); to live (so long); to take (as snuff, tobacco, wine, &c.); to absorb (as oil); to fit or lean on (as a beam); to play some games; to get the better of, &c. &c.

chiáh kúi-lâng, how many guests, &c., do you have at table?

chiáh pē-bú, to live on one's parents (v. pē). **chiáh thâu-ke**, to get our food from our employer, at his expense. **chiáh ka-kī**, to find one's own food, not getting it from employer. **ka-kī-chiáh**, to eat alone, cooking one's own food, or having it cooked separately from others. **chiáh-kiá^{n} chiáh-sun**, to live on one's sons or grandsons. **chiáh kiá^{n}-sun**, id.; also said of an old man who survives all his descendants.

bōe-chiáh--tit, not eatable; too powerful to let us get money out of him; nothing can be got out of him. **chiáh--i bōe-tó**, his work is too heavy or too difficult for me. **chiáh--i m̄-ta**, do.; also, I can't get the money out of him (v. ta). **chiáh--i bōe-noā^{n}**, I have not ability or strength for his work. **chiáh--i kè-kè**, to have quite the upper hand of a man; to be able to overcome him with the utmost ease. **chiáh--i sa^{n}-tù-thàu**, do. (figure from gambling). **goá chiáh-tit-i-kàu**, I can hold my own against him; I am not afraid of him. **ná^{n} chiáh-tit-i-kàu, chiū-thang**, if you are quite able to hold your own against him, then you may venture. **chiáh--i khah-kàu**, well able to get the better of him; not at all afraid of him. **khit--i péh-péh-chiáh**, to be oppressed or fleeced by him without power of resistance.

chiáh kiáu-tâng, to live by gambling. **chiáh-tâng chiáh-thih**, to live on others by bold wicked means. **chiáh chhim-tsúi**, to screw money improperly out of people with whom he has no connection. **chiáh-thi^{n}-lō͘** (live on dew), to have uncertain means of living; to live by one's wits, as poor literati who make people pay money by threatening with lawsuits. **chiáh-thien-tông**, to get one's money by improper means, as underlings of yamuns (v. thien). **chiáh-tsoā, phè hó͘-huih** (serpents with tiger's blood), said of a very wicked daring man. **chiáh-chhàu-bí**, to be an employé in a yamun (v. chhàu). **chiáh-pit-bé**, to live by writing documents for lawsuits, as meddling literati. **chiáh jîn-bēng**, to take money for the settlement of a case about a death. **chiáh hōng-lòk**, to have official salary. **chiáh-niû^{n}**, to be a soldier. **chiáh-chhèng**, to be a soldier who uses a gun. **chiáh-pâi**, do using a shield. **chiáh-keng**, to be an archer, in army.

chiáh kùi-bí, to be suffering from dearth. **chiáh-pún**, to live on one's capital. **siu-tso͘ chiáh-soá^{n}**, to live on the rents of property. **chiáh-kha chiáh-chhiú**, to live by the labour of one's own limbs; said also of a mandarin severely punishing his own underlings. **liu-chhiu chiáh-bák-chiu**, a man must use his eyes sharply (v. chhiu).

chiáh-tsó͘, to eat the feast in the ancestral temple. **chiáh-kī**, to eat a feast on anniversary of birth or death of the deceased. **chiáh-si^{n}-jit**, to eat a birth-day feast of a living friend. **chiáh pùt-si^{n}-jit**, to have a feast on an idol's birth-day. **chiáh-tiā^{n}**, to have a feast when the money and presents are sent, after betrothal, but before the marriage. **chiáh i-ê-si^{n}**, to take his surname and worship his ancestors, as a weak village does to a powerful one, to get their assistance. **chiáh-kàu**, phrase used by the heathen for "becoming a Christian," but not a good phrase. **chiáh-chhài**, to be a vegetarian. **chiáh sa^{n}-lák-káu**, to abstain from animal food on the days ending in 3, 6, and 9.

chiáh-hun, to smoke (tobacco). **chiáh-phī^{n}-hun**, to take snuff. **chiáh-ngó͘-ien**, to take snuff, tobacco, and opium. **chiah-o͘-hun**, to smoke opium. **chiáh-tiâu**, become an inveterate opium-smoker. **chiáh-phah-phûn**, to smoke only a little opium, not yet inveterate. **chiáh-chiú**, to take wine, &c. (v. chiú). **chiáh-tê**, to drink tea.

chiáh-tsúi, to drink water. **tsûn chiáh-tsúi**, the vessel draws (so much) water. **khui-khang hō͘--i chiáh-tsúi**, to show him an opening for squeezing money out of some one.

chiáh-iû, to absorb oil, as a thing steeped in it, &c. **chiáh-tsō**, to be dyed with sulphate of iron. **chiáh-chiu^{n}**, to be starched, as cloth or clothes.

chiáh-hong, to take in wind, as a sail well placed to catch the wind. **chiáh-thih**, to attract iron, as the load-stone. **chiáh-soa^{n}**, to make gradual progress, gaining on the land, as a vessel in successive tacks.

chiáh-jī, to take the bait, as fish. **chiáh-tiò**, to bite the hook. **chiáh-pn̄g**, to eat rice; to take food (v. pn̄g). **chiáh thit-thô**, to eat something for mere amusement, or by the way. **chiáh--bē**, have you eaten? how do you do? **chiáh-khoà^{n}**, to taste. **toā-chiáh**, eating much. **sòe-chiáh**, eating little. **chiáh-beh-sí**, very greedy at food (v. sí). **chiáh-bōe-khì**, unable to eat more, as when full, or when meat is very fat. **péh-péh-chiáh**, to eat rice without condiments (v. péh). **kéng-chiáh**, very nice (too particular) about one's food, always wishing the very best. **mih^{n}-chiáh**, confections, sweetmeats, &c. **ū-chiáh-sit**, to live well on good food (v. sit).

chiáh-pá, to have eaten enough, or till satiated; to be saturated, as with oil (v. pá). **chiáh-liáu**, to eat up the whole, leaving nothing. **chiáh--liáu**, after having eaten. **chiáh--liáu sán**, always lean, whatever he eats. **chiáh--liáu thit-thô**, doing nothing but eat and amuse himself. **chiáh--liáu, bô-siá^{n}-sū**, id. **chiáh oá^{n}-lāi, kóng oá^{n}-goā**, eats his food, but speaks ill of him behind his back (v. oá^{n}). **chiáh-khó chiáh-kà**, whether eating better or worse food (rice thicker or thinner). **chiáh-khó chiáh-kà, tióh chit--ē pêng-chêng**, whatever they have or have not to eat, the members of a family should be at peace among themselves.

thàn-chiáh, to earn one's food (v. chiáh). **tsoán-chiáh**, to get one's food any way, either by earning or by begging. **khit-chiáh**, to beg; a beggar (v. khit). **pun-chiáh**, id. **pun--chiáh**, to make arrangements for having meals separate from others. **pun-khui-chiáh**, id. **thiah-chiáh**, id. **háp-teh-chiáh**, taking meals regularly together. **tsú-chiáh**, to cook (v. tsú).

chiáh tn̂g-hè-siū, to enjoy long life (v. hè). **i beh-chiáh khah-kú**, he hopes to live longer. **chiáh á-bē kàu-lāu**, not old yet. **ū-pn̄g, chiáh kàu-lāu; bô-pn̄g, chiáh kàu-sí**, may you lose your riches, and be very poor in old age!

sa^{n}-chiáh-à^{n}, fitting well together, as parts of an article of furniture; friendly; of one mind. **chiáh-chhēng**, food and clothes (v. chhēng). **sa^{n}-chiáh-chhēng**, fitting well together. **bô-sa^{n}-chiáh**, not agreeing well together, as essay to text, or as evidence. **chiáh-tôe**, agreeing well with the text, as essay.

chiáh m̄-tióh tsúi-thó͘, to be injured in health by the climate.

tham-chiáh, gluttonous; small-pox very thick on the body (v. tham).

chiáh chit-ki ê-lát, leans on this beam for support, as a smaller beam does, or as a set of rafters on a great beam. **chiáh koái^n-á ê-lát**, to lean one's weight (more or less) on a staff. **chiáh tó-kháu ê-lát**, wind in such a direction that the oar held in the left hand must be rowed with more force.

chiáh-ngī^n, bô-chiáh-nńg, determined to carry out our purpose in spite of any opposition. **chiáh-phiah**, having an obstinate temper; dogged and crotchety. **chiáh i-ê-phiah**, id. **chiáh-i chit-ê-phiah**, id. **chiáh-kiū^n**, of set purpose taking the very opposite way to that which others wish or advise. **chiáh-kiēn**, id. **chiáh-thâu**, harbouring revengeful feeling (v. thâu). **kap--i chiáh-khì**, id. **chiah-kōe** (C.), insubordinate.

chiáh-tù, to win stakes in gambling (v. tù). **goá kā--lí chiáh--khì**, you win the stakes from me. **chiáh-tit**, to play a game called "tit," *q.v.* **chiáh-jí-á**, a game with bits of tile (v. jí).

chiáh gûn-tsúi, to get so much less than the price would be counted in mixed (good and bad) cash, because it is paid in silver. **chiáh phái^n-chî^n-tsúi**, id. **khah-chiáh-kè**, paying a little over the price willingly.

chiáh-ki^n, to lose money by acting as surety and having to pay; or as by doing a commission for another, and having the goods thrown on our hands.

thòe--lâng chiáh-tsōe, to bear the responsibility of another's crime or fault.

hō--i kā-chiáh, to be scolded by him very violently.

ōe-chiáh chhàu-bah khí--lâi, able to remove putrefying flesh, as a medical application.

chiak (C.), = A. chiok. **chiak-iák**, a sort of flower.

chiak (C.), = A. chiok, a sort of cup; a rank of nobility.

chiak (C.), = A. chiok. **chim-chiak**, to consider carefully.

chiák — **chiák-sit** (C.), = A. tiók-sit, the real facts of a case.

chiam [R. to look up to]. **sa^n-chiam**, to observe each other carefully, as two men on a road avoiding running against each other; or as two vessels sailing together, taking care not to part company; or as two men on an unknown or dangerous road.

chiam [R. to divine by lot], a cent; to prognosticate; to settle a balance. **chit-chiam**, one cent.

sa^n-chiam-tsāu, to settle a small balance (either way) from a payment. **sa^n-chiam**, id.; also, three cents. **chiam joā-tsōe chî^n-bé**, what balance?

thâu-chiam, the bearer who occupies the first place in front in carrying an idol.

chiam i-ê-bāng, to interpret his dream. **chiam-koà**, a sort of divination (v. koà).

chiam [R. tsam], (Cn. tsam; C. tsom, in some phrases), a lady's hair-pin. **chiam-á**, id. **sek-thn̂g-chiam**, a sort used (superstitiously) by elderly women. **téng-kó-chiam**, upper hair-pin in female head-dress. **hô-lô-chiam**, those worn at the sides, with heads of the "hô-lô" shape.

kim-chiam, a beautiful red flower somewhat like Amaryllis (Hemerocallis!); also used as a vegetable. **kim-chiam-hoe**, id. **kim-chiam-chhài**, do. as a vegetable. **gék-chiam**, the tuberose. **giók-chiam**, id.

chiam (R. id.), a surname.

chiam (R. id.), pointed; sharp-pointed; a point; an extremity, esp. pointed. **chiam-chiam**, sharp-pointed. **chiam-lāi**, very sharp. **chhùi chiam, chih lāi**, a great talker; a chatterer.

si^n bák-chiam, to have a stye on the eyelid. **liú-chiam**, shoes with only one rib in front. **hia-chiam**, the toe of a boot. **pit-chiam**, the point of a pen or hair-pencil. **soa^n-chiam**, a mountain peak. **jîn-jī-chiam**, a roof made with a ridge (not flat). **tsúi-chiam**, a fish with a pointed mouth. **ngó-chiam**, the head, feet, and wings of a bird. **khì-ngó-chiam**, to cut off head, legs, and wings of a fowl before cooking it (or head and feet of a beast); to cut off the head, hands, and feet of a criminal.

siu-chiam, to sharpen to a point. **khioh-chiam**, to pile up (in pyramidal shape) to a point, as stones, bricks, &c. **put-chiam**, to heap up earth, lime, &c., in a pointed mound of pyramidal shape. **chiam-thâu**, pointed at the end, as a pole (s. needle). **chiam-chhùi--ê**, a rat. **chiam-chhùi** (C.), = khoah-chhùi, a pickaxe. **chiam-hî**, a fish with a very sharp head. **n̂g-chiam-lí**, a sort of yellow plum. **chiam-á-bí**, the best sort of rice. **chiam-tāu**, a small round bean.

sa^n-chiam lák-kak, all points, corners, and angles; very irregular in shape; very angular; quite opposed to our views and expectations, as language of a man to whom we apply for something. **chiam-kha iù-chhiú**, hands and feet delicate, as of woman or literary man, or son of rich man. **thâu chiam, phī^n tuh**, face long and nose sharp; counted good-looking.

chiam (R. chiam, chim), (Cn. tsam), a needle; used in the names of instruments having a needle or a tube.

kan-chiam, a mariner's compass. **kín-bān-chiam**, regulator of watch or clock. **hong-ú-chiam**, a barometer. **hân-sú-chiam**, a thermometer. **pió-á-chiam**, hand of watch. **sî-chiam**, hour-hand of watch or clock. **khek-chiam**, minute-hand. **biáu-chiam**, second-hand.

pín-chiam, a foreign pin. **siù-chiam**, the smallest sort of needle for embroidering and fine needle-work. **hoe-chiam**, id. **toā-pò-chiam**, a large needle. **jī-pò-chiam**, a smaller sort. **sa^n-pò-chiam**, a sort still smaller.

chiam-tsái^n, a thimble. **chiam-phī^n**, the eye of a needle. **chiam-khang**, the hole made by a needle. **chiam-bé**, point of needle. **chiam-chí**, needle-work and embroidery (v. chí). **chiam-kha iù**, the needle-work is fine. **chiam-áh**, a small needle-case. **chiam-khoeh**, a small box for needles. **chiam-tâng**, a small cylindrical vessel for do. **chiam-pau**, a paper of needles. **chit-pau-chiam**, one paper of needles. **chiam-soà^n**, needle and thread. **chiam-thâu soà^n-bé**, do. **bô-chiam, put-ín-soà^n**, without a proper introduction it cannot be properly managed.

hái-tóe bong-chiam, to feel for a needle at the bottom of the sea. **kau-chiam**, to sew with very close stitches. **kau-chiam tèng, bát-liú poà^n**, very careful; over careful or minute in money matters (v. bát).

chiâm [R. to go deep or secretly]. **tîm-chiâm**, self-collected; thinking deeply or carefully before speaking or acting. **chiâm-sim** (R.), diligent and earnest in study.

chiám (R. chím). **chiám-thâu**, = chím-thâu, a pillow.

chiàm (R. id.), (cf. chiam, chhiàm), to take unjust possession of; to interfere to separate combatants.

chiàm-pan-gî, to compel a man to sell cheap. **ka-kī chiàm-teh-kóng**, to talk right on, maintaining

厦英大辭典

that we are all right (as when found fault with), letting no one else get in a word. **chiàm-tāi-seng**, to take the first place for one's self somewhat rudely.

chiàm-tsòng, to take unjust possession of a grave. **chiàm-tōe**, to take unjust possession of land. **chiàm-chhân**, id. **chiàm lâng-ê-bó**, take unjust possession of another man's wife.

pà-chiàm, to usurp; to take unjust possession either of throne or of any possessions, *e.g.* house or land. **kiông-chiàm**, do. by violence. **su-chiàm**, to take illegal possession of public property for one's self. **chhim-chiàm**, to encroach upon; to take unjust possession of (as of land). **chhim-chiàm koaⁿ-tōe**, to encroach on land that is government property.

chiàm--lâng, to interfere to separate combatants or men quarrelling; to try to stop a scrimmage. **saⁿ-chiàm**, id. **chiàm--i**, to interfere to keep him from being beaten, as in a quarrel, or as a child that parents are beating. **sio-chiàm** (C.), to assist one of two parties quarrelling.

chiàm — **sio-chiàm** (P.), = A. saⁿ-oá, leagued together, as two friends who make common cause in all cases.

chiām (R. id.) **chiām-chiām**, by degrees; gradually. **chiām-chìn**, make gradual progress.

chiām (R. id.) **chiām-sî**, temporarily; in the meantime. **chiām-sî-á**, only for a short time. **chiām-toà**, to stay for a short time. **chiām-chhiáⁿ**, just for a short time let —. **chiām-koân**, to be a temporary substitute; to use as such, esp. in some work or office. **chiām-koân teh-ēng**, using it or him temporarily till a better can be got.

chian (in several tones), better, "chien" (q.v.)

chiang [R. tiong, to stretch out], (C. tiang). **koāi-chiang**, very stubborn and obstinate; determined to have his own way or say, esp. as inferior.

chiang [R. chiang, Cn. chiong], (Cn. cheng). **chiang-chiu**, Chang-chew. **chiang-se**, thin mixed silk stuff made at Chang-chew. **chiang-pán**, blocks cut there. **chiang--ê**, made at Chang-chew.

chiang-tsoân, Changchew & Chinchew. **chiang-tsoân-piàⁿ**, a feud between Chang-chew and Chin-chew men. **hok-kièn oân-oân, m̄-tah chiang-tsoân**, in all Fuh-kien, Chang-chew and Chin-chew are the best places.

chiang [R. chiong, an essay], (C.), = A. chiong, a surname, &c. **pió-chiang** (C.), = A. pió-chiuⁿ, a memorial to the emperor.

chiang (C.), = A. chiong, to use (as instrument); sign of future; often R.

chiáng [R. chióng, = col. chiúⁿ, an oar]. **pat-chiáng-tsûn**, eight-oared boats used by custom-house officials. **pat-chiáng-á**, id.

chiáng [R. chióng, to praise]. **po-chiáng**, to praise an inferior so as to encourage him to more exertion.

chiáng [R. tióng, to grow, to increase; by change of tone from "tiông," long], to rise, as the price of anything. **gûn-kè chiáng**, the value of the dollar has risen. **bí-kè chiáng**, the price of rice has risen. **chiáng-chìn** (C.), = A. chióng-chìn, to grow rich (v. chìn).

chiáng [R. chióng, the palm of the hand; to rule]; (Cn. chióng). **chiáng-koán**, to rule; to have authority over. **chip-chiáng**, to have (power or authority). **chiáng-kùi**, the man in a hong who has charge of the silver.

chiáng-kiō, to hold the poles of the sedan of a high mandarin. **chiáng-siⁿ**, a large fan carried before very high mandarins.

chiàng [R. chiòng, a military officer]. **láu-chiàng**, a soldier. **hàn-chiàng**, a tall fat man. **hó-hàn-chiàng**, id. **chiàng-iâ**, low custom-house officials (not in the office) like tide-waiters.

Also (C.), = A. chiòng (military officers, idols, &c.)

chiàng — **lāi-chiàng** (C.), = A. lūi-chiòng, an eye disease.

chiàng (R. tiòng). **hūn-chiàng**, falsified, as a document; confused, or out of order, as the management or settlement of an affair. **chòe-sū hūn-chiàng**, to manage a matter in a confused or disorderly way. **saⁿ-hūn-chiàng**, confusedly mixed, as good or bad, or as things belonging to different owners.

chiāng (P.), = iāng, = chiāⁿ, to carry on the back, as a man or child.

saⁿ-chiāng (T.), to stand back to back, as two houses or villages. **saⁿ-chiāng kha-chhng** (T.), id.

chiap (R. id.), to receive; to succeed to; to join; to set, as a broken bone; to splice or lengthen, as rope; to add a piece of paper, cloth, &c.; to make larger.

put-chiap-it, matters not going well; said euphemistically of death.

èng-chiap, to receive, as guests. **chiap-èng**, id.; also, to assist as with troops. **chiap-láp**, to receive, as persons. **chiap-hong** (R.), to give a feast to a friend on his coming home. **pí-chiap** (Cn.), to meet and try to arrange a quarrel.

chiap āu-siū, a widower marrying a virgin. **chiap pâng-hūn**, to keep up the succession, as an adopted son. **chiap i-ê-kheh** (C. khoeh), to fill the vacancy left by him; to succeed him. **chiap-ūi**, to succeed to the throne. **chiap-jīm**, to succeed to a mandarin's office. **chiap-ìn**, id. (receiving the seals).

ū-chiap-chhah, to have proper connection, as a literary composition (v. chhah). **saⁿ-chiap**, connected, as in close succession; adjoining to. **soà-chiap**, to succeed to, as inheritance, &c. **chiap-soà**, closely connected, as following clause; to succeed. **saⁿ-chiap-soà**, closely connected in succession, as sentences or events. **sêng-chiap**, to inherit; to succeed to, as property, &c. **chiap-siòk**, in close succession; connected without interruption or intermission. **ū-chiap-siòk**, do. as clauses in context, or as train of reasoning. **saⁿ-chiap-siòk**, id.; said also of money coming in constantly. **chîⁿ-gûn chiap-siòk**, money coming in from time to time in considerable quantities. **saⁿ-chiap-siòk-thàn**, id.

kau-chiap, to associate, as friends. **kau-chiap óng-lâi**, id. **kau-thâu chiap-jíⁿ**, to talk in whispers, "*tête-à-tête.*" **chih-chiap**, to associate or receive, as friend or visitor, or business connection. **kap--i chih-chiap**, do.; to have direct dealings with him in business.

chiap-chhiú, to settle a bargain. **saⁿ-chiap-kha**, to follow in succession, as in walking; to supply a man's place, as in gambling. **saⁿ-chiap-kha lâi**, one coming in as another goes out.

chiap-ki, to graft. **chiap-soh**, to splice or lengthen a rope. **chiap-ûi**, to set up the parts of a foreign mast. **chiap-thih**, to weld iron. **chiap-sún**, to dovetail; to join by tenon and mortice. **gâu chiap-sún-khak**, skilful at saying what corroborates another's story (false or conjectural); talking as if we knew all about a matter which we do not know. **chiap kàu ū-**

ki ū-hio̍h, one man adding a tissue of inventions to what another (truly or falsely) says, so as to give all the appearance of manifest truth.

chiap-hûn, the seam or joint, as where one piece of cloth, timber, &c., is joined to another. **chiap-le̍k-bah**, the meat of the soft loin (v. le̍k).

chiap (R. id.), (Cn. tsap), juice, sap, gravy, &c. **tsúi-chiap**, watery juice. **lin-chiap**, milk flowing in small quantities from the teat. **sái-chiap**, watery excrement as in diarrhœa, esp. of young children.

kôe-chiap, brine of salt or pickled fish, &c. **bah-chiap**, gravy; sauce from the meat.

chiap (R. chiet). **ba̍k-chiap-mn̂g**, better "ba̍k-chiah-mn̂g," eye-lashes.

chia̍p (R. chiet), fast; quick. **chia̍p-chia̍p**, often; constantly; diligently. **chia̍p-chia̍p-o̍h**, constantly learning or practising. **chia̍p-chia̍p-kóng**, constantly talking. **chhùi chia̍p-chia̍p-tân**, too talkative.

kín-chia̍p, rapidly. **kín-chia̍p-khoài**, nimble; very quick, as at work. **kín-thin chia̍p-lim** (pour and drink quickly), to manage a matter very rapidly. **liâm-chia̍p**, quick; prompt; active; energetic. **lia̍p-chia̍p**, id **kha-chhiú liâm-chia̍p**, hands and feet nimble. **kóng-ōe chia̍p-lut-lut**, to talk very fast.

chia̍p — **chia̍p chhùi-tûn**, to smack the lips. **chhùi chia̍p-chia̍p-kiò**, sound of smacking the lips. **chhùi chia̍p-chia̍p-háu**, id.

chiat, **chia̍t**, better chiet, chie̍t, *q.v.*

chiau (R. tso). **chiau-that** (esp. T.), = tsau-that, to maltreat, &c.

chiau [R. bright, manifest]. **thien-lí chiau-chiau**, Heaven's judgments very plain and manifest, as calamities on the wicked. **thien-tō chiau-chiau**, id.

chiau [R. name of several plants, sometimes = col. chio]. **liên-chiau**, sort of red arum with large leaves. **liên-chiau kiet-kó**, may the arum have fruit, felicitous words at marriage, represented by two stalks of arum and a cake of dried limes. **pa-chiau-sìⁿ**, an ancient sort of fan (v. pa).

chiau [R. certain parts of the body]. **sam-chiau-hé**, the hot principles of the upper, middle, and lower parts of the body. **sam-chiau-hé toā**, these hot principles very powerful, &c.

chiau [R. scorched, grieved]. **sim-koaⁿ būn-chiau-chiau**, grieved, as at leaving relatives or friends. **chiau-tsu̍t**, a sort of medicine treated with fire.

chiau [R. to invite, a confession, = col. chio]. **chiau-jîn**, to confess guilt on trial. **put-táⁿ put-chiau**, unless beaten he will not confess. **khut-táⁿ sêng-chiau**, to beat violently and force to confess.

chiau-iâu, to circulate exciting tidings, as about rebellion or others faults (v. iâu). **chiau-pâi**, a signboard or trade mark. **chiau-tsâi-ông**, the god of wealth.

chiâu (R. tsoân, = col. tsn̂g), complete; regular; even; well mixed, as dough.

chiâu-tsn̂g, complete. **chiâu-pī**, id.; all ready. **chiâu-lâi**, all have come. **chiâu-kàu**, all have arrived. **chiâu-ûn**, regularly in good measure, as rain or work (v. ûn). **chiâu-hó**, all right and ready, as something prepared. **m̄-chiâu-liáu**, not wholly finished. **á-bē chiâu-liáu**, id.

chiâu-chiâu, all alike. **chiâu-chiâu beh**, all of them desire. **chiâu-chiâu-á-toā**, all of the same size. **chiâu-chiâu hiah-toā**, id.

siá-khi-chiâu, write evenly. **boah-khi-chiâu**, spread it (as lime) evenly all over. **lia̍p hē-i-chiâu**, work it up (as clay or dough) with the hands, till it is well mixed and of uniform consistency.

chiâu [R. wood for fuel]. **gû chiâu, keng tho̍k** (r.), fishermen, wood-cutters, farmers, and scholars.

chiâu [R. grieved], (cf. chiau, chhiau). **chiâu-sim peh-pak**, sorely grieved and distressed, as at things all going wrong. **chiâu-tsō**, grieved and vexed in mind. **chiâu-tsūi**, miserable and mournful looking.

chiáu (R. niáuⁿ), a bird. **chiáu-á**, do. **chiáu-chiah**, birds in general. **chiáu-chεh** (C.), id. **koe-chiáu**, fowls and birds in general.

chiáu-chiⁿ, a malicious demon in the form of a bird; a person who is too sharp and cunning. **hé-chiáu**, an ill-omened bird supposed to appear about a fire; a boy who is over sharp, cunning, forward, or impudent. **gán-chiáu**, a man who is more knowing or skilful, or better at talking than others, and so naturally takes the lead. **thâu-ba̍k-chiáu**, do. but with more influence.

teh chiáu-á-koà, to divine by a bird picking out one lot from several. **tiau-hoe khek-chiáu**, to carve wood in general. **chiáu-lâi**, a wild pear. **chiáu-ta̍h-chhì**, a thorn with a yellow leguminous flower. **chiáu-á-hún**, white pigment for the face, in small bits. **chiáu-kha**, legs without calves. **khiàng-chiáu**, appearance like squinting, when the skin of the eye is drawn up at the corner; cross-eyed. **ba̍k-chiu tso̍h-chiáu**, id. **ba̍k-chiu phah-chiáu**, id. **phah-chiáu**, to shoot birds. **bāng-chiáu**, to catch birds by a net.

chiáu-kang, a male bird. **chiáu-kak**, id. **chiáu-bú**, a female bird. **chiáu-bôe**, a decoy bird. **chiáu-chhèng**, a small-bore fowling-piece. **chiáu-tauh**, a sort of snare for birds. **chiáu-siū**, a nest. **chiáu-lâng**, a cage. **chiáu-lúi**, a bird's cup. **chiáu-ta̍h**, a roost, as in a cage.

chiáu-tsûn, a junk, with picture of bird on stern. **chháu-chiáu**, boats that carry grass and shrubs for fuel; boats like them in size and shape. **chiáu-chhùi**, a bird's beak or bill; the two projections at the bow of a junk, between which the windlass is placed. **chhiⁿ-chiáu-chhùi**, a junk with blue bow (Cantonese). **chiáu-chhùi, gû kha-chhng** (bird's beak, but cow's posteriors), little coming in, but much going out.

chiáu (R. chiá). **chiáu-hu**, = chí-hu, husband of elder sister. **goán-chiáu--ê**, my elder sister's husband.

chiáu (R. tiáu). **lān-chiáu**, the penis.

chiàu (R. id.), an imperial decree. **chiàu-tsu**, id. **chiàu-si** (C.), id. **pan-chiàu**, to publish abroad an imperial decree. **sià-chiàu**, an imperial decree of pardon. **chih-chiàu**, to receive the imperial commands with ceremonies, as the mandarins do. **ûi-chiàu** (R.), imperial last will and testament.

chiàu [R. to shine, = col. chiò; to protect], according to.

chiàu-kò, to protect; to take care of; to take charge of. **chiàu-èng**, to assist and befriend. **chiàu-koán**, to take charge of, as a house. **chiàu-iāu**, to assist (as by influence) and make prosperous (v. iāu).

chiàu-kū, as formerly; as before. **chiàu-goân**, id. **chiàu-siông**, according to the usual manner.

chiàu-sit, to tell the truth. **chiàu-sit-kóng**, to speak truthfully. **lóng-bô chiàu-kóng**, not according to the truth. **chiàu-khí-kang**, according to what is right, orderly, or proper. **chiàu-kiâⁿ**, id. **chiàu-tsòe**, doing work diligently and well. **chiàu-iūⁿ**, according to the pattern. **chiàu-khoán**, id.

chiàu-ûn, in regular turn, as in play. **chiàu-pái**, in one's proper turn. **chiàu-lûn**, by turns; in regular and proper succession. **chiàu-lûn-liû**, id. **chiàu-oe**, id. **chiàu-pâi**, arranged in proper order. **chiàu-kah**, mixed in proper proportions, as good and bad cash. **chiàu-phòe**, in proper proportion. **chiàu-pun**, dividing equally among all; in equal parts. **chiàu-khui**, to divide into equal parts. **chiàu-thoa^n**, to divide expenses in fair proportions.

chiauh — **chiauh-khok-jí**, to toss up small rounded stones, as children in play. **chiauh jí-á**, id. **chiauh-kun**, id.

chiauh (C.), = A. chiáuh. **chiauh-chiauh-háu**, incessant talking, &c.

chiáuh (C. chiauh). **chiáuh-chiáuh-háu**, incessant talking; sound of mouth in eating. **chhùi-chiáuh-chiáuh-háu**, id.

chien [R. thick rice-gruel]. **tá^n-chien**, to take a meal (as a mandarin) at a road-side stage; said politely by inn-keepers to travellers.

chien [R. carpet; felt, = col. chi^n]. **mê^n-chien**, a sort of coarse hairy stuff. **tē-chien**, a carpet. **tōe-chien**, id. **jiông-chien**, a hairy rug. **téng-chien ē-jiòk**, soft mattresses and coverlets, above and below, as in bed of a rich man.

chien (R. id. = col. tsoa^n, chi^n), to fry with little fat; to melt (as silver) in purifying. **chien-iû**, to fry in little fat. **chien-khi-se**, fry till crisp. **chien-ké**, to fry steamed cakes. **chien-chhá**, to fry crisp by stirring constantly. **chien-tsoán**, to fry and then boil (v. tsoán).

chien-poâ^n, a flat frying-pan. **chien-sî**, a spoon for stirring things in frying. **chien-te**, sort of fried cake. **boán-chien**, sort of cake rolled up and fried. **koán-chien**, id. **koán-chien-ko**, id.

kheng-chien, to fuse and cast large quantities of (sycee) silver in pieces (phòng-sim) of ten taels each; formerly done in Amoy; not done now. **kheng-chien-hâng**, a sort of mint (licensed by the mandarins) for this work. **khui-kheng-chien**, to have such a mint; said of the company or firm that holds such a license. **lòh-chien**, to melt (as silver) in purifying.

chien [R. unlucky]. **tso-chien**, to meet with bad luck. **tun-chien** (R.), unlucky, as a man.

chien (R. id.), fine glossy paper in large sheets (of various colours), used for scrolls, &c. **chien-tsoá**, id. **chiang-chiu-chien**, do. from Chang-chew. **se-chien**, do. from Soo-chow. **lâh-chien**, a very smooth waxed sort of paper.

chiên [R. = col. chêng, before]. **chiông-chiên**, formerly. **gán-chiên**, at present. **hong-chiên-chiok** (candle before the wind), said of an old man's life. **ku-chiên-chhâu**, plantago (v. ku). **ú-chiên** (before the rain), a sort of tea (young Hyson ?).

chiên-têng, persons who have a degree, civil or military. **chiên-pòe**, persons one generation (or more) above us in the genealogical tree, as parents, uncles, and their cousins, &c. **chiên-hē** (r.), before and after. **chiên-iâ^n**, the van of the army (one of the five divisions); the commander of it. **chiên-thia^n**, his assistant.

chiên [R. a coin; money, = col. chî^n]. **chiên-kok su-iâ**, the mandarin's private secretary and adviser who attends to the land-tax and grain (v. kok). **iú-chiên--chiá seng, bû-chiên--chiá sú**, money decides life or death, said of bribes.

chién (R. id.) **chién-hêng**, to give a man a parting feast, before he makes a long journey, or goes abroad. **chién-hêng ê chiú-toh**, such a parting feast.

chién (C.), = A. chit. **chién--ê**, this; these. **put-chí chién--ê**, very —, said as an elliptical expression, when the speaker does not just know how to end the sentence, or wishes to suggest "very bad" or "very improper" without exactly saying so.

chién —. **chién-á**, the book-worm, that eats books and clothes. **chién-á-thâng**, id. **chién-tsoáh**, id.

chién (R. id.), to cut with shears or with a hinged knife; to buy, as cloth and medicines. **chién-jiông**, to buy stag's horn medicine; also, a sort of flower. **chién-iòh**, to buy a dose of medicine; to cut down medicinal plants small with a hinged knife. **chién-som**, to buy ginseng. **chién-pò**, to buy cotton cloth. **chién-nî^n**, to buy woollen cloth.

chién-liú, a pickpocket. **chién-chè**, to prepare medicinal plants by cutting and by fire.

ka-chién, scissors. **siù-chién**, small scissors used by dressmakers, sempstresses, &c. **chek-chién**, candle-snuffers. **gûn-chién**, strong shears for clipping silver. **iòh-chién**, a knife on a hinge for slicing medicines.

chièn [R. an arrow, = col. chì^n]. **jit-goát jû-so: kong-im sū-chièn**, days and months are like a shuttle; days and nights like an arrow.

chièn (R. id.), to recommend or introduce, as for a situation. **kú-chièn**, id. **chièn--lâng**, id. **ín-chièn**, id. **ngī^n-chièn**, to recommend very urgently for a situation, generally engaging to be security for him. **tit-thâu-chièn**, id.

bit-chièn, fruits preserved with sugar, &c., for idolatrous worship. **bit-chièn thn̂g-kó**, id. **ta-chièn**, dry sorts, wrapped in paper or put on a tray. **tâm-chièn**, preserves, jellies, &c. (same use), put on a frame or basket. **chièn-áp**, a few sweet things offered to idols (v. áp).

chièn [R. to fight; to shake and tremble]. **kau-chièn**, to fight in battle. **tá^n-chièn**, id. **cheng-chièn**, id. **chhut-chièn**, to go out to war or battle. **toā-chièn**, a great battle or series of battles. **tsúi-chièn**, a naval battle. **chièn-tsu**, a challenge to battle. **hā chièn-tsu**, to send a challenge. **thó-chièn**, to challenge to battle. **koat-sí-chièn**, to fight for life or death. **tsō-chièn**, to help in battle. **chièn-tīn**, to be engaged in battle, as armies.

chièn-kah, a coat of mail. **chièn-tsûn**, a ship of war. **hé-hun-chièn**, a war steamer. **chièn-kó**, a war-drum. **lûi chièn-kó**, to beat the war-drum. **chièn-bé**, a war-horse. **chièn-peng**, soldiers for battle, better than those for garrison. **chièn-hiòng**, this better class of soldiers, drawing more pay.

chièn-kioh, good at fighting, as a soldier; good at any work, as workman. **chièn-chiòng**, good at warfare, as a military officer; bold and skilful at managing any affair.

sim kia^n, tá^n chièn, very much terrified. **chhiú chièn** (R.), hand shaking.

chièn (R. id.), (C. tsàn). **chièn-pâng**, a storehouse; a godown. **chièn-pâng-sè**, rent or charges for use of storehouse or godown. **thiap chièn-pâng-sè**, to pay warehouse dues or charges. **tê-chièn**, a godown or storehouse for tea.

chiēn (R. id. = col. tsoā^n), mean; low and coarse; my (in some phrases) in polite expressions.

iàm-chiēn, to reject with disgust.

chiēn-bêng, my name. **chiēn-miâ^{n}**, id. **pi-chiēn**, in a low or humble position. **hā-chiēn**, mean, as employment or station. **pîn-chiēn**, very poor. **chit--ê chiēn-jîn**, what a low fellow! said in scolding an inferior for acting very improperly. **phoat-chiēn**, fond of scolding and quarrelling, said only of a woman. **chhàu-chiēn**, very mean and low, as character; very worthless, as a thing. **chhàu-chiēn-kut**, having a mean manner or appearance, as a rich man wearing mean clothes, or associating with low characters; also said of an over-humble manner, as of a man who will not accept our hospitality in full, *e.g.* sleeping on floor when asked to take a bed, or sitting on a stool instead of a chair. **chhàu-chiēn-siòng**, id. **chiēn-kut-siòng**, id.; also said of oneself (when reproving an idle inferior), "I go through hard work."

chiēn, to play as children, rather in a troublesome way. **chiēn-thâng** (troublesome insect!), said in scolding a child. **chiēn-chhiú**, over-playful and troublesome, restless and mischievous, as a child. **chiēn-kha chiēn-chhiú**, id. **kha-chhiú chiēn**, id.

chhiú chiēn, fond of pilfering small things, &c.

gâu-chiēn (C.), joking; practical jokes; mischievous. **bô-gâu-chiēn** (C.), this is a serious matter; this is no joke; dangerous or serious, as state of affairs.

chiet [R. a joint, a term, circumstances or items, chastity, moderation, = col. tsoeh, tsat.]

sù-sî pat-chiet, the four seasons and eight principal terms of the year.

chiet-tsàu, to memorialize or report to the emperor. **pháu-chiet**, to carry an express despatch from a high mandarin to the emperor.

koan-chiet, having secret underhand dealings with officials, so as to have one's matters settled. **thong koan-chiet**, id. **siáu-chiet-bòk**, unimportant, as of matters, money, &c. **chêng-chiet**, circumstances of a case. **liòk-chiet**, all the circumstances, particulars, or reasons of an affair, very minutely and plainly. **to-chi-chiet**, troublesome or confused with many details, as an affair; troublesome to deal with, as a man who is changing his mind or plans, or raising some new troublesome item. **kāu-chi-chiet**, id. **toá^{n}-toá^{n} chi-chiet**, id. **chi-chhi chiet-chiet**, id.

chiet-khiām, careful and economical. **bô-chiet-chè**, too free and lavish in the use of money (v. chè). **ū khì-chiet**, to have such self-respect or conscience, as not to meddle with shameful or improper matters. **liâm-chiet**, correct in behaviour, not covetous or improper. **tiong-hàu liâm-chiet**, faithful, filial, pure, and not covetous. **chiet-chhò** (R.), keeping one's character free from stain. **bêng-chiet**, good character. **pāi-bêng sit-chiet**, to ruin one's own character for ever, as by adultery, or some very great and shameful wickedness. **oân-bêng tsoân-chiet**, reputation perfectly good in life and death; esp. of a widow or a mandarin; said also of an affair managed well from first to last, and brought to a good termination.

cheng-chiet, pure and chaste, as a virgin, or as a widow refusing to marry again. **chiet-hàu**, do. and remarkably filial (v. hàu). **chiet-hng**, an archway in memory of such a lady. **chiet-hū**, a widow who never marries again. **chiú-chiet**, to remain always so. **chiet-lú**, a perpetual virgin, as on account of the death of her betrothed, or some other important reason. **chiet-hū liėt-lú**, constant widows and suicidal virgins. **chiet-liėt**, committing suicide for such a cause, as virgin or widow. **chīn-chiet**, to commit suicide, as a widow; or as a mandarin in the hands of enemies, &c. **kái-chiet**, to marry again, as a widow.

chiet [R. to break, to deduct], to reduce (as money) from one denomination to another; to take off discount; to make a composition for a debt, by money or goods; to contradict to one's face.

iáu-chiet, short-lived. **chiet-hok**, to diminish the fated portion of one's own good fortune; said of a man taking his full swing of the power, honour, or pleasure within his reach; or of a too fastidious man, refusing good common food; or of a careless thoughtless fellow, living above his income.

chiet--lâng, to contradict a man to his face. **tng-bīn chiet--lâng**, id. **kóng-ōe chiet--lâng**, id. **chiet lâng-ê-ōe**, id.

chhut-bí-chiet, to pay money in lieu of rations to solders. **chiong-mih^{n} chiet-gûn**, to compound for a debt by goods or articles valued at so much. **chiong-mih^{n} chiet-chî^{n}**, id.

chiet-khe-sia^{n}, to reduce to dollars (v. sia^{n}). **chiet-gûn**, to reduce to dollars or taels. **chiet-chî^{n}-sia^{n}**, to reduce from taels or dollars to cash. **chiet-chî^{n}**, id. **chiet phái^{n}-chî^{n}-tsúi**, to allow a due measure of discount when all the cash are good, because custom allows several bad cash in each hundred.

chhú-chiet, to pay only a percentage or composition. **chhí-chiet** (C.), id. **chhú-chiet hêng--i**, to make a composition for the debt. **kā--i chhú-chiet**, id. **hē--i chhú-chiet**, to accept a percentage as payment of the debt. **chhú-pat-chiet**, to pay 80 per cent.

thėh-chiet, to accept a percentage as payment. **liàh-chiet**, to take off discount, as on price of goods. **pat-chiet**, taking off or allowing 20 per cent. discount, or reckoning a composition at 80 per cent. (s. joint). **tsòe-pat-chiet-sǹg**, id. **tsòe-poeh-chiet-poà^{n}**, taking off 15 per cent. discount. **chiet-siàu**, to take a composition on a debt.

phah-chiet, to take off discount, as on price of goods, or as on a dollar that has some fault. **phah-chiet-thâu**, id. **bô-chiet-thâu**, an enormous discount taken off, *e.g.* about half the price on goods slightly damaged. **bōe--liáu, bô-chiet-thâu**, to sell at a great loss. **iáu-ū chiet-thâu**, the discount though large is not ruinous, causing little or no loss on the cost price.

thó-chiet, to collect or demand a percentage on a debt that cannot be paid in full. **thó kúi-chiet**, what percentage have you recovered? **thó ū-kúi-chiet**, id. **thó-poàn-chiet**, to get 50 per cent. **thó-chhit-chiet**, to get 70 per cent.

chiet, rancid; having a tainted smell. **bī chiet-chiet**, the smell is tainted or rancid. **chhàu-chiet**, having a tainted smell, as salted fish, &c. **chiet-bī**, id. **àu-chiet**, id.

chiet — **bòk-chiet** (T.), a shell-fish like the "thē-poe," but larger.

chiet (R. id.) **chiet-kang**, Chekiang province. **bân-chiet**, the two provinces of Fuh-kien and Chekiang.

chiėt [R. quick]. **liáu-chiėt**, quick, as at seeing what course is best in the case; good at determining and acting with decision; ready at understanding when the case is hopeless, accepting the situation and making the best of it. **kín-chiėt**, quick in general. **bín-chiėt**, clever, talented, skilful, or energetic.

liên-chiėt, passing rapidly up from one honour or office to another in succession. **kán-chiėt**, abridged, for clearness or brevity; in summary.

chiét [R. to cut off, to obstruct, = col. tsàh, tsòeh]. **chiét-tō chhiú^n^-kiap**, highway robbery. **chiét-tiông pó-toán** (to cut the long to mend the short), to make up what is deficient in one by what is over in another, *e.g.* to excuse a man's faults for his other excellencies. **chiét-chí**, to terminate, as a stated payment at a fixed date. **chiét lâng-ê-ōe**, to interrupt a man when speaking (v. ōe). **poàn-chiét-bėh**, stockings of two colours or stuffs joined in middle. **poàn-chiét-i**, a dress of which the body and skirt are of different stuffs. **poàn-chiét-tó**, half wood and half plastered (above and below), as a partition; half wood and half glass, as a door.

bát-chiét, securely closed; closely shut up, so that one cannot see in or steal.

chih (R. chiap), to receive, esp. with ceremony. **chih--lâi**, id. **chih-chiap**, to receive, as a friend or customer (v. chiap). **ngiâ-chih**, to go out and receive, as a friend or visitor. **tán-chih**, to go out and wait for (v. tán). **chih lâng-kheh**, to receive visitors or guests. **chih-sîn**, to receive the spirits when they come down again on 1.4. **chih-pùt**, to receive (with offerings, &c.) an idol carried in procession. **chih-pán**, to receive the coffin into the house. **chih hoán-tsú**, to receive the tablet after the burial. **chih-chiàu**, to kneel and receive the imperial commands.

chih-tsài-bōe-tiâu, too heavy to bear, as a load or a disease. **chih-koa^n^-têng**, sheds for mandarins resting on journeys.

chih — **chih-tsuh**, mischievous, properly said only of children.

chih (R. chiap? liap?), to fold; to turn down, as a leaf. **chih-kim**, to fold idolatrous imitation gold paper. **chih-tsoá**, to fold paper. **chih-sa^n^**, to fold clothes. **chih-hûn**, a crease; a mark left by folding.

chhiú-chih, a small memorandum-book for the pocket, folded back and forwards. **chhiú-chih-á**, id. **khioh-chih**, made to fold in alternate folds, as a bamboo sail. **chhia chit-chih**, take out one reef of such a folding-sail.

chih (Cn.), **chih--gê**, = chit-ê, this.

chih (R. siét), the tongue. **chih-ē**, the part of the mouth below the tongue. **chih-thâu**, the root of the tongue; the tongue. **chih-thâu ngī^n^**, thick indistinct speaking. **chih-bé**, the point of the tongue. **tioh chih-bé**, to lisp and speak somewhat indistinctly. **tiuh chih-bé**, id. **tiuh chih-kun**, to speak very indistinctly, having great difficulty in getting out the words, the initial consonant being indistinct or wanting altogether. **tioh chih-kun**, id. **chih-kun té** (string of tongue short), said of man about to die. **kóng-ōe, té-chih-kun**, stuttering or stammering. **liàh lâng--ê chih-kun**, to catch peoples' meaning from casual hints in their talk, as fortune-tellers, &c. **oàn-kúi thiu-chih-kun**, said of a man unexpectedly manifesting his own guilt before a mandarin. **têng-chih**, stuttering or stammering. **toā-chih-káu**, speaking with difficulty and indistinctness, as from a large tongue, or in great sickness. **toā-chih-kiet**, id.

chih-á, the uvula. **hé-chih**, a tongue of flame. **niau^n^-chih**, a cat's tongue; a sort of edible fish. **hó-chih-lòe**, a coarse file (lit. tiger's tongue). **hó-chih-tauh**, the self-acting bolt of a latch or lock, such that a key is needed to open it. **koe-chih-táu**, projections below the ends of beams in roof of a Chinese house (lit. fowl's tongue). **ke-chih-á** (C.), a sort of spear with a straight flat blade.

thó-chih, to protrude the tongue. **tsoâ thó-chih**, self-acting bolt of a lock; also, the end of a beam projecting through a wooden pillar; also, the sloping pavement at the gate of a yamun. **nà^n^-chih**, to put out the tongue for a moment, as in wonder or fear. **koah-chih**, to cut out the tongue in punishment; also, an enchanter's trick.

gâu-tńg chih-koan, good at putting the best face on a story, or a new face on an argument, when pressed hard, without any regard to truth. **goá kā--lí liàm-chih**, I will pull out your tongue (said to children, &c., when talking improperly). **m̄-kia^n^--i liàm-chih**, I am not afraid of his finding fault with what I say. **bô-lâng-tī^n^ goá-ê-chih**, there is no one who can keep me silent.

chhùi-chih, the mouth and tongue. **ū-chhùi-chih**, good at making polite talk, as with visitors, &c. **ìn-chhùi ìn-chih**, always taking the last word. **òh-chhùi òh-chih**, to repeat a man's words in his presence in a mocking way; to repeat to a man what has been said against him behind his back. **boâ-chhùi boâ-chih**, to talk a great deal to no purpose. **chhùi chiam, chih lāi**, too fond of talking, often so as to give offence without meaning it. **chhùi ti^n^, chih kùt**, words soft and deceitful. **chhit-chhùi poeh-chih**, equivocating and lying. **lún-chhùi khiū^n^-chih**, to restrain one's appetite or one's anger so as to keep silent. **khang-chhùi pē-chih** (chewing one's tongue in an empty mouth), to make false, deceitful promises. **chit-chhùi thoân-chit-chih**, to pass from mouth to mouth, as a report. **chhùi kap-chih ū-sî sa^n^-khàp** (or "sa^n^-gāi"), even friends and relatives sometimes quarrel.

chih (R. chiet), to break. **at-chih**, to break, as a stick, &c. **chih-lī-lī**, broken quite asunder. **chih-hûn**, mark of a fracture, esp. after it is mended. **chih-thâu**, broken at the head (s. tongue). **chih-bé**, broken at the point or tail (s. tongue). **phī^n^-oa^n^ chih**, nose naturally too flat between the eyes (v. phī^n^). **phah-chih lâng--ê ké-pì^n^**, to cut short a man's talk so that he does not gain his end. **kut chih, bah lih**, flesh and bones broken. **kha khê, chhiú chih**, foot distorted and arm broken.

tsoān--chih, to break by twisting, *e.g.* a key in a lock. **tsàm--chih**, to break by stamping on. **tsām--chih**, to sever by one blow of a chisel. **tsām chih**, the chisel is broken. **kng--chih**, to break (as a pole) by too heavy a weight in the middle. **tàng--chih**, to pinch off, as a flower. **hiàp--chih**, to break by bending back and forwards, as a nail. **khàp--chih**, to break by accidentally running against. **khò--chih**, to break by accidentally pressing upon. **chē--chih**, do. by sitting on. **teh--chih**, do. by falling on. **ûn--chih**, do. by coming against.

chim [R. to pour out gently, careful], to kiss. **sa^n^-chim**, to kiss. **kha sa^n^-chim**, toes turned inwards in walking. **chim i-ê-kha**, to kiss his feet. **chim-chhùi**, to kiss the lips. **chim chhùi-tûn**, id. **chim chhùi-phóe**, to kiss the cheek.

chim chit-tiám-á, to taste a very little, as wine (cf. "lim" and "chip").

chim-chiok, to consider carefully; to be cautious, as in examining well before acting.

chim [R. moral maxims], (C. tsom). **chim-giên** (R.), moral maxims; (X.) the book of Proverbs. **siú koan-chim** (R.), following the proper rules of mandarin action. **i--ê koan-chim hó**, his conduct as a mandarin is good.

chîm [R. sîm, to search], C. = A. jîm, to feel in one's pocket for a thing.

chîm (R. sîm), a crab. **se-khak-chîm**, a good firm, full crab. **chîm-jîn**, eggs or roe in the crab. **chîm-ko**, soft yellowish meat in male crab. **chîm-m̂**, the round excrescence on belly of female crab. **chîm-kóng**, crab's pincers. **chîm-kóng-bah**, the large thick muscle between a man's thumb and finger, said to be wanting in men who have a tendency to leprosy. **chîm-kóng-ngéh**, surrounding an enemy by two troops meeting.

pàng-chîm, to put out wicker-work baskets to catch crabs. **chîm-hé**, a sort of fish that feeds on crabs.

chím [R. a pillow], (Cn. chiám).

āu-chím, the projecting part of the back of the head just where the neck joins. **thâu-khak-chím**, id. **chím-thâu-kut**, the bone at that place. **chím-kut**, id. **thâu-āu-chím** (Cn.), that part of the head. **chím-tsu**, a large boil or carbuncle on back of neck. **chím-āu-eng** (C.), id. **ut-chím**, neck stiff and sore from sleeping in a constrained position.

khò-chím, the cushioned back of a ceremonial couch (slightly raised) for resting the elbow. **tîn-chím**, a rattan pillow. **oan-iu^n-chím**, a pair of pillows given to a young couple, as symbol of love (v. iu^n).

chím-thâu, a pillow. **chím-thâu-siu^n**, a long narrow box made to be used as a pillow, and for holding valuables. **chím-thâu-tē**, a pillow-case (foreign). **chím-thâu-thò**, do. without ends. **chím-thò**, id.

chím (R. id.), (C. sím), wife of father's younger brother; title of elderly women. **á-chím**, do. in addressing her. **m̂ chím**, aunts-in-law, in general.

sió-chím, wife of younger brother, when said of a man; wife of husband's younger brother, when said of a woman. **chím-pô**, wife of paternal grandfather's younger brother; form of addressing an old woman.

chìm (R. id.), to soak, to steep, to soak in. **chìm-khi-thàu**, soak it thoroughly. **chìm-tsúi**, to soak in water. **chìm-tsúi-chhâ**, wood that is water-logged or saturated with water. **chìm-chiú**, to soak in liquor, as medicine. **chìm-mih^n ê-chiú**, liquor in which things have been steeped to improve the flavour. **chìm tê-á-iû**, to steep fragrant things in camellia oil to make hair-oil. **chìm thn̂g-sng**, to dissolve sugar-candy in water.

chìm-tsù, quite soaked, as a field with constant rains. **chìm-tâm**, soaked by being steeped. **chìm--sí**, to be drowned.

chìm-lé (X.), baptism by immersion (lit. by soaking). **chìm-lé-kàu** (X.) the Baptist church or system.

chìm-khī, the yellow persimmon.

chìm— **tsúi-chìm** (T.), name of a bird = "tsúi-khām-chhe^n," or "hî-chhiok."

chīm (T.), = A. jīm, in the names of many places, *e.g.* "chióh-chīm."

chin [R. tin, precious]. **chin-tsu**, a pearl.

chin (R. id.), real; correct; really true; very —. **chin-sit**, true. **chin-chià^n**, really, truly. **chin bô-ióh**, certainly there is no resource. **chin-sim**, a true heart. **chin-ké**, real and counterfeit (v. ké). **chin-sí**, really dead.

tàng-chin, certainly. **téng-chin**, of first-rate excellence (as things); very strict, as a master (or man with whom we have dealings) who will not let faults pass. **têng-chin**, to write out the fair copy from a scroll. **kó-chin** (r.), certainly. **jīn-chin**, diligent in one's duty and proper work. **ū kì^n-chin ê-sé-tsāi**, sufficient proof of the truth can be given. **khêng-chin**, to examine into the real facts, as of a rumour (v. khêng). **thia^n-bô-chin**, to make a mistake in hearing. **lí tióh-thia^n-khi-chin**, take care that you hear exactly.

chin-hó, very good.

goá chin-á m̄-tsai, really I do not know. **goá chin-tiu^n m̄-tsai**, id. **bô-chin-tiu^n**, not certainly. **bô-chin-tiu^n beh-khì**, he does not seem to intend to go. **kì^n-chin-tiu^n**, when it comes to the reality (not mere talk). **kì^n-chin-tiu^n, chiū m̄-ká^n**, when it comes to the reality, then he dares not. **chin-kim put-phà^n-hé**, real gold does not fear the fire. **hè chin, kè sit**, the articles are good and the price fixed.

chin chhó, thoàn lē, four sorts of Chinese characters.

kàng-chin, incense used in the worship of "thi^n-kong." **kàng-chin-hiu^n**, id.

chin-bú tè-kun, name of an idol, = hiên-thien siōng-tè. **sun-chin-jîn**, a Tauist priest of the surname "sun," deified as god of medicine. **tiu^n-chin-jîn**, another idol. **tiu^n-chin-kun**, id. **khé-chin-jîn**, another idol of surname "khé." **gê-chin-jîn**, another (v. gê).

chin [R. seng, to ascend; a measure], a small measure, $\frac{1}{10}$ of a "táu;" sometimes called a pint or a catty, but not exactly. **bí-chin**, a small rice-measure. **chit-chin-bí**, one "chin" of rice.

tsúi-chin, a dipper for a bath, for lading out water, made with one straight handle.

chin [R. a ferry; to moisten]. **thien-chin**, the city Tien-tsin (Cn. thien-tin). **bô-chin-ėk**, wanting moisture in mouth and throat (v. ėk).

chin— **koa^n-chin**, a large reed used in making partitions, &c. (v. koa^n).

chin— **chhi^n-chin**, a sudden start or impulse; acting in a sudden impulsive way.

chin— **tsúi chin, hî-hiān**, when the water is clear the fish appear (better "chheng"); innocence will come clear at last.

chîn (C.), = A. cheng. **kut-chin-hóe**, a sort of disease; v. cheng.

chîn (R. sêng); a line for use in building, &c., for making a straight line; a plummet or chalk-line, &c. **chîn-soh**, id. **chîn-soà^n**, id. **hún-chîn**, a chalk-line, used by tailors, &c. **bák-thâu-chîn**, a line used with a black powder; an ink line.

khan-chîn, to stretch a line, as a building-line or ink-line, &c. **toā^n-chîn**, to touch the stretched line with the finger, so as to make the mark. **tūi-chîn**, to apply the plumb-line, making it hang down. **tùi-chîn**, made according to the prescribed rule or proper pattern. **ōe-tùi-chîn**, sure to succeed, as a request, &c.

tsún-chîn, a pattern or rule (fig.) **ū-tsún-chîn**, accurate, as instrument or workman; truthful or correct, as conduct. **bák-chiu ū-tsún-chîn**, able to measure at a glance, or to touch any point one may wish.

chîn (R. id.), the state of Tsin, at the N.W. of the empire, one of the greatest states of the Chow dynasty; the dynasty that overthrew the Chow; a surname; to be carefully distinguished from "chìn."

chîn-tiâu, the Tsin dynasty, between the Chow (chiu) and the Hàn. **chîn-sí-ông**, the tyrant who overthrew the Chow dynasty, changed the feudal empire into a centralized empire, and built the great wall.

chín (R. thién). **pō-chín thien-bùt**, to use things wastefully, = pe-chéng thien-bùt.

chín (R. id.) **chín-chè**, to assist by alms.

chîn (R. id.) **chîn-kiù** (R.), to deliver. **chîn-khí** (R.), to bring into prosperity (as a god); to become prosperous and flourishing.

chìn (R. id.), a state of the Chow dynasty, not nearly so famous as "chîn," from which it is to be carefully distinguished; a dynasty.

chìn-tiâu, the Chin or Tsin dynasty, divided into the Eastern and Western Tsin, A.D. 265–419.

chìn-kang, the district (Hien) in which Chin-chew city (tsoân-chiu-hú) stands. **chìn-kang-koāi**^{n}, id. **chìn-kang-lí**, said of a very stingy miserly man.

chìn (R. id.), one of the eight diagrams. **chìn-koà**, id.

chìn (C.), = A. chèng, witness.

chìn [R. to enter]; to advance (lit. or fig.); to pay (as tribute); to offer (as ceremonial offerings); to become a graduate.

chìn-chêng, to advance; formerly. **sái-bōe-chìn**, to make no progress in sailing, as from contrary tide. **chiām-chìn**, to make gradual progress. **chìn-pō͘**, to make progress, as in learning or excellence. **chìn-tek**, to make progress in learning. **chìn-iah**, to advance in wealth, &c. **chìn-ek**, to make progress in literary excellence. **thiam-teng chìn-tsâi**, get more sons and more wealth. **chìn-chí**^{n} (Cn.), a bird like a small magpie (= tsúi-khām-chhɛ̂^{n}), supposed to be an omen of increasing wealth.

chióng-chìn, to grow rich, from a state of poverty, by one's own exertions. **put-chióng-chìn**, idle and ill-behaved, without sense of shame, so as to be of no use in the world; said especially of the unworthy descendants of diligent and honoured parents. **put-chióng-chìn-hàn**, id.

āu-chìn, the back part of a house; posterity, esp. good. **phái**^{n}**-āu-chìn**, bad descendants. **hó-chìn**, posterity who are a credit to their parents or ancestors.

chìn-tsòe, to marry a wife and stay for a time in her father's house. **chìn-pâng**, to enter the bridal chamber, as the bride does about the beginning of the marriage rites at the husband's house.

chìn-kòng, to pay tribute. **chìn-chiok**, to obtain a higher grade of nobility; to present a cup in worshipping the spirits. **chìn-chiú**, to bring forward wine in worship. **chìn-siēn**, to bring forward offerings of rice, &c., for the spirits. **chìn-hiu**^{n}, to bring the incense-stick to the principal worshipper, that he may present it in worship; to bring incense from a more sacred temple. **chìn-tsú**, to introduce an ancestral tablet into the ancestral hall. **chìn-tsòng**, to place the coffin in the grave.

ín-chìn, to introduce; to recommend, as a person or a friend, as for employment. **ín-chìn thâu-lō͘**, to get a situation for another.

chìn-sū, a graduate of the third degree; a Tsin-sze (v. sū). **chìn-tiòng**, to get a degree, in general. **chìn-òh**, to become a Sew-tsae (siù-tsâi). **chìn-bûn-òh**, to become a literary Sew-tsai. **chìn-bú-òh**, to become a military Sew-tsai. **pī-chìn** (lit. ready for entering), candidates for the Sew-tsae degree whose essays are good enough, but who fail to get the degree because the legal number is made up; they are expected to graduate next year.

chìn-thè, to advance and to retire. **chìn-chìn thè-thè**, hesitating in manner. **chìn-put-chìn, thè-put-thè**, in a very troublesome dilemma. **chìn-thè lióng-lân**, id. **chìn-thòe lióng-lân**, id. **tsai-chìn-thòe**, knowing what should be done or not done in given circumstances. **chìn-chêng thè-āu**, to go forward or draw back, as troops, or as a party in a quarrel. **chìn-m̄-chìn, thè-m̄-thè**, very irresolute in purpose; will not choose either way. **lát-hí hó-chìn, m̄-chìn; bé-ka hó-thè, m̄-thè**, the "lát" could easily push on through the net, as its head is large; the "bé-ka" could draw back, as its head is small: but each tries the opposite, and is caught; said of a man in trouble doing just the worst thing he could.

chīn (R. id.), to complete; to exhaust; exceedingly; to the utmost.

tsū-chīn, to commit suicide. **chīn-chiet**, to commit suicide, as a widow; or as a mandarin fallen among enemies. **siū-sè kai-chīn**, the fated time having come, one must die.

chīn-thâu, to the very end; to the utmost. **chīn-bé**, the very end. **chīn-tsâi**, exceedingly. **chīn-hó**, exceedingly good. **chīn-chit**, to fulfil all the duties of one's office. **chīn-tiong**, thoroughly faithful. **chīn-sim**, with all the heart. **chīn-lát**, with all the strength. **hùi-chīn sim-lát**, to exert one's self very much, as in managing an affair. **chīn-chêng**, to exert one's self to the utmost for another.

chīn-hoat-pān, to examine into and punish a crime with the full rigour of law. **siū-chīn hong-song**, much exposed to wind and frost, as travellers. **chīn-hong sái**, to sail as near the wind as is possible with full sails. **chīn-phâng sái**, id.; said also of exerting one's influence to the very utmost. **m̄-thang chīn-liōng**, do not use your influence, &c., to the very utmost. **chīn-liāng-kú** (C.), very very long time. **chīn-kun**, leaving no power of redemption, as in sale of property.

liáu-chīn, all expended. **bô-liáu bô-chīn**, endless; inexhaustible. **bōe-chīn**, boundless. **kóng-bōe-chīn**, subject inexhaustible. **kám-un put-chīn**, thanks boundless. **bô-kiông-chīn**, without limit or end. **bû-kiông-chīn**, id. **bû-kiông bû-chīn**, id. **tsâi kiông, lèk chīn**, strength and resources all spent.

chio [R. chiau, plantain, arum, &c.] **gêng-chio**, the plantain; the banana. **keng-chio**, id. **gê-chio** (C.), id. **chit-ki gêng-chio**, a whole stalk of plantains; the whole produce of one plant. **chit-pî gêng-chio**, one whole bunch making a complete circle round the stem, which is cut across. **chit-ê gêng-chio**, one single fruit of plantain. **chit-tiâu gêng-chio**, id. **chit-tsâng gêng-chio**, one plant of plantain.

pa-chio, a tree like plantain with a large leaf (v. pa). **bí-jîn-chio**, a sort of red arum. **ún-tsúi-chio**, a medical plant (sort of arum?). **ín-tsúi-chio**, id. **chio-hióh**, leaf of plantain or arum.

chio-koah, a very strong yellowish stuff (colour of plantain), made of cotton and coarse silk mixed; it is hard, rough, and absorbs perspiration, so as to be cool though thick. **chio-á-pè**, id. **chio-á-sa**^{n}, dress made of it. **chio-sa**^{n}, id. **chio--ê**, made of this stuff.

chio (R. chiau). **hô͘-chio**, pepper. **hô͘-chio-kóng**, a pepper-box. **hô͘-chio-hoe**, a pattern like small flowers, cut on wood-work, or printed on foreign calico. **chio-liāu**, spices for cooking. **hoa-chio**, a sort of white pepper. **hoe-chio**, id.

chio (R. chiau), to invite; to call; to beckon; to enlist, as soldiers; to call in, as confederates or converts; a written confession of guilt; a beacon set on a rock or bank; to get a son-in-law who adopts the surname of the family he marries into.

chio-bē, to enlist (soldiers). **chio gī-bîn**, to enlist volunteers or militia. **chio-ióng**, id. **chio-kun bóe-bé** (enlist an army and buy horses), said in scolding children for making noisy play with companions.

chio-hē, to propose a sort of subscription club for mutual help. **chio gâu-lâng**, to invite wise men to take office or employment.

chio kiáⁿ-sài, to take a man into the family as son-in-law, so that he changes his surname. **hē-lâng-chio**, to marry thus, taking the surname of the bride, and becoming a member of their family. **chio-hu ióng-tsú**, to get a second husband that he may take care of the children.

chio sió-tī, to invite a younger brother to be born, as the elder children are supposed to do. **chio-hûn**, to invite the soul of the dead (shortly after death), as is always done. **chhit-jit chio-hûn**, to do so on the seventh day after death.

chio-ín, to invite, as to do something. **chio-chip**, to call together, as for some enterprise. **saⁿ-chio-io**, to lead one another to do anything (v. io). **khah-kōe-chio**, readily going along with others when asked (good or bad). **chio-hø**, to talk in a polite and hospitable manner to visitors or customers. **chio-kheh**, to invite customers by polite talk. **chio-bóe chio-bōe**, to invite to buy and sell. **chio-pâi**, a sign-board with characters or emblems.

ūi-chio, to sign a confession, as of a capital crime.

chhah-chio, to set up a beacon, *e.g.* a branch stuck on a sand-bank.

chió (R. siáu), few; to diminish or take fewer. **tsōe-chió**, many or few; much or little, in quantity; number or quantity, in the abstract; more or less; how many, or how much. **m̄-tsai tsōe-chío**, don't know how many or how much. **chió-lâng-chiáh**, few people eat it. **chió-kheh**, very abundant; very numerous; sometimes said somewhat ironically. **chió-khoeh** (C.), id. **té-chió**, deficient; not enough. **chió-chhùi-chih**, a man of few words.

kiám-chió, to diminish; to make fewer or less. **chió joā-tsōe**, how much less? how many fewer? how many are wanting? **chió chit-ê**, one fewer; there wants one. **chió chit-ē**, one blow fewer. **beh-chió lâng-chîⁿ**, wishing to pay people less than was promised, or than ought to be paid. **bōe-chió--tit**, cannot be made less; no reduction can be made. **kam-goān chió-théh**, willing to take less, *e.g.* a composition on a debt.

chió (Cn.), in some phrases = tsáu, to walk: better tsió, *q.v.*

chiò (R. chiàu), to shine; to illuminate; to see or make a reflection, or image, or shadow; to be opposite (as wall, &c.); a passport, clearance, or diploma.

chiò-bīn, to look in a mirror; to illuminate the face. **chiò-kiàⁿ**, to look in a mirror. **chiò chhien-lí-kiàⁿ**, to look with a telescope. **chiò hàm-kiàⁿ**, to look with a microscope. **chiò-kìⁿ**, to look carefully at a thing, as by the light of a lamp, or as in a mirror. **chiò-kìⁿ lâng-iáⁿ**, to see a man's shadow cast by a lamp. **chiò-lâng-iáⁿ**, to reflect a man's figure in water; to cast a man's shadow, as a lamp. **chiò-lâng-ńg**, id. **chiò-tsúi-iáⁿ**, to reflect (as one's self) in the water. **jit chiò-iáⁿ**, the sun casts a shadow, of anything. **chiò-jī-ńg**, to cast the shadow of a word (on a rock, &c.), so as to trace its outline for cutting. **chiò-hé-iáⁿ**, id.; also to use for our own use the light from a neighbour's lamp. **chiò-hé**, to illuminate, as by lamp or candle. **chiò-hóe** (C.), = A. chioh-hé, to warm one's self at a fire. **chiò-kng**, to shine; to reflect light. **jit chiò**, the sun shines on —. **chiò-jit**, to be illuminated by the sun, as a mirror or the surface of water. **sai-chiò-jit**, illuminated by the light of the western sun, as a room.

bák-bé chiò--chit-ē, **chiū-tsai**, to understand by a single side glance.

chiò-chhiûⁿ, the "reflecting wall" placed right opposite the chief gate of a temple or yamun (v. chhiûⁿ). **tùi-chiò**, to be right opposite as such a wall, or as one house opposite another, or as the spider called "bái-kúi," that causes a sort of nightmare(!). **khit-i-chiò**, to be so affected by that spider. **tò-chiò**, to reflect light; said of a house on opposite side of a court. **ē-chiò**, to be right opposite, but on a lower level, as a building.

koan-chiò, to have reference to, as one passage of a book to another, &c.

chip-chiò, a passport; a license for trade; a diploma of purchased rank issued by local mandarins. **pē-chiò**, a diploma of purchased rank issued by the Board of Office. **kip-chiò**, a diploma of purchased rank; a certificate or deed for public ground sold by mandarins; and such like documents; to give a clearance to a ship or a license to a man. **kiáu-chiò**, to give in the ship's papers on arrival. **tsûn-chiò**, a port clearance. **niáⁿ tsûn-chiò**, to get the clearance, before leaving harbour. **pâi-chiò**, the papers of a vessel, the register and the clearance; smaller local junks need only the clearance (chiò), without the "pâi."

chiò (R. chiàu), Tauist rites of thanksgiving to obtain good fortune or avert calamity. **sam-tiau-chiò**, these rites celebrated for three days. **tsòe-chiò**, to perform such rites. **tsòe-chheng-chiò**, to fast and have these rites. **tsòe-hō-chiò**, to have them as thanksgiving for rain. **hó-chiò**, rites to keep away tigers, or in expiation for having killed a tiger, to appease the spirit of the tiger. **tsòe-hó-chiò**, to do so. **tsúi-chiò**, rites performed on the water to appease the spirits of drowned men. **hé-chiò**, rites after a destructive fire, to ward off fires. **pêng-an-chiò**, rites to ward off calamity and get prosperity. **thiⁿ-kong-chiò**, such rites in honour of Yuh-hwang Shang-ti.

phah-chiò, to have these rites (as sailors do) in a temple on shore specially engaged for the purpose, to which the idol from their junk is carried for the time.

chiò-toâⁿ, a room or gallery for a shrine made across a street (raised above a man's height) for these rites. **kè-chiò-toâⁿ**, to be consecrated in such a shrine, as an amulet. **chiò-pńg**, a bill put out by the Tauist priests stating when the rites are to be held; it is beautifully written like printing, contains the names and subscriptions of the principal subscribers, and is burned as an intimation to the spirits after men have seen it long enough.

chiō (R. chiāu), (C.), to chew the cud. **hoán-chiō**, id.

chioⁿ, in all the tones; (P.), = A. chiuⁿ.

chioh (R. chià), to borrow; to lend; to take lodgings; (politely used in asking).

chioh-ēng, to borrow for use; to use in a figurative or metaphorical sense.

chioh-kè, please let me pass. **saⁿ-chioh-mn̄g**, to ask polite questions, as on meeting.

chioh-khiā, to take lodgings, or ask permission to stay a short time. **chioh-toà**, id.

chioh-toaⁿ, a promissory note. **thai-chioh-jī**, a

厦英大辭典

deed assigning a vessel or some property as security for a loan (v. thai).

hē-lâng-chioh, to lend to people. **chioh--lâng**, id. **chioh--i**, lend to him. **chioh--khì**, to lend.

kā-lâng-chioh, to borrow from people. **chioh--lâi**, id. **la-chioh**, id. (v. la). **chioh-chè**, id. (v. chè). **chioh-pún**, to borrow capital.

seng-chioh, to get money in advance; to advance money. **saiⁿ-chioh** (T.), id. **sia-chioh**, to buy on credit and to borrow money. **sia-chioh bién-giên**, no credit given here. **î-chioh bién-giên**, id. **î-chioh**, to borrow. **oaiⁿ-chioh**, to be constantly borrowing money before paying what is due, or asking help (under the name of borrowing) from friends who have money.

chioh-to sat-jîn (to kill with a borrowed sword), to use a third party to do an injury.

chioh, to cut down (as small trees).

chioh (R. chek). **mîⁿ-chioh**, a cotton quilted coverlet in a net-work of cross-threads. **phah mîⁿ-chioh**, to make such a coverlet.

chioh — **nāⁿ--chioh** (T. Cn.), to stay over a night.

chioh (R. sek), (C. chiò). **chioh-sio**, to warm one's self, as at a fire. **chioh-hé**, to warm one's self at the fire; to warm a thing slightly at the fire. **chioh hé-thang**, to warm one's self with a portable basket-stove. **chioh-jit**, to warm one's self in the sun. **lòh-sng, ū-jit-chioh: ə-koâⁿ, sí-bô-iòh**, in frost one has the sun to warm himself, but cold wet weather is deadly without remedy.

chioh — **ng-chioh** (Cn.), a seed-bed for young rice.

chioh (= chhioh), (P. chiah). **kha-chioh-tóe**, the sole of the foot. **kha-chioh-té** (C.), id.

chioh — **tóe-chioh**, the foundation, as of an affair; the original history, as of a house, &c.; *e.g.* to whom it originally belonged, how bought, &c.; the good-luck of a house, others having had good health or prosperity in it; the good-luck of a shop, as to its position or good name, &c. **ū-tóe-chioh**, to have some property; to be in good health; safe and good, as title-deeds or a business or a property. **hó-tóe-chioh**, id. **phah--khì hó-tóe-chioh**, to make good arrangements or good rules from the beginning, so that all goes on well afterwards.

chioh — **lôe-chioh**, the lower horizontal part of a plough, on the end of which the share is fixed. **lê-chioh** (C.), id. **lê-āu-chioh** (C.), id. **thoa-chioh** (C.), id.

chioh (P.), = A. C. chek, younger uncle. **saⁿ-chioh**, third brother of father, younger than he; (but "saⁿ-chioh" (A.), to lend or borrow, becomes "sio-chioh").

chiòh (R. sék), a stone; a rock; granite; a surname; a measure, = ten "táu."

chiòh-tsām, a chisel for cutting stone. **khui-chiòh**, to quarry rocks. **phah-chiòh**, to work stone in any way. **chiòh-kang**, stone-cutters. **phah-chiòh sai-hū**, a stone-cutter. **phah-chiòh-sai**, do. **phah-chiòh-sai**, to make a stone lion. **chiòh-sai**, a stone lion.

chiòh-khang, a hole in or among rocks. **chiòh-tsoâⁿ**, a fountain among rocks. **chiòh-tāng**, stone ballast. **chiòh-ki**, a stone foundation. **chiòh-pâi**, a small stone tablet, as at a grave. **chiòh-pi**, a large stone tablet, as with a long inscription. **chiòh-kài**, a boundary-stone. **chiòh-tsu**, stone base of pillar. **chiòh-gîm**, a long stone step round a house. **chiòh-hák**, a stone vault. **chiòh-hàk**, a medicine (v. hák).

chiòh-iù, dust and very small chips from stone-cutting. **chiòh-phè**, chips of stone. **chiòh-kak**, large broken pieces of stone. **chiòh-thâu**, a stone; a rock of a massive or rounded form. **chiòh-poâⁿ**, a large flat rock. **chiòh-phê**, a large low flat rock. **chiòh-pē** (C.), a large stone or piece of rock (v. pə). **chiòh-sún**, a tall pillar-shaped rock. **chiòh-sún**, a stone tenon. **chiòh-n̄g**, pebbles or stones worn round by water. **toā-liáp chiòh-n̄g**, large water-worn stones used in rough form for seats. **chiòh-lan**, a hard knot or nodule in a stone or rock. **chiòh-tún**, a short cylindrical stone (v. tún). **chiòh-lún**, a stone roller.

to-chiòh, a whet-stone or grindstone. **boâ-chiòh**, id. **pó-chiòh**, a gem, a jewel, a precious stone. **pó-chiòh-lâm**, a very fine rich blue; ultramarine. **chhiⁿ-táu-chiòh**, green granite. **chiòh-chhiⁿ-sek**, dull-green, like the Amoy green granite. **hé-chiòh**, flint. **he-chiòh**, lime-stone, **chiòh-he**, lime made from lime-stone. **hip-chiòh**, the load-stone. **gûn-chiòh**, a touch-stone for rubbing silver on. **sìn-chiòh**, arsenic. **siàh-chiòh**, marble. **hún-chiòh**, a stone from which face-powder is made.

chiòh-liú, a yellow wood for furniture. **chiòh-tek**, a thin hard bamboo with short joints. **chiòh-ko**, a cooling medicine. **chiòh-hoe**, a sea plant from which a cooling gelatinous drink is made. **chiòh-kàng**, a large sort of frog. **chiòh-soeh**, a small green crab that creeps into crevices.

chiok (R. id.), (C. chiak). **chiok-iòk**, a sort of peony. **chhiah-chiok**, the red peony (used medicinally). **pėh-chiok**, white peony. **pėk-chiok**, id. **hâng-chiok**, peony from Hang-chow, counted very good. **kui-kiong chiok-tē**, the four medicines called "sù-bu̍t."

chiok [R. a candle, = col. chek], also (P.), = chek, a candle. **hong-chiên-chiok**, a candle before the wind, said of the uncertainty of an old man's life. **hiong-hoa teng-chiok**, incense, flowers, lamps, and candles, in honour of idols.

chiok (P.), = chek, a younger uncle, &c.

chiok [R. a foot, enough], enough; full measure, or a little more.

chiok-kièn, evidence enough that —.

chiok-giàh, enough. **tsáp-chiok**, quite sufficient; complete. **chhiong-chiok**, abundant; having abundance. **hiet-khì chiok**, having a full-blooded constitution.

tsū-chiok, self-sufficient; proud. **chiok-goān**, having all one's desires fulfilled. **moáⁿ-chiok sim-ì**, id. (v. ì). **ti-chiok**, contented. **sim ti-chiok**, id. **put-ti-chiok**, covetous, greedy, unsatisfied and discontented, &c. **jîn-sim put-chiok**, man's heart is never satisfied.

chiok-ēng, sufficient for use. **î-sit chiok-ēng**, food and clothing sufficient. **chiok-tāng**, full weight. **chiok-chhìn**, just correct in weight. **chiok-siâⁿ**, of highest purity, as silver (v. siâⁿ). **khùn kàu chiok-bîn**, to have had a thoroughly good sleep (v. bîn).

hù-chiok, having enough and to spare; wealthy. **hù-chiok**, to supply enough for use, as for one's family, or for persons in our employment. **hù-chiok hē-i-ēng**, id. **hù-chiok i-ēng**, id.

khah-chiok, rather more than full amount, as of

time, measure, weight, &c. (generally put at the end of a clause), *e.g.* **chit-tn̂g khah-chiok**, fully ten feet, a very little more. **tsáp-táu chiok**, fully ten of the measure "táu," or a little more.

heng-tē, jû siú-chiok, brothers are like our hands and feet. **hù-kùi tsāi-chhiú-chiok**, wealth and honour are shown by the hands and feet, in fortune-telling.

chiok (R. id.), to invoke a blessing; a surname. **chiok-hok**, to pray for a blessing on another; to invoke a blessing. **chiok-hok-khì**, id. **chiok-siā**, to give thanks to a god. **chiok-bûn**, a written prayer, read aloud and then burned, as in worship of Sages. **chiok-siū**, to express good wishes for a man's long life on his birth-day, as by visit, letter, card, or presents.

chiok [R. a ceremonial cup, a rank of nobility], (C. chiak). **chìn-chiok**, to get a higher grade of nobility; to bring in a cup of wine to present to the spirits in worship. **chiú-chiok**, a large wine-cup with three legs, used in sacrificial offerings. **lé-pân-chiok**, wine-jug and wine-cup, used at ancestral rites, &c.

kong-chiok, rank of duke. **hê-chiok**, rank of marquis. **pek-chiok**, rank of earl. **tsú-chiok**, rank of viscount. **lâm-chiok**, rank of baron.

chiok [R. to order]. **chiok-thok**, to intrust with, as a message or commission, or affair. **chiok-hù** (r.), to give special instructions for work or message. **chhien teng-lêng, bān chiok-hù**, very careful and repeated instructions. **mái^n-chiok**, to bribe or suborn in any way; to hire for any bad purpose, *e.g.* villains to injure another by violence, or false witnesses, &c. **mái^n-chiok jîn-sim**, to buy or steal the hearts of the people by improper means. **ûi-chiok-jī** (R.), last will and testament.

chiok [R. to pour out], (C. chiak). **chim-chiok**, to be careful to consider well before deciding or acting; to act deliberately and thoughtfully. **chim-chim chiok-chiok**, id.

chiok— **chiok-koán** (T.), = A. chek-koán, as you please.

chiong— **hiong-chiong**, hurried and careless; reckless from haste. **hiong-hiong chiong-chiong**, id. **hiong-chiong-chiong**, id.

chiong [R. end; to the end]. **lîm-chiong**, to come to the end of life. **siēn-chiong**, an easy death by old age or by a disease that is not painful. **kun-tsú oát-chiong; siáu-jîn oát-sú**, in the case of a good man it is called "end;" in the case of a bad man "death."

chiong-sin, all one's life long. **chiong-jit**, the whole day. **chiong-sì-lâng** (T.), one's whole life long. **siēn-ok, chiong iú-pò**, the good and bad have their recompense at last. **chiong-kui**, in the long run; to the last; always said in scolding or finding fault, *e.g.* **chiong-kui, sī chit--hō ê-lâng**, to the last he will be that sort of fellow, will never improve, but be as bad or worse.

sí-chiong, beginning and end. **sí-chiong jû-it**, constantly the same from first to last. **tsū-sí chì-chiong**, from the first to the last. **bû-sí bû-chiong**, without beginning or end.

chiong [R. a chapter, = col. chiu^n], (C. chiang), a surname. **tô-chiong**, a seal.

chiong [R. about to], (C. chiang), particle used for introducing a noun in the clause before that which contains its verb, almost like "ēng," *e.g.* **chiong-sim pí-sim**, to judge of another's feelings by our own. **chiong chit--ê tāi-chì, kā-i-kóng**, tell him this matter.

chiong-kun, the Tartar general of province; title of some idols (v. **kun**).

chiong-kūn, nearly the same; almost synonymous; near in time, or meaning, or amount. **chiong-chiū**, to take what we can in default of better (v. chiū). **kə-put-chiong**, to do a thing we do not wish, because there is no other way possible; to take a plan that is unpleasant or bad, because it cannot be avoided, or to avoid a greater evil, = "put-tek-í." **kə-put-kì-chiong**, id. **kə-put-jî-chiong**, id.

chiong-lâi, afterwards. **chiong-sìn chiong-gî**, half believing, half doubting.

chiong [R. a bell? a cup?], a surname. **chiong-kûi**, a spirit that rules demons or ghosts (v. kûi).

chiong (P.), in several words in the several tones, = A. cheng.

chiông [R. to follow; from]. **chiông-tiong**, from among them, among them. **chiông-lâi** (r.), hitherto. **chiông-kim í-āu**, henceforward.

chiông-koân, to act somewhat beyond one's authority, under the pressure of necessity or very urgent circumstances. **chiông-koa^n**, to be in the mandarin's hands, as a case.

chiông-tông hia^n-tī, second cousins (v. tông). **chiông-it-phín**, the lower section of the first or red-button mandarins (v. phín).

chiông-siòk, to follow usual customs (v. siòk). **i-o chiông-sū**, to follow blindly the leading of another. **khiok-kì siong-chiông**, to follow another's will, putting a restraint on one's own desires. **giên thèng, kè chiông**, his words are obeyed, and his plans followed. **kái-ok chiông-siēn**, to reform the evil and follow the good. **ték kî-siēn, jî chiông--chi**, to choose the good and follow it. **jîn iú siēn-goān, thien pit-chiông--chi**, Heaven certainly fulfils the good desires of men.

chióng [R. tióng, to increase; by change of tone from "tiông" long], (C. chiáng). **chióng-chìn**, to grow rich out of poverty (v. chìn).

chióng [R. seed, = col. chéng]; also (C.), = A. chéng, seed. **hit-chióng-mn̂g ê-lâng**, that sort of people (depreciatory).

sió-chióng, Souchong tea. **chióng-pōe**, a sort of Souchong. **chióng-ki**, a cheaper sort with small stalks in it. **bêng-chióng-tê**, very fine Souchong. **bêng-sek-chióng**, id. **khé-koe-chióng**, Souchong from the place called "khé-koe."

chióng (Cn.), = A. chiáng. **po-chióng**, to praise and encourage, as an inferior, &c. **pə-chióng**, id.

chióng (Cn.), = A. chit; this, these.

chióng [R. the palm of the hand, = col. chiú^n, to rule, = col. chiáng]. **hiet-chióng**, the palm of the hand naturally red (v. hiet). **háp-chióng**, to place the palms together as in worship. **háp-chióng pài**, to worship by putting the palms together and so bowing. **háp-chióng-bō**, a cap with a ridge in the centre, like hands so placed; worn by Buddhist priests, and by children for good luck.

chióng-koán (esp. Cn.), = A. chiáng-koán, to rule, to have the management of.

chiòng (R. id.), (C. chiàng). **lūi-chiòng**, blindness caused by the eye getting covered with white; sometimes also protruding.

chiòng [R. tiòng, to hit the mark; by change of tone from "tiong," middle], (C. tsòng). **put-chiòng-**

iōng, very dull in intellect, so as to be useless, as a man.

chiòng [R. all, = col. chèng]; also (C.), = A. chèng, all. **hô-chiòng**, having the power of living harmoniously with all. **tóng-chiòng**, to collect a crowd of people for some bad purpose. **tsó-tō hék-chiòng**, deceiving the multitude by false teachings, as Tauist priests. **iòng-chiòng** (R.), crowded together, as persons. **lâng-bé iòng-chiòng** (r.), people in great crowds. **chiòng-kun sat-jîn, tsōe kip tsú-sòe**, if any one in the army kill a man, the responsibility is on the general; a superior is responsible for the evil that he allows his inferiors to do.

sī-chiòng, to warn all men by the terrible example. **kê--teh sī-chiòng**, put in the cangue as a warning to others. **kùi--teh sī-chiòng**, hung up as a terrible warning, as the head of a criminal.

tāi-chiòng-iâ, a hideous paper figure, the chief of the "all souls" of the rites called "phó-tō;" some say the aggregate of these spirits (s. officer). **tāi-chiòng-iâ** (C.), = A. chèng-kong-má, temples containing tablets that have no descendants. **hàu tāi-chiòng-iâ**, (C.), to worship all the spirits of these tablets at once.

chiòng (C.), = A. chèng, to sow seeds carefully.

chiòng [R. a high military officer), (C. chiàng), a word forming many titles of high military officers and of idols. **tāi-chiòng**, a high military officer. **béng-chiòng**, a brave do. **ló-chiòng**, an old do. (v. ló). **lú-chiòng**, a female warrior; said also of a woman who is too bold and forward in speaking to men. **chham-chiòng**, = chham-hú, an officer about rank of colonel. **hù-chiòng**, the next rank (= hiàp) above that. **chiòng-siòng**, very high civil and military mandarins, as generals and ministers of state. **chiòng-sòe**, high military officers, as generals and commander-in-chief. **chiòng-lēng**, a general's orders. **chiòng-tâi**, a raised platform at review-ground, where an officer stands to give orders.

chièn-chiòng, skilful in military matters, as military officer; skilful and bold in the management of any sort of matter. **put-chí chièn-chiòng**, very skilful and successful in managing matters.

chiòng-iâ (Cn.), = A. chiàng-iâ, underlings of the customs.

ө-chiòng, gambling cards with the word "chiòng" in black. **âng-chiòng**, such cards with "chiòng" in red.

hó-chiòng, an image of a tiger that is worshipped (v. hó). **chiòh-sîn-chiòng**, stone figures at graves.

sù-tāi-chiòng, four idols (attendants on Tāi-tō-kong) worshipped together; gamblers trust much to their incense; one of them is specially powerful; so they say, "lâm-siū-keng ê tāi-chiòng; chit-sien chiàh, saⁿ-sien siòng" (v. siòng). **tāi-chiòng-iâ**, any one of these four idols; also (T.) a deified tiger (s. all). **koan-chiòng-iâ**, images made with a sword as body, and only a human head instead of the handle; placed as attendants on idols, esp. on "ông-iâ." **koan-chiòng-thâu**, do. esp. five such. **saⁿ-tsàp-lák koan-chiòng**, the thirty-six attendants of "tāi-tō-kong." **koan-chiòng**, spirit soldiers sent by the gods to assist their votaries. **kun-chiòng**, id. **pàng-kun-chiòng**, to send these spirit soldiers to assist. **khò-chiòng**, to make offerings to them.

chiōng [R. tsōng]. **chiōng-goân**, the highest literary degree; the highest name on the list of new Han-lin members (hān-lîm) on each occasion (v. goân).

chip, to sip with the lips. **chip-chit-chhùi**, to sip a little. **chip--teh, chip--teh**, sipping little by little (all with lips).

chip (Cn.), = A. jip, to chase. **chip-siang** (P.), = A. jip-siong, to object to a house being built, &c., because of the injury to the "hong-súi." **chip** (P.), = (C.) jip, = A. tòng, to come forward with claims, &c., when a property is sold. **cheng-chip** (P.), id.

chip (P. jek), to squeeze out, as matter from a boil.

chip [R. to hold; to hold firm or obstinately]. **chip-siú**, to observe and keep, as a rule. **chip-hoat**, to adhere firmly to strict rules, as mandarin. **chip-chiáng**, to exercise, as power or authority.

chip-sū, the tablets and instruments carried before a mandarin; also (X.) a deacon (v. sū). **chip-thiap--ê**, the man in a yamun who has charge of calling cards.

chip-áu, very obstinate (v. áu). **kó-chip**, do. **khu-chip**, do. **chip-ì**, do. **chip-phiah**, id. **chip-it**, id. **chip-sí-pán**, extremely obstinate (v. pán). **chip-sí-soah**, id. **chip-sí-koat**, do. **chip-bê**, obstinate in error or in some bad course of action. **chip-bê put-ngō**, do. without the least repentance. **chip-m̄-tit** (Cn.), obstinately refusing to have the quarrel settled.

chip (R. chek), a sort of census roll (= chek), according to which men are counted to belong to their ancestral districts, *e.g.* **hok-chiu-chip**, belonging by descent to Fuh-chau, so as to go there for examinations, &c.

chip (R. id.) **tsū-chip**, to assemble. **chio-chip**, to call together, as for some enterprise or special purpose. **tsôe-chip**, to assemble in full numbers for some special purpose, *e.g.* graduates for an examination; rowdies for a disturbance, or enemies for a feud. **chê-chip**, id.

chip (R. id.? chek?). **chip-chēng** (R.), very lonely and quiet, as a place.

chit [R. natural constitution, simple, to cross-examine]. **pún-chit**, original constitution of mind or body, as to strength, elegance, activity, skill, or intelligence, but not as to morals. **tsu-chit**, natural talents, esp. as to literature. **tsâi-chit**, natural talents or ability. **khì-chit**, mental or bodily character (original or acquired), as to talents, appearance, manner, temper, &c., but not as to morals. **khì-chit put-chí-hó**, of good talents or general ability. **pièn-hoà khì-chit**, whole manner and appearance gradually changed (as a country fellow come to town), so as to get a polite and cultivated look, even face, &c., changed.

chit-phak, quiet in taste, and indisposed to display.

chit-sìn (R.), to examine the parties face to face, as a mandarin.

chit (R. id.), official duty, station, or rank. **chit-jīm**, id. **chit-hūn**, id. **koaⁿ-chit**, mandarin rank or office. **bô-phín-chit**, not having official rank. **jīn-chit**, to perform one's official duties diligently. **chīn-chit**, fully execute one's office. **siú-chit**, attend to one's duties.

kek-chit, to depose from office, and degrade more or less in rank. **sit-chit**, to fail in duty. **pi-chit** (R.), I myself, said by a mandarin.

chit (R. chek). **chit-hí**, a very common small fresh-water fish. **chit-á-hí**, id. **chit-hí-á**, do. esp. the small ones. **hoan-chit-á**, a salted sort from Siam, &c.

chit (R. chek), this; these. **chit--ê**, id. **chit--**

dê (or chid--ê), id. **chit-pē**, now. **chit-tiáp**, id. **chit-sí**, id.

chit [R. sek, a house]. **tsāi-chit-lí** (C.), = A. tsāi-sek-lú, a virgin.

chit — **im-chit** (C.), = A. im-chek, meritorious works.

chit (R. id.), to weave. **chhái-chit**, to weave coloured figures in cloth. **chit-gím**, to weave flowered silk. **chit-pò͘**, to weave cotton cloth. **chit-tsoá**, woven paper made at Eńg-chhun. **chit-chhiȯh**, to weave mats of reeds.

chit-ko, a stuff like coarse white flannel, from the north. **chit-kui**, a loom.

chit-pé, to darn finely (without a patch), by stitches in both directions crossing each other.

chit-lú, the "weaving girl," a star (in Lyra) which is worshipped on 7·7 along with "gû-nn̂g."

chit [R. the back-bone, = col. chiah; the ridge of a hill or house].

soa^{n}-chit, the very ridge of a mountain. **lêng-chit**, the long ridge of a hill gradually descending so as to end in a small eminence; counted very auspicious.

ka-chiah-chit, the back-bone; the seam down the back of a dress.

tiong-chit, the ridge of a roof. **tiong-chit-î^{n}**, the ridge-pole. **chhio-chit**, the ridge of the roof turned up and pointed at the ends. **chhù-chit**, the ridge of a roof. **chhù-chit-thâu**, the points at the two ends of the ridge. **chhù-chit-bé**, on the raised ridge of a roof (any part of it), *e.g.* said of drying or sunning things on it.

chit (R. id.), (Cn. chėk). **chit-lê**, a thorny shrub (Tribulus?) used medicinally for eruptions, &c.

chit [R. a disease, = chėk]. **tài-chit**, any severe chronic or inveterate disease or malformation. **seng-khu tài-chit**, to have such a disease. **lī-chit**, dysentery. **hòe-chit** (T. hòe-chėk), incurable and useless, as a man who is lame, blind, maimed, a leper, or having some severe incurable disease, often venereal.

chit (R. id. = chėk). **chit-tò͘**, envy; some say, chėk-tò͘, esp. Cn.

chit (R. it), one; having only one (instead of a pair). **chit-bák**, having only one eye. **chit, nn̄g, sa^{n}**, one, two, three. **thâu-chit-ê**, the first (v. thâu). **sam khi-lióng; lióng khi-chit**, three oppress two, and two oppress one. **chit-ê**, one. **chit-lâng**, one man. **chit-poa^{n}**, alike. **chit-poa^{n}-iū^{n}**, id. **chit-iū^{n}**, id.

chit-tsōe, all at once. **chit-tui**, one heap or company (v. tui). **tsòe--chit-ē kàu**, to arrive or come all at once. **chit-ē-khoà^{n}**, at one glance.

chit-pi^{n}, on one side. **chit-pi^{n} . . . chit-pi^{n}**, both . . . and at the same time. **chit-hī jip, chit-hī chhut**, in at one ear, out at the other. **chit-lâng chit-lē**, not having any connection with each other's affairs, as two persons whom you would expect to keep together, *e.g.* two brothers, or as man and wife. **chit-lâng siū^{n}-chit-lē**, wishes and aims quite different or opposite. **chit-hó kah-chit-gâi; bô-nn̄g-hó sa^{n}-pâi**, a good or good-looking man has a bad or ugly wife, seldom are both good; sometimes (fig.) said of other things.

chiu (R. id.), an alluvial island in a river or at its mouth. **chiu-chhân**, flat fields in an alluvial island. **jip-chiu**, just where an alluvial delta meets the sea.

chiu (R. id.), a department; often used in the name of a Foo, *e.g.* "chiang-chiu-hú" (v. hú), or simply "chiang-chiu," &c.; but by itself it means properly a department (chow) less honourable, and generally smaller and less ancient than a Foo, though not under the Foo, but equally governing districts (koāi^{n}), and immediately responsible to the Tau-tai, *e.g.* Lêng-nâ-chiu, and Eńg-chhun-chiu. **ti-chiu**, the mandarin of such a department. **hun-chiu**, assistant mandarin of do.

chiu [R. to give charity]. **chiu-tsē**, to assist with money. **chiu-tsān** (T.), id. **chiu-chè** (r.), id. **chiu-kip** (R.), to assist those who are in want.

chiu [R. all round, complete], a surname; the Chow dynasty; a segment, as of a cake.

chiu-ûi, all round about. **chiu-bit**, kept close, as a secret or private affair; very careful or well arranged, so that there is no flaw. **jîn-ien chiu-bit**, the smoke of men (of cooking fires) closely crowded; population numerous, as in a village or region. **chiu-chì**, all complete, none wanting, as the furnishings of a room, &c.; without a flaw or fault, as a deed, or document, or arrangement. **chiu-tsoân**, to arrange so as to be without flaw, as a quarrel, or as a sale of property, or other affair. **chiu-soân**, to arrange for another, as a quarrel or troublesome affair that had become dangerous.

chit-chiu, one segment or section, as of a cake. **tsóeh tsòe-sì-chiu**, cut into four pieces by two cuts at right angles, as a flat cake. **sù-chiu-á**, a sort of persimmon, very good to eat, having four divisions, and few seeds.

chiu-tiâu, the Chow dynasty. **chiu-kong**, Duke Chow. **chiu-ék**, the Yih-king, or classic of changes. **chiu-chhong-iâ**, the companion of Kwanti. **chiu-chiong-kun**, id.

chiu [R. a boat, a junk]. **chiu-san**, the island of Chusan. **iú-lō͘, bók-teng-chiu**, if there be a road by land, don't go into a boat. **sūn-tsúi hêng-chiu** (sailing with the tide), all going on well.

chiu — **bák-chiu**, the eye (v. bák).

chiú (R. id.) **sàu-chiú**, a broom or besom for sweeping (v. sàu).

chiú [R. siú, to guard], to guard; to keep carefully. **chiú-kè** (r.), to guard. **chiú-chhân**, to watch the crops in irrigated fields. **chiú-chî^{n}-lê**, a miser.

chiú-koá^{n}, a widow (v. koá^{n}). **chiú-chiet**, to remain a widow determinedly, refusing to be married again. **chiú khang-pâng** (to keep the empty bedroom), to be a widow. **iú^{n} chit-ê-kiá^{n} lâi-chiú**, a widow adopting a son.

chiú-ki^{n}, to keep watch, as watchman; a watchman. **chhià^{n}-chhát chiú-ki^{n}**, to have a thief as watchman (proverb). **tsòe-chhát chit-ki^{n}; chiú-chhát chit-mî^{n}**, the thief comes in one watch only, but we must keep guard the whole night. **káu chiú-chhát**, the dog guards against thieves.

chiú (R. id.), spirituous liquor in general; distilled or fermented liquor; generally from rice or potatoes.

iâ-chiú, cocoa-nut milk. **péh-chiú**, a fermented (undistilled) liquor, made from glutinous rice and sugar. **péh-chiú hé-hu**, a white powder used for scouring. **ti^{n}-chiú**, sweet wine or spirit, &c., in general. **chiú-ti^{n}** (C.), liquor fermented, but not yet distilled. **ló-chiú**, a fermented (not distilled) liquor made from rice. **tsúi-chiú**, weak liquor. **khì-chiú**, a weak liquor (mixed with water) made in Amoy. **sio-chiú**, hot liquor; spirits; warmed liquor. **hé-sio-chiú**, strong spirits (from the north) that can burn. **hé-chiú**, id. **siang-liāu-chiú**, strong spirits made in Amoy. **thiām-chiú**, spirits in which glutinous rice has been steeped (v. thiām). **phû-tô-chiú**, wine; wine made from grapes. **io̍h-chiú**, medicated alcoholic preparations. **kok-kong-chiú**, a medicated liquor invented by Sái Kok-kong. **chiú-thâu**, the liquor of the first distillation, very strong.

chiú-khut, dimples in the cheek near the corners of the mouth, when laughing. **chiú-chî^{n}**, payment for the carriage of a letter or small parcel. **chiú-tsu**, id. **hō͘--lí bóe-chiú** (lit. buy some liquor with it), take this small reward, as above. **chiú-lé**, offerings of liquor made to the gods or spirits of the dead. **chiú-liāu**, things eaten along with liquor. **chiú-iên**, a feast with liquor. **chit-se̍k-chiú**, one feast with liquor. **chiú-phoh**, refuse from making liquor. **chiú-bú**, the whole mass of materials (as rice, potatoes, sugar, &c.), all ready for fermenting. **chiú-pê**, id. **chiú-tsau**, the refuse of spirit-making.

kek-chiú, to distil spirits; to invite and excite one another to take liquor. **gô-chiú**, to distil liquor (v. gô). **un-chiú**, to warm liquor. **phè-chiú**, to take some condiment or cakes, &c., along with liquor; to be so used. **tiēn-chiú**, to make a libation of liquor. **tah-chiú**, to buy liquor. **hoàt-chiú**, to make the loser in a game give liquor as a forfeit to the winner. **kèng-chiú**, to call on guests to drink bumpers (as host, or as one guest to another), with bowing, &c. **sa^{n}-pièn-chiú**, three cups of liquor drunk before eating. **sam-sûn-chiú**, id.

chhiá^{n}-chiú, to invite guests to a feast with liquor. **chhiá^{n} chhun-chiú**, to invite friends to a drinking feast in the new year's holidays. **chhiá^{n}-chiú-hì**, a play performed for the amusement of the guests at a feast. **chia̍h-chiú**, to drink liquor; to be at a feast; to have a feast. **chia̍h-si^{n}-jit-chiú**, to partake of a birth-day feast. **chia̍h-hí-chiú**, to be at a feast on some joyful occasion, *e.g.* when a friend gets married or obtains an office. **chia̍h-sán-chiú**, to drink liquor without any sufficient condiment. **chia̍h-chiú-tsùi**, to get drunk (v. tsùi). **tsùi-chiú**, drunk; spoiled, as pine-apple.

tsau-chiú, enervated by drink; constitution broken down by drink. **chiú-sek**, wine and women; drink and lust (v. sek). **chiú-sien**, a drunkard; one of the genii fond of liquor. **hoat-chiú-hông**, mad with drink. **hoat-chiú-hong**, to have red eruptions from liquor. **chiú-bī**, smell of liquor. **ū-chiú-bī**, under the influence of liquor. **chiú-ì**, manner of a man who has been drinking a little, so as to be somewhat forward, excitable, or incautious. **chiú-liōng**, a man's capacity for liquor. **chiú-liōng koāi^{n}**, he can take a great quantity of liquor. **chhiú-liōng chhién**, has small capacity for liquor. **chiú-tek**, the manner in which a man is affected by liquor (v. tek).

chiú-lêng, a machine for heating liquor. **chiú-thiu**, a syphon for liquor. **chiú-lâu**, a sort of funnel for filling bottles. **chiú-kàu**, a measure for liquor. **chiú-táu-á**, a small measure for lading it out. **chiú-tiàm**, a liquor shop. **chiú-khè**, a large liquor shop. **chiú-lâu**, an upper-room in a liquor shop where guests are served. **chiú-lóng**, a spirit shop (foreign).

chiú-thâm, a sort of jar for liquor (v. thâm). **chiú-tho̍h**, a small jar for liquor. **chiú-àng**, a large jar for liquor. **chiú-pân**, a sort of jug or decanter for do. **chiú-tê-e**, another sort (v. tê). **chiú-kan**, another sort like a bottle. **chiú-kip-sio**, a small thin earthen kettle for warming liquor. **chiú-au**, a small cup for liquor. **chiú-chiok**, a large cup used in idolatrous offerings. **chiú-cheng**, a very small cup for liquor. **chiú-tsoá^{n}**, a larger sort. **chiú-poe**, a large cup for liquor.

chiù (R. tsù), worm-eaten; moth-eaten; holes made by insects; to decay; decayed, as wood, teeth, &c. **chiù-thâng**, the insect that eats bamboo; it is supposed that teeth also are eaten by an insect. **chiù-iû^{n}**, a small insect that destroys grain in granaries. **chiù-khang**, holes eaten by insects; cavities in decayed teeth. **chiù-khí**, decayed teeth. **chiù-hu̍t**, a sort of the lichi (nāi^{n}-chi) fruit that has a small stone. **pu̍t chiù**, the idol is worm-eaten.

chiù — **chiù-khàng**, to make wearisome repeated demands for something refused, as children; to find fault with a man behind his back, as for niggardly or exacting conduct.

chiù (R. id.), to make spells, imprecations, &c. **chiù-tsoā**, to swear (v. tsoā). **chiù-mē^{n}**, to curse and scold. **chiù-mā^{n}** (T. Cn.), id. **chiù-tsé** (R.), to make imprecations against. **chiù-liām**, to make imprecations. **chiù-lóe**, id. **liām-chiù**, to mutter spells or make incantations, as sorcerers (tâng-chí) when trying to become possessed, or as priests in rites. **chhui-chiù**, to repeat the incantations when the spirits have not obeyed the former incantations.

chiù-chhàm, heavy imprecations. **hû-chiù**, written and spoken Tauist charms and spells.

chiū (R. id.), to approach; according to (in a few phrases); (to accomplish); a connective particle, then, therefore, or immediately.

chiong-chiū, the best that can be got in the circumstances; to put up with the best of a bad case. **bóng-chiong-chiū**, put up with it, as it cannot be helped, at least in the meantime.

sêng-chiū, to complete and accomplish an affair. **kong-bêng sêng-chiū**, official rank attained. **seng-lí tsòe-put-chiū**, trade does not prosper.

chiū lâng-ê-ōe, to take up a man's words and answer or convict him out of his own mouth. **chiū-phiò niá^{n}-gûn**, to draw money on presenting a bank-note, &c. **chiū-i-thô tsoh-i-chhiû^{n}** (lit. build the wall according to the mortar); to make the things for him according to the money he allows.

chiū-hà chhoā (T.), = A. sūn-hà chhoā, to marry just after parents' death.

chiū-sī, that is; just so (v. sī). **hó, chiū-hó**, if you think it well, just let it be so (though I do not think so).

chiū-kūn, to approach; to draw near. **chiū-oá**, id. **sái-khì-chiū--i**, sail right up to him. **lak-kè lâi-chiū--i**, let down the price to come nearer his offer. **kàng-kè lâi-chiū--i**, id.

chiu^{n}, this syllable, in all the tones, becomes chio^{n} in many parts of Chang-chew, esp. P.

chiu^{n} (R. chiong), a chapter. **chiu^{n}-tsat**, chapters and verses. **téng-chiu^{n}**, the preceding chapter.

bûn-chiu^{n}, a literary essay (v. bûn).

tsàu-chiu^{n}, a memorial or report to the throne. **pió-chiu^{n}**, id. **piáu-chiu^{n}**, id.

chiu^{n} (R. chiong), starch; to starch; fluid matter of small-pox or cow-pox; (said of various things like liquid starch).

thô-bê-chiu^{n}, deep slushy mud. **thô-chiu^{n}**, id. **tāu-chiu^{n}**, soft bean-curd not yet pressed. **koàn-chiu^{n}**, full of matter, as a pock. **gû-lin-chiu^{n}** (C.), milk.

bí-chiu^{n}, a sort of pulp made by grinding rice with water. **ám-chiu^{n}**, liquid rice-starch, rice water. **hún-**

8

chiu^n, wheat-starch. **hún-chiu^n-kə̂**, wheat-starch made ready like paste. **chiu^n-ám**, to starch with rice-water. **chiu^n-sa^n**, to starch a coat or long dress. **chiu^n-sóe**, to wash and starch, as clothes; to scold violently; to speak to a man in a very disrespectful way. **chiáh-chiu^n**, to be starched. **khí-chiu^n**, to take out starch, as by soaking the dress in water.

chiu^n (R. chiong). **chiu^n-ló**, camphor. **chiu^n-lə́** (Cn.), id. **chiu^n-ló-iû**, sap of the camphor-tree. **chiu^n-chhiū**, the camphor-tree. **chiu^n-chhâ**, camphor-wood.

chiu^n (R. chiong). **chiu^n-hî**, a sort of cuttle-fish that has no bone in it.

chiu^n (R. chiong). **chiu^n-tsû**, a sort of toad (used medicinally).

chiû^n [R. siông, skirt, petticoat]. **i-chiû^n**, clothes in general. **in-chiû^n**, id. **in-chiû^n-thûi**, a wooden mallet (like a club) for washing clothes.

chiú^n (R. chióng), a surname.

chiú^n, an animal like a large tortoise; its feet are like fins or paddles instead of the claws of the turtle.

chiú^n, the large red-deer of Formosa.

chiú^n (R. chióng), the palm of the hand (or sole of foot); the paw of a bear, &c.; a webbed-foot.

chit-pa-chiú^n, one hand held up with fingers expanded, meaning 5 or 50, or 500, &c. **nn̄g-pa-chiú^n**, both hands held up expanded, meaning 10 or 100, or 1000, &c. **sien-pa-chiú^n**, a small prickly cactus, much cultivated on roofs to keep off evil influences.

hó-chiú^n, a tiger's paw. **hîm-chiú^n**, a bear's paw, counted a delicacy. **gô-chiú^n**, a goose's web-foot. **gô-kha-chiú^n**, id. **ah-kha-chiú^n**, duck's web-foot. **ah-chiú^n**, id. (s. oar).

chhiú-chiú^n, the palm of the hand. **koat-chhiú-chiú^n**, to slap a child's palm with our own. **kha-chiú^n**, the sole of the foot. **kha-chêng-chiú^n**, the front part of the sole at and near the toes. **chiú^n-sim**, the middle of the palm. **chiú^n-hûn**, lines on the palm. **khoà^n-chiú^n**, to examine the palm, as a fortune-teller. **tn̄g-chiú^n**, having a line quite across the palm; lucky for men, but very unlucky for women.

chiú^n (R. chióng), an oar. **chiú^n-bé**, the blade of an oar. **chiú^n-hióh**, id. **chiú^n-chhiú**, the other half of the oar which contains the handle. **chiú^n-chhêng**, id. **chiú^n-pə̄**, the band which splices these two parts into the one oar. **chiú^n-thâu**, the oar-handle. **chiú^n-tiah**, the small cross-piece of the oar-handle. **chiú^n-tiam**, an oar-pin. **chiú^n-tiam-kek**, the small cross-piece of wood that keeps the lower end of the oar-pin steady. **chiú^n-khau**, the loop by which the oar is hung on the oar-pin.

chit-hù-chiú^n, a pair of oars. **siang-chiú^n**, a two-oared boat. **siang-chiú^n-tāi**, the boatman of a two-oared boat. **poeh-chiú^n**, eight-oared boats (used by custom-house officers, &c.)

kò-chiú^n, to row by pushing (done standing, but to pull sitting is "pien"). **kah-chiú^n**, put on the oars (as when the wind falls) to begin rowing. **phái^n-chiú^n-lə̄**, inconvenient arrangement for rowing. **jī-chiú^n**, the oar on the left side of a two-oared boat held in the right hand. **bé-chiú^n**, id., the stern oar. **khah-bé-chiú^n**, to row hard with that oar, so as to turn the boat's head to the right. **ah-bé-chiú^n**, id. (v. ah). **khah-jiû-chiú^n** (C.), give a stroke with the oar very gently.

chiù^n [R. chek, this]. **chiù^n-pêng**, on this side; here. **chiù^n-tsá-khí** (said in Quemoy), this morning. **chiù^n-ê-hng** (in Quemoy), this evening. **àn-chiù^n-sì** (T. Cn.), thus.

chiù^n (R. chiòng), a sort of sauce or condiment.

chiù^n-chiù^n, thick and miry, as roads. **iû^n-iû^n chiù^n-chiù^n**, all softened and spoiled by wet, as things; all miry, as roads. **chiù^n-chiù^n siû^n-siû^n**, softened and spoiled, as by damp.

tāu-chiù^n, sauce made from beans and flour. **ə-chiù^n**, a dark sort. **chiù^n-chheng**, the thinner part of tāu-chiù^n. **iâm tsau, chiù^n chhə**, four condiments used in cookery. **hoan-kiu^n-chiù^n**, this sauce seasoned with cayenne pepper. **ti^n-mûi^n-chiù^n**, a preparation from yellow plums and sugar. **lə̄-hê-chiù^n**, a sauce made from pickled shrimps.

chiù^n-liāu, various sorts of vegetables preserved in tāu-chiù^n. **chiù^n-koe**, pumpkins so preserved. **chiù^n-kiu^n**, ginger so preserved. **chiù^n-mī^n-chià**, wheaten dough balls in this sauce.

chiū^n — **chiū^n-chî^n**, troublesome behaviour of children wishing to be fondled and made of (v. chî^n).

chiū^n (R. ióng), to itch. **chiū^n-iah-iah**, very itchy; very eager for some bad gratification, as gambling or seeing plays, &c., so that he will not be kept from it. **chiū^n--tè m̄-pê; m̄-chiū^n--tè, pê kàu-huih-lâu** (won't scratch the itchy place; but where is no itch, scratches till the blood flows), to neglect important matters, while very busy about what does not concern him. **chiū^n--tè m̄-pê; m̄-chiū^n, khòng-khòng-pê**, do. **pê-chiū^n**, to scratch an itchy spot. **hī-khang chiū^n; ká^n-sī ū-lâng teh-liām goá**, my ear itches, surely some one is speaking of me.

chiū^n (R. siōng, =col. chhiū^n, siū^n), above, upon, upper, superior, former; to ascend, to go up, to come up to, or go above; to go to a place of superior rank; to raise; to place upon, or write down.

mn̂g-chiū^n, a mandarin's secretary. **thâu-mn̂g liām-chiū^n--ê**, the first wife (as to time) married by a man. **thâu-chiū^n--ê**, first-born child. **thâu-chiū^n-kiá^n**, id.

chiū^n-bīn, upper side; overhead; to come out on the face, as emotion or disease. **hoat-chiū^n-bīn**, to break out on the face. **chiū^n-thâu chiū^n-bīn**, devoid of shame and modesty, as a slave girl too impudent towards her mistress, or as a child demanding money from its parents, &c.

chiū^n-tsúi, to land goods from a ship; to discharge cargo. **chiū^n-mí^n**, the edge (as of a knife) becoming sharp (v. mí^n). **chiū^n-tsng**, to add to personal beauty by dress and ornaments, as young woman. **chiū^n-khàu**, to put fetters on the limbs. **chiū^n-niû^n**, to put the ridge-pole of a house in its place. **chiū^n-hé**, to light the lamps, as in market streets, or in great idolatrous celebrations, at night. **chiū^n-pún**, to present a memorial to the throne; also, the previous volume of a book, or the first of two volumes.

khoà^n-chiū^n-bák, to think well of; to respect. **m̄-chiū^n-bák**, to think unimportant; to despise. **khoà^n--lâng m̄-chiū^n-bák**, to despise people.

m̄-chiū^n chit-géh-jit, not quite a month. **bē-chiū^n chit-géh-jit**, id. **bē-chiū^n-kun**, not up to a catty in weight. **chiū^n-kun-koe**, a fowl over a catty in weight. **chiū^n-gûn**, to come up to an amount counted in silver, as price, or account run up to so much. **m̄-tát chiū^n-kúi-ê-î^n**, not worth more than a few cash. **bē-tát chiū^n-kúi-ê-î^n**, id. **chiū^n-kè** (C.), = A. tióng-kè, to rise in price.

chiū^n-toh, to be placed on the table, as the articles in a feast (v. toh). **liáh-chhát chiūⁿ-tsng**, in catching a chief get the stolen goods, as evidence of guilt.

chiūⁿ-chiàⁿ, to write out a fair clean copy. **chiūⁿ-chheh**, to insert in a list; to write down in a book. **chiūⁿ-ke-kah**, to be enrolled in a census, as present inhabitants. **miâⁿ-jī chiūⁿ-tsoá**, to have one's name recorded formally or officially. **chiūⁿ-khòe**, to set down (as additional items) in a deed of sale, &c. **chiūⁿ-sǹg**, to insert in an account, as an item. **bô-chiūⁿ-sǹg**, not counted in the number, *e.g.* as foreigners in a Chinese census; not fit to be counted, as a disabled or useless man or thing; need not put it down in the account, as a small thing given extra. **ōe-kham--tit chiūⁿ-sǹg**, fit to be counted, as being really fit for use. **chiūⁿ-siàu**, to enter as an item in an account. **ki-chiūⁿ-siàu**, id.

chiūⁿ-kang, to begin work, as on each day. **chiūⁿ-jīm**, to enter on office. **chiūⁿ-pan**, to take one's turn of duty, as underlings of yamun, &c. **chiūⁿ-lō͘**, to begin a journey. **chiūⁿ-kiō**, to begin the journey (in sedan) from her parents' house to her new home, only on that *one* occasion, and only of the bride. **chiūⁿ-mn̂g chhoā**, bridegroom going in person to the bride's house to conduct her to his own house.

chiūⁿ-lóh, to ascend and descend; to go and come. **chiūⁿ-koâiⁿ**, to get higher rank; to go northwards. **chiūⁿ-tsûn**, to embark. **chiūⁿ-bé**, to mount a horse (v. bé). **chiūⁿ-pîⁿ**, to mount the stage. **chiūⁿ-tsō**, to go on the sacred seat (as in seventh moon) to perform certain rites. **chiūⁿ-hák** (vulg.), to go to stool. **chiūⁿ-chhè**, id. **chiūⁿ-āu**, id. **chiūⁿ-soaⁿ**, to ascend a mountain; to go ashore; to go to the fields from a village, as for field-work. **khoà-chiūⁿ-soaⁿ**, to be stranded.

chiūⁿ-sin, to be possessed by a spirit. **chiūⁿ-tâng**, do. in the case of the "tâng-chí," or sorcerers.

chiūⁿ-pak, to go to the north. **chiūⁿ-sa**, to set sail on voyage to North China. **chiūⁿ-kiaⁿ**, to go to the metropolis. **chiūⁿ-séng**, to go to the provincial capital. **chiūⁿ gê-mn̂g**, to go to a mandarin's office. **chiūⁿ-tn̂g**, to appear before the tribunal. **chiūⁿ-tiâu**, to go to have an audience of the sovereign. **chiūⁿ-tiēn**, do. of the emperor. **chiūⁿ-thiⁿ**, to ascend to heaven. **chiūⁿ se-hong**, to go to the (Buddhist) western heaven.

pé-bōe-chiūⁿ, unable to refund or repay enough. **kang-hu óh-chiūⁿ-chhiú**, the trade (work) thoroughly learned. **kā lóng-bōe chiūⁿ-tsoā**, though taught, he cannot do it well.

chiūⁿ-chhiú, the title-deed by which the seller proves his right to sell. **chiūⁿ-chhun**, early in spring. **chiūⁿ-nîⁿ**, the former year. **tsó-chiūⁿ**, distant ancestors.

chiūⁿ-si, high officials. **chiūⁿ-ūi**, upper place or seat, *i.e.* more honourable.

chiūⁿ-kiuⁿ, the roof of the mouth; the palate. **ǹg-chiūⁿ**, upwards. **toà--tióh i-bīn-chiūⁿ**, in consideration for him (as doing a favour to a third party). **bé-chiūⁿ**, on horse-back. **lō͘-chiūⁿ**, on the road (v. lō͘). **beh-kàng goá-sin-chiūⁿ**, about to come on my person, as calamity.

chiūⁿ-siaⁿ, the shang tone; the second of the four tones. **chiūⁿ-piâⁿ** (C. téng-pêⁿ), the upper first or upper ping tone. **chiūⁿ-khì** (C. téng), the upper third tone. **chiūⁿ-jip** (C. téng), the upper fourth tone.

chiuh — **chiuh-chiuh-háu**, to squeak, as a rat (cf. kiuh).

chiuh (cf. kiuh: kiúh). **tâm-chiuh-chiuh**, very wet, as house, &c. **bát-chiuh-chiuh**, very crowded, as a street when there is a play in it.

chiúh (cf. kiúh; khiúh). **nńg-chiúh-chiúh**, very soft, as dough, &c.

chng, in several tones; better tsng, &c., q.v.

cho, **cho͘**, **chö**, in several tones; better, tso, tso͘, tsö, &c., q.v.

choa, **choaⁿ**, **choah**, **choāi**, **choan**, **choat**, in several tones; better, tsoa, tsoaⁿ, tsoah, tsoāi, tsoan, tsoat, &c., q.v.

choe, **choeh**, **choh**, **chöh**, **chok**, **chom**, **chong**, in several tones; better, tsoe, tsoeh, tsoh, tsöh, tsok, tsom, tsong, &c., q.v.

chöng (Cn.), = A. cheng, in some tones and words.

chu, **chü**, **chut**, in several tones; better, tsu, tsü, tsut, &c., q.v.; sometimes ju, jü, esp. T.

chuh, **chui**, **chuiⁿ**, **chun**, **chut**, in several tones; better, tsuh, tsui, tsuiⁿ, tsun, tsut, &c., q.v.

chwa, **chwaⁿ**, **chwah**, **chwāi**, **chwan**, **chwat**, in several tones; better, tsoa, tsoaⁿ, tsoah, tsoāi, tsoan, tsoat, &c., q.v.

CHH.

Before a, ng, o, o͘, ö, u, ü, the sound of this initial is often between chh and ts'h; and sometimes (esp. in T. and Cn.) the sound is almost or quite ts'h.

chha — **toā-chhi-chha**, great profusion of food at a feast, &c. (v. chhi).

chha [R. to differ, to send; cf. col. chhe, "to send"], (C. generally chhɛ), to differ; different; wrong.

cheng-chha, difference; gen. difference from what is right. **ū-cheng-chha**, it is different; not correct. **cheng-chha lâi cheng-chha khì**, variations this way and that way. **chha-chhok**, error; fault. **chit-sî chha-chhok**, sudden unpremeditated fault. **chha-biū** (R.), a mistake or fault (v. biū). **kiâⁿ-chha-lō͘**, to behave wickedly, as gambling, lasciviousness, and drink.

bô-chha, quite correct; the same. **ū-chha**, different; wrong. **toā-chha**, very far wrong; very different, as from pattern. **chha-tit-hn̄g**, id. **chha-khi-hn̄g**, id. **chha bô-hn̄g**, nearly alike; nearly correct. **chha iú-hiēn**, id.

chha-put-to, nearly the same; nearly correct; tolerable; it will do (in this one phrase C. is also "chha").

chha (R. id.), (C. chhɛ), to overlap. **chha-oá**, to make (a dress) overlap, without buttoning. **chha-chhiú**, to put each hand into the sleeve of the other; to cross the hands on the breast. **chhiú chha--leh**, do.; the hands laid together. **chhiú chha--lâi**, id.

chha — **tiūⁿ-chha**, a piece of cloth (usually embroidered or ornamented) for holding a bed-curtain close to the bed-post when drawn open. **chha-oá**, to fasten the bed-curtain to the bed-post in this way.

chhâ (R. tsa), (C. chhɛ̂), to search minutely; to

investigate; to examine into. **chhâ-khoàⁿ**, id. **tsa-chhâ**, id. **chhâ-bāi** (Cn.), id. **chhâ-mn̄g**, to inquire into a matter, as a superior. **chhâ-khó**, to investigate (v. khó).

chhâ-koe, a sort of policeman who examines the streets and markets; belongs to the office of the military mandarin. **chhâ-koe koán-hú**, id. **bú-iâⁿ chhâ-koe**, id. **chhâ-iā**, to make search or investigation in the night, as police or soldiers. **chhâ lāi-hô**, to search the harbour and adjoining creeks (as near Amoy) for pirates or smugglers.

chhâ [R. tea, = col. tê]. **chhâ kái-būn** (R.), tea dispels sadness.

chhâ (R. chhâi). **chhâ-ê**, a medicine (v. ê).

chhâ (R. chhâi), wood; firewood; a surname; stiff. **chhâ-bák**, a knot in wood. **chhâ-miâⁿ**, resinous wood, as in fir roots. **chhâ-thâu**, a block of wood. **long-á-chhâ**, an unsplit billet of wood. **chhâ-pêng**, a split bit of fire-wood. **chhâ-khe**, a bundle of fire-wood. **chhâ-chí**, a very small bundle of fire-wood. **chhâ-tsúi**, fire-wood and water for cooking. **chhâ-liâu**, timber. **tsáp-chhâ-á-tiàm**, a shop for wooden utensils, as oars, &c. **chhâ-kiáh**, wooden-soled shoes.

chhâ-chhâ, stiff and unmoved, as eyes, or limbs, or features; as man about to die, or in catalepsy; or as an idle lazy fellow; or as an idol. **chhâ**, id. **chhâ-chhâ bōe-tín-tāng**, id. **bák-chiu chhâ-chhâ**, eyes fixed and motionless, as when about to die; or as naturally so; a look of unconcern or foolishness. **bák-chiu chhâ-chhâ tiàu-tiàu**, eyes fixed, glazed, and staring upwards, sign of death at hand.

chhâ-kang, tall and large-boned, ungainly and somewhat clumsy-looking, as a man. **chhâ-kang-siⁿ**, id.

phāiⁿ-kha-chhâ, ill-formed, as girls' feet; esp. from having been ill bound. **pák--khí phāiⁿ-kha-chhâ**, feet (of girl) ill bound.

chhâ [R. tsâi, materials]. **koaⁿ-chhâ**, a coffin (v. koaⁿ). **khí-chhâ-thâu**, to worship the coffin outside the door, just before it is carried to the grave.

chhá (R. chháu), to fry or parch on frying-pan, with little or no fat. **kan-ta-chhá**, do. without any fat or water (s. annoy). **chè-chhá**, to prepare medicines by parching thus. **chien-chhá**, to fry and parch. **chhá-khi-se**, fry till crisp. **jiét-jiét-chhá**, to fry with little fat. **jiét-chhá**, a small bowl of fried meat, at an eating-house. **kúi-jiét-chhá**, how many of them. **jiét-chhá-oáⁿ**, a small bowl for holding this eatable. **sió-chhá**, pork cut in very long, thin, narrow slices, and fried dry. **sió-chhá-bah**, id. **mīⁿ-chià chhá-bah**, wheat dough cooked with pork. **póh-phìⁿ-chhá**, fried slices of meat (pork) about an inch broad.

chhá (R. chháu), to make a disturbance; to annoy by noise and clamour. **chhá-lā**, id. **ká-chhá**, id. **ká-lá-chhá**, id. **chhá-jióng**, id. **chhá kàu-loān**, make a great confusion and disturbance, as by clamour. **kiáu-chhá**, to annoy; to make a disturbance. **chhá-jiók**, to make a noise, scolding and insulting.

chhà (R. chháu, = col. chhá). **táⁿ-chhà**, to annoy; to disturb by noise and clamour.

chhà (= chhā). **chhà-chhà-háu**, sound of water.

chhà [R. chhàu, paper money, &c.] **chíⁿ-chhà**, money in general. **chíⁿ-chhá ân**, hard pressed for money.

chhā — **chhā-chhā-háu**, sound, as of rain or waterfall, or constant talking. **chhā-chhā-lāu**, sound as of water dropping from a leak. **tsúi kún chhā-chhā**, water boiling violently. **chhī-bú chhī-chhā**, confused indistinct sound of talking. **loān-chhī-chhā**, confused or crowded, as mind with many matters; or as a busy market or crowd. **toā-chhī-chhā--chit-ē**, a tremendous turmoil, as on occasion of fighting, or arrival of mandarins or robbers.

chháⁿ — **kap--i chháⁿ-chhiú**, to throw out one's arms to fend off a blow.

chhāⁿ — **chhāⁿ-chhāⁿ-háu**, confused noise of gongs, drums, &c. **lô-kó chhāⁿ-chhāⁿ-tân**, gongs and drums making a loud confused noise. **chhîm-tih-chhāⁿ**, sound of various instruments. **phah-chhîm-tih-chhāⁿ**, to strike things (to amuse a child) as if they were musical instruments.

chhah (R. chhap). **thâu-chhah**, ornaments worn in women's hair. **chiam-á thâu-chhah**, ornaments for women's head in general.

chhah (R. chhap). **chhah-kak**, to piece (esp. with a triangular bit of cloth), generally at the corner; done in making a garment, from want of material, or to save it; also, an operation in the mensuration of fields of very peculiar shape, so as to calculate the odd corners. **chhah-koh**, to put in a triangular piece of cloth in the arm-pit of a dress. **chhah-ńg**, to put in triangular pieces in the inner side of the arm of a dress as it gets broader. **toā-chhah**, a large triangular piece, as in the seat of trousers. **sió-chhah**, a small triangular piece in a dress.

chhah (R. chhap), to insert; to set up, as in a socket; to plant slips, as of sugar-cane. **chhah-jip**, to insert.

kah-chhah, suiting well together, as the several parts of dress, &c. **chhēng-chhah**, manner of dress, as good or bad (v. chhēng). **ū-chiap-chhah**, to have proper connection, as the several parts of a literary composition. **chiap-chhah lâng-kheh**, to receive and pay attentions to guests. **gâu-chiap-chhah** (Cn.), good at any work, esp. at assisting a superior.

chhah-teh-khiā, to live alone, or almost alone, in a place, among a people quite different from us, *e.g.* among a different surname. **chhah-tī-hia khiā**, id. **chhah-ku** (r.), id. **chhah-ki** (C.), id. **an-chhah**, to arrange, as troops in garrisons and stations; to distribute those who have been rebels or pirates, and have made submission, putting them in small numbers here and there. **chhah kúi-ê**, to place a few such men separate from their old comrades.

chhah-kó, to join a mercantile firm, taking a small share (v. kó).

chhah-chhêng, to stick up branches of banyan on 5.5. **chhah-chhêng, khah-kiāⁿ-lêng: chhah-hiāⁿ, ōe tn̂g-miāⁿ**, sticking up banyan branches, we grow stronger than dragons; and the artemisia, we get long life. **chhah-hiāⁿ, ōe-khin-kiāⁿ**, &c., and we get strong and vigorous. **chhah-chhiⁿ**, to stick up green twigs (as on a field when the owner or farmer owes money) as a sign that the land or crop is claimed; or as on a house on occasion of rites for good luck, or in time of sickness (by sorcerer's instructions), to warn strangers away; or as on 5.5. **chhah kam-chià**, to plant out slips of sugar-cane.

chhah-io, to put the hands on the hip-joints. **chhah-chhiú**, id.; or, to put the hands in the pockets or into the folds of one's dress for warmth. **chhah-kiō**, to assist in carrying a sedan, as a third bearer; to hold the poles of a mandarin's sedan. **hû-chhah**, to hold up by the arm-pits, as when helping to walk.

chhah-hoe, to put flowers in the hair, as women do; to put flowers in a glass, &c.; an additional side-sail (like a studding-sail) in a junk. **chhah hoe-kan**, to put flowers in a flower-jar. **chhah-chek**, to put a candle on the stick that serves instead of a socket. **tsûn chhah-chek**, vessel sunk to the bottom, leaving only the end of the mast visible.

chhah-hiu^{n}, to stick an incense-stick in the old ashes in the censer that stands before an idol. **chhah-hû**, to stick written charms in the hair. **chhah-to**, to wear a knife or sword at one's side; the 18th radical when written at the side. **chhah-kî**, to stick up a small flag. **chhah-pio**, to stick up the prize that serves as a goal for the dragon-boat race. **chhah-pit**, to put a hair-pencil in its stand.

chhai (R. id.), a riddle; to guess one. **chhai-bī**, to guess a riddle. **chhai-khoà^{n}**, to try a guess. **chhai-tio̍h**, to guess rightly. **si-chhai**, a sort of gambling by lines of poetry. **teng-chhai**, puzzles put on transparent lanterns at the doors of scholars. **teng-chhai-bûn**, do. **chhai-gî** (R.), to suspect a man or a matter; to have suspicions.

chhâi [R. tsâi, to cut, to regulate, to diminish], (C. tsâi), to cut the edges of paper; to disband soldiers because too many; to diminish the number of officers to a command or division, not as punishment, but permanently for economy.

tsú-chhâi, to determine definitely; to settle authoritatively.

toā-tsóng-chhâi, the examiner for the Tsin-sze degree.

sèng-chhâi, ground-rent levied by military mandarins on government ground, esp. on the sea-beach.

chhâi-hông, a tailor. **chhâi-hông-chhiū^{n}**, a mandarin's tailor. **chhâi-chhioh**, the foot-measure used by tailors, longer than that used by carpenters and masons (v. chhioh).

chhâi khah-chió, to diminish the number, as of soldiers or officers.

chhâi-to, a knife for cutting even the edges of paper. **chhâi-tsoá**, to cut the edges of paper even. **chhâi-chheh**, to cut even the edges of a book, as in binding.

chhâi (R. id.) **chhâi-lông**, a wolf.

chhâi [R. tsâi, materials]. **chhâi-liāu**, materials.

chhâi [R. just at the time]. **chhâi-chhâi-chiah-lâi**, arrived just now.

chhái [R. coloured ornaments; ornamental hangings; an omen; a present, esp. with idea of good-luck].

sîn-chhái, expression of face, esp. as to health or intelligence. **ū-sîn-chhái**, to have a look of vigorous health, animation, or intelligence. **sîn-chhái chiok**, id. **bô-sîn-chhái**, having a spiritless, aimless look. **bô-sîn bô-chhái**, id.

chheng-chhái, clear, bright, and fair, as weather; genteel and polite in appearance, as wealthy or literary man. **khì-siōng chheng-chhái**, happy, cheerful look (of men or things). **khah chheng-chhái**, in better health now. **pak-té-lāi khah-chheng-chhái**, feeling better.

chhái-tiāu, an omen. **hó-chhái-tiāu**, a good omen. **chhái-thâu**, an omen. **thâu-chhái**, id.; red cloth put on the bow of a junk at the new-year for good luck. **hó-chhái-thâu**, a good omen. **phái^{n}-chhái-thâu**, a bad omen.

tsok-chhái, to make a present of money to a man that he may have good-luck. **sàng-chhái**, to present a long piece of red stuff (silk or woollen), as to a mandarin on some joyful occasion; to perform rites on the occasion of burning the idol "ông-iâ." **kat-chhái**, to hang up ornamental hangings, as at idolatrous celebrations. **kat chhái-lâu**, to make a temporary pagoda of bamboo and wood, ornamented with bright colours, and at night hung all over with lamps; a great idolatrous concourse is held for several days. **chhái-lâu**, this temporary pagoda; also (r.), an ornamental upper room, as for women. **chhái-lē̍**, street full of coloured hangings at an idolatrous display. **iû-soa^{n} chhái-lē̍**, to have the idol carried in a procession through the country, and also to have these hangings in the streets. **chhái-kiō**, a red bridal sedan. **chhái-pe̍h-tiàm**, a shop for the clothes used in burial.

chhái-chit, to weave coloured figures. **chhái-ūi**, to paint in various colours. **chhái-sek**, vari-coloured. **ngó͘-chhái**, having five colours; variegated. **ngó͘-chhái-hûn**, a five-coloured variegated cloud. **khí-ngó͘-chhái**, to reflect bright colours, as a diamond, &c.

kong-chhái, bright as a mirror, or as the sky when the sun is about to come out; bright as a healthy red or ruddy face; also (R.), very richly decorated. **hoa-chhái** (R.), very richly decorated.

chhái (R. id.) **ū-chhiù-chhái**, paying attentions, as to a visitor (v. chhiù).

chhái [R. chháu, to annoy, = col. chhá]. **kái-chhái**, to annoy, to tease; to torment by annoyances.

chhái (R. id.), to pluck, as flowers or tea-leaves; (to buy), (worth while), (perhaps), (a spindle). **chhái-hoe**, to pluck flowers; to sip honey from flowers, as bees. **chhái-tê**, to gather tea-leaves.

chhái-pān, to select and buy, as goods. **chhái-bóe**, id. **chhái-tiáh**, to send out and buy grain from many places, as merchant or mandarin. **phài-chhái-mái^{n}**, to levy forced contributions from rich men under the name of buying rice.

thih-chhái, a thin iron spindle on which the thread is rolled by the spinning-wheel. **chhái-tsûn**, the leather-guard on it separating the thread from the endless band.

chhái-liên-koa, a song sung at the procession of the idol "ông-iâ." **chhiù^{n} chhái-liên**, to sing this song at the procession. **chhái-liên-thâu**, the principal subscriber for a boat (ông-tsûn) for that idol. **tsng-chhái-liên**, to dress him up in great splendour on the occasion. **chhái-liên-kha**, the other contributors.

chhìn-chhái, at random; no matter how; any way; carelessly (v. chhìn). **kiám-chhái**, perhaps; if perhaps. **khiám-chhái**, id. **thiám-chhái**, id. **tiám-chhái**, id. **tú-chhái**, id.

bô-chhái, alas! how unfortunate! said of the death of a person or of a thing being destroyed. **chin bô-chhái**, how very unfortunate! (as above). **bô-chhái hit-ê-lâng**, alas for that man, as when dead or having committed some very shameful action, making him infamous for ever. **bô-chhái hit-ê-mih^{n}**, said of a thing quite lost or spoiled. **bô-chhái-chhùi**, talking is of no use. **bô-chhái-kang**, not worth the trouble; to lose one's pains. **bô-chhái kha-kut, thó-kha khit-lē̍-kiâ^{n}**, a long walk to no purpose. **bô-chhái in-pē-bú si^{n}--i**, it was not worth while for his parents to get such a son.

chhài (R. id.), vegetables, esp. mustard plant and

cabbage; meat or any condiment to rice; vegetarian food as opposed to animal food.

chhài-thâu, a long sort of turnip; the head man of a vegetarian hall and society.

chhài-gėk, false jade-stone.

chhài-iû, ground-nut oil. **sng-chhài**, pickles. **chhài-kap**, the common pigeon, not the carrier (v. kap). **chhài-ièn**, a native sea-weed (used to make a jelly like bird's-nest).

chhài-bú, a very salt kind of sauce. **chhài-tsúi**, juice of vegetables. **chhài-tà^n**, a load of vegetables carried to market. **chhài-koái^n**, a stalk of a vegetable, esp. of mustard. **chhài-pau**, minced long turnips mixed with various things (meat, &c.), rolled up in a thin cake and fried. **chhái-pó**, long turnips sliced and salted. **kiâm-chhài**, the leaves of the mustard plant salted for food. **khòng-chhài**, long turnips salted and boiled soft. **chhìn-chhài**, cold vegetables; to weigh vegetables. **liàm-chhài**, to pick off leaves and other refuse from vegetables before cooking. **tòh-chhài** (C.), id. (v. tòh).

chhài-chî^n, money paid for various condiments, meat, vegetables, &c., and all except the rice. **chhài-kheng**, a basket for buying meat, &c., for household use. **tsú-chhài**, to cook meat, vegetables, &c., all except rice. **bóe-chhài**, to buy meat and all sorts of condiments, animal or vegetable; a comprador who provides provisions. **pān-chhài--ê**, a man who makes meals or feasts for sale. **kā--lâng pān-chhài**, to make ready such meals. **pān-chhài**, to procure and prepare food, as for guests. **àn-chhài**, please eat! **piēn-chhài**, common ordinary fare; pot-luck; a plain common meal. **chhe-chhài piēn-pn̄g**, id. **lō-chhài**, dried or salted meat and other condiments for use on a journey. **sàng-lō-chhài**, to present such meat or condiments to a friend or mandarin on his starting for a journey.

chho-chhài, animal food and vegetarian diet as contrasted. **chheng-chhài**, vegetarian diet. **chiảh-chhài**, to be a vegetarian. **chiảh-tn̂g-chhài**, to be a strict vegetarian at every meal. **chhài-kàu**, the vegetarian sect. **chhài-tn̂g**, a vegetarian hall or lodge. **pān-chhài-toh**, to prepare a vegetarian meal. **chhài-pùt**, idols that have no animal food offered to them. **chhài-pn̄g**, cheap and poor offerings to the spirits (v. pn̄g). **chhài-kong**, a vegetarian keeper of temple, appointed by priests to cook for them, but not himself a priest.

chhài-soe, vegetables in general. **chháu-chhài**, vegetables and other small plants. **chhài-koe**, a long soft sort of cucumber. **chhài-tāu**, a bean with a very long pod; used in the pod. **tāu-chhài**, sprouted beans. **chhài-hoe**, cauliflower (v. hoe). **koà-chhài**, the mustard plant. **pėh-chhài**, cabbage. **ko-lê-chhài**, foreign cabbage. **chhài-ki**, **sì-bák sa^n-tùi**, one should be equitable in dealings (fig. from embroidery).

chhài — **bé-ka-chhài**, young "bé-ka" fish, a few inches long.

chhāi — **bák-sîn chhāi-chhāi**, eyes looking firmly and intently.

chhāi — **ām-kún chhāi-chhāi**, neck very short, stout, and stiff.

chhāi, to set; to place; to place firmly; to be placed, as an idol. **chhāi-pút**, to set up an idol; to have an idol in the house. **chhāi sîn-tsú**, to set up ancestral tablets. **chhāi-í**, to set a chair. **chhāi-toh**, to set a table. **chhāi teng-hé**, to set a small lamp.

ka-nn̂g-jit chhāi ti-chia, all day here, without ever going away! as an idle fellow; or as a petitioner urgently asking and refusing to go away. **tiā^n-tiā^n chhāi--teh-chē**, id.; sitting (either as idle man, or person urgently pressing something).

chhāi (T. sái, Cn. sāi). **chhāi phoà-noā^n**, very urgent and quite devoid of shame or self-respect, in trying to get what one wants; as child taking no denial; or as a beggar that you may scold, insult, or beat, but he won't desist; or as poor relative or acquaintance who will have something from us whether we will or no, = siet-nāi^n.

chhāi (= sái). **chhāi àm-tók**, to conspire against a man; to cause evil or trouble to a man by secret plots.

chhai^n (T.), = A. chheng, a thousand.

chhâi^n (T.), = A. chhâm. chhêng, silk-worm, &c.

chhái^n (T.), = A. chhéng, a sort of dusting brush; to dust or brush with it.

chhái^n (T.), = A. chhéng, to waste lavishly.

chhái^n (= chhái). **chhái^n-ūi**, to paint in colours.

chhài^n — **chhài^n-sek**, to work in colours, as in painting or embroidery, &c. **chhài^n-pėh**, some white put on a ground of another colour. **chhài^n koá-âng**, put on a little red. **beh-chhài^n sím-mih-sek**, what colour do you wish to put on?

chhak, a scroll (as a map or picture) for hanging up. **chit-pak-chhak**, one scroll. **chhak-koái^n**, the rollers of scrolls. **chhak-tsoá**, thick paper used for scrolls. **pè-chhak**, thick paper used for scrolls.

chhak — **chhak-khiā**, stiff, as well-starched clothes, or as thick paste-board.

chhák (R. chhók), to cut with a chisel; to pierce or stab; (a chisel). **chhák-á**, a chisel. **poe-chhák**, a broad chisel, about two inches. **chhùn-chhák**, a chisel one inch broad. **hun-chhák**, a narrow chisel, from one-tenth to four-tenths of an inch. **sì-hun-chhák**, a chisel four-tenths of an inch broad. **kńg-chhák**, a gouge. **pí^n-chhák**, a broad chisel with thin edge.

chhì-chhák, to grieve, as if piercing the heart; pained and dazzled (eyes) by the sun. **ka-lé-chhák**, close fighting hand to hand. **chià^n-chhák tò-phut**, cutting, slashing, and piercing, as in close combat; cutting the material so as to spoil and waste it, as an unskilful workman.

ngī^n-chhák, too hard, as fur or hair; too stiff and determined, as language.

chhák-he, to caulk. **chhák he-tsoā**, id. **chhák pé-lāu**, to caulk and stop leaks. **chhák-hoe**, to carve flowers; to carve. **chhák-khang**, to make a mortice. **chhák-sún**, to make a tenon.

chham (R. id.), to mix; to report an officer's misconduct, as his superior does, accusing him to a still higher superior.

chham-siông, to deliberate together.

chham-hú, a military or naval officer, below a "hiāp;" sometimes called a colonel. **chham-chiòng**, id. **chham-bô**, an officer who assists in planning battles, &c.

kah-chham--teh, mixed together. **sa^n-lām-chham**, mixed, as good and bad, of the same sort of article. **chham-lam**, mixed. **chham-chhu**, mixed in confusion. **chham-chhi**, id. **chham-lâi chhap-khì**, id. **chham-chhùi**, mixed in confusion, as several sorts or sizes, when all ought to be uniform; or as room all in disorder.

hó chham-phái^n, good and bad mixed. **hó-phái^n**

厦英大辭典

chham-poàn, good and bad mixed in about equal proportions. **chham-thn̂g**, to mix some sugar. **thâu-mn̂g chham-pe̍h**, hair partly gray. **chham khah-po̍h**, to dilute, as tea or liquor.

chhâm [R. the silkworm], (C. chhêng, T. chhâiⁿ, Cn. chhûiⁿ). **chhâm thò-si**, the silkworm vomits silk. **khiong-chhâm**, a medicinal preparation of preserved silkworms.

chhâm (cf. khâm, chhiâm, chhîm). **phah toā-chhâm**, to beat large cymbals. **toā-chhâm-ké**, a pair of large cymbals along with drums. **chit-hù toā-chhâm**, a pair of large cymbals.

chhám (R. id.), wretched; miserable. **chhám-chhoeh**, id. **chhiⁿ-chhám**, do. **chhiⁿ-chhiⁿ chhám-chhám**, very miserable and wretched. **chhiⁿ-chhám lo̍k-phek**, id. **ai-oàn chhiⁿ-chhám**, bewailing one's miserable fate. **ai-chhám**, deeply grieved. **chhám--ah**, alas!

chhám-tām, affairs all gone wrong; countenance or sky overcast. **chhám-sòng**, wretchedly poor. **tio̍h-chhám**, to meet with calamity. **tng-chhám**, just now become very miserable. **chhám-chhut**, a tragedy.

chhám (R. chham?). **chhám-pe̍h**, gray, as beard or hair, white and black mixed.

chhàm (R. id.), to foretell; to prognosticate. **chhàm-gú**, a prophecy. **chhàm i-ê-hó**, to prognosticate good fortune for him. **chhàm i ōe-hó**, id.

chiù-chhàm, imprecations and curses; incantations against others. **liām-chiù liām-chhàm**, to perform incantations against others.

chhàm [R. to repent, rites for the dead, &c.] **keng-chhàm**, Buddhist religious books. **chin-keng chin-chhàm**, true books of religion (Buddhist). **che-chhàm**, Buddhist rites for the dead (v. che). **pài-chhàm**, to perform such rites. **pài-chhàm-tsòe**, id. **pài-tsn̂g-chhâm**, to perform very expensive rites for the dead for several days.

chhām — **chhām-chhām**, long continued, as rain or tears. **ba̍k-sái chhām-chhām-lâu**, tears flow in streams. **hē chhām-chhām-lo̍h**, rain for several days steadily.

chhan (R. id.), to murmur, as water running, or as kettle simmering. **tsúi chhan**, water murmuring.

chhan, to groan; to moan. **aiⁿ-aiⁿ-chhan**, to groan sadly. **hāiⁿ-hāiⁿ-chhan**, id. **chiap-chiap-chhan**, to groan incessantly, as a sick man. **hiⁿ-hiⁿ-chhan**, id. **hēⁿ-hēⁿ-chhan**, id.

iau chhan, pá chhan; chia̍h-pá, kiò kan-lân, always grumbling and complaining, even when just having eaten enough. **khàu-chhan**, to complain without cause, or for insufficient cause. **gâu khàu-chhan**, always murmuring and complaining without cause; falsely complaining of poverty, &c., only said in scolding people for being dissatisfied. **lí teh-khàu-chhan**, you dissatisfied murmuring fellow!

chhan (C.), = A. chheng, a thousand.

chhan (R. id.) **chhan-jio̍k**, having no powerful influence to back one, and therefore weak in a quarrel or feud.

chhan [R. a feast, a meal]. **it-jit sam-chhan**, to have three meals a-day. **boán-chhan** (X.), the Communion; the Lord's Supper. **hòe-chhím bông-chhan** (R.), to forget to eat and sleep, as from grief.

chhân (C.), a silkworm.

chhân (T.), a large hank of yarn or hemp fibres.

chhân [R. chhan, feeble, weak]. **chhân-chhoāⁿ**, a small sort of eel.

chhân (R. tsân), cruel. **chhe-chhân**, violent or cruel; fond of fighting, striking, or injuring people. **sim chhe-chhân**, cruel-hearted. **sim put-chí-chhân**, cruel, pitiless. **chhiú put-chí-chhân**, fond of fighting and striking. **chhân-chhiú**, id. **chhân-thâu**, rough and violent, as a coarse low fellow, ready for anything bad (s. field).

chhân — **chhân-chháu** (C.), = sin-chháu, a plant from which a cool jelly is made.

chhân — **chhân-iⁿ**, a dragon-fly.

chhân (R. tiân), an irrigated field; a surname. **chit-khu-chhân**, one irrigated field. **chhân-iûⁿ**, a flat plain of rice fields. **chhân-khu**, irrigated fields in general. **chhân-bé**, fields in general. **chhân-hn̂g**, cultivated fields, either wet or dry. **chhân-tī** (Cn. T.), id.

chhân-hoāⁿ, raised boundaries of irrigated fields (v. hoāⁿ). **chhân-keh**, subsoil of a field (v. keh). **chhân-gia̍p**, landed property. **chhân-tse**, rent of fields. **chhân-khòe**, deed of sale of fields. **chhim-chhân**, deep miry rice fields.

tsoh-chhân, to cultivate fields, esp. irrigated fields. **tsoh-chhân-lâng**, a farmer. **khui-chhân**, to begin to cultivate waste land, laying it out for irrigation. **èng-chhân**, to manure fields. **pè-chhân**, to plant out the young rice from the seed-plot.

chhân-tsû, yams. **chhân--ê**, grown in wet fields, as potatoes. **chhân-kap-á**, a sort of frog.

chhân-thâu-má, title of the spirits of a shrine or small temple holding the tablets of persons who have no posterity. **chhân siùⁿ-kang**, an idol of the surname "chhân."

sán-chhân gâu-sò-tsúi (barren dry fields absorb much water); debts eat up gains; lean men eat much (prov.)

chhán (C.), = A. chhéng, a duster

chhán — **phah-chhán** (C.), = A. phah-chhéng, to use wastefully.

chhàn (R. id.) **chhàn-lān**, splendid, dazzlingly beautiful.

chhàn — **ôe-chhàn**, the inner sole of a shoe, close to the foot. **chhàn-phê**, leather inner sole of shoe.

chhang — **lin-chhang**, the teat and the part of the breast close to it, of man or woman.

chhang (R. chhong), an onion or leek; a socket or ferule or such tube; colour of onion leaf, dull blue of common Chinese cotton cloth.

chhang-kn̂g, a ferule; a funnel for a lamp; a cover for point of pen; or such sort of tube. **chek-chhang**, a candle-socket. **khí-chhang**, porous, as lava, or as leavened cakes.

chhang-chhài, onions, leeks, &c. **hong-chhang**, a sort of leek, good for colds. **chhang-thâu**, onions (root). **chhang-tsu**, onions (roots) cut down for eating. **chhang-pe̍h**, white part of onions near the root. **jiet-iû-chhang**, onions cooked in fat.

chhang, a sort of sweetmeat drawn out in long crisp porous sticks. **thn̂g-chhang**, id. **pe̍h-thn̂g-chhang**, white sort.

chhang (R. chhiong). **chhang-pô**, the Acorus, hung up as a charm on 5. 5.

chhang (R. chhong). **chhang-miâⁿ**, clever, intelligent, talented.

chháng — **chháng-péh**, very white gray, almost white.

chháng (cf. chhiáng). **jû chháng-chháng**, entangled, involved, perplexed.

chhàng, to hide, as a tiger among reeds, or as a thief or other bad character among promiscuous company in his resort. **chhàng-làng tī-hia**, he usually resorts and hides there. **chhàng-ke** (T.), the head of a gang of robbers.

chhàng (R. id.) **chhàng-chháng**, all in disorder, as hair. **chhàng-mn̂g**, hair dishevelled; feathers ruffled, as a bird when ill; to erect the feathers of the tail, as a turkey-cock. **chhàng-bé**, to erect its tail, as cat or tiger. **chhàng-chhiu**, moustaches on end with rage.

hòng-hòng chhàng-chhàng (C.), incautious or reckless in doing a thing.

chhap, to meddle with, to have to do with, as with a person or affair; to shuffle, as cards.

chhap-lap, to meddle with, to associate with, as with promiscuous company, esp. with persons of suspicious character; to associate with, rather improperly or incautiously; to mix up, as cards in shuffling. **chhap-lap--i**, don't have anything to do with him.

kau-chhap, to be associated or connected, as in business, so as to be involved in his responsibilities or losses. **bô-sa^n-kau-chhap**, not at all involved in his affairs.

chhap pâi-á, to shuffle cards.

chhap-tsáp, mixed in confusion. **chhap-jióng**, all in confusion; great confusion and noise. **chham-lâi chhap-khì**, confusedly mixed.

chhap-chhùi, to talk when we have no business to talk. **chhap-chhap chhùi-chhùi**, in a disorderly state, as room, &c. **chhap-chhùi-chhéng**, all in disorder or confusion, as things or affairs. **chhap-chhùi ê seng-lí**, a miscellaneous small business.

m̄-chhap, will not meddle with the matter; will have nothing to do with it. **m̄-chhap--i**, will have nothing to do with him, one way or another. **goá-m̄-chhap**, it is no affair of mine; I will not meddle at all. **m̄-chhap-lí-tn̂g**, **m̄-chhap-lí-té**, will not meddle with your affair in any way. **bòh--tit chhap--i**, have nothing to do with him, either for or against him. **chhap-sū**, to meddle with other people's matters. **chhap tāi-chì**, id. **ài-chhap-sū**, fond of meddling in other people's affairs. **chhap-êng-sū**, to meddle with what is no concern of ours.

chhap (R. id.) **chhap-hiet hōe-bêng**, to make a league or confederacy by mixing each other's blood in liquor and drinking it (forbidden by law), esp. for rebellious ends. **chhap-hiet tông-bêng**, id. **chhap-huih kiet-bêng**, id.

chhat [R. to investigate]. **séng-chhat**, to examine into. **siông-sè séng-chhat**, do. very minutely and carefully. **tsa-chhat**, to investigate officially, as the messengers of a mandarin. **hóng-chhat**, to make official investigation (somewhat secretly), as mandarin.

àn-chhat-si, the provincial judge. **àn-chhat-hâm**, having the rank of provincial judge without the office.

sit-kak-chhat, to neglect one's duty (as mandarin, or as person in charge of something), so that much injury ensues.

chhat (R. id.), to blot out; to score out. **chhat-siau**, id. **chhat-siàu**, to mark an account settled; to score off an account. **chhat chit-jī**, to blot out a character.

chhat (R. chhek), varnish; lacquer; to varnish. **sái-chhat**, to varnish. **chhit-chhat**, id. **tsú-chhat**, to boil varnish, in preparing it. **ká-chhat**, to strain and press out the prepared varnish in making "sèk-chhat."

iû-chhat, paint and varnish; to paint or varnish, in general. **iû-chhat sai-hū**, a painter and varnisher; a painter. **chhat sai-hū**, id. **kêng-iû pù-chhat**, paint must be put on thin; but varnish may be thick, several coats.

hé-chhat, a cement like wax, melted by a heated iron. **he-chhat**, varnish mixed with lime, as a cement for crevices. **chhat-mī^n**, a very strong cement made of flour and varnish. **chhi^n-chhat**, unprepared varnish, duller colour. **sek-chhat**, prepared varnish. **kan-chhat**, unmixed varnish, without any colour.

chhat-chhiū, the varnish-tree, from the juice of which varnish is made; the leaves are beautifully red in winter. **chhat-liāu**, material for varnish, ready for use. **chhat-seh**, a brush for varnishing or painting; a paint-brush. **chhat-khì**, varnished or lacquered wares.

chhat-kim, to make idolatrous paper in imitation of gold. **chhat-kim pè-póh**, id. **chhat-lėk**, to varnish light green. **chhat-chhi^n**, to varnish a bluish green. **ūi-ơ chhat-péh**, to scribble and scrawl black and white; said also of a dirty face, esp. of a boy.

khit-chhat-kā, to get a sore from the effect of varnish; the exhalation from it is enough to affect some constitutions.

chhát [R. chėk, a robber?]. **péh-chhát**, a lie. **péh-chhát-ōe**, id. **péh-péh chhát-chhát**, all lies together. **kóng-péh-chhát**, to tell a lie.

chhát (R. chėk), a robber, a thief; a bandit; a rebel. **chhát-thâu**, a head of thieves, robbers, pirates, or rebels. **chhát-hé**, one of a gang of thieves, pirates, &c. **chhát-á**, a young or raw thief or pirate. **chhát-lá**, id. **chhát-bôe**, a thief's spy.

chhát-bé, thieves, robbers, or pirates. **hó-bé-chhát**, a skilful thief, robber, &c. **hiáng-bé-chhát**, great highway-robbers. **hái-chhát**, a pirate. **hoán-chhát**, rebels. **chhát-húi**, banditti. **chhát-khò**, rebels, banditti, or great bands of robbers. **cheng-piàng ê-chhát**, a housebreaker; a burglar. **kiap-chhát**, a robber. **kiông-kiap-chhát**, a burglar; a highway-robber. **kiông-kòng-chhát**, a burglar. **chhú-chhát-á**, a pilferer; a thief who steals small articles, as clothes, &c. **liông-sim-chhát**, a thief or robber who leaves a good deal not stolen. **kun-tsú-chhát**, a thief who looks like a respectable man (so that you would not suspect him), who steals small and valuable things; said also of a man who has an intrigue with another's wife.

chhát-chhi^n, a rascal or scoundrel who injures or cheats, or plunders others. **chhát-phe**, an abandoned lad on the way to become a robber. **soa^n-chhát** (C.), a tiger.

chhát-bák, a covetous eye. **chhàt-sim**, a covetous heart. **chhát-sim chhát-hēng**, covetous heart and conduct. **chhát-hêng**, coarse large uncultivated appearance. **chhát-siòng**, id. **chhát-mih^n**, stolen goods. **chhàt-hè**, id. **chhát-siū**, a den of robbers or resort of thieves, pirates, &c. **chhát-chêng bēng-àn**, cases of robbery and murder.

chhát--ah, thief! thief! **hiàm-chhàt**, to call out "thief!" **jióng-chhát**, to make a loud outcry and

厦英大辭典

shouting after a thief. **thong-chhát**, to be in league with rebels or robbers, &c. **tsáu-chhát**, to flee from robbers or bandits. **tsáu-chhát gū-tiòh-hó**, fleeing from robbers meets a tiger; out of the frying-pan into the fire. **tng-chhát**, to wait to catch a thief. **chhiō-chhát**, to search for thieves with a light. **tiàu-chhát**, to tie up a thief by his hands. **tún-chhát**, to fasten a thief to a large stone (as punishment). **phiáh-chhát**, to crucify a robber. **cheng-chhát**, to go in force to attack piratical or robber villages. **tsòe-chhát chit-kiⁿ**, **chiú-chhát chit-mîⁿ**, though the thief comes only in one watch, we must be on guard all night (v. chiú). **chhát kiap-chhát**, one robber robbing another of his booty (said of a cheat being cheated in his turn). **chhát piàⁿ-chhát**, thieves or bad men quarrelling among themselves. **chhát hoah-chhát**, a thief shouting out "stop thief!" that he may himself escape detection (said of a bad man condemning in others the very things that he does himself).

chhau [R. chho, to hold, to exercise], to drill; to exercise. **saⁿ**, **chhau--khí-lâi**, to hold up one's clothes with the hand, as when crossing a stream, walking on wet road, or going down a steep path.

chhau-ién, to drill; to exercise. **chhau-liēn**, do. **chhau-peng**, to exercise soldiers. **khui-chhau**, to commence the (half-yearly) drill or review. **lòh-chhau**, to go to drill or review, as troops. **tsúi-chhau**, a naval drill or review. **soaⁿ-chhau**, drill or review on land. **toā-chhau**, a large review. **sió-chhau**, small do. (s. copy).

chhau [R. chiau or chiâu, grieved, scorched, = col. chhiau]. **chhau-sim peh-pak**, heart sorely distressed, agitated, and ready to break with distress and anxiety. **chhau-sim**, id.

chhau (Cn.) **chhe-chhe chhau-chhau**, in great numbers or quantities, = lāu-jiėt. **chhe-chhau**, id. **jiėt-chhau-chhau**, in great numbers or crowds, as persons.

chhau (R. id.), to copy a writing. **chhau-jī**, id. **chhau-siá**, to write out a copy, *e.g.* as clerk in public office. **àm-chhau**, to write out a passage of a book from memory. **chhau-pún**, a manuscript copy. **chhiú-chhau--ê**, copied by hand, as a book. **chhiú-chhau** (C.), = chhiú-chhih, a memorandum-book. **chhau-siàu**, to transcribe an account. **chhau-chiàⁿ**, to write a fair copy. **sió-chhau**, manuscripts containing copies of official documents and news (esp. from the capital), sold in the provinces from the want of newspapers.

chhau (= chhâu, tsâu, chhiau), to exterminate.

chhâu (= chhau, &c.) **chhâu-biėt**, to exterminate. **chhâu sam-tsók**, to kill an offender along with his family, and the families of his wife and mother.

chhâu (Cn.), = A. chhiâu, to alter (slightly) the place or position of a thing.

chháu [R. chhiáu, slightly]. **chháu-chháu**, but small; of small extent; said (*e.g.*) politely in speaking of one's own business.

chháu (R. id., = col. chhá, chhái). **chháu-lāu**, to wrangle; loud clamour; to make an uproar in order to cause annoyance or trouble. **chháu-nāuⁿ**, id. **chháu-chháu-jióng**, constant brawling or violent noisy disputing. **chháu-táh**, to cause trouble and disturbance, as at a house or shop (v. táh).

chháu [R. thó, head, = col. thâu]. **lát-chháu**, strength.

chháu [R. chhó, the state of Tsoo, under the Chow dynasty]. **chháu-pà-ông**, name of a famous king of that state; a usurper.

chháu — **chháu-tsōng** (esp. C.), to pretend that a thing exists that has no reality.

chháu [R. khó, the mouth, = kháu]. **chiáh toā-chháu**, determined to have a large fee, as doctor or mandarin's people. **hó-chhī-chháu**, a good trade at good price and many customers. **hó-chháu-hâm** (C. T. hó-kháu-hâm), able to eat anything with good appetite and good digestion; voracious. **uih-koe-ko, phah chháu-lô**, a child's game (v. uih).

chháu — **niūⁿ-chháu**, provisions; provender.

chháu (R. chhó), grass; herbs; weeds, reeds, small shrubs or brush-wood, ferns, &c. (fur); said also of some coarse or inferior things. **chit-phō-chháu**, a large bunch of growing grass, weeds, or small shrubs. **chit-ki-chháu**, a stalk of grass, &c. **chháu-ki**, a stalk of grass; a straw. **chháu-ki poáh-tó-lâng** (a straw makes a man fall), great disasters come from small causes.

hoan-chháu, to chew the cud. **thoáⁿ-chháu**, to cut up grass and small plants for fuel. **khau-chháu**, to root out grass, weeds, &c., for any purpose. **tsat-chháu**, to pack with straw (as furniture) by wrapping straw round it. **liáh-chháu**, to thatch. **khàm-chháu**, to cover loosely with straw.

chháu-chiâu, a boat that carries grass and brushwood for fuel. **chháu-á-liâu**, a shop where they sell grass, &c., for fuel (v. liâu). **chháu-tsáh**, an instrument for chopping straw, as to mix with lime.

chháu-lâng, a figure of a man made of straw, &c., as for "tāi-sin" in superstitious rites, or for use as a scare-crow. **chháu-pau**, a bag made of straw or grass-matting; a stupid fellow. **chháu-in**, a wisp of straw. **chháu-chèng**, a straw or reed mat. **chháu-siⁿ**, id. **chháu-sim**, the best sort of reeds for mats. **chháu-phí**, a small sod of turf. **chháu-phí-á**, id. **chháu-phiáⁿ**, a sod of turf; also, straw beaten small and made into round cakes for mixing in mortar. **chháu-phiáⁿ-he**, mortar made with lime and these straw cakes (with little sand and little or no clay) for the surface of good walls. **chhiah chháu-phiáⁿ**, to dig up sods of turf for laying turf. **thoáⁿ chháu-phiáⁿ**, to tear up turf for fuel. **chháu-he**, mortar made of mud (only) mixed with coarse cut straw.

chháu-iòh, vegetable medicines. **chháu-thâu**, roots of grass and small plants.

chháu-pán, coarsely cut blocks for printing. **chháu-nîⁿ**, an inferior (local) sort of the medicinal plant called "nîⁿ."

chháu-pe, a grassy piece of ground; a meadow, a grassy plot. **chháu-tiûⁿ** (C.), grassy ground. **hó-chháu-tiûⁿ** (C.), fine grassy ground suitable for grazing cattle. **chháu-tē** (F.), = soaⁿ-tiûⁿ, the country, as opposed to the town.

chháu-á-sèng, quick-tempered; a quick temper (like grass that rapidly catches fire and as rapidly goes out).

hoâiⁿ-chháu bô-niⁿ, **tit-chháu bô-liàm**, very gentle; very honest.

chháu-meh, a grasshopper. **chháu-kâu**, an insect like a large grasshopper. **chháu-hî**, a fish that feeds on grass.

phê-chháu, fur of animals, as used for dress, &c. **hê-lî-chháu**, foxes' fur. **mn̂g-chháu**, fur; hair or wool or fur; feathers on the bird.

9

chhàu [R. chhò͘, to meet with]. **chhàu-khám,** unexpectedly and suddenly; accidentally, by chance. **chhàu-tú-khám,** id. **sa^{n}-tàu-chhàu,** accidentally and fortunately met. **chhàu-khiáu,** accidentally and fortunately. **chhàu-chhi^{n}-kia^{n},** suddenly starting, as at a ghost.

chhàu (R. hiù), bad-smelling; suppurating; rotten; vile; (deaf); much said in vile scolding. **àu-chhàu,** rotten and bad-smelling. **phang-chhàu,** sweet-smelling and bad-smelling. **m̄-bat phang-chhàu,** not able to distinguish good and bad.

chhàu-lâng, deaf. **chhàu-hī-lâng,** id.

chhàu-thâu, scabbed head. **chhàu-bīn,** face having sores; unpleasant countenance (v. bīn). **chhàu-bák,** eyes sore and suppurating, or ulcerated (chronic). **chhàu-kha,** leg having a bad sore or ulcer. **chhàu chhùi-kak,** corners of mouth suppurating.

chhàu-sim, having a very bad heart, always trying to injure people; having a rotten heart, as fruit or potatoes. **chhàu-sim tók-hēng,** heart and conduct very wicked and injurious. **chhàu-hēng,** very wicked injurious conduct. **chhàu-chiēn,** very mean and low (v. chiēn). **chhàu-miâ^{n},** having a vile reputation; notoriously bad. **chhàu-chî^{n},** money got by vile means. **chiáh-chhàu-bí,** said of the underlings of yamuns, esp. of customs.

chhàu-hōe, wild aloes.

chhàu-lāu, appearing much older than he really is.

sio chhàu-ta, to singe or scorch; burned taste. **chhàu-hé,** having a smoky taste. **chhàu-hé-hun,** id. **chhàu-hé-lo-bī,** having a singed burned taste (v. lo). **chhàu-thô͘,** having an unpleasant earthy taste or smell, as tea or water. **chhàu-iû,** having an unpleasant oily smell or taste, as food ill-cooked. **chhàu-chho,** strong unpleasant smell, as of fish. **chhàu-chhi^{n},** bad tasted because too raw, as ground-nuts not fired enough. **chhàu-sng,** sour from being kept too long. **kam-chià chhàu-bák,** sugar-cane bad tasted. **chhàu-hiu^{n} han-tsû,** potatoes having faults in them. **chhàu-hièn,** heavy smell, as of meat. **chhàu-hiam-hiam,** very stinking. **chhàu-sioh,** rather bad-smelling, as fish about to spoil.

m̄-thang-lā; chit-lā chit-chhàu, don't raise the matter; if raised it will be very unpleasant.

chhàuh [R. táp, constantly]. **chhàuh-chhàuh,** = tàuh-tàuh, constantly.

chhe (R. chhui), (C. chhoe, Cn. chhö), to cook by steaming. **chhe-ké** (C. chhoe-kóe), to cook cakes by steaming. **chhe-tháng,** a large wooden vessel used for steaming rice. **chhe-pe͘,** a bamboo frame used in cooking by steam. **chhö-tsoah** (Cn.), a bamboo frame for steaming and cooking (v. tsoah).

chhe (C.), = A. chhoe, beginning. **tng-goân-chhe** (C.), at the beginning (s. send).

chhɛ (C.), = chɛ, chhê, = A. tsa, to investigate.

chhe [R. chha, a fork, to fork or branch out; crossed, as strokes or hands; to overlap], (C. chhɛ), a cross made in shape of St. Andrew's cross; one of the notes of Chinese music.

Also, **chhɛ** (C.), = A. chha, to overlap.

khui-chhe, to branch out, as a tree or branch, &c. **sim-koa^{n} khui-chhe,** mind distracted by having to attend to two separate pieces of work or business, each being important and engrossing. **hî-bé-chhe,** shaped like a fish's forked tail. **siang-chhe-lō͘,** road dividing into two. **sa^{n}-chhe-lō͘,** road dividing into three making four in all. **sì-chhe-lō͘,** place where four roads meet.

phah-chhe, to make a mark in shape of St. Andrew's cross, as in a book or document, &c. **phiet-chhe,** to mark (as bad or blundered) by such a cross; to be at variance with; to have a slight quarrel. **phoat-chhe,** id.

chhe-chhiú, to put each hand into the sleeve of the other.

chhe-á, a forked pole. **thih-chhe,** a trident-shaped weapon. **thô͘-lêng-chhe,** a sort of trident-shaped weapon, for catching a sort of eel called "thô͘-lêng." **bâ-chhɛ-á** (C.), a three-pronged trident used in hunting. **kong-chhɛ** (C.), sort of three-pronged fork for spearing wild animals.

chiáh--liáu toā-chhe, taking too much of the meat and condiments at a meal (opening the chop-sticks too wide, and taking large lumps).

chhe [R. chha, divergent streams], (C. chhɛ). **siang-chhe-hô,** confluence of streams.

chhe — **chhe-chhe chhau-chhau,** in great quantities; abundant, as food at a feast. **chhe-chhau,** id.

chhe — **jiėt-chhe-chhe,** very desirous of something. **hê-chhe-chhe,** = hê-chhè-chhè, managing matters very carelessly.

chhe [R. chha, to differ, to send], (C. chhɛ), to send (a person); (to employ, as messenger or servant); constables or police.

chhe-khién, to send (a person). **chhe-ēng,** to employ, as a servant; a servant. **chhe-kah,** to employ, as a servant. **chhe-kiò,** id. **chhe-sái,** to employ, or use (as person), or send messages. **hōng-chhe,** to be sent, as by a superior or person in authority. **bōe-chhe--tit,** not fit to be employed or sent on such business.

chhe-tsûn, mandarin vessels used for action against pirates or smugglers. **chhe-sū,** the business on which any one is sent officially.

khim-chhe, imperial messenger, as any commissioner or ambassador. **hù-chhe,** an assistant messenger, great or small. **kè-chhe,** persons used to convey criminals to their place of punishment, &c. **niû^{n}-chhe,** collector of land-tax.

goân-chhe, constables who are sent out with warrants. **kai-chhe,** the constables for a particular day. **tō-chhe,** constables employed by the Tau-tai. **sêng-chhe,** the "keng-sêng" and the constables. **chhe-sêng,** id. **chhe-iáh,** constables and police, &c. **khoài-chhe,** servants kept at yamun for going short distances with messages. **chhe-kha,** hangers-on who go along with constables to serve warrants. **tsáp-chhe,** servants in a yamun for going messages, and doing odds and ends of work; servants occasionally engaged at temples, &c. **tsáp-chhe-pâng,** room in yamun where these servants stay. **thèng-chhe,** messengers in a civil yamun, at the call of any of the principal employés, to be sent messages. **tng-thèng-chhe,** to have this employment. **pang-chhe,** unauthorized assistants of the constables. **chhe-tsóng,** head of the police, &c. **chhe-lé,** gratuity given to the constables when they serve a warrant.

kau-chhe, to hand over a man to the constables to keep in ward, as mandarin does. **pí-chhe,** to beat the constables for failure in duty, as mandarin does. **áu-chhe,** to beat constables, as unruly people when a warrant is served on them. **thek-chhe,** to order out constables on special duty. **tng-chhe,** to be employed in the service of mandarins. **tng-kong-chhe,** to be employed on distant official business, *e.g.* carrying despatches, or arresting a criminal at a distance. **tng-lāi-chhe**, to have one's work within a yamun, as servant. **tng-goā-chhe**, to be employed in yamun for going messages (name not enrolled). **teh-tng toā-chhe**, said fig. of having some heavy expenses to bear, as of idolatrous feast.

pān-chhe, to make all the preparations for lodging, food, &c., of a high mandarin coming on a visit (and for his attendants), as the local mandarins do; to prepare the furniture and fittings of a yamun for a new mandarin, as smaller mandarins do for their superior; and as the constables do for a small mandarin.

ko-chhe, a man who watches the boys of a band of actors (for the man who hires them out), seeing that they do not run away.

chhɛ (C.), = A. chha, different, in most phrases, *e.g.* **cheng-chhɛ**, to differ, &c.

chhe (R. chhui), (C. chhoe, Cn. chhö), to blow, as the wind does; a wind-instrument, a pipe; a kite; distinguish from "pûn," to blow with the mouth or with instrument.

chhe-sit-hé, to blow out a light, as the wind does of itself. **chhe-hong**, blowing (as the wind); to be blown upon by the wind. **hong chhe**, the wind blows. **hong-chhe** (C. kong-chhɛ), a paper-kite. **pàng-hong-chhe**, to fly a kite. **hong-chhe-teng**, a lamp tied to tail of kite. **hong-chhe-lién**, a toy that turns with the wind.

hun-chhe, a tobacco-pipe. **a-phièn hun-chhe**, an opium pipe. **tsúi-hun-chhe**, a pipe for smoking tobacco through water. **chhiⁿ-hun-chhe**, a tobacco-pipe with a mouth-piece and a brass bowl. **kòng-káu hun-chhe**, a short pipe with a very heavy head. **phuh-hun-chhe**, to blow the smoke from one's mouth. **hun-chhe-tē**, a bag for holding the pipe. **hun-chhe-thàu**, a probe for cleaning the stem of a pipe. **hun-chhe-thâu**, the bowl of a pipe; the end of a pipe at the bowl; it is a great insult to strike with it.

kó-chhe, drums and wind-instruments; one drum and two pipes. **pûn kó-chhe**, to play these instruments. **chit-tīn kó-chhe**, a band of them. **chit-tīn-chhe**, id. **bé-chiūⁿ-chhe**, a band of music on horseback, as at idolatrous processions. **pat-im-chhe**, a band with eight sorts of instruments. **chhe-pan**, mandarin's band of musicians.

pûn-chhe, to play a sort of wind-instrument. **toā-chhe**, a sort of clarionet.

chhe [R. a wife; cf. chhoe]. **hu-chhe** (R.), husband and wife. **chhe-kū**, wife's brother. **chhe-kīm**, wife of wife's brother. **tek-chhe**, the legal wife. **hiân-chhe**, my good wife! **it-chhe it-chhiap**, one wife and one concubine. **chhe-tsú sū i-hók**, wife and child are like one's clothes. **cheng-chhe toát-tiân, kièn-sú jû-biân**, in defence of wife and lands, look on death as a sleep. **seng, tsok bān-jîn-chhe; sú, tsok bû-hu-kúi**, said of a bad woman, in life having connection with many men, after death belongs to no husband. **hân-tan-chhe, sat kiú-hu**, the wife of Hân-tan was betrothed to nine bridegrooms who all died. **hân-tan-chhe**, said of a woman whose horoscope is deadly to those betrothed or married to her, or to connections.

chhê (R. sûi), (C. chhôe; Cn. chhö), a long thin rod of wood or bamboo. **chhê-á**, id. **ko-chhê**, a long thin bamboo pole. **mīⁿ-soàⁿ-chhê**, cross bars of a frame for drying macaroni. **hé-chhê**, a poker. **kiò-koaⁿ-chhê**, to call out for mercy while being beaten in court. **gâu-kiò koaⁿ-chhê**, said of a child crying much when struck quite gently. **iau-koe m̄-ùi-chhê; iau-lâng, m̄-kò bīn-phê** (or, "bô-sioh bīn-phê"), a hungry hen does not fear the stick; a starving man does not care for his character.

chhê (C.), = A. chhôe, to crawl on hands and feet.

chhê — **khám-chhê** (T.), = A. khâm-chhēⁿ, cymbals.

chhɛ̂ (C.), = A. chhâ, to investigate.

chhé (R. id., perhaps two words), to fold together with a loose tie; to tie a loop, gen. loosely; a noose, a slip-knot; a small hank of thread; (to take at an average).

chhé-á, a small hank, as of thread or twine.

chhé-chhiú, bridle; reins. **bé-chhé-chhiú**, id.

saⁿ-chhé, intertwined, as the coils of two ropes. **chhé tsòe-chit-tui**, to fold together, as a pair of stockings. **chhé tsòe-chit-ē**, id. **chhé-lé tsòe-chit-ē**, tie all (loosely) together. **chhé-khi-ân**, make the knot tight.

chhé-chhiam, to bend one knee (as to a superior), but not so far as to touch the ground.

khan-chhé, to accuse of being art and part, as in our own fault or crime.

khien-chhé-ûn--khì, to take things at an average, good and bad mixed (v. ûn). **chhé-lâi chhé-khì**, to take at an average (as things or persons) what is better in one making up for defect in another.

chhé (R. chhúi); (C. chhóe; Cn. chhö̆), marrow; brains. **thâu-khak-chhé**, brains. **kut-chhé**, marrow. **pháiⁿ kàu-jip kut-chhé**, very wicked. **thiàⁿ kàu-jip kut-chhé**, pain very severe. **lêng-koaⁿ hōng-chhé**, dragon's liver and phœnix brains; said of most expensive food.

chhè (R. id. by change of tone from "chhiet"). **it-chhè**, all at once, entirely, all.

chhè (= chhe). **hō-chhè-chhè**, managing matters very carelessly.

chhè (R. id.); (C. chhɛ̀), a necessary. **chhè-tī**, id. **lòh-chhè**, to go to stool. **chiūⁿ-chhè**, id.

chhè (cf. chhē). **lûi chhè**, thunder rattling very loud. **chhè-chhè-háu**, sound of a rushing stream, or of rain running in torrents from the roof. **hō-lòh kàu chhì-chhì chhè-chhè**, rain in torrents, as on the roof. **chhì-chhè-háu**, id.

chhè (R. chhùi), brittle, crisp, as toasted food; crank, as a vessel. **chhè-tàuh-tàuh**, exceedingly brittle. **tsûn chhè-chhè**, the vessel is very crank, and ready to upset.

chhè (C.), = A. chhòe, to scrub.

chhē (cf. chhè); (C. chhɛ̄). **chhē-chhē-tò**, falling abundantly, as tears, rain, or water. **tsúi chhē-chhē-tò**, water falling abundantly, as in a cataract, or heavy rain from roof. **bàk-sái chhē-chhē-tò**, tears falling profusely. **bàk-sái chhē-chhē-lâu**, id. **bàk-sái chhē-chhē-tih**, id. **hō chhē-chhē-lâi**, heavy lashing rains.

chhē (= chhɛ̄ⁿ). **tsúi-khám-chhē**, a small bird (the magpie robin?).

chhē (C. chhōe; Cn. chhö̆), to search; to look for, as for something lost; to demand payment, as from a security; to demand assistance in a matter, as from a surety.

chhiau-chhē, to search carefully, as for something lost. **tsāu-chhē**, id. **chhē-khoàⁿ**, to search for. **chhē-tióh**, to find by searching. **chhē-ū**, id. **chhē-bô**, to search but not find. **chhē-m̄-kìⁿ**, id.

pé-chhē (C. pόe-chhōe), to search diligently for something. **pé-chháu chhē-chhin** (to search in the grass for relations), said of a man very good at finding out relations. **moá^{n}-siâ^{n} chhē-siā-hia^{n}** (to search the whole city for a fellow-villager), to look for what is hopeless to find (as "a needle in a hay-stack"). **chhē thâu-sū**, to try to find a clue to an affair.

chhē-khang chhē-phāng, to look for an opportunity, as of extorting money, or of slandering or injuring another. **chhē sí-lō**, to act so as to bring death and ruin on one's self, by any wicked courses. **chhē-sîn**, to call the spirits of the dead. **chhō-sià^{n}** (Cn.), to consult a sorceress who calls up spirits.

chhē [R. tsō, to sit; cf. col. chē, chhāi]. **ām-kún chhē-chhē** (C. chhōe; Cn. chhō), = **ām-kún chhāi-chhāi**, neck very short and thick.

chhē-giàh (C.), = A. chē-giàh, to accept responsibility for payment, as of expenses which we had authorized. **chhē** (C.), = A. chē, to accept responsibility or stand security; but in other phrases chē is both C. and A.

chhē (= chhe, chhɛ^{n}), one of the Chinese musical notes.

chhɛ^{n} (C.), = A. chhi^{n}, when the final of the reading form is **eng**; *e.g.* green; indigo; raw; star.

chhɛ̂^{n} (T. chhê). **chhɛ̂^{n}-á**, small cymbals. **khám-chhɛ̂^{n}-kó**, musical instruments used at funerals (cf. chhɛ^{n}).

chhɛ́^{n} (C.), = A. chhí^{n}, to waken; feeling the sexual impulse, as a female animal; said, in vile obscene scolding, of women.

chhɛ́^{n} — **chhin-chhɛ́^{n}** (C.), = A. chhin-chhí^{n}, pretty.

chhɛ̄^{n} (cf. chhe, chhē), one of the Chinese musical notes.

chhɛ̄^{n} (T. chhê, in most phrases). **chhɛ̄^{n}-chhɛ̄^{n}**, sound of small gongs. **khâm-chhɛ̄^{n}-chhɛ̄^{n}**, sound of gongs and cymbals. **pûn â^{n}-m-chhɛ̄^{n}** (C.), sound of wind-instruments.

chhɛ̄^{n}-lô, a small gong about eight inches across (v. lô). **khám-chhɛ̄^{n}**, a pair of cymbals. **khám-chhɛ̄^{n}-kó**, a pair of cymbals and a small drum, used for funereal music. **phah khám-chhɛ̄^{n}**, to strike cymbals, only in funereal music; also, a vile scolding phrase among women with women.

chhɛ̄^{n} (= chhē). **tsúi-kham-chhɛ̄^{n}**, a small bird. **sái-khām-chhɛ̄^{n}**, id. (khàm?).

chheh (R. chhoat); (C. chhoeh; Cn. chhöh), to sip, as gruel, &c. **chheh-thng**, to sip soup. **chheh-khùi**, to take a great mouthful of air, as on suddenly meeting a strong wind.

chheh [R. chhek, thin tablets, a list]; (C. chhɛh), a book; a list; a record; (not used in Cn. except for "a list;" while "tsū" is always used for a book).

hāu-peh-chheh, venetian blinds or shutters.

chiū^{n}-chheh, to insert on a list or record; to be formally recorded or put in a list.

ôe-chheh, a book for holding threads of many colours for embroidery of all sorts.

keng-chheh, classical books. **goā-chheh**, other sorts of books. **tsu-chheh**, books. **chit-pún-chheh**, one book.

chheh-teh, a weight of metal or heavy wood, for keeping a book open. **chheh-chhiam**, title pasted on outside of book. **chheh-gán**, do., also title-page. **chheh-chih**, paste-board cover for several volumes. **chheh-phê**, book-cover. **chheh-kun**, cloth in which school-boys fold up their books. **chheh-pau**, bundle of books thus folded up. **chheh-tû**, a book-case, esp. with doors; a book-press. **chheh-kè**, book-shelves.

chheh-miâ^{n}, name given by teacher to the scholar. **chheh-mn̂g**, themes for the third Kujin examination.

chheh-á, a book with superstitious receipts for diseases. **khoà^{n}-chheh-á**, to consult it, in case of sickness. **chheh-á-tsoá**, various sorts of idolatrous paper, mixed up according to the prescriptions of that book, for certain diseases. **poa^{n}-chhia sin-chheh-á kū-làh-jit**, raking up old stories (quite out of date) against people.

khoà^{n}-chheh, to read a book silently. **thák-chheh**, to read a book aloud; to learn and study a book. **thák-chheh ê-lâng**, a scholar; a literary man. **thák-sí-chheh**, to read words, learning the sound without understanding the meaning. **thák-bô-chheh**, not making progress in study. **thák chêng-sì-chheh**, to learn a book very quickly, as if having read it in a former life.

liām-chheh, to recite the lesson. **siū-chheh**, to give out a lesson. **siū^{n}-chheh**, id. **un-chheh**, to revise a lesson. **iáh-chheh**, to turn over the leaves of a book. **tù-chheh**, to compose a book. **kap-chheh**, to bind a book. **pun-chheh**, to distribute books. **khoán-chheh**, to select books, as in making up a set or selecting a number to take out. **thōng-chheh**, to pile up books in an even pile.

chheh [R. chhoat, to take up with the fingers], (C. chhoeh, Cn. chhöh). **chit-chheh-á**, a very small quantity, as of food.

chheh (C.), = A. chhoeh, sad; exclamation of grief and surprise, as at some injustice, misfortune, or great wickedness.

chhèh (C. chhɛ̍h), to sink down, as a wall on a bad foundation; to come down, as a sail when the rope breaks, &c. &c. **chhèh--lòh-lâi**, to come down, as a sail when rope breaks, or as a kite; to settle down, as house on bad foundation, or as a door settling down so that the hinges will not work well.

chhèh--lòh-khì, very far gone in sickness, as when constitution is broken. **chhèh-tóe**, to have the bottom leaky and ready to fall out, as a bucket.

chhèh^{n} — **phoà-chhèh^{n}**, sound of a broken hoarse voice.

chhɛ̍h^{n}, noise, as of crockery dashed together, or such loud sound. **chhɛ̍h^{n}-nɛ̍h^{n}-nɛ̍h^{n}**, sound of loud thunder. **lûi chhɛ̍h^{n}-nɛ̍h^{n}-nɛ̍h^{n}**, thunder rolling loudly.

chhek [R. chhiok, to gore, to meet with, as misfortune, &c.; cf. "tak"], to meet with, as a bad omen. **chhek-tióh-kúi** (lit. meet a demon), to meet with an unexpected difficulty (as by the opposition of some one not thought of) which quite upsets our plans. **chhek-soe**, to meet with a demon or sickness, or some bad omen or bad luck. **chhek-ò**, to offend the majesty of a god by unclean conduct in his presence; to draw down calamity on another by impure conduct (v. ò).

chhek, to tie a loose knot. **chhek--teh**, tied very loosely. **chhek oáh-kat**, to tie a very loose knot, that is easily opened. **chhek khah-tn̂g**, tie a loose knot at greater length, as to keep a thing from being in the way; make the piece to be broken off longer than you were going to make it. **chhek khah-té**, tie the loose knot at a shorter length.

chhek [R. chhiok, to press close; this group perhaps belongs to two words], to make shorter. **chhek-oá**, to press very close to. **chhek oá-oá**, id.

chhui-chhek, to come gradually to each others' terms (s. fathom). chhek--lòh-lâi, to come down to a lower price. chhek-kē--lòh-lâi chiū--i, to come down near his price.

chhek-kha--lòh-lâi chiū--i, to come down towards his position, as a superior showing condescension to an inferior, as making explanations to him, or dispensing with ceremony; to come down to a lower price to meet his offer.

chhek-kē, to bend one's body (but keeping head straight up), as in order to pass through a low door. chhek-khah-kē, id.

chhek [R. chhiok, to hurry, urgent]. pek-chhek, too urgent and too hard on people.

chhek [R. chhiok, to cut]. chhek-thâu kóe-bé, to make an old article (of furniture) as good as new by a thorough repair; said figuratively of other things. chhek-thâu oā^{n}-bé (T.), id. of anything.

chhek [R. chhiok, a small bird]. chhek-chiáu-á, a small bird like a sparrow. kim-si n̂g-chhek-chiáu-á, a small yellow bird.

chhek [R. a foot, = col. chhioh]. chhek-chhùn put-ī, not needing to be changed at all (not a foot or an inch). chhek-tók, a book of models for letters and such documents (s. fathom).

chhek (R. id.) kè-chhek, a scheme; a plan or plot. sok-chhiú bû-chhek, arms folded on breast, and having no plan to get out of the difficulty.

chhek [R. connections by the female line and by marriage]. chhin-chhek, relations and connections in general. chhin-chhek kə-kū, id. chhin-chhek-kan, among relations and connections. chhin-chhek-kan bô-lūn, accounts are not kept too strictly among connections. bô-chhin bô chhek, having no relations or connections alive. lāi-chhin goā-chhek, relations and connections by blood and by affinity. goā-chhek, relations by female line and connections by marriage.

chhek [R. the knee, C. chhip]. lâm-tsú chhek-hā, iú hông-kim (there is yellow gold below a man's knee), a man should not lightly or basely kneel.

chhek (R. id.) giû-chhek, = giû-chhip, a medicinal plant (v. giû).

chhek (R. siok), (P. chhiok), rice in ear; growing rice; paddy; rice in the husk.

bí-chhek, rice in general. bí-chhek hi-bî, rice-crop scanty. chhek-chéng, seed-rice. chhek-gê, dried sprouted rice. chhek-mí^{n}, the awn of rice.

chhek-thâu, light empty refuse rice that does not separate from the husk in the mill called "thə-lâng;" it is used for feeding animals.

phà^{n}-chhek, empty rice. phà^{n}-chhek-hiu^{n}, a plant used to give fragrance to liquor. hong chhe phà^{n}-chhek (wind blows away empty rice), said of ill-fated persons taking an epidemic. hong chhe phà^{n}-chhek, pòk-hok--chiá siū, id.

chhek-siā^{n}, a large boarded receptacle for rice, as in a granary. chhek-chhng, a rice granary. chhng-chhek, rice from public granaries not good. koa^{n}-chhek, id.

phi-chhek, to spread rice in the sun to dry. oe-chhek (P. e-chhiok), to separate the husk from the rice by the "thə-lâng." ké-chhek, to winnow rice.

chhek [R. to fathom]. chhui-chhek (r.), to consider carefully (s. shorten).

bōe chhek-tók--tit, cannot be searched and found out, as the heart. put-chhek, unexpectedly bad, evil, or dangerous. put-chhek ê-tāi, unexpected evil, calamity, or danger. sim put-chhek, his heart is very wicked. tsûn-sim put-chhek, secretly plotting evil in his heart.

chhek [R. red, = col. chhiah]. chhek-sin lō-thé, naked or nearly so, *e.g.* perhaps short drawers on. kūn-tsu--chiá, chhek; kūn-bėk--chiá, hek, he who comes near vermilion gets red, near ink gets black.

chhek (P.), = A. chhiok, in some words.

chhėk (P. chhiók), to shake, as pencils or chopsticks, to make them even; to shake up and down, as a sedan, or as on horseback; to shake or jerk, as a bag of rice to make it hold more, or as a bundle to get it right on the shoulder; to compare evidence, or discuss each other's claims (as the two parties) face to face.

chhėk-tsôe, to shake even, as pencils or books; to arrange a matter so that both sides are satisfied; all the parties arrived. chhėk-khah-khí, to replace a bag or bundle that was falling from the shoulder, by a jerk of the body. chhėk-gû-lin, to shake milk (in a bottle) to make butter.

tùi-chhėk, the two parties in a dispute discussing their affair together, so as to settle it.

chhiau-chhėk, in high spirits, exulting with delight, as a child boisterously happy; also, shaken about (as in a sedan or boat) so as to feel uncomfortable in the stomach.

thiô-kha-chhėk (T.), to hop.

chhėk (cf. jiók), to work up in the hands, as dough, or as clay for an image.

chheng [R. blue, green, = col. chhi^{n}]. chheng-i, a blue dress worn by Sew-tsae graduates. lâm-chheng, id. chheng-liên, a purplish blue colour. ūi tan-chheng, to paint in colours (lit. blue and red).

chheng-phî, a medicinal skin like orange or citron skins. chheng-tāi, a green medicinal salt. lėk-chheng (R.), bitumen.

chheng [R. chhin, self, one's own]. chheng-teng, the clerk who keeps the account of goods shipped and delivered; a sort of assistant supercargo. chheng-teng-thâu, id.

chheng (R. id.) chheng-hə, to address by an honourable designation; to style. chheng-tsàn (R.), to praise. thong-chheng, general appellation politely added to another's name, *e.g.* ko, chek, peh, chím, tāi-jîn, &c. tsū-chheng, to style one's self in a boasting or egotistic way. tsun-chheng, to give an appellation which is indeed customary, but rather higher than is strictly correct. chheng-ông chheng-tè (lit. styling kings and sovereigns); to be one's own master, as man of independent means, or who has a business of his own; or of an employé when his master allows him to do as he pleases.

chheng (R. chhien), (T. chhai^{n}, Cn. chhüi^{n}, C. chhan, but P. chheng), a thousand. chheng-it, eleven hundred. chheng-bān, ten millions. kúi-nà bān chheng-kun ê-lát, strength of several myriads of thousands of pounds.

chheng [R. chhoan, to perforate; cf. chhng]. chheng-soa^{n}-lêng, a sort of gingall.

chheng (P), = A. chhiong in some tones and words.

chheng (R. id.), clear, pure, clean; to clean; only; to pay off, as an account; clear and bright, as sky, or as red colour; (vegetarian); free from care or anxiety or need of toil; comfortable; fair and just; the Manchoo dynasty; cooling in its effect, as food or medicine.

sam-chheng, the Tauist trinity. tāi-chheng,

the Manchoo dynasty. **chheng-tiâu**, id. **chheng-bêng**, the "feast of tombs;" correct and clear (v. bêng).

koe-nñg-chheng, white of (hen's) egg. **thn̂g-chheng**, sugar melted in warm water. **chiùⁿ-chheng**, a salt sauce (v. chiùⁿ). **thâu-chheng**, opium refuse made up for smoking. **jī-chheng**, the refuse of the "thâu-chheng" made up again for smoking (very poor and bad).

chheng-tsá, very early in the morning. **hiēn-chheng** (C.), at present.

jit-chheng, a journal or day-book in business. **chhó-chheng**, a rough scroll-book or sale-book in which sales are entered at the time, to be afterwards copied into the day-book.

chheng-chhó, settled, as account; clear, distinct, and accurate, as a statement. **chheng-chhé**, id. **bô-thang-chheng**, unable to pay off the score. **chheng-siàu**, to pay off, as account (v. siàu). **chheng-hoân**, id. **khioh tsòe-chit-ē chheng**, to settle a number of old scores at once, either of money or of grounds of offence and quarrel.

chheng-liâm, pure and uncorrupted by avarice, as mandarin. **tsòe-koaⁿ chheng**, to be pure in his official duties. **lâi chheng, khì bêng**, all clear, open, and correct, as a ready-money transaction. **chheng-pék**, unspotted in character. **it-sin chheng-pék**, whole life blameless. **ke-hong chheng-pék**, family of blameless reputation for some generations. **chheng-pék-ke**, id. **sam-tāi chheng-pék**, do. for three generations. **chheng-thien pék-jit**, in broad daylight; weather fine, clear, and sunny; just and fair, as mandarin (said by himself).

chheng-khì, clean. **chheng-khì-siùⁿ**, id. **sóe-chheng**, to wash clean. **sam-kang-tsúi sóe-bōe-chheng**, the water of the three great rivers could not wash it clean. **piàⁿ-chheng**, to clear out thoroughly. **chheng-tî**, to clean out a pond. **chheng kau-á**, to clean out a ditch.

ke-sū chheng, very poor. **ke-sū chheng-tām**, id. (v. tām).

chheng-chheng, only, simply, merely. **chheng-chheng-m̄**, decidedly refusing; doggedly refusing; often without reason or without giving a reason. **chheng-chheng-beh**, decidedly or persistently desirous; often without good reason.

chē-chheng, to settle and become clear, as a liquid. **têng-chheng**, to settle, as muddy water (v. têng). **chheng-chēng**, very pure. **tsúi chheng, hî-hiēn** (when the water becomes clear the fish are seen), the trick will out at last, and a man's character be cleared. **chheng-tsúi, tsú pėh-bí** (white rice cooked in clear water), candid and truthful.

chheng-chhài, vegetarian diet. **tsòe-chheng-chiò**, to fast and perform the rites called "chiò." **chiáh-chheng**, to take food or medicine that has a cooling tendency (not as to warmth). **chiáh-chheng khùn-keng**, to eat vegetarian food and sleep in a temple; to have an easy life of it; said also of a man who lives on his parents or his property without any cares, or of a man who has no family cares.

chheng-êng, free from care, anxiety, or need of toiling; in easy circumstances (v. êng). **chheng-hân** (R.), id. **it-jit chheng-hân, it-jit sien**, such a man is as happy as one of the genii. **chheng-khò**, having a little money or property so as to be in no need of toiling to earn money. **hê-siūⁿ put-chí-chheng**, Buddhist priests are very free from care (with perhaps an inuendo at their vegetarianism). **chheng-sim**, mind untroubled and free from cares, having no wants and no cause for anxiety. **chheng-sim-toāⁿ**, taking it easy and amusing one's self; rather jolly. **lí teh-chheng-sim**, you are taking it far too easy, *e.g.* refusing to take responsibility that you ought to take, or amusing yourself and keeping jolly or easy when you ought to be sad. **ké-chheng**, pretending to be joyful when really sad or anxious; pretending to be very good, and finding fault with the very sins that he himself commits.

thiⁿ chheng-chheng, sky serene. **chheng-liâng**, agreeably cool, as weather; cooling, as medicine. **chheng-hong**, sky clearing up with wind. **chheng-hong bêng-goát**, wind pleasant and moon bright; fine cool moonlight night. **chheng-chhái**, bright and unclouded, as sky; in a state of comfort and prosperity (v. chhái). **chheng-sóng**, comfortable, clean, and neat; pleasant, as a place; at ease and leisure. **chheng-hiu**, neat and comfortable, as a house. **chheng-kéng**, comfortable and well got up, as house; comfortable in mind and circumstances. **chheng-chhun-sî**, period of blooming youth (v. chhun). **chheng-hé**, making great manifestations of delight; feeling quite comfortable and at ease; to remove the hot principle so as to bring down fever or inflammation. **teh-chheng-hé**, very much pleased, and showing it outwardly (said half in joke). **chheng-siù**, elegant and gentlemanly, as a man who is rather thin and of cultivated manners. **chheng-phang**, pleasantly fragrant, not too strong-smelling.

chheng-âng, bright red.

chhêng (R. iông), (C. chhiông), (sometimes, esp. T., chêng), the banyan-tree. **chhêng-chhiū**, id. **chhêng-chhiū-chí**, its fruit (useless). **chhêng-chhiū-ông**, the god of the banyan. **chhah-chhêng**, to stick banyan branches on the door on 5.5 (v. chhah). **ti-bú-chhêng**, a tree somewhat like a banyan. **thái-ko-chhêng**, a tree like a banyan. **chhêng-chhiu**, abortive roots of banyan.

chhêng (R. siông), (C. chhiông; Cn. chêng; T. chêng, chhiûⁿ). **chhêng-peh**, the common fir-tree. **chhêng-peh-iên**, resin from do. **chhêng-peh-lûi**, fir-cones. **thái-ko chhêng-peh**, a diseased fir-tree. **thái-ko chhêng-peh chhut-miāⁿ** (lit. it produces resinous matter), said of a notoriously bad man.

chhêng-hê, leaves of fir-tree. **chhêng-hê-chhiu**, id. **chhêng-lin**, resin, as taken from the tree.

chhêng— **khût-chhêng**, scraggy and ill-formed; of unpleasant and repelling temper (v. khût).

chhêng (cf. sông, chhiâng). **pūn-chhêng**, corpulent or thick-set and awkward; thick and unwieldy; clumsy, coarse, and ugly, as man or thing.

chhêng— **chiúⁿ-chhêng**, that half of a Chinese oar that has the handle.

chhêng, a sort of narrow spade or hoe; to dig up with it, as oysters. **thih-chhêng**, a sort of narrow spade. **thê-chhêng**, id. **pùn-chhêng**, a sort of spade or hoe for removing dirt. **ô-chhêng**, a narrow spade for gathering oysters. **chhêng-ô**, to gather oysters with it.

chhêng [R. chhâm; C. (R.) chhân, the silk-worm]; (also, **chhêng** (C.), = A. **chhâm**, the silk-worm).

soa-chhêng (T. soa-chhâiⁿ), an edible mollusc, found in sea-sand.

chiáh kim-chhêng, to be bewitched by a charm connected with golden silk-worms (that have wonderful magical power), so as to become their slave; done by secretly mixing poisonous charms with food. **chiáh**--

tióh kim-chhêng, id. chhāi kim-chhêng, to set up an incense vessel for the worship of them, as the sorcerers do.

chhéng [T. chháiⁿ; Cn. chhúiⁿ; C. sometimes, chhán); to dust; to flap its wings as a bird throwing off dirt; a sort of brush. **chhéng-á**, a soft brush for dusting. **tsang-chhéng**, a brush made of palm fibre. **koe-mn̂g-chhéng**, a dust-brush made of feathers. **tek-chhéng**, a bamboo scrubbing-brush.

chhéng-he, to whitewash. **chhéng-thûn**, to sweep away the soot of a year in the twelfth moon. **chhéng-sàu**, to dust and sweep. **chhéng-thê**, to flap its wings so as to throw off dirt, as a fowl does. **chhap-chhùi-chhéng**, all in disorder, as things or affairs. **thâu-mn̂g chhap-chhùi-chhéng**, hair dishevelled or in disorder; *e.g.* when working very hard with no time to comb.

chhéng (T. chháiⁿ; C. chhán). **phah-chhéng**, to use lavishly, as money; to waste and abuse (in use), as things.

chhéng (C. chhoán), to act in a bragging manner. **siàu-liân teh-chhéng**, a young fellow acting in a bragging manner. **chhéng-pang**, to act or speak in a proud or big way; to brag. **chhéng-pang-tsúi**, id.

chhéng — **phók-phók-chhéng**, to palpitate. **phiák-phiák-chhéng**, id. **chhih-chhih chhéng-chhéng**, playing about, as an idle boy.

chhéng [R. to invite, to request, = col. chhiáⁿ]. **chhéng-an**, to salute. **chhéng-kong**, to request a reward for meritorious services to the state. **chhéng-kàu** (polite), I beg you to instruct me. **chhéng-bēng**, to ask the commands of a superior. **chhéng-chí**, to request to know the imperial will.

chhèng [R. id. (by change of tone from chheng, to name or style); to fit, to suit]. **chhèng-ì**, to suit one's wishes. **bêng chhèng-kî-sit**, having a good reputation and deserving it. **put-chhèng**, not suiting well with another thing or things, *e.g.* articles of dress with each other, or as furniture with house. **bô-chhèng**, id. **bô-chhèng-chit**, not fit for the office. **put-chhèng-chit**, id.

chhèng (R. chhiòng), (P. chhiòng); a gun, a cannon, musket, pistol, &c. **chit-mn̂g-chhèng**, one gun or cannon, &c. **saⁿ-mn̂g-chhèng**, three guns fired as a salute to a mandarin of considerable rank. **an-kiⁿ-chhèng**, the one signal gun fired at the first watch (v. kiⁿ). **jī-mn̂g-chhèng**, the two shots fired at second watch. **khui-lē-chhèng**, the gun in the early morning, signal for opening the city gates. **liân-hoân-chhèng**, many guns (muskets, &c.) fired in rapid succession.

pn̄g-sî-chhèng, a very poisonous serpent, probably a cobra. **chhèng-ki-chìⁿ**, a rocket. **chhiú-chhèng**, solitary lasciviousness.

bé-chhèng, a pistol. **sió-chhèng**, do. **sió-chhèng-á**, id. **hoan-á-chhèng**, foreign fire-arms (often said of pistols). **gō-pak-chhèng**, a five-barrelled revolver. **siang-pak-chhèng**, a double-barrelled gun or pistol. **toaⁿ-pak-chhèng**, a single-barrelled gun or pistol. **toā-pak-chhèng**, a gun of large bore. **chiáu-chhèng**, a gun, a musket. **toā-chhèng**, a large cannon; an opium pipe. **giâ-toā-chhèng** (lit. carry large cannon on shoulder), to be an opium smoker; to meet with some very great calamity, or severe disease, esp. venereal. **lêng-kòng-chhèng**, a very large cannon. **hé-chhèng**, a sort of gingall with tiger's head. **hō-goá khì-giâ-hé-chhèng**, you set me to a very difficult task. **káu-tsat-chhèng**, a sort of gingall with nine rings like joints. **tek-chhèng**, a bamboo gun, used by children.

chhèng-kè, frame of a cannon, instead of a gun-carriage. **chhèng-chhn̂g**, stock of a gun. **chhèng-sin**, barrel of gun. **chhèng-koāiⁿ**, id. **chhèng-hī**, touch-hole. **chhèng-tauh**, sort of lock that holds the match of a matchlock. **chhèng-khang**, a port-hole in fort or vessel. **chhèng-iēn**, port-holes in a vessel (v. iēn). **chhèng-bé-to**, a bayonet. **chhèng-chí**, a bullet, shot. **chhèng-chí bat-lâng**, the bullet knows the (fated) man; every bullet has its billet. **chhèng-thok**, a ramrod. **chhèng-thuh**, id. **chhèng-ióh**, gunpowder. **chhèng-tháng**, small barrel for carrying ammunition for the guns. **chhèng-kėk**, an arsenal for fire-arms.

chhèng-tūi, a company of musketeers or riflemen. **chhèng-siú**, an artillery-man, a gunner. **chhèng-peng**, a musketeer or rifleman. **chiáh-chhèng**, to be a soldier who uses a gun, to be a musketeer or rifleman. **keng pâi chhèng**, the three sorts of soldiers, who use bows, shields, and guns respectively; the bow is the highest.

phah-chhèng-siâⁿ (T.), rites to get a soul out of that part of hell where those who have been shot are confined.

chhèng-pé, a target for musket or rifle practice. **khó chhèng-pé**, to practise shooting with guns. **khó-chhèng**, to drill or review at shooting (gun-practice), as mandarins. **khoe-chhèng-bō**, sort of soldier's cap.

phah-chhèng, to shoot with a gun or fire-arms. **sià-chhèng**, to discharge a gun (just to let it off) without an aim. **pàng-chhèng**, to shoot with fire-arms, in general. **khui-chhèng**, id. **tióh-chhèng**, to be shot or hit by ball or bullet, or shot. **tióh-chhèng--sí**, to be shot dead. **chhèng-siong**, a gun-shot wound.

chhèng — **chhèng-kám-pang**, the (loose) boards that make the false deck of a Chinese junk, laid above the real water-tight deck.

chhèng — **chhèng-éng**, to manifest great delight by gesticulation, as a person in inferior position on getting power or influence.

chhèng (C. chhiòng); to spout or jet out from an opening, as steam or vapour, or a torrent; to emit steam, as lime in slaking; to ascend, as the vapour of a sacrifice; to affect or be affected by, as a vapour or malarious influence; to scent by placing some fragrant thing near; to build a little higher; to cook very dry with little water, as rice or potatoes.

chhèng--tióh, to affect as a vapour, steam, or odour; to come violently upon, as a torrent. **chhèng-lèng--tióh**, id.

chhèng-phīⁿ, to blow the nose. **chhèng-phoà lâng-phīⁿ-khang**, said of a very strong odour (pleasant as of cooking, or very unpleasant, as of rotten things) coming strongly on the nostrils.

chhèng-téng, the head all covered with a disgusting soft eruption. **siⁿ-chhèng-téng**, id.

chhèng-koán, to sing very high notes, as boys. **chhèng-bōe-koâiⁿ**, unable to sing very high notes; unable to build up high, or to spout up high. **chhèng-khah-koâiⁿ**, to build higher, as a house (as by adding a story to an old house); to spout up higher, &c. **chhèng-koâiⁿ**, to spout up, as steam or smoke in a jet. **hé-hun chhèng-koâiⁿ**, the smoke rising in a jet. **ien chhèng--khí-lâi**, steam suddenly spouts up.

chhèng-tê, to flavour tea with sweet herbs or flowers. **chhèng-hún**, to scent hair-powder with flowers. **chhèng-hiu**^{n}, to scent things by laying them beside incense.

chhèng-khì, to be affected by some vapour or exhalation, good or bad. **chhèng-thô-khì**, to be affected by exhalations from the earth; to be cooled by the damp air of the ground, as medicine set to cool on the ground that its effects may be less heating. **chhàu-mih**^{n} **chhèng--lâng**, bad smells coming to one's nose or affecting one. .

chhèng iû-pn̄g, to boil rice dry in a peculiar way (v. pn̄g). **chhèng han-tsû**, to boil potatoes dry with the skins on.

chhēng (P. chhiōng), to wear or put on, as clothes (but not hat or cap). **chhēng-sa**^{n}, to put on coat, shirt, or any dress of upper part of body. **ke-chhēng-sa**^{n}, to put on or wear more coats, &c. **chhēng sa**^{n}**-á-khò**, to put on coat and trousers. **chhēng-ôe**, to put on or wear shoes. **chhēng ôe-béh**, to wear or put on shoes and stockings.

chhēng-sún, to put a tenon and mortice together. **chhēng-mn̂g**, to hang a door on its hinges. **giâ-lâi-chhēng**, bring (the door) and put it on its hinges. **sa**^{n}**-chiáh-chhēng**, to fit well together. **chiáh-pē chhēng-bú**, fed and clothed by parents.

chhēng-sin, to wear new clothes. **sin-chhēng**, good dress (on one's body). **ū-sin-chhēng**, to have on good dress. **tsòe-sin-chhēng**, to have clothes made for self or for family. **sin-chhēng hóng-hóng**, very finely dressed. **chhe-chhēng**, common every-day dress.

khah-ū-chhēng, has more wear (or a great deal of wear), as shoes or dress. **kim-chhēng** (C.), having very good wear, as clothes. **khiām-chhēng tit-sin**, take care of clothes and they are as good as new.

gûn-chhēng-kah, a sort of waistcoat with pockets at the side. **gûn-chhēng**, id.

chhēng-bōe-tiâu, unable to bear so many clothes because of heat.

chhēng-chhah, manner of dress, as fine or simple, good or bad. **ū-chhēng-chhah**, well-dressed. **hó-chhēng-chhah**, id.

kiáu-kùn chhēng kî-koa^n**-ngóeh**, a skilful gambler grown so poor that he has to crouch between the supports of a flag-staff for warmth. **hàm kàu-bōe-chhēng báng-tà**, lies so big that even a mosquito-curtain could not cover them. **thoa-moâ**^{n} **chhēng-soh**, to wear coarse ropes of raw hemp-bark round the waist, as son or daughter-in-law at funeral; those who have done so should never be put away though they were only adopted.

chhēng — **lō--nih**^{n} **chhēng--tióh**, to meet on the road.

chhi — **só-chhi**, the spring and wards of a Chinese padlock. **bî-chhi**, lock gone wrong.

chhi — **mn̂g-kńg-chhi kiâ**, hair standing on end, as from fear or cold.

chhi (R. su). **hî-chhi**, the gills of a fish. **chit-hî chiáh-tsúi, chhi-ē kè**, the fish called "chit" drinks water, but it goes out below the gills (said of a man forgetful who did him a kindness or favour).

chhi (R. su). **gê-tsô-chhi**, the part of the cheek at the roots of the molar teeth (v. tsô). **bî-chhi**, slight obstruction in the throat (v. bî), (s. wards of lock).

chhi (cf. chhu). **chham-chhi**, all in confusion; confusedly mixed. **chham-chham chhi-chhi**, id.

toā-chhi-chha, great profusion of food at a feast. **lāu-jiėt chhi-chha**, very crowded and bustling.

chhi (R. id.) **chhi-tsoat**, stupid, awkward. **chhi-gâi**, stupid, silly.

chhi (C.), = A. chhu (R.), female.

chhi (C.), = A. chhu, a larva or animalcule.

chhi, to make a hissing sound, as a frying-pan; to sail under press of sail, hissing through the water. **chhi-chhi-háu**, to make a hissing sound, as frying in a frying-pan. **tsúi teh-chhi**, water making a hissing sound in boiling. **chhi-chhi lā-lā**, the sound of meat frying in melted fat. **chhi--chit-ē**, to parch or fry on a frying-pan with little or no fat. **chhi-chhi-kún**, sound of water boiling (said also of a child restlessly impatient to see or get something); sound of frying.

tit-tit-chhi, to make way rapidly through the water with a hissing sound, as vessel under press of sail. **ngī**^{n}**-liâu-chhi**, id. **chhi--lâi**, to come along at full speed, as vessel coming close up to us. **chhi-oá**, to run rapidly alongside so as to attack a vessel. **chhi-oá, beh-lâi-phah--goá**, he ran up rapidly close to me to beat me.

chhî, damp, as hair, cakes, floor, &c. **chhiū**^{n}**-chhî**, to grow damp. **iâm chhiū**^{n}**-chhî**, the salt grows damp. **chhî-kauh-kauh**, very damp, as cakes or room. **lâu-koā**^{n} **chhî-chhî**, slight perspiration on skin.

chhî [R. to hold with the hand]. **hû-chhî**, to aid, to assist, as gods. **chi-chhî**, to give some little help to keep a matter from going all wrong. **tsú-chhî**, to have the full management of an affair. **pá-chhî**, shrewd, difficult to get round. **khim-chhî**, very shrewd and skilful, as in managing affairs or giving advice about them, so that it is hard to get round him, and that what he does generally comes right.

chhiá^n**-chhî--teh**, pausing a little to consider before deciding, *e.g.* before beginning a quarrel. **î-chhî**, to use temporarily in hope of improvement; to keep up or take care of, as an interim arrangement; to stay for a time in an unsuitable place till a better can be got, or waiting for repairs, &c. **bóng-î-chhî**, id. **chhiá**^{n}**-î-chhî**, id. **î-chhî kè-jit**, to put up with temporarily (as with employment, place, or person) till something better can be got.

ùt-pāng siong-chhî, gû-jîn tek-lī (prov.), when people go to law the mandarins and their underlings get their money.

chhî (R. sû), (A. chhî, sû; Cn. sû), a surname.

chhí (R. id.) **chhia-chhí**, prodigal extravagance or luxury.

chhí [R. a tooth, = col. khí]. **kā-gê chhiet-chhí**, to gnash the teeth in rage or pain. **chhí pék, tûn hông**, teeth white and lips red (said of a pretty face).

chhí (C.) **khe-chhí**, small flat boats of very small draught for shallow sandy streams.

chhí (C.), = A. chhú, rat, mouse, &c. **lé-chhí**, = A. niáu-chhú, a rat.

chhí (C.), = A. chhú, to select, &c.

chhí (C.), = A. chhú, to reside, to manage.

chhí (C.), = A. chhú, a piece of wood for mixing mortar. **cheng-chhí**, a sort of pestle.

chhì (R. id.) **kî-chhì**, flags and streamers of an army. **kî-chhì sien-bêng**, the flags all new and beautiful.

chhì (R. sì), to try; to tempt; to make trial of. **chhì-khoà**^{n}, to try; to make an experiment; to see how it will do. **chhì-bāi** (esp. T.), id. **chhì-êng**, to use on trial. **chhì-chiáh--chit-ē**, to taste so as to try. **chhì-chiáh-khoà^n**, id. **chhì-siū^n**, to consider carefully.

chhì lâng--ê ōe-ì, to try to find out a man's meaning. **thâu-mn̂g chhì-hé**, to rush into evident danger (lit. try fire with our hair). **chhì-liēn** (r.), afflictions, trials, or persecutions (X.)

chhì — **chhiō-chhì**, to light a lamp near a corpse. **chhì-iû**, the oil burned in a lamp beside a corpse (used afterwards for incantations). **boah-chhì-iû**, to sprinkle (secretly) with this oil, supposed to cause a quarrel with husband. **kì^n-chhì**, to come suddenly in sight of a corpse, coffin, or funeral.

chhì [R. a fin]. **hî-chhì**, fishes' fins for food, esp. sharks' fins.

chhì [R. a sort of fish]. **chhì-hî**, a sort of fish very full of bones. **chhì-liu**, id.

chhì — **chhì-chhè-háu**, sound of heavy rain on the roof (v. chhè).

chhì [R. chhù, to pierce, to taunt; interchanged with the next word]. **ki-chhì**, to ridicule; to taunt; to make sarcastic remarks. **chhì-khek**, to assassinate or attempt to assassinate a sovereign or very high mandarin by a dagger.

chhì (R. chhù), a thorn; a prickle; a thorny plant. **chhì-chhì**, very prickly. **khí-chhì**, rough and uneven, as a surface. **giah-chhì**, to extract a thorn.

chhì-chhák, to grieve and pierce the heart; to dazzle the eyes (v. chhák).

chhì-á, a thorn. **chhì-phè**, id. **chháu-chhì**, thorny plants. **chhì-tsâng**, a thorny plant. **chhì-loáh**, a thorn-hedge. **chhì-phè-loáh**, id.

chhì-kiû, a ball with iron pricks (used by sorcerers to wound themselves). **chhì-kiû-á**, round thorny wild fruits. **mê-thâng-chhì**, a sort of prickly sea-worm (v. thâng). **chhì-som**, prickly biche-de-mer. **chhì-koe**, a cucumber. **chhì-tek**, a sort of bamboo full of thorns. **tek-chhì**, a long thin bamboo branch; a bamboo thorn. **sut tek-chhì**, to whip with a thin long bamboo branch.

chhoa^n-chhì, causing annoyance or trouble by constantly raising objections or finding fault; very peevish. **chhoa^n-chhì-lê**, do.; also said of an affair that involves many troublesome details difficult to set right. **kāu-chhoa^n-chhì**, do. do. to a great extent. **chhit-chhoa^n poeh-chhì**, id. **bô-chhoa^n bô-chhì**, there is no flaw or danger of trouble about the affair; no fear (*e.g.*) of extra expenses or unforeseen difficulties. **khí-chhoa^n-chhì**, to raise trouble when there is no need; to cause mischief by raising objections, &c.; to pick a quarrel. **khí-chhoa^n khí-chhì**, id.

noā^n-thô bô-chhì (soft mud with no thorns), a man who bears injuries without resisting or retaliating.

tsō-chhì, a medicine. **hé-hāng-chhì**, a sort of cactus. **pêng-an-chhì**, do., used much on 5.5. **úi-tô-chhì**, another cactus (upright and tall). **gû-kak-chhì**, a sort of hard-wood. **koe-kak-chhì**, the thistle. **koe-kang-chhì-thâu**, the root of a sort of thistle (used as a cooling medicine). **toā-chhì-thâu**, a medicine. **chhì-thâu-hiu^n**, a medicine, &c. &c.

chhī (R. id.), a market-street; a street with shops; forms the last word in the names of many market-towns or large trading towns.

chhī-thâu, street or streets of shops in a village. **koe-chhī**, a market-street; a street of shops. **koe-thâu-chhī-bé**, the whole market. **siâ^n-chhī**, a city with its suburbs (v. siâ^n). **hî-á-chhī**, a fish-market.

chhin-chhī, a sort of silk (v. chhin).

pā-chhī, united shutting of all the shops (of a town or ward) as a demonstration against the mandarins for some injustice. **hù-chhī**, to arrive at the market in good time. **khui-chhī**, to begin the sales of the day; to begin business, as a new shop, or as after the holidays.

hó-chhī-chháu, good trade, purchasers numerous and prices good. **hó-chhī**, id. (s. feed). **lī-chhī**, good sale; good trade. **ka-iáh lī-chhī**, id. **tāi-kiet lī-chhī**, good-luck in trade (somewhat superstitious phrase). **pāi-chhī**, bad sale; trade not good. **khah-phái^n-chhī**, id. (s. feed). **kơ-mn̂g tók-chhī**, the only house that has any special article.

chhī — **loān-chhī-chhā**, crowded or confused, as a crowd, or as the mind (v. chhā). **chhī-chhī-kún**, sound of men in great numbers swaying about.

chhī-bú chhī-chhū, whispering.

chhī — **khùn-chhī-chhī**, to sleep very sound.

chhī — **chhiò-chhī**, smiling pleasant appearance of countenance.

chhī — **pờ-chhī-á** (C.), the young rice-plants that are planted out from the seed-beds.

chhī (R. sū), to feed (active), to nourish; to bring up; to rear; to supply food to; to become food for; to temper, as iron.

iú^n-chhī, to feed; to support; to bring up. **hó-io-chhī**, good-tempered and healthy, as child easily fed and tended and growing well. **hó-chhī**, id. (s. market). **phái^n-chhī**, difficult to rear and bring up, as delicate child (s. market).

chhī tsa-bó, to keep a concubine. **chhī tsa-bó-kiá^n**, to bring up a daughter. **chhī-gín-á**, a young boy who serves as a servant (almost like a slave) for food and clothing only. **chhī-lí-toā**, feeds (or has fed) you till grown up. **chhī thit-thô**, to keep (as birds) for amusement merely. **chhī-lâng**, to employ or support people.

chhī bát-sat, to let bugs breed abundantly. **chhī-hî**, may you be drowned and become food for fishes! also, to feed fish. **chhī-chhèng**, to be food for powder. **chhī-toā-chhèng**, id. **chhī pán-tsô**, id. **gê-béng chhī-báng**, the boy named gê-béng got the mosquitoes to bite him so as to spare his parents. **chhī-hó**, be devoured by a tiger; said of a useless fellow, or of reckless running into danger; said also to frighten children. **thâu-khak boah phí^n-sng, khì-chhī-hó**, to try to poison tigers by one's own head smeared with arsenic.

chhī-chiáu, he-hé liáu, the keeping of fancy birds for amusement wastes one's property. **chhī cheng-si^n**, to keep or feed domestic animals. **chhī-chhiū^n** (esp. T.), id. (v. chhiū^n). **chhī-káu, pūi ka-kī**, to keep a dog that barks at ourself. **chhī-tsoâ, kā koe-bú**, to nourish a serpent that eats the hens; to have a secret enemy in our house. **chhī niáu-chhú kā pờ-tē**, to nourish a rat that eats our bags (same meaning). **chhī-kiá^n, bô-lūn pn̄g; chhī pē-bú, siàu-tǹg**, sons get rice without stint, but what parents eat is counted up and grudged. **chhī hāu-si^n, iú^n lāu-sê; chhī tsa-bó-kiá^n, pát-lâng-ê**, if you bring up a son he will nourish his old father, but the daughter whom you rear goes over to others. **lâng chhī-lâng, sin chit-ki-kut; thi^n chhī-lâng, pûi lut-lut**, with all man's feeding he is nothing but bones; but, if Heaven feed him, he is very fat. **thi^n ná^n-beh khit-lâng-chhī, chhòng thih-thûi kòng-bōe-sí**, if Heaven will have a man live, you cannot kill him even with a hammer.

chhī-thih (C. chhū), to temper iron in water. **chhī-tsúi**, id. **chhī-chhùi**, to temper the edge, as of a stone-chisel.

chhi^n [R. chheng, pure]. **chhi^n-miâ^n** (C. chheng-bêng), the "feast of tombs," about April 5th. **tàh-chhi^n**, to keep that day by going to the graves and worshipping; repairs are usually made about that time, gen. a day or two before.

chhi^n [R. seng, to produce, living, raw, = col. si^n], (C. chhɛ^n), raw, uncooked, unacquainted; (wild, irascible); unbroken, as horse; in some phrases gives the idea of haste or touchiness or sickishness.

chhi^n-sə, unacquainted with a thing, person, &c.; unskilled, inexperienced; ill-composed and unsuitable, as a literary composition. **lō chhi^n**, ignorant of the road. **chhi^n-chheh**, a book that we are not familiar with.

chhi^n-kông, acting very impulsively and hastily. **chhi^n-chin**, making a sudden start; do a thing very impulsively. **chhi^n-kia^n**, to be startled. **chhàu-chhi^n-kia^n**, sudden start, as at a ghost. **phah-chhi^n-kia^n**, to startle; to scare away, as birds.

chhi^n-hoan, savages. **chhi^n-bé**, an unbroken horse; a wild, unreasonable, ungovernable man. **chhi^n-bé-khùi**, irascible; always ready to quarrel; having violent temper; passionate.

chhi^n-bīn, touchy; readily taking offence, *e.g.* taking offence at a joke, as if it were in earnest. **kōe-chhi^n-bīn**, id. **chit--ē chhi^n-bīn**, to take offence suddenly when not meant, as a touchy man. **pì^n-chhi^n-bīn**, id. **chhi^n-bīn-hó**, a very touchy man (lit. tiger).

chhi^n-gî, feeling a tendency to vomit, as from a bad taste; suddenly taken aback and feeling suspicious, as at what seems dangerous, or at apparent signs of improper conduct; harbouring suspicion or distrust. **chhi^n-áu**, feeling of sickness, bringing up a little sour watery stuff. **chhi^n-iau**, incessant craving for food of a diseased stomach. **phah-chhi^n-iau**, to have this feeling.

chhi^n-chhìn, chilly cold feeling (v. chhìn).

chhi^n-lȧt-peng, fresh troops.

chhi^n-khîm oáh-liáh, to take alive, as a prisoner; very urgent about a matter (v. liȧh).

chhi^n-thih, unwrought iron. **chhi^n-iòh**, raw materials for medicine. **chhi^n-tsoá**, unglazed paper. **chhi^n-iâm**, a large-grained sort of salt (med.) **chhi^n-hoân**, raw alum. **chhi^n-chhat**, varnish not fully prepared.

chhi^n (R. seng). **chhàu-chhi^n**, having a heavy raw or unpleasant odour, as fish, or bad smelling things, or as ground-nuts not toasted enough. **chhi^n-chho**, animal diet, as opposed to vegetarian. **hî-chhi^n**, edible marine animals, in general.

chhi^n (R. chhe). **chhi^n-chhám**, wretched, miserable.

chhi^n (R. sien); fresh (not tainted), as fish; fresh and unfaded, as flowers; clean and stiffly starched, as clothes or new cloth.

chhi^n-hoe, natural flowers. **chhi^n-chhioh**, fresh and nice looking, as new cloth or fresh flowers. **chiu^n-khi-chhi^n**, starch it stiff. **hî chhi^n**, the fish are fresh. **chhi^n gû-lin**, milk curdled but not yet salted.

chhi^n (R. chheng); (C. chhɛ^n). **chhi^n-mî^n**, blind.

chhi^n (R. chheng); (C. chhɛ^n); the Chinese indigo plant. **chhi^n-tiā^n**, blue dye. **hoan-chhi^n**, foreign indigo. **soa^n-chhi^n**, a wild plant, not any sort of indigo.

phah-chhi^n, to work up the indigo in the vat to extract the colour. **chhi^n-tháng**, a large tub or vat for steeping indigo. **chhi^n-kng**, an earthen vat for dyeing with indigo. **khiā chhi^n-kng**, to have such a dye-vat in one's shop.

chhi^n (R. chheng); (C. chhɛ^n); green; said also of various shades of blue and purple.

chhi^n-kun, veins as they appear blue on the skin (v. kun).

tâng-chhi^n, verdegris; a green paint made from verdegris. **tâng-chhi^n-hī** (having green ears), a sort of fowl supposed to drive away white ants.

chhi^n-si, a thin silk stuff, of various colours. **chhi^n-si-á**, a small yellow bird. **chhi^n-ioh**, a small green frog. **chhi^n-thî**, green moss.

chhi^n-á (F.), the areca palm. **chhi^n-á-chí**, betel-nut from Formosa, green and soft.

chhi^n-liāng, the transparent blue button of third-class mandarins.

chhi^n-kim, gold of greenish colour. **chhi^n-tâng**, brass.

hoat-chhi^n, to put out green leaves. **tāu-chhi^n**, short sprouted (edible) peas. **kàu tn̄g-chhi^n**, till no green thing remains, as in great drought. **chhah-chhi^n**, to put up green branches on a house or field (v. chhah). **kìm-chhi^n**, to prohibit cattle from the green crops, done by having a play.

chhi^n-táu-chiòh, the common green granite of Amoy. **chiòh-chhi^n-sek**, the dark dull bluish green of green granite. **ah-nn̄g-chhi^n**, very light blue, colour of duck's egg. **liû-chhi^n-sek**, nearly the same colour. **chhi^n-chhùi**, verdant. **chhi^n lang-lang**, bright green, as fields. **phû-tô-chhi^n**, purplish blue, colour of grapes. **thien-chhi^n**, a dull purple. **hoan-á-chhi^n**, dark blue. **hāu-huih-chhi^n**, light dull blue, colour of the blood of the king-crab. **sam-kong-chhi^n**, a sort of violet-coloured silk.

chhi^n-n̂g, pale, as the face of a sick man. **bīn chhi^n-n̂g**, face of that pale greenish yellow colour. **tài-chhi^n-n̂g**, id. **bīn chhi^n-pėh**, face greenish white, as of sickly constitution. **bīn chhi^n-sún-sún**, face pale with sickness or sudden fear. **phah ə-chhi^n**, to beat black and blue.

chhi^n-chhòng pėh-chhòng, not well made; to manage ill and spoil, as affair.

chhi^n (R. seng); (C. chhɛ^n), a star. **chhi^n-sîn**, stars (many). **chhi^n-siù**, the stars and constellations. **pe-chhi^n**, a falling star.

kə-chhi^n, the Pleiades. **chhit-chhi^n**, id. (v. chhit). **khé-bêng-chhi^n**, the morning star. **pak-táu-chhi^n**, the Great Bear. **sàu-chiú-chhi^n**, a comet. **thoa-bé-chhi^n**, id. **chhoah-sái-chhi^n** (vulg.), a meteor or falling star. **tn̂g-bé-chhi^n**, a comet; also, a son who brings evil on his father. **tn̂g-bé-chhi^n-á**, said in scolding a disobedient boy who is always causing trouble.

phái^n-chhi^n, a comet; a very wicked injurious man, as a bad mandarin, or a robber or seducer. **phái^n-chhi^n jip-kéng**, such a wicked hurtful man coming to a place. **hoân--tióh phái^n-chhi^n**, to come suddenly on some one whom we wish not to meet; to meet with something that unexpectedly thwarts our plans; to suffer injury from some wicked man or malignant spiritual power.

chhát-chhi^n, a rascal who plunders or injures others.

hó-chhì^{n}, a deliverer or benefactor. **kiù-chhì^{n}**, a man who delivers us from a very pressing danger. **ū-kiù-chhì^{n}**, there is some one to deliver us from the danger. **hó-kiù-chhì^{n}**, id.

hé-chhì^{n}, a spark. **hé-kim-chhì^{n}**, a fire-fly.

chhi^{n} [R. chhin, related]; (C. chhɛ^{n}). **chhi^{n}-ḿ**, the mothers of bride and bridegroom, as related to each other; the wives of the "chhin-ke."

chhí^{n} [R. chhién, shallow]; light blue, the colour of common Chinese blue cotton cloth. **tìm-chhí^{n}**, somewhat darker blue, as that cotton when new and starched. **chhiò-chhí^{n}**, somewhat lighter blue. **chhí^{n}-bō**, a light blue cap, worn in secondary mourning.

chhí^{n} (C. chhé^{n}). **chhin-chhí^{n}**, pretty. **chhut chhin-chhí^{n}**, to have small-pox.

chhí^{n} (R. séng), (C. chhé^{n}), awake; having the sexual feeling, only said of the females of lower animals, esp. pigs and cats.

chhí^{n}-chhùi, to give an appetite, as a relish does.

jîm-chit-chhí^{n}, to doze for a few moments, as with head on hand.

m̄-tsai-chhí^{n}, very soundly asleep. **kiò-chhí^{n}**, to awaken another. **phah-chhí^{n}**, to awaken a man unintentionally. **phah-chhí^{n}-bîn**, id. **chhí^{n}-bîn**, to awake from sleep; also, to keep one's self awake, as by drinking tea. **khùn-chhí^{n}**, to awake from sleep. **poà^{n}-chhí^{n} poà^{n}-khùn**, half-asleep. **chhí^{n}-chhí^{n} bô-khùn**, wide awake. **oà^{n}-khùn tsá-chhí^{n}**, late to bed and rising early.

tiám-chhí^{n}, to warn (by a hint) of a plot or other danger, as a friend; or as a god, by a dream or vision, &c. **chhí^{n}-gē̤** (X.), to awaken as to the knowledge of a doctrine; to begin to understand it. **chhí^{n}-ngē̤**, id.

chhì^{n} (R. chhù), to pierce (= chhì), either literally or figuratively of grief at heart.

chhī^{n}, an instrument used in making nets. **bák-chhī^{n}**, a wedge-shaped piece of wood, used by carpenters for dipping in ink and drawing lines on wood. **bih-chhī^{n}**, do. made of bamboo split small like a brush.

chhia (R. ku), a carriage; a windlass or capstan; instruments with a wheel, as a lathe, a spinning-wheel, &c.; to turn such a wheel; to turn in a lathe; a surname.

tià^{n}-chhia, windlass for anchor, on bow of junk. **phâng-chhia**, windlass for sail, at mast. **tsúi-chhia**, a chain water-wheel for irrigation. **tsúi-chhia-iáp**, the paddles of a chain water-wheel. **chià-chhia**, a sugar-mill. **iû-chhia**, an oil-press. **chhiú-chhia**, a spinning-wheel. **pháng-chhia**, do. **pháng-chhia-lûn**, the wheel of a spinning-wheel. **sái pháng-chhia-lûn**, to make one's arms go round like a wheel.

gû-chhia, a cart drawn by oxen. **bé-chhia**, a cart or carriage drawn by a horse. **hè-chhia**, a cart. **hé-hun-chhia**, a railway train. **lêng-chhia hōng-lién**, imperial carriage and sedan. **chē-chhia**, to ride in a carriage or cart. **koá^{n}-chhia**, to drive it. **thoa-chhia**, to draw a cart or carriage.

tsáp-lák-chhia, the smaller poles used in carrying a coffin; so called, though usually only eight bearers are employed. **chhòng-chhia**, to fit these poles for a coffin.

chhia-khoan, a capstan bar. **chhia-hu**, a charioteer; a driver. **chhia-soh**, a carriage rope; the endless band of a spinning-wheel. **pháng-chhia-soh**, the endless band. **chhia-lûn**, a carriage-wheel. **chhia-lûn-kì^{n}**, a spoke. **chhia-kì^{n}**, id. **chhia-lûn-sim**, the boss of a wheel. **chhia-lûn-sng**, the axle. **chhia-sng**, id.

chhia-tià^{n}, to raise the anchor. **chhia-phâng**, to spread the sail by raising it. **chhia-tsan**, to raise (by windlass) a square net set on a pivot on rocks by the sea. **chhia-se**, to transfer the thread from the iron spindle to the wooden spools, or what stand for bobbins. **chhia-ké̤-pô**, a man dressed as a woman, who beats the drum at an idol procession (v. ké̤).

chhia-kui, a turning-lathe. **chhia-kang**, the expense of turning; men employed as turners. **chhia-gê**, to turn in ivory. **chhia-gê sai-hū**, a turner in ivory. **chhia-gėk**, to turn jade in a lathe. **chhia-chhâ**, to turn in wood.

chhia-poā^{n}, to say the same thing wearisomely over and over in a discussion; endless weary repetition of the same arguments. **ū-hoan-chhia**, able to accommodate one's self to the circumstances; versatile. **pak-lāi tióh-ōe hoan-chhia**, you should be willing to change your mind and plans, on being spoken to reasonably. **tē̤-lāi lóng-bōe hoan-chhia**, too stiff and unable to accommodate one's self to circumstances. **bô-hoan-chhia**, id.

chhia — **péh-chhia-kû**, a white material from a shell, used for opaque white official buttons (v. kû).

chhia — **chhia-låt**, to be very serious, as a matter of pressing importance.

chhia — **lô-chhia**, an idol in form of a little boy (= tiong-tân goân-sòe) holding a spear, attendant on Tāi-tō-kong, and some other idols. **lô-chhia thài-tsú**, id.

chhia (R. id.) **chhia-chhí**, lavish; prodigal in gaudy display and expenditure; wasteful and extravagant in vanities or pleasures. **chhia-hoâ**, id.

chhia (C. chhu), to gnaw or eat up by making holes, as ants and such insects. **péh-hiā chhia**, the white ants eat it. **khit-thâng-chhia**, to be eaten through by insects.

chhia (R. chhui), to push; falling in floods, as water. **chhia-tó**, to push over; to overset; to upset. **sa^{n}-chhia**, to push each other, as in wrestling or struggling.

lāi chhia-bú, bú chhia-lāi, compound interest accumulating.

thap-thâu-chhia, to fall head-foremost. **chhia pha-lìn-táu**, to make a somerset. **hō̤ chhia-teh-pià^{n}**, rain coming down in floods. **hō̤ chhia-teh-tò**, id. **chhia**, a waterfall; put after the name of the place, *e.g.* **táng-á-chhia**, the waterfall near the village "táng-á," near Chang-poo.

chhia — **poa^{n}-chhia**, to move things about, as in looking for something; to talk over and over the very same thing with wearisome iteration, as in arguing. **poa^{n}-chhia sin-chheh-á kū-låh-jit** (prov.), to rake up old out-of-date faults or reports against a man.

chhiâ (R. siâ), oblique; slanting; sloping. **oai-chhiâ**, oblique. **khi-chhiâ**, leaning over, as a vessel, or as a wall about to fall.

jit chhiâ, the sun about to set. **géh chhiâ**, the moon about to set.

chhiâ-bûn, drills or twilled cloth (v. bûn). **chhiâ-thong**, the sloping beams of a roof which support the rafters.

chhiâ-thé̤, the thirty-second radical, as written at the side. **chhiâ-giòk**, the ninety-sixth radical, as written at the side. **chhiâ-ông**, id.

chhià (R. siâ), steep; steeper than "bîn," but less steep than "kiā;" about half a right angle.

chhia^n — **bé-chhia^n** (C.), the thick bristles of a horse's tail.

chhia^n (R. chheng). **hok-chhia^n**, Fuh-tsing Hien, near Fuh-chau. **bân-chhia^n**, Min-tsing Hien, near do.

chhiâ^n (R. sêng), (dist. from chiâ^n), to make complete; to repair thoroughly; to help a man to complete a thing; to give valuable assistance. **chhiâ^n-bé**, to complete properly what had been unfinished. **chhiâ^n-mih^n**, to make a thing all right that was imperfectly made. **chhiâ^n hō-i-hó**, id., &c.

kóe-chhiâ^n, to repair or correct thoroughly. **chhiâ^n-ke**, to take care of a household so as to make it prosper, as a good wife does. **chhiâ^n--lâng**, to assist a man to get on in life, as a friend does by setting him up in business, or lending him money; or as a benevolent spirit does to his votaries. **chhiâ^n-lâng-hó**, to help a man to prosper yet more than before. **chhiâ^n-tī**, to bring up children till they are married, or can take care of themselves. **chhiâ^n--i chiâ^n-lâng**, to rear and take care of him till he gets married. **tńg-chhiâ^n**, to become of marriageable age, as boy or girl.

chhiá^n — **pùn-chhiá^n**, a coarse shovel-shaped scoop for gathering up sweepings.

chhiá^n (R. id.), just let —; please just —; now just —; just for a short time —. **bóng-chhiá^n**, id. (v. bóng).

ké-chhiá^n, remissly; carelessly; inaccurately. **kïó-chhiá^n** (Cn.), id. **chiām-chhiá^n**, just temporarily let —; just for a short time —. **chhiá^n-bān**, wait a little. **chhiá^n-bān--chiah**, id. **chhiá^n-lēng--teh**, just wait a little before doing it. **chhiá^n-kià--lí**, I intrust this thing to you to keep for me for a short time.

siōng-chhiá^n, yet notwithstanding; almost always followed by "hô-hòng," or such a phrase, giving the sense "even when . . . yet, . . . how much more" (v. siōng).

chhiá^n (R. chhéng), to invite; to engage, as a teacher; good-bye. **chhiá^n-mn̄g**, to ask politely. **chhiá^n-chē**, please take a seat; please don't go away. **chhiá^n-tê**, to invite to take a cup of tea. **chhiá^n-hun**, to offer a smoke. **chhiá^n-thiap**, invitation cards. **chit-chhiá^n chit-chhui**, to invite, and afterwards urge more strongly.

chhiá^n sien-si^n, to engage a teacher. **phèng-chhiá^n**, to make a present to a wise man, and invite him to be a minister of state, &c. (v. phèng).

chhiá^n-lēng, to ask orders from a military superior, as for an expedition, or for beheading. **chhiá^n-pâi**, to ask a license for a pawn-shop, &c. (v. pâi). **poa^n-chhiá^n**, to get one's family to move, esp. a mandarin's family moving to his seat of office.

chhiá^n-put, to invite an idol to come from one place to another; to call the spirit of an idol to come into the body of an enchanter. **chhiá^n-lêng**, to invite the spirit of the dead to come and stay in the "lêng-chhù" during the rites for the dead. **chhiá^n-sîn**, to invite the spirits to come to some ceremony. **chhiá^n-ông**, to invite the spirit "ông-iâ" to come. **chhiá^n bók-tsú**, to invite the ancestral tablets to change their place. **thau-chhiá^n**, to steal an idol or ancestral tablet. **chhiá^n-hé**, to bring sacred fire from a greater temple to an inferior one. **chhiá^n-kǹg**, to get an amulet from an idol.

sa^n-chhiá^n, to invite friends. **sa^n-chhiá^n bô-lūn**, when inviting friends we don't count how much they eat. **chhiá^n-toh**, to give a feast. **chhiá^n chhun-chiú**, to invite to a feast in the new-year's holidays (v. chiú).

chhià^n (R. chhèng), to hire, as a boat or servant, or workman (but not said of a teacher). **sa^n-chhià^n**, id. **kè-chhià^n**, id. **chhin-chhiū^n kè-chhià^n**, like a hireling (said in blaming a relative for giving too little care to what we intrusted him). **tiau-chhià^n**, to hire specially. **tit-chhià^n**, id. **chhià^n-kang**, to hire labourers; a hired labourer.

iang-chhià^n, to intrust a message or commission to a man. **chhià^n-chhiu^n** (to hire a spear), to engage a man to write an essay for us for the examination.

chhiah [R. chhek, the side]. **chhiah-bák-khoà^n**, to look with a side-glance angrily, displeased, or enviously. **sái-chhiah-bák**, id.

chhiah [R. chhek, = chhù, col. chhì, to pierce], to sew or embroider; to brand; to make, as a net; to pierce; to dazzle; to dig, as turf; to stir, as the fire.

chhiah-huih, to pierce so as to bring blood, as in killing a pig. **chhiah--tiòh chit-ki-chhoa^n**, pierced by a small thorn or splinter. **chhiah-tiòh-chhì**, pierced by a thorn. **chhiah-jī**, to stamp characters on criminals; to brand.

chhiah bák-chiu, to dazzle the eyes, as the sun; to excite desire, as things seen. **chhiah-iàh**, an uncomfortable feeling of body, as from dirty clothes, profuse perspiration, or prickly heat; uncomfortable disappointed feeling, as from some loss or cross. **phah chhiah-sng-eh**, to belch with a bad sour taste and smell.

chhiah-hoe, to embroider finely with short stitches, the hand keeping on one side of the cloth. **chhiah-siù**, to embroider by passing the needle right through and then back. **thio-hoe chhiah-siù**, to embroider; embroidering in general. **chhiah-ôe**, to sew shoes in making. **chhiah-bāng**, to make a net. **chhiah tsang-sui**, to make a rain-coat of palm fibre.

chhiah-hé, to stir the fire. **chhiah-thô**, to stir the earth, as with a spade (s. red). **chhiah chháu-phiá^n**, to dig sods of turf. **chhiah koá chháu-phí**, to dig a few sods.

chhńg-chhiah, looking out avariciously for every chance (right or wrong) for making money.

chhiah [R. chhek, red], brownish-red; naked; very poor, as man or place; rude, coarse, or wild, as persons. **o-âng, chhiah pe̍h-le̍k**, the five colours.

chhiah-bah, the lean of meat (v. bah). **chhiah-lī**, the brown mucous discharge of dysentery.

âng-thi^n, chhiah jit-thâu, very hot cloudless sky.

chhiah-bí, a red sort of rice. **chhiah-khak-tsút**, the best sort of glutinous rice.

chiok-chhiah-kim, pure unalloyed gold. **chhiah kàu ná^n le̍k-kim**, shining as if inlaid with gold; said also of a man very poor.

chhiah-koái^n-koái^n, very very poor. **chhiah-khiū-khiū**, id. **chhiah kàu jip-jiông** (T.), most extremely poor (lit. to the quick). **sòng-chhiah** (Cn.), very poor. **sàn-chhiah**, very poor; sometimes has the idea of daring to do any bad action to get money. **iá-chhiah**, very wild and rude. **chhiah-á**, roughs, rowdies, and vagrants. **phè-chhiah** (Cn.), the rowdies of a ward. **chhiah-tsa-bó**, a forward, vulgar, and impudent woman, ready to dispute and quarrel shamelessly with men.

chhiah-kha, feet naked; bare foot. **chhiah-tiâu-tiâu**, stark naked. **chhiah-sin lō-thé**, naked body.

chhiah-kháu-jit, certain days that are unlucky, so that matters begun on them will cause much troublesome discussion.

chhiah-kiuⁿ, a sort of brown cricket (v. kiuⁿ). **chhiah-kiú**, a small round fish. **chhiah kàu náⁿ chhiah-kiú--nihⁿ**, said of a man who is very poor, or a woman very impudent, or child very troublesome. **chhiah-tsang-á**, a small fish two or three inches long. **chhiah-hái** (F.), a fish of brilliant red colour.

chhiah-phê, a sort of hard wood (used for furniture). **chhiah-chhài**, a sea-weed (used in making idolatrous paper). **chhiah-jîn-thô**, a sort of reddish clay. **chhiah-thô**, id. (s. pierce).

chhiáh (C.), = A. siàh, a sort of spoon or ladle. **chhiáh-á**, id. **chhâ-chhiáh**, a sort of wooden ladle.

chhiak (C.), = A. chhiok. **kim-chhiak-hoa**, a beautiful yellow flower.

chhiák — **chhiák-chhiák-chhiák**, sound of dollars shaken. **chhiák-chhiák-háu**, do.; also said of a young person or inferior talking on loud and big when he should be quiet. **chhiák-chhiák-kiò**, id.

chhiák, to start suddenly. **chhiák--chhit-ē**, id. **chhiák-chhiák-tiô**, to palpitate, as the heart; to jump up and down noisily and angrily. **chhiák-chhiák-thiàu**, to jump and frisk about incessantly.

ài-chhiák, fond of display and expense; making a great appearance of exultation, self-importance, or bravado. **siuⁿ-chhiák**, making too much display, bravado, &c.

chhiam (R. id.), long narrow slips of wood (used as lots); potatoes or dough made into long thin slips. **chhiam-á**, a long thin wooden lot. **iô-chhiam-á**, to shake the cylinder holding the lots before drawing one. **iô-chhiam-á thàn-chiáh**, to live by this style of fortune-telling (the lowest sort). **hiàm chhiam-á**, to gamble by drawing lots—twenty-five in number—five lots for each of the five colours. **thiu-chhiam**, to draw lots, as in fortune-telling. **chhiam-si**, colloquial verses on slips of paper, drawn by lot in temples. **tsoa-chhiam**, to get by lot, as an office; appointed to office by lot.

chhiam-tâng, a cylinder for holding the lots.

hé-chhiam, a tally given to a mandarin's messenger, as proof of the special urgency of the commands.

tāu-chhiam, a sort of dough cut up into long narrow thin slips. **han-tsû-chhiam**, potatoes cut into long narrow slips and dried.

chhiam — **chhiam-taⁿ**, a pole sharp at each end for carrying fuel; it often has iron points, but not always.

chhiam [R. chham, to mix]. **chhé-chhiam**, to bend one knee to a superior without touching the ground.

chhiam [R. all]. **chhiam-kí** (C.), to give a united recommendation, as several persons.

chhiam [R. to write, as one's name; a narrow slip of paper with writing]. **chhiam-ah**, to write the date (and some other marks) in red ink on an official document (v. ah). **chhiam-miâⁿ**, to sign or put down one's name; to put down another man's name by his authority. **chhiam-miâⁿ ūi-hō**, to write one's name (or have it written) and make the legal mark.

chheh-chhiam, the long narrow title pasted on the outside of a book.

chhiâm (= chhîm). **bák-sái chhiâm-chhiâm-lâu**, tears flowing abundantly.

chhiâm (esp. C., = chhiâng), a close-skinned or coolie orange.

chhiâm (= chhâm). **toā-chhiâm-kó**, large cymbals and drums.

chhiám (R. id.), a fork; a fork-shaped instrument; to pierce; to sew (esp. the edge) by short longitudinal stitches; to hem; to thrust in, as a carrying-pole into a bundle of fuel.

chhiám-á, a fork; an instrument for twirling the ball of opium in the flame before smoking. **to-chhiám**, knife and fork. **thih-chhiám**, an iron fork (used in cooking). **a-phièn-hun-chhiám**, a cleaner for the bowl of the opium-pipe.

phah-chhiám, to put a sharp instrument into things to examine them, as custom-house officers do. **thn̂g-chhiám**, a hollow-pointed instrument for taking a sample of sugar without opening the bag. **chhiám-thn̂g**, to take a sample of sugar out of a bag by inserting this instrument through the bag. **bí-chhiám**, a pointed hollow instrument for inserting in a rice-bag so as to take out a sample without opening it. **chhiám-kóng**, id.

chhiám-hoe, to stick flowers on thin bamboo slips, for wearing in the hair. **chit-chhiám-hoe**, a thin slip of bamboo with flowers stuck on it. **hoe-chhiám**, a hair-pin for flowers.

chhiám-oá, to fasten together (as the boards of a door) by long bamboo pins.

chhiám ôe-lí, to sew the edges of the lining of shoes, in sewing them on. **chhiám-piⁿ**, to hem a dress.

kha chhiám--tióh, the foot hurt by coming against something sharp. **chhiám-bâ** (C.), to spear wild animals with a sort of spear or fork.

chhiám (R. id.), the keel of a vessel. **thâu-chhiám**, the fore-part of the keel. **bé-chhiám**, the after half of the keel. **teh-chhiám**, to lay down the keel with idolatrous ceremonies. **an-chhiám**, do.

chhiàm — **lék-chhiàm-chhiàm**, very green, as fields after rain; having a green shade, as inferior black cloth.

chhiàm (R. id.) **chhiàm-koân**, to usurp authority. **chhiàm-chheng**, to assume or use a high title without any right to it. **chhiàm-chhùi**, to inform against a man to his superior, though we have no direct duty in the matter.

chhiàm — **chhiàm-to**, a sort of knife or graving-tool for cutting blocks for printing.

chhian, in all the tones; better chhien, *q.v.*

chhiang [R. chhiong, a spear, = col. chhiuⁿ]. **niáu-chhiang**, a gun; a musket. **thai-chhiang**, a sort of large gun worked by two men.

chhiang (C.), = A. chhiong. **chhiang-kông**, violent and hasty.

chhiang (C.), = A. chhiong (a prostitute); to scold with vile impure epithets.

chhiang (C.), = A. chhiong. **bûn-chhiang**, the god of literature.

chhiâng (r.), = chhiûⁿ, to winnow.

chhiâng [R. tiông, bowels, = col. tn̂g]. **ien-chhiâng**, sausages.

chhiâng [R. siông, constantly]. **chhiâng-tsāi**, constantly present, as at his post.

chhiâng (R. siông), (C.), to repay; to pay a debt.

chhiâng, to sweep away soil, as a torrent. **kún-chhiâng-chhiâng**, boiling violently, as water.

chhiâng [R. tiông, an area, an arena, = col. tiûⁿ]. **pâi-chhiâng**, gaudy. **kóng-ōe, ài-pâi-chhiâng**, talking very big.

chhiâng (= chhiâm), the close-skinned or coolie orange.

chhiâng (= chhêng). **pūn-chhiâng**, too fat and awkward in gait; awkward-looking, from having on too many clothes, or clothes ill put on; vulgar in talk.

chhiáng, to walk with much difficulty, as with a lame or sore leg; to get along by a sort of hopping with a stick or a crutch. **ûn-á-chhiáng**, to walk along slowly, as with a painful leg. **chhiáng-kha**, do.; sometimes with a sort of hop. **chhiáng-ke-le** (Cn.), to hop, as a child.

chhiáng [R. jióng, confused, involved]. **jû-chhiáng-chhiáng**, very intricate, entangled, or involved. **jí-chhiáng-chhiáng** (C.), id. (cf. chháng).

chhiàng — **chhiàng-chhiàng-tsáu**, to run very fast.

chhiàng (C.), = A. chhiòng, (to be first).

chhiàng [R. chhiòng, to sing, to call loud, cf. col. chhiùⁿ], to call out with a loud voice in a formal manner; to make express stipulation verbally, as for price or wages. **kap-lí-chhiàng**, make a distinct arrangement or agreement with you.

tsáu-chhiàng, to go about, as itinerant ballad-singer for money; a street-singer. **tsáu-chhiàng ê-lâng**, a street ballad-singer.

chhiàng-miâⁿ, to call out a name loud, as in calling a roll of names. **chhiàng-miâⁿ--ê**, the man in a yamun whose duty it is to call out loud for whatever subordinate is wanted. **chhiàng-lé**, to call out the name of each offering and of each rite to be performed, as the master of ceremonies does at solemn offerings. **chhiàng-kè**, to call out the price, as an auctioneer. **chhiàng-lí-lék**, to state verbally (to superior officer) one's own birth and history (v. lék).

chhiàng-khí-thâu, to be the first to propose a matter or to raise a subject (perhaps this phrase belongs to the previous word).

chhiāng — **chhiāng-chhiāng-kún**, to make a noise, as a number of people, or as water boiling (cf. chhiâng).

chhiāng (cf. chhiáng), (C.) **chhiāng-kha-ke**, to hop.

chhiap [R. a concubine]. **it-chhe it-chhiap**, one wife and one concubine. **khì-chhe thióng-chhiap**, to put away the legal wife, and take a former concubine as wife, punishable by transportation. **bī-chhū-chhe, sien chhū-chhiap**, to take a concubine before marrying a wife; against Chinese law, and counted highly improper by the people.

chhiat, chhiát; better chhiet, chhiét (*q.v.*)

chhiau — **chhiau-chhē**, to search, as for a thing lost. **chhiau-khoàⁿ**, to search, as a person or house for stolen articles. **chhiau-ke**, to search a mandarin's family residence (at home), to see if he has embezzled or squeezed seriously; it generally includes the idea of confiscation. **chhiau-ū**, to find by searching. **chhiau-bô**, to look, but not find.

chhiau — **chhiau-poâⁿ** (= chhia-poâⁿ), to talk over the same thing with wearisome reiteration.

chhiau (= chhau). **chhiau-sam-tsók**, to put to death a criminal with his relatives, and those of his mother and of his wife.

chhiau, to mix by stirring, as a powder with a fluid or semi-fluid, as dough, mortar, &c. **chhiau-thô**, to mix mortar. **chhiau-kàⁿ**, to mix leaven. **chhiau-ké**, to mix the materials for the cakes called "ké." **chhiau mīⁿ-hún**, to work up wheaten dough. **chhiau-chhòe**, to make rice-dough. **chhiau-tiⁿ**, to mix sugar in dough, for making sweet cakes or sweetmeats. **chhiau-tsúi**, to mix water with a powder, such as lime, flour, &c. **chhiau-iû**, to mix oil as above.

chhiau — **bé-chiúⁿ chhiau--leh**, move the stern-oar like a helm, with a slight motion.

chhiau [R. to excel, to raise]. **chhiau-seng**, to save a soul out of punishment, so that it is again born into this world. **pit-hā chhiau-seng**, the pen writes down that the criminal may live. **chhiau-tō**, to save a soul out of hades; to get again born into this world.

chhiau-poát, having an appearance of intelligence and talent; also (R.) to rescue a soul from hades to be again born into the world. **chhiau-thoat**, easy, off-hand, and unconstrained in manner; also (R.) to get a soul again born into the world. **chhiau-chhék**, exulting manner; in high spirits.

chhiau-soán, to choose the best, as goods or men. **chhiau-kûn** (R.), to have surpassing talent or excellence of any sort, mental or physical, or in external appearance. **chhut-chiòng chhiau-kûn** (R.), id. **chhiau-téng**, the ten competitors who get the highest prizes at the (giok-pin) Amoy local examinations.

chhiau (= chiâu). **chhiau-sim peh-pak**, sorely grieved and distressed.

chhiâu, to move a thing slightly so as to get it into the right place or position; to alter slightly for the better; to set to the right time, as a watch; to give a slight twist to a statement or message for a purpose; to adjust by a small change; to adjust a dispute, esp. in money matters, by getting each party to abate something of his demands; to get a man put out of his situation by statements not strictly true.

bōe-chhiâu--tit, it is fixed or settled, so that it cannot be altered in the least, so that it cannot be mended, *e.g.* a demand that will be insisted on, or an incautious statement made in evidence, or an inconvenient promise or agreement, that we are held to. **chhiâu-tām-póh**, to alter slightly, as the terms of a bargain, or agreement, or settlement, &c. **hō-goá chhiâu-tām-póh**, allow me to have somewhat better terms, *e.g.* let me have a little more money than was promised; let me alter it slightly according to my views of what is better.

chhui-chhiâu, to adjust a difference in money matters; to discuss a bargain till the price is fixed; to haggle. **chhiâu kè-chîⁿ**, to adjust the price by mutual concessions. **kap-i-chhiâu**, to come to an agreement with him, by each yielding a little. **goá kā-lín-chhiâu**, I will adjust and arrange your dispute so as to bring you to an agreement.

chhiâu-poah, to put a matter (that was in a bad state) into a better state. **chhiâu khah-hó-thiaⁿ**, to alter slightly our report of an affair, or a message given us, so as to make it sound better. **chhiâu khah-hó**, id. **chhiâu khah-pháiⁿ**, to alter the report slightly, so as to make the affair seem worse than the reality.

chhiâu chió-chîⁿ, to get the price a little lowered. **m̄-hō--lí chhiâu-chió-chîⁿ**, won't let down his price or monetary demands in the least for you.

chhiâu i--ê thâu-lō, to make him lose his situation by making misrepresentations against him to his superior. **khit--i chhiâu--khì**, to lose one's place through his misrepresentations.

chhiâu-kut, to set a bone that was displaced. **chhiâu-í chhiâu-toh**, to move furniture (chairs and tables) into proper positions by slight changes. **chhiâu-khi-chià^n**, alter it a little so as to make it quite even or correct.

chhiáu — **chhín-chhiáu**, mischievous, behaving badly, as troublesome child. **chhín-chhiáu-chhiáu**, id.

chhiáu (C.) **chhiáu-chhiáu khah-toā**, just a little larger.

chhiàu [R. siàu, C. (R.) chhiàu, to laugh, = col. chhiò]. **soat-chhiàu**, to jest and joke, to talk laughable things. **chhiàu-tâm**, jocular talk. **kóng chhiàu-tâm**, to make or tell jests and jokes; to talk foolish talk.

chhiauh, a bamboo instrument used as an accompaniment in some songs. **phah-chhiauh**, to beat it at the set times while singing. **teh-chhiauh**, id.

chhiauh — **chhih-chhiauh**, mischievous, behaving in a disorderly manner, as children or women.

chhiauh — **chhiauh-chhiauh-tiô**, to jump up and down angrily; to dance about, as a Tauist sorcerer (tâng-chí) in ecstacy. **khì kàu chhiauh-chhiauh-tiô**, dancing with rage.

chhiáuh (cf. chiáuh). **chhiáuh-chhiáuh-háu**, clattering sound, as of shoes worn loosely; said of a man (esp. an inferior) talking on long when he should stop. **chhùi chhiáuh-chhiáuh-háu**, talking on when he should stop. **chhiáuh-chhiáuh-liām**, to talk on in a low discontented tone, when he should be satisfied. **chhiáuh-chhiáuh-nih^n**, to wink or blink constantly, as from custom or from state of eyes.

chhien (R. id.), to migrate; to change one's residence. **chhien-î**, id. **chhien--khì pât-sé-tsāi**, id. **chhien-soá** (r.), id. **chhien-ku** (r.), id. **chhien-ki** (C.), id.

kái-kò chhien-siēn, to reform one's faults and return to virtue. **pièn-chhien**, to change for the worse, or passing away. **sè-sū pièn-chhien**, affairs all changing for the worse.

chhien (R. id.); (T. chhien, chhin). **chhien-chhiu**, a swing. **hiù-chhien-chhiu**, to swing a swing. **hì^n-chhien-chhiu**, id.

chhien [R. a thousand, = col. chheng]. **chhien-kim** (polite), a daughter. **chhien-kim-tūi**, a medicinal plant. **chhien-jit-hông**, a sort of everlasting flower.

chhien-ke-lē, commodities that are in constant use by every one, so as to be very safe to trade in. **chhien-tsóng**, a mandarin who commands (nominally) a thousand men, but really few. **chhien-lí-kià^n**, a telescope. **chhien-lí-bé**, a courier.

chhien-bān, most earnestly— (said in urging or entreating). **chhien-bān m̄-thang**, on no account do so. **kóng-chhien kóng-bān**, to entreat or exhort very earnestly. **chhien-giên bān-gú**, a vast deal of talk. **chhien-chin bān-chin**, most certainly true. **chhien-pièn bān-hoà**, all sorts of changes and transformations (v. hoà). **chhien-gûn bóe-chhù, bān-gûn bóe chhù-pī^n**, it is ten times easier to buy a good house than to get good neighbours.

chhiên [R. tiên, a field, = col. chhân]. **chhiên-kap-á**, bits of paper which children play with (v. kap).

chhiên, to delay. **iên-chhiên**, id. **ke-chhiên-jit**, to delay longer. **chhiên i-ê-kang**, to interrupt and delay his work.

chhiên-ūi, to refuse to sit down till the other sits down, or urging the other to take a higher seat. **sa^n-chhiên**, id. or asking one another to take precedence in walking.

chhién — **khioh-chhién**, to pile up cakes, fruit, &c., very high on a flower-pot by means of a stick as a back-bone; done in the seventh moon for worship of the spirits. **ka-nn̂g-chhién**, a whole pile of eatables so arranged.

chhién (R. id.), shallow; simple and easy, as doctrine or instruction.

chhién-á, a small bamboo wicker dish. **chhién-poah**, a shallow earthen basin. **chhién-tsûn**, a very shallow flat-bottomed boat for shallow streams. **chhién-tià^n**, an anchor with only one fluke. **chhién-thoa**, slippers without heels.

ke-chhién, a small bamboo basket with offerings to the dead, in general; (poor men go and eat them). **pah-jī-chhién**, a hundred and twenty of these small baskets with offerings; if more numerous they are in the same proportion.

chhién-liōng, having but small capacity for drinking liquor (said by one's self); also, standing too rigorously on one's rights. **chhién-kièn**, of shallow understanding. **chhién-hák**, of small scholarship. **chhién-hiēn**, plain and easy, as a character, or as doctrines or purpose; open and exposed, as a house. **chhién-pòh**, shallow and thin. **iû-chhién jip-chhim**, to proceed from the easy to the difficult.

chhién [R. to manifest, to explain]. **chhién-bêng** (R.), to comment upon; to explain, as books or doctrine. **sù-su chhién-tsù**, a commentary on the commentary on the Four Books.

chhién [R. chiên, cash; said in imitation of the mandarin sounds and tones, = col. chî^n]. **it-tiàu-chhién**, one string of cash. **ang hién, tē-tsú liáu-chhién** (C.), when the idol is powerful, his votaries have to spend money.

chhiet (R. id.), to cut, to slice in pieces; urgent. **chhiet-chhiet**, earnestly; urgently. **chhiet-iàu**, important. **khún-chhiet**, earnest, urgent. **pek-chhiet**, id. **chhiet put-khó**, certainly it will not do at all. **sim kien, ì chhiet**, purpose of heart determined.

khak-chhiet, true and important, as proof. **chhiet-sit**, sincere, safe, very honest, as person or words; quite correct and as it should be, according to pattern or promise.

chhiet-mī^n, to cut dough into long strings, to be cooked. **kā-gê chhiet-chhí**, to gnash the teeth.

ū-koan-chhiet, important in relation to some matter or thing; to count of importance so as to give diligence to it. **put-chí koan-chhiet**, very important. **bô-koan-chhiet**, not important to, or not concerning us. **koan-chhiet tī-hit-hāng**, specially important as having relation to that matter. **tióh khah-koan-chhiet**, you should count it of more importance.

chhiét, sound of going slip-shod, with shoes that are too loose. **chhiét-chhiét-háu**, id.

chhih, to bend down; to stoop. **bih-chhih**, keeping out of the way, as afraid to meet people. **sì-kòe-chhih**, wherever he goes he falls asleep; said of a child. **hé kiàh-khah-chhih**, hold the torch more down, to make it burn better.

chhih-thâu, having its head pressed down, as a boat with men sitting on the bow. **chhih-thâu chhih-náu**ⁿ, keeping one's head bent down. **thâu-khak chhih-chhih**, id.

chhih — **lāu-jiėt chhih-chhih**, very crowded (with persons). **bô-êng chhih-chhih**, very busy; having no leisure. **chit-jit bô-êng chhih-chhih**, no leisure all day. **bô-êng chhih-chhih; chien-chîm chhá-chhih, ə-koe sáh-pih**, so busy cooking that I have no leisure, said figuratively.

chhih — **ok chhih-chhih**, very overbearing or tyrannical.

chhih — **chhih-chhiauh**, mischievous; behaving in a disorderly way, as children or women. **chhih-chhih-kún**, swaying back and forwards, as a crowd. **chhih-chhih-kńg** (T.), id. **chhih-chhih chhéng-chhéng** (C.), playing about, as an idle boy.

chhih (= sih). **chhih-chhoah** (esp. Cn.), lightning flashing.

chhih (= chhihⁿ). **chhih-chhih-thî**, to sob. **chhih-chhih-háu**, to sob; to make a hissing sound, as a vessel sailing rapidly.

chhih — **chhih-chhih-háu**, to stutter or stammer; to talk on in a low displeased tone. **chhih-chhih-kiò**, to talk on in a low displeased tone.

chhih — **lok-chhih-chhih**, very wet, as roads. **tâm-chhih-chhih**, all wet, as with dew.

chhih (R. chiėt), the spotted crab or craw-fish. **chhih-jîn**, eggs or roe in it. **chhih-ko**, soft meat in the male. **chhih-hoe**, cluster of its spawn on outside. **hoe-kha-chhih**, a large speckled sort. **ti-bú-chhih**, a sort (= hái-ka-to) with two very large long claws, and the rest very small and short.

pun-chhih-kha (lit. to divide a crab's leg); to insist on the division of a small thing that might well be left undivided; to make two bites of a cherry.

chhih (= jih), to crush; to press with the hand. **chhih-píⁿ**, to crush flat. **kiông-kiông-chhih**, to force a man by strong pressure to do something against his will. **at-chhih**, id.; also, to prevail on the underlings of a yamun (by strong influence) not to issue a warrant that has been ordered.

lāi chhih--lòh-khì tsòe-bú, compound interest counted.

lòk-chhih lòk-chhih, having a terribly broken-down look, as an opium-smoker.

chhihⁿ (= chhih). **chhihⁿ-chhihⁿ-thî**, weeping and sobbing bitterly. **chhihⁿ-chhihⁿ-kiò**, making a hissing sound, as vessel sailing fast.

chhim, deep. **chhim-bô-tóe**, bottomless. **chhim long-long**, very deep. **chhim-ə̂**, deeply concave, as a bowl. **chhim-khín**, deep and shallow; depth in general (v. khín). **iû-chhién jip-chhim**, proceeding from the easy to the difficult.

chiáh chhim-tsúi, to meddle with other people's matters so as to get money out of them, though he has really nothing to do with them. **khiā chhim-tsúi**, pleased to see our enemies quarrelling with each other, or doing something wicked that will bring trouble on themselves. **lòh-chhim**, to get into deep water, as vessel. **chhim-tīn**, to venture into great danger, esp. run great risk in a venture in trade.

chhim-chíⁿ, the open court in centre of a house (v. chíⁿ). **chhim-kui-lú**, a virgin. **chhim-soaⁿ**, far among the mountains. **chhim-khiⁿ**, a deep abyss or chasm (v. khiⁿ). **chhim-chhân**, deep wet miry fields. **chhim-bák**, deep-set eyes. **chhim bák-u**, id.

kiⁿ-chhim, late in the night. **nîⁿ chhim**, near the year's end. **niⁿ-kú gėh-chhim**, for a very long time, *e.g.* ten or twenty years, or for one's lifetime.

chhim-tîm, very profound; very cautious or scheming (v. tîm). **chhim-siūⁿ**, to think deeply. **chhim-sìn**, to believe firmly. **jī-bák put-chí-chhim**, well acquainted with books; learned. **chhim-ti kî-siông**, intimately acquainted with the matter, *e.g.* some business, or a man's character and history.

chhim [R. chhím, to sleep]. **chhim-i hok-kun**, dress and hood for a corpse.

chhim (R. id.), to embezzle; to encroach upon or take unjust possession; to spend one's own reserved earnings; to get into debt; to retain too long a balance due to another; to use secretly or in advance the money of employer or partners, but not necessarily dishonestly.

chhim-chiàm, to take unjustly, as land (v. chiàm). **chhim tōe-ki**, to take another's ground unjustly, to build on. **chhim-hoān--tiòh**, to offend, as a person; to encroach on, as land or territory.

chhim-ēng, to embezzle; expenses beyond income. **chhim-thòeh**, to embezzle. **chhim-chhú**, id. **chhim-chhí** (C.), id. **chhim-khə̀**, to embezzle from the national treasury. **chhim-bô-tin**, to have embezzled so much that he cannot give a plausible account of the whole. **chhim--lòh-khì**, to get deep in debt. **chhim-khiàm**, to be in debt by having got large advances, or having used employer's money or goods. **chhim-khiàm tsòe-i-khì**, absconded for debt. **chhim-thām--khì**, to spend all one's reserved money; to get deep in debt.

chhîm [R. sîm, to search]. **chhîm-chhiòh**, to draw out information gradually (v. chhiòh).

chhîm (cf. chhâm, khâm), sound of cymbals clashing. **toā-chhîm-kə́**, large cymbals and drums. **chit-hù toā-chhîm-kə́**, large cymbals and gongs with two sorts of drums. **chhîm-tih-chhāⁿ**, sound of several sorts of instruments (v. chhāⁿ).

chhîm (= chhiâm). **bák-sái chhîm-chhîm-lâu**, tears flowing abundantly.

chhím (R. id.) **ûn-á-chhím**, to walk slowly, as man unable to go quick. **chhím-khoàⁿ**, to feel one's way slowly with the feet, as in the dark, or when fording a river. **chhím-kha-kiāⁿ**, to walk slowly with short steps, as in descending a steep hill, or when lame.

chhím [R. to sleep]. **hòe-chhím bông-chhan** (R.), to neglect food and sleep, as with great sorrow.

chhím, just having —. **chhím-chhím**, id. **chhím-kàu**, having just arrived. **chhím-khì**, having just gone. **chhím-nîⁿ**, just about the end of the year. **nîⁿ chhím**, id.

chhím-chiah-lâi, just come. **chhím-chiah-kóng, liâm-piⁿ bōe-kì--tit**, I have just told you, and you have forgotten. **thiⁿ chiah-chhím-kng**, just at first dawn. **jit chiah-chhím-àm**, just getting dark. **jit chhím-chhím-àm**, id. **chhím-chhím-á-kàu**, just exactly enough; just arrived. **chhím-chhím-á khì**, has just left.

chhin (= sin), (C. chhân, T. sien). **chhin-chháu**, a plant from which a cooling coagulated jelly is made, called chhin-chháu-tàng.

chhin [R. jîn, a man]. **kong-chhin**, a sort of arbiter who tries to get the parties to agree, but without authority.

chhin (T.), = A. chhien. **chhin-chhiu**, a swing.

chhin — **chhin-chhí^n**, pretty (v. chhí^n).

chhin [R. sin, new]. **chhin-chhī**, a sort of cream-coloured silk, of medium thickness, but good and strong. **chhin-chhī tn̂g-sa^n**, a long dress made of it.

chhin (R. id.), related; a relative; (near); affectionate or intimate; self; one's own; (used in many phrases about marriage).

chhin-chhiū^n, alike, similar, same kind as if (v. chhiū^n).

chhin-teng, confidential attendant of a mandarin, gen. from his own home. **chhin-teng** (C.), = A. chheng-teng, a sort of supercargo or purser in a vessel. **si-chhin**, the near relative of a man found dead under suspicious circumstances, to whom explanation or reparation must be made.

chhin-kūn, to approach (a person) in order to have intercourse. **chhin-bit**, closely united, as in friendship. **chhin kàu-jip-kut**, very affectionate, as friends. **chhin-jiėt**, warm in friendship. **chhin-hō͘**, very friendly; associating very intimately. **chhin-hò͘-hò͘**, id. **kì^n-tiòh-lâng chhin-hò͘-hò͘**, id. **chhin-tauh-tauh**, id.

chhin-pêng, relations and friends. **chhin-pêng kò͘-iú**, id. **chhin-soe**, relatives and strangers. **pōe-chhin ǹg-so͘**, to leave relatives and go to strangers. **pōe-chhin hiòng-so͘**, id. **pé-chháu chhē-chhin**, good at finding out relatives at a distance (as if in grass). **toàn-lí, put-toàn-chhin**, to judge justly, not according to the influence of relatives.

chhin-sin, one's self. **chhin-bák-khoà^n**, to see with one's own eyes. **chhin-chhiú**, with one's own hand. **chhin-pit-chek**, own hand-writing. **goá-chhin-khì**, I myself will go. **chhin-lîm**, to go in person, as a mandarin to arrest criminals. **chhin-thiô**, to choose in person, as things or men (v. thiô).

liòk-chhin, the six relationships: all the near relations, including sisters and the nearest connections by marriage of other surnames. **chhin-phài**, closely related, as ancestors for four or five generations and their descendants of the same surname only. **kai-chhin**, a relative; relations. **tsòk-chhin**, a very distant relative of the same surname. **chhin-chhek**, relations (v. chhek). **chhin-lâng**, relations by the male line. **chhin-tông**, cousins and other relatives of same surname (v. tông). **chhin-chiâ^n**, connections by marriage (v. chiâ^n). **bó-thâu-chhin**, wife's relations. **ien-chhin**, connections by marriage. **piáu-chhin**, relations by the mother's side. **ū-chhin**, to be related. **bô-chhin**, no relation. **sì-bák bô-chhin**, having no relations.

koa^n-chhin, mandarin's relations. **chhin-koàn**, wife and near connections of a mandarin. **chhin-ông**, a near relative of the emperor; a near prince of the blood, but not a son. **kiong-chhin-ông**, Prince Kung. **hiong-chhin**, a fellow-villager.

chhin--ê, a real relative of same surname (not adoptive), and of the nearest form that the phrase alluded to will allow, *e.g.* a real brother, cousin-german, uncle, &c., and not any of the more distant relations called by the same name. **chhin-hia^n-tī**, brothers by the same father. **chhin-ko͘**, father's sister. **chhin-peh**, father's elder brother. **chhin-chek**, father's younger brother. **chhin-si^n-kiá^n**, one's own real son. **chhin-hiet-bėk**, one's own real sons or posterity. **chhin-kut-hėk**, said of son or brother by birth, not by adoption. **má-chhin**, grandmother. **bú-chhin**, mother. **chhin-bú**, id. **hū-chhin**, real father. **chhin-pē**, id. **song-chhin**, father and mother. **thien-tē, kun chhin su**, in the whole universe the most important relations are sovereign, parent, and teacher. **thien-hā, kun chhin su**, do. (in the whole world).

kiû-chhin, to be looking out for a wife for one's son, &c. **tùi-chhin**, to settle a contract of betrothal for one's daughter. **phòe-chhin**, to settle the contract of betrothal. **tēng-chhin**, id. **phèng-chhin**, id. **tsòe-chhin**, do.; also, to have affinity, as the parents of the couple. **kiet-chhin**, to contract affinity, as the relations of the couple. **sêng-chhin**, to complete the nuptial relation by intercourse. **hóe-chhin**, to break off a match after betrothal. **thè-chhin** (esp. C.), id. **jī-hun-chhin**, second marriage of a woman.

chhin-ke, the fathers of bride and bridegroom in relation to each other; said also of any near relations of the couple. **tsòe-chhin-ke**, to fix a contract of marriage between each other's children. **chhin-ke-mn̂g**, near connections by marriage. **chhin-ke-chek**, younger brother of "chhin-ke." **chhin-ke-peh**, his elder brother. **chhin-ke tùi-mn̂g, lé-sò͘ goân-tsāi**, though next-door neighbours and having the closest affinity, yet proper ceremonies should be observed. **tùi-thâu chhin-ke**, the fathers of the couple, when there was previously a connection of affinity between the two families. **chhin tháh-chhin**, parties marrying from families already connected by affinity.

chhin-gêng, the bridegroom going to the bride's house to escort her to his house. **sàng-chhin**, the bride's elder brother accompanying her to the bridegroom's house. **hōe-chhin**, son-in-law invited by mother-in-law soon after marriage.

chhín — **chhín-chhiáu**, mischievous, as a child.

chhìn (R. chhèng), a steelyard; to weigh by a steelyard; a sort of lever.

chhìn-á, a steelyard. **o͘-chhìn**, the movable arm of a well-sweep (v. o͘). **tōe-chhìn**, a very strong lever for raising heavy weights. **chhien-kun-chhìn** (lit. lever for a thousand catties) an arrangement of several levers for raising great weights.

chhìn-miā^n, to calculate the weight of a man's good or bad fortune, as fortune-tellers do. **chhìn-tāng**, to weigh by steelyard. **chhìn--khí-lâi**, to prise up a heavy thing by a strong lever.

chhìn-thûi, the weight of a steelyard. **chhìn-liâu**, the cord of a steelyard. **chhìn-kau**, its hook. **chhìn-koái^n**, beam of steelyard. **chhìn-koá^n** (C.), id. **chhìn-hoe**, the white dividing points on the beam.

kàu-chhìn, a steelyard that makes things appear a little lighter than they are. **tāng-chhìn**, a fraudulent steelyard making things seem much lighter than they really are. **khin-chhìn**, a fraudulent steelyard making things much heavier than the reality. **mn̂g-kháu-chhìn**, sort of steelyard used by pedlars (also in houses), two ounces heavier than the usual steelyard. **kun-jī-chhìn**, id.; according to the "pah-lák-tô." **táu-chhìn kong-pî^n**, measures and weights just. **chiok-chhìn**, just correct in weight.

tèng-chhìn, to mark the divisions on the beam of a steelyard. **kah-chhìn**, to test a steelyard by comparing it with another. **sih-chhìn-thâu**, to lose in trade by customers always demanding rather over-weight. **tah-chhìn-thâu**, to give good weight, so that the beam turns. **chhìn-khah-khí**, id. **chhìn ū-khí-sì**, just having turned the beam.

chhìn — **chhìn-chhâi**, anyhow; of no consequence; just as you please, all the same, carelessly; well, that may do. **chhìn-chhái-lâng**, any person. **chhìn-chhái sé-tsāi**, any place.

chhìn, cold. **koâ^{n}-chhìn**, very cold; unpleasantly cold, as weather. **chhìn-piang-piang**, very cold, *e.g.* as cold tea. **chhìn-sng-sng**, ice-cold. **chhìn-pi-pi**, very cold. **chhìn-thih-thih**, id. **chhìn-tih-tih**, id. **chhìn-tsúi**, cold water.

chhìn-sim, having lost heart about a matter. **chhìn-chhiò**, a sarcastic smile (v. chhiò). **chhìn-bīn**, a sullen countenance. **chhi^{n}-chhìn**, feeling of shivering fear, as passing graves or a lonely mountain in a dark night; desolate, chill, and lonely feeling, as in a large house with almost no one in it. **chhi^{n}-thâu chhìn-bīn**, putting on an angry look at first sight, as when going to scold. **chhi^{n}-chhìn-hong**, a raw, cold, piercing wind, making one shiver.

phah-chhìn, to get a cold or ague. **chhìn-méh^{n}-nah^{n}**, a slight red eruption (v. nah^{n}).

chhiu-chhìn, pleasantly cool, as weather, wind, or place. **sim-lāi chhiu-chhìn**, highly pleased, as at good news or at constant good-fortune. **tú--tióh i teh-bô-chhiu-chhìn**, to fall on a time when he is out of temper, and so at once gets angry with us. **tú-tioh-i bô-chhiu-chhìn ê-sî**, id.

chhio, having a sharp edge for a point, as bow of Chinese boat, or pointed end of the up-turned ridge of a roof. **biô-chhio**, tapering, as the bow of a light boat, or end of a bamboo pole. **chhio-chit**, ridge of roof turned upwards and pointed.

chhùi chhio, always quarrelling with one's mouth.

chhio-tiô, active and lively, as child; strong, and active, and lively (often to excess), as a young man; active and lively, as beasts or birds.

chhio-giô (C.), (vulg.), impudent and swaggering (perhaps belongs to next word).

chhio, having the sexual feeling (of the male); strong; lustful. **koá^{n}-chhio**, burning with lustful passion, as the male when excited. **khí-chhio**, the male sexual feeling excited. **chhio-koe**, a cock fowl (entire, as opposed to a capon); its flesh is supposed to excite lustful feelings.

chhiô [R. giâu, =col. giô, a cockle]. **ka-chhiô**, a small edible shell-fish.

chhiò (R. siàu), to laugh; to smile; to laugh at; light-coloured, esp. of blue; the lettered side of a cash, when turned up; turned with the concave side up, when that is the reverse of the usual position, as the palm turned up, or as an inverted lid.

chhiò-sek, light-coloured, esp. of blue. **sek put-chhí-chhiò**, the colour is very light. **chhiò-chhí^{n}**, light indigo blue, as blue cotton that has been worn long and often washed. **chhiò-âng**, light red.

chhiò-tā^{n}, a pleased, cheerful, or smiling look, as the usual expression of countenance. **chhiò-iông**, id. **chhiò-bīn**, id. **tì^{n}-chhiò-bīn**, falsely put on a pleased look. **chhiò-bīn-hó** (a smiling tiger), pretending friendship while plotting grievous injury. **chhiò-thâu chhiò-bīn**, usual pleased cheerful look. **chhiò-sîn**, id. **chhiò-chhī**, pleasant smiling countenance, in holding intercourse with people.

hó-chhiò, laughable. **khó-chhiò**, id. **pio-chhiò**, to joke, laugh, or jest, or take undue liberties. **kún-chhiò**, to jest, to make fun. **kóng-chhiò-ōe**, to jest. **soat-chhiò**, jesting. **hō--lâng seh-chhiò**, to be a laughing-stock, because of some disgraceful action. **lāng-i-chhiò**, to sport with him and make him laugh. **thí-chhiò**, to laugh at, to make ashamed. **léng-chhiò**, scornful sarcastic smile. **chhìn-chhiò**, id. **tì^{n}-chhìn-chhiò**, to smile sarcastically. **khiên-chhiò** (Cn.), to put on a smiling look while really hating.

chhiò-ba-ba, to smile pleasantly. **chhiò-bi-bi**, id. **bi-bi-chhiò**, id. **ba-bún-chhiò**, to smile. **chhiò-bun-bun**, id. **chhiò-bún-bún**, id. **bî-bî-á-chhiò**, id. **chhiò-hā-hā**, loud laughing. **chhiò-khah-khah**, id. **chhiò-lih-lih**, to laugh with the mouth wide open. **chhiò kàu-sí--khì**, to laugh constantly and immoderately. **ōe-chhiò, chhiò kàu-bōe-chhiò**, to laugh (till one can laugh no more) immoderately. **chhiò-bī-sī**, to smile, as on hearing something, esp. when we don't wish to give any opinion of what was said, or when we did not understand it. **chit-jit chhiò-bī-sī**, said of a man who lets nothing trouble him. **m̄-tsai-thâu m̄-tsai-bé, chhiò-bī-sī**, smiling, but not understanding the matter at all. **bát-sat chhiò-chhiū-gūi**, the bed-bug laughs at the tree-bug; pot laughing at kettle.

hō͘ chhiò-tsàu (Cn.), the fire blazing up very brightly in the cooking-place, an omen of guests coming.

thán-chhiò, lying with face up, or inverted with concave side up. **tó-khioh-chhiò**, to lie on one's back with face up. **péng-chhiò**, to invert so as to have the concave side up, when naturally it is down, as a cover or lid inverted. **péng-khioh-chhiò**, id., also to lie with one's face up when lying down or reclining. **chhiò-chhiú**, holding the hand with the palm upwards. **sái-chhiò-chhiú**, to turn the palm up. **chhiò-tsô**, the long furrows of a tiled roof.

sái-khui-chhiò, to sail a boat with two masts with the sails set on the opposite sides of the respective masts, as with wind right astern. **khui-chhiò**, the sails arranged so; also, to take off the hand (in odds and evens) and show the cash with its face up. **lióng-phak khui-chhiò**, to try to keep about half-way or neutral between two parties or opinions, as arbiter, or as in giving an opinion, or in action, or by keeping our purpose and opinion secret; an affair still unsettled, and uncertain how it may go. **siang-phak khui-chhiò**, id. **phak-chhiò**, odds and evens; tossing cash; sort of gambling. **khap-chhiò**, id. **teh phak-chhiò**, to cover a cash and let it be guessed odds or evens. **lién-phak-chhiò**, to twirl a cash and guess odds or evens. **sang-chhiò**, both evens, as in tossing cash (v. sang). **chhiò-poe**, the throw of the divining blocks, when each has the flat side up.

chhiō [R. chiàu, to shine, =col. chiò], to illuminate; to make light shine on some thing or place. **chhiō-kng**, id. **chhiō-chhát**, to take a light and look for a thief (v. chhát). **chhiō-chhì**, to light a lamp near a corpse. **chhiō chhân-lê** (T. Cn.), to catch snails by torch-light.

chhie^{n}, in all the tones (P.), = A. chhiu^{n}.

chhioh (R. sek), to bite venomously, to sting, as insects. **chhioh-pùi-á-thâng** (C.), a sort of caterpillar.

chhioh, to damp slightly. **chhioh-tâm**, id. **chhioh-tsúi**, id.

chhioh — **chhí^{n}-chhioh**, young, as person. **chhi^{n}-chhioh**, fresh and nice-looking, as fresh flowers or new cloth.

chhioh (R. chhek), a Chinese foot, generally a very little shorter than the English foot; a measuring rule.

khut-chhioh, a carpenter's square (v. khut). **ko-**

厦英大辭典

chhioh, a wooden measuring rod (gen. ten feet long) used by carpenters for houses or junks. **pái-chhioh**, a pendulum. **keh-chhioh**, a ruler (not round) for ruling lines. **àh-chhioh**, a straight edge for ruling lines or cutting paper even. **thiⁿ-chhioh**, a quadrant or sextant.

lé-pan-chhioh, the common foot, used by masons and carpenters; ten feet want about two inches of ten English feet. **chhâi-chhioh**, the foot used by tailors, considerably longer than the lé-pan-chhioh.

ū-chhioh-thâu, to have a little more than the strict measure. **niūⁿ-chhioh**, to measure by a foot-rule. **chhùn-chhioh**, feet and inches (v. chhùn). **chhioh-it**, one foot and one-tenth, *i.e.* one foot one inch, Chinese. **chhioh-jī**, one foot two (Chinese), one foot and a fifth.

koh-chit-chhioh ê-jit, in a very short time (lit. the shadow cast by the sun travelling one foot).

chhioh (cf. chioh, chiah). **kha-chhioh-tóe**, the sole of the foot. **kha-chhioh khah-tn̂g**, (his) foot is very long.

chhioh (R. chhiok), the pancreas or sweet-bread of a pig; in other animals it is called "ih." **ti-chhioh**, id., only of pig.

chhioh, ducks or geese eating.

chhio̍h — **chhîm-chhio̍h**, to get information gradually out of people, especially avoiding anything that would raise suspicion of the object.

chhio̍h (R sók), a mat. **bih-chhio̍h**, a bamboo mat. **tîn-chhio̍h**, a rattan mat. **ka-bûn-chhio̍h**, a fine reed mat, imported from the Straits. **kiâm-chháu-chhio̍h**, a mat made (local) from reeds that grow in salt or half-salt water, much inferior. **teng-sim-chhio̍h**, mats (imported) made from fresh-water reeds. **chiáⁿ-tsúi-chhio̍h** (C.), id. **chhio̍h-chháu**, reeds for making mats. **chháu-chhio̍h-pau**, a coarse grass mat bag.

phah-chhio̍h, to make mats. **chhu-chhio̍h**, to spread a mat. **chhio̍h-ló-tia**, said contemptuously of a petty military officer, as hāu-iōng, &c.

chhio̍h (C.), = A. chhio̍k, slushy, as road.

chhiok (R. id.) **hí-chhiok**, the magpie, counted a bird of good omen.

chhiok [R. id., = col. chhek, a small bird], (C. chhiok, chhiak). **khóng-chhiok**, the peacock. **khóng-chhiok-bé**, peacock's tail. **tsu-chhiok**, one of the four spirits of the four quarters. **kim-chhiok-hoe**, a beautiful yellow flower (genista?)

chhiok [R. to lay hold of]. **pē-hong chhiok-éng**, to take up and spread baseless stories (lit. wind and shadows). **chhiok-náⁿ** (R.), to arrest, as a criminal.

chhiok [R. superabundant, leisurely]. **chhiok-hō**, a nickname or familiar name, given from personal appearance.

chhiok [R. to gore, to oppose, to come suddenly against, = col. chhek, chhok, tak].

chhiok-hoān, to come unintentionally on a person, in an ill-omened way, or so as to offend him. **chhiok--tio̍h**, id. **chhiok--tio̍h i--ê siū-khì**, unintentionally provoke a man's anger. **chhiok lâng-ê-toán**, to talk openly about a man's faults. **chhiok lâng-ê-phàiⁿ**, id.

chhiok-khoàⁿ, to examine at random, or "ad aperturam," the other having no warning what is to be asked or examined. **tiâu-tì beh-lâi chhiok--i**, to go specially, in order to catch a man in the act of which we suspect him, *e.g.* opium-smoking. **chhiok-kéng** (Cn.), = A. chhok-kéng, to try one's luck, as at lots, &c. **chhiok-kéng seng-chêng**, some circumstance reminding us of a beloved friend or place, and calling up warm emotions.

chhiok [R. id., = col. chhek]. **pek-chhiok** (R.), very urgent.

chhiok (P.), = A. chhek, rice in the husk; rice in the ear.

chhiok — **chhiok-kha-köe** (L.), to hop.

chhio̍k (T. jio̍k, C. chhio̍h, jio̍k), slushy, as roads. **lō͘ chhio̍k**, the road very wet and slushy.

chhio̍k (same as above?). **chhio̍k--tio̍h**, to spatter by stepping in mud, &c. **chhio̍k hái-thê**, to dirty one's self by walking on the muddy sea-beach. **chhio̍k-tsúi**, to spatter up water unintentionally in walking.

chhio̍k (P.), = A. chhe̍k, to shake even, as pencils, &c.

chhiong (R. id.), (C. chhiang). **chhiong-pô**, the acorus or flag (v. pô).

chhiong [R. id. by change of tone from "chiông," to follow]. **chhiong-iông**, taking things calmly and easily; not agitated or bustled (v. iông).

chhiong [R. violent], (C. chhiang). **chhiong-kông**, behaving very violently, urgently, or absurdly, almost as if mad.

chhiong [R. to rush against]. **chhiong-tn̄g**, to run against unintentionally. **chhiong-tōng**, do.: to come against violently, as a flood. **chhiong-pōng**, careless hurried manner, so as to spoil things [or is this the former word?].

chhiong-soaⁿ, to run a vessel aground. **chhiong-oá**, id. **chhiong-hoān-tio̍h-kúi**, to meet with a demon.

chhiong--chhut-lâi, rushing out with great force [what word?].

chhiong--tio̍h i--ê bé-thâu (lit. to come before his horse's head, *i.e.* of a mandarin, which causes a beating), said of provoking the anger of a powerful person.

chhiong [R. to ascend, as steam; to infuse]. **chhiong-tê**, to infuse tea.

saⁿ-chhiong, directly opposed, as purposes or wishes of two persons. **chhiong-sim hūn**, to hate a man so violently, as to feel enraged whenever he appears.

chhiong--tio̍h, to injure the good fortune, as of a grave or house. **tùi-chhiong**, directly opposite, so as to injure good fortune of house or grave; coming in collision with the horoscope (v. tùi).

chhiong-thiⁿ, to mount to sky or heaven, as vapour or rage. **hé-kng chhiong-thiⁿ**, the bright flames mounting to heaven, as at a conflagration. **khùi chhiong-thiⁿ**, rage very great and strongly manifested. **lō͘-khì chhiong-thiⁿ**, id. **lō͘-khì chhiong-thien**, id. **chhiong-thien**, to mount to heaven, as rage or guilt, &c. **phâu-hūn chhiong-thien** (R.), harbouring very deep enmity in the heart. **chhiong-thien ê-chì-khì**, purpose of distinguishing one's self greatly. **chhiong-thien-koan**, a royal crown with nine dragons looking up towards heaven.

chhiong [R. a prostitute], (C. chhiang). **chhiong-ki**, a prostitute. **chhiong-á**, do., said in vile scolding. **chhiong-bâ**, id. **chhiong-piáu**, to scold a woman as one. **chhiong-iu lō͘-tsut**, four classes whose sons cannot become mandarins.

chhiong (R. id.), (C. chhiang). **bûn-chhiong**, the god of literature; properly, a certain star or its spirit. **bûn-chhiong tè-kun**, id. **bûn-chhiong-hōe**, an assembly of the literati of a place.

chhiong [R. full, to transport, to confiscate or contribute funds]. **chhiong-sēng**, very abundant. **chhiong-chiok**, id. **chhiong-moá^n**, id. **khok-chhiong** (R.), to develop and increase knowledge.

chhiong iâ^n-ngó͘, to enlist in the army or navy. **chhiong-kun**, to transport to the military frontiers, in N.W.

chhiong-kong, to contribute funds or property to some public object, fund, or company. **chhiong-koa^n**, to confiscate property; sometimes a disputed property is thus voluntarily given up to the imperial exchequer. **chhiong-lȯh-koa^n**, id. **chhiong lȯh giȯk-pîn**, to confiscate on behalf of the Amoy academy, called "giȯk-pîn."

hoā-péng chhiong-ki, to paint a loaf in order to stay hunger.

chhiông [R. chiông, to follow; cf. chhiong]. **iông-chhiông**, to indulge (another); too indulgent, not punishing faults.

chhiông [R. to wound, = col. chhông]. **chhiông-chėk**, to injure one's self by wicked courses.

chhiông (C.), = chhêng, the banyan-tree.

chhiông (C.), = A. chhêng. **chhiông-pɛh**, the fir-tree.

chhióng [R. chhiòng, to begin]. **chhióng-sū**, to raise quarrels or feuds; to breed mischief. **tsū-chhióng kî-hō**, to draw calamities on himself.

chhiòng [R. to set loose, to indulge]. **chhiòng-hêng**, wicked and violent conduct. **hòng-chhiòng**, to give loose to one's passions or lusts; unbridled licentiousness; to allow inferiors to behave wrong without check.

chho-chhiòng tsū-jû, master of one's own actions, as person who manages his own business, not employed or ruled by another.

chhiòng (R. chhiong). **jiȯk-chhiòng-iông**, a medicinal plant (v. iông).

chhiòng (=chhiàu). **soat-chhiòng**, foolish talking and joking.

chhiòng [R. to sing, = col. chhiàng, chhiù^n], (C. chhiàng). **chhiòng-hō** (R.), to sing and respond, as in making poetry extempore.

chhiòng [R. to be first], (C. chhiàng). **chhiòng-sí** (R.), to be the first to speak of a thing; to raise the subject. **chhiòng-siú**, id. **hu-chhiòng hū-sûi** (husband leading and wife following), said of husband and wife being harmonious and affectionate.

chhiòng (C.), = A. chhèng, a gun, a cannon. **chhiòng-á-chí** (lit. gun-shot), a low shrub with small white flowers and edible berries; root good for inflammation.

chhiòng (C.), = A. chhèng, to spout out, &c. **chhiòng-lâu**, to add an upper story to a house, or make it a little higher.

chhiōng (C.), = A. chhēng, to wear or put on, as clothes.

chhip, barnacles. **o-chhip**, id. **tsûn-tóe si^n-chhip**, boat's bottom getting covered with barnacles.

chhip, incrustations forming in some sorts of vessels. **tê-chhip**, incrustations on inside of old tea-pots. **jiō-tháng-chhip**, incrustation in urine buckets.

chhip — **chhip-chhip-á-tsúi**, a very small quantity of water, as in a stream or in cooking.

chhip — **thâu-chhip**, a bow-sprit.

chhip (R. chek). **chhip-chhip-kiâ^n** (C.), to walk slowly with short steps.

chhip (R. chhek), (= chhip). **giû-chhek**, a medicinal plant (v. giû).

chhip (C.), = A. chhek, [R. the knee]. **hȯh-chhip**, = A. hȯk-sek, ornaments for the knees. **hȯk-chhip**, id.

chhip [R. chhím, (?) to sleep]. **chhip-àn**, to lay up the papers of a case; case at rest.

chhip [R. to join; to pursue; to apprehend]. **chhip-ná^n** (R.), to apprehend secretly. **chhip-húi** (R.), secretly apprehend bad characters. **chhip-hóng** (R.), to send messengers secretly to search for and apprehend a criminal.

chhip, a net on a bamboo frame worked (with both hands) by a man up to the neck in the sea; to catch (as shrimps, &c.) with such a net. **oe-chhip**, to work this sort of net. **lu-chhip**, id. **chhip-hê**, to catch shrimps with it.

chhit [R. giet, to eat; cf. mandarin "chīh"]. **mauh^n-chhit**, to embezzle money, as when intrusted with a commission.

chhit, seven. **chhit-jī-pêng**, dollars full weight, *i.e.* 7 mace 2 candareens according to the "khò-tô," = 7 mace 6 candareens of the "hā-tô."

chhit-chhi^n, the Pleiades. **thiàu chhit-chhi^n**, a child's game, making seven circles with a stone in each, and hopping about to kick the stones out. **chhit-niû^n**, the goddess of the Pleiades and of young unmarried girls. **chhit-niû^n-má**, id. **chhit-siàh**, the evening of 7.7. **chhit-gėh**, the seventh month, when the spirits of the dead in general are let out of Hades, and are specially worshipped. **chhit-gėh-poà^n**, the 7.15, = tiong-goân, great day for the worship of ancestral tablets. **chhit-gėh-poà^n-kúi**, you hungry ghost! (said to a man too eager for eating). **chhit-gėh-poà^n ah-á m̄-tsai-sí**, said of a man acting wickedly in spite of impending calamity. **chhit-gėh koai^n-bô-liáu**, you demon, whom they forgot to shut up at end of the seventh month! (said in scolding a child). **chhit-jit chio-hûn**, to call back the soul of the dead seven days after death.

chhit-lí-hiong, a sweet-scented flower (v. hiong). **sam-chhit**, a medicine stewed with food; specially given to young persons about coming of age. **thó sam-chhit**, = chhiu^n-to-iȯh, a thick-leaved medicinal plant.

chhit-pó-tâng, very fine sort of copper or brass. **phah chhit-hiáng**, to play on a musical instrument made with five pieces of metal like saucers. **chhit-khiàu**, the seven openings in the heart causing intelligence (v. khiàu). **jîn-seng u-sè, chhit-sip kó-lâi-hi**, from of old, few people reach the age of seventy.

put-tap put-chhit, full of blunders and unfit for use, as a document. **chhit-thó poeh-thó**, very rude and vulgar. **chhit-chiàh poeh-chiàh**, eating voraciously. **chhit-khai poeh-khai**, lavish expense. **chhit-oai poeh-tsoāi**, all wrong together. **chhit-soah poeh-pāi**, everything going wrong (v. soah). **chhit-chhiú poeh-kioh**, touching persons or things in a too familiar way (v. kioh).

chhit (R. sek; C. (R.), sit), to wipe. **chhit-ta**, to wipe dry. **chhit-chhat**, to varnish.

chhit (C.), = A. thit. **chhit-thô**, to play (often with a bad meaning).

chhiu [R. thiu, to draw out]. **phah-chhiu-hong**, to ask money, &c., from friends for one's self, separately from others.

chhiu (R. id.), autumn. **chhiu-thi^{n}**, id. **tiong-chhiu**, the 8.15 of lunar year (specially sacred to thó-tī-kong). **jip-chhiu**, the first day of autumn by solar year, August 7th or 8th. **lip-chhiu**, id. **chhiu-hun**, the autumnal equinox.

chhiu-chhìn, cool (v. chhìn). **chhiu-liâng**, cool autumn weather. **chhiu-āu-joáh**, warm weather in autumn after a break of cool weather.

chhun-chhiu, one of the five classics; history by Confucius of part of the Chow dynasty. **chhun-chhiu tsó-toān**, the commentary on it.

chhiu-bō, a light cap for autumn or summer. **chhiu-á-béh**, stockings of thin material, often short. **chhiu-gān**, a sea-bird that comes in autumn. **chhiu-ûi** (R.), the examination for the Kujin degree. **chhiu-kiô** (C.), great tides in autumn. **it-jit put-kièn, jû sam-chhiu**, one day without seeing (him) is like three years.

chhiu (R. id.) **chhien-chhiu**, a swing (v. chhien).

chhiu — **liu-chhiu, chiáh bák-chiu**, a man ought to be able to understand at a glance what he should do, as to be firm or to yield, to escape or remain, to ask much or little, to be quick or slow; because it is to his eyes that he must trust to get on in life. **ta-pe-kiá^{n}, liu-chhiu, chiáh bák-chiu**, id.

chhiu (T. liu), to rub or tickle another's cheek with the point of the finger, esp. done to children; if to a man, it is very contemptuous and insulting. **ùi-lâng-chhiu**, afraid to have his cheeks tickled, as child. **kia^{n}-lâng-chhiu**, id.

chhiu (R. su), beard, moustaches, whiskers, antennae; tendrils, tassels, fringe, &c.; weeds on a boat's bottom.

lâu-chhiu, to grow a beard, &c. **chhàng-chhiu**, moustaches on end with rage.

chhùi-chhiu, beard and whiskers, or part of them. **chhùi-chhiu-thâu**, stumps of beard. **ē-táu-chhiu**, beard, as distinguished from whiskers. **lí-phiet-chhiu**, moustaches. **ní^{n}-phiet-chhiu**, id. **nñg-phoat-chhiu**, id. **téng-tûn-chhiu** (C.), id. **pìn-chhiu**, whiskers when hanging down long and straight separate from beard. **hê-chhiu**, beard and whiskers all thick and in one. **ngé-pē-chhiu**, whiskers, moustaches, and beard, all quite distinct, as on images of Kwanti.

kì-chhiu, hairs growing from a mole.

péh-chhiu--ê, having a white beard. **péh-chhiu-pò**, a storm on the birthday of thó-tī-kong (who has a white beard) in eighth moon. **péh-chhiu-kong**, a sort of white shrimp.

jit-chhiu, rays from the sun.

si-chhiu, silk fringes or tassels. **báng-tà-chhiu**, fringes of mosquito-curtains. **tiù^{n}-chhiu**, fringes of curtains. **hau-pau-chhiu**, tassels at the clasp of a sort of purse.

tsoâ-chhiu, a snake's forked tongue. **lêng-chhiu**, a dragon's beard. **lêng-chhiu-chháu**, a medicinal plant. **lâu-lêng-chhiu**, to let one's beard, whiskers, &c., grow in a year of which the dragon is the presiding animal in the cycle of twelve. **hê-chhiu**, the beard of a shrimp or prawn. **hê-chhiu-á-soà^{n}**, a sort of fine twine, good for very small parcels.

giâ-kang-chhiu (centipede's whiskers), a defence put on junks to keep off pirates. **iû^{n}-káng-chhiu**, a goat's beard. **tióh iû^{n}-káng-chhiu**, to have a sort of eruption on the chin, as children; sometimes also on the upper lip. **tióh iû^{n}-kong-chhiu**, id.

hó-chhiu, a tiger's whiskers. **pùih-hó-chhiu**, a game of chance. **liu-hó-chhiu**, to draw lots to determine which man is to pay for some common expense, *e.g.* a feast.

chhêng-chhiu, abortive pendulous roots of the banyan. **chhêng-hê-chhiu**, the sharp leaves of the fir-tree (used as fuel). **hoe-chhiu**, stamens and pistils of flowers. **chhài-koe-chhiu**, tendrils of cucumbers. **khiû, kah ná^{n} chhài-koe-chhiu**, as crooked as a cucumber tendril; very crooked in dealings. **tit, kàu ná^{n} chhài-koe-chhiu**, do. (lit. as straight, &c.) ironically. **tit, ná^{n} chhài-koe-chhiu--nih^{n}**, id.

chhiu — **tsúi-chhiu**, spray. **hē-á-chhiu**, small rain.

chhiu, a troop or detachment of troops, esp. as sent off from the army in battle for some special service. **chit-chhiu-peng**, a troop of soldiers, gen. a few tens or hundreds. **toā-chhiu**, a large troop. **sòe-chhiu**, a small troop.

chhiû [R. sorrowful]. **siau-chhiû kái-būn** (R.), to dispel sadness and melancholy.

chhiû [R. chiû, to grasp firmly], to pull toward us, as a rope; to haul in, esp. with alternate hands; to unwind, as a thread; to use a clue to find out more.

chhiû-soh, to haul in a rope. **chhiû-soà^{n}**, to unwind a thread, pulling it towards us. **chhiû-tià^{n}**, to haul in the anchor. **chhiû-tiò**, to haul in a fishing line.

chhiû kun-goân, to investigate carefully (having got the clue) so as to find the real root and origin of the matter. **bān-bān chhiû--chhut-lâi**, to draw out gradually, as a secret. **bán-koe chhiû-tìn**, to get at the truth step by step, often by round-about way (v. tìn).

chhiú [R. chhú, to take]; (T. chhiú^{n}), to redeem from pawn or mortgage; esp. Cn., = A. thó.

chhiú khan-thâu, to redeem an article that is pawned. **chhiú-sa^{n}**, to get a coat out of pawn, &c. **chhiú-chhân**, to redeem fields. **chhiú-chhù**, to redeem a house.

chhiú cheng-sîn (Cn.), = A. chhiú^{n} cheng-sîn, idolatrous rites for bringing back good health.

chhiú [R. siú, the head]; classifier of odes or hymns. **chit-chhiú-si**, one hymn or ode. **tē-it-chhiú**, first hymn.

chhiú-bú-nñg, a fowl's first egg (v. nñg).

chhiú-sek, ornaments for women's hair and head.

chhiú (R. siú), the hand; the arm; (an assistant, &c.)

chhé-chhiú, bridle reins. **chiú^{n}-chhiú**, that half of a Chinese oar which has the handle. **bōng-chhiú**, the outer rim of a grave, like two arms. **bō-á-chhiú**, the projection on the rim of the upper mill-stone into which the driving-hook fits.

thâu-chhiú, a head-workman; the head man of several workmen at one work. **jī-chhiú**, an assistant. **chhiu^{n}-chhiú**, a man who composes essays for students. **pang-chhiú**, to assist; an assistant (v. pang). **hù-chhiú**, an assistant. **tsān i--ê āu-chhiú**, to help him to do what he could not well have done alone (v. āu). **chhiú-ē**, persons under our authority, as servants, dependants, assistants, children, &c., esp. assistants. **ē-chhiú**, id.

bé-chhiú, the end, afterwards; at last. **chiūⁿ-chhiú**, the previous one, as a deed, &c. **téng-chhiú**, done by a former hand, begun by another person, said specially of the deed by which the seller shows his own right to the property which he sells. **téng-chhiú ê-khòe**, the title-deed by which the seller got the property. **téng-chhiú ê-lâng**, the former possessor of a property; the former holder of an office, &c.

tùi-chhiú, able to be his match, as enemy; a fellow-labourer (v. tùi). **tsòe-chhiú**, counterfeit. **kang-hu óh-chiūⁿ-chhiú**, to have learned a trade well. **hun chit-chhiú**, slack the rope a little.

ńg-chhiú, compliant, as in a dispute; inclined to come to terms. **ngīⁿ-chhiú**, will not yield at all; determined to keep up the quarrel. **sat-chhiú**, fond of fighting, as soldier; not afraid to act in a dangerous matter; venturing to treat a disease in a way that will kill or cure. **sék-chhiú**, a skilful hand. **tun-to chhut lāi-chhiú**, a blunt knife makes a skilful hand. **soe-chhiú**, unsuccessful at play. **ōng-chhiú**, successful in gambling. **hó-chhiú**, having a good hand, at cards. **khang-chhiú**, nothing in the hand; having nothing. **toā-chhiú-bīn**, liberal; not niggardly; open-handed. **khah-khoàⁿ-chhiú**, using money freely. **hièn-chhiú**, very liberal; very free in the use of money. **tsáu-chhiú**, hastily; without much care (v. tsáu). **khah-khin-chhiú**, not using much force with hand (v. khin). **tāng-chhiú**, using the hand heavily. **tāng-chhiú**, to begin fighting or quarrelling (v. tāng "to move"). **seng chhut-chhiú**, to be the first to use violence, as in striking or plundering, so as to begin a quarrel. **khí-chhiú**, to begin a work or quarrel (v. khí). **lòh-chhiú**, at the first putting hand to work. **khah-lòh-chhiú**, somewhat better able to do it now (v. lòh). **hē-chhiú**, to use violence, as in striking or fighting. **hē-ták-chhiú**, to deal heavy murderous blows, as in violent attack or murder; to make very violent false accusation before mandarins. **hē-tók-chhiú**; id. (v. tók). **sit-chhiú**, to make a slip with the hand so as to do injury (v. sit). **chhò-chhiú**, to kill by mistake when only meaning to beat. **thêng-chhiú**, to pause in working or writing. **sūn-chhiú**, taking the opportunity when doing something. **thàn-chhiú**, id.; also, all going well. **tè-chhiú**, immediately (v. tè "to follow"). **toà-chhiú**, to bring or take away in the hand (v. toà). **sûi-chhiú**, to take in one's hand at once (v. sûi "to follow"). **sûi-chhiú**, to let the hands hang down by the sides; to set down a sedan (v. sûi, "to hang down"). **sok-chhiú**, to fold the hands on the breast, in the sleeves or under the other arms (v. sok). **tiàu-chhiú**, to let the hand move easily, as in writing large characters. **chhun-chhiú**, to stretch out the hand. **chhng-chhiú**, id. **chhun-tn̂g-chhiú** (to stretch out a long arm), said of a beggar, or man always asking money or things. **iap-chhiú**, to put the hands behind the back (v. iap). **iét-chhiú**, to wave the hand up and down, or rather inwards with the palm down and turned inwards, as in calling a person to come to us. **iô-chhiú**, to move the hand from side to side with fingers up and palm forwards, as in declining, refusing, or warning not to do. **hè-chhiú**, to toss the hand upwards, with palm up, in sign of displeasure (v. hè). **pí-chhiú**, to gesticulate with the hand (v. pí). **kí-chhiú**, to point with the hand.

chiap-chhiú, to make a bargain. **khui-chhiú**, to give some extra money at first (v. khui). **oāⁿ-chhiú**, to change hands, lit. or fig. **kè-chhiú**, to pass from one to another (v. kè). **kàu-chhiú**, to come to hand, as thing sent. **chih-chhiú**, to receive in the hand, as things. **jip-chhiú**, to be received, as money, gains or income. **khan-chhiú**, to hold each other's hands; to hold another's hand. **tùn-chhiú**, to shake hands (as foreigners). **poàh-chhiú**, matters not going well (v. poàh).

chhit-chhiú poeh-kioh, touching persons or things too familiarly (lit. seven hands and eight feet, v. kioh). **kha-chhiú**, hands and feet; assistants. **tàu-kha-chhiú**, to assist; to lend a hand. **hó-kha-chhiú**, a useful helper. **bô-kha-chhiú**, a useless fellow; having no one to assist him. **bô-kha bô-chhiú**, id. **chhe-kha-chhiú**, coolies for coarse rough work, as at a hong. **thīⁿ-kha thīⁿ-chhiú**, to add lies to a story fundamentally true. **siⁿ-kha siⁿ-chhiú**, id. **phê-kha sáng-chhiú**, to flatter. **tīⁿ-kha poàⁿ-chhiú**, to be in the way, as ropes or furniture; to be an encumbrance, keeping a man *e.g.* from leaving home, as family. **kiⁿ-kha kiⁿ-chhiú**, id. **khiau-kha khè-chhiú**, legs drawn up and arms rested on something; making one's self very much at ease. **chhut-kha chhut-chhiú**, very restless, as a child. **kha sng, chhiú-ńg**, limbs weak with sickness or exhaustion (v. ńg). **kha tn̂g, chhiú toā**, limbs full sized, said in scolding a grown-up person for being idle and useless. **chhiú bâng, kha loān**, in a great bustle or hurry.

chhiú-thâu, power, authority (v. thâu). **hó-chhiú-sì**, all going on well, as the management of pupils, or as the course of a disease. **hó-chhiú-sè**, in a suitable posture or position for doing something. **hó-chhiú-sì** (C.), id. **chhiú-lē**, workmanship, as good or bad (v. lē). **chhiú-gōe**, handicraft. **chhiú-toāⁿ**, ability in cooking (v. toāⁿ). **chhiú-phīⁿ khah-ngīⁿ**, determined to have no compromise, but carry on the feud to the bitter end; not afraid to cause people severe injury or even death. **gán cheng, chhiú khoài**, able to play tricks of legerdemain or to deceive people.

chhiú-bé (the end of the arm), clothes and small articles of personal property left at death. **chhiú-bé-chîⁿ**, a cash tied to the wrist by a white string (superstitious). **ū chhiú-bé-lát**, to have great strength in one's arms, *e.g.* able to hold a heavy weight with the arm stretched straight out. **tu chhiú-bé**, to try each other's strength, by pushing a bar against each other's wrists. **thuh chhiú-bé**, id. **kek chhiú-bé**, id. **áu chhiú-bé**, to try strength by pulling each other's arms bent at right angles. **pien chhiú-bé**, id.

chhiú-sng-chîⁿ, a small gratuity given as a reward for some slight service. **chiàⁿ-chhiú**, the right hand. **toā-chhiú-pêng**, the left-hand side. **tò-chhiú-pêng**, id. **chhiú-ìn**, the mark of the inked hand on a document, &c. (v. ìn). **chhiú-pit**, hand-writing. **chhiú-chhia**, a spinning-wheel. **chhiú-teng**, a small lamp for carrying in the hand; a road-lamp. **chhiú-pó**, a small hand-hatchet. **chhiú-kù**, a small hand-saw. **chhiú-pún**, a folded blank book of red paper for writing petitions (v. pún). **chhiú-chih**, a small folding memorandum-book for pocket. **chhiú-chhau** (C.), id. (v. chhau). **chhiú-kun**, a napkin or handkerchief. **chhiú-phè-á**, a handkerchief for wrapping small things in. **chhiú-lông**, gloves. **chhiú-lok**, the gloves put on a corpse when buried. **chhiú-siū**, sort of mits (without fingers) for the wrist. **chhiú-khoân**, armlets. **chhiú-sóh**, flat armlets. **chhiú-chí**, a finger-ring (v. chí).

chhiú-kut, the arm; the bone of the arm. **chhiú-tsat**, one of the two parts of the arm, esp. the lower

海上絲綢之路文獻集成　科技與文化編

arm. chhiú-ē-tsat, the lower arm. chhiú-ti-á, the fleshy part of the upper arm. chhiú-tó, the fleshy part of the lower arm; the calf of the arm. chhiú-ké (C.), id. chhiú-thn̄g, the arm from elbow to wrist, only when mutilated, as by loss of hand, or as a fragment separated from the body (v. thn̄g). chhiú-āu-ti^n, the elbow. chhiú-āu-nn̄g, id. sái chhiú-āu-nn̄g tò-tn̄g, to strike backwards with the elbow. chhiú-oan, the inner part of elbow (v. oan). chhiú-khiau, the elbow bent at an acute angle (v. khiau). chhiú-oá^n (T.), the elbow-joint. chhiú-khū, the wrist; a sort of mortar (v. khū). chhiú-tôe, the inner side of the wrist, at the root of the palm; the carpus (v. tôe). chhiú-lûn, the wrist-joint. chhiú-mēh^n, the pulse at the wrist. chhiú-bák, the protuberance at the wrist-joint; the knuckles. chhiú-poā^n, the back of the hand. chhiú-pòe, id. chhiú-chiú^n, the palm. chhiú-sim, the middle of the palm. chhiú-tiong-sim, id. chhiú-bīn, the palm. toā-chhiú-bīn, liberal. chhiú-bīn thàn-chiáh, earn one's living by one's own labour. kap-khit-chiáh pé-chhiú-bīn, to quarrel with him will be troublesome and shameful (like with a beggar), and with no possible advantage (v. pé). chhiú-phāng, the interstices between the fingers. chhiú-tsái^n, a sort of thimble; also (r.) a finger. phái^n-chhiú-jiáu^n, to pilfer (v. jiáu^n). chhiú-to, the side of the hand at the little finger, when held flat like a knife. chhiú-hûn, wrinkles on the hand; mark left by the hand when pressed down. chhiú-sióh, slight perspiration or moisture on the hand.

chhiù (R. id.) m̄-chhiù--i, to show him no politeness or attention; will have nothing to do with him. bô-lâng beh-chhiù--i, no one will have anything to do with him. m̄-chhiù-chhái, will have nothing to do with him; showing we cannot be troubled with him; unwilling to meddle with the matter; will show him no attention; the cut direct. m̄-chhiù m̄-chhái, id. bô-chhiù-chhái, id. bô-chhiù-bô-chhái, id. ū-chhiù-chhái, receiving with politeness and kindly manner, as towards an inferior, or a person asking a favour.

chhiū [R. iông, the plum], (C. chhiū^n). chhiū-m̂, the fruit commonly called arbutus, really a myrica (v. m̂).

chhiū (R. sū), a tree. chhiū-tsâng, id. chit-tsâng-chhiū, one tree. chhiū-bák, trees in general. chhiū-nâ^n, a wood; a forest. chhiū-sim, the heart of a tree. chhiū-phê, the bark; hollands and linen stuffs. chhiū-khak, the rough outer bark. chhiū-pak, a hollow in the trunk of a decayed tree. chhiū-ki, a branch; a twig. chhiū-oāi^n, a large branch of a tree, esp. one of the primary divisions of the trunk. chhiū-bé, the top of a tree. chhiū-sin, the stem. chhiū-sin khiā-tit-tiāu, m̄-kia^n chhiū-bé iô-hong, if the trunk stand firm the top shaking in the wind is no matter; said of a fearless upright man. chhiū-thn̄g, the trunk of a tree. chhiū-tūi^n (C.), id. chhiū-bú, the main stem, as opposed to suckers or secondary stems. chhiū-thâu, the stem near the root. ké-chhiū-thâu, an old stump; said also of a man very small for his age. chhiū-kha, near the tree; below the tree.

lī-chhiū, to fall from the tree, as fruit. chhiū-n̂g, cool shade of tree. chhiū-iá^n, shadow of tree; reflection of tree in water. chhiū-lin, the juice of a tree; india-rubber, gutta-percha, &c. chhiū-ni^n, id.; said of a juice used for making varnish hold well.

chhiū-gūi, the tree-bug (v. gūi). chhiū-siēn, the cicada. chhiū-lân, a sweet flowering shrub. chhiū-kiu^n, a sort of fern. chhiū-bî-hoe (= chhiû^n), a sort of rose.

toā-chhiū, phoà ū-chhâ, a large tree if cut up must yield wood; said of something large, which does not seem of much use, but out of which a good deal can be got. chî^n-chhiū khui-hoe (the money-tree blooms), said of getting much money, especially of a prostitute at the age when she brings in much money to her owner.

chhiu^n (in all the tones), becomes "chhie^n" in Changpoo and many parts of Changchew.

chhiu^n (R. chhiong). chióh-chhiu^n-pê, a sort of acorus used medicinally (v. pê).

chhiu^n [R. siōng, form, appearance]. phái^n-bīn-chhiu^n, sullen or sulky appearance of countenance, such as to repel or frighten people.

chhiu^n (R. chhiong). chhiu^n-hî, a flat reddish fish of a roundish square shape (the pomfret fish?).

chhiu^n (R. chhiong), a spear. chhiu^n-koái^n, the shaft of a spear. chhiu^n-pī^n, butt end of spear. chhiu^n-á-pī^n, id. chhiu^n-bah, iron point of spear. chhiu^n-á-bé, point of spear. khau-liâm-chhiu^n, a sort of halbert (v. liâm). siâ-mâu^n-chhiu^n, a spear with a crooked blade.

chhià^n-chhiu^n, to hire a man to write an essay for the examinations, so as to deceive the examiner. tsòe-chhiu^n, to be so employed. chhiu^n-siú, the man who thus writes the essay for the candidate. chhiu^n-chhiú, id.

kiàm-chhiu^n (lit. sword and spear), a wooden railing made with the points of the rails projecting above the cross-bar. kiàm-chhiu^n-mn̂g, a door made with this sort of railing; used for public buildings, offices, &c. kiàm-chhiu^n-goā, outside the railing, esp. of space in front of yamun.

chhiu^n-to, spears and swords. chhiu^n-to-ióh, a medicinal plant (= thó-sam-chhit), with succulent leaves somewhat like the house-leek. chhiu^n-to bák-pê, warlike weapons. pâi chhiu^n-to-hâng, to arrange files of spears and swords, as at an execution. chhiu^n-to ê tsai-ê, the calamities of war, rebellion, &c. to-chhiu^n ê tsai-ē, id.

chhiû^n — kng-chhiû^n, bright, as lamp; cheery and bright, as room. àm-chhiû^n, dark and dismal, as a house.

chhiû^n (R. chhiông). chhiû^n-bî-hoe, a sort of rose, esp. double and sweet-scented.

chhiû^n — chhiû^n-peh (T.), = chhêng-peh, the fir-tree.

chhiû^n (R. iông), to winnow (as wheat), by pouring out from a height in the wind (or by fanners). chhiû^n-hong, id.; in the wind. chhiû^n-béh, to winnow wheat by pouring out in the wind. chhiû^n hong-ké, to winnow by fanners. chhiû^n hong-kūi (C.), id.

chhiû^n (R. chhiông), a wall. chhiû^n-lē, a line of wall (v. lē). chit-lē-chhiû^n, one wall, in building. chit-phì^n-chhiû^n, id.

tháng-chhiû^n, the staves forming the sides of a barrel, tub, bucket, &c.

chhiû^n-piah, walls in general (v. piah). siâ^n-chhiû^n, a city wall. chiò-chhiû^n, the wall built opposite the main gate of a yamun or temple. chiò-chhiû^n-lāi, in the space between this wall and the main gate. ûi-chhiû^n, to surround with a wall; a surrounding wall. **tsáu-ûi-chhiû^{n}**, a surrounding wall. **chhiû^{n}-ûi**, a wall round a terrace (v. ûi).

tsoh-chhiû^{n}, to build a wall. **cheng-chhiû^{n}**, to make a wall of clay and mortar by a frame, beating it hard; to build a mud wall or cob-wall. **chhiû^{n}-khòeh**, the frame used for building such mud or mortar walls. **chhiû^{n}-hák**, id. (v. hák).

chhiû^{n}-kha, at the foot of the wall; near the wall. **chhiû^{n}-thâu**, top of wall. **chhiû^{n}-thâu-téng**, on the top of the wall, *e.g.* where flower-pots are often kept. **sīn koá-chhiû^{n}-thâu**, nothing remains but some ruined walls.

chhiú^{n} [R. chhióng, a shed, a public depôt or store]. **gī-chhiú^{n}**, place where coffins are furnished gratis to the poor. **kun-kong-chhiú^{n}**, government arsenal and dock for war vessels. **tah-chhiú^{n}**, to make a sort of shed for the rites (khiā-hà) for the worship of the spirit soon after death; to build a shed for work. **chhiú^{n}-koa^{n}**, a figure set as steersman in the mock ship of the idol "ông-iâ."

chhiú^{n} (R. chhióng), to snatch; to plunder. **chhiú^{n}-kiap**, to rob; to plunder. **kiông-chhiú^{n}**, id. **chhiú^{n}-téh**, to snatch away. **chhiú^{n}-thèh** (C.), id. **chhiú^{n}-pak**, to rob and strip. **chhiú^{n}--lâng pak--lâng**, to rob and strip people. **chhiú^{n}-hoān**, forcibly rescue a prisoner. **chhiú^{n} jîn-bēng**, to plunder the house where a suspicious death has taken place. **chhiú^{n} hé-sio**, to plunder at a fire. **ná^{n}-chhiú^{n} hé-sio**, said of eating very hastily and ravenously. **chhiú^{n}-chiáh**, to eat too hastily and voraciously.

chhiú^{n}-chhoah, to do work too hurriedly and carelessly.

chhiú^{n} bīn-chêng-kng, to try to put on a good face though making it worse at the last, *e.g.* telling many lies to hide one. **niáu-chhû thau-chiáh-iû, chhiú^{n} bák-tsâi^{n}-kng** (T.), the rat drinks up the oil and has no more light, said of a man keeping up appearances by means that only make matters worse.

chhiú^{n} [R. chhú, to take]. **chhiú^{n} cheng-sîn** (= Cn. chhiú), idolatrous rites for bringing back good health.

chhiú^{n} (T.), = A. Cn. chhiú, to redeem, as from pawn, &c.

chhiù^{n} (R. chhiòng), to sing, as a song. **chhiù^{n}-koa**, to sing a song. **chhiù^{n}-khek**, id. **chhiù^{n} lâm-koán**, to sing colloquial songs. **chhiù^{n}-pak-koán**, to sing mandarin songs. **sió-chhiù^{n}**, to sing, as young boys, with very high notes. **tsáu-chhiù^{n}**, street ballad-singers. **chhiù^{n}-liām-hó**, to sing and recite well, as an actor, or as a man reciting bits of plays.

chhiù^{n}-koâi^{n}-tiāu, to ask an exorbitant price. **ké-khek, chhiù^{n}-bōe-lóh-âu**, to tell transparent lies that can't be swallowed.

chhiù^{n} (R. ip). **chhiù^{n}-jiā**, to make a bow. **chhiù^{n}-hiā**, id.

chhiù^{n} — **àm-chhiù^{n}**, dark, as night.

chhiù^{n} — **phah-ka-chhiù^{n}**, to sneeze. **phah-kha-chhiù^{n}** (r.), id. **hat-chhiù^{n}** (Cn.), id. **hah-chhiù^{n}** (C.), id. **heh-chhiù^{n}** (C.), id.

chhiū^{n} — **chhiū^{n}-thâu**, superstitious rites performed just before marriage, both on males and females; if neglected then must be performed afterwards, otherwise in the next world they would be boys and girls, and not adults.

chhiū^{n} [R. siōng, above, to ascend, which in a different sense becomes col. chiū^{n}], (to cause to ascend, to bring up), to set up, as doors; to store up, as goods; to sew on, as soles of shoes; to raise, as water; to produce, as damp, mist, white ants, &c.

chhiū^{n}-bōng, to make offerings and worship at graves. **chhiū^{n}-bē**, id. (esp. Cn.)

chhiū^{n}-keng, to string a bow. **chhiū^{n}-mn̂g**, to set a Chinese door on its hinges. **chhiū^{n} tiàm-thang**, to set up the boards of a shop-window. **chhiū^{n}-ôe**, to sew together the soles and uppers of shoes. **chhiū^{n}-béh**, to sew together the soles and legs of stockings.

chhiū^{n} péh-hiā, to become infested with white ants. **chhiū^{n}-è**, a white film forming on the eye. **chhiū^{n} tâng-sien**, to get covered with verdigris. **chhiū^{n}-chhî**, to grow damp, as salt, &c. **chhiū^{n} iâm-sî^{n}**, to grow white with saline incrustations (v. sî^{n}). **chhiū^{n}-phú**, to grow mouldy. **chhiū^{n} chhi^{n}-thî**, to get covered with green moss (v. thî). **chhiū^{n}-pan**, to get spotted, as with the sun or with mould, as damp clothes or books. **chhiū^{n}-bū**, mist gathering. **chhiū^{n}-hûn**, clouds rising and thickening.

chhiū^{n}-tsúi, to draw water. **chhiū^{n} tiàu-e**, to raise water by a well-sweep.

chhiū^{n}-tsng, to buy goods cheap, and store them up waiting for a rise in price. **chhiū^{n}-niū^{n}--khí-lâi**, id. **chhiū^{n} gē-kak**, to store up large quantity of grain for a rise in price. **chhiū^{n}-tiáh**, to buy and store up grain for a rise in price.

chhiū^{n} moâ^{n}-khí (C.), to catch small crabs in rivers by torch-light.

chhiū^{n} [R. siōng, an image, likeness]. **chhin-chhiū^{n}**, like; alike; similar; as if. **chiâ^{n}-chhin-chhiū^{n}**, exactly alike. **chhin-chhiū^{n} kàu bô-jī**, exceedingly like. **i kap-lâng bô-chhin-chhiū^{n}**, he has a bad disposition, worse than other people.

khah-chhiū^{n}, more like. **iáh-chhiū^{n}**, rather like.

chhiū^{n} [R. siōng, a figure, an elephant], an elephant. **chhiū^{n}-gê**, ivory. **chhiū^{n}-phī^{n}**, proboscis of elephant. **chhiū^{n}-kán**, elephant's keeper. **chhiū^{n}-kî**, a sort of chess having twelve pieces on each side; some of them are called "elephant." **hé-pà sai-chhiū^{n}**, tigers, panthers, lions, and elephants.

chhiū^{n} [R. thiok, domestic animals]. **chhī-chhiū^{n}**, to feed domestic animals, esp. pigs and poultry. **ū-chhī-chhiū^{n}**, having abundance of domestic animals all getting on well. **bô-chhī-chhiū^{n}**, domestic animals not getting on well. **bô-chhī bô-chhiū^{n}**, not keeping any domestic animals. **bô-chhī bô-chhiū^{n}, ke-hé tsòe-bōe-chiū^{n}**, without keeping domestic animals a family does not get rich. **chhī-chhiū^{n}, ke-hé chiū^{n}**, to keep domestic animals increases the wealth of a family.

chhiū^{n} [R. chhiōng, a workman, an artificer]. **bák-chhiū^{n}**, a carpenter. **thô-tsúi-chhiū^{n}**, a builder; a mason; a bricklayer. **thih-chhiū^{n}**, a worker in iron; a smith. **gûn-chhiū^{n}**, a silver-smith. **thì-thâu-chhiū^{n}**, a mandarin's barber. **chhâi-hông-chhiū^{n}**, a mandarin's tailor.

chhiū^{n} (R. siōng), a large sort of tree.

chhiū^{n} [R. iông, the plum]. **chhiū^{n}-m̂** (C.), = A. chhiū-m̂, the so-called arbutus (v. m̂).

chhng [R. chhun, a village], (C. chhui). **hiu^{n}-chhng**, a village. **chhng-lâng-thâu**, you rustic! said in scolding. **chhng-hàn** (r.), a rustic; a clownish-looking fellow.

chhng (R. chhong), a granary. **gī-chhng**, a public granary. **chhng-khò**, granaries and treasuries. **chhek-chhng**, a granary for rice. **chhng-chhek**, paddy from public granaries, not good. **chhng-bí**, rice from do., not good.

niû^{n}-chhng, cubical mensuration.

chhng (R. chhong), the hold of a vessel. **tsûn-chhng**, id. **tsúi-chhng**, the part of the hold for the bilge-water. **chhng-tóe**, the bottom of the hold; the last of the cargo from a vessel, inferior quality.

khui-chhng, to open the hold; to open the hatches. **khui-chhng-jī**, a document giving permission to open the hatches. **chhng-kháu**, the hatches. **koán chhng-kháu**, to watch the hatches and mark down what is taken in or out, as supercargo or clerk does. **chhng-kháu-phō͘**, book in which goods shipped and delivered are noted down. **chhng-kháu-toa^{n}**, a vessel's manifest. **chhut-kháu ê chhng-kháu-toa^{n}**, export manifest. **jip-kháu ê chhng-kháu-toa^{n}**, import manifest.

chhng (R. chhoan), (C. chhui^{n}), to pass through or press through a hole.

chhng-khang, to make a hole, as insect. **chhng-chiam**, to thread a needle. **lâm-sám-chhng**, to go improperly through private places, *e.g.* through the private apartments of a house. **chhng--kè-khì**, to go through, as through a house, using too much freedom.

chhng-tîn, to make wicker-work with rattan. **chhng-bih**, to make bamboo wicker-work. **chhng sì^{n}-hio̍h**, to put on the paper on a fan in making it. **chhng-soa^{n}-lêng**, a sort of gingall.

leng-chhng, the orifice of a teat.

chhng (C. chhui^{n}). **kha-chhng**, the posteriors; the buttocks; the anus; the hollow on which a cup (or bowl, incense vessel, &c.) stands; the obverse of a coin, opposed to "bīn;" the wrong side, as of paper.

kha-chhng-táu, the hips, the posteriors. **kha-chhng-chiam**, the part of the hips that makes the corner when bent. **kha-chhng-phóe**, the hip. **kha-chhng-thâu**, the lower end of the back where the posteriors begin. **kha-chhng-phāng**, the depression between the hips. **kha-chhng-khang**, the anus. **phah kha-chhng**, to beat in punishment, as before the tribunal.

tsoá-kha-chhng, the wrong side of paper, rougher than the other side.

kha-chhng-āu, close behind a person. **iô kha-chhng-hoe**, to shake one's hips from side to side, as an awkward walker. **khin-kha-chhng**, ready to do acts of politeness and service, as a polite willing boy, or as a man forgetful of his dignity. **chhùi kiū^{n}, kha-chhng ńg**, talking bold and big, but really much afraid and powerless. **sa^{n}-kēng kha-chhng**, two persons combining (standing back to back) to resist or injure another. **sa^{n}-chiāng kha-chhng** (T.), placed back to back, as two houses or villages.

chhng (R. chhong), an ulcer, especially venereal.

tī-chhng, piles at the anus. **pán-chhng**, large blotches of itch on the posteriors.

kan-chhng, venereal ulcers. **kam-chhng**, id. **to̍k-chhng**, id. **ok-chhng**, id. **sì^{n}-chhng**, to have venereal ulcers. **chhng-jiah**, mark left by them. **chhng-hûn**, id. **chhng-hong**, syphilis in its later forms.

chhng — **phī^{n}-chhng** (P.), = phī^{n}-sng, arsenic.

chhng [R. sin, = col. chhun], to stretch out, as the hand. **chhng-chhiú**, to stretch out the hand.

chhn̂g (R. chhông), a bed; a couch.

chhèng-chhn̂g, the stock of a gun.

bîn-chhn̂g, a bedstead. **mn̂g-chhn̂g**, id. **bûn-chhn̂g** (C.), id. **bîn-chhn̂g-kong**, guardian god of marriage-bed. **bîn-chhn̂g-pô**, guardian goddess of it. **chhn̂g-bú**, female spirits that take care of infants (like nurses) shortly before and after birth. **chhn̂g-chiá-bú**, id. **bîn-chhn̂g-bî**, wooden ornamental work across the top of the front of a bed. **chhn̂g-bî**, id. **bîn-chhn̂g-tō**, the broad flat board which makes the front of a bed, for sitting on. **chhn̂g-tō**, id. **bîn-chhn̂g-hoā^{n}**, id. **chhn̂g-tóe**, the body of a bedstead, including the feet. **chhn̂g-teh** (C.), a bamboo frame for the bottom of a bed. **chhn̂g-kè**, shelf in bedstead. **chhn̂g-ûi**, the curtain below the bed. **chhn̂g-jio̍k**, a mattress. **bîn-chhn̂g ta̍h-táu**, a bed and the long stool that stands at front below (v. ta̍h).

pó-chhn̂g, a couch for use in gambling with the lién-pó. **tiàu-chhn̂g**, a hanging bed or couch; a hammock. **tîn-chhn̂g**, a rattan couch or sofa. **khòng-chhn̂g**, a state-couch for guests (v. khòng). **siên-chhn̂g**, a couch with arms at each end. **siên-chhn̂g-í**, an arm-chair. **siên-chhn̂g-toh**, a table with a rim on three sides. **chhn̂g-kūi**, a long chest for storing things, used as a couch or bed. **kūi-chhn̂g**, id. **to̍k-sūi-chhn̂g**, a bedstead fit for one person (v. sūi). **toā-chhn̂g**, a large bedstead fit for two or three persons.

tó-chhn̂g, to be so unwell as not to be able to rise; confined to bed; bed-ridden. **tó-tsāi-chhn̂g**, id.

chhńg (C. chhúi^{n}), to suck a thing inside the mouth, as bones, kernels, &c. (but "tsńg" is to suck as a teat); to get money by intimidation or other improper means. **chhńg-kut**, to suck bones. **chhńg-hu̍t**, to suck kernels. **chhńg koe-chí**, to suck melon-seeds.

chhńg-sit, to dress its wings with its bill, as a bird.

chhńg-khang, constantly looking out for any chance (right or wrong) to make money. **chhńg-phāng**, id. **gâu-chhńg ôe-phāng**, fond of picking holes in what people say. **chhńg-chhiah**, avariciously taking every opportunity (right or wrong) of making money. **chhńg lâng-ê-chî^{n}**, to get money from people by threatening to accuse them before the mandarins, as is done by subordinates at yamuns and by many of the literati. **hō͘--lâng chhńg-chî^{n}**, to be done out of money thus.

chhǹg (C. chhùi^{n}). **chhǹg-jip**, to rush in hurriedly. **chhǹg-chhut**, to rush out hurriedly. **chhǹg--tsáu**, to rush on with head bent down.

chhǹg (C. chhùi^{n}). **chhǹg-khang**, to bore a hole.

chhǹg (R. chhoàn), (C. chhùi^{n}), to string together; a small string of beads, pearls, &c., strung together (a larger is "koā^{n}"). **kui-chhǹg**, a complete string, as of beads. **chhǹg-tsu-á**, to string beads or pearls.

chhngh, to snuffle with the nose, only outwards (but "sngh" is inwards), as when the nose is stuffed, or as a child when dissatisfied or ill-pleased or half angry. **chhngh phī^{n}-khang**, id. **chhngh phī^{n}-hong**, id.

chho (R. id.), animal food, including also eggs, garlic, and onions (not eaten in fasts nor by vegetarians). **chhi^{n}-chho**, flesh and fish in general. **chho-chhài**, animal food and vegetarian diet respectively. **chia̍h-chho**, to eat animal food; not to be a vegetarian. **khui-chho**, to break off vegetarianism.

hî-chho, flesh and fish in general. **chhàu-chho**, strong-flavoured fish; strong, unpleasant smell, as of fish. **ùi chhàu-chho**, not liking to eat strong-smelling fish. **hái-tsúi chhàu-chho**, the waters of the sea having

12

an unpleasant smell; sign of bad weather. **chhàu-chho siâⁿ-sín** (strong-smelling fish alluring flies), said of a bad woman much ornamented alluring lads.

chho [R. to hold firmly], (Cn. chhe). **chho-chhiòng tsū-jû**, master of one's own actions; not under the control or direction of another.

chhó — **chit-chhó**, ten thousand. **chiâⁿ-chhó**, about ten thousand.

chhó — **chhó-jī-táu**, a measure (about 1·2 of a common "táu" measure) used for measuring uncleaned rice, chhò-bí; (sound probably changed from "chhò").

chhó (R. chhé). **chheng-chhó**, = chheng-chhé, settled, as account; well and accurately done.

chhó [R. só, small, minute], (T. só). **chhó-chhùi**, miscellaneous; troublesome and difficult to set right, as an affair in a confused and involved state that will require much discussion; to wrangle; disputing over and over without coming to an agreement; troublesome to deal with, as a man fond of disputing and always making objections. **kap--i teh-chhó-chhùi**, having much violent disputing with him without coming to an understanding.

chhó [R. plants, the 140th radical], (Cn. chhé). **sì-chhó**, the essay that wins a degree, printed for private circulation among friends.

chhó [R. plants; coarse, rough draft; running hand; = col. chháu], (Cn. chhé), pith for fancy work.

chhó-bók, trees and plants (v. bók). **chhó-pún**, herbaceous (not shrubby), as a plant. **pún-chhó**, the Chinese book of botany and pharmacopeia. **chhó-á-thâu**, the 140th radical, written at the top.

chhó-hoe, artificial flowers, made of pith. **thong-chhó**, the plant (aralia) from which it is made (v. thong). **chhó-e**, aconite. **chhó-siau**, a plant used as a purgative medicine. **kam-chhó**, liquorice. **chià-chhó**, liquorice sliced and dried, medicinal. **liên-chi-chhó**, a fabulous good-omened plant. **chhó-kó**, a medicine (*Amomum medium?*).

chhó-su, running hand. **chhó-jī**, id. **chhó-kó**, a rough draft or scroll. **chhó-chheng**, a scroll-book in which sales are entered as they are made. **chhó-sut**, carelessly; in an off-hand manner; without much care. **ló-chhó**, id. **ló-chhó-siá**, to write a scroll or rough copy.

phah hoe-chhó, to strike one's own arms, thighs, and body, as a beggar does.

chhò (R. id.), to cut in small pieces; to mince; to fell, as a tree.

chhò-chhiū, to fell a tree. **chhò-ûi**, to cut away a mast. **chhò-chhâ**, to cut fire-wood.

chhò-bah, to mince meat, esp. pork. **chhò-bah-sîⁿ**, id. **chhò-bah-oân**, meat balls. **chhò-hî-oân**, minced fish balls.

chhò-bé--ê, having the head cut off, as sugar-cane. **chhò-bé-káu ké-lòk** (a dog with cropped tail pretending to be a stag), a man pretending to dignity when he has none.

káⁿ thâi-phah-chhò, daring to beat and cut violently (said of a daring robber or ruffian). **bān-to-chhò**, may you be cut small by ten thousand knives!

chhò — **chhò-khîm**, to strike the harp.

chhò [R. to sing loud, as birds]. **chhò-hī**, to din the ears; to stun the ears. **chhò-jiáu**, to cause trouble, anxiety, or expense to another. **chiáu-á chhò-nâⁿ-pê**, a large flock of birds making a loud noise in the wood (said of a number of children or inferiors making a great noise by talking or otherwise).

chhò [R. id., by change of tone from "chho" to hold]. **chiet-chhò** (R.), very correct in conduct.

chhò (R. id.) **chhò-bí**, rice separated from the husk by the mill, but not yet beaten white in the mortar which separates the bran. **bí chhò**, the rice is still entire, not having the bran beaten off it. **tsúi-tùi bô-chhò-bí**, a pounding-mortar driven by water leaves none of the rice uncleaned (said of a man who is too knowing to be easily cheated).

chhò [R. chhok, mistake]. **sit-chhò**, a mistake; a fault. **chhò-gō**, a mistake. **bô-chhò**, certainly it is so; no mistake! yes indeed. **tsai-chhò**, to know one's fault. **jīn-chhò**, to confess a fault or error. **kóng-chhò**, to say a wrong thing by mistake. **siūⁿ-chhò**, to make a mistake in thinking or planning. **thiaⁿ-chhò**, to make a mistake in hearing. **bóe-chhò**, to buy a wrong article by mistake.

chhò-to, a mistake in anything (originally, with a knife). **chhò-sū**, faults in conduct, esp. gambling and licentiousness. **kiâ-chhò-sū**, to commit gambling or lewdness. **chhò-sí**, to die from carelessness or neglect, *e.g.* from taking poison or wrong medicine accidentally, or from drowning when assistance might have been given, or of a disease which could have been easily cured. **chhò-chhiú**, to kill a man accidentally when it was intended only to beat him. **chhò-kûn**, to kill or wound a man very severely in boxing, unintentionally.

chhò — **thèh--khì chhò-chhùi**, (T.) take it there and eat it (said in scolding a child).

chhe (R. id.), coarse, rough, common, vulgar, cruel, violent.

toà-chhe, to be in deepest mourning, for parents or grand-parents. **chhe-pè-saⁿ**, dress of common cotton stuff. **chhe-hoaihⁿ hoaihⁿ**, very coarse, as cloth.

chhe-siap, coarse and rough, as a surface. **chhe-phê**, a granulated rough surface of skin (like a small eruption), chronic.

chhe-kha, unbandaged feet, of women. **chhe-siók**, vulgar in manner; very cheap and inferior. (v. siók). **chhe-lé**, wanting in refinement; rather uncultivated in manner. **chhe-pūn**, clumsy, ill-formed, awkward-looking. **chhe-phoh**, large and rough-looking, as man. **chhe-tāng**, rough hard work in which one must exert strength. **chhe-lâng**, a coarse or vulgar labourer, as a coolie or chair-bearer. **chhe-teng**, a man who works at rough hard work, as farmer or workman. **chhe-kang**, coolies, workmen, or labourers for rough work. **chhe kha-chhiú**, coolies for rough work (as in a hong). **chhe-kioh**, id. (v. kioh). **chhe-khì**, coarse, rough, or unpolite in manner or appearance.

chhe-chhēng, every-day clothes. **chhe-chhài piēn-pn̄g**, a common every-day dinner; pot-luck.

chhe-chhùi, vulgar vile scolding with abominable phrases. **chhe-ōe**, vile language. **chhe-kún**, wrestling, striking, or coarse play together, such as readily passes from play to a real quarrel; improper talk or liberties with women.

chhe-sim, cruel heart. **chhe-chhân**, cruel or violent in character; fond of fighting, striking, or injuring people. **ēng-chhe-hoat**, to act violently, as striking, &c.; said also of very high-handed violent proceedings. **tāng chhe-hoat**, id., as striking, &c.

chhe-khng, rice-chaff (v. khng). **hō put-chí-chhe**, the rain is very heavy.

chhe͘-ngī^{n}, too hard and stiff, as a fur; too stiff in shape, as a written or printed character.

chhe͘-hî iù-tē͘, a coarse fish with a good inside; said of a man with rough exterior but good abilities.

chhe͘ (R. id.), ordure; excrement; solid manure. **chhe͘-pûi**, id. **chhe͘-jiō**, excrement and urine; solid and liquid manure. **chhe͘-tsûn**, boat carrying manure. **chhe͘-tháng**, buckets for carrying manure. **chhe͘-hia**, ladle for lading out manure.

chhe͘ [R. beginning, = col. chhoe, C. chhe]. **chhe͘-chhe͘**, at the first; just lately begun. **chhe͘-chhe͘ khì-khiā**, very soon after beginning to live there. **khí-chhe͘**, the beginning. **tng-goân-chhe͘**, at the commencement or beginning. **jîn-chi-chhe͘** (lit. man's beginning), the Chinese trimetrical primer, = sam-jī-keng.

chhe͘ (Cn.). = A. chho, (R.) to hold firm.

chhé͘ (R. id.), the kingdom of Tsoo, in the Chow dynasty; about the present Hoo-nan. **chhé͘-kok**, id. **chhé͘-pà-ông**, a famous usurper, king of Tsoo. **khé͘-chhé͘**, to torment.

chheng-chhé͘, = chheng-chhó, completely paid; all clear and settled.

chhè͘ (R. id.), vinegar. **sng-chhè͘**, id. **bí-chhè͘**, vinegar made from rice. **ló-chiú-chhè͘**, vinegar made from the fermented liquor called ló-chiú. **chhè͘-lâ**, mother of vinegar. **chhè͘-tsau**, dregs of vinegar (v. tsau). **chhè͘-kiu^{n}**, a condiment made of vinegar, ginger, and sugar.

chhè͘ (Cn.), = A. chhò, in some cases.

chhö (Cn.), in several words of several tones, = A. chhe.

chhoá [R. tsū, to collect, to assemble]. **khah-chhun-chhoá**, making a little money now so as to accumulate.

chhoá — **loá-chhoá**, acting carelessly, remissly, or lazily; working in an untradesmanlike way; to procrastinate in managing an affair. **noá^{n}-chhoá**, id.

chhoá (C.) **chhoá-chhoá**, slim, not strong, as cloth.

chhoà [R. chhài, a surname, name of a kingdom], a surname.

chhoā [R. tō, to lead; cf. col. thoā], to lead; to conduct; to guide the way. **ín-chhoā**, to lead. **chhoā-lē͘**, to guide; to conduct in the way. **chhoā-káng**, a pilot; to pilot. **io-chhoā--i**, to lead him about and show him attention.

thau-chhoā, to run off with, as a child; to abduct; to kidnap (child). **chhoā-tsáu**, to abduct, esp. female child or slave. **sa^{n}-chhoā-tsáu**, to run off together, esp. to elope.

chhoā-kiá^{n}, to lead out (as fowl) her chickens to walk.

chhoā-jiō, to pass water involuntarily, as children (v. jiō).

chhoā [R. chhū, chhù, to marry], to marry a wife. **chhoā sin-niû^{n}**, id. **chhoā-chhin-chiâ^{n}**, id. **chhoā-bó͘**, id. **kā--i chhoā-bó͘**, to get a wife for him, to get him (*e.g.* one's son or grandson) married. **chhoā chit-ê-bó͘ hē--i**, id. **chhoā--bē**, are you married? **kè-chhoā**, to marry (man or woman) in general. **jī-chhoā**, to marry a second time, as after death of first wife. **āu-chhoā**, id. **chiū^{n}-mn̂g chhoā**, bridegroom going in person to the bride's house to conduct her to his house.

chhoa^{n} [R. soan, a wooden pin, = col. sng], a splinter; a small thorn or prick; to prick, as a thorn or splinter; to take away some small thing against the owner's will; also (vulg.), to copulate. **chhoa^{n}--tio̍h**, to be pierced by a splinter. **chhoa^{n}-chhì**, very troublesome; causing much trouble (v. chhì).

chhoâ^{n} [R. tsân, to wound, cruel], to cut away, as some branches or other parts of plants.

chhoá^{n} — **noá^{n}-chhoá^{n}**, lazy; careless; utterly without spirit or energy, as opium-smoker (v. noá^{n}). **noā^{n}-chhoá^{n}**, id.

chhoá^{n} [R. sién, eruptions or dirt on skin]. **káu-chhoá^{n}**, an eruption on the skin like ringworm or scrofulous eruptions. **tio̍h hong-chhoá^{n}**, to have a sort of itching eruption.

chhoá^{n} [R. chhán, to smooth off], to smooth off a small bit of wood; to turn the boat's head in a slightly different direction. **chhoá^{n} chit-tè**, to smooth off a bit of wood. **chhoá^{n} hē-i-pī^{n}**, id.

chhoà^{n}, very ready to take offence and get up a quarrel; unwilling to take advice or warning; reckless of consequences.

chhoà^{n} (R. chhoàn). **chhoà^{n}-tō**, to cross the road just in front of a mandarin and his retinue. **phah-hoâi^{n}-chhoà^{n}**, to attack an enemy by a flank movement.

chhoà^{n} — **chhoà^{n}-tn̄g lâng-ê-ōe**, to stop short a man's talk by interrupting him.

chhoà^{n} [R. soan, = col. sng], (P. chhoè^{n}), a bolt; to bolt, as a door. **mn̂g-chhoà^{n}**, a door-bolt. **chhoà^{n}-mn̂g**, to bolt a door. **chhoà^{n} téng-chhoà^{n}**, to bolt the upper bolt of the two usual bolts of a Chinese door. **chhoà^{n}-ē-chhoà^{n}**, to bolt the lower bolt. **chhoà^{n}-lo̍h-kúi**, to let down the small secret pin that keeps the bolt shut and fastened.

chhoà^{n}-kun, a cross piece of wood sunk into two planks or pieces of wood to hold them together.

chhoā^{n} [R. siēn, an eel], a small sort of eel. **chhân-chhoā^{n}**, a very small fresh-water eel having soft eatable bones. **ngī^{n}-kut-chhoā^{n}**, a salt-water sort with numerous hard bones, not good to eat.

chhoah — **bák-chiu chhoah**, eyes twitching nervously.

chhoah, to tremble; to have spasms; to flash, as lightning. **sih-chhoah**, skin twitching slightly; glancing, as lightning. **chhih-chhoah** (esp. Cn.), id. **lûi-tân chhih-chhoah**, thunder pealing and lightning glancing.

bah-chhoah, flesh twitching or trembling. **kha-chhiú bah-chhoah**, limbs all trembling, as with fear, &c. **lák-lák-chhoah**, id. **khéh-khéh-chhoah**, id. **géh-géh-chhoah**, id. **ngiáuh-ngiáuh-chhoah**, id.

chhoah [R. chhiap, to steal]. **lí ū-chhoah--goá**, you have deceived me, and made me pay far too dear.

chhoah, to pluck out, as hair or feathers; to give a sudden jerk or sharp pull, esp. so as to break, as a rope; to snatch. **chhoah--khì**, to snatch and break away, as something from another. **chhoah-hiet-kák**, to pull out and throw away, as gray hair, or as ends of threads. **chhoah-tn̄g**, to break by a sudden pull, as chain or rope. **chhoah--khí-lâi**, to hoist up, as taking a boat on board; to take off, as a sculling oar, &c.

chhoah-chhiu, to pull another's beard, a very great insult; said in scolding an old man. **chhoah chhùi-chhiu**, id. **chhoah-sit**, to pluck the wings, as of a fowl. **chhoah chit-tsâng**, to pull up a small plant by the roots. **chhoah jiû-hî**, to catch the fish called "jiû," by giving a rapid pull as soon as it bites.

chhiúⁿ-chhoah, to do work too hurriedly and carelessly.

chhoah, a grater, as for long turnips; to grate down, esp. into long strips. **chhài-thâu-chhoah**, a fine grater for long turnips. **han-tsû-chhoah**, a coarse grater for sweet potatoes. **chhoah han-tsû**, to grate down potatoes. **chhoah chhài-thâu tsòe-si**, to grate long turnips into long strips.

chhoah — **chhoah-nn̂g**, to spawn or lay eggs in vast abundance, as fish or butterflies.

chhoah [R. siet, diarrhœa]. **chhoah-sái**, to have diarrhœa; to have a loose motion; to be purged. **chhoah-sái-chhiⁿ** (vulg.), a falling star. **chhoah--lòh-khì**, to fall suddenly, as a meteor.

chhoah (Cn.), to lend money for a very short time. **î-chhoah**, to borrow for a very short time.

chhoàh [R. siâ, oblique, = col. chhiâ], (C. tsoàh, in some cases), awry; off the straight; squinting.

moâⁿ-phang-chhoàh (C. tsoàh), diagonal lattice-work. **oai-chhoàh**, awry (v. oai). **chhoàh-kak**, diagonal; slanting; not at right angles. **tiàu-kak-chhoàh**, slanting, as at a corner; esp. as to folding, drawing, &c. **ka-chhoàh**, to cut (cloth) awry, as a bad tailor.

thán-chhoàh, diagonal; awry. **bú-thán-chhoàh**, id. **chē bú-thán-chhoàh**, to sit awry. **chē thán-chhoàh**, id. **thán-chhoàh-bák**, squinting. **chhoàh-bák**, id. **bák-chiu chhoàh-chhoàh**, id.

chhoan [R. tsoân, a sacrificial victim]. **sam-chhoan ngó-bī**, all sorts of very good eating.

chhoan (= soan), (Cn. chhun). **chhoan-tîn**, to send out suckers.

chhoan [R. to press or put into a small opening, = col. chhng].

chhoan-tn̂g, the inner room in a yamun, just behind the public hall of judgment. **chhoan-sim**, the pin of the lock that runs up into the (foreign) key. **chhoan-tiông-tī**, fistula. **chhoan-san-kah**, the scales of the (lâ-lí) pangolin (or manis?).

chhoan-chhòk, unnecessarily involved, as the management of an affair (v. chhòk).

chhoan [R. a river; in the names of things means "from Sze-chuen"]. **san-chhoan** (R.), mountains and rivers. **poát-siáp san-chhoan** (R.), travelling far over hills and rivers.

kòng-chhoan, very strong smooth good writing paper.

sù-chhoan, the province of Sze-chuen. **chhoan-nîⁿ**, a cooling medicine from Sze-chuen. **chhoan-hông**, inferior bezoar from do. **chhoan-lêng**, best sort of China-root from it. **chhoan-kiong**, a medicine (v. kiong). **chhoan-kién**, a sort of silk from Sze-chuen. **chhoan-pòe**, a medicine (v. pòe).

chhoân [R. toân, to deliver an order], to summon to court (as a graduate), in a less peremptory way than by the usual warrants.

chhoân-kiong (C.), = A. thoân-keng, the interpreter in a mandarin's office.

chhoân (R. id.), to select or choose, as persons or things, to be ready for some special purpose. **chhoân-pān**, to select and make ready, as materials or other things, or as men. **chhoân-piēn**, id. **chhoân-tsôe**, to select and make fully ready, and all in order for a purpose; all fully prepared. **chhoân-lâng**, to get the persons all ready for something to be done. **chhoân-liāu**, to select and get ready the materials. **tiâu-chhoân--ê**, specially selected.

chhoân, to plot against; to take secret action so as to injure a man. **chhoân-chhòk**, id.; also, to make preparations, or manage a matter (v. chhòk). **chhoân--lâng**, to plot against a man, and take secret action to his injury.

chhoán (R. chhún), to pant; to breathe, esp. to breathe hard. **chhoán-jip**, to inhale breath. **chhoán-chhut**, to breathe out breath. **chhoán-khùi**, to breathe. **chhoán-toā-khùi**, to draw a long breath; quite out of breath. **toā-khùi-chhoán** (C.), asthma.

hēⁿ-hēⁿ-chhoán, to pant hard, as with running or with a heavy load. **phih^n-phih^n-chhoán**, id. **phī-phī-chhoán**, id. **phīⁿ-phīⁿ-chhoán**, id. **hāⁿ-hāⁿ-chhoán**, id.

chhit-khang bô-hù-chhoán, said of a man who is very miserable, in great want of money.

chhoán-kihⁿ-kàⁿ (C.), panting very hard; making one's self very big and behaving improperly.

chhoán (same word?). **siàu-liân-chhoán**, a young fellow making himself very big by words or actions.

chhoán (C.), = A. chhéng, to behave in a big bragging way.

chhoàn [R. koàn, accustomed]. **chhoàn-kóng bô-jī-ōe**, all he says is baseless talk. **chhoàn-kóng bô-hó-ōe**, constantly talking bad language. **chhoàn-kiâⁿ bô-hó-tāi**, all his actions are improper. **chhoàn-kiâⁿ hiám-lō**, he is always going in dangerous courses. **chhoàn-kiâⁿ sī-hiám-lō**, id. **chhoàn-tsòe sī-phái^n-tāi**, he does nothing but wicked actions. **chhoàn-chhut sī-chhát**, it breeds robbers (or pirates) abundantly, as a place. **chhoàn-kau sam-ko liòk-pô**, constantly consorting with nuns, female sorcerers, &c.

chhoàn [R. to string, as beads; connected; a receipt for house-tax].

koàn-chhoàn, mutually connected, as the parts of a composition or of reasoning.

chhoàn-thong, to conspire with enemies against our superior or employer (said of persons in employment or specially related). **chhoàn-keng**, to prompt a man under examination before a mandarin, suggesting to him what to say (very improper).

chhoàn-kun, the part of a document left in the book when it is torn off for use, *e.g.* of a receipt for land-tax, or pawn-ticket. **tē-tso-chhoàn**, a receipt for the Amoy ground-tax on houses. **chhut-chhoàn**, to issue these forms to the tēpó.

liòk-chhoàn, a strong silk stuff, generally of a light bluish-white, but sometimes black or other colour.

chhoàn (R. id.), to usurp; to supplant. **chhoàn-ūi**, to usurp the throne. **chhoàn-koân**, to usurp authority.

saⁿ-chhoàn, to get a business or situation by supplanting a rival; to undersell or supplant. **chhoàn-lâi chhoàn-khì**, each trying to undersell or supplant the other. **chhoàn-thâu-lō**, to supplant a man in his employment. **chhoàn-pái**, forcibly take the turn before our turn has come.

chhoàn-tông, to come circling round from the back to the front of the grave, as an amphitheatre of hills (v. sa).

chhoàn [R. to rush away hurriedly]. **chhoàn--chhut-khì**, to rush out hurriedly. **chhoàn--jip-khì**, to rush in in great haste. **tit-tit chhoàn-jip**, to bolt right in. **tit-chhoàn--jip-lâi**, to come rushing in hurriedly. **gâu-chhoàn**, fond of running about very fast in sport, as horse, dog, or pig. **phāu-thâu chhú-chhoàn**, to cover one's face with hands and run away (in shame) like a rat.

chhoàn (R.), to compile, as a book. **chhoàn-chheh**, (R.), to compile a book.

chhoàn — **chhoàn-gê**, a tooth projecting far out of its proper place. **tùi-piⁿ--thâu chhoàn-chhut**, to project at the side, as a tooth.

chhoàn (R. id.) **chhoàn-á**, a lance like a sword with a long handle. **tn̂g-chhoàn**, a long lance on a bamboo shaft.

chhoàn [R. to cook]. **hun-chhoàn**, to have their meals separately regularly. **tsū-chhoàn-tiàm** (R.), an inn where each cooks for himself.

chhoàng, gaudy, richly ornamented, finely-dressed, showy, pretty (often with the idea of improper conduct). **chhoàng-tiám**, beautiful, as dress; good-looking and finely-dressed, as person.

tsòe-koaⁿ-chhoàng, very intimate with mandarins. **hì-chhoàng**, fond of going to plays; intimate and spending money with the actors who represent women (often includes the idea of lascivious intercourse).

chhoàng-hiaⁿ, a fast licentious young fellow. **chhoàng-kùn**, a fellow fond of low vicious pleasures, who leads others into vice and is fond of quarrels and rows.

chhoe [R. chhe, the beginning], (C. chhe). **khí-chhoe**, the beginning. **tng-chhoe**, at the beginning. **tng-goân-chhoe**, id. **tng-chhoe-sî**, id.

chhoe--nih, in the first ten days of the month. **gêh-chhoe**, the first decade of the month. **chhoe-it**, the first of the month. **chhoe-jī**, the second. **chhoe-tsáp**, the tenth day of the month. **chhoe-kúi**, which of the first ten days is it?

chhoe [R. chhe, wife]. **hu-chhoe**, husband and wife.

chhoe (C.), = A. chhe, to cook by steam. **tiông-chhoe-kóe**, twice-steamed cakes.

chhoe (C.), = A. chhe, to blow a pipe, &c.

chhôe (C. chhê), to crawl on hands and feet, as a child, or as a lame man. **chhôe-chhôe**, id. **thê-kha--nihⁿ chhôe**, id. **gîm bák-kiáh-tsoe**, **toà-teh-chhôe**, a cripple crawling on the ground with things like wooden clogs in his hands (often said in cursing, may you come to that plight!).

chhôe (C.), = A. chhê, a thin stick.

chhóe (C.), = A. chhé, marrow, brains.

chhòe, rice-dough; rice-flour. **chhòe-hún**, rice-flour. **ta-bí-chhòe**, id. **bí-chhòe**, rice-dough made from soaked rice. **cheng-chhòe**, to beat soaked rice into dough. **chhiau-chhòe**, to mix rice-dough. **noáⁿ-chhòe**, to knead and work up rice-dough.

chhòe [R. soat, a brush; to scrub, = col. seh], (C. chhè), to scrub; to scour, as with a wet cloth or with a hard brush and water; to rub smooth, as with sand-paper or with rough leaves or fish-skin. **tiáⁿ-chhòe**, a scrubbing-brush for cleaning rice-boilers.

chhōe (C.), = A. chhē, to search.

chhōe (C.), = A. chhē, thick and short, as the neck.

chhoeh [R. chhek, grieved], (C. chheh), sad, sorrowful; repining. **chhám-chhoeh**, id. **khé-chhoeh**, id. **chhoeh-sim**, repining. **oàn-chhoeh**, displeased at one's self or at one's fate (v. oàn). **oàh-oàh chhoeh--sí**, to die of vexation (lit. or fig.) **bōe-chhoeh bōe-píⁿ**, he will neither repent nor reform.

chhoeh-chhoeh-thî, to sob.

chhoh, to scold with obscene language. **saⁿ-chhoh**, id. **chhoh-mēⁿ**, id. **chhoh-chhoh-háu**, id. **chhoh-kàn-kiāu**, id. **chhoh--lâng**, to scold people obscenely.

chhöh (Cn.), = A. chheh, to sip. **tò-chhöh** (T.), to take in a long breath after a great burst of sobbing.

chhöh (Cn.), = A. chheh. **chit-chhöh-ngá**, a very small quantity, as of tea, salt, vermicelli, &c., taken up in the hand.

chhok [R. chhoat, to take up in the fingers; a pinch], (= col. chheh). **chit-chhok-á**, a small quantity of something, especially taken up with the fingers. **chit-chhok-á-hé**, a little fire for kindling. **chit-chhok-á-mn̂g**, a small tuft, as of feathers.

chhok (R. id.) **ok-chhok**, filthy, dirty.

chhok [R. chhiok, to meet with; to come upon accidentally, = col. chhek], (Cn. chhiok), to try a man's character by giving him an opportunity of stealing or deceiving us. **chhok lâng--ê sim-sū**, id.

chhok-kéng, to try one's luck by some superstitious rite. **chhok chit-ê-kéng**, id. **chhok-jī-sè**, to try one's luck by pulling out lots, each having a character on it.

chhok-khoàⁿ, to examine at random (*ad aperturam*). **chhok-tsong**, to give (or take) what comes to hand without selection (v. tsong).

chhok [R. to mistake]. **chha-chhok**, a mistake (v. chha). **chhok-gō** (R.), to mistake. **chhok-jīn**, to mistake one thing (or person) for another. **tng-bīn chhok-kè**, to let slip an opportunity. **chiong-chhok chiū-chhok**, having made a mistake not try to alter it, but just make the best of it.

san-tin hái-chhok, the delicacies of land and sea. **chhok-gók** (R.), to start suddenly.

chhok — **sái-chhùi-chhok**, to make a signal by a slight movement of the mouth.

chhók (R. id.), a large seal used by the tēpó of a ward; a seal used in yamun for stamping petitions and complaints. **chhók-kì**, id. **tǹg-chhók**, to stamp with this seal. **pó-tiúⁿ-chhók**, the tepo's seal. **tê-kì-chhók**, the stamp put on petitions in yamun.

chhók [R. to chisel, = col. chhák]. **chhoan-chhók**, to make much needless work in the management of a matter, making it no better, but rather injurious; ill-composed, as a sentence too elaborate or awkwardly involved, so as to be indistinct.

chhók — **chhoân-chhók**, to take secret action against a man; to intrigue or plot against a man. **lâng beh chhoân-chhók--lí**, people are secretly preparing to act against you (same as next word?)

chhók — **chhoân-chhók**, to get ready persons or things, making arrangements to be ready for some special matter, or to manage some affair. **chhoân-chhók kha-chhiú**, to get ready bearers of sedans and of luggage for the journey, or for such work. **chhoân-chhók lâng-sek**, to get ready the persons who are to act in a matter, as parties, witnesses, assistants, &c., for a trial.

chhong [R. a granary, = col. chhng]. **chhong-jíⁿ**, a thorny seed (Xanthium?) used in medicine. **chhong-jíⁿ-chí**, id.

chiu-chhong-iâ, the companion of Kwanti; worshipped along with him. **koan put-lī chhong**;

hân-sìn put-lī koái-thong, said of a man always consulting an intimate friend about whatever he does.

chhong [R. green, flourishing]. **chhong-tsùn**, beautiful, well-formed, of a person (v. tsùn). **súi-chhong**, how very fine! how beautiful! (ironically for "how very ugly!") (v. súi).

chhong-tsút, a medicine (v. tsút).

chhong [R. a window, = col. thang]. **tông-chhong**, a fellow-student. **tông-chhong pêng-iú**, id. **chhong-iú**, id. **tông-chhong hia^{n}-tī**, id. **chhong-hā-kó**, essays written in preparing for examinations, to be corrected by teacher. **chhong-hā-khè**, id. **chhong-chiên, khûn-khó thók; má-siōng, gím-i hôe**, study hard at the window, and you will come back (a graduate) on horseback with flowered dress.

chhong (R. id). **chhu-chhong**, obsequious; fawning on a man of power or influence.

chhong [R. onions, = col. chhang]. **lòk-chhong-hoe**, a sort of lily with small blue flowers.

chhong — **chhong-pōng**, rash, hurried, or careless, so as to run against and spoil or break things, or to spoil a good case. **chhong-hông**, hurried and bustled (v. hông).

chhong [R. intelligent]. **chhong-bêng** (P.), = A. chhang-miâ^{n}, intelligent. **chhong-bêng tsâi-nî^{n}-bók**, intelligence and talent are shown by the appearance of the ears and eyes, as in fortune-telling. **chhong-bêng tsū-gō**, his own genius spoils him, as a man who gives up regular study and trusts to his talents, or as a man who trusts too much to his own wisdom in managing matters, instead of consulting others.

chhông (R. id.), gluttonous, to eat gluttonously, said in scolding. **gâu-chhông**, you glutton! **tham-chhông**, gluttonous. **tham-chhông chiâ^{n} ngō-kúi**, a glutton becomes a hungry ghost. **toā-chhông**, very gluttonous. **ài-chhông**, do. said in scolding. **lí kah-hiah sòe-chhông**, why do you eat so little? said in scolding a child when it does not eat enough.

chhông [R. chhiông, to wound]. **chhông-chék**, shortening one's life by vice.

chhông (R. a couch, = col. chhn̂g). **siâ-chhông-tsú**, a medicinal plant (Cnidium?). **siâ-chhông**, id.

chhóng (C.) **bóng-chhóng**, rash and reckless. **bóng-chhóng-chhóng**, id.

chhòng [R. to make], to repair, to mend; to make up, as false reports.

chhòng-tsûn, to repair a boat. **chhòng-sin**, to repair till it is as good as new. **chhòng-khì-sin**, repair it and renew it. **chhòng-sin--ê**, newly made. **chhòng-tsō**, to make. **chhi^{n}-chhòng péh-chhòng**, made or managed ill; done imperfectly; made in an untradesmanlike way. **chhòng-khau**, to get ready the lots; the others draw them, and the last one remains with the man who got them ready.

chhòng chit-ê-kiá^{n}, to buy or adopt a son. **chhòng--ê**, an adopted son.

chhòng-kéng, to deceive by false reports. **chhòng-tī** (Cn. thòng-tī), to play tricks upon; to molest slightly or annoy. **chhòng-sū**, to cause trouble intentionally, often false. **chhòng-sū sa^{n}-loā**, to involve others (intentionally) in our own faults or troubles. **chhòng-giên tsō-gú**, to invent lies and false reports.

chhu — **chhu-chhu**, sloping, inclined, with considerable declivity, as steps off the level. **thán-chhu**, laid down sloping, a good deal off the level. **kiā-á chhu-chhu**, the steps (as of an old stone stair) sloping very much, so as to be difficult or dangerous to walk on.

chhu, to spread out as a mat or coverlet. **chhu-chhiòh**, to spread a mat. **chhu-phē**, to spread out a coverlet. **chhu-pang**, to lay down boards so as to make a level surface, as for a bed or for the floor or deck of a boat. **chhu-lâi chhu-khì**, to lay such boards, moving them back and forwards till they fit and are level.

chhu [R. to run fast]; (C. chhi; Cn. chhü). **chhu-chhong**, obsequious, fawning, as a parasite or flatterer. **chhu-sî**, to follow the fashion. **chhu-sî siáp-sè**, to follow the fashion, and fawn upon the powerful. **chhu-kiet pī-hiong**, to choose the lucky and avoid the unlucky.

chhu (= chhi); (Cn. chhü). **chham-chhu**, confusedly mixed.

chhu (R. id.); (C. chhi; Cn. chhü); animalcules, larvæ or small insects of such shape in water. **toā-thâu-chhu**, a sort with a large head. **chhu-thiông**, small worms in decaying things (v. thiông). **hún-chhü** (Cn.), = tsúi-sau, a small fresh-water insect good for feeding fish.

chhu-hó, a figure like a lizard, carved on furniture.

hê-chhu, to catch larvæ and such water-insects with a small hand-net. **hia-chhu**, id. **chhu-hia**, a net on a pole for catching them. **chhu-tē**, the bag of such a net.

chhu — **béh-chhu**, prickly heat. **toā-béh-chhu**, id.

chhu [R. male], (C. chhi, Cn. chhü). **chhu-hiông** (R.), male and female (v. hiông).

chhu (C.), = chhia, to eat, as white ants.

chhû [R. a fault, as in a gem]. **siáu-chhû**, over strict and exact to the very last cash or the most minute particulars.

chhú (R. id.), (Cn. chhṳ́; cf. C. chhí), a stick like a pestle for mixing mortar, &c.

chhú [R. to take, to select]; (C. chhí). **khó-chhú**, fit to be praised or chosen; commendable; having good qualities. **bû-it-tiông khó-chhú**, having no good quality at all. **bû-tiong chhú-iú**, to make the best of a bad lot.

tsū-chhú-jiók, to get one's self insulted or brought to disgrace by one's own folly. **chhú-tsōe** (R.), to contract guilt (s. adjust).

chhú-pó, to demand security or bail. **chhú-siók**, to redeem; to ransom. **chhim-chhú**, to embezzle. **chhú-keng**, to seek out and bring sacred books, as from a distant country. **chhú-phien**, to take a secondary wife.

chhṳ́ (Cn.) **lêng-chhṳ́**, = lêng-khó, rather than that, better that —.

chhú (Cn.), = A. chhúi. **chhú-chhú**, very small, as pimples, pearls, or beads.

chhú [R. this, these]. **chhú-sî**, now. **chhú-jî-kim** (R.), id. **chhú-hiēn-tsāi**, id. (v. hiēn). **chhú-pē**, id.

chhú-tiong ê tō-lí, the principle of this affair. **khí-iú chhú-lí**, how can this be right? **khiú-chhú-lí**, id. **khiú-chhú chêng-lí**, id. **tō-toā^{n} tsāi-chhú**, a Tauist priest lives here. **hông-hông tò-chhú**, may the phœnix come here (v. hông).

chhú [R. to dwell, to adjust an affair, by change of tone from "chhù," a place], (C. chhí, Cn. chhṳ̄), to adjust a quarrel, as arbiter, &c.

chhú-sú (C. chhí-sí), the term about the 23d of August.

jī-jī ū-chhut-chhú, every word has good literary authority, as in a composition.

siong-chhú (C. siang-chhí), well acquainted and associating with a person. **kó-siong-chhú**, old friends. **ōe-siong-chhú--tit**, fit to be associated with; fit to be a friend. **hó-siong-chhú**, id. **phái^{n}-siong-chhú**, not fit to be made a companion of.

chhú-chiet, to pay a composition on a debt (v. chiet). **ū-khui-chhú**, there is a way open for an amicable settlement, by one or more of the parties being willing to make reasonable terms. **chhú-sū**, to adjust (or try to adjust) a quarrel, dispute, or feud, by a sort of informal arbitration. **chhú-hô**, to arbitrate (not like our arbitration) in a quarrel, so as to end it. **tiāu-chhú**, to adjust an affair, or try to do so, as third parties, appointed by the parties, but without power to bind by their decision. **gī-chhú**, id. **chhú-tī** (R.), to settle by a judgment, as mandarin. **chhú-tsōe** (R.), to punish crime (s. take).

chhú [R. a rat, mouse, squirrel, and some other animals], (C. chhí, Cn. chhü). **niáu-chhú**, a rat (v. niáu). **bâ-chhú** (cats and rats), (v. bâ). **chhú-chhát-á**, a thief who steals small things; a pilferer. **phāu-thâu chhú-chhoàn**, to run away terribly ashamed (v. chhoàn).

chhú-báng, eyes small and half-closed (as man), with eyebrows drawn down, and gen. near-sighted. **bák-chiu chhú-chhú**, id. **kâu-thâu chhú-hī** (monkey's head and rat's ears), said of a man who is very ugly or ill-bred. **kâu-thâu chhú-bīn** (face), id.

chhú-bé (dragon's tail), a great whirlwind; a water-spout at sea. **khí-chhú-bé**, a whirlwind or water-spout occurring. **chhú-bé-hong**, a sudden great whirlwind, more violent than kńg-lê-hong.

chhiah-chhú, a weasel; a clever thief who steals small things. **tsúi-chhú**, a water-rat. **chhân-chhú**, a field rat. **gûn-chhú**, a white mouse. **hui-chhú**, an animal that yields a fine fur. **chî^{n}-chhú**, a sort of rat that has such a strong smell that cats don't like to catch it. **hé-chhú**, a squirrel. **pàng hé-chhú**, to set off a sort of squib.

tek-chhú, a sort of firework that jumps about when lighted; a squib. **pàng tek-chhú**, to set off a squib.

chhú-kōe (Cn.), = A. chhài-koe, a sort of cucumber.

chhú [R. tsū, to assemble]. **chhú-tsôe**, to assemble all together at a fixed place; all fully assembled, as for a procession.

chhù, a house. **chhù-thèh**, house and yard; houses in general (v. thèh). **bô-ūi-chhù**, having no place, *e.g.* no house.

chhù-lāi, wife. **chhù-pi^{n}**, a neighbour. **chhù-pi^{n} thâu-bé**, the neighbours on each side. **chhù-pi^{n} chêng-āu**, id. **chheng-gûn bóe-chhù, bān-gûn bóe-chhù-pi^{n}**, it is ten times harder to get good neighbours than a good house.

lêng-chhù, paper houses burned for the dead. **tsó--chhù**, an ancestral hall. **sip-chhù**, sort of shed or small house in which coffined corpses are laid till a fortunate grave and day are found. **hō--chhù**, the two smaller houses built at the two ends of the principal house, separated from it by a narrow court, and facing it. **chit-keng-chhù**, one house. **chit-tsō-chhù**, one block of houses. **piēn-chhù chhut-sè**, a house to let.

khí-chhù, to build a house. **kìm-chhù**, to forbid any one except the family (for superstitious reasons) to enter the house, for three, five, or seven days; as after the rites of consecrating a new house, or in sickness. **tńg-chhù**, the bride going to make a short call at her parents' house, on the fourth day after the marriage.

chhù-tsú, owner of house; landlord. **chhù-tiēn**, tenant of house. **chhù-tat**, plan of a house (v. tat). **chhù-kè**, scaffolding for building. **chhù-tōe**, a site where an old house had stood. **chhù-tē** (C.), id. (s. order). **chhù-kak**, the corner of a house. **chhù-kak-thâu**, id. **chhù-chit**, the ridge of a house (v. chit). **chhù-koà**, the roof. **chhù-téng**, on the roof; the roof, as a place. **chhù-téng-bé**, up on the roof.

chhù [R. second, order]. **khah-chhù--ê**, second class; of inferior quality. **chhù-lē--ê**, id. **chhù-sū**, order. **chhù-sī** (C.), id. **chhù-tē**, successive order.

chit-chhù, once. **āu-chhù**, next time. **sè-chhù**, several times. **lúi-chhù**, often.

chhù (R. id.) **chhù-bī**, agreeable; pleasant. **iú-chhù**, attractive; taking the fancy, as things. **sek-chhù**, taking the fancy; games of chance played for amusement, sometimes including the drinking some liquor together to pass the time. **chin-sek-chhù**, very taking to the fancy; very interesting to look at or to hear. **kan--á sek-chhù**, well, indeed it is interesting or pleasant. **tāi-ke teh-sek-chhù**, they are amusing themselves with games of chance, no money, or very little, being used. **sek-chhù-á**, games such as chess, or games of chance played for amusement; also said by euphemism of other improper amusements (esp. gambling or opium), when found at it, "it is only a little amusement, not our usual habit." **lâi sek-chhù-á**, come and have some amusement, said of gambling and opium.

chhū — **chhī-bú chhī-chhū**, whispering.

chhū, to slide; to slip. **chhū--lóh-khì**, to slide down a slope. **chhū-chhi^{n}** (T.), a falling star.

chhū [R. to marry a wife, = col. chhoā]. **siók-chhū**, to marry a second wife, as a widower. **bī chhū-chhe, sien chhū-chhiap**, to take a concubine before marrying a wife, counted highly improper.

chhū (C.), = A. chhī, to temper metal in water.

chhuh — **chhuh--chit-ē**, to go off without much noise, as a bad cracker, or gun with insufficient charge. **hóe chhuh--chit-ē** (C.), make the smouldering match blaze by a puff. **hóe-chhuh-kóng** (C.), a small joint of bamboo for extinguishing and keeping a match.

chhuh — **chhuh tī-thô--nih^{n}**, to ground on soft mud, as a boat. **chhuh tī thô-phiâ^{n}**, to ground on the muddy bank or shore.

chhui [R. lofty, mountainous], a surname.

chhui (R. id.), to urge; to hasten (active), to dun for payment.

chhui-tiâ^{n}, a second petition sent in to a mandarin, when the first has not been effectual; to send in such a second complaint or petition. **chhui-chiù**, to repeat the incantations when the spirits have not answered the first. **chit-chhiá^{n} chit-chhui**, to invite and afterwards to urge strongly to accept.

chhui-chhiâu, to drive a bargain; to haggle. **chhui-chhek**, do.; coming gradually to each other's terms (s. calculate).

chhui-thó, to demand urgently the payment of a debt. **chhui-pek**, to urge to do anything very quickly (v. pek). **chhui-koá^{n}**, id. **chhui-kín**, id.

chhui-ân, to press very urgently.

chhui-siⁿ-io̍h, medicine that assists in parturition.

chhui — chhui-ân, to tighten. chhui--sí, to strangle to death. chhui-oá, to gather, in sewing.

chhui (R. thui, chhui), to calculate, as a date; to rub smooth, as plaster.

chhui-úi (R.), to make excuses, as for not doing something; to put the blame on another.

chhui-sǹg, to calculate mentally. chhui-chhut, to draw an inference; to infer. chhui kah-chí, to calculate the cyclical characters, as for a day. chhui nîⁿ-kō, to calculate the cyclical characters for a year. chhui-lâi chhui-khì, to calculate minutely, as a lucky day. chhui-lâi chhui-khì, bô hit-hō-jit, though calculating back and forwards cannot find a good day. chhui-chhek (R.), to consider carefully (s. urge).

chhui-tsun, to make a man (by common consent) the chief person in a company; to give the place of honour to a man.

chhui-piah, to rub plaster smooth with a smooth stone, but not so smooth as "gē."

chhúi (Cn. chhú). chhúi-chhúi, very small, as pimples, beads, pearls, &c. hoat-liáp chhúi-chhúi, to have an eruption of numerous small boils or pimples.

chhúi [R. to investigate; to feel about]. chhúi-mê (R.), to investigate, as from many facts or books. chhúi-bêng (R.), to think out clearly, as meaning of a book. chhúi-to̍k (R.), to draw inferences from evidence.

chhùi (R. id.) chhiⁿ-chhùi, green. chhùi-lâm, bright light-blue. húi-chhùi, a bird with brilliant blue feathers. húi-chhùi-ge̍k, a greenish-blue sort of jade. chhùi-joán, the finest feathers of the húi-chhùi (used for females' head-dress). chhùi-chiáu-mn̂g-hoe, artificial feather flowers.

chhùi, the mouth; the edge, as of a knife; a mouthful.

chit-chhùi-á, a small quantity, as of food. kúi-nà-chhùi, several mouthfuls.

hong-chhùi, the edges of paper where it is pasted up. hong-chhùi, a pimple. báng-chhùi, mark of mosquito bite. siu-chhùi, the edges of a wound closed up. kap-chhùi, joint of two boards; seam in dress.

chiáu-chhùi, a bird's beak; the bow of a junk (v. chiáu). koe-chhùi, a T-headed pin for fastening ropes. ah-bú-chhùi, a duck's bill; a small hook worn on the dress for carrying small things (v. ah).

phâng-chhùi, the rope that fastens the lower end of the sail to the mast. poh-chhùi, the splice of an oar (s. scold). bóe-bō-chhùi, deceitful (traders) mouth; two bowls placed mouth to mouth, but not exactly meeting; the leaves of a two-leaved door laid to, but not shut. khoah-chhùi, a pick-axe. kiā-chhùi (C.), id. chiam-chhùi (P.), id.

hun-chhe-chhùi, the mouth-piece of a pipe. tê-koàn-chhùi, mouth of tea-pot. to-chhùi, edge of sword or knife.

thâu-chhùi, mouths in a family. kúi-ê thâu-chhùi, how many mouths are there in the family? bōe-bó bōe-kiáⁿ, chió-thâu-chhùi, sell wife and children so as to have fewer mouths to feed (said in joke). hó-thâu-chhùi, good at using the regular conventional phrases on meeting people; making profitable voyages, as vessel sailing well without damage.

phīⁿ-ba̍k-chhùi (nose, eyes, mouth), the features in general. chhùi-chih, mouth and tongue; the mouth in general (v. chih). khiû-chhùi, to pout the lips. chhùi-khí, the teeth (v. khí). chhùi-chhiu, the beard, whiskers, &c. (v. chhiu). chhùi-phóe, the cheek. chhùi-tûn, the lips (v. tûn). chhùi-kak, the corners of the mouth. chhùi-khang, the orifice of the mouth (v. "that," to shut up). chhùi-kháu, the mouth (v. kháu).

phah chhùi-kó, to talk idle talk (as if mouth like a "drum"). koat chhùi-kó, to slap a child's cheek (said in scolding). sái chhùi-chhok, to make a signal by a slight change of the mouth.

chhùi-ē-táu, the chin. toā-chhùi-táu, asking a very large sum, as for managing an affair. pháiⁿ-chhùi-táu, scolding or cursing with vile language; foul-mouthed. chhe-chhùi iá-táu, id. pháiⁿ-chhùi-phīⁿ, id. chhùi-thâu, the mouth (figuratively). chhùi-thâu khin, willing to take a low price. chhùi-thâu giám-ngīⁿ, doggedly refusing to make up a quarrel. saⁿ-tak-chhùi, having a slight altercation (v. tak). poh-chhùi, two persons beginning to scold; slight angry altercation. kiūⁿ-chhùi, very doggedly refusing to admit an undeniable mistake or fault. siàⁿ-chhùi, said of a man whose guesses as to the future come true. sí-chhùi, unable to reply (v. sí). chhùi tsōe, talkative. chhùi ba̍t, cautious in speaking. chhùi lī-hāi, good at talking over and deceiving people. hó-chhùi, speaking so as to please the hearer; speaking kindly so as to avoid irritating. hó-chhùi-súi, good at polite or flattering talk (v. súi). ū-chhùi-hoe, good at speaking politely to those we meet. kāu-chhùi-hoe, full of flattering or pleasant ingratiating talk.

kiò-chhùi, a young servant (boy or girl) kept for messages and small bits of work (v. kiò). saⁿ-tùi-chhùi, the parties themselves arranging a matter without using any go-between or middle-man. tùi-chhùi ìn--i, answering him at once. m̄-sī i--ê tùi-chhùi, unable to contend with him in arguing, disputing, bickering, or scolding. gâu-ìn-chhùi, fond of answering again, as an impudent servant to master. chhap-chhùi, to take part in a conversation with which we have no concern (s. broker). chhut-chhùi, to be spoken out, as a proposal or order (v. chhut). thàn-chhùi, to accept a price or condition offered (v. thàn). thiaⁿ i-ê-chhùi, to follow what he says. tè-chhùi-bé, to repeat a teacher's words in learning; to repeat a man's words, as in ridicule or pretending to obey.

khui-chhùi, to begin to speak of a matter; to make the first proposal of a price. khui-chhùi-thiaⁿ, an open central hall with no partition to separate it from the court in front.

chit-chhùi siang-thâu-chhut, said of a tale-bearer or great talker of scandal. chit-chhùi pe̍h-chha̍t, all he says is false. kō chit-ki-chhùi, to have nothing to rely upon but one's own power of talk and strength of assertion, as a man who has neither truth nor influence on his side. tiuⁿ chit-ki-chhùi, id.; all mere talk.

chhùi-ta, thirsty. chhùi pe̍h, having a bad appetite, as child, or as man long unwell. chhùi siap, having a bad taste in mouth and disinclined to eat, as man slightly unwell. chhùi pho, do. slightly. lún-chhùi, to refrain from eating a thing for fear of sickness. kìm-chhùi, to forbid indiscriminate eating or certain sorts of food, as in sickness. chhíⁿ-chhùi, to give an appetite, as a relish.

chhùi (R. id.), broken to shivers; in small quantities; by retail. chhùi-chhùi, id.

lân-chhùi, miscellaneous. lùi-chhùi, id. chhùi-

chhùi-bōe, to sell in small quantities by retail. **bōe-chhùi-hō͘** (Cn.), to sell miscellaneous goods, as general store or shop.

chhó-chhùi, miscellaneous; difficult to set right, as affair needing much disputing (v. chhó). **só-chhùi** (T.), troublesome to deal with, as affair; much wearisome discussion, = A. chhó-chhùi.

thiah-chhùi, to tear to pieces. **chhùi-bí**, broken rice (v. bí).

chhùi-bang-bang, broken very small. **chhùi-sap-sap**, id. **chhùi-ióh-ióh**, id. **saⁿ**, **thiah kàu chhùi-ióh-ióh**, clothes torn to tatters. **chhùi-iâm-iâm**, broken down small. **chhùi-kê-kê**, id. **sim-koaⁿ chhùi-iáp-iáp**, the mind very anxious about many matters.

gûn-chhùi, broken dollars. **chhùi-gûn**, id. **hún-chhùi**, broken bits of face-powder. **ièn-chhùi**, broken bits of raw bird-nest. **pò-chhùi**, cuttings of cloth. **chhun koáⁿ pò-chhùi**, a few cuttings of the cloth remain.

chham-chhùi, mixed in confusion or disorder. **chhap-chhùi ê seng-lí**, a miscellaneous small business (v. chhap). **tsáp-chhùi ê-seng-lí**, id.

chhuiⁿ (C.), = A. chhng, to press into a hole.

chhuiⁿ (C.), = A. chhng, a village.

chhuiⁿ (C.) **kha-chhuiⁿ**, = A. kha-chhng, the posteriors; wrong side of paper, &c.

chhüiⁿ (Cn.), = A. chheng, a thousand.

chhüiⁿ (Cn.) **chhüiⁿ-miâⁿ**, = A. chhiⁿ-miâⁿ, the feast of tombs.

chhûiⁿ (Cn.), = A. chhêng, the silk-worm.

chhúiⁿ (C.), = A. chhńg, to suck in the mouth. **chhúiⁿ-chhiah**, too minute and particular about work, &c., done for us, so as to cause much trouble to people.

chhûiⁿ (Cn.), = A. chhéng, to dust; a brush.

chhùiⁿ (C.), = A. chhǹg, to rush in hurriedly; to bore a hole; to string things; (more than one word).

chhun (R. id.), spring; (sexual appetite). **chhun-thiⁿ**, spring. **chhun-hun**, the vernal equinox. **lip-chhun**, the beginning of spring, about 4th of February. **jip-chhun**, id. **chiūⁿ-chhun**, in the beginning of spring. **sin-chhun**, early days of spring. **hō-sin-chhun**, to make the New-year's congratulations. **chhiáⁿ-chhun-chiú**, to invite to a New-year's feast. **ngiâⁿ-chhun**, rites on the festival of lip-chhun. **chhun-gû**, the earthen cow used at these rites (v. gû). **ū siang-chhun**, having that festival twice in one year, as year with intercalary month. **sió-iông-chhun**, a false spring in winter.

chhun-lēng, the general sort of weather in spring (v. lēng). **chhun-hō͘**, spring rains. **chhun koâⁿ, hō͘ náⁿ-tsoāⁿ**, when it is cold in spring, the rain comes in torrents. **chhun-im** (R.), the cold dark weather (more or less rainy), common in spring. **chhun-hong**, spring winds. **khah-chhun-hong**, looking better off; now at leisure and free from care, as a man when his work is done. **moáⁿ-bīn chhun-hong**, face having the look of good health and comfortable circumstances; pleasant appearance, as of man in prosperous condition. **chhun-ûi** (R.), the examinations of the Tsìn-sze degree.

ūi-chhun-kiong, to draw lascivious pictures. **chhun-hng**, medicine used to give strength for lascivious pleasure. **chhun-sim tāng**, person (male or female) longing for sexual gratification. **su-chhun** (R.), female desiring sexual intercourse.

chheng-chhun-sî, time of early youth, about 20. **tsáp-poeh jih-jī, chheng-chhun siàu-liân-sî**, about 18 years of age to 22, the bright spring season of life.

thâu-chhun ê-tê, tea of the first crop. **thâu-tsúi-chhun**, id.

chhun-chhiu, one of the five classics (v. chhiu). **chhun-hē chhiu-tang**, the four seasons. **thien-sù pêng-an hok; jîn-gêng hù-kùi-chhun**, Heaven gives peace and happiness, men receive the spring time of wealth and honour.

chhun-tiû, a silk stuff (v. tiû). **tiū-chhun**, a beautiful red flower, like a rose. **tiū-chhun-hoe**, id. **bān-liân-chhun**, Ficus Afzelii. **jit-jit-chhun**, a flower that blossoms all the year round, has a red tubular corolla.

chhun (R. id.) **ien-chhun**, a quail. **phah ien-chhun**, to make quails fight; to gamble with quails. **liáh ien-chhun**, to hold fighting quails in the hand, in training and feeding them. **ien-chhun-tē**, a bag for keeping fighting quails. **ien-chhun-khoân**, a tub for them fighting in. **ien-chhun-khoan**, id.

chhun, surplus; remainder; to remain over, as a balance. **chhun-chîⁿ**, cash over; balance remaining. **khah-chhun-chhoá**, accumulating a little money. **chhun-tiông**, accumulating, as wealth, esp. as money at interest. **chhun-tñg**, id. **saⁿ-pun, chiáh ū-chhun; saⁿ-chhiúⁿ, chiáh bô-hūn**, in a dispute, each should yield a little to others, or none will have anything.

chhun (R. sin), (= chhng), to stretch out; to stretch; to straighten. **chhun-chhiú**, to stretch out the hand (v. chhiú). **chhun-tit**, to stretch out straight. **chhun-ûn**, to stretch one's self, as when tired or slightly unwell (v. ûn). **chhun-kha**, the wings of a large house facing the court on each side, in the same line with the hō͘--chhù, but lower.

chhun--cheh kiu--cheh, almost doing the thing and then drawing back; very irresolute. **chhun--chit--ē, kiu--chit-ē**, id. **bōe-chhun bōe-kiu**, neither able to stretch out or draw in, as a palsied man.

chhun (Cn.) **chhun-tîn**, = A. chhoan-tîn, to send out suckers, as a plant.

chhûn, to inform a superior or a friend of what we mean to do. **saⁿ-chhûn**, to treat each other with politeness, esp. each declining what the other offers, or by consulting on an intended action. **tsun-chhûn**, to inform a superior or friend before doing some action. **chhûn-kèng**, to show respect to, as a superior or friend, as by making presents, or by respectfully consulting on what we mean to do. **saⁿ-chhûn-kèng**, id. **toā, chhûn-toā; sòe, chhûn-sòe**, to consult with others (higher or lower) instead of acting of our own sole purpose.

chhûn [R. tsûn, to remain over, to continue]. **chhûn liông-sim**, to obey conscience, as in the treatment of others. **ū-chhûn-ì**, to have a long cherished desire or fixed purpose secretly in the heart only waiting for an opportunity, *e.g.* determined to have a great feud on any small occasion when a convenient time comes. **ū-chhûn-tsō-ì**, id.

bô-chhûn beh-hó, you do not think of right conduct or amendment. **bô-chhûn-pān**, without any previous thought about it, as something coming unexpectedly. **bô-chhûn-pān beh-khì**, having had no idea of going, but suddenly having to go.

bô-chhûn tsú-kè, to treat a friend or customer

ill (as for some small temporary gain), so as to lose his custom or friendship. **chhûn āu-pē**, to keep something in reserve for the future, as money, strength, power, or influence, not using them to the utmost, or keeping our purpose secret, so as to be able to change if desirable, or having another plan in reserve; not too much committed to one plan or party. **chhûn chit-ê āu-pē**, id. **bô-chhûn āu-pē**, not taking due care for the future, not making preparation for possible emergencies; taking an apparent present good and so losing what is far better; *e.g.* charging too dear and so losing a customer entirely. **bô-chhûn āu-lâi ê-tāi-chì**, id. **bô-chhûn-āu**, id. **bô-chhûn kàu-āu-lâi**, id. **bô-chhûn āu-tńg**, id.

chhún [R. contrary]. **bēng-tē to-chhún**, my fate is very bad; I am fated to misfortune.

chhún (R. id.) **gû-chhún**, stupid. **chhún-pūn**, awkward and vulgar (v. pūn).

chhún [R. to consider]. **chhún-tók** (R.), to examine into the thoughts and purposes of one's self or of others.

chhùn (R. id.), an inch; the Chinese inch, one-tenth of a Chinese foot, therefore larger than the British inch.

chhùn-jī, one inch and two-tenths. **chhek-chhùn put-ī**, quite correct; not needing to be changed at all. **chhùn-chhioh**, inches and feet. **bô-chhùn-chhioh**, making a thing carelessly, different from pattern or quite out of proportion, or wasting the material. **bô-hun-chhùn** (lit. not by inches and tenths), making no proper measurement or examination; careless or inaccurate in doing things.

chhùn-pē lân-hêng (can hardly go one inch more), walking very slowly and with difficulty.

saⁿ-chhùn-khùi-tn̄g, to expire, in allusion to the length of the throat. **chit-chhùn-á-jit**, a very short time, allusion to the shadow cast by the sun on the ground. **chit-chhùn-á ê jit-iáⁿ**, id. **koh chit-chhùn-á-jit**, after a very short time. **khiàm chit-chhùn-á-jit**, it wants a few moments. **it-chhùn kong-im, it-chhùn-kim**, a moment of time is an inch of gold.

lák-chhùn-á, thick tiles six inches (about seven English) broad. **chhùn-kim-tsó**, a confection.

phah-chhùn, a game (tipcat) played by striking a small shuttle-shaped bit of wood on the end, so that it leaps away. **chhùn-chí**, the cat, or small stick, thus struck. **chhùn-ko**, the longer stick by which it is struck; the bat.

chhūn, to pinch with the fingers.

chhut (R. id.), an act of a play; one of the successive acts of offering in the rites called "chiò." **chhut-thâu**, id. (s. go out). **hì-chhut**, an act of a play. **chit-chhut-hì**, one act of a play. **tiah-chhut**, to select a play. **khó-chhut**, a tragedy. **chhám-chhut**, id. **hoa-chhut**, a lascivious play. **siâ-chhut**, id. **poaⁿ-siâ-chhut**, to play a lascivious play.

chhut (R. id.), to go out; to issue; to come or go out from; to go out to; to come out to; to give out; to produce; to be produced; to have some diseases that make special marks on skin; to offer a price, as buyer; to be more than —.

chhut-jip, to go in and out (v. jip). **chhut--lâi**, to come out. **chhut--khì**, to go out. **chhut-khì**, to lose the auspicious influence, as a grave (v. khì). **chhut-lâng**, to supply labour, self or others. **chhut-lâng**, to suppurate. **chhut-kè**, to be married, as a virgin. **chhut-kè**, to offer a price, as the buyer (v. kè, price). **chhut-kim**, to produce gold. **chhut-kim**, the helm getting out of gear. **chhut-chîⁿ**, to give out or offer money, esp. copper cash. **chhut-chîⁿ**, to have projecting eaves, as a house.

chhut-tāng, rather more than the weight, *e.g.* one or two per cent. **chhut-tsáp**, days of moon from the 11th to about the 14th. **chhut-jih**, days of moon from 21st onwards.

chhut-kì, very strange. **chhut-siu**, to have a crop better than the average. **chhut-chiòng chhiau-kûn** (R.), to surpass others, as in talent, &c. **khah-chhut-tioh**, excelling other persons or things. **chhut-miâⁿ**, famous. **chhut-thâu**, to become distinguished; to get office; to undertake or assume responsibility. **chhut-sin**, to attain to rank, office, or wealth; to act as head in a dangerous matter (v. sin). **chhut-sū**, to become a mandarin. **chhut-kòng**, to become a graduate of the title "kòng-seng."

chhut-sìn, to come forward to the trial, as a party in a case. **chhut-sím**, id. **chhut-sè**, to come forward and enter a formal answer to an accusation. **chhut-siù**, to give information against a man (v. siù). **chhut-khó**, to go to the examinations. **chhut-kun**, to go to war, as soldiers or mandarins. **chhut-chièn**, to go out to battle. **chhut-sàu**, to go out to attack pirates. **chhut-tīn**, to go to battle; to go out in procession; to march in rank and file.

chhut-hái, a supercargo. **chhut-tsúi**, to take goods from the warehouse to the vessel; to repolish a stone with a dull surface; water coming out (v. tsúi). **chhut-tsûn**, to start in a vessel for a long voyage. **chhut-goā**, to go from home, esp. to live a while. **saⁿ-chhut-lē**, to miss each other on the road. **chhut-lē teh-toà--ê**, things we take with us when we go from home. **chhut-koe**, to go to market. **chhut-iûⁿ**, to go to sea, as mandarins after pirates. **chhut-soaⁿ**, to bury. **chhut-tsōe**, to be banished or transported.

chhut-sì, to be born. **tek-chhut--ê**, born of the principal wife. **sù-chhut--ê**, born of an inferior wife. **chhut-ūn**, to get out of an unlucky period of life into a lucky one.

chhut-hiēn, to become manifest; to appear plainly. **hién-chhut**, to manifest. **chhut-phoà**, to become known, as a secret. **chhut-hì**, to begin a play.

hoat-chhut, to produce; to give forth; to grow, as buds. **chhui-chhut**, to draw an inference. **siūⁿ-chhut**, to think out. **khoàⁿ-chhut**, to discover or perceive by looking at. **khoàⁿ-m̄-chhut**, cannot make it out.

chhut-siàu, to lend or sell on credit. **chhut-tse**, advertised for lease, as a house to let. **chhut-sè**, id. **chhut-tién**, to be in the market for mortgage, as a property.

chhut-ke, to become a Buddhist priest, monk, or nun. **chhut-kè**, to be married, as a virgin. **chhut-kui**, id. **jī-chhut-lâng**, a woman married a second time. **jī-chhut--ê**, id. **chhut-sū**, to give a child to another man to be adopted.

chhut-chhùi, to be said by one's mouth, as an order or advice, or the first proposing of a matter. **ōe kóng-chhut-chhùi**, the word has been spoken and cannot now be recalled. **chhut-chhùi ū-jī**, to use a great many book-phrases in conversation.

chhut hī-khang, to be very attentive. **seng-chhut-chhiú**, to be the first to do a violent act with one's hand, as in plundering or in beginning a quarrel. **chhut-kha chhut-chhiú**, restless, as a child.

chhut-lát, to exert strength (v. lát). **chhut-kang**, to furnish labour or labourers. **chhut-sia^n**, to call out loud.

chhut-kiong, to go to stool. **chhut-mn̂g**, to go out of the house for a longer or shorter time (v. mn̂g). **chhut-hêng**, to go out of the house on a lucky day (v. hêng). **chhut-chhù**, to go out of a house. **chhut-kiō**, to alight from a sedan. **chhut-kàu**, to leave a religion; to apostatize. **chhut-óh**, to go out of the school-room; to get out of the jurisdiction of the "ló-su," by becoming a high graduate.

chhut-kè, to offer a price, as buyer (v. kè). **chhut jī-tsáp**, to offer twenty (*e.g.* cash), as the price or wages. **chhut--i joā-tsōe**, how much was he offered? **chhut-tù**, to lay stakes (v. tù).

chhut-jī, to give or issue a formal document, esp. deed of sale for land or slave. **chhut pîn-kù**, to produce proof. **chhut kò-sī**, to issue a proclamation. **chhut-phiò**, to issue a warrant.

chhut-pún, to invest capital (v. pún). **chhut-hiòng**, to pay soldier's pay. **chhut chî^n-niû^n**, id. **chhut-gûn**, to pay money; to produce silver. **chhut-hè**, to bring out goods, as from vessel or from warehouse (v. hè). **tī-sî beh-lâi-chhut**, when will you take delivery of your goods? as from ship or hong.

chhut-jîn-bùt, to produce distinguished men. **chhut-chhát**, to produce robbers or pirates, as a place. **chhut hó-kiá^n-sun**, to have good descendants.

chhut-sek, the good colour coming out beautifully, as in painting or dyeing. **chhut-bī**, giving a good taste, as meat well cooked. **chhut-koā^n**, to perspire by a medical application; to become damp, as a rock or wall in the south wind.

chhut-khēng, a rainbow appearing. **chhut-jit**, sunrise; sun breaking out from among clouds. **chhut-gėh**, moon rising or appearing from among clouds. **gėh chhut**, id.

chhut-tsu, to take small-pox. **chhut-hóng**, id. **chhut-chhin-chhí^n**, id. **chhut-phiáh**, to take measles. **chhut-pan**, to take a very severe fever like typhus. **chhut-tan**, another dangerous fever.

chhwá, **chhwa^n**, **chhwah**, **chhwan**, **chhwàng**, in several tones; better, chhoá, chhoa^n, chhoah, chhoan, chhoàng, &c. (*q.v.*)

D.

Some words with initial **l** are sometimes heard with an initial **d**, or a sound very like it, so that names beginning in English with **d** are often imitated by the Chinese by initial **l**.

dê, sometimes heard after final t, = ê, the sign of the genitive. **hit--dê**, = hit--ê, that. **hid--dê**, id. **chit--dê**, = chit--ê, this. **chid--dê**, id. **chit-dê**, = chit-ê, one.

dz, sometimes heard (T. Cn.) in place of **j** in the lower series of tones, *e.g.* **dzoáh** (T.), = joáh, hot. **dzū** (Cn. T.), = jū, tsū, in some cases.

E.

e (C. oe), a small earthen or metal pot. **e-á**, id. **hûi-e**, a small earthen pot. **tê-e**, small earthen tea-kettle. **chiú-tê-e**, a sort of wine-jug. **toā-e**, a large earthen pot for boiling water. **tīm-e-á**, a small earthen vessel for putting in an outer vessel of boiling water for stewing. **e-koà**, lid of a small earthen pot.

tâng-e, a small brass pot. **si^n-e**, a small pot of pot-metal. **loán-e**, a brass or pewter vessel for keeping food warm by burning charcoal put inside. **joán-e**, id.

e (= o), (Cn. ö). **tang-e-chhài**, parsley.

e (C. oe). **e-chhài**, lettuce.

e (R. oe). **e-hoan**, Japanese. **ok kàu ná^n-e--nih^n**, as violent and cruel as a Japanese.

e, an interjection. **e--lah**, exclamation of men working together, as at a heavy pull or lift, answering to "o--lah," the call of the leader.

e (T. ö). **e-lê**, very troublesome, fretful, and fractious, as a young child, **e-e lê-lê**, id.

e (C.), = A. oe, to jostle; to turn a mill.

ê [R. kî, he, she, it], (Cn. gê), sign of the genitive; final particle, forming adjectives out of nouns, or binding several words into a single term; a general classifier, which may be applied very widely; most properly used as classifier of men and cash; sometimes, after final **t**, becomes lê, dê, or kê; often enclitic. **goá-ê**, my, mine. **i-ê**, his. **lâng-ê-kha**, a man's foot.

kim--ê, golden. **hó--ê**, a good one; some good article. **tsong--ê**, of same surname, but not a relative.

hit--ê, that. **chit--ê**, this. **chit-ê**, one. **chit-poà^n-ê-á**, scarcely any. **bô-poà^n-ê** (not half a one), none at all.

ê [R. bêng, dark; night, = col. mî^n], (C. ê). **ê-hng**, evening. **ê-hui^n** (C.), id.

ê (C.), = A. ôe, a shoe. **ê-té**, = A. ôe-tóe, the sole of a shoe. **ê-té-hî**, = thoah-se, the sole (fish).

é (R. á), (C. é, Cn. ó, ek). **é-káu**, dumb (v. káu). **é-sia^n**, indistinct, broken, or hoarse voice, as from sickness, or from weeping or long talking. **khàu kàu é-sia^n**, hoarse with weeping and sobbing. **gûn-sia^n é-é**, the dollar has a bad sound, as a cracked dollar or one of inferior silver.

é— **é-é**, sound used in ordering, as scolding children. **é-é m̄-thang-háu**, don't cry there!

é (C.), = A. óe, short in stature.

è (R. id.), (C. ì), a white film that forms in the eye (amaurosis?). **khí-è**, to have this disease of the eye. **chhiū^n-è**, id.

è [R. òe, to defile, filthy], (Cn. ō). **è--tiòh-lâng**, to infect. **è-lâ-sâm**, to make very dirty and troublesome to clean, as by filth or water. **è-sè**, to make a litter, as by bits of paper, wood shavings, &c. (v. sè).

è-ờ, to be unclean, filthy; to defile (in a superstitious sense). **è-ờ thi^n-tōe**, to offend against the purity of heaven and earth, as by leaving a corpse unburied on the ground. **è-ờ sîn-bêng**, to defile the sanctity of the gods, as by some impure act or exposure in their presence, or as a Buddhist priest taking a wife.

è (R. id.), (C. ì). **hē-è**, posterity; descendants. **hīō-è** (Cn.), id.

ē — **phài-ē**, a large division of a clan. **siók tá-lóh chit--ê phài-ē**, to which branch of the family or clan do you (or does he) belong?

ē (R. hā), (C. ɛ̄), below; after; classifier of blows; (an occasion; a plan), one of the musical notes.

téng-ē, above and below. **téng-ē-jit**, on one or other of two or three successive days. **thi^n-téng tōe-ē**, heaven above and earth below. **soa^n-téng hái-ē**, on land or on sea (or river) (v. hái).

hái-ē, on sea or on a river. **thi^n-ē**, under heaven; all under heaven; the Chinese empire. **hiu^n-ē**, among the villages.

ē-tóe, below. **tóe-ē**, id. **ē-thâu**, id. **ē-bīn**, id.; the lower surface or side. **ē-kha**, the lower part. **ē-sin**, the lower part of one's body; lower down, as a place. **ē-sì**, on the southern side, on the lee side, &c. (v. sì). **lâu-ē**, the ground-floor. **ē-lóh**, the front division of a house. **ē-chiò**, a building right opposite the principal house, but lower down. **ē-kim**, the lower support of the helm. **bák-ē**, at present. **bák-ē ê-lâng**, the men of this time.

ē-si, inferior officials (v. si). **ē-chhiú**, dependants, inferiors, assistants. **chhiú-ē**, id.

ē-pơ, the afternoon. **ē-pái**, next time. **ē-tang**, the second rice harvest; latter part of year. **ē-nî^n**, the year following; a following year. **ē-gėh**, next month. **ē-chit-gėh**, one month afterwards. **ē-jit**, a day after; four or five days after. **ē-chit-jit**, one day after. **ē-pún**, the next volume.

chit-ē, one blow. **phah-chit-ē**, to strike once. **chit-ē-khoà^n--kì^n**, at one glance. **tsòe-chit-ē**, making one lot; all at once; all in one. **pun tsòe-kúi-nà-ē kià**, send it in several successive lots or portions.

chêng-ē, a former occasion. **toā-ē**, exceedingly —; very abundantly. **sa^n-ē-toā**, thrice as large.

ē-siàu, a plan; a contrivance, as regards its advantage or otherwise. **ɛ̄-sùi^n** (C.), id. **hó-ē-siàu**, it is a good plan or state of matters; it can be managed in this way. **phái^n-ē-siàu**, it cannot be so done or will go wrong; no way of managing it well. **bô-ē-siàu**, id. **phái^n-ē**, very awkward and inconvenient, as a bad mistake, or as a man failing to pay what was counted upon; state of matters making one feel quite ashamed, *e.g.* some one coming on us in undress. **chin phái^n-ē** (esp. Cn.), matters in a very bad state.

ē [R. hā, a mansion]. **ē-mn̂g**, Amoy. **ɛ̄-mûi^n** (C.), id. **ē-mn̂g-soa^n**, the island of Amoy.

ē (R. hō). **tsai-ē**, calamity (v. tsai). **ē-toan**, a matter that breeds troubles. **ē-kàu**, when calamity comes. **ē-lâi**, id. **jiá-ē**, to bring calamity on one's self. **khí-ē**, id. **gín-ná khí toā-lâng-ē**, quarrels begun by boys involve old men.

ē (= lē). **háu-ē-ē**, to chirp, as a cicada.

ē (C.), = A. ōe, able.

ɛ^n (R. eng), (T. i^n). **ɛ^n-á** (Cn. sōe-ká^n), an infant. **ū-ɛ^n-á**, to be pregnant. **tsa-bó-ɛ^n**, you little girl.

ɛ^n (R. eng), (T. i^n). **ɛ^n-ɛ^n-háu**, sound of an infant crying.

ɛ^n [R. hā, below], (= ɛ̄^{n}), one of the Chinese musical notes.

ɛ^n (C.), = A. i^n. **chhân-ɛ^n**, a dragon-fly.

ɛ^n [R. eng, a hero], (C.), = A. i^n, colloquial form of the proper name "eng."

ɛ̂^{n} (C.), = A. î^n, a beam; a rafter.

ɛ̄^{n} [R. hā, below], (= ɛ^n, ē), one of the Chinese musical notes.

eh [R. lek, C. (R.) ek, a narrow pass, calamity], (C. ɛh). **tsai-eh**, calamities (v. tsai). **khó-eh**, id. **eh-ūn**, an unlucky period of one's life. **ū-eh-ūn**, to be very unfortunate. **tsoâ-siong hó-eh, thi^n-tōe-sờ**, injuries by snakes and tigers are decreed by heaven and earth.

eh (C. ɛh, T. Cn. öh), (cf. uh). **phah-eh**, to hiccup; to belch. **kí^n-kui phah-eh**, to hiccup from eating too fast or too much. **phah chhàu-sng-eh**, to belch, leaving a sour taste, or bringing up a little sour bad-smelling stuff. **phah chhiah-sng-eh**, id.

eh-sng, to bring up a little sour or acid stuff. **eh-tsúi**, to bring up a little watery stuff.

khơ-eh, to hiccup. **khơ-sái-eh**, to hiccup; of a child only.

thó-eh, to belch; done politely, as an indication of having eaten enough. **ìn-öh** (Cn.), id. **bô-chiáh, ké thó-öh; bô-chhēng, ké chhiau-cheh** (T.), though not having eaten, yet belching as if full; though with almost no clothes, yet putting on a comfortable pleased appearance.

ɛh (T. ɛh^n), exclamation of surprise at something curious.

ėh (C. óeh, Cn. ōh), (A. also óeh). **khng-ėh**, small chaff or coarse bran of rice, coarser than "bí-khng."

tê-ėh, small broken bits of tea-leaves. **hî-pó-ėh**, refuse and small fragments of dried fish.

ėh (cf. aih^n, ùt). **kāu-ėh**, uncomfortable feeling, as from much dirt on the skin or dirty clothes; uncomfortable, murmuring, discontented feeling. **ai-ėh**, grieved and murmuring internally. **àu-ėh**, displeased or discontented unhappy state of mind; discontented or displeased look; full of superstitious fears from some bad omen.

ėh (C.), = A. óeh, narrow. **ėh-tėh**, id.

ėh (C.) **phah-ėh**, = phah-eh (also C.), to belch or hiccup.

ɛh^n (T.), = A. ɛh, interjection of surprise.

ɛ̇h^n, to make a slight sound, as an infant on awaking.

ek [R. to force, grieved, = col. ah]. **ut-ek**, much vexed and grieved. **ek-lėk**, to compel.

ek [R. to increase, to benefit, = col. iah]. **lī-ek**, benefit; profit; advantage; to benefit; to do good to. **ū-lī-ek**, beneficial; useful; advantageous. **bô-lī-ek**, of no use; useless. **bû-ek**, id. **iú-ek**, advantageous; beneficial. **iú-sún bû-ek**, both useless and positively injurious. **chìn-ek**, to make progress in literary excellence. **ek-bú-oân**, pills used for women shortly after confinement.

ek (R. id.) **ek--chhut-lâi**, to spill over, as water; too full; to make a sudden sally or sudden attack. **ek-lâi ek-khì**, to spill (as water), by shaking back and forwards; to surge back and forwards, as a battle, or as a crowd, or as waves. **ek-kè-lâi ek-kè-khì**, to surge

厦英大辭典

back and forwards, as crowd or battle. **ek-lin,** to let milk drop down, as child in sucking.

ek (Cn.) **ek-káu,** = A. é-káu, dumb.

ėk (R. id.), (C. iȧh, Cn. hėk). **un-ėk,** pestilence; epidemic. **un-ėk-pīⁿ,** id. **un-ėk-khì,** miasma; pestilential influence. **un-ėk-kúi,** demons that cause pestilence. **un-ėk-kúi chhut-lâi-iā,** the demons come out scattering the seeds of pestilence. **khu-siâ tiȯk-ėk,** to expel the evil influence that causes pestilence.

ėk [R. secretions]. **bô-chin-ėk,** wanting moisture in throat and mouth, as when slightly feverish. **ū-chin-ėk,** having sufficient moisture in the mouth, so that the voice is good.

ėk [R. a wing, = col. sit]. **tsó-iū-ėk** (R.), the wings of an army. **ėk-tiúⁿ,** an assistant on the general's staff for consultation on plans.

ėk (R. id.) **hoan-ėk,** to interpret.

ėk [R. to change]. **î-ėk,** to alter. **keng-ėk,** id. **thiet-pán put-ėk,** fixed so as not to be changed (as if on iron plates), as purpose or orders. **kau-ėk** (R.), to buy and sell.

chiu-ėk, the Yih-king, = iȧh-keng.

ėk (R. id.) **ėk-jī-thâu,** the 56th radical.

ėk (R. iȯk), (Cn. hėk, ėk). **sóe-ėk,** to bathe by throwing water over the body. **tsâng-ėk,** id. **ėk-tî,** a bath; a bath-room. **bȯk-ėk-têng,** a paper imitation bath-room, used in the rites of "khiā-hà," for worshipping the recently deceased.

ėk (P.), = A. iȯk in some words, *e.g.* lust.

eng [R. hero, excellent], a surname. **eng-hiông,** a hero. **cheng-eng,** lively; intelligent. **bô-cheng-eng,** dull; wearied; having a spiritless look.

tāi-eng-kok, Britain. **eng-kiet-lī** (r.), id. **eng-lê** (Cn.), id.

kim-eng, the large single white rose. **kim-eng-ko,** a black extract from its fruit, used as a medicine, and for adulterating opium.

eng — **sù-eng,** the small white jessamine.

eng [R. a vase or jar]. **eng-sek-hoe,** the poppy (v. sek).

eng — **eng-thô,** a large red fruit (v. thô).

eng [R. an infant, = col. ɛⁿ]. **iȯk-eng-tông,** a foundling hospital. **eng-jî** (R.), an infant.

eng (R. id.) **eng-kai,** ought, should (v. kai).

eng (R. iong), (C. iong), an abscess, carbuncle, or large boil in any place where there are large muscles or sinews; applied also to fistula, &c. **eng-á,** id. **lin-eng,** abscess or cancer in female breast. **leng-eng,** id. **chē-bé-eng,** a large boil or abscess about the division of the legs. **khiâ-bé-eng,** id. **phang-siū-eng,** a large carbuncle or boil opening in many places, esp. on inside of arm or thigh. **siēn-eng,** abscess in the scrotum. **tē-tsâi-eng,** boil near the navel. **té-eng,** an abscess in a fleshy part. **kun-eng,** a boil where the muscles are strong, as on the neck or near a joint.

eng-lāu, fistula in the anus.

eng, flying dust; dust getting into the eyes, or on furniture, &c. **eng-ia,** id. **eng-eng,** all dusty. **eng--khí-lâi,** dust rising and flying about. **eng kàu-àn-niⁿ,** so very dusty. **bȧk-chiu eng,** dust got into the eye. **eng--tiȯh bȧk-chiu,** id. **bȧk-chiu eng-tiȯh-soa,** sand getting into the eye. **eng i-ê-bīn,** dust blowing in his face. **soa eng--lâi,** sand blown in clouds. **phōng-phōng-eng,** flying about in great quantities, as dust. **eng-phōng-phōng,** id. **eng phóng-phóng,** id. **phū-phū-eng,** id.

eng [R. parrot]. **eng-bú,** a parrot. **eng-ko,** id. (s. eagle). **eng-ko-kè,** a torturing machine, used in yamuns. **chiūⁿ eng-ko-kè,** to be tortured on it.

eng (R. id.) **eng-á,** a sparrow.

eng [R. eagle, hawk]. **eng-chiáu,** an eagle; a hawk. **kap-eng,** a sort of hawk or falcon.

eng-ko, a figure of an eagle painted on the stern of a junk (s. parrot). **eng-ko-pîn,** the boarding on stern of junk on which it is painted. **tèng eng-ko-pîn,** to nail that boarding on.

tsoá-eng, a paper kite in the shape of a hawk or eagle; a rough paper figure of a bird thrown or blown about by children. **chih eng-á,** to fold these coarse paper birds for children.

eng-jiáuⁿ-hoe, a very strong-smelling flower of a green colour, shaped like an eagle's claw.

eng (P.), in several tones and words, = A. iong.

êng (R. hân), (T. âiⁿ, Cn. ûiⁿ, C. ân; but P. êng), leisure; at leisure (idle); (what does not concern us). **êng-êng,** at leisure. **êng-sî,** when at leisure. **thàn-êng,** taking the opportunity of having leisure. **êng-jit,** a holiday; a day on which no work is done. **khah-êng sat-bú** (more idle than a louse), I am doing nothing. **bô-êng-kang,** very busy; no leisure; no spare time. **bô-êng,** id.; also, have to go to ease myself. **bô-êng chhih-chhih,** having no leisure at all (v. chhih).

chiáh êng-bī, to live on other people. **êng-sin,** well off, and not needing to do any sort of work. **êng-êng chheng-chheng,** at ease and comfort, with nothing to trouble him. **chheng-êng,** in comfortable circumstances, having a competency; quite free from care and anxiety, and not needing to work. **chheng-chheng êng-êng,** id. **chheng-êng-miāⁿ,** id. **êng-kha bóng-kiâⁿ,** strolling about at leisure. **chin-êng-kha,** id., esp. of going to talk over a matter that is finally settled, having the walk to no purpose. **êng-kha-kut,** id.

êng-lâng, a man who has no connection with the affair in hand; a by-stander. **lē-kièn put-pêng, khì--sí êng-jîn,** injustice so flagrant that passers-by are indignant. **êng-hoân-ló,** unnecessary trouble or anxiety of mind, as in meddling in other people's affairs. **êng-tāi,** other people's matters, that we have nothing to do with. **êng-sū,** id. **chhap-êng-sū,** to meddle with what does not concern us. **hèⁿ-chhap êng-sū,** a meddler. **ài-chhap êng-sū,** id.

êng-ōe, gossip, chat; idle or unimportant talk. **kóng êng-á-ké,** to tell idle stories, and talk empty useless talk. **êng-á-mihⁿ,** superfluities; things of no real use, as curiosities and ornaments. **êng-mihⁿ,** id. **êng-chîⁿ,** unemployed money. **êng-keng,** an empty room, as for guests; a public room (in a village) where people come together idly for talk or play. **êng-keng-á,** such a public room in a village.

êng (C. esp. P.), = A. iông. **êng-īⁿ,** = A. iông-īⁿ, easy.

êng [R. to scheme; a camp, = col. iâⁿ]. **keng-êng,** diligent; actively engaged, as in business for a livelihood. **put-chí keng-êng,** very diligent, as at work.

êng [R. full]. **êng-moáⁿ** (r.), full, as the number of things or days. **la-êng,** too jolly; too fond of idleness, sport, and pleasure, often licentious pleasure (v.

la). **êng-hēng**, behaving in an overbearing and unjust or proud and consequential manner; often said of a proud self-willed child; but (C.), only "rather idle."

êng (R. id.) **êng-kng**, glory, splendour. **êng-hoâ hù-kùi**, very prosperous. **êng-hién** (R.), illustrious. **hién-tsó êng-tsong**, to add glory to one's ancestors, as a high mandarin. **êng-éng, tì koe-mn̂g-chhéng**, boastful and bragging.

éng [R. a shadow, = col. iáⁿ]. **lâi bô-tsong, khì bô-éng**, to come and go without any one knowing. **pē-hong chhiok-éng** (grasp wind and shadows), to take up and spread baseless rumours. **ū-éng-hióng**, to have some foundation in fact (but gen. not much), as a rumour. **éng-hióng iá-bô**, not having the shadow of a foundation, as an utterly baseless rumour or calumny.

siáu-éng, a miniature or small-sized portrait. **khioh siáu-éng**, to draw a small portrait. **tāi-siū siáu-éng**, large and small portraits.

thuh éng-á (T.), = A. thok kéng-á-hì, a play somewhat like a magic lantern.

éng [R. kéng, a landscape; circumstances]. **chhèng-éng**, manifesting great delight by gesticulation or outward manner, when getting power, influence, or great success (said of inferiors).

éng — **êng-éng, tì koe-mn̂g-chhéng**, said of a boastful bragging fellow; lit. wearing a feather dust-brush, as if it were a peacock's feather.

éng [R. to bubble up or dash about, as water], (P. ióng), a wave. **hái-éng**, id. **éng-niāⁿ**, swell on the sea. **toā-éng**, a great wave. **thê-pô-éng**, the great waves in an estuary, esp. when wind and tide are contrary; the bore in a river's mouth. **hong-éng**, wind and waves. **hong-éng thàu**, wind and waves boisterous and stormy. **hong-éng toā**, id. **hong chīⁿ, éng pīⁿ**, wind and waves fallen. **tam-hong tam-éng**, exposed to wind and waves, as a traveller.

khioh-éng, to turn the boat's head to a coming wave. **thìm-éng**, to dip into the waves, as the bow of a boat in rough weather.

éng (R. id.), perpetual; eternal; always. **éng-éng**, id. **éng-oán**, perpetual; eternal. **éng-bô**, never! **éng-ū**, certainly there is or there are.

éng-sî, often or always (in the past). **éng-siông-sî**, id. **éng-nîⁿ**, every year (in the past). **éng-kòe** (C.), usually, over and over (in the past). **éng-kó** (Cn.), id.

èng (R. iòng), (C. iòng). **èng-chhài**, sort of convolvulus grown in water.

èng (R. iòng), to manure. **èng-pùn**, id. **èng-pûi**, id. **èng-chhân**, to manure irrigated fields.

èng [R. to answer, to recompense, to fulfil, = col. ìn]. **èng-báu**, to answer to the roll, as soldiers, &c. **èng-sìn**, to make appearance at a trial, as persons (though not parties) whose names are in the documents (v. sìn). **tah-èng**, to promise verbally. **èng-sêng**, to promise verbally to grant, as a request (v. sêng). **èng-ún**, to promise. **èng-ín**, id.

èng-siû, to hold friendly intercourse by visits or ceremonial presents. **èng-sè**, do., or by proper polite phrases. **èng-chiap**, to receive, as guests or visitors, treating them properly. **chiap-èng**, id.; also, to assist, as a body of fresh soldiers. **ngó-kok hong-sêng, hē-tsúi chiap-èng**, rain and grain abundant.

chiàu-èng, to take care of; to assist; to befriend. **gōe-kong lōe-èng**, treachery within helping the attack from without.

pò-èng, to recompense (as the gods do) by reward or punishment. **lêng-èng**, powerful and able to answer prayers. **kám-èng**, id. **ū-kám-èng**, id. **iú-èng**, id. **iú-kiû pit-èng**, prayer (as to some special divinity) will be answered. **bān-èng-kong**, the spirit of a shrine for tablets that have no posterity. **bān-èng-ko**, a sort of plaster, said to be good for a vast number of diseases.

èng-giām, to fulfil or be efficacious, as prayer or medicine. **èng-hāu**, to be efficacious, to be fulfilled, as a votive prayer.

sûi-sî èng-piàn, to act according to the circumstances. **sûi-ki èng-piàn**, id. **ū-èng-piàn**, good at adapting one's plans and procedure to the circumstances.

èng-hūn, the portion that belongs to a man on the division of an inheritance. **èng-hūn ê-giáp**, id. **èng-hūn ê ke-giáp**, id. **chit-keng sī i--ê èng-hūn**, this house is his portion of the inheritance.

ēng (R. iōng), (C. iōng), to use; to spend; with (with an instrument). **ēng-to koah**, cut with a knife. **ēng-gûn bóe**, to buy with silver. **ēng-pit siá**, to write with a pen or pencil.

lē-ēng, a use. **ū-lē-ēng**, useful. **bô-lē-ēng**, useless. **toā-lē-ēng**, very useful. **ū sím-mihⁿ lē-ēng**, of what use is it? **bōe-ēng--tit**, not fit for the purpose. **m̄-ēng**, will not use it; there is no need of (esp. said in Cn. in place of "m̄-sái").

bô-ēng, it is better not to —; stronger than "m̄-sái," but not so strong as "m̄-thang." **bô ēng** —, not using —. **bô-ēng-lâng** (T.), I am a good-for-nothing man; said politely to mean, I am a plain honest man, and cannot help in bad schemes.

khai-ēng, to spend money; to use money. **hùi-ēng**, id. **sái-ēng** (not in Cn.), expenditure; to use; to spend (money). **thām-ēng**, to use more than our income. **chhim-ēng--lâng**, to embezzle. **lām-ēng**, very lavish of money, as for bad purposes, or of other people's money. **kam-ēng**, not afraid to spend money on proper occasion (v. kam). **káⁿ-ēng**, rather too liberal or lavish. **khiām-ēng**, economical. **kiám-ēng**, to use somewhat less. **séng-ēng**, to use more sparingly; to manage to get on without using so many.

lán ke-ēng--i kúi-ê-chîⁿ, we get a few cash better exchange from him, as by paying in silver instead of in copper cash.

chhe-ēng, to employ as a servant, in general; a servant.

bóng-ēng, only tolerable; middling; will just do, for want of better. **hó-ēng**, good for use. **thong-ēng**, universally current. **iàu-ēng**, to require for use for some special purpose; specially needed; indispensable. **kàu-ēng**, enough for use; having enough to use. **chioh-ēng**, to borrow for use (v. chioh). **hē-teh-ēng**, lay it down to be ready for use, as it is wanted.

ēng-sim, to apply the mind. **ēng-kang**, to work diligently; worked or made with care; carefully.

G.

This initial is often interchanged with **ng** (*q.v.*); very frequently the reading form is in **ng**, while the colloquial is **g**.

gâ [R. a tooth, ivory, = col. gê], (C. gê). **gâ-koan bōe-khui** (the teeth will not open), as in a faint or near death.

gā (R. id.), (Cn.), to suspect; to feel suspicious. **gî-gā**, id.

gâi (R. id.), stupid, foolish. **gâi-chîⁿ**, bad cash. **khò-gâi**, miserably poor. **chhi-gâi**, silly; very dull and stupid; foolish. **gâi-gām-gōng**, very stupid (said in scolding). **gâi-káu** (C.), said of a man who interrupts or browbeats another when speaking, or will not listen to reason.

gāi (R. id.), (T. ngāiⁿ). **ū-kan-gāi**, there is some impediment. **kan-gāi--tio̍h lí**, it may (slightly) involve you. **gāi--tio̍h**, to tend to involve or compromise a man; to affect injuriously. **bô-kan-gāi**, there is no impediment, no danger or obstruction. **bô-gāi**, id. **bô-saⁿ-gāi**, not having any injurious or obstructive influence on each other. **bô-siong-gāi**, not having injurious influence (esp. on good luck); there is no impediment; not hurt, as in a fall.

gāi-gio̍h, feeling uncomfortable. **gāi-ba̍k**, to offend the eye, as some wicked thing. **chhùi-kap-chih ū-sî saⁿ-gāi**, the best friends (like mouth and tongue) sometimes fall out.

koà-gāi, to be anxious about, as a person or affair. **khoà-gāi**, id. **bô-koà-gāi**, there is no danger or impediment; need not be anxious.

ga̍k (R. id.) **ga̍k-hū** (R.), wife's father. **ga̍k-bú** (R.), wife's mother. **lēng-ga̍k** (R.), your wife's father.

ga̍k [R. music]. **ga̍k-khì**, musical instruments. **tāng ké-ga̍k**, to play joyful music. **kìm ké-ga̍k**, to forbid music, as during mourning for the emperor. **hōng-kìm ké-ga̍k**, to receive orders from a superior forbidding the use of music. **lé-ga̍k** (R.), ceremonies and music. **tsok-ga̍k** (R.), to make music with instruments. **ga̍k-koaⁿ**, minister of music in ancient times.

ga̍k [R. a high mountain peak]. the great temple (esp. agricultural) outside the east gate of a city. **tang-ga̍k**, id. **ga̍k--nihⁿ**, id.; in that temple. **ga̍k-kháu**, the door or front of that temple. **lia̍h kàu ga̍k-kháu**, to drag a departed soul to that temple, where giâm-lô-ông judges the dead.

ga̍k-tè, the chief god of the tang-ga̍k temple. **tang-ga̍k-tè**, id. **ga̍k-ông** (C.), id.

ga̍k (C.), = A. ge̍k (a prison), in some phrases. **tē-ga̍k**, hell.

gâm [R. a steep rock or cliff; cf. col. giâm]. **tsâm-gâm**, strong, firm, and well made. **lin-gâm**, an abscess or cancer in the (female) breast. **leng-gâm**, id.

gâm — **n̂g-gâm-gâm**, very yellow, as ripe fruit, &c. **n̂g-gâm n̂g-gâm**, id.

gām, foolish, stupid, as a man. **gām-gām**, id. **gām-siⁿ**, having a stupid manner. **gām-ba̍k**, having a dull unintelligent eye. **tàm-gām**, appearance of dullness and want of ability, *e.g.* head hanging down, &c.

gām, = ngām. **gām-áu-á**, a small sort of fish. **gām-áu-hî**, id.

gân [R. the face], a surname. **gân-sek**, complexion; countenance. **gân-iông**, complexion. **liông-gân** (R.), the face of the emperor; lit. of dragon. **hông-gân, to po̍k-bēng**, beautiful women are often unfortunate.

gân [R. gêng, to congeal], chilly and cold, as weather; cold and benumbed, as hand held long in cold water. **thiⁿ-khì gân-gân**, weather very cold and chilly. **thâu-khak gân**, head cold and chilled. **chhùi-khí gân**, teeth chilled and sore, as with drinking very cold water. **chhiú gân, kha gân**, hands and feet benumbed with cold.

gân (C.), = A. giên (to speak). **gân-gí**, = A. giên-gú, language, talk.

gán [R. the eye; a joint]. **siⁿ-gán**, the joint of a fan. **sí-gán**, a fixed rivet. **oa̍h-gán**, a joint made to allow free motion.

jī-gán, a book-phrase. **chheh-gán**, title-page of a book; title pasted on a book.

póng-gán, the second name on the list of new members of the (Hān-lîm) Imperial Academy. **siang-gán-lêng**, a peacock's feather with two eyes. **chhien-lí-gán** (eye seeing a thousand li), an attendant of the idol Má-tsó-pô.

gán-chiáu, a man more acute, skilful, or daring than others, and fond of meddling in matters, so as to be naturally a leader though not appointed. **kong-gán**, very bright, too sharp for his years, as a lad about eighteen (v. kong "bright"). **hó-gán-sîn**, eye having an appearance of intelligence (v. sîn). **ū-gán-le̍k**, good at discerning good from bad at a glance. **hó-gán-le̍k**, id. **hó-gán-sek**, skilful at discerning by a glance. **gán cheng, chhiú khoài**, eye and hand very quick, as of a thief or juggler. **kò-gán put-tsài**, able to repeat after one reading. **gán-khóng toā**, so proud and haughty as not to salute or notice people; not deigning to speak, &c.

tsùi-gán, eyes naturally having a soft and swimming look, as if drunk (v. tsùi). **gán-lūi** (R.), to shed tears. **sńg-gán**, injurious to the eyes, as late writing or sewing, or some sorts of food. **jî-sun boán-gán**, large posterity seen before death. **khai-gán**, to touch an idol's eyes with the red pigment called "sîn-se," in consecrating it. **khai-gán-tsoá**, yellow paper with rude pictures of horses and chariots, burned to hasten the spirits to come to the sorcerer.

gán-chêng (C. gién-chêng), at present. **gán-chiên**, id.

gán-kiàⁿ, spectacles (v. kiàⁿ). **gán-khe**, eye diseases (v. khe).

gán (C.), = A. géng, to grind in a sort of mortar.

gàn, to cool, as in water, or as by applying a piece of cold iron; to temper. **gàn-tsúi**, to cool or temper in water. **gàn-kǹg**, to temper steel. **gàn-ba̍k**, to cool the eyes, as by a piece of rock-crystal or a cold knife or bit of steel.

gān [R. a sea wall or dyke, = col. hoāⁿ] **po̍k-gān**, a low broad wall or bank built at the foot of a wall or embankment to strengthen or protect its base; the parapet wall of a terrace, as on house-top.

gān (R. id.) **hái-gān**, a sea-goose. **chhiu-gān**,

sort of goose that comes in autumn. **hông-gān**, a sort of sea-bird (said to be used for carrying letters).

kə-gān, a widow or widower (said because the wild-goose is supposed to remain so).

gān — **gān-chí-tsng**, small fine bricks for ornamental work.

gāng (cf. gōng). **gāng-gāng**, having a stupified and bewildered look, as at sudden bad news, or as when unable to reply to a severe rebuke. **gāng-gāng teh-khiā**, standing with a bewildered look.

chhiú gāng-gāng, out of work and having no money.

gap (C. ap), to swallow water, as a fish. **gap-tsúi**, id. **chî^{n} khit--i gap--khì**, to be swindled of money by him.

gâu [R. hiên], (T. gâu, ngâu^{n}), clever; wise; skilful; good at —. **gâu-tsá**, you are early up. **gâu-toā**, growing fast, as boy tall for his age. **gâu-kún**, playing practical jokes or tricks (v. kún). **gâu-lâng**, a wise man. **gâu tsòe-lâng**, polite and kind. **ké-gâu**, to pretend to be clever.

bōe-gâu--tit, the matter is so fixed by Heaven's decree that the most skilful man cannot change it.

gāu (Cn.), = ngāu, fond, as of pleasure.

gê [R. hâ, red clouds, = col. hê], (C. gê). **bīn âng-gê**, face ruddy and healthy-looking.

gê (R. gâi), (T. gô), in great perplexity; mind confused, as with grief, madness, or liquor. **gê soáh-soáh**, in very great perplexity.

gê (Cn.) **gê--lâng**, to act so as to make another displeased. **gê-sí-lâng**, to irritate a man very much.

gê [R. gâ, a tooth], (C. gê), a tusk, as of boar or elephant; ivory.

gê-tsô, the lower jaw (v. tsô). **gê-kam**, a very severe disease of the jaw. **chhoàn-gê**, a very protruding tooth. **gê-khí** (C.), the teeth. **kā-gê chhiet-chhí**, to gnash the teeth in pain or rage.

nńg-gê, to come down in one's talk after being very violent. **lí hèng peh-gê**, you are very fond of opening your jaws (when talking of what should not be mentioned).

gê-lâng, a broker or middleman for small transactions (lit. one who uses his teeth and mouth), esp. for domestic animals. **gê-hâng**, a shop or firm that transacts brokerage. **tsòe-gê--ê**, to be a broker. **ti-á-gê**, a shop or broker's office where pigs are bought and sold. **chhâ-gê**, do. for sale of fire-wood. **gê-chî^{n}**, brokerage or small commission. **thiu gê-chî^{n}**, to take a small percentage for brokerage, as broker or weigher. **khioh gê-chî^{n}**, to levy a small rate on gambling, or opium-shops, &c., as underlings of yamuns do.

toā-gê, the tiller of a helm. **lêng-gê** (lit. dragon's teeth), several upright pins on the bow of a junk, between which the anchor cables run.

gê-jit, the 2d and 16th of each month. **bé-gê**, the 12.16, specially sacred to thó-tī-kong. **toā-gê** (C.), id. **sió-gê** (R.), the 2d and 16th of each month, except the last. **thâu-gê**, the 2.2, birth-day of thó-tī-kong. **tsòe-gê**, to keep the 2d and 16th of each month with worship of mn̂g-kháu-kong.

gê-sek, cream-colour or yellowish-white, like ivory long exposed to the air. **gê-pâi**, dominoes for games of chance. **gê-tī**, ivory chop-sticks. **chhiū^{n}-gê**, ivory; elephant's tusk. **thǹg-gê**, to shed the tusks, as elephant.

gê (C.), **gê-chio**, = **gêng-chio**, the plantain.

gê (R. gâ), (C. gê), a young sprout. **puh-gê**, to sprout. **hoat-gê**, id. **thun-gê**, esculent sprouts of the "thun" tree. **kiu^{n}-gê**, ginger sprouts. **béh-gê**, barley sprouted so that the sprouts and roots are all interlaced, and dried in slices for medicine. **chhek-gê**, dried sprouted rice (med.) **tāu-gê** (C.), = A. tāu-chhài, sprouted peas.

gê-siau, a white medicine.

gê (C.), = A. gôe, a surname.

gê [R. kì; he, she, it], numeral for one article when followed by a fraction; also (Cn.), = A. ê, sign of genitive; classifier of men and some things.

gê-poà^{n}, one and a half. **gê-poà^{n}-chî^{n}**, one copper cash and a half, as in calculating prices. **gê-goā-chî^{n}**, worth a good deal more than one cash. **gê-jī**, 1$\frac{2}{10}$ = 1$\frac{1}{5}$th of anything, esp. of a cash. **gê-jī-chî^{n}**, 1$\frac{1}{5}$th of a cash.

gê-gê (Cn.), one by one; each and every one. **chiḣ--gê** (Cn.), this. **hiḣ--gê** (Cn.), that.

gê (R. gâ), (C. gê). **gê-mn̂g**, a yamun; a mandarin's office, court, and official residence. **koa^{n}-gê**, id. **gê-mn̂g-lâng**, an attendant, assistant, or underling in a mandarin's court. **gê-iàh**, messengers and lower assistants in do. **gê-lāi**, within the yamun. **gê-kháu-tiâ^{n}**, the paved court before the great gate of yamun. **tō-iâ-gê**, the Tau-tai's yamun. **thê-tok-gê**, general's or admiral's yamun.

pâi-gê, to arrange the assistants, &c., to receive the newly arrived mandarin. **pé-gê**, to guard the gate of yamun in the daytime; the door-keeper of yamun. **khiā-gê-mn̂g**, to be on duty staying in yamun of naval mandarin (as some of the marines).

gè (C.) **chhun-chhiú, bô hē-gè**, having no money or property.

gē (R. id.) **kang-gē**, handicraft. **chhiú-gē**, a handicraft or art. **tsòe gē-niū^{n}**, to do a bit of work half for amusement to pass the time. **tsò-gē** (C.), to idle about, as child at play, or as idle fellow pretending to work. **sù-tsú chhien-kim, put-jû kàu-tsú it-gē**, better teach your son one trade than give him a thousand pieces of silver.

gē (C. gē). **ū-gē**, the anchor taking hold of the ground; the anchor home; to be glad and pleased, as at getting some favour we had asked, or as looking at curious or interesting things (this last sense esp. C.) **tāi-chì gē--lah**, the parties are now willing and the object attained. **pha-bô-gē**, the anchor will not catch. **bōe-gē**, id. **bô-gē**, id.; also feeling ashamed and displeased, as at failing to get an expected favour, or losing hope of success, or at meeting one whom we wished to avoid; feeling of ennui in bad weather with no amusement (these last senses esp. C.) **phah--lâng bô-gē**, to make a man feel quite ashamed, as by disrespect or scolding, or taking no notice of him, or refusing what he confidently expected. **thun bô-gē-oân** (swallow a bitter pill), to feel very much ashamed at want of success. **bô-gē-oân**, id. **phái^{n}-gē** (C.), unpleasant state of feeling, as when a man gets angry with us without cause, or insists on paying for a gift or favour.

tòng-bōe-gē, opposition utterly unsuccessful. **kóng bōe-gē**, utterly unsuccessful in a request.

gē, to rub very smooth the second time, so as to polish (as wood, horn, or ivory). **ûn-á gē**, to rub and polish very carefully so as to polish. **kè-gē**, very well polished.

gē — **léng-gē**, to speak sarcastically or ironically to a man.

gē (C.) **toā-gē** (= A. koh), a large frame with incense and boys dressed as girls, carried in idolatrous processions. **gē-pē**ⁿ, id. **gē-toàⁿ**, the boys dressed as girls who sit on it. **tsng-gē**, to make up and ornament this frame. **ngiâ-gē**, to carry it in procession.

ū chhut-chîⁿ, bô kng-gē (A.), to subscribe money, but get no fame or advantage from it (lit. and not carry the ornamental frame).

geh (T.), = A. giet (C. gėh), to joke roughly at a person.

gėh (= khėh). **gėh-gėh-tiō**, to shiver, as from cold or fear.

gėh (R. goa̍t), (C. gòeh, T. Cn. gȫh), the moon; a month. **gėh-niûⁿ**, the goddess of the moon.

gėh-pėh, white with a slight bluish tinge. **gėh-sek**, id.

âng-gėh, the bull's-eye of a target (red), often three of them perpendicularly. **gėh-toh**, a round table. **gėh-thang**, a round window. **gėh-pó**, an axe with a convex semicircular edge. **gėh-khîm**, a sort of stringed musical instrument.

jit-gėh, sun and moon; days and months (v. jit). **nîⁿ-gėh**, years and months (v. nîⁿ). **gėh-kè-gėh**, from month to month.

siⁿ-gėh, the month of one's birth. **théh siⁿ-gėh**, to get the horoscope (poeh-jī) of the proposed bride or bridegroom. **phoà-gėh**, the cyclical name of natal month disagreeing seriously with the name of the year; if a girl, it has a deadly effect when married on her husband; if a boy, it will have a deadly effect on his wife's relations, therefore not so important! **gėh-lēng**, the cyclical name of a month (for divination), consisting of two characters, the first varying with the year, the second fixed for the same month in all years.

khiā-gėh, the bride spending some days (or a month) with her parents soon after marriage. **sūn-gėh**, within a month before the time of child-birth. **moáⁿ-gėh**, one month after confinement. **gėh-lāi**, within a month after confinement; also (in general), within the month. **gėh-lāi-lâng**, a woman within the month after confinement. **gėh-lāi-pâng**, the room where the child was born, so called during the first month only. **gėh-lāi-hong**, the woman's sickness in that season. **tsai i--ê gėh-lāi, phah i--ê pâng-mn̂g** (knowingly to knock at the door of that room in that month), to talk to a man's face of his secret faults or shame. **gėh-keng**, the menstrual discharge.

gėh-chhoe, the first ten days of a month. **gėh-thâu**, the beginning or first part of a month. **gėh-bé**, the last few days of month, about 26th to end. **gėh-poàⁿ**, about 14th, 15th, or 16th. **gėh-poàⁿ-jit**, a month and a half. **chhit-gėh-poàⁿ**, the middle of the seventh month, 7. 15, = tiong-goân (v. chhit). **n̄ng-gėh-jit**, a period of two months long. **jī-gėh**, the second month of the year. **chiaⁿ-gėh**, the first month. **lūn-gėh**, an intercalary month. **lūn-gō-gėh**, intercalary month just after the fifth month, usually called "intercalary fifth month." **toā-gėh**, a month in which a great deal of business is done. **gėh toā**, the month has thirty days. **gėh sòe**, the month has 29 days. **chit-gėh sī-toā á-sòe**, has this month 30 or 29 days?

gėh chiūⁿ, the moon ascending. **gėh tng-kiā**, moon at zenith. **gėh tiong-kiā**, id. **gėh tùi-tiong**, id. **gėh chhiâ**, moon about to set. **sit-gėh**, eclipse of moon. **gėh tńg-îⁿ**, the moon become round again after eclipse (it is counted lucky to see this). **gėh îⁿ**, the moon full. **gėh-pêng**, half-moon. **gėh-bâi**, crescent moon, at first or last. **gėh-hoâ**, sort of lunar halo of five colours (a spirit is supposed to be in it bestowing blessings). **gėh ûi-khơ**, the moon has a halo of usual kind. **gėh tì-lòeh**, a small circle of clouds round the moon. **gėh ûi-khơ, khit-hō ak; tì-lòeh, khit-jit phák**, the one get drenched with rain, the other get scorched by the sun. **gėh hoáⁿ**, the moon giving little light, either small or clouded. **gėh-hoáⁿ-á**, id. **gėh-àm-miⁿ**, a moonless night. **gėh-iáⁿ**, shadow from moon; moonlight on water, &c. **siúⁿ-gėh**, to gaze at the bright moon.

gėh (C. gòeh, T. gȫh). **chhin-chiâⁿ gō-gėh** (C. chhin-chhek gơ-gòeh), relations, connections, friends, and neighbours. **bô-chhin-chiâⁿ gō-gėh**, having no relatives or friends. **kóng tsáp-tsoh gō-gȫh** (T.), to talk in an involved way about a great many matters, esp. to avoid directly answering an inconvenient question.

gėh (C.), cf. A. giet, giȯh (T. geh). **giȯh-gėh** (C.), to taunt, or jest and jeer at.

gėk (R. id. = col. khėh), to rebel, disobey, or offend seriously. **gėk-hong**, wind contrary. **hêng-gėk**, perverse; very wicked. **pōe-gėk**, to rebel against. **ngó-gėk**, disobedient to parents. **bê-hoán tāi-gėk**, rebellion and treason.

gėk-thien, to offend against Heaven. **gėk-lí**, to transgress Heaven's laws. **gėk-chí**, to disobey the imperial orders. **liông-iȯh khó-khó; tiong-giên gėk-níⁿ**, good medicine is bitter; faithful words offend the ear.

gėk (R. giȯk), (C. giȯk), jade-stone. **pó-gėk**, very precious jade. **ké-gėk**, false jade. **chhài-gėk**, id. **sơ-gėk**, fine white jade with a slightly yellowish tinge. **âng-gėk**, red jade.

gėk-áh, a casket made of jade-stone. **gėk-khì**, articles made of jade.

gėk-chiam-hoe, a sort of lily (v. chiam).

gėk [R. giȯk, a prison], (C. giȯk, gȧk). **lô-gėk**, a prison. **kaⁿ-gėk**, id. **gėk-koaⁿ**, a small mandarin who has charge of a high mandarin's prison. **chē-gėk**, to lie in prison. **kùiⁿ-gėk** (Cn.), to imprison. **liēn-gėk**, purgatory.

tē-gėk, hell. **tē-gėk-siâⁿ**, id. **tōe-gėk** (Cn.), id. **lòh tē-gėk**, to go to hell. **kè tē-gėk**, to pass through hell (Buddhist). **phah tē-gėk**, to deliver a soul from hell, as Buddhist priests do. **khui tē-gėk-mn̂g**, to open its gates (on 7. 1) to let the ghosts out for a month. **koaiⁿ tē-gėk-mn̂g**, to shut them in again on last day of seventh moon.

gėk (Cn.), = A. jiȯk, a cushion, &c.

gêng (R. id.), to coagulate; to lie heavy on the stomach. **gêng chit-tè**, coagulate into a mass. **gêng chit-oán**, feeling of indigestion like a ball on the stomach. **chiáh--liáu, gêng--leh**, id. after eating. **gêng tī-sim-koaⁿ-thâu**, id. **huih gêng--teh**, blood coagulated, as when shed. **hiet-khì gêng--leh**, blood supposed to be internally coagulated, and not acting properly, as in tumours, &c. **huih-khì gêng--teh**, id.

gêng (C. gê). **gêng-chio**, the plantain; the banana (v. chio).

gêng [R. liông, a dragon]. **gêng-géng**, the dragon's eye, or lung-yen fruit (v. géng). **gêng-á-koaⁿ** (C.), dried lung-yen.

gêng [R. to receive ceremoniously]. **gêng-sin**,

khì-kiū (R.), to take to the new and forsake the old, as a fickle-minded man. **jîn gêng hù-kùi chhun**, man receives wealth and prosperity like spring (from heaven).

géng [R. gán, the eye], (T. gái^n, Cn. güi^n, C. kán, kéng). **gêng-géng**, the dragon's eye, or lung-yen fruit (Dimocarpus Longan!). **hok-géng**, a large sort. **liú-á-géng**, a small sort. **gêng-géng-koe**, a beautiful insect somewhat like a butterfly. **lêng-kéng-ke** (C.), id. (v. ke).

géng (R. gién), (T. ngái^n, Cn. ngüi^n, C. gán, gién), to grind with a wheel in a mortar; to roll out, as dough; to roll and polish smooth, as cloth; to press or mould with finger or palm, as a swelling to be reduced.

géng-poah, a long trough-shaped sort of mortar. **géng-tsô**, do. **géng-lûn**, the wheel worked in the trough. **géng-thûi**, a roller for dough; a sort of pestle. **géng-chioh**, a large smooth stone for pressing and polishing cotton cloth. **géng-pè-chioh**, id. **géng-pè**, to press and polish cloth, by two men standing on the two ends of the stone, by a see-saw motion. **géng-ioh**, to grind medicine in a trough. **géng-boah**, to grind to powder. **géng-iù**, id. **géng-mi^n**, to roll out dough into thin cakes. **géng-piá^n**, id.

ûn-á géng-chhut, gradually get out facts more and more fully after the clue has been found.

toà-teh-géng, standing deriding or jesting at people.

géng-tn̄g, to sunder, by working the hand or some instrument back and forwards; to bite asunder, by moving the teeth or toothless gums back and forwards. **bóng-géng**, barely manage to bite it with toothless gums, as old man or child.

gēng [R. id. by change of tone from "gêng," to receive ceremoniously]. **chhin-gēng**, to go to the bride's house in person to take away his bride, as bridegroom does if he wishes to show great respect for his relatives.

gēng — **gēng-chio**, better gêng-chio, the plantain (v. chio).

gî [R. ceremony], a small ceremonial present or fee. **chit-ê-gî**, do., especially at betrothal. **chit-pau-gî**, do. in silver. **sàng lé-gî**, to make the ceremonial presents, as at betrothal. **phèng-gî**, presents to bride's parents from bridegroom's parents.

tsoeh-gî, presents made to a teacher at some of the terms. **kiō-gî**, hire of sedan for teacher, paid by scholars; sometimes do. for friend. **hō-gî**, a congratulatory present. **sîn-gî**, presents to Kujin on going to the capital, and such like.

sit-gî, to fail in ceremony proper to a superior. **ui-gî** (R.), dignified manner, causing reverence or awe.

gî (R. pî, id.) **gî-pê**, the loquat or pîpê fruit (v. pê).

gî (R. pî, id.) **gî-pê**, a four-stringed guitar, shaped like the loquat (v. pê).

gî (C.), = A. gû, a surname.

gî (C.), = A. gû, foolish.

gî — **gî-pân** (T.), = A. tók-pân, a bright green sort of bettle.

gî (C.), = A. gû, to catch fish (R.)

gî — **gî-gê**, a thorny shrub (v. gê).

gî (R. id.), to doubt; to suspect. **gî-ngâi**, id. **giâu-gî**, id. **gî-hêk**, id. **tî-gî** (R.), to have suspicions or doubts so as to delay; very uncertain in purpose, not knowing how to act. **tì-gî**, to have suspicions or distrust. **gî-gā**, to suspect; to be suspicious. **chhai-gî** (R.), id. **to-gî**, full of suspicions. **gî-tang gî-sai**, id. **gî-sîn gî-kúi**, id. **hâm-gî**, to harbour suspicion. **toà-gî**, id. **tài-gî**, id. **koà-gî**, id. **gî-sim**, suspicious mind. **gî-sim tāng**, suspicions rising in the mind. **gî seng-koài**, suspicion makes one more and more suspicious (v. koài). **poà^n-sìn poà^n-gî**, half believing, half doubting. **chiong-sìn chiong-gî**, id. **khó-gî**, suspicious, as affair. **hoān-gî**, to be suspected. **kièn-gî**, id.

bô-gî-gē, unexpectedly; before one is aware or has any thought of it.

chhi^n-gî, nauseated, as at bad taste; ready to vomit; suddenly taken aback and suspicious of danger.

gî [R. right, ought]. **háp-gî**, proper, right, as it should be. **lông-tām tek-gî** (R.), dress just proper, not shabby or gaudy.

kiā^n-gî, behaviour. **in-sî chè-gî**, to fit one's actions to the circumstances.

pan-gî, cheap, a good bargain. **pan-gî--lâng**, to insult a man, or scold him violently when he dares not retort. **chiàm--lâng pan-gî**, to act in an overbearing way. **chiàm-pan-gî ê-lâng**, a man who acts so. **tok--lâng pan-gî**, to cheapen too much, to drive too hard a bargain. **tàu-pan-gî**, to undersell.

lióng-gî, the Yin and Yang (im-iông), especially as represented by a circle divided into two equal halves, of different colours, by a wavy line made by two semi-circles meeting at the centre.

gî-lí-sī (C.), certainly ought to be —; surely will —; should exert yourself to —. **gî-lí-sī tioh àn-nē^n** (C.), indeed you should do so.

gí (C.), = A. gú, talk, words. **gân-gí**, = A. giên-gú, id.

gí [R. to give judgment, to sentence]. **gí-tsōe**, to pronounce sentence; to condemn to punishment. **gí sí-tsōe**, to condemn to death. **gí-ká**, to sentence to be strangled. **gí-liû**, condemn to banishment, &c. **gí-tiā^n**, to give sentence. **gí tiā^n-tioh**, id.

pí-gí (R.), to compare.

gī [R. gōe, handicraft]. **tsòe-gī-niū^n**, to make things just to pass the time or for amusement.

gī [R. intimate friendship]. **kiet-gī**, to form sworn friendship and alliance, as persons. **kiet-gī hia^n-tī**, sworn brothers. **gī-heng-tē**, id. **sè-gī**, allied for several generations, as families. **ū-sè-gī**, id.

gī [R. to discuss or consult]. **gī-chhú**, to discuss and arrange a dispute, as third party by his good offices. **it-jîn tì, put-jû lióng-jîn gī**, one man's wisdom is not so good as two men's consultation. **siong-gī**, to discuss or talk over a matter together. **gī-lūn** (r.), id. **àm-gī** (r.), to consult secretly, as conspirators.

pē-gī, the decision of any one of the Supreme Boards (liòk-pē) on a matter sent to them by the emperor for consideration and to be reported on.

gī — **gī-gī**, pleased and happy appearance, almost laughing. **gī-gī-chhiò**, to laugh in a grinning manner; to titter.

gī (= gih). **gī-gī-chhoah**, to tremble, to shake with fear.

gī (C.), = A. gū, to lodge. **gī-sé**, = A. gū-sé, a lodging, esp. of students come to examinations.

gī (C.), = A. gū, imperial.

gī (C.), = A. gū, to meet.

gī (R. id.), justice, gratefulness; (free, as school), (adopted, as relative), (meaning, as of book).

jîn-gī, benevolence and justice. **jîn-gī lé-tì-sìn**, the five cardinal virtues. **kong-gī**, just. **thien-hā**

海上絲綢之路文獻集成　科技與文化编

厦英大辭典

kong-gī, universally regarded right and proper. **put-gī**, unjust, unfair. **tiong-gī**, upright, just, and faithful, esp. of mandarin to sovereign. **tiong-sîn gī-sū**, faithful ministers and literati who act rightly. **chheng-gī** (X.), to justify, to pronounce righteous. **gī-lí**, the principles of justice; the meaning, as of a book.

ì-gī, the meaning, as of a book.

gī-thióng, a free burying-ground. **gī-chhiúⁿ**, a place where coffins are given gratuitously. **gī-óh**, a free-school. **gī-chhng**, a public granary. **gī-bîn**, volunteers. **gī-ióng**, id.

khí-gī, to propose and take the lead, as in a subscription, or in some enterprise. **gī-khì**, readiness to assist relatives or persons in distress, or to requite favours (dist. ngīⁿ-khì).

ū-gī, grateful, as to friend or benefactor; showing thankfulness by trying to requite favours. **ū-chêng-gī**, id. **ū-chêng ū-gī**, id. **káu ū-gī**, the dog is grateful to his master. **bô-gī**, ungrateful, unthankful, and forgetful of favours. **bô-chêng-gī**, id. **hớ bô-gī**, the tiger is utterly devoid of gratefulness. **ka-tsui bô-gī**, the turtle-dove is ungrateful (v. tsui). **a iú hoán-pē chi-gī**, the crow shows gratitude (to its parent) by carrying food. **put-chí liām-gī**, manifesting much gratefulness for favours done to self or parents, &c. **pōe-gī**, to act ungratefully; not requiting kindness. **bōng-un pōe-gī**, id. **ke-un hū-gī**, id.

gī-tsú, a sort of adopted son. **gī-hū**, a sort of adoptive father.

gī-hiaⁿ, the paramour of a bad woman, or a sodomite.

giâ [R. gâ, a tooth], (C. hâ). **giâ-lan**, crimson (v. lan).

giâ — **lâ-giâ**, a large spider, like tarantula. **lâ-giâ-si**, its web. **lâ-giâ-mơ̍hⁿ**, the white woolly film that incloses the eggs of that spider, used as application to a sore skin.

giâ (R. gô), = gô, a goose, in general. **giâ-kak**, a gander.

giâ (C. An.), = A. iâ, the cocoa-nut.

giâ (R. ngơ̂). **giâ-kang**, the centipede (s. carry). **hái-giâ-kang**, a marine insect like a centipede.

giâ-kang-bāng, to mend a tear by cross-stitches. **giâ-kang-thui**, a ladder made of one long piece of wood, with steps nailed on it and projecting on each side. **giâ-kang-chháu**, a sort of fern. **giâ-kang-ông**, an idol. **giâ-kang-kha**, pointed poles at stern of junk, for keeping off pirates. **giâ-kang-khí** (lit. teeth), a long wavy cavity in a door, made so as to allow the bolt to be fastened or opened from the outside. **giâ-kang-pîⁿ**, a long narrow jointed flexible platform that can wind through narrow crooked streets, used in incense processions.

khí-giâ-kang, a severe disease of the gums (v. khí, "tooth").

giâ (T. kiâ, Cn. kâ), to carry a large bulky thing (as a chair) with both hands (sometimes resting also on the shoulder); to raise up (as boat aground) by pushing backwards with one's back; to raise the lid of a pot or kettle, as the steam does when boiling violently; to wear, as the cangue; to get the help of an influential person to assist our cause.

giâ-kang, coolies carrying heavy things with both hands, each separately (s. centipede). **giâ-khui**, to lift out of the way, as a chair. **giâ--teh**, carrying a heavy thing (as above). **giâ-teh**, pressed down by the weight of the heavy thing carried so.

giâ-kê, to wear the cangue. **giâ-í-kê**, to carry a chair by putting one's head into it from below. **giâ-kiō**, to carry an empty sedan, as one man.

khì ài-giâ--khí-lâi, feeling in throat like a slight coughing or tendency to bring up phlegm. **sēng-ti giâ-tsàu**, a pig allowed to have its own way burrows under the cooking place (v. tsàu).

giâ jîn-bēng, falsely charge a man with responsibility for a death. **giâ sè-thâu**, to get the help of an influential man, as in a yamun; or to use one's own power or influence. **giâ sè-kờ**, id.

giâ (R. gêng), = ngiâⁿ (*q.v.*), to go in an idolatrous procession, &c.

giah (R. kek), (T. Cn. kiah), to extract, as a thorn or splinter; to pick out, as stitches; to take out, as the entrails of fish after cutting open.

giah-khui, to open a small thing by leverage. **giah-phoà**, to open, as a small boil by a lancet. **giah lâng-huih**, to let out blood and matter from a small boil by puncturing. **giah-chhì**, to extract a thorn. **giah bát-sat**, to take out bugs from a crevice, as with knife. **giah mn̂g-chhoàⁿ**, to pick open a door-bolt. **giah mn̂g-sui**, to part the hair on a woman's forehead.

giah-pan, to puncture the spots of the fever called "chhut-pan."

giȧh, = kiȧh. **giȧh-thâu**, to lift up the head.

giȧh, the proper quantity, complement, or number of men or things. **giȧh-siàu**, id. **siàu-giȧh**, id. **kàu-giȧh**, enough. **chin kàu-giȧh**, well, that *is* quite enough!—said on meeting with something quite unexpected and unpleasant. **chiok-giȧh**, enough. **goân-giȧh**, the original quantity (as of money or things) or state (as of health). **hȧp-giȧh**, just the thing; it just suits. **hūn-giȧh**, the fit allotted portion, as of property or duty.

giȧh-goā, a petty officer, like a sergeant, between "goā-úi" and "hāu-iōng;" more than is necessary; out of one's proper business.

chē-giȧh, to bear the responsibility for a payment. **tsāi-giȧh**, to be regularly engaged, as assistant.

hó-giȧh, rich. **ū hó-giȧh-tóe**, to be of a rich family. **ū-giȧh**, rich. **khoàⁿ--liáu ū-giȧh**, on looking at it there seems a great deal, as something loosely wrapped up, or larger than we expected. **bô-giȧh**, poor; not enough; not sufficient. **khui-bô-giȧh**, unable to account fully for the money intrusted to us. **khui-khòng bô-giȧh**, to embezzle or spend funds improperly without entering it on the books, so that a deficit appears that cannot be accounted for. **khai-khong bô-giȧh**, id.

lâng-giȧh, the complement or number of men. **tìn nn̄g-lâng ê-giȧh**, to take up the space or place of two men. **beh-phài kúi-lâng-giȧh**, for how many men will you make provision? **ke-phài chit-lâng-giȧh**, make provision for one man more.

phài-giȧh, to make provision for, as for a specified number. **phài i-ê-giȧh**, to make provision for him.

joā-tsōe keng-giȧh, how many rooms? **khêng gûn-giȧh**, to count up carefully how to account for money intrusted to us, so as to balance right (v. khêng). **sǹg-giȧh**, to count the number, as of things; to count how many; to include (as an item) in the calculation, esp. of something faulty or inferior that might have been left out of count.

that-giȧh, to fill a place, as a substitute; to make up for loss or damage, as money or other article; to supply such a vacancy or deficiency. **pó-giȧh**, id.

tî-giàh, id. (v. tî). tú-giàh (C.), id. tàu-oáⁿ-giàh, to use some inferior bowls to make up a set; said also fig. of men or things in general.

giak — chhơ-giak-giak, very coarse.

giàk (cf. giòh, gèh), to make jokes at a man who has met with some misfortune or failed in some endeavour; to make game of. kóng-giàk, to talk ironically or sarcastically.

giàk (C.), = A. giòk (R.), cruel; tyrannical.

giâm (R. id.), rigid, stern, strict; a surname. giâm-hàt, rigid, stern, strict. giâm-kín, rigidly careful; very strict in a matter. ui-giâm, majestic, stern, dignified. giâm-lē (R.), too dignified and stern in manner.

ka-giâm (R.), my father. giâm-hū chhut hàu-tsú, a strict father makes obedient children. giâm koaⁿ-hú chhut kāu-chhàt, a severe mandarin makes robbers abound.

giâm (R. iâm), a surname. giâm-lô-ông, the judge of the dead, or emperor of Hades. giâm-lô, id. giâm-lô-n̂g, id. giâm-lô thien-tsú, id. giâm-kun, id. (the Indian Yama).

giâm (R. id.), a mountain temple, esp. at a cave. soaⁿ-giâm, id. giâm-īⁿ, id.

giám, a cluster of fruit (as grapes or lung-yen) or of flowers. chit-giám-á, a small cluster of them.

giám (R. id.), giám-ngīⁿ, strong, brave, lusty, as a strong young man; stiff, as a bamboo or piece of wood. giám-jiên, like as; as if.

giām (R. id.), to make official examination, search, or inspection. giām-khoàⁿ, id. khàm-giām, id. tsa-giām, id. kè-giām, to be officially examined, &c.; to have an official inspection.

èng-giām, to fulfil; to accomplish, as prayer, prophecy, or medicine. lêng-giām, able to answer prayers. hāu-giām, to be efficacious, as medicine, prayers, or superstitious rites.

giām-si, to hold an inquest on a corpse. giām-siong, officially examine a wound. giām chhiⁿ-siong, to examine fresh wounds officially. giām siong-hûn, examine wounds more or less healed. giām-hè, to examine goods, as customs officers. giām-tsûn, examine a vessel, as customs. giām-hiông, id. giām-hong, to examine the seal of a package of government money on its way to see if it be sealed safe. giām-toaⁿ, a certificate given by customs officer stating the amount of goods found on board. sè-giām-toaⁿ, id.

gian (in several tones), better gien (*q.v.*)

giang (R. gien). súi giang-giang, very pretty.

giang (R. gien). giang-á, a small hand-bell used by priests, &c. sai-kong-giang, sort used by Tauist priests. gin-gong-giang, sound of such a bell. gin-giang, id.

giáng (C.), = A. gióng (R.), to look up.

giàng, projecting, as a tooth, or as a nail not driven home, or as rocks on a hill or out of the water. giàng-giàng, id.

giàp (R. id.), property; heritable or landed property. keng-giàp, diligent, industrious. sū-giàp, property enjoyed in turn by relations on condition of performing ancestral rites (from "sū," sacrificial offering). sū-giàp (R.), occupation, business, profession (from "sū," business). su-giàp, private property. kong-giàp, property held in common. ke-giàp, property. ki-giàp, heritable property (v. ki). û-giàp, paternal or ancestral inheritance. tsó-giàp, ancestral property. chhân-giàp, landed property. sán-giàp, property, estate.

giàp-tsú, the owner of a property. pun-giàp, to divide a property, as among heirs. hak-giàp, to buy a property. bóe-giàp, id. hùi-giàp, to waste an inheritance. kièn-kong lip-giàp, to obtain wealth and estate by one's own exertions.

giàp — giàp-miāⁿ, toilsome, wretched, ill-fated life. giàp-chè, miserable life as recompense for great wickedness in a former life. hong giàp, the wind very unfavourable.

giat, giàt. better, giet, giêt (*q.v.*)

giâu (R. id.), the ancient emperor Yau or Yaou. giâu-sùn, Yaou and Shun, the two great ancient emperors. giâu-sūn, id. giâu-thien sùn-jit, the golden age of Yau and Shun.

giâu — giâu-gî, to doubt, to suspect. hoān-giâu, suspected; raising suspicions. tâu-á giâu, one die lying on the top of another when thrown in gambling.

giauh (cf. ngiáu). giauh-giauh-háu, to say the same thing over and over, as a troublesome fellow.

giên (esp. T.), = kiên, to congeal.

giên (T.), = A. gîn, to give an angry look with the eyes.

giên [R. language; to speak], (C. gûn). tâm-giên, to chat (v. tâm). iâu-giên, idle talk and false rumours (v. iâu). loān-giên, to talk at random. kék-giên (R.), extremely strong form of expression, generally somewhat exaggerated. kó-lâng-giên, a saying of the ancients.

ngó-giên-si, odes in lines of five syllables or words. chhit-giên-si, odes in lines of seven syllables.

bô-giên-sû, not good at speaking (v. sû). giên thèng, kè chiông, words obeyed and plans followed. giên tiōng, your advice is much valued; advice followed or attended to. giên kheng, I fear my words are light and will not be attended to (often politely said in self-depreciation); our advice not followed. goá-ê-giên khin, id.

giên-gú (C. gûn-gí), language, talk, idle talk. giên-gú put-tông, language different. kāu-giên-gú, fond of talking very much, as a tattler. chhien-giên bān-gú, a vast deal of talk. siⁿ-giên tsō-gú, to invent false reports. chhòng-giên tsō-gú (R.), id. iá-giên tòk-gú, vile abusive language. òe-giên tòk-gú (R.), id.

sia-chioh bién-giên, no credit given here (v. bién). khó-chhut tāi-giên (R.), speaking very proud boastful words. it-giên hòng-chhut, sù-má lân-tui, four horses cannot catch a word once uttered. giên-to pit-sit, among many words some mistake is sure to occur.

gién [R. gán, the eye]. gién-chêng (C.), = A. bàk-chêng, at present.

gién (C.), = A. géng, to grind in a sort of long mortar.

gién [R. lién, liám, the face]. siáu-phí-gién, very mean, despicable, and niggardly, so as to insist on every cash.

gièn, craving for indulgence of some low appetite; lean. gièn-gièn, id. sán-gièn, very lean; skin and bone. ài-gièn, feeling the terrible craving. kè-gièn, to get over the craving, as by indulgence or by medicine. sùh-gièn, broken down and low-spirited.

厦英大辭典

a-phièn-gièn, terrible craving for opium; opium horrors, esp. of an emaciated smoker. **hun-gièn**, id. **gièn a-phièn**, feeling the opium horrors. **gièn-hun**, do.; having a strong craving for a smoke. **gièn-chiú**, having a strong craving for intoxicating liquor. **gièn tsa-bó**, feeling strong sexual impulse, as man. **gièn-kiáu**, feeling a strong craving for gambling.

giēn — **tsùi-giēn-giēn**, quite drunk. **sòng-giēn-giēn** (esp. T.), extremely poor.

giet (R. iet). **giet-á**, a scorpion. **giet-lá**, id. **giet-á-thâng**, id.

giet [R. to eat up]. **hē-lí bōe-giet--tit**, will not let you swallow the money you expect to get out of him.

giet (esp. T.), = giėt, to joke and jest at a man. **giet--lâng**, to joke ironically at a man's appearance, or at what he has done; to jibe at him. **giet--lâng phiet--lâng**, to speak contemptuously or insultingly to an inferior, so that he is put to shame; to scold severely. **phiet-phiet giet-giet**, to talk on in a scolding way. **phiet kàu-giet**, to scold violently.

giėt (T. giet), to jest or jibe at a man. **giėt-siet**, id. **giėt-siet ê-ōe**, such talk (cf. next word).

giėt (R. id.), very wicked or vicious. **giėt-ōe**, talk about vile lascivious matters. **giėt-tiāu**, a very bad omen. **giėt-būt**, you vile wretch! **giėt-thiok**, you vicious brute! said in scolding a very wicked boy or girl. **iau-giėt**, how monstrously wicked! said in scolding a very bad boy, or at something very extraordinary, unexpected, and unaccountably bad. **tsok-giėt**, to act very wickedly. **tsū-tsok-giėt**, to bring death on one's self by great wickedness. **tsōe-giėt**, great crime. **giėt-tsú**, a wild wicked boy, precocious in lust or crime. **giėt-tsú thiàu-hàn**, a wild, idle, ill-behaved boy. **giėt-tsú-kiáⁿ**, you wicked mischievous boy! **ok-chhe giėt-tsú, bû-hoat khó-tī**, wicked wife and sons, whom we cannot rule or restrain.

giėt — **giėt-kièn**, to play shuttle-cock.

gih (cf. khih, nglhⁿ). **gih-gih-chhoah**, to tremble, as with fear. **gih-gih-tsùn**, do., or with cold or sickness.

gih [R. kû, lean, = col. khih, ngiàuhⁿ]. **sán-gih-gih**, very lean. **sòng-gih-gih**, very poor.

gîm (R. id.), to sing, esp. in a sort of chant, with a very long loud note at the end. **gîm-si**, to chant odes.

gîm — **tîm-gîm**, to think silently and deeply, as in planning something.

gîm (R. id.) **gîm-kîⁿ**, the long broad stone step like a basement running along one or more sides of a house. **gîm-koe**, id. **gîm-ke** (C.), id. **chiȯh-gîm**, id. **gîm-ē**, in front of that stone step. **gîm-khàm-ē** (C.), id. **gîm-chiȯh**, the stones of that long broad step.

gím, to talk over a man by specious talk, *e.g.* to buy too dear, or what he does not need, or so as to do something to his own injury. **kap--lâng poâⁿ-chhùi-gím**, to have a good deal of discussion and dispute about a matter.

gím — **tsúi-gím**, a beautiful flower (sort of mallow?) **sàu-chiú-gím**, a white flower.

gím (Cn. kím), flowered silk. **chit-gím**, to weave flowered silk. **siȯk-gím**, flowered silk from Sze-chuen. **gím-tiû**, flowered silk. **gím-siù**, flowered and embroidered silk. **náⁿ gím-siù**, like them (said of a fine essay). **lîn-lô gím-siù**, splendid silks and satins. **gím-sim siù-khó**, fine mind and accomplished mouth. **tsō gím-lông**, to make a shrewd guess of the future (v. lông, a bag). **gím-tún**, a rich silk cushion, used at court by privileged ministers. **gím-siōng thiam-hoa** (flowers added to flowered silk), said of very great wealth or literary talent. **má-siōng gím-i hôe**, to return on horseback wearing flowered silks, as a high literary graduate.

gím-ló, a savoury bowl of mixed meats. **gím-ló-tiàm**, an eating-house where it is sold. **tsȧp-gím**, an inferior sort. **tsȧp-gím-thng**, this sort with its soup. **pièn-tē-gím**, a small plant like clover, often round the roots of pot-flowers. **gím-tsoâ**, a variegated harmless snake, used in mèdicine.

gím, to grasp; to take in the hand.

gīm — **n̂g-gīm-gīm** (T.), very yellow, as fruit.

gin — **gin-gong-giang**, sound of small bells or jingling ornaments. **gin-giang**, id.

gîn (Cn. gûn, T. giên), to frown and look with the white of the eye. **bȧk-chiu gîn**, id. **gîn--goá**, to look so at me.

gîn (C.), = A. gûn, silver.

gîn (C.) **pe-gîn-á**, a plant used for making medicinal plasters.

gín (C. kín, Cn. kán). **gín-á**, a young boy; a male child; said for "I" by a man examined by a mandarin. **gín-ná**, id. (Cn. kán-ngá, kán-ngiá, kán-káⁿ). **gín-ná-sek**, behaviour of a child or boy (v. sek). **gín-ná-thûn**, a lad about fifteen. **gín-ná-ui**, the caul or after-birth. **tsa-bó gín-ná**, a girl. **chhī-gín-ná**, a very young boy who serves for food and clothing without wages. **gín-ná-lâng**, a young lad; a lad unacquainted with the ways of the world.

gín (C.) **tē-gín**, = A. thō-ún, the earth-worm.

gīn (Cn. gūn). **gīn--lâng**, causing a feeling of disgust and displeasure in any one who sees it, &c. **khoàⁿ--liáu chiū-gīn--lâng**, the sight of it (or of him) causes disgust and aversion, and makes one look displeased; *e.g.* of a man somehow connected with us who will do wrong regardless of advice. **khoàⁿ--liáu chiū-gīn**, id. **khoàⁿ chiū-gīn**, id. **khoàⁿ--liáu chiū-gīn--goá**, the sight of him makes me utterly disgusted. **goá hō--i khoàⁿ-tiȯh chiū gīn--i**, if I let him see me, it will excite his displeasure. **khoàⁿ--kìⁿ, chiū gīn-sîn**, disgusted at the very sight of him (or it). **kap--i gīn-sîn**, all the more determined to do it because he is opposed and displeased. **kap--i lāng-gīn**, id. **lāng-gīn**, to speak or act intentionally so as to displease, disgust, or spite a man; to ridicule a man so as to spite him. **put-chí lāng-gīn**, quite out of humour; very much annoyed, as when teased or spited, or as at numerous mosquitoes or flies.

bȧk-chiu gīn-gīn, to give an angry displeased glance or frown.

giô — **ò-giô**, a sort of fig, from the seeds of which a cooling jelly is made. **ò-giô-chí**, its seeds. **ò-giô-tàng**, the jelly made from it.

giô (R. giâu), a cockle. **giô-á**, id.; also (vulg.), the female pudenda. **giô--ê**, a namesake (same name compared to the two similar shells).

giô (R. giâu). **giô-poe**, a paddle for a boat.

giô (C.), (cf. tiô). **chhio-giô** (vulg.), very impudent and swaggering in manner.

giō (R. kiāu), (C. kiō). **lē-giō**, a sort of leek.

gioh, an enclitic word, sometimes used in terminating a statement (esp. T.)

giȯh, id. (?).

gio̍h [R. ge̍k (?), to offend]. **gāi-gio̍h**, uncomfortable, as in mind, or in any part of the body, often from some slight annoyance. **ngāiⁿ-gio̍h**, id. **thiaⁿ--liáu, put-chí ngāiⁿ-gio̍h**, feeling very uncomfortable after hearing it.

gio̍h (C. ge̍h, T. gio̍h, ge̍h), to jeer, jest, or jibe; to mock, taunt, or jest ironically at a man, esp. for some old fault. **gio̍h--lâng**, id. **gio̍h-sio̍h**, id. **kap-i-gio̍h**, to jest or jeer at him. **saⁿ-gio̍h**, jest and jeer at one another. **gio̍h-lâi gio̍h-khì**, id. **gio̍h-ge̍h** (C.), to jeer or mock at.

gio̍k (R. id.), (C. gia̍k). **pō-gio̍k**, to tyrannize; cruel and tyrannical (as sovereign or very high mandarin).

gio̍k (C.), = A. ge̍k (prison, hell, &c.)

gio̍k [R. jade-stone, = col. ge̍k], also (C.) colloquial = A. ge̍k, in all phrases.

gio̍k-chiam-hoe, a sort of lily. **gio̍k-ièn**, a beautiful small bird. **gio̍k-pîn**, a sort of academy in Amoy where literary prizes are competed for, but not for degrees. **gio̍k-hông**, the idol Yuh-hwang (v. hông). **gio̍k-tè**, id. **gio̍k-chí**, his commands.

gióng (R. kióng). **gióng-chhiú**, = kióng-chhiú, to join one's own hands and shake them as a salutation.

gióng [R. to look upwards], (C. giáng), turned somewhat upwards, said of the lower support (ē-kim) of a Chinese helm. **gióng-bōng** (R.), to look upwards.

gip (R. id.) **gip-gip**, in danger of falling, as over a precipice, or on a steep slope.

giû [R. a cow, = col. gû], a surname. **giû-tsong**, New-chwang. **giû-hông**, cow bezoar; biliary calculus of cow. **giû-chhek**, a medicinal plant (Pupalia geniculata, and other Amaranthaceæ?). **giû-chhek-chháu**, id. **giû-chhip**, id.; the medicine made of it.

giú, to snatch suddenly. **giú--lâi**, to take a thing suddenly, *e.g.* lay hold (in sport) of a man's money, as if going to appropriate it. **khit-goá-giú--lâi**, got by me suddenly and unexpectedly, as money or things.

giuh (C.), = A. khiuh. **sòng-giuh-giuh**, very poor.

gô (R. gô, ngô), a goose, = giâ. **gô-kak**, a gander. **gô-chiúⁿ**, goose's web-foot.

gô (R. id.) **gô-á-chhài**, a plant used for plastering up sores, and for feeding ducks.

gô, = gô. **seng-gô** (C.), = A. tô-seng, a sort of cedar or pine.

gô (R. id.), to distil. **gô-chiú**, to distil spirits. **gô-chiú-tháng**, a Chinese still, made like an alembic. **gô-chiú-tsúi**, the water used for condensing in distillation.

gô (T.), = A. ngô. **âu-gô**, cancer (?) in the throat.

gô [R. id., cf. kô, kō], to whirl round (neuter); to revolve on its axis, as a top or a globe. **îⁿ-îⁿ-gô**, id. **lin-lin-gô**, id. **hoang-gô** (T.), = A. hong-chhe-lién, a toy that whirls round by the wind.

gō (R. id.), to starve (neuter). **gō--sí**, to die of starvation. **iau-gō**, hungry and starving. **iau-koâⁿ-gō**, cold and starving. **phièn-chhiáⁿ hāi-gō** (deceitfully invite to eat so as to starve him), said of deceitfully breaking a promise. **chit-jit, chiah saⁿ-tǹg: chit-mîⁿ, gō kàu-kng**, eat three meals in the day and starve all night (said in joke).

gō (R. id.), = ngō. **kiau-gō**, proud.

gô͘ (R. id.), = ngô͘ (T. kô͘). **pe̍h-gô͘**, a large white fish, very fond of leaping. **gô͘-hî**, id. (r.), said by landsmen. **âng-gô͘**, a fish like a shark; some say a large sort of shark.

gô͘ (R. ngô͘, gô͘), a surname; the ancient kingdom of Woo, about Che-kiang and Shanghai. **gô͘-chin-jîn**, an idol of that surname, = tāi-tō-kong, a native of Pe̍h-ta, near Hái-chhng.

gô͘ — **gî-gô͘**, a thorny shrub with white blossoms, somewhat like the sloe, used medicinally.

gô͘ (C.) **siong-gô͘**, = seng-gô, = A. tô-seng, a sort of pine like a cedar.

gô͘ (R. id.) **gô͘-tông**, a tree with large leaves, Dryandra or Sterculia platanifolia?

gô͘ (R. id.) **gô͘-khî**, the leech.

gô͘, v. ngô͘ (several words).

gō͘ (R. ngó͘), five. **chhin-chiâⁿ gō͘-ge̍h**, relatives and friends (v. ge̍h). **gō͘-ge̍h**, the fifth month, counted unlucky for beginning matters, because "gō͘" also means to mistake and to injure. **gō͘-ge̍h-tsoeh**, the 5.5. **gō͘-si-su**, slips of paper pasted on doors on that day.

gō͘-kak, = ngó͘-kok, the five grains, now used to include potatoes, &c., also. **gō͘-phâng**, a large long river-boat covered with five mats. **gō͘-tsáng-thâu**, the principal part of an affair, &c. (v. tsáng).

gō͘-tsa̍p, fifty. **it-gō͘ it-tsa̍p**, the series of 5, 10, 15, &c. **it-gō͘ it-tsa̍p kā-i-kóng**, tell him minutely and particularly. **chiong-sam kóe-gō͘**, to deceive (lit. change 3 to 5, easily done in Chinese). **sam-put-gō͘-sî**, occasionally; sometimes; from time to time.

gō͘ (R. ngó͘). **gō͘-sî**, from 11 A.M. to 1 P.M. **gō͘-sî-chiàⁿ** exactly at noon; 12 o'clock noon.

gō͘ (R. id.), to lead into loss or disaster; to injure and delude, as by bad teaching. **gō͘ lâng--ê tsú-tē**, to spoil or ruin other people's children, as by neglecting their instruction, by incompetent or bad teaching, or by leading them into vice. **gō͘--lâng liáu-chîⁿ**, to lead a man into a losing concern, either intentionally or by mistake. **gō͘-sū**, to spoil a case; to ruin an affair, as by mismanagement. **tsū-gō͘**, to injure one's self, as by neglecting and losing a rare opportunity. **tam-gō͘**, to disappoint the trust placed in us, as by forsaking a wife, or by dying shortly after marriage.

gō͘ (R. id.) **sit-gō͘**, mistake. **chhò-gō͘**, id. **tùi-thâu-gō͘**, mistake and misunderstanding on both sides. **lióng-gō͘**, a misunderstanding either on one or both sides. **saⁿ-gō͘**, to fail in keeping an appointment or a promise; to disappoint, from mistake, or carelessness, or set purpose. **saⁿ-tāⁿ-gō͘**, mistake as from not hearing plainly, &c. **saⁿ-gō͘-tāⁿ** (T.), id. **chhiet-chhiet bu̍t-gō͘**, be most careful to make no mistake. **gō͘-thok**, to put mistaken confidence in a man. **gō͘-siong**, to wound accidentally. **gō͘-sat**, to kill accidentally. **gō͘-hoān**, to offend unintentionally. **gō͘-ta̍h--tio̍h**, to tread on by mistake, &c. &c.

gō͘ [R. to meet with]. **bô-gî-gō͘**, quite unexpectedly.

gō͘ [R. to awaken], = ngō͘. **liáu-gō͘** (R.), to awake to a sense of the vanity of the world (a Buddhist phrase). **chhíⁿ-gō͘** (X.), to awake to the knowledge of a truth.

gō͘ (R. ngó͘). **gō͘-tsoh**, a coroner.

gō͘ (T.), = A. gô, mind confused and perplexed.

goá (R. ngó͘), I, me. **goá-ê**, my; mine. **lí-goá**, you and I.

goā (R. gā), exclamation of astonishment. **goā-piāng** (T.), id. **goā-pē** (Cn.), id. **goā-káⁿ** (Cn.), id. **goā-kiāⁿ** (Cn.), id.

goā (R. gōe), out; outside; besides; more than; excepting; by female side, of relations and connections.

goā-kang, the provinces where mandarin is spoken (v. kang, a river). **goā-úi**, a petty officer, like a sergeant-major, just below "pé-tsóng." **giàh-goā**, a sergeant (v. giàh).

goā-chheh, second-rate books, *i.e.* all books except the classics and their commentaries; some also except the great historical works. **goā-tsâi**, external polite accomplishments, &c. (v. tsâi). **put-chí goā-khì**, fond of outward display; dashing. **khah-ū goā-khì**, id. **khah-ū goā-khùi**, id. **kek goā-khùi**, to affect display or a dashing manner, when quite beyond his circumstances, *e.g.* a man of no consequence talking very big. **goā-phê**, external. **goā-kháu**, outside (v. kháu). **goā-bīn**, outside. **goā-thâu**, id. **goā-sin**, farther out, as compared with another place. **goā-pêng**, the outside. **mn̂g-goā**, outside the door or gate. **chhut-goā**, to go from home, esp. to emigrate. **goā-kheh**, a travelling merchant from a distance; visitors not nearly related, as at funeral ceremonies.

hūn-goā, beyond our sphere of duty. **tsàp-goā**, more than ten; generally nearly twenty. **tsàp-goā-goā**, a great deal more than ten, as about twenty. **chheng-goā**, above a thousand, &c. &c. **chheng-goā-lâng**, more than a thousand men. **lēng-goā**, besides this; in addition. **í-goā**, besides; except. **goá í-goā**, besides me; excepting me. **tû-sí í-goā**, excepting death. **tùi-tû-goā**, balance, on either side (v. tû).

goā-sì^n, of a different surname. **goā-kong**, maternal grandfather. **goā-má**, maternal grandmother. **goā-tit**, son of wife's brother. **goā-tit-sun**, son of wife's brother's son, or son of brother's daughter. **goā-sun**, daughter's child. **goā-ke**, a woman's own relatives, said after she is married. **Lí--ê goā-ke tī tá-lòh**, where do your own relations live? (said to a married woman).

lāi-goā, in and out. **poà^n-lāi-goā**, half in, half out; not plainly and definitely choosing one's line of action. **chhut-jip lāi-goā**, said of an experienced person. **ū-lāi ū-goā**, properly divided, as house with outer and inner rooms for men and women; attending to act with propriety towards various classes of persons. **lāi-chhin goā-chhek**, connections by blood and by marriage (v. chhek).

goân [R. hiên, dark-coloured, profound]. **goân-som**, a very cheap sort of ginseng, not really a Panax. **goân-sun**, great-great-grandson. **goân-bú**, = hiên-bú, a spirit worshipped by Tauists.

goân [R. oân, round, an official]. **úi-goân**, = úi-oân, a smaller mandarin sent out by a superior with a commission for some special temporary purpose. **goân-chhe**, police runners or constables, who serve and execute warrants and seize criminals.

goân (R.), a large turtle or tortoise spoken of in the classics. **goân-gô** (R.), two such animals. **goân-ngê** (R.), id. **sù-su, thák thàu-thàu: bōe-hiáu-siá goân-ngê ku-pih-tsàu**, having read the four books all through, but unable to write these five characters (very like and complicated).

goân [R. commencement, principal]. **khiau-kha goân**, this character, so called to distinguish it from the following word.

goân-tiâu, the Yuen dynasty; the Mongol dynasty. **goân-sòe**, a commander-in-chief (v. sòe). **goân-sí thien-tsun**, the supreme God of the Tauists. **goân-pó**, a silver ingot; a sort of idolatrous paper. **chiu-goân**, the sort of cash specially used for divining by tortoise-shell.

chiōng-goân, the senior wrangler of the Han-lin Imperial Academy, the highest literary rank. **tsōng-goân**, id. **chiōng-goân pài-siòng**, said of his becoming prime minister, as sometimes happens. **chiōng-goân-tiû**, a game of chance (v. tiû). **chiōng-goân-chhi^n**, = bûn-khiok-chhi^n, a very auspicious star. **chiōng-goân-tōe**, a grave-site good enough to produce an imperial senior wrangler. **hōe-goân**, the highest of the Tsin-sze (chìn-sū) graduates. **kài-goân**, the highest of the Kujin graduates. **à-goân**, a Kujin graduate somewhat lower on the list. **tiòng sam-goân**, to gain these three highest honours, kài-goân, hōe-goân, and chiōng-goân, in succession. **liên-tiòng sam-goân**, may you in rapid succession win the highest possible literary honours. **poàt-goân**, title given to a "lím-seng" selected once in twelve years out of each Hien.

goân-tàn, New-year's morning. **goân-siau**, the feast of lanterns, on the evening of 1.15. **siōng-goân**, the 1.15. **siōng-goân-î^n**, small sweet rice-balls, now used at any time. **tiong-goân**, the 7.15. **hā-goân** (R.), the 10.15.

goân-khì, one's fundamental constitution. **goân-khì sit**, constitution become feeble. **goân-khì ōng**, very strong and healthy. **kò-goân-khì**, to take care of one's health and constitution. **sún goân-khì**, to injure one's constitution, as by lust or any excess. **pó goân-khì**, to restore the constitution, as by strengthening medicine. **goân-sìn**, natural constitution, as strong or weak (v. sìn). **siū-goân**, longevity, in some phrases (v. siū).

goân [R. origin, beginning, to forgive]. **goân-chêng**, to forgive or treat with forbearance one who has committed a fault; having a forgiving disposition. **goân i-ê-chêng**, to treat him with forbearance; to forgive him.

goân-kò, the plaintiff. **goân-pī**, plaintiff and defendant. **goân-lâng**, the principal party in a bargain or dispute. **goân-ūi**, original place. **goân-lō**, the same road by which we went. **goân-kè**, prime cost. **goân-giàh**, the original quantity or state. **goân-mih^n**, the original articles unchanged. **goân-tsng-hè**, goods as originally made, not dressed up or flavoured for the market. **goân-hong put-tōng**, goods in the original package unopened. **goân-jīm**, holding the same office for a second term. **chiàu goân-jit**, according to the date originally fixed. **goân-sèng put-kái**, bad nature not reformed. **iû-goân**, as formerly. **chiàu-goân**, id. **goân-kū**, id. **goân-iû**, origin, as of an affair. **goân-thâu**, id. (s. fountain). **pún-goân**, origin. **goân-pún**, id.; originally. **goân-lâi**, originally. **tng-goân-chho**, at the beginning. **tng-goân-chhoe**, id. **chhiû kun-goân**, to search for the origin of the matter (or next word?). **goân, siu, chhut, tsûn**, balance in one's cash-book, &c. **goân-phòe**, the wife whom a man marries first of all.

khut-goân, the ancient worthy whose death is commemorated on 5.5.

goân [R. a fountain-head]. **tsúi-goân**, a fountain-head. **goân-thâu**, id. (s. origin). **tsúi-goân, bók-pún**, a tree has a root, water has a fountain-head; so men should honour and reverence the fountain of their being, their parents. **súi-goân bók-pún**, id.

bók-pún súi-goân, id. **kun-goân**, root or origin (or last word).

goán, we; us (excluding the person or persons spoken to); I; our: my. **goán-ê**, our; ours; my; mine. **goán-pē**, my father. **goán-tau**, my home. **goán-ê-lâng**, one of my or our relatives or party (not yours).

goán [R. to amuse one's self with]. **kó-goán**, toys; playthings. **goán-khì**, id. **koan-san goán-súi**, to go about for amusement looking at scenery. **goán-sióng** (R.), to look at, as a view. **sióng-goán** (R.), id.

goān (R. id.), a vow. **hē-goān**, to make a vow in a formal way, as before an idol (v. hē). **hoat-goān**, to vow, esp. by mere language, as in sudden danger. **hoat-phái^n-goān**, to vow to commit a crime. **sè-goān** (r.), to make a solemn vow. **siā-goān**, to perform one's vow, esp. said when the vow was in the more formal way of "hē-goān." **hêng-goān** (r.), id. **kóe-goān**, to perform a vow, esp. of the less formal "hoat-goān."

goān [R. willing; desire; would that]. **kam-goān**, willing to make no opposition. **sim-goān**, the desire of the heart. **chêng-goān**, heartily willing. **kam-sim chêng-goān**, heartily willing. **lióng-goān**, both parties quite willing, satisfied, and pleased. **chiok-goān**, having all one's desire gratified. **jû-goān**, one's wishes or desires accomplished. **jû-goān jû-ì**, id. **sûi--lâng ì-goān**, to fulfil a man's wish. **thàn--goá ì-goān**, it came out just as I wished. **thien-chiông jîn-goān**, Heaven fulfils men's desires. **jîn iú siēn-goān, thien pit-chiông--chi**, Heaven certainly fulfils men's good desires. **koa^n toàn, put-jû bîn-goān**, the voluntary obedience of the people is better than the judgment of mandarins.

goát [R. the moon, = col. gėh]. **jit-goát**, the two side-boards of a coffin; also (R.), the sun and moon. **jit-goát jû-so**, days and months are like a shuttle. **chheng-hong bêng-goát**, pleasant cool wind and bright moon. **liók-goát-song**, a sort of cooling medicine. **goát-á-pêng**, the 74th or 130th radical when written at the side, though properly the 130th is not "goát" but "jiók." **goát-lí sióng-ngô**, a beautiful lady (in the moon). **sióng-goát** (R.), to gaze at the moon.

goát (Cn.), = A. oát (R.), to say.

goe, to rub against, as a boat or rope, &c. **goe--tio̍h**, id. **goe-tn̄g**, to get broken by rubbing, as a rope.

gôe (R. gô), (Cn. gôe; C. gô), a surname.

gōe (Cn.) **kap-gōe**, a young frog. **kap-gōe-kui**, a tadpole.

gōe (R. id.) **gōe-seng**, a sister's son. **gōe-seng-lú**, a sister's daughter.

gōe [R. out, outside, = col. goā]. **lōe-siong gōe-kám**, internal predisposition to disease developed by a cold or chill. **kek-gōe** (R.), exceedingly, extraordinarily (only with verbs). **ì-gōe ê-tāi-chì** (r.), things quite beyond expectation.

gōe [R. gō, handicraft], = gō. **kang-gōe**, handicraft; workmanship. **chhiú-gōe**, id. **kì-gōe**, skill at handicraft. **tsòe-gōe**, to make small things at leisure time for amusement. **bú-gōe**, military arts and exercises. **hó-bú-gōe**, well-trained in military exercises. **pí bú-gōe**, to teach or exercise or make trial of skill in military exercises, as fencing, archery, &c.

go̍eh (C.), = A. gėh, the moon, a month. **go̍eh têng**, the moon at the zenith. **go̍eh thêng**, id.

gö̍h (Cn.), = A. gėh, the moon; a month.

go̍k (R. id.), the sea eagle. **go̍k-chiáu**, id.; also, a man well acquainted with the management of affairs and not afraid to act as a leader. **siā-go̍k**, a man who is a leader in his village, not by appointment, but just because all fear him. **lâng-go̍k**, id. **tsòe-lâng-go̍k**, to act very imperiously, as such a man.

go̍k (R. id.) **go̍k-hî**, the crocodile or alligator.

go̍k (R. id.) **chhok-go̍k** (R.), to start suddenly. **chhok-go̍k--chit-ē**, id. (r.)

gong — **gin-gong-giang**, sound of jingling bells, as in Buddhist rites.

gông — **gông-ngia̍h**, suddenly surprised; startled and afraid.

gōng (R. id.), stupid; foolish and dull; slightly giddy; sometimes put before names of men in a familiar colloquial form. **gōng-tit**, rather too blunt and simple. **gōng-tá^n**, rash. **gōng-thu̍h-thu̍h**, wanting in ability; foolish-looking. **gōng-tho̍h** (C.), id. **khám-gōng**, foolish and somewhat rash in speaking or acting. **am-khám-gōng**, id. **gû-gōng** (r.), foolish. **gōng-thâu gōng-bīn**, foolish; stupid-looking. **tien-gōng**, idiotic (v. tien). **siáu-gōng**, fond of gambling, low jokes, or foolish pleasures. **tòng-gōng**, having a dull or foolish-like manner, as an old man. **lāu-tòng-gōng**, old man of dull appearance. **gōng-sîn**, stupid-looking; having the appearance of dull stupidity. **gōng-lâng**, you foolish fellow! **lí teh-gōng**, you are acting or going to act foolishly. **lí-gōng**, nonsense! you know nothing about it! **i-chia̍h lí-gōng**, he profits by your stupidity. **gōng-siū^n**, foolishly purposing or planning; said politely in giving our advice or opinion. **gōng-jip, bô gōng-chhut**, pretending not to understand (as in counting money) so as to gain, but taking good care not to lose. **ēng-gōng-chî^n**, to waste money foolishly on self-indulgence; spend fool's pence. **ēng gōng-á-chî^n**, id. **poa̍h-gōng-kiáu**, stupidly gambling away money, as a dupe. **gōng kàu ná^n sí-lâng**, as stupid as a corpse. **gōng khah-chhám-sí**, your extreme stupidity is worse than death.

hîn-gōng, giddy, dizzy. **hîn-gōng-gōng**, id. **thâu-khak gōng-gōng**, head slightly giddy, as with weakness or sickness.

hái-lâm-gōng, a large bird (from Hai-nan) like a pelican; said of a big dull simple-looking fellow. **gōng-á-soa**, the large shark.

gōng [R. gō, proud]. **khòng-gōng**, having a proud bearing.

gû (R. giû), a cow; an ox; anything put under a lever to serve as a fulcrum. **toā-gû**, the large beam from which a coffin hangs when carried, this great beam being supported by numerous ropes and poles, called "chhia." **tîn-gû** (T.), a small instrument making a humming noise, attached to a kite.

chhun-gû, the earthen cow carried in procession and broken at the spring festival. **chhun-gû-tô**, the common Chinese sheet almanac. **tōe-gû**, the great cow under the earth that bears up the world. **tōe-gû oā^n-keng**, that cow shifting its shoulders, so causing earthquakes.

n̂g-gû, the common cow. **chhiah-gû**, id. **súi-gû**, the water buffalo (s. fish). **sai-gû**, the rhinoceros. **iá-gû**, a wild ox. **gû-káng**, a bull. **súi-gû-káng**, also (T.), a thin variegated beetle, about an inch long,

厦英大辭典

with long antennæ. **soaⁿ-gû-káng** (A.), id. **gû iûⁿ bé**, cows, goats, and horses. **bô-gû sái-bé**, if you can't get a cow, use a horse. **gû-iâ bé-iâ**, two idols with heads of a cow and horse respectively, attending on Giâm-lô-ông, and sometimes on Sêng-hông-iâ. **gû-thâu bé-bīn**, id. **gû-chiong-kun**, the cow-headed one.

gû-thâu liòk-tsut, clownish fellow, said in scolding. **chhiⁿ-mîⁿ-gû** (blind cow), an illiterate clown. **lâng sim-koaⁿ, gû pak-tó** (man's heart, cow's belly), very covetous or ambitious.

gû-tsàu, a slaughter-house for cattle. **gû-noâⁿ**, a fold for cattle. **gû-tiâu**, a stall for cattle. **gû-bō**, a mill turned by oxen. **gû-chhia**, a cart drawn by oxen. **gû-liâu**, a rope by which a cow is led or tied. **gû-kǹg**, a ring for nose of ox; a sort of worm. **gû-kak**, horn. **gû-kak-kóng**, a sort of horn blown by priests. **gû-tē**, tripe. **gû-lin**, milk; sometimes said of salted curdled milk. **gû-leng**, id. (v. leng). **gû-niⁿ**, id. **gû-lin-chiuⁿ** (C.), milk. **gû-lin-iû**, butter.

ǹg-gû, to tend cattle, as herd-boy. **koà-gû**, to yoke cattle for ploughing. **kà-gû**, to train a cow or ox yet untrained.

gû-nn̂g, a star worshipped along with "chit-lú." **gû-kak-chhì**, a very hard wood. **gû-bé-hî**, a sort of fish, = tek-kah.

gû [R. a fish, = col. hî]. **súi-gû** (Cn. sûi-hû), a flat brass plate with a hole, that falls on the staple for the padlock of a door or drawer. **ng súi-gû**, to play at blindman's buff. **bók-gû**, a wooden drum, shaped like a fish.

gû [R. to fish], (C. gî; Cn. gû). **gû-ong** (polite), a fisherman. **ùt-pāng siong-chhî, gû-jîn tek-lī**, when the oyster and the bird catch each other, the fisherman gets gain (said of the expenses of lawsuits.)

gû [R. foolish], (C. gî). **gû-tsoat**, foolish, stupid (said politely of one's self). **gû-chhún**, stupid, foolish. **gû-thún**, id. **gû-gōng** (r. X.), id. **gû-tû**, stupidly dogged and rough (v. tû). **gû-thû**, id. **gû-bîn**, the ignorant people. **phah-bó, chin sī-gû**, he who beats his wife is certainly a fool.

gû [R. to be on one's guard, to be prepared for], (C. gî), a surname. **hong-súi put-gû**, sudden, unexpected, unavoidable calamity, as by sudden and terrible wind, waves, floods, rains, storms, fire, robbers, &c. **hong-súi put-gû, goá bô kā-lí-pó**, I will not take the responsibility of insuring you against such sudden casualties.

gú [R. speech, a saying], (C. gí, Cn. gû). **giân-gú** (C. gân-gí), language, conversation, talk (v. giân). **im-gú**, language. **im-gú put-siong-tông**, language different. **siòk-gú**, a common phrase; a common proverb or saying. **sêng-gú**, a phrase originally literary which has become colloquial or nearly so. **kháu-thâu-gú**, usual phrases for commencing a sentence, as used commonly in special places or by particular persons. **thò-gú**, polite salutations and questions about health, weather, &c., used on meeting friends or in letters, &c. **thò-thâu-gú**, id. **tiòng-hong put-gú**, a very sudden and fatal disease which at once deprives of the power of speech.

phoe-gú (C. phe-gí), a mandarin's written answer to a petition. **chhàm-gú**, a prophecy. **ún-gú**, a phrase with a hidden meaning, as an inuendo or a play upon words, either a set phrase or made on the occasion. **chià chhùi-gú**, to pretend to have a verbal order so as fraudulently to get possession of things for one's self.

gū [R. imperial], (C. gī, Cn. gū). **gū-sú**, imperial censors at Pekin, one for each province. **gū-tsn̄g**, an accusation before the supreme tribunal at the metropolis. **gū-hùi**, the personal names of emperor or princes, which must not be written or spoken. **gū-lîm-kun**, the palace guards. **gū-kà**, the imperial equipage. **gū-kà chhin-cheng**, the emperor going to war in person.

gū [R. to lodge], (C. gī, Cn. gū). **gū-sé**, a lodging-place; lodgings.

gū (R. id.), (C. gī), to meet with. **gū--tiòh**, to meet with. **gū-bô-tiòh**, not manage to meet with, though having tried. **tú-gū-tiòh**, to meet with by chance. **tú-gū chit-jit**, it chanced one day. **tú-gū i-lâi**, when I thought of going to him, he came to me. **tsáu-chhàt gū-tiòh-hó**, fleeing from robbers met a tiger (out of the frying-pan into the fire). **ngó-gū-jiên**, unexpectedly (v. ngó).

kéng-gū, circumstances good or bad, as of a man or of a family or place. **tso-gū**, fortune, luck, circumstances or opportunity, as good or bad. **hó-tso-gū**, a fortunate opportunity, favourable circumstances. **pháiⁿ-tso-gū**, unfavourable state of matters. **bô-tso-gū**, id. **i--ê tso-gū**, his opportunity.

gū — **án-gū**, words said to a baby. **á-gū**, an insect like a small cicada, named from its shrill voice.

gûi (R. id.) **gûi-hiám**, dangerous; danger. **gûi-kip**, very urgent and pressing (and dangerous to delay), as an affair. **lîm-gûi**, to come into great and imminent danger.

gûi [R. deceitful, false]. **tsà-gûi**, very cunning and deceitful.

gūi (R. id.), name of an ancient state, Wei; a surname.

gûi (R. id.) **a-gûi**, assafoetida.

gûi (cf. bûi, pûi). **chhiū-gûi**, the tree-bug. **bát-sat chhiò chhiū-gûi**, the bed-bug laughing at the tree-bug (the pot calling the kettle black).

gûiⁿ (Cn.), = A. géng. **gêng-gûiⁿ**, = A. gêng-géng, the dragon's-eye or lung-yen fruit.

gûn (R. id.), (C. gîn, Cn. gûn), silver, money. **gûn-á**, small silver coins, &c. **gûn-khì**, silver articles. **gûn-hāng**, silver; money. **bûn-gûn**, sycee silver (v. bûn). **chiok-siâⁿ-gûn**, pure silver. **gûn bô-sím-mihⁿ-koâiⁿ**, the silver is not very good. **kē-gûn**, impure silver, with much alloy. **ké-gûn**, spurious silver. **kè-gûn** (C. kè), value or price in silver. **kè-gûn** (C. kòe), to transmit silver to a superior mandarin (v. kè, to send under escort). **kè-gûn** (C. kòe), to hand over silver. **tâng-gûn**, silver heavily adulterated with brass or copper. **tâng-gûn bóe tsoá-hia**, bad silver buying paper boots; cheaters cheating each other. **chhùi-gûn**, broken dollars or silver. **gûn-chhùi**, id. **gûn-iù**, id. **hoe-gûn**, dollars much stamped. **lân-san-gûn**, a few loose dollars, not up to ten, or not put in a roll. **toā-gûn** (L.), good large dollars. **hut-thâu-gûn**, Spanish dollars. **chiáu-á-gûn**, Mexican dollars. **koáiⁿ-á-gûn**, Bolivian dollars.

nn̄g-gûn, dollars counted a little lighter. **hiēn-gûn**, ready money. **iên-gûn**, money subscribed. **tsāi-gûn**, freight. **tiāⁿ-gûn**, earnest-money. **teh-tōe-gûn**, money advanced on a lease, to be repaid if the house be taken back. **hiòng-gûn**, money received

15

for customs dues; pay of soldiers, marines, &c. **tiōng-gûn** (= C. hàp-tek, = gê-chî^n), commission or brokerage for selling goods. **pèng-gûn**, commission or brokerage paid by the buyer.

gûn-thâu, money in silver; a silver head. **gûn-thâu ōng**, money abundant, as in village or hong. **chî^n-gûn**, money in general. **tsài-chî^n tsài-gûn**, to carry a very valuable cargo. **chit--ê gûn-chî^n**, one silver coin; one dollar. **gûn-tiā^n**, silver ingots shaped liked an hour-glass. **gûn-khò**, silver ingots of semi-circular shape (v. khò). **gûn-khờ**, a treasury. **khờ-gûn**, money of the state treasury. **gėh-gûn**, monthly wages or salary.

kim-gûn, gold and silver; money; paper used for idolatrous burning (v. kim). **gûn-pȯh**, tin-foil. **gûn-bīn**, silver-plated or silvered. **gûn-pâi**, a silver medal. **gûn-tsúi**, percentage of a few cash allowed to buyer when payment is made in silver (v. tsúi). **gûn-hun**, difference of light and heavy dollars (v. hun). **gûn-kè**, value of a dollar in cash according to varying exchange. **gûn-chiȯh**, a touchstone for rubbing silver upon. **gûn-soa**, a very fine white sort of sand from Quemoy. **gûn-chhēng-kah**, a sort of vest with side pockets for money. **gûn-siō**, a strong box for carrying treasure (v. siō). **gûn-kūi**, a man in a hong who has charge of the money; a cashier; a large strong box for keeping money.

khoà^n-gûn, to examine dollars to see if they be good. **bat-gûn**, skilled in examining dollars. **tú-gûn**, to deduct so much from a payment (v. tú). **niá^n-gûn**, to receive money. **jip-gûn**, to get silver in change for cash; to pay money on account.

tūi-gûn, to get silver in exchange for cash or for gold. **tùi-gûn**, to transfer money to or from a distance by a bill, draft, cheque, &c. **bōe-gûn**, to sell so much as that the payment is in silver (v. bōe). **chiū^n-gûn**, to come up to a sum payable in silver, as a price or an account. **kheng-gûn**, to melt silver (v. kheng).

súi-gûn, quicksilver; mercury. **gûn-tsu**, vermilion; cinnabar; red ink. **gûn-hēng**, a white medicinal nut. **gûn-hô**, the milky way. **gûn-hî**, a small edible worm-shaped fish.

gûn [R. the gums]. **khí-gûn** (R.), the gums.

gûn (Cn.), = gîn, to look angrily at one.

gún, = goán, we, us (excluding the person or persons spoken to).

gūn (Cn.), = A. gīn, to cause a feeling of disgust or aversion, &c.

gwá, gwā; better, goá, goā (*q.v.*)

gwân, **gwán**, **gwān**; better, goân, goán, goān (*q.v.*)

gwàt; better, goàt (*q.v.*)

H.

h, in the reading form, often becomes **k** in colloquial, and in some words **ph**. Sometimes it is dropped.

h, in some colloquial words, comes from **l** in the reading form, especially when the preceding word ends in **n**, and in the Cn. dialect, *e.g.* hoân-hô, sin-hô. Sometimes it comes from **g**.

ha, to breathe out gently. **ha-sio**, to warm by breathing on. **ēng-chhùi ha**, to breath gently on, *e.g.* to moisten or warm a thing.

ha (cf. hah). **ha-ha-chhiò**, to laugh loud with mouth open. **chhiò ha-ha**, id. **ha-ha toā-chhiò**, do. very loud.

ha — **ha-lā-nî^n**, a sort of woollen cloth (v. lā).

hâ (R. id.), (C. hê), a flaw, as in pottery or as in a gem. **hâ-hûn**, id. **hâ-hûn**, dim and cloudy, as night when the moon gives little light. **bô-hâ**, faultless, as a gem, &c. **ū-hâ**, having a flaw, as gem.

hâ, to bind round; to gird. **hâ-oá**, to tie loosely together. **hâ chháu-á**, to bind grass or small brushwood loosely for fuel. **hâ thâu-pờ**, to put on a turban or head-band; to wear it. **hâ ơ-kun**, to put on a broad black ribbon on the head, as women. **hâ-niá^n**, to put on a collar. **hâ tớ-koā^n**, to tie on a pouch (like a sporran) on the belly. **hâ-io**, to gird the loins. **hâ io-toà**, id.

hâ [R. gâ, a tooth]. **hâ-lan** (C.), = A. giâ-lan, crimson.

hâ [R. a shrimp, a toad], (C. hê). **hâ-bô**, dried toads (medicinal).

hà [R. hàu, filial duty], mourning worn for superiors. **ū-hà--teh**, to wear mourning. **ū-hà**, to wear mourning; also (esp. C.), to act in a filial manner towards parents. **sng-hà**, mourning dress. **hà-sa^n**, id. **hà-hók**, id. **ū-hà-hók**, to be in mourning. **hà-hók bē-moá^n**, period of mourning not yet ended. **hà-bé**, short time before end of mourning. **thǹg-hà**, to put off mourning. **toà-hà**, to wear mourning. **chhēng-moā^n toà-hà**, to be in very deepest mourning. **koà-hà**, to hang white sack-cloth at the door. **khiā-hà**, to have offerings and rites (in the house) for a person recently deceased. **sa^n-nî^n-hà**, mourning for twenty-seven months. **tùi-nî^n-hà**, one year's mourning, as for brother. **sūn-hà-chhoā**, to marry immediately after parent's death, so that the bride may join in the funeral rites. **chiū-hà-chhoā** (T.), id. **hà-thǹg**, a stick with white paper on it carried by a son at funeral.

hâ [R. id., leisure, = col. hē], (C. hɛ̂, T. hâu). **hân-hâ**, leisure; at leisure.

hā (= hah). **hā-sau**, opening out in chinks between planks, &c., as floor or bucket.

hā [R. summer, = col. hē; China], (C. hɛ̄), a surname; the Hea dynasty. **hoa-hā** (R.), China. **hā-tiâu**, the Hea dynasty. **hā-pờ** (R.), summer-cloth; grass-cloth. **poàn-hā**, a medicine for cough.

hā [R. a mansion, Amoy], (C. hɛ̄). **hā-bûn** (R.), Amoy, = col. "ē-mn̂g." **hā-tô**, the Amoy steelyard rates, making one dollar weigh seven mace and six candareens (v. tô).

hā (= hoā, = kā). **hā-hā-kún**, to be noisy at play.

hā [R. low, to lower, to descend, = col. ē, kē], (C. hɛ̄). **su-hā**, secretly, private. **hā-chiān**, mean, low, as employment or station, *e.g.* of slaves, actors, &c. **hā-tsoh**, mean and shameful, as actions. **goá bô-beh hiah-hā-tsoh**, I will not demean myself so much, *e.g.*

to ask a favour from such a man. **hā-liû put-siàu**, mean, worthless (person). **hā-têng**, inferior quality (men or things). **hā-pòe**, persons lower in genealogical rank. **hā-siòk ê-lâng**, people of very mean condition (v. siòk, common, mean). **i--ê hā-siòk**, persons under his special control, *e.g.* inferior officers (v. siòk, to belong to).

siōng-tiong-hā, top, middle, and bottom; three qualities—best, medium, and inferior; first, second, and third, when there are only three. **khòa-siōng, put-khòa-hā** (looking above, but not below), leaving various parts of a matter not attended to, so that it goes wrong. **siōng put-chèng, chek hā-oai**, when superiors are wicked, so are their inferiors. **siōng put-chèng, chek hā-bān**, a wicked superior gets no respect. **hā-goân** (R.), the 10.15.

chhiá^n hòng-hā, just leave that over till other matters are first settled. **chhiá^n-àn-hā**, id. **hā chièn-tsu**, to send a challenge to battle. **pit hā chhiau-seng**, the pen writes down, "Let him live." **hā-san-hó**, a tight vest with many buttons (v. hó).

hā-hiet, to have dysentery. **tāi-siáu-piēn ū-hā**, to have a motion and pass urine, as sick man under treatment. **hā-siau**, seminal diseases, esp. spermatorrhœa (v. siau).

bōe-tit--thang hā-tâi, cannot manage to conclude the matter suitably (lit. to get down from the terrace); unable to get out of the matter with dignity, honour, or prestige. **thien-sîn hā-kàng**, the 12.25, when the celestial spirits come down (v. sîn). **hông-kiâu, su hā-má**, one should dismount at a bridge. **khî-hó chi-sè, put-tek-hā**, one who rides on a tiger cannot come down (started a dangerous matter which he cannot stop or control).

hâ^n, what did you say? (when one has not heard plainly); when pronounced very long and drawn out, it indicates that what has been said is displeasing or disregarded, or shows unwillingness to hear; also, to talk loud in an overbearing, bullying manner, in order to intimidate. **hâ^n--ah**, what do you say? **hâ^n, sím-mih^n**, id.

hâ^n [R. "hâp," to join; or "hâm?"]. **hâ^n-e**, when it is nearly dark.

hâ^n [R. hâm, together]. **jit hâ^n-soa^n**, the sun very near the horizon, so as almost to touch it.

hâ^n (cf. hâm, hiên). **hâ^n--teh**, matter left unsettled, *e.g.* offer made, but neither accepted nor rejected. **poà^n-lâm-hâ^n**, hung up unsettled, as affair. **poà^n-liâm-hâ^n**, id. **poà^n-liâm poà^n-hâ^n** (Cn.), id. **pàng-poà^n-lâm-hâ^n**, to leave a matter in an unsettled state, either temporarily or for ever.

há^n (= háng), to menace; to threaten; to intimidate by violent language.

hā^n, to growl, as a dog. **hā^n-hā^n-chhoán**, to part hard. **hā^n-hā^n-háu**, to growl or snarl, as dog; to hum, as bees or flies; to express approval of whatever is said, "Yes, yes." **káu hā^n--lâi**, the dog comes on growling.

hā^n, to lift the foot or leg over another. **sio-hā^n**, putting their legs over each other, as children. **hā^n--liáu, bōe toā-hàn**, having put one's leg over (child) he will never grow tall! **m̄-thang hā^n--kè**, don't step over it, as over printed or written paper.

hā^n — **khui hā^n-hā^n**, become loose, as joints or seams in furniture, making the article useless or nearly so; open very wide, as mouth. **chhùi khui-hā^n-hā^n**, said of a man covetously asking for too much for land, or for winding up a case. **toā-chhùi, khui hā^n-hā^n**, demanding an extravagant price. **chhoán kàu chhùi khui hā^n-hā^n**, gasping for breath.

hah — **hah-hì**, to gape; to yawn. **hah-hah-chhiò**, to laugh out loud. **chhiò hah-hah**, id.

hah (Cn. T.) **hah-sa**, = A. sau-hong, gaping in chinks, as wood [last word ?].

hah (C.) **hah-chhiù^n**, = A. phah-ka-chhiù^n, to sneeze.

hah (= hiah). **hah-kú-á**, for some little time (past).

hah, to affect, as vapour, exhalation, or heat; to warm, as by breath or vapour; to extend to and affect powerfully, as the influence of a powerful man. **hah-tio̍h-khì**, injured by some vapour, miasma, or subtle influence. **hah--tio̍h to̍k-khì**, injured by poisonous vapour, &c. **hah-tio̍h-jit**, injured by the sun, as in a sun-stroke. **hah--kàu**, to reach and influence so far, *e.g.* influence of heat or of exhalation, or of powerful man.

ha̍h — **hàng-ha̍h**, boasting falsely or with exaggeration. **kóng-ōe chin hàng-ha̍h**, talk in a very boastful exaggerated style.

ha̍h [R. hia̍p, to agree]. **ha̍h-ūn**, to agree in rhyme or metrical harmony.

ha̍h [R. ha̍p, to join; to unite], to fit; to suit (lit. or fig.) **ha̍h-ha̍h**, closed tight, as door, &c. **m̄-ha̍h**, not agreeing well, as men. **ōe-ha̍h--tit**, can fit well or act harmoniously, as men or things. **ha̍h-koán**, in tune, as instruments agreeing with each other. **ha̍h-ì**, agreeing with one's inclination. **ha̍h-lâng**, pleasing to a person. **ha̍h-lâng-ēng**, fit for the purpose; fit for use. **ha̍h-ēng**, id. **ū-ha̍h-ēng**, id. **bô-ha̍h-ēng**, useless; unfit for the purpose. **ha̍h-pî**, suiting one's stomach. **ha̍h-chhùi**, pleasant to taste; suiting one's taste. **ha̍h-kha**, to fit the foot. **ha̍h-su**, fitting well, as dress. **m̄-ha̍h-su**, not fitting well, as dress. **m̄-ha̍h-sin**, id.

ha̍h — **thi^n thiah-ha̍h**, morning dawn breaking. **tang--sì thiah-ha̍h**, id. [next word ?].

ha̍h — **kah-ha̍h**, large sheathing-leaves at bamboo joints. **tek-ha̍h**, smaller do. **chià-ha̍h**, outer leaves of sugar-cane (v. chià). **tsang-ha̍h**, the outer sheathing-leaves of the palm called "tsang." **ha̍h-lo̍eh**, sun-hat made of bamboo leaves.

ha̍h [R. hia̍p, the sides of the chest]. **heng-ha̍h**, the breast and sides at the ribs; the chest.

ha̍h (C.), = hâ, to gird, as with a girdle.

hah^n (= hah), to influence or affect, as a vapour or exhalation (gen. unpleasantly or injuriously). **hah^n-sio**, to warm again (as cold food) near the fire. **hah^n-tio̍h-hé**, somewhat injured by being near the fire. **lâng-khì hah^n**, the strong smell and heat of a crowd affecting one unpleasantly, as in hot weather.

ha̍h^n — **ha̍h^n-ha̍h^n**, wanting in substance, as ground-nuts.

ha̍h^n (cf. hâ^n). **ha̍h^n-ha̍h^n**, yes, I hear what you say (but giving no opinion or promise). **i ha̍h^n-ha̍h^n**, he only said "ha̍h^n-ha̍h^n," giving no indication of his purpose.

ha̍h^n, to approach very close, as boat alongside a ship. **ha̍h^n-soa^n**, to hug the shore.

hai, very large; immense.

hâi [R. bones, limbs]. **kut-hâi**, bare human bones. **hêng-hâi**, appearance and form of body. **sù-chi pek-hâi**, the members of the body.

biėt-hâi, to make away with the bones of a grave when taking unjust possession. **biėt-hâi chiàm-tsòng**, id. **kap-goá beh-biėt-hâi**, he is determined to have a hot quarrel with me.

hó-khe-hâi (C. khoe), good at pacing back and forwards (as actor) on the stage. **hó-khe-hâi chhàu-pak-lāi**, putting on a very good and kind appearance, but really very wicked and injurious. **hū-jîn-lâng ê khe-hâi**, feminine in manner (said of a man too minutely neat in dress, &c.) **kāu khe-hâi**, too minute, particular, and over-cautious in a matter, so as to be troublesome, *e.g.* constantly starting additional objections; changeable, inconstant, and unreliable.

hâi (R. id.) **ē-hâi**, the lower jaw.

hâi [R. a boy, a child]. **hâi-jî-á**, a clay child (used as a toy). **hâi-jî-á-sek**, flesh-coloured. **kah ná^{n} hâi-jî-á**, as pretty as a doll (said of a pretty child). **hâi-jî-bīn-tsoá**, large sheets of paper of clay or flesh colour. **hâi-jî-tê**, cutch, catechu.

hâi [R. hāi, a weapon]. **khì-hâi**, weapons of war; deadly weapons. **hâi-tè**, to fight with deadly weapons. **hâi-tiò** (Cn.), id.

hâi (R. id.) **hô-hâi**, harmonious, as music.

hái (R. id.), the sea; the ocean; a lake or large stream or large expanse of water. **sù-hái**, the four seas (v. sù). **soa^{n}-hái**, land and water (v. soa^{n}).

bȧk-hái, a small brass vessel holding cotton saturated with ink.

hái-hông, assistant mandarin of a Foo (the Haifang). **hái-koan**, chief-collector of customs (often incorrectly said for a consul). **hái-lē**, customs duties, port dues, &c. **hái-iû^{n}**, a pirate. **hái-chhȧt**, id.

hái-sū, an island. **hái-thô**, sea-mud. **hái-kha**, the sea-shore. **hái-kî^{n}**, id. **hái-tē**, ground reclaimed from the sea. **iên-hái**, along the shore, as a series of places. **hái-phiâ^{n}**, space between high and low water mark. **hái-thoa^{n}** (R.), soft muddy sea-beach. **hái-pơ**, high dry flat part of sea-beach, not overflowed, or only at highest tides. **hái-bīn**, surface of sea. **poà^{n}-hái**, half way on a voyage in the middle of the sea. **hái-kháu**, mouth of the bay or harbour. **chhun, khoà^{n} hái-kháu; tang, khoà^{n} soa^{n}-thâu**, in spring look out to sea (for signs of weather), in winter look at the hills. **hái-ē**, on the sea or on a large river. **soa^{n}-téng hái-ē**, on land or on water.

hái-liōng (capacity like the sea), very generous; magnanimous. **hái tiōng**, very high tides.

hái-lêng-ông, the god of the sea. **hái-koe-bú**, a sort of broker who deals with ships (v. bú); also, a sort of sea-bird. **hái-bī**, marine animals (in general), used for food (v. bī). **hái-tang** (Cn.), the take of fish, as in a year or season. **bô-hái-lē**, almost no fish to be caught (at a particular time). **hái-chhài**, agar-agar. **hái-som**, biche-de-mer. **hái-hún**, a green sea-weed (dried for food). **hái-lông**, a marine animal with fine fur (v. lông). **hái-bé**, the seal. **hái-ang**, the whale. **chhiah-hái** (F.), a bright red fish. **hái-á**, an animal like a small crab (= phê-oá).

thó-hái, to fish. **thó hái-á**, to catch marine animals when the tide is out; if said of fishing from a boat, it is disrespectful. **thó sió-hái**, id. **lȯh-hái**, to go into the water; to go and catch fish, &c., at low water; to go in a small boat peddling among vessels. **chhut-hái**, the supercargo, esp. in a junk going a shorter distance (for longest voyages it is "tsûn-tsú"), opposed to "chē-soa^{n}--ê," the owner or charterer. **thiām-hái**, may you be drowned! (v. thiām). **kè-goā-hái** (cross the outer sea), said of a candidate getting the Kujin degree by having an essay conveyed to his cell in the stream of water, a plan that needs great bribery.

hài — **hái-hái**, easy and not exacting in dealings. **tsòe-lâng hái-hái**, id.

hái (= hái^{n}), get out of the way! (said to dogs).

hài (= hài^{n}), exclamation of grief.

hāi (R. id.) **hāi-tsāi**, a fabulous animal (v. tsāi).

hāi — **hāi-tsāi**, firm and steady in character; not afraid in time of danger (v. tsāi).

hāi (R. id.), a cyclical character. **hāi-sî**, from 9–11 P.M.

hāi (R. id.), to hurt; to injure. **sa^{n}-hāi**, to injure one another. **siong-hāi**, to wound. **sún-hāi**, to act injuriously, as food, &c. **siū-hāi**, to be severely injured by men. **tsai-hāi** (R.), calamities sent by Heaven.

lī-hāi, dangerous; much to be dreaded, as man, or animal, or weapon; very clever.

ta^{n} hāi--lah, now it is quite spoiled, as a thing; now it is all up, as affair quite ruined. **hāi-sí**, to kill; to cause a man's death. **hāi-lán-chhám**, makes us very miserable. **hāi--lâng tó-àn**, to be the cause of a man losing his case. **hāi-jîn, chek hāi-kí**, who injures another injures himself. **hāi-lâng, chek hāi-kí**, id.

hai^{n} — **hai^{n}-hai^{n}-chhan**, to groan sadly.

hâi^{n} (T.), = A. hêng, to give back; to restore or pay back.

hái^{n} — **hái^{n}-lō-sō**, doing work in a superficial way, without energy or care.

hái^{n} (= hái), noise made in driving away animals.

hài^{n} (= haih^{n}, hài), exclamation of displeasure, distress, or grief for others, as at their actions.

hāi^{n} (T.), = A. hēng, to make a present.

hāi^{n} — **hāi^{n}-ló-sō**, cry of men working together, as in sculling a boat; to assent to, or follow whatever a man says or does, good or bad.

hāi^{n}, exclamation of great pain or weariness. **hāi^{n}-hāi^{n}-háu**, sound of groaning. **hāi^{n}-hāi^{n}-chhan**, id. **hāi^{n}-hāi^{n}-chhoán** (T.), sound made in bearing a very heavy load. **thó-khùi pūn-hāi^{n}**, to sigh bitterly in distress of mind. **tháu-khùi hī^{n}-hāi^{n}** (C.), id.

hāi^{n} — **nńg-hāi^{n}-hāi^{n}**, very wearied and sleepy; weak in body, as a man who has not much strength, though without any decided disease.

haih^{n} (R. hat), an exclamation of displeasure at another's conduct, or of distress or grief for him.

hak, to buy, especially land or houses. **hak-giȧp**, to buy land or houses.

hak, to distil spirits. **hak-chiú**, id.

hak — **pàng-hak-kȧk**, = pàng-hiet-kȧk, to throw away.

hȧk [R. a school, to learn, = col. "ȯh"]. **hȧk-sip**, to learn thoroughly; accustomed to: practised in. **hȧk-hoat**, to learn Tauist arts. **hȧk-būn**, scholarship; learning (v. būn). **chhién-hȧk**, shallow in scholarship. **tāi-hȧk**, one of the four books. **hȧk-seng**, a scholar; a student. **hȧk-hū**, father of scholars. **lí-hȧk**, title conferred on some very learned men, who are then worshipped by the literati. **hȧk-tâi**, the literary examiner of a province. **hȧk-ī^{n}**, id. **tāi-hȧk-sū**, four high chancellors at Pekin, about the rank of prime ministers. **hiȧp-pān tāi-hȧk-sū**, one grade lower. **hȧk-sū-í**, a sort of easy arm-chair.

hák [R. a vault], a necessary. **sái-hák**, id. **khû-hák**, to go to stool. **lòh-hák**, id. **chiū^{n}-hák**, id. **ta^{n}-hák**, to carry away the manure from it.

chiòh-hák, a stone vault for money (s. measure, medicine). **tsáp-goā hák-gûn**, more than ten vaults full of silver.

hák (R. id.), a measure, = ten "chiòh," or one hundred "táu;" a frame for building walls of mud, or of earth and lime. **chhiû^{n}-hák**, the frame for building mud walls, &c. **cheng kúi-hák-chhiû^{n}**, of how many successive layers do you make the wall? (each layer being the height of the frame).

chiòh-hák, a shell like a limpet (medicinal), outside black, inside shining (s. vault). **kim-chiòh-hák**, a medicine like yellow dried straw or rushes. **tsúi-chiòh-hák**, a plant like rushes (Dendrobium or Triticum?).

hák — **hák-hî**, a sort of fish, smaller than the "bé-ka."

ham (R. id.) **ham-bān**, stupid; unskilful; ignorant how to act; inefficient.

ham (R. id.) **tsùi ham-ham** (esp. C.), drunk. **chiú chiáh kàu-ham-ham**, to drink liquor till drunk.

ham — **bák-chiu ham-ham**, eyelids red and swollen, as from weeping, sleeping, or inflammation, or naturally so. **si^{n} bák-ham**, to have a red swelling on the eyelid (not on the edge, which is "bák-chiam").

ham — **téng-ham**, the upper bone inclosing the eye or the mouth. **ē-ham**, the lower bone inclosing the eye.

ham (R. id.), a cockle, especially a large cockle. **ơ-ham**, a small black cockle. **ham-khak**, a cockle-shell. **ham-khak-chháu**, a creeper with leaves like cockle-shells. **ham-khak-chî^{n}**, a cockle-shell, as used in games of chance by children, or as used for rubbing a sick man. **ham-khak-á-chî^{n}**, id.

hâm [R. all], a surname. **hâm-hong**, the reign of Hien-fung.

hâm (R. id.) **hâm-siàu**, a sort of magnolia (fuscata?) with a very sweet smell. **hâm-siàu-hoe**, id.

hâm [R. to contain, to guide, rank]. **koa^{n}-hâm**, official rank and title. **khang-hâm**, mere title of rank without office, like brevet rank. **hōe-hâm**, to put their names and official titles side by side, as two mandarins issuing a joint proclamation.

pien-hâm, the grooves in which a sliding lid, cover, or door works; groove or overlapping edge, by which two boards are fitted together to avoid the risk of chinks.

hâm-toâ^{n}, the hole under the deck, where the foot of the mast is fixed. **hâm-thoâ^{n}**, id. (this and following words have the characters often doubtful or interchanged).

hâm [R. to inclose, to hold in the mouth], along with. **pau-hâm**, to include; inclusive; general or indefinite, as language. **hâm-lâm**, all together; all counted in one. **hâm-gûn, iáh thóeh--khì**, and took away the silver also.

hâm-hê, intentionally talk ambiguously or indistinctly. **hâm-hâm hê-hê**, id. **kóng-ōe hâm-hâm**, intentionally talk of a matter in general or indefinite terms.

hâm--teh, put together, but not yet locked, as a Chinese padlock; still shut, but just about to open, as a bud just bursting; folded and put in the envelope, but not yet sealed, as a letter; laid over, and nothing being done in it, as a case. **hoe hâm-hâm**, bud just bursting, but not yet open. **hâm-lúi**, a half-opened flower.

hâm-kháu-sǹg, to calculate mentally (as if holding the account in one's mouth).

hâm-hūn, to harbour resentment or enmity. **hâm-jīm**, to conceal anger and bear with an offender, because it would be dangerous to deal with him now, but intending to have it out of him again.

siá lâi-hâm, to write the inscription on the inside of an ancestral tablet.

hâm-lêng, small rattles with balls inside, especially used on horses. **hâm-lân** (Cn. T.), id.

hâm-bîn, to talk in one's sleep. **hâm-bîn hâm-tak**, only half wakened and hardly knowing what he is doing; also said of doing a thing very carelessly. **ké-hâm-bîn**, pretending to be foolish, when really cunning or knowing. **lí teh-hâm-bîn**, you are telling a falsehood.

hâm — **hó-chháu-hâm**, able to eat anything. **hó-kháu-hâm**, id. **toā-kháu-hâm**, not content with small gains, as a mandarin or his underling.

hâm (R. id.) **hâm-sau**, slightly cracked, as crockery (v. sau). **hâm-hěh^{n}**, sound of coughing or of cracked crockery (v. hěh^{n}), **hâm-he**, id.

hâm — **hâm-sek-hong** (Cn.), a very dangerous venereal disease.

hám (R. kám), to eat in large mouthfuls without chewing.

hám (R. id.), (T. hán). **hám-oan**, to make a loud noise in order to call for redress from a mandarin, = háu-oan.

hám — **âng-hám-hám**, very red.

hám (C.), = A. hḿ, to strike downwards with a weapon or instrument.

hàm (R. id.; cf. hàng), swollen, as in disease. **hàm-chéng**, id. **hàm-phúh**, id. **hàm-n̂g**, swollen and yellow, as in jaundice. **hàm-tām**, swollen and flabby, as face. **kha hàm**, foot swollen (&c.)

hàm-kià^{n}, a microscope.

hàm (R. id.), vain and empty, as boasting; inflated, false, or exaggerated; untruthfully boastful. **hàm-ōe**, exaggerated talk. **hong-hàm**, exaggerated, as talking very big. **hơ-hàm**, id. **kóng chiah-hàm**, how exaggerated and inflated (talk). **hàm-kớ**, false wonderful stories. **hàm-káu**, reckless and careless in managing matters. **káu-hàm**, id. **hàm-khoā-khoā**, id. **tsòe-sū hàm**, to manage a matter carelessly, so as to leave flaws. **hàm kàu bōe-chhêng--tit báng-tà**, a lie so big that mosquito-curtains could not cover it.

hām — **hām-lām**, together; taken together.

hām — **chhùi hām-hām**, mouth kept quite shut, refusing to speak (= hīm).

hām (P.), = A. ā^{n}, contents of cakes, tarts, &c.

hām [R. a pit; to fall into; to injure], to fall into great calamity. **hong-hām**, very great calamity, as to persons or city. **hiong-hām**, id. **teh-beh-hām**, about to meet with a great calamity. **hām-lòh**, to fall into, as a fault or crime. **hām--lòh-khì**, to fall down, as a landslip, or as man falling down a precipice. **táh-hām**, to tread on a place that is undermined, and so falls down. **pang-hām**, to give way, as an embankment; to fall, as a landslip; to break down suddenly, as a man's health or wealth. **hām--khì**, to fall down, as a landslip.

thê-hām, a pitfall; a deep pit, made by a torrent or by digging. tōe-hām, a covered pit for catching an enemy or wild beast. hām-khiⁿ, a pitfall for catching wild beasts or enemies; a deep pit worn away by a torrent, &c. bé-hām-khiⁿ, a pitfall for catching horse and rider together. khui-hām khui-lang, to make deep pits, as for traps or for security (v. lang).

hām-hāi, to injure very severely, often injure to death.

han [R. hoan, foreign]. han-tsû, sweet-potatoes, = hoan-tsû (v. tsû).

hân [R. leisure, = col. "êng"]. hân-hā, leisure; at leisure. hân-hāu (T.), id. hân-hāu (C.), to wait for a person. an-hân tsū-tsāi, mind and body quite easy and at rest; comfortable, without any need of toil or anxiety. siau-hân (R.), going about at leisure. chheng-hân (R.), in easy and comfortable circumstances (v. chheng).

hân [R. to guard]. hông-hân (R.), to keep careful watch over (as younger relatives) so as to restrain them from bad courses. hông-hân tsú-tē, id.

hân (C.), = A. hiân. hân-thien siōng-tè, one of the great gods.

hân (C.), = A. hêng, to give back (but P. hêng).

hân [R. cold, = col. "koâⁿ," my, in some polite phrases]. hân-soan, very niggardly, over-cautious, mean, or shy (v. soan). pîn-hân (R.), very poor. tám-hân, much afraid.

hân-ka, my surname (polite). hân-sià, my house (polite).

hân-lē, a term about October 8th. tāi-hân, term about Jan. 20, always a fortunate day for making or repairing graves, or for inspecting or removing bones. siáu-hân, the term two weeks before "tāi-hân," *i.e.* about Jan. 5th.

hân-sú-chiam, a thermometer. hong-hân sú-sip, four classes of diseases (v. sú). hân-chèng (R.), colds and such like diseases. siong-hân, having become ill through a chill or a cold. tńg-hân, to become suddenly very cold and dangerously ill, as in the course of an illness. ūi-khì hân, having a tendency to vomit sourish water. pak-lāi hân, cold feeling in the belly, to be relieved by warm drinks. chiūⁿ-bé-hân, a deadly venereal disease. má-siōng-hân (Cn.), id.

hân (R. id.), an ancient kingdom; a surname. hân-kok, the kingdom of Han. hân-tan chhe, a woman whose bridegrooms died (v. "chhe," wife).

hân [R. bêng, bright, morrow]. hân-á-tsài (C.), = A. bîn-á-tsài, to-morrow.

hán [R. seldom, rare]. hán--tit, rarely; seldom or never. hán--tit tī-sî, occasionally. hán-iú, rare. hi-hán, rare, few, costly. hi-hán-kiáⁿ, an only son, much valued. hán-kiàn, rarely to be seen; rarely met with. hán-hông, have you seldom met with it? it is quite common. hán-hông, sái kiaⁿ-bô, you may seldom have seen it, but it is quite common.

hán — saⁿ-thàn saⁿ-hán, to follow other people's example; to follow each other's example. saⁿ-thàn-hán, id.

hán [R. hám, to shout loud]. hán-hoā, loud noise or indistinct hum of a crowd, with noisy talk; to be in an excited state, as a community, when rebels or banditti are said to be near. hán-hoah, loud shouting and noisy disturbance; to make a loud shouting, *e.g.* in junks when a storm is rapidly coming on. hán-oan (T.), = háu-oan, = hám-oan, to call loudly and noisily on a mandarin for redress.

hàn [R. the Han dynasty; Chinese], (a person). hàn-tiâu, the Han dynasty. hàn-ko-tsó, its founder, worshipped by the heads of wards (tē-pó), as he was originally a Tepo.

hàn-lâng, a Chinaman, as opposed to Tartars. hàn-peng, Chinese (not Tartar) troops. hàn-sek, a feast in Chinese style. hàn-jī, Chinese characters. boán-hàn, Manchoo and Chinese (v. boán).

lô-hàn (Cn. lê-hàn), a Lohan; one of the eighteen great disciples of Buddha. lô-hàn-kha, a wandering man, generally idle or ill-behaved; a rowdy or loafer, a tramp. lô-hàn-tsáⁿ, a dress made of two sorts of stuff, in the body and the skirt. lô-hàn-i, id.

lâm-tsú-hàn, a man, not a woman, said only in a few phrases. tōng-tōng lâm-tsú-hàn, you big fellow! said in scolding a grown-up fellow for fawning on people or begging from them. hàn-chiàng, a tall fat man (v. chiàng). hó-hàn, fat, stout (rarely said of animals). sòe-hàn, young, as a child or boy; very short, as a man. toā-hàn, grown up, as an adult; tall, or full-grown. toā-bú-hàn, tall. toā-bóng-hàn (C.), id. ài-toā-hàn, fond of flattery; fond of being counted of consequence. i toā-hàn ê só-tsāi, the place where he lived from youth till grown up. chhng-hàn (r.), a rustic. iá-hàn, uncultivated clownish-like man. thó-hàn, id. tsùi-hàn, a drunkard. chiàh-chiú-hàn, id. thiàu-hàn (T. hān), a troublesome, idle, unruly boy.

hān [R. perspiration, = col. "koāⁿ."]. hoat-hān, to perspire in disease, for recovery. hān-kun, a cloth for wiping off sweat.

hān [R. a pen]. hān-lîm, the Imperial Han-lin Academy; a member of it (v. lîm).

hān (R. id.), (cf. ān), a limit; to limit, as a time of grace for payment. kài-hān, a limit, of place. bô-kài-hān, unbounded. bô-hān-liōng, immense; illimitable.

hān-tiāⁿ, to limit; to set a limit or fixed time, esp. extended period for payment. hān tī-sî, set what time as the limit? hān sî-khek, to limit to the moment. kè-hān, to pass the proper time or quantity; rites for making a man pass from a bad fate to a good fate. tsáp-hān, káu bô-iáⁿ, of ten promises to pay, nine are not kept. bōe-hān--tit (T.), = A. bōe-ān--tit, cannot appoint a future time; you must pay now.

thiàu-hān (T.), = A. thiàu-hàn, an idle, unruly, troublesome boy.

hān [R. drought, = col. "oāⁿ."] hān-lē, road by land. khòng-hān, severe drought. hān-poàt, the demon of drought; a paper image of him. tsoá-kê hān-poàt, paper image of him. thâi-hān-poàt, Tauist ceremony of beheading the image so as to get rain. hān-poàt-chhùi, constantly saying unlucky words (unintentionally), as about sickness or death.

hang (R. hong), to dry or warm at the fire; to toast. hang-hé, id., either self or things. hang-ta, to dry at the fire. hang-sio, to warm at the fire. hang-chhiú, to warm one's hands. hang hé-thang, to warm one's self with a small portable stove in a wicker basket. hang bīn-pau, to toast bread.

hang-lô, a small portable earthen stove, as for boiling water for tea.

hang (R. hong), the skate-fish. hang-hî, id. n̂g-hang, the yellowish sort, counted best. o-hang, the dark-coloured sort, counted worse.

hang-kiàm, the long spike of the skate. **hang-chhì**, the pair of spikes at its tail. **it hang, jī hê**, the "hang" and the "hê" are the fishes that make the worst wounds.

hâng (R. id. by change of tone from "kàng" to descend), to surrender on condition of impunity, generally taken into service; to make submission on terms. **hâng-hòk**, to make submission; to subdue. **tâu-hâng**, to surrender on condition of impunity or reward, or being taken into the service of the government. **tsà-hâng**, to make feigned submission. **hâng-mô-thú**, a baton for quelling demons.

hâng (R. id., variation, with tonal mark, from "hêng," to go), a row; a column, as of words or of figures; to quilt, as a dress or a coverlet; a large mercantile firm or hong; properly only a great hong that issues securities (kiet) for junks belonging to other firms.

hâng-ngê, gaudy; splendid.

sek-hâng, skilful, experienced.

sù-hâng, the four lictors, holding chains or bamboos, who stand or walk before a mandarin.

hâng-kau, a large trading firm; a wholesale mercantile house; a hong (v. kau). **toā-hâng**, a large trading firm. **sió-hâng**, a small one. **hâng-ke**, head or manager of a firm. **hâng-hē**, a wholesale merchant or head of the house. **hâng-siong**, id. **hâng-tiú^n**, the hired manager of a hong. **iû^n-hâng**, house trading in foreign goods. **káu-poeh-hâng**, a commission agent taking two per cent. commission. **gê-hâng**, sort of broker or commission agent. **khui-hâng**, to have a warehouse or hong, as merchant. **khui-hâng chē-tiàm**, to have hongs or shops. **hâng tó**, bankrupt.

hâng-kiet, the security given to the mandarins by a registered hong (*e.g.* kim-éng-chhiong) for a junk of another firm (v. kiet). **hâng-tiōng**, commission charged by commission agent, &c. **hâng-chêng**, market price. **hoā^n hâng-chêng**, to fix the market price of goods, as a leading firm does, so that the other firms follow; also, to have the authoritative voice in a hong for buying or selling. **i khah-tsai hâng-chêng**, he is specially acquainted with the price of goods. **i khah-ū hâng-chêng**, he is very fair in the prices that he names (as broker or merchant), so that people apply to him to value goods.

hâng-thâu, a hong in relation to the sending of goods to it. **kià sím-mih^n hâng-thâu**, to which hong is it to be sent, by ship? **thèh hâng-thâu-gûn**, to borrow money from the hong with which our vessel does business.

hâng-hiû, to quilt a coat. **hâng khah-khin-chhiú**, quilt it more loosely.

hâng (R. id.) **hâng-chiu**, Hang-chow. **hâng-chiok**, a medicine from it. **so-hâng**, Soo-chow and Hangchow.

háng (R. hōng), to threaten; to frighten by talk; to intimidate. **háng-phièn**, to frighten and cheat, as sorcerers or Tauist priests, or underlings of yamuns. **háng-phièn-sút**, id. **háng lâng-ê-chî^n**, to cheat and frighten people out of their money, as mandarins' underlings.

háng-hoah, to scold and threaten; to intimidate by talking loud. **háng-hip**, id. **háng-sau** (C. háu-sau), to scold loudly; to wrangle in a loud overbearing way. **háng-sè**, to boast or brag of one's power or influence. **ū háng-thâu**, using big words; talk in a bragging, boastful, or blustering way. **háng-thâu toā**, id.

hàng (R. hèng, cf. phàng, phòng, hàm), to swell, as from a blow or a poisonous bite; swollen; (to brag). **hàng-hàng**, covered with itching swellings, as from insects' bites; slightly swollen. **hàng-chéng**, a swelling. **kha hàng--khí-lâi**, foot swollen. **hàng-lin**, female breast swollen, as by disease; also (T.), naturally grown large, as of girl coming of age; also (T.), grown fat on milk, as infant.

hàng-lâu, tide broken by rocks, as in chow-chow water.

hàng-hàh, very boastful (v. hàh).

hāng — **hāng-tāng**, heavy and cumbrous; ponderous; severe, as sickness; heavy manner of walking, setting down foot heavily. **kóng-ōe hāng-tāng**, to talk in a loud voice so as to show that the matter is important, or pretending so.

hāng (R. id.), a lane. **hāng-á**, id. **hāng-lē**, a private lane; a passage in a house. **thong-hāng**, a public lane used as a thoroughfare. **hāng-á hāng-sut**, a very out-of-the-way corner of a lane. **bô-bé-hāng**, a *cul-de-sac*. **hāng-thâu**, the spaces at the corners of the central house in a Chinese large house. **khut-chhioh-hāng**, a lane with a right angle bend. **oan-koe phiah-hāng**, crooked and unfrequented streets and lanes. **hāng chhim, káu ok**, very hard of access.

hāng (R. id.), a kind, a sort. **bô-chit-hāng**, not anything of any sort. **bōe kui-hāng**, to sell wholesale (v. kui). **chiâ^n-hāng**, in considerable quantities. **ka-nn̄g-hāng**, id. **goá bô ka-nn̄g-hāng-chî^n**, I have not large quantities of money.

siàu-hāng, an account of a sum due. **hiòng-hāng**, money of customs duties. **chî^n-hāng**, money. **gûn-hāng**, silver; money; treasure in silver. **chit-tiâu gûn-hāng**, one item in account, or considerable sum due, counted in silver.

tng sím-mih^n hāng-tàng, what office (subordinate) have you? as in yamun. **bong sím-mih^n hāng-tàng**, what is your business?

hāng — **hé-hāng**, the cactus, especially the common coarse cactus.

hāng (R. hiēn). **hāng-chhài** (T.), = A. hēng-chhài, a sort of vegetable.

hap, to speak falsely; to give an uncertain statement as if it were certain truth; to go beyond the truth. **gâu-hap**, fond of talking so. **chhùi lām-sám-hap**, id. **lâng hap-hap**, the man is not to be relied upon.

hàp (R. id.), to join; united; fitting well; to shut; one round, as in a fight; one pair or set of some things.

sa^n-hàp, joined together; fitting together. **sa^n-hô-hàp**, agreeing well, as persons. **khè-hàp** (R.), joined in close friendship. **hàp-kiōng**, all united; sum total. **hû-hàp**, agreeing well, as evidence or documents. **hàp-tâng**, agreement about division of family property (v. tâng). **khàm-hàp**, the words "khàm-hàp" stamped or written on a document where it is to be torn or cut in two, or on the two parts of a tally, or on two documents, to be used in comparing them as evidence. **tǹg-khàm-hàp**, to stamp these words. **tùi khàm-hàp**, to examine if they correspond on the two parts. **hàp-iok**, a bond or agreement in duplicate, the character "hàp" being stamped on both at once, to serve as proof.

hàp-kai-tiòh, ought to —. **hàp-sit**, fit; fitting; becoming. **m̄-hàp-lí**, improper. **hàp-ì**, to suit one's mind. **hàp i--ê sè-ēng**, fit for his use.

háp-hé, to join stock in trade, with about equal shares. **háp-sit**, to take meals regularly together. **háp-toh**, the feast of the bride with her female friends. **háp-hun**, to consummate a marriage. **phòe-háp**, joined in marriage. **kau-háp**, to have sexual intercourse.

háp-thàn, to gain cent. per cent. **thiu háp-tek** (C.), to take off a small sum for brokerage (v. "tek," to get).

háp-á, a dollar made of base metal coated with silver.

chit-háp, a pair, as of knives; a set, as a nest of small pots with covers inside each other. **chit-háp-toh**, a pair of tables.

iā-háp, the magnolia. **pek-háp**, a medicinal root (squills?) like garlic. **pek-háp-hoe**, a sort of lily (or Amaryllis?) with a great many petals (Lilium tigrinum, or = pe̍h-kok-pie̍t, white Amaryllis?).

hat — **hat-á**, a long bag with dollars tied round the waist. **hat-lá**, id. **hat-pŏ** (T.), a cloth for strapping a child on the back.

hat (R. id. = col. "hoah"), to speak loud and angrily, as in finding fault with a man, or in saying, I will have nothing to do with it. **hat-lat**, id. **hat--lâng**, id. **hat-thâu**, to scold or reprove violently.

hat — **hat-chhiùⁿ** (Cn.), to sneeze.

hat [R. to rule, to govern]. **koán-hat**, to rule; to manage authoritatively. **hun-hat**, to order to their several duties. **hə-hat**, to give orders to inferiors somewhat imperiously. **thóng-hat**, to govern, rule, or manage the whole, as a mandarin. **tī-goá hat-ē**, under my authority, as an inferior.

hát [R. hān, to limit], to limit in quantity; amount very limited or barely enough. **hát tiāⁿ-tio̍h**, to limit a certain quantity. **hát joā-tsōe-chîⁿ**, how much money has he fixed? **chîⁿ-thâu hát**, money very scarce, or hardly enough. **chîⁿ khah-hát**, id. **hát-tsúi**, to use water sparingly, either from scarcity, or for keeping the due proportion, as in cooking, or in mixing medicine. **tsúi put-chí-hát**, water very scarce.

giâm-hát, very stern or strict, as teacher, master, or mandarin.

hát, a ganglion; a small swelling on the nerves or under the skin, which can be moved about, and does not suppurate. **khan-hát**, to have such a swelling.

hau — **bīn hau-hau**, face having thick-skinned spots, as when affected by varnish, or as at commencement of leprosy, &c.

hau [R. hə? to call out, to lie; or hong? fabulous; or some of the phrases may be imitation of mandarin]. **hau-lák**, to tell lies; to exaggerate enormously; what a story! **hau-siâu** (vulg.), what a great lie! **gâu-hau** (T.), always telling lies. **hau-tông**, **bô-iáⁿ-chiah sòng** (T.), = A. hong-tông, &c., fabulous stories, as of Tang and Sung dynasties.

hau (R. o). **hau-pau**, a sort of purse or small pouch. **hau-pau-toà**, the string for drawing it shut. **hau-pau-sok**, a bit of shell or pretty stone through which the cord runs. **hau-pau-chhiu**, two tassels where it is fastened.

hâu [R. hə̂, = col. "kâu," a monkey], a surname, = kâu.

hâu [R. hiên, to hang up], (Cn.), = A. hâuⁿ, to procrastinate; to put off.

háu (R. hə́), to cry; to chirp, sing, low, bellow, roar, &c., as almost any animal; to make a noise, of many sorts. **pak-lāi háu**, sound of wind in the belly. **thî-háu**, to sob bitterly (v. thî). **háu-kiò**, to cry or call out loud, as in pain (v. kiò). **háu-iau**, to cry for food, as a child. **háu-oan**, to make a loud noise in calling on a mandarin for redress. **háu-hoah**, to talk very loud, in scolding, reproving, or threatening. **háu-sau**, to scold with a loud voice; to wrangle in a loud overbearing way.

chiuh-chiuh-háu, to squeak, as a rat. **hāⁿ-hāⁿ-háu**, to snarl, as dog. **hoā-hoā-háu**, to make a loud noise, as waves or many persons. **ki-ki-háu**, constantly crying. **ngáuh-ngáuh-háu**, to grumble indistinctly, as a discontented man afraid to speak out. **khiáuh-khiáuh-háu**, to make a constant noise, as constant beating a stone, or constant talking, &c. (v. khiàuh).

hàu (R. id.), filial duty; filial piety; to worship by offerings; to act in a filial manner. **hàu-kèng**, id. **hêng-hàu**, to perform filial duty. **hêng-hàu pē-bú**, to act in a filial way to parents. **hàu-pē-bú**, id. **hàu-hēng**, filial conduct. **hàu-sim**, filial heart. **hàu-sūn**, filial and obedient. **chīn-tiong chīn-hàu**, dutiful and filial to the utmost. **ū-hàu**, filial and dutiful to parents. **put-hàu**, unfilial, disobedient, undutiful or ungrateful to parents. **tāi-put-hàu**, extremely undutiful to parents. **sēng-kiáⁿ put-hàu**, a spoiled child becomes disobedient (v. sēng). **hàu-keng**, the classic of filial piety.

hàu-mihⁿ, to worship with offerings. **hàu-pn̄g**, to make offerings (of rice, &c.) to the spirit of a person recently buried, in the rites called "khiā-hà," before the image called "hûn-sin;" done on the 1st and 15th for a year; or for 40, 60, or 100 days; said also as a coarse joke to a man eating rice. **hàu-chhài-pn̄g**, to make offerings of food in the worship of the spirits called "mn̂g-kháu-kong."

hàu mn̂g-kháu, to worship the wandering spirits at the door, as in the seventh moon; or on the 2d and 16th of each moon. **hàu-pu̍t**, to worship idols by offerings. **hàu thiⁿ-kong**, to worship Heaven by offerings on 1.9. **hàu-kə**, to make offerings to a spirit that has no descendants; said also in scolding (v. kə). **hàu koaⁿ-chhâ-thâu**, to make offerings at the coffin (said in a proverb).

hàu-lâm, a son in deepest mourning for a parent while acting as mourner at the funeral and some special rites; said also in scolding a man who looks very foolish, dull, and unintelligent: "You look as if in mourning for a parent." **thùh-thùh náⁿ-hàu-lâm**, looking terribly dull and stupid. **hàu-lú**, a daughter (&c.) in deepest mourning at funeral rites. **hàu-sun**, a grandson in mourning at funeral ceremonies. **hàu-tsú-hng**, a memorial archway put up by imperial authority in memory of a very filial son. **hàu-tsú-têng**, a shed over a tablet for do. (less honourable). **chiet-hàu-hng**, memorial archway in honour of a lady distinguished for purity and filial piety.

hàu — **lāu-hàu**, a sort of nutmeg, larger and coarser than "tə-khə̀." **lāu-hàu-chí**, a nutmeg. **lāu-hàu-khak**, its husk. **lāu-hàu-hoe**, nutmeg flowers, medicinal.

hāu [R. hə, after]. **hāu-siⁿ**, a son. **hāu-siⁿ-ke**, a young lad. **khit hāu-siⁿ**, to buy a boy and adopt him as a son. **goán-hāu--ê**, my son.

hāu (R. hə), to wait for. **hāu-goá**, wait for me. **hāu siau-sit**, waiting for news. **hāu-sím**, to wait for the trial coming on, as parties and witnesses. **hāu-phoe**, to wait for the mandarin's official answer to a petition. **chí-tiến hāu-siòk**, to close a pawn-shop, and wait a time to let the goods be redeemed.

hāu-pé, having got the rank (like brevet-rank) and orders from the supreme board to have the office as soon as a vacancy occurs. **hāu-pé ti-hú**, expectant or designate prefect.

hāu-bēh, to feel the pulse the second time. **hāu-mēhⁿ**, id.

pài-hāu, to pay a ceremonial visit; to call upon, as a friend. **thèng-hāu** to wait, for a time. **hân-hāu** (C.), id. **su-hāu**, = su-hə, to wait upon or wait for, as attendants on a mandarin when he comes out (v. hə). **sî-hāu** (r. esp. C.), time.

hāu [R. hā, leisure]. **hân-hāu** (T.), = A. hân-hā, at leisure.

hāu [R. to exert one's self; interchanged with the next word]. **hāu-iōng**, a small military official, who has a gilt button but no office. **sió-sim hāu-lô**, extremely attentive, as servants (v. lô). **hāu-lèk** (r.), to be diligent in military service, as soldiers or petty officers giving assistance to superiors. **eng-kai--tiòh hāu-lèk**, it was my duty to assist you, said politely when thanked for a service.

hāu [R. to accomplish; to copy; efficacious]. **hāu-giām**, effective in accomplishing its end, as medicine, predictions, prayers or superstitious rites. **èng-hāu**, id., especially of vows. **kong-hāu**, efficaciousness, as of medicine, or plan, or labour. **ū-kong-hāu**, to be efficacious, as medicine, &c. **bô-kong bô-hāu**, having no good result, as agricultural toil when weather delays or spoils the crop.

hāu-iû, to imitate bad example.

hāu [R. oá, a tile, = col. hiā, hoā]. **hāu-hiaⁿ-phè**, broken bits of tiles, as at a ruined house. **hāu-phiaⁿ-phō** (T.), id.

hāu (T.) **khùt-hāu**, a small piece of a rainbow in mid sky.

hāu (R. id.), the king-crab. **hāu-huih-chhiⁿ**, light dull blue, like its blood. **hāu-peh-chheh** (its overlapping scales), venetian shutters. **hāu-bé-to**, a bayonet. **hāu-khak**, the shell of the king-crab. **hāu-phiô**, a skimmer made of the shell. **hāu-siàh**, a small scoop or ladle made of it. **hāu-hia**, a large ladle made of it. **hāu-hiàh**, having a large forehead (v. heng, "breast").

soaⁿ-hāu (vulg.), a rough boorish fellow; a dull awkward fellow. **tsòe-chhàt tsòe-hāu**, to be thieves and robbers. **liàh hāu-á**, to seize men and extort money. **liàh-hāu**, to seize in the act of vile lust. **chit-ngauh-hāu**, two persons in the act of impurity, esp. of unnatural lust.

tsúi-hāu, a fresh-water insect that lives long after being caught. **tsúi-hāu-ang**, a toy containing one of them that moves the arms and head of the figure. **ah-bú chiàh tsúi-hāu** (the duck gobbles up the insect, which lives long after), said in joke of a man feeling anxious and grieved.

hāu-kha-chhì, a low trailing thorny shrub, with glossy leaves and black edible berries. **hāu-á-chhì**, id. **hāu-á-chí**, its berry. **hāu-á-thâu** (P.), its root, used as medicine.

hauⁿ, = hàuhⁿ, sound as of a dog growling. **hauⁿ-hauⁿ-háu**, id.

hâuⁿ [R. hiên, to hang up], (Cn. hâu), to put off too long; to delay improperly.

háuⁿ — **háuⁿ-háuⁿ-pūi**, sound of a dog barking long.

hàuⁿ [R. hòⁿ, "to desire," by change of tone from hóⁿ, "good"], to take pleasure in, as improper pleasures.

hauh — **hauh-khak**, peeling off, as paint, skin, or scab. **hauh--khí-lâi**, id.

hauhⁿ (C. hop; Cn. nauhⁿ; T. nauhⁿ, ngauhⁿ), to catch suddenly in the mouth, as a dog; to snap up or bite suddenly. **hauhⁿ--tiòh**, id.

hàuhⁿ — **pit-hàuhⁿ-hàuhⁿ**, all splitting into cracks, as wood in drought.

hàuhⁿ (cf. khàuh), under-cooked, as potatoes or vegetables (not flesh); bad, as potatoes that cannot be cooked well. **ngīⁿ-hàuhⁿ**, too hard, as cakes, &c.

hàuhⁿ, = hauⁿ. **hàuhⁿ-hàuhⁿ-háu**, sound of dog growling. **hàuhⁿ-hàuhⁿ-pūi**, id.

he (C. hɛ). **he-ku**, asthma. **hâm-he**, sound of coughing.

he (= hí, = hit-ê), that, demonstrative pronoun, only in combination when unaccented.

he [R. hoa, a flower, = col. "hoe"]. **khè-he-sek**, = khè-hoe-sek, light grayish purple.

he (R. oe, hoe), (C. hoe; Cn. hö), lime; plaster (for wall); mortar; cement. **he-hún**, powdered lime. **he-chiòh**, limestone. **chiòh-he**, lime from limestone. **ô-khak-he**, lime from oyster-shells. **he-thâu**, refuse lime, riddled out. **he-phí**, thin scales of plaster peeling off walls. **lak he-phí**, these peeling and falling off. **he-phiáⁿ**, large masses of plaster from walls.

he-sek, light gray colour. **he-tsoā**, a line of caulking. **he-chhat**, varnish and lime mixed, for filling crevices. **he-iô**, a lime-kiln. **he-sî**, sort of trowel for building, with the handle placed as on a shield. **he-thûi**, an instrument for beating and mixing lime.

kan-he, mortar of pure lime with no mixture. **lām-he**, well mixed with lime, as good mortar. **thang-iû-he**, cement made of lime and the oil of the "thâng" tree. **tsoá-kun-he**, fine plaster made with finely chopped paper. **chháu-he**, plaster made of clay or mud mixed with chopped straw, but no lime. **chháu-phiáⁿ-he**, plaster made of lime and earth with finely beaten straw (v. chháu). **soa-he**, mortar of lime and sand. **he-soa**, lime and sand, ready to be mixed. **he-soá**, mortar of lime and very stiff clay. **he-thô**, mortar of lime and clay or earth.

oà-he, to pour water on quick-lime. **hoat-he**, to slack lime, whole process. **cheng-he**, to beat mortar hard and smooth, as on a floor, by a pestle. **koat-he**, to beat cement smooth with a sort of trowel. **kuih-he**, to rub cement into crevices. **chhák-he**, to caulk. **boah-he**, to plaster. **chhéng-he**, to white-wash. **phiák-he**, to dash the lime on.

hê, an interjection of sudden astonishment.

hê (R. hâ), (C. hê). **âng-hê**, red clouds (s. shrimp). **hûn-hê** (T.), id. **khí âng-hê**, red clouds appearing, as at sunset. **chhut âng-hê**, id. **hōng-koaⁿ hê-pòe**, head-dress and ornamental girdle of wealthy lady (v. koaⁿ, koan, "a cap").

hê (C.), = A. hâ, a flaw, as in a gem.

hê (R. hôe), (C. hôe, sometimes hê; T. hō), to return a thing; to carry a message back or forwards; to accompany another on a musical instrument; to slack the tiller-rope so as to let the vessel go somewhat off the wind.

āu-hê, afterwards; on another occasion.

hê-ōe, to interpret between two persons. **hê-lâi hê-khì**, to take messages back and forwards. **jip--khì hê**, to go in (as into the yamun) and give the mes-

16

sage. **hê hō͘-i-tsai**, id. **hê-hok**, to make report to him who sent us. **hê-phoe**, to send a letter in answer. **hê-bûn**, to answer an official letter. **hê-thiap**, to send a card in return; a return card. **hê-pài**, to return a visit. **hê-thâu-kiō**, a return sedan. **hoat-hê**, to send back, as goods sent for inspection but not chosen, or as presents not accepted, as in general those from mandarins.

hê-sim tńg-ì, to change one's mind. **hê-lâm àh-sai**, north wind falling and veering round to south-west; after sudden anger, changing suddenly to friendly feeling. **hê-lâm**, to change to a south wind; anger suddenly changing. **hê lâm-hong**, id. id.

goá-chhiùⁿ lí-hê, I sing, and you accompany on an instrument.

hê [R. hē, summer]. **lóh-hê-bê**, long-continued drizzling rains about the time of "jip-hē."

hê (R. hâ), (C. hê), a shrimp; a prawn; grubs of some kinds. **phang-hê**, the grub of the bee.

lêng-hê, the lobster. **káu-hê**, a small sort of shrimp. **gē-chhiu-hê**, a small white shrimp. **âng-hê**, red shrimps (s. clouds). **péh-hê**, white shrimps. **péh-hê-á**, id. **soa-hê**, shrimps from sandy beaches. **thô-hê**, small shrimps from sea-mud. **chhân-hê** (C.), a sort from rice-fields. **lō͘-hê**, pickled shrimps from Shantung. **lō͘-hê-chiùⁿ**, brine from them. **hê-bí**, very small shrimps. **hê-ko**, a very large sort (v. ko).

hê-chhiu, beard of shrimp (v. chhiu). **hê-kô**, a trap for shrimps. **hê-lāng** (C.), id.

tng-hê, to lay a trap for shrimps. **khan-hê**, to catch shrimps by pulling along a net (tsan), as by boat and raft. **khan-káu-hê**, id.

ngiauh-hê, quite dead (said of a man somewhat as a joke).

hiuⁿ-hê, bags of cotton and incense on idol's forehead, shaped like shrimps.

hê [R. hô, harmonious, concord], (C. hôe), not too hot, as tea or water. **hê-siūⁿ**, a Buddhist priest; a sort of crab (v. siūⁿ). **hê-hoan**, to go and make peace with (Tartar) foreigners (v. hoan). **chhut-pún hê-hoan**, to pay money in advance for a friend (v. hoan).

hê [R. hā, below; to come down], to let down, as a sedan, or as one's temper; become gentle, as wind. **hong hê-hê**, wind blowing gently. **hong khah-hê**, wind become gentle. **kè-sò khah-hê**, the price has fallen somewhat. **hō͘ khah-hê, chiah-khì**, wait till the rain has abated before you go. **hê--lóh-khì**, let it down, as sedan. **sèng-tē pàng-khah-hê**, let your temper down a little.

hê [R. to take up or lead by the hand]. **thê-hê**, to assist a man in straits, as by lending money or giving work, or helping to get a situation.

hé [R. hó, colleague, comrade, company], (C. hóe; Cn. hō͘). **hé-tiúⁿ**, captain of a large junk or ship. **toā-hé**, captain, as of a foreign ship. **jī-hé**, first mate. **saⁿ-hé**, second mate. **sió-hé**, private business of his own (done by a hired manager in a hong, with the funds of the hong, and on the premises). **tsòe-sió-hé**, to transact his own private business thus. **háp-hé**, to join stock and capital in about equal shares. **chhát-hé**, one of a company of thieves, robbers, or pirates.

hé-kì, a partner or assistant; a fellow-workman; often said to a man in addressing him (Cantonese "fokee"); sometimes, my wife. **liên-tsâi hé-kì**, partners in a firm. **thiah hé-kì**, to dissolve partnership. **tàu-hé-kì**, to be partners in a business. **saⁿ-nîⁿ, chhut chiōng-goân: saⁿ-nîⁿ, chhut bô-chít-ê hó-hé-kì**, once in three years one man gets the highest literary degree, but a good partner is not found so often.

chit-hé ê-lâng, persons of one class, company, or faction. **in-chit-hé ê-lâng**, a man of their class, sort, &c. **kap--i tsòe-chit-hé**, to be of one class with him.

hé (C. hóe; Cn. hō͘), often interchanged with the previous and following words.

hé-sit, food, as used or prepared (v. sit).

ke-hé, property of any sort. **pun-ke-hé**, to divide the property and goods, as after father's death.

pān kong-hé-á, children playing at an imitation feast with broken bits of bowls, &c.

hé (R. hóⁿ), (C. hóe; Cn. hō͘), fire; a lamp; the hot or inflammatory principle in the constitution.

hé-hāng, the cactus. **hé-kim-chhiⁿ**, the fire-fly. **hé-iâⁿ** (Cn.), id. **hé-soān**, a first-class diamond. **hé-chiáu**, a certain ill-omened bird; an over-cute boy (v. chiáu).

hé-sîn-iâ (C. hóe-ông), the god of fire. **hiuⁿ-hé**, small bags of incense ashes with idols' names on them (used as charms).

hé-jī-kha, the 86th radical (fire) when written as four dots below the rest of the character.

hé-thâu, a cook. **sio-hé**, id.; sometimes said for "my wife." **chhàu-hé-lo-bī**, singed taste. **bô-kàu chhâ-hé**, not sufficiently fired in cooking. **iû-hé-hun**, expense of tobacco and of oil of lamp for it (v. iû). **hé-chiú**, strong spirits that can burn. **hé-thúi**, ham.

hé-khì, the hot principle in the human constitution; inflammatory or feverish tendency. **hé-seng**, having much of the hot principle in one's constitution; having a tendency to a red face, and not daring to eat heating things. **hé-sèng**, a fiery temper. **sim-hé**, internal heat, as slight feverishness (v. sim). **sim-hé tòh**, rage stirred up. **iok-hé**, the fire of lustful passion. **thâm-hé**, tendency to (cancerous?) swelling of the throat. **chheng-hé**, to remove feverishness or inflammation; comfortable or delighted (v. chheng). **thè-hé**, to remove feverishness or inflammation. **khì-hé**, id. **hu-hé** (C. hi-hóe), feeling slightly feverish, *e.g.* mouth dry and skin somewhat hot. **ut-hé**, feeling uncomfortable and unwell (v. ut). **kan-hé**, feverish state, supposed to come from the liver (v. kan). **pak-lāi ū siâ-hé**, much fevered. **hong-hé**, wind and fire (diseases of the nature of swellings, inflammations, and fevers). **hong-hé kek**, caused by these diseased tendencies. **kín náⁿ-hong-hé**, as quick as wind and fire.

kúi-hé, *ignis fatuus.* **hé-thai**, exceedingly sultry weather.

hé-sok, very quickly, as in executing orders. **hé phiò**, a warrant for the very speedy arrest of a man. **hé-pâi**, id. (v. pâi). **hé-chhiam**, slips of wood given to the messenger to show the urgency of the warrant.

hé-hu, ashes in powder (v. hu). **hé-ien**, colourless smoke or steam. **hé-hun**, smoke (v. hun). **hé-ńg**, place in shade from a lamp or candle (v. ńg). **hé-iām**, a flame. **hé-chih**, a tongue of fire. **hé-chhiⁿ**, sparks. **hé-hoe**, sparks, as from a match (v. hoe). **hé-sái**, spots from a lamp-wick; snuffings. **hé-sio-chhù**, a conflagration; a house on fire. **hé-sio--ah**, fire! fire! **thiah hé-lō͘**, to tear down houses in order to subdue a fire. **hé-chíⁿ**, a vault for keeping things secure from fire. **hé-khò**, a fire-proof store.

hé-chiòh, flint. **hé-hiā^{n}**, tinder. **hé-to**, a steel for striking fire. **hé-poe**, a sort of iron like a poker with a crooked end (used red-hot for melting cement, &c.) **hé-kńg**, a hollow bamboo for blowing the fire. **hé-khî^{n}**, tongs. **hé-ngoeh**, slim tongs with curved points. **hé-tī**, two iron rods used as tongs. **hé-chhê**, a poker. **hé-iām**, a shovel.

teng-hé, a small lamp made with a small saucer. **chit-pha-hé**, one lamp or light. **hé-oá^{n}**, a metal dish with a very large wick, used at plays. **hé-táu**, a three-sided screen for a lamp, used at plays. **hé-lô**, a stove; a furnace; a fireplace. **hé-thang** (C. hóe-lang), a small charcoal stove in a basket, for warming the hands, or putting under one's clothes. **hé-tiá^{n}**, the pan for cooking rice; a rice-boiler. **kúi--ê hé-tiá^{n}**, how many families?

hé-koe, the part of the gun that holds the match. **hé-lêng**, match for matchlock. **hé-pau**, a ball full of powder thrown in war. **hé-koàn**, a "stink-pot" used by pirates. **tē-lûi hé-phàu**, sort of mines in war. **hé-iòh**, gunpowder. **hé-chhat**, a sort of cement that is melted when used.

ien-hé, fireworks. **pàng ien-hé**, to let off fireworks. **péh-hé**, a sky-rocket. **hé-bé**, a firework like a horse, made of bamboo. **pàng hé-bé**, to set off this firework. **hé-sai**, firework like a lion. **hé-ku**, one like a turtle. **tsū-lâi-hé** (r.), lucifer matches. **hoan-á-hé**, id. **tsoá-lién-hé**, a lighted match of twisted paper.

khiet-hé, to strike fire with a flint. **phah-hé**, to strike fire. **phah-hoa-hé**, to extinguish fire (v. hoa). **phah-sit-hé** (T.), id. **sit-hé**, to set on fire accidentally. **khí-hé**, to light a fire. **hiâ^{n}-hé**, to add more fuel (v. hiâ^{n}). **ín-hé**, to take a light from another light; to catch fire (v. ín). **hoà-hé**, to be completely burned; to burn, as paper. **chiū^{n}-hé**, to light many lamps, as in markets at night, or as at idolatrous illuminations. **pûn-hé**, to blow the fire; to blow out a lamp; to blow a match into flame. **chiò-hé**, to give light, as by a lamp hung up. **chioh-hé**, to warm one's self, or a thing, at the fire. **hìm-hé**, to cover up and extinguish embers, to be kept for use. **ìm-hé**, id. **tâu-hé**, to fly into the flame, as a moth. **thiàu-hé-phûn**, to leap through a large pile of burning wood, as on 1.15. **sio-hé-phûn**, to have this ceremony. **kè-hé**, to go through a charcoal fire, as necromancers with an idol, at any time. **táh-hé**, id. **chhiá^{n}-hé**, to bring sacred fire with incense ashes (and carrying idols) from a greater temple to a less important one. **khat-hō͘** (Cn.), id.

hé, an emphatic interjection used before a negative sentence. **hé-m̄-sī**, no, indeed! it is not so at all! **hé m̄-thang**, you must on no account. **hé, kám-m̄-sī àn-ni^{n}**, well, is it not so!

hé (C.), = A. hóe (angry glance).

hè (R. sòe), (C. hòe, Cn. hō͘), a year (of age) counted from New Year, not from birthday (but "nî^{n}" is a year of time). **nî^{n}-hè**, years of age. **hè-siū**, length of life (v. siū). **ke-chiáh chit-hè**, to live one year more. **tsáp-lák-hè-lāi**, under the 16th year; not above 14, by our reckoning. **hè-thâu iáh-tsōe**, yet he is of considerable age. **kúi-hè**, in what year of his age? **sa^{n}-hè**, in his third year; two years old. **sa^{n}-hè gín-ná**, a mere child; might sometimes be only a few days more than one year old. **sa^{n}-tâng-hè**, of the same age. **pî^{n}-hè**, id. **lāu-hè**, an old man. **lín-lāu-hō͘** (T.), your father. **lín lāu-hō͘-ngá** (Cn.), id.

hè (R. hò^{n}), (C. hòe, Cn. hō͘), goods. **siá^{n}-hè**, what thing? what is the matter?

hè-hè, very slim and inferior, *e.g.* too cheap furniture. **lám-hè**, inferior goods. **hè-tóe**, remnant of a lot of goods. **hè-bé**, id. **tó-tōe-hè**, worthless goods that no one wants. **teh-tóe-hè**, id. **hè-bút**, goods. **hè-sek**, sorts or qualities of goods. **hè-pān**, a sample. **tsáp-hè**, mixed goods (v. tsáp). **iû^{n}-hè**, foreign goods (v. iû^{n}). **liáh su-hè**, to seize smuggled goods.

hè-tsú, owner of goods or of cargo. **hè-kheh**, a travelling merchant or commercial traveller buying or selling. **hè-toa^{n}**, an invoice, bill of lading, or bill of sale (v. toa^{n}).

chhut-hè, to sell goods; to unlade goods; to discharge cargo, or deliver goods out of the warehouse, &c. **chhut-hè-toa^{n}**, an order from the Hong to deliver goods at vessel or warehouse (v. toa^{n}). **chhut-jip-hè**, to buy and sell goods. **tì-hè**, to buy goods. **pān-hè**, to buy goods for sale or on commission (v. pān). **sia-hè**, to buy goods on credit. **khí-hè**, to unlade. **pok-hè**, to trans-ship goods into smaller vessel or lighter (v. pok). **tsài-hè**, to transport goods. **tah-hè**, to send goods. **kià-hè**, to send or consign or intrust goods. **tsng-hè**, to pack up goods. **goân-tsng-hè**, goods in the original state as made, not made up to look better for sale. **tún-hè**, to store up goods.

hē [R. hā, leisure], (C. hē). **pàng-hē**, to dismiss school, at each time of each day, usually three times a day (s. below).

hē (R. hōe), (C. hōe). **lô-hē**, aloes (v. lô).

hē [R. connected, succession], (C. hē). **sè-hē**, a genealogical table (C. sì-hē).

hē [R. to be, connected], (C. hē). **kó-hē**, really so (v. kó). **m̄-tsai tí-hē**, to know nothing about the matter at all. **m̄-tsai hit--ê tí-hē**, id. **koan-hē**, relation to consequences, esp. as to responsibility or danger (v. koan). **kan-hē** (r.), id.

hē [R. hā, summer, China], (C. hē, in all cases = A. hā, hē), summer. **hē-thi^{n}**, summer. **hē-chì**, midsummer day. **jip-hē**, beginning of summer; May 6th or 7th. **lip-hē**, id. **hē-lēng**, the usual sort of summer weather. **chhun-hē chhiu-tang**, the four seasons. **chhun lâm, hē pak; bô-tsúi thang boâ-bák**, south wind in spring and north wind in summer do not bring one drop of rain. **hē-ko-chháu**, a medicinal plant (v. ko).

hē (C.), = A. hōe. **mô-hē**, a crab. **mn̂g-hē** (P.), id. **hē-á**, small crab found in fields.

hē (R. hā), (C. hē, in every case = A. hā, hē), to lower; to let down; to lay down; to mix, as manure, salt, or poison; to ship; to invest; to vow; often at the end of a clause almost untranslatable, indicating a downward motion.

ū-hē-lòh, well behaved; safe to meddle with (v. lòh). **ū sím-mih^{n} hē-lòh**, what news of him?

hē-goān, to vow formally, as before a god. **hí-hē** (C.), id. **kiû-hē**, id. **tâu-hē** (r.), id. **tàu-hē**, to vow together. **hē-pút**, to make a vow to an idol. **hē-sîn thok-pút**, to vow to spirits and idols. **hē-tsoá**, to make incantations and imprecations (for the injury of others) with burning paper; done for money by childless old hags, because persons with a family dare not, for fear of calamity coming on their family. **hē-tsoá tsòe-khiò**, id. **khit--lâng hē-tsoá**, to be injured by such incantations. **hē-lí-than, hē-lí-ô; kàu-sí, mih^{n} to-bô**, said of promising to reward a man if he gives help, but failing to keep the promise; said of the idol thé-tī-kong (v. tī).

kì-hē--teh, to write down. **siu-hē**, to lay up, or lay away, as goods. **siu-hē--teh**, id. **chek-hē**, to collect more and more, as things. **tiu-hē** (Cn.), to throw away. **pàng-hē**, to lay down (s. leisure). **pàng-hē--teh**, id. **bák-chiu pàng-hē-hē** (C. kē-kē), eyes looking down, as very sad, ashamed, or reverential. **chhiá^n-hē--teh**, just lay it down. **hē--teh bîn-á-tsài**, lay it down for to-morrow's use.

hē-hè, to put goods on board, or into a godown, &c. **hē-tsāi**, to put cargo on board. **hē-iâm**, to ship salt; to sprinkle salt on meat, so as to preserve it. **hē-pûi**, to manure. **hē-tók**, to give poison secretly. **ká^n-hē tāng-ióh**, not afraid to prescribe very powerful medicine, that may kill or cure.

hē-pún, to invest money. **hē-lē̍**, to give a bribe. **hē-soeh** (T.), to give a bribe to one person.

hē-chhiú, to use violence in striking, or in a feud (v. chhiú). **hē sí-thûi**, to strike with a murderous club. **hē-bāng**, to set a net. **hē-phâng** (C.), to lower sail. **hē-khah-kē** (C.), to take in sail.

hē [R. hōe, a society, to meet]; (C. hōe, which is also A. in some phrases), to consult together, to discuss or confess.

hē-thâu, the head manager of a club for mutual benefit. **chio-hē**, to propose subscriptions for such a club. **iô-hē**, to raffle for the loan of money in it.

hoe-hē (C. hoa-hōe), a sort of gambling, or rather two sorts, one by an octangular teetotum with five to eight characters; the other, which is much worse, has thirty-seven characters, and is played by shaking dice without a teetotum. **iô-hoe-hē**, to shake the dice in the worse sort. **hoe-hē-tiû^n**, a gambling place (in a village) for this worse sort. **hoe-hē-tâu**, the teetotum of the less hurtful sort. **lién hoe-hē**, to twirl it, as the keeper of the gambling-house does. **teh-hoe-hē**, to gamble with it, as the player. **hoe-hē-pang**, board used for this sort.

hē-ōe, to discuss or talk over a matter, with explanations. **hun-hē-ōe**, id. **hun-hē**, id. **bô-hun bô-hē**, without any explanations, *e.g.* doing a thing without stating before, or before allowing explanation. **lí-hē**, to discuss a matter with another. **biēn-hē**, to meet together and discuss a disputed matter. **hē-siàu**, to meet and examine an account. **sa^n-pé-hē** (C. sio-póe-hōe), to discuss a matter so as to come to an agreement, generally by each party yielding a little. **kap--i pé-hē**, to discuss the matter with him. **hē-tsōe**, to meet together in order to take common action, *e.g.* to go together for some purpose.

hē-m̄-tióh, to go to a man and confess being wrong, so as to make it up. **hē-m̄-sī**, id. **hē-put-sī**, id. **kā--lâng hē-m̄-tióh**, id. **kā-i-hē**, id. **hē jîn-chêng**, to claim credit or thanks for a favour done, either done by one's self or by another whom we say we have influenced to it. **hē khang-jîn-chêng**, to claim credit for it falsely, *e.g.* for what we would have done at any rate, or for what another did quite independently of us.

hέ^n (=heh^n), interjection used in reproving. **hέ^n m̄-thang àn-ni^n**, you must not on any account act so.

hὲ^n (=hn̂g), yes! (I hear what you say); yes sir!

hε̄^n (cf. hāi^n, hī^n). **hε̄^n-hε̄^n-chhan**, to groan incessantly, as a sick man.

heh (T.), = A. hεh^n. **sa^n-heh**, to stir up one another to do something.

heh [R. hā, to lower], (C. hε̄). **heh-phâng**, to lower the sail (taking it in).

hεh (C.), = hah. **hεh-chhiù^n**, to sneeze.

heh (cf. heh^n), interjection of wonder or surprise, sometimes with displeasure. **heh tsái^n-iū^n**, how ever is this? **heh m̄-thang**, that will never do.

heh^n (=hέ^n), interjection used in sudden reproving.

hεh^n [R. kek, to incite, to provoke], (T. heh). **sa^n-hεh^n**, stirring up each other to do something dangerous, expensive, or difficult. **hεh^n-lâi hεh^n-khì**, id. **hōng-hεh^n**, several persons thus inciting each other to act together. **tàu-hōng-hεh^n**, id. **hōng-hōng hεh^n-hεh^n**, acting hurriedly on the spur of the moment, without full consideration.

hεh^n (C.), = A. hioh, to rest. **toà-hεh^n**, to stay, as a guest or visitor, for some time.

hέh^n, noise, as of things broken, or of crockery-ware struck that has a crack in it. **oá^n hέh^n-hέh^n**, the bowl gives a bad ring, showing that it is cracked. **hâm-hέh^n**, sound of coughing or of cracked crockery. **hâm-hέh^n ka-sàu**, sound of severe coughing, as in consumption.

hek [R. black]. **hek-kiu^n**, ginger root burned into charcoal for medicinal use. **hek-pék put-hun** (black and white not distinguished), innocent person unable to prove his innocence (v. pék). **kūn-tsu--chiá, chhek: kūn-bék--chiá, hek**, contact with vermilion makes one red, with ink makes one black; a man becomes like his companions.

hek (R. id.) **hién-hek**, glorious and illustrious, as a god or spirit that answers prayer.

hek (better "hiet"). **pàng-hek-kák**, to throw away.

hék (R. id.) **hék-chiá**, perhaps. **hék-sī**, perhaps it is —. **hék-ká^n sī àn-ni^n** (T.), I should think it may be so.

hék [R. to doubt; to deceive]. **gî-hék**, to doubt; to suspect, as a person or affair. **bê-hék**, to lead astray. **iú-hék**, id. **iâu-giên siēn-hék**, to deceive by false and crafty words. **tsó-tō hék-chiòng**, to deceive the multitude by wicked arts, as the Tauist priests.

hék [R. jiók, flesh]; also (Cn.), = A. bah, flesh, pork.

hék-sin, the body. **chhin-kut-hék**, one's own relations, by blood (not adoptive), as son or brother. **hia^n-tī ná^n kut-hék**, brothers are like our own flesh. **siah-kut lòh-hék**, very very lean. **e-lâm-hék**, meat of a sort of shell-fish. **thê-kúi-hék** (T.), id.

hék [R. a place]. **siū-hék**, a grave-site prepared before death.

hék [R. gék, to oppose, = kéh]. **hoâi^n-hék**, violent, overbearing, and unjust.

hék (Cn.), = A. iáh. **un-hék**, pestilence, epidemic.

hék (Cn.), = A. ék. **sōe-hék**, to bathe by throwing water over one's self.

heng [R. elder brother, = col. hia^n]. **pau-heng**, elder brother by same father. **lēng-heng**, your elder brother (polite). **sè-heng**, teacher's son (lit. small elder brother). **heng-tē**, elder and younger brothers (v. tē).

heng [R. to prosper; to rise], (C. hin). **heng-ōng**, to prosper. **teh tng-heng**, in great repute for power, as idol. **tiong-heng**, coming to prosperity after a difficult beginning, as a dynasty. **heng-khí**, to raise up or make to flourish; to spring up, as a great man. **heng-soe**, to prosper and to decay. **kōe-heng kōe-thè**, rapidly prospering and as rapidly decaying. **sîn-put heng, tē-tsú kêng**, when the idol prospers, its votaries are poor.

siāu-heng, Shau-hing-Foo (v. siāu). **heng-hoà**, Hing-hwa-foo. **heng-tsoân-éng-tō**, the Amoy Tautai, ruling Hing-hwa, Chin-chew, and Yung-chun.

heng [R. successful]. **heng-thong** (R.), to be successful and prosperous, as a man.

heng [R. hiong, the breast]. **heng-háh**, the chest. **heng-chêng**, the breast or bosom. **heng-keh**, the chest; the parts inclosed by the ribs. **heng-khám-keh**, id. **heng-khám**, the breast. **heng-khám-kut**, the breast-bone. **khiú heng-khám**, to seize a man by the neck of his dress at the breast. **khiú-heng-á**, id.

hiàn-heng, to expose the breast uncovered; to open the outer dress so as to let the inner one appear. **tah-heng**, to strike the breast with the palm, as in promising to be security. **tṅg-heng**, to strike one's breast violently with the palm, as sign of great displeasure, or determination to quarrel; also (C. **siàng-heng**), to beat the breast with a large stone, as beggars do. **tûi-heng**, to beat the breast with the fist (v. tûi).

koe-heng, breast projecting like a fowl's. **koe-heng hāu-hiáh; m̄-sí, iáh-tsòe khit-chiáh**, with a breast like a fowl's, and a large forehead like a king-crab, if he don't die, he will be at least a beggar.

phan-heng-thâu (T.), the upper corner of the flap of dress where it buttons at the neck.

heng (P.), = hiong. **sòng-heng**, = sòng-hiong, poor.

hêng [R. hiông, male]. **ah-hêng**, a young drake (s. form). **ah-hêng-sia^{n}**, broken voice of a young lad just coming of age. **sàu-liáu ah-hêng-sia^{n}**, deep consumptive sound of voice.

hêng [R. constant, continual]. **hêng-hô**, the Ganges. **hêng-hô sa, sè-hut** (Buddhist phrase), Buddhas are innumerable as the sands of the Ganges.

hêng [R. the ancient feudal state of Hing], a surname.

hêng [R. to walk, to go, to act; the elements, = col. kiâ^{n}]. **hêng-tōng kú-chí**, behaviour. **hêng-chí**, id. **bô-hêng-chí**, devoid of good conduct. **bô thi^{n}-lí, kah bô hêng-chí**, utterly devoid of good principles or conduct. **hêng-kèng**, behaviour. **hêng-siēn**, to live morally. **hêng-hiong**, to commit crimes of violence (v. hiong). **hêng-hêng sù-chí**, wicked disorderly conduct. **hêng-i**, to practise medicine; to act as a doctor (s. return). **hêng-hiet**, purifying for the blood, as medicine. **hêng-pông** (R.), to have sexual intercourse with wife or concubine.

kú-hêng, to take action in a matter; to make a beginning of it. **thong-hêng**, universally prevalent or current; can be used anywhere. **kong-hêng**, publicly and openly. **liû-hêng**, to go on in regular course, as nature's operations; to act far and wide, as epidemic. **sù-kùi liû-hêng**, the seasons roll on. **un-ék liû-hêng**, epidemic prevailing. **thien-tē hêng-tsai**, Heaven and earth send calamities. **thien-tsai hêng-hō**, calamities sent by Heaven.

ngó-hêng, the five elements. **ngó-hêng phòe-tah**, the five elements (metal, wood, water, fire, earth) duly proportioned in a man's horoscope or appearance, said in fortune-telling.

hêng-lí, baggage. **bî-hêng**, to go incognito, as mandarin. **chhùn-pō lâu-hêng**, cannot go one inch further. **pan-hêng thien-hā**, to publish all through the world, as a decree. **hêng-hiu^{n}**, to go in procession to offer incense, as mandarins (v. hiu^{n}). **chhut-hêng**, to begin to go from home on a lucky day, esp. at New-Year season. **chhut-hêng-jit**, a lucky day for that purpose, or for an idol visiting its native place. **sì-hêng**, to leave a card when leaving home for a distance, esp. as mandarins and kujin do, in order to get presents of money in return (s. return). **sàng-hêng**, to see a man off on a journey. **sòng-hêng**, id. **chién-hêng**, to give a parting feast to a man (v. chién). **sūn-tsúi hêng-chiu**, sailing with the tide; all going well.

hó-hêng-tsé (Cn. chió), graceful gait and demeanour (v. tsé). **hêng-thâu**, fine clothes. **bô-hêng-thâu**, having no nice clothes to wear. **kúi-niá^{n} hêng-thâu**, how many fine dresses? **ū-hêng-thiô** (Cn.), having fine clothes to wear (v. thiô).

hêng-su, the more regular form of the current hand.

hêng (R. id.), form; shape; the embryo in an egg. **hêng-tsōng**, outward form (v. tsōng). **hêng-siōng**, form (of man). **hêng-hâi**, shape or appearace of person. **hêng-iōng**, id. **hêng-thé**, external form. **hêng-tō**, a likeness for detecting a criminal. **hêng-sè**, shape or form, especially of a hill, as regards its good or bad luck. **soa^{n}-hêng**, shape of hills. **lâng-hêng**, form of a man. **jī sū jîn-hêng**, a man's writing is like his appearance. **bīn-hêng**, form of the face.

chêng-hêng, condition and circumstances, as of a matter. **hêng-chek**, traces (v. chek). **ū-hêng-iá^{n}**, to have some reality or some foundation in fact (v. iá^{n}), = ū-éng-hióng.

bú-hêng, feminine look. **bú-hêng-thé**, id. **tsa-bó-hêng**, id. **chhát-hêng**, very coarse, large, and rough in appearance (like a robber). **ok-hêng**, unpleasant natural appearance of face, as if bad-tempered (v. ok). **kúi-hêng**, fiend-like. **ui-hêng**, stern awe-inspiring manner and bearing. **bô sím-mih^{n} ui-hêng**, not very dignified or terrible in appearance. **ui-hêng chin-tāng**, manner exceedingly stern.

piàn-hêng, to change one's manner from friendly to unfriendly appearance; to change one's appearance, as when just about to die.

ū-hêng, there is an embryo in the egg. **ah-hêng**, embryo in duck's egg (s. male).

hêng — **sēng-hêng**, spoiled, as a child; determined, as a beggar [last word or following word ?]

hêng [R. cross, perverse, = col. hoâi^{n}], (Cn. hûi^{n}, hêng). **hêng-gék** (Cn. hûi^{n}-gék), very wicked, vicious, violent, or perverse; especially injurious to others. **chhiòng-hêng**, id. **hêng-hêng sù-chì**, very wicked disorderly conduct.

hêng [R. to punish; punishment]. **hêng-hoát**, to punish; punishment. **tāng-hêng**, severe punishment. **khok-hêng**, cruel, unjust, and oppressive (punishment); severe (torture). **hêng-khū**, instruments for punishment or torture, as in yamun.

hêng-pō, the board of punishments, at capital; the minister of justice. **hêng-pâng**, the official in a yamun who attends to that department of business. **hêng-bêng**, the secretary (su-iâ) who attends to legal cases. **hêng-bêng su-iâ**, id. **hêng-bêng chiên-kok**, the two principal secretaries in a yamun, managing respectively legal cases and revenue. **tng-hêng-tiōng**, to have the office of beating criminals, &c. (v. tiōng).

hêng (R. hoân), (T. hâi^{n}, Cn. hûi^{n}, tûi^{n}, C. hân,

P. hêng), to return a thing; to pay back; to repay; to send back a thing. **sì-hêng**, to return, as a present or part of a present that one does not accept (s. walk). **sì hêng--i**, to decline a thing and return it to him (to the sender). **thè-hêng**, to send back, as part of goods not wanted. **thoaⁿ--hêng**, to pay a percentage, as in general average. **phiⁿ-hêng**, to pay by instalments. **tui-hêng**, to send and catch a thief so as to get back stolen property, as mandarins do. **hêng-bōe-khí**, unable to raise enough to pay, as for another. **hêng--i**, return it to him. **hêng-chè**, to pay a debt. **hêng-siàu**, to pay an account.

héng — **héng-héng**, with all one's heart; quite in the spirit of a thing; full of desire to do something at once. **héng-héng saⁿ-kap-khì**, went with him with all his heart. **khí-thâu héng-héng, bé-chhiú léng-léng**, at first very warm for it, afterwards very cool. **héng-héng tī koe-mn̂g-chhéng** (fond of wearing a dust-brush instead of a feather in his cap), said of a mean fellow making himself very consequential (cf. hèng).

hèng [R. id. by change of tone from "heng," to prosper], (C. hìn), to delight in; to have a fancy for; to desire strongly, often in a somewhat bad sense. **hèng-oan-ke**, quarrelsome. **hèng-siá-jī**, fond of writing characters. **hèng-chiah**, fond of eating it, as some special sort of food.

kau-hèng, to desire very much; have a fancy for. **ū-hèng-thâu**, having a strong desire to. **sim-sek-hèng**, have a fancy for something or some pleasure; to take a fancy to. **tioh-i sim-sek-hèng, chiah-beh**, must wait till the fancy strikes him, and then he will do it. **hoat-hèng**, to get quite into the spirit of a thing. **chit-tsúi-á hoat-hèng**, quite warm in a matter for a short time.

hô-hèng, fond of, as some pleasure; in full spirits for —. **hǒ-hèng** (Cn.), id. **hô-hèng-lim**, fond of drinking. **hô-hèng khì soaⁿ-giâm**, setting off in high spirits for a walk to hill temples.

sit-hèng, dispirited; dejected; having lost heart about a matter.

hêng (T. hāiⁿ, Cn. hūiⁿ), to make a present. **saⁿ-hêng**, id. **kap--i saⁿ-hêng**, giving and receiving presents, as intimate friends. **hêng-ké**, to make presents of cakes and the other offerings after they have been offered to ancestors or spirits. **hêng iû-pn̄g**, to present rice to friends who call soon after birth of a child (v. pn̄g).

hēng [R. to get by chance or bad means]. **hiau-hēng**, by chance; by good-luck, often when not deserved; by bad means; not keeping one's promise. **hiau-hēng lâng-chîⁿ**, to swindle people. **hēng-gū siong-hông** (R.), fortunately met.

hēng [R. fortunate]. **hēng-tit**, fortunately. **put-hēng**, unfortunately; by bad-luck.

hēng — **êng-hēng**, behaving in an unjust or overbearing way (v. êng). **siūⁿ-hēng**, lazy; idle. **siūⁿ-té-hēng**, to neglect one's work or do it in a slip-shod inefficient manner. **kek-hēng**, lazy; idle; unwilling to give any assistance. **sǹg-hēng**, lazy; unwilling to give any assistance beyond what our employment compels us to. **kāu-hēng**, lazy and idle; always finding excuses for negligence or overreaching; refusing to do more than can be avoided, or to tell what one ought; cunning, as child good at making excuses for disobedience. **óe-lâng kāu-hēng**, short people are lazy and selfish. **óe-lâng bô-hēng, thiⁿ-ē thài-pêng**, if short people were not lazy and selfish, the world would be peaceful and happy.

hēng [R. conduct; behaviour; by change of tone from "hêng" to walk]. **phín-hēng**, behaviour. **tek-hēng**, id. **ū tek-hēng**, of good character. **bô-tek-hēng**, of bad character. **hó-tek-hēng**, good character and conduct.

siu-hēng, to reform and live morally. **hàu-hēng**, filial piety. **toán-hēng**, wickedly and secretly injuring others. **chhàu-hēng**, wickedly injuring people.

sim-hēng, character of heart, as good or bad. **ū sim-hēng**, good at contriving how to do anything. **toā-sim-hēng**, avaricious, covetous, venturous. **chhàu-sim-hēng**, wickedly injuring others. **pháiⁿ-sim tók-hēng**, very wicked and injurious in heart and conduct. **hó-sim hó-hēng**, of good character and conduct. **hó-sim hó-hēng, bô-saⁿ thang-chhēng**, well-behaved people have no clothes to wear.

hēng [R. the almond]. **hēng-jîn**, almonds. **kam-hēng**, do., as medicinal. **hēng-hoe**, the almond plant or flower. **hēng-hoa** (C.), id. **khó-hēng**, kernels of the bitter peach (medicinal). **gûn-hēng**, a white medicinal nut (gingko? Salisburia adianthifolia ?), = peh-ké-á.

hēng (R. hiēn), (T. hāng, Cn. hūiⁿ). **hēng-chhài**, a sort of vegetable (Chenopodium ?).

hi [R. good fortune or happiness]. **hō sin-hi**, to make congratulations in the first days of the year.

hi [R. glory or prosperity]. **khong-hi**, the reign of Khang-hi. **khong-hi-kun**, the emperor Khang-hi. **khong-hi jī-tién**, the Imperial Chinese Dictionary.

hi (R. id.) **hok-hi**, Fuh-hi, one of the most ancient emperors.

hi [R. to heat; to roast]. **tsu-hi**, Choo-he (Chu-hi), or Choo-foo-tsze, the great commentator. **tsu-hi-kong**, id.

hi [R. a pleasing appearance]. **chhiò hi-hi**, smiling pleased look. **hi-hi-chhiò**, to laugh with pleased look and mouth open.

hi — **hi-hi-háu**, to make a constant talking.

hi — **àn-hi**, = àn-niⁿ, thus (rare and local phrase).

hi (C.), = A. hu, empty.

hi (R. id.), few; scanty. **hi-bî**, id. **hi-hán**, rare (v. hán). **hi-bê**, very thin-boiled rice. **bê hi-hi**, the rice very thin boiled. **chhit-sip kó-lâi-hi**, from ancient times few men reach seventy years.

hi (R. hu), = hu, a market held on fixed days; a market-village. **sì-hi**, a market-day. **hi-tiûⁿ**, market-place. **hi-tǒ**, a passage-boat to or from a market. **ti-á-hi**, a pig-market.

koáⁿ-hi, to come to market. **lȯh-hi**, id. **hù-hi**, to reach the market in good time. **hi soàⁿ**, the market broken up.

hî (R. gû), (T. hû, Cn. hû), a fish. **kui-á-hî**, a tadpole. **bák-hî**, the cuttle-fish. **gûn-hî**, a long white worm-shaped fish (*not* silver fish). **kim-hî**, gold fish or silver fish. **kim-hî-soe**, floating weeds in jars of gold or silver fish.

péh-hî, a sort of edible fish. **tiò-péh-hî**, a sort of game; to play at it. **khiā-péh-hî**, to stand on one's hands with head down. **péh-hî-á** (C.), the book-worm.

siⁿ té-hî, to have a long sore on the calf of the leg.

hî-jī, a fish-bait. **hî-chhiⁿ**, edible marine animals in general. **hî-kî**, dorsal fins. **hî-iét**, pectoral fins. **hî-sit**, fins. **hî-chhì**, shark's fins (edible). **hî-n̄ng**,

海上絲綢之路文獻集成　科技與文化編

roe, spawn. **hî-chí**, dried and salted roe. **hî-pa**, dried fish. **hî-koa^n**, id. **kiâm-hî**, salted fish. **hî-siū^n** (Cn.), id. **hî-pé**, small dried fish, slightly salted and moist. **hî-bé-chhe**, a fish's forked-tail. **ôe, chhēng kàu ná^n hî-bé-chhe--nih^n**, shoes worn till like a fish-tail.

thó-hî, to fish. **pha-hî**, to fish with large nets. **tsan-hî**, to fish with the smaller net called "tsan."

chit-bé ná^n-hî--nih^n, having on no clothes whatever. **tsúi chheng, hî hiēn**, said of a man's innocence getting justice at last. **chiá^n-tsúi-hî jip kiâm-tsúi-káng**, quite out of his element.

hí (R. pí), (= hit), that, those (pronoun). **hí-tau**, there. **tī-hí-lāi**, inside there. **tī-hí toh-téng**, on that table. **àn-hí** (T. C.), thus.

hí [R. hú, to promise]. **hí-hē** (C.), to make a vow.

hí [R. to rejoice, joy]. **hoa^n-hí**, to rejoice; to be pleased. **hoa^n-hoa^n hí-hí**, very much pleased, and manifesting it. **hoa^n-hí kàu tio̍h-poa̍h**, so full of joy as to stumble. **kiò-hoa^n-hí**, to call out and give orders solely for the pleasure of giving orders. **hoah-hoa^n-hí**, id., or as calling out on a hill for amusement in exuberant spirits.

kiong-hí, to congratulate; I congratulate you, sir! **hō-hí**, to congratulate. **tàu-hí**, to make a call of congratulation. **pò-hí**, to announce specially good news, esp. as omen (v. pò). **hí-chhiok**, = kheh-chiáu, a sort of magpie; a good-omened bird. **ngiâ hí-sîn**, an idolatrous procession of military mandarins in spring. **tsòe-hí-khèng**, Tauist rites for good luck on joyful occasions (v. khèng). **chia̍h-hí-chiú**, to be at a feast on some auspicious occasion, esp. a marriage. **hí-sū**, matter for much congratulation, *e.g.* birth of son. **ū hí-sū**, said of wife conceiving. **song-hí-sū**, births, deaths, marriages, &c., with their ceremonies. **jip-mn̂g hí**, to have a son as soon as possible in course of nature after the marriage. **chhut-bûn kièn-hí**, to meet with a good omen or good news on going out of doors.

hí-siá, to give joyfully, as alms (v. siá).

hì (R. hùi), (Cn. hùi), the lungs; the lights of an animal. **hì-kn̂g**, the wind-pipe. **hì-iong**, a deep abscess near the lungs. **hì-hú**, the lungs and another great internal organ (v. hú). **lūn-hì**, to mollify the lungs, so as to cure coughing or want of voice.

ti-hì, pig's lights.

hì — **hah-hì**, to gape. **hì-hì-chhiò**, to smile and laugh (pleased) with mouth open.

hì [R. to sport, a play], a play. **chit-pî^n-hì**, one play. **chit-chhut-hì**, an act of a play.

hì-hiok, to talk bad language and low jesting together, esp. of women or children. **hì-hiauh**, id. **hì-lāng**, to make improper jokes and gestures, &c., towards a woman, as a man with bad intention.

kun-tiong bû-hì-giên (no jokes in the army), it is too serious a matter for joking. **hui tông-jî-hì** (R.), this is no child's play. **khûn iú-kong, hì bû-ek**, diligence is useful, but amusement is useless.

poa^n-hì, to act a play. **poa^n-kâu-hì**, to have a play with monkeys (as beggar), or a play in which a pig and a monkey are represented. **chhut-hì**, to begin a play. **thò-hì**, to rehearse a play. **tsng-hì**, to follow the business of an actor. **pák--lâng tsng-hì**, to apprentice and hire out (as one's son) for a long term of years to an actor. **khoà^n-hì**, to look at a play. **tiah-hì**, to select the play for performance. **chéng-hì**, to engage a company to play for us. **tè-hì**, to be fond of seeing plays, esp. following one particular company; often includes the idea of lasciviousness. **toà-hì**, to keep a theatrical company at one's house, hiring them out for plays.

tn̄g-hì-koà, to observe what sort of a play one chances to meet with, and take an omen from it for one's fortune. **hoa̍t hì-toh**, to exact as a forfeit the expense of a play and a feast.

tsòe-pá-hì, jugglery; idle play (v. pá). **tsok kéng-á-hì**, transparencies like magic lantern. **tsoá-iá^n-hì**, id. **ka-lé-hì**, puppet-shows (v. lé). **pò-tē-hì**, another sort of puppet-shows. **sèng-siū-hì**, plays on birthday of emperor or empress. **chià^n-im-hì**, plays in mandarin dialect. **toā-hì**, colloquial plays by adults. **lāu-hì**, id. **tàu-lāu-hì**, actors clubbing together in a company without a head, and leaving when they choose; fig. of man and woman cohabiting without marriage, just so long as they like. **hì-á**, a play in the Chin-chew dialect by boys. **hoe-hì**, a play of a lascivious character.

hì-chî^n, money subscribed for idolatrous plays. **hì-phûn**, plays for the dead (v. phûn). **hì-toa^n**, a list of plays from which the idol selects one. **hì-pî^n**, a stage for temporary use. **hì-pî^n-kha**, round about the stage, as among the spectators. **hì-tâi**, a permanent stage, as before a temple. **hì-koán**, a house where actors lodge. **hì-ho̍k**, theatrical dresses. **hì-láng**, sort of box for carrying them.

hì-pan, a company of actors. **hì-á-pan**, young actors. **hì-kioh**, an actor, esp. of mandarin dialect and of lower class. **chhit-kioh-hì pò bān-peng**, seven actors saying they are ten thousand soldiers; said of a little money or a few things going a great way. **hì-seng**, a male character. **hì-toà^n**, a female character (always done by men). **hì-khôeh**, a sort of clown in a play; a man who talks or acts ludicrously to make people laugh. **hì-siu^n**, a man who doats on a company of actors, esp. on those who represent females (v. siu^n). **hì-chhoàng**, id. **hì-tü** (T.), id.

hiâm-hì bôh-chhiá^n; chhiá^n-hì bôh-hiâm, if you don't like them don't hire them, if you hire them don't find fault. **sek-sek-hì poa̍h-lo̍h pî^n-kha**, the most skilful actor sometimes falls from the stage.

hî (C.) **hui^n-hî**, waste and uncultivated, as land.

hī (R. jí^n, ní^n), the ear; handles of a jar or hod, &c. **chhèng-hī**, touch-hole of a gun. **àng-hī**, handles of a large jar. **la̍k-hī**, the two supports of a mast at the side. **thê-lâng-hī**, projection on rim of mill for cleaning rice, having a hole for the hook by which it is turned. **sa^n-hī-á**, a sort of basket used in building. **kau-nái^n-hī**, the 163d or 170th radical, as written at the side (v. kau).

kau-hī, an ear-pick (v. kau). **hī-kau**, an ear-ring. **hī-tūi**, id. **hī-khoân** (T.), id. **hī-to**, small knife for cleaning the inside of the ear. **hī-chì^n**, arrows stuck in the ears of delinquent soldiers.

hī-á, the ear, as a whole. **hī-á-kun**, the veins at back of ear. **hī-á-kî^n**, rim of the ear. **hī-á-āu**, the part of the head covered by the flap of the ear behind. **hī-á-tûn**, large lobe of ear. **hī-tûn**, id. **hī-kià^n**, tympanum of the ear. **hī-khang-kúi**, id. **phah-phái^n hī-khang-kúi**, to injure the tympanum by too much picking. **hī-khang-kúi ki-ki-háu**, a ringing in the ears. **hī-khang háu**, id. **hī-khang**, the orifice of the ear; the ear, in relation to hearing. **hī-àng-á**, the cavity of the ear. **hī-hio̍h**, the large flap of the ear. **hī-tsu**, the lower lobe of the ear. **hī-tì**, the small lobe that almost covers the orifice.

chhàu-hī-lâng, deaf. **iû^n-hī**, ear always moist and needing to be cleaned. **si^n hī-àng-á**, ear suppurating. **chhàu-hī-àng-á**, id. **si^n-hī-that**, to have a growth in the ear, stopping it. **hī-that**, flaps of coarse yellow mourning cap covering the ears, signifying that the mourner is to have no ear for worldly matters.

hī-khang khin, ready to believe or follow whatever one is told, however absurd. **hī-khang tāng**, dull of hearing. **hī-khang lāi**, sharp at hearing. **hī-khang-lāi**, within the ear.

poā^n-hī, to shake the ears (v. poā^n). **chi^n hī-á**, to pull the ears. **khǹg-hī**, to bore the ear (as of a pig) for a ring. **tsǹg-hī**, to bore the human ear. **lién-hī**, to brush the ear, as barber. **chhò-hī**, to stun the ears. **kóng kàu toā^n-phoà lâng-hī-khang**, to talk so much about what a man wishes not to hear, as to split his ears. **phah-chih lâng hī-khang-mn̂g**, to speak to a man so unjustly or unreasonably as to make him very angry. **kéh--chih lâng hī-khang-mn̂g**, id. **kéh-tūi^n lâng hī-khang-mê^n** (C.), id. **phah-kéh lâng** &c. (C.), id. **kéh-hī**, making people unwilling to listen, as unreasonable talk. **thia^n--liáu kéh-hī**, unwilling to listen to what has been said. **thia^n kàu pá-hī**, having heard so much that we don't wish to hear more. **bô-jip-hī ê-óe**, what one does not like to hear. **chit-hī jip, hit-hī chhut**, in at one ear and out at the other. **thia^n-lòh-hī**, to hear and understand distinctly. **thia^n bô-lòh-hī**, to hear indistinctly. **thia^n--liáu tā^n-hī** (Cn.), to hear indistinctly, so as to mistake. **ui hī-khang**, to pick the ears. **ui hī-khang, chēng-chēng-thia^n**, clean your ears, and listen attentively (may include the idea of not speaking or meddling).

ū-hī bô-chhùi, hear but must not report; said to a child. **chhiû^n-piah ū-hī**, walls have ears, take care what you say. **thia^n-hī thia^n-piah**, to listen secretly, as an eaves-dropper. **goá-koà tī-hī-á bé-liu**, I hang it at the corner of my ear; I don't care much for what you say. **goá-kùi** &c., id. **tī-thâu-chhùi pùn-ki-hī**, mouth like a hoe and ears like a hod; I am not good at speaking nor able to understand what is said (humble language).

koâi^n-kē-hī, ears of different size. **hī-á toā-tùi**, ears large, sign of good luck in making money. **thâu chiam, hī-tûn pȯh**, face long and ears thin, supposed not to get rich. **thâu chiam, hī pȯh**, id. **kâu-thâu chhú-hī** (monkey's head and rat's ears), very ugly. **thâu phoà, hī ùih**, head severely wounded. **chhàu-thâu noā^n-hī**, head all over boils, &c.

hó͘-hī-chháu, a small plant used in pots round the roots of other plants (the leaf is like a tiger's ear), used for diseases of the ear; said also of a daughter brought up, as just in order to look well, though she might very well be dispensed with.

hi^n — **hi^n-hi^n-chhan**, to groan. **chhan hi^n-hi^n**, id.; sound of sobbing, as of children. **hi^n-hi^n-háu**, sound of child crying or constantly asking for things; sound of flies or mosquitoes. **háu-hi^n** (vulg.), said in scolding children for crying or people for asking things.

hi^n (C.), to sob, as a bride on leaving her mother.

hi^n (T.) **àn-hi^n**, = àn-ni^n, thus.

hî^n [R. hiên, a string]. **hî^n-soe**, the reed of a loom. **hî^n tsàng**, the reed and the perpendicular threads (v. tsàng). **hî^n-soe khàu-tsàng**, id. **hî^n-so**, a shuttle. **hî^n-kui** (C.), a loom.

khiā-hî^n--ê, stake-nets, = khiā-bāng.

hí^n [R. pí, = col. hit, &c.] **àn-hí^n àn-hiù^n** (C.), unsettled in purpose, varying back and forwards. **àn-hí^n** (T.), thus, in this way, said in giving orders to do so and so.

hì^n (T.) **àn-hì^n-sī**, that way. **àn-hì^n, á-sī àn-chì^n**, shall it be this way or that way?

hì^n (C.) **mɛ^n-hì^n**, a small cricket that makes this sound, = chhiu-siên.

hì^n, to toss up or throw away. **hì^n-hiet-kák**, to throw away. **hì^n--khí lâi**, to toss up. **hì^n-lóh-hái**, to toss into the sea. **hng-hng hì^n-hì^n**, all in disorder, as a room.

iô-kha hì^n-chhiú, to swagger about, moving one's limbs excessively. **lō͘-nih^n-hì^n**, to swing or shake from side to side. **hì^n chhien-chhiu**, to swing a swing.

pàng-hì^n-tā^n (Cn.), to throw away. **hì^n-tā^n** (An. L.), id. **hì^n-tàn-tā^n** (An. L.), id.

hī^n (R. hiēn), an ink-stone, for rubbing down ink. **siàh-hī^n**, a marble ink-stone. **khui-hī^n**, to make an ink-stone. **pit-bák-hī^n**, pen, ink, and ink-stone. **pit-bák tsoá-hī^n**, do. and paper.

hī^n-áh, case for ink-stone. **hī^n-tî**, hollow for the water in it. **hī^n-ê**, do. in large stone for writing large characters. **hī^n-tsô** (C.), id.

hī^n (cf. hi^n). **hī^n-hī^n-chhoán**, to pant and gasp. **thé-khùi hī^n-hāi^n** (esp. C.), to groan, sob, and pant bitterly.

hia (R. id.), a boot. **hia-tháng**, the leg of a boot. **hia-àng**, id. **phê-hia**, leather boots. **iû-hia**, boots with soles soaked in "thâng" oil. **chièn-hia**, boots for defending the leg in war. **oân-thâu-hia**, boots with round toes, used by civil mandarins. **chiam-bé-hia**, boots with sharp toes, used by military officers. **phoà-hia-tóng**, broken-down literati, who make a living by frightening people, and sharing money with underlings of yamuns.

hia, a ladle, a scoop, a very small hand-net; to catch with a small hand-net. **tsúi-hia**, a scoop for lading out water. **chhe-hia**, one for lading out manure. **pùn-hia**, bucket on a pole for manure. **hāu-hia**, a ladle made of the king-crab shell. **pû-hia**, a ladle made of a gourd, or of wood. **chhâ-hia**, a wooden one. **chhâ--ê pû-hia**, id. **hî-hia**, a small hand-net shaped like a ladle. **bāng-hia**, one for scooping fish out of a large net. **báng-hia**, hand-net for catching mosquitoes. **chhu-hia**, one for catching larvæ.

hia-chhu, to catch larvæ in a small hand-net. **hia-báng**, to catch mosquitoes thus.

hia [R. pí, that, those, there], there. **tī-hia**, id. **hia-ê**, those.

hia [R. hoa, a flower]. **hia-pai**, ostentatious, dashing, gaudy (v. pai). **hia-pai^n** (T.), id.

hia — **hia-chia**, very cumbrous, as large piece of furniture.

hia (T.) **sek-hia pùt-tsé**, = sek-kia, Shakyamuni or Buddha.

hiā (= jiā). **chhiù^n-hiā**, to make a bow; to bow.

hiā (R. oá), (Cn. hoā), a tile, for roof. **chhù-hiā**, roof-tiles. **hiā-iú^n**, outer and inner tiles for roof. **tsng-phiáh-hiā**, tiles and bricks of all sorts. **hoe-thâu-hiā**, tiles with a point turned down, used at eaves. **thi^n-thang-hiā**, tiles with bit of glass or oyster-shell in the middle, for light.

hiā-hoe, fragile partition with wide spaces made of tiles placed diagonally, as on the top of a wall. **hiā-**

iô, a tile-work. **hiā-tsô**, a boat carrying tiles. **hiā-tsô**, alternate rows (raised and depressed) of tiles on a roof. **hiā-tâng**, semicylindrical tiles for roofs. **hiā-thâng**, id. **hiā-to**, a bricklayer's trowel for breaking and laying bricks, &c. **hiā-sien**, small worms like centipedes. **hiā-san** (Cn.), id.

chhù-hiā-phè, broken bits of tiles. **hiā-phia^n-phòe** (C.), id. (v. phia^n).

khioh-hiā, to lay tiles on a roof, in the usual Chinese way. **nī^n-hiā**, id.

hiā (R. gî), an ant. **thâng-hiā**, ants and other creeping things. **âng-hiā**, red ants. **káu-hiā**, the common small ant. **káu-hiā-phang**, a small but venomous wasp. **káu-hiā pài thi^n-tōe**, ants worshipping Heaven and earth; a man of low condition, as quite unworthy to see a man of very high rank. **n̂g-sng-hiā gâu-phī^n-chē**, good at finding what is for one's own interest (v. phī^n). **pe̍h-hiā**, white ants. **chhiū^n pe̍h-hiā**, to breed white ants. **pe̍h-hiā-thô**, the covered ways made by white ants. **tio̍h-hiā**, to have white ants in it. **toā-tsúi-hiā**, winged ants that appear in or before wet weather. **hong-hiā**, id. **lâm-hong-hiā**, id. **kan-hiā** (C.), white ants breeding in roof without communication with the ground.

hia^n (R. heng). **hia^n-hia^n**, very strong-smelling, as new paint, or as a very strong-smelling flower. **phī^n--liáu hia^n-hia^n**, it smells very strong. **hia^n-loa̍h**, strong-scented and pungent; having much wealth or influence. **miâ^n-jī hia^n-loa̍h**, held in much reputation, as a rich, influential, or famous man. **chhàu-hia^n-lo** (T.), having a smoked taste.

hia^n (R. heng), an elder brother (used as a suffix to names of men); a cousin, or man of the same genealogical rank, older than we. **toā-hia^n**, eldest brother. **jī-hia^n**, second eldest brother. **chhin-hia^n**, real elder brother by same father. **tông-hia^n**, elder cousin or man of same genealogical rank, of same surname. **piáu-hia^n**, cousin of different surname. **siā-hia^n**, a fellow-villager (v. siā). **hia^n-só**, elder brother's wife. **hia^n-bē**, elder brother and his younger sister (*e.g.* speaking of only these two remaining of the family).

thâu-hia^n, head of a gang of thieves. **sai-hia^n**, an elder apprentice or elder Tauist priest, said by the younger. **chhoàng-hia^n**, a dandy fast licentious young fellow. **khè-hia^n**, paramour of a bad woman, **khòe-hia^n**, id. **gī-hia^n** (esp. C.), id. **hia^n-ko**, id. **hia^n-thâu**, id.

hia^n-tī, brothers, in general; also said of cousins, esp. of same surname; members of the same society. **pêng-iú tī-hia^n**, all you gentlemen and friends! **bô-hia^n bô-tī**, having no brothers at all. **chhin hia^n-tī**, brothers by the same father. **phah-hó͘, tio̍h chhin-hia^n-tī**, in hunting tigers brothers should be used as assistants. **phah-hó͘ lia̍h-chha̍t, tio̍h chhin-hia^n-tī**, do., or in seizing robbers. **siang-pak hia^n-tī**, brothers by the same parents. **chek-peh hia^n-tī**, cousins (of same surname), or wider. **chhin-tông hia^n-tī**, cousins of same surname; men of same surname and of equal genealogical rank. **tông-hia^n-tī**, id. **chiông-tông hia^n-tī**, second cousins of same surname. **keh-kai^n hia^n-tī** (T.), first or second cousins of same surname. **piáu-hia^n-tī**, cousins of different surnames.

hōe-hia^n-tī, members of a society. **oā^n-thiap hia^n-tī**, men who have exchanged cards to make sworn brotherhood. **bêng-hia^n-tī**, sworn brothers and confederates. **kiet-gī hia^n-tī**, id. **kiet-pài hia^n-tī**, do. still more intimate, looking on each other's parents as their own. **hó-hia^n-tī**, title of spirits worshipped in the "phó͘-tō͘" ceremonies in 7th month.

toā-thâu-hia^n (C.), sometimes said euphemistically for a tiger.

hia^n (T. phia^n). **hāu-hia^n-phè**, broken fragments of tiles.

hiâ^n (R. hông). **kia^n-hiâ^n**, to fear greatly; much frightened.

hiâ^n, to add more fuel; to warm up. **hiâ^n-hé**, to put on more fuel. **hiâ^n-chhâ thi^n-hé**, id. **hiâ^n-kún**, to cause to boil. **hiâ^n-sio**, to warm up, but not so hot as "kún." **koh hiâ^n-sio**, to warm up again. **hiâ^n sio-tsúi**, to warm water.

hiâ^n, a bulk-head in a boat or junk. **tiām-hiâ^n**, timbers that are placed across the keel. **it-á-hiâ^n**, the front bulk-head. **thâu-hiâ^n**, id. **lāi-kiâ^n-hiâ^n**, id. **thâu-kap-á-hiâ^n**, the second bulk-head. **toā-tó͘-hiâ^n**, the bulk-head at the widest part. **a-pan-hiâ^n**, the middle bulk-head. **bé-hiâ^n**, the flat stern of the boat.

hiá^n (cf. hiah^n). **hiá^n-ba̍k**, to catch the eyes, as gaudy goods. **hiá^n-tiû^n**, flurried, losing presence of mind, as at examinations, or before a superior, or when meeting with several persons for business.

hiá^n-hiá^n (Cn.), too hurried and off-hand in doing things.

hià^n [R. hiòng, to lean towards; formerly; = col. ǹg, hiù^n], to lean over; to lean, as a tottering wall. **hià^n-hià^n**, leaning to one side; off the perpendicular (of men or things). **hià^n-sin**, leaning backwards. **khah-hià^n**, id. **hià^n-āu**, leaning backwards; to fall behind the rest of the row, as one house in a street; said also of woman's hair all combed back. **hià^n-chêng**, leaning forwards, as wall. **hià^n-khui**, to lean backwards to avoid something, as child unwilling to be embraced; to draw back from what one has promised.

tsúi hià^n, the tide just beginning to ebb. **hià^n-lâu**, id.

hià^n-sî, at that time (past); formerly.

hiā^n (R. ngāi^n), a plant (Artemisia) used for cauterizing and for tinder. **chhi^n-hiā^n**, id. **hiā^n-ho** (C.), id. **chhah-hiā^n**, to hang up Artemisia on 5.5 (v. chhah).

hé-hiā^n, tinder. **hé-hiā^n-khoeh**, a tinder-box.

hiā^n (C.) **nâ^n-hiā^n**, = A. kiā^n, the bent handle of a basket.

hiah (Cn. hoah), so—; just so—. **hiah-tn̂g**, so long (linear). **hiah-tsōe**, so many. **kàu-hiah-tsōe**, so very many! **kah-hiah-tsōe**, id. **m̄-sái hiah-tsōe**, no need of so many. **hiah-kú**, so long (in time), (v. kú).

hia̍h (R. ge̍k), the forehead. **thâu-hia̍h**, id. **hia̍h-chêng**, id. **hia̍h-hûn**, wrinkles on forehead. **hia̍h-kak**, the projecting parts of the forehead above the outer corners of the eyes. **hia̍h-bâi**, the part of the forehead just above the eyebrows; an ornament worn on the forehead by women, children, and actors. **pa̍k hia̍h-bâi**, to wear the ornament called "o͘-kun-khò͘" on the forehead. **pau hia̍h-bâi**, to tie a black ribbon (o͘-kun) on the brow, as women. **hia̍h-kha**, the middle of the forehead just below the boundary of the hair. **hia̍h-kha tsôe**, the dividing line of the hair nearly level across the brow, counted beautiful in women. **hia̍h-kha khàm-khàm**, the hair growing far down on the forehead, making it seem low and small. **thâu-hia̍h khàm-khàm**, id., sign of a toilsome miserable life. **thâu-mn̂g khàm-hia̍h**, id.

khok-hiáh, having a very projecting forehead. **liû-hiáh**, bald on forehead and crown of head. **hāu-hiáh**, having a projecting forehead like a king-crab (v. heng, "breast"). **tok-hiáh**, to wound the forehead with a stone (as beggar) to excite compassion. **phoà-hiáh**, id. **kiáh pê-put, ka-kī kòng-hiáh**, to raise a matter that injures one's self.

tsàu-hiáh, the flat top of a cooking-place round the rice-boiler (v. tsàu).

hiah^n, to carry with the hands or arms, esp. with both (but not by placing them evenly below, which is "phâng"). **hiah^n-sa^n**, to carry clothes; to go away with clothes. **thau-hiah^n**, to steal, as clothes. **chit toā-hiah^n**, a large quantity (as of clothes, &c.), such as must be carried between the arms.

hiah^n [R. hek, to threaten, frightened], (cf. hiá^n), to start suddenly; to get a start. **hiah^n--chit-ē**, to start suddenly. **tah-hiah^n**, to start. **chhi^n-kia^n tah-hiah^n**, id. **hō--lâng tah-hiah^n**, to make a man start.

hò-hiah^n, careless; hurried; acting thoughtlessly or flurried, so as to spoil or break things. **hóng-hiah^n** (C.), id. **táng-hiah^n**, id. **bô-hò-hiah^n**, careful or thoughtful in action. **hò-hò hiah^n-hiah^n**, very careless, thoughtless, or flurried.

hiah^n— **chhiú hiah^n-khui**, to throw out one's arms rapidly, as in excited discourse.

hiáh^n, = hiah^n, to start suddenly.

hiak (C.), = A. hiok. **hì-hiak**, to sport or joke in a low vile way.

hiam— **chhàu-hiam-hiam**, very stinking.

hiam (Cn. An.), = A. iam. **hō-hiam**, = hé-iam, a fire-shovel.

hiâm (R. id.), to find fault with; to censure; to blame; to scold. **sa^n-hiâm**, to dislike each other. **hoān-hiâm**, to excite suspicion; to be found fault with; to meet with censure. **hiáp-hiâm**, to harbour quarrelsome feeling. **hiâm-kùi**, to object to it as too dear. **hiâm-sòe**, to find fault with it as too small. **bô-hiâm tióh-boâ**, willing to take any trouble to get it done. **hiâm-hì bóh-chhiá^n, chhiá^n-hì bóh-hiâm**, if you dislike the play, don't hire them; if you hire them, don't find fault.

hiám (R. id.), dangerous; in danger of; almost (of harm or danger). **hiám-hiám**, id. **hiám-phoà**, in imminent danger of being broken. **hông-hiám**, dangerous; in great danger, as affair or disease. **gûi-hiám**, dangerous. **hiám, chiah-sī hiám**, the danger was very great indeed. **lāng-hiám**, to risk. **lîm-hiám**, to get into great and imminent danger.

hiám-iàu, important, as a pass. **hiám-ài**, id. **kù-hiám**, to guard an important pass.

kan-hiám, dishonest, roguish. **hiau-hiám**, id.; ungrateful, returning evil for good; very dangerous, as affair. **kan-hiau-hiám**, very dishonest, ungrateful, and scheming, as a rogue. **tsûn-sim kan-hiau-hiám**, constantly and desperately wicked.

hiàm (R. hám), to shout loud; to bawl out. **hoah-hiàm**, id., as to a man at a distance. **hiàm-sia^n**, id. **hiàm-kiò**, id. **kiò-hiàm**, id. **hiàm-tò-tńg**, to shout and call back. **hiàm-oan**, to make a loud shouting and noise in calling on a mandarin for redress.

hiàm-chhát, to shout, "Thief!" **hiàm-kiù**, to shout for help. **hiàm-kiù-lâng**, id. **hiàm-kiù-hō** (Cn.), id.

hiàm chhiam-á, to gamble by drawing lots and calling out.

hian, hiân, hián, hiàn, hiān; better hien, hiên, hién, hièn, hiēn (*q.v.*).

hiang [R. hiong, a village, = col. hiu^n]. **hiang-tâm** (Cn. hiong-tâm), local dialect. **lī-hiang, put-lī khiang**, one may leave his native place, but can't get rid of his native dialect.

hiang (C.), = A. hiong (village).

hiang [R. hiong, incense, fragrant]. **hiang-iû**, fragrant oil, edible. **hiang** (C.), = A. hiong, incense, fragrant.

hiang (C.) **khau-to-hiang**, shavings planed from wood.

hiáng (R. hióng), to resound; to sound loud and long, or echo. **hiáng-liāng**, clear and loud; far-sounding. **hiáng-keng**, a small humming instrument on a paper kite. **hiáng-tsoá^n**, a small gong used by Buddhist priests; a musical instrument made with five little bells like cups. **phah chhit-hiáng**, to play on these five musical cups. **jîn, put-soat put-ti; ké, put-tá^n put-hiáng**, said of a man not acknowledging a great favour done him.

hiáng— **hiáng-bé**, a highway-robber who levies black-mail. **hiáng-bé-chhát**, id.

hiáng (C.), = A. hióng, to enjoy.

hiàng (C.), = A. hiòng, towards. **chē-hiàng**, direction of house or grave.

hiàng (C.), = A. hiòng, customs' dues.

hiap, to refuse to return a thing lent or intrusted, or money due. **hiap--lâng**, id. **kiông-hiap**, do., because we are more powerful. **kiông-kiông-hiap**, id.

hiap (C.), = A. hip, to cover up.

hiap (P.), = hip. **hiap-chióh**, the loadstone.

hiáp [R. the ribs; to intimidate]. **hiáp-kut**, the ribs. **pek-hiáp**, to compel a man, under great pressure, to do something wrong, *e.g.* to join an illegal society.

hiáp [R. to carry under the arm; to hide in the bosom; to extort; cf. col. ngóeh].

hiáp-chè, to force a man, by intimidation or by improper pressure of influence, to do what he does not like. **kiông-kiông hiáp--khì** (= hiap), to refuse to pay a debt, &c., manifestly due, simply trusting to one's power.

hiáp-oàn, to harbour enmity. **hiáp-hūn**, id. **hiáp-hiâm**, to cherish in one's mind the determination to have a quarrel with a man.

hiáp [R. to bend or break], to shake or bend back and forwards in order to loosen or break. **hiáp-chih**, to break by bending back and forwards. **hiáp-khui**, to unfasten by shaking so. **hiáp--khí-lâi**, to loosen by shaking back and forwards so as to pull it out, as a nail or post. **hiáp hō-i-lō**, id., as a plant to be pulled up.

hiáp [R. united, harmonious], a colonel, or nearly so, one grade above "chham-hú," and just below "tìn-tâi." **hiáp-tâi**, id. **heng-hoà-hiáp**, the "hiáp" in command at Hing-hwa. **hiáp-toà**, an officer who assists the officer (tsóng-toà) in command of a body of troops. **hiáp-pān**, an assistant mandarin for some special matter; assistant mandarin in custom-house or some other public offices. **hiáp-pān tāi-hák-sū**, certain high officials at the court (v. hák).

hô-hiáp, of one mind and acting together (in lawful things). **hiáp-hô** (R.), id. **tâng-sim hiáp-lék**, with one heart and united strength.

bô-hiáp, not executed melodiously, or not harmonious, as music.

hiat, hiát; better, hiet, hièt (*q.v.*)

hiau — **hiau--tó**, to over-set by first slightly raising up (while "chhia" is a mere horizontal motion). **hiau-hiet-kák**, to throw away, as out of a tray by tossing it upwards.

hiau (R. id.) **hiau-hēng**, got by chance or by bad means (v. hēng).

hiau [R. a very wicked bird]. **hiau-hiông**, cunning, roguish, and wicked.

hiau [R. id. ? perhaps more than one word; cf. also the two words above], wicked, perverse, crafty; deceitful, unfaithful; refuse to perform duty, as to pay a debt or fulfil a promise; (warped, as wood).

hiau-hiòh, warped, as wood. **hiau-than**, very much warped, as wood (more than "hiau-hiòh"); faithless and deceitful; disappointing our trust. **khah-hiau than-khak**, as little to be trusted as the shell of the "than" shell-fish, which cuts the hand that holds it. **hiau--khì**, to swindle away, as money. **hiau-hoán**, to break and disregard a promise or agreement. **hoán-hiau**, id. **hiau-pōe**, to break an agreement; to act very deceitfully (v. pōe). **hiau-chè**, to refuse to pay just debts. **hiau lâng-ê-chè**, id. **hiau-thun**, to swallow another's money or property wrongfully. **hiau-hū**, to refuse to pay what is due; to keep back what belongs to another. **hiau-hū lâng-ê-un**, very ungrateful. **hiau-sim**, faithless and ungrateful in money matters. **hiau-hiám**, very ungrateful and injurious (v. hiám).

hong-hiau, dangerous or unlucky, as the state of matters.

hiâu, lewd, lascivious (only said of vile women). **hiâu-kháng**, id. **hiâu-siáu**, id. **hiâu-lin-long**, exceedingly lascivious (woman). **lāu-hiâu**, an old and lewd woman.

hiáu (R. id.) **hiáu--tit**, to understand. **hiáu-ngē**ⁿ (R.), id. **ū-hun-hiáu**, understanding well one's duty or business. **hiáu-lí**, understanding the principles of a question, or the way of managing a matter. **hiáu-lí ê-lâng**, a man who understands matters well.

hiàu — **hiàu-liàu-khì**, to sell off at a great sacrifice. **siòk-siòk-hiàu**, id. **sa**ⁿ**-tàu-hiàu**, underselling each other at ruinously low prices.

hiàu (C.) **hiàu-khak**, = A. hiauh-khak, to peel off, as paint or white-wash.

hiauh (= hauh), (C. hiàu), to scale or peel off, as skin or paint, or white-wash. **hiauh--khì**, id. **hiauh-khak**, id.

hiauh (R. hiok), to jibe or jest at misfortunes or peculiarities, esp. indirectly by inuendoes (often in low vile language). **hì-hiauh**, low bad joking, as by women or children.

hid (cf. hit). **hid--ê**, that (pronoun). **hid-dê**, id., = hit-ê.

hien (R. id.) **tsu-hien** (R.), a school, an academy. **ko-hien** (R.), your school.

hien (R. id.), to open, as a book, lid, or door-screen; to draw aside, as a veil. **hien-khui**, to open, as a book or lid. **hien--khí-lâi**, to open, as a lid. **hien-koà**, to take off a lid.

thàu-hien, to make a new roof.

hien ɵ-kun, to raise the veil of the bride, as the bridegroom does at marriage. **hien chhiú-phè** (C.), id.

hiên [R. wise, = col. gâu]. **hiên-jîn**, a wise man, or sage of inferior class. **sèng-hiên**, sages and wise men. **kèng-ló tsun-hiên**, reverence the aged, and honour the wise. **hiong-hiên-sû**, temple for the most distinguished literati of a district, at the side of the Confucian temple. **jip-hiong-hiên**, to be canonized among these worthies by imperial command.

hiên-hōe, gentle and affable in receiving guests, said only of a woman. **hiên-chhe**, my good wife; my dear wife.

hiên [R. a bow-string]. **keng-hiên**, a bow-string.

hiên [R. string for a musical instrument], a string for a guitar, &c.; a sort of guitar. **chit-tiâu-hiên**, one string. **chit-ki-hiên**, one guitar. **hiên-koán**, stringed and wind instruments (v. koán). **hô-hiên**, to tune the guitar. **jī-hiên**, a guitar with two strings. **jī-hiên-keng**, a bow for it. **jī-hiên-lák**, a drill worked by a bow. **sam-hiên**, a guitar with three strings. **toà**ⁿ **sam-hiên**, to play it. **pak-hiên**, a northern guitar, sometimes has copper wire instead of strings. **kóng-á-hiên**, a guitar with few strings and a small bamboo cylinder. **kiáh kóng-á-hiên**, to try to get money out of a man (said in allusion to the word "oaiⁿ," which means either to play on a guitar, or to get money out of people). **hiên-soàⁿ**, a guitar string. **khîm-hiên**, strings of harp.

siòk-hiên, a widower's second wife (lit. extra string for guitar !).

hiên [R. to hang up, to suspend]. **hiên--teh**, laid to sleep, as a case on which all action is suspended. **chhiáⁿ-hiên--teh**, just let it alone for a time. **sim-koaⁿ hiên--teh**, purpose quite unsettled; halting between two opinions.

hiên [R. dark-coloured; the private name of Kang-hi], (C. hân, in some cases). **hiên-thien siōng-tè**, the god of the north star. **hiên-toàⁿ-kong**, the idol called also "Tiō goân-sòe." **hiên-bú**, one of the four spirits (Tauist) of the four quarters; the four are "pèk-hó, chheng-liông, tsu-chhiok, hiên-bú."

hiên-som, = goân-som, an inferior sort of ginseng.

hiên (R. id.) **si**ⁿ **hoâi**ⁿ**-hiên**, to have a large venereal sore about the middle of the groin, below the navel. **si**ⁿ **noā**ⁿ**-hiên**, id.

hién (C.), = hit. **hién--ê**, that, these.

hién [R. hám, to shake], to shake backwards and forwards (neuter), as a man; to roll, as a vessel (but to pitch is "thîm"). **lē-lē-hién**, to shake, as a table or as a drunk man. **khōng-khōng-hién**, to shake about, as an unsteady chair or restless child; very restless. **kōng-kōng-hién**, id. **ōe-hién**, apt to shake about, as table, &c.; in danger of shaking about (s. manifest).

hién [R. to manifest, illustrious]. **hién-chhut**, to manifest. **hién-bêng**, id.; famous. **hién-jiên**, openly; publicly.

hién-tát, to become a mandarin or very illustrious (v. tát). **hién-iāu** (R.), glorious (v. iāu). **hién-iông** (r.), fine or grand in appearance, as house. **êng-hién** (R.), illustrious (v. êng). **hién-pí**, deceased mother. **hién-khó**, deceased father.

hién-hek, powerful and glorious, as a god. **lêng-hién**, able to answer prayers. **hién-sèng**, to appear in a visible form in answer to prayers for assistance. **ōe-hién**, powerful and efficacious, as an idol (s. shake). **ang hién, tē-tsú lòk-lién** (C.), when the idol is powerful its votaries grow poor. **ang hién, tē-tsú liáu-chhién**, do. do. spend their money.

ngé-hién-tè, an idol of the surname Iû^n, with three eyes. **ngé-hién-tāi-tè**, id. **ngé-hién-biō**, his temple.

hièn — **chhàu-hièn**, heavy unpleasant smell, as of fish. **ka-tsoàh-hièn**, bad smell of cockroaches. **chhàu-ka-tsoàh-hièn**, id. **iû^n-ko-hièn**, strong bad smell of new sheep-skin. **chhàu-iû^n-ko-hièn**, id. **chhàu-iû^n-bah-hièn**, smelling strong of goat mutton, as butcher, or as man who has been eating it.

ah-hièn, small feathers at a duck's tail, used for ear-brushes; two small bad-smelling balls near the duck's tail. **nn̄g-liáp-hièn**, these two balls.

hièn (R. id), to offer; to make an offering. **hièn-chè**, to make a sacrificial or ceremonial offering to a god or spirit. **chè-hièn**, id. **hièn-tsoá**, to offer burning paper, as at grave or to demons. **hièn-kèng**, to make offerings of many things (all together) at noon. in the rites called "chiò."

hièn-chhut, to produce openly, as man or thing. **hièn jîn-chêng**, to do a favour. **hièn-chêng**, id. **hièn-kong**, to put, as gains, into the common stock. **hièn-lòh-kong**, id. **hièn sio-koah**, to bring in slices of roast pig, the last dish of a feast.

hièn-siâ^n, to surrender a city. **hièn-khang-siâ^n** (to leave the city open to the enemy), said of leaving one's house open and unguarded.

hièn, to open out, as clothes on breast; opening out wide, as the mouth of a trumpet; shallow, as a saucer; bevelled, as a door or window; (boastful, liberal).

chhùi hièn-hièn, mouth opened very wide. **khah-hièn**, rather shallow and open, as a cup (opp. to "chhim-é," deep), &c. **hièn-heng**, to open the clothes so as to show the breast, or the inner dress. **hièn-kah**, to show the side of the breast near the shoulder (skin or inner dress) by unbuttoning part of dress. **hièn-khui**, to open out, as the dress. **hièn-khui-khui**, dress opened quite wide.

hièn-chhiú, liberal; open-handed; very free in the use of money. **toā-hièn**, id. **toā-hièn ê-ōe**, boastful talk; big words. **hièn-táu**, boastful, in manner or in exaggerated or false talk (v. táu). **hièn-thâu**, id. **gâu-hièn**, id.

hièn tsòe kúi-nà-hièn, to cut up into several pieces, as meat for sale; to make a great display out of little; to boast of power or excellence far beyond the truth. **sa^n-niú^n-bah tsòe sì-hièn** (cut three ounces of pork into four pieces), to make a great display or pretence with very little foundation.

āu-hièn (Cn.), the back half of the large central hall of a house, when it is divided by a transverse partition. **āu-hièn-pîn** (Cn.), that partition.

hièn (R. id.) **hièn-si**, high civil mandarins, as Tautai and above. **hièn-kiō**, a large broad sedan without sides, having a lion for footstool, used by high mandarins at the spring festival, and on going to war.

hiēn [R. hān, a limit], (C. ān). **iú-hiēn**, few; small in quantity.

hiēn [R. id. by change of tone from "kièn," to see], to appear; plain; manifest; (now, present). **hoat-hiēn**, to appear; to become manifest. **chhut-hiēn**, id. **lō-hiēn**, id. **tù-hiēn**, to manifest.

khoà^n-hiēn-hiēn, to see a thing very plainly. **thia^n-bô-hiēn**, not to hear plainly, as what is spoken too low or indistinctly. **chhién-hiēn**, plain and easy, as a word, a purpose, or a doctrine; open and exposed, as a house on the road or main street.

hiēn-kóng, talk of it at once. **hiēn-kim**, now; at present. **hiēn-sî**, id. **chhú-hiēn-sî**, id. **hiēn-chheng** (C.), id. **hiēn-chêng** (Cn.), id. **hiēn-chiâ^n**, id. **hiēn-tsāi**, now; present. **chhú-hiēn-tsāi**, now. **chit-tiáp hiēn-tsāi**, id. **chhú-hiēn-pē** (C.), id.

hiēn-gûn, ready money. **hiēn-chî^n**, id. **hiēn-kau-koan**, ready-money transaction. **hiēn-bóe hiēn-bōe**, id. **chit-chheng sia, m̄-tàh poeh-pah-hiēn**, a thousand (cash) for credit are not so good as eight hundred ready money.

hiēn — **hiēn-sì**, descendants of prosperous ancestors become very poor, robbers, or wretched and miserable. **kiá^n-sun hiēn-sì**, id. **kiá^n-sun teh hiēn-sì**, id. **hiēn-sì--tiòh tsé-kong**, to bring disgrace on our ancestors in this way.

hiet (cf. hì^n), to throw. **hiet-kák**, to throw away. **pàng-hiet-kák**, id. **hiet-tiu** (T.), id. **hiet--lòh-khì**, to throw down. **hiet-liet--khì**, to throw away; to leave off, as an affair. **hiet khut-lá**, game of throwing cash into a small hole.

hng-hng hiet-hiet (Cn.), all in disorder, as a house in a litter.

hiet — **hoe-hiet**, gaudy; showy; beautifully painted and ornamented, as house; beautifully laid out for sale, as showy goods; too specious and plausible, as words that sound well but mean little; when said of women it is too gaudily ornamented, as if for bad purposes.

sok-hiet (Cn.), = A. sok-kiet, neat and tidy.

hiet [R. blood, = col. huih]. **hiet-liû**, a bloody tumour. **hiet-lī**, bloody dysentery. **hiet-lîm**, bloody urine. **hiet-pheng**, flow of blood from female organs. **hiet-peng** (C.), id.

hiet-chióng, palm of the hand red (counted a good omen).

hiet-kiet, dragon's blood.

hā-hiet, to have bloody dysentery. **liâng-hiet**, cooling for the blood, as food or medicine. **hêng-hiet**, making the blood more abundant, healthy, and active, as medicine. **phò-hiet**, to diminish the blood injuriously, as some condiments are supposed to do. **chhit-khóng liû-hiet**, blood flowing from mouth and nose, as in severe fever or from poison.

hiet-khì, the vital principle of flesh and blood; animal spirits. **hiet-khì put-hêng**, vital principle not acting well, as in some diseases. **hiet-khì gêng--teh**, blood supposed to be arrested in its action, as in tumours, &c. **hiet gêng--teh**, id. **hiet-khì chiok**, in good vigorous health; having a full-blooded constitution. **hiet-khì ūn-tōng**, the vital principle moving about to the several organs in the successive hours of day and night, supposed to make one complete revolution in twenty-four hours, has no connection with the real circulation of the blood (v. tōng).

chhin hiet-bėk, one's own real son, not adopted (v. bėk). **cheng-hiet chhiong-chiok**, in strong vigorous health, as a man in the full vigour of his whole bodily powers. **lâm cheng, lú hiet**, generative principles of male and female. **hū cheng, bó hiet**, do. of father and mother.

hiėt [R. a cave], classifier of graves. **tsâu-hiėt**, a den of wild beasts or bad men. **hiėt-tōe**, location for a grave. **chit-hiėt hong-súi**, one site for a grave; one grave. **tâng-hiėt**, buried in the same grave. **siāng-hiėt**, id. **tiám-hiėt**, to lay down the exact place and position of a grave after the site itself has been chosen. **tiám hiėt-tiû^n**, id.

hih — **hih-hih-chhiò**, to giggle. **hih-hih hū-hū**, sound of wind or of a mill, &c. (v. hū).

hih (Cn.) **hih--gê**, = hit-ê, that.

hihⁿ— **hih**ⁿ**-hih**ⁿ**-thí**, to sob and cry. **hih**ⁿ**-hih**ⁿ**-háu**, to cry, as a child or as a man with a heavy burden.

him, to talk in an overbearing or threatening manner. **him-hoah**, to bawl angrily; to scold a man so as to silence him. **toā-sia**ⁿ**-him**, id. **toā-him**, id. **toā-him sái gâi-chîⁿ**, to talk loud and pass bad cash.

him [R. to like, to be pleased]. **him-bē**, to long for; to desire much. **him-soān**, id.; to delight in. **him-siēn**, id.

hîm (R. hiông), a bear; a baboon; a surname. **lâng-hîm**, a baboon. **soa**ⁿ**-hîm**, a bear. **hîm-táⁿ**, bear's gall (medicinal). **hîm-chiúⁿ**, a bear's paw, counted very strengthening food. **hoah-hîm hoah-hé**, calling out in great terror at sudden danger.

that-hîm, a game in which one boy keeps seven bits of brick, trying to kick the other boy who must snatch them all away. **hîm-chí**, these bits of brick, representing bears' cubs.

hìm — **hìm-hé**, to smother embers in a jar, for future use.

hīm (= hām). **chhùi hīm-hīm**, mouth shut; unwilling to speak; sullenly silent.

hin (= hit). **hin-pêng**, = hit-pêng, that side.

hin (C.), = A. heng, to prosper. **khoài-hin khoài-thè**, rapidly prospering and rapidly declining.

hin [R. sin, the body]. **hin-su** (C.), the body. **hin-sin** (C.), id.

hîn (R. hiên), giddy; dizzy; sick with giddy feeling. **hîn-tsûn**, sea-sick. **hîn-kiō**, sickened by using a sedan. **hîn-soa**ⁿ, made sick by coming on shore. **hîn-gōng**, giddy; dizzy. **hîn-gōng-gōng**, id. **ē-àm-hîn**, blind with giddiness. **thâu-khak-hîn**, head giddy or swimming. **hîn-bòng-bòng**, head swimming and things seeming to turn round. **bōng-bōng-hîn**, id. **khì-thâu-hîn**, to cure giddiness.

hîn (R. hiên). **iûⁿ-hîn**, epilepsy.

hîn [R. hiông, male]. **hîn-hông**, a drug used as a medicine and charm; realgar (v. hông).

hìn (C.), = A. hèng, to desire. **kau-hìn**, id.

hīn (C.), = A. hūn, to hate.

hiô (Cn.), = A. hê, a marquis; a feudal lord.

hiô (Cn.), = A. hê, frivolous; floating.

hiò (C.), a cry for driving away birds.

hiō (K.), = A. hē, rain.

hiō (Cn.), = A. hē, to wait.

hiō (Cn.), = A. hē, after. **jiên-hiō**, afterwards. **jit-hiō**, id.

hiō (Cn.), = A. hē, queen.

hiō (Cn.), = A. hē, thick, grave, serious, &c.

hioⁿ (P.), in all the tones, = A. hiuⁿ; and so in many parts of Changchow.

hioh [R. hiet, R. sek], (C. hehⁿ), to rest. **hioh-kang**, to rest from work. **hioh-khùn**, to rest from work or walking; to lie down. **hioh-siēn**, to rest because tired. **hioh-chhoán**, to rest to take breath. **hioh-hē**, to take shelter from rain. **hioh-ńg**, to take shelter from heat in the shade. **hioh-ki**, to perch on a branch, as a bird. **hioh-koaiⁿ**, to roost, as in a cage. **hioh-tiàm**, to lodge a night, as in an inn. **tâu-hioh**, to stay a night at a place. **an-hioh-jit** (X.), the Sabbath-day.

hioh (R. iáp), a leaf (not of a book); the paper of a fan; the blade of an oar. **chhiū-hioh**, the leaves of trees; foliage. **ké-hioh**, leaves used for wrapping cakes when steamed. **phâng-á-hioh**, bamboo leaves used in making sails.

hiau-hioh, to be warped, as wood.

kim-hioh, a thin plate of gold used for inlaying; used also as a portable sort of treasure. **hī-hioh**, the flap of the ear. **mn̂g-hioh**, the leaf of a door. **chiúⁿ-hioh**, an oar-blade. **toā-hioh**, the blade of the helm. **sìⁿ-hioh**, the paper of a fan ready to be pasted on the ribs of the fan. **chit-ki-hioh**, one paper for a fan.

lì-hioh, to strip off leaves. **thùi-hioh**, to shed leaves and grow new ones.

ki-hioh, branches and leaves. **kāu-ki-hioh**, making a great many words about a matter; too minute about objections or conditions. **kim-ki gėk-hioh** (branches and leaves of gold and jade), said of the children of mandarins or wealthy men, who do not need to do hard work. **siⁿ-ki hoat-hioh**, the foundation of the story true, but false in its details. **kóng kàu ū-ki ū-hioh**, to describe details so minutely that a lie looks just like truth. **tsō kàu ū-ki u-hioh**, id. **siⁿ kàu** &c., id. **chiap kàu ū-ki ū-hioh**, one man adding a tissue of lies to the statement (true or false) of another so as to make it appear all true.

hioh (R. hiau). **bā-hioh**, the kite. **boàh-hioh**, id. **lāi-hioh** (C.), id. **nāiⁿ-hioh** (T.), id. **lā-hioh** (Cn.), id.

lāi-hioh-kha, waddling and awkward in walking; shaking from side to side. **lāi-hioh-chhì**, the thistle. **lāi-hioh-chhì-thâu**, thistle roots (medicinal). **lāi-hioh-chhì-kū**, a thorny shrub with a yellow flower. **m̄-koaiⁿ koe-bú, phah lāi-hioh**, said of a man not restraining his own dependants, but finding fault with others for trouble.

hiok (R. id.), (C. hiak). **hì-hiok**, to make vile low jokes. **hì-hiok ê-ōe**, jibes or calumnies evidently false and ridiculous.

hiong (R. id.), ill-omened; inauspicious; unlucky. **kiet-hiong**, lucky and unlucky. **hiong-hām**, very great and severe, as calamity. **hiong-sîn ok-soah**, malicious demons. **hiong-hók** (R.), mourning dress.

hiong (R. id.), wicked; vicious. **hiong-ok**, do.; cruel. **hiong-sin**, a murderer who commits the act with his own hands (s. village). **hiong-sin-phe**, not afraid to risk one's life in some dangerous attempt. **hiong-siú**, a murderer. **hiong-hoān**, id. **hêng-hiong**, to fight or strike or assault very violently, so as to wound or murder, &c. **káⁿ-hêng-hiong**, very violent; ready for fighting or murder. **kiông-hiong kėk-ok**, very powerful, wicked, and dangerous. **phēng-hiong**, appearance as if about to fight. **kap-goá phēng-hiong**, he appears as if he would fight me (when I would get him to pay what he is due).

hiong (cf. hiông). **hiong-kúi-kúi**, extremely ugly in face. **hiong-pa lí-láu**, very ugly (v. láu).

hiong, hasty, hurried. **hiong-hiong**, id. **hiong-chiong**, hurried and careless (v. chiong). **hiong-kông**, too hasty and urgent in manner; so impulsive as to be almost violent.

hiong (P. heng). **sòng-hiong**, very poor.

hiong [R. fragrant, incense, = col. hiuⁿ], (C. hiang). **hiong-káng**, Hongkong. **chhit-lí-hiong** (fragrant at seven li distant), a shrub with sweet white flowers and small fruit. **lī-kun-hiong**, = thô-hiu^{n}, a small aromatic plant. **hiong-hû**, a medicine made from the root of the thô-hiu^{n} (Cyperus?). **hūi-hiong-hû**, this medicine from Hūi-an. **siông-hiong** (Cn.), = siông-ka, resin. **ut-kim-hiong-chiú**, a fragrant wine (v. ut).

hoa-hiong-tê, tea flavoured with flowers to conceal its inferior quality (orange pekoe?). **hoa-hiong**, id. **hiong-hoa teng-kó**, incense, flowers, lamps, and drums, as in idolatrous procession, or sometimes in honour of a virtuous retiring mandarin. **hiong-hoa teng-chiok**, incense, flowers, lamps, and candles, used in honour of idols.

hiong [R. a village, = col. hiu^{n}], (C. hiang). **hiong-sin**, graduates and gentry (s. wicked). **hiong-chhin**, fellow-villager (a courteous salutation). **hiong-ióng**, village braves. **hiong-sì**, the examination for the Kujin degree. **hiong-hiên-sû**, temple for the canonized literati of a district (v. hiên). **su-hiong** (r.), to long for home. **bōng-hiong-tâi**, a place in Hades from which the dead can see their house and family.

biên-hiong, of the same village; villages combining, *e.g.* to oppose a powerful opponent in a clan feud, or against rebels, &c. **liên-hiong**, id. **liên-hiong-kiet**, an agreement made with the mandarins, in which several villages stand security for each other's good conduct.

hiong-tâm (Cn.), = A. hiang-tâm, local dialect.

hiong [R. the breast, = col. heng]. **ū-sim-hiong**, prudent and shrewd; having good common sense and tact; *e.g.* ready with an answer for anything, or well able to adapt action to the circumstances, or to guard against danger. **toā-sim-hiong**, desirous to get large gains; having one's mind set on much money, as merchant who runs great risks in the hope of large profits, or as a thief who steals valuable things but despises articles of small value.

hiông [R. a bear, = col. hîm], a surname.

hiông [R. male, brave, = col. hêng, hîn]. **hiông-hiông**, very violent or urgent in manner; ugly, large, and coarse-looking, as face. **hiông-hiông-thóeh**, to take away what the other is unwilling to give. **hiông-hiông-tsáu**, to run on, as in urgent haste.

eng-hiông, a hero. **kan-hiông**, cunning and roguish. **hiau-hiông**, very roguish, deceitful, and wicked.

chhu-hiông (R.), male and female, esp. of birds. **chhi-hiông** (C.), id. **kièn-chhu-hiông**, to try which is stronger, as in a feud. **chhu-hiông-kiàm**, two knives making a pair. **chhu-hiông-gán**, eyes of unequal size, said somewhat in joke.

hiông-kài-kài, very fierce-looking; large and coarse-looking, as man. **hiông-kúi-kúi**, as ugly as a demon (of face).

hióng [R. loud-sounding, = col. hiáng, hiú^{n}]. **ū-éng-hióng**, having some foundation in truth, as a rumour.

hióng (Cn.), = hit. **hióng-gê**, = hit-ê, that, those.

hióng (C. hiáng), to enjoy. **hióng-siū**, id. **hióng-hok**, to enjoy good fortune. **hióng-chè**, to accept sacrificial offerings. **phòe-hióng**, to share in receiving offerings or worship, as secondary spirits conjoined with the chief object of worship in the ceremony.

hiòng [R. id., = col. hiù^{n}, ǹg], (C. hiàng), towards; facing; formerly; a surname.

hiòng-lâi, formerly; up to that time.

tùi-hiòng, right opposite, as house or grave, &c. **tsō-hiòng**, direction, as of a grave, fixed by the geomancer. **hun-kim tsō-hiòng**, id.

ì-hiòng--i, to have our mind towards a person.

hiòng-iông, in an airy healthy situation. **hiòng-tang**, facing the east. **hiòng-chêng**, facing forwards, as in advancing. **hiòng-thien**, looking towards the sky. **bīn hiòng-thien**, face towards the sky. **hiòng-thien-sai**, figure of a lion looking up (said of a man with his face looking up).

hiòng-jit-kûi, the sun-flower.

hiòng (R. id.), (C. hiàng), customs' dues; soldier's pay. **kháu-hiòng**, customs' dues. **hiòng-hāng**, money collected for customs. **hiòng-gûn**, id., soldier's pay. **hiòng-koán**, a custom-house, esp. a branch custom-house; the official in charge of it. **hiòng-koán toā-iâ**, an inspector at a branch custom-house, as for inspecting vessels entering the harbour.

hiòng-tién, a pawn-shop.

niá^{n}-hiòng, to receive pay, as a soldier; to draw his pay; to draw the money for the army from the provincial treasury. **niá^{n}-hiòng-bé**, to draw the balance of military pay. **chhut-hiòng**, to pay soldier's pay. **chièn-hiòng**, superior class of soldiers with more pay. **siú-hiòng**, inferior soldiers with less pay. **niá^{n} siú-hiòng**, to draw that pay.

tāng-hiòng, subject to heavy duty. **phah-hiòng**, to levy dues, to collect customs. **thiu-hiòng**, id. **teng-hiòng** (C. tin-hiàng), id. **ah-hiòng**, to convey government money to the superior city under escort. **giām-hiòng**, to search (as a vessel) to see what is liable to duty. **liàh-hiòng**, to seize goods for duty. **láp-hiòng**, to pay duties or customs. **oân-hiòng**, id. **pò-hiòng**, to give in a statement of goods liable to duty (v. pò). **tsáu-hiòng**, to smuggle. **lāu-hiòng**, id.

hip (R. id.), (cf. him). **háng-hip**, to frighten by scolding; to threaten or intimidate. **kiông-kiông-hip**, to intimidate or terrify into doing something.

hip — **tò-hip**, to turn round on an assailant and overcome him; to shut up an opponent in argument by a sharp retort or counter-charge, either true or false [word above? or below?].

hip (R. id.), (C. hiap, hip), very close, with little or no air; to smother; to suffocate; to hatch by artificial heat. **hip-au**, a tea-cup with a cover. **hip-tê**, to infuse tea in a covered cup. **hip-siōng**, to take a photograph. **hip ah-nn̄g**, to hatch duck eggs by artificial heat. **hip--sí**, to smother to death.

hip [R. siap, to manage, to seize, = liap], (C. hiap). **hip-chióh**, the loadstone.

hit [R. pí, = col. hí, hin, hiù^{n}, &c.], (Cn. hióng, C. hién), that, those. **hit-ê**, that, that one. **hit-dê**, id. **hit-lâng**, that man. **hit-pái**, that time, that occasion. **hit-hō**, that sort. **hit-ki**, that one, of things classified under "ki" (and so with other classifiers). **hit-tá**, there, that place. **hit-á**, id. **hit-lá**, id.

hit (cf. hì^{n}), to oscillate; to shake about, as pendulum. **lē-nih^{n}-hit**, to swing from side to side. **lē-nì^{n}-hit**, id.

hiu [R. to cease; to divorce]. **hiu-tsu**, a written divorce. **hiu-lí** (R.), to divorce. **bô-sí-hiu**, without any stop, as a continual feud. **pàng--i kan-hiu**, to let him off without punishment.

hiu [R. deep and dark, elegant]. **chheng-hiu**, neat and comfortable, pleasant and retired, as a house.

hiû (R. kiû), a warm coat or jacket. **mî^{n}-hiû**, a warm dress quilted or wadded with cotton. **kiap-hiû**, a warm dress lined but not wadded. **koeh-hiû**, id. **köh-hiû** (Cn.), id. **chit-ko-hiû**, warm dress lined with sort of flannel or woven wool. **iû^{n}-ko-hiû**, one lined with sheep-skin. **phê-á-hiû**, one lined with fur. **phoà-hiû-kong**, a very old wadded coat (*e.g.* twenty years old or so), said in joke. **chiàh-pē-pn̄g, chhēng bú-hiû**, fed and clothed by one's parents.

hiú (R. id.) **hiú-noā^{n}**, rotten. **noā^{n} hiú-hiú**, very soft or rotten. **hiú-bók put-khó-tiau**, rotten wood cannot be carved (said of a fellow of whom nothing can be made).

hiú — **hiú-hiú-háu**, to whizz.

hiù (cf. hì^{n}). **hiù-chhien-chhìu**, to swing a swing.

hiù, to sprinkle. **hiù-tsúi**, to sprinkle water. **hiù-phâng**, to throw water on a sail in order to keep it from being injured by the heat.

hiù [R. bad smelling, stinking, = col. chhàu]. **ûi-hiù bān-liên**, to leave a name of bad reputation for a myriad years.

hiu^{n} — **hiu^{n}-hiu^{n}**, weak and sickly, as a child.

hiu^{n} (R. hiong), a village. **hiu^{n}-lí**, id. **hiu^{n}-siā**, id. **hiu^{n}-chhng**, id. **toā-hiu^{n}**, a large village. **pún-hiu^{n}**, native village. **siāng-hiu^{n}-lí**, of the same village. **hiu^{n}-kan**, among the villages. **hiu^{n}-ē**, id. **hiu^{n}-tâm** (Cn.), = hiang-tâm, local dialect. **sū-hiu^{n}** (Cn.), = su-hiong, home-sick.

hiu^{n} (Cn.) **péh-phī^{n}-hiu^{n}**, an animal like a small stag with a white nose.

hiu^{n} (R. hiong), incense; perfume; (various drugs). **chit-ki-hiu^{n}**, an incense-stick. **sái sa^{n}-ki-hiu^{n}**, to sail within the time that three incense-sticks burn. **n̄g-tiâu-hiu^{n}** (two incense-sticks), a fore-and-aft schooner. **n̄g-ki-hiu^{n}**, id.

báng-hiu^{n}, a composition burned to keep off mosquitoes. **phà^{n}-chhek-hiu^{n}**, a drug used for flavouring liquor, &c. **ut-kim-hiu^{n}**, a sort of drug (v. ut). **siā-hiu^{n}**, musk. **jú-hiu^{n}**, frankincense. **tîm-hiu^{n}**, aloes (v. tîm). **toâ^{n}-hiu^{n}**, sandal-wood. **thiâ^{n}-hiu^{n}-sek**, light grayish-purple. **phī^{n}-hiu^{n}**, snuff. **teng-hiu^{n}**, cloves. **tsúi-teng-hiu^{n}**, a marsh plant, with bright blue flowers and arrow-shaped leaves, used for snake-bites. **teng-hiu^{n}-á**, a small red bird. **àn-sek-hiu^{n}**, gum benzoin. **lô-liâm-hiu^{n}**, a sort of adhesive gum. **bák-hiu^{n}**, putchuk (v. bák "wood"). **pêh-gîn-hiu^{n}** (C.), an evergreen-tree with large bunches of scarlet berries. **pêh-jîn-hiu^{n}** (C.), id. **poeh-kak-hiu^{n}**, anise seed. **soa^{n}-hiu^{n}** (C.), a wild medicinal plant. **thê-hiu^{n}**, a weed used for medicine (Cyperus esculentus?), = hiong-hū. **tê-hiu^{n}** (Cn.), id. **sūi-hiu^{n}**, a beautiful flower (v. sūi). **chhì-thâu-hiu^{n}**, a medicinal root.

chēng-hiu^{n}, powdered incense (used for ceremonial cleansing). **kàng-chin-hiu^{n}**, incense used to bring down "thi^{n}-kong" in worship (Laka?). **phà^{n}-sok-hiu^{n}**, a fine sort of incense. **soà^{n}-hiu^{n}**, a long incense-stick with no bamboo in it. **tek-á-hiu^{n}**, a long slip of bamboo covered with incense. **bih-hiu^{n}**, id. **tiông-siū-hiu^{n}**, long incense-sticks for birth-days.

hiu^{n}-chháu, fragrant plants (used for scenting hair-oil). **hiu^{n}-chhâ**, sandal-wood. **hiu^{n}-ke**, sort of mushroom. **hiu^{n}-î^{n}**, the citron. **hiu^{n}-sim** (Cn.), sort of tree.

hiu^{n}-thâu, bits of incense. **hiu^{n}-hé**, incense-bag worn as amulet. **hiu^{n}-hê**, incense-bags (like shrimps) hung on idols. **hiu^{n}-pau**, bags of incense worn only for the smell. **hiu^{n}-tē**, id. (esp. in 7th month). **hiu^{n}-ôe**, do., shaped like shoes. **hiu^{n}-thiap**, do., worn on women's hair-pins. **hiu^{n}-seh** (C.), do. in women's hair. **hiu^{n}-tsu**, perfumed beads. **hiu^{n}-oân**, perfume-balls. **hiu^{n}-khoân**, long spiral roll of incense (lasting sometimes several weeks) burned in temple. **hiu^{n}-thah**, id. **hiu^{n}-pâi**, tablet made of several incense-sticks for marriage and other ceremonies. **hiu^{n}-sok**, paper bundles of incense-sticks (v. sok). **hiu^{n}-soà^{n}-lok**, long paper bag for holding a number of incense-sticks. **hiu^{n}-nâ^{n}**, basket with burning incense. **hiu^{n}-tà^{n}**, two small frames carried at the ends of a pole with incense burning in one; also, a load of incense carried for sale by a pedlar. **hiu^{n}-oà^{n}**, an incense-table (v. oà^{n}). **hiu^{n}-lê**, a standing censer; a vessel full of incense-ashes in which burning incense-sticks are stuck. **hiu^{n}-tī**, sticks for arranging the incense on the censer. **hiu^{n}-sî**, spoon for pressing down the incense-ashes. **hiu^{n}-hu**, incense-ashes. **hiu^{n}-ien**, incense-smoke. **hiu^{n}-ien put-toān**, incense always burning without ceasing, as in temple. **hiu^{n}-tîn**, a procession carrying incense. **chit-tîn-hiu^{n}**, id. **hiu^{n}-tiâu**, yellow bills announcing incense processions; long sticks of incense. **hiu^{n}-piá^{n}**, cheap hollow sweet cakes.

sio-hiu^{n}, to burn incense. **sio hó-hiu^{n}, chiàh hó-chhài**, to be wealthy and get everything of the best. **chhah-hiu^{n}**, to stick incense-sticks in the ashes. **ngiâ-hiu^{n}**, to carry idols and incense in procession. **koah-hiu^{n}**, id. **sûi-hiu^{n}**, to follow such a procession. **hêng-hiu^{n}**, to go in procession to the temples to worship, as mandarins do on taking office, and on 1st and 15th of each month. **hêng-hiu^{n} hòng-kò**, to go to worship in procession and give notice that the office is open for accusations, as newly-arrived mandarin. **chìn-hiu^{n}**, to bring an incense-stick to the worshipper that he may use it in worship; to bring incense from a greater temple to a less. **liam-hiu^{n}**, to worship by offering an incense-stick (v. liam). **'thia^{n}-hiu^{n}**, to listen for the first word heard after offering incense, as an omen (v. thia^{n}). **tsòe-hiu^{n}**, to make incense-sticks.

han-tsû chhàu-hiu^{n}, potatoes having faults and holes in them.

pún-tōe-hiu^{n} bōe-phang, incense made in the neighbourhood is not sweet-scented; foreign things are most valued.

hiú^{n} [R. hióng, loud-sounding, = col. hiáng]. **hong pū-pū-hiú^{n}**, the wind howling loudly. **khiang-khiang-hiú^{n}**, to sound loud, as a brass thing when struck.

hiú^{n}, said in Tiô-thoà for "háu," to make a noise.

hiù^{n} (= hit). **hiù^{n}-pêng**, on that side. **àn-hiù^{n}-sì** (T. C.), in that way; thus. **àn-hiù^{n}** (T.), id. **àn-hì^{n} àn-hiù^{n}** (C.), of very unsettled purpose.

hiù^{n} [R. hiòng, towards, = col. ǹg, à^{n}]. **hng-hiù^{n}**, direction, as of a house or grave; quarter to which it looks. **tēng hng-hiù^{n}**, to fix by compass the lucky direction for house or grave. **tang-hiù^{n}**, towards east. **chē hiù^{n}-tang** (T. old dialect), facing east. **hun-kim chē-hiù^{n}**, geomantic direction of house or grave. **tsō-hiù^{n}** (R.), id. **chē-hiù^{n}** (T.), id. **hiù^{n}-siú^{n}** (T.), direction, as of house or grave, or of persons sitting at table. **hó-hiù^{n}-siú^{n}** (T.), good direction for it.

hiuh — **póh-hiuh-hiuh**, very thin.

hiùh (= khiùh). **sòng-hiùh-hiùh**, very poor.

hm̂ (R. mûi^{n}), (C. bûn). **hm̂-lâng**, a go-between in making marriages. **hm̂-lâng-kong**, id. **hm̂-lâng-pô**, a woman who buys and sells female slaves, and makes irregular marriages by sale. **hm̂-lâng-lé**, fee of the go-between in marriages.

hm̂-lâng-soàⁿ, a thread with which cloth is very loosely sewed at first (taken out when the firm sewing is completed).

hm̂ (R. bâu, mâuⁿ). **hm̂-chháu**, sort of grass used for thatch and for medicine. **hm̂-á-chháu**, id. **hm̂-á-kun**, its root. **hm̂-á-koaⁿ**, this grass dried.

hm̂ (= m̂). **tih-tùh-hm̂**, a toy that makes a humming noise.

hm̂, exclamation of surprise.

hḿ (C. hám), (cf. hmh), to strike hard with an instrument or stone held in the hand; noise made to stop children's noisy play. **hḿ--sí**, to strike dead, as with a club.

hm̄ — **hm̄-hm̄-háu**, to buzz; to growl, as a tiger. **hm̄-hm̄-kiò**, to growl, as a tiger.

hmh (= hḿ), to strike with some heavy thing held in the hand; a sound made to stop children's noise.

piah-hmh, a large beetle that comes flying against walls and people; said also of a useless dull awkward fellow.

hm̍h (cf. hîm). **hm̍h-hm̍h**, keeping one's mouth shut and saying nothing.

hng [R. hong, a region; means, plans, or prescriptions]. **tōe-hng**, a region or tract of country. **sì-hng**, in every direction. **pak-hng**, the north (&c.) **hng-hiòⁿ**, direction, as of grave or house (v. hiòⁿ). **thien-tek-hng**, an auspicious hill near the grave (v. tek).

hng-thâu, a medical prescription, usually with directions for use. **iòh-hng**, id. **khui-iòh-hng**, to write out a prescription. **pì-hng**, a secret medical prescription. **chhun-hng**, medicine for lascivious purposes.

hng [R. hong, waste, desert, famine], (C. hng, huiⁿ). **ki-hng**, famine; dearth (C. id.) **iau-hng**, voracious; only said in scolding a child that is always eating, esp. cakes and sweetmeats.

pha-hng (C. pha-huiⁿ), to lay waste. **hng-hòe** (C. huiⁿ-hùi), desolate; laid waste. **hng-hng hìⁿ-hìⁿ** (C. huiⁿ), all in disorder, as room or house. **hng-hng hiet-hiet** (Cn.), id.

hng (R. hong). **chiòh-hng**, a stone memorial archway. **chiet-hng**, one in honour of a lady of great purity and excellence. **chiet-hàu-hng**, one to a lady of purity and filial piety. **khiā-hng**, to set up such an archway by imperial permission. **hng-kha**, at the foot of the memorial arch.

hng [R. hun, dark, dusk, twilight], (C. huiⁿ). **ê-hng** (C. ê-huiⁿ), evening. **bîn-hng** (T. Cn.), id. **tsā-hng**, yesterday evening. **jī-káu ê-hng**, the last night of the year (though really the 30th).

hng — **hng-hng-háu**, sound of flies or mosquitoes; sound of a child repeating songs, &c. **hng-hng-kiò**, sound of mosquitoes, &c.

hn̂g, what? (said in answer to a question or instructions not distinctly heard).

hn̂g (R. hông), (C. hûiⁿ). **liû-hn̂g**, sulphur. **jiû-hn̂g**, id.

hn̂g (R. oân), (C. hûiⁿ), a dry field; a field not much irrigated; a garden; an orchard. **chhân-hn̂g**, fields of all sorts, wet and dry; fields and gardens; cultivated land in general. **hoe-hn̂g**, a flower-garden. **ké-chí-hn̂g**, an orchard. **kam-chià-hn̂g**, a field of sugar-cane. **bèh-hn̂g**, a field of wheat or barley. **soa-hn̂g**, a plot of dry sandy ground. **soaⁿ-hn̂g**, dry fields on hills. **hn̂g-pho**, dry hilly fields (in general), as distinguished from irrigated fields. **lòk-hn̂g** (X.), paradise (lit. garden of pleasure).

khui-hn̂g, to make a garden or dry field. **tsoh-hn̂g**, to cultivate a dry field or garden. **kùt-hn̂g**, to dig it. **koáⁿ-hn̂g**, to take up a whole field (as of potatoes) at once.

hn̂g-bèh, wheat or barley from dry fields. **hn̂g-tsû** (C. hûiⁿ-chî), sweet-potatoes from dry fields. **hn̂g--ê**, id.

hńg [R. hóⁿ, good, = col. hó]. **hô-hńg** (P.), = hô-hó, friendly. **hńg** (P.), a man's name.

hńg, interjection of displeasure or contempt.

hǹg, interjection of anger, disappointment, or disdain (pronounced with more emphasis, and rather deeper than the next word).

hǹg (cf. hèⁿ), yes! yes, sir!

hn̄g (R. oán), (C. hūiⁿ), far; distant. **hn̄g lo-lo**, very far. **lī-hn̄g**, far separated; far distant. **tsoáh hn̄g**, difference great. **tsáp-pē chiah-hn̄g**, ten times as far.

hngh (A. esp. T.), (cf. hǹg), yes, I observe what you say.

hn̍gh (Cn.), = A. hàhⁿ, hehⁿ, — yes! I have heard what you say, and observe it.

ho, an interjection. **ho-ho-ho**, sound made by men (*e.g.* boatmen) working together. **ho-lo**, id. **hoah-ho**, to call out "ho," as to a man at a distance. **hoah-ho--chit-ē**, id.

ho [R. hok, = col. hoh], to scorch, as the sun; very sultry, as weather. **chhùi ho**, the mouth very dry and thirsty. **jit ho--lâng**, the sun scorching people.

ho [R. ko, tall herbs]. **hiāⁿ-ho** (C.), a plant used as tinder (v. hiāⁿ).

ho — **ho-lin-tāu**, green pease (probably originally "hô-lân," Dutch).

ho — **ka-kī khai-ho**, to boast of one's own talents, success, or prosperity.

ho [R. hō, a mark, a sign]. **chhut-ki-ho**, to make a secret sign by sound or gesture, which none but a confederate will recognize.

hô (R. id.), (Cn. hô, hô), a large river; a canal. **lāi-hô**, the canals in a plain; harbour and creeks (near Amoy). **chhâ lāi-hô**, to search these creeks and straits for pirates and smugglers. **hô-á**, a canal; a ditch. **chheng hô-á**, to clean out a canal, &c. **keh-hô**, separated by a large river.

gûn-hô, the Milky Way. **thien-hô**, id. **thien-hô-pán**, a ceiling (= thien-lô-pán). **iû thien-hô**, to take his journey on the heavenly river, as the idol "ông-iâ" when he is burned. **iû tē-hô**, to be sent to float away on the sea, as ông-iâ.

hô-lâm, Honan province; often said also for Hunan. **hô-ti**, a porcupine.

hô (R. id.), (Cn. hô). **hô-kau**, a moat.

hô (R. id.) **pók-hô**, peppermint plant. **pók-hô-iû**, oil of peppermint. **póh-hô-iû**, id.

hô [R. hô, the water-lily]. **hô-liên**, a sort of water-lily. **hô-lân**, Holland (v. lân).

hô (R. id.), (Cn. hô). **sien-hô** (C. san-hô), coral. **sien-hô-ki**, a coral ornament for the hair.

hô [R. grain]. **ka-hô-lí**, a polite name for Amoy.

hô [R. what, who], (Cn. hô). **hô-hōng**, how much the more? **hô-kò**, why? **in-hô**, id.; how? **hô-khó**, why trouble yourself? **hô-tek-khó**, id. **chiong-**

hô jî-chhú, how can this matter be managed? **bû-nāiⁿ-hô**, having no other resource; no alternative.

hô (R. id.), (Cn. hə̂), harmonious; to unite; to mix in due proportions. **hô-hiân**, to tune a guitar. **hô-ioh**, to mix medicine with food, for strengthening. **hô-lát**, to unite strength in one effort.

hô-hó, at peace and harmony. **saⁿ-hô**, id. **hô-khì**, harmony. **hô-hiáp**, of one mind and acting together. **hô-chiōng**, good at living in harmony with all. **hô-pêng** (R.), peace and harmony. **hô-sūn**, harmonious and submissive, said of wife and husband. **hô-tâng**, harmonious, as persons of the same mind; agreeing, as evidence, or as things with the pattern. **hô-tông**, id. **hô-iok**, to make an agreement; a treaty of peace. **hô-sek-tiāⁿ**, a joint petition by the parties saying that the quarrel is settled (v. sek).

liáh-hô, a drawn game; to arbitrate by splitting the difference; to join in a plot in order to attack a third party, especially when the two were formerly at feud with each other. **liáh tiong-hô**, to split the difference, as in bargaining or settling a quarrel. **chhú-hô**, to arbitrate a quarrel and so bring it to an end. **khǹg-hô**, to exhort men to peace. **khoàn-hô**, id. **kóng-hô**, to talk over conditions of settling a quarrel; to have agreed on a settlement; to combine, as two persons against a third. **káng-hô**, to discuss and arrange a peaceful settlement (esp. between nations).

un-hô, temperate and genial, as climate; gentle, as temper (v. un). **hô-hâi**, harmonious, as music. **tiau-hô**, mixed well, as medicine or food; harmoniously adjusted, as music, &c., mixed in proper proportions. **im-ūn tiau-hô**, music harmonious.

thài-hô-koe, a small fowl, like a bantam.

hô [R. hoâ, flower, splendid]. **hô-piáu**, a memorial archway (v. piáu).

hô [R. valorous, heroic], (Cn. hə̂). **hô-kiát**, having great courage, talents, or wisdom, along with a kind disposition.

hô (Cn. hə̂). **hô-hèng**, fond of, as pleasures; in full spirit for (v. hèng).

hô [R. fine hair, a small weight], a small weight one-tenth of a lî; also one-tenth in value of a copper cash. **hun-hô**, very little, in negative phrases. **hun-hô bô phah-sńg**, not a particle lost. **hun-hô m̄-khéng**, utterly unwilling. **hun-lî hô-hut**, in very minute quantities; niggardly. **sǹg kàu hun-lî hô-hut**, very niggardly and sharp in calculation. **hô-lî m̄-thang**, you must by no means. **chit-si-hô, to bōe-tsòe--tit**, it will not do at all.

kúi-hô-chîⁿ, how many tenths of a cash? **chhit-hô-chîⁿ**, seven-tenths of a cash.

pék-hô, a sort of tea (Pekoe?).

hô [R. lô, to toil]. **sin-hô**, = sin-lô, wages for labour.

hó (Cn.) **hoân-hó**, = A. hoân-ló, sorrow; anxiety.

hó (R. hóⁿ), (Cn. P. hə́, hó), good; well; friendly; kind; completely made or finished; by good luck; prospering; (alive); as an answer it often means "yes;" but often only "well, I observe what you say," without being an affirmative answer.

hó-pháiⁿ, good and bad. **bô-hó bô-pháiⁿ**, of medium quality, tolerably good, as men or things; all about one and the same quality, as a lot of things. **hó-lâng**, a good man; a man in good health. **khah-hó**, better, in goodness or in health; rather more. **bōe-hó**, cannot recover. **lāu-pē hó**, while father is alive. **m̄-hó**, bad; dead. **m̄-hó--khì**, has died. **m̄-hó chit-ê-sun--khì**, lost a grandson. **kūn-lâi hó**, have you been well of late? how do you do? **chiah-kú hó--má**, id.

tng-hó, just now prosperous; just while in good fortune, or on good terms with a man (v. tng). **lí náⁿ-teh-hó**, you are constantly prospering more and more. **hó i--ê tsó-kong hién-sèng**, fortunately his ancestor miraculously appeared and delivered him. **hó-lâng koáⁿ-kàu**, by good luck some one suddenly came up, *e.g.* saving a man from robbers. **hó kiù-chhiⁿ**, id. **hó-chhiⁿ**, a deliverer or benefactor. **hó-tāi-chì**, auspicious matters, as birth, marriage, &c. (with no idea about morality). **hó-jit**, a lucky day. **kóng hó-ōe**, to speak auspicious words.

hó-chhiò, laughable; ridiculous. **hó-kiâⁿ**, good for walking on; safe for travelling upon. **hó-khoàⁿ**, beautiful; looking well; easily seen. **tôe khah-hó-khoàⁿ**, make a subscription that will look better. **hó-sè** (C. sòe; Cn. sə̀), easy to rent. **hó-sè** (C. sì), proper; suitable (v. sè, power). **hó-thák**, easy to read; so composed as to read well aloud.

hó-bé (C. bé), a good walker. **hó-bé** (C. bóe; Cn. bə́), good termination of an affair. **hó-kha hó-chhiú**, skilful, active; a good helper. **hó-thâu hó-bīn**, good-looking. **hó-chhùi**, talking politely, often mere empty fair words. **hó-lé**, politeness. **hó-lé-á** (C.), take care! **hó-sé-kiâⁿ**, easy and friendly, not wishing much ceremony, but taking ordinary treatment in good part. **kap-i-hó**, on good terms with him; if said of man and woman, generally implies improper relations. **hó-lâi hó-khì**, mutually doing good offices. **tsòe-lâng-hó**, to treat kindly. **hó-iú**, close friends. **siong-hó**, intimate, friendly. **hô-hó**, friendly, at peace. **bóe-hó**, to give money so as to get a judge or arbiter or influential person on our side, in settling a dispute or managing a matter. **hó--gê** (Cn.), "my good friend," said as on asking the road.

óh-hó, fully learned, as a task. **iáu-bē-hó**, not yet finished, as a work; not quite made, as a thing. **tsòe-hó**, to behave well; to have finished, as a work, or as a thing we were making. **siá-hó**, I have written it all.

pìⁿ-hó, to change from bad to good. **hó-sim**, kind, benevolent (v. sim). **khǹg-lâng-hó**, to exhort men to good behaviour.

hó-táⁿ, bold. **hó-thiⁿ**, good weather. **hó-giáh**, wealthy. **hó-kheh** (C.), id. **hó-pān**, wealthy; making a good profit; of a good form or pattern; easy to manage, as an affair. **hó-siu**, good harvest.

iā-hó, middling; will barely do; just tolerable; name often given to a daughter. **chiáh sím-mihⁿ, to-hó**, eat what comes to hand. **hó chiū-hó**, well, as you say it is well, let it be, but it is barely tolerable.

hō [R. id. by change of tone from "hô," harmonious]. **hō-lō-sō**, to assent, without consideration, to another's opinion. **hù-hō**, id. **saⁿ-hù-hō**, all saying yes! yes! and approving of the plan or of what was said.

hō-si (R.), to respond, in making extempore poetry. **chhiòng-hō** (R.), to sing and respond alternately in making extempore poetry.

hō [R. misery, calamity, = col. ē], (Cn. hə̄). **hō-hok**, bad and good fortune. **hui-hō**, sudden calamity (lit. flying). **thien-tsai hui-hō**, sudden calamity sent by Heaven. **thien-tsai hêng-hō**, id. **tsai-hō** (C.), = A. tsai-ē, calamity. **hō-toan**, (C.), = A. ē-toan, source or cause of misfortune or calamity.

hō [R. great and wide, extensive], (Cn. hə̄). **hō-**

18

hō tōng-tōng (R.), great and majestic, only said of Heaven.

hō (R. id.), (Cn. hɵ), a mark, a signal, a kind or sort; name of a firm; (to set a mark or name); day of foreign month. **hō-miâ^{n}**, to give a name, as to a child. **tsóng-hō**, a general name or term. **tē-hō-miâ^{n}**, name of a place. **tōe-hō-miâ^{n}**, id. **thé-hō-miâ^{n}**, a name taken from personal appearance. **thé-hō**, id. **thɵ́-hō**, a nickname; a colloquial name for a man. **chhiok-hō**, a nickname; to give a nickname.

kok-hō, the name of a reign, commonly called name of emperor, *e.g.* tō-kong (Tau-kwang), tông-tī (Tung-chih), &c.

sìn-hō (C.), the soft place on a child's head.

hit-hō, that sort or kind. **hit-téng-hō**, id. **hit-hō-lâng**, that sort of man.

jī-hō, a mark (a word); a trade-mark (by words); a designation of a firm or "chop." **hâng-hō**, name of a firm or Hong. **tiàm-hō**, name of a shop or small firm. **àm-hō**, a secret mark or signal. **kì-hō**, a mark. **kî-hō**, a distinctive mark or signal (as of troop or nation) made by a flag (v. kî). **hō-phàu**, signal gun (mandarin). **hō-lēng**, an order to soldiers by signal. **pàng hé-hō**, to set off fire signals. **hoat hé-hō**, id. **kê-hō**, the inscription on the cangue (v. kê, the cangue).

hō-pâng, a lodge at a high mandarin's gate for cards and letters; also, the office in a military mandarin's yamun for receiving complaints and doing general business with the people. **koa^{n}-gûn-hō**, the customs' banker. **lāi-hō**, a small private stamp used by a mandarin for documents of which he has personal cognizance. **kè-lāi-hō**, to be stamped with it. **hō-siu**, phrase used in the foreign customs for receipts (v. siu).

hō-thâu, a trumpet with a curved mouth; the number of a chapter or lesson, &c., either marked by numbers, or by the thousand-character-classic, or otherwise. **pien hō-thâu**, to mark things or volumes by the successive words of a book or of a sentence. **hō-siú**, a long trumpet with a narrow up-turned mouth. **pûn-hō-siú**, to blow these trumpets at the head of funerals and some other processions; the men who blow them.

hō-i-koà, a military coat or jacket.

jī-tsáp-hō, No. 20 (&c.); said also (especially at the Straits) for the day of the European month, to distinguish from the day of the Chinese moon.

phah-hō, to make a mark. **phah-jī-hō**, to make a mark by characters, as on goods. **ūi-hō**, to make one's mark at one's name, as a signature. **khí-hō**, to re-open a shop after holidays; sometimes to open a shop at the first.

hō (R. id.) **hō-hí**, to make a formal congratulation. **kiong-hō** (R.), to make presents and congratulations on joyful occasions. **khèng-hō** (R.), id. **khià^{n}-hō** (Cn.), id. **hō-siū**, to make congratulations, with presents (or a play), to a man on his birth-day. **hō-jīm**, do. to mandarin on his taking office. **hō-tsoeh**, make visits and presents on festivals. **hō-nî^{n}**, make visits, or send cards, on last day of year. **hō-chia^{n}**, make visits in the first days of new-year. **hō sin-chhun**, id. **hō sin-hun** make congratulatory presents after a marriage. **hō-lé**, to make congratulatory presents, as after a marriage, or getting office, &c.

hō-gî, money given on such an occasion, as a congratulation.

hɵ [R. to breathe out; to call; to order], to make a verbal bargain or agreement. **bêng-hɵ**, to promise plainly; to make a verbal bargain. **chheng-hɵ**, to address by an honourable appellation. **chio-hɵ**, to talk politely, as to visitors or customers.

hɵ-khip, breathing, used in medical phrases (v. khip).

hɵ-im, to give the sounds, to pronounce the sounds clearly, as in learning to read.

hɵ-hat, to give orders to inferiors, somewhat imperiously. **hɵ-hoàn**, to order, as a servant. **hɵ-lɵ̂ hoàn-pī**, to have menials and slaves at one's command.

ɵ-hɵ (R.), phrase used in mourning for the dead. **ɵ-hɵ ai--tsài** (R.), id. **it-tàn ɵ-hɵ**, one may die (and be mourned for) any morning; if I (or any one) should suddenly die some day.

hɵ — **hɵ-soat**, to tell lies. **kóng-hɵ**, id. **lām-sám-hɵ**, id. **gâu-hɵ**, fond of telling lies. **hɵ-hàm** (= hong-hàm), exaggerated language, talking very big. **hɵ-hoah**, to tell falsehoods in a loud overbearing way. **hɵ-thi^{n} hɵ-tōe**, to tell very great lies; *e.g.* accusing people falsely.

hɵ̂ (R. id.), (Cn. hīô), a marquis; the second of the five ranks of nobility; a feudal prince. **hɵ̂-iâ**, a marquis. **tsu-hɵ̂**, feudal princes. **ông-hɵ̂**, kings and feudal princes. **kong-hɵ̂**, dukes and marquises; lords. **hong-hɵ̂**, to creat a marquis.

hɵ̂ (R. id.), (Cn. phû). **hɵ̂-lî**, a fox. **hɵ̂-lî-chháu**, fox fur. **hɵ̂-kûn káu-tóng**, a set of vile abandoned men, leading each other into all wickedness. **hɵ̂ ká hɵ́-ui** (R.), mandarin's attendants making themselves very big (lit. fox using the tiger's majesty). **hɵ̂-gî**, suspicious, and therefore undecided.

hɵ̂ (R. id.) **hɵ̂-sîn**, house-flies (v. sîn). **hɵ̂-se-á** (P.), a small stinging insect.

hɵ̂-tiàp, hinges (v. tiàp).

hɵ̂ — **hɵ̂-liu**, a very small sort of fish (v. liu).

hɵ̂ (R. id.) **hɵ̂-chio**, pepper.

hɵ̂ (R. id.) **hɵ̂-lɵ̂-pû**, a gourd (v. lɵ̂).

hɵ̂, to lift a small thing out of the water with a dipper or strainer; to gather, as water-lily roots. **hɵ̂--khí-lâi**, id. **hɵ̂-sau**, to catch larvæ with a small net. **hɵ̂-chhu**, id. **hɵ̂-pn̄g**, to lift out boiled rice with a dipper that strains it. **hɵ̂-phiô**, to gather duck-weed with a strainer.

hɵ̂ [R. floating], (Cn. hîô). **hɵ̂-hoân**, unfounded, groundless, as rumour (v. hoân). **hɵ̂-sam put-lám** (floating wood not tied), said of men or things (v. lám). **hu-hɵ̂** (R.), empty and false, as boastful talk.

hɵ̂ [R. paste, = col. kɵ̂; confused]. **hɵ̂-tɵ̂**, careless, negligent; dishonest, equivocating (v. tɵ̂). **hɵ̂-sàm**, roughly made and ill-finished, as furniture, dress, &c. **hɵ̂-hūn**, confused and somewhat untrue, as language; ill-mended or corrected (not sufficiently like the original); a lot having some articles mixed which are worse or not uniform. **hɵ̂-sáp-sáp**, in a disorderly state, as dishes spattered with food, or as a tangled dirty beard. **hɵ̂-chhe-chhe**, careless in managing or doing something. **hɵ̂-chhè-chhè**, id. **hɵ̂-nà^{n}-sah**, id.

hâm-hɵ̂, to talk indistinctly and ambiguously of set purpose, or manage things in a confused way so as to mislead.

hɵ̂ [R. a lake, = col. ɵ̂]. **hɵ̂-si**, raw silk from Central China (Hoo-chow? or Hoo-peh?). **hɵ̂-si-kheh**, silk merchants from Central China. **khah-kùi hɵ̂-si**, dreadfully expensive, as goods. **hɵ̂-lâm** (R.), = ɵ̂-lâm, Hoo-nan province.

hɵ̂ [R. beard, whiskers]. **hɵ̂-hɵ̂-hɵ̂**, having large

厦英大辭典

bushy whiskers. **hê̤--ê**, all hairy round below the chin. **hê̤-chhiu**, beard and whiskers. **chhêng-hê̤-chhiu**, pointed leaves of the fir-tree. **chhêng-hê̤**, id. **hê̤-sai-káu**, a shaggy little dog.

hê̤ [R. a deep bowl, = col. ê̤]. **jiō-hê̤** (esp. Cn.), = jiō-ê̤, a chamber-pot. **iā-hê̤** (Cn. T.), id. **hông-tè iā-hê̤** (Cn.), said in coarse joke of a man who is too knowing, in allusion to "kok-pih."

hê̤ (C.) **san-hê̤**, = A. sien-hô, coral.

hê̤ (Cn.), = A. hô, a river.

hê̤ (Cn.), = A. hô, harmonious.

hê̤ (Cn)., = A. hô. **hê̤-hèng**, to desire very much.

hê̤ (Cn.), = A. hô, what? who? why? and so with some other words.

hé̤ (R. id.) **hé̤-phek**, amber.

hé̤ [R. hú, the bank of a river]. **hé̤-thî**, a sort of edible sea-weed. **hé̤-soe**, sort of sea-weed fried in fat.

hé̤ [R. hé̤ⁿ, fire, = col. hé]. **hé̤-m̄**, the wild raspberry (v. m̄).

hé̤— **hé̤-kū**, name of a bird (v. kū).

hé̤, to cheat out of money; to take money in an overbearing way or by force.

hé̤ (Cn. P.), = hó, good.

hé̤ (R. id.), a tiger. **hé̤-khí**, tiger's tooth hung up as an amulet. **hé̤-kut**, tiger's bones. **hé̤-kut-ka**, jelly from tiger's bones (very strengthening). **hé̤-lô**, a tiger-trap. **hé̤-lê̤** (P.), id. **hé̤-tû** (T.), id.

lin-hé̤, a deep abscess in the breast. **leng-hé̤**, id. **chhut-mn̂g-hé̤**, a large boil or carbuncle on the back of the neck where the hair ends.

hé̤-lo̍k, outwardly good, but inwardly very bad (v. lo̍k). **pu̍ih hé̤-chhiu**, a game of chance (v. chhiu). **phak-tē-hé̤**, a catamite. **saⁿ-kha-hé̤** (vulg.), a man who limps (said in scolding).

tháng-hé̤, a hooked instrument for pulling on the hoops of barrels, &c. **hā-san-hé̤**, a thick strong vest with many buttons on the breast, made very tight. **hā-san-hé̤-hiû**, do. wadded.

hé̤-chhèng, a sort of gingall. **hé̤-bō**, a sort of child's cap. **hé̤-á-ôe**, sort of shoes for children. **hé̤-chih-lòe**, a coarse iron file (v. chih). **hé̤-bāng**, a sort of fish-net (v. bāng). **hé̤-kháu**, the space between the thumb and the fore-finger (v. kháu). **hé̤-mn̂g**, Bocca Tigris, on the Canton river. **hé̤-ui**, majesty of a mandarin (v. ui). **hé̤-pan-tiám**, marked with long large streaks like a tiger's skin. **hé̤-chiò**, Tauist rites for keeping away tigers, or for atoning for the killing of a tiger. **hé̤-sa**, the hills stretching from behind a grave round on the right hand (v. sa).

lêng-hé̤-pn̂g, official list of successful candidates for the literary degrees of Kújîn and Chìn-sū (lit. roll of the dragon and tiger). **lêng-hé̤-chíⁿ**, the front space at a temple, with figures of dragon and tiger. **lêng-hé̤-kî**, flags of very high mandarin, with figures of them. **lêng-hé̤ pé tsúi-kháu**, the dragon and tiger guard the entrance of the harbour, as at Amoy by the "hé̤-thâu" and "lêng-thâu." **pe-lêng pe-hé̤**, flying dragon and tiger on flags carried before high mandarins. **lêng-hé̤ kau-chièn, ku-pih siû-tsai**, when the great quarrel the small suffer. **hé̤-lêng pà-piu**, very violent and wicked men. **thien liông, tē hé̤** (C.), the dragon in heaven and the tiger on earth are the great powers. **pe̍k-hé̤, chheng-liông, tsu-chhiok, hiên-bú**, the (Tauist) spirits that preside over the four quarters. **liông seng liông-tsú, hé̤ seng pà-jî**, children are like their parents in excellence.

pe̍h-hé̤, a white tiger. **hé̤-iâ**, the deified tiger; the god of gambling. **hé̤-chiòng-iâ**, id. **hé̤-sài-iâ**, id. **hé̤-chiòng-kong** (esp. T.), id. **hé̤-sèng-kong**, earthen image of a tiger carried on 1. 14 or 15 to collect wood for the fires called "hé-phûn." **thien-hé̤** (C.), tigers sent by heaven (v. thien). **sîn-hé̤** (C.), a tiger which is really a spirit in the shape of a tiger, from which it is impossible to escape.

hé̤-thâu, a very bad man, who is always acting as the head and patron of people who cause trouble. **hé̤-thâu-pâi**, a shield with a tiger's head painted on it. **hé̤-thâu-kaⁿ**, a dungeon at Fuh-chau. **hé̤-thâu, niáu-chhú bé**, boastful at first, but a coward at the last.

chio̍h-hé̤, a sort of wild cat. **chîm-hé̤**, a fish that devours crabs. **tsoá-hé̤**, the book-worm. **tāu-hé̤**, a small winged beetle that wastes peas, beans, &c. **hê̤-sîn-hé̤**, a small insect about the size of a pea. **piah-hé̤**, = siēn-lâng, the common lizard. **chhu-hé̤**, a figure like a lizard carved on furniture. **chhi-hé̤** (C.), id.

hé̤-sai, tigers and lions (v. sai). **hé̤-sai**, a sort of crab. **hé̤-se**, a sort of sole. **hé̤-soa**, a large spotted dangerous shark. **hé̤-hî**, id. **it hang, jī hé̤**, this and the skate make bad wounds (v. hang). **hé̤-hī-chháu**, a small plant used for medicine (v. hī), (v. phoāⁿ).

chhī-hé̤, to rush foolishly into danger; a worthless wretch (v. chhī). **béng-hé̤**, a fierce tiger. **béng-hé̤ bōe-tùi--tit kâu-kûn**, a tiger cannot beat a crowd of monkeys. **pek-hé̤ siong-jîn**, to drive a tiger to bay will hurt men, said of driving a man too hard; said also of an unlucky grave (v. sa). **pák-hé̤ iông-ī; chhiòng-hé̤ lân**, to bind a tiger is easy, the trouble is to let him loose. **khî-hé̤ chi-sè, put-tek-hā**, he who rides a tiger cannot dismount (v. hā). **chhiò-bīn-hé̤**, a tiger with a smiling face; pretending friendship while plotting our ruin. **chhiⁿ-bīn-hé̤**, absurdly touchy. **ū, tsòe-hé̤ tsām: bô, tsòe-hé̤ thìⁿ-ām**, having money he is voracious as a tiger; without money he stretches out his neck looking up like a tiger.

hè̤ (R. id.) **hè̤-tháng**, a large bucket for irrigation, swung on two ropes between two men. **hè̤-táu**, a smaller bucket for water; also, having one's lower jaw projecting too much. **ē-táu hè̤-hè̤**, lower jaw very prominent. **ē-táu khah-hè̤**, id.

tò-hè̤--kè, to make a somersault forwards. **hè̤-chiūⁿ hè̤-lo̍h**, to climb about up and down, as a restless boy.

hè̤-chhiú, to toss the hand out and upwards with the palm open upwards, as expression of displeasure. **hè̤-chhiú hè̤-kioh**, to toss one's arms upwards, and shake about one's legs in disputing.

hè̤-tsúi, to raise water by a bucket swung between two men. **hè̤ lêng-ba̍k**, to wash the eyes of the dragon-boats before the race.

hè̤ (T. he̤). **sip-jī-hè̤**, tied in the shape of a cross. **sip-jī-hè̤ pák--teh**, to tie by strings at right angles, as a bundle. **phah sip-jī-hè̤**, id. **si-liām-hè̤**, id. **tiàu-kak hè̤--teh**, tied diagonally, as a bundle tied in a napkin by its four corners.

hè̤ [R. hòng, to let loose, = col. pàng]. **hè̤-hiahⁿ**, flurried; hurried (v. hiahⁿ).

hè̤ [R. he̤, thick, = col. kāu]. **chhin-hè̤-hè̤**, very intimate, as friends.

hē̤ [R. to guard; to protect]. **pó-hē̤**, to protect. **kiù-hē̤**, to save or deliver from great danger, as man or idol. **hiàm-kiù-hē̤**, to call out loud for help.

hō͘-sàng, to convoy. **hō͘-sin-kiàⁿ**, a breast-plate (v. kiàⁿ).

hō͘--chhù, the two houses at the ends of the principal house, facing towards it. **hō͘-lêng** (T.), id.

úi-hō͘, name of an idol. **hō͘-hoat**, = khiā-lîm-iâ, an idol. **hō͘-hoat-iâ**, id. **hō͘-kài-kong** (Cn.), id., he has long hair.

kim-kng hō͘-sîn (Cn.), several idols named and worshipped together, set in front of Shakya-muni (sek-khia).

hō͘ [R. a door; a single-leaved door; a family; master of a family or of a business, &c.]

hō͘-tēng, threshold. **hō͘-tāiⁿ** (T.), id. **thong-hō͘-kūi**, shop-counter at door of shop. **hō͘-tiáp**, hinges (gen. so written, but properly hô͘-tiáp). **mn̂g-hō͘**, doors in general; a door. **mn̂g-hō͘ saⁿ-tùi**, families of about equal rank. **mn̂g-pang hō͘-sìⁿ**, all the doors and their fittings, as in stating whether they are in good order or not. **mn̂g-sîn hō͘-ùi**, the guardian spirits of doors, civil and military respectively. **phah toā-mn̂g, khui toā-hō͘**, to do wicked things openly, as keeping a public brothel openly.

hō͘-kháu, a household, in regard to a sort of census of families. **tsō hō͘-kháu**, to make such a list of families, done by mandarins and tepo. **ka-ka hō͘-hō͘**, every household. **phài hù-hō͘**, to levy contributions from rich houses.

tsûn-hō͘, junks, as to their number; the owner of a junk (v. tsûn). **hâng-hō͘**, owner or partner of a hong. **kau-hō͘**, do. of smaller firm. **tiàm-hō͘**, a shop-keeper (s. rain). **phò-hō͘**, a shop; a shop-keeper (v. phò). **tiēn-hō͘**, the tenant of a farm. **tūiⁿ-hō͘** (Cn.), id.

kah-hō͘, a group of about twelve houses, making a subdivision of a small ward (pó). **kúi kah-hō͘**, how many such groups are there in one "pó?" **hō͘-thâu-miâⁿ**, the name under which a group of fields or houses is entered in the register-books of the tax-collectors; generally it is the name of some ancestor which remains unaltered for many generations. **siâng-hō͘-thâu**, having one's field or house in the same group in the books with some other man's. **khiā sím-mihⁿ hō͘-thâu-miâⁿ**, what is the name under which your property stands on the register?

hō͘-pō͘, the Board of Revenue at Pekin; the president of it, like chancellor of exchequer. **hō͘-pâng**, the revenue department in a yamun, esp. of the land-tax; the secretary who has the management of it.

hō͘ [R. empress or queen; a ruler], (Cn. hiō). **hông-hō͘**, empress by marriage. **thài-hō͘**, empress-mother; validi-sultana; empress-dowager. **hông-thài-hō͘**, id. **thài-hông thài-hō͘**, emperor's grandmother.

hō͘-chek, the god of agriculture. **hō͘-thó**, id., the spirit of the earth, viewed as consort of Imperial Heaven (v. thó). **thien-hō͘ niûⁿ-niûⁿ**, the goddess of sailors, = má-tsó-pô.

hō͘ [R. after, = col. āu], (Cn. hiō). **hō͘-è**, posterity. **hō͘-ì** (C.), id. **hō͘-sû**, posterity; heirs. **hō͘-chìn**, descendants who are a credit to their ancestors. **hō͘-thè**, descendants who are a disgrace to ancestors. **hō͘-sè**, after generations. **hō͘-tāi**, id. **hō͘-jit**, on a future day. **sū-hō͘**, afterwards, at some future time, only from this time forward, never used when speaking of what was once future, but is now past. **hō͘-sin**, afterwards. **hō͘-lâi**, id. **sien-hō͘**, before and after. **chiên-hō͘** (r.), id.

hō͘ (Cn.) **hō͘-liâm**, very quickly, very speedily, esp. said in urging some one to be quick.

hō͘ [R. to wait, = col. hāu, pō͘], (Cn. hiō, C. hāu). **su-hō͘**, to wait ready (as yamun people) to accompany the mandarin when he comes out. **hoah su-hō͘**, to call the underlings to get ready to wait on and accompany the mandarin. **goá su-hō͘--lí**, I am waiting till you are ready (said to a man who is too busy to attend to us, but for whom we are resolved to wait till he is ready).

hō͘ (R. ú), rain. **hong-hō͘**, wind and rain. **tsòe-hong lòh-hō͘**, wind and rain come. **hō͘-lâi-thiⁿ**, rainy weather. **thiⁿ-khí hō͘-ì**, appearance of rain about to fall. **tsòe-hō͘-ì**, id. **kip-sì-hō͘**, seasonable rain. **àm-hō͘ tiâu-mî**ⁿ, rain late in the day lasts through the night. **hō͘ chhia-teh-piàⁿ**, rain falling in torrents. **hō͘ sì-lâm-sûi**, rain overflowing everywhere. **chìm-tsù-hō͘**, long-continued soaking rains. **chhiⁿ-kông-hō͘**, heavy squall of wind and rain. **sai-pak-hō͘**, north-west rain-storm, soon clears off.

ien-bū-hō͘, gloomy rainy weather. **hûn-hō͘**, a brief passing shower of very limited range. **kè-soaⁿ-hō͘**, a heavy passing shower on the hills. **siēn-hō͘**, long weary rains, not very heavy. **lòh-siēn-hō͘**, to have such long rains.

bông-chéng-hō͘, rain on the term called "bông-chéng" (v. chéng). **chhiūⁿ-m̂-hō͘** (C.), rain at the time the arbutus (Myrica) ripens.

hō͘-tsūn, a shower. **hō͘-á-mng**, drizzling rain. **hō͘-á-chhiu**, id. **phùn--tiòh hō͘-hoe**, to get some drops of rain on one. **hō͘-tsúi**, rain-water; rain. **kāu hō͘-tsúi**, rain abundant. **hō͘-tsúi sūn-siòk**, rain in due season from time to time. **sîn hō͘-tsúi**, to catch rain-water in a vessel.

lòh-hō͘, to rain. **lòh-hō͘-bê**, drizzling rain. **pàng-hō͘**, to rain in small quantity. **tih-hō͘**, to have rain dropping from the roof.

hō͘ chìⁿ, the rain cleared off.

thàu-hō͘, through the rain. **chiâⁿ-thàu-hō͘**, rain enough to saturate the ground (v. thàu). **khit-hō͘**, to pray for rain. **tsáu-hō͘**, to take shelter from rain. **tiàm-hō͘**, id. (s. door). **hioh-hō͘**, id. **oân-hō͘**, to spread a mat or sail, as cover from rain. **siòng-hō͘-phāng**, taking advantage of a break in the rain.

hō͘-soàⁿ, an umbrella (v. soàⁿ).

thiⁿ bô-hō͘, lâng bô-lō͘, if Heaven give no rain man has no resource.

hō͘ (R. ú), (Cn. thò), to give; to cause; also, = khit, sign of the passive in some phrases.

kau hō͘--i, hand it over to him. **m̄-thang hō͘--i**, don't give it him. **soà tióh-chîⁿ hō͘--i**, and must also give him money.

hō͘-i-phah, to be struck by him. **i hō͘--lí poàh-bōe-tó**, you cannot beat him in argument.

hō͘-lí-chē, you must be responsible for the payment. **hō͘-i-kóng**, let him speak. **hō͘-lí-kóng**, you may speak; please say on. **hō͘--lâng tah-hiahⁿ**, to make a man start.

káⁿ-sí hō͘--lâng, not afraid to kill one's self in order to make an enemy responsible for the death.

hō͘ [R. thick, = col. kāu], (Cn. hiō). **tiong-hō͘**, honest; faithful; upright. **hō͘-tō**, honest, fair, and safe to have dealings with. **sûn-hō͘**, honest, well-behaved, and pleasant to deal with. **hong-siòk sûn-hō͘**, customs of a place excellent. **phok-sit tun-hō͘** (R.), honest, straightforward, and simple in tastes. **hō͘-tiōng**, grave, quiet, and sedate; large and fat in person.

chhin-hō͘, associating intimately (v. chhin).

hù-hō͘, very rich. **hō͘-lī**, very profitable, as trade.

iông-iông to hə̄-hok, common ordinary people usually have much happiness.

hə̄-phak, a very thick sort of bark, used to cure a dyspeptic or bilious feeling.

hə̄ (R. id.), a word used in the names of many places. **chhim-hə̄**, Chimmo, near Chinchew. **hə̄-bé**, the native name of the town at the settlement of Tam-suy, in Formosa.

hə̄ [R. interlocking like two hooks, mutual]. **saⁿ-kau-hə̄**, hooking into each other in the form of the character "hə." **se-hə̄**, a frame shaped like that character, for making hanks of yarn. **se-hə̄-toh**, a table of which the feet come separate from the top, and fold up like a folding chair. **se-hə̄-kha--ê**, id. **hə̄-se**, to make hanks of yarn on the frame.

hə̄ (T.) **sì-liām-hə̄**, = A. sì-liām-hə̀, tied crossing at right angles, as the string of a parcel.

hə̄ (Cn.), = A. hō, a kind; a sort; a mark.

hə̄ (Cn.), = A. hō, misery; calamity.

hö (Cn.), = A. he, lime.

hö̂ (Cn.), = A. hê, to return.

hö́ (Cn.), = A. hé, fine. **hö́-m̄**, = A. hé-m̄, the Chinese raspberry.

hö́ (Cn.), = A. hé, comrade, company, &c.

hö́ (Cn.), = A. hé. **hö́-sit, ke-hö́**, &c.

hȫ (Cn.), = A. hè, year of age.

hȫ (Cn.), = A. hè, goods.

həⁿ, to bray, as an ass. **həⁿ-həⁿ-háu**, to buzz; to snore. **həⁿ-həⁿ-kiò**, id. **khùn-kàu həⁿ-həⁿ-kiò**, to sleep and snore.

hə̂ⁿ, an interjection used at the end of a statement, followed by a pause, to let what has said be fully considered, suggesting the idea "is not that so?" or "is not that a good reason?"

hə́ⁿ [R. fire, = col. hé]. **kim-bo̍k-súi hə́ⁿ-thə́**, metal, wood, water, fire, earth: the five elements. **bêng-hə́ⁿ kiap-lio̍k**, housebreaking and robbery with lighted torches. **toān-súi-hə́ⁿ--sí**, to put to death by prohibiting the use of fire and water, *i.e.* by starvation.

hə́ⁿ (cf. hə̀). **hə́ⁿ-hə́ⁿ hiáⁿ-hiáⁿ**, much flurried.

hə̀ⁿ [R. to desire, to be fond of, by change of tone from "hə́ⁿ," good]. **hə̀ⁿ-sū**, a meddler; a busybody; a tattler and talebearer. **hə̀ⁿ-chhap êng-sū**, id. **hə̀ⁿ-îm**, lascivious. **hə̀ⁿ-ko**, ambitious. **hə̀ⁿ-sèng**, domineering; fond of being superior. **hə̀ⁿ-siēn**, to delight in virtue and goodness.

hə̄ⁿ — **hə̄ⁿ-hə̄ⁿ-chhoán**, to pant hard.

hoa, to extinguish or go out, as fire. **hé hoa**, the fire is gone out. **tè-hé-hoa**, may life go out as a lamp (sometimes said as an oath for confirmation). **tng teng-hé hoa**, may my life go out like this lamp before me! **phah-hoa**, to extinguish. **ìm-hoa**, to extinguish by covering up. **ak-hoa-hé**, extinguish fire by water. **pûn-hoa**, do. by blowing. **kiù-hoa-hé**, to put out a (dangerous) fire.

hoa--khì, to be fully cured and so disappear, as a cutaneous disease.

tih-beh-hoa, about to die, as a very sickly child.

hoa (R. id.) **soan-hoa** (R.), noisy disturbance; noisy talk or clamour. **kìm-chí soan-hoa** (R.), no noise allowed here; written up at offices, &c.

hoa [R. a flower, often has the idea of licentiousness, = col. hoe; but in C. both R. and col. are "hoa"].

hoa-phùn, dressing gaudily, boasting, and making one's self of importance. **hoa-hùi**, to spend lavishly (v. hùi). **hu-hoa**, lavish expense; dissolute. **hi-hoa** (C.), id. **hong-hoa**, dissolute. **ien-hoa ê sé-tsāi**, a house of ill-fame. **ien-hoa ê-lâng**, a prostitute. **hoa put-bê-jîn, jîn tsū-bê**, it is not beauty that deludes men, men delude themselves.

gím-siōng thiam-hoa, an addition to great wealth or learning (flowers upon flowered silk). **thien-hoa-hún**, a seed used medicinally. **thien-hoa-pán**, = (better) thien-lô-pán, a ceiling. **lo̍k-hoa liû-súi** (flowers fallen and floating away), extremely miserable. **lo̍k-hoa-seng** (R.), = lo̍k-kha-seng, ground-nuts. **hoa-chio**, white pepper. **hoa-hiong-tê**, tea flavoured with flowers (v. hiong).

hoa-kî-kok, the United States (v. kî).

hoa [R. hoâ, splendid]. **hoa-hā** (R.), China. **tiong-hoa**, id. **hoa-chhái** (R.), richly ornamented.

hoâ [R. splendid]. **êng-hoâ hù-kùi**, very prosperous. **chhia-hoâ**, lavish; gaudy.

ge̍h-hoâ, vari-coloured halo of the moon, supposed to be an omen of great good.

hoâ [R. àn, according to, to examine], (T. hoâⁿ). **hoâ-khoàⁿ**, to calculate by a rough guess at sight, without measurement. **hoâ-sǹg**, to make a rough calculation of quantity, but more careful than "hoâ-khoàⁿ." **hoâ-sǹg-khoàⁿ**, id.

hoâ-soah (Cn.), = (T.), hoāⁿ-soah, to get people to make up a quarrel, as neighbours do.

hoà [R. to change, to renovate, to beg, as priests; to digest; luck or fortune], (C. hoè), to change, as the transformations of nature; to rot away.

siau-hoà, to digest. **hoà-hé**, to be accidentally consumed, as paper or clothes. **hoà-tsòe hé-hu**, to be burned away to ashes.

hoà-hoà, naturally taking things quite easy; not much affected by good or bad news. **thoat-hoà**, easy-minded; not anxious about danger or trouble; not particular about ceremony; taking things as they come. **sim bōe-hoà**, grief hard and long to remove.

hūn-hoà, quite alike and undistinguishable, as a mend or a counterfeit. **khah-hoà**, having the edges shading gradually (a beauty in painting, but a fault in writing).

tiám-hoà, to instruct or warn, as a spirit does in a dream. **kám-hoà**, to renovate, as doctrine or spiritual influence. **kàu-hoà**, to instruct and lead to better conduct. **hong-hoà**, influence of superiors on character, esp. for good. **hó-hong-hoà**, good example and influence.

pièn-hoà, natural changes; to be transformed (v. pièn). **hoà-siⁿ**, produced from a chrysalis, &c. **bān-bu̍t hoà-seng**, all things are produced by natural changes. **hoà-sin**, to die and become a Buddha. **hoà-sin-tōng**, a cave where beggars die (v. tōng).

hoà-iên (C.), = A. hòe-iên, to beg, as Buddhist priests.

tsō-hoà (R.), to make and transform. **hó-tsō-hoà** (C. hó-tsū-hoè), good luck; good fortune. **tsō-hoà sī**, id. **tsō-hoà m̄-sī**, bad luck. **pháiⁿ-tsō-hoà**, id. **phòng tsō-hoà**, to make a trial or attempt with some hope (but not much) of success; to make a venture, *e.g.* at examination, or asking for a situation, &c. **tú tsō-hoà**, id. **tə́ tsō-hoà**, id. **tú lí--ê tsō-hoà**, I will try my best for you, but with much doubt of success. **phēng lí--ê tsō-hoà**, id. = phòng &c. = tàu &c. **tàu tsō-hoà**, to make a venture along with another, as partners in a trading speculation.

hoā [R. speak, words, = col. ōe]. **hoā put-tê-**

厦英大辭典

ki, poàn-kù to, when what is said is not agreeable half a sentence is too much.

hoā, noisy play; turmoil or disturbance. **hoā-hoā**, id. **hoā-hoā-kún**, id. **hoā-hoā-háu**, id. **hoā-hoā-tiō**, to move about in great excitement, as a crowd (v. tiō). **hán-hoā**, indistinct noise or hum of a crowd, with more or less noisy talk; to be in an excited state, as a community when there are rumours of rebellion. **kóng-hoā kóng-chhiò**, to joke and jest and talk loudly.

hoā [R. to paint or draw, = oā]. **hoā-phɵ́**, a book of drawing lessons. **hoā-kong** (C. oē-kong, oāi-kong), an ornamental painter, as of flowers, &c. **hoā-péng chhiong-ki**, to paint a loaf to appease hunger. **hoā-hɵ́ put-sêng, hoán ûi-kɵ́**, try to paint a tiger, but make it a dog (v. hoán).

hoā (Cn.), = A. hiā, a tile.

hoā (Cn.) **hoā-lâng**, Spaniards, said esp. by people who have been at Manila.

hoa^n (R. hoan). **hoa^n-hí**, to be glad or pleased (v. hí).

hoâ^n, to snore.

hoâ^n (T.), = A. hoâ, to make a rough guess or calculation.

hoâ^n (C.), = A. hoâi^n, across.

hoâ^n (C.), = hoâi^n. **ɵ̄-hoâ^n-si**, a plant used in making cakes.

hoá^n (cf. hoà^n), careless; inattentive to business. **hoá^n-hoá^n**, id.; without determination; colour indistinct. **hoá^n-hoá^n kè--khì**, negligently let matter pass without proper attention.

ɵ-hoá^n, dull or grayish black; dim, as light. **âng-hoá^n**, light red. **hoá^n-âng**, id. **n̂g-hoá^n n̂g-hoá^n**, light yellow. **gėh hoá^n**, moon not giving much light, as at beginning or end of month, or when the sky is clouded. **gėh hoá^n-hoá^n**, id.

hoà^n (R. hoàn). **hoà^n-hoà^n**, not caring much about a matter; not giving attention (cf. hoá^n). **tiu^n hoà^n-hoà^n**, to pretend indifference.

hoà^n [R. tàn, the morning]. **bîn-hoà^n**, after this time; afterwards; on a future day. **tiám-hoà^n** (Cn.), just lately; a very short time ago.

hoā^n — **khí-hoā^n**, the gums. **chhùi-khí-hoā^n**, id.

hoā^n (R. gān), an embankment; a dyke. **tē-hoā^n**, a sea-dyke, inclosing reclaimed land. **hái-hoā^n**, id.; a sea-wall. **hô-hoā^n**, dyke on a great river. **ùn-hoā^n**, embankment of a pool that is overflowed at high-tide. **thūn-hoā^n**, to make the dyke higher or stronger. **oá-hoā^n**, to approach the embankment; to come near the mark (v. oá), (s. lean).

bîn-chhn̂g-hoā^n, the broad board on front of a bed, for sitting on.

hoā^n — **chhân-hoā^n**, the raised divisions between irrigated fields. **chhân-hoā^n-lɵ̄**, a road on the narrow banks between rice-fields. **chhân-hoā^n-chî^n** (P.), money paid, once for all, for the right of cultivating common fields so that they cannot be taken away.

hn̂g-hoā^n, raised divisions between dry fields.

hoā^n [R. àn, to lay the hand on], to lay the hand heavily upon, so as to steady or to lean upon; to manage, as household or accounts.

hoā^n-bėh, to feel the pulse.

hoā^n-toā, to steer a vessel.

sa^n-hoā^n, hands leaning on each other's shoulders. **hoā^n keng-thâu**, to lean on another's shoulder by the hand. **hoā^n hɵ̄-i-tiā^n**, steady it with the hand. **hoā^n-khi-tiā^n**, id. **hoā^n-tiā^n**, to keep one's mind at ease (v. tiā^n). **tah-hoā^n**, to lay one's hand on something to steady one's self; to depend upon another, as widow, orphan, &c. **bô-tah bô-hoā^n**, having no one to look to for support. **bô-té thang-oá-hoā^n**, id. **bô-lâng thang-oá-hoā^n**, id.

hoā^n-ke, to manage household affairs. **hoā^n ke-sū**, id. **hoā^n hâng-chêng**, to fix the market price (v. hâng). **hoā^n-poā^n**, to have the authoritative voice in a business, as manager (ke-tiū^n) or shroff. **hoā^n-siàu**, to keep the accounts.

hoā^n sìn-tē, to have a small military district.

hoā^n-soah, to try to get people to make up a quarrel, as neighbours or friends.

hoā^n-phek, the man in a band of music who beats the "phek." **hoā^n sù-koán**, to play musical instruments of all sorts. **hoā^n hiên-koán**, to play joyful music.

hoā^n, to solder. **hoā^n-iȯh**, id. **tâng-hoā^n**, soldering with hard solder. **siah-hoā^n**, soldering with soft solder.

hoah (Cn.), = A. hiah, thus, this, these.

hoah (R. hat), to shout loud; to bawl. **hoah-loah**, id. **hoah-hiàm**, id. **tàu-hoah**, to call out loud, encouraging each other to do something. **hán-hoah**, loud shouting or noise; noisy disturbance. **him-hoah**, to reprove so as to silence. **háng-hoah**, to frighten; to call loud in a threatening way; to bully. **háu-hoah**, to talk loud in reproving or threatening. **hoah hoa^n-hí**, to shout out for amusement, as on the hills; to call out loud to inferiors just for the pleasure of ordering. **hoah-chia hoah-hia**, calling out in great terror and perturbation, as at sudden danger. **hoah-hîm hoah-hɵ́**, id. (as if at bears and tigers!)

hɵ-hoah, to tell lies and make a great noise. **hɵ-thi^n hoah-tōe**, id. (often with the idea of slander).

hoah iû-o, man who calls out "iû-o" before a mandarin to clear the road. **hoah-tō**, id. **hoah hɵ́-ui**, shouting loud as the mandarin ascends the tribunal. **chhȧt-hoah-chhȧt**, a thief calling out "stop thief!" (v. chhȧt).

hoah-soa^n, to call the auspicious influence of the mountain to the grave, at burial (v. soa^n). **hoah-thɵ́**, to perform rites before beginning to build or repair a house or grave.

hoah-kûn, to play at morra (v. kûn). **hoah lê-lang**, an auction. **hoah lê-long**, id.

hoah-kè, to put an extra price on an article, as from change in supply or demand.

hoah thâu-sia^n, to make the proposal which the rest of the company follow; to be in the habit of taking the lead in arranging what is to be done. **hoah ōe-tāng**, his words are usually followed. **tāi-ke hoah-thang**, all at once gave their assent.

hoah-soah, to order inferiors and make them stop a quarrel, between themselves or with others.

hoȧh — **soah-hoȧh**, to determine and decide what is to be done, as the leader or principal party in an affair.

hoȧh [R. hān, a limit, = col. ān, hȧt]. **tsat-hoȧh**, to use an average moderate amount, as of strength, or of food, &c.

hoȧh [R. hoȧt, to subdue, to stride], a stride: one step; to take one good step. **toā-hoȧh**, a very long step. **n̄ng-hoȧh chit-pɵ̄**, two steps make one pace. **sa^n-pɵ̄ tsòe-n̄ng-hoȧh**, in a tremendous hurry (making two steps as long as three paces). **chiâⁿ-pah-hoah-kha**, about a hundred steps = fifty paces. **hoah--kè-khì**, to take a long step across.

hoai, or hoɛ (P.), = A. hoe, a flower. **hoai-kī-kō**, variegated, = A. hoe-lī-lō.

hoâi [R. id., = col. iû]. **hoâi-chhiū**, a tree with yellow flowers (Sophora?). **hoâi-hoe**, its flowers used as a dye for staining wood a greenish yellow.

hoâi [R. to carry in the bosom, heart, or womb, = col. kûi], (P. hôɛ). **hoâi-hūn**, to cherish enmity. **hoâi-liām** (R.), to cherish a feeling in the heart. **sim-hoâi** (R.), the breast (inside). **khai-hoâi thiòng-ím**, jolly over the wine-cups. **hoâi-thai**, to be pregnant. **hoâi-īn** (R.), id.

hoâi [R. name of the river Hwai in the north of Ngan-hwui, and of a city, Hwai-ning foo, in Honan]. **hoâi-soaⁿ**, = soaⁿ-iòh-tsû, a medicinal root from Hwai-ning and North China (Dioscorea?). **hoâi-san**, id.

hoâi [R. hâi, the bones of the chin]. **ē-hoâi**, the lower jaw-bone. **ē-hoâi-kut**, id. **bô-ē-hoâi**, having a very small lower jaw and almost no chin.

hoāi (R. id.) **pāi-hoāi**, to spoil. **sún-hoāi**, id. **húi-hoāi**, id. to destroy. **phah-hoāi**, id. **phah-hoāi-sū**, to ruin an affair or business by mismanagement. **hoāi-sū**, id. **hiú-hoāi**, to rot away. **tó-hoāi**, to fall down, as a house. **pang-hoāi**, to fall, as a landslip, or as an embankment giving way.

hoâiⁿ (R. hêng), (Cn. hûiⁿ; C. hoâⁿ), across, crosswise; (horizontal); wicked, unfair; especially, unfair and overbearing when having an influential protector.

hoâiⁿ-tsâi, wealth got by mere good luck, or by unjust means. **hoâiⁿ-tsāⁿ**, to get large gains suddenly. **hoâiⁿ-kō**, id. **hoâiⁿ-kō ê seng-lí**, making enormous gains in trade.

hoâiⁿ-kèh, opposed to right and justice; disobedient and unruly (v. kèh). **hoâiⁿ-hék**, violent, overbearing, and unjust. **áu-hoâiⁿ**, unfair, oppressive, and injurious, as a man who has powerful influence at his back; to get people's money out of them by an overbearing and violent manner. **hoâiⁿ-peh-peh**, id.

thán-hoâiⁿ, crosswise, transverse; horizontal as opposed to perpendicular. **tháⁿ-hoâiⁿ** (T.), id. **tó thán-hoâiⁿ**, lying across. **sim-koaⁿ thán-hoâiⁿ**, heart perverse and wicked.

hoâiⁿ-tit, straight and cross-wise; in every direction. **hoâiⁿ-khǹg tit-khǹg**, to entreat and exhort by every means. **hoâiⁿ-kiâⁿ tit-tn̂g**, not afraid to go anywhere. **hoâiⁿ-chháu bô-niⁿ, tit-chháu bô-liàm**, very gentle, very honest.

hoâiⁿ-tē, a ferry-boat. **kiâⁿ hoâiⁿ-iûⁿ**, to cross to Formosa (v. iûⁿ). **phah-hoâiⁿ-chhoàⁿ**, to attack by a flank movement. **hoâiⁿ-thâu-toh**, a table at the side of a room. **hoâiⁿ-phi**, an inscription written horizontally, as over a door or at the top of a scroll. **hoâiⁿ-bah-bīn**, repulsive distorted face. **hoâiⁿ-chhâ, giâ jip-tsàu** (to put wood crosswise in the fireplace), perverse and contrary in temper.

hoâiⁿ (T.), = A. hoân, to spread out, as a mat.

hoâiⁿ [R. hêng, name of a plant], (C. hoâⁿ). **ē-hoâiⁿ-si**, a fibrous plant used in making the soft steamed cakes called "ké."

hoaihⁿ, sound of creaking or of breaking. **tāng-hoaihⁿ-hoaihⁿ**, very heavy. **chhe-hoaihⁿ-hoaihⁿ**, very coarse, as cloth. **tēng-hoaihⁿ-hoaihⁿ**, very hard, as cakes.

hoan [R. soân, to go round; to twine]. **hoan-hoe**, a convolvulaceous creeping plant, with light purple flowers, that spreads very rapidly (Calystigia?).

hoan [R. foreign, a time], foreign; barbarian; rude and clownish and foolish.

kúi-hoan (R.), how often?

hoan-hoan, rude, ignorant, and unreasonable. **gín-ná hoan-hoan**, the child is very exacting, unreasonable, and hard to please. **hoan-ti-tu** (clownish spider), a man who is absurdly unreasonable. **hoan-kong-thé**, very rude and ignorant, while affecting knowledge (v. thé).

thé-hoan, aborigines, as in Formosa. **sek-hoan**, civilized aborigines or foreigners. **pîⁿ-pe-hoan**, aborigines in Formosa (near the limit of the plains) who have submitted to the Chinese. **chhiⁿ-hoan**, uncivilized savages. **biâu-hoan**, unsubdued aborigines (Miau-tsze) in some parts of China, esp. north of Kwang-tung and Kwang-si provinces. **e-tē-hoan**, an ancient tribe of barbarians mentioned in the "sam-kok-chì."

hoan-lâng, a foreigner; a barbarian. **hoan-á**, do. (more disrespectful), (s. flag). **hoan-ná**, id. **hoan-á-hoán**, foreigners rebelling against China. **kim hoan-á-thâu**, a gold coin of considerable size. **hoan-thâu**, a Spanish dollar (s. turn). **hoan-ah**, a sort of duck (v. ah). **hoan-thong-sū**, an interpreter. **hoan-pang**, a foreign country. **hoan-pêng**, foreign parts. **hoan-tsû**, = han-tsû, sweet potatoes. **hoan-beh-sūi**, maize; Indian corn. **hoan-koah**, a plant with a root somewhat like a turnip (v. koah). **hoan-ké-chí**, = lién-bū n, the rose-apple.

kè-hoan, to go abroad. **kiâⁿ-hoan**, to travel abroad. **hoàn-hoan**, to go abroad trading. **hê-hoan**, to go and make peace with foreigners, as the Princess Chiau-kun, married to the king of the (kim) Kin Tartars. **chhut-pún hê-hoan**, to lay out money in advance for a friend, as on a commission for goods which he has asked us to execute for him, or as in paying expenses on his account.

hoan (R. id.), to turn over. **hoan-loan**, to turn over and over. **koh hoan--lâi**, to relapse, as in sickness. **hoan-lâi hoan-khì**, to toss restlessly, as sick man on bed. **hoan-kiau**, to roll on the ground, as a horse. **hoan-soa**, id. **hoan-lìn-tńg**, to turn upside down; immediately (v. lìn).

hoan-sin, immediately; in a moment. **hoan-thâu**, to turn one's head round; immediately (in indicative sentences), in speaking of coming back (s. foreign). **hoan-thâu chiah-lâi**, will come back immediately. **tsúi hoan-thâu**, the flood-tide just beginning to flow.

hoan-tsoán, versatile (v. tsoán). **û-hoan-chhia**, id. (v. chhia). **kap-lâng-hoan**, to draw back from a promise, agreement, or engagement. **hoan-bōe-tit**, will not be pleased, as a child that cries for something else as soon as it gets what it asked before.

hoan-àn, to bring up a case again; to reverse the former decision of the court or of a lower court. **hoan-khòng**, to raise again a case that had been settled. **hoan-kài**, to repair a house by taking down the roof and part (at least) of the walls (v. kài). **hoan-pán**, to cut new blocks for a book. **hoan-chháu**, to chew the cud. **hoan-the**, the child moving in the womb just before birth. **hoan-thien** (T.), to come in by the roof, as a thief. **hoan-thien hok-tē**, to make great confusion, as in rebellion, &c. (v. hok). **tsúi hoan-káu**, water gathering a scum when kept too long. **hoan chhân-thê**, to turn up the soil in preparation for another crop. **pah-poaⁿ seng-lí-lē, m̄-táh**

hoan chhân-thê, agriculture is the safest and best of all occupations.

hoan-kih-kā, so confused as to be unintelligible (v. kā).

hoan (R. id.) **hoan-ék**, to interpret, to translate.

hoan [R. a sort of flag or streamer]. **hoan-á**, streamers attached to a circular frame used at funerals. **kiâh hoan-á**, to carry it, as chief mourners at funeral. **ín-hûn-hoan**, white streamers for calling back the spirit of a man who has died abroad. **tông-hoan**, set of streamers on a triangular rim, used as an ornament of idols and at funerals of vegetarians. **khiā-hoan**, to set up streamers at the ceremonies of "kong-tek" for the dead. **khiā-hoan pàng-sià**, to set up these streamers and burn paper images.

hoan [R. hun, to command]. **hoan-hù**, to order; to command; to give a message (v. hù).

hoân [R. to return; to repay, = col. hêng; in some phrases "hoān" (*q.v.*); also C., = A. hêng].

chheng-hoân, to clear off, as an account. **hoân-chè** (esp. C.), to pay a debt. **hoân--i** (C.), pay him.

hoân-hûn, to revive from a swoon, faint, or apparent death (v. hûn). **hoân-tiàu**, to go and pay respects, sometimes with gifts (in return), to a man who has worshipped our parent (tiàu-tsoá) shortly after death.

chit-pō͘ hoân-chit-pō͘, taking slow and careful steps in walking; to manage a matter very carefully, step by step, making sure of one step before taking another. **chit-kù hoân-chit-kù**, each clause spoken separately and distinctly.

hoân (cf. oân), (T. hoâiⁿ), to open out, as something rolled up; to spread out, as a mat. **hoân-chhiòh**, to spread out a mat. **hoân mn̂g-lî**, to open out a hanging door-screen. **hoân báng-tà**, to put up mosquito-curtains.

hoân — **hoân-phê**, to prepare leather for use, as a tanner.

hoân [R. all; every, = col. hoān, the world]. **kàng-hoân**, to come from heaven to be born into the world, as a god. **thoat-hoân**, to die, as Buddhist priest; to have one's mind not set on the world's affairs, as any man.

hoân — **liân-hoân-chhèng**, many guns fired in rapid succession so as to make a running fire. **tńg-liân-hoân**, to fire them thus.

hoân [R. thoân, a round mass; a company]. **liân-hoân-kiet**, an agreement made by all the households of a street or ward to keep away bad characters, all being responsible for each.

hoân (R. id.), alum. **péh-hoân**, id. **sek-hoân**, prepared alum. **chhiⁿ-hoân**, raw alum. **chheng-hoân** (R.), copperas (?) **tám-hoân**, sulphate of iron; copperas, esp. the refined sort from abroad. **tsō-hoân**, do., esp. coarse native sort. **hoân-tsúi**, a solution of alum.

hoân-tsoá, paper sized with alum. **chhiⁿ-kāu-hoân**, a sort of thick paper treated with alum.

hoân [R. troubled; anxious]. **hoân-ló**, sorrow; grieved; anxious about the future. **hoân-hó** (Cn.), id. **êng hoân-ló**, unnecessary anxiety. **hoân-sim**, mind grieved and anxious. **hoân-sim peh-pak**, sorely distressed and anxious. **sim-hoân ì-loān**, mind disturbed and anxious about a multitude of matters.

hoân-sîn, I beg to trouble you, sir; I have given you a vast deal of trouble (v. sîn). **lô-hoân--lí**, I beg to trouble you. **hoân--lí sàng chit-ê-mih**ⁿ, I will trouble you to hand this (to another) for me. **hoân lí--ê tāi-kà**, I beg to trouble you, sir.

tam-hoân, to have great anxieties, as about troublesome matters (v. tam). **put-tān-hoân**, willing to take any pains to get it done. **ùi-hoân**, to dislike being troubled; to decline troublesome duty.

hoân (R. id.), a surname.

hoân, growing soft and bad, as tiles.

hoán (R. id., = col. péng), to turn back (or bring back); to change, as purpose; to rebel; rebellion; but; on the other hand. **tùi-hoán**, opposite in meaning or purpose. **hoán-tńg**, but; on the other hand. **hoán-m̄**, to change one's purpose and refuse or reject; but now he will not. **lōng-kháu hoán-tsoat**, to try to be knowing but act as a fool. **hoā-hó͘ put-sêng, hoán ûi-kó͘** (try to paint a tiger but make it a dog), said of a most miserable failure, so utter that it would have been far better never to have tried it at all.

hoán-hóe, to repent; to change one's purpose. **hoán-hòe** (C.), id. **hoán-koà**, to break one's promise. **hoán-hiau**, to betray trust in money matters. **hiau-hoán**, to break an agreement; to betray trust. **hoán-pān**, to send goods inferior to the sample. **hoán-keng**, to retract the confession or evidence given in court (v. keng). **hoán-kàn-kè**, to use secret plots and calumnies against a man (v. kè, "a plan").

hoán-hok, changeable in purpose; fickle (v. hok). **hoán-siông**, to change rapidly from good to bad, or from friendship to enmity (v. siông). **hoán-bīn**, to change countenance, as in sudden anger. **hoán-biēn bû-siông**, fickle, inconstant in friendship; touchy (v. siông). **hoán-biēn bû-chêng**, inconstant in friendship; ungrateful; fickle.

hoán-sek, to change colour; to become rancid by heat, as meat. **hoán-pak**, to turn the stomach; vomiting. **hoán-chiō** (C.), to chew the cud.

hoán-loān, to rebel. **hoán-poān**, id. **tsō-hoán**, id. **bē-hoán**, id. **kap-pán-hoán**, the war between Britain and China in 1842. **sio-to-hoán**, the Triad insurrection. **hoán-chhát**, rebels. **hoán-kut**, a man determined to rebel as soon as possible. **tsáu-hoán**, to flee from insurrection. **pī-hoán**, id.

óng-hoán, going and returning, as on a journey. **hoán-tsú**, to bring back the tablet from the funeral. **hoán-tiāu**, to give a sort of mournful turn up at the end of a line in a tune. **im-iông hoán-pōe**, turning day into night and night into day. **hoán-bûn** (T. páiⁿ-bûn), the 66th or 67th radical, written at the side on the right hand.

hoàn (R. id.) **hoàn-lām** (R.), a vast flood or deluge.

hoàn [R. floating, vague, negligent], (Cn. hoàng). **hoàn-hoàn**, working without heart or decided purpose; not careful; not particular how a thing is done; vague and general; insincere. **tsòe-lâng hoàn-hoàn**, to act so. **khah-hoàn**, in a rather general way, not giving many particulars. **kap--lán hoàn-hoàn**, very easy in his dealings with us; not very particular.

hoàn — **hu-hu hoàn-hoàn**, quite uncertain or utterly false, as a story. **hoàn-hoàn-tāi**, not very clear how the matter stands, but not of much consequence. **hê-hoàn**, groundless, unsubstantial, as a rumour. **hê-hê hoàn-hoàn**, id. [perhaps some phrases belong to the previous word].

hoàn (R. id.) **hø-hoàn**, to order, as a servant (v. hø).

hoàn [R. to sell goods; to be a pedlar, = col. phoà^{n}.] **hoàn-á**, a pedlar. **hoàn-á-péh**, secret dialect, or slang used by pedlars. **tsòe-hoàn**, to be a pedlar. **chhài-hoàn**, a pedlar who sells vegetables. **ah-hoàn**, pedlar who sells ducks.

hoàn--chhut-lâi, to trade in bringing produce from the interior. **hoàn-hoan**, to trade abroad, either in person or by sending agents. **hoàn-tsô**, a medium-sized junk, as about 800 or 1000 peculs.

hoàn-sau, a dealer in slaves and children. **hoàn-sau-keng**, shop of such a dealer.

hoān [R. an official]. **bêng-hoān-sû**, temple to canonized mandarins of district or department (stands beside the Confucian temple).

hoān (R. id.), to transgress; to offend against; a criminal; to meet with, as calamity or bad omen.

hoān-hoat, to break the law. **hoān-tsōe**, to contract guilt; to commit a crime. **hoān-kìm**, contraband; strictly forbidden by law or regulation; to break such a prohibition. **hoān-àn**, to be accused of crime; to be involved in a lawsuit. **hoān-hùi**, to offend against a sacred name, as of Sage or Emperor. **hoān-iā**, to go about without a lamp, and at forbidden time of night.

hoān-lâng, a criminal. **tsōe-hoān**, id. **tiōng-hoān**, a great criminal. **ka^{n}-hoān**, an imprisoned criminal. **siû-hoān** (R.), id. **liû-hoān**, a transported convict. **kê-hoān**, a criminal wearing the cangue. **hiong-hoān**, a murderer. **chhát-hoān**, an apprehended robber. **khim-hoān**, a state prisoner arrested by imperial command. **sí-hoān**, you condemned criminal! (scolding); also, a prisoner who has died in prison. **tsáu-hoān**, an escaped prisoner. **láu-hoān**, a prisoner who has been in prison several years. **sin-hoān**, a recent prisoner.

chhiú^{n}-hoān, to rescue a criminal by force. **tiàu-hoān**, to order up a criminal to be tried. **kè-hoān**, to send a prisoner to a higher court to be tried or punished. **koat-hoān**, to behead a criminal.

chhim-hoān, to offend against (a person) so as to displease him; to encroach upon, as grave, or land, or territory. **chhiok-hoān**, to come unintentionally on a man in an unlucky, ill-omened, awkward, or troublesome manner. **hoān--tio̍h**, to offend against; to meet with, generally (but not always), unpleasant or hurtful things.

hoān-hong, to meet with a heavy gale. **hoān-hiâm**, liable to blame. **hoān-giâu**, to excite suspicion; to be suspected. **hoān-gî**, id. [some say that this paragraph belongs to the next word].

hoān [R. calamity]. **hoān-lān** (R.), calamity; to have suffering or calamity.

hoān-soah, to be under the evil influence of the demons called "soah-sîn," as a house or grave. **hoān-sam-soah**, id.; sometimes said of a person.

hoān-tio̍h-pī^{n}, become unwell. **hoān-tio̍h-kúi**, injured by meeting with a demon. **chhiong-hoān-tio̍h-kúi**, id. [some say this paragraph belongs to the previous word].

hoān [R. a rule; a pattern]. **keng-hoān**, to taunt; to jeer at, especially at personal appearance. **ti-io-hoān**, kidney-shaped. **tê-au-á-hoān**, shaped like a tea-cup. **gûn-tiā^{n}-hoān**, shaped like a silver ingot or hour-glass. **moâ^{n}-phang-hoān**, lozenge-shaped; diamond-shaped. **moâ^{n}-tê-hoān** (C.), id.

hoān [R. hoân, to return; to repay; some are also pronounced "hoân"]. **lí hoān-lí, goá hoān-goá**, you and I have no connection in our affairs. **lí-ê, hoān lí-ê; goá-ê hoān goá-ê**, yours and mine are quite distinct. **hoa-kî, hoān hoa-kî; hô-lân, hoān hô-lân**, the Americans and the Dutch are quite distinct (people or nations). **lāi, hoān--tit sī-lāi; goā, hoān--tit sī-goā**, inside and outside (as of a house) must be kept quite distinct.

hoān [R. hoân, the world; all]. **hoān-kan**, the world. **hoān-nā^{n}**, in every case that —. **hoān-sū**, in all affairs; in any matter. **hoān-tsòe-sū**, in all matters that we do, &c.

hoang (Cn. T.), = A. hong, "wind" (only in phrases strictly colloquial, while in reading phrases that have become colloquial it remains "hong," *e.g.* "hong-siók).")

hoang-gô (T.), = A. hong-chhe-lién, a toy made to turn with the wind.

hoang (Cn.), = A. hong, waste; fabulous.

hoáng, a Dutch coin.

hoàng (Cn.), = A. hoàn, without heart; without decided purpose.

hoat [R. the hair of the head]. **kiet-hoat**, the wife whom a man marries first of all; opp. to the one married after her death or divorce, who is "āu-bǿ" or "siók-hiân."

lâu tsoân-hoat, to let the whole of one's hair grow long, as women. **hoat-jī-á-thâu**, the 190th radical, written at the top.

hoat (R. id.), a rule; a law; a means; black arts, esp. Tauist; to manage; French.

siâ-hoat, Tauist magical arts. **hoat-sút** (v. sút), id. **iau-hoat**, id. **hoat-le̍k**, powerful influence of an idol. **hoat-le̍k ko-kiōng**, the power of the idol is very great. **iám-sin-hoat**, the art of becoming invisible. **hû-hoat**, rites to secure the success of a charm. **hoat-soh**, a magical rope used by Tauists. **hoat-chí**, the commands of Lau-tsze. **hoat-su**, complimentary title of Tauist priest. **hoat-koa^{n}**, sort of Tauist enchanter. **hoat-tiú^{n}**, head of a company of boys at an idolatrous procession. **hoat-tiû^{n}**, a place where magical rites are performed; also, an execution ground. **ha̍k-hoat**, to learn black arts and Tauist rites. **sái-hoat**, to use magic. **tsok-hoat**, id. **tàu-hoat**, to try which is superior in magic.

hø̄-hoat-iâ (Cn.), an idol (v. hø).

hoat-tø̄, a rule; a law; a plan; a method. **hoat-lu̍t**, a law, as of the state. **lu̍t-hoat**, id. **hoat-kài** (R.), id. (v. kài, "prohibition"). **hoat-kài** (R.), the region where Buddha lives (v. kài, "boundary"). **kok-hoat**, the laws of the kingdom. **hong-hoat**, a plan; a method; means. **chèng-hoat**, to execute a criminal; a just and right plan. **ēng-chèng-hoat**, to act in a perfectly fair and just way. **chià^{n}-hoat**, the fit way to accomplish an end. **chêng-lí-hoat**, the proper plan in the circumstances of the case (v. chêng). **put-hoat**, lawless.

tīn-hoat, military manœuvres. **ka-hoat**, regulations of a family (v. ka). **i-hoat**, rules of medicine. **chiàu-kun-hoat**, according to military rules. **seng-lí-hoat**, the rules and regular practices of trade. **soàn-hoat**, arithmetic. **sêng-hoat**, multiplication (v. sêng). **hoat-thiap-jī**, a sort of copy-book.

ēng-ke̍k-hoat, to use very strong or severe measures; going to extremities. **ēng-kek-hoat**, to talk to a man so as to incite him to take up a matter quite willingly and heartily. **ēng-chhø-hoat**, to act vio-

19

lently (v. chhe). **tio̍h-hoat**, to hit on the right way of doing a thing. **tek-hoat**, to hit on the right way; quite correct; to manage a matter successfully. **siet-hoat**, to put matters in right order or in a proper train. **siú-hoat**, to act properly; to be of good behaviour; to observe the laws. **ti-hoat phà^{n}-hoat**, they who know the law should obey it (said in finding fault with literati or underlings of yamuns, who break the laws); also, "I know the law, and will certainly obey it."

hoat-lo̍h, to manage an affair; to arrange or determine what is to be done.

bô-hoat--i, cannot manage it; cannot do anything with (him); quite beyond (my) power. **kék bô-hoat--i**, cannot manage it at all. **kék bô-hoat--tit**, id. **bô-hoat--i tâ-oâ**, having no resource; quite helpless and unable to resist or to accomplish. **bô-hoat--lâng tâ-oâ**, unable to resist or overcome him. **bô-hoat--lâng ê-tâ-oâ**, id. **beh-siá^{n}-hoat--i**, what resource is possible? nothing can be done. **beh-siá^{n}-hoat--goá tâ-oâ**, what resource (has he) against me? **lí ū-siá^{n}-hoat--goá**, what ever can you do to me? (as to compel me or to prevent me). **goá bô-sím-mih^{n} i-hoat**, I have no way to make him submit. **bô-hoat-pu̍t, kāng hê-siū^{n}**, unable to punish the principal offender, but taking revenge on his subordinates.

iâm-hoat-tō, the salt commissioner.

hoat-lân-se, France. **hoat-lông-se**, id., often pronounced "hô-lân-se." **tāi-hoat-kok** (R.), id. **tāi-hoat** (R.), id.

hoat (R. id., = col. pauh, puh), to produce; to sprout; to begin to grow; to come out, as eruptions, sweat, &c.; to ferment; to pay out, as money.

it-hoat, all the more.

hoat-si^{n}, to produce; to grow or bear, as fruit, &c. **hoat-chhut**, to produce. **hoat-hiēn**, to appear; to become manifest. **hoat-pauh**, to come out, as a secret or a plot. **hoat-tsoh**, to break out, as a disease showing itself on the body; to come to pass, as a plot; to come to light, as a secret; to begin to grow into a man, as a lad (v. tsoh). **hoat-kak**, to come to light, as a secret (v. kak, "to know"). **hoat-kak**, to grow horns (v. kak, "a horn"). **hoat-chhi^{n}**, to put out green leaves. **hoat-í^{n}**, to bud; to sprout. **hoat-gê**, to sprout and shoot out (longer than "í^{n}"). **hoat-chháu**, to grow grass and small plants. **hoat-mn̂g**, to grow hair or feathers, as animals; to begin to grow hair, as a wound or scabbed place when healing. **hoat-chhùi-chhiu**, beard beginning to grow. **hoat chhùi-khí**, to get teeth; teething. **hoat-khí**, id.

hoat-jie̍t, to take fever; to have a feverish attack. **hoat chiú-hong**, to have small red eruptions, from drinking liquor. **hoat-hông**, to get swollen, as from a venomous bite (v. hông, "swollen"). **hoat-hông**, burning with rage or passion (v. hông, "heated"). **hoat-hōng**, face flushed; to blush. **hoat-lia̍p**, to grow pimples or boils. **si^{n}-thâu hoat-bé**, to have pimples, boils, or eruptions. **hoat-chiū^{n}-bīn**, to break out on the face, as eruption. **hoat-koā^{n}**, to perspire by use of medicine, &c., in disease. **hoat-hān**, id. **hé tn̂g-hoat**, frantic with rage; sudden severe fever or inflammation; conflagration raging with great violence. **hoat-kông**, mad; wild; extravagantly absurd, as man. **hoat-sèng**, to get suddenly angry (naturally). **hoat-lát**, to show anger by loud voice or gesticulation, *e.g.* striking the table.

hoat-sim, to show kindness. **hoat-sè**, to make a solemn oath. **hoat-goān**, to make a sudden vow by language without any formal rite.

hoat-hok, fat and good-looking; getting on well in business. **tng hoat-hoe**, making money at the time (v. hoe). **hoat-tsâi**, to grow rich. **hoat-chî^{n}**, id. **hoat-tát**, to prosper in wealth or office, &c., as person or family. **hoat-chek**, to rise from obscurity to high station. **hoat--ah**, may it prosper! said at the rites of "chēng-iû" by Tauist priests. **în tsòng, báu hoat**, as soon as the body is buried the auspicious influence of the grave begins to operate.

hoat-he, to slake lime. **hoat-kà^{n}**, to ferment. **hoat-ké**, a sort of cake made with a sort of yeast.

khai-hoat, to distribute money, as wages; to punish slightly on the spot, and set free at once. **hun-hoat**, to distribute money, as wages; to separate the items of some difficult piece of business, to be taken up in succession; to send out employes or members of family to different places to make their living. **chî^{n} hoat-hō--i**, give him the money.

chhòng ké--ê, lâi hoat--lâng, to cheat people by selling them bad articles. **khit--i hoat--khì**, to be taken in by him selling us bad articles.

hoat-thoat, to clear off the stock; to sell off at any price; to escape secretly, or help to escape (v. thoat). **hoat-bōe**, for sale. **hoat-tôe**, for sale, as goods. **hoat-hê**, to send back, as goods not liked, or as a rejected present.

hoat-tiâu, the main-spring of a watch or timepiece.

hoat-m̄-chiâ^{n} sai-pak, north-west wind suddenly rising and falling, with almost no rain. **bān-lō-chî^{n} tsôe-hoat**, numerous calamities coming at once (v. lō, "a cross-bow"). **ngó-lō chê-hoat**, id. (v. lō, "a road").

hoa̍t [R. to subdue rebels]. **cheng-hoa̍t** (R.), to go to war, and chastise or subdue rebels.

hoa̍t [R. to punish], to fine; to mulct; to punish, as by fine or forfeit; to break, as a horse.

hêng-hoa̍t, to punish; punishment. **gâu hêng-hoa̍t--lâng**, fond of punishing people; fond of causing people great trouble or expense. **chek-hoa̍t**, to punish, as a god. **hoa̍t-hōng**, to mulct of official salary. **hoa̍t-gûn**, to fine. **hoa̍t-chî^{n}**, id. **hoa̍t-hì-toh**, to make a man stand the expense of a play and a feast, as a forfeit. **hoa̍t-toh**, make him forfeit a feast. **hoa̍t-chiú**, make him forfeit some liquor.

kè-hoa̍t, to be broken, as a horse. **put-chí-pà, tio̍h kè-hoa̍t**, he is very disobedient and ill-behaved (lad), and must be broken in like a horse.

hoa̍t [R. to be deficient or in want]. **khoat-hoa̍t** (R.), in want. **khat-hoa̍t** (r.), id.

hoa̍t [R. alive, active, = col. oa̍h]. **hoa̍t-phoat**, active and lively (as man); graceful and flowing, as written characters. **liēn kàu hoa̍t-hoa̍t**, to work up very thoroughly and carefully, as mixing material for pills or such medicine. **liēn-khi-hoa̍t**, work it up well. **liēn-hoa̍t**, thoroughly worked and mixed up.

seng-hoa̍t-kè, a means of livelihood.

to̍k-hoa̍t, a medicinal root. **khiong-hoa̍t**, a medicinal root from Se-khiong (Angelica?).

hoe (C.), = A. he, lime.

hoe (R. hoa), (C. hoa, P. hoai, hoe), a flower; a flowering plant; a blossom; variegated; dim, as eyesight; in many phrases means "licentious."

mî^{n}-hoe, raw cotton. **hoan-hoe**, foreign cotton. **khè-hoe**, mace (v. khè). **chhài-hoe**, cauliflower or brocoli. **kú-chhài-hoe**, flower-stalks of celery.

kan-hoe, pig's liver. **tāu-hoe**, soft bean-curd, not

yet shaped. **chióh-hoe**, a pleasant cooling jelly made from a plant (like Ceylon moss or Irish moss). **chióh-hoe-pâi**, this gelatinous substance boiled into a sweet confection, somewhat stiff. **chióh-hoe-phìⁿ**, do. cut into thin slices.

lêng-hoe, the feathers of an arrow. **khau-to-hoe**, shavings of wood made by a plane. **hiā-hoe**, fragile work (on the tops of walls, &c.) made of thin tiles placed diagonally and leaving open spaces. **hoe-thang-chhí**, ornamental tiles for use in open trellis-work. **bān-jī-hoe**, the figure called "bān," worked in large quantities, as in the open work of screens.

chhih-hoe, clusters of spawn of the craw-fish. **hé-hoe**, sparks as from a match. **lak hé-hoe**, to let sparks fall. **teng-hé-hoe**, large lumps on the wick of a lamp. **teng-hé khui-hoe**, the lamp gathers large spots on the wick; when very large they are auspicious.

chek-hoe, ornamental flowers on candles (v. chek). **siù-teng-hoe**, to embroider flowers on the gauze frame of a lamp.

chhìn-hoe, white dots on the beam of a steelyard for marking the weight.

tsúi-hoe, spray. **phah tsúi-hoe**, to splash spray. **phùn--tióh hō-hoe**, to get some drops of rain on one's self. **lâu koāⁿ-hoe**, to have perspiration in small drops on the skin.

jit-hoe, a ray through a chink; rays through clouds or through the leaves of trees. **chhut jit-hoe-á**, rays breaking through the clouds.

sim-hoe khui, delighted at something. **ū chhùi-hoe**, good at speaking in a polite or insinuating manner (v. chhùi). **iô kha-chhng-hoe**, to shake about one's hips in walking. **lāng koái-á-hoe**, to brandish his stick with delight, as beggar (v. koáiⁿ).

khui-hoe, to bloom; to blossom. **chîⁿ-chhiū khui-hoe**, making a great deal of money (often said of a prostitute). **tng hoat-hoe**, beginning to be prosperous. **teh-hoat-hoe**, making a great deal of money. **lāng-hoe**, to protrude the flower, as corn or grass. **siúⁿ-hoe**, to admire flowers. **chhái-hoe**, to gather food from flowers, as butterflies or bees. **bōe-hoe**, to sell flowers; a flower-seller. **chhah-hoe**, to stick flowers in the hair; a studding-sail.

khek-hoe, to carve wood into any sort of figures. **tiau-hoe khek-chiáu**, id. **chhák-hoe**, id. **siù-hoe**, to embroider (v. siù). **chhiah-hoe**, to embroider finely (v. chhiah). **thio-hoe**, id. (v. thio).

oāⁿ-hoe, to change the colour of the flowers on a woman's tree of fate (in the invisible world) from red to white, so that she may have male children instead of females; said also of a bride's younger brother visiting her three days after marriage. **tsai-hoe oāⁿ-táu**, superstitious rites for curing female barrenness. **khit-hoe**, to pray for children. **hoe-kong hoe-pô**, two deities (male and female) that give out these flowers—red for females, white for males. **hoe-kong-pô**, id.

thàm-hoe, the third in rank of the new Hanlin (hān-lîm) graduates. **kim-hoe**, gilt flowers (tinsel) used by a new-made sew-tsae or higher graduate, and at some other ceremonies; Turkey opium. **kim-hoe-âng**, a sort of opium. **chhó-hoe**, artificial flowers.

hoe-âng, money wrapped in red paper, given in engaging an assistant, clerk, or manager for a shop.

hoe-hiet, prettily painted or coloured; gaudy, as goods, buildings, and such things; too gaudy, as women; specious and flattering, as words (v. hiet).

hoe-lêng, a peacock's feather with one eye. **hoe-thiaⁿ**, reception-room for visitors, as in a yamun. **hoe-kiō**, a red bridal chair.

hoe-tiám, spotted with small spots. **hoe-pan**, speckled; spotted; freckled. **hoe-lòk-lòk**, variegated; mottled (like a stag). **hoe-lī-lō**, variegated; mottled; indistinct in colour; all in confusion, as money matters; not managing properly; not treating persons of various rank as they should be treated relatively. **hoe-lō-lō**, id. **hoe-káu**, a spotted dog. **hoe-bé**, a piebald horse. **hoe-teng**, a flowered lantern. **hoe-phè**, a flowered or variegated cloth used for wrapping up clothes, &c. **hoe-pò͘**, flowered, spotted, or variegated cotton cloth. **ìn-hoe-pò͘**, printed cotton. **toā-hoe-pò͘**, large-flowered do. **sió-hoe-pò͘**, small-flowered do. **ìn-iûⁿ-hoe-pò͘**, foreign printed cotton; chintz. **chí-hoe-pò͘**, nankeen.

hoe-gûn, dollars all covered with stamps.

hoe-bák, flowers and shrubs (v. bák). **hoe-lúi**, a blossom. **hoe-m̂**, a flower-bud. **hoe-tsâng**, a flowering-plant. **hoe-hún**, flowers and paint for the face. **hoe-chhiám**, a pin for flowers in the hair (v. chhiám). **hoe-thô͘**, earth in a flower-pot. **hoe-tâi**, a terrace built up for flower-pots. **hoe-nâⁿ**, a flower-basket, as in a room. **hoe-pân**, a flower-jug for artificial flowers, or for water and cut flowers. **hoe-kan**, do. with cut flowers and water. **hoe-khaⁿ**, a flower-pot. **hoe-phûn**, do. of finer ware, as porcelain. **hoe-thâng**, insects that prey on flowers; caterpillars. **hoe-sîn**, spirits of flowers (v. sîn). **hoe-hn̂g**, a garden.

hoe-chio, white pepper. **hoe-bî**, a bird that talks and fights. **hoe-thiâu**, the mud-fish. **hoe-ki**, a large spotted sort of cuttle-fish. **chháu-hoe-tsoâ**, a variegated harmless snake.

bák-chiu hoe, eyes dim. **bák-hoe**, id.

hoe-hē (C. hoa-hōe), two sorts of gambling (v. hē). **bóe-hoe-tn̂g** (Cn.), = A. teh-hoe-hē, to gamble in this way.

hoe-keng, a house of ill-fame; a brothel. **ien-hoe-chhùi** (harlot's mouth), you great liar! (vile scolding). **hoe-théng**, boats used as brothels (Cantonese). **hoe-hì**, a lascivious stage-play. **hoe-chhut**, id. **hoe-toàⁿ**, a character in a mandarin play representing a beautiful and cheerful young woman.

hôe, to wipe the feet, as on a mat; to rub or scrape the feet. **hôe-hôe**, id. **hôe--sí**, to kill by rubbing with the foot, as a worm.

hôe (R. id.) **tāi-hôe**, = poeh-kak, anise-seed. **toā-hôe**, id. **sió-hôe**, a sweet-smelling seed like a grass, = phàⁿ-chhek-hiuⁿ (fennel? coriander?), used for its smell or flavour. **siáu-hôe**, id.

hôe [R. to turn back, to return, Mahomedan], (in some phrases interchanges with "hô͘"), a section of a book.

hôe-hôe-kàu, Mahomedanism, so named from the Uigours. **hôe-hôe**, Mahomedan.

hôe-jiông, a sort of velveteen (v. jiông).

óng-hôe, to go and return. **hôe-thâu**, to turn back; to come back. **thiet-hôe**, to disband, as volunteers or militia. **hôe-lé**, to make a visit or perform a ceremony in return for the other having first done so to us. **hôe-pài** (C.), = A. hô͘-pài, to return a ceremonial visit. **hôe-hok** (C.), = A. hô͘-hok, to make a report. **hôe-oā** (C.), = A. hê-ōe, to interpret verbally between two persons.

goân-toaⁿ pok-hôe, bill protested. **hôe-lêng**, the ridge of a hill conducting the auspicious influence and carrying it round till the grave directly faces the origin (soaⁿ-bú) of the influence.

hôe-hûn, to revive, as from a swoon, from death, or from despair. **hôe-iông**, to return to life. **khí-sú hôe-seng**, to restore the (almost) dead to life (said of a very skilful doctor).

siòk-hôe, to ransom; to redeem. **hôe-sim tńg-ì**, to alter one's mind. **bán-hôe sim-chì**, to reform one's heart. **bán-hôe thi^{n}-ì**, to influence Heaven to favour, as by virtuous conduct. **bōe bán-hôe--tit**, the matter so bad or so far settled that it cannot now be altered or set right.

liên-hôe, miserable and destitute, as a man of utterly ruined reputation who cannot get into better circumstances. **liên-liên hôe-hôe**, id. **ûn-á liên-hôe**, may you be constantly and irretrievably miserable and ruined! **liên-hôe sì-chèng**, id., disgraced for ever by some vile act of himself or of some near relative.

hôe-pī (R.), to keep out of the way of a mandarin.

hôɛ (C.), = A. hoâi, to hold in the bosom, &c.

hóe (C. hé). **hóe-bák**, to give an angry glance. **bák-chiu hóe**, id.

hóe (R. id.) **hoán-hóe** (C. hoán-hòe), to repent and amend; to change one's purpose and conduct. **hóe-ngē**, to repent. **hóe--chiá tî**, it is then too late to change one's mind. **tsòe-chit-sî hóe**, to change one's mind at once.

hóe-chhin, to break off a betrothal.

thè-hóe (C.), to find out our mistake, and be sorry or repent having done it.

hóe [R. bribery]. **hóe-lē kong-hêng** (R.), mandarins taking bribes openly.

hóe (C.), = A. hé, fire. **àm-hóe**, at dark. **hóe-ông** (C.), = A. hé-sîn-iâ, the god of fire.

hóe (C.) **hóe-sit**, = A. hé-sit, food, &c.

hóe (C.), = A. hé, a partner. **tsò-hóe**, to act or do anything together.

hòe (R. id.), (C. hùi), to destroy; to annul; to pass away. **hòe-bô**, to make void; to cause to cease. **hòe--khì**, to pass away, as a custom or rule become obsolete. **hòe-tūi**, fallen into decay. **hòe-sí**, to cease to be done, as a rite or course of action. **poàn-tô jî-hòe**, to stop half-way and fail utterly.

hong-hòe, laid waste; dilapidated: desolate. **hng-hòe**, id. **hòe-giáp**, useless unclaimed ground, as ruined house or inundated land. **hòe-hûn**, deserted graves. **hòe-siā**, to destroy a village, as mandarins, or as enemies in a feud. **hòe-hiu^{n}**, id., as mandarins. **hiu^{n}-siā hòe--khì**, the village is ruined and deserted.

hòe-jîn, a useless fellow, as a cripple, or maimed; a worthless fellow, idle or wicked. **hòe-chit**, incurable and useless, as a cripple, lame, leprous, or blind, &c. **hòe-chek** (T.), id.

hòɛ [R. hoà, to influence and renovate], (C. hòɛ, also = A. hoà, to renovate].

hòe-iên, to beg, as Buddhist priests.

tek-hòe, the city of Teh-hwa, in the prefecture of Yung-chun (éng-chhun).

hòe (C.), = A. hóe. **hoán-hòe**, to repent; to change one's purpose and conduct. **thè-hòe**, to be grieved and repent of what one has done, often of what cannot now be changed. **siū^{n}-thè-hòe**, id.

hòe (C.), = A. hè, goods. **hòe-mih^{n}**, = A. hè-bu̍t, goods and things in general.

hòe (C.), = A. hè, a year of age.

hōe — **hōe-koán**, a sort of exchange rooms, where merchants meet to consult on prices, &c.

hōe (R. id.), (sometimes interchanges with "hē;" sometimes "hōe" and "hē" interchange in C. and A., or vice-versa); an assembly; a society or association; to meet together; to combine together.

ki-hōe, an opportunity.

hōe-toa^{n}, a bill of exchange.

hōe-goân, the highest of the new Tsin-sze (chìn-sū) graduates. **hōe-khoe**, those of the new Tsin-sze who rank from second to tenth on the list. **hōe-sì**, the examinations for the Tsin-sze degree (v. sì).

ti-hōe, to notify. **thé-hōe**, to examine the meaning, or a man's purpose, till we thoroughly understand it. **lí-hōe** (esp. C.), = lí-hē, to talk over a matter so as to come to an understanding about its settlement. **hōe-ì** (r.), to understand the meaning. **hū-hōe**, to express assent, often mere empty words. **hun-hōe** (C.), = A. hun-hē, to make one's statement or discuss a question making explanations.

hōe-siàu (= hē-siàu), to meet, examine, and settle accounts. **biēn-hōe**, to settle a matter by discussing it face to face. **hōe-bīn**, to meet face to face, for any purpose. **hōe-biēn**, id. **hōe-chhin**, son-in-law visiting father-in-law soon after marriage. **pài-hōe**, to visit on equal terms, as mandarins. **hiên-hōe**, affable and polite to visitors (said of ladies). **tsū-hōe**, to meet together. **chī-hōe** (C.), id. **tsòe-hōe**, to meet together; to form a society. **siong-hōe**, to meet one another. **hù-hōe**, to come in time to a meeting. **hōe-tsôe**, to assemble for taking united action. **hōe-bêng**, to confederate. **hōe-tóng**, to combine together for bad purposes. **hōe-tē**, the villages of a region combining, as to put down feuds or plundering. **hōe-lé**, civil and military mandarins gathering soldiers and going together to seize criminals. **hōe-hâm**, two or more mandarins jointly issuing a proclamation.

bûn-bú-hōe, a meeting of civil and military graduates. **siù-tsâi-hōe**, a meeting of sew-tsae graduates to consult on some matter. **tsòe-bûn-chiu^{n}-hōe**, a literary society for writing essays. **liû-li-hōe**, a society that worships liû-lî-kong. **bêng-pē-bú-hōe**, a club for the burial of parents. **kong-hōe**, a public society or association. **sió-to-hōe**, the Triad society (rebellious). **siang-to-hōe** (C.), id. **thien-tē-hōe**, id. **pat-koà-hōe**, a similar illegal society (some say, the same). **tāi-siáu-sèng-hōe**, small clans or villages banded to oppose greater ones. **sèng-hōe**, the church (the society, not the building). **kàu-hōe**, id., a sect. **hoa-hōe** (C.), = A. hoe-hē, two sorts of gambling (v. hē).

jip-hōe, to enter a society. **hōe-iú**, members of a society; friends engaged on the same literary work, &c. **hōe-hia^{n}-tī**, id. **hōe-tiú^{n}**, head man of a society or association, good or bad. **hōe-thâu**, head of a society; *e.g.* head of the Triad rebels, either of the whole society or of those at one place; also (C.), = A. hē-thâu, head of a mutual benefit club.

hōe (R. id.) **chhàu-hōe**, wild aloes. **lô-hōe** (C.), = A. lô-hē, aloes.

hōe (R. hāi), (C. hē; Cn. hōe), the hairy crab or craw-fish. **mê-hōe**, id. (C. mê-hē), (Cn. mn̂g-hōe). **kim-chî^{n}-hōe**, a smaller sort.

hōe [R. hō, a mark]. **sìn-hōe** (Cn.), = sìn, the soft place on a child's head.

hōɛ (C. P.), = some words in "hoāi" and "hoā."

hoeh (C.), = A. huih, blood.

hoh (R. hok), = ho, to scorch, as the sun.

hoh, = huh, to cook on a dry frying-pan.

hòh (R. hòk), a stork. **pêh-hòh**, a white stork.

sien-hòh, a stork said to live a hundred years. **hòh-têng**, the crest of the stork, used for rings and amulets. **hòh-sìⁿ**, a large oval fan carried before idols and high mandarins. **hòh-á chek-tâi**, candlestick shaped like a stork.

hòh (C.) **hòh-lêng-ko**, = A. hók-lêng-ko, a sweet cake, somewhat medicinal.

hòh [R. hō, to protect]. **hòh-chhip** (C.), = A. hók-sek, ornaments for the knees.

hoh̄ⁿ [R. hóⁿ, good, well], (cf. hòⁿ, hôⁿ), interjection placed at a pause, directing attention to what has been said; "observe and take note of this;" also, in answer to what another has said, as if saying, "yes, I observe and understand," but without giving any opinion for or against; this use of it is only by superiors or equals; if said by an inferior, it is improper.

höh (Cn.) **höh-chē**, to sit and rest.

hok [R. a roll of paper or cloth, = col. pak]. **chhim-i hok-kun**, dress and hood of a corpse, according to the Ming pattern.

hok [R. hok = hók; to repeat, to report; = col. koh]. **hê-hok**, to report to him who sent us; to give an answer on inquiry, as a commissioner. **hôe-hok** (C.), id. **pín-hok**, to give in a report, as an inferior to a superior official. **hok-bûn**, to answer an official letter. **hok-chí**, to report to the emperor the accomplishment of his commands.

hok-sím, to examine the case in court over again another time. **hok-sìn**, id. **koh hok-khoàⁿ**, look over it again carefully. **hok-siàu**, to look over an account again to see if there be any error; to check an account. **sam-koan ngó͘-hok**, to examine over and over again very carefully [some phrases interchanged with the next word].

hok [R. to overturn; to cover; to repeat], (some phrases interchanged with the previous word).

hoán-hok, indeterminate in purpose; fickle; changeable in intention; back and forwards. **hoán-hoán hok-hok**, id. **hoán-hok bû-siông**, fickle, as to promises or friendship.

sam-hoan ngó͘-hok, very deliberate and careful (revolving the matter over and over) before making up one's mind.

hoan-thien hok-tē, to put things all in confusion, *e.g.* as boys or servants when their superior is absent; to behave in a very disorderly manner; to make disturbance or rebellion (lit. turn heaven and earth upside down). **chhut-tsāi-lí; hoan-thien hok-tē, goá bô-chhap**, whatever you may do, I will not meddle at all.

hok [R. hù, to cover, by change of tone from "hok," to overturn]. **hok-ìm**, to benefit descendants, as by wealth or official merit; to assist, as a powerful friend (v. ìm).

hok [R. two-fold, as a dress with lining]. **tiông-hok**, tautology, as in an essay. **hok-sèng**, a surname consisting of two characters, as su-má, su-tô͘, au-iông, &c.

hok [R. a bat]. **pién-hok**, a bat, = bít-pô. **hûn-hok**, wavy figures like bats or clouds on flowered silk stuffs, &c.

hok [R. speedy; a certain high mountain], a surname.

hok (R. id.), good fortune; happiness; Fuh-chau. **hok-khì**, good fortune; happiness. **hok-hūn**, one's whole allotted measure of good fortune. **hó-hok-hūn**, great good fortune. **iú-hok put-khó chīn-hióng**, do not use good luck to the utmost. **iú-hok, m̄-thang chīn-hióng**, id. **hióng-hok**, to enjoy good fortune. **ū-hok**, id. **sioh-hok**, to restrain one's self from taking the full swing of power or pleasure; to refrain from taking all the pleasure or dignity, or exercising all the power one could have had. **m̄-sioh-hok**, to take one's full swing of pleasure, &c.; to live fast or lavishly. **chiet-hok**, to cut down one's fated measure of good fortune by a too free use of what we have, as by proud overbearing conduct, by fast or lavish living, or by fastidiousness and waste of food or clothing, so as to provoke Heaven to cut short the measure of fortune.

pòk-hok, ill-fated; having bad luck; also said politely of one's self, "I am not worthy of such good fortune;" having a hard life with little good fortune. **thien-tē hêng-tsai, pòk-hok--chiá siū**, heaven-sent calamities fall on the ill-fated. **hong chhe phàⁿ-chhek, pòk-hok--chiá siū**, rice-chaff is blown by the wind, and the ill-fated take epidemics. **iông-iông, to hē-hok**, common ordinary people usually have a good deal of good fortune.

hoat-hok, to grow fat. **hok-siòng**, plump, fat, and good-looking.

tsòe-sîn-hok, to make abundant offerings on great festivals or idols' birth-days, as hongs do. **khai-sîn-hok**, to lay out the expenses for such feasts. **pn̄g-sîn tsok-hok**, to have a good feast on the occasion of making offerings to an idol. **tsok-ui tsok-hok**, to have a proud haughty manner (v. ui).

chiok-hok, to pray for blessings on another. **thok-hok**, I enjoy good fortune by your favour or influence (a polite phrase).

hok-sîn, the god of the ground; the guardian spirit of graves. **hok-tek chèng-sîn**, id. **hok-tek-iâ**, id. **hok-tē**, a good grave. **hok-tē, hok-jîn ku**, fortunate persons get fortunate graves. **hok-jîn ku-hok-tē**, id.

ngó͘-hok, the five blessings; all sorts of good fortune and happiness; variously enumerated, in Amoy generally, "hù-kùi tsâi-tsú-siū," wealth, honour, talent, posterity, and long life. **ngó͘-hok lîm-bûn**, may all prosperity come to this house. **hok-lòk**, good fortune and official rank (salary). **hok-lòk-siū saⁿ-jī-tsn̂g**, good fortune, official salary, and long life, all complete. **hok-lòk-siū-tsoân**, id.

hō-hok, calamities and good fortune. **tâng-hō-hok**, joined in fortune (good or bad), whatever may come. **hok bû-song-chì, hō put-tan-hêng**, happy events do not come in pairs, but calamities never go singly.

hok tsū-thien-lâi, good fortune comes from Heaven's appointment. **thien-sù pêng-an hok**, Heaven bestows peace and good fortune. **thien-koan sù-hok**, the idol "thien-koan" gives good fortune, as on 1.15. **iók-kiû thien-siōng-hok, su-tiám hút-chiên teng**, if you wish blessings from Heaven light lamps before Buddhas.

hok-kièn, Fuh-kien province. **hok-chiu**, Fuh-chau. **hok-chiu-mn̂g**, an outer-door close to the inner, made with bars in the upper half and close boards in the lower half. **hok-géng**, large dragon's-eye fruit. **hok-oân**, dried do. **hok-oân-bah**, do. dried without stones or skin. **hok-lèk**, green cloth from Fuh-chau. **hok-âng**, very bright red cloth from Fuh-chau. **hok-chhiaⁿ**, Fuh-tsing, between Fuh-chau and Hing-hwa. **hok-lêng**, Fuh-ning-foo.

hók (R. id.) **bâi-hók**, to lie in ambush. **hók-peng**, soldiers in ambush.

hók-hi, Fuh-he or Fuh-hi, an ancient emperor before the historic period.

hók — **téng-hók**, the lintel of a door or window. **ē-hók**, the lower cross-timber of the frame of a door (or window), on which the threshold (hē-tēng) is laid down. **mn̂g-hók**, upper or lower cross-timber of door-frame. **thang-á-hók**, do. of window-frame. **chit-ki-hók**, one of them ready to be fitted into the other timbers to make the frame.

hók (R. id.), dress; (relationship); mourning-dress; to submit or obey; (to subdue); to swallow, as a drug.

hók-sāi, to serve; to worship. **kèng-hók**, to reverence and obey. **sìn-hók** (R.), to believe and submit or obey. **sūn-hók**, to submit; to make submission. **hui-hók**, to make submission, as a rebel or enemy. **hâng-hók**, to subdue; to make submission, as a rebel or enemy. **hâng-hók tī-i**, make submission to him. **jīn-hók**, to own one's self beaten or inferior. **m̄-jīn-hók**, will not own himself beaten. **giâ-kang kap-á-tsoâ, sam put-hók**, the centipede, the frog, and the snake, each not afraid of the other; said of three persons not agreeing well (frog said not to fear the centipede, nor the centipede the snake, and yet the snake eats the frog).

hók-tsōe (R.), to confess guilt.

put-hók tsúi-thó, the climate not agreeing with one.

hók-ióh, to take medicine. **hók-tók**, to take poison. **hók-tók--sí**, to poison one's self.

i-hók, dress; clothes. **hók-sek**, id. (s. next word). **hók-chè**, form of dress prescribed by the dynasty (v. chè). **tiâu-hók**, court dress. **kong-hók**, official dress or uniform of mandarin, worn on ceremonial occasions. **lé-hók**, ceremonial dress. **piēn-hók**, undress (not in uniform), as of an official. **sò-hók**, plain dress, as of man at end of mourning with no mourning on, but yet nothing gaudy or ornamental. **kiet-hók**, ordinary dress, as opposed to mourning. **hì-hók**, actor's dresses. **ká-lé-hók**, dress for puppets.

pièn-hók, to put on mourning. **ū-hók**, to wear mourning, as for a relative sufficiently near. **hiong-hók**, mourning-dress. **hà-hók**, id. **song-hók**, deep mourning. **moâⁿ-hók**, sackcloth dress of deepest mourning, as of sons at funeral. **tōe-á-hók**, a sort of mourning for a near relative. **ki-liên-hók**, one year's mourning, as for a brother. **tám-hók**, mourning worn three months after the regular three years (v. tám). **khí-hók**, to begin the rites of "khiā hà" for the dead. **sêng-hók**, to put on deep mourning either at first, or on occasion of these rites. **khoat-hók**, to fulfil the period of mourning.

ngó-hók, the five degrees of relationship for which mourning is worn (only of the same surname, and does not include sisters). **ngó-hók-lāi**, related in the direct line within five generations. **ngó-hók-goā**, only a distant relative, for whom mourning is not worn.

hók [R. hō, to protect]. **hók-sek**, ornaments for the knees (s. dress). **hók-chhip** (C.), = C. hòh-chhip, id.

hók (R. id.) **pau-hók**, a bundle of clothes or other small things tied up in a napkin or cloth. **pau-hók-kun**, a cloth folded round clothes, &c.

hók (R. id.) **thó-hók**, China root (Smilax China) used for scurvy, &c. **hók-lêng**, id. (v. lêng). **hók-sîn**, China root having woody fibre in the middle of the tuber.

hók [R. to repeat; to give back; cf. hok], to obtain again, as an office. **hók--khí-lâi**, id. **hók i-ê-koaⁿ**, recovers his office. **hók koaⁿ-chit**, id. **hók-tò**, to recover what is lost (as in war) or taken away unjustly. **hók-tò-tńg**, id. **chit-sì-lâng bōe-hók-tò-tńg**, can never recover it all his life, as good name ruined by some scandalous crime, or as fortune hopelessly ruined. **khek-hók**, to be recovered, as a city from rebels, or as lands or houses from those who had taken unjust possession.

hong (R. id.), (Cn. hoang, in strictly and originally colloquial phrases, but "hong" in those adopted from the literary style), wind; (rumour); usages; gay; dissipated.

hong-siok, customs; habits (v. siok). **hong-lē**, a custom. **hong-thó jîn-chêng**, customs of place and character of people. **hong-khì**, habits or present character of the people in a place (not of such long standing as "hong-siok"), *e.g.* custom of opium-smoking. **ím-hong**, licentious customs, as of a place. **khó-koan-hong**, to examine the literati of a place not a Foo or Hien. **bûn-hong**, literary character of a place (v. bûn, "literary"). **ui-hong**, majestic appearance (v. ui). **sit-hong**, to lose prestige. **kó-hong**, virtuous and kind. **mn̂g-hong**, reputation of a family. **ke-hong**, id. **pē-bú ke-hong**, reputation of parents.

hong-siaⁿ, rumour, report. **thàu-hong**, to give secret information. **lāu-hong**, to let out a secret. **bûn-hong sòng-tám**, courage failed at hearing it.

khiā-hong, to keep watch so as to give timely warning, as a sentinel (*e.g.* on a hill or outside the door) set by conspirators or others doing some illegal or secret action, *e.g.* some work of cruelty, plunder, or lust. **sûn-hong**, a sort of military policeman (v. sûn).

hong-hoa, dissipation; vanity and low pleasure; wanton. **hong-so**, constantly rambling about, as for low pleasures. **hong-liû**, dissipated, as a fast young fellow (v. liû), (s. inflammation). **liàh-hong jip-iáⁿ**, to pursue empty shadows and vanities.

hong-chhe (C. kong-chhɛ), a paper kite. **hong chhe** (C. hong chhoe), the wind blows. **hong-mn̂g**, the touch-hole of a gun (s. seal). **hong-kó**, fanners. **hong-kūi**, a sort of bellows (v. kūi); also (C.), fanners. **hong-ú-chiam**, a barometer. **hong-chhang**, a sort of leek, used for colds.

pîn-hong, a fixed wooden screen or partition (= tn̂g-tsàh) across the central hall of a house. **khan-hong**, a sort of boat a little larger than an ordinary rowing-boat, but not so large as a small junk; also, to work Chinese bellows.

hong-súi, a grave, esp. as regards good luck (v. súi). **hong-sai**, image of a lion and rider, put on roofs to ward off bad luck. **hong-soah**, deadly influence of inauspicious wind on a house or grave. **hong-soàⁿ**, an unhealthy influence (like palsy) caused by demons (v. soàⁿ). **hong-chhùi**, very small red eruption (s. seal). **hong-hé**, wind and fire; an inflammatory or feverish tendency (v. hé). **àu-hong**, a tainted smell.

siong-hong, to have a cold. **kám-hong**, id. (v. kám). **ùi-hong**, feeling somewhat shivering and unwell; feeling afraid of a draught. **ín-hong**, to cause cold or rheumatism, as fat food; to cause a draught, as a wind-sail (v. ín). **sahⁿ-hong**, to be slightly out of sorts (less than "kám-hong"), supposed to be caused by a draught. **koàn-hong**, to blow into (as into a bag), to inflate it; to make ill by the influence of wind. **koài-**

hong, a strange sudden violent wind. **khit-koài-hong phah,** to have an incurable palsy, that appears on the face. **kúi-á-hong,** a sudden strange strong gust or squall. **khit-kúi-á-hong phah--tio̍h,** may the demons strike you with a destructive wind! **tiù^{n}-hong,** full of wind, as a sail, or as belly after eating beans. **phòng-hong,** the belly swollen. **tiòng-hong put-gú,** a disease that at once causes dumbness, and is very speedily fatal. **hong-thâm pè-sim,** a fit of dull madness (v. thâm).

hong-hē, wind and rain (v. hē). **hong-jit,** wind and sun. **hó-hong-jit,** fine weather. **hong-jit chin-hó,** weather very good. **khit-hong-jit phak,** weather-beaten and sun-burnt. **hong-hân sú-sip,** wind, cold, heat, and damp. **hong-pêng lōng-chēng,** wind and waves still. **tn̄g-poà^{n}-tih-hong,** not the least wind or rain. **tn̄g poà^{n}-tiám-hong,** id. **hong chī^{n},** wind died away; become calm. **tiām-hong,** no wind. **chheng-hong,** sky clearing with wind, as after rain. **tsòe-hong,** there is wind. **hong thàu,** the wind very strong (v. thàu). **hong-éng,** winds and waves (v. éng). **hong soà-soà, tsúi toā-toā** (T.), said of a man on whom no reliance or confidence can be placed.

hong-sî, a squall. **hong-tsūn,** id. **chit-tsūn-hong,** id. **chhú-bé-hong,** a terrible squall or whirlwind. **kông-hong,** a violent wind. **pò-thâu-hong,** a strong north-east wind. **lo̍h-soa^{n}-hong,** a squall from the hills. **hong-thai,** a typhoon. **chhun-hong,** spring winds (v. chhun). **chhiu-hong,** autumn wind, esp. dry north-east wind without rain (s. abundant).

hong-bīn, direction of the wind; the direction from which the wind comes. **bô-hong-bīn,** a wind that cannot be used for the course. **pì^{n}-hong-bīn,** to change from friendliness to anger or displeasure. **tńg-hong-bīn,** wind changing; to change from anger to friendliness. **oát-hong-bīn,** wind changing; veering about. **hong-thâu,** the part from which the wind comes. **phi-hong-thâu,** to hang up to dry in the wind, as washed clothes. **khùn-hong-thâu,** to sleep in a draught. **hong-bé,** the direction towards which the wind blows; the lee side of a vessel.

ka-chiah-āu-hong, wind aft. **téng-sì-hong,** id. **ē-sì-hong,** a head wind. **ge̍k-hong,** against the wind; a head wind. **tu-hong,** to go against the wind. **sūn-hong,** favourable wind (v. sūn). **chiap-hong,** to give a feast to a friend on his return from a voyage. **hoān-hong,** to meet with a heavy gale. **tsûn khit-hong phah,** driven out of course by violent wind. **khau-hong,** to tack. **sái-hong,** to sail by wind. **chīn-hong-sái,** to sail as near the wind as possible with sails full. **tak-hong,** to lay to. **bōe-chia̍h--tio̍h hong,** so near the wind as hardly to move.

pàng-hong, to pass wind; to make threats against a man to third parties, so that he may hear of it and be frightened (v. pàng). **thong-hong,** having free circulation of air. **khe-hong,** to make a whistling sound, as by flying or blowing. **hong-hong-kiò,** sound in the ears, as of wind, *e.g.* when covered by the hand. **kien-hong,** hardened by the wind, or by exposure to the air. **sau-hong,** cracked by drought, as wood. **jia-hong,** to keep off the wind; the boards at back and ends of a bed (v. jia). **tsáh-hong,** to ward off wind. **siám-hong,** to avoid the wind. **tô-hong,** do., as vessel running into harbour. **iėt-hong,** to make wind by fanning. **iā^{n}-hong,** waved or agitated by the wind. **chhiū-bé iô-hong,** top of the tree shaken by the wind (v. iô).

hong [R. to roast or toast, = col. hang]. **hong-lô** (esp. T.), = hang-lô, a small portable earthen stove.

hong (R. id.), inflammatory, rheumatic, venereal, and some other affections. **tio̍h-hong,** to have rheumatic or venereal pains; but (C.) only venereal. **hong-to̍k,** sores arising from venereal or rheumatic causes (v. to̍k).

bâ-hong, leprosy. **hong-tien,** mad. **hong-tsūn,** convulsions, as in a child (s. wind). **kín-keng-hong,** sudden convulsions of children (v. keng). **bān-pî-hong,** a very dangerous disease of children—dull, weak, exhausted, and very sleepy, with belly somewhat distended. **hong-ba̍k,** inflamed eye. **hong-lâu,** a sort of swelling that does not suppurate, and readily goes away (s. wind). **hoat-chiú-hong,** to have a small red transient eruption, from the use of liquor. **tio̍h hong-chhoá^{n},** to have a sort of itching eruption.

hong thià^{n}, rheumatic pains. **hong-khì,** a sort of rheumatic affection (s. wind). **hong-khì thià^{n},** id. **lio̍h-lio̍h-á hong-khì,** having a slight rheumatic pain. **thâu hong,** rheumatic pains in head. **chhiú hong,** do. in hand or arm. **kha hong,** do. in leg. **khì-hong,** to remove rheumatic pains.

hông-hong, a medicine (Libanotis?) used for removing inflammation and feverishness. **hông-hong siên-thòe,** this drug along with the shells of cicadas.

ge̍h-lāi-hong, a female's illness after delivery. **hā-siau-hong,** spermatorrhœa, gonorrhœa, and such diseases. **sek-hong,** a very severe venereal disease. **tsa-bó-hong,** id. **chhng-hong,** syphilis, in some forms. **ún-hong,** a sort of venereal disease. **chiū^{n}-bé-hong,** a sort that comes on, and is often fatal in the very act. **lo̍h-bé-hong,** a sudden fatal sort just after the act.

hong [R. good-looking]. **hong-tsu,** appearance of the face, as to health (v. tsu). **hong-sîn,** expression of countenance (s. seal). **phah--lâng bô-hong-sîn,** to put a man to shame before others (v. sîn).

hong [R. abundant]. **hâm-hong,** the reign of Hien-fung. **hong-sēng,** very abundant. **ngó-kok hong-sēng,** harvest very abundant; grain very plentiful. **ngó-kok hong-teng,** id.

phah-chhiu-hong, to ask money from friends for one's self.

hong [R. the point of a weapon]. **.sien-hong,** a military officer sent on before a higher mandarin to make preparations for him.

hong [R. a mountain peak]. **ngô-hong** (R.), a sort of academy or college at Fuh-chau.

hong [R. square, a region, a plan, just then = col. hng, pang]. **sù-hong,** square; the four regions; everywhere. **sù-hong pat-ta̍t,** in all places; everywhere. **sù-hong khah-tn̄g,** rectangular, but not quite square. **sù-hong khah-lò,** id. **toan-hong sù-chèng,** all correct and proper, as conduct. **toan-hong sì-chià^{n},** id.; well arranged, as a thing set straight and even, not awry or uneven.

hong-chí, a square bit of wood with which mandarins strike the table on the tribunal (v. chí, "a son"). **hong-khang** (r.), port-holes. **hong-thien-kek,** a sort of halbert. **ngó-hong-kî,** small triangular flags of five colours.

hong-biēn, liberal in gifts, rewards, &c., and fond of appearing so (v. biēn). **tāi-hong,** generous and liberal in money matters; large, fat, and well-formed, as man or child. siⁿ-tsōe tāi-hong, naturally large, fat, and well-formed.

se-hong, the western paradise (Buddhist). tē-hong, = tōe-hng, a place; a region (v. tē). iû-hong hê-siūⁿ, a travelling Buddhist priest (v. iû).

hong-hoat, a plan; a method or means. pí-hong, a comparison; for example. tan-hong tȯk-bī, a medicine that is taken alone, without any mixture with other drugs.

hong-chhâi-chiah-lâi (R.), just arrived.

hong (T.), = A. sièn, to slap on the face. (The following phrases are A.) goá hong--chit-ē hē--lí, I give you a slap on the face! (said to a child). chhùi goá-kā-lí-hong, I give you a slap on the face! chhùi goá kā--lí hong--lȯh-khì, id. chhùi-phóe siang-pêng-hong, I give you a slap on each cheek! [perhaps the next word, "to seal up"].

hong (R. id.), to seal or paste up, as a letter, box or small parcel; to seal by affixing papers, as the house of a criminal, or as boats temporarily impressed by the government for transports; classifier of letters and small parcels; to appoint to rank or office, as the emperor does; to confer a title on a god or spirit or deceased man, as emperor does; to invest a tributary sovereign or feudal inferior.

hong-khò, honorary titles conferred on the wife or ancestor of a high mandarin. khò-hong, id. thek-hong, specially appointed (by emperor) to posthumous honour. hong-sîn-toān, a book of ancient fabulous stories and myths, esp. of early part of the Chow dynasty; much used by the (kóng-kó) men who read stories publicly; (said of any groundless absurd story); one who talks at random; a fickle changeable man. kóng hong-sîn, to tell lies and baseless stories.

phi-hong, a sort of cape worn by mandarin ladies. hong-phiau, a small paper with the name of the shop, or of the maker, pasted or wrapped round small articles sold (v. phiau).

pau-hong, to paste or seal up carefully, as a parcel, or as a letter inclosing others; or as articles sold in the package without being opened. goá-bō pau-hong, I sold it to you open, not sealed up; I am not answerable for its quality, and will not now take it back. pau-hong bóe-bōe, to buy in a package or by sample, without examination. goân-hong put-tōng, the goods in the original package unopened. chit-hong-gûn, a roll of dollars rolled up in paper. giàm-hong, to examine a package of government money (on the way) to see if the seal be unbroken.

hong-mn̂g, to close a door by an official stamped red paper (s. wind). hong-tiâu (Cn. T. pang-tiâu), an official red paper pasted on a door or vessel when confiscated or temporarily taken possession of for government purposes. hong-ìn, to close the (seals of the) public offices in the holidays. hong-chhùi, edges of paper where pasted together (s. wind). hong-phoe, to paste up a letter; to close a letter.

hong [R. fragrant, = col. phang]. liû-hong pek-sè, to leave a fragrant memory for a hundred generations. hong-kaⁿ (Cn.), a sort of bitter orange.

hong [R. id., = col. hng], (Cn. sometimes "hoang"), waste; fabulous. hong-hòe, laid waste; ruined; desolate; uncultivated, as fields. hong-soaⁿ khòng-iá, a wilderness of lonely mountains.

hong-pòng, to raise or spread groundless reports, as of the spread of rebellion, &c. hong-tông, fabulous stories; fabulous (v. tông, Tang dynasty).

hong [perhaps two words]. sim-koaⁿ hong, heart dissipated and confused by pleasure, as a young person.

pìⁿ-hong, become idle and fond of plays and low vile pleasures, as boy or lad about sixteen. pìⁿ-khi-hong, id. kūn-lâi pìⁿ-hong, lately grown idle, truant, or ill-behaved, as boy.

gû teh-hong, a bull in an excited state for the cow.

hong [R. the bee, = col. phang]. hong-gí sek kun-sin (R.), bees and ants know the relation of kings and ministers.

hong — hong-hàm, exaggerated language.

hong [next word?]. hong-hiau, dangerous and unlucky, as the state of matters.

hong [R. hiong, ill-omened, unlucky]. hong-hām, very great and severe, as a calamity to person or place. hong-sîn ok-soah, malicious demons.

hong [cf. hiong, "hurried"]. hong-kông, = hiong-kông, very hasty and urgent in manner (v. hiong).

hông [R. to fear, = col. hiâⁿ]. chhong-hông, hurried, as with great press of business. chhong-hông-tsáu, to rush on in a great hurry. hông-hông bông-bông, carelessly; hurriedly.

hông-khióng (R.), lest; for fear that —.

hông [R. the fosse or moat outside a wall]. sêng-hông-iâ, the tutelary god of a city or fort; he has dominion in the spirit-world over all the spirits of the dead of the Foo or Hien, just equal to the mandarins over the living. tø-sêng-hông, the guardian spirit of the capital, having rank like that of the emperor over all the others. sêng-hông-biāu, temple of the tutelary god of the city. sêng-hông-biō, id. kò-sêng-hông, to give in to the Tauist priests a written complaint against oppressors, to be read and burned before sêng-hông-iâ. khùn-sêng-hông, to sleep in his temple so as to get dreams proving guilt, as mandarins sometimes make an accused man do, and judge him next morning in the temple. kúi bong sêng-hông-iâ ê-thâu, will a weak man dare to meddle with a powerful man!

hông (R. id.), imperial. hông-siōng, the emperor. hông-tè, id. kóng-thiⁿ, seh hông-tè, to talk idly about all sorts of strange things. hông-hō, the empress (v. hō). hông-hui, imperial concubine. hông-chhin, imperial relatives. hông-tsú (R.), son of emperor. hông-thài-tsú, heir-apparent. hông-kiong, imperial palace (residence). hông-un, imperial favour.

sam-hông, the three ancient (mythical) emperors, hȯk-hi, sîn-lông, and n̂g-tè. giȯk-hông, the idol Yuh-hwang Shang-ti. giȯk-hông siōng-tè, id., he was a man of the Hàn dynasty, of the surname Tiuⁿ. hông-thien hō-thó, the sovereign powers Heaven and Earth.

hông [R. vast, great, and wide, as a flood]. hông-hok (R.), great happiness. hông-súi (R.), the Chinese flood in the time of the great Yu (ú).

hông [R. a wild goose, vast]. hông-gān, a large sea-bird (v. gān).

hông [R. vast; far-reaching, as sound]. khoan-hông tāi-liōng, magnanimous; generous; liberal. khoan-hông tē-liōng, id.

hông [R. the female phœnix]. hōng-hông, the phœnix.

hông [R. a medicinal plant; luxuriant, as herbage]. hông-lâi-tó, the dwelling of the genii (sien), (v. lâi).

hông [last word ?]. **káu-kā-hông**, a plant (like a dock) used for curing the bite of a dog. **toā-teng-hông**, plant used for reducing inflammation. **koe-chih-hông**, a plant with a leaf like a bird's tongue. **chhú-bé-hông**, a sort shaped like a rat's tail. **kāu-boàh-hông** (C.), a medicinal plant.

hông [R. yellow, = col. ńg], sulphur. **liû-hông**, sulphur. **siau-hông**, nitre and sulphur. **tâng-hông**, verdigris on the article. **chhiū**ⁿ **tâng-hông**, to get covered with verdigris. **hîn-hông**, a yellow drug used on 5.5, mixed with wine or water, for expelling demons from houses; realgar. **hîn-hông-chiú**, do. mixed in wine. **tan-hông**, a reddish-yellow paint (an oxide of lead ?), (s. red).

tāi-hông, rhubarb (medicinal).

giû-hông, cow bezoar; biliary calculus of the cow. **chhoan-hông**, inferior bezoar from Sze-chuen, not from the cow.

hông-hun, twilight. **hông-tsoân**, the invisible world (v. tsoân). **hông-kim**, jars holding old bones collected from graves.

hông-hô, the Yellow River (the Hwang-ho). **hông-hô têng-chheng**, when the Yellow River grows clear (v. têng).

hông [R. red, = col. âng]. **áu-hông**, to vomit blood. **hông-tan**, red-lead. **tan-hông**, red paper, such as is used for making visiting cards (s. yellow). **hông-phièn-ko**, a confection. **boán-tông-hông**, a hanging candelabrum with many lamps.

it-tiōng-hông, the hollyhock (lit. ten feet long of red). **it-tōng-hông**, id. **chhien-jit-hông**, a sort of everlasting flower.

chhí pėk, tûn hông, teeth white and lips red (said of a beauty).

hông — **hoat-hông**, burning with rage (s. swollen). **hoat-kiáu-hông**, mad upon gambling; much excited in gambling (esp. to win what has been lost), so that he will not stop though urged to stop.

hông [R. swollen]. **hoat-hông**, swollen, as with a poisonous bite or bite of dog, or from inflammation (s. last word). **hoat-tsúi-hông**, to become inflamed, as a wound from the application of cold water. **thè-hông**, to reduce inflammation or swelling.

hông-thán, jaundice, as in children.

hông (R. id.) **hông-thiông** (R.), a locust.

hông [R. to sew, = col. pâng, phāng]. **chhâi-hông**, a tailor. **tsâi-hông** (Cn.), id.

hông [R. to meet with]. **siong-hông** (r.), to meet with, as a person (s. guard). **hēng-gū siong-hông** (R.), happily met.

hán-hông, rarely met with indeed! (ironical), (v. hán).

hông [R. to guard against]. **tî-hông**, to be on one's guard against; to guard against. **thê-hông**, id. **hông-chhát**, to be guarding against thieves, robbers, rebels, &c. **hông-tė́**, to guard an important place when war or rebellion is near. **hông-hân** (R.), to take great care of (as children or nephews), that they may not become bad (v. hân). **koan-hông**, to be on one's watch, and guard a house against loss or thieves; to watch that no suspicious characters come in; also, the seal of an oblong form used by some mandarins, as the Tau-tai and Governor-general.

hái-hông, the Hai-fang, or assistant mandarin of a Foo, usually stationed at some important place, *e.g.* at Amoy. **sìn-hông**, station of a small military officer. **tsoan-hông**, a petty officer who guards a city gate; he also assists the Show-pei (siú-pī) in managing the whole division (iâⁿ) of the army. **tsoan-hông-thia**ⁿ, id. **tsoan-hông-sìn**, id.

hông-hong, a medicine (v. hong, rheumatism).

àn-kiàm siong-hông, mutually on the watch against each other (lit. hands on swords). **àm-kiàm siong-hông**, id. **ka-chėk lân-hông**, it is hard to guard against a thief within the household. **chek-kok hông-ki**, to gather up corn against time of famine.

hông — **hông-hiám**, dangerous, as disease, or as state of matters.

hông (contracted from hō-lâng). **hông-phah**, to be struck or beaten. **hông-hiâm**, to be found fault with.

hông [R. hóng, shining, splendid]. **put-chí-hông**, very gaudy.

hông [R. bōng, dark, = col. phông]. **àm-hông**, too dark, as house or room; giving very little light, as lamp, &c.

hóng (R. id.) **hóng-hut**, similar (v. hut, "similar").

hóng (R. id.) **hóng-hut**, confused and frightened (v. hut).

hóng (C.) **hóng-hiah**ⁿ, = A. hō-hiahⁿ, bustled; flurried.

hóng (R. id.), to imitate or copy, as a map, picture, or style of writing; to draw or paint a likeness. **hóng lâng--ê pit-chek**, to imitate a man's writing, especially for an exercise in writing. **hóng lâng--ê jī-thé**, id. **hóng lâng--ê chhiú-pit**, id.

hóng [R. hòng, = hóng, to meet with, the more], what a man meets with; circumstances of a man or state of an affair. **hó-kéng-hóng**, good fortune; prosperous state of matters. **phái**ⁿ**-kéng-hóng**, bad fortune.

hóng [R. shining, splendid], (esp. Cn. T.), gaudy, showy, or splendid, as dress, &c. **chhēng khah-hóng**, finely dressed. **sin-chhēng hóng-hóng**, id. **khoà**ⁿ**-hóng**, to gaze on beautiful things, as pictures, curiosities, or plants set out only to be looked at.

chhut-hóng, to have small-pox.

hóng [R. random, false]. **tám-hóng**, to take a thing or money, pretending that the owner has commissioned us to borrow or get it.

hóng [R. to inquire, to investigate]. **hóng-chhat**, to investigate officially and somewhat secretly. **àm-hóng**, to make secret official search, as incognito, or by confidential secret messengers. **tsa-hóng**, to investigate officially, as constables or tepo. **chhip-hóng** (R.), to search secretly for a criminal, as men sent to seize him.

hòng [R. hòng, = hóng, to meet with, the more]. **hô-hòng**, how much the more; so much the more; all the more. **hòng-kiam**, do., when the original idea has something added to it.

hòng [R. to let loose, to set free, = col. pàng]. **hòng-hòng**, free from care; too careless and thoughtless; taking things too easy. **pàng-hòng-hòng**, id. **khah-hòng**, id. **sim tioh-pàng khah-hòng**, don't be so anxious about the matter. **hòng-hòng chhàng-chhàng** (C.), incautious; careless. **hòng-sim**, free from anxiety. **sim hòng**, heart full of bad desires. **sim-koa**ⁿ **hòng**, heart full of vanity; given to carelessness and pleasure. **hòng-tōng**, loose and irregular in conduct. **hòng-tá**ⁿ, utterly without fear of consequences; often foolhardy. **hòng-chhiòng**,

20

giving loose to one's passions or desires; loose and irregular in behaviour; to allow inferiors to behave ill. **hòng-sù**, disrespectful; impertinent.

hòng-kò, to open the (mandarin's) office for receiving accusations (v. kò). **hòng-seng**, to save the life of an animal for Buddhist merit. **hòng-seng-tî**, a pond in temples, for keeping fish alive. **it-giân hòng-chhut, sù-má lân-tui**, four horses cannot catch a word once spoken. **chhiá**ⁿ**-hòng-hā**, just leave that matter alone for the present, till more pressing matters are first arranged.

hōng [R. official salary]. **hōng-lòk**, salary of officials. **hoát-hōng**, to mulct of his salary.

hōng — **hoat-hōng**, face flushed, as with rapid walking or with illness; to blush. **hōng-hōng-jiėt**, very hot, as from fever or inflammation, or from heat. **jiėt hōng-hōng**, id. **sio-hōng-hōng**, id.

hōng [R. loud sound of voices]. **hōng-hōng-kiò**, buzzing sound, as of a crowd, or of a steamer, or as a ringing sound in the ears. **hōng-hōng-háu**, id.

hōng [R. kiōng, together, = col. kāng], to stir up or encourage another to do something he is not quite sure about. **tàu-hōng**, id. **hōng-hɛh**ⁿ, several men inciting each other to act (v. hɛh). **hōng-hōng hɛh**ⁿ**-hɛh**ⁿ, to do on the spur of the moment. **tāi-ke hōng--ê**, done in common by several men, as a play thus subscribed for.

hōng (R. id.), the phœnix. **hōng-hông**, do.; properly the male and female phœnixes. **hōng-hông tò-chhú**, may the phœnix come here (words pasted up at marriages). **loân-hōng**, male and female phœnixes. **loân-hōng siong-sûi**, a pair of phœnixes going together (said of a married couple).

lêng-chhia hōng-lién, imperial carriage and sedan. **hōng-koa**ⁿ, ornamental head-dress worn by mandarin ladies and at marriages (v. koaⁿ). **hōng-koan hê-kòe** (C.), sort of head-dress for females at marriages (v. koan). **hōng-kè** (C. kòe), id.

kim-hōng, the balsam (flower). **kim-hōng-hoe**, id. **kim-hōng-chí**, = kip-sèng-chí, its seed. **hōng-bé-chháu**, the fern. **hōng-bé-nî**ⁿ, fern roots, medicinal.

hōng [R. to receive or present respectfully with both hands, to reverence, = col. phóng, phâng]. **kèng-hōng**, to worship; to reverence by making offerings to. **hōng-sêng**, to treat with great respect and attention and politeness, as distinguished visitors or superiors; sometimes with flattery. **hōng-chí**, to receive imperial commands; sometimes said in joke, "I have got my orders." **hōng-bēng**, to receive orders. **hōng-chhe**, to be sent by a superior. **hōng-kìm**, to receive an interdict from a superior. **hōng-kàu**, Roman Catholic phrase for entering the church.

hop (C.), (= A. ngauh, hauhⁿ), to catch in the mouth, as a dog; to take money very covetously. **hop-lop chiȧh-liȧh--khì**, to take a quantity of money avariciously and improperly.

hu [R. a man, a male, husband, = col. pơ]. **kang-hu**, work. **kang-hu-pī**ⁿ, consumption. **kang-hu-lâng**, an artisan; a journeyman; a skilled workman. **khah-kang-hu**, of very fine or skilful workmanship. **kang-hu-tê**, Congou tea. **siōng kang-hu**, best Congou. **tiong-kang-hu**, medium quality of Congou. **ū-kang, chiū ū-hu**, if there be work there will be wages. **ū-kang, tȧt--lí ū-hu**, I must have my wages for each day's work.

hu-jîn, the wife of a mandarin like the Tau-tai. **tsun-hu-jîn**, your wife (polite phrase). **tek-hu-jîn**, a wicker-work frame like a large pillow, for sleeping cool with the arms stretched out on it. **chî**ⁿ**-kháu hu-jîn**, the goddess of the eaves. **hu-jîn-má**, the goddess of childbirth. **lîm-súi hu-jîn**, do. in temple of Sêng-hông-iā. **tî-thâu hu-jîn** (T.), id.

bú-hu, phrase used in disparagement of a military mandarin. **iông-hu siȯk-tsú**, a common rough-like illiterate man. **kan-hu**, an adulterer.

tiōng-hu, husband (v. tiōng). **chí-hu**, elder sister's husband. **chiá-hu**, id. **chiáu-hu**, id. **bē-hu**, younger sister's husband. **māi**ⁿ**-hu** (C.), id. **hu-hū**, husband and wife (v. hū). **hu-chhe**, id. (v. chhe). **hu-chhoe**, id. **liėt-lú put-kà jī-hu**, a chaste widow does not marry a second husband. **chio-hu ióng-tsú**, to marry a second husband to take care of the children. **chio-hu ióng-tsú, sè chhut bû-nāi**ⁿ, do., because she has no other resource.

koán-hu, a man who keeps a cook-shop, and supplies feasts to order. **tsúi-hu**, water-carrier for a yamun or examination hall. **chhia-hu**, driver of a carriage. **koa**ⁿ**-hu**, mandarin's chair-bearers. **kiō-hu**, a chair-bearer; a chair-coolie (addressed as "kong-siā"). **hu-kè**, pay of mandarin's chair-coolies. **sió-hu**, common chair-coolies. **sa**ⁿ**-miā**ⁿ**-hu**, three chair-coolies, as for one chair. **hu-thâu**, man who lets out sedan chairs; also, man who has charge of all the chair-coolies and porters when a mandarin's family is removing. **ah-hu**, overseer of many coolies carrying loads or sedans. **kioh-hu**, a coolie; a porter. **thiau-hu**, id. **ki**ⁿ**-hu**, a public watchman who watches the streets.

hu [R. hiu, to remove, to divorce]. **hu-jîn-lí**, a sort of plum, very good to eat.

hu (R. id.), (C. hi; Cn. hü), empty; hollow; false; vain. **hu-sit**, empty or solid; false or true. **hu-jī** (R.), a particle, in grammar.

khiam-hu, humble, humble-minded. **hu-sim** (R.), id.

khang-hu, empty, vain, hollow. **pak-lāi khang-hu**, hungry; illiterate; internally weak, as a consumptive man, or sick man without appetite. **tơ-lāi khang-hu**, illiterate; feeling weak or giddy with hunger, or as a convalescent; hungry.

lōe-hu, a dangerous disease, when the patient is very weak though he looks fat, and has large abdomen. **hu-tóe**, naturally of a weak constitution. **hu-lám**, weak and emaciated; in weak health. **hu-hé**, slightly feverish. **hu-jiėt**, typhus or typhoid fevers. **hu-sún**, consumption. **hu-lô ê-chèng**, id. **hu-lô kó-kek**, three (or four) very dangerous chronic diseases. **hu-lô kó-keh**, id.

hu-hoa, vanity; foolish expenditure; dissipation. **hu-hùi**, to waste, as money; lavish expenditure.

hu-hu hoàn-hoàn, utterly false, as a story. **hu-sû**, false, as words. **hu-hê** (R.), false and empty, as the talk of a boaster. **hü-hiô** (Cn.), id. **it hu, pek hu**, one part being proved false, it is evidently all false (lit. the hundred are false).

hu [R. hui, lime, ashes, dust, = col. he], ashes; things broken down to powder; decayed or worm-eaten and falling into powder; growing soft and bad, as meat kept too long. **hu-hu**, reduced to ashes, decayed and turning to powder. **hu-hu--khì**, burned to ashes, or wasted to powder, &c. **sio-hu**, to burn to ashes.

tsng-á-hu, powdered bricks or tiles, used for scouring metal. **tsang-hu**, small broken down fibre of the "tsang" palm.

hé-hu, ashes in fine powder. **péh-chiú hé-hu**,

the ashes of a plant, used for sharpening knives, and for making rice white in pounding it. **hé-hu-sek**, light purplish gray, not so much red as "khė-hoe-sek."

kim-hu, ashes of the idolatrous paper that represents gold and silver. **chîⁿ-lê-hu**, id. **bóe chîⁿ-lê-hu**, to buy these ashes; pedlars who pretend to buy it, but really buy stolen and broken articles. **hiuⁿ-hu**, ashes of incense, used medicinally. **tsoá-hu**, ashes of paper. **jī-tsoá-hu**, ashes of written or printed paper.

hu (R. id.) **béh-hu**, wheat or barley parched and pounded small.

hu [R. skin]. **phê-hu**, skin and muscular flesh close under the skin; also, very shallow and scanty, said of information, instruction, essay, or other composition. **hó-phê-hu**, healthy condition of body, so that a wound heals well. **pháiⁿ-phê-hu**, unhealthy state of body, so that a wound is hard to heal.

hu, sound of a strong wind. **hong hu-hu-háu**, the wind howling. **hu-tu**, the sound of blowing a horn.

hu— **hu-hu-hu**, to rub gently, in a circular way, as a sore place on a child, in order to please him; sometimes also breathing on the place.

hu (R. id.), = hi, a market. **hu-chhī**, id. **hu-tiûⁿ**, market-place.

hu [R. sufficient]. **put-hu**, not enough. **chîⁿ-giàh put-hu**, money not sufficient. **khai-khong put-hu**, to embezzle and use up part of the money entrusted, so as to be unable to account for the whole.

hû [R. id. = col. phû]. **hû-iông-hoe**, the tree mallow; Hibiscus.

hû (T.), = A. hî, a fish (Cn. hû). **sûi-hû** (Cn.), = A. sûi-gû, the broad clasp that falls over the staple for a padlock.

hû [R. to help to rise; to assist, = col. phô], to lift up, as by supporting under the arms. **hû-khí hû-tó**, to assist in rising and lying down, as a sick or old man. **hû-chhah**, to support by holding up the arm-pits.

hû-tsō, to assist, as with funds. **hû-chhî**, to protect or assist, as the gods. **hû-tî** (C.), id. **hû-tsò**, to assist the sovereign, as a good mandarin.

hû-kiō, to hold the poles of a mandarin's sedan at the sides.

hû (R.), to fit together and correspond; a stamp or tally that fits to another; a written Tauist charm.

hû-háp, corresponding well, as evidence. **liên-māu put-hû**, his age and appearance do not correspond with the description.

tso-koaⁿ-hû, to litigate; to be engaged in a lawsuit; to be at law.

hû-chiù, written and spoken charms and incantations. **hû-hoat**, rites for using a charm. **hû-lēng**, the word "hû" written on a bit of green bamboo with a piece of red cloth at the top, used as a charm. **hû-tsúi**, water charmed by the ashes of a burned charm, blown out from the mouth of the Tauist priest.

thô-hû, charms made of peach leaves or branches. **pêng-an-hû**, a charm to cause good fortune. **sai-kong-hû**, a Tauist charm. **tek-hû**, a short peg of bamboo with a charm written on it and a bit of red cloth tied at the top, used as a charm. **chhiⁿ-tek-hû**, id. **an chhiⁿ-tek-hû**, to pin down this charm.

tèk-hû ê sù-chiá, spiritual messengers who carry the messages of priests to and from the gods and spirits.

ūi-hû, to write charms. **kat-hû**, to tie a charm in one's hair, on the queue. **kê-hû**, to paste up charms. **tah-hû**, id. **an-hû**, id.

hú [R. a department; the palace of an imperial prince], a department; a Foo; the prefect of a department; his office; the chief city of a department; (forms titles of several other officials).

sèng-hú, a clan. **sèng-hú tân**, my surname is Tân. **tāi-sèng-hú**, a large clan.

im-hú, the spiritual world; Hades. **tē-hú** (Cn.), id. **ông-hú**, the palace of a prince of the blood. **ngó-hú liók-pō**, the great offices of state at the metropolis.

koaⁿ-hú, mandarins in general; a mandarin. **chham-hú**, an officer like colonel or major-general, below "iû-kek," and above "chhien-tsóng." **iū-hú**, the officer of that rank who commands the right wing. **tiong-hú**, commander of the centre; (&c.) **tiong-kun-hú**, = toā-thiaⁿ-iâ, an idol (v. thiaⁿ).

ti-hú, the prefect of a department; the Foo mandarin. **hú-thài-iâ**, id. **hú-koaⁿ**, id. **hú-tsun** (R.), id. **toā-hú**, id. **pún-hú**, the prefect of *this* department. **hú-tō**, the prefect and the Tau-tai. **hú-koāiⁿ**, the Foo and Hien mandarins; the prefect and sub-prefect. **jī-hú**, assistant mandarin of a department, = hai-fang (hái-hông). **hun-hú**, do. or the following (sam-hú); the region placed under his special supervision. **sam-hú**, second assistant of the prefect, of smaller importance, *e.g.* at Chióh-bé and at Bé-hāng.

ē-chiu-hú, phrase used in speaking of Java, as opposed to Singapore. **chiang-chiu-hú**, the city of Chang-chew; the department of Chang-chew; the prefect of Chang-chew. **hú-hūn**, the department. **kè-hú**, to pass from one department to another. **hú-siâⁿ**, the Foo city. **chiūⁿ-hú**, to go to the Foo city. **hú-gê**, the yamun of the prefect. **hú-kháu**, the large space in front of his yamun. **hú-óh**, the academy or college of the department; the literary mandarin who is its principal or president.

hú [R. great; a particle used in polite designations]. **koán-hú**, experienced soldiers who wait as assistants at the military yamuns.

hú [R. the lower intestines]. **liók-hú**, the six lower intestines, the gall, the stomach, the bowels and the urinary organs, with the "chiau." **ngó-tsōng liók-hú**, the great internal organs. **hì-hú**, the lungs and the "hú." **hùi-hú**, id. **hì-hú tn̂g-tō**, the intestines in general. **kám-jip hùi-hú**, thankful to the bottom of the heart. **hì-hú ê-ōe**, words spoken from the bottom of the heart. **khoàⁿ--kìⁿ lí--ê hùi-hú**, to see your inmost feelings and desires.

hú [R. flesh prepared and dried, = col. pó]. **bah-hú**, meat (pork) boiled, dried, and reduced to fine fibres. **lók-hú**, stag's flesh prepared thus.

hú (R. id.), (Cn.), = A. bú. **hú-īⁿ**, = A. bú-īⁿ, the governor of one province. **hú-tâi**, id.

hú [R. to promise; a surname, = khó], (Cn. hú, C. hí). **èng-hú** (Cn.), to promise; to engage.

hù [R. hū, a teacher, = col. pò]. **thài-hù**, a very high rank at court; one of the highest ministers of state. **thài-tsú thài-hù**, tutor of heir-apparent.

hù [R. rich, = col. pù]. **pîn-hù**, poor and rich. **hù-kùi**, rich and honourable; very comfortable and happy (v. kùi). **hù-hō**, rich. **hù-jū**, id. **hù-ka**, a wealthy family. **hù-chiok**, wealthy (a. hand over). **kiap-hù tsè-pîn**, to plunder the rich and help the poor (by selling their booty cheap), as robbers and pirates say. sip-hûi, kiú hù; put-hù, tēng-sī siáu-phí-ku: of ten fat people, nine are wealthy; if not wealthy, certainly he has small hips!

hù [R. to announce a death]. **hù-im-thiap** (R.), a letter announcing a death to a near relative.

hù (R. id.), to arrive in good time; to be in good time for anything. **i lâi hù-hù**, he came in very good time. **m̄-hù**, too late. **bōe-hù**, id. (no use of trying). **bōe-tit-hù**, id. **hù-bô-tsûn**, arrived too late for the boat. **hù-hi**, to attend the market. **hù-hōe**, to be in time for the meeting. **hù-lâu-tsúi**, to catch the tide. **hù-sî hù-khek**, just in time. **bô-hù-chhoán**, said of a very poor man (v. chhoán).

hù — **sio-hù-hù**, very hot.

hù [R. a surname; = col. pô]. **hù-iét**, a builder who became prime minister of the founder of the Hàn dynasty, worshipped by builders.

hù (R. id.) **hoan-hù**, to command; to order; to give a message or deliver a commission. **hun-hù**, id. **chhien teng-lêng, bān chiok-hù**, giving very careful and repeated orders.

hù [R. to assist; a second], a second copy; a duplicate; a set of articles. **chià^n-hù**, the principal document and the duplicate, &c. (v. chià^n). **hù-chhiú**, an assistant. **hù--lâng āu-chhiú**, to help a man to do what he could not well have done alone (v. āu). **hù-tià^n**, a spare anchor.

tsâi-hù, a book-keeper in a vessel.

hù-iâ, a small military officer (under a "tsóng-iâ"), often stationed at a subdivision of a Hien district. **hù-chiòng**, = hiáp-tâi, a military officer (like adjutant?) one grade above the "chham-hú." **hù-chhe**, assistant-messenger or commissioner, great or small. **hù-tsú-khó**, assistant-examiners for the Kújîn degree. **hù-pn̂g**, the list of those candidates for the Kújîn degree whose essays are good, but whose degree is put off till the next time.

kui-hù, a complete set of articles. **chit-hù**, one set; often ten articles. **chit-hù-oá^n**, a set of bowls. **chit-hù-chiú^n**, a pair of oars.

chit-hù cheng-sîn, in quite good spirits.

hù [R. to hand over]. **kau-hù**, to hand over; to intrust to one's care; to deliver to one's charge. **hù-thok**, to intrust to one's care, as money, or things, or child. **hù-chiok**, to supply with what they need, as family or employers (v. chiok), (s. rich).

hù [R. hū, near]. **hù-hō**, to assent to another's opinion (v. hō).

hù [R. poetry; taxes; sometimes col. hū]. **si-hù** (R.), various sorts of poetry or hymns. **si-sû ko-hù**, four sorts of metrical composition. **gîm-si tsòe-hù**, to make and chant several sorts of poetry.

iòh-sèng-hù, medical rhymes or rhythmical phrases for receipts, &c.

hū [R. hù, poetry; taxes], a receipt for land-tax. **tē-tsô-hū**, receipt for house-tax in suburbs of some cities. **tōe-tsô-hū**, id. **chî^n-niû^n-hū**, a receipt for land-tax. **pun chî^n-niû^n-hū**, to distribute these papers to the collectors, as the officials of the yamun do. **chî^n-hū** (Cn.), a receipt for a mace or more of silver for land-tax. **hun-hū** (Cn.), do. for a candareen or more. **tsoân-hū** (Cn.), receipt in full for land-tax.

hū [R. near; in one phrase, "hù"]. **hū-kūn**, near; in place. **kūn-hū**, id. **kui-hū**, to join one's self to, as a weaker party to a stronger party. **hū-hōe**, to express assent, often without really meaning it.

hū-sin, to possess a man, as a demon does; to go and reside in an idol, as the spirit of another man (not the idol's own spirit) is supposed sometimes to do. **hū-sîn** (C.), id. **hū-ki**, to possess a man, for the purpose of writing oracles, as a spirit does.

hū-óh, to attend school as an extra scholar, additional to those whom the patron (tong-ka) provides. **hū-khò**, the third class of candidates in competitions for literary rewards (v. khò).

hū (R. id.) **hiong-hū**, a medicine made from thô-hiu^n (v. hiong).

hū (cf. pū). **hū-hū-kiò**, loud sound, as of thunder or of a steamer. **hih-hih hū-hū**, sound as of wind howling, or as of mill for cleaning rice; said also of a man in a great hurry and flurry.

hū (R. id.) **hū-tsòng**, to bury in the same grave side by side with a relation buried before.

hū [R. hú, crushed; rotten or pulpy]. **tāu-hū**, bean-curd shaped into squares (from the pulpy "tāu-hoe"), but not yet pressed (v. tāu).

hū (R. id). **hū-má**, son-in-law of the emperor.

hū [R. a teacher; in one phrase "hù," = col. pô], (sometimes "sai-hū" is improperly written with "hū," a mound).

su-hū, respectful title given to Buddhist priests.

sai-hū, a mechanic; a skilled workman; a journeyman; a teacher of songs, some sorts of gymnastics, or boxing, &c. **sai-hū-kioh**, a journeyman. **sai-hū-thâu**, a master tradesman; a head mechanic. **khek-sai-hū**, a teacher of songs. **thûi-á sai-hū**, a man who teaches the use of the long club called "thûi." **thì-thâu sai-hū**, a barber (&c.)

put-chí sai-hū, talking in a way of indirect hints, so as to avoid giving offence; not speaking straight out.

hū [R. father, = col. pē]. **hū-chhin** (r.), father. **gī-hū**, adoptive father. **kè-hū**, step-father. **gák-hū** (r.), wife's father. **sien-hū**, deceased father. **tông-pau ī^n-hū**, of same mother, but different father. **hák-hū**, scholar's father. **sîn-hū**, Roman Catholic title for priest; spiritual father.

hū-tsú, father and son. **hū-bó**, father and mother (v. bó). **hū-bió** (Cn.), id.

teng hū-iu, to be in mourning for father. **sêng-hū koán-giáp**, to succeed to one's father, and have control of the property.

hū [R. a woman; properly a married woman, = col. pū, bó]. **hū-jîn-lâng**, a woman. **hū-jîn** (R.), id. **ta-po hū-jîn** (r.), men and women. **lâm-hū ló-iù**, male and female, old and young. **hu-hū**, husband and wife. **hu-chhiòng hū-sûi**, husband and wife very harmonious.

tē-hū, younger brother's wife. **chiet-hū**, a widow who refuses to marry again. **îm-hū**, a lewd woman; an adulteress. **hū-khe**, diseases of women. **sip-hū kiú-tô**, of ten wives, nine dislike concubines.

hū [R. to carry on the back (= col. pē); to owe money; ungrateful]. **hū-sim**, ungrateful. **ko-hū**, to reject or requite ill, as kindness (v. ko). **hiau-hū**, to keep back what belongs to a man (v. hiau). **khui-hū**, to act ungratefully and injuriously; to betray trust, as in money matters.

khi-hū, to treat ill and oppress; to treat with injustice, as a more powerful man who quite despises the power of the man whom he wrongs. **toā-siā khi-hū sió-siā**, a large village constantly plundering or oppressing a smaller village that is quite unable to resist.

huh, to cook in a frying-pan (tiá^n) without water or oil, over a slow fire.

hùh, exclamation used in driving away fowls.

厦英大辭典

hui [R. a concubine]. **hông-hui** (R.), an imperial concubine. **thien-hui**, a title of the idol má-tsó-pô.

hui, to clean a medicinal powder by washing, as "tiû" is said of other powders.

hui [R. to move with the hand], to copy stone-cut characters by rubbing a sheet of paper over them. **hui-jī**, id. **hui-kim jû-thó** (R.), to spend gold like dirt.

hui [R. to fly, = col. pe]. **hui-hō**, sudden calamities (v. hō). **hui-khîm tsó-siù**, birds and beasts. **hui-chhú**, an animal (from the north) with a fine fur. **gák-hui**, a famous statesman and general (Yoh-fei) in the end of the Sung dynasty. **gák-hui-biō**, temple of Yoh-fei, with chained figure of Chîn kòe, who falsely accused him and got him put to death.

hui [R. is not, no, it is not; wrong]. **hui-siông**, unusual; extraordinary. **sī-hui** (r.), right or wrong. **tû-hui tioh** —, the only way is to —. **phàⁿ-sí, hui tiong-sîn**, he who fears death is not a faithful statesman.

hui-ûi, to act very wickedly. **hui-ûi tsok-tái**, id. **ûi-hui**, id. **ûi-hui tsok-tái**, id. **thong-tông ûi-hui**, to work wickedness together. **thong-bô ûi-hui**, to plot together to work wickedness. **hòng-tōng ûi-hui**, to work all sorts of wickedness.

hûi (R. tsû), earthenware; pottery, stoneware; crockery. **hûi-khì**, id. **hûi-iô**, a pottery. **sio-hûi**, to bake earthenware; to make pottery. **sio-hûi--ê**, a potter. **hûi-sai-hū**, id. **hûi-sio--ê**, made of stoneware or pottery. **sio-hûi chiáh-khih**, potters use the damaged ware (and sell the good).

hûi [R. fat, = col. pûi]. **hûi-jî-oân**, sort of pills for strengthening children (v. oân).

húi (R. id.) **húi-chhùi**, a bird with beautiful feathers (v. chhùi).

húi (R. id.), to destroy. **húi-hoāi**, id.; ruined; destroyed. **húi theh-theh** (Cn.), utterly ruined, as a house.

húi [R. to revile]. **húi-pòng**, to revile; to slander; to calumniate; to blaspheme. **húi-māⁿ** (T.), to revile and scold violently.

húi [R. robbers, ruffians]. **húi-lūi**, ruffians; rowdies; thievish low fellows; thieves and vagabonds. **chhát-húi**, banditti; brigands; violent robbers. **thó-húi**, local rebels, bandits, or robbers not connected with any great rebellion. **liám-húi**, the Nienfei rebels.

hùi (R. id.), to spend; to expend; often with idea of spending much or lavishly. **hùi-ēng**, id. **phoà-hùi**, to waste one's property, as by needful expenditure on sickness, or lawsuits, &c., or by lavish prodigality. **khai-hùi**, to spend money; expenses. **sé-hùi**, expenses. **sé-hùi-tāng**, expenses heavy: expensive. **sú-hùi** (C.), expenses. **peng-hùi**, military expenses, viewed in relation to the expense to government. **lō-hùi**, expenses, as of a journey. **poāⁿ-hùi**, id. **poāⁿ-tīⁿ lō-hùi**, id. **poāⁿ-chīⁿ sé-hùi**, id. **hu-hùi**, to spend lavishly. **hoa-hùi**, id. **ke-hùi**, household expenses. **ke hùi joā-tsōe**, spend how much more? **hùi-oân-oân**, all spent, as money. **hùi-giáp**, to waste or dissipate property. **hùi-chhân hùi-giáp**, id. **hùi-chhùi hùi-chih**, a great deal of talk without any good effect. **hùi-chīn sim-lát**, to put forth all one's energies, often to no purpose. **óng-hùi sim-sîn**, to exert one's mind uselessly. **hùi-sim-sîn** (to spend much thought), very troublesome, as affair. **hùi-sim**, many thanks! you have taken a great deal of trouble for me. **hō--lí hùi-sim**, id. **hùi-sîn**, to put one's self to much trouble or expense; troublesome, as an affair needing much thought or exertion; I am much obliged to you for your trouble; I have given you a great deal of trouble, sir! **m̄-thang hùi-sîn**, do not put yourself to trouble or expense for me (said by a guest, &c.)

hùi-khì, requiring much labour; very troublesome, as an affair that is involved and difficult; hardly worth the trouble. **bô-siáⁿ-hùi-khì**, not needing much trouble to set it right.

hùi (R. id.), a name that must not be pronounced, sometimes must not even be written; a tabooed name, as the "small name" of a sage, emperor, deceased father, &c. **hùi-miâⁿ**, id. **sèng-hùi**, small name of a sage or emperor. **gū-hùi**, do. of emperor or of imperial prince. **khī-hùi**, to reverence such a name by avoiding the writing or pronouncing of it. **pī-hùi**, id. **hoān-hùi**, to offend by pronouncing such a name, or writing that of the emperor. **tuh--tióh lâng--ê hùi-bú**, to speak openly of what makes another terribly ashamed, as a secret shameful act or flaw in genealogy.

hùi (Cn.), = A. hì, the lungs.

hùi (C.), = A. hòe, to abolish or make void. **huiⁿ-hùi**, = A. hng-hòe, laid waste; become desolate.

hūi (R. id.), the warp of a web. **kiⁿ-hūi**, warp and woof. **keng-hūi** (R.), id.

hūi (R. id.) **tì-hūi**, wisdom.

hūi (R. id.) **un-hūi**, favour; grace; gratuitous kindness. **siū-hūi** (R.), I feel obliged for your kindness, sir!

hūi-oaⁿ, the city and district of Hui-an. **hūi-hiong-hū**, the root of "thô-hiuⁿ," from that region.

huiⁿ (C.), = A. hng, waste, desolate. **khui-huiⁿ**, laid waste and uncultivated, as fields. **huiⁿ-hī**, id. **huiⁿ-chhân**, fields fallen out of cultivation, as from feuds or failing population. **huiⁿ-hìⁿ-hìⁿ**, all in disorder, as a room.

huiⁿ (C.) **huiⁿ-huiⁿ**, very wicked. **o-huiⁿ**, a very poisonous black serpent.

huiⁿ (C.) **ê-huiⁿ**, = A. ē-hng, evening. **tsá-huiⁿ**, yesterday.

hûiⁿ (C.), = A. hn̂g, a dry field; a garden.

hûiⁿ (C.) **liû-hûiⁿ**, = A. jiû-n̂g, sulphur.

hûiⁿ (Cn.), = A. hêng, to return a thing; to repay.

hûiⁿ (Cn.), = A. hoâiⁿ, transverse. **hûiⁿ phiah-phiah**, very wicked. **hûiⁿ-gék**, = A. hêng-gék, very wicked and injurious.

hūiⁿ (C.), = A. hn̄g, far.

hūiⁿ (Cn.), = A. hēng, a sort of vegetable.

hūiⁿ (Cn.), = A. hēng, to make a present.

huih (R. hiet), (C. hoeh), blood. **huih-khì**, principle of animal life. **huih-khì chiok**, full-blooded; in vigorous health. **huih-khì gêng--teh**, the blood supposed to be arrested in its action, as in a tumour and other diseases. **huih-liû**, a bloody tumour. **huih-méhⁿ**, the pulse. **huih-kun**, veins or arteries.

huih-tsúi, the serum of the blood. **huih-tsúi-á**, a very little blood, as trickling from a wound. **huih-tái**, blood in small quantities, as on the skin. **huih-tô**, clotted blood in large quantity; soft clotted gore. **huih-táng**, id. **huih-pa**, hardened blood, as on the skin or on clothes from a sore.

huih-tî, a pool in the Buddhist hell, for women who die within one month after childbirth.

phah--tióh huih-lō, to strike a man in a dangerous place, where it will at least be very painful, or make him unwell, if not kill him. **tiám i--ê huih-lē**, do. with the point of the finger.

lâng-huih, human blood. **lâng-huih**, blood and matter. **koah-lâng-huih**, to cut a large boil or abscess with a knife, so as to let out blood and matter. **giah-lâng-huih**, to open a small boil with a pin or needle.

koah-huih, to cut and let blood. **chhut-huih**, to bleed (neuter), especially in small quantity, as a bruise or small cut. **lâu-huih**, to bleed profusely. **lék-huih**, to press blood from a wound. **chí-huih**, to staunch blood. **phùi-huih**, to spit blood. **siūⁿ kàu-beh-phùi-huih**, so anxious as almost going to spit blood; looking very anxious. **siūⁿ kàu-beh thó-huih**, till almost going to vomit blood; or "áu-huih," to vomit blood.

huih phō-sim, the blood supposed to collect at the heart so as to cause death.

huihⁿ — **huihⁿ-huihⁿ-thî**, weeping and sobbing bitterly.

hun [R. sin, to stretch, to state a case]. **hun-sò**, to make a statement, defence, or explanation to superior or judge. **hun-hē**, do.; to discuss a matter making explanations (v. hē). **hun-hōe** (C.), id.

hun (R. id.) **sin-hun**, a marriage. **hō sin-hun**, to make congratulatory marriage presents. **chiáh sin-hun-chiú**, partake of a marriage feast. **hun-in**, a marriage. **hun-ien**, id. (s. tobacco). **hun-iên** (r.), a marriage feast. **chiú-hun-toh**, a repast spread in the nuptial chamber for bride and bridegroom. **háp-hun-toh**, id.

háp-hun, to consummate a marriage. **kiet-hun**, to settle a marriage. **têng-hun**, to betroth. **têng-hun**, marriage when either party has been married before. **jī-hun-chhin**, marriage when the bride has been married before. **thè-hun**, to break the betrothal. **thè-thâu-hun**, marriage when one of the parties had been espoused before, but that espousal had been broken by death; counted unlucky, as the spirit of the deceased betrothed still counts the betrothal binding, and the marriage existing.

hun-tsu, slips of red paper used as a marriage contract, given by the parents of the bride and bridegroom to each other. **tsú-hun**, the superiors (parents or guardians) of the bride and bridegroom, who arrange the marriage.

hun-phòe (C.), to give away in marriage, as one's daughter or concubine (s. divide). **hun-phòe--lâng** (C.), id.

hun [R. to divide; a small division, = col. pun], a small part, especially one-tenth; $\frac{1}{10}$th of an inch; a minute; a small weight, a candareen, $\frac{1}{10}$th of a mace (chîⁿ), $\frac{1}{100}$ of a tael (niúⁿ); (commission or percentage); to allow a small change of position or quantity; to slacken a rope a little, *e.g.* to let a boat pass, or in order to sail a little further from the wind.

hun-bêng, plain, clear, distinct. **ū-hun-hiáu**, understanding well one's duty or business, as instructed. **hun-piet**, to distinguish. **hun-piēn**, to make distinctions, as in argument or in vindicating one's self or another. **hun-lūi**, to sort. **hun kui-lūi**, id. **kàu-bé, hek-pék tsū-hun**, at last the right and wrong will come plain (v. pék).

hun-phòe, to apportion, as soldiers to stations, or as so much salt to be bought by each shop (s. marriage C.) **hun-phài**, to appoint to special duty, as each of several persons. **hun-hat**, id. **hun-poah**, to divide, as things to be sent to several persons; to send to different men who were formerly together.

hun-thiah, to dissolve partnership; to arrange to have meals separate; to explain minutely. **hun-chhoàn**, to cook and eat separately. **hun-soàⁿ**, all dispersed or distributed in different directions, as men or things. **tsō-tē hun-tsng**, to be a receiver of stolen goods.

hun-bién, to be delivered of a child. **hun-boán** (C.), id.

chhun-hun, the vernal equinox. **chhiu-hun**, the autumnal equinox. **chhiu-hun, mîⁿ-jit pîⁿ-pun**, at the autumnal equinox day and night are equal.

hun-hú, a part of a Foo department placed under the special care of an assistant-mandarin; that assistant himself, as "hái-hông" or "sam-hú." **hun-chiu**, similar division or assistant-mandarin of a Chow department. **hun-koāiⁿ**, similar division, or assistant-mandarin of a Hien district. **hun-si**, a still smaller assistant official.

hun-kim, small variation, as from pattern, or as from cardinal points in position of a grave or house (v. kim). **hun-kim**, alloyed gold.

khah-hun lî-lî-á, move it a very little further; rather a smaller quantity; slack the rope a very little. **tióh-hun--lòh-lâi**, let it down a very little more (by slacking the rope), as in carrying some heavy thing. **hun khah-lēng**, slack the rope a little. **hun chit-chhiú**, slack the rope (of the sail) a little.

hun-hô, in the very smallest degree; used in negative phrases (v. hô). **chit-hun ê jit-iáⁿ**, a very short time; a moment (as while the shadow moves one-tenth of an inch). **bóe-bōe sǹg-hun**, in buying and selling, men count small fractions.

kàu-hun, just up to the exactly proper quantity, *e.g.* in infusing medicines; just exactly ripe, as fruit; mellow; at the best. **bē-kàu-hun**, not yet fully ripe, as fruit. **kè-hun**, too ripe, as fruit; too much, as in making an infusion.

hun-thâu, a small commission or percentage on a transaction. **thiu-hun**, to take off a small percentage.

gûn-hun, difference on light and heavy dollars. **thiap gûn-hun**, to pay the sum necessary to make up the value of a full-weight dollar. **pó gûn-hun**, id. **khek-liám gûn-hun**, to make an unfair profit by paying the full number of dollars, but too light.

hun-siaⁿ, the denomination of candareens. **hun-hū** (Cn.), a receipt for one candareen or more of land-tax.

bô-hun-chhùn, very inaccurate, as in work (v. chhùn). **hun-chhák**, a chisel from one-tenth to four-tenths of an inch broad.

pat-hun, the sort of writing also called "lē-su," because it is eight-tenths like "khai" characters, and two-tenths like "thoàn" characters.

tsáp-hun-hó, most excellent. **tsáp-jī-hun-hó**, id.

chit-hun-lāi, interest at one per cent. each month, or 12 per cent. per annum (13 when there is an intercalary month). **nn̄g-hun-lāi**, 24 per cent. **saⁿ-hun-lāi**, 36 per cent.

hun [R. entangled; confused], confused; in disorder. **hun-hun**, id. **hun-loān**, id. **hun-hun put-it**, all in confusion and not agreeing, as opinions.

hun-bê, deceived and deluded. **sim-koaⁿ hun-hun**, mind disturbed and confused. **hun-sim**, id. **bêng-lī hun-sim**, fame and wealth delude and confuse the mind.

hun [R. confused and indistinct, as thoughts]. **pī^n kàu-hun-hun**, so ill as to be about unconscious; often talking incoherently. **pī^n kàu hun-hun m̄-tsai**, so ill as to be unconscious.

hun [R. dark, as evening, = col. hng]. **hông-hun**, dusk; evening twilight. **hông-hun-àm**, id.

hun [R. id., = col. hoan]. **hun-hù**, to command; to give orders or commissions.

hun (R. ien), smoke; tobacco; opium. **hun-iû**, tobacco oil. **hun-hio̍h**. tobacco leaves; cigars. **phī^n-hun**, snuff. **chia̍h phī^n-hun**, to take snuff. **se̍k-hun**, prepared tobacco. **chhi^n-hun**, a yellowish sort of tobacco. **kāu-hun**, strong-flavoured tobacco. **po̍h-hun**, weak tobacco. **tsúi-hun**, tobacco mixed with arsenic, smoked through water.

o͘-hun, black smoke; opium. **a-phièn-hun**, opium. **hun-thô͘**, crude opium. **o͘-hun-thô͘**, id.

báng-hun, a mixture burned to keep off mosquitoes (v. báng).

hé-hun, smoke. **hé-hun-tsûn**, a steamer. **hé-hun-chhia**, a locomotive and train. **kek hé-hun**, to get up steam. **chhàu-hé-hun**, unpleasant smoky taste or smell. **iû hé-hun**, expenses of oil (of lamp) and tobacco for visitors.

hun-ien, tobacco smoke (s. marriage). **hun-chhe**, a tobacco-pipe (v. chhe). **hun-pau**, a tobacco-pouch. **hun-tē**, id. **hun-kóng**, a box furnished with the materials for smoking. **hun-kui**, a press for pressing tobacco very hard. **hun-tà** (r.), a cover for the top of a chimney.

hun-keng, an opium shop. **hun-sái**, refuse of smoked opium, made up again for smoking at a cheaper rate. **hun-tóe**, id. **sio-hun-phā**, to make the pellet of opium burn in the flame of the lamp.

kóe-hun, to reform from opium-smoking. **kài-hun**, to refrain from opium-smoking. **tiâu-hun**, enslaved to opium so as not to be able to do without it unless by medicine.

chhiá^n-hun, to invite to smoke tobacco. **pàng-hun**, to sell a smoke of a pipe (for two or three cash). **hō͘--lí bóe-hun**, take this as a small reward or cumshaw (lit. to buy tobacco). **chia̍h-hun**, to smoke tobacco or opium (v. chia̍h). **suh-hun**, id. **jip-hun**, to fill the pipe, as with tobacco. **tsng-hun**, to pack tobacco; to put opium on the pipe. **tsòe-hun sai-hū**, a tobacconist. **chit-poa̍h-hun**, one pipeful.

hun-o͘, to blacken with smoke. **hun-báng**, to smoke out mosquitoes [do these two phrases belong to the next word?].

hun [R. smoke], to smoke, as meat or liquor. **hun-bah**, smoked meat (pork). **hun tāu-iû**, to smoke soy. **kè-hun**, to be smoked (as liquor) in a close cemented jar, by chaff piled round it and burned.

hun (R. id.) **kong-hun** (R.), merit, as deserving reward from the emperor for services done to the state. **kong-hun tō-tek**, great merit and virtue. **khai-kok goân-hun**, the merit of having helped the dynasty to the throne; title of Aǹg Sêng-tiû of Lâmoa^n, who invited Shun-chih (sūn-tī-kun) to take the throne when he entered Pekin.

hun (R. id.), animal food (= chho), including also onions, &c., as opposed to strict vegetarian diet.

hun [R. sin, the body]. **hun-su** (C.), = hin-su, the body.

hûn (R. id.) **hûn-bōng**, a grave. **tsó͘-hûn**, ancestral graves. **hòe-hûn**, deserted graves.

hûn (R. id.), a scar; a cicatrix; a wrinkle; a crease; a mark left by an indentation, or scratch, or blow, or of a joint or joining; a flaw or crack in the form of a line; a mark left by water, &c.; a line drawn as a mark.

hâ-hûn, a crack or flaw, as in a gem or in a piece of crockery (s. clouds).

to-hûn, scar left by a cut when healed. **siong-hûn**, scar of a wound; mark left by a blow or bruise. **chiap-hûn**, mark of a joining, as in carpenter's work. **khih-hûn**, having a flaw or notch in the edge, as crockery. **chih-hûn**, a crease. **chih-hûn**, a crack made by a stroke, esp. after mending. **pit-hûn**, slightly cracked, as wood or crockery; a small crack in do. **tiam-hûn**, an indentation; to make an indentation. **lòe-hûn**, scratches made by rubbing.

ūi-hûn, to paint a line (as for a mark), as with ink or paint. **uih-hûn**, to score or draw a line, as with chalk, or bit of brick, or knife, or nail.

chhiú-hûn, wrinkles on the hand; mark left by the hand pressed down. **chiú^n-hûn**, wrinkles on the palm of the hand. **tsńg-thâu-á-hûn**, lines on the fingers; impression made by the fingers. **tsńg-kah-hûn**, marks made by the finger-nails. **chhùi-khí-hûn**, marks left by the teeth in a bite. **hia̍h-hûn**, wrinkles on the forehead. **phī^n-pi^n-hûn**, the hollows at the side of the nose and down towards the mouth. **im-chek-hûn**, lines on the face showing benevolence and portending good luck (v. chek).

tsúi-hûn, mark left by high water, or by water in a jar, &c., when it was at its highest. **tsúi lek-hûn**, tide just beginning to ebb. **tsúi-pho-hûn**, wavy lines, as at the foot of a mandarin's robe.

kau-hûn, hooked pattern made on the edge or corner of a dress, wall, floor, &c. **ūi kau-hûn**, to paint or draw this pattern on a floor or wall, or on cloth to be cut out for sewing on. **khûn kau-hûn**, to lay on braid in this form, and then paste and sew it on firmly.

hûn [R. the soul]. **sîn-hûn**, the soul. **kia^n kàu sîn-hûn sì-soà^n**, suddenly terrified and taken aback, so as to be unable to do anything (lit. souls scattered). **sîn-hûn, khì chit-tiâu**, having lost one of our (three) souls, as by sudden fear or grief: Tauist priests bring it back. **lêng-hûn** (R.), the soul. **im-hûn**, a soul in Hades. **ko͘-hûn**, a disembodied spirit with no one to make offerings to it. **bông-hûn**, a disembodied spirit. **hûn-phek**, the soul and the animal spirits, or spirit and soul (v. phek).

hoân-hûn, life returning after apparent death. **hoân-hûn-chháu**, a medicine used by the genii (sien) for bringing the dead to life; also, a medicine for curing a swoon or faint. **hôe-hûn**, to revive, as from a swoon, despair, or death. **chio-hûn**, to call the soul of a corpse soon after death (v. chio). **ín-hûn**, to call back (by rites performed on the shore) the soul of a man who has died at a distance. **bê-hûn-io̍h**, anaesthetic medicine (v. bê).

hûn-pe̍h, a tablet covered with white cloth (used in rites while the body is unburied, and then changed for the permanent ancestral tablet). **hûn-sin**, a rude image made to represent the soul in certain rites (v. sin). **hûn-têng**, open chair with a canopy, like a sedan, for carrying the ancestral tablet. **hûn-bé**, papers burned to become horses for the spirits ascending and descending on 12.24 and 1.4 (s. cloud).

hûn (R. id.), a cloud; the clouds. **hûn-hō͘**, a passing shower. **hûn-bū**, mist. **hûn khui**, clouds breaking up. **hûn soà^n**, the clouds dispersed. **hûn tà-bát-bát**, sky cloudy all over. **làng-hûn**, clouds opening and showing clear sky. **phû-hûn**, floating clouds. **ngó-chhái-hûn**, five-coloured or variegated clouds. **ngó-sek-hûn**, id. **hâ-hûn**, dim and cloudy, as night when the moon gives little light (s. sear). **àm-hûn**, cloudy and dark, as night when clouds quite hide the moon and stars. **chhiūⁿ-àm-hûn**, to be dark with clouds, as night; to grow dim, as the surface of a brass mirror needing to be polished again. **chhiūⁿ-hûn**, clouds gathering. **chiūⁿ-hûn**, to mount the clouds, as gods. **thêng-hûn kà-bū**, id. **pe-jip hûn-siau** (to fly up among the clouds), said of a man terribly afraid. **poàⁿ-thiⁿ hûn-bé**, very high up in the clouds.

hûn-hok, wavy figures like clouds or bats on some sorts of cloth.

hûn-thui, scaling ladders.

ū-hûn ū-iáⁿ, really it is so; that is true. **bô-hûn-bô-iáⁿ**, utterly false. **bô-hûn-iáⁿ**, id.; also said of finding no trace of a man at his house. **ū-hûn bô-iáⁿ ê-ōe**, false deceitful words.

hûn-lâm (C. ûn-lâm), the province of Yun-nan. **koan-hûn-tióng**, = koan-tè, the "god of war."

hún (R. id.), powder; dust; flour; vermicelli; (some preparations like arrow-root); pigment or powder for the face; tender, as pig's liver well cooked.

hún-âng, reddish; florid (like red mixed with white). **hún-tiû**, sort of white silk. **hún-chiáu**, a good sort of dove or pigeon. **hún-chhū** (Cn.), a small fresh-water insect.

hún-pâi, a white-painted writing-tablet. **hún-soàⁿ**, a chalk-line (used by tailors). **hún-chîn**, id. **hún-piah**, to plaster a wall smooth in Chinese way; a whited wall.

thô-hún, dust. **hún-thô**, yellow clay (used for colouring playing-cards). **hún-chióh**, chalk-stone, from which face-powder is made. **he-hún**, powdered lime. **hoe-hún** (C.), id. **hoe-hún** (C. hoa-hún), flowers and face-powder.

phòng-hún, face-powder in round balls. **tsúi-hún**, do. in cylindrical form. **chiáu-á-hún**, do. in small balls. **koe-nñg-hún**, do. like eggs. **ū-hún-thâu**, nice-looking, as woman well adorned. **hó-hún-thâu**, nice-looking and finely adorned, as woman; sometimes with bad idea. **chhèng-hún**, to scent face-powder with flowers. **so-hún**, to rub powder on the face or skin. **boah-hún**, do. with much care. **phah-hún**, do. rather thick. **koat-hún**, do. still thicker.

kòng-hún, fine-powdered loaf-sugar. **ióh-hún**, powdered medicine. **sù-sîn-hún**, a medicinal powder of four drugs mixed (v. sîn). **kheng-hún**, a very powerful drug (v. kheng, light). **thih-hún**, iron rust or very small filings (medicinal). **iên-hún**, white lead.

hún-chiuⁿ, starch. **hún-ké**, a white jelly in diamond-shaped pieces, made from small green peas.

mīⁿ-hún, wheaten flour (v. mīⁿ). **béh-hún**, meal. **chhòe-hún**, rice-flour. **ko-á-hún**, rice-flour for making cakes called "ko-á."

bí-hún, rice-flour vermicelli. **bí-hún-tiâu**, id. **bí-hún-koaⁿ** (Cn.), id. dry. **liâng-hún**, vermicelli in a cool syrup. **soaⁿ-tang-hún**, fine vermicelli from Shantung.

hái-hún, a green sea-weed dried for food, like vermicelli.

ngāuⁿ-hún, flour from water-lily roots; said also of arrow-root. **han-tsû-hún**, potatoe-flour from the sweet potatoe. **keh-hún**, a powder like arrow-root, from the root of the "keh" plant. **koah-hún**, do. from root of the "koah" plant. **pek-háp-hún**, flour (like it) from root of "pek-háp-hoe," said to be good for coughs.

tang-hoa-hún, a plant (tapioca?) with large palmate leaves (are some of the above identical?).

hún [R. ardour, zeal]. **hoat-hún** (R.), to be very zealous at a work.

hùn [R. to make an exertion]. **hùn-chì** (R.), to act with energy and earnestness; to exert one's self much. **jiát-sim hùn-chì**, id. **hùn-ióng** (R.), to make a tremendous effort.

hùn [R. to teach; to instruct]. **kàu-hùn**, instruction. **bô-kàu-hùn**, ill-behaved and rude. **put-siū kàu-hùn**, incorrigible and refractory, as boy or lad.

hùn (R. hoàn), to stretch on a last; to make a hole larger by driving in wedges. **ôe-hùn**, a shoemaker's last. **hùn-thâu**, id. **hùn-ôe**, to stretch shoes on a last.

hùn-pit--khì, to split by wedging too tight, as wood. **hùn-khah-chhut**, to take in a little more than the original limits, *e.g.* a little more ground than is in the deed, perhaps enough to set the walls on. **hùn--chhut-lâi**, do.; also, to enlarge gradually, as a growing village.

hùn— **hùn-lâng**, to gather matter (pus); to suppurate.

hūn— **siⁿ-hūn**, unacquainted or strange, as a man; shy, as child. **sɛⁿ-hūn** (C.), id. **siⁿ-hūn-lâng**, a stranger.

hūn [R. hūn = hûn, undistinguishable]. **hūn-chiâⁿ**, just alike; undistinguishable, as a mend, or as a counterfeit or imitation. **hūn-hoà**, id.

hūn-hūn, not readily distinguished. **bōe-hūn--tit**, cannot pass off the bad as good. **hūn bōe-tit-kè**, id.

hūn [R. confusion; to confound; chaos]. **hūn-tūn**, chaos. **hūn-loān**, confusedly mixed; all in disorder. **hūn-tsáp**, mixed, as persons (v. tsáp). **saⁿ-hūn**, confusedly mixed, as good and bad, or as things belonging to different persons.

hê-hūn, confused, indistinct, and somewhat untrue, as language; having some inferior articles mixed; mended or corrected, but not agreeing with the old.

hūn-chiàng, confused, as the management of an affair; falsified, as a document (v. chiàng). [the previous word?]

hūn— **hūn--khì**, to faint or swoon away. **lâng hūn-hūn**, in a state of giddiness and almost fainting.

hūn [R. id. by change of tone from "hun," to divide], a part; a portion. **chit-hūn**, one part, one tenth. **bān-hūn ê chit-hūn**, ten thousand to one. **tsáp-hūn thiu-chit-hūn**, take off ten per cent. **chhit-poeh-hūn m̄-sī**, seven to three, or eight to two, it is not so. **sì-hūn-chit**, a quarter. **tiuⁿ-hūn**, to divide into equal parts and lay them out. **pun-hūn**, to divide into shares, as men who have bought a lot of goods in common, or as underlings in a yamun, dividing their gains at the end of the year. **saⁿ-chiⁿ, pun toā-hūn**, to take the lion's share.

kè-hūn, to take more than belongs to us; to take too much upon us, *e.g.* scolding people who have no connection with us. **kè-hūn--lâng**, to treat people unjustly or in an overbearing way; to meddle officiously with what does not concern us. **bô-jīn-hūn**, does not keep his place, as an uppish inferior.

hūn-goā-kùi, exorbitantly dear. **hūn-goā ê-sū**, matters that do not concern us, that do not belong to us.

pún-hūn, duty; one's proper business. **sioh pún-hūn**, to attend to one's duty, to keep one's place (v. sioh). **siú pún-hūn**, id. **siú-hūn**, id. **an-hūn**

siú-kí, to do one's duty and keep from meddling in improper things. **siú-kí an-hūn**, id.

iên-hūn, marriage viewed as fated (v. iên). **hok-hūn**, fated portion of good fortune.

èng-hūn, portion which a man should have at division of property. **chiap-pâng-hūn**, to succeed and keep up the succession, as adopted son. **hūn-giāh**, allotted portion, as of property or money; allotted duty.

chit-hūn, office, station, or rank, as of an official. **bêng-hūn**, station, rank; duties of station. **tsûn-hūn**, employment as boatman or sailor (engaged). **thó-hūn**, to ask for a situation, employment, or work. **sin-hūn**, rank, wealth, or position in life; size of body (v. sin). **seng-khu-hūn**, size of body.

séng-hūn, a province. **hú-hūn**, a department; a Foo. **koāi^{n}-hūn**, a district; a Hien. **phè-hūn**, a ward or district of a town (v. phè).

hūn (R. id.), (C. hìn; Cn. hūn), to hate. **oàn-hūn**, to hate, to repine at or envy. **oàn-hūn miā^{n}-phái^{n}**, to repine at one's lot. **hūn-miā^{n}-phái^{n}**, id. **hūn-lâi hūn-khì, hūn-miā^{n}-phái^{n}**, id. **hūn-sim**, heart full of hatred. **hūn--lâng jip-kut**, to hate violently or exceedingly. **khó-hūn**, odious; hateful; detestable. **àm-hūn**, to hate secretly, especially when one dares not show it.

hūn-khì, hatred; rage. **tháu chit-tiám hūn-khì**, to relieve one's anger, either in words or by getting vengeance or punishment inflicted. **tháu chit-pak hūn-khì**, do. by getting the offender punished. **moá^{n}-pak hūn-khì, bô-tè thang-tháu**, full of rage, but without means to vent or gratify it.

iàm-hūn, to be disgusted at; to abhor; esp. one's own bad conduct. **thòng-hūn**, to hate exceedingly (v. thòng). **thiòng-hūn**, id. **tiòng-hūn** (R.), id. to be deeply grieved for our own fault.

khioh-hūn, to harbour or cherish enmity and watch for an opportunity of revenge; to keep up a grudge. **khioh-hūn bâi-oàn**, id. **hoâi-hūn**, to harbour enmity. **hâm-hūn**, id. **phâu-hūn** (R.), id.

hut [R. confused]. **hóng-hut**, absent in mind; quite inattentive to, or forgetful of what is said or done; almost out of one's mind (s. similar). **hóng-hóng hut-hut**, mind confused, frightened, or unsettled; mind changing frequently at very short intervals. **sim-sîn hóng-hut**, absent in mind; quite inattentive to what is going on; confused and almost out of one's mind, as from excessive grief or illness. **cheng-sîn hóng-hut**, id. **thia^{n}--liáu hóng-hut**, quite inattentive to, and forgetful of what is said. **khoà^{n}--liáu hóng-hut**, had only an indistinct glance of it.

hut [R. similar]. **hóng-hut**, similar; very difficult to distinguish; indistinctly known or remembered, as from looking hastily, or from lapse of time, or forgetfulness (see the previous word; some of the phrases perhaps interchanged).

hut [R. a very small fraction; sudden; to slight], a very small weight, one-tenth of a "hô," one-thousandth of a "hun." **hun-lî hô-hut**, the very minutest quantities (v. hô).

hut-jiên, suddenly. **hut-jiên-kan**, do. in a moment.

hut-liók, to slight, to treat with disrespect, to do a thing without much attention (v. liók). **sơ-hut** (R.), careless.

hut (R. id.) **hut lâng--ê ì-sù**, to oppose or thwart a man's wishes, as by refusing to hear or to gratify him.

hut (R. id.) **gėk-hut** (R.), = col. tsàu-pán, a flat tablet like a leaf held in the hand by some idols, formerly used by ministers of state at audience.

hut (R. id.) **hong hut-hut-háu**, wind murmuring or howling.

hůt (R. hėk), the stone, as of a fruit; a lump, as in paste. **hůt-hůt**, having hard lumps in it, as tumour or boil. **kui-hůt kui-hůt**, all full of lumps, as paste ill-mixed.

hůt-thô, the walnut. **thô-á-hůt**, a peach-stone. **ka^{n}-ná^{n}-hůt**, stone of the Chinese (false) olive, much used for carving ornaments. **chiù-hůt**, a sort of li-chi (lāi-chi) having a small stone. **chiù-hůt lāi-chi**, id. **lān-hůt**, the testes.

hůt [R. Buddha, = col. pút]. **sêng-hůt**, to become a Buddha. **tsòe-hůt-sū**, to have Buddhist priests doing rites for the dead. **hůt-bûn**, the Buddhist sect, priests and nuns. **jip-hůt-bûn**, to become a Buddhist priest or nun. **ang-hůt** (C.), = A. pút, idols in general.

hůt-bú, an idol with eighteen hands. **tsún-thê hůt-bú**, id. **o-mî-tô-hůt**, Amida Buddha, often said as a prayer or charm. **sek-kia-hůt**, Shakyamuni, the historical Buddha. **sóe-hůt**, an idol carried about to give good luck to shops.

hůt-thâu-gûn, Carolus dollars; Spanish dollars. **hůt-siú-kam**, the fingered citron.

sim kien, chek-sī hůt, a man of firm purpose is just as powerful as a Buddha. **iók-kiû thien-siōng hok, su-tiám hůt-chiên teng**, if you wish to ask good fortune from Heaven, light lamps before Buddha.

hwa, hwâ, hwà, hwā; better hoa, hoâ, hoà, hoā, *q.v.*

hwa^{n}, hwâ^{n}, hwá^{n}, hwà^{n}, hwā^{n}; better hoa^{n}, hoâ^{n}, hoá^{n}, hoà^{n}, hoā^{n}, *q.v.*

hwah, hwáh; better hoah, hoáh, *q.v.*

hwai, hwâi, hwāi, hwâi^{n}, hwaih^{n}; better hoai, hoâi, hoāi, hoâi^{n}, hoaih^{n}, *q.v.*

hwan, hwân, hwán, hwàn, hwān, hwang, hwáng, hwàng; better hoan, hoân, hoán, hoàn, hoān, hoang, hoáng, hoàng, *q.v.*

hwat, hwát; better, hoat, hoát, *q.v.*

I.

i (R. id.), (C. ui, when a verb), to heal; to try to heal; to cure. **i-tī**, id. **hêng-i**, to practise healing. **i-pī^{n}**, id. **pau-i**, to treat a case to be paid only if successful. **i-hó**, to cure. **i-bōe-hó**, not cured; incurable. **bô-i**, cure not attempted; incurable. **i-sí**, to kill instead of curing. **oáh-lâng i-kàu-sí**, to doctor a healthy man to death, as a quack. **sòe-lih, i kàu toā-lih**, to make bad worse.

i-seng, a doctor, a physician or surgeon. **tiáp-tá^{n} i-seng**, a surgeon for falls and wounds. **ká-mē^{n} i-seng**, a quack. **iông-i** (R.), an incompetent doctor. **sîn-i**, a very skilful doctor. **sî-i**, a doctor in good practice. **bêng-i**, a celebrated physician. **jû-i**, a learned physician. **sè-i**, a doctor whose ancestors were doctors. **thài-i**, imperial physician. **i-seng koâi^{n}**, the doctor is skilful.

i-koán (f.), a hospital. **i-seng-koán**, id. **óh i-tō**, to learn the rules of medicine. **san i bêng, pok siòng**, arts of medicine and divination (v. siòng). **ûi jîn-tsú, put-khó put-ti i**, every one should know something of medicine.

i (R. id.), (cf. in, ui), dress; clothes. **i-hók**, id. **i-chiû^{n}**, id. **hō-i**, a soldier's jacket. **hō-i-koà**, id. **soat-i**, a sort of warm dress. **âng-soat-i**, a sort of red dress (or with red border) worn by mandarins on expeditions, and at executions. **poàn-chiét-i**, a dress of which the upper and lower parts are of different stuffs. **piēn-i**, common dress; every-day dress. **sò-i**, a plain dress; not full dress. **siù-i**, embroidered dress. **hoe-i**, flowered dress worn by women, children, and mandarins. **tiâu-i**, court dress. **bān-jîn-i**, a robe with the names of the people who subscribe on it, given to a retiring mandarin when much liked. **i-koan khîm-siù**, dressed like a gentleman but acting like a brute (said of graduates or mandarins acting wickedly), (v. koan, "a cap").

siū-i, grave-clothes made before death, supposed to lengthen life. **koan-kok i-khim**, coffin and grave-clothes. **keng-i-sé**, a room for visitors changing clothes when they come to worship the dead. **keng-i-tsoá**, paper pictures of clothes, burned for the use of the spirits of the dead. **tsu-i-kong**, an idol attendant on Bûn-chhiong (v. tsu, "red").

i-sit, clothes and food (v. sit). **i-siu^{n}**, a trunk or box for clothes. **i-kè**, a low clothes-stand.

i (R. id.), he; she; they; him; them; rarely it; (often enclitic, when not emphatic). **i-ê**, his; her; hers; their; theirs; rarely its. **phùi i-ê-noā^{n}**, to spit contemptuously while speaking against him. **bô-hoat--i**, cannot manage it at all (v. hoat). **kap--i phēng soe-ōng**, to make a venture with the goods. **m̄-koán--i**, no matter; don't mind.

i-lê, the province of Ili, in Turkestan.

i [R. to rely upon; according to]. **i-kiū**, as formerly; as before. **i-o**, to assent to or follow another without examination (v. o.)

i-oá, to rely upon, to depend upon (v. oá). **lông-pōe siong-i**, two persons helping each other in what each is deficient in.

i [R. a sound such as "i"]. **i-i o-o**, sound of several men exerting their strength together, or of children playing together. **i-i a-a**, sound, as of playing a flute.

i (C.), = A. u (R.), in; at.

î (R. id.), maternal aunt; mother's sister; polite affix to woman's name. **goán-î**, my maternal aunt; our maternal aunt. **án-î**, aunt! **î-bú**, maternal aunt. **bú-î**, id. (s. tea).

toā-î, wife's elder sister. **sió-î**, wife's younger sister. î-á, id. **î--ah**, said in addressing one's elder brother's wife. **î-pô**, grandmother's sister. **î-bú-pô**, id.

î-tiū^{n}, husband of maternal aunt, or of mother's cousin. **î-piáu hia^{n}-tī chí-bē**, sons and daughters of maternal aunts. **kө-î kū-kīm**, all aunts and other relatives and connections of wife, mother, or grandmothers (v. kө).

sòe-î, concubine or wife of secondary rank. **î-niû^{n}**, secondary wife or concubine of a mandarin.

ang-î, a sorceress who pretends to hold intercourse with departed spirits. **má-î** (T.), id.

î [R. iên, to delay]. **î-oān**, to delay, so as to give more time (v. oān).

î [R. only], (C. ûi). **bān-poa^{n}, kai hā-phín: î-iú thók-su ko**, all sorts and conditions are of low rank, only the literati are high.

î [R. to connect]. **î-chhî**, to use, stay, or manage temporarily, while waiting for something better (v. chhî).

î (R. id.), to remove; to change; to borrow. **î-ék**, to alter; to change; to make different. **chhek-chhùn put-î**, so well made that it cannot be improved. **thiet-pán put-î**, certainly fixed and determined.

î-chioh, to borrow (v. chioh). **seng-î**, to get payment in advance. **î-chhoah** (T.), to borrow money for a short time.

î-soá (r.), to remove; to change residence. **chhien-î**, to change residence, esp. of a number of persons. **î-khui**, to remove out of the way. **î-oát**, to move a thing; to change one's purpose (v. oát). **î-si**, to move a corpse to another man's house, so as to involve him in the responsibility. **î-soa^{n} tó-hái**, to move mountains and seas. **î-san tó-hái**, id.

î (R. id.) **á-î** (T.), = am-pө-chê, the cicada.

î [R. constant rule of virtue]. **bú-î-soa^{n}**, the Bohea hills. **bú-î**, Bohea tea.

î (R. id.), a barbarian (any one except a Chinaman); a savage (much worse than "hoan"). **î-ték**, id. **goā-î**, outer barbarians. **sù-î**, all the barbarians on all sides of China.

î (C.), = A. û, a surname.

î (C.), = A. û, surplus. **khó î-teng**, = A. khó iû-teng, to examine candidates for the position of soldiers.

í (R. id.), a seat; a chair; a stool; a bench. **poà^{n}-chē-í**, a low seat. **í-thâu**, a stool. **í-á**, a stool or small chair. **kha-táh-í**, a footstool. **phoân-thúi-í**, a large broad stool. **í-liâu**, a bench. **pán-í**, a broad bench made of one board. **khîm-í**, a shorter broad bench with a sort of frame round it. **siên-chhn̂g-í**, a long bench with back and arms, used at temples. **bé-í**, a small wooden bench, used as a tressel for a tressel-bed or sawyer's bench. **teng-í**, a tall square-topped stool, used as a step-ladder, or as a support for scaffolding. **kó-í**, a drum-shaped stoneware seat. **í-kó-á**, a round or octagonal stoneware seat.

kau-í, a chair. **tek-í**, a bamboo chair. **tîn-í**, a rattan-bottomed chair. **tit-pòe-í**, a square straight-backed chair. **oan-pòe-í**, a chair with a round back. **pùn-táu-í**, a square arm-chair. **poà^{n}-the-í**, a sort of easy chair. **phi-í**, a chair that draws out for reclining on. **tsùi-ong-í**, a sort of lounging chair (lit. for drunk man!). **hák-sū-í**, a large easy arm-chair. **thài-kàm-í**, a small arm-chair with a low back. **phê-í**, a folding chair with leather seat. **tsáh-í**, id.

í-kiō, a chair closed in front for small children; gen. with wheels (v. kiō).

í-bīn, the seat of a chair or stool. **í-koai^{n}**, the rounds of a chair. **í-kha**, leg of a chair. **í-pè**, back of chair. **í-pòe** (esp. C.), id. **í-the**, id. **í-tsū**, a cloth or skin spread on the back and seat of a chair (v. tsū). **í-tiām**, a chair-cushion, usually of leather. **í-jiók**, a cloth chair-cushion, usually partly on the back, and part hanging down in front. **í-phi**, cloth cover for back of chair.

í-toh, chairs and tables; furniture. **giâ-í**, to carry a chair. **giâ-í-kê**, to carry a chair over the head (head inside) like a cangue.

í [R. to cause, to use, by means of]. **khó-í**, it will do. **í-tì-kàu**, having the (unwished-for) effect that —. **só͘-í**, therefore, so that —. **só͘-í--chiá** (r.), on account of that circumstance. **só͘-í-jiân**, reason why; cause of a matter; rationale of an event. **i-ê só͘-í-jiân**, its reason, or cause, or rationale.

í-kip, also; together with; and also in addition. **í-chiū^{n}**, above that limit (this and the following phrases after the limit). **sa^{n}-hè í-chiū^{n}**, from two years old and upward. **í-siōng**, above that limit. **í-hā**, below that limit. **í-ē**, id. **í-chiên**, before it. **í-chêng**, id. **í-āu**, from that time onwards. **í-hō͘**, id. **í-lâi**, from that time till now, only of time already past.

í [R. to finish]. **í-keng**, already. **put-tek-í**, could not help it; had no resource.

í [R. to lean upon, = col. oá]. **í-tiōng**, to commit the whole management of a matter to, as to a man in whom we have full confidence.

í (C.), = A. ú, rain.

í (C.), = A. ú, with; to give.

í (C.), = A. ú, the emperor Yu.

ì (R. id.), purpose; meaning; intention. **ì-sù**, id. (v. sù). **bô-ì**, without desire or purpose; aimless (person). **bô-ì-tì**, having no heart about it (v. tì). **ì-khì**, purpose as manifested in one's manner. **ì-khì siong-tâu**, agreeing in opinion. **ì-sìn**, appearance or manner, as of acting or speaking, as showing one's purpose (not so strongly shown as "ì-khì"), (v. sìn). **sîn-ì** (r.), id. **chêng-ì**, disposition (v. chêng). **sim-ì**, bent of mind or purpose. **sa^{n}-sim nn̄g-ì**, vacillating. **ì-goān**, settled will or desire. **ì-ài**, to wish much; to desire. **goá--ê ì-tiong**, in my purpose. **ì-goā**, beyond expectation.

ì-gī, meaning; signification. **ì-bī** (r.), deep meaning, as of a book or sentence. **tāi-ì**, general meaning or purpose; speaking generally.

chí-ì, imperial will; sovereign decree. **tsú-ì**, determination; purpose; to determine (v. tsú, "lord"). **tsù-ì**, with fixed purpose; fixed on one subject; attentive. **tì-ì**, intent on something. **lip-ì**, to determine; with fixed purpose. **koat-ì**, decided in purpose; determined (mind). **kè-ì**, purposely. **tiâu-kè-ì**, id. **tiâu-ì-kè**, id. **chhiet-ì**, with very earnest purpose. **sim-kien ì-chhiet**, id. **khún-ì**, pressing earnestly (as asking a guest to stay when he is leaving). **tsûn-ì**, cherishing a purpose. **chhûn-ì**, id. **tsō-ì**, id.; planning to gratify a secret desire. **siá-ì**, idle and neglectful (v. siá). **koà-i**, anxious. **khoà-ì**, id.

khoài-ì, pleased; happy. **khiap-ì**, manifestation of unfriendly feeling. **biâu-ì**, kind and friendly manner or temper. **kó͘-ì**, good, kindly, and gentle (like the ancients!). **chiú-ì**, manner of one who has been drinking a little. **tsùi-ì**, manner of a drunk man.

thi^{n}-ì, Heaven's purpose or decree (v. thi^{n}). **tsòe hō͘-ì**, appearance as if about to rain. **ū-thiap-ì**, said of characters written in the style of copy-lines.

khiok-ì, to reject a man's kindness (v. khiok, "to refuse"). **khiok-ì**, to bend one's will (v. khiok, to bend). **jīm-ì**, to follow one's own desires, gen. stubborn or bad. **sûi-ì**, to follow one's own desires (v. sûi). **sūi-ì**, matters falling out just as we would desire. **chiok-ì**, desires satisfied. **sim-moá^{n} ì-chiok**, all our wishes gratified. **moá^{n}-chiok sim-ì**, id. **jû-ì**, everything as we would wish (v. jû). **tek-ì**, to obtain one's wishes; much pleased. **tèng-ì**, just suiting one's wish; just to one's taste. **háp-ì**, in accordance with one's wish. **hàh-ì**, id. **kè-ì**, pleased with a thing or event. **kòe-ì** (C.), id. **seng-ì**, interesting; amusing; pleasing; taking the fancy.

ì (R. id.) **ì-jîn**, grain from a plant (Coix?) very like pearl-barley; said for "pearl-barley."

ì — **ì-chì**, soiled; dirty.

ì (C.), (R. ù), to soil; to dirty; to infect by coming in contact. **sio-ì**, id. **chhàu-kam sio-ì**, a rotten orange infects the rest (one black sheep infects the flock).

ì (R. ùi). **mûi^{n}-sîn hō͘-ì** (C.), = A. mn̂g-sîn hō͘-ùi, words or figures on doors (v. ùi).

ì (C.), = A. è. **hō͘-ì**, descendants.

ì (C.), = A. è, a white film in the eye.

ī [R. easy, by change of tone from "ėk," to change]. **iông-ī** (better, iông-i^{n}), mediocre; easy. **pêng-ī**, cheap; (some other phrases better "i^{n}" *q.v.*)

bêng-ī, a sort of oil that is mixed with varnish to make it dry fast.

ī [R. i^{n}, different; strange], in most phrases, better "i^{n}" (*q.v.*)

tông-pau ī-hū, having the same mother, but different fathers. **tông-bó͘ ī-hū**, id.

î^{n} (R. cheng), (C. ε^{n}). **chhân-i^{n}**, the dragon-fly. **chhân-i^{n}-bák** (T.), eyes glazed and staring, as of a dying man.

î^{n} [R. eng, a hero; British], colloquial form (C. ε^{n}) of "eng," as a man's name; also (Cn.), = A. ia^{n}, name of a flower, a sort of rose.

sù-i^{n} (Cn.), = A. sù-eng, white jessamine.

î^{n} [R. eng, a sound]. **i^{n}-i^{n}-háu**, sound of a child crying. **o͘^{n}-i^{n}**, sound used in lulling a child to sleep. **o͘^{n}-i^{n}-khùn**, id.

î^{n} [R. eng, an infant]. **i^{n}-á** (Cn. An.), = A. ε^{n}-á, an infant (only said in some places). **goán i^{n}-ká^{n}** (An.), my little boy. **a-i^{n}** (Cn.), said by father to boy, "my boy."

í^{n} [R. êng, entangled]. **í^{n}-tî^{n}**, entangled or involved and troublesome, as an affair; very troublesome to deal with, as a man.

í^{n} (R. êng), (C. έ^{n}), a beam; a rafter. **í^{n}-á**, id., especially a small one. **toā-ki-í^{n}**, a large beam or rafter. **í^{n}-bé**, the smaller end of a beam. **í^{n}-phè**, bits of stone or brick laid on the wall to support the ends of the beams and keep the wall from cracking. **í^{n}-phák**, pieces of wood nailed on a sloping beam to keep the rafters from sliding down. **í^{n}-tú**, a wooden pillar supporting a beam or rafter. **khoà-í^{n}**, to lay the beams or rafters in their places. **í^{n}-kak**, rafters and lath for nailing the tiles on.

î^{n} (R. iên). **hiu^{n}-î^{n}**, the large round citron.

î^{n} (R. oân), round; circular or globular. **géh î^{n}**, the moon full. **î^{n}-lin-lin**, globular. **î^{n}-lin-lìn**, id. **î^{n}-long-long**, circling round, like a wall or line. **î^{n}-kùn-kùn**, round, as a plump and fat limb, or as round leg of table (v. kùn). **î^{n}-oan-oan**, circular or semi-circular. **î^{n}-kó͘ î^{n}-kó͘**, round, as a rope, or pencil, or fleshy limb; said also of a round face. **kó͘-á-î^{n}**, id., of the face. **î^{n}-tī^{n}**, quite round and plump, as a very fat man; quite full and round, as a good grain of rice. **î^{n}-lauh^{n} î^{n}-lauh^{n}**, fat and plump, as the face.

î^{n}-kho͘, a circle; a hoop. **î^{n}-khoân**, a circle; a ring. **î^{n}-oai^{n}-toh**, a folding-table. **î^{n}-si**, sycee silver.

î^{n}-î^{n}-tn̂g, to turn round and round; to turn quite round. **î^{n}-î^{n}-sėh**, to go quite round, as in a circle. **î^{n}-î^{n}-gô**, to revolve on the axis. **î^{n}-î^{n}-kō**, to roll along; rolling over and over, as a ball.

toâ^n-î^n, completed (said of the consummation of a marriage or the reunion of a scattered family, as in the finale of a play, or of an unbroken family). **toâ^n-toâ^n-î^n**, id. **so-î^n**, to rub, or roll, or knead till it becomes round; to set right a matter that has become troublesome (s. balls). **so-î^n tī^n-pí^n**, to adjust or inflame a quarrel just as we please. **m̄-tsai sī-î^n, á-sī pí^n**, not understanding a matter. **chē-î^n, bô-chē-pí^n**, to take praise for all that goes well, but refuse to be responsible for what goes wrong.

î^n (R. oân), a small ball, globule, pellet, or pill. **î^n-á**, a small ball, as of dough. **ióh-î^n**, a pill. **bí-î^n**, small balls made of rice. **mī^n-î^n**, do. of flour.

so-î^n, to make balls or pills; to make balls for eating on 6.15 and other festivals (s. round). **î^n-á-thng**, soup made with these balls. **chiáh-î^n**, to eat balls of rice or dough, as at some festivals. [perhaps two words.]

î^n (R. chiên, = col. chî^n), a copper cash (esp. Cn.), used only after numbers, or in asking how many. **kúi-ê-î^n**, how many cash? **kúi-î^n**, id. **chit-ê-î^n**, one cash. **chit-î^n**, id. **bô-poà^n-ê-î^n**, not even half a cash!

í^n [R. iōng, a bud; a pattern, = col. iū^n], a bud when it first appears (shorter than "gê"); a side bud or sprout of a plant. **puh-í^n**, to sprout or bud. **pauh-í^n** (C.), id. **hoat-í^n**, id. **thó-í^n**, just beginning to bud.

sim-koa^n-í^n (middle of breast), endearing phrase used to young children. **goá--ê sim-koa^n-í^n**, said by mother or nurse to small baby. **thià^n ná^n sim-koa^n-í^n**, said of loving very dearly.

ì^n (R. ièn). **ì^n-á**, a swallow. **kim-ì^n**, a small sort of swallow with bright feathers. **o-ì^n**, a dark-coloured swallow; the black skate-fish. **o-ì^n-hî**, the black skate. **ì^n-bé**, the back part of a young woman's hair made sharp like the keel of a boat.

ì^n [R. eng, a sound, = col. i^n]. **ì^n-ì^n-háu**, sound as of a child crying or of a man groaning under a heavy load.

ì^n— **ì^n-ò^n**, to speak indistinctly, as from an impediment; to haggle or wrangle (v. ò^n).

ī^n [R. different; strange, = ī]. **ī^n-toan**, false doctrine. **ī^n-sèng**, of a different surname. **ī^n-pang** (X.), Gentile nations. **tāi-tông siáu-ī^n**, mostly alike, but slightly different. **tông-hū ī^n-bú**, by same father, but different mother. **tông-bú ī^n-hū**, of same mother, but different father. **tông-pau ī^n-hū**, id.

kî-ī^n, wonderful; strange. **kî-tin ī^n-pó** (R.), rare and precious things. **koài-ī^n** (R.), strange.

ī^n (better īh^n). **ī^n-áih^n**, discontented state of mind (v. áih^n).

ī^n (R. iēn), temples and public buildings of several kinds. **am-ī^n**, a Buddhist monastery or nunnery. **sī-ī^n**, large mountain-temples. **giâm-ī^n**, id. **tsu-ī^n**, a college. **kòng-ī^n**, the examination-hall in provincial capital for the Ku-jin degree.

hān-lîm-ī^n, the Imperial Han-lin Academy. **ióng-chè-ī^n**, sort of public poor's-house.

bú-ī^n, the governor of one province, sometimes called the lieutenant-governor. **hák-ī^n**, the literary examiner for the province.

ī^n [R. easy, by change of tone from "èk," to change, = ī]. **iông-ī^n**, easy. **pêng-ī^n**, mediocre; ordinary; easy. **kè-chî^n pêng-ī^n**, cheap. **kheng-ī^n**, easy to manage, as an affair; somewhat hasty and incautious in action, either on one's own idea or at the suggestion of another. **bô-hiah-kheng-ī^n**, not so easy as you suppose, as managing a matter or inviting an influential man.

ia (R. ai). **eng-ia**, dust.

iâ [R. a final particle]. **iâ-so**, Jesus (v. so).

iâ [R. èk, to serve; a servant, = col. iàh]. **toā-iâ**, an assistant in a yamun, as a secretary or head of one of the sub-offices (s. next word). **mn̂g-thâu toā-iâ**, = mn̂g-thâu, the confidential secretary of the mandarin. **khoà^n-koán toā-iâ**, the jailor of the prison called "koán." **toā-iâ piah-long**, form of cursing a "toā-iâ" (v. long).

chiàng-iâ, custom-house officers (not in the office), like tide-waiters, who examine vessels, &c.

iâ (R. id.), honourable title in the names of gods, sovereigns, mandarins, &c.; sometimes "father," said by sons of mandarins or rich men; also (C.), mother.

bān-sòe-iâ, the emperor. **chhien-sòe-iâ**, younger brother of emperor. **ông-iâ**, title of an imperial prince; also, name of a number of idols (v. ông). **kong-iâ**, a duke (v. kong). **hô-iâ**, a marquis. **siòng-iâ**, prime minister. **thài-su-iâ**, id. **su-iâ**, legal adviser and confidential secretary of a mandarin. **tō-iâ**, Tautai. **thài-iâ**, title of small mandarins (as hun-koài^n or sûn-kiám), lower than "ló-iâ." **hú-thài-iâ**, the prefect of a department (not said in speaking to him). **ló-iâ**, title used in addressing a kujin or a mandarin of medium rank (sometimes politely said to a much lower man). **toā-ló-iâ**, your worship; your honour (said only in addressing a mandarin of medium rank, higher than "toā-ló," but lower than "tāi-jîn"). **koan toā-ló-iâ**, the god Kwanti. **tsóng-iâ**, a military officer *supposed* to command a thousand soldiers. **hù-iâ**, a small military officer (v. hù). **pah-iâ** (Cn.), a petty officer, like drill-sergeant.

siōng-tè-iâ, the god also called "hiên-thien siōng-tè." **tè-iâ** (T.), the god Kwanti. **hok-tek-iâ**, = thó-tī-kong, the god of graves and fields. **hé-sîn-iâ**, the god of fire. **bé-sài-iâ**, images holding horses at temple gates. **péh-káu-iâ** (T.), a deified dog. **hó-chiòng-iâ**, a deified tiger. **hó-iâ**, id. **tāi-chiòng-iâ**, a hideous paper figure worshipped in the seventh month (v. chiòng, "all"). **tāi-sū-iâ**, paper image of the king of ghosts (v. sū). **sêng-hông-iâ**, the tutelary god of a city (v. hông). **poeh-iâ káu-iâ**, two attendant images of his. **goân-sòe-iâ**, four attendants of Má-tsó, &c. **toā-thia^n-iâ**, an idol that serves as an attendant on some great idols (v. thia^n).

toā-iâ-peh, eldest brother of a mandarin. **jī-iâ-peh**, second do. **iâ-sià**, title given to sons, grandsons, &c., of high mandarins. **siàu-iâ**, son of a mandarin. **ko-iâ**, title of mandarin's son-in-law. **á-iâ**, title given to a mandarin by his child. **án-iâ**, id. **kū-iâ**, brother of mandarin's wife; also, nephew or younger brother of bride at marriage time (v. kū). **piáu-iâ**, a cousin of different surname (somewhat polite).

in-iâ (C.), his mother.

iâ (R. id.), (C. An. giâ), the cocoa-nut. **iâ-phê**, cocoa-nut husk. **iâ-khak**, cocoa-nut shell. **iâ-oá^n**, cup made of it. **iâ-phiô**, scoop or ladle made of it. **iâ-bah**, meat of cocoa-nut. **iâ-chiú**, cocoa-nut milk. **iâ-iû**, cocoa-nut oil.

iá [R. to melt, bedizened, = col. iá^n]. **iám-iá** (R.), gorgeous; splendid, as flowers, or as a finely-dressed person.

iá (R. id.), wild, violent, wicked, dishonest, greedy, ill-behaved, rude.

khòng-iá, a wilderness. **hong-soa^n khòng-iá**, wild waste mountains. **iá-siù**, wild beasts. **soa^n-khim iá-siù**, wild birds and beasts.

iá-bī, a bad taste; also (R.), venison; flesh of wild animals in general. **iá-chéng**, said of various plants of inferior quality, *e.g.* an inferior sort of lāi-chi fruit.

chhe-chhùi iá-táu, a vile scolding railing mouth. **iá-giên tók-gú**, vile abusive language. **iá-chhiah**, very rude and ill-behaved, especially of women. **sàn-iá**, very rude and uncultivated, almost like a rowdy. **san-iá**, id. **iá-siók**, rough, rude, and uncultivated. **iá-hàn**, a rough ignorant clownish fellow. **khah-iá-chhát**, more roguish than a thief. **khah-iá hái-iû^n**, do. than a pirate.

iá (same as above?). **the-sû iá-kè**, to decline for feigned reasons.

iá [R. an initial or final particle, = col. iáu]. **iá-bē**, not yet. **iá-bô**, no more; there is no more. **iá-ū**, there is more yet.

iá [R. ek, or else, = col. á]. **sī àn-ni^n, iá-m̄-sī**, is it so or not?

ià [R. iàm, to loathe], surfeited; to loathe. **chiàh--liáu, ià**, disgusted at a bad taste; feeling nauseated and unwilling to eat it.

ià (R. ì), wearied; fatigued; sickish; unwell. **ià-siēn**, tired. **ià-lái**, id. **ià-lán**, id. **ià-sin**, spiritless, or slightly unwell from great exhaustion. **seng-khu ià**, very much exhausted; unwell. **seng-khu teh-ià**, id. **kan-ta-ià**, wearied with doing nothing; feeling ennui. **ià kàu-beh-sí**, utterly worn out and exhausted. **ià kàu-beh sit-sîn**, so exhausted that we cannot think or listen.

lâng kōe-ià, very fickle or flighty; taking up things and soon letting them drop.

ià (= ioh). **âi--ià**, exclamation of sudden grief or surprise.

iā, to strew or scatter with the hand, as seed, sand, &c.; to throw or lay about without order. **iā soà^n-soà^n**, to strew or scatter about. **sì-kòe-iā**, scattered about in all directions, as seed, &c. **iā-khng**, to strew chaff. **iā-soa**, to scatter sand with the hand. **iā-chéng**, to scatter seed; to sow seed. **iā-ng**, to sow rice in a wet seed-bed to raise young plants for transplanting. **iā-ng chìm-chéng**, to soak rice and sow it thus.

un-ék-kúi chhut-lâi-iā, demons scattering the seeds of pestilence or epidemics.

soá^n-iā, running about with no one to control him, as a spoiled child (v. soá^n).

iā (cf. iá, iáh), also. **iā-hó**, not very good; not bad; passable. **iā-bô**, there is no more.

iā [R. night]. **tiù-iā** (R.), day and night. **chhâ-iā**, to search about at night, as police, soldiers, or mandarins. **sûn-iā**, id. **hoān-iā**, to go out at night without a lamp at forbidden hours.

iā-háp, the Magnolia fuscata. **iā-hê** (Cn. T.), a chamber-pot.

ia^n (R. eng), a tassel; (a mane). **bō-ia^n**, a tassel of a cap. **âng-ia^n-bō**, mandarin's servants, and messengers, who wear a cap with a red tassel. **lé-lóeh-ia^n**, a horse-tail tassel on a summer cap. **bé-ām-ia^n**, tassels hanging below a horse's neck.

bé-ia^n, a horse's mane. **sai-ia^n**, a lion's mane.

ia^n — **toā-ia^n**, a large instrument like a chisel used for housebreaking (s. rose).

ia^n [R. iông, bright, = col. iā^n]. **kng ia^n-ia^n**, = kng iā^n-iā^n, shining brightly, glittering.

ia^n [R. eng, a hero, British, = col. i^n], (Cn. i^n). **ia^n-hoe**, the rose. **ia^n-á-hoe**, id. **toā-ia^n**, the large white single rose (s. instrument).

iâ^n [R. êng, the fire-fly]. **hé-iâ^n** (Cn.), = A. hé-kim-chhi^n, the fire-fly; the glow-worm.

iâ^n (R. êng), a camp; a division of an army; one-fifth part of an army.

bú-iâ^n, a military mandarin in general.

gō-iâ^n, the five divisions of an army. **chêng-iâ^n**, the van. **āu-iâ^n**, the rear. **tiong-iâ^n**, the centre. **iū-iâ^n**, right wing. **tsó-iâ^n**, left wing. **iâ^n-ngé**, garrison of soldiers or marines at the station of a military mandarin. **chhiong iâ^n-ngé**, to enlist in army or navy. **iâ^n-bé**, army horses for mandarins or soldiers.

kun-iâ^n, camp of an army. **iâ^n-poâ^n**, a military station. **iâ^n-lúi**, a fortified camp. **iâ^n-chē**, an encampment. **an-iâ^n**, to encamp. **an-iâ^n tsat-chē**, id. **tsat-iâ^n**, id. **tah-iâ^n**, id. **bê-iâ^n**, to plan a secret attack on a camp.

thái-ko-iâ^n, a lazar-house. **khit-chiàh-iâ^n**, a place where the beggars live together. **péh-tsúi-iâ^n**, the village of Pechuia (lit. market of the boat-women).

iâ^n [R. êng, surplus; to conquer], to win; to be victorious; to excel. **khah-iâ^n**, id. **iâ^n-kè**, to excel; to surpass. **su-iâ^n**, to lose or win (v. su). **iâ^n chit-tîn**, to gain one victory.

iâ^n-chî^n, to win money, as in gambling or in a dispute. **iâ^n-gûn**, id. **iâ^n-kiáu**, successful gambling (v. kiáu). **thâi-iâ^n**, to conquer in battle. **chì^n-iâ^n**, to get the better in a dispute. **pok-iâ^n**, id.

iá^n [R. éng, = col. ńg], a small shadow, as of hand or of man; shadow, as of a lamp; a reflection in water or mirror, esp. of things or other persons; a reflection of bright light from water or mirror.

iá^n-iá^n, shadowy; indistinct, as something far away, or rapidly passing, or seen with dim eyes. **e-iá^n**, dim, indistinct, shadowy appearance of a thing seen dimly when it is dark or nearly so.

jit-iá^n, a shadow cast by the sun; sunlight reflected from water or mirror, &c. (either image of the sun or merely brightness). **lóng-bô jit-iá^n**, the sun does not shine in at all, as in thick dense foliage. **chit-chhùn-á jit-iá^n**, a very short time; a very few moments. **chit-hun-á ê jit-iá^n**, id., very short. **géh-iá^n**, shadow from moon; moonlight on water, &c. **tsúi-iá^n**, image reflected in water; light reflected from water playing on a roof or wall. **lâng-iá^n**, a man's image, as in water; a man's shadow, as when moving, or as cast by a lamp. **chiò-hé-iá^n**, to use for one's self the light thrown by another man's lamp (v. chiò). **tsoá-iá^n-hì**, shows of transparencies, like a dark magic-lantern.

tsai-iá^n, to know how to do a thing; expert; skilful. **khah-tsai-iá^n**, more skilful. **m̄-tsai-iá^n**, inexperienced; not knowing how to do it. **liàh-iá^n**, to pretend to know what we know nothing or very little about, and only make a guess of; to spread false stories either heard or invented. **tà-iá^n**, to meddle in matters that do not concern us, so as to get money improperly. **chhòng chit-ê-iá^n tiā^n-tiā^n**, to make an unsubstantial, hollow appearance, that cannot last long.

ū-iá^n, that is true; quite true; quite correct (as report). **bô-iá^n**, that is false; quite false and groundless. **bô-iá^n-chiah**, id. (v. chiah). **kàu-sî, khioh bô-iá^n**, when the time comes, it turns out to be false; to break one's word. **khui-chhùi, chhut bô-iá^n**, all he says is false. **ū-sia^n bô-iá^n**, having sound but no shadow, as wind; report utterly false. **lâi, bô-sia^n**;

khì, bô-iá^n, coming and going stealthily and noiselessly. **hong-sia^n pòng-iá^n**, false or exaggerated reports going about against people. **ū-hêng-iá^n**, = ū-éng-hióng, having at least some foundation in fact. **bô-hêng-iá^n**, utterly baseless. **bô-sin-iá^n**, utterly false (v. sin). **ū-hûn ū-iá^n**, really it is so (v. hûn).

iá^n [R. kióng], said in Yung-chun (éng-chhun), for A. iāng, to carry on the back.

iá^n [R. iá, to melt, bedizened]. **iām-iá^n**, beautiful, as shops or things (not said of persons), (v. iām).

ià^n — **ké-ià^n**, fictitious; to pretend or feign. **ké-ià^n-khùn**, feigning to sleep.

ià^n [R. iòng, cf. ia^n], to shine, as fire. **kng-ià^n-ià^n**, shining brightly; glittering.

iā^n [R. iông, to winnow or shake with wind, = chhiû^n], to toss up in the wind; to clean grain by pouring it out or throwing it up in the wind. **iā^n-bí**, to toss up rice in the wind to clean it.

iā^n-hong, to be moved by the wind. **iā^n-tióh-hong**, id. **sa^n teh-iā^n**, clothes shaken by the wind. **iā^n-iā^n-pe**, floating in the air, as dust.

iah [R. ek, to benefit]. **chìn-iah**, to make progress in anything; to be prosperous. **iah--lâng**, to be advantageous to a man. **phoà-chî^n iah-miā^n**, to lose money but so get long life. **iah goā-kéng**, to attend to distant matters, while neglecting or injuring one's own. **péh-bák-put iah-goā-kéng**, the idol Keh-sèng-ông assists other people but neglects his own relations, who are very poor.

iah [R. oat, = col. uih, ui], to scrape a hole; to scrape up or out, as with the finger or with a small trowel or stick; to rake up, as a man's old faults. **iah--khí-lâi**, id., raising it up by slight leverage. **iah bák-chiu**, to scoop out an eye. **iah hī-khang**, to pick the ears. **iah-khang**, to scrape a hole, as in a wall. **iah-piah**, to scrape a hole in the wall of a house. **ui-khang iah-piah**, id. **iah koa^n-chhâ**, to rifle a coffin, as for ornaments. **iah-thô**, to scrape a hole in the ground. **iah-kô**, to take up a quantity of paste with a spoon or broad stick. **iah han-tsû**, to take up potatoes with a trowel. **han-tsû-iah**, a trowel for lifting potatoes.

chiū^n-iah-iah, very itchy; restlessly itching for some bad gratification.

pê-iah, to scrape up (as sand), as children do. **toà--teh pê-khàng-iah**, doing nothing but scratch holes in his skin (said of an idle fellow). **beh tá-lòh khì-khàng-iah**, where can I ever scrape it together? as a very poor man ordered to furnish a great amount of money, or as a man ordered to find a small thing that has been lost.

iah-khàng, to rake up a man's old faults, or things he would be ashamed to hear of. **i iah--i**, he raked up his old faults, &c. **iah lâng-ê-phái^n**, to bring up a man's unknown or forgotten faults. **iah lâng--ê kun-tóe**, to rake up something bad or shameful about a man's early antecedents.

iah — **bâng-iah-iah**, mind in a state of great perplexity.

iàh (R. ék). **un-iàh** (C.), = A. un-ék, a pestilence; an epidemic.

iàh [R. ék, some sorts of disease]. **chhiah-iàh**, uncomfortable feeling of body, as from perspiration or dirty clothes or prickly heat; uncomfortable and unhappy state of mind, as from a loss or disappointment.

phī^n-iàh, nose diseased and decaying, usually venereal. **si^n phī^n-iàh**, the nose decaying and falling in from venereal disease. **phī^n si^n-iàh**, id. **si^n-iàh**, id. **khí-iàh**, id. **tióh-iàh**, id.

iàh [R. iáp, a leaf; a surname, = col. hióh], the leaf of a book; to turn over the leaves. **iàh-chheh**, to turn over the leaves of a book. **iàh-khoà^n**, id., either looking at the contents or searching for insects, &c. **iàh--kè-lâi**, to turn over the leaves forwards. **iàh-kè-lâi**, to turn over the leaves backwards.

bé-iàh, the last leaf (s. butterfly). **chheh-iàh-kim**, very thin plates of gold, almost like paper. **siàu-iàh**, to count the leaves of a book. **thiàu-iàh**, to pass over a leaf.

iàh [R. ék, to change; to trade], a surname. **iàh-keng**, the Yih-king, or book of changes.

iàh [same word?]. **ka-iàh**, to take well in the market; a good sale. **ka-iàh lī-chhī**, a good sale. **ka-iàh, bōe-bô-chî^n**, wares much in demand are all sold on credit (said of doing a service to a friend and getting nothing for it).

iàh — **iû-iàh**, having the look of prosperity, as person, family, or kingdom; in a prosperous state; looking sleek and healthy.

iàh [R. ék, also; even, = col. iā], also; nevertheless. **iàh-hó**, yet it will do; not bad; just tolerable; name often given to female children. **chióh-sai, iàh-kia^n lâng-kò**, even a stone lion is afraid of being accused before a mandarin.

iàh [R. ék, to serve; a messenger, = col. iā]. **chhe-iàh**, constables or police who serve warrants, apprehend criminals, &c. **soá^n-iàh**, assistants engaged by the constables but not recognized by the mandarins. **goā-iàh**, messengers, lictors, &c., who carry insignia before the mandarin when he goes out. **gê-iàh**, any or all of these regularly employed underlings, lictors, messengers, constables, &c. **lī-iàh**, writers, clerks or secretaries, and these lictors, messengers, and constables (both classes).

iàh [R. ék, a stage for couriers, &c.] **iàh-tsām**, a stage for couriers, &c., where horses are kept (v. tsām). **koán-iàh**, (?) government stations for relays of couriers.

toà-iàh-bé, fated to lead a licentious life; said by fortune-tellers.

iàh [R. ék, a sort of insect]. **iàh-á**, a small insect (winged white ant) that burns itself at lamps in summer, it devours grain; farmers kindle large fires to attract and destroy them.

iàh [R. tiáp, a butterfly]. **bé-iàh**, a butterfly or moth (s. page). **bóe-iàh** (C. id.) **bé-iàh-hoe**, = soa^n-koa^n-lân, a wild flower like a butterfly. **bé-iàh-ien**, down of butterflies' or moths' wings, supposed to be poisonous. **bé-iàh-siû^n**, do. when it dirties one's hands. **ô-bé-iàh**, name of a passage-boat carrying a black butterfly as its flag. **péh-bé-iàh**, passage-boat with white butterfly (&c.)

niû^n-á-iàh, the moth of the silk-worm. **tsúi-iàh**, the large butterfly or miller that hovers near water. **toā-tsúi-iàh**, id.

bông-chéng-iàh, thó bô-chiàh, the insects that come out after the term called "bông-chéng" come too late to get food.

iak (C.), = A. iok, to promise; an agreement.

iàk (C.), = A. iòk, to leap. **thiàu-iàk**, lively and cheerful, as a healthy child.

iam [R. id., = iàm, satiated]. **bû-iam**, inordinately covetous; never having enough. **sim bû-iam**, id. **chin bû-iam**, id.

iam [R. im, female; the Yin; chilly]. **ka-iam,** chilled and shivering with cold. **ka-iam-koā^n,** id. **poà^n-iam-iû^n,** a hermaphrodite; an imperfectly developed male.

iam (R. id.), to castrate. **iam-ti,** to castrate a pig; a castrated pig; a man whose occupation is to do it. **iam-gû,** a cut bull. **gû-iam** (C.), id. **iam-iû^n,** a wether. **iam-koe,** a capon (v. koe).

iam [R. hiam, a shovel]. **hé-iam,** a shovel. **iam-chî^n,** to take out a quantity of cash from one's pocket in the hand. **iam-gûn,** do. with silver. **iam té-koā^n,** to put one's hand into the pouch (sporran), and take out loose money. **iam té-tē,** id.

iam — **thâu-bé iam--teh,** anchored stem and stern.

iâm [R. iám, to cover]. **ti-koa^n-iâm,** the piece of fat beside a pig's liver.

iâm (cf. iû^n). **chhùi-iâm-iâm,** broken to shivers; broken into very small pieces.

iâm (R. id.), salt. **iâm-sî^n,** white deposit on walls or clothes (v. sî^n). **iâm-siau,** salt kept till it is bad; a white incrustation on walls and floors (v. siau). **iâm-lē,** moisture from salt in wet weather. **lē-iâm,** slightly salted. **chhi^n-iâm,** salt prepared specially for medicinal purposes. **iâm-sng-chháu,** a sort of oxalis.

iâm-khu, salt pans. **iâm-tiâ^n,** id. **iâm-tiû^n,** id. **iâm-tiû^n-koa^n,** a small mandarin who has charge of salt pans. **iâm-tō,** the salt commissioner of a province. **iâm-hoat-tō,** id. **iâm-toā-sài,** deputy salt commissioner appointed by him. **iâm-sûn-noâ^n,** men employed like excisemen to prevent salt smuggling. **iâm-sàu,** id. **iâm-koán,** a government salt store; the small official who has charge of it. **pák iâm-koán,** to farm the salt trade of a (Hien) district. **iâm-tsûn,** a boat or junk carrying salt. **iâm-ûn,** a large sea-going salt junk. **iâm-siong,** a salt contractor who farms the salt revenue from government. **phài-iâm-siong,** to assign the salt to them, bound to take so much annually. **liáh iâm-siong,** id. **tng iâm-siong,** to farm the salt revenue. **phòe-iâm,** to compel the people to buy so much salt each year from a particular salt store. **phòe iâm-koán,** id. **liáh-iâm,** to seize smuggled salt. **liáh su-iâm,** id. **su-iâm,** smuggled salt. **koa^n-iâm,** salt legally made and sold under the government monopoly.

phah-iâm, to manufacture salt. **phák-iâm,** to make salt by evaporation. **phoah-iâm,** to scoop up salt-water into the salt-pans. **hē-iâm,** to load a vessel with salt; to put salt on meat, &c. **lóh-iâm,** to put salt into anything. **soah-iâm,** to sprinkle salt. **tiām-iâm,** to pickle with much salt.

iâm-bí, salt and rice mixed, used to counteract inauspicious influences met by chance. **siak-iâm-bí,** to throw salt and rice with force. **iā-iâm-bí,** to scatter it about.

iâm (R. id.), a hard wood, used for helms, from Formosa. **iâm-tê** (?), a sort of tree. **pê-iâm,** a shrub with large pinnate leaves, and large loose panicle of white flowers.

iám [R. to cover up, to conceal, = col. iap]. **jia-iám,** to screen; to shelter; to hide (lit. or fig.) **iám-bát,** to cover up; to conceal. **iám-hong,** sheltered from the wind. **ū-iám,** to have shelter, as an anchorage.

iám-sek, to conceal under a false exterior, as a bad action (v. sek, "to adorn"). **iám-jîn ní^n-bók,** to delude people by plausible pretences while acting very wickedly. **iám-kî sit-kó** (flags hid and drums silent), said of a secret attack or underhand doings. **iám-sin-hoat,** a sort of legerdemain for making one's self invisible.

iám-chhàu, to cover up a bad-smelling thing, esp. to bury a body without the usual ceremonies. **iám-thó,** to cover up with earth. **iám-soà^n,** to dip the state umbrella, as when mandarins or idols pass one another.

iám-mn̂g, a trap-door; to close a door without quite shutting it; to lay a door to. **poà^n-iám-mn̂g--ê,** a married woman who privately receives men, as a bad house. **iám chit-sì^n,** to close one-half of a folding-door. **thang-á-iám,** an outer shutter for a window made of one piece, hanging by hinges above, and supported by a prop when opened.

iám-á, a small bit of cloth sewed on any article of dress, to strengthen it at that point, *e.g.* where a button is sewed on, and the cloth is too weak. **iám-té** (C. Cn.), = té-koā^n, a broad pouch or sporran worn on the belly.

iám [R. hurtful demons causing nightmare, &c.] **chè-iám,** to expel hurtful demons.

iàm [R. ap, to restrain]. **iàm-khì,** able to ward off the hurtful influence of demons, as some charms, *e.g.* a stamp of a high mandarin's seal, esp. of the provincial criminal judge; or as a teacher's red brush hung up in a bedroom (s. loathe).

iàm [R. to loathe]. **iàm-ò^n,** to hate or dislike with much disgust, as a bad man. **iàm-hūn,** to hate and abhor; to be discontented at one's own fate; to feel disgusted, as at one's own conduct. **iàm-chiēn,** to loathe; to reject with disgust and contempt. **iàm-khì,** to loathe (s. previous word). **chiáh kàu iàm-khì,** to eat to surfeit and loathing.

iām (R. id.), a flame; to blaze. **hé-iām,** a flame. **jit iām,** the sun scorching. **iām-thi^n,** scorching weather. **iām-thi^n chhiah-jit-thâu,** id. **iām-joáh,** very sultry weather. **thi^n-khì iām-jiét,** id. **ná^n-tóh ná^n-iām,** blazing more and more fiercely. **iām-phông-phông, pha-pha-tóh,** blazing fiercely. **hé-chih iām-phòng-phòng,** id. **kng-iām** (r.), brilliant, as flame.

sè-iām, influence and prestige great, as through intimacy with powerful or influential people.

iām [R. beautiful, luxuriant, = col. ām]. **iām-sek** (R.), splendidly beautiful, as colour, or woman decked out; gaudy. **hoe-khui iām-iām,** flowers very beautiful. **iām-iá** (R.), dazzlingly beautiful, as flowers, or as woman too gaudy. **iām-iá^n,** gorgeous, as shops or things, not said of persons. **hè-sek iām-iá^n,** goods in the shop very fine-looking.

kim iām-iām, brilliant, like gold.

iām [R. iám, to cover]. **ló-iām,** the bit of hard wood spliced on a sculling oar, where it works on the pin (v. ló).

ian, iân, ián, iàn, iān; better, ien, iên, ién, ièn, iēn (*q.v.*)

iang [R. iong, middle, to intrust, = col. ng], to wind, as silk or yarn; also (esp. C.), to intrust with a commission.

se-iang, a wooden frame on which yarn is wound to be ready for weaving. **sɛ-iang** (C.), id.; also, = noā^n-sim, a sort of tree. **iang-se,** to wind yarn on the frame. **iang-si,** to wind silk thus.

iang-chhià^n, to engage a man to go a message (this group is specially C.) **iang-lâng-khì,** id. **lí hē-**

goá iang--teh, I cause you too much trouble by this.

iang (C.), = A. iong, calamity.

iâng [R. iông, a sheep or goat, = col. iûⁿ]. **biên-iâng**, a sheep-skin with the wool on; a sheep. **san-iâng**, a goat-skin with the wool on. **jú-iâng**, a sort of fur with very fine curly wool. **iâng** (C.), also = A. iông.

iâng [R. iông, male, the Yang, = col. iûⁿ]. **hōng-iâng**, the city of Fung-yang. **hōng-iâng-pô**, female jugglers, pedlars, or beggars from it. **iâng** (C.), = A. iông.

iâng (C.), = A. iông, to spread, as fame.

iâng (C.), = A. iông, a sort of disease.

iâng [R. iông, a willow, a surname, = col. iûⁿ]. **iâng-kong-khit**, = hun-kim-khit, a stick or peg with "iông-kong" written on it (all these are only C.) **tèng-iâng-kong**, to stick this peg in the ground when making a grave. **chhāi iâng-kong**, to set such a peg in a measure full of rice, when going to build a house or temple. **siā iâng-kong**, to make offerings to him at the end of the rites.

iáng (C.), = A. ióng, to nourish.

iāng [R. kióng], (Cn. chiāⁿ, P. āiⁿ, chiāng; Eng-chhun, iāⁿ; as a verb), to carry on the back, as a person. **iāng pau-hỏk**, to go travelling with one's bundle on one's back.

phē-iāng, a cloth for carrying a child slung on the back. **iāng-kun**, id.

iap [R. iám, to cover, to conceal], to conceal about the person; to put behind the back, as one's hands; (to do a thing stealthily). **ng-iap**, to conceal behind the back or about the dress. **thau-iap**, to take stealthily, and put behind back or about dress. **iap-siam--khì**, to put a thing stealthily out of the way. **iap-chîⁿ hō͘--i**, to give him some money without others seeing it. **iap chit-pún hō͘-i-khoàⁿ**, secretly hand him a book.

iap-chhiú, to fold the hands behind the back. **chhiú iap-āu**, id. **chhiú hō͘-lâng-pảk iap-āu**, to have one's hands tied behind the back, as a caught thief. **iap-bé**, to put the tail between the legs, as dog. **náⁿ iap-bé-káu--nihⁿ** (like a dog with his tail so), said of a man very much afraid or ashamed.

iap-siap, retired and out of the way, as a house; clandestine; keeping out of sight, for concealment in some bad purpose, as a thief or spy; shrinking from view, as a modest person, or as man carrying such a thing as manure. **khah-iap-thiap**, keeping out of view, as something dirty, or of which we feel ashamed (v. thiap).

iap-sit, small additions to the side houses belonging to a large house (v. sit).

iảp [R. a leaf; a surname, = col. hiỏh, iảh], the surname Yeh; the spoke of a wheel; petals of flowers. **hoe-iảp**, petals of flowers. **pah-iảp**, double, as a flower. **toaⁿ-iảp**, single, as flower.

chhia-iảp, spokes of a wheel. **tsúi-chhia-iảp**, leaves of a water-wheel.

chheh-iảp-kim, very thin plates of gold.

iảp (same word?). **sim-koaⁿ chhùi iảp-iảp**, said of a man anxious about many things. **sim-koaⁿ tsōe-tsōe-iảp**, having a great many plans; rather too cunning and planning.

iảp (same word?). **iảp-iảp-sī**, in great crowds; multitudes collected together.

iat, **iảt**; better, iet, iẻt (*q.v.*)

iau (R. hiau), hungry. **iau-gō**, starving. **khat-khó iau-gō**, willingly bear hunger. **iau-koâⁿ**, hunger and cold. **iau-koâⁿ-gō**, cold and starvation. **iau-loān**, stomach disordered by hunger. **chhiⁿ-iau**, morbid hunger of diseased stomach. **phah-chhiⁿ-iau**, to have that morbid craving. **chin-iau-hng**, said in scolding a child always eating sweetmeats, &c. **chiảh kōe-iau**, hungry just after eating. **iau-kúi**, a hungry ghost; said also in scolding a fellow eating constantly or greedily. **háu-iau**, to cry for food, as a child. **khàu-iau**, id. **tī-iau**, to allay hunger (said in joke), (s. demons). **iau-ki sit-tn̂g**, to let (one or more) meal-time pass without eating, from any cause; to be very hungry. **iau--khì kè-ki**, exhausted or sick from not getting food at the usual time. **iau--khì siuⁿ-kè-ki**, very much so.

iau-pá, hungry or satisfied. **m̄-chiâⁿ iau-pá**, between hungry and full. **iau chhan, pá chhan**; **chiảh-pá, kiò kan-lân**, said of a lazy, complaining fellow. **iau-lâi pá-khì**, he comes when hungry, and goes as soon as satisfied.

iau-koe m̄-ùi-chhê; iau-lâng m̄-kò͘ bīn-phê, a hungry fowl does not fear the stick: a starving man does not care for his reputation or honour. **chhìn-bē tng iau-lâng**, cold rice catches a hungry man.

iau (R. id.) **iau-kiau** (R.), beautiful and richly adorned, as woman with bad purpose.

iau (R. id.), malignant demons or imps; magical. **tiỏh-iau**, bewitched; to be bewitched. **liảh-iau**, to catch demons, as Tauists. **tī-iau**, to drive away demons (s. hunger).

iau-koài, spectres and demons. **iau-hoat koài-sút**, magical arts (v. koài). **iau-sút**, id. **iau-chiⁿ**, a ghost or malignant imp. **iau-chiaⁿ** (C.), id. **iau-chiaⁿ sì-sóe** (C.), said of a woman behaving indecently.

siáu-iau, you little imp! (said in scolding other people's children). **iau-giẻt**, most extraordinary! (said on meeting with something most unexpected and inexplicable); also, very wicked (said in scolding children). **iau-tō**, a crafty magic-working Tauist priest.

iâu [R. a precious gem]. **iâu-tî**, the dwelling-place of the genii (sien), ruled by Se-ông-bú.

iâu (R. id.) **iâu-giên**, idle talk; gossip; false reports. **iâu-giên húi-pòng**, slanders and calumnies. **iâu-giên siên-hẻk** (R.), deluding into wickedness by crafty malicious words.

iâu [R. to shake; to agitate, = col. iô]. **iâu-tōng**, agitated, excited, and almost in commotion, as the people when hearing reports of rebellion, &c. **tōng-iâu**, id. **iâu-tōng jîn-sim**, to disturb the minds of the people by such rumours. **iâu-tōng bîn-sim**, id. **siuⁿ-iâu-tōng**, making too great a display of one's wealth, so as to draw the notice of robbers or mandarins.

chiau-iâu, spreading rumours of what should not be spoken about, as of rebellion coming near, or about money or valuable goods in a house, so as to incite to robbery. **chiau-iâu hīⁿ-bỏk**, to seduce people's ears and eyes, as great show of wealth attracting robbers, or as highly-adorned women alluring men.

iâu [R. distant]. **lō͘-tô͘ iâu-oán**, very far distant; road very long. **siau-iâu**, to wander about at will, as for pleasure or healthy amusement. **siau-iâu tsū-tsāi**, going about amusing one's self, with nothing to trouble the mind. **siau-iâu-soáⁿ**, sort of medicine for removing uneasy feeling.

iâu (R. id), a surname, = iô.

iâu [R. giâu, a cockle, = col. giô]. **kang-iâu-tsū**, preserved flesh of a certain marine animal.

厦英大辭典

iáu (cf. iá), still; yet. **iáu-kú**, id. **iáu-ū**, there still remain. **iáu-bô**, no more. **iáu--ê**, the remainder; the rest. **iáu-hó**, tolerable; passable; (&c.)

iáu [R. short-lived]. **iáu-chiet**, short-lived; dying young. **iáu-siū**, id. **iáu-siū-á** (you short-lived wretch!) said in scolding a lad who cheats or injures people). **kóng-ōe iáu-siū-khoán**, talking so indefinitely that nothing can be got out of him. **iáu-siū-khoán**, beginning troublesome things (as feuds or legal cases) and leaving them unsettled, so as to cause great injury to others, while he gets out of the way and avoids responsibility. **iáu-siū-á-pē̍**, id.; said also of making furniture in a very unsubstantial way.

ke-pîn-iáu, having no relatives, poor, and short-lived. **ke-pîn-iáu saⁿ-jī-tsn̂g**, all these three calamities at once! **ke-pîn-iáu, saⁿ-jī tio̍h-chiàm-chit-jī**, must have one of these three as his fate, as a payment to Heaven and to the demons for being skilful at black arts. **ke-pîn-iáu saⁿ-jī tio̍h niáⁿ-chit-jī**, id.

iàu [R. important]. **iàu-kín**, important. **bô-iàu-kín**, unimportant; not counting it of importance. **pàng bô-iàu-kín**, to treat as of no consequence. **kín-iàu** (r.), important. **bô-koan kín-iàu** (r.), of no consequence. **chhiet-iàu**, urgently important. **iàu-ēng**, specially required; important or indispensable for the purpose; to require for a special purpose. **hiám-iàu**, very important, as a pass.

iāu [R. to shine; illustrious]. **hién-iāu tsó-kong**, to reflect glory on one's ancestors. **hién-iāu bûn-bî**, to become illustrious, as a mandarin, or high graduate, or very wealthy man (lit. splendid gate). **iāu-bú iông-ui**, a man's bearing showing himself of importance (v. ui). **chiàu-iāu**, to assist and make prosperous, as by influence. **hok-seng chiàu-iāu** (may the auspicious star favour you), said of assistance by influence.

iāu [R. iāu, iâu], (Cn.), a large fierce bird.

iauⁿ, to mew, as a cat.

ien (R. iam). **ien-chhun**, a quail (v. chhun).

ien [R. an abyss]. **ien-hái**, the deep ocean. **chhim-ien**, id.

ien [R. how?]. **tsū-kí put-lêng-pó, ien-lêng pó tha-jîn**, can't protect himself: how can he protect others?

ien [R. in; marriage]. **ien-chhin**, connections by marriage. **hun-ien**, marriage (s. smoke).

ien [R. smoke; steam; vapour; tobacco; opium; soot; sepia], steam; clear vapour.

hé-ien, steam. **phū-phū-ien**, steam rushing out in abundance. **ien-bū**, mist (v. bū).

ien-n̄g, dim, as eyes (v. n̄g).

chia̍h ngé-ien, to use opium, arseniated tobacco, raw and prepared tobacco, and snuff. **kài-chiú toān-ien**, to abstain from liquor, opium, and tobacco. **hun-ien**, smoke of tobacco or opium (s. marriage).

ien-hé, fire-works. **ien-thúi**, a ham. **ien-chhiâng**, sausages.

chhèng-ien, smoke of a gun. **hiuⁿ-ien**, smoke of incense (v. hiuⁿ). **jîn-ien chiu-bit**, smoke of men (of cooking fires) crowded; population numerous. **bô-jîn-ien**, utterly desolate; without an inhabitant, as a wilderness or a deserted village. **ien-tâng**, a chimney. **ien-tun**, mandarin beacons. **ien-thûn**, soot. **e-ien**, id., lampblack. **e-ien-iû**, soot mixed with oil, as black paint. **e-ien pe̍h-pāng**, calamities suddenly coming on (v. pe̍h).

bák-hî-ien, paint from the cuttle-fish; sepia. **bát-tsát-ien**, id.

ien-hoa ê sé-tsāi, a brothel (v. hoa). **ien-hoe-chhùi**, a harlot's mouth (said in scolding).

ien (same word?). **ien-thâu**, the gloss, as of new cloth. **sin-ien**, having the original gloss yet on, as new cloth or other new articles.

bé-iáh-ien, the down on the wings of butterflies, said to be poisonous.

ien (R. id.) **ien-chi**, rouge (v. chi).

ien [R. the throat]. **ien-âu** (r.), the throat; an important pass.

iên (R. id.) **iên-chhiên**, to delay. **iên-tî**, id. **iên-oān**, id. **oe-iên** (r.), to delay; to procrastinate. **oe-iên kè-jit**, to procrastinate day after day. **iên-chhiên kè-jit**, id.

iên [saliva, = col. siên]. **thâm-iên**, phlegm and spittle. **chhêng-peh-iên**, resin naturally flowing from fir-trees (but "siông-ka" is manufactured). **liông-iên-hiuⁿ**, a medicine (v. liông, a dragon).

iên [R. a feast]. **iên-sia̍h**, a feast; an entertainment. **iên-toh**, id. **chiú-iên**, a feast with liquor. **chē-iên**, to sit at a feast. **siet-iên**, to make a feast. **pān-iên**, id. **thiet-iên**, to remove the remains of a feast.

iên (R. oân). **iên-sui**, coriander.

iên [R. along, continuous]. **iên-hái**, along the sea-shore. **iên-lē̍**, along the road. **iên-lē̍ chia̍h**, to eat while walking (counted vulgar).

iên, a layer, as of stones or bricks in building; a range, as of beams; a pile, as of books; classifier of decks (cf. ûn; see also the following word).

chit-iên chit-iên, row after or upon row; in successive rows or piles, &c. **saⁿ-iên-pūn**, third deck. **jī-iên-pūn**, second deck. **jī-iên-á** (P.), a very young pig.

iên [R. a cause, a reason; purpose of Heaven as to marriage; a subscription; the border of a dress].

iên-kè, a reason, a motive, a purpose. **iên-iû**, id.

ū-lâng-iên, to have the faculty of taking people's hearts; to be much liked, so as to be readily followed, approved of, or employed; cunning or captivating in manner. **ū-iên**, to be liked; to be captivating; to have a heaven-decreed marriage connection. **bô-iên**, marriage unhappy. **thien-iên**, happy, heaven-appointed, and unplanned arrangement of marriage (sometimes said of friendship). **in-iên**, a marriage, as fated to be happy. **in-iên tsù-tiāⁿ**, marriage decreed by fate. **in-iên gē̍-pah-nîⁿ-chêng tsù-tiāⁿ**, marriage fated five hundred years before. **iên-hūn**, marriage viewed as a fated period. **iên-hūn kàu**, the fated time of marriage come. **iên-hūn moáⁿ**, marriage ended by death; said also of illicit intercourse broken off. **iên-tâu**, a young dandy, esp. having illicit connections (v. tâu).

tôe-iên, to make a subscription. **kau-iên**, to pay the subscription. **siu-iên**, to collect the subscription-money. **hoà-iên**, to beg money, as Buddhist priest. **hòe-iên**, id.

iên-phē̍, subscription-book, as for a temple or charitable object. **iên-gûn**, money subscribed (s. lead). **iên-chîⁿ**, cash subscribed (s. lead).

iên-pán, a perpendicular board under the eaves of a house (v. pán).

iên (R. id.), lead. **pe̍h-iên**, zinc; spelter. **iên-hún**, white lead. **iên-pit**, a black-lead pencil. **iên-chí**, a bullet. **iên-tūi**, a leaden weight, as for a clock, or for a sinker for net or sounding-line. **iên-chîⁿ**,

22

counterfeit leaden cash; also, small cash fastened in the dress of bride and bridegroom, and put in their water-jar, supposed to make them love each other (play on the previous word), (s. subscription). **iên-gûn**, dollars adulterated with lead (s. subscription). **iên-tâu**, loaded dice (s. previous word).

koàn-iên, to pour melted lead into anything to make it heavy, as pendulum, or to adulterate, as dollars. **pé-iên**, to fill up with lead, as a hole made in a dollar. **so iên-sái**, to fill up dollars with lead by means of quicksilver.

ién [R. ióng, to nourish, = col. iúⁿ]. **ién-lāu-sê** (prov.), to nourish one's old father (v. sê).

ién — **lô-ién-sê**, a group of persons (usually twelve boys) in an idolatrous procession shaking rings with metal bells attached (v. sê).

ién [R. to exercise]. **chhau-ién**, to drill or exercise, as soldiers. **ién ke-si**, to exercise or fence with weapons. **ién tîn-pâi**, to exercise with the shield. **ién-bú-têng**, a stand from which mandarins look at reviews.

ién [R. to lie or throw down]. **saⁿ-ién**, to wrestle together. **ién-tó**, to throw down; to upset, as in wrestling.

ién [R. to overflow, abundant]. **iû-ién** (R.), to ramble at leisure. **sàn-ién**, spending money foolishly; lavish expense; very poor, and daring to commit any crime. **káⁿ lām-sám-ién**, spending far too much money (beyond one's means), as in food, dress, or pleasures.

ièn [R. a feast]. **sam-jit tāi-ièn; ngó-jit siáu-ièn**, great and small feasts every three and five days (said of a wealthy man constantly giving entertainments).

ièn [R. iàm, to loathe]. **ièn-khì**, mean or miserly.

ièn [R. a swallow, = col. ìⁿ]. **ièn-o**, edible bird's-nests. **chhài-ièn**, a native sea-weed, making a jelly very similar. **kòng-ièn**, bird's-nests sent to Pekin for the emperor's table. **pān kòng-ièn**, to send such bird's-nests, as the great Hongs at Amoy have to do. **koaⁿ-ièn**, a very good sort. **mê-ièn**, an inferior sort, but genuine. **ièn-tsoáⁿ**, pieces of raw bird's-nest shaped like a cup or Chinese spoon. **ièn-si**, thin strips of it. **ièn-chhùi**, small broken bits of it.

hó-thâu ièn-ām, head like a tiger's and neck like a swallow's (said of a noble-looking man). **giòk-ièn**, a beautiful small bird.

iēn [R. iên, a cause], to work the border of a dress more ornamentally than "kún" (esp. T.). **siuⁿ-kún-iēn**, to put ornamental borders of various sorts on women's dress. **iēn-niáⁿ** (C. T.), to work an ornamental border near the neck of a woman's dress.

iēn — **chhèng-iēn**, a port-hole in a junk. **ūi chhèng-iēn**, to paint false port-holes.

iet [R. a scorpion, = col. giet]. **tsoân-iet**, salted scorpions (used as a medicine for dyspepsia).

iét [R. to be pleased], (C. oát). **hù-iét**, the god of builders (v. hù, a surname).

iét [R. to look over; to examine], (C. oát). **iét-lék**, experienced; well skilled.

iét [R. amusement; easy; self-indulgence]. **phiau-iét**, lively, easy, self-confident, and unconstrained in manner.

iét, to dye (said only of old silk stuffs).

iét [R. sièn, a fan; to fan; to wave], to fan; to wave; to beckon with the hand, palm downwards, moving the fingers towards us; to call a person to us.

iét-sìⁿ, to fan. **iét-hong**, id. **iét-hé**, to fan a flame. **iét-sit-hé**, to put out a flame by fanning. **iét kún-tsúi**, to fan a fire for boiling water. **iét-báng**, to fan away mosquitoes. **iét hong-ké**, to work fanners. **iét-hong-kūi** (C.), id. in shops. **iét-kî**, to wave a flag.

iét-phâng, to change the sail to the other side of the vessel. **iét-lìn-tńg**, id.

iét-chhiú, to beckon with the hand, palm downwards and fingers moved towards one's self, in calling a man to come, as if drawing him towards us. **iét-tī-á**, a small tail on the side of a little boy's head, supposed to beckon a new brother to come. **kúi teh-iét--lí**, the demons are beckoning you; you are going in a wicked course that will end in ruin.

hî-iét, pectoral fins of fish.

ih — **ih-oat**, much involved, as an affair; also (C.), winding, as a road.

ih (= ihⁿ). **ih-út**, grumbling and dissatisfied.

ih — **péh-ih**, sort of Chinese soap.

ih (R. î), the sweet-bread or pancreas of the cow or sheep (in the pig it is called "chhioh"). **gû-ih**, sweet-bread of cow. **iûⁿ-ih**, sweet-bread of sheep or goat.

ih (next word?). **làh-ih**, honey-comb after the honey is removed. **phang-ih**, id.

ih — **chiâⁿ-ih**, united in a mass, as a quantity of grass, or as hair long uncombed. **kui-tsong kui-ih**, in considerable quantities, as goods.

ihⁿ (cf. nihⁿ). **ihⁿ-ihⁿ-tán**, to wait anxiously, as for news, or for a person. **ihⁿ-ihⁿ-khoàⁿ**, to look for very earnestly, as for some one who has delayed very long. **ihⁿ-ihⁿ-lâu**, to flow abundantly, as tears. **ihⁿ-ihⁿ-siá**, to write constantly.

ihⁿ — **tāng-ihⁿ-ihⁿ**, very heavy.

ihⁿ — **ihⁿ-ihⁿ oáihⁿ-oáihⁿ**, sound of furniture creaking.

ihⁿ — **ihⁿ-áihⁿ**, dissatisfied state of mind or expression; grumbling manner. **ihⁿ-út**, = ih-út, id.

im (R. id.), the female or negative principle in nature; the Yin; often has the idea of bad luck, or illness, or darkness, or decay. **im-khì**, id.; said of a place that is damp and unhealthy. **khiàm-im**, having too little of the Yin in one's constitution, and too much of the hot Yang principle. **lòh-im**, in a low, dark, damp, unhealthy, or unlucky situation. **im-chèng**, a sort of painful swelling, as in the thigh (v. chèng).

im-iông, the positive and negative principles; the Yin and the Yang (v. iông).

thài-im (R.), the moon. **thài-im-niû**ⁿ, the goddess of the moon; the moon as a goddess.

tsu-im, causing a cool feeling, and removing feverishness (v. tsu). **im-léng**, shady; pleasantly cool (v. léng). **thiⁿ im**, sky dark and cloudy. **thiⁿ o-im**, id. **o-im**, id. **o-im-koâⁿ**, dark, cloudy, cold weather. **poàⁿ-im poàⁿ-chíⁿ**, clouds, rain, and sunshine mixed in succession. **chhun-im** (R.), the cold, dark, cloudy, rainy weather of spring. **im-sim**, dense, as the foliage of trees.

im-thim, crafty; designing (v. thim). **im-tim**, id.

im-kan, Hades. **im-si**, Hades; the ruler of Hades. **im-hûn**, the soul or spirit in the spirit-world. **kui-im**, to die. **hù-im-thiap**, a notification of a relative's death. **im-tōe**, a place for a grave. **im-tē**, id. **im-tōe put-jû sim-tōe**, a good heart is better than a

厦英大辭典

good grave-site. **hàu im-kong**, to worship the ghosts of Hades, as in 7th month, and on the 2d and 16th of any month (v. kong, "brightness").

im-kong, meritorious virtue deserving Heaven's favour (v. kong, "merit"). **im-chek**, id. (v. chek).

im-bùt (r.), the female organs. **im-mn̂g**, id.

im-jī, characters cut in; also, white characters on a black ground, printed from blocks so cut. **im-poe**, both of the divining sticks falling with the convex sides up (unfavourable).

kong-im (R.), time (lit. light and darkness). **sioh kong-im**, to be careful in the use of time. **jit-goat jû-so: kong-im sū-chièn**, days and months are like a shuttle; light and darkness like an arrow. **it-chhùn kong-im, it-chhùn-kim**, one inch of time is an inch of gold.

ìm, to flood; to inundate; tide or flood rising high. **im-chhân**, to overflow the rice-fields. **im-tsúi**, to flood with water. **im--sí**, drowned by an inundation. **im-lim--sí**, id. **tsúi im**, the tide rising. **tsúi im-phóng-phóng**, the water rising very high. **tsúi im-ām**, the flood up to the neck (said of a very great and imminent danger).

kàng-kè lâi-im--i, to sell low so as to compel him to sell low, so as to injure him, or secretly further our own ends. **pàng-kè lâi im--i**, id. **chêng-thâu bóe, āu-thâu im**, to lose much money on a large lot of goods by the price falling.

im (R. id.), sound: a sound. **siaⁿ-im**, a sound, voice, or tone. **im-ūn**, cadence; rhythm; quality of voice (v. ūn). **sit-im**, to lose voice, as in consumption, &c. **hø-im**, to give the sounds, as in learning to read.

im-gú, language. **thó-im**, vernacular or colloquial language. **koaⁿ-im**, sound of a word in the mandarin dialect. **chiang-im**, sound of a word in the Chang-chew dialect. **tsáu-im**, sound different (as in another dialect), or ill-pronounced. **tsoàh-im**, id. **tûn-im**, labials. **sip-ngó-im**, the native dictionary of the Chang-chew dialect.

pat-im, the eight tones; also, the eight kinds of music made by eight sorts of instruments.

im-sìn, news by letter, as of a relative or friend. **ti-im**, to know the meaning fully; to know how to act. **hok-im** (X.), the gospel.

koan-im, the goddess Kwan-yin, = koan-im hùt-tsó, = koan-im tāi-sū, = koan-sè-im phø-sat, = (Cn.) koan-im-má.

îm (R. id.), lascivious; lewd; to debauch; lewdness. **îm-loān**, lewd; lewdness, especially the worst forms. **kan-îm**, adultery, properly with a married woman. **îm-hū**, an adulteress. **îm-hong**, lascivious customs of a place. **îm-iok**, lust; lascivious passions. **hòⁿ-îm**, fond of lewdness. **îm lâng bó-kiáⁿ**, to debauch other people's wives and daughters. **bān-ok, îm ûi-siú**, of all sins lewdness is the chief.

ím [R. to drink]. **ím-sit**, food and drink (v. sit). **thiòng-ím**, drinking much liquor. **khai-hoâi thiòng-ím**, making jolly over the cups. **phiâu tó ím**, whoredom, gambling, and drinking.

ìm [R. shade, to protect, to cover up, to extinguish by covering]. **ìm-ńg**, the shade, as of a tree. **chhiū-ìm-ńg**, the shade of a tree.

ìm-sīⁿ, drysalted peas, prepared by covering up close. **ìm-hé**, to extinguish a fire by covering it up. **ìm-hoa**, id. **hé ìm-sit**, id. **ìm hé-thoàⁿ**, to extinguish charcoal by covering it up. **ìm-kńg**, a joint of bamboo used as an extinguisher for extinguishing a match. **hé-ìm-kńg**, id. **hé-ìm-kóng**, id.

hong-súi ìm-khoàⁿ, to bury the bones of a pig in a jar or small coffin, to try whether the soil of a grave-site is good: if after some years the bones remain hard and brown, the soil is suitable.

tì-ìm, to protect; to assist by power or influence. **ìm chhin-chhek**, to protect one's relations. **siū-ìm**, to receive such protection. **ìm-seng**, the son of a high mandarin who gets office readily because of his father. **ìm-sin** (C.), id. **ìm chit--ê miâⁿ-jī**, to give protection to a person, as sub-officials in yamuns do. **ìm chit--ê báu-miâⁿ**, do., by putting a man's name (as a nominal employé) on the books.

hok-ìm, to assist or protect, as an influential friend; sometimes by money; to benefit, as ancestors by their wealth or merit in government matters. **hok-ìm kiáⁿ-sun**, to benefit descendants, as parents or ancestors, by accumulated wealth, or by the meritorious services they have rendered to the state, &c. **siū-lí hok-ìm**, I have to thank you for your powerful assistance. **bāng-lí hok-ìm**, I hope to have the shelter of your powerful influence. **pn̄g lí--ê hok-ìm**, I take the advantage of your influential assistance.

in [R. a cause, from a cause or occasion]. **in-ūi**, because of. **in-hô**, why? **in-sî chè-gî**, to fit our actions to the state of the case.

khí-in, the cause or original commencement of an affair. **in-iû**, a cause. **in-toaⁿ**, id. **in-toaⁿ khí-lí, sī tsáiⁿ-iūⁿ**, under what circumstances did this matter originate. **hō-i bô-in**, give him no opportunity to meddle. **kap-goá bô-in**, I have nothing to do with it.

in [R. a thick mat]. **in-tîn**, wormwood; Artemisia.

in, to wind; to twine; a wisp, as of straw; a ball or tightly rolled reel, as of yarn. **in-soaⁿ**, to wind thread. **in kè-á-lê**, to wind one's tail in a knot behind the head. **in khah-ân**, wind it more tightly. **in-in khah-siap-tiap**, id. **in-in tāu-tîn**, said of a long story with intricate details and no clue (lit. of pea-stalks). **in-in tāu-tîn chit-toā-thoa**, id.; also said of meddling with what is not our business.

chháu-in, a wisp of straw. **chit-in-chháu**, id. **soàⁿ-in**, a ball or reel of thread. **chit-in-soàⁿ**, id. **chit-in soh-á**, a ball of cord. **kiâm-chhài ū chit-in**, (salted vegetables are tied in a bundle), said in allusion to "in," a cause, the matter has some origin.

in [R. relationship; marriage]. **hun-in**, a marriage. **in-iên**, decrees of fate about marriage (v. iên).

in, they; them; their; his. **in-ê**, theirs; their; his. **in-tau**, their house (residence); his house or place. **in-chhù**, id. **in-pē**, his father; their father.

in (C.), = A. un, grace; favour.

in (C.) **in-khîn**, = A. un-khûn, kind to visitors.

in (C.) **in-chiûⁿ**, = i-chiûⁿ, clothes.

in [R. chhin; related]: **saⁿ-in-chhiūⁿ** (Cn.), = saⁿ-chhin-chhiūⁿ, alike.

în (R. id.), a cyclical and horary character. **în-sî**, from 3 to 5 A.M. **în tsòng, báu hoat**, as soon as the body is buried, the auspicious influence of the grave is exerted.

în (R. iên). **în-oān**, = iên-oān, to delay; to procrastinate.

în (C.), = A. hûn (R.), clouds. **în-lâm**, = A. hûn-lâm, the province of Yun-nan.

ín (R. ún), to consent; to promise. **ín-beh**, to

promise that (he) will. **ín--lâng**, to promise to some one. **ín-lâng-kang**, to promise to do work for some on. **ín-hè**, to promise goods to the buyer. **ín-iûⁿ-hè**, to promise to sell goods for exportation.

ín (C.) **tē-ín**, = A. tē-ún, a worm.

ín (C.), = A. ún, secret (only in some phrases).

ín (Cn.), = A. án, ńg; prefix to names of relationships. **ín-tia**, = A. án-pē, papa! **ín-iâ**, = A. áu-néⁿ, mamma!

ín (R. id.), to lead; to quote. **chio-ín**, to invite to go with one, to good or bad. **ín-iú**, to allure, esp. to evil. **ín-lō͘**, to guide in the way. **ín-chhoā**, to lead; to guide (lit. or fig.) **ín-thoā**, to lead a man to imitate us, esp. bad (v. thoā).

ín-chìn, to introduce to favour, or for notice, or for employment, as a friend does. **ín-chièn**, id. **khan-ín**, id. **ín-kièn**, a high mandarin having an audience of the emperor on getting higher rank or new office.

ín-hé, to light one lamp from another; to catch fire, as from a spark; fire spreading. **ín-teng** (T.), to light one lamp from another. **ín-hong**, to cause a draught of wind; to cause a cold or rheumatism, as a draught of air, or as eating fat food. **phoà-siⁿ ín chheng-hong**, a broken fan can make a cool breeze.

ín-hûn, to bring back the spirit of a man who has died away from home. **ín-kúi jip-thèh**, to bring demons or ghosts into a house.

bô-chiam put ín-soàⁿ (without a needle one cannot draw a thread through), without an introduction or beginning made, the matter cannot be arranged.

ín-khí, to introduce a subject; to quote. **ín chheh-kù**, to quote a book-phrase. **ín kò-tién**, to quote ancient ceremonies, books, or antiquities.

ín-kheh, to procure passengers for a vessel, as a broker does, for a commission—gen. about ten per cent. **ín-tsāi**, to ship goods for another in another man's vessel, taking them in and forwarding them, for a commission; to collect cargo for a vessel from various quarters, as broker or commission-agent; to do the business of a shipping-agent. **thòe-goá ín-tsāi**, to collect goods as cargo for my vessel, as a broker, &c. **kā-goá ín-tsāi**, id.

tsúi-ín, a conduit for water. **ióh-ín**, a medicine mixed with other things, especially one co-operating with other medicines. **lō͘-ín**, a sort of passport. **tsoá-ín**, a paper match. **hé-ín**, id. **hiuⁿ-ín**, an incense-stick used as a match.

ín-tsn̂g, an awl. **ín-khèng**, a sort of musical instrument (v. khèng). **ín-tsúi-chio**, a medicinal plant (v. chio).

ìn [R. èng, to fit or correspond; to answer], to answer. **ìn-tap** (R.), id. **ìn-siaⁿ**, to answer with the voice; to echo a word distinctly. **ìn-ōe**, to give a verbal answer. **gâu-ìn-chhùi**, answering a superior insolently. **ìn-chhùi ìn-chih**, determined to have the last word. **ìn-öh** (Cn.), to give a slight belch politely to show we have eaten enough.

kiò-ìn, to call and to answer. **kiò-bōe-ìn**, to call, but get no answer; said also of a man near death. **saⁿ-kiò-ìn**, to rhyme; to correspond, as sentences, clauses, or words in prose; to echo; to answer one another, as in scolding, or when junks beat gongs. **hó-kiò, m̄-hó-ìn**, though speaking kindly to him, he will not hear. **soaⁿ-téng bô-hó-kiò; soaⁿ-ē bô-hó-ìn**, said of mutual reviling. **kiò-thiⁿ, thiⁿ m̄-ìn; kiò-tōe, tōe bô-thiaⁿ**, to call on heaven and earth, but get no answer.

ìn-thīn, well proportioned to each other, as two articles (v. thīn). **ìn kha-pō͘**, the step of each bearer agreeing with the step of the other, as of two men carrying a sedan or one load.

ìn (R. id.), a stamp; a seal; a mould (used by stamping); to stamp; to print; to mould, as bricks. **ìn-sìn**, the stamp put on any document to make it trustworthy. **ìn-siū** (R.), seals of office and girdle. **ìn-thek**, yellow roll fastened to an idol's seal (v. thek). **ìn-thit** (C.), id. **ìn-sek**, the red ink used in stamping with a seal. **ìn-sek-áh**, the small box holding it. **ìn-áh**, case for a seal. **ìn-kui**, small frame in which a seal is firmly wedged while being cut.

koaⁿ-ìn, official seal or stamp. **chiàⁿ-ìn-koaⁿ**, a civil mandarin who uses a square seal, as the provincial judge, the treasurer, the foo, and the hien, who govern the old original divisions of the country. **phien-ìn--ê**, mandarins who use oblong seals, holding offices of more recent institution, as governor-general, governor, tau-tai, fun-foo, and fun-hien. **tiàm-hō-ìn**, a stamp with the name of a shop or firm upon it. **siáh-ìn**, a seal made of marble. **gėk-ìn**, a seal made of jade-stone.

kau-ìn, to hand over the official seal to the successor. **chiap-ìn**, to receive it, as the new mandarin does. **tiah-ìn**, to take away the seal from a degraded mandarin. **khoàⁿ-ìn**, to have temporary charge of the seals of office, and do routine work for the mandarin when he is absent for a short time. **pài-ìn**, to bow to the official seal and worship it on receiving it. **hong-ìn**, to close the public offices for the holidays. **khui-ìn**, to open them at end of holidays.

phah-ìn, to stamp or seal in general. **tεh-ìn** (C.), id. **tn̍g-ìn**, to seal or stamp, esp. as private persons. **khàm-ìn**, do. as officials. **phah-chhiú-ìn**, to stamp irrevocably with the impression of one's hand wet with ink. **phah kha-ìn chhiú-ìn**, do. of hand and foot, as in selling a wife.

ìn-chheh, to print books. **ìn-pán**, wooden blocks for printing. **khek-ìn-pán ê-ōe**, words that will not be changed; a set phrase, as forms of salutation used by all. **ìn-kim**, to print idolatrous paper (v. kim). **ìn-hoe-pò͘**, printed cottons (v. hoe). **ìn-si-tsoá**, thin large semitransparent paper.

ìn thô͘-kat, to mould unburned bricks. **ku-ìn**, a mould for making turtle-shaped cakes. **ìn-ku**, to make such cakes. **ìn pút-á**, to mould small clay images, each side done separately and then joined together.

īn (R. id.) **hoâi-īn** (R.), pregnant. **ū-sin-īn**, to be pregnant. **toà-sin-īn** (Cn.), id. **toā-īn** (Cn.), id.

īn [R. ūn, to move; to transport], to re-echo; to echo with reverberations. **soaⁿ īn--khí-lâi**, long re-echoing among the hills.

io [R. hiau, to invite], to invite and lead another, especially to lasciviousness. **io-chhoā--i**, to lead him about, showing him attentions, as for pleasures. **io--lâng thit-thô**, to invite a man to go idly strolling about, esp. to bad things. **saⁿ-io saⁿ-chio**, leading one another about, as to amusement or idolatry. **saⁿ-chio saⁿ-io**, id. **chio-io**, id. **saⁿ-chio-io**, id.

io [R. iòk, to nourish], to cherish fondly or nourish up, as a child. **io-lin**, to give suck, as a nurse only. **io-kiáⁿ**, to nourish children. **io-kiáⁿ-bú**, a wet-nurse. **io-i-khùn**, to carry away a child and put it to sleep. **hó-io-chhī**, easily managed, as a healthy good-tempered infant.

io [R. iau, small], the throw of one in playing dice; an ace. **io-khang**, the dice giving only the ace; a bad throw. **io-jī-sa**ⁿ, the throw of the dice, 1, 2, and 3 respectively. **io-jī-sam**, id.

io (R. iau), the waist; the loins; kidneys (of meat). **poàⁿ-io**, the waist. **téng-poàⁿ-io**, the body above the waist or loins. **ē-io**, the part of the body just below the waist. **lám ē-io**, to seize one's opponent (in wrestling) by the waist so as to throw him down: thus a little man may get the better of a tall man. **niū̍ⁿ--lí lám ē-io**, I will even let you take me by the waist, and yet you cannot overcome me; I am not the least afraid of you. **sin-io**, the waist, in relation to its shape. **sin-io tn̂g**, having a long waist. **sin-io té**, having a short waist; so also, sin-io khoah, sin-io toā, sin-io sòe. **io-kut**, the lower part of the back-bone.

io-chí, kidneys (said of pigs). **gû-io**, cows' kidneys. **iûⁿ-io**, sheeps' kidneys. **ti-io**, pigs' kidneys.

àⁿ-io, to bow. **hâ-io**, to gird one's self; to put on a girdle. **hâ io-toà**, id. **sơ-io**, stooping in gait, as old man or yamun people. **phak-io** (T.), id. **chhah-io**, to put one's hands on the hip-joints. **tûi-io**, to shampoo the loins. **tó-io**, to throw back the head and make the belly project, as child throwing cymbals, or as a man about to stand on his hands. **pán-io** (C.), id.

hoâiⁿ-io, a strong cross-bar, such as runs along below the windows of a wooden verandah. **soaⁿ-io**, a path along a ledge half-way up a mountain between steep parts above and below. **phīⁿ-io**, the bridge of the nose between the eyes; it includes a little way down the nose. **sn̂g-io**, narrowed at the middle, as an hour-glass or insect. **nahⁿ-io**, id. **ti-io-hoān**, kidney-shaped.

io-pau, a purse worn at the side. **io-tớ**, a long broad leather girdle with pockets. **io-pêng**, a money-bag with a flap cover like a pocket, hung at side from girdle. **io-phêng**, id. **io-to**, a sword worn at the girdle (v. to). **io-toà**, a girdle or waist-band. **io-tháng**, a tub used for accouchement.

io, in several tones, used in Tiô-thoà and Koàn-kháu for A. ơ; *e.g.* "black."

iô (R. iâu), a surname.

iô (R. iâu), a kiln; a pottery. **he-iô**, a lime-kiln. **hoe-iô** (C.), id. **hûi-iô**, a pottery. **oáⁿ-iô**, a pottery for making bowls. **hiā-iô**, a brick-kiln. **hoā-iô** (Cn.), id.

iô (R. iâu), to shake about; to scull; to shake dice; to wag, as tail; to swagger or swing from side to side in walking; to ring, as a hand-bell. **chhiū iô-hong**, the tree is shaken by the wind. **hong iô-chhiū**, id.

iô-tsoah, excited, as the populace, by rumours of insurrection or incitements to tumult, &c.

iô **tâu-á**, to rattle the dice. iô **chhiam-á**, to shake the divining lots (v. chhiam). **iô-hē**, to raffle for help in a mutual assistance club.

iô **giang-á**, to ring a small hand-bell. **iô tsáp-sè**, to go along shaking a small hand-bell, as a pedlar. iô **thih-pán**, to make a similar signal by a bit of iron or brass, as people who go about mending metal articles. **iô tâng-pán**, id.

iô-tsûn, to scull a boat. **iô-lớ**, id.

iô-nâⁿ (C.), = A. ơ-nâⁿ, a cradle.

iô-pái, to walk in a swaggering way, or swinging from side to side; to shake, as a boat by wind or waves. iô **pái-pái**, id. **iô-thâu pái-bé**, gestures of great delight, as at deliverance from danger. **iô-thâu**, to shake one's head. **iô-bé**, to wag the tail. **iô-chhiú**, **to shake the hand** (bent back with the palm outwards) on the axis of the wrist, or from side to side, as a sign of declining, refusing, forbidding, or warning. **iô-chhiú** **nihⁿ-bák**, to shake the hand and wink, as giving a secret signal. **iô-kha hìⁿ-chhiú**, to swagger about. **iô kha-chhng-hoe**, to make one's hips swing from side to side in walking. **iô seng-khu**, to swing one's self from side to side. **kiâⁿ iô-iô**, to walk in a swaggering way. **phû-phû iô-iô**, id. **sam-pán-iô**, self-important strutting manner (lit. like a boat sculled). **iô-lâng bô-tsâi, iô-ti khì-thâi**, a swaggering fast sort of man can't get rich; a restless pig is soon killed. **iô-sai**, little children shaking their heads about (v. sai, "a lion"). **khang-chhiú pėh-iô** (T.), to come and go empty-handed, as on a fruitless errand when money was expected, or as an idle fellow who will not carry anything, or as a guest who should have left some gift.

ió [R. ó, to strike, = col. áu], to strike a side blow with a stick, as on the waist. **ió--chih**, to break by a side-blow, as a man's leg. **kha-kut ió-chih**, leg broken thus.

ió (R. iáu), Cn. = A. iúⁿ, to bale or lade out, as water. **ió-chiú** (Cn.), to buy wine.

iơⁿ (P.), in all the tones, = A. iuⁿ.

ioh [R. ek, a hundred thousand; to guess], to guess. **ioh-jī**, to guess a character. **ioh-bī**, to guess riddles, as children. **ioh-chiâ-khōng**, to play a game of chance by guessing which end of a stalk of sugar-cane will be longer when broken. **tsáp-ioh, káu m̄-tióh**, guesses are ten to one wrong.

ioh [R. iok, to make an agreement]. **toàn-ioh**, to make a definite agreement. **saⁿ-toàn-ioh**, id.

ioh — **chhiⁿ-ioh**, a green frog, larger than "chhân-kap-á," but smaller than "súi-koe."

ioh (= iā). **âi--ioh**, exclamation of sudden pain (v. âi).

ioh — **ioh-ioh**, too thin, as jelly that will not coagulate; soft and flabby, as the flesh of a too fat man.

ioh (R. iok), (Cn.), a very small quantity; one-tenth of a "kap."

ioh (Cn.) **phû-phû ioh-ioh** (= A. iô), walking in a swaggering way.

io̍h (R. io̍k), a lock; to lock. **mn̂g-io̍h**, a door lock. **io̍h-mn̂g**, to lock a door. **io̍h-kúi**, the bolt of a lock.

io̍h — **chhùi io̍h-io̍h**, broken down very small (v. chhùi). **tsú kàu io̍h-io̍h** (T.), to cook, as rice, till very soft. **beh-io̍h-lio̍h--khì** (T.), to get broken down small, as cakes or such eatables kept too long, or as rice very much boiled. **io̍h--khì** (C.), to grow bad, as coagulated food.

io̍h (R. io̍k), medicine; a remedy; a drug. **bô-io̍h**, no remedy; no resource, in general. **bô-io̍h thang-tī**, id.

piáⁿ-io̍h, a sort of alkaline lye, like "kiⁿ." **oáⁿ-io̍h**, a mineral used for glazing earthenware. **kim-io̍h**, paint used for making idolatrous paper. **chhèng-io̍h**, gunpowder. **siau-io̍h**, id. **hé-io̍h**, id. **hé-io̍h-kóng**, a powder measure. **niáu-chhú-io̍h**, poison for rats; arsenic. **kâu-io̍h**, poison (esp. arsenic) for killing the "thơ-kâu" insect. **káu-io̍h**, medicine for a dog's bite; drugs given by thieves to dogs.

ko-io̍h, sort of medical plaster. **kơ-io̍h**, id. **ơ-ko-io̍h**, black plaster, gen. blistering. **phah-kûn, bōe kơ-io̍h**, to wound one's self, and put on a plaster, as quacks do. **phah thih-piⁿ, bōe kơ-io̍h**, do. with iron lash. **kơ-io̍h**, to put on a green medical preparation of herbs, like a poultice. **soa-io̍h**, medicine for colic or cholera, taken like snuff. **pớ-io̍h**, strengthening medicine. **jiét-iȯh,** heating medicine. **léng-iȯh,** cooling medicine.

iȯh-tsâi, medicines in the original natural state. **chhi^n-iȯh,** medicines slightly prepared, but still in a rough raw state. **sek-iȯh,** prepared medicine. **chháu-iȯh,** plants used for medicine. **chháu-iȯh-thâu,** medicinal roots. **iȯh-thâu,** first infusion or decoction of medicine. **iȯh-che,** second one. **iȯh-thng,** a medical infusion or decoction in general. **iȯh-tê,** a medicinal infusion; medicinal tea. **iȯh-chiú,** medicated alcoholic liquors. **iȯh-phoh,** solid refuse of medicine after infusion or decoction. **iȯh-tái,** thick dregs of it. **iȯh-î^n,** a pill. **iȯh-oân,** id. **iȯh-tan,** very concentrated powerful medicine; very small strong pill. **iȯh-hún,** medicinal powder. **phah-piàⁿ-iȯh,** medicine that will kill or cure. **ká^n-hē tāng-iȯh,** venture to prescribe very powerful medicine.

hoā^n-iȯh, to solder.

chè-iȯh, to prepare drugs, esp. in large quantities, changing them from "chhi^n" to "sek." **tsoa^n-iȯh,** to boil medicine. **phàu-iȯh,** to infuse medicine. **chién-iȯh,** to cut down medicine, in preparing it; to buy a dose of medicine. **kap-iȯh,** to buy medicine (to be mixed) according to a prescription. **thiah-iȯh** (T.), id. **hô-iȯh,** to prepare food along with a medical prescription. **tīm-iȯh,** to stew medicine, either alone or with food. **pûn-iȯh,** to blow in a medicine with a quill. **hȯk-iȯh,** to swallow medicine. **chiȧh-iȯh,** id. **phài-iȯh,** to prescribe medicine. **kng-pùt thó-iȯh,** to bring an idol and ask it what medicine to take. **pùt-iȯh,** medicine prescribed by an idol.

iȯh-hng, a medical prescription. **iȯh-toa^n,** do. written out for the apothecary. **iȯh-ín,** a medicine that is used for mixing with others. **chit-thiap-iȯh,** a dose of medicine. **iȯh-sèng,** the nature of a medicine. **iȯh-sèng-hù,** a book of medical prescriptions, &c., in rhyme. **iȯh-chheh,** medical books. **iȯh-téng,** a small steelyard. **iȯh-chién,** machine for cutting down medicines small. **iȯh-ông,** Shin-nung, the god of medicine. **iȯh-tsâi-ông,** id.

iok [R. to bind; an agreement; about so much, = col. ioh], (C. iak), an agreement; a treaty; a bargain or lease; to make an agreement.

iok-sok, to restrain.

iok-liȯk, in general; about (so much); more or less, calculating roughly. **iok-liōng,** id. **liōng-iok,** id. **tāi-iok,** id.

iok-jī, a written agreement. **háp-iok,** an agreement or bond in duplicate, the word "háp" being stamped on both so as to make them tally. **hô-iok,** a treaty of peace; to make an agreement. **siong-iok,** to make an agreement or contract. **lip-iok,** to make a contract. **toàn-iok,** to make a definite agreement or arrangement. **pōe-iok,** to break a contract or agreement. **iok-liáu bô-iá^n,** to promise but not fulfil. **àm-iok,** to make a secret arrangement. **su-iok,** a private agreement. **kong-iok,** a public agreement, as by mandarins or the head men of villages. **kìm-iok,** a public agreement of all the people of a place to forbid some practice (sometimes originating with superiors).

sin-iok (X.), the New Testament (lit. new agreement or covenant). **kū-iok** (X.), the Old Testament.

iȯk [R. to nourish; to bring up, = col. io]. **seng-iȯk,** to get a child (said of either parent). **iȯk-eng-tông,** a foundling hospital.

iȯk [R. to bathe by throwing water over one's self]. **tsai-kài bȯk-iȯk,** to fast and bathe ceremonially (v. tsai).

iȯk (R. id.) **chiok-iȯk,** a flower like a peony.

iȯk [R. to wish; to desire]. **iȯk-kiû thien-siōng-hok,** whoever wishes to ask happiness from Heaven (v. hok). **iȯk-kan iȯk-sat,** determined to be at feud. **su-iȯk** (R.), all sorts of evil passions and desires, including covetousness, anger, lust, &c. **khí-su-iȯk** (R.), these desires or passions excited.

iȯk [R. lustful desire]. **îm-iȯk,** lascivious desire or passion. **sek-iȯk,** id. **iȯk-hé,** the fire of lust. **iȯk-hé teh-tȯh,** lustful desire arising. **khí iȯk-hé,** id.

iong [R. an abscess, carbuncle, or very bad boil, = col. eng], (also C., = A. eng, id.) **lin-iong,** an abscess or deep boil at the side of the teat. **tō͘-iong,** a large boil on the belly. **hì-iong,** a deep abscess near the lungs. **iong-tsu hoat-pòe,** sloughing carbuncle on the back.

iong [R. middle; to intrust with a commission, = col. iang, ng], (C. iang). **iong-thok,** to commission; to intrust with a matter.

iong [R. calamity], (C. iang). **tsai-iong,** calamities. **siū-tso-iong** (r.), to meet with terrible calamities, as rebellion, &c.

iông [R. liông, a beam]. **tiòng-iông,** better "tiòng-liông," important, as a person or matter.

iông [R. the face; to bear with; easy]. **iông-ún,** to bear with; to tolerate. **khoan-iông,** to bear long with; indulgent; long-suffering. **pau-iông** (R.), id. **iông-chhiông,** to indulge; not find fault with. **thien put-iông,** Heaven will not endure it (said of wicked plotting).

iông-ī^n (P. êng-ī^n), easy.

chhiong-iông, taking things calmly, quietly, easily, or leisurely; not bustled, frightened, or agitated; not too urgent; calm and easy in manner. **chhiong-iông tsū-tsāi,** do.; calm and self-possessed.

bīn-iông (r.), countenance. **iông-māu^n,** id. **gân-iông,** complexion. **iu-iông,** a sad expression of face. **tài-iu-iông,** having a morose or sulky look. **chhiò-iông,** a happy look of face. **hêng-iông,** appearance of person.

iông [R. constant, common, = col. iû^n]. **tiong-iông,** the due medium; the Chung-yung or doctrine of the Mean. **iông-i,** an incompetent doctor; a quack. **iông-i sat-jîn,** a quack kills people. **iông-hu siȯk-tsú,** common rough illiterate people. **iông-iông to hō͘-hok,** ordinary people commonly have much happiness. **iông-siô** (C.), = A. iû^n-siû^n, very useless, as a man.

iông (R. id.) **phû-iông-hoe,** the Hibiscus rosa sinensis. **phû-iông,** id. **hû-iông-hoe,** id. **jiȯk-chhiòng-iông,** a strengthening medicine, esp. for venereal complaints.

iông [R. to display; to publish abroad], (C. iâng). **hién-iông,** grand or fine looking, as a house. **ì-khì iông-iông,** proud bearing of a successful or prosperous man. **iāu-bú iông-ui,** said of a man having a proud consequential manner (v. ui).

pò-iông, to publish abroad; to proclaim widely. **lōng-iông,** to spread injurious reports, either true or false. **m̄-thang lōng-iông,** don't let this matter be known. **bêng iông sù-hái,** very famous and illustrious (v. bêng, "name").

iông [R. id., = col. iû^n], (C. iâng), the masculine or positive principle or influence of nature; the Yang, having relation to warmth, light, life, and prosperity. **iông-**

khì, id. **pé-iông**, strengthening the positive influence in the human constitution (opposed to "tsu-im"). **hiòng-iông**, in a good airy healthy situation.

thài-iông, the sun. **thài-iông-kong**, the sun, as an object of worship. **tiông-iông-tsoeh**, the 9.9 (lit. double masculine, as 9 is a masculine number), when Khoe-seng is specially worshipped. **tiông-iông**, id. **sió-iông-chhun**, warm genial weather in winter. **chí-iông**, name of an academy in ē-mn̂g-káng.

au-iông, a surname.

iông-kan, the present life; the visible world. **hôe-iông**, to return to life. **iông-ku**, a dwelling-house, opposed to "im-tē," a grave.

iông-jī, large embossed characters, as on a sign-board (v. jī).

iông-bùt, the penis. **hoat-iông**, erection of it. **tó-iông**, loss of virility, as in an old man. **tsòng-iông ê-ióh**, medicine for aphrodisiac purposes.

im-iông, the Yin and Yang; the negative and positive, or feminine and masculine, influences or principles of nature. **im-iông-si**, an idol (in the temple of the tutelary god of a city) having the two sides of his face red and black respectively; he has authority in both worlds. **im-iông hoán-pōe**, turning day into night. **im-iông-tsúi**, warm and cold water mixed, just so warm as can be taken into the mouth. **kiáu im-iông-tsúi**, to mix hot and cold water thus.

iông [R. a sheep or goat, =col. iûⁿ], (C. iâng). **biên-iông**, a dressed lamb-skin. **lêng-iông**, a sort of antelope. **lêng-iông-kak**, its horns, of a white colour (used medicinally). **lêng-iông sai-kak**, id.

kong-iông-toān, a book on the "chhun-chhiu" record of Confucius.

iông [R. an ulcer; a suppurating sore, =col. iûⁿ], (C. iâng). **iông-mûiⁿ**, a bubo.

ióng [R. to nourish, =col. iúⁿ], (C. iáng). **ióng-liâm**, salary of a mandarin (lit. nourishing administrative purity). **ióng-siām**, share kept by a father for himself when dividing his property among his sons (v. siām).

tiâu-ióng, to take care of, as one's own health. **pó-ióng**, id.; also, to take care of a child for another person, as to bodily wants. **pôe-ióng**, to foster, nourish up, train, and educate carefully, as children; to take care of, as one's own health.

ióng-bú, adoptive-mother, who has brought up a child; foster-mother. **phāu-ióng--ê**, son adopted from infancy. **bú-ióng**, to nourish carefully and bring up, as a child. **ióng-seng-tn̂g**, a foundling hospital. **ióng-jî thāi-ló**, to bring up a son, expecting his help in old age. **chio-hu ióng-tsú**, to get a second husband to bring up the children.

ióng (P.), =A. éng, a wave.

ióng (R. id.), strong; strong and well; a brave; a militiaman or volunteer. **ióng-kiāⁿ**, strong, as a man. **ióng-sin-miāⁿ**, in good health. **ióng-tsòng**, strong and vigorous, as a young grown-up man. **ióng-ōng**, lusty and vigorous. **tng-ióng**, to be a brave or militiaman; to be just about come to one's full strength, as about eighteen or twenty. **pé-ióng**, to eat strengthening medicine.

peng-ióng, soldiers in general. **gī-ióng**, militiamen, volunteers, or braves (v. gī). **liēn-ióng**, a sort of volunteers. **hô-lâm-ióng**, soldiers from central China, especially Hu-nan. **ióng-kah**, a soldier's jacket with the word "ióng" on it.

ióng-béng, brave. **tiong-ióng-sû**, temple to distinguished military officers who have died for their country. **iú-ióng bû-bô**, brave without wisdom. **hòⁿ-ióng**, a bully. **tó-ióng**, two men trying which is stronger, or each boasting of superior courage and strength. **hùn-ióng** (R.), to make great efforts. **pāi-peng chi-chiòng, put-kám giên-ióng**, the commander of defeated soldiers does not dare to speak of valour.

kī-ióng, a stone used for trying the strength of candidates at the military examinations. **phah kī-ióng**, to exercise with it. **phō kī-ióng**, to lift it and lay it on one's breast. **khó-kī-ióng**, to try candidates with this exercise.

iòng (R. id.) **iòng-chiòng** (R.), to crowd together, as persons.

iòng [R. to shine, to reflect], (C. iàng). **iòng-jit** (R.), facing the sun.

iòng (P.) **iòng-chhài**, =A. èng-chhài, a vegetable grown in water.

iōng [R. to use, =col. ēng], (also C., =A. ēng). **bōe-iōng-sîn--tit**, not fit to be employed (as man) for some purpose. **tiòng-iōng**, skilful; useful, as a man. **put-tiòng-iōng**, dull, stupid, awkward, and useless, as a man. **put-chiòng-iōng**, id. **put-tsòng-iōng** (C.), id. **kɛ-iōng** (C.), household expenses.

kong-iōng, for public use ("kong," public). **kong-iōng**, great usefulness and efficacy, as of a medicine or plan, but not of a person ("kong," merit, efficacy). **ū-kong-iōng**, to be of great use, as a medicine or plan.

hāu-iōng, a soldier who has got the lowest button, but no office yet; somewhat about a corporal.

ip (R. id.) **tsok-ip**, to make a low bow with folded hands. **pài-ip**, id., as to a superior, or to one whom we treat as a superior.

ip [R. id., a city]. **siāⁿ-ip**, a Hien district or county.

ip (R. id.) **ip-á**, a small hand-net on a long pole (smaller than "tsan") for rivers or ponds.

ip (R. id.), to catch with a small hand-net, as fish or shrimps. **ip-hê**, to catch shrimps thus.

ip (Cn.), =A. hip. **ip iû-pn̄g**, to cook rice with water and fat till dry. **ip-pn̄g**, id. **ip bí-ko**, to cook diamond-shaped cakes of rice with fat till dry.

it [R. ek, to increase]. **it-hoat**, all the more; so much the more; more and more.

it [R. ek, to recollect, to think upon]. **it--tióh**, to think upon with pleasure; to desire much. **it--tit**, to recollect.

it (R. id.), one of the cyclical characters, used to indicate a person not named. **kah-it**, Mr. A. and Mr. B.

it [R. one, first, entire, single, alike, =col. chit].

tē-it, the first. **tōe-it**, id. **kài-tē-it**, the very first, highest, or greatest. **kài-it-toā**, the very greatest. **tē-it-toā**, id. **it-téng**, first-class. **thâu-it-téng-lâng**, a man of first-rate rank, wealth, power, or influence. **thâu-it-téng--ê**, first-rate, first-class, as man or thing; of very great influence; of first-rate position or rank. **it-phín**, first-rank (of mandarins). **it-póng**, rank of Kújîn. **tī-hí it-āu**, at the very furthest back part, as of premises. **it-á-hiâⁿ**, front bulkhead of a boat.

chhoe-it, first day of month. **chhe-it** (C.), id. **tsáp-it**, eleven. **it-tsáp**, ten. **it-jī-tsáp-ê**, between ten and twenty. **it-jiáp**, id. **it-jiáp-goā**, a little over twenty. **ka-it-thàn**, to gain ten per cent.

chip-it, obstinate; determined; dogged. **it-tēng**,

certainly. **it-tit**, straightforward; determined on a course. **tsoan-it**, exclusively at one thing (v. tsoan). **it-iūⁿ**, of one pattern; alike. **sí-chiong jû-it**, constant from first to last. **put-it**, not agreeing. **hun-hun put-it**, id. **put-chiap-it**, matter not going on well (v. chiap).

it-thé, all alike; equally (v. thé). **it-khài**, entirely; altogether. **it-thóng**, the whole, as of a dominion (v. thóng). **it-seng**, one's whole lifetime.

it-bȯk, a one-eyed man. **it-kiok**, a man lame of one foot. **it-tiōng-hông**, the hollyhock (v. hông, "red"). **bān bū it-sit**, not one mistake in a myriad.

it-jī-pîⁿ, made as level as the character "it" (a horizontal stroke). **it-jī-boah**, laid quite level and even, as several books. **it-jī-bâi**, having one's eyebrows connected and all in one straight line (counted an omen of good luck, esp. of having many brothers); colloquial name of a man having such eyebrows.

iu [R. sad, displeased, mourning]. **iu-būn**, sad; grieved. **iu-ut** (R.), sad and disquieted; vexed. **iu-lū**, grieved and anxious. **iu-liu tsòe-chit-pé**, brow wrinkled with grief, anxiety, discomfort, or displeasure. **iu-khé**, very sorrowful. **iu-thâu khé-bīn**, having a displeased look. **bīn-iu bīn-jiâu**, face wrinkled with vexation, or anger and grief. **bīn iu-iu**, face looking sad. **bȧk-chiu-thâu iu-iu**, corners of the eyes having a sad or anxious expression. **bȧk-bâi iu-iu**, knitting the brows. **iu-iông** (r.), a sad countenance.

teng-iu, mourning for parents or grand-parents, esp. by officials. **pò teng-iu**, to report the death of a parent or grand-parent to his superior, as a mandarin or graduate does. **teng hū-iu**, in mourning for father. **teng bú-iu**, in mourning for mother. **teng kok-iu**, mourning throughout the empire for emperor or empress. **kok-iu**, id.

sit jîn-chi-lȯk, tam jîn-chi-iu, if you eat a man's wages, you should bear his troubles.

iu [R. extra, to dally, an actor]. **iu-jiû koáⁿ-toàn**, undecided in purpose. **iu-kòng**, one form of the degree of "kòng-seng" (v. kòng). **chhiong-iu, lē-tsut**, harlots, actors, and low underlings in yamuns, the most degraded classes.

iû [R. alike, doubtful]. **iû-goân**, as formerly; as before. **iû-ū put-koat**, undecided in purpose. **iû-thài** (X.), Judaea.

iû [R. û, superfluous], (C. û). **khó iû-teng**, to examine candidates to be ready for the vacancies that may occur among the soldiers. **thiáu-iû-teng**, to choose new soldiers out of these men previously examined.

iû [R. to float or drift, satisfied]. **iû-iȧh**, having the look of health and prosperity (v. iȧh).

iû (R. id.), to ramble about for amusement. **iû-goán**, to ramble at pleasure. **sì-kòe-iû**, id. **iû-siúⁿ**, to go about looking at things for amusement. **iû-hȧk**, a travelling scholar. **iû-hong hê-siūⁿ**, a travelling Buddhist priest holding a certificate; said also in scolding a man who is always idly going about his friends' houses. **iû-tsûn**, to make an excursion in a boat, esp. at the dragon-boat festival. **iû-kang**, spectators going about in boats to look at idolatrous festivals. **iû hái-bīn**, to go about for pleasure in boats.

iû-hái, an idol carried in state in a boat. **iû-soaⁿ iû-hái**, do., on land or on water. **iû-soaⁿ**, to carry about an idol (esp. ông-iâ) in procession on land. **iû-soaⁿ chhái-lē**, to do so, and have coloured hangings in the streets. **iû thien-hô**, to choose to be burned. as "ông-iâ." **iû-tē-hô**, to choose to be sent off to sea in his state-boat, as "ông-iâ."

iû-kiong, imperial conjugal intercourse.

iû-kek, a military officer about the rank of lieutenant-colonel.

iû [R. excessive; wickedness; to resent], a surname. **hāu-iû**, to follow bad example. **oàn-thien iû-jîn**, to murmur at Heaven and hate men.

iû [R. from; cause; origin; to permit; to pass through]. **in-iû**, antecedents of a matter; reason or cause. **iên-iû**, id. **goân-iû**, origin, beginning, as of a matter. **chêng-iû**, cause or circumstances of an affair. **kê-iû**, statement of the crime for which a man is made to wear the cangue, written on the cangue.

iû-chhién jip-chhim, to go on from the easy to the difficult. **poàn-tiám put-iû-jîn**, nothing comes from men (but all from fate), (v. bēng, "fate"). **thèng-thien iû-bēng**, to submit to the will of Heaven. **iû-koāiⁿ chiȧh-koāiⁿ; iû-hú chiȧh-hú**, said of a high mandarin (as viceroy or examiner) living on the districts he visits.

iû — **tsá-iû**, early rice of the summer crop, esp. from Formosa. **iû-á-bí**, id.

iû [R. hoâi]. **iû-hoe**, a tree (sophora) that yields the yellow dye called "hoâi-hoe."

iû (R. id.) **iû-hî**, a sort of fish, like trout.

iû [R. iông, the ocean, = col. iûⁿ]. **iû-âng**, = iûⁿ-âng, rich crimson (s. next word).

iû (R. id.), oil, fat, grease; oil-paint; to paint with oil-paint, or stain (as wood) with oil.

bȧk-iû, mucus from the eye. **bīn-iû**, sweat and dirt mixed with sweat on the face. **iû-káu**, oily stain or dirt from the hair. **chhàu-iû**, unpleasant oily taste or smell. **iû-khì**, having fat, as meat.

iû-láng, an oil-jar made of wicker-work and oiled paper. **iû-lâu**, a funnel used for pouring oil. **iû-siȧh**, sort of small measure or spoon for lading out oil. **iû-kàu**, a small oil measure. **iû-kau** (Cn.), a hanging lamp. **iû-ki**, a long roll of paper dipped in oil, or bamboo rolled round with paper, used for a light. **iû-chhia**, an oil-press. **iû-chiⁿ-ôe**, shoes soled with oiled felt. **iû-hia**, boots with such soles. **iû-tsoá**, oiled paper.

iû-phoh, the browned residue when a mass of fat is fried down. **iû-khe**, the refuse from making tea-oil (v. khe). **iû-tái**, dregs of oil. **iû-chɛ** (C.), id. **iû-chhang**, onions fried in fat. **iû-pn̄g**, rice cooked dry with fat, &c. (v. pn̄g).

iû-tiû, a glossy sort of cloth from Canton. **iû-lėk**, rich glossy green cloth. **iû-lê**, a small glossy blackish gray snail.

iû-chhat, paint and varnish; to paint or varnish (v. chhat). **iû-o**, to paint black. **iû-âng**, to paint red (s. previous word). **kan-iû**, oil, unmixed with paint, used for varnishing or staining wood. **kim-iû**, sort of paint made with comminuted gold or brass, so as to shine like gilding. **o-ien-iû**, oily soot; black paint made of lamp-black.

chhì-iû, oil burned in lights beside a corpse (v. chhì). **chêng-iû**, idolatrous rites of purification (v. chêng).

gû-lin-iû, butter. **gû-iû**, tallow. **ti-lâ-iû**, hog's lard (v. lâ). **koe-kè-iû**, fat about pig's sweet-bread, &c. **bāng-se-iû**, fat near the mesentery of the pig. **iû-jī**, fat, as edible. **kheng-iû**, wax from the tallow tree.

tāu-iû, soy. **o-tāu-iû**, dark-coloured soy. **seng-**

iû, the common oil from ground-nuts. **tê-á-iû**, oil of tea or camellia. **tê-iû**, id. **moâⁿ-iû**, oil from hemp-seed (v. moâⁿ). **hun-iû**, tobacco oil. **iâ-iû**, cocoa-nut oil. **póh-hô-iû**, oil of peppermint. **hiuⁿ-iû**, fragrant oil. **hiang-iû**, id. **thâng-iû**, oil made from the "thâng-chí" (v. thâng). **tē-pi-iû**, castor-oil. **lê-hē-iû**, oil of aloes.

tah-iû, to buy oil; to lade out oil. **phah-iû** (T.), to buy oil. **bóe-iû** (Cn.), id. **thiⁿ-iû**, to replenish a lamp with oil. **pheng-iû**, to cook in fat or oil. **chìⁿ-iû**, to fry in a large quantity of melted fat. **chiⁿ-iû**, to press oil out of seeds by wedges. **khoeh-iû**, to press out oil in an oil-press. **ngâuⁿ-iû**, to melt down fat slowly so as to purify it. **siau-iû**, to help to digest fat (as arsenic). **bak-iû**, to soil with oil or grease. **tiám-iû**, to light an oil lamp, as opposed to candles. **goá kā-lí tiám-iû**, I will remember this against you, = goá kā-lí tiám-iû, tsòe kì-hō. **tiám-iû tsòe kì-hō**, to remember a quarrel till it can be paid.

iû hé-hun, tobacco and oil for the lamp for visitors taking a smoke. **phīⁿ-thâm-noāⁿ oāⁿ iû-hé-hun**, said of a fellow sorning on us and giving us no benefit (v. noāⁿ).

iú (R. id.) **pêng-iú**, a friend. **chhin-pêng kè-iú**, relatives and old friends. **hó-iú** (r.), close friends. **hōe-iú**, fellow members of a literary society. **siā-iú**, id. **e-hun-iú**, associates in opium-smoking. **chhong-iú**, fellow-students. **thák-chheh-iú**, literary friends. **iú-ài** (r.), to love dearly, as brothers.

iú (R. id.), a cyclical character. **iú-sî**, from 5 to 7 p.m. **tiám-teng-iú**, that hour, namely, the time when people light lamps. **tiám teng-hé iú**, id.

iú (R. id.) **ín-iú**, to allure to evil. **iú-hėk** (r.), to tempt and lead astray. **koái-iú**, to kidnap, as a child; to allure into evil.

iú [R. to have, = col. ū]. **iú-kong**, having merit for services to the state. **iú-tsōe**, guilty. **iú-khùi**, ashamed of one's self. **iú-chhù**, attractive; taking the fancy. **iú-sêng**, to become a man of note or usefulness (said of a boy that he will be so). **iú-èng**, powerful in answering prayers or vows, as an idol.

iú-hiān, few; limited. **iú-sò**, not many. **hán-iú**, rare.

iú-bû, to have and not to have. **iú-sún bû-ek**, injurious without any benefit. **iú-ióng bû-bē**, brave without wisdom. **bû-tiong chhú-iú**, to take what is inferior when the best cannot be had. **bû-tiong seng-iú** (R.), to raise groundless rumours.

iù (R. id.), small; fine; broken down small. **iù-siau**, small, slim, and delicate. **iù-siù**, delicate, refined, polite. **iù-chíⁿ**, young and tender, as child; fine, as cloth. **iù-boáh-boáh**, in fine powder. **iù-boah-boah**, id., also, very smooth, as skin of child or of melon. **iù-seh-seh**, broken down small, as eatables. **iù-mng-mng**, very fine, as powder. **iù-bang-bang**, id. **iù-but-but**, very small, as boy or domestic animal. **iù-liáp-mihⁿ**, goods that have great value in small bulk.

kim-iù, powdered gold or brass, for making ornamental paper, &c. **chióh-iù**, dust and small chips from stone. **chhâ-iù**, small chips and shavings of wood. **piáⁿ-iù**, crumbs of cakes or of bread.

iù-lē, fine workmanship. **iù-kha**, bandaged small feet of women. **iù-kán**, a beautiful and accomplished female slave. **iù-pè**, fine cotton or linen cloth. **iù-tê**, fine tea, in leaf. **siⁿ iù-bah**, new good flesh forming in a wound or sore. **tsòe tāi-chì chin-iù**, the deceit arranged very carefully, so that it is very long of being detected, if at all.

iù-tông, a very young candidate for a degree. **iù-hák**, rudiments of learning; a young scholar. **iù-teng**, a little lad, as under sixteen. **lâm-hū ló-iù**, male and female, old and young. **lâm-toā lú-iù**, id.

iū [R. right-hand side; secondary]. **iū-pêng** (r.), the right-hand side. **iū-chhiú** (r.), the right hand. **iū-iâⁿ**, the right wing of an army. **iū-hú**, the officer (as chham-hú) who commands it.

iū-siòng, the second prime minister (Chinese, not Tartar). **iū-tn̂g**, the second (literary) mandarin of a city.

lîn-iū, neighbours.

tsó-iū, left and right; more or less; about so much; on an average or rough calculation. **tsó-iū-lîn**, the neighbours on each side. **tsó-sí iū-sí**, on either side is death. **phien-tsó phien-iū**, going to one side or the other of the road.

iū (R. id.) **pì-iū**, to protect, as a god does.

iū [R. hóe, wealth; to bribe]. **siū-iū**, to receive a bribe. **siū lâng-ê-iū**, to receive a bribe from a man.

iū (R. id.), also; in addition; again. **iū-koh**, id. **iū-kam**, a small green fruit of which the taste changes from sour to sweet in the mouth.

iū [R. iú, the time from 5—7 P.M.] **àm-iū** (Cn.), very late at night, after that hour, *e.g.* 8, 9, or 10.

iū (R. id.) **sià-iū** (R.), to pardon.

iū (R. id.), the pumelo or shaddock, Citrus decumana. **iū-á**, id. (C. also "nūiⁿ-á"). **âng-iū**, the red pumelo. **péh-iū**, the white pumelo. **bit-iū**, a very sweet kind. **bûn-tàn-iū**; **phīⁿ-soaⁿ-iū**, very good sorts, named from the places that produce them.

iū [R. io̍k, medicine, = col. ióh]. **iū-á-chí** (C.), a seed used for stupifying fish.

iuⁿ— **iuⁿ-siūⁿ**, to keep a child in good temper; to be very kind, as to a stranger (v. siūⁿ).

iuⁿ [R. iong, sort of insect]. **oan-iuⁿ**, an insect like a wasp. **oan-iuⁿ-siū**, its nest. **oan-iuⁿ-thê**, the stuff of which its nest is made. **oan-iuⁿ thoa ka-tsoáh**, the wasp dragging along a cockroach (said of a child with a heavy load). **oan-iuⁿ kā ka-tsoáh**, id. (lit. bites).

iuⁿ [R. a sort of bird]. **oan-iuⁿ**, the mandarin-duck, a small variety, emblem of conjugal love. **tsúi-oan-iuⁿ**, a sort of duck. **oan-iuⁿ-chím**, a pair of pillows (often embroidered with figure of this duck) given to a young couple as an emblem of affection. **oan-iuⁿ-sia, têng-thâh-khiàm**, to get goods on credit, and borrow money deeper and deeper from the same creditor.

iûⁿ (R. iông), a sheep; a goat. **iûⁿ-káng**, a ram. **iûⁿ-bú**, a ewe or she-goat. **soaⁿ-iûⁿ**, a goat. **miⁿ-iûⁿ**, a sheep. **biên-iûⁿ**, id. **iam-iûⁿ**, a wether (s. masculine).

iûⁿ-hîn, epilepsy. **iûⁿ-bák**, eyes that do not close in sleep.

iûⁿ-ko, a sheep; a sheep-skin with the wool on; a sheep-skin dress. **iûⁿ-ko-thò**, a dress worn over a sheep-skin dress. **iûⁿ-phê**, sheep-skin; vellum. **iûⁿ-phê-kim**, strong gilt-paper. **iûⁿ-mn̂g**, wool.

iûⁿ-pî, the sweet-bread of a sheep or goat. **iûⁿ-ih**, id. **iûⁿ-bah**, mutton. **thâi-ti tó-iûⁿ**, to have pigs and goats killed in great numbers, as for sacrificial offerings or great entertainments. **gû-iûⁿ-bé**, cows, sheep (or goats), and horses.

23

iû^n mĕh^n-mĕh^n, words used in calling goats. **iû^n-tài-lâi** (Cn. C.), a plant with prickly seeds.

iû^n [R. iông, sheep? willow?]. **iû^n-tô**, the Carambola, an angular fruit (v. tô).

iû^n [R. iông, a willow; a surname], the surname Yang. **iû^n-liú**, the willow. **iû^n-moâ^n**, hemp (v. moâ^n).

iû^n— **âng-iû^n** (Cn.), = khớ-koe, the bitter cucumber.

iû^n— **chiù-iû^n**, a small insect that devours grain in granaries. **iû^n-meh^n** (C.), a sort of small grasshopper. **iû^n-kóng-sai** (Cn.), = am-pơ-chê, the cicada.

iû^n [R. iông, the Yang or masculine principle; the sun]. **jia-iû^n**, a small additional roof over a shop-front to keep off the sun. **poà^n-iam-iû^n**, hermaphrodite.

iû^n (R. iông), the ocean; foreign; (a plain). **chhân-iû^n**, a flat plain of irrigated fields, larger or smaller. **pî^n-iû^n**, id. **pí^n-iû^n khòng-thớ**, a vast level plain. **hō-lóh kàu-pî^n-iû^n**, rain so heavy that the whole plain is under water. **hớ lóh pêng-iû^n, pī-khién khi**, a tiger in the plain is molested by dogs.

hái-iû^n, a pirate.

goā-iû^n, the ocean; the open sea. **toā-iû^n**, id. **pàng-toā-iû^n**, to go out to sea out of sight of land.

pàng-iû^n, to go to sea, as a trading junk. **chhut-iû^n**, to go to sea, as mandarin against pirates. **kiâ^n-iû^n**, to travel abroad by sea. **kiâ^n hoâi^n-iû^n**, to cross the sea, as to Formosa. **hoâi^n-iû^n ê-tsûn**, a junk trading to Formosa. **chit-ki^n-iû^n**, average distance that a junk sails in three hours.

iû^n-tsûn, a junk trading abroad or to very distant ports. **iû^n-hâng**, a hong engaged in foreign trade, &c. **iû^n-kheh**, a Chinaman who goes abroad to trade. **iû^n-hè**, foreign goods; goods for the foreign market. **în iû^n-hè**, to promise goods to a merchant to be sent abroad. **pān iû^n-hè**, to prepare or deal in goods to be sent abroad. **pān iû^n-tsng**, id. **iû^n-som**, foreign ginseng. **iû^n-âng**, a rich red colour from abroad. **iû^n-n̂g**, a rich foreign yellow.

sai-iû^n, the Western Ocean; Western regions; Europe and America; foreign cotton-stuffs. **sai-iû^n-pò**, foreign cotton-stuffs. **pèh-sai-iû^n**, white shirtings. **pún-sek sai-iû^n**, gray shirtings. **tang-iû^n**, Japan.

iû^n [R. iông, an ulcer or suppurating sore]. **iû^n-iû^n**, all suppurating, as a sore or ulcer. **iû^n-hī**, a suppurating ear; an ear constantly needing to be cleared of wax and moisture.

iû^n (cf. iâm). **chhùi iû^n-iû^n**, broken down small, as dry things; broken to shivers (cf. next word).

iû^n (R. iông), to melt. **gâu iû^n-chî^n**, fond of squandering money. **iû^n-thih**, to melt iron. **iû^n-thn̂g**, to melt sugar. **lí m̄-sī tsoá-kơ̂, kám-ōe iû^n--khì**, are you made of paper pasted! why are you afraid of rain as if you should melt!

iû^n-iû^n, grown soft and melting; pulpy or broken down small. **iû^n-iû^n chiù^n-chiù^n**, spoiled by being soaked to a pulp; slushy, as roads. **iû^n kơ̂-kơ̂**, grown soft and pulpy, as sweetmeats. **phah kàu iû^n-kơ̂-kơ̂**, to beat very severely (lit. to a pulp); to break to shivers.

iû^n-iû^n siû^n-siû^n, grown damp and soft, as eatables (v. siû^n).

iû^n [R. iông, constant; common]. **iû^n-siû^n**, rather dull, slow, and mediocre in ability; without temper, vivacity, or energy.

iú^n (R. iáu), (Cn. ió), to lade out (as water or oil) with a spoon, cup, ladle, &c.

iú^n (Cn. ngiú^n), thin flat tiles for roofs, laid between the boards and the outer tiles. **iú^n-á**, id. **phơ-iú^n**, to put on these inner tiles. **hiā-iú^n**, outer and inner roofing tiles.

iú^n (R. ióng), to nourish; to feed; to bring up, as a child. **iú^n-chhī**, id. **thi^n-si^n tōe-iú^n**, heaven gives life, earth nourishes. **pôe-iú^n**, to foster and tend, as children. **pó-iú^n** (C.), to take care of, as a child. **chhī hāu-si^n, iú^n lāu-sê**, to bring up a son to nourish his old father.

iú^n-pē, a foster-father. **iú^n--ê**, bought and brought up from childhood, as adopted son or slave. **an-iú^n** (Cn.), to bring up, as bought child. **tsn̂g-sōe an-iú^n** (Cn.), id. **iú^n chit-ê-kiá^n lâi-chiú**, to adopt a son, as a widow sometimes does.

iū^n [R. iōng, to feed, = col. iú^n]. **káng-iū^n** (Cn.), to worship by offerings. **kūi^n-iū^n** (Cn.), id.

iū^n [R. iōng, = col. ī^n], a form; pattern; model; manner; example; a shoot from a tree; a prolongation of last year's growth. **hoat-iū^n**, to bud at the end of a shoot; to begin to prosper. **puh-iū^n**, to bud at end of shoot. **n̂g-moâ^n-iū^n**, sprouts of hemp, used as a vegetable.

iū^n-siù^n, form; manner; appearance. **bơ̂-iū^n**, pattern; example; manner. **tsng-bơ̂ tsòe-iū^n**, to make a false pretence. **tsòe-iū^n**, to make an unsubstantial and brief show of good, &c. **tiu^n-iū^n**, to feign a false appearance (v. tiu^n).

tsái^n-iū^n, how (v. tsái^n). **tsoá^n-iū^n** (C.), id. **tsūi^n-iū^n** (Cn.), id.

thàn-iū^n, to follow the pattern or example. **khoà^n-iū^n**, to look at the pattern; to follow the pattern; to copy. **sa^n-khoà^n-iū^n**, to copy one another. **tāi-ke sa^n-khoà^n-iū^n**, all copying each other. **chiàu-iū^n**, according to the pattern. **ka-iū^n**, to cut out a pattern with scissors. **ka-ôe-iū^n**, to cut the shoe-pattern, as the betrothed daughter-in-law does at betrothal, and gives to her future mother-in-law.

siāng-iū^n, alike; of same form. **tâng-iū^n**, id. **tâng-chit-iū^n**, of same form; of same sort; alike. **chit-iū^n**, id. **it-iū^n**, id. **chit-poa^n-iū^n**, all the same; in the same manner. **pī^n-poa^n-iū^n**, id.

koh-iū^n, different; unlike; strange; unwell. **nn̄g-iū^n**, two sorts; different. **kī-iū^n**, formed curiously or different from what is usual (generally better). **khá-iū^n**, finely made. **sin-iū^n**, of a new shape, as better because more fashionable, &c. **chiâ^n-iū^n**, good or good-looking, as person or thing; correctly formed. **hó-iū^n**, of good behaviour. **pì^n hó-iū^n**, to reform one's habits; to change for the better, as man. **sió-iū^n**, rather mean in actions. **kúi-iū^n**, how many sorts or kinds? **kúi-iū^n**, very ugly or wicked (lit. like a demon). **lâng-iū^n**, form of a man. **m̄-chiâ^n lâng-iū^n**, not good-looking, as man.

厦英大辭典

J.

In some words sounded very like **l**, or interchanged with it. Sometimes, especially when nasal, very like **n**. Sometimes, as in the syllables **ji**, **jiau**, the forms that are nasal and not nasal are interchanged, for which reason I have in such cases mixed them instead of separating them as usual.

In the tones of the lower series, **j** is sometimes heard like **dz**, especially in Cn. T. before **o** and **u**, *e.g.* **dzoáh**, **dzū**, for **joáh**, **jū**.

jê (C. jôe), to rub with the hand, as in washing; to crush by turning the foot, as a worm. **jê--sí**, to crush to death, as by turning the foot or by the hand. **jê bák-chiu**, to rub the eyes. **jê-saⁿ**, to rub clothes in washing. **jê-tâm**, to wet by rubbing, as clothes in washing. **jê-ta**, to rub dry, as with hand or foot.

jek (P. in some places), = C. jiok, = A. jip, to pursue; to overtake.

jek (P.), = A. chip, to squeeze out, as matter from a wound.

jék (P.), = A. jiók, to work up, as clay.

jêng [R. formerly]. **jêng-kiū** (R.), as formerly.

jêng (P.), = A. jiông, the quick of the nail, &c.

jî — **bâ-jî-tek**, a fine sort of bamboo (v. tek).

jî [R. and, but]. **sam put-jî-sî**, occasionally. **kə put-jî-chiong**, no alternative; no other resource. **put-jî-kò** (esp. C. T., rare in A.), only. **tsū-jiên jî-jiên** (R.), self-existing.

jî-kim (r.), now; at present. **jî-āu** (C.), afterwards. **jî-bóe** (C.), at last.

jî [R. a child, a son; an affix to nouns, like col. á]. **sia-jî-á**, a very little quantity. **thih-bâ-jî**, a sort of iron anchor with three prongs.

hâi-jî-á, small toy figures of men (v. hâi). **hâi-jî-tê**, cutch or catechu; terra japonica. **jî-tê**, id. **tē-jî** (C.), a drug like a bit of child's flesh (said to spring from the ground, and to be found when ploughing!).

kán-jî, a female slave. **hui tông-jî-hì**, this is no child's play; it is a serious matter. **pó-jî**, you whoreson! (said in vile scolding).

siáu-jî, my little boy. **lâm-jî**, a male person (v. lâm). **lú-jî**, a female child; a daughter. **eng-jî** (R.), an infant. **hûi-jî-oân**, pills for making children fat. **jî-khe**, doctor who gives himself to children's diseases.

jî-sun, posterity. **jî-sun boán-gán**, numerous posterity seen before death. **kiáⁿ-jî**, children; sons; sons and daughters. **kiáⁿ-jî sim-pū**, sons, daughters, and daughters-in-law. **kiáⁿ-jî chit-toā-koah**, an immense family. **hāi-kiáⁿ hāi-jî**, to injure one's children, as ill-behaved parent.

ióng-jî thâi-ló: chek-kok hông-ki, bring up children to take care of us in old age; store up corn against famine. **liông seng liông-tsú, hó chhut pà-jî**, dragons and tigers produce their like; superior men have superior children.

jî (C.), = A. jû, a surname.

jî (C.), = A. jû, as.

jî (C.), = A. jû, tangled.

jî (C.), = A. jû, the class of literati.

jî (T.) **lê-jî**, = A. lê-chí, the cormorant.

jí (C.), = A. jú, milk.

jí [R. tsú, a lord]. **bók-jí** (C.), = bók-chí, = A. bók-tsú, ancestral tablets.

jí [R. tsú, a son; a piece in a game, = col. chí]. **thê-jí**, small, flat, rounded bits of tile (used by children in games). **jí-á**, id. **thê-jí-á**, id. **tok jí-á**, to make them. **khó jí-á**, to play by throwing them. **chiáh jí-á**, a game played with five bits of tile, one larger (bú, the mother), held in the hand, and the four others (kiáⁿ), smaller, thrown up in the air.

ə-pėh-jí (= chí), a sort of chess which has 32 men on each side. **khok-jí**, small globular bits of stone or tile like marbles (used in children's play) (v. khok).

jíⁿ [R. tsú, a son, = col. chí, jí]. **tô-jíⁿ**, = tô-chí, weights for scales.

jíⁿ [R. = níⁿ, thou; you, = col. lí]. **kap-lí bô-jíⁿ-ngó**, I will be quite open, honest, and truthful with you (v. ngó).

jíⁿ (R.), = níⁿ, the ear (v. níⁿ).

jī [R. two; second]. **tē-jī**, the second. **tōe-jī**, id. **kí-jī** (R.), id. **bé-jī--ê**, the second last (v. bé). **jī-tsáiⁿ**, the forefinger. **jī-chhoā**, widower marrying again. **jī-chhut--ê**, a woman married the second time. **jī-hun-chhin**, marriage when the bride has been married before, as widow or sold or divorced wife. **tsòe jī-hun-chhin**, to marry such a woman. **chiáh jī-chheng**, to smoke the refuse of opium made up a second time.

jī-pí, the two parties in a dispute. **jī-kâu**, that one of the dice that has two dots. **jī-sim**, double-minded. **ū-jī-sim**, id.

bô-jī, having no peer or equal (s. word). **chì-toā bô-jī**, the greatest of all; having none equal. **chhin-chhiūⁿ, kàu bô-jī**, exceedingly like.

jī-kúi, how many above twenty? which day of the last decade of the month? **jī-tsáp**, twenty; the 20th of the month. **jī-tsáp-it**, twenty-one. **jī-it**, id.; the 21st of the month. **jī-káu**, twenty-nine; the 29th of the month (v. káu). **it-jī-tsáp-ê**, near twenty. **jī-pah**, two hundred. **tsáp-jī**, twelve. **jih-jī**, twenty-two; the 22d. **tsáp-poeh jih-jī**, from 18th to 22d year (blooming period of youth). **jī-poeh**, twenty-eight. **sì-sì, tsáp-lák: jī-poeh, iáh-sī tsáp-lák**, four times four make sixteen: so also twice eight; it is just the same any way you take it.

ka-jī-thàn, to gain twenty per cent. (v. ka). **jī-pat-thiu**, to take twenty per cent. commission (v. pat).

jī [R. id., = jū], a word; a character; a style of writing; a document; one point of the Chinese compass.

miâⁿ-jī, a name. **bô-miâⁿ-jī**, name not in the books or documents. **jī-ûn**, the special characters used in families for indicating degrees of relationship (v. ûn). **jī-hō**, a character or phrase used as a mark or sign.

chit-jī, one word or character; one point of the Chinese compass; one twenty-fourth of the circumference = 15 degrees. **poàⁿ-jī**, half a point of the Chinese compass = 7½ degrees. **bô-poàⁿ-jī**, not even half a word; not a bit of a word. **teh sang-jī** (T.), = A. sang-chhiò; both evens, in tossing cash.

jī-ūn, one's fate or fortune, good or bad (v. ūn). **poeh-jī**, the eight words of a man's horoscope: year, month, day, and hour of birth (v. poeh). **jī-sò**, mode of using words for fortune-telling (v. sò).

jī-péh, a placard or hand-bill pasted up as a notice or advertisement, &c. **jī-thâu-á**, an open note, chit, or memorandum. **iok-jī**, a written agreement or bond for any purpose. **thai-jī**, a document assigning a vessel or property as security for a loan (v. thai). **bōe-jī**, a deed of sale. **liên-jī**, ornamental scrolls with sentences.

ū-jī, to have a character, as a spoken word that can be written down; to have it on black and white, as a statement or evidence; to have a document. **bô-jī**, to have no document or documentary evidence; to have no equivalent character, as some colloquial words. **bô-jī-ōe**, empty talk that cannot be depended on. **bô-jī bô-bák**, destitute of written proof (v. bák, "ink"). **siūⁿ kàu-lóng-bô-jī**, cannot think out any plan; find it impracticable. **siūⁿ--khì, ū-jī á-bô**, have you thought out a plan.

jī-gán, a literary phrase. **jī-bák chhim**, good at reading and writing (v. bàk, "the eye"). **kāu jī-sái**, full of tautology and redundant words, as a composition. **jī-bú**, a radical of a character; a letter of the alphabet. **jī-pêng**, the phonetic or formative half of a character. **khoàⁿ jī-pêng chiū-ioh**, to guess the sound from looking at the phonetic half. **ioh jī-pêng**, id. **jī-thé**, form of a word, as written ill or well. **jī-kut**, id. **bô-jī-kut**, not neatly written, as to the minute elegance of the strokes. **pak jī-kut**, to examine minutely the meaning of a difficult character. **pok jī-kut**, id. **gâu-pok jī-kut**, fond of examining things too minutely and always finding fault. **bô-jī-hoat**, ill-written, the parts quite ill-proportioned and worse than "bô-jī-kut." **bô-jī-tīn**, words not written in proper line, or not of equal size. **jī-tīn m̄-hó**, id. **jī-ùih**, strokes in characters, as regards the form of writing. **jī-ùih nńg**, characters too slim in form. **jī-ūi**, words and pictures, as on fans, scrolls, &c. **jī sū jîn-hêng**, a man's writing is similar to his bodily form.

chiàⁿ-jī, the mandarin dialect; the reading sound of characters. **péh-jī**, words written in a colloquial style. **tn̂g-jī**, Chinese characters. **hàn-jī**, id. **boán-jī**, Manchoo characters. **hoan-jī**, foreign characters. **khái-jī**, the common square form of characters used in books. **sòng-thé-jī**, the form (nearly the same) used in the Sung dynasty. **thoàn-jī**, the seal character. **chhó-jī**, current hand. **sòe-jī**, small characters (s. careful). **toā-jī**, large characters. **bé-jī**, the last word (s. second). **thiap-jī**, characters written in the style of copy slips. **tiáp-jī**, to repeat a word, as in poetry; to write two words in a space where there should only be one.

siá-jī, to write characters; to write. **liān-jī**, to practise writing. **chhiah-jī**, to brand with characters. **tsām-jī**, to stamp characters, as on metal (v. tsām). **lóh-jī**, to omit a word by mistake in writing (v. lóh). **khoàⁿ-jī**, to read or look at characters silently; to examine writing. **tiâⁿ-jī**, to examine a scholar's writing, correcting what is bad. **sûi-jī thák**, to read aloud, pronouncing each word separately. **chiàu-jī thák-jī**, to conform strictly to the terms of a written agreement. **bat-jī**, to be able to read. **m̄-bat-jī**, unable to read. **jī m̄-bat-goá**, do., said in joke. **péh-tsoá, siá ơ-jī: i bat-goá, goá-m̄-bat i**, black words on white paper: they may know me, but I don't know them!

thap-jī, words cut sunk, as on a block or slab; if on a block, they print white on a black ground. **im-jī**, id. **koah im-jī**, to cut blocks with sunken characters. **im-iông-jī**, black and white characters on the same block or page, as sometimes done in commentaries or dictionaries. **iông-jī**, the usual style of characters cut in relief.

jī-tién, a dictionary. **jī-lūi**, a vocabulary. **jī-phō**, a copy-book. **jī-keh**, ruled paper for writing on, or copy to be traced. **jī-tsoá**, written or printed paper. **jī-tsoá-láng**, basket for collecting it. **jī-tsoá-lô**, furnace for burning it. **sàng jī-tsoá**, solemnly carry the ashes, and commit them to the water. **kèng jī-tsoá**, to reverence paper with characters on it. **jī-tsoá-têng**, a large well-built furnace (with ornamental top) for burning it. **kèng-jī-têng**, id.

sip-jī-kè, a cross (v. sip). **it-jī-bâi**, eyebrows in a straight line (v. it). **sòe-jī-kî**, a general's flag with the word "sòe" on it. **jin-jī-chiam**, an ordinary roof, not flat (v. jîn). **bûn-jī-khak**, the 169th radical (v. khak). **kong--jī, bô chhut-thâu**, the word "labourer" does not put out its head (v. kong).

saⁿ-jī-tsn̂g, all the three words in their full meaning; said in various phrases, *e.g.* **si khè jī, saⁿ-jī-tsn̂g**, good at poetry, essays, and writing. **hok lȯk siū, saⁿ-jī-tsn̂g**, having good fortune, rank, wealth, and longevity.

jī — **giâ-lan-jī**, a wood like rose-wood, used for anchors. **ka-lan-jī**, id.

jī [R. bí, rice]. **chhó-jī-táu**, a rice measure about one-fifth larger than the usual measure.

jī [R. fat]. **iû-jī**, fat, as edible. **jī-nn̂g**, the layer of fat between the skin and the flesh, as in a pig (v. nn̂g).

jī — **sòe-jī**, careful; take care (s. word). **sè-jī** (C.), id.

jī (R. id.), a bait for fishing. **hî-jī**, id. **chiáh-jī**, to take the bait. **péh-hî-jī**, the long flat fish "péh-hî" cut up into bits for bait.

jī (C.), = A. jū (R.), to order; to explain. **pí-jī**, a comparison.

jī (C.), = A. jū (R.), abundant; affluent.

jia [R. chia, which is also col.], to cover or shelter from. **jia-khàm**, to cover up; to conceal. **jia-iám**, to screen, shelter, or hide. **jia-tsáh**, to ward off; to intercept, as a view. **jia-keh**, to ward off blows, as shield. **jia-moâⁿ**, to deceive by concealing. **jia-pè**, to cover or overshadow hurtfully; to becloud, as the mind.

jia-àm, to overshadow and darken, as clouds, buildings, &c. **jia-jit**, to shelter from the sun. **jia-hō**, to shelter from rain. **jia-hong**, to shelter from the wind; the panelling at the end of a bed. **jia-hong-tó**, that panelling. **jia-hong-pang**, id.

moaⁿ-jia, the sloping roof of an open shed or verandah. **jia-iûⁿ**, the additional projecting roof at front of shop.

jiá (R. id.), to excite and draw upon one's self, as calamity or anger. **jiá siū-khì**, to draw another's anger upon ourself. **jiá-sū**, to bring trouble on one's self. **jiá-ē**, to bring calamity on one's self.

jiá — **oát-jiá**, still more; all the more (v. oát).

jiá — **jîn-jiá**, affable, good-tempered, polite, gentle, and modest; amiable; said of women and young persons.

jiā (R. ip, = col. hiā). **chhiùⁿ-jiā**, to make a bow; to bow.

jiah (R. chek, = col. chiah), a trace; a scar or mark left by a wound, tumour, &c. **kha-jiah**, a footstep. **kha-jiah-tóe**, sole of the foot. **siàⁿ-jiah**, manifesta-

海上絲綢之路文獻集成 科技與文化編

tions of power and efficacy by an idol. **sîn-jiah** (X.), a miracle.

jiák (C.), = A. jiók, weak.

jiám (R. id.), a surname.

jiám [R. to dye, to taint, to pollute, to be infested, = col. nī^{n}]. **jiám-sek**, to paint in colours, as above a black and white sketch, or on a white ground. **tsong-jiám**, id. **gâu tsong-jiám**, good at painting so; also (Cn.), fond of talking in a false or exaggerated way, or putting on a false appearance.

jiám-tio̍h-hân, have got a bad cold or fever from getting wet. **jiám-tio̍h-pī^{n}**, to get unwell. **jiám--tio̍h sî-khì-chèng**, to take an infection or epidemic. **m̄-thang jiám--tio̍h**, don't get polluted, as by some wicked course of life.

jiân, better, jiên (*q.v.*)

jiáng (C.), = A. jióng, to bawl or shout loud. **jiáng-kó**, = A. chéng-kó, to make a loud noise with gongs, &c., at the beginning of a play.

jiáng [R. jióng, in confusion, = col. chháng, chhiáng]. **jû-jiáng-jiáng**, all in confusion (Cn. jióng). Also, **jiáng** (C.), = A. jióng, in confusion.

jia̍p (=jī-tsa̍p), twenty. **it-jia̍p**, near twenty. **jia̍p-jī**, twenty-two (&c.)

jiat, **jia̍t**, better; jiet, jie̍t (*q.v.*)

jiâu — **jiâu-sa** (r.), sal-ammoniac.

jiâu (R. jiàu, = col. jiâu^{n}, jiàu^{n}), wrinkled; crumpled. **phah-jiâu**, to crumple. **áu-jiâu**, id. **bong-jiâu**, to crumple by touching. **bīn jiâu**, face wrinkled. **jiâu-bīn-phê**, id. **bīn-iu bīn-jiâu**, face sad and wrinkled with sorrow or anxiety. **khiau-khiau jiâu-jiâu**, crooked, as a piece of wood, &c.

jiâu-piēn, the cracked appearance of the surface of fine old china. **jiâu-hûn**, marks of crumpling.

jiâu^{n} (=jiâu), crumpled; wrinkled.

jiâu [R. abundance; to pardon], to spare, as life. **jiâu-miā^{n}**, to spare life. **jiâu sì^{n}-miā^{n}**, id. **jiâu-bēng**, id. **jiâu-sù** (R.), to forgive, as a superior does.

jiâu-jū, have great abundance of wealth.

jiáu^{n} (C. tsáu, T. lék). **jiáu^{n}-súi**, the ornamental brackets and rim below the edge of a Chinese table. **jiáu^{n}-súi-teng**, small iron nails, such as are used for nailing it on; used also for other purposes.

jiáu^{n} (R. jiáu), (Cn. niáu^{n}), claws. **kha-jiáu^{n}**, claws. **chhiú-jiáu^{n}**, finger-nails. **phái^{n}-chhiú-jiáu^{n}**, to pilfer; a thief.

eng-jiáu^{n}-hoe, a strong-scented green flower, like eagles' claws. **köe-jiáu^{n}-chhiú** (T.), fingers drawn together, as in severe illness, or near death (like hen's claws). **köe-jiáu^{n}-kha** (T.), toes drawn together in like manner.

jiáu (=jiáu^{n}), claws.

jiáu (R. id.), (Cn. niáu^{n}). **jiáu-loān**, disturbance; turmoil; riot; confusion and uproar. **teh-jiáu**, to be in an excited and disturbed state, as the people of a place. **kiáu-jiáu**, to make disturbance; to annoy, as by noise or turmoil, or by constant coming. **chhò-jiáu**, to cause trouble, expense, or anxiety to another. **jiáu-hāi** (r.), to cause confusion and injury, as unruly people.

jiáu^{n} (=jiáu), id.

jiáu — **jiáu-a**, a large gong, used before mandarins and idols.

jiáu^{n} — **jiáu^{n}-a**, id.

jiàu^{n} (=niàu^{n}). **jiàu^{n}-ām**, having a scar on the neck, as from a sore or wound.

jiàu^{n} (R. jiáu, jiâu), to scratch; a scratch. **jiàu^{n}-soa**, to scratch up the sand, as a dog. **siáu-káu jiàu^{n}-soa** (excited dog scratching the sand), said of idle bad fellows looking about where there are women. **sán-káu jiàu^{n}-soa**, id. **sán-káu jiàu^{n}**, id.

jiàu (=jiàu^{n}), to scratch.

jiàu [R. wrinkled; some read "chhiù"; = col. jiâu, jiâu^{n}, jiàu^{n}]. **jiàu-se**, crape. **soà^{n}-jiàu**, silk camblet. **jiàu-pò**, a cotton stuff, wrinkled like crape, used for women's head-dresses. **jiàu-kim**, brass foil beaten thin and pasted on paper (so as to look crumpled) for idolatrous use. **o-jiàu-som**, a rough sort of biche-de-mer.

jiàu^{n} (=jiàu). **jiàu^{n}-se**, crape (&c.)

jiên [R. to light up; so; an adverbial particle]. **pún-jiên**, originally; naturally. **tsū-jiên**, naturally; certainly; self-existent (v. tsū). **thien-jiên**, naturally; certainly. **kó-jiên**, certainly; of course.

kai-jiên, as it ought to be; according to what is right. **liáu-jiên**, understanding clearly; plainly understood. **oán-jiên**, alike; like as. **tsám-jien**, exceedingly; very. **tsn̂g-jiên**, entirely. **tsoân-jiên**, id. **hut-jiên**, suddenly. **tu̍t-jiên**, id.

sui-jiên, although. **kì-jiên**, already; inasmuch as. **kèng-jiên**, yet after all. **kiù-kì-jiên**, on examining into the real state of the case. **bók-koài kì-jiên**, no wonder it is so, for it is quite natural; there is no cause for displeasure. **sé-í-jiên**, the rationale or cause of an event or affair.

jiên-āu, = liên-āu, next; then; in immediate succession after that.

jiên-teng-hu̍t, a Buddha much earlier than Amida Buddha, o-mí-tô-hu̍t.

jiet (C.) **jiet-á**, = chién-á, the bookworm.

jie̍t [R. hot, feverish, ardent, crowded, = col. joa̍h], hot and feverish; having a heating tendency, as food or medicine; fever. **sio-jie̍t**, hot and feverish; feeling heated when violently scolded. **sò-jie̍t**, having a heating tendency, as some sorts of food. **jie̍t-mih^{n}**, food that has a heating effect. **jie̍t-io̍h**, heating medicine, for diseases that are counted "cold." **jie̍t-chhá**, a small bowl of fried meat (v. chhá).

jie̍t-khì, the hot principle or humour in the constitution; feverish heat; inflammation. **léng-jie̍t**, the cold and hot principles. **léng-jie̍t put-hô**, the cold and hot principles not duly tempered; a sort of disease; climate not good. **hōng-hōng-jie̍t**, very great heat, as of fire or of disease; violent fever or inflammation. **jie̍t-hōng-hōng**, very hot. **iām-jie̍t**, scorching hot, as sultry day. **thi^{n}-khì iām-jie̍t**, weather dreadfully hot.

jie̍t-chèng, fever. **jie̍t-chèng-pī^{n}**, id. **jie̍t-pī^{n}**, id. **hoat-jie̍t**, to become fevered or feverish. **thè-jie̍t**, to remove fever or inflammation, as medicine. **jie̍t thè**, the fever abated or gone. **jie̍t-kōng**, delirium in fever. **hu-jie̍t**, typhus and typhoid fevers. **koâ^{n}-jie̍t**, fever and ague. **phah-koâ^{n} phah-jie̍t**, to have fever and ague fits. **koâ^{n}-jie̍t-tsūn**, the periodical fit of fever and ague. **koâ^{n}-jie̍t-kúi**, an irresolute fellow who will neither say yes nor no. **koâ^{n}-jie̍t-io̍h**, medicine for fever and ague; esp. quinine. **jie̍t-kat-á**, small boils.

jie̍t-kún-kún, very numerous, as a crowd; very desirous of a thing, as pleasure or amusement, or as soldiers for battle; very hot and fevered in illness.

jiėt-chhau-chhau (Cn.), very crowded, as men. **lāu-jiėt**, crowded; a great gathering, large party, or assemblage. **lāu-jiėt chhi-chha**, extremely so. **lāu-jiėt chhih-chhih**, id.

jiėt-sim, earnest; diligent; keen about it; hearty or zealous. **jiėt-chhe-chhe**, very desirous of anything. **chhin-jiėt**, intimate and warm in friendship. **taⁿ-láng khah-jiėt tsng-toàⁿ**, the bearers of the actors' baggage more keen about it than the actors (said of parties not concerned taking more interest in a matter than the principals).

jih [=jī-tsáp, =jiáp, twenty]. **jih--nihⁿ**, in the last decade of the month, from the 20th onwards. **chhut-jih--nihⁿ**, id. **jih-it**, the 21st of month. **jih-jī**, the 22d (v. jī), (&c.)

jih (cf. chhih), to crush; to squeeze down; to break by crushing; to squash. **jih-píⁿ**, to crush flat. **jih-tiàu**, to strangle one's self; to hang one's self. **jih-tiâm**, to press down in water or brine (v. tiâm). **jih--lȯh-khì**, to crush or squeeze down. **jih-khîm**, to play a piano, harmonium, concertina, &c. **jih-hoa-hé**, to crush out fire. **beh-phah beh-jih**, striking a man, and squeezing his neck, or going to do so; quarrelsome.

at-jih, to urge a party to come to an arrangement, as mutual friend trying to settle a quarrel; to get proceedings stopped or stayed by giving money to underlings. **kiông-kiông-jih**, to urge an unwilling man. **ah-jih**, id. **khit-kúi-jih**, to have a sort of nightmare. **khit-kúi jih--lȯh-khì**, to have a sudden fainting feeling, so as to fall down, as a man in weak health (supposed to be done by a demon!); to do most unaccountably something which we well know to be very dangerous.

jîm (R. id.), one of the cyclical characters; often used in men's names.

jîm [R. id., by change of tone from "jīm," office, to bear], a surname.

jîm [R. sîm, to search for, =col. chhîm, chîm], (C. T. chîm), to feel for things, as in pocket, pouch, or dark hole. **chîm-bô-chîⁿ**, to feel in one's pocket and find no money.

jím [R. to endure; to bear; cruel, =col. lún]. **jím-siū**, to endure patiently. **jím-ki siū-ngō͘**, to endure hunger patiently and willingly. **jím-khì kiû-tsâi**, to control one's anger so as to get wealth. **jím-khì thun-seng**, to repress emotion and voice, as before superior (v. thun). **jím-nāiⁿ** (R.), to bear patiently. **put-jím**, cannot bear to —; dislike to do —. **bōe-jím--tit**, cannot bear. **hâm-jím**, to bear with an offender for a time, because it would be troublesome or dangerous to punish or quarrel with him now.

tsân-jím, cruel. **jím-sim** (r.), cruel heart. **jím-sim hāi-lí** (r.), cruelty outrages Heaven's rules.

jīm (R. sīm), (T. chīm), a word entering into the names of many places, where navigation by junks ends, *e.g.* **chióh-jīm**, the harbour of Tâng-oaⁿ. **koaⁿ-jīm**, one near Tâng-oaⁿ, and one above Pechuia.

jīm [R. office; to entrust with]. **sìn-jīm**, to trust and employ confidentially, without minutely examining what he does. **jīm-ì** (r.), to do as one pleases. **jīm-m̄-khí**, I have not the ability for such an office. **jīm-bōe-khí**, id.

chek-jīm, responsibility, as in care of an affair. **chit-jīm**, office. **chit-jīm**, one term of office, for three years. **liên-jīm**, to continue in office after the first term has ended. **goân-jīm**, id. **liû-jīm**, to make petition to have the mandarin remain so (as people sometimes do). **kek-chit liû-jīm**, to degrade from rank or office, yet leaving temporarily in the office. **kek-jīm**, to put out of office. **kái-jīm**, to remove an official from one office to another, because of some small fault making him unsuitable where he was. **lī-jīm**, to go out of office. **sià-jīm**, to hand over one's office fully to successor. **chiap-jīm**, to succeed to office. **chiūⁿ-jīm**, to enter on office. **tò-jīm**, to arrive at seat of office, as new mandarin. **sin-koaⁿ tò-jīm**, id. **sit-jīm**, really having the office, not merely titular or temporary. **sûi-jīm**, wife and family (sometimes also mother) of mandarin following him to his seat of office. **hō-jīm**, to make presents to a newly arrived mandarin.

jīm-sé, official place or position, as regards emolument. **hó jīm-sé**, a profitable office. **pháiⁿ jīm-sé**, an office where there is not much money to be made. **jīm-lāi**, during his term of office. **hāu jīm-khoeh** (C.), waiting for a vacant office to take.

jîn [R. a man; another man; a person (either male or female), =col. lâng]. **jîn-bu̍t**, distinguished men, as belonging to a place (v. bu̍t). **jîn-phín**, behaviour; conduct. **jîn-tsâi**, air; mien; dignified manner (v. tsâi). **ti jîn-sū**, come to the years of discretion (v. sū). **jîn-sū**, a small present as a reward (v. sū).

jîn-chêng, kindness; favour (v. chêng). **ûi-jîn lân**, it is difficult to act kindly and pleasantly to every one. **jîn-tsú** (R.), a man's son; (X. Son of man). **ûi jîn-tsú**, to act as a son. **ûi jîn-tsú, put-khó put-ti-i**, every one should know something of medicine.

jîn-lûn, the human relationships. **jîn-ke**, a family. **jîn-ien chiu-bit**, population thick. **jîn-teng**, male members of a family; male inhabitants. **jîn-bēng**, a human life (v. bēng). **jîn-tē lióng-sơ**, place and people both strange to us. **bān-jîn-soàⁿ**, an honorary umbrella given to a good mandarin by the people on his leaving.

jîn-tiong, the hollow in the middle of the upper lip just below the nose (v. tiong). **jîn-som**, gin-seng. **jîn-sim** (T.), id.

jîn-sim put-chiok, the human heart never knows satiety. **bóe jîn-sim**, craftily gain the hearts of people. **tōng jîn-sim**, to excite desire, as wealth, &c. (v. tōng). **thien ko, bī-sī ko; jîn-sim, tsat-tsat ko**, Heaven, though high, yet is not high; it is man's heart that always aims higher.

thien-tē-jîn, heaven, earth, and man. **sun-chin-jîn**, a god of medicine, of surname Sun. **ngô͘-chin-jîn**, =tāi-tō-kong, a god of medicine, surname Ngô͘ (Woo). **kim-kah sîn-jîn**, sort of angels sent by Yuh-hwang (v. sîn).

jîn-jī-chiam, an ordinary roof, not flat; a gable roof. **jîn-jī-kè**, the couples of a gable roof. **jîn-jī-thong**, the great horizontal beam of a couple. **jîn-jī-tú**, the smaller horizontal beam of a couple.

tāi-jîn, an image made to ward off evil (v. tāi, "instead of"). **tāi-jîn**, a high mandarin (v. tāi "great"). **siōng-jîn**, superior mandarins (said by inferior mandarins). **kú-jîn**, a graduate of the second degree, like M.A. **sèng-jîn**, a canonized sage or saint. **sien-jîn**, deceased ancestors; the ancients. **jîn-sîn**, a minister of state. **jîn-kun**, a sovereign. **sià-jîn**, a man whose father or elder relative is a mandarin or high graduate.

hū-jîn-lâng, a woman (v. hū). **hu-jîn**, wife of a high mandarin; title of some idols (v. hu). **an-jîn**, wife of lower mandarins and wealthy men. **bí-jîn**, a beautiful woman. **ka-jîn** (R.), a beautiful woman

(v. ka, "beautiful"). **ka-jîn**, a household slave (v. ka, "a household").

siáu-jîn, a worthless fellow (v. siáu, "small"). **siáu-jîn**, ashamed (v. siáu, "ashamed"). **hòe-jîn**, a useless fellow, *e.g.* maimed or crippled; a worthless man, *e.g.* lazy or wicked. **kong-jîn**, an arbiter (without power like our arbiters). **un-jîn**, a benefactor. **siû-jîn**, an enemy. **tsōe-jîn** (r.), a criminal (v. tsōe).

hāi-jîn lī-kí, to injure others to benefit one's self (v. kí). **tsòe kàu-khì-jîn**, drawing down people's deserved hatred (v. khì).

jîn (R. id.), benevolence; love; a kernel; yolk of egg; ball of eye, &c.

jîn-ài, benevolence; love of kindness; affectionate; kind. **jîn-tek**, benevolence; kindness; affection. **jîn-tsû**, affection of parents or superiors. **jîn-gī, lé tì-sìn**, the five cardinal virtues. **put-jîn**, unfeeling; cruel. **jîn-jiá**, polite; affable (said of young folks).

chîm-jîn, roe of crab. **chhih-jîn**, eggs or roe in a craw-fish.

koe-nn̄g-jîn, yolk of hen's egg. **nn̄g-jîn**, yolk of egg. **ah-nn̄g-jîn**, yolk of duck's egg.

bák-chiu-jîn, the ball of the eye. **bák-chiu pe̍h-jîn**, white of the eye. **pe̍h-jîn**, id. **bák-chiu o-jîn**, the iris. **o-jîn**, id. **ang-á-jîn**, the pupil. **bák-chiu ang-á-jîn**, id.

hēng-jîn, almonds; almond kernels. **sa-jîn**, a medicinal fruit like almonds (v. sa). **hu̍t-thô-jîn**, walnut kernels. **moâⁿ-jîn**, hemp-seed. **hu-jîn-lí**, a sort of plum.

bák-kiàⁿ-jîn, the glasses of spectacles. **pó-jîn**, dice used in gambling with the "pó-táu."

chhiah-jîn-thô͘, a reddish clay used for building.

jîn--ê (T.), very good large, clear, bright cash.

jîn (R. id.) **ì-jîn**, seeds of water-lily.

jîn [R. gûn, the gums]. **chhùi-khí-jîn**, the gums. **kā chhùi-khí-jîn**, to gnash one's teeth in anger. **chhun hit--ê khí-jîn**, nothing left but his gums (said of old toothless man).

jîn [R. gûn, C. gîn, silver]. **pe̍h-jîn-hiuⁿ** (C.), = pe̍h-gîn-ngiuⁿ, an evergreen shrub with red berries (v. hiuⁿ).

jīn (R. id.), to confess; to recognize; to acknowledge. **sêng-jīn**, to confess or acknowledge. **saⁿ-jīn**, to recognize one another. **jīn-khoàⁿ**, to recognize by looking at. **kì-jīn**, a mark for recognition, as a scar or other indelible mark on the body. **jīn-chhin**, to recognize relations; to treat relations as such.

jīn-chin, diligent in one's duty; doing one's duty or work diligently. **jīn-chit**, id. **jīn-lō͘**, id. **bô-jīn-hūn**, not keeping his place, as inferior who tries to rule or obstruct, or who is too uppish.

tam-jīn, to take the responsibility for; to stand security for. **pó-jīn**, id. **pó-jīn-lâng**, man who stands security. **sìn-jīn**, to give verbal security to some small extent for a man whom we recommend. **jīn-tiēn**, to go security for a man renting house or land. **jīn-tūiⁿ** (Cn.), id.

chhut-mn̂g, m̄-jīn hè, will not take back goods after they are out of the shop.

chiau-jīn, to make confession in court. **láu-sit-jīn**, to confess truly, as a fault. **jīn-tsōe**, to confess guilt. **jīn-keng**, to make a statement before a mandarin, as in answering his questions. **jīn m̄-tio̍h**, to confess being in the wrong. **jīn-ho̍k**, to confess being excelled or beaten (v. ho̍k). **jīn-chhò**, to confess a fault or mistake.

jiō (R. jiāu), urine. **khēng-jiō**, slight rain after the appearance of a rainbow. **chheng-jiō**, pure urine. **chho͘-jiō**, urine mixed with dung. **jiō-tháng**, a bucket for urine. **jiō-kó͘**, a chamber-pot. **jiō-ô͘**, id. **jiō-pih**, a finer sort of do.

pàng-jiō, to make water. **tsoāⁿ-jiō**, do. in a large stream. **chhoā-jiō**, to pass urine involuntarily, as children, &c. **chhoā-jiō-bāng**, an empty baseless dream. **siàm-jiō**, to make water in small quantities, with difficulty. **si-jiō**, to induce an infant to make water. **tìⁿ-jiō**, to make a great effort to pass urine. **lún-jiō**, to keep in urine too long.

jio̍h (R. jio̍k). **jio̍h-jio̍h**, weak and exhausted, as by work, walking, or wounds; soft and wanting in stiffness, as a dress that has lost its starch or was not starched sufficiently; all crumpled and breaking into shreds, as paper.

jiok (C.), = A. jip, to pursue.

jio̍k [R. to insult]. **lêng-jio̍k**, to insult; to abuse (generally including bad treatment). **jio̍k-bo̍k**, to insult; to treat with contempt; to abuse a person. **pê͘-jio̍k**, to insult by abusive language. **pō-jio̍k** (T.), id. **chhá-jio̍k**, to make a disturbance, scolding and insulting. **áu-jio̍k**, to beat and insult. **jio̍k-mēⁿ**, to insult and scold violently. **tsū-chhú-jio̍k**, to bring insult or disgrace on one's self by one's own folly, as by meddling in other people's matters, or going where we are sure to be insulted.

jio̍k (R. id.), (Cn. gek), a mattress; a pillow or cushion; a rug for sitting on. **jio̍k-á**, id. **í-jio̍k**, a light cushion for back and seat of a chair. **í-jio̍k-tiām**, thick cushion for seat, and thinner one for seat and back. **kiō-jio̍k**, sedan cushion. **chhn̂g-jio̍k**, long cushion or mattress for couch or bed. **phē-jio̍k**, coverlet and mattress. **hó͘-phê-jio̍k**, tiger's skin used for a seat for idols and first-class mandarins.

jio̍k (cf. chhek), (P. je̍k), to work up and mould in the hands, as clay; to crumple up, as paper. **jio̍k tsòe-chit-bê͘**, to work up into a lump, as clay or dough. **jio̍k tsòe-chit-tui**, to crumple up, as paper.

jio̍k (T. Cn.), = A. chhio̍k, slushy, damp, as roads.

jio̍k [R. flesh, = col. he̍k]. **jio̍k-sin**, the body. **kut-jio̍k chi-chhin**, near relations by blood. **chhin-kut-jio̍k**, son or brother by birth, not by adoption.

liên-jio̍k, white lobes of water-lily seed. **oán-chì-jio̍k**, the plant called "oán-chì" after the fibres have been pulled out.

jio̍k-kùi, cinnamon (v. kùi). **jio̍k-khò͘**, nutmeg (v. khò͘).

jio̍k [R. weak, = col. jio̍h, chiáⁿ]. **loán-jio̍k**, weak; feeble, as in body or in influence. **soe-jio̍k**, feeble; debilitated. **nō͘ⁿ-jio̍k**, spiritless and lazy; without energy. **ló-jio̍k-peng**, the old and the feeble among the soldiers. **jiû-jio̍k** (R.), too weak, gentle, and yielding in disposition. **jio̍k-pâng**, a division of a large family or clan, that is smaller or has less power than another division. **kiông-jio̍k**, the strong and the weak (= béng-lám), esp. as to power or influence. **kiông khi-jio̍k**, the strong oppress the weak. **kiông-pâng khi-hū jio̍k-pâng**, the more powerful branch of a clan oppressing the weaker branch.

jiông [R. plants growing luxuriantly; sort of deer's horns], (P. jêng), the quick of a nail; sort of deer's horns. **tsńg-kah-jiông**, the quick of the nail. **jip-jiông**, to hurt the quick. **tsńg-kah jip-jiông**, the nail broken or cracked so as to hurt the quick. **chhiah kàu-jip-jiông** (T.), miserably poor.

lȯk-jiông, young horns of stag covered with a soft down. **lȯk-kak-jiông**, id.; it is cut down small and used as an invigorating medicine. **khī-jiông**, a somewhat inferior sort. **iûⁿ-jiông**, do. from abroad. **chién-jiông**, to buy these stag horns, to use as medicine (s. velvet).

jiông (R. id.), silk velvet; floss silk; minced very small, as meat; stewed very soft. **jiông-jiông-jiông**, minced very small. **phah kàu jiông-jiông**, to beat (a man) to a jelly.

hái-jiông, a sponge. **moâⁿ-jiông**, sort of oakum made from old sacks and ropes.

kim-jiông, a native cotton stuff, fine, soft, and strong. **kim-jiông-pè**, id. **hoe-jiông**, flowered velvet. **hôe-jiông**, a thin velvety stuff; velveteen, or thin fustian.

jiông-soàⁿ, velvet thread. **jiông-niáⁿ**, a silk-velvet collar. **jiông-chien**, sort of hairy rug. **jiông-chiⁿ**, id. **jiông-thán**, a rug or coverlet made with a long hairy nap.

tsoán-jiông, the mule-pink or sweet-william. **chién-jiông**, id. (s. previous word). **chién-jiông-hoe**, id.

jiông-koe, a small sort of fowl with fine white feathers, supposed to keep away white ants by its odour; a fowl stewed very soft. **jiông-ah**, a duck stewed very soft.

soàn-jiông, pounded garlic. **chhò-bah-jiông**, to mince meat small.

jiông (R.), the tribes on the western frontier of China. **se-jiông** (R.), id.

jióng [R. confused, entangled, = col. chhiáng, jiáng], (C. jiáng). **jû-jióng**, perplexed in mind; all in confusion, as things.

jióng (R. id.), (C. jiáng), to bawl; to shout or cry loudly or riotously; to make a clamour. **chhap-jióng**, making a noise and confusion. **chhá-jióng**, to make a noise and disturbance. **chháu-chháu-jióng**, noisy brawling. **hoā-hoā-jióng**, id. **kiù-kiù-jióng**, id. **kiauh-kiauh-jióng**, make a row about a thing by loud and rude talk. **jióng-nāuⁿ**, to make a noise and disturbance. **jióng-lāuⁿ**, id.

jióng-chhát, to make a loud shouting after a thief. **jióng kan-khé**, to make loud noisy complaints about one's troubles.

jip (R. id.), (C. jiok, P. jek), to pursue; to chase. **jip-tiòh**, to overtake. **jip-tsûn**, to chase a vessel. **tui-jip**, to pursue; to chase.

niáu-chhú-jip, sort of squib that jumps about. **chhiáⁿ, m̄-kiâⁿ: tà phè-á-kun lâi-jip**, would not accept when politely asked, but now runs after him with veiled head, eager to get it (fig. from bad woman); said of any sort of matter. **âng-teng sì-kiō, kng-m̄-kiâⁿ: tà phè-á chiah-lâi-jip**, id. (lit. with red lamps, and chair with four bearers, as at marriage).

jip (C.), (P. chip), to come forward and make claims on a property, as after some one has sold it.

jip (R. id.), to enter; to put in; to stuff in; to come in. **ōe-tit jip-thâu**, able to make a favourable beginning. **ū jip-sit**, truthful; honest (as man); correct and safe, as affair. **kàu-jip-kiók**, so as to be fit for the purpose intended, good or bad (v. kiók). **jip-chêng jip-lí**, according to correct principles. **jip-tôe**, answering well to the text or thesis. **chhut-keng jip-tién**, according to classical style.

chhut-jip, to go out and in. **chhut-chhut jip-jip**, constantly going out and in. **chhut-jip lāi-goā**, said of an experienced man. **chhut-siⁿ jip-sí**, exposing one's self to great danger. **ū-chhut bô-jip**, having expenses, but no income. **ū-jip bô-chhut**, miserly. **chit-chhiú jip, chit-chhiú chhut**, spending money just as we get it.

jip-tiûⁿ, to enter an examination. **jip-òh**, to begin to go to school. **jip-phoàn**, to become a Sew-tsai. **jip-hōe**, to enter a society or association. **jip-kàu**, to enter the church. **jip-kî**, to become a Manchoo bannerman, as a Chinaman sometimes does. **jip-báu**, to get one's name put on the books of a mandarin's office, as if an employe, for protection (v. báu). **jip-tsòe** (R.), to marry, and go to live with the wife's parents for some time, yet keeping one's own surname (v. tsòe). **jip-siòng**, to become prime minister.

jip-koaⁿ, to be confiscated. **jip-siàu**, to receive part payment. **jip-lāi**, to pay interest (v. lāi, "interest"). **jip-lāi**, to go inside (v. lāi, "inside"). **jip-gûn**, to get silver in exchange for cash; to pay money on account. **chiong-chîⁿ jip-gûn**, to get silver for cash. **jip-chhiú**, to be received, as money.

jip-iòh, to put in powder, as into a gun. **jip-tsúi**, to leak, as a boat; to put in water, as into a bottle or can. **jip-hun**, to fill a pipe, as with tobacco. **jip-mîⁿ**, to put in a large quantity of cotton, as into a pillow.

jip-liȧp, the grain well formed in the ear. **jip-sún**, to put a tenon into a mortice. **jip sìⁿ-hiòh**, to put the paper on the frame of a fan, as in making it.

jip-tiâⁿ, to enter a formal written complaint or accusation in court.

jip-sim, to go to the heart. **kám-siā jip-kut**, exceedingly grateful (v. kut). **jip-chhùi**, to enter the mouth; to put in the mouth.

jip-siaⁿ, the tone called "juh" or "jip;" the fourth tone, upper or lower, ending in p, t, k, or h. **ē-jip**, the lower jip tone. **chiūⁿ-jip**, the upper jip tone. **téng-jip** (C.), id.

jip-chhun, the beginning of spring, about 4th February. **jip-hē**, beginning of summer, about 5th or 6th of May. **jip-chhiu**, beginning of autumn, about 7th or 8th August. **jip-tang**, beginning of winter, about 7th November.

jit (R. id.), the sun; a day; daytime; (time), (weather). **jit-chí**, a day. **phah-sńg jit-chí**, to waste one's days. **jit-sîn**, a day as named by two cyclical characters, and in regard to good or bad fortune (v. sîn). **toā-jit**, a very auspicious day, when many persons get married, &c. **toā-jit-sîn**, id.

jit-thâu, the sun; a day. **jit-thâu-kong**, the sun, as an object of worship. **tng jit-thâu tī--teh**, if what I say is false, may I die as this sun goes down! **tè-jit-lòh**, id. **tng jit-thâu kóng-ōe**, to use that form of oath. **jit-thâu té**, the days are short, as in winter.

jit-khò, a card given by a fortune-teller telling the auspicious day for a marriage. **jit-khòe** (C.), id. **sàng jit-thâu**, to send that card by a go-between to the espoused bride. **sàng-jit**, id. **théh-jit**, to go and get a lucky day from a fortune-teller. **khoàⁿ-jit**, to choose a lucky day (v. khoàⁿ). **tek-jit-su**, a man who chooses lucky days (v. su).

kóe-jit, to assign a different day from that first appointed. **ān-jit**, to appoint a fixed day, as in limiting an extension of time. **àn-jit**, day by day, as each day requires. **kè-jit**, to pass the day. **jit-kè-jit**, from day to day. **oh kè-jit**, hard to get a living. **kōe kè-jit**, easy to get a living. **ke-chhiên-jit**, to delay longer.

âng-thi^{n} chhiah-jit-thâu, hot, rainless, cloudless sky. **hó-hong-jit**, fine weather (v. hong). **chheng-thien pėk-jit**, bright sunny day; clear weather; in broad daylight, *e.g.* in speaking of a robbery; also, just and fair (said by a mandarin of himself in exhorting the people). **pėk-jit seng-thien**, to ascend to heaven in clear daylight (said also of rapid and unexpected preferment).

jit--sî, daytime. **jit-tà^{n}--sî**, id. **jit-mî^{n}**, day and night. **mî^{n}-jit**, id. **bô-khàng mî^{n}-jit**, day and night without any (long) intermission.

si^{n}-jit, a birth-day (v. si^{n}). **lé-pài-jit**, Sunday; Sabbath. **bit-jit** (R.), id. **an-hioh-jit** (X.), Sabbath. **thien-sià-jit**, four days (changed each year) which are counted very lucky. **giâu-thien sùn-jit**, the golden age of Yaou and Shun.

put-jit, not fixing what day; any day; soon. **kūn-jit**, a near day, before or after. **tsá-jit**, formerly. **tsā-jit**, yesterday. **tsā-bē-jit**, id. **tsòh--jit**, day before yesterday. **sùn--tsòh-jit** (Cn.), the second day before yesterday. **lòh--tsòh-jit** (T.), id. **chêng-jit**, a former day. **ē-jit**, a later day, esp. four or five days after (v. ē). **bîn-ná-jit**, to-morrow. **āu--jit**, the day after to-morrow. **lòh-āu--jit**, the second day after to-morrow. **āu-jit**, a future day. **jit-āu**, on some future day; after to-day. **jit-hiō** (Cn.), id.

chiong-jit, the whole day. **kui-jit**, id. **kúi-jit**, how many days? **jit-jit**, day by day. **jit-sit**, daily food (v. sit). **sî-jit**, hours and days; time (v. sî). **chit-chhùn-á-jit**, a very few moments (v. chhùn). **koh chit-chhioh ê-jit**, after a very short time (v. chhioh). **sa^{n}-géh-jit**, three months long. **chit-géh-jit**, one month's time. **jit-géh**, sun and moon; days and months. **si^{n}-sî jit-géh**, the eight characters of a man's nativity. **jit-géh chhui-pek, lâng kōe-lāu**, days and months press on, and man soon grows old. **jit-goát**, the two side-boards of a coffin; also (R.), sun and moon. **jit-goát jû-so, kong-im sū-chièn**, time is like a shuttle or an arrow. **pàng jit-á-chî^{n}**, a very heavy sort of usury (v. pàng).

chhien-jit-hông, a sort of amaranth. **jit-jit-chhun**, a wild herbaceous plant with red tubular corolla (somewhat like periwinkle) that flowers all the year round.

jit-pún, Japan.

jit chhut, sunrise; the sun breaking out of clouds. **chhut-jit**, sun breaking out of clouds. **jit khí**, the sun rising higher. **jit chiū^{n}**, id. **jit-chiū^{n} sa^{n}-ki tek-ko koâi^{n}**, late in the morning when the sun is the height of three bamboo poles. **jit tàu**, noon. **jit tiong-tàu**, id. **jit tiong-kiā**, sun at zenith. **jit lòh**, sunset. **jit-lòh-sin**, the double hour "sin" when the sun sets. **jit-chhut-sîn**, the double hour "sîn" when the sun rises. **sit-jit**, eclipse of the sun. **jit-kng**, sunlight. **jit toā**, the sun very hot. **jit iām**, the sun scorching hot. **jit phû ti-hái-bīn**, sun just appearing on the sea, as in early morning.

jit-kui, a sun-dial. **jit-iá^{n}**, shadow thrown by the sun; sun's image or brightness on water or in mirror, &c. (v. iá^{n}). **jit-hoe**, a ray of sunlight through clouds, leaves, chink, &c. (v. hoe). **jit si^{n}-kha**, rays streaming through clouds.

chiò-jit, to shine bright in the sunlight, as mirror or water (v. chiò). **chioh-jit**, to warm one's self at the fire. **phák-jit**, to dry in the sun. **tsà^{n}-jit**, do. for a short time. **thî^{n}-jit**, dazzled by sunlight.

jiû — **koe-jiû**, a tree like an elm, with small leaves and rough crooked branches. **ke-jiû** (C.), id.

jiû (R. id.) **jiû-hî**, a fish like the cuttle-fish, but boneless and better.

jiû (R. id.) **un-jiû**, gentle; meek; yielding; soft in disposition. **un-jiû siông-sè**, gentle and cautious. **un-jiû siong-chè** (Cn.), two parties each yielding a little so as to make up a quarrel. **kong-jiû siong-chè**, firmness and gentleness well united; strictness and merciful consideration well tempered. **poà^{n}-kong-jiû**, id. **iu-jiû koá^{n}-toàn**, undecided in intentions or plans; purpose not fixed. **jiû-jiók** (R.), too yielding and gentle in disposition.

khah-jiû--chit-ē, omit one stroke in rowing. **khah-jiû-chiú^{n}** (C.), give a stroke very gently in rowing. **khah-jiû** (C.), id.

jiû, to rub with a wet cloth (with more strength than "chhit"), as body, furniture, floor, &c. **jiû thê-kha**, to wipe the floor with a wet cloth.

jiû (R. liû). **jiû-n̂g**, sulphur.

joā [R. jiók, if, = col. loā, oā], how many? how much? (interrogative or interjection); so much! **joā-tsōe**, how many? **ū joā-tsōe**, how many are there? there are a good many. **bô-joā-tsōe**, not very many. **bô-joā**, id. **kàu-joā-tsōe**, how many? **sái joā-tsōe-tsûn**, sail how far? **joā-tsōe-lō͘**, how far is the road? **ke-kiâ^{n} joā-lō͘**, walk so much or how much further. **joā-lâng**, how many men? **khoà^{n} joā-tsúi**, look how much water there is.

beh-joā, how many or how much do you wish? **beh-goá joā-tn̂g joā-toā**, how much money do you wish from me? **joā-iá^{n}**, how much superior? **khoà^{n}-lí joā-á-béng**, we will see how brave (or powerful) you are. **joā-kú**, how long? so very long (time), &c.

joáh [R. jiėt, but used in a somewhat different sense], hot, as weather; the hot season of summer; thin grass-cloth. **pàng-joáh**, to give holidays or vacation in the hottest part of summer. **khah-joáh**, further on in summer (said in beginning of summer); hotter, as weather.

sio-joáh, very hot, as weather. **joáh-ták**, sultry; oppressively hot. **ut-joáh**, sultry and oppressive (v. ut). **thi^{n}-khì iām-joáh**, sun scorching hot. **ōe-joáh--má**, do you feel the weather hot? **bōe-joáh**, not hot. **ùi-joáh**, afraid of heat, as man who wears few clothes (v. ùi). **tham-joáh**, fond of heat, as man who wears many clothes even in hot weather (v. tham).

joáh-pè, thin grass-cloth. **pėh-joáh**, white grass-cloth. **o͘-joáh**, black grass-cloth. **kang-sai-joáh**, grass-cloth from Kiangsi province (first-class).

joáh-bō, a mandarin's summer cap with button. **joáh-lóeh**, a broad ceremonial cap with tassels (v. lóeh). **joáh-sa^{n}**, a summer coat. **joáh-khò͘**, very thin trousers for summer.

joán [R. tsoán, to turn, = col. tńg]; = tsoán, to turn round with the hand, as the handle of a door.

joán (R. id.) **joán-joán**, to rub with the fingers of one hand.

joán [R. soft, flexible]. **nńg-joán**, soft, fine, and delicate, as fur or cakes, or as soft hand of a man who does not do hard work. **chhùi-joán**, feathers of the bird called "húi-chhùi," used for women's head-dress. **an-joán**, to glue on these feathers. **pho͘-joán**, id.

joán (C.), = A. loán (R.), warm.

joán [R. loán; ceremonial present of food to a superior]. **joán-pâng** (C.), = A. thàm-pâng, younger brother or nephew of bride bringing presents to her on the day after marriage.

24

jôe (C.), = A. jô, to rub or scrape with the foot.

jû (R. id., = jū), (C. jî). **jû-jû**, tangled; intricate; involved. **thâu-mn̂g jû-jû**, hair dishevelled. **sim-koa^{n} jû-jû**, mind perplexed and confused. **jû-jû sù-sù**, all in disorder (v. sù). **jû-loān**, perplexed; entangled; in disorder. **jû-jû loān-loān**, id. **sim-koa^{n} jû-loān**, mind confused.

jû-bé-bé, confused in mind. **jû-kà-kà**, intricate and involved, as affair. **jû-chháng-chháng**, confused; tangled; all in confusion; intricate. **jû-chhiáng-chhiáng**, id., or perplexed in mind. **jû-jióng**, id. **jû-kông-kông**, mind confused and perplexed, as with a multitude of affairs; also (T. Cn.), very urgent for anything to have it done in a tremendous hurry.

jû [R. as, like as], (C. jî, T. dzû). **put-jû**, not equal to; there is no better way than to.

tsū-jû, fully recovered; quite well again. **chho-chhiòng tsū-jû**, one's own master; not under the control of another. **jû-jiên**, quite well again. **jû-goān**, matters falling out just as one would wish. **jû-ì**, according to our desire. **bān-sū jû-ì**, everything just as we would desire.

jû-chhú (R.), thus. **ìn-tap jû-liû**, fluent at answering. **kièn-sú jû-biên**, to look on death as a sleep (v. biên). **tâng-kiâ^{n}, jû tâng-miâ^{n}**, fellow-travellers ought to assist each other in the dangers of the road.

jû-lâi, a name of Buddha (v. lâi).

jû [R. literary], (C. jî, T. dzû). **jû-kàu**, Confucianism. **jû-i**, a learned physician, who is a good scholar.

jû [R. name of a tree]. **chí-jû-chhâ**, a hard yellowish brown wood, good for furniture. **tē-jû**, a wood used for medicine.

jû [R. name of a plant]. **hiu^{n}-jû**, a medicinal plant. **hiu^{n}-jû-tê**, an infusion of it.

jû (R. id.) **tsu-jû**, a medicinal plant (v. tsu).

jû (R. id.), (C. jî), a surname, said to be originally related to the surnames "thê" and "û," of which the characters are very similar.

jú [R. decaying, as fish], (Cn. jû). **jú-jú**, separating into its fibres, as a cord worn away and about to break, or as the end of a cord.

jú [R. id., = col. ná^{n}]. **jú-kú jú-hó**, the longer (in time) the better.

jú (R. jú, jû). **tek-jú**, the outside of green bamboo scraped off; infused as a cooling medicine.

jú [R. milk], (C. jí). **jú-bú**, a wet-nurse. **tông-pau kiōng-jú**, of the same father and mother. **iông iú kūi-jú chi-un**, the lamb kneels for its milk, showing its sense of parental favour.

jú-miâ^{n}, the name originally given to a child by its parents.

jú-hiu^{n}, frankincense. **tāu-jú**, a preparation of beans, made into curd and salted in small squares.

jú — **jú-á**, a fine curly sort of fur; a dress made of it. **jú-iâng**, id. **ơ-jú-á**, black do. **pėh-jú-á**, white do.

jū [R. a written or printed word, = col. jī, tsū]. **jū-miâ^{n}**, = tsū-miâ^{n}, the name taken at marriage or when grown up.

jū [R. a statement], (C. jī). **phì-jū**, a comparison; for instance; supposing that. **pí-jū**, id.

jū [R. a command], (C. jī). **sèng-jū**, the "Sacred Edict" of the Emperor Kang-hi (khong-hi). **siōng-jū**, an order or decree issued directly by the emperor. **tn̂g-jū**, an order issued by the mandarin on the judgment-seat, written by himself with red ink. **chhut tsu-jū**, to issue such an order in red ink, as mandarin.

jū [R. abundant], (C. jī). **hù-jū**, affluent; very rich. **ko-jū**, id. **kơ-jū** (Cn.), id. **jiâu-jū**, having abundant wealth.

jūn [R. jūn, lūn, soft]. **nńg-jūn**, soft and delicate, as cakes.

jūn [R. joán, loán], tough, as meat; elastic; not easily split or broken. **jūn-jūn**, id. **kun-jūn**, tough; elastic; hard or narrow, as man unwilling to pay out money. **jūn-pé**, shrivelled, as cucumber too long plucked. **jūn khiùh-khiùh**, tough and elastic, as india-rubber or some cakes. **jūn-thn̂g**, sugar worked up into a tenacious form, as a sweet-meat.

jūn (R. id.), (T. lūn, as also sometimes A.), moistened; damp, as with rain. **sip-jūn**, very slightly softened by damp, as ground, or as some other things. **jūn-tėk** (R.), well watered; full of fresh vigorous health and pretty well off. **jūn-tiōng** (R.), to mollify the bowels and cure costiveness, as medicine or food.

hē--lí jūn-pit (this is to moisten your pen), said to a friend who writes a document for us, on giving him a small sum.

jwā, jwȧh, jwán, better joā, joȧh, joán (*q.v.*)

K.

k in many words corresponds to **h** of the reading style.

ka (R. kau), glue; isinglass; some sorts of jelly made from animals; resin. **tsúi-ka**, common glue. **gû-phê-ka**, glue made from cow-hide. **hî-piō-ka**, sort of isinglass (v. piō). **a-ka**, a medicinal jelly made from turtles' bones. **ku-ka**, jelly made from turtles. **hó-kut-ka**, strengthening jelly from tigers' bones. **lȯk-kak-ka**, do., from stags' horns.

siông-ka, resin from the fir-tree.

tiàu-ka, to glaze cloth with glue. **tiàu ka-tsúi**, id. **liâm-ka**, to glue. **thè-ka**, the glue parted, as in furniture. **ngâu-ka**, to manufacture glue for sale. **tsú-ka**, to melt glue (by heat) for use.

ka (= kui). **ka-n̂g**, entire; complete (v. n̂g). **ka-ní^{n}** (C.), id.

ka — **ka-iȧh**, to take well in the market.

ka — **ka-liô**, words used in calling a dog.

ka — **ka-lí-lô**, not yet; not yet finished; yet distant; wide of the mark. **ka-lí-lien-lô**, id. **ka-lí-lien**, id. **ka-lô--lah**, id.

ka — **ka-láu ka-lé**, to talk indistinctly of a matter (v. láu).

ka [R. kúi, id.] **ka-lé-hì**, puppet-shows used in idolatry (v. lé).

ka — **ka-lak**, a windlass, as at a well; a block in a vessel.

厦英大辭典

ka (Cn. pa; C. kha). **ka-chiah**, the back (v. chiah).

ka (R. kau), to cut with scissors. **ka-chién**, shears; scissors. **ka-to**, id. **hái-ka-to**, sort of crab with two very long claws. **ka-tn̄g**, to cut separate by scissors (s. add). **ka-iū^{n}**, to cut out a pattern (v. iū^{n}). **ka-sa^{n}**, to cut out a coat, shirt, &c. **sa^{n}-thap-ka**, to cut cloth so as to lose as little as possible (v. thap).

ka [R. id., the sound of a bird; by change of tone from "ngáu," to bite]. **ka-lâ-pa**, Batavia (v. pa).

ka [R. kài, to cover, = col. khàm, koà, khap]. **péng ka-lán-phak**, to lay on its face or mouth, as an inverted cup. **péng ka-lién-phak**, id.

ka [R. khap, kháp, to strike against]. **ka-láuh**, to fall, to drop, as an inanimate object (v. láuh). **phah-ka-soa** (C.), id., as of small things dropping from the table.

ka [R. khap, to shut the eyes, = col. kah, khoeh]. **ka-chē**, to nod in sleep; drowsy. **tuh-ka-chē**, id. **ka-tsōe** (C.), id.

ka — **ka-iam**, shivering; chilled (v. iam). **ka-lún-sún**, to shiver with cold or fear; shivering feeling from eating something sour.

ka — **phah-ka-chhiù^{n}**, to sneeze. **tiòh-ka-tsák**, slight obstruction in throat or nostrils (v. tsák). **tiòh-ka-tsáuh** (C.), id. **tiòh-ka-sàu**, slight obstruction caused by food half swallowed, making one cough it up. **hâm-hèh^{n} ka-sàu**, sound of severe coughing, as in consumption or old age.

ka — **ka-tsáu**, a flea (v. tsáu). **ka-chê** (Cn.), a cicada.

ka — **ka-tsoàh**, a cockroach (v. tsoàh).

ka [R. kang, a large river]. **ka-chhiô**, a small boneless marine animal. **ka-tsúi-á** (T.), a fish like the cuttle-fish (v. tsúi).

ka [R. kau, name of a fish]. **bé-ka**, a very good sort of fish. **bé-ka-hî**, id. **ka-láh-hî**, another good fish.

ka [R. kau, name of a bird]. **ka-lēng**, a bird very like the magpie (v. lēng).

ka (R. khiu). **ka-tsui**, the dove (v. tsui).

ka [R. kam, sweet]. **ka-tang-chhiū**, a large tree with useless wood.

ka — **ka-tia^{n}**, the mangrove and similar water-shrubs (v. tia^{n}).

ka (= giâ). **ka-lan-jī**, a hard wood, used for anchors.

ka [R. kɵ, = col. kam]. **ka-mn̂g** (esp. Cn. T.), = kam-mn̂g, a very poisonous plant.

ka [R. kiet, fortunate]. **ka-poà**, cotton (v. poà). **ka-pók-mî^{n}**, raw cotton with the seeds in it, used for quilting.

ka (kā?). **ka-boàh-chhài** (Cn. kūn-toàh), a sort of vegetable.

ka [R. a reed]. **ka-pék-sún**, the edible shoots of a water vegetable (v. sún).

ka (R. kau). **ka-būn-chhiòh**, a fine woven mat made from reeds. **ka-tsù**, a coarse straw bag (v. tsù). **ka-chì** (C.), id. **ka-chèng**, a very coarse mat of reeds or straw. **ka-tsài^{n}** (T.), id. **ka-tsūi^{n}** (Cn.), id.

ka — **ka-liàh**, a very large round bamboo wicker-work tray, used for drying things, or exposing them for sale. **ka-lôe** (esp. T.), id. **ka-ló**, a deep wicker-work bamboo vessel, almost half globular.

ka [R. a household, a family, one's self, or one's own, = col. ke], (C. kɛ, excepting "ka-kī").

ka-kī (C. ka-ti), self: one's self; alone. **goá ka-kī**, I myself. **ka-kī-kiâ^{n}**, to walk alone. **ka-kī ê-lâng**, one of my own relations. **ka-kī, tùi ka-kī**, feud between relatives or fellow-villagers.

hân-ka, my surname. **ka-hū**, my father. **ka-bú**, my mother. **ka-bió** (Cn.) id. **lú-ka** (R.), the bride's own relations.

bē-ū sek-ka, not yet married, said by another. **tī-sek-ka**, married. **pék-siú sêng-ka**, out of poverty become rich. **sɵ-ka**, to confiscate, especially the property of a mandarin. **kheng-ka**, to lose all one's property (v. kheng).

tong-ka, the owner or manager of a school who engages the teacher; said also by a teacher of the father of his pupils. **ɵ-ka**, a receiver of stolen goods. **o-ka**, id.

bîn-ka, the households of the people. **koan-ka ê tsú-tē**, young brothers, sons, and nephews of mandarins. **hù-ka**, a rich family. **bêng-ka**, an illustrious and good family. **sè-ka**, family honourable for generations back. **sè-ka-tóe**, sprung from such a family of mandarins or graduates.

ka-siòk, wife and family. **ka-têng ê tāi-chì**, private domestic matters (v. têng). **ka-phoe**, a letter for or from home. **ka-sìn**, id. **ka-teng**, a boy hired or indentured as household servant for a long period (v. teng). **ka-jîn** (r.), a household slave (s. beautiful). **ka-sán**, family property or wealth (v. sán). **ka-tsâi**, id. **hó-ka-tàng**, very wealthy.

ka-ka hē-hē, house by house.

ka-hoat, rules of a household, as good or bad. **hó-ka-hoat**, well taught, ruled, and regulated, as a family. **hó-ka-kàu**, id. **siáu-ka-sɵ̀**, family not flourishing. **sió-ka-sɵ̀**, id. **tāi-ka-sɵ̀**, family flourishing and wealthy, having good rank and respectability. **sêng-ka-sɵ̀**, become wealthy and flourishing, as family.

háp-ka pêng-an, may the whole family enjoy peace and comfort. **ka-chèk lân-hông**, it is hard to guard against a thief in the household.

ka [R. a sort of dress], (C. kia). **ka-se**, a gown without arms, used by Buddhist priests (v. se).

ka [R. beautiful], (C. kɛ). **ka-jîn** (R.), a beautiful young woman (s. household).

ka [R. good, happy], (C. kɛ). **ka-khèng**, the reign of Kia-king, father of Tau-kwang. **ka-hô-lí** (R.), Amoy island.

ka [R. to add, to increase, = col. ke], (C. kɛ). **ka-thiam**, to increase (active). **ka-kip**, to raise a degree in rank (v. kip). **ka-un**, to forgive a crime or bestow a very great favour.

ka-tn̄g, to wash and rinse (s. cut).

ka-pē (C. kɛ-pōe), double, as in quantity. **ka-it-thàn**, to gain ten per cent. (v. thàn). **ka-jī-lāi**, twenty per cent. on one venture (*e.g.* on one voyage), not counted by time.

ka-bū, to accuse falsely. **kau-ka**, to have monetary dealings with a man. **kap--i kau-ka**, to have transactions with him.

ngó-ka-phî, a yellow wine from the north flavoured with a drug (with Aralia palmata?). **ngó-ka-pî**, id.

kâ (Cn.), = A. giâ, to carry, as a heavy thing.

ká [R. false, pretended, to feign, = col. ké], (C. ké). **ká-chià**, to make underhand or improper use of another's name or influence. **ká-mē^{n}**, to assume falsely, as name or character (v. mē^{n}). **ká-sū**, false stories. **ká-jîn ká-gī**, feigned virtue. **ká-kong hêng-su**, pretending zeal for public ends to advance one's private interests. lōng-ká sêng-chin, sportive pretence become a sad reality.

ká [R. id., by change of tone from "kà," price], (C. kè), a surname.

ká [R. káu, a violent disease of the bowels]. **kiau-ká**, severe colic or spasms in the bowels, as if entangled. **kiau-ká-thiàⁿ**, id. **pak-té-tn̂g kiau-ká**, id. **pak-té-lāi kiau-ká**, id.

ká (R. káu), to twist; to strangle, especially by twisting a rope tight. **ká-lá**, to twist much, as a rope. **ká-ân**, to twist or wring tight. **kúi-nà-tsáp-tiâu ká-lá tsòe-chit-tui**, many troublesome matters all coming on one at once to be set right.

ká--sí, to strangle by putting a rope round the neck and twisting it tight. **gí-ká**, to condemn to strangulation in this way. **tsám-ká**, beheading and strangulation (the second is less dishonourable).

ká-pang, to unite in one fleet, company, or convoy for mutual protection. **ká-pâi**, to make a raft (v. pâi). **ká-soh**, to make very thick ropes by twisting several together. **ká ti-lâ-si**, to remove spiders' webs with a stick. **ká hong-chhe**, to entangle the strings of two kites, as a game. **hong-chhe saⁿ-ká**, id.

ká-chhat, to strain out prepared varnish in making it. **ká-chiap**, to press out juice, as from sugar-cane.

lêng ká-tsúi, a great fall of rain from a waterspout. **tò-ká-lâu**, tide broken and eddying at rocks. **ká-lê-hong** (C.), a whirlwind.

ká-chí, a rod used for twisting a noose tight; a man used by both parties, and on whom both throw the blame. **liáh-goá tsòe ká-chí**, you are making me take a vast deal of thankless trouble for you.

ká (cf. kái, kiáu). **ká-chhá**, to make noisy disturbance, as boys at play. **ká-lá-chhá**, id. **gâu-ká--lâng**, fond of annoying people, as a troublesome infant.

kà [R. to be married to husband, = col. kè], (C. kè). **liét-lú put-kà jī-hu**, a chaste widow will not marry a second husband.

kà (R. kàu), to teach; to instruct; to train. **kà-sī**, id., often including the use of correction. **kà-koai**, to tame, as by beating. **kà-lâng tsòe-hó**, to teach men to live well. **kà kiáⁿ-sun**, to keep one's descendants in good order. **kà sai-á**, to teach apprentices. **kà lóng-bōe chiūⁿ-tsoā**, quite unable to learn (fig. from a cow). **kà-gû**, to train an unbroken cow or ox for ploughing. **kà-tiûⁿ**, the review-ground (v. tiûⁿ).

kà-óh, to teach a school. **kà-óh sien-siⁿ**, a schoolmaster. **kà-ōe-tó**, well able to teach, as a teacher. **kà-chheh**, to teach the books. **kà-khek**, to teach songs.

kà, thin and watery, as gruel, soup, boiled rice, or paste. **kà-kà**, id. **khó-kà**, thick and thin, as such things. **chiáh-kà**, to eat very thin boiled rice; to be very ill off (v. chiáh).

tâm-kà-kà, all wet, as a leaky house or boat; slushy, as road. **kà-lóng-lóng**, thin, as rice paste, &c. **kà-lok-lok**, id. **kà-kê-kê**, id.

kà [R. káu (?), to twist; tangled, = col. ká]. **jû-kà-kà**, entangled and confused, as an affair. **loān-kà-kà**, id.

kà-lòk-lòk, all gone wrong, as an affair, so that it is past remedy [or is this the previous word ?].

kà [R. an equipage; to ride in one], (C. kè). **thêng-hûn kà-bū**, to ride on the mist and clouds, as spirits and genii.

tsun-kà (R.), sir! **hoân-lí tāi-kà**, I beg to trouble you, sir!

chiàⁿ-kà, the boat of a high mandarin. **tāi-jîn ê-tsō-kà**, the admiral's vessel. **loān-kà**, the imperial equipage. **gū-kà**, id. **chih-kà**, ceremoniously receive the imperial equipage. **kiù-kà**, to save the life of the emperor. **pó-kà**, to take care of the emperor when he goes out, as a high military officer does.

kā (cf. hā, hoā). **kā-kā-kún**, to be noisy at play. **kih-kih kā-kā**, indistinct sound of talk, such that one cannot make it out. **hoan-kih-kā**, so confused that it cannot be understood or made anything of. **khoàⁿ--liáu hoan-kih-kā**, having seen it, can make nothing of it.

kā [R. kiōng, along with; together, = col. kāng, kap], (Ch. kāng), a preposition, used with persons only, meaning to, from, for: it is often the converse of "hō͘," and must be used with great care according to fixed usage.

kā-i-kóng, tell him. **goá kā-lí-kóng**, I tell you. **kā-lâng-khǹg**, to exhort people.

kā-i-khui, to open it for him, as a door. **kā--i kah-phē**, give him a coverlet to sleep under. **kā--lâng phah-phái**ⁿ, to spoil another's property, or let it be spoiled in our hands.

goá kā-lí-chē, I am responsible to you for payment.

kā-i-chioh, borrow from him. **kā-i-thó**, demand from him. **kā-i-bóe**, buy from him. **kā-i-tn̂g**, mortgage from him. **kā-i-thóeh**, take or receive from him.

kā (= ka, kāu). **kā-boáh-chhài**, a sort of vegetable.

kā (R. ngáu), to bite; to chew slightly, as a confection; to kill by biting, as dog or tiger does; to fight, as quails or crickets; to cause a sore, as varnish. **kā tiâu-tiâu**, to bite and hold fast; very dogged. **kā niáu-chhú**, to kill a rat, as cat. **kā--sí**, to bite to death. **khit-hó͘-kā**, to be killed by a tiger. **kā--chih**, to break by biting. **kā-chih**, to bite one's tongue. **kā-chih--sí**, to kill one's self by biting off the tongue.

bé-kā-kiuⁿ, the bit of a bridle. **káu-kā-hông**, a plant good for a dog's bite.

niáu-chhú-kā, articles stolen by persons employed in the house. **bóe niáu-chhú-kā**, to buy such things, as men who pretend to be pedlars. **chhī-niáu-chhú, kā pè-tē**, to have a pilfering servant.

kā sek-sut, to set crickets to fight. **kā ien-chhun**, to set quails to fight. **kā chhiên-kap-á**, to blow bits of paper against each other, as children do (v. kap). **sū-káu saⁿ-kā**, to set dogs to fight; to set people a-quarrelling. **hō͘--i kā-chiáh**, to be scolded very violently by him, as on going to ask a favour.

khit-chhat-kā, to get a sore from poisonous varnish. **ōe kā-chhùi**, leaving a harsh bad taste in the mouth, as unripe fruit.

kā chhùi-khí-kun, to clench one's teeth, as in pain or displeasure. **kā chhùi-khí-kun ín--i**, to give consent with clenched teeth when quite unwilling but consciously powerless to prevent it. **kā-chhùi-khí-kun ún-i-soah**, agreed to let the matter take end, but under compulsion. **kā chhùi-khí-kun, lún-thiàⁿ**, to clench the teeth in pain. **chhùi-khí kā-ân-ân**, to clench the teeth firmly, as child in convulsions or man near death. **kā-gê chhiet-chhí**, to gnash the teeth, as in pain or rage.

kā-phang, to eat well-flavoured things (for the

taste), as a child. **thóeh tām-póh, lâi kā-phang**, take a small sum (*e.g.* a few hundred cash) for your trouble, as a middleman for renting a house. **kā thn̂g-á**, to chew or taste confections.

hē sè-sū kā-lā--khì, to have all one's gains eaten up by the customary expenses of festivals, ceremonies, idolatrous rites, &c. **ōe-kā, kā-bōe-háu** (or **pūi**), said of taking strong measures rapidly without talking about it, *e.g.* getting his enemy apprehended at once without warning.

ka^n [R. kam, to inspect; a prison], a prison; a jail. **ka^n-lô**, id. **ka^n-koán**, prisons in general. **ka^n-hoān**, a prisoner. **ka^n-siû**, id. **ka^n-lé**, fees paid to jailer.

kè-ka^n, to guard a prison. **khoà^n-ka^n**, id. **khoà^n-ka^n toā-iâ**, a jailer. **koán-ka^n**, to have superintendence of prison, as small mandarin for great mandarin. **koai^n-ka^n**, to imprison. **koai^n-jip-ka^n**, id. **kìm-ka^n**, id. (v. kìm). **siu-ka^n**, id. **chhut-ka^n**, to get out of prison. **phoà-ka^n**, to break open a prison.

ka^n (originally "ká^n", = kiá^n, a son). **ka^n-ná^n-sun**, a great grandson.

ka^n [R. kám, name of tree]. **ka^n-ná^n**, the Chinese olive (not a real olive), Canarium Pimela. **ka^n-ná^n-sî^n**, salted olives. **ka^n-ná^n-hút**, olive stones (used for carving into ornaments).

ka^n (Cn.), = kam, a loose-skinned orange. **âng-ka^n**, id. **hong-ka^n**, a sort of yellow bitter orange. **sien-ka^n**, a very large sort of orange. **hé-thâu-ka^n**, id.

ka^n — **ka^n-nâ^n** (T.), = A. kau-nâ^n, a small simple round basket with semicircular handle.

kâ^n [R. hâm, to hold in the mouth; together, = col. hâ^n, khâ^n, kâm], to hold in the mouth on one side; to inclose, as a ball in a rattle; to hold within the closed hand or under the arm; (to pilfer); to fasten by soldering, or by small metal pins soldered in; to join two pieces of cloth by making them overlap, or by a piece put under, on which both are sewed. **kâ^n-oá**, to join, as pieces of a broken cup by metal pins soldered in; to sew together, as overlapping pieces of cloth. **kâ^n-tiâu**, to keep from falling (as a weak partition) by double props on each side; to sew together firmly by overlapping.

thau-kâ^n, to pilfer; hiding under one's clothes. **kâ^n-kâ^n kòeh-kòeh**, carrying a number of things between the arms and the body.

sàu-kâ^n-huih, to cough and bring up a little blood.

ká^n (Cn.), = A. kiá^n, a son; also sometimes = A. á, affix of nouns. **tán chit-ká^n**, wait a little. **liōng khah-tn̂g chit-ká^n**, a very little longer (as a thing). **thāi-ká^n**, a short time ago. **to-ká^n**, a son. **to-ká^n** (An.), a knife.

ká^n (R. kám), to dare. **ká^n-sī**, I rather think it is so; I suppose it is. **ká^n-m̄-sī**, I think it is not so. **ká^n-bô**, I think there is none. **ká^n-tióh**, I presume it is right. **ká^n-tióh-khì**, I think (you) should go. **iáh-ká^n**, perhaps it is so (said at end of a statement); he will also dare.

m̄-ká^n, I dare not; he dares not; well-behaved; not acting violently or wickedly. **āu-pái ká^n--má**, will you dare to do it again? (said in beating a child). **ká^n--lah**, yes, I dare!

ká^n-ēng, using money very freely or lavishly. **ká^n-chiáh**, rather too lavish in spending money for food; to dare to eat a thing. **ká^n-tng**, to dare to bear responsibility. **ká^n-sí**, not afraid of death; very fearless. **ká^n-sí ká^n-oáh** (lit. ready for death or life), said of a daring robber or ruffian. **ká^n-thâi-phah-chhò**, id. (lit. not afraid to wound in any way). **ká^n-thàn ká^n-sih**, clever and daring; willing to risk great loss for the sake of large gains.

ká^n (= kah, kàu). **iá ká^n-ná^n-chhát**, as greedy and unjust as a robber!

kà^n — **kà^n-kà^n-kiò**, to snore. **kà^n-kà^n-háu**, to snore; to growl, as a tiger. **chhoán-kih^n-kà^n** (C.), panting very hard (v. chhoán).

kà^n (= kà). **loān-kà^n-kà^n**, confused and involved.

kà^n (R. kàu), leaven. **kà^n-bú**, id. **ké-kà^n**, leaven for cakes. **chhiau-kà^n**, to mix the leaven. **hoat-kà^n**, leaven rising.

kah [R. kàu, to teach; to order, = col. kà], to order; to tell to do; to cause a man to do. **chhe-kah**, to order and employ in general, as servants, messengers, employés, &c. **khoài-kah**, ready to do what one is asked or told, as friend or inferior. **kiông-kah--i**, force him to do, as by commands or threats. **kah--i m̄-thang**, tell him he must not. **kah-i-tsòe**, order or tell him to do or make. **kah-i-lâi**, tell him to come.

kah-i-bóh, let him take his own course; it is no matter to me; I am not afraid about it.

kah (R. id.), the first of the cyclical characters; the first in a list of names, Mr. A.; a small division of a ward, consisting of (tsàp-hē) ten houses; (a census or list of names); a finger-nail; a vest; a coat of mail; (the region of the shoulder).

kah-it, the first and second in a list of names, Mr. A. and Mr. B. **kah-chí**, the first year of the cycle of sixty years; the mode of calculating by the cycle. **koh chit-ê kah-chí**, again another initial year of the cycle. **lâng bô-chiàu thien-lí, thi^n bô-chiàu kah-chí**, if men follow not Heaven's laws, Heaven will not follow the usual course, as of the seasons.

ò-kah, the overseer of a harbour. **kah-tiú^n**, the head-man of a group of ten houses. **kah-hē**, a group of ten houses (v. hē). **ke-kah**, a census. **tsō-ke-kah**, to make a census. **chiū^n ke-kah**, to be enrolled in a census.

kho-kah, having got a literary degree by merit. **kho-kah chhut-sin**, to advance by merit through the literary examinations. **kho-kah put-toān**, successive generations all taking degrees. **kho-kah liên-teng**, to become Kujin and Tsin-sze in rapid succession.

tsńg-kah, finger-nails (v. tsńg). **tsái^n-kah** (T.), id. **kha-kah**, toe-nails. **oā^n-kah**, to shed a nail. **kah-pi^n**, the quick at the side of the nail. **si^n kah-pi^n**, to have a sore beginning at the side of the nail, often making the nail fall off.

kah-háh, strong outer sheathing-leaves of bamboo at joints. **tek-kah-lóeh**, a strong sort of hat used by boatmen.

keng-kah, the whole region about the shoulder. **hièn-kah**, to let the part of the breast near the shoulder appear (either the skin itself or an inner dress) by leaving coat or jacket unbuttoned. **sià-poà^n-kah**, to take off one arm of a coat, shirt, or jacket, leaving that shoulder bare. **phoáh-kah**, crossed over the shoulder, as a scarf (v. phoáh).

chièn-kah, a coat of mail. **khoe-kah**, helmet and coat of mail. **kah-á** (T. kaih-á), a waistcoat; a vest. **tek-kah**, a vest made of small bits of bamboo on netting, worn next the skin in hot weather (s. fish). **soe-thâu kah-á**, a short coat worn by women at toilet. **gûn-chhēng-kah**, a large waistcoat with pockets for money. **boán-hàn-kah**, a vest (with several rows of foreign buttons) broadly bordered with black velvet. **ióng-kah**, a soldier's jacket with the word "brave" (ióng) upon it. **niá^{n}-kah**, a Chinese article of dress like a narrow vest or cape. **mî^{n}-bėh, kóe kah-á** (making a vest out of a pair of stockings), reduced to great straits.

phi-kah, Manchoo soldiers. **phi-kah-peng**, id. **kim-kah-sîn**, spirit-messengers of Giók-hông Siōng-tè (v. sîn). **chhoan-san-kah**, the scaly otter or ant-eater (its scales?) = lâ-lí.

kah (R. kap). **kah-ko**, the yards of a foreign vessel.

kah [R. kàu, to compare]. **kah-khoà^{n}**, to test, as a steelyard, by comparing it with others (s. fit). **kah-khoà^{n} ū-tsún**, id. **kah-chhìn**, to test a common steelyard. **kah-téng**, to test a small steelyard.

kah [R. khap, to shut the eyes, = col. ka, khoeh]. **tuh-kah-chē**, to dose or nod in sleep.

kah — **kám-kah**, skilful at any sort of work.

kah [cf. kap, with; to fit together], to fit; to suit; to fit together; to add on; also; in addition; to mix in proper proportions; to put on splints on a limb; engaged, as boat hired for ship. **kah-khoà^{n}**, to put together, as the parts of a thing not fully finished, to see if it will suit and fit well together (s. compare).

kah-kha, to fit the foot, as a shoe. **kah-chhùi**, suiting one's taste, as food or drink. **kah-ì**, just to one's mind. **m̄-kah-ì**, unsatisfactory. **bô-kah lí-ì**, does not suit or please you. **kah-sim**, just to one's mind; the front part of a carcase (as of goat or pig) for food, making about one-third of the whole.

phòe-kah, fitting each other well, as articles of dress (v. phòe). **kah-chhah**, corresponding well, as dress to one's station, or as one part of dress to another. **kah-chiú^{n}**, to put on the oars when going to row. **ū-kah-kan**, the bottle goes along with the liquor. **kah-tsûn**, small-boat engaged to wait on a ship or large junk. **kah-tiā^{n}-tiòh**, engaged regularly, as such a boat. **ēng-chhâ kah--teh**, spliced by tying on a piece of wood, as a broken limb.

kah-chham--teh, mixed together. **am-lâi kah-khì**, taking good and bad on an average, as things or work. **chiàu-kah**, following the due allowed proportion in mixing, as good and bad cash, or as a few inferior articles in a lot. **kah phái^{n}-chî^{n}**, to mix the allowed number of bad cash among good ones. **goá bô-khah-ke kah--lí**, I do not mix more bad cash for you than the fair usual rate. **chit-hó, kah chit-gâi**, one good joined with one bad (v. chit).

sńg-sîn, kah bô-bîn, to injure one's self and lose sleep by turning night into day (v. sîn). **bô thi^{n}-lí, kah bô-hêng-chí**, without any regard to the laws of Heaven, or to the rules of good conduct. **kau-chiam tèng, kah bát-liú** (sew very close and full of buttons), said of a man painfully minute and accurate.

kah — **kah-sì^{n}-khí**, building by boards or lath and plaster work between wooden pillars (v. sì^{n}).

kah [R. kài, to cover, = col. khàm, khap, ka], to put on, as a coverlet. **kah-phē**, to have a quilt or coverlet over one's self. **kā--i kah-phē**, give him a coverlet to sleep under. **hē-i-kah**, give him something to sleep under. **bô-thang-kah**, has nothing to sleep under.

kah —, the rim of a basket, &c. **poà-ki ê-kah**, the rim of a winnowing tray. **poà-ki-kah**, a very poisonous snake, so called from the markings on its body.

kah — **tek-kah**, a long thin sort of fish (s. vest).

kah (= kàu). **kah-chiah** —, so very —! **kah-hiah** —, id. **kah-hiah-tsōe**, so very many! too many! **iá, kah-ná^{n}-chhàt**, as greedy and wicked as a robber.

kàh (Cn.), = A. kiàh, to hold in the hand, as a stick, umbrella, sword, &c.

kai [R. all]. **bān-poa^{n}, kai hā-phín**, all sorts (of trades and professions except the literati) are of low rank.

kai [R. ought; proper; connected; aforesaid]. **kai--tsài**, fortunately! **put-chí kai--tsài**, how very fortunately!

eng-kai, ought. **eng-kai--tit**, id. **eng-kai-tiòh**, ought; ought to. **kai tit--tiòh**, ought to get. **kai-jiân**, according to what is right. **hàp-kai**, according to what is right. **kai-sí**, you should die! (said in scolding). **kai-sí ê-lâng**, id. **siû-sò kai-chīn**, the fated time having come, one must die. **sì^{n}-thâu phah--lâng bōe-thià^{n}; ì-sù put-kai**, it will not do at all to strike with a fan, though it gives no pain; the action, though slight, has a very improper meaning and cannot be allowed.

kai-chhe, the constables of a civil mandarin for the particular day. **kai-pan--ê**, id. **kai-pan**, to come to one's turn for the day, as constable.

kai-chhin, relations.

kai-koat (r.), inclusive; what is contained (v. koat).

kái (cf. ká, kiáu), to tease; to annoy; to molest. **kái-chhái**, to annoy; to play tricks upon.

kái [R. to separate a thing into its parts; to untie; to loose; to deliver from calamity; to compose a quarrel; to explain, = col. kóe; and by change of tone, kài, kè]. **tsù-kái**, to explain by writing notes or comments on.

khai-kái, to explain, as a book or doctrine; to comfort a man who is very sad or anxious, by making explanations, &c.; to propose a way of settling a dispute, as a mutual friend or mediator. **put-tek khai-kái**, no way of making such explanations as to get the quarrel amicably settled. **khui-kái** (T.), to make a satisfactory settlement of a dispute, as a mediator or arbiter. **khoàn-kái**, to exhort men to make up a quarrel. **oan khó-kái**, a quarrel ought to be settled amicably (v. oan). **pâi-kái**, to adjust or try to adjust (a quarrel) for another, as by speaking to the other party, or by interceding with his displeased superior. **pâi-kái bōe-chiâ^{n}**, to try to do so, but not succeed. **pâi-kái bô-sū**, to help to settle a quarrel, as a friend or mediator.

kái-ûi, to compel the enemy to raise a siege (v. ûi). **kái-tók**, to cure a diseased state of body caused by eating something unwholesome. **kái-ut**, to cure a dyspeptic or bilious feeling. **siau-tsai kái-eh**, to remove or ward off calamities (v. siau). **kái-liên-keng**, a yellow paper burned for removing calamity (v. liên, "calamity").

kái-chiet, a widow marrying again.

tek-kái (esp. C.), to be very glad and happy.

siáu-kái, to make water (polite phrase). **kái-pì^{n}**, the hollow between the thigh and the belly.

kái [R. to correct; to alter, = col. kóe]. **kái-jīm**, to change a mandarin's place of office because of some small fault, disagreement, or unsuitableness.

ti-kò pit-kái, when you know a fault you should certainly correct it. **kái-ok chiông-siēn**, to reform what is bad and follow the good. **kái-kò chhien-**

siēn, to reform and turn to virtue. **goân-sèng put-kái,** the original bad character is not yet reformed.

kài [R. a boundary]. **sè-kài** (r.), the world. **hoat-kài** (R.), the dwelling-place of Buddha (s. command). **hē-kài-kong** (Cn.), an idol (v. hē).

sam-kài-kong, the three idols presiding over heaven, earth, and water. **sam-kài-kong-siⁿ,** their birth-days, viz.; 1.15, siōng-goân; 7.15, tiong-goân; 10.15, hā-goân. **sam-kài-khien,** cakes made in the form of a chain (v. khien). **sam-kài-teng,** a pair of lamps with a lamp called "thien-teng" between them. **sam-kài-lê,** an incense vessel hung up in the house, and used on their birth-days. **khah-siàⁿ sam-kài,** always efficacious or coming true, as good medicine, or as man whose warnings or guesses always come true; or as food that always disagrees with us, as we were warned. **thiⁿ-tōe khah-siàⁿ sam-kài,** the natural signs of weather and such laws of the seasons are much more sure than the most powerful idols.

kài-chí, a boundary stone or mark (s. warn). **chióh-kài,** a stone boundary. **kài-hān,** a boundary (v. hān). **pien-kài,** frontiers. **kéng-kài,** boundary of province or territory (s. warn). **tōe-kài,** boundary of a country, region, or property. **kau-kài,** a boundary. **sâng-kau-kài,** having a common boundary; adjoining, as region. **saⁿ-kau-kài,** id. **āu-kài,** vacant ground at back of a large house, within the inclosing wall. **āu-kài-thê,** id.

kài [R. id., = khài], to smooth the top of a measure with a stick. **táu-kài,** a stick for making level what is in a measure. **bí-kài,** id., for rice. **kài-bí,** to smooth the rice in a measure. **kài-béh,** to smooth wheat or barley in a measure. **kài-tāu,** do. with pulse. **kài-chhân,** to roll a field smooth with a large wooden roller.

kài [R. koài; strange, a demon]. **hiông-kài-kài,** very fierce or fierce-looking.

kài [R. to cover; a cover; to excel; to put on the last finish, = col. khàm, koà, &c.]

kám-kài, to treat with kindness or leniency (v. kám).

khí-kài, to build a house. **hoan-kài,** to repair a house, at least new roof and a good part of the walls new. **hoan-kài-khí,** id.

phe-kài, mats, coverlets, &c., used as bedding in travelling.

kài-sè-kan, the best in the world; to surpass the whole world. **kài-tiûⁿ,** to be the best in a contest or examination. **kài-ē-mn̂g--ê,** the best in Amoy; superior to any in Amoy. **kài-it-toā,** the very largest or greatest. **kài-it-hó,** the very best. **kài-tē-it,** the very best or first or first-class. **kài-tē-it-toā,** the very largest or greatest. **kài-tē-it-hó,** the very best (&c.)

kài-bīn, to put on the last finish, or a new surface. **kài-sek,** to put on colour on another colour, or on a white ground. **kài-chhái-sek,** to paint with various colours. **kài-ngé-sek,** id. **kài-láh,** to wax, as paper; to rub smooth with wax, or put on a waxy surface.

kài [R. to hand over; by change of tone from "kái," to loose, = col. kè, kóe]. **kài-goân,** the highest of the Kujin (kú-jîn) graduates.

kài [R. to beg]. **kài-siú-thâu,** the head of the beggars in a place.

kài (R. id.) **kap-kài,** an animal used in medicine.

kài [R. an assistant; an individual; to be anxious, = col. koà]. **ke-kài,** unsociable; disobliging; unneighbourly; of a solitary or misanthropic temper, *e.g.* unwilling to assist, or to give a lodging, and difficult to agree with. **ke-kài-khì,** id. **ke-kài-phiah,** id.

kài [R. mustard, = col. koà]. **kài-loáh,** powdered mustard. **kài-boáh,** id., used as a medicine. **péh-kài-chí,** mustard-seed.

keng-kài, a thorny plant (sort of Salvia?), used as a febrifuge. **keng-kài-chháu,** id. **keng-kài-chí,** its seed. **keng-kài-sūi,** its spike. **hông-hong keng-kài,** this and another medicine often combined.

kài [R. a residence for officials]. **kong-kài,** the whole inclosed extra grounds of a yamun.

kài [R. commandments, esp. prohibitions; sometimes interchanged with the next word]. **kài-lút,** fixed commandments. **hoat-kài** (R.), id. (s. boundary). **tsáp-tiâu-kài,** the ten commandments.

kài [R. to warn; to prohibit; to refrain from]. **kéng-kài,** to punish slightly; to chastise gently; to try to deter men from evil, *e.g.* warning them by the example of those who have been punished for it (s. boundary). **kéng-kài-á,** to give a few blows as a chastisement, as father or mandarin. **kài-thek,** to reprimand or chastise slightly, esp. as literary mandarin (v. thek).

kài-chiú, to abstain from alcoholic liquors. **kài-hun,** to abstain from opium. **tsai-kài bók-iók,** to fast, abstain, and perform ceremonial ablutions (v. tsai).

siu-kài, to enter formally the number of regular Buddhist priests by a sort of consecration, cauterizing part of the brow, &c. **toā-kài-thâu,** head of a great recognized community of Buddhist priests, who can consecrate priests. **kài-tsú,** id.

kài-chí, a square piece of wood with which Buddhist priests strike the table between and at end of some prayers; also (R.), a finger-ring (s. boundary).

kaiⁿ [R. kam, an orange]. **chhàu-kaiⁿ-á** (T.), = chhàu-kiô-á, a solanaceous plant.

kaiⁿ (T.), = A. keng, a room; classifier of houses and buildings.

kaiⁿ (T.), = A. keng (shoulder). **kaiⁿ-thâu,** the shoulder. **keh-kaiⁿ hiaⁿ-tī,** first or second cousins. **keh-kaiⁿ--ê,** id.

káiⁿ (T.), (= Cn. káng, kūiⁿ). **káiⁿ-iūⁿ,** to worship by offerings, as ancestors.

káiⁿ (T.), = A. kéng, to choose.

káiⁿ (T.), = A. kéng, an aqueduct or conduit; to lead water by such a conduit.

kàiⁿ [R. kàn, to intermit; by change of tone from "kan," between]. **kàiⁿ-tn̄g,** to intermit. **kàiⁿ-jit,** each alternate day; passing over one day. **kàiⁿ-chit-jit,** to omit one day.

kàiⁿ-sek, vari-coloured.

kāiⁿ (T.), = A. kēng, to assist; to push, as a boat with a bamboo pole.

kaih (T.), = A. kah, a vest; a waistcoat.

kak [R. kok, grain]. **gō-kak,** = ngó-kok, the five grains; corn, rice, and grain in general; originally "tō liông siok bek sú," but now including all sorts, and even potatoes. **gō-kak ū-siu,** a good harvest.

kak [R. to know]. **hoat-kak,** to come out, as a secret (s. horn). **sit kak-chhat,** to fail in one's duty by negligence, so that evil results (v. chhat). **put-kak** (R.), unawares; suddenly and unexpectedly. **sîn put-ti, kúi put-kak,** very secret, hidden even from the spirits.

kak (R. id.), lath or clap-boards on which tiles are laid. **kak-á,** id. **kak-ki,** id. **îⁿ-kak,** beams and lath for a roof. **tèng-kak**, to nail on the lath on the beams to be ready for the tiles.

kak — **kak-phang**, a large sort of wasp.

kak, a male or cock bird. **koe-kak**, a cock. **koe-kak-kong**, a very large cock. **koe-kak-á**, a small cock chicken. **ah-kak**, a drake. **gô-kak**, a gander.

kak [R. kàu, =kak, to compare; to dispute]. **ài kap-lâng ke-kak**, fond of quarrelling. **kap-lâng kak-khé**, quarrelling with people. **kap-lâng khé-kak**, id.

kak (R. id.), a horn; a corner; a small bit; the tenth-part of a dollar; a trumpet; a part of a place; a division of a clan living together in one place, not necessarily genealogical. **lêng-kak**, dragon's horns. **lêng-kak**, a sort of Trapa with edible fruit. **lêng-kak**, China-root broken into bits (v. lêng). **lêng-kak**, horn made thin and transparent for lanterns. **bêng-kak**, id. **bêng-kak-teng**, a lamp of thin translucent horn. **kak-toà**, an ornamental girdle worn by ladies of rank (v. toà). **kak-soe**, a horn comb. **kak-tiⁿ**, a shoe-horn. **kak-thöeh** (Cn.), id.

hoat-kak, to grow horns (s. know). **kak-tsang**, a little boy's tail. **gû-kak**, a cow's horn. **gû-kak-chhì**, a medicinal plant. **gû-kak-kóng-chhì**, id. **gû-kak-ké-chhì**, id. **niáu-chhú jip gû-kak** (rat in a horn), to get into a road that has no outlet, a cul de sac.

sàu-kak, a trumpet. **pûn-kak**, to blow a trumpet.

chit-kak, ten cents. **chit-kak-gûn**, id. **kak-jī**, twelve cents.

chióh-kak, a large broken piece of stone.

kak-thn̂g, loaf-sugar. **kak-tsúi**, fine syrup from white loaf-sugar. **kak-tsoá**, a sort of strong paper that does not easily tear.

chhut-thâu chhut-kak, to meddle in other men's matters. **chhut-thâu sńg-kak**, to take responsibility and so injure one's self.

kek-kak, to the utmost (v. kek). **siám-kak**, quiet and retired, as a place. **tiàu-kak**, slanting (esp. at a corner), as in folding or drawing (not said of placing things). **tiàu-kak-chhoáh**, id. **tiàu-kak hé-teh**, tied by the four corners, as a handkerchief inclosing things. **chhoáh-kak**, diagonal; slanting; not at right angles. **chhah-kak**, to piece in making a dress; a sort of mensuration (v. chhah). **sê-kak**, a corner out of proportion to the rest. **mîⁿ-kak**, having sharp edges, as table, &c. (v. mîⁿ). **phah-khih-kak**, having a flaw in the edge. **oat-kak**, to turn a corner; a corner or turning of a road.

kak-thâu, a corner; a part of a village or region. **pun kak-thâu**, to allot the several parts of a village or region to different families, &c., as for monopoly of carrying loads, or sedans, &c. **kiông-pâng ngīⁿ-kak**, a most powerful portion of a powerful family. **i teh-khiā ū-kak**, he is very powerful in that place, so that no one ventures to oppose him.

hiáh-kak, the projecting corners of the forehead above the eyes. **pìn-kak**, the temples (said of women). **bák-kak**, the outer corners of the eyes. **chhù-kak**, the corner of a house (v. chhù). **piah-kak**, corner between two inner walls. **thiⁿ-piⁿ hái-kak**, the most distant parts of the world (of heaven and of the sea). **thiⁿ bô-piⁿ, hái bô-kak**, the extent of the world is vast and boundless.

saⁿ-kak, triangular; thirty cents. **sì-kak**, four-cornered; square; forty cents. **sì-kak-kak**, square; four-cornered. **thài-sì-kak**, very straightforward and unbending as to principles of right, or too unbending (according to the idea of the speaker). **sì-kak-sin**, very unbending as to the principles of justice and integrity, as mandarin, &c. **lák-kak**, hexagonal. **saⁿ-chiam lák-kak** (six corners and three points), very roughly and clumsily made; troublesome to deal with, as a crotchety man who likes to thwart other's wishes. **poeh-kak**, octagonal; anise-seed stars; a sort of paper kite with the 8 diagrams on it.

kak (Cn.), = A. kek, the chrysanthemum.

kák (T. sometimes "kók"), to throw. **kák chióh-thâu**, to throw a stone. **hiet-kák**, to throw away. **pàng-hiet-kák**, id. **tìm-hiet-kák**, id. **tsóh-hiet-kák**, id. **phuh-hiet-kák**, to puff away the smoke without swallowing it. **soa-hiet-kák** (C.), to drop and get lost, as small things from a table. **khioh-kák**, utterly useless, as man or thing; a loafer, thief, or ne'er-do-well. **chit-sì-lâng khioh-kák**, utterly useless his whole lifetime. **thek-kák** (esp. C.), id.

kam [R. sweet, willing], a surname. **kam-tiⁿ**, sweet. **kam-kút**, pleasant to eat and swallow; pleasant to hear, as sweet words (v. kút).

kam-siok, Kan-suh province. **kam-chiu**, Kan-chow in Kan-suh. **siám-kam**, Shensi and Kan-suh.

kam-goān, willing; make no further opposition. **kam-sim chêng-goān**, heartily willing; thoroughly pleased, as to do a work or give a gift. **kam-sim**, heartily willing. **kam-sim siū-khé**, happy to undergo the toil to get the object. **m̄-kam-sim**, unwilling; discontented, as at having to do or give something under pressure, or at having lost something. **m̄-kam**, unwilling; niggardly.

kam-kiet, a bond taken by mandarins, esp. stating that a case is finally settled. **kam-ēng**, spending money freely. **kam-ēng, m̄-kam-chhēng**, using money freely or lavishly for other purposes, but dressing too shabbily.

kam-chià, esculent sugar-cane. **kam-chhó**, liquorice. **kam-á-bit**, a condiment chewed with betel-nut and siri leaf. **kam-hēng**, almonds, as medicinal. **kam-kek**, chamomile. **kam-sék**, a medicinal stone (v. sék). **iū-kam**, a small, round, hard, green fruit: its taste changes from sour to sweet in the mouth.

kam [R. sort of disease]. **kam-chek**, a disease of children caused by over-eating. **tióh-kam**, to have this disease. **gê-kam**, a severe disease of the jaws —some say, a bad gumboil; some say, like cancer—the gums wasting away and the roots of the teeth laid bare. **tióh gê-kam**, to have this disease.

kam [R. kan, lasciviousness]. **kam-chhng**, venereal ulcers.

kam (R. ké), (Cn. ka). **kam-mńg**, a very poisonous plant. **kam-múiⁿ** (C.), id.

kam (R. id.), (Cn. kaⁿ), a mandarin orange; a loose-skinned orange. **âng-kam**, a red orange. **hé-thâu-kam**, a very large and fragrant sort of orange. **hút-siú-kam**, the fingered citron. **kam-bān**, a lobe of an orange. **kam-phê**, the skin of an orange; raw orange-peel.

kam [R. id., =col. kaⁿ, a prison], to oversee so as to watch a man for faults and report him to his superior, as a man does who is appointed for that purpose, but without power himself to rule the other; also, to take a kindly care of a person in our employment committed to our care (*e.g.* son of a friend), helping him when his duties are difficult. **kam-lâi kam-khì**, to watch one another, as two mandarins of nearly equal rank, or as two men used together for some work set to keep an eye on each other. **chiong-kun kam tsóng-tok**, the Tartar general watches the Viceroy.

kam-tsám, to witness an execution, as mandarin (v. tsám). **kam-kok**, to act as regent. **kam-kok tāi-sîn**, regent.

kam-tok (r.), to oversee; (X.), a bishop.

kam [R. kan, dry, = col. koa^n]. **kam-bī-tiàm**, a sort of grocery shop (v. bī).

kam (C.), = A. kā^n, to join cloth at a seam by overlapping. **sio-kam**, id.

kâm [R. hâm, to join; to hold in the mouth, = col. hâ^n, kâ^n, khâ^n], to hold in the mouth; to hold shut, as the mouth. **chhùi kâm--teh**, mouth held shut. **kâm-tûn**, to take the lips between the teeth, as infants. **kâm-lin**, to hold the teat in the mouth, as child sucking. **kâm-pn̄g chhī-kiá^n**, to feed a child with rice from one's own mouth. **chit-ê-chhùi kâm chit-ê-chih** (mouth contains nothing but a tongue), not able to speak a word when it is needed. **ōe, kâm tī-chhùi--nih^n**, speaking very indistinctly. **kóng-ōe kâm--teh**, to talk indistinctly. **kâm-huih phùn-thi^n** (to spit blood at Heaven), to accuse falsely of enormous crimes.

kâm-tsúi, swollen with damp, as wood. **kim-kâm**, a sort of sugar confection.

sa^n-kâm, jointed together, as the overlapping boards of a partition, or as mortice and tenon.

kám, the fixed convex water-tight cover of the hold in a vessel below the movable boards of the false deck. **kám-á-kau**, the gutter between the side of a boat and the convex cover of the hold. **kám-kak**, at the corner of that convex cover of the hold. **chhèng-kám-pang**, the movable boards which make the (false) upper deck for treading upon [the groups of this and following words are doubtful].

kám — **tiá^n-kám**, the lid of a Chinese frying-pan or rice-boiler. **tiá^n-kám-koà**, id.

phâng-kám, a bamboo mat or hurdle, made like a bamboo sail, used as a cover for a boat or for a shed.

ôe-kám, the part of a shoe-sole that is next the foot and above the rest of the sole.

kám, to cover (as coffin) with clay or earth, not deep.

kám (R. id.) **kám-thâu**, a sort of mourning-hood worn by women at funerals. **moâ^n-kám-thâu**, id., made of coarse hempen cloth, in deepest mourning. **moâ^n-kám**, id. **tōe-á kám-thâu**, cover for head, one grade less deep mourning.

kám — **kám-á**, a shallow wicker basket (without handle), much used for holding eatables at shop doors, and for woman's work-basket. **tîn kám-á**, do. made of rattan. **bih-kám**, do. made of bamboo wicker-work. **bí-kám**, shallow bamboo basket for holding rice for sale. **kám-ô**, a large and rather deep wicker vessel for holding rice, dough, &c.

kám [R. to dare, = col. ká^n, kiám], an initial interrogative particle which asks a question meant to be answered in the negative, thus equal to a strong affirmation of the opposite.

kám-kah, skilful at work, manual or literary. **kám-tong**, daring to take the responsibility (v. tong). **khí-kám**, how can I dare! you honour or flatter me too much.

kám-chhái, = kiám-chhái, perhaps; it may be that—.

kám-ōe (= "kiám-ōe," and so in following phrases), how can —? how could —? surely it cannot be. **kám-bōe** —, how can — not? surely it is. **kám-beh** —, how can it be that (you) will —? surely will not. **kám-ū àn-ni^n**, surely it is not so. **kám-sī àn-ni^n**, id. **kám-m̄-sī**, surely it is so; surely he is; how could it be otherwise!

kám [R. to influence, as by moral influence or by kindness]. **kám-kài**, to treat with kindness and leniency, as an inexperienced or favourite servant, not exacting much from him; to help kindly, as an inferior, by influence or money, or by assisting him in his work.

kám-hong, to have a cold; slightly feverish. **kám-tio̍h-hong**, id. **kám--tio̍h**, id. **kám-léng**, id. **kám-mē^n**, id. **kám-mn̄g** (C.), id. **têng-kám**, relapse, in disease.

kám-siā, to thank. **kám-un**, grateful for favour; to give thanks for favour. **kám lâng--ê un-chêng**, grateful to a man. **kám jip hì-hú**, grateful from the bottom of the heart.

kám-hoà, to influence or affect the heart with renovating or transforming energy, as a sage or a spirit. **kám-tōng**, to affect the heart with emotion or influence. **kám-kek**, id.

lêng-kám, powerful; efficacious, as idol that can answer prayers. **kám-èng**, to answer prayers and give protection. **kám-èng-phien**, the book of recompenses, a famous Tauist book.

kàm [R. to oversee, by change of tone from "kam"]. **kàm-pún**, the square regularly-formed characters, as commonly printed or written.

kàm-chhat, to examine, as a superior. **kàm-la̍p**, to accept with favour, as a sacrifice or oblation.

kàm-seng, a purchased degree nearly equal to siù-tsâi. **koan-kàm**, to buy it. **la̍p-kàm**, id. **kok-tsú-kàm**, the ancient university of Pekin, which sells the degree of "kàm-seng." **khim-thien-kàm**, imperial astronomer.

kiong-kàm, an imperial eunuch. **thài-kàm**, id. **thài-kàm-í**, a sort of low arm-chair.

kàm [R. a mirror, = col. kià^n]. **kong-kàm**, the national history from first to last. **í-kó ûi-kàm**, to use ancient history as a mirror.

kām (cf. gām). **ko-kām-á** (C.), a fish like a nail, with large head and small body.

kan [R. kat, to cut, = col. koah]. **io̍k-kan io̍k-sat**, = io̍k-kat io̍k-sat, determined to have a feud.

kan [R. kien, firm]. **kan-lo̍k**, = kien-lo̍k, a spinning-top.

kan [R. the liver, = col. koa^n]. **kan-hoe**, pig's liver. **kan-hé**, a feverish state of body, shown by slight inflammation of eyes, dryness of mouth or sleeplessness, supposed to come from the liver. **kan-hé tōng**, slight redness of eyes and sleeplessness, either from illness or simply from much thought and anxiety. **kan-hé sēng**, id.

kan [R. dry; only; harden, = khiên, = col. kien, kiên, koa^n], a word used at the beginning of a sentence, introducing a new or different thought, but can hardly be translated; also (C.), not watered, as butcher-meat.

kan-ta, only; merely (v. ta). **m̄-pàng--i kan-hiu**, will not let him off; will not let the matter drop. **kan-á**, well indeed —, introducing a statement that seems antecedently improbable. **kan--á hó**, well it is really good; well then it will do well, though at first it seemed unsuitable. **kan-ōe**, well, after all, I suppose he is able; yet he can or it can be. **kan-á-**

ōe, id. **phah-sǹg-bōe, i kan-á-ōe,** contrary to expectation he is able.

kan-kiȯt, over-strict, as master; bad for making money, as a place (v. kiȯt).

kan-ki^{n}, a mariner's compass. **kan-tsam,** id. **kan-chiam,** id.

kan-ơ, dark black, without any gloss of other colour. **kan-chhat,** varnish unmixed with colour. **kan-iû,** oil used for staining wood, &c., not mixed with paint. **kan-he,** mortar made of pure lime without earth.

kan-chēng, clean; dry and clean. **put-tek kan-chēng,** cannot get out of trouble.

kan-niû^{n}, dry provisions, as for a journey. **kan-bī,** dried flesh, &c. (v. bī). **kan-ké,** dried eatables (v. ké). **kan-kiu^{n},** parched ginger used medicinally. **kan-koah,** a medicinal root (v. koah).

kan-hiā (C.), white ants that breed in roofs.

kan (Cn.) **sek-kan-tsû,** = A. sù-kun-tsú, a medicine used for worms.

kan [R. a shield; cyclical characters; witness; to have relation to: to offend]. **tāng-khí kan-ko** (to begin to move shield and spear), to begin a feud (v. ko).

kan-chèng, witness; proof; to give evidence. **tsòe-kan-chèng,** to give evidence.

ū-kan-kè, it has reference to (us, &c.); (we) are concerned or involved in it (s. difficult). **ū-kan-kòe** (C.), id. **bô-kan-kè,** it does not concern or involve. **kap-lí bô-kan-kè,** has nothing to do with you; none of your business. **kan-siáp,** to have connection with, as affair. **bô-kan-siáp,** having no relation or relevancy, as matter that does not concern us.

put-siong-kan, not setting a good example to inferiors, as ill-behaved parent or master. **ū-siong-kan,** of importance, as affair. **bô-siong-kan,** it does not concern; of no consequence; it does not matter; no matter. **kap-lí bô-siong-kan,** it does not concern you. **bô-siong-kan ê-sū,** an unimportant matter; a matter that does not concern us. **bô-siong-kan ê-lâng,** a worthless fellow; a man of no importance; man who has no connection with us or with the matter in hand.

bô-kan-gāi, there is no impediment or fear of trouble from it (v. gāi). **kan-hoān** (R.), to offend against, as a law.

thien-kan (R.), the smaller cycle of ten used in making the cycle of sixty. **thien-kan tē-chi** (R.), the cycles of ten and twelve; all the cyclical characters.

siā-kan-thâu, the root of the plant called soa^{n}-koa^{n}-lân (Pardanthus or other iridaceous plant). **siā-kan,** medicine made from it.

kan-koah, a medicinal root (better, kan, "dry," but generally written "shield"), (v. koah).

kan [R. traitorous; unfaithful; intriguing; craftily; deceitful]. **kan-tsà,** deceitful; intriguing; crafty. **kan-chè** (C.), id. **kan-khiáu,** id.; dishonest (v. khiáu). **kan-khiet** (R.), id. **kan-hiám,** fraudulent; dishonest and intriguing. **kan-hiau-hiám,** id. **kan-siâ,** id. **kan-hiông,** crafty and roguish. **kan-kúi,** deceitful rascal, esp. deceiving both sides for one's own gain.

poà^{n}-kan-tiong, of very doubtful fidelity. **tāi-kan,** a traitorous minister; a very cunning, crafty, intriguing man. **kan-sîn,** a traitorous minister. **kan-sîn-tóng,** a traitorous minister and his fellow-conspirators, esp. mandarins; said also of employes or servants banded together to cheat their employer or master. **kan-tóng,** id., id.

kan (R. id.) **kan-îm,** lasciviousness; impure in conduct; properly adultery. **kan-hu,** an adulterer. **kan-chiâ^{n},** a legal case of adultery, as brought into court. **thong-kan,** to hold illicit intercourse. **tè-kan,** lewd fellows fighting for a woman. **kiông-kan,** rape. **ke-kan,** sodomy. **māi^{n}-kan,** to keep a brothel. **kan lâng-bó-kiá^{n},** to debauch the wives and daughters of others. **kan-lâu,** venereal ulcers. **kan kūn-sat,** he who commits adultery is in danger of being killed.

kan [R. keng, classics, &c.] **kan-kí,** (T.), = A. keng-kí, a man's employment or means of livelihood.

kan [R. a post; a stake, = col. koa^{n}]. **lân-kan,** a railing; a balustrade; a sort of lace or border.

kan (R. id.), a bottle; a tall jug or glass of stoneware or glass, especially with narrow neck. **kan-á,** id. **po-lê-kan,** a glass bottle. **hoe-kan,** a flower-glass; a tall fine flower-jar. **tsúi-kan;** a water-jug. **kok-kong kan-á,** a stoneware bottle for the liquor called "kok-kong-chiú," suitable for holding medicine. **ū-kah-kan,** the bottle is given or sold with its contents.

kan [R. between; among; in; a room; = col. keng], also (C.), = A. keng, classifier of houses, &c.

sè-kan, the world. **sì-kan** (C.), id. **iông-kan,** the present world. **hoân-kan,** id. **im-kan,** the world of spirits; hades.

tiong-kan, among; between; in the middle. **soa^{n}-kan** (among the hills), the hilly country. **hiu^{n}-kan,** in the country among the villages. **chhin-chhek-kan,** among one's relations. **jit--kan,** in the daytime. **mî^{n}--kan,** night-time; at night. **ū-kan--á ū** (C.), sometimes there are. **ū-kan--á bô** (C.), sometimes there are not.

kan [R. calamity; suffering; difficult]. **kan-kè,** difficult to accomplish; in want or poverty (v. kè, "plan"), (s. shield, related).

kan-lân, pain; suffering (v. lân). **kan-khó,** misery; suffering; grief; miserable; sore trouble; troublesome; difficult. **kan-khó-kóng,** troublesome or difficult to speak about. **jîn bû kan-khó-kè, lân-tek sè-kan-tsâi,** no gains without pains.

kán [R. kám, to dare, = col. ká^{n}], (esp. T.) **kán-ōe,** how can that be! **kán ōe-àn-ni^{n},** id.

kán (C.), = A. kién. **kán-tiû,** a sort of silk.

kán [R. gán, the eye]. **lêng-kán** (C.), = A. gêng-géng, the lung-yen fruit.

kán — **toā-kán-tsan,** a sort of war junk (v. tsan).

kán [R. concise; to choose, = col. kéng], a surname; abbreviated; concise; simple in taste; without display; also (C.), = A. kéng, to choose.

kán-chiȯt, carefully abridged. **kó-kán,** remissly; carelessly. **kán-séng,** abridged; abbreviated; doing hurriedly or at less expense. **kán-sé^{n}** (C.), id. **kán-séng-siá,** to write with contracted or abbreviated characters. **kán-tóh** (C.), to choose out.

kán [R. kién, a son], a female slave; a concubine. **kán-jí,** id. **tsa-bó-kán,** id. **tsa-bó-kán-kiá^{n},** a child born of a concubine. **iù-kán,** a beautiful and accomplished female slave. **lāu-kán,** an old female slave. **sûi-kè-kán,** a female slave given to a daughter at her marriage.

chhiū^{n}-kán, an elephant's keeper. **chhun-gû-kán,** the boy represented in the picture in almanacs as tending the cow; a figure of that cow-herd used at the spring festival.

kán-ngá^{n} (Cn.), = A. gín-ná, a boy. **kán-ngiá^{n}** (Cn.), id. **kán-ká^{n}** (Cn., esp. An.), id.

kàn [R. the trunk of a tree; business; skilful]. **lêng-kàn**, having a great capacity for business. **kàn-pān**, to manage an affair for another. **kàn-pān--ê**, got by money and management (not by merit), as a degree. **kàn-soân**, to put right, or try to arrange (as a troublesome matter) with considerable trouble.

kàn [R. kan, a shield, related to]. **lí kàn-tn̄g**, why have you brought this trouble on yourself? (v. tn̄g). **beh kàn-tāi-chì** (Cn.), what would you be at? what ever do you want? **bô-kàn** (Cn.), of no consequence.

kàn [R. kan, adultery, fornication], to commit fornication, adultery, &c.; a vulgar word, much used in vile scolding.

kàn (R. id. ?) **kàn-á**, = thə̂-kúi, a small bivalve shell-fish. **kàn-á-kôe**, do., pickled. **kàn-á-kôe-bák**, having (naturally) very small eyes that look almost shut.

kàn [R. to reprove a superior]. **kàn-chèng**, to warn a superior (as sovereign or father) of his faults, and exhort him to reform. **kàn-kun** (R.), to exhort one's sovereign to reform his bad conduct.

kàn [R. id., by change of tone from "kan", between, = col. kài^{n}]. **kàn-tn̄g**, to break a constant succession (T. kài^{n}-tn̄g; Cn. kūi^{n}-tn̄g).

hoán-kán-kè, to plot secretly against a man (v. kè, a plan).

kang [R. kong, name of a fish]. **kang-hî**, a small sort of fish.

kang— **kang-bé**, a tree having soft light wood, palmate leaves, and berries in large corymbs: soles for shoes are made from it, and potash is made from its ashes. **kang-bú**, id.

kang [R. kong, public; duke; male; cf. ang, káng, kak], male (of animals). **kang--ê**, a male. **kang-bú**, male and female. **kì^{n}-kang-bú**, determined to have out the quarrel, and see who wins. **gû-kang**, a bull. **ti-kang**, a male pig; a boar. **kang-ti--ê**, flesh of a male pig. **chiáu-kang**, a cock-bird.

siù^{n}-kang, a mandarin's secretary or confidential assistant; polite appellation of a kujin, or of a gentleman or literary man. **lāi-kūi siù^{n}-kang**, clerks in custom-house (v. kūi). **chhân-siù^{n}-kang**, an idol of the surname "chhân:" he was minister of music in the Tang dynasty, and is much worshipped by actors. **siù^{n}-kang-tia**, id. **siù^{n}-kang-iâ**, id.

ng chhi^{n}-mî^{n}-kang, to play at blind-man's-buff [same word ?].

kang (R. id.), a large river; the Yang-tse-kiang; a surname. [distinguish from "káng," a channel.]

kang-san sit, the empire lost (lit. rivers and mountains); a man losing all he possesses. **put-chí kang-ə̂**, very careful to avoid phrases that would give offence (v. ə̂).

iû-kang, spectators going about in boats looking at idolatrous festivals. **chè-kang**, to sacrifice at a river, *e.g.* to a man drowned there, or for a safe passage. **kang-thâu**, the upper end of an inlet, as far as boats go (s. work). **kang--thâu**, name of a place on Amoy island.

sam-kang, three great rivers near Soo-chow. **sam-kang ngó-ə̂**, the three rivers and the five lakes (v. ə̂). **sam-kang-tsúi sóe-bōe-chheng**, the waters of the three great rivers cannot wash it out.

goā-kang, the provinces in whose names the word "kang" occurs. **goā-kang-lâng**, a man from those parts, or beyond (where mandarin is spoken). **kang-so**, Kiang-soo. **kang-sai**, Kiang-si. **kang-lâm**, Kiang-nan. **tìn-kang-hú**, Chin-kiang, near Nan-kin. **chìn-kang**, the Hien district of Chin-chew city. **lō-kang** (R.), Amoy island.

kang (R. kong). **giâ-kang**, a centipede (v. giâ), (s. work).

kang (R. kong), work; a day's work; a hired workman, in relation to his work; (leisure), (cf. khang).

giâ-kang, coolies carrying loads on their shoulders, &c. (s. centipede). **kng-kang**, do. carrying between two on a pole. **ta^{n}-kang**, do. carrying each separately on a pole (v. ta^{n}). **thô-kang**, builders; masons. **bák-kang**, a carpenter. **lú-kang**, a female worker; a sempstress or embroiderer. **ūi-kang**, painters of ornaments, pictures, &c., as hired.

lâng-kang, a labourer; a porter; a coolie. **tn̂g-kang**, a labourer engaged for a long time, as a field labourer. **pak tn̂g-kang**, to hire a man for a long time (v. pak). **bē-tn̂g-kang** (C.), to bind one's self for a long term to a master. **té-kang**, a man engaged for a short period of work; work for a short period, not constant. **chhià^{n} té-kang**, to engage workmen for a short time. **sió-kang**, the very lowest class of labourers or assistants in coarse work. **thó chit--ê sió-kang**, to ask the post of the lowest sort of labourer. **kang-kioh**, coolies for carrying burdens and such coarse heavy work (v. kioh). **kioh-á-kang**, id. **chhe-kang**, id.

khiàm-kang, in want of labourers. **kè-kang**, to hire labourers. **chhià^{n}-kang**, id. **tok-kang**, to oversee workmen.

bô-kang, no leisure. **bô-êng-kang**, id. **êng-kang**, leisure.

kang-hu, work; Congou tea (v. hu). **siōng-kang**, best Congou. **kang-chêng**, work, as regards its amount. **kang-chêng toā**, the work is very great. **bô-sím-mih^{n} kang-chêng**, does not require much work; quite easy. **bô-khó-sái kang-chêng**, id. **kang-tiā^{n}**, a piece of (not coarse) work, esp. literary work. **kang-bé**, the end of a piece of work. **kang-thâu**, the beginning of a piece of work (s. river). **kang-gōe**, handicraft. **kang-gē**, id. **kang-khòe** (C., = A. khang-khè), work. **kang-tiû^{n}** (C.), work.

chit-kang, one man's work for one day. **nn̄g-kang**, one man's work for two days, or two men's work for one day. **chit-tiám-kang**, about one-third of a day's work (v. tiám).

ēng-kang, carefully. **tiâu-kang**, of set purpose. **chiàu-kang**, according to the amount of work done, as in making a charge. **chiàu-khí-kang**, done according to proper rule; according to justice; performing one's duty fully and faithfully. **khí-kang**, to begin work, as work suspended for some time, or as work that is done at one season, *e.g.* shoe-making or dyeing. **tāng-kang**, to begin work at the very commencement of a whole piece of work. **chiū^{n}-kang**, to begin work on each successive day. **ke-kang**, additional work, need more work. **bô-ke-kang**, without any more trouble, as doing a favour which is quite easy for us. **chhut-kang**, to give one's work, as in a partnership.

thoa-kang, to put off work; to procrastinate. **poah-kang**, to suspend work for a little, so as to attend to something else. **thêng-kang**, to stop work for a time. **hioh-kang**, id. **pàng-kang**, id. **khàng-kang**, to intermit work, as one-third of a day or more; at leisure (v. khàng).

piān-kang, easy work (not needing much thought) given to an inferior workman, all ready to be done, *e.g.* copying or sewing when the pattern is cut out. **tsáp-**

jī-gėh-kang, the time at the end of the 12th moon, when no one has leisure.

kang-chìⁿ, wages. **kang-tsu**, id. **kang-pâng**, the department (in a yamun) for public works, corresponding to the "kong-pɵ" at the metropolis.

chhâ-kang-siⁿ, coarse and awkward-looking, as a large-boned man.

káng (cf. kang). **gû-káng**, a bull (v. gû). **iûⁿ-káng**, a ram.

káng [R. kiong, to serve or supply; cf. kūiⁿ], (T. káiⁿ). **káng-iūⁿ** (Cn.), to worship with offerings, as idols or ancestors.

káng — **káng-bān**, a myriad or more; by myriads or several myriads. **káng-chheng**, by thousands. **káng-chheng káng-bān**, by thousands and tens of thousands. **káng kúi-nà-bān**, several myriads.

káng [R. to discourse; to explain by discoursing or lecturing, = col. kóng], also (Cn.), = A. kóng, to discourse or discuss, but not "to say" (v. kóng).

khai-káng, to explain to scholars, as a book or doctrine. **káng-lūn**, to discuss and explain, as a book or affair, &c. **káng-chheh**, to explain books orally. **káng-kàu**, to preach doctrine. **káng-hô**, to discuss matters till peace is made, esp. of nations. **tùi-káng**, parties arranging a matter by themselves without an intermediate party.

káng-kiù, to investigate or inquire into, as doctrine.

káng (R. id.), a channel; a strait; an arm of the sea or wide estuary; a harbour of that form. [dist. "kang," a great river.]

káng-kha, a port (said only of distant ports, *e.g.* Singapore). **káng-kháu**, a port (of considerable trade). **káng-lɵ̄**, the channel for navigation. **phien-káng**, smaller ports, *e.g.* any in Formosa excepting Tâi-oân, Lók-káng, and Tām-súi; also, unusual dollars, *e.g.* Bolivian. **hiong-káng**, Hong-kong.

chhoā-káng, a pilot. **pàng-káng**, id. **chhut-káng**, to go to sea. **kìm-káng**, to forbid vessels going out and in, or forbid trading in some article. **jip-káng**, **sûi-oan**, do in a place as others do (v. sûi).

kàng — **chióh-kàng**, a sort of toad. **khiⁿ-kàng**, id.

kàng [R. to descend; to send down; to degrade]. **kàng-lîm**, to descend, as a god. **kàng--lóh-lâi**, id. **kàng-lóh**, to come down or send down, as a spirit. **kàng-ki**, to come down on the enchanter or medium that he may give written oracles, as the spirit is said to do. **kàng-chin-hiuⁿ**, incense supposed to bring down the spirits. **thien-sîn hā-kàng**, the celestial spirits coming down on 12.25 (v. sîn). **kàng-hoân**, to come down from heaven to be born into the world. **kàng-sè**, id.

sng-kàng, the term on or near Oct. 23d (v. sng, frost).

kàng-kip, to degrade in rank. **kàng-kè**, to sell at a very low rate (v. kè).

kàng [R. inundation]. **káu-kàng-tsúi**, the very high tides in the 8th and 9th months. **káu-kàng-hong**, the strong winds usual about that time, esp. about 9.18.

kàng [R. khòng, a pit or hole, = col. khàng]. **thê-kàng-phang**, sort of bee that makes its nest in a hole in the ground.

kāng [R. kiōng, together, = col. kā], (together); alike; to tease; to annoy, molest, persecute, or injure another; also (Cn.), = A. kā, in relation to, &c.

bô-kāng, not alike; quite different. **tàu-saⁿ-kāng**, to assist one another.

kāng--lâng, to annoy, molest, or injure people.

kāng-i-khui (Cn.), open it for him. **kāng-i-sōh** (Cn.), = A. kā-i-kóng, say to him.

kap (R. id.), a pigeon (never "kap-á," a next word). **kap-eng**, a sort of hawk. **kap-tû**, a pigeon-house (v. tû). **kap-long**, a horn whistle tied to a pigeon's tail. **chhài-kap**, a pigeon of the common sort used for food (not a carrier-pigeon). **chhài-kap-bák**, dull of apprehension, as a man (fig. from a pigeon not fit to be used as a carrier).

kap (R. id.) **kap-á**, a small land frog. **chhân-kap-á**, id. **chhiên-kap-á**, id.; also, bits of paper which children cut out and blow at each other's on a table: that one which turns over is beaten. **pûn chhân-kap-á**, to blow these bits of paper. **kā chhiên-kap-á**, id. **pûn kap-á**, id.

kap-lûi, a small sort of shell-fish. **kap-kài**, an animal used in medicine.

kap-koɛ-á (C.), a tadpole. **kap-gōe** (Cn.), a young frog.

kap — **kap-pán**, a foreign square-rigged ship or vessel (v. pán).

kap (R. kiap). **kap-bān**, a strong chest for keeping money. **kap-pān** (C.), id.

kap — **tsòe kap-tsoh**, to be a carpenter who makes furniture (v. tsoh).

kap (cf. kāng, kah, hàp), with; along with; to unite; to join together; to bind, as a book; to buy medicine prescribed.

saⁿ-kap, together. **kap--i saⁿ-kap-khì**, to go along with him. **kap-i-kóng**, speak with him.

kap-oá, to sew together, as cloth; to put or fasten together, as the parts of a thing. **kap-chhùi**, a seam, as in a dress; a joint where two boards are united. **kap-chheh**, to bind a book. **kap-béh**, to sew together the soles and legs of stockings. **kap-soàⁿ**, to make thread (of more than one strand) from yarn. **kap-kɵ́**, to join several ropes or strands to make one rope; to join stock-in-trade. **kap-pâng**, to unite in the bridal chamber.

kap-ióh, to buy the medicines prescribed in a prescription. **kap hɵ́-ióh**, to conspire against a man (lit. tiger's medicine) by false witness, &c. **kap--lâng kap-khang**, to conspire with bad men to prey on others.

kap [R. hàp, to unite], (Cn.), a small measure, one-tenth of a "chin."

kat (R. kek). **thê-kat**, unburnt sun-dried bricks. **ìn thê-kat**, to mould unburnt bricks.

kat (R. kiet), to tie a knot; a knot; to fit up, as hangings. **sí-kat**, a hard knot. **oáh-kat**, a bow-knot. **tsa-bɵ́-kat**, a loose knot. **bɵ́-kat**, id. **kat-thâu**, a knot. **chhē kat-thâu**, to search for the clue (lit. or fig.) **kat-á**, a knot. **jiét-kat-á**, small painful boils. **pùi-kat** (T.), pimples and eruptions, as on child's head.

tháu-kat, to loose a knot. **kiù-kat**, to get entangled. **phah-kat**, to tie a knot. **phah-kat-kiû**, all tangled. **bák-bâi phah-tsòe chit-kat**, eyebrows drawn together, as in great sorrow or anxiety.

kat-sí-kè, regular unchanging rate of wages or price, *e.g.* of boat-hire. **kat-ân**, to tie tight and firm. **kat-tiâu**, to tie so that it does not hang loose. **kat saⁿ-á-toà**, to give certain presents to children (v. toà).

kat-chìⁿ, to tie cash on a string. **chit-kat-chìⁿ**,

a few cash thus tied together, *e.g.* a few tens or about a hundred; not so many as "koāⁿ."

kat-toāⁿ, to fit up a temporary shrine. **kat-chhái-lâu**, to fit up a temporary pagoda (v. chhái). **kat-káu-tiâu**, to put up hangings for rites soon after a death (v. tiâu). **kat-lêng**, to put up a paper and cloth house for the dead. **kat-teng**, to hang up lanterns in some rites (v. teng).

kat [R. name of a plant, = col. koah]. **tsu-kat**, name of the ancient hero Khóng-bêng. **tsu-kat-teng**, fire-balloons.

kat [R. to cut, = col. koah]. **kat-tn̄g**, to break off or have no intercourse (v. tn̄g). **kat-toān**, id. **kat-tsoát**, id. **kau-kat**, to dissolve partnership.

kat-lé (X.), circumcision.

iòk-kat iòk-sat, determined to have a feud.

kat-kèk, illiberal; narrow; stingy; unwilling to do what one is asked.

kau (Cn.) **put-tek khai-kau** (= A. kiau), cannot be put right (as quarrel), so as to leave all on good terms.

kau (R. id.) **hâng-kau**, a firm, hong, or company, for wholesale trade. **hâng-kau phò-hē**, hongs, warehouses, and shops. **kau-hē**, owner or partner of a small hong. **káu-poeh-kau**, a commission agent who takes 2 per cent. from the seller and the same from the buyer. **bí-kau**, a wholesale rice-store. **hú-kau**, a firm having trade with Tai-wan-foo. **lòk-káng-kau**, one trading with Lók-káng.

tàu-kau, to join a large firm (s. associate).

kau (R. kɵ), a ditch; a small canal or channel for irrigation; a drain. **kau-á**, a drain. **kau-âm**, a covered drain or gutter. **hiā-kau**, the channels between the rows of tiles on a roof. **kám-á-kau**, the gutter between the side of a boat and the arched cover of the hold. **tsúi-kau**, a ditch; a water-channel. **tsùn-kau**, a channel for irrigation. **han-tsû-kau**, the hollow between two beds of potatoes. **khiⁿ-kau**, the channel of the stream in a ravine. **hô-kau**, a city moat.

phîⁿ-ê-kau, the Formosa channel.

kau-khut, ditches and pools (v. khut). **khan-kau kè-khiah** (to help over ditches and ravines), to help over troubles, dangers, and difficulties, as the gods do.

téng-kau-tsûn, junks from near Chin-chew, &c. (v. tsûn).

kau (R. id.) **kau-lêng**, a dragon or sea-monster supposed to cause floods. **khí kau-lêng**, to cause such an inundation.

kau (R. id.) **kau-chiu-soân**, felt caps from "kau-chiu," brought by junks from Shantung.

kau (R. kɵ), a hook; to hook; a down-stroke with a hook at the bottom; to mark a scroll or proof-sheet with a long curved stroke, to show that words or clauses are to be transposed. **tò-kau**, hooked; barbed. **chit-kau**, a down-stroke hooked at bottom.

chhìn-kau, the hook of a steelyard. **niūⁿ-kau**, hook of large steelyard. **niáⁿ-kau**, the hook of a Chinese collar. **thê-lâng-kau**, the hook of a mill for separating rice from chaff (v. lâng). **hái-lâng-kau**, a sea-bird with a very long bill. **tah-kau**, a boat-hook. **bah-kau**, a hook for hanging meat on, as in a butcher's shop. **hī-kau**, an ear-ring.

kau-hī, an ear-pick; to pick the ears with it. **kau-hī-oáⁿ**, spoon-shaped end of it. **kau-hī-chiam**, woman's hair-pin with ear-pick on it. **tsó-kau-hī**, the contracted form of the 170th radical. **iū-kau-hī**, do. of 163d radical. **kau-hī-á**, either of 163d or 170th radical. **kau-náiⁿ-hī**, id.

kau-hûn, a hooked pattern worked on the border of a dress (v. hûn). **kau-tiò**, a good-sized fish-hook (v. tiò).

kau-oá, to pull by a hook, as a boat pulled to the jetty by a boat-hook. **kau-saⁿ**, to steal clothes by a hook, as from roof or through window. **kau--tó**, to make a man fall by hooking his leg, as by our foot. **kau--poàh**, id. **kau-kè-lâi**, to mark a passage to be transposed in reading or copying. **kau-lâi kau-khì**, much ravelled or involved, as a thing or affair (s. associate).

kau [R. kɵ, to mark with a hook, &c., often interchanged with the previous word], to cancel an account by making a mark on it (esp. Cn.) **kau-siau**, id., as by writing the word "oān" over it and making a large circle. **kau-phoà**, a tonal mark written on the corner of a character.

kau-tàng, an affair, business, or matter.

kau-tîn, a fabulous (Tauist) animal (s. associate).

kau (Cn.) **iû-kau**, a hanging oil-lamp.

kau [R. ko, fat, rich]. **kau-liâng-sio**, a strong sort of spirits (v. sio).

kau [R. ko, high]. **kau-hèng**, to be very fond of or desire eagerly, as pleasures. **kau-hìn** (C.), id.

kau (R. id.) **kau-í**, a chair. **kau-í-bīn**, the seat of a chair. **kau-í-pīⁿ**, the arms of an arm-chair. **kau-í-the**, the back of a chair. **kau-í-pè** (C. pòe, T. pē), id.

kau — **khih-kau-thâu**, the projecting corners of the cheeks below the eyes. **koeh-kau-thâu** (C.), id. **hih-kau-thâu** (Cn.), id. (hí ?). **bô-kɵ̀ khih-kau-thâu**, having no regard to one's own good name and character (v. kɵ̀).

kau (R. id.), to associate or have intercourse with; to hand over.

kau-kài, a boundary (v. kài).

kau-nâⁿ, a basket (with no divisions) having a semicircular handle. **kau-tháng-á**, a sort of bucket with a semicircular handle. **kau-chiam tèng, bát-liú poâⁿ** (lit. sewing done very close), over-cautious (v. bát).

kau-chièn, to join battle. **kau-piàⁿ**, very hot and fierce combat, while victory is still in suspense.

kau-háp, to have sexual intercourse. **saⁿ-kau**, to copulate (said only of the lower animals).

tsoán-kau, to hand over to another according to instructions. **kau--i**, hand over to him. **kau-lí-kɵ̀**, I hand it (or him) over to you to take care of. **kau-tāi**, to hand or deliver over. **kau-hù**, id. **kau-kē**, to intrust with, as business or article. **kau-poāⁿ**, to transfer, as commercial business or office, to another. **kau-oāⁿ**, to interchange. **kau-tiāⁿ**, to give the earnest money. **kau-iên**, to pay a subscription. **kau-lûn**, to give over to another in his turn, as land held in common. **kau-lîn** (T.), id. **kiò-kau-thòe**, a ghost calling a man to be drowned or to kill himself (v. thòe).

kau-koan, to have mercantile intercourse. **kau-siong**, id. (v. siong). **ū-kau-siáp**, to have close connection in business or friendship (v. siáp). **kau-chhap**, so connected as to be involved in his affairs (v. chhap). **kau-ka** (C. kɛ), to have monetary dealings with. **kau-khâⁿ**, involved, as affair; avoiding to commit one's self to a decided opinion (v. khâⁿ). **kau-khê** (C. khê), not yet straight, as involved and troublesome affair. **kau-tīⁿ**, troublesome and involved, causing much loss of time. **kau-tìn**, said by the front chair-bearer to warn the hinder one of some obstacle in the way (s. mark). **kau-thong**, to have intercourse with improper or suspicious persons. **kau-lâi kau-khì**, holding mutual intercourse together (s. hook). **kau-chiap**, to have familiar intercourse with. **kiet-kau**, to make friendship with. **kau-kiet pêng-iú**, id. **kau-hoan**, to have intercourse with foreigners. **kau-koaⁿ, kêng**, they who have intercourse with mandarins grow poor. **kau-pôe**, to associate with. **kau-poe**, bride and bridegroom exchanging cups after tasting. **kau-pài**, bride and bridegroom saluting each other. **it-biēn chi-kau**, having met only once, or very seldom. **kau-lâng**, to be intimate with people. **kau-lâng bô-bé**, short and changeable in one's friendships. **sim-kau ê-lâng**, a very intimate friend. **khóng-kau**, fond of entertaining people; hospitable. **chhoàn-kau**, constantly consorting with (v. chhoàn). **lām-kau**, to have indiscriminate intercourse with all sorts of people. **lâ-kau**, unsafe to deal with, as a man who does not return or repay what he borrows. **lāu-hì tàu-kau**, actors forming a company.

soàⁿ-kau, to break up, as a company of actors. **tsoát-kau**, to break off an acquaintance. **kau-koah**, to separate one's affairs from another's (v. koah). **kau-kat**, id.

kau — **kau-kè**, to mark the divisions of an essay.

kâu — **kâu--lâi**, to hold in a man (either by force or by strong influence), so as either to make him do what he is unwilling to do, or to restrain him from doing something dangerous which he wishes to do, or to keep him from leaving us.

kâu [R. tê, dice, = col. tâu]. **tàu-kâu**, a set of three dice. **thiàu-kâu**, id. **tiàu-kâu** (T.), id. **poàh-tàu-kâu**, to gamble with a set of three dice. **mə-tàu-kâu**, id., especially of the first player. **jī-kâu**, the throw of the die with two dots. **sè-gē-kâu**, to get one 5, and the other two equal to each other (by the second player). **lák-kâu**, the throw when one has six dots, and the other two are equal to each other. **poàh lák-kâu**, to get that throw of the dice.

kâu [R. hê, a marquis, = col. hâu], a surname. **kâu-koaⁿ**, one of the Hien districts of Fuh-chau city.

kâu (R. hê), a monkey; a sort of insect; (said of a licentious man). **kâu-kui**, the projecting throat of the monkey.

teng-kâu, a bamboo frame for an oil-lamp (v. teng).

phah kâu-kûn, to strike or wound one's self, as a beggar or quack (v. kûn). **piⁿ-kâu-lāng**, legerdemain; to play tricks. **poaⁿ-kâu-hì**, to play a kind of play for the dead. **ti-ko kâu**, figure of boar and monkey in the "hì-phûn" played for the dead. **pùih kâu-bé** (T.), children going in a row, each holding on by the coat of the one before. **kâu-thâu** (T.), the leader of the string of boys. **thuh phō-kâu** (T.), a game (v. thuh).

kâu-bīn, a mask like a monkey's face; a face as ugly as a monkey. **bīn kâu-kâu**, face like a monkey's, chin and forehead projecting. **kâu-thâu chhú-hī** (monkey's head and rat's ears), very ugly (v. chhú). **soaⁿ-lāi-kâu chiáh chhiū-chí** (a rustic monkey feeding on seeds of trees), said of a raw rustic just come to town.

kâu chè-thien, the monkey which made offerings to Heaven; the monkey-king, ancestor of British, Americans, and other foreigners! **siet-sien, poaⁿ kâu-chè-thien**, to make a pretence.

liáh-kâu, to catch a monkey; to catch a man with a woman. **khan-kâu**, to lead a monkey; to lead a man to a bad house; also (T.C.), children running in a string, each holding by the coat of the one before, = pùih-kâu-bé.

chháu-kâu, a large sort of grasshopper. **tē-kâu**, an insect like a wingless grasshopper, very destructive to crops. **kâu**, id. **thê-kâu** (Cn.), id. **kâu-ióh**, arsenic, much used for poisoning it. **kâu-ún** (L.), = A. tə-ún, the earth-worm.

káu [R. kə́, dirt]. **káu-koeh-sien**, indurated dirt on the skin. **káu-koeh-san** (C.), id. **iû-káu**, greasy mark made by the hair of the head. **chhàu-iû-káu**, smelling bad, as the hair itself, or as pillow dirtied by the hair. **tsúi-káu**, the dirty film that gathers on water kept too long. **tsúi hoan-káu**, this film forming on water. **káu-chhoáⁿ**, sort of eruption supposed to be caused (from confusion of the word) by eating from a bowl that a dog has licked, or by food which we touched after touching a dog. **káu-sién**, id.

káu [R. ngáu, to bite]. **má-káu**, Macao. **má-káu-lâng**, a Portuguese. **má-káu-tsûn**, a Portuguese lorcha.

káu — **káu-hiā**, an ant, but not a white ant (v. hiā).

káu — **káu-hê**, a small sort of shrimp (v. hê).

káu (R. kə́), a dog. **siáu-káu**, a mad dog. **sē-káu**, a wild animal like a small wolf. **láh-káu**, a hunting-dog; a wandering man (v. láh). **hoan-káu**, you foreign dog! (abusive epithet applied to foreigners). **hoan-á-káu**, id. **hàm-káu**, careless and reckless in managing matters. **káu-hàm**, id. **pháiⁿ-káu**, a vile, disorderly, ill-behaved, low fellow; a rowdy or rough. **hê-kûn káu-tóng**, a set of vile, wicked, low fellows. **tsòe saⁿ-kha-káu pê--tsáu**, to crawl away like a wounded dog on three legs (said of a man beaten severely, or dreadfully ashamed). **thāu-káu**, to poison a dog, as thieves do. **káu-ióh**, medicine for a dog's bite; also, drugs used by thieves for stupifying dogs. **ti koe káu**, pigs, fowls, and dogs. **káu-siū**, a kennel. **káu-khang**, a hole in a door for a dog; a small door in one leaf of a large door or gate, *e.g.* in a street-gate. **káu-khang-mn̂g**, small door for the hole in the large door.

káu-soh, a large rope or cable (fastened at both ends in the bottom of the sea) to which boats are tied in a row. **tâi káu-soh**, to fasten it at both ends in the sea-bottom. **káu-ūi**, the space occupied by that rope and the boats. **siang-chiúⁿ ê-káu**, the rope to which small boats are tied in a row. **mn̂g-káu** (T.), = A. mn̂g-kúi, a secret bolt to keep a door-bolt shut.

péng-káu-pêng, the contracted form of the 94th radical, at the side. **péng-káu**, id. **péng-káu-á**, id.

tâng-tsoâ thih-káu, the serpent and dog of Hades. **péh-káu-iâ** (Cn. T.), a deified dog.

bīn koāⁿ-káu-á (T.), the skin of a man's neck flabby and making large wrinkles just below the cheeks. **bīn koāⁿ-káu koāⁿ-káu**, id.

káu-kang, a male dog. **káu-bú**, a female dog; a bitch. **káu-bú-tsoâ**, a sort of lizard. **káu-bú-hî**, sort of fish. **káu-bú-soa**, a large sort of shark (v. soa). **káu-bú-tāi** (T.), an animal like a large lizard. **káu-á-thâng**, a hairy caterpillar, said to be poisonous (v. thâng). **kim-káu-á**, a plant with a quantity of hair at the crown of the root (Aspidium Baromez?). **kim-káu-á-mn̂g**, its hair, used for stanching blood.

海上絲綢之路文獻集成 科技與文化編

hāng chhim, káu ok, said of a man very difficult of access. **káu-kā niáu-chhú; lô, jî bû-kong,** a dog killing a rat has toil but no thanks, because he overturns or breaks things (said of a meddler getting no thanks though the affair comes right). **káu-kā niáu-chhú, bô-kong,** id. **beh-chiáh-káu, bōe-tit--thang káu-sí** (wishing to eat a dog, but unable to get it killed), trying to get something, but unable. **ū-chîⁿ, táh kim-sai; bô-chîⁿ, káu iā-lâi,** a wealthy man gets a gilt lion as a footstool (becomes a high mandarin), but a poor man has only a dog to kick; a man without money must put up with what he can get.

káu (R. kiú), nine. **jī-káu,** twenty-nine; the 29th day of the month. **jī-káu ê-hng,** the last evening of the year, even though it be the 30th. **káu-kàng-hong,** heavy gales about the ninth month (v. kàng). **chiáh saⁿ-lák-káu,** to abstain from animal food on the nine days of the month ending in 3, 6, and 9.

káu-poeh-hâng, a commission agent or firm that takes two per cent. from seller and buyer (v. poeh). **káu-ńg,** a very low pawn-shop that levies enormous usury (v. ńg). **káu-tiâu,** part of a room screened off for the rites of "kong-tek" (v. tiâu). **káu-tsat-chhèng,** a sort of swivel-gun.

káu [R. khó, the mouth, = col. kháu]. **é-káu,** dumb; ill-developed, as ears of corn almost empty, that will not open in cleaning; said also of a flower-bud that withers away without opening. **é-káu** (C.), id. **é-káu** (Cn.), id. **ek-káu** (Cn.), id. **é-káu-seh,** blundering translation of characters (v. seh).

toā-chih-káu, speaking with difficulty, as from an impediment, or in sickness or great fear. **gâi-káu** (C.), rude in answering or interrupting; refusing to listen to reason or good advice. **kéh-káu,** difficult to read off, as a sentence ill put together. **káu-kéh** (C), id.; also, said of persons discussing a matter together but not agreeing.

kā-káu (T.), a flat fish very good for eating, like the "pîⁿ-hî" but larger.

káu — **káu-khê,** at variance with people (v. khê).

káu [R. crafty; deceitful]. **káu-tsà,** crafty; intriguing; deceitful. **káu-kòe,** id. **káu-koài,** id. (v. koài). **káu-kut,** id. **káu-kút,** id. **káu-khiet** (R.), id. **káu-nāiⁿ,** very impudent and troublesome (v. nāiⁿ).

kàu [R. to teach; a sect, = col. kà], doctrine; instruction; a religious or philosophical sect. **kàu-hùn,** instruction (v. hùn). **kàu-hoà,** to renovate by instruction. **kàu-tok,** to instruct and keep in good order, as our inferiors. **káng-kàu,** to preach or explain doctrine. **ka-kàu,** family instruction (as to its goodness). **hó-ka-kàu,** having good family instruction; well-ordered family. **pháiⁿ-ke-kàu,** having no rule or method in training one's family. **lòh--lâng ke-kàu,** to receive submissively the rule of the family she enters, as bride or affianced bride. **chhéng-kàu** (polite), I beg to be instructed. **léng-kàu** (R.), I have received your instructions.

jip-kàu, to enter a sect or church. **chhut-kàu,** to leave it. **chiáh-kàu,** phrase used by the heathen in speaking of entering the church (not a good phrase).

siâ-kàu, a false religion; a heretical sect. **chèng-kàu,** a correct doctrine or sect. **sèng-kàu,** the doctrine of the sages; sacred doctrine or religion. **sam-kàu,** Confucianism, Tauism, and Buddhism. **jû-kàu,** Confucianism. **tō-kàu,** Tauism. **sek-kàu,** Buddhism. **pùt-kàu,** id. **hôe-hôe-kàu,** Mohammedanism. **thien-tsú-kàu,** Romanism. **thien-chí-kàu** (C.), id. **iâ-so-kàu,** Protestantism (v. so).

kàu-mn̂g, a school of fencing or boxing. **kàu-mn̂g-lâng,** a Mohammedan. **kàu-hōe,** the church. **kàu-tsú,** the founder of a religion or sect. **kàu-thâu,** the head of a religious body; sometimes said of missionaries, chaplains, &c. **kàu-su** (T.), a teacher of boxing or gymnastics; also (R.), a religious teacher or missionary. **kàu-sip,** a drill-sergeant. **kàu-liān--ê,** thoroughly instructed, as in boxing or other things.

kàu [R. to compare; to measure strength, &c.; to dispute; to contest]. **khó-kàu,** a literary examination. **kàu-khàm,** to examine carefully into a matter; very minute and exacting. **pí-kàu,** to compare two things to see which is better; to make trial of one's skill, knowledge, ability, &c. (of any sort), with another.

kàu-nāuⁿ, angry clamorous disputation; to make a row about a matter. **kè-kàu,** to dispute somewhat violently; to wrangle.

kàu — **peh--kàu,** determined to get something that is difficult to be got.

kàu (R. tò), to arrive at; till; to a place, time, or quantity; enough; to win at cards.

bô-kàu, insufficient; has not arrived. **ēng-bô-kàu,** insufficient for use. **bē-kàu,** not yet arrived; not enough yet. **bat-m̄-kàu,** do not know it sufficiently. **tì-kàu,** having the (injurious) effect to —. **beh-kàu,** about to arrive; almost. **tú-á-kàu,** just arrived.

kàu-tsûn, when the boat arrives; the boat has arrived; to arrive at the boat. **kàu-tè,** arrived at the place (v. tè). **kàu-chhiú,** come to hand, as a thing sent.

kàu-tsúi, just in proper season (v. tsúi). **kàu-sî,** when the time comes. **kàu-i tò--lâi,** when he returned. **kàu-bé,** at last; to the end. **thâu kàu-bé,** from first to last. **siàu-liân kàu-lāu,** from youth to age.

kàu-giàh, enough. **kàu-tāng,** heavy enough; up to weight. **kàu-kè,** up to the market price. **siuⁿ-kàu-kè,** rather too high a price. **kàu-lé,** politeness quite up to the mark. **kàu-ēng,** enough for use. **kàu-chiáh kàu-sái,** having enough to eat and use.

kàu-chhìn, a steel-yard that makes a thing a little lighter than it is.

chiáh-tit-i-kàu, able easily to overcome him, because we are much more powerful. **chiáh--i khah-kàu,** to be more powerful than he (v. chiáh). **kàu kúi-moáⁿ,** how many games of cards has he won? **phah-chit-ki lâi-kàu,** to lay down such a card that the other wins (said of a man telling another of a good opportunity for making money).

koáⁿ-kàu, to arrive at with speed (v. koáⁿ). **tui-kàu,** to overtake. **bô-siūⁿ--kàu,** did not consider so far (v. siūⁿ). **hah--kàu,** reaching to, as the heat of a fire or influence of exhalation, or influence of a powerful man. **jit-chiò--kàu,** the sun shines so far as to shine on it. **bô-beh kiâⁿ-kàu,** will not go or walk to it, as to a house. **bô-sîn-kúi kiâⁿ-kàu,** no need of fear, no trouble will come; nothing will be lost. **iok--kàu, kiâⁿ--kàu,** he keeps to his word. **phah--kàu, liáh--kàu,** whatever place they capture they also seize the people.

kàu (C. kàuh), a funnel or measure, as for oil or spirits. **iû-kàu,** an oil measure; a funnel for filling in oil. **chit-kàu-iû,** one measure (kàu) of oil; about seven or eight catties. **chiú-kàu**, a small measure for liquor, not of fixed size.

kāu [R. hə], thick; abundant; full of —; strong in flavour, as tea (infused) or liquor. **kāu-pȯh**, thick and thin; strong and weak, as liquor or tea. **kāu tut-tut**, very thick. **kāu-láu**, very thick, as paper, cloth, &c. **kāu-tāng**, very fat, as man; thick and heavy, as a thing (v. tāng). **kāu-bīn-phê**, brazen-faced.

kāu-hēng, lazy; doing as little as can be avoided (v. hēng). **kāu-ėh**, uncomfortable from dirt on clothes or skin; discontented, murmuring, and uncomfortable in mind. **kāu-ōe**, too fond of talking or murmuring. **kāu chhoaⁿ-chhì**, giving all manner of trouble; raising all sorts of difficulties. **kāu-khôe**, peevish and bad-tempered, as crying child that will not be pleased, whatever you try. **kāu-khê** (C.), id.

kāu khoán-thāi, to treat very kindly. **kāu-lé**, very polite. **kāu khièn-sńg**, very superstitious. **kāu-thàn**, to make very good profits. **it-hoat kāu-siàu**, getting deeper and deeper into debt. **kāu sū-lē**, having very many affairs to attend to, or many successive illnesses. **kāu-soh-lē**, having many ropes or affairs (v. soh). **khah-kāu-kang**, with much more (or too much) labour. **kāu hō-tsúi**, a great deal of rain. **kāu-chhát**, full of robbers or pirates. **kāu-kut**, full of bones, as a fish. **kāu-báng**, mosquitoes very numerous.

kāu-hun, a strong kind of tobacco. **kāu-hoân-tsoá**, a thick paper made with alum. **chiàⁿ-kāu-tsoá**, sort of large and thick white paper. **chiàⁿ-kāu**, id. **tiong-kāu**, a thinner sort.

kāu (cf. kā, ka). **kāu-boȧh-chhài**, a vegetable like lettuce. **kāu-boȧh-hông** (C.), a medicinal plant (v. hông).

kāu (T.), = A. kȧuh, kō; to roll along.

kauh, thick cloudy mist. **kauh-bō**, id. **thiⁿ kauh-kauh**, id. **thô-kauh** (T.), very thick mist.

kauh (= kȧuh). **o-kauh-kauh**, very black.

kauh, to become soft, mouldy, and bad, as rice or other eatables lying too long; to rot away into manure, as grass.

tâm-kauh-kauh, all quite damp or wet. **chhî-kauh-kauh**, quite damp, as house, or as cakes.

nńg-kauh-kauh (= kȧuh), too soft, as eatables not good to eat.

kauh, to mix eatables, especially putting one inside another; classifier for cakes or pies wrapped up in thin cakes or paste. **kauh pȯh-piáⁿ**, to mix and roll up eatables in thin soft cakes. **pėh-thn̂g-chhang, kauh pȯh-piáⁿ**, a white sugar confection wrapped in a soft cake. **pȯh-piáⁿ-kauh**, eatables so wrapped up. **ké kauh-piáⁿ**, a thick cake wrapped in a thin one.

kúi-kauh, how many such pies? **chit-kauh pȯh-piáⁿ**, one of that sort of pie.

kȧuh — **chiáⁿ kȧuh-kȧuh**, very insipid, tasteless, or fresh (without salt). **nńg-kȧuh-kȧuh**, very weak, as a mat; very feeble in body; also (= kauh), too soft, as eatables (opp. ngiⁿ-khȧuh-khȧuh).

kȧuh (= kauh). **o-kȧuh-kȧuh**, very black.

kȧuh (T. kāu). **kȧuh-kȧuh-lìn**, to roll about, as a ball (cf. kō).

kȧuh (C.), = A. kàu, a measure for oil, &c.

ke (C. kɛ). **ke-ōe**, to wrangle; to dispute.

ke — **ài kap-lâng ke-kak**, fond of quarrelling.

ke (C.) **gîm-ke**, = A. gîm-koe, the long stone step running along a house.

ke (C.), = A. koe, a street.

ke [R. a fowl; a hen, = col. koe]; also (C.), = A. koe, a fowl; a hen. **ke-kan**, sodomy.

kim-ke soá-kha (C.), the golden hen changes her leg, causing an earthquake. **lêng-kéng-ke** (C.), a beautiful insect somewhat like a butterfly or dragon-fly. **kha náⁿ lêng-géng-ke**, foot like it (said of a woman's very beautiful small feet).

ke (C.), = A. koe, to moor vessels close alongside.

ke (C.) **âng-ke**, = A. âng-koe, a sort of fish.

ke — **phah-kȯk-ke**, the cackling of a hen before laying an egg.

kɛ (C.), = A. ka (R.), good. **kɛ-khèng**, the reign of Kia-king.

kɛ (C.), = A. ka (R.), beautiful.

ke (R. ka), (C. kɛ, which also stands for A. ka), to increase; to add to the number or quantity. **ke-thiⁿ**, id. **ke-kiám**, to increase or diminish; more or less (v. kiám). **bô-ke**, no more.

tiȯh-ke chit-pah, must give a hundred more. **khah-ke**, still more. **khah-ke chit-chheng**, more than a thousand. **beh khah-ke-chîⁿ**, he wishes more money. **phah ke-ē**, to beat still more strokes. **ke-kang**, more work or workmen; needing more work (v. kang). **ke-lâng**, more men. **ke-gûn**, more money, &c.

ke-khui, asking too much money for expenses. **ke-chhēng-saⁿ**, to put on more clothes. **ke-chiȧh chit-hè**, to grow one year older. **ke-i chit-hè**, one year older than he.

ke (R. ka), (C. kɛ, which also stands for A. ka), a household; a family; used in some phrases for "person."

oan-ke, to quarrel; a feud (v. oan). **kong-ke**, public; common. **tāi-ke**, all (only of persons); all of you. **tȧk-kɛ** (C.), id.

ta-ke, husband's mother. **toā-kɛ** (C.), id. **ta-ke ū-chhùi, sim-pū bô-chhùi**, the mother-in-law may order as she pleases, the daughter-in-law has nothing to say. **ke-koaⁿ**, husband's parents (v. koaⁿ). **chhin-ke**, fathers of bride and bridegroom (v. chhin).

hâng-ke, the head or manager of a firm. **thâu-ke**, the head of a firm, business, or shop. **thâu-ke-niûⁿ**, his wife. **tsú-lâng-ke**, an innkeeper; a man who calls a doctor for self or for one of his family. **pó-ke**, a security or surety; insurance office or agency (v. pó). **siàu-liân-ke**, a young man. **hāu-siⁿ-ke**, id. **toā-lâng-ke**, an old man.

tsó-ke, ancestral home (v. tsó). **goā-ke**, a woman's own blood-relations (said after she is married). **lú-ke**, the bride's relatives. **lâm-ke**, the bridegroom's relatives. **jîn-ke**, a family in general. **ke-ke hō-hō**, family by family; all the families. **thong-ke**, the whole family (v. thong). **kui-ke-kháu**, all the persons in a family (v. kháu). **kɛ-sèⁿ** (C.), a clan.

ke-lāi, wife; wife and children. **ke-āu**, wife. **ke-koàn**, wife; wife and children. **ke-tiúⁿ**, head man of a village; manager or shroff in a hong (v. tiúⁿ). **ke-kah**, a census (v. kah). **ke-hùi**, family expenses. **kɛ-iōng** (C.), id. **ke-giȧp**, family property. **ke-hé**, family property of all sorts. **kɛ-hóe** (C.), id. **ke-sū**, family affairs, as to wealth, &c. (v. sū). **ke-sîn-pâi**, broad ancestral tablets with several names.

ke-si, instruments; implements; furniture; weapons (v. si). **ke-kòe**, tools; implements for work or fighting (v. kòe).

ke-ūn, the fated period of a family getting on well or ill. **ke-sì**, state of a family as to behaviour and prosperity. **ke-sì-bé,** family declining and coming to utter ruin, as when all its members act improperly. **hó-ke-sì,** family prospering by the good behaviour and wealth of its members. **phái^{n}-ke-sì,** family all disobedient, wasteful, and ill-behaved, so that all goes wrong. **hó-ke-tàng,** wealthy. **hó-ke-kàu,** having good order in the family (v. kàu). **pē-bú ke-hong,** parent's reputation.

hoā^{n}-ke, to manage the affairs of the family. **lí-ke,** id., as wife does. **chhiā^{n}-ke,** to increase family property, as wife does by care of household. **phoà-ke,** to waste family property; to injure the good luck of the family, as a bride having a bad horoscope. **phoà-ke-kiá^{n},** a wasteful son. **phoà-ke-tiāu,** omen of house going to ruin, as bad conduct of self or of family. **chhiau-ke,** to search a mandarin's house, as his ancestral home, so as to confiscate what he has embezzled.

chhut-ke, to become a Buddhist priest or nun. **khiā-ke,** to have one's family living at a place. **tiù-ke** (Cn.), id.

kê (cf. khê). **kê--teh,** somewhat obstructed, as a drawer or sliding-door; delayed, as an affair, because something else must first be arranged. **kê--tióh** (T. tê--teh), involved in delays because of something that must be done before our affair. **ū sím-mih^{n} kê--tióh,** what is it that hinders, *e.g.* hinders door from shutting. **kî^{n}-kî^{n} kê-kê,** ill-arranged and obstructing the way, as furniture in a room, or as a load to be carried. **ki-ki kê-kê,** id.

tü-kê (T.), = A. ti-tsâh, a barrier for keeping pigs from getting out of a yard.

kê (R. kâ), (C. kê), the cangue, a heavy square block fastened round a criminal's neck; to put the cangue on a man; to put a man's feet in a sort of stocks. **kha-kê,** sort of stocks for the feet (used by villagers). **siang-liên-kê,** a large cangue with holes for two criminals at once. **kê-hoān,** a criminal wearing the cangue. **kê-hō,** inscription on the cangue giving name, crime, and length of punishment. **kê-iû,** id. **kê-tiâu,** id.

giâ-kê, to wear the cangue. **giâ-í-kê,** to have a chair put on one's head in joke. **pàng-kê,** to take off the cangue. **phah-kê,** to beat and put on the cangue. **kê-chhàt,** to put the cangue on a thief. **kê hit-ê-lâng,** put the cangue on that man's neck. **kê i-ê-kha,** put his feet in a sort of stocks.

kê (C.), = A. kôe, pickled-fish or shell-fish.

ké (C. kóe; Cn. kö), to put something under a piece of furniture so as to make it steady, or to raise it higher. **ké-toh,** to put something below the foot of a table so as to steady it. **ké-kha,** to use something (as a stool) so as to reach higher (s. false). **ké-khi-tsāi,** make it steady by putting something under.

ké (C.), = A. kóe, to correct; to change. **ké-hó,** to change for the better; to reform (s. A. false).

ké (C.), = A. kóe, to explain, &c. **ké-soeh,** = A. kóe-seh, to interpret book-language in colloquial.

ké (C.), = A. ká, a surname.

ké (R. ká), (C. ké; also = A. ká), to feign; to pretend; to forge; feigned; forged; counterfeit. **chin-ké,** real and counterfeit. **ké-ià^{n},** feigned; pretended. **ké-ì,** deceitful purpose. **ké-tsòe,** feigned; feigning; pretending. **ké-tsòe m̄-tsai,** pretend not to know; feigning ignorance. **ké-bô,** to pretend not to be what one is. **ké bô-khoà^{n}--kì^{n},** pretend not to see; to wink at faults.

ké-kha, making women's large feet look like small feet by small shoes on the toes (s. support). **ké-hó,** hypocrisy (v. hó). **ké lâng-ê-miâ^{n},** to pretend to be such a man, either by word or by forgery. **ta-pơ ké-tsa-bó,** a man in woman's dress. **hoan-ná ké-tn̂g-lâng,** a foreigner pretending to be a Chinaman, as by wearing the Chinese dress.

ké-khiên, sportive caressing by children. **ké-kiēn-koai,** making a pretence of disobedience or resistance while knowing it to be quite useless. **ké-khek, chhiù^{n}-bōe-lòh-âu,** said of a man telling transparent lies.

ké (R. kó), (C. kóe, Cn. kö), a cake, especially a soft cake; pastry; various things offered to idols. **chit-sn̂g-ké,** one large steam-cooked cake. **chhiau-ké,** to mix and work up dough for cakes. **hèng-ké,** to make presents of cakes and various other things that have been offered to the spirits.

kan-ké, dried eatables of various kinds, as dried flesh, salted fish, and miscellaneous vegetable condiments, but not sweetmeats, except walnuts and some dried fruits. **kan-ké-tiàm,** a shop for such articles.

ké-koa^{n}, dried cakes. **ké-kà^{n},** leaven for cakes. **ké-ā^{n},** stuffing of cakes. **ké-thng,** sort of soup made with sliced cakes. **ké-kun,** a cloth or bag used for wrapping cakes in steaming. **ké-hióh,** leaves used for this purpose.

hún-ké, a white jelly, in diamond shape, made from the pea called "lėk-tāu." **khī-ké,** persimmons dried flat. **hoat-ké,** sort of leavened cake. **ti^{n}-ké,** sweet cakes. **ku-ké,** turtle-shaped and other sorts of cakes.

ō-ké, cakes made of rice and taro. **bí-so-ké,** shuttle-shaped cakes (v. so). **bí-ké,** cakes made of rice dough. **mī^{n}-ké,** cakes made of wheaten flour. **mī^{n}-pit-ké,** sort of fermented cake that splits open. **thn̂g-ké-á,** sweetmeats of sugar and rice-flour. **káu-têng-ké,** sweetmeats with wavy lines in nine layers or so. **bėh-te-ké,** cakes fried in fat with meal, &c. **boán-chien-ké,** a sort of twisted fried cake. **iû-chià-ké,** another sort. **oá^{n}-ko-ké,** cakes made in cups. **sang-ko-ké,** cakes made of sugar and parched rice. **chhài-thâu-ké,** sort of cake made with grated long turnips.

ké [R. kó, fruit], (C. kóe, Cn. kö). **ké-chí,** fruit. **ké-chí-hn̂g,** an orchard. **ké-chí-thėh,** an inclosed orchard near a house. **ké-chí-thâu,** the first fruit of the season, said of the (pí-pê) loquat.

pėh-ké-á, a white medicinal nut (= gûn-hēng), about size of hazel (Salisburia?).

kè (R. kà), (C. kè), price. **kè-sờ,** id. **kè-sờ kàu-tá-lòh,** what is the price? **kè-chî^{n},** price. **kè-gûn,** id., as in silver (s. cross, s. send). **ū-kè,** to have a good rate (of price). **oā^{n} ū-kè,** to change at a good profit or rate. **bōe-ū-kè,** to sell at a good rate. **bōe-bô-kè,** to sell without much profit. **bô-kè-pó,** very costly; worth a vast amount. **hè chin, kè sit,** the articles are good and the price fixed.

gûn-kè, value of the dollar in cash according to the state of exchange; the value of silver. **gûn-kè khah-lòh,** the value of silver has fallen. **chî^{n}-kè khah-tióng,** the value of copper cash has risen. **hu-kè,** the hire of a mandarin's chair-bearers. **iû-kè,** the price of oil; (&c.) **sí-kè,** the current price. **chiàu-sí-kè,** according to the current price. **kiet-sí-kè,** to fix an unvarying price, as for something we are constantly buying from a man. **kat-sí-kè,** do., or as recognized unchanging rate of price or wages. **put-têng-kè,** at different prices, as articles of the same sort, but of various sizes or excellence. **goân-kè,**

26

prime cost. **siók-kè**, a low price; cheap. **phái^n-kè**, id., said by the seller. **tó-tōe-kè**, an extraordinarily low price that cannot be expected to get lower.

phah-kè, to propose a price to the seller; to state the proper price, as a third party. **ké-kè**, to estimate the price (v. kè), (s. frame). **chhiàng-kè** (f.), to call out the price loud, as at auction. **toàn-kè**, to agree on the price after discussion. **kóng-kè**, to ask more than the price, gen. as preparation for being brought lower. **liām-kè**, id. **hoah-kè**, to put an extra price on an article, as from change in supply and demand. **gâu-phan-kè**, skilful at getting a high price for one's goods.

kàu-kè, up to the current market price (v. kàu). **khah-chiáh-kè**, to pay (willingly) rather more than the price. **kō-kè** (Cn.), too high a price offered. **thi^n-kè**, to increase the sum one offers. **khí-kè**, to rise in price. **tióng-kè**, to rise in price; to charge a little more because articles are of picked quality. **chiū^n-kè** (C.), to rise in price. **phòng-kè**, price charged more than was paid (v. phòng), (s. head-dress).

lak-kè, to lower the price; to fall in price. **lòh-kè**, to fall in price. **siu^n-lòh-kè**, too cheap. **siū^n-lòh-kè** (C.), to regret or repent of having done anything. **kàng-kè lâi-chiū--i**, let down the price, to come nearer his offer. **kàng-kè lâi-têng--i**, to undersell him. **kàng-kè lâi-im--i**, to sell cheap in order to compel him to lower his price too (v. im).

chhut-kè, to offer a price (as buyer), generally less than is asked, and less than he is really expecting to give (s. marry). **bô-chhut-kè**, does not haggle by offering a price lower than is asked, as a good customer; does not allow any haggling, as a shop with fixed prices which they will not lower. **chhut-m̄-chiâ^n-kè**, to offer a price too low to be accepted. **kè chhut-chiâ^n--liáu**, the bargain is fully made.

kè [R. kà, leave of absence; furlough], (C. kè). **pàng-kè**, to dismiss a school for the holidays. **kò-kè**, to request leave of absence on furlough, as a mandarin (s. connected). **kè-kè** (Cn.), id. **kò-toā-kè**, to ask to be relieved of office for a very long time, as a mandarin with a severe chronic disease.

kè (C.), = A. kòe, itch and similar cutaneous diseases.

kè [R. a thistle; name of a city], a surname.

kè [R. kò, a sort of fish], (Cn. kō; C. kè). **kè-hî**, a reddish fish. **kè-á-hî**, id. **pak-kè-á**, dried fish of this sort from the North.

kè (C.), = A. kà. **tāi-kè**, you, sir! (polite).

kè (C.), = A. kòe. **sì-kè**, in all directions. **tsò-sì-kè**, to do field-work; to cultivate the fields. **ū-sì-kè**, to have fields. **toā-bóng sì-kè**, very abundant (v. bóng).

kè (R. kà), (C. kè), to marry a husband; to give a daughter in marriage. **kè-chhoā**, to marry or be married, in general; marriage. **kè-ang**, to be married to a husband. **chhut-kè**, id., said only of a virgin. **kóe-kè**, to marry a second husband, as a widow. **tsài-kè**, id. **āu-kè**, id.

kè tsa-bó-kiá^n, to give one's daughter in marriage.

kè-tsng, marriage outfit given to a daughter. **sûi-kè-kán**, female slave given to a daughter at marriage. **sûi-bú-kè--ê**, a child that goes with its widowed mother when she is re-married. **sàng-kè-m̂**, a matron who accompanies the bride at marriage to instruct her in her duties. **sàng-kè-chí** (T.), id. **toā-kū sàng-kè**, bride's elder brother accompanying her to the husband's house (on horseback), (only occasionally done by wealthy persons).

kè-koe, tè-koe pe; kè-káu, tè-káu tsáu (if married to a fowl or a dog, you must fly or run), wife must share the toils and troubles of husband.

kè [R. to connect in succession]. **kip-kè**, very diligent.

kò-kè, to be adopted as son, generally from the same clan (s. furlough). **kō-kè** (Cn.), id. (s. price). **kè-sû**, to be adopted as a son, in order to continue the line of succession. **hō--i kè-sû**, give over (a son) to him to be adopted for that purpose.

kè-tsú, son of wife (who was a widow) by her former husband (said in relation to the second husband), (s. cross). **kè-tsú-á**, adopted son (said in scolding). **kè-heng-tē**, half-brother by either parent re-married after death of the other parent. **kè-hū**, step-father. **kè-bú**, step-mother.

kè [R. kài, to send, as money or criminal under escort; by change of tone from "kái," to loose], (C. kòe). **kè-sàng**, to send under guard, as a criminal, esp. to a superior mandarin. **kè-hoān**, id. **kè-chhe**, men who conduct the criminal to the office of the mandarin who is to try or punish him. **kè-gûn**, to transmit silver to a superior mandarin (s. price; s. cross). **kè-gûn-siō**, transmit boxes of silver to superior mandarin. **kè-gûn chiū^n-séng**, id., to provincial capital. **kè-hiòng-gûn**, to transmit customs money thus. **kè-chî^n-niû^n**, transmit land-tax thus.

phah-tē-kè, to send a criminal under guard from another Hien district to his own district mandarin to be punished. **phah-tōe-kè**, id.

kè [R. id., head-dress of woman; man's queue; cock's comb], (C. kòe; Cn. kō). **kè-á**, an ornament of artificial hair worn on a woman's head. **thâu-kè**, id. **thâu-tsang-kè**, id. **kō-thuh**, (Cn.) id. **hōng-kè**, a large ornamental head ornament worn by mandarin's ladies, and at marriages. **kim-kè**, a small sort worn at marriages. **phòng-kè**, a sort of female head-dress (s. price). **moâ^n-kè**, head-dress of coarse yellow hemp, worn at a funeral by widow or daughter-in-law. **kut-kō** (Cn.), all a female's head ornaments. **kè-soh**, a band for woman's hair ornaments, generally red. **kè-tsam** (T.), a hair-pin. **kè-ké-tsam** (T.), hair ornaments in general.

tì-kè, to put on or wear this sort of head-dress, as at marriage. **thǹg-kè**, to take it off, three days after marriage. **pák-kè**, to make this sort of ornament (s. cross). **pák thâu-tsang-kè**, id. **pák-kō** (Cn.), to fasten on the ornament on the top of a woman's hair. **chiàu-pē soe-thâu, chiàu-bú pák-kè**, imitate parents (lit. as to hair).

kè-á-bé, string at end of a man's queue. **in kè-á-lê**, to make the queue into a knot at the back of the head (said also of other things of same form). **tî^n kè-á-lê**, id. **tî^n kè-á**, id. **kè-á-tsang**, small queue at side of child's head. **kō-liu** (Cn.), a man's queue.

koe-kè, a cock's comb. **ke-kòe** (C.), id. **koe-kè-hoe**, the cock's-comb flower. **koe-kè-iû**, the fat about the sweet-bread of a pig.

kè [R. a plan; to plan; to sum up; sum total; all]. **kè-bō**, to plan or scheme; a scheme or plot. **thong-bō tsō-kè**, to conspire against a man. **siet-kè**, to plan. **kè-tì**, a plan or scheme (v. tì). **kè-chhek**, id. **àm-kè**, a secret plot. **tiòng-kè**, to be ensnared by a scheme; to fall into a plot. **kè-kiông**, all his scheming come to nothing. **giên thèng, kè chiông**, his counsels are followed.

seng-hoàt-kè, means of livelihood.

put-kè kì-sò, innumerable. **kè-sǹg joā-tsōe**, count up the sum total. **kè-kiōng**, sum total. **kiōng-kè**, id. **kè--ê tióh-pīⁿ**, all are ill. **kè--ê thiàⁿ**, all are pained. **kè--chit-ē hó**, all are well. **kè-sī-àn-niⁿ**, they are all so. **kè-ōe-kóng--tit**, either or any of them may be said.

kan-kè, taking a long time to get done; difficult to accomplish; in want (s. cross). **kan-kè toā**, growing with difficulty, as a child. **ū sím-mihⁿ kan-kè**, what difficulty is there in that? **jîn bû kan-khó-kè, lân-tek sè-kan-tsâi**, no gains without pains. **hoán-kàn-kè**, to use trickery to set men at enmity; to plot secretly against a man, as by insinuating false accusations; to lead into danger and then turn against him. **ēng hoán-kàn-kè**, id. **sái hoán-kàn-kè**, id.

kè-kàu, to wrangle; to dispute violently or scold one another. **ēng-sim kè-kàu**, to try every means to get what our heart is set upon.

kè (R. kò), (C. kòe; Cn. kù), to cross; to go through or over; past; gone; to infect by contagion; an occasion or time; classifier of so many times; to burn away to ashes, as wood or coals; to overpass or go beyond bounds; often sign of passive, or of work done on a thing.

āu-kè, next time. **chit-kè**, once. **chit-kè**, this time. **chit-kè poàⁿ-kè**, scarcely if ever (lit. half a time). **chit-poàⁿ-kè**, very rarely. **tsáp-jī-kè**, twelve times.

tsòe-kè, to have done. **ˏkìⁿ-kè**, to have seen. **bat-kiâⁿ-kè**, to have had experience of it. **kè-liáu**, already past. **kè-āu**, id. **kè-sin**, past; dead. **kè--khì**, gone; dead; past. **kè-óng**, to die, as man; past, as affair. **kè-sì**, to die. **kè-khùi**, id.

kè-tsú (C. kòe-chí), to be cooked. **kè-tsú** (C. kòe-tsú), to change owners, as property (s. connected). **tsú siuⁿ-kè-hé**, cooked too much. **kè-boâ**, to be sharpened. **kè-mîⁿ**, to become sharp, as edge (v. mîⁿ). **kè-phiò**, to have been bleached. **kè-tiû**, to be washed or filtered out, as powdered articles. **kè-giâm**, to make search, as customs officers.

kè-tsúi, to be slightly washed; to cross the water in a boat; across the water; small roofs built at the two front corners of the large central house, connecting it with the side houses. **kè-tiáⁿ**, to be cooked in a frying-pan or rice-boiler. **kè-tē-gék**, to endure the Buddhist hell, passing through it into another state.

kè saⁿ-sûn, to perform the third set of rites for the dead (done by a married daughter or son-in-law).

kè-âu, to be swallowed. **kè-chhiú**, to pass from one man to another, as money, &c. **hāi--lâng bōe-kè-chhiú**, unable to do some one the injury we wish.

kè-sit, a fault; a sin.

kè-tō, too much (v. tō). **kè-tō**, to cross by a ferry. **kè-thâu**, too much. **kè-hūn**, taking more than our share; acting in an overbearing or unjust manner (v. hūn). **kè-hun**, too ripe, as fruit; too strong, as medical infusion. **kè-sék**, too ripe. **tióh-boâ kè-koà**, to labour far beyond one's strength, so as to hurt one's self. **kè-tsoa**, opportunity quite lost. **kè-kòng**, id. **kè-hān**, delay beyond set time. **kè-ān**, id. **kè-ān bô-hêng**, delay payment beyond set time. **kè-sî**, to pass the proper time. **kè-sî-láh-bī**, an old affair that need not be raised again (v. láh, "almanac").

tùi-m̄-kè, unable to overcome him. **chiáh--i kè-kè**, easily able to overcome him, so that he has no chance. **sài-kè**, to be better than. **khah-sài-kè**, id. **sái ōe-kè-bīn**, can be used, as bad money, or as a plan somewhat improper, or a falsehood. **sái ōe-kè-bé**, it can be passed, as a bad article, or as bad money. **sái ē-kòe-bé** (C.), id. **sái-kè-bé**, to pass a bad article, &c. **khit-i-liáh kè-bé**, to be seized by an enemy in battle, and dragged over to his horse; to be so much inferior to a man (in strength, skill, wisdom, &c.), as to submit to him without resistance. **phien-phiaⁿ-sî sái-tit-kè**, to be able to pass without injury certain very unlucky days (v. phiaⁿ).

kap-goá bô-kan-kè, it does not concern me (v. kan, "a shield").

goá-bat kè-bák, I have looked at it. **hō-goá kè-bák**, let me have a look at it. **hit-ê-mihⁿ ū-kè goá-bák**, I have seen it. **m̄-kè lâng-bák**, not pleasant to look at, as a thing or an action.

kè-ì, pleased; glad; to rejoice. **m̄-kè-sim**, cannot bear the thought of it, *e.g.* of leaving one's family to go abroad; to feel very much grieved and dissatisfied with one's self for what one has done, *e.g.* for injuring one's own children. **kè bōe-tit-khì**, id.

sio kàu-kè-kè, to burn quite away to ashes. **se-sim iáu-bē-kè**, the lamp wick is not yet burnt out. **chek bô-joā-kú ōe-kè**, the candle will not last long.

kè-jit, to pass the day (v. jit). **kè-geh**, next month; either calendar month, or from a fixed day. **tan-teng kè-tē**, each generation having only one son. **bóng-kè**, just getting on so and so (v. bóng).

kè-siàu, to pay by giving a bill on some one who owes us (v. siàu). **kè-tiāⁿ**, to pay the earnest money. **kè-gûn**, to pay over silver, consummating a purchase, &c. (s. price; s. send).

kè-bâi, a cross bar (wood or stone) over the lintel of a door or window.

kè-liâu, to change the rate of a tune. **kè-liâu**, to pass the sheet from one side of the vessel to the other in tacking; to get over a difficulty, as by borrowing a little money (v. liâu). **kè-ki**, to make a new plant by tying mud on a branch; adopted from another surname; to pass from branch to branch, as birds. **kè-ki**, to pass the usual meal time without eating (v. ki, "opportunity").

kè-pâng, to be adopted, generally by man of same clan. **kè-pâng hiaⁿ-tī**, adoptive brothers. **kè-pâng toā-chí**, elder sister in the family into which one is adopted.

ài-kè-lâng, infectious. **kè-tióh**, infected by contagion, as itch, &c.

chioh-kè, please let me pass. **kiâⁿ--kè-khì**, to pass by or through. **thàu-kè**, to pass through, as in boring a hole, or as liquid soaking through. **phah-thàu-kè**, to make a door, passage, or access through and through. **thiàu-kè**, to leap over. **keng-kè**, to go through, as on a journey, or as an experience.

kè-lō, to pass along the road. **kè-chhù kè-thèh**, to pass from house to house, as busybody. **kè-hú**, to go into another Foo department. **kè-koāiⁿ**, to go into another Hien district. **kè-hoan**, to go abroad; to emigrate. **thok--lâng kè-chhùi**, to ask another to speak for us.

kè (R. kà), (C. kè), a frame; a stand; scaffolding or shelves. **kè-á**, a small frame or set of shelves, &c. **sip-jī-kè**, a cross. **jîn-jī-kè**, the couple for a gable-roof. **phâng-kè**, frame on which the sail rests when taken down. **bāng-se-kè**, frame on which nets are hung in a junk, as a guard against bullets. **chhèng-kè**, frame on which a cannon is mounted; a gun-carriage. **phàu-kè**, id. **to-kè**, a stand for swords and spears, &c., at gate of city or of yamun. **saⁿ-á-kè**, a high clothes-stand. **i-kè**, a low clothes-stand. **ui-kè**

(C.), bride's clothes stand. **chheh-kè**, a set of book-shelves; an open book-case. **chhài-kè**, frame or shelves at shop door for eatables set out for sale.

pit-kè, a small rest for the ends of pens. **kha-kè**, a large footstool. **chhù-kè**, scaffolding for building. **tah-kè**, to put up scaffolding. **eng-ko-kè**, a torturing machine used in yamuns.

kè-pang, shelf in upper part of bed.

gû-kè-á (C.), a wooden muzzle with wooden spikes, for keeping calves from sucking.

kē [R. hā, below, low. = col. ē, hē], (C. kɛ̄), low; unskilful; impure, as metal much alloyed. **koâi^n-kē**, high and low (v. koâi^n). **lóh-kē**, to go lower. **kē-kim**, impure gold. **kē-gûn**, impure silver. **kiáu kē**, unskilful at gambling. **bák-chiu pàng-kē-kē** (C.), = A.----hē-hē, eyes cast down.

kē (C.), = A. kōe, easy.

kɛ^n (C.), = A. ki^n, a cyclical character.

kɛ^n (C.), = A. ki^n, a watch of the night.

kɛ^n (C.), = A. ki^n, the warp; to weave.

kɛ^n (C.), = A. ki^n, soup.

kɛ^n (C.), = A. ki^n. **kɛ^n-tit**, one of the terms.

kɛ́^{n} [R. kéng, to choke, as with a bone], (T. Cn. kéh). **kɛ́^{n}--tióh**, to have something sticking in the throat. **kɛ́^{n}--sí**, to die of choking, as from a bone in the throat. **kɛ́^{n}-kui**, feeling of discomfort (causing hiccup, &c.) from eating too fast or too much.

kɛ́^{n} (C.), = A. kí^n, a flail.

kɛ̀^{n} (C.), = A. kì^n, rods of abacus; spokes of wheel. **lō-kɛ̀^{n}**, a small road; a path. **tsáh i--ê lō-kɛ̀^{n}**, lie in wait for him.

kɛ̀^{n} (C.), = A. kì^n, a row of rafters.

keh [R. kek, the diaphragm]. **heng-khám-keh**, the upper part of the trunk inclosed by the ribs; the chest. **heng-keh**, id. **heng-keh thià^n**, the breast all pained.

keh-sit, a severe chronic disease (internal cancer?) in which one always vomits food when half swallowed.

thun bōe-lóh ē-keh, said of unlawful gains immediately lost, or slipping from one's grasp when apparently certain.

keh [R. kek, to investigate, to calculate, a pattern, a frame; a line, as a rule], (C. kɛh). **keh-sek**, pattern; model, as for a document; proper way of writing a man's title, as to the words and their position; proper rule or style for an accusation, petition, &c. **háp-keh-sek**, made according to geomantic rules, as a grave. **jī-keh**, ruled paper; a ruled copy-book. **keh-chhioh**, a ruler (not round) for ruling lines.

siú^n-keh, a proclamation offering a reward, as for apprehending a man or killing a tiger.

keh-ki^n, to apply the compass to determine the luck of a grave, &c. **keh lô-ki^n**, id.

ē-keh, the lower part, as of a set of shelves, or as of the trunk, about the belly. **téng-keh**, the upper part of the trunk; the chest.

ū kùi-keh, face giving omen of wealth. **phín-keh** (r.), general bodily form of a man. **kut-keh**, general form of the body. **hó-kut-keh**, body well formed. **kut-keh lóng-thià^n**, all one's bones pained. **moá^n-sin-keh**, one's whole body, *e.g.* in pain. **toā-keh-koe**, fowl of large sort, as from Shanghai.

bān-jī-keh, open work, as of a screen, in the form of the figure called "bān."

kì^n thi^n-keh (lit. seeing the framework of the skies), said of a clear cloudless sky.

keh (C. kɛh). **chhân-keh**, the hard subsoil of a field. **kì^n chhân-keh**, subsoil visible. **chhèng kàu-kì^n-keh**, to lay bare the subsoil, as a flood. **keh-thô**, the subsoil, of a reddish-brown colour. **thô-keh**, id. **ū thô-keh**, to have such a subsoil, as a grave dug down to it, as is proper.

keh [R. khiet, = col. koeh], (C. kɛh, keh). **keh-á** (esp. C.), a reaping-hook.

keh [R. kek, a bamboo division], (C. kɛh). **nâ^n-keh**, horizontal division of a basket. **tek-kɛh** (C.), a stiff bamboo screen hung outside of a door.

keh [R. kek, to partition, to separate], (C. kɛh), to separate, as a wall or river; to have an interval, as of days, or as passing a night.

keh-tn̄g, to separate, as a wall, &c. **tsé-keh**, to obstruct. **keh-hô**, separated by a canal or large river. **keh-soa^n**, separated by a mountain. **keh chit-ê-soa^n**, id.

keh-piah, next door neighbours.

keh-mî^n, to pass the night. **keh-chit-jit**, after one free day has intervened; on alternate days; day after to-morrow; letting one day pass without doing something done each other day. **keh-sa^n-jit**, after three clear days have intervened.

keng-keh, rooms made by partitions; separate rooms in a house. **joā-tsōe keng-keh**, how many rooms has the house.

keh-kai^n hia^n-tī (T.), first or second cousins. **keh-pak hia^n-tī**, sons of same father by different mothers.

keh (R. kek), (C. kɛh), to parry; to ward off. **keh-khui**, id.; to separate with the hands, as parties quarrelling. **jia-keh**, to ward off, as blows with a shield.

keh (R. kok), (C. koeh; Cn. köh), the surname Kwoh. **keh-sèng-ông**, an idol, = kóng-ték tsun-ông, born in the interior near Ankoi, to whose tomb there are great pilgrimages.

keh (C.) **tāu-keh**, = A. tāu-ngoeh, long legumes.

keh [R. khoat, an edible plant], (C. koeh). **keh-hún**, a flour like arrow-root made from the root of a plant. **keh-hún-pau**, a confection made from it.

keh [R. kek, a sort of vegetable], (C. kɛh). **keh-nâ^n-chhài**, a vegetable like cabbage or greens. **kɛh-mê^n-chhài** (C.), id.

kėh (= ke, onomatopoetic sound), (C. kɛ̍h^n). **kėh-kėh-háu**, to cackle, as a hen; said also of a boy or woman disputing, and talking too loud or too much.

kéh (Cn. T.), = A. kɛ́^{n}, to stick in the throat, as a bone.

kéh — **kéh--tó**, to trip; to stumble.

kéh (R. gėk), (C. kéh), to oppose, esp. oppose or resist a superior. **ûi-kéh**, to oppose a superior. **sa^n-kéh**, to oppose each other. **tùi-kéh**, in direct opposition to a man's wishes or plans. **hoâi^n-kéh**, opposed to what is right and just; disobedient, as conduct or language. **hoâi^n-hoâi^n kéh-kéh**, id.; all in confusion.

kéh-kiū^n, refusing to obey; obstinately opposing. **kéh-phiah**, stubborn; obstinate in disposition. **kéh-káu**, difficult to read or recite, as a sentence ill put together. **kéh-hī**, making people unwilling to listen, as unreasonable talk (v. hī).

phah-kéh, to act diametrically opposite to the wish of a superior or partner (&c.) in order to show displeasure and make a quarrel; to spite him. **phah-kéh m̄-chiáh**, to refuse to eat just to spite him. **phah-kéh m̄-khì**, determined not to be put away, as wife or concubine. **phah-kéh beh-khì**, determined to leave, and acting so as to make our superior (or partner) displeased with us, and willing to let us leave; or as wife or slave-girl acting so as to make her husband or master willing to divorce or sell her. **phah-kéh beh-thiah**, constantly acting contrary to partner's wishes in order that he may be willing to dissolve the partnership.

kɛ́h^n [R. gėk, to oppose, = col. kėh]. **kōng-kɛ́h^n**, not on good terms; slightly at variance; not getting on well together, as in a family; always ready to find fault and make little quarrels; out of tune with each other, as two instruments.

kɛ́h^n (cf. khɛ́h^n, kėh). **kih^n-nih^n kɛ́h^n-nɛ́h^n**, sound of things breaking or rattling together, as if ready to break. **kih^n-kih^n kɛ́h^n-kɛ́h^n**, id. **lûi kɛ́h^n-nɛ́h^n-nɛ́h^n**, great sound of thunder. **lûi-tân kɛ́h^n-nɛ́h^n-nɛ́h^n**, id.

kɛ́h^n-kɛ́h^n-háu (C.), = A. kėh-kėh-háu, cackling of a hen.

kek [R. the diaphragm, = col. keh]. **kek-sit**, a deadly internal disease that causes food to be vomited as soon as it is taken. **hu-lô kớ-kek**, this and other deadly diseases.

siu^n-pá-kek, feeling a surfeit.

kek (R. id.), a halbert; a halbert-shaped spear. **hong-thien-kek**, id. **to-chhiu^n kiàm-kek**, swords and spears.

kek — **chiú^n-tiam-kek**, the lower piece of wood that keeps an oar-pin steady.

kek [R. to strike]. **kong-kek**, to attack; to fight against (s. expel). **kek-kớ**, to strike the drum in a yamun in order to draw attention to some urgent case of violence, &c.

iû-kek, a military officer somewhat like a colonel or lieutenant-colonel.

kek (R. id.), (P. kiok), to expel; to drive away. **kek-chhut**, to expel, as from a village, family, or society. **kek-tiók**, id. **kong-kek**, to drive away unitedly and publicly (as a robber), so as not to allow him to harbour among them; done by all the people of a village (s. strike).

kek-niû^n, to dismiss a soldier. **kek-chit**, to depose from office, and more or less degrade in rank. **kek-chit liû-jīm**, to degrade in rank but leave in the office. **kek-jīm**, to put out of office, not affecting his rank.

kek [R. id., = col. keh], to put up a partition; to partition off. **kek bát-pîn**, to put up a close partition. **kek-khám**, to divide into small divisions; to be on bad terms with people (v. khám). **kek-tsân**, to partition into horizontal layers.

kek (R. kiok), (C. kiok, T. Cn. kak), the chrysanthemum and such flowers. **kek-hoe**, id. **bān-siū-kek**, the marigold. **chháu-kek-á**, a small flower like chrysanthemum.

kam-kek, camomile. **pėh-kek-hoe**, white chrysanthemum; camomile.

kek (P.), = A. kiok, in the case of some words.

kek (R. id.), (P. sometimes "kiok"), to dam up, as water; (to suffocate); to raise steam or make great heat; to distil; to make a special effort; to put on airs or affect some manner; to stir up to emulation or anger; to provoke.

kek-tsúi, to dam up water. **tò-kek**, to dam up, as water, so as to make it flow in the opposite direction. **kek-lîm**, great difficulty in passing urine, as in disease (v. lîm).

kek--sí, to be drowned or suffocated, as by smoke; to cause a man's death by irritating or threatening him. **ēng-ōe kek--sí**, to make a man die of rage or fear. **hé-hun kek--sí**, to be suffocated by smoke. **khit-tsúi kek--sí**, to be drowned.

hong-hé kek, caused (as a disease) by a hot or feverish state or tendency of body. **kek âng-kun**, veins red and inflamed. **hé kek-kàu chin-âng**, to make a furnace very hot.

kek hé-hun, to make steam, as in boiler of engine. **kek-chiú**, to distil spirits; to incite each other to drink liquor by mutual pledging, &c. **sa^n-kek-chiú**, to incite each other to drink liquor.

chhàu kàu kek--lâng, very bad-smelling. **chhàu kàu kek-phī^n**, id.

sa^n-kek, to stir up, provoke, or irritate one another. **sa^n-kek-khí**, to stir up each other by emulation to do something. **chhòng-ōe sa^n-kek**, to excite or stir up by talking, *e.g.* to do a favour, or to a quarrel. **ēng kek-hoat**, to use sarcasm, praise, or contemptuous inuendo, &c., so as to get a man to take up willingly what he had meant not to do. **ōe-kham--tit kek**, can bear much provocation, &c. **kek siū-khì**, to stir up rage. **kek-liét**, using very extreme or violent language, as in reproving. **kek ām-kún-kun teh-kóng**, to get into a sudden rage and speak incautiously.

kek-ngī^n, to make as stiff as possible, as one's limb or neck. **kek-lớ**, to exert one's self very much in sculling a boat. **kek-lát**, to clench the hand firmly, as child or as boxer. **kek chhiú-bé**, to try strength by pressing against one another's hands. **kek-toā-sia^n**, to speak of set purpose in a specially loud and unnatural tone of voice. **kek sòe-sia^n**, to speak intentionally in a very low (not natural) tone.

kek-kha, to press and hurt the foot, as tight shoes.

kám-kek, to influence by kindness, favour, grace, &c.

kek-tiām, to put on the feigned appearance of being very quiet and well-behaved. **kek sì-kiâ^n**, to charge a high rate of fees (as doctor), &c., just in order to raise one's fame. **kek-khang**, to put on haughty airs without having any foundation for it. **kek phài-thâu**, to put on the airs and manner (and talk) of a man of consequence while having no position at all. **kek goā-khùi**, affecting grandeur or gaudiness in dress or house; an awful swell. **kek-khùi**, do., or in talk; to put on airs like a man of rank or wealth. **kek kàu-bô-khùi**, so full of smoke (as room) that one cannot breathe; almost drowned or suffocated.

kek-kut, doing or saying something just in order to be contrary to others, *e.g.* by ironical or sneering talk, or by walking in a different road from that used by others; or trying to show one's skill by doing a thing in a way different from the usual way, gen. making a mess of it. **kek-kut ê-ōe**, ironical or sarcastic language; language intentionally contradicting what another has said, *e.g.* "very cold;"..."not at all!" **kóng-ōe kek-kut**, to talk so.

kek [R. to investigate to the utmost; to calculate, = col. keh], to calculate roughly. **kek-sǹg**, id. **kek-sǹg m̄-chhut**, unable to conjecture; events coming out quite different from expectation. **kek-lí**, to think out or infer the state, origin, or real principle of a matter from various circumstances, as by circumstantial evidence or by induction; to think out the proper way of managing an affair. **kek lí-khì**, id. **kek chit-ê lí-khì**, id. **kek lí-phè**, id. **chiáh-pá teh-kek-kớ**, to sit after eating, talking all sorts of queer stories, old or imaginary (s. strike).

kek-gōe (R.), exceedingly; extraordinarily (only used with verbs). **kek-gōe si-un**, to bestow extraordinary favour or grace.

kiàm-kek, very minute, strict, and exacting in calculating prices or expenses.

kek-hēng, idle and lazy.

kék (R. id.), extremity; extremely. **teng-kék**, to begin a reign; to ascend the throne. **thài-kék**, name of a star: also (R.), the original state of existence from which the universe was produced. **bû-kék**, boundless.

pok-kék, the north pole. **pak-kék**, id. **lâm-kék**, the south pole (v. lâm).

kék-kí, extremely —; exceedingly —. **kàu-chì-kék**, to the utmost extent; to the utmost. **kàu-kék**, id. **kék-mn̂g**, do., as of misery, or as of ultimatum in price, or in offer to settle a quarrel. **kàu-kék-mn̂g**, id. **kóng kàu-hia kék-mn̂g**, to speak very determinately or doggedly, so that no abatement or compromise can be made; to lay down the matter with great definiteness and distinctness. **kék-thâu**, to the utmost; to the last extremity, often meaning that no plan now remains. **kék-kak**, to the utmost; quite full of meat, as shell of crab. **kàu-kék-kak**, to the very utmost. **kàu-chia kék-kak**, come to the utmost stage (as of misery or poverty), or as affair in so bad a state that no more can be done. **kék-kak-hó**, extremely good. **kék-kak-tēng**, quite full of meat, as shell of crab. **kék-piⁿ ê sé-tsāi**, most distant and out-of-the-way parts. **kék-phín**, highest rank of mandarins.

ēng-kék-hoat, to use extreme measures. **kék-kék bô-hoat--i**, utterly unable to do anything with him or it (v. hoat). **siūⁿ kàu-jip-kék--khì**, to think very carefully or minutely. **lók-kék, pi-seng**, sorrow comes at the time of greatest joy.

kék (C.), = A. kiák. **kék-kék-háu**, said of a young man talking too big.

kék [R. kiók], (C. kiók), general name for arsenals and some sorts of local government offices or boards; classifier of games of chess; very poor; mean.

kat-kék, illiberal; stingy; too hard and mean in money matters; unwilling to do a favour.

kî-kék, a chess-board with the men set on it in some special form (v. kî). **pâi tit-kék**, to set out a board for the gambling called "tit."

chîⁿ-kék, a government bank. **chîⁿ-niûⁿ-kék**, office of land-tax collectors for a sub-district; that company of tax-collectors. **sè-khòe-kék**, office for stamping deeds of sale. **lî-kim-kék**, a board or office for collecting the "lî-kim" tax. **thô-kék**, do. for collecting the opium revenue.

kun-tsong-kék, an arsenal for warlike stores. **hé-ióh-kék**, a powder magazine or manufactory. **chhèng-kék**, arsenal for guns or cannon.

kék-oân, a mandarin at the head of some special local board or office, such as the "lî-kim."

bô-kék (T.), = A. bô-kiók, feeling lonely, or full of ennui, or want of interest.

keng (R. id.) **keng-hî**, the whale. **keng-hî-kut**, whalebone. **keng-hî-iû**, train-oil.

keng [R. bêng, dark; night; Hades, = col. mîⁿ]. **keng-i-tsoá**, paper pictures of clothes burned for the dead. **sio keng-i**, to burn them.

keng [R. to change; a watch of the night, = col. kiⁿ]. **keng-ék**, to alter; to change.

keng-i-só, a room for visitors putting off their usual dress and putting on mourning, and vice versa, when they call to worship the dead.

keng [R. warp of web (= col. kiⁿ); to pass straight through; to manage; correct; finished; the menses], classical or sacred books. **keng-chheh**, classical books. **keng-tsu**, id. **keng-toān**, id. **keng-kù**, a sentence from a classic. **ngó-keng**, the five classics. **iáh-keng**, the Book of Changes. **su-keng**, the historical classic. **si-keng**, the Book of Odes. **sam-jī-keng**, the trimetrical classic. **sèng-keng**, sacred books; Scriptures. **put-keng**, Buddhist classics. **keng-chhàm**, sacred books and charms of Buddhists (v. chhàm). **liām-keng**, to recite sacred books; to read prayers, as priests. **siōng-keng**, id. **cheng-sîn-keng**, a yellow paper, with characters, tied on the figure called "thòe-sin," and burned. **kái-liên-keng**, a larger paper, tied and burned along with it, to remove calamity.

keng-khoe, title of several kújîn, from the second downwards.

ū-keng-chè, correctly composed, as a literary composition in a good style. **chhut-keng jip-tién**, id.

chèng-keng, honest; virtuous; correct as to morality (v. chèng).

í-keng, already.

keng-kè, to pass through, as a region, or as an experience. **keng-chhiú ê-lâng**, a man through whose hands money is paid or anything sent; a broker, go-between, or agent. **kap-i keng-chhiú**, act as go-between, &c., for him in managing a matter or transferring money or goods. **sī-i keng-chhiú**, it is he who acted as go-between, &c.

hiet put-kui-keng, the blood does not go in its proper course (not said of the circulation), *e.g.* when one sits up too late. **tá-lóh--chit-ê keng-lók**, in what part of the body (is the disease)? **cheng-sîn tsāi-keng**, having all one's wits about one; keeping one's presence of mind. **goân-sîn tsāi-keng**, id.

keng-kí, business, occupation, or means of livelihood (T. kan-kí, C. kin-kí, = keng-kí). **keng-êng**, diligent; engaged in business for livelihood. **keng-giáp**, diligent; industrious.

keng-koán, subordinate officials (esp. "keng-sêng") in a yamun who have charge of some parts of the work. **tng-keng-koán**, to be a clerk or assistant-secretary in a yamun. **sī lí--ê keng-koán**, it is your business to attend to it (originally of yamun business, but used in general). **keng-sêng**, the official in a yamun who receives accusations and defences (tiāⁿ), and prepares warrants.

gėh-keng, the menses of a woman. **keng-kî**, the period of the menses. **kiāⁿ-keng**, to have the menstrual flux.

keng [R. kiong, to provide; to offer; to give evidence], (C. kiong). **tn̂g-keng**, verbal evidence or confession given in court. **kháu-keng**, id. **hó-kháu-keng**, giving evidence in a good self-possessed way; knowing well what to say on examination; said also (half-joking, half-scolding) of a man who is too good at answering and disputing with us. **hoán kháu-keng**, to recant or withdraw one's confession or evidence. **hoán-keng**, id. **jīn-keng**, to make a statement or give evidence in court when examined by a mandarin. **thò-keng**, to rehearse evidence beforehand. **chhoàn-keng**, to suggest to the witness or party under examination what he should say (very improper). **thoân-keng** (C. chhoân-kiong), interpreter in a yamun. **khit-lâng-keng**, to be accused or inculpated by a man under examination in his verbal evidence. **khit--i keng--tio̍h**, id.

ū-keng-siēn, to get his food as well as his salary, as a school-teacher sometimes has.

keng [R. kien, the shoulder], (Cn. küi^{n}, T. kai^{n}, sometimes koai^{n}). **keng-thâu**, the upper part of the shoulder. **keng-thâu tsún-lō͘, hō͘-lâng-kiâ^{n}**, one's shoulders like a road for others (said of chair-bearers). **keng-thâu thóeh-thóeh**, shoulders high and lean, whether naturally so, or from opium-smoking, &c. **kek-thóeh-keng**, to shrug one's shoulders.

khí-keng, to help another to raise a load or sedan on his shoulder (s. temple, s. cultivate). **sa^{n}-phoáh-keng**, arms on each other's shoulders. **tńg-keng**, to change the load from one shoulder to the other, as a coolie or porter. **oā^{n}-keng**, id. (s. room). **tōe-gû oā^{n}-keng**, the cow that supports the earth changing her shoulder, and so making an earthquake.

keng-kah, the whole region of the shoulder (v. kah). **keng-páng**, the outer side of the arm, close to the shoulder-joint.

têng-keng, the border of the dress at the neck, made of double thickness, or corded, so as to be strong. **ui têng-keng**, to cut out the place for the neck in making a dress.

keng [R. to cultivate]. **keng-tsoh**, to cultivate land. **khí-keng**, to take away land from the tenant who has been cultivating it, either for one's own use or for letting to another (s. temple, s. shoulder).

keng — **keng-thóe**, to jeer at a man, or give him a nickname, from his personal appearance or conduct (v. thóe). **keng-hoān**, id.

keng [R. kan, a room; a dwelling; between], (C. kan, P. keng, T. kai^{n}, Cn. küi^{n}), a room; classifier of houses, buildings, or rooms; the space in a house that would be sufficient for one room.

keng-keh, a room partitioned off (v. keh). **sa^{n}-keng-chhù**, three houses. **chhù ū sa^{n}-keng**, the house has three rooms, or room for three. **pâng-keng**, a room. **bō-keng**, a house used as a mill. **êng-keng**, an empty room, as for guests; a public room in a village for talking or amusement (v. êng). **kiáu-keng**, a gambling-house. **hoe-keng**, a brothel. **tsa-bó͘-sun-keng**, id. **phái^{n}-kiá^{n}-keng**, id.

keng (R. kiong), (C. kiong), a temple. **keng-biō**, a temple; temples. **keng-tiēn**, imperial residence and hall of audience. **léng-keng**, prison of imperial harem. **kìm-lo̍h léng-keng**, to confine one of the inmates of the imperial harem there, and hold no intercourse with her.

chià^{n}-keng, the empress. **phien-keng**, an imperial concubine.

keng-kong, a temple-keeper. **keng-tiâ^{n}**, a paved court before a temple. **chit-keng-keng**, one temple. **chit-kai^{n}-keng** (T.), id. **chit-kan-kiong** (C.), id. **khí-keng**, to build a temple (s. shoulder, s. cultivate).

báng-keng, a folding mosquito-curtain on a frame, making a semicircle over the bed when set up (v. báng).

chhi^{n} kè-keng, a star falling or shooting (from its place) across the sky.

keng [R. a thorn]. **keng-kài**, a medicinal plant (v. kài). **chí-keng**, a tree with a magnificent scarlet flower in large bunches. **chí-keng-hoe**, its flower.

keng [R. to fear, = col. kia^{n}]. **tāi-keng siáu-koài**, much terrified and in great perturbation, as at sudden danger, robbers, ghosts, &c. **kín-keng-hong**, sort of convulsions taken by children. **keng-hong-soá^{n}**, medicine for preventing such starting or convulsions.

keng [R. a man's age; one of the cyclical characters, = col. ki^{n}]. **kùi-keng** (polite), what is your age, sir? **liên-keng**, the cyclical characters for the year of a man's birth. **théh seng-keng**, to take the natal characters of a proposed pair to see if they suit for good fortune.

tiông-keng (R.), the evening-star. **tiông-keng-chhi^{n}** (R.), id.

keng (R. kiong), (C. kiong), a bow. **tek-keng**, id. (made of bamboo). **chit-tiu^{n}-keng**, one bow. **keng-chì^{n}**, bow and arrows (v. chì^{n}). **keng-hiên**, a bow-string. **keng-tē**, a bag for keeping a bow in.

chiáh-keng, to be one of the company of archers in an army (superior to the others). **keng, pâi, chhèng**, the three classes of soldiers. **bé-keng-siú**, archers on horseback. **pō͘-keng-siú**, archers on foot.

khiā-keng, to practise the attitude for archery. **óh-keng**, to learn archery. **pan-keng**, to draw a bow. **khui-keng**, to draw the bow in shooting. **thoa-keng**, to draw an empty bow (as if with arrow in it) for exercise. **tiau-keng**, to practise pulling a strong bow without the arrow. **tiau-keng sai-hū**, a man who makes bows. **tiu^{n}-keng**, to string a bow. **chhiū^{n}-keng**, id. **khiâ-bé chē, bán-keng chiáh**, to sit with legs apart (as if on horseback) and eat with arm stretched out (as if in archery), (said of sitting and eating in a very awkward or too free-and-easy manner, esp. of a lad).

keng-ôe, very small shoes for women (v. ôe). **oân-keng-bé**, the raised round stem of a junk. **phâng-kám-keng**, a long split piece of bamboo bent into a semicircle to support the mat cover of a boat.

hiáng-keng, a small instrument, making a humming noise, attached to a kite.

keng (= gêng, gê). **keng-chio**, plantains, = gêng-chio.

keng, to stretch smooth and tight, as a rope or a cloth. **keng hō͘-i-ân**, id. **keng-pa**, to stretch out on a bamboo pin, so as to dry in the sun, as a duck.

thâu-bé-keng, moored stem and stern, as a vessel. **siang-thâu-keng**, id.

keng [R. a stalk, as of grain], a stalk or loose spike or panicle of flowers not very numerous; classifier of anchors. **chit-keng-tià^{n}**, = chit-mn̂g-tià^{n}, one anchor.

keng [R. to compassionate; careful; proud]. **kiau-keng**, proud and bragging, in manner or talk.

keng (P.), in some words, = A. kiong.

kêng [R. kiông, limit; extremity; exhaust; poor; = col. khêng], extremely poor. **kêng-sán**, id. **kêng-kúi**, a poor devil; wretchedly poor fellow. **kêng kàu-sí**, most miserably poor. **khah-kêng sí-lâng**, id. **kêng sí tsáu, bô-thang-thó**, nothing can be got from the poorest, the dead, and the absconder. **kau-koa^{n} kêng**, they who associate with mandarins become poor (v. kau).

soa^{n} kêng, hái kiėt, land and sea barren and poor; place very bad for making a living. **kêng-chhù, bô-kêng-lō͘**, though poor at home, one cannot do without money on a journey. **kêng-iû pù-chhat**, paint must be thin, but varnish may have many coats. **kêng bûn, pù bú**, literary graduates often come from poor families, military graduates usually from the rich. **beh-pù, kêng chiū-kàu**, when just getting rich poverty suddenly comes. **bē-pù, chhut pù-jî; bē-**

kêng, chhut kêng-si, before growing rich, one has skilful and thrifty sons; before growing poor, one's sons are as mean and niggardly as corpses.

kéng [R. éng, a shadow, = col. iá^n]. **thok-kéng**, to make a sort of play by shadows, somewhat like a magic lantern. **thok kéng-á-hì**, id. **thuh-éng-á** (T.), id. **khoà^n-thok-kéng**, to look at them.

kéng [R. kióng, kiong], a surname.

kéng [R. kién, a chrysalis; a cocoon; sort of silk, *q.v.*], a chrysalis; a cocoon of the silk-worm.

kéng [R. to warn; to alarm and arouse]. **kéng-kài**, to chastise, not very severely; to deter from evil by the example of chastisement (v. kài), (s. district).

kéng [R. kién, a conduit], (T. kái^n). **tsúi-kéng**, a conduit or aqueduct for water, either of bamboo or stone, &c. **tek-kéng**, bamboo pipes used as a conduit for water. **nî^n-chî^n-kéng**, do., at the eaves of a house.

kéng (R. kán), (C. kán; P. kéng; T. kái^n; Cn. kŭi^n), to choose; to select. **kéng-soán**, id.

kéng [R. name of plant], (Cn. kí^n). **kiet-kéng**, = kiet-kĕng, a medicinal plant.

kéng [R. gán, the eye]. **lêng-kéng** (C.), = A. gêng-géng, the dragon's eye or lung-yen fruit.

kéng (R. kán), (Cn. kŭi^n), a fold or plait, as in a dress; a wrinkle, as on face. **kûn-kéng**, folds of a petticoat. **pah-kéng-kûn**, a dress with a hundred plaits or folds, worn by northern men. **khioh-kéng**, to plait folds, as in a dress or an edging. **bīn khioh-kéng**, face wrinkled, as of an old person. **bák-bâi-thâu khioh-kéng**, id., as old person. **bák-chiu-thâu phah-kéng**, corners of the eyes wrinkled, as by grief or care. **bák-chiu-thâu put-sî phah-kéng**, you constantly look grieved and anxious.

kéng (R. id.), a district; a ward or subdivision of a town. **kéng-kài**, borders or limits; region (s. warn). **kéng-lāi**, within the ward or district. **kéng-chèng**, common to a whole ward, as idol or rites. **hap-kéng pêng-an**, may the whole ward enjoy prosperity. **péh-bák-pùt iah goā-kéng**, Keh-sèng-ông takes care of other people but neglects his own relatives.

kéng-tsú, the guardian idol of a ward, chosen by the people. **kéng-tsú-kong**, id. **tòng-kéng**, id.

kéng [R. circumstances; aspect; appearance; landscape], scenery; appearance of landscape. **kéng-tì**, scenery; fortune, luck, or circumstances, as of man or of place. **kéng-hóng**, circumstances, as of man, place, or affair (v. hóng). **kéng-gū**, id. **chêng-kéng**, id. **sè-kéng**, existing circumstances, as of a place. **kàu-chit--ê sè-kéng**, matters have gone from bad to worse, even to this state. **kong-kéng**, landscape; scenery; circumstances, as of man or place. **hó-kong-kéng**, fortunate and prosperous. **phái^n-kong-kéng**, unfortunate state of matters; all going ill.

bé-kéng, one's circumstances in the concluding period of life. **hó-bé-kéng**, prosperous at last, esp. after a hard and toilsome life. **phái^n-bé-kéng**, closing period of life unfortunate and miserable, esp. after a fortunate life.

sūn-kéng, affairs all going well. **chheng-kéng**, well got up; comfortable, as house or garden; in comfortable circumstances without anxiety, as man. **bô-tùi-kéng** (Cn.), unsuitable for the purpose.

kéng-siōng, an aerial phenomenon or meteor; appearance of sky as to clouds, rain, or other weather. **ú-kéng**, the appearance of rain in a picture.

phûn-kéng, arrangement of flowers in pots, so as to look neat and nice. **phoā^n-phûn-kéng**, to improve the appearance of a pot plant, as another small plant (v. phoā^n).

siet-kéng, to make a carefully arranged plot to deceive by a whole tissue of lies, pretences, false appearances, and deceitful actions. **chhòng-kéng**, to annoy; to make a fool of; to deceive by false reports. **chhok-kéng**, to try one's fortune by lot or such superstitious rite (v. chhok). **chhiok-kéng** (Cn.), id.

chhiok-kéng seng-chêng, to meet with circumstances that call up deep, warm, solemn, and somewhat sad emotions, *e.g.* old remembrances of friends now dead or far off, or recollections of our own former experiences. **kièn-kéng siong-chêng**, feeling sympathy arising at the sight of misery or distress.

kèng [R. a mirror, = col. kià^n]. **bêng-kèng**, your honour, whose mind is as clear and just as a mirror! (said to a mandarin). **toā-ló bêng-kèng**, id., to a mandarin to whom "toā-ló" is the proper address.

kèng [R. finally; to exhaust or examine to the bottom]. **kiù-kèng**, in fine, as in a brief summary of the whole matter; at last, as the due accomplishment of a whole course of action, though long delayed and apparently frustrated. **kèng-jiên**, but after all —; yet, though it appeared unlikely to be so.

kèng [same as next word?]. **kèng-oá^n**, a set of various sorts of eatables, offered all at once in the rites called "chiò." **chhòng kèng-oá^n**, to make these offerings. **pān kèng-oá^n**, id. **pān-kèng**, id.

chhài-kèng, a set of vegetable offerings thus presented in worship.

kèng [R. kiòng, to make offerings; by change of tone from "kiong," to supply, to provide]. **pài-kèng**, to kneel and make offerings at the Tauist "chiò" ceremonies. **hièn-kèng**, to offer a number of miscellaneous articles, as ornaments, flowers, money, and other valuables; it is done just at noon, making the middle offering of the series in the "chiò," in Amoy usually seven. **tsòe-kèng** (T.), = A. tsòe-chiò, to perform these rites of "chiò" in general.

kèng (R. id.), to reverence; to worship; to honour; to treat with due respect or politeness (applied both to human and divine things, so that it is hard to distinguish). **kèng-ì**, respectful feelings or intention. **kèng-khiên**, devout; reverential. **kiong-kèng**, id. **sêng-kèng**, very reverential, as towards the idols.

kèng-tiōng, to respect; to reverence. **kèng-hōng**, to worship. **kèng-pài**, to do reverence; to worship. **kèng-hók**, to reverence and obey.

hàu-kèng, to serve filially; to worship by offerings. **khim-kèng**, to reverence; to venerate, as man of great influence or excellence. **tsun-kèng**, to honour. **chhûn-kèng**, to show respect to a friend or superior, as by consulting him about what is to be done, or by presents (v. chhûn).

sa^n-kèng, to treat another politely; to treat one another politely (not necessarily mutual). **siong-kèng**, id. **siong-kèng put-jû chiông-lēng**, I will at your desire relax the strict rules of politeness, *e.g.* allowing the guest not to drink.

kèng-chiú, to invite one another to drink liquor at a feast.

kèng jī-tsoá, to honour written or printed paper, by keeping it from pollution. **kèng thi^n-tōe**, to worship Heaven and earth. **kèng pē-bú**, to serve or honour parents filially. **kèng-ló tsun-hiên**, to honour the aged and the wise. **kèng lâng-kheh**, to treat guests with proper politeness.

kèng [R. more, still more, by change of tone from "keng," to change, a watch]. **kèng-khah,** still more—. **kèng-koh-khah,** id.

kèng [R. a road, a path, = col. kiⁿ]. **hêng-kèng,** behaviour. **hó-hêng-kèng,** good behaviour. **pháiⁿ-hêng-kèng,** bad conduct.

lō͘-kèng (a path), a means or plan of doing something. **ū lō͘-kèng,** to have a business, or means of livelihood. **bô-siāng-lō͘-kèng,** having different trades or professions from each other.

kēng (= khēng). **kēng-tsoá,** a sort of paper used for drawing paper, and in the rites called "chiò." **toā-kēng,** the largest and best sort, from Soo-chow. **tiong-kēng,** medium do. **sió-kēng,** inferior do. **sėk-kēng,** a good sort. **chhiⁿ-kēng,** an inferior sort.

kēng (T. kāiⁿ, Cn. kūiⁿ), to put in a support to keep a thing from falling; to press against a thing, as to support it or to keep it from moving, sometimes so as to injure it slightly; to obstruct, as some small thing keeping a door from moving; to assist by giving a little money. **kēng--tio̍h,** to press against.

saⁿ-kēng kha-chhng (standing back to back), two men combining to protect one another from a third party or others, or to injure him.

tàu-kēng, to assist a man by a small gift, so as to keep him from being ruined. **kō͘-kèng,** id. **tāi-ke kō͘-kèng,** several doing so. **kēng-koá-chîⁿ hō͘--i,** assist him by a little money.

kēng [R. kéng, name of a plant]. **kiet-kēng,** = kiet-kéng, a medicinal root.

ki [R. hunger; famine]. **ki-hng,** famine. **ki-hân** (R.), hunger and cold. **iau-ki sit-tǹg,** to lose a meal or more; hungry or starving. **chí-ki,** to appease slightly the cravings of hunger, but not satisfy. **hoā-péng chhiong-ki,** paint a loaf to satisfy hunger. **chek-kok hông-ki,** collect grain to guard against famine. **jím-ki siū-ngō͘,** endure hunger patiently and willingly.

ki [R. chi, the 65th radical; to branch; a tribe]. **hun chit-ki,** one part of a clan dividing off into a separate family division.

ki [R. few; somewhat; nearly]. **sù-ki** (R.), probably; very nearly; strongly expecting that —. **sì-ki** (C.), id.

bô-ki, not many. **ke bô-ki,** not much additional. **ke iáh-bô-ki,** id. **chhun iáh-bô-ki,** only very few remain. **bô-ki-chîⁿ,** only a few cash. **bô-ki ê-chîⁿ,** id.

ki [R. chi, a mere mark of sound]. **pek-ki,** a coarse woollen stuff like baize, generally red; long ells.

ki — **âng-ki-ki,** very red.

ki (R. id.) **ki-chhì,** to deride a man; to jeer at; to satirize.

ki [R. a wicker basket, hod, or tray]. **pùn-ki,** a basket or hod for mortar.

poà-ki, a flat wicker tray for winnowing grain by throwing it up in the wind. **poà-ki-kîⁿ,** the rim of such a tray.

poà-ki-kah, a very venomous variegated snake, marked like the rim of that tray.

ki — **hoe-ki,** a large sort of cuttle-fish (s. flower).

ki — **ki-ki kê-kê,** all in confusion and disorder, as furniture (v. kê).

ki [R. muscular flesh]. **ki-hu,** muscular flesh and skin. **bô-ki-hu,** very lean; has no flesh on his bones.

ki [R. the full revolution of a year]. **ki-liên-song,** mourning for one year, as for uncle or brother. **ki-liên-hók,** id.

ki (R. kī). **chhiong-ki,** a harlot. **chhiang-ki** (C.), id. **ki-lú,** id.

ki (C.), = A. ku, to dwell.

ki (C.), = A. ku, the corners of a dress.

ki (C.), = A. ku, a carriage, &c.

ki [R. a secret; a contrivance; a machine; a loom; an opportunity, = col. kui]. **kè-ki,** to pass meal-time without eating (s. branch). **iau--khì kè-ki,** to be hungry and exhausted from losing a meal (v. iau). **sēng-ki,** to take advantage of an opportunity. **ki-hōe,** an opportunity or suitable occasion.

ki-bit, secret, as affair; managing secretly, as a man. **chhut ki-ho,** to make a secret sign (by sound or gesture) that only our confederates understand. **tiám-ki,** to give intelligence by a few words which the hearer can supplement, often unintelligible to others.

ki-khiàu, intelligence; cleverness; quickness of mind (v. khiàu). **ki-tauh-á,** a trap, as for birds. **ki-kúiⁿ-á** (C.), instruments moved by secret springs or wheels, &c.

ki-koan, ability to adapt one's plans to new circumstances; curious contrivances with secret springs, wheels, &c., as in toys, watches, &c. **ki-koan kiàn-sek,** intelligence and acuteness. **ū-ki-koan,** skilful at adapting one's conduct or plans to new circumstances or emergencies; versatile; shifty (good or bad); crafty. **toā-ki-koan ê-lâng,** id. **lāu-siet ki-koan,** to let out a secret. **lāu-siet thien-ki,** to let out Heaven's plans or secrets. **thien-ki put-khó lāu-siet,** Heaven's secrets must not be let out (said by fortune-teller when he is asked to explain minutely what he has said vaguely; said in joke by a man who will not tell a secret). **lāu-siet kun-ki,** to let out military secrets (said also figuratively in general). **kun-ki-bō,** a cap sometimes worn by military mandarins.

ū sim-ki, good at planning or thinking out. **ū-ki-piàn,** able to act according to sudden emergencies or change of circumstances; versatile. **sûi-ki èng-piàn,** to act according to the circumstances or emergency.

kóng thàu-ki, to tell fully, with all the circumstances, keeping back nothing. **kóng--khì thàu-ki,** id.

tâu-ki, to agree in opinion. **kóng tâu-ki,** to say what is pleasing to another, by agreeing with his opinion. **kap-goá tâu-ki,** of the same opinion or views with me. **giên-gú tâu-ki,** agree in opinion and statements. **oā put-tâu-ki, poàn-kù to,** when what one says is not pleasing, half a sentence is too much. **hoā put-tâu-ki,** &c., id.

ki-pėk, superfine white grass-cloth. **ki-siōng-pėk,** id.

ki [R. foundation]. **tōe-ki,** a foundation carried generally some feet above the ground. **ki-tōe,** id. **chio̍h-ki,** a stone foundation. **chhiûⁿ-ki,** foundation of a wall, esp. of a mud or cement wall.

khí-ki, origin or commencement of an affair; to begin an affair or business. **khai-ki,** to originate, as a family, or as a firm or business (said in looking back after it has long existed). **khai-ki-tsó͘,** first ancestor or founder of a family or clan. **khai-ki sí-tsó͘,** id. **khai-ki chhòng-giap,** to lay the foundation of a family's wealth.

ki-giap, an inheritance.

ū kun-ki, will be strong and fortunate, as child

27

with good horoscope. **kun-ki tiâu-tsòng**, having a very good horoscope. **bô kun-ki**, having a bad horoscope; will be sickly or unlucky, as child; often counteracted by giving the child to be son to another man, or even assigning it as son to a man already dead. **kun-ki phû**, id. **kun-ki phû-phiò**, id.

ki [R. chi], a branch; a twig; classifier of long straight things, as pencils, poles, masts, pine-apples, playing-cards, small rolls of the more valuable sorts of cloth. **chit-ki-toān**, a roll of satin. **tiuⁿ chit-ki-chhùi**, all mere talk, without power or reason (v. chhùi).

ki-hiòh, branches and leaves (v. hiòh).

chháu-ki, a stalk of straw, grass, &c. **hoe-ki**, stalk of a flower (s. cuttle-fish). **chhiū-ki**, branch or twig of a tree or shrub. **san chhiū-ki**, to prune and thin out branches or twigs. **sien-hô-ki**, coral ornament for hair. **bih-ki-á**, splinter of bamboo. **kak-ki**, lath.

tê-ki, tea-leaves with the ends of the small twigs mixed. **chióng-pōe-ki**, sort of Sou-chong with small twigs mixed.

iû-ki, a long roll of paper dipped in oil; or oiled paper rolled round a thin piece of bamboo (used for a light). **chhèng-ki-chìⁿ**, a sky-rocket. **tek-á-ki**, a tube of thin dried bean-curd (v. tek).

chiap-ki, to graft. **kè-ki**, to make a new plant by tying wet earth on a branch (T. tŏh); also, adopted from another surname; to pass from branch to branch, as bird (s. opportunity). **thèh kè-ki--khì**, stolen and passed from one man to another, so that it cannot be found.

ki-kut, general shape of person. **hó-ki-kut**, well-formed in bodily shape, esp. woman. **pháiⁿ-ki-kut**, so ill-formed naturally that no fine dress or ornaments can make her good-looking. **ki-kut hó-khoàⁿ**, limbs gracefully formed. **ki-kut thiau-lāng**, id. (v. lāng). **ki-kut siⁿ-tsòe-hó**, naturally well-formed in body, though perhaps at present ugly from poverty or illness. **chhe-ki toā-kut**, large-boned and strongly made, but clumsy or ungainly in appearance, as man. **phiaⁿ-ki-kut**, rib of animal. **pak ki-kut**, to make a framework of thin split bamboo, as for a gauze lamp-frame, or for a paper image; to set in proper train or order at first, as in beginning to teach a boy, or as in making the plan of an essay, accusation, or petition; also (Cn.), to make the model of a house to be built.

siⁿ-tsòe chit-ki-á, slender, pretty, and graceful in form.

saⁿ-ki-ûi, a full-rigged ship (v. ûi). **ki-poàⁿ-poàⁿ**, a three-masted schooner.

ki [R. divination, esp. by writing]. **ki-tông**, a sorcerer who pretends to be possessed by a spirit. **tâng-ki**, id. (v. tâng). **ki-kha** (Cn.), id.

koan-ki, to mutter prayers and incantations so that the afflatus may come on the medium for writing oracles. **koan-ki tiô-tâng**, to make incantations and come into an ecstatic state by the afflatus, either for a sorcerer who cuts himself like a fakeer, or for writing oracles. **kàng-ki**, the spirit coming down to possess the medium for writing. **chiūⁿ-ki**, the spirit taking possession of him. **chhut-ki**, to get the afflatus for writing oracles. **hū-ki**, the spirit coming on a man and possessing him, either on a sorcerer like a fakeer, or on the men who hold a branch to write under the afflatus. **khan-ki**, to hold a forked-branch (gen. peach), as two men do, while the third end traces words on bran. **khan-ki chhut-jī**, id. **kiáh-ki**, id. **kiáh-chiàⁿ-ki**, to be the principal holder of that branch. **kiáh-tò-ki**, to be the assistant holder of it.

kî [R. a ghost or demon, = kî; also, a shrill sound; perhaps these are two different words].

á-ki, name given to foreigners (said to be from the shrillness of their voices, like ghosts).

ki-ki-háu, crying disagreeably; a ringing in the ears. **chhit-gėh-poàⁿ-kúi ki-ki-háu**, you are crying like a ghost on 7.15 (said to a child constantly crying for things). **ki-ki-thiu**, to cry, as a ghost, or as a child constantly asking for things. **ki-ki-kiò**, always crying and calling out. **ki-ki-tân**, to whizz. as a bullet; sound of whistling. **chhùi ki-ki-tân**, whistling with the mouth.

ki-ki kū-kū, twittering. **hong thàu ki-ki**, wind howling. **hī-khang ki-ki ê-siaⁿ**, a ringing in the ears.

kî (R. id.) **kî-lîn**, the sacred animal called "kilin" (v. lîn).

kî [R. spirit of the earth]. **thien-sîn tē-kî**, the spirits of heaven and earth.

kî [R. to pray]. **kî-kiû**, to beseech; to pray. **kî-tó** (R. and X.), to pray to a god. **kî-jī-pêng**, the 113th radical (R. sī), written at the side.

kî [R. chess]. **kî-chí**, chess-men. **an kî-chí**, to set out the chess-men ready for beginning the game. **kî-phó**, a book of chess lessons. **chhiūⁿ-kî**, sort of chess having twelve pieces on each side. **kî-poâⁿ**, a chess-board. **kî-kėk**, a chess-board with the men set out ready for a problem. **pâi kî-kėk**, to set out chess-men on the board ready for gambling; to arrange a plan all ready that a man may fall into the snare. **kî-kėk chiú-liōng**, there are many different degrees of ability, better and worse (lit. for chess and drink).

tioh-kî, to play chess. **kiâⁿ-kî**, to play the sort called "chhiūⁿ-kî." **ûi-kî**, to play at the sort called o-pėh-jīⁿ. **kî koâiⁿ**, skilful at chess.

kî (R. id.) **kî-lâm**, a sort of wood (v. lâm).

kî [R. name of an herb]. **ng-kî**, a medicinal herb in its raw state. **chià-kî**, do. prepared. **kiâm-kî**, do. salted.

kî [R. kiû, a hornless dragon]. **kî-liông**, a dragon without horns. **kî-liông-toh**, a long narrow table with these dragons carved on it; narrower than "oàⁿ-toh." **kî-liông sì-sien**, this table along with a small square one.

kî [R. a fixed day]. **jit-kî**, a set day; a fixed date. **sî-kî**, a fixed day, as in a series, *e.g.* special days for special business at an office. **chhit-jit chit-kî**, once in seven days. **sam-pat-kî**, the days ending with 3 and 8, for entering complaints, accusations, and answers, at yamuns. **ngó-sip-kî**, the days ending in 5 or 0. **keng-kî**, the time of the menses of a woman.

kî-siàu, a debt or account payable at a fixed time or times. **chheng-kî-siàu**, to pay in full at the time fixed; to pay the last instalment. **kî-toaⁿ**, a bill fixing a time for payment. **bô-tùi-kî**, not yet due, as a bill. **bē-kàu-kî**, not yet come to the time, in general. **kàu-kî**, the fixed time come; at the fixed time. **thoa-kè-kî**, to delay beyond the fixed time.

kî (R. id.), a flag; a banner; one of the Manchoo banners; an instrument used in making nets, used as a measure for making the meshes all of one size.

kî-chhì, flags and banners of army (v. chhì). **kî-hō**, distinctive mark, as of nation or troop, made by a flag. **lí-khoàⁿ i--ê kî-hō**, you are fawning on him. **kî-koâiⁿ**, a common flag-staff. **kî-koaⁿ**, official flag-staffs, in pairs (v. koaⁿ).

kî-ē, under the flag. **kî-ē-lâng**, Manchoo Tartars;

bannermen. **jip-kî**, a Chinaman becoming a Manchoo bannerman.

hong-kî, a flag used as a vane. **lēng-kî**, a flag used for giving commands by mandarin or idol. **pó-tók-kî**, sort of flag used by generals. **sòe-jī-kî**, a flag (of general or idol) with the character "sòe" (commander-in-chief) on it. **ngó͘-sek-kî**, triangular flags of various colours. **ngó͘-hong-kî**, five flags of five colours in a set.

hoa-kî-kok, the United States of America. **hoe-kî-kok**, id. **hoa-kî**, American (of U. S. A.) **sip-jī-kî**, the Danish flag.

seng-kî, to hoist a flag. **chhah-kî**, to stick up a flag, as in a socket or in one's hair, &c. **khiā-kî**, to erect a flag with flag-staff. **iét-kî**, to wave a flag. **chè-kî**, to make offerings to a flag. **iám-kî sit-kó͘**, not using the flags and drums, as in ambush or on a secret march. **kiàh-kî**, to carry a flag in the hand. **kàu-hit-sî**, **kiàh hit-kî**, act according to the circumstances.

kî [R. the dorsal fin]. **hî-kî**, the dorsal fin of a fish.

kî (C.) **ke-kî**, = A. koe-kû, a street of shops.

kî (C.) **pe̍h-chhia-kî** (= A. kû), white stone used for buttons of mandarin caps.

kî [R. strange; rare; clever]. **kî-khá**, ingenious; crafty; with great skill and beauty of work. **kî-khiáu**, skilful at work. **kî-īⁿ**, strange (v. īⁿ). **kî-iūⁿ**, of different form from what is usual (generally better); strangely formed. **kî-koài**, strange; extraordinary. **kî-hêng koài-tsōng**, strange uncommon form. **chin-kî-sū**, a strange affair indeed!

kiàn-kî, superior to others, as in skill or excellence. **bô-sím-mih kiàn-kî**, not superior to others; quite mediocre, as things or workman, or as a doctor, &c. **goá--ê tiōng-kî**, that in which I am specially skilled or proficient (v. tiōng). **chhut-kî**, wonderful; very strange; much superior to others. **jú-chhut jú-kî**, each successive time the better or more successful, *e.g.* in disputes or lawsuits, or sons more and more talented; said also ironically of getting worse and worse.

kî [R. he, she, or it; sometimes very like the definite article]. **kî-sit**, in reality. **kî-û**, surplus; remaining. **kî-î** (C.), id. **put-kè kî-sò͘**, innumerable. **kīn-ti kî-it, put-ti kî-jī**, knowing only a very little of the matter. **tek-kî-tiong**, to hit on the proper medium (v. tiong).

kék-kî, exceedingly —.

kiù-kî-jiân, on examining into the real state of the case (v. jiân).

ko͘-put-kî-chiong (esp. C.), = ko͘-put-chiong, having no other alternative. **put-kî-sî** (C.), = put-si, at any time.

kí [R. chí, the finger; to point], to point; to point out, as with the finger. **kí-tsáiⁿ**, the fore-finger. **sûi-jī kí**, to point out word by word. **kí-thiⁿ**, to point to Heaven, as witness in swearing; to call Heaven to witness. **kí-thiⁿ kí-tōe**, to call Heaven and Earth to witness.

kí [R. name of a plant]. **kó͘-kí**, a small red or black berry used as a cooling medicine (Lycium sinense? Berberis Lycium?), brought from the north; there is also another sort native near Amoy. **kó͘-kí-sim**, the bud of a small erect shrub a few inches high, that grows near Amoy; used also as a vegetable for mixing with oysters, &c. **kó͘-kí-thâu**, its root (native), medicinal. **kó͘-kí-kū** (P.), id.

kí [R. a small table]. **kí-toh**, a small square table; a teapoy. **tê-kí**, id. **khòng-chhn̂g-kí**, the small stool-shaped table set on a state-couch between the two seats. **kí-siōng-kí** (lit. a small table on a teapoy), said of a very mean and low menial, as the servant of a mandarin's attendant, or the slave of a female slave.

kí [R. to record; a history; a period of twelve years; to rule], a surname. **nîⁿ-kí**, years, in regard to age. **nîⁿ-kí joā-tsōe**, how many years old? **chit-kí**, a period of twelve years. **chit-kí-nîⁿ**, id.

keng-kí, employment; business; means of livelihood. **kan-kí** (T.), id. **kin-kí** (C.), id.

kí [R. one's self, = col. kì]. **tsū-kí** (r.), one's self. **ti-kí ê-lâng**, a very intimate friend. **siú-kí** (r.), to restrain one's self from evil (v. siú).

khek-kí thāi-jîn, to put one's self to inconvenience for others (v. khek). **sún-jîn lī-kí**, to injure another for one's own benefit. **hāi-jîn lī-kí**, id. **hāi-jîn, chek hāi-kí**, to hurt another is to hurt one's self. **hāi-lâng, chek hāi-kí**, id.

kí — **ló͘-kí**, a Cantonese harlot. **ló͘-kí-á**, id.

kí (C.), = A. kú, to choose. **chhiam-kí**, to make a united recommendation of a man for some post or office.

kí (C.), = A. kú (R.), a carpenter's square.

kí — **kí-kí kiáuh-kiáuh**, noise of birds or of children.

kì [R. a record; to remember; a mark; often at the end of the name of a firm], to write down. **kì-hō**, a mark. **kì-jīn**, a mark by which a thing may be recognized, esp. a scar or such indelible mark on the person. **ûi-kì**, a note or mark by which a house (&c.) may be recognized; a memorial given by friends at parting, often after illicit connection. **chhók-kì**, official stamp put on petitions, &c. **tó͘-kì**, a mandarin's official seal (v. tó͘).

sú-kì, annals or history of a state. **lé-kì**, the Book of Rites. **chhòng-sè-kì** (X.), Genesis.

kì--teh, to write down. **kì--lóh-khì**, id. **kì-hē--teh**, id. **kì-hē** (C.), id. **kì-tsài**, to record; to write down. **kì-miāⁿ**, to write down a name. **kì-keng**, to write down verbal evidence given in court. **kì-siàu**, to write accounts; to put down in an account. **kì-chiūⁿ-siàu**, to put in the account, as item. **teng-kì**, to take notes at the time, as in an account or memorandum book; to note down. **sûi-sî teng-kì**, to take down a note of it at the very time. **tsûn-kì-phō͘**, a book containing entries of business transactions, kept for future reference. **kì-sū** (R. and X.), the clerk of a meeting, or of presbytery, &c.

kì--tit, to remember. **bōe-kì--tit**, to forget. **kì-tiâu-tiâu**, to remember perfectly. **kì-liām**, to think of with pleasant and grateful remembrance (v. liām). **kì-sìⁿ**, memory, the mental power of memory. **kì-tî**, id. **kì-sim**, to treasure up in the heart; to remember carefully. **kì tī-sim--nih**, id. **kì-tsāi-sim**, id. **kì-sim kì-koaⁿ**, id. **bô-kì-sim**, forgetful.

tek-kì, Tait & Co. **hô-kì**, Boyd & Co. **î-kì**, Ellis & Co.

kì [R. past; already]. **kì-jiân**, already; as it is already; inasmuch as.

kì (R. chì), a mole or natural spot on the skin. **o͘-kì**, a black mole, counted unlucky. **âng-kì**, a red mole, lucky. **tsu-se-kì**, id. **àm-kì**, a mole on some place covered by the dress. **kì-chhiu**, the hair-on a mole. **tiám-kì**, to touch a mole with medicine in order to remove it.

kì [R. kè, a plan; to calculate]. **hé-kì**, an assistant or partner in trade; a fellow-workman (v. hé).

kì (C.) **kì-lí-ài**, = A. kù-lí-ài, just as you please.

kì (C.), = A. kù, proof.

kì (C.), = A. kù; a saw; to saw.

kī [R. kí, one's self], (C. tī). **ka-kī**, self; one's self (v. ka).

kī [R. skilful; ingenious]. **kī-ióng**, a stone used at military examinations (v. ióng). **kī-gōe**, skill in handicraft. **kī-gē** (C.), id.

kī (C.) **hoai-kī-kō**, variegated; mottled; indistinct in colour, &c.

kī (C.), = A. kū, to reject (in some phrases).

kī (C.), = A. kū. **khì-kī**, an instrument or implement, &c. &c.

kī (C.), = A. khī (R. khū), to fear.

kī [R. to dislike; to have a superstitious horror of, = col. khī], days for ancestral worship, esp. the anniversary of ancestor's death; also (C.), = A. khī, to dread and avoid.

tsòe-kī, to worship and feast on the anniversary of a man's death. **tsòe-bién-kī**, to worship and feast on the anniversary of birth. **bién-kī**, anniversary of birth, for ancestral worship. **chiàⁿ-kī**, anniversary of death. **kī-jit**, id. **kī-sîn**, id. **tsé-kī**, general worship of ancestors in ancestral hall.

sin-kī, the first *ordinary* celebration of the anniversary of parent's death: it is on the second anniversary, for the rites of the first anniversary are quite extraordinary.

kong-kī, common worship (and feast) of paternal grandfather or great-grandfather. **kong-pô-kī**, anniversaries of death of ancestors. **chiáh kong-pô-kī**, to partake of the feast at their worship. **kong-pô sì-kī**, all the days for the worship of ancestors along with the (sì-tsoeh) other festivals. **kong-pô sì-kī, nī^{n}-tang gêh-tsoeh**, id.

kī-khek (C.), = A. khī-khek, to stand in dread of, as of another man.

kî^{n} [R. keng, a cyclical character], (C. kε^{n}), one of the cyclical characters in the denary cycle.

kî^{n} [R. keng, a metropolis, = col. kia^{n}], (C. kε^{n}). **kî^{n}-tit**, the term when insects come out, about 5th or 6th of March.

kì^{n}, to copulate (said only of the lower animals, especially of cats). **sa^{n}-kì^{n}**, id.

kì^{n} — **kì^{n}--tióh**, to have something (as a rope) come across us so as to dirty our trowsers or cause some slight inconvenience. **kì^{n}-kha**, to be in the way, so as to entangle or come against one's legs, as ropes on road, or as too much furniture in room. **kì^{n}-lâng-kha**, id. **kì^{n}-kha kì^{n}-chhiú**, to be in the way of one's limbs, as ropes or furniture; to be an incumbrance, as a family.

kì^{n} ti-tu-si, to brush away spiders' webs, as with a stick (s. weave). **kì^{n} ti-lâ-si**, id.

kì^{n} (R. keng), (C. kε^{n}), soup. **hî-kì^{n}**, fish-soup. **gû-bah-kì^{n}**, beef-soup. **tsáp-o-kì^{n}**, remnants of meat mixed and cooked as a condiment.

kì^{n} (R. kiam), a sort of alkali or lye. **piá^{n}-ióh-kì^{n}**, id. **kì^{n}-tsúi**, water in which this alkali is dissolved. **kì^{n}-tsàng**, a sort of confection.

sio-kì^{n}, to burn shrubs to make this alkali. **chiáh-kì^{n}**, to injure one's self, as by becoming surety for a man and having to pay, or doing a commission for him and having the goods thrown on our hands.

kì^{n} (R. chi). **n̂g-kì^{n}**, the Gardenia, a low shrub with large white sweet-scented flowers; the fruit (becho ?) is used as a yellow dye for cloth and for bean-curd. **n̂g-kì^{n}-hoe**, id. **ûi^{n}-kì^{n}** (C.), id.

kì^{n} [R. keng, to change; a watch], (C. kε^{n}), a watch of the night (longer in winter than in summer); one fifth part of the night.

an-kì^{n}, the first watch, about dark. **jī-kì^{n}**, the second watch, about 9 o'clock. **gō-kì^{n}**, the fifth watch, about dawn. **kúi-kì^{n} kúi-tiám**, what watch and what part of it? **kì^{n}-chhim**, far on in the night. **chit-kì^{n}-tsûn**, the distance that a junk will sail on an average in one watch; about eleven miles. **chit-kì^{n}-iû^{n}**, id.

kì^{n}-hu, a public watchman in the streets. **chiú-kì^{n}**, to keep watch; a watchman (v. chiú). **koe kiò-kì^{n}**, fowls crowing all through the night (not near morning).

kì^{n}-teng, a watchman's lantern; a fixed lantern at watch stations. **kì^{n}-khòk**, a watchman's rattle. **kì^{n}-kó**, a large drum on which the watches are struck, at yamen or city gate. **kì^{n}-lô**, a gong beaten by watchman. **kì^{n}-pâng**, a sentry-box. **kì^{n}-liâu**, watch-house in street or at city gate; small hut or shed for watching fields. **kì^{n}-lâu**, a watch-tower for guarding against feuds, as at entrance of village, or at boundary of two hostile clans.

kì^{n} [R. keng, the warp; to go through; classical books; a compass], (C. kε^{n}), the warp of a web; to weave. **kì^{n}-hûi**, warp and woof.

kì^{n}-á-lóeh, a light broad ceremonial cap, with red tassel.

kan-kì^{n}, the magnetic compass. **lô-kì^{n}**, the compass used by geomancers. **khan lô-kì^{n}**, to take bearings with compass for geomantic purposes. **pâi lô-kì^{n}**, id. **keh-kì^{n}**, id.

kì^{n}-pò, to weave cotton cloth. **thó-kì^{n}-pò**, very coarse cotton cloth woven at home. **kì^{n}-si**, to spin silk, as the silk-worm does; to weave mischievous plots in order to cause trouble; very much involved and difficult to settle, as an affair. **kì^{n} ti-tu-si**, to weave spiders' webs (s. entangle).

kap-lâng-kì^{n}, to cause unceasing trouble to a man; to be always dunning (as relative) for help, or constantly asking more than is just. **kì^{n}-bōe-tit**, cannot be easily settled, as a quarrel or involved affair where both parties are deceiving or otherwise in fault (said also of a man always borrowing and not paying).

kî^{n} — **kî^{n}-kî^{n} kê-kê**, very ill-arranged, as furniture that blocks the way, or as a load so ill-arranged that it can hardly be carried through the streets. **kî^{n}--tó**, to trip or stumble, as on a rope.

kî^{n} (R. khiên), edge, border, rim, &c., as of sea, table, dress, &c. **kî^{n}-á**, edge or border, as of table, dress, &c.

lîm-kî^{n}, just at the edge; in a very dangerous position (v. lîm).

gîm-kî^{n}, the long stone step or curb-stone along the side of a house, below the eaves. **hái-kî^{n}**, the sea-shore. **toh-kî^{n}**, the edge of a table.

bák-kî^{n}, the edges of the eyelids. **âng-bák-kî^{n}**, the edges of the eyelids watery and inflamed; blear-eyed. **tâm-bák-kî^{n}**, id.

kún-kî^{n}, to sew on the border on a dress, of different colour from the dress (v. kún). **kûn-kî^{n}**, the border of a woman's petticoat. **ôe-kî^n**, the raised border of a shoe. **oá^n-kî^n**, the edge of a bowl. **lûn-kî^n**, rim of wheel.

kí^n (Cn.) **kiet-kí^n**, a medicine, = A. kiet-kéng.

kí^n (C. ké^n), a flail. **ké^n-á** (C.), id. **bèh-kí^n**, a flail for wheat or barley. **liān-kí^n**, a flail. **ná^n liān-kí^n**, said of beating very severely, as a slave. **phah-kí^n**, to thresh with a flail. **kòng-ké^n** (C.), id.

kì^n (cf. chhì^n). **kì^n-á**, a sort of pin or bodkin for weaving nets. **bāng-kì^n** (Cn.), id.

kì^n [R. kèng, a road; a path], (C. kè^n). **sǹg-poâ^n-kì^n**, the rods on which the balls of an abacus move (v. sǹg). **chhia-lûn-kì^n**, the spokes of a wheel.

kì^n (C. kè^n), a row of cross rafters between two great beams. **lák-kì^n**, bed or mosquito curtains large enough for one person. **poeh-kì^n**, do., barely large enough for two. **tsáp-kì^n**, do., of good size for two.

kì^n (R. kièn), to perceive, especially by seeing; to have an audience or interview, as with a superior; to meet with; whenever met with.

bat-kì^n-kè, have seen it; have met with it. **kì^n-chî^n-sí**, very covetous. **kì^n--tióh chit-ê-chî^n, ná^n sì^n-miā^n**, looks on one cash as a matter of life and death.

tsòe-chèng-kì^n, to witness to what one has seen. **thi^n-tsai tōe-kì^n**, Heaven and earth know that what I say is true.

kì^n-thi^n, open to the sky; a small back court (v. thi^n). **kì^n-kúi**, you are telling a lie (lit. have seen a ghost). **lí kì^n-kúi**, id. **kì^n-soa^n**, to perceive land from sea, esp. first sight of land.

sa^n-kì^n, to meet with one another. **kì^n-bīn**, to meet with a man (lit. see face). **kì^n--tióh**, to visit a superior or a man of whom we ask a favour. **kì^n-koa^n**, to have an interview with a mandarin. **pài-kì^n**, to pay a ceremonial visit. **khàu-kì^n**, to have an audience of a very high mandarin. **pín-kì^n**, a graduate or lower official visiting a higher official on business. **tiâu-kì^n**, to have an audience of the sovereign. **ùi-kì^n-lâng**, afraid to see people; shy, bashful, or ashamed (v. ùi). **ōe-kì^n-chèng--tit**, fit to be looked at publicly, as man or affair all correct (v. chèng, "all").

khoà^n--kì^n, to see (lit. look and perceive), (v. khoà^n). **thia^n--kì^n**, to hear (v. thia^n). **kia^n--kì^n**, to fear; lest. **bāng--kì^n**, to dream. **chiò-kì^n**, to look at a mirror, or by lamplight (v. chiò). **chhē-m̄-kì^n**, to search for but not find. **phah--m̄-kì^n**, to lose; lost. **m̄-kì^n** (C.), id.

kì^n-chin, to see which of the two is right. **kì^n-chin-tiu^n**, when it comes to be reality (v. chin). **kì^n-su-iâ^n**, determined to lose or win. **kì^n-si^n-sí**, determined to conquer or die. **kì^n-kang-bú**, determined to have out the quarrel and see who wins (lit. male or female).

kì^n-i kì^n-hó, whenever he prescribes, the patient recovers. **kì^n-tsóh kì^n-tióh**, hits the mark every time. **kì^n-thák kì^n-bat**, whatever he reads he remembers and knows. **kì^n-khoà^n kì^n-bat**, can understand anything at a glance; can read a book anywhere you choose to try him.

gèh-kì^n, the monthly rose. **gèh-kì^n-hoe**, id.

kia (R. id.) **sek-kia**, Shakya, a name of Buddha, = sek-khia (v. khia).

kiâ (R. id.) **kiâ-lâm**, name of a Buddhist idol.

kiâ (esp. T.), = giâ, to carry with the hands or on shoulder without using a pole, as a heavy thing; also (T.), to push off a boat (that has grounded) with one's back.

kiâ [R. kî, a promontory], a syllable used in the names of many places on promontories. **ko-kiâ**, a village on Amoy island. **āu-kiâ-bé**, a suburb of Amoy.

kià (R. kì), to send (a thing, never a person); to send, as goods by a man; to intrust, as with a thing to be kept carefully for us, or with a commission; (to remain for a time); to intermit, as rites for the dead.

kià-tah, to send, as goods or letter. **kià-phoe**, to send a letter. **kià-bāi**, to send a salutation. **kià-māi^n** (C.), id. **kià-sia^n**, to spread a report that we had heard; to send a message by word of mouth.

kià-hè, to intrust or consign goods to be kept, sold, or sent. **thok-kià pān-hè**, to employ as agent to buy goods for us at another place (v. pān). **chhiá^n-kià--lí**, I intrust this to your care to keep for me for a short time. **kià-lok--teh**, to deposit; to intrust to a man's care, as goods or valuables for safe keeping. **sa^n-kià**, to intrust a man with a commission. **kià-tek, put-kià-sit**, people intrust things to others to be kept safe, not to be lost. **kià-tit, put-kià-sit**, id.

kià-óh, to hand over a graduate to the literary mandarin (óh-koa^n) for custody or punishment.

kià-téng, to take away a mandarin's button temporarily, suspending him from his rank till his case can be examined fully. **kià-pn̄g**, to intermit the rites for the dead for a few days. **kià kúi-jit**, how many days of interval in the rites are there?

kià-kha, to stay at a place for a short time. **sè-chhù kià-kha**, to rent a house for a short temporary residence. **pún sī kià-kha, ta^n sī tsāi-giáh**, at first had temporary employment (*e.g.* getting only one's food), but now regularly engaged for wages. **thó kià-kha**, to ask to be allowed to stay and have food (with no wages) for work. **kià-chiáh kià-toā**, to lend one's boy to another man to serve him for food and clothes till he be grown up.

kià-si^n, a parasitic plant, as misletoe; a sort of marine animal (v. si^n).

kià-tià^n, to anchor for a short time, as when waiting for wind or tide. **kià sa^n-kó**, to put out a small rope to fasten to another vessel or to the shore.

kiā (R. kī), steep; perpendicular, or nearly so; a stone stair or flight of steps built up or cut in rock; at zenith, as sun, moon, or star; standing on end, as hair.

kiā-á, a stone or brick stair, or flight of steps. **chióh-kiā**, a flight of stone steps; a stone stair. **chit-kiā chit-kiā**, one step after another of a flight of stone or brick steps. **chiū^n-kiā**, to go up a flight of stone or brick steps. **lóh-kiā**, to go down it.

mn̂g-kńg-chhi kiā, hair standing on end, as with fright or cold.

jit tiong-kiā, sun at zenith, at noon. **jit tng-kiā**, id. **gèh tiong-kiā**, moon at zenith. **gèh tng-kiā**, id.

āu-piah-soa^n kiā (the hill behind is steep), said of a man who has powerful helpers; also of a man in business who has property, so that he is greatly independent of his business.

kiā — **kiā-pē**, a very small sort of crab.

kiā (C.) **kiā-chhùi**, = A. khoah-chhùi, a pick-axe.

kia^n (R. keng), to fear; to be afraid of —; to be afraid; lest; to terrify. **kia^n-hiâ^n**, to fear; to be much afraid. **kia^n-kháuh-kháuh**, shaking with fear. **kia^n-sim**, a fearful heart. **sim kia^n, tá^n chièn,**

very much terrified. **kia^n-thâu kia^n-bé**, irresolute through fear of possible consequences. **hē-lâng-kia^n**, to frighten people. **ùi-kia^n**, shy and easily frightened, as child. **chhi^n-kia^n**, to be suddenly startled (v. chhi^n). **teh-kia^n**, fearing; being afraid. **teh kia^n**, to keep down fear; to put in good spirits, as by medicine.

kia^n i-seng, to make the doctor afraid, as some dangerous slow disease, that does not strike an unskilful observer; also, to be afraid of a doctor, as a child. **khí-peng lâi-kia^n--i**, to raise soldiers to terrify them. **ōe-kia^n-tsoâ**, having the power of frightening serpents, as some animals are said to have.

kia^n--lâng, to terrify people; to be afraid of people. **kia^n-lâng**, dirty. **bak-kia^n-lâng**, to soil; to dirty. **phah-kia^n-lâng**, id. **kia^n-sí-lâng**, very very dirty. **kia^n-sí tī-lâng**, id.

kia^n--sí, to die of fear. **kia^n-sí**, to fear death; to be very much afraid. **kia^n kàu-beh-sí**, terribly frightened.

kia^n-ùi, lest. **kia^n--kì^n**, id. **kia^n--liáu**, id.

kia^n (R. keng), the metropolis. **kia^n-siâ^n**, id. **pak-kia^n**, Pekin. **lâm-kia^n**, Nankin. **chiū^n-kia^n**, to go to the metropolis. **kia^n-khòng**, to appeal to one of the supreme boards at the capital. **kia^n-pò**, the Pekin Gazette. **kia^n-bák**, very fine ink, said to be from Pekin. **kia^n-liāu**, articles from Pekin; first-rate goods of some sorts.

kiâ^n (R. hêng), to walk; to travel; to begin to move, as a boat that had stuck fast; to act; to behave; to perform; to be efficacious. **chiàu-kiâ^n**, doing one's work diligently and well. **bōe-kiâ^n**, unable to walk; cannot succeed, as a plan. **bōe-kiâ^n--tit**, ought not to be done. **ōe-kiâ^n**, able to walk; will probably succeed, as plan, petition, &c. **sái ōe-kiâ^n--bōe**, can it be used to advantage? as a challenged dollar, or as a man's influence.

kiâ^n-lāi, to be at interest, as money (v. lāi). **kiâ^n-khì**, to have good effect, as medicine, or as a lucky grave; the animal spirits acting well in the body; to succeed, as a request for a favour. **hong-súi kiâ^n-khì**, the influence of the grave comes into action, causing good fortune to the descendants of the dead. **kiâ^n-keng**, to have the menstrual flow. **kiâ^n-tāng**, to die; to go to stool.

sî-kiâ^n, fashionable; much sought after (v. sî). **kiâ^n-sî**, making money in good practice, as physician.

kiâ^n-táh, behaviour; manner of walking, as to elegance, vigour, &c. **kiâ^n-pàng**, behaviour. **kiâ^n-gî**, id. **sé-kiâ^n**, behaviour. **hó-sé-kiâ^n**, easy and unconstrained in manner of intercourse; not insisting on ceremony, but kindly accepting familiar treatment; very good-natured, letting small insults (or things not just right) pass easily.

kiâ^n-hó, to act rightly or virtuously. **kiâ^n-phái^n**, to act wickedly or viciously; to commit impurity. **kiâ^n kan-îm**, to commit adultery, &c. **kiâ^n-pâng**, to have lawful conjugal intercourse.

kiâ^n-lé, to salute ceremoniously; to perform ceremonies. **kiâ^n tē-lí**, to practise geomancy. **kiâ^n-kûn**, to practise boxing without an opponent. **kiâ^n-kî**, to play a sort of chess. **kiâ^n-tit**, to play the game called "tit."

kiâ^n-tsûn, to be employed on a vessel. **kiâ^n-lō**, to walk on a road. **kiâ^n-bô-lō**, to lose one's road. **kiâ^n-tsoā**, to walk back and forwards, as after a meal (v. tsoā). **kiâ^n-soá**, to take a walk. **kiâ^n-niâ^n**, id. **bóng kiâ^n-kiâ^n**, id. **khì kiâ^n-kiâ^n**, id. **kiâ^n-lâi kiâ^n-khì**, to walk backwards and forwards. **kiâ^n-khui**, to get out of the way. **bān-chiah-kiâ^n**, stop a little. **tò-thè-kiâ^n**, to walk backwards, with face backwards. **kan-ta-kiâ^n**, to have a walk in vain. **thó-kha kiâ^n**, id. **khang-kiâ^n**, to walk on foot, or not carrying anything, or getting no good result. **kha-kiâ^n**, to walk on foot. **pō-kiâ^n**, id. **khá-kiâ^n**, you seldom visit us: surely you have some business or some favour to ask, as you come. **phái^n-kiâ^n**, unsafe for travelling on, bad for walking on, as a road. **hó-kiâ^n**, good or safe for travelling on. **hó-kiâ^n-tsáu**, in good order for walking, as dress; good for walking on, as road.

kiâ^n, the rim, as of a sieve, &c. **thai-táu-kiâ^n**, the rim of a sieve. **poà-ki-kiâ^n**, the rim of a shallow wicker tray used for winnowing.

kiâ^n (R. kêng), the stiff curved handle (about semicircular) of a basket or lamp. **nâ^n-kiâ^n**, semicircular handle of basket. **nâ^n-á-kiâ^n**, id. **teng-kiâ^n**, semicircular handle of a Chinese hand-lantern. **ū koà-kiâ^n**, having a handle of a semicircular form.

kiá^n [R. kién, =col. kán, á, gín], (Cn. ká^n), a son; a child. **sai-kiá^n**, a lad to whom we have taught a trade; an apprentice; adopted son of a Buddhist priest. **khit-ê-kiá^n**, a son bought and adopted. **bêng-ê-kiá^n**, id. **kè-pâng ê-kiá^n**, son adopted from another branch of the family.

gû-kiá^n, a calf. **chhoā-kiá^n**, to lead chickens to walk, as hen does. **ō-kiá^n**, young roots of taro that grow in a cluster round the old root.

kiá^n-jî, children; sons and daughters (v. jî). **kiá^n-sun**, descendants; posterity (v. sun). **tsa-bó-kiá^n**, a daughter; a girl. **tsáu-kiá^n** (C.), id. **kiá^n-sài**, son-in-law (v. sài). **kiá^n sim-pū**, son and his wife.

pē-kiá^n, father and son. **bó-kiá^n**, wife and children. **bú-kiá^n**, mother and son. **bú-kiá^n tùi pē-kiá^n**, marriage of two children by former marriage of widow and widower respectively, who themselves marry.

toā-kiá^n, eldest son. **sòe-kiá^n**, younger son; a young boy or child. **soah-bé-kiá^n**, youngest son. **soah-bé-kiá^n chiáh-ū-leng**, the youngest son gets plenty of milk to drink, *i.e.* is a favourite (in allusion to the Chinese custom of giving milk for two or three years). **mńg-kiá^n**, son got in old age, having had none before. **tsá-kiá^n**, child of very young parents. **sim-thiàⁿ-kiá^n**, a favourite child. **sim-koa^n-kiá^n**, id. **sēng-kiá^n**, to spoil a child; a spoiled child. **kheh-kiá^n**, in want of sons, *e.g.* none, or only one or very few. **hi-hán-kiá^n**, an only child. **ko-kiá^n**, an only son.

si^n-kiá^n, to get a son; to get a child born. **toa^n-si^n-kiá^n**, only son. **chhin-si^n-kiá^n**, one's own son (not adopted). **si^n-kiá^n-bú**, a midwife; a woman who has children. **thó-si^n-kiá^n**, a child born abroad of Chinese father and foreign mother. **lí-ko si^n-kiá^n, lūi chèng-lâng**, when a nun has a child it implicates many in suspicion; one wicked man involves many innocent. **ōe-si^n kiá^n-sin, bōe-si^n kiá^n-sim**, can get a son, but cannot make a filial heart.

bô-kiá^n-chè, usury so heavy that Heaven denies children to the usurer.

liù-tsú-kiá^n, a wicked boy about 15–20 years old. **sió-kiá^n**, a sodomite. **phái^n-kiá^n**, a lascivious person; a robber or rowdy. **phái^n-kiá^n-keng**, a brothel. **phái^n-kiá^n-lō**, lascivious conduct. **phái^n-kiá^n-chèng**, venereal disease. **phái^n-kiá^n-thâu**, a man who bargains for giving immunity from robbers to those who pay him money and get a flag from him.

kiâ^n [R. kì, to deposit; to remain, = col. kià]. **kiâ^n-si^n**, = kià-si^n, a parasitical marine animal.

kià^n (R. kèng), a mirror. **hī-kià^n**, the tympanum of the ear. **ūi-kià^n**, a framed picture. **hē-sin-kià^n**, a breast-plate. **hē-sim-kià^n**, a small ornament placed on the breast at burial. **hàm-kià^n**, a microscope. **chhien-lí-kià^n**, a telescope. **gán-kià^n**, spectacles. **ba̍k-kià^n**, id. **koà-ba̍k-kià^n**, to wear spectacles. **ba̍k-kià^n-kheng**, frame of spectacles. **ba̍k-kià^n-jîn**, glasses of spectacles. **kūn-sī-kià^n**, spectacles for near-sighted eyes.

bīn-kià^n, a mirror. **soe-tsng-kià^n**, a woman's mirror. **chhiú-kià^n**, a small mirror with handle. **tiàu-kià^n**, a mirror suspended on wall or stand. **khiā-kià^n**, a mirror or picture fixed on a stand without any joint.

chiò-kià^n, to look in a mirror. **chiò-sin-kià^n**, a full-length mirror. **chiò-hàm-kià^n**, to examine with a microscope. **boâ-kià^n**, to polish a brass mirror.

kià^n-pîn, a mirror fixed on a stand without any joint. **kià^n-tâi**, stand for a mirror. **kià^n-bīn**, face of a mirror. **kià^n-bīn-ní^n**, woollen cloth with a very smooth surface. **kià^n-bah**, the glass of a mirror, or of a framed picture, as distinguished from the frame. **kià^n-tē**, the wooden back of it. **kià^n-a̍h**, a small case containing a mirror.

ô-kià^n-thang, window made of oyster shells (v. ô). **lāi-kià^n-hiâ^n**, front bulkhead of a boat. **thâu-lāi-kià^n**, id.

kiā^n (R. kiēn), classifier of many sorts of articles, as clothes, &c. **mih^n-kiā^n**, a thing; an article. **ān-kiā^n**, a lawsuit. **tiâu-kiā^n**, particulars, as in an agreement.

sǹg-kiā^n-sia^n, to count articles by the number of units. **joā-tsōe kiā^n-sia^n**, how many articles are there? counting by units, *e.g.* not by hundreds nor by weight. **kúi-kiā^n-sa^n**, how many articles of dress? **ta̍k-kiā^n**, each article. **khoán-kiā^n**, to put in order a set of articles (v. khoán). **ū-kiā^n ū-chî^n**, so much money for each article.

kiā^n [R. kiēn, strong]. **ióng-kiā^n**, strong and vigorous. **ióng-kiā^n, khah-khoài-sí**, strong people die sooner than others. **kiā^n-sin**, strong in body, in good health; having a good constitution, so as to recover readily from sickness or accident. **chhi^n-kông-kiā^n**, strong, vigorous, and lusty, as lad or young man. **khah-kiā^n-lêng**, stronger than a dragon (v. lêng). **khin-kiā^n**, strong and vigorous. **kha-chhiú khin-kiā^n**, limbs nimble and strong. **kha-chhiú kūn-kiā^n** (Cn.), id.

kiā^n — **goā-kiā^n** (Cn.), exclamation of great astonishment.

kiah (R. kek, = col. giah). **kiah-tsâi**, the 64th radical (the hand) when written at the side. **kiah** (Cn. T.), = A. giah, to extract, as a thorn, &c.

kiah (T.) **kiah-chhùi**, to protrude the lips, as a secret sign (cf. khiàu).

kia̍h — **chhâ-kia̍h**, wooden-soled shoes or clogs, with uppers of cloth or leather like common shoes. **chhâ-kia̍h-ôe**, id. **ba̍k-kia̍h**, wooden clogs with only a strap of leather or coir. **tsang-ba̍k-kia̍h**, clogs fastened with only a strap of coir from the "tsang" palm. **tsang-kia̍h**, id. **âng-ba̍k-kia̍h**, wooden clogs with uppers or broad strap of red leather. **ba̍k-kia̍h-cheh**, wooden heels for women's small shoes. **ba̍k-kia̍h-tsoe**, an instrument like a wooden clog held in the hand by a cripple crawling on the ground (v. tsoe).

kia̍h [R. kiŏk, = col. kia̍k]. **kiau-kia̍h**, active, graceful, and cheerful in manner; having an intelligent look; fresh and blooming, as flowers after rain (v. kiau).

kia̍h (Cn. kàh), to carry in the hand, as umbrella, stick, sword, lamp, &c.; to hold, as a pen; to hold up, as head; to turn up, as eyes; to calculate by the abacus; a perpendicular handle, and some sorts of supports. **kia̍h-pē**, sort of halbert held by some idols.

kia̍h-koâi^n, to hold up high, as hand, or something in the hand, &c. **chhiú kia̍h-koâi^n**, to lift one's hand high; to be gentle, easy, and lenient, as a superior, or as the successful party in a lawsuit. **kia̍h-khí**, to hold up, as head; to raise up, as the eyes. **toā-tîm kia̍h-khí; khin-khin pàng-lo̍h**, lifting the rod, as for a severe blow, but striking very gently; as when bribed to beat gently, or as parent frightening the child. **thâu kia̍h-m̄-khí**, will not lift up his head, as from sorrow, shame, or sickness.

kia̍h-thâu, to carry the head high; two small additions (one on each side) in front of a house. **kia̍h-ba̍k**, to lift up the eye; to gaze or look attentively. **kia̍h-ba̍k-khoà^n**, to look attentively or earnestly. **kia̍h-tsan**, to raise up a square net hinged on the bow of a boat by walking up the ladder attached. **kia̍h-teng**, to carry a lantern. **kia̍h-pit**, to take up or hold a pen. **kia̍h-koái^n-á**, to carry a stick. **kia̍h-tiû**, to receive the tally along with the bale to be carried, as the cooly does. **kia̍h-kî**, to hold up a flag (v. kî). **kia̍h-ki**, to hold a stick for writing oracles (v. ki, divination).

kia̍h sǹg-poâ^n, to take up the abacus and calculate by it. **kia̍h-khoà^n**, calculate (with abacus) and see how much it is.

kia̍h kóng-á-hiân (to carry a small guitar), said of a man coming to get money out of another (play on the meaning of the word "oai^n").

teng-kia̍h, a pillar-shaped lamp-stand. **tháng-kia̍h**, a straight handle of a bucket rising straight from the side. **khut-chhioh-kia̍h**, wooden knees for supporting a boat's bulwarks (one limb nailed to the deck and the other to the bulwarks). **pūn-kia̍h**, id.

kiak (C.), = A. kiok (R.), foot.

kia̍k (= khia̍k). **ok-kia̍k-kia̍k**, very fierce. **kia̍k-kia̍k-háu** (C. kék), talking in a forward or unbecoming way, as inferior or young fellow talking too much. **kia̍k-kia̍k-kiò**, id.

kia̍k [R. kiŏk, = col. kia̍h]. **kia̍k-siak**, lively and active in manner.

kiam (R. id.), along with; to hold or exercise together, as two offices. **sa^n-kiam**, id. **bōe-kiam--tit**, they cannot be held or done at once. **kiam-koán**, to manage several offices or duties at once. **tsâi-tì lióng-kiam**, having both ability and skill. **hó kiam-phái^n**, good mixed with bad.

hòng-kiam, so much the more (said when the original object compared is added to, but not changed).

kiam toā-tiû (Cn.), to be set at a small angle from one of the four points of the compass (v. tiû).

kiâm (R. hâm), salted; salt-tasted; brackish; salted vegetables, &c., used as condiments; niggardly. **kiâm-siap**, bad-tasted; niggardly (v. siap). **kiâm-tok-tok**, very salt. **kiâm-sí-sí**, id.

kiâm-chiá^n, salt and fresh (v. chiá^n). **tì^n-kiâm, chia̍h bô-hiâm**, will take whatever comes to hand, and find no fault. **kiâm-sng-ti^n**, a confection combining several tastes. **kiâm-sng-chháu**, the oxalis plant.

tū-kiâm, to salt or pickle by plunging in brine.

sīⁿ-kiâm, to pickle; to salt. **soah-kiâm**, to put in a little soy or such salt condiment.

kiâm-tsúi, salt-water; said also of black-looking dollars. **kiâm-tsúi-chháu**, reeds from salt-marshes, not good for mats. **kiâm-chháu**, id. **kiâm-chhài**, salted vegetables, especially mustard-plant. **kiâm-lē**, all sorts of salted meat, fish, &c., or brine from them. **tāu-kiâm** (Cn.), = A. tāu-jú, salted bean-curd.

kiám [R. kám, to dare, = col. káⁿ]. **kiám-chhái**, perhaps; if perhaps. **kiám-ōe**, can it be possible that —, = kám-ōe (*q.v.*)

kiám (R. id.), to diminish in number or quantity. **kiám-chió**, id. **kiám--koá**, a few less. **khah-kiám**, fewer; less. **kiám-séng**, more sparing in expenses.

ke-kiám, more or less; to add or diminish. **ka-kiám**, id.

kiám-liáu, to have narrowly escaped losing money, *e.g.* by not having sent goods meant to be sent by a vessel that was wrecked. **kiám-chhun joā-tsōe**, how much less surplus is there than was expected? **kiám-phah**, to beat fewer blows than he said, or than was usual. **kiám-ēng**, to use somewhat less. **khah-kiám-chíⁿ**, cheaper than before, or than something else. **khah-kiám-kè**, offering to give it for less money. **kiám-kháu**, to diminish the population, as an epidemic (v. kháu). **kiám hè-siū**, to have one's life shortened by Heaven for wickedness. **kiám-chiáh**, to eat less. **kiám toā-tǹg**, to abstain from breakfast, as women often do on the 1st and 15th of the month (v. tǹg).

kiám [R. to arrange; a pattern; to examine]. **kiám-tiám**, to make a list or inventory; to examine the circumstances carefully; not hastily taking up a statement or report. **ka-kī kiám-tiám**, to examine carefully for one's self; not trusting to others. **sit-kiám-tiám**, to neglect something in the inventory; to take too little care of things intrusted to us, so that they are lost.

tsa-kiám, to examine a list or inventory to see if all be there. **se-kiám**, to search the candidates for examination, to see that they do not carry in anything on their persons. **kiám-si**, to investigate the cause of death (as coroner) when the body is decayed to the bones.

sûn-kiám, an assistant to the Hien mandarin, lower than "hun-koāiⁿ," about = "hun-si:" he is not appointed from among the graduates, but after a time can rise to higher office; a graduate does not kneel to him.

kiám-tsng, box containing ladies' shoes, trousers, feet-bandages, &c., for wedding (v. tsng).

kiàm (R. id.), a double-edged sword or long dagger. **hang-kiàm**, the long spike of the skate-fish. **pó-kiàm**, a magical or miraculous sword. **siang-ké-kiàm**, a double-bladed dagger. **sang-ké-kiàm**, id.

kiàm-sok, a scabbard. **kiàm-toà**, a ribbon with a pointed end. **kiàm-chhiuⁿ**, a railing with the heads of the rails projecting (v. chhiuⁿ).

lāi kiàm-kiàm, as sharp as a sword (for cutting), said of teeth.

bú-kiàm, to brandish a sword. **pùih-kiàm**, to draw a sword. **àn-kiàm siong-hông** (watching each other with hands on swords), meditating mutual injury. **àm-kiàm siong-hông**, id. **kiàh-to kiàh-kiàm** (holding drawn swords), said of a new-born babe whose horoscope will cause the death of some near relative; such children are sometimes killed to avert the calamity.

kiàm — **kiàm-kek**, very strict and exacting in calculations about money matters.

kian, kiân, kián, kiàn, kiān; better kien, kiên, kién, kièn, kiēn (*q.v.*)

kiang — **liu-kiang**, to get out of the way, to escape some duty or danger which we ought to share (v. liu).

kiâng (C.), = A. kiông, violent.

kiáng (C.), = A. kióng (R.), to force; to compel.

kiàng — **hong kiàng-kiàng-háu**, the wind howling loudly.

kiāng — **chhùi kiāng**, obstinate in argument; will not submit to be scolded, or admit that he is beaten, or confess a fault. **sèng chin-kiāng**, temper very obstinate and stubborn.

hong thàu kiāng-kiāng, wind boisterous and howling.

kiap (R. id.), to plunder; to rob; also (R.), a fated time of great calamity; a Buddhist kulpa.

kiap-àn, a (legal) case of robbery. **kiap-liáh**, to plunder and seize people. **bêng-hé̤ⁿ kiap-lio̍k**, to rob with lighted torches. **chhiúⁿ-kiap**, to rob. **chiét-tē chhiúⁿ-kiap**, highway robbery. **phah-kiap**, to be in the habit of plundering, as a robber village. **kiông-kiap**, violent robbery. **kiông-kiap-chhát**, burglars or highway-robbers. **kiap-chhát**, robbers.

kiap-iâⁿ, to plunder an enemy's camp and carry off the spoil.

kiap-sè, any fated time of terrible calamity. **kiap-sè lân-tô**, great fated calamities cannot be avoided. **tso-kiap**, to meet with some great calamity, as plunder or slaughter. **kè-kiap**, to pass through some terrible calamity, *e.g.* some long and dreadful disease or imprisonment. **boàt-kiap**, the Buddhist last day.

kiap [R. warm lined coat]. (Cn. köh, Cn. T. koeh). **kiap-hiû**, a lined warm coat, not wadded.

kiap [R. to take under the arm; to squeeze; to take on both sides, = col. ngoeh], to torture by the instrument for squeezing the feet. **kiap-kùn**, the instrument for squeezing and torturing the feet.

kiap-kong, to attack on both sides. **lióng-pêng kiap-kong**, id., = lióng-le kiap-kong. **lāi-goā kiap-kong**, to attack both from within and from without. **lōe-gōe kiap-kong**, id.

kiap-sim, the horizontal timbers with grooves for the boards of a partition, above and below.

kiap [R. a legume or pod, = col. ngoeh]. **bêng-kiap-chháu**, a fabulous sensitive plant.

kiat, kiát; better kiet, kiét (*q.v.*)

kiau — **kiau-so**, to instigate.

kiau [R. ke, a channel, = col. kau], (Cn. kau). **put-tek khai-kiau**, cannot find any way to set the quarrel right, so as to leave all on good terms.

kiau — **hoan-kiau**, to roll about on the ground, as a horse.

kiau [R. kiu]. **kiau-ká**, violent pains in the bowels (v. ká).

kiau [R. beautiful], bright and decided, as a colour; pretty (said in scolding or jesting to persons). **kiau-lāi**, bright and distinct, as a colour. **sek-tsúi kiau**, id.

kiau-á, licentious pictures. **iau-kiau** (R.), beautiful and finely adorned, as woman fitted to seduce.

kiau (R. id.), proud; to treat proudly; unwilling to listen or obey. **kiau-gō**, proud. **kiau-ngē**, id.

kiau-thâu, id. **kiau-keng**, proud and bragging, as in manner or talk. **kiau pit-pāi**, the proud will be worsted. **kiau-peng pit-pāi**, id. (fig. from soldiers).

kiau-kiàh, graceful, cheerful, and intelligent looking; not at all dull or depressed; active, lively, and neat; fresh and looking up, as flower vigorous, blooming, and healthy-looking after rain.

kiâu [R. a bridge, = col. kiô]. **hông-kiâu, pit hā-má** (R.), on coming to a bridge dismount (be cautious).

kiâu [R. name of a plant]. **liên-kiâu**, a sort of medicine.

kiáu [R. piáu, to paste]. **kiáu-pè** (Cn. T. piáu-pō), to paste paper together.

kiáu [R. to bend or straighten]. **kiáu-kióng** (R.), doing a thing in an unnatural, unreasonable, or absurd manner (v. kióng).

kiáu [R. to disturb; to annoy], to mix, as liquids; thank you, sir! as for things given.

kiáu-chî^{n}, I thank you for these cash (s. gamble; s. report). **kiáu--lí**, thank you, sir, for these things (lit. I have annoyed you!).

kiáu-jiáu, to annoy; to tease; to make a disturbance. **kiáu-lā**, to make a disturbance, as at a man's house (v. lā). **kiáu-chhá**, to make a disturbance. **loān-tsú kiáu**, id. **lām-sám kiáu**, id. **kiáu-lâng-bîn**, to startle a man so as to awaken him.

kiáu-tsúi, to mix with water. **kiáu-iû**, to mix with oil. **kiáu-thn̂g**, to mix sugar. **tsúi-kiáu**, a confection like a tart, made with meat, &c.

kiáu (R. tô), gambling. **poàh-kiáu**, to gamble. **poàh-kiáu-chē**, sitting cross-legged (unmannerly). **poàh-kiáu-sien**, a confirmed gambler. **poàh-kiáu lōng-tōng**, abandoned; dissolute; gambling. **poàh-gōng-kiáu**, unskilled in gambling; to gamble foolishly, as a victim. **poàh-toā-kiáu**, to gamble for a large stake. **poàh sió-kiáu**, to gamble for a small stake. **poàh iâ^{n}-kiáu**, to win in gambling. **poàh su-kiáu**, to lose in gambling. **su-kiáu**, id. **poàh-kiáu, lông-kun: bóe-bōe, chhàt**, there is honour among gamblers, but traders are thieves. **poàh-kiáu, ham-khak khí; tsòe-chhàt, thau-mi^{n}-bí**, gambling begins with shells, and stealing with a little rice. **iâ^{n}-kiáu su-kiáu-tiāu**, to win in gambling is the sure prognostic of losing.

kiáu-ti, a foolish fellow (pig) always losing in gambling. **kiáu-kúi**, a confirmed gambler. **kiáu-kùn**, a very skilful gambler. **kiáu-kha**, a gambler, especially in regard to the gambling place he frequents. **sī chia--ê kiáu-kha**, he is a regular gambler at this place. **kiáu-bōe**, a decoy for luring men to gamble. **kiáu-koa^{n}**, the keeper of a gambling-house or place (s. report). **kiáu-thâu**, id. **kiáu-thâu-ke**, id.

kiáu-keng, a gambling-house. **kiáu-tiû^{n}**, a gambling place, as out of doors. **kiáu-kū**, any sort of furniture or instruments used for gambling. **kiáu-lē**, money paid to the underlings or mandarins for tolerating gambling-houses. **kiáu-chî^{n}**, money got by gambling; a gambling debt (s. thank, annoy; s. report). **kiáu-chî^{n} bōe-tsòe--tit ke-hó**, gambling gains cannot make lasting wealth.

pâi-kiáu, to keep a gambling place. **tsôe-kiáu**, to unite capital to set up a gambling place. **gièn-kiáu**, craving for gambling. **hoat kiáu-hông**, to get excited in the game, so as to gamble on madly without any restraint. **chiàh-kiáu-tâng**, to live by gambling. **chin-gâu liàh kiáu-sat**, fond of finding fault whenever fault can possibly be found.

kiáu (R. id.), to report or give in to a mandarin, as a document or funds. **kiáu-bûn**, to give in a document to a mandarin. **kiáu-tiâ^{n}**, to send in a petition or report to a superior. **kiáu-lēng**, to give in a report to a superior military officer. **kiáu-chí**, to make report to the emperor of having executed his commands. **kiáu-chî^{n}**, to give in money to mandarin, as Tēpó does (s. gamble; s. thank, annoy). **kiáu kun-su**, to pay in the squeeze called military contributions.

kiāu (cf. kiauh, ngiauh), to move by a lever. **kiāu-khui**, to open by leverage. **kiāu--tó**, to upset by leverage, &c. **kiāu--khí-lâi**, to raise by leverage.

kiāu — **kàn-kiāu**, to scold with vile language, calling abominable names, &c. **chhoh-kàn-kiāu**, id. **kiāu** (C.), id.

kiauh (cf. kiāu, ngiauh), an upstroke in writing. **kiauh--khí-lâi**, to raise one's self up. **kiauh-khí**, to rise from one's seat.

kiauh (T.), = A. ngiauh; to lift up some small thing, as with the finger-nail.

kiauh — **kiauh-kiauh-jióng**, speaking loud and rudely; to make a row by talking very loud. **kiauh-kiauh-háu**, to talk on rudely when one ought to be quiet.

kiàuh — **kiàuh-kiàuh-kiò**, sound of voices, especially indistinctly objecting or murmuring at what is ordered. **ki-kí kiàuh-kiàuh**, sound, as of birds chirping; noisy, as children.

kiàuh^{n} — **kōng-kiàuh^{n}**, out of harmony; not getting on well together, as family or friends.

kiàuh^{n} — **tāng-kiàuh^{n}** (C.), a small sort of frog.

kien [R. the shoulder, = col. keng]. **kien-thiau pòe-hū**, to carry on the shoulder and on the back, as porters and pedlars. **phi-kien**, an ornament for the shoulders, worn by mandarins and Kujin.

kien (R. gien), pretty; too pretty; often said in joke of a person, with an inuendo of bad character. **hè-sek put-chí-kien**, the goods are very beautiful; said also of a woman who is too gaudy, as for bad purpose.

kien [R. kan, dry; to harden, = khiên, "heaven," = col. koa^{n}]. **kien-hong**, hardened and dried by the wind. **kien-koa^{n}**, to dry articles of food till quite dry. **kien-tāu-koa^{n}**, bean-curd dried quite hard. **siu-kien**, so far healed (as sore or ulcer), that the scab is about to form. **kien-phí**, the scab forming or formed. **kien-pa**, to dry, as meat. **gō kàu-beh kien-pa--khì**, terribly hungry (as if going to be dried).

kien-ta, = kan-ta, only (v. ta).

kien ōe, = kan ōe, yet indeed he is able (v. kan). **àn-ni^{n} kien thong**, it is indeed a good plan. **kien hó** (T.), = kan hó, though it seemed not good (or not well), yet after all it is so. **kien-á** (T.), = A. kan-á, well indeed —.

kien (R. id.), firm; steady. **kien-kò**, firm; steady; steadfast. **kien-tsòng**, strong; firmly made, as a thing, *e.g.* furniture, or as a city. **kien-tēng** (C. kin-tēng), strongly made, as thing. **kien-sim**, with fixed purpose. **sim-kien ì-chhiet**, id. **sim kien, chek-sī hùt**, a man of firm purpose is as powerful as a Buddha.

kien-lîn (r.), parsimonious; niggardly; stingy.

kien-lòk, = kan-lòk, a spinning-top.

kien (C.) **kien-tê**, = A. koan-tôe, to subscribe money. **kien-kàm**, to buy the degree of kàm-seng.

28

kiân (T. giân), to congeal or coagulate. **kiân-sng**, to congeal; to freeze. **kiân-tàng**, to coagulate.

kiân [R. kan, khiân, = col. kan, kien, koaⁿ], dry and parched, as tongue or throat in fever. **bīn lóng-kiân--khì**, face all become dark, as by sickness or opium-smoking.

kién [R. a cocoon; a chrysalis], (C. kán), a sort of silk from Sze-chuen province. **chhoan-kién**, id. **kién-tiû**, a yellowish white silk, which afterwards grows white. **péh-kién**, a fine thin white silk stuff.

kièn [R. to establish; to make firm, or build up]. **kièn-tì**, to purchase for one's self. **kièn-lip** (R.), to set up; to establish. **kièn-kong**, to obtain merit, by some great service to the state.

hok-kièn, Fuh-kien province. **kièn-liân**, water-lily seeds from Fuh-kien. **thien-hā piàn-piàn, m̄-tàh hok-kièn**, no place in the world is equal to Fuh-kien.

kièn — **kièn-chí-bah**, meat cut from the ham.

kièn [R. to perceive; to meet with; on every occasion; sign of the passive, = col. kìⁿ].

kièn-siàu, ashamed (v. siàu). **kièn-koài**, to be offended, as at small faults (v. koài). **kièn-kòe**, to be offended, esp. slightly. **kièn-tiông**, that in which one is specially skilful or excels others (v. tiông). **kièn-kì**, superior in quality (v. kì). **kièn-gî**, to be suspected.

kièn-sek, knowledge; wisdom (v. sek). **ì-kièn**, opinion. **bô-têng-kièn**, changeable in purpose. **chhién-kièn**, of shallow understanding; contracted in his views. **toán-kièn**, going to kill one's self (v. toán). **siáu-sé-kièn**, having but little experience; not acquainted with the world; having rarely met with influential people. **siáu-sé-kièn, to kî-koài**, he who has seen little is easily astonished. **kièn-tāi-sek-biēn**, acquainted or having mixed with influential people.

hán-kièn, rarely seen or met with. **chiok-kièn**, evidence enough that —. **lō-kièn put-pêng**, to see a case of gross injustice on the road (v. pêng). **put-kièn tsū-bêng**, of course it is so; unmistakably true. **tà put-kièn-thien**, to put up awnings so as quite to hide the sky (fig. of a man declining to see us or to help), (v. tà).

ōe-kièn-chèng--tit, can safely appear in sight of all men, as an honest and clear transaction (v. chèng, "all"). **kièn-tiâu**, to attend the regular daily audience of the emperor. **ín-kièn**, to have an audience of the emperor, as high mandarin on getting higher rank. **chì-kièn-lé**, fee paid on first calling a doctor or engaging a teacher.

kièn-chhu-hiông, to try which will conquer (lit. male or female). **kièn-ko-te**, id. (lit. high or low).

kièn-tsòh kièn-tiòng, hits the mark every time. **kièn-liāu, kièn-tiòh**, every guess comes true. **kièn-i kièn-hó**, curing by every prescription. **kièn-khùn, chiū bāng--kìⁿ**, every time I fall asleep I dream. **kièn-phoà**, wherever it is torn or broken.

kièn [R. ièn, a swallow, = col. ìⁿ]. **giét-kièn**, to play at shuttle-cock, done with the feet. **hiet-kièn**, id. **that-kièn**, id.

kiēn [R. vigorous and healthy]. **tsòng-kiēn**, robust, strong, and vigorous (of man). **khong-kiēn**, robust in old age.

kiēn-tiu, active, nice-looking, pleasant, and open in manner, as a child (v. tiu).

kiēn (cf. kiūⁿ), stubbornly refusing to acknowledge being in the wrong or to take advice. **kap-goá kiēn**, doggedly refusing to do what I wish. **chiàh-kiēn**, of set purpose doing the very contrary to what is asked or desired. **kiēn-lô**, you obstinate slave! (said in scolding a son or inferior who tries to be disobedient and obstructive). **kiēn-koai**, very dogged and crotchety; fond of opposing and obstructing others' wishes or plans; of set purpose going against what others desire. **ké-kiēn-koai**, making a show of disobedience and dogged resistance while quite aware that resistance is impossible. **ké-kiēn** (C.), id.

bōe-siau-kiēn--tit, unwilling to obey, but quite unable to make effectual resistance. **bōe-siau-kiēn**, id. **m̄-káⁿ siau-kiēn**, id.

kiēn (R. id.), (C. kīn), the gizzard. **ah-kiēn**, duck's gizzard. **koe-kiēn**, hen's gizzard.

kiet (R. id.) **chheng-kiet**, (R.), clean.

kiet (R. id.), (C. kit), auspicious; of fortunate omen; lucky. **kiet-hòk**, ordinary dress, as put on when mourning is put off. **kiet-hiong**, good and bad fortune; lucky and unlucky. **hiong-kiet**, id. **hiong-kiet-sū**, lucky and unlucky matters, as all sorts of festivals, anniversaries, &c. **hiong-kiet sî-sū**, id. **kiet-hiong bī-lâi, sien iú-tiāu**, omens come before good or bad fortune.

kiet-siông jû-ì, may you have happiness according to your desires (this and the following phrases are often pasted up). **tāi-kiet lī-chhī**, may this shop have great prosperity. **tāi-kiet tāi-lī**, id. **khai-tiong tāi-kiet**, id. **pêng-an tāi-kiet** (peace and great prosperity), small incense bags on which this is written. **liân-chiau kiet-kó**, may all be auspicious and happy (phrase used at marriages).

kiet (R. id.), (C. kit). **kiet-á**, a lime. **kim-kiet**, preserved limes. **soaⁿ-kiet-á**, a small wild shrub, not a lime at all.

kiet [R. name of a plant], (C. kit). **kiet-kēng**, a medicinal plant. **kiet-kéng**, id. **kiet-kíⁿ** (T. Cn.), id. (Platycodon ?).

kiet — **pì-kiet**, costiveness.

kiet (R. id., = col. kat), to form into a knot, lump, or mass; to join, as relationship or league; to sum up and balance; to wind up an affair; a sort of bond or security, as for good behaviour, or for closing a dispute; a certificate given by a mandarin to a man under his jurisdiction when appointed to any office; hard and strong, as a good rope.

kiet-liet, to form into a knot, mass, or league; to balance up; to wind up an affair, &c. **kiet-chiâⁿ**, to form into and become —, as in a relationship, &c. **kiet-tsòe chit-tè**, to form into one mass; to coagulate. **kiet ka-nn̄g-tè**, id. **kiet-bāng**, to make a net-work, esp. for a dress.

kiet-hun, to settle a marriage definitely. **kiet-chhin**, to arrange a marriage contract; to contract affinity (said of the relatives of the couple, or of the couple themselves). **kiet-tsòe ang-bó**, to become man and wife. **kiet-kau**, to associate with; to form a friendship. **kiet-kau pêng-iú**, id. **kau-kiet pêng-iú**, id. **kiet-pài**, to form the connection of sworn brothers, who look on each others' parents as their own. **kiet-pài hiaⁿ-tī**, such sworn brothers. **kiet-siā**, to make a literary society for writing essays. **kiet-tóng**, to form a clique or conspiracy for bad purposes. **kiet-oan**, to be at open enmity and feud. **kiet-oàn**, to cherish deep enmity in the heart.

kiet-hoat, the wife whom a bachelor marries first of all.

kiet-sūi, the ear of grain forming, after the flower is past. **kiet-ké-chí**, the fruit forming; to bear fruit. **kiet hoe-lúi**, to form flower buds or flowers.

kiet-sit, neatly and tightly tied or sewed up; real and certain, not empty pretence (said of words or an affair); also (R.), to bear fruit. **kiet-sok**, neat and tidy; neatly fastened up, as box, basket, parcel, &c.; not loose, as dress well fastened by girdle. **sok-kiet**, id.; said also of a house or room, small but neat and comfortable. **kiet-tēng**, strong; firm.

pa-kiet, skilful at managing matters; hard to get round; ingratiating one's self with influential persons (v. pa).

kiet-kó, final circumstances of a man, esp. as result of his life; to kill (v. kó). **kiet-kiók**, finished up, completed, as an affair. **kiet-àn**, to close up a case, by the parties signing a bond called "kiet." **kiet-tsñg**, the bond or deed that settles up a case. **kam-kiet**, a bond finally winding up a lawsuit; a bond signed by the people promising (to the government) to do or refrain from something. **pó-kiet**, a document giving security for a man, or promising to hold an arrangement final. **liên-hoân-kiet**, a bond of mutual security given by the people of a ward (v. hoân). **hâng-kiet**, a security given by a great privileged hong for the junk of another firm, which is required before the official papers are given to the junk. **chhut hâng-kiet**, to issue this bond. **tǹg hâng-kiet**, to stamp it with the seal of the hong. **tǹg-kiet**, id.

tsóng-kiet, the summing up and balancing of a whole account, as at the end of the year, or at the closing up of a business or affair or of whole set of accounts. **nî^{n}-kiet**, the balancing up at end of year. **gėh-kiet**, do., at end of month. **kiet-siàu**, to sum up and balance an account, as at the end of the month; to sum up and balance an entire account. **kiet tsóng-siàu**, to make up an account, as at the end of the year, or of a whole affair.

kiet-liú, the silk or cotton knob of a Chinese cap. **hiet-kiet**, the gum called dragon's blood. **toā-chih-kiet**, speaking with much difficulty or indistinctness, as from malformation of the tongue, or as in fever, &c.

kiėt [R. to exhaust; to exert to the utmost], too severe and exacting, as a master; bad for getting a livelihood, as a place. **ke-sū kan-kiėt**, very poor. **soa^{n} kêng, hái kiėt** (land and sea barren), very hard to make a living there.

chin-sim kiėt-lėk (R.), to exert one's self to the utmost. **kiėt-chīn sim-lėk** (R.), id.

kiėt (R. id.), the tyrant Kieh of the Hia dynasty, with whom it ended. **hā-kiėt**, id. **kiėt-tiū**, the two great tyrants, Kieh and Chow (v. tiū).

kiėt [R. eminent in talents or virtue; a hero], pleasant and intelligent, as a child. **hô-kiėt**, having great ability and magnanimity; clever, courageous, and disinterested. **kớ-kiėt**, very nice-looking and neat; well made and small, as man or article; useful and desirable (as thing), though not intrinsically precious; pleasant and intelligent, as child. **kớ-kiėt kớ-kiėt**, id.

kiėt (cf. khiėt, khiák). **phah kàu kiėt-kiėt-háu**, to make the blows ring on his skin, as in beating a boy.

kih, to pile up wood in a pile or stack, especially by laying down two pieces and then two above them at right angles, and so on: to pile up, as bricks, tiles, stones, &c., in a pile. **kih-lih--khí-lâi**, id. **kih chhâ-thah**, to pile up a pile or stack of timber.

kih gîm-kî^{n}, to build a long stone step along the wall of a house. **kih-chhiû^{n}**, to build up a wall with stone or brick.

kih [R. kek, a cackling sound]. **kih-kih-háu**, talking on so as to weary one. **kih-kih-kiò**, id. **hoan-kih-kā**, so indistinct that nothing can be made of it (v. kā).

kih — **kih-kih kiùh-kiùh**, to twitter, as a bird; to squeak, as a rat; to chatter, as children.

kih^{n} — **chhoán-kih^{n}-kà^{n}** (C.), panting very hard (v. chhoán).

kih^{n} — **kih^{n}-kih^{n} koáih^{n}-koáih^{n}**, sound, as of boards creaking. **kih^{n}-nih^{n} kėh^{n}-nėh^{n}**, sound of things breaking or rattling (v. kėh^{n}).

kim [R. now, at present, = col. kin]. **kim-mî^{n}**, to-night. **hiān-kim**, at present. **tong-kim**, id. **jî-kim** (R.), id. **chhú-jî-kim** (R.), id.

bák-kim, at present. **bák-kim, chî^{n} tsòe-lâng**, at present the only thing people count important about a man is wealth, not caring for justice or even relationship. **chiông-kim í-āu**, henceforward. **kim-sì tsòe, kim-sì siu**, recompense comes in this present life (v. sì).

kớ-kim, ancient and modern times. **óng-kớ lâi-kim** (R.), from of old till now. **kim put-tông-kớ**, the present cannot compare with the past. **tâm-kim soat-kớ**, to talk idly of things ancient and modern. **soat-kớ tâm-kim** (r.), id.

kim — **oá^{n}-kim-kơ-lėh**, the broken bottom of a bowl. **oá^{n}-kim-kơ-le** (T.), id.

kim — **ē-kim**, the lower support of a helm. **kim-sng**, the wooden bolts fixing it into the stern. **chhut-kim**, to get out of its groove, as helm striking the bottom (s. gold).

kim — **kim-chhēng** (esp. C.), lasting, as dress having much wear in it. **kim-iōng** (C.), do. of other things.

kim (R. id.), gold; idolatrous gilt paper; (some sorts of money); bright; shining; intently (as gazing); jars containing old bones; a surname (but many give "kim" as their surname, who are really of the "kim-tun" branch of the surname "ñg"); also (esp. in Hái-têng), to look angrily at a man.

sok-kim, a teacher's salary. **sin-kim**, wages (not salary). **phèng-kim**, money sent by bridegroom's parents to bride's parents. **bêng-kim**, good copper cash. **kim-pien** (Cn.), sort of large good cash (v. pien).

kiò-kim, to sound a gong to call the spirits to come, as when a junk goes out or in; or on the 1st and 15th of the month. **bêng-kim siu-kun**, to give the signal for retreat of army.

kim-tan, = sien-tan, the fabulous elixir of immortality. **sù-tāi kim-kong**, name of four great idols often at entrance of temples.

hông-kim, jars containing (or for containing) the bones of the dead. **kim-tāng**, id. **kim-táu**, id. **tâi kim-táu**, to bury bones in jars. **tsòng-kim**, id. **khang-kim**, empty jars for bones. **tâi khang-kim**, to bury these empty jars in a grave site (as if with bones) to prevent others getting the site.

lâm-jî chiok-hā, iú hông-kim, there is yellow gold beneath a man's leg (he does not like to be always kneeling). **kim kha-thâu-u**, seldom having to kneel

(v. u). **chin-kim put-phà^n-hó^n**, real gold does not fear the fire.

kim-téng, a brass button worn by small officials and by gentry. **kim-póng**, the rank of Tsin-sze (chìn-sū). **kim-pn̂g**, id. **kim-hoe**, tinsel flowers worn by a new graduate; Turkey opium (v. hoe).

chhien-kim (polite), your daughter. **sù-tsú chhien-kim, put-jû kàu-tsú it-gē**, better teach your son a trade than give him a thousand dollars.

kim-kiá^n, a very dear child, loved rather too much. **bān-kim-kiá^n**, heir of a wealthy family. **ná^n kim-ang-á** (like a golden image), said of son of rich parents, esp. if only child or much loved. **kim-tiàu-tháng**, said of a man who will not assist when asked. **kám-siā lí--ê kim-giên** (polite), thanks for your excellent words (often said in joke). **kim-liên**, small-bound feet of women. **kim-liēn**, a metal chain for suspending a pouch.

tēng hun-kim, to fix the angle at which a house or grave stands from one of the cardinal points. **hun-kim tsō-hiòng**, the geomantic direction of it. **hun-kim chē-hiù^n**, id. **hun-kim-soà^n**, the string with a cash at the end of it, used (along with the compass) in geomancy. **hun-kim-khit**, the peg used in the same operation. **hun-kim-á-tsoáh**, a very small divergence, as from a pattern, or from even regularity in a piece of work.

hun-kim, alloyed gold. **chiok-hun-kim**, pure gold. **chiok-hun kim-hiòh**, very fine gold in thin plates. **chiok-siâ^n-kim**, pure gold. **chiok-chhiah-kim**, id. **chhiah-kim**, id. **kē-kim**, gold much alloyed; very impure gold. **ké-kim**, false gold; imitation gold. **n̂g-kim**, yellow gold. **chhi^n-kim**, gold with a greenish hue, as Japanese gold.

o-kim, dark, as the skin of a man much in the sun; getting on well in the world; making a good deal of money. **o-kim-chhat**, fine black varnish.

kim-bīn, gilded or plated with gold. **pau-kim**, to plate thickly all over with gold by putting on a solid plate. **tō-kim**, to gild or plate another metal with gold very thinly (done by melting). **tō kim-tsúi**, do. still more thinly (not with real gold). **an-kim**, to gild with gold-leaf, as wood or earthenware. **siu^n-kim**, to inlay with gold. **lèk-kim**, to plate with gold by melting, as on silver or other metal.

tāi-kim-kok, the country of the Kin Tartars, who once ruled North China. **kim-soa^n**, a gold-producing country (said of Australia, California, and Borneo). **sóe-kim**, to wash gold out of sand.

kim-gûn, gold and silver; idolatrous paper representing gold and silver. **kim-gûn-tiàm**, a shop for selling idolatrous paper. **kim-gûn-hoe**, honeysuckle. **kim-pau-gûn**, the best sort of glutinous rice from Ankoi (said to take a whole year to ripen); infused as a medicine.

kim-tiá^n, a sort of censer or tripod for burning idolatrous paper. **kim-lô**, a furnace for burning it; a furnace for refining gold. **kim-láng**, a basket for holding that paper. **kim-tsoá**, idolatrous paper representing gold. **kim-chí^n**, id., yellow. **kim-khô**, bundles of it. **kim-thàh**, a pile of it. **kim-thah**, id.; also, name of a country (v. thah). **kim-iòh**, paint used for making idolatrous paper. **kim-iû**, a gold-coloured paint used to give the appearance of gilding (not for idolatrous paper). **kim-hiu^n-chek**, idolatrous paper, incense, and candles. **toā-kim**, large bundles of that paper burned at once. **jiàu^n-kim**, brass foil pasted on paper so as to look crumpled (idolatrous). **siū-kim**, idolatrous paper with the word "longevity" (siū) on it. **ìn-siū-kim**, to stamp that word on it. **ìn-kim**, to stamp idolatrous paper. **chih-kim**, to fold it. **chhat-kim pè-pòh**, to make it by painting and pasting. **sio-kim**, to burn it (v. sio).

kim-thâu, the gloss of new cloth, &c. **kim-kim**, bright; shining; smooth. **boâ-kim**, to polish or furbish bright. **kim siám-siám**, shining, as a polished surface. **kim siak-siak**, id. **kim siàk-siàk**, id. **kim-nà^n-sà^n**, id. (v. nà^n). **kim-iām-iām**, brilliant, like gold.

kim-kim-siòng, to look very intently or earnestly. **kim-kim-khoà^n**, id. **bák-chiu kim-kim**, eyes glancing; eyes very bright or looking very intently. **tiám-tiám kim**, very knowing; careful in business; hard to cheat.

kim-iù, powdered gold for making ornamental paper. **kim-soa**, gold-dust; a sort of fine sand. **kim-pòh**, tin-foil coloured to look like gold-leaf. **kim-mòh^n**, gold-leaf, true or false. **kim-hiòh**, thin plates of gold, much used as a portable private treasure, esp. by mandarins. **chheh-iàh-kim**, very thin plates of gold, much used for portable treasure. **chheh-iàp-kim**, id. **iû^n-phê-kim**, very strong well-gilt paper, used for making ornaments. **pán-kim**, strong stiff gilt-paper (for ornamental work) with the gilding very smooth.

kim-tiā^n, a gold ingot about four ounces; a bundle of idolatrous paper. **kim-tiâu**, a bar of gold about ten ounces. **kim-poàt-á**, a small gold coin about size of a sovereign. **kim hoan-á-thâu**, a larger sort.

kim-si-chiáu, a beautiful small yellow bird. **kim-hî**, gold or silver fish. **hé-kim-chhi^n**, fireflies. **kim-sîn**, the large blue-bottle fly (v. sîn). **kim-ku**, a very small beetle (v. ku).

kim-koe, the pumpkin. **kim-chhiok-hoe**, a beautiful yellow flower. **kim-hōng**, the balsam. **kim-eng**, the large, white, single rose (v. eng). **kim-tsó**, preserved limes. **kim-kiet**, id. **kim-chiam**, a flower and vegetable (v. chiam). **ut-kim-hiu^n**, a fragrant medicinal plant (v. ut). **pièn-tē-kim** (Cn.), a small white water-lily. **bé-tôe-kim**, a medicinal compound. **kim-kong-tāu**, sort of confection.

kím (Cn.), = A. gím, variegated or flowered silk.

kím (Cn.), to make game of.

kìm [R. to forbid; to imprison], to forbid; to interdict; to prohibit. **kìm-chí**, to prohibit. **kìm-chí**, a jailer; door-keeper of a prison (from "chí," a son). **kìm-siâ^n**, the innermost city in Pekin. **kìm-tiâu**, prohibitory proclamations on long narrow slips of paper. **kìm-iok**, a mutual agreement among the people of a place to forbid some practice. **kong-kìm**, id.

khu-kìm, to restrain a man by force; to hold in durance. **siû-kìm** (R.), to imprison. **kìm-ka^n**, to imprison; to keep in prison. **kìm-lòh-ka^n**, to imprison.

kìm-khī, to avoid a thing from medical or superstitious reasons (v. khi). **kìm-chhùi**, to forbid some sorts of food, in disease. **kìm-kháu-lī**, a severe disease of the bowels, which takes away appetite. **kìm-chhù**, superstitious prohibition of strangers entering a house (v. chhù). **kìm-tô**, to forbid the killing of animals, as in drought. **kìm kó-gák**, to forbid music, as for imperial mourning. **kìm-káng**, to forbid vessels sailing, or forbid export. **kìm-kô** (r.), to disable from taking degrees or office (v. kô). **kìm phái^n-chí^n**, to forbid the use of bad cash. **kìm-chhe^n** (C.),

厦英大辭典

villagers agreeing to prohibit the pasturing of cattle in the fields when near harvest-time: the agreement is made known and ratified by a play.

hoān-kìm, contraband; forbidden. **lē-kìm**, forbidden by the code of laws. **hōng-kìm**, to receive a prohibition or interdict from superior. **ûi-kìm**, to break a prohibition. **khui-kìm**, to take off a prohibition. **put-kìm, jî tsū-kìm**, to restrain one's self though not prohibited.

kīm (T.), to hold in the hand; to take in the hand. **kīm-béh**, to feel the pulse.

kīm-thn̂g, bô-sóe-chhiú (A.), extremely intimate with each other.

kīm (R. id.), wife of maternal uncle, or of wife's brother. **á-kīm**, id. **kīm-á** (of a man), wife of his wife's younger brother; (but of a woman), wife of her younger brother. **kīm-pô**, wife of maternal grandmother's brother; also said in scolding with a bad meaning. **kɵ-î kū-kīm**, aunts and their husbands; brothers of wife or mother, &c. (v. kɵ).

bú-kīm, mother's brother's wife. **bó-kīm** (C.), id. **bɵ́-kīm**, wife's brother's wife. **chhe-kīm**, id. **sòe-kīm**, wife's younger brother's wife. **toā-kīm**, wife's elder brother's wife; wife of oldest maternal uncle. **jī-kīm**, wife of second oldest maternal uncle.

kīm-piáu hiaⁿ-tī (T.), son of maternal uncle.

kin [R. kim, now; present]. **kin-á-jit**, to-day. **kin-ná-jit**, id. **kin-nîⁿ**, this year. **kin-toàⁿ** (r.), now (v. toàⁿ).

kin (C.) **kin-têng**, = A. kien-tōng, strongly made, as things.

kin (C.) **kin-tu**, = A. kun-tu, yet after all the same.

kin (C.), = A. kun, a root. **chhiông-pɛh-kin**, a short red snake found in fir-roots.

kin (C.), = A. kun, a napkin.

kin (C.), = A. kun, a catty.

kin (C.), = A. kun (R.), to follow.

kin (C.), = A. kun, a sinew; a nerve. **kin-nɛⁿ**, the small fibrous parts of the sinews or nerves (v. nɛⁿ).

kin (C.) **kin-kí**, = A. keng-kí, business, trade, or occupation.

kin (F.) **kin-chio**, = gêng-chio, the plantain.

kīn (C.), = A. tīn, to pour off, as pure water from sediment or muddy water, or as medicinal infusion, or as liquid from food.

kín [R. tight; urgent], fast; quick; prompt; tight; firmly tied. **put-chí-kín**, very quick; very tight. **kín-kín**, id.

kín-mɛ́ⁿ, quick. **koáⁿ-kín**, quick! to hasten. **pàng-kín-kiâⁿ**, to walk fast. **thàn-kín**, id. **pek-kín**, to urge on quickly, as a matter. **chhui-kín**, id. **kín-khoài**, easily done; quick. **kín-sèng**, quick-tempered. **kín-sèng-tē**, id. **kín-bâng-bâng**, in a tremendous hurry. **kín suh-suh**, very quick. **kín-bān**, quick and slow (v. bān). **kín-oān**, id. **kín-lâi**, come quick!

iàu-kín, important. **kín-iàu** (r.), id. (v. iàu). **kín-kip**, urgent and important; pressing, as want.

bô-táⁿ-kín, good-natured and pleasant to deal with; kind and considerate, not too exacting, as master; diligent, well-behaved, and pleasant to have in employment, as servant. **beh-siáⁿ-táⁿ-kín**, of what consequence is it? (said as in making light of a matter which we have asked and been refused).

chhùi kā kín-kín, teeth clenched very tight, as in a faint or near death. **kín-sin-á**, a close-fitting warm jacket.

kín (C.), = A. ún (R.), a worm. **tē-kín** (Tt.), a worm.

kín (C.) **kín-ná**, = A. gín-ná, a boy; a young lad.

kín [R. careful; circumspect; cautious]. **kín-sīn**, to be cautious, circumspect, or watchful against; to take great care against some danger. **giâm-kín**, rigidly careful; very strict. **khûn-kín**, diligent, careful, and laborious. **kín-kiuⁿ**, id.

kìn (R. koàn), sort of very thin cheap silk stuff, almost like silk-gauze. **péh-kìn**, white do. **hoe-kìn**, flowered do. **kìn-sìⁿ**, a fan made of paper pasted on it.

kīn [R. just barely]. **kīn-kīn**, just barely, but no more. **kīn-ū**, just barely so much or so many, but almost falling short. **kīn-ti kî-it, put-ti kî-jī**, knowing only a very small part, but not the important facts or principles of the matter.

kīn (C.), = A. kūn, near.

kīn (C.), = A. kiēn, the gizzard.

kiô [R. kiâu, name of a grain]. **kiô-béh**, buck-wheat.

kiô (R. kâ), the egg-plant; the brinjal. **kiô-sek**, a light-gray with a dash of lilac or of light-purple, darker than khɵ̀-hoe-sek. **n̂g-tsúi-kiô**, a poisonous solanaceous plant with large white fruit, used in medicine externally, for boils, &c. **n̂g-chhí-kiô**, id. **chhàu-kiô-á**, a solanaceous plant with small berries.

kiô (R. kiâu), a bridge. **kiô-so**, the piers of a bridge. **kiô-kha**, at the foot of the bridge.

oaⁿ-kiô, the wooden framework of a Chinese saddle. **to-kiô**, a bridge of knives used by sorcerers. **kè to-kiô**, to cross it. **tiàu-kiô**, a draw-bridge. **phû-kiô**, a floating-bridge; name of a stone-bridge at Chinchew, where originally there was a floating-bridge. **tah phû-kiô**, to make a floating-bridge. **chhâ-kiô**, a wooden-bridge; a wooden jetty on piers. **ún-ku-kiô**, a bridge having the roadway steep, but not necessarily arched.

phɵ-kiô, to make a bridge, or a great repair of one. **phɵ-kiô tsō-lō͘**, to make bridges and roads. **siu-kiô tsō-lō͘**, to repair bridges and make roads. **tsō-kiô**, to make a bridge (v. tsō).

kiô [R. tiâu, the tide]. **chhiu-kiô** (C.), great tides and floods in autumn.

kió (Cn.), = A. kɵ́ (R.), remissly; carelessly; illicit.

kió (Cn.) **kió-kí**, = A. kɵ́-kí, a medicinal plant (v. kí).

kió (Cn.), = A. kɵ́ (R.), a dog.

kiò (R. kiàu), to call; to name; to be named; to sound or make a noise. **saⁿ-kiò**, to rhyme. **saⁿ-kiò-ìn**, to call and answer; to rhyme (v. ìn).

kiû-kiò, to call upon, as in prayer. **kiò-thiⁿ**, to call on Heaven. **kiò-mn̂g**, to call out at a door to get it opened. **kiò-bô-mn̂g**, to call out, but get no one to open the door.

kiò-kim, to beat gongs, as several junks do at once when a junk is entering or leaving the harbour; done also on the 1st and 15th of the month. **kiò-kim kiò-kɵ́**, to beat drums and gongs inviting the spirits to offerings.

kiò kau-thòe, a ghost tempting a man to commit suicide, that it may get back to life (v. thòe). **khit-kúi kiò--khì**, said of a man formerly well-behaved, but now enticed to evil by bad men (v. kúi).

kiò-chhùi, a young boy or girl who is at our call, for work or messages. **chhī chit-ê, thang kiò-chhùi**, to bring up or hire a young boy or girl for messages or small bits of work. **sa^n-kiò-chhùi**, so far reconciled as to speak to one another. **chhe-kiò**, to order about and use for work, as a servant. **kiò-i-lâi**, call him here. **kiò-kang**, call men to do the work. **kiò-kiō**, to call a sedan.

hiàm-kiò, to call out loud to a person. **âu-kiò**, to shout very loud; to yell. **háu-kiò**, to cry out, as under pain (as child), or under a strong sense of wrong. **gâu háu-kiò**, said of a man constantly talking and troubling people, or of a child crying when beaten, or of a pig or dog making a constant noise. **kiò-hoa^n-hí**, to call out (*e.g.* giving orders) for the mere pleasure of it. **kiò-koe--ê**, blind beggars who call in the streets, especially at night. **kiò m̄-ká^n**, to call out, "I'll not do it again," when beaten. **kiò-loa** (T.), = A. khơ-toa^n, hen cackling before laying an egg. **lèh-lèh-kiò**, sound of thunder quick and loud. **khiét-khiét-kiò**, scraping sound of a dipper or ladle emptying a jar or rice-boiler nearly empty; (so with many such phrases of noise).

phien-kiò, to give too low a title, *e.g.* calling one's father "á-chek," as from superstitious motives. **miâ^n-kiò**, his name is —. **lí-kiò sím-mih^n**, what are you called? **lí-kiò sím-mih^n-miâ^n**, what is your name?

kiō (R. kiāu), a sedan-chair. **chit-téng-kiō**, one sedan. **chit-pé-kiō**, id. **bé-kiō**, horses and sedans.

í-kiō, a small chair for children, often made with wheels. **tek-í-kiō**, id. **phah í-kiō**, two men crossing hands and so carrying another. **phah-chhiú-kiō**, id. **chē teng-kiō**, to sit in a sedan full of nails, as sorcerer.

lién-kiō, an idol's sedan. **sió-kiō**, a sedan with two or three bearers. **toā-kiō**, sedan with four or more bearers, used by mandarins and high graduates. **sì-kiō**, sedan with four bearers. **âng-kiō**, a bridal sedan. **hoe-kiō**, id. **chhái-kiō**, id. **hièn-kiō**, large sort of sedan used by high mandarins (v. hièn). **thoa-tóe-kiō**, a sedan so long that the feet can be comfortably rested inside. **se-thang-kiō**, sedan with gauze windows. **hê-thâu-kiō**, a sedan returning empty (can be hired cheaper). **kè-soa^n-kiō**, a paper sedan set outside the door of a person newly died and not yet buried.

kng-kiō, to carry a sedan. **giâ-kiō**, to carry an empty sedan, as one man does. **phah chit-téng-kiō**, to get ready a sedan. **pák chit-téng-kiō**, to engage a sedan for a long journey, as for several days. **kiò-kiō**, to call a sedan. **kè-kiō**, to hire a sedan. **chhià^n-kiō**, id. **chē-kiō**, to sit in a sedan; to travel by sedan. **jip-kiō**, to enter a sedan. **chiū^n-kiō**, the bride beginning the journey (in sedan) from her parent's house to the husband's house, on the marriage-day.

liáh-kiō, to take hold of the pole of a sedan to help the bearers to get it on their shoulders. **tsah-kiō**, to steady the poles of a sedan, as attendants. **chiáng-kiō**, to hold the poles of the sedan of a superior officer. **khî^n-kiō**, to lay hold of a mandarin's chair in order to present a petition. **noâ^n-kiō**, id.

kiō-kha, sedan-bearers; chair-bearers. **kiō-hu**, do. for mandarins. **kiō-pan**, mandarin's company of bearers. **kiō-gî**, sedan hire, as for teacher. **kiō-kǹg**, poles of sedan. **kiō-ta^n**, the cross-bars between the poles, which rest on the shoulder; but (C.) the separate small poles used in a sedan, with four or eight bearers. **kiō-táu**, the place below the seat, for holding small things. **kiō-lî**, the blind or curtain of a sedan. **kiō-tiù^n**, the curtains at front of mandarin's sedan. **kiō-ûi**, the screen hung up before the legs. **kiō-jiók**, sedan cushion. **kiō-thâu**, knob on top of sedan. **kiō-liú**, id. **kiō-thang**, window of sedan. **kiō-pè**, back of the chair in the sedan. **kiō-pòe** (C.), id.

kiō (C.) **lơ̄-kiō**, = A. lơ-giō, a sort of leek.

kiơ^n, in several tones; (C. esp. P.), = A. kiu^n.

kioh, a final enclitic particle. **tsai--kioh**, to know; knowing that. **m̄-tsai--kioh**, I don't know. **kóng--kioh**, saying that —; an expletive phrase, sometimes gathering up the thread of what was said before, but often a meaningless expletive. **bòh-kioh**, how then can —? a phrase following "liên," or "siōng-chhiá^n" in the previous clause (v. bòh).

kioh [R. kiok, the foot], an individual, especially said of coolies and actors.

lùt-chhiú lùt-kioh, to bare one's arms and legs. **hò-chhiú hò-kioh**, to toss about one's arms and legs, as in disputing, reproving, or showing displeasure. **chhit-chhiú poeh-kioh**, touching other people's persons or things in a too familiar way. **goá-m̄-sī chhit-chhiú poeh-kioh**, I am not able for so much work as you put upon me.

koe-kioh, a small shell-fish shaped like a turtle's foot.

chièn-kioh, good at fighting, as soldier; skilful at work, as workman. **kioh-siàu**, number of hands employed in some work; number of actors, esp. full number for a play. **hó-kioh-siàu**, good at work, as workman. **kúi--ê kioh-siàu**, how many actors? **tsng sím-mih^n kioh-siàu**, what character does he act in the play?

kioh-sek, a man's appearance, as indicating his trade, profession, &c. **m̄-sī kioh-sek**, unfit for the position, work, or business entrusted to him. **sím-mih^n kioh-sek**, what employment or position has he? in what way is he fit to be employed? **tsng sím-mih^n kioh-sek**, what character in the play does he act? **tsng seng ê-kioh-sek**, acts the part of a man in the play. **m̄-sī seng-lí ê-kioh-sek**, he does not look like a man that is a merchant.

hì-kioh, an actor (v. hì). **thiú-kioh**, the clown in a play.

tsòe-kioh, to be a coolie, porter, or rough labourer. **tsúi-kioh**, a water-carrier. **kioh-hu**, a coolie; a man who carries burdens, or coarse heavy work. **kang-kioh**, id. **kioh-á-kha**, id. **kioh-á-kang**, id.; said also of the men who carry a coffin. **chhơ-kioh**, a coolie for rough work. **tsng chhơ-kioh**, to act the part in a play of a common soldier or coolie. **tsng iù-kioh**, to act the part of a polite or wealthy man. **sai-hū-kioh**, an apprentice just turning into a journeyman.

kiok [R. the foot, = col. kioh, kha], (C. kiak). **lióng-kiok tiâu-thien**, fallen on the back with feet to the sky. **sam-kiok-phòng**, a sort of gambling with cards. **it-kiok thiàu liông-bûn**, the one-footed man enters the palace (said in joke of a lame man, in allusion to a lame native of Quemoy who became a high mandarin).

kiok (C.) **kiok-hoa**, = A. kek-hoe, the chrysanthemum.

kiok (P.), = kek, to drive away.

kiok (P.), = kek, to drown.

kiok [R. to bend the body]. **kiok-kiong**, to

厦英大辭典

make a bow, when the hands have been put together. **siang-kha khiā-tsôe, siang-chhiú kiok-kiong,** standing with feet even and making a respectful bow.

kiȯk [R. a game; an affair, especially in reference to its completion or suitableness; an arsenal or public office; an association or company; mean or poor, = col. kėk], very poor.

siáu-kiȯk, niggardly and mean, as man; made too small, as a thing. **sió-kiȯk,** scant in size, as a dress.

bô-kiȯk, dull and uninteresting; not at all pleasing; lonely, out of the way, and dull, as a residence; feeling dull, lonely, or troubled with ennui; feeling somewhat ashamed, as at failing to get a request, or at being found fault with. **toaⁿ-kiāⁿ bô-kiȯk,** walking alone, and so feeling dull and wearisome. **kə-toaⁿ chit-ê, bô-kiȯk,** all alone, so as to feel ennui and dulness. **ū-kiȯk,** having power to please and interest, as novel, beautiful, or curious things. **ū-kiȯk-sè,** getting on better now, as business or lawsuit that formerly was not getting on well. **ū-kiȯk-bīn,** id.

oân-kiȯk, fully settled, as an affair. **kiet-kiȯk,** to finish up, as an affair or discussion. **sìⁿ-miāⁿ kiet-kiȯk,** term of life ended. **bōe-soah-kiȯk,** cannot be wound up or settled, as a troublesome dispute or feud. **bô-liáu-kiȯk,** cannot be brought to an end, as quarrel which we wish settled.

jip-kiȯk, brought so far as to be suitable for the purpose (good or bad) intended. **tsòe kàu-jip-kiȯk,** to make it so as to fit for the purpose. **ín--i jip-kiȯk,** to lead him into some bad company, gang, or conspiracy.

kiong [R. id., = col. keng], (also C., = A. keng, a palace; a temple), a palace.

hông-kiong, an imperial palace; the imperial residence. **ông-kiong,** a royal palace. **kiong-tiān,** imperial residence and audience hall. **bêng-kiong** (R.), the heavenly palace of the gods.

kiong-kàm, imperial eunuchs. **kiong-ngê,** female slaves of the empress, &c., in the harem. **kiong-ngê bí-lú,** imperial concubines and female slaves of empress, &c. **kiong-lú,** women of the imperial harem (slaves of empress, &c.), excepting a few who are specially selected for favour.

kiong-teng, lanterns used at marriages (like those used at temples), given by bride's friends to bridegroom.

iû-kiong, imperial conjugal intercourse. **ūi-chhun-kiong,** to draw lascivious pictures.

chhut-kiong, to go to stool.

báng-kiong (C.), = A. báng-keng, a portable folding mosquito curtain.

kiong (C.), = A. keng, soup. **thiau-kiong,** = A. thng-si, a spoon for soup.

kiong [R. rigid like a corpse], (C. kiang). **kiong-si,** a corpse in a coffin left long in a shed or temple unburied; supposed to be covered with white hair; fond of chasing, catching, and killing passers-by.

kiong [R. frontier or boundary of country], (C. kiang). **sin-kiong,** the distant north-west frontiers of the empire, about Ili and Turkestan.

kiong [R. to respect; to venerate; respectful; courteous]. **kiong-kèng,** to venerate; reverential. **kiong-hí,** to congratulate; congratulatory salutation. **kiong-hō** (R.), to make congratulations and send presents on special occasions.

kiong-chhin-ông, Prince Kung.

kiong [R. the body]. **kiok-kiong,** to make a bow (v. kiok).

kiong [R. to provide; to supply; to offer; to give evidence, = col. keng], (also C., = A. keng, verbal evidence in court).

kiong-kip, to supply with food, as a teacher or guest. **ū-kiong-kip,** to have one's food as well as salary, as a teacher.

chhoân-kiong (C.), = A. thoân-keng, the interpreter at a mandarin's office. **kháu-kiong** (C.), = A. kháu-keng, verbal evidence or confession, &c., before a mandarin.

kiong [R. name of a plant], (C. khiong). **chhoan-kiong,** a medicine used for strengthening the blood; comes from Sze-chuen (Tormentilla?). **kui-kiong chiok-tē,** this drug, along with tong-kui, pėh-chiok, and siȯk-tē.

kiông [R. violent; overbearing; strong; superior], (C. kiâng). **kiông-kiông,** violent; fierce; overbearing. **kiông-hiong** (R.), fierce; violent. **kiông-hiong kėk-ok,** very powerful, wicked, and dangerous. **kiông-pō** (R.), oppressive; tyrannical. **sái-kiông,** to act in a violent overbearing manner; to act oppressively and injuriously, as a man who has strong influence at his back. **sái-kiông-liông,** id.

kiông-jiȯk, the powerful and the weak; the strong and the defenceless (v. jiȯk). **kiông-pâng,** a powerful branch or family of a clan. **kiông-pâng ngīⁿ-kak,** specially influential and powerful, as a man belonging to the most powerful part of the most powerful branch.

kiông-tō (r.), a robber; a highwayman (from "tō," a robber). **kiông-tō beh,** doggedly determined on it, so that no entreaties or reasonings will move him (from "tō," road; doctrine). **kiông-tō m̄,** doggedly refusing.

ko-kiông, very strong or skilful, especially of physical strength or skill. **hoat-lėk ko-kiông,** the power of the idol's charm is very great. **bú-gē ko-kiông,** very skilful at military arts and exercises. **pún-sū ko-kiông,** very skilful, esp. at boxing and military exercises.

kiông-sû, doggedly refuse to admit fault or mistake. **kiông-kiû,** to beseech very urgently. **kiông-khit,** to beg money very importunately, as beggar. **kiông-tsoán,** id. **kiông-oaiⁿ--lâng,** to extort money from a man, as by threatening a false accusation. **kiông-pek,** to urge a man violently (with great pressure) to do something, so as to compel him. **kiông-kiông-kah,** to compel, as by commands or threats. **kiông-kah--i,** id. **kiông-tê,** to plot and injure by overwhelming influence. **kiông-chiàm,** to usurp. **kiông-pà,** id.

kiông-pak, to strip and rob of clothes. **kiông-kiap,** to rob forcibly (v. kiap). **kiông-chhiúⁿ,** id. **kiông-kòng,** housebreaking. **kiông-liȧh,** to take captive, as in a feud, or as robbers. **kiông-kan,** rape; to ravish.

kiông [R. limit; to exhaust; poor, = col. kêng, khêng]. **bô-kiông-chīn,** without limit or end (v. chīn). **kè kiông,** all his plots come to nothing.

kiông-kip, very pressing, as poverty or danger. **chin-kiông,** very poor and miserable. **pîn-kiông,** very poor and miserable. **oȧt-kan, oȧt-khiáu, oȧt pîn-kiông,** the more crafty and cunning he becomes the more poor and wretched.

kióng [R. to join one's hands]. **kióng-chhiú,**

to join one's own hands and shake them in making a Chinese bow.

kióng [R. to force; to compel; by change of tone from "kiông," violent], (C. kiáng). **bién-kióng**, to force; to compel. **bién-kióng, sêng tsū-jiên**, after having with great difficulty got one's self to do it, it becomes natural. **áu-kióng**, to urge another violently or very urgently to do as we wish. **kiáu-kióng** (R.), doing a thing of set purpose in an unreasonable, absurd, or unnatural way, knowing it to be quite different from what it ought to be.

kióng [R. kiong, kióng, = col. kéng], a surname.

kiōng [together with, = col. kāng, kā], taken together. **háp-kiōng**, taken altogether; the whole amount or sum total is. **lóng-kiōng**, id. **thong-kiōng**, id. **kè-kiōng**, id.; in total. **kiōng-kè**, id. **tông-pau kiōng-jú**, having the same mother and fed by the same milk; generally means having the same father and mother.

kip [R. hasty; urgent; in extremity]. **tiòh-kip**, in very great haste; not willing to wait a moment, as as in some very urgent matter. **tiòk-kip**, id. **kióng-kip**, very urgent and pressing, as poverty, or as imminent danger. **gûi-kip**, very dangerous, urgent, and pressing, as disease or danger. **kín-kip**, urgent, important, and pressing, as wants or business. **kín-kip-sū**, very urgent matters. **kín-kip-chèng**, a very sudden and dangerous disease, *e.g.* cholera. **kip-kip, jû lùt-lēng**, very swift, like the demon of thunder; words written on Tauist charms, to show that they are speedily efficacious; said also figuratively of anything to be done in great haste, *e.g.* money to be paid to a poor man in great need of it.

kip-kè, diligent.

kiù-kip, to relieve urgent distress or severe sickness; to save from pressing danger. **chiu-kip** (R.), to give alms to a man in want. **lîm-kip**, in very urgent want or danger, that must be speedily relieved or put right, if at all; come to a crisis, as a case just going to be heard by a mandarin.

kip-sio, a small thin flat-bottomed earthen kettle for warming things quickly. **kip-sèng-chí**, balsam seed.

kip [R. a degree in rank; a head, = col. khip]. **siú-kip**, a head cut off (said in speaking of the number beheaded).

phín-kip, rank of a mandarin. **kàng-kip**, to degrade in rank. **ka-kip**, to elevate in rank, with or without office. **ka-hu-kip**, to bestow mere titular or brevet rank. **seng-kip**, to rise in rank and office. **liên-seng saⁿ-kip**, raised three degrees of rank in very rapid succession, *e.g.* in a month or two. **thiàu-kip-seng**, promoted several degrees at once.

kip [R. to bestow]. **kip-pâi**, to give the papers, as to a ship. **kip-chiò**, id.; also certain official documents, as diplomas, licences, &c. (v. chiò). **kip-sài**, = bú-phoàⁿ, an assistant of the (sêng-hông) tutelary god of a city.

kiong-kip, to supply with food, as teacher (v. kiong). **chhut siúⁿ-kip**, to issue a proclamation offering a reward for the apprehension of a criminal. **kip-siúⁿ**, to give that reward.

kip [R. to arrive at; to reach to]. **î-kip**, and also in addition; and even — too. **put-kip**, not sufficient; to be inferior to; not up to the mark; faulty by defect. **put-kip--i**, inferior to him; not up to him. **ì-sióng put-kip**, unexpectedly; beyond expectation.

kip-sî, coming at the fitting or needed time. **kip-sî-hō͘**, rain at the due season when needed. **kip-kàu hit-sî**, when the time came (only of the past). **kip-chì kàu-hit-sî**, id.

sam-kip-tē, the highest three of the new Han-lin graduates (v. tē).

kip [R. name of a plant]. **péh-kip**, a very poisonous medicinal plant, said to preserve from moths; used also as a glue.

kit (C.), = A. kiet, auspicious; fortunate.

kit (C.), = A. kiet, a lime.

kit (= khit). **kit-kit**, boiled very thick, and nearly dry, as rice. **khó-kit-kit**, very thick, as rice, or as boiled preserves.

kiu [R. kiû, sort of dragon; to wriggle]. **thô͘-kiu**, = thô͘-sún, an edible worm found in the sea.

kiu (cf. kiù), to shrink, as man, or as cloth. **kiu-kiu**, shrinking up; drawing up one's arms and legs, as in cold weather; drawing one's self into a heap. **kiu-liu**, id. **kiu--tsáu**, to draw back from an affair, as when it becomes dangerous. **kiu-kiu ngóeh-ngóeh**, shrinking and frightened appearance. **kiu-kóeh**, very much afraid to meddle with a matter or to spend a cash; having a frightened, servile, cringing manner in the presence of a superior or of a powerful man. **kiu-kiu kóeh-kóeh**, id., especially cringing and frightened in manner. **kiu-köeh** (Cn.), naturally high-shouldered or shrugged up, as shoulders (v. köeh).

kiu-thâu-tiàm, to keep out of the way so as to avoid meeting a man, or to avoid responsibility. **kha kiu--khí-lâi**, legs drawn up. **kiu-kha teh-chē**, sitting with legs drawn up. **kiu-kha**, to draw back from what we had promised to do or were committed to. **kiu-kha-tiàm**, to keep out of the way, as to avoid responsibility, &c. **kiu-kha kiu-chhiú**, legs and arms drawn up, as with cold or illness; not venturing to take responsibility; very quiet, with frightened appearance, in the presence of a superior. **kiu-chhiú**, to draw one's arm out of the wide sleeve below the dress, as in cold weather.

lun--cheh, kiu--cheh (lit. stretching and contracting), half-willing and half-unwilling; extremely cautious and unsettled in purpose; very much afraid to take either course decidedly. **lun--chit-ē, kiu--chit-ē**, id. **kiu--cheh, lun--cheh**, id. **lun-lun kiu-kiu**, id. **chhun--cheh, kiu--cheh**, id. (v. chhun).

kiû [R. to beseech; to seek for], to pray; to pray to; to beseech. **kî-kiû**, to pray; to beseech. **kiû-khit**, to beg for. **khit-ai kiû-lîn**, to beg hard for a favour to one's self because of distressed condition. **khún-kiû**, to beseech earnestly. **kiông-kiû**, to beseech with great urgency. **pín-kiû**, to beseech by a written petition to a superior official. **kiû-kiò**, to pray and cry to; to make very earnest request. **kiû-hē**, to vow and pray. **kiû-poe**, to ask direction by the divining blocks. **kiû-thiⁿ pài-tōe**, to worship and pray to Heaven and Earth. **iú-kiû pit-èng**, if there be prayer, it will be answered (written on idol shrines, &c.)

kiû-chhin, to be looking out for a wife for one's son or junior relative. **kiû miâⁿ-siaⁿ**, to seek for fame. **lún-khì kiû-tsâi**, to restrain one's anger for the sake of gain.

kiû (R. id.), a ball (interchanged with the following word).

phah-kat-kiû, all tangled.

海上絲綢之路文獻集成 科技與文化編

phah-kiû, to play at ball with the hand. **that-kiû**, to play at ball with the foot.

chhì-kiû, a straw ball, stuck full of sharp points, with which sorcerers or fakeers (tâng-chí) lash themselves. **chhì-kiû-á**, round thorny wild fruits.

siù-kiû-teng, a round lantern with figures on it, made to roll along the ground when lighted. **siù-kiû-hoe**, a plant with white flowers tipped with red, much grown as a shade from the sun. **phau siù-kiû**, to throw the embroidered ball, said to have been a way in which a high mandarin's daughter (in ancient times) chose a husband.

kiû [R. a ball, especially of precious stone, which is the radical; often interchanged with the previous word], a bunch, as of grapes.

tē-kiû, a terrestrial globe; also a triangular mark, like a ball, at which mounted archers shoot while riding past.

liû-kiû, the Loo-choo islands.

kiû (R. id.) **kiû-siû**, an enemy.

kiú — **chhiah-kiú**, a small round fish (v. chhiah).

kiú [R. long, as to time, = col. kú]. **tiông-kiú**, lasting long, as a situation or office. **bān-liân kiú-oán**, lasting for ever. **put-kiú**, before long. **sîn put-kiú-thêng** (a spirit does not stop long), said of a man waiting a very short time.

kiú [R. nine, = col. káu]. **it-kiú thàn**, to gain one-ninth of profit. **kiú-kui soàn-hoat**, the rules of arithmetic by the abacus (v. kui). **kiú-liû**, all sorts of priests, nuns, sorcerers, &c. (v. liû). **kiú-liân-khoân**, the Chinese puzzle, made with rings and rods. **kiú-tsoân tōe-ē**, the world of spirits. **kiú-bûn thê-tok**, the military governor of Pekin. **kiú-liông** (R.), nine dragons (v. liông).

kiù (R. id.), to save; to deliver. **kiù-hē**, to assist out of great danger (v. hē). **kiù--ah**, help! help! **chín-kiù** (R.), to deliver.

kiù-kip, to save from very pressing danger. **kiù-khó kiù-lān**, to save from calamities (said especially of Kwan-yin). **kiù-hé**, to extinguish a conflagration. **kiù-hoa-hé**, id. **oán-súi lân-kiù kūn-hé**, help far off is of no use.

kiù-miāⁿ, to save life. **kiù sìⁿ-miāⁿ**, id. **kiù-i-oàh**, to save his life. **kiù-kà**, to save the emperor's life. **kiù-sè**, to save the world. **kiù-sè-tsú**, Saviour of the world. **kiù-tsú**, saviour. **kiù-chhiⁿ**, one who delivers us from pressing danger (v. chhiⁿ). **phoà-kó kiù-géh**, a broken drum may save the moon (from eclipse); don't despise a broken thing or a man who seems useless. **tsō-sī put-kiù**, to sit and look without giving any help to one in danger.

kiù [R. to investigate to the bottom]. **kiù-khàm**, to make minute inquiry into a matter; to investigate thoroughly. **káng-kiù** (r.), id. **kiù-pān**, to take action, investigate, and settle judicially. **kiù-tui**, to take vigorous action to recover stolen property, as mandarin. **kun-kiù**, to compel a man to appear by legal action, especially by strong measures against his relatives, &c. (v. kun).

kiù-kèng, in fine; yet after all (v. kèng). **kiù-kí-jiân**, but according to the real state of matters, as found on examining into the facts of the case. **kiù-kí-sit**, id.

kiù (cf. kiu), having a wrinkled look; to shrink, as cloth; to shrink with fear, as a man. **kiù-kiù**, having a wrinkled surface, as face, either naturally or from age. **kiù-liù**, to shrink, as cloth, or as man through fear. **kiaⁿ--chit-ē kàu-kiù-kiù**, limbs drawn up and shaking with fear.

kiù-soàⁿ, a sort of velvet.

kiù (R. kiu). **kiù-kat**, to get entangled, as a string.

kiù — **kiù-kiù-jióng**, noisy brawling. **kiù-kiù-háu**, to talk on in a grumbling discontented way.

kiū [R. old; former, = col. kū]. **i-kiū**, as formerly; as before. **jêng-kiū** (R.), id.

kiū [R. a maternal uncle, = col. kū]. **kok-kū**, a brother of the empress.

kiū (R. id.), a coffin containing a corpse. **koan-kiū**, id. **chit-khu-kiū**, one coffin containing a dead body.

kiū [R. a fault; to blame]. **kui-kiū**, to charge with a fault or crime, either truly or falsely.

kiuⁿ (in all the tones and words, C. kioⁿ, especially in P.)

kiuⁿ (R. kiong), ginger; ginger-root. **kiuⁿ-bú**, hard dry ginger-root (much used for medicine). **kiuⁿ-bú-tê**, infusion of it. **kiuⁿ-bú-thn̂g**, a small square confection made of sugar and ginger. **kiuⁿ-si**, ginger cut into thin strips. **kiuⁿ-ko**, preserved ginger (large pieces in syrup). **bêng-kiuⁿ**, very good preserved ginger. **chiùⁿ-kiuⁿ**, ginger in a sort of sauce (v. chiùⁿ). **chhò-kiuⁿ**, a mixture of vinegar, ginger, and sugar.

pû-kiuⁿ, to roast ginger on burning charcoal so as to char the outside; ginger thus treated used in medicine. **hek-kiuⁿ**, ginger-root burned into charcoal (medicinal). **kan-kiuⁿ**, ginger-root dried very thoroughly (medicinal). **chhiⁿ-kiuⁿ**, raw ginger-root (not prepared any way, so called when prescribed as medicine. **chí-kiuⁿ**, young esculent shoots of ginger. **chíⁿ-kiuⁿ**, id. **tsúi-kiuⁿ** (Cn.), id.

kiuⁿ-n̂g, turmeric (rad. curcumae), dark-yellow with a tinge of brown. **chhiū-kiuⁿ**, a sort of parasitic fern. **hoan-kiuⁿ**, red pepper. **hoan-kiuⁿ-chiùⁿ**, the sauce called "chiùⁿ" seasoned with red pepper. **pê-kiuⁿ**, a medicinal herb (much used for adulterating tea). **pê-kiuⁿ-tê**, an infusion of its leaves just drank like ordinary tea. **pê-kiuⁿ-thâu**, its roots (used medicinally). **pê-kiuⁿ-tāu**, a sort of pea (used for a medicinal infusion).

kiuⁿ [R. chiong], a small animal like a stag, with tusks like a hog, found abundantly near Yung-chun (éng-chhun); counted very good eating. **kiuⁿ-á**, id. **soaⁿ--nihⁿ, chià-ko kiuⁿ; hái--nihⁿ, bé-ka chhiuⁿ**, the best eating of land and sea animals are these —.

kiuⁿ (R. kiong). **chhiah-kiuⁿ**, a small brownish cricket, as distinguished from the black sort. **chhiah-kiuⁿ-á**, id. **chhiah-kiuⁿ--ê**, id.

kiuⁿ — **chiūⁿ-kiuⁿ**, the roof of the mouth; the palate. **ē-kiuⁿ**, the part of the mouth between the tongue and the lower teeth.

kiuⁿ [R. kiong, a bridle]. **bé-kā-kiuⁿ**, the bit of a bridle.

bé-kiuⁿ (T.), a shuttle-shaped fish.

kiuⁿ [R. keng, a thorn]. **kiuⁿ-á-chhâ**, a sort of hard wood.

kiuⁿ — **kín-kiuⁿ**, active and diligent. **kiuⁿ-khíⁿ**, very diligent at work; not readily getting tired or stopping.

kiūⁿ (R. kiōng), disobedient; obstinate; dogged; intentionally contrary to others; (rather).

29

kiū^n-peh-nì^n, to force one's self to act. **kiū^n-nè^n-kóng** (C.), to talk very big; to brag. **kiū^n-kut**, obstinately or stoically refusing to admit pain or weariness, *e.g.* forcing ourself to work at what is too hard work for us; wearing little dress in cold weather; or as a man who is poor, but puts on the appearance of better circumstances. **kiū^n-phiah**, doggedly opposing others; fond of acting opposite to others' wishes. **kiū^n-chhùi**, doggedly refusing to admit error even when it has brought us into trouble, or events have proved it. **chhùi kiū^n**, id., or not admitting fear, though really very much afraid. **chhùi kiū^n, kha-chhng nńg**, talking boldly, but really much afraid and powerless. **chiáh-kiū^n**, intentionally taking the very opposite course from what others wish or advise. **kéh-kiū^n**, obstinately refusing to obey lawful authority; disputing doggedly with a superior. **kùn-kiū^n**, id., obstinate in wrong. **kùn-kiū^n, phah ke-ē**, if you do not submit I will beat you still more.

khah-kiū^n hit-hō, yet it is better than that sort, though barely tolerable. **khah-kiū^n kè-hit-hō**, id. **khah-kiū^n-i**, after all better than he (the only other alternative), though not so good as could be wished. **khah-kiū^n toà-teh-chē**, it is better than sitting idle, though by no means a profitable employment. **siók-siók-hiàu, khah-kiū^n khiàm-siàu**, better even to sell at a loss than to be in debt.

kiū^n (T.) **kiū^n-soe**, = sàu-soe, a coarse bamboo brush.

kiuh (cf. koeh). **kiuh-siù-á**, a small dagger, as for assassination (v. siù).

kiuh — **sng-kiuh-kiuh**, very sour. **nńg-kiuh-kiuh**, soft, as dough (cf. kiùh).

kiuh (= kiù, cf. kiùh, chiuh). **kiuh-kiuh-háu**, talking on when one should be quiet, as boy or inferior.

kiùh (cf. khiùh, kiuh, chiùh). **nńg-kiùh-kiùh**, soft, as dough.

kiùh (cf. kiuh, chiuh). **kiùh-kiùh-háu**, chirping of a bird or squeaking of a rat; rumbling sound in one's belly. **kih-kih kiùh-kiùh**, squeaking or twittering (v. kih).

kng (R. kong), (C. kui^n), light; brightness; shining; glossy; polished; smooth; bare; empty; naked. **kng-kng**, do., only as adjective.

êng-kng, glory. **chhiú^n bīn-chêng-kng**, to try to put a good face on matters, though only making it worse at the last, *e.g.* borrowing when hopelessly in debt.

kng-liāng, lucidly transparent, as crystal. **thang-kng**, fully understanding a matter; bright and cheery, as a well-lighted house. **kng-thang**, do. do.; also, having the threads too far apart, as inferior cloth. **bák-kng ê-lâng**, a man who can see; not blind.

kng-iām, brilliant, as a flame. **kng-chhiū^n**, shining brightly, as a lamp; bright and cheerful-looking, as a room or house. **chiò-kng**, to shine. **nà^n-kng**, to glitter; dazzling. **kng sih-sih**, exceedingly bright and glittering. **jit-kng**, daylight. **thi^n kng**, dawn (daylight in early morning). **thi^n beh-kng**, early dawn. **thi^n chiah-chhím-kng**, just at dawn. **thi^n phú-phú-kng**, dawn (v. phú).

kng-si^n, smooth and clean, as skin, or as other surfaces. **kng-koeh**, smooth, as a surface. **kng-tsñg**, smooth and even, as a dress, or as the surface of a wall. **kng-kút**, very smoothly polished, as a surface (v. kút). **kng khút-khút**, quite smooth and bare, as tree, hill, head, &c.; without money or relatives (v. khút). **chit-bé kng-thiâu-thiâu**, very poor; quite naked. **kng-khō-khō**, naked, or having only on short drawers; having no relatives alive. **kng lìn-lìn**, having no near relatives alive. **kng liu-liu**, quite bare and naked. **kng liù-liù**, quite bare, as tree without leaves, or as forehead without hair; naked (without any clothes at all); having no relatives. **kng-thâu**, having no hat or cap on; bare-headed. **liù-kng-thâu**, id. **siang-bīn-kng**, smooth on both sides.

thn̄g-kng, to glaze, as pottery. **thǹg kng-kng**, to strip (one's self) naked. **pak kng-kng**, to strip (another) naked, as in robbing a man even of his clothes. **sø kng-kng**, all taken away, as by mandarins or by thieves, &c. **so-kng**, to rub smooth.

kng [R. kong, hard, firm, unyielding]. **kim-kng** (T.), = A. kim-kong-hút, name of an idol. **kim-kng-iâ** (T.), id. **kim-kng hō-sîn** (Cn.), several idols usually named together (v. hø, "to guard"). **kim-kng táh sió-kúi** (Cn.), said in warning a man of little power or influence to avoid quarrelling with a powerful man.

kng [R. kong, work, labour, = col. kang]. **ah-kng**, a ship's carpenter (often written as the next word].

kng (R. kong), to carry on a pole between two men or more; to carry, as a sedan, by two or more bearers. **kng-kiō**, to carry a sedan. **kng-lién**, to carry an idol's sedan. **kng-koh**, to carry an idolatrous ornamental platform (v. koh). **kng sím-mih^n-lâng**, who is in the sedan you are carrying? **kng-khui**, to move a little out of the way while carrying so. **kng-khui--khì**, to carry out of the way, as two or more men do. **kng-kang**, coolies engaged to carry things on poles between two men.

kng — **kng-tāu**, the two great longitudinal timbers in the middle of a boat (v. tāu).

kng (R. kong), a large-mouthed earthen jar. **toā-kng**, a large wide-mouthed jar. **toā-kng sòe-àng**, large and small jars. **tsúi-kng**, a large water-jar. **chhì^n-kng**, a large earthen vessel for dyeing with indigo (v. chhì^n). **phun-kng**, a jar for refuse rice-water. **jiō-kng**, an earthen jar for urine.

kńg [R. koán, a roll; a scroll], a roll, as of matting. **chit-kńg-chhiòh**, a roll of matting. **chit-kńg-tsū** (Cn.), = A. chit-pún-chheh, one book; one volume.

kńg (R. koán), (C. kúi^n), to roll up. **kńg-lê-hong**, a whirlwind. **tsúi teh-kńg-lê**, water eddying strongly. **kńg-tsñg**, eddying, as of water at a rock, or of wind whirling. **kńg-lien**, to curl up, as leaves in drought (v. lien). **kńg-chhák**, a curved chisel; a gouge.

kńg (T.), = A. kún, to move about in an excited state. **chhih-chhih-kńg**, many persons swaying back and forwards, or moving about rapidly, as a crowd.

kńg [R. kóng, broad], (C. kúi^n). **kńg-tang**, Canton; Quang-tung; Kwang-tung. **kńg-sai**, Kwang-si province. **ø-kńg**, Hoo-kwang, comprehending Hoonan and Hoo-peh.

kńg--ê, Cantonese, from Canton, as goods. **kńg-liên**, water-lily seeds from Canton.

kńg (Cn.), (r.), metallic ore. **si^n-kńg**, iron ore (v. si^n). **gûn-kńg**, silver ore. **kút-tiòh-kńg**, to meet with ore in digging (cf. C. koá^n).

kńg [R. koán, to rule; a tube], (C. kúi^n), a tube; a measure, half a "chin." **bí-kńg**, a small rice measure.

hé-kńg, a tube for blowing the fire. **ìm-kńg**, a small joint of bamboo for holding and extinguishing a match. **chhang-kńg**, a small short tube or ferule, as for mouth-piece of pipe, for end of a staff, or funnel for a lamp, &c.

bêh-kńg, the place at the wrist where the pulse is felt. **mēhⁿ-kńg**, id. **mn̂g-kńg** (r.), the pores of the skin. **mn̂g-kńg-chhi kiā**, hair standing on end, as with fear or cold. **mn̂g-kńg-chhi lóng-kiā**, hair all on end, as with great cold or terror.

nâⁿ-âu-kńg, the windpipe; the gullet. **âu-kńg**, id. **hì-kńg**, the windpipe. **ngīⁿ-kńg**, id. **nâⁿ-âu n̄ng-tiâu-kńg** (the throat has two pipes), one should not be too stiff on his supposed rights. **sái phīⁿ-khang-kńg**, to talk in a displeased nasal tone.

só-kńg, a sort of cuttle-fish. **sió-kńg**, id. **sió-kńg-kôe**, salted do.

kǹg (R. kong), steel. **kǹg-thih**, id. **chiàʳ-kǹg**, real genuine good steel. **to-kǹg**, the steel edge and point of a knife or sword. **to ū-kǹg**, the knife (or sword) has steel edge or point. **to bô-kǹg**, it has no steel.

kǹg (R. kòng), a large round pole, used for carrying heavy things between two or more bearers; the poles of a sedan; classifier of large heavy packages carried by two bearers. **kǹg-á**, a round carrying pole. **kǹg-á-thûi**, a short, thick, round carrying pole. **kiô-kǹg**, the poles of a sedan. **lién-kǹg**, the poles of an idol's sedan. **koaⁿ-chhâ-kǹg**, two thick bamboo poles tied by ropes to a coffin when it is carried.

láng-kǹg, a large wicker-work frame, fitted with poles like a sedan, used especially for carrying mandarin's baggage or public money (one such frame often carries a number of separate packages). **chit-kǹg láng-kǹg**, one such large heavy package. **chit-kǹg-siāⁿ**, one large tray (like a basket) with presents, carried on a pole between two men.

kǹg (R. koàn), (C. kùiⁿ). **gû-kǹg**, a ring for the nose of an ox or buffalo.

kǹg [R. koàn, to make a hole or string together; connected], (C. kùiⁿ), to bore a hole, as for a ring to hold; to string together on a string; to put in a ring, as in the nose of an ox.

kǹg-chîⁿ, to string cash together (a. amulet). **kǹg-hī**, to bore a hole in the ear for a ring, as in a pig's ear. **kǹg-phīⁿ**, to make a hole in the nose (as of an ox), and put in a ring. **lâng sìn-jī, gû kǹg-phīⁿ**, as an ox has a ring put in its nose, so a man believes and is held by a written document.

chîⁿ-kǹg, the common sort of string or twine used for stringing cash.

kǹg (R. koàn), (C. kùiⁿ), a sort of amulet with names of gods or goddesses on it, especially worn by children on a string. **kǹg-chîⁿ**, id. (s. string). **gûn-kǹg-chîⁿ**, that amulet made of silver or imitation silver. **gêk-kǹg-chîⁿ**, do. of jade-stone. **koāⁿ kǹg-chîⁿ**, to wear the amulet by a string round the neck. **koāⁿ-kǹg**, id. **koà-kǹg** (T.), id. **chhiáⁿ-kǹg**, to get the amulet from an idol. **chhiáⁿ i-ê-kǹg**, to get the amulet from that idol.

má-tsó-kǹg, an amulet with the name of Má-tsó-pô on it. **chhit-niûⁿ-kǹg**, amulet having on it the name of chhit-niûⁿ.

kǹg [R. koàn, a volume], (C. kùiⁿ), a folded paper prepared for writing an examination essay upon; the essay when written. **chit-pún-kǹg**, id. **chhiú-kǹg**, specimen of well-written characters to be copied, generally from some old fine writing. **khó-kǹg**, collections of successful essays, printed and sold to be studied as models. **tsu-kǹg**, an essay that has gained the degree of Kujin or Tsin-sze, printed for private circulation among friends (written with red ink).

kǹg-toaⁿ, a ticket of admission to the examination; on giving it in, a paper (kǹg) is given for the essay to be written upon.

niáⁿ-kǹg, to receive the blank paper on giving in the ticket. **kau-kǹg**, to give in the essay when written. **khoàⁿ-kǹg**, to read and examine the essay, as the examiner does.

ko [R. kho, a rule; a class; examination]. **ko-chhioh**, a wooden measuring rod or rule several feet long.

ko [R. a pole, especially of bamboo]. **tek-ko**, a bamboo pole. **tek-ko-kúi**, said of a very tall thin fellow. **teng-ko**, a pole with a lamp at the end, set up in superstitious rites. **khiā teng-ko**, to set it up. **pè-ko**, tall poles for hanging cloth when dyed. **tsûn-ko**, a boat-pole (said by landsmen). **chhùn-ko**, the stick used for striking the cat in tip-cat (v. chhùn). **kah-ko**, a ship's yards.

ko-chhê, a thin bamboo stick.

ko — **ko-chhe**, the man who has charge of the boy actors in a company (v. chhe).

ko [R. a spear; the 62d radical]. **tāng kan-ko**, to have a determined feud or war (lit. move shield and spear), either by fighting or by accusation in court. **tāng-khí kan-ko**, to begin a feud or war. **tó-ko**, the 62d radical.

ko [R. a sheep]. **iûⁿ-ko**, a sheep; a sheepskin (v. iûⁿ). **chit-ko**, a coarse woven woollen stuff from the north, like very coarse blanketing. **ko-tùt-biên**, a foreign smooth woollen stuff. **ko-to-biên**, id.

ko — **chióh-ko**, powdered gypsum, used as a cooling medicine.

ko [R. fat; ointment; extract of unctuous consistency, = col. kau, ko]. **ko-ióh**, medical plaster (v. ióh). **ióh-ko**, medical salve. **siau-ko**, black medical plaster. **bān-èng-ko**, a sovereign plaster for many diseases. **tan-ko oân-sán**, four sorts of medicines (v. sán).

bák-ko, thickened ink on ink-stone. **bák-sái-ko**, thickened matter about the eye. **so-bák-ko**, water-colour paint made from sapan-wood. **a-phièn-ko**, extract of opium. **thô-ko**, opium in its coarse state in the ball when opened. **kim-eng-ko**, a black extract from the fruit of the wild rose (v. eng). **chîm-ko**, soft yellowish substance in the male crab. **chhih-ko**, do. in the craw-fish. **koe-ko**, soft yellowish dung of fowls. **uih koe-ko**, a child's game (some say it is "song"), (v. uih).

pēng jip-ko-bông, the disease has reached the vital parts, and is incurable. [Perhaps add **ko**, jam, jelly, and the phrases under it.]

ko [R. an ode; a song, = col. koa]. **si-sû ko-hù**, four sorts of elegant metrical compositions.

ko — **thái-ko**, leprosy (v. thái).

ko [R. o, a frying-pan]. **ko-pa-phí**, incrustation on a rice-boiler (as in a junk) after long use.

ko (P.) **ko-chhɛⁿ**, = A. ko-chhiⁿ, the Pleiades.

ko [R. high], (Cn. ko, except the surname, which remains "ko"); a surname.

ko-kùi, too high-priced, as goods; making one's goods or services too high-priced (v. kùi). **ko-kiông**, very strong or skilful, especially of physical strength (v. kiông). **goá-beh ko-phan--lí**, will you kindly come with me, sir?

tsū-ko, proud. **hòⁿ-ko**, ambitious. **ko-seng**, promoted to high office. **kièn-ke-te**, determined to try which conquers. **kûn-thâu, ko-ko tsāi-siōng**, though very skilful there are others still more so (originally said of boxing). **thien ko, bī sī-ko; jîn-sim tsat-tsat-ko**, Heaven, though high, is not very high; it is man's heart that always wishes higher.

ko-sèng (polite), what is your surname, sir? **lí--ê ko-tê**, your scholar. **ko-hien** (R.), your school.

ko-tsó, great great-grandfather. **teng-ko-jit**, the 9.9 day (v. teng). **ko-san tsùn-léng** (R.), lofty mountains.

ko-lê, Corea (v. lê). **ko-phi** (f.), coffee (v. phi).

ko [R. kong, grandfather; male; duke, = col. kang]. **ti-ko**, a boar, as used for covering. **khan-ti-ko**, to lead a boar for a sow. **chhī-lâng, chiâ^n ti-ko**, said of a man being very lean.

ko (R. id.), an elder brother; also a respectful appellation, as an affix to a name (often enclitic), much like "hia^n," but perhaps a little more respectful, *e.g.* iáp-ko.

toā-ko, elder brother (esp. T.); also, polite form of addressing a stranger. **a-ko**, son of first-class mandarin. **a-ko-sià**, sons and grandsons of mandarins, in general.

hia^n-ko, paramour of a bad woman; but in Tiô-thoà, used for "elder brother." **bé--ko**, servant in a bad house.

ko — **eng-ko**, the figure of an eagle on the stern of a junk (s. parrot).

ko (R. id.) **eng-ko**, a parrot (v. ko), (s. previous word).

ko (R. id.), jam; jelly; preserves; thick syrup. **ké-chí-ko**, jam; jelly; preserves. **sng-tsó-ko**, a sort of Chinese preserve (v. tsó). **lâi-á-ko**, preserved pears. **lí-á-ko**, preserved plums. **tsú-ko**, to boil preserves or extracts in making them. **béh-lê-ko**, a thick glutinous inspissated syrup, made from new sugar and other ingredients. [This group is generally written with the following word "cake," but probably should be the same as "fat, ointment, extract."]

ko [R. a cake, especially made by steaming]. **ko-á**, a small cake, made with rice-flour. **ko-á-hún**, rice-flour mixed with sugar for making cakes. **at ko-á** (lit. break a cake), to divide profits equally. **ko-piá^n**, small cakes, in general. **koe-nn̄g-ko**, sponge-cake. **ke-nūi^n-ko** (C.), id. **lėk-tāu-ko**, short white cakes made with a stuffing of meal of small green peas. **bí-ko**, a cake made of rice and sugar, generally sold in diamond shapes. **chhèng bí-ko**, to prepare them by steaming.

tēng-ko--ê, good mealy potatoes. **m̄-tsai toā-phà^n tēng-ko**, cannot distinguish good and bad (lit. potatoes).

oá^n-ko-ké, cakes made in small cups. **oá^n-ko**, id. **teh-kóng sím-mih^n oá^n-ko**, what *are* you talking about? **tsòe sím-mih^n oá^n-ko**, what *are* you doing? **á-sī sím-mih^n oá^n-ko**, or whatever it be. **beh-poàh sím-mih^n oá^n-ko**, how can I (or he) gamble, having no money? **bô-chí^n, beh-bóe chit--ê oá^n-ko**, having no money, how can I buy anything? **lóng-bô oá^n-ko bí-so**, nothing can be had to eat. **ū sím-mih^n oá^n-ko bí-so**, what eatables have you got? as for a lunch or hurried meal. **thó chit--ê oá^n-ko bí-so**, got nothing for my pains; *e.g.* fruitless attempt to recover a debt.

kô [R. kó, a basket-work trap for fish], to put in a basket, as a pig. **kô-ti**, to catch a pig and put it in the basket. **ti-kô**, a large basket for carrying pigs. **hî-kô** (Cn.), a bamboo trap for catching fish, made like basket work, with a round mouth and a circle of converging sticks which allow entrance but not exit. **hê-kô** (C.), do., for catching shrimps, in fields.

kô [R. gô, to whirl; cf. kō], to stir, as with a spoon. **kô-lâi kô-khì**, to stir about. **kô chit-sin-thô**, to get one's self all bemired by falling into mud.

oai-kô, awry. **oai-oai kô-kô**, id. **oai-kô lȧh-chhoȧh**, id.

nn̂g-kô-kô, very soft.

kó [R. a steamed cake, = col. ké]. **bit-chièn thn̂g-kó**, a number of sweetmeats used in idolatrous offerings.

kó — **chhó-kó**, a medicine used as a diuretic (s. stalk; draft).

kó (R. id.), a stalk of grain or reed, including the ear; the rough draft of a composition. **chhó-kó**, a rough draft (s. medicine). **phah chhó-kó**, to write the roughly written copy, to be afterwards copied out neatly. **phah-kó**, id. **khí-kó**, id. **tsú-kó**, to manage this in a yamun. **sàng-kó**, to send in the draft of a document to be inspected by the mandarin; done by the "keng-sèng" in a civil yamun. **chhong-hā-kó**, essays made to be corrected by teacher (v. chhong, "window").

tiū-kó, rice stalks (v. tiū). **chit-kó-tiū**, a stalk of rice. **lê-sóe-kó**, a stalk of millet. **moâ^n-kó**, a stalk of hemp, dried and peeled. **béh-kó**, a stalk or straw of wheat or barley, without the ear. **béh-kó-thâu**, stubble of wheat or barley. **béh-kó-lôeh**, a straw hat for summer.

kó (T. kó). **lô-kó-chiȯh**, a coarse sort of coral.

kó [R. to wrap up]. **pau-kó** (C.), = pau-hȯk, a bundle (as of clothes, &c.) wrapped in a cloth.

kó [R. the result; truly; interchanged with the next word], (Cn. kó). **kó-jiên**, truly; certainly; indeed. **kó-chin**, id. **kó-hē**, really; truly. **kó-hē sī àn-ni^n**, truly it is so.

kiet-kó, fully settled so that all is quiet, as a quarrel; final state of a man's circumstances just before death, often with the idea of a Nemesis, good or bad (s. fruit). **éng-ū kiet-kó**, certainly there will be a just retribution, good or bad. **hó-kiet-kó**, comfortable circumstances at end of life, and an easy death, passing gently away. **phái^n-kiet-kó**, great misery at or near death. **sí^n-miā^n kiet-kó**, he is dead now. **sèng-bēng kiet-kó**, id. **kiet-kó i--ê sí^n-miā^n**, to kill him in an unlawful manner. **kā--i kiet-kó--sí**, id.

kó [R. fruit, = col. ké; interchanged sometimes with the previous word], (Cn. kó). **chheng-kó-sí^n**, salted olives. **sù-kó-thng**, an infusion of four sorts of dried fruits. **bû-hoa-kó**, the fig. **liên-chiau kiet-kó**, may all be auspicious and fortunate (said at marriages and at the Tauist rites called "chiò").

kò [R. classifier of men]. **tan-tan it-kò**, only one person; all alone.

kò [R. to inform; to accuse], (Cn. kò), to sue at law; to enter an accusation. **kò-sò**, to enter an accusation or an answer to one. **ū-kò ū-sò**, the accusation and reply have both been entered. **sa^n-kò**, to go to law. **kò-tiā^n**, the accusation put in by the plaintiff. **kò-tsn̄g**, to enter an accusation (v. tsn̄g). **khòng-kò**, to lay an accusation before a mandarin. **bû-kò**, to accuse unjustly. **mē-kò**, id. **hòng-kò**, to open the courts for receiving accusations, as after a new mandarin has arrived, or after the holidays. **hòng-kò-**

pâi, a notice hung up telling that accusations may now be entered. **kò koa^{n}-hú**, to enter an accusation before a mandarin. **kò sêng-hông**, to give in a written complaint to be burned before the tutelary god of the city (v. hông). **tâu-kò thi^{n}-tōe**, to lay one's wrongs before Heaven and Earth.

goân-kò, the plaintiff. **pī-kò**, the defendant. **phō-kò**, a man who comes forward in a lawsuit as the representative of a person who may not lawfully be beaten in examination, *e.g.* of a woman, or of an old man or Kujin.

kò-sī, an official proclamation by a mandarin. **kò-pèk**, a hand-bill or proclamation posted up. **kò-pèh**, id.

kò-ló, to ask to be allowed to retire from office on the plea of age. **kò-pī^{n}**, to ask a period of rest (as mandarin) on account of severe sickness. **kò-kè**, to ask leave of absence, as mandarin (s. pass).

kò [R. to pass; to go over; to exceed; a crime, = col. kè, koà], (Cn. kə̀). **tsōe-kò** (r.), a crime. **kái-kò**, to reform one's faults. **kái-kò chhien-siēn**, id. **ti-kò pit-kái**, on learning a fault, one should certainly correct it.

put-kò, only; no more than. **put-jî-kò** (esp. C.), id. **thài-kò**, far too much; excessively. **kò-po** (R.), to flatter highly. **sim-su kò-tə̄**, to think or scheme too deeply (v. tə̄).

kò-kè (Cn. kö-kè), to be adopted, as a son, generally from family of cousins or second cousins (s. inform). **kò-gán put-tsài**, able to repeat at one reading.

kò, to row (a boat) by standing and pushing the oars; (the European mode of rowing is "pien"). **kò-chiú^{n}**, id. **kò siang-chiú^{n}**, to row a two-oared boat. **kò-tsûn**, to row a boat in that way. **kiám-kò--chit-ē**, to omit one stroke in rowing.

kō [R. hō, a mark]. **nî^{n}-kō**, a year, as a date.

kō— **hoai-kī-kō** (C.), variegated; indistinct. **hoɛ-kī-kō** (C.), id.

kō (cf. kô, gô), to roll along a round thing, as a ball. **î^{n}-î^{n}-kō**, to roll along; rolling over and over, as a ball. **kō-kō-lìn**, id. **kō--lòh-khì**, to roll down, as over a precipice. **kō-lâi kō-khì**, to roll about, as in bed. **kō-moâ^{n}**, to cover a cake or sweetmeat with hemp-seed. **tiàm--tī thô-kha kō**, to roll about on the floor, as a child.

hoâi^{n}-kō, getting great gains suddenly or improperly (v. hoâi^{n}).

kō thô-bê, to roll and wallow in mud. **kō chit-sin-thô** (= kô), to get all bemired in mud.

ko͘ [R. rotten wood; dried and shrivelled]. **ko͘-tâ**, dried and shrivelled; dried up for want of moisture. **seng-khu ko͘-sò**, skin dry and hot, and having small eruptions slightly itchy.

ko͘ (R. id.) **ko͘-kut**, old rotten human bones. **sí--lâng ko͘-kut** (T.), old bones of dead men. **ko͘-lô**, id. (v. lô).

ko͘ [R. an angular ceremonial vase; angular]. **tek-á-ko͘**, bamboo spikes, used for impeding the advance of an army. **pàng-ko͘**, to place these spikes where an attack is expected.

ko͘— **toā-ko͘**, a large cargo-boat; a large boat propelled by sculling (s. aunt). **ko͘-á**, a smaller sculling-boat. **ko͘-á-tāi**, the boatman of a sculling-boat.

ko͘ (R. id.), paternal aunt; sister or female cousin of father, though a distant cousin, if of same surname (used in titles of nuns, &c.)

ko͘-put-chiong, having no resource but to do it; no alternative (v. chiong). **ko͘-chiâ^{n}**, = kə̀-chiâ^{n}, to coax.

chhin-ko͘, father's sister. **tông-ko͘**, father's female cousin of same surname, near or distant. **á-ko͘**, paternal aunt, &c.; said also by a wife (when she has a son) to her husband's sister, naming her as her own son would do. **án-ko͘**, id. **ńg-ko͘**, id. **toā-ko͘**, father's eldest sister (s. scull-boat). **jī-ko͘**, father's second oldest sister, &c. **toā-niû^{n}-ko͘**, husband's elder sister. **sió-ko͘**, husband's younger sister. **ko͘-pô**, paternal grand-aunt; paternal grandfather's female cousin (near or distant) of same surname.

ko͘-tiū^{n}, husband of paternal aunt. **ko͘-piáu hia^{n}-tī chí-bē**, cousins whose relationship is by their paternal aunt. **ko͘-piáu sa^{n}-thīn**, two families already connected by marriage forming another marriage connection. **chhin-chhek ko͘-kū**, relatives in general. **ko͘-î kū-kīm**, near relations and connections of wife, mother, and grandmother, as aunts, &c. **ko͘-î kū-kīm, lāi-chhin goā-chhek**, relations and connections in general. **ko͘ thià^{n}-sun, siāng-jī-sì^{n}**, a paternal aunt is fond of a nephew or niece because of having the same surname.

tō-ko͘, a Tauist nun. **sai-ko͘** (esp. Cn.), a Buddhist nun. **lî-ko͘**, a Buddhist nun (not polite in speaking to one). **kau lî-ko͘, tò tāng-á bí**, a woman who consorts with nuns must empty out her rice-jar. **sam-ko͘ liòk-pô**, nuns, female conjurors, witches, fortune-tellers, mediums, &c.

ko͘-niû^{n}, a mandarin's daughter; an unmarried lady of a good family; some unmarried ladies of exemplary character are worshipped by this title. **ko͘-iâ**, title of the husband of a mandarin's daughter.

sien-ko͘, a fairy (v. sien). **ko͘-chhi^{n}** (P. ko-chhɛ^{n}), the Pleiades. **chhit-ko͘-chhi^{n}**, id.

ko͘— **oá^{n}-ko͘-lèh**, the broken bottom of a bowl. **oá^{n}-ko͘-le** (T.), id. **oá^{n}-kim-ko͘-le** (T.), id. **oá^{n}-ko͘-lö** (T.), id. **oá^{n}-ko͘-tsui** (C.), id. **oá^{n}-kim-ko͘-tsui** (C.), id.

ko͘ [R. a sort of fish]. **ko͘-tai**, a sort of fish (s. high). **thap-bák-ko͘**, a small flat fish with a sunken eye. **thap-bák ko͘-hî**, id. **ko͘-kām-á** (C.), a sort of edible fish.

hê-ko͘, a large sort of shrimp. **hê-ko͘-chháu**, a medicinal plant (Lophanthus?).

ko͘ (R. id.) **ko͘-lê**, a sort of shell-fish.

ko͘ [R. a sort of insect]. **ka-lak-ko͘** (T.), the firefly. **kan-á-ko͘** (T.), id., because it is often kept in a bottle.

ko͘ [R. crooked; to make a mark, = col. kau]. **ko͘-tîn**, = kau-tîn, a fabulous animal like a winged dragon.

ko͘ [R. name of a bird]. **chià-ko͘**, the partridge. **chē-ko͘**, (C.), id.

ko͘— **ko͘-n̂g-chiáu**, the great owl. **ko͘-n̂g**, id. **ko͘-ûi^{n}-chiáu** (C.), id.

ko͘ [R. solitary; an orphan]. **ko͘-ko͘**, solitary; alone. **ko͘-toa^{n}**, id. **ko͘-toa^{n} chit-lâng**, one person alone. **ko͘-ko͘ chit-lâng**, id. **ko͘-khia**, one odd article of a pair. **ko͘-kiá^{n}**, an only son. **ko͘-teng**, having no brother or son. **ko͘-sin**, a solitary person with no relations. **ko͘-gān**, said of a widow or widower. **tsòe ko͘-pô**, to be an old maid. **ko͘-nḗ^{n}**, a solitary old man having the privilege of begging (v. nḗ^{n}). **ko͘-pîn-iáu**, a man who has no relatives, very poor, and short-lived (v. iáu). **ko͘-sèng**, having no one of the same surname in the place. **ko͘-sì^{n}**, id.

ko͘-khùt, solitary without relatives; unsociable; unneighbourly. **kɵ-khut-siòng**, unsociable and unneighbourly. **kɵ-kài**, of unpleasant temper; unwilling to answer or assist (v. kài). **kɵ-tåk**, selfishly unneighbourly, unsociable, and disobliging. **kɵ-tȯk** (R.), solitary, as an orphan, &c. **kɵ-sng**, unneighbourly and unfriendly, *e.g.* unwilling to lend or to do a favour; selfish and disobliging. **kɵ-sí-sng**, exceedingly unneighbourly and disobliging.

kɵ-koáⁿ, orphans and widows (v. koáⁿ). **thok-kɵ**, to intrust our son to a guardian to be taken care of after our death.

kɵ-ɵ, the best throw in the sort of gambling called "lién-pó" (v. ɵ).

kɵ-hûn, a ghost that has no relations to make offerings to it. **hàu-kɵ**, to make offerings to such a ghost; said also in joke to a man eating. **chè-kɵ**, to make sacrificial offerings to such a ghost; said also in scolding a man eating. **kɵ-chhién**, a sort of basket used in the offerings made to the dead in general. **kɵ-pîⁿ**, a shed or awning set up with the offerings to ghosts that have no posterity. **tah kɵ-pîⁿ**, to set it up. **chhiúⁿ kɵ-pîⁿ**, to scramble for these offerings at the end of the rites; said also in scolding children for snatching food. **chhiúⁿ-kɵ**, id.

kɵ — **kɵ-pô-ɵ̄**, a wild plant like taro (v. pô).

kɵ (R. id.), mushrooms, fungus, mould, lichens, &c. **hiuⁿ-kɵ**, edible mushrooms (esp. dried) of best-flavoured sorts. **soaⁿ-tsû-kɵ**, a medicinal fungus that grows at tree-roots. **siông-kɵ**, a fungus that grows on tree-roots, much eaten by vegetarians. **sam-kɵ**, useless and poisonous mushrooms growing on the "sam" tree, &c. **chhâ-kɵ**, id. **ti-sái-kɵ**, id., whether on dung or in other places.

hoat-kɵ, to grow mouldy. **siⁿ-kɵ**, id. **siⁿ-kɵ chhiūⁿ-phú**, id. **chih siⁿ-kɵ**, tongue furred, as when unwell.

kɵ — **chhiáng-kɵ-le** (Cn.), to hop, as a child.

kɵ [R. ko, high], (also Cn., = A. ko). **kɵ-tai-chîⁿ**, large bundles of idolatrous paper (representing money) torn into very long shreds.

kɵ [R. ko, fat; ointment; rich], (also Cn., = A. ko, id.) **kɵ-iȯh**, = ko-iȯh, medicinal plaster (v. iȯh).

kɵ-jû (Cn.), wealthy. **kɵ-dzû** (Cn.), id.

kɵ (Cn.), = A. ko; in several other words.

kɵ [R. a crime; ungrateful]. **kɵ-hū**, to behave ungratefully; to requite ill, as kindness or favour. **kɵ-hū un-tién**, to act ungratefully after receiving kindness, favour, or grace. **kɵ-un**, id. **kɵ-un hū-gī**, id.

bû-kɵ (R.), innocent. **bû-kɵ siū-khut**, oppressed or treated ill without cause. **kò pó-kɵ**, to enter an accusation against a man who has beaten another so as to endanger his life; if the man die within forty days the accusation is valid for compensation for his life.

kɵ [R. to buy]. **kɵ-chiú** (C.), to buy spirituous liquor.

kɵ̂ [R. kɵ, aunt]. **kɵ̂-chiâⁿ**, = kɵ-chiâⁿ, to coax.

kɵ̂ [R. hɵ, = col. khɵ], paste; to paste; to paste or plaster up, as a crevice; to put on a poultice; to put on (face-paint) too thick; a sort of stiffly-starched cloth.

kɵ̂-iȯh, to put on a plaster of herbs like a poultice. **kɵ̂-liâng**, to put on a cooling plaster, as on a boil. **kɵ̂-he**, to plaster up with lime or cement, as a crevice. **kɵ̂-bōe-tiâu**, the paste does not hold. **tsoá-kɵ̂--ê**, made of paper pasted together

kɵ̂-kēng, to assist a man with a little money (v. kēng).

kɵ̂-tsoá, to paste paper for idolatrous purposes. **kɵ̂-teng**, to make a lantern by pasting. **kɵ̂-phoe**, to seal up a letter with paste or rice. **kɵ̂-liên**, to paste up antithetical sentences. **kɵ̂ mn̂g-sîn**, to paste up antithetical phrases on doors.

kɵ̂-tōe, stiffly-starched grass-cloth. **toā-chhân-kɵ̂**, do. from Tāi-tiên. **éng-chhun-kɵ̂**, do. from Yung-chun. **kɵ̂-khit** (Cn.), a peg covered with coarse starch, over which that stuff is drawn in starching it.

bėh-kɵ̂, paste made from wheat; it is eaten. **hún-chiuⁿ-kɵ̂**, starch or paste made (ready for use) from rice. **tsu̍t-bí-kɵ̂**, paste made from glutinous rice. **moâⁿ-chî-kɵ̂**, paste made from the confection called "moâⁿ-chî," boiled down soft.

khièn-kɵ̂, to stir paste in making it. **khu̍t-kɵ̂**, id. **boah-kɵ̂**, to put on paste; to smear with paste. **uih-kɵ̂**, to take up a small quantity of paste, as on the finger or on small thin slip of wood, *e.g.* for closing a letter. **iah-kɵ̂**, to take up a large quantity of paste, as with a spoon or large broad piece of wood.

kɵ̂-kɵ̂, gelatinous; sticky. **chhu̍i-kɵ̂-kɵ̂**, broken down small. **noāⁿ-kɵ̂-kɵ̂**, very soft, as cooked food, or as something soaked and spoiled by rain. **sȧh siuⁿ-kɵ̂**, to boil too soft, as vermicelli or potatoes. **iûⁿ-kɵ̂-kɵ̂**, all bruised, beaten, or melted to a pulp; broken to shivers (v. iûⁿ). **nn̂g-kɵ̂-kɵ̂**, very soft, as dough, &c. (v. nn̂g). **kà-kɵ̂-kɵ̂**, thin and watery, as boiled rice.

kɵ̂ — **pėh-kɵ̂** (T.), = A. pėh-gɵ̂, a large white fish.

kɵ́ (R. id.) **tê-kɵ́**, an earthen tea-kettle, sometimes used as a coarse tea-pot. **tâng-tê-kɵ́**, a brass tea-kettle. **chiú-tê-kɵ́**, a sort of wine-jug. **chiú-kɵ́** (T.), an earthen vessel for boiling spirituous liquor. **jiō-kɵ́** (esp. Cn.), a chamber-pot with a stroop.

kɵ́ [R. ancient, antiquity], stories about ancient times, read or delivered.

kɵ́-tsá, long ago; ancient. **bān-kɵ́** (R.), extremely ancient times. **bān-kɵ́ liû-thoân**, handed down from the remotest times. **bān-kɵ́ chheng-nî**, extremely ancient times; thousands of years ago. **chiâⁿ-bān-kɵ́**, id. **kɵ́-kim**, ancient and modern times (v. kim). **í-kɵ́ ûi-kàm** (R.), to use ancient history as a mirror. **kɵ́-lâng-giên**, a saying of the ancients, esp. a proverb.

kɵ́-koài, strange; eccentric (v. koài).

kɵ́-ì, of excellent character; good, kind, and upright. **kɵ́-hong**, id. **kɵ́-kiėt**, neat, small, and well made (v. kiėt). **kɵ́-tsui**, pleasant and nice-looking, as a child. **kɵ́-kɵ́-tsui**, pretending to have far more knowledge or ability than one has. **kɵ́-pán-lâng**, a man of quiet, simple, honest, old-fashioned ways (v. pán).

kɵ́-chè, old-fashioned, as things. **kɵ́-lē**, ancient laws or customs. **kɵ́-chek**, ancient relics, monuments, &c.; antiquities. **kɵ́-ūi**, old pictures. **kɵ́-goán**, old curiosities. **kɵ́-tóng**, id. (v. tóng).

kɵ́-siong-chhú, old friends. **kɵ́-siang-chhí** (C.), id. **éng-kɵ́** (Cn.), always or very generally in the past.

kɵ́-lauh-phauh, old, as man; ancient, as curio, old-fashioned, as dress, &c. **kɵ́-lɵ́-chhiū**, a sort of low straggling tree with large leaves and soft wood. **kɵ́-ló-chhiū**, id. **kɵ́-chhiū-thâu**, an old stump almost dead.

kɵ́-ló-sien, = kok-ló, one of the genii.

kóng-kɵ́, to tell or read ancient stories from books (generally historical novels), as men do to make money. **kóng-kɵ́-sien**, a man who makes this his business.

kóng-hàm-kớ, to tell incredible stories. **kóng êng-á-kớ**, to talk idle useless stories and empty talk. **phàⁿ-kớ**, empty baseless stories. **thiaⁿ-kớ**, to listen to these sort of stories. **pien-kớ**, to tell stories invented at the time, as an improvisatore, &c.; to talk scandal, mainly fictitious. **teh kek-kớ**, talking and inventing strange stories (v. kek), (s. drum). **phah-chih lâng--ê kớ-piⁿ**, to cut short a man's talk so as to defeat his purpose (play on the word "kớ," a drum). **kớ-chheh**, books of old stories (used by men for reading aloud), somewhat like historical novels. **kớ-tiûⁿ**, a place where people meet (bringing out benches for the purpose) to hear these old stories.

kớ (= kó). **ló-kớ-chióh**, = ló-kó-chióh, a coarse sort of coral.

kớ [R. name of a shrub], (Cn. kió). **kớ-kí**, a medicinal shrub (v. kí).

kớ [R. koán, a tube; a horn; to rule, = col. kńg, kóng]. **gû-kak-kớ-chhì**, a thorny leguminous shrub and medicine. **chhâ-chek-kớ**, an imitation candle with a lamp at the top. **chek-kớ** (Cn.), id.

kớ (C.) **kớ-lê-hong**, = kńg-lê-hong, a whirlwind.

kớ [R. carelessly; irregularly; illicitly; if], (Cn. kió). **kớ-chhiáⁿ**, remissly; carelessly; inaccurately. **kớ-kán**, id. **kớ-hàp**, illicit sexual intercourse.

kớ [R. a dog, = col. káu], (Cn. kió). **hoán ûi-kớ**, but after all he makes it only a dog; a miserable failure (v. hoán).

kớ [R. dropsy]. **kớ-tiòng**, dropsy in the abdomen, = tớ-tiòng. **kớ-chèng**, id. **hu-lô kớ-kek**, several very severe chronic diseases (v. hu).

tiòng-tsoâ-kớ, to be bewitched so as to have dropsy (v. tsoâ).

kớ (R. id.), to estimate or fix a price; to appraise or value. **kớ-kè**, id. (s. drum). **kong-kớ**, publicly fix the price, done by several men together. **kớ loā-tsōe-chîⁿ**, value at how many cash? **kớ-lớ--khì**, assign at estimated value, as goods to creditor, &c. **kớ hō--i**, give it him at a valuation, as payment for a debt.

kớ (Cn.) **piⁿ-kớ**, = gû-taⁿ, a yoke for a cow or ox.

kớ (Cn.), = A. kó, in several words.

kớ (R. id.), a drum or similar instrument; to winnow with fanners; said of some round things; word used by coolies to mean 100 cash. **kớ-tñg**, said by coolies to mean 150 cash.

ñg-kớ-á, coarse paper painted yellow for making into mock-money for the worship of spirits (sîn). **péh-kớ-á**, do. left white for the worship of ghosts (kúi). **kớ-á-tsoá**, either kind.

chióh-kớ, solid broad wheel-shaped stones on each side of the door of a temple or yamun. **thñg-kớ**, a large confection used at marriages. **kớ-phàu**, a large drum-shaped frame full of crackers, used at marriages. **óe-kớ óe-kớ**, short and stout, as a man. **kớ-á-bīn**, face plump and round. **kớ-á-îⁿ**, id. **î-kớ-á**, an octagonal or round, drum-shaped, hollow, earthenware seat. **kớ-á-í**, id. **kớ-í**, id. **îⁿ-kớ-í**, id. (s. limb). **hûi-kớ-í**, id.

kớ-chhek, to winnow rice with fanners. **kớ-lớ**, to winnow with fanners. **hong-kớ**, a machine like fanners, for winnowing. **iét-hong-kớ**, to work the fanners; to winnow.

tsùn-kớ, an ornament (in women's head-dress) that shakes on a spiral wire. **chîⁿ-kớ**, a tambourine. **lāng chîⁿ-kớ**, to play the tambourine. **bák-kớ**, a wooden drum shaped like a fish. **chièn-kớ**, a war-drum. **kiⁿ-kớ**, a large drum at a yamun or city gate for beating the watches. **lin-long-kớ**, a pedlar's rattle; a rattle used by children. **piak-kớ**, a sort of drum with skin on one end only. **phiāng-kớ**, a long hollow bamboo with skin on one end, used by beggars and quacks (v. phiāng). **tâng-kớ**, a pedlar's rattle with brass at the ends. **iô-tâng-kớ**, to shake it. **thè-tâng-kớ**, to draw back from an affair we had taken in hand (fig. from sorcerer), (v. thè). **thong-kớ**, a sort of drum suspended from the neck. **chhiú-kớ**, a small drum with a handle, used in processions. **khám-chhēⁿ-kớ**, pair of cymbals and one hand drum (v. chhēⁿ). **toā-chhâm-kớ**, large cymbals and drums. **toā-khâm-kớ** (Cn.), large cymbals, drum, and gong. **lô-kớ**, gongs and drums. **tāng-lô-kớ**, to beat gongs and drums in superstitious rites. **kớ-gák**, drums and other music (v. gák). **kớ-chhe**, a drum and two pipes (v. chhe).

lûi-kớ, to beat a large drum quick, loud, and long (v. lûi). **phah-kớ**, to beat a drum. **phah chhùi-kớ**, to talk about unimportant matters; to have an idle talk; to gossip (s. limb). **phah piⁿ-kớ**, to give a man a secret hint. **kek-kớ**, to beat the drum in a yamun, to call for justice in a very urgent case. **chéng-kớ**, to beat drums just before a play. **tân-kớ** (C.), id. **jiáng-kớ** (C.), id. **khí-kớ**, to begin beating the drum at rites for the dead; also (Cn.), = A. chéng-kớ, to beat drums before a play. **piⁿ-kớ**, to make a drum by stretching the skin on the drum. **táⁿ-hoa-kớ**, a man dressed as a woman, who beats a drum and sings at a play. **chhia-kớ-pô**, do. at an incense procession. **chhia-kớ-kong**, a man in male dress doing so.

kớ-thûi, a drum-stick. **kớ-lâu**, a tower for holding a drum. **kớ-têng**, a shed for musicians, at the side of the gate of a high mandarin; a canopy containing a drum carried at idolatrous processions. **kớ-kè**, a frame or stand for a drum (s. estimate).

kớ [R. a limb, esp. the thigh], a strand of a rope; a share in business; a division of an essay; (said of a partner or companion).

sit-kớ, wings (v. sit). **méhⁿ-kớ**, the place where the pulse is felt at wrist or temples, especially at the wrist. **chhiú-kớ** (C.), the calf of the lower arm. **chhiú-kớ kièn-chí-bah**, said of a man well off, with arm fat and strong. **koat chhùi-kớ**, to beat the cheeks (said in scolding a child), (s. drum).

îⁿ-kớ îⁿ-kớ, round, as a rope, or as shaft of brush, or pencil, or leg of table, or fat fleshy well-formed limb (s. drum). **îⁿ-kớ-piⁿ**, round braid or narrow thick tape.

sang-kớ-kiàm, a double-bladed dagger. **téng-kớ-chiam**, the upper hair-pin in a woman's head-dress.

saⁿ-kớ, a rope made with three strands. **kià saⁿ-kớ**, to put out this rope from a junk in order to fasten it. **chit-kớ-soh**, one strand of a rope. **thoàⁿ-kớ**, the strands of a rope or queue opening out of themselves. **tháu-kớ**, to open out a rope (intentionally) into its strands; said also of getting a dispute set right (v. tháu).

kap-kớ, to join several ropes or strands to make one rope; to join capital in trade. **khiā-kớ**, to have a share in a business. **tàu-kớ**, to have shares in a joint business. **pun-kớ**, to divide profits according to shares. **thiah-kớ**, to dissolve partnership. **chhah-kớ**, to join a partnership, taking a small share. **chhah-chit-kớ**, id. **chit-kớ seng-lí**, one share in the business. **hè, tsòe-nñg-kớ khui**, to have two equal shares in the trade. **kớ-bê**, to take the lead in starting a joint business.

hó-kha-kớ, a pleasant boon companion in low pleasures. **tàu sī kha-kớ**, a good companion or partner for business or pleasure. **bô hit--ê kha-kớ**, there are not enough of persons ready, either to assist in work, or to take parts in a game, &c.

poeh-kớ, the eight divisions of an essay, according to the old plan. **la̍k-kớ**, the six divisions of a modern essay. **kau-kớ**, to mark the divisions of an essay. **tsa̍h-kớ**, id. **tiám-kù tsa̍h-kớ**, to punctuate and mark the divisions of essay.

kờ (R. id.), to hire, as workman or boat. **kờ-chhiàⁿ**, id. (v. chhiàⁿ). **tiau-kờ**, to hire specially for the purpose. **kờ-lâng-oàn**, to draw feelings of dislike on one's self, as by manner or appearance. **thē kờ-hê tsòe-ba̍k** (the medusa using the shrimp as an eye), one man idly or ignorantly making use of another's knowledge or skill in managing matters.

kờ [R. firm, obstinate]. **kien-kờ**, firm; steady. **kờ-siú**, to guard and watch carefully, as house, &c.

kờ-ì, on purpose; intentionally. **tiâu-kờ-ì**, id. **tiâu-ì-kờ**, id. **tsoan-ì-kờ**, id. **kờ-chip**, obstinate.

kờ [R. to fuse; to keep from office]. **kìm-kờ** (r.), to disable a man from getting a degree or office or rank. **kìm-kờ chiong-sin** (r.), to disable a man for life from all rank, office, or degrees.

kờ (Cn.), = A. kò (R.), to pass —. **put-kờ**, not more than; only.

kờ (Cn.), = A. kò, to accuse; to inform.

kờ (R. id.), to guard; to take care of; a surname. **chiàu-kờ**, to take care of. **khàn-kờ** (r.), id. **koán-kờ**, to watch and take care of; to oversee; to manage for another in his absence. **kau-lí-kờ**, I intrust it to you to take care of. **kờ-tiâu-tiâu**, to keep and guard carefully.

tsú-kờ, a customer, as of a shop. **toā-tsú-kờ**, a large customer. **hó-tsú-kờ**, a customer who does not drive hard bargains. **bô-chhûn tsú-kờ**, to take improper or unwise advantage of a man, so as to lose his custom or friendship, *e.g.* cheating a good customer, or ill-using a friend.

ōe-kờ--tit, well enough to do what is wanted, though not strong; having time to attend to the matter, along with what we were doing before. **bōe-kờ--tit**, very ill; very poor; much grieved or pained; very painful, so as to be intolerable; having no time to attend to the matter, because fully occupied with other things. **kàu-bōe-kờ--tit**, to the utmost, exceedingly (said of some feelings and emotions). **ōe-kờ--tit chêng, bōe-kờ--tit āu**, quite unable to attend to all the parts of a complicated affair, so that from one side or another disaster is sure to come. **ōe-kờ--tit tang-ga̍k, bōe-kờ--tit sêng-hông**, must let one of the two objects drop (as man not having time to worship at both temples). **kờ-siōng, put-kờ-hā**, attending only to half one's duties, so that the other part goes all wrong. **thâu-bé bōe-saⁿ-kờ**, cannot attend at once to both parts of the affair, so that the whole goes wrong, *e.g.* an army defeated because one part is lost. **thâu-bé bô-saⁿ-kờ**, the beginning and the end not agreeing together, as of evidence, of essay, or discourse.

kờ-pún, careful of one's capital in trade, avoiding rash ventures, and keeping to safe investments; thrifty; avoiding dangerous matters; respectable and careful of one's character. **khah-kờ-pún**, id. **tio̍h-kờ-pún**, you should avoid dangerous matters, not meddling in other people's disputes. **kờ-thé-biēn**, to be careful of one's reputation, respectability, and prestige. **kờ-liâm-thí**, modest and conscientious. **kờ-bīn-phê**, to take care of one's character. **kờ-sìⁿ-miāⁿ**, to take care of one's own life; to spare one's self.

kờ-lim-chia̍h, caring for nothing but eating and drinking. **kờ chit-ê-chhùi**, id. **kờ-sái-tsûn**, attend to the working of the vessel. **kờ-iûⁿ**, to tend sheep or goats; a shepherd. **kờ-kha**, take care of your feet! warning by the front chair-bearer that something on the road might hurt the feet.

kờ [R. old; reason; cause; affairs; death]. **iên-kờ**, a reason; a cause; a motive. **the-sû iá-kờ**, to decline for a feigned reason.

sū-kờ, an affair or business to be attended to. **the sū-kờ**, to decline a request, or refuse to do something on fair but false pretexts or excuses (v. the). **thok-sū-kờ**, id. **ū sū-kờ**, there are matters to be attended to, so that there is no time for other affairs. **sè-kờ**, influence (v. sè, "power").

sin-kờ, he has died (said only in announcing a death).

kờ-kū, old; original; long acquainted. **chhin-pêng kờ-iú**, relatives and old friends. **kờ-tsoá**, old paper (medicinal). **kờ-tién**, the manner or style of the ancients, as to customs, &c. (v. tién). **tsng kờ-sū**, to dress up in the character of ancient personages (v. tsng). **kờ-chek**, an old disease that has come back again and again.

kơ̄ [R. kớ, remissly; carelessly]. **bô-khoà-cheng, kơ̄-lap** (to tread the rice-pestle carelessly, not attending to clean the rice), said of doing anything in a great hurry without care.

kơ̄ [R. hơ, kơ, to trust in]. **kau-kơ̄**, to intrust, as business or thing. **beh-kơ̄ sím-mih̍ⁿ-lâng**, to whom will you intrust this matter? **kơ̄ chit-ki-chhùi**, to have nothing to trust to but one's own power of talking, strength of assertion, or tissue of plausible lies, *e.g.* when one has no real power or influence to back him, or not even the truth of the case. **kơ̄ hit-ê-chhùi**, id.

kơ̄ [R. hơ, time; to wait, = col. hāu, pơ]. **chhûn-āu-kơ̄** (C.), = chhûn-āu-pơ, to have something over (as surplus money) for emergencies.

kơ̄ [R. hō, a mark]. **nî-kơ̄** (Cn.), = A. nîⁿ-kō, a year, as a date.

kō͘ (Cn.), = A. ké, to support by something put under to make it higher.

kō͘ (Cn.), = A. ké. **kō͘-chí**, fruit.

kō͘ (Cn.), = A. ké, cakes.

kō͘ (Cn.), = A. kè, a woman's head-dress. **kut-kō͘**, the whole set of a woman's hair-pins, &c.

kō͘ (Cn.), = A. kè, to cross; to pass over. **kō͘-kè**, to be adopted from a related family. **kō͘-kè**, too high a price.

kō͘ (Cn.), = A. kè, name of a fish.

koa (R. ko), a song having a regular number of words (usually five or seven) in each line. **koa-khek**, songs of various sorts, of regular and irregular structure. **koa-koat**, mnemonic rhymes. **chit-tè-koa**, one song. **khit-chia̍h-koa**, sort of songs sung by beggars. **chhiùⁿ-koa**, to sing a song. **pien koa-á**, to compose a song.

koa [R. kok, to pause; to delay, = col. koh], to pause or rest at a place in passing, especially going slightly out of the way to do so. **koa-oaⁿ**, to lie for a

厦英大辭典

short time at a port or anchorage, as a vessel. **koa-khì-hia**, to go slightly out of the way to stop at that place. **koa-chia koa-hia**, stopping here and there in passing. **koa--khì pát-sé-tsāi**, to go slightly out of the way to stop (for some purpose) at another place. **koa-kha**, to pause or rest at a place on the way or a little out of the way.

koa [R. ko, by change of tone from "kò," to cross; to pass, = col. kè, koà]. **chiaⁿ koa** (Cn.), the New-Year season over, as after the 16th of the first month, or about the 20th. **koa-chiaⁿ** (T.), id. (v. chiaⁿ).

koa, too hard and fibrous, as fruits, vegetables, ginger, or bamboo-shoots, that are too tough for good eating; having lost the freshness and bloom of youth.

koa-sò, dry and hard, as one's skin (v. sò). **bīn-phê khah-koa**, the face having lost the fresh look of youth. **koa-bih-bih**, too old and hard, so as to be unpleasant to eat, as vegetables, &c.

koa [R. kho, a branch], a surname.

koa [R. a melon, cucumber, &c., = col. koe], (also C., = A. koe).

bók-koa, the quince. **tē-koa** (R.), potatoes.

koa (C.) **âng-koa**, = A. âng-koe, a sort of fish.

koâ (R. hô), a large tree with very showy and beautiful white flowers. **koâ-chhiū**, id. **koâ-hoe**, a shrub with beautiful clustered white flowers, somewhat like laurustinus.

koá [R. koáⁿ, solitary; few], (T. koáiⁿ), a small quantity; often enclitic. **kiám--koá**, a few less. **pān--koá**, make ready a little. **pān-koá-liāu**, have made ready a few things, *e.g.* for eating or for other purposes. **tn̂g-koá-chîⁿ**, to have a small balance of cash over, as after executing a commission (v. tn̂g, "long"). **koá lâi-jip-siàu**, a little money given as part payment.

koà [R. khoà, to straddle]. **khiā-koà**, to stand or sit practising the proper attitude, as for archery or riding. **khiâ-bé-koà**, to practise sitting in the proper attitude for riding. **koà siang-thâu-bé**, pretending to be on each side, and injuring each party by information got from the other.

koà [R. kài, the mustard-plant]. **koà-chhài**, the mustard-plant.

koà [R. kò, to cross; a crime, = col. kè]. **chē-koà**, a crime; a sin.

kè-koà, too hard, as work; very severe, as disease; too much, as exerting one's self. **tióh-boâ kè-koà**, to work far beyond one's strength.

koà — **hoán-koà**, to break one's promise.

koà [R. kài, an assistant; to be anxious]. **koà-ì**, to be anxious or grieved about matters.

koà [R. to hinder; an impediment, = col. khoà]. **koà-gāi**, to be anxious about a matter (v. gāi); this word and the previous word are often interchanged with the following.

koà (R. id.), to suspend; to wear suspended, as a chain; to wear, as various ornaments, *e.g.* in the cap or on the neck; to have attached, as leaves on end of stalk, or as handle on basket.

koà-sim, to be anxious. (this group, = khoà). **koà-lū**, id. **koà-liām**, id. **koà-tiàu sim-koaⁿ**, deeply distressed and anxious, *e.g.* afraid of the death of an absent friend.

goá-koà tī hī-á bé-liu (I hang it at the tip of my ear), I don't care much for what you say.

koà-hà, to hang up white cloth at doors, &c., in mourning. **kā--i koà-âng**, to give some red thing as a present to a man who does some unlucky thing for us (v. âng).

koà-liēn, to wear a chain; to chain. **koà-thih-liēn**, id. **koà-hiuⁿ-hé**, to wear amulets made with incense. **koà-kǹg** (T.), = A. koāⁿ-kǹg, to wear an amulet of metal (v. kǹg). **koà-bé-long**, to wear a sort of bell, as a horse.

koà-bák-kiàⁿ, to wear spectacles. **koà-chhiú-khoân**, to wear bracelets. **ài-koà-súi**, fond of wearing ornaments (v. súi). **koà-niáⁿ**, to put on or wear a collar. **koà-lêng**, to wear a peacock's feather in the cap, as high mandarin.

koà-gû, to yoke an ox or cow for ploughing. **koà-oaⁿ**, to wear a saddle (v. oaⁿ).

koà-bāng, to set a net.

koà-thn̄g, glazed, as pottery. **koà-khak ê-béh**, wheat or barley with the rough outside not yet ground off. **koà-bé--ê**, having the bunch of leaves at the end still attached (not yet cut off), as a stick of sugar-cane, &c. **koà-iaⁿ**, to have a tassel attached, as cap. **ū-koà-kiāⁿ**, having a (curved) handle attached, as basket. **koà-the-mn̂g**, still having on the hair that was on the fœtus, as a child in the first month before it is shaved.

koà-kūi, to be pregnant, as one of the lower animals.

koà-báu, to have one's name on the books of a yamun for protection.

koà [R. kài, to cover; a cover, = col. khàm], (T. sometimes "koài"), a cover; a lid. **hien-koà**, to raise the lid.

chhù-koà, a roof. **siāⁿ-koà**, the hatches. **tiáⁿ-koà**, the lid of a rice-boiler. **tiáⁿ-kám-koà**, id.

ū-tóe ū-koà, done quite properly, as a document or an affair (v. tóe).

koà, and along with (over and above). **kiâm-koà-siap**, very niggardly. **hong koà-hō͘**, wind and rain. **tsûn koà-chiúⁿ**, oars along with the boat. **koà-chham--teh**, added in addition, *e.g.* adding another man's name in accusation.

koà [next word?]. **má-lí-koà**, name of a flower with a head of flowers like a ball.

koà [R. an outer jacket or short coat]. **bé-koà**, an outer jacket, with arms not very long, buttoning up the middle of the breast. **n̂g-bé-koà**, a yellow coat, sometimes bestowed by imperial special favour. **kun-ki-koà**, jacket buttoning at the side and faced with a different colour. **thài-pêng-koà**, jacket buttoning in middle of breast, with long narrow arms. **tek-sèng-koà**, jacket with many foreign buttons, fastened at side. **pó-koà**, outer jacket worn by a mandarin or kujin, bearing the insignia on a square on the breast. **hō-i-koà**, a sort of military coat.

phàu-koà, both the long robe and the jacket worn over it.

koà — **tsam-koà**, to invest a new-made Sew-tsai with gilt flowers and red sash, as used to be done; now they go ready dressed out.

koà [R. the "diagrams" of Chinese divination], (C. koè). **pat-koà**, the eight diagrams of Fuh-hi, often worked as an octagonal figure. **pat-koà-lâu**, an octagonal tower, for superstitious purposes. **pat-koà-hōe**, a rebellious society like the sió-to-hōe.

koà-sîn hó, the answer by tortoise-shell divination is good. **koà-sîn phái**ⁿ, do. is bad. **chhiam-siàⁿ koà-tiāⁿ**, my instruments of divination are sure and certain.

30

pok-koà, to divine by tortoise-shell. **poàh-koà**, id. **khì poàh-koà**, to go and inquire at a diviner. **khì pok-koà**, id. **poàh-ku-koà**, to divine by six trials with three cash, called "chiu-goân," put in the shell of a turtle or tortoise. **teh chiáu-á-koà**, to divine by seeing which of the lots a bird pecks up.

chiam-koà, another sort of divination. **chiam-bí-koà**, to divine by rice grains. **liam-bí-koà** (T.), id. **tn̄g-hì-koà**, to try one's luck by the part of a play that we first meet with. **tn̄g-chhùi-koà** (Cn.), = thia^n-hiu^n, to listen for the first word heard after offering incense, on 1. 15. or 8. 15.

koà (T.) **àm-koà-chiáu**, = àm-kong-chiáu, a sort of owl.

koā (C.), to hate; to be much displeased at a man for not doing what he promised; to try to injure a man, as an idol does if a vow be not paid.

koa^n (R. kan), the liver. **sim-koa^n**, the heart and liver; the heart as the seat of thought and affections. **sim-koa^n-khut**, the soft depression near the middle of the breast. **sim-koa^n-tì**, id. **sim-koa^n-thâu**, the lower part of the breast at the pit of the stomach. **sim-koa^n-thâu khui**, sorrow or anxiety somewhat allayed. **sim-koa^n-thâu peh-peh**, feeling of heaviness and indigestion.

sim-koa^n thiàu, palpitation of the heart in great terror or anxiety. **sim-koa^n chiâ^n-oân**, heart choking in great grief.

bô-sim-koa^n, thoughtless; forgetful. **sim-koa^n sòe**, satisfied with small gains. **ū-chit-tiám sim-koa^n**, to have some settled purpose, as of affection or of sincerity; desiring something earnestly. **sim-koa^n bô-thàn-chhùi**, he does not think as he speaks. **sim-koa^n-kiá^n**, a favourite child. **goá--ê sim-koa^n-í^n**, an endearing phrase said by mother or nurse to baby (v. í^n).

siū^n-sim siū^n-koa^n, to think out a selfish or improper plan (v. siū^n). **boâ-sim boâ-koa^n**, to exert one's mind very much.

ti-koa^n, pig's liver. **ti-koa^n-sek**, the red colour like pig's liver. **ti-koa^n-chhiū**, a tree with bright red berries like holly berries.

koa^n [R. koan, a cap], (C. koan). **hōng-koa^n**, an ornamental head-dress worn by mandarin ladies, and also at marriage by other ladies. **hōng-koa^n hê-pòe**, ornaments for head and girdle worn by mandarin ladies or wealthy ladies at marriage.

koa^n [R. kan, a flag-staff; a post]. **kî-koa^n**, a fixed flag-staff. **kî-koa^n-táu**, a projection, like a box, near the top of a Chinese flag-staff. **kî-koa^n-ngòeh**, the two side supports for a flag-staff. **kî-koa^n-tâi**, a square pediment about two feet high for supporting the flag-staff of a Tsin-sze or very high mandarin.

koa^n [R. kan, a rod or staff]. **tiò-koa^n**, a fishing-rod. **ơ-koa^n**, the long thin bamboo of a well-sweep that supports the bucket. **ơ-koa^n-chhìn**, that thin bamboo and the movable beam of the machine.

koa^n [R. kan, dry; dried, = khiên, = col. kiân, kien], dried eatables. **koa^n-bah**, the eatable part of dried fruit. **kien-koa^n**, dried, as eatables. **phåk-koa^n**, to dry in the sun, as eatables.

tāu-koa^n, bean-curd, boiled, salted, and pressed, in large squares. **ké-koa^n**, steamed cakes dried hard. **piá^n-koa^n**, biscuit. **bîn-thâu-koa^n**, hard-dried biscuits. **bák-koa^n**, dried cuttle-fish. **bát-koa^n**, id. **hî-koa^n**, dried fish. **lē-koa^n**, sort of dried fish.

mī^n-koa^n (Cn.), = A. mī^n-soà^n, vermicelli made from wheat. **bí-hún-koa^n** (Cn), = A. bí-hún, vermicelli made from rice-flour.

koa^n [R. koan, a coffin]. **koa^n-chhâ**, a coffin. **koa^n-chhâ-kn̄g**, two bamboo poles tied by ropes to the coffin when carried. **koa^n-chhâ-khut**, the pit of an old grave from which the coffin has been removed. **koa^n-chhâ-chiáu**, a bird with a beautiful crest. **oàh, m̄-chè nâ^n-âu; sí, chiah-beh-hàu koa^n-chhâ-thâu**, will give him no food in life, but after death will make offerings at the head of the coffin. **koa^n-chhâ tèng-teng, chiū kóe-pì^n**, will never reform till his coffin is nailed up.

koa^n [R. kan, name of an herb]. **koa^n-lân**, a flower somewhat like an iris. **koa^n-lân-hoe**, id. **soa^n-koa^n-lân**, a wild sort of flower like the above, but coarser; it produces the medicine "siā-kan."

koa^n (R. koan), a tall coarse sort of reed. **koa^n-chin**, stalks of this reed. **koa^n-chin-piah**, a partition made of these reeds interlaced and plastered. **koa^n-bâng**, stalks of the reed, used for brooms. **koa^n-thâu**, stubble of this reed (s. mandarin). **koa^n-chèng**, a coarse under mat made of this reed.

koa^n —. **koa^n-chià**, the common sugar-cane, grown to make sugar, as distinguished from the esculent "kam-chià."

koa^n (C.), = A. koai^n, a cross-bar in furniture. **toh-koa^n**, the cross-bars between the feet of a table.

koa^n (C.), = A. koai^n, to shut.

koa^n (R. koan), a mandarin; mandarin rank or office; belonging to government; public; affix to some names of relationships and superiors; respectful affix to names of women.

koa^n--lâng, mandarins in general. **koa^n-lâng**, master of a female slave. **koa^n-lâng niû^n-á**, master and mistress of female slave. **khiàm-koa^n-niû^n**, to be in arrears of land-tax. **koa^n-niû^n**, affix to name of husband (used by a slave or beggar in naming a married woman), *e.g.* **tsà-koa^n-niû^n**, the wife of the man whose name (not surname) is "tsà." **gîn-koa^n**, polite way of naming a woman whose name (not surname) is "gîn" (said by an inferior or stranger).

án-koa^n, master! (said by a slave). **ta-koa^n**, husband's father. **toā-koa^n** (C.), id. **ta-ke-koa^n**, husband's father and mother. **ke-koa^n**, id. **ū-ke ū-koa^n**, to have them, as daughter-in-law has. **kèng-ke-koa^n**, to reverence them as she ought to do. **goán-koa^n**, my husband's father. **chek-koa^n**, younger brother of husband's father. **peh-koa^n**, elder brother of husband's father.

kheh-koa^n, said by inn-keeper to his guests. **kiáu-koa^n**, the keeper of a gambling-house. **pó-koa^n**, keeper of a place where the "lién-pó" gambling is carried on. **hoat-koa^n**, a sort of Tauist enchanter. **tiám-tsú-koa^n**, the man who dots an ancestral tablet with red, at the grave.

phoà^n-koa^n, an idol attendant on the tutelary god "sêng-hông" (v. phoà^n). **sià-koa^n**, a paper image of a mandarin, burned in rites for the dead. **ơ-koa^n-iâ** (Cn.), a deified dog.

koa^n-hú, a mandarin. **chit-thia^n-koa^n**, one mandarin, *e.g.* as managing some business alone (v. thia^n). **koa^n-oân**, mandarins in general (v. oân). **bûn-bú pah-koa^n**, all the mandarins, civil and military. **bûn-koa^n**, a civil mandarin. **bú-koa^n**, a military or naval mandarin. **tūi-koa^n**, officer of some tens of soldiers. **sòe-koa^n**, a small mandarin. **toā-**

koaⁿ, a great mandarin. **toā-koaⁿ** (C.), = A. ta-koaⁿ, husband's father. **koāiⁿ-koaⁿ**, the mandarin of a Hien or district. **pē-bú-koaⁿ**, id. **gėk-koaⁿ**, small mandarin who has charge of the prison of a high mandarin. **pē-koaⁿ**, a member of one of the supreme boards at the metropolis. **ȯh-koaⁿ**, the literary mandarin of a department or district.

koaⁿ-chhin, mandarin's relatives. **koaⁿ-gê**, a mandarin's official residence; a yamun. **koaⁿ-thâu**, a confidential assistant of a mandarin in his yamun (s. reed). **koaⁿ-mûiⁿ**, a sort of female jailer (v. mûiⁿ). **koaⁿ-hu**, mandarin's chair-bearers. **koaⁿ-peng**, soldiers of the army of the government. **koaⁿ-bé**, government horses; used by soldiers or mandarins. **koaⁿ-tsō**, sort of mandarin barge. **chiȧh-koaⁿ-pn̄g**, to be in mandarin's employment.

koaⁿ-chit, official position; office. **koaⁿ-hâm**, official title. **koaⁿ-chiok** (r.), title of official rank. **koaⁿ-miâⁿ**, name assumed by a mandarin when he takes office; said also of the name taken by a graduate when he gets his degree. **koaⁿ-thé**, suitable behaviour and style of a mandarin, as in conduct, dress, &c. **bô-koaⁿ-tsâi**, wanting in the dignity of manner suitable to a mandarin. **kek-koaⁿ-phài**, to affect the manner or style of mandarins or of mandarin families.

ū-koaⁿ-sin, to be a mandarin. **ū-koaⁿ thang-tsòe**, to have the office of mandarin. **tsòe-koaⁿ**, to be a mandarin. **seng-koaⁿ**, to rise in office (v. seng). **koan-koaⁿ**, to purchase office or official title. **koan hit-ê-koaⁿ**, he has purchased that title. **sí-koaⁿ**, to resign office, retaining rank. **liáu-koaⁿ**, to be deposed from office and rank. **lut-koaⁿ**, id. **hȯk i-ê-koaⁿ**, to recover his office. **koaⁿ iáu-kú tī--teh**, his official rank is still left him.

chhiong-koaⁿ, to confiscate (v. chhiong). **bu̍t-koaⁿ** (r.), to be confiscated. **jip-koaⁿ** (r.), to be confiscated. **chiông-koaⁿ**, to be in the mandarin's hands, as a case already begun. **tso-koaⁿ-hû**, to litigate; to go to law. **phah-koaⁿ-si**, id.

koaⁿ-ōe, the "mandarin" dialect, *i.e.* the vernacular of Northern and Western China. **koaⁿ-im**, the sound of a word according to the mandarin dialect. **koaⁿ-lō͘**, a great road. **koaⁿ-phò͘**, a measure of ten lí (about three miles). **koaⁿ-tōe**, government land. **koaⁿ-táu**, the regulation bushel (táu) used in rice-shops. **koaⁿ-iâm**, salt from government stores legally bought (not contraband). **koaⁿ-chhek**, rice from government granaries.

koaⁿ-thiaⁿ, the cabin of a junk for richer passengers; a waiting-room in a yamun or temple (v. thiaⁿ). **koaⁿ-iè̍n**, birds'-nest of fine quality. **koaⁿ-kùi**, best cinnamon.

ti-koaⁿ káu-koaⁿ, mandarins cruel and unjust like pigs and dogs. **tham-koaⁿ ù-lī**, avaricious mandarins. **koaⁿ-toàn put-jû bîn-goān**, better that the people be willing than that the mandarin force the matter by a judgment.

koâⁿ (R. hân), cold (of weather or of feeling). **toā-koâⁿ**, great cold. **sng-koâⁿ seh-tàng**, extremely cold (lit. like frost and snow). **koâⁿ-kàu**, the cold weather or the ague fit has come. **ōe-koâⁿ**, are you cold? **bōe-koâⁿ**, I do not feel cold.

koâⁿ-léng, very cold. **koâⁿ-chhìn**, very cold, as weather. **koâⁿ-joȧh**, cold or hot, as weather. **koâⁿ-jiėt**, fever and ague (v. jiėt). **ka-iam-koâⁿ**, chilled; shivering. **ùi-koâⁿ**, chilled; shivering; afraid of a chill, so as to put on more clothes (v. ùi). **iau-koâⁿ**, cold and hungry (v. iau).

koâⁿ-thiⁿ, cold weather. **o͘-koâⁿ**, dark cold weather, as in winter or spring. **o͘-im-koâⁿ**, id. **o͘-koâⁿ-hō͘**, cold, dark, rainy weather.

koâⁿ-saⁿ, clothes for cold weather. **koâⁿ-bō**, a mandarin's warm cap with the button on.

koáⁿ [R. solitary; few, = col. koá], a small quantity. **koáⁿ-á**, id. **iu-jiû koáⁿ-toàn**, undecided in purpose.

ko͘-koáⁿ, orphans and widows. **ko͘-koáⁿ ê-lâng**, id. **ko͘-pîn-koáⁿ**, widows, orphans, and poor. **koan-koáⁿ ko͘-tȯk**, widows, bachelors, orphans, and others who have no relatives.

chiú-koáⁿ, a widow. **chiú-kóɛⁿ** (P.), id. **chiú-koáⁿ-lâng**, id. **chiú-koáⁿ ê hū-jîn-lâng**, id. **koáⁿ-hū**, id. **koáⁿ-ku**, to be a widow, especially a young widow remaining so. **teh-koáⁿ-ku**, id. **tsn̂g-siàu-liên koáⁿ-ku kàu-taⁿ**, has been a widow from youth till now, *i.e.* till old age.

koáⁿ-jîn (r.), said by a sovereign in speaking of himself, "I, the solitary man."

koáⁿ [R. koán, to rule; a tube]. **tsóng-koáⁿ**, a sort of boatswain formerly employed on large sea-going junks; not now used. **tso͘-koáⁿ**, a rich man's factor, who collects rents.

koáⁿ (R. kán), to chase away; to drive; to hasten, esp. another; to assemble at market.

koáⁿ-chhia, to drive a chariot or carriage. **koáⁿ-ah**, to feed a flock of ducks.

koáⁿ--khì, to drive away. **koáⁿ-soàⁿ**, to drive away and scatter. **koáⁿ-chhut**, to drive out. **koáⁿ-tiȯk**, expel, as a bad character from village, society, or employment. **tui-koáⁿ**, to chase.

koáⁿ-kín, to hasten. **koáⁿ-kàu**, to arrive by making speed. **hó-lâng koáⁿ-kàu**, by good fortune some one suddenly came up and saved from the danger. **chhui-koáⁿ**, to hasten a man still more; to urge him to do something very quickly. **goá--beh koáⁿ--i**, I will hasten him. **koáⁿ-lâng-siⁿ koáⁿ-lâng-sí, koáⁿ-lâng-chiȧh bô-thiⁿ-lí**, don't hurry a man at his meals.

koáⁿ-lō͘, to travel in great haste along the road. **koáⁿ-tsām**, id. **koáⁿ-hi**, to assemble at the market at the market-time. **koáⁿ-lâu-tsúi**, to travel in haste to catch the tide. **koáⁿ-phoe**, to be very busy getting a letter ready for an opportunity, so that we have no time to spare. **koáⁿ-hn̂g** (Cn.), to clear a field thoroughly of its crop, esp. potatoes. **koáⁿ-chhio**, excited with sexual passion, as the male.

koáⁿ (C.), = A. koáiⁿ. **chìⁿ-koáⁿ**, an arrow-shaft without feathers or shod.

koáⁿ (C.) **thih-koáⁿ**, iron ore (cf. Cn. kńg).

koàⁿ (R. koàn), a large Tauist temple for the worship of Yuh-hwang Shang-ti. **thiⁿ-kong-koàⁿ**, id. **koàⁿ-tsú**, the chief idol of such a temple, said not to be "thiⁿ-kong," who has no image.

koāⁿ (R. hān), sweat, perspiration. **lâu-koāⁿ**, to perspire; to sweat. **lâu-koāⁿ-hoe**, perspiration coming out in small drops on the skin. **koāⁿ-lâu moáⁿ-bīn**, face covered with perspiration. **chhìn-koāⁿ**, a cold perspiration. **lâu-chhìn-koāⁿ**, to have a cold sweat. **hoat-koāⁿ**, to perspire under medical treatment in illness. **chhut-koāⁿ**, perspiration coming at last in a disease; to grow damp, as wall or rock in south wind; to perspire.

hip-koāⁿ, to cover up warmly (as in illness) so as to cause perspiration. **sò-koāⁿ**, to absorb perspiration, as a dress.

koā^{n}, to carry a thing hanging down from the hand, as a basket; (to suspend round the neck); a large string of beads, pearls, cash, &c., strung together; a handle (attached at two places), as of basket or bucket, for carrying it; (string for fastening a hat); [perhaps these make more than one word].

koā^{n}-khí, to take up with the hand a thing that hangs down like a basket; to bring forward a subject. **koā^{n}-sa^{n}**, to lift up one's dress with the hand, as in crossing a stream. **koā^{n}-sàng**, to carry food, as to a man in prison (v. sàng). **koā^{n}-tsúi**, to carry water in a bucket or pitcher hanging down. **koā^{n}-hoe**, to carry a basket of flowers.

koā^{n} kha-lô, to have one's feet manacled (v. lô). **koā^{n}-kn̂g**, to wear a sort of amulet called "kn̂g" suspended round the neck.

koā^{n}-kui, having the crop very full and hanging down heavily, as a fowl; to have one's dress hang too loosely on the breast (v. kui). **bīn koā^{n}-káu** (T.), the cheek swollen, or very fat just below the eyes.

té-koā^{n}, a pouch like a sporran, worn on the belly, suspended from the neck. **gûn-koā^{n}**, a chain worn round the neck for suspending the pouch, &c. **ām-koā^{n}**, a child's bib; also (Cn.), a string of various things (esp. amulets) suspended from a child's neck.

chit-koā^{n}, a large string of beads, pearls, cash, &c. (much larger than "chhn̂g"), strung on a string. **chit-koā^{n}-chî^{n}**, a string of several hundred cash, (but a few cash tied together make "chit-kat.")

teng-koā^{n}, a handle fixed by its two ends on the top of a lantern. **tháng-koā^{n}**, a handle (as of rope) of a bucket, by which it can be hung or carried. **lóeh-á-koā^{n}**, a string for tying on a sun-hat. **bō-koā^{n}**, a string for fastening on a hat.

koā^{n}-mn̂g, fastenings of rattan, like ropes, by which the sail when spread is fastened to the mast. **sái-oá-koā^{n}**, to sail on the tack that brings the sail close on the mast. **sái-khui-koā^{n}**, to sail on the tack which makes the sail go as far as possible from the mast, held by these fastenings.

koah (R. kat), to cut, especially by drawing the knife along, or back and forwards; to wound, as by cutting; to reap; to slice, especially horizontally; to buy, as flesh meat; to undermine (a wall) or carry away (crops), as a flood; (to cut off, as intercourse).

koah tn̂g-tō͘, to hurt the bowels, as poison; to wound the heart, as severe grief (v. tn̂g). **koah-bah tn̂g-thiàn^{n}**, to make one cut, and have it over (said of some very painful matter that has to be done but once), (v. thià^{n}). **koah-bah**, to cut a criminal in pieces; to cut the flesh surgically. **koah chit-tè-bah**, to buy a piece of pork. **koah-âu**, to cut one's throat. **koah-koe**, to kill a fowl, by cutting the neck. **koah-huih**, to cut, so as to bring blood, as a fowl; or as a sorcerer does (v. huih).

koah-siá, to break off intercourse, especially said of man and woman, or of near relations. **kau-koah**, to dissolve partnership or business connections. **kap--i kau-koah**, to have finished up our business with him, so as now to have no responsibility. **kui-koah**, the share of the business reverting to another.

koah-tn̄g, to cut off; to cut separate. **koah-chháu**, to cut grass, &c. **koah-tiū**, to reap rice (v. tiū). **koah thâu-tsang**, to cut off the queue. **koah hī-á**, to cut off the ears. **koah kha-kun**, to cut the tendons of the heel, sometimes done as a punishment. **koah-chih**, to cut off the tongue; to cut the tongue, as sorcerers. **san-koah**, to prune, as branches; to cut away some, as grass.

koah im-jī, to cut sunk characters, as on wooden blocks, &c.

koah chhiû^{n}-kha, to undermine a wall, as a flood. **kiô khit-tsúi koah--tó**, the bridge was broken down by the flood.

moâ^{n}-koah, a stick with a hooked iron blade at the end, used for catching eels. **koah-moâ^{n}**, to plunge this instrument in the mud, and draw it up for eels.

sio-koah, meat cut from a roast pig. **hièn-sio-koah**, to present this meat to the guests, the last course of a feast in Manchoo style.

kòng-koah, common Chinese letter-paper.

koah, a company, clique, crowd, or herd. **oang-koah**, a set, company, or clique of persons (generally for somewhat bad purposes). **i--ê oang-koah**, his set of intimate associates or friends. **kui-oang kui-koah**, making a company, league, or confederacy; in cliques or companies. **kui-koah**, in herds or companies; a whole company. **kui-kûn kui-koah**, in herds or companies. **chit-toā-koah**, a great crowd or lot at once.

koah-hiu^{n}, to carry incense in procession.

koah [R. kat, name of a plant; Dolichos?], the plant from which grass-cloth is made. **koah-pò͘**, grass-cloth. **chēng-tsúi-koah**, common white grass-cloth.

ōng-lâi-koah, coarse summer cloth made from pine-apple leaves. **chio-koah**, a coarse yellow stuff of silk and cotton (v chio).

pėh-koah-koah, white, as complexion.

hoan-koah, a plant with a white edible root, somewhat like a turnip; has a palmate leaf in seven divisions. **teh-kóng sím-mih^{n} hoan-koah**, what ever are you talking about!

koah-hún, flour made from the root of the "koah" plant, somewhat like arrow-root. **kan-koah**, the same root sliced; it is infused to make a cooling mucilaginous drink.

koai, tame; gentle. **kà-koai**, to tame, as by beating or scolding. **bē-bat kà-koai**, not yet tamed, as a wild lad. **gín-ná koai-koai**, the child is very good. **beh-ōh-koai, pì^{n}-chiâ^{n}-gōng**, trying to be very clever at something, but spoiling it, as a lad or boy. **koai-lâi**, bright and intelligent, as a child. **koai-khá**, obedient and clever, as a child. **léng-lī koai-khá**, id. **koai-khá gín-ná**, a boy crafty, impudent, and foul-mouthed beyond his years. **koai-khá pì^{n}-chiâ^{n}-gōng** (C.), trying to play a clever part, but showing himself a fool, as a boy [same as following word?]

koai [R. disobedient; cf. koāi]. **kiēn-koai**, very dogged and crotchety; fond of opposing the wishes of others (v. kiēn).

koai (P.), = A. koe, a melon, cucumber, or pumpkin; better "koe."

koái (R. id.), to swindle; to kidnap; to seduce or decoy into evil. **koái--khì**, to kidnap or decoy away. **koái-lâng-khì**, id. **koái-tài**, to allure a woman or child to elope and run away. **koái-phièn**, to swindle; to kidnap; to allure to run away. **koái-iú**, to seduce into evil; to kidnap.

koái lâng-ê-chî^{n}, to swindle people out of their money. **pái--lâng koái--lâng**, id.

koái-lōng, to poison a man's mind against another; to delude into a quarrel with another.

koái-kùn, a swindler; a kidnapper; a great rogue. **koái-ông**, a swindler or man who leads lads into wicked courses.

koái [R. a staff, = col. koái^{n}], (also C. Cn., = A. koái^{n}). **lí thok-koái** (A.), one of the eight genii (sien) represented as a beggar; worshipped specially by beggar ballad-singers. **lí thek-koái** (Cn.), id. **thok-koái-sien** (C.), id. **kiàh-koái** (Cn.), = A. kiàh koái^{n}-á, to carry a staff.

koái [R. a sort of rush or grass; a surname]. **koái-thong**, a man of the Han dynasty who was a great talker. **koái-thong-chhùi**, a great talker.

koài (T.), = A. koà, a cover. **chit-koài-á-bí**, a small cover full of rice.

koài [R. strange; singular; a sort of demon; to be displeased, = col. kòe].

kièn-koài, to be somewhat displeased or offended, as at a slight fault or want of politeness. **bóh--tit kièn-koài**, do not be offended; forgive this fault. **goá bô-koài--lí**, I am not offended at you. **bōe-koài--tit**, he cannot well be found fault with, as his failure was unavoidable, &c. **bók-koài kî-jiên**, there is no reason for being offended, or taking it ill, as it is quite natural and proper.

kî-koài, strange (v. kî). **ku-koài**, id. **chhit-ku poeh-koài**, very strange. **ku-koài-phiah**, having a very strange peculiar temper or disposition, perverse, or apt to take notions. **koài-phiah**, id. **kó-koài**, eccentric; very peculiar in temper, *e.g.* not willing to do a friendly turn; very different from what was expected, as a thing. **khá-koài**, very strange or singular, as a discovery or invention; strange and unexpected, as result of illness or of affair. **káu-koài**, crafty and intriguing; changing one's conduct, so as to injure people unexpectedly. **koài-sū**, a very strange affair. **koài-ī^{n}** (R.), strange.

tāi-keng siáu-koài, suddenly much terrified (v. keng). **gî seng-koài**, suspicion makes a man more and more suspicious, = gî, chek seng-koài, = gî lêng-seng-koài.

tsok-koài, to injure, as a demon causing trouble, or as a man making secret opposition; to behave in an idle and wicked way, as young man. **poeh-jī koài-koài**, the combinations of the horoscope very extraordinary, so that the ordinary rules do not apply. **koài-hong**, a strange sudden violent wind (v. hong). **koài-sút**, magical diabolical arts. **koài-bùt**, a very wicked demon which once was an animal, and now works mischief in the shape of that animal.

kúi-koài, spectres, ghosts, demons, &c. **tsòe-kúi tsòe-koài**, very crafty and injurious, with pretence of honesty or friendship. **kúi-kúi koài-koài**, id. **kì^{n}-kúi kì^{n}-koài**, utterly false. **iau-siâ kúi-koài**, diabolical or magical arts, spectres, &c. **iau-koài**, spectres, goblins, demons, elves, fairies, &c. **liàh iau-koài**, to catch them, as priests do.

koāi [R. koai, stubborn; contrary in temper], (C. kōe, in some phrases), to sprain, as the foot, especially by unexpectedly stepping lower than we thought. **koāi--tiòh**, id. **kha koāi--tiòh**, the ankle sprained.

koāi-koāi, not agreeing well; not as we could wish. **koāi-phiah**, of a somewhat perverse or contrary disposition. **koāi-tsūn**, perversely disobedient; intentionally bad-tempered and disobliging (worse than "koāi-phiah"). **kap-goá koāi-tsūn**, disobedient or doggedly contrary to me. **koāi-chiang**, obstinate in disputing; determined to have his own way; very stubborn; esp. said of an inferior. **koāi-tiang** (C.), id. **koāi-lién**, changed to the opposite mind (from having been of our mind) so as to disobey, distrust, or thwart us.

koai^{n} (C. koa^{n}), a cross-bar, as in furniture; a roost. **hioh-koai^{n}**, to roost.

í-koai^{n}, the cross-bars or rounds connecting the feet of a chair or stool; small bits of wood or bamboo in the arms of an arm-chair. **toh-koai^{n}**, cross-bars connecting the feet of a table. **chhn̂g-koai^{n}**, cross-bars at head or foot of a bedstead. **jia-hong-koai^{n}**, id.

koai^{n} [R. koan, a gateway; to shut a door], (C. koa^{n}; Cn. kūi^{n}), to shut, as a door; to imprison. **koai^{n}-ka^{n}**, to imprison in the worse prison (v. ka^{n}). **koai^{n}-koán**, to confine in the less uncomfortable prison. **koai^{n} thang-á**, to shut a window. **koai^{n}-mn̂g**, to shut the door. **koai^{n} tah-tah**, to shut quite close, as door (v. tah).

koai^{n} (T.), = kai^{n}, = A. keng, the shoulder.

koâi^{n} (C. koân; Cn. kûi^{n}), high; skilful, as doctor, or at games, &c.; good, as silver; powerful, as magic. **koâi^{n}-kē**, high and low; skilful and unskilful. **koâi^{n}-lâu**, a high building of more than one story.

koâi^{n}-tioh, skilful at anything; superior to others in skill. **i-seng koâi^{n}**, the doctor is skilful. **kûn-thâu koâi^{n}**, skilful at boxing. **kî koâi^{n}**, good at chess. **kiáu koâi^{n}**, skilful at gambling. **gûn bô-sím-mih^{n}-koâi^{n}**, the silver is not very good.

chit-tsoā koâi^{n}, one voyage in the year (is made by the junk) to the north (v. tsoā).

chhiú pàng-koâi^{n}, to act more gently or more mercifully towards a man than we had intended, or than he deserves. **chhiú kiàh-koâi^{n}**, to reach up high with the hand; to act gently or mercifully (v. kiàh).

koái^{n} (R. kán), (C. koá^{n}; Cn. kúi^{n}), a stalk of grain or vegetables; (shaft of arrow or pen; beam of steelyard, &c.) **chhài-koái^{n}**, stalk of vegetable. **chhèng-koái^{n}**, the barrel of a gun. **kî-koái^{n}**, a small flag-staff; a flag-staff of a simple kind without boxes, supports, &c. **pit-koái^{n}**, shaft of a Chinese pen. **chhiu^{n}-koái^{n}**, shaft of a spear. **chì^{n}-koái^{n}**, shaft of arrow, without shod or feathers. **chhun chit-ki-koái^{n}**, having quite lost its point, as a Chinese pen.

chhìn-koái^{n}, the beam of a steelyard. **téng-á-koái^{n}**, beam of small steelyard.

koái^{n} (R. koái), (C. Cn. koái), a staff; a stick. **koái^{n}-á**, a walking-stick. **tuh koái^{n}-á**, to feel one's way with a stick in walking. **thuh koái^{n}-á**, to lean on a stick. **thok koái^{n}-á**, id.; also to feel one's way with it. **lí-thok-koái^{n}**, one of the genii. **kiàh koái^{n}-á**, to carry a stick.

lāng koái^{n}-á-hoe, to flourish one's stick with joy, as a beggar (said in derision of a man making too much demonstration of joy, or of actors). **khit-chiàh lāng koái^{n}-á-hoe**, id.

koái^{n}-á-gûn, Bolivian dollars. **beh-siú^{n} koái^{n}-á-gûn**, said in joke of a man going to strike another with a staff.

chhiah koái^{n}-koái^{n}, very poor. **chhun chit-ki-koái^{n}**, very poor and having no relations at all (s. "stalk," to which perhaps this last group may belong).

koái^{n} (T.), = A. koá, a small quantity (enclitic).

koài^{n} (R. koàn), (C. koàn; Cn. kùi^{n}), accustomed; habituated. **ōe-koài^{n}**, he will get accustomed to it. **ta^{n} koài^{n}--lah**, now he has got accustomed to it. **kóng-koài^{n}**, said constantly, as a phrase or word commonly used. **m̄-koài^{n}**, not accustomed. **m̄-koài^{n}-sì**, id. **koài^{n}-sì**, accustomed; habituated; experienced and accustomed to. **koài^{n}-sì sêng tsū-jiân**, habit become a second nature.

koāi^{n} (R. hiēn), (C. koān; Cn. küi^{n}), a Hien city, or district, or mandarin of it; a county or district. **hái-têng-koāi^{n}**, the city or district or mandarin of Hái-têng.

koāi^{n}-siâ^{n}, the chief city of a county or district. **koāi^{n}-koa^{n}**, the district mandarin. **koāi^{n}-tsú**, id. **koāi^{n}-óh**, the Confucian temple of a district; the literary mandarih of the district. **hun-koāi^{n}**, the mandarin of a subdivision of a district; the Fun-hien. **koāi^{n}-sêng**, id. **hú-koāi^{n}**, department and district; prefect and district mandarin.

koāi^{n} (C. kōe). **oai^{n}-koāi^{n}**, to get a little money out of a man (without any idea of repayment) by constant asking or begging; to extort small sums, as underlings of yamuns. **lán bô-oai^{n} bô-koāi^{n}**, we don't ask a cash of his money; we feel quite independent of him and his wealth. **chhit-oai^{n} poeh-koāi^{n}**, to get money out of people in all sorts of ways.

koàih^{n}, noise, as of breaking wood. **koàih^{n}--chit-ē**, sudden sound, as of a piece of wood breaking. **koàih^{n}-koàih^{n}-kiò**, sound of a creaking lid or door, or of a chair creaking, when a man does not sit still. **koàih^{n}-koàih^{n}-háu**, id.

bòh-tit-koàih^{n}, don't talk in that way! esp. said to an inferior speaking of what should not be spoken of at all, or talking on when he should stop.

kōng-koàih^{n}, not agreeing well together, at variance, as persons; legs of unequal length.

koàk, sound of drinking.

koan [R. an old bachelor or widower]. **koan-koá^{n} kə-tòk**, the four classes of solitary persons to be compassionated, viz.: an old man with no wife; a widow; an orphan; a childless old man, with no near relatives.

koan [R. name of a bird]. **tə̄-koan**, a sort of bird; a kind of red flower. **tə̄-koan-hoe**, that flower. **âng-tə̄-koan**, id.

koan [R. kun, an army]. **koan-chiòng**, spirit soldiers of the gods (v. chiòng).

koan [R. to look at carefully; to observe], to observe carefully with a view to certain actions, *e.g.* to watch the stroke-oar or the state of the waves; to watch against thieves or loss.

koan-im, the goddess Kwan-yin (v. im).

koan-khoà^{n}, to look at attentively, as a view or a man's conduct. **sam-koan ngə́-hok**, to examine over and over very carefully. **koan lâng--ê ì-sù**, to make out a man's intention by observing his conduct carefully. **koan thâu-chiú^{n}**, to observe the stroke-oar (in China the bow-oar) so as to take the stroke correctly. **koan éng-sè**, to observe the state of the waves, as in rowing.

koan-san goán-súi, to go about looking at scenery for amusement. **koan thien-siōng**, to look at atmospheric phenomena or the heavenly bodies. **biēn-biēn siong-koan**, looking speechlessly at one another, as when unable to ward off imminent danger.

khó-koan-hong, to examine the literati of a place, giving bursaries or scholarships (not examination for degrees).

koan [R. id., = col. "koai^{n}," to shut], a gateway; a barrier or pass with a gate, as of a custom-house; relating to; a surname; to perform certain Tauist incantations for calling spirits; to talk over, seduce, or wheedle by plausible talk.

koan-ki, to perform Tauist incantations (burning paper, reciting prayers, &c.), to call the spirit of an idol to the mediums who write oracles by a peach branch (v. ki). **koan-tâng**, to make incantations to call the spirit to a (tâng-chí) sorcerer. **koan-pùt**, do., either for writing or for a sorcerer, in presence of an idol. **koan-lién**, to recite prayers and burn paper to bring the spirit of the idol to the image in its sedan.

gâu-koan--lâng, skilful at talking over people (formerly unwilling) to do what one wishes, as a plausible swindler, or as a seducer (fig. from the priest getting the spirit to consent by his incantations). **khit--i koan--khì**, to be persuaded at last by his plausible talk to go to do some bad or ruinous thing, though at first unwilling.

toā-láu-koan, a great swindler with very plausible ways.

kau-koan, to have intercourse with in trade. **ki-koan**, an intricate contrivance; versatility and ability to adapt one's plans to emergencies (v. ki).

thong-koan, to remove a feeling like dyspepsia by medicines taken like snuff (v. thong).

kè-koan, to pass the custom-house, as a document; to get safely through certain critical periods when the influence of malicious spirits is very dangerous to infants. **chiàh bōe-kè-koan**, unable to swallow.

koan-soah, demons very dangerous to infants at certain periods called "koan." **pah-jit-koan**, the crisis at one hundred days after birth, very dangerous to infants. **hoān--tiòh pah-jit-koan**, to be unwell at that crisis. **hoān--tiòh lûi-koan**, child in danger of being struck by lightning.

sú-bûn-koan, the gates of the invisible world. **kúi-bûn-koan**, id. **jip kúi-bûn-koan**, to die; to be as good as dead, as a man in most imminent danger without any hope of life; or as a man who is quite gone to the bad in wicked courses.

lə̄-koan, a journey as regards its course or route; a bill pasted up telling the time and route of an idolatrous incense-procession. **lə̄-koan-pâi**, a tablet of wicker-work and paper giving that information. **tah lə̄-koan**, to paste up such a bill. **chhau lə̄-koan**, to copy such a bill. **lə̄-koan-kə́**, the drum that heads the procession and leads the way.

koan-sim, to count important; to have one's mind much set upon a thing; careful and attentive, as at work or study. **ū-koan-sim**, carefully remembering or considering and making exertion. **ū-koan-chhiet**, having importance in relation to a matter or thing (v. chhiet). **koan-chiet**, to have underhand dealings, as with mandarins (v. chiet). **bô-koan kín-iàu** (r.), of no consequence.

koan-chiò, to have reference to, as one passage of a book to another, &c.

koan-siàp, related to; having connection with. **bô-koan-siàp**, having no connection with it (cf. kan-siàp). **koan-hē**, relation to consequences, esp. evil or dangerous; responsibility for an action. **sī lí--ê koan-hē**, the responsibility is yours. **bô-koan-hē**, not involving any responsibility or danger of bad consequences. **ū-koan-hē**, of grave importance, as a matter that has or may have serious consequences. **koan-hē put-siáu**, the consequences are or may be very serious. **koan-hē siong-tiōng**, id.

hái-koan, a custom-house (only said of the more important custom-houses); chief commissioner or collector of customs at a port (often applied improperly to consuls). **sin sè-koan**, the new foreign custom-house.

hoan-koan, id. **koan-sè**, customs duties. **chē-koan**, to be on duty at the custom-house at the hours of business, as a customs officer.

koan-ài, a pass having a gate. **koan-mn̂g**, the gate of a pass or barrier. **koan-hông**, to watch or guard carefully, as against thieves or robbers, or against loss; the oblong seal of some mandarins, as Tautai and others, of more recent institution than those having a square seal. **pé-koan**, to guard a pass or barrier-gate. **siú-koan**, id.

gâu-tńg chih-koan, skilful at putting the best face on a story or argument, so as to suit the circumstances, with no regard to truth. **gâ-koan bōe-khui**, the teeth locked, as in a faint, or when near death.

koan-tè, Kwanti, the god of war (much worshipped by merchants and shopkeepers). **koan-tè-iâ**, id., = koan-tè-kun, = koan-sèng-tè. **koan-kong**, id., = koan-ló-iâ, = koan-hūn-tióng. **koan-pêng**, his adopted son, who attends him. **koan-to**, a peculiar hooked spear or halbert. **bú toā-ki koan-to** (to wield a large spear), said of having considerable influence or a good business. **kiáh toā-ki koan-to**, id. **koan-to-teng**, a lantern with a hook in front (much used by children at the feast of lanterns).

koan [R. a coffin, = col. koa^n]. **ūn-koan**, to convey home the coffined corpse of a man who has died far from home. **thêng-koan**, to keep a coffined body long unburied waiting for a lucky time and place. **khǹg-koan**, id. **hē-koan**, to have such coffins lying in it, as a dead-house. **tsòng-koan**, to bury a body in a coffin; opposed to "tsòng-kim," burying a jar of bones. **kiap-koan**, to plunder ornaments, &c., from graves.

koan-kok, a coffin (properly outer and inner coffin). **koan-kok i-khim**, coffin and shroud. **koan-kiū**, a coffin containing a body. **si-siá koan-bók**, to give coffins gratuitously. **koan-tà**, a pall. **koan-khut**, the cavity of an old grave from which the coffin has been removed.

koan-thâu, the head of a coffin. **koan-thâu-tsoá**, idolatrous paper presented to the relatives after a death. **sàng koan-thâu-tsoá**, to make presents of it, as friends do. **koan-bé**, the foot of a coffin.

koan [R. a cap, = col. koa^n]. **i-koan put-chéng**, clothes and cap ragged or dirty. **i-koan put-chê**, id. **i-koan khîm-siù**, said of a graduate acting wickedly and lasciviously like a beast. **sien tiōng-i-koan, hō tiōng-jîn**, to value men according to their dress. **koan-tài** (R.), cap and belt of mandarin. **ka-koan chìn-lók** (R.), may you rise to high rank (written on doors). **kiú-liông-koan**, a royal crown with nine dragons. **chhiong-thien-koan**, id. **hōng-koan hê-kòe** (C.), female head-dress used at marriage. **lêng-koan hōng-kòe** (C.), id.

koan [R. to subscribe money; to purchase a degree or rank]. **koan-tôe** (C. kien-tê), to subscribe money. **koan kun-su**, to promise to pay so much of contributions for government purposes.

koan-pan, to purchase a degree or office. **koan-koa^n**, to purchase official rank. **koan-kòng**, to purchase the title of kòng-seng. **koan-kàm**, to purchase the title of kàm-seng.

koan [R. a mandarin; a ruler, = col. koa^n]. **ngó-koan**, the features, namely, the ears, eyes, eyebrows, nose, and mouth. **ngó-koan put-chê**, having some ugly blemish, especially about the features. **ngó-koan toan-chiá^n**, features regular and without any blemish. **sù-chi ngó-koan**, the members of the body, including the head. **ngó-koan sù-chi**, id.

thien-koan, the spirit that rules the sky or heaven; his birthday is 1.15. **thien-koan tāi-tè**, id. **thien-koan sù-hok**, may the ruler of heaven give happiness. **tē-koan**, the spirit that rules earth and hell. **tē-koan-si^n**, his birthday on 7.15. **súi-koan**, the spirit that rules the sea; birthday is 10.15. **sam-koan tāi-tè**, these three rulers, = sam-kài-kong.

koan-ka tsú-tē, younger brothers, sons, and nephews of mandarins, when young. **tham-koan ù-lī**, avaricious mandarins. **koan iú lióng-khó**, a mandarin has two mouths (in allusion to the form of the character, which is like two mouths under one cap). **koan-chim** (R.), proper rules of official conduct (v. chim). **it-sè koan, kiú-sè oan**, nine generations at enmity because of the wicked conduct of their ancestor when in office.

koân (C.), = A. koâi^n, high.

koân (R. id.), authority; power; (to act according to circumstances or beyond instructions). **ū-koân**, to have authority. **bô-koân**, having no power or authority. **koân-lêng**, authority. **koân-pèng**, id. **koân-sè** (C. si), id.

peng-koân tsāi-chhiú, to have authority to manage matters for others, *e.g.* in a company. **ū peng-koân**, do.; also, to have military authority. **chiáng peng-koân**, id. (both senses).

koân-pièn, going somewhat beyond one's authority in order to accommodate one's action to an urgent emergency. **chiông-koân**, id. **hêng-koân** (R.), id.

koân--ê, temporarily acting as a substitute or in a vacancy till a new man be appointed (said, *e.g.*, of employé, or teacher, or official. **chiām-koân**, to be acting as a temporary substitute (v. chiām). **chhiàm-koân**, to usurp authority. **chhoàn-koân**, id. **tsoan-koân**, having the sole management of an affair or business (v. tsoan). **tong-koân**, having the control or management at the time; having much influence just then.

lōng-koân, to make a bad use (as for his own ends) of authority committed to him, or of the influence he has with a powerful superior who has confidence in him, yet keeping within the letter of the law. **lōng i-ê-koân**, id.

koán (R. id.), a public hall or office; a school; a lodging; a prison for minor offences, or for simply confining without punishment.

tsō-koán, to rent a lodging. **kong-koán**, a sort of hotel for mandarins and literati (said politely for "your inn"). **kheh-koán**, an inn; a lodging-house. **lí--ê kùi-koán**, your school; your lodgings or hotel. **koán-tē**, school premises. **koán-tē tá-lòh**, where is your school? **ū koán-tē**, to have a school or school premises. **bô-koán-tē**, to have no school or no premises for one. **khek-koán**, a place for teaching songs. **kûn-thâu-koán**, a school for boxing. **keng-chì^n-koán**, a school for archery. **khiā-koán**, to teach boxing, &c., at one's own gymnastic school.

hōe-koán, a sort of club-house or exchange; the meeting-house of a society called a "hōe." **tê-koán**, a refreshment-room for drinking tea. **i-koán** (f.), an hospital. **hì-koán**, an actor's lodging-house. **tèk-jit-koán**, stall or shop of a man who chooses lucky days.

ka^n-koán, prisons in general, the more and less uncomfortable. **khoà^n-koán**, to have charge of the less uncomfortable prison. **khoà^n-koán toā-iâ**, the keeper of it. **siu-koán**, to imprison in it (s. rule; manage). **siu-lóh-koán**, id. **lóh-koán**, id. **koaiⁿ-koán**, to keep imprisoned in it. **ah-koán**, id. **tsô-khoài-koán**, the rooms for the underlings on each side at the outermost part of a yamun.

hiòng-koán, a custom-house (v. hiòng). **iâm-koán**, government salt-store and custom-house for salt; the official in charge of it. **pò-sè-koán**, an office at the custom-house where vessels report themselves. **pò-toaⁿ-koán**, id. **bûn-su-koán**, a sort of post-office, properly for official despatches.

koán-hu, a man who provides and cooks feasts to order; keeper of a cook-shop.

koán [R. koan, to subscribe money]. **ū-koán-kok**, to have one's food as well as salary, as the teacher has in some schools.

koán [R. to roll up, =col. kńg, boán]. **koán-chien**, a sort of fried cake (v. chien).

koán [R. to rule; a tube, =col. kńg, kóng, kə́, koáⁿ], to rule; to manage; to control; wind instruments; some kinds of songs.

put-koán, no matter which. **put-koán sím-mih-lâng**, no matter who or whom. **m̄-koán**, no matter which. **m̄-koán--i**, no matter; don't mind (him or it). **chek-koán**, as it pleases you. **chek-koán kóng**, speak out fearlessly; say what you please. **m̄-sái lí-koán**, you need not meddle. **thèng-koán--i**, you may rule or punish him as you please.

chit-hāng koán chit-hāng, one part (as of a dose) corrects one part (as of the disease).

koán-lí, to have the management; to manage, as a business or affair. **chiáng-koán**, id. **chióng-koán**, id. **koán-hat**, to rule; to govern. **koán-kə̀**, to oversee and manage for another; to watch over and take charge of. **tsóng-koán**, to have the general management over a number of persons employed, as a wealthy man's steward. **chiàu-koán**, to oversee or take charge of, as a house. **siu-koán**, to have authority over, as things (v. siu), (s. prison). **sêng-koán**, to succeed to and have control over, as property (v. sêng). **kiam-koán**, to manage two offices or duties at once.

keng-koán, subordinates in a yamun, at the head of the several departments of business (v. keng). **koán-hú**, a soldier of good standing; he often has three or four raw men under him. **koán-kaⁿ**, to superintend a prison, as a very small mandarin does for a high mandarin.

koán-sū, a steward, as in a foreign house. **koán-ke**, head-servant or steward. **koán-ke-pô**, a housekeeper. **koán-siàu**, a steward who manages accounts. **koán-gûn**, a man who has charge of the money.

hiân-koán, stringed and wind instruments. **oaiⁿ hiân-koán**, to make joyful music on them. **hoāⁿ hiân-koán**, id. **thit-thô hiân-koán**, to amuse one's self with them. **phín-koán**, an instrument like a flute along with three sorts of guitars, namely, pí-pê, sam-hiân, and jí-hiân. **tōng-koán**, a clarionet along with these three guitars.

háh-koán, in tune, as instruments, with each other or with the voice. **chhèng-koán**, to sing very high notes. **pak-koán**, songs in the mandarin dialect. **lâm-koán**, songs in the local dialect. **phah lâm-pak-koán**, to play all sorts of musical instruments.

koàn [R. to string together; to connect, = col. kǹg]. **koàn-chhoàn**, logically connected, as the context, or as the parts of a discourse or composition. **lāi-chîⁿ koàn bú-chîⁿ**, compound interest. **tsōe-ok koàn-boán** (r.), measure of wickedness come to the full.

koàn [R. accustomed to; habituated, =col. koàiⁿ], (also C., = A. koàiⁿ). **koàn-sio̍k**, experienced and very skilful; thoroughly acquainted with a matter or business, &c. (s. family). **koàn-liān**, id. **koàn-sèk** (P.), id.

sip-koàn, sêng tsū-jiân, what is constantly practised till habitual becomes natural.

koàn [R. koân, the cheek-bones], the projecting part of the cheek at the cheek-bone. **koàn-kut**, the cheek-bone. **i-ê-koàn khah-toā**, his cheek-bones project very much.

koàn [R. to pour; to make a libation], to pour into the throat or similar aperture; to stuff into the throat; to pour (melted lead) into a cavity; to come through a passage or hole, as wind.

koàn-kūi, filled with water, as the wall of an ill-built house. **koàn-lâng**, to gather matter, as a boil or abscess.

koàn-hong, to be blown upon by a draught of wind, as some diseases are said to be caused. **hong tùi-tá-lóh koàn--lâi**, from what place does that draught of wind come?

koàn-iân, to pour melted lead into a cavity; dollars thus adulterated. **chhia-koàn--ê**, a dollar hollowed out and filled with lead.

koàn-chiú, to pour liquor down the throat, as in large quantities, or down another's throat. **koàn-io̍h**, to pour medicine down the throat, as of another. **koàn-tsúi**, to pour water into the bowels of an animal that has been killed, so that it is absorbed into the flesh and makes it heavier for sale. **koàn-tsúi ê-bah**, pork that has been made thus to absorb water, as adulteration. **koàn-kui**, to put heavy things into the crop of a fowl to make it weigh heavier for sale. **koàn-soa**, to put sand thus into a fowl's crop. **koàn-thih-sái**, to make a fowl swallow a sort of heavy stones for this purpose.

koàn-tiān (R.), to pour out a libation in worship. **koàn-tōe**, to pour a libation on the ground. **ēng-chiú koàn-tōe**, to make a libation of spirituous liquor.

koàn [R. a jug, vase, or small jar]. **tâng-koàn**, a brass jug or jar. **siah-koàn**, a pewter jug.

hé-koàn, a jar full of inflammable matter (called a "stink-pot") thrown into vessels by pirates.

tīm-koàn, an earthenware vessel used for stewing things, placed within an outer dish of boiling water. **thâm-koàn**, a spittoon. **chhâ-khe koàn-á**, a small earthen vessel that holds a little wood and rice presented to idols. **lêng-koàn**, an earthenware vessel for water, shaped like a kettle, with dragons on it. **tsúi-koàn**, a jug or small jar for water; a ewer. **kún-tsúi-koàn**, a jug for hot water. **io̍h-koàn**, a small jar for medicine. **iû-koàn**, an oil-jug. **thn̂g-koàn**, a sugar-dish. **ba̍k-tsúi-koàn**, an ink-bottle.

tê-koàn, a tea-pot. **tê-koàn-sui**, the spout of a tea-pot. **tê-koàn-chhùi**, the very end of the spout. **tê-sim-koàn**, a tea-canister.

koàn [R. to take care of; to love; family]. **ke-koàn**, wife and children. **ū-ke ū-koàn**, to have a family. **lāu-ke-koàn**, my old wife. **sió-ke-koàn**, a concubine. **chhin-koàn**, mandarin's wife and connections by marriage.

koàn-sio̍k, wife and family (s. accustomed).

koàn [R. to cap; to be superior; by change of tone

厦英大辭典

from "koan," a cap]. **koàn-tiûⁿ**, to be the best essay in the examination; to overcome in a contest, as a horse in a race, or as a game-cock or quail at a fight, &c.

koàn [R. koàn, koán, a roll; a volume, = col. kǹg, kńg], a small volume or section of a volume. **tē-jī-koàn**, second volume or second division of large volume. **koàn-jī**, id.

koàn [R. koàn, khoàn]. **khòe-koàn**, deeds of sale or mortgage.

koān (C.), = A. koāiⁿ, a district or hien city, county, or mandarin.

koān [R. wearied; exhausted]. **koān-sîn koān-sîn**, dull and wanting animation, as man when unwell or much exhausted, or depressed by some calamity. **phî-koān** (R.), exhausted; faint. **khùn-koān** (R.), id.

koat [R. to pare; to scrape]. **koat-siėt**, a tongue-scraper.

koat — **koat-tsoȧt**, to cut off intercourse.

koat [R. to determine; to behead]. **koat-toàn**, determined. **koat-ì**, id. **iû-ū put-koat**, undecided; wavering. **koat-sí-chièn**, to fight for life or death.

koat-hoān, to behead a criminal.

koat — **koat-bêng**, a medicine used for inflamed eyes and for boils (v. bêng).

koat [R. a rule or receipt for doing some difficult or secret sort of work], mnemonic rhymes or antithetic sentences, as for medical prescriptions, or for teaching children the shapes of words. **liām-koat**, to repeat such mnemonic sentences. **koa-koat**, mnemonic rhymes for any purpose. **pì-koat**, secrets, esp. trade secrets, taught only to the initiated. **siong-thoân ê pì-koat**, secrets of business or profession handed down from one generation to another, esp. medical or surgical.

tek-koat, to hit on the right plan; all right and just as we would wish it; suitable to effect the purpose. **m̄-tek-koat**, not arranged as it should have been, as an affair; not suitable for the work or business. **ēng-i, m̄-tek-koat**, he is not the suitable man to use.

chip-sí-koat, obstinate. **liȧh-sí-koat**, id. **tsō-sí-koat**, id. **sí-koat ê seng-lí**, a steady moderate trade, that does not need much skill, and that has regular though small profits.

koat, to slap; to clap on, as mortar. **koat-chhiú**, to clap the hands. **koat chhiú-chiúⁿ**, to slap a child's palm with our palm. **koat chhùi-phóe**, to slap the cheek. **koat hī-á**, to slap the ears.

koat-he, to clap cement (as on a floor) with a sort of trowel, so as to make it smooth and hard. **koat-thô͘**, to clap mortar on a wall. **koat-hún**, to paint one's face very thick.

pėh-koat-koat, very white, as whitewash.

koat [R. to include]. **pau-koat**, to include; inclusive. **kai-koat** (r.), all that is contained in a thing; all that is included. **kai-koat tsāi-lāi** (r.), id.

koat (C.), = A. khiet. **kúi-koat**, deceitful.

koe — **súi-koe**, a large edible frog. **súi-ke** (C.), id. **kap-koɛ-á** (C.), a tadpole.

koe — **koe-lun**, an edible gray sea-slug.

koɛ (C.), in several tones and words, = A. koa.

koe [R. kui, a tortoise, = col. ku]. **koe-kioh**, a small marine animal shaped like a tortoise's foot.

koe — **koe-bîn** (C.), = A. hâm-bîn, talking in sleep. **lí teh-koe-bîn** (C.), you are telling what is not true.

koe — **koe-liu**, very mean and low in money matters.

koe (R. ke), (C. ke, Cn. köe), a fowl; a hen or cock. **sio-koe**, roast fowl.

hé-koe, the lock of a gun; a turkey. **khī-koe**, a pheasant. **thī-koe**, id. **tī-koe**, id. **chhân-koe-á**, a small bird somewhat like a partridge or quail.

tsàu-koe, a small speckled cricket, found in cooking places.

koe-bú, a hen that has laid eggs. **hái-koe-bú**, a sort of ship-broker (v. bú). **koe-kak**, a cock. **koe-kak-chhì**, the thistle. **chhio-koe**, an entire cock. **iam-koe**, a capon. **iam-koe-kiâⁿ**, to walk in a crouching attitude with slow steps; to walk on one's hands. **iam-koe thàn-hōng-pe**, a capon trying to fly like the phœnix! **koe-á**, a young chicken. **chhut-sì koe-á**, a chick lately hatched. **koe-noāⁿ**, a young fowl, as one that has not yet hatched chickens. **koe-thô-á**, chickens not yet weighing one Chinese pound. **chiūⁿ-kun-koe**, a good-sized fowl, weighing above a Chinese pound.

toā-keh-koe, a large sort of fowl from Shanghai. **tiàu-koe**, id. **thài-hô-koe**, a small sort of fowl like a bantam. **óe-kha-koe**, id. (lit. short-legged). **iù-mn̂g-koe**, a sort of white fowl. **jiông-koe**, id. (v. jiông), also, to stew a fowl very soft.

koe-mn̂g, hen's feathers (v. mn̂g). **koe-kū**, a cock's spur. **koe-kè** (C. ke-kòe), a cock's crest or comb (v. kè). **koe-kha-lân**, a sweet flower shaped like a hen's foot (v. lân). **koe-tȧ**, a basket without bottom for covering fowls like a coop. **koe-tàu**, id. **koe thí**, the cock crows (v. thí). **koe-tâi**, an insect that lives on fowls. **koe-ko**, soft yellowish fowl's dung (v. ko). **koe-sái**, dark-coloured fowl's dung, harder than the above. **koe-sái-tîn**, a bad-smelling medicinal creeper.

koe-bȧk, fond of sleep, and going soon to bed. **koe-heng**, having a projecting breast (v. heng). **koe-chih-táu**, projecting ends of beams below the roof, shaped like a fowl's tongue. **koe-chhùi**, a double-headed pin for making a rope fast. **tiô-kha-koe**, to hop, as children do. **thiàu-kha-koe**, id. **chhiāng-kha-ke** (C.), id.

koe (R. koa), (C. koa; P. koɛ, koai), a melon, pumpkin, or cucumber. **koe-pîⁿ**, a trellis for cucumbers, &c. **koe-chí**, melon seeds, sold salted. **koe-liām**, a cut of a melon. **chit-liām-koe**, id. **chiùⁿ-koe**, condiment made of the pumpkin called "am-koe" and the sauce called "tāu-chiùⁿ."

si-koe, the water-melon (v. si). **chhài-koe**, the long soft cucumber, much used as a vegetable. **chhū-koe** (Cn.), id. **chhài-koe-chhiu**, cucumber tendrils. **kim-koe**, the pumpkin. **chhì-koe**, the cucumber. **khó͘-koe**, the rough bitter cucumber. **am-koe**, a long sort of pumpkin, much used salted. **siau-koe** (Cn.), id. **tang-koe**, a very long pumpkin almost like a cucumber (Cucurbita Pepo); a preparation of it in sugar. **tang-koe-liāu**, this fruit prepared with sugar as a sweetmeat. **âng-koe** (F.), a small red edible fruit.

koe sòe, chí sek (melon small, but seeds ripe), said of a short man who looks younger or less knowing than he really is.

koe (R. ke), (C. ke, Cn. köe), a street. **koe-lô͘**, id. **koe-chhī**, a street of shops; a market in a street. **koe-kû**, id. **ke-kì** (C.), id. **goā-koe**, streets in the suburbs. **lāi-koe**, streets within the walls of a city. **sip-jī-koe**, a place where two streets cross at right angles.

chhâ-koe, a policeman. **tsáu-koe-á**, street fortune-tellers, quacks, &c. **tsáu-koe-á-sien**, id.

koe [R. kai, stone steps], (C. ke; Cn. köe). **gîm-koe**, the stone step at the foot of the wall of a house.

koe (C. ke; Cn. köe), to moor vessels close side by side in one mass, by anchors at stem and stern and cables fastening the vessels together. **koe-pang**, id. **koe chit-pang**, id. **koe-oá**, to join a vessel in this way to another, or to the whole mass of vessels.

thâu-koe, the rope at a boat's head, used for tying the boat to the common rope called "káu-soh."

koe (C. koa). **âng-koe-hî**, a red edible fish, = (Cn.), kim-lêng-hî. **âg-koe-hî** (T.), id.

âng-koe-hî khit-chhùi-gē, said of a man scolding or talking foolishly so as to injure himself, when silence would have left him safe; for this fish makes a sound which attracts the fisherman.

koe (C. ke). **koe-jiû**, a tree somewhat like the elm (v. jiû).

kôe [R. hâi, a sort of fish], (C. kê; Cn. kõe), salted or pickled fish or shell-fish (the name of the fish or shell-fish is prefixed). **kôe-chiap**, brine of pickled fish or shell-fish. **sīⁿ-kôe**, to pickle, as fish or shell-fish. **hî-kôe**, pickled fish. **hê-kôe**, pickled shrimps. **hê-kôe-phoà**, do. broken down small.

kóe [R. kái, to separate the parts of a thing; to untie; to loose; to deliver; to cure; to explain], (C. ké; Cn. kõe), to counteract, as incantations; to loose from a vow; to explain, as a word or clause.

kóe-seh (C. ké-soeh), to explain, as the meaning of a book; to translate book phrases into colloquial. **tiòh-kóe chiah-ōe-bêng**, it must be explained to be understood, *e.g.* an inuendo or a pun. **kóe-bêng**, to explain, as a phrase. **khui-kõe** (Cn.), to explain plainly.

kóe-khǹg (C. ké-khùiⁿ), to exhort to reconciliation, or not to grieve too much.

kóe-goān, to perform a vow of the form "hoat-goān" (v. goān). **kóe-tsoā**, to take away the binding power of an oath by ceremonies. **kóe-khiò**, to counteract incantations by other rites.

kóe-ûi, to compel the enemy to raise a siege; also, to deliver from trouble, as by frightening the opponent, &c. (v. ûi). **siau-tsai kóe-eh**, to remove or prevent calamities. **kóe-būn**, to remove sadness, *e.g.* by amusement (v. būn). **kóe-tók**, to remove eruptions, &c., supposed to be caused by some unhealthy food.

kóe [R. kái, to correct], (C. ké; Cn. kõe), to correct; to repair; to alter; to change. **kóe-chhiâⁿ**, to mend thoroughly; to repair and make all right. **kóe-pīⁿ**, to reform one's self (v. pīⁿ). **kóe-oāⁿ**, to change, esp. for the better. **kóe-miâⁿ oāⁿ-sìⁿ**, to change one's name and surname. **kóe-sim oāⁿ-hēng**, to reform one's heart and life. **kóe-thâu oāⁿ-bīn**, to make an old thing look new, as furniture, house, or character; to change from wicked to good conduct. **kóe-thâu oāⁿ-bé**, to make an old thing look quite new by a thorough repair. **chhek-thâu oāⁿ-bé**, id., *e.g.* as furniture. **kõe-sak** (Cn.), to cast off, as bad habits.

kóe-kè, to marry again, as a widow. **kóe-chiàⁿ**, to correct and write out a fair copy of a document. **kóe-chheh**, to correct or alter a book. **kóe-jit**, to appoint a different day. **chiong-sam kóe-gō͘** (to change 3 to 5), to deceive.

kóe (C.) **kóe-chí**, = A. ké-chí, fruit.

kóe (C.), = A. ké, cakes.

kóe (C.), = A. ké, to prop up slightly.

kòe [R. koài, strange; to be displeased], (C. kòɛ), to be offended at. **kièn-kòe**, to be offended at, esp. slightly. **kòe--lâng**, to be angry at a man; to bring trouble or evil on a man, as idols or demons when displeased. **hō͘-lâng-kòe**, to give offence to a man; to provoke his displeasure, either intentionally or unintentionally. **m̄-thang saⁿ-kòe**, do not be offended, as at him or at me. **bòh-tit-kòe**, do not be offended. **goá put-chí-kòe--i**, I am much offended at him. **bōe-kòe--tit**, do not be offended at him, for he was not to blame, and should not be found fault with. **bōe-kòe--tit-i**, id.

kòe [R. crafty]. **káu-kòe**, cunning and constantly intriguing.

kòe (R. kài), (C. kè; Cn. kõe), the itch and similar cutaneous diseases (but never "itchy; to itch," which is "chiūⁿ"). **kòe-iòh**, medicine for itch. **sīⁿ-kòe**, to have the itch. **soa-kòe**, itch in small patches all over the skin. **noāⁿ-kòe**, large sores of itch. **kòe-thê** (C. kè-thôe), large spots of itch about size of a dollar. **kòe-thê-á**, do. rather smaller.

kòe — **lâu-kòe**, debris floating on the surface of the tide.

kòe [R. kài, a boundary; a world], (C. kè; Cn. kõe). **sì-kòe**, in the four quarters; everywhere; from every side; in every direction. **toā-sì-kòe**, everywhere; very abundant. **toā-bú sì-kòe**, id. (v. bú). **toā-m̄-siak-kõe** (Cn.), id. **sì-kòe-kiâⁿ**, to go about everywhere or in every direction. **sì-kòe-tsáu**, run about everywhere.

kòe [R. hāi, instruments]. **ke-kòe**, instruments; tools; implements; weapons. **ién ke-kòe**, to fence; to exercise with weapons. **ke-kòe-thâu**, tools; implements.

kòe [R. a sort of tree]. **kòe-peh**, an evergreen shrub like juniper. **kòe-liû**, a tree somewhat like an elm. **kòe-chhiū**, a large tree from which planks are made. **kòe-chhâ**, wood from it, very large and straight.

kòe (C.), = A. kè, to cross over; an occasion. **éng-kòe**, usually (said of past time). **siâng-kòe**, usually. **kòe-tsúi**, = A. kè-tsúi, to cross the water, &c. &c.; also, = A. léng-lông, the covered sides of the middle court of a house.

kòe (C.), = A. kè, a female's head-dress; the queue, esp. of a woman; crest of a cock, &c.

kòe (C.), = A. kè, to send under escort to a mandarin, as a criminal or money.

kōe [R. īⁿ, ī, easy; by change of tone from "ėk," to change, = col. iàh], (C. kē; Cn. kõe), easy; quickly. **kōe-iau**, getting soon hungry after eating. **kōe-àm**, getting soon dark, as a cloudy or rainy day. **khah-kōe-chio**, readily going with another when asked, either to good or bad. **khah-kōe-kóng**, readily doing what one is asked, right or wrong. **lâng kōe-lāu**, man soon grows old. **tán-lâng kōe-lāu**, when waiting for and expecting a man, a short time seems an age.

kōe (C.) **oaiⁿ-kōe**, = A. oaiⁿ-koāiⁿ, to defraud or get money out of people.

kōe (C.), = A. koāi, to sprain; perverse. **chiàh-kōe**, insubordinate.

kóɛⁿ (P.) **chiú-kóɛⁿ**, = A. chiú-koáⁿ, a widow; but other phrases remain "koáⁿ."

koeh — **ɵ-koeh**, a fish like the ka-lâh, but shorter and darker. **koeh-hî** (C.), a sort of fish.

koeh [R. koat, to scrape], (C.) to strip off the bark, as from stalks of hemp; also, = A. kuih, to rub hard in curing a disease.

koeh [R. kiap, a pod or legume], (Cn. T.), = A. ngoeh. **tāu-koeh** (Cn. T.), a long-podded legume.

koeh (T.), = A. ngoeh, to take up with pincers, tongs, &c.

koeh (C.), = A. keh, a surname.

koeh [R. khiet, a sort of knife; cf. kiuh], (C. keh, kɛh). **koeh-á**, a reaping-hook; a pruning-hook. **koeh-á-to**, id. **chháu-koeh**, a knife for cutting grass and brushwood for fuel. **chhâ-koeh** (esp. Cn.), a cleaver for wood. **koeh-siò-á** (T.), a sheath for a grass-cutter's knife.

koeh [R. kiet, clean]. **kng-koeh**, smooth; not hairy; not rough. **káu-koeh-sien**, dirt hardened on the skin. **káu-koeh-san** (C.), id.

koeh (Cn. T.) **koeh-hiū**, = A. kiap-hiū, a lined warm coat.

koeh (C.), = A. kɵih. **koeh-kau-thâu**, the projecting corners of the cheeks below the eyes. **koeh-kau-kut**, the corner of the cheek-bone.

koeh (C.), = A. keh. **koeh-hún**, a sort of flour like arrow-root.

kóɛh (C.) **hàm-kóɛh-kóɛh**, telling great lies.

kòeh — **kiu-kòeh**, very narrow about money matters, or afraid to meddle in an affair (v. kiu).

köeh (Cn.), = A. thòeh. **küiⁿ-thâu kiu-köeh**, shoulders high, either naturally or shrugging. **küiⁿ-thâu köeh-köeh**, id.

kòeh (Cn.), = A. ngòeh, to take under the arm. **kâⁿ-kâⁿ kòeh-kòeh**, carrying many things under the arms.

koh [R. kok, the part of a dress below the arm]. **koh-ē**, the part of a dress just below the arm (s. next word). **tiàu-koh**, arms of dress too tight at the armpits. **chhah-koh**, to put in triangular pieces of cloth in the armpits of a dress in making it.

koh [R. kok, the armpit]. **koh-ē**, the armpit (s. previous word). **koh-ē-lang**, id. **koh-ē-khang**, id.

koh (R. hok, = hòk, = hù, to repeat], again; also, a second time; besides; (different).

koh-tsài, again; a second time; over again. **tsài-koh**, id. **têng-koh**, over again. **iū-koh**, also. **koh-lâi**, to come again. **koh-oáh**, to live again. **koh saⁿ-jit**, on the third day (only two clear days intervening). **beh-koh**, going to do it again. **beh-koh-tê**, will you have some more tea? **bô-koh**, not a second time.

koh-khah-hó, still better, &c. **kèng-koh-khah-hó**, yet better still. **kèng-koh-khah-thang**, all the more ought.

koh-chit-ê, one more; another, in the sense of one additional (but another, in the sense of a different one, is "pát-ê").

koh-iūⁿ, different; strange; unwell. **siâng-bú koh-pē**, having the same mother but different father. **sâng-pē koh-bú**, same father but different mother.

koh [R. kok, to wait; to delay, = col. koa]. **tam-koh**, to waste one's time (v. tam).

koh [R. kok], an ornamental platform, or small upper story of one room.

lōe-koh, the imperial council, like the cabinet or privy-council. **jip-koh**, to become a member of the cabinet. **loán-koh**, the tribunal where a mandarin sits.

lâu-koh, upper stories of several rooms or of one room. **khí-lâu khí-koh**, to build finely ornamented upper stories. **khui-chhùi-koh**, a small upper-room open on one side.

tsng-koh, an ornamental platform with finely-dressed young girls, or boys dressed as girls, carried in an idolatrous procession. **koh-pîⁿ**, id. **koh-toàⁿ**, girls, or boys representing them, carried on such a platform. **kng-koh**, to carry it in procession.

köh (Cn.) **köh-hiū**, = A. kiap-hiū, a warm-lined coat or jacket.

köh (Cn.), = A. keh, a surname.

kok [R. kok, kek, name of a plant]. **kok-tát-pín**, very coarse bamboo wicker-work like hurdles (v. tát).

kok [R. an ornamental platform, = col. koh]. **kok-hā**, your excellency; your honour (polite phrase used to a superior).

kok (R. id.) **kok-tan**, the red Amaryllis; the red lily. **âng-kok-piét**, id. **kok-piét-hoe**, the Amaryllis, esp. the white variety.

kok [R. a valley]. **soaⁿ-kok** (R.), a valley. **soaⁿ-piⁿ kok-lok-phāng**, in a deep valley or glen far among the mountains.

kúi-kok-tsú, a famous diviner who lived in the time of Mencius, now worshipped by diviners. **kúi-kok sien-siⁿ**, id., = kúi-kok sien-seng. **kúi-kok sien-tsé**, id.

kok [R. an outer coffin]. **koan-kok**, a double coffin (ancient form), outer and inner (v. koan).

kok [R. grain, = col. kak]. **ngé-kok**, the five grains; grain of all sorts in general; the crops. **ngé-kok-ông**, the god of agriculture (= hɵ-chek), made with a blue face. **ngé-kok tāi-tè**, id. **ngé-kok sien-tè** (T.), id. **ngé-kok hong-sēng**, crops abundant. **chek-kok hông-ki**, to collect grain against famine. **chiên-kok su-iâ**, the private secretary (of a mandarin), who attends to land-tax and grain. **hêng-bêng chiên-kok**, the two private secretaries in yamun, who attend to legal cases and to the land-tax respectively.

kok-ú (rain for grain), the term that falls on or about April 20th. **ū-koán-kok**, to have food in addition to salary, as teachers in some schools who get their rice. **kok-cheng**, a medicine. **kok-cheng-chí**, id. **kok-cheng-tsū** (T.), id.

kok [R. wide, large]. **ē-kok**, the chin.

kok [R. the walled suburb of a city]. **iú-hok, ku sêng-kok**, the wealthy live in cities and suburbs (v. sêng).

kok (R. id.), each. **kok-lâng**, each man. **kok-iūⁿ**, each kind. **lēng-ku kok-sit**, living separately, and each having his own meals.

kok (R. id.), a kingdom; a state; a country. **pang-kok**, id. **kok-tē**, id. **kok-ka**, a kingdom viewed as a family. **goā-kok**, foreign kingdoms or countries. **hoan-kok**, id. **pún-kok**, one's native country. **pè-kok** (R.), my native land. **kùi-kok** (R.), your honourable country. **bān-kok**, all nations. **liét-kok**, the several feudal kingdoms and states under the Chow dynasty. **sam-kok**, the three kingdoms; the time when China was split into three warring states. **sam-kok-chì**, the book giving an account of that time mixed with much romance.

kok-ūn, the fortune of a kingdom or of a dynasty. **kok-tiâu**, the reigning dynasty. **kok-ông**, a king; a sovereign. **kok-kun**, id. **kok-tsú** (r.), id. **kok-bú**, the mother of the sovereign. **kok-tiōng**, father-in-law of the sovereign. **kok-hoat**, the laws of the kingdom. **kok-khò**, government revenues. **kok-thé**, the dignity of the kingdom (v. thé).

siòng-kok, a prime minister. **khai-kok goân-hun**, the merit of having helped the dynasty to the throne, said of âng sêng-tiû, a native of Lâm-oaⁿ. **khai-kok kong-sîn**, a title given to him.

kok-pih, very knowing, or rather too knowing (v. pih). **kok-ló**, the chief of the genii (v. ló).

kok bû-jī-ông, a kingdom has not two kings. **cheng-thien toȧt-kok**, to aim at the throne. **tiong-kun pò-kok**, extremely loyal to his sovereign and grateful to the dynasty, *e.g.* meeting great danger or death. **chīn-tiong pò-kok**, id., loyally faithful to the sovereign and dynasty. **sún-hoāi kok-pó**, to injure or deface coins.

kok-jī-khak, the 31st radical, inclosing the phonetic part; called "ûi" in the dictionaries.

kȯk (T.), = A. kȧk, to throw away.

kȯk [R. kok, lȯk], chuckling or cackling noise made by a fowl. **phah-kȯk-ke**, hen cackling before laying an egg. **kȯk-kȯk-kiò**, cackling of a hen. **kȯk-kȯk-háu**, id., said also of a person talking on too much without ever stopping.

kong — **oân-kong-mn̂g**, a door with an arched top (v. oân).

kong [R. an important rope; a bond of society]. **lám-kong**, the rope which draws the top of the sail close to the top of the mast; it lies along the mast. **lám-kong-soh**, id.

sam-kong, the three great relations or headships of king, father, and husband. **sam-kong ngé-siông**, the three headships and the five relationships of life.

kong-kàm, the national history (of China).

kong [R. name of a star]. **thien-kong-sîn**, the thirty-six heavenly spirits used as messengers of the supreme Deity. **saⁿ-tsȧp-lȧk thien-kong**, id. **thien-kong tē-soah**, the good and bad spirits of heaven and earth, in all a hundred and eight. **thien-kong-chhiⁿ**, stars where they reside, especially at or near the Great Bear.

kong [R. the bladder]. **pông-kong** (R.), id., politely used for the scrotum.

kong (C. keng). **toā-bú sì-kong-kòe**, in great abundance. **toā-bú-kong-keng**, very large, as a house.

kong [R. firm, strict]. **kong-jiû siong-chè**, firmness and gentleness well combined (v. jiû). **sèng-tē khah-kong**, temper rather quick, rough, or stiff.

sù-tāi kim-kong, the four giants that guard the entrance of a large Buddhist temple. **kim-kong-hu̍t** (T. kim-kn̂g), certain idols that have a very bold and brave look (different from the above).

kong [R. steel, = col. kǹg]. **kim-kong-tsǹg**, a good steel awl.

kong [R. kiong, a temple or palace, = col. keng]. **kong-tsú**, the daughter of a king (s. duke).

kong [R. to strike; to attack]. **kong-kek**, to attack (s. public). **kong-táⁿ**, to attack, as a city. **kong-siâⁿ**, to attack a city (v. siâⁿ). **kong-phoȧ**, to take, as a city. **kiap-kong**, to attack on both sides (v. kiap). **gōe-kong lōe-èng**, enemies without, and treacherous help within. **huih kong-sim**, much flurried or excited, as with running hard or press of business (v. sim).

kong [R. an earthen jar, = col. kng]. **sam-kong-chhiⁿ**, a sort of violet or deep purple-coloured silk.

kong — **kong-tāi**, a sort of shell-fish, like the (than) spout-fish.

kong — **tāi-kong**, a steersman; the captain of a small junk: sometimes said to the assistants in foreign Hongs, as the heads of the Hongs used to be captains of receiving ships.

kong [R. to carry on a pole between two men, = col. kng]. **kong-siā**, sedan-bearers.

kong [R. hong, wind]. **kong-chhɛ** (C.), = A. hong-chhe, a paper kite (s. next word).

kong — **kong-chhɛ** (C.), a sort of three-pronged fork, used in hunting (s. previous word).

kong [R. name of a tree]. **kong-lông** (F.), a plant like a palm or sago-palm (v. lông).

kong [R. efficacious work; merit]. **kong-lô**, merit. **kong-hun** (R.), merit for services to the state. **kong-hun tō-tek**, great merit and virtue. **kong-tek**, (meritorious conduct), rites for the dead (v. tek). **kong-bêng**, rank, civil or military (v. bêng).

kong-iōng (r.), efficacy, as of medicine (v. iōng), (s. public). **kong-hāu**, efficacy, as of a method or medicine (v. hāu).

im-kong, works of supererogation, deserving reward from Heaven; meritorious virtues (s. light). **ū im-kong**, to have such merit as to deserve rewards from Heaven. **kun-kong**, merit for military success or assistance in military operations. **chiong-kong pé-tsōe**, to make up for faults by one's merit. **iú-kong**, to have merit for services to the state. **khûn iú-kong**, diligence has useful results. **lô jî-bû-kong**, hard toil, and no thanks for it (said of a dog killing a rat).

sêng-kong, to carry out any work to a successful issue. **chhéng-kong**, to request a reward for meritorious services to the state. **hō-kong**, to congratulate a man (with presents, &c.) for the reward by government of his meritorious services. **kièn-kong**, to get merit by some great service (esp. military) to the state; also, to make much money, as by going abroad. **kièn-kong lip-giȧp**, to set up an estate, or grow wealthy by personal work or diligence. **kièn-kong-giȧp**, id.

tėk-jit ê-kong-tsô, special spirits for each day (v. tsô).

kong [R. work, = col. kang], one of the musical notes. **kong-pē**, the Board of Works at the metropolis; the president of it. **kun-kong-chhiúⁿ**, an arsenal for marine stores, and place for building war-junks, &c.

oā-kong, a painter of pictures.

thé-kong, men who dig graves, put the corpse in the coffin, and carry it to the grave; rude and vulgar. **hoan-kong-thé**, very rude and ignorant, esp. affecting knowledge; unpolite or ill-bred (v. thé).

cheng-kong, of very good workmanship; fine and accurate, as work; very skilful, as at work, or at managing an affair.

jîn-lėk pé thien-kong, human strength improving upon nature's work, *e.g.* by levelling a field, or

厦英大辭典

making a road; or as a man not naturally talented becoming distinguished through hard study; or as a man lengthening his life beyond the usual period by great care.

kong-jī-tú, a short beam placed as a support crosswise between two beams, as in a floor where there is an opening for a stair or trap-door; named from being in the form of the character "kong." **kong--jī bô-chhut-thâu**, the character "kong" (work) does not put out its head, which would change it into the character "thô" (earth or land); a labourer does not easily become a wealthy man.

kong [R. id., = col. kang, "male," ang], grandfather; duke; public; common; public funds or property; title of many gods, sages, officials, &c.; Patna opium.

kong-su, public and private; just and selfish (v. su). **kong-tō**, fair; just; equitable. **kong-pìⁿ**, id. (v. pìⁿ). **kong-pêng**, id. **kong-gī**, do., as a judge or official.

kong-thoaⁿ, to divide fairly, as expenses. **kong-toàn**, to judge justly or publicly (v. toàn). **kong-phoàⁿ**, to decide to whom a thing belongs, as arbiter.

kong-àn, the table used as the tribunal of a mandarin. **kong-tsō-toh**, id. (v. tsō). **kong-tn̂g**, judgment-hall (v. tn̂g). **kong-hòk**, official dress.

kong-ke, public; common to all the parties, esp. to relatives. **kong-chèng** (C. chiòng), public; common; possessed in common. **kong-hêng**, public; publicly; openly. **kong-jiên**, id. **kong-tông**, publicly; in the presence of all interested.

kong-phêng, to discuss openly a matter in dispute, as several persons met together. **kong-kek**, unitedly expel (v. kek), (s. attack). **kong-iōng**, for public use. **kong-ēng**, id. **kong-tòe**, subscribed for a public purpose. **kong-kú**, to make a united recommendation of a man for an office.

kong-koán, a hotel; an inn (v. koán). **kong-thiaⁿ**, the public central hall of a house, when used in common by several families. **kong-si**, a firm; a trading company. **kong-hōe**, a public society or association. **kong-sài tāi-sîn**, a foreign ambassador. **kong-sū**, public business. **kong-giàp**, property in which several persons have a share.

kong-chhin, a sort of arbiter, having much less power than our arbiters; almost like a mediator, who endeavours to make the parties agree. **kong-jîn**, id. **tsòe kong-tō-lâng**, to act as a sort of arbiter, as about prices.

chhiong-kong, to put money into a public or common fund. **hièn-kong**, id., quite voluntarily.

kong-kī, anniversary of death of paternal grandfather or great grandfather. **tiòh-kong**, to have the turn of attending to the common ancestral worship. **tiòh toā-kong**, to have the turn for attending to the more important ancestral rites for ancestors.

kong-pô, ancestral tablets (v. pô). **kong-má**, grandfather and grandmother (v. má). **khǒ-kong** (Cn.), to worship ancestral tablets. **án-kong**, grandfather! **á-kong**, id. **thài-kong** (Cn.), = A. tsó, great grandfather. **tsó-kong**, ancestors. **chek-kong**, paternal grandfather's younger brother, or cousin of any degree; polite address to an old man (v. chek). **peh-kong**, paternal grandfather's elder brother or cousin (v. peh). **lāi-kong**, paternal grandfather. **goā-kong**, maternal grandfather. **kū-kong**, grandmother's brother (v. kū). **kū-kong**, old Patna opium.

lāu-kong-á, an old man (not said to himself). **goán lāu-kong-á**, my husband (said by an old woman). **sien-siⁿ-kong**, teacher's father.

sai-kong, a Tauist priest. **su-kong**, adoptive father of the adoptive father of a Buddhist priest (all priests). **tsú-kong**, a patron who assists and protects dependants, and whom they obey and aid. **hm̂-lâng-kong**, a woman who arranges a marriage. **pó-tiúⁿ-kong**, the tepo or head man of a ward. **kó-kong**, the secretary of a military mandarin. **keng-kong**, a temple-keeper appointed by the people (not a priest). **chhài-kong**, temple-keeper employed by priests, but not a priest. **pn̄g-tiàm-kong**, the keeper of an eating-house, esp. old man. **sien-kong**, a beggar. **mê-kong**, you vile lascivious wretch! (said in vile scolding).

koe-kak-kong, a large cock-fowl. **tū-kong** (Cn.), a large (male) hog. **chháu-mehⁿ-kong**, a large grasshopper. **báng-á-kong**, a mosquito (said in joke). **phoà-hiû-kong**, an old wadded coat (said in joke). **téng-kong-á** (T.), a small dragon-fly.

kong-chiok, the rank of a duke. **kong-iâ**, a duke. **bé-kong-iâ**, an idol of the surname "má." **kong-kheng** (R.), very high mandarins, esp. ministers of state (v. kheng). **kong-tsú**, son of a very high mandarin or nobleman (s. palace). **kong-tsú** (Cn.), id. **kong-hô**, dukes and marquises; feudal princes. **kong-hô pek-tsú-lâm**, the five orders of nobility. **ông-kong**, kings and dukes.

chiu-kong, Duke Chow. **khóng-tsú-kong**, Confucius. **tsu-bûn-kong**, Choo-he, the commentator (v. bûn). **kok-kong-chiú**, a medicinal wine made in Amoy, originally by a man called "kok-kong." **kok-kong kan-á**, earthenware bottles for it; much used also for other medicines.

thiⁿ-kong, the god of heaven, = Giòk-hông Siōng-tè (v. thiⁿ). **tōe-kong**, the earth, as a god (v. tōe). **siōng-tè-kong**, = hièn-thien siōng-tè, the god of the north star. **sam-kài-kong**, the gods of heaven, earth, and water (v. kài). **tāi-tō-kong**, = pó-seng tāi-tè, the god of medicine. **tè-kun-kong**, id. **koan-kong**, Kwanti, the god of war. **lûi-kong**, the god of thunder. **thó-tī-kong**, the god of agriculture. **thó-tē-kong** (C.), id. **jit-thâu-kong**, the sun, as an object of worship. **thài-iông-kong**, id. **tsàu-kun-kong**, the god of the hearth or fire-place. **chîⁿ-kháu-kong**, the god or guardian spirit of the eaves. **sù-tāi kim-kong**, the four large idols placed as gate-keepers at the gate of a great temple; they have great power over spirits. **sèng-ông-kong**, = Keh-sèng-ông. **tsó-su-kong**, name of several idols (v. su). **iâng-kong** (C.), an ancient builder, worshipped when making a grave or house.

kéng-tsú-kong, the guardian idol of a ward or region. **sien-kong**, any one of the genii, said esp. in regard to dreams. **ang-kong** (C. T.), an idol in general (v. ang). **bān-èng-kong**, collective title for the spirits of a shrine for persons who have no posterity. **phó-tō-kong**, = tāi-sū-iâ, a large hideous paper image worshipped at the rites of phó-tō (v. phó). **hàu mn̂g-kháu-kong**, to worship the spirits at the doors on 2d and 16th of each month. **hàu lāu-toā-kong**, id., and at some other times.

hó-sèng-kong, the deified tiger, the god of gamblers. **hó-chiòng-kong**, id. **sī-chiá-kong** (C.), a large harmless sort of snake that is worshipped. **chiòh-thâu-kong**, a large shapeless stone worshipped at Chang-chew. **ti-tiâu-kong**, the guardian spirit of a pig-sty. **gû-tiâu-kong**, the guardian spirit of a cow-house.

kong [R. bright; light, = col. kng]. **sam-kong**, the three lights, sun, moon, and stars. **kong-im** (R.), time (v. im). **àm-kong-chiáu**, the small owl.

kong-kéng, a landscape; state or circumstances (v. kéng).

kong-chhái (R.), very bright or shining; very richly decorated. **boán-thien-kong**, a hanging lamp with several wicks. **bán-thien-kong**, id.

khai-kong, to dot an idol's eye with blood or with a red composition, on consecrating it. **kong-gán**, intelligent, esp. of boys. **kong-gán-lâng**, a sharp or intelligent fellow. **kong-kùn**, a rogue; a swindler (v. kùn). **put-sit ngiû^n-khién, kong-bêng put-hién**, without eating cows or dogs, intelligence is not manifested (said in joke).

tō-kong, the reign Tau-kwang. **kong-tiong ê-chî^n**, cash from Cochin-China, &c., current at Amoy (but not at Fuh-chau, &c.), having the characters "kong-tiong;" or cash like them.

tap-siā un-kong, to give thanks to a powerful spirit for help. **tap-siā im-kong**, thanks to all the ghosts (written on idolatrous lanterns, esp. in 7th moon). **hàu-im-kong**, to worship the spirits in the 7th moon. **kèng-im-kong**, id. **tēng-kong-hút**, an idol with very long ears, originally Tauist, but became Buddhist. **tēng-kong-sien**, id. **tāi-ní^n tēng-kong-sien**, do. (said in joke of a man with long ears).

kông (R. id.), violent; mad; acting hastily on the spur of the moment. **kông-kông**, id. **hong-kông**, in a great hurry or too urgent, so as to be hasty or careless. **hong-hong kông-kông**, id. **hiong-kông**, id. **chhiong-kông**, acting violently, boisterously, imperiously, or too urgently. **kông-pō**, violent and hasty in temper, esp. of a man in authority. **kóng-ōe khah-kông**, to speak in a violent overbearing way.

kông soàh-soàh, quite madly or violently. **kông phia^n-phia^n**, in a tremendous hurry, greatly flurried.

jû kông-kông, mind confused and perplexed with a great deal of very troublesome business.

hoat-kông, to go mad; mad. **teh-siáu-kông**, mad. **tien-kông**, id. **khit-kúi phah--khì teh-kông**, you have been beaten by demons till you are mad! (said in scolding).

chhi^n-kông, very impulsive; hasty in action. **chhi^n-kông-tsáu**, to rush on hurriedly or thoughtlessly. **chhi^n-kông-kiā^n**, very strong, lusty, and vigorous, as a lad or young man. **chhi^n-kông-lát**, working very vigorously, as a strong young man who does not economise his strength, sometimes too roughly or rashly.

kông-hong, a sudden violent wind; a squall.

kông (R. id.) **jiét-kông**, delirium in fever.

kông, to fasten a man's legs in the stocks, or in a similar way.

kông — **mn̂g-kông**, a strong upright bar, fastened inside of a door, for keeping out robbers. **khiā-kông**, id. **hoâi^n-kông**, a strong transverse bar for a door.

kóng (R. káng), to say; to talk; to discourse upon; to discuss; to explain by discoursing (Cn. "káng," to discourse or discuss; Cn. "söh," to say, to talk).

kóng-kè, to ask more than the proper price, gradually letting it down through haggling. **kóng-hô**, to discuss matters till agreed, as persons at feud, or as two men plotting against a third.

kóng-phoà, to tell the particulars. **kóng-chheh** (Cn. káng-tsü), to discourse on a book, explaining it. **kóng tō-lí**, to discourse on doctrine; to preach. **kóng-kó͘**, to tell stories about ancient times (v. kó͘). **kóng sèng-jū**, to discourse or preach upon the "sacred edict," explaining it.

kóng-ōe, to speak (v. ōe). **i-ê-ōe kóng**, what he says is —. **kā-i-kóng** (Cn. kāng-i-söh), say to him. **kap-i-kóng**, id. **tùi-i-kóng**, id. **lí kap--i tùi-kóng**, speak to him yourself, not through another. **goá-kóng lí-thia^n**, I tell you that you may hear. **kóng-chhò**, to make a mistake in speaking. **kóng-tā^n**, id. **bóng-kóng**, to talk at random; to say a thing without exactly meaning it, or without a definite purpose. **kóng kàu-bô-pān**, to talk recklessly and with great exaggeration; to ask far too high a price. **chiàn^n-kóng tò-kóng**, to talk at one time on one side, and soon after on the opposite side. **lóng-bô chiàu-kóng**, not according to the truth.

kóng-khí, to raise a question. **kóng-khí-lâi, ōe-thâu tn̂g**, to talk of this matter would take a long time. **kóng-bōe-liáu**, cannot be fully told, as it is so great or long. **kóng-bōe-lâi**, cannot express it properly; cannot speak so as to accomplish the purpose (v. lâi). **oh-tit-kóng**, hard to tell. **oh-kóng**, hard to persuade. **khah-kōe-kóng**, easily talked over; ready to do whatever (good or bad) one is asked. **khoài-kóng**, id.

kóng [R. broad, = col. kńg]. **kóng-khoah**, broad and wide.

lióng-kóng tsóng-tok, the governor-general of Canton, *i.e.* of the two Kwang provinces, Kwang-tung and Kwang-si. **kóng-chiu-hú** (R.), the city or department of Canton.

kóng-tāi bû-pien, illimitably great (said of the laws of Buddha). **sîn-thong kóng-tāi**, miraculous powers very great (said of a spirit or an idol). **kóng-ték tsun-ông**, = keh-sèng-ông, an idol much worshipped in Fuh-kien.

kóng — **âng-kóng-á**, the smallest sort of good cash. **âng-kóng-á-chî^n**, id.

kóng — **am-kóng-tsûn** (C.), the cicada, = A. am-po͘-chê. **àm-kóng-tsûn** (Cn.), id. **iû^n-kóng-sai** (Cn.), id.

kóng — **oá^n-kóng-le** (T.), the bottom of a broken bowl, = oá^n-ko͘-léh.

kóng [R. koán, a tube; to rule, = col. kńg, kó͘, koá^n], a short tube, or hollow horn, or tubular case, &c. **toā-bú-kóng**, thick and tubular, as a joint of a large bamboo or large claw of a crab. **toā-kóng-chháu** (Cn. T.), large coarse grass, as on sea-shore, &c.

phī^n-kóng, the nose, esp. the part near the nostrils (v. phī^n). **chím-kóng**, a crab's pincers (v. chím). **gô-mn̂g-kóng**, a goose-quill. **gû-kak-kóng**, a polished hollow horn used by priests (v. kak).

tek-kóng, a hollow piece of bamboo used for any purpose; either one joint, or two or three feet long. **a-phièn-kóng**, an opium-pipe. **chhiám-kóng**, an instrument used for taking samples of rice out of unopened bags. **hé-ióh-kóng**, a powder-measure for one charge. **pit-kóng**, a cover for the point of a Chinese pen. **tsoá-lién-kóng**, a bamboo tube for extinguishing and keeping a paper match. **phâng-kóng**, a bamboo instrument for throwing water on a sail.

pat-sien-kóng, a long-shaped bamboo case for carrying some of a barber's instruments. **hê-chio-kóng**, a pepper-box.

kóng-á-hiên, a small guitar made with a bamboo cylinder.

phòng-kóng, full of air-bubbles, as ill-pasted paper, or as lime too loose on a wall. **phok-kóng**, id. **puh kóng-á**, bubbles rising in water, as from crabs in wet sand or mud, or bubbles from something decaying or fermenting. **puh tsúi-kóng**, id.

chhàu-tsúi-kóng, very wet, hard, and bad-tasted, as potatoes left long in water, or that cannot be boiled dry and mealy; bad-tasted, as water out of a bamboo vessel that has lain long in water. **chhàu-tsúi-kóng-bī**, id.

kòng [R. kò, to pass; to cross, = col. kè, koà]. **kè-kòng**, the opportunity quite lost, *e.g.* affair gone so far wrong that it cannot now be set right, or as doctor coming when the patient is just dying; extremely hard, as work; very severe, as disease.

kòng — **kim-kòng-thûi**, a sort of mace carried before idols and mandarins (T. kim-koe-kòng).

kòng [R. kàng, red colour], (C. khòng). **âng-kòng-kòng**, very red.

kòng — **toā-kòng**, a large cannon. **tâng-kòng**, large brass cannon (s. tribute). **lêng-kòng-chhèng**, a large sort of cannon.

kòng, to strike or beat with an instrument or implement, &c. **kòng-cheng**, to strike a bell (or gong having a boss) with a stick.

kiông-kòng, housebreaking; burglary. **kiông-kòng-chhát**, a housebreaker. **lim-thîn kòng-phah**, fond of drinking and fighting.

kòng-khòk, to beat the rattle; to conspire to gamble a man out of his money, or to fleece him; to tell empty stories or jokes, often licentious. **kòng-báng**, to conspire together to fleece another. **saⁿ-kap kòng-báng**, id. **kòng-báng-sìⁿ**, a fan fit only for beating mosquitoes (said in joke of a coarse or worn-out fan). **kòng-chîⁿ**, to squeeze money, allotting so much to each to pay. **kòng-chia kòng-hia**, to strike about restlessly, as child at play; to squeeze money from various villages, &c., as mandarins.

kòng-kòng-háu, loud sound, as of rice-mortar worked by the foot, or as of the wind howling loud.

kòng (R. id.), tribute; used in the names of some things of special excellence; also in name of satin and of fine sugar; used in the names of some literary degrees.

chìn-kòng, to pay tribute. **lâp-kòng**, id. **tiâu-kòng**, to present tribute in person. **pān-kòng**, to prepare tribute to be sent. **kòng-hông-tè** (Cn.), to pay tribute to the emperor. **kòng-ông** (Cn. T.), to worship the idol "ông-iâ" with offerings; also fig. of giving much food to an ungrateful man.

kòng-ièn, best bird's-nests, such as are sent as tribute from Amoy.

kòng-koah, common Chinese letter-paper. **kòng-chhoan**, superfine thick Chinese letter-paper.

kòng-thn̂g, finest loaf-sugar. **kòng-péh**, id. **chiàⁿ-kòng-péh**, id. **kòng-hún**, finest white sugar in powder.

kòng-toān, satin. **o-kòng-toān**, black satin. **hoe-kòng**, flowered satin.

kòng-īⁿ, the examination-hall (in the provincial capital) for the Kujin degree. **kòng-seng**, literary degree or title just below Kujin, generally those who come nearest to getting the Kujin degree in the examination. **hù-pńg-kòng**, the highest class of Sew-tsai, just about to become Kujin. **iu-kòng**, the degree of "kòng-seng," when given partly for some merit in examination, and partly for money. **un-kòng**, that degree given on occasion of accession or of the birth of a prince, &c. **poát-kòng**, one "lîm-seng" graduate, chosen once in twelve years out of each Hien district. **sòe-kòng**, title given after twelve years to those "lîm-seng" graduates who do not become "poát-kòng." **chhut-kòng**, to become a "kòng-seng" as a lîm-seng does. **bóe-kòng**, to buy the title of kòng-seng. **koan-kòng**, id. **tâng-kòng** (copper graduates), said of those who have bought the degree (s. cannon).

kōng [R. kiōng, together, = col. kāng, kā, hōng]. **kōng-kéhⁿ**, slightly at variance, and ready to quarrel or find fault; not getting on well together (v. kéhⁿ). **kōng-kiáuhⁿ**, id. **kōng-koáihⁿ**, id.; also, one foot shorter than the other.

kōng (= khōng). **kōng-kōng-hián**, to shake about, as an idol when carried.

kōng, prayers used by Siamese Buddhist priests. **liām-kōng**, to mutter such prayers, curses, or incantations.

ku [R. kó, ancient]. **ku-koài**, strange (v. koài).

ku [R. khu, the body]. **sin-ku**, the body; better sin-khu (v. sin).

ku — **he-ku**, asthma.

ku (R. ku, kû). **ku-là** (T.), a sort of child's cap.

ku (R. kui), a turtle or tortoise; a turtle-shaped cake; used in the names of some insects such as beetles. **ku-pih**, turtles and tortoises. **ku-kiáⁿ**, a young tortoise. **ku-á**, id.; a sort of beetle. **ku-sîn**, a small dark sort of aphis. **chià-ku**, a small edible grub found in roots of sugar-cane. **gû-sái-ku**, a beetle that lives on cow-dung (said of a man who comes awkwardly knocking against people or things). **kim-ku**, a small insect like a beetle or lady-bird. **kim-ku-séh**, a toy in which these insects make a wheel turn. **kim-ku-gô**, id. **it--tióh kim-ku, hāi--liáu sìⁿ-miāⁿ**, to injure one's self very much by covetousness. **tsúi-ku**, a small fresh-water insect. **kak-phang, khoàⁿ-tsòe tsúi-ku** (to mistake a wasp for it), said of being injured by a familiar friend supposed to be harmless.

bé-ku, a paper kite made like a tortoise with a long tail. **pàng-bé-ku**, to fly such a kite. **âm-khang-ku**, said of a shy man who seldom stirs out of his door.

bōng-ku, the mound of a grave, whether made of turf or of cement. **siū-ku**, large turtle-shaped cakes made on birth-days. **ku-á-piáⁿ**, small cakes of that shape. **bí-ku**, do. made of rice. **mīⁿ-ku**, do. made of flour. **tsúi-chiⁿ-ku**, do. with white stuffing of pulse. **ku-ké**, cakes of various forms. **ìn-ku**, to make turtle-shaped cakes. **tsòe-ku**, id. **chhe-ku**, to steam them. **hang-ku**, to toast them. **pun-ku**, to distribute them. **cheng-ku**, to beat rice for them.

ku-tsang, a woman's queue. **ku-khak**, the shell of a turtle or tortoise (entire); a small cabin built on a boat, *e.g.* on a passage-boat, or on those used by foreigners. **poàh ku-koà**, divining by three cash in the shell of a tortoise (v. koà). **ku-ka**, jelly made from turtles.

ku [R. a cart or chariot, = col. chhia], (C. ki, Cn. kü). **ku-chiên-chháu**, a medicinal plant; plantago. **ku-chiên-chí**, its seed, used as a cooling medicine.

chí-lâm-ku (R.), the mariner's compass.

ku [R. the flap of a dress], (C. ki, Cn. kü). **saⁿ-á-ku**, the corner of the flap of a dress at the bottom. **toā-ku**, the large flap, as on the breast of a coat. **lāi-ku**, the inner flap. **chêng-ku**, the front flap of a long dress (generally said only of the lower corner). **bīn-chêng-ku**, the front flap of a dress. **āu-ku**, the lower corner of the hinder flap of a dress, at the side.

sē-ku, having one flap too long. **tiàu-ku**, having one flap too short. **khih-ku**, the division of the flaps at the side. **khih-ku lih**, torn at the division of the flaps at the side.

ku [R. to dwell; to reside], (C. ki; Cn. kü). **iông-ku**, a dwelling-house; opposed to a grave. **pè-ku** (polite), the place where I reside.

koáⁿ-ku, to be a widow, esp. young (v. koáⁿ). **ku-song**, to be in mourning for a parent

ku-ke-lâng, the general settled orderly part of the population living in their own homes. **lēng-ku kok-sit**, to live and have meals all separate. **kì-ku**, to live in a place for a short time. **phû-ku**, id. **chhah-ku** (r.), to live alone (or almost alone) among a large population of a different clan or race. **chhien-ku**, to migrate. **sì-kòe-ku**, to go about as a vagrant, with no settled dwelling. **ku sím-mihⁿ tōe-pē**, what is his present rank, as mandarin?

ún-ku san-lîm, to dwell in retirement among mountains and woods, as a good statesman or sage who has retired from the world in disgust and hopelessness (s. humpbacked). **ún-ku soaⁿ-nâⁿ**, id.

hok-jîn ku hok-tē, a fortunate man gets a good grave, so that his descendants profit by it.

ku (R. ku, kû). **ún-ku**, humpbacked; a hunchback (s. dwell); a bridge, of which the road-way is greatly arched, as in pleasure-grounds. **ún-ku bōe sì-chiàⁿ**, a matter bad at the first cannot be mended. **ún-ku sang-tiám-lē**, even the deformed gets sustenance from Heaven (fig. as if "two drops of dew" lodge in the angles of the hump!).

khiau-ku, humpbacked; a hunchback. **ku-pòe**, id. **ku-pòe tiâu-thien-tsú**, the hunchback had an audience of the emperor, *i.e.* became a great mandarin.

tuh-ku, nodding, as a sleepy, old, or sick man. **lâng ku-ku**, going with a stooping gait. **ku-sio**, to sit crouching in some warm place, as in a sunny sheltered spot, or near a fire.

ku [R. kē, the leg; a limb]. **siáu-phí-ku**, having small hips (said in joke, in imitation of the mandarin).

kû [R. a street], (C. ki; Cn. kü). **koe-kû**, a street of shops; a market street (C. ke-ki).

kû (R. id.), (C. ki). **pèh-chhia-kû**, the white opaque shell of the shell-fish called "ham," from which white official buttons are made. **chhia-kû-téng**, a white official button of the sixth rank. **tì-chhia-kû**, to wear that button. **tì pèh-chhia-kû**, id.

kú (R. kiú), long (in time); yet; still. **iáu-kú**, yet; notwithstanding; still. **m̄-kú**, id.; but yet. **kú-ū**, there yet remains. **siōng-kú**, yet (v. "siōng," yet). **siōng-kú**, at the longest (from "siōng," above).

kú-kú, a long time; long ago. **kú-tn̂g**, for a long time; lasting. **kú-kú tn̂g-tn̂g**, lasting a very long time, or perpetual. **tn̂g-tn̂g kú-kú**, id. **hiah-kú**, for some time back; of late. **ū-hiah-kú**, id. **hiah-kú-á**, quite lately. **chiah-kú**, of late. **hah-kú-á**, in a short time (future). **khah-kú-á**, in a very short time. **chit-bák-nihⁿ-kú**, in a moment. **nīⁿ-kú gèh-chhim**, for many years long. **kú-nīⁿ--ê**, belonging to a time many years ago. **náⁿ-kú náⁿ-hó**, the longer the better. **tàu-kú**, to try which can longest do or bear something (v. tàu).

kú [R. kiú, a leek]. **kú-chhài**, leeks. **kú-chhài-hoe**, flower-stalks of leeks; counted very good. **kú-chhài-pē**, the narrow hem on a man's dress.

kú [R. a carpenter's square], (C. kí; Cn. kü). **kui-kú**, a rule; correct rules (lit. compass and square). **chiàu-kui-kú**, according to proper rules; to behave properly. **siú kui-kú**, to behave properly. **kui-kú ê-lâng**, a man who acts properly. **sûn-kui tō-kú**, correct and orderly in conduct.

kú [R. to elevate; to recommend; to select; to speak of, or raise a matter], (C. kí; Cn. kü). **kú-khí**, to make a first proposal or motion, as in a meeting; also (R.), to lift up on high, as a very heavy weapon or weight by a hero. **kú-chièn**, to recommend for a situation or office. **pó-kú**, to recommend and stand security for. **kong-kú**, to make a united recommendation of a man for some office or employment.

kú-jîn, a Kujin, = M.A. **kú-tsú** (R.), id. **bú-kú**, a military Kujin. **it-kú sêng-bêng, thien-hā ti**, on becoming a Kujin all the empire knows of it.

kú-tōng, behaviour; conduct (v. tōng). **kú-hêng**, to commence action in a case, as mandarin. **thai-kú**, to assist a man, as by buying his goods, or giving custom. **khai-kú**, id.

kú-thê sam-chhek, iú sîn-bêng, look up three feet, and the spirits are present (v. thê, "head").

kù (R. id.), a sentence; a clause. **chit-kù-ōe**, one short sentence. **kù-tāu**, clauses and sub-clauses (v. tāu). **kù-tē**, id. **tiám-kù**, to punctuate, as a writing or book. **tiám-kù tsáh-ké**, to punctuate and mark the divisions of an essay.

keng-kù, a sentence from a classic. **ín chheh-kù**, to quote book phrases. **ēng tsu-kù**, id. **têng-kù**, to repeat clauses in a stammering way.

kù [R. kiù; cf. col. ù], to cauterize. **ēng-hiuⁿ kù**, to cauterize with burning incense. **kù-hûn**, to make lines with a red-hot iron.

kù [R. to hold firm; proof], (C. kì; Cn. kü). **pìn-kù**, proof; evidence. **chhut pìn-kù**, to give evidence; to give proof. **bô-pìn bô-kù**, no evidence. **chèng-kù**, evidence of eye-witness. **ū-sìn-kù**, to have good, certain, and sure proof. **sit-kù**, evidence true, good, relevant, and sufficient for the purpose. **khòe-kù**, a deed of sale or mortgage adduced as evidence.

kù-hiám, to guard an important or narrow pass.

kù-lí-ài, just as you please: as you like. **kù-tsāi-lí**, just as you please. **kù-tsāi-i**, as he pleases. **bóng-kù-tsāi--i**, just let him alone; let him have his own way.

kù (R. id.), (C. kì; Cn. kü), a saw; to saw. **liâu-kù**, to do sawyer's work.

kù-á, a saw. **chhiú-kù**, a short hand-saw. **toā-kù**, a long saw worked by two men. **kù-to**, a saw with a stiff fixed back. **kù-sut**, saw-dust.

kù [R. ill-mannered]. **kù-ngōⁿ**, rude, proud, and uncivil; *e.g.* taking no notice when spoken to, or when another comes in; or putting on the manner of a superior.

kū — **lū-kū**, uncivil in reply; answering gruffly and laconically (v. lū).

kū [R. to reject], (C. kī; Cn. kü). **kū-tsoát**, to reject; to cast away; to abandon. **khòng-kū**, to resist a superior disobediently or rebelliously; unruly and insubordinate.

kū [R. great; large]. **tāi-tsong kū-tsòk**, very large and numerous clan. **bêng-kong kū-kheng**, high and illustrious mandarins (said in relation to the place or clan from which they are sprung).

kū — **ām-kún-kū**, the prominent lump in the front of the throat.

kū [R. spur of a cock, &c.], (T. khū). **koe-kū**,

the spur of a cock. **koe-kha-kū**, id. **lāi-hióh-chhì-kū** (C.), a thorn (leguminous) with yellow flowers and strong thorns.

hó-kū (P.), tiger's claws (s. sound of birds).

kū — **kó-kí-kū** (P.), a small medicinal shrub (v. kí).

kū (R. kiū), brother of mother or of wife. **á-kū**, id. **kū-piáu**, son of maternal uncle. **chhin-chhek ke-kū**, relatives in general. **ke-î kū-kīm**, aunts, maternal uncles, and their wives, &c. (v. ke).

bú-kū, maternal uncle. **bó-kū** (C.), id. **kū-kong**, grandmother's brother [also old Benares opium]. **thi^n-téng**, **thi^n-kong**: **tōe-ē**, **bú-kū-kong**, a mother's elder brother must be treated with great respect, (almost like a god!)

bó-kū, wife's brother. **chhe-kū** (r.), id. **kū-á**, wife's younger brother. **sōe-kū** (Cn.), id. **toā-kū**, wife's elder brother. **bōe-bó**, **tsòe toā-kū**, said in derision of a man selling his wife, as if she were a sister, so that he became brother-in-law of the new husband. **kū-iâ**, brother of mandarin's wife. **sa^n-jit kū-iâ thàm-pâng**, bride's younger brother or nephew taking presents to her on the day after marriage. **sa^n-jit kū-á**, &c., id.

kū, sound of birds. **kū-kū-háu**, to coo, as doves, &c. **ki-ki kū-kū**, twittering sound of birds.

hó-kū, a bird that calls "khū-khū," somewhat like the ke-n̂g-chiáu (sort of owl?), (s. spur). **hó-kū-chiáu**, sort of bird; id. (?).

hó-kū (C.), a long-legged insect, like a large grasshopper.

kū (R. kiū), old; former; opposed to "new" (not as opposed to "young"). **sin-kū**, new and old. **ngiâ-sin khì-kū**, to receive the new and reject the old, improperly. **chiàu-kū**, in the same way as before. **goân-kū**, id.

kū-nî^n, last year. **kū-siù^n**, looking faded, as an old dress. **kū-lē**, an old law or custom. **kū-khoán**, an old form or custom. **kū-pán**, old printing blocks; an old edition. **kū-iok** (X.), the Old Testament.

kū [R. prepared; to present; all together; an instrument, = col. khū], (C. ki). **kū-miâ^n**, to put down a name or names, as in a letter, or as parties in an official document [also, "old name"]. **kū-thiap**, to write a ceremonial card.

khì-kū, an instrument (s. old). **kiáu-kū**, any sort of furniture or instrument used for gambling.

kui [R. to return], to revert to; to fall to. **chiong-kui**, to the last; in the long run; said in scolding (v. chiong). **koh-kui**, to revert again to, as property.

kui-im, to die. **kui-sien**, id. **kui-thó**, to return to dust; to die.

khì-siâ-kui-chèng, to reform one's self. **kui-hók**, to submit. **kui-oá**, to attach one's self to, as to a man; to revert, as property (v. oá). **kui-hū**, to lean upon a powerful man or party, joining one's fortunes to his.

kui-lē, to set one's self diligently to one's work. **bô-kui-lē**, not working with a will; trying to do many things and doing none of them well; not making a definite choice between two courses. **kui-tiók**, correctly settled or put in a good train for settlement, as an affair.

kui-ūi, to return to one's proper place (v. ūi). **kui-lūi**, to assort (v. lūi).

hong kui-sin, the wind settled and steady. **thi^n-sî kui-sin**, weather settled and fine. **kui-sin-thi^n**, settled weather.

kui-tiong, to be in the very middle; also, a medicine, = tong-kui. **tong-kui**, a soft medicinal root, said to be good for the blood (Aralia? Levisticum?). **thó-tong-kui**, another medicinal plant (Angelica?).

kiú-kui soàn-hoat, the rules of arithmetic. **óh kiú-kui**, to learn the elements of arithmetic on the abacus. **kiú-kui-khak**, the first elements of it. **kui-tû**, division. **kui-tû sêng-hoat**, multiplication and division. **sêng-hoat kui-tû**, id.

kui-tsōe, to lay the blame upon —. **kui-tsōe--i**, to blame him for it. **kui êng-kng**, to give glory to.

boán-tsāi êng-kui, to return prosperously with full cargo, as a vessel; said also of emigrant coming home rich.

kui (cf. ka). **kui-ê**, complete, as a thing that wants none of its parts. **kui-phō**, a complete set, as a book having all the volumes; a large bunch or tuft, as of grass from one root or in one mass. **bô-kui-phō**, the set (of volumes) not complete. **kui-hù**, a complete set or suit. **kui-siang**, a pair. **kui-chhn̂g**, a whole string, as of beads strung together. **kui-kûn**, a large company; a whole crowd.

kui-tsong, all the goods of a particular sort (v. tsong). **kui-tsú bóe**, to buy all the goods of one owner on the premises of a commission agent. **kui-hāng**, in considerable quantities. **bōe kui-hāng**, to sell wholesale. **bóe kui-hāng**, to buy wholesale.

bô-kui-sim, not with one's whole heart; not with fixed attention. **kui-seng-khu**, the whole body. **kui-jit**, the whole day. **kui-phièn**, a whole piece or slice. **kui-liėt**, making a whole row (v. liėt). **sí kui-phiáh**, all in a place dead. **siám kui-pêng**, all go to one side of the road, so as to leave the other side quite clear for others to pass. **kui-bê**, become one mass (v. bê).

kui-n̂g (esp. T.), = ka-n̂g, complete; both forms are used both in A. and T.

kui [R. ki, a contrivance; a machine; a loom; a secret], a loom; a frame, as for embroidery, &c.; a press; to press in a press.

kui ôe-tóe, to press shoe-soles. **kè-kui**, pressed tight, as goods that have been through the press. **pi^n-kui**, to stretch out on the frame, as embroidery.

chit-kui-pò, a web of cotton cloth, about a hundred feet long.

chhia-kui, a turning-lathe. **hun-kui**, a press for pressing tobacco very tight. **mī^n-soà^n-kui**, a frame for drying vermicelli, in making it. **siù-kui**, a frame for embroidery.

chit-kui, a loom. **pò-kui**, id. **hî^n-kui** (C.), id. **toā-kui**, id. **chit toā-kui**, to weave broad cotton cloth, as women do at and near Amoy. **toā-kui-pò**, broad cotton cloth (native). **kui-á-pò**, narrow (native) cotton cloth.

kui [R. a pair of compasses; a rule]. **kui-kú**, a rule; a regulation or custom (v. kú). **kui-kí** (C.), id.; finished. **tēng-kui**, to settle a rule; a fixed rule (v. tēng). **tiâu-kui**, regulations or stipulations. **kui-lē**, a regular fee, as at government office (v. lē). **pang-kok kui-bê** (R.), laws and rules of the state.

ìn-kui, a frame in which a seal is tightly wedged while being cut.

kui — **jit-kui**, a sun-dial.

kui [R. ku, to dwell]. **lēng-kui kok-sit** (Cn.), = A. lēng-ku kok-sit, to live and have meals all separate.

kui [R. the women's part of a house]. **kui-lú**, a

32

virgin. **chhim-kui-lú**, id. **chhut-kui**, to be married the first time, as a virgin.

kui — **láng-khò-kui**, the slits (like pockets) in boatmen's wide outer-trousers [next word ?].

kui, the crop of a bird. **ām-kui**, the front part of the neck (v. ām). **kâu-kui**, the projecting neck of the monkey.

toā-pak-tó-kui, enlarged spleen.

chhiú-ńg-kui, the inside of a sleeve.

kéⁿ-kui, unpleasant feeling from eating too fast or too much. **koàn-kui**, to stuff a fowl's crop to make it sell well. **chìⁿ-kui**, id. **tiùⁿ-kui**, crop very much distended, either from voracious eating or from fraudulent stuffing (v. tiùⁿ).

koāⁿ-kui, crop (of fowl) very full and hanging down; having one's dress hanging too loosely on the breast. **bó-kiáⁿ teh-koāⁿ-kui**, family being an encumbrance, so as to prevent a man leaving home. **hō-goá put-chí koāⁿ-kui**, makes me extremely uncomfortable, as some very painful matter which cannot be set right or got rid of, *e.g.* great misconduct of a very near relative.

kui — **kui-hî**, a sort of fish good for food.

kui — **kui-á-hî**, a tadpole. **kap-kui** (Cn.), id. **kap-gō͘e-kui** (Cn.), id.

kui [R. a tortoise or turtle, = col. ku]. **kui-lêng hók-soàn**, may you live as long as the tortoise and stork.

o͘-kui, a brothel-keeper; a cuckold; man whose wife or daughter is a prostitute.

kui (cf. pui). **thút-kui**, built with ridge of roof in the same line as that of another house, but lower; also, eaves carried out very wide at a lower level than the eaves close to the roof, with a perpendicular connection, as is often seen in temples.

kûi [R. the jaw-bone; place where roads meet]. **chiong-kûi**, the ruler of ghosts; a Tsin-sze graduate of the Tang dynasty. **chiong-kûi tī siáu-kúi**, said of a bold influential man guiding and ruling other men. **chiong-kûi tī-kúi**, id.

kûi (R. id.) **kûi-koe**, the sun-flower. **hiòng-jit-kûi**, id.

tsu-kûi, a famous grave-digger. **khì-chhē niauⁿ-tsu-kûi** (gone to look for pock-marked Tsu-kûi), said of a man just dying; also, in scolding a lazy man who is always sleeping.

kûi [R. hoâi, the bosom; to hold in the bosom, = col. kûi], to put, fold, or hold in the bosom within the dress. **thau-kûi**, to secrete in the bosom under one's dress. **kûi-kûi tsah-tsah**, to carry some things (or a child) in one's bosom, and other things about other parts of the dress (v. tsah). **kûi gín-ná**, to cover a child with the flap of our dress in the bosom, so as to keep it warm.

bák-chiu kûi-tsúi, eyes slightly swollen (kûi ?).

kúi [R. khúi, deceitful, intriguing]. **kan-kúi**, very deceitful and rascally, esp. of a man who deceives both sides for his own gain.

kúi (R. id.), a ghost; the spirit of a dead man; a demon; a wretch; a secret spring or bolt; (used to express deceit, intrigue, and very strange things).

soaⁿ-kúi, a mountain spirit; a man who acts as agent for buying sites for graves. **tē-hong-kúi**, a spirit supposed to rule a particular region (said in joke of a very tall man). **tek-ko-kúi**, a very tall thin fellow. **hoan-kúi**, foreign ghost or demon (rarely said except in imitation of Cantonese "fan-kwei"). **o͘-kúi**, an assistant or servant in a shop (v. o͘).

o͘-kúi-kúi, very black, as a man. **hiông kúi-kúi**, very ugly, as face.

chiú-kúi, a drunkard. **kiáu-kúi**, a confirmed gambler. **a-phiàn-kúi**, a confirmed opium-smoker. **hong-so-kúi**, a lascivious fellow. **hong-liû-kúi**, id. **thiàu-kúi**, a mischievous, troublesome boy. **té-miāⁿ-kúi**, you shall not live long! (said in scolding).

kúi-kúi tsúi-tsúi, very deceitful and intriguing. **kóng kúi-ōe**, to talk deceitfully. **pí-i koh-khah-kúi**, even more crafty and cunning than he. **siang-bīn-to-kúi**, a double-tongued man, who excites quarrels by speaking to each party against the other. **kìⁿ-kúi**, to see a ghost; to tell lies. **phièn-kúi**, do you think you can deceive me thus? (v. phièn). **tsòe-kúi**, to be a ghost or demon; to cause trouble secretly. **lōng-kúi**, to be prime mover in a deceitful and injurious plot. **ke nn̄g-ê-kak, chiū-sī-kúi** (if he had two horns he would just be a demon), very knowing, so as not to be easily cheated, deceived, or over-reached. **chhiáⁿ-kúi i-pīⁿ**, to ask a man to assist in a matter, who puts it all wrong. **phāiⁿ-kúi ui-pēⁿ** (C.), id. **ín-kúi jip-thêh**, to call ghosts into the yard; also, to give a man his first introduction into a place where, afterwards, he proves very injurious. **kap-kúi tsòe-chhù-piⁿ**, said of keeping company with a very dangerous man. **kah-goá khì liàh-kúi**, telling me to try to catch a man of whom no trace can be found. **kap-kúi pé-chhiú-bīn** (warding off demons with the hand), said of a man whom it is very dangerous to oppose. **kap--i ngó-kúi tùi-chhiong**, to be at irreconcilable feud with him. **chhek-tiòh-kúi**, to meet with an unexpected difficulty that upsets our plans. **tú-tiòh-kúi**, id. **tú--tiòh phāiⁿ-kúi**, unexpectedly come across some one who throws all our plans wrong. **kúi-kap-bé háu** (ghosts and horses making a noise), meddling where one has no business (v. bé). **pak-tó-lāi theh-theh-kúi**, very suspicious about everything.

kúi-thâu, a head or ruler of demons. **tsòe-kúi-thâu**, to be the leader of a plot to injure people, or to lead a man into vicious courses. **kúi-ông**, a prince or ruler of demons, *e.g.* giâm-lô-ông, tāi-sū, or chiong-kûi. **kúi-á phièn kúi-ông**, said of an inferior vainly trying to deceive his master.

kúi-sîn, ghosts and spirits (v. sîn). **sîn-kúi**, id. **kúi-á**, a little ghost or demon; a common inferior ghost. **kúi-koài**, ghosts and goblins (v. koài). **kúi-siâ**, id. **siâ-kúi**, wicked demons. **phāiⁿ-kúi**, id. **ok-kúi**, malicious demons. **mô-kúi**, a devil. **iau-kúi**, a hungry ghost. **un-ek-kúi**, demons that cause pestilence. **un-kúi**, a spirit that requites favours by making a man a Kujin.

oan-kúi, ghost of an unavenged murdered man (v. oan). **tiàu-kúi**, ghost of man who hanged himself (v. tiàu). **bô-thâu-kúi**, ghost of beheaded man. **tsúi-kúi**, ghost of a drowned man. **tsúi-kúi giâ tāng-kê**, do., wearing a heavy cangue. **tsúi-kúi kiò-kau-thòe**, ghost of drowned man tempting a man to kill himself (v. thòe).

khit-kúi kiò--khì, to be unexpectedly enticed into evil by wicked men, as a man formerly well-behaved. **kúi kiò--lí**, those whom you are following are wicked men luring you to ruin, or you yourself are going on a ruinous course. **kúi teh-kiò--lí**, id. **kúi teh-iét--lí**, id. **kúi teh-thó-miāⁿ**, a demon is taking your life (said of a man dying whose death is supposed to be somehow connected with his own wickedness). **jip kúi-bûn-koan**, to die (a Buddhist phrase).

ū-kúi, to be haunted. **kúi-siū**, a haunted place.

jit--sî m̄-thang kóng-lâng, mî^n--sî m̄-thang kóng-kúi, don't talk of a man by day, or of a ghost by night, or he will come.

oàh-kúi, secret springs, bolts, or joints skilfully arranged in a machine. **oàh-kúi-á**, id. **àm-kúi**, id., *e.g.* secret bolt in a door or drawer. **mn̂g-kúi**, secret bolt for keeping the bolt of a door shut. **mn̂g-kúi** (P.), = A. mô-kúi, a devil. **só-kúi**, the spring in a Chinese padlock which catches the tongue of it when inserted. **ióh-kúi**, id. **chhoà^n-lóh-kúi**, let down the secret bolt (of the door-bolt, &c.) **hī-khang-kúi**, the tympanum of the ear (v. hī).

kúi-hé, ignis fatuus. **kúi-á-hé**, id. **kúi-á-hong**, sudden, strange, and violent squall or gale (v. hong). **kúi-á-phùi**, soap-bubbles blown by children. **toà-kúi-thai**, stomach distended so as to give the unreal appearance of pregnancy.

bái-kúi, a large spider, supposed to cause an oppressive feeling in sleep. **thê-kúi** (T.), = A. kàn-á, a sort of shell-fish. **thê-kúi-hèk**, = A. ô-lâm-hèk, meat of a sort of shell-fish.

siáu-kúi-bīn, lock of door or drawer; very ugly, as face. **pô-tē-kúi**, an image made with a sack over the head, and having a head on the breast or belly.

kúi-jī-kha, the long legs forming the lower part of the character "kúi."

kúi-kok sien-tsé, a famous diviner now worshipped (v. kok, "a valley").

kúi (R. kí), how many? a few (only used in combination).

kúi-ê, how many? **kúi-jit**, how many days? **kúi-lâng**, how many men? **kúi-kiā^n**, how many articles? **kúi-bé**, how many animals, classified by "bé" (and so with the other classifiers and measures). **kúi-khô**, how many dollars? **kúi-tiám-cheng**, what o'clock? **kúi-siâ^n-gûn**, what is the degree of purity of the silver?

tē-kúi, which in order? (answered by "first," "second," &c.) **tōe-kúi**, id. **pài-kúi**, which day of the week? **chhoe-kúi**, which day in the first nine days of the month? **tsáp-kúi**, what number between ten and twenty? which day of the second decade in the month? **jī-kúi**, which day of the last decade of the month? **jī-chheng-kúi**, how many hundreds above two thousand? **khô-kúi**, how many ten-cents above a dollar?

kúi-nā^n, several. **kúi-nā^n-lâng**, several persons. **kúi-liáp-á**, a few grains, as of rice. **bô-kúi-ê**, only a very few (so with other classifiers). **bô-kúi-lâng**, only a very few persons.

kùi (R. id.), a cyclical character, the 10th and last in the cycle of ten.

kùi [R. one of the four seasons; the youngest of a family, or last of a number; the noble house of Ki, in the kingdom of Loo in the time of Confucius].

ún-kùi, the second rice-harvest, towards the end of the year. **chit-kùi-béh**, one crop of wheat or barley. **chèng sa^n-kùi**, to have three crops in a year.

sù-kùi (C. sù-khùi), the four seasons. **sù-kùi liû-hêng, bān-bùt hoà-seng**, the seasons revolve, and all things are produced. **sè-chhù, tsòe-sì-kùi thòeh**, rent of a house to be taken each quarter. **chiáh sì-kùi-tsúi**, to grow through the four seasons before ripening (said of the rice called kim-pau-gûn).

kùi — **tsòe-kùi**, wanton jesting or gestures between men and women. **bīn ū-kùi ū-kùi**, face pretty (said of a woman who looks of doubtful character).

kùi [R. cinnamon; cassia]. **kùi-hoe**, cassia flowers (Olea fragrans?). **kùi-ki**, twigs of cinnamon. **jiók-kùi**, cinnamon. **jiók-kùi-phê**, id., in the form of bark. **koa^n-kùi**, the best cinnamon.

kùi-lîm, very fine, large, long sort of the lāi-chi fruit. **kùi-lîm-koa^n**, do. dried.

tan-kùi, a small red flower. **chhiú-phan tan-kùi** (R.), to grasp a twig of it, *i.e.* become a Tsin-sze graduate or higher. **chhiú-phan tan-kùi tē-it-chi**, to become the chiōng-goân.

gô sam-kùi, Woo San-kwei, the Chinese general who invited the Manchoos to enter China.

kùi (cf. koà), to suspend a thing, as on a wall, or from the roof. **kùi-teng**, to hang up a lamp. **kùi-bō**, to hang up a cap or hat on a pin. **kùi-sa^n**, to hang up a coat, &c., by the neck.

kùi [R. kòe, to cut off]. **kùi-tsú-siú**, an executioner.

kùi (R. id.), honourable; noble; costly; dear in price. **tsun-kùi**, of high rank; honourable; noble (in rank). **kùi-khì**, costly; highly valued; honourable. **kùi-kùi khì-khì**, very much so. **hù-kùi**, rich and honourable; very comfortable and happy. **hù-kùi pîn-chiēn**, rich and poor; honourable or plebeian. **kùi-chiēn**, id. **bô-lūn kùi-chiēn**, no matter whether rich or poor. **tāi-kùi, pit-iú tāi-chiēn**, a man who is very rich or high in rank must afterwards become very poor and low; a very dear commodity soon becomes very cheap by glutting the market. **kùi-tsoā^n**, dear and cheap.

àm-kùi, a secret mark (as a wart) on the skin (said by fortune-tellers). **ū-kùi-keh**, appearance of face giving omens of wealth.

ko-kùi, high-priced, as goods. **mih^n ko-kùi**, goods are very dear (in that shop). **teh-ko-kùi**, asking too much, as for goods or for one's services. **kàu-chiah-ko-kùi**, said in finding fault with an inferior who is unwilling to help or to come when called.

kùi-sèng (polite phrases), your surname. **kùi-kok**, your native kingdom. **kùi-hú**, your native place.

teng-tsâi-kùi, sa^n-jī tsn̂g, male posterity wealth and rank in full measure. **tsâi-teng-kùi**, &c., id.

kūi (R. id.), a chest; a shop-counter; used in the names of various parties having the care of money or accounts.

siàu-kūi, a book-keeper (v. siàu). **siàu-kūi-toh**, a shop-counter. **chiáng-kūi**, man who has charge of the money in a hong. **gûn-kūi**, a large strong money-chest; a shroff, or man in a hong who has charge of the money. **peng-kūi**, a confidential agent of the Tartar general (not himself a mandarin), who is stationed in the office of the Chinese commissioner of customs (hái-koan) to watch and report what he does. **lāi-kūi siù^n-kang**, clerks or secretaries within the custom-house, who have charge of the money. **goā-kūi siù^n-kang**, clerks in the outer part of the custom-house who stamp documents, &c. **kūi-su**, a collector of taxes for a division of a hien district who goes about the country as assistant of the hô-pāng.

chî^n-kūi, a large long chest for money, esp. copper cash. **chî^n-kūi-á**, a smaller sort. **chî^n-kūi-á-tiàm**, a money-changer's shop. **chî^n-kūi-á-toh**, a money-changer's table. **chî^n-kūi-toh**, id. **liên-kūi**, a shop-counter. **thong-hô-kūi**, do. outside the door, or partly inside it. **thong-lô-kūi**, id. **toh-kūi**, a table with drawers in it. **toh-kūi-á**, do.

smaller. **pâi toh-kūi-á**, to have a table as a stall in the street, as fortune-tellers, street money-changers, or men who write documents for a small payment. **toh-kūi-thoah**, a drawer in a small table.

oā^{n}-kūi, to change one's style of dress at beginning of summer or winter. **kūi-á**, a small chest, esp. for clothes. **chhn̂g-kūi**, a long chest that serves as a bed or couch. **kūi-chhn̂g**, id.

hong-kūi, the Chinese substitute for bellows, a cylinder with a piston; also (C.), fanners. **khan hong-kūi**, to work the piston of Chinese bellows. **iėt hong-kūi** (C.), to winnow with fanners. **chhiû^{n} hong-kūi** (C.), id. **lô-kūi**, bellows for a forge (cylindrical). **tsúi-kūi**, a water-tank for a vessel.

kūi (R. id.), to kneel; to kneel to. **kūi hông-tè**, to kneel to the emperor. **kūi thi^{n}-tōe**, to kneel and worship Heaven and Earth. **kūi-tiâ^{n}**, to kneel and present a petition to a mandarin, as on the road.

kūi-pài, to kneel and do reverence or worship. **khiàm-chit-kūi**, to do everything but kneel (said of very urgent entreaty). **poà^{n}-kūi**, bend low, almost kneeling. **phah-poà^{n}-kūi**, id. **siang-kha kūi tah-tah**, kneeling on both knees very humbly. **khòk-khòk-kūi**, to kneel over and over. **phak-tē kūi**, to kneel and prostrate one's self, as to a very high official. **kūi phak-tē**, id. **kūi-phak**, id. **sam-kūi kiú-khàu**, to kneel thrice, and knock the forehead nine times. **kūi-jú** (R.), to kneel in sucking, as a lamb.

kūi [R. hoâi, the bosom; to contain, = col. kûi]. **koà-kūi**, pregnant; not said of a woman, but only of animals, esp. pigs; swollen with the ear, as the blade of grain about to burst, just before "chhut-sūi."

kūi-tsúi, slightly dropsical and swollen, as limbs, or as diseased yellow face. **koàn-kūi**, full of water that leaks in, as ill-built wall.

kui^{n} (C.), = A. kng, bright; light.

kûi^{n} (Cn.), = A. keng, a room; classifier of houses (distinguish from "keng," a temple, which remains unchanged in Cn.)

kûi^{n} (Cn.), = A. keng, the shoulder.

kûi^{n} (Cn.), = A. koai^{n}, to shut, as door or window.

kûi^{n} (Cn.), = A. koâi^{n}, high.

kúi^{n} (C.), = A. kńg, to roll up.

kúi^{n} (C.), = A. kńg, a tube. **ām-kúi^{n}**, = A. ām-kún, the neck.

kúi^{n} (C.), = A. kńg. **kúi^{n}-tang**, Canton. **kúi^{n}-sai**, Kwangsi.

kúi^{n} (C.) **ki-kúi^{n}-á**, snares, traps, or curious contrivances, worked by secret wheels, springs, &c. **tiu^{n} oáh-kúi^{n}** (A. kúi), to use such contrivances.

kúi^{n} (Cn.), = A. kéng, to choose.

kúi^{n} (Cn.), = A. kéng, a fold in a dress.

kúi^{n} (Cn.), = A. koái^{n}. **chhin-kúi^{n}**, the beam of a steelyard, &c.

kúi^{n} (Cn.) **kûi^{n}-iū^{n}**, to worship ancestors by offerings (T. kái^{n}).

kùi^{n} (C.), = A. kǹg, an essay, &c.

kùi^{n} (C.), = A. kǹg (several words); to make a hole; to string; a string, as of pearls; a ring for nose of ox, &c.

kùi^{n} (Cn.), = A. koài^{n}, accustomed.

kùi^{n} (Cn.), = A. kàn, to break the regular succession, as of days, &c.

kūi^{n} (Cn.), = A. koāi^{n}, a Hien district or city; its mandarin.

kûi^{n} (Cn.), = A. kēng, to assist, &c.

kuih (C. koeh), to scratch with the hand or with an instrument; to rub hard, as in shampooing to relieve pain or sickness; to rub in, as cement; to clean, as a small-tooth comb. **thui-kuih**, to shampoo with long and short rubs ("kuih" is the shorter rub, and done with more force). **kuih ham-khak-á-chí^{n}**, to rub hard with a shell, as in sickness; also (T. uih), to make a shell turn upside down by pressing it with the nail, as children do in play. **kuih--khí-lâi** (cf. uih), to take up with the finger, as paste. **kuih-he**, to rub lime or cement into a crevice. **kuih tsng-phāng**, do. into the crevices of a tiled floor or roof.

kuih po-lê, to break off a small bit of glass by scratching it with a diamond.

kuih (cf. kúi). **o kuih-kuih**, very black, as a person.

kun (Cn. kün). **khat-kun**, willing to do something difficult, troublesome, or expensive (v. khat).

kun — **tsoá-kun**, paper cut into long strips, as for making matches, or for mixing in mortar. **tsoá-kun-he**, fine plaster for walls or ceilings, having finely cut paper mixed in it.

kun [R. equally]. **kun-tu** (C. kin-tu), yet all the same after all. **kun-nih^{n}**, id. **kun--tit**, id. **kun--tit bōe-ōe**, after all quite unable, however you may teach, or he may try. **kun-tu sī àn-ni^{n}**, no difference after all; "six and half-a-dozen;" though it may appear different, yet really it is much the same, *e.g.* salary more, but expenses greater. **kun-tu bô-beh-thia^{n}**, yet after all one tries he will not hear.

kun-pêng, equal and undecided, as a drawn game.

kun [R. koan, a barrier]. **thâu-kun-ta**, the large rock (Cornwallis Rock) near ē-mn̂g-káng.

kün (Cn.) **kün-toàh-chhài**, = ka-boàh-chhài, a vegetable.

kun (R. id.), a sovereign, king, emperor, reigning duke, &c. **kun-ông**, id. **jîn-kun**, id. **kok-kun**, id. **kun-sîn**, sovereign and minister (v. sîn). **tiong-kun pò-kok**, loyal to his sovereign, and grateful to the dynasty (v. tiong). **khi-kun**, treason. **gėk-chí khi-kun**, id. **sèng-kun**, an emperor who acts as a sage. **sèng-kun hiên-siòng**, emperor and prime minister very wise, good, and just.

tong-kun, the owner of a school, or man who supplies the funds, and engages the teacher. **lông-kun**, a polite phrase for a young man; sometimes said of a husband (v. lông).

kun-tsú, a man of superior excellence; a good man. **sien siáu-jîn, hō kun-tsú**, first bargain strictly, and afterwards you can be courteous. **kun-tsú-só**, a very small padlock. **kun-tsú-siâm**, wrestling or embracing, as if wrestling for amusement. **kun-tsú-chhát**, a thief who looks respectable, and steals valuable things; said also of an adulterer (v. chhát).

sòe-kun, the name of a year expressed by cyclical characters, as used for divination.

sù-kun, four important medicines, viz. sim, lêng, tsút, chhó. **sù-kun-tsú** (R. sú-kun-tsú; Cn. sek-kan-tsū), a medicine much used for worms in children; fruit of Quisqualis sinensis.

tè-kun, title of Kwanti and of Wên-chang; said also in addressing Tāi-tō-kong. **bûn-chhiong tè-kun**, Wên-chang, the god of literature. **tsú-tòng tè-kun**, id. **ná^{n} tsú-tòng tè-kun**, said of a very elegant good-looking man. **chin-bú tè-kun**, = Hiên-thien siōng-tè. **tè-kun-kong**, a title of Tāi-tō-kong.

giâm-kun, = giâm-lô-ông, the judge of the dead. **tsàu-kun-kong**, the god of the fire-place (v. tsàu). **pak-táu seng-kun**, the star-god of the Great Bear. **tiuⁿ chin-kun**, an idol of the surname (tiuⁿ) Chang. **tiuⁿ thien-kun**, id.

kun (R. id.), an army (properly 12,500 men on paper); to banish to the frontiers. **kun-liû-tē**, three sorts of banishment; banishment or transportation in general. **chhiong-kun**, to banish to the military frontiers, or to a distance of from four to eight thousand lí. **chhiong-kun mn̄g-liû**, transportation and banishment. **chhiong-goā-kun**, to transport to the most distant frontiers.

chiong-kun, the Tartar general stationed at each provincial capital. **chiòh-chiong-kun**, stone figures of men at graves **bé-chiong-kun**, an idol with a horse's head, attendant on Giâm-lô-ông. **gû-chiong-kun**, cow-headed do. **siⁿ-mn̂g chiong-kun**, a shrub with bunches of rich purple flowers. **chiong-kun-tiùⁿ**, a pair of curtains hung before a general or other high mandarin (civil or military) when administering justice. **chiong-kun bô-tī--teh, sió-kun phah-làh**, when the general is away, the soldiers go to hunt; cat away, mice play.

sió-kun, a common soldier. **chiòng-kun** (R.), the whole army (v. chiòng, "all"). **kun-bîn**, soldiers and people. **kun-bîn jîn-téng**, id. **kun-peng**, soldiers. **kun-sū** (R.), soldiers and petty officers. **kun-su**, an officer on the staff skilful at planning battles (v. su, "teacher"). **kun-su** (C. kun-si), war taxes or contributions so called (v. su, "to need").

kun-chêng, circumstances or affairs of an army. **lāu-siet kun-ki**, to let out secrets. **kun-ki-bō**, a cap sometimes worn by military mandarins. **kun-hoat**, military rules and regulations. **kun-lēng**, military orders. **kun-khì**, weapons and ammunition; munitions of war. **kun-tsong**, id. **kun-tsong-kėk**, an arsenal chiefly for warlike stores. **kun-kong-chhiúⁿ**, arsenal and dock for building war-vessels.

gū-lîm-kun, the imperial body-guard. **sam-kun**, the imperial army in three divisions.

chêng-kun, the van. **āu-kun**, the rear. **tsó-kun iū-kun**, the wings. **tiong-kun**, the centre. **tiong-kun-hú**, = toā-thiaⁿ-iâ, name of an idol (v. thiaⁿ).

bé-kun-iâ, two images, attendants of Kwanti or of Sêng-hông, holding horses. **lėk-bé-kun**, id. **pàng-kun-chiòng**, to send spirits to help their votaries, as powerful idols do. **khò-kun**, to make offerings of food to the spirit soldiers sent to guard a place.

chhut-kun, to go to war, as army. **siu-kun**, to make a retreat or call back the army. **hôe-kun**, id. **tâu-kun**, to enlist; to enter the army. **chio-kun bóe-bé**, said in scolding noisy children. **loān-kun-tiong**, in the turmoil of battle. **kun-tiong bû-hì-giên**, serious talk in serious matters.

kun (R. id.), (C. kin; Cn. kün), a napkin; a towel; a cloth; a band for the head. **chheh-kun**, a cloth for wrapping round books. **ké-kun**, a bag for steaming some cakes, &c. **lū-kun**, a cloth for straining the materials in making bean-curd.

khàm-kun, the cross timber on the bow of a boat or junk, on which the anchor rope or cable runs.

thâu-kun, a cloth worn on the head by women. **thâu-kun-téng**, the top-sail of a junk. **thâu-mn̂g-kun**, the cloth that is tied on a man when he is being shaved. **kha-kun**, cloth tied round the loins, as substitute for short trowsers; cloth for drying the feet (s. sinew). **chhiú-kun**, a handkerchief; a napkin. **bīn-kun**, a small handkerchief used for washing the face. **ɵ-bīn-kun**, a black cloth worn on the head by old women. **ɵ-kun**, a small black scarf or handkerchief, tied round woman's head. **ɵ-kun-khɵ**, ornament worn on woman's forehead. **hien ɵ-kun**, to raise the bride's vail slightly, as bridegroom does on the marriage day. **phè-á-kun**, sort of cloth worn on the head, esp. by bad women. **báng-kun**, sort of head-band used by women in the Ming dynasty, now seen in plays. **chhim-i hok-kun**, dress and hood of the dead according to the Ming form. **hoe-kun**, a checked or variegated handkerchief, used for wrapping things; also a thin checked cloth sometimes worn on the head by women, esp. by Cantonese bad women (s. root). **tà-hoe-kun**, to wear it on the head; worn also in Tâng-oaⁿ by middle-aged women. **jiàuⁿ-se-kun**, a long band of crape, or stuff like crape, used by men as a turban, or for tying round the waist; or worn by women on the head.

kun (R. id.), (C. kin; Cn. kün), a catty; a Chinese pound, = about 1⅓ pounds, = 16 taels (niúⁿ). **kun-niúⁿ**, catties and taels. **kun-jī**, one catty and two taels (&c.) **bē-chiūⁿ-kun** (C. bōe-chiɵⁿ-kin), not up to one catty in weight.

chhien-kun-tūi, = lám-kong, the rope that draws the top of the sail close to the mast. **chhien-kun-chhìn**, an arrangement of several strong levers for raising a great weight (v. chhìn). **chit-pah-kun-làt**, able to carry a hundred catties.

chiauh-kun, to throw up small round stones, as children do in play. **phek-kun**, id.

kun [R. the heel; to follow], (C. kin; Cn. kün), to get hold of a man by first getting hold of one of his relatives, &c. **kun-chhut**, to force a man to compear by laying hold of a relative or connection, and keeping him or punishing him till he gets the other to deliver himself up. **kun-tiòk**, id. **kun-kiù kàu hit-ê-lâng chhut--lâi**, id. **khit--i kun--khì**, to be forced to come forward by our relative being seized or getting into trouble.

kun-tè (C. kin-tòe), to follow; to wait upon, as attendant. **kun-sûi**, id. **kun-koaⁿ**, to follow a mandarin, as an attendant. **kun-pan**, a mandarin's attendant who goes on foot after his sedan

kun [R. a sinew? the heel?].

phah-kun-táu, to make a somerset.

kun (R. id.), (C. kin; Cn. kün), a root. **hoe-kun**, a flowering plant (s. napkin). **kun-tîn ōng**, having numerous posterity that live. **ū-kun-ki**, said of a child whose luck is to grow well and to prosper (v. ki, "foundation").

kun-tsat, careful and cautious, as in managing matters (v. tsat). **ū-bák-kun**, able to see quickly what should be done in any circumstances, esp. as to politeness (s. vein).

chhoàⁿ-kun, a piece of wood sunk crosswise into two planks or timbers to hold them together.

chhoàn-kun, the part of a document (*e.g.* receipt for land-tax) left in the book when the document is torn off and used.

tsáng-kun-thâu, the most important item, or principal manager, of a matter. **tsóng-kun-thâu**, a central place from which many roads diverge. **tsòe tsóng-kun-thâu**, to be the principal agent or manager in a matter.

kun-pún, origin. **kun-tóe** (C. kin-té), origin or beginning, as of an affair; antecedents of a man, or his original circumstances (v. tóe). **kun-tì**, id. **kun-bú**, the crown of the root of a plant; the root principle, origin, or most important part of an affair. **chhiû kun-goân**, to follow the clue to search out the real root of the affair. **tn̄g-kun** (C. tūi^n-kin), to cut up by the root, as a disease or bad habit. **bóe-chīn-kun**, to buy in perpetuity. **bōe-chīn-kun**, to sell without power of redemption. **chīn-kun-bōe**, id.

si^n-kun, to send out roots. **si^n-kun tèng-tiâu**, apparently fixed permanently in a situation or residence (as if rooted or nailed firm); said also in scolding a man who does not rise politely when a visitor comes in.

kā chhùi-khí-kun, to clench the teeth, as in pain or impotent displeasure (v. kā).

chhiah-kün-chhài (T.), = pe-lêng-chhài, a sort of vegetable.

kun (R. id.), (C. kin; Cn. kün), a sinew or tendon; a muscle; a nerve; a vein or artery.

kun-jūn, tough and elastic; narrow and unwilling to pay money. **kha-chhiú kun kiā^n** (Cn.), arms and legs strong.

huih-kun, veins or arteries. **kun-mêh^n**, the veins as appearing on the skin **hī-á-kun**, the veins at the back of the ear. **bák-kun âng**, eyes red, as with liquor (s. root). **kek âng-kun**, veins red and swollen, as with inflammation. **chhi^n-kun phû**, veins appearing swollen on the skin. **chhi^n-kun hiên**, id. **chhi^n-kun tiù^n-ām**, veins of the neck swollen (said of a man calling out loud and long).

kun-le, the small branching nerves or sinews in men or animals. **kun-thâu**, thick muscular parts of the limbs and breast. **kun-thâu ân**, rheumatic pains in the muscles. **tùi-kun-thâu leh**, to twitch the thick muscular parts, in shampooing. **kun-eng**, a boil or abscess where the muscles are thick and strong. **tsoáh-kun**, a very severe sprain. **siau-kun**, cramp. **kha siau-kun**, cramp in the leg. **kha-kun siau**, id. **kha-kun**, the large tendon at the heel (tendon Achilles), or in the bend of the knee (s. napkin). **pàng-kha-kun**, to cut the tendon of the heel. **koah kha-kun**, id. **kha-āu-kun**, the great tendon or sinew in the bend of the knee. **toā-pán-kun**, id. **chih-kun**, the string of the tongue (v. chih).

lòk-kun, stag's sinews, edible. **soa^n-bé-kun**, sinews of horses (edible), generally counterfeit. **gû-kun**, cow's tendons, for bow-strings. **thèng-kun**, stirrup-straps. **gē-kun-chháu**, = ku-chiēn-chháu, the medicinal plantago; leaf has five veins.

kûn, to boil very thoroughly in water. **kûn-thng**, to make a soup or decoction. **kûn-bah**, to boil pork very soft. **kûn-noā^n**, to boil very soft; to boil to rags.

kûn (R. id.), a petticoat. **sa^n-á-kûn**, woman's gown and petticoat. **tn̂g-sa^n sàm-kûn**, long gown and flowing skirt, the full dress under the Ming dynasty (still said of full dress, though not now worn). **bóng-kûn**, dragon-embroidered petticoat of mandarin's wife. **siù-kûn**, embroidered petticoat.

kûn-thâu, waist of petticoat (s. fist). **kûn-toà**, band for tying on the petticoat at the waist. **kûn-kéng**, folds of petticoat.

phâng-kûn, extra sail below the main-sail. **ē-kûn**, the cross timber below the main folding-doors of a central hall.

ûi-su-kûn, an apron. **ûi-sin-kûn**, id. **tē-kûn**, a pouch tied over the bride's abdomen when she goes to be married.

kûn [R. koân, khoân, the fist; the closed hand]. **kûn-thâu**, the fist; boxing with the fist (s. petticoat). **kûn-thâu-bú**, the fist. **kûn-thâu sai-hū**, a teacher of boxing **kûn-thâu-pē**, the arts or tricks of boxing (v. pē). **kûn-thâu koâi^n**, good at boxing. **kûn-thâu kē**, unskilful at boxing. **liēn kûn-thâu**, to practise boxing. **liēn-kûn**, id. **pí-kûn**, to go through boxing exercise, either alone or with another. **pí-kûn-thâu**, id. **pí kûn-thâu-bú**, to shake one's fist at a man. **kiâ^n kûn-thâu**, to gesticulate, showing how we can box; to beat the air in boxing exercise. **kiâ^n-kûn**, id. **liáh kûn-thâu**, id. **liáh-kûn**, id.

phah-kûn, to strike one's self hard with the fist, as men do in the streets for a show, or as quacks, &c. **phah-kûn, bōe ke-ióh**, to wound one's self by beating and then apply a plaster, as quacks do to get a good sale. **phah kâu-kûn**, id. **kâu-kûn**, a peculiar sort of boxing. **éng-chhun tát-tsun, thài-tsó kâu-kûn**, said of Sòng thài-tsó, the founder of the Sung dynasty, who was a great boxer.

khí-kûn, to raise the fist, as when going to strike. **chhò-kûn**, to wound severely or kill unintentionally. **tsān-kûn**, to assist in thrashing a man. **tûi-kûn liáh-lêng** (Cn.), to shampoo, &c., as barbers do.

kûn-thò, the arts or tricks of boxing. **kúi-nā^n thò-kûn**, several boxing tricks.

hoah-kûn, to play at morra, guessing the number of fingers the other holds up. **chiáh-chiú hoah-kûn**, to drink and play at morra.

kûn (R. id.), a flock; a herd; a large company of persons or animals, even of fish. **iû^n-kûn**, a flock of sheep or goats. **chit-kûn-iû^n**, id. **lâng-kûn káu-tóng**, "birds of a feather flock together," rather in bad sense. **hê-kûn káu-tóng**, a set of vile wicked people.

kui-kûn, a whole flock or herd; a whole large company; in large numbers. **kui-kûn kui-koah**, in large companies or flocks, as men or animals. **tsòe-kûn**, to consort with, as companion. **tàu-kûn**, to go in a company. **chhiau-kûn** (R.), superior to others in something (v. chhiau). **koá^n-kûn** (r.), to run about in noisy troops, as boys. **khí-kûn** (T.), to have a desire for the male, as female cattle.

kún (C. kúi^n). **ām-kún**, the neck (v. ām).

kún, to sew on an ornamental border (on the very edge of a dress) of different colour or stuff; to face or trim a dress with some stuff. **siu^n-kún**, to ornament clothes by sewing on a border of a different stuff on the very edge, or a little way off the edge ("siu^n" is a little off the edge, leaving a rim of the original stuff visible; "kún" is on the very edge), (s. boil). **siu^n-kún-iēn**, do. in various ways on women's dress.

kún-sa^n, to face or trim the edge of a dress. **kún-niá^n**, to put on a double thickness of cloth at the collar. **kún-kí^n**, to sew on a border or facing of different stuff. **kún toān-kí^n**, to face with satin. **kún-toān**, id. **kún-pè**, to face or bind the edge with cotton cloth. **kún-jiông**, to face with velvet.

kún-liâu, a narrow band of some stuff to be used as a border or edging of dress, cap, &c. **toān-kún**, a satin border or edging. **pè-kún**, border or edging of cotton cloth.

kún (R. id.), to boil; to be boiling, as water (not said of the things that are boiled in the water); boiling; to bubble in boiling; to be noisy. **hiâ^n-kún**, to make to boil; to set a boiling, as water. **hiâ^n kún-tsúi**, to boil water. **kún-tsúi**, boiling water. **iét kún-tsúi**, to blow the fire (with a fan) so as to make the water boil. **siu^n-kún**, too hot and boiling (s. border).

sio kún-kún, very hot, as hot water, or as in the sun. **jiét kún-kún**, very hot and fevered, as in illness; very crowded and numerous, as a multitude; very desirous of something, *e.g.* of pleasure or of battle.

loān-loān-kún, very noisy and busy, as many persons. **hoā-hoā-kún**, bawling and making a great noise, as a crowd. **chhiāng-chhiāng-kún**, making a great noise, as a multitude, or as water boiling. **kún chhiâng-chhiâng**, boiling violently.

pak-tó kún--chhut-lâi, having a tendency to vomit; unable to repress a smile or a laugh.

kún, to joke; to laugh and jest; to make sport or play tricks by word or actions. **kún-chhiò**, id. **chhø-kún**, coarse play (wrestling or fighting for fun), such as may easily grow to a real quarrel; improper liberties in talk or action, as with females. **gâu-kún**, making practical jokes or playing tricks. **bô-gâu-gún**, this is a serious affair, and no joke. **m̄-thang gâu-kún**, don't play tricks so; don't make such unseasonable sport or jesting. **m̄-thang-kún**, id.

kún (cf. kùn). **kún-lún-tsūn**, to struggle, as in escaping; to writhe or wriggle, as in pain, or as a snake; much twisted, as a rope, or as the root of a tree (v. tsūn).

kùn — **kùn-kiūⁿ**, obstinate (v. kiūⁿ). **kùn-tsūn**, to struggle to get free from one who holds us; to take means to avoid paying expenses (v. tsūn). **kùn--tsáu**, to escape by struggling violently. **kùn-lùn--tsáu**, id. **kùn-lèng--tsáu**, to struggle violently with body and limbs to get off (v. lèng). **khit--i kùn--khì**, to have let him escape by struggling.

kùn (R. id.), a club; the wooden stick by which punishment is inflicted in military yamens; to strike with a heavy stick; (used in many phrases describing rascals and rogues).

kong-kùn, a rogue; a swindler. **láu-kong-kùn**, a great rogue. **toā-kong-kùn**, id. **kong-kùn-thûi**, a man too sharp to be taken in by any rogue; sometimes himself too cunning for others. **koái-kùn**, a kidnapper. **kiáu-kùn**, a very cunning skilful gambler. **siōng-kùn**, a pettifogging lawyer who constantly incites to lawsuits. **khan--i siōng-kùn**, to accuse him of being such a pettifogger. **tē-kùn**, a man who takes a lead in evil, as in a village. **thé-kùn**, id. **chhoàng-kùn**, a man fond of low vicious pleasures and rows, and who leads others into them.

īⁿ kùn-kùn, fat and plump, as the arm; round, as the leg of a table. **īⁿ-kùn īⁿ-kùn**, id. **īⁿ-kùn** (C.), plump and fat, as a man. **chhēng kàu īⁿ-kùn-kùn**, having on a great many clothes, so as to look quite fat.

chhâ-kùn, a large club or staff. **bók-kùn**, id. **tîn-kùn**, a heavy rattan-stick for punishment in military yamen. **kiap-kùn**, an instrument for torturing the feet.

kùn kúi-ē, beat how many blows in military yamen. **kùn jī-tsáp**, beat twenty blows. **phah jī-tsáp-ē kùn**, id.

kūn (R. id.), (C. kīn, Cn. kūn), near, in place or time. **kūn bih-bih**, very near, in place. **kūn-hū** (r.), id. **hū-kūn** (r.), id. **pek-kūn**, to press near; to press upon. **oá-kūn**, to approach. **kūn-oá**, id. **kūn-chêng**, to come forward and approach. **chiū-kūn**, to approach. **chhin-kūn** (r.), to come near and have intercourse with a person.

kūn-sī, near-sighted.

chiong-kūn, almost; nearly; very similar to.

kūn-jit, a day not far distant, before or after. **kūn-lâi**, lately; recently; not long ago. **kūn-lâi hó--ma**, have you been well of late? how do you do?

oán-chhin put-jû kūn-lîn, a neighbour at hand is better than a relative far off (v. oán).

kūn-tì--chiá, hiên, they who keep company with the wise grow wise. **kūn-tsu--chiá, chhek; kūn-bék--chiá, hek**, near vermilion becomes red; near ink, black.

kut (R. id.), a bone; the ribs of a fan; the pieces of wood that make up a window ready for the glass or for the venetian slips. **kut-thâu**, a bone. **kut-hâi**, fleshless bones of the dead. **kø-kut**, rotten old human bones (v. kø). **kun-kut**, sinews and bones.

kha-kut, the bone of the leg; the leg. **chhiú-kut**, the bone of the arm; the arm. **nńg-kut**, gristle; also, impotent in the legs (without any definite disease or injury), so as to be quite unable to walk.

kāu-kut, full of bones, as a fish. **chit-ê-bīn kut-kut**, face naturally lank and lean, with bones prominent. **kut-bīn kut-bīn**, id. **bīn lóng-sī kut-lø̄**, id.

khah-ū kut-lø̄, solid, well-connected, and full of matter, as an essay. **khah-ū kut-khì**, id.

kut-keh, general form of body (v. keh). **ki-kut**, id.; framework, as of a lamp, &c. (v. ki). **thih-kut-á-siⁿ**, short and firmly set, as man. **tâng-sin thih-kut**, not afraid of cold or of a beating (v. thih).

pháiⁿ-kut-tè, giving signs that he will be an idle and useless fellow if he grows up (said of a bad boy). **pháiⁿ-kut-phe**, id. **pháiⁿ-kut-tsoe**, id. **pháiⁿ-kut**, id. **pháiⁿ-kut-thâu**, id.

sek-kut, precocious and intelligent, as young child [perhaps this phrase belongs to the second following word, "kut," = kùt].

toāⁿ-kut, lazy. **pîn-toāⁿ-kut**, id. **lø̂-moāⁿ-kut**, an idle dissolute fellow (v. moāⁿ). **kiūⁿ-kut**, stoically indifferent to pain, toil, &c. (v. kiūⁿ). **poān-kut**, a man who sides with his employer's enemies. **thiáp-kut-sit** (T. Cn.), regular and proper in behaviour. **khit-chiáh-kut**, a mean or mean-looking fellow, like a beggar. **chiēn-kut-siōng**, making one's self too low or humble in manner or appearance, *e.g.* wearing dress too mean for one's position, or not accepting comforts offered (v. chiēn).

kek-kut, ironical, sarcastic, or jibing and contradictory (v. kek). **pē-thâu bú-kut**, said of vile scolding by applying abusive epithets to a man's parents.

jī-kut, the style or hand in which a word is written (v. kut).

kut-lûn, a large joint, as of the limbs. **kut-bák**, the enlargement at a joint, as at ankle or knuckles; one of the smaller joints, as in feet or hands. **kut-tsat**, one bone (esp. a small bone) between two joints. **kut-chhé**, marrow.

bē tńg-kut, not come to puberty, as a boy (the bones are supposed to supply the masculine principle). **beh tńg-kut**, about to come to that age.

chhin-kut-jiók, one's own blood relations (not adoptive), as son or brother (v. jiók). **chhin-kut-hék**, id. **tâng-kut-hék**, near blood-relation. **kut-bah**, bones and flesh (v. bah). **bah-kut**, pig's bones. **bah-siau, kut-hiēn**, flesh wasted away and bones appearing.

sán-kut lòh-hiòh, very very lean. **chit-têng-phê, piⁿ chit-têng-kut**, skin and bone.

hūn--lâng jip-kut, hating heartily. **hūn--lâng kàu-jip-kut**, id. **thiàⁿ kàu-jip-kut**, to be extremely painful; to love very affectionately, as husband and wife, or as parent and child. **chhin kàu-jip-kut**, very affectionate, as friends.

sì^n-kut, the ribs of a fan. **n̂g-moâ^n-kut**, peeled and dried hemp-stalks. **siēn-hî-kut**, work like a closely-jointed watch-chain (like eel's back-bone). **lêng-kut**, a sort of mineral (fossil bones? Belemnite?), (v. lêng). **kut-kō** (Cn.), the whole set of a woman's hair-pins, &c.

tē-kut-phî, a cooling medicine. **hó-kut-ka**, jelly from tigers' bones (medicinal). **ngâu^n-kut**, to boil bones into jelly or glue.

pn̄g-sî-kut, the shoulder-blade. **gî-pê-kut**, inner shoulder-bone. **io-kut**, lower end of back-bone. **ka-chiah-kut**, the back-bone. **heng-khám-kut**, breast-bone.

kut [R. chhut, to go out; to put out]. **kut-la̍t**, to exert strength.

kut [R. ku̍t, crafty; cf. ku̍t]. **káu-kut**, crafty; deceitful; intriguing. **kè-kut**, over-sharp in dealings. **ké-kut**, pretending to be knowing and cunning. **kut-kut** (Cn.), precocious and intelligent, as child.

khiáu-kut, lively and open, as child. **sek-kut**, precocious and intelligent, as child [or does this phrase belong to "kut," a bone?]

ku̍t (R. id.) **káu-ku̍t**, = káu-kut, crafty; intriguing.

ku̍t (R. id.), slippery; very smooth. **ku̍t-ku̍t**, id.; savoury, as food well-cooked with much fat. **ku̍t-lu̍t-su̍t**, slippery. **ku̍t liu-liu**, id., as road. **ku̍t liù-liù**, id.

kng-ku̍t, polished very smooth, as a surface; very smooth, as a man's skin; specially polished more than once, or worn very smooth by use. **kam-ku̍t**, very sweet and pleasing, as flattery, or words of praise, or politeness, either true or false; very pleasant to eat, as fruit just ripe, or food well-cooked. **chhùi-tì^n chih-ku̍t**, smooth, flattering, and deceitful in talk. **chhùi ku̍t-ku̍t**, too talkative.

ku̍t--lo̍h-khì, to slide down a slippery incline. **ku̍t--tó**, to slip or slide so as to fall. **ta̍h-ku̍t--khì**, to stumble by treading on a slippery or slushy place.

ku̍t [R. high and eminent, like a solitary peak]. **ku̍t-khí**, to begin to be prosperous, as a man whose ancestors and parents have not been any way distinguished.

ku̍t (R. id.), to dig. **ku̍t-thô**, to dig in the earth. **ku̍t-gûn**, to dig up silver (said of trade extremely prosperous). **thàn-chî^n, ná^n ku̍t-kim**, making a vast deal of money, like digging up gold. **khah-hó khì ku̍t-kim**, id. (lit. better than digging gold).

ku̍t [R. name of a medicine]. **ku̍t-sek**, a sort of medicine.

kwa, kwâ, kwá, kwà, kwā; better koa, koâ, koá, koà, koā (*q.v.*)

kwa^n, kwâ^n, kwá^n, kwà^n, kwā^n; better koa^n, koâ^n, koá^n, koà^n, koā^n (*q.v.*)

kwah; better koah (*q.v.*)

kwai, kwái, kwài, kwāi; better koai, koái, koài, koāi (*q.v.*)

kwai^n, kwâi^n, kwái^n, kwài^n, kwāi^n; better koai^n, koâi^n, koái^n, koài^n, koāi^n (*q.v.*)

kwa̍ih^n; better koa̍ih^n (*q.v.*)

kwa̍k; better koa̍k (*q.v.*)

kwan, kwân, kwán, kwàn, kwān; better koan, koân, koán, koàn, koān (*q.v.*)

kwat; better koat (*q.v.*)

KH.

kha [R. hoa, a flower]. **lo̍k-kha-seng**, the ground-nut or pea-nut; arachis.

kha (C.) **kha-chiah**, = ka-chiah, the back.

kha (T.) **khih-kha-thâu**, = A. khih-kau-thâu, the corners of the cheek-bones below the eyes.

kha (Cn.), = A. khia, one article, esp. one article of a pair without the other.

kha (Cn.) **su-kha**, = A. sai-khia, private.

kha [R. kiok, = col. kioh], the foot; the leg; at or near the foot of — (after the word); used in many phrases for an assistant, a worker, or a place.

kha-chhiú, hands and feet; arms and legs; assistants (v. chhiú). **kha-á**, an assistant, esp. for low or coarse work. **chha̍t-kha-á**, the assistants of a head thief or robber. **koh chit-kha**, one more hand (is wanted), as chair-bearer or gambler. **phái^n-kha**, a bad customer, who pays ill; a cunning gambler, hard to be fleeced, or who pays ill. **hó-kha**, a good customer; a gambler who readily pays his debts; a pleasant boon companion. **hó-kha-ké**, a pleasant companion in low pleasures (v. ké). **kiáu-kha**, a gambler, esp. in relation to his usual gambling haunts (v. kiáu). **tùi-kha poa̍h**, two persons gambling together. **kə-tùi-kha**, id. **thit-thô-kha**, a young fellow fond of low vicious pleasures. **kiō-kha**, a chair-bearer. **kong-siā-kha**, do., esp. counting the number in a shop. **siâ^n-lāi-kha**, chair-bearers from the city, *e.g.* from Chin-chew. **lién-kha**, bearers of an idol's chair. **chhái-liên-kha**, secondary subscribers to the "ông-iâ" procession, &c. **tsúi-kha**, a water-carrier. **phöe-kha** (Cn.), a courier. **lô-hàn-kha**, a tramp; a wandering man without friends or relatives, generally idle and vagabond. **ki-kha** (Cn.), a sorcerer who pretends to be inspired.

tsàu-kha, a kitchen. **thô-kha**, an earthen or tiled floor; the ground viewed merely as a surface (v. thô). **hái-kha**, the sea-shore. **káng-kha**, a seaport (said only of distant ports). **sòng-kha**, Luzon (v. sòng).

ē-kha, the lower part, as of any place. **pìn-kha**, the place near the temples, where the hair (of women) stops. **hia̍h-kha**, the middle of the forehead just where the hair ends (v. hia̍h). **mn̂g-kha**, id. **mn̂g-kha**, at the very door, just inside (v. mn̂g, "door"). **lâu-kha**, the ground floor of a house. **kiā-á-kha**, the foot of a stair. **pî^n-kha**, the foot of a stage; round or near the stage. **chio̍h-hng-kha**, near the foot of the memorial arch. **siâ^n-kha--nih^n**, at the foot of the city wall. **chhiû^n-kha**, the foot of the wall. **chhiū-kha**, near the foot of the tree; below the tree. **tī-hé-kha--nih^n**, just below the lamp. **tī-sio̍ng-kha**, almost up to the rank of prime minister. **hia̍p sī tìn-kha**, the officer called "hia̍p" is the next below the "tìn-tâi." **thi^n-kha-ē**, all under heaven.

pē-bú kha-tau, parent's house or home. **hông-tè kha-tau**, the metropolis; the imperial capital. **tī-**

厦英大辭典

lí--ê kha-tau, just at your feet; just where you stand.

toh-kha, the foot or leg of a table. **khò-kha,** legs of trowsers. **khí-kha,** the roots of the teeth. **khí-kha,** to lift one's foot. **bān-jī-kha,** the character "bān" worked at the foot, as of a dress, or of a curtain, or of wood-work. **hé-jī-kha,** the 86th radical written at the foot of the character. **khoàⁿ-hé siⁿ-kha,** to see rays from a lamp or candle, as in a peculiar state of the eyes. **jit siⁿ-kha,** rays of the sun shining through the clouds.

ơ-kha (C.), the tide just beginning to ebb.

chhun-kha, sort of small wings projecting in front of a house.

chiam-kha iù, the needlework is fine.

kha-pān, the measure of one's foot. **che-m̄-sī kha-pàng,** behaviour very bad, *e.g.* gambling, licentiousness, &c. **kiâⁿ--khì, m̄-sī kha-pàng,** id. **kha-pō͘,** a step, as to the manner of walking (v. pō͘). **chit-pah-hoáh-kha,** one hundred strides; fifty paces.

pái-kha, lame. **luh-kha,** to limp in walking. **kiu-kha,** to draw up the legs; to draw back from what we promised to do (v. kiu). **liam-kha,** to walk softly. **soá-kha,** to shift the position of the feet, as for a change (v. soá). **khiau-kha,** to put one leg over the other knee (v. khiau). **khoà-kha,** to rest the leg stretched out, as on a chair. **khè-kha,** to support the foot, as on a stool. **ké-kha** (C. kóe; Cn. kó͘), to use a stool or other support to get up higher; to support one leg of a table. **ké-kha** (C. ké), a woman's large foot made to look like a small foot. **khiā-kha,** to take temporary work for food, or very small wages (v. khiā). **kià-kha,** to dwell in a place for a short time. **hioh-kha,** to rest for a short time. **thêng-kha,** to pause in walking. **thǹg-chiah-kha,** barefooted (v. thǹg). **tǹg-kha,** to stamp the foot. **khioh-khí-kha chiū-kiâⁿ,** to get up (from sitting or lying), and get on one's legs ready to walk. **kha-kiâⁿ,** to go on foot. **saⁿ-chiap-kha,** to follow in a line (v. chiap). **êng-kha-kut,** walking to no purpose. **chin-êng-kha,** id. **khiàm-kha-chè,** to have a journey in vain. **thó-kha khit-lō͘-kiâⁿ,** id. **kiâⁿ bōe-khui-kha,** unable to go far from home because of family matters. **pe bōe-khui-kha,** to hover (as hawk) over some animal that it is going to seize. **thiàu-kha-koe,** to hop. **tiô-kha-koe,** id. **chhiāng-kha-ke** (C.), id.

iù-kha, small bandaged feet of women. **chhơ-kha,** unbandaged feet of women. **toā-kha,** having large feet, either merely larger than the feet of others, or women's unbandaged feet. **pháiⁿ-kha-chhâ,** feet of girl ill-formed, from not having been well bandaged at first. **chiáu-kha,** a bird's leg (said also of a person whose legs have no calves). **chhàu-kha,** a leg with a bad sore or ulcer. **kha hong,** foot or leg having rheumatic pains.

lióng-kha-khiâ, to keep neutral; to act or speak without making a decided choice. **saⁿ-kha-tiam,** forming a triangle, as three villages. **saⁿ-kha-liâu,** sailing with wind about a-beam. **sì-kha--ê,** quadruped. **chîⁿ sì-kha: lâng nn̄g-kha,** money has four feet, but man only two: hard to get it.

kha-bé, the foot. **nìⁿ-kha-bé,** to stand on tiptoe. **kha-bé-chek,** candles burned at the foot of a corpse. **kha-kut,** the leg-bone; the leg. **kha-kut ū sì-ki, chiū thang-khì,** if you have four legs you may venture to go. **kha-thúi,** the thigh. **kha-phāng,** the opening between the legs, or in the bend of the knee. **kha-chhng,** the posteriors; the hollow bottom of a cup or bowl (v. chhng). **kha-tâng,** the leg from knee to ankle. **kha-liâm,** the shins. **kha-phīⁿ-liâm,** id. **kha-tó,** the calf of the leg. **kha-āu-tó,** id. **kha-thn̄g,** piece of the leg from knee to ankle, when the foot is gone (v. thn̄g). **kha-thâu-u,** the knee (v. u). **kha-oan,** the hollow in the bend of the knee (v. oan). **kha-bák,** the ankle. **kha-khū,** the ankle in regard to cutting off (v. khū). **kha-poâⁿ,** the upper surface of the foot; the instep. **kha-āu-tiⁿ,** the heel. **kha-āu-tsan** (r.), id. **kha-kun,** the tendon of the heel (v. kun, a sinew). **kha-kun,** a long cloth for the loins, &c. (v. kun, a napkin). **kha-tsńg-thâu-á,** a toe. **kha-kah,** nails of toes. **kha-chiúⁿ,** the sole of the foot (v. chiúⁿ). **kha-jiah,** a footstep. **kha-jiah-tóe,** the sole of the foot. **kha-chiah-tóe,** id. **kha-chioh-tóe,** id. **kha-chhioh-tóe,** id. **kha-tôe,** the hoof of an animal. **kha-sióh,** soft dirty moisture of the sole.

kha-péh, a bandage for the feet (used by women). **kha-béh,** wadded leggings with no feet (used by women). **kha-tháng,** a foot-pail (v. tháng). **kha-táh,** a foot-stool, especially one belonging to its own couch. **kha-kè,** a large footstool. **kha-khè,** id. **kha-kê,** a sort of wooden stocks for the feet. **kha-khóeh,** id. **kha-khàu,** iron fetters for the feet. **kha-lô,** id. **kha-liâu,** id. **kha-lô chhiú-khàu,** manacles and fetters for hands and feet. **kha-liâu chhiú-khàu,** id.

khâ (Cn.), = A. khiâ, to ride.

khá [R. kháu, = col. khiáu], ingenious; elegant; strange. **kí-khá,** ingenious; crafty; beautiful. **khá-koài,** wonderful; unexpected and strange (v. koài). **chin-khá,** a strange affair indeed! **chin khá-sū,** id. **khá-khoán,** of peculiarly beautiful or ingenious workmanship, esp. some new form or pattern; also, what a singular and improper way of acting! **chin-khá-khoán,** what extremely irregular and improper conduct! **khá-bī,** fine taste; delicate taste. **bô sím-mihⁿ-khá,** just tolerably good; not at all above the common. **kóng-khá-ōe,** to talk in a humorous ludicrous way (often with low jesting or use of unusual phrases). **khá-ê-ōe,** such talk.

koai-khá, bright, intelligent, and obedient, as boy or child (v. koai). **bák-thâu khá,** able to see and learn at a glance.

khá-kiâⁿ, you seldom visit us, surely you must have some business or some favour to ask.

khà [R. khò, to strike; to cut off, = col. khàu], to strike; to rap (more gently than "kòng"); to knock, *e.g.* as a pipe, to get something out of it; to cut off part of the length of a dress or of a sleeve.

khà-mn̂g, to knock at the door. **khà hun-chhe,** to strike a pipe on the ground so as to knock out the tobacco and ashes. **khà ham-khak-chíⁿ** (T.), = A. tèng . . . , to throw one shell at another so as to turn it upside down, as in a boy's game.

khā [R. hā, leisure, = col. hē]. **bô-khā** (C.), no leisure.

khā (Cn.), = A. khiā, to stand.

khaⁿ (R. kham), an earthen pot. **toā-khaⁿ,** a large earthen pot. **pn̄g-khaⁿ,** a coarse earthen dish for cooked rice. **hoe-khaⁿ,** a flower-pot.

khâⁿ [R. hâm, to contain; joined, = col. hâⁿ, kâⁿ]. **khâⁿ-tiâu,** glued or cemented. **khâⁿ--teh,** mended, as with glue; loosely attached, *e.g.* as loose papers sticking in the leaves of a book; stopped, as straws on a stream by slight obstacles over which a stronger current would carry them.

33

kau-khâⁿ, involved, as an affair; concealing one's purpose by avoiding a direct categorical answer. **ū-kau-khâⁿ**, involved, as a property on which there is a burden. **lóng-bô kau-khâⁿ**, having no burden or disputed right on it. **saⁿ-kau-khâⁿ**, much involved and hard to set right, as an affair; *e.g.* when both parties are somewhat wrong, or because every possible settlement injures men of influence, or with whom we wish to be friendly. **kap-i ū-saⁿ-kau-khâⁿ**, to be involved in his troubles because of having some relation or connection with him.

lióng-kau-khâⁿ, double-minded and double-tongued; undecided and shuffling about, so as not to commit one's self on either side; one foot in and one foot out.

khah (R. khiok), (T. khaih), a round small-mouthed wicker-basket used by fishermen. **khah-á**, id. **tek-khah**, id.

khah, more — (adverb, joined to verbs and adjectives), sign of the comparative; still more; rather —; too —; sometimes sign of superlative. **khah-tn̂g**, longer; too long. **khah-ok-hó͘**, more cruel than a tiger, &c. **khah-kùi--ê, saⁿ-pah tiāⁿ-tiāⁿ**, the dearest cost only 300.

koh-khah, still more —. **kèng-koh-khah**, yet still more.

khah-tit, a little better than before, though far from well; better than something else, but yet only tolerable. **khah-sī**, rather it is —. **khah-sī**, quicker. **khah sī-lâi**, come quicker. **khah-iâⁿ**, to conquer; to be superior or better. **khah-su**, to be beaten; to be inferior; can't help it (v. su). **khah-thiⁿ**, add still more. **khah-bô**, rather not so. **khah-ū goā-khì**, rather fond of display. **khah-thêng-á**, after a little.

khah (= hah). **chhiò-khah-khah**, to laugh very loud.

kháh (cf. khák, ka). **phah-kháh-chhiùⁿ**, to sneeze.

kháh (cf. khók, khàuh). **kháh-kháh**, incessantly; constantly. **kháh-khah-lâi**, constantly coming. **kháh-kháh-kóng**, constantly speaking. **kháh-kháh-tó** (T.), constantly falling, as a child.

kháh — **khe-kháh**, to procrastinate idly, as a messenger. **sì-kòe-kháh**, id.; to gad about idly; to get obstructed and settle down here and there, as bits of wood or straws on a stream.

kháh, to come near, as door or boat, &c.; to lose ground in tacking against wind and tide. **kháh--lòh-lâi**, to lose ground in tacking.

saⁿ-kháh, to come together, as two boats floating. **kháh-oá**, to bring near, as boat or door; to run a boat close to shore, or to another boat. **kháh-mn̂g**, to lay a door to. **mn̂g kháh-oá**, door shut, but not fastened. **mn̂g kháh--teh**, id.

kháh-pái, to come to the jetty and wait for passengers in regular turn, as boats do at night.

khan-kháh, to involve others somewhat in our quarrel, *e.g.* by an incidental remark when conversing on something else, or by putting their names in a legal document as witnesses to be called, or as having some connection with the matter.

khai [R. thai, to carry]. **khai-kú**, to help by giving custom. **khai-kí** (C.), id.

khai [R. to open; to begin; to explain, = col. khui], to spend. **khai-hoat**, to pay out, as money; to punish slightly and summarily and then set free. **khai-un**, to pardon a fault; to forgive a debt in whole or in part.

khai-kong, to dot the eyes of an idol with blood (or a red mixture) in consecrating it. **pu̍t khai-kong**, id. **khai-gán**, id. (v. gán). **khai-lō-sin**, a frightful paper image carried before funerals to terrify demons. **thien-bûn-khai**, the day (6.7) when the door of heaven is open (v. bûn).

khai-niûⁿ, to expel a soldier from the army. **khai lāu-peng**, to discharge old soldiers at 60 years of age.

ka-kī khai-ho, to boast of one's own talents or success. **khai-hoâi thiòng-ím**, to make merry over wine.

khai-pit, the formation of the world out of Chaos (v. pit). **khai-ki**, to originate, as a family or firm (v. ki). **khai-kok**, to set up a dynasty (v. kok). **khai-tiong**, to open a new shop (v. tiong). **khai-khún**, to begin to cultivate, as waste land.

khai-kái, to explain, as a book or doctrine, to scholars; to propose a good way of settling a dispute, as third party (v. kái). **khai-káng**, to explain a book, as teacher does to scholars. **khai-khiàu**, to teach a pupil so as to develop his mind well. **put-tek khai-kiau**, affair so involved that no satisfactory amicable solution can be found.

khai-siàu (r.), to note down disbursements.

khai-siau, to spend money (v. siau). **khai-chîⁿ**, id. **khai hō--i**, pay him, as wages or price. **khai-goá joā-chîⁿ**, how much paid out on my account. **khai-hùi**, expenses; to spend money. **khai-ēng**, to spend money. **toā khai-ēng**, to spend lavishly; very heavy expenditure. **chhit-khai poeh-khai**, to spend lavishly and unnecessarily. **khai-khong put-tin**, to embezzle so as not to be able to account for the money (v. tin). **khai-khong put-hu**, id. **khai-khong bô-giàh**, id.

khái (R. id.) **khái-jī**, the common square printed character. **khái-su**, id. **toan-khái**, written or cut very square and nice-looking, as characters.

khài [R. to make even; altogether, = col. kài]. **it-khài**, altogether —. **tāi-khài**, generally speaking; not exacting all that is due; gentle in punishing.

khài — **khì-khài**, a man's appearance and manner of conducting himself (as to outward matters, not as to good and evil). **toā-khì-khài**, having an open, liberal, and somewhat big manner. **sió-khì-khài**, having a rather mean or stingy manner. **siàu-liên khì-khài**, manner of a young fellow, fond of fine clothes and rather dashing in appearance.

khài (R. id.) **khóng-khài**, liberal; magnanimous; open-handed; having an easy confident air. **khóng-khài jip--khì**, to go in with an easy self-confident look, *e.g.* on going to visit a superior. **khài-jiên**, too boldly and fearlessly, *e.g.* wanting in the respect due to a superior, or fearlessly doing wicked things openly.

khaiⁿ (T.) **thô-khaiⁿ**, = thô-kha, an earthen or tiled floor.

khaiⁿ, the sound of a gong. **khaiⁿ-khaiⁿ-háu**, to sound loud, as a gong.

kháiⁿ (T.) **saⁿ-kháiⁿ**, to rub intentionally against each other in passing. **kháiⁿ-tioh**, id. **kháiⁿ-lâi kháiⁿ-khì**, id.

khàiⁿ (T.), = A. khàm, to cover.

khàiⁿ (T.) **nńg-khàiⁿ**, = A. nńg-khàm, the soft part of the side between the ribs and the thigh.

khaih (T.), = A. khah, a small-mouthed small wicker basket.

khak [R. certain; sure; firm]. **tek-khak**, cer-

海上絲綢之路文獻集成　科技與文化編

tainly. **khak-khak sī àn-niⁿ**, certainly it is so. **khak-sit**, true; truthful, as proof. **khak-chhiet**, true and important, as proof.

khak [R. kiok, khiok, sort of yeast or medicine]. **sin-khak**, a medicine made at Chin-chew, counted good for many diseases. **toā-khak**, half-fermented grain, ready for distillation. **peh-khak**, a sort of yeast, made from grain (a shell). **âng-khak**, a red preparation of grain, for giving a red colour to eatables. **táu-bí táu-khak ê-chiú**, a good sort of spirit made from a half-and-half mixture of fresh and fermented rice.

khak (R. id.), a shell; a husk; a case, as for watch or steelyard; (said of some of the radicals of words). **than-khak**, the shell of the spout-fish (v. than). **hāu-khak-á**, a ladle made from the shell of the king-crab.

ku-khak, the shell of a tortoise; sort of cabin on a passage-boat, or such small boat.

khang-khak, hollow; empty. **hiauh-khak**, to shell or peel off (neuter), as paint, plaster, skin, or label. **hauh-khak**, id.

kiú-kui-khak, the first elements of arithmetic, by the abacus.

gâu-chiap sún-khak, skilful at saying what fits into and confirms another's story, generally false or conjectural.

bih-khak, the soft inside of the bamboo, useless for wicker work.

só-khak, the body of a Chinese padlock. **joáh-lòeh-khak**, a broad ceremonial cap without tassels (v. lòeh). **pió-á-khak**, the case of a watch. **téng-á-khak**, case for a small steelyard. **teng-khak**, frame of a lamp. **to-khak** (C.), a scabbard. **tû siuⁿ-khak**, to make a deduction, allowing for the weight of the box in which goods are packed.

chhiū-khak, rough outer bark of a tree. **tāu-khak**, husks of pease or beans (v. tāu). **eng-sek-khak**, poppy-pods.

kok-jī-khak, the 31st radical, containing the phonetic part. **pēng-jī-khak**, the 104th radical. **bûn-jī-khak**, the 169th radical. **tham--jī, pîn-jī-khak**, the character "tham" (covetous) is very like the form of the character "pîn" (poor).

sái-khak (Cn.), a very coarse sort of cotton, refuse of cotton after beating. **sái-khak-mîⁿ** (Cn.), id.

khak (= khȧk). **khak-thâm**, to expectorate; to bring up phlegm.

khȧk (cf. khâm, khēhⁿ, khak), to clear the throat; the noise of clearing the throat. **khȧk-thâm**, to expectorate; to clear the throat of phlegm. **khȧk-hông** (r.), to bring up blood.

kham [R. to sustain; worthy; fit for]. **put-kham**, cannot be endured (said in scolding). **ōe-kham--tit**, fit for; worthy; able to bear or to hold. **ōe-kham-tit-kek**, can bear much provocation. **bōe-kham--tit**, unworthy; unfit; unable to bear. **bōe-kham-tit-phah**, unable or afraid to endure beating (*e.g.* an old or sick man), so as to be willing to make a false confession. **bōe-kham--tit lí-phah**, it is not *your* place to beat *me*. **bōe-kham--tit i-kiû**, cannot long bear the urgency of his request, and so grants it.

kham-û-sien (R.), a geomancer.

kham (R. id.), a shrine for an idol or tablet, &c. **pùt-kham**, shrine for a Buddhist idol. **kong-pô-kham**, a shrine for keeping ancestral tablets.

sèng-jîn-kham, a binnacle.

piah-kham, a niche in a wall, as for a cupboard or shelves, &c. **piah-kham-á**, id.

khâm [R. kham, rough and uneven, as ground]. **khâm-khiėt**, rough and bad for walking on, as road.

khâm [R. khài, to clear the throat; cf. col. khȧk]. **khâm-sàu**, to clear the throat. **toà-teh-khâm**, in the act of clearing his throat.

khâm (C.) **khâm-khê**, tedious and difficult to heal, as a disease.

khâm — **ơ-khâm-khâm**, all black, as with a crowd of people, or with smoke, or as a great swarm of bees. **hun kàu ơ-khâm-khâm**, all black with smoke, as kitchen.

khâm (cf. chhâm; khám), (C. khôm). **sió-khâm**, small cymbals. **tiong-khâm**, cymbals of medium size. **toā-khâm**, large cymbals. **toā-khâm-kó** (Cn.), a drum, a gong, and a pair of large cymbals.

phah-khâm, to beat cymbals. **khâm chhēⁿ-chhēⁿ**, sound of gongs and cymbals.

khám (cf. khâm). **khám-chhēⁿ**, a pair of cymbals, used in funereal music (v. chhēⁿ). **khám-chhê** (T.), = A. khâm-chhēⁿ.

khám [R. a pit; a hole]. **khám-khó**, troublesome to deal with, as affair; always miserable, sick, or in great trouble, as man.

khám, a notch [the groups of all these words "khám" are uncertain]. **khek-khám**, to cut notches. **kap--i khek-khám**, to be on bad terms with him (probably simply a variation of sound from "kek"). **kap--i kek-khám**, not getting on well with him; not agreeing with him.

kek chit-khám chit-khám, to divide or partition into several small divisions, *e.g.* the shelves of a cupboard.

khám, classifier of shops. **chit-khám-tiàm**, one shop. **thiàu-khám**, to pass over one shop, when distributing things equally among all; *e.g.* presents of cakes on some occasions.

khám (R. id.), to fell, as a tree; to slash; to chop. **khám-chhiū**, to fell a tree. **khám-chhâ**, to fell trees for fuel or timber.

khám — **chiàu-khám-tsām**, according to rule; properly (v. tsām).

chhàu-khám, unexpectedly (v. chhàu).

khám (cf. khàm). **chit-khám-á**, a very low step up or down, with much less difference of height than the ordinary steps of a stair; a small sudden change of level, as on a road. **chit-khám** (C.), one step, as of a stair. **khám-á** (C.), id.

khám (C.) **khám-mēⁿ**, = A. kím-mēⁿ, quick; be quick!

khám — **heng-khám**, the breast (v. heng).

khám [R. ham; cf. col. kham], foolish, absurd, and almost like a madman, in saying or doing things (more active than "gōng," which has more of dull stupidity). **am-khám**, id. **am-khám-gōng**, foolish or stupid. **khám-gōng**, id. **khám-sîn**, having a foolish or mad-like manner. **poàⁿ-khám**, talking at random or acting foolishly. **khong-khám**, stupid; wanting in sense.

khàm (R. id.), to inspect or examine minutely, as a mandarin. **khàm-mn̄g**, id. **khàm-giām**, to inspect officially the state of a place or person, esp. as to injuries. **tsa-khàm**, to make careful investigation (personally or by deputy), as a mandarin, or head of a village or firm.

kàu-khàm, to examine minutely and carefully into the state of any matter (as any one); very strict, minute, and exacting. **khêng-khàm**, to examine minutely, as account or affair.

khàm-háp, the two words "khàm-háp" written or stamped where a document is torn in two, to be used as proof (v. háp).

khàm [R. kài, = col. koà, kah, khap], (C. khèng, only in sense of "cover"), to cover; to cover with; to conceal; to defraud or embezzle small sums; to stamp.

khàm-ìn, to stamp, as a seal or mark.

khàm-làm, to cover up. **khàm-chhiòh**, to cover with a mat. **khàm-chháu**, to cover loosely with straw, &c. **thâu-hiàh khàm-khàm**, hair growing far down on forehead, omen of bad luck (v. hiàh).

jia-khàm, to cover over, as a matter; to conceal.

àm-khàm, to get secret gains by concealing part of the business, esp. at expense of employer. **bô-àm-bô-khàm**, no secret or improper gains in the matter. **khàm lâng-ê-chîⁿ**, to embezzle part of money intrusted, or of gains which the employer should have got. **khit--i khàm--khì**, to have some of our money fraudulently kept back by him. **phiⁿ-khàm**, to defraud of small sums by charging too much ("phiⁿ" is rather by an overbearing manner, "khàm" by deceit). **hoâiⁿ-kéh phiⁿ-khàm**, id. **phiⁿ--lâng khàm--lâng**, id.

khàm (cf. khám, foolish). **khàm-khàm**, having a dull foolish appearance. **khàm-thâu khàm-bīn**, unable to distinguish when people are pleased or displeased, as a man who foolishly asks prices absurdly high, or who bears to be scolded violently without taking any notice.

khàm (R. id.), (cf. khám), a cliff or precipice; a change of level, as in terraced fields; (a step, as of a stair). **chit-khàm**, one step of a stair. **gîm-khàm**, the long stone step along the wall of a house. **gîm-khàm-ē** (C.), just before that stone step. **khàm-á-kha** (C.), id.

soaⁿ-khàm, a precipitous bank or cliff. **chióh-khàm**, a rocky cliff. **téng-khàm**, an upper terrace, as in fields on a hill-side. **ē-khàm**, lower terrace, do. **koâiⁿ-kē-khàm**, sudden change of level, as on a road, or on terraced hill-side, or at a waterfall.

tsúi-khàm-chhē, name of a bird.

khàm (T. khàiⁿ). **nńg-khàm**, the soft part of the side between the ribs and the thigh.

khàm [R. kàm, khàm, red colour]. **âng-khàm-sek**, dark brownish-red colour. **âng-khàm-âng-khàm**, id.

khām (cf. khàp, kháh). **khām--tióh**, to come striking or bumping against, as man, or boat, or other things. **khām-oá**, do. especially of boat or door; to close a door, as hand or wind. **saⁿ-khām**, to jostle one another, as men carrying burdens (usually unintentionally, but not always so); to come knocking together, as boats, or as articles in a boat tossed by waves.

khan (R. khien), to lead by the hand; to catch by the hand so as to raise up or assist; to drag along, as a net; to seize, as a vessel; to stretch out, as a line; to draw out long, as voice (or as an affair); to work Chinese bellows; to involve in another affair; classifier of disputes and affairs (also T. Cn. more general); to tighten the tiller-rope so as to sail nearer the wind.

khan-thâu, an article pawned. **tǹg-khan-thâu**, to pawn a thing. **thó-khan-thâu**, to redeem a thing from pawn. **chit-khan-sū**, one dispute or affair. **hit-khan** (Cn.), so-and-so (said of well-known person, thing, or affair, to avoid naming). **hióng-khan** (Cn.), id.

jī-khan-á, a long slip of paper (with name) hanging down to mark a lot of the same or related things, *e.g.* books in shop or accounts in office.

khan-siaⁿ, to draw out one's voice loud and long, as in reciting or singing. **khan sìⁿ-miāⁿ**, to drag out a miserable life, as in great poverty or pain. **bóng-khan bóng-kè**, to get on just barely tolerably. **hō--i bōe-khan-bán--tit**, make him unable to refuse paying the money due (v. bán).

khan-thoa, to accuse falsely of a fault (v. thoa). **khan-chhé**, to accuse of being one's accomplice. **khan-kháh**, to involve others in our quarrel (v. kháh). **khan-liên**, name involved in a legal case (v. liên). **khan i-ê-miâⁿ**, to put his name in an accusation or defence, as involved in the case. **khan--i siōng-kùn**, to accuse him of having incited to and conducted the lawsuit.

khan-hát, to have a small swelling under the skin. **khan-tîn**, to throw out long trailing shoots or suckers.

khan-kiⁿ, to take compass-bearings (v. kiⁿ). **khan-chîn**, to stretch a line, as a chalk-line. **khan-soàⁿ**, id. **khan-se**, to cover a cotton quilt with the crossed threads. **ti-tu khan-si**, the spider weaves its web.

khan-thiu, a broad border sewed on (v. thiu).

khan-hong, a boat (with one sail) rather larger than a large sampan, between 30 and 40 feet long.

khan-hong, to work the piston of the cylinder used as Chinese bellows. **khan hong-kūi**, id. **khan-siⁿ**, to melt iron in a furnace (v. siⁿ).

khan-bông, to bring up the spirits of the dead by rites, as a medium does. **khan-ki**, to write oracles before an idol, as a medium does (v. ki). **khan-tsn̄g**, rites for the soul of a woman who dies within one month after delivery, done by a praying-wheel, &c. (v. tsn̄g).

saⁿ-khan, to stand or walk hand in hand. **chhiú saⁿ-khan**, id. **saⁿ-khan--khì**, to walk away hand in hand. **khan-chhiú**, to take by the hand; to lead by the hand. **goán khan-chhiú--ê**, my wife. **khan-i-khì**, to lead him by the hand without force. **khan--i khí--lâi**, take his hand and raise him up, as child fallen or man kneeling. **mn̂g tióh-khan--lâi**, draw the door nearly shut.

khan-ín, to introduce for some employment. **khan-khioh**, to assist, as by money, or by getting work or a situation for him. **khan-sêng**, to assist, as in business, till he can get on well himself. **khan-kau kè-khiah** (lit. help over ditches and ravines), to help over dangers and troubles, as idols do.

khan-tsan, to drag along the smaller net called "tsan" (*q.v.*) **khan-bāng**, to drag along a large net, as many men together. **khan-hî**, to draw together a large net on floats, inclosing the fish. **khan káu-hê**, to catch shrimps by a net drawn by two men.

khan-gû, to lead a cow. **thau-khan-gû**, to steal a cow. **thau-khan-bé**, to steal a horse. **khan-tsûn**, to take a vessel, as pirates.

khan-kâu, to lead a man (lit. monkey) to a brothel. **khan-ti-ko**, to lead about a boar for sows.

khan (R. id.) **khan-pán** (R.), to cut characters on wooden blocks for printing. **ū khan-pán á-bē**, has it been cut for printing yet?

khán (C., esp. P.), = A. khéng, willing.

khàn [R. to look, to watch, = col. khoàⁿ]. **khàn-kè**, to watch over. **khàn-siú**, to watch and guard. **sè-chêng, khàn-léng-loán**, the world's way is to look at warm or cold, *i.e.* at wealth or poverty. **khàn-**

厦英大辭典

siōng, look up! (said by a chair-bearer when there is some obstacle above).

khàn (R. khèng), a Buddhist musical instrument like a bell with its mouth up. **tâng-khàn,** id. **cheng-khàn,** a bell and this sort of instrument.

khàn [R. khàm, to examine officially]. **tn̂g-khàn,** the mandarin on the tribunal deciding which side of the case agrees best with the verbal evidence.

khang [R. kong, work, = col. kang]. **khang-khè,** work (C. kang-khòe). **khang-khè-tiū^{n},** any place where work is going on, *e.g.* carpenter's work or house-building. **khang-khè-liâu,** a workman's shed, esp. carpenter's or builder's.

khang [same as next word? or R. khóng?], a hole; an aperture; a mortice; an opportunity of making money, or of finding fault. **khang-sún,** mortice and tenon (v. sún).

khang-kháu, the mouth of a hole. **khang-kháu ok,** fierce and bold at the mouth of his hole, as a dog; fig. of a man at his own home. **khang-khiah,** holes and crevices; a place to find fault with; a slight blemish in character, &c. (v. khiah). **khang-phāng,** chinks or crevices ("khang," larger; "phāng," smaller), a flaw; an opportunity for finding fault or getting money out of people. **ū-khang-phāng,** there is a place for finding fault, &c. **chhē khang-phāng,** to seek an opportunity for injuring another. **siū^{n}-khang siū^{n}-phāng,** to watch for an opportunity, as of injuring another, or of getting money out of people.

ū-khang, to have a hole; to have an opportunity. **chhak-khang,** to make a hole, as with a chisel. **iah-khang,** to bore a hole, as in a wall. **uih-khang,** id. **khui-khang,** to make a hole; to give or point out an opportunity to another. **khui-khang hō͘--i chiáh-tsúi,** to show him an opportunity of squeezing money out of some one, esp. of yamen people. **phah-khang,** to help a man to a way of getting money, *e.g.* by pointing out some flaw that will enable him to extort money, or by helping him to get a loan. **phah-khang hō͘--lâng thàn-chiáh,** to make an opening for a man to make a living. **tsòe-khang,** to conspire to deceive or injure. **kap--lâng kap-khang,** to plot with bad men to prey upon others. **gâu-lién-khang,** good at getting money out of people (v. lién). **gâu-pì^{n}-khang,** good at finding means of earning money, as at a trade; often with the idea of cunning or intrigue. **hó-khang,** a good opportunity, as of getting money easily.

chêng-khì āu-khang (to go forward, but leave an undefended place in the rear), to gain less than we lose. **chhit-khang bô-hù-chhoán,** very miserable or poor (v. chhoán).

hī-khang, the hole of the ear; the ear (v. hī). **phī^{n}-khang,** the nostrils. **that chhùi-khang,** to stop one's mouth. **koh-ē-khang,** the arm-pit. **po-pì^{n}-khang,** scupper-holes for water from deck. **chhèng-khang,** port-holes; mouth of a gun. **soa^{n}-khang,** a cave or cavity in a mountain. **soa^{n}-khang-tóe,** an out-of-the-way place among the mountains. **chî^{n}-khang,** the hole in a cash (v. chî^{n}). **káu-khang,** dog's hole; small door in a street-gate (v. káu). **âm-khang,** a small covered drain for water.

khang (R. khong), hollow; empty; vain; false. **khang-khang,** id. **khang-hu** (r.), id. (v. hu). **khang-so͘-so͘,** quite empty. **khang-lo͘-so͘,** id. **khang-khak,** hollow. **khang-phà^{n},** empty; hollow, as chaff, or an empty fellow.

io-khang, the ace in dice; the worst throw of all.

ân-khang, having no money. **khang-chhiú,** empty-handed. **khang-chhiú péh-theh,** bringing no presents. **khang-sin,** not carrying any valuables. **khang-sim,** stomach empty. **khang-hâm,** a mere official title without office. **khang-kim,** empty jars for bones (v. kim).

khang-kiâ^{n}, to walk on foot; to travel without baggage, or without carrying anything; to get no good results from going.

khang [R. khong, the socket of the eye, = col. kháng]. **bák-khang,** the socket of the eye. **bák-khang òeh,** envious. **bák-khang toā,** expecting much more than is offered, so as to refuse the reward, wages, or present that is offered.

kháng [R. khong, the socket of the eye, = col. khang]. **bák-kháng-khū,** the socket of the eye. **bák-kháng òeh,** envious. **bák-kháng toā,** not content with the sum offered for favour or service done; will not look at such a sum. **toā-bák-kháng,** id.; also, having the eyes much sunken, either from illness, or from the sockets being naturally deep.

kháng [R. khong? a square frame, = col. kheng]. **bīn-kháng,** the appearance of the countenance. **ū-bīn-kháng,** having a pretty face. **hó-bīn-kháng, phái^{n}-tē-tháng,** having a pleasant friendly look, but cherishing wicked and injurious purposes. **kāu-bīn-kháng,** utterly shameless. **bô-bīn-kháng,** ugly; ashamed to see a person. **bô-bīn-kháng thang kì^{n}-lâng,** dares not look a person in the face. **phái^{n}-bīn-kháng,** very ugly (said in scolding); displeased or unwilling look, somewhat sidewise. **pì^{n} kàu hit--ê bīn-kháng,** looking so very much displeased!

kháng — **hiâu-kháng,** very lascivious (said only of a woman).

khàng [R. khòng, a pit, = col. kàng]. **thê-khàng,** a deep pit in the earth.

khàng [R. khòng, vacant ground; wilderness]. **khàng-tōe,** an open vacant piece of ground suitable for building upon, &c. **khàng-po͘,** a large piece of ground quite unused; an open common.

khàng [R. khòng, to leave a space; by change of tone from "khong," empty, = col. khang], to intermit; to intermit work for at least one-third of a day's work (a shorter time of rest or intermission is "hioh" or "thêng").

khàng-chit-khiah, to have a depression between two level or higher parts, as on a road, or a piece of ground, *e.g.* a site for a house.

bô-khàng-mî^{n}-jit, day and night without any long intermission. **khàng-kang,** to intermit one's work for a considerable time; at leisure. **m̄-thang khàng-kang,** don't stop your work. **lí-ū thang khàng-kang,** when you can get some leisure. **khàng-kang chiah-lâi,** come when you are at leisure, or can stop work for a while. **khàng chit-tiám-kang,** to lose or intermit one-third of a day's work (v. tiám).

khàng — **khàng-khū,** fittings and utensils of a vessel.

khàng (R. khòng), a brick couch (with a fireplace in it) that can be heated, such as is used in North China. **khùn-khàng,** to sleep on that sort of bed.

khàng, to scratch or scrape away with one's nails. **khàng-phí,** to pick off scabs. **toà--teh pê-khàng-iah,** doing nothing but scratch himself! (said of an idle fellow).

iah-khàng, to rake up a man's faults, or old stories about things of which he will be ashamed.

chiù-khàng, to make constant complaints (behind his back) of a man's narrowness or exacting ways; to make incessant wearisome crying for something refused, as child.

khap [R. to shut; all]. **khap-hā pêng-an** (R.), may all Amoy enjoy peace and quiet! **khap-hā chiu-ti**, all Amoy knows it.

khap [R. kài, a cover; to cover, = col. khàm, koà, kah, ka], inverted, as a bowl, &c.; the plain side of a cash lying up; a surname.

péng-khap, to invert (as a bowl, plate, cup, or dish, that naturally has its mouth up), turning its mouth down; to turn down the side of a cash which has the inscription (never said of men). **péng-thán-khap**, id. **kìⁿ-khap khioh**, to win the cash each time the plain side turns up. **khap-chhiò**, the two sides of a cash (odds and evens), as in gambling. **teh-khap-chhiò**, to gamble, by covering a cash and guessing it. **lién-khap-chhiò**, to gamble by twirling a cash. **poáh-khap-chhiò** (C.), id.

kháp [R. to knock against; cf. khām]. **kháp--tiòh**, to come striking against, or jostling unintentionally; said also by chair-bearers as a warning. **kháp--chih**, to be broken by accidentally coming in contact. **saⁿ-kháp**, to knock against each other. **chhùi-kap-chih ū-si saⁿ-kháp**, the best friends sometimes come in collision.

put-chí tak-kháp, very unfortunate; everything going wrong; constantly unlucky and miserable. **lap-kháp**, id. **koe-nn̄g kháp-chiòh**, utterly unable to contend with him (as egg with stone).

kháp-thâu, to knock the forehead on the ground in reverence or supplication. **thòe-lâng-kháp**, to beg very earnestly on behalf of another. **tùi-i-kháp**, to beg earnestly from him.

khat, to lade or bale out, as water; to take food out of a rice-boiler (tiáⁿ) with a spoon; to take fish out of a larger net with a small hand-net. **khat-tsúi**, to bale out water; to lade out water with a dipper. **khat-pn̄g**, to take hard-boiled rice out of the rice-boiler **khat-bê**, to take out soft-boiled rice.

khat (Cn.) **khat-hō**, = A. chhiáⁿ-hé, to bring fire from a greater temple to a less important one; also (in some places), to strike fire with a flint.

khat [R. khek, to sustain; adequate; to conquer]. **khat-kun**, to consent to do or give something, or to spend money (though really unwilling or hardly willing) because it is very urgently asked, or because it cannot well be helped; to put a pressure or restraint on one's self to do or bear something. **khat-kun chioh--i**, to lend it to him (though unwilling) because it would be awkward to refuse, or for very urgent request. **bōe-khat-tit-kun**, cannot bring one's self to endure it any longer, or only under very great pressure and with much unwillingness and impatience; very highly displeased; cannot restrain one's self or bring one's self to it. **bōe-khat--tit**, id. **bōe-khat-tit-khó**, unable to endure the suffering, so as to do something weak or wrong which we would not otherwise have done, *e.g.* do what the torturer desires. **khat-khó**, to put a pressure on one's self so as to bear an injury, or to do unpleasant or distasteful work; to toil patiently, or quietly endure great hardships; either unwillingly through fear, or for gain, as a servant; or quite willingly, as a student or workman for his own benefit. **khat-khó iau-gō**, willingly endure hunger rather than submit or do anything shameful.

khat [R. khek, to subdue, to oppress or destroy]. **saⁿ-khat**, the horoscope disagreeing with that of a relative or connection, or one part of it with another part, so as to be unlucky. **poeh-jī saⁿ-khat**, horoscope at conflict with that of a relative. **nîⁿ-géh saⁿ-khat**, the year of nativity disagreeing with the month in horoscope. **sî-jit saⁿ-khat**, natal day and hour so disagreeing. **khat-sî**, id.

khat [R. thirsty, = col. khoah]. **chí-khat**, to slake thirst.

khat [R. khoat, to want]. **khat-hoát** (r.), in want.

khau [R. to strike], to plane; to scrape, as tongue or as roots; to tack ship; to pull up, as plants; to strike, as a bell. **khau-cheng**, to ring a large bell, as Buddhist priests (only).

khau-siet, to jeer at; to make game of a man.

khau-khek gûn-hun, to deduct a small fraction from the value of silver (v. khek).

khau--khí-lâi, to erase a word; to lift a plant either in order to transplant it or as a weed; to pull up by the roots. **khau-chháu**, to pull up plants or weeds by the roots, as weeds, or for medicine, or for fuel, &c.

khau-tsûn, to tack in sailing. **tsûn khau-hong**, the vessel is tacking.

khau-to, a carpenter's plane. **khau-to-hoe**, wood shavings. **khau-to-lien** (C.), id. **oan-khau**, a curved knife for smoothing the inside of buckets, &c. (v. oan). **khau-á**, a sort of scraper for taking the skin off coarse cucumbers (s. hook). **chih-khau-á**, a tongue-scraper.

khau-tiáⁿ, to scrape a rice-boiler. **khau-chih**, to scrape the tongue. **khau-phê**, to scrape off skin, as from roots. **khau han-tsû**, scrape potatoes (so with "chhài-thâu," &c.)

khau [R. kə, a hook, = col. kau]. **khau-liâm**, a sort of halbert with a crooked blade like a sickle (v. liâm). **khau-á**, a sort of hook for cleaning drains; also (C.), a sort of spear for hunting or fighting (s. plane).

khau [R. khə, a loop, cf. col. khàu], a hank of yarn or thread; a tie-stone placed crosswise to bind together two lines of stones.

chiúⁿ-khau, the loop which fastens the oar to the oar-pin. **chit-khau-soàⁿ**, one hank of thread.

khau-teng, ends of bricks left projecting on a wall, so as to bind on another wall if afterwards built. **lâu khau-teng**, to leave such projecting bricks.

khau (R. id.), a lot; lots. **liam-khau**, to draw lots. **khioh-khau**, id. **thiu-khau**, id. **liu-khau**, id. **chhòng-khau**, to make ready the lots; he who does so gets that one of the lots which is left when the rest have drawn.

lûn-khau, to take turns by lot. **khau-hūn**, portion got by lot.

khau-su, a document fixing the division of family property (a copy is given to each party) made either before or after the father's death. **khau-su háp-tâng**, id.

kháu [R. khə, the mouth], a mouth or opening (only in certain phrases); a mouthful, as of betel-nut; (said of persons in numbering).

kháu-bīn, at the outside, as of door or port, &c. **kháu-sin**, outside, as a place. **goā-kháu**, at the outside. **goā-kháu-kháu**, at the very outside. **pak-kháu-goā**, the country near Ili on the northern frontier.

mn̂g-kháu, space about the outside of a door. **tiàm-kháu**, do. of shop door. **keng-kháu**, do. of temple door. **chîⁿ-kháu**, space about covered by the eaves (v. chîⁿ). **chhng-kháu**, hatches (v. chhng). **chhèng-kháu**, muzzle of a gun. **ńg-kháu**, mouth of a sleeve; cuffs. **hái-lông siū-kháu**, do. made of a sort of a skin. **hái-lông-kháu**, id. **khoàⁿ-kháu**, wide-mouthed, as sleeves or pocket. **khoàⁿ-kháu**, to watch the mouth of a harbour, as at a branch custom-house. **pùn-kháu**, the anus. **hó-kháu**, the space between the thumb and fore-finger. **hó-kháu-mn̂g**, id.

tsúi-kháu, place where water runs off from a grave; mouth of a drain, as when it runs into the sea. **ài-kháu**, a narrow pass. **khang-kháu**, mouth of a hole. **káng-kháu**, a trading-port. **hái-kháu**, mouth of the bay or estuary. **toā-kháu**, a busy port; the wider entrance to the harbour. **sió-kháu**, a small port; the smaller entrance to the harbour. **jip-kháu**, to enter harbour. **jip-kháu-hiòng**, import duties. **chhut-kháu**, to leave the harbour. **chhut-kháu-hiòng**, export duties. **chhut-kháu-toaⁿ**, a port clearance. **tsûn pò-chhut-kháu**, the vessel has notified that she is going out (no more cargo can then be taken on board). **kháu-lē**, port dues; tonnage dues.

khiuⁿ-kháu, a dialect. **poâⁿ-kháu**, the price first asked by a hong for a new lot of goods (v. poâⁿ).

khoa-kháu, to boast. **hó-phûn-kháu**, generally successful in gambling. **hó-kháu-bún**, good at talking in a very winning pleasing way. **kāu-kháu-siėt**, requiring or raising much dispute and discussion (v. siėt). **chhiah-kháu-jit**, days that will cause much disputing about any matter begun on them. **tak-kháu**, to be somewhat at variance; having a slight altercation (v. tak). **tò-kháu**, to wrangle loud. **tàu-kháu**, id. **hâm-kháu-sǹg**, to calculate mentally. **kháu-keng**, verbal evidence in court (v. keng). **kháu-thâu-gú**, words used in commencing a conversation or sentence, differing with different places and persons. **kháu-thâu-ōe**, id.

chhùi-kháu, the mouth, at the lips. **chhùi-kháu-teng**, small hard boil on the lip. **to-chhùi-kháu**, the edge of a knife or sword. **mihⁿ kàu-chhùi-kháu, hō--i ka-láuh--khì**, there's many a slip between the cup and the lip. **chhùi-kháu-so**, small short round cakes (v. so).

kháu--so (Cn.), so and so, said of person, thing, or affair, which the hearers will understand, to avoid mentioning the name.

lī-kháu, to please the taste, so as to excite appetite in a patient disinclined to eat. **sóng-kháu**, pleasing the palate (in general). **hó-kháu-hâm** (T. C.), = A. hó-chháu-hâm, having a voracious appetite and good digestion. **kìm-kháu-lī**, severe chronic dysentery that takes away appetite. **lok-kháu**, to gargle. **sóe-kháu**, to wash the mouth. **sek-kháu**, id. (v. sek). **soá-kháu** (C.) id. **sóe-kháu-thn̂g**, a confection used at marriages. **kháu-khì**, the odour of the breath; a man's purpose as shown in his manner of speaking (s. clever). **chhì i--ê kháu-khì**, to observe carefully how he speaks, so as to get at his idea. **kháu-khì tāng**, smell of breath very bad, as of a very sick man. **chhàu-kháu-khì**, breath smelling ill, as from eating bad-smelling things, or from not washing the mouth, or when slightly unwell.

hō-kháu, a household, in reference to a census (v. hō). **kháu-tsàu**, a household, as in counting the households of a village. **kúi--ê jîn-kháu**, how many persons (old and young, male and female) altogether are there in the family? **chit-ke kúi-kháu**, id. **kui-ke-kháu**, a whole family. **chit-ke-kháu**, id. **khàu-ke-kháu**, a widow weeping and lamenting for her husband. **toā-ke kháu-chèng**, very large household. **kiám-kháu**, to diminish the number of the people, as Heaven does by epidemics, &c. **kiám-kháu-ông**, a leader of rebels, by whom Heaven destroys the people.

kháu-niûⁿ, soldiers' daily pay.

bé-kháu-thih, tin-plate.

kháu [R. clever; skilful; = col. khá, khiáu]. **lōng-kháu sêng-tsoat**, to try to be very clever, but only show one's self stupid. **lōng-kháu hoán-tsoat**, id.

bé-kháu, dressing gaudily and walking in a swaggering way; *e.g.* wearing a large turban, mouth full of betel-nut, jacket half-open, carrying a big pipe, and ready to quarrel. **bóe-kháu** (C.), id.

kháu-khì, very troublesome, inconvenient, and awkward, as an affair (s. mouth). **kháu-khìⁿ** (T.), troublesome to deal with, as a man who is not straightforward.

kháu — **âng-kháu**, reddish. **n̂g-kháu**, yellowish.

kháu — **tó-kháu**, the oar on the port or right-hand side of a boat, held in the left hand. **kò-tó-kháu**, to row with this oar. **khah tó-kháu**, to give a stroke, or row strongly with it. **chiàh tó-kháu ê-lát**, wind in such a state that this oar must be rowed with more strength.

khàu [R. khò, to strike]. **khàu-kìⁿ**, to have audience of a very high mandarin. **khàu-siā**, to give thanks by knocking the head on the ground, as by a subordinate to a very high mandarin; said also politely to a superior, "I thank you very much." **khàu-thâu**, to knock the forehead on the ground, in reverence or supplication. **sam-kūi kiú-khàu**, three kneelings and nine knockings of head, before the emperor or to Heaven; the kotow ceremony (Cn. khiò, in some phrases).

khàu (R. khò), (Cn. khiò), to subtract; to deduct, as from wages or price. **khàu-tû**, to deduct or cut down, as price or wages (v. tû). **khàu-khí**, id. **khàu-sin-lô**, to cut wages. **khàu-kang-chîⁿ**, id. **khàu-chîⁿ**, id., or price. **khàu-tsāi**, to deduct from the freight, as for damage. **khàu-tô-tóe**, to deduct a very small discount from the price of goods, *e.g.* one mace on a hundred dollars (v. tô).

khàu [R. khò, cf. col. khau], (Cn. khiò). **liú-khàu**, the loop used instead of a button-hole.

chìⁿ-khàu, the notch of an arrow for the string. **chìⁿ bô-jip-khàu**, the arrow has not got the string in its notch.

khàu (R. khò). **khàu-tsàng**, the perpendicular threads of a loom, which work up and down (v. tsàng).

khàu — **poe-khàu** (T.), the divining blocks. **sìn-khàu** (Cn.), id.

khàu (R. khok), to make loud lamentation; to cry and wail, especially for the dead. **thì-khàu**, to lament with sobs and cries. **toā-thî sòe-khàu**, children large and small crying and sobbing loud. **khàu-iau**, to cry for hunger, as a starving child. **gâu-khàu-chhan**, always complaining without reason (said only in scolding dissatisfied people) (v. chhan). **sí kàu-bô-lâng-khàu**, may all your relatives die till none remains to lament for your death!

khàu-pē, to make loud lamentation for father's death; said also in scolding; what are you making such a noise about? as if you were lamenting your father's death. **khàu-pē khàu-bú** (lit. for parents), said in scolding, as above; or of a man groaning sorely in great pain. **khàu-bú**, to lament loudly for mother's death. **khàu-kiáⁿ**, lament for son's death.

khàu (R. khok), (Cn. khīò), manacles; fetters; to manacle; to handcuff. **kha-khàu**, fetters for the feet. **chhiú-khàu**, manacles; handcuffs. **kha-lô chhiú-khàu**, fetters and manacles for feet and hands. **kha-liâu chhiú-khàu**, id. **liâu-khàu**, id.

khàu--khí-lâi, to put on fetters or manacles. **khàu-kha-khàu**, to put fetters on the feet. **chiūⁿ-khàu**, to put fetters on. **só-khàu**, id., to lock them on.

kháuh, to boil a liquid slowly till it becomes thicker. **khàuh khah-thiám** (T.), boil it down still thicker.

kháuh (cf. khók, khiáuh). **ngīⁿ khàuh-kháuh**, too hard and stiff, as a seat, or as eatables not enough cooked; stiff with cold, as limbs. **tēng-khàuh-kháuh**, too hard, as seat or eatables.

khih-khih khàuh-kháuh, constant slight noise, as of knocking in making repairs, or as rats.

kháuh [R. gȯk, to fear; to tremble; cf. col. khéh]. **kiaⁿ kháuh-khàuh**, shaking with fear. **kháuh-kháuh-tsùn**, to shudder or shiver; shaking with fear or cold.

kháuh (cf. kháh, khók). **kháuh-kháuh-lâi**, constantly coming. **kháuh-kháuh-pūi**, constantly barking. **kháuh-kháuh-háu**, always crying. **kháuh-kháuh-thí**, sobbing bitterly. **kháuh-kháuh-tó**, constantly falling, as man in fits or in great pain, or as a child. **kháuh-kháuh-kóng**, constantly talking; loquacious.

khe [R. to examine into], (C. ke). **khe-khó**, to investigate, as history, or doctrine (v. khó). **khe-tsa**, to investigate, as a mandarin (C. ke-chɛ).

khe [R. kho, class; order; literary examinations; department in mandarin's office], (Cn. khö), (C. kho, in all but the first two phrases).

khe-chíⁿ, to collect the usual contributions which the people impose on themselves for various purposes. **khe-phài**, to allot and collect the contributions required to be paid, as mandarin, or as head-men of a village for common purposes.

pâng-khe, the six offices in a yamun, for the duties of the six Supreme Boards; the officials in charge of them. **lák-pâng-khe**, id. **tē-tsɵ-khe**, the office for house-tax in Amoy; the official who manages it, over the "tē-pó," and under the "hái-hông."

khe-tiûⁿ, the literary examinations. **khe-ūn**, fated time of literary success. **un-khe**, gracious grant of extra examinations. **khe-nîⁿ**, the year for the Kujin examinations. **toā-khe-nîⁿ**, do., or for Tsin-sze. **tá-lóh chit-khe**, on which year did (you) graduate. **téng-khe chin**, got his degree (of Sew-tsai) at last year's examinations.

goā-khe, external diseases. **goā-khe i-seng**, a surgeon. **lāi-khe**, internal diseases. **lāi-khe i-seng**, a physician. **hū-khe**, female diseases. **jî-khe**, attending to children's diseases. **gán-khe**, eye diseases. **tsoan-tī gán-khe**, only attends to eye diseases.

khe (C. khoe). **kāu-khe-hâi**, over-cautious in a matter, and constantly changing one's mind, so as to be troublesome and unreliable (v. hâi).

khe (C.), = A. khoe, a river; a stream. **khe-chhí**, shallow boats for shallow streams.

siông-khe, a sort of tea (Twan-key ?).

liông-khe (A. = C.), the Hien district of Lung-ki, in which Chang-chew city stands; also, a market-town and region in the district of Lâm-chēng (Nan-tsing).

khe [R. kho, name of a plant], (C. khoe; Cn. khö). **khe-tîn**, a creeping plant (used medicinally).

khe (R. kûi), (C. khoe), a sort of palm-tree. **khe-síⁿ**, a sort of fan made of a palm-leaf.

khê (cf. kê), (C. khê), entangled, so as to retard or prevent motion; involved, as affair; jammed, as anchor. **khê--teh**, involved and troublesome, as affair; choking with something in the throat. **tiàⁿ khê tī-chióh--nihⁿ**, anchor jammed among rocks. **tiàⁿ khê--teh**, id.

kau-khê, not yet straight, as a troublesome and involved affair. **káu-khê**, at variance. **kap--lâng káu-khê**, at variance with people. **kap-i-khê**, having a quarrel or feud (great or small) with him. **khê-khang**, at variance, as persons. **khê-phûn**, id.

khê-pê, to clog or retard the harrows, as weeds (C. khê, or khê). **tiū-kó-thâu teh-khê-pê** (stubble clogging the harrows), said of a man secretly putting obstructions in the way of some business (C.)

khê (R. kâ), (C. khôe), deformed, as hands or feet; sprained and distorted. **khê-kha**, leg or foot distorted, or very different in length from the other. **khê-chhiú**, hand distorted, withered, or dwarfed. **khê chit-chhiú**, one hand so. **kha khê, chhiú chih**, leg distorted and arm broken.

khê (C.) **kāu-khê**, = A. kāu-khôe, peevish; bad-tempered, as child.

khé (C. khóe; Cn. khö̃), to bow with hands near the body, as a woman does.

khé [R. to open]. **khé-bêng-chhiⁿ**, the morning-star.

khè [R. kà, a frame, = col. kè]. **kha-khè**, a foot-stool. **khè-kha**, to rest the foot, as on a footstool. **khè-kha khè-chhiú**, to rest one's limbs lazily or luxuriously, as an idle fellow. **khiau-kha khè-chhiú**, lazily drawing up the legs, and resting the arms.

khè [R. khò, an essay, exercise, or task-work], (C. khòe; Cn. khö̃), literary essays. **chit-phiⁿ-khè**, one essay. **tsòe-khè**, to compose an essay. **thák-khè**, to read essays aloud in a loud rhythmical tone. **chhong-hā-khè**, essays composed by students for teacher's correction (v. chhong). **si-khè-jī saⁿ-jī-tsñg**, well able to write odes, essays, and characters.

khí-khè, a sort of divination; much less minute than "pok-koà."

khang-khè (C. kang-khòe), work of any kind (v. khang).

khè [R. khò, by change of tone from "kho," sort; examination], (Cn. khö̃), a crucible.

khè [R. united; a deed or document, = col. khòe], (also C., = A. khòe, a deed).

khè-háp (R.), united in closest friendship; quite of the same mind.

khè-hiaⁿ, = khòe-hiaⁿ, the paramour of a bad woman.

khè (C.), = A. khòe, to gnaw.

khɛⁿ (C.), = A. khiⁿ, a ravine. **khɛⁿ-lang-á**, a narrow valley.

khɛ̂ⁿ— **khîⁿ-khîⁿ khɛ̂ⁿ-khɛ̂ⁿ**, all in disorder, as things, or as an affair.

kheh [R. khoat, = col. khih], (C. khoeh; Cn. khöh), to be wanting; to be deficient; a vacancy. **kheh-kheh**, deficient. **kheh-goá joā-tsōe**, how much of a balance is still due me? **khiàm-kheh**, to be in

海上絲綢之路文獻集成 科技與文化編

want; deficient. **kheh-khiàm**, id. **té-kheh**, deficient in quantity; not enough, esp. money; supply insufficient. **kheh-kiá^n**, in want of sons, having none, or very few.

chió-kheh, very numerous; very abundant.

pé-kheh, to appoint a man to a vacant post. **pé i-ê-kheh**, to get the place left vacant by him; to succeed him. **bô-kheh thang-pé**, there is no vacancy to be filled up; no post ready for him. **bô-kheh thang-khui**, id. **khui-kheh**, to leave a vacancy, as mandarin on leaving a post. **téng i-ê-kheh**, to succeed to the vacancy left by him. **téng-thòe i-ê-kheh**, id. **chiap i-ê-kheh**, id. **that-kheh**, id. **pàng-kheh**, to send a mandarin to fill a vacant post. **hāu-kheh**, to wait for a vacancy to get office. **hāu-jīm-kheh** (C.), id.

sit-kheh, real office; not mere titular rank.

kheh (C.), = A. khoeh, to jostle.

kheh (C.), = A. khoeh, to press out, as oil, &c.

kheh (C.), = A. khoeh, to shut, as the eyes. **bak kheh**, the eyes shut.

kheh (C.) **kheh-á**, = A. khoeh-á, a small box, &c.

kheh (T.), = khit, sign of the passive (in some cases).

kheh (R. khek), (C. khɛh), a stranger; a visitor; a guest; a passenger; a customer; a Hakka.

tsòe-kheh, to go on a visit of some days at least to her own relatives, as a married woman does; to be married, as a virgin.

lâng-kheh, a guest; a visitor **chhiá^n lâng-kheh**, to invite guests. **kheh-thia^n**, reception room for guests; parlour or drawing-room. **thàm-kheh**, to go and visit friends, as a new graduate or mandarin. **pài-kheh**, do., generally expecting presents. **bát-sat chiáh-kheh** (the bug eats up his guests), said of a man getting more from his guests than he gives them.

kheh-thâu, a coolie broker; a man who levies dues on passengers by passage-boats. **hó-khɛh-thâu** (C.), pleasant to do business with.

sin-kheh, a new-comer. **hân-soan-kheh**, a man who is extremely shy, mean, or afraid to act (v. soan). **toā-ti-kheh**, a dull foolish-looking fellow (lit. like a pig). **bīn-thâu-kheh**, you are as stupid as a man in deep mourning (v. bīn).

kheh-lâng, a Hakka man. **kheh-ōe**, the Hakka language or dialect, nearly allied to the mandarin: spoken in Ting-chow (theng-chiu), Kia-ying-chow (ka-eng-chiu), and some other parts.

kheh-chiáu, the magpie. **kheh-chiáu pò-hí**, the magpie gives a good omen.

kheh-koán, an inn. **kheh-tiàm**, id. **kheh-koa^n**, phrase used by an inn-keeper to his guests.

kheh-tē, a passage-boat. **tah-kheh**, a passenger in a boat. **kheh-bôe**, the passenger who first takes his seat in a boat (v. bôe). **lòh-kheh**, to be taking in passengers, as just before sailing. **ín-kheh**, to get passengers for a boat, as broker.

tiàm-kheh, the tenant of a shop. **tūi^n-kheh** (Cn.), id. **chhân-kheh** (Cn.), tenant of fields. **phiâu-kheh**, a whoremonger.

goā-kheh, a travelling merchant from a distance; visitors (as at funeral ceremonies) who are not nearly related. **tsú-kheh**, a regular customer, either buyer or seller (v. tsú). **hó-kheh**, a customer very pleasant to deal with, *e.g.* who offers the price he means to give. **hó-khɛh** (C.), a wealthy man. **hó-kheh-chêng**, polite and kind to guests or visitors (v. chêng). **phái^n-kheh**, a bad customer, who tries to get things at very low prices, or to return things bought, or who is bad at paying. **ok-kheh**, a customer who drives a very hard bargain. **bóe-kheh**, a customer; a buyer. **bōe-kheh**, a travelling merchant selling goods in bulk or by sample. **kheh-siong**, a travelling merchant (v. siong). **toā-siong-kheh**, id., dealing in great quantities. **iû^n-kheh**, a Chinaman who goes abroad to trade. **pak-kheh**, a Chinaman who travels, trading between Amoy and North China. **hoan-kheh**, a Chinaman who has returned from foreign parts. **hè-kheh**, a merchant travelling with goods either on his own account or for others; a large customer of a hong from distant parts. **tê-kheh**, a travelling tea-merchant from the tea-districts. **tsúi-kheh**, a man who carries small goods great distances for sale. **phoe-kheh**, a man who collects letters, and brings them from great distances. **kheh-mn̂g put-chí-ōng**, great many people having dealings with the shop or hong, from distant places.

khèh [R. gok, to fear; to start, = col. kháuh, khiáuh], (T. khōh). **khèh-khèh-chhoah**, to quake and shake with fear or cold. **khèh-khèh-tiō**, id. **khèh-khèh-tsùn**, id.

khèh (= khɛ́h^n). **khèh-lèh**, loud noise, as of thunder.

khèh (= khɛ́h^n), (C. khɛ́h), to press hard with the open hand between thumb and fingers, as on a man's throat.

khɛh^n (= khɛ́h^n), sound of coughing.

khɛ́h^n [R. khek, cf. col. khɛ́h^n], sound of a harsh voice, or of coughing or hoarseness, or of things breaking. **tit-tit-khɛ́h^n**, constant coughing, as in consumption. **khɛ́h^n-nɛ́h^n**, loud noise, as of thunder. **khɛ́h^n-khɛ́h^n-háu**, sound as of severe coughing; also (C.) as of carpenter's work.

khɛ́h^n (= khèh), to press between thumb and finger with hand open, as throat.

khek (R. id.), to carve, as characters or ornaments in wood; a quarter of an hour. **tiau-khek**, to carve, as in wood. **khek-tiâm**, to cut characters cutting into the wood. **khek-phû**, to cut in relief. **khek-hoe**, to carve ornaments in wood. **tiau-hoe khek-chiáu**, id. **khek-ìn-pán**, to cut blocks for printing. **khek-to**, a knife for such carving. **khek-khám**, to cut notches (v. khám).

khì-khek, to fear and dread, as a person, or as a calamity. **kī-khek** (C.), id.

khek-pak, to extort money oppressively. **khek-pók**, selfishly exacting; too hard or stingy in money matters.

chit-khek, a quarter of an hour. **sì-khek**, one hour's time. **sî-khek**, constantly. **sî-sî khek-khek**, id. **bô-lī sî-khek**, never stopping or abandoning. **oān-sî oān-khek**, to procrastinate.

lip-khek, immediately. **bô-thêng-khek**, id. **khéng-khek-kan**, in a moment; immediately.

khek-chiam, the minute-hand of a watch or clock.

khek [R. to subdue; to oppress; to destroy]. **khek-khui**, to treat unjustly and wrongfully. **khek-liám**, to embezzle, as pay, drawing all and paying only a part. **khau-khek gûn-hun**, to take off a small percentage from the value of the silver received in payment, *e.g.* as pawnbrokers when articles are redeemed, or as officials when taxes, &c., are paid. **khau-khek gûn-tsúi**, to give rather less than the regular amount of cash in change for silver in some payments.

saⁿ-khek, to be at variance so as to cause bad luck, as the horoscopes of two persons. **poeh-jī saⁿ-khek**, id. **khek--sí**, to cause the death of a relative by our horoscope being unlucky for him. **khek-pē**, horoscope of son injurious to his father. **khek pē-bú**, do. to parents. **khek-pē khek-bú**, id. **khek ka-kī**, to injure one's own fortune by having a bad horoscope.

khek [R. to sustain; adequate; to conquer]. **khek-khûn khek-khé**, very diligent, laborious, and economical. **khek-khûn khek-khiām**, id.

khek-hȯk, to be retaken, as a city, or recovered, as lands, houses, or such property.

khek-kí thāi-jîn, to stint one's self or put one's self to inconvenience for the sake of others.

khek [R. khiok, crooked, = col. khiau], a song in irregular metre, made for changes of rate (liâu) and with pauses for beating the "phek." **koa-khek**, songs of both sorts. **khek-phé**, a song-book. **khek-tiāu**, a song-tune. **khek-thò**, a song-tune. **chit-thò-khek**, a set of songs such as are sung at a stretch. **chit-tè-khek**, one song. **sòe-tè-khek**, a short song. **sió-khek**, id.

thiaⁿ-khek, to listen to songs. **pien-khek**, to compose a song. **chhiùⁿ-khek**, to sing songs. **ké-khek, chhiùⁿ-bōe-lȯh-âu**, said of telling manifest lies. **phah-chih lâng--ê khek-pìⁿ**, to cut short a man's talk so as to frustrate his purpose.

khek-sai-hū, a teacher of songs.

khek [R. a guest; a stranger, = col. kheh]. **kùi-khek** (polite), my honoured guest! **ū-khek-thò**, using a great deal of ceremony to visitors (v. thò).

chhì-khek, to assassinate a sovereign or high mandarin with dagger or sword.

khek (by change of sound from "kek," which is better). **khek-khám**, to be at variance.

kheng [R. to turn over; to pour out; cf. khêng], to melt, fuse, or purify metal. **lȯh-khi-kheng**, put it (the metal) in the crucible to melt it. **kheng-gûn**, to melt, fuse, or purify silver for any purpose. **kheng-kim**, to melt gold. **kheng-siah**, to work tin-mines.

kheng-chien, to melt sycee silver into pieces of ten taels.

kheng-ka, to lose all one's property in any way. **kheng-ka tōng-sán**, do. esp. by luxury, excesses, &c., or by legal cases.

kheng [R. a great noble or officer of state]. **kong-kheng** (R.), very high mandarins, esp. ministers of state. **kong-kheng tāi-hu**, high mandarins, esp. at court. **kiú-kheng** (R.), the nine nobles of the Chow dynasty. **sam-kong kiú-kheng**, the high officers of the Chow dynasty; now said of the highest mandarins, esp. at court. **bêng-kong kū-kheng**, great and illustrious first-class mandarins (said in relation to the places which produce them, or to the metropolis where they congregate).

kheng (R. khong), a small basket. **kheng-á**, id. **kheng-thâu**, id. **cheh-kheng**, basket for flax fibres. **chhài-kheng**, basket for carrying home meat, &c., bought in market for household use.

kheng (R. khiong), the back of an axe or knife at the eye, where the handle is inserted. **to-kheng**, id. of a knife. **pé-thâu-kheng**, id. of an axe.

kheng [R. khong, a square frame], a frame, as of door, spectacles, &c. **bȧk-kiàⁿ-kheng**, frame of spectacles. **mn̂g-kheng**, a door-frame. **toh-kheng**, frame of a table at the top. **pó-táu-kheng**, a square brass vessel for gambling, made of two parts, upper and lower.

bīn-kheng, the shape of the face (cf. bīn-kháng).

khui-kheng, joints opening and gaping in the frame of a piece of furniture.

kheng (R. khéng). **kheng-moâⁿ**, a weak sort of hemp (v. moâⁿ).

kheng [R. light; unimportant, = col. khin]. **giên kheng**, my words will not have weight. **put-sek kheng-tiōng** (R.), not understanding to distinguish important and unimportant things, or good and bad men.

kheng-bān, to slight; to treat lightly. **kheng-pók**, light and frivolous, or somewhat mean; to jest at (v. pók). **kheng-thiau**, light and frivolous in manner (v. thiau). **kheng-īⁿ**, easy, &c. (v. īⁿ).

kheng-hún, a very poisonous drug, used for stopping the putrefying of a sore.

khêng (R. keng). **khêng-hî**, the whale, = keng-hî (*q.v.*)

khêng [R. kheng, to pour out; to melt; cf. kheng], to purify by melting, as silver. **khêng-siah**, to melt down broken bits of pewter, or ashes of burned idolatrous paper gathered together, so as to get a mass of metal.

khêng [R. kiông, limit; exhaust; extremely poor; investigate fully, = col. kêng], to investigate or calculate the state of a matter; to gather up carefully, as the grain after winnowing. **khêng-lêng**, to collect and gather up, as things scattered or mixed with others, or as money subscribed or due. **chhut-khì-khêng**, to go round and collect, as subscriptions, &c., not yet fully paid up.

khêng-giȧh, to examine (for our own satisfaction) that our balance is correct. **khêng gûn-giȧh**, id. **khêng-siàu**, to make a calculation of the state of our own accounts and balances, gen. for temporary purpose, or roughly, to see that all is going right.

khêng-khàm, to examine minutely, as account or affair. **khêng kàu-tóe**, to investigate to the very bottom, as an affair. **khêng-sit**, to investigate carefully, so as to get at the real facts of the case. **khêng-chin**, id. **khêng-chin-tiuⁿ**, id. **khêng-chin-tiuⁿ, bô-iáⁿ**, on full investigation it is found to be a baseless story.

khéng [R. a moment]. **khéng-khek-kan**, in a moment.

khéng (R. id.), (T. khín; C. khán), willing. **m̄-khéng**, unwilling. **chêng-kan put-khéng-khì** (R.), unwilling to go in fair weather.

khéng (P.), = A. khióng, to fear, &c.

khèng (R. id.) **khèng-hō** (R.), to congratulate, esp. by presents. **tsòe-hí-khèng**, Tauist rites for good luck on joyful occasions, as births, marriages, graduation, &c. **tsòe-khèng-sêng**, such rites when the building or repairing of a temple is completed.

ka-khèng, the reign of Kea-king, the father of Tau-kwang.

khèng (R. id., = col. khàn), a triangular musical instrument. **gėk-khèng**, one made of jade-stone. **ín-khèng**, a musical instrument, = hiáng-tsoáⁿ. **phah-ín-khèng**, to play it.

khèng-teng, sort of triangular lanterns.

khèng [R. spent; exhausted]. **khèng-khong**, all spent, as property (v. khong).

khèng (C.), = A. khàm, to cover, &c.

khēng (R. khiū), (P. khiōng), the tallow-tree.

khēng-chhiū, id. **khēng-á**, id. **khēng-chí**, berry or fruit of it, from which the vegetable tallow or wax is made. **khēng-á-chí**, id. **khēng-iû**, the vegetable wax or tallow.

khēng (=kēng). **khēng-tsoá**, a sort of paper (v. kēng).

khēng (R. hông), a rainbow. **chhut-khēng**, a rainbow appearing; there is a rainbow. **chit-tsoā-khēng**, one rainbow. **chit-tiâu-khēng**, id. **khēng-jiō** (lit. urine of the rainbow), a slight fall of rain on the appearance of a rainbow.

khi [R. to deceive or cheat; to oppress]. **khi-phièn**, to deceive. **khi-moâⁿ**, do., by concealing faults.

khi-hū, to oppress; to treat unjustly (v. hū). **kiông khi-jiòk**, the strong oppress the weak. **sam khi-lióng; lióng khi-chit**, three oppress two; two oppress one.

khi-bóng (R.), to treat a superior with disrespect, or neglect his orders. **khi-báng**, id. **khi-kun**, treason (v. kun). **lê khi-tsú**, a slave insulting his master (v. lê). **hó͘ lòh pêng-iûⁿ, pī-khièn-khi** (a tiger in the plain has to bear insults from dogs), said of a man powerful at home, but of small importance elsewhere. **jîn siēn, phī-jîn-khi: má siēn, phī-jîn-khî**, as a good horse is ridden, so a good-hearted man is deceived and oppressed.

khi (R. id.), leaning over; inclined; head on one side. **thán-khi**, leaning over; slanting. **thán-khi khùn**, to sleep on one's side. **tó-thán-khi**, to lie on one's side. **tó thán-khi-sin**, id. **khi-sin**, body leaning to one side. **khi-thâu**, having one's head bent slightly downwards on one side. **tsûn khi**, boat leaning over, as in a gale.

khi-phîn, leaning to one side, as man or wall; having one shoulder higher than the other. **khi-chhiâ**, leaning over, as vessel or wall. **khi-phóe**, having one cheek or side sloping more than the other.

i teh-khi, he is smoking opium. **nn̄g-ê teh-khi**, the two are smoking opium together.

khi-khiau, crafty; not straightforward; touchy; easily getting angry without cause [same word?].

khi — **khiau-khi**, capricious and peculiar in temper; readily taking offence, and misconstruing others' words or actions; not straightforward in business; rough and troublesome to travel, as a road. **kóng-ōe ū-khiau-khi**, to talk in a way not plain or straightforward, *e.g.* giving hints of threats; or as half scolding, half joking. [cf. previous word.]

khi (R. id.) **khi-khu** (r.), rough and difficult, as a mountain road.

khi [R. khù, to go, =col. khì], a particle used in imperative phrases, &c., *e.g.* **kóng-khi-bêng**, speak plainly!

khî (R. kî). **gô-khî**, a leech. **ngô-khî**, id. **moâⁿ-khî** (C.), a small sort of crab, like "kiā-pô." **chhiūⁿ moâⁿ-khî** (C.), to catch them by torchlight.

khî [R. to ride, =col. khiâ]. **khî-hó͘ chi-sè, put-tek-hā**, when riding a tiger it is hard to get off (said of an unpleasant or dangerous affair, which we cannot set right or get clear of). **má siēn, phī-jîn-khî** (r.), a good horse is ridden upon (v. khi).

khî — **siⁿ-khî**, to have a peculiar sort of swelling or tumour on the forehead or temples. **chit-liàp-khî**, such a mark in the form of a round swelling. **chit-jiah-khî**, the mark left by it, on which hair will not grow.

khí [R. kí, to record; a period of twelve years; a surname]. **koh chit-khí-níⁿ** (= kí), after twelve years to come. **toā-goá chit-khí-níⁿ**, twelve years older than I.

khí [R. how? = col. thái]. **khí-kám**, how can I dare (to accept so much honour)? you honour me too much. **khí-iú chhú-lí**, how *can* this be right?

khí [R. chhú, to dwell; by change of tone from "chhù," a place]. **khiā-khí**, to dwell; to reside.

khí (R. chhí), a tooth; barb of hook; fluke of anchor; projections of key for the wards of a lock.

tiàⁿ-khí, the fluke of an anchor. **tiò-khí**, the barb of a hook. **tò-kau-khí**, the barb, as of a hook or of a harpoon. **giâ-kang-khí**, a sort of arrangement for the bolt of a door (v. giâ).

chhùi-khí, a tooth. **khí-phāng**, the interstices between the teeth. **chhùi-khí-phāng**, id. **khí-hoāⁿ**, the gums. **chhùi-khí-jîn**, id. **chhùi-khí-thâu**, the stump or root of a tooth. **khí-kha**, roots of teeth (s. raise). **kā khí-kun**, to clench the teeth, as in pain or impotent displeasure (v. kā). **khí-siông**, the tartar of the teeth.

chiù-khí, a decayed tooth. **khí-pau**, a gum-boil. **sεⁿ-khí-sau** (C.), to have a gum-boil. **khí-giâ-kang**, a very severe disease of the gums or jaw. **chhùi-khí-thiàⁿ**, toothache (v. thiàⁿ).

hoat-khí, to get teeth (s. rise). **lak-khí**, to lose one's teeth. **oāⁿ-khí**, to change the teeth, as children. **bán chhùi-khí**, to pull a tooth. **pó͘ chhùi-khí**, to insert a tooth. **thok-khí**, to pick the teeth. **thak-khí**, id. **soeh-khí**, food sticking between the teeth. **thǹg-khí**, teeth sore from something hot. **tàng-khí**, teeth sore or chattering with cold, or with some cold thing (v. tàng). **tak-khí**, teeth rapidly shut, or chattering with cold. **pauh-khí**, the two upper incisors projecting too much.

āu-tsan-khí, the back-teeth. **āu-khí**, id. **tiong-khí**, the fore-teeth. **chêng-khí**, the front-teeth. **thâu-chêng-khí**, id. **thâu-tsan-khí**, id. **gê-tsô-khí**, the canine teeth.

thih-khí, obstinately refusing to admit a manifest fault, and telling lies to cover it. **thih-chhùi-khí**, id. **tâng-gê-tsô, thih-chhùi-khí**, id. **gê-khí** (C.), a tooth.

khí-thok, a tooth-pick. **khí-bín**, a tooth-brush.

bé-khí-tāu, a sort of bean (v. tāu). **bé-khí-soa**, coarse sand; fine gravel (v. soa).

khí (R. id.), to rise; to raise; to begin; to build; to take away (only a few phrases); classifier of lawsuits, &c.; used as an auxiliary to express ability.

khí-keng, to build a temple. **khí-kiong** (C.), id. **khí-keng**, to help another to lift a load or sedan on his shoulder. **khí-kaiⁿ** (T.), id. **khí-kťiⁿ** (Cn.), id. **khí-keng**, to take back land from a tenant who has been cultivating it.

khí-chhù, to build a house. **khí-kài**, id. **hông-kiong-khí**, built in style of a palace, as temples of some great canonized idols. **tè-tiēn-khí**, id. **kah-siⁿ-khí**, to build with wooden pillars, filling up the panels with weaker work (v. siⁿ).

khí-kè, to rise in price. **tit-thàu-khí**, to rise rapidly, as price of an article (v. thàu).

khí-hè, to unlade, as goods from vessel. **khí-tsûn**, to disembark. **khí-soaⁿ**, to step ashore. **bōe-khí-chhn̂g**, confined to bed. **khí-ūi**, to rise from one's seat, as on visitor entering, &c. (v. ūi). **khí--lâi**, to rise up; to get up (often enclitic); to lose a situation, or have to give it up. **khí--khì**, to go up, as an ascent. **khùn-khí**, to rise from sleep. **khùn khí**, sleeping and waking. **chhìn ū-khí-sì**, just enough to turn the steelyard; good weight. **khí-thâm** (raising phlegm), gurgling in throat of man about to die. **khí-tāng--lí**, I beg to trouble you to —; thank you, sir! (v. tāng). **kiàh-khí**, to lift up, as eye or staff, &c. (v. kiàh).

khí-chhì, rough; uneven; troublesome, as affair (v. chhì). **khí-chhang**, porous. **khí-pan**, the spots appearing in the fever called "chhut-pan." **khí-è**, a white film growing on the eye.

khí-peng, to raise soldiers. **khí-lâng**, to hire men to help, as in a feud.

khí-sū, to raise trouble. **gín-ná khí toā-lâng-ē**, young persons make troubles that involve their seniors. **khí-hō**, to begin business, esp. after the New-Year's holidays. **khí-hòk**, to begin the rites (khiā-hà) for the recently dead. **khí-kó͘**, to begin beating a drum at rites for the dead; also (Cn.) before a play. **khí-lô͘**, to light the oven. **khí-hé**, to kindle a fire; to take fire, as at beginning of a conflagration. **khí-gī**, to propose and take the lead, as in a subscription or enterprise. **khí chhâ-thâu**, to worship the coffin outside the door when about to be carried to the grave. **khí-thêng**, to begin a journey. **khí-sin**, to begin, esp. a journey. **khí-kang**, to begin work (v. kang). **khí-ki**, commencement, as of affair; to begin a business or affair. **khí-tóe**, first beginning or origin; originally; to make the first beginning, as of a custom or family. **khí-in**, cause; origin. **in-toa^{n} khí-lí**, id. **khí-chhoe**, the beginning; at first. **khí-chhe͘**, id. **khí-seng**, id. **khí-thâu**, id. **khí-chhiú**, to begin a work or quarrel. **khí-chhiú chiū-iâ^{n}**, at the very beginning (of the game) he wins. **khí-chhiú, chiū phah-phái^{n}**, as soon as he began (the work) he spoiled it.

khí-kha, to lift the foot (s. tooth). **khí-kûn**, to lift the fist, as when about to box.

tsá-khí, early in the morning (v. tsá).

phah-khí, to make a beginning; to be the first to do something. **kin-ná-jit phah-khí**, begin to-day **tùi-chia phah-khí**, begin at this point. **têng-thâu phah-khí**, do it all over from the beginning. **kóng-khí**, to raise a question. **thê-khí**, id. **koā^{n}-khí**, id.; also to take up in the hand (as a basket) by a handle. **sǹg-khí**, to count such a time as the commencement of an engagement or calculation.

thâu-khí, prospering, as business. **khah-thâu-khí**, having special influence, esp. having the confidence of a powerful person, and easy access to him. **thâu-khí ê-lâng**, a man of special influence and importance, *e.g.* well acquainted with mandarins. **lí m̄-sái teh-thâu-khí**, there is no reason why *you* should take the lead in this matter.

kúi-khí, how many legal cases or disputes? **tsòe-kúi-khí**, how often are the soldiers changed? **hit-khí ê-lâng**, all the persons concerned in that legal case or dispute, *e.g.* parties, persons managing the affair, &c.

khí chhàu-bah, to remove the putrid flesh from a wound or sore, as medicinal application. **ōe-chiàh chhàu-bah khí--lâi**, able to remove it. **khí-chiu^{n}**, to take starch out of dress, &c., as by water.

khoà^{n}-lâng m̄-khí, to treat a man with contempt (not looking at him). **jīm-m̄-khí**, I have not the ability for such an office. **tng-m̄-khí**, unable to bear such honour; you are too polite or too kind to me. **tng-bōe-tit-khí**, id. **bōe-tng-tit-khí**, id. **tôe-bōe-khí**, unable to raise so much by subscription. **hêng-bōe-khí**, unable to repay, for another.

chiah-ōe-ēng-tit-khí, and by that means it becomes fit to be used; *e.g.* a bad cash mixed with the due proportion of good ones.

khì [R. id., = col. khùi], vapour; odour; flavour; breath; physical constitution; animal spirits; principles of life, health, or strength; character; anger; influence of malaria, or of good or bad luck.

khì-bī, odour; flavour, &c. (v. bī). **iû-khì**, having fat, as meat. **khì-chiú**, a weak spirit made in Amoy, mixed with water.

chheng-khì, clean; pure (v. chheng).

kháu-khì, smell of a man's breath; purpose as shown by manner of speaking, &c. (v. kháu). **kháu-khì**, very troublesome, awkward, and inconvenient, as a matter.

sip-khì, dampness (communicated). **tsúi-khì**, damp (natural). **sú-khì**, scorching heat of summer. **tōe-khì**, influence of ground or locality, as in relation to health, climate, or geomancy. **thi^{n}-khì**, weather. **lêng-khì**, auspicious influence, as of hill or grave; appearance of cleverness, as in a boy (v. lêng). **lâng-khì**, odour or influence of many persons being together, *e.g.* as to warmth, or as to keeping away demons.

hé-khì, the hot principle in the constitution; tendency to fever or inflammation. **jiėt-khì**, heat, as of fever or inflammation. **léng-khì**, cold, the cold principle in the constitution. **chhìn-khì**, id.

hiet-khì, vital principle or animal spirits (v. hiet). **huih-khì**, id. (v. huih). **seng-khì**, principle of life (v. seng), [also, to grow angry]. **goân-khì**, constitution of a man (v. goân). **péng-khì**, natural constitution as to strength (v. péng). **im-khì**, the female or negative principle (v. im). **iông-khì**, the masculine or positive principle (v. iông). **tông-khì** (R.), brothers by the same father.

hùi-khì, very laborious or troublesome (v. hùi). **kiâ^{n}-khì**, to be successful, as a request, medicine, or grave (v. kiâ^{n}). **sàn-khì**, feeling of warmth and comfort, caused by pepper, liquor, &c. (v. sàn). **thong-khì**, making a through draught of air; causing a comfortable feeling, as medicine taken in the nose. **teh-khì**, to remove pain in the breast or stomach; to keep down a tendency to vomit, cough, or pant, as medicine. **khì ài-giâ--khí-lâi**, feeling like slight choking in the throat, with tendency to cough up phlegm. **ut-khì**, feeling of biliousness or dyspepsia.

tūi-khì, swollen legs.

hong-khì, rheumatic pains, &c. (v. "hong," sort of disease). **hong-khì**, present customs or character of a community or place (from "hong," wind). **un-ėk-khì**, pestilence; epidemic. **sî-khì-chèng**, id. **tòk-khì**, id., or influence of some hidden poison in the system.

khì-mėh^{n}, the pulse (v. mėh^{n}). **sim-khì-thià^{n}**, pain about the pit of the stomach; dyspepsia.

khì-chit (r.), temper or character; habit of body (v. chit). **khì-khài**, outward mein or manner (v. khài). **khì-sek**, complexion, as indicating bodily constitution. **khì-siōng**, one's manner or appearance, as indicating feeling or purpose, or as an omen; appearance of sky, as sign of weather (v. siōng).

siù-khì, elegant in manner; finely formed, as man. **soa^{n}-tiû^{n}-khì**, rustic, as manners of men or style of dress, &c. **sip-khì**, customs and manners, as of a place (v. sip). **khah-ū goā-khì**, fond of outward display; dashing (v. goā).

chì-khì, purpose of will; self-respect (v. chì). **ū-khì-chiet**, having such self-respect, honour, or conscience, as not to demean one's self by meddling in improper matters, &c. **ì-khì**, purpose as manifested outwardly. **sèng-khì phái^n**, temper bad. **phái^n sìn-khì**, awkward state of matters, so as to make one feel ashamed. **ū khì-phiah**, to have a peculiar temper. **khì-liōng sòe**, too particular about small matters (v. liōng).

hô-khì, harmony, of persons. **bêng-khì**, very fair or generous in one's dealings (v. bêng); (s. instrument) **gī-khì**, honourable and generous in dealings; readiness to requite favours or assist relatives, &c. (v. gi). **ngī^n-khì**, very honest, blunt, or outspoken; unwilling to accept assistance (v. ngi^n) **lī-khì** (r.), unwilling to accept favours. **khah-lī-khì**, very distant, as place (v. lī, "to leave"). **siáu-khì**, meanness, smallness of mind. **ièn-khì**, mean and miserly.

siū-khì, anger; angry. **oàn-khì**, hatred; revengeful feeling. **hūn-khì**, id. (v. hūn). **tē-khì**, wrangling altercation (v. tē). **tè-khì**, id. **sat-khì**, rage for slaughter in battle; very brave natural appearance of countenance. **kap--i chiáh-khì**, to harbour revengeful feeling against him. **thâu-khì**, harbouring displeasure or resentment. **thâu-khì**, very much involved, as affair (v. thâu). **seng-khì**, to grow angry. **cheng-khì, put-cheng-tsâi**, have dispute or feud for anger or feeling, not for money. **toā-tîm khì--sí**, very deeply grieved or angry. **goá chin-khì--sí**, I am sorely grieved or displeased. **hō--i khì--sí**, to be deeply grieved and displeased at his conduct; generally without means of setting matters right. **beh-hō--lí khì--sí**, he does it of set purpose to grieve, annoy, and distress you. **hō--i oáh-oáh khì--sí**, to make him dreadfully and impotently grieved and angry. **khì-sí-goá**, he makes me almost die of grief or rage. **khì-kàu-sí**, deeply grieved all one's life for another's bad conduct, and unable to set it right; *e.g.* wife for husband, or parent for son. **khì kàu-poà^n-sí**, half dead with grief or displeasure.

lún-khì, to restrain one's anger (v. lún). **jím-khì** (r.), id. (v. jím). **chē-siên ūn-khì**, to sit cross-legged without eating, speaking, or feeling emotion, as Buddhist priest.

ūn-khì, fortune, good or bad, in relation to a fated period (v. ūn). **khì-ūn**, id. **hok-khì**, good fortune, prosperity, happiness. **tsâi-khì**, success in making money (v. tsâi).

ōng-khì, making money in great abundance; always winning at gambling; temperament strong and warm, as of a young or vigorous man (v. ōng). **soe-khì**, becoming very poor, from better circumstances; numbers in family or village rapidly diminishing; everything going wrong and failing (v. soe). **chhut-khì**, to lose flavour; to lose lucky influence, as grave. **hong-súi chhut-khì**, the grave has lost its auspicious influence on the posterity. **sit-khì**, to lose influence, power, or good luck; to fall from wealth to poverty; to lose health; to lose power or feeling, as finger or limb, for a longer or shorter time. **thè-khì**, to lose the auspicious influence, as a grave.

iàm-khì, able to ward off the malign influence of evil spirits, as a charm (v. iàm), (s. reject).

lí-khì, the rationale or real principle of some matter (v. lí).

chit-nî^n, jī-tsáp-sì-khì, a year has twenty-four terms, arranged according to the solar year. **cheh-khì** (C.), = A. tsoeh-khùi, these terms.

khì [R. an instrument]. **khì-kū**, an instrument. **khì-khū**, id. **khì-hâi**, weapons.

kùi-khì, precious; valuable; honourable. **chiâ^n-lâng sêng-khì**, to get set up in the world, as by getting into a good business or getting married.

hûi-khì, pottery; earthenware. **chhat-khì**, lacquered ware. **pó-khì**, precious things; valuables. **gûn-khì**, silver ornaments, esp. for female head-dress. **goán-khì**, toys; play-things. **bih-khì-tiàm**, a shop for wicker-work. **peng-khì**, warlike weapons and stores. **kun-khì**, id. **lāi-khì**, sharp instruments; edged tools. **lī-khì**, id. (s. vapour). **tiâu-têng ê-bêng-khì**, mandarin insignia of rank and office.

khì [R. to reject; to abandon]. **khì-tsoát**, to reject; to abandon. **khì-sak** (Cn.), id. **iàm-khì**, to loathe (v. iàm), (s. vapour). **tsòe kàu-khì-jîn**, to draw down people's disgust and hatred on one's self by bad conduct. **tsòe chiâ^n khì-jîn**, id.

khì-siâ kui-chèng, to forsake the evil and return to the good. **ngiâ-sin khì-kū**, to leave the old for the new; fickle.

tsū-pō tsū-khì, to throw away invaluable opportunities to our own great injury.

khì [R. khù, to go; to leave; cf. col. khi], (Cn. khū; T. khù, khū), to go; to go to; to go away; to remove or cure (some diseases), as medicine; to lose (some things); one of the four tones, the "departing" tone, or third great tone-class, both upper and lower. **khì** is often enclitic, as also the phrase lâi-khì.

khì-hong, to remove rheumatic pains, &c. **khì-hé**, to remove fever or inflammation. **khì-thâm**, to remove phlegm. **khì-thâu-hîn**, to remove giddiness.

khì-tià^n, to lose the anchor. **khì-ûi sit-toā**, to lose mast and helm. **sîn-hûn, khì-chit-tiâu**, having lost one of our three souls by sudden terror (v. hûn). **khì-ngé-chiam**, to cut off head, arms (or wings), and feet (v. chiam).

khì-ok kui-siēn, to leave the bad and return to the good (better "khù"), (s. "khì," to reject).

khì-sia^n, the "khì" or departing tone-class, either upper or lower; the third great tone-class, including also the sixth or seventh, according to other modes of numbering. **ē-khì**, the lower third tone or lower khì, called also by some the sixth, by some the seventh. **chiū^n-khì**, the upper third tone or upper khì, called also the third tone when all the seven or eight are separately numbered. **téng-khì** (C.), id.

chit-khì, m̄-hôe-thâu, to go away and never return. **kóng-ōe, khì-khì tò-tò**, to talk indefinitely, saying both yes and no (v. tò).

lâi-khì, to come and go; let us go; when enclitic, almost like "lâi," to come. **jip--lâi-khì**, come in. **chiū^n--lâi-khì**, come up. **lâi-khì-khoà^n**, let us go and look. **lâi-lâi khì-khì**, coming and going constantly. **lâi-khì, lóng-sī lí--ē m̄-tióh**, from first to last you are in the wrong; it is all your fault. **chham-lâi chhap-khì**, confusedly mixed. **lâi chheng, khì bêng**, all plain and open, as a ready-money transaction, &c. **ū-khì bô-lâi**, all expenses and no receipts; all go, and none come back. **ū khì-lō, bô lâi-lō**, a road to go, but no way back again.

chiū^n--khì, to ascend. **lóh--khì**, to descend. **tò--khì**, to go back. **túi^n--khì** (C.), id. **kè--khì**, to cross over. **chhut--khì**, to go out, &c. &c.

bô--khì, to perish; to cease to exist; to be lost. **bô-lô--khì**, id. **hō--i chhoán--khì**, to be supplanted by him. **chhoán-bô--khì**, situation lost through another supplanting us. **chhoán-bô-khì**, supplanting attempted but not successful. **chiáh-bōe-khī**, cannot eat anything near the whole; great abundance to eat and much still over.

khī [R. the persimmon or Chinese fig, not a true fig]. **âng-khī**, the red persimmon. **teng-khī** (Cn.), id. **chìm-khī**, the yellow persimmon.

khī-tì, the dried calyx of the persimmon (v. tì). **khī-ké**, dried persimmons. **khī-chî** (Cn.), id. **khī-song**, dust or bloom which gathers on dried persimmons (used in medicine). **khī-song-hún**, id. **khī-á-chiap**, persimmon juice (used in making umbrellas). **khī-á-tsoá**, paper treated with it.

khī-jiông, inferior sort of medicinal stag's horn (said to be the interior part).

khī [R. tī, = col. thī]. **khī-koe**, the pheasant (v. thī).

khī [R. khū, to fear]. **sù-bû-khī-tān**, quite without any fear; recklessly wicked, without fear of superiors.

khī [R. kī, to dislike; to have a superstitious horror or fear of; days sacred in memory of relative's death, &c.], (C. kī), to fear, stand in awe of, or avoid, especially from medical or superstitious reasons. **tò-khī**, envious. **khī-khek**, to fear; to dread, as person or calamity. **khī-hùi**, to refrain from pronouncing or writing a tabooed or sacred name. **khī-chiáh**, to avoid eating something on account of health. **chhùi bōe-khī--tit**, cannot restrain one's self from eating what is hurtful.

kìm-khī, to fear or avoid for medical or superstitious reasons, or as nauseous food. **bô-kìm-khī**, having no danger of causing bad luck, as an auspicious day. **bô-kìm-khī ê-lâng**, a man above such superstitious fears. **bô-kìm bô-khī**, id., *e.g.* not afraid though a man in mourning should come to a marriage. **bô-kìm bô-khī, chiáh pah-jī**, living to 120 years of age though above superstitious fears. **pek-bû-kìm-khī**, having no such fears at all; phrase written up when some work is begun which might have inauspicious effects; said also of a man who has no respect for superiors, or who does wicked things openly without fear.

khiⁿ (R. kheng), (C. khɛⁿ), a ravine; a dell; a narrow valley. **khiⁿ-kau**, the channel of a stream in a ravine or dell. **hām-khiⁿ**, a pitfall (v. hām).

khiⁿ-kàng, a sort of toad.

chhim-khiⁿ, a very deep ravine or chasm. **chhim-khiⁿ nâⁿ-tóe**, deep ravines and dense forests. **bô-tóe chhim-khiⁿ**, a tremendously deep (bottomless) chasm. **chhùi sī bô-tóe chhim-khiⁿ**, his mouth is a bottomless abyss; insatiable, or spending large sums on food and drink. **pak-tó sī bô-tóe chhim-khiⁿ**, id. (his belly, &c.) **poáh-lóh bān-tn̄g chhim-khiⁿ** (to fall into an abyss a hundred thousand feet deep), to commit some great crime or dreadful mistake, or begin some terrible quarrel that can scarcely ever be set right again.

khiⁿ (T.) **kháu-khiⁿ**, not straightforward; troublesome to deal with, as a man.

khîⁿ — **khîⁿ-khîⁿ khɛ̂ⁿ-khɛ̂ⁿ**, all in disorder, as things or affair.

khîⁿ (R. khîm), to seize; to grasp tightly. **khîⁿ--lâi**, to catch and pull towards one. **khîⁿ-kiō**, to lay hold of the poles of a mandarin's sedan, to present a petition irregularly. **ū-khîⁿ-khip**, to have property or family on which a creditor can have a hold (v. khip). **khîⁿ-tit-tiâu**, manage to keep from falling by grasping something; the price will stand in market; the house or firm will just manage to avoid bankruptcy; the family just managing to get on without a total loss. **khîⁿ-chhiûⁿ peh-piah**, to climb and clamber on walls, as thief or restless child.

khîⁿ [R. khiâm, pincers, &c.], (C. khîⁿ, khiâm). **khîⁿ-á**, large pincers; tongs. **hé-khîⁿ**, tongs. **hé-thâu-khîⁿ**, pincers curved inwards at the point. **tháng-khîⁿ**, instrument for knocking the hoops firmly on a barrel.

khîⁿ [R. khiên, to venerate; devout; sincere]. **kiuⁿ-khîⁿ**, very diligent at work; not easily tired or led to stop.

khia (= khiâu), to demand an extortionate price or wages because of a man's urgent need.

khia (= khiā). **khia-lâm-iâ**, name of an idol.

khia [R. ka, = col. kia]. **sek-khia**, Buddha, Shakya-muni, said to be the same as Julai; also, the custard-apple. **sek-khia-hùt**, Buddha.

khia (Cn. kha). **sai-khia**, private, as property; one's own. **su-khia**, id.

khia (Cn. kha), odd (not even); one of a pair; classifier of boxes, baskets, and of odd articles from a pair. **ke-khia**, an odd article (one of a pair). **toaⁿ-khia**, id. **chit-khia-siuⁿ**, one box.

tī-khia, one single chop-stick.

khiâ (R. khî), (Cn. khâ), to ride. **khiâ-bé**, to ride a horse. **khiâ-bé-long**, to sit across, as on a bench or wall; or on a person, as in play, or when beating him.

lióng-kha khiâ, keeping neutral; having two strings to his bow. **khiâ-lêng**, placed on the sloping descent of a hill (as a house or grave), across the line of auspicious influence. **saⁿ-khiâ**, to copulate, as quadrupeds.

khiâ [R. khiok, crooked, = col. khiau, khiâu, khia], to refuse to pay money due. **kā--lán khiâ--leh**, refusing to pay us our money.

khiā (cf. khia). **khiā-lâm**, name of a Buddhist idol. **khiā-lâm-iâ**, id. **khiā-lâm-sîn**, id.

khiā (Cn. khā), (cf. kiā), to stand; to stand upright; to set upright; to erect, as a pole or tablet; perpendicular; a perpendicular stroke; (a door-post); to dwell; to reside; to hold an office, post, or share. (Cn. "to stand; perpendicular," &c., khā: but "to dwell," tiù, in many phrases.)

chit-khiā, a perpendicular stroke without any hook. **chit-khiā chit-ùih**, one perpendicular stroke and one horizontal stroke, as in the character "sip," the figure of a perpendicular cross. **mn̂g-khiā**, a door-post. **teng-khiā**, an upright stand for an oil-lamp (v. teng).

chhak-khiā, very stiff, as starched clothes.

thán-khiā, perpendicular. **khiā-tit**, id.; to stand erect. **khiā-khi-khí**, stand up! **tó-tó khiā-khiā**, lounging about. **khiā-khùn**, to sleep while standing (v. khùn). **khiā-sin**, in a standing position (specially said of an idol). **khiā-sin ló-tia**, said of the interpreter, who, standing before the mandarin, acts as if he were mandarin. **khiā-pan**, to stand in attendance on a judge, as his retainers.

khiā-pîn, a standing screen at a door. **khiā-kiàⁿ**, a mirror or picture fixed upright on a stand, without any joint. **khiā-âm**, a perpendicular water-pipe. **lê-khiā-chiàⁿ** (C.), the upright timber of a plough.

khiā-ûi, to set up a mast. **khiā-thiāu**, to set up a pillar. **khiā-pi**, to set up a stone tablet. **khiā-kî**, to set up a flag-staff. **khiā teng-ko**, to set up a

厦英大辭典

bamboo with a lamp at the top, covered with a cap (superstitious). **khiā-hoan**, to set up a frame with streamers after a death.

khiā chhiⁿ-kng, to have (in the shop) a vat for dyeing blue.

khiā-hà, to have in the house offerings (of food, paper, houses, and furniture, &c.) for the dead for many days in succession. **khiā-lêng**, id.

khiā-tsāi, to stand firmly. **khiā-tit-tiâu**, I can stand my ground; am not afraid of him. **oā-thâu-khiā**, to lay to (as ship), so as not to move, or scarcely move. **khiā-siám**, to stand out of the way. **khiā-khui**, id. **khiā-n̂g**, to wither, as a transplanted plant (v. n̂g).

khiā-tháng, to stand in a cage with head out till starved to death. **khiā-tû**, id.; the cage so used.

khiā-koà, to practise attitudes, as for archery or riding (v. koà). **khiā-keng**, id. for archery. **khiā pėh-hî**, to stand on one's hands with head down. **tò-khiā-thêng** (C.), id.

khiā-hong, to keep watch, so as to give notice to confederates in a bad work, *e.g.* as sentry set by gamblers or conspirators. **khiā chhim-tsúi**, to look on when others are quarrelling, or doing something bad, without checking them, or giving information to their superiors, but rather pleased that they thus get into trouble. **pâi-bīn-chêng-khiā**, to put on an appearance of diligence, obedience, or very good behaviour in presence of master, or of some one whom we wish to please.

kap-i ū-pîⁿ-khiā, to be able to associate with him, as in similar station or position in society. **kap-i ū-chē-khiā**, id. **tāi-ke pîⁿ-chē-khiā**, all of similar class, circle, or position in society, *e.g.* all mandarins, or of mandarin families. **kap-lâng bô-chē-khiā**, unfit to associate with respectable people, *e.g.* because of one's self or one's parents having done something very disreputable.

khiā-khí, to dwell; to reside. **chioh-khiā**, to lodge; to take lodgings. **saⁿ-kap-khiā**, to live together. **siāng-khiā-lāi**, living in separate rooms of the same premises. **sāng-khiā-lāi**, id. **khiā-ke**, to have one's family living in a place. **khiā-chhù-á**, to stay in a house four months free of rent after notice to quit. **khiā-òh**, to keep a school, as a teacher. **kap--i khiā-kha**, to stay with a man, working for him for food, and little or no wages, while waiting for a better situation. **khiā-sìn**, to occupy a military or police station. **khiā-pō͘**, to have office in one of the Supreme Boards.

khiā-kó͘, to have a share in business. **khiā chit-kó͘**, to have one share. **khiā kúi-pah-khó͘**, how many hundred dollars has he in the business as his share?

khiā thiⁿ-lō͘, to have no house to live in, as very poor man. **khiā sang-keng-chhù**, to have one's feet put through a hole in the wall and fastened there, as in stocks, so as to die if not ransomed, *e.g.* as a captive in a clan feud. **khiā-gėh**, to spend some time (often a month) at her parent's house, as bride does soon after marriage.

khiaⁿ [R. kheng, light, = col. khin]. **khiaⁿ-pôh**, having hands, face, &c., small and insignificant looking (said to be a bad omen).

khiaⁿ (T.), = A. khien, the handles of a box.

khiàⁿ [R. khèng, to congratulate]. **khiàⁿ-hō** (esp. Cn.), to make congratulatory presents.

khiah (R. khek), a crevice; a notch; an aperture; a flaw; a breach, as in a wall; a ravine.

khang-khiah, holes and crevices; a small blemish (or apparent blemish), as in character; a flaw or point for finding fault. **ū-khang-khiah**, there is a flaw or place to find fault with. **bô-khang bô-khiah**, no place to find fault. **chhē-khang-khiah**, to search for a flaw, or fault, or place to reprove, find fault with, accuse, or injure. **chhē-khiah**, id.

khui-khiah, to make a small opening, as in an embankment, so that water may flow out for irrigation. **ū-khui-khiah**, to have a way open for setting a matter right. **khan-kau kè-khiah**, said of idols helping people over difficulties. **chit-khiah pháiⁿ**, one step is bad, as in a set of stone or brick steps. **siâⁿ-khiah**, the interstices in the battlements of a wall; breaches in a wall. **sam-pan-khiah**, the interstices in the battlements. **sam-poan-khiah** (C.), id. **káu-kiâⁿ sam-pan-khiah** (a dog walking on the ledge of the battlements), said of a man taking a roundabout road when he might go straight, or spending far more labour than is needed.

khiak (cf. khiàk), very strong, as paper; skilful and successful at managing matters.

khiak (= khiet). **bàk-chiu sek-khok sek-khiak**, eyes glancing rapidly all about.

khiak (Cn.) **khiak-hō͘**, = A. khiet-hé, to strike fire with a flint.

khiak (C.), = A. khiok, indeed; to refuse, &c.

khiàk (cf. kiàk, khiėt, khiak), strong, stiff, and good, as cloth or paper. **pò͘-sin iáu-khiàk**, the cloth is pretty strong.

khiàk-khiàk-háu, sound of stiff paper or cloth when shaken, or of striking an empty water-jar, or of beating a boy.

ok-khiàk-khiàk, very fierce, bold, overbearing, or imperious.

khiam (R. id.) **khiam-sùn**, humble, as in manner. **khiam-pi**, id. **khiam-hu**, id. **tsū-khiam**, speaking humbly; politely using humble phrases.

khiâm (C.) **khiâm-á**, = A. khîⁿ-á, tongs, pincers.

khiâm (C.) **tháng-khiâm**, = A. tháng-khîⁿ, an instrument for knocking down the hoops on a barrel.

khiám [R. kám, to dare, = káⁿ, kiám]. **khiám-chhái**, = kiám-chhái, perhaps.

khiám [R. kín, quick, = col. kím]. **khiám-mé̤ⁿ** (C.), be quick!

khiàm [R. name of a plant]. **khiàm-sit**, a medicine used for indigestion (Euryale?). **khiàm-sìn**, id.

khiàm (R. id.), to be deficient; to be wanting or in want of; to owe, as money. **khiàm-kheh**, to be in want; deficient. **kheh-khiàm**, id. **thau-niⁿ thau-liàm, chit-si-lâng kheh-khiàm**, thieves are always in want. **khiàm-ēng**, to require or be in want of for use (whether obtained or not). **khiàm-chit-kūi**, to try every means short of kneeling in making a very urgent request. **bōe-khiàm--tit**, cannot allow the debt to be contracted or to remain unpaid. **khiàm-chit-hun**, to be deficient in weight one candareen; to want one minute, &c.

kū-khiàm, an old debt. **thoa-khiàm**, to be very long of paying. **sia-khiàm**, to be in debt for things bought on credit. **chhim-khiàm**, to owe (esp. to employer) what one has got or taken (v. chhim). **khòng-khiàm**, to refuse to pay what one owes.

têng-thåh-khiàm, to get deeper in debt to the same creditor. **oan-iuⁿ-sia, têng-thåh-khiàm**, to borrow money and get goods on credit from the same man so as to get deeper in debt. **khiàm-siàu**, to owe an account. **khiàm-chè**, to owe a debt (v chè). **khiàm-chîⁿ**, to owe money. **khiàm--lâng gûn-hāng**, to owe dollars. **hō-lâng-khiàm**, to have money owing to us. **khiàm-toaⁿ**, a note of hand, as proof of a debt. **tùi-tû-goā siōng-khiàm**, balance showing a deficiency.

khah-khiàm-sîn, naturally having a dull unexcitable manner or unintelligent appearance, often having the appearance of not observing or attending to what is said or done, but not necessarily implying more than the external manner and appearance.

khiām (R. id.), economical, as person, to use sparingly or economically. **khiām-liám**, very sparing in what one uses. **thài-khiām**, miserly. **gâu-khiām**, economical, as person. **gâu-khiām-ke**, economical in household expenses, as wife. **khiām-ēng**, temperate, economical, or careful in using or eating. **bōe-khiām--tit**, cannot be dispensed with; must be had, *e.g.* good food for sick man. **bōe-hiáu-khiām**, lavish; careless of expense.

khiû-khiām, rather niggardly. **chiet-khiām**, careful and economical. **khûn-khiām**, id., and diligent. **khek-khûn khek-khiām**, extremely so. **khiām-phak**, economical, as person. **khiām-séng**, to use money very sparingly. **khiām-sɛ́ⁿ** (C.), id. **khiām-khoeh** (T.), very economical; parsimonious. **khiām-khóeh** (T.), id.

khiām-chiáh, moderate in eating. **khiām-chiáh lún-chhùi**, very sparing in eating. **khiām-chhùi**, moderate in eating. **khiām-chhēng tit-sin**: **khiām-chiáh tit-chhun**, take care of clothes, and they are as good as new; be moderate in eating, and there is a surplus.

khian, **khiân**, **khián**, **khiàn**; better khien, khiên, khién, khièn (*q.v.*)

khiang (R. khien), sound as of crockery broken. **khiang-liang**, clear ringing sound, as of a good dollar. **khiang-khiang**, sound of bell or tambourine, or of metal struck. **khin-khin khiang-khiang**, id. **khiang-khiang-hiúⁿ**, ringing sound, as of brass when struck.

khōng-khiang, unsteady gait, as of a woman having small feet.

tsong-khiang (C.), making a false pretence or show by outward appearance or plausible talk.

khiang [R. a dialect, = col. khiuⁿ]. **khun-khiang**, songs in the mandarin dialect (v. khun). **lî-hiang, put-lî-khiang**, one can leave his home, but can't get rid of his local dialect.

khiang (C.), = A. khiong, a surname.

khiang (C.) **khong-khiang-á**, a small sort of fish.

khiâng [R. kiông, strong; violent]. **láu-khiâng-tâu**, said in scolding a man who is too exacting in money matters (v. tâu).

khiáng [R. káng, to discuss; to talk, = col. kóng], to dispute. **gâu-khiáng**, fond of disputing. **khiáng-lâi khiáng-khì**, disputing violently and scolding each other; talking mandarin together, as Fuh-kien people.

khiáng-chiàⁿ-jī, to talk the mandarin colloquial dialect.

khiàng — **khiàng-chiáu**, sort of squinting appearance from the skin of the eye being drawn up at the corner, as if in shooting.

khiàng, bold, in good or bad sense; strong and firmly made, as house, ship, or other article; skilful at managing an affair or work. **béng-khiàng-khiàng**, bold and quarrelsome or overbearing. **khiàng-táu**, extremely sharp, as at business or law; too sharp to have to do with, or at least hard to be imposed upon.

khiap, spoiled, as a thing. **phah-khiap**, to spoil; to injure; to impair. **khah-khiap chhiong-kun mn̄g-liû**, worse than transportation, esp. of having to emigrate far and long without getting home.

khiap-sì, ugly.

khiap-ì, unfriendly in manner or behaviour; display of unfriendly or displeased feeling. **khí-khiap-ì**, to show such feeling by unfriendly treatment.

khiap [R. cowardly]. **khiap-táⁿ** (Cn.), cowardly (r.)

khiap [R. khiām, economical]. **khiap-sái**, miserly; stingy.

khiàp [R. hiàp, to force, = col. ngóeh, khiâu], to take selfish advantage of the scarcity of supply, or of another's troubles or necessities, esp. by asking too high a price; to demand too much money, as underlings of mandarins; to be very troublesome, as a child insisting on getting much attention. **beh-khiàp khah-tsōe-chîⁿ**, insisting on getting far too much money, as we are in urgent need.

khiat, **khiát**; better khiet, khiét (*q.v.*)

khiau — **tåh-khiau**, to walk on stilts. **tåh-khiau kiâⁿ-soh**, to walk on stilts and on the tight-rope.

khiau (= khiâu, khiàp), to demand too high a price from one who can't help giving it.

khiau — **khiau-khi**, rough, as a road; capricious and ready to take offence (v. khi).

khiau [R. khiok, crooked, a song, = col. khek, khiàu], crooked. **khiau-ku**, hump-backed. **bīn khiau-khiau**, forehead bent down and chin turned up.

oan-khiau, crooked; deceitful (v. oan). **bû-khiau, put-sêng-sû** (C. sî), must go about the bush to accomplish this matter.

áu-khiau, to bend and make crooked. **khiau-sí**, long spoon-shaped appendages of the Ming cap called "se-bō."

khiau-lâi khiau-khì, bent in different directions at different parts. **khiau-kè-lâi, khiau-kè-khì**, having got twisted or bent in different directions at the two ends, as a thing originally straight. **i khiau-lâi, lán khiau-khì**, if he act unfairly to us, we will do so to him. **i khiau--chit-ē kè-lâi, lán khiau--chit-ē kè-khì**, id.

chhiú-khiau, the arm bent to an acute angle at the elbow. **khùn-chhiú-khiau**, to sleep with one's head on the elbow for a pillow. **sái-chhiú-khiau tò-tōng**, to strike back with the bent elbow.

khiau-kha, to put up one leg across the other knee. **khiau-kha khè-chhiú**, legs drawn up, and arms resting on them or on something else. **khiau-kha-goân**, the character "goân," which has two level strokes and two long legs. **ka-tiong bû-bâ niáu-chhú khiau-kha**, when there is no cat in the house the rats play.

tit-tit-chhâ, thâi kàu-khiau, said of a good case mismanaged till it is spoiled, *e.g.* by telling transparent lies.

khiâu [R. hiàp, to force, = col. khiàp, khia, khiâ,

海上絲綢之路文獻集成 科技與文化編

khiau], to refuse to do what one is ordered, as insolent man or spoiled child; to screw money out of people, as yamun underlings; to demand too high a price when we alone have the article wanted. **khiâu-tiàu**, id. **khiâu-khò**, to drive too hard a bargain. **khiâu-khé**, to take advantage of a man's necessities, as by making enormous demands or refusing to do what we are well able. **khiâu--lâng**, id.; said also of a superior always finding fault or demanding presents, or of a man too particular about having everything just to his mind, or of a child always crying for this or that. **khiâu-lâi khiâu-khì**, to give a vast deal of trouble, as by constantly changing one's mind (esp. after promising), or by being extremely particular about minute matters. **khiâu-tang khiâu-sai**, id. **khiâu-chit-hāng, khiâu-hit-hāng**, causing constant trouble, as yamun people extorting one thing after another endlessly; very exacting, as a man who is extremely particular, or as a troublesome child.

khiáu [R. kháu, = col. khá], clever; crafty. **kî-khiáu**, skilful at work. **ké-khiáu**, trying to do something in a different way from others, but making a mess of it.

khiàu-sin, pretty and pleasant-looking, as child or girl. **khiáu-kut**, lively, open, and intelligent (not shy), as child. **khiáu-lē**, skilful, as workman; clever and intelligent-looking, as child; well-formed, beautiful, as thing or man; when said of a woman it makes a bad inuendo.

chhàu-khiáu, suddenly; unexpectedly.

kan-khiáu, cunningly wicked; roguish and plotting. **oát-kan oát-khiáu, oát pîn-kiông**, the more crafty the poorer. **kan-kan khiáu-khiáu, thien put-iông**, Heaven will not endure crafty plotters. **kan-khiáu, tò-tí thien put-iông**, id. at the last.

khiàu [R. openings in the heart, supposed to cause intelligence]. **chhit-khiàu**, the seven openings in the heart of the most intelligent men.

ū-khiàu-sîn, healthy, strong, good and intelligent looking, as child; very interesting and pleasant to look at, as things beautiful, new, or strange. **ū-khiáu-biāu**, very clever; skilfully made; attractive, interesting, or excellent, as a thing. **chit-khoàⁿ, chit-ū-khiàu**, the more you look at it, the more it pleases.

it-khiàu put-thong, very stupid. **bô-khiàu**, dull of apprehension. **bô-ki-khiàu**, id. **ki-khiàu**, intelligence; quickness of apprehension, &c. **sim-koaⁿ ū-ki-khiàu**, very clever and intelligent, having mental powers well developed. **ū-khiàu**, id. **ū-sim-khiàu**, id. **ū-lêng-khiáu**, id.

khui-khiàu, to develop a scholar's intellectual powers by education, so that he becomes intelligent and can think and study for himself; to become intelligent, as a scholar after several years of good education. **khui-sim-khiàu**, id. **khui i--ê lêng-khiàu**, id. **khai-khiàu**, id. **hē--i ka-kī khui-khiàu**, to bring him to the point that he can study and think for himself.

khiàu [R. id., by change of tone from "hiau," fortunate, by chance], (Cn. khiò). **khiáu-tiāu**, superstitious and magical arts.

khiàu [R. khiok, crooked, bent back, = col. khiau, khek]. **phīⁿ-khiàu**, the depressed part of the nose just between the eyes. **khiàu-chhùi**, upper lip turned up (permanently). **chhùi khiàu-khiàu**, lips protruded in scorn or displeasure. **chhùi-tûn khiàu-khiàu**, id. **chhùi-tûn khiàu-tú-phīⁿ**, id., till the upper lip almost meets the nose! (either naturally or in bad temper or displeasure); how very bad-tempered you are!

siang-thâu khiàu-khiàu, both ends turned up, as of a bamboo pole for carrying loads. **káu-bé khiàu-khiàu**, dog's tail bent.

tó khiàu-khiàu, to lie or fall down straight on bed or ground, as when wearied, or by tripping. **sí-khiàu-khiàu**, quite dead. **péng-khiàu-chhiò** (C.), lying flat on the back.

khiàu (cf. kiauh, ngiauh). **khiàu--khí-lâi**, to turn over, as a chair; to turn up, as the beam of a balance or steelyard. **khiàu--lòh-khì**, to turn very much down, as its beam. **khiàu-khi-khí**, to be raised, as its beam. **chhìn-kàu-khiàu-khiàu**, to get the full turn of the steelyard.

khiáuh (cf. khàuh, khok), the sound of striking a stone or bamboo, &c. **khiàuh-liàuh**, dull sound, as of bad silver, &c. **tēng-khiáuh-khiáuh**, very hard, as stone or wood. **khih-khih khiáuh-khiáuh**, making noise and confusion, as boys. **khiáuh-khiáuh-kiò**, sound as of wood struck, or of wooden clogs, or shoes on wooden floor, or of children striking things in play. **khiáuh-khiàuh-háu**, id., or of a child constantly talking.

khiáuh (cf. khàuh, khéh). **khiáuh-khiáuh-tsùn**, to quake for fear; to shake and shiver with cold or illness.

khiáuh — **ta-khiáuh-khiáuh**, very dry and parched.

khien (R. id.) **chhoà-khien**, a famous pirate of the surname Chhoà. **khah-iá chhoà-khien**, more wicked or violent than that pirate.

khien [R. to lead or draw along, = col. khan], a ring used as a handle for door or drawer, or for a knocker; a staple or ring for a hook or latch, &c.; sort of cakes made like rings; to put a hook in its staple; to latch a door.

khien-chhé, taking things at an average in the gross, good and bad mixed. **khien-chhé ûn--khì**, id.

khien-mn̂g, fasten the door by putting the hook in its staple. **khien--teh**, shut as a door, in that way. **khien-á**, a staple or hook for it, &c. **khien-ná**, id. **só-khien**, the staple for a Chinese padlock. **siuⁿ-khien**, do., for padlock of box; rings used as box-handles. **mn̂g-khien**, a ring on a door used as handle and knocker. **khīⁿ-mn̂g-khien ok**, very brave and big when holding one's own door handle.

khu-khien, over-ceremonious, both in one's own conduct and requiring it from others.

sam-kài-khien, cakes made in the form of chains of rings (or round), esp. for worship of sam-kài-kong. **sam-kài-kong-khien**, id. **tsòe-khien**, to make these cakes.

khiên, fretful, disobedient, and bad-tempered, as a child. **khiên-leh-leh**, to fret, as a child. **ké-khiên**, caressing, as a child to its parents when wishing a favour.

khiên-chhiò (Cn.), smiling deceitfully while really hating.

khiên [R. to venerate; devout; sincere, = col. khīⁿ]. **khiên-kèng**, devout; reverential. **kèng-khiên**, id. **khiên-sêng**, id. **khiên-sim**, id.

khiên, a sort of net on small stakes, used in shallow water. **chhiⁿ-khiên**, id. **khiā-khiên**, to set it.

khiên [R. heaven; a sovereign; firm; by change of tone from "kan," dry]. **khiên-liông**, the reign of the Emperor Kien-lung. **khiên-khun** (R.), heaven and earth.

khién [R. a dog]. **siáu-khién**, my little pup, politely said of one's own son. **siáu-khién-á**, id. **péng-khién**, the contracted form of the 94th radical, written at the side. **hó lóh pêng-iûⁿ, pī-khién-khi**, a tiger in a plain is molested by dogs (v. khi). **put-sit giû-khién, kong-bêng put-hién: sit-liáu giû-khién, tē-gék lân-bién**, without eating cows and dogs one does not become eminent, but then it is hard to escape hell.

khién (R. id.) **chhe-khién**, to send, as a man. **siau-khién**, to stroll about at leisure, as for health or amusement. **sì-kòe siau-khién**, id.

khién (T.), = A. khín, willing.

khièn (R. id.) **khièn-chek**, to punish, as the gods.

khièn, to mix glutinous things by stirring, as paste or dough. **khièn-phang**, a pleasant odour rising from the frying-pan, as when ginger, onions, &c., are put in. **khièn-lé**, to mix in some brine from pickles, while eatables are being fried. **khièn-iû-chhang**, to mix onions with fat, &c., on a hot frying-pan, so as to raise a fragrant smell.

khièn-kê, to stir paste, in making it. **khièn-khi-thâu**, stir (the paste) till it is all of uniform thickness.

khièn-hún (Cn. and Quemoy), = A. ô-á-tau, preparation of oysters in potato starch.

khièn — **khièn-sńg**, superstitious rites or notions (not said in Cn., where "siâ-sút," "khiò-tiāu," or some such phrases are used). **kāu-khièn-sńg**, very superstitious. **tsòe-khièn-sńg**, to perform superstitious rites. **sióh-khièn**, superstitious.

khièn-siùⁿ, very narrow, niggardly, or exacting about money.

kāu-khièn, very particular about having everything according to the usual rites (more from habit than belief), and easily taking offence if all be not what he counts correct.

khiet (R. id.) **chhong-khiet**, the inventor of writing.

khiet [R. solitary]. **khiet-jiên it-sin**, left all alone, without relatives or friends.

khiet (T.) **khiet-kiâⁿ**, = khí-lâi-kiâⁿ, to begin a journey.

khiet [R. to take up in the hand]. **khiet-thiap**, a placard vilifying a man, true or false.

khiet [R. to interrogate, as a superior does]. **gâu-pok-khiet**, fond of finding fault whenever the least opportunity can be found; examining very minutely; questioning and cross-questioning. **pok-khiet ê-lâng**, a man of that sort, whom it is hard to get round. **chin-pok-khiet**, very much so.

khiet [R. to speak of secrets or faults]. **lih-khiet**, very cunning, deceitful, and dangerous, as a man who secretly injures people while pretending friendship.

khiet (R. id.), (C. koat). **káu-khiet**, artful; intriguing; deceitful. **khúi-khiet**, id. **kan-khiet** (R.), id. **poan-khiet** (C.), id.

khiet (= khiak). **bák-chiu sut-khok sut-khiet**, eyes glancing about rapidly, seeing all that happens around.

khiet (Cn. khat, khiak, khök). **khiet-hé**, to strike fire with a flint.

khiėt — **o-khiėt**, dark-coloured, as face, not from sickness.

khiėt — **khâm-khiėt**, rough and bad for walking on, as a road.

khiėt (cf. kiėt, khiàk, kiàk), strong and stiff, as cloth or paper. **khiėt-khiėt-kiò**, sound, as of a dipper in a water-jar or rice-boiler when nearly empty. **khiėt-khiėt-háu**, id.; also, sound of strong stiff paper or stiffly starched cloth when shaken. **phah-kàu khiėt-khiėt-háu**, to beat (a boy), making the blows ring on his skin.

khih [R. khoat, having a flaw; deficient, = col. kheh], having a flaw in the edge, as pottery. **khih-hûn**, id. **khih-khih lih-lih**, having flaws and cracks, as pottery.

khih-chhùi, hare-lipped. **khih-ku**, the division of the flaps of a dress, at the side (v. ku).

phah-khih, to break a small bit out of the edge, as of crockery or of a knife. **phah-khih-kak**, id., a larger piece. **sio-hûi chiáh-khih**, a potter uses for his own table those bowls that have flaws.

khih [R. kiap, the cheek], (C. koeh; Cn. hih). **khih-kau-thâu**, the projecting corners of the cheeks (v. kau). **khih-kha-thâu** (T.), id.

khih (cf. gih, ngihⁿ). **khih-khih khiàuh-khiàuh**, making a noise, as boys. **pak-tó-lāi, khih-khih khū-khū**, sound, as of wind in the belly. **khih-khih khók-khók**, noise of stone-cutting, or of horses or chariots on a road. **khiâ-bé khih-khók**, to ride along making a clatter with hoofs.

khih [R. kû, lean; cf. gih, ngiàuh]. **khih-khih**, very lean; emaciated. **sán khih-khih**, very very lean.

khim [R. imperial; to reverence]. **khim-kèng**, to venerate; to reverence.

khim-chhe, imperial envoy, commissioner, or ambassador. **khim-hoān**, a prisoner arrested by imperial command. **khim-sù**, granted by the emperor, as degree. **khim-tiám--ê**, appointed by imperial command, as mandarin. **khim-thien-kàm**, imperial astronomer.

khim [R. khim, keng, to compassionate; careful; proud]. **khim-chhî**, very shrewd and skilful at managing a matter (v. chhî).

khim [R. sort of coverlet or shroud]. **koan-kok i-khim**, coffin and shroud.

khim [R. the flap, collar, or cape of a dress]. **sin-khim**, the literati of a place, who have taken degrees.

khim-tit, son of wife's sister.

tùi-khim, a coat opening in the middle of the breast.

khîm (R. id.), a harp (said also of a piano, organ, harmonium, concertina, &c.) **géh-khîm**, a harp with a circular sounding-board. **tâng-soàⁿ-khîm**, harp made with brass wires. **hong-khîm**, an organ, harmonium, or concertina. **khîm-sek** (R.), harps; guitars, &c.

khîm-soàⁿ, string of a harp. **khîm-hiên**, id. **khîm-phó**, tune-book for harp. **khîm-kî su-ūi**, harp, chess, scrolls with sentences, and pictures.

toâⁿ-khîm, to play the harp. **chhò-khîm**, id. **jih-khîm**, to play the piano, harmonium, &c.

khîm-í, a sort of seat (v. í).

khîm [R. a bird]. **khîm-siù**, wild beasts and birds (v. siù).

khîm [R. name of a plant]. **ñg-khîm**, a bitter medicinal plant, febrifuge and diuretic (Scutellaria ?).

khîm [R. to apprehend, as a criminal, = col. khîⁿ].

厦英大辭典

khîm--lâi, to apprehend or arrest. **khîm-liȧh**, id. (v. liȧh). **khîm-chhȧt, seng khîm-ông**, first catch the ringleader.

khin (R. kheng), light; unimportant; frivolous; nimble; active. **khin-tāng**, light and heavy (v. tāng). **khin-tsōe**, light guilt or crime. **khin-gûn**, light dollars.

khin-sang, feeling fresh and comfortable in body, *e.g.* after a good sleep. **khin-kiāⁿ**, strong and vigorous (v. kiāⁿ).

khin-sńg, light and active, as man; small and light, as thing. **khin-báng-báng**, very light. **khin-khó**, light, as a load, or as work. **khin-phiò**, light, as baggage, or as the build of a boat (v. phiò). **khin-pȯh**, frivolous and shallow in manner; small and light, as things (v. pȯh).

khin-khoài, readily induced to help or to do a favour; willing to help. **sim-koaⁿ khin**, easily persuaded; ready to believe or follow what others say. **hī-khang khin**, id. **chhùi-thâu khin**, easily persuaded to promise or say things. **khin-kha-chhńg**, ready to do acts of service or politeness, as a polite boy, or as a man forgetful of his dignity.

khoàⁿ-khin, to despise. **goá-ê-giên khin**, my words would not have weight.

khin-á-khoàⁿ, to give a rapid glance. **khin-khōng-khoā**, in very great or too great haste. **khin-khoā-khoā**, id.

khin-chhìn, a steelyard that makes things seem heavier than they really are.

khin-chhiú, careful and gentle in doing fine work with the hands. **khah-khin-chhiú**, id. **hâng khah-khin-chhiú**, quilt it more loosely. **khah-khin-lȧt**, using less strength; done with too little strength, as cloth woven too loose. **khah-khin-á-lȧt** (C.), id. **khin-kha-kiāⁿ**, to tread lightly. **tiȯh khah-khin-kha**, tread more lightly.

khin (R. khien). **khin-khin khiang-khiang**, sound of vibrating strings, &c.

khîn (C.), = A. khûn, diligent.

khîn (C.), = A. khûn, a sort of tree.

khín [R. chhién, = col. chhíⁿ], shallow; shallows in sea or stream; light, as yellow. **chhim-khín**, deep and shallow. **phah-chhim-khín**, to take soundings. **khoà-khín**, aground on the shallows.

khín-tháⁿ, shallow, as a dish, or as learning; easy. **khín-pȯh-lâng**, man who boasts much of any small success. **khín-bîn**, sleeping lightly, and easily wakened. **khín-n̂g**, light-yellow.

khín (C.), = A. khéng, willing.

khín — **khín-khín khòng-khòng**, much noise, as of repairs, or of things moved about, or of children at noisy play, or of rats running about.

khīn — **khīn-khōng**, sound as of noisy children, or of moving heavy things.

khió (Cn.), = A. khó͘, kháu, the mouth; (in some book phrases).

khiò (R. khiàu), (Cn. khīò), magical or diabolical arts; black arts. **tsòe-khiò**, to practise black arts. **hē-tsoá tsòe-khiò**, id. **khit--lâng tsòe-khiò**, to be injured by such incantations and imprecations. **tsòe lâng-ê-khiò**, to practise black arts to injure others. **tsòe bó͘-lâng ê-khiò**, do. to injure Mr. So-and-so.

kóe-khiò, to remove the hurtful effect of such incantations by counter rites done by Tauist priests. **tháu-khiò**, id.

khïò-tiāu (Cn.), superstitious practices, magical charms, incantations, &c. **khïò-tiō** (Cn.), id.

khïò (Cn.), = A. khàu, to deduct, as wages.

khïò (Cn.), = A. khàu, manacles, &c.

khïò (Cn.), = A. khàu, khò͘, to knock the forehead on the ground.

khïò (Cn.), = T. khàu, a loop for a button.

khiò, a pipe for water; to lead water or have water flowing in such a pipe. **tek-khiò**, a bamboo conduit for water, generally only half a pipe, but may be whole. **tsúi-khiò**, do. of any material. **nîⁿ-chîⁿ-khiò**, such a gutter at the eaves.

khiò-tsúi, to have water running in a pipe or conduit. **tsúi khiò--lȯh-lâi**, id.

khioⁿ (C. esp. P.), = A. khiuⁿ, in all the tones.

khioh, to pick up; to gather; to collect; to draw a likeness; to get a child born; to sharpen, as saw or razor; (to smooth a surface); to treasure up, as dislike. **khioh-lioh**, to pick up or gather many things; to sharpen. **saⁿ-chiⁿ-khioh**, to snatch, as many persons snatching things. **khioh-seh**, to gather fragments; to glean. **khioh-sip**, to gather up carefully; habitually careful that nothing be lost. **khioh-lok--teh**, to take up and store up. **khioh-kut-thâu**, to collect bones into jars. **khioh-tsāi**, to be taking in cargo for voyage. **khioh-chîⁿ**, to collect money. **khioh sai-khia-chîⁿ**, to appropriate what should have been divided among others.

khui-khioh, to apportion the sums levied from each, which he must pay for a common expense.

khioh-khau, to draw lots.

khan-khioh, to assist a man out of great want, as by giving or lending some money, or by getting employment for him.

khioh gín-ná, to have a child born. **khioh-chiá**, a midwife. **khioh-chiá-bú**, id.

khioh siáu-éng, to draw or paint a miniature likeness from life. **khioh ang-á**, id. **khioh tāi-siū**, to draw a full-length likeness. **khioh-siòng**, to draw a likeness from life.

khioh-bīn, to make the surface smooth, as of a stone, &c.; to take a miniature likeness. **khioh-chiam**, to pile up in a conical or pyramidal form, as stones or bricks. **khioh-hiā**, to lay a sloping roof with thin tiles, not cemented.

khioh-kéng, to make folds or plaits, as in a dress; to get wrinkled, as face of old person. **khioh-chih**, a bamboo sail made so as to fold down; to fold such a sail in taking it down, as in taking in sail.

khioh-tiāⁿ, to raise the anchor.

khioh-khoán, to treasure up causes of displeasure till the whole comes to a point at once. **khioh-khoáⁿ**, id. **khioh-oàn**, to harbour deep resentment. **khioh-hûn**, to cherish enmity and watch for an opportunity of revenge (v. hûn).

khioh-kȧk, utterly useless, as person or thing (v. kȧk).

khioh-liȧp-bē, rice boiled soft, but yet having the grains whole and separate.

péng-khioh-chhiò, to lie, turn, or recline with the face upwards (v. chhiò). **khioh-éng**, to turn the boat's head to the waves. **khioh-tsāi-phīⁿ**, to shift sail so as to have the wind well on the quarter. **khioh-khí-kha chiū-kiāⁿ**, to get up, from sitting or lying, and begin to walk.

khioh [R. khiok, to refuse; an initial particle], an initial particle somewhat like "indeed," or "well then," often conveying the idea that matters have taken an unexpected turn. **khioh-ū** —, well, there are —, or there is —.

ta^{n} **khioh-bô--khì**, suddenly to lose what one had, or find we have not what we supposed we had. **liâm-pi^{n} khioh-bô--khì**, id. **āu-lâi, khioh-bô-khì**, change one's mind and refuse to go. **āu-lâi, khioh-m̄-khì**, id. **kàu-sî, khioh-bô-iá^{n}**, turns out false when the time comes. **liâm-pi^{n} khioh-chiâ^{n}**, is suddenly and unexpectedly accomplished, quite beyond hope. **khioh-m̄-chiâ^{n}**, yet the matter could not be accomplished. **khioh-phoà-pī^{n}**, unexpectedly got unwell. **ta^{n} khioh-léng-tām**, now his affection has changed into cold-heartedness.

khiok [R. to refuse; an initial particle, = col. khioh], well then —; indeed —. **khiok sī** —, indeed it is —. **khiok ōe-àn-ni^{n}**, well, then, it can or may be so. **khiok-seh**, well, it is said that —, phrase used for introducing a story from the "kə́-chheh," or novels (v. seh).

khiok-ì, to nullify a man's good intentions, *e.g.* by refusing a present (s. crooked). **khiok lâng-ê-ì**, id.

khiok [R. crooked, a song, = col. khiau, khiàu, khek]. **khut-khiok**, very crooked, as a lane, or as a piece of wood.

úi-khiok, crooked, deceitful, as ways of working; too much cunning and roundabout planning; much involved, confused, or intricate, as an affair. **ū úi-khiok**, much involved, as an affair that has several causes of trouble in it. **úi-khiok--lâng**, to injure people craftily.

khiok-ì siong-chiông, to follow another's will against one's own desires. **khiok-ì chiông-siòk**, to follow the customs of a place against one's own feelings or opinions.

bûn-khiok-chhi^{n}, a very auspicious star, incarnate in Pau Bûn-chín, of the Sung dynasty.

khiong (C. khiang), a surname.

khiong (C. khiang). **se-khiong**, a part of Tangut, in Central Asia. **khiong-chhâm**, a medicine made of preserved silk-worms. **khiong-hoàt**, a medicinal root (v. hoàt), (cf. kiong).

khióng [R. to fear], (P. khéng). **hông-khióng**, for fear that —; lest. **khióng-ùi**, id., very much afraid. **put-chí khióng-ùi**, too much afraid to venture. **pah-hāng khióng-ùi**, afraid and suspicious of everything. **chit-pah-hāng khióng-ùi**, id.

khióng (C.) **tsúi-khióng**, = A. tsúi-kéng, a conduit for water.

khiōng (P.), = A. khēng, the tallow-tree. **khiōng-á**, id., = A. khēng-chhiū.

khip (R. kip), = kip, classifier of degrees of rank.

khip [R. to draw water], a surname.

khip [R. to breathe]. **hə-khip**, breathing (said in medical matters). **hə-khip kúi-chì**, how many beats of the pulse has he for one expiration or inspiration?

khip — **khip--teh**, catching firmly. **ū-khî^{n}-khip**, to have some one who stands security; to have family, or relatives, or property on which a creditor can have a hold as a security; some responsible party can be found in the case, so that the matter can be got hold of. **ū-khî^{n} ū-khip**, id. **ōe-khî^{n}-khip--i**, can have a hold on him, *e.g.* on relative or security of a debtor. **tùi-in-chhin-lâng khî^{n}-khip**, to get hold of the matter by acting on his relatives. **ū thang-khî^{n}-khip**, to have some hold on the man or affair, *e.g.* by having a receipt, or by being able to get hold of his relatives or property. **bô-khî^{n}-khip**, to have no property, relatives, &c., on which a creditor could lay hold; also said of an affair in which no responsible party can be found who is of any use for the purpose. **bô-khî^{n} bô-khip**, id.; said also of a large box or stone that cannot well be got hold of, as it has no handles or projections.

khit (R. id.), to beg; to ask earnestly; to buy, as a son or wife; also (Cn.), to betroth. **khit-ū**, to have got a good deal by begging. **kiû-khit**, to beg or entreat earnestly (v. kiû). **kiông-khit**, to beg with great urgency, as a beggar. **khit-hoe**, to pray for children, as woman. **khit-hə̄**, to pray for rain in procession. **khit-jiâu-miā^{n}**, to beg for life.

khit-hāu-si^{n}, to buy a boy to be a son. **khit-bə́**, to buy a wife, a less regular way of getting married. **khit sim-pū** (Cn. and Quemoy), to get a daughter-in-law. **khit-tiā^{n}-tiòh** (Cn.), betrothal settled.

khit-chiáh, a beggar; to beg, as beggar. **khit-chiáh-pô**, an old beggar woman. **khit-chiáh-thâu**, a man who has the charge of the beggars in a ward. **khit-chiáh-toa^{n}**, a ticket given by him to shops that pay an annual rate, securing them against beggars troubling them. **khit-chiáh-iâ^{n}**, place where beggars live. **khit-chiáh-kut**, a mean-looking fellow.

khit [R. kip, to give; to cause], sign of the passive, with the agent expressed. **khit-lâng-phah**, to be struck by a man. **khit-chhát-thau**, to be stolen by a thief. **khit--i tsáu--khì**, to have your man escape when you thought he was in your power. **khit--i bû-lí--khì**, scolded or driven away by him in an unjust and improper manner. **m̄-thang kàu-sî khit--i bô-iá^{n}**, take care that he do not cheat you when the time comes.

bōe-khit-i-iau, not hungry though not satisfied, *e.g.* having staved off hunger by a lunch or by a light meal. **thó-kha khit-lə̄-kiâ^{n}**, all the travelling is in vain.

thèh--chit-ē khit--i, give him (a beggar) something. **thi^{n} nā^{n}-beh khit-lâng-chhī**, if Heaven will nourish a man (v. chhī).

khit — **ə-khit**, a black sort of bird, somewhat like a magpie.

khit (= kit). **khó-khit-khit**, very thick, as a liquid, or as boiled rice.

khit (R. ėk), a peg; a wooden pin; a small stake; to fasten with a peg. **tèng-khit**, to drive in a peg or stake, as into the ground. **chhâ-khit**, a wooden peg. **gû-khit**, a stake for tethering a cow. **hun-kim-khit**, a peg used in laying down the auspicious direction of a house or grave. **iâng-kong-khit** (C.), id. **kə̂-khit** (Cn.), a peg over which cloth is drawn while starching it.

khiû [R. kiû, a ball or globe]. **liû-khiû**, = liû-kiû, the Loo-choo islands (s. curled).

khiû [R. kiû; cf. kiu, kiù], curled; curly; penurious; very economical and rather niggardly.

khiû-liu-liu, curly or entangled, as tendrils or long hair. **khiû-khiû liu-liu**, id. **khiû-mn̂g**, curly hair.

khiû-chhùi, to pout the lips. **khiû kha-chhiú**, to draw one's self up, in order to keep warm. **khiû-khiû teh-khùn**, to sleep with limbs drawn together for warmth. **kia^{n} kàu-khiû-kha khiû-chhiú**, sitting with limbs drawn up, and shaking with terror, as at robbers.

厦英大辭典

khiû-khiâm, extremely economical; penurious. **liû-khiû**, determined to keep up the dispute or feud, as a man who always finds some new demand or objections when it seemed almost settled; too urgent for getting things, as a child (s. Loo-choo). **liû-khiû-ok**, id. **khiû kàu-lán bàt-sat-pé**, as niggardly as a dried up little bug!

khiú (cf. liú, giú), to grasp and pull towards one; to seize violently; to lay hold of roughly. **saⁿ-khiú**, to struggle or wrestle together. **khiú-lák**, to lay hold of violently, so as to injure. **khiú heng-khám**, to seize a man by his dress at the neck or the breast near the neck. **khiú thâu-tsang-bé**, to seize a man's queue.

khiú (= khí-iú). **khiú-chhú chêng-lí**, how *can* this be right!

khiū — **khiū-khiū**, tenacious; viscous, as a thick jelly.

khiū (cf. khiùh). **chhiah khiū-khiū**, extremely poor.

khiuⁿ [R. khiong, khiang], a dialect; a cognate language. **khiuⁿ-kháu**, id. **hó-khiuⁿ-kháu**, talks the dialect well. **tsáu-khiuⁿ**, a different dialect or language, but related; pronunciation different. **goā-kang-khiuⁿ**, the mandarin dialect.

khah-khiuⁿ, rather different from the dialect spoken here. **khiuⁿ-khiuⁿ-khiuⁿ**, very different in dialect; very hard to understand.

khiūⁿ [R. khiām, moderate; economical], to restrain our appetite from what does not agree with us. **khiūⁿ-chhùi**, id. **chhùi m̄-sái-khiūⁿ**, may eat anything. **lún-chhùi khiūⁿ-chih**, to restrain passion and keep silent; to refrain from eating, *e.g.* from economy, &c.

khiūⁿ-siùⁿ, very careful of one's clothes; taking care of them so that they wear well.

khiùh (cf. kiùh, chiùh, khiū). **nńg-khiùh-khiùh**, very soft, as dough. **jūn-khiùh-khiùh**, tough, as cakes; tough and elastic, as india rubber.

sòng-khiùh-khiùh, very poor.

khng [R. khong, peace], a surname. **khng goân-sòe**, a red-faced idol, attendant on má-tsé, &c.

khng (R. khong), rice; chaff; bran from rice; small, like fine chaff. **khng-khng-khng**, very small, like chaff or bran.

bí-khng, bran from rice, worked off the grain by the mortar. **chhe-khng**, coarse rice husks, rice chaff, worked off in the "thê-lâng." **chhe-khng-hoe**, = chhien-jit-hông, a sort of everlasting flower. **khng-éh**, small chaff of rice; coarse rice bran. **khng-óeh** (C.), id.

khǹg [R. khoan? khoat? cf. col. khoah, khoàⁿ, khoaⁿ]. **khoah-khǹg**, wide, as a piece of ground. **khoàⁿ-khǹg**, large, as a house.

khǹg, to store up; to conceal. **khǹg-nǹg**, id. **siu-khǹg**, to lay past; to conceal, as men or things. **khǹg-bát**, to hide away. **lâu-khǹg--teh**, to reserve and keep, as a part or remainder. **khoán-khǹg--teh**, stowed away carefully in order. **chek-chek khioh-khǹg--teh**, to store up large quantities of things.

khǹg-pē, to conceal part, as of our plans, or of the circumstances of a matter; to teach in a slovenly way.

khǹg-siū-khì, to harbour angry feeling. **khǹg-iu-būn**, to cherish feelings of deep sorrow.

khǹg (R. khoàn), (C. khùiⁿ), to exhort. **khǹg-nǹg** (C. khùiⁿ-nùiⁿ), id., at some length. **saⁿ-khǹg**, to exhort another. **kā-i-khǹg**, exhort him. **kiông-khǹg**, to exhort very urgently. **khé-khǹg**, to exhort earnestly. **kóe-khǹg**, to exhort to reconciliation, or to desist from some bad purpose, &c.; to comfort and soothe by exhortation. **khǹg-hô**, to exhort to peace. **khǹg-lâng-hó**, to exhort men to virtue. **hoâiⁿ-khǹg tit-khǹg**, to exhort in every way.

khǹg (Cn.), [R. khòng, = col. khàng, kàng]. **thê-khǹg**, a vaulted opening at the end of a large grave made ready to have the coffin shoved in. **bē-khǹg**, id. **chìn-khǹg**, to shove the coffin endwise into such a cavity. **phoà-bē-khǹg**, the hole of a broken-down grave.

kho [R. class; order; literary examination, = col. khe], (also C. sometimes = A. khe). **teng-kho**, to get a degree. **kho-kah**, having got a degree by merit in examination, not bought (v. kah). **kho-ūn**, the fated time for literary success.

kho — **péh-kho**, a sort of white wood used for the blades of oars.

kho (Cn.), = A. o, to cook in a pan nearly dry.

khô — **khô-khô**, strutting along proudly, as a literary man. **kiâⁿ-lē khô-khô**, id. **khô--teh khô--teh**, id. **kek-khô**, to put on this bearing.

khó (R. id.), (Cn. khéⁿ), to examine, as students or candidates, especially for degrees.

chhâ-khó, to investigate carefully, as any matter. **bô-chhâ-khó**, without asking any questions or making any inquiry. **khe-khó**, to examine and investigate carefully, *e.g.* history, or old deeds, or the origin of an affair, or doctrines. **bô-tè thang-khe-khó**, cannot be found by investigation; said also of great numbers or wealth.

khó-sì, examinations for degrees. **khó-kàu**, id. **sòe-khó**, the triennial examination of Sew-tsai graduates. **khó-pîⁿ**, the examination-hall for the Sew-tsai degree.

chhut-khó, to go to the examinations, as a student. **pā-khó**, all the literati refusing to go to examination. **khó--tióh thâu-miâⁿ**, to be at the head of the list.

khó-bûn, examine for literary rank. **khó siù-tsâi**, to examine candidates for the degree of Sew-tsai (and so with other degrees). **khó koan-hong**, to examine the literati for prizes or bursaries, not for degrees. **khó-bú**, to examine for literary rank. **khó iû-teng**, to examine candidates for the situation of soldier, to be ready for any vacancy. **khó-chhèng**, competition in gun-practice. **khó-chhèng-pé**, id. **khó chìⁿ-pé**, competition in archery. **khó-chìⁿ**, id. **khó-pé**, competition either with archery or with guns.

toā-tsú-khó, chief examiner for the Kujin degree. **chiàⁿ-tsú-khó**, id. **hù-tsú-khó**, assistant-examiner for do.

khó — **khó tsúi-phi** (C. phe tsúi-phe), to throw stones along the water, making them skim along bounding several times. **ēng-gûn khó tsúi-phi**, to spend money lavishly.

khó [may or can be], (Cn. khé), used in many phrases with verbs in the sense of "fit to be —." **khó-í**, it will do. **put-khó** (R.), must not.

khó-kiàn, hence it may be seen that —. **khó-chhú**, fit to be commended (v. chhú). **khó-èⁿ**, abominable; hateful. **khó-è**, id. **khó-hūn**, hateful; to be detested. **khó-chhiò**, laughable.

khó-lîn, to pity; alas! **khó-liân**, id. **khó-siong**, to be lamented; alas! what a pity! **khó-sioh**, alas! what a pity! **khó-sek** (C.), id.

khó (Cn. khé). **khó-oā**

khó (Cn. khé). **khó-oāⁿ**, great drought (C. khòng-hān).

khó [R. hú, to permit; a quantity; a little; a surname, = col. khé, khoá]. **khin-khó**, light, as a load; light and easy, as work. **siáu-khó**, small and unimportant, as an affair.

khó [R. rugged; uneven]. **khám-khó**, troublesome to deal with, as an affair; constantly unfortunate and miserable, as a man who is constantly getting sick or falling into troubles, or when whatever he undertakes goes wrong.

khó (R. id.), to ebb, as the tide; thick, as fluids. **khó-khó**, very thick, as a liquid almost like a paste or jelly, or as thick-boiled rice. **khó-thâu-bê**, rice boiled till thick and adhesive. **khó-kà**, thick and thin, as fluids or rice. **khó táuh-táuh**, very thick, as boiled rice. **khó pih-pih**, id. **khó kit-kit**, id. **khó khit-khit**, id.

khó-tut-tut, very crowded, as animals; very thick, as rice, paste, or mud. **khó tsút-tsút**, very numerous, as men or animals crowded together; very thick, as rice, &c.

tsúi khó, ebb-tide; tide beginning to ebb; tide ebbing. **tsúi-khó, sím-mihⁿ-sî**, when does ebb-tide begin? **lòh-khó**, to go down with the ebb tide.

khó-tî (T.), to empty out a pond, as in order to catch fish.

khò [R. khok, cruel; excessive], to hurt one's shoulder, as by a rough carrying-pole. **khò-gâi**, miserably poor. **khiâu-khò--lang**, to drive too hard a bargain. **khò--lâng pan-gî**, id.

khò [R. id., = col. khoà]. **khò--tiòh**, to ground accidentally, as a vessel on a bank or on the shore.

khò [R. id., = col. khoà], (Cn. khè), to lean upon; to trust upon. **oá-khò**, id. **sìn-khò** (r.), to believe and trust upon.

khò-chím, the pillow-shaped rim at the back of a state-couch for resting the elbow. **khò-pán**, the cross-bar for the arms to rest upon in a large (mandarin's) sedan. **khò-chhiú-pán**, id.

khò-siòk, very free and easy, dispensing with polite conventional forms (v. siòk).

tùi-thâu ū-khò, there are powerful persons backing each side. **āu-piah-soaⁿ ū-khò**, your adversary has powerful supporters.

khò--chih, to break accidentally, as by pressing upon. **khò--tiòh**, to injure by coming against, as by rubbing when carried past or coming down from above.

khò [R. to give a largess], (Cn. khè). **khò-siúⁿ**, to give a largess to soldiers, as after a victory. **khò-sióng**, id. **khò-sióng sam-kun**, do. to the whole imperial army. **khò-lō**, to reward soldiers by largesses. **khò-chiòng**, to make offerings to the spirit-soldiers of the gods. **khò-kun** (esp. T.), id.

khò [R. an essay; exercise; work, = col. khè], the classes or divisions of a list of candidates. **lāi-khò**, first division of the successful candidates for bursaries or prizes. **goā-khò**, second division, having smaller rewards. **hū-khò**, third class, who get no rewards, but have their names published.

jit-khò, a document given by a fortune-teller fixing the fortunate days for all the ceremonies connected with a marriage.

khò, an ingot shaped like a boat; classifier of small ingots; bundles of idolatrous paper. **gûn-khò**, an ingot of silver shaped like a boat; a quantity of idolatrous paper. **kim-khò**, a boat-shaped ingot of gold. **kim-gûn-khò**, idolatrous paper made up in bundles. **chit-khò oân-pó**, one ingot of silver. **chit-khò-gûn**, id., of various sizes, generally about forty or fifty taels; also said of idolatrous paper. **chit-khò kim-tiāⁿ**, one ingot of gold.

kok-khò, government revenue, esp. money from taxes and customs. **khiàm-kok-khò**, to be in arrears for customs or taxes.

khò [R. an order; a patent of rank]. **khò-hong**, titles of rank conferred by imperial authority on ancestors or wife of mandarin. **hong-khò**, id. **chhiáⁿ hong-khò**, to make application for do. **chih-hong-khò**, to receive the patent of rank with great ceremony. **khò-thek**, the roll containing this document.

khò — **chheng-khò**, having a little property, so as to have no need of toiling to get a living.

khō — **kng khō-khō**, naked, as a man wearing only short trousers; quite solitary, as a man with no relatives; having nothing that can be laid hold of, as a large heavy stone or box.

khe (R. id.), a hoop; a circlet; a circle; a halo; a dollar; a billet of firewood; (a neighbourhood); to put on a hoop, as on a bucket.

e-kun-khe, an ornament worn by women on the forehead. **bō-á-khe**, a sort of circlet worn by boys, like a skull-cap without the crown. **pat-thoân-khe**, a round pattern much used on flowered silk.

toā-khe-thâu, very large and corpulent, as a man.

chhâ-khe, a billet of firewood.

thih-khe, an iron hoop. **bih-khe**, a bamboo hoop. **tháng-khe**, a hoop for a bucket or tub. **khe-tháng**, to put a hoop on a tub or bucket (not said in T.) **khe-lòh**, bamboo hoop and ropes for carrying loads; a coolie who carries loads (v. lòh).

han-tsû-khe, sweet-potatoes sliced and dried. **ien-tâng-khe**, tubular tiles for chimney.

îⁿ-khe, a circle. **lâu mn̂g-khe**, to have a circle of hair unshaven round the queue, to be afterwards braided into it. **géh-khe**, a lunar rainbow. **géh ûi-khe**, the moon has a halo. **ûi-khe**, to make a circle. **phah-khe**, to make a hoop, as of bamboo. **phah-toā-khe ûi**, to make a great circle, as in walking, running, or flying. **séh chit-toā-khe ûi**, id.

âng-bák-khe, eyes very red, as with weeping. **bák-chiu-khe**, edges of the eyes. **bák-chiu-khe thiàⁿ**, edges of the eyes sore. **bák-chiu-khe toā-ê**, too proud to take notice of people, as man who was once poor himself. **bák-chiu-khe toā-bóng-lúi**, id.

chit-khe, one dollar. **chit-khe-gûn**, id. **khe-siaⁿ**, the denomination of dollars. **khe-saⁿ**, one dollar and thirty cents. **kúi-khe**, how many dollars? **khe-kúi**, how many tens of cents above one dollar?

chit-khe-á-ûi, this neighbourhood. **chit-khe** (Cn., but not T.), this neighbourhood; this place. **chit-khe-ngá** (Cn.), id.

khe [R. hu, bran; husk; refuse, = col. phe]. **tê-khe**, the refuse of camellia seeds after the oil has been pressed out (used as soap). **iû-khe**, id. **iû-khe-boáh**, do. broken small. **tê-khe-boáh**, id. **tāu-khe**, refuse of beans (from North China) after oil-making, made into round cakes of "bean-cake;" used as manure, &c. **moâⁿ-khe**, cakes of refuse from hemp-seeds after oil is pressed out. **seng-khe**, do. from ground-nuts.

khe [R. he, to call or make a sound], to call, as

厦英大辭典

animals; to call troops by trumpet. **khe-káu**, to call a dog. **khe-koe**, to call fowls. **koe-bú khe koe-á** (the hen calling the chickens), said of a powerful man inviting others to come under his protection.

khe-toaⁿ, to cackle, as a hen about to lay an egg (T. kiò-loa).

khe-hong, to make a noise, as the kite does; to whistle for the wind, as sailors. **khe-sùt-á**, to give a signal by a sort of whistling or hissing sound. **khe-tûi**, to make a trumpet-call to call troops together.

khe-eh, to hiccup (v. eh).

khe [R. ke, to copulate], (T.), = A. kàn, to commit lewdness (used in vile scolding; for which reason "khe-tháng" must not be said in T.)

khê [R. hê, paste; glutinous; confused, = col. kê], to adhere unpleasantly, as paste or glutinous things; to fasten loosely with paste; to dirty one's self, as with lime, paint, or paste; to procrastinate. **khê-chhùi**, to adhere unpleasantly to the mouth, as some sort of cakes, *e.g.* "ké."

khê-kháh, to procrastinate idly. **khâm-khê** (C.), slow and tedious to heal, as a disease.

khê-lâng (C.), to be forming matter, as boil not yet quite ripe.

khó [R. kó, fruit; really]. **bô-khó beh-tsòe** —, not caring to do —. **bô-khó sái-kang**, it does not require much work to do it. **m̄-khó sái-kang**, id. **m̄-khó-káⁿ**, scarcely venturing. **goá m̄-khó-tsai**, I do not know certainly. **bōe-khó ōe-iâⁿ**, cannot well conquer.

khó [R. khó, able; can], (also Cn., = A. khó). **lêng-khó**, it is better that —; better — than —.

khó (Cn.) **khó-oāⁿ**, = A. T. khó-oāⁿ, a drought.

khó (Cn.), in some words, = A. khó.

khó [R. hú, to permit; a small quantity, = col. khó, khoá], a surname. **khó chin-jîn**, name of an idol.

khó — **khó-mn̂g**, the small short hair all over one's body. **khó-phê**, the thin skin that peels off at the side of a wound or sore when it is healing. **tn̂g-khó-phê**, wound healed to this state.

khó [R. the mouth, = col. kháu], (Cn. khió). **boán-khó èng-sêng**, mouth full of fair promises. **koan iú lióng-khó**, a mandarin has two mouths (said in allusion to the shape of the character "koan").

khó-siét ê-sū, a matter causing much wrangling. **kāu-khó-siét**, id. **kap-lâng kak-khó**, quarrelling in altercation. **kap-lâng khó-kak**, id. **kun-tsú tāng-khó, put-tāng-chhiú**, a superior man uses his mouth, not his hands, in a quarrel or dispute.

khó-á-pêng, the 30th radical (mouth) when placed at the side.

khó (R. id.), bitter; wretched; distressed; (very earnest); to grieve about; to murmur or fret at. **tiⁿ-khó**, sweet and bitter (v. tiⁿ). **khó-ióh**, bitter medicine.

khiâu-khó, to take advantage of another's need to make exorbitant demands. **khó-chhó**, to torment; to oppress severely. **khó-tók**, to treat harshly or severely, *e.g.* woman beating a female slave (v. tók).

oáh-oáh khó--sí, to die of vexation; vexed to death, literal or figurative. **goá-khó--i poàh-kiáu**, I am grieved for his gambling. **teh-khó bô-thang-chiáh**, anxious about having nothing to eat.

khat-khó, to put a pressure or restraint on one's self, so as to do or endure patiently something toilsome, hard, or distasteful (v. khat).

khó-sim, very diligent, *e.g.* at study, or at teaching. **khó-khǹg**, to advise or exhort very earnestly. **khûn-khó**, very diligent and laborious. **khek-khûn khek-khó**, extremely diligent, laborious, and economical. **chhong-chiên khûn-khó thók**, to study very diligently at a window. **khó-thák**, to study under great difficulties, or to great exhaustion. **lô-khó**, severe or toilsome.

kan-khó, miserable; wretched; difficult (v. kan). **tsai-khó**, to experience misery, or feel calamity. **khó-lān**, calamity; misery (v. lān). **khó-eh**, calamities. **khó-thàng**, painful; miserable (v. thàng). **khó-chhoeh**, sad; deeply grieved. **iu-khó**, very sorrowful (v. iu). **khùn-khó**, miserable; wretched. **sin-khó**, painful (v. sin), **seng-khó**, id. **khó-chhut**, a tragedy. **khó-toàⁿ**, a tragic female character in a play.

khó-koe, the bitter cucumber. **khó-tê**, wild uncultivated tea. **khó-thô**, the bitter peach. **khó-chháu**, a plant like a dock. **khó-lēng**, a tree with lilac flowers (v. lēng). **khó-nâⁿ-poāⁿ**, a shrub with white flowers that grows in ditches and streams.

khò (R. id.) **tē-khò**, nutmeg, in general (smaller and finer than lāu-hàu?). **tāu-khò** (C.), id. **jiók-tē-khò**, nutmeg kernels; nutmegs. **jiók-khò**, id. **tē-khò-hoe**, mace.

péh-tē-khò, cardamom.

khò-hoe-sek, light grayish purple, or light lilac colour. **khò-he-sek**, id.

khò (R. id.) **chhát-khò**, great robbers, banditti, or rebels.

khò (Cn), = A. khò, to trust. **i-khò** (r.), to trust or rely upon.

khò [R. a treasury; a magazine; a store], a treasury. **gûn-khò**, id. **khò-pâng**, treasurer in a mandarin's office; treasury of a hong. **khò-gûn**, national money. **khai khò-gûn**, to spend money from the public purse. **phoaⁿ-khò**, the provincial treasury.

chiú-khò, a wine or spirit store; a large liquor shop. **hé-khò**, a fire-proof vault.

khò-tô, said of the scale of weights making one dollar = 7 chīⁿ 2 hun (v. tô). **khò-pêng**, id.

khò-koaⁿ, image of a treasurer, burned in certain rites. **khò-chíⁿ**, paper with long scolloped incisions, burned for the dead; a small quantity is supposed to represent myriads of cash. **khò-chíⁿ-tsoá**, paper for making it.

khò (R. id.), trowsers; drawers, &c. (the classifier is "niá;" but in C. Cn. "tiâu"). **saⁿ-khò**, coat and trowsers. **saⁿ-á-khò**, id. **kûn-khò**, petticoat and trowsers.

sek-khò, women's short trowsers. **tà-sek-khò**, to put them on.

tsúi-khò, short trowsers like bathing drawers. **khò-tn̂g**, id. **khò-thúi**, leggings. **khò-thúi-khò**, large warm leggings (double or padded and tied at the foot) worn by old men. **mīⁿ-khò**, id. **láng-khò**, wide outside trowsers or overalls, worn by boatmen, &c. **láng-khò-kui**, the slits like pockets (not real pockets) in them for the hands. **khui-kha-khò**, children's wide trowsers, made with no seat, so that they never need be let down. **khui-tóe-khò**, id.

khò-thâu, the top or waistband of trowsers. **khò-thâu-lêng**, a long hollow band for tying round the waist to hold up the trowsers, and also serving as a purse. **khò-toà**, a simple string or tape for holding up trowsers. **khò-tóe**, seat of trowsers. **khò-kha**, legs of trowsers.

tsah-khɵ̀, to pull up trowsers at the waist, letting more hang down over the band, so as to shorten the legs.

teng-khɵ̀, cylindrical frame of a lantern.

khɵ̄ [R. hɵ, after, = col. āu]. **khɵ̄-liâm** (Cn.), = hɵ-liâm, very quickly.

khɵ́^{n} (Cn.), = A. khó, to examine, as at the literary examinations.

khö (Cn.), = A. khe, to investigate, &c. **khö-chhâ** (T.), to collect wood from many families for idolatrous rites.

khö-goā ê-tāi-chì, things with which one has no business to meddle. **kō-khö ê-tāi-chì**, id.

khō͘ (Cn.) **khō͘-sì^n**, = A. khê-sì^n, a fan made from a sort of leaf.

khō͘ (T.) **thiô-kha-khō͘**, to hop.

khō͘ (Cn.), = A. khé, to bow in a certain way; to worship, esp. ancestors. **khō͘-kong**, to worship ancestral tablets.

khoa (R. id.) **khoa-kháu**, to boast. **tsū-khoa**, to boast of one's self. **khoa-toā**, to boast of one's own greatness. **khoa-pù tàu-gâu** (L.), to boast of one's wealth and wisdom.

khoá [R. hú, to permit; a small quantity; a surname, = col. khó, khɵ́]. **sió-khoá**, small; unimportant; in small quantity; few in quantity. **sió-khoá-kúi**, a man who gets highly delighted at a very small gain or loan, &c.

khoà [R. khò, to run aground], to run aground. **khoà-ta**, to ground on shallows. **khoà sió-tsúi**, to get aground when the tides are growing smaller, so that it cannot get afloat till as long after neap tide. **tsûn khoà**, boat or vessel run aground.

khoà [R. khò, to lean or trust upon], to lean; to rest on; to recline; to lay down a thing steadily. **khoà-tiâu**, resting steadily on something. **khoà-thâu-khak**, to rest the head, as on a pillow. **khoà-kha**, to rest the leg, stretched out, as on a chair.

khoà--chih, to break accidentally by pressing on a thing.

khoà-î^n, to lay beams or rafters in their place. **ōe-khoà-mih^n**, things can be laid on it, *e.g.* on a chair, though it be broken. **chhiá^n khoà--teh**, please lay it down!

khoà (= koà), (C. khoè). **khoà-sim**, to be anxiously thoughtful. **khoà-liām**, id. **khoà-lī**, id. **khoà-lū**, id. (v. lū). **khoà-gāi**, anxious, as about a person or an affair (v. gāi).

bô-khoà-cheng, **kɵ̄-lap**, to be careless in doing something (v. cheng).

khoà— **bô-khoà-chiàh**, having no time even to eat, as man occupied with work or amusement. **bô-khoà thang-khì**, no leisure to go. **bô-khoà** (esp. C.), no leisure.

khoà (T.) **sang-khoà-khoà**, well-cooked and mealy.

khoā (cf. hoā). **khoā-khoā-háu**, the indistinct hum of a multitude, or of waves. **khoā-khoā-kiò**, id. **khoā-lâi khoā-khì**, surging back and forwards with an indistinct hum.

hàm-khoā-khoā, talking in an exaggerated or unreliable way; managing a matter in a careless or too easy way.

khoā-khoā-tán, to wait a long long time, as for news, &c.; generally with the idea of unwillingness or want of leisure.

khoā-khoā-lâi, to come in great numbers, as men or insects.

khin-khoā-khoā, in very great or too great haste. **khin-khōng-khoā**, id.

khoā-khoā-lìn, to roll about, as a ball, or as a child on the floor.

khoa^n [R. khoan, broad; to delay; forbearing]. **khoa^n-khoa^n**, slowly; leisurely. **khah-khoa^n-sī**, more leisurely. **khah-khoa^n-kiâ^n**, walk slower.

khoá^n [R. khoán, a sort]. **kúi-nā^n-khoá^n**, several times. **khioh-khoá^n**, to collect causes of displeasure till we have it out all at once.

khoá^n— **bīn ɵ-khoá^n**, face covered with large dark spots, as old man. **chhiū^n ɵ-khoá^n**, id.

khoà^n [R. khoài, easy; comfortable, = col. khoài^n], (Cn. khūi^n). **khoà^n-oàh**, comfortable.

khoà^n [R. khoan, khoat; cf. col. khoah, khoa^n], wide; large and spacious; extensive, as a piece of ground, or as a roomy house. **khoà^n-khn̂g**, spacious, as a house. **khui-khoà^n**, wide, open, and unobstructed, as a situation; broad; having plenty of spare room. **khoà^n-khoà^n**, id.; also, rather loose, as clothes, or as something tied loosely. **khoà^n-lòng-khoà^n-lòng**, too large and loose, as clothes. **khoà^n-long-long**, id.; also, large and spacious, as house that looks large and empty, or having abundance of room for guests. **khoà^n-kháu**, wide-mouthed, as sleeves or pocket.

khah-khoà^n-chhiú, using money freely. **khoà^n-pak tɵ̄-liōng**, liberal; generous; magnanimous. **tɵ̄-liōng khoan-khoà^n**, kind and liberal in manner.

khoà^n (R. khàn), to look; to look at; to regard; to watch; to guard; to read silently; to try; to examine, as a disease, or as fortune.

khoà^n--kì^n, to see. **khoà^n-kì^n-kì^n**, to see very plainly. **khoà^n-m̄-kì^n**, to look but not see. **khoà^n-bô-kì^n**, id. **khoà^n--lâng bô-kì^n**, to disdain to look at people, not recognizing them. **khoà^n-bô**, not able to see it. **khoà^n-bô-tiòh**, did not manage to see it; *e.g.* from coming too late, or not being near enough, &c., though it really was there. **khoà^n-bōe-tiòh**, unable to see it; *e.g.* from something obstructing the view.

khoà^n-khin, to despise. **khoà^n-lâng m̄-khí**, to treat a man with contempt. **khoà^n-chiū^n-bák**, to count of importance.

khoà^n--khí-lâi, to infer; to conclude from premises. **khoà^n-chhut**, to make out. **khoà^n-m̄-chhut**, cannot make it out. **khoà^n-phoà**, to see through, as an artifice or hollow appearance. **khoà^n-phoà sè-chêng**, to see through the vanity of the world. **khoà^n thàu-thàu**, to see clearly.

khoà^n-thâu, to keep watch, as sentry set by persons secretly engaged in some illegal, impure, or improper action; to protect from piracy, as pirates do for a yearly sum; to protect for a consideration, as a powerful patron does for a gambling-house, &c. **khoà^n-soa^n**, to protect fields from being plundered, as a powerful man does for a consideration, like a sort of black-mail. **khoà^n-bāng**, do. for nets at sea. **khoà^n-ka^n**, to guard a prison (v. ka^n). **khoà^n-koán**, to guard the outer prison. **khoà^n-mn̂g**, to watch a door. **khoà^n-tiàm**, to watch a shop. **khoà^n-ìn**, to take temporary charge of a mandarin's seals, using them for him in his absence.

khoà^n-sam-sek, to look neutral, waiting to see which side begins to win so as to join that side. **tāi-ke sa^n-khoà^n-iū^n**, following one another's example (v. iū^n). **tāi-ke sa^n-khoà^n**, id.; also, each waiting for the other to act first.

厦英大辭典

khoàⁿ-pīⁿ, to examine a patient's disease. khoàⁿ-chèng, id. khoàⁿ-lē̤, to pick out one's road in walking, as when wet or dark. tsáu-bé, khoàⁿ chin-tsu (to seek for pearls while riding fast), to miss seeing things because of haste.

khoàⁿ-miāⁿ, to tell fortunes. khoàⁿ-jit, to choose a lucky day. khoàⁿ-jit--ê, a fortune-teller who chooses lucky days.

khoàⁿ-thiⁿ thàn-chîⁿ, to do a fair business, not taking unjust gains. khoàⁿ-thiⁿ chiȧh-pn̄g, to live on honest gains. kiȧh-thâu khoàⁿ-thiⁿ, to act rightly; refusing to do wrong when it would seem advantageous. teh-khoàⁿ-thiⁿ, said of a man waiting idly, having no work to do. khoàⁿ-thiⁿ-sî, to look at the state of the weather.

khoàⁿ-chheh, to read a book silently. khoàⁿ pu̍t-jī, to examine and interpret the oracles written by a medium before an idol. khoàⁿ-hì, to look at plays. khoàⁿ-sin-niûⁿ, visitors going to see the bride for a day or two after marriage.

hó-khoàⁿ, beautiful; that looks well. pháiⁿ-khoàⁿ, ugly; bad-looking.

thau-khoàⁿ, to look stealthily; to peep. koan-khoàⁿ, to look steadily or attentively. khoàⁿ-kè̤, to watch over.

sûn-khoàⁿ, to inspect; to go round and examine. chhìm-khoàⁿ, to feel one's way very carefully, as in an affair (v. chhìm). liȧh-khoàⁿ, to measure by spans (v. liȧh, "to seize"). liȧh-khoàⁿ, to make a rough calculation. sǹg-khoàⁿ, to try a calculation. phēng-khoàⁿ, to compare two things so as to observe likeness or unlikeness. pí-khoàⁿ, id. chiȧh-khoàⁿ, to try the taste. siá-khoàⁿ, to try a pen or a man's skill in writing. chhì-khoàⁿ, to try; to make a trial; to try of what sort he or it is. khoàⁿ-bāi, id. thàm-khoàⁿ, to make inquiry or investigation, as a guide for action.

khoah [R. khoat, = col. khoàⁿ], broad, wide. khoah-toā, great and wide; to make wide-spread. kóng-khoah, widely extended, as region. khoan-khoah, spacious, as a house (v. khoan). khui-khoah, wide-spread; wide. khoah bóng-bóng, immense, as a flood. khoah-khǹg, large and wide, as a piece of ground. khoah-lòng, too large, as clothes. khoah-pak toā-liōng, very liberal and easy to have business dealings with. khoah-chhùi--ê, having a broad mouth (s. pick).

khoah (C. kiā). khoah-chhùi, a pick-axe (s. broad). khoah-chhùi-á, id., smaller.

khoah [R. khat, thirsty]. chí-khoah, to slake thirst. iau-khoah, hungry and thirsty. chhùi-khoah, thirsty. âu ta, chhùi khoah, very very thirsty. âu ta, chih khoah, id.

khoái [R. khoat, to stumble]. kiāⁿ-lē̤ khoái-khoái, always shaking to one side in walking, as lame or awkward man. khoái--chit-ē, khoái--chit-ē, id. pái-khoái, gone all wrong, as an affair mismanaged and ruined; to take an attitude of opposition or disobedience after being friendly or submissive. kap-goá teh-pái-khoái, he now disobeys or opposes me, contrary to what he used to do.

khoài [R. easy, pleased, comfortable, = col. khoàiⁿ, khoàⁿ, khùiⁿ], easy; quick; hasty in action, either on advice by another or on one's own idea. khoài-khoài, quick; be quick! mé̤ⁿ-khoài (C.), quickly; easily done. kín-khoài, easily done; can be easily done. khah-kín-khoài, be quick! kín-chiáp-khoài, nimble, active, vigorous, and ready in anything. khin-khoài, ready to help, do a favour, go together, &c., when asked. khoài-kóng, easily talked over; easily led to do a thing by asking; readily promising or granting a favour. khoài kóng-ōe, readily granting a favour or promising. bé, khoài-tióh-kiaⁿ, the horse readily starts. khoài-tsòe, easily done. khoài-piēn, easy; convenient; speedy at work (v. piēn).

khoài-sàu, a customs-boat; officer of such boat. khoài-théng, a swift mandarin lorcha. khoài-chhe, servants kept at yamuns for short messages. bé-khoài, the head of the police (or of the thieves!) in a ward, who catches thieves or recovers stolen property. khoài-pan, the low underlings of a yamun who have rooms on the left hand as you enter. khoài--pêng, that side of the yamun. tsô-khoài-pan, these underlings on both sides of the yamun. tsô-khoài-koán, all their rooms.

sóng-khoài, comfortable. thiòng-khoài, pleased and happy, as at some amusement or success. khoài-oȧh, comfortable (but in P. has a bad meaning). khoài-lo̍k, glad and happy. khoài-ì, pleased and joyful.

khoaiⁿ (cf. khoāiⁿ), sound of a gong. khoaiⁿ--chit-ē, shrill sound of a gong. khong-khoaiⁿ, noise of gongs in idolatrous rites.

khoàiⁿ [R. khoài, easy, = col. khoàⁿ, khùiⁿ]. khoàiⁿ-oȧh, comfortable.

khoāiⁿ (cf. khoaiⁿ), loud sound of a gong. khoāiⁿ--chit-ē, id., once. khoāiⁿ-khoāiⁿ-háu, loud sound of gongs.

khoan [R. broad; mild; indulgent; not severe, urgent, or exacting, = col. khoaⁿ, khoàⁿ]. khoan-khoan, deliberately; leisurely. chhiáⁿ-khoan--leh, take it easily, don't be in a hurry; let the matter lie over for a little. chhiáⁿ-khoan--chit-pē̤, id. chhiáⁿ pàng-khoan--teh, id. khoan-sim, mind quite easy; not anxious. chhiáⁿ-khoan-sim, keep your mind quite easy! khoan-ān, to allow further delay, as for work or payment. khoan-oān, id. khoan-sù, to act leniently (v. sù). khoan-iông, to allow, as slight faults; to let alone, as offender; long-suffering. khoan-liōng, to treat with indulgence or forbearance. khoan-hông tāi-liōng, id. (v. liōng).

khoan-khoah, large and spacious, as house or ground. tē̤-liōng khoan-khoah, liberal and kind; magnanimous. tē̤-liōng khoan-khoàⁿ, id.

khoan — chhia-khoan, capstan bars.

khoan (= khoân). ien-chhun-khoan, sort of tub for fighting quails.

khoân [R. poân, a bason; coiled up; cross-legged; = col. phoân, poâⁿ, phûn], (T. khûn). thiáp-khoân teh-chē, sitting cross-legged (= thiáp-phoân). kha thiáp-khoân, cross-legged.

khoân (R. id.), a circle; to mark with circular marks; to coil up, as a rope. îⁿ-khoân, a circle or loop.

khoân--khí-lâi, to coil up, as a rope. thiáp-khoân, to pile up, as several coils of rope one above another (s. cross-legged). khoân-lìn-tn̂g, to make a round or circle, coming back by a different way.

to-khoân, a sword-hilt. hiuⁿ-khoân, a spiral roll of incense which burns for several days. chháu-khoân, a small round straw cushion, used for kneeling on, or worn by beggars on the head. ien-chhun-khoân, a deep tub used as a pit for quails fighting. kiú-liên-khoân, a puzzle made with rings.

khoân-thò, a snare or trap.

khoân-tiám, to mark a book with dots and small circles at side of characters.

36

khoân (R. hoân). **chhiú-khoân**, a large ring, worn as an armlet. **kha-khoân**, rings worn by children round the ankles. **koà chhiú-khoân**, to wear armlets. **hī-khoân** (esp. T.), sort of ear-ring.

khoán (R. id.), appearance; manner; form; mode; pattern; sort; kind; to select or make up in sets; to get ready, as luggage.

khoán-thāi, to treat well or ill, esp. well (v. thāi).

khoán-sit, form; manner; pattern. **khoán-sek** (C.), id. **khoán-chè**, pattern; form; character or behaviour. **siāng-khoán**, alike. **hó-khoán**, of good behaviour. **chiâ^n-khoán**, id. **m̄-sī-khoán**, all wrong; conduct or work very bad. **sî-khoán**, customary fashion of the time. **khá-khoán**, beautifully or ingeniously made; very improper conduct (v. khá). **lâng-khoán**, a man's manner or conduct.

tiâu-khoán, stipulations or articles of an agreement.

pì^n-khoán, to change one's character or conduct for the worse. **tiu^n-khoán**, to put on a feigned appearance, *e.g.* of an emotion one does not feel. **lòh-khoán**, to write down (on an ornamental scroll of writing) one's own name, or the name of the friend to whom it is given. **lòh toa^n-khoán**, to write on it only the name of the writer. **lòh siang-khoán**, to write one's own name and the name of the friend to whom they are given, respectively on a pair of scrolls.

khioh-khoán, to collect causes of displeasure or hatred, till all come out at once.

khoán-kiā^n, to put in order a number of articles, either to be stowed away, or to be sent to some place. **khoán-khoà^n**, to examine all the things, and see if the number be correct. **khoán--khi chiâu-tiòh**, get the things all ready in proper order. **khoán-khǹg--teh**, packed away carefully in order. **khoán-lòh-siu^n**, put carefully into the box, article by article. **khoán-chheh**, to select books, *e.g.* making up a set, or arranging them when in confusion.

khoàn [R. to exhort, = col. khǹg]. **khoàn-siēn**, to exhort to virtue. **khoàn-sè-bûn**, Buddhist tracts. **khoàn-hô**, to exhort to peace. **khoàn-kái**, id.

khoat [R. to shut a door; to terminate]. **khoat-hók**, to fulfil the period of mourning.

khoat [R. to be wanting, = col. kheh, khih]. **khoat-hoát** (R.), in want.

khoe (R. id.), a helmet. **chit-téng-khoe**, one helmet. **khoe-kah**, helmet and coat of mail; defensive armour. **khoe-chhèng-bō**, a sort of soldier's cap.

thâu-khoe, a coarse yellow hemp cap, worn by sons at funeral of parent. **moâ^n-khoe**, id.

khoe [R. the pole-star; the god of it; a chief or first of a class]. **khoe-seng**, the god of the north star, attendant on Wen-chang, the god of literature; also much worshipped by literary men. **khoe-seng-kong**, id. **khoe-seng that-táu**, do. represented as kicking the dipper (measure). **khoe-seng-lâu**, pagoda for his worship, close to Confucian temple. **thiàu-khoe-seng**, to hop about on one leg, as he is represented.

bûn-khoe, any literary Kujin. **bú-khoe**, any military Kujin. **à-khoe**, Kujin from the second to the tenth or twelfth on the list. **keng-khoe**, do. from second to about the fifth. **hōe-khoe**, Tsin-sze graduates from second to tenth on list. **tāi-khoe thien-hā**, to become "chiōng-goân," the very highest literary rank.

khoe-thâu, the head end of a coffin. **khoe-bóe** (C.), foot end of do. **khoe-thâu-bóe** (C.), the two ends of it.

khoe, to scrape, as with a knife. **khoe-mn̂g**, to scrape the hair off an animal to be cooked (s. river). **khoe-tiá^n**, to scrape a frying-pan.

khoe — **khoe-sóe**, to get small sums of money, or some food, tobacco, &c., from a man, by sorning on him against his will.

khoe (R. khe), (C. khe; Cn. khöe), a river; a stream. **khoe-pe̍**, uncultivated river banks liable to be flooded. **khoe-mn̂g**, the mouth of a valley (s. scrape). **khoe-lâu**, the current of the river.

khoe-phiàh, sort of flat-bottomed river-boat with a mast. **khöe-pih** (Cn.), very shallow boat for poling up rivers.

khoe (C.) **khoe-sì^n**, = A. khe-sì^n, a fan made of a sort of palm-leaf.

khoe (C.) **kāu-khoe-hâi** (= A. khe), inconstant and unreliable, &c. (v. hâi).

khôe (C. khê). **kāu-khôe**, peevish; fretful; bad-tempered, esp. of child that will not be pleased whatever you do.

khôe (C.), = A. khê, deformed or shrivelled, as a limb.

khóe (C.), = A. khé, to bow as a woman, with the hands near the body.

khòe (C. khè; Cn. khöe), to gnaw. **bah, hē-lâng-chiàh; kut, m̄-chiâ^n hē-lâng-khòe**, said of allowing a friend to be slightly injured, but defending him against great violence or oppression.

khòe (C. khoà; P. khoè), luxuriant, as grass or herbage, or as green growing corn, or as hair.

khòe (R. khè), (C. khè; Cn. khöe), a deed of sale or of mortgage.

khòe-pē, a man taken as a sort of patron, somewhat like an adoptive father, but not so intimate a relation. **khòe-bú**, woman somewhat like adoptive mother. **khòe-kiá^n**, young man taken under protection, somewhat like adopted son, but not so close. **khòe-toā-chí**, woman treated like adoptive elder sister. **khòe-sió-bē**, id., younger. **khòe-bē**, id. **khòe-án-hia^n**, man taken as sort of elder brother. **khòe-sió-tī**, id., younger. **kiet-khòe** (r.), to make agreement to treat as brother or sister.

khòe-hia^n, paramour of bad woman. **khöe-tē** (Cn.), a sodomite.

lip-khòe, to make a formal deed of sale, or mortgage, or bottomry bond. **chiū^n-khòe**, to write additional particulars in a deed, *e.g.* about large trees on ground, or large articles in a room, or such pendicles. **chīn-khòe-bé**, to sell without power of redemption.

khòe-koàn, deeds of sale or mortgage. **khòe-kù**, do. used as evidence. **tsé-khòe**, a deed inherited from ancestors. **sin-khòe-jī**, deed of sale of a slave girl. **chhân-khòe**, deed for fields. **chhù-khòe**, deed for house. **tién-khòe**, deed of mortgage. **sè-khòe**, deed of sale having the mandarin's stamp on it (v. sè). **pèh-thâu-khòe**, an unstamped deed. **âng-khòe**, document affixed as proof of registration.

khòe [R. khò, an essay, exercise, work, &c.] **jit-khòe** (C.), = A. jit-khò, a document given by a fortune-teller fixing the auspicious days for the rites connected with marriage.

kang-khòe (C.), = A. khang-khè, work of any sort.

khoè (C.), = A. khoà. **khoè-hē**, to lay down, as a thing.

厦英大辭典

khŏe [R. khoài, easy]. **khŏe-piēn** (Cn.), having an easy delivery, as a woman (to be distinguished from "khoài-piēn," which has the same meanings as in A.)

khoeh [R. khap, id., = col. kah, ka], (C. kheh; Cn. khöeh), to shut, as the eyes. **khoeh-bák**, to shut the eyes. **bák-chiu pàng-khoeh**, id. **bák-chiu khoeh-khoeh**, eyes almost shut, as very sleepy or in some disease. **sí-liáu, bák-m̄-khoeh** (though dead, the eyes will not close), the affair, though now quiet, will come up again and cause trouble. **sí, bák m̄-goān-khoeh**, id.

khoeh [R. kiap, to squeeze; to take up with pincers, = col. ngoeh, ngeh, hiahⁿ], (C. kheh; Cn. khöeh), to press, as between two boards, or between the nails, or in a sugar-mill or oil-press; to split peas by putting them through a sort of loose-set mill; crowded, as men; to jostle.

oe-khoeh (C. e-kheh), to crowd and jostle. **oe-oe khoeh-khoeh**, id.; very crowded and pushing each other. **ȯeh-khoeh**, much crowded, so as to be scant of room.

khoeh-iû, to press oil out of seeds. **khoeh-chià**, to press sugar-cane in a mill. **khoeh sat-bú**, to kill a louse between the nails.

khoeh [R. kiap, a sort of box], (C. kheh; Cn. khöeh). **khoeh-á**, a small box, *e.g.* with a sliding lid. **hé-hiāⁿ-khoeh**, a tinder-box. **chiam-khoeh**, a very small box for needles. **chièn-áp-khoeh**, a small box with compartments, for offerings of sweetmeats, fruits, &c.

khoeh (C.), = A. kheh, to want.

khoeh (= khȯeh). (T.) **khiām-khoeh**, very economical.

khȯeh (cf. ngȯeh), to be pinched or crushed, as by a door or by the boards of a bed. **saⁿ-khȯeh**, to be crushed by each other, *e.g.* as fruits in a bag. **khȯeh-lâi khȯeh-khì**, id. **khit-mn̂g khȯeh--tiȯh**, to be pinched by a door.

khȯeh tī-tiong-ng, to lie closely pressed between them, as a small house, district, or state between two larger ones.

khȯeh (cf. ngȯeh). **kha-khȯeh**, sort of wooden stocks for the feet. **khȯeh kha-bák**, to torture the ancles by squeezing [same as former word ?].

khȯeh (R. hák). **chhiûⁿ-khȯeh**, a frame used for building mud-walls.

khȯeh — **hì-khȯeh**, a sort of clown in a play, = thiú (said of a man who makes so much ceremony as to provoke laughter, or who talks ludicrously to amuse others).

khȯeh (= khoeh). (T.) **khiām-khȯeh**, very parsimonious.

khȯeh (C.), to boil down a fluid, making it thicker. **khȯeh-khȯeh**, well-boiled and soft, as rice neither too thick nor too thin.

khöh (T.) **kiaⁿ-khöh-khöh**, shaking with fear (cf. gėh, khȧuh, &c.)

khok [R. to weep and lament, = col. khàu]. **khok-san-tiōng**, mourning-staff carried by widower at wife's funeral (v. tiōng). **khok-lāi seng-tsú**, to beget a child in the hundred days of deepest mourning for a parent, considered criminal.

khok — **khok-jí**, small rounded (spherical) bits of stone or tile, like marbles, used by children in play. **chiȯh-khok-jí**, id. **chiauh khok-jí**, to throw them up in play.

khok [R. sound of a hard stone]. **tēng khok-khok**, very hard, as strongly-made furniture, or as a hard cake, &c. **khok-khok-tân**, sound of a hard thing struck.

khok (R. id.) **bák-chiu sut-khok sut-khiet**, eyes glancing about rapidly. **bák-chiu sek-khok sek-khiak**, id.

khok — **nn̂g-sng-khok**, coming to the point very gradually, as in a bargain, &c. (v. nn̂g).

khok [R. to expand; to enlarge]. **khok-chhiong** (R.), to expand, as knowledge.

khok [R. wide, large; to enlarge]. **khok-thâu**, having an unusually projecting forehead. **khok-hiȧh**, id. **thâu-khok khah-toā**, forehead projecting very much.

khok-á-lȧ, sort of large cap worn by children.

khok [R. khak, a shell]. **pėh-thâu-khok**, a small white-headed bird (= C. pėh-thâu-á).

khok [R. cruel; excessive, = col. khȯ]. **khok-hêng**, severe, as torture; cruel or oppressive, as mandarin. **khok-tȯk**, very cruel towards an inferior, esp. to female slave or daughter-in-law.

khok--lâng pan-gî, to drive too hard a bargain, cheapening down too much. **khok-lí-kùi**, he is forcing you to pay too much because you urgently need what he only can furnish.

khok (Cn.), = khȯk. **phah-khok**, to beat the watchman's rattle.

khök (Cn.) **khök-hō͘**, = A. khiet-hé, to strike a light with a flint.

khȯk (cf. khȧuh, khȧh). **khȯk-khȯk-kiû**, to beg hard over and over for a thing. **khȯk-khȯk-pài**, to bow low over and over. **khȯk-khȯk-kūi**, to kneel over and over. **khȯk-khȯk-hė**, teeth chattering (v. hė).

khȯk (Cn. khok, khȯk), a hollow instrument of wood or bamboo, somewhat like a rattle, used by watchmen and priests. **kiⁿ-khȯk**, a watchman's rattle. **chiú-kiⁿ-khȯk**, id. **phah kúi-kiⁿ-khȯk**, how many strokes does the watchman strike? equal to the number of the watch. **phah-khȯk**, to beat the rattle.

kòng-khȯk (to beat the rattle), to conspire to gamble or otherwise swindle a man out of his money; to talk empty stories or jokes, often licentious.

cheng-khȯk, bell and rattle used by priests; also those hung at a child's wrist to keep off evil influences. **cheng-khȯk-á**, those used by children. **khȯk-thûi**, the clapper of a watchman's rattle.

khȯk — **saⁿ-khȯk**, to come knocking together with a sharp ring. **thâu-khak saⁿ-khȯk**, heads knocking together, as in the dark. **khȯk-khȯk-khȯk**, said of a hammer striking gently on a chisel, *e.g.* to break a tile, &c.

khih-khih khȯk-khȯk, sound of stone-cutting, or of horses and chariots, &c. **khiâ-bé khȯk-khȯk**, to ride along, making a noise with the hoofs. **khiâ-bé khih-khȯk**, id.

khȯk, to talk together in an improper, idle, or licentious manner, as man and woman. **toà-teh-khȯk**, engaged in such an improper conversation.

lȯk-khȯk, abandoned to licentious ways; idle and pleasure-seeking. **lȯk-lȯk khȯk-khȯk**, id.; gadding about, often to improper places; very unsafe to deal with, as a man who does not keep his promises. **lȯk-khȯk-bé, bô-koà-oaⁿ** (horse sporting about with no saddle), said of a young idle fellow going about doing what he pleases, with no one to keep him in order, generally fond of bad pleasures.

khok — **khok-hî**, the fish on which Khoe-seng is represented standing as it saved him from drowning; a small figure of it worn by children. **khok-á-hî**, small figure of a fish, worn by children, of the same shape as the "bók-gû" of Buddhist temples. **pûi náⁿ-khok-á-hî**, as fat as that figure of a fish (said of man or pig). **chiáh kah-náⁿ khok-á-hî**, said of a man who is very fat and strong.

khom (P.), **khom-siū**, = A. thong-siū, to put the hands into the opposite sleeves.

khôm (C.), = A. khâm, large cymbals.

khong [R. peace; excellent; a surname, = col. khng], a surname, = khng. **khong-goân-sòe**, an idol, attendant on Tāi-tō-kong.

khong-hi, the reign of the Emperor Kang-he (v. hi).

khong-kiēn, strong and healthy (said of an old man).

khong — **khong-khiang-á** (C.), a very small fish, like the "hoe-thiâu," but smaller.

khong (C.) **khong-siū**, = A. thong-siū, to put the hands into the sleeves of the other hands.

khong — **khong-khoaiⁿ**, sound of gongs in idolatrous ceremonies.

khong [R. ignorant; simple]. **khong-khám**, stupid; wanting in ability.

khong [R. hollow; empty, = col. khang], name applied by the vegetarians to the object of their worship, perhaps the empty expanse of heaven. **thien khong, tē khong, jîn iàh-khong**, heaven, earth, and man are all emptiness, a vegetarian phrase. **poàn-khong-tiong**, in mid-heaven, in the sky, as birds, or as spirits. **thêng-khong**, to ascend to the sky.

khai-khong bô-giàh, to embezzle or mis-spend employer's money, so as not to be able to give an account of it (v. khai). **khèng-khong**, quite spent and exhausted, as property. **it-chîn khèng-khong**, all one's money and property lost or spent. **sam-tāi liàp-chek, it-tàn khèng-khong**, the accumulations of three generations spent in one morning.

khong, to put on a hoop or edging of metal; to paste paper round, as round a stick of fine incense. **khong-tâng**, to put on a hoop or edging of brass. **khong-kim**, to put on a gold edging, as round a picture. **khong-thih**, to fasten with an iron hoop or band.

khóng [R. open; excellent; a surname], a surname. **khóng-tsú**, Confucius. **khóng-hú-tsú**, id. **khóng-bēng**, Confucius and Mencius. **khóng-bêng**, a famous man in the time of the three kingdoms (v. bêng).

khóng-chhiok, the peacock (v. chhiok).

chhit-khóng, the seven orifices of the head: the mouth, eyes, ears, and nostrils. **chhit-khóng liû-hiet**, blood flowing from mouth and nose (v. hiet).

khóng [previous word? cf. khang, kháng]. **gán-khóng toā**, haughty (v. gán).

khóng — **bân-khóng**, firmly fixed; strongly made and lasting, as a piece of work; safe, as a mercantile house.

khóng (R. id.) **khóng-khài**, liberal in spending money; having an easy self-confident bearing. **khóng-kau**, hospitable; fond of giving or attending entertainments.

khòng — **lòng-khòng**, too large and wide, as clothes (v. lòng).

khòng [R. the sound of stones striking together; cf. col. khōng]. **khín-khín khòng-khòng**, noise, as of repairs, or of children, &c. (v. khín).

khòng (cf. khōng, khok). **khòng-khòng-pūi**, loud constant barking. **khòng-khòng-pê**, scratching one's self hard and constantly. **khòng-khòng-lâi**, always coming. **khòng-khòng-pài**, to be making a great many bows. **gōng kiáⁿ-sài, jip-mn̂g khòng-khòng-pài**, said of a bridegroom making his first visit to his wife's relatives and bowing to everyone.

khòng (C.) **âng-khòng-khòng**, = A. âng-kòng-kòng, very red.

khòng [R. a pit; a mine, = col. khàng, khàng], the pit of a grave. **bōng-khòng**, id. **bōng-khòng-khang**, the cavity of an old grave. **thô-khòng**, pit of grave made with earth without lime. **he-khòng**, id., made with lime. **khòng-khut**, the rough opening of a grave, esp. of old grave (v. khut).

khui-khòng, to dig a grave. **lòh-khòng**, to lay (the coffin) in the grave. **siāng-khòng**, buried in the same grave.

kim-khòng, a gold mine.

khòng [R. waste; desert; unoccupied, = col. khàng]. **khòng-iá**, a wilderness (v. iá). **pîⁿ-iûⁿ khòng-thé**, an extensive plain.

khòng [R. khong, empty, = col. khang], a cypher, used in speaking, as a cypher is in writing. **sì-pah khòng-saⁿ**, four hundred and three. **thiu khòng-ngé**, to take off a commission of 5 per cent.

khui-khòng bô-giàh, to embezzle, so as to be unable to account for all the money.

khòng [R. to cook by roasting; a heated couch, = col. khàng], to boil or stew very soft. **khòng-khi-noāⁿ**, boil it very thoroughly, till it is quite soft. **khòng-tôe**, pig's feet boiled soft. **khòng-chhài**, long turnips boiled and salted.

khòng-chhn̂g, a couch made for two persons to sit on, used as an honourable seat for guests; said also of a sofa. **khòng-chhn̂g-kí**, the small low broad table like a stool set on the couch between the guests.

khòng [R. khong, ignorant; simple]. **khòng-gōng**, having a proud bearing.

khòng (R. id.) **khòng-hān**, = khó-oāⁿ, a great drought.

khòng [R. to oppose; to refuse; to resist], to deduct from rent or wages, &c.; to refuse to pay it. **khòng-khiàm**, to refuse to pay what one owes. **khit--i khòng--khì**, to lose money on a bad debt. **khòng-niûⁿ**, to refuse payment of land-tax. **khòng-chhù-tsoe**, to deduct a sum from the rent, *e.g.* for repairs.

khòng-kū, to oppose a lawful authority rebelliously or disobediently.

khòng [R. to enter an accusation]. **khòng-kò**, to institute a legal process against another. **hoan-khòng**, to raise again a case that has been settled. **siōng-khòng**, to raise an action in a superior court (like an appeal). **kiaⁿ-khòng**, to enter an accusation in one of the supreme boards at the capital, as an appeal.

khòng [R. the throat]. **toā-âu-khòng**, having a voice that can be heard at a distance. **ū-âu-khòng**, id. **bô-âu-khòng**, having but little voice and unable to sing high notes. **kek-âu-khòng**, to exert one's self so as to speak with an unnaturally loud voice, as an actor.

khōng — **ioh chià-khōng,** to guess the lengths of the pieces of a bit of sugar-cane broken as a game.

khōng (cf. khòng). **khīn-khōng,** sound of heavy things moved about, or of noisy children. **khīn-khōng-háu,** id. **khin-khōng-khoā,** in great haste, or too great haste.

khōng-táu, a sieve shaped like a basket which shakes about in a mill. **khōng-khiang,** unsteady gait, as of a woman with bound feet.

khōng-khōng-háu, sound, as of a rice-mortar, or of door or window shaking, or of beating moderately hard on a table. **khōng-khōng-hién,** to shake about, as an unsteady table or a restless child. **khōng-khōng-pài,** constantly making ceremonial bows (v. pài).

khu (R. khiu), a surname.

khu [R. the body]. **sin-khu,** the body (v. sin). **seng-khu,** id.

khu [R. to grasp; to restrain; to adhere obstinately]. **khu-sok,** to keep under strict discipline, as pupil, younger relative, or slave. **khu-ah,** to keep in ward, as a criminal, or as a party in a case. **khu-kìm,** to hold in durance; to keep from doing something, either by actual force or by intimidation. **tiā^n-tiā^n khu-teh,** kept under very strict discipline, as children, pupils, or apprentices, not allowed to go out, &c.

khu-chip, obstinate. **u-khu,** dogged and troublesome to deal with; unsociable, not caring to go about with friends; very cautious and afraid of taking action. **khu-khien,** too strict about ceremonies. **bô-khu-lé,** not standing on ceremony. **put-khu-lé,** id. **put-khu,** no matter which. **put-khu-sî,** at any time. **put-khu-tsúi,** mix just as much water as you please, as in medicine.

khu (R. khiu), a small piece of ground; classifier of fields. **chhân-khu,** rice-fields in general. **iâm-khu,** salt-pans made on the sand for natural evaporation. **sa^n-khu-chhân,** three irrigated fields; name of the garden jetty on Kolongsoo.

khu [R. to drive away]. **khu-siâ,** to expel evil influences (v. siâ).

khu [R. rough and hilly]. **khi-khu** (R.), rough to walk upon, as a mountain path. **soa^n-niá^n khi-khu,** rough mountain paths.

khû, to sit on one's haunches; to squat or crouch; to go to stool. **kia^n kàu-khû-kha,** so much afraid as to draw one's self together. **khû-hák,** to go to stool outside. **khû-tháng,** do. in the house.

khū (R. kú). **koe-kha-khū** (T.), = A. koe-kū, a cock's spur.

khù (T.), = A. khì, to go (said especially in the villages of Amoy island and the adjoining parts of the mainland, elsewhere shading into "khì" or "khū").

khū (Cn. T.), = A. khì, to go.

khū [R. to fear], (C. kì). **ùi-khū** (R.), to fear greatly. **khū-phà^n,** id.

khū — **khū-khū-tân,** sound as of thunder. **khū-khū-háu,** id.; also, to purr, as a cat; sound of phlegm in the throat that cannot be brought up; sound of wind in the belly. **pak-tó-lāi khih-khih khū-khū,** rumbling sound of wind in the belly.

khū (R. kiū), classifier of coffins.

khū (R. kiū), a mortar only for cleaning rice by pounding or working up dough (not for triturating); the socket of a door, &c. **tùi-khū,** a large stone mortar for cleaning rice (worked by the foot). **cheng-khū,** a stone mortar for pounding, worked by the hand, for rice or dough. **chióh-cheng-khū,** id. **cheng-khū-á,** a small do. **cheng-khū-thûi,** a pestle for such a mortar.

lut-khū, to dislocate. **chhiú-khū,** the wrist when used to press one's weight on something by the wrist (some say the elbow); also, a hand-mortar for pounding. **chhiú-khū-á,** a hand-mortar. **kha-khū,** the ankle in regard to cutting off. **tái^n kha-khū,** to cut off the foot at the ankle, as of a robber. **ām-kún-khū,** the prominent lump at the back of the neck where the back-bone joins. **bák-kháng-khū,** the socket of the eye.

mn̂g-khū, the lower socket of a Chinese door (used instead of a hinge). **mn̂g-āu-khū,** id. **mn̂g-téng-khū,** the upper socket at the lintel. **chē-khū,** the lower socket worn away so much (or the pivot of the door worn away), so that the door settles down too much.

khū [R. kū, an instrument]. **khì-khū,** implements; instruments. **khàng-khū,** fittings and instruments of a vessel. **hêng-khū,** instruments of torture.

khúh — **khúh-khúh-sàu,** constant coughing.

khúh — **ûn-á-khúh,** to let a thing boil slowly after it has been brought a-boil (by taking away some fuel), so as to boil it down to greater consistency. **hē-i-khúh,** id. (cf. khóeh).

khui (R. khai), to open; open; to begin; to make out, as an account or a money-charge, or a prescription; to dig, as a well or grave; to set sail; to remove, as a prohibition; to prepare for use, as a fruit, by taking off the skin; to fire a gun.

khui-lō͘, to open a road. **khui-tō,** to clear the way before a mandarin going out. **hûn khui,** the clouds breaking up.

khui-hī^n, to make an ink-stone. **khui-khang,** to make a hole or opportunity (v. khang). **khui-hiėt,** to dig a grave. **khui-khòng,** id. **khui-chí^n,** to dig a well.

khui-chhe, to branch into two (v. chhe). **khui-kheng,** joints (as of a table) opening out. **khui-chhiò,** the sails of two masts set on the opposite sides of the masts (v. chhiò). **khui-bé,** having an open stern (as boat) instead of having boards as bulwarks there. **khui-kha-khò͘,** wide trousers for children with no seat. **khui-pō͘ kiâ^n,** to walk with long strides (v. pō͘).

khui-sia^n, to speak distinctly and clearly. **khui-sia^n thák,** to read with a clear voice. **khui-sia^n khàu,** to lament for the dead with a loud voice.

khui-chhùi, to begin to speak of a matter; to make the first offer of a price (v. chhùi). **khui-chhiú,** to give something extra on engaging a man for some work, *e.g.* entrance-fee to teacher. **khui-chhiú-lé,** the extra sum thus given. **khui-chhiú chiū-phah,** he struck him at once without allowing him to make any explanation. **khui-pit-lé,** the first fee to a teacher when he begins to draw out the first accusation in a legal case (v. pit). **khui-chhân,** to begin cultivating the ground. **khui-tsûn,** to set sail. **khui-pî,** whetting the appetite (v. pî). **khui-pî^n,** to play a play without being paid, as a company of actors do on coming to a place to show what they can do. **khui-chhau,** to commence a military review. **khui-óh,** to open a school; to start a school. **khui-chhī,** to commence the sales of the day or of the year. **khui-tiàm,** to set up a shop. **khui-hâng,** to open or have a warehouse (v. hâng).

khui-ìn, to take up business again in a court after the holidays. **khui-kìm,** to remove a prohibition. **khui-tē,** to remove the prohibition of killing animals. **khui-chho,** to give up vegetarianism.

khui-chhèng, to fire a gun. **khui-keng**, to draw a bow in order to shoot.

khui-hoe, to flower. **sim-hoe khui**, pleased; delighted. **sim-koa^n m̄-khui**, heart very anxious or sad. **sim-koa^n khah-khui**, grief or anxiety somewhat allayed.

khui-thiah, to explain. **khui hō͘-i-thia^n**, explain to him the reasons for settling the dispute. **ū-khui-chhú**, a way is open for a reasonable and amicable settlement (v. chhú). **khui-kōe** (Cn.), to explain more minutely. **khui-khiàu**, to develop a pupil's mind well (v. khiàu).

khui-miâ^n, to report names, as to an official. **khui io̍h-hng**, to write out a prescription. **khui-toa^n**, to make out an account. **khui-khioh**, to apportion the sums which each must pay for some common object. **khui bô-giàh**, unable to account fully for money or goods intrusted, as from forgetting, or from having given too good weight in selling; with no idea of dishonesty. **khui bô-tin**, do. do. **khui-khòng bô-giàh**, do. with idea of embezzlement. **kong-khui**, to share the expenses. **kong-ēng kong-khui**, to use in common and share expenses. **bô-ke-khui**, not charging more than the real price or sum spent. **ū-siàu chiàu-khui**, to put down all the items honestly, as of goods sold or of expenses paid. **chiàu-khui**, id.; also, to divide into equal parts.

khui-khoah, wide; wide-spread. **khui-khoà^n**, wide open and unobstructed, as a place.

the-khui, to decline politely to meddle with an affair. **pun-khui**, to divide; to separate. **lī-khui**, to leave; to go away; to be distant. **lī khui-khui**, very far distant. **chhoe-gō͘ kè-khui**, after the 5th of the month is past. **khiā-khui**, to stand out of the way. **siám-khui**, to get out of the way. **tsáu-khui**, to run out of the way. **giâ-khui**, to carry out of the way, as a chair, &c. **that-khui**, to kick out of the way; to kick open. **peh-khui**, to break open with the hands. **phoà-khui**, to burst open (v. phoà).

khui [R. deficient; to injure]. **khek-khui**, to treat unjustly, especially as to money matters. **khek-khui chit-poà^n**, each bearing half the loss, as of something broken or lost. **siū-khui**, to suffer injustice. **khui-sún**, to injure. **khui-hū**, to betray trust; to act injuriously and ungratefully (v. hū). **khui-pún**, to sell for less than cost price, so as to lose capital.

khui-sim, very unfair, wicked, and faithless, *e.g.* refusing to pay debts, or abandoning one's wife. **khui-sim-sū**, extremely injurious behaviour, *e.g.* great frauds, scattering of families, adultery, &c. **khui-sim-tāi**, id.

khúi (R. id.) **khúi-khiet** (R.), deceitful; intriguing. **khúi-tsà** (R.), id.

khùi [R. ashamed]. **iú-khùi**, ashamed of one's self. **péng-sim bû-khùi**, of unimpeachable integrity, having no cause for shame. **khùi-sú bû-tē** (R.), very much put to shame before the world.

khùi (C.) **sù-khùi**, = A. sù-kùi, the four seasons.

khùi [R. khì, vapour; odour; flavour; breath; physical constitution, character, &c.], breath, &c. **sng-khùi sng-khùi**, having a sour smell or flavour.

khùi-thâu, ostentatious, as in dress or manner; appearance of a wealthy or influential man. **ū-khùi-thâu**, to have a strong pleasant odour, as tea; to have power or influence, or the appearance of it. **kek-khùi**, to put on too haughty an air, as a man of wealth, rank, or influence; or to make one's self appear of importance. **kek-goā-khùi**, to make one's self seem important, as by fine clothes, &c. (v. goā).

tsoeh-khùi (C. cheh-khì), the 24 terms of the solar year at half-monthly intervals.

khùi-la̍t, strength (v. la̍t). **khùi-be̍h** (T.), = A. khì-me̍h^n, the pulse. **bô-khùi bô-me̍h^n**, very weak, as old or sick man; quite exhausted, as with hard running.

chhoán-khùi, to breathe (v. chhoán). **pûn-khùi**, to blow out one's breath. **thó͘-khùi**, to sigh. **tháu-khùi** (C.), id. **hip kàu-bô-khùi--khì**, covered up so as to have no air, as under a coverlet, or as in a close confined crowded room or cabin. **tsáu kau-bô-khùi--khì**, to run till very much exhausted and out of breath. **tsáu kàu chêng-khùi chiap-m̄-tio̍h āu-khùi** (= chih-m̄-tio̍h), to run till the one breath cannot overtake the other, till quite out of breath. **chhiò kàu-bōe-tńg-khùi**, to laugh till quite out of breath. **tit-khùi**, a very long inspiration or expiration. **ien tit-khùi**, steam coming out in a strong steady jet. **pûn tit-khùi**, to give a long expiration. **tit-khùi--khì**, panting with long expirations and short inspirations, as when about to die, &c. **chia̍h tit-khùi**, to take a very long inspiration, as in smoking.

sah^n sim-khùi, mind very much moved with desire for a thing, good or bad. **phō sim-khùi**, to have a sudden feeling of pain at heart, like stoppage of breath, or almost fainting, as in great and sudden fear or anxiety at a critical moment, or just after the excitement of the crisis has passed; often so as to perplex or confuse, and unfit one for the very thing that should be done.

lún-khùi, to repress the manifestation of anger. **khùi chhiong-thi^n**, very very angry, and showing it. **chhi^n-bé-khùi**, having violent passions or irascible temper, so as to be ungovernable, or always quarrelling.

chit-khùi-á, a very short time. **thêng-khùi**, to pause for a short time.

kè-khùi, to die. **tn̂g-khùi**, id. **khùi-tn̂g**, just dead. **khùi-tsoa̍t**, id. **sa^n-chhùn-khùi-tn̂g**, id. (lit. the three inches of breath). **chit-tiâu-khùi iáu-bē-tn̂g**, just a breath between him and death, as very old or sick man.

khūi^n (Cn.) **khūi^n-oàh**, = A. khoài^n-oàh, comfortable.

khun [R. earth; the feminine or Yin principle]. **khiên-khun** (R.), heaven and earth. **lêng-khun-tan**, sort of pills used for diseases of females.

khun [R. to scrape off], to shave a second time, so as to make quite smooth; to go over a second time where wood has been cut, gleaning up all that is left.

khun [R. an elder brother]. **khun-tiōng**, brothers, elder and younger.

khun [R. name of a mountain; name of the city of Kwen-shan, near Shanghai, of great literary fame]. **khun-lûn-soa^n**, the Kwen-lun mountain, near the source of the Yellow River, the most sacred of mountains.

khun-khiang, songs in mandarin colloquial. **chhiù^n-khun**, to sing them. **chhiù^n-khun-khiang**, id.

khûn (R. id.), (C. khîn), diligent; laborious. **khûn-sim**, id. **khûn-kín**, id. **khûn-khiām**, diligent and economical. **khûn-khó͘**, extremely diligent (v. khó͘). **khûn-kang**, diligent at work. **khûn ēng-kang**, to study or read long and diligently. **khûn-tha̍k**, to study hard. **khûn-sim-tha̍k**, id. **khûn iú-kong**, diligence has benefit.

un-khûn, courteous and kindly, as in receiving guests.

khûn (C. khîn), a tree with a bunch of large glossy pinnate leaves at the top.

khûn (R. id), (C. khîn). **khûn-chhài**, celery. **chhái-khûn** (R.), to become a Sew-tsai.

khûn (T.) **thiáp-khûn teh-chē** (= A. khoân), to sit cross-legged.

khûn (R. id.), to coil, as a rope or snake; winding, as road; to work figures in braid; a stack, as of corn, hay, or wood.

tiū-khûn, a heap or stack of cut rice.

khûn-khûn--teh, coiled up, as a rope, &c. **un-lun-khûn**, coiled up, as a snake, or as a cat or dog lying with its tail turned round to its head.

khûn kau-hûn, to lay on braid in the form of hooked or looped figures (of different colour) on the border of a dress; it is then pasted on, and sewed down firmly; the sewing is properly "tèng," but the whole operation is called "khûn-kau-hûn." **khûn bān-jī**, to work figures of braid in the form called "bān-jī."

khún (R. id.), to bind with a cord, as a bundle; a bundle, sheaf, or bale. **khún-pák**, to bind with a cord, as hands or feet. **pau-khún**, to wrap and tie up. **pau-khún-khi-hó**, wrap and tie it up tight. **khún-soh**, to tie up with a rope, as a parcel or box; a sort of rope used for this. **khún-chhiòh**, to tie up a number of mats (gen. about fifty) in one bundle.

khún-á, a small bundle tied up. **bėh-khún**, a sheaf of wheat or barley. **chit-khún-tsoá**, several bundles of paper tied together.

khún [R. to cultivate new land]. **khai-khún**, to clear waste land, and bring it into cultivation.

khún [R. importunate, to beg earnestly]. **khún-kiû**, to request very earnestly. **khún-chhiet**, earnestly; urgently. **khún-ì**, pressing a guest to stay when he is leaving.

khún [R. straitened; distressed; urgent]. **khún-pek**, to harass; to persecute. **khún-tiòk** (R.), to expel; (X.), to persecute. **khún--lâng**, to force a man to pay too much for goods or labour, because we have the only supply of what he needs.

khún (R. thún). **khún-khún** (T.), = A. pûi-thún, short, stout, and corpulent. **khún-tàu-khún-tàu** (T.), id.

khùn [R. miserable; confined], to besiege. **ûi-khùn**, to surround or besiege, as an army or a city.

khùn-khé, very miserable. **khùn-koān** (R.), very tired and exhausted.

khùn, to sleep; to lie at rest; to sleep on or in. **hioh-khùn**, to rest or stop a little. **heh^{n}-khùn** (C.), id. **khiā-khùn**, to sleep standing. **chiah-kú teh-khiā-khùn**, a long time out of employment.

khùn khí, sleeping and waking; at all times. **khùn-khí**, to rise from sleep. **khùn-chhí^{n}**, to wake from sleep (v. chhí^{n}). **khùn-pá**, having slept enough. **tsá-khùn**, to go to bed early. **oà^{n}-khùn**, to go to bed late. **ài-khùn**, sleepy. **mí^{n}-mí^{n}-khùn**, always falling asleep as soon as wakened. **khùn-chhī-chhī**, sleeping very sound. **toā-khùn sió-sí**, very very sleepy. **tāng-bîn-khùn**, to sleep soundly. **khùn-bōe-lòh-bîn**, lying, but unable to sleep. **hó-khùn**, to sleep well; good for sleeping in or on. **phái^{n}-khùn**, restless in sleep; unpleasant to sleep in or on.

ōe-khùn kúi-lâng, for how many persons is there room to sleep? **khùn-tsa-bó**, to sleep with a bad woman.

khùn-bāng, to sleep so as to get an oracle in a dream. **khùn-sien-kong-bāng**, id., in the temple of the genii. **khùn-sêng-hông**, to sleep in the temple of the tutelary god of the city to get evidence about a crime (v. hông). **khùn-bōng**, to sleep in the hollow of a grave in order to get a prophetic dream. **chiàh-chheng khùn-keng**, to live at ease in temples; to have an easy life (v. chheng). **khùn-chhiú-khiau**, to sleep with one's own elbow for a pillow. **khùn-thi^{n}-lē**, to sleep in the open air. **khùn-hong-thâu**, to sleep in a draught. **khùn-tui**, to pass the night at a police watch-house, as soldiers on duty. **khì-chhē in-má khùn**, he is dead (lit. gone to sleep with grandmother). **khah-ún kap-in-má khùn**, safer than a child in grandmamma's lap.

khut (R. id.), a hole in the ground; a pool; a small pit. **khut-á**, a small pool, or puddle, or hole in ground. **khut-lá**, id. **thâm-khut**, ponds and pools, larger and smaller. **hāi--lâng lòh-thâm-khut**, to bring people into great trouble. **kau-khut**, ditches and pools. **tsúi-khut**, a small pool of water. **soa^{n}-khut**, a small pool on a hill. **chiòh-khut**, a pool or cavity in a rock.

thê-khut, a piece of ground lower than the surrounding ground, sometimes of considerable extent. **koan-khut**, cavity of an old grave from which the coffin has been removed. **khòng-khut**, the pit of a grave roughly dug (before the lime is put in), where the coffin is to be laid, or of an old grave from which the coffin is removed. **koa^{n}-chhâ-khut**, cavity of deserted grave.

chiú-khut, the dimples of the cheek near corner of mouth when one laughs. **sim-koa^{n}-khut**, the soft depression near the middle of the breast. **sim-koa^{n} tì-á-khut**, id.

lap-khut, sunk into depressions, as a floor or road that should be level. **hiet-khut-á**, game of throwing cash into small holes.

khut [R. to bend; to treat very unjustly]. **khut--lòh-lâi**, to bend down one's body; to stoop down by bending forward. **kha khut--lòh-khì**, to bend one knee almost to the ground. **khut-kha**, to bend one or both legs, *e.g.* in preparing to shoot. **khut-kha-jîn**, the tenth radical. **khut-khiok**, bent, crooked, as a piece of wood, or as a lane. **khut-chhioh**, a carpenter's square. **khut-chhioh-kiáh**, a timber "knee" in boat-building. **khut-chhioh-hāng**, a lane with a right angle in it.

khut-kí thāi-jîn, to humble or deny one's self for the sake of others. **siū-khut**, to suffer severe injury or oppression. **bû-kø siū-khut**, do. without fault. **bû-oan siū-khut**, id. **khut-tá^{n} sêng-chiau**, to beat violently so as to force a false confession. **un-khut**, to accuse unjustly of crime; to oppress grievously by an unjust judgment on a false charge. **oan-khut** (R. and C.), id. **oai--lâng khut--lâng**, to raise or spread slanderous accusations against people.

óng-khut, an expression of astonishment with grief or displeasure, often with the idea that one would never have expected anything so wicked or so foolish of him; sometimes to treat unjustly. **ka-kī óng-khut**, to throw away one's opportunities; to ruin one's own prospects. **m̄-thang óng-khut--lâng**, you should not treat people unjustly. **óng-khut i-ê-kang**, alas that his labour is of no avail! **óng-khut i--ê kong-lô**, alas that his merit fails of reward! **óng-khut i--ê tsâi-chêng**, alas! he throws away his talents, as by low pleasures. **chin óng-khut**, what a pity that labour should be thus lost! either from his own fault or otherwise. **óng-khut hē-lí chiah-toā-hàn,** what a big useless fellow you are! **óng-khut lí-tsòe siù-tsâi,** what a shame that you (who act so ill) are a graduate!

khut-goân, the man in memory of whom the feast of dragon-boats (5.5) is kept.

khůt [R. short, as feathers of a bird], short, as a tail. **khůt-khůt,** stunted or scraggy, as an ill-formed tree; bare, as a rocky hill. **bé khůt-khůt,** the tail is very short. **khůt-bé,** having lost its point, as a hair-pencil. **té khůt-khůt,** very short. **khůt-hāu** (T.), a small bit of a rainbow seen up in the sky, less distinct than "phoà-phâng."

khůt-thâu-hāng, a road that ends abruptly, leading nowhere; a cul de sac.

khůt — **kə-khůt,** having no relations; unsociable; unneighbourly (v. kə). **kng khůt-khůt,** smooth and bare, as tree with few or no leaves or branches, or as hill without vegetation; without hair, as scabbed head; solitary, as man without relatives, without money or goods.

khůt — **khůt-chhêng,** of very unpleasant temper; unwilling to assist; fond of answering gruffly and laconically; unsocial and uncommunicative; scraggy and stunted, as a tree; too much clipped, as a sentence. **kóng-ōe khůt-chhêng,** to speak in a too laconic, gruff, and repelling manner.

khůt — **khůt-kə̂,** to stir paste in making it. **khůt khah-kà,** make it thinner, as paste. **khůt-thûi,** a stick for stirring paste.

khwa, khwá, khwà, khwā; better khoa, khoá, khoà, khoā (*q.v.*)

khwaⁿ, khwáⁿ, khwàⁿ; better khoaⁿ, khoáⁿ, khoàⁿ (*q.v.*)

khwah; better khoah (*q.v.*)

khwái, khwài; better khoái, khoài (*q.v.*)

khwaiⁿ, khwàiⁿ, khwāiⁿ; better khoaiⁿ, khoàiⁿ, khoāiⁿ (*q.v.*)

khwan, khwân, khwán, khwàn; better khoan, khoân, khoán, khoàn (*q.v.*)

khwat; better khoat (*q.v.*)

L.

l is often interchanged with **n** and **j**.

Many words beginning with l are mere reduplications of the previous word with the initial letter changed, *e.g.* kóng-lóng, kheng-leng.

la (cf. lâ), (T. la, le), too jolly or full of sport; amusing one's self too lightly, sometimes improperly or licentiously. **teh-la,** too jolly and full of fun; taking too great liberties with superiors, or too great licence in pleasures. **phah-la,** to amuse one's self idly, as by empty jokes, by laughing at passers-by, by throwing stones at mark, &c. **sēng-khi-la,** to spoil, as child or slave-girl, by allowing too great liberties.

la-êng, too jolly or fast; having too much of his own way, as a spoiled child or fast youth; too exuberant in spirits, or too fond of pleasures, often low or licentious. **chiáh-liáu la-êng,** full-fed and fond of pleasure or idleness, often in the way of insulting others or of wanton amusement. **thàn--khi la-êng,** having earned so much money as to get saucy, amusing himself, enjoying the "dolce far niente," putting on airs, despising small gains and refusing to take a job, as a coolie. **tsoán--khi la-êng,** id., or as a beggar. **khit--khi la-êng,** id., only of a beggar who has got so much that he stops begging to get jolly.

la (cf. lâ). **li-la,** unsafe to have dealings with, as a deceitful man who looks fair at first, but becomes dangerous, or borrows from friends and does not pay. **kóng-ōe li-la,** to talk in a way not to be depended on.

la — **li-li la-la** (C. lɛ), indistinct prattle of a child; also, to earn something more than one's wages or salary by miscellaneous bits of work. **chhùi la-la-háu,** said (in praise) of a child beginning to talk a good deal, or (in blame) of a man who talks too much.

la, to draw, as a bow or a boat. **la-keng,** to draw a bow. **la-tsûn,** to draw or pull a boat. **la-oá,** to pull close (as a boat) by a rope. **la-khui,** to pull it away from something else.

la-chioh, to borrow money. **sì-kòe-la, sì-kòe-chioh,** to go about borrowing money everywhere.

lâ — **soa-lâ,** a shell-fish somewhat like a cockle. **lâ-á,** id. **kiâm-lâ,** id., salted.

lâ (C.), = A. giô, a cockle.

lâ (R. lêng). **lâ-lí,** the scaly ant-eater; the pangolin.

lâ — **lâ-giâ,** a very large spider (v. giâ). **ti-lâ-si,** spiders' webs.

lâ (C. â). **lâ-sâm,** dirty; filthy (v. sâm).

lâ (cf. la). **lâ-kau,** unsafe to have dealings with, as man who does not repay what he borrows. **lâ-lâ kau-kau,** id.

lâ (cf. la, liâ). **kóng-lâ-liâng,** to joke and jest.

lâ — **pá-lâ,** very corpulent; full-fed and too full of jollity, esp. making fun of other people. **chiáh--khi pá-lâ,** having eaten to the full, and amusing one's self in a too loose or exuberant way [= the following word? or the former word?].

lâ (R. lô, liâu). **iû-lâ,** animal fat; lard. **ti-lâ,** hog's lard. **ti-lâ-iû,** id. **pán-lâ-iû,** the mass of fat at the animal's side; leaf fat.

lâ — **chhə̀-lâ,** mother of vinegar.

lâ, Benares opium (imitation of the accented syllable "na" of Benares). **kū-lâ,** old Benares opium.

lâ (R. liû), (C. lâu). **ka-lâ-pa,** Java; Batavia.

lâ — **lâ-lûn-sio,** lukewarm (v. lûn).

lâ — **lâ-sē,** spiritless; hanging down (v. sē).

lâ — **lâ-lē,** the low cross-beams on which the boards of the upper deck rest.

lâ (T. C.) **lâ-ták,** sort of harrows used instead of a plough for wet fields.

lâ (Cn.) **lâ-ták,** = A. nâ-pók, carrots. **lâ-pák,** id.

lá, = á, affix to nouns; used after words ending in *t*; *e.g.* **chhát-lá, giét-lá, khut-lá,** &c.

là, reduplication of "thà," &c. (v. thà).

là — **khok-á-là,** a large sort of cap worn by children. **ku-là** (T.), a hood like a "hong-bō" worn by children.

厦英大辭典

là; better "lah," final enclitic particle in indicative sentences.

lā — **ha-lā**, a very fine sort of woollen cloth. **ha-lā-nīⁿ**, id.

lā (T.) **bô-lā-oā**, = A. bô-tā-oā, no other resource; could not be avoided.

lā (T.) **chhi-chhi lā-lā**, sound of meat frying in melted fat. **tsú kàu lí-lí lā-lā**, to have a vast deal of cooking going on, as for numerous guests.

lā (Cn.) **lā-hiȯh**, = A. bā-hiȯh, the kite.

lā, to stir, as paste or water; to poke about with a stick, or as a bird with its bill; to make trouble or disturbance; to search about, as for employment; to make a remark, to suggest an idea, or raise a subject.

saⁿ-lā, fence with sticks, swords, &c. **lā niáu-chhú-khang**, to feel a rat's hole with a stick. **chhá-lā**, to annoy; to cause disturbance. **kiáu-lā**, id. **kiáu-lā--lí**, I am giving you a great deal of trouble.

lā **hō͘-i-tsai**, to give the first inkling or intelligence of an affair to him. **lā chit--ê ōe-thâu**, to make a remark that may lead a man to speak of a matter which we wish to ask, but don't like to ask directly. **m̄-thang-lā**; **chit-lā chit-chhàu**, don't stir that matter, for it will be very unpleasant to hear. **lā kun-le**, to make round-about inquiries to find out the secret origin of a matter, or, *e.g.* the facts about a theft. **lā thâu-lō͘**, to search for employment. **soáⁿ-lā**, to look about in all directions for odds and ends of work, earning a little here and there. **ah-bú-chhùi bóng-lā** (duck's bill feeling about in mud), to make a request with small hope of success, but may just as well try.

lah, enclitic particle at the end of a sentence, especially of an indicative sentence; sometimes marks the completion of an action.

lah (T.) **lah-lún**, too soft, as eatables insufficiently dried.

lah (T.), = A. lȧp, to sew the soles of stockings or shoes.

lah (An.), = A. tá, tah. **chit-lah**, here. **hit-lah**, there.

lȧh (R. lȧp, liȧp), bees'-wax. **n̂g-lȧh**, yellow wax. **pėh-lȧh**, white wax. **lȧh-chek**, a wax candle.

kài-lȧh, to rub with wax, so as to make smooth with a waxy surface. **lȧh-chien**, sort of drawing paper, with waxed surface.

lȧh (wax?). **pėh-lȧh-sȧh**, very white.

lȧh [R. lȧp, liȧp, the 12th month]. **lȧh-mûiⁿ**, a sweet yellow flower, Chimonanthes fragrans, which blooms in the 12th month.

lȧh (R. lėk). **lȧh-jit**, an almanac. **kè-sì lȧh-jit ê-tāi**, an affair quite past and forgotten. **kè-sì lȧh-bī**, id. **poaⁿ-chhia sin-chheh-á kū-lȧh-jit** (v. chheh).

lȧh [R. lȧp (?), mixed in confusion]. **oai-kô lȧh-chhoȧh**, awry; not even or square.

lȧh (R. lȧp, liȧp). **phah-lȧh**, to hunt. **chiong-kun bô-tī--teh, sió-kun phah-lȧh**, when the general is away, the soldiers play. **lȧh-káu**, a hunting dog; a man who is seldom to be found at his own house.

lȧh [R. lėk; to rein; to compel]. **ah-lȧh**, to force; to compel, = ek-lėk.

lȧh — **hong-lȧh**, a sort of disease in new-born infants. **tiȯh-lȧh**, to have that disease. **lȧh-chháu**, herbs used for its cure.

lȧh (R. liȧp), (C. lėh). **ka-lȧh**, a fish that tastes slightly like salmon. **ka-lȧh-hî**, id.

lȧh — **lūn-lȧh**, having a slight pleasant moistness or softness of surface, as face of man in good health and well off, or as skin of sleek horse, or as surface of a pill that is not too dry; gentle in manner, not readily angry but ready to settle a dispute; well-formed, easy and flowing, as written characters.

lȧh (Cn. esp. An.) **kúi-lȧh**, = A. kúi-nāⁿ, several.

lâi [R. weeds, thistles]. **hông-lâi**, the dwelling of the genii, the Tauist paradise. **hông-lâi-tó**, id.

lâi (R. id.), to come; at the end of a phrase it expresses motion towards the agent, or the accomplishment of the object; at the beginning of a clause following another, it is often a mere connective, carrying on the sense, answering to the connective particle "jî" in the literary style.

khí--lâi, to rise up (v. khí). **lâi-khì**, to come and go (v. khì). **óng-lâi**, to go and come; to have intercourse with (v. óng).

thó-lâi, to get back by asking for. **pān-bōe-lâi**, unable to arrange the matter, because it is so difficult. **tsòe-bōe-tit-lâi**, unable to accomplish it. **tng-bōe-lâi**, unable to undertake so difficult an office or business. **kóng-bōe-lâi**, cannot express it properly, as from want of ability or ignorance of the language; unable to speak to purpose so as to accomplish our object. **kóng ōe-tit-lâi**, to have such influence that our words are successful; to state a matter so clearly that it is well understood.

thėh-lâi, to bring in the hand, as a small thing. **giâ-lâi**, to bring, as a chair, &c. **kng-lâi**, to bring by carrying on a pole between two men (and so with the other ways of carrying).

lâi-lėk, history of a person or affair from the beginning; account of the origin. **lėk-lâi**, always hitherto for a long time back. **goân-lâi**, originally; formerly. **pún-lâi**, id. **chiông-lâi** (r.), hitherto.

chiong-lâi, afterwards; after this. **chiang-lâi** (C.), id. **āu-lâi**, afterwards. **chit-sì lâi-sè**, this life and that of the next birth by transmigration.

jû-lâi, a name of Buddha or Sek-khia. **jû-lâi-hút**, id.

lâi [R. lê, lî, a pear]. **lâi-á**, a pear. **lâi-á-chhiū**, a pear-tree. **tsúi-lâi**, a sort of pear. **hiang-tsúi-lâi**, do., from North China. **tsang-pau-lâi**, a large sort. **seh-lâi**, white winter pear from Shan-tung. **chiáu-lâi**, a small wild yellowish (useless) pear.

ōng-lâi, a pine-apple (v. ōng). **bān-jī-lâi**, a rough-skinned fruit (not a pear) shaped like a finger, or like the character "bān," used medicinally.

pàng-toā-lâi, to set off a firework (like pear-blossom), that spouts for a while with a bright light. **lâi-á-hoe**, id.

lâi (C.) **lâi-bâ**, a sort of wild animal like a fox (cf. lî).

lái [R. lán, spiritless; lazy, = col. noāⁿ]. **ià-lái**, wearied out; quite exhausted.

lái — **lí-lái**, spoiled, as things; in a bad state, as an involved affair hard to put right; troublesome or dangerous to have as an associate, as a man who cannot be depended on.

lái — **o͘-lái**, dirty dark reddish coloured, as common coarse pottery or clotted blood.

lāi (R. lī). **lāi-á-bah**, boiled flesh of a very small sort of cockle.

lāi [R. lī, clever; intelligent]. **lêng-lāi**, ingenious; clever, esp. precocious and intelligent, as child.

37

chhùi bô-lêng, hī-khang bô-lāi, not good either at speaking or hearing. **koai-lāi**, bright and intelligent, as child.

lāi (enclitic; cf. tāi). **beh--lāi**, what is the matter? what do you want?

lāi (C.), = A. bā, = Cn. lā. **lāi-hio̍h**, the kite.

lāi (R. lōe), within; inside; interior. **lāi-goā**, inside and outside (v. goā). **ba̍k-lāi-ū**, to esteem; to respect. **ba̍k-lāi-bô**, to despise. **o̍h-lāi**, a Sew-tsai graduate. **pak-lāi**, within the belly or heart; entrails (v. pak). **lāi-tsâi**, good mental powers and talents, as acquaintance with classics and literary ability. **lāi-khe**, internal diseases (v. khe). **soaⁿ-lāi**, among the mountains (v. soaⁿ), (s. interest).

lāi-sin, inside, as of a place. **lāi-bīn**, inside. **goán-lāi-bīn**, the inside of our house; my wife. **lāi-thâu**, inside; one's wife. **chhù-lāi**, wife. **ke-lāi**, wife; family. **ke-lāi-lâng**, id. **sāng-khiā-lāi**, living in the same house (v. khiā).

lāi-kong, paternal grandfather. **lāi-má**, paternal grandmother. **lāi-sun**, son's son.

sit-lāi, exact measurement within, as within the walls of a house. **tsāi-lāi**, inclusive; included in it. **pau-tsāi-lāi**, id. **pau-koat tsāi-lāi**, id. **put-tsāi-lāi**, not included in the sum or amount. **bô-tsāi-lāi**, id.

lāi [R. lī, sharp; benefit; interest], sharp; strongly acrid, as alkaline solution; very cold, as water; interest of money; auspicious, as position of house.

lāi-khì, sharp instruments. **chiam-lāi**, sharp, as point and edge (v. chiam). **lāi-to**, a sharp knife or sword.

kiau-lāi, bright and distinct, as a colour. **tun-to chhut lāi-chhiú**, a blunt knife shows the skill of the workman.

lāi-nîⁿ, a lucky year for some particular position. **bô-lāi**, the direction is not auspicious. **kin-nîⁿ sī-lāi**, this year the position referred to is auspicious for a house. **ū sím-mihⁿ-lāi**, which is the auspicious direction for building? **tang-sai lāi**, the lucky direction (this year) is to face the west.

lāi-chîⁿ, interest of money. **lāi-sit** (C.), id. **ka-jī-lāi**, interest at 20 per cent. on a whole voyage or single venture, not counted by time. **chit-hun-lāi**, interest at 1 per cent. a month, or 12 per cent. a year. **nn̄g-hun-lāi**, 24 per cent. a year. **sì-hun-goā-lāi**, more than 48 per cent. **tāng-lāi**, heavy interest; usury. **pàng-tāng-lāi**, to lend on heavy usury. **soaⁿ-lāi**, ordinary interest on the security of property on shore, or to man living on shore (s. inside). **pàng-soaⁿ-lāi**, to lend on such interest. **tsúi-lāi**, very high interest on goods shipped: if the vessel be lost both interest and principal are lost. **sīⁿ-lāi**, to be producing interest, as money. **kiâⁿ-lāi**, id. **chioh-chîⁿ kiâⁿ-lāi**, to borrow money, and have to pay interest. **jip-lāi**, to receive interest for money.

bú-lāi, principal and interest. **beh-lāi, liân-bú bô**, to lose the principal by trying to get interest. **lāi-chîⁿ koàn bú-chîⁿ**, compound interest. **lāi chhia-bú, bú chhia-lāi**, id. **lāi chhih--lo̍h-khì tsòe-bú**, id.

lâiⁿ, lāiⁿ, better, nâiⁿ, nāiⁿ (*q.v.*)

láiⁿ, reduplication of pháiⁿ. **pháiⁿ-láiⁿ**, become very bad; quite spoiled.

lak [R. thok, a bag, = col. lok]. **lak-tē**, a pocket; a small cotton bag. **lak-á**, id.

lak (= lok). **phīⁿ-lak-kóng**, the nose, esp. the middle part of the nose, excluding the tip and the bridge.

lak (T.) **sún-lak**, elegantly made, as a piece of furniture; elegantly formed, as a limb, or as the whole person.

lak (= la̍k). **lak-lak-háu**, sound, as of silver shaken.

lak— **ə-lak**, a long dark-gray sea-slug.

lak [R. ló, name of a fish], (C. láu). **pa-lak-hí**, a small edible fish (v. pa).

lak, reduplication of a previous word. **bak-lak**, to soil or dirty much. **phak-lak**, many things or persons lying on their faces; quantity of grain laid with rain.

lak, to drill a hole. **lak-tsǹg**, a drill worked by a string. **jī-hiân-lak**, a drill worked by a bow. **lak-soh**, the string of a drill. **ti-lak-soh**, a rope for catching pigs.

lak— **lak-khoàⁿ**, to stamp a hole nearly through a dollar by a strong sharp stamp (not taking away any of the silver), to see if it be a good dollar.

lak [R. lók, a rut; a sort of wheel]. **ka-lak**, a block, as in a ship, or for a pulley. **ka-lak-piáⁿ**, a sort of cake with a hole in the middle. **ka-lak-kə** (T.), = A. hé-kim-chhiⁿ, a fire-fly.

lak [R. lók, = col. lóh, lok, làu], to fall, as leaves, over-ripe fruit, or fetters; to shed, as hair; to fall, as price; to let fall or lose (only in some phrases); to let out the sheet (liâu-bú) of a sail much more than "hun."

lak-kè, to fall in price; to lower the price. **lak-lién**, to lose reputation, or influence, or prestige. **lak-bīn**, id. **lak i--ê thé-biēn**, to put him to shame before others.

lak-sún, joints of furniture opening out. **sún lak**, id. **lak-jī**, to omit a word or words by mistake in writing. **lak chit-jī**, to omit one word so. **lak-khí**, to lose one's teeth. **lak hé-hoe**, to let sparks fall, as from a match. **lak hō-tiám**, small rain falling. **lak-tsúi**, to put in water, as cloth or dress. **sim-koaⁿ siūⁿ kàu-beh-lak**, to think so hard as to be like to fall down.

lak chit-piⁿ, lay the matter aside for the present. **lak-khui--khì**, let the boat out further from shore.

la̍k (= lak). **la̍k-la̍k-háu**, sound of silver shaken.

la̍k [R. lek, to tremble]. **la̍k-la̍k-chhoah**, to shake and tremble with fear.

la̍k (R. lio̍k), six. **la̍k-pâng**, the six sub-offices in a mandarin's office. **la̍k-kak**, hexagonal (v. kak). **la̍k-kâu**, that throw of the dice when two have equal numbers, and the other is 6. **chiáh saⁿ-la̍k-káu**, to abstain from animal food on the nine days of the month ending in 3, 6, and 9. **la̍k-jī**, large good cash of Kien-lung, of a reddish brown metal.

toā-la̍k-lō, a very large house, having the central hall divided by a partition, and having the full complement of side-houses. **la̍k-lō-khí**, built in this style. **sió-la̍k-lō** (esp. T.), somewhat smaller, but of similar style.

la̍k-gėh-péh, a whitish fruit with a fine bloom on it. **la̍k-gėh-ə**, a sort of fruit (v. ə). **sòe-kiáⁿ bô-la̍k-gėh** (there is no hot month for a child), a child should wear plenty of clothes even in the hottest months.

la̍k [R. lio̍k, to seize, = col. liáh], to grasp or lay hold of violently, as man or wild animal. **khiú-la̍k**, to grasp violently. **saⁿ-khiú saⁿ-la̍k**, to seize and pull each other about violently, as in a quarrel. **la̍k-lâi la̍k-khì**, id.

la̍k, to take up a small thing in the fingers pointing

海上絲綢之路文獻集成 科技與文化編

厦英大辭典

downwards; to catch with the fingers from above, as a falling ball (but from below is "sīn"); a small quantity, as of meal taken up in the fingers from above.

chit-lák, a small quantity taken up in the fingers from above. **chit-lák-á**, id.

chhìn-chhái-lák, to take up small things improperly, *e.g.* money; to talk in a random improper way, *e.g.* false, disrespectful, or impudent. **lām-sám-lák**, to tell lies or exaggerated stories. **hau-lák**, id.; not quite so bad as "peh-chhàt."

lák--khí-lâi, to catch from above and lift up, or pull up to keep from falling; to hold up, as legs of trousers or skirt; to pull up, as sleeve; to give some assistance to set right an affair that had become dangerous. **lák bé-soh**, to hold a bridle or halter. **lák tâu-á**, to take up the dice in the fingers, as gamblers. **lák tām-póh**, to take a small quantity of something in the fingers. **lák chit-pé**, id. **thau-lák**, to steal small things. **thau-lák mīⁿ-hoe**, to steal a little cotton; said also of improperly touching another's person with bad intentions. **lák-sái lák-jiō**, to remove excrement and urine with the hand from an infant, as mother or nurse does.

lák — lák-hī, the two long boards at the side of a mast, which support it.

lam (C.), = A. am, a sort of basket. **ke-lam**, = A. koe-am, a basket for fowls. **ah-lam**, a basket for ducks.

lam (reduplication). **chham-lam**, mixed together.

lâm [R. male], a baron. **kong hô, pek tsú lâm**, the five ranks of nobility. **lâm-chiok**, the rank of a baron.

lâm-lú, male and female (v. lú). **lâm-hū ló-iù**, male and female, old and young. **lâm-teng**, a male person. **lâm-tsú**, id. **lâm-tsú-hàn**, id. **lâm-jî**, id., especially a young man or child.

hàu-lâm, a son mourning at his parent's funeral; said also in scolding a fellow who looks dull and stupid (you look as if you were mourning for your father). **hèⁿ-lâm-hong** (r.), sodomy. **lâm-sek**, id. (s. blue).

lâm (R. id.), a sort of tree with good hard wood, imported from Singapore. **lâm-á-chhâ**, this wood. **lâm-pang**, a board of it.

kî-lâm, a heavy costly wood (used for incense, and as a diuretic). **kî-lâm-hiuⁿ**, id.

lâm (R. id.), south. **lâm-pak**, north and south (v. pak). **tang-lâm**, south-east. **chhut-tang-lâm**, a south-east wind rising. **sai-lâm**, south-west. **tsòe sai-lâm**, a violent south-west storm or gale rising. **toā-sai-lâm**, a very strong south-west monsoon. **o-kha sai-lâm**, a sudden black south-west storm with heavy rain and great floods.

hê-lâm, to turn to a south wind (v. hê). **tiàu-lâm**, to beat against the south wind in sailing south. **tiàu-lâm--lóh-lâi**, id. **bīn ǹg-lâm** (face looking south), said of a sovereign or mandarin.

lâm-kiaⁿ, Nankin. **an-lâm**, Cochin-China, Annam. **hûn-lâm**, Yunnan. **kang-lâm**, Kiangnan. **o-lâm**, Hoonan. **hái-lâm**, Hainan. **hái-lâm-gōng**, a large sea-bird (v. gōng), (and so in many local names). **lâm-táu**, a southern constellation of six stars (v. táu). **lâm-kék sien-ông**, the guardian spirit of the south pole.

lâm-koán, songs in Amoy colloquial. **lâm-tsûn**, junks from Chang-poo (chiuⁿ-phó) and such places southward from Amoy. **lâm-á-tsûn**, id. **lâm-á-lâng**, men from Tong-san (tâng-soaⁿ), Swatow, or Canton. **ē-lâm-lâng**, people of Amoy, Chang-chew, Chin-chew, &c.

lâm (R. id.) **lâm-lúi**, tattered, ragged, slovenly.

lâm (T. liâm). **poàⁿ-lâm-hâⁿ**, hung up unfinished, as an affair (v. hâⁿ).

lâm — **o-lâm-hék**, flesh of a sort of shell-fish.

lâm — **khiā-lâm-iâ**, the name of an idol (v. khiā).

lâm (R. id.), deep blue. **mêⁿ-lâm**, id. **àm-lâm**, dark blue; the colour of the opaque blue button. **sam-lâm**, a very deep dark blue. **jī-lâm**, a shade not quite so deep. **pó-chióh-lâm**, a very rich blue (ultramarine). **thien-lâm**, a dark brownish purple, much used for (bé-koà) jackets. **it-phín-lâm**, a very bright blue with a purplish tinge. **chhùi-lâm**, bright light blue. **lâm-sek**, blue colour (s. male). **lâm-chheng**, the dress of a Sew-tsai. **lâm-téng**, the opaque blue button of the fourth rank of mandarins. **lâm-lêng**, an artificial feather worn by some mandarins.

lâm [R. lîm, to drench], to pour water upon, as on one's head, or as hot water into a hole of vermin; to pour melted metal over a thing, &c. **lâm--lóh-lâi**, to flow down abundantly on, as water on a water-wheel. **sì-lâm-sûi**, flowing all over, as tears or a flood (v. sûi). **lâm-tsúi**, to pour water on one's self in bathing. **lâm bàt-sat**, to pour hot water into a bug's nest to kill them.

lâm-phí, to pour a pint of parched beans over a person just recovering from small-pox, when the scabs fall off, done on a lucky day before an idol, and the beans are divided to children to eat to keep away small-pox.

lâm-thn̄g, to put on the glazing on pottery. **lâm gûn-tsúi**, to pour melted silver on some other metal to coat it. **lâm gûn-bīn**, to put a silver coating on a baser metal. **lâm siah-bīn**, to put a coating of tin or pewter.

lám (R. id.), to embrace; to take in the arms. **pau-lám**, to monopolize; to take the entire management of an affair. **pau-lám-bé**, to engage to make up the deficiency, as in a subscription. **lám-bé**, id. **lám-tsāi-jī**, a bill of lading in foreign vessels. **lám tah-tah**, to embrace closely, as a child, or as in joke. **lám ē-io**, to seize a man by the waist, as in wrestling (v. io).

lám [R. lám, lām, a large rope; to fasten with a rope]. **lám-kong**, a rope which draws the head of the sail close to the mast (v. kong). **toā-lám**, = toā-lām, a cable for lashing wood or bamboos to the sides of a junk. **toā-lám-soh**, id.

hê-sam put-lám (floating wood not tied), said of a useless ill-behaved fellow of whom no one takes care, or of very ill-made useless articles. **poàⁿ-lám-phû**, hanging up, as a matter without a definite settlement.

lám [R. lâm, ragged; tattered]. **lám-noāⁿ**, slovenly in person or dress.

lám (R. lién), weak; not strong, as man or thing; in bad health; having little or no power or influence; polite phrase (depreciatory) in speaking of what belongs to ourselves; inferior in quality.

lám-lâng, a man who has no power or influence to back him. **béng-lám**, powerful and weak, as clans or families; influential or uninfluential; having or not having prestige. **phín-béng-lám**, to boast of power and influence.

soe-lám, very weak, as old man, or as man with weak constitution and always ill. **hu-lám**, weak and emaciated. **lám sin-miāⁿ**, in delicate health.

lám-sai-hū, an inferior workman. **lám-kang-hu**, inferior ill-done work. **lám-tê**, tea of inferior quality. **lám-hè**, inferior goods. **lám-mih^n**, id.; also, "my poor articles." **lám sé-tsāi**, my poor house. **goán--ê lám-chhù**, id.

làm (cf. lòng, long, làng). **làm-làm**, hanging too loosely about one, as dress too loose or long, or as sleeves. **siu^n-làm**, id. **làm-sin**, the body of the dress hanging too loosely about one.

làm (cf. lop), (C. lòm). **làm-chhân**, very wet fields.

lām [R. a flood; excessive; disorderly; to waste]. **hông-súi hoàn-lām** (R.), a great deluge.

lām-kau, associating too freely with all sorts of people. **lām-êng**, to use too freely; lavish expense. **khah-lām-êng**, id. **lām-sám**, disorderly; at random; in any way whatever comes; without settled plan or arrangement; false; vicious; corrupt. **lām-sú** (C.), id. **lām-sám-sám**, very disorderly or improper. **lām-sám-kóng**, to talk at random; to speak falsely. **lām-sám kan-chèng**, false witness. **lām-sám chiù-tsoā**, random or false swearing. **lām-sám-kiâ^n**, to behave in an improper or disorderly way; to walk about without any definite plan.

lām, to mix. **sa^n-lām**, id. **lām-lām**, mixed together. **lām-tsām**, id., especially as good and bad of the same sort of article. **chham-chham lām-lām**, id. **sa^n-lām-chham**, id. **lām-he**, to mix up lime in mortar. **lām tsòe-chit-tui**, to put together in a heap.

lâm — **bô-lâm**, having no companion. **sio-lâm** (C.), to join and make one company, as two companies in a procession. **phoā^n-lâm** (C.), to keep company with; to go as companion.

lām [R. lām, lám, a large rope; to fasten with a rope]. **bih-lām**, a large bamboo cable. **lām-soh**, a cable such as is used for lashing wood on the sides of a junk. **toā-lām**, id.

lan — **giâ-lan**, crimson; carmine. **hâ-lan** (C.), id. **giâ-lan-bí**, cochineal. **giâ-lan-jī**, a hard, heavy, red wood, like rosewood, much used for anchors. **ka-lan-jī**, id.

lan, induration of the skin on foot or hand; a corn. **chhiú-lan**, a hardening on the hand caused by work. **kha-lan**, a corn. **siu kha-lan**, to extract corns. **koe-kha-lan**, hard places on a fowl's foot.

chiòh-lan, a hard nodule or knot in a stone.

lân [R. name of several flowers]. **lân-hoe**, a tree with a small sweet flower, Olea fragrans. **lân-hoe-bí**, these flowers plucked, without the stalk. **chhiū-lân-hoe**, small yellow sort, specially fragrant in the morning. **sè-sim-lân**, a variety (or species) with the centre nearly the same colour as the petals. **koe-kha-lân**, very small sweet flower on stalks like a hen's foot (Chloranthus inconspicuus). **koa^n-lân**, a flower like an iris (v. koa^n). **chhiah-lân** (C.), a beautiful evergreen shrub. **chhiah-lân-á** (C.), id.

hô-lân, Holland. **hô-lân-tsû**, potatoes, not sweet potatoes. **hô-lân-se**, France. **hoat-lân-se**, id., generally confounded with Holland by the Amoy people.

lân [R. difficult; painful; sometimes used in the sense of "cannot"]. **kan-lân**, pain; suffering; painful. **seng-khu kan-lân**, sick or sorely pained in body. **iau chhan, pá chhan: chiàh-pá, kiò-kan-lân**, always complaining.

lân-ûi, to maltreat, as by compelling to pay money unjustly, or to do too much work. **thiau-lân**, to cause trouble to another intentionally or maliciously, *e.g.* by unreasonably finding fault, making exorbitant demands, or refusing to give proper help, &c.

lân-tô, cannot escape (v. tô). **oán-súi lân-kiù kūn-hé**, distant water cannot help a fire close at hand. **ka-chèk lân-hông**, it is hard or impossible to guard against a thief in the household. **it-giên hòng-chhut, sù-má lân-tui**, four horses cannot catch back a word once spoken. **lân-tek** (R.), difficult to get.

ûi-jîn lân, it is hard to please every one. **chhiòng-hé lân**, but it is the setting loose a tiger that is the trouble (v. hé). **khì-tò lióng-lân**, in a sad dilemma, feeling unable to go on or draw back. **chìn-thè lióng-lân** (= thòe), id. **pah-poa^n, khí-thâu lân**, all things are difficult at the beginning. **chhùn-pē lân-hêng**, walking slowly and with difficulty.

lân (R. lêng). **lân-kan**, a railing; a balustrade. **sa-lân**, the railing outside the gate of a yamun. **sa-lân-goā**, outside the yamun railings.

lân (same as above?). **lân-kan**, a sort of lace, edging, or border.

lân [R. lâm, south]. **lân-thân**, plays in the Swatow or Chau-chau dialect.

lân (R. lêng), a small remainder or excess; over and above; odd in number; a word used in speaking equivalent to a cypher in writing. **lân-chhùi**, miscellaneous; retail, not wholesale. **lân-san**, in small quantities. **lân-san-bōe**, to sell in small quantities; to sell by retail. **lân-san-bah**, an excrescence on the body, *e.g.* a superfluous finger. **lân-san-gûn**, a few dollars (less than ten). **ài-kóng lâng lân-san-ōe**, fond of raking up old stories about people's bad actions.

chit-pah lân-káu, 109. **sa^n-phè-lân**, above 30 li. **làk-tsàp-lân nî^n**, rather more than 60 years.

lân [R. lêng, lēng, to cut], (esp. C.), to pull off the leaves of sugar-cane; also (C.), to take off superfluous leaves or twigs. **lân chiá-hàh**, to cut off the outer leaves of sugar-cane. **lân--koá khí--lâi**, to remove a few, as leaves or twigs.

lân (R. lîn), a scale, as of a fish. **hî-lân**, fish-scales. **sàu-lân**, to scrape off scales. **phah-lân**, id.

lân (T.), = A. lêng, a small bell, &c. **bé-lân** (A. T.), = bé-long, sort of bells worn by horses. **hâm-lân** (T.), id.

lán (= ná^n), (Cn. lín), like; similar to. **lán-chhin-chhiū^n**, id.

lán [R. id., = col. lái, noá^n, noā^n]. **lán-lán**, spiritless; without purpose or energy. **lán-tō**, lazy. **lán-thán**, indisposed to take trouble. **ià-lán**, quite tired, wearied, and exhausted.

lán (= lién). **péng ka-lán-phak**, to invert, as a cup

lán, you and I; you and we; we, including the person or persons spoken to; sometimes may refer to "you" alone, as a polite form of expression, but rarely, if ever, to the first person alone (in Cn. "lán" and "lín" change places). **lán-lâng**, you and I; you and we. **lán-tau**, our house.

lān (R. id.) **chhàn-lān**, brilliant; splendid; dazzlingly bright.

lān [R. id., by change of tone from "lân," pain; suffering]. **tsai-lān**, great calamity or affliction. **khé-lān**, great misery. **kiù-khé kiù-lān**, to save from misery and calamity. **hoān-lān** (r.), to meet with or suffer calamity; calamity. **tso-lān**, to meet with calamity. **pī-lān** (r), to avoid calamity. **tô-lān**, to flee from calamity.

lān (R. lin), the male organs, especially the penis. **lān-chiáu**, the penis (much used in vile scolding). **lān-pha**, the scrotum. **lān-hut**, the testes. **iá-lān**, said in coarse scolding of a man who wishes far too great gain in trade. **hiēn-lān**, so short as to show the secret parts, as a coat. **thǹg-khè-lān**, not wearing trowsers; naked below the waist, as child or fisherman.

lang — **khui thê-lang**, to make or have a deep pit with a narrow mouth, for catching animals or men, or for hiding goods. **khui-lang**, id. **khui-hām khui-lang**, id., for catching animals, &c.

lang — **koh-ē-lang**, = koh-ē-khang, the armpits.

lang (C.) **lang-á**, a narrow valley. **soaⁿ-lang**, id. **soaⁿ-lang-á**, id. **khɛⁿ-lang-á**, id.

lang (cf. long; to run away). **lang--khì**, to steal, as small things.

lang (more usually "long"). **hoah-lê-lang**, an auction.

lang — **chhiⁿ-lang-lang**, brightly green, as verdant fields or foliage.

lang — **pa-lang-hî**, a small fish like trout.

lang (C.) **hóe-lang**, = A. hé-thang, a small hand-stove in a basket.

lâng (R. jîn), a man; a person; people; other persons, as opposed to one's self; one's own body; often used indefinitely, like the German "man," French "on," or English "they," or untranslated in phrases which we would express by the passive, as lâng-kóng, it is said. **hō-lâng-phah**, to be struck. **thâi-lâng**, to kill people; to kill. **chioh--lâng**, to lend money. **pák--lâng tsng-hì**, to apprentice (one's boy) to actors for a number of years. **chèng-lâng**, all people; every one. **ok--lâng**, to behave in a proud overbearing way.

kiaⁿ-lâng, filthy.

tiūⁿ-lâng, wife's father. **koaⁿ-lâng**, master of female slave. **koaⁿ--lâng**, mandarins in general (v. koaⁿ). **toā-lâng**, a married man; a grown-up man; also (C.), a Kujin graduate. **tńg-toā-lâng**, to become a full-grown man. **toā--lâng ê-kiáⁿ**, son of the legal wife, opposed to sons of secondary wives. **chhiāⁿ-lâng**, to get married (v. chhiāⁿ).

lâng-kheh, a guest; a visitor. **kheh-lâng**, a Hakka. **tn̂g-lâng**, a Chinaman. **êng-lâng**, a man who has no connection with the affair. **sin-lâng**, a newly-arrived man (said in joke). **thih-lâng**, a man not afraid of anything, who can stand all weathers, or daring and dangerous. **lám-lâng**, a man who has no powerful relatives to back him. **núiⁿ-lâng** (C.), id. **chhng-lâng-thâu**, you clown!

lâng-bé, persons in general. **lâng-kang**, a coolie; a porter; a labourer.

chháu-lâng, a scarecrow.

m̄-sī-lâng, a bad man; inhuman or vicious. **i kap-lâng bô-chhin-chhiūⁿ**, he has a bad disposition (not like others). **i-ê-lâng kiau-gō**, his manner or bearing is proud. **tsòe-lâng**, to behave; to behave kindly; behaviour. **tsòe-lâng-hó**, to behave kindly or well. **tsòe-lâng-pháiⁿ**, to behave wickedly or cruelly. **gâu-tsòe-lâng**, kind and hospitable; treating others well. **tsòe-lâng-n̂g**, to act imperiously or overbearingly. **tsòe-lâng-gók**, id. (v. gók). **bák-kim, chîⁿ tsòe-lâng**, at present it is wealth that is valued in a man.

lâng-khì, the strong odour or warmth of a crowd; the influence of a number of persons in restraining demons. **lâng-huih**, human blood (s. matter). **lâng-hêng**, the form of a man.

lâng m̄-ài, unwell; indisposed. **lâng m̄-tsai**, insensible, as in a swoon, or from a fall, &c.; also, people do not know. **hó-lâng**, in good health; also, a good man. **lâng lóng-ià**, in very weak health; also, all the people are tired. **lâng tiòh-lòh-hái**, get into the water yourself! (said to a boatman who is making ineffectual attempts to effect the object without going out of the boat); or, the people should go into the sea.

lâng [R. thiông, a reptile, = col. thâng]. **siēn-lâng**, a lizard, = C. sīn-thâng. **sīn-lâng** (T.), id.

lâng [R. lông, deaf]. **chhàu-hī-lâng**, deaf. **chhàu-lâng**, id.

lâng, to pierce or stab with a sort of indirect thrust, moving the point round after it is inserted.

lâng [R. liông, sort of mill]. **thê-lâng**, a machine like a mill worked by hand, for removing the husk from grain. **oe thê-lâng**, to work it. **oe-lâng**, id. **thê-lâng-khí**, its teeth, of hard wood. **thê-lâng-ê**, the lower half of it. **thê-lâng-hī**, the projection on the edge of the upper half, with a hole for the hook. **thê-lâng-kau**, the hook by which it is worked.

hái-lâng-kau, a sea-bird with a long bill (like the hook) and a shrill cry.

lâng [R. lông, = col. láng], a cage. **koe-lâng**, a cage or coop for hens; Kelung, in Formosa. **koe-lâng-soaⁿ**, a hill shaped (conical) like a hen-coop, as at Kelung, and one near Anhái. **chiáu-lâng**, a bird-cage. **chiáu-táh-lâng**, a trap for birds, made to fall on them. **táh-tùi-lâng**, do. for birds or beasts.

lâng-sn̂g, a frame for cooking by steam (v. sn̂g). **bé-lâng-thâu**, = lông-thâu, a horse's head-stall. **bé-lâng-soh**, the rope fastening it on the horse's head.

lâng (R. lông), matter from a sore; pus. **lâng-huih**, matter and blood mixed (v. huih), (s. man). **siⁿ-lâng**, to suppurate. **chhut-lâng**, to emit matter, as a boil. **pū-lâng**, to come to a head, as a boil. **hùn-lâng**, to begin to gather matter, before it comes to a head. **koàn-lâng**, matter forming and filling up. **tiùⁿ-lâng**, to be full of matter, as boil about ripe. **ūn-lâng**, to suppurate again in a new place. **khê-lâng** (C.), matter forming, not yet ripe.

láng [R. lóng, clear]. **bêng-láng**, distinct, clear, as a sound, or as meaning.

láng — **áng-láng**, stupid, sour-tempered, or obstinately dull (v. áng).

láng [R. lông, a cage, a basket, = col. lâng], a basket; a wicker-work trunk. **kim-láng**, a tall cylindrical basket for holding idolatrous paper. **jī-tsoá-láng**, basket for collecting printed or written paper. **hì-láng**, trunks for actor's dresses. **ka-lé-láng**, trunks for carrying puppets. **láng-tsú**, the man who hires out a company of actors.

iû-láng, a wicker-work oil-jar, made tight by oiled paper. **tê-láng**, a water-proof tea-basket. **pîⁿ-láng**, a flat wicker-work trunk. **bih-láng**, a wicker-work trunk. **tsu-láng**, a basket or wicker-work trunk for books. **hé-sit-láng**, a small basket used by travellers for carrying some provisions. **thih-láng**, an iron cage. **siuⁿ-láng**, boxes and baskets.

láng-pe, a wicker frame used in cooking by steam. **láng-kn̂g**, a large wicker frame-work on poles for carrying many things (v. kn̂g).

òh poàⁿ-láng-bí, to learn a thing only half (v. poàⁿ).

láng (cf. lóng), to put together loosely, as the staves of a bucket before fixing them; to hold up with the hand, as trowsers legs, to keep them out of the mud; to help in carrying a sedan, as a third bearer does. **tàu-láng**, to assist in lifting or carrying a sedan.

tsóng-láng, to sum up in a rough general way. **láng-khoàⁿ**, to make a rough calculation (esp. mentally) of the sum total.

láng chit-ê-phe, to make a beginning of a matter to be afterwards carried out. **seng-láng**, to put together loosely before fastening firmly together. **láng tsòe-chit-tui**, to put together loosely, either merely temporarily, or to be afterwards fastened firmly. **láng tsòe-pû**, id.

láng-khò͘, outer trowsers or overalls, worn especially by boatmen (v. khò͘).

láng khò͘-kha, to hold up the legs of trowsers with the hand.

tà-láng-sáng (T.), doing things very carelessly.

làng (cf. lòng, long, lāng, làm), (T. lāng), to leave a space. **làng-khui**, to move out a little from the land, as a boat. **bô-làng-chit-jit**, without intermitting one single day. **làng-khang**, to leave an empty space. **làng-phāng**, to leave a space, as in writing; to take the opportunity to make off (v. phāng). **soe-làng**, of loose texture, as cloth; set well apart, as trees, houses, or characters. **soe-làng-soe-làng**, id. **làng-hûn**, clouds scattering and clear sky appearing. **khah-làng-hong**, having a good free circulation of air, or more free circulation, *e.g.* dressing loosely, or piling sheaves, &c., so as to let the air circulate, or as house with plenty of openings.

làng (C.), = A. lèng, to kick.

lāng (cf. làng). **pò͘ lāng-lāng**, the threads of the cloth too far apart or irregular. **pò͘ lāng-li lāng-li**, id. **lāng-lö lāng-lö** (T.), id. **lāng-thang**, loose in texture, as gauze, &c. (v. thang). **thiau-lāng**, airy, as a room; having plenty of space between, as houses, trees, characters, &c. **ki-kut thiau-lāng**, limbs well-formed and graceful. **kha-chhiú thiau-lāng**, id.; also, walking gracefully. **bák-sîn oáh-tāng, ki-kut thiau-lāng**, eyes full of fire and intelligence, and limbs graceful.

lāng-toā, to pull up the rudder, as in shallow water. **chhia khah-lāng**, hoist the sail a little higher. **lāng-hoe**, to flower, as grain or grass.

lāng (T.), = A. làng.

lāng (R. lōng), to brandish; to gesticulate, especially so as to make sport, as a fool.

lāng-hiám, to run a risk; to venture. **lāng-hiám-tsòe**, id.

lāng-gīn, to speak or act so as to make a man feel displeased or disgusted (v. gīn). **lāng-gûn** (Cn.), id. **hì-lāng**, to make improper gestures or lewd talk, as man with woman or depraved boys. **lāng-i-chhiò**, to sport so as to make him laugh. **pìⁿ-lāng**, to annoy, cause trouble, or work mischief, as man; to amuse itself with toys, as child. **hō͘--i pìⁿ-lāng**, give it some toys to amuse itself. **pìⁿ-kâu-lāng**, to work sleight of hand; legerdemain.

bú-lāng, to practise gymnastics or fencing; to gesticulate with arms and legs. **bú-bú lāng-lāng**, id. **lāng-sit**, to shake its wings, as a fowl. **lāng-sai**, to act the artificial lion, in an idolatrous procession. **lāng-to lāng-kiàm**, to brandish swords. **lāng chhíⁿ-ké**, to play the tambourine. **lāng nâⁿ-poàh**, to play with cymbals. **lāng-lâu**, do., as Buddhist priest. **lāng koáiⁿ-á-hoe**, flourishing his stick in delight, as a beggar.

lāng — **tī-lāng**, a cylindrical vessel for holding chop-sticks.

lāng (C.) **hê-lāng**, a sort of basket-work trap for shrimps, set in fresh water.

lāng [R. hāng, the neck; a sort]. **tāu-lāng**, the lower part of a pig's neck (v. tāu).

lap (cf. chhap), to mix or shuffle, as cards. **chhap-lap**, to meddle; to associate promiscuously and rather improperly (v. chhap). **lap-lâi lap-khì**, to carry on trade with little capital of our own, by constant borrowing and paying. **lap pâi-á**, to shuffle cards.

lap — **lap-sap**, dirty, as things or conduct.

lap [R. thap, depressed; to sink down, = col. nahⁿ], concave; to sink, so as to make depressions or holes; to become concave; to step unintentionally into a hole; to fall into danger or a trap or evil, or to delude another into it; to trample or kick with the sole of the foot.

thap-thap lap-lap, sunk or fallen in, as a road that once was level, or a bad roof, or as an old hat. **lap--lóh-lâi**, to become thus flattened, dinted, or depressed. **lap-tóe**, having the bottom fallen out, as a basket. **lap-phīⁿ**, having lost one's nose by disease. **lap-u**, concave, as a hole or a depression; situation (as of a house) too low, lower than the surrounding ground. **lap-o**, id. **lap-khut**, sunk into depressions, as floor, road, or ground.

lap-kháp, matters all going wrong. **lap-pún**, to lose money in trade. **lap-lién** (C.), to lose character, influence, or prestige.

lap-tsúi, to step unintentionally into water. **lap-pē͘**, to take a step down, as into a hole, or down a step. **lām-sám-lap**, to step about awkwardly or incautiously, as in the dark; to walk carelessly, so as to soil one's shoes, or dirty something with our shoes. **lap--lóh-khì**, to step unintentionally into a hole, or fall into a snare or plot. **lap--lâng**, to ensnare an unsuspecting man into danger or evil; also, to kick a man with the sole.

lap-tùi, to work a rice-mortar with the foot. **lap-béh** (T. C.), to pound barley in a mortar (worked by the foot) to remove the awn. **lap kiâm-chhài**, to tread salted mustard-leaves till solid. **lap--sí**, to trample to death. **lap-tióh-lâng**, to step unintentionally on a man's foot, as in the dark or in a crowd.

láp [R. to sew or stitch together; to patch], (T. lah). **láp ôe-tóe**, to sew the several parts of a shoe sole into one piece, ready for the uppers. **láp béh-tóe**, to stitch the thick stiff sole of a Chinese stocking into one piece, ready to be sewed on the leg. **láp-tóe**, having such thick soles, as Chinese stockings.

láp [R. to receive; to pay]. **chiap-láp**, to receive, as a person. **kàm-láp**, to receive and accept (an offering), as a god or spirit does. **ōe-siau-láp**, able to digest.

oān-láp, to pay in full any taxes, dues, &c. **koan-láp**, to pay for a title of rank. **láp-kàm**, to buy the title of kàm-seng. **láp-kòng**, to pay tribute. **láp-hiòng**, to pay customs' dues. **láp chîⁿ-niûⁿ**, to pay land-tax. **láp-sè**, to pay rent.

láp — **láp-láp-háu**, sound of eating (imitation of the sound?).

láp [R. mixed; confused, = col. láh]. **láp-tsáp-tsáp** (C.), mixed in confusion. **láp-láp tsáp-tsáp** (C.), id.

lát (R. lek). **lát-chí**, chestnuts. **lát-chí-chhiū**, the chestnut-tree.

làt, a knife-shaped fish (about ten inches long) full of small bones (edible, but said to cause boils or itch !). **làt-á-lêng**, fine nets for catching them.

làt [R. lėk, but the character is unauthorized]. **sit-làt**, Singapore. **sit-làt-pho**, id.

làt (C.) **làt-pàt**, = nâ-á-poàt, the guava.

làt (R. lėk). **lí-làt**, scrofulous sores on the neck. **bí-làt**, id.

làt (R. lėk), strength. **làt-thâu**, id. **làt-chháu**, id. **khùi-làt**, id. **sńg-khùi tio̍h-làt**, causing or requiring a great deal of toil or trouble.

tio̍h-làt, to have to exert one's self very much (v. tio̍h). **ēng-làt**, to exert one's self. **chīn-làt**, to exert strength to the utmost. **tìⁿ-làt**, to collect one's strength for some great effort, as a lift or strain. **hô-làt**, to unite strength in one effort. **kek-làt**, to clench the hands, as a child, or as a boxer preparing to strike. **ū-làt**, strong; powerful; when said of a medicine it refers to the nature of the substance, not to the strength of the dose or mixture. **chhia-làt**, requiring much exertion, as a matter in a critical or urgent state. **hoat-làt**, to show anger, as by loud voice, by striking the table, or by gesticulation. **lé-làt**, thank you ! (v. lé). **chhut-làt**, to exert one's self. **chhut-sí-làt-phah**, to make a very violent attack, striking very violently. **toā-làt-pùih**, to pull out or up with great force.

chiàh hit-ki ê-làt, to rest on that large beam, as the rafters, &c., do. **pìⁿ-pìⁿ chiàh-làt**, each equally bearing the strain, as two ropes or two supports.

pē-bú-làt, one's natural strength of body. **i--ê pē-bú-làt khah-toā**, he is naturally stronger in body. **chīn-bú-làt**, to exert all one's physical strength. **chiàh-niⁿ-làt soà-chhut**, id.

làt-siùⁿ, energetic, active, diligent at work. **chheng-kun-làt**, a thousand pounds of strength. **chhìⁿ-làt-peng**, fresh troops.

lau (cf. lâu, láu), to get secret information out of a man by talking of a matter as if we knew all about it, or by taking him at unawares. **lau--chhut-lâi**, id. **lau-i-kóng**, id. **lau--lâng**, id.; also, to get a thing fraudulently by pretending to be commissioned by the owner.

lau (reduplication of pau). **pau-lau**, to wrap up.

lâu [R. liû, a tumour or wen], a swelling on the head such as is made by a blow. **thâu-lâu-á**, small boils on child's head. **hong-lâu**, a sort of swelling which subsides of itself without suppurating. **phah chit-lâu**, to strike on the head so as to cause a swelling.

lâu — **au-lâu**, ugly and filthy in face (v. au). **lâu-siông**, slovenly, as person or room.

lâu (R. liû), a surname.

lâu (C.) **ka-lâu-pa**, = ka-lâ-pa, Java (said to be from a Javanese word).

lâu [R. nâuⁿ, cymbals, = col. nâⁿ]. **lâng-lâu**, to play with cymbals, as Buddhist priests. **lâu-poàh** (C. T.), = A. nâⁿ-poàh, cymbals.

lâu (R. liû), to detain; to remain over; to keep; to detain forcibly, as in a feud, or for debt; to allow to grow, as beard or queue. **lâu-khǹg--teh**, to keep over, as a part of anything. **lâu ti-thâu**, to set apart a pig's head to be used as an offering.

lâu-i-toà, get him to stay longer.

lâu chhùi-chhiu, to grow a beard; to have a beard. **lâu thâu-tsang**, to cultivate a queue, *i.e.* letting it grow while the rest of the head is shaved. **lâu tsoân-hoat**, to let the whole of one's hair grow long, as women.

lâu bīn-phê, to keep one's respectability by avoiding shameful actions. **bô-lâu-liōng**, to go to too great an extreme (v. liōng). **lâu tōe-pē**, to leave one's self some plan or force yet unused, to be ready for an emergency (v. pē). **bô-lâu û-tōe**, to put a man too much to shame, as by severe scolding before others (v. û).

lâu (R. lô), a tower; a house with an upper story; an upper story, esp. with more than one room. **lâu-koh**, upper stories in general (v. koh). **poàⁿ-lâu**, a small garret; a small low second story carried only half across the room. **saⁿ-tsàn-lâu**, a third floor; a house of three stories, &c. **soe-tsng-lâu**, upper room for women. **chiú-lâu**, a drinking room in a tavern. **bé-lâu**, sort of platform or cabin at stern of junk. **tsáu-bé-lâu**, the space round the central opening in the upper floor of a large Chinese house; an upper verandah.

lâu-thui, a ladder (v. thui). **lâu-chíⁿ**, an opening for a trap-door. **lâu-pang**, the floor of an upper story. **lâu-ē**, downstairs; the ground-floor. **lâu-kha**, id. **lâu-téng**, upstairs; the upper story. **lâu-bé-téng**, id. **chiūⁿ-lâu**, to go upstairs. **khí-lâu**, to build a house or tower of more than one story. **ū-lâu**, to have an upper story.

siâⁿ-lâu, tower at a city gate. **siâⁿ-mn̂g-lâu**, id. **kiⁿ-lâu**, a watch-tower, as at entrance of village or at boundary of clans. **kó-lâu**, a large tower within a city; a drum-tower. **chhái-lâu**, an ornamented temporary pagoda (v. chhái). **pat-koà-lâu**, octagonal tower, gen. connected with a temple. **thô-lâu**, a very large house with many stories, built of earth mixed with lime (often made like a fort).

lâu (R. liû), to flow; the tide; to carry away, as a stream or tide; the current of a stream or of the tide. **khoe-lâu**, the current of the river. **lâm-lâu**, the flood-tide from the south, as at Amoy. **bô-lâu**, there is no tide. **lâu teh-kiâⁿ**, there is tide, either ebb or flood. **khó-lâu**, ebb-tide. **khó-lâu-thâu**, the first of ebb. **lâu-thâu**, the first of the tide, esp. of ebb. **tn̂g-lâu-thâu**, the first of flood. **lâu-tsúi**, the tide. **hó-lâu-tsúi**, a favourable tide. **toā-lâu-tsúi**, spring-tides. **sió-lâu-tsúi**, neap-tides. **hù-lâu-tsúi**, to be in time for the tide. **koáⁿ lâu-tsúi**, hastening to catch the tide. **bô-lâu bô-tsúi**, unsuitable tide. **tu-lâu**, to sail against the tide. **lím-lâu**, close on the time of tide, so that no time should be lost. **iú-hong, put-phàⁿ-lâu**, having the wind we don't fear the tide (said figuratively).

m̄-sī lâu-pái, not suitable time for doing something (v. pái).

pun-lâu, the tide or current divided, as by an island, &c. **tò-pūn-lâu**, tide broken by rocks and eddying. **lâu-pūn**, id. **tò-ká-lâu**, id. **hàng-lâu**, id. **hoan-lâu**, a back current of the tide, as in a side channel.

lâu-kòe, debris floating on the tide.

tsúi-lâu phoà-pò͘, said of a man negligent and dilatory about what has been intrusted to him (like floating rags). **tsúi lâu-lâng**, flood drowns and carries away people. **lâu-sí-lâng**, id.

lâu-lo̍h, having no relative or friend on whom we can lean; to flow down.

tīⁿ lâu-lâu, full and overflowing, as a liquid.

lâu-koāⁿ, to perspire (v. koāⁿ). **lâu-huih**, to bleed (neuter); to lose blood. **lâu-lâng**, to have matter flowing out. **lâu-phīⁿ**, the nose running. **lâu bàk-sái**, to weep (v. sái).

láu [R. ló, old, skilful, = col. lāu, lauh, niáu], spoiled, or almost spoiled by keeping, as fruit or vegetables; to talk with fluency, as a different dialect or language; experienced, as at work. **láu-pún**, skilful from long experience. **láu-liān**, practised; experienced. **sèk láu-láu**, id. **chin-láu-chhiú**, very skilful, as at fine workmanship, or at literary work. **khah-láu-chhiú**, id. **láu chiàⁿ-jī**, to talk mandarin with fluency. **láu khiuⁿ-kháu**, to be able to talk a dialect. **láu-khi-sèk**, talk it (another language) till you get fluency.

láu-sit, honest, faithful.

láu-chiàng, a trained soldier. **láu-hoān**, a prisoner who has been some years in prison.

tsau-láu, worn out and spoiled.

láu (cf. lau, làu), to swindle; to get things by deceit, as by pretending to have an order from the owner; to cheat, as by false jewels or bad silver. **láu-phièn-siet**, to deceive and defraud in all ways.

láu-á, a thief. **láu-á-tsáiⁿ**, the third finger. **toā-láu-koan**, a great plausible swindler. **toā-láu kong-kùn**, a great rogue and swindler. **láu-kong-kùn**, id.

láu — **láu--tiòh**, to sprain or overstrain one's self by too great or too rapid exertion. **láu-tiòh-kun**, id.

láu (= náuⁿ). **láu-thâu tsūn-ām**, to shake about or bend one's neck, as an impudent or disobedient child.

hiong-pa lí-láu, very ugly, as a painted face, or as very bad writing.

láu — **pa-lun pa-láu**, to bolt one's food; to talk of a matter indistinctly (v. lun). **ka-láu ka-lé**, to talk of a matter indistinctly, either intentionally, or as a lad who does not know how to speak about matters.

láu (a mere reduplication). **áu-láu**, to crumple up. **kāu-láu**, very thick.

láu [R. ló, name of a fish]. **pa-láu-hí**, a sort of fish (edible). **poa-láu-hí** (C.), id.

láu (R. ló). **láu-hiòh**, siri or betel leaf. **láu-hiòh-chí**, betel-nut. **tsúi-láu** (P.), a water-plant with a leaf very like betel-leaf.

láu [R. liáu, name of a plant]. **láu-hoe**, a brittle confection made of sugar, rice, &c. **moâⁿ-láu**, a similar confection made with hemp-seed. **bí-láu**, a confection.

làu (=nàuⁿ, cf. láuⁿ). **àu-làu**, displeased, vexed, or angry feeling.

làu [R. lòk, to fall, = col. lòh, lok, lak, láuh], to shed or let fall off, as leaves or scabs; to open out of itself, as a knot or joint; to run before the wind; to have diarrhœa and such diseases.

làu-hiòh, to shed leaves in great abundance. **làu-phí**, scab (of small-pox) falling off.

sún-teng làu-tsâi, to lose male children or nephews, &c., and also lose money.

làu-sún, joints opening out and getting loose, in furniture. **khún--khì làu-làu**, you have tied it far too loose, so that it opens out of itself. **làu-hûn** (Cn.), the clouds opening and dispersing.

làu-tsûn, to run before the wind, as a vessel. **làu-lâm-hong**, to run with a fair south wind.

làu-pak, diarrhœa. **làu-sià**, id. **làu-thò**, purging and vomiting; cholera. **thò-làu**, id. **áu-làu** (C.), id. **làu toā-tn̂g-thâu**, internal piles protruding at time of stool. **làu-the**, to have a miscarriage (said only of quadrupeds). **làu--khì**, id.

làu — **khah-làu-bák**, having very long joints, as bamboo or sugar-cane. **ū-làu-bák**, not knotty, as wood; knots far apart.

làu [R. ló, old; skilful, = col. lāu, láu]. **sèk làu-làu**, well skilled; well acquainted with, as with road or with work.

làu (cf. lau, láu), to inveigle; to get a secret out of a man in some way; to lead a man into danger by deceitful promises. **chhòng chit-kù-ōe lâi-làu--i**, say something to him so as to draw out from him what he wished to keep secret. **làu-i-kóng**, id.

lāu [R. noise or confusion, as of a crowd, = nāuⁿ]. **lāu-jiet**, crowded; bustling (v. jiet). **lāu-joàh**, id. **lāu-tōng**, much noise and confusion, as of a crowd.

chháu-lāu, to make an uproar of set purpose; to cause confusion and trouble. **jióng-lāu**, id. **lāu-tâi**, to make a great noise of music just before a play, esp. in mandarin colloquial play. **lāu kong-tn̂g**, to make a great noise or disturbance in a mandarin's court so as to get him to attend (in an irregular way) to some case of murder or violence.

lāu-sū, to raise troubles by improper conduct.

lāu [R. lə, ulcers or scrofulous sores]. **eng-lāu**, fistula. **kan-lāu**, venereal ulcers. **kan-îm-lāu**, id. **siⁿ-chhng phah-lāu**, to have such venereal diseases.

lāu (R. lə), to leak out; to filter, as sugar; to steal a small quantity out of a large quantity, so that it may not be observed; (to smuggle); a funnel or filter.

lāu-á, a small funnel. **chiú-lāu**, a funnel for pouring liquor. **iû-lāu**, a funnel for pouring oil. **tê-lāu**, a small strainer hung from the mouth of a tea-pot for straining the tea as it is poured out. **bí-lāu**, a square box with a funnel, used in a machine for cleaning rice. **thn̂g-lāu**, a conical vessel for refining sugar.

lāu-thn̂g, to filter sugar in refining it.

lāu-thng, to have juice oozing out, as crushed or rotten fruit. **siàm-lāu**, to leak a little or ooze out. **tiâm-lāu**, to leak seriously so as to cause much damage. **ū-lāu**, it leaks. **liàh-lāu**, to examine (*e.g.* a roof) to find and stop the leaks. **that-lāu**, to stop a leak; to caulk.

lāu-siet, to let out, as a secret (v. siet). **lāu-hong**, id. **ûi-lāu** (R.), to omit, as an item in an account.

thau-lāu, to steal things, either larger or as in very small quantities, so that they may not be missed, as an employé. **bô-thau bô-lāu**, not stealing in either way. **lāu-hiòng**, to smuggle. **lāu-sè**, id.

lāu [R. ló, = col. láu, làu, lauh], old; aged; also (P.), to die. **lāu-tsau**, worn-out and useless, as old shoe. **chhàu-lāu**, appearing much older than he really is. **lāu ngiauh-ngiauh**, old and worn out, as feeble old man. **lâng kōe-lāu**, man soon grows old (v. kōe). **lāu-hì**, plays in colloquial, played by grown-up men (v. hì).

lāu-pún, dowager portion. **tiuⁿ-lāu**, to prepare (while alive) clothes, &c., to put on when buried (v. tiuⁿ). **lāu--khì** (P.), to die.

lāu-toā, an elder or head-man in a place. **thài-lāu**, title of the father of a graduate or mandarin. **lāu-tia** (Cn. T.), = A. ló-tia, a mandarin.

lāu-hè, aged (v. hè). **níⁿ lāu**, id. **lāu-pē**, father. **lāu-bú**, mother. **lāu-sè** (T.), father, in some phrases. **lāu-ūn**, last part of an old man's life. **lāu-lâng**, an old man. **lāu-lâng chiâⁿ sòe-kiáⁿ**, old man in second childhood. **lāu-put-siu**, you old wretch!

lāu — **lāu-hàu**, a sort of large nutmeg (v. hàu).

lāu (= làh). **lāu-mûiⁿ**, the yellow sort of the flower mûiⁿ-hoe.

láuⁿ [R. ló, angry; displeased, = col. náuⁿ; cf. làu, nàuⁿ]. **àu-láuⁿ**, vexed angry feeling.

海上絲綢之路文獻集成　科技與文化編

láuⁿ, = náuⁿ (*q.v.*)

lauh [R. ló, old, = col. lāu, láu]. **kó-lauh-phauh**, ancient; old-fashioned (v. kó).

láuh [R. lók, to fall, = col. lòh, lok, lak, làu]. **ka-láuh**, to fall, as things. **phah-ka-láuh**, to let fall. **saⁿ ka-láuh, sì tióh-poáh**, all going wrong. **ka-láuh-jī**, to omit a word or more by mistake, in writing. **ka-láuh chit-jī**, do., one word. **ka-láuh-the**, to have an abortion. **ka-láuh-sin**, id.

lauhⁿ— **î**ⁿ**-lauh**ⁿ **î**ⁿ**-lauh**ⁿ, fat and plump, as face.

le (C. nεⁿ). **kun-le** (C. kin-nεⁿ), small branching sinews or nerves. **lā kun-le**, to make roundabout inquiries to find the real truth of a matter.

le (C.) **o-le**, words used in beginning to say something.

le (Cn.) **chhiáng-ke-le**, to hop, as a child.

le (T.), = A. **la**, light amusement, &c. (cf. lê, lû). **le-le**, having much leisure and full of fun. **chit-jit le-le-le**, having nothing to do all day but to amuse one's self. **le kàu-phah-tsoah**, much too jolly.

lε (C.), = A. la. **li-li·lε-lε**, prattle of children.

le (T.), = léh, lö. **oáⁿ-ke-le**, the bottom of a broken bowl (v. ke).

lê — **hoah-lê-long**, an auction. **hoah-lê-lang**, id.

lê (C. lε̂), to talk long without stopping, especially in defending one's self, saying that all was quite right. **lê-lê-háu**, id. **chin-gâu-lê**, very fond of talking so. **lî-bú lî-lê**, talking on far too much.

lê (cf. la, le). **phah lê-á**, to chatter; to talk empty foolish stories and jokes; to talk idly instead of working. **chhùi náⁿ-phah-lê-á**, id.

lê— **lê-á**, the small rings in the front of a baby's chair. **phah-lê-á**, to make them turn by striking them to amuse the child. **pa-lê**, metal rings with small balls inside, shaken at idolatrous processions to make a jingling noise.

lê (R. lî). **po-lê**, glass.

lê (C.), = A. lôe, to bend down the head and rush on.

lê [R. a plough, = col. lôe]; also (C.), = A. lôe, a plough; to plough. **lê-khiā-chiàⁿ** (C.), the upright stick of a plough.

i-lê, the province of Ili in Turkestan, on the N.W. borders of the Chinese empire.

lê, very thin; tearing easily, as cloth. **sán lê-lê**, id.

lê (T. lô). **e-lê**, troublesome and fractious, especially of a fretful child (v. e.)

lê [R. lē, elegant; excellent]. **ko-lê**, Corea, = tiâu-sién. **ko-lê-chhài**, cabbage.

lê [R. name of a plant]. **chit-lê**, a thorny medicinal plant (Tribulus?). **chék-lê** (Cn.), id.

lê [R. têng, the dragon-fly]. **pē-lê**, the largest kind of dragon-fly. **pók-lê** (C.), id. **toā-lε̂** (C.), the cicada, = **am-po-chê**.

lê [R. gâ, a sprout, = col. gê]. **béh-lê-ko**, a sort of thick glutinous syrup.

lê (= lē), to prune off small twigs.

lê [R. lô, a snail or univalve, = col. lê], (Cn. lô), a snail; any spiral univalve shell-fish; a spiral. **lê-á**, a snail or univalve. **lê-khak**, its shell. **lê-phí**, white inner layer of the shell (v. phí). **lê-tì**, the cover of the mouth of the shell. **lê-hék**, dried flesh of such shell-fish. **lê-phièn**, a slice of it.

kńg-lê-hong, a whirlwind (v. kńg). **ká-lê-hong** (C.), id. **ké-lê-hong** (C.), id. **séh bé-lê**, to put off settling a matter, &c. (v. séh). **in kè-á-lê**, to make the queue into a knot at the back of the head (v. kè). **lê-si-teng** (C.), = A. lê-si-teng, a screw-nail.

chhân-lê, field snails. **lē-lê**, snails. **ka-tiaⁿ-lê**, a yellow sort of univalve. **tek-lê**, a long tapering sort. **hoe-lê**, a variegated sort. **iû-lê**, a glossy blackish-gray sort. **ōng-lê**, a large good sort. **béh-lê**, a small sort. **tsu-lê, bah-lê, chióh-lê, ka-tsui-lê**, &c., various other sorts.

lé [R. lûi, to injure, as in fight], (Cn. lô). **ka-lé-hì**, puppet-shows. **ka-lé-láng**, trunks for carrying them. **ka-lé-koán**, house where men live who exhibit puppet-shows. **ka-lé-hók**, dresses for puppets. **ka-lé-chhák**, hard fighting hand to hand, with cutting and slashing, &c. **ka-lé-kha**, having the feet much turned outwards; also, a double angle (both right angles) in opposite directions in a moulding, as where a higher house is joined to a lower, or where a door in a wall is higher than the rest of the wall. **poaⁿ ka-lé**, to play or have a puppet-show. **thiu ka-lé**, to pull the strings of the puppets. **tiàu-ka-lé**, to commit suicide by hanging. **tiàu-ka-lé--sí**, id.

lé (T. lô). **ka-láu ka-lé**, to talk indistinctly about a matter (v. láu).

lé (C.) **hó-lé-á**, take care!

lé (C.), = A. lóe, né (mother). **niûⁿ-lé** (C.), mother.

lé (C.), = A. lóe, to scold; to revile.

lé [R. ló, old, = col. lāu, láu]. **lé-chhí** (C.), = A. niáu-chhú, a rat.

lé (C.) **lé-khang**, to make a hole.

lé — **pa-lé**, a padre; imitation of the Spanish word. **lû-sòng pa-lé** (Cn.), said of an overbearing domineering man, who is always correcting others, but won't take correction himself (lit. a Manila padre). **lû-sòng pa-lé, kong-ka-kī-tō** (Cn.), id.

lé (R. id.), ceremony; propriety; politeness; a fee; a small present. **ū-lé**, polite. **bô-lé**, unpolite; unbecoming. **bô-háp-lé**, id. **hó-lé**, politeness. **lé-lē**, politeness; proper ceremonies; a ceremonial present on any occasion. **chit--ê lé-lē**, a suitable present for the occasion. **kap--i kiâⁿ lé-lē**, to perform the proper ceremonies, or give the fitting present to him. **sàng lé-gî**, to make the customary presents at betrothal. **lé-sò**, ceremony; politeness (v. sò). **lé-māuⁿ**, polite deportment; to treat with respect (v. māuⁿ). **lé-pài**, ceremonial worship; a week (v. pài).

lé-pē, the Board of Rites; the President of it. **lé-kì**, the Book of Rites. **chiu-lé**, the book of the rites of the Chow dynasty. **lé-seng**, the master of ceremonies in solemn rites, *e.g.* funerals, great rites of ancestral worship, &c. **chhiàng-lé**, to call out (as he does) what is to be done at each rite. **lé-thiap**, a document sent along with the presents at betrothal, stating the presents (v. thiap). **lé-hók**, ceremonial dress. **lé-pân** (Cn.), a wine-jug used at ancestral rites, &c.

chit-tsoā-lé, one ceremonial visit. **chit-hong-lé**, money wrapped in paper, and given to a teacher or doctor. **chit-pau-lé**, id. **pau-lé hō--i**, wrap up a fee and give it him.

seng-lé, offerings of flesh made to idols or spirits. **chiú-lé**, offerings of liquor thus made. **sóe-lé** (X.), baptism.

chhe-lé, fee given to constables when they serve a warrant. **kaⁿ-lé**, fee to jailer. **phèng-lé**, money and other presents sent by bridegroom's parents to bride's parents. **siā-lé**, a small reward for trouble to a friend. **sai-kong-lé**, fee of a Tauist priest. **tiong-lâng-lé**, commission paid to the middleman, as in buying house or land. **hm̂-lâng-lé**, fee paid to the go-between in a marriage. **tê-lé**, a small present given on getting a cup of tea, as to a priest, or as to new-married bride.

sit-lé, to make a mistake in regard to politeness; to fail in politeness; I beg your pardon for my rudeness. **bô-khu-lé**, not standing on ceremony. **kiâ^{n}-lé**, to salute; to perform a ceremony. **hôe-lé**, to return a ceremony or ceremonial call. **tap-lé**, to make a present, or do a ceremony in return for the like. **tîn-lé**, to make ceremonial presents to the great. **hō-lé**, to make congratulatory presents, as at marriage, graduation, taking office, &c. **tsōe-lé**, very polite. **kàu-lé**, politeness up to the mark. **kāu-lé**, too polite and ceremonious. **lé to, jîn pit-tsà**, a very polite man must be cunning. **giên to, pit-sit: lé to, pit-tsà**, in much talk there will be some mistake; in much politeness there is surely some cunning.

poàn-lé-pêng, the 113th radical when written at the side; said also of the 145th radical. **poàn-lé**, id.

siáu-lé (C.), = A. siáu-lóe, ashamed.

lē [R. to exert; to incite]. **bién-lē**, to incite to good actions; to stir up zeal.

lē [R. sharp; to sharpen]. **giâm-lē** (R.), very stern; too dignified in manner.

lē (C.), = A. lōe, a file.

lē [R. lī, to rule; an officer; a subordinate]. **chhiong-iu lē-tsut**, prostitutes, actors, and underlings of yamuns, whose sons cannot become graduates or mandarins.

lē [R. laws; regulations; tariff], (C. lī), fees paid to officials. **lu̍t-lē**, a code of laws. **tāi-chheng lu̍t-lē**, the criminal code of the Manchoo dynasty. **hong-lē**, a custom. **kó͘-lē**, ancient rules and regulations. **chek-lē**, a tariff. **hái-lē**, customs and port dues. **kháu-lē**, port dues; tonnage dues. **kui-lē**, a regular fee, as at yamun or custom-house. **kui-lē-chî^{n}**, id. **lē-chî^{n}**, squeezes levied by government underlings for tolerating things forbidden by law. **kóng lē-chî^{n}**, to promise to pay such moneys for illegal toleration. **gû-bah-lē**, money levied for winking at the killing of cows. **kiáu-lē**, do. from gambling-houses. **piáu-lē**, do. from brothels. **lē-kìm**, forbidden by the laws.

lē [R. subject; inferior]. **lē-su**, the common square form of the Chinese characters. **chin-chhó thoàn-lē**, four forms of writing.

tit-lē, the province of Chih-li.

lē, = lē (T. lȫ), to prune off small twigs; to cut off the tops and side shoots of sugar-cane.

lē [R. name of a fish, = col. lōe]. **lē-hî** (esp. C.), a round fish with black spots. **lē-koa^{n}**, this fish dried.

lē [R. name of a shell-fish]. **bó͘-lē**, a medicine made from a shell. **bó͘-lē-khak**, the shell of a long-shaped bivalve. **bó͘-lē-hún**, do. powdered.

lē (cf. lē), (C. lɛ̄). **háu lē-lē**, to make a noise, as a cicada. **lē-lē-háu** (C.), id. **toā-lɛ̄** (C.), a large cicada.

lē (C.) **lē-chi**, = A. lāi-chi, nāi^{n}-chi, the fruit called lichi.

lē (R. id.) **pūi^{n}-lē** (C.), = A. tsoá^{n}-lī, a strainer for lifting out boiled rice.

lɛ̄ (P.) **ám-lɛ̄**, a useless soft-wooded tree, with glossy pinnate leaves, which grows abundantly by streams. **tsúi-lē**, id.

leh, an enclitic, often used at the end of a sentence.

leh (Cn. lōh), to pinch or twitch, especially for curing disease. **leh-soa**, to pinch one's neck to cure a colic. **khit-kúi leh--khì**, said of a thing suddenly stolen, or of a child dying very suddenly.

leh (T. lȫh). **khiên leh-leh**, to fret, as a child. **lí-leh**, very troublesome, as a young boy; fond of talking and joking with men, as woman.

lân-san lí-leh, in small quantities; not in full sets or large quantity. **lí-lí leh-leh**, id.

le̍h [R. jio̍k, weak], soft and flabby, as skin of fat man; too soft and doughy, as cakes; soft and easily broken, as a string.

le̍h (T. lȫh). **liām-liām le̍h-le̍h**, constant talking in a querulous way; *e.g.* a woman talking on about a matter quite ended. **gâu-liām-le̍h**, id.

le̍h [R. le̍k, noise of thunder, &c., = col. neh^{n}], (C. nɛh^{n}, nɛ̍h^{n}). **khe̍h-le̍h**, loud and quick sound of thunder. **le̍h-le̍h-kiò**, id. **le̍h-le̍h-tân**, id. **nih^{n}-nih^{n} le̍h-le̍h**, sound of rattling or shaking things together carelessly. **le̍h-le̍h-háu**, id., or of thunder, or of beating metal. **sai-lâm le̍h-le̍h-háu**, the south-west monsoon roaring.

le̍h [R. lie̍t, to tear; to crack, = col. li̍h]. **le̍h-sū**, the island called Little Quemoy. **oá^{n}-ke-le̍h**, the broken bottom of a bowl. **oá^{n}-kim-ke-le̍h**, id.

le̍h (C. lɛ̍h), to rip up; to slit up or slit open, without cutting separate. **le̍h-khui**, to slit open, as with a knife. **le̍h-tō͘**, to rip the belly, so as to remove the entrails. **le̍h chit-khang**, to slit up and make an opening. **chit-le̍h**, one long cut with a knife. **thâi chit-le̍h**, to give a long slash or cut.

le̍h (C.), = A. lo̍eh, a broad sun-hat.

lɛ̍h [R. le̍k, a sort of oak]. **pe̍h-lɛ̍h-á** (P.), a sort of oak; the acorn is sometimes eaten.

lɛ̍h (C.), = A. lie̍t, wide open, as door.

lɛ̍h (C.) **ka-lɛ̍h**, = A. ka-la̍h, name of a fish.

le̍h (C. lɛ̍h), (mere reduplication). **pe̍h-le̍h-se̍h**, very white.

lek— **lêng-lek**, to insult, as by abusive words. **khit-i-lek** (T.), to be sorely insulted by him, with words.

lek [R. le̍k, to bridle; to compel]. **lek-sek**, = le̍k-sek, to extort money.

lek— **lek-phī^{n}**, the nose wrinkled in displeasure. **lek-phī^{n} lek-ba̍k**, to wrinkle nose and eyes, by a frown, in anger.

lek, to make a line, as a mark; to make a fold, as in a dress where a plait is to be sewed. **tsúi lek**, the water just beginning to ebb, just making the tide-mark. **tsúi lek-hûn**, id. **lek-hûn**, to make a line or fold, as a mark, or as a disease does; to make a fold, as in a dress. **lek chit-sûn**, to make a fold or plait, as on dress or cap (v. sûn).

phak-lek-soà^{n}, sort of bead-moulding.

lek— **lek-lēng**, to slacken, as a rope (v. lēng).

lek— **lek-chhiú**, to stop striking or fighting, as on the intervention of others.

lek— **lek--lo̍h-lâi**, to sink down ill or fainting. **lek--lo̍h-khì**, id.

lek— **bīn lek-sek**, face pale (losing colour), as from fear or shame.

lek (cf. neh^{n}). **lek-tá^{n}**, to lose courage. **lún-lek**, to be afraid to do a thing.

lek— **pe̍h lek-lek**, very white, as cloth.

厦英大辭典

lėk [R. to bridle; to restrain; to compel]. **lėk-bé**, to rein in a horse. **lėk-bé-kun**, images holding horses, as at temple of Sêng-hông, &c. **lėk-tē**, a certain rope in a vessel (v. tē). **bé-lėk-tē**, saddle-girth. **bé-lėk-soh** (C.), bridle reins. **lėk-soh** (C.), id.

ek-lėk, to oppress; to compel improperly. **lėk-sek**, to extort money; to squeeze money (s. green).

lėk--chhut-lâi, to press out, as blood or matter from a wound. **lėk-huih**, to press blood from a wound.

nī^n-lėk-hùt, the fat Buddha. **bī-lėk**, id. **pûi-lėk**, id.

lėk (cf. lȧk), to pull up, as one's sleeves, or the legs of trowsers. **lėk-khah-khí**, id.

lėk [R. the ribs]. **chiap-lėk**, the soft part of the loin on the hind quarter. **chiap-lėk-bah**, meat from that part.

lėk — **âng-lėk-kôe**, a sort of salted shell-fish from North China.

lėk [R. liȯk, a green plant; interchanged with the next word]. **lėk-tāu**, a small sort of pea (v. tāu). **lėk-tek**, a sort of bamboo; the shoots are much eaten.

lėk (R. liȯk), light green; yellowish green. **lėk-sek**, id. (s. oppress). **lėk-chhiàm-chhiàm**, bright green, as fields after rain, or ugly green tinge of what was meant to be black. **kim-ku-lėk**, a rich deep green (almost black), like a beetle. **hoe-hiȯh-lėk**, rich green, like the leaves of plants. **hoe-âng liû-lėk**, gaudily adorned with red and green; too gaudy in dress. **chhêng kàu hoe-âng liû-lėk**, gaudily dressed, as woman.

tâng-lėk, verdegris (verditer?). **lėk-tê**, green tea.

soa-lėk, green without any gloss. **soa-lėk-pò͘**, green cloth without gloss. **iû-lėk**, glossy green; glossy green cloth. **hok-lėk**, green cloth from Fuh-chau.

lėk [R. to drop or drip]. **lėk-chheng** (R.), a bituminous substance.

lėk [R. liȯk, dry land]. **lėk-lō͘**, road by land. **lėk-lō͘-koa^n**, an officer in the army. **lėk-lō͘ thê-tok**, a general. **lėk-lō͘ tsúi-su**, military and naval.

bô-chî^n, kiam lėk-lō͘ (a long land journey and no pay), said of having a great deal of trouble and little benefit. **bô-chî^n, kah lėk-lō͘**, id.

lėk [R. to sink; to love to excess]. **lėk-ài**, to love excessively, as son, &c. (v. ài).

lėk (next word?). **tîm-lėk**, to hide and keep for one's self, as another's property; *e.g.* money sent to one's care from abroad and secretly embezzled.

lėk [R. to conceal; clandestine; to hide]. **ún-lėk**, to hide and keep secret, as a thing, affair, or person. **lėk--khí-lâi**, id. **lėk-siàu**, to keep a sale secret, not putting it in the books, so as to embezzle the price (s. copy).

lėk (R. liȯk), to copy out, as items from an account-book. **lėk-siàu**, to copy out the items in our books which refer to each customer, *e.g.* in order to collect debts (s. conceal). **siàu tiȯh-lėk--khí-lâi**, copy out these items. **tiȯh-lėk-lėk--khì**, id.

bȯk-lėk (Cn. P.), = A. bȯk-liȯk, a table of contents.

lėk — **lėk-kim**, to plate a metal (especially silver) with gold, by the use of molten gold.

lėk — **lėk-tn̂g lėk-tē**, very much exhausted with any work, mental or bodily (v. tē).

lėk — **lėk-súi** (T.), = A. jiáu^n-súi, the ornamental work between the legs of a table.

lėk [R. sound, as of thunder]. **phek-lėk**, great rattling sound of thunder. **toā-phek-lėk**, id.

lėk — **nî^n-lėk-to** (T.), a small sort of reaping-hook.

lėk [R. strength, = col. lȧt]. **hoat-lėk**, powerful influence of an idol; magical arts of Tauists (v. hoat). **hó-gán-lėk**, able to distinguish good and bad at a glance. **khah-hó tám-lėk**, rather courageous. **sè-lėk**, influence and power. **ū sè-lėk**, to have influence to back him and also ability. **tsâi-sè-lėk sa^n-jī tsn̂g**, abundant wealth, influence, and ability. **tsâi kiông, lėk chīn**, money and strength all exhausted. **tâng-sim hiàp-lėk**, with united heart and strength. **lėk-liōng**, the measure of one's strength or ability, esp. wealth and ability to pay. **toā-lėk-liōng**, of considerable wealth or ability. **sûi-lâng ê-lėk-liōng**, according to a man's ability, as to subscribe. **jîn-lėk pó͘ thien-kong**, art improving on nature (v. kong).

lėk [R. to pass through; in succession; to experience]. **lėk-tāi**, in successive ages or generations. **lėk-nî^n**, in each successive year. **lėk-lâi**, from a long time back always till now. **lâi-lėk**, the history of a person or affair from the first; the account of the origin and antecedents. **lâi-lėk put-bêng**, antecedents not clear, *e.g.* some flaw or doubt about the title-deeds of the seller; or as some blot or want of clearness about a man's genealogy or early history. **lí-lėk**, a document stating the particulars of one's birth, literary rank, official rank, &c., given in to a superior officer, as on taking office, on rise in rank, or on visiting a high superior. **thiên lí-lėk**, to write such a statement. **tâu lí-lėk**, to give it in to the superior. **chhiàng-lí-lėk**, to make such a statement verbally on having an audience of a superior.

iėt-lėk, experienced in affairs; having seen much of the world. **kè-iėt-lėk**, id. **oȧt-lėk** (C.), id.

leng [R. nái, mother, teat, milk, = col. né, lóe; lin, ni^n], (T. lin), teat; udder; breasts of woman; nipple; a knob, as for a handle; milk; juice of trees, &c.

leng-thâu, a teat. **leng-chhng**, the orifice of a teat. **leng-eng**, abscess in the female breast. **leng-hó͘**, id., somewhat different form. **leng-gâm**, another variety of abscess. **leng-niau^n**, a smaller sort. **bong-leng**, to touch a woman's breast; if allowed, is a sign of consent to illicit connection.

leng-bú, a wet-nurse. **chhī-leng**, to feed with one's milk, as mother or nurse; to suckle. **chiȧh-leng**, to live on milk. **suh-leng**, to suck milk. **lùt-leng**, to milk. **tn̄g-leng**, to wean. **gû-leng**, cow's milk; soft salted curd. **kiâm-gû-leng**, soft salted curd. **chhi^n-gû-leng**, cow's milk, generally curdled, but not yet salted. **gû-leng-chiu^n** (C.), cow's milk. **gû-leng-iû**, butter. **gû-leng-piá^n** (f.), cheese.

ti-bú-leng, an edible plant (v. ti). **chhiū-leng**, juices of trees used for valuable purposes, *e.g.* India-rubber, gutta-percha, &c. (one sort used for making varnish adhere well). **pui^n-leng** (C.), the juice of the "pui^n," or liquid-amber tree (used in gilding).

lêng [R. a sort of net], a net for catching fish in the meshes as they try to swim through. **pàng-lêng**, to set such a net, as in a rapid stream or strong tide-way. **bé-ka-lêng**, net with large meshes for catching the bé-ka. **lȧt-á-lêng**, a finer sort with smaller meshes for the lȧt-á-hî.

lêng [R. id., = col. lîn]. **lêng-tiû**, a sort of thin silk stuff.

lêng [R. liông, the ridge-pole of a house, = col. niû^n].

phī^{n}-lêng, the ridge of the nose (s. dragon). **hē-lêng** (T.), = A. hē--chhù, the houses at the two ends of a large house.

lêng [R. bêng, to engrave]. **lêng-cheng**, a banner at a funeral, with name and titles of deceased.

lêng [R. bêng, clear, plain]. **lêng-kak**, horn made thin and transparent, for lanterns (s. Trapa; s. China root).

lêng [R. sort of Trapa]. **lêng-kak**, Trapa natans or bicornis; the fruit is eaten; it is red outside but white inside (s. clear; s. China root).

lêng [R. China root]. **hok-lêng**, China root (Smilax China?). **hok-lêng-kak**, id., broken small. **lêng-kak**, id. (s. clear; s. Trapa). **hok-lêng-phì^{n}**, China root in large slices. **lêng-phì^{n}**, id. **hok-lêng-ko**, a sort of sweet cake made with it. **hoh-lêng-ko**, id.

chhiah-lêng, a red-coloured sort. **chhoan-lêng**, the best sort from Sze-chuen.

lêng [R. name of a vegetable]. **pe-lêng-chhài**, a vegetable like spinach (Convolvulus reptans?). **poe-lêng-chhài** (C.), id., = T. chhiah-kūn-chhài.

lêng [R. name of an insect]. **bêng-lêng--ê**, a child that is bought and adopted.

lêng — **lêng-sit**, to clip the wings. **lêng chit-tè** (T.), cut off a small bit, as of meat.

lêng [R. to insult; to disgrace], a surname. **lêng-jio̍k**, to insult. **lêng-lek**, to insult by abusive words.

lêng-tî, to put to death by cutting in pieces while alive (v. tî). **lêng-tî--lâng**, to annoy people very much (said of a child that won't sleep, or of a master who makes his hands or servants miserable).

lêng [R. able; power], (Cn. lêng). **koân-lêng**, authority; power. **tsâi-lêng**, ability; skill. **lêng-kàn**, skilful; expert; having much capacity for business (should not be said in Amoy, as it suggests a bad meaning). **ū lêng-ûi**, able to do a thing (v. ûi). **bô-lêng** (polite), I have not sufficient ability. **bû-put-lêng**, able to do all things; almighty. **bû-só put-lêng**, id.

lêng [R. spiritual; intelligent; efficacious, as prayers or divinities, or geomantic position].

lêng-hûn (R.), the soul or spirit. **lêng-chhù**, paper houses burned for the dead. **lêng-ûi**, the place where the "hûn-sin" is placed in the rites for a person recently deceased; the spirit is supposed to stay there during the rites; it is made of paper, sometimes like a house, sometimes like hangings. **lêng-chêng**, the place in front of the hangings round the "hûn-sin." **lêng-toh**, the table placed there. **kat-lêng**, to put up the paper or cloth house or hangings (lêng-ûi) round the "hûn-sin." **tì-lêng**, to set up the hûn-sin, put up the screen or cloth partition round it, and make all things ready for the rites of "kong-tek." **an-lêng**, to begin these rites, as relatives and priests do. **chhiá^{n}-lêng**, to invite the spirit of the dead to come and stay in the "lêng-chhù" during these rites. **khiā-lêng**, to perform these rites. **tû-lêng**, to take away and burn the hûn-sin, with all the fittings, at the end of the ceremonies. **thiet-lêng**, id.

lêng-lâi, precocious and intelligent (v. lâi). **lêng-thong**, of great mental discernment. **ū lêng-khiàu**, well educated; having mental powers well developed. **chhi^{n}-mî^{n} cheng, é-káu lêng**, blind men and dumb men are very sharp (v. cheng). **kháu lêng, siét piên**, mouth clever and tongue ready, never at a loss for an answer some way or other, so as to get out of a difficulty. **bān-bu̍t chi-lêng**, the most intelligent of all things (said of man).

lêng-khì, appearance of intelligence, as in child or young boy; powerful influence for good fortune, as of a mountain as a site for a grave, house, or village. **chit-tiám lêng-khì**, a good deal of cleverness (said as of boy at school); auspicious influence, as of grave, &c.

pàng-lêng, to lead down the auspicious influence of a hill, as some forms of rocks or ridges do. **tùi-chia lo̍h-lêng**, the auspicious influence descends this way. **ū lêng-lo̍h**, to have a good way for the auspicious influence of the fung-shuy (hong-súi) coming down the ridge from the highest peaks to the site of a house, city, or grave. **ū-chit-ki lêng-lo̍h**, do. of grave or house; also, beautiful in appearance, as person. **lêng-mêh^{n}**, veins in the hills that lead along the auspicious influence. **lêng-chit**, a long ridge descending gradually and ending in a small eminence, counted a very lucky form. **lêng-sin**, place about the middle of the declivity of a hill where there is good luck for a grave or house-site. **khiā-lêng**, placed about midway on the sloping ridge of a hill, as grave or house. **hôe-lêng**, facing the origin of the auspicious influence, as a grave-site (v. hôe). **hoah soa^{n}-lêng**, to call the good influence of the hill to come to the grave; done at time of burial by the geomancer (standing on rising ground apart, with sword and compass in hands), with shouting and gesticulations, with guns, crackers, &c. **tåh soa^{n}-lêng**, to search for a good grave site on the hills, as geomancer. **liåh soa^{n}-lêng**, id.

ui-lêng, majesty and power of an idol or god. **ui-lêng-kong**, the guardian idol of a Foo or Ting. **lêng-tan**, the Tauist elixir of immortality. **lêng-sià^{n}**, powerful, as an idol. **lêng-kám**, id. **lêng-hiën**, id. **lêng-giām**, id. **lêng-èng**, id.

pit-lêng, a sort of bird that imitates the song of several birds. **pek-lêng**, id. **ná^{n} pit-lêng**, said of a man who is good at talking and telling lies to make a case good. **lêng-áu**, a sort of fish. **kim-lêng-hî** (Cn.), = A. âng-koe, a sort of fish.

lêng (R. liông), (C. often liông), a dragon. **liåh-lêng**, to shampoo. **siù^{n}-lêng**, born in a year of which the dragon is the sign. **si^{n} phī^{n}-lêng**, to have a polypus in the nose.

toā-lêng, the tiller-rope for the helm. **khê-thâu-lêng**, a long narrow purse made so as to tie round the waist to hold up trowsers, and at the same time to hold money.

tsúi-lêng, a fire-engine. **chiú-lêng**, a portable machine for boiling wine.

hé-lêng, a match for a gun. **hé-lêng-pau**, a pouch for carrying the match. **tauh hé-lêng**, to light the powder with the match. **chheng-soa^{n}-lêng**, a sort of gingall. **chhi^{n}-soa^{n}-lêng** (T.), id. **chhùi^{n}-soa^{n}-lêng** (Cn.), id. **lêng-kòng-chhèng**, a large sort of cannon.

lêng-gê, upright sticks in the bow of a junk between which the anchor cable runs. **lêng-chhiu**, a dragon's beard (v. chhiu). **lêng-kut**, a mineral, esp. from Sze-chuen, like belemnite or fossil bones of a saurian.

lêng-ông, the god of the sea. **lêng-ñg**, id. **hái-lêng-ông**, id. **lêng ká-tsúi**, a waterspout from the sky. **thiâu-lêng**, pillars with dragons carved on them, as at temples. **lêng-pê**, a flowing robe embroidered with dragons. **lêng-koàn**, a water-jug (like a kettle) with dragons on it.

lêng-hé-chî^{n}, the space just outside a temple door (v. hé). **lêng-chhia hōng-lien**, imperial equipages.

chhah-chhêng, khah-kiā

chhah-chhêng, khah-kiāⁿ-lêng, we put up banyan branches, and are stronger than dragons.

lêng-tsûn, a dragon-boat, used on 5.5. **pê lêng-tsûn**, to paddle them in racing. **lêng-tsûn-hoe**, a bright red flower (Clerodendron) that blooms about 5.5. **lêng-tsûn-pak**, a very strong north wind for several days about that time. **lêng-tsûn-kut**, the back-bone. **thàu-lêng** (T.), the whole back-bone of a pig. **hè-lêng-bák**, to wash the eyes of the dragon-boats.

lêng-kéng (C.), = A. **gêng-géng**, the dragon's-eye or lung-yen fruit. **lêng-kán** (C.), id. **lêng-táⁿ-chháu**, a febrifuge medicine.

lêng-hê, a lobster. **thê-lêng**, a sort of eel. **thê-lêng-chhe**, sort of trident for spearing it. **chháu-lêng**, an animal like a lizard with a snake-like body. **kau-lêng**, a sea-monster (v. kau). **ɵ-lêng**, a small black cricket.

lêng (R. id.), (T. lân). **lêng-á**, a small bell used by children and Tauists. **kap-lêng**, bells on pigeons' wings. **hâm-lêng**, rattles containing small balls, worn by horses and dogs; also hung at child's wrist. **koà-hâm-lêng**, to wear them. **io-lêng**, to shake a small bell.

lêng (R. id.), to grasp tight and keep from moving away, as man or animal; also, to move by putting the hands below (one man or many), as a large heavy box or cupboard. **lêng--lâi**, to grasp firmly and pull towards one's self. **lêng-tiâu**, to grasp very tight, so that he cannot escape. **lêng-i-tiâu**, id. **tùi-phīⁿ kā--i lêng--nih**, catch it by the nose, as cow. **tióh-lêng gû-thâu, m̄-thang lêng gû-bé**, if a man owes you money you must take a fitting time to demand it back, *i.e.* when he has some money.

tàu-lêng, unitedly move (as a heavy chest) by putting the hands below.

lêng [R. rest; quiet; peace; rather than]. **lêng-khé**, the best way is to —; better to — than —. **lêng-chhū** (Cn.), id.

lêng-khun-tan, a medicine (v. khun). **thiⁿ chheng-chheng, tōe lêng-lêng**, the influences of heaven and earth all propitious (said by Tauist priest in benediction).

lêng-pho, Ningpo. **hok-lêng**, Fuh-ning-foo, between Fuh-chau and Wen-chau.

lêng [R. name of a bird]. **chek-lêng** (R.), a bird said to be a pattern of fraternal affection.

lêng [R. a mound], a long raised bed in a cultivated field. **kui-lêng**, the whole of such a long raised bed or beds; said also of the large fat folds on the neck of a corpulent man. **ka-nn̂g-lêng**, the whole bed of vegetables. **han-tsû-lêng**, a long raised bed of potatoes (Cn. siuⁿ). **tāu-á-lêng**, do. of beans.

lêng [R. a sort of goat]. **lêng-iông**, a sort of antelope (v. iông).

lêng [R. age]. **kui-lêng hók-soàn** (R.), may you live as long as the turtle and stork.

lêng [R. a feather]. **chìⁿ-lêng**, the feathers of an arrow. **lêng-hoe**, id.

hoe-lêng, a peacock's feather with one eye. **siúⁿ hoe-lêng**, to give permission to wear it in the official cap, a high honour. **siang-gán-lêng**, peacock's feather with two eyes, very high honour. **ɵ-a-lêng**, an artificial feather, much less honourable than hoe-lêng. **lâm-lêng**, id. **lêng-téng**, having a feather in his official cap, given for special service. **sù-lêng**, to give permission to wear such a feather. **koà-lêng**, to wear a feather so.

lêng [R. to order or command]. **teng-lêng**, to order or instruct gradually over and over again. **chhien teng-lêng, bān chiok-hù**, frequent and repeated commands and instructions.

léng [R. lióng, two; a pair; a tael, = col. niúⁿ, nn̄g], (T. lióng). **léng-lông**, the covered sides of the court of a Chinese house connecting the front and back parts of the house.

léng [R. lêng, clever; an actor]. **léng-lī**, neat and clean; well and neatly done; intelligent, as child; pretty (v. lī).

léng [R. a mountain pass, = col. niáⁿ]. **ko-san tsùn-léng** (R.), lofty mountains.

léng [R. to receive; to lead; to govern or manage; a collar; = col. niáⁿ]. **léng-kàu** (R.), I have received your instructions. **léng-chêng chiū-sī**, no, I thank you; said in declining a present (lit. having received your kind intention is enough). **tsoân-léng**, to accept the whole, as a present.

tài-léng, to lead soldiers, as a commanding officer. **léng-sū-koaⁿ**, a consul.

hó-pún-léng, having much ability, talent, or skill. **bô-pún-léng**, not having sufficient ability.

léng (R. id.), cold or cool, as water or food; cooled, as affection. **léng sih-sih**, very cold, as food. **léng peng-peng**, ice-cold. **peng-léng**, id. **piang-piang-léng**, very cold or cool. **liâng-léng**, cool; pleasantly cool. **koâⁿ-léng**, very cold. **im-léng**, shady and pleasantly cool. **thiⁿ-khì im-léng**, pleasant, cool, cloudy weather. **léng-jiét**, hot and cold principles (v. jiét). **poàⁿ-sio-léng**, tepid, as water; half-cold, as food.

léng-tām, grown cold-hearted; feeling dreary or heartless (v. tām). **léng-chēng**, lonely; desolate. **léng-lòh** (C.), decayed or desolate, as place or family. **léng-chhiò**, sarcastic laugh. **léng-gē**, to speak sarcastically. **léng-keng**, the prison of the imperial harem (v. keng). **kìm-jip léng-pâng**, said of a man who has several wives leaving one without intercourse.

kám-léng, having a cold, slightly feverish. **ùi-léng**, having a slight shivering feeling; also (C.), ague (v. ùi).

lèng (C. làng, liòng), to kick right out with the sole of the foot. **kha-lèng chhiú-lèng**, pushing away with hands and feet, as child resisting when carried away. **kùn-lèng**, to struggle hard with hands, feet, and body, as to get off. **gâu-kùn-lèng**, good at struggling and kicking, so as to escape from one's grasp. **kùn-lèng--khì**, to break away by struggling, and run off. **kùn-lèng--tsáu**, id. **lèng--tsáu**, id.

lèng (T.), = A. lìm, to doze for a short time. **lèng chit-chhìⁿ**, id.

lēng — **péh-lēng-si**, the paddy-bird; the white egret.

lēng — **ka-lēng**, the magpie; more properly the black and white mina: it can learn to speak a little.

lēng (R. liēn), (T. nāiⁿ; Cn. nūiⁿ). **khé-lēng**, a tree with lilac blossoms (Melia Azederach?). **lēng-á**, id. **khé-lēng-chhiū**, id.

lēng [R. to order or command; to cause; honourable; polite phrase for "your" in reference to relatives].

tsú-lēng, a man who commits a crime by the instrumentality of another.

bēng-lēng, a command; also (r.), to command. **kun-lēng**, military orders. **chiòng-lēng**, a general's order. **ông-lēng**, the imperial commission to a high mandarin, which gives him the power of life and death. **kiàh ông-lēng**, to carry triangular flags with the word "lēng" before some idols (*e.g.* ông-iâ), as is done by thirteen little boys. **tok-lēng**, the boy who acts as head of that band, carrying a large flag. **lēng-kî**, a flag given to a messenger who carries the special orders of a high mandarin or of an idol. **lēng-chìⁿ**, an arrow given to a messenger by a very high mandarin, to show that his orders are extremely urgent. **hoat lēng-chìⁿ**, to give this arrow. **hō-lēng**, an order given to soldiers by a signal. **thek-lēng**, Tauist charms in unintelligible characters on yellow paper. **hû-lēng**, a charm made of green bamboo with the character "hû" written on it, and a bit of red cloth at the top.

chhut-lēng, to issue a military command. **hoat-lēng**, id. **thoân-lēng**, to transmit or deliver military orders given by a superior (v. thoân). **siong-kèng put-jû chiông-lēng**, I will (as you desire it) relax a little the rules of strict politeness according to which I should treat you.

gèh-lēng, the cyclical name of a month (v. gèh). **sì-lēng** (r.), the things that should be done and said in the four seasons. **chhun-lēng**, the usual sort of weather in spring. **tang-thiⁿ**, **kiâⁿ chhun-lēng**, warm spring weather in winter. **taⁿ kiâⁿ chhun-lēng**, the weather is now (in spring) the usual spring weather. **hē-lēng**, the usual summer weather.

lùt-lēng, the demon of thunder, who hastens the thunder on its way. **kip-kip jû-lùt-lēng**, as swift as the thunder-spirit (v. kip).

lēng-jîn khó-ài, very lovable (lit. causing people to be able to love).

lēng-lông, your son. **lēng-ài** (r.), your daughter. **lēng-siok**, your father's younger brother. **lēng-pek**, do. elder. **lēng-tsun**, your father. **lēng-tông**, your mother. **lēng-tsé**, your grandfather (all polite phrases).

lēng, the long mark left by the blow of a rod. **phah chit-lēng**, strike, so as to leave a long mark or scar. **phah kàu-e-bah-lēng**, to beat till black and blue in long streaks.

lēng [R. besides; in addition]. **lēng-goā**, besides this; in addition; separately; exceedingly. **lēng-goā-khiáu**, exceedingly clever. **lēng-goā-chiàh**, to have one's meals alone; to eat separately from others. **lēng-ku kok-sit**, to live and have meals apart. **lēng-ke kok-sit**, id. **lēng-oáⁿ lēng-tī**, separate bowls and chopsticks, as for a vegetarian, or man with contagious disease. **séng--tit lēng-lê, khí-tsàu**, one is enough (lit. one cooking place), no need of more.

lēng [R. liōng, measure; liberal], loose; not tight. **chhiáⁿ-lēng--teh**, delay, or wait a little, as before doing something. **khah-lēng--leh**, id. **khah-liâu-lēng**, less severe, as disease; mind more at ease; not so urgent, as affair; less scarce, as money; having a good deal of ready money, and not needing to work hard. **chîⁿ-thâu liâu-lēng**, money less scarce. **chîⁿ-tsúi liōng-lēng**, money pretty abundant. **pàng-lēng**, to loosen, as a rope. **hun khah-lēng**, to let out, as a rope made looser. **lek-lēng**, id. **ōe lek-lēng--tit**, elastic; also, it can be put off a little without injury, as work or business. **khah-lēng** (C.), = khah-liōng, a little more, better, or larger.

lēng (C.), = A. niāⁿ (C. also "liōng"). **soaⁿ-lēng**, the sloping shoulder of a hill.

li (T. lö). **pè lāng-li lāng-li**, the threads of the cloth too far apart.

li (cf. lî). **póh li-li**, very thin. **li-á-hn̂g**, a very short distance. **li-á-niauⁿ**, slightly pock-marked, &c.

li— **hong li-li-á**, wind gentle.

li— **li-li lo-lo**, glancing about everywhere, as eyes of thief; constant chattering, and long, empty, useless talk (v. lo). **li-la**, unsafe to associate or have dealings with, as man who evades payment (v. la).

li— **lê-li-lien**, words called out at the beginning of a play (v. lien).

lî (R. id.), a small weight, one-tenth of a "hun;" an atom or very small part of a thing; mean in dealings about money. **lî-lî-á**, a very little; slightly. **lî-boát**, small and unimportant, as trade or gains. **lî-si**, a very small quantity. **chit-lî-si-á**, id. **bô-lî-si**, not the very least. **hô-lî**, a very small quantity (v. hô). **hun-lî hô-hut**, very small divisions; niggardly.

phí-lî, mean in money matters (v. phí). **iáu-lî**, rather stingy and grasping. **in khah-lî**, they are very minute and stingy about money. **chìn-kang-lî**, said of a mean stingy fellow, as the Chin-chew people are generally poorer.

li-kim, the impost called "lekim" or "lekin." **lî-kim-kėk**, office for collecting it.

lî-téng, a small steelyard for weighing silver or fine medicines; generally marked so as to make a dollar = 7 chîⁿ 2 hun.

lî— **lô-lî-thi**, involved and confused, as a matter; not straightforward, as man (v. thi). **lî-bú lî-lê**, talking on far too much. **lî-lôh** (T.), id. **chi-chi lî-lî** (R.), very intricate and difficult to settle well, as an affair with many troublesome details; very impracticable, as man talking over and over on unimportant matters.

lî (R. id.) **liû-lî**, a translucent material like glass (v. liû).

lî (R. id.) **tsoáⁿ-lî**, a strainer for lifting out boiled rice.

lî [R. liâm, a screen]. **mn̂g-lî**, a bamboo door-screen made to roll up; hung specially before doors where families live. **pàng-mn̂g-lî**, to let down the door-screen. **pè-lî**, a cloth curtain or blind (single) hung at a door or window. **kiō-thang-lî**, curtain or blind of sedan-window made of cloth or bamboo.

lî [R. a fence]. **lî-á**, a fence of bamboos or thorns, or of dead reeds. **tek-lî**, a bamboo fence or railing, gen. dead. **lî-pa** (R.), a fence, as round a field.

lî [R. a pear-tree, = col. lâi]. **hoa-lî-bòk**, a very fine hard-grained wood for furniture (rosewood?).

lî [R. heavy rains]. **lîm-lî**, long heavy rains. **hē lîm-lî**, id. **liâm-lî**, id.

lî (R. id.), to divorce, as a wife. **hiu-lî** (R.), id. **lî-bé**, to divorce a wife; a divorced wife. **lî-tsu**, a bill of divorcement.

lî [R. nî, to agree]. **lî-ko**, a Buddhist nun (v. ko).

lî (R. id.) **hê-lî**, a fox.

lî [R. lû, a door]. **bâ-lî**, a sort of small cabin in a junk. **lî** (C.), = A. lû (a door).

lî (C.), = A. lû, an ass.

lî (Cn.), = A. jî, in some words.

lí [R. a Chinese mile; a village], a Chinese lí or mile, about one-third of an English mile; but varies in different places. **saⁿ-lí**, three lí, about one English mile (s. dress). **saⁿ-lí-lē**, id. **bān-lí**, ten thousand lí (v. bān). **chhien-lí-bé**, a courier. **chhien-lí-kiàⁿ**, a telescope.

hiu^{n}-lí, a village. **siā-lí**, id. **ka-hô-lí** (R.), a name for Amoy.

lí [R. lióng, two; a pair, = nn̄g, nī^{n}]. **lí-phiet-chhiu**, moustaches.

lí [R. inside], lining. **lí-bīn**, id. **sa^{n}-lí**, the lining of a dress (s. mile). **pò-lí**, cotton lining. **thùt-lí**, the lining too full, so that it appears at the edges. **tiù^{n}-lí**, to make a dress of two plies; to put in a lining (v. tiù^{n}). **tiò-lí**, id. **kim-hoe piáu-lí**, richly ornamental dress, worn by mandarins; also at marriages; an imitation is worn at the idolatrous rites called "chiò."

goát-lí siông-ngô^{n}, the beautiful lady in the moon (v. ngô^{n}).

ná^{n}-lí ōe àn-ni^{n}, how can it be so (said in imitation of mandarin). **ná^{n}-lí ū àn-ni^{n}**, id.

lí [R. the carp]. **lí-hî**, a sort of fish; the carp. **chhi^{n}-lí-hî**, the blue fish, sign of some passage-boats, *e.g.* Chióh-bé; and so with other colours.

lí — **lâ-lí**, the scaly ant-eater, manis, or pangolin.

lí (C.), = A. teh, the sign of the present in verbs; in the very act of —. **lí-beh**, = A. tih-beh, about to —.

lí (C.), = lú, female; woman.

lí (C.), = A. lú, stranger; visitor.

lí (R.), doctrine; reason; principle; right principle; (to manage or rule). **ū-lí**, to be reasonable, as a proposal; to be in the right in a quarrel or discussion. **bô-lí**, to be wrong in a dispute, &c. **bû-lí**, to scold violently or insult (improperly). **khit--i bû-lí--khì**, unjustly and improperly scolded or driven away by him. **hiáu-lí**, understanding how to do a thing (v. hiáu). **put-chí ti-lí**, knowing and doing his duty well, esp. as inferior. **khí-iú chhú-lí**, how can this be right? **toàn-lí, put-toàn-chhin**, to judge according to the right, not by relationship.

tō-lí, doctrine; principle of an affair (v. tō). **gī-lí**, the principles of justice or righteousness; the meaning, as of a book. **thien-lí**, the laws or principles of Heaven's justice (v. thien). **thi^{n}-lí**, id. (v. thi^{n}). **tē-lí**, geomancy, geography (v. tē).

seng-lí, trade (v. seng).

bûn-lí, polite; elegant, as person, words, or manner. **bûn-lí-lí**, very polite. **seng-sêng bûn-lí**, person of good appearance. **bûn-lí-khì**, having a polite or elegant manner or style.

siu-lí, to repair. **chéng-lí**, to arrange neatly. **liāu-lí**, to manage. **tī-lí**, to govern; to rule. **pān-lí**, to manage; to put right, as an affair. **koán-lí**, to oversee. **tsóng-lí**, to rule or have the general management. **chi-lí**, to be responsible for, as for management of affair or payment of another's debt. **goá bô-beh chi-lí**, I will not take the responsibility. **tùi-goá chi-lí**, apply to me, as finally responsible.

lí-hōe, to discuss a matter together, so as to come to an understanding about its settlement. **lí-hē**, id. **lí-lòh**, to manage well, especially household. **lí-ke**, to manage the house well, as wife. **lí-bōe-tit**, the matter cannot be set right; I have not the ability to set it right.

sū-lí, any matter or affair in relation to its cause and to the proper way of setting it right. **tí-lí**, original cause and origin of an affair that has become involved. **in-toa^{n} khí-lí**, the origin of an affair.

gî-lí-sī (C.), certainly you ought to —.

lí-khì, the real principle or hidden rationale of a particular case. **kek-lí-khì**, to infer the real origin, principle or state of a matter (v. kek). **ū lí-khì**, to be reasonable and fair, as an argument or proposal. **kóng-ōe ū-lí-khì**, to speak according to the principles of fairness. **lí-lō**, the right way of action. **ū-lí-lō**, right; proper. **lí-lō tit**, right course, as of speaking or doing.

chêng-lí, the right principles of action, as in some particular case. **jîn-chêng bùt-lí**, the right principles of all affairs. **jip-chêng jip-lí**, reasonable, as a matter. **ū-chêng-lí**, id.; to have the right on our side. **bô-chêng-lí**, unreasonable. **bat chêng-lí**, knowing what is right, as in cases of dispute and their settlement. **kóng chêng-lí**, to speak of the proper principles for settling a case. **poàh chêng-lí**, to discuss the principles of justice in regard to a dispute (v. poàh). **chêng-lí-hoat**, the real facts, right principles, and proper plan, in any particular matter. **chêng-lí-hoat, sa^{n}-jī tsn̂g**, all these three things correct and complete. **kóng chêng-lí-hoat**, to state all these correctly, as in a dispute.

lí-hák, a high title conferred on some very learned deceased men (like canonizing), who are then worshipped by the literati.

lí [R. a plum], a surname. **lí-á**, a plum. **lí-á-chhiū**, a plum-tree. **lí-á-pêng**, a confection made of halved plums. **lí-á-sng**, sort of preserved plums. **n̂g-chiam-lí**, a sort of plum. **tsu-lí**, a very small sour sort (s. shoe). **tsu-lí-á**, id. **hu-jîn-lí**, a very good sort of plum. **thô chiap-lí**, to graft a plum on a peach.

hêng-lí, baggage; traveller's luggage.

lí ló-kun, the philosopher Lau-tszc. **lí thok-koái^{n}**, one of the genii. **lí sien-tsé**, id.

lí [R. a shoe; to walk]. **lí-lėk**, an account of one's self given in when taking office or getting promotion, &c. (v. lėk). **tsu-lí** (R.), red shoes of very high mandarins (s. plum).

lí [R. lûi, scrofula, &c., = col. bí]. **lí-lát**, scrofulous sores on the neck.

lí — **lí-lái**, spoiled, as things; very troublesome or bad to have as an associate (v. lái). **hiong-pa lí-láu**, very ugly (v. láu). **lí-leh**, behaving improperly; a small quantity (v. leh). **lí-loá**, to work in a negligent or dilatory way (v. loá).

lí (R. nī^{n}), (T. lú), thou; thee; you. **lí-goá**, you and I. **lí-ê**, your; yours; thy; thine. **goá beh-lí chiáu-á-gûn**, I want you to pay me in Mexican dollars.

lí — **ka-lí-lô**, not yet; far from the end; not nearly finished; a long time yet (v. ka).

lí (T.) **tsû kàu lí-lí lā-lā**, to have a vast deal of cooking going on (v. lā).

lì, to strip off, as bark, skin, or leaves; to skin; to flay. **lì-phê**, to flay; to skin. **lì-phoà**, to tear and destroy, as clothes, or as sedan. **lì-hióh**, to strip off leaves. **lì-moâ^{n}**, to pick hemp bark into fine fibres, for making ropes. **lì-tsang**, to pick palm fibre into long thin fibres.

lì-liù, over-sharp in dealing, somewhat cheating, as a boy (v. liù).

lī — **hoe-lī-lō**, variegated; mottled; indistinct.

lī — **lī-khì** (r.), unwilling to accept a favour or monetary help (s. sharp).

lī (C.), = A. lū, to strain out.

lī (C.), = A. lū, a surname. **lī-sòng**, Manila; the Philippines.

lī (C.), = A. lū, to be anxious.

lī (C.), = A. lē, laws, taxes, &c.

lī [R. to rule; an officer; a subordinate; = col. lē].

lī-pō͘, the board of office at Pekin, which appoints mandarins; the president of it. lī-pâng, the office in a yamun which manages that department, *e.g.* having charge of inferior mandarins, and issuing certificates (kiet) to men of the district who get office; the secretary who manages it, who also often has charge of the treasury of the yamun, and acts as a check on the "hō͘-pâng," as his own original department is very light. tham-koaⁿ ù-lī, avaricious mandarins. khò͘-lī, a small official who has charge of the treasury of the provincial treasurer; a treasury clerk. tién-lī, a degree and title got by men who make out documents in criminal cases in the yamuns of high mandarins; having this degree he can be made sûn-kiám or sûn-si, without the usual literary examinations, and may thus rise to higher office. lī-iah, mandarin's writers and messengers.

pó-lī, a man employed by the keeper of a "lién-pó," gambling house.

lī [R. dysentery, &c.] lī-chek, dysentery. lī-chit, id. péh-lī, white mucous discharge in dysentery. chhiah-lī, brownish do. pàng-lī, to pass such mucous discharge; to have dysentery (s. leave). tsòe-lī, to have dysentery. sió-lī, slight mucous dysentery. hiet-lī, bloody dysentery. tsòe-hiet-lī, to have it. a-phièn-lī, bowel complaint caused by trying to give up opium. kìm-kháu-lī, a severe bowel complaint which takes away appetite and voice.

lī [R. clever; expert; = col. lāi]. léng-lī, pretty; clever and intelligent, as child; neatly finished, as a piece of work; clean and neat, as room; settled properly, as an affair. léng-lī koai-khá, clever and obedient (said of a boy or very young girl). pān kàu léng-lī, to settle up a matter all perfectly straight, leaving no cause of future trouble. chheng-khì léng-lī, clean and neat, as a place, or as a woman; settled altogether satisfactorily and honourably, as an affair. piàⁿ put-chí léng-lī, clean it out quite clean, as room.

sóng-lī, comfortable and pleasant, as one's person, or as house or garden (v. sóng).

lī [R. sharp; benefit; gain; interest; dangerous; = col. lāi]. lī-khì, sharp instruments; edged tools. lī-hāi, very clever; rather too clever; dangerous to have as an enemy.

lī-piēn, convenient, as place or thing (v. piēn). lī-kháu, pleasing the palate, as giving appetite to invalid. lī-pí, to agree with the stomach. lī-súi, to be diuretic. lī-ek, benefit; to benefit (v. ek). hāi-jîn lī-kí, to injure others and benefit one's self (v. kí).

lī-sek, interest of money.

hō͘-lī, very profitable, as a business. tek-lī, profitable. ōe-tek-lī, advantageous, profitable, as a business transaction. toā-tek-lī, bringing great gains. tek-lī-chîⁿ, profits in trade. tek-lī--ê, id. lī-chhī, prosperous business; a good sale (v. chhī). lī-lō͘, business; employment. hó-lī-lō͘, a good business.

sè-lī ê-lâng, a man who meanly hangs on the rich or powerful. tsâi-lī, gain; wealth; riches. kiû-tsâi-lī, to seek for wealth. bêng-lī, fame and wealth. kiû-bêng kiû-lī, to seek for fame and wealth. bêng-lī hun-sim, fame and wealth delude the heart. ūi-bêng ūi-lī, for the sake of fame and wealth, or wealth. put-ūi-bêng, chek ūi-lī, if not for fame, then it is for money.

put-lī, disadvantageous; unlucky. put-lī jit-chí, an unlucky day. toā-tîm put-lī, causing very heavy loss. put-lī tang-sai: tāi-lī lâm-pak, east and west is unlucky, north and south auspicious; as in some years.

lī (R. id.), to leave; to be distant from. lī-khui, id. (v. khui). saⁿ-lī, to separate from each other; to be distant. khah-lī-khì, very distant, as a place; *e.g.* house from place of work or from a friend's house. lī-hn̄g, to be far distant. lī oá-oá, not far off. lī-phāng, to open into chinks. khah-lī--teh, move slightly from the place; delay a little.

lī-piet, to bid farewell to; to take leave of. pun-lī, to leave; to go away; to separate from one another. pàng-lī, to let go; to let off; to abandon (s. dysentery). tsáu-lī, to run away and escape. thoat-lī, to escape (v. thoat).

lī-jīm, to leave a place where one has held office. lī-sin, to escape from danger; to get away from some business that detains us. bōe-tit lī-sin, unable to get away, as from business. bô-chit-sî thang lī-sin, I cannot get any leisure at all. ōe-tit lī-sin chiah-lâi, come as soon as you can get away. bô-lī-lâng, never without some one present. put-lī-lâng, id. koe-lō͘ put-lī-lâng, street always full of people. m̄-thang lī-lâng, there must always be some one present.

ta-lī, quite dry, not damp. khah-ta-lī, getting on now a little better in the world (v. ta).

tó lī-lī, fallen down flat on the ground, as man or house; quite bankrupt (v. tó). chih lī-lī, broken quite in two. kóe lī-lī, quite cured, as of opium. kóe-bōe-lī, unable quite to break it off, as opium-smoking.

liâ (= lâ). kóng-liâ-liâng, to joke and jest.

liah, to break off, as a splinter. liah chit-tè, id. liah--khí-lâi, to break off with the hand, as splinter; to split off (neuter). liah-bīn, to break off small splinters from a piece of wood slightly smoothed.

liah [R. liók, a small quantity; in average, in general, or by rough calculation, = col. lióh]. liah-siàu, to make a rough examination of an account to see if it be correct; *e.g.* comparing a few places at random with vouchers or other accounts. liah-khoàⁿ, id.; also, to take a rough estimate of our gains or losses, or of the state of an account (s. seize).

liah (R. lèk?) ka-liah, a very large round bamboo tray. phah ka-liah (T.), to make one's body go like a wheel round and round with feet and hands.

liah (R. liók), to seize; to arrest; to apprehend; to lay hold of; to force to do something; to lay on loosely, as thatch or tiles; to plait, as queue; to shampoo; to help men to get a sedan on their shoulders; to measure by spans; a span length; to regard or consider as —.

kúi-liah, how many spans? liah-khoàⁿ, measure by spans (s. general). pí-liah-khoàⁿ, id.

liah-tâng, to become possessed by a demon, as an enchanter. liah soaⁿ-lêng, to look for auspicious grave-sites, as geomancer. liah-lêng, to shampoo. tûi-kûn liah-lêng (Cn.), id. liah-kûn, to beat the air in boxing exercise (v. kûn). liah-soa, to pinch, &c., for the cure of colic or cholera.

liah iên-chhun, to hold in the hand and feed quails for gambling. liah-kiō, to help the bearers to get the sedan on their shoulders.

liah-lāu, to examine a roof or a vessel to find and stop leaks. liah kiáu-sat, to find fault wherever possible (v. sat). liah i--ê péh-chhat, to catch him telling a lie.

liah tsòe-àn-niⁿ, to suppose it to be so. liah-hó tsòe-pháiⁿ, to count good to be bad. liah-n̂g tsòe-chhiah, to mistake yellow for red.

liah-chiet, to take off discount on goods. liah

tiong-hô, to split the difference (v. tiong). **liáh-hô**, to join together against another (v. hô). **liáh sí-koat**, to be very obstinate. **liáh ngī^n-phī^n**, to sail on one tack right on with a strong wind; very dogged and immovable, listening to no advice or entreaty. **liáh-tn̂g pé-té**, to make up for defects (lit. short) by counterbalancing points of superior excellence.

liáh-chháu, to thatch. **liáh chháu-chhù**, id. **liáh-liáh**, to lay on loosely without fastening, as tiles. **liáh thâu-tsang**, to plait the queue.

liáh-iâm, to seize smuggled salt. **liáh-iau**, to seize evil spiritual influences, as an idol carried about, or as a sorcerer. **liáh-hái**, to catch sea animals, esp. at low water.

liáh-lâng, to take a prisoner or a captive; to seize or kidnap people. **thau-liáh**, to seize or catch secretly; to kidnap. **thau-liáh-koe**, to steal a fowl. **khîm-liáh**, to arrest; to seize. **ū-khîm-liáh**, to have some property or relatives, &c., which make some security to a creditor. **chhi^n-khîm oáh-liáh--khì**, to take alive, as a prisoner in war; said also of a man dying very suddenly, as if carried off by demons. **chhi^n-khîm oáh-liáh**, id.; also, to urge a man very hard to come to a place or to do something. **liáh-i tsòe-thâu**, to press him to take the lead and the chief responsibility (as all the persons associated do) in a subscription or work done in common. **liáh iâm-siong**, to compel a man to farm the salt revenue. **kiông-liáh**, to seize violently, as a prisoner; to compel the rich to make contributions to government; to compel a man by strong pressure to do something much against his will. **khit--i liáh-kè-bé**, to be so much weaker that we yield to him without thought of resistance (lit. dragged on his horse). **kiap-liáh**, to plunder and take captives, as highway-robbers.

liáh-pūi^n (C.), = A. phâng pn̄g-táu, to bring in the bucket or large dish of boiled rice for a meal.

liák (C.), = A. liók (R.), to seize.

liam — **liam-liam**, walking softly and noiselessly. **kiâ^n-lē liam-liam**, id: **liam-kha**, id. **liam-kha-kiâ^n**, id., so as to avoid making a noise, as in presence of a superior. **liam-kha bih-chhiú**, advancing secretly and noiselessly so as to be unobserved.

liam [R. id., = col. ni^n], to take up or catch a small thing between finger and thumb. **liam-khau**, to draw lots. **liam-hiu^n**, to take up incense-sticks and offer them in worship, as in the phé-tē rites, and as by mandarins twice a month. **liam-keng tah-chì^n**, to take the bow and draw the arrow. **liam chhân-i^n**, to catch a dragon-fly between finger and thumb.

liam — **khah-liam**, rather less than —. **khah-liam chit-pah**, rather less than a hundred, *e.g.* 97 or so.

liâm [R. lîm, to come down; to arrive]. **liâm-pi^n**, immediately. **liâm-mi^n**, id. **liâm-pi^n kóng**, **liâm-pi^n kiâ^n**, done as soon as said. **liâm-pi^n hó-hong**, **liâm-pi^n phái^n-hong**, at one moment a fair wind. and immediately a contrary wind. **liâm-sî**, immediately; suddenly. **liâm-sî liâm-tsūn**, id. **liâm-tong-sî**, id.

hē-liâm (Cn.), very speedily; very soon. **khē-liâm** (Cn.), id. **khah-hē-liâm** (Cn.), be quick! **tsá-liâm-ngá** (Cn.), a very short time ago.

liâm [R. liên, connected, = col. liáp]. **kha-chhiú liâm-chiáp**, hands and feet nimble (v. chiáp).

liâm (= lâm). **poâ^n-liâm-hâ^n** (esp. T.), hung up unfinished, as affair (v. hâ^n).

liâm (R. id.), to glue; to paste; to paste on; clammy; adhesive; to fasten together, as by paste or by hooks; a surname.

liâm-liâm, adhesive; adhering closely. **liâm-lô**, id. **lô-liâm-hiu^n**, sort of adhesive gum. **liâm thi-thi**, adhering or sticking very closely. **sa^n-liâm**, joined together (lit. or fig.) **sa^n-liâm tì-toà**, united closely, as relations, or as parts of the body; very much involved (as an affair) with other people's affairs.

si^n-liâm, to grow soft and damp, as cakes or sweetmeats just before growing mouldy.

liâm-he, to plaster with mortar. **liâm pui-thâu**, to make the gable-head with lime. **liâm-ka**, to glue together.

liâm (cf. nî^n-chî^n, eaves). **hui-liâm tsáu-piah**, to climb over eaves and walls.

liâm [R. a sort of halbert]. **khau-liâm**, a sort of halbert, with a shaft about five feet long and blade about one foot long, crooked like a sickle. **khau-liâm-to**, id. **khau-liâm-chhiu^n**, a spear with two prongs, one crooked and one straight. **liâm-á** (C.), a crooked knife for cutting grass and fuel.

kha-liâm-to, the foot used as a hook for tripping up another.

liâm [R. the shin or lower leg]. **kha-liâm**, the shin. **kha-phī^n-liâm**, id. **chhàu-kha-liâm**, having a sore or ulcer on the shin. **chhàu-phī^n-liâm**, id. **chhàu-kha-phī^n-liâm**, id. **si^n kha-phī^n-liâm**, to get such an ulcerous sore.

liâm [R. lîm, rain; constant dropping]. **hē liâm-lî**, constant heavy rains.

liâm [R. bride's toilet or trousseau]. **tsng-liâm**, marriage portion given to a daughter (gen. of clothes and such articles; sometimes includes landed property).

liâm [R. sparing; pure; uncorrupted], a surname. **chheng-liâm**, pure and uncorrupted by avarice, as a mandarin. **ū-liâm-thí**, to have a strong sense of propriety and respect for one's own character (v. thí). **tiong-hàu liâm-chiet**, faithful, filial, pure, and correct in conduct.

ióng-liâm, a small sum added to a mandarin's theoretical salary, said to be paid in order to keep him from extortion and bribes. **ióng-liâm ê-gûn**, id. **iáng-liâm** (C.), id.

liâm [R. name of a fish]. **liâm-hî**, a large fish from Siam and Cochin-china, counted very good. **toā-liâm**, the largest sort of it. **sió-liâm**, the smallest. **tiong-liâm**, medium-sized do.

liám [R. the cheek, = col. lién]. **liám-biēn**, character; respectability; prestige (v. biēn).

liám [R. to dress a corpse for the coffin], (C. liām). **siu-liám**, to put a corpse in the coffin. **jip-liám**, id.

liám [R. to gather; to collect]. **liám-séng**, very sparing and economical in the use of money. **liám khah-chió**, to use fewer or a smaller quantity. **khiām-liám**, very sparing in what one uses. **ná^n-liám, ná^n-lī**, by taking less and less you will gradually get free from the habit, *e.g.* of opium-smoking.

khek-liám, to embezzle by paying less money than should be paid, and pocketing the balance. **khek-liám ka-kī**, to deny one's self in a matter of expense, or for the benefit of others. **khek-liám gûn-hun**, to pay a man the correct number of dollars, but worse or lighter, and pocket the difference. **khek-liám lâng-ê-chî^n**, to pay a man less than he should have, while drawing the whole. **khek-liám i--ê chiáh-**

39

chhēng, to give him less food and clothing than he is entitled to. **khek-liám kun-niû**ⁿ, to embezzle soldiers' pay. **khek-liám ke-sū**, to give one's family too little money and squander it on one's self. **khek-liám khah-séng**, to be too stingy in the expenses we allow to others. **khek-liám jit-sit**, to be very sparing in expenses for daily food, as for economy, or as starving his family for his own bad pleasures. **khek-liám lâng--ê jit-sit**, to embezzle part of the money intrusted to us for feeding others, giving them too little.

liám (=lám). **pau-liám-bé**, to be responsible for any deficiency in a subscription.

liàm (R. id.), to pinch; to pinch off; to pluck with the fingers. **liàm-hiet-kák**, to pinch off and throw away. **liàm-chhài**, to pick off the skin, leaves, &c., from vegetables before cooking. **liàm-khang**, to make a hole with fingers, as in a cap.

liàm-miâⁿ, to get one's name withdrawn from a case (as by a payment) so as not to be further involved. **liàm-bōe-tn̄g**, cannot well break off the connection (v. tn̄g).

liàm-chih (lit. to catch the tongue), said in scolding a child, &c. (v. chih). **thau-niⁿ thau-liàm**, constantly stealing (v. thau). **hoâiⁿ-chháu bô-niⁿ, tit-chháu bô-liàm**, said of a very gentle or very honest man.

liām [R. to reflect upon; to repeat], to recite or repeat, as a lesson or prayer; in consideration of —. **liām--tiòh**, out of consideration for —. **liām--tiòh i-ê-chêng**, in consideration of his kindness. **put-chí liām-gī**, showing much gratefulness, as for favour done to one's self or to relatives, &c. **tài-liām**, on account of; in consideration of —. **siàu-liām**, to think of with warm affection, as relative or friend; to remember kindness with gratitude. **kì-liām**, to think of with grateful remembrance, as of some favour or kindness, or as of parents' instructions. **koà-liām**, to think anxiously about. **khoà-liām**, id. **sim liām**, to bear on the mind, esp. a desire to do something. **sim-sim liām-liām**, id. **hoâi-liām** (R.), to cherish some feelings, *e.g.* affection. **tui-liām** (R.), to meditate on kindness shown long ago.

liām-kè, to ask too high a price.

liām-chheh, to recite books. **oát-liām**, to say a lesson with one's back to the teacher. **thiu-liām**, to take a passage at random (ad aperturam) for the scholar to recite. **liām-tsáiⁿ**, to practise songs. **chhiùⁿ-liām-hó**, to sing well. **liām-phó͘**, to repeat the notes of a tune by name. **liām-keng**, to recite religious books; to say off written prayers, *e.g.* Buddhist. **liām-kōng**, to say certain Buddhist prayers or incantations. **liām-sò͘**, another sort. **liām-chiù**, to mutter spells (v. chiù). **chiù-liām**, to curse. **lóe-liām**, to swear at one.

tsáp-liām, to talk incessantly (said in scolding); incoherent or delirious talk. **liām-liām lèh-lèh**, constant discontented talk (v. lèh). **ngáuh-ngáuh-liām**, to grumble by talking indistinctly when not daring to speak out. **ngiáuh-ngiáuh-liām**, id. **m̄-thang-liām**, do not mention it, as some inauspicious word. **ū-lâng teh-liām--goá**, some one is speaking of me (said when the ear itches).

liām, a handful, as of grass or grain taken in the hand when cutting. **chit-liām**, one do. **sì-liām-hò͘**, crossed twice, as usual form of the string on a parcel. **sì-liām-hō͘** (T.), id. **phah-sì-liām-hò͘**, to tie a string so.

thâu-mn̂g liām-chiūⁿ--ê, the first wife ever married by a man.

liām, a bit, as of a melon. **chit-liām**, one do. **kim-koe-liām**, a bit of a pumpkin.

liām (C.) **siu-liām**, = A. siu-liám, to put a corpse in the coffin.

lian, liân, lián, liàn, liān; better lien, liên, lién, lièn, liēn (*q.v.*)

liâng — **kóng-lâ-liâng**, to joke and jest. **kóng-liâ-liâng**, id.

liâng (R. id.), cool. **liâng-léng**, id. **chheng-liâng**, pleasantly cool, as weather; having a cooling influence on the system (not merely cool to the touch), as food or medicine. **chhiu-liâng**, cool autumn weather. **liâng-hiet** (T. liông), cooling for the blood, as some eatables. **kò͘-liâng**, to plaster (as a boil) with herbs to make it cool. **liâng-pîⁿ**, an awning spread for coolness. **liâng-têng**, id. **liâng-hún**, a sort of vermicelli swimming in syrup, for hot weather.

liâng (C.), = A. liông, good.

liâng (C.), = A. liông, to consult.

liâng (C.), = A. liông, sort of grain.

liáng (C.), = A. lióng, two.

liāng (R. id.), transparent or translucent. **kng-liāng**, brilliant and translucent, as a gem. **bêng-liāng**, bright, as a lamp; transparent, as glass (s. clear voice). **péh-liāng**, transparent colourless crystal button, of fifth rank. **chhiⁿ-liāng**, transparent blue button, of third rank.

liāng (R. id.), clear and loud, as voice in shouting or singing. **hiáng-liāng**, loud and wide-echoing, as sound. **bêng-liāng** (C.), clear and distinct, as voice (s. transparent).

liāng (C.), = A. liōng, capacity; measure. **chin-liāng-kú**, very long, in time.

liāng (C.), = A. liōng (to suppose).

liap [R. to whisper], a surname.

liap [R. to work up with the fingers, as clay, = col. liáp], to make fraudulent use of a name. **mō͘ⁿ-liap**, id. **liap-miâ**ⁿ, id.

liáp (R. liap), to work or mould in the hands, as clay; to work the fingers gently on the palm, as a child; to take a thing in the hand, closing the fingers gently. **thô͘-liáp--ê**, formed of clay, as idol. **m̄-thang-liáp**, don't take or catch it in your hand, as some delicate, fragile, or beautiful article (said to a child). **liáp-sái liáp-jiō**, cleaning away an infant's excrements and urine with the hand, as parent or nurse.

liáp [R. liâm, to adhere]. **put-chí-liáp**, very intimate with a person.

liáp [R. liên, connected, = col. liâm]. **kha-chhiú liáp-chiáp**, quick at any work.

liáp (R. lip), a grain, as of wheat, rice, &c.; classifier of balls, grains, round fruits, small insects, stars, and large rocks in water.

toā-liáp, very large, said of any of such things very large and fat, or as man. **toā-bú-liáp**, very tall fat man. **toā-liáp-béng**, very powerful and influential. **toā-liáp-hō͘**, rain in very large drops. **sió-liáp-chí**, said of a little man. **khah-sòe-liáp**, less powerful; having less influence to back him; smaller, as anything classified by "liáp."

iù-liáp-mihⁿ, goods having great value in small bulk.

liáp-chek, to gather up, as wealth, little by little (v. chek). **kúi-liáp-á**, a small quantity.

jip-liàp, the grain well formed in the ear. **bí-liàp**, rice grains. **pn̄g-liàp**, grains of boiled rice used as paste.

liàt, better liėt (*q.v.*)

liau, stiff, as limbs drawn up from cold, numbness, or fear, or as near death. **kha liau, chhiú liau**, limbs weak and stiff and drawn up, as through fear or illness. **kha-chhiú liau**, id.

ngīⁿ-liau, too stiff and hard, as point of pen, or as boards of bed, or eatables, or dress, &c.; too stiff in discussion, or in ordering others, or in pressing one's claims.

liâu [R. a companion]. **tông-liâu** (R.), a mandarin who is a friend or companion of another official.

liâu [R. a hut]. **tah-liâu**, to erect a hut or rough shed. **liâu-á**, a hut. **chháu-liâu**, a straw hut. **chháu-á-liâu**, a shed for selling fuel. **tek-liâu**, a store where bamboos are sold. **pùn-liâu**, a place where manure is stored and sold. **khang-khè-liâu**, a shed for workmen, as a house building, or at a carpenter's yard. **kiⁿ-liâu**, a straw hut for watching crops; a shed for the watch, as in street, or near city gate.

liâu [R. a rope; to bind]. **liâu-soh**, small ropes attached to the sail, all meeting in the main sheet. **phâng-liâu-soh**, id. **liâu-á-soh**, id. **liâu-bú**, the large rope in which the others meet; the main sheet. **toā-liâu**, id.; also, the man who has charge of the ropes in a large junk. **thâu-liâu**, these ropes of the foremast.

kè-liâu, to pass the ropes from the one side of the vessel to the other in tacking; to get over a difficulty, as by borrowing a little money (s. voice). **hē--i kè-liâu**, lend him a little to help him over the difficulty. **pàng-hē--i kè-liâu**, to let off, as a man who has committed some fault. **kè-liâu--khì**, opportunity quite lost.

saⁿ-kha-liâu, sailing with wind about abeam. **ngīⁿ-liâu**, sailing near the wind with press of sail. **ngīⁿ-liâu-chhi**, id.

liâu [same word?]. **kha-liâu**, iron fetters for the feet. **kha-liâu chhiú-khàu**, fetters and manacles.

liâu [R. an initial particle; careless; to depend upon]. **khah-liâu-lēng**, less severe, as disease or scarcity, &c. (v. lēng). **liâu-chhiáⁿ** (R.), using temporarily, though not very suitable. **liâu-thien liâu-thien**, easy-minded (s. run off).

bû-liâu, having a feeling of weariness or ennui from having nothing to do, or no friend or companion; feeling lonely and dull.

liâu [R. distant]. **liâu-á-sī**, slowly and cautiously. **liâu-á-kiâⁿ**, walk slowly.

liâu-tang, the part of Manchuria (Liau-tung) where New-chwang stands, on the east of the river Liâu.

liâu [R. anxious; grieved]. **liâu-bāng**, to watch earnestly for, as friend or foe.

liâu [R. tiâu, a branch; anything long and slender], a long strip; said of walls and of lines of work in building, &c.; to tear along a fold, as paper; to saw up longitudinally, as wood.

î-liâu, a wooden bench. **chiòh-liâu**, a long stone slab used for a seat; a stone bench. **kún-liâu**, a narrow band for the border of a cap or dress. **khan-thiu-liâu**, a broad band sewed on like a hem. **pè-liâu**, a narrow strip of cloth. **tsoá-liâu-á**, long strips of paper torn evenly. **moâⁿ-liâu**, a long-shaped confection made with hemp-seed (v. moâⁿ). **chit-liâu-bah**, a large thick slice of pork, that can be cut into several slices. **chit-liâu-á**, said of a man's face when very thin.

liâu-kù, to do sawyer's work. **liâu-chhâ**, to saw up timber longitudinally. **liâu-tsoá**, to tear paper along a fold or crease, or along a straight edge.

liâu, to run off (in thieves' slang). **liâu--lâi**, to come (esp. by the roof), as a thief. **liâu--khì**, to go so. **liâu-thien**, to run away, as a thief, esp. by the roof (v. thien), (s. careless).

liâu — **liâu-lô**, banditti; a band of robbers (v. lô).

liâu — **phiaⁿ-liâu**, the middle part of an animal (*e.g.* of a pig), including the ribs (v. phiaⁿ). **liâu-bah**, the flesh of this part.

liâu [R. sound of the voice, &c.] **tńg-liâu**, to change the time or rate in music. **kè-liâu**, id. (s. rope). **at-liâu-phek**, according to proper rules and time, as any work (v. phek). **kàu-liâu**, minute and exact in business, or in managing matters. **kàu-liâu kàu-siàu**, just come to the time exactly proper for doing something; preparing just the proper quantity, neither too much nor too little. **bô-liâu bô-siàu**, managing matters in a careless or random way. **ū-liâu ū-tiāu**, good at singing. **ū-liâu ū-siàu** (C.), id.

liâu, to wade. **liâu-tsúi**, to wade through water; to ford a stream. **liâu-tėh**, to wade over the wet seabeach. **liâu chhân-hoāⁿ**, to wade through the wet parts of the raised boundaries between rice-fields.

liâu (T.), = A. jiâu. **khiau-khiau liâu-liâu**, crooked and uneven, as a piece of wood.

liáu (R. id.), to finish; finished; after; to spend; used to give a perfect or pluperfect sense to verbs. **kóng-liáu chiū-khì**, go after speaking. **sí-liáu**, after death. **sí liáu-āu**, id. **chiáh--liáu**, after having eaten. **chiáh-liáu**, to eat up the whole (v. chiáh). **pāi--liáu**, all lost! **kè-liáu-sî, soah-liáu-tāi**, old affairs that are quite past, and should not be brought up again. **bô--liáu**, all spent, finished, or gone; nothing remains. **bô-liáu bô-chīn**, endless. **bô-liáu-sî**, id. **bô-liáu-kiók**, cannot be brought to an end, as a troublesome quarrel. **kóng-bōe-liáu**, cannot manage to tell the whole.

liáu-koaⁿ, to be deposed from office and rank. **liáu-chîⁿ**, to spend money. **ke-hé liáu**, property all spent. **kan-ta liáu**, all lost or spent uselessly. **péh-péh liáu**, id. **liáu-chīn**, quite spent; all used or done. **liáu theh-theh** (Cn.), id.

liáu-liáu, altogether; in great numbers or quantities. **sí liáu-liáu**, they are all dead. **lâng liáu-liáu**, there are men in great numbers.

liáu-jiên, understanding clearly; plainly understood. **it-bòk liáu-jiên**, seeing all at one glance. **liáu-chiėt**, quick at observing the real state of a case, or forming a resolution without vacillation (v. chiėt). **liáu-gō** (R.), to awake to know the emptiness of the world.

liāu (R. id.), a surname. **liāu-lāi**, Rhio, in the Dutch possessions.

liāu [R. liâu, a rope]. **chhìn-liāu**, the rope or string of a steelyard. **gû-liāu**, the rope by which a cow is tied or led. **gû-liāu-soh**, id. **bé-liāu-soh**, rope by which a horse is tied or led.

liāu [R. materials; to expect; to manage], materials, of any sort. **bô-liāu**, without materials; did not think of it beforehand; would not have expected it. **liāu--tiòh**, to expect beforehand. **kièn-liāu kièn-tiòh**, all his guesses or predictions come true. **liāu-chhut**, to conjecture correctly beforehand. **liāu-sióng put-tò**, did not consider before so far as that. **put-chhut ngé-sé-liāu**, it is exactly as I expected or reckoned.

liāu-lí, to manage, as affair or business.

phín-liāu, materials. **chhâi-liāu**, id. **liāu-toaⁿ**, a list of materials to be used, *e.g.* for building. **m̄-chiâⁿ-liāu**, insufficient, as a remnant of material. **m̄-chiâⁿ chhâi-liāu**, id.; also of a useless man. **pān-liāu**, to prepare materials, as for building a house. **pān koá-liāu**, I have made ready a few things for you to eat. **kiaⁿ-liāu**, articles from Pekin, or of very good quality.

liāu--ê, imitations, as of gems or of silver. **liāu-si-teng**, sort of lantern (v. si). **siang-liāu**, a very strong double-distilled spirit, made in Amoy. **siang-liāu-chiú**, id.

âng-liāu, bricks and tiles of all sorts. **chhâ-liāu**, timber. **bák-liāu**, id. **sam-liāu**, timber of the fir wood called "sam." **sek-liāu**, colours (prepared) or materials for colours. **chhat-liāu**, materials for making varnish. **ióh-liāu**, medicines in an unprepared state. **chio-liāu**, spices. **chiùⁿ-liāu**, various condiments made with "tāu-chiùⁿ" (v. chiùⁿ). **chiú-liāu**, things to be eaten with liquor. **tê-liāu**, tea-bread, &c. (v. tê). **thn̂g-liāu**, sweetmeats. **tang-koe-liāu**, thin bits of sugared cucumber. **chháu-liāu**, provender. **pak-té bô-sím-mihⁿ-liāu**, very little in one's stomach; *e.g.* said when asked to go a long way. **pak-té-lāi bô-sím-mihⁿ-liāu**, having no ability for literary composition.

liàuh, expression of sudden surprise, as on breaking something or letting it fall.

lien [R. liên, a mere sound]. **lê-lien**, words called out while the music is being made at the beginning of a play. **lê-lien liú-lien**, id. **lê-liú-lien**, id. **lông-liú-lien**, id. **liú-lông-lien**, id. **lē-li-lin** (T.), id. **lê-li-lien**, id. **toà--teh lê-li-lien**, waiting doing nothing, either as having nothing to do, or as when wilfully idle. **toà--teh lông-liú-lien** (C.), id.

lien [same word?]. **ka-lí-lien**, not yet near the end (v. ka).

lien, to curl up, as leaves in drought, or as the edges of a grass-cloth dress. **kńg-lien**, id. **khau-to-lien** (C.), shavings of wood.

liên (R. id.) **liên-hî**, a sort of large fish.

liên [R. lîn, to compassionate; to pity]. **khó-liên**, alas! what a pity!

liên [R. biên, liên, united; in succession; scrolls with antithetic sentences], ornamental scrolls in pairs, with antithetic sentences, hung on walls, or pasted on doors.

liên-lòk, united, as the people of a region under a head man (v. lòk). **liên-hiong**, villages combining; of the same village (v. hiong).

liên-pâi, antithetical scrolls, as for hanging on walls. **liên-tùi**, id. **chit-tùi-liên**, a pair of them. **toā-pak-liên**, very large scrolls for wall. **mn̂g-liên**, antithetical inscriptions pasted on doors or door-posts. **mn̂g-khiā-liên**, do., on door-posts.

liên [R. united; connected, = col. nn̂g, nîⁿ], connected; a surname; and even; even also. **saⁿ-liên**, connected. **saⁿ-liên-toà**, id. (v. toà). **kiet-liên**, joined, as in one enterprise or confederacy. **liên-āu**, afterwards. **liên-soà**, doing several things in succession. **liên-tháh**, in rapid succession (v. tháh). **liên-liên**, successively; in rapid succession. **liên-liên-phah**, to strike several blows in rapid succession. **liên-chiét**, rapidly passing from one literary degree to another. **kho-kah liên-teng**, to become Kujin and Tsin-sze in rapid succession. **liên-hoân-chhèng**, a running fire (v. hoân).

liên-lūi, to involve in the consequences. **khan-liên**, involved in another's (legal) case, as by name appearing in a document or in spoken evidence. **liên-hoân-kiet**, a joint bond made by several householders (v. hoân).

pí-liên, conterminous, as fields; having a common wall, as houses. **pī-liên** (T.), id. **liên-kūi**, a shop-counter.

liên-oáⁿ iáh-chī, he licks even the bowl, said of a greedy man. **beh-lāi, liên-bú bô**, trying to get interest he loses the principal too.

chit-tn̄g khah-liên, rather more than ten feet long.

liên-hôe, destitute, miserable, and of ruined character, without any hope of getting into a better way of life (v. hôe).

liên (R. lêng), a word used like a cipher in writing, = khòng. **nn̄g-pah liên-saⁿ**, 203. **chit-chheng liên sì-tsáp**, 1040.

liên [R. lêng, name of a plant]. **liên-chi-chhó**, a fabulous plant of good omen.

liên [R. the water-lily and such plants], (T. nâiⁿ, Cn. nûiⁿ, in some phrases). **liên-hoe**, the water-lily. **hô-liên**, small white water-lily. **gē-sî-liên**, a water-lily that opens at mid-day. **pek-tsú-liên**, a flower like a lily with a tall stalk and a large bunch of beautiful blue flowers (lit. hundred); the Agapanthes. **chhit-hióh-liên**, a medical plant with large pinnate leaves, somewhat like the elder. **tò-tiàu-liên**, a small green bird, fond of hanging by its feet; a plant that grows abundantly hanging down on cliffs and old walls. **liên-chiau**, the red-flowering arum.

chheng-liên, a rich bluish purple, of medium darkness, like the flowers of the pek-tsú-liên. **kim-liên**, women's small feet. **chhái-liên-thâu**, the chief subscriber to an "ông-tsûn" (v. chhái).

liên-chí, seed of water-lily. **liên-chí-sim**, the sprout or germ in the centre of it. **kńg-liên**, water-lily seeds from Canton. **kièn-liên**, do., from Fuhkien. **liên-jiòk**, lobes of the seed. **liên-pê**, its seed-vessel. **liên-hoe-pê**, id. **liên-ngāu**, water-lily roots.

liên (R. id.) **tah-liên**, a double bag hung over the shoulder. **pē tah-liên**, to carry it. **phāiⁿ tah-liên** (C.), id.

liên [R. a year, = col. nîⁿ]. **siàu-liên**, young. **siàu-liên-lâng**, a young man. **siàu-liên-liên**, very young. **siàu-liên ló-sêng**, young but wise like an old man. **tiong-liên**, of middle age, about 30 to 40. **ló-liên**, aged. **sam-liên-song**, mourning for three years (v. song). **liên-keng**, the cyclical characters for the year of one's birth. **liên-māuⁿ**, age and appearance of face (v. māuⁿ). **ûi-hiù bān-liên**, to leave a bad memory for ten thousand years.

liên [R. lân, misery; painful]. **kái-liên-keng**, a yellow paper with characters on it, tied to the "thôe-sin" and burned to avert calamity.

liên (C.) **liên-chi**, = A. lāi-chi, the fruit called lichi or lai-chi.

lién [R. to tread]. **pē-lién**, to walk on foot. **tit-tit-lién**, to go on foot right on.

lién — **lién-būn**, = hoan-ké-chí, a fruit from the Straits and Formosa.

lién (= lám). **pau-lién-bé**, to engage to make up whatever may be wanting in a subscription.

厦英大辭典

lién [R. the cheek, = col. liám]. **phí-lién,** impudent; brazen-faced. **ngó-sek-lién,** a wild violent rough character. **koāi-lién,** taking up a position of disobedience or opposition, as one (esp. an inferior) who had formerly always agreed or assisted. **siáu-phí-lién,** despicably mean and miserly in dealing, holding to the last farthing. **siúⁿ-lién,** to give a favour out of respect to a third person. **bô-kè-lién,** utterly careless of character; willing to do any shameful thing for a little gain. **sit-lién,** to lose one's reputation or prestige; not daring to hold up one's head, on account of something wrong, *e.g.* a great defeat in some quarrel. **lak-lién,** to lose one's respectability, influence, or prestige. **lap-lién** (C.), id. **lok-lién,** to become very poor or in low circumstances.

lién (R. id.), to twirl; to get money out of people improperly, esp. by threats. **lién-hī,** to brush the inside of the ears after shaving. **lién phīⁿ-khang,** to clean or tickle the nostrils, as with a bit of wood.

lién-pó, a sort of gambling (v. pó). **lién hoe-hē,** to twirl the teetotum, as keeper of gambling-house (v. hē). **lién phak-chhiò,** to twirl cash for odds and evens. **péng-ka-lién-phak,** to invert, as a cup. **lién-chîⁿ,** to twirl a cash (s. sedan).

lién-á, an instrument for twirling opium in the flame. **hong-chhe-lién,** a toy made to turn with the wind. **tsoá-lién,** small rolls of twisted paper (used as matches). **tsoá-lién-hé,** do. lighted. **so tsoá-lién,** to make them. **tsoá-lién-teng,** same dipped in oil and used as a light; also (without oil) used for binding books. **tsoá-lién-kun,** do. for binding books.

gâu lién-khang, good at getting money out of people in all ways, as by cheating, intimidation, and various pretexts. **gâu lién-tsoān,** id. **gâu lién-chîⁿ,** id. **lién lâng-ê-chîⁿ,** to get money out of people by all means; to extort money on false pretences, esp. as underlings of mandarins and mean literati. **lo-lién,** to get money out of people by hook or by crook, as by urgent dunning or by intimidation. **gâu lo-lién,** good at getting money or getting a situation for one's self by such means.

lién (R. id.), sedan of emperor or idol. **khang-lién,** an empty idol's sedan. **lién-kiō,** a carved sedan for an idol. **pút-lién,** id. **lêng-chhia hōng-lién,** imperial carriage and sedan.

lién-kha, persons who carry an idol in its chair. **lién-kn̂g,** poles of an idol's sedan. **lién-chîⁿ,** a wheel used for grinding in a long trough-shaped mortar; a solid wheel without spokes; a single wheel (though with spokes), as in a wheel-barrow (s. twirl).

koan-lién, to perform rites to call the spirit to the image in the sedan. **kng-lién,** to carry the idol's sedan. **lôe-lién,** to run along carrying it.

lièn (C.), = A. lìn, to trundle about; to stir about with the hand. **lièn--lòh-khì,** to roll and tumble down, as a precipice. **îⁿ-lièn-lièn,** quite round. **pēⁿ kàu-îⁿ-lièn-lièn,** very unwell.

liēn [R. a chain]. **thih-liēn,** an iron chain. **gûn-liēn,** a white metal chain (used for suspending the pouch). **gûn-liēn-á,** id. **koà-liēn,** to wear a chain; to be chained. **koà só-liēn,** id. **toà-liēn,** id.

liēn — **liēn-kîⁿ,** a flail (v. kîⁿ). **liēn-kéⁿ** (C.), id.

liēn (R. id.), to prepare in the fire, as gold, or as the elixir of immortality. **thoàn-liēn** (r.), to try in the fire, as gold or silver (v. thoàn). **liēn-tan,** to prepare the Tauist elixir of immortality. **siu-liēn,** to follow the Tauist rules for virtue and health. **tsoan-liēn,** to be skilful at one special kind of work [is this next word?].

liēn (R. id.), to practise; to drill; to exercise one's self at a thing (sometimes said of beating). **láu-liēn,** well practised in a thing; experienced. **liēn-tát** (r.), id. **liēn kàu-sėk,** to practise till we can do it well. **liēn-sėk,** experienced; practised. **náⁿ-liēn náⁿ-sėk,** practice makes perfection. **bat kè-liēn,** to have been drilled; experienced; well-trained. **kàu-liēn--ê,** thoroughly taught and skilful (as artisan or boxer), and able to teach others. **liēn-jī,** to practise writing. **chhau-liēn,** to exercise, as soldiers. **thoân-liēn,** method of dividing a town into small districts (about one street), each having a head man, and furnishing some volunteers to be ready in case of rebellion or disturbance. **liēn-ióng,** the braves or volunteers thus supplied. **liēn-tiúⁿ,** the head man of such a subdivision. **liēn-tsng** (Cn.), the head men of several villages united to put down plundering, &c. (v. tsng).

liēn-khi-hoát, to work up very carefully, as pills (v. hoát).

ták-jit teh-liēn, constantly beating, as an apprentice or daughter-in-law. **ēng-kîⁿ lâi-liēn,** thresh with a flail.

liėt [R. lėk, wide open], (C. lėh). **khui liėt-liėt,** quite fully wide open, as door or window. **khui khah-liėt,** open more fully wide. **peh-sì-liėt,** opened quite square and wide. **mn̂g khui sì-liėt,** door opened so.

liėt [R. to arrange; several], a row; a rank. **kui-liėt,** making a whole row; the whole length of the row. **lâng chē kui-liėt,** the people sit in a row.

pâi-liėt, to arrange in order.

liėt-kok, the several kingdoms; the feudal states of the Chow dynasty. **liėt-ūi,** polite phrase in addressing several persons. **lín liėt-ūi,** id. **liėt-ūi pêng-iú,** id.

liėt [R. burning; ardent]. **chiet-liėt,** so pure and chaste as to commit suicide, as a widow who will not marry a second time, or as a virgin. **liėt-lú,** id. **liėt-lú put-kà jī-hu,** a chaste woman will not marry a second husband. **tiong-liėt-sû,** a temple (at the side of the Confucian temple) set up by government for canonized mandarins who died for their country. **tiong-liėt-biō,** do. set up by private persons.

kek-liėt, using very strong or violent language, as in disputing.

liėt-liėt-háu, loud sound, as of the wind, or of stiff paper shaken, or of metal-plate struck, &c.

lih — **lih-khiet,** very deceitful, intriguing, and injurious, as a man.

lih [R. liėt, to tear, = col. lėh], to tear; a rent; to open out, as a seam or joint. **thiah-lih,** to tear open, as a letter; to tear, as cloth or paper. **thoa-lih,** to tear asunder, as by horses. **phoà-lih,** to rend asunder. **lih-phoà,** id. **lih-khui,** to open out, as a joint or seam. **khih-khih lih-lih,** having flaws and cracks, as pottery. **lih-kè-lâi, lih-kè-khì,** to tear alternately on opposite sides, as in making a strip of paper into a long string.

toā-lih, a large rent. **sòe-lih,** a small rent. **sòe-lih i-kàu-toā-lih,** to make bad worse. **taⁿ lih--lah,** now it is quite spoiled or ruined, as thing or affair; now it is all up.

chhiò-lih-lih, to laugh with the mouth open all its length. **kut-chih bah-lih,** bones broken and flesh torn. **soaⁿ-pang tōe-lih,** mountains falling and earth rending, as in earthquake.

lim, to drink, especially in small quantities, or slowly (but "chiàh" is far more commonly the translation of "drink"); to sip. **kan-ta-lim,** to drink without eating. **sahⁿ-sim-lim,** to gulp down in great quantities. **hèⁿ-lim,** fond of drink. **lim-thng,** to drink warm soup. **lim-chiàh,** to eat and drink. **lim-thîn kòng-phah,** fond of drinking and fighting. **lim-ta,** to drink till empty, as a cup. **lim-bô-ta,** to drink but not empty.

lîm [R. a forest, = col. nâⁿ], a surname. **hān-lîm,** the Han-lin or Imperial Academy at Pekin; a member of it. **hān-lîm-īⁿ,** that academy. **jip hān-lîm,** to become a member of it. **thiáu hān-lîm,** to choose members of it from among the Tsin-sze. **hān-lîm-liók,** list of members when new ones are added.

ún-ku san-lîm, to dwell solitary in mountains and forests (said originally of a sort of hermits); said also of a man who has money living in learned ease and retirement. **gū-lîm-kun,** the palace guards.

lîm (reduplication of tîm). **toā-lîm,** = toā-tîm, exceedingly —. **tîm-lîm,** to sink down, as in water.

lîm [R. name of disease]. **kek-lîm,** passing urine bloody or with difficulty, as from calculus or other diseases, often from bad diseases. **hiet-lîm,** urine bloody or dark. **soa-lîm,** the disease of urinary calculus.

lîm [R. to descend; to arrive at]. **kàng-lîm,** to descend, as a spirit or a god. **lîm-kàu,** id. **chhin-lîm,** to go in person to a place to manage a case, as a mandarin. **ngó-hok lîm-bûn,** may all sorts of happiness come on this house.

sū lîm-sin, serious trouble come upon (him). **tāi-chì lîm-sin,** id. **tsai-ē lîm-sin,** great calamities come on (him). **kàu-lîm-sin,** when it (trouble, &c.) comes on him, &c. **lîm-chiong,** near death. **lîm-tīn,** to go into battle. **lîm-tiûⁿ,** to come to the place of battle, or of examination (as scholar). **lîm-kip,** come to a crisis; in great or urgent danger or need (v. kip). **lîm-gûi,** in imminent and great danger. **lîm-hiám,** id. **lîm-phûn,** to be in childbirth. **lîm-súi hu-jîn,** the goddess of childbirth.

lîm-thiap, to copy from copy-books containing copies of ancient characters.

lîm [R. rain]. **chhiu-lîm,** autumn rains in great quantities for several days. **kam-lîm** (R.), rain in season of need, as after drought.

lîm [R. to drip; to pour upon; to soak, = col. lâm]. **lîm-lî,** long-continued heavy rains. **chêng-kan, put-khéng khì; su-thâi ú-lîm-lî,** if you won't go in fine weather, you will have to wait (when you wish to go) till the heavy rains are over.

lím [R. a granary]. **lím-seng,** the literary rank just above a Sew-tsai. **lím-pó,** id., so called because his recommendation is necessary for the candidates for the degree of Sew-tsai. **pang-lím,** to become a lím-seng.

lím [R. to fear; to reverence]. **ui-hong lím-lím,** very terrible and majestic, as a mandarin or warrior.

lím — **lím-lím-á,** just barely enough. **lím-lím-á-kàu,** id. **lím-lím-á chiah-kàu,** has just this moment arrived. **lím-lím-á chiah-khì,** has just this moment gone away. **lím-chiah,** just a few moments ago. **lím-lâu,** close on the time of tide. **lím-kîⁿ,** near the edge; ready to fall over; in a dangerous position.

lìm (T. lèng), to take a very short dose, either lying down, or only leaning the head on the hand. **lìm-khì,** to fall into such a short sleep or dose. **lìm-chit-chhíⁿ,** to dose a short time.

lin, a long narrow net dragged along the bottom. **khan-lin,** to draw this net, so as to inclose the fish.

lin — **lin-long,** running about, as at play (v. long).

lin [R. lêng, a tinkling sound], (C. lîn). **lin-long-ké,** a rattle used by pedlars and children.

lin (cf. lìn). **lin-lin-gô,** to whirl round (neuter). **lin-lin-tńg,** to roll, as a ball. **lin-lin-sèh,** to revolve, as in orbit. **îⁿ-lin-lin,** globular.

lin — **hoe-lin-niauⁿ,** of variegated colours.

lin [R. nái], = leng, niⁿ (v. leng), milk; a teat; a knob on a door or window, used as a handle. **gû-lin,** cow's milk, &c. (v. leng). **lin-chiap,** milk dropping from the teat in small quantities. **lin-bé,** about the end of giving milk. **io-lin,** to give suck, as a nurse. **hàng-lin** (T.), grown very fat on milk, as infant; breasts grown, as of girl about age.

lin-thâu, a teat; the beginning of giving milk. **lin-pê,** the breast (the whole projecting part) of female or male. **lin-chhang,** the part of the breast close to the teat within the black circle. **lin-hé,** an abscess or deep boil in the female breast near the centre. **lin-iong,** id., more to the side.

chhêng-lin, resin from trees.

cheng-lin, the knob of a gong. **mn̂g-lin,** a knob on a door; a round door-handle. **thoah-lin,** round handle of drawer.

thē-lin, the part of the medusa (edible) from which the arms radiate. **chióh-lin,** an animal like the sea-anemone, which clings to rocks in the sea. **ô-lin,** a red roundish sea-slug (cf. lun).

lîn (R. id.) **kî-lîn,** the fabulous auspicious beast called kilin, sometimes translated unicorn. **pha kî-lîn,** to roll one's body sidewise like a wheel, with legs and arms like spokes.

lîn [R. lûn]. **kau-lîn** (T.), = A. kau-lûn, to hand over to a man in his turn, *e.g.* land cultivated in turn by relatives. **chiàu-lîn** (C.), = A. chiàu-lûn, by turns.

lîn [R. id., = col. liên]. **lîn-bín,** to pity; compassion; merciful. **khó-lîn,** to pity; alas! **thòe-i khó-lîn,** to pity him. **khó-lîn--i,** id. **khit-ai kiû-lîn,** to beg for some favour to one's self in distress.

lîn (R. id.) **lîn-iû,** neighbours. **chhù-piⁿ lîn-iû,** neighbours in general. **tsó-iū-lîn,** the neighbours on each side. **oán-chhin put-jû kūn-lîn,** a neighbour at hand is better than a friend at a distance.

lîn (R. lêng), (Cn. lêng), a thin glossy sort of silk stuff. **lîn-á,** a very thin glossy silk. **pėh-lîn,** thin white glossy silk. **âng-lîn,** red do. **ú-lîn,** cheap glossy stuff of wool and cotton (v. ú). **lîn-toān,** thin glossy silk and satin. **lîn-lô gím-siù,** rich and variegated silks and satins (v. lô).

lîn (C.) **lîn-lông-ké,** = A. lin-long-ké, a sort of rattle (v. long).

lín, you; ye; your (in Cn. "lín" and "lán" almost change places). **lín-ê,** your; yours. **lín-tau,** your house.

lín (Cn.), = A. lán, náⁿ, like.

lìn — **lìn-lìn lòng-lòng,** loud noise or turmoil, as of knocking or moving heavy things (v. lòng).

lìn (T.) **lē-li-lin,** = A. lê-li-lien, words used at the beginning of a play.

lìn (cf. lin), to roll, as a ball. **îⁿ-lìn-lìn,** round, as a ball or egg. **kng-lìn-lìn,** having no near relatives. lə̄-lìn-hit, = lə-nì^n-hit, to swing from side to side. lìn--lòh-khì (C. lièn), to roll and fall down, as a precipice, ravine, or bed. sì-kòe-lìn, to roll itself about back and forwards, as a ball, or as a child on the floor; said also of a child or young lad going about with no one taking care of him. khoā-khoā-lìn, to roll itself about, as a ball, or as child on floor. kō-kō-lìn, to roll about, as a ball. kàuh-kàuh-lìn, id. lìn-hê-lê-būn, to throw the dice on a sort of paper in gambling (v. būn).

hoan-lìn-tńg, to turn upside down; immediately. hoan bōe-lìn-tńg, unable to turn, as in nightmare, &c. poàh-lìn-tńg, to turn right round, as a thing; to turn one's self round so as to let another pass; to pretend that a man said what we ourselves said. poàh-lìn-tńg-thâu, to turn quite round about. sim-koa^n poàh-lìn-tńg, to change one's mind quite round, esp. from affection to coldness in a near relative. péng-lìn-tńg, to invert; to turn upside down, as hand or thing, or as in bed. pán-lìn-túi^n (C.), id. oàt-lìn-tńg, to turn one's self round; to look round; to turn and go back. oàt bōe-lìn-tńg, unable to turn round. iét-lìn-tńg, to shift the sail to the other side. pha chit-lìn-tńg, to make a complete circuit, as in walking. chhia pha-lìn-táu, to make a somerset.

ô-á-lìn, a preparation of oysters and potatoe flour.

līn (R. id.) kien-līn (r.), parsimonious; stingy; niggardly. līn-sek (R.), id.

lio (reduplication of sio). sio-lio--khì, to be burned and quite consumed.

liô — ka-liô, words used in calling a dog; also sometimes said in imitation of the name Carlo.

liô, to slice horizontally; to skim.

lió (= lioh), to give a rapid glance. lió--chit-ē, id.

liò (Cn.), = A. lò, tall.

liō (K.), = A. lə̄, a road.

liō (Cn.) liō-cheng, = A. tūi-cheng, gonorrhœa.

lioh (reduplication of khioh). khioh-lioh, to collect; to gather; to smooth a surface, &c.

lioh (= lió), to glance or make a rapid look at something. bàk-chiu lioh, id., to make a sign by a glance. bàk-chiu lioh, chiū-tsai, to know at a glance or on one rapid reading; very talented.

liòh [R. liòk, to write]. têng-liòh (Cn.), = A. têng-liòk, to copy out in red the essay of a candidate for the Kujin degree.

liòh [R. liòk, small quantity]. liòh-liòh-á, slightly; a little.

liòh [R. jiòk, weak, = col. jiòh, lèh]. ńg-liòh, elegant and graceful (not coarse, fat, or angular), as hand or foot; very weak and exhausted, as from illness or severe exercise.

liòk [R. six, = col. làk], one of the musical notes. liòk-chiet, full particulars; all the circumstances plainly and minutely stated. liòk-chhin, near relatives. liòk-bû, having no near relations (said in reviling), (v. bû). liòk-ngâu^n, the diagram "ngâu^n." liòk-pə̄, the six boards at Pekin. ngə́-tsōng liòk-hú, the intestines. sam-kə liòk-pô, nuns and dangerous old women (v. pô). liòk-thiok, the domestic animals. liòk-siù, spirits of six animals, propitiated by Tauist priests. liòk-sîn, id., said by the priests. gû-thâu liòk-tsut, a clownish fellow.

liòk-pat-phêng, the rate of counting dollars, as 6 chí^n 8 hun by the khə̀-tô weight = liòk-pat-pêng (v. pêng). liòk-goàt-song, a sort of cooling medicine (v. song).

liòk — liòk-chhoàn, a strong sort of silk stuff (v. chhoàn).

liòk [R. dry land; six, = col. lèk]. liòk-lə̄, by land; military, as opposed to naval. liòk-lə̄ thê-tok, a general. liòk-thê (r.), id.

liòk-siòk, in continuous succession, but small quantities; moderate, as gains, &c. (v. siòk).

liòk [R. to kill]. sat-liòk, to slaughter; to massacre.

liòk [R. to seize], (C. liàk). bêng-hə́^{n} kiap-liòk, housebreaking and robbery with torches, generally having faces disguised with paint.

liòk [R. to write down carefully; to record], (P. lèk). bók-liòk, index or contents of a book; a list or catalogue. pò-liòk, official notification to a man who has got a degree. têng-liòk, to transcribe in red ink an essay for the Kujin degree (v. têng). siù-tsâi-liòk, list of new Sew-tsai graduates printed for sale. kú-jîn-liòk, do. of new Kujin. chìn-sū-liòk, do. of new Tsin-sze.

liòk [R. small quantity, = col. liòh], (C. liàk). iok-liòk, in general or on an average; speaking roughly and generally. tāi-liòk, id. phó-liòk-á, slightly; to a small extent. phə́-liòk-á, id. phə́-liòk-á tsai, to know a little of it.

hut-liòk, to do a thing without much care or attention; to slight; to treat with want of respect or attention, *e.g.* taking no notice of a man when he comes or goes.

liông [R. a dragon; imperial, = col. lêng], (also C., = A. lêng). kiú-liông-pau, a pouch for ammunition. kiú-liông-tīn, an army divided (for battle) into nine parts. kiú-liông-koan, a royal crown with nine dragons. kiú-liông-poâ^n, a wooden tray with nine divisions. liông-sa, hills like an arm behind a grave on the left hand (v. sa). pék-hə́ chheng-liông, two of the great Tauist spirits (v. hə́). liông-gân (R.), the face of the emperor. it-kiok thiàu-liông-bûn, the lame man crossed the imperial threshold. liông-bûn-soa, a sort of shark (edible).

ə-liông, Oo-long tea; also a small black cricket or "sek-sut;" the reddish sort is called "chhiah-kiu^n." kî-liông, a hornless dragon (v. kî). soa^n-liông-á (C.), a reptile like a snake with four feet. chhâu-liông-á (C.), id. liông-thiông (T.), a sort of marine worm or mollusc. liông-iên-hiu^n, a medicine. liông-siên-hiu^n, id.

liông [R. liōng, to measure, = col. niû^n], (C. liâng). siong-liông, to consult together.

liông [R. good], (C. liâng). liông-bîn, good subjects. siēn-liông, good, as man. sûn-liông, well-behaved, trustworthy, and safe. liông-iòh khə́-khə́; tiong-giên gék-ní^n, good medicine is very bitter; faithful words displease the ear.

liông-sim, conscience, especially as to duties among men. liông-sim-chhàt, a thief who steals only a part, leaving what he could have taken. thien-lí liông-sim, Heaven's law agreeing with conscience; I am perfectly honest and truthful. tiòh thien-lí liông-sim, should act in good conscience. ū thien-liông, conscientious, just, and fair in dealings. tsûn liông-sim, id.

liông (reduplication of kiông). sái-kiông-liông, to act violently and wickedly towards another.

liông [R. a beam, = col. niû^n]. tiòng-liông,

important or useful, as person or thing, &c. **tòng-liông**, id.

liông [R. eminent; glorious; abundant, = col. liōng]. **khiên-liông**, the reign of the Emperor Kien-lung. **liông-sēng** (better "liōng"), in very great abundance (v. sēng).

liông [R. lông, a wolf]. **liông-pōe**, = lông-pōe, very poor and miserable.

liông [R. a sort of grain], (C. liâng). **kau-liông**, a sort of distilled liquor. **tō-liông-siok, bék-sú-chek**, the six grains.

liông [R. liâng, cool]. **liông-hiet** (T.), cooling for the blood.

lióng [R. two; both; a tael, = col. nñg, niú^n, nǹ^n, lí, léng], (C. liáng). **lióng-goān**, both parties quite willing and pleased. **lióng-gē**, a misapprehension, so as to fail of doing what was expected. **lióng-kau-khâ^n**, unsettled in purpose; double-minded or trimming (v. khâ^n). **lióng-kha-khiâ**, telling only half one's mind; concealing one's schemes and seeming neutral. **lióng-phak khui-chhiò**, trimming between two opinions or courses (v. chhiò). **koan iú lióng-khé**, the character "mandarin" (koan) has two mouths. **chìn-thòe lióng-lân**, to go on and to draw back are both difficult or dangerous (v. lân). **siēn-ok put-lióng-lip**, good and bad cannot stand together. **siâ-chèng put-lióng-lip**, if you employ bad men, the good will leave you. **jîn-tē lióng-se**, people and place both strange to us.

lióng-gî, the emblem of the Yin and Yang, by a circle divided equally by two half-sized semicircles. **lióng-póng**, the rank of Tsin-sze. **lióng-kiok tiâu-thien**, fallen on the back, with feet towards the sky. **lióng-lông** (T.), = A. léng-lông, the two covered ways on the sides of the central court of a Chinese house. **sam khi-lióng**, three men oppressing two (v. khi). **it-to lióng-toān**, said of at once determining a matter long unsettled (v. toān). **it-jîn tì, put-jû lióng-jîn gī**, the counsel of two is better than one man's wisdom.

liòng (C.), = A. lèng, to kick or push away with the sole of the foot.

liōng [R. liông, eminent; abundant]. **liōng-sēng**, very abundant, as money or grain, &c. (v. sēng). **chî^n-tsúi liōng-lēng**, his money very abundant (v. tsúi).

liōng [R. to suppose, excuse, or assist], (C. liāng). **iok-liōng**, about (the quantity). **liōng-iok**, id. **liōng-pit**, I should say it must —; I should say that —. **ōe-liōng--lâng**, considerate and gentle, as towards inferiors or person in fault. **liōng lâng-ê-chêng**, id. **liōng-chêng**, to forgive or act with consideration and forbearance, as towards a man who is in fault; gentle, kind, and long-suffering. **khah-ōe liōng-chêng**, of a rather gentle or forgiving disposition.

liōng [R. jiōng, to yield, = col. niū^n], (C. niū^n). **liōng--chit-ē**, omit one stroke of the oar; pause a little, as in striking or in a legal process; stop a little, *e.g.* said by the bearer of our baggage asking us to let him rest a little.

liōng [R. a measure, = col. liâng, niû^n], (C. liāng, except in one or two phrases). **liōng-tsá** (C. liōng), a good deal earlier than is absolutely necessary. **khah-liōng** (C. liōng, lēng), a little larger; slightly more; rather better, as in sickness.

liōng-tāi-siáu, to use more or less as we please (v. siáu). **bô-hān-liōng**, boundless.

hó-liōng, liberal; generous; forbearing. **ū-liōng**, id. **ū-tē-liōng**, id. **tē-liōng toā**, id. **tē-liōng khoan-hông**, id. **toā-liōng**, generous. **tāi-liōng**, id. **khoan-hông tāi-liōng**, id. **hái-liōng**, exceedingly generous (like the sea!). **chhién-liōng**, too rigorous for one's rights; also (said by one's self), not able to drink much liquor. **chiú-liōng**, ability to drink liquor (v. chiú). **lėk-liōng**, measure of one's ability (v. lėk). **chì-liōng toā**, having high aims, *e.g.* for high literary rank. **khì-liōng toā**, aiming at considerable matters; not too particular about small things. **khì-liōng sòe**, having small aims; too minutely careful about small things, *e.g.* small sums, or reproving for small faults. **khoan-liōng**, to treat people with indulgence or forbearance. **bô-lâu-liōng**, to go to too great an extreme, *e.g.* spending all one's income, exerting one's strength or influence to the very utmost, or taking too much liquor. **iú-sè, put-khó chīn-liōng**, do not use your power or enjoy your good fortune to the utmost.

liōng (C.), = A. niā^n. **soa^n-liōng**, the shoulder of a mountain, rising higher than the connecting ridge. **soa^n-liōng-á**, id.

lip (Cn.) **lip-lip-á**, = A. lím-lím-á, all but —.

lip [R. to stand; to set up]. **siet-lip**, to set up; to appoint or ordain. **kièn-lip** (R.), to set up or establish firmly. **kièn-kong lip-giàp**, to establish one's merit and fortune. **put-lióng-lip**, cannot stand together, as good and bad (v. lióng).

lip-khek, immediately.

lip-sim, to determine one's intention; fixed purpose. **lip-ì**, id. **lip-chì**, id. **kien-sim lip-chì**, id.

lip-chhun, the term about Feb. 4th. **lip-hē**, about May 5th or 6th. **lip-chhiu**, about August 7th or 8th. **lip-tang**, about Nov. 7th.

lit, = lùt (C. bit), the rope that hauls up a Chinese sail, like halyards. **lit-á-soh**, id. **chit-thia^n-lit**, one such rope. **chit-tiâu-lit**, id. **lit-chí^n**, the upper end of this rope, where it is fastened to the sail.

liu (Cn.) **táh-liu**, to stumble.

liu [R. chhiu, name of a fish]. **hê-liu**, a small fish, a few inches long, that lives in ditches and pools. **thê-liu**, id. **chhì-liu**, a sort of salt-water fish.

liu (T.), = A. chhiu, to tickle with the finger, as the face.

liu — **khiû-khiû liu-liu**, curled or tangled, as long hair (v. khiû).

liu [R. thiu, to draw out, = col. chhiu]. **liu-khau**, to draw lots. **liu hé-chhiu**, to draw lots to see which man is to pay the principal share of some common expense.

liu, to steal small things; to steal away secretly. **tsòe-i-liu**, he has gone off suddenly and unexpectedly. **liu--kè-khì**, to make off suddenly, as from a creditor or from a man trying to catch him. **liu--tsáu**, id. **liu-kiang**, to get out of the way so as to escape from danger, or shirk duty and responsibility. **liu-kiang kiâ^n-tāng**, id. **tsòe--i liu-kiang**, he has run off so. **chit-jit liu-liu-khì**, absent the whole day, as servant or scholar. **chit-jit liu-liu-tsáu**, id.

kō-liu--khì (Cn.), quite lost, as opportunity gone beyond recall.

liu — **koe-liu**, very mean and low in money matters and in doing business.

liu — **kut liu-liu**, very slippery, as road. **kú liu-liu**, very long (time). **sam-jit put-kiàn, kú liu-liu**, three days without seeing (him) is very long. **kng liu-liu**, quite bare and naked. **theh liu-liu** (Cn.), naked; nothing whatever left, as by robbers.

liu (cf. niuⁿ). **bé-liu**, the utmost end; the extremity. **soaⁿ-bé-liu**, the very top of a hill; the extremity of the base of a hill. **teh-beh liu-bé**, about to come to an end, as a family of bad sons. **kō-liu** (Cn.), a man's queue.

liu — **liu-chhiu, chiáh bák-chiu**, a man should know by a glance what he has to do (v. chhiu).

liû [R. to flow; to run on in course; to transmit; a sort; = col. lâu], to banish, as from the province; to choose out, as good or bad from a mixed lot; to lead about, as a horse for exercise. **phiau-liû**, carried away, as by a flood (v. phiau). **liû-chhiⁿ-sek**, light greenish-blue, like duck's egg. **liû-seng-thûi**, an ancient weapon (v. seng). **liû-put-thài-sòe**, the demon that causes eclipses (v. put).

liû-bé, to lead about a horse, as for exercise.

liû phái"-chîⁿ, to choose out bad cash. **kè-liû**, carefully selected out of a lot.

lûn-liû, in rotation (v. lûn). **saⁿ-liû-lông**, id. **liû-hêng**, to go on acting widely, as nature's operations, or as an epidemic (v. hêng). **liû-thoân**, to transmit, as from one age to another (v. thoân). **liû-toân** (T.), id. **ìn-tap jû-liû**, fluent at talking.

hā-liû, very mean. **hā-liû put-siàu**, a good-for-nothing fellow. **kiú-liû**, all sorts of priests, nuns, and sorcerers. **sam-kàu kiú-liû**, a jack-of-all-trades. **put-jip-liû ê-lâng**, a useless fellow unfit for any work. **bē-jip-liû**, said of a very small mandarin.

hong-liû, dissipated; too fond of gaiety and pleasure. **hong-liû-lâng**, a dissipated man. **sì-kòe-liû**, to go about associating with bad or low characters. **liû-lók**, to wander about with no settled dwelling or occupation, as a man in great poverty. **sì-kòe liû-lók**, id. **lók-hoa liû-súi**, in great poverty and misery. **liû-súi**, a sort of scroll-book for entering sales (v. súi).

liû-tê, to banish or transport, in general. **gī-liû**, to condemn to banishment, as to another province. **mn̂g-liû**, id. **chhiong-kun mn̂g-liû**, to exile or transport. **khah-khiap chhiong-kun mn̂g-liû**, worse than transportation (v. khiap). **liû-hoān**, to banish a criminal; a banished criminal. **chioh liû-hoān-chè**, to borrow at heavy usury from banished criminals (those at Amoy are usually from the north). **liû-bîn**, a vagabond; a wandering fellow with no settled occupation. **liû-bîn-ná**, id. **liû-bîn-ná-thiⁿ**, pleasant warm weather in winter.

liû (cf. chhiû), to unwind; to draw in the slack of a rope gently.

liû [R. to retain; to detain; to keep over, = col. lâu]. **tau-liû**, to detain forcibly, as men or things, *e.g.* for ransom, or to get payment of debt; to keep in confinement, as an enemy in a feud. **siu-liû**, to receive and entertain in one's house, as guest or lodger. **liû-tsûn**, to reserve; to keep in reserve. **liû-jīm**, to make application to get a good mandarin reappointed (v. jīm).

liû-sim, attentive; to pay close attention; to keep the mind on a thing. **liû-sim tì-ì**, id.

liû [R. id., = jiû]. **liû-hông**, sulphur. **liû-n̂g**, id.

liû (R. id.) **bián-liû**, a square-topped crown with pendants, worn by sovereigns and idols. **tsu-liû**, the set of pendants of a crown or coronet.

liû (R. id.) **liû-lî**, a translucent material like glass, but different. **liû-lî-thâu**, a bald head (said in joke). **liû-lî-teng**, a sort of lamp used in temples; a scabbed head (said in scolding or jeering). **liû-lî-kong**, an idol specially worshipped by vegetarians (said to have been the spirit of a lamp). **liû-lî-hōe**, a society for the worship of liû-lî-kong.

liû — **liû-khiû**, fond of keeping a feud or dispute open, as man; fractious, as child (v. khiû).

liû [R. name of a tree]. **siàh-liû**, the pomegranate. **chióh-liû** (Cn.), id. **sėh-liû** (C.), id. **péh-siàh-liû**, a white variety with light greenish fruit (good for dysentery). **kim-siàh-liû**, a plant used for dysentery. **soaⁿ-siàh-liû**, a wild shrub with a white flower.

liû [R. id., = col. lâu], a tumour, wen, or swelling on the neck. **bah-liû**, id. **huih-liû**, such a tumour red and full of blood. **hiet-liû**, id. **che-liû**, one soft and round, and white when cut. **tāu-che-liû**, id. **toā-ām-liû**, a large tumour on the neck. **sìⁿ-liû**, to have a wen on the neck. **ām-kún sìⁿ-liû tú--tióh**, it can't be helped any more than a tumour on the neck. **phah-chit-liû**, to raise a lump by striking.

liû [R. jiû, name of fish]. **liû-hî**, a fish like the cuttle-fish, but counted better.

liú — **liú-lōng-lien**, words called out at the beginning of a play. **lōng-liú-lien**, id.

liú (R. id.), a willow; a surname. **liú-ki**, a willow branch. **liú-chiam**, shoes with only one rib on the toe. **liú-tiâu-thang**, a window made with long thin slips of wood. **liú-tiâu-pîn**, a partition made with such slips. **liú-tiâu-pò**, gingham.

chióh-liú, a willow with hard white wood. **kòe-liú**, a tree like the elm. **iûⁿ-liú** (r.), the willow. **sûi-si-liú**, the weeping-willow.

hoe-âng liú-lėk, gaudily dressed (v. lėk). **hoa-ke liú-hāng**, said of a house of bad fame.

liú [R. id., cf. col. khiú, giú], to grasp and pull towards one, as a rope or tail; to haul. **liú-oá**, to pull near by a rope, as a boat. **liú--lâi**, to grasp and pull towards one. **liú-tiàⁿ**, to pull in the anchor-rope by hand, as to raise the anchor. **liú-chìn**, to pull up closer, as boat, by rope attached to the bow.

liú (cf. liù), a hank, as of thread. **chit-liú**, one hank.

liú (R. id.), a button, properly a twisted knot on end of a cord (used as a button); to button. **liú-saⁿ**, to button a dress. **chién-liú**, a pickpocket. **liú-pīⁿ**, sort of round cord (v. pīⁿ). **liú-á-géng**, a small sort of lung-yen fruit (gêng-géng) with little pulp.

liú-khàu, the loop which serves as a hole for a Chinese button. **liú-phàn**, double piece of cord sewed on a dress, either to receive the button, or twisted into a knob (Chinese button), or ending in a loop used as a button-hole. **pâi-á-liú**, a button of foreign shape. **liú-pâi**, buttons in general. **pīⁿ-liú**, a flat button of foreign shape. **pè-liú**, a knot of cotton cord used as a button. **phah-pè-liú**, to make one. **kiet-liú**, the knob on a Chinese cap. **kiō-liú**, the knob on the top of a sedan.

bát-liú-liú, very close or crowded.

liú (cf. liu, liù). **pīⁿ-liú-liú** (Cn. T.), very smooth and level, as road.

liù (cf. liú), to catch with a running noose or lasso; to allure a man to some bad course. **liù-káu**, to catch a dog with a noose. **liù-ti**, to catch a pig with a noose. **liù--lâng khì-poàh**, to allure people to gamble, as

40

companions. **chhòng mīⁿ-soàⁿ khì liù-ah** (to make a vermicelli noose to catch ducks), to try to do a thing with quite insufficient means.

liù— **sá-liù**, skilful; cunning. **lì-liù**, over-sharp in dealing (cheating somewhat), esp. said of a boy. **lì-liù-á-pē̤**, too sharp practice.

liù— **liù-tsú-kiáⁿ**, a wicked boy or lad, as 15 or 20 years old.

liù, to take off, as a hat. **liù-bō**, to take off one's hat. **liù-e̤-kun**, to take off the bride's vail at marriage, as the bridegroom does. **liù-phê**, the skin grazed, as by a stroke; the skin peeling off, as at the edges of a sore when healing. **liù-hiàh**, bald on the forehead and crown of the head. **liù-kng-thâu**, having no cap or hat on; bare-headed.

kut-liù-liù, very slippery, as road. **kng liù-liù**, quite bare or naked (v. kng).

liù [R. liû, to flow, = col. lâu]. **bô-sūn-liù**, very unpleasant and quite contrary to expectation, *e.g.* all that is said being in favour of our enemy when help is asked.

liū, to soften in a covered rice-boiler (tiáⁿ), as cakes. **liū-ké**, to soften hard cakes by steaming thus.

liùh [R. liòk, six, = col. lák], one of the musical notes, = liòk.

liúh— **liúh-liúh-á**, slightly; better lióh-lióh-á (*q.v.*)

lo (cf. lu, tho), to dabble in mud, as a duck. **ah-bú-chhùi bóng-lo**, may as well ask for it, though with almost no expectation of success.

lo, to ask over and over in a coaxing way (*e.g.* surely you won't refuse me); to ask importunately, as for money or employment, or a favour for self or other; to get money or a favour by constant asking. **lo-chîⁿ**, to ask over and over for money. **lo-lién**, to get money by hook or by crook (v. lién). **tit-tit-lo**, to ask right on, taking no denial. **kap-i-lo**, to ask thus from him. **bōe-kham--tit i-lo**, could not resist his importunity.

lo (= lô). **lo-so**, troublesome, as a man constantly talking or asking or making difficulties. **lo-lo so-so**, id.

lo— **li-li lo-lo**, glancing about rapidly in every direction, as the eyes of a thief; empty talk, as mere formal expressions, or idle useless chattering, or repeated asking.

lo— **hn̄g lo-lo**, very distant.

lo [R. lòk, to roast or burn]. **chhàu-hé-lo**, a burned or singed taste, when something gets dried and singed in cooking. **chhàu-hé-lo-bī**, id. **chhàu-lo chhàu-lo**, id. **chhàu-hiaⁿ-lo** (T.), id. **chhàu-tiáⁿ-lo**, singed in the frying-pan.

lo (mere reduplication). **po-lo-so**, to praise very much. **ho-lo**, an interjection used in calling out to a man, like ho! ho!

lô (R. id.) **lô-chhia**, name of an idol (v. chhia).

lô— **ka-lí-lô**, not yet completed; far from the end yet (v. ka).

lô (R. id.) **lô-siong**, consumption. **lô-chèng**, id. **hu-lô ê-chèng**, id. (v. hu).

lô [R. toil, trouble], (Cn. lê̤). **kong-lô**, merit, esp. for services to the state. **sin-lô**, wages. **sió-sim hāu-lô**, to be exceedingly attentive to a man, as servant to master, or as attendant to sick man, or as a parasite fawning on an influential person. **lô jî-bû-kong** (r.), toil and no profit (v. kong).

lô-sim, thinking deeply or anxious about some matter. **lô-sim--ê**, caused by anxiety or mental labour (said of the cause of a disease.) **lô-sim peh-pak**, much vexed or anxious about matters. **lô-sim kè-tē̤**, to give a great deal of thought and anxiety to the planning or management of a matter. **lô-sim kò-tē̤**, id. **lô-sim lô-lèk**, to exert one's mind and strength very much. **lô-lèk**, to labour very hard, or with all one's strength.

lô-lòk-miāⁿ, a severe toilsome life. **lô-khé̤**, severe or toilsome, as labour. **lô-bîn siong-tsâi** (R.), to oppress the people and take their money.

lô-tōng, I will trouble you, sir, to —; I have given you a vast deal of trouble. **lô-hoân--lí**, id. **lô-sìn** (R.), thank you, sir, for your trouble.

pit-lô, a small, lean, harsh-voiced bird, said to be unfilial. **pek-lô**, id. **chhī-koe, chiâⁿ pit-lô**, the fowls one feeds are as small and lean as the pit-lô.

lô— **lô-so**, troublesome, as a man; better "lo-so" (*q.v.*)

lô— **liâm-lô**, adhesive; sticky. **lô-liâm-hiuⁿ**, a sort of adhesive gum used for making incense.

lô-thi-thi, very much involved, as an affair hard to put right, or as indefinite talk (v. thi).

lô, muddy; turbid, as a liquid; of a dull or indistinct colour, as foreigner's eyes.

lô— **o-lô-sô**, very black.

lô [R. hô, a great river]. **thien-lô-pán**, = thien-hô-pán, a ceiling.

lô [R. a net], (P. sometimes lê̤), a sort of gauze used for mosquito-curtains; a surname. **péh-lô**, white stuff for mosquito-curtains. **thih-soàⁿ-lô**, a very stiff stuff used for that purpose. **lîn-lô si-toān**, silks, satins, and net. **lîn-lô gím-siù**, fine variegated silks, &c. **lô-phè**, a sort of kerchief worn by women. **to-lô-nîⁿ**, a sort of woollen stuff.

lô-bûn-tsoá, a sort of lined paper. **lô-táu**, a fine sieve in a flour-mill (v. táu).

hé̤-lô, a trap for tigers. **lô-bāng**, a net (figuratively). **lô-bóng** (R.), a net (v. bóng).

lô-kiⁿ, a geomancer's compass (v. kiⁿ).

giâm-lô, the judge of the dead. **giâm-lô-ông**, id. **siām-lô**, Siam; Siam and Laos. **lô-hàn**, Buddhist saints or Lohans (v. hàn), (Cn. lê̤-hàn). **pho-lô-bit**, the jack-fruit tree.

lô— **se-lô** (C.), a brass wash-basin.

lô (R. id.), a flat gong without a boss (but "cheng" has a boss). **lô-á**, a small gong (used by pedlars). **sió-lô**, two small gongs set in a wooden frame. **lô-kó̤**, gongs and drums. **chhēⁿ-lô**, a small gong (about 8 inches broad) with a shrill sound. **chhēⁿ-lô-á**, a very small sort. **lô-ién-sê** (T. lê̤-ién-chê), a band of about a dozen boys at idolatrous processions.

lô-thûi, the clapper for a gong. **phah-lô**, to strike a gong. **thoân-lô**, to give information by beating a gong.

lô [R. id., = col. loâ], a large round wicker-tray; to clean grain by shaking it in such a tray. **bí-lô**, a flat round bamboo tray for shaking rice so as to separate the clean rice from the chaff or the rice still having the husk. **bí-lô-á**, a small one. **lô-lô**, to shake (as rice) in a tray. **lô-bí**, to shake rice thus so as to clean it. **lô-bí thai-chhek**, to clean rice by shaking or riddling.

thn̂g-lô, a large round wicker-tray or frame for drying sugar.

lô [R. a mere sound]. **liâu-lô**, banditti; also, the south-east corner of Quemoy island.

lô (R. id.), a mule. **hái-lô**, a sort of seal (or beaver?).

lô [R. ê, coral, = col. hô]. **sien-lô-chhiū**, a coral-tree.

lô [R. a creeping plant]. **lú-lô**, a sort of creeper (dodder?).

lô [R. name of a tree]. **lô-bák**, a hard blackish wood. **lô-bák-chhâ**, id.

lô [R. a prison], (Cn. lê). **kaⁿ-lô**, a prison. **lô-gék** (r.), id. **tsúi-lô**, a sort of dungeon like a well. **thien-lô**, the imperial prison (s. net).

lô (R. liâu ?). **kha-lô**, fetters for the feet. **kha-lô chhiú-khàu**, fetters and manacles. **koāⁿ kha-lô**, to have one's feet fettered. **náⁿ-koāⁿ kha-lô** (as if fettered), said of being impeded in travelling, as by leading a child.

ló [R. old, aged, = col. lāu, láu, lauh, niáu], affix to a man's name (not surname) in speaking to him or of him with some respect. **lâm-hū ló-iù**, male and female, old and young. **ló-liên**, aged. **ló-sêng**, having the good sense and staid manner of an old man, though only middle-aged. **ló-sêng-jîn**, id. **siàu-liên ló-sêng**, young in years but wise and staid. **ló-tông**, an aged candidate. **ló-jiók-peng**, old and feeble soldiers. **ló-mēⁿ**, aged and infirm. **ló-ong** (R.), a polite phrase for addressing an old man. **jîn phàⁿ-ló**, all men are afraid of old age (v. phàⁿ). **ióng-jî thāi-ló**, to bring up a son to prepare for old age (v. ióng). **tiông-seng put-ló**, long life without growing old; a Tauist phrase.

ló-tia (Cn. lāu-tia), a mandarin (v. tia). **toā-ló**, title of medium-rank mandarins. **ló-iâ**, title of Kujin or medium-rank mandarin (v. iâ). **sì-ló** (C.), assistant mandarin of the district (koāiⁿ) mandarin. **ló-su**, title of the literary mandarin of a department or district; polite title for a learned instructor (v. su). **tiúⁿ-ló** (X.), an elder (v. tiúⁿ). **ló-chiòng**, an old military officer. **hông-tiong, lāu-ló-chiòng**, Hwang Chung, though old, was vigorous (said of a hale old man).

kok-ló, the chief of the genii (sien); also (R.), a sort of prime-minister. **ló-kun**, Lau-tsze, the founder of Tauism. **thài-siōng ló-kun**, id. **lí ló-kun**, id. **ló-kun-kong**, id. **ló-kun-iâ** (T.), id. **ló-tam** (R.), id.

ló-chiú, a fermented and smoked liquor made from rice. **ké-ló-chhiū**, an old stump; also (esp. C.), a sort of straggling soft-wood tree with large leaves. **ló-kong-su**, a sort of plant (v. su).

ló [R. a wicker-work vessel]. **ka-ló**, a half globular bamboo wicker vessel for holding rice.

ló [R. anxious; angry; vexed, = col. láu, lâu], (Cn. hó). **hoân-ló**, anxious; grieved; to be anxious about something, especially future. **hoân-ló-chiàh**, anxious about what is to be had to eat.

ló [R. name of a stone]. **bé-ló**, cornelian. **bé-ló-chiòh**, id. **âng-bé-ló**, id. (red). **bé-ló-tsu**, cornelian beads.

gím-ló, a bowl of savoury mixed meats (v. gím).

ló — **ló-kó-chiòh**, coarse coral. **ló-ké-chiòh**, id.

ló [R. brains, = col. náuⁿ], (Cn. lé). **chiuⁿ-ló**, camphor.

ló [R. a torrent; careless]. **ló-chhó**, in a careless off-hand manner (v. chhó).

ló — **o-ló**, to praise. **gâu o-ló**, fond of flattering people.

ló — **hāiⁿ-ló-sō**, to follow or assent to whatever (good or bad) a man says or does; cry of men working together, as in sculling a boat.

ló (reduplication of "hó"). **chit-ke hó-ló-ló**, the whole household is now quite well.

lò (R. id.), (Cn. liò), tall, as man; long-shaped, as an oblong seal or a long parallelogram; long, as an oar-pin, or as the limbs. **lò-ām**, having a long neck. **lò-kha lò-chhiú**, having long arms and legs.

lò (better "lòh," *q.v.*) **lò-āu--jit**, the day after to-morrow.

lō [R. to reward for labour; by change of tone from "lô," labour]. **khò-lō**, to give a largess to soldiers to incite them to courage.

lō — **sio-lō**, pleasantly warm, as weather, dress, or food.

lō (mere reduplication). **tsō-lō**, to blacken, as in blotting out a word or sentence.

hō-lō-sō, to express assent without consideration.

lō — **háiⁿ-lō-sō**, to do work without spirit or energy.

lō — **hoe-lī-lō**, variegated; mottled; indistinct. **hoe-lō-lō**, indistinct; in disorder, as an affair; unable to manage properly.

lō (cf. lōng), a strong horizontal bar quite across a door; to bar the door with it, fastening its ends in the wall or in iron hoops. **mn̂g-lō**, such a horizontal bar for a door. **lō-mn̂g**, to fasten a door with this bar. **mn̂g lō--khi-lah**, the door is firmly barred thus.

lō [R. ló, a wicker vessel], a wicker-work vessel containing about four, five, or ten "táu;" sometimes used for measuring rice in husk (chhek) or ground-nuts. **iû-lō**, a large wooden large-mouthed tun (of fixed size) for holding oil; the quantity is measured by the depth. **chhek-lō**, a large tun or receptacle for holding rice in husk. **bô-chhek, bōe-kah-lō**, how can I be expected to buy when I have no money.

lō [R. liâu, lō]. **hī-khang lō-lō**, a ringing sound in the ears.

le — **khang le-se**, quite empty.

lé [R. ló, an itchy place or sore]. **tiòh-le**, to be mangy, as cat or dog.

le (C.), ashes of burned paper or weeds. **hóe-le**, ashes at end of an extinguished paper match.

lê (R. id.) **lê-hē**, aloes. **lê-hōe** (C.), id. **lê-ōe** (C.), id. **lê-hē-iû**, the juice of the aloe leaf; oil of aloes. **lê-hē chit-phòe**, one leaf of the aloe.

lê [R. name of a fish]. **lê-hî**, a large fish, white and spotted on the back. **lê-moâⁿ**, a conger-eel (v. moâⁿ).

lê [R. lô, a snail or spiral shell, = col. lê]. **lê-si-teng**, a screw-nail (v. si).

lê (R. id). **lê-pók** (R.), a male slave. **lê-pī** (R.), male and female slaves (v. pī). **lê-tsâi**, a male slave, said in scolding; used also as an interjection of distress at matters going wrong. **kiēn-lê**, you stubborn slave! said in scolding a son or inferior trying to be disobedient and obstructive. **chiú-chîⁿ-lê**, a slave to money; a miser. **bé-lê**, a slave acting as ostler, said only in jeering or scolding. **lê khi-tsú**, a slave insulting his master; said in scolding an insolent employé.

lê [R. sound, as of birds chirping], (cf. lông, lōng). **lê-lien**, words used at the beginning of a play (v. lien).

lê [R. an old skull-bone]. **ke-lê**, old rotten human

bones. **ko-lô͘-kut**, id. **siu ko-lô͘**, to collect and bury such old bones, as a meritorious work.

lô͘ (R. id.), a surname.

lô͘ — **óe-kha-lô͘**, a low sort of cock's-comb (flower).

lô͘ (R. id. = col. lo). **lô͘-tek**, a reed. **lô͘-úi** (R.), id.

lô͘ [R. a gourd]. **hô͘-lô͘**, a sort of gourd, much larger at the one end than the other; ornamental gourd-shaped ends of palings, or mortar ornaments on roofs; gourd-shaped vessel for holding drugs. **hô͘-lô͘-pû**, that sort of gourd; a man talking falsely. **hô͘-lô͘-á**, a small knob on a string (as of a screen that draws up) for making it fast. **hô͘-lô͘-tūi**, a pendulum weight. **hô͘-lô͘-kha**, the foot of a table turned with beads. **hô͘-lô͘-toaⁿ**, tickets sold to shops by the head of the beggars, to keep away beggars. **hô͘-lô͘-būn**, a paper with figures on it, used in gambling (v. būn). **iô kim-hô͘-lô͘**, to get much gain by bad means, esp. by prostitution. **m̄-tsai hô͘-lô͘-lāi sī-sím-mihⁿ-ióh**, I don't know what his secret idea or purpose is (lit. what drug is in the bottle).

lô͘, to tie tight, as an anchor cable, by a small rope wound many times round and round it. **tiàⁿ-lô͘**, the small rope used for thus fastening the cable when enough of it is paid out.

lô͘ (R. id.) **lô͘-chî**, the cormorant. **chhân-lô͘**, a sort of bird with a long bill.

lô͘ [R. a stove, furnace, oven, or fire-place; a vessel for burning incense]. **hé-lô͘**, a stove; a furnace; a fire-place. **hé-lô͘-toh**, a mantel-piece. **hong-lô͘**, a small movable earthen stove, as for boiling water for tea. **hang-lô͘**, id. **hang-lô͘-kè**, the frame on which it is set when used. **hang-lô͘-sìⁿ**, a small fan for blowing the fire. **tê-lô͘**, a small hand-stove for boiling water for tea. **pē-lô͘**, a large broad low stove for drying tea, drugs, or tobacco. **pek-lô͘**, an oven for cakes, &c. **piak-lô͘**, id. **piáⁿ-lô͘**, an oven for bread or cakes. **thih-lô͘**, a smith's forge. **chhiú-lô͘**, a small covered brass stove for warming the hands; a small incense vessel held in the hand by Buddhist priests, at some rites. **táh-lô͘**, a sort of stove put in a footstool in cold weather. **hiuⁿ-lô͘**, a vessel for burning incense. **téng-lô͘**, a small-mouthed incense vessel on legs (v. téng). **tâng-sien-lô͘**, a broad-shaped brass incense vessel. **tâng-soan-lô͘**, id. **sam-kài-lô͘**, an incense vessel hung up in a house, used on the birthdays of sam-kài-kong. **jī-tsoá-lô͘**, a furnace for reverentially burning written or printed paper. **kim-lô͘**, a furnace for refining gold; a vessel for burning idolatrous paper. **chîⁿ-lô͘-hu**, ashes of idolatrous paper. **tan-lô͘**, a place where the genii make the elixir (sien-tan) of immortality.

lô͘-kūi, the instrument used for bellows at a forge. **lô͘-tóe**, dollars somewhat dark-coloured, considered of slightly inferior quality; said to be from the bottom of the crucible.

lô͘-tsú, the man who has charge (in turn) of the idolatrous rites in a ward (keng), &c., or who is acting as head of a guild. **thâu-ke-lô͘**, the incense vessel of which he has temporary possession, as his badge of office.

ûi-lô͘ (surrounding the cooking-place), a feast held by each household on the last day of the year. **kè-lô͘**, to be put in the incense vessel while the idol is being worshipped, a means of consecrating a charm. **khí-lô͘**, to light a stove or oven, &c.

lô͘ (T.) **lô͘-ién-chê**, = A. lô-ién-sê, a company of boys at idolatrous processions.

lô͘ (Cn.), = A. lô, toil; labour. **lô͘--lí**, many thanks for the trouble I have given you.

lô͘ (Cn.), = A. lô, consumption.

lô͘ (Cn.), = A. lô, a prison.

lô͘ (Cn. in reading phrases, and P. sometimes only), = A. lô, a net. **lô͘-hàn** (Cn.), = A. lô-hàn, a Lohan or Buddhist saint (v. hàn).

lô͘ [R. lô, a creeping plant]. **lô͘-tîn** (C.), a creeper, shaped like ropes, used for stupifying fish.

ló͘ (R. id.), a sculling oar; a boat-scull. **tsûn-ló͘**, id. **piⁿ-ló͘**, a scull worked on the side of a boat. **ló͘-bīn**, the larboard, left, or port side of a junk. **ló͘-iām**, the bit of hard wood spliced on the scull to work on the pin. **ló͘-iām-khang**, the cavity of the scull which works on the pin. **ló͘-tê-khang**, id. **ló͘-tê**, the pin or knob on which the scull works. **ló͘-tiam**, id. **ló͘-lān** (very vulgar), id. **ló͘-khang**, the hole in the stern through which the scull goes.

iô-ló͘, to work the scull; to scull. **sái-ló͘**, to scull a boat or junk. **lóh-ló͘**, to put on the scull (s. brine). **kek-ló͘**, to exert strength very much in sculling.

ló͘ [R. to exert strength]. **ló͘-lát**, to thank for trouble taken; thank you! **hō͘--lí ló͘-lát**, thank you! I beg to trouble you. **ló͘ lí-ê-lát**, thank you! **ló͘-lí-ê**, "and thank you!" said in return to a man who has said "ló͘-lát." **séng-ló͘-lát**, to lessen the labour. **ùi-ló͘-lát**, to be afraid of toil or trouble, and so avoid a matter. **tióh-khah-ló͘-lát**, it will take more trouble or labour.

ló͘ (R. jiòk). **ló͘-lòeh**, a cap made of material like rattan, with horse-hair tassel. **ló͘-bō** (T.), id. **ló͘-lòeh-iaⁿ**, the tassel of such a cap.

ló͘ [R. salt; careless or vulgar; = col. lo], a sort of brine. **ló͘-thng**, sort of brine. **ló͘--ê**, slightly pickled; not so salt as "sìⁿ." **lóh-ló͘**, to put into brine, as eatable to be pickled (s. scull). **phah-ló͘**, to make a sort of sauce, with flour, fat, spices, &c. **khièn-ló͘**, to mix some salt sauce or brine while things are frying.

chho-ló͘, wanting in refinement; somewhat vulgar in manner, but not intentionally. **ló͘-bóng**, acting in a hurried, careless, or somewhat reckless manner.

ló͘ [R. to seize]. **hōe-ló͘**, civil and military mandarins together going with soldiers to arrest and punish criminals.

o-ló͘-pà, Europe (v. pà). **se-ló͘**, the Russians. **sai-ló͘**, id. **chhiáⁿ--goá khì-tu se-ló͘**, it is a very difficult and dangerous thing you ask me to assist in. **i-chhiáⁿ--lí khì-tu-se-ló͘**, he is asking you to assist him in a very troublesome and dangerous affair.

ló͘ (R. id.), the kingdom of Loo; a surname. **ló͘-pan**, the god of carpenters. **ló͘-pan-kong**, id. **ló͘-pan-chhioh**, the Chinese foot used by masons and carpenters; ten feet want about two inches of our measure (v. chhioh).

pa-tô͘-ló͘, a Manchoo title of high military rank. **o-ló͘-bók-chê**, Urumutsi, a place of severe transportation (v. chê).

ló͘ [R. ló, old, = col. lāu, láu, &c.]; (also sometimes Cn., = A. ló). **ló͘-kí**, a Cantonese harlot. **ló͘-chhú** (Cn.), = A. niáu-chhú, a rat.

ló͘ — **kó͘-ló͘-chhiū**, a sort of low straggling tree, = kó͘-ló-chhiū.

ló͘ (Cn.) **chiuⁿ-ló͘**, = A. chiuⁿ-ló, camphor.

ló͘ (C.) **tê-ló͘**, = A. tê-lo, old used tea-leaves.

lō͘ [R. ho, a door]. **thong-lō͘-kūi**, = thong-ho-kūi, a sort of shop-counter.

lō͘ [R. lô, a reed]. **lō͘-sóe**, a sort of millet.

lō͘ (C. ló͘). **tê-lō͘**, used tea-leaves.

lɵ̄ [R. rude in behaviour]. **thɵ́-lɵ̄**, rude; clownish. **phí-lɵ̄** (R.), mean and low in conduct.

lɵ̄ [R. lɵ́, salt], to salt slightly; to grow damp, as salted things. **iâm-lɵ̄**, salt that has melted by exposure to damp air; brine dripping from salted fish, &c., in damp weather. **si^{n} iâm-lɵ̄**, to grow damp, as salted fish. **tò-lɵ̄**, id.

lɵ̄-iâm, slightly salted. **lí-á-lɵ̄**, put on a little salt. **chhòng-iâm kā-i-lɵ̄**, salt it slightly. **lɵ̄-hê**, pickled shrimps. **lɵ̄-poá^{n}**, the "poá^{n}" fish slightly salted. **kiâm-lɵ̄**, all sorts of salted meat, fish, &c.; brine from it. **bah-lɵ̄**, brine from salted pork. **hî-lɵ̄**, brine from salted fish.

lɵ̄ — **lɵ̄-lê**, snails.

lɵ̄ [R. a cross-bow]. **bān-lɵ̄-chì^{n}** (arrows from many cross-bows, as from an ambush), many enemies coming at once from all sides; many troubles or calamities coming all at once. **bān-lɵ̄-chì^{n} chê-hoat**, numerous calamities coming at once. **bān-lɵ̄-chì^{n} tsôe-hoat**, id. **bān-lɵ̄ chê-hoat**, id.

lɵ̄ [R. bribery]. **hē-lɵ̄**, to give a bribe, especially to one person. **pɵ̀-lɵ̄**, to bribe, esp. a number of persons. **sái-lɵ̄**, to bribe. **hóe-lɵ̄ kong-hêng** (R.), bribery practised quite openly.

lɵ̄ [R. lɵ́, to shake about], to be unsteady or shaky; light in behaviour. **lɵ̄-lɵ̄**, id. **sim lɵ̄-lɵ̄**, heart unsteady. **lɵ̄-lɵ̄-hién**, to shake, as a table. **lɵ̄-nih^{n}-hit**, to shake or swing from side to side. **lɵ̄-nih^{n}-hì^{n}**, id. **lɵ̄-nì^{n}-hit**, id. **lɵ̄-lìn-hit**, id.

lɵ̄ (T.) **lɵ̄-li-lìn**, = A. lɵ̂-li-lien, words used at beginning of a play.

lɵ̄ [R. dew; to be manifested], dew. **lɵ̄-hiēn**, to appear; to come to light. **chhut-thâu lɵ̄-bīn**, to appear openly in public (as a woman), as at games or plays. **siet-sin lɵ̄-thé**, naked. **chhek-sin lɵ̄-thé**, id. **chhiah-sin lɵ̄-thé**, id.

lɵ̄-tsúi, dew. **lɵ̄-tsúi chiàh-khi-chhim**, to get money by meddling with the affairs of men with whom one has no connection. **pėh-lɵ̄**, the term about Sept. 7th or 8th. **hân-lɵ̄**, the term about Oct. 8th. **lȯh tāng-lɵ̄**, heavy dew. **tàng-lɵ̄**, to cool in the dew. **phiò-lɵ̄**, to bleach in the dew. **hong chêng, ú lɵ̄**, wind, calm, rain, and dew. **chit-tiám-lɵ̄**, one drop of dew. **ún-ku sang-tiám-lɵ̄**, a hunchback gets two drops of dew from Heaven.

chiàh-thi^{n}-lɵ̄, to have uncertain means of livelihood, as by jobs now and then; to take advantage of people's troubles or liability to accusation to squeeze money out of them, especially as informers or pettifogging literati who meddle in yamun business. **khùn-thi^{n}-lɵ̄**, to have no place to lodge in, as vagabonds or very poor men; or to sleep in the open air for coolness. **toà-tī hit-thi^{n}-lɵ̄--nih^{n}**, to have no place to lodge. **khiā-thi^{n}-lɵ̄**, id.

lɵ̄-chêng (Cn.), exclamation when something is spoiled, &c. (v. chêng).

lɵ̄ (R. id.) **lɵ̄-giō**, a sort of leek. **lɵ̄-kiō** (C.), id.

lɵ̄ [R. anger; angry]. **lɵ̄-khì chhiong-thien**, very great rage (lit. mounting to heaven).

lɵ̄ [R. sort of crane]. **pėh-lɵ̄-si** (R.), the small white egret or paddy-bird (v. si). **lɵ̄-tó** (R.), Amoy island. **lɵ̄-kang** (R.), id.

lɵ̄ — **lɵ̄-si-teng**, screw-nails; better lɵ̂-si-teng (v. si).

lɵ̄ (R. id.), a road; a way; a journey; a groove, as the road for a lid, &c.; a method or style of work.

toā-lɵ̄, generous; liberal; having a gentlemanly bearing; a great road; a main road. **tsoân-chiu toā-lɵ̄**, the main road to Chin-chew. **sió-lɵ̄**, a small road; a path; a side road. **koa^{n}-lɵ̄**, a great highway. **mn̂g-lɵ̄**, a doorway. **koe-lɵ̄**, a street. **chhái-lɵ̄**, streets ornamented with coloured hangings (v. chhái). **sip-jī-lɵ̄**, streets or roads crossing at right angles. **sa^{n}-chhe-lɵ̄**, place where three roads meet (v. chhe).

káng-lɵ̄, the channel for navigation. **tsúi-lɵ̄**, way or journey by water. **soa^{n}-lɵ̄**, route or journey by land. **liȯk-lɵ̄**, id. (v. liȯk). **lėk-lɵ̄**, id. **hān-lɵ̄**, id. **ngɛ̄^{n}-lɵ̄** (C.), id. **bé-lɵ̄**, a road for horses practising on, especially one on a review-ground. **sì-kòe-ngɵ́-lɵ̄**, in every direction. **ngɵ́-lɵ̄-lâng**, people from all parts. **ngɵ́-lɵ̄ chê-hoat**, persons or troubles coming in numbers at once on a man from all directions. **ngɵ́-lɵ̄-tsôe-hoat**, id.

bô-lɵ̄, there is no road or no means; to have no employment. **chìn-chêng bô-lɵ̄; thè-āu bô-pɵ̄**, can go neither way; no resource at all. **ū-lɵ̄**, there is a road or way; to have a means. **put-chí ū-lɵ̄**, to have a strong passion for or delight in a thing, as for pleasures or business. **chiàh a-phièn, put-chí ū-lɵ̄**, to have a strong passion for opium.

tùi-lɵ̄, pleasing to a person; suitable; acceptable; by road, not by water. **m̄-tùi-lɵ̄**, it does not please him; not a suitable or proper way. **kap--i bô-tùi-lɵ̄**, it does not please him; he does not get on well with him. **ōe-tùi-lɵ̄**, will be successful, as request, or as medicine. **hȧh-lɵ̄**, pleasing to a person. **kui-lɵ̄**, to be diligent at one's work (v. kui). **jīn-lɵ̄**, diligent at duty or at work.

chiàⁿ-lɵ̄, well-behaved; of good conduct. **chhù-lɵ̄--ê**, second-rate. **ū phoà-pī^{n}-lɵ̄**, faulty, as character or work (v. pī^{n}). **khiáu-lɵ̄**, skilful; clever; well-formed; beautiful. **iù-lɵ̄**, fine work. **chhiú-lɵ̄**, workmanship, as good or bad. **chhiú-lɵ̄ chhɵ**, work coarse and inferior. **phái^{n}-chiú^{n}-lɵ̄**, inconvenient arrangement for rowing. **hó-to-lɵ̄**, a good cut of meat.

ū-lɵ̄-ēng, to be useful (v. ēng). **ū-lɵ̄-iōng** (C.), id. **ū-lɵ̄-sái** (C.), id. **bô-lɵ̄-tn̂g**, utterly without ability (v. tn̂g). **gâu-siū^{n}-lɵ̄**, skilful and intelligent in managing matters.

lí-lɵ̄, the right way of action (v. lí). **lé-lɵ̄**, politeness; a ceremonial present (v. lé). **lī-lɵ̄**, employment; business (v. lī). **kāu-sū-lɵ̄**, having a great many matters to arrange; having many diseases one after another. **chhoa^{n}-chhì-lɵ̄**, said of a very troublesome business. **oȧh-lɵ̄**, a regular means of livelihood; means of deliverance from terrible danger (v. oȧh). **seng-lɵ̄**, means of avoiding death. **si^{n}-lɵ̄**, id. **sí-lɵ̄**, conduct that leads to ruin or destruction (v. sí). **kiâ^{n} té-lɵ̄**, to commit suicide (v. té). **kiâ^{n} àm-lɵ̄**, to behave very wickedly and licentiously. **phái^{n}-kiá^{n}-lɵ̄**, lascivious conduct.

thâu-lɵ̄, employment; business; a regular situation. **thâu-lɵ̄ tit**, straightforward and honest in dealings and business; *e.g.* keeping promises and engagements at proper time. **kap--lâng chiàu-thâu-lɵ̄**, to act fairly in dealings. **tsòe-thâu-lɵ̄ kap--lâng bô-tit**, not straightforward in dealings. **bā thâu-lɵ̄**, to look out for an employment or situation.

chhien-ke-lɵ̄, trade in articles that are sure to find a market, as things in constant use by people. **pɵ̀-lɵ̄**, the matter of buying cloth (s. bribe). **bô-hái-lɵ̄**, almost no fish to be caught, as at some particular time.

huih-lɵ̄, a place where a blow is dangerous (v. huih).

kut-lō͘, general shape of one's body. **ū-kut-lō͘**, lean, as face; solid, as essay (v. kut). **soh-lō͘**, ropes (in position), in relation to number and direction (v. soh). **khui pang-lō͘**, to make a groove in a long piece of wood for the ends of partition-boards. **lâ-lō͘**, the cross-beams on which the boards of a boat's upper deck rest.

chhiûⁿ-lō͘, a wall, in regard to its building, position, or direction. **siāng-chhiûⁿ-lō͘**, having a common wall, as two houses. **chit-lō͘-chhiûⁿ**, one wall, as in building. **kúi-lō͘ jîn-jī-kè**, how many sets of couples in or for the roof? **toā-lák-lō͘**, a very large sort of house (v. lák).

poàⁿ-lō͘, half-way (v. poàⁿ). **joā-tsōe-lō͘**, how far? **saⁿ-lí-lō͘**, three lí, about a mile.

lō͘-ke soàⁿ-thèh, family scattered in all directions. **ū-lō͘ bô-chhù**, said of wandering vagrant, or very poor man, who has no place to live. **lō͘ tn̄g**, holding no intercourse; having no means of livelihood. **lō͘ tūiⁿ** (C.), id. **kap--i tn̄g-lō͘**, having no more intercourse with him (v. tn̄g; C. tūiⁿ).

lō͘-tn̄g, a much frequented road (v. tn̄g). **lō͘-tō͘** (r.), a road. **lō͘-koan**, a placard telling the day and route of an idolatrous procession (v. koan). **lō͘-tsām**, a stage on a road; a stage of a road. **lō͘-thêng** (r.), a stage; a journey (v. thêng). **lō͘-têng** (C. T.), id. **lō͘-thâu**, a landing-place; a jetty; the beginning of a journey. **lō͘-thâu-sit**, work of porterage at a landing-place. **lō͘-thâu-thiap**, a placard, notice, or bill posted up. **lō͘-thâu-ang**, a man who cohabits habitually with a woman without marriage. **lō͘-thâu-bó**, such a woman. **lō͘-bé**, end of road; end of matter or affair (v. bé). **lō͘-piⁿ**, roadside. **lō͘-pông-si**, a corpse at the roadside. **lō͘-hùi**, expenses of journey. **lō͘-chhài**, dried or salted meat for journey (v. chhài). **lō͘-chîⁿ**, black-mail; money levied on travellers by villagers on road. **bóe-lō͘-chîⁿ**, id. (v. chîⁿ). **lō͘-teng**, a lamp on a pillar, or wall, or road (v. teng). **lō͘-ìn**, sort of passport.

sūn-lō͘, quite on our way. **bê-lō͘**, to lose one's way. (v. bê). **bat-lō͘**, to know the road. **lō͘ sek**, well acquainted with the road. **lō͘ chhiⁿ**, ignorant of the road. **chhoā-lō͘**, to guide. **ín-lō͘**, id. **saⁿ-chhut-lō͘**, to miss each other on the road (v. chhut). **saⁿ-thut-lō͘**, id. **koáⁿ-lō͘**, to travel on the road with haste. **siu-lō͘**, to repair a road. **siu-kiô tsō-lō͘**, to repair bridges and make roads.

hông-tsoân lō͘-siōng, the invisible world. **hông-tsoân lō͘-chiūⁿ**, id. **thiⁿ-lō͘** (X.), the heavenly road (s. dew). **ū-khì-lō͘, bô-lâi-lō͘**, there is a way to go, but none to return.

lö (T.), = A. li. **pè lāng-lö lāng-lö**, the threads of the cloth too far separate or irregular.

lö (R. liėt). **oáⁿ-kóng-lö** (T.), = A. oáⁿ-kó-lėh, the bottom of a broken bowl.

lö̂ (T.) **ö-lö̂**, = A. e-lê, fractious and bad-tempered, as child.

lö́ (Cn.) **ka-lö́**, = A. ka-lé, puppets; puppet-shows.

lȫ (T.). = A. lē, to prune off shoots.

loa (T.), = A. n̄g-toaⁿ, small eggs in the ovary. **kiò-loa** (T.), = A. khe-toaⁿ, cackling of hen about to lay an egg.

loa (mere reduplication). **thoa-loa**, to drag along; to draw out, as out of water.

loâ (R. lô), a flat round bamboo wicker tray. **bí-loâ**, a flat round bamboo tray for holding rice.

loá (cf. noáⁿ). **loá-chhoá**, acting very carelessly or absurdly; idle and mismanaging matters; lazy and procrastinating. **lí-loá**, to do a thing in a rough-and-ready manner without much minute care (it may be quite properly). **ōe lí-loá--tit**, it need not be done with much care; rough work will do quite well for the purpose. **lí-loá kè-jit**, to work in a very dilatory lazy way.

loā, to lay on loosely, as tiles temporarily laid on a roof when rain suddenly comes on before it is finished. **chhiáⁿ-loā--teh**, id.

loā [R. lāi, to lean or trust on], to charge falsely with a fault or crime; a surname. **bû-loā**, to accuse falsely. **chhòng-sū saⁿ-loā**, to involve others in our own troubles or faults. **beh-loā--lâng**, to try to frighten people into giving money by threats. **sí-loā--lâng**, to kill one's self so as to cause trouble to our opponent; also, fig. of too urgent entreaty. **loā jîn-bēng**, to accuse falsely of liability for a death.

oá-loā, to rely upon, usually in some improper sense; to sorn and live upon a man.

loā — **chiâⁿ-loā**, making a small raised swelling on the skin, as the bite of an insect, or some eruptions.

loā [R. jiók, as, how many? = col. joā, oā], how many? how much? so much or many! (v. joā).

loā (R. lāi), a rapid on a river.

loā (T. noāⁿ). **chhiⁿ-loā**, a large green caterpillar.

loā (Cn.). **köe-loā**, = A. koe-noāⁿ, a young fowl.

loah (mere reduplication). **hoah-loah**, to speak loud or angrily; to scold.

loah, to rub gently back and forwards with short rubs, as to ease pain; to rub in, as salt into a fish, &c. **loah-iâm**, to rub with a little salt, as flesh or fish, in curing it.

loȧh (R. loȧt), to stroke with long strokes all in one direction; to stroke, as the beard; to smooth by stroking, as fur of animal, or as a dress. **loȧh-tit--khì**, to smooth by stroking, as dress or thread. **so-loȧh**, to stroke gently in one direction; to get round a man by saying sweet things, by fine talk and flattery; to fondle, as child: to put a matter to rights, by settling a quarrel and reconciling enemies. **so--lâng loȧh--lâng**, to get a man to do as we wish by saying sweet things to him, "stroking him down." **chit-ē-loȧh, pîⁿ-pho-pho**, he can put it straight with a touch (v. pho). **chit-ē-loȧh, chiū tsáu-tsoȧh**, if he touches a man's arm he makes him ill, as a skilful boxer (v. tsoȧh).

loȧh--lâi, to pull things straight towards one's self with finger points turned down, as cash on a table.

chhùi-chhiu-loȧh, a small comb for the beard.

loȧh — **soaⁿ-loȧh**, a large serpent (said to be quite harmless).

loȧh (R. loȧt), pungent. **hiaⁿ-loȧh**, strong-scented and pungent (v. hiaⁿ). **chhàu-hé-loȧh** (T.), having a smoked taste from bad cooking.

kài-loȧh, mustard (not the plant, which is "koà-chhài"). **kài-loȧh-hún**, powdered mustard. **loȧh-chhài**, flower-buds of mustard plucked and covered up close so as to become very pungent.

loȧh (R. loȧt), to harrow a field before planting the rice.

loȧh — **chhì-loȧh**, a hedge of thorny plants. **hn̂g-loȧh**, a hedge round a dry field or orchard. **chhì-phèⁿ-loȧh** (C.), a hedge of thorny plants.

loân [R. small bells; imperial]. **loân-kà**, the imperial equipage; said also of some high divinities. **kim-loân-tiān**, the imperial hall of audience.

厦英大辭典

loân [R. the female phœnix]. **loân-hông**, female and male phœnix (v. hông).
toà-kə-loân, fated to be a solitary widow.

loân [R. to desire exceedingly]. **tham-loân**, to hanker after or doat upon, as wealth or improper things. **loân-loân** (R.), very much attached to and unable to bear the thought of separation. **loân-loân put-siá**, loving with warmth and constancy (may be said of friends).

loán [R. warmth, as of the sun]. **loán-koh**, the part of the judgment-seat where the mandarin sits.

loán [R. warm, as fire], (C. joán). **loán-e** (C. joán-oe), a dish with burning charcoal inside for keeping food warm. **sè-chêng, khàn-léng-loán**, said of looking at a man's circumstances, as to wealth or poverty, &c.

loán [R. food presented to superiors]. **loán-siū**, a man's sons and daughters-in-law visiting him on the evening before his birth-day.

loán [R. weak, = col. nńg, joán]. **loán-jiók**, weak; feeble.

loān, confused, disorderly, rebellious. **loān-sîn**, confused and almost out of one's mind from sad news, anxiety, or fear. **jû-loān**, entangled, perplexed (v. jû). **thâm-loān**, crazy (dull quiet madness). **thâm-loān-siáu**, mad (said only in scolding). **bâng-loān**, in great hurry and bustle (v. bâng). **bê-loān**, deceived by vicious pleasure (v. bê). **sim-hoân ì-loān**, mind confused and distressed by numerous matters. **tsau-loān**, utterly confused and perplexed in mind by troublesome or painful matters, or by multiplicity of business. **loān-tsau-tsau**, id. **loān-bé-bé**, confused in mind. **loān-kà-kà**, involved; confused. **loān-kàⁿ-kàⁿ**, id. **loān-chhī-chha**, confused, as mind, or as a crowded market. **hūn-loān**, confused. **hun-loān**, id., especially as the mind. **loān-tsú**, in a disorderly manner (v. tsú). **loān-giên**, talking away at random. **loān-loān-kún**, struggling to break away. **loān-peng**, soldiers in the confusion of route.
tso-loān, feeling of dull pain in the stomach (v. tso).
iau-loān, stomach disordered by hunger.
îm-loān, lewd; lascivious. **loān-lûn**, incest.
hoán-loān, rebellion; insurrection; to rebel. **jiáu-loān**, turmoil; riot; disturbance. **lōe-loān**, feud in a family; disturbance in a state. **loān-sè**, times of rebellion or civil war. **pī-loān**, to flee from rebellion or civil war.

lôe (R. lô, = col. loâ). **ka-lôe** (esp. T.), = ka-liâh, a large round bamboo tray used for drying things.

lôe (R. lê), (C. lê; Cn. lôe), to plough; a plough. **lôe-pē**, plough and harrows. **lôe-thâu**, the ploughshare. **lôe-thâu-siⁿ**, metal used for ploughshares. **lôe-chioh**, the low horizontal stick on which the share is fixed (v. chioh). **lôe-ñg** (C. lê-ûiⁿ), the crooked body of the plough. **lôe-pìⁿ**, the plough handle. **lôe-āu-tsō**, the cross-stick at the back of the plough.
tiuⁿ-lôe, to make a plough. **sái-lôe**, to plough. **lôe-chhân**, to plough rice-fields. **lôe han-tsû**, to take up a whole field of potatoes either with plough or hoe.

lôe (C. lê), to rush on with all one's might, esp. blindfold or with head bent down; to run against or come in collision; to strike on a bank or rock, as vessel. **lôe-jip lôe-chhut**, to rush rapidly out and in. **lôe-lién**, to rush on rapidly carrying an idol in its chair.
saⁿ-lôe, to come in collision, as boats. **lôe-tiòh**, to come in collision or run aground. **lôe-tiòh-tsûn**, to run against another boat. **lôe-chiūⁿ-soaⁿ**, to run aground.
gâu-lôe, asking over and over, with pleasant talk and plausible reasons, for some favour which the other is unwilling to grant; *e.g.* to get things cheaper, or get delay in payment.

lóe [R. náiⁿ, mother; milk], (C. lé). **niûⁿ-lóe** (r.), mother. **náⁿ-lóe-máⁿ--nihⁿ**, said of a woman who is too imperious, violent, and troublesome (said in allusion to the character of an imperious old housekeeper in a play). **lin-lóe** (T.), a milk-nurse (often has a bad sense).

lóe (R. li), (C. lé; Cn. lóe), to scold. **lóe-mēⁿ**, to scold violently. **lóe-māⁿ** (T.), id. **lóe-thiⁿ mēⁿ-tōe**, to speak in a scolding and displeased way of heaven and earth. **lóe-liām**, to swear at one. **chiù-lóe**, to make imprecations and incantations against.

lóe (R. id.) **lóe-chi**, dispirited; to lose heart entirely.

lóe [R. lé, ceremony], (C. lé). **siáu-lóe**, ashamed; shy. **ùi-siáu-lóe**, shy. **pê siáu-lóe**, to pay a fine or forfeit (as money, or a feast or play, &c.) in acknowledgment of having done something wrong; *e.g.* to pay a sum of money for permission to break an agreement after the earnest-money has been paid (C. pôe siáu-lé). **pê--lâng siáu-lóe**, id.

lòe (C. lē; T. lōe), a file; to file; to grate down, as potatoes or turnips; to rub with a cloth, or with a rough leaf or skin, as substitute for sand-paper. **lòe-á**, a file. **kù-lòe**, a file for sharpening saws. **hé-chih-lòe** (r.), a coarse file. **tsām-lòe**, to make or sharpen a file.
lòe-hûn, marks made by scratching. **lòe-hún**, to grate or rub down small, as potatoes or stone. **lòe siàh-hún**, to rub down marble into powder.

lōe [R. in, inside, = col. lāi]. **lōe-tiong**, in the affair or matter. **lōe-koh**, the cabinet or privy-council. **lōe-tit**, son of wife's brother. **lōe-loān**, quarrelling in a family; disturbances within a kingdom. **lōe-siong**, a deep internal disease. **lōe-chèng**, id. **lōe-hu**, looking fat and well, but in very weak health. **gōe-kong lōe-èng**, enemies without and treachery within.

lōe, = lē (C. lē; Cn. lōe). **lōe-hî**, a sort of fish. **lōe-koaⁿ**, do. dried, from Siam.

lōe — **teh-pa-lōe sím-mihⁿ**, what are you engaged about? **bô-sím-mihⁿ thang pa-lōe**, nothing to do.

lōe (T.), = A. lòe, a file; to file.

lóeh (R. lip), (C. léh; Cn. lōeh), a broad cap or hat nearly flat, for sun, rain, or ceremony; the head of a nail. **kiⁿ-á-lóeh**, a light broad ceremonial tasselled cap made of rattan, covered with satin or other fine stuff (worn by gentry). **lé-lóeh**, a tasselled summer cap (v. lé). **chháu-lóeh**, a broad flat cap made of leaves. **béh-kó-lóeh**, id., made of straw. **joàh-lóeh**, a broad ceremonial cap with tassels. **joàh-lóeh-khak**, id., without its tassels (worn at funeral rites). **lóeh-thò**, the bamboo or rattan work inside such a cap, which fits tight on the head.
teng-lóeh, the head of a nail. **teng-á-lóeh**, id. **khah-toā-lóeh**, having a larger head, as nail. **géh tì-lóeh**, a small circle of clouds close round the moon (v. géh).

loh, = lah, a final enclitic particle at the end of an indicative sentence.

lòh [R. lók, a camel], a surname.

lóh [R. lók, joy; rejoice]. **tiô-lóh,** the city and district of Chang-loh, near Fuh-chau.

lóh [R. lók, united]. **khe-lóh,** a bamboo hoop and ropes for carrying loads; a cooly who carries loads. **khe-lóh-soh,** these ropes. **lóh-á-soh,** id. **lóh-á,** these ropes fastened to the bamboo hoop. **poeh-lóh,** sort of rope much used by porters. **poeh-lóh-soh,** id.

lóh [R. lók, to lop off], to prune away branches (C.)

lóh — **koe-thî thâu-lóh,** the first cock-crowing. **koe-thî jī-lóh,** the second cock-crowing.

lóh [R. lók, to fall, &c., = col. lak, loh, lâuh, làu], to descend; to come down; to go down into; to lay down or write down; (a place); one compartment of a house.

tá-lóh, where? **tó-lóh,** id. **tá-lóh-ūi,** what place? **tī-tá-lóh,** where? **tī-tá-lóh chit-ê,** which one? **tá-lóh chit-ê,** id. **tó-lóh chit-ê,** id. **tá-lóh-lâng,** to what place does he belong? **beh tá-lóh-khì,** where will you go?

āu-lóh, the back compartment of a Chinese house, generally separated from the front part by a court. **chêng-lóh,** the front part, on the street or road. **ē-lóh,** id. **tiong-lóh,** the middle part, where there are three, separated by two courts. **saⁿ-lóh,** these three parts. **ū-lêng-lóh,** to have a good site in respect of Fung-shuy.

lóh tsòe-sì-thúi, cut up into the four quarters, as carcase of pig or sheep.

lóh-āu--jit, the day after to-morrow. **lóh-āu-nîⁿ,** the year after next. **koh-lóh chit-jit,** yet one day later. **lóh-tsóh--jit** (T.), = A. sùn-tsóh--jit, the second day before yesterday.

ū hē-lóh, well-behaved; correct in conduct, esp. as to money matters; safe to deal with; of respectable position or character, so that he will not do anything very bad; having a pretty good foundation, or a fair chance of success, as an affair. **tsòe-sū ū-hē-lóh,** safe to deal with. **pān kàu ū-hē-lóh,** to manage an affair till it becomes pretty safe or straight. **pān kàu ū chit--ê hē-lóh,** id. **pān--liáu ū-hē-lóh,** well managed and settled properly. **kià--khì ū-hē-lóh,** to send (as letter or parcel) by a safe mode of conveyance. **chhâ kàu ū-hē-lóh,** to examine till we get at the real state of the case. **iáu-bē ū-hē-lóh,** don't yet know the real state of the matter. **chhâ chit--ê hē-lóh,** to examine so as to find the real state and circumstances of the case, as to safety, &c. **ū sím-mihⁿ hē-lóh,** what news of him, or it? **m̄-tsai i--ê hē-lóh,** don't know where he lives, or how he is situated, or what are his circumstances and antecedents. **i--ê hē-lóh sī tsáiⁿ-iūⁿ,** what are his circumstances and antecedents? **lóng-bô hē-lóh,** no news at all. **bô-hē-lóh,** disreputable, as man; unprincipled; of bad character; untrustworthy; unimportant and useless, as a thing. **bô-hē bô-lóh,** id. **kiaⁿ--liáu bô-hē-lóh,** I fear the affair will go wrong, or that the thing sent is lost and cannot be traced. **kià--khì bô-hē-lóh,** to have sent a thing by an unsafe mode of conveyance, so that it is quite lost without any trace.

hoat-lóh, to manage or arrange an affair. **lí-lóh,** to manage well, esp. household matters. **bô lí-lóh,** does not manage well, as household. **siet-bōe-lóh,** unable to establish, as a custom or rule.

chiūⁿ-lóh, to ascend and descend. **lóh--lâi,** to come down. **lóh--khì,** to go down. **chhim--lóh-khì,** to get heavily in debt. **chiáh--lóh-khì,** to swallow down (&c.) **pàng-lóh,** to lay down, as a thing; to repress, as a passion or emotion. **jit lóh,** sunset (v. jit). **chhiⁿ lóh-tōe,** a star setting. **ke-chhiⁿ lóh-tōe** (T.), the Pleiades setting.

lóh-pit, to begin to write. **lóh-lé,** to put on the sculling oar. **lóh-chhiú,** at the very first putting one's hand to a thing. **lóh-chhiú, chiū phah-pháiⁿ,** at the first touch he spoiled it. **lóh-chhiú chiū-iâⁿ,** he won as soon as he began to play. **khah-lóh-chhiú,** better acquainted with the way of doing a thing than at first.

lóh-khoán, to put down a name on an ornamental scroll (v. khoán). **lóh-miâⁿ,** to write down a name. **lóh chit-jī,** write down this word. **lóh hit-jī,** write down that word.

lóh chit-jī, to omit one word in writing by mistake. **lóh-jī,** do. (one or more). **lóh-sin,** to have a miscarriage (v. sin). **sit-lóh,** to lose (v. sit). **lóh-sih,** to lose capital; to lose in trade.

lóh-kè, to become cheaper (v. kè). **lóh-chîⁿ,** to become much poorer, though still having some wealth. **lóh-póh,** to sink from affluence into poverty. **lóh-im,** in a low, dark, damp, unhealthy situation. **lâu-lóh,** to flow down; having no friends or relations to take care of us. **léng-lóh** (C.), desolate or decayed, as place. **lóh-sún,** to fall into consumption.

lóh-sún, to fit a mortice joint (v. sún). **lóh-ngáuhⁿ,** to agree well together, as persons. **lóh--lâng ke-kàu,** to receive submissively the rule of the family she enters, as a bride. **lóh-nn̂g,** to come nearer the terms of the other party.

lóh-âu, to be swallowed (v. âu). **thiaⁿ-lóh-hī,** to hear distinctly (v. hī). **lóh-chhim,** to get into deep water. **lóh-khó,** to come down with the ebb-tide. **beh-lóh-sai,** about to set in the west, as the sun. **lóh-tsûn,** to embark. **lóh-óh,** to go to school, as thrice each day. **lóh-hi,** to go to the market. **lóh-hák,** to go to stool.

lóh-soaⁿ, to come down from a hill; to set behind a hill, as the sun. **lóh-kiā,** to come down a flight of steps. **lóh-bé,** to dismount (v. bé). **lóh-pan,** to retire from duty, after having taken one's turn, as underling in yamun. **lóh-sa,** to come from the north of China to Amoy, as junk.

lóh-kheh, to be taking in passengers, as vessel. **lóh-hō͘,** to rain. **lóh-seh,** to snow. **lóh-sng,** to have hoar-frost; to snow. **lóh-sng lóh-seh,** to snow and have hoar-frost. **lóh-iâm,** to put salt on a thing or into a dish. **lóh-pùn,** to manure. **lóh-pûi,** id. **lóh-kiō,** to set down a sedan.

löh (T.) **lí-löh,** = A. lí-leh, very troublesome, as boy, &c.

lö̍h (T.), = A. léh. **liām-lö̍h,** talking far too much. **lí-lö̍h,** id.

lok [R. lók, to descend or lay down, = col. lóh, lak, lâuh, &c.], to lay down; decayed and sunk, as fruit, or as leg with sores in it. **lok--teh,** to lay down. **kià-lok--teh,** to deposit; to commit to a man's care, as money or some article.

lok-chì, quite dispirited and faint-hearted, from bad luck or want of success. **lok-sōng,** appearance of being in very reduced circumstances. **lok-lién,** to become very poor and in bad circumstances.

lok-tsúi, to step unintentionally into water. **lok--lóh kau-á,** to step by mistake into a ditch or drain. **lok--lóh chhim-chhân,** to step by mistake into deep miry irrigated fields.

lok-lok, very slushy, as road; having places sunk and decaying, as over-ripe fruit or diseased leg. **noāⁿ-noāⁿ lok-lok,** sunk and decaying, as limb. **tâm**

lok-lok, very wet and slushy, as roads. **lok-chhih-chhih**, id. **kà-lok-lok**, very thin, as rice paste. **lok-thúi**, thigh full of sores. **phah kàu-lok-thúi**, to beat till great sores form on the thighs, as before a mandarin. **phah kàu-lok-lok-lok**, to beat till it makes open sores.

lok (=lak). **phī^{n}-lok**, the nose. **phī^{n}-lok-kóng**, id.

lok [R. thok, a bag, =col. lak], a small bag. **tsoá-lok**, paper bags, used in shops. **chit-lok-hún**, one small bag of face-powder. **hiu^{n}-soà^{n}-lok**, a long bag for holding a number of incense sticks.

chhiú-lok, sort of gloves put on the hands of a corpse when buried.

lok — **lok-kháu**, to gargle the throat and mouth.

lok (mere reduplication). **kok-lok-phāng**, a deep glen or dell (v. kok).

lòk [R. connected, =col. lòh]. **liân-lòk**, sort of combination of the people of a town under head-men of each street or so, to prevent rebellion, riots, or plundering, each house or two furnishing a volunteer. **biân-lòk**, id. **liân-lòk-thâu**, the head-man of a town thus banded together.

keng-lòk, the part of the body where some disease has its seat. **tá-lòh--chit-ê keng-lòk**, in what part of the body?

lòk [R. a sort of wheel, =col. lak]. **kan-lòk**, a spinning-top. **kien-lòk**, id. **tèng-kan-lòk**, to throw down a top to spin.

lòk [R. id.; also, a surname, =col. lòh]. **lòk-tô**, a camel.

lòk (R. id.), a deer; a stag. **lòk-tû**, a cage for carrying criminals. **hoe lòk-lòk**, mottled, spotted, variegated.

lòk-jiông, young stag's horns, medicinal (v. jiông). **lòk-kun**, stag's sinews. **lòk-kak**, stag's horns; also, =lêng-gê, the upright sticks on the bow of a junk, between which the anchor rope runs. **lòk-kak-chháu**, a small plant (med.) with leaves like horns. **lòk-chhong-hoe**, a sort of flower (v. chhong), said to be =soan-chháu.

hé-lòk, very deceitful, as by words, appearance, or actions. **hé-hé lòk-lòk**, id. **hé-lòk-chhùi**, deceiving by lying words. **chhò-bé-káu ké-lòk** (a dog with cropped tail aping a stag), said of aping the appearance of dignity. **chí-lòk ûi-má** (to point at a stag as a horse), to accuse falsely.

lòk [R. to descend; to fall, =col. lòh, làuh, lak, lok]. **ū-tiòk-lòk**, to be depended on, as a man; safe or sure, as a matter of which there is sufficient evidence (v. tiòk).

kà-lòk-lòk, quite spoiled past remedy, as an affair. **liû-lòk**, to wander about, as poor man with no employment (v. liû). **lòk-phek**, miserable (v. phek). **lòk-hoa liû-súi**, very miserable.

lòk-kha-seng, ground-nuts, =thé-tāu.

lòk [R. rocky; toilsome; miserable]. **lô-lòk-miā^{n}**, a toilsome miserable life. **lô-lòk-chè**, miserable life because of sins in a former life. **lòk-chhih lòk-chhih**, having a very miserable broken-down look, as opium-smoker.

lòk [R. joy; glad]. **khoài-lòk**, enjoying great pleasure; very happy. **tsok-lòk**, to show delight by gestures or appearance. **an-lòk** (R.), happy and comfortable. **an-an lòk-lòk**, in comfort and ease, with nothing to trouble one. **kék-lòk ê-sè-kài**, a Buddhist phrase for heaven. **lòk kék, pi-seng**, sorrow comes when joy is at the full. **thiòng-lòk**, delighted; pleased (often has a bad sense). **lòk-thiòng**, going about idly and fond of low pleasures (v. thiòng). **lòk-khòk**, licentious (v. khòk). **tsāi-si^{n} m̄-lòk; sí, tiòh kā-kúi koā^{n}-pau-hòk**, he who is always melancholy in life shall carry bundles for the ghosts after his death.

lòk [R. official salary]. **hōng-lòk**, the official salary of a mandarin. **hok-lòk**, good fortune and rank (v. hok). **lòk-ūi**, a tablet set up in honour of a good mandarin in his lifetime (v. ūi). **sit jîn-chi-lòk, tam jîn-chi-iu**, he who lives on a man's money should share his sorrows.

ông-lòk, a travelling doctor, quack, or fortune-teller. **ông-lòk-sien**, id.; also said in scolding a liar; you quack! **ông-lòk-chhùi**, deceitful lips.

lom (P.), the worst part of a prison; a dungeon or inner prison. **lom-á-té**, id.; in the dungeon. **siu-lom**, to be imprisoned in it.

lóm (P.) **óm-lóm**, to collect into a mass.

lòm (C.), =A. làm (cf. lop). **lòm-chhân**, soft muddy fields. **lòm-thê**, id.

long (cf. lang, nng), to shove endwise into a hole, as a stick, or as a pillow into its case, or as a pen into its cover; said also in a bad sense in vile foul scolding. **long--kè-lâi**, to push in, as a beam through a window or hole. **long hit-tsàu-khang**, to shove into the stove, as a stick of wood.

thàu-piah-long, to put the feet of a captive through holes in a wall, as a sort of stocks. **toā-iâ piah-long**, may your uncoffined corpse be pushed through a hole in the yamun wall! (done to any of the subordinates), (said in scolding an underling of a yamun).

long--kè-khì, to run off stealthily and unobserved (as if through a hole). **long--jip-khì**, to enter stealthily and unobserved; to draw one's arm into the sleeve of one's dress. **lut-long chhiú-tsáu**, to steal away unobserved and unexpectedly in an undignified manner, so as to be out of the way. **lut-long tsòe-i-khì**, id.

long-pang, to work one's passage in a vessel.

long (cf. lòng, làm). **chhim-long-long**, very deep, as water, or as a large house. **khoà^{n}-long-long**, very spacious, as a house; too loose, as clothes (v. khoà^{n}). **khoah-long-long**, very loose and wide, as sleeves.

long — **î^{n}-long-long**, circling round, as wall or line; long and round, as a stick. **long-á-chhâ**, an unsplit billet of wood.

long — **lin-long**, running about, as children at play. **séh-lin-long**, to run round in a circle, as children. **pha chit-lin-long tńg**, to make a complete circuit, as in a walk. **hiâu-lin-long**, very licentious (said only of a woman).

long [R. liông, lông], (C. lông). **lin-long-kó**, a rattle used by pedlars and by children. **long-long-háu**, to rattle (neuter), as the sound of a rattle.

long [R. tong, sound of water]. **long-long-háu**, sound of a rushing stream of water, as in a gutter or torrent. **tsúi long-long-háu**, id. **long-long-kiò**, id.

long — **kap-long**, small horn whistles tied to pigeons, sounding as they fly. **bé-long**, sort of bells on horses. **koà-bé-long**, to wear such bells, as horse.

long — **khiâ-bé-long**, to sit astride on a person, as in play, or as when beating him.

long (=lang). **hoah-lê-long**, an auction; to sell by auction.

lông [R. a young man; a gentleman, = col. nn̂g]. **lēng-lông** (polite), your son. **pók-chêng-lông**, a man who abandons a woman. **hó-lông-kun**, my good husband. **lông-kun tsú-tē**, a rich and handsome young fellow. **hó-lông-kun tsú-tē**, id., said in reference to a bride being affianced to such a desirable youth. **poáh-kiáu lông-kun, bóe-bōe chhát**, there is honour among gamblers, but traders are thieves. **lông-kun-iâ**, an idol of the surname Bēng, worshipped by song-singers. **jī-lông-sîn**, a military idol different from the above. **jī-lông-kun** (Cn.), id. **jī-lông tè-kun** (Cn.), id. **jī-lông-biō**, his temple.

lông [R. a basket, = col. lâng, láng], a muzzle; to muzzle; to put on a horse's head-stall. **lông-thâu**, a horse's head-stall. **bé-thâu-lông**, id. **bô-koà-lông-thâu bé**, a lad who goes about doing what he pleases under no control.

lông [R. a bag; to put in a bag]. **chhiú-lông**, gloves. **phoe-lông**, an envelope. **thiap-lông**, envelope for a card. **tsō gím-lông**, to make a shrewd guess of the future. **goá kā-lí-tsō gím-lông**, I will tell you what will be the sure result of your action; I warn you of the misfortunes you will bring on yourself.

lông-lông khǹg-tī-pē̍-tē, stow away in a bag.

lông (R. id.) **phau-lông** (R.), the scrotum, = lān-pha.

lông [R. a sort of palm-tree, = col. nn̂g]. **kong-lông** (F.), a plant of the palm tribe (Cycas? or like a date-palm?).

lông — **saⁿ-liû-lông**, acting in turn; in rotation.

lông — **tō-lông**, to help one out of great trouble or poverty.

lông [R. id., cf. col. liông]. **chhâi-lông**, wolves. **hé-lông pà-piu**, very fierce and wicked men. **hái-lông**, a northern animal with very fine, dark, soft fur (beaver?). **hái-lông-bō**, a cap made of its fur. **hái-lông-kháu**, cuffs made of it.

lông-pōe, in great poverty (v. pōe). **lông put-lông, siù put-siù**, quite unfit for work; out of employment and miserable.

lông [R. matter from a sore, = col. lâng]. **thúi-thâu-lông**, a large boil on the buttocks. **àu-lông**, very stinking (said in vile scolding).

lông (R. id.), strong, nourishing, and heating, as food; opposed to "chheng" of a light and cooling nature. **sek-tī lông-lông**, the colour is very deep. **bák boâ kàu-lông-lông**, rub down the ink till it is thick and black. **m̄-thang siuⁿ-lông**, don't make it too thick. **tê phàu-khah-lông** (esp. C.), make the tea stronger.

lông [R. a covered portico; a cloistered or covered way]. **léng-lông**, the two covered ways (under the broad eaves) on the opposite sides of the court of a house, connecting the front and back premises. **liáng-lông** (C.), id.

lông (R. id.) **lông-hu** (r.), a farmer. **sū-lông kong-siong**, the four classes of employments: scholars, farmers, workmen, and traders. **sîn-lông**, Shin-nung, the god of drugs, worshipped in medicine-shops. **sîn-lông tāi-tè**, id.

lông (C.), = A. long. **lîn-lông-ké**, a sort of musical instrument. **lîn-lîn lông-lông**, the sound of it.

lông (cf. lōng, lê). **lông-liû-lien**, words used at the beginning of a play.

lóng — **chiú-lóng**, a foreign wine and spirit shop.

lóng (cf. láng, tsóng), all. **lóng-tsóng**, id. **lóng-hó**, all are good; all is right. **lóng-ū**, all these are present; have them all. **lóng-bô**, not at all; have none of them. **lóng-m̄-sī**, certainly it is not. **lóng-m̄-thang**, you must not on any account.

lóng (cf. lok). **kà-lóng-lóng**, very watery, as soup or thin rice paste.

lóng (mere reduplication). **kóng-lóng**, to talk away; to talk idly or tautologically.

lòng — **lìn-lìn-lòng-lòng**, loud noise and turmoil, as of heavy things moved about, or of men treading heavily, or of loud rapid knocking. **lìn-lòng**, do., but not so loud. **lìn-lòng-háu**, id. **lìn-lòng-kiò**, id. **éng lòng-lòng-háu**, the waves roaring.

lòng (mere reduplication). **kòng-lòng-phoà**, to dash in pieces by striking.

lòng, to strike with a heavy stone, or with the end of a heavy beam, as with a battering-ram. **lòng-khui**, to burst open (as a door) in that way. **lòng-mn̂g**, to batter a door thus, in order to open it.

lòng (cf. long). **lòng--kè-khì**, to run off. **sì-kòe-lòng**, to travel about in all directions to considerable distances, as for trade or amusement.

lòng (cf. long, làm). **khoah-lòng**, too large and loose, as clothes. **khoàⁿ-lòng-khoàⁿ-lòng**, id. **lòng-khòng**, id. **lòng-khòng-toā**, id. **lòng-lòng-khòng-khòng**, very spacious, as a house; too large and loose, as clothes.

lōng (cf. lō), a great bar across a door or window, fastened at the two ends in the walls or frame; to fasten a door or window by such a bar, horizontal or perpendicular. **khiā-lōng**, a perpendicular bar for a door, fastened in the threshold and lintel. **mn̂g-lōng**, a horizontal bar quite across a door. **thang-á-lōng**, a perpendicular bar for a window.

lōng [R. flaming]. **hé-lōng**, a sort of congreve rocket for use in war.

lōng — **hī-khang lōng-lōng-háu**, ringing sound in the ears. **lōng-lōng-háu**, id.

liú-lōng-lien, words said at beginning of a play.

lōng [R. a wave; dissipated, = col. nn̂g]. **pho-lōng** (R.), waves. **ké-lōng-sū**, the island of Kolongsoo or Kulangseu. **hong thiâm, lōng chēng**, winds and waves quiet. **hong pêng, lōng chēng**, id. **pêng-hong chēng-lōng**, id. **kông-hong tāi-lōng** (r.), wind and waves stormy.

lōng-tōng, profligate; ill-behaved (v. tōng). **lōng-liáu**, money all wasted in folly.

lōng [R. to brandish; to instigate, = col. lāng], to egg on (esp. by falsehoods), as to injure others, or to begin a quarrel, or to come into great danger; to instigate to evil, especially to feuds and quarrels. **bú-lōng**, to make a fool of (v. bú, to insult). **bú-lōng**, to brandish (v. bú, to brandish). **lōng-thûi**, an instrument like a club, for beating and stirring indigo in the vat. **lōng-chhiⁿ**, to work up indigo with it. **phah-lōng**, to whip up (a horse) to its utmost speed.

lōng-koân, to make improper and selfish use of authority committed to us, or of trust placed in us. **lōng-pè**, to manage secretly something improper, as in a legal case. **lōng-kúi**, to be the prime mover in a plot for deceiving people. **lōng-iông**, to spread bad reports (v. iōng). **lōng--lâng**, to instigate a man secretly against another. **khit--lâng lōng--khì**, to be imposed upon so as to injure others, get into a feud, or into great danger. **chit-pêng lōng-kè-lâi, hit-pêng lōng-kè-khì**, egging on each party against the other. **pái-lōng**, to instigate to enmity or feud by false reports or accusations. **koái-lōng**, id. **sái-lōng**, id. **tsok-lōng**, to impose upon by false reports; to play tricks on; to befool; to possess or injure, as a demon. **poan-lōng**, to poison a man's mind by lies against another, and so cause strife (v. poan). **ohháu-lōng-tsōng** (esp. C.), to make a false pretence about some matter which does not exist at all.

lōng-kháu sêng-tsoat, to try to do something very clever, but turn out stupid (v. kháu). **lōng-ká sêng-chin**, a jest or practical joke turned into a sad reality.

lōng (Cn.), = A. lêng, able.

lop (cf. làm), wet and soft, as ground. **lop-lop**, id. **lop-tsúi** (C.), to step into water carelessly, as children, &c.

lu (cf. tu), to push a thing away from one's self, or towards another, as with hand, foot, or stick.

lu (cf. lū). **thâu-khak lu**, keeping one's head bent down and forward. **chhùi lu-lu**, mouth naturally projecting. **tsûn-thâu lu-lu**, the boat's head low and projecting forward, instead of turning up. **lu-lâi lu-khì**, to rush back and forwards through the rain or dark night. **thàu-hō͘ lu--lâi**, to come running with head down through the rain.

lu (= lo). **bóng-lu**, to make an attempt to get a favour, though with very small hope of success.

lu — **lu-chhip**, to work a small net by going into the sea neck-deep.

lû [R. a gate], (C. lî; Cn. lû). **hién-iâu bûn-lû** (R.), to become highly distinguished, as a high graduate or mandarin (lit. splendid gate).

lû (R. id.), (C. lî; Cn. lû), an ass. **lû-tô**, asses, as used for carrying burdens. **hái-lû**, a sort of seal. **thut-lû** (a bald ass), said in scolding a Buddhist priest.

lú (T.), = A. lí, thou; you; thee; ye (said also in the villages on Amoy island).

lú [R. female: a daughter], (C. lí; Cn. lú). **lú-tek**, female character (v. tek). **lú-sek**, female beauty, esp. as inciting to lust. **lú-ôe**, women's small shoes. **lú-kang**, a female worker; a sempstress or milliner, &c. **lú-chiòng**, a female warrior (v. chiòng). **lú-pī** (r.), = tsa-bó͘-kán, a female slave; a concubine. **kiong-lú**, female slaves of the empress in the harem (v. kiong). **ki-lú**, a harlot.

tsāi-sek-lú, a virgin. **kui-lú**, id. **chhim-kui-lú**, id. **cheng-lú**, a virgin who remains so to the last. **chiet-lú**, id., refusing to marry, as because of the death of her betrothed, or other good reason. **liét-lú**, a widow who commits suicide rather than marry again (v. liét).

lú-jî, a daughter. **siáu-lú** (polite), my daughter. **hàu-lú**, a daughter mourning for parent, &c., in the ceremonies. **tit-lú**, a brother's daughter. **gōe-seng-lú**, a sister's daughter. **lú-sun**, a granddaughter.

lâm-lú, male and female; men and women. **it-lâm it-lú**, one man and one woman. **chin-lâm ké-lú**, a man pretending to be a woman, as actor. **lâm-toā lú-iù**, male and female, old and young. **lâm-jîn lú-thóe** (C. lí-thé), man with effeminate or feminine look or manner. **lâm-ke lú-ke**, the relatives of the bridegroom and bride respectively.

sien-lú, a fairy. **chit-lú**, a star (lit. the weaver), worshipped on 7.7. **lú-o**, the woman who made the sky. **lú-jîn-kok**, the kingdom where all the people are females.

lù (R. lū), to scour or rub bright, as with a cloth or fish skin (like sand-paper), but not with a brush; to grate down. **lù-hún**, to grate down sweet potatoes for making starch. **lù-kng**, to polish bright by rubbing. **lù-tâng**, to polish brass. **lù-gék**, to polish jade-stone. **lù-to**, to polish a knife by rubbing something on the knife.

lū (R. id.), (C. lī; Cn. lū), to filter out; to strain out by a cloth. **kè-lū**, to be filtered or strained. **lū-kun**, a cloth for straining or filtering through, as in making bean-curd.

lū (= lu), to rush on blindly.

lū (C.), = A. lu, to dabble in mud. **lū-lâi lū-khì**, to dabble about in mud.

lū — **lū--lòh-lâi**, to slip or slide down, as from one's seat, or as a thing from a place where it had been lying steady.

lû [R. lûi, the handle of a plough, &c.] **lû-pê** (T.), a sort of rake or grubber for agriculture. **lû-chháu** (T.), to grub up weeds from among growing crops with it. **lû-chhân** (T.), id.

lū (R. id.), (C. lī; Cn. lū), a surname. **lū-sien-tsé**, one of the genii (sien), worshipped by barbers. **lū tōng-pin**, id.

lū-sòng, Luzon; the Philippine Islands (v. sòng).

lū (R. id.), (C. lī; Cn. lū). **khoà-lū**, to be anxious about: to feel anxious for. **koà-lū**, id. **iu-lū** (r.), grieved and anxious. **lū-tñg lū-té**, anxious about everything. **khoà-tñg lū-té**, id.

lū [R. lazy; indisposed to act]. **lū-kū**, answering gruffly; ill-mannered in reply, either in refusing or consenting; *e.g.* when told what to do, answering, "I know that already." **lū-tū** (C.), id.

luh (R. lút), to limp. **luh-kha**, id. **luh--chit-ē**, to make a limping step.

lui, a knob or boss, as on a gong; a round lump or swelling, as on the head. **cheng-lui**, the boss of a gong.

lui — **pûi-lûi-lui**, very fat.

lui (T.) **lui-lui tui-tui** (= A. lûi), troublesome, involved, or not straightforward.

lui (Cn.) **táh-lui**, to stumble and fall backwards.

lûi (cf. lui, liû). **chit-lûi**, a swelling on the head caused by a stroke.

lûi (some say "lui"), (T. lui). **lûi-tui**, troublesome and involved, as affair; talking in a way not straightforward, or untruthful; confused and dirty (v. tui).

lûi (R. id.), to triturate: to grind to powder in a mortar. **lûi-boáh**, id. **lûi-ióh**, to triturate medicines. **lûi-poah**, a stoneware mortar for triturating. **lûi-thûi**, a pestle for it.

m̄-sái kap-i-lûi, you need not waste words with him about it.

lûi [R. lî, a sort of shell-fish; cockle?]. **kap-lûi**, a small edible shell-fish.

lûi [R. fruit or seed of a tree], a fir-cone. **chêng-peh-lûi**, id. **chhêng-peh-lûi**, id. **tō͘-seng-lûi**, the large sort of fir-cone. **chhâ-lûi**, a fir-cone. **png-lûi**, the fruit of the liquid-amber (png) tree. **seng-gô-lûi** (C.), a sort of excrescence on a fir-tree.

lûi — **thé-lûi,** blind because the eyeball projects enormously.

lûi (R. id.), thunder (including the idea of the destructive power of lightning); electricity; a surname. lûi-khì (r.), electricity. **lûi-tân,** the thunder sounding. **lûi-tân sih-nà^n,** thunder and lightning. **lûi chhè,** thunder rattling very loud (v. chhè). **lûi chhe̍h^n-ne̍h^n-ne̍h^n,** great sound of thunder. **lûi-hé-sio,** burned by lightning. **thi^n-lûi,** thunder. **hō thi^n-lûi phah--sí,** to be killed by lightning. **khí-lûi,** to be the place where lightning strikes. **khí ngé-lûi,** tremendous thunderstorm; said also of people coming and making a great row. **hō ngé-lûi phah--sí,** may the five thunders kill (if the oath be false), (said in adjuring or swearing to witness the truth). **ngé-lûi ê-hû-lêng,** a Tauist charm on a slip of bamboo by which the five thunder-spirits drive away demons. **lûi-phia^n,** a god of thunder. **lûi-kong,** the great thunder-god; thunder and lightning, as a destructive agent; thunder. **lûi-kong tiēn-bú,** the god of thunder and the goddess of lightning. **lûi-kong khū-khū-tân,** thunder making a loud noise. **lûi-kong phah-sí-lâng,** lightning killing a man. **ti-ko-phī^n lûi-kong-chhùi** (pig's nose and thunder-god's mouth), very ugly.

hó-sim khit-lûi-phah (a good man struck dead by lightning), I meant it well, but you scold me! **ná^n-ah thia^n-lûi** (like a duck hearing thunder), not knowing what all the noise is about. **lûi kòng-tit,** thunder on the term called ki^n-tit (v. tit). **la̍k-ge̍h chhit-lûi chí káu-thai,** thunder in the 6th moon keeps off nine typhoons (v. thai).

tē-lûi, a mine (in war) for blowing up: a child's toy that makes a loud noise by pulling a string. **tē-lûi hé-phàu,** a mine in war. **tâi tē-lûi,** to set a mine.

lúi (R. id.), classifier of flowers. **hoe-lúi,** a blossom; a flower. **kiet hoe-lúi,** to produce flowers. **khui-hoe chiâ^n-lúi,** id. **hâm-lúi,** a half-opened bud.

lúi, classifier of eyes. **tī^n-toā-lúi,** to stare angrily (v. tī^n). **bák-chiu toā-sòe-lúi,** treating people with partiality.

lúi — **chiáu-lúi,** a bird's cup for water and food. **chiáu-á-lúi,** id. **chiáu-lúi-á,** id.

lúi, to try whether two things be of equal weight, or to make them equal. **lúi-tāng,** id. **lúi-khoà^n,** try if they be the same weight. **lúi hō-i-pī^n,** weigh and adjust till of equal weight.

lúi (R. lú). **lâm-lúi,** slovenly or tattered, as dress. **lâm-lâm lúi-lúi,** id.

lúi — **o-lúi-lúi,** very black.

lúi — **ut-lúi,** = ut-lút, title of the spirit of a man of the Tang dynasty, whose name is written on doors.

lúi [R. a heap of stones; to heap up], to build a wall of loose stones; to build a rubble wall; to pile up, as bricks or stones; to heap up. **lúi--khí-lâi,** id. **lúi-tn̂g,** to run up a wall in a slim manner in order to separate a place. **chio̍h-lúi--ê,** built of rough stones laid together.

lúi-lúi tsòe-chit-tui, to gather into a heap. **lúi-chek** (R.), to gather more and more, as money.

iâ^n-lúi, a fortified camp.

lúi [R. lú, constantly: cf. col. lùi]. **lúi-lúi,** constantly over and over again. **lúi-chhù,** several times; frequently.

lùi (cf. lúi). **lùi-chhùi,** miscellaneous.

lūi [R. tears]. **gán-lūi** (r.), to shed tears. **chek-lūi,** candle-droppings.

lūi (R. id.), to beat loud and long, as a drum. **khí-lūi,** to begin beating the drum, as at the first watch. **lūi-kó,** to beat a large drum quick, loud, and long. **khau-cheng lūi-kó,** to sound bells and drums, as Buddhist priests. **lūi-chiàn-kó,** to beat a war-drum thus in war or at review.

lūi, to throw or push (a stone) downwards, so that it rolls down, as from roof or hill; to roll down, as a large stone.

lūi (R. tūi), to let down or draw up by a rope. **lūi--lo̍h-khì,** to let down by a rope. **lūi--khí-lâi,** to draw up by a rope; to hoist up.

lūi (R. id.), to involve, as in debt, responsibility, or trouble. **lūi--tio̍h,** id. **liân-lūi,** id. **thoa-lūi,** id. **lūi-thūi,** to cause obstruction or impediment, as family, &c. **siū-lūi,** to be involved in another's affairs. **pī-lūi,** id. **khit-lâng-lūi,** id. **lūi--lán hō-lâng-tâu,** involving us so that people come and complain to us. **thòe--i pê-lūi,** to have to pay expenses for him because of being somehow connected with him, much against one's will and often with small hope of repayment. **hāi-goá pê-lūi,** his action has compelled me (unwillingly) to pay out money for him. **bô-hó-hia^n lūi sió-tī,** an ill-behaved elder brother involves his younger brother in trouble. **ka-tsáu tsòe-sū, lūi sat-bú,** the flea does the mischief and involves the louse.

lūi (R. id.), a sort, a class, or kind. **tóng-lūi,** an illegal association or confederacy. **húi-lūi,** vagabonds; ruffians; rowdies; rabble. **kiá^n-lūi,** descendants. **chéng-lūi,** id. **jîn-lūi,** mankind. **siù-lūi,** quadrupeds, esp. wild beasts. **tâng-lūi,** of one sort. **siāng-lūi,** id. **kui-lūi,** to arrange in order; to sort. **pun-kui-lūi,** id. **hun-kui-lūi,** id. **hun-lūi,** id.

lūi (R. id.) **jī-lūi,** a small dictionary; a vocabulary. **tùi-lūi,** a small book with antithetic words or phrases learned by children.

lūi [R. lōe, inside, = col. lāi]. **lūi-chiòng** (C. lāi-chiàng), blindness caused by a white formation (v. chiòng).

lun [R. sin, to stretch out, = col. chhun], to stretch out stealthily (as the head) to take a look or listen secretly. **lun--chhut-khì,** id., as from a door or window. **lun--chhut-lâi,** id., said by those towards whom the head is protruded. **thau-lun--chhut-lâi,** id. **lun-thâu teh-khoà^n,** putting out the head to take a secret look. **lun-thâu bih-ām,** appearance of listening or looking stealthily. **lun--cheh kiu--cheh,** afraid, or very cautious and unsettled in purpose (v. kiu).

lun, to draw straight back without turning, as head, or as a boat; to push straight backwards, as a boat. **lun--chit-ē,** id. **lun--tsáu,** to move slightly so as to keep out of sight. **lun--lo̍h-khì tē-tóe,** to go down at once to the hold, as on going on board a junk. **lun-kha lun-chhiú,** drawing in one's limbs for fear; keeping very quiet in the presence of a superior, in a respectful or frightened manner; afraid to meddle in a dangerous matter. **pàng-lun,** to let (a boat) go right astern. **tò-bé-lun,** to push or draw a boat right backwards. **tò-lun,** id.; to draw straight back, as head, or whole person, &c. **thâu-khak tò-lun,** to draw in one's head. **tò-lun--jip-khì,** to draw back the head or person in a stealthy or frightened way (said by an observer outside). **lun--jip-khì,** id.

lun — **chē kàu lun-lun,** to sit with the back somewhat bent, so that the head hangs down a little.

lun — **pa-lun tsn̄g-chih,** to lick one's lips, as when thirsty, or as when there is a pleasant taste on the lips. **pa-lun pē-chháu,** to chew the cud or ruminate, as the cow. **pa-lun pa-láu,** to bolt one's food without chewing; to talk about a matter indefinitely and indistinctly, intentionally avoiding clear expressions. **pa-lun--lo̍h-khì,** to bolt one's food; to swallow without chewing, as a pill. **pa-lun-thun,** id. (v. thun). **pa-lun-thâu** (C.), to cover up one's head in bed in the coverlet. **poa-lun-thâu** (C.), id.

lun (cf. lin). **koe-lun,** a truncated sea-slug, edible, and of dark-gray colour.

lun — **giâ-se̍k-lun,** a composition like glass with particles of gold in it, used for making small ornamental bottles.

lûn (R. id.) **lûn-liû,** by turns; in rotation. **chiàu-lûn-liû,** id. **chiàu-lûn** (C. lîn), id. **lûn-khau,** to take turns by lot. **kau-lûn** (C. lîn), to give over to another in turn. **lûn-tng** (Cn.), to have charge by turn, as of some special duty.

lûn (R. id.), a wheel. **chhia-lûn,** the wheel of a cart or carriage (v. chhia). **géng-lûn,** the wheel used in a long mortar. **lûn-kîⁿ,** the rim of a wheel. **îⁿ-lûn îⁿ-lûn,** quite round.

lûn-hôe, transmigration.

kut-lûn, the larger joints of the body. **thúi-lûn,** the thigh-joint. **chhiú-lûn,** the wrist-joint. **thut-lûn,** to dislocate a joint. **tńg-lûn,** to turn, as the eyes. **chhun-lûn** (T.), = A. chhun-ûn, to stretch one's self.

lûn [R. name of a mountain, = col. lūn]. **khun-lûn,** the sacred mountain Kwen-lun (v. khun).

lûn — **lâ-lûn-sio,** lukewarm. **lâ-lûn,** id. **lâ-lûn-á,** id. **lâ-lûn-tsúi,** lukewarm water.

lûn [R. relationships]. **jîn-lûn,** the five human relationships. **ngó͘-lûn,** id. **thien-lûn,** the three natural relationships (parent and son, husband and wife, brothers). **thien-lûn chi-lo̍k,** family unbroken by death or emigration. **thien-lûn lo̍k-sū,** id. **loān-lûn,** incest. **ge̍k-lí pāi-lûn,** to commit incest. **bêng-lûn-tn̂g,** the great hall in a Confucian temple.

lûn (R. id.) **tîm-lûn,** to perish.

lûn (Cn.) **pe-lûn-chhài,** a sort of vegetable.

lún [R. a large roller; to use it], to roll with a large stone roller. **chio̍h-lún,** a large stone roller in the form of a truncated cone, used for rolling grain or seeds. **lún-khe,** to crush cakes of bean-cake with this roller. **lún-be̍h,** to separate chaff from wheat (or barley) by it.

lún (cf. lūn, jūn). **lah-lún** (T.), insufficiently dried and too soft, as eatables. **lún-pé** (T.), = A. jūn-pé, shrivelled, as cucumbers too long kept after plucking.

lún [R. loán, warm]. **lún-poah** (Cn.), = A. e, a small earthen pot for cooking.

lún (R. jím), to be patient; to endure. **thun-lún,** id. **chhiáⁿ-lún--i,** just have patience; don't get into a quarrel so quick. **bóng-lún,** just bear it as well as (you) can. **bōe-lún--lit,** impatient; cannot be borne. **lún-iau,** to bear hunger. **lún-koâⁿ,** to bear cold patiently. **lún-thiàⁿ,** to bear pain. **kā chhùi-khí-kun, lún-thiàⁿ,** to clench one's teeth in severe pain. **lún-jiō,** to keep in urine very long. **lún-khùi,** to repress the manifestation of anger. **lún-khì,** id. **lún-khì thun-siaⁿ,** to repress one's feelings and keep quiet (v. thun). **lún-khì kiû-tsâi,** to repress anger for the sake of money. **lún-chhùi,** to curb one's appetite for fear of illness. **lún-chhùi khiūⁿ-chih,** to restrain one's feelings and keep silent; to curb one's appetite. **khiām-chia̍h lún-chhùi,** to be very sparing in eating.

lún, to flinch; to be startled; to be afraid of. **ka-lún-sún,** to shiver, as with fear, cold, &c. (v. ka). **m̄-sái-lún,** no need of fear. **lún--lâng,** to be afraid of people. **goá put-chí-lún--i,** I don't wish to have anything to do with him, afraid that he will cause trouble. **lún-lek,** to be afraid to do a thing. **lún-nɛhⁿ,** afraid to meddle with a matter (v. nɛhⁿ). **lún-thàng,** to be much afraid of going somewhere (v. thàng).

lún — **kún-lún-tsūn,** struggling, writhing, or twisted (v. tsūn).

lùn — **kùn-lùn--tsáu,** to burst away by violent efforts. **khit--i lùn--tsáu,** to lose hold of a man (from his struggling), so that he escapes. **khit--i lùn--khì,** to fail over and over in attempts to get him to pay the expenses that he is expected to bear. **lùn-kàu-bién,** to refuse over and over to pay such expenses, so as at last to get free of them.

lūn [R. intercalation]. **lūn-ge̍h,** an intercalary month. **lūn-gō͘--ge̍h,** the intercalary fifth month, just after the ordinary fifth month, &c. **saⁿ-nîⁿ chit-lūn,** in the third year there is an intercalary month. **gō͘-nîⁿ tsài-lūn,** in the fifth year (the second after) there is another intercalary month. **bô-bí, kiam lūn-ge̍h,** no food to eat, and then it is an intercalary month, when no money is received of the usual income. **lūn-jit,** an intercalary day.

lūn [R. to discuss]. **phì-lūn,** a comparison; for example; suppose that —. **pí-lūn,** id. **pí-tn̂g lūn-té,** to be extremely minute in finding fault, as in a piece of work or in money matters. **káng-lūn,** to discourse upon, as on doctrine or on a book. **gī-lūn,** to discuss; to reason with another. **tâm-lūn,** to converse. **phêng-lūn,** to criticize, as conduct or character, generally, but not always, unfavourably. **lūn-kàu** (r.), in regard to; concerning.

put-lūn, no matter which —. **bô-lūn,** id. **khah-bô-lūn,** easy, liberal, or generous, as in business transactions, or as in entertaining guests. **saⁿ-chhiáⁿ bô-lūn,** when entertaining friends we don't count how much they eat. **chhī-kiáⁿ bô-lūn-pn̄g,** you feed your children without stint (v. chhī).

lūn [R. moist], = jūn. **lūn-te̍k** (R.) = jūn-te̍k, well watered (v. jūn). **lūn-hì,** to mollify the lungs (v. hì). **lūn-tiông,** to cure costiveness.

lūn — **lūn-la̍h,** having a pleasant slight moisture, as face; gracefully formed, as characters; gentle in manner (v. la̍h).

lūn [R. jūn, lūn, soft; delicate; supple], = jūn, tough. **lūn-piáⁿ,** thin tough cakes like scones. **siang-ko-lūn,** a cake of two or three layers of different colours; best made at Hái-têng. **sang-ko-lūn,** id.

nńg-lūn, soft and delicate, as the skin of the hand of a fat man, or of a man not engaged in manual labour; or as fine fur, silk, or dough.

lūn-pn̄g (T.), = A. būn, to cook rice dry.

lūn [R. lûn, name of a mountain]. **soaⁿ-lūn,** a long low flat hill without any marked feature. **chit-lūn-soaⁿ,** id. **lūn-á-bé,** at the end of the long low spur of the hill. **kè-lūn,** to cross such a low ridge.

lūn (mere reduplication). **hūn-lūn sit-lit--khì,** to faint away.

lut (cf. thut, thu̍t), to slip out of place; to be loosened, as a knot; to lose an office or situation; to loosen and strip off, as hair or feathers, by scalding; to swindle. **lut--khì**, to slip out of its place; to get loosened by accident, as a knot; to lose an office or situation. **lut--lo̍h-khì**, to fall off, as a shoe, feathers, &c.; to fall down, as trowsers. **phah-lut**, to let something slip out of its place, as by careless use. **thâu-lē phah-lut**, situation lost.

lut-koa^{n}, to lose office, as mandarin. **lut-khū**, to dislocate, as joint. **lut-tsō**, to get out of the socket. **lut-mn̂g**, to lose hair or feathers that do not grow again, as animal growing old; to lose the hair, as a fur, or sheep-skin, or velvet, &c.; to loosen, as hair or feathers, by scalding with boiling water. **lut thâu-mn̂g**, hair, of old man, falling off. **lut-miâ^{n}** (C.), to buy off a man who threatens to accuse us before a mandarin.

lut-á, a swindler. **lut--lâng**, to swindle people. **lut-long chiū-tsáu**, to steal away secretly and noiselessly (v. long).

lut — **kng lut-lut**, smooth, glossy, and shining. **kóng-ōe chiap-lut-lut**, to talk very fast.

lut (T. tut). **pûi-lut-lut**, very fat.

lut (Cn.) **lut-hō͘**, to take a light from another light.

lut (mere reduplication). **thut-lut**, to rub hard with the hand or foot, as in washing, &c. (v. thut).

lu̍t — **ku̍t-lu̍t-su̍t**, very slippery.

lu̍t — **lām-sám-lu̍t**, to talk in a random improper way, as false or disrespectful impudent talk. **chhùi lām-sám-lu̍t**, id.

lu̍t (R. id.) **lu̍t-lē**, the code of laws (v. lē). **lu̍t-hoat**, laws; a code of laws. **hoat-lu̍t**, id. **kài-lu̍t**, id. **àn-lu̍t**, according to the laws. **chiàu-lu̍t thák-lu̍t** (Cn.), to act justly in public matters, as judgment or arbitration.

lu̍t-lēng, the demon of thunder (v. lēng).

lu̍t, to stroke in one direction with the closed hand, as a man's arm or queue; to bare the arm; to squeeze out with the hand, as blood; to milk. **lu̍t-leng**, to milk. **lu̍t-lin**, id. **lu̍t-ni^{n}**, id. **lu̍t-chhiú**, to pull up one's sleeve. **lu̍t chhiú-kut**, id. **lu̍t chhiú-n̂g**, id. **lu̍t-chhiú lu̍t-kioh**, to bare one's arms and legs, as for fighting, or for hard or dirty work. **chhiú tio̍h-lu̍t--khí-lâi**, bare your arm! **lu̍t--khí-lâi**, to bare, as the arm. **chhiú-n̂g lu̍t--lo̍h-khì**, let down the sleeve again.

lu̍t (R. id.) **ut-lu̍t**, = ut-lúi, name of a very powerful spirit (v. ut).

lu̍t, = lit, a rope serving as halyards.

lu̍t, = u̍t. **lu̍t-pāng siong-chhî**, said of people ruining themselves by litigation (v. pāng).

lwa, lwâ, lwá, lwā; better loa, loâ, loá, loā (*q.v.*)

lwah, lwa̍h; better loah, loa̍h (*q.v.*)

lwân, lwán, lwān; better loân, loán, loān (*q.v.*)

M.

M and B are not distinguished by the Amoy people. Many words are spelled indifferently with either letter. In many cases the colloquial form in M comes from a reading form in B.

Many of the words may be written with or without a nasal; therefore no distinction is here made in the alphabetical order.

m̂, a flower-bud. **hoe-m̂**, id. **phah-m̂**, to produce flower-buds.

thô͘-m̂ (T.), a clod of earth.

m̂ [R. mûi^{n}, bôe, the plum]. **m̂-á**, a small yellow plum. **o͘-m̂**, small yellow plum dried and smoked.

chhiū-m̂, the fruit usually called arbutus (properly Myrica sapida). **chhiū^{n}-m̂** (C.), id. **âng-chhiū-m̂**, the red edible arbutus. **pe̍h-m̂**, the white do. **pe̍h-bit chhiū-m̂**, id. **chhiū-m̂-piá^{n}**, arbutus dried and sugared. **chhiū^{n}-m̂-hō͘** (C.), rains at the time when the arbutus is ripe.

m̂ (= hm̂). **tih-tu̍h-m̂**, a toy that makes a humming noise.

m̂ (Cn.) **ko͘-m̂**, = A. ko͘-n̂g, the great owl.

ḿ, a round excrescence on the belly of a female crab. **chîm-ḿ**, id. **chhih-ḿ**, do. of craw-fish.

ḿ [R. hū, woman; female]. **ḿ--ê**, female, said of some animals, as crabs; sometimes said in a depreciatory way of one's own daughter; also (T.), said of pigs and some other animals. **kang-ḿ** (T.), male and female, said of many animals.

ḿ (R. bó), wife of father's elder brother. **peh-ḿ**, father's elder brother and his wife. **ḿ-chím**, wives of paternal uncles. **chím-ḿ**, id. **chek-peh-ḿ**, id.

tiū^{n}-ḿ, wife's mother. **chhi^{n}-ḿ**, mother of son-in-law or of daughter-in-law. **ḿ-pô**, wife of paternal grandfather's elder brother; polite address to a very old woman. **m̀--ah**, polite address to old woman. **sàng-kè-ḿ**, a matron who goes for a few days with a newly married bride.

ḿ (Cn.) **toā-ḿ-siak-kōe**, = A. toā-bú si-kòe, very abundant or numerous.

m̄ — **hé-m̄**, the Chinese raspberry: it grows on a low trailing shrub. **hō͘-m̄** (Cn.), id. **toā-pún hé-m̄**, a sort of rasp that grows on an erect shrub.

m̄ [R. put, not], not; will not: to refuse; to be unwilling; sometimes used at the beginning of a clause with a very slight meaning, somewhat like "but," or "yet," or "well then."

bô-m̄ —, certainly; without exception or doubt. **m̄-nā^{n}**, not only (v. nā^{n}). **m̄-tān**, id. **m̄-sī**, is not; bad or false (v. sī). **kám-m̄-sī**, is it not? (v. kám). **m̄-koán**, it is no matter (v. koán). **m̄-sái**, it is not needed; no I thank you. **m̄-bién** (Cn.), id. **m̄-ká^{n}**, dare not; inoffensive; well-behaved; I'll never do it again. **m̄-thang**, must not; you must not. **m̄-tsún**, will not permit; said in scolding dogs.

m̄-hó, bad; dead (v. hó). **m̄-ba̍t**, not managed so as to keep the secret. **m̄-bat**, I don't know. **m̄-ún**, unsafe. **m̄-koāi^{n}**, not accustomed. **si^{n}-tsòe m̄-koāi^{n} m̄-kē**, stature neither tall nor short. **m̄-tio̍h**, wrong.

phah-m̄-kì^{n}, to lose (v. kì^{n}). **khoà^{n}-m̄-kì^{n}**, to look but not see it. **thia^{n}-m̄-kì^{n}**, not hear. **tùi-m̄-kè**, unable to overcome him. **tng-m̄-khí**, I cannot bear such honour.

goá-m̄, I will not. **koat-toàn-m̄**, certainly I will

not; to refuse absolutely. **m̄-khì**, will not go; refuse to go. **m̄-tih**, does not wish; do not care for. **beh-m̄**, will you or will you not? **beh á-m̄**, id. **lí náⁿ-beh, goá náⁿ-m̄**, the more you wish, the more I refuse. **iáh náⁿ-beh, iáh náⁿ-m̄**, half willing, half unwilling. **á náⁿ-beh, á náⁿ-m̄** (à?), id.

m̄-kú, yet; notwithstanding. **m̄-á**, but indeed —; yet now —. **lí-beh, goá m̄-á m̄**, you are willing, but I will not allow it. **m̄-á tióh-khì**, but yet (you) should go; after all, should go. **m̄ tióh-khì**, id. **m̄--tióh** —, you had better —. **m̄--to** —, id.; well, after all —. **m̄--tóh** —, id. **m̄--chiah**, id. **m̄--chiū**, id. **m̄--chiū bōe-tit-khì**, well then I cannot go. **m̄-tsóng tióh-khì**, no help for it, but must just go (v. tsóng).

m̄-lāu--lah, is not he old! **chit--ê m̄-té**, but this is too short! (as a rope).

maⁿ (cf. màⁿ, bong). **ɵ maⁿ-maⁿ**, very dirty and black; very dark, as place with no light.

maⁿ — **maⁿ-maⁿ-khàu**, to sob very loud and bitterly, esp. child. **maⁿ-maⁿ-háu**, constantly crying or asking for something.

maⁿ (cf. bong, bông). **tsùi-maⁿ-maⁿ**, quite drunk. **maⁿ-chiú**, id. **chiú chiáh kàu-maⁿ-maⁿ**, id.

mâⁿ (C. P. sometimes), = A. moâⁿ, hemp. **ûiⁿ-mâⁿ**, = A. n̂g-moâⁿ.

mâⁿ (T.) **mâⁿ-nîⁿ**, = A. mêⁿ-nîⁿ, next year.

má [R. a horse, a surname, = col. bé]. **hū-má**, son-in-law of the emperor. **chhien-lí-má**, an express courier. **pat-tsùn-má**, a picture of eight fine horses.

má--siōng, very speedily; immediately. **má--siāng**, id. **má--siōng beh** —, immediately will —. **má--siōng khui-tsûn**, boat just about to start. **má-siōng gím-i hôe**, to return on horseback with flowered robes, as a new graduate. **it-giên hòng-chhut, sù-má lân-tui**, four horses cannot catch back a word once spoken.

má, an enclitic interrogative particle; often written "mah."

má, better "m̄-á;" a particle used at the beginning of a sentence, with somewhat of the sense of "but," or "after all," or "well then."

má (mere imitation of the sound). **má-káu**, Macao (v. káu).

máⁿ (T.), = A. moáⁿ, full; only used in some special phrases.

má (R. id.), grandmother. **lāu-má**, id. **má-chhin** (r.), id. **án-má**, grandmother! **n̂g-má**, id. **lāi-má**, father's mother. **goā-má**, mother's mother. **toā-má**, principal wife of grandfather (said in relation to grandson descended from a concubine). **sù-má**, the concubine who is his real grandmother. **jī-má**, id. **thài-má**, mother of mandarin or graduate. **sien-siⁿ-má**, mother of teacher; a female doctor. **siàⁿ-má** (Cn.), a sorceress; a witch. **má-î** (T.), id. **náⁿ lóe-má--nihⁿ**, said of a woman who is too imperious and violent (v. lóe). **khì-chhē in-má khùn**, is dead.

kong-má (grandfather and grandmother), ancestral tablets. **chèng-kong-má**, a temple for the tablets of persons who have no posterity. **bān-sîn-má** (Cn.), collective title of female ghosts that have no posterity. **tsu-kong-má**, the god and goddess of small-pox. **tsu-niûⁿ-má**, the goddess who protects children from small-pox. **chhit-niûⁿ-má**, the goddess of the Pleiades, and of unmarried girls. **má-tsó-pô**, the queen of heaven and goddess of the sea (v. tsó). **koan-im-má**, the goddess of mercy. **hu-jîn-má**, the goddess of child-birth. **chhân-thâu-má**, the spirit of a shrine for tablets that have no posterity. **thó-tī-má**, a goddess of the earth. **tōe-má** (Cn.), the earth as a goddess. **thiⁿ-má** (Cn.), name of a goddess (v. thiⁿ).

màⁿ (= maⁿ). **ɵ màⁿ-màⁿ**, very black.

māⁿ (T. Cn.), = A. mēⁿ, to scold; to revile. **húi-māⁿ** (T.), to scold very violently.

mah (better má), enclitic interrogative particle.

mahⁿ (Cn.), = A. bah, flesh; meat; said quite rarely, usually "hèk."

mâiⁿ (P. Cn.), = A. bê, rice cooked soft.

máiⁿ [R. to buy, = col. bóe]. **máiⁿ-chiok**, to bribe; to suborn (v. chiok). **máiⁿ--chiá put-bêng, māiⁿ--chiá tī-tong**, the seller bears the responsibility, and not the buyer. **phài-chhái-máiⁿ**, to compel rich men to pay large contributions, under the name of money for buying rice.

māiⁿ [R. to sell, = col. bōe]. **māiⁿ--chiá tī-tong**, the seller bears the responsibility. **māiⁿ-kan**, to keep a brothel (lit. sell lewdness).

māiⁿ — **māiⁿ-siáp**, a very durable light reddish wood.

māiⁿ (C.) **kià-māiⁿ**, = kià-bāi, to make a salutation to a person at a distant place.

māiⁿ (C.), = A. bē (younger sister). **māiⁿ-hu**, husband of younger sister. **goán-māiⁿ--ê**, the husband of my younger sister.

mâuⁿ (R. id.), (T. bâu), a sort of helmet worn at the ceremony of "sng-kàng." **thâu-mâuⁿ** (R.), id.; a helmet. **chhēng-kah tì-mâuⁿ**, to wear a coat of mail and helmet.

mâuⁿ [R. a sort of spear]. **siâ-mâuⁿ-chhiuⁿ**, a sort of crooked spear.

ka-kī mâuⁿ-tún, to contradict one's self.

mâuⁿ — **mâuⁿ-mâuⁿ**, not particular in calculating or inquiring; letting things pass easily; without much spirit or energy. **kap--i mâuⁿ-mâuⁿ**, taking it easily with him; letting him off without much examination. **mâuⁿ-mâuⁿ-tāi**, the matter is of small importance, and may be let pass, *e.g.* said by a third party to men disputing. **siuⁿ-mâuⁿ**, too easy and negligent. **chit--ê m̄-thang-mâuⁿ**, this matter must not be treated carelessly, or allowed to pass, as of small importance. **bōe-mâuⁿ--tit**, it cannot be allowed to pass; it will not do to put it among the rest, bad among good; he will not let anything pass that is not up to the mark. **bóng-mâuⁿ**, just let it pass; take it, though not so good as it should be. **kā--lí bóng-mâuⁿ**, well I will just let your work (or thing, &c.) pass. **chhìn-chhái, kā-lí-mâuⁿ**, id. **kā-i-mâuⁿ--khì**, let him off easily, in anything. **kā-goá-mâuⁿ--khì**, just take it off my hands, though it is inferior. **beh-mâuⁿ--khì**, willing to let the matter pass easily, *e.g.* buyer taking a worse article among good ones.

mâuⁿ [R. mêⁿ, hair, = col. mn̂g]. **mâuⁿ-pēng**, a fault; a defect; something wrong.

mâuⁿ (R. id.) **mâuⁿ-chháu**, a large sort of grass or reed.

māuⁿ (R. id.) **bīn-māuⁿ**, appearance of the face or countenance. **iōng-māuⁿ** (R.), id. **siōng-māuⁿ**, cast of countenance. **goā-māuⁿ**, one's manner and outward behaviour. **liên-māuⁿ**, a man's age and the appearance of his face, as written down when he is enrolled as a candidate for degree, or as a soldier. **liên-**

māu^n put-hû, his age and look do not agree with the description. **lé-māu^n**, polite deportment; polite in manner; politeness; to treat politely, or with respect. **bô-lé bô-māu^n**, disrespectful; impertinent.

māu^n [R. mə^n, to feign, forge, or pretend]. **māu^n-sit**, pretending to know things of which he is quite ignorant; acting as an impostor. **māu^n-sit-kúi**, a barefaced impostor.

mauh^n, to eat or munch slowly, as a toothless child or old man does; also to embezzle money, as part of money entrusted, or as price of goods sold, but not marked down (Cn. T. in this second sense only "pauh"). **ûn-á-mauh^n**, to munch slowly, as a toothless person. **mauh^n-chhit**, to embezzle money intrusted, and pretended to be paid.

mɛ^n (C.), = A. mi^n, to take up with the fingers.

mɛ^n (C. mėh^n), the bleating of a goat. **iû^n mɛ^n-mɛ^n**, words used in calling goats. **mɛ^n-á** (C.), a lamb. **mɛ^n-hi^n** (C.), a small cicada that makes this sound.

mê^n [R. bêng, bright, morrow, = col. bîn], (T. mâ^n). **mê^n-nî^n**, next year.

nî^n mê^n (C.), within about ten days of the end of the year. **nî^n mê^n-tau**, id. **mê^n-chè** (C.), = A. tə-chè, exactly one year after birth.

mê^n (C.) **chhɛ^n-mê^n**, blind, = A. chhi^n-mî^n.

mê^n (C.), = A. mî^n, night.

mê^n (C.), = A. mî^n, sharp.

mê^n (C.), = A. mî^n, the awn of grain. **bėh-mê^n** (C.), = A. bėh-chhiu, the beard of barley or wheat.

mê^n (C.) **kɛh-mê^n-chhài**, = A. keh-nâ-chhài, a sort of vegetable.

mé^n [R. béng, fierce; violent; brave, = col. mí^n]. **kín-mé^n**, quickly; be quick. **kím-mé^n**, id. **thám-mé^n** (r.), id. **thiám-mé^n**, id. **mé^n** (C.), quick. **mé^n-mé^n** (C.), id. **khám-mé^n** (C.), id. **khiám-mé^n** (C.), id. **khah-mé^n** (C.), quicker! **mé^n-khoài** (C.), quickly; easily done.

mē^n (R. mā), (Cn. T. mā, mā^n), to scold; to revile; to rail at; to curse. **lóe-mē^n**, id. **jiók-mē^n**, to scold insultingly. **thek-mē^n**, to reprove an inferior very violently. **chiù-mē^n**, to curse. **phah-mē^n**, to strike and revile, or scold. **mē^n chit-tiû^n**, to scold or rail at great length. **mē^n-thi^n oàn-tōe**, to grumble and rail at heaven and earth.

mɛh^n (C.) **mɛh^n--tsài**, this morning. **mɛh^n--tsài ē-hui^n**, morning and evening.

mɛh^n (T. nih^n). **chháu-mɛh^n**, a grasshopper. **iû^n-mɛh^n** (C.), a small sort of grasshopper.

mɛh^n (C.), = A. mng. **iù-mɛh^n-mɛh^n**, small, as a very small boy.

mėh^n (C.), = A. mɛ^n, sound of sheep or goats bleating. **iû^n mėh^n-mėh^n**, words used in calling goats.

mėh^n — **mėh^n--chit-ē**, to start suddenly; much slighter than "hiah^n."

mėh^n [R. bėk, the pulse], (Cn. T. béh), the pulse. **huih-mėh^n**, id. **khì-mėh^n**, id. **ū-khì-mėh^n**, healthy. **bô-khì-mėh^n**, sickly; delicate; of feeble constitution or temperament. **bô-khùi bô-mėh^n**, id. (v. khùi). **khì-mėh^n khah-kiâ^n**, the blood acting more freely, as after a good walk, or after some sorts of medicine. **khì-mėh^n khah-chiâu-kiâ^n**, id. **sí-mėh^n**, state of the pulse just before death. **mėh^n thoat**, pulse gone, as of a dying man. **mėh^n tîm**, the pulse in such a state that you must press before feeling it. **mėh^n phû**, the pulse such that it is felt on the first touch. **bong-mėh^n**, to feel the pulse. **hoā^n-mėh^n**, id. **khoà^n-mėh^n**, id. **hāu-mėh^n**, to feel the pulse the second time. **kúi-chì-mėh^n**, how many beats of the pulse?

mėh^n-kńg, the place where the pulse is felt at the wrist. **mėh^n-kə́**, id., or at temple, but specially at wrist. **chhiú-mėh^n**, the pulse of the hand. **kun-mėh^n**, veins, as appearing on the skin. **mėh^n-lí**, the doctrine of the pulse.

tōe-mėh^n, veins or strata in the earth, in geomancy. **lêng-mėh^n**, veins in the hills supposed to lead along the auspicious geomantic influence.

mi^n (C. mɛ^n), to take up in the hand by putting all the fingers below, as small things. **chit-mi^n-á**, a small handful. **mi^n-thoa^n**, a sort of gambling (v. thoa^n). **mi^n chhiam-á**, to draw a bamboo lot. **mi^n-bak**, to gain a little money on a transaction in a surreptitious way (v. bak). **mi^n-iâm sī^n-sim-koa^n**, be content with what has taken place and can't be improved. **mi^n-oá**, to draw in one's fingers towards the palm, almost close shut. **thau-mi^n-bí**, to steal a small quantity of rice.

mi^n — **liâm-mi^n**, = liâm-pi^n, immediately.

mî^n [R. bêng, dark], (C. mê^n), night. **mî^n--sî**, night-time; at night. **mî^n-tà^n--sî**, id. **mî^n--kan**, id. **mî^n-thâu tn̂g**, the night is long, as in winter. **mî^n-jit**, day and night (v. jit). **jit-mî^n**, id. **àm-mî^n**, dark night. **géh-àm-mî^n**, a moonless night. **kim-mî^n**, to-night. **bîn-ná-mî^n**, to-morrow night. **tsā-mî^n**, last night. **poà^n-mî^n**, midnight; about midnight. **téng-poà^n-mî^n**, the first half of the night. **ē-poà^n-mî^n**, the latter half of the night. **chiâ^n-mî^n**, about a whole night. **thàu-mî^n**, the whole night; through the night; said of something that takes a good part of the night, *e.g.* a long night-journey. **àm-hē tiâu-mî^n**, late rain lasts through the night. **keh-mî^n**, to pass the night.

mî^n [R. biên, connected; enduring], earnest and importunate, as in entreaty. **mî^n-chi^n**, very urgent and importunate, or earnest and persevering (v. chi^n). **kàu-chiah-mî^n**, so very importunate! **mî^n-mî^n-kiû**, to ask importunately. **mî^n-mî^n-beh**, id. **mî^n-noā^n**, very earnest and importunate. **mî^n-noā^n-kiû**, to ask importunately. **kóng-ōe mî^n-noā^n**, very urgent in pressing a request.

mî^n — **mî^n-mî^n-khùn**, falling asleep over and over again as often as awakened.

mî^n (R. bêng), (C. mê^n). **chhi^n-mî^n**, blind. **chhi^n-mî^n-gû**, an unlettered illiterate clown (lit. cow). **chiah-mî^n**, unable to see clearly at night (s. earnest).

mî^n (R. bông), (C. mê^n). **chhek-mî^n**, the sharp awn of rice.

mî^n (R. bông), (C. mê^n), the sharp edge, as of a knife. **to-mî^n**, the sharp edge of sword or knife. **ū-mî^n**, it is sharp. **bô-mî^n**, edge blunted, as by use. **tó-mî^n**, having the edge turned so as to be blunted. **chiū^n-mî^n**, the edge becoming sharp. **boâ kàu-chiū^n-mî^n**, to sharpen till the edge is very sharp. **boâ kàu-kè-mî^n**, id.

kè-mî^n-kak, well-finished, as an essay or any sort of work; very intelligent and sharp at searching out everything, as a man. **kè-mî^n kè-kak**, id. **ū-mî^n-kak**, having sharp edges (not rounded), as a table.

mî^n (= bî, mí). **o-mî^n-tô-hút**, name of Buddha.

mî^n (T.) **bák-chiah-mî^n**, = A. bák-chiah-mn̂g, the eyelashes.

mî^n (R. biên), cotton. **mî^n-hoe**, raw cotton.

hoan-mî^n, foreign raw cotton. **ka-pók-mî^n**, a coarse sort of raw cotton, not yet cleared from the seed, used for quilting and stuffing. **mî^n-pê**, cotton just as gathered with the seeds in it. **mî^n-tiâu**, raw cotton in pieces of about a foot long, ready for spinning. **mî^n-bé**, id. **mî^n-á-bé**, id. **kńg mî^n-á-bé**, to make ready these long pieces of raw cotton. **mî^n-se**, cotton-yarn, esp. native. **pháng mî^n-se**, to spin cotton. **mî^n-se-tsoá**, a sort of thin, soft, tough paper. **mî^n-tsoá**, id. **mî^n-á-tsoá**, id. **mî^n-tiû**, a fine and strong stuff of silk with some cotton mixed. **si-mî^n**, a mass of cotton and silk mixed in a soft thick form, used for absorbing ink for stamping, or for a sort of ink-box for examinations; also for quilting.

pê-mî^n, small threads on the surface of cloth. **tsoá-mî^n**, paper broken down into dust; also (C.), ashes of a half-burned match. **hóe-mî^n** (C.), = A. hé-hiā^n, tinder.

phah-mî^n, to beat cotton with a bow and string. **phe-mî^n**, wadded or quilted with cotton, as dress or coverlet. **jip-mî^n**, to put in a large quantity of cotton, as into a pillow. **pháng-mî^n**, to spin cotton.

mî^n-sim, cotton wicks. **mî^n-chioh**, a warm quilted cotton coverlet, not in a cover. **mî^n-phē**, do. in a cover. **mî^n-phōe** (C.), id. **mî^n-hiû**, a coat or jacket wadded with cotton. **mî^n-phàu**, a long quilted robe.

mî^n-chhiū, the cotton-tree.

mî^n [R. béng, fierce; quick, = col. mé^n]. **kím-mî^n**, quickly; be quick!

mí (R. bí, mí). **o-mí-tô-hút**, Amida Buddha (v. hút).

mī^n (R. biēn), dough; thin flat strips of wheaten dough, used like maccaroni. **mī^n-tiâu**, these wheaten strips. **phah-mī^n**, to make it. **chhiet-mī^n**, to cut it into these strips. **sáh-mī^n**, to boil it. **bāu-mī^n**, to mix it with other eatables. **chhi^n-mī^n**, raw strips of dough. **sék-mī^n**, do. cooked. **bah-mī^n**, do. cooked with shrimps and pork-fat. **tau-mī^n**, potato-starch cooked with oysters (v. tau). **hún-mī^n**, dough in strips (mī^n) mixed with rice-vermicelli (bí-hún) in a bowl ready to be eaten.

mī^n-soà^n, vermicelli made from wheat. **mī^n-koa^n** (Cn.), id. **mī^n-soà^n-kui**, a frame for drying vermicelli in making it. **mī^n-soà^n-chhê**, cross-bars of that frame. **mī^n-thai**, a sieve for straining boiled vermicelli or maccaroni, &c. **mī^n-phi**, frame for drying boiled do.

mī^n-hún, wheaten flour. **mī^n-tsoe**, wet dough. **mī^n-chià**, small lumps of raw glutinous wheaten dough (v. chià). **mī^n-thi**, gluten made from wheat. **mī^n-ké**, wheaten cakes. **mī^n-pau**, bread. **mī^n-thô**, an imitation peach made of flour, offered to idols. **mī^n-ku**, do., like a turtle.

mī^n-toa^n, tickets for getting one or more meals, given on mandarins' birth-days.

chhat-mī^n, a very strong cement made of flour and varnish, used for filling crevices of coffins, &c.

mī^n-sī (Cn.), = A. tāu-chiù^n, a sort of salt sauce.

mī^n [R. bí, a tail, = col. bé], classifier of oysters. **toā-mī^n-ô**, a large oyster.

mī^n, = bī, a word used at the beginning of a sentence, esp. in Cn.

mī^n (R. bī, mī^n). **thiám-mī^n** (R.), to flatter.

miâ^n [R. bêng, name; fame; reputation], a name, but not a surname; classifier of persons, esp. soldiers or chair-bearers. **kúi-miâ^n**, how many persons? as coolies, &c.

miâ^n-sia^n, fame; reputation, good or bad (v. sia^n). **chhut-miâ^n**, famous; illustrious. **àu-miâ^n**, having a bad reputation.

miâ^n-jī, name of person (v. jī). **lâng-miâ^n**, a man's name. **tōe-hō-miâ^n**, name of a place (v. hō). **thó-miâ^n**, the common colloquial name of a man or place when it differs totally from the literary name, having different characters. **tsóng-miâ^n**, a general term or name. **tsûn-miâ^n**, name of a vessel, as that on the vessel. **pâi-miâ^n**, the name by which a vessel is registered, different from the above. **hùi-miâ^n**, a name that must not be pronounced, sometimes not even written, *e.g.* name given at birth, afterwards disused. **jú-miâ^n**, name used in childhood. **jū-miâ^n**, name taken when grown up (often at marriage), by which a man is usually named. **tsū-miâ^n**, id. **chheh-miâ^n**, name given by teacher to pupil. **koa^n-miâ^n**, name assumed on becoming a mandarin or graduate. **miâ^n-thiap**, one's calling-card with writing on it saying that he pays his respects.

miâ^n-sì^n, name and surname. **kóe-miâ^n oā^n-sì^n**, to change one's name and surname. **oā^n-miâ^n kóe-sì^n**, id. **oā^n-miâ^n kóe-sèng**, id.

pien-miâ^n, to give a fancy name, as to goods. **hō-miâ^n**, to give a name. **kì-miâ^n**, to record a name or names, as in a list. **lóh-miâ^n**, to put down a name. **tiám-miâ^n**, to mark names, as in a list.

miâ^n [R. bêng, clear; distinct; = col. bîn, mê^n]. **chhang-miâ^n**, very intelligent; clever.

chhi^n-miâ^n, the "feast of tombs," when the graves are visited, having been repaired; about April 5th.

miâ^n, the resinous part of wood, which very easily ignites; esp. from the roots of fir-trees. **chhâ-miâ^n**, id. **miâ^n-tī**, a pair of chop-sticks made of resinous wood, given with a bit of onion (chhang) to a boy on first going to school, that he may be "chhang-miâ^n."

miā^n [R. bēng, to command; fate; fortune; life], the decree of Heaven; fate; fortune, good or bad; life.

sì^n-miā^n, life. **tn̂g-miā^n**, long life; long-lived. **té-miā^n**, short-lived. **jiâu-miā^n**, to spare life. **jiâu sì^n-miā^n**, id. **kiù-miā^n**, to save life. **tô-miā^n**, to escape alive. **bóe-miā^n**, to buy long life, by burning idolatrous paper. **tì-miā^n ê-sé-tsāi**, a vital place. **tí-miā^n**, to pay life for life. **pê-miā^n**, to make satisfaction for a death by money or by death. **thó-miā^n**, to require the death of the murderer, as the *ghost* of the murdered man. **phe-miā^n**, to risk one's life (v. phe). **pià^n-sì^n-miā^n**, id. **thoa-miā^n**, to labour very hard (as in weak health) at the risk of health or life. **sí-lâng beh-miā^n**, unexpectedly getting back what we had given up for lost, as something stolen (or trace of it), or a bad debt. **sa^n-hun-miā^n**, only three-tenths of an average life-time. **kiâ^n-tsûn-lâng sa^n-hun-miā^n**, sailors are very short-lived. **kiâ^n-tsûn tsáu-bé, sa^n-hun-miā^n**, sailors and horsemen are so.

sin-miā^n, state of bodily health or constitution. **lám-sin-miā^n**, in delicate health. **ióng-sin-miā^n**, strong and well. **m̄-chiâ^n sin-miā^n**, in delicate health; to have on very ragged clothes. **chhut sin-miā^n**, to exert one's self very much or to the utmost. **ká^n-chhut sin-miā^n**, not afraid of fighting, or law-suits, or dangers. **chit-sin chit-miā^n**, one whole life long. **thoa-sin boā-miā^n**, to exert one's strength very much. **thoa-sin thoa-miā^n**, do., to the utmost, when quite unfit for such exertion. **siá-sin siá-miā^n**, to exert one's self to the utmost. **chit-sin chit-miā^n**, one's whole life-time. **oàn-sin chhoeh-miā^n**, to murmur at one's fate.

42

oàn-thiⁿ chhoeh-miāⁿ, to murmur at Heaven and fate. hūn-miāⁿ-pháiⁿ, to repine at one's lot (v. hūn). pháiⁿ-miāⁿ, unlucky, esp. all one's life; bad luck! pháiⁿ-miāⁿ-chè, miserable life because of sins in a former life. giàp-miāⁿ, having a painful toilsome life. lô-lòk-miāⁿ, id. hó-miāⁿ, good fortune, esp. for lifetime; fortunate, as man. chheng-êng-miāⁿ, having an easy comfortable life.

ū-miāⁿ, having still life in him, as man just escaped from great danger or recovering from an almost fatal disease. i-seng i ū-miāⁿ-lâng, doctors heal men fated to live. ū-kiáⁿ-miāⁿ, to be fated to have a son. bô-miāⁿ, dead; as good as dead. tek-khak bô-miāⁿ, he is just as good as dead; *e.g.* a great criminal when apprehended. sîn-sien bōe-kiù bô-miāⁿ-lâng, spirits and genii cannot save a man not fated to live.

miāⁿ-ūn, long-continued fortune, good or bad (v. ūn). miāⁿ-chheh, fortune-tellers' books. miāⁿ-tsu, a paper telling one's fortune. tâng-miāⁿ, sharing one another's fortunes, as emigrants who keep together. tâng-kiáⁿ jû-tâng-miāⁿ, id. bat miāⁿ-lí, to be acquainted with the art of fortune-telling. khoàⁿ-miāⁿ, to tell fortunes; a fortune-teller. khoàⁿ-miāⁿ mn̂g-koà, to divine and tell fortunes. oá-ūn khoàⁿ-miāⁿ, said of flattering a prosperous man, saying that he will prosper. sǹg-miāⁿ, to tell fortunes (v. sǹg). siōng-miāⁿ, to tell fortunes by the appearance of the face and one's manner of acting or resting. siàng-miāⁿ (C.), id. chhìn-miāⁿ, to tell a man's fortune by calculating the weight of his natal characters. miāⁿ put-chí-tāng, the weight of his fate is great (said either of very good or very bad). chheng-kun-lát m̄-táh sì-niúⁿ-miāⁿ, a thousand pounds weight of strength are not so good as four ounces of fated fortune.

mihⁿ (cf. beh, mihⁿ). mihⁿ-sái, why? implying some fault-finding or that no proper answer can be given. mihⁿ-kan-siáp, whatever has he to do with it! mihⁿ-tióh-khì, what reason can there be for going! lí mihⁿ-ōe-hoat--goá, what can you manage to do to me! mihⁿ--nah, what would you be at! (said by a superior, somewhat finding fault). mihⁿ-tāi-chì, id.; what is the matter now? beh mihⁿ-tāi-chì, id.

bé-mihⁿ-lâng, Mr. So-and-so. bé-mihⁿ--ah, Mr. —! mihⁿ-á-mihⁿ, whatever thing. bô-mihⁿ-hn̄g, not very far.

sìⁿ mihⁿ, miâⁿ mihⁿ, what is your surname and your name? sím-mihⁿ, = sím-mihⁿ, what?

mihⁿ (cf. mihⁿ). sím-mihⁿ, what? which? sím-mihⁿ, id. siáⁿ-mihⁿ (C.), id. sím-mihⁿ-lâng, who? sím-mihⁿ-mihⁿ, what thing? ū sím-mihⁿ-pháiⁿ, what is bad or wrong about it?

bô-sím-mihⁿ —, not very —. bô-sím-mihⁿ-hó, not very good; rather bad. bô-sím-mihⁿ-pháiⁿ, not very bad.

mihⁿ (R. bu̍t), (Cn. T. mn̂gh), a thing; an article; especially meat or other condiments used with rice. mihⁿ-kiāⁿ, a thing; an article. bān-mihⁿ, all things. pah-hāng-mihⁿ, all sorts of things. tiuⁿ-lāu-mihⁿ, various things prepared (before their death) for the burial of parents. hòe-mihⁿ (C.), goods.

m̄-chiâⁿ-mihⁿ, not very good; does not come to much, as something inferior. pát-mihⁿ, a different thing (v. pát).

mihⁿ-phè, condiments; whatever is eaten along with rice or potatoes. mihⁿ-chiáh, cakes; confections, &c. chiáh-mihⁿ-chiáh, to eat cakes, &c., not a regular meal.

mng (C. sometimes mɛhⁿ, muiⁿ). mng-mng, very small. iù-mng-mng, id. hē-á-mng, small drizzling rain. hē-á mng-mng, id.

mng — chháu-á-mng, very small grass and such small plants.

mng — ta-mng, a small edible green sea-weed that grows on rocks overflowed by the tide.

mng, a sort of fern, especially brake. soaⁿ-mng, id. koah-mng, to cut brake for fuel.

mn̂g (R. bûn), (C. mûiⁿ), a door; a gate; a gateway; classifier of guns, crackers, anchors, helms, fishing-hooks, &c.

kék-mn̂g, to the utmost extremity, as of misery or want (v. kék). khah-toā-mn̂g, more on that side, of reasons or ideas; more probably —. khah-toā-mn̂g m̄-sī, more probably it is not.

kàu-mn̂g, Mohammedanism; a school of boxing or fencing. hit-chióng-mn̂g ê-lâng, that sort of people, depreciatory.

ōe-mn̂g té, not able to say much, as when reproved (v. ōe).

kheh-mn̂g put-chí-ōng, having a great many customers and callers from distant places. sí-mn̂g ê-seng-lí, a quiet small trade (v. sí). tn̂g-mn̂g ê-seng-lí, a safe steady trade, that lasts long, as in articles which people are always using. khah-tn̂g-mn̂g, giving good or steady profits, as such a business; more profitable, as a situation with more pay. khah-ū tn̂g-mn̂g, to be steady, as such a trade; to be lasting, as friendship.

tâng-mn̂g, men married to sisters. tâng-mn̂g--ê, husband of one's wife's sister. tâng-mn̂g-tiūⁿ, id. chhin-ke-mn̂g, the nearest connections by marriage. bē kè-mn̂g (C. bōe-kòe-mûiⁿ), not yet married, though betrothed. jip-mn̂g hí, to have a son at the earliest natural time after marriage.

khoe-mn̂g, the mouth of a valley. sam-tə-mn̂g, the region of Sam-tə. (&c.) ē-mn̂g, Amoy. kim-mn̂g, Quemoy.

sìn-mn̂g, the soft place on a child's head where the sutures join. hé-kháu-mn̂g, the space between the thumb and the fore-finger. hong-mn̂g, the touch-hole of a gun. im-mn̂g (r.), the female organs.

gê-mn̂g, a yamun or yamen; a mandarin's office and official residence (v. gê). mn̂g-thâu, a mandarin's confidential secretary for general business. mn̂g-chiūⁿ, id.

tsúi-sien-mn̂g, the gangway. tsúi-mn̂g, a gate on a canal where it enters a city wall. táu-mn̂g (Cn.), flood-gates. táng-mn̂g (C.), id. siāⁿ-mn̂g, a city gate. koan-mn̂g, a gate in a pass. ài-mn̂g, a gate in a street. ài-mn̂g-khang, a small door in one leaf of a street gate.

chit-têng-mn̂g, one gate in a series. toaⁿ-sìⁿ-mn̂g, a single-leaved door or gate. siang-sìⁿ-mn̂g, folding doors or gates. soaⁿ-mn̂g, the outer gate of a hill temple. toā-mn̂g, the principal door of a house or yamun. thâu-chêng-mn̂g, front door. āu-bé-mn̂g, back door. āu-mn̂g, id. jī-mn̂g, the second gate of a yamun, counting from outside. thiaⁿ-mn̂g, hall-door. théh-mn̂g, gate of court-yard.

tsng-mn̂g, a door or gate faced with thick tiles for safety. thang-á-mn̂g, a window or window-shutters opening with hinges like a two-leaved door. géh-thang-mn̂g, a doorway made quite round, as in ornamental grounds. poàⁿ-mn̂g-á, a small door, as in one leaf of a gate. mn̂g-tsáh-á, a small half-door, as a wicket in a shop. **poàⁿ-tsah-mn̂g** (T.), id. **oân-kong-mn̂g**, a doorway with arched top. **oân-mn̂g-á** (esp. T.), id. **oân-mn̂g** (T.), = A. oân-bûn, side gates of the inclosure in front of a yamun. **kaⁿ-koán-mn̂g**, a large high outer door of a house, like a gate. **kiàm-chhiuⁿ-mn̂g**, a gate made like a railing, with the tops of the rails projecting. **hok-chiu-mn̂g**, an outer door made with the lower half solid, and the upper half only bars (v. hok).

iám-mn̂g, a trap-door; to lay a door to (v. iám). **kháh-mn̂g**, to shut a door, laying it to, but not fastening it. **koaiⁿ-mn̂g**, to shut a door. **khien-mn̂g**, to latch a door by a hook on a staple. **tú-mn̂g**, to place a prop behind a door to keep it shut (v. tú). **tū-mn̂g**, id. **hong-mn̂g**, to seal up a door by pasting red paper. **tiuⁿ-mn̂g**, to make a door to fit the doorway. **chhēng-mn̂g**, to put a door on its (Chinese) hinges. **chiūⁿ-mn̂g**, id. **phê-mn̂g**, to lift a door off its hinges. **thǹg-mn̂g**, id. **chhut-mn̂g**, to go out of one's door, as for a short time, or for a journey. **chhut-mn̂g bô-jīn-hè**, goods not changed (not acknowledged) after they leave the shop.

mn̂g-thoah, a sliding door. **mn̂g-hē**, doors in general (v. hē). **mn̂g-ak**, an outer gateway or porch.

mn̂g-kháu, space at the door outside. **mn̂g-kháu-kong**, the spirits worshipped at the doors in the 7th month, and on the 2d and 16th of each month. **mn̂g-kháu-chhìn**, = pah-lák-tô, the sort of steelyard used by pedlars. **mn̂g-kháu-kha**, close to the door just outside. **mn̂g-kha**, close to the door just inside (s. hair). **khiā-mn̂g-kha**, to stand there, as women do, looking at things outside. **mn̂g-lē**, doorway.

mn̂g-chhoàⁿ, a door-bolt on the door. **mn̂g-tauh**, a latch or clasp for a door. **mn̂g-kúi**, a secret small bolt, to keep the bolt (chhoàⁿ) shut. **mn̂g-káu** (T.), id. **mn̂g-khien**, a ring on a door, often used as a knocker. **mn̂g-ióh**, door-lock. **mn̂g-kông**, a great upright bar inside a door. **mn̂g-thn̄g**, id., generally upright. **mn̂g-lō**, a great bar across the whole of a large door, fastened on the walls. **mn̂g-lōng**, id. **mn̂g-tú**, a large bar set end on against a door to keep it shut. **mn̂g-siⁿ**, the leaf of a door. **mn̂g-kheng**, door-frame. **mn̂g-hók**, lintel or threshold of the door-frame. **mn̂g-bâi**, lintel. **mn̂g-tēng**, threshold. **mn̂g-tūiⁿ** (Cn.), id. **mn̂g-khū**, socket for Chinese door, instead of hinge. **mn̂g-sún**, the projection of the door that fits into it. **mn̂g-lî**, bamboo screen hung down at a door. **mn̂g-pìn**, standing screen at door. **mn̂g-liên**, inscriptions on doors or door-posts (v. liên). **mn̂g-sìn**, inscriptions on the leaves of a door (v. sìn).

mn̂g-hong, the reputation or estimate formed of a family by neighbours.

mn̂g (R. mɵⁿ), (C. mɵⁿ), hair; feathers; wool. **mn̂g-chháu**, hair or wool on a fur; fur; feathers on the bird. **pè-mn̂g**, small threads on cloth. **tsoá-mn̂g**, paper worn down to dust or small shreds. **koe-mn̂g**, hen's feather. **gô-mn̂g**, feather of a goose. **gô-mn̂g-kóng**, a quill. **iûⁿ-mn̂g**, wool.

âng-mn̂g, red-haired or red bristled; said vulgarly for British or English (v. âng).

khé-mn̂g, the short hair all over the body. **kì-mn̂g**, the hair on a mole. **the-mn̂g**, infant's hair when born (v. the). **tiah bīn-mn̂g**, to pluck out the hair from the face. **thâu-mn̂g**, the hair of the head. **thâu-mn̂g chhì-hé**, to rush into needless danger. **thâu-mn̂g-bé**, the end of the queue. **thâu-mn̂g-bé-soàⁿ**, the tassel at its end. **thâu-mn̂g-sng** (T.), a plant with prickly seeds. **thâu-mn̂g-chhì** (T.), id. **tn̂g-thâu-mn̂g**, the Taipings. **tn̂g-mn̂g**, id. (s. door).

siⁿ-mn̂g, to grow hairy, as articles growing mouldy. **hoat-mn̂g**, to grow hair or feathers, as animal; to begin to grow hair again, as place where there was a wound or scab. **thùi-mn̂g**, to moult. **thǹg-mn̂g** (C. thùiⁿ-mɵⁿ), to shed hair or feathers (s. door). **lut-mn̂g**, to lose hair finally, as animal, or as fur or velvet; to take off feathers or hair with hot water (v. lut). **thut-mn̂g**, having lost one's hair.

mn̂g-kha, the middle of the forehead, just below the place where the hair ends (s. door). **mn̂g-khɵ**, a circular rim of hair left unshaven. **mn̂g-sui**, do. grown longer, but not yet plaited into the queue; also, hair at side of woman's head (v. sui). **mn̂g-kńg-chhi kiā**, hair standing on end (v. kńg). **mn̂g-káu-á-thâng**, a sort of hairy caterpillar.

mn̂g — **koāⁿ-mn̂g**, the rattan bands which fasten the sail to the mast.

mn̂g [R. biên, to sleep, = col. bîn]. **mn̂g-chhn̂g**, a bedstead; a large bed.

mn̂g (Cn.) **koe-mn̂g-tsoá**, = A. mîⁿ-se-tsoá, a soft, thin, tough sort of paper.

mn̂g (Cn.) **mn̂g-hōe**, = A. mɵ̂ⁿ-hōe, a sort of crab. **mn̂g-hē** (P.), id. (C. mɵⁿ-hē).

mn̂g [R. mɵ̂ⁿ, a demon]. **mn̂g-kúi** (P.), = A. mɵ̂-kúi, the devil (s. door).

mn̂g [R. mɵ̂, to rub or feel about]. **mn̂g-se** (P.), Moses; and so with some other Scripture names, *e.g.* **thê-mn̂g-thài** (P.), Timothy.

mńg [R. boán, = col. ún], (C. múiⁿ), late, either as to day, or year, or proper time. **siuⁿ-mńg**, too late. **tsá-mńg**, morning or evening (v. tsá). **mńg-pɵ**, the latter part of the afternoon, about 4 to 5 o'clock. **mńg-tǹg** (Cn.), supper. **mńg-kiáⁿ**, a son born to his father in old age, when he has had no son, or at least none alive.

mńg [R. bún, name of a plant], (C. múiⁿ). **ka-mńg**, a very poisonous shrub with a yellow flower, and a leaf somewhat like siri leaf; it is said that goats eat it with safety. **kam-mńg**, id. **kam-mńg-thâu**, its root.

mn̄g (R. būn), (C. mūiⁿ), to ask a question (never to ask for a thing); to interrogate. **mn̄g-jī**, to ask the meaning of a character. **mn̄g-lē**, to ask the road. **saⁿ-chioh-mn̄g**, to make polite inquiries, as on meeting. **mn̄g-pok**, to consult a man who divines by tortoise-shell. **khoàⁿ-miāⁿ mn̄g-koà**, fortune-telling.

sím-mn̄g, to make official examination in court, as mandarin. **sìn-mn̄g**, id. **chhiong-kun mn̄g-liû**, to condemn to transportation or banishment (v. liû).

chheh-mn̄g, themes for the third Kujin examination.

mn̄g (P.) **kám-mn̄g**, = A. kám-mɵⁿ, to have a cold; feverish.

mn̍gh (Cn. T.), = A. mìhⁿ, a thing.

mɵⁿ [R. bɵ̂, to touch, = col. bong; cf. Cn. bɵ], to make the first play in gambling; the second is "sè." **mɵⁿ--lí**, I make the first play in gambling with you. **mɵⁿ sip-pat**, to play with six dice. **mɵⁿ thiàu-kâu**, to make the first play with three dice (v. kâu).

mɵⁿ (cf. bong). **àm-mɵⁿ-mɵⁿ**, very dark, as night.

mɵⁿ (C.), = A. mng, sort of reeds or grass for fuel, esp. brake. **ta-mɵⁿ**, = A. ta-mng, sort of edible green sea-weed.

mêⁿ [R. pông, a crab], (Cn. P. mn̂g). **mêⁿ-hôe,** a sort of crab or craw-fish. **mêⁿ-hē** (C.), id.

mêⁿ [R. a demon or devil], (P. often mn̂g). **mêⁿ-kúi,** a devil. **iau-mêⁿ kúi-koài,** malignant demons and devils. **hâng-mêⁿ-thú,** a baton for conquering demons.

mêⁿ — **mêⁿ-kong** (vulgar), a vile lascivious man (only said in vile scolding).

mêⁿ [R. to rub; to feel about], (P. sometimes mn̂g). **tát-mêⁿ-hút,** name of a Buddha; Dharma. **tát-mêⁿ tsó-su,** id. **mêⁿ-se** (X.), Moses (P. mn̂g-se).

chhúi-mêⁿ (R.), to investigate, as by comparing many things or books.

mêⁿ [R. to grind; by change of tone from "bō," a mill, = col. boâ]. **ok-jîn, tsū-iú ok-jîn mêⁿ,** wicked oppressive men are certainly ground down in turn by others.

poát-mêⁿ tsó-su, an idol brought from India.

mêⁿ [R. bû, not, none, = col. bô]. **mêⁿ-sîn** (C.), mad; you are mad; you are talking sheer nonsense. **mêⁿ-sîn-káu** (C.), a mad dog.

mêⁿ [R. coarse hair; bristles, = col. mâu, mn̂g], (also C., = A. mn̂g, hair), gross weight, as opposed to net; a surname.

mêⁿ-tāng, gross weight; opposed to "chēng," net. **mêⁿ joā-tsōe,** how much by gross weight?

mêⁿ-ièn, inferior birds'-nests.

mêⁿ-lâm, a rich deep blue. **mêⁿ-o-pò,** black cotton cloth. **mêⁿ-tāi-siáu,** elastic, as woollen socks. **ú-mêⁿ,** camblets, alpacas, and such stuffs. **mêⁿ-chien,** a carpet; coarse rough stuff like carpeting. **siⁿ-mêⁿ-thâng,** a sort of hairy caterpiller (v. thâng).

mêⁿ-si (C.), the book of odes, the Shi-king, = A. si-keng.

mēⁿ [R. mêⁿ, to feel]. **tát-mēⁿ,** = tát-mêⁿ, the Buddha called Dharma.

mēⁿ [R. extremely aged]. **mēⁿ-mēⁿ,** dull and without animation; aged and infirm, as old man whose senses have grown dull. **ló-mēⁿ,** aged and infirm.

mēⁿ [R. to feign or make a false pretence, = col. bō]. **mēⁿ-liap,** to make fraudulent use, as of a name. **mēⁿ-kò,** to accuse falsely at a mandarin's office. **mēⁿ-bêng,** to assume a man's name falsely; to lay claim falsely to talents, reputation, &c. **mēⁿ-tsàu,** to memorialize the emperor improperly. **ká-mēⁿ,** to assume or use improperly, as a name. **ká-mēⁿ lâng-ê-miâⁿ,** to make false use of another's name. **ká-mēⁿ jī-hō,** make false use of another's mark or title.

kám-mēⁿ (P. kám-mn̄g), to take a cold.

mēⁿ-tok--lí, I beg to trouble you, sir (v. tok).

moaⁿ, a cloak without sleeves; a loose cape; a shawl or plaid. **toā-moaⁿ,** a large sleeveless cloak or shawl. **hoan-moaⁿ,** foreign do.

moaⁿ, to put on or wear thrown over the shoulders, as an article of dress that has no sleeves, or not putting the arms in the sleeves if there be any; to lay one's arms on another's back or over his shoulders. **moaⁿ-saⁿ,** to throw a coat or shirt over one's shoulders without putting the arms in the sleeves. **moaⁿ--lóh-khì,** to put on any article of dress in this way. **moaⁿ tsang-sui,** to put on a rain-cloak of native manufacture.

saⁿ-moaⁿ, to put one another's arms on each other's shoulders, or round each other's neck. **sio-moaⁿ,** id. **moaⁿ-moaⁿ chit-bīn,** all covering the face, as dishevelled hair. **moaⁿ-moaⁿ tī-chhiûⁿ-thâu,** spreading loosely all over old walls, as creepers.

moaⁿ — **moaⁿ-îⁿ,** with rounded edges, as furniture.

moaⁿ — **moaⁿ-jia,** the sloping roof of an open shed or open verandah. **moaⁿ-chia,** id. **siâ-moaⁿ,** a small shed built at a wall. **moaⁿ-siâ-á,** id. **moaⁿ-phiâⁿ,** an open shed leaning on a house or wall; the 53d radical. **moaⁿ-phiaⁿ** (C.), id. **tah moaⁿ-phiâⁿ,** to put up such a shed.

bōng-moaⁿ, the circular back of a grave.

moâⁿ [R. mâ, = col. bâ], (T. boâ; P. mâⁿ), hemp; hemp-seed; coarse hempen cloth worn in deepest mourning. **iûⁿ-moâⁿ,** hemp. **soaⁿ-iûⁿ-moâⁿ,** a medicinal plant, said (in Cn.) to be good for dysentery. **seng-moâⁿ,** a medicinal plant (v. seng). **n̂g-moâⁿ,** common hemp. **kheng-moâⁿ,** a weak sort of hemp (almost like flax) that does not stand water. **o-moâⁿ,** black seeds of hemp. **péh-moâⁿ,** white seeds of hemp.

moâⁿ-tek, a sort of bamboo with large leaves and long joints.

lì-moâⁿ, to pick hemp-bark into fibres for making ropes.

moâⁿ-khe, refuse from making oil from hemp-seed. **moâⁿ-iû,** oil made from hemp-seed. **o-moâⁿ-iû,** dark hemp-oil, counted strengthening. **péh-moâⁿ-iû,** clear hemp-oil. **pi-moâⁿ-iû,** castor-oil. **moâⁿ-kut,** dried peeled hemp-stalks. **moâⁿ-kó,** id. **moâⁿ-phôe,** hemp-bark peeled off but not yet torn up small. **moâⁿ-jiông,** sort of oakum made from old sacks and ropes, &c. **thiah moâⁿ-jiông,** to pick old sacks, &c., into oakum. **moâⁿ-jîn,** hemp-seed. **moâⁿ-liâu,** a long-shaped confection made with hemp-seed. **at moâⁿ-liâu,** a sort of gambling by breaking one. **moâⁿ-chî,** a sort of confection (v. chî). **moâⁿ-láu,** another sort. **moâⁿ-tsó,** another sort. **moâⁿ-phang,** a diamond-shaped confection. **moâⁿ-phang-chhoáh,** lattice-work. **moâⁿ-tsoáh** (C.), id. **moâⁿ-tê-tsoáh** (C.), id. **moâⁿ-tê-hoân** (C.), lozenge or diamond shaped, **moâⁿ-tê** (C.), a small diamond-shaped confection. **sat-bú náⁿ-moâⁿ--nihⁿ,** lice very numerous.

moâⁿ-pò, coarse yellowish hempen sackcloth. **moâⁿ-saⁿ,** funeral dress of deepest mourning made of it. **moâⁿ-hók,** id. **moâⁿ-khoe,** mourning cap for sons, &c. **moâⁿ-kè,** mourning head-dress of it, worn by widow or daughter-in-law at funeral. **moâⁿ-kám,** sort of hood worn at funeral. **moâⁿ-tsoâ,** long twisted piece of coarse hempen-cloth tied round men's caps at funeral. **moâⁿ-nîⁿ,** short piece of hempen-cloth hung from lintel of house in deepest mourning. **moâⁿ-teng,** lanterns bound round with coarse hempen-cloth hung up in deepest mourning. **tiàu moâⁿ-teng,** to hang them up, as after parent's death (said by children in scolding). **moâⁿ-teng-chè,** debts to be paid when father dies. **chhēng-moâⁿ toà-hà,** to wear very deep mourning. **thoa-moâⁿ,** to tie round one's waist long strips of hemp-bark (twisted like coarse rope) hanging down behind, as son, daughter, or daughter-in-law at funeral. **thoa-moâⁿ chhêng-soh,** id., said by daughter-in-law or adopted son, if it be proposed to put them away, meaning, "I have done the most solemn funeral rites just like a child."

moâⁿ (R. boân), to deceive by concealment or false appearance. **saⁿ-moâⁿ,** id. **m̄-sái saⁿ-moâⁿ,** you need not try to deceive me. **moâⁿ-phiàn,** to deceive (v. phiàn). **jia-moâⁿ,** to deceive by concealment. **khi-moâⁿ,** id. **ún-moâⁿ** (r.), id. **moâⁿ siⁿ-lâng-bák,** to put on a false appearance in a man's presence.

moâⁿ (R. bân), a large sort of eel; a conger-eel.

moāⁿ-hî, id. **hái-moāⁿ**, id., from the sea. **ə-hî-moāⁿ**, a river eel. **chhiⁿ-moāⁿ**, a sort with greenish head. **lê-moāⁿ**, a very large fresh-water conger (said to be very lazy in the daytime). **lê-moāⁿ-kut**, a lazy fellow who lies about idly all day, generally indulging in low pleasures. **náⁿ-lê-moāⁿ**, said of such a fellow.

moāⁿ-koah, a stick with an iron hook at the end for catching eels (v. koah).

moâⁿ [R. məⁿ, hair]. **moâⁿ-khî** (C.), a small sort of crab.

moáⁿ (R. boán), (T. sometimes máⁿ), full; crowded; the whole of —; to complete, as a term of office (but never "to fill" with anything, nor "full of"); classifier of games of chance. **kàu-kúi-moáⁿ**, how many games of cards has he won?

sió-moáⁿ, a term about May 21st or 22d.

moáⁿ-gėh, a full month, esp. of woman after delivery. **tsòe-moáⁿ-gėh**, to perform rites and make presents to the parents at that time. **moáⁿ-jīm**, to complete one's full term of office. **saⁿ-nîⁿ-koaⁿ nn̄g-nîⁿ moáⁿ**, said of a man not staying long in a place.

moáⁿ--chhut-lâi, overflowing, as a liquid. **tīⁿ kàu-moáⁿ--chhut-lâi**, full to overflowing. **tīⁿ moáⁿ-moáⁿ**, very full of a liquid. **tìn-moáⁿ**, crowded, as room, with persons or things. **pá-moáⁿ**, stuffed full, as of food. **chhiong-moáⁿ**, quite full; very abundant. **tsōe-bī-moáⁿ**, very abundant.

moáⁿ-moáⁿ-sī, everywhere in great abundance. **moáⁿ-sì-kòe**, everywhere. **moáⁿ-tōe**, all over the ground. **moáⁿ-thê-kha**, id. **moáⁿ-bīn**, all over one's face; one's whole face. **moáⁿ-poāⁿ**, the whole business (v. poāⁿ). **moáⁿ-soaⁿ**, all over the land. **moáⁿ-hái**, all through the sea. **moáⁿ-seng-khu**, over the whole body. **moáⁿ-seng-khu siⁿ-thiàⁿ**, all over sores. **moáⁿ-pak**, whole heart full (v. pak). **moáⁿ-sim hoaⁿ-hí**, to rejoice with one's whole heart. **moáⁿ-sim oàn-hūn**, to hate with one's whole heart. **moáⁿ-chiok sim-ì**, desires satiated (v. ì).

moâiⁿ (C.), = A. bê, soft-boiled rice.

moāiⁿ (C.) **sió-moāiⁿ**, = A. sió-bē, younger sister.

môɛⁿ (P.), = A. bê, soft-boiled rice.

məhⁿ, drooping and nearly withered, as leaves of a tree; feeling very uncomfortable from hunger. **məhⁿ-məhⁿ**, id. **məhⁿ--lȯh-khì**, to subside, as a swelling. **iau kàu-məhⁿ-məhⁿ**, feeling extremely hungry.

məhⁿ — **məhⁿ--khì**, to steal, as small things.

mə̇hⁿ (R. bȯk), thin cuticle of the skin; thin film on peas, nuts, &c. **mə̇hⁿ-mə̇hⁿ**, very thin, as paper, or as slip of bamboo; very small and light, as a bundle. **phê-mə̇hⁿ**, the cuticle of the skin. **lâ-giâ-mə̇hⁿ**, the white woolly membrane inclosing the eggs of the tarantula. **tāu-mə̇hⁿ**, the thin pellicle of a pea or bean. **tek-mə̇hⁿ**, the inner lining of the bamboo. **phín-á-mə̇hⁿ**, a thin bit of bamboo used as the tongue of a flute.

kim-mə̇hⁿ, gold-leaf, real or false; brass-foil.

tsȧp-mə̇h, slightly colded, unwell, or out of sorts; feel dull, anxious, uncomfortable, or grieved from being harassed with many troublesome affairs. **tiȯh-chhìn-mə̇hⁿ-nahⁿ**, a sort of eruption (v. nahⁿ).

mə̇hⁿ [R. bȯk, wood; tree, = col. bȧk]. **tsȧp-mə̇hⁿ-hiȯh**, miscellaneous leaves used for adulterating tea (v. tsȧp).

muiⁿ (C.) **muiⁿ-muiⁿ**, = A. mng-mng, small, as rain or dust.

mûiⁿ [R. bî, soft-boiled, as rice, = col. bê, bôe], very soft, as food cooked very soft and tender.

mûiⁿ [R. bê, a frog] **ām-mûiⁿ** (esp. T.), a young frog or tadpole.

mûiⁿ [R. mûiⁿ, bôe, a plum, = col. m̂]. **mûiⁿ-hoe**, a sweet-scented flowering shrub like an almond. **pėh-mûiⁿ**, the white sort. **lȧh-mûiⁿ**, the yellow sort, Chimonanthus fragrans. **lāu-mûiⁿ**, id. **hún-mûiⁿ**, another sort.

peng-mûiⁿ, yellow plums preserved in sugar. **tiⁿ-mûiⁿ-chiùⁿ**, a condiment made of sugar and pounded yellow plums.

iông-mûiⁿ, a bubo.

mûiⁿ [R. a go-between, = col. hm̂], (C. also bûn, bôe). **koaⁿ-mûiⁿ**, a sort of female jailer for females: she also arranges marriages when the mandarin orders parties to be married. **hoat-lȯh koaⁿ-mûiⁿ**, to hand over (a woman) to her care, as men are given over to the "goân-chhe."

mûiⁿ-lâng (C.), = A. hm̂-lâng, a go-between for making a marriage.

mûiⁿ (C.), = A. mn̂g, a door.

mûiⁿ (R. mûiⁿ, bôe). **mûiⁿ-thoàⁿ** (R.), coals.

múiⁿ (R. id.), each. **múiⁿ-lâng**, each man. **múiⁿ-pái**, each time.

múiⁿ (C.) **chiȯh-múiⁿ**, a shrub like sloe with a corymb of small edible berries; the stem is very full of knots, and is much used for pipe-stalks.

múiⁿ (C.) **kam-múiⁿ**, = A. ka-mńg, a very poisonous shrub.

mūiⁿ (C.), = A. boán, mńg, ùn, late. **múiⁿ-tang**, = A. ùn-tang, the harvest in or about the 10th month. **soah-múiⁿ**, well on in the afternoon; not far from sunset. **soah-múiⁿ-á**, id.

múihⁿ [R. bê, a frog or toad; cf. mûiⁿ]. **ām-múihⁿ**, a young frog.

N.

Many words in **n** are also written with l, and others with j.

Words in **ng** are placed under a separate initial, and not under **n**.

Many words in **n** are mere reduplications of nasal words.

nâⁿ (R. lîm). **chhiū-nâⁿ**, a forest; a wood. **chhiū-nâⁿ-pê**, a dense forest (v. pê). **tek-nâⁿ**, a bamboo grove. **soaⁿ-nâⁿ**, mountain forests. **chhim-soaⁿ nâⁿ-tóe**, in the depths of forests and mountains. **chhim-khiⁿ nâⁿ-tóe**, in deep woods and ravines.

nâⁿ — **nâⁿ-âu**, the throat (v. âu).

nâⁿ (T.), to take fire accidentally. **hō͘ nâⁿ-tsoâⁿ** (T.), suddenly taking fire accidentally. **hóe nâⁿ-tsoâⁿ** (C.), id.

hé nâⁿ-tsoâⁿ (A.), sort of eruption on children. **hō͘ nâⁿ-toaⁿ** (T.), id.

nâⁿ (R. lâm), (T. nâiⁿ), a basket; a surname; where this is the prevailing surname, a basket is not called "nâⁿ," but "kheng." **nâⁿ-kiâⁿ**, the handle of a basket. **nâⁿ-keh**, the horizontal divisions of a basket in several layers.

nâⁿ-táu, a basket with no handle. **nâⁿ-táu-á**, id. **siāⁿ-nâⁿ**, a basket made in several layers or compartments one above the other. **ê-nâⁿ**, a cradle. **iô-nâⁿ** (C.), id. **kau-nâⁿ**, a basket with semicircular handle and no divisions. **kaⁿ-nâⁿ** (T.), id. **píⁿ-nâⁿ** (Cn.), id. **tîn-nâⁿ**, a rattan basket. **bih-nâⁿ**, a bamboo basket. **chhat-nâⁿ**, a painted basket. **tiûⁿ-nâⁿ**, a basket used by students going to the examinations. **koe-nâⁿ**, basket for carrying fowls.

teh-nâⁿ, to send some small thing back in the basket that brought presents (v. teh).

nâⁿ— **nâⁿ-tâu**, the Pandanus or screw-pine: appearance a good deal like the pine-apple plant.

nâⁿ [R. lô, name of a plant]. **nâⁿ-pók**, carrots. **nâⁿ-pók-chhài**, id. **nâⁿ-ták**, id. (s. harrow).

nâⁿ — **keh-nâⁿ-chhài**, a vegetable like a Savoy cabbage, but it does not form a heart (C. keh-mêⁿ-chhài).

nâⁿ — **khé-nâⁿ-poâⁿ**, a sort of shrub (v. poâⁿ).

nâⁿ— **nâⁿ-á-pùt**, the guava (v. pùt). **nâⁿ-á-poát**, id. (C. làt-pát; T. nâiⁿ-á-poát).

nâⁿ [R. nâuⁿ, lâuⁿ, cymbals]. **nâⁿ-poàh**, cymbals (v. poàh).

nâⁿ — **nâⁿ-ták**, sort of harrows used in wet fields (v. ták), (s. carrot).

nâⁿ [R. gâm, a steep rocky hill, = col. giâm]. **lêng-nâⁿ**, the city or department of Lung-yen-chow.

nâⁿ (C.), = A. noâⁿ, to hinder. **nâⁿ-tsáh**, to separate by using the hands, as men quarrelling. **nâⁿ-khui**, id.

náⁿ [R. jú, the more —]. **náⁿ — náⁿ —**, the — the —. **náⁿ-kú náⁿ-hó**, the longer the better. **lí náⁿ-beh, goá náⁿ-m̄**, the more you wish, the more determined am I against it (v. m̄).

náⁿ (= lán), like; similar to. **náⁿ-chhin-chhiūⁿ**, id. **náⁿ-pe--nihⁿ**, as if flying. **náⁿ-hî--nihⁿ**, like a fish. **náⁿ-ū**, it would seem as if there are —.

náⁿ [R. to take, to seize]. **chhiok-náⁿ** (R.), to arrest, as criminal. **chhip-náⁿ** (R.), to arrest quietly.

náⁿ [R. that; there; what? which? = col. tá, tó]. **ná-lí** (R.), how? where? (v. lí, "inside").

náⁿ (R. lám). **kaⁿ-náⁿ**, a Chinese olive (not the real olive), (v. kaⁿ).

náⁿ [R. kién, a son, = col. kiáⁿ, kán, á, ná, &c.] **kaⁿ-náⁿ-sun**, great grandson.

náⁿ, a final particle or affix of nouns, sometimes used instead of the usual **á**, especially after words ending in n. (cf. lá; cf. Cn. ngáⁿ, ngiáⁿ, káⁿ, therefore originally = kiáⁿ, a son, and same as former word.)

gín-ná, = gín-á, a son; a boy. **kin-ná-jit**, = kin-á-jit, to-day.

nàⁿ, to protrude rapidly, as the tongue. **nàⁿ-chih**, to put out the tongue for a moment, as in wonder or fear. **chih nàⁿ--chhut-lâi**, id.

nàⁿ [R. tiēn, lightning], to flash, as lightning; to glance brightly, as something glittering.

sih-nàⁿ, lightning (v. sih).

nàⁿ-kng, to glitter. **kim-nàⁿ-sàⁿ**, shining; glittering. **kim-nàⁿ-nàⁿ**, id. **kim-sàⁿ-nàⁿ**, id. **o-sàⁿ-nàⁿ**, black, glossy, and shining.

hê-nàⁿ-sàⁿ, doing things very carelessly. **hê-nàⁿ-sahⁿ**, id.

nàⁿ, to singe or burn slightly. **nàⁿ--tióh**, id. **khit-hé náⁿ--tióh**, to get singed by fire.

nàⁿ, to sun for a short time. **nàⁿ-jit**, id. **phák-nàⁿ** (T.), id.

nāⁿ [next word?]. **kúi-nāⁿ**, several (v. kúi). **hoān-nāⁿ**, in every case that —; every one who —.

nāⁿ [R. jiók, if, like], if; supposing that —. **nāⁿ-sī**, if it be (s. only). **nāⁿ-bô**, if not so; if there be none. **lí nāⁿ-beh**, if you wish (nāⁿ is generally thus placed second in the clause).

nāⁿ [R. tān, only]. **nāⁿ-sī**, only (s. if). **nāⁿ-ū**, there is only; there are only. **nāⁿ-sái**, all that is needed is —. **nāⁿ chia-ê**, only these. **nāⁿ-tiāⁿ**, only; said at the end of the clause. **m̄-nāⁿ**, not only. **m̄-tān-nāⁿ**, id. **khah-m̄-nāⁿ**, a good deal more.

nāⁿ, to wait at a place; to stay for a short time. **nāⁿ--teh**, id. **nāⁿ--chioh**, id.

nāⁿ, to singe, scorch, or burn slightly, as by powder or fire. **khit-hé nāⁿ--tióh**, to be slightly singed or burned, as a dress, or as one's skin.

nah, = lah, a final enclitic particle, especially after a nasal. **mihⁿ--nah**, what would you be at!

nahⁿ [R. thap, concave; to sink down, = col. lap], concave; having a deep hollow in it, as a sunken face; sunken, as a surface. **chit-nahⁿ**, a small hollow, as on the face, or on any surface. **nahⁿ-io**, having the middle narrower than the rest of it, as an hour-glass.

nahⁿ— **tióh-chhìn-méhⁿ-nahⁿ**, to have a reddish eruption like flea-bites; it lasts but a short time. **khí chhìn-méhⁿ-nahⁿ**, id.

nahⁿ (C.), to do bits of work in an irregular way. **nahⁿ--chit-ah, nahⁿ--hit-ah**, id.

nahⁿ (C.), to interrupt a speaker, as by an explanation or contradiction.

naiⁿ (T.), (cf. nāiⁿ), to droop, as leaves in drought. **naiⁿ--lóh-khì**, id. **hióh naiⁿ-naiⁿ**, the leaves are drooping.

nâiⁿ (T.) **nâiⁿ-hoe**, = A. liên-hoe, the water-lily.

nâiⁿ (T.) **nâiⁿ-á-poát**, = A. nâⁿ-á-pùt, the guava.

nâiⁿ (T.), = A. nâⁿ, a basket. **pàng-nâiⁿ**, to lay basket-work traps for crabs. **chhih-nâiⁿ**, basket-work traps for crabs. **hû-nâiⁿ**, do. for fish.

náiⁿ [R. mother; milk, = col. né, lóe, niⁿ, leng]. **náiⁿ-náiⁿ**, title of the wife of a district (Hien) mandarin; also (C.), of the wife of a Kujin, who in Amoy is called "thài-thài."

náiⁿ [R. truly; also]. **kau-náiⁿ-hī**, the contracted form of the 163d or 170th radical (v. kau).

nāiⁿ [R. a resource; how? = col. tāi, tā]. **bû-nāiⁿ**, having no alternative; having to do it, or accept or submit, though not as we would wish.

chio-hu ióng-tsú, sè-chhut bû-nāiⁿ, having no other resource, marries another husband, taking him into the family to take care of her children. **sè chhut bû-nāiⁿ**, it was because in the circumstances no other alternative was possible. **bû-nāiⁿ-hô** (r.), = bô-tāi-oā, no other resource; no alternative.

nāiⁿ [R. lāi, to trust; to depend on; to sorn; to accuse falsely, = col. loā]. **siet-nāiⁿ**, very forward and impudent, as a beggar, or brazen-faced woman. **káu-nāiⁿ**, very impudent and troublesome, as man who makes much loud talking and row, or who will not pay a debt, or confess an unquestionable fault.

海上絲綢之路文獻集成　科技與文化編

nāi^n [R. to endure; patient]. **jím-nāi^n** (r.), patient; patience.

nāi^n (R. lē), (C. lē; Cn. liên, nūi^n). **nāi^n-chi,** the fruit called li-chi or lai-chi; Dimocarpus Litchi.

nāi^n (T.) **khé-nāi^n-chhiū,** = A. **khé**-lēng, a tree with lilac flowers.

nāi^n (T.) **nāi^n-hióh,** = A. bā-hióh, the kite (v. hióh).

nāi^n (cf. nai^n). **nn̂g-nāi^n-nāi^n** (T.), drooping, as leaves in drought.

náu^n [R. ló, angry; anxious; displeased, = col. láu]. **hoat-náu^n**, to get angry. **àu-náu^n**, displeased and vexed; impatient and displeased.

náu^n [R. ló, brain]. **thâu-náu^n**, person or item of principal importance in an affair. **chhut-thâu chhut-náu^n**, to take the initiative or responsibility. **bô-thâu bô-náu^n**, no one taking the responsible management, so that nothing can be done. **kúi-thâu kúi-náu^n**, very cunning, crafty, and false (lit. demon's head).

náu^n (= láu). **náu^n-thâu tsūn-ām,** to shake one's head and neck about in a light and improper manner.

nāu^n [R. lāu, noise or confusion]. **jióng-nāu^n**, to make a noise and disturbance. **kàu-nāu^n**, violent angry disputation.

nauh^n (esp. T. Cn.), = A. ngauh^n, hauh^n, to snap up, as a dog.

nɛ^n (C.), = A. le. **kin-nɛ^n**, the fine fibrous parts of nerves or muscles. **thi^n ē-tsai^n lán--ê kin-nɛ^n kut-kɛh,** Heaven knows even our muscles and bones.

nɛ^n (C.) **àn-nɛ^n**, thus, = A. àn-ni^n.

nɛ̂^{n} (C.), = A. nî^n, to spread out, as clothes: to lay, as roof tiles. **nɛ̂^{n}-tsoâ,** a very poisonous sort of serpent.

né [R. nái, mother; milk, = col. lóe, lin], (C. nɛ́^{n}; T. nî^n). **án-né,** mamma! **ńg-né,** id. **in-né,** his mother; often has an improper meaning.

nɛ̀^{n} (C.), = A. nì^n, to exert one's self. **kiū^n-nɛ̀^{n}-kóng,** to talk very big; to brag.

nɛ̄^{n} (C.) **khah-nɛ̄^{n}**, rather more than —. **chit-tn̄g khah-nɛ̄^{n}**, somewhat more than ten feet (cf. lēng, "besides").

nɛ̄^{n} (C.) **phī^n-khang àng-nɛ̄^{n}**, nose stuffed, as with a cold.

nɛh^n (cf. lek). **lún-nɛh^n**, afraid, *e.g.* afraid to meddle with a matter. **lún-lún nɛh^n-nɛh^n**, id. **lún--chit-ē, nɛh^n--chit-ē,** id.

nɛ́h^n (cf. lėh). **kɛ́h^n-nɛ́h^n**, great noise, as of striking or of thunder (v. kɛ́h^n). **chhɛ́h^n-nɛ́h^n-nɛ́h^n**, loud sound of thunder (v. chhɛ́h^n).

ni^n (= leng, lin), milk (v. leng). **ni^n-bú,** a wet nurse. **chiáh-ni^n-lát soà-chhut,** to exert all the strength one has got from sucking days onwards.

ni^n [R. lėk, = col. nih^n]. **ni^n--sí,** to kill by strangling with the hand.

ni^n [R. lėk, to drop]. **a-ni^n**, a sort of distilled spirit. **a-ni^n thàu ló-chiú,** this spirit mixed with a weaker fermented liquor; said in an altercation when the other insists on something being done "àn-ni^n" ("thus"), when this play on the word is sometimes made.

ni^n (R. liam), to take up a small thing between finger and thumb. **thau-ni^n thau-liàm,** stealing (v. liàm). **ni^n-tang ni^n-sai,** to take up small quantities of things in the fingers, *e.g.* as an acquaintance looking at things in a shop.

nì^n (C. nɛ^n), (T. ni^n, hi^n, hî). **àn-ni^n**, thus. **àn-ni^n-si^n**, id.

nî^n (R. liên), a year. **nî^n-hè,** a year of age. **pah-nî^n-hè-āu,** after one is dead. **nî^n-kí,** years of age (v. kí). **nî^n-kō,** a year, as to date. **hó-thi^n-nî^n**, a year of abundance. **phái^n-thi^n-nî^n**, a year of dearth. **nî^n-géh,** years and months. **nî^n-kú géh-chhim,** for a long time, *e.g.* twenty years or so. **nî^n-tsoeh,** a year and its terms (v. tsoeh).

nî^n-bé, end of the year. **nî^n-chhím,** near the year's end. **nî^n-chhim,** id. **chhim-nî^n**, id. **nî^n-tau,** the last few days of the year, *e.g.* for about two weeks. **nî^n-tau-pi^n**, close to the end of the year. **tsòe-nî^n-tau,** to perform the rites for the end of the year. **tsòe-poà^n-nî^n**, to keep the 6.15. **nî^n-tang,** harvest (v. tang). **nî^n-kiet,** a balance at the end of the year.

kin-nî^n, this year. **kū-nî^n**, last year. **tsá-nî^n**, a former year. **chêng-nî^n**, id. **chiū^n-nî^n**, the former year. **tsûn--nî^n**, year before last. **lóh-tsûn--nî^n**, three years ago. **óng-nî^n**, in past years; year by year in the past. **éng-nî^n** (C.), id. **siâng-nî^n** (C.), id. **āu--nî^n**, the year after next. **āu-nî^n**, in some future year, either next year or later. **mê^n-nî^n**, next year. **mâ^n-nî^n** (T.), id. **sin-nî^n**, the year about to come in, said near the end of the old year. **goân--nî^n**, first year of a reign. **jī--nî^n**, second year of reign. **nn̄g-nî^n**, two years. **tâng-nî^n**, having taken the degree of Kujin (or higher) in the same year. **lāi-nî^n**, a lucky year for some special position of house or grave.

tiòh-nî^n, our year come (in turn) for some duty or office, esp. for having charge of some idolatrous rites. **tng-nî^n**, id. **tùi-nî^n**, same day in next year, esp. one year after death (v. tùi). **tsòe-sa^n-nî^n**, to perform rites on second anniversary of death. **hō-nî^n**, to pay visits or send cards on last day of year. **sî-nî^n**, to take leave of the year with rites. **kè-nî^n**, to pass from one year to another; to enter on a new year. **nî^n kè-nî^n**, year after year. **kè-nî^n-pn̄g,** some rice cooked on the last day of the year, and eaten next morning; so as to have food all the year. **kè-nî^n-chhài,** a bit of vegetable, &c., thus cooked and eaten. **sio kè-nî^n-pùn** (C.), to burn small heaps of earth and rubbish at end of year.

nî^n (C.) **boeh-nî^n**, whatever are you about? what do you want now? **boeh-tsò-nî^n**, what can I do? (seem to have no resource). **tsoá^n-nî^n-iū^n**, how?

nî^n, **toā-nî^n**, large shrimps from Manila. **tiong-nî^n**, a smaller sort.

nî^n — **toā-nî^n**, = toā-lêng, the tiller rope.

nî^n (R. liâm). **nî^n-chî^n**, the eaves of a house (v. chî^n).

nî^n [R. liên, united; connected], a sort of medicine. **n̂g-nî^n**, a fern used as a bitter cooling medicine (Chelidonium?). **chhoan-nî^n**, that medicine from Sze-chuen (justicia?). **hōng-bé-nî^n**, a medicinal fern root (or justicia?) from Sze-chuen. **thé-nî^n**, an inferior native sort, fern root. **thé-n̂g-nî^n**, id. **soa^n-n̂g-nî^n**, id. **chháu-nî^n**, id.

to-nî^n, a wild azalea, with an edible fruit like a small grape. **tiong-nî^n** (Cn.), id. **tsúi-to-nî^n**, a plant (not edible) with large leaves and large purple flower.

nî^n (C.) **ka-nî^n**, = A. ka-nn̂g, complete.

nî^n [R. to agree, = col. lî]. **tiong-nî^n**, the name of Confucius.

nî^n (cf. bî, bî). **nî^n-lėk-hùt,** one of the Buddhas (v. lėk).

nî^n, woollen cloth; tweeds; flannel; broad-cloth;

Spanish stripes, &c. **tsúi-nî^n**, flannel. **ə-nî^n**, black broad-cloth. **kiā^n-bīn-nî^n**, very smooth cloth. **sió-nî^n**, thin woollen stuffs, as cassimeres, &c. **chhə-nî^n**, coarse woollen stuffs. **ha-lā-nî^n**, thick superfine cloth. **to-lô-nî^n**, a sort of cloth.

nî^n-ú, camblets, broad-cloths, and woollen stuffs in general. **nî^n-ú tiû-toān**, silks, satins, and good woollen stuffs.

nî^n (C. nê^n), to hang out loosely, as clothes or netting (but "pì^n" is to stretch out tight); to lay tiles on a roof. **nî^n-sa^n**, to hang out clothes to dry. **nî^n-hiā**, to put on tiles on a roof. **nî^n-nî^n**, id.

nî^n [R. liâm, a screen, = col. lî]. **moâ^n-nî^n**, a short piece of coarse hempen cloth hung from the lintel of a house in deepest mourning. **bih-nî^n** (T.), a bamboo screen at a door. **nî^n** (T.), = A. lî, a hanging screen.

nî^n [R. liâm, a reaping-hook]. **nî^n-lėk-to** (T.), a small reaping-hook, smaller than "koeh-á."

nî^n (R. jiám), to dye. **nî^n-sek**, id. **nî^n-pâng**, a dye-work; a dyer's shop. **tsòe-nî^n--ê**, a dyer. **pėh-pėh-pè nî^n kàu-ə**, said of bearing false-witness against the innocent.

nî^n, = jí^n [R. the ear, = col. hī]. **nî^n-bȯk**, ears and eyes (v. bȯk). **kau-thâu chiap-nî^n**, to talk in whispers with mouth to ear, as for some secret and improper purpose.

sūn-hong-nî^n, one of the attendants of má-tsó-pô. **tāi-nî^n tēng-kong-sien**, a large-eared idol (v. kong).

bȯk-nî^n, a vegetable substance (a fungus?) stewed with food to make it less heating; brought from the north. **chhong-nî^n**, a medicinal plant (burdock?). **kāu-nî^n** (C.), a good-sized tree with red flowers.

nî^n [R. thou; you], = jí^n (*q.v.*)

nî^n [R. lióng, two; a pair, = col. nn̄g, niú^n, &c.], (C. lī). **nî^n-phiet-chhiu**, moustaches (v. chhiu).

nî^n (C.) **hán--nî^n tī-sî**, = A. hán--tit tī-sî, rarely.

nî^n (T.) **tiah-nî^n**, = ngeh-á, pincers.

nî^n (T.), = A. né, mother.

nì^n (cf. tì^n), (C. nè^n), to stand on tiptoe; to exert one's self. **kiū^n-peh-nì^n**, to exert one's self very much to do something. **toā-pē-nì^n**, to exert one's self and walk with long steps. **nì^n-kha**, to stand on tiptoe. **nì^n-kha-bé**, id. **nì^n-koāi^n**, id. **nì^n-kha khoà^n**, to stand on tiptoe to look.

nì^n (= nih^n). **lē-nì^n-hit**, to oscillate or shake about.

nī^n [R. lī, name of a plant]. **bȧk-nī^n**, white jessamine. **bȧk-nī^n-hoe**, id.

nī^n (cf. mī, bī), a connective particle with a very slight meaning.

niâ^n [R. liông, liûng, a lady, = col. niû^n], (Cn.), mother. **in-niâ^n**, his mother (Cn.)

niâ^n (mere reduplication). **kiâ^n-niâ^n**, to walk about; to take a walk.

niá^n [R. ná, where? how? = col. tá, tó]. **niá^n-ōe** (Cn.), how can it possibly be?

niá^n (C.), = ná^n, the — the — (r.) **niá^n-kú** (r.), the longer — the —.

niá^n (R. léng), a collar; classifier of articles of clothing; to receive; to bail out; to lead, as soldiers.

kúi-niá^n, how many articles of clothing?

niá^n-thò, a Chinese article of dress of a very narrow and straggling form, fastened under the elbows, worn above the other clothes to keep the queue from soiling them. **niá^n-kah**, another article of dress like a narrow vest or cape. **niá^n-tau**, the collar of a dress. **niá^n-tāu**, id. **niá^n-kau**, the hook of a Chinese collar. **oân-niá^n**, the large round collar of a robe worn by Sew-tsai graduates. **hong-niá^n**, a collar turning up for warmth. **nn̂g-niá^n**, do. made of soft fur, &c. **ām-á-niá^n**, the fixed collar of a coat, &c. **ām-kún-niá^n**, id. **koà-niá^n**, to put on or wear or have a collar. **hâ-niá^n**, to put on a collar.

niá^n-peng, to lead soldiers. **niá^n-lâng**, to bail out a man. **niá^n-chhut**, to get out, as man or thing, by standing security for him or it. **niá^n-tsn̄g**, a document by which a man binds himself as security, as in giving bail. **pau-niá^n**, to guarantee or stand security for. **pó-niá^n**, id. **tam-niá^n**, id.

niá^n--lâi, to receive, as things, esp. pay or rations. **niá^n-gûn**, to receive money. **niá^n-hiòng**, to receive soldier's pay (v. hiòng). **niá^n-bí**, to receive rations of rice. **niá^n-kǹg**, to receive a blank form for an examination essay. **niá^n sóe-lé** (X.), to receive baptism. **niá^n-pîn**, to receive a sort of official certificate (v. pîn). **niá^n chit-jī**, to get a word of fate (fortune-teller's phrase).

niá^n (R. léng), a mountain-pass or road over a pass. **soa^n-niá^n**, id. **niá^n-kha**, the foot of the pass, or of the road up the hill. **chiū^n-niá^n**, to ascend the steep road. **lȯh-niá^n**, to descend it. **tȧh-niá^n**, to walk up a hill with slow measured step, as chair-bearers. **koâi^n-soa^n tsùn-niá^n**, lofty hills and steep passes. **soa^n-thâu niá^n-bé**, mountains and steep hills. **poâ^n-soa^n kè-niá^n**, to cross steep mountains.

niā^n (R. lēng), (C. liōng). **soa^n-niā^n**, the shoulder of a hill higher than the intervening part; a swelling hump on the side of a hill. **khí-niā^n**, to have such a swelling shoulder, as a mountain.

niā^n — **gû-niā^n**, the hump at a cow's neck. **éng-niā^n**, the swell of the sea.

niah^n [R. hek, to frighten, = col. hiah^n]. **tah-niah^n**, to be suddenly startled. **sim-kia^n tah-niah^n**, id.

niau^n — **ə niau^n-niau^n**, very black with dirt, or with a great many black spots. **hoe-lin-niau^n**, variegated in colour.

niau^n [R. biâu, a cat, = col. bâ], a cat; pock-marked; to look earnestly; a sort of abscess; a catamite. **niau^n-bî**, sound used in calling cats. **niau^n-chih**, a fish like a small "bé-ka." **niau^n-thâu-chiáu**, a sort of owl. **kê-niau^n**, to put on a plaster of cat's flesh (good for a wound made by a tiger, which some call euphemistically "toā-chiah-niau^n.") **niau^n chhia-tó-ám, kā-káu tsòe-sì^n-jit**, said of unintentionally doing another a good turn.

niau^n-tsô, the hole in which the foot of a mast rests.

leng-niau^n, a small abscess in the breast.

tsòe-niau^n, to be a catamite. **sí-niau^n**, you vile catamite (or sodomite). **chhàu-hièn-niau^n**, you stinking catamite.

niau^n-niau^n-khoà^n, to look very intently at a person, or very earnestly for him.

niau^n-pan-tiám, marked with small spots; pock-marked. **niau^n--ê**, a pock-marked man. **niau^n pà-pà**, much pock-marked. **niau^n pi-pa**, id. **bīn niau^n**, face pock-marked. **chhùi-bí-niau^n**, marked with small pock-marks. **niau^n-kun**, the pock-marked man named Kun, &c.

niáu^n (Cn.), = A. jiáu^n, a claw or talon; so also with some other words in "jiáu^n."

niáu [R. a bird, = col. chiáu]. **niáu^n-chhiang**,

厦英大辭典

a musket. niáu^n-siù (R.), birds and beasts. pek-siét-niáu^n (hundred-tongued bird), a man who is never at a loss in argument (v. siét).

niáu [R. ló, old, =col. láu, lāu, &c.], (Cn. lé; C. lé, niáu). niáu-chhú, a rat; the lowest custom-house underlings who keep watch at landing-places. niáu-chhú-á, a small rat (or mouse); said also of these customs underlings. pe̍h-niáu-chhú, a white mouse. niáu-chhú-io̍h, arsenic. niáu-chhú-tauh, a rat-trap. niáu-chhú-tû, box with small tread-mill worked by mice or rats. niáu-chhú-chhák, a pointed stick for rats. niáu-chhú-jip, sort of squib that jumps about. niáu-chhú jip-gû-kak, said of getting into a cul-de-sac, or road with no outlet. pò niáu-chhú-á-oàn, to repay a slight injury by another. niáu-chhú-kā, articles stolen by persons in the house (v. kā). káu kā-niáu-chhú, a dog killing a rat (v. káu). niáu-chhú-khang, ui kàu-chiâ^n oân-kong-mn̂g (to enlarge a rat's hole to a round-headed doorway), a small affair become very great. niáu-chhú chia̍h-iû, ba̍k-chiu kng (the rat drinks the oil, and has light only so long), said of a man who keeps up a false appearance without thinking of the denouement.

niàu^n (Cn.), =jiàu^n, the scar of a wound.

nih^n (cf. nî^n, "pincers"). ba̍k-nih^n, the place at the keel where the foot of the mast is made fast.

nih^n, to wink; to twinkle; to glance and shimmer, as a glow-worm, or as distant lightning. nih^n--chit-ē, id. nih^n-ba̍k, to wink. iô-chhiú nih^n-ba̍k, to give secret signals to another, as by beckoning and winking. pí-chhiú nih^n-ba̍k, id. ba̍k-nih^n-kú, a moment. chit-ba̍k-nih^n-kú, id. ba̍k-nih^n-á-kú, id. sih-nà^n teh-nih^n teh-nih^n, distant lightning glancing.

nih^n (=nî^n, lîn). lō-nih^n-hit, to shake from side to side; to oscillate. lō-nih^n-hi^n, id.

nih^n (cf. ih^n). nih^n-nih^n-khoà^n, to gaze intently for a long time; to look long and earnestly, as for some one coming. nih^n-nih^n-háu, sound of children crying long. nih^n-nih^n-khàu, constant crying. ba̍k-sái nih^n-nih^n-lâu, weeping profusely.

nih^n (R. nî^n), an enclitic particle, used esp. in comparisons and interrogations. m̄-tsai--nih^n, I don't know. sím-mih^n--nih^n, what is the matter? ná^n-hî--nih^n, like a fish. ná^n-pe--nih^n, as if flying.

nih^n (T.) chháu-nih^n, =A. chháu-meh^n, a grass-hopper.

nih^n (cf. nih^n, nî^n), a particle with a very slight meaning. mih^n--nih^n hó: kè--nih^n pan-gî, the articles are good and the price low.

nih^n [R. lí, inside; in], (Cn. nn̄gh), in; on; usually enclitic. lō--nih^n, on the road. kha--nih^n, on the foot. hái--nih^n, in the sea. tī-hái--nih^n, id. chhoe--nih^n, in the first ten days of a month. jih--nih^n, within the days from the 20th to end of month.

chit-nih^n, here; this place. hit-nih^n, there; that place.

kun-nih^n, yet after all it is just the same (v. kun).

nih^n [R. le̍k, a bridle; to force; to strangle; =col. nî^n, la̍h], (C. tē^n), to grasp or squeeze in the hand; to knead between the fingers; to take up a small thing with the fingers downwards. nih^n-oá, to squeeze in the hand. nih^n--khí-lâi, to take up in the hand with fingers down. nih^n-nih^n tām-po̍h, to take some secret unjust gains in a transaction. nih^n-phoà, to break by squeezing. nih^n--sí, to strangle with the fingers or hand. nih^n ām-kún, to seize by the neck. hân-soan-kheh, nih^n kia^n-sí, pàng kia^n-pe, said of a man afraid to say either yes or no (lit. afraid the bird will die if he hold it, or fly away if let go).

nih^n — nih^n-nih^n le̍h-le̍h, sound of rattling or shaking things together.

nio^n (C., esp. P.), in all the tones, =A. niu^n.

niu^n (cf. liu, "small"), a man's name. niu^n-niu^n, very small in quantity. sòe-niu^n-niu^n, very small, as a thing. the̍h chit--ê niu^n-niu^n-á, to take a very small quantity. tsûn-á-niu^n (C.), a very small boat.

niû^n [R. liâng, lady; mother; woman; title of some goddesses]. tsu-niû^n, a woman. tsu-niû^n-lâng, id. ke-niû^n, an unmarried lady, esp. mandarin's daughter; some ladies are worshipped by this title; said by slaves to their masters' daughters. sin-niû^n, a bride. sien-si^n-niû^n, a teacher's wife. thâu-ke-niû^n, wife of the head of a firm. koa^n-niû^n, affix to name of a woman's husband to designate her; said by slave or beggar (v. koa^n).

niû^n-pē, father. niû^n-lóe (r.), mother. niû-lé (C.), mother. in-tia-niû^n, his parents.

niû^n-niû^n, title of empress. thien-hō-niû^n-niû^n, empress of heaven, title of má-tsó-pô. má-tsó-niû^n (Cn.), id. tsù-si^n niû^n-niû^n, the goddess of child-birth. chhit-niû^n-má, the goddess of the Pleiades (v. chhit). thài-im-niû^n, the goddess of the moon. gê̍h-niû^n, id. súi kàu-ná^n-gê̍h-niû^n, as beautiful as that goddess.

niû^n-á, mistress of a slave (a. silkworm). án-niû^n, said by slaves to their master's mother; said also by a son to his mother. lín-niû^n, your master's mother (said to a slave girl). in-niû^n, her master's mother. in tsú-lâng-niû^n, said of a slave's mistress. lāu-niû^n, grandmother or mother of slave girl's master or mistress.

âng-niû^n, a small red fish.

niû^n [R. liâng, liông, provisions; land-tax; soldier's pay]. chî^n-niû^n, land-tax. niû^n-chhe, collectors of land-tax. chî^n-niû^n-chhe, id. niû^n-tō, the commissioner (at provincial capital) who disburses the money for the pay of the imperial forces. chî^n-niû^n-ke̍k, company of land-tax collectors for a sub-district; their office. chî^n-niû^n-hū, a receipt for land-tax. siu chî^n-niû^n, to collect the land-tax. khòng-niû^n, to refuse to pay the land-tax. khiàm-koa^n-niû^n, to be in arrears for land-tax. oân-niû^n, to pay land-tax. oân-chî^n-niû^n, id. pí chî^n-niû^n, to flog (or threaten it) for non-payment of land-tax. chia̍h-niû^n, to be a soldier. chia̍h chî^n-niû^n, id. soà^n-niû^n, to pay soldiers. soà^n-chî^n-niû^n, id. chhut-niû^n, id. chhut chî^n-niû^n, id. sí-niû^n, to leave the army, as a soldier selling out. kek-niû^n, to expel a soldier. khai-niû^n, id. khek-liám kun-niû^n, to embezzle soldier's pay, as by paying only a part. kháu-niû^n, soldier's daily pay.

bí-niû^n, provisions. niû^n-chháu, provisions; provender. tsai-niû^n, vegetables and condiments used by Buddhist priests and vegetarians. ūn-niû^n, to transport provisions for an army. ūn-niû^n-koa^n, an officer of the commissariat. bē hêng-kun, seng hêng-niû^n, count the cost before engaging in an affair (send provisions before the army).

niû^n — sim-koa^n-niû^n thià^n, the heart deeply pained, as a mother when punishing her child severely, or as a man having broken some very valuable thing, or having lost heavily in gambling.

niû^n (R. liông), a great beam or ridge-pole in a house;

a surname. **tiong-niû^n**, the ridge-pole. **thong-niû^n**, the great horizontal beam of a couple for a gable-roof; the great beams which support the rafters of a floor or flat roof. **chiū^n-niû^n**, to set up the ridge-pole with ceremonies. **niû^n-thiāu**, a pillar built to support a great beam, with a hole in it for the beam. **niû^n, thiāu**, great beams and pillars.

phī^n-niû^n, the ridge of the nose. **só-niû^n**, the straight pin of a Chinese padlock, which goes through the staple.

niû^n (= niū^n). **oan-ke niû^n-chè**, to have a violent feud (v. niū^n).

niû^n [R. liōng, a measure; to measure, = col. liông, niū^n], to measure, either length or capacity. **niû^n-chhng**, cubical mensuration. **niû^n-bí**, to measure rice. **niû^n tsōe-chió**, to measure quantity. **niû^n-tn̂g-té**, to measure length. **niû^n-tn̄g**, to measure how many "tn̄g" of ten feet each. **ēng-kha niû^n-khoà^n**, measure by paces.

su-niû^n, to consult together. **chit-lâng tsú-tiu^n, m̄-tát nn̄g-lâng su-niû^n**, two consulting is better than one deciding.

niû^n [R. liâng, cool]. **niû^n-soà^n**, a state umbrella, carried before mandarins or idols (v. soà^n).

niû^n — **niû^n-á**, the silkworm (s. lady). **niû^n-á-hióh**, mulberry leaves. **niû^n-á-si**, silk, as spun by silkworms.

niú^n [R. lióng, two; a pair; a tael; = col. nn̄g, léng, ní^n], a tael; about an ounce and a third, = ten "chí^n;" it is one-sixteenth of a "kun;" a tael of silver is about 6s. 8d. **kun-niú^n**, catties and taels. **niú^n-sia^n**, the denomination of taels. **nńg-niú^n**, counting the tael a very little lighter. **ngī^n-niú^n**, allowing no discount or allowance at all.

niú^n — **bô-niú^n-siú^n**, much smaller than was expected; shrinking very much, as vegetables, &c., when cooked (v. siú^n).

niū^n (= niû^n). **oan-ke niū^n-chè**, to have a violent quarrel or feud. **oan-kɛ niū^n-toā-chè** (C.), id.

niū^n [R. liōng, to measure, = col. niû^n, &c.], a large steelyard for heavy weights (but "chhìn" is a smaller steelyard); to weigh with it. **niū^n-tô**, its weight. **niū^n-kau**, its hook.

niū^n (R. jiōng), to yield; to give way; to give place. **sa^n-niū^n**, to yield or give place to another, or to one another. **niū^n-ūi**, to abdicate the throne; to give place politely to each other. **niū^n--i**, to give place, or yield situation, &c., to him. **thè-khui niū^n--i**, to get out of the way, so as to avoid disputing with him. **niū^n-lí seng-kiâ^n**, I will let you walk first. **niū^n-chhiú**, to relax one's attack a little, as in striking, or in entering an accusation. **chit-niū^n, chit-ū-phā**, if you yield a little he will be all the more exacting.

niū^n — **tsòe-gī-niū^n**, to make things for amusement, or just to pass the time. **tsòe-gē-niū^n**, id. **bô-gī-niū^n**, without any work whatever to do, however slight; so idle as to take to games.

nng (cf. long, nǹg), (C. nui^n), to shove endwise into a hole, as some long thing; to creep in, as into a hole. **nng-khang**, to creep into a hole, as insect. **nng--jip-khì**, to shove a long thing into a hole, *e.g.* a billet of wood into the mouth of a stove, or as one's arm or leg into coat, trowsers, or boots. **nng hit-tsàu-khang**, to put (a long bit of wood) into the mouth of the stove; to creep into it, as rat or cat.

nn̂g [R. lông, a young gentleman, &c.] **sī-nn̂g**, the vice-president of a Supreme Board. **gû-nn̂g**, a star worshipped on 7.7 along with "chit-lú;" these are two stars in a diamond-shaped group of four.

nn̂g — **tsû-nn̂g**, a wood which dyes reddish brown; also used medicinally.

nn̂g [R. lông, a sort of palm]. **pin-nn̂g**, the areca palm; the betel-nut (a Malay word). **pin-nn̂g-sū**, Penang island; said also of a small rocky island shaped like a betel-nut.

nn̂g — **bah-nn̂g**, the fat mixed among the lean of meat. **bah-nn̂g-iû**, the fat mixed with the lean of pork, just below the skin. **jī-nn̂g-iû**, id. **jī-nn̂g**, the thin layer of fat between the skin and the flesh, esp. of the pig (s. next word). **jī-nn̂g-bah**, this layer of fat with a little lean in it. **hàm-jī-nn̂g**, a swelling on the abdomen (supposed only skin deep, while "ké-tiòng" is very serious).

nn̂g, the soft inside, as of a pumelo-skin or of bamboo. **tîn-nn̂g**, the softer inside part of rattan. **bih-nn̂g**, the softer inside layer of the bamboo (but not the innermost), used for wicker-work, but much inferior to the "phê" or outside. **nn̂g--ê**, made of this softer part. **iū-jī-nn̂g**, the soft white lining between the lobes and skin of a pumelo. **jī-nn̂g**, id. (s. previous word).

nn̂g [R. liên, united; connected], to stitch very loosely together, just sufficiently to hold together and in place till sewed more firmly (esp. Cn.)

nn̂g [R. thoân, a globular mass; united; complete, = col. toâ^n, thn̂g], (C. nûi^n, nî^n). **ka-nn̂g**, complete; entire; undivided. **kui-nn̂g**, id. **ka-nn̂g-tiâu**, one whole long piece, *e.g.* of cloth. **ka-nn̂g-siu^n**, a whole boxful. **ka-nn̂g-tè**, one lump or mass. **kiet ka-nn̂g-tè**, to coagulate or form into one lump or mass.

nn̂g (T.) **jiû-nn̂g**, = jiû-n̂g, sulphur.

nńg (R. joán, loán), (C. núi^n), soft; tender; delicate; yielding; merciful; flexible; weak; weary. **ngī^n-nńg**, hard and soft, &c. (v. ngī^n). **nńg--lòh-khì**, to sink, as an ill-made foundation. **hióh nńg--khì**, leaves drooping, as in drought.

nńg-pe, the afternoon drawing towards sunset. **jit khah-nńg**, the sun less powerful, as in afternoon, or late in year, or clouded.

nńg-chiá^n, delicate; feeble; weak as to power or influence. **nńg-lūn**, soft and delicate, as fur, or silk, or hand (v. lūn). **nńg-jūn**, soft and delicate, as cakes. **nńg-lióh**, elegant; delicate, as hand (v. lióh). **nńg-áu**, soft and unpleasant, as a dress that has lost its starch; drooping, as leaves in drought. **nńg-sè**, weak, as wicker-work or thin boards. **nńg sìm-sìm**, weak and elastic, as boards of floor or bed; elastic, as iron wire. **nńg sē-sē**, soft and watery, as dough.

nńg chî-chî, soft and tenacious, as a cake; weak, as a child that cannot stand though old enough. **nńg-kê-kê**, very soft, as dough; very weak and delicate, as child difficult to bring up or that cannot stand for weakness. **sin-miā^n nńg-kê-kê**, of delicate constitution, as man. **nńg-kô-kô**, very soft, as dough. **nńg ô-ô**, id. **nńg-khiùh-khiùh**, id. **nńg-kiùh-kiùh**, id. **nńg-kiuh-kiuh**, id. **nńg-chiùh-chiùh**, id. **nńg-káuh-káuh**, very weak in constitution; too soft and unpleasant to eat, as eatable. **nńg-kauh-kauh**, id. **nńg hāi^n-hāi^n**, very weary and sleepy so as to be nodding; too soft and useless, as man; too soft, as dress that has lost its starch. **nńg nāi^n-nāi^n** (T.), drooping, as leaves.

nńg-lâng, a man who belongs to a weak clan or family. **khah-nńg-pâng**, a weak (or weaker) branch of a family. **nńg-sim**, compassionate; merciful; readily granting a favour or request, or assisting the miserable. **sim-koa^n nńg ná^n-mî^n**, very compassionate or merciful (lit. soft as cotton). **nńg-gê**, to come down in one's talk after being very determined and violent. **khah-nńg-chhùi**, more willing to come to a settlement. **khah-nńg-lē**, easy and pleasant to deal with in a business. **lóh-nńg**, to come nearer the terms of the other party. **chhiá^n-pàng-khah-nńg**, let down your terms a little, as in a dispute. **nńg-niú^n**, giving a very small discount by counting the tael somewhat lighter. **nńg-gûn**, id.

sng-nńg, weak and worn out; in a state of lassitude; all weary and aching. **sng-nńg-thià^n**, id. **nńg-sng-khok**, doing business very slowly. **ûn-á kap--i nńg-sng-khok**, id., *e.g.* gradually offering more for a thing, or making cautious and prudent advances to a man in some delicate and doubtful or dangerous matter. **kha sng, chhiú nńg**, limbs weak and sore with sickness, or hunger, or weariness. **kha nńg, chhiú nńg**, id., or as from fear or sad news. **chhiú pàng-nńg**, to relax the muscles of the arm. **nńg-kha**, having weak legs, as congenital or from long sickness. **chìm kàu-nńg-kha**, to stand or work in water till one's legs are weak. **kia^n kàu-nńg-kha**, terribly afraid, as at imminent danger, or in order to keep out of danger. **nńg-kut**, gristle; impotent in legs, so as not to be able to walk. **nńg-khàm**, the soft part of the side, between the thigh and the ribs.

pûi-nńg, fat and plump (v. pûi). **tiû-nńg**, soft silks. **nńg-tsoe**, soft dough. **jī-úih nńg**, the written character too slim in form.

nn̂g (cf. nng), (C. nùi^n), to creep or rush in or out. **nn̂g--khì**, to creep or rush through or into. **nn̂g--kè-khì**, to creep or rush through. **nn̂g-tsáu**, to creep through and escape when just almost caught, as through a crowd or a secret passage. **nn̂g-hé**, to rush through a fire, as house on fire. **nn̂g-hé-tsáu**, to rush through the fire and escape. **nn̂g-hé-phāng-tsáu**, id. **nn̂g-hé-khe**, to rush through a circle of fire, as at a theatrical play.

nn̂g-tsn̂g, skilful at scheming for making money, &c. (v. tsn̂g). **nn̂g-chî^n-khang**, id. **gâu-nn̂g-khang**, id.

nn̂g (mere reduplication). **khǹg-nn̂g**, to hide; to lay past.

nn̂g (mere reduplication), (C. nùi^n). **khǹg-nn̂g**, to exhort much (C. khùi^n-nùi^n).

nn̄g (R. loán, tān), (C. nūi^n), an egg; spawn. **chióh-nn̄g**, a stone rounded by water. **kha-āu-nn̄g**, the under part of the heel. **chhiú-āu-nn̄g**, the elbow. **bé-nn̄g**, a preparation of dough, eggs, &c.

si^n-nn̄g, to lay eggs, as fowls or other birds. **chhoah-nn̄g**, to lay great quantities of eggs at once, as butterflies. **pàng-nn̄g**, id. **sáh-nn̄g**, to boil an egg. **sa^n-liáp-nn̄g**, three eggs.

hî-nn̄g, fish spawn or roe. **pih-nn̄g**, tortoises' eggs. **kap-nn̄g**, pigeons' eggs (&c.) **nn̄g-toa^n**, embryo egg in ovary. **nńg-nn̄g**, a large egg about ready to be laid, but with the shell still soft. **chhiú-bú-nn̄g**, the first egg laid by a fowl; when a boy goes first to school the teacher makes him roll it before Khoe-seng; if it roll straight he is to be clever.

koe-nn̄g, a hen's egg (C. ke-nūi^n). **koe-nn̄g-chheng**, white of hen's egg. **koe-nn̄g-jîn**, yolk of do. (v. jîn). **koe-nn̄g-ko**, sponge-cake. **koe-nn̄g-bīn**, a well-formed, healthy, plump face, neither too round nor too long. **koe-nn̄g bát-bát, to ū-phāng**, the closest affair has some hole in it. **ah-nn̄g**, a duck's egg. **ah-nn̄g-chheng**, the white of a duck's egg. **ah-nn̄g-chhi^n**, very light pale-blue. **poáh ah-nn̄g**, to play a game with painted duck-eggs. **hip ah-nn̄g**, to hatch duck-eggs by artificial heat in husks of grain.

nn̄g [R. lióng, two; a tael; = col. niú^n, léng, nī^n], (C. nō^n), two (but never "second"). **nn̄g-iū^n**, two sorts; different. **sa^n-sim nn̄g-ì**, purpose unstable. **nn̄g-sa^n**, two or three; about three. **sa^n-nn̄g**, about two. **nn̄g-pah**, two hundred. **chit-pah khòng-nn̄g**, a hundred and two (but 120 is "pah-jī").

nn̄g (R. lōng). **pho-nn̄g**, waves. **tiām-hoang chī^n-nn̄g** (T.), winds and waves still.

nn̍gh (Cn.), = A. nih^n, in (a place), (usually enclitic).

nó^n [R. ló, old, = col. láu, lāu, &c.] **ko-nó^n**, a solitary old man who gets a ticket from the district mandarin allowing him to beg for money, not subject to the head of the beggars. **kip ko-nó^n-pâi**, to give this ticket. **ko-nó^n-ī^n**, an old men's asylum. **ko-nó^n-sū** (Cn.), id.

nō^n (C.), = A. nn̄g, two.

nō^n (R. id.) **nō^n-nō^n**, without spirit or energy; taking things too easy; letting things take their course. **nō^n-jiók**, spiritless; without energy.

noâ^n (R. lân, = col. â^n), to hinder; to keep off. **noâ^n-chí**, to prevent; to hinder. **noâ^n-tsó**, to hinder or prevent something just about to be done. **noâ^n-khui**, to separate, as combatants. **noâ^n-tsáh**, to hinder by stretching out our hands, as in separating combatants. **noâ^n-lō**, to stop the road. **noâ^n-kiō**, to lay hold of a mandarin's chair in order to hand in a petition.

iâm-sûn-noâ^n, sort of salt excisemen.

noâ^n (R. lân), a fold, pen, or inclosure for animals, usually with no roof, but not always. **chí^n-noâ^n**, a well-curb. **gû-noâ^n**, a fold for cattle; a cow-pen. **iû^n-noâ^n**, a fold or barrier for sheep or goats. **bé-noâ^n**, a stall or inclosure for horse, with or without a roof.

noâ^n — **liáh-tiong-noâ^n**, to split the difference, as in a quarrel or bargain.

noá^n, to knead and work up, as dough, &c.; to press with the hands in kneading; to roll with the hands, as tea-leaves. **noá^n-sa^n**, to knead and squeeze down clothes in washing. **noá^n kiâm-chhài**, to press out the juice from salted mustard leaves before putting them into jars. **noá^n-ké**, to knead and roll dough in making cakes. **noá^n-mī^n**, to knead wheaten dough. **noá^n-chhòe**, to knead rice-dough.

phah-noá^n, to handle too roughly so as to crumple or damage, as some fragile thing. **khah-ū phah-noá^n**, having a good deal of wear in it, as strongly made dress or furniture. **bōe-kham--tit phah-noá^n**, cannot bear to be moved about much, as a sick man.

noá^n — **poâ^n-noá^n**, to hold friendly intercourse, as in business or friendship. **sa^n-kap poâ^n-noá^n**, id. **poâ^n-noá^n put-chi-kú**, long intimate.

noá^n [R. lán, lazy; idle, = col. noā^n]. **noá^n-chhoá^n**, lazy, careless, or negligent at work; doing work in a perfunctory, idle, or untradesman-like way; utterly without energy, as opium-smoker. **noá^n-**

chhoá, id. **noá^n-chhoá^n chiū-kè--khì**, quite forgetful of the matter, from not having given attention at the time.

noà^n, to writhe and struggle to get free; to roll about on the floor in play or pain, as child or dog. **tó-teh-noà^n**, rolling on the ground so.

noā^n (R. lān), rotten; putrid; boiled very soft and tender; lazy, useless, or easy-tempered. **noā^n-tsoā^n**, very cheap; very abundant (v. tsoā^n).

phoà-noā^n, all torn and ragged, as dress (s. urgent). **chhēng phoà-noā^n**, to wear very ragged things.

noā^n-**léh**, too soft, as doughy cakes, &c. **noā^n kê-kê**, very soft, as cooked food; soaked all through, as by rain. **tsú-noā^n**, to boil soft; to boil to rags. **kûn-noā^n**, id.

chhàu-noā^n, putrid. **chhàu-thâu noā^n-hī**, face covered with boils and eruptions. **hiú-noā^n**, rotten. **noā^n hiú-hiú**, very soft or rotten. **noā^n-noā^n lok-lok**, full of rotten sores, as a sore leg. **noā^n-bák**, eyes with sores on the eyelids or just below the eyes. **kha-bák noā^n**, a disease of the ancles of girls when the feet are being compressed. **noā^n-sién**, soft scurf; ring-worm. **noā^n-sim**, having the heart decayed, as a vegetable; also (Cn.), a tree somewhat like an ash, with light pinnate leaves and trunk that easily decays.

lám-noā^n, slovenly, esp. in dress or person. **noā^n-sèng**, very easy-minded; taking things too easy, *e.g.* neglecting duty or passing over injuries. **lâng noā^n-noā^n**, lazy useless man, with no energy. **noā^n-thô**, soft mud (said of a soft, gentle, submissive temper). **noā^n-thô bô-chhì**, said of a gentle easy man, who receives injuries without resistance.

chiáh--i bōe-noā^n, I have not strength or ability for his work; often includes the idea that he is too hard a master.

noā^n [R. lán, idle; lazy]. **noā^n-chhoá^n**, = noá^n-chhoá^n, negligent; lazy; perfunctory, &c.

noā^n [R. liēn, a young fowl], (Cn. loā). **koe-noā^n**, a young fowl that has not yet hatched chickens.

noā^n [R. lāi, to lean upon; to sorn; to accuse falsely, = col. loā]. **mī^n-noā^n**, very urgent and importunate in beseeching (v. mī^n). **phoà-noā^n**, shamelessly urgent, as beggar who won't go without getting money (s. rotten). **chhāi-phoà-noā^n**, id. (v. chhāi). **sái-phoà-noā^n** (T.), id. **sāi-phoà-noā^n** (Cn.), id.

noā^n, saliva; spittle. **péh-phéh-noā^n**, white saliva at the mouth, as in disease. **thâm-noā^n**, phlegm. **kāu-phī^n-thâm-noā^n**, quantities of mucus flowing from the nose. **phī^n-thâm-noā^n oā^n iû-hé-hun**, said of a man who is always getting little benefits from us (as a meal or a smoke) and making no return. **phùi-noā^n**, to spit (v. phùi). **thun-noā^n**, to swallow one's saliva. **kut-lát chiáh-lát: pîn-toā^n thun-noā^n**, the active lives by his exertion, the idle has only his saliva to swallow. **khoà^n-lâng-chiáh kàu-thun-noā^n**, mouth watering at seeing others eating. **ài-chiáh kàu-lâu-noā^n**, mouth watering for food. **ài-chiáh kàu-tih-noā^n**, id. **lâu-noā^n**, saliva running from the mouth.

noā^n (T.) **chhi^n-noā^n**, = A. chhi^n-loā, a large green caterpillar.

nui^n (C.), = A. nng, to creep through.

nūi^n (Cn.) **nūi^n-chi**, = A. nāi-chi, the fruit called li-chi or lai-chi.

nûi^n (Cn.), = A. liên. **nûi^n-hoe**, the water-lily. **tsúi-nûi^n-hoe**, a small white sort, used medicinally.

núi^n (C.), = A. nńg, soft. **núi^n-bú**, walking like a woman (said in scolding).

nùi^n (C.), = A. nǹg, to creep through.

nùi^n (mere reduplication). **khùi^n-nùi^n** (C.), = A. khǹg-nǹg, to exhort much.

nūi^n (C.), = A. nīg, an egg.

nūi^n (C.), = A. iū, a pumelo. **nūi^n-á**, id.

NG.

In the words which consist of **ng** alone (in the several tones) there is an indistinct vowel sound heard in the nasal consonant, neither before nor after it.

The words that have **ng** as their initial are often interchanged with those having initial **g** (*q.v.*)

ng (R. iong) **tiong-ng**, middle (v. tiong).

ng (= ńgh). **ng-ng-kiò**, to whine, as a child. **ng-ng-háu**, id.

ng (R. iong), (Tt. ə), young rice plants, raised in a seed-bed to be planted out. **ng-tiā^n**, a seed-bed for young rice. **ng-chioh** (Cn.), id. **iā-ng**, to sow rice in the seed-bed. **tsai-ng**, to plant out the young rice.

ng' (C. ui^n), to cover up, as with the hand, or with a cloth; to hide by covering up; to cover up an affair, that it may not be known.

ng **pak-tó**, to hold one's belly, as when in great pain.

ng-iap, to hide a thing behind our back or about our dress. **ng-bīn**, to cover up the face. **ng-chhùi**, to cover the mouth. **ng-hī**, to stop one's ears so as not to hear. **ng hī-khang**, id. **ng phī^n-khang**, to cover or close the nostrils. **ng bák-chiu**, to cover the eyes.

n̂g (R. hông), (C. ûi^n), yellow; a surname. **n̂g-sek**, yellow. **kim-n̂g**, a rich golden yellow. **tāng-n̂g**, id. **kiu^n-n̂g**, dark yellow with a tinge of brown; turmeric. **tîn-n̂g**, gamboge. **khín-n̂g**, light yellow. **bit-n̂g**, honey-coloured; a bright light yellow. **n̂g-hoá^n-hoá^n**, yellowish. **tām-n̂g**, yellowish. **n̂g-phā-phā**, yellow, as fruit. **n̂g-gâm-gâm**, very yellow. **n̂g-phih-phih**, yellow, as face. **n̂g-gīm-gīm** (T.), very yellow.

chhi^n-n̂g, pale, as face in disease (v. chhi^n). **n̂g-sng**, yellow and emaciated; having a sickly look (v. sng). **n̂g-sán**, yellow and wasted. **n̂g--lòh-khì**, to grow yellow and sickly. **khiā-n̂g**, to have its leaves yellow and withered, as a plant in drought, or when just transplanted. **chit-jit soá-tsai, sa^n-jit khiā-n̂g**, it takes three days before a plant loses its withered look after being transplanted; a man who moves into a new place is not at first very comfortable or successful.

n̂g-ki^n, a yellow dye. **n̂g-si**, a wood very good for oars. **n̂g-gû**, the common cow or ox. **n̂g-phang**, the honey-bee. **kə-n̂g-chiáu**, the great owl. **kə-n̂g** (Cn. kə-m̂), id. **n̂g-koe-hî**, = âng-koe-hî, a good sort of fish.

n̂g-pńg, an imperial proclamation. **n̂g-kim**, gold; yellow gold. **n̂g-kim-tsoá**, yellow paper. **n̂g-sē-tsúi**, thin matter from a wound.

n̂g (R. hông), (C. ûiⁿ). **n̂g-chéng**, jaundice. **hàm-n̂g**, id. **n̂g-thán**, a disease of children (v. thán).

n̂g, = ôe; answer to a call; yes, sir!

n̂g (R. hông), (C. hûiⁿ). **liû-n̂g**, sulphur. **jiû-n̂g**, id., = hông.

n̂g [R. ông, a king]. **tsòe-lâng-n̂g**, to act imperiously towards others, as an older child towards the younger. **lêng-n̂g**, = lêng-ông, the god of the sea.

giâm-lô-n̂g (Cn.), = A. giâm-lô-ông, the judge of the dead; the god of Hades. **kòh-sèng-n̂g** (Cn.), = A. keh-sèng-ông (v. keh).

n̂g [R. oân, crooked, bent], (C. ûiⁿ). **lôe-n̂g** (C. lê-ûiⁿ), the crooked body of a plough.

ńg [R. éng, a shadow; = col. iáⁿ], the shade; shade from heat; a shadow, esp. a steady deep shadow, as of a house, hill, or tree.

ìm-ńg, the shade. **hioh-ńg**, to rest in the shade. **tiàm-ńg**, to keep in the shade.

lâng-ńg, a man's shadow or reflection in the water. **chhiū-ńg**, the shade of a tree. **chiò-jī-ńg**, to cast the shadow of a character on a rock so that its shape may be traced on it (v. chiò). **hé-ńg**, the parts which the lamp's light does not reach; the places that are in shade from the lamp. **soeh hé-ńg**, to creep along stealthily in the places that lie in shade from the lamp. **pn̄g i--ê hē-soàⁿ-ńg** (rely on the shade of his umbrella), to take advantage of a man's travelling to get cheaper, more easily, or more safely, &c. **pn̄g lâng niûⁿ-soàⁿ-ńg** (of his state parasol), to depend on a man's influence to get our affair set right.

ńg (C. úiⁿ). **ńg-á**, a small basket used for selling or weighing things.

ńg (C. úiⁿ). **káu-ńg**, a very low sort of pawnshop where they lend 90 cash, counting them as 100, and take very heavy usury; they often receive stolen goods. **káu-ńg-á**, id. **káu-ńg-á-tiàm**, id. **goá-tn̂g poeh-ńg**, I am so poor that the lowest pawnshops (káu-ńg) will not take my things; if I have to pay I must pawn at a lower pawnshop *than exists.*

ńg (C. úiⁿ), a sleeve. **chhiú-ńg**, id. **pih chhiú-ńg**, to turn up the sleeves. **chhiú-ńg-tóe**, in the inside of the sleeve. **chhiú-ńg-kui**, the inside of the sleeve where things can be carried secretly. **chhiú-ńg-sok**, an outer sleeve, serving as a cover to the sleeve.

bé-tôe-ńg, cuffs made in the form of a horse's hoof for ceremonial dress. **khoah-ńg**, wide sleeves. **khoah-ńg-saⁿ**, a dress with wide sleeves. **óeh-ńg-saⁿ**, dress made with narrow sleeves, esp. worn by women.

ńg-kháu, end of sleeve; cuffs. **ńg-siū**, women's cuffs. **ńg-thò**, outer sleeve, used as a cover for the sleeve.

chhah-ńg, to put in a triangular piece in the inside of a sleeve in making a dress. **chiap-ńg**, to join a piece to make a sleeve long enough. **chiap ńg-kháu**, id. **chiap ńg-bé**, id.

ńg (C. úiⁿ), to take things under the arm.

ńg (R. goán), (C. úiⁿ), a surname.

ńg, = án, prefix to some names of relations when addressing them. **ńg-né**, mother! **ńg-má**, grandmother! **ńg-ko**, paternal aunt!

ǹg (R. hiòng), to face towards; to look towards; to have a desire towards; to expect; to watch or tend, as animals.

saⁿ-ǹg, facing each other. **sim saⁿ-ǹg**, sympathizing with each other.

ǹg-bāng, to hope for; to expect. **bô-ǹg**, having none to look to, as parents whose sons are all dead or have gone wrong; no hope of reforming, returning, or again prospering.

ǹg-tn̄g, self-willed, obstinate, and idle, as child or young person who will not do what is ordered. **ǹg-tǹg**, id.

ǹg-gû, to tend cows when at grass. **ǹg-iûⁿ**, to watch and tend sheep or goats, as shepherd.

ǹg-thiⁿ, looking towards heaven. **ǹg-hia khì**, go in that direction. **ǹg-téng**, facing upwards. **ǹg-chiūⁿ**, id. **ǹg-ē**, facing downwards. **ǹg-chêng**, facing forwards. **ǹg-āu**, facing backwards. **ǹg-pak**, facing north, &c. **chē-pak ǹg-lâm**, having its back to the north and facing south, as a house (v. lâm).

n̄g [R. ūn, obscure; a halo], (C. ūiⁿ), dim, as eyes from long looking, or from glare of sun, or when just risen from sleep, or from leaning on the hand, sometimes seeing motes dancing.

goèh n̄g-n̄g, the moon dim, not bright.

ien-n̄g, eyes dim, so as to see quite indistinctly, as from long looking; or from long writing, esp. by lamplight; or in weak health; or when but half awake; or from being dazzled. **bák-chiu ien-n̄g**, id. **bák-chiu n̄g**, id. **bák-chiu n̄g-n̄g**, id. **bák-chiu-thâu ien-n̄g**, said of some very urgent matter in which we cannot bear delay, esp. being terribly short of money and quite unable to get any. **khoàⁿ kàu ien-n̄g**, to look till our eyes are dim.

ǹgh (= ng). **ǹgh-ǹgh-háu**, to whine. **ǹgh-ǹgh-kiò**, id.

ngá (R. id.), (C. ngé), elegant, as a literary composition. **bûn-ngá**, literary; polite; elegant. **put-ngá** (r.), unpolite.

ngá (Cn.), = A. á, suffix of many nouns; also, enclitic suffix in names of boys.

pē-ngá, = A. pē-kiáⁿ, father and son. **to-ngá**, a son. **to-ngá**, a knife. **tsa-bó-ngá**, a daughter.

hoan-ngá, a foreigner.

hoan--ngá, the boy called "hoan."

ngáiⁿ — **gî-ngáiⁿ**, to doubt; to feel suspicion.

ngáiⁿ (T.), = A. géng, to grind.

ngáiⁿ (T.), = A. géng. **gêng-ngáiⁿ**, the dragon's-eye or lung-yen fruit.

ngāiⁿ (T.), = A. gāi, impediment, &c.

ngām, = gām. **ngām-á-hî**, a small fish.

ngâu (R. id.), one of the eight diagrams. **liòk-ngâu**, id.

ngâu (R. gô), to stew or boil to a jelly. **ngâu-ko**, to make (medicines or preserves) into a jelly. **ngâu ióh-ko**, make a medicinal jelly. **ngâu-ka**, to manufacture glue or gelatine. **ngâu-kut**, to boil bones to a jelly. **ngâu-iû**, to melt fat slowly in order to purify it.

ngâuⁿ (T.), = gâu. **bô-ngâuⁿ-kún**, no joke; quite a serious matter.

ngáu — **ngáu-ngáu-pūi**, barking away, as a dog.

ngāu (= ngáuh). **ngāu-ngāu-háu**, grumbling secretly in a low tone of voice.

ngāu [R. id., by change of tone from "lòk," to rejoice], (Cn.), = gāu, fond of —, to delight in —, as pleasure, good or bad. **ngāu sio-chiú**, fond of spirits.

ngāu [R. ngó]. **liân-ngāu**, water-lily roots.

ngāu-tsat, id., sliced and prepared with honey. **ngāu-hún**, powder made from water-lily roots; said also of arrow-root.

ngauh, to catch in the mouth, as a dog does.

ngauh [R. ngé, a pair]. **chit-ngauh**, a pair in lasciviousness. **chit-ngauh-hāu** (lit. a pair of king-crabs), said of unnatural lust.

ngáuh (cf. ngāu). **ngáuh-ngáuh-háu**, to grumble; to show dissatisfaction by indistinct words when afraid to speak out. **ngáuh-ngáuh-kiò**, id. **ngáuh-ngáuh-liām**, id. **toà-teh-ngáuh**, standing grumbling so.

ngáuh — **lòh-ngáuh**, to agree well together, as relatives, or as men working together.

ngáuhⁿ — **tāng-ngáuhⁿ**, a sort of frog that makes a very loud noise.

ngέⁿ (C.), = A. ngá, elegant; polite.

ngε̄ⁿ (C.), = A. ngīⁿ, hard; stiff.

ngεh, = ngoeh (R. kiap), (C. T. only ngεh; Cn. ngöeh), to take up with pincers or chopsticks, &c. **ngεh-á**, = ngoeh-á, pincers; tongs; splints for setting a fracture. **tiah-ngεh** (esp. T.), nippers; pincers. **bák-bâi-bé ngεh hō-sîn**, the wrinkles at the outer corner of his eyes could catch flies (said of a wrinkled old man).

ngεh (C.), = A. ngoeh, pods of peas, beans, &c.

ngèh, = ngöeh (R. hiàp), (C. ngὲh; Cn. ngöeh), to carry under the arm; to catch with toes, or between the knuckles, &c. **ngèh-khi-tiâu**, take it firmly (in that way). **chîm-kóng-ngèh**, surrounding an army or troop by two bodies of soldiers, like crab's claws.

ńgh — **ńgh-ńgh-háu**, to whine. **ńgh-ńgh-kiò**, id.

ngīⁿ (R. gēng, kēng), (C. ngε̄ⁿ), hard; stiff; daring; determined not to yield a jot; strong, as wind.

ngīⁿ-ńg, hard and soft; firm and yielding. **poàⁿ-ngīⁿ-ńg**, at due medium between too much firmness and too much yielding. **chiáh-ngīⁿ**, **bô chiáh-ńg**, quite determined not to yield in the least.

ngīⁿ tú-ngīⁿ, neither party willing to give in the very least. **ngīⁿ-chhiú**, determined to have the quarrel out; will not make any compromise in the feud. **ngīⁿ-sèng**, very stiff temper. **ngīⁿ-phiah**, id. **ngīⁿ-sim**, id.; heart hard and unrelenting. **sim-koaⁿ khah-ngīⁿ-thih**, heart harder than iron (in the sense of showing no pity, or refusing to make up a dispute). **sim-koaⁿ khah-ngīⁿ-chiòh**, do. than stone. **kiông-pâng ngīⁿ-kak**, the most powerful section of the most powerful division of a clan.

giám-ngīⁿ, strong, lusty, and bold (as a strong young man); powerful; stiff, as a bamboo or piece of wood. **chhùi-thâu giám-ngīⁿ**, doggedly determined, as refusing to make up a quarrel, or determined to get a great deal of money out of people. **chhùi-thâu ngīⁿ**, id.

ngīⁿ-liâu, sailing as near the wind as possible (v. liâu). **sái-ngīⁿ-phìⁿ**, to sail right on, on one tack, with a strong wind; very dogged and obstinate, listening neither to advice nor entreaty. **liáh-ngīⁿ-phìⁿ**, id. (both senses).

ngīⁿ-chiàn, to recommend very urgently for employment. **ngīⁿ-pó**, very urgently demand to be accepted as bail or security for a man accused (v. pó).

ngīⁿ-khì, very honest; of great integrity; very open, blunt, straightforward, or plain-speaking; not afraid to tell a man his faults to his face (dist. gī-khì). **ngīⁿ-tit**, straightforward, and not afraid to give offence (v. tit).

ngīⁿ-liau, too stiff and hard (v. liau). **chhe-ngīⁿ**, too hard and rough, as cloth or fur; too stiff in form, as written or printed characters. **ngīⁿ-chhák**, too stiff, as fur, or as language. **ngīⁿ-chiāⁿ**, stiff, as starched cloth; strong, hardy, and ready for hard work. **ngīⁿ-háuhⁿ**, too hard, as cakes. **ngīⁿ-khàuh-khàuh**, too hard, as a couch, or as eatables; stiff with cold, as limbs.

ngīⁿ-niúⁿ, counting the tael at its exact weight, and allowing no discount. **ngīⁿ-tsoâⁿ**, a strong perennial spring that runs even in long drought. **ngīⁿ-piah**, a solid partition (v. piah). **ngīⁿ-tōe**, hard soil (shallow?). **ngε̄ⁿ-lō** (C.), = A. soaⁿ-lō, road by land.

chih-thâu ngīⁿ, speech thick and indistinct.

ngiâⁿ [R. gêng, to go out to receive ceremoniously], = giâ. **ngiâⁿ-chih**, to receive ceremoniously, as a visitor. **ngiâⁿ-sin khì-kū**, to take to the new and forsake the old; fickle. **ngiâⁿ-sàng**, to go out to meet on arrival, and accompany on departure; to treat with great respect.

ngiâⁿ-pút, to carry idols in procession. **ngiâⁿ-ang** (C.), id. **ngiâⁿ-hiuⁿ**, to carry incense in procession. **ngiâⁿ-gε̄** (C.), to carry a richly ornamented frame in idolatrous procession. **ngiâⁿ-tūi** (P.), id. **ngiâⁿ-teng**, to carry lamps in procession in honour of idols called "ông-iâ." **ngiâⁿ-sng-kàng**, the procession at the beginning of frost. **ngiâⁿ-hí-sîn**, procession of military mandarins in spring.

ngiáⁿ (Cn.), = A. á, final affix of some nouns, especially diminutive, = ngá.

ngiáh (R. gòk). **gông-ngiáh**, very much astonished; suddenly surprised.

ngiau, to tickle. **ngiau-ngiau**, sensation of tickling. **nâ-âu-tóe ngiau-ngiau**, feeling of irritation in throat, as when about to cough or to vomit. **ùi-ngiau**, easily tickled. **bōe-ùi-ngiau**, not easily tickled. **ùi-ngiau kiaⁿ-bó**, a henpecked husband. **ùi-ngiau-chháu**, the sensitive plant.

ngiáu (cf. giauh, ngiáuhⁿ). **ngiáu-ngiáu**, unintelligible, as foreign speech or indistinct talk; the sound of a dog's bark. **kóng-ōe ngiáu-ngiáu**, to talk indistinctly and unintelligibly.

ngiauh (cf. kiāu, kiauh), (T. kiauh), to prise up with a lever; to lift a small thing with the finger-nail; to carry *one* load on the end of a pole over the shoulder; to give a gentle stroke with an oar; an upstroke in writing. **ngiauh lâng-ê-phái**ⁿ, to bring up a man's faults. **ngiauh pát-lâng khí**, to get another man put out of his situation. **ngiauh--chit-ē**, to give a gentle stroke with an oar, &c. **ngiauh han-tsû**, to dig potatoes. **ngiauh--khí-lâi**, to rise up from lying down; to lift up things, as in searching for something, &c.

ngiauh — **ngiauh--lah**, he is dead and gone (said of a man). **hit-ê-lâng ngiauh--khì**, id. **ngiauh-hê**, id. (lit. as dead as a shrimp). **ngiauh-than**, id. (as shell-fish).

lāu-ngiauh-ngiauh, worn out and useless, as a feeble old man.

ngiauh (cf. khiàu), to protrude the lips. **ngiauh-tûn**, upper lip naturally turned up. **chhùi-tûn ngiauh-ngiauh**, id. **ngiauh-chhùi** (T. kiah-chhùi), to protrude the lips, as a secret sign.

ngiáuhⁿ — **ōe-ngiáuhⁿ**, still able to move by a muscular twitching, as animal not quite dead.

ngiáuh^{n}-ngiáuh^{n}-chhoah, to tremble with fear. **ngiáuh^{n}-ngiáuh^{n}-tsùn**, id. **ngiáuh^{n}-ngiáuh^{n}-tāng**, to be in constant motion; always at work; restless.

ngih^{n}-ngih^{n} ngiáuh^{n}-ngiáuh^{n}, restless motion, or sound of it (as of child or animal); indistinct talking, as of men secretly consulting, or of a man displeased, but unwilling or afraid to speak openly. **ngiáuh^{n}-ngiáuh^{n}-háu**, unintelligible talk, as of a foreign language, or of many confused voices. **ngiáuh^{n}-ngiáuh^{n}-liām**, to talk indistinctly, as when making light of a thing.

sán-ngiáuh^{n}-ngiáuh^{n}, very lean and emaciated.

ngih^{n} (cf. khih, gih). **ngih^{n}-ngih^{n} ngiáuh^{n}-ngiáuh^{n}**, in restless motion; talking with intentional indistinctness (v. ngiáuh^{n}).

ngió (Cn.), = A. ngó͘ (R.), image; suddenly.

ngiu^{n} (C.) **pe̍h-gîn-ngiu^{n}**, = pe̍h-jîn-hiu^{n}, a sort of tree (v. hiu^{n}).

ngiú^{n} [R. jiú, to bend]. **tsūn-thâu ngiú^{n}-tāu**, to shake about one's head and neck, as disobedient boy, or as light and ill-behaved girl.

ngiú^{n} (Cn.), = A. iú^{n}, thin tiles.

ngô͘, = gô͘. **pe̍h-ngô͘**, a large white fish (v. gô͘).

ngô͘ (R. gô͘). **ngô͘-tông**, = gô͘-tông, a sort of tree.

ngô͘ (R. gô͘). **ngô͘-tsu-jû**, a medicine, said to be heating; so called because brought from the country anciently called Gô͘ (Woo).

ngô͘ (R. gô͘). **ngô͘-khî**, the leech.

ngô͘ (T. gô͘). **âu-ngô͘**, a very dangerous swelling of the glands of the throat (cancerous?), gen. fatal in about a week. **nâ-âu-ngô͘**, id. **si^{n} âu-ngô͘**, to have this fatal disease; often said in swearing or adjuring, that this deadly disease may come on the lying throat. **siang-ngô͘**, this disease when there is a swelling on each side of the throat.

ngô͘ (R. gô͘, ngô͘). **goa̍t-lí siông-ngô͘**, the beautiful lady in the moon (said of a beauty). **kiong-ngô͘**, female slaves, &c., of the empress (v. kiong).

ngô͘ (R. gô͘, ngô͘). **goân-ngô͘** (R.), two ancient animals like turtles (v. goân).

ngô͘ (R. gô͘, ngô͘). **í-ngô͘ thoân-ngô͘**, error (as a false report, &c.), spread from one to another, and so on.

ngó͘ [R. five, = col. gō͘]. **ngó͘-lō͘-lâng**, men from all parts. **ngó͘-tè**, five idols with three eyes (v. tè). **toan-ngó͘**, the 5.5. **toan-ngó͘-jit**, id. **ngó͘-lûn**, the five relations of men. **ngó͘-siông**, id. (v. siông). **ngó͘-ho̍k**, the five degrees of relationship (v. ho̍k). **ngó͘-hok**, the five blessings (v. hok). **sam-koan ngó͘-hok**, to look over and over very carefully. **ngó͘-kok**, the five grains. **ngó͘-keng**, the five classics (v. keng). **ngó͘-hêng**, the five elements. **ngó͘-sek**, the five colours, variegated (v. sek). **ngó͘-chhái-hûn**, variegated clouds (v. chhái). **ngó͘-hong-kî**, five-coloured flags, either on one flag or one of each colour. **ngó͘-bī**, the five flavours (v. bī). **ngó͘-seng**, the five sorts of offerings. **ngó͘-koan**, the features of the face, with the ears (v. koan). **ngó͘-tsōng lio̍k-hú**, the internal organs. **ngó͘-chiam**, the five extremities of man or fowl (v. chiam).

ngó͘-toán-si^{n}, short and stout; hands, legs, and neck all short, but well-formed. **ngó͘-toán si^{n}-tiu^{n}**, id. **sip-ngó͘-im**, the native dictionary of the Chang-poo form of the Chang-chew dialect. **ngó͘-ka-phî**, a medicine (v. ka, to increase).

ngó͘ [R. a rank, properly of five men], a surname. **iâ^{n}-ngó͘**, the garrison at station of military mandarin (v. iâ^{n}). **tūi-ngó͘**, ranks of soldiers; rank and file. **tūi-ngó͘ chéng-tsôe**, ranks in good order. **bô-tūi bô-ngó͘**, not keeping good order, as troops.

hāng-ngó͘, gaudy.

tsāi-ngó͘, calm, self-possessed, and collected, as in danger or before a mandarin or superior.

ngó͘ (R. id.), a cyclical character, = gō͘ (mid-day). **ngó͘-sî** (R.), from 11 A.M. to 1 P.M. **tiong-ngó͘**, noon; 12 o'clock at noon. **tsú-ngó͘**, midnight and mid-day; quite straight opposite; the pole-star. **tsú-ngó͘-chhi^{n}**, the pole-star. **tsú-ngó͘ tùi-chhiong**, quite opposed in purposes and desires. **kap-goá tsú-ngó͘-chhiong**, quite opposed to me in desires and wishes. **bô-chiàu tsú-ngó͘**, doing things in an improper way, not according to proper rules. **bô-tsú-ngó͘**, id.

ngó͘-bûn (r.), the side-doors near the front of a palace.

ngó͘ [R. I, me, = col. goá]. **bô-jî^{n}-ngó͘**, without partiality for one's self; quite fairly and honestly, making no distinction between you and myself. **kap-lí bô-jî^{n}-ngó͘**, I act quite openly and honestly towards you, without any deceit. **bô-hun jî^{n}-ngó͘**, having complete community of interests and desires. **put-chhut ngó͘ sé-liāu**, it does not differ the least from what I reckoned before.

ngó͘ (R. id.) **ngó͘-gèk**, disobedient to parents.

ngó͘ (R. id.) **ngó͘-hî**, a good sort of fish (mullet?). **it, ngó͘: jī, âng-sa: sa^{n}, chhiu^{n}: sì, bé-ka**, the "ngó͘" is the best of fish; the second, third, and fourth best are —, &c.

ngó͘ (R. id.), (Cn. ngió). **ngó͘-siōng** (R.), a human image; an idol. **ngó͘-chhiāng** (C.), id.

ngó͘-jiên, by chance; suddenly and unexpectedly. **ngó͘-gū-jiên**, id. **ngó͘-gū--tio̍h**, to meet with unexpectedly. **ngó͘-jiên-thia^{n}**, to hear by chance.

ngō͘^{n} [R. gō, to starve]. **jím-ki siū-ngō͘^{n}**, to endure hunger patiently and willingly. **tham-chhōng chiâ^{n} ngō͘^{n}-kúi**, a glutton becomes a hungry ghost.

ngō͘ — **ông-ngō͘**, a pettifogging lawyer; a literary man who is always engaged in lawsuits or inciting and assisting others in them. **tsòe-ngō͘**, to be such a character.

ngō͘ [R. gō͘, to awake]. **hiáu-ngō͘**, to understand; to come to understand. **hóe-ngō͘**, to repent. **chip-bê put-ngō͘**, doggedly persisting in his wicked ways.

ngō͘ [R. gō, proud]. **kiau-ngō͘**, proud. **kù-ngō͘**, proud and uncivil in bearing, *e.g.* taking no notice when we go in, or rude in not answering when spoken to.

ngoeh (R. kiap), (C.T. ngeh; Cn. ngóeh; A. ngeh, ngoeh), to take up with tongs, chop-sticks, pincers, &c. **ngoeh-á**, pincers. **hé-ngoeh**, tongs with curved points.

ngoeh (R. kiap), (C. ngeh, keh; T. koeh). **tāu-ngoeh**, pods of beans or pease, including the pease or beans. **toā-ngoeh**, large pod. **sòe-ngoeh**, small pod. **chit-ngoeh**, one pod (entire).

ngóeh (R. kiap, hiáp), (T. nge̍h), (cf. nge̍h, khóeh), to catch or squeeze, as between claws of a crab, or knuckles, or a half-split piece of wood; to hold tight, as with pincers; to carry a thing under the arm or between the arm and the breast; to hold tightly, as a package strapped between two bamboo poles to be carried; to lie between two places (as a region), filling up the intermediate space; (the supports of a flag-staff; an instrument for torture).

khit-chhâ ngóeh--tio̍h, to be caught by a half-split piece of wood. **ngóeh--tio̍h**, id., or as by a crab. **ngóeh--khí-lâi**, to pull out, as a tooth. **ngóeh-oá**, the two halves (as of pincers) uniting. **siang-pêng ngóeh-oá**, id. **n̄g-pún sa^n-ngóeh**, two open books half-shut so as to keep each other open. **ngóeh-phoà**, to break by pressing, as between the knuckles, or as fruit or eggs crowded together.

keng-thâu ngóeh-ngóeh, the shoulders high, either naturally so, or from leanness, or from opium-smoking. **kiu-kiu ngóeh-ngóeh**, having a shrinking frightened manner.

ngóeh kha-bák, to torture the ankles by a sort of wooden screw or vice. **pàng-ngóeh**, to take off that torturing instrument from the feet. **kî-koa^n-ngóeh**, the stone supports on each side of a flag-staff. **kiáu-kùn chhêng kî-koa^n-ngóeh**, a skilful gambler become so poor that he has to crouch for shelter between these supports for lack of clothes.

ngúi^n (Cn.), = A. géng, to grind.

O.

Including **o͘** and ö.

o͘ is by others written **o'**.

Many words in **o** are by others written with **w**, *e.g.* oa, oa^n, oai, oai^n, oan, oang, oa̍h, oa̍k, oa̍ih^n, oat, in their various tones. In these words the **o** must not be pronounced too strongly, and it often approaches very near **w**.

O [R. a nest; a den; a hole; cf. col. o͘, u]. **iàn-o**, edible birds'-nests. **o-ka**, a receiver of stolen goods.

lap-o, situation, as of a house, lower than the surrounding ground; a considerable piece of ground lower than the rest, as among hills.

O (C.) **tiàu-o**, = A. tiàu-o͘, a well-sweep for raising water.

O [R. hô, the water-lily]. **o-hoe**, the water-lily. **o-liên** (R.), id.

O [R. ho, name of vegetable, = col. e], (Cn. ö). **tang-o**, parsley. **tang-o-chhài**, id.

O [R. oa, name of a person], (Cn. o͘). **lú-o**, the lady who made or mended the heavens with mosaic-work. **lú-o niû^n-niû^n**, id.

O (Cn. kho), to bake (as a fowl), as in an oven with no water, or with only a very little sauce. **o-koe**, to bake a fowl thus. **o-ah**, to bake a duck so (&c.) **tsáp-o-ki^n**, odds-and-ends of food (remnants) mixed and made up as a condiment.

O [R. an exclamation; to assent; to flatter]. **o-ló**, to praise. **o-sī** (Cn.), id., rather flattering. **i-o** (Cn. i-o͘), to follow or assent to another implicitly. **i-o chiông-sū**, to follow another's guidance implicitly without inquiring whether it be right or wrong (generally wrong). **kap--i tàu-i-o**, id.

o-bî-tô-hu̍t, Amida Buddha.

chhùi o-o-háu, calling out loud, as child, or as man in great delight or not in his right mind. **o--lah**, exclamation made by the first of several men working together, which the rest answer by crying "e--lah." **o-le** (C.), phrase used in beginning a sentence.

Ô (R. hô), an oyster (classifier mi^n). **ô-khak**, oyster-shells. **ô-khak-he**, lime from oyster-shells. **ô-kià^n-thang**, a window made with oyster-shells. **ô-kià^n-thang-teng**, a lantern made with them. **ô-te-chì^n**, oysters, rice, &c., fried in a mass. **ô-á-bê**, oysters boiled with rice. **ô-á-lìn**, preparation of oysters and potato-starch. **ô-á-tau**, do. boiled to a paste. **toā-mī^n-ô**, a large oyster. **phoà-ô**, to gather oysters. **ô-lin** (T.), a round red sea-slug.

Ô (cf. kô). **nńg-ô-ô**, very soft.

Ó (R. id.) **ó-á**, a bridal dress. **âng-ó**, id. **sin-niû^n-ó**, id. **siù-ó**, embroidered do. **ó-á-kûn**, upper and lower bridal-dress. **bóng-ó**, sort of female dress embroidered with dragons, worn by mandarins' wives and at marriages of the wealthy.

toā-ó, Tauist priest's robe embroidered with dragons, used at the most solemn ceremonies. **sió-ó**, dress of Tauist priest at usual rites. **sai-kong-ó**, red, black, or yellowish green robe of Tauist priest. **hê-siū^n-ó**, robe of a Buddhist priest for some rites. **pô-chiá gûn-ó**, paper mock money and figures of dresses cut out in paper and burned in bundles by women in the worship of the goddess of child-birth.

Ó, exclamation used in calling to another, esp. when his name is not known. **ó-ó**, id.

Ó (C.), = A. ut. **kha ó--tio̍h**, foot sprained. **ó--khì**, id. **ām ó--khì** (= ut--tio̍h), neck stiff and painful, as from sleeping in a constrained position.

Ò — **âi--ò**, an exclamation of sudden pain or grief (v. âi).

Ò — **ò-soà^n**, to twirl the state umbrella when idols meet and salute each other. **kap-i ū-ò-soà^n**, to have friendly relations with him. **goá kap-i bô-ò-soà^n**, I have no dealings with him.

Ò — **ò-giô**, a fruit like a small fig. **ò-giô-tàng**, a gelatinous dish made from its seeds, much used in summer.

Ò [R. a harbour; an anchorage; a dock, = col. ù]. **ò-kah**, the overseer of a harbour. **tsûn-ò** (esp. T.), = A. tsûn-ù, a dock.

lâm-ò, Namoa.

Ò (R. id.) **ò-biāu**, mysterious and profound. **chhim-ò** (r.), id.

Ò (Cn.) **ò-hî**, = A. pe̍h-hî, a sort of fish. **ò-siū^n**, = A. kiâm-pe̍h-hî, id., salted.

O͘ (C. o). **tiàu-o͘**, a well-sweep for raising water, like the Egyptian shaduf. **chhiū^n tiàu-o͘**, to draw water with a well-sweep. **khiā tiàu-o͘**, to set up a well-sweep at first. **o͘-thiāu**, the fixed pillar of the well-sweep. **o͘-tháng**, its bucket. **o͘-thiu**, the thin bamboo by which the bucket hangs. **o͘-koa^n**, id. **o͘-koa^n-chhìn**, this thin bamboo and the movable arm or beam. **o͘-chhìn**, the beam or arm of the well-sweep which moves on the pivot. **tek-o͘**, id. **chhiū^n tek-o͘** (T.), to draw water with it.

O͘ [R. an interjection]. **o͘-ho͘** (R.), an interjection used in lamenting for the dead (v. ho͘).

O͘ — **o͘-lô-pa**, Europe. **o͘-ló-pà**, id.; cotton goods. **o͘-ló-pà-éng** (lit. European), sort of cotton goods.

o͘ [R. o, a nest or den]. **o͘-ka**, a receiver of stolen goods.

o͘ [R. name of a place], a surname.

o͘ (Cn.), = A. o, a depression, as in the ground.

o͘ (Cn.), = A. o. **lú-o͘**, = A. lú-o, the lady who made or mended the sky.

o͘ (Cn.), = A. o. **i-o͘ chiông-sū**, to follow another implicitly, right or wrong. **o͘-bí-tô͘-hu̍t**, invocation of Buddha.

o͘ (in Tiô-thoà), = A. ng, young rice.

o͘ (R. id.), black. **o͘-sek**, id. **kan-o͘**, deep dark black without any gloss. **o͘-kim**, shining black or dark colour; getting on well in the world (v. kim). **o͘-sàⁿ-nàⁿ**, black, glossy, and shining. **o͘-khâm-khâm**, all black or dark with crowds of men, &c. (v. khâm). **o͘-maⁿ-maⁿ**, very dirty and black; very dark, as place with no light. **o͘-màⁿ-màⁿ**, very black. **o͘-lúi-lúi**, id. **o͘-kúi-kúi**, very black, as person (lit. like a demon), (+). **o͘-kuih-kuih**, id. **o͘-niauⁿ-niauⁿ**, very black, dirty, or spotted (v. niauⁿ). **o͘-bák-bák**, very black (+). **o͘-thih-thih**, id. **o͘-tiù-tiù**, id. **o͘-tè-tè**, id. **o͘-lô-sô**, id. **o͘-sô-sô**, id. **o͘-lái**, dirty dark reddish colour. **o͘-tè**, dark and dull, as red; spotted and dirty (v. tè). **o͘-sien**, grayish black. **o͘-tēng**, having a dark complexion and face somewhat lean, or at least not fat. **o͘-tâ**, dark appearance of face when in bad health. **o͘-khiėt**, dark coloured, as face naturally so, and not unwell. **bīn o͘-khoáⁿ**, face covered with large black spots, as old man. **o͘-áu**, black and withered, as leaves; black and beaten, as man. **phah-o͘-chhiⁿ**, to beat black and blue. **phah kàu o͘-bah-lēng**, to beat so as to leave long dark marks of stripes. **o͘-âng-bīn**, face painted black and red, as in plays or processions. **o͘-bīn-lâng**, a black man, as negro or Malay, &c. **o͘-bīn-ông** (C.), an idol whose face got black from choking on a fowl.

o͘-bák, black ink (+). **o͘-bák**, ebony. **o͘-bák-tsoâ**, a short black venomous snake; said also of a very dangerous man. **o͘-phiáh**, well-burned bricks. **o͘-hun**, opium. **o͘-bí pėh-bí**, opium and rice (said of the two wants of an opium-smoker). **o͘-kun**, a black scarf worn as head-dress by women (v. kun). **o͘-âng-bō**, the four lictors of a mandarin, two with black caps and two with red. **o͘-thn̂g**, unrefined sugar in its coarsest form, raw sugar. **o͘-jîn**, the iris of the eye.

o͘-kúi, an under-clerk or assistant-salesman in shop (said only by the man himself), (+). **tng o͘-kúi**, I am an assistant in a shop. **tng--lâng o͘-kúi**, id. **o͘-kúi-á** (vulg.), a black man.

hun-o͘, black with smoke; to blacken with smoke. **o͘-àm**, dark, as room or night; incipient giddiness. **o͘-àm-hîn**, dizzy; giddy; giddiness. **o͘-àm pėh-pāng**, calamity coming suddenly. **o͘-ien pėh-pāng**, id. (v. pėh). **thiⁿ o͘-im**, sky overcast and rainy-looking (v. im). **thiⁿ o͘-o͘**, id. **thiⁿ tsòe-o͘**, id. **sì-tsa̍p-káu-jit-o͘**, 49 days of rainy weather in spring. **hâⁿ-o͘**, when it is nearly dark in the evening. **o͘-kha sai-lâm**, a very black south-west storm (v. sai). **o͘-kha** (C.), water just beginning to ebb.

sim-koaⁿ o͘, fond of injuring people.

tùi-o͘, to hit the mark. **ko͘-o͘**, the best throw of the lién-pó gambling, the cash being found opposite the word "pó" on the die.

o͘-a, a crow (v. a). **o͘-hí**, a fish like trout. **o͘-á-hí**, id. **kiâm-tsúi-o͘**, id., from the sea (best). **chiáⁿ-tsúi-o͘**, id., from fresh water (inferior). **o͘-îⁿ**, a black coloured skate-fish. **o͘-lak**, a long gray sea-slug. **o͘-liông**, a small black cricket. **o͘-á**, a small dark sweet Arbutus (Myrica) at end of season. **o͘-á-m̂**, id. **lák-gėh-o͘**, a dark red fruit. **siù-o͘**, a plant taken (internally) to make the hair black. **chhó-o͘**, aconite.

ô͘ (cf. o͘, a well-sweep). **ô͘-nâⁿ**, a cradle, usually made of bamboo.

ô͘ (R. hô͘), a jar (wide-mouthed), especially an earthen jar. **ô͘-ô͘**, shaped like a jar, deeply concave. **chhim-ô͘**, deeply concave, as a bowl. **tô͘-ô͘**, a game of throwing sticks into a jar. **tê-ô͘**, a covered bowl for infusing tea. **sai-ô͘**, a small coarse earthen jar with the figure of a lion as the handle on the lid. **kám-ô͘**, a large deep wicker vessel for holding rice, &c. **tâng-ô͘**, a brass jar, such as used to be made a clepsydra. **jiō-ô͘**, a chamber-pot. **kim-hî-ô͘**, a large earthenware tub from Shanghai, such as is used for a bath-tub (lit. for gold-fish). **chit-ô͘ kim-hî bōe-kham--tit chit-bé tiong-pan**, one bad intriguing fellow causes trouble in a whole household.

ô͘, to work an oar backwards; to row backwards. **ô͘--lâi**, back your oars! as when in risk of collision.

ô͘ (R. hô͘), a surname.

ô͘ (R. hô͘), a lake; a roundish or basin-shaped valley or small plain. **hīⁿ-ô͘**, a cavity in a large ink-stone for writing large characters. **khoàⁿ-ô͘**, a sort of gambling with cards. **poáh-khoàⁿ-ô͘**, id.

ô͘-lâm, the province of Hoo-nan. **ô͘-pak**, Hoo-peh province. **ô͘-kńg**, the old province of Hoo-kwang, now divided into these two. **ô͘-pit**, pencils from Hoo-chow. **ngó͘-ô͘ sù-hái**, the great lakes and rivers. **sam-kang ngó͘-ô͘** (R.), the great rivers and lakes. **kiâⁿ-kang-ô͘ ô͘-lâng**, travelling quacks, fortune-tellers, &c. **kóng-ōe kang-ô͘**, careful to avoid phrases that would give offence, *e.g.* avoiding any proverb alluding to step-mothers in a house where there is a stepmother. **put-chí kang-ô͘**, id.

ô͘ [R. hô͘, name of a plant]. **chhâ-ô͘**, a root used for feverish colds (Radix Bupleuri octoradiati?).

ó͘, to prize up with a lever; to take up, as roots, by a trowel or spade, or by the hand; to scoop out, as eyes. **ó͘--khí-lâi**, to prize up things, or lift roots. **ó͘--chhut-lâi**, to scoop out, as eye. **ó͘ han-tsû**, to take up a few potatoes. **ó͘ bák-chiu**, to scoop out an eye.

ó͘ (Cn.) **ó͘-káu**, = A. é-káu, dumb.

ò͘ [R. id., by change of tone from "ok," bad, = òⁿ]. **è-ò͘**, unclean; to defile (v. è). **ò͘-tò͘**, to envy. **khó-ò͘**, odious; abominable. **chhek-ò͘**, to insult the majesty of a divinity by unclean conduct, or by placing something ceremonially unclean in his presence; to cause bad luck by unclean conduct (morally or ceremonially), esp. by things connected with a woman's confinement. **chhek-ò͘ thiⁿ-tōe**, to offend heaven and earth by unclean conduct. **chhek-ò͘-kúi**, said to a man beginning to talk some very vile lascivious talk, or bringing in some vile stinking thing, or of man coming in stark naked. **khit--lâng chhek-ò͘--tióh**, to meet with bad luck by coming upon some ill-omened person or thing in a marriage, or such ceremony, which ought to be entirely auspicious.

ò͘ (Cn.) **ò͘-biāu**, = A. ò-biāu, mysterious.

ō͘ (R. ū), taro. **pėh-ō͘**, a white sort. **âng-ō͘**, a sort with reddish skin. **tek-ō͘**, taper-pointed sort. **pin-nn̂g-ō͘**, a sort common at Amoy, much sold in halves ready boiled. **káu-tôe-ō͘**, another sort. **tsúi-ō͘**, a wild plant like taro, used medicinally and for feeding pigs: the leaves are used for wrapping things; sometimes grown in ponds as shelter for gold fish, &c. **ko͘-**

pô-o͘, a wild plant like taro, medicinal. **káu-kā-o͘** (Cn.), a sort used medicinally. **o͘-hoāi^{n}-si**, a stringy plant used in making cakes. **o͘-pû** (T.), = A. hoe-táu-pû, a sort of gourd.

o͘-pêng, taro cut in halves, sold ready cooked. **o͘-ké**, cakes made with rice and taro. **o͘-thâu**, a whole full-sized root of taro, the original root of a cluster. **o͘-bú**, the original root of a cluster. **o͘-pô**, id. **o͘-kiá^{n}**, the young tubers. **o͘-á**, id.

o͘ (C.) **lām-sám o͘--lâng**, to raise or repeat false evil reports against a man.

o͘ (C.) **sio-o͘**, to assist a man with whom another is quarrelling.

o͘^{n} — **o͘^{n}-i^{n}**, sound used in lulling a child to sleep.

ò͘^{n} — **kap-lâng-ò͘^{n}**, to haggle about payment after buying. **ò͘^{n}-ò͘^{n}-háu**, to talk indistinctly, as in a great hurry for something urgent, or as man half asleep. **ì^{n}-ì^{n} ò͘^{n}-ò͘^{n}**, to talk indistinctly, as from great haste, or from malformation of mouth or throat making an impediment, or from unwillingness to say some unpleasant truth, or ask something distasteful; to wrangle doggedly. **ì^{n}-ò͘^{n}**, to talk unintelligibly; to dispute about payment after the thing is bought. **tāi-ke ì^{n}-ò͘^{n}**, disputing doggedly, each denying what the other says. **toà-teh-ò͘^{n}**, id. **ò͘^{n}-ò͘^{n}-kiò**, noisy disputing or wrangling. **ò͘^{n}-ò͘^{n}-háu**, id.; also, to talk unintelligibly, as in sudden hurry, &c. **ò͘^{n}-ò͘^{n}-jióng**, very noisy disputing.

ò͘^{n} [R. ò, to hate; by change of tone from "ok," bad]. **khó-ò͘^{n}**, odious; abominable. **iàm-ò͘^{n}**, to loathe. **oàn-ò͘^{n}**, to loathe and abhor. **ò͘^{n}-tò**, to envy.

ö (T. Cn.), in several words in the several tones, = A. e, esp. when the Changchew dialect changes to "oe."

ö (T.) **ö-lô**, = A. e-lê, fretful and troublesome.

ö (Cn.) **tang-ö-chhài**, = A. tang-e-chhài, parsley.

ö̆ (Cn.) **ö̆--tio̍h**, to infect.

oa [R. a frog]. **chéng-tí-oa** (a frog at bottom of a well), said of an inexperienced fellow.

oa (C.), = A. oāi^{n}, a large branch of a tree, especially one of the primary divisions of the trunk.

oa [R. a beautiful woman]. **hā-oa** (X.), Eve.

oâ [R. hô, what? which?], a surname. **oâ--chhù**, a town on Amoy island.

bô-tā-oâ, having no other resource; having no alternative; cannot help it. **bô-tāi-oâ** (C.), id. **bô-tā-tit-oâ**, id. **bô-hoat--i tā-oâ**, id. **bô-hoat--lâng tā-oâ**, have no resource against some one. **sái-hoat--goá tāi-oâ** (C.), what ever can I do!

oá — **phē-oá**, a sort of crab. **pō-oá** (T.), id.

oá [R. í, to lean upon], (Cn. oá, ūi^{n}), to lean upon; to rely or depend upon; to incline to; near; to come near; to join or attach one's self to; to come up to very near a sum, as a subscription or value. **sa^{n}-oá**, to lean on or draw near one another; to be very close or near, as two places; to combine for some purpose. **sa^{n}-oá-pn̄g**, to live together, as man and woman without any form of marriage.

khah-oá, nearer. **lī oá-oá**, not far off. **oá-ì**, nearly correct, as a guess. **oá-ūn**, to guess or come near the mark; to rhyme (v. ūn). **oá-ōng khoà^{n}-miā^{n}**, saying that a man has good luck when he is manifestly prospering. **oá sa^{n}-tsa̍p**, nearly thirty. **oá n̄ng-tiám-cheng**, near two o'clock; nearly two hours. **oá-hái**, near the sea. **oá-piah**, near the wall; leaning on the wall of a room, as an article of furniture. **chē oá-hé**, to sit near the fire. **oá-pi^{n}**, to approach the side (v. pi^{n}). **giâ-oá--lâi**, to lift up and bring near, as a chair or table. **kha̍h-oá**, to close, as a door, but not fastened; to come close, as boat to shore or other boat. **sak-oá**, to push shut. **chhek-oá**, to press close, as on a man. **pek-oá**, to press near. **lâng tit-tit-oá**, people are crowding near and pressing on. **khiā-oá**, to stand close to the side, as of a road, to let one pass. **siám-oá**, to get out of the way, as by going close to a wall, or to side of road. **hâ-oá**, to tie loosely together. **ngoeh-oá** (= ngeh), to close, as pincers.

oá-hoā^{n}, to approach the river-bank or sea-wall (hoā^{n}), as boat. **oá-hoā^{n}**, to lean on for support, as widow or orphan (v. hoā^{n}, "to lean"). **lóng-bô oá-hoā^{n}**, quite away from the text, as a composition; offering a price still very far from what can be accepted.

oá-lâi oá-khì, of unstable purpose. **oá-khò**, to trust upon. **oá-loā**, to sorn on. **i-oá**, to rely upon; to trust upon. **bô-i-oá**, having no relations, &c., to depend upon for support or protection, as widow or orphan. **bô-i bô-oá**, id. **oá-sè**, to depend on another's influence and power. **oá-sì** (C.), id. **oá-i-chia̍h**, to have one's meals cooked by him or his household, at our own expense. **oá-i-bōe**, to intrust goods to him (or them) to sell for us, as dealer or vessel. **oá-tsāi**, to give our goods to a Hong, &c., to be shipped for us (v. tsāi). **oá-hâng**, to deal with a Hong, as ship or dealer in produce, esp. to intrust whole cargo to them for sale. **tsûn oá-hâng**, the ship is consigned to the Hong, or does its business with it. **tsûn oá sím-mih^{n}-hâng**, with which Hong does the ship transact its business? **hâng oá-tsûn**, the Hong has vessels consigned to it. **hè oá--lâng**, to intrust goods to a commission agent to sell for us. **kui-oá**, to make submission and attach one's self to, as to an enemy in war, or as a party in a feud or lawsuit leaving his friends and going over to the other side; to attach one's self to a protector; to revert, as to one person, as property or business formerly shared by others. **kui-oá--i oân**, the (land) tax all falls to him to pay, *e.g.* the others who had shares having all died or left the place. **siang-pêng-oá**, trying to keep neutral. **si-koe, oá toā-pêng**, said of liking to follow the stronger side.

oà [R. àn, to lean, according to, = col. hoā^{n}, &c.], to lean heavily upon with the hand. **chhiú oà--i**, id. **seng-khu oà--i**, resting one's whole weight on it by the hand.

oà [R. hoat, to emit, send out, or produce]. **oà-he**, to slake lime.

oā [R. hoā, to paint]. **oā-kong**, a painter of pictures.

oā [R. jio̍k, if, as, = col. joā, loā]. **bô-oā**, not many; only a few or a little; not enough, as price offered.

oā [R. hoā, words; language, = col. ōe], (also C. = A. ōe, language). **oā put-tê-ki, poàn-kù to**, when what is said is not agreeable, half a sentence is too much (A.)

oā, to lay to, as a ship. **oā-i-sí**, to lay to so as not to move at all, or as little as possible. **oā-thâu-khiā**, id.

oa^{n} [R. an, a saddle]. **bé-oa^{n}**, a saddle. **bé-oa^{n}-tsū**, piece of leather put on horse's back below the saddle. **bé-oa^{n}-tîn**, the wild convolvulus, with purple flowers and saddle-shaped leaves, that grows on sandy banks; also a salve made from it. **oa^{n}-kiô**, the wooden body of a Chinese saddle. **koà-oa^{n}**, to wear a saddle. **lo̍k-kho̍k-bé, bô-koà-oa^{n}**, said of a fast young fellow, with no one to control him (v. kho̍k). **kim-oa^{n}**, a gilt saddle. **pėh-bé koȧ-kim-oa^n**, a white horse with a gilt saddle, said of the "chiōng-goân."

Oa^n [R. at, the bridge of the nose]. **phī^n-oa^n**, a high bridge of the nose, not usual among the Chinese. **bô phī^n-oa^n**, nose low and flat between the eyes, without any ridge. **phī^n-oa^n chih**, id.

Oa^n [R. an, peace], a surname. **tâng-oa^n**, Tungngan (or Tông-an) city or district. **lâm-oa^n**, Nanngan, or Nan-an. **oa^n-hái**, Anhai.

oa^n-pâi (T.), = A. an-pâi, arranged in order.

Oa^n, an anchorage. **oa^n-ù**, an open harbour, haven, or anchorage. **soa-oa^n**, a sandy beach suitable for landing. **pak-hong-oa^n**, a small bay sheltered from the north wind. **lâm-hong-oa^n**, id., sheltered from the south wind. **koa-oa^n**, to lie at a port or anchorage, as vessel. **kàu-oa^n**, to reach the anchorage, as vessel.

chit-oa^n-tsûn, the distance which junks usually make in one tide; *e.g.* from Amoy to Chiȯh-bé, or to Quemoy (kim-mn̂g).

Oâ^n (T.), to borrow.

Oá^n (R. oán), a bowl; a bowlful. **thâu-khak-oá^n**, a skull. **bȧk-chiu-oá^n**, the socket of the eye. **kau-hī-oá^n**, spoon-shaped end of ear-pick. **phêng-oá^n**, the scales of a balance. **tô-oá^n**, id. **thien-pêng-oá^n**, id., of large balance. **hé-oá^n**, a lamp with a large wick made of many wicks on a flat metal dish, used at plays. **tâu-á-oá^n**, a bowl for shaking dice. **iâ-oá^n**, a cocoa-nut cup. **kim-hî-oá^n**, a large sort of bowl. **toā-phín-oá^n**, a very large bowl. **oá^n-thâu**, a large bowl. **kèng-oá^n**, a set of offerings made in the rites of "chiò" (v. kèng).

oá^n-bō, a skull-cap. **oá^n-ko**, sort of small cakes (v. ko). **oá^n-thô**, clay for making bowls. **oá^n-iȯh**, a mineral used for glazing earthenware. **oá^n-u**, the hollow in the bottom of a bowl. **oá^n-kə-lėh**, the broken bottom of a bowl (v. kə). **oá^n-poâ^n**, bowls and plates. **oá^n-tih-tī**, bowls, small plates, and chopsticks.

phak-oá^n, to lay down a bowl inverted. **tàu-oá^n-giȧh**, to put in an inferior man or article to make up the set or required number. **chiȧh oá^n-lāi, kóng oá^n-goā**, to eat a man's food and speak ill of him behind his back. **chiȧh-kín, phah-phoȧ-oá^n**, more haste the less speed; to overreach one's self in seeking gain.

Oá^n [R. oán, some joints of the arm or leg, = col. oan]. **kha-thâu-oá^n**, the knee-pan. **kha-thâu-u-oá^n**, id. **chhiú-oá^n** (T.), the elbow-joint.

Oà^n [R. àn, a long table; the table before a judge; a legal case]. **oà^n-toh**, a long high narrow table, usually placed against a wall. **kong-oà^n-toh**, a mandarin's table of judgment. **hiu^n-oà^n-toh**, a long table for incense. **hiu^n-oà^n**, id. **tang-sai-oà^n**, the two priests (Tauist or Buddhist) on the right and left hand of the presiding priest at any ceremony.

tâng-oà^n, graduates who have taken the degree of Sewtsai at the same time. **khó kū-oà^n**, to examine the Sewtsai graduates of former year, after the other examinations.

Oà^n (R. àn), late; too late. **tsá-oà^n**, early and late, = tsá-àm (*q.v.*) **khah-oà^n chiah-lâi**, come later. **chiȧh-pn̄g-oà^n**, soon after breakfast. **toā-oà^n**, some time after breakfast, but before noon. **àm-oà^n-chiáu** (T.), = àm-kong-chiáu, a sort of owl.

Oā^n [R. hān, drought]. **toā-oā^n**, a very great drought. **khó-oā^n**, a great drought. **khə́-oā^n** (Cn.), id., = C. khòng-hān. **oā^n chin-hn̄g**, the drought extends over a vast region.

Oā^n (R. hoān), to change; to exchange; to shift. **sa^n-oā^n**, to change or exchange mutually. **oā^n-sin**, to change an old thing for a new one. **koh-oā^n**, to change over again, at least a second time. **tsài-oā^n**, id. **têng-tsài-oā^n**, id. **têng-oā^n**, id. **têng-thâu-oā^n**, id., completely over again.

kóe-oā^n, to change for the better; to correct (v. kóe). **piàn-oā^n**, to change. **pì^n-oā^n**, id. **tùi-oā^n**, to exchange; to barter. **pái-oā^n**, id. **kau-oā^n**, to exchange or interchange, as goods or documents. **thùi-oā^n**, to put an inferior article (or person) deceitfully in place of a better; to mend by putting in an entirely new piece (v. thùi). **thòe-oā^n** (C. thè), to change, as men doing work or holding office in succession. **lûn-liû thòe-oā^n**, do., in turn.

oā^n-âng, to put on one's usual dress again after mourning. **oā^n-sa^n**, to change one's dress, especially coat or jacket. **oā^n-kūi**, to change one's dress for the season. **oā^n-hoe**, rites to make a woman have male children instead of female; also visit of bride's younger brother, three days after marriage (v. hoe). **oā^n-chhiú**, to change hands, as house or land bought or mortgaged; to get a fresh hand, as in work or gambling; to change from one hand to the other, as in carrying a heavy basket. **oā^n-tsú**, to change owners, as house or land. **oā^n-pan**, to change garrison, guard, &c. (v. pan). **oā^n-ūi**, to alter one's place, office, &c.; to alter the place of a thing. **sa^n-oā^n-ūi**, to transpose or mutually change places. **oā^n kè-ūi**, to change the place, as of a thing or of one's residence. **oā^n-keng**, to change a load from one shoulder to another (v. keng). **oā^n-keng**, to change or move to another room. **oā^n pȧt-keng**, id. **oā^n-thiap**, to exchange cards in vowing perpetual friendship (v. thiap). **hè-oā^n-hè**, to barter. **oā^n-gûn**, to change a dollar, getting cash for it. **chí^n oā^n-gûn**, to give cash for silver. **oā^n ū-kè**, to change money at a good rate. **hó oā^n-phái^n**, to change good for bad. **goá kā-lí-oā^n phái^n-chí^n**, give me good cash for these bad ones.

oȧh (R. hoȧt), alive; living; often said in the sense of movable or active (in Chau-an district used meaning "to kindle," instead of "tȯh," which is not there used in that sense). **bōe-oȧh**, not alive; cannot live. **ōe-oȧh**, able to come to life or to remain alive; able to move, as the bolt of a door, or as the hand so placed as to move freely in writing. **koh-oȧh**, alive again. **koh-tsài-oȧh**, id.

khoà^n-oȧh, comfortable (in some parts of C. has rather a bad sense). **khoài^n-oȧh**, id. **khùi^n-oȧh** (Cn.), id. **hō͘ i-ê-sim oȧh**, to lead him to form expectations.

oȧh-tāng, active; lively; constantly moving; said of body or mind. **oȧh thiàu-thiàu**, strong and active, as a fish. **oȧh-kat**, a bow-knot. **oȧh-pán**, movable types. **sái oȧh-kúi**, to use contrivances with springs or secret wheels, &c. **oȧh-tsúi**, running water. **oȧh-tsoā^n**, a spring of flowing water.

oȧh-lō͘, a way of escape from death or imminent danger; a constant and regular employment or business. **bô-oȧh-lō͘**, having no regular business or employment, living on one's money or property. **ū oȧh-lō͘**, to have a regular business. **oȧh-lō͘-chí^n**, money got in a steady regular business, either on one's own account, or employed by others. **khui oȧh-lō͘**, to deliver from death or great danger; *e.g.* by forgiving a heavy debt that was just ruining him, or by opening a way of paying it. **hó i-khui chit-tiâu oȧh-lō͘**, by good fortune, he showed or gave a way of escape.

ká^n-sí-oȧh. not afraid of life or death (said of a daring robber or ruffian). **ká^n-sí ká^n-oȧh**, id. **beh-sí beh-oȧh**, pressing one's request or demand very urgently, as child that will take no denial, or as beggar or suppliant who will submit to any indignity and maltreatment to gain his desire; said also of a man very miserable, as in extremest poverty or having an enormous carbuncle, &c.; also, threatening to kill one's self. **pī^n kàu-beh-sí beh-oȧh**, disease very severe and dangerous, hanging between life and death. **chì^n-sí chì^n-oȧh**, to dispute most doggedly or determinedly, denying what is asserted. **sí-lâi oȧh-khì**, in great pain or distress. **pī^n kàu sí-lâi oȧh-khì**, sick almost to death. **boā kàu sí-lâi oȧh-khì**, toiling extremely hard. **chhut-sí jip-oȧh** (r.), to get from death to life. **sí-lâng oȧh-hó͘**, a dead man is like a living tiger, as much an object of fear. **sí-lâng i-kàu-oȧh, oȧh-lâng i-kàu-sí**, said of quackery. **oȧh-oȧh khó͘--sí**, to die of grief (lit. or fig.) **oȧh-oȧh chhoeh--sí**, id. **hō͘--i oȧh-oȧh khì--sí**, to make him terribly grieved and distressed at his conduct, *e.g.* a wicked son. **oȧh-oȧh phah--sí**, to kill outright, as a child.

oai, crooked; awry; distorted; off the straight. **oai-oai tsoāi-tsoāi**, id. **oai-kô**, awry. **oai phîn-phîn**, much off the perpendicular, as wall much to the side, or as one's head. **oai-chhoȧh**, awry; diagonally. **oai-kô lȧh-chhoȧh**, id. **oai-chhoȧh--khì**, not able to come to an agreement; to break off relations abruptly. **bōe-oai-chhoȧh--tit**, no opportunity of getting any secret improper gains on the transaction. **oai-ām**, wry-necked; very troublesome by resisting authority, &c. **oai-chhùi**, wry-mouthed. **oai-phóe**, having one cheek awry, or one side projecting more than the other (v. phóe). **oai chit-pêng**, one side projecting more than the other. **oai chit-pi^n**, placed at one side; out of due proportion with other things. **tiau-oai**, to make crooked by tying, as a tree. **tiàu-oai**, hung up off the perpendicular. **siōng put-chèng, chek hā oai**, when superiors are wicked, then inferiors are crooked and bad.

oai [R. oan, to oppress], to accuse falsely of a crime; to charge falsely with a debt. **oai--lâng**, to defraud people by false accusations, private or public. **tò-oai--lâng**, to deny one's fault and turn round accusing the accuser.

oái, to sprain or strain, as a limb. **oái-chit-tó**, to give one's foot a slight twist so as to fall. **kha oái--tiȯh**, the foot sprained. **chhiú oái--tiȯh**, arm sprained.

oāi (P.) **oāi-kong**, = A. hoā-kong, a painter of pictures.

oāi (P.), = A. ōe, words; language.

oai^n, the long creaking sound of a door or of an oil-mill, &c. **oai^n-oai^n-háu**, to creak in this way.

oai^n [R. ai, to push back and forwards, to delay, = col. oe]. **oai^n jī-hiân**, to play on the two-stringed guitar. **oai^n kóng-á-hiân**, to play on another sort of guitar.

oai^n [R. oan, bent; crooked]. **í^n-oai^n-toh**, a folding-table.

oai^n (cf. oai), (T. oā^n), to extort money from a man, as by pretending that he owes it; to live on another man unfairly. **lām-sám oai^n--lâng**, id. **oai^n-koāi^n**, to get small sums out of people improperly (v. koāi^n). **oai^n-chioh**, to ask money importunately under the name of borrowing, *e.g.* without hope of paying, or without paying former loan. **tò-oai^n chiȧ^n-oai^n**, to make false or over charges right and left.

oāi^n [R. a, a branch], (C. oa; P. oɛ), the first great divisions of a tree; the largest branches. **chhiū-oāi^n**, id. **toā-oāi^n**, a very large branch.

oaih^n (cf. oai^n, oák, ók), noise of a door, &c., creaking. **oáih^n-oáih^n-háu**, creaking sound of mill or door, or of furniture. **ih^n-ih^n oáih^n-oáih^n**, noise of chair or table creaking, or of children making a noise.

oȧk (cf. ȯk), to cry, as a crow or raven, duck or frog; to croak. **oȧk-oȧk-háu**, id. **toȧ-teh-oȧk**, croaking, as a raven; said of a man making a secret sign to entice another to go with him to some bad pleasure.

oan [R. to oppress: cf. un, oai, oai^n]. **oan-óng**, to oppress; to treat unjustly. **oan-khut** (R.), to oppress; to slander grievously (also C. colloquial), (v. khut). **toā-oan**, great oppression.

oan-iâ^n, to win in a feud or quarrel. **oan-su**, to be overcome in it. **oan-ke**, a feud; a state of enmity. **oan-ke niū^n-chè**, a great feud. **oan-kɛ niū^n-toā-chè** (C.), id. **tsòe-oan tsòe-ke**, constantly raising needless quarrels about small matters; said also of a child difficult to please. **oan-ke lō͘-óeh**, said of meeting one's enemy unexpectedly. **tùi-thâu oan-ke-tsú**, the very party with whom we have the feud or quarrel. **oan ū-ke, tùi ū-tsú**, the quarrel concerns the two parties alone and no one else. **ū oan-siû**, to have a feud or quarrel on account of another or others, generally from ancestors. **kiet oan-siû**, to become at feud; to have a feud. **kiet-oan**, id. **bô-oan-siû**, (you) have no feud with him. **kap-lí bô-oan bô-siû**, not at feud with you. **oan-oan siong-pò**, feud continued by mutual revenges and injuries. **pò-oan**, to take revenge; to execute vengeance (by a private party), as for murder of relative, great plundering, or such grievous injury. **háu-oan**, to make complaint to a mandarin about some very grievous injury, by striking the drum in court. **hám-oan**, id. **hiàm-oan**, id. **hán-oan** (T.), id. **sè-oan**, to make defence against a false accusation. **sè-oan-óng**, id. **sin-oan**, to redress a wrong. **iú-oan bû-sin**, to suffer wrong and have none to redress it. **hâm-oan** (r.), to cherish secretly the purpose of revenge for a great wrong. **oan khó-kái, put-khó-kiet**, a quarrel should be made up, and not become a long feud.

oan-kúi, the unavenged ghost of a murdered man haunting the murderer. **goá--ê oan-kúi**, a man who is always troubling me and thwarting my plans. **chêng-si-oan** (a feud formed in a former life), said of a man killing another with whom he was at friendship.

gâu-oan, very fretful or peevish, as a child that cannot be pleased any way. **ài-oan--lâng**, id. **beh-oan--lâng phō**, insisting to be carried, as child that cries till it is done.

oan [R. oán, a joint of arm or foot, = col. oá^n]. **chhiú-oan**, the hollow inside the elbow-joint. **chhiú-oat-oan**, id. **chhiú-āu-oan** (C.), id. **kha-oan**, the hollow inside the knee-joint. **kha-oat-oan**, id.

oan (R. id.), a bay; a bend in a river or channel. **hái-oan**, a bay. **jip-hong sûi-siók, jip-káng sûi-oan**, do at Rome as Rome does.

oan (R. id.) **oan-oan**, crooked. **oan-oat**, id. **sim-koa^n oan-oat**, very cunning. **chhit-oan poeh-oat**, very crooked. **oan-khiau**, crooked (lit. or fig.); deceitful; going about the bush. **bô-oan-khiau**, truthful and straightforward.

í^n-oan-oan, circular or semicircular. **oan-kong-**

厦英大辭典

mn̂g, an arched door-way. **koe-sit-ké-oan**, zigzag or very crooked, as a road. **bák-bâi oan**, eyebrows arched. **oan-pòe-í**, a chair with a curved back.

tsoán-oan, to try to settle a dispute by skilfully adapting the plan to the circumstances, *e.g.* by putting a new face on the matter or partly explaining it away, generally with some measure of falsehood, especially done by a third party. **bōe-hiáu tsoán-oan**, not adapting one's self to circumstances; very stiff and blunt in dealings. **khà-oan**, to clinch, as a nail.

oan-to, a sort of convex plane for smoothing the inside of buckets, &c. **oan-khau**, id. **oan-to khau tháng-lāi**, said of a lazy fellow living on his relatives or employers without earning anything. **oan-khau khau tháng-lāi**, id. **oan-ām** (lit. crooked neck), said of meeting a man we wish not to meet, or of affair difficult to manage, or with many blunders. **oan-koe phiah-hāng**, crooked and unfrequented streets and lanes.

oan [R. name of bird]. **oan-iuⁿ**, the small duck called the mandarin duck (v. iuⁿ).

oan — **oan-iuⁿ**, sort of wasp (v. iuⁿ).

oân [R. oan, a bay]. **tâi-oân**, Formosa; Tai-wan-foo. **tâi-oân-hú**, the city or department or prefect of Tai-wan-foo. **tâi-oân-koāiⁿ**, the district or sub-prefect of Tai-wan-hien. **kè-tâi-oân**, to cross to Formosa from the mainland; said also for "dead" by a play on the words "buried and finished."

oân [R. the side-gates of a yamun]. **oân-bûn**, the east and west gates of the railed inclosure in front of a yamun. **oân-mn̂g** (T.), id. **tang-oân-bûn**, the east one. **sai-oân-bûn**, the west one. **oân-bûn-lāi**, within the space inclosed by them. **oân-bûn-kháu**, just outside one of these gates. **oân-bûn siùⁿ-kang**, secretary in admiral's office. **khiā oân-bûn**, to be on duty at admiral's yamun, as marines.

hien-oân, = n̂g-tè, one of the three ancient emperors.

oân [R. long robes], a surname.

oân [R. goân, origin, Yuen dynasty]. **oân-pó**, = goân-pó, a large ingot or shoe of sycee silver, about 50 taels weight. **chit-chiah oân-pó**, one such ingot. **chit-khò oân-pó**, id.

oân [R. complete, finished], to pay in full, as taxes or account; completed, as period or work. **oân-tsoân**, complete and in right order (v. tsoân). **oân-pī**, id. **oân-chiâⁿ**, fully completed or accomplished, as affair (v. chiâⁿ). **oân-kiók**, fully settled and ended, as affair. **oân-boán**, completed, as work or fixed time; fully paid, as money. **hùi-oân-oân**, all spent, as money. **oân-bêng**, settled, as account. **tǹg-oân**, to receipt an account by stamping the word "oân." **oân-siàu**, to pay an account. **oân-la̍p**, to pay in full, as taxes, dues, &c. **oân-niûⁿ**, to pay land-tax.

oân [R. hoân, a pellet or pill]. **ióh-oân**, a pill. **tsoá-oân**, a paper pellet, as for a pop-gun. **thun bô-gē-oân**, said of a man very much ashamed at want of success or at being scolded. **lio̍k-bī-oân**, a medicine made of sù-sín and two other drugs. **phâu-liông-oân**, sort of pills from Canton. **hûi-jî-oân**, pills for making children fat. **chí-ū hûi-jî-oân**, his only care is that his children be strong (with no care for his parents).

oân [R. round; classifier of officers, = col. goân], classifier of balls, as of raw sugar.

koaⁿ-oân, mandarins in general. **bûn-bú koaⁿ-oân**, civil and military mandarins. **úi-oân**, a deputy sent by a superior mandarin. **seng-oân** (R.), a Sew-tsai. **seng-oân-tsø**, rents of property left to be enjoyed only by those descendants who take a degree. **oân-niáⁿ**, sort of collar worn by Sew-tsais.

hok-oân, dried lung-yen (gêng-géng) fruit. **hok-oân-bah**, do. dried without stones or skins. **thn̂g-oân**, balls of dark raw sugar: some of them should be sent back in the empty basket in which a present was sent. **oân-thn̂g**, to make raw sugar into balls. **bah-oân**, balls made with minced pork. **bah-oân-bīn**, a broad fat face. **chiâⁿ-oân**, to be formed into a ball, as raw sugar; to form into lumps, as flour or other powders. **chiâⁿ-oân--ê**, globular, as lumps of raw sugar. **mīⁿ-hún chiâⁿ-oân**, flour getting full of lumps. **sim-koaⁿ chiâⁿ-oân**, feeling of choking or oppression at heart, as with great grief. **sim-koaⁿ kek-kui-oân**, do. with grief or sickness. **gêng chit-oân**, feeling of indigestion like a ball in the stomach.

oân [R. round; to interpret, as dreams; = col îⁿ], to spread out, as a semicircular cover; to interpret, as a dream (this word and the previous in the sense of "round" are often interchanged).

oân-bāng, to interpret a dream (v. bāng). **oân-sien-bāng**, to go and dream in the temple of the genii or with their incense. **chhiáⁿ--lâng oân-sien-bāng**, to ask a man to interpret such a dream.

thoân-oân (R.), round and unbroken, as family. **chit-ke thoân-oân**, family still unbroken.

oân-phâng, to spread a bamboo sail or stiff mat, as a cover (arched). **oân-hē**, do., as a protection from rain.

oân-thâu-hia, round-toed boots of civil mandarins. **oân-keng-bé**, rounded stern of junk raised above the deck. **oân-kong-mn̂g** (= oan ?), a door-way with arched top. **oân-mn̂g-á**, id. **oân-kong-thâu**, the rounded top of such a door-way or arch.

oân-téng, to have one's head shaved entirely, as Buddhist priest or nun.

chit-oân-soàⁿ, a ball of thread or thin twine. **chit-oân-thô**, a lump of mud.

oân — **oán--teh**, to tie tight. **oán-sí**, to tie very tight. **oán-tiâu**, id.

oán [R. alike]. **oán-jiên** (r.), similar; like as.

oán [R. winning; complaisant]. **oán-tsoán**, managing by some indirect or roundabout manner (v. tsoán). **kóng-ōe khah-úi-oán**, to talk in a somewhat gentle or winning manner, avoiding what is offensive or disagreeable, or stating it indirectly, so that advice or reproof may be more readily taken. **úi-oán-khǹg**, to exhort in a winning manner without directly naming the fault. **úi-oán lâi-khǹg**, id.

oán [R. goán, to look at, *q.v.*]. **koan-san oán-súi**, to take a walk looking at scenery.

oán [R. distant, = col. hn̄g]. **éng-oán**, lasting very long; perpetual; eternal. **bān-liên kiú-oán**, id. **lō-tô iâu-oán**, road very long. **tiâu-oán**, very distant, as places. **oán-súi lân-kiù kūn-hé**, distant help is of no use. **oán-chhin put-jû kūn-lîn**, a neighbour is of more use than a relative living far away.

oán-chì, a medicine (v. chì).

oàn (R. id.), to hate; to repine at; to envy. **oàn-hūn**, to hate; to repine; to envy; to be displeased (v. hūn). **oàn-òⁿ**, to hate and loathe; to abhor. **oàn-tò**, to envy. **oàn-chhoeh**, to be displeased at one's self or at one's fate. **oàn-thiⁿ chhoeh-miāⁿ**, to murmur at Heaven and Fate. **oàn-sin chhoeh-miāⁿ**, id. **mē-thiⁿ oàn-tōe**, to murmur and find fault with Heaven and Earth. **oàn-thi^n oàn-tōe**, id. **oàn-thien iû-jîn**, to repine at Heaven and envy men. **ai-oàn**, to repine bitterly against Fate, Heaven, or men. **ai-oàn chhi^n-chhám**, repine at one's miserable fate. **oàn-khì**, violent hatred or enmity. **oàn-khì chhiong-thien**, hatred boiling up to heaven. **oàn-jip-kut**, hatred rooted in one's very bones; very deep hatred.

chek-oàn, to harbour enmity. **bâi-oàn**, id. **khioh-hūn bâi-oàn**, id. **khioh-oàn**, id. **kiet-oàn**, to cherish deep enmity in one's heart. **kè-lâng-oàn**, inspiring dislike by one's appearance, action, or manner. **pò-oàn**, to retaliate. **pò niáu-chhú-á-oàn**, to pay a small insult or injury in the same way. **oàn-kúi thiu chih-kun**, said of guilt unexpectedly coming out plain in examination before a mandarin.

oān [R. id. = col. bān]. **oān-oān**, slowly; leisurely. **kín-oān**, fast and slow. **tî-oān**, to delay; to procrastinate. **iên-oān**, id. **în-oān**, id. **î-oān**, to delay (as affair) to allow more time. **bōe-î-oān--tit**, it cannot be delayed or put off at all. **khoan-oān**, to grant delay, as for a payment. **oān-jit**, to delay some days. **oān-sî**, to delay. **oān-sî oān-khek**, id.; to procrastinate. **oān-sî-khek**, id. **bô-oān-khek**, not delaying a moment.

oān [R. a sort of robe]. **oān-á** (C.), = lâm-chheng, a long dress worn by Sew-tsai graduates.

oang — **tàu-oang**, to join in one company of associates. **kap-in sa^n-oang**, keeping company with them, good or bad. **oang-koah**, a set or clique of persons (v. koah). **ū-oang-tóng**, to have a clique or set of associates, who assist each other in any case (v. tóng).

oang [R. hoan, a loud cry]. **oang-oang-háu**, cry of a sea-goose.

oat — **oan-oat**, crooked (v. oan). **chhiú-oat-oan**, the inside of the bent elbow. **ih-oat**, involved, as affair; also (C.), winding, as a road. **phiet-phiet oat-oat**, walking with feet turned outwards, and swaying about slowly in a self-important manner. **kiā^n-lē oat-oat**, walking with feet too much turned inwards. **kha oat-oat**, feet so turned.

oat-kak, to turn round a corner; a turning or corner of a road. **tńg-oat chiū-sī**, turn off at that point and you are at the place. **oat--lóh-khì chiū-sī**, id. **oat-tńg-chhiú chiū-sī**, id. **oat-tò-chhiú**, turn to the left, as on a road. **oat-tò-tńg**, to turn back, as on a road. **tò-oat--lâi**, to come back to where we started from. **oat chit-pêng**, take the road turning off on this side. **oat--kè-lâi**, to turn off to the side, as on a road. **oat-kè-lâi, oat-kè-khì**, to wind back and forwards, as a road. **oat-lâi oat-khì**, id. **oat-kè-tang**, to turn off towards the east. **oat-kè chiā^n-chhiú-pêng**, to turn off to the right hand.

oàt [R. to cross over; more], to turn round in the opposite direction. **oát-jiá**, still more (from some additional cause); all the more. **oát-jiá siong-tiōng**, worse and worse, as sorrow from more bad news, or as disease from mistaken treatment. **oát-kan, oát-khiáu, oát pîn-kiông; kan-khiáu tò-tí thien put-iông**, the more crafty, the poorer and more miserable, for at last Heaven will not endure such cunning.

oát-liām, to say a lesson with back to teacher. **oát-thâu**, to turn the head. **oát-bīn**, to look to the side, turning the face round. **oát-hong-bīn**, wind changing or veering about. **oát chit-phi^n-phâng**, to change to another tack. **koh-oát chit-phi^n**, to make one tack more. **oat-lìn-tńg**, to turn round (v. lìn). **oát-tńg-lâi**, to turn (a thing or one's self) round (v. tńg). **oát-tńg-chhiú**, immediately. **oát-lâi oát-khì**, to turn back and forwards several times, as one's self, or head, or thing. **oát--kè-lâi**, to turn in the opposite direction, as one's face or a thing. **oát-kè-lâi**, id. **oát-kè-lâi-khoà^n**, to turn round and look at. **oát-kè-lâi, oát-kè-khì**, to turn one's face, or a thing, back and forwards several times. **oát-chit-sèh** (T.), to take a short walk and come back.

î-oát, to move things to other places; to change a purpose, or plan, or promise, or engagement. **bōe-î-oát--tit**, it cannot be altered, as a plan.

toâ^n-oát-tsú (Cn.), man who gave the site or endowment for a temple (v. toâ^n).

oát (C.) **oát-lék**, = A. iét-lék, experienced.

oát (C.), = A. iét (R.), to be pleased.

oe [R. ai, to push backwards and forwards; to delay, = col. oai^n], (C. e; Cn. öe), to jostle or rub against in passing; to turn a hand-mill; (to take in turn); to put off, as business.

sa^n-oe, to jostle. **oe--tióh**, to strike or rub against with elbows or arm. **oe-khoeh**, to jostle (v. khoeh). **oe-loe--chhut-lâi**, to come out jostling each other, as crowd. **oe-oe sak-sak**, pushing about in a crowd; getting on with difficulty. **oe-lâi sak-khì**, id. **sa^n-oe-sin**, to rub against each other, as two men crossing each other in a narrow path. **oe-tó**, to push over by jostling. **lâu oe--jip-lâi**, the tide carries us inwards out of our course.

bóng-oe bóng-kè, to get on with difficulty: barely getting on in the world. **oe-iên** (r.), to delay (v. iên). **ōe-oe--tit**, can be put off, as a troublesome business. **oe hō-pát-lâng**, to put off on another, as a work to be done. **sa^n-oe-the**, id. **oe-thoe kè-jit**, to do very little work while drawing the pay.

oe jī-hiên, to play the two-stringed guitar.

chiàu-oe, in regular turn.

oe-bō, to turn a hand-mill. **chià^n-oe**, to turn it round in same direction, as hands of watch. **tò-oe**, to turn it in the opposite direction. **oe-chhek**, to clean rice from the husk by a sort of mill. **oe-béh**, to clean wheat or barley thus. **oe mī^n-hún**, to grind flour. **oe-chhòe**, to make dough by a hand-mill. **oe-chhip**, to work a sort of hand-net neck-deep in the sea. **thàn-chî^n ná^n teh-oe-kim**, to make money, as if grinding gold from a mill.

oe (C.), = A. e, a small earthen jar. **chiú-tê-oe**, a sort of wine-jug. **tiá^n-oe**, = A. hûi-tiá^n, a large thin shallow covered earthen dish for cooking in.

oe (C.), to scrape with a knife, as in making a bucket or smoothing things.

oe (C.), A. e. **oe-chhài**, a reddish vegetable. **âng-oe**, a very red sort. **péh-oe**, a whitish sort.

oe (C.), = T. ōh, to cut some grain before it is ripe; *e.g.* when in urgent want of money, cutting our grain too soon. **thau-oe**, to cut and steal unripe grain.

oɛ (C.), = A. ui, uih, to bore a hole.

oɛ (P.), = A. oāi^n = C. oa, a large branch.

ôe, the answer to a call; yes, sir!

ôe — **ôe-lôe--chhut-lâi**, to come rushing out suddenly, as crowd from a house (cf. oe).

ôe (R. hâi), (C. ê; Cn. ôe), a shoe. **hiu^n-ôe**, small shoe-shaped bags of incense, used as amulets. **keng-ôe**, smallest shoes of women; also small models of shoes full of incense, used on 5.5. **lú-ôe**, small shoes for women. **siù-ôe,** embroidered shoes for women. **khùn-ôe,** women's small shoes made without heel-taps, for sleeping in. **ché-á-ôe,** shoes for large-footed women. **boán-á-ôe,** id., with sharp upturned point and very narrow sole. **pau-á-ôe,** small shoes with soft cloth soles, for children. **chhâ-kiáh-ôe,** wooden-soled shoes. **tsoá-tóe-ôe,** shoes with paper soles. **iû-ôe,** oiled shoes. **iû-chiⁿ-ôe,** shoes made with soles of oiled felt, for wet weather. **phê-ôe,** leather shoes. **pê-ôe,** shoes made of the plant called pê-chháu.. **chháu-ôe** (straw shoes), sandals. **kā-lí-thǹg chháu-ôe,** I give you a feast on the occasion of your return from your long journey.

ka ôe-iūⁿ, to cut the pattern of the shoe, as the betrothed daughter-in-law does and gives to her future mother-in-law. **í-keng ka-ôe-iūⁿ,** the daughter-in-law is fully fixed.

chhiah-ôe, to make shoes. **tsòe-ôe,** id. **chhiūⁿ-ôe,** to stitch the uppers to the soles. **tàu-ôe,** id. **poāⁿ-ôe,** to work the border of a shoe with thread (v. poāⁿ). **ūi-ôe,** to paint on a shoe the pattern to be embroidered. **tiam-ôe,** to mend shoes. **hùn-ôe,** to stretch a shoe on the last. **thoa-ôe,** to walk slipshod with heels turned down, or with old shoes that don't catch on the heels. **púih-ôe,** to draw up the heels of shoes that have been on slipshod.

ôe-béh, shoes and stockings. **kha-péh ôe,** women's shoes and the bandages used in place of stockings.

ôe-chheh, a book for holding the many-coloured threads for embroidery of any sort. **ôe-hùn,** a last. **ôe-bín,** a shoe-brush. **ôe-púih,** a shoe-horn. **ôe-thóeh,** a bit of cloth at the heel for pulling on a shoe. **ôe-phe,** shoes shaped, but unfinished. **ôe-thâu,** the toe of a shoe. **ôe-āu,** back of shoe. **ôe-āu-tiⁿ,** heel of shoe (below). **ôe-kám,** the inside of the sole, next to the foot. **ôe-chhàn,** inner sole of shoe. **ôe-tóe,** sole of shoe. **ôe-lí,** lining of shoe. **ôe-bīn,** uppers of shoe. **ôe-phìⁿ,** the two side pieces of the uppers. **ôe-phīⁿ,** the rib or ribs in the middle of the toe. **siang-phīⁿ-ôe,** shoes with two such ribs in front. **toaⁿ-phīⁿ-ôe,** shoes with only one rib. **ôe-phàn,** strip of cloth between the two ribs at the toe; also, loops of woman's or child's shoe (v. phàn). **ôe-bôe** (T.), the loops of women's shoes.

óe (R. ái), (C. é; Cn. ŏe), short, as a man; somewhat dwarfish. **óe-tóe,** id. **óe-lâng,** a short man; a dwarf. **óe-ké óe-ké,** short and stout. **óe-pûi óe-pûi,** id. **óe-kha-koe,** a sort of fowl with very short legs. **óe-kha-lê,** a low sort of cockscomb (flower).

òe [R. dirty, defiled, = col. è]. **ù-òe,** dirty. **òe-giân tók-gú** (r.), vile abusive language.

òe, to take in the hand. **òe-mih,** to take things in the hand.

ōe [R. hōe, to assemble; to understand; able], (C. ē; Cn. ŏe), able; can; to be able. **ōe-bōe,** can you, or can you not? can you? **ōe-koāⁿ,** are you cold? **tsòe ōe-tit-lâi,** able to effect the result. **óh-ōe,** to learn till able to do a thing (s. word). **káⁿ ōe-bô,** I think it will not be so. **ōe-lóh-hō͘,** it may probably rain. **ōe-sái--tit,** it will do (not said in Cn.) **ōe-tsòe--tit,** id. **ōe-ê-lâng,** a man of ability.

ōe [R. to guard]. **sī-ōe,** imperial guards of the highest class, chosen from the military Tsin-sze (chìn-sū), as the Han-lin are chosen from the literary Tsin-sze. **jip-sī-ōe,** to be chosen into their number.

ōe (R. hoā), (C. oā; P. oɛ̄, oāi), language; speech; a spoken word. **péh-ōe,** colloquial language; the vernacular. **koaⁿ-ōe,** the "mandarin dialect," or colloquial language of North China. **hó-ōe,** fair promises; plausible talk; auspicious words or phrases regularly pronounced at marriages, &c. **pháiⁿ-ōe,** vile or ill-omened language. **giét-ōe,** talk about vile lascivious matters. **kóng kúi-ōe,** to make groundless threats or deceitful statements. **bô-jī-ōe,** empty or exaggerated talk that cannot be depended on. **chhùi-chêng-ōe,** conventional phrases used on meeting people. **kháu-thâu-ōe,** common phrases for special uses (v. kháu). **thò-thâu-ōe,** polite phrases used on meeting, &c. (v. thò). **chit-kù-ōe,** one sentence; a few words. **ōe tiⁿ-bit-bit,** words sweet, flattering, and deceitful. **ōe sī-hong, jī sī-tsong,** words are wind, but writing remains.

ōe-tū, giving a sharp or gruff answer (v. tū). **ke-ōe,** to quarrel. **kāu-ōe,** fond of disputing, esp. talking about other people's affairs. **tsōe-ōe,** very talkative when one should not speak. **óh-ōe,** to take up and spread a report (s. able). **kóng-ōe,** to speak; to talk. **söh-ōe** (Cn.), id. **kóng toā-ōe,** to talk proudly, big, or boastfully. **hit-ê-lâng put-chí pháiⁿ-kóng-ōe,** he is very hard to talk over. **kóng lán-ê-ōe,** to talk on our side of the question. **lóng-sī i-ê-ōe,** talking as if most unquestionably in the right. **hē-ōe,** to make explanations or apology when found fault with. **hê-ōe,** to interpret spoken language, as in a court. **thoân-ōe,** id.

ōe-ì, the meaning of the words. **ōe-mn̂g té,** not able to say much for one's self, as when reproved. **ōe-mn̂g iáu-tn̂g,** I have still a great deal to say. **gâu-liáh ōe-sat,** fond of catching at some small error in speaking. **gâu-chhn̂g ōe-phāng,** id. **phah-chih lâng--ê ōe-piⁿ,** to cut short a man's talk, so that he does not gain his end. **chiét lâng-ê-ōe,** to interrupt a man when speaking; to cut short another's long story. **chiét lâng--ê ōe-thâu,** id. **tsáh lâng--ê ōe-thâu,** id. **lā chit--ê ōe-thâu,** to make a remark that will naturally lead a man to speak of a matter which we don't like to ask directly. **kóng-khí-lâi, ōe-thâu tn̂g,** it would take a long time to talk over this matter. **ōe-thâu ōe-bé,** the beginning or end of a talk, *e.g.* a place where an (apparently) incidental remark can be made, so as to ask a favour, or speak against a man, &c. **ang-î sūn ōe-bé,** a sorceress catching up one's ideas from the questions asked, so as to give suitable answers; said of taking the cue from what a man says, and speaking so as to please him.

ōe (C.), = A. ūi, to paint or draw.

ōe (C.) **lê-ōe,** = A. lê-hōe, aloes.

ōɛ (P.), = A. ōe, = C. oā, words; speech.

ōɛ (P.) **ōɛ-á-hí,** a small sort of fish.

oeh (C.), to brush away with the hand, as water or earth from a table.

oeh (P.) **oeh ham-khak-á-chíⁿ,** = A. kuih, &c., a game which children play with shells.

o̍eh (R. hiáp), (C. éh; Cn. ŏeh), narrow. **o̍eh-tóeh,** id. **khoah-o̍eh,** broad and narrow. **o̍eh-khoeh,** much straitened for want of room. **o̍eh-soeh,** id. **o̍eh-sòe,** small, as a place. **oan-ke lē-o̍eh,** to meet unexpectedly one whom we would like to avoid (v. oan).

o̍eh (cf. éh). **khng-o̍eh,** coarse bran, or fine chaff.

o̍eh (C.), = A. úih, a stroke of the pen.

o̍eh (C.), to fall away, as ground on river bank undermined by the water. **o̍eh--khì,** id.

óeh (C.) **phah-óeh**, sort of belching.

oh [R. ok, bad], difficult; slow. **oh-tit-tsòe**, difficult to do. **phah oh-tit-sit**, difficult to extinguish. **oh-kiâ**ⁿ, slow at walking. **tán-mih**ⁿ **oh-kàu**, when waiting for a thing time looks long.

óh (R. hák), to learn; a school; to imitate or follow example; to practise so as to learn.

óh-lāi, a Sew-tsai graduate. **chìn-óh**, to become a Sew-tsai (v. chìn). **bú-óh**, a military Sew-tsai. **chhut-óh**, to go out of the school-room; to get out of the jurisdiction of the literary mandarin, by becoming a Kú-jîn, or a Kòng-seng. **hú-óh**, the Confucian academy (or college) and temple of a Foo city; the principal or president of it. **koāi**ⁿ**-óh**, do. of a Hien (koāiⁿ) city. **óh-koa**ⁿ, the principal of the Foo or Hien academy, who has authority over the graduates and students. **kià-óh**, to hand over (a graduate) to him for custody or punishment. **khóng-tsú-óh**, a Confucian temple and academy.

óh-tn̂g, a school-house. **óh-pâng**, a school-room or study. **toā-óh**, a school for grown-up pupils; an academy or college. **jip-óh**, to enter school for the first time. **lóh-óh**, to go to school each time, usually three times a-day. **kà-óh**, to teach a school (v. kà). **khiā-óh**, to have a school, as teacher. **soà**ⁿ**-óh**, to dismiss a school at the end of the year. **the-óh**, to play truant. **chéng-óh**, to prepare a room and engage a teacher, as the patron (tong-ka) of a school does. **hū-óh**, to go as an additional scholar, not one of those connected with the person who engages the teacher.

óh-bú, to learn military exercises, as candidates for military degrees. **óh-siá-jī**, to learn writing. **óh-kang-hu**, to learn work. **kang-hu óh-chiū**ⁿ**-chhiú**, to have learned a manual trade. **óh-ōe**, to take up and spread a report without evidence: to repeat whatever another says. **óh-oā** (C.), id. **óh-ōe** (r.), to learn till able. **óh-ē** (C.), id. **óh-hó**, to learn thoroughly. **chiáp-chiáp-óh**, to learn diligently by practising over and over. **óh--i**, to follow his example. **óh i-ê-khoán**, id. **óh i-ê-phái**ⁿ, to imitate his wicked conduct. **óh-chhùi óh-chih**, to repeat a man's words to his face, making joke of them, as an unmannerly lad; to repeat to a man what has been said against him behind his back.

öh (Cn.) **ìn-öh**, to give a slight belch so as to show that we have eaten enough.

öh (Cn.), = A. eh, in some words.

ö̍h (T.), to cut a man's grain before it is quite ripe, as robber (cf. C. oe). **thau-ö̍h**, id. **ö̍h i--ê tiū-á-bé**, said of a sort of adulterous intrigue, = A. koah i--ê tiū-á-bé (v. tiū).

ok [R. ak, dirty]. **ok-chhok**, filthy; extremely dirty, as things or language.

ok [R. wicked, bad, = col. oh], fierce; cruel; overbearing; domineering; over-strict; to treat roughly or in an overbearing manner, often so as to cheat or oppress. **siēn-ok**, good and bad (v. siēn). **hiong-ok**, wicked; cruel. **sip-ok tsāi-lāi**, having all sorts (lit. ten) of wickedness. **tsōe-ok** (r.), wickedness and guilt. **tsōe-ok koàn-boán**, measure of guilt full. **ok-tók**, very wicked or cruel (v. tók). **ok chhih-chhih**, very fierce or overbearing. **ok kiák-kiák**, id. **ok khiák-khiák**, id. **ok-chek**, guilt accumulated so as to call down Heaven's vengeance. **ok-siók**, wicked customs. **ok-sim**, a wicked cruel heart; malicious. **ok-sèng**, bad-tempered, as child. **ok-hêng**, having an unpleasant ugly look, as if bad-tempered; passionate, overbearing, or bad-tempered; self-willed, disobedient, and troublesome, as boy. **ok-kúi**, a malicious demon. **ok-tóng**, a wicked confederacy or clique.

tàu-ok, to quarrel loudly and violently, each trying to be more overbearing. **ok--lâng**, to treat others in a domineering overbearing way, relying on our power or influence. **ok-lâng**, an overbearing imperious man. **ok-bé, ok-lâng khiâ**, a wild horse gets his match as a rider. **ok-jîn, tsū-iú ok-jîn mô**ⁿ, oppressors are oppressed (v. môⁿ). **ok-kheh**, a customer who drives a very hard bargain. **hāng chhim, káu ok** (lane deep and dog fierce), very difficult of access.

ók (cf. oák). **ók-ók-háu**, to croak, as a frog or toad.

óm (P.) **óm-lóm**, to collect into a mass.

ong [R. an old man]. **ló-ong** (R.), a respectful address to an old man. **si-ong** (R.), a poet. **sien-ong**, an aged genie. **lâm-kèk sien-ong**, the spirit of the South Pole. **tsùi-ong-í** (r.), a sort of long lounging-chair.

ông (R. id.), a king; an imperial prince of highest rank; a surname (Wang); title of many idols. **kok-ông**, a king; a sovereign. **kun-ông**, id. **jîn-ông** (r.), id. **tè-ông**, an emperor; emperors and kings. **lú-ông**, a sovereign queen in her own right. **lí-ông** (C.), id. **chhin-ông**, an imperial prince. **ông-hú**, palace of imperial prince.

hong-ông, to appoint, as a tributary king. **hoan-ông**, a foreign sovereign. **hoán-ông**, a rebel chief. **chhát-ông**, a rebel king or robber chief. **khîm-chhát, seng khîm-ông**, first catch the ringleader. **pà-ông**, a usurper (v. pà). **kiám-kháu-ông**, a rebel chief used by Heaven as a "scourge of God" to slaughter the wicked people, but not himself reaching the throne.

ông-lók, a travelling doctor (quack) or fortune-teller (v. lók). **ông-ngē**ⁿ, a literary man skilled in the business of law-courts, who lives by exciting trouble and managing lawsuits; a pettifogging lawyer. **koái-ông**, a swindler; a man who entices lads to plays, gambling, or bad houses.

ông-lēng, imperial commission giving the power of capital punishment; also an idolatrous symbol (v. lēng). **ông-hoat**, the laws of the kingdom. **ông-hoat bû-chhin**, the law is impartial. **ông-kiong**, a royal palace, especially the harem.

chheng-ông chheng-tè, said of having an independent fortune (v. chheng).

ông-kong, kings and dukes; feudal sovereigns; also (C.), title or name of several idols, esp. Tûn sèng-ông and Keh sèng-ông. **sèng-ông-kong**, the idol Keh sèng-ông. **ông-iâ**, title of imperial princes; name given to a great many idols. **sio ông-iâ**, an idol of the surname Sio, and so with some other surnames.

ông-tsûn, a junk built for the worship of "ông-iâ," and sent round the country with his image. **chhiá**ⁿ**-ông**, to invite ông-iâ to come. **giâ-ông**, to carry him in procession. **sàng-ông**, to burn the "ông-tsûn" or set it to float away, done with great ceremonies. **sàng-ông khí-sin**, to burn the image of ông-iâ (by land or water); said also of happily getting rid of a man who had been living on us and troubling us, but whom we could not ask to go away, *e.g.* the deputy of a superior mandarin. **kòng-ông** (Cn.), to worship him with offerings.

giâm-lô-ông (Cn. fig), the judge of the dead. **chiau-tsâi-ông**, the god of wealth. **ngó-kok-ông**, the god of grain, = hō-chek. **ióh-ông**, = Shin-nung, sîn-lông (v. ióh). **lêng-ông**, the god of the sea (v.

lêng). **kúi-ông,** a prince of demons (v. kúi). **keh-sèng-ông,** a famous idol of surname Keh (Cn. köh sèng-ûg). **kóng-ték tsun-ông,** id. **tân sèng-ông,** an idol of surname Tân. **chhêng-chhiū-ông,** the god of the banyan-tree. **hóe-ông** (C.), = A. hé-sîn-iâ, the god of fire.

chhiâ-ông, the 96th radical (giȯk), when written at the side, so called because its contracted shape is almost the same as the character "ông."

óng [R. to go; to depart; past in time]. **kè-óng,** to die. **kè-óng ê-sū,** affairs that are past and out of date. **kè-óng ê-tāi-chì,** id. **óng-jit,** every day formerly (it was so, &c.) **óng-géh,** each month formerly. **óng-nîⁿ,** year by year in past years. **óng-sî** (r.), in past time.

óng-hôe, to go and return. **óng-hoán,** do., as a messenger or sedan. **óng-lâi,** to go and come; to have intercourse, as friends. **lâi-óng,** id. **kau-chiap óng-lâi,** to have frequent friendly intercourse. **ū lâi-óng-siàu,** to have an account current (money or goods), each sometimes in debt to the other.

thong-óng, to have a secret intimacy, as with improper or suspicious characters, as for low amusements, improper gains, or injuring one's master, *e.g.* giving information out of the family to enemies. **lāi-bīn ê-lâng kap--i thong-óng,** some one within the party or family has such intercourse with bad purpose. **ōe-thong-óng--tit,** safe for travelling on, as road. **goá kap--i bô-thong-óng,** I have no dealings or intercourse with that man.

óng (R. id.) **oan-óng,** to treat unjustly; to wrong greatly or oppress; oppression or a great wrong (v. oan). **óng-toàn,** to judge unjustly and oppress, as mandarin. **óng-sí,** to be killed by very unjust judgment; to be murdered; to commit suicide. **óng-sí-siâⁿ,** the part of Hades for those who have died violent deaths; they must have committed some very great crime in second previous life.

óng-khut, an expression of astonishment with grief or displeasure (v. khut). **óng-hùi sim-sîn,** to spend one's labour (esp. mental labour) uselessly.

ōng (R. id.), to prosper. **heng-ōng,** to prosper. **hin-ōng** (C.), id. **ióng-ōng,** strong and vigorous, *e.g.* not afraid of heat or cold. **siaⁿ put-chí-ōng,** voice very loud. **hé ōng,** the fire is burning well. **kun-tīn ōng,** having numerous living posterity. **poeh-jī ōng,** horoscope good. **ūn-khì ōng,** in great prosperity (v. ūn). **lâng-khì ōng,** temperature warm and pleasant, as when men sleep together for warmth, or as when many people are in a room; influence of numerous inhabitants so strong that demons do not dare to injure. **ōng-khì,** making money in great abundance; always winning at gambling; temperament strong and warm, as of a strong young man. **ōng-chhiú,** a skilful hand, as at gambling. **oá-ōng khoàⁿ-miāⁿ,** saying that a man has good luck when he is manifestly prospering.

soe-ōng, to decline and to prosper. **phēng soe-ōng,** to make a venture, esp. in trade or feud. **phēng lí--ê soe-ōng,** I will try to do what I can for you (as going to ask a favour, &c.), but feel very doubtful of success. **kap-i-phēng soe-ōng,** I am making a venture, as with a lot of goods.

ōng-lê, a fine sort of univalve shell-fish.

ōng — **ōng-lâi,** a pine-apple. **chit-ki ōng-lâi,** one pine-apple. **ōng-lâi-sng,** a condiment made from pine-apples.

op (P.), = A. gap, to gulp water, as a fish. **op-op-kiò,** sound made by small frogs.

P.

In many words corresponds to initial H of the reading form.

pa [R. mark left by a wound?], a dried clot. **huih-pa,** dried blood on the skin or clothes, as from a sore. **kui-pa,** in large dried masses, as dried blood or matter, or as starch laid on too thick and dried in a mass (s. palm).

pa — **ko-pa-phí,** incrustation on a rice-boiler. **ko-pa,** id.

pa [R. dried meat], dried; emaciated. **pa-pa-pa,** dried and shrivelled, as dried meat; very lean and emaciated. **pek-pa,** to dry over the fire, so as to keep a long time. **piak-pa,** id. **phák-pa,** to dry in the sun, as meat or fish: to be scorched, as by the sun, or by long drought. **náⁿ phák-sí-pa,** said of man standing or working in a very hot sun. **keng-pa,** to stretch out by a stick of bamboo and dry in the sun, as a duck cut open. **kien-pa,** to dry, as meat, without stretching.

hî-pa, dried fish. **ah-pa,** dried duck. **koe-pa,** dried fowl. **bah-pa,** dried meat, esp. pork. **gû-phê-pa,** dried untanned cow-hides.

pa [R. to slap with the palm; an exclamation of surprise; an ancient state in Sze-chuen]. **chit-pa-chiúⁿ,** the expanded hand, meaning five, or fifty, &c. (v. chiúⁿ). **niauⁿ-pi-pa,** all over pock-marked. **kui-pa,** in large masses or patches (like palm of hand), as itch or eruption (s. clot).

pa-kiet, skilful at managing business; hard to get round; to ingratiate one's self with a superior, by flattery, &c. **gâu-pa-kiet,** good at ingratiating one's self with a powerful man by flattery, sycophancy, and such mean arts. **teh-pa-lōe sím-mihⁿ,** what are you engaged about? (v. lōe).

e-lô-pa, Europe (v. e).

pa — **pa-lun-thun,** to bolt, as food or medicine (v. lun). **hiong-pa lí-láu,** very ugly (v. láu).

pa [R. sound made by children]. **pa-siâⁿ,** Batavia. **ka-lâ-pa,** Java. **ka-lâu-pa** (C.), id.

pa [R. the banana and such plants], a plant (arum?) like a plantain, with large leaf and beautiful red flower. **pa-chiau-sìⁿ,** a large leaf-shaped fan, used by the ancients and by the genii.

pa-tāu, the croton-oil bean or plant. **pa-tāu-jîn,** croton-oil beans.

pa [R. a bamboo fence]. **lî-pa,** a fence of plants or railing of reeds round a field or garden; a hedge (C. lî-loa).

pa (C. poa). **pa-lak-hî** (C. poa-láu), a good edible fish. **sék-pa-lak,** cooked do. (sold cooked). **pa-lang-hî,** another sort, larger. **pa-láu-hî,** another sort.

45

pa — **pa-lê**, metal rings with balls inside (v. lê).

pa (Cn.) **pa-chiah**, = A. ka-chiah, the back.

pá [R. to hold in the hand, = col. pé, pah]. **pá-chhî**, shrewd; difficult to get round; able and confident in one's powers. **pá-pèng**, determined in purpose (v. pèng).

pièn-pá-hì, jugglery. **pî^n-pá-hì**, do.; idle play; idle and full of sport, as a playful boy. **tsòe-pá-hì**, to sport about, as a boy hopping, leaping, or at gymnastics, or playing with some small animal he has caught.

pá (R. páu), satiated; satisfied; full. **iau-pá**, hungry and full (v. iau). **siu^n-pá-kek**, much surfeited. **pá-tiù^n**, surfeited. **chiáh-pá-tiù^n**, to surfeit one's self. **chiáh-pá**, to eat till satisfied; I have eaten enough. **chiáh-pá teh-chē**, having nothing to do (but eat). **chiáh-pá chiū-khùn**, only eats and sleeps. **iû tióh-chiáh-khi-pá**, make it absorb oil till saturated. **chiáh kàu-pá-tong-tong**, I have eaten quite enough.

pá-tī^n, stuffed full. **pá-moá^n**, id. **pá-tsát**, closely packed or crammed together; fully understanding a thing. **pá-tsúi**, well filled, as fruit or grain. **chit-phè pá-pá**, fully ten li. **khùn-pá**, having slept quite enough. **chhùi pá, bák m̄-pá**, though having eaten to the full, the eyes are not yet satisfied. **thia^n kàu-pá-hī**, id.; feeling that we have heard quite enough, and don't wish to hear any more.

pá-lâ, very corpulent; also, amusing one's self too much, as lads too fond of pleasures, or when meddling with other people's matters and troubling them.

pà (R. id.) **a-pà**, Papa!

pà (R. id.), a leopard. **hó-pà**, tigers and leopards. **hó-pà sai-chhiū^n**, do., and lions and elephants. **hó-lêng pà-piu**, said of men of very violent disposition (v. piu). **hó seng pà-jî**, the tiger has cubs like leopards.

niau^n pà-pà, very much pock-marked.

pà (R. id.), to usurp. **pà-chiàm**, to take violent and unjust possession. **kiông-pà**, id. **pà-sèng**, crabbed and bad-tempered, as children. **à-pà**, id. **put-chí-pà**, very disobedient and ill-behaved, as a bad young lad. **pà-tō**, violent and oppressive. **ēng pà-tō**, by violence, or threats of violence. **ēng pà-hoat**, to use force, or show determination to use it if resisted, as in taking possession of something.

pà-lâi pà-khì, very busy; always managing matters, or diligently seeking for work; also (C.), striking right and left with his paws, as tiger. **sì--kòe pà--lâng**, borrowing everywhere, but not paying.

pà-chháu-meh^n, to catch grasshoppers, as with both hands, or with a hand-net.

pà-ông, a usurper. **chhó pà-ông**, a famous king of Tsoo. **chháu pà-ông**, id.

pà — **bé-pà-thâu**, the small of the back. **bé-pà**, id.

pà [R. pa]. **o-lé-pà** (Europe), cotton goods (v. o).

pā [R. pō, violent; to strike, = col. pāu, phāu], to strike the head with the open hand. **pā thâu-khak**, id. **khit-lûi pā--tióh**, to be somewhat stunned by lightning; said also of a man talking in a random reckless way.

pā [R. to stop; to cease]. **pā-chhī**, to shut the shops (of a street, or ward, or town), as a protest against some action of the mandarins. **pā-khó**, the whole of the literati refusing to go to the examinations, as a demonstration against the mandarins. **pā--liáu**, no more of this! the matter is ended now.

pā^n (T.), = nā^n, to singe, as fire or lightning.

pah [R. pek, = col. peh], (C. peh), a hundred. **nn̄g-pah**, two hundred. **jī-pah**, id. **pah-jī**, a hundred and twenty. **pah-bān**, a million.

pah-iū^n, all sorts. **pah-hāng-mih^n**, all sorts of things. **bûn-bú pah-koa^n**, all mandarins. **pah-nî^n-hè-āu**, dead. **pah-iáp**, double, as a cultivated flower.

sa^n-pah-lák-si, a sort of very thin paper. **tsòe-pah-jit**, to finish the ceremonies of khiā-hà, after burial.

pah [R. pá, to hold in the hand, = col. pé], (C. peh). **pah-iâ**, a petty officer of land troops (like naval tūi-koa^n), said to command about thirty soldiers, especially cavalry; he is not counted a mandarin; also (Cn.), a sort of drill-sergeant. **pah-tsóng** (Cn.), = A. pé-tsóng, a captain of about 100 men (v. tsóng).

pai [R. pan, a company or relay], (T. pai^n). **hia-pai**, fond of gaudy display, as in dress, house, &c.; ostentatious; dashing; fond of intercourse with mandarins or wealthy people. **ài-hia-pai**, id., or fond of giving feasts. **kóng-ōe ài-hia-pai**, in the habit of talking very big.

pâi (R. id.), to arrange in order; to set in regular rows; classifier of tiers, &c. **sa^n-pâi**, to set out things over against each other. **chiàu-pâi**, arranged in regular order. **pî^n-pâi**, arranged in an even orderly manner. **an-pâi**, to tidy up. **an-pâi pè-tì**, all nicely arranged. **pâi-khui**, to spread out, as a number of articles. **pâi-liét**, to arrange in order.

pâi-chhiâng, extravagantly ornamental; gaudy, as house or dress. **pâi-chí**, id.; also, proud and self-satisfied in bearing, as on growing rich or getting much success. **pâi-piét**, having much display, as a spectacle.

pho-pâi, to treat with respectful attention; to arrange things in nice order (v. pho).

pâi-pí, to arrange or adjust matters: to make preparations for some one. **pâi-kái**, to adjust a dispute, &c., for another (v. kái).

pâi-gê, to arrange all the servants and employés of a yamun, as on the arrival or return of a mandarin. **pâi chhiu^n-to-hāng**, to arrange files of soldiers, as at an execution. **pâi-tīn**, to arrange the ranks of an army. **pâi-tūi**, id. **pâi-peng pè-tīn**, id. **pâi-toh**, to set the table for a meal. **pâi oá^n-tī**, id. **pâi-mih^n bōe**, to set out things for sale. **pâi kó-tóng**, to arrange ornaments or curios, &c., as for sale or as for ornament. **pâi-kiáu**, to keep a gambling house or place. **pâi-thoa^n**, to set out a Cantonese sort of gambling. **pâi-toâ^n**, to set up a temporary shrine with a great many ornaments. **pâi-chè**, to come (as friend) to worship the dead with a great quantity of offerings.

pâi (R. id.), a raft. **tek-pâi**, a bamboo raft or catamaran, as for fishing, &c., or a raft of bamboos brought down the river. **sam-pâi**, a raft of timber. **ká-pâi**, to make a raft. **ká sam-pâi**, make a raft of timber.

pâi (R. id.), a tablet; a sign-board; (cards or dominoes); (a shield); a licence, warrant, or pass-port, ship's papers, &c.

hún-pâi, a white painted board for writing on, used as a slate, washing off the ink with water. **tsúi-pâi**, large white painted tablet on which notices are written at yamun gate. **koà-tsúi-pâi**, to hang up this board with intimations. **koà-pâi**, to hang up a memorial tablet; to hang up an intimation of cases to be tried at yamun. **hòng-kò-pâi**, a tablet with intimation that complaints may now be entered, as after holidays, or by new mandarin. **pâi-pién**, a tablet put up above a door; a sign-board. **chiau-pâi**, a shop-sign; a trade-mark. **pâi-sū**, the inscription in small letters at corner of wooden tablet. **tn̂g-kha-pâi**, tablets on long handles with titles of mandarins or idols, set up at gate of yamun or temple, and carried in procession. **lē-koan-pâi**, a wicker tablet covered with paper telling the route of an incense procession. **ke-kah-pâi**, a census tablet containing the names of the members of the family (often put up at door of house). **ke-sîn-pâi**, a large ancestral tablet with several names (v. sîn). **liên-pâi**, scrolls with sentences for hanging on walls. **teng-pâi**, a very long lantern with inscription.

chióh-pâi, a small stone tablet with inscription, smaller than "pi." **chióh-pi-pâi**, engraved stone tablets. **bōng-pâi**, a tombstone. **khiā-pâi**, to set up a head-stone at a grave. **khiā bû-ték-pâi**, said of a cock or cockchafer that beats all competitors.

gûn-pâi, a medal. **liú-pâi**, buttons in general. **pâi-á-liú**, buttons of foreign shape. **gék-só-pâi**, a jade amulet worn by child, in shape of a flat padlock. **io-pâi**, a ticket worn at the waist by a soldier out of the yamun.

hé-pâi, an express warrant, especially for ordering or summoning a mandarin. **pâi-phiò**, a warrant. **úi-pâi**, credentials given to a mandarin appointed to some duty, or to a deputy (úi-oân) sent to manage some affair. **koaⁿ-pâi**, a ship's papers, renewed at short intervals. **pâi-chiò**, ship's papers (two), the register and the clearance. **âng-pâi**, a ship's register. **pâi-miâⁿ**, the name by which a vessel is registered. **tsûn-pâi**, a vessel's register given in each time the vessel enters port. **giâm tsûn-pâi**, to examine a vessel's papers. **niáⁿ tsûn-pâi**, to get back the register when about to leave port again. **niáⁿ-pâi**, id. **oāⁿ-pâi**, to have ship's register changed, as on change of owner, or great repairs, or change of usual line of voyage; to have vessel's papers changed. **chhiáⁿ tsûn-pâi**, to make application for the register when a junk is built and ready for sea. **chhiáⁿ-pâi**, id., or when thoroughly repaired; to ask a licence for a pawnshop.

tîn-pâi, a shield. **pîn-pâi**, id. **chhiú-pâi**, id. **chit-bīn-pâi**, one shield. **hó-thâu-pâi**, shield with tiger's head on it. **chiáh-pâi**, to be one of the soldiers who carry shields (v. chiáh). **ién tîn-pâi**, to use a shield. **sái pîn-pâi**, id. **pâi-toà**, a long sword used in war.

pâi-á, playing cards. **chit-ki pâi-á**, one card. **poáh pâi-á**, to play at cards. **phah pâi-á**, to throw down a card. **kut-pâi**, dominoes made of bone. **gê-pâi**, do. of ivory. **phe gê-pâi**, to lay them out in playing.

pâi-thâu-tia, an idol attendant on Sêng-hông-iâ (v. tia).

pái, to talk plausibly so as to represent a thing better than it is: to talk over a man by plausible words. **gâu-pái**, skilful at deceiving by plausible talk. **kap-ì-pái**, talking him over, so as to swindle or cheat him, or secretly instigate him against another. **kap-goá teh-pái**, making very plausible excuses for not doing what I tell him. **pái-lōng**, to instigate by slanders, as to hatred, feud, or injury. **pái-lâi pái-khì**, to delude men into mutual enmity by maliciously slandering each to the other. **pái-kè-lâi, pái-kè-khì**, id., = chit-ki-chhùi, pái-kè-lâi pái-kè-khì [perhaps this word and all the other "pái" are really the same, from the root idea of shaking from one side to the other].

pái, to exchange, as similar things (esp. Cn. Ank.); also (Ank.), to borrow money. **pái-chiⁿ**, to exchange, as good for bad cash which we had given in payment; also (Ank.), to borrow money. **pái-oāⁿ**, to exchange. **pái-poah**, to exchange, as places, duties, or persons; esp. to send subordinates to a different place for a short time; to assist, as gods do (v. poah). **saⁿ-pái**, to exchange, as things (s. time). **pái-lâi pái-khì**, id. **pái-kè-lâi pái-kè-khì**, id. **pái kúi-îⁿ** (Ank.), to borrow a little money.

pái [R. to arrange; to set out], to shake about. **pái-lâi pái-khì**, to shake from side to side, as boat at anchor in a swell. **pái--chit-ē, pái--chit-ē**, to shake about in walking, as lame man or man who walks ill. **pái--cheh pái--cheh**, id. **pái-toā**, to take a step to the left, as chair-bearer. **pái-sió**, to take a step to the right. **iô-pái**, to strut; to walk ostentatiously; to shake about (v. iô). **pái-chhioh**, the pendulum of a clock.

pái-pè, to use underhand means (as intrigues, influence, or bribes) to advance one's own ends or injure another; to help over a difficulty, as the gods; to represent a man to his superior as worse than he really is. **pái-pē** (T.), id. **pái-pè bô-sū**, to assist out of trouble, as the gods. **khit--i pái-pè**, to suffer from the intrigues of another. **kap-goá teh-pái-pè**, trying to delude me by deceitful intrigues. **kāng-goá pái-pè**, id.

pái — **pái-kha**, lame; limping in walking. **kha pái-pái**, id. **pái-kha pái-chhiú**, feet lame and hands disabled, &c. **pái-pōe**, lame in leg or arm; all gone wrong (v. pōe). **pái-khoái**, mismanaged and all gone wrong, as affair that is gone wrong beyond mending; to change to strong opposition (v. khoái). **o-a kiò pái-sūi**, the crow called lame Sūi to his ruin (v. a).

pái, a turn, time, or occasion. **pái-pái**, every time; constantly. **ták-pái**, each time. **só-pái**, every time; over and over (v. só). **bô-siàu-pái**, a great many times. **chit-poàⁿ-pái**, only once, or very seldom. **chit-pái-á**, id. **saⁿ-pái**, thrice (s. exchange). **kúi-pái**, how often? **sêng chhit-pái**, to multiply by seven, esp. on the abacus. **āu-pái**, the next time. **chêng-pái**, on a former occasion.

chiàu-pái, in proper turn. **i-ê-pái**, his proper turn. **chhoàn-pái**, forcibly take one's turn before the proper time. **kháh-pái**, to come to the jetty and wait for passengers in regular turn, as boats do at night in turn. **saⁿ-pái-thòe**, to work by turns.

thàn-lâu-pái, to take advantage of the opportunity (fig. from time of tide). **hó-lâu-pái**, a favourable opportunity. **m̄-sī lâu-pái**, this is not the proper time for doing it. **che-sī sím-mihⁿ lâu-pái**, what sort of time is this? (I am too busy, or the time is quite unsuitable). **koáⁿ-kín ê-lâu-pái**, a time when great haste must be made.

tn̂g-pái, a junk that plies with goods and perhaps a few passengers, not every day.

pài (R. id.), to do reverence to; to worship; to pay a ceremonial visit; to pay respects to; to take as one's instructor or patron. **kèng-pài**, to worship. **kūi-pài**, to kneel and do reverence to. **pài-ip**, to make a bow, as to a superior. **kau-pài**, bride and bridegroom saluting each other. **tùi-pài**, id. **khók-khók-pài**, to bow low over and over. **phak-teh-pài**, to kneel and bow very low. **phak--teh khōng-khōng-pài**, to kneel and bow very often. **tùn-siú pài**, to bow the head in reverence or worship.

pài-thok, to request a friend, or man of similar station, to do a commission or give a message.

pài-kì^{n}, to pay a visit. **pài-hāu**, id. **pài-hōe**, visit of equal mandarins. **pài-chia^{n}**, to pay visits at new-year time. **pài-siū**, to make a congratulatory visit on birthday. **pài-kheh**, to visit acquaintances, as new graduate or mandarin, generally expecting to get presents. **pài-siā**, to give thanks ceremonially (v. siā). **siā-pài**, to go and pay respects to a man who has come and worshipped our deceased relative. **hàu-lâm siā-pài**, a son doing so after father's death (said only in scolding). **hê-pài**, to return a visit. **hôe-pài**, id. **tap-pài**, id., or a bow.

pài-kèng, to kneel and make offerings at the rites called "chiò." **pài-chhàm**, to perform certain Buddhist rites for the dead (v. chhàm). **pài-tùi**, to worship Confucius or Khoe-seng by antithetic sentences, as young scholars.

pài-toa^{n}, to send a card instead of calling. **pài-pió**, to present or forward a memorial to the emperor. **pài-pún**, id. **pài-pn̂g**, id. **pài-siòng**, to become prime minister (v. siòng).

pài-toā, to draw up the helm and lay it flat on deck.

pài sai-hū, to engage one's self or be engaged to a master, as apprentice. **pài sien-si^{n}**, to study under a teacher. **pài-báu**, to have one's name put on the books of an official in a yamun for protection (v. báu). **pài-sien** (C.), id. **pài tō-su**, to have one's name thus put on the books of the Tau-tai's yamun. **pài--lâng tsòe khòe-bú**, to take a woman as a sort of adoptive mother or patroness. **kiet-pài hia^{n}-tī**, men who agree to look on each other's parents as their own.

lé-pài, ceremonial worship; a week. **lé-pài-jit**, Sunday; Sabbath. **lé-pài-tn̂g**, a chapel. **pài-tn̂g**, id. **pài-it**, Monday. **pài-jī**, Tuesday, &c. **pài-kúi**, which day of the week?

pài-tiām, a cushion for kneeling on. **pài-thiap**, a card of invitation, or card with some polite phrase.

pāi (R. id.), to decay; to go to ruin; to be defeated; to ruin. **pāi-hoāi**, to ruin. **pāi--liáu**, undone! all gone wrong! **chhit-soah poeh-pāi**, all gone wrong. **pāi-pán**, damaged, as goods, or as affair all gone wrong. **pāi-chhī**, bad sale. **phoà-pāi**, ruined and bankrupt; all lost or squandered; wasted away, as family (v. phoà). **pang-pāi**, quite ruined and bankrupt, as firm or shop. **pāi i-ê-lō͘**, to damage ruinously a man's plans of action or means of livelihood. **pāi-ke**, to ruin a family, as a wicked son or bad wife, &c. **pāi-kok**, to ruin a nation or kingdom; said also of one man by his wickedness bringing shame on all his relations, or by his imprudence ruining a whole affair. **pāi hong-súi**, to injure the good luck of a place. **pāi tē-lí**, id. **siong-hong pāi-siòk**, to ruin the morals of a place, as a very wicked man or bad custom. **gék-lí pāi-lûn**, to commit incest. **pāi-bêng sit-chiet**, to commit some great and shameful crime (esp. adultery among relatives), so that one's name can never be clean again.

thâi-pāi, to be defeated in battle. **pāi-tīn**, id. **pāi-pok** (R.), id. **pāi-tsáu**, to be defeated and routed; to be put to flight. **pāi-peng**, defeated soldiers; to be defeated in battle. **ēng chit-ê, khì-pāi-peng**, we have lost our case by employing this fellow. **pāi-peng chi-chiòng, put-kám giên-ióng**, a defeated general dares not talk of courage.

pai^{n} [R. pan, spotted]. **chhiū^{n}-pai^{n}** (Cn.), get spotted with mould, as books or clothes.

pai^{n} (T.) **hia-pai^{n}**, = A. hia-pan; gaudy, fond of display, &c.

pai^{n} (T.), = A. pan, a man's name.

pâi^{n} (T.), = A. pêng, a side.

pái^{n} (T.), = A. péng, to turn. **pái^{n}-bûn**, = A. hoán-bûn, the 66th radical, at the side.

pāi^{n} (Cn.) **goā-pāi^{n}**, = goā-piāng, exclamation of great surprise.

pak (R. hok), the belly; the seat of the mind and feelings; (the barrel of a gun); the hollow, as of a decaying tree. **pak-tó**, the belly, or seat of mind.

chhiū-pak, the hollow in a tree. **àu-pak**, having a decayed hollow in the trunk, as tree. **toā-pak-chhèng**, a gun of large bore. **siang-pak-chhèng**, a doubled-barrelled gun or pistol.

tsát-pak, stupid; solid, not hollow. **sim-pak ê-lâng**, a very intimate friend and trusty confidential adviser. **sim-pak-lâng**, id. **moá^{n}-pak hūn-khì**, full of rage. **moá^{n}-pak bûn-chiu^{n}**, very learned, as to essays, &c. **moá^{n}-pak tō͘-liōng**, very compassionate and generous. **khoà^{n}-pak tō͘-liōng**, liberal; magnanimous. **tháu chit-pak hūn-khì**, to let out one's anger by expressing it in words. **lâng-sim-koa^{n}, gû-pak-tó**, very covetous. **peh-pak**, anxious grieved state of mind. **chhau-sim peh-pak**, id. **chiâu-sim peh-pak**, id. **lô-sim peh-pak**, id. **hoân-sim peh-pak**, id. **pak-tó bô-poà^{n}-tiám bák-tsúi**, has no learning or power of literary composition at all.

pak-lāi, within the belly, or mind, or heart; also, the entrails, as of a pig. **bóe pak-lāi**, to buy the entrails. **hó-pak-lāi**, very clever and intelligent. **pak-lāi khang-hu**, hungry; with empty stomach but no appetite, as sick man; said also of a man of weak and consumptive constitution, though outwardly looking well; illiterate.

pak-tsâi, the navel. **pak-tó-pi^{n}**, the soft part of the side below the ribs. **phoà-pak**, to rip up the belly; to tell one's whole mind. **ng pak-tó**, to hold one's belly, as in great pain. **làu-pak**, looseness of bowels. **tsáu-pak**, id. **sià-pak**, id. **phái^{n}-pak-tó**, severe diarrhœa. **hoán-pak**, stomach turned; vomiting. **thun-lóh-pak**, to swallow down. **chiáh-lóh-pak**, to swallow, as smoke.

toā-pak-tó, pregnant. **siang-pak hia^{n}-tī**, sons of same father and mother. **keh-pak hia^{n}-tī** (T.), sons of same father by different mothers.

péh-pak, a good edible fish, like the "bé-ka." **khoah-pak**, a sort with broad belly, not so good.

pak (R. hok), classifier of ornamental scrolls for hanging on walls. **chit-pak-pò͘**, a roll of cloth. **chit-pak-pút**, one scroll with picture of idol. **chit-pak-jī**, one scroll with written characters. **chit-pak tsâi-tsú-siū**, a scroll with picture of the impersonations of Wealth, Posterity, and Longevity.

pak (R. id.), to skin; to strip off; to plunder clothes from a man's back; to remove soil so as to make the ground lower and level. **khek-pak**, to extort money by oppression. **pak-phê**, to skin; to flay. **kiông-pak**, to strip and plunder of dress. **pak-sa^{n}**, id. **chhiú^{n}-pak**, to plunder and strip. **pak kng-kng**, to strip a man quite naked. **thǹg-pak-theh**, naked. **pak-theh-theh**, id. **pak kàu-chit-sin kng-liù-liù** (= liu), to strip stark naked, as a robber; said also of a bad fellow gambling away all that he has, even to his clothes.

pak-siap, feeling of pain and emptiness; very poor and wretched; dry and unpleasant, as food (v. siap).

pak (R. pok), north. **lâm-pak**, south and north. **tang-sai lâm-pak**, east, west, south, and north. **lâm-pak tùi-chhiong**, south and north right opposite, as in site for grave or house. **chhun lâm, hē pak; bô-tsúi thang boâ-bák**, south wind in spring and north wind in summer don't bring water enough to rub ink. **tang-pak**, north-east. **sai-pak**, north-west; a N.W. wind (v. sai). **hong pak**, the wind is from the north. **lêng-tsûn-pak**, a strong N. wind for several days about the beginning of the 5th month.

chiūⁿ-pak, to go to the north. **ǹg-pak**, facing the north. **bīn ǹg-pak**, to be a private individual.

pak-táu, Ursa Major (v. táu). **pak-kék**, the pole-star. **pak-kiaⁿ**, Pekin. **toā-pak**, the north of China, *e.g.* Shantung and beyond. **sió-pak**, parts of China a long way north from Amoy, but not so far; *e.g.* about Shanghai. **pak-thâu**, the north of China. **pak--sì**, on the north; northern region. **pak-kháu-goā**, the regions beyond the N.W. borders of China proper; *e.g.* Sin-kiong and I-lê, used as places for banishment. **pak-á**, a man of North China. **pak-kheh**, a Chinaman who trades between Amoy and the North of China (a native of either). **pak-tsûn**, vessels trading with North China. **pak-hè**, goods from the north. **pak-tāu**, beans or pease from the north. **pak-hiên**, sort of guitar. **pak-koán**, songs in the mandarin dialect (v. koán).

pak [R. variegated; to discuss, = pok]. **pak-tsáp**, having various colours mixed indistinctly together; skilful at a great many things. **pak jī-kut**, to examine minutely into the meaning of a character; examining too carefully and minutely into a matter.

pák (R. pók), to tie; to bind. **siuⁿ-pák**, too tight, as dress. **pák-ki-kut**, to make a framework, as for a lantern; to set a matter in proper train (v. ki). **pák-lâng-sn̂g**, to make a large wicker frame for cooking by steam. **pák-kè**, to change the front oar to the other side of the boat. **pák-kè**, to make the female head-ornament called "kè" (v. kè). **pák-kha**, to bind the feet of women. **beh-kè, chiah pák-kha**, to begin preparation when too late.

sok-pák, behaving properly, esp. avoiding too free manners, under the restraint of the presence of another, esp. a superior. **khit--i pé-pák**, afraid or unable to do something because restrained by another's commands or wishes. **pé-pák--teh**, do., or unable to go somewhere because of household cares or business. **hē-hong-siók pé-pák**, to have to do something (against one's own wish or views) because of the general custom. **hē-mê-kúi pé-pák**, to be enslaved by the devil to some bad course.

pák, to hire or rent for a long time; to charter or apprentice; to farm, as revenue. **pau-pák**, to farm a monopoly from the government. **pē-pák--ê**, having a monopoly of a trade from a supreme board; said also to a man acting in an overbearing way and trying to prevent another selling some article. **lí m̄-sī pē-pák--ê**, have not you a monopoly from Pekin? (said to such a man). **pák bé-á**, to farm the revenue, as of opium, &c. **pák pe-thâu**, to farm the monopoly of some article at a place. **pák iâm-koán**, to farm the salt monopoly for a district.

pák-tsûn, to charter a vessel. **pák-chhân**, to rent land for farming. **pák chit-téng-kiō**, to hire a sedan for a long journey. **pák tn̂g-kang**, to hire a labourer for a long period. **pák--i tn̂g-kang**, to be thus hired by him. **pák lê-tsâi**, to hire a boy, almost like a slave, for several years. **pák--lâng tsòe-lê-tsâi**, to hire out (as one's son) to be like a slave to another for so long; to be so hired out or bound so. **pák--lâng tsng-hì**, to apprentice out a boy to actors for a long term of years.

pák (Cn.) **lâ-pák**, = A. nâ-pòk, carrots.

pan [R. name of disease]. **chhut-pan**, to have a severe disease that makes dark spots on the body. **chhut o-pan**, a very dangerous fever (typhus?) with black spots. **chhut âng-pan**, a sort with red spots, less dangerous. **khí-pan**, these spots appearing. **giah-pan**, to puncture the spots, for healing.

pan [R. to publish by authority]. **pan-chiàu**, to publish an imperial decree. **pan--chhut-lâi**, to publish everywhere by imperial authority. **pan-hêng thiⁿ-ē**, do. to all the world. **pan-hêng thien-hā**, id. **pē-pan--ê**, published by order of a supreme board, as imperial decree.

pan [R. pān, piēn, ready]. **pan-gî**, cheap (v. gî).

pan (cf. pien, to pull). **pan-chí**, a ring worn on the thumb, esp. by archers, also for ornament. **gėk-pan-chí**, an ornamental thumb-ring of jade-stone.

pan [R. poan, pan, name of insect]. **pan-bâ**, a small beetle like the Spanish fly; blistering-plaster is made from it.

pan (C.) **pan-chi-hoa**, = A. pien-chi-hoe, the bombax-tree.

pan (C. poan). **sam-pan-khiah**, the interstices between the battlements of a wall.

pan [R. a company; relays in order], a relay or company acting in turn. **koan-pan**, to purchase rank or office; purchased office or rank. **lán chit-pan ê-lâng**, we this sort of people (said by police or actors).

a-pan, a sailor who climbs the mast; also, unreasonable in money matters, *e.g.* refusing to pay enough, but not so bad as "áu-bân." **kap-goá teh-a-pan**, refusing to pay me all that is due. **a-pan-hiâⁿ**, the middle bulk-head of a boat.

lé-pan-chhioh, the foot-measure used by carpenters and masons (v. lé; v. chhioh).

hì-pan, a company of actors. **hì-á-pan**, young actors. **toā-pan-hì**, plays in mandarin dialect by grown-up men. **sòe-pan-hì**, do. by young actors.

pan-thâu, head-men of mandarin's attendants and lictors, one for each side of the yamun, and more in larger yamuns. **pan-thiaⁿ**, central room of the house in a yamun where the police, &c., sit waiting. **pan-pâng**, side-rooms of do.

bûn-pan bú-pan, ranks of civil and military mandarins in attendance on emperor at audience. **tsō-pan**, mandarin's attendants and lictors. **kun-pan**, mandarin's servants. **kiō-pan**, mandarin's chair-bearers. **chhe-pan**, musicians who play at meal-time in yamun; military musicians.

khiā-pan, to stand before the mandarin's tribunal (as his attendants) when the court is held. **tsàn-pan**, do., or when the mandarin goes out or in. **chiūⁿ-pan**, to enter on one's term of duty, as lictors, police, &c. **tioh-pan**, to come to one's turn or time of duty about yamun. **kai-pan**, do., of civil mandarins only (v. kai). **lòh-pan**, to retire from duty on ending one's term. **kè-pan**, turn of duty passed to another. **ē-pan**, the next time our turn comes. **oāⁿ-pan**, to change the garrison or watch of soldiers. **oāⁿ-pan-peng**, a company of soldiers who change the garrison of Formosa. **toà-**

pan-peng, to lead soldiers to relieve others, as garrison of Formosa.

pan (R. id.) **pan-pan**, speckled or spotted, as animal. **pan--ê**, pock-marked man. **chit-ê-bīn pan-pan**, face all pock-marked. **hoe-pan**, speckled; spotted. **chhiūⁿ-pan**, spotted by sun or age (not by illness); spotted with black spots of mould, as clothes from damp. **pan-tiám**, spotted; slightly pock-marked. **niauⁿ-pan-tiám**, marked with small spots; slightly pock-marked. **hó-pan-tiám**, marked with large long streaks like a tiger. **hó-pan**, id.

tiong-pan, a very small fresh-water fish, abundant in the èng-chhài-hô at Amoy. **tiong-pan-hî**, id.

pân — **tók-pân**, a sort of bright green flying beetle (s. jar). **tē-pân** (C.), id. **gî-pân** (T.), id.

pân (C.), = A. pêng, side (P. pêng).

pân [R. pin, a sort of earthen jar]. **tê-pân**, a teapot, especially tall and narrow. **chiú-pân**, a wine jug. **lē-si-pân**, a tall small-necked wine-jug, used on ceremonial occasions. **hoe-pân**, a tall jug or glass jar for cut flowers in water, or for artificial flowers. **chit-pân-hoe**, a bouquet of cut flowers for a flower-glass. **tók-pân**, an earthen vessel for flowers (s. beetle). **tē-pân** (C.), id. **lé-pân** (Cn.), a wine-jug used at ancestral worship and such ceremonies. **lé-pân-chiok** (Cn.), do., and cups for these ceremonies.

pán (R. id.), a board; a coffin; a bamboo for beating; classifier of blows in punishment. **sam-pán**, a small boat; a female slave with large feet (v. sam). **tsàu-pán**, a flat ornament held in the hand in ancient times at audience (v. tsàu). **pán-tsô**, a sort of breech-loading gingall. **pán-kim**, stiff gilded paper, used for ornamental work.

toā-pán-kun, the great sinew in the bend of the knee. **pán-lâ-iû**, the large mass of fat at an animal's side. **pán-chhng**, large blotches of itch at the posteriors.

siū-pán, a coffin made ready during life. **pán-tiàm**, a coffin shop. **pán-phe**, an unfinished coffin.

toā-pán, the large bamboo for beating with. **sió-pán**, the small one. **phah toā-pán**, to beat with the large bamboo. **phah sió-pán**, do. with the small. **khiā-pán**, to beat with the edge of the bamboo. **phah kúi-pán**, how many blows of the bamboo? (in yamun). **ēng to-pán siau**, to strike with the flat of a sword (v. to).

tek-pán, bamboo split into strips suitable for use as boarding. **an tek-pán**, to lay down bamboo boarding, esp. on threshold. **tek-pán-í**, a seat made of bamboo laid horizontally.

pán-í, a broad bench, on which one can sleep. **pán-pîⁿ**, a flat wooden terrace. **tē-pán**, a wooden floor on ground-floor. **tōe-pán**, id. **thien-hô-pán**, a ceiling. **thien-lô-pán**, id. **thien-hoa-pán**, id. **mn̂g-siⁿ-pán**, the leaf of a door before it is put on, or when taken off for some purpose. **khò-pán**, cross-board for elbows in large sedan. **iên-pán**, perpendicular boarding carried round below the eaves to cover the ends of the clap-boards.

pán (R. id.), blocks for printing; types [this word is often interchanged with the former]. **in-pán**, blocks for printing. **chheh-pán**, id. **khek-pán**, to engrave blocks for printing (v. khek). **khan-pán** (R.), id. **oáh-pán**, movable types. **tâng-pán**, copperplate. **chháu-pán**, ill-cut blocks. **kū-pán**, old blocks; old edition. **sơ-pán**, printed at Soo-chow. **chiang-pán**, printed at Chang-chew.

pán [R. pān, to manage; a pattern; a sample]. **pán-tsú**, supercargo or owner of junk, esp. in junks trading south. **pāi-pán**, damaged, as goods or anything; unsuccessful and ruined, as affair. **chip-sí-pán**, very obstinate in keeping to one's own way. **chip kó-pán**, to adhere obstinately to old customs or patterns. **chiàu-kó-pán**, according to ancient customs or pattern, *e.g.* rather coarsely made though strong and good, or made without using the latest improvements. **kó-pán-lâng**, a man who is quiet and straightforward, moderate and simple in his tastes, not fond of display or amusements, or new-fangled ways.

pán (R. id.) **kap-pán**, a square-rigged vessel (from Malay, "kapel"). **kap-pán-tsûn**, id. **kap-pán-á**, a boat of foreign build, or small yacht. **kap-pán-hoán**, the war of 1842.

pán [R. hoán, to turn over, = col. péng], (also C., = A. péng, to turn over).

pán-bûn, the 66th or 67th radical written at the side.

pán (C.) **pán-sit**, = A. pién-sit, a cake of dough containing minced meat (v. sit).

pān [R. hún, pān, to dress up]. **táⁿ-pān**, style of dress; dress; fashion of place or time; to dress one's self just "comme il faut." **gâu-táⁿ-pān**, fond of dressing one's self just in strict propriety according to one's station. **soe-tsng táⁿ-pān**, to adorn one's self, as woman.

pān (R. pān, piēn), = bān, a lobe of an orange, lemon, or pumelo, &c.

pān (C.) **kap-pān**, = kap-bān, a sort of strong chest.

pān (R. id.), pattern; sample; manner; form; to manage or take action; (to prepare; a manager).

bô-chhûn-pān, without having had any previous thought of it (v. chhûn). **pān-phoe** (C.), to conjecture or calculate beforehand. **bô-pān-phoe** (C.), unexpectedly. **bô-phài-pān** (C.), id.

bô-pān, no regularity; all various. **kóng kàu-bô-pān**, to talk falsely, or at least with great exaggeration and recklessness; to make exorbitant demands. **toā-pān**, liberal; frank and open; self-composed and at ease when meeting with strangers or superiors; dignified in manner; wide and flowing, as dress; large in body. **khah-toā-pān**, more so; also getting on better in business, or looking better off. **siⁿ-tsòe toā-pān**, large in body.

hó-pān, easy to manage or settle; good of its sort; of good form or pattern; wealthy; making a good profit.

pān-thâu, a sort: a sample; a muster of goods. **chiàⁿ-pān**, a fair profit; properly made. **siōng-pān**, first-rate. **tiong-pān**, of medium quality. **hā-pān**, inferior quality. **chiàu-pān**, according to sample or pattern. **chiàu-pān-bóe**, to buy by sample. **sûn-pān**, all alike, and like the pattern. **khoàⁿ-pān**, to look at the pattern or sample, so as to follow it. **pí-pān**, to compare the pattern. **tsoáh-pān**, to differ from the pattern or sample. **tsáu-pān**, id. **hoán-pān**, to send goods inferior to the sample. **hè-pān**, a sample or muster of goods. **tê-pān**, a sample or muster of tea, as in a paper, or in a small box.

kha-pān, the measure of one's foot. **khoàⁿ-jit-pān**, to observe how far the sun's shadow has gone. **tsúi-pān**, the state of the tide; the depth of water; also, a piece of stone or brick which marks how much water may be taken from a common stream. **phah tsúi-**

厦英大辭典

pān, to take soundings with lead or pole. **sím-mih**ⁿ **pān-sia**ⁿ, how many fathoms deep?

su-pān, a clerk in a mandarin's office. **tsū-pān** (Cn.), id. **hiáp-pān**, an assistant mandarin in the customs or other office (v. hiáp). **tāi-pān**, an agent or temporary substitute authorized to act for his principal, either in business, or for a mandarin; to act temporarily, as such a substitute, or as agent. **thòe--i tāi-pān**, to act temporarily in his place. **bóe-pān**, a servant who buys provisions for a hong; a ship's steward. **beh-khì bóe-pān**, I am going to buy things for household use.

pān-hè, to buy goods in order to sell them again, either on one's own account or on commission. **thok--lâng pān-hè**, to commission a man to buy goods for us. **thok-kià pān-hè**, do. from a place a good way off. **pān-tê**, to buy up tea where it is grown. **chhái-pān**, to select and buy goods.

pī-pān, to prepare; to make ready. **chhoân-pān**, to make all ready (persons or things). **pān-chhe**, to prepare food, lodging, servants, bearers, &c., for a mandarin who is coming (v. chhe). **pān-kòng**, to prepare tribute for emperor. **pān-toh**, to prepare a feast. **pān-chhài**, to prepare and cook food for guests (v. chhài). **pān-chiú**, prepare liquor for guests. **pān-chiú chhiáⁿ--lâng**, to invite people to such a feast.

pān-lí, to manage an affair. **pān-lí tek-hoat**, do. successfully. **pān-sū**, to manage affairs. **kàn-pān**, to manage an affair for another (v. kàn). **kiù-pān**, to take vigorous action in a case, as a mandarin. **pau-pān**, to take up a case (for large payment) and manage it one's self, merely using the name of the real party, as vile intriguing pettifogging literati do (considered a serious crime); also, to roll up a sample for examination.

pang [R. hong, square]. **bīn-bé sì-pang**, face full and well-proportioned. **sì-pang hō-tiōng**, grave and sedate (opp. khin-phiò); fat and full-faced.

pang — **chhéng-pang**, to behave or speak in a proud bragging way. **chhéng-pang-tsúi**, id.

pang [R. hong, to seal]. **pang-tiâu**, long slips of paper pasted on the door of a house where a mandarin is temporarily living, telling his surname, rank, and titles; also (Cn. T.), = A. hong-tiâu, slips of red paper by which mandarins seal up houses or take possession of vessels.

pang (R. id.), a state; a kingdom; a country. **pang-kok**, id. **bān-pang**, all nations. **bān-pang bān-kok**, id. **hoan-pang**, foreign nations. **goā-pang**, id. **īⁿ-pang** (X.), Gentile nations.

pang [R. peng; cf. pheng], to slip down, as a landslip; to burst, as an embankment; to scale off, as paint or plaster. **pang-lang**, id. **pang-hoāi**, to break down, as embankment or landslip. **pang-hām**, to break down suddenly, as man's health or wealth, or as a landslip or embankment. **pang-pāi**, utterly ruined and bankrupt, as shop or firm. **pang chit-khiah**, a part having fallen, as of a wall. **tsúi pang--khì**, embankment burst. **pang hông-hô**, banks of the Yellow River given way. **soaⁿ pang**, the mountain falls in a landslip. **soaⁿ pang, tōe lih**, mountains falling and earth splitting. **tsúi pang-soaⁿ**, said of a man suddenly becoming poor from a state of wealth, or of a man's constitution suddenly breaking down in a few days. **huih pang-soaⁿ** (esp. C.), = hiet-pheng, a flow of blood from the female organs.

pang (R. id.), to help; a fleet or company travelling together; a lot, as of letters sent by one opportunity, or such like. **long-pang**, to work one's passage in a vessel.

āu-pang, another time. **thâu-pang**, the first company, as of persons or vessels. **thâu-pang-phoe**, the first letter sent on some special subject (as by a vessel or passenger), said after it has arrived. **āu-pang-phoe**, a following letter (as one with more details), gen. said before it comes. **jī-pang-phoe**, the second letter. **chit-pang-phoe**, the letter by this opportunity. **chit-pang-phoe**, a lot of letters for one place arriving by one opportunity. **chit-pang-tsûn**, a fleet; a number of vessels sailing together. **ká-pang**, to join in one fleet or company for a voyage or journey. **koe-pang**, to fasten many junks together in one mass.

pang-lím, to become a graduate of the rank called "lím-seng." **khó toā-pang-phoe**, do., said of the Sew-tsai who stands at head of list.

saⁿ-pang, to help one another; to give assistance. **tàu-saⁿ-pang**, id. **pang--i**, help him. **pang-tsō** (r.), to help. **pang-tsān** (r. and X.), id. **pang-chhiú**, to help; an assistant. **tàu-pang-chhiú**, to help. **chîⁿ pang--i**, to help with money. **pang-thiap**, to give a regular allowance, as to widows, &c. **pang-chhe**, unauthorized assistants of the constables (goân-chhe) or police.

pang (R. hong), a plank; a board. **chhu-pang**, to lay down boards so as to make a level surface. **khau-pang**, to plane boards. **khui pang-lō**, to make a groove in a long cross piece of wood for the ends of the boards of a partition.

pò-pang, sort of pasteboard made of old clothes (used for shoe-soles). **póh-pang**, thin planks or lath. **póh-pang boah-he**, lath and plaster. **lâu-pang**, floor of upper story. **tiām-pang**, boards of the floor of a boat. **pìn-pang**, boarding used as a partition. **pang-tó**, a wooden partition. **kè-pang**, the shelf on the upper part of a bed. **jia-hong-pang**, board at head of bed. **bān-thien-pang**, board on top of bedstead. **toā-pang**, long footstool along side of bed (below), with three drawers in it. **táh-pang**, id. **chiūⁿ-táh-pang, soà-beh-chiūⁿ bîn-chhn̂g**, if he get on the step he will get on the bed. **tah thiàu-pang**, to put up a scaffolding for building, &c. (v. thiàu).

pâng (R. pông), a room; a bed-room; a primary division of a clan or family. **pâng-thâu**, a primary division of a family or clan. **pâng-tiúⁿ**, head of such a branch or division. **kiông-pâng**, a powerful branch of a family (v. kiông). **toā-pâng khi-hū sòe-pâng**, a large branch oppresses a smaller one. **béng-pâng lám-thiāu**, a weak subdivision of a powerful branch of a family. **tó-pâng**, a branch of a family become extinct (s. sew). **kè-pâng**, to be adopted, as a son (v. kè). **chiap pâng-hūn**, to keep up the succession, as adopted son.

lák-pâng, the six offices or departments in a yamun corresponding to the six supreme boards at capital; the secretaries in charge of them. **pâng-khe**, the six officials in charge of these six departments in a yamun. **piaⁿ-pâng**, the office or official for military matters. **hêng-pâng**, do. for punishments. **kang-pâng**, do. for public works. **hō-pâng**, do. for revenue, especially land-tax. **lī-pâng**, do. for matters concerning inferior mandarins and candidates for office; often has also charge of the treasury of the yamun. **lé-pâng**, do. for ceremonies. **khò-pâng**, a treasury; a treasurer. **pò-pâng**, office where high graduates, &c., give in their names (v. pò). **pió-pâng**, office and officer in a great yamun for sending despatches to the throne. **hō-pâng,** lodge at gate of great yamun for cards, letters, &c.; also, office in military mandarin's yamun for general business. **pan-pâng,** rooms in yamun occupied by police, &c. **tsáp-chhe-pâng,** rooms in yamun occupied by various messengers and underlings.

tū-pâng, a mandarin's cook.

ki^n-pâng, a sentry-box. **óh-pâng,** a school. **tsu-pâng,** id. (v. tsu). **ní^n-pâng,** a dyer's shop. **bō-pâng,** a house used as a flour-mill. **chièn-pâng,** a store-house; a godown. **siù-pâng,** a shop for embroidery; a woman's chamber (v. siù). **bé-pâng,** a stable. **bit-pâng,** honey-comb.

pâng-keng, a room. **khùn-pâng,** a bed-room. **kiâ^n-pâng,** to have sexual intercourse with wife or concubine. **phien-pâng,** a concubine. **léng-pâng,** said of wife or concubine out of favour (v. léng). **chiú-khang-pâng,** to be a widow. **phoā^n-pâng,** an aged female accompanying the bride to the husband's house (v. phoā^n). **chìn-pâng,** the bride entering the bed-room about beginning of marriage rites. **thàm-pâng,** younger brother or nephew of bride taking presents to her a day or two after marriage (v. thàm). **joán-pâng,** (C.), id.

pâng (R. hông), to sew with cross stitches over a rough edge, generally close and fine, often over and over; to overcast in sewing. **khiā-pâng,** to overcast without folding in the edge. **tó-pâng,** to overcast after folding in the rough edge (s. room).

pâng (R. bông). **pâng-se,** borax; used in melting gold or silver (cf. pêng-se).

pâng [R. pêng, interchanged with "pêng," proof], a surname.

pâng [R. a high house], a surname.

pâng [R. hông, to meet]. **hó-lâng sa^n-pâng,** may good men keep company; only said in Tauist rites.

páng [R. to tie; cf. col. póng], to bandage with splints, as a broken leg or arm.

páng — **keng-páng,** the outside of the arm close to the shoulder joint. **keng-páng,** manner of stretching one's arm for archery. **chhiú-páng,** id. **keng-páng súi,** manner of stretching arm for archery very good.

pàng (R. hòng), to let go; to let loose; to set free; to set off, as gun or crackers; to sail a vessel outwards; to lend on interest. **pàng-chhut,** to set at liberty, as prisoner. **bô-pàng-chhut,** does not now lend money any more, as near the end of the year.

kiâ^n-pàng, behaviour. **che m̄-sī kha-pàng,** this is very bad conduct, *e.g.* gambling or licentiousness.

pàng-tsá, early in the morning. **pàng-kín kiâ^n,** to walk fast.

pàng-tiò, to fish with hooks (v. tiò). **pàng-hî,** to put young fish in a pond for breeding; to use nets or lines in deep-sea fishing. **pàng-chîm,** to set wicker-work traps like baskets to catch crabs. **pàng-lêng,** to set the nets called "lêng" (+). **pàng-tók,** to put poison in food or drink. **pàng-pī^n,** to make a patient ill or keep him ill, so as to get more fees, as Chinese doctors sometimes do.

pàng-hé, to set on fire; arson. **pàng-chhèng,** to fire a gun or cannon. **pàng-pé,** to shoot at a mark at full distance. **pàng-phàu,** to set off crackers (v. phàu). **pàng-tiáp,** to burn paper prayers. **pàng-sià,** to burn paper images at rites for the dead. **pàng-tsoá,** to scatter paper before the coffin as it is carried to the grave. **pàng-ke,** to scatter sharp-pointed things, as impediments for an enemy.

pàng-pio, to offer the prize for the dragon-boat race (v. pio). **pàng hong-chhe,** to fly a kite. **pàng-tsûn,** to set sail. **pàng-iû^n,** to go to sea, as trading junk (v. iû^n). **pàng-tsúi-teng,** to launch a lamp on the water, for the spirits. **pàng-káng,** a pilot.

pàng-tiû, to give out tallies (to coolies) along with the bales. **pàng-thiap,** to distribute cards of invitation. **pàng-hun,** to sell a smoke of tobacco for two or three cash.

pàng-lêng, to lead down the auspicious influence of a hill to a house, grave, &c. (+). **pàng-hō͘,** to rain in small quantities. **pàng-tsúi,** to let out water, as from a reservoir or irrigated field, &c.

pàng-bit, to make honey, as the bee. **pàng-nn̄g,** to lay numerous eggs, as moths, &c. **pàng-jiō,** to make water. **pàng-sái,** to have a motion of the bowels. **pàng-pùn,** id. **pàng-lī,** to have (mucous) dysentery (+). **pàng-âng,** to pass blood; bloody dysentery. **pàng-phùi,** to pass wind.

pàng-hong, to pass wind; to throw out a threat, in order to frighten a man, by saying it to third parties who are expected to repeat it. **sì-kòe pàng-hong,** to circulate such threats. **pàng-sia^n,** to warn a man that we will punish or accuse him if he do so and so. **pàng-tiau,** to threaten. **pàng-tiau pàng-tńg,** id.

bák-chiu pàng-khoeh, to shut the eyes. **pàng-toā-sòe-bák,** to wink at faults.

pàng-bô-khoà^n--ki^n, to pretend not to see. **pàng-bô-thia^n--ki^n,** pretend not to hear. **pàng-bô-iàu-kín,** to treat a matter as of no consequence. **pàng-kù-tsāi,** let him have his own way. **pàng-hō͘--i ka-kī,** to leave him to himself, without help. **pàng-hō͘-i-sí,** intentionally leave him to die of neglect, as sick man.

pàng-sak, to reject or abandon. **pàng-hiet-kák,** to throw away. **pàng-lī** (r.), to let go (+). **pàng-ke-hé,** to bequeath property. **pàng-i-khì,** let him go. **thau-pàng,** to release secretly. **pàng-soah,** to make an end of a matter (v. soah).

pàng-kun-chiòng, to send spiritual officers and soldiers to help their votaries, as idols. **pàng-peng,** id. **pàng-pia^n** (T.), id. **pō͘-pàng--ê,** directly appointed by the supreme board of office, as a mandarin. **thi^n-pàng--ê,** Heaven-sent, as a calamity, *e.g.* tigers.

pàng-tá^n, confident and courageous. **pàng-sim,** to put one's mind at ease. **chhiú pàng-koâi^n,** to treat a man more gently than we had intended, or than he strictly deserves. **pàng-chhiú,** to let one's hand fall by one's side. **bōe-pàng-pō͘,** only able to take very short steps, as man who is sick or has a sore leg. **pàng-lòh,** to lay down, as a thing; to let down, as the hands, or as temper. **pàng-hē** (C.), to lay down (+).

pàng-hē (C. hē), to dismiss school, several times each day. **pàng-kè,** to dismiss school for the holidays. **pàng-kè,** to lower the price, in selling. **pàng-tang,** to dismiss school for short vacation at harvest time. **pàng-jòah,** do., in the hottest part of summer. **pàng-kang,** to cease work for a time. **bô-pàng-chit-jit,** without intermitting one single day.

pàng-lēng, to slacken; to slack out. **pàng-sang,** id. (v. sang). **pàng-nńg,** to let soft or loose, as muscles of limb (v. nńg). **pàng-kha-kun,** to cut the tendon of a man's heel. **pàng-lun,** to let a boat go astern. **pàng-mn̂g-lî,** to let down a door-screen. **pàng-só,** to take off a man's chains. **pàng-kê,** to take off the canque. **pàng-ngóeh,** to remove the torture instrument from the feet. **pàng-soán**, do., from the hands. **pàng-sīⁿ**, to save alive an animal bought for the purpose (superstitious).

pàng-siàu, to give credit, esp. for goods. **pàng-chè**, to lend money on interest. **pàng-chè ê-lâng**, a money-lender, who makes it his business. **pàng-tāng-chè**, to lend on heavy usury. **pàng-tāng-lāi**, id. **pàng-lāi**, to lend on interest. **pàng-lāi-chîⁿ**, id. **pàng-lī-sek**, id. **pàng-tsúi-lāi**, to lend for a venture on a voyage, at very high rate. **pàng-tsûn-thâu**, id. **pàng tiáⁿ-kám-phû**, to lend to gamblers, getting interest three times in one day. **pàng jit-á-chîⁿ**, to lend a few hundred cash, counted as a thousand, and take back about ten each day till all is paid up.

pāng — **pîⁿ-pāng**, level.

pāng [R. pō, sudden; violent]. **ơ-àm pėh-pāng**, very sudden, as calamity. **ơ-ien pėh-pāng**, id. (v. pėh).

pāng (R. id.), a short club. **toā-thûi toā-pāng**, large sticks and clubs; sometimes said of a large coarse-looking man. **kiáh-thûi kiáh-pāng**, said of a man fond of quarrelling.

pāng — **pāng-sióh**, spoiled with damp or heat, as food.

pāng (R. id.), name given to two sorts of shell-fish, the pearl-oyster, and a very large bivalve (found in the neighbourhood), the shell of which is used as a spoon. **pāng-khak**, mother-of-pearl, or shell of the native "pāng." **pāng-khak-tsu**, false pearls, made of mother-of-pearl or other shell. **ùt-pāng siong-chhî, gû-jîn tek-lī**, when the bird and the shell-fish seize each other, the fisherman makes gain (said of mandarins and underlings making gain of the people's lawsuits). **lút-pāng**, &c., id.

pat [R. eight, = col. poeh]. **pat-jī-kha**, walking with toes much turned out. **sù-sî pat-chiet**, the four seasons and eight terms. **pat-chiet**, counting as 100 when really only 80 (v. chiet). **jī-pat thiu**, to get commission, &c., of 20 per cent. **jī-pat ka-jîn** (R.), a beautiful girl about sixteen years old. **mơ sip-pat**, to play a game with six dice.

pat-sien, the eight genii, &c. (v. sien). **pat-koà**, the eight diagrams (v. koà). **pat-thoân**, a pattern common on flowered silk (v. thoân). **pat-hun**, = lē-su, the simpler form of the seal character. **pat-tsō**, a sedan with eight bearers. **pat-tâi**, a mandarin entitled to use eight bearers. **pat-chiáng-tsûn**, eight-oared boats used by customs (v. chiáng).

chhit-thong pat-tát, road clear of obstacles, so as to be good for travelling. **sù-ûi pat-tát**, all round; everywhere; in all places. **sù-hong pat-tát**, id.

pat (T.), = A. bat, to know.

pát [R. piét, piet, to distinguish; difference; of another sort], another, only in the sense of different, not the same, like Latin "alius," French "autre" (but never in the sense of "one more," which is "koh chit-ê," like French "encore un," German "noch ein"); used with any of the classifiers, *e.g.* **pát-chiah, pát-ki, pát-ê**, a different one. **pát-hāng**, a different sort. **pát-hō**, id. **pát-jit**, a different day.

pát-mihⁿ, a different thing; different. **pát-mn̂gh** (Cn. T.), id. **pát-mihⁿ-tāi**, quite a different matter; quite another thing. **bô-pát-mihⁿ**, nothing else; nothing but this. **bô-pát-mihⁿ-tāi**, id. **bô-pát-hāng**, id.

pát-lâng, a different man; another person. **pát-lâng ê-kiáⁿ sí-bōe-liáu**, said of using other men's sons for dangerous work. **pát-lâng--ê kûn-thâu-bú, cheng-bōe-thiàⁿ**, hitting with another's fist we feel no pain.

pát (C.) **lát-pát**, = A. nâⁿ-á-pút, the guava.

pau [R. placenta; uterine]. **pau-thai**, the caul (of the womb). **pau-the**, id.

pau-chek, father's younger brother. **pau-siok**, id. **pau-peh**, father's elder brother. **pau-heng**, elder brother by same father. **pau-tē**, younger do.

tông-pau, having same mother. **tông-pau kiōng-jú**, from same mother and same milk. **tông-pau hiaⁿ-tī**, brothers by same parent. **tông-pau chí-bē**, sisters by do. **tông-pau īⁿ-hū**, of same mother by different father. **tông-pau ī-hū**, id.

pau — **khí-pau**, a gum-boil. **sīⁿ khí-pau**, to have a gum-boil.

pau (R. id.), to wrap up; to inclose or include; to plate with metal; to surround, as an enemy; to guarantee or insure; a package or bale; classifier of packages; a sort of round soft cake; a surname. **pau-lau**, to wrap up, include, or guarantee, &c. **pau-hong**, to close, paste, or seal up carefully, as a parcel or letter inclosing others (v. hong). **pau-iông** (R.), to endure, or indulge, or be patient with another, in regard to his conduct. **tò-pau**, to cut off and surround an enemy.

pau-tsoá, to wrap up in paper. **pau-kim**, to plate thickly with gold. **tâng-pau**, dollars filled with brass. **pau-tâng**, id. **pau-thn̂g**, to inclose sugar, as in a pie or cake. **pau-āⁿ**, inclose stuffing of mince, &c. (v. āⁿ). **pau-chheh**, to wrap up books.

pau-hâm, to include; vague or ambiguous, as language. **pau-koat** (r.), to include. **pau-lám**, to monopolize; to take the whole management. **pau-lám-bé**, to engage to make up what may be wanting in a subscription. **pau-liám-bé**, id. **pau-lién-bé**, id. **pau-pák**, to monopolize a trade by farming it from government. **pau-tsāi**, to carry goods in large quantity, making one charge for the lot. **pau-pān**, to take the whole management of a lawsuit, as a deceitful intriguing lawyer (v. pān). **pau-pè**, to favour the guilty for bribes, as yamun people; to defraud one's employer, &c. (v. pè). **pau-i**, to engage to heal a man, taking no payment unless the cure be effected.

pau-niáⁿ, to warrant; to insure; to guarantee. **pau-pó** (r.), id. **goá kā-lí-pau**, I guarantee it for you. **pau-soaⁿ pau-hái**, daring to take the responsibility of anything (lit. in sea or land).

io-pau, a purse worn at the girdle at the side. **phoāⁿ-pau**, do. usually ornamented. **phoāⁿ-pau sìⁿ-tē**, do. and fan-case. **hau-pau**, a sort of purse (v. hau). **hun-pau**, a tobacco-pouch. **hiuⁿ-pau**, incense bags, used only for the smell. **hé-pau**, powder wrapped up and thrown in war; a "stink-pot." **hé-lêng-pau**, pouch for carrying the lighted match for a match-lock. **kiú-liông-pau**, a pouch used by soldiers for carrying powder and bullets. **chheh-pau**, books tied in a napkin or cloth, *e.g.* used by scholars. **chháu-pau**, a grass-mat bag; a stupid fellow. **ka-tsù-pau**, coarse matting, used for bags. **chhài-pau**, vegetables, &c., wrapped in thin cakes and fried. **bah-pau**, minced meat wrapped up and fried. **bīn-pau**, bread. **mīⁿ-pau**, id. **pau-á**, sort of soft cakes. **pau-á-ôe**, small shoes with soft cloth soles for infants. **pau-á-běh**, soft socks for children.

pau-hók, a bundle of clothes, &c. (used by travellers, &c.) **pau-kó** (C.), id. **pau-phê**, the wrapper

46

or covering of goods or dollars, subtracted in calculating the nett amount. **jīn pau-phê**, to acknowledge the wrapper or envelope, as evidence of the quantity or of the identity in making an exchange. **sái thùi-pau**, to cheat by giving a bad article for a good one, or an inferior bride or bridegroom (v. thùi).

pau-thâu, a bag full of goods, esp. dried eatables; a small paper package, as of tobacco; mist on the hill-tops; to wrap a cloth round one's head. **pau-thâu-tiàm**, a shop that only sells whole bags, as of dried fruits, &c., above 100 pounds weight or so. **pau-thâu seng-lí**, this sort of wholesale business. **tsòe-pau-thâu**, to carry on such a business. **pau thâu-péh**, to wear a white cloth on the head, in deepest mourning for parents.

pau (R. id.), (cf. pâu), a surname; a sort of round fish, good for the eyes and for the kidneys. **pau-hî**, this sort of fish.

pâu (R. pau), = pau, a surname.

pāu [R. pō, violent, to strike, = col. phāu, pā], to strike the upper part of the head with the hand somewhat closed. **pāu thâu-khak**, id. **ng-thâu kù-i-pāu** (putting one's hands to the head, and waiting quietly to be struck), said of a man yielding so far that he is ready to endure any injury or indignity.

pauh (cf. puh). **pauh-khí**, the two upper incisor teeth projecting too much. **pauh--chhut-lâi**, to burst out, as something (*e.g.* grain) in a package tied too tight. **hoat-pauh**, to come out, as a secret. **chhut-pauh**, id. **tāi-chì hoat-pauh**, the affair is come out now. **pauh** (C.), = A. puh, to bud. **pauh liáp-á** (C.), to have small pimples, &c.

pauh (Cn. T.), = A. mauhⁿ, to embezzle a portion of money.

páuh (= bâuh), to take a rough average, as in bargain or calculation; to buy in a lot, &c.

pe (R. hui), (C. poe; Cn. pö), to fly. **pe-le--khì**, to fly away. **iāⁿ-iāⁿ-pe**, floating, as dust in the air. **pe-tsoâ**, an eruption in lines of small pustules. **pe-toà**, an arched band (of wood or clay) behind and above the head of some idols, supposed to assist them in flying. **pe-chhiⁿ**, a falling star.

chhùi pe-pe, to talk wildly or incoherently, as in delirium or intoxication.

pe [R. pa, to collect or gather], (C. pɛ), to scrape up the rice from the bowl with chopsticks. **pe-pn̄g**, to eat rice with chopsticks.

pe [R. po, name of vegetable], (C. poe). **pe-lêng-chhài**, a vegetable like spinach (Convolvulus reptans?)

pe (C.) **chìⁿ-pe**, an arrow-head.

pe (C.) **tek-pe**, = A. tek-poe, a flat bamboo for beating scholars.

pe (C.) **pe-chhák**, = A. poe-chhák, a broad chisel.

pê [R. pâ, a guitar], (C. pɛ̂). **pî-pê**, the four-stringed guitar. **gî-pê**, id. **pî-pê-kut**, name of a bone.

pê [R. pâ, name of a fruit], (C. pɛ̂). **pî-pê**, the loquat fruit (s. guitar). **gî-pê**, id.

pê [R. pâ, same as last word?], (C. pɛ̂). **bák-pê**, a three-pronged weapon like a trident. **chhiuⁿ-to bák-pê**, warlike weapons.

pê (R. pâ), (C. pɛ̂). **thih-pê**, a heavy weapon like a trident. **pê-thâu**, id.

pê (R. pâ), (C. pɛ̂). **tek-pê**, a bamboo rake. **lū-pê** (Cn.), a sort of rake for agriculture.

pê (C. pɛ̂), a sort of harrow worked by the hand (but "pē" is drawn by a cow). **thoa-pê**, to harrow. **khê-pê**, to clog or obstruct the harrow (v. khê). **pê-put-á**, a sort of wooden implement like a hoe or shovel (v. put).

pê (R. pâ), (C. pɛ̂), to crawl or creep, as a child; to scratch with all the fingers; to paddle. **pê lêng-tsûn**, to paddle the dragon-boats. **tsòe-saⁿ-kha-káu pê--tsáu**, to crawl away like a crippled dog (v. káu).

pê-chiūⁿ, to scratch an itchy spot (v. chiūⁿ). **khòng-khòng-pê**, to scratch hard, as itch. **pê-iah**, to scrape up, as sand (v. iah). **pê kau-á**, to clean out a drain with a hook. **pê pùn-sò**, to scrape dirt together. **pê-chháu**, to gather grass for fuel.

pê (R. pôe), (C. pôe; Cn. pö̂), to make restitution or compensation; to make up loss or deficiency. **pê-pó**, id. **pê-tiām**, to make up what we have stood security for. **thòe--i pê-lūi**, involved with him so as to have to pay expenses for him. **pê-chîⁿ**, to make up a loss or injury by paying money. **pê-miāⁿ**, to make satisfaction for a death, usually by money.

pé [R. pá, to hold in the hand: to guard], (C. pɛ́), a handful; a sheaf of corn; (a target); classifier of sedans. **pé-siú**, to guard, as soldier. **pé-koan**, to guard a gate in a pass. **pé-mn̂g**, to guard a gate or great door, as door-keeper. **pé-mn̂g--ê**, door-keeper at yamun or large hong.

pé-tsóng, a commander of (nominally) 100 men; a centurion or lieutenant. **pɛ́-tsóng** (C.), = pɛh-iâ.

hé-pé, a torch. **chhâ-pé**, a small bundle of wood for fuel, tied with straw or grass. **chhài-pé**, a bundle of vegetables. **chit-pé-chhài**, id. **iu-liu tsòe-chit-pé**, brow wrinkled, as with grief (v. iu).

khit--i pé-pák, unable to do something because restrained by another (v. pák).

chhèng-pé, a target for gunnery. **chìⁿ-pé**, a target for archery. **khó chìⁿ-pé**, to compete at archery. **khó-pé**, to compete with guns or bows. **tun-pé**, to practise shooting at a mark close at hand. **pàng-pé**, to shoot at full distance.

pé (C. póe), to ward off with the hand; (to search for); to take up, as earth-nuts. **pé thô-tāu**, to dig up earth-nuts (arachis). **pé han-tsû-kau**, to glean from the furrows between potato-beds.

pé-lâi pé-khì, to talk long together without a definite result; to struggle together, as in wrestling or boxing. **saⁿ-pé-hē** (C. sio-póe-hōe), to discuss a matter in order to come to an agreement (v. hē). **pé-chhē** (C. póe-chhōe), to search for (v. chhē).

pé-khui, to ward off with the hands. **pé-chhiú**, do.; to use the hands in pushing or slight striking, as in the beginning of a quarrel. **kap--i pé-chhiú-bīn** (to ward off his blows from our face), to have a long and violent dispute with him, as in dunning for a debt. **kap-kúi pé-chhiú-bīn**, don't try a quarrel with that man: it would be as dangerous and useless as fighting with a demon. **kap-khit-chiáh pé-chhiú-bīn** (like quarrelling with a beggar), dispute troublesome and dangerous, and with no possible benefit.

bōe-pé--tit, cannot easily be got round or overcome by cunning; nothing can be got out of him, as a very sharp man or a customer who beats down the price too much; no profit to be got in the business; opposition to his plan will not squeeze any money out of him. **hē--lâng bōe-pé--tit**, said of a master so strict that his employés cannot make anything extra out of him.

pè [R. pöe, pòe, the back], (C. pòe; Cn. pö̀), the

back of a chair. **kau-í-pè**, id. **kiō-pè**, the back of the chair in a sedan.

siⁿ-pè, to have a carbuncle on the back. **phang-siū-pè**, a large carbuncle on the back, breaking out in many places.

pè [R. to cover]. **jia-pè**, to overshadow or cover injuriously; to becloud or delude, as the mind. **hong-thâm pè-sim**, having a fit of dull madness (v. thâm).

pè [R. spoiled; bad, = col. pē]. **tsok-pè**, to hinder a matter secretly while all seems smooth. **lōng-pè**, to use secret and improper means, as in a legal case. **pau-pè**, to delude, defraud, or deceive one's employer or superior officer, as by concealing from him faults of which he should have been informed, or by prejudicing him in favour of the guilty, or by secret and improper use of his authority or influence. **bú-pè** (r.), id. **iú-su-pè**, getting improper advantage (for one's own profit) of a commission or of delegated powers, *e.g.* secretly appropriating part of the money intrusted for some purpose.

pè [R. mean; low; politely used in some phrases for "my"], (C. pì). **pè-ku** (R.), the place where I reside. **pè-kok** (R.), my native kingdom or state. **pè-sià** (R.), my poor house.

pè (C. pòe, Cn. pŏ), to paste, as paper. **kiáu-pè**, id. **piáu-pŏ** (Cn. T.), id. **pè-tsoá**, to paste paper. **pè-tsoá-phe**, to make pasteboard. **pè-pòh**, to paste tinfoil, &c., on paper (v. pòh). **pè-piah**, to paper a wall.

pè (R. pà), (Cn. T. pŏ), a mound or embankment for damming up water. **tsoh-pè**, to make such an embankment to dam up water.

pè (Cn.) **koân-pè** (r.), authority; power.

pē [R. pā, a harrow], (C. pɛ̄). **thih-pē**, sort of iron harrows. **lôe-pē**, plough and harrows.

pē (R. hū), (C. pɛ̄), father. **lāu-pē**, id. **niûⁿ-pē**, id. **chiàⁿ-pē**, actual father. **siⁿ-pē**, id. **siⁿ-lán ê-pē**, our actual father. **āu-pē**, stepfather. **iúⁿ-pē**, one who brings up a child like a father; a foster-father. **khòe-pē**, a man whom another engages to treat as a sort of adoptive father. **sai-pē**, a Buddhist priest who buys a boy as a son.

khek-pē, natal characters of son's horoscope coming into collision with those of his father (v. khek). **sí-pē**, to lose one's father (by death); one's father having died; said also in scolding a man who looks dull and foolish: you look as dull as if your father were dead!

pē-kiáⁿ, father and son. **pē-bú**, father and mother; parents. **pē-bú-koaⁿ**, the mandarin of a Hien district. **pē-bú kha-tau**, paternal home. **i--ê pē-bú-lát khah-toā**, he is naturally stronger in body. **pē-thâu bú-kut**, vile scolding by applying abominable epithets to parents. **mɛ̄ⁿ--lâng pē-thâu bú-kut**, to scold so. **pē-pn̄g bú-hiû**, parents' food and clothes, as given to their children. **chiàh pē-pn̄g, chhēng bú-hiû**, to be fed and clothed by our parents. **chiàh-pē chhēng-bú**, id. **chiàu-pē soe-thâu, chiàu-bú pák-kè**, to follow parents' example. **bú-kiáⁿ tùi-pē-kiáⁿ**, children (by former marriages) of widow and widower engaged when their parents marry. **bú-á tùi-pē-á** (T.), id.

pē [R. mə̄ⁿ, = pōe]. **tāi-pē**, = tāi-pōe, tortoise-shell.

pē [R. pōe, so many fold], (C. pōe; Cn. pŏ). **têng-pē**, twofold; double in size, quantity, &c. **ka-pē**, id. **n̄ng-pē**, id. **bān-pē-toā**, a thousandfold greater.

pē [R. spoiled; bad, = pè]. **pē-pēng**, blemish; fault; depravity (v. pēng).

pē [R. pōe, pòe, the back, = col. pè]. **saⁿ-pē**, to stand back to back, as houses or villages. **pē-bé**, to harness and saddle a horse. **tāu-koaⁿ-pē**, a square frame like a sieve on which bean-curd is dried over the fire.

pē [R. hū, to carry on the back; to owe], (C. pōe), to carry on the back or shoulder, as a heavy thing. **phah-pē**, to fasten wood or bamboo on the outside of a junk by ropes. **sià-pē**, to unlade it. **pē-soh**, the ropes for tying it on. **pē-sam**, to carry pine-wood thus. **pē-tek**, to carry bamboo thus. **thâu-chêng-pē**, the fastenings near the bow. **bé-āu-pē**, the fastenings near the stern.

pē [R. pōe, to wear at the girdle], (C. pōe). **pē-kiàm**, to wear a short sword hung from the shoulder. **pē io-to**, to wear a sword at the girdle, as military mandarin.

pē (R. pōe), (Cn. pŏ), to toast (as food) on or at the fire; to fire, as tea-leaves. **pē-ta**, to dry at the fire. **ta-pē**, too dry, as surface of the face, or of eatables, &c. **pē-lô**, a stove or furnace for firing tea, or drying drugs or tobacco. **pē-tê**, to fire tea. **pē-iòh**, to dry medicinal herbs by a stove.

pē— **pē-si-pêng**, = pōe-si-pêng, the 120th radical written at the side.

pē [R. steps of a throne]. **pē-hā** (R.), your majesty.

pē (T. pŏ), a sort of sculling-oar used for steering a boat, as at the dragon-races.

pē, to manure with solid manure in agriculture.

pɛⁿ (C.), = A. pien, to draw out, as a peg or stiff drawer; also, = A. piⁿ, to pull aside, &c.

pɛ̂ⁿ (C.), = A. pîⁿ, a stage or light framework.

pɛ̂ⁿ (C.), = A. pîⁿ, level; even; also, = A. piâⁿ, the tones called the Ping or first tones. **têng-pɛ̂ⁿ**, = A. chiūⁿ-piâⁿ, the upper ping or upper first tone. **ē-pɛ̂ⁿ**, the lower ping or lower first tone (v. piâⁿ).

pɛ̀ⁿ (C.), = A. pìⁿ, a handle.

pɛ̄ⁿ (C.), = A. pīⁿ, disease; unwell.

peh [R. pek, a senior uncle; an earl], (C. pɛh), father's elder brother, or father's elder cousin of same surname, however distant; *i.e.* any man of same clan who is one grade in genealogy above us, and older than our father. **chek-peh**, paternal uncles in general, or men of same clan and same genealogical rank with our father (v. chek). **á-peh**, uncle! (said also colloquially for "father!") **peh-ḿ**, senior paternal uncle and his wife. **peh-kong**, grandfather's elder brother, &c. **peh-kong-tsó**, great-grandfather's elder brother.

pau-peh, father's elder brother. **chhin-peh**, id. **peh-tia**, id.; also, sometimes a respectful address to an old man. **tōng-peh**, elder son of paternal granduncle, or one of father's senior cousins, more or less distant, of same surname. **chhin-tōng peh**, do. one or two degrees distant. **chiông-tōng-peh**, father's distant senior cousin of same surname. **piáu-peh**, elder son of grandaunt, or of grandmother's brother.

toā-peh, husband's elder brother (it is not counted proper for his younger brother's wife to converse with him). **toā-peh--ah**, eldest brother of father. **tōng-toā-peh**, elder cousin of husband. **toā-iâ-peh**, elder brother of a mandarin (v. iâ). **peh-koaⁿ**, elder brother of husband's father. **jī-peh**, second eldest senior brother of father. **jī-pɛh** (C.), id.; also, second eldest brother of husband. **saⁿ-peh**, third eldest senior brother of father. **tiūⁿ-lâng-peh**, elder brother of wife's father.

chhin-ke-peh, elder brother of the man to whose child our child is married.

tāi-sū-peh, an incarnation of Kwan-yin, worshipped in the 7th moon.

peh [R. pek, the fir or pine-tree], (C. pɛh). **chhêng-peh**, the fir-tree (v. chhêng). **chêng-peh** (T.), id. **chhiông-pɛh** (P.), id. **chhiông-pɛh-kin** (C.), a very poisonous short red snake, bite said to be incurable. **píⁿ-peh**, an ornamental dwarf-tree (juniper? cypress?), often grown in flower-pots. **kòe-peh**, a larger tree, like juniper. **n̂g-peh**, a cooling medicine (Pterocarpus flavus?).

peh [R. pek, to urge], (C. pɛh). **kiūⁿ-peh-nìⁿ**, to force one's self to act. **peh--kàu**, determined to have what is difficult to be got, or to see what is far off or difficult to see.

peh — **hoâiⁿ-peh-peh**, very overbearing or oppressive (v. hoâiⁿ).

peh — **piⁿ-peh**, in great want of cash. **ke-sū piⁿ-peh**, pecuniary affairs of household in a very bad state. **peh-púih**, very miserable through poverty (v. púih).

peh (R. phek), (C. pɛh). **peh-khui**, to break open, as with the hands. **peh-phoà**, to break asunder with the hands. **peh--sí**, to kill by clawing, as tiger or cat does. **peh-phê**, to peel off with the hand without a knife. **peh-khak**, to peel off a soft shell with the hand, as the li-chi fruit.

peh-pak, grieved (v. pak). **peh-sim peh-koaⁿ**, id. **sim-koaⁿ peh-kàu-phoà**, extremely grieved and distressed, heart almost breaking. **sim-koaⁿ peh kàu-beh-phoà**, id.

sim-koaⁿ-thâu peh-peh, feeling of heaviness and indigestion. **sim-koaⁿ-thâu peh-peh chek-chek**, id.

peh-si-liét, opened quite square and wide, as a door.

peh — **peh-khui**, to open (neuter), as the eyes. **bák-chiu peh-khui, chiū tióh-chiah-ê-chîⁿ**, so much cash are absolutely necessary for every day's wants.

peh — **peh-khui**, to open, as the mouth. **lí-hèng peh-gê**, you are very fond of talking about what should not be mentioned.

peh — **hāu-peh-chheh** (overlapping scales on the belly of the king-crab), venetian blinds or shutters.

peh (R. pek, a hundred, = col. pah], (C. pɛh, also = A. pah, a hundred). **peh-sìⁿ**, the people (lit. the hundred surnames); the people, as distinguished from rulers. **kū-nîⁿ peh-tsài** (T.), long past and out of date, as an affair.

pɛh-tsóng (C.), = A. pé-tsóng, an officer (nominally) commanding 100 men. **pɛh-iâ** (C.), id.

peh (C. pɛh), to climb. **peh--khí-lâi**, to climb up; to rise up, *e.g.* from lying down, or in order to salute a stranger who comes in. **peh-koâiⁿ peh-kē**, to climb about everywhere, as a too active child. **khîⁿ-chhiûⁿ peh-piah**, to climb walls (v. khîⁿ).

peh (T.) **tē-peh**, a small insect that burrows, like a cricket.

peh (C.), = A. poeh, eight. **peh-pɛh**, = A. poeh-pah, 800. **pɛh-peh**, = A. pah-poeh, 180.

péh — **ɵ-ien péh-pāng**, said of calamities or very troublesome disputes suddenly coming on. **ɵ-ien péh-pōng**, id. **tsáu kàu ɵ-ien péh-pōng**, running in great fear and confusion, as from rebels. **ɵ-àm péh-pāng**, said of very sudden calamities. **ɵ-hûn péh-pāng**, do., as robbers, &c.

péh — **péh-tiō-á**, feeble stooping appearance of old or weak person.

péh (C.), = A. púih, to pull out or up.

péh [R. pék, silk stuff; wealth], (C. péh). **hûn-péh**, a tablet covered with white cloth, used before burial (v. hûn). **chhái-péh-tiàm**, a shop where grave-clothes, &c., are sold; an undertaker's shop. **thâu-péh**, a white head-band worn at funerals. **kha-péh**, a bandage for the feet, worn by females. **kha-péh-sún** (C.), a sort of water vegetable.

péh (R. pék), (C. péh), white; plain and distinct; colloquial or plain, as speech; (solely or unmixed); fat of meat; a surname.

péh-péh, very white, plain, or distinct; gratuitous; (unmixed). **péh-péh hō--lâng**, to give gratuitously. **péh-péh sià-bién**, to forgive without any reparation. **kóng-ōe péh-péh**, to speak distinctly and intelligibly. **péh-péh-chiáh**, to eat rice without condiments. **péh-péh chiáh--i**, to take presents or pay or food from a man without doing work or making any return. **to péh-péh**, the knife or sword is bright and sharp.

péh-ōe, the colloquial language. **chhát-á-péh**, thieves' slang. **taⁿ-tàⁿ-péh**, colloquial phrases used by porters. **kng-kiō-péh**, id., by sedan coolies. **hoàn-á-péh**, do., by pedlars. **seh-péh**, to talk such a slang or private colloquial; to talk prose in a play (as distinguished from poetry). **péh-jī**, characters written according to the colloquial, without regard to classical usage. **khang-tsoá péh-jī**, said of a letter with fair words but no material help. **tsò-péh-jī** (C.), to have a play in colloquial. **péh-bûn**, the text of a book, as distinguished from notes and comments.

péh-sin-lâng, a private individual. **khang-chhiú péh-jī**, bringing no presents.

péh-chhát, a lie; a falsehood.

péh-chiáⁿ bô-bī, tasteless. **chhùi péh**, want of appetite; not caring to eat much, as child, or as man after long sickness.

péh-láh-sáh, very white. **péh-léh-séh**, id. **péh-léh-séh** (C.), id. **péh-siak-siak**, brilliantly white. **péh-seh-seh**, very white. **péh-theh-theh**, id. **péh-lek-lek**, white, as cloth, or as child's skin. **péh-koah-koah**, white, as complexion. **péh-koat-koat**, very white, as white-washed wall. **géh-péh**, white with a very slight bluish tinge.

chhiⁿ-péh, pale and sickly looking. **bīn chhiⁿ-péh**, face having a greenish paleness, as of sickly constitution. **chhiⁿ-chhòng péh-chhòng**, made ill or roughly, as an article made in an untradesmanlike way.

pûi-péh, fat and fair.

chháng-péh, almost quite white, with very little black. **chhám-péh**, white and black mixed; gray, as hair. **thâu-mn̂g chham-péh**, some gray hairs among the black. **thâu-mn̂g poàⁿ-péh**, hair gray, about half white. **péh-chhiu--ê**, having a white beard (v. chhiu).

péh-tiō, white mark on skin left by a healed wound. **péh-bīn**, white-faced. **péh-bīn-lâng**, a white man. **péh-bīn-á**, a sort of wild cat, or similar animal.

péh-bah, the fat of meat. **péh--ê**, id. **poàⁿ-chiaⁿ-péh**, half fat, half lean.

péh-jîn, white of eye (v. jîn). **péng-péh-bák**, to turn up the white of the eye, as in pride or anger.

bák péh, to miss stays, in tacking.

jī-péh, a placard or hand-bill pasted up. **kò-péh**, id. **kòng-péh**, finest white sugar, esp. in shape. **chhang-péh**, white part of onion stalk near the root.

soàn-á-péh, root and white foot of garlic stalk cut small. **lák-géh-péh**, a whitish fruit like a plum or peach (two sorts?) with a fine bloom on it; also (T.), a long white legume like chhài-tāu, but shorter.

toà-péh, to be in deep mourning. **phiò-péh**, to bleach, as cloth. **thiò-péh**, id. **cheng-péh**, to beat till white, as rice in a mortar. **thí^n-péh**, eyes dazzled, as by looking at a bright white wall.

péh-chí^n, white idolatrous paper, for the worship of the "kúi." **péh-liāng**, transparent crystal button of mandarin of fifth grade. **péh-gék**, white jade-stone. **péh-tâng**, sort of white metal (v. tâng). **péh-thé-thê**, chalk (v. thê). **péh-hé**, a sky-rocket for a signal. **péh-khak**, white shell, &c. **péh-khak**, sort of yeast. **péh-chiú**, a liquor fermented from glutinous rice (v. chiú). **péh-thiām**, a strong sweet spirit (v. thiām). **e-péh-chí**, chessmen having thirty-two of each colour. **e-péh-jí**, id. **âng-péh**, red and white (said of a great system of clan feuds with red and white flags).

péh-lē, the term that falls about September 7th or 8th. **péh-tóe**, sort of boat (with white bottom) like a small "khan-hong." **péh-thâu-khòe**, a deed of sale without any official stamp. **péh-tsúi-pô**, a boat-woman, esp. living in fishing-boat (v. tsúi).

péh-hiā, white ants. **péh-hî**, sort of fish; sort of game (v. hî). **péh-gê**, a large white fish (v. gê). **péh-hóh**, a white crane. **péh-lēng-si**, the white egret or paddy-bird.

péh-phê, Malwa opium. **péh-chhài**, white cabbage. **péh-léh-á** (P.), a sort of oak; its acorn is sometimes ground down and mixed with rice.

pek [R. id. = col. peh, a senior paternal uncle], an earl; the third rank of nobility. **pek-chiok**, the rank of earl.

pek-lô, a small harsh-voiced bird (v. lô).

pek — **pek-ki**, long ells; a woollen stuff somewhat like baize.

pek (R. id., = col. piak), to roast, toast, or warm at the fire. **pek-hé**, to injure one's self (*e.g.* small boils or sore eyes) by keeping too near the fire, as in cooking. **pek-jiét**, id. **pek-pa**, to dry at the fire, so as to be fit for keeping long. **pek-lê**, sort of oven for cakes, &c.

pek (R. id.), to press against: to urge to do something; to dun; urgent. **pek-kūn**, to press near. **pek-oá**, id.

pek-kín, to hasten on a matter. **pek-chhiet**, urgent. **pek-chhek**, extremely urgent; too urgent and hard on people. **pek-chhiok** (R.), very urgent. **kiông-pek**, to compel by strong pressure. **pek-hiáp**, to compel thus to do some wrong thing, *e.g.* to join an illegal society. **thài-pek**, extremely urgent, as time, or as creditor. **lâng-khì thài-pek**, oppressive feeling from many people being crowded together in hot weather. **chhui-pek**, to urge to do something very quickly, as work or payment. **sa^n-chhui sì-pek**, id. **jit-géh chhui-pek**, days and months press on rapidly. **pek--sí**, to dun very hard; to torment to death (lit. or fig.) **oáh-oáh pek--sí**, id. **chit-sì chit-pek**, incessantly dunning and driving at a man to do something. **pek-ân**, to press very urgently, as for payment. **pek-thó**, to demand payment very urgently. **pek-chè**, id.; to dun for a debt. **pek-siàu**, id.

khún-pek, to persecute or harass. **pek-tiòk**, to expel and drive away, as relatives or superiors do. **pek-hé siong-jîn**, to make a tiger stand at bay injures people.

pek [R. a hundred, = col. pah, peh]. **pek-pēng**, all diseases. **sù-chi pek-hâi**, the members of the body. **liû-hong pek-sè**, to leave a fragrant memory for a hundred generations. **it-hu, pek-hu**, one thing being proved false, all is false. **it-lí thong, pek-lí thiet**, one thing being learned, all is understood.

pek-háp-hoe, a sort of flower (v. háp). **pek-tsú-liên**, the Agapanthes, with a large head of blue flowers. **pek-siét-niáu^n**, a bird that learns many tunes, &c. (v. siét). **pek-lêng**, a small bird; some say same as above.

pék [R. silk; wealth, = col. péh]. **tsâi-pék**, wealth and treasure in general.

pék [R. white, = col. péh]. **chheng-pék**, unsullied in character (v. chheng). **pék-jit**, in broad daylight (v. jit). **pék-siú sêng-ka**, to become rich out of poverty.

bêng-pék, clearly understood; to comprehend plainly; finished. **bêng-bêng pék-pék**, very clearly understood; quite completed. **m̄-bêng-pék**, intentionally leaving things in an unsettled state, *e.g.* debts not paid, or flaws left that may cause trouble, or getting more money than is proper.

hek-pék put-hun, good and bad (black and white) are not distinguished; the matter is not clear, innocence fails to prove itself, or justice is disregarded. **kàu-bé hek-pék tsū-hun**, right will come right at last.

kò-pék, a placard or hand-bill pasted up. **ki-pék**, superfine white grass-cloth. **ki-siōng-pék**, id. **thài-pék-chhí^n**, the evening-star. **jîn-tiong-pék**, incrustation of urine jars, prepared as a medicine. **pék-chiok**, a medicine (v. chiok). **pék-tài**, a running disease of the female organs. **pék-lók**, the white stag, worshipped. **pék-hô**, a sort of tea.

pék (same word?). **ka-pék-sún**, edible shoots of a water vegetable (v. sún).

peng (R. id., = col. pia^n), a soldier. **peng-teng**, id. **peng-á**, a common soldier. **peng-ióng**, soldiers and militia in general. **peng-bé**, soldiers. **sàu-peng**, a low sort of tide-waiters (v. sàu). **chhèng-peng**, a soldier who uses a gun. **siú-peng**, soldiers (inferior) for garrison. **chièn-peng**, soldiers for battle (superior). **bé-peng**, cavalry. **ló-jiók-peng**, old and feeble soldiers. **boán-peng**, Manchoo soldiers. **hàn-peng**, Chinese soldiers. **tô-peng**, a deserter. **pāi-peng**, defeated soldiers (v. pāi). **loān-peng**, routed soldiers in disorder. **tāi-peng**, a very large body of soldiers.

thien-peng, the armies of the gods: offerings made to them, as well as to the gods, through Tauist priests or sorcerers. **sîn-peng**, id. **pàng-peng** (T. pàng-pia^n), to send them out to assist the votaries.

tng-peng, to be a soldier. **bōe-peng**, to sell the position of a soldier. **khí-peng**, to raise soldiers. **thi^n-peng**, to increase the number of troops. **tiám-peng**, to mark those present at muster. **thiu-peng**, to select a special proportion of soldiers for some purpose. **chhut-peng**, to send out soldiers. **niá^n-peng**, to lead or command soldiers. **ēng-peng**, to do battle. **siu-peng**, to draw off soldiers to retreat.

tsóng-peng, a lieutenant-general, like "tìn-tâi." **tsáp-sa^n-seng, kàu tsóng-peng**, on rising thirteen degrees one becomes tsóng-peng. **chiáng peng-koân**, to have military command; to have the responsible management of an affair (v. koân). **peng-hùi**, soldier's pay, in reference to its being paid out by the mandarins. **peng-khì**, military weapons and stores. **to-peng ê-tsai-ē**, calamities of war and rebellion.

peng-tsu chièn-chheh (r.), books on military matters.

peng (R. id., = col. piang, pi), ice; very cool, as jellies; made cool, as eyes by bathing with water. **peng-léng**, ice-cold (v. léng). **léng peng-peng**, id. **put-chí-peng**, very cooling and pleasant to eat (as jellies) in hot weather.

peng-sng, ice and frost. **kiên-peng**, to freeze. **peng-hô**, to freeze a river. **peng-hái**, to freeze the sea.

peng-phièn, Baroos camphor. **peng-thn̂g**, sugar-candy. **peng-mûiⁿ**, yellow plums preserved in sugar.

peng [R. pêng, level; peace; balances, = col. pîⁿ, &c. **peng-kūi**, a confidential agent of the Tartar general, who acts as a spy on the Hái-koan.

peng [R. pheng, to fall as a mountain, = col. pang]. **hiet-peng** (C.), = A. hiet-pheng, a flow of blood from the female organs.

pêng [R. piēn, piên, convenient; ready, = col. pan]. **pêng-īⁿ**, cheap; mediocre; easy (v. īⁿ). **pêng-ī**, id.

pêng (cf. pâng). **pêng-se**, borax.

pêng [R. a friend], (Cn. pông). **pêng-iú**, a friend (v. iú). **chhin-pêng kò-iú**, relations and old friends (v. chhin). **hó-pêng--ê**, my good friend (said in asking the way, &c.)

pêng (R. pêng? phîn? cf. phin). **pêng-kó**, the apple. **pêng-kó-chhiū** (r.), the apple-tree.

pêng [R. level; even; uniform; usual; equal; just; peace; balances; = col. pîⁿ, piâⁿ, phêng], to restore to a peaceful state, as after rebellion; balances (of moderate size); to weigh in balances; when affixed to the weight fixed for dollars, it means according to the rate called "khò-tô," agreeing with the weights usually used for balances. (In the sense of "balances," T. pêng, C. phêng, A. pêng or phêng.)

pêng-sò, heretofore; usually (in the past). **pêng-sî**, id. **pêng-jit**, id. **pêng-seng**, during one's whole past life; all one's life usually. **seng-pêng**, id. **pêng-siông**, ordinary; usually; mediocre (v. siông).

pêng-téng, of same class; of equal rank. **pêng-pòe**, of equal genealogical rank, at equal distance from the common ancestor. **kun-pêng**, a drawn game.

kong-pêng, just and fair; equitable. **put-pêng**, indignant at injustice done to another. **chèng-lâng put-pêng**, every one is indignant at such injustice. **thòe--i put-pêng**, indignant at the wrong done to him (a third person). **lō-kiàn put-pêng**, indignant at a wrong which we happen to observe by the way. **lō-kiàn put-pêng, khì--sí êng-jîn**, injustice or oppression so flagrant that casual passers-by are most indignant.

pêng-an, peace and quiet (v. an). **pêng-tiāⁿ**, quiet; free from disturbance; to pacify or quiet, as a region. **pêng-chēng**, quiet, as the sea, or as a region (v. chēng). **thài-pêng**, great peace and prosperity; Taipings. **thiⁿ-ē thài-pêng**, the whole empire enjoying peace and prosperity. **thài-pêng-koà**, a jacket with long narrow sleeves, and opening at middle of breast. **pêng-tē, khí hong-pho**, to accuse a man falsely, and cause great trouble to him without any cause.

pêng-iûⁿ, a level plain (v. iûⁿ).

pêng-tāng, to weigh in balances, as money. **kè-pêng**, to be weighed in balances. **thien-pêng**, large balances. **thien-pêng-chhìn**, beam of large balances. **thien-pêng-chiam**, needle of do. **thien-pêng-oáⁿ**, scales of do. **pêng-oáⁿ**, id. **teh pêng-tóe**, to deduct a small discount from the price of goods paid in silver. **thiap pêng-tsúi**, to pay a small premium (about three or four mace on $100) on duties paid into customs, &c.

sî-pêng, the current local rate for weight of dollars in the special branch of business. **si-pêng** (r.), the rate of weight or sort of balances authorized by the provincial treasurer, esp. for payments to government. **khò-pêng**, rate of weights making $1 = 7 mace 2 candareens, as at Changchew, about five or six per cent. heavier than the Amoy rate. **chhit-jī-pêng**, dollars at full weight (by the khò-pêng), at 7„2. **liòk-pat-pêng**, rate of (nominal) light dollars, counted at 6„8 of the khò-tô, = 7„2 of the Amoy hā-tô. **liòk-liòk-pêng**, rate of dollars counted at 6„6 of the khò-tô.

koan-pêng, the adopted son of Kwanti. **pêng-hô**, the district of Ping-ho. **an-pêng**, Anping, the port of Taiwanfoo.

pêng (T. phêng). **io-pêng**, = io-phêng, a purse with a flap as a cover, worn at the side on the girdle or band that holds up the trowsers.

pêng (C. pân, pêng; T. pâiⁿ, pîn; Cn. pûiⁿ), a side; one-half of a thing cut in two. **siang-pêng**, both sides; both parties. **chit-pêng**, one side; one-half of a split thing. **chit-pêng**, this side. **chiùⁿ-pêng**, id. **hit-pêng**, that side. **sòe-pêng**, the right-hand side. **toā-pêng**, the side of honour, the left-hand side; the larger half. **si-koe, oá toā-pêng**, people like to favour the stronger side (lit. larger half of a melon).

hoan-pêng, foreign regions.

toh-pêng, one-half of a double table. **thiāu-pêng**, a half pillar; a pilaster. **ō-pêng**, half a root of taro. **lí-á-pêng**, preserved split plums. **tāu-pêng**, split pease. **chhâ-pêng**, split billets of wood. **phoà-pêng**, to cut or split into two halves. **phoà tsòe-nn̄g-pêng**, id.

jī-pêng, the half of a character; the phonetic half (v. jī). **péng-káu-pêng**, the contracted form of the 94th radical. **phō-sim-pêng**, the 61st radical written at the side. **poàn-lé-pêng**, the 113th radical written at the side; sometimes the 145th. **pē-si-pêng**, the 120th radical at the side. **pōe-si-pêng**, id. **pīⁿ-si-pêng**, id. **tāi-jī-á-pêng**, the formative part made of a horizontal stroke crossed by one sloping to the left (not a radical), like the 37th radical without its right-hand stroke.

péng (R. hoán), (T. páiⁿ; Cn. pûiⁿ; C. pán; P. péng), to turn; to turn over; to invert; to be upset, as boat; to cheat out of money; to sew two pieces of cloth together, turning the rough edges inwards so as to make a smooth seam on the outside. **péng--chhut-lâi**, to turn inside out. **péng bé-koà**, to turn a jacket and wear it inside out. **péng kiàm-toà**, to make a pointed sash, sewing the edges so as to turn inside. **péng-chhiú**, to turn the hand over, esp. Buddhist or Tauist priests turning it over and over in some rites. **bàk-chiu péng-péh**, turning the white of the eyes, as in anger or when about to die. **péng-káu-á**, the 94th radical at the side (v. káu). **ám-péng-sui-khang**, holes for running water off the deck.

péng--khí-lâi, to turn over; to turn upside down. **péng-lìn-tńg**, to invert (v. lìn). **péng-khap**, to invert, as bowl (v. khap). **péng-phak**, to turn on the belly; to invert, with mouth down, as bowl (v. phak). **péng-chhiò**, to invert, turning up the concave side of something that naturally has the concave side down, as a lid or cover (v. chhiò). **péng-tó**, to turn a thing upside down. **tò-péng**, inverted. **tò-péng-kóng**, to speak ironically, saying the opposite of what is meant. **tùi-péng**, on the other hand.

péng--lâng, to cheat people out of money. **péng-pī^{n}**, to find some new way of living when the old way fails. **péng-lâi péng-khì**, to say yes and no at different times; saying contradictory things to different men or at different times. **chhùi péng-lâi péng-khì**, id. **péng-tàng** (C.), very troublesome, as child.

péng [R. to hold; to maintain]. **péng-kong**, acting with equity. **péng-kong pān-sū**, to decide a case justly. **péng-sim bû-khùi**, integrity of heart unimpeachable, so as to have no cause for shame. **péng-sim lâi-kóng-ōe**, to speak openly and honestly.

péng [R. pín, to receive from a superior]. **péng-sèng**, natural disposition or temper. **péng-khì soe-pòh**, natural constitution (as of child) weak. **péng-khì kāu-pòh**, the strength or weakness of our natural constitution as to health.

péng [R. a loaf, = col. piá^{n}]. **oā-péng chhiong-ki** (to stay hunger with a painted loaf), to disappoint by false grounds of hope. **hoā-péng chhiong-ki**, id.

péng (T.) **péng-sit**, = A. pién-sit, a sort of cake.

pèng [R. a handle; authority, = col. pì^{n}]. **koân-pèng**, authority; power. **ū-pá-pèng**, having determination and ability (carrying out one's purpose in spite of opposition). **bô-pá-pèng**, very changeable in purpose. **thòe--lâng pá-pèng**, to help a man (gen. secretly and rather improperly) to accomplish what he could not do alone, as by exerting some secret influence or advising him how to act. **tek-khak ū-lâng teh-pá-pèng**, certainly some one must be secretly making opposition.

pèng [R. along with; to compare; really], commission on goods bought.

pèng-bô, there is not; there is no such thing or person. **pèng-m̄-sī**, certainly it is not —. **pèng-sī àn-ni^{n}**, certainly it is so.

pèng-gûn, commission paid by the buyer to the commission-agent. **ka pèng-gûn**, to pay it. **ke-pèng--lòh-khì**, id. **pèng-tiōng**, commission paid by buyer and seller, about two per cent. (v. tiōng).

pēng [R. a disease, a fault, = col. pī^{n}]. **pē-pēng**, a blemish, fault, or flaw; depravity. **ū-pē-pēng**, having a blemish, physical or moral. **ū pē-pēng-lē**, having a blemish, as character; having a flaw, as affair. **mâu^{n}-pēng**, a blemish. **pek-pēng**, all sorts of diseases. **tài-pēng**, while unwell (in reference to action). **tài-pēng chhut-mn̂g**, to go out while really too unwell to go, by putting a pressure on one's self. **kiú-pēng sêng liông-i**, long illness makes one a good doctor; long experience makes a man skilful at what he never formally learned; *e.g.* a man long troubled by lawsuits learns how to manage them. **kiú-pēng sêng i-seng**, id. **tsū-pēng put-lêng-i**, does not know his own faults; manages other people's business better than his own. **pēng-jī-khak**, the 104th radical.

pi — **pûn pi-á**, to whistle.

pi [R. peng, ice, = col. piang]. **chhìn-pi-pi**, very cold, as a thing.

pi — **niau^{n} pi-pa**, pock-marked.

pi [R. name of a plant]. **pi-moâ^{n}-chí**, seeds of the castor-oil plant. **pi-moâ^{n}-iû**, castor-oil. **tē-pi-iû**, id. **tē-pi-chí**, the seeds.

pi [R. sad; sorrowful]. **pi-siong**, grieved; sorrowful. **siong-pi**, id. **pi-ai** (R.), id. **tsû-pi**, tenderly affectionate, as a parent or superior. **lòk kèk, pi seng**, grief comes at the height of joy. **lòk kèk, seng-pi**, id.

pi [R. low; humble]. **khiam-pi**, humble-minded. **pi-chiēn**, in a humble, low, or mean position. **tsun-pi**, high and low, in rank. **ū-tsun-pi**, treating superiors (esp. elder relatives) with due respect. **khah-bô tsun-pi**, not showing proper respect and ceremony to superiors.

pi [R. name of an insect]. **gû-pi**, an insect that attacks cows: its blood is used as a glue. **gû-pi, ū-jip bô-chhut**, said in scolding a man who is miserably mean (the insect is said to have no excrement).

pi-bâ (Cn.), = A. pan-bâ, the blistering-fly.

pi [R. a stone tablet]. **chiòh-pi**, a large stone tablet for an inscription, larger than "pâi." **chiòh-pi-pâi**, engraved stone tablets. **khiā-pi**, to set up a stone tablet with an inscription, as at road-side.

pi (R. id.), a weir or dam on a river, especially for a large sluice. **pi-á**, a smaller one. **pi-thâu**, the raised ground on each side at the dam. **tsoh-pi**, to make a dam or weir.

pî (R. id.) **pî-pê**, the loquat fruit (v. pê).

pî (R. id.) **pî-pê**, a guitar (v. pê).

pî [R. phê, skin; bark, = col. phê]. **ngé-ka-pî**, = ngé-ka-phî, sort of yellow wine.

pî — **chit-pî**, one bunch, as of plantains. **chit-pî gêng-chio**, one circular bunch of plantains made by cutting the stalk across above and below.

chit-pî hî-chí, one piece of fish-roe, *i.e.* the whole mass at one side; the half of what one fish has [next word ?].

pî (R. id.), an internal organ near the stomach; the pancreas or sweetbread in some animals, called "chhioh." **iû^{n}-pî**, the sweetbread of the sheep or goat. **pî-ūi**, the pancreas and the stomach (v. ūi). **pî-thé**, constitution of a man's stomach. **pî-thé hó**, having a good appetite and able to digest well.

pó-pî, tonic; assisting digestion. **pó-pî lī-súi**, tonic and diuretic. **háh-pî**, to agree with the stomach. **lī-pî**, id. **khui-pî**, the appetite returning after sickness; whetting the appetite. **put-chí khui-pî**, very good for whetting the appetite. **chiah-kú khah-khui-pî**, have had more appetite of late. **khui-pî-thng**, a medicinal infusion for giving appetite. **sún-pî**, to disagree with the stomach. **siong-pî**, id. **sit-chek siong-pî**, ill from over-eating, as child. **sí-pî**, a disease causing great indigestion and loss of appetite. **khùn kàu sí-pî--khì**, idly sleeping at all hours of the day instead of working. **bān-pî-hong**, a very dangerous disease of children (v. hong).

pí [R. pí, contiguous; conterminous], (T. pí). **pí-liên**, contiguous, conterminous, as fields, or as adjoining houses having a common wall.

pí [R. that; those, = col. hit]. **pí-tong-sî**, just at that (past) time. **pí-chhú** (R.), that and this.

pí (R. id.) **hién-pí**, title given to a deceased mother on gravestone and at offerings.

pí [R. pī, ready; to prepare]. **pâi-pí**, to prepare, arrange beforehand, or put in order.

pí (R. id.), to compare; compared with; to practise, as gymnastics or military exercises; to gesticulate or make signs with hand, &c.; to beat officially so as to get payment, &c. **pí-jū**, a comparison; for example. **pí-hong**, id. **pí-lūn**, id. (v. lūn). **pí-phēng**, to compare. **sa^{n}-pí**, id. **lâi-pí**, come and measure and compare the two. **pí-khoà^{n}**, to compare, as two things, to see the likeness. **pí-pān**, to compare with the pattern. **pí-kàu**, to compare two things to see the difference or to try which is better; to try which is the stronger or more skilful at anything.

bōe-pí--tit, cannot be compared with. **put-pí**, not so good as —; not equal to —. **lí put-pí-i**, you cannot be compared with him. **chì-toā bô-pí**, the very greatest beyond compare. **ū-chí^{n} kàu-bô-pí**, surpassingly rich. **pí-goá khah-hó**, better than I. **pí-lí khah-toā**, greater than you.

jī-pí, the two parties in a dispute. **pí-chiap** (Cn.), to meet and endeavour to arrange a quarrel.

tāi-pí ê-nî^{n}, the year of the great examinations, as for the degree of chìn-sū. **pí bú-gōe**, to practise military arts, as archery, fencing, &c. **pí ke-si**, to practise fencing, &c. **pí kûn-thâu**, to exercise in boxing (v. kûn). **pí-sè**, to hold a weapon, as if about to strike; to gesticulate so as to show another how to do a thing. **pí sè-bīn**, id. **pí-pē**, to gesticulate, as in teaching or practising steps, boxing, fencing, or as in threatening a child. **pí-pē beh-phah--i**, put one's self in attitude, as if going to strike him. **pí beh-phah--i**, id. **ēng-chhiú teh-pí**, making a sign to another with the hand. **pí-chhiú**, to beckon or make a sign with the hand, shake the fist, &c. **pí-chhiú kā-i-kóng**, to let him know by a sign made by the hand. **pí-chhiú sut-bák**, beckon and wink. **pí-chhiú nih^{n}-bák**, id. **pí-kha tāng-chhiú**, moving one's limbs in a boisterous or disorderly way, as troublesome boy or unruly man. **pí tsńg-thâu-á**, to make secret signs with fingers.

pí-tui, to beat a thief or a responsible person (*e.g.* the bé-khoài) till stolen articles are recovered. **pí-tsng**, id. **pí-chhe**, to beat the constables or police for neglect of duty. **pí chí^{n}-niû^{n}**, to flog for arrears of land-tax. **sàng pí-tiâu**, to send in a statement that some one should be thus beaten (sent from the keng-sêng).

pì [R. to protect]. **pó-pì**, to protect or help, as gods. **pē-pì** (Cn.), id. **pì-iū**, id.

pì [R. secret]. **pì-koat**, secrets, as of trade (v. koat). **pì-hng**, a secret medical prescription. **pì-thoân**, secrets handed down from ancestors, as in medicine or manufactures; to hand down such a secret.

pì [R. to seal or shut up]. **pì-kiet**, costiveness. **pì-bát**, to keep very close, as a secret, or as something carefully hidden away; secret; hidden. **pì-bát-bát**, carefully concealed, as a secret or a hidden thing.

pì (R. id.), benumbed; sleeping, as hand or foot. **kha pì**, foot sleeping. **chhiú pì**, hand sleeping. **bâ-pì**, satiated with sexual indulgence (sometimes used in the following senses). **lim--khì chin-bâ-pì**, having drunk so much liquor as to feel somewhat elevated, but yet having command of one's self. **thàn--khì bâ-pì**, greatly delighted at having gained a good deal of money. **seng-khu bâ-pì**, feeling of somewhat painful weariness, as after hard work. **khùn kàu bâ-pì**, having slept so snug and cozy as to sleep too long, or feel inclined to sleep too long, in the morning.

pì [R. the arm]. **tsó-pì** (r.), the left arm. **iū-pì** (r.), the right arm.

pì (C.) **tek-pì**, small shoots of bamboo at side of large stem.

pì (C.), = A. pè. **pì-kok** (polite), my native land.

pī (R. id.) **lú-pī**, a female slave; a concubine. **lê-pī** (R.), male and female slaves or menials. **hê-lê hoàn-pī**, to have many slaves and menials at one's call.

pī [R. phī, to cover; a coverlet; sign of the passive, = col. phē, phī]. **pī-kò**, the defendant. **goân-pī**, the two parties, plaintiff and defendant. **pī-lūi**, to be involved by another. **khit--i pī-lūi**, id. **pī-pién** (R.), to be degraded from office.

pī (R. id.), to avoid; to get out of the way. **siám-pī**, id. **tsáu-pī**, id. **tô-pī**, to run away; to abscond; to get out of the way (good or bad). **phiah-pī**, to get out of the way and conceal one's self for a short time. **thòe-pī**, to keep at a respectful distance from a superior. **thè-pī**, id. **hôe-pī** (R.), clear the way (words on a board carried before a mandarin).

pī-hùi, to avoid the use of a sacred or tabooed name. **pī-sú**, to avoid the heat. **pī-hoán**, to flee from a place in a state of rebellion or anarchy. **pī-loān**, id. **pī-lān**, to keep out of the way of great calamities, as war or rebellion.

pī [R. to prepare; complete]. **siú-pī**, a military officer between chhien-tsóng and tē-si; (a lieutenant-major?). **siú-pī-thia^{n}**, id. **pia^{n}-pī-tō**, a Tautai who has also the management of the funds for military and naval expenses.

chek-pī, to reprove.

chiâu-pī, complete. **tsâu-pī** (Cn.), id. **tsôe-pī**, all complete, as a number of articles. **chê-pī**, id. **oân-pī**, all complete and in proper order.

pī-pān, to prepare; to make ready. **tsún-pī**, ready prepared, as person. **ū-pī**, id., to get ready beforehand. **pī-chìn**, candidates who were good enough for the Sew-tsai degree, but who failed because the allowed number of graduates was complete (v. chìn).

pī (T.) **pī-liên**, = A. pí-liên, immediately adjoining or conterminous, as fields or houses.

pī (C.) **pī-si-pêng**, = A. pi^{n}-si-pêng, the 120th radical at the side.

pi^{n} (R. pien), the side. **phien-pi^{n}**, at the side. **pi^{n}-á**, id. **pi^{n}--thâu**, id. **pi^{n}-thâu-lâng**, bystanders. **chit-pi^{n}**, on one side. **lak chit-pi^{n}**, lay the matter aside for the present. **khah-soe chit-pi^{n}**, rather more distant in relationship. **chit-pi^{n} — chit-pi^{n}**, at the same time — at the same time. **chit-pi^{n} chiàh-hun, chit-pi^{n} siá-jī**, smoke and write at once. **chit-pi^{n} hoan-hù, chit-pi^{n} bô-beh-thia^{n}**, though I order him yet he will not listen or obey. **chit-pi^{n} sī-kau, chit-pi^{n} sī-tsùn** (a ditch on each side), either alternative will offend a friend or be very unsuitable. **nn̄g-pi^{n}**, the two parties in a dispute.

goā-pi^{n}, the outside. **chhù-pi^{n}**, a neighbour (v. chhù). **lō-pi^{n}**, the road-side. **sin-pi^{n}**, at one's side; at the side. **sim-pi^{n}**, id. **soa^{n}-pi^{n}**, far among the mountains (v. soa^{n}). **pìn-pi^{n}**, near the temples; the parts near the temples. **hiap-pi^{n}**, the side at the ribs. **kái-pi^{n}**, the hollow between the thigh and the belly. **kah-pi^{n}**, the quick at the side of the nail (v. kah). **thi^{n}-pi^{n}**, very far-off places. **thi^{n}-pi^{n} hái-kak**, the most distant regions (v. kak). **thi^{n} bô-pi^{n}**, heaven is of vast extent. **kėk-pi^{n} ê sé-tsāi**, the most distant and out-of-the-way places.

nî^{n}-tau-pi^{n}, about the end of the year.

siám-pi^{n}, to go to the side to avoid. **thè-pi^{n}**, to keep to the side to let a man pass (v. thè). **oá-pi^{n}**, to approach the side. **sái oá-pi^{n}**, to sail near the shore.

pi^{n}-lô, a sculling oar at the side of a boat. **phah pi^{n}-kè**, to give a secret hint.

pi^{n} — **liâm-pi^{n}**, immediately (v. liâm).

pi^{n} (C. pɛ^{n}), to pull or stretch out straight and tight, as paper, or cloth, or skin, or a rope, or as the edge of a dress; to stretch paper or cloth on a frame or in making an umbrella; to stretch a rope from the mast to the shore so as to tow a boat. **pi^n--chhut-lâi**, to pull out with some force, as a stiff drawer. **pi^n-khui**, to pull a boat away from the shore or from another boat, by means of a rope. **pi^n-pè**, to stretch cloth, as on a screen or frame. **pi^n-kui**, to stretch work on a frame, as for embroidery. **pi^n-kó**, to stretch the leather on a drum (s. side). **pi^n-phoà**, to tear by stretching tight, as dress or paper, &c. **siang-chhiú pi^n**, to pull on hard with both hands, as a tight stocking. **pi^n-ân**, to stretch out tight. **phê pi^n-khi-ân**, make your skin tight and ready for a thrashing. **beh kā--lí pi^n-phê**, I will stretch your skin for you (will beat you), said to a boy. **bô-chit-têng thang pi^n-phê**, having no clothes to put on, = bô-chit-niá^n thang pi^n-phê, = bô-chit-tsoā thang pi^n-phê, id. **sán kàu chit-têng-phê pi^n chit-têng-kut**, nothing but skin and bone.

pi^n tek-than, to dredge for a sort of spout-fish.

pi^n-peh, in great want of money (v. peh). **pi^n-púih--lâng**, to throw one's self for support on a very poor man, so as to make him miserably poor (v. púih).

pì^n (R. pien), a whip; a switch. **bé-pì^n**, a whip or switch for a horse. **tîn-pì^n**, a whip or scourge made of rattan. **thih-pì^n**, a square iron rod used as a club in war. **phah thih-pì^n bōe ko-ióh**, to beat one's self with an iron scourge and sell plaster (after showing its virtues on one's self), as quacks do.

pî^n (R. pêng), (C. pê^n), level; even; smooth; (equal; alike; just). **pî^n-pî^n**, quite level; equal; equally. **pî^n-pî^n-toā**, of equal size. **pî^n-toā**, id. **pî^n-poa^n-iū^n**, in same manner; quite alike. **pî^n-téng**, of equal rank (s. stage). **pî^n-hè**, of same age, as persons. **pî^n-tú-theng**, neither party able to overcome the other. **kap-i ū-pî^n-khiā**, able to associate with him, as in somewhat similar station.

kong-pî^n, fair; honest, as in trade (not of servant); just; equitable, as judge, judgment or business. **táu-chhìn kong-pî^n**, measures and weights fair and just.

pî^n-tit, pretty level and straight, as road; tolerable; mediocre (v. tit). **pî^n-chià^n**, ordinary; of medium quality; fair (v. chià^n). **pî^n-siû^n**, of usual or common quality; mediocre.

pî^n-tiā^n, peaceful, quiet, as region with no disturbance. **hong chī^n, éng pî^n**, wind and waves quiet.

thán-pî^n, lying flat or level; to fall down flat. **pî^n-thá^n**, level, as road. **pî^n-pāng**, level. **it-jī-pî^n**, quite level, as a straight line. **pî^n-pho-pho**, level, as road (v. pho). **pî^n-liú-liú** (Cn.), id. **pî^n-pî^n-lē poáh-tó-lâng** (a level road makes men fall), an affair going all wrong that seemed quite safe. **pî^n-po**, a level plain (v. po). **pî^n-iû^n khòng-thó**, id. (v. iû^n). **sàu-pî^n**, to level down; to raze to the ground. **siu-pî^n**, to repair so as to level. **tiên-pî^n**, to level ground by filling it up. **pho-pî^n**, to spread out level and even.

pî^n (= tî^n). **pî^n-poà^n**, to encumber or entangle (v. tî^n).

pî^n (R. pêng), (C. pê^n), a stage; an awning; a canopy; classifier of plays and of companies of actors. **khó-pî^n**, examination hall for graduation. **tsàu-pî^n**, cooking-place in a junk. **pán-pî^n**, a flat wooden terrace. **tsng-pî^n**, a flat tiled roof or terrace. **pò-pî^n**, a tent; an awning; canopies over streets in idolatrous rites. **liâng-pî^n**, an awning put up for coolness; also, pieces of cloth at the ends of a sedan that can be stretched out to shade from the sun. **ko-pî^n**, a covered shed with offerings to ghosts that have no posterity (v. ko). **tah-pî^n**, to erect a stage or awning. **tah-teng-pî^n**, to make an idolatrous illumination with a vast number of lamps, &c. **giâ-kang-pî^n**, a long jointed flexible frame used at some idolatrous processions.

hì-pî^n, a stage for a play (v. hì). **chit-pî^n-hì**, one play, as acted. **bān-siū-pî^n**, temporary stage at yamun for emperor's birthday. **khui-pî^n**, to make a first performance without payment, as a newly arrived company of actors. **pî^n-téng ū-he-lâng**: **pî^n-ē iáh-ū he-lâng**, said of some action so shameful that one would think it could only be in a play.

pí^n (R. pién), flat; thin; flattened. **pí^n-poe pí^n-poe**, flat-shaped. **pí^n-siu^n**, a long flat low box. **pí^n-láng**, do., of wicker-work. **pí^n-tsǹg**, an instrument like a flat-headed drill, used by robbers for making holes in walls. **pí^n-thâu**, flat at the end. **pí^n-thâu-á**, man with flat forehead. **pí^n-chhùi**, having a flat bill, as a duck (v. ah, "duck"). **ta^n pí^n-chhùi**, he has a long mouth now, as a man quite defeated in argument and silenced so that he cannot answer; or as man who used to laugh at others' calamities but who has met with great calamity himself. **chhùi pí^n**, unable to answer a word.

táh-pí^n, to flatten by treading upon. **tûi-pí^n**, to beat flat, as with hammer or fist. **chhih-pí^n** to press flat, as with the hand. **thán-pí^n**, turning the flat side, as of a sword. **chē-í^n, bô-chē-pí^n**, to take praise but not blame (v. í^n).

pí^n-tāu, a medicinal bean (v. tāu). **pí^n-peh**, a sort of tree grown in flower-pots (v. peh). **pí^n-hî**, a flat-fish like turbot, very good. **pí^n-hî-koa^n**, do. dried, much used.

pì^n (Cn.) **pì^n-kó**, = gû-ta^n, a yoke for a cow or ox.

pì^n (R. pèng), (C. pè^n), a handle (straight or nearly so), as of a knife or plough. **to-pì^n**, handle of sword or knife. **chhiu^n-pì^n**, butt end of spear. **káu-í-pì^n**, arms of arm-chair. **lôe-pì^n**, handle of plough. **tháng-pì^n**, straight handle of bucket, rising straight from the side. **phah-chih lâng--ê khek-pì^n**, to cut short a man's talk (lit. his song) so that he does not effect his purpose. **phah-chih lâng--ê ōe-pì^n**, id. **phah-chih lâng--ê kó-pì^n**, id. (lit. his story).

pì^n (R. pièn), to change; to be altered (gen. gradually), usually for the worse. **pì^n-bīn**, to change countenance, becoming angry or displeased; to frown. **pì^n-hong-bīn**, to change from friendliness to displeasure. **kūn-lâi pì^n-hong**, of late he has become a bad, idle boy. **pì^n-báng**, beginning a bad course of life, as a young lad (v. báng). **pì^n-khoán**, to change for the worse. **pì^n-phái^n**, id. **pì^n-phái^n-khoán**, id. **pì^n-hó**, to change for the better. **pì^n-hó-khoán**, id. **pì^n-hó-iū^n**, id. **kóe-pì^n**, to reform one's self. **hoán-hóe kóe-pì^n**, to repent and reform. **koa^n-chhâ tèng-teng, chiū kóe-pì^n**, will not reform till his coffin is nailed. **bōe-chhoeh bōe-pì^n**, he will neither repent nor reform. **chiū^n-kiō, tsáp-poeh-pì^n**, the bride entering the bridal sedan should make eighteen changes of character for the better.

tńg-pì^n, to become of marriageable age, as about sixteen.

péng-pì^n, easily finding a new means of livelihood when the former way fails. **pì^n-kâu-lāng**, legerdemain; jugglery (v. lāng). **pì^n-pá-hì**, id.; idle play.

pī^n (R. pēng), (C. pē^n), sick; unwell; a disease. **pī^n-pī^n**, constantly in weak health; having a dull lazy manner with no animation. **pī^n-thià^n**, disease; illness. **pī^n-chèng**, id. **pī^n hó**, recovered from illness. **chit-**

47

pī^n soah-chit-lâng, people die of many different diseases.

jie̍t-pī^n, fever. sún-pī^n, consumption. kú-tn̂g-pī^n, a severe chronic disease. kú-tn̂g-pī^n, bô hàu-tsú, in a long chronic disease sons prove undutiful. sin-tsù-pī^n (Cn.), a natural disease, not caused by demons.

pàng-pī^n, intentionally make the patient worse. ū-pī^n, unwell. tio̍h-pī^n, id.; to become unwell. jiám-tio̍h-pī^n, to take a disease. tì-pī^n, id. toà-pī^n, to be unwell (said in relation to what one does though unwell). toà-pī^n khì, to go though unwell. toà-pī^n pān-sū, managing the matter, though really too ill to do so. thoa-pī^n tsòe-kang, to do work by great exertion, when quite too ill to do anything (much worse than toà-pī^n). thoa-pī^n khì, to go though extremely ill, and quite unable for it. the-pī^n, to refuse on the pretence of sickness. phoà-pī^n, very unwell; a fault or flaw in character or in any work. ū phoà-pī^n-lē, faulty, as character or work.

pī^n (R. piēn), to plait, braid, or twine; a plaited lace; braid. pī^n-á, narrow braid, a lace, generally silk; a Chinaman's queue. î^n-ké-pī^n, a round lace; round cord. liú-pī^n, id. liú-si-pī^n, a round silk lace. pí^n--ê pī^n-á, flat braid; a flat lace.

pī^n thâu-tsang, to plait the queue; to wear a queue.

pī^n (cf. pē), (C. pī). pī^n-si-pêng, the 120th radical at the side (esp. T.)

pia^n [R. peng, a soldier, military; cf. phia^n]. pia^n-pē, the Board of War at the capital; the President of it. pia^n-pâng, the office in a yamun that manages military matters; the official at the head of it. pia^n-pī-tō, title of the Tautai, because he disburses the pay of the troops. pàng-pia^n (T.), = A. pàng-peng, to send spirit soldiers to help their votaries, as the gods do.

pia^n, to throw, as stones, at something, or as throwing away sulkily. pia^n-lâi pia^n-khì, to throw backwards and forwards. tùi-bīn ká^n-pia^n--goá, you dare to behave sulkily to my face! said to slave or child. pia^n-hiet-ka̍k, to throw away. pia^n-í pia^n-toh, to strike chairs and table in anger. siū-khì siū-toa̍h, pia^n-oá^n siak-tī, to throw down bowls and chopsticks in a sulk, pet, or rage. pia^n-pia^n sak-sak, m̄-chêng m̄-goân, throwing things about in a pet or rage.

piâ^n (cf. poâ^n), to copy, as a document. piâ^n-jī, to transcribe a document. piâ^n chit-tiu^n, take one copy of the document.

piâ^n [R. pêng, level, even, = col. pî^n], (C. pê^n). piâ^n-sia^n, the tones called "ping," or even, though only one of them is now really even; the first tone, or first and fifth. piâ^n-cheh, the "ping" tones, and the tones that are not "ping;" the method of metrical composition according to the rules for tones. bô-piâ^n-cheh, not composed according to these rules, as colloquial rhymes. chiū^n-piâ^n (C. téng-pê^n), the upper first, or first tone. ē-piâ^n, the lower first, also called the fifth tone.

piá^n (R. péng), one of the cyclical characters.

piá^n (R. péng), a cake; a biscuit. ko-piá^n, small cakes in general. tāu-piá^n, bean-cake, imported from North China chiefly for manure. lék-tāu-piá^n, white cakes with stuffing, made of pease-meal. ā^n-piá^n, cakes with such stuffing. khang-khak ê-piá^n, hollow cakes with empty cavity. thn̂g-piá^n, a very cheap hollow sort with a little sugar inside, but almost empty. ka-lak-piá^n, sort with hole in the middle, for stringing them on a string. lūn-piá^n, thin tough cakes like scones. po̍h-piá^n, very thin cakes, almost like paper. po̍h-piá^n-kauh, eatables wrapped in them. hiu^n-piá^n, a cheap empty sort of sweet cake. bah-piá^n, a cake with bits of pork in it. bah-piá^n-bīn, a broad fat face, not good-looking. ná^n bah-piá^n, said of an ugly pock-marked face. tiong-chhiu-piá^n, cakes made in the 8th month.

chhiū-m̂-piá^n, dried sugared arbutus (Myrica) fruit.

piá^n-lô, an oven. piá^n-io̍h, sort of alkaline lye. piá^n-ah, small basket or box for carrying cakes, &c. piá^n-sut, crumbs of cakes or biscuits. piá^n-iù, id. piá^n-koa^n, biscuits.

pun-piá^n, to distribute cakes, a way of combining in a secret confederacy.

pià^n [R. pèng, to compare; to risk life in battle], to join battle; to quarrel. sa^n-pià^n, id. kap--i sa^n-pià^n, quarrelling, scolding, or fighting with him. toā-pià^n, a great battle. chiang-tsoân-pià^n, a feud between men from Chang-chew and Chin-chew, as in Formosa. pià^n-tīn, the battle raging fiercely, as in a general engagement. pià^n-lâi pià^n-khì, the battle swaying back and forwards. pià^n-thi^n-ūi, to attack the throne by rebellion. pià^n-sí^n-sí, to engage in mortal combat, or in a feud that will ruin one party at least. pià^n-sì^n-miā^n, to risk one's life, as in some dangerous work. siā pià^n-siā, villages fighting. chha̍t pià^n-chha̍t, robbers or bad men quarrelling with each other. phah-pià^n, to fight for life or death; to risk all on one venture (as in battle, feud, or trade), which, if lost, all is ruined. toā-phah-pià^n, id.; very dangerous or deadly. phah-pià^n-io̍h, medicine that will kill or cure. chit-thiap-io̍h kap--i phah-pià^n, to use such dangerous medicine. m̄-ká^n phah-pià^n, terribly afraid of meddling in a matter. kau-pià^n, contest very fierce and still doubtful, as in battle, boxing, &c. koà^n-joa̍h kau-pià^n, weather just changing, but not yet settled, as from cold to hot weather. sin-kū kau-pià^n, the old just going out, and the new just coming in, as corn.

pià^n, to pour out, as a liquid; to clean out; to empty out, or pour in a large quantity (as of water) rapidly; to put in order, as a bed in the morning. pià^n-chhut, to empty or clean out. pià^n-lâi pià^n-khì, to empty back and forwards, as buckets (s. fight). pià^n-tām-po̍h, to pour a small quantity rapidly in or out. pià^n-ta, to pour out quite empty. pià^n-chheng, to clear or clean out thoroughly. pià^n-sàu, to sweep, and clean out, and make tidy, as a room. hō chhia-teh-pià^n, rain in torrents.

pià^n lâng--ê pn̄g-oá^n, to get a man out of his situation. tsòe--chit-ē pià^n, to pour out the whole at once; to tell all one's mind, as to a confidential friend; or as in scolding, in the excitement of the quarrel saying all we feel, which we would not have done when cool. ōe pià^n-niā^n-chhut, do., as in scolding.

piah (R. phek), a partition wall. chhiû^n-piah, walls in general. chhiû^n-piah ū-hī, walls and partitions have ears. thia^n-hī thia^n-piah, to listen secretly, as an eaves-dropper. khí^n-chhiû^n peh-piah, to climb walls (v. khí^n). chhiû^n-piah-tîn, a creeper of the fig tribe. chio̍h-piah, a stone partition. ngī^n-piah, a solid partition, as stone, brick, or well-limed composition. pang-piah, a wooden partition of a room. koa^n-chin-piah, a partition made of reeds.

keh-piah, next door; near neighbours. āu-piah,

behind, in place. **āu-piah-soa**ⁿ, said of powerful influence assisting a man (v. soaⁿ).

piah-to, a large flat trowel with handle on the back as on a shield. **piah-tú**, a prop for a wall. **piah-tû**, a cupboard or press in a wall. **piah-kham**, a niche in a wall with no door. **thàu-piah-long**, to have the feet through a partition, as captive (v. long). **piah-kak**, at the corner between two walls. **piah-kha-pi**ⁿ, secret places. **piah-pi**ⁿ, id.

piah-hé, a sort of lizard. **piah-hmh**, a sort of beetle (v. hmh). **piah-sien-si**ⁿ, the cockroach (counted useful in medicine).

hún-piah, to plaster a partition smooth and white; a white-plastered wall. **chhui-piah**, to rub the plaster on it smooth. **iah-piah**, to make a hole in a wall, as thief. **kùi-piah**, to hang on the wall. **tah-piah**, to paste on the partition (as a bill); to lean against a wall. **pè-piah**, to paste paper on a partition. **tú-piah**, to prop up a partition. **chhun-chhiú, tú-tióh-piah**, having no money and no way of getting it.

piak (R. pek), to roast or toast (v. pek).

piak (cf. phiāng). **piak-kó**, a sort of drum with skin on one end only.

piak, to burst and fall to pieces, as a gun, jar, or barrel. **piak--khui**, to split up and fall separate, as things that had been glued or joined together. **sim-koa**ⁿ **beh-piak--khui**, heart bursting with grief or distress. **sim-koa**ⁿ **beh-piak--phoà**, id. **tāi-chì piak--phoà**, the affair has become public; the feud has begun, so as to cause great trouble and evil, *e.g.* by a secret leaking out, or by one party entering a complaint at the yamun, or the negotiations otherwise failing.

piák, sound as of glass cut or broken, or of fire, or of water falling on melted fat, or of salt or charcoal splitting in the fire, or of wood cracking in dry weather; sound of crackling or cracking. **piák-piák-háu**, to crackle or give a cracking sound (as above). **pih-pih piák-piák**, sound as of coals or charcoal crackling in the fire.

pian, **piân**, **pián**, **piàn**, **piān**; better pien, piên, pién, pièn, piēn (*q.v.*)

piang — **pók-piang pók-piang**, sound of beating raw cotton. **pók-piang-thûi**, rod for beating raw cotton.

piang [R. peng, ice, = col. pi]. **chhìn-piang-piang**, very cold, as tea. **piang-piang-léng**, very cool or cold.

piàng [R. pèng, to compare, to combat, = col. piàⁿ]. **tsòe--chit-ē piàng**, to have it out in scolding, &c. (v. piàⁿ).

piàng — **cheng-piàng**, housebreaking. **cheng lâng-ê-piàng**, id.

piàng (C. piāng). **pìn-pìn piàng-piàng**, loud noise of heavy steps, or of steps on an unsteady floor, or of carrying heavy things. **pìn-piàng-háu**, id. **piàng-piàng-háu**, id.

piāng (C.), = A. piàng. **pìn-piāng-háu**, loud sound of steps, &c. &c.

piāng, the sound of a gun.

piāng (cf. pāiⁿ). **goā-piāng** (T. Cn.), exclamation of great surprise.

piāng — **piāng-kó**, = phiāng-kó, a long thick bamboo with a skin over one end only, used by beggars and quacks as a drum.

piat, **piát**; better piet, piét (*q.v.*)

piau [R. top branch; signal; label; beautiful; = col. pio, phiau]. **piau-tì** (r.), beautiful, as person. **hù-piau-thong**, wealthy, good-looking, and talented. **hù-piau-thong, sa**ⁿ**-jī tsn̂g**, very much so.

piau [R. fat, = col. pio]. **phauh-piau**, plump, fat, and good-looking.

piáu [R. the outside of a dress; to manifest; a memorial to the throne; a pattern], to give a name; appellation of relatives by the mother's side. **piáu-miâ**ⁿ, to give a name. **piáu-bêng**, to illustrate, exemplify, or typify. **it-piáu ê jîn-bût**, a man of elegance and beauty. **piáu-chiu**ⁿ, a memorial to the throne. **hô-piáu**, a memorial archway. **pàng-hô-piáu**, to make fireworks in the shape of such an arch.

kim-hoe piáu-lí, said of some splendidly ornamented dresses (v. lí).

piáu--ê, a relative by the mother's side. **piáu-chhin**, id. **in-piáu**, his relative (especially cousin) by the mother's side. **piáu-iâ**, cousin of different surname. **piáu-hia**ⁿ, elder son of aunt or of maternal uncle. **piáu-sió-tī**, younger do. (so also with terms for sisters, &c.) **piáu-tit**, son of cousin of different surname. **piáu-sun-á**, id. **piáu-tit-sun**, grandson of such cousin. **piáu-peh**, elder son of grandaunt or of grandmother's brother. **piáu-chek**, younger do. **kū-piáu**, son or daughter of maternal uncle. **bú-kū-piáu**, id. **kīm-piáu hia**ⁿ**-tī** (T.), son of maternal uncle. **î-piáu hia**ⁿ**-tī**, son of maternal aunt. **î-piáu chí-bē**, daughter of do. **kσ-piáu hia**ⁿ**-tī**, son of paternal aunt (v. kσ).

piáu (R. id.), a prostitute; a harlot. **piáu-thâu**, a brothel-keeper. **piáu-keng**, a brothel. **piáu-kiá**ⁿ, you whoreson! (scolding). **piáu-tsú-kiá**ⁿ, id. **phiâu-piáu**, to commit whoredom. **chhiong-piáu**, to revile by calling a person a whore.

piáu (Cn.), = A. kiáu, to paste paper, as in making scrolls for hanging up. **piáu-pō**, id.

pien (C. pan). **pien-chi-hoe**, the bombax-tree, with large red flowers.

pien [R. side, boundary, = col. piⁿ]. **pông-pien**, at the side. **pông-pien ê-lâng**, a bystander; one who has nothing to do with the matter. **pien-hâm**, grooves for a sliding lid or door, or in the edges of planks morticed together. **kim-pien-chíⁿ** (Cn.), large good cash with bright edges. **kim-pien**, id. **hoa-pien**, a dollar (only said in joke in imitation of mandarin).

pien-kài, frontier of a state. **kék-pien ê só-tsāi**, most distant parts. **kóng-tāi bû-pien**, great and wide without limit (said of the laws of Buddha). **hoat-lék bû-pien**, idol's power very great.

pien — **gû-pien**, a bull's pizzle. **lók-pien**, stag's do. (used medicinally).

pien [R. to string together; to arrange materials; to compose], to give a specially-invented name, as a fancy name to goods; to compose, as a song. **pien-miâ**ⁿ, to invent and give a fancy name or sort of nickname. **pien hō-thâu**, to mark successive volumes or houses (or such like) with the successive words of a book or sentence. **sin-pien--ê**, newly made, as a song. **pien-khek**, to compose a song. **pien-kó**, to invent and tell stories or scandal. **pien chit-hō ê-péh**, to make or use a sort of secret slang, used by each class of people.

pien (cf. pan), (C. pεⁿ, pan), to pull out, as a stiff peg or drawer: to row by pulling the oar as Europeans do (but "kò" is by pushing); to grasp with the hand, as in climbing. **pien-khui**, to pull open with force, as a stiff door or drawer. **pien-chhut**, to draw out, as a stiff drawer. **pien--khí-lâi**, to draw out with the hand, as a peg; to pull off with some force, as a stiff cover. **pien-chih**, to break by pulling. **pien chhiú-bé**, to try each other's strength by pulling each other's arms at right angles.

piên (T. H.), =pîn. **piên-toā^{n}**, =pîn-toā^{n}, lazy.

pién (R. id.) **pién-hok**, a bat, commonly called "bit-pô."

pién [R. a flat tablet or sign-board]. **pâi-pién**, a sign-board, as of a shop. **chhut pâi-pién**, to put up a sign-board. **pién-jī**, large characters, as on a complimentary tablet. **khiā-pién**, a tablet with a perpendicular column of characters, as at door of yamun or of a Chiōng-goân. **koà-pién**, to hang up a tablet, as at the door of a Kujin or higher graduate, or in a temple, as a tablet given by the people to a good mandarin, &c. **sàng-pién**, to present an honorary tablet, as to a successful doctor or to a good mandarin when his term of office is expired.

pién [R. flat, =col. pí^{n}, pin]. **pién-tāu**, a legume used as medicine for diarrhœa (Dolichos Lablab ?). **pién-sit** (C. pán; T. péng), a thin cake of flour inclosing minced-meat (v. sit).

pién (R. id.), to degrade or remove from office, as a mandarin. **pī-pién** (R.), to be degraded from office.

piàn [R. to go all round or over; everywhere], classifier of successive times, as of reading over, infusing, drinking, sewing, playing games, painting several coats, &c. **piàn-piàn**, all over a place. **kiâ^{n} piàn-piàn**, to walk or travel all over. **piàn-sin**, all over the body; the whole body. **piàn-tōe**, all over the earth or land.

thâu-piàn, the first time, as of an infusion, &c.; the first coat of paint. **tē-jī-piàn**, the second do. **koh-tháh chit-piàn**, to put on another coat, as of varnish. **su chit-piàn**, to lose one game. **kúi-piàn**, how many times? as of painting, drinking wine, &c. **thák kúi-piàn**, how many times have you read (the lesson) over aloud? **thák sa^{n}-piàn**, read it three times. **sa^{n}-piàn-chiú**, three times drinking liquor at a feast.

piàn (=poàn). **piàn-sūi**, =poàn-sūi, palsy.

piàn (R. id., =col. pì^{n}), to change, generally for the worse. **piàn-oā^{n}**, to change.

piàn-bōe, to sell.

piàn-hoà, to be transformed, as in the changes in nature. **chhien-piàn bān-hoà**, all sorts of changes, permutations, or transformations, as in the processes of nature, or as the action of spirits and gods; having applications to all varied circumstances, as the doctrines of the sages; said also of a man managing to carry on business with almost no capital by all sorts of cunning plans. **jī, chhien-piàn bān-hoà**, characters can be used in many various ways and senses according to the connection.

piàn-pē̍, to change one plan for another when the first fails. **sûi-sî èng-piàn**, to act according to circumstances (v. èng). **piàn-thong**, versatile (v. thong). **ū-ki-piàn**, id. (v. ki). **tsoán-piàn**, changing one's plans or language to suit new circumstances. **koân-piàn**, going somewhat beyond our authority in an emergency (v. koân). **piàn-pá-hì**, jugglery.

piàn-chhien, to change and pass away; changing for the worse (v. chhien). **piàn-khoán**, to change one's manner, appearance, or conduct, esp. for the worse. **piàn-siòng**, to change to an unfriendly bearing. **piàn-hêng**, id.; also, to change appearance, as when about to die. **piàn-sek**, to change colour, as men, things, or sky (v. sek). **piàn-hók**, to put on mourning. **kɛ piàn** (C.), a family or village of one surname at feud within itself.

piān (R. id.), ready; prepared; (convenient; usual); then (in that case). **chhòng-piān**, to make ready. **chhoân-piān**, to select and make ready. **put-piān**, unsuitable; inconvenient. **thàn-piān**, to take advantage of the opportunity. **sûi-piān**, in any way; all the same; just as you please. **sūn-piān**, without any special additional trouble, as doing something just on one's way while doing something else. **khoài-piān**, easy; convenient; speedy at work, so as not to give trouble; said of a woman having a rapid and easy delivery. **lī-piān**, convenient, as a thing or a place. **lī-lâng-piān**, to help at once when asked; to pay a debt or give a loan, &c., at once, without making any trouble.

piān-hók, undress, as of a mandarin. **piān-i**, usual everyday dress. **piān-tsòe**, ready-made. **piān-chhài**, a simple dinner; pot-luck. **chhe-chhài piān-pn̄g**, id. **piān-thò-ōe**, conventional phrases (v. thò).

tāi-piān, going to stool; motion of bowels. **tāi-siáu-piān ū-hā**, having motion and able to pass urine, as sick man. **siáu-piān**, to make water. **piān-tók**, a swelling near the groin, often does not come to a head for months, or not at all.

piān [R. biēn, the face, surface, =col. bīn]. **jiâu^{n}-piān**, beautiful appearance of the surface of old china, all over like small cracks. **jiâu^{n}-piān-hûi**, china-ware of that appearance.

piān [R. to distinguish; to discuss]. **piān-lūn**, to discuss. **piān-pok**, to dispute. **sa^{n}-piān**, to discuss together. **piān-iâ^{n}**, to overcome in argument. **piān-tó**, id.; to shut up our opponent. **hun-piān**, to make an explanation in argument; to answer defending one's self from some charge. **piān-piet** (r.), to discriminate. **piān chin-ké**, to discuss or investigate the right and wrong, true and false, on both sides; to show in action that we so distinguish. **tan-ko oân-sán, chin-sien lân-piān**, all in confusion (lit. drugs), so that even one of the genii could not distinguish.

piān [R. name of a place; a rule], a surname.

piet (R. piet, by change of tone from piėt). **hun-piet**, to distinguish; to discriminate clearly; to perceive clearly. **piān-piet** (r.), id.

piėt [R. piėt, to distinguish; to part; different; =col. pát, piet]. **lī-piėt**, to take leave of; to bid farewell to. **sa^{n}-piėt**, id. **sàng-piėt**, to accompany a friend a short way when he leaves. **pài-piėt**, to take respectful leave.

pâi-piėt, having a good deal of display and grandeur, as a mandarin coming out, or such spectacle.

piėt [R. pėk, white, =col. pėh, bat]. **kok-piėt**, the Amaryllis lily, esp. the white. **kok-piėt-hoe**, id. **âng-kok-piėt**, the red sort.

pih (R. piet), a very small sort of turtle. **sáh-pih**, boiled do. **sí-pih, beh-bōe sa^{n}-tsáp-jī**, will make no deduction at all. **khöe-pih** (Cn.), very shallow flat boats for poling up shallow streams.

pih — **jiō-pih**, a small sort of chamber-pot of finer material, used by women.

pih, to roll or fold up, as sleeves, &c. **pih-tsah**, to draw up trowsers and fold up sleeves to be ready for walking or work (v. tsah). **pih chhiú-ńg**, to fold up one's sleeves. **pih khè-kha**, to roll up the legs of foreign trowsers.

pih [R. pit, to assist]. **kok-pih,** rather too knowing; skilful at almost anything, esp. of a child or lad too clever by half. **ké kok-pih,** said of trying to improve what is well enough already.

pih — khó pih-pih, thick, strong, and good, as soup, or as boiled rice.

pih, sound, as of a man falling down, or of a rat falling from the roof. **pih--chit-ē,** id.

pih — pih-pih piak-piak, sound of coals, charcoal, or twigs crackling in the fire. **pih-pih pók-pók,** id.

pin (R. id.), (C. pun). **pin-nn̂g,** the areca palm; the areca or betel-nut (v. nn̂g).

pin [R. a guest], a surname. **lū tōng-pin,** = sien-tsé, one of the genii worshipped by barbers. **bē-pin** (R.), = su-iâ, a private secretary in a yamun. **se-pin** (R.), a teacher in relation to the "tong-ka" who engages him.

pin (R. id.) **pin-pin ché-ché** (R.), neat, elegant, and polite.

pin [R. pién, flat, = col. píⁿ], (T. pín; C. pun). **pin-taⁿ,** a carrying-pole for the shoulder (v. taⁿ).

pîn (esp. T.), = pêng, side.

pîn (C. pûn; T. H. piên, pîn). **pîn-toāⁿ,** lazy; idle. **pîn-á-thâng** (Cn.), a lazy fellow.

pîn (R. id.) **pîn-kiông,** poor (v. kiông). **pîn-chiēn,** poor and in low circumstances. **pîn-hân** (R.), extremely poor. **ko-pîn-koáⁿ,** orphans (or having no relations), poor, and widows. **ko-pîn-iáu,** without relations, poor, and short-lived (v. iáu). **siá-sì pîn-bîn,** to give alms to the poor. **sip-sán, kiú-pîn,** of ten lean men nine are poor.

pîn [R. proof; an official certificate, &c.; on the evidence of; according to]. **pîn-kù,** proof; evidence (v. kù). **pîn-sìn,** sufficient proof (v. sìn). **ū-sìn-pîn,** trustworthy.

pîn-sim, fair in dealing. **pîn-liông-sim,** id.

pîn-lí-kóng, according to what you say; supposing what you say to be true. **pîn-toaⁿ,** on the evidence of a receipt or such document. **pîn-tsāi-lí,** conduct the matter just as you please. **pîn-tsāi-goá,** I will act just as I please in the matter, no one else has any business what I do. **pîn hó-jī-ūn,** trusting to his own good luck.

pîn-tsún, a certificate or good documentary proof (v. tsún). **bûn-pîn,** a document given to a mandarin as proof of his office. **niáⁿ-pîn,** to receive such a commission from the governor-general, when appointed to a new position. **niáⁿ kan-khó-pîn lâi chhut-sì,** to get misery as one's lot to be born into.

pîn (R. id.), (cf. pín), a standing screen; a wooden partition. **eng-pîn,** a boarding on the stern of a junk with picture of eagle. **giòk-pîn,** a sort of government academy at Amoy where the literati compete for prizes.

pîn-pâi, a shield (v. pâi).

ûi-pîn, a standing screen, either stiff or folding. **khiā-pîn,** a standing screen, as at door. **mn̂g-pîn,** standing screen opposite a door. **kiàⁿ-pîn,** a mirror fixed upright in a frame (without any joint) on a stand. **bát-pîn,** a close wooden partition. **kek bát-pîn,** to make one. **soe-pîn,** a partition of lattice-work or of upright bars at small distances. **liú-tiâu-pîn,** partition made with very thin slips of wood very close to each other (v. liú). **thiaⁿ-pîn,** a cross partition dividing the central hall into front and back halves (v. thiaⁿ). **pîn-pang,** a wooden partition. **pîn-té,** id.

pîn-hong, a fixed wooden partition across central hall. **pîn-mn̂g,** a door in a partition, esp. at sides of central hall.

tsúi-pîn (C.), a small wash-stand in bride's outfit. **tsúi-pîn ui-kè** (C.), this wash-stand and a small frame for clothes.

pîn [R. jiên, so, an adverbial particle]. **pō-pîn,** suddenly.

pín (R. pìn), a bamboo screen. **pín-á,** a small hanging bamboo screen. **tek-pín,** id. **bih-pín,** a stiff bamboo screen, hung at a door. **thiⁿ-thang-pín,** a cover for a sky-light, often made of oyster-shells. **kok-tát-pín,** coarse bamboo wicker-work material (like hurdles) used for making coarse partitions, &c.

pín (T.) **pín-taⁿ,** = A. pin-taⁿ, a carrying pole (v. taⁿ).

pín [R. a petition; to receive from Heaven; cf. péng], a petition or memorial; to petition. **pín-thiap,** a petition or memorial. **pín-toaⁿ,** a report given in to a superior officer, as by police or by tē-pó. **pín-kìⁿ,** to visit a superior officer (or graduate visiting a mandarin) on business. **pín-kiû,** to petition by a written petition. **pín-hok,** to report to the superior officer. **pín-ti** (R.), to inform superior officer by a document. **pín-tò,** to report that the parties in the case have arrived (v. tò). **pín ló-tia,** to petition or report to the mandarin.

pín-sèng, natural character.

pín, a pin; to pin loosely; to baste very loosely in sewing. **pín-chiam,** a foreign pin.

pìn, to comb. **sat-pìn,** a small tooth comb (lit. for lice). **sat-pìn-thak,** an instrument for cleaning it. **pìn-thâu-tsang,** to comb the queue. **pìn-thâu,** id.

pìn — ū-pìn-poàⁿ, to be on terms of intimacy with a person (v. poàⁿ). **teh-pìn-poàⁿ,** there is some impediment.

pìn, to pull to the side, as the fore-sail. **thâu-phâng pìn,** pull the fore-sail to the side, as in tacking.

pìn [R. the temples]. **pìn-piⁿ,** the temples and parts close to them; at the temples. **pìn-kak,** the place at the temples where the corner of the hair ends (said of women). **pìn-kha,** the part near the temples (of women), close to the limit of the hair. **pìn-súi,** the hair worn by women on the side of the head. **pìn-chhiu,** long hanging whiskers, separate from the beard. **pìn-soh,** a thread going round a woman's head and held in her teeth at toilet. **poàⁿ-pìn-soh,** id.

pìn — pìn-pìn pòng-pòng, loud sound of heavy footsteps, or of moving heavy things (v. pòng). **pìn-pìn piàng-piàng,** id. (v. piàng). **pìn-pìn piāng-piāng** (C.), id.

pīn — pīn-pīn pōng-pōng, dull heavy noise of man walking heavily, or of moving heavy things (v. pōng).

pīn — o-ien pīn-pōng, smoke filling the room in great quantities; confused hurrying, as on the approach of rebels or such sudden calamities.

pio [R. piau, a branch; a spear or signal; a label; beautiful; cf. phiau], a javelin; a dart; a harpoon; to catch with a harpoon; a pole stuck in the sand, as the goal and prize of the dragon-boat race. **pó-pio,** a small arrow sold by a man who guarantees that the bearer (man or vessel) shall not be molested by robbers or pirates in a certain dangerous part of road or sea. **tn̂g-pio,** a sort of javelin. **té-pio,** a short deadly dart. **chhiú-pio,** id. **chhɛⁿ-tek-pio** (C.), a venomous snake, said to have long feelers. **bé-ka-pio,** a trident-shaped harpoon. **háh-hî-pio,** a harpoon with the prongs very near. **pio bé-ka,** to catch the bé-ka fish with a harpoon.

pàng-pio, to offer the prize for the dragon race, as some wealthy man. **chhah-pio,** to set up the prize as a goal, sticking the pole in the sand; to stick the prize on the bow of the successful boat. **chhiú^n-pio,** to snatch the prize on reaching the goal. **chhiú^n thâu-pio,** to seize the first prize in the race. **ài-chhiú^n thâu-pio,** fond of putting one's self forward to take the lead. **m̄-sái chhiú^n-thâu-pio,** you need not be always putting yourself forward thus.

pio (esp. Cn.), to play or joke. **pio-chhiò,** to joke and jest; unfounded, as thing said in jest. **kóng pio-chhiò,** to joke and jest.

pio [R. piau, fat], very fat, as a horse.

pio = pió, a watch.

pió [R. piáu, outside; to manifest; a memorial to the emperor; a watch]. **pió-chiu^n,** a memorial to the emperor. **pió-chiang** (C.), id. **pài-pió,** to forward or present a memorial to the emperor. **pió-pâng,** office and official (in the yamun of a high mandarin who is in constant communication with the throne) for preparing memorials to the throne.

pió-á, a watch. **sî-pió,** id. **sî-sîn-pió** (Cn.), id. **pió-á-chiam,** hand of a watch. **pió-á-tsoān,** watch-key. **pió-á thêng,** the watch has stopped.

piō (R. piáu). **hî-piō,** isinglass just as got from the intestines of the fish. **hî-piō-ka,** prepared isinglass. **âng-koe-piō,** isinglass from the âng-koe, the best sort.

pit (R. id.), a pen; a pencil. **soān-pit,** a glazier's diamond. **ô-pit,** hair pencil from Hoo-chow, very good. **iên-pit,** a lead pencil (foreign).

bók-pit-hoe, name of a beautiful flower. **bók-pit,** id.; also a female head-ornament shaped like that flower. **kúi-pit,** a cooling medicinal plant, like a mushroom, reddish with black point.

tāi-pit, an amanuensis for writing a deed or important document. **ko-pit** (R.), your handwriting. **hó-pit-bék,** fine handwriting. **pit-chek,** handwriting (v. chek). **chhiú-pit,** id. **hóng lâng--ê chhiú-pit,** to copy or imitate a man's writing, *e.g.* for exercise. **chhiú ū gûn-tsu-pit,** palm has a line straight to one of the divisions between the fingers, will become a graduate. **chhiú ū bûn-pit,** id.

kiáh-pit, to take up a pen, as in order to write. **ùn-pit,** to dip it in ink. **chìm-pit,** to soak it, so as to soften it, when ink had got hardened in the point. **bē-pit,** to press out the superfluous ink, and smooth the point of the pen for writing. **boah-pit** (Cn.), id. **lóh-pit,** to begin to write. **hē-pit,** id. **pàng-pit,** to lay down the pen. **sit-pit,** to make a slip in writing; a lapsus pennæ. **chhah-pit,** to put the pen into the stand. **phoà-pit,** to go first time to school. **khui-pit,** to write characters for the first time in a new year. **khui-pit-lé,** first fee to a teacher when he begins to write the first accusation or defence for us in a legal case that requires a good deal of such work before it is over. **hē--lí jūn-pit,** said on giving a small fee to a man who writes a document for us (lit. to moisten your pen!)

pit-sim, the hair that makes the point of a Chinese pen. **pit-sim lut--khì,** the hair has all dropped out in a piece. **pit-chiam,** the point of a pen. **pit-bé,** id. **pit thut-bé,** the point has lost its sharpness. **chiáh pit-bé,** to live by fomenting lawsuits, as a pettifogger. **tsng pit-á-bé,** id. **pit-siau,** the stem of the pen, as distinct from the hair. **pit-koài^n,** id. **pit-kóng,** cover for end of pen. **pit-thap,** id. **pit-that,** id. **pit-tē,** bag or case for pen or pencil. **pit-tâng,** cylindrical stand for holding pens when not used. **pit-kè,** a small serrated rest for laying pens nearly level when wet. **pit-kè-soa^n,** name given to some mountains that have several peaks close in a line near the top. **pit-bák-hī^n,** pen, ink, and inkstone.

pit (Cn.) **tē-pit,** an insect like a cricket, that burrows in the ground (T. tē-peh).

pit (R. id.) **pit-jiên** (R.), certainly; must be so. **pit-tēng** (R.), id. **pit-tiā^n,** I think it certainly is. **pit--tióh** (r.), must. **pit-sī,** certainly it is so. **liōng-pit,** I should think that —. **put-pit,** it is better not to —; better that it should not —. **bē-pit,** I think it is not so, or should not be done. **bī-pit,** id. **bī-pit-jiên,** id. **bē-pit-jiên,** id.

pit, to crack; to open into chinks. **pit-khui,** id. **pit-hûn,** a small crack or flaw; cracked, as wood or crockery. **chhiú pit,** hands chapped, as with cold. **pit háuh^n-háuh^n,** all splitting, as wood in drought. **mi^n-pit-ké,** sort of fermented cake that splits open.

pit [R. sound of fire]. **pit-pok-háu,** sound, as of crackers, &c.

pit [R. pek, a hundred, = col. pah, peh]. **pit-lêng,** a bird that learns to sing many things (v. lêng). **pit-háp-hoe** (T.), = pek-háp-hoe, a white lily with great many petals.

pit [R. name of bird]. **thok-pit-á,** a small bird much kept by children. **pit-á** (T.), id.

pit [R. pek, elder brother, earl, = col. peh], (T. phit). **pit-lô,** a sort of small bird (v. lô).

pit (T.) **a-pit-tó,** = A. **áh-put-tó,** a round-bottomed doll.

pit [R. to open]. **khai-pit,** the formation of this present world. **khai-thien pit-tē,** id. **tāi-pit** (X.), David.

pit (cf. pit). **pit-pit pók-pók,** crackling of fire on twigs, &c.

piu (R. id.), a fierce animal like the hyaena. **hé-lông pà-piu,** said of very fierce and wicked men. **hé-lêng pà-piu,** id. **hé-liông pà-piu,** a company of bad fellows going about doing all sorts of wickedness and low amusements.

tit-tit-piu, to run away in great haste, as man or animal.

png [R. hong, square, a place, = col. hng, pang], (C. pui^n), a surname. **png-chhân,** name of a village near Pechuia.

png (R. hong), (C. pui^n), a high tree with deeply indented leaves, which take beautiful colours in the fall; the Liquidambar Formosana; a sort of gum is obtained from it. **png-lûi,** its fruit (useless). **png-kià-si^n,** the misletoe, parasitic on this tree. **png-thâng,** a large green caterpillar found on it, from which a strong gut is made.

png [R. pang, to assist; to join together], to join together by iron hoops, as two pieces of wood in making a mast, or in making a thick pillar; to join in trade a man or company that has far more capital than we. **sa^n-png,** to assist each other, as two or more persons, in trade, or in managing a matter for longer or shorter time. **goá png-i,** I, having little capital, join in trade him who has much more.

png-thiap, to give a regular allowance, as to poor relatives (v. thiap).

png (same as above?), to lay down a stake on another man gambling. **png-tù**, id. (v. tù). **png--lí**, I lay down this stake on your game.

pńg (R. póng), a list (posted up), as of successful candidates for degree; said also of some sorts of proclamations and idolatrous bills. **ñg-pńg**, an imperial proclamation. **pńg-pûn**, the text of an imperial proclamation. **tsàu-pńg**, a memorial to the emperor. **pài-pńg**, to present a memorial to the emperor.

chiò-pńg, a bill issued by Tauist priests announcing the performance of the rites called chiò (v chiò). **tah-pńg**, to put up such a bill, as for the rites of "kong-tek."

chhut-pńg, to issue the official list of new graduates. **tâng-pńg**, having taken the degree of Kujin (or Tsin-sze) in the same year. **kim-pńg**, rank of Tsin-sze. **lêng-hó-pńg**, official list of new Kujin, or higher degree. **hù-pńg**, list of candidates for Kujin degree who have done well, but whose degree is put off till the next examination. **hù-pńg-kòng**, highest class of lím-seng graduates, who will soon be Kujin.

pńg (Cn.), = A. pún, a volume; capital (only said in some phrases, esp. those most simply colloquial: "pún" is also used). **pńg-chîⁿ**, capital. **chit-pńg-tsṳ**, one book.

pńg (T.) **pńg-sit**, = A. pién-sit, a sort of cake.

pn̄g (R. hoān), (C. pūiⁿ), boiled rice, boiled dry and whole. **bê-pn̄g**, cooked rice in general (v. bê). **chhìn-pn̄g**, cold rice. **tsá-khí-pn̄g**, breakfast. **jit-tàu-pn̄g**, dinner. **chit-chhùi-pn̄g chit-bé-hî kàu** (must have one fish for each mouthful of rice), asking fully sufficient, and allowing no abatement.

chhài-pn̄g, food of the cheapest sort, offered to spirits. **chhài-kiⁿ-pn̄g**, id. **chhe-chhài piēn-pn̄g**, a simple every-day dinner.

hàu-pn̄g, to make offerings to the spirit of a man newly buried (v. hàu). **kià-pn̄g**, to intermit these rites for a few days. **thêng-pn̄g**, id. **soah-pn̄g**, to end these rites. **pn̄g-têng**, a small paper house for the spirit at these ceremonies.

iû-pn̄g, rice cooked with hemp-seed, oil, and ginger till it becomes dry; used at any time, but especially for some days (three to thirteen) after the birth of a child, sent by parents to their friends, who have come to make inquiry. **hēng iû-pn̄g**, to make these presents. **chhèng iû-pn̄g**, to cook rice in this way, especially for various rites. **ip iû-pn̄g** (Cn.), id. **ip-pn̄g** (Cn.), id.

tsú-pn̄g, to boil rice. **būn-pn̄g**, to cook rice with little water. **sàng-pn̄g**, to take food to a prisoner. **thiⁿ-pn̄g**, to fill the bowl with rice. **tóe-pn̄g**, id. **pe-pn̄g**, to use chopsticks in eating rice. **phè-pn̄g** (C. phòe-pūiⁿ), to eat as a condiment along with rice; to be used as a condiment with rice. **saⁿ-oá-pn̄g**, to cohabit, as man and woman without any form of marriage.

chiáh-pn̄g, to eat food; to take a meal. **chiáh-pn̄g--bē** (have you had food?), how do you do? **khoàⁿ-thiⁿ chiáh-pn̄g**, to live by honest means. **chiáh-koaⁿ-pn̄g**, to be in mandarin's service. **chiáh lâng-ê-pn̄g**, to be in a man's employment, or depending on him. **chiáh hit-ê-pn̄g**, to follow that sort of employment. **chiáh sí-pn̄g**, to eat merely to live (as an idle rich man); to be of no use in the world. **chiáh lâng--ê sí-pn̄g**, to take wages, but do no work, or almost none, for it.

pn̄g-tiàm, an eating-house. **chiáh pn̄g-tiàm**, to take a meal in an eating-house. **pn̄g-sî**, a rice spoon (v. sî). **pn̄g-táu**, a wooden dish for boiled rice.

pn̄g [R. pōng, pông, near; to depend upon], to rely upon; to trust to. **saⁿ-pn̄g**, to join together and assist each other. **saⁿ-pn̄g-pòh**, mutually assisting each other (v. pòh). **saⁿ-pn̄g khùi-lát**, to assist each other by strength or influence, as in fighting or in a legal case. **saⁿ-pn̄g hok-khì**, to join, as partners in trade, or in some particular speculation. **saⁿ-pn̄g tsâi-khì**, to join capital in trade. **pn̄g lí--ê hok-khì**, I join you to get the benefit of your large capital in trade. **pn̄g i--ê khùi-lát**, leans on his powerful influence. **pn̄g lí--ê hok-ìm**, I take advantage of your influence and assistance, as in some danger, or to get some benefit, or on going to see some influential man. **pn̄g i-ê-sè**, to take undue advantage of his power or influence. **pn̄g-i-khì**, to take advantage of a man's travelling (or going to see some person) to go along with him. **pn̄g i--ê hō-soàⁿ-ńg** (get shelter of his umbrella), take advantage of his travelling to travel safer, cheaper, or free (v. ńg). **kâu pn̄g hó-ui**, the monkey using the influence of the tiger's majesty (v. ui). **pn̄g-sîn tsok-hok**, to have a good feast on the occasion of an idol's birthday or some other occasion of worship.

po [R. to praise], (Cn. pe), to praise too much; to flatter. **po--lâng**, to praise people too much. **ài-lâng-po--i**, fond of being praised. **po-chiáng** (Cn. pe-chióng), to praise an inferior, as his superior does, to encourage him and incite him to further effort. **po-so**, to cajole; to flatter; to plead with flattery. **po-lo-so**, to flatter much; to cajole. **siuⁿ-kè-po**, you flatter me too much. **kò-po** (R.), to praise over-much. **khoàⁿ-miāⁿ bô-po, chiáh-tsúi iáh-bô**, a fortune-teller must praise the man's luck, or he will not even earn a drink of water; said also of flattery in general.

po (Cn. pe), the bulwarks of a vessel or boat. **tsûn-po**, id. **po-kîⁿ**, the rim of the bulwarks, out or in. **po-piⁿ**, the part of the deck near the bulwarks; close to the bulwarks. **po-piⁿ-khang**, scupper-holes for running water from deck; sometimes said of port-holes. **po-téng**, on the top of the bulwarks, *e.g.* sitting or standing on them. **chhiⁿ-po**, having green sides, as vessel (so with other colours).

po (R. id.) **po-lê**, glass.

po (C.) **po-tiú-á**, = pe-tiú-á, the lark.

pô [R. old woman; mother]. **lāu-pô**, an old woman. **hoan-pô**, a foreign woman (not polite). **ang-pô**, husband and wife. **sau-pô**, woman who lives in a boat. **pêh-tsúi-pô** (C.), a boat-woman. **hm̂-lâng-pô**, a woman who deals in female slaves and in making low marriages by sale. **hōng-iâng-pô**, female pedlar or juggler from Fung-yang. **sam-ke lióк-pô**, nuns and several such sorts of questionable women, such as flower-sellers, washer-women, female-barbers, match-makers, &c. **chhoàn-kau sam-ke lióк-pô**, always associating with such characters (not good). **tsòe-ke-pô**, to be an old maid ("ke," solitary).

ke-pô, paternal grandfather's sister, or any old woman of same clan and same genealogical rank; respectful address to old woman of same surname. **î-pô**, grandmother's sister. **m̄-pô**, wife of paternal grandfather's elder brother. **chím-pô**, wife of paternal grandfather's younger brother. **kīm-pô**, wife of grandmother's brother (v. kim).

ĕ-pô, the original tuber of taro, from which the young ones are produced.

kong-pô, ancestral tablets. **kong-pô-kī**, days for special worship of them. **sî kong-pô**, to take leave of the ancestral tablets (v. sî). **hoe-kong-pô**, male and female deities which bestow children (v. hoe). **tsu-kong-pô**, the god and goddess of small-pox. **tsu-pô**, goddess of small-pox. **má-tsó-pô**, the queen of heaven and goddess of the sea (v. má). **thó-tī-pô**, the goddess of the earth. **bîn-chhn̂g-pô**, the guardian goddess of the marriage-bed. **pô-chiá**, numerous spirits that watch over infants about the time of birth. **pô-chiá-bú**, id. **pô-chiá gûn-ó**, paper dresses and paper money burned by mothers in worshipping these spirits.

pô — **thô-pô**, a mud-fish like the cuttle-fish or chiuⁿ-hí, but with no bone (tsûn) in it.

thô-pô-éng, the bore or great waves at the mouth of a river. **khí thô-pô**, to raise these great waves.

tėk-pô, an edible fish, the skin of which is used like sand-paper.

pô (Cn. pô). **bit-pô**, a bat.

pô — **ko-pô-ĕ**, a wild medicinal plant like taro. **ko-pô-hióh** (C.), leaves of a plant like taro, used for wrapping things, as cakes or fish.

pó [R. to take care of; to protect; to guarantee], (Cn. pó), to guarantee; to be surety or security for; a ward in a town or group of villages. **tsȧp-poeh-pó**, the eighteen wards of Amoy and Emngkang. **pó-tiúⁿ**, the head man of a ward. **pó-tiúⁿ-kong**, id. **tē-pó**, id. **tē-pó-koaⁿ**, id. **tsóng-pó**, the head man of the villages of Amoy island; nominally also the head of the eighteen wards of Amoy, but the tepos of these wards are not really controlled by him. **lím-pó**, a lím-seng graduate (v. lím). **tiong-pó** (r.), a middle man who stands security; (X.) a mediator. **thài-pó**, guardian of heir-apparent.

pó-niáⁿ, to guarantee; to warrant; to stand security for. **tam-pó** (r.), id. **pau-pó** (r.), id. **pó-jîn**, to stand security and be responsible for a man. **pó-kiet**, written security given by one man for another's conduct; a written agreement promising to hold a settlement final. **pó-jī**, a written security. **pó-ke**, a surety; an insurance office. **pó-ke-jī**, a policy of insurance. **pó-ke-toaⁿ**, id. **pó-pio**, a small arrow sold as guarantee against molestation by robbers or pirates (v. pio). **thó-pó** (r.), to demand security. **chhú-pó** (r.), to require security or bail. **kò pó-ko**, to enter an accusation for beating to danger of life (v. ko). **ngīⁿ-pó**, to insist on being bail for a man charged with a crime, so as to bail him out. **ngīⁿ-pó--chhut-lâi**, to succeed in thus getting him out on bail. **pó-kú**, to recommend for office or employment, being in some measure security for him. **pó-tsàu**, to memorialize the emperor proposing a man for office, or praying that he may not be punished.

pó-pì, to protect or defend, as gods. **pó-sioh**, to love, cherish, and take care of. **pó-ióng**, to take care of, as one's own health; to take care of a child (not including training) for a friend or relative. **pó-iúⁿ** (Cn.), to take care of, as a child. **ka-kī pó-tiōng**, to take care of one's own health. **pó-tsoân**, to take care of; to keep safely that it be not injured. **pó-tsoân bêng-chiet**, to keep her character pure, as widow who remains a widow. **tsū-kí put-lêng-pó, ien-lêng-pó tha-jîn**, how can one take care of others who can't take care of himself?

pó [R. precious; treasure]. **pó-pòe**, precious; precious things. **tin-pó**, precious. **kî-tin îⁿ-pó**, rare and precious things. **bô-kè-pó**, very costly; extremely precious. **tsâi-pó**, treasures (v. tsâi). **tsu-pó**, pearls and other very costly things. **oân-pó**, a large ingot of sycee silver (v. oân). **goân-pó**, id.; said also of idolatrous paper. **sún-hoāi kok-pó**, to injure or deface coins. **sûi-sin-pó**, very valuable articles always carried with one (v. sûi). **oȧh-pó**, some imaginary animated source of good fortune for a place or family. **chhū-pó**, to search for a source or principle of good luck.

pó-khì, precious things. **pó-chióh**, a precious stone; a gem (v. chióh). **pó-gėk**, precious jade-stone. **pó-tsu**, fine pearls. **pó-to**, a very valuable sword. **pó-kiàm**, a magical or miraculous sword. **pó-ūi**, a royal throne. **pó-tók-kî**, a general's flag. **pó-thah**, a pagoda.

sam-pó, the Buddhist triad. **pat-pó-soáⁿ**, a medicine compounded of eight drugs. **bûn-pông sù-pó**, the four implements for writing, viz. pen, ink, paper, and ink-stone.

teh-hó-pó, you count it very precious! (ironically); it is very little worth. **tién-pó** (C.), to boast and brag.

lién-pó, a sort of gambling by a small cube shaken in a square box. **teh lién-pó**, to gamble with it. **pha lién-pó**, id. **poȧh lién-pó**, id. **poȧh-pó**, id. **pó-táu**, the instrument used for this gambling. **pó-táu-jîn**, the die used for it. **pó-jîn**, id. **pó-táu-khak**, the square brass box in which the die is put. **pó-táu-kheng**, id. **pó-táu-koà**, its cover. **tsòe-pó**, to join capital so as to set up a place for this gambling. **tsòe-pó**, to put the die into the box all ready for the gambling. **phâng-pó**, id. **chhut-pó**; **jip-pó**, two different positions of the game when examined. **piⁿ-á-pó**, the sort of lién-pó played at small places on the streets for small sums. **chîⁿ-pó**, id. **gûn-pó**, the kind played only for silver, generally for very large sums. **pó-tiûⁿ**, a gambling place for the lién-pó. **pó-chhn̂g**, a couch for use in this gambling. **pó-koaⁿ**, the keeper of the gambling place. **pó-thâu-ke**, id. **pó-lī**, assistant of the gambling-house keeper.

pó — **pó-jî**, you whoreson! (said in scolding).

pó (C.) **am-pó-chê**, = A. am-po-chê, the cicada.

pò [R. pòe, pò, a violent wind or typhoon]. **pò-thâu**, a sudden stormy wind; a heavy gale. **pò-thâu-hong**, id. **pò-bé**, the end of a strong north-east gale (s. inform). **chhun, pò-thâu: tang, pò-bé**, a spring storm is worst at the beginning, a winter storm at the end. **má-tsó-pò**, a gale about the time of the birth-day of má-tsó. **thiⁿ-kong-pò**, a storm about 1.9. **péh-chhiu-pò**, storm near birth-day of thó-tī-kong, in 8th month. **tāi-tō-kong-pò**, storm near birth-day of pó-seng tāi-tè. **pùt-tsó-pò**, one about birth-day of Kwan-yin. **pùt-á-pò**, gales on birth-days of some small divinities, about 4th moon.

pò (R. id.), (Cn. pò), to inform; to make a formal statement; to recompense, reward, or punish. **pò-bé**, an express courier (s. storm). **kiaⁿ-pò**, the Pekin Gazette. **pò-tsúi**, to give information of a criminal's hiding-place. **pò-sin**, to give sad intelligence. **pò-hí**, to announce good news, esp. birth of first son or some high honour. **kheh-chiáu pò-hí**, the magpie gives a good omen. **it-kiⁿ pò-hí, jī-kiⁿ pò-sí**, cock-crowing in first watch is a good omen, in second watch is an omen of death. **ū-pò** (T.), said when more cocks than one crow at an unlucky hour, which takes away the bad omen. **pò-lâng-tsai,** to inform a man. **pò hē-i-tsai,** to inform him.

pò-toaⁿ, a ship's manifest, or similar document. **khí-hè ê pò-toaⁿ,** an application for leave to land goods. **pò-hiòng,** to give in a statement of goods on board liable to duty. **pò-hiòng-toaⁿ,** a ship's manifest. **pò-toaⁿ-koán,** office at custom-house where vessels report themselves on arrival and before sailing. **pò-sè-koán,** id. **pò-pâng,** an office at capital or provincial capital, which issues official notifications of degrees and titles of rank. **pò-tiâu,** diploma or notification to a man (issued by the pò-pâng) that has got a degree or title of rank. **pò-liòk,** id. **pò-kú-jîn,** to notify a man that he has got the Kujin degree. **pò-siù-tsâi,** do. of Sew-tsai. **chhit-kioh-hì pò-bān-peng** (seven actors say they are ten thousand soldiers), can't believe all you say.

pò-tap, to recompense; to reward. **pò-èng,** to reward or punish; to recompense justly, as the gods do. **pò-siúⁿ** (r.), to reward. **pò-oàn,** to retaliate, often quite small. **pò-oan,** to take vengeance for murder or great injury; to revenge (v. oan). **pò-siû,** id. (v. siû). **siēn iú siēn-pò, ok iú ok-pò,** good and bad have their just recompense. **siēn-ok chiong iú-pò,** at the last good and bad certainly have due recompense. **thiⁿ-tōe bô-pò,** said of the wicked prospering and escaping punishment. **pò-un,** to make returns for favours or benefits. **ti-un pò-pún,** to recompense the favours of those from whom we spring (our parents). **siū-un put-pò,** to fail in gratitude for favours. **tiong-kun pò-kok,** loyal to sovereign and dynasty (v. tiong).

sok-pò-si (T. sek-phè-si), an attendant of the idol sêng-hông (v. si).

pîⁿ-pò-phûn, yielding returns barely sufficient to pay expenses (v. phûn).

pò [R. to sow seed, = col. pò], (Cn. pò). **pò-iông,** to spread abroad, as fame or doctrine.

pō [R. scorching; violent; sudden; to strike with the hand, = col. phák, pō, pō, pāu, phāu], (Cn. pō). **pō-kí-jiên,** suddenly. **pō-pîn,** id. **pō-chín thien-bùt,** to use things wastefully. **tsū-pō tsū-khì,** to throw away invaluable opportunities; to reject one's own good fortune. **sò-pō,** violent, rude, and headstrong. **kông-pō,** violent and hasty in temper, esp. as man in authority. **kiông-pō** (R.), tyrannical, violent, and oppressive. **pō-giòk,** to tyrannize; tyrannical, as sovereign or high mandarin. **pō-jiòk** (T.), = A. pō-jiòk, to insult, as by abusive language.

pō (T.) **pō-oá,** = A. phē-oá, a sort of crab (cf. kiā-pō).

pò͘ (R. id.), half a day, especially the afternoon. **ē-pò͘,** the afternoon. **téng-pò͘,** the forenoon. **chit-pò͘-kú,** half a day; a long while. **chiâⁿ-pò͘-kú,** about half a day. **pò͘-lâu,** the afternoon tide. **n̂g-pò͘,** the latter part of the afternoon, about four or five o'clock. **m̂ng-pò͘,** id. **múiⁿ-pò͘** (C.), id. **poàⁿ-pò͘,** about half through the afternoon. **chhit kiā, poeh tó, káu pò͘, tsáp lòh** (T.), the Pleiades are in the 7th month high at zenith at daybreak, in 8th month some way down, in 9th low like afternoon sun, in 10th just setting.

pò͘ — **chhe-pò͘,** a bamboo frame for steaming food. **láng-pò͘,** id.

pò͘ [R. pò͘, a port]. **pò͘-thâu,** a port for trade. **phah pò͘-thâu,** to make a new landing-place and market. **pák pò͘-thâu,** to farm the monopoly of some article in a port or district. **pò͘** (Cn.), the market or busy streets with shops in a village, as distinguished from the rest of the village.

pò͘ (R. id.), a plain; a level (or gently sloping) piece of ground. **hái-pò͘,** the part of the sea-beach which is only flooded at high tides. **khoe-pò͘,** the grassy banks of a stream which are sometimes overflowed. **khoe-soa-pò͘,** sandy bed of a stream. **soa-pò͘** (Cn.), = A. soa-pho, a sandy beach. **soaⁿ-pò͘,** gently sloping or level grassy place on a hill. **chháu-pò͘,** a level (or nearly level) grassy piece of ground. **khàng-pò͘,** a common; a large piece of unused ground. **kà-tiûⁿ-pò͘,** review-ground. **chē-pò͘,** open grassy ground near a fort. **pîⁿ-pò͘,** a plain. **pîⁿ-pò͘-hoan,** Formosan aborigines who have submitted to Chinese rule and learned to speak Chinese. **hòe kàu-chiâⁿ pîⁿ-pò͘,** to raze to the ground, so that all traces of houses disappear. **sio kàu-chiâⁿ pîⁿ-pò͘,** to burn to the ground. **tó kàu-chiâⁿ pîⁿ-pò͘,** utterly ruined, as village with no trace remaining. **sí kàu-chiâⁿ pîⁿ-pò͘,** depopulated and become waste (as a region) with rebellion or pestilence.

pò͘, to grow rotten, as wood; decayed and rotten, as wood. **pò͘--khì,** to rot away thus, as decaying wood. **pò͘-lò͘--khì,** id.

pò͘ [R. hu, a man; a male; a husband]. **ta-pò͘,** a male person (v. ta). **tsa-pò͘** (C.), id. **chí-pò͘** (Cn.), = A. chí-hu, husband of elder sister.

pò͘ (better pē, *q.v.*) **pò͘-tiú-á,** the lark.

pò͘ (better pē, *q.v.*) **am-pò͘-chê,** the cicada.

pò͘ — **pò͘-lûn-chhài** (Cn.), a vegetable. **pò͘-gîn-ná** (C.), a medicinal plant (v. gîn).

pò͘ (Cn.), = A. po, the bulwarks of a boat.

pò͘ (Cn.), = A. po, to flatter.

pē̍r — **chit-pê chit-pê,** all curly, as hair in curly locks.

pê [R. bê, a mould; a pattern]. **bīn-pê,** shape of face.

pê (same word?). **chiú-pê,** the whole mass of materials prepared for fermentation. **tāu-sī-pê,** black beans boiled, dried, and kept till mouldy, for making soy. **tāu-chiùⁿ-pê,** white beans boiled into a mass, and kept till mouldy. **tāu-pê,** either of these two preparations.

mîⁿ-pê, raw cotton in lumps, just as gathered with the seeds in it.

pê — **liên-hoe-pê,** the seed-vessel of the water-lily. **liên-pê,** id.

pê — **lin-pê,** the breast (of male or female) near the teat.

pê [R. pông, a room, = col. pâng]. **bit-pê,** honey-comb.

pê — **chhiū-nâⁿ-pê,** a thick wood or forest. **chhò-nâⁿ-pê,** to make a great noise in the forest, as flock of birds (v. chhò). **chhì-nâⁿ-pê,** a thick-set thorn hedge, or thick mass of thorny plants.

pê — **pê-kiuⁿ,** a herb from which an aromatic or medicinal tea is made (v. hiuⁿ). **pê-iâm,** a sort of shrub (v. iâm).

pê — **pê-tiú-á,** the lark.

pê [R. hû, sort of cicada], (some say "pò͘"]. **am-pê-chê,** the cicada.

pê [R. the sweet-flag], a surname. **chhang-pê,** the Acorus, or sweet-flag. **pê-chháu,** id. **chhiong-pê,** id., especially when spoken of as a medicine.

48

chióh-chhiu^n-pê, root of Acorus terrestris, medicinal. pê-ôe, shoes made of this plant. kha--nih^n chhēng pê-chháu, wearing these shoes (said in a rhyme about a swaggering fellow).

pê [R. same as above, but used as a name]. **pê-chhân**, the district of Pu-tien, in which Hing-hwa-foo (heng-hoà) stands.

pê [R. pō, violent, tyrannical, &c., = col. pə, pāu, &c.], to insult; to twit a man, as for a fault. **pê-jiok**, to insult by abusive language. **pê--lâng**, to twit or jibe at a man. **khit--i pê--khì**, to be insulted by him.

pê — **lêng-pê**, an ancient flowing dress with dragons, worn by sovereigns and by some idols.

pê [R. hông, to sew, to hem, = col. pâng, phāng], a hem or border of a dress. **áu-pê**, to fold a hem; to make a hem. **áu-toā-pê**, to make a broad hem or border, as on women's dress. **toā-pê**, the broad border of women's dress. **kú-chhài-pê**, the narrow hem of men's dress. **ē-kha-pê**, the broad border at the bottom of a dress. **sièn-pê**, broad facings, hem, or border of women's dress. **sù-pê**, ravelled edges of dress, in deepest mourning. **sàn-pê**, id. **sàm-pê**, id. **sàm-pê-sa^n**, a dress having the hem opened out, and ravelled almost like a fringe, worn in deepest mourning, ravelled in front for father, behind for mother.

pê (C.) **pê-tô**, = A. phû-tô, the vine; grapes.

pê (Cn.) **bit-pê**, = A. bit-pô, a bat.

pé [R. hú, mandarin's robe]. **pé-koà**, robe worn by a mandarin, with an embroidered square on the breast. **hāi-tsāi-pé**, robe of a high military mandarin, with the lion-unicorn on the breast.

pé [R. hú, an axe]. **pé-thâu** (C. pú-thâu), an axe; a hatchet. **toā-pé**, a large axe. **chhiú-pé**, a small hand-hatchet. **gêh-pé**, an axe with convex semi-circular edge. **kiáh-pé**, sort of halbert held by attendant images of idols. **tiám-pé**, to drive two or three nails in nailing up a coffin, as graduate or mandarin does for a fee. **to-pé-siú**, an executioner.

pé [R. hú, dried flesh], dried and shrivelled, as leaves or fruit in drought; not juicy, as orange. **pé-pé koa^n-koa^n**, quite dried, as herbs for medicine. **jūn-pé**, shrivelled and not juicy, as cucumber or sugar-cane too long cut. **lún-pé** (T.), id. **chhài-pé**, long turnips salted and dried. **hî-pé**, small dried fish slightly salted and moist. **chiâ^n-lâng-pé**, become very lean, as a man. **pì^n-chiâ^n lâng-pé**, id. **khiû kàu-lán bàt-sat-pé**, as niggardly as a little dried bug.

pé (R. id.), to mend or repair, by putting in a new piece; to make up for; to make up a deficiency; strengthening, as medicine or food. **pê-pé**, to make up for. **pé-tsō**, to help; to make up a deficiency. **tiām-pé**, to make up a deficiency, as in a subscription. **tiēn-pé**, to pay up a deficiency, as a third party: to increase or renew capital in trade for another. **thiên-pé**, id. **thák-pé**, to study enough to make up arrears of study. **pé-thi^n**, to make up a deficiency. **pé-thī^n**, mending and sewing. **pé-thùi**, to put in an entire new piece by the old seam or joining. **thùi-pé**, id. **pé-thak**, to mend, as a wall, or as a dress, with great neatness (v. thak). **pé-thap**, to mend, as a dress, by changing a bit of cloth. **pé-that**, to repair, by filling up cracks or leaks. **chhák-pé-lāu**, to recaulk a leak. **uih-pé**, to correct a writing, by cutting out a bit, and pasting in the correction. **chit-pé**, to mend, by darning finely in both directions without change or addition of cloth. **siu-pé** (T. Cn.), to mend neatly, esp. as a small thing. **pé-bōe-chiū^n**, unable to repay enough.

pé-ióh, medicine that strengthens the system. **put-chí-pé**, very strengthening, as medicine or food. **sò-pé**, heating and strengthening, as medicine. **tsu-im-pé**, medicine or food that strengthens the system, and allays feverishness (v. im). **chiáh-pé**, to take strengthening medicine or food. **pé-ióng**, id. **pé-iông**, to strengthen the positive principle in one's constitution. **pé-pì**, to give strength to the stomach; tonic. **pé-sīn**, strengthening the kidneys and the eyes.

pé-kheh, to appoint a man to fill a vacancy (v. kheh). **hāu-pé**, men who have got official rank, and have orders from the capital to get office as soon as there is a vacancy.

pé-ūn, to improve one's destiny. **pé-tiâ^n**, to enter an additional complaint when the first has not led to action. **pé gûn-hun**, to make up the deficiency in weight of a light dollar. **pé-iên**, to fill up a hole in a dollar with lead. **pé chhat-mī^n**, to mend with a sort of cement like varnish. **pé chhùi-khí**, to insert a false tooth. **chiong-kong pé-tsōe**, to make up for (one's own) faults by merit, as a mandarin; sometimes said figuratively. **jîn-lėk pé thien-kong**, human strength making improvement on nature's work.

pè [R. cotton cloth; to spread out; to arrange; to spread widely; to bribe], cotton or linen cloth, or grass-cloth.

pè-chèng, the provincial treasurer. **pè-chèng-si**, id. **pè-si**, id.

pè-tì, to arrange in order, as things (v. tì). **pè-tīn**, to arrange troops in ranks or battalions for battle. **pâi-peng pè-tīn**, id. **kóng-pè** (R.), to publish abroad. **pè-sì**, to give a largess, as to the poor or to employés. **pái-pè** (T. pái-pə), to intrigue, as by bribes, influence, calumnies, &c. (v. pái). **pè-tah**, to give small bribes, as to underlings of yamuns. **pè-lō**, to bribe (from lə, "to bribe"). **pè-lō**, the matter of buying cloth (from lə, "a road").

toā-pè-chiam, a large needle (v. chiam). **jī-pè**, the second size of needle. **sa^n-pè**, a still smaller sort.

pè-pang, pasteboard made of old clothes. **pè-phit**, piece goods, cotton or linen. **pè-ko**, tall poles for drying cloth when dyed. **pè-pì^n**, an awning or tent (v. pì^n). **pè-tē**, a bag or sack (v. tē). **pè-liâu**, a narrow strip of cloth. **pè-lí**, cotton lining. **pè-mn̂g**, small threads that come off cloth. **pè-mî^n**, id. **pè-mê^n** (C.), id. **pè-bák**, the interstices between the threads of cloth. **jip pè-bák**, deeply ingrained into the cloth, as a stain. **ū-chî^n, chhut ū-pè-bák**, the more money you spend you will have the better piece of work, though it could be done cheaper, but not so good.

ki^n-pè, to weave cotton or linen cloth (v. ki^n). **chit-pè**, id. **chién-pè**, to buy cotton, &c. (lit. cut it with scissors).

bīn-pè, a cloth for wiping the face. **ə-bīn-pè**, a large black cloth worn (by old women) on the head, the ends hanging down. **béh-pè**, a cloth worn under the stocking. **toh-pè**, a cloth for wiping the table.

ka-poà-pè, native cotton cloth. **jiàu^n-pè**, rough cotton cloth with a surface somewhat like crape. **niàu^n-pè**, id. **kui-á-pè**, narrow native cotton cloth. **pak-pè**, narrow cotton cloth from Shanghai and the north. **sán-pè**, a thin slim cloth (v. sán). **chhiâ-bûn-pè**, twilled cotton (v. bûn). **ìn-hoe-pè**, printed cottons (v. hoe). **pún-sek-pè**, unbleached cottons.

koah-pè, grass-cloth. **joáh-pè**, id. **hā-pè**, id. **tōe-pè**, white grass-cloth. **tōe-á-pè**, id. **moā^n-pè**, coarsest yellow hempen stuff for sacks, &c. **phâng-**

pờ, sail-cloth; canvas. **si-pờ**, cloth of mixed silk and cotton.

pờ [R. pò, to sow seed; to publish abroad], to plant out, as young rice-plants (never to sow seed). **pờ-tiū**, to plant out young rice. **pờ-chhân**, id. **pờ-chhân-hoe**, the large single white rose. **pờ-chhī-á** (C.), young rice-plants.

thoân-pờ (R.), to proclaim, as doctrine. **soan-pờ** (R.), id.

pờ [R. hù, hū, a teacher], a surname.

pō͘ [R. hə, to wait, time, = col. bə, hāu]. **chí-pō͘**, now; just now (s. pace). **chit-pō͘**, id. **chhú-pō͘**, id. **chhú-hiēn-pō͘** (C.), id.

chhûn āu-pō͘ (C. kə), to reserve some strength, plan, or money for future exigencies.

pō͘ (R. id.), a pace; two steps; a contrivance, resource, or plot. **chit-pō͘**, one pace; one step in an affair. **chit-pō͘ hoân-chit-pō͘**, step by step, *e.g.* walking at a moderate pace with slow steps; scheming to get a thing done bit by bit, step by step, in managing a matter. **chhiáⁿ-khoan chit-pō͘**, just wait a little in the matter. **chí-pō͘**, to halt (s. wait, time). **tåh-pō͘**, to walk with slow measured step up a hill, as chair-bearers. **lap-pō͘**, to step down, as down a step or into a hole. **soá-pō͘**, to walk with short steps, as child, or as man with chain on foot (v. soá). **thap-pō͘-kiāⁿ**, to measure the ground by the lengths of our foot. **toā-pō͘-kiâⁿ**, to walk with long steps. **khai-pō͘**, to take a long step, esp. chair-bearer. **khui-pō͘ kiâⁿ**, to walk with long steps. **khui-pō͘ tsáu**, to run with long strides. **khah-khui-pō͘**, take longer steps. **chhùn-pō͘ lân-hêng**, to walk slowly and with difficulty; hardly able to walk an inch further. **tò-thè-pō͘**, to step backwards (v. thè). **chìn-pō͘** (r.), to advance, as in learning or excellence. **siā-pō͘**, to make a visit of thanks to a man who had come on certain ceremonies (v. siā).

kha-pō͘, steps, as to manner of walking or exercise. **kiâⁿ kha-pō͘**, to practise one's steps, as for gymnastics or military exercise. **kha-pō͘ hó**, having a good step, as actor. **kha-pō͘ chhiú-lō͘ chin-hó**, movements of limbs all good, as actor or teacher of boxing. **pí-pō͘**, to gesticulate, as in teaching or learning boxing, fencing, &c. (v. pí). **kûn-thâu-pō͘**, feints or tricks in boxing. **ēng kûn-thâu-pō͘**, to use unexpected feints or secret plans to thwart or injure people.

pō͘-lién, to walk on foot. **pō͘-kiāⁿ**, id. **pō͘-peng**, infantry. **pō͘-chìⁿ**, archers on foot. **bé-pō͘-chìⁿ**, cavalry and infantry archers.

pō͘-sờ, a contrivance or plot, as for managing a matter, or for boxing, &c. **hó-pō͘-sờ**, having a good plan (for a special case) how to get round people or manage an affair. **ū-pō͘-sờ**, id. **hó-pō͘**, a good plan or advice how to do a thing. **bô-pō͘**, having no resource. **chìn-chêng bô-lō͘, thè-āu bô-pō͘**, no way of escape backwards or forwards; no resource at all in any way. **ū siáⁿ-pō͘**, what *can* be done? there is evidently no resource. **iáu-siū-á-pō͘**, to begin affairs and not settle them, so as to cause great trouble to others. **piàn-pō͘**, to try a new plan when the first has failed; to use some artifice, intrigue, or cunning scheme. **pìⁿ-pō͘**, id. **khǹg-pō͘**, to conceal part of our plans, or of a story or affair; to teach in a slovenly way. **gâu-siūⁿ-pō͘**, good at contrivances; ingenious; fruitful in resources; scheming. **sái tók-pō͘**, to use some wicked scheme against a man. **sái àm-pō͘**, id. **pái-pō͘** (T.), = A. pái-pờ, to calumniate a man to his superior (v. pái).

tōe-pō͘, rank or relative position (only used in some such phrases as the following). **tē-pō͘**, id. **toā-tōe-pō͘**, high rank or station, or great wealth. **kàu-hit--ê tōe-pō͘**, having reached that position or rank; the affair having come to that position. **kàu sím-mihⁿ tōe-pō͘**, what rank has he reached? (as mandarin). **ku sím-mihⁿ tōe-pō͘**, what is his present rank? **ū sím-mihⁿ tōe-pō͘**, what rank, position, or wealth has he reached? **bô-sím-mihⁿ tōe-pō͘**, wanting in ability, so as not to prosper. **i--ê tē-pō͘ iáu-bē kàu hit--ê sé-tsāi**, he has not yet reached such a position, as of rank, office, &c.

lâu-tōe-pō͘, to have some plan or thing in store for an emergency; not exhausting one's self or one's resources; not pressing matters to the utmost. **kā-i-lâu chit--ê tōe-pō͘**, to leave him some respectability or dignity, *e.g.* do not reprove or punish him so much as to leave him no respect in the eyes of others.

pō͘-ūi, rank (v. ūi), (s. vital part).

pō͘ — **kiā-pō͘**, a small sort of crab (cf. pō͘-oá, phô͘-oá).

pō͘ — **chiúⁿ-pō͘**, the band which splices the blade of an oar to the handle.

pō͘ — **toā-pō͘-bú**, the thumb; the big toe. **kha toā-pō͘-bú**, the big toe. **chhiú toā-pō͘-bú**, the thumb. **toā-pō͘-bú-phāng**, the opening between the thumb and the finger.

pō͘ [R. to seize; to grasp]. **pō͘-hong chhiok-éng**, to take up and spread baseless stories (lit. wind and shadows).

sûn-pō͘, an assistant or aide-de-camp of a high mandarin (v. sûn). **pō͘-thiaⁿ**, an assistant mandarin of the Hien or Foo mandarin. **sàu-pō͘**, sort of excisemen or tide-waiters for salt revenue.

pō͘ (C.) **chiòh-pō͘**, a broken bit of stone or rock. **toā-chiòh-pō͘**, a large piece of rock, as about size of fist. **chiòh-pō͘-á**, quite a small bit of rock or stone.

pō͘ (R. id.), to chew. **chiåh bô-pō͘**, to eat without chewing. **pō͘ thun--lòh-khì**, chew and swallow. **pa-lun pō͘-chháu**, to chew the cud. **khang-chhùi pō͘-chih**, to make an empty promise, with no intention to keep it. **a iú hoán-pō͘ chi-gī**, the crow gives food in gratitude (to its parent).

pō͘ [R. a division or class, as of characters under one radical; a set, as of books; the Supreme Boards at Pekin, = col. phō͘]. **pō͘-lūi**, the group of characters belonging to one radical. **jip sím-mihⁿ pō͘-lūi**, to which radical does the word belong? **siòk sím-mihⁿ pō͘-lūi**, id. **sim-pō͘**, the radical "sim," as forming a group of words in the dictionary.

liòk-pō͘, the six Supreme Boards at Pekin. **ngé-hú liòk-pō͘**, all the great offices at Pekin. **lé-pō͘**, the Board of Rites; its president. **lī-pō͘**, the Board of Office; its president. **hō͘-pō͘**, the Board of Revenue; its president. **kong-pō͘**, the Board of Works; its president. **hêng-pō͘**, the Board of Punishment; its president. **piaⁿ-pō͘**, the Board of War; its president. **jip-pō͘**, to become a member of one of these boards. **pō͘-koaⁿ**, the members of the boards. **pō͘-siòk**, lower officials of the boards. **pō͘-gī**, the opinion of a board reporting to the emperor on a subject sent down for its consideration. **pō͘-bûn**, a decree issued by a board by imperial command. **pō͘-tsat**, do. when quite small, generally about one single particular. **pō͘-pan--ê**, published by a supreme board, as a decree. **pō͘-pàng--ê**, directly appointed by the Board of Office, as a mandarin. **tùi-pō͘ pák**, granted by authority of a supreme board, as a monopoly; it may be granted by a high mandarin who has delegated authority to do so. **pe̍-pak--ê**, id. (v. pak).

pe̍-ūi, a vital spot in the body where one blow is fatal (s. pace). **pe̍-poâⁿ**, the groin. **pe̍-poâⁿ-téng**, the part between the navel and the groin. **pe̍-poâⁿ-piⁿ**, at the side of that part.

ngé-pe̍-chhiu, beard, whiskers, and moustaches all distinctly separate.

pe̍ (C. pók). **pe̍-lê**, the largest sort of dragon-fly.

pe̍ [R. pō, violent, tyrannical, &c., = col. pāu, pô, &c.] **pe̍-chéng thien-bu̍t**, to use things wastefully.

tsu̍-pe̍ tsu̍-khì (Cn.), to injure one's self by throwing away invaluable opportunities (and so in other phrases, Cn., = A. pō).

pe̍ [R. bó, male of some animals]. **pe̍--ê** (T.), the male (said of pigs).

pö (Cn.), = A. pe, to fly.

pö̂, Cn., = A. pê, to repay; to make up a deficiency.

pö̀ (Cn.), = A. pè, to paste paper. **piáu-pö̀**, = A. **kiáu-pè**, id.

pö̀ (T.), = A. pòe, pè, the back (in some phrases).

pö̀ (T.), = A. pè, a mound for damming up water.

pö̌ (Cn.), = A. pē. **saⁿ-pö̌ kha-chhng**, set back to back, as two men, houses, or villages; assisting each other against all others, as men. **hat-pö̌** (T.), a cloth for strapping a child on one's back.

pö̌ (Cn.), = A. pē, so many fold, &c. **saⁿ-pö̌**, three times as many.

poa (C.) **poa-láu**, = A. pa-láu, a sort of fish.

poa (C.) **poa-lun-thâu** (= pa), to cover up one's head in the bed-clothes.

poà (R. pò), to throw away (by a slight shake of the wicker tray) the light rice and chaff which has already been separated by a different sort of motion. **poà-hiet-kák**, id. **poà-ki**, the flat shallow tray used for this purpose (v. ki). **poà-chhek-thâu**, to throw away the light empty rice in this way. **poà-bí**, to separate rice from chaff, &c., in this way.

poà [R. pòe, precious]. **ka-poà**, raw cotton; the cotton plant; native cotton cloth (imitation of the Indian or Persian name "karpasi"). **ka-poà-pe̍**, native cotton cloth.

poaⁿ [R. poan, a sort, kind, or manner]. **chit-poaⁿ**, alike (especially said at the end of a sentence). **chit-poaⁿ-iūⁿ**, all alike; just the same. **bān-poaⁿ**, all sorts or kinds. **pah-poaⁿ**, id. **pah-poaⁿ, khí-thâu lân**, all things are difficult at the beginning.

poaⁿ [R. poan, to remove; to excite enmity], to remove; to move things; to change one's dwelling. **poaⁿ-chhia**, to move things back and forwards; to talk the same story over and over, as in discussion (v. chhia). **poaⁿ-tiàh**, to keep up a long discussion. **poaⁿ-lâi poaⁿ-khì** (move back and forwards), to repeat people's sayings to others.

poaⁿ-chhù, to change one's dwelling. **koáⁿ-i-poaⁿ**, to evict him from the house. **poaⁿ-khang**, to clear out all the things, as from room or house. **poaⁿ-chhut-hè**, to take out the goods, as from store or vessel. **poaⁿ-soá**, to move away elsewhere (v. soá). **poaⁿ--khì**, to move away. **poaⁿ-chhiáⁿ**, to get one's family to come and live together, as mandarin to his official residence.

poaⁿ, to act a play. **poaⁿ-hì**, id. (v. hì). **siet-sien, poaⁿ kâu-chè-thien**, said of making false pretences.

poâⁿ, to mix together, as dry powders, *e.g.* flour and sugar. **poâⁿ-khi-thàu**, mix them (the powders) thoroughly.

poâⁿ [R. poân, a great rock]. **chióh-poâⁿ**, a large flat rock. **thiāu-poâⁿ**, a large flat stone sunk in the ground, as a foundation for a pillar.

poâⁿ [R. pêng, a chessboard; a game at chess], classifier of games at chess. **kî-poâⁿ**, a chessboard.

poâⁿ — **kha-poâⁿ**, the upper surface of the foot; the instep. **chhiú-poâⁿ**, the back of the hand.

poâⁿ [R. poân, a plate; to calculate; to hold friendly intercourse; to discuss; = col. phoân], a plate; a platter; a saucer; a tray; to calculate, as a lucky day.

poâⁿ-sǹg, to calculate, as a lucky day.

thong-poâⁿ, all alike (v. thong).

chit-poâⁿ seng-lí, the whole of a mercantile business (said in regard to transferring it, or temporarily handing it over to another to manage). **kui-poâⁿ**, id. **moáⁿ-poâⁿ lóng-kau--i**, handed over the whole business to him. **moáⁿ-poâⁿ ê-sū**, the whole affair from beginning to end. **kau-poâⁿ**, to hand over to another, as an office or business, or one's share in a business. **hoā-poâⁿ**, to have the authoritative voice in a business, *e.g.* as the manager or shroff. **poâⁿ-kháu**, the price asked at first for goods, as by a wholesale hong (afterwards it may be lowered). **khui chit--ê poâⁿ-kháu**, to propose a first price (to open the market), as the seller does.

poâⁿ-chîⁿ, expenses of a journey. **poâⁿ-tîⁿ**, id. **poâⁿ-hùi**, id. (v. hùi).

iâⁿ-poâⁿ, a military station, as a sìn-hông, or larger one.

sǹg-poâⁿ, an abacus. **kín-bān-poâⁿ**, the regulator of watch or clock. **táh-poâⁿ**, the frame on which a sail rests when it is lowered.

pe̍-poâⁿ, the groin (v. pe̍). **thē-poâⁿ**, the white meat of the body of a medusa.

thâng-poâⁿ, a tray. **tê-poâⁿ**, a salver for a teapot, not for cups. **teh tê-poâⁿ**, to give a small present on taking tea (v. tê). **chien-poâⁿ**, a flat frying-pan. **téng-á-poâⁿ**, the scale of a small steelyard. **oáⁿ-poâⁿ**, bowls and plates. **poâⁿ-tih**, large and small plates. **chhâ-poâⁿ**, a large wooden platter, used for exposing things for sale. **ngé-seng-poâⁿ**, platter for presenting idolatrous offerings. **kiú-liông-poâⁿ**, a wooden tray with nine divisions, as for marriage presents. **poâⁿ-áp**, round wooden basket with horizontal divisions.

poâⁿ-noáⁿ, to hold friendly intercourse (v. noáⁿ). **chhiau-poâⁿ**, to talk the same thing over and over endlessly in discussion. **chhia-poâⁿ**, id. **poâⁿ-chheh**, to discuss books in a friendly way to try each others' learning. **poâⁿ-ōe**, to wrangle on violently without stopping, *e.g.* raking up old quarrels. **poâⁿ chhùi-tûn-phê**, to have a wordy dispute. **kap--lâng poâⁿ-chhùi-gím** (= poaⁿ), to have a great deal of discussion with a man about some matter.

poâⁿ (same word?), to copy or transfer, as accounts (cf. piâⁿ). **poâⁿ-siàu**, to transfer accounts from one book to another.

poâⁿ (R. boân), to climb over. **poâⁿ-jip**, to climb in. **poâⁿ-chhut**, to climb out; to overflow, as very full tide overflowing the fields. **poâⁿ-kè**, to climb over. **poâⁿ-chhiûⁿ**, to climb over a wall. **poâⁿ-soaⁿ**, to cross a mountain. **poâⁿ-soaⁿ kè-niá**, to cross lofty mountains.

poâⁿ-tsai, to transplant.

海上絲綢之路文獻集成 科技與文化編

poâ^n — **poâ^n-ôe**, to work (with needle in thread) the raised border of a shoe. **poâ^n ôe-kî^n**, id. **poâ^n ôe-phī^n**, to work the raised ridges on the toe of a shoe. **kau-chiam tèng, bát-liú poâ^n**, said of being over-cautious (v. bát).

poâ^n — **khé-nâ^n-poâ^n**, a shrub with white flowers that grows by ditches, &c.

poá^n — **poá^n-hî**, a sort of fish. **poá^n-á-hî**, id. **lō-poá^n**, do., salted.

poá^n [R. pán, poán, an embankment against water], a word entering into the names of many villages, *e.g.* **lāu-poá^n**, near Amoy; **āu-poá^n**, near Chang-chew.

poà^n (R. poàn), a half. **chit-toā-poà^n**, the greater part. **sòe-poà^n**, the smaller part. **poà^n-lâu**, a small half upper story. **poà^n-lâu**, half tide. **poà^n-jit**, half a day. **poà^n-sî**, one hour's time. **poà^n-pe**, half through the afternoon. **poà^n-mî^n**, midnight (v. mî^n). **poà^n-soa^n**, half-way up the mountain. **poà^n-hái**, half-way across the sea, in mid-ocean. **poà^n-thi^n**, up in the sky; among the clouds. **poà^n-piah**, half-way up the partition wall. **poà^n-lō**, on the way; on the road; half-way. **poà^n-lō khàu**, to lament on the way, as daughter for parents. **hāi poà^n-lō-chiū^n**, to lead into danger and then injure or leave to suffer. **poà^n-tiong-tè soah--khì**, to fail after beginning. **poà^n-tiong-tn̂g soah--khì**, id.

poà^n-lâm-hâ^n, hung up half-finished, as affair (v. hâ^n). **óh poà^n-lám-phû**, to learn a thing (as business or trade) only half well (v. phû). **óh poà^n-láng-bí**, id. **tsú poà^n-láng-bí**, half-cooked. **poà^n-sí**, half-dead. **poà^n-tsá^n**, a sword about two feet long, handle and blade about equal length. **tùi-poà^n-thàn**, to gain cent. per cent. **poà^n-lâi-goā**, half out half in. **hó-phái^n chit-poà^n**, about half good half bad. **siá chit-poà^n**, to write one half; said also of a son half transferred to a person whom his widowed mother marries, the son worshipping the ancestors both of him and of his own father.

poà^n-chiah, one half of a thing of which "chiah" is the classifier. **poà^n-tè**, half of a thing classified by "tè." **chit-poà^n-ê-á**, perhaps just one, but of no consequence. **chit-kè poà^n-kè**, scarcely, if ever; very rarely (v. kè). **bô-poà^n-lâng**, not a single man. **poà^n-tih-tsúi iá-bô**, not the least drop of water remains.

gê-poà^n, one and a half, of anything. **khe-poà^n**, a dollar and a half. **chit-khe-poà^n**, id. **ki-poà^n-ûi**, a schooner (lit. one mast and a half). **ki-poà^n-poà^n**, a three-masted schooner.

poà^n [R. poàn, a sort of rope; to entangle]. **poà^n--tióh**, to trip up a man, as a rope. **poà^n-tióh-soh**, to trip on a rope. **poà^n-tó**, to trip on ropes or make another trip. **poà^n-bé-soh**, ropes placed so as to make the enemy's cavalry fall. **tî^n-tî^n poà^n-poà^n**, all involved and entangled, as an affair (v. tî^n). **pî^n-poà^n**, id. **poà^n-pìn-soh**, a thread used by women at toilet (v. pìn).

ū-pìn-poà^n, to be on terms of friendly intercourse. **kap--i ū-pìn-poà^n**, do., with him. **chiah-ê teh-pìn-poà^n**, there are some obstacles, *e.g.* as one's family making it difficult to take a journey. **bô-pìn-poà^n**, having no entanglements or impediments. **kap--i bô-pìn-poà^n**, not on terms of acquaintance with him.

poā^n (R. hut), to dust; to shake off the dust or dirt; to strike with a stick or cloth so as to dust. **poā^n-sàm thâu-mn̂g**, to dishevel the hair. **poā^n-báng**, to drive away mosquitoes, as with a brush. **poā^n seng-khu**, to beat or shake one's dress gently to remove the dust. **poā^n kia^n-lâng**, to beat or shake to remove dirt or dust. **phah-poā^n** (Cn.), to clean by striking, as a dress. **poā^n-mn̂g**, to shake its feathers, as a hen, or its hair, as a dog. **poā^n-hī**, to shake the ears, as cow or dog. **iô-thâu poā^n-hī**, to shake one's head, as on hearing of some wicked deed or unsafe character. **siū-khì kàu iô-thâu poā^n-hī**, in a great rage.

poah [R. poát, cymbals, &c. = col. poáh]. **hê-siū^n thuh-poah**, the Buddhist priest supporting a tambourine on a bamboo pole that rests on his head or palm.

poah [R. poat, an earthen dish; a mortar], a shallow earthen dish; a small earthen basin. **poah-á**, id. **hûi-poah**, id. **chhián-poah**, a very shallow sort. **kha^n-poah**, deep and shallow earthen jars and dishes. **lún-poah** (Cn.), = A. "e," a small thin earthen pot for cooking.

bák-poah, a large dish like a bowl for holding ink for writing large characters. **lûi-poah**, a round mortar, of stone or stoneware, for triturating with a pestle. **géng-poah**, a long-shaped mortar worked by a wheel.

poah (R. poat), to separate into lots or divisions; to allot or tell off for particular duties. **poah-kang**, to intermit work in order to attend to something else. **chhiâu-poah**, to put a matter in a better state. **poah-chî^n hêng--lâng**, to make an effort to get money to pay a debt, *e.g.* taking money that was required for some less urgent purpose. **pái-poah**, to lend for a short time, as money, or goods, or persons in employment; to assist, as the gods; to change places, duties, or office temporarily, or order subordinates to do so. **sa^n-pái-poah**, to exchange places, duties, or persons temporarily, or take several duties for a time. **pái-poah bô-sū**, to assist out of trouble, as gods. **tāi-sū, poah siáu-sū; siáu-sū, poah bô-sū**, to make great troubles less and remove small troubles, as a powerful divinity. **phài-poah**, to appoint men to their several duties. **hun-poah**, to separate into portions to be sent to different persons: to allot separate pieces of work to men who were together. **poah sé-tsāi**, to allot the places for each person. **poah-khui**, to put separate, esp. by moving one's hands apart without violence; to open the way in a crowd, or separate combatants. **phái^n-lâng poah-khui**, may bad men be kept away (said in Tauist worship).

poáh (R. poát), to stumble so as to fall; to fall or cause to fall; to throw down, as a dollar to try its sound. **hiám-hiám-poáh**, to stumble so as almost to fall. **poáh-tó**, to fall; to make to fall. **poáh chit-tó**, to fall down. **chháu-ki poáh-tó-lâng**, a straw may make a man fall. **pî^n-pî^n-lō poáh-tó-lâng**, a matter that seemed safe and sure to succeed may cause great trouble. **poáh-lóh**, to fall down from a place somewhat higher. **poáh-lóh-bé**, to fall from a horse. **tn̄g-poáh-chē**, to fall on one's posteriors, as when a chair has been taken away, or as going down a steep place. **poáh--sí**, to die of a fall. **tiàu-bah poáh-sí-niau^n**, said of tantalizing people (v. tiàu). **kau--poáh**, to make a man fall by hooking his leg. **phah-poáh**, to cause to fall, as a child. **put-chí phah-poáh**, extremely restless and uncomfortable, as a sick man tossing about; to exert one's self very much and have a vast deal of trouble in managing an affair.

poáh-chhiú, matters not going well, not succeeding at all, or very troublesome. **bô-poáh-chhiú**, all going on smoothly. **sa^n ka-láuh, sì tióh-poáh**, matters all going wrong.

poáh (same word?). **poáh chêng-lí**, to discuss

the principles of justice in relation to a dispute. **tò-poáh--i**, to pretend that he said what we said, or to make some charge against him as a set-off against a charge we cannot answer. **poáh-tó sien-sin**, to pose a teacher, as by a rare character. **i hē-lí poáh-bōe-tó**, you cannot overcome him in argument. **chêng-lí poáh--tó thài-san**, truth and right can overthrow in argument even the mountain Thài-san.

poáh — **poáh-tńg**, to turn a thing round so as to get it into a better position. **poáh-tńg-lâi**, id. **poáh-tńg-sin**, to turn one's self about so as to be in a better position. **poáh-lìn-tńg**, to turn right round (v. lìn).

poáh [R. poát, to pull, = col. phoáh, pu̍ih]. **poáh-tit--khì**, to draw up (cloth) and stretch it away from one's self, as in measuring or looking at it. **poáh thán-hoāin**, to draw it out and stretch between one's hands at arm's length, as for a rough measurement.

poáh-tháng, a bucket for drawing water (C. phoáh = poáh, in all this paragraph). **poáh-tháng bōe-lī--tit ké-chín** (the bucket can't leave the well), said in exhorting near relatives not to quarrel, as their interests cannot be separated. **chit-poáh-tsúi**, one bucketful of water drawn from the well.

poáh (T.) **san-poáh-kong**, = A. san-phoáh-sià, two idols represented as if wrestling with each other.

poáh, a pinch of tobacco, snuff, or opium. **chit-poáh-hun**, one pipeful (as of tobacco) taken up in the fingers. **toā-poáh**, a large pipeful, as of tobacco or opium; a large dose of opium, as smoked (s. cymbal). **chiáh sòe-poáh**, to smoke a small quantity of tobacco or opium.

poáh, to gamble; to play a game of chance (sometimes to divine or draw lots). **poáh-kiáu**, to gamble; gambling (v. kiáu). **poáh su-iân**, to gamble. **poáh-chiáh-thit**, gambling, drunkenness, and lewdness. **tùi-poáh**, to gamble with each other. **poáh sim-sek**, to play a game of chance for amusement, not for money. **poáh thit-thô**, do., or for very small stakes. **poáh tâu-á**, to gamble with dice. **poáh thiàu-kâu**, to gamble with three dice (v. kâu). **poáh pâi-á**, to gamble with cards. **poáh sù-sek**, gamble with cards of four colours. **poáh siang-hù**, gamble with two sets of cards at once. **poáh ah-nn̄g**, gamble for duck-eggs, as boys. **poáh bé-khí-tāu**, gamble for a sort of bean.

poáh-toan, to draw by lot (in presence of idol) which play is to be played. **poáh-koà**, to divine by tortoise-shell (v. koà). **poáh-poe**, to divine by bamboo roots (v. poe).

poáh (R. poát), cymbals. **toā-poáh**, large cymbals (s. pinch). **nâin-poáh**, cymbals used at funerals. **lâu-poáh** (C.), id. **phah nâin-poáh**, to play with cymbals. **hiet nâin-poáh**, to toss up the cymbals in playing them. **hìn nâin-poáh**, id. **lāng nâin-poáh**, to play with cymbals. **nâin-poáh-kó**, cymbals and drum used at funerals.

nâin-poáh-chí, seeds used for poisoning fish (not the guava).

poan [R. to remove, to excite enmity, = col. poan]. **gâu-poan**, fond of injuring people by raising stories. **poan-thio**, to raise false or greatly exaggerated reports so as to set people at variance, as a tale-bearer. **poan-lâi poan-khì**, to do so on both sides. **poan-lōng**, to poison a man's mind against another so as to stir up enmity. **poan--lâng lōng--lâng**, id. **poan-khiet** (C.), deceitful and intriguing.

poan [R. a sort, = col. poan]. **bān-poan, tē sī-bēng**, all is fixed by fate (v. bēng).

poan (C.), = A. pan. **sam-poan-khiah**, the interstices in the battlements of a wall.

poàn [R. a half, = col. poàn]. **poàn-tô jī-hòe**, to fail half-way. **poàn-khong-tiong**, in mid-heaven. **poàn-chiét-i**, a long dress made of two stuffs above and below. **thó poàn-chiet**, to get 50 per cent. on a bad debt. **poàn-kong-su**, half public half private. **poàn-thun poàn-thò**, telling only part of what one knows. **hó-pháin chham-poàn**, good and bad about half-and-half. **poàn-sien**, half a genie (v. sien). **poàn-lé-pêng**, the 113th radical written at the side (v. lé).

poàn-hā, a medicine used for the cure of coughs.

poàn (= piën). **poàn-sūi**, palsy.

poān (R. id.), to rebel; to revolt. **pōe-poān**, id. **hoán-poān**, id. **poān-sîn**, a rebellious statesman. **poān-kut**, a traitor; a man who sides with our enemies or speaks against us behind our back, though in our employment or connected with us. **poān-lâi poān-khì**, to change allegiance back and forwards, as in war.

poát [R. to pull out, to select, = col. pu̍ih, poáh, phoáh], to select a graduate to become a poát-kòng. **soán-poát**, id. **poát-kòng**, title of one lím-seng graduate selected from each Hien district once in twelve years. **poát-goân**, id.

chhiau-poát, having an appearance of talent and intelligence, as a scholar; also (R.), to deliver souls from torment and get them born again into the world. **thê-poát**, to help a man to get employment or office.

poát-mô tsé-su, name of an idol introduced from India (v. su).

poát [R. to cross over, to stumble, = col. poáh]. **poát-siáp san-chhoan** (R.), to travel far over mountains and rivers.

poát (R. id.) **hān-poát**, the demon of drought (v. hān).

poát [R. cymbals, = col. poáh, pu̍t]. **nân-á-poát**, = nân-á-pu̍t, the guava (v. pu̍t). **kim-poát-á**, a small gold coin like a sovereign.

poe (R. id.), a large cup like a bowl (not a tea-cup); divining blocks made of split bamboo roots. **chiú-poe**, a large wine-cup. **poe-poân**, large cups and platters. **sóe-chhiú-poe**, a finger-bowl. **kau-poe**, bride and bridegroom exchanging cups after tasting.

hé-poe, a long iron like a poker, crooked at the end, used heated for melting some sorts of cement.

poe-sìn, divining blocks, made of bamboo roots. **siūn-poe**, id. (v. siūn). **poe-khàu** (T.), id. **sìn-poe** (C.), id. **chit-siūn-poe**, the throw when one has the convex side up and the other the flat; the best throw. **chhiò-poe**, both with flat side up. **im-poe**, both with convex side up. **kiû-poe**, to ask direction by the divining blocks. **poáh-poe**, to throw up the blocks so as to divine by them. **poáh kàu-ū-poe**, to throw them till a favourable answer is got (said of constantly asking till consent is given). **poáh poe-á**, to gamble by throwing three cash on the ground. **siàng-poe-á**, id. **poe-si** (T.), divination before an idol by lots that direct to verses of poetry. **poáh poe-si** (T.), to divine in this way, esp. before thó-tī-kong.

poe (C. pe). **tek-poe**, a flat bamboo rod for beating criminals or scholars. **thoa tek-poe**, to carry bamboo rods before a mandarin's chair, larger than those actually used for beating.

poe-chhàk, a broad chisel about two inches broad.

poe — **giô-poe**, a boat's paddle. **pīⁿ-pīⁿ poe-poe**, flat in shape, as anything. **thê-poe** (T.), a long-shaped shell-fish somewhat like the ka-chhiô. **thê-poe m̄-si sam-seng-tsâi** (T.), said of a man of very small ability (lit. not fit to be used in offerings).

poe (C.), = A. pe, to fly.

poe (C.) **poe-lêng-chhài** (= A. pe), name of a favourite vegetable.

pôe (R. id.) **kau-pôe**, to keep company; to associate with. **saⁿ-pôe**, to keep company, as sitting or drinking together. **pôe-phoāⁿ**, id. **pôe lâng-kheh**, to sit and keep company with guests or visitors. **pôe-lí-chē**, to sit in company with you. **sit-pôe**, excuse me (said on leaving company or on refusing to eat). **pôe-sàng**, to accompany a friend when he sees a visitor off, as a third person does. **pôe-pài**, to make bows, &c., along with a visitor who comes to worship our lately deceased parent, or to pay his respects to our parent on birth-day.

pôe [R. to earth up; to assist; to foster]. **pôe-iúⁿ**, to tend, foster, and nourish up, as children. **pôe-ióng**, to train up, as children; to take care of, as one's own health. **tsai-pôe** (R.), to cultivate carefully, as trees or plants; to bring up and train carefully, as child.

pôe (C.), = A. pê, to repay or make restitution.

póe (C.), = A. pé, to ward off with the hand; to dig up, as ground-nuts.

pòe (R. id.) **pó-pòe**, precious. **pòe-jī-kha**, the 154th radical at the bottom.

pòe [R. name of a medicine; also written with the previous character "precious"]. **pòe-bú**, a medicine for coughs. **pòe-bó**, id. **chhoan-pòe**, do., from Sze-chuen.

pòe [R. pōe, girdle ornaments]. **hōng-koaⁿ hê-pòe**, ornaments for head and girdle, worn by wealthy ladies (v. koaⁿ).

pòe (R. id.), a sort or class of people, especially as to genealogical position. **pòe-siàu** (C.), position in genealogical rank. **pêng-pòe**, of the same genealogical rank, *i.e.* equally distant from the common ancestor. **chiên-pòe**, persons one or more generations nearer the common ancestor. **tióng-pòe**, superior in genealogical rank; includes also an elder brother. **téng-pòe**, our parents and their equals in genealogical rank. **khah-koâiⁿ chit-pòe**, one generation higher in the genealogical line, &c. **ē-pòe**, persons lower in genealogical rank, as sons, nephews, &c. **hā-pòe**, id. **āu-pòe ê-lâng**, the next generation (said in relation to something to be done by or for them).

ngó-pòe--ê, of our class (said by the literati). **boán-pòe**, polite phrase for "I," in speaking to an old man or to a teacher.

pòe (C.), = A. pè, to paste paper.

pòe [R. pōe, pòe, the back; to turn the back, = col. pē, pè], (T. sometimes pō). **ku-pòe**, hunchbacked. **iong-tsu hoat-pòe**, sloughing carbuncle on back of neck. **kien-thiau pòe-hū**, to bear on the shoulder or the back, as coolies and pedlars. **pòe-āu** (r.), behind one's back.

chhiú-pòe, the back of the hand. **tsoá-pòe**, the wrong side of paper. **to-pòe**, the back of a knife. **tit-pòe-í**, a chair with a square straight back. **tsòe tit-pòe**, to make a chair of this sort. **oan-pòe-í**, a chair with a curved back.

kau-í-pòe (C.), = A. kau-í-pè, the back of a chair. **kiō-pòe** (C.), = A. kiō-pè, back of the chair in a sedan.

pōe [R. pōe, pòe, the back; to turn one's back upon; to oppose or turn away from]. **siong-pōe**, each side breaking their engagements with the other. **saⁿ-pōe**, id. **hiau-pōe**, to treat a man ill from whom we have received benefits; to break an agreement; to embezzle money intrusted. **pōe-biū**, to offend against, as against instruction or doctrine. **im-iông hoán-pōe**, turning night into day. **bōng-ùn pōe-gī**, very ungrateful. **pōe lâng-ê-un**, to act ungratefully towards a man. **pōe lâng-ê-chêng**, id. **pōe-tsó**, to transgress ancestral customs. **pōe-chhin hiòng-so**, to leave near relatives and take up with strangers or distant connections.

pōe (R. id.), to rebel against. **pōe-gėk**, to rebel; to disobey a sovereign or good doctrine; rebellious. **pōe-poān**, to rebel.

pōe-goān, to break a vow.

pōe [R. name of a fabulous animal; very miserable]. **liông-pōe**, very poor and miserable; having lost all resources; ruined. **lông-pōe**, id. **lông-pōe siong-i**, two persons (each deficient in what the other has) helping each other; figure from two animals said to lean on each other so as to be able to walk.

pái-pōe, leg or arm lame or distorted, so as to make walking or work difficult; all gone wrong, as an affair. **kha pái-pōe**, leg lame; very shaky, as the legs of a table or chair. **tē-lāi pái-pōe**, uncomfortable feeling in stomach, as if about to vomit. **chhùi-khí pái-pōe**, teeth very ugly, irregular, and out of line.

pōe (= pē, piⁿ). **pōe-si-pêng**, the 120th radical at the side.

pōe (R. moⁿ, pōe, = col. pē). **tāi-pōe**, = tāi-pē, tortoise-shell (s. toast).

pōe [R. to toast; to fire, as tea-leaves; = col. pē]. **tāi-pōe**, a sort of tea (s. tortoise-shell). **sió-chióng-pōe**, a sort of Sou-chong tea. **chióng-pōe-ki**, a sort with small ends of twigs in it.

pōe [R. so many fold, = col. pē]. **ngó-pōe-chí**, a seed used for killing parasitical animals and for dyeing an inky colour like the clothes of Buddhist priests.

kúi-pōe (C.), = A. kúi-pē, how many fold? (and so in the other phrases, C., = A. pō).

pōe (C.) **siāⁿ-pōe-téng**, on the top of a city wall; the walk on the wall.

pōe (C.) **pōe io-to** (= A. pē), to wear a sword at the girdle.

poeh (R. pat), (C. peh), eight. **poeh-jī**, the eight characters of a man's nativity or horoscope, namely, two for year, month, day, and hour. **pâi-poeh-jī**, to write them out in a tabular form for divination. **théh-poeh-jī**, to take the horoscope of a couple to be betrothed to see if they agree well. **poeh-jī tùi-chhiong**, some of these characters conflicting with those of a near relative. **poeh-jī tāng**, horoscope good, so as not to need to fear demons or unlucky days, &c. **poeh-jī khin**, very apt to be injured by unlucky days, sights, &c., as by seeing an execution, or by any evil spiritual influence.

káu-poeh-hâng, commission-agent taking a commission of two per cent. **káu-poeh-kau**, id. **thiu káu-poeh**, to take that commission on goods. **tsáp-tsáp poeh-poeh**, all in confusion. **chhit-soah poeh-pāi**, all going wrong (v. chhit).

poeh-kak, eight-cornered; anise-seed; a sort of paper kite. **poeh-lòh**, a sort of rope (v. lòh). **poeh-**

si-á, a very thin stuff like satin, of very little strength (v. si).

poeh [R. phà", to fear]. **poeh-sí**, feeling ashamed (v. sí).

pòeh (C. Cn.), = A. pùih, to pull up or out.

poh [R. pok, to dispute; to discuss]. **toà-teh-poh**, disputing, scolding, or wrangling together. **m̄-sái-poh**, don't wrangle so. **poh-chhùi**, slight angry altercation (s. splice). **poh-lâi poh-khì**, to have such an altercation.

poh — **poh-chhùi**, the splice of an oar (s. dispute).

poh [R. pok, north, defeated, = col. pak]. **phah-poh**, to engage in a very dangerous conflict; to make a venture in trade, which, if unsuccessful, will be ruinous. **sì"-miā" kap--i teh-phah-poh**, to engage in mortal combat with him; to do or die.

pȯh (R. pȯk), thin, as paper, cloth, skin, &c.; weak, as tea. **kāu-pȯh**, thick or thin. **pȯh hiuh-hiuh**, very thin. **pȯh li-li**, id. **lȯh-pȯh**, to fall into poverty from affluence. **soe-pȯh**, scanty, as small crop of fruit, &c.; or as a small quantity of pocks in a case of small-pox. **chhién-pȯh**, shallow and thin. **khín-pȯh-lâng**, a man who boasts much of any slight success or good fortune. **khin-pȯh**, frivolous and shallow in manner, *e.g.* too fond of joking and laughing, or too much elated at success; light and thin, as paper, leaves, or bad cash. **khin-pȯh-siòng**, readily getting angry or pleased, *e.g.* getting angry about one cash. **khia"-pȯh**, having a thin and delicate look; hands and face small and insignificant looking; said also by fortune-tellers of an unlucky man. **pȯh-phê**, thin-skinned, very sensitive to pain, or crying readily when scolded.

tām-pȯh, a small quantity of anything. **tām-pȯh-á**, id.

pȯh-hô-iû (= pȯk), oil of peppermint.

pȯh — **chhì"-pȯh**, sort of shallow stake-nets, inclosing much less space than the net called "khiên."

pȯh (R. pȯk), metallic foil. **kim-pȯh**, false gold-leaf, made of tin, coloured for idolatrous paper. **siah-pȯh**, tin-foil. **gûn-pȯh**, do. uncoloured, to represent silver. **pè-pȯh**, to paste tin-foil on paper, so as to make idolatrous paper. **chhat-kim pè-pȯh**, to make such paper.

pȯh — **sa"-pn̄g-pȯh**, mutually helping each other, as in a joint business, or as in drawing up a document.

pok (R. id.), to divine by tortoise-shell. **pok-koà**, id. (v. koà). **m̄ng-pok**, to consult a diviner who divines by tortoise-shell. **būn-pok**, id. **bī-pok sien-ti**, I know before you tell me (lit. before divining). **san i bēng, pok siòng**, geomancy, medicine, fortune-telling, and divination by tortoise-shell, and by marks on and appearance of body (v. siòng).

pok [R. north, defeated, = col. pak, poh]. **pok-kèk**, the pole-star, or heavenly north pole (v. kèk). **tong-se lâm-pok**, east, west, south, and north. **pāi-pok** (R.), to be conquered in battle.

pok [R. to discuss; vari-coloured; to trans-ship or lighter; = col. pak, poh], to make objections; to dispute; to give an unfavourable answer to a petition; to lighter. **piēn-pok**, to argue against; to make objections. **pok-khiet**, fond of minutely cross-questioning. **pok-tó**, to overcome in argument (v. tó). **pok-iâ"**, id. **pok-su**, to be beaten in argument.

phoe-pok, answer to the petition (to mandarin) unfavourable. **pok-bûn**, to find fault with a document sent up by an inferior mandarin, as his superior does. **pok-tò-tn̍g**, to refuse to receive, as insufficient fee or disrespectful petition; to protest, as a bill. **goân-toa"**. **pok-hôe**, bill protested.

pok jī-kut, to examine minutely the meaning of a character (v. jī).

pok-hè, to take cargo out of a vessel into a smaller vessel or lighter, or to take a small quantity of it ashore. **pok-á**, a smaller junk or schooner for carrying cargo to some neighbouring port. **tsoân-chiu-pok**, a medium-sized junk that carries goods to and from Chin-chew. **î-kì-pok**, a schooner belonging to Ellis & Co. for trading with some near port, *e.g.* with Formosa.

pok — **pok--chhut-lâi**, to come out of the socket, as an eye hopelessly blind that protrudes very much.

pok [R. noise of fire]. **pit-pok-háu**, crackling sound of burning bamboos, or of crackers, &c.

pȯk (R. id.) **lê-pȯk** (R.), a male slave.

pȯk [R. bȯk, wood, = col. bȧk]. **ka-pȯk-mî"**, coarse cotton with the seeds in it, used for stuffing pillows, &c. **pȯk-piang-thûi**, an instrument for beating raw cotton.

pȯk [R. thin, = col. pȯh]. **khek-pȯk**, stingy and unkind, niggardly and exacting. **kheng-pȯk**, light, trivial, or frivolous in conduct; niggardly, but not so bad as khek-pȯk. **kheng-pȯk--lâng**, to jest at people.

pȯk-chêng, ungrateful to a friend; grown cold in friendship. **pȯk-chêng-lông**, a man who abandons a woman with whom he has cohabited. **hông-gân, to pȯk-bēng**, beautiful women are usually ill-fated.

tām-pȯk (P.), = tām-pȯh, a small quantity.

pȯk-hô, peppermint. **pȯk-hô-iû**, = pȯh-hô-iû, oil of peppermint.

pȯk (same word?). **pȯk-gān**, a low basement, built at the foot of a wall or embankment to support it; a parapet on a terrace.

pȯk [R. name of a plant]. **nâ"-pȯk**, carrots.

pȯk (cf. phȯk). **pȯk-pȯk-thiàu**, to jump about, as a flea. **pit-pit pȯk-pȯk**, crackling sound, as of fire or twigs. **pih-pih pȯk-pȯk**, id.

pȯk (C.) **pȯk-lê**, = A. pe̍-lê, a large sort of dragon-fly.

pông [R. name of a plant]. **giû-pông**, a medicinal plant. **giû-pông-chí**, its seeds.

pông [R. the side]. **pông-pien**, at the side, as by-standers (v. pien). **lō-pông-si**, a corpse at the road-side. **lō-pông**, id.

pông [R. a room, a bedroom, = col. pâng]. **bûn-pông sù-pó**, the four valuables of a literary room, pen, ink, paper, and inkstone. **hêng-pông**, to have sexual intercourse with wife or regular concubine. **pông-sū**, such connubial intercourse.

pông (R. id.) **pông-kong** (R.), the scrotum.

pông [R. tông, the Tang dynasty; sudden; Chinese; = col. tn̂g]. **pông-tût**, coming suddenly and unexpectedly.

póng (cf. páng), to splice on an additional piece, as on a mast or wooden pillar (as by iron hoops), either in first making or in mending, because the other piece is not thick or strong enough; to mend a wooden article by putting in new wood; to mend a dress by putting in a new piece below, without cutting out the old. **póng-**

ûi, to put on an extra piece of wood on a mast by iron hoops.

póng [R. an official list, =col. pn̂g]. **tông-póng**, having taken the Kujin degree at the same time. **it-póng**, rank of Kujin. **lióng-póng**, rank of Tsin-sze. **kim-póng**, id. **póng-siú**, the first in the list of new graduates in any degree. **póng-gán**, the second of the Han-lin graduates.

pòng (=phòng). **ke-pòng-tāng**, to charge over-weight.

pòng [R. to slander]. **húi-pòng**, to slander. **iâu-giân húi-pòng**, id. **pòng--lâng**, to slander people. **hong-pòng**, to raise false rumours, as of rebellion breaking out. **hong-sian pòng-ián**, false or grossly exaggerated reports spread abroad injuriously.

pòng (T. sometimes pōng). **pìn-pìn-pòng-pòng**, loud sound, as of heavy steps, or of moving about heavy things. **pìn-pòng-háu**, such sounds made. **pòng-pòng-háu**, id. **pòng-pòng-kiò**, id.

pōng— **pīn-pīn pōng-pōng**, dull heavy sound, as of a man walking heavily in next house. **pōng-pōng-háu** (T.), = A. pòng-pòng-háu, making a loud noise, as with feet. **pōng-pōng-kiò** (T.), id.

pōng (cf. phōng, phóng). **pōng-pōng-sin**, breeding and multiplying abundantly, as animals or men.

pōng (cf. pāng). **ɵ-ien pīn-pōng** (smoke in great quantity suddenly filling the room), calamities suddenly coming; people rushing away in great fear from calamities. **ɵ-ien péh-pōng**, calamities or troubles coming on very suddenly (v. péh).

pōng— **chhong-pōng**, too hurried and careless, so as to run against people or break things; acting rashly, so as to spoil a matter. **chhiong-pōng**, id.

pōng (=phōng). **pōng-song**, loose and bulky, as parcel or address.

pōng [R. phong, sound of a stone falling; used colloquially "pōng," in imitation of the foreign word], a foreign pound weight. **beh-kè-pōng**, I will have it weighed to see how many pounds it is.

pōng (Cn.), = A. pêng. **pōng-iú**, a friend.

pu, to blow the fire with the mouth; to blow with a shell, as a man selling pork. **pu-hé**, to blow the fire with the mouth.

pû (R. pâu), to bake or roast in ashes or with a slow fire, as potatoes or taro; to treat with fire, as some drugs; to heat in the fire, as an iron; to cook rice soft (bê) in a small earthen pot. **pû-kiun**, to roast ginger on burning charcoal so that the outside is charred. **pû-tsām**, to heat red-hot the wedges used for splitting granite, so as to make them ready for use again. **pû-bê**, to cook a little rice soft (especially in a small earthen vessel called e-á), as a poor or solitary man. **pû e-á-bê**, id. **pû e-á**, id. **pû--sí**, to be roasted to death, as in a burning house.

pû (R. pâu), a sort of gourd. **pû-á**, id. **hê-lê-pû**, a sort of gourd much larger at one end; a man talking falsely. **hoe-táu-pû**, the common large light green variegated gourd. **ē-pû** (T.), id. **bān-siū-pû**, the Papaya (it has male and female plants); its milky juice counted good for lactation. **pû-hia**, a calabash; also (T.), a wooden scoop or bowl made of one piece of wood. **pû-khak**, the empty shell of a gourd.

pû (T. sometimes bû). **ka-n̂g-pû**, a whole heap; in the whole mass. **chit-pû-thô**, a heap or small mound of earth. **chháu-pû**, a luxuriant clump of grass or plants; a heap of cut grass, &c. **tiū-pû** (C.), a heap of cut rice. **be̍h-pû** (C.), a heap of cut wheat or barley.

tsòe-pû, to come together or assemble, as two or more persons; sometimes said of sexual intercourse; to consummate the marriage with a daughter-in-law brought up in the house, often done in an irregular way (these phrases are not at all used in Cn., and not much in A.) **tsò-pû** (C.), id. **tsòe chit-pû**, id. **tsòe-pû lâi**, all met together or assembled; all of them come. **tsòe-pû kóng**, to tell the whole matter at once without concealing any part. **tsòe-pû teh-kóng**, to talk all at once. **tsòe-pû khiā**, to live together.

pû (C.) **pe̍h-pû**, a plant with flowers in catkins and leaves downy beneath.

pú (C.) **pú-thâu**, = A. pó-thâu, a hatchet or axe.

pù (R. hù), rich. **pù-táu**, id. **toā-pù**, very rich. **sió-pù**, rich, but not very rich. **thó-pù**, rich, but ignorant; without culture or rank. **kêng-iû pù-chhat** (v. kêng).

pū (R. pāu), to sit on eggs or chicks; to hatch. **pū-n̄g**, to hatch eggs. **pū koe-á**, to sit on chicks.

pū— **pū-lâng**, to suppurate, as matter forming in a boil.

pū— **chìm kàu-pū-pū-pū**, soaked till quite saturated with water, as wood that is water-logged.

pū (cf. hū). **hong pū-pū-hiún**, wind howling very loud.

pū (cf. tū). **àu-pū-pū**, morose and sulky.

pū [R. hū, a woman; a married woman; = col. bó]. **sim-pū**, a daughter-in-law. **sim-pū-á**, a little girl taken into the family in order to become daughter-in-law afterwards. **sun-sim-pū**, grandson's wife. **ta-ke ū-chhùi, sim-pū bô-chhùi**, the daughter-in-law must obey her mother-in-law. **sin-sim-pū sóe tsàu-hiâh**, new brooms sweep clean.

puh [R. hoat, to produce; to emit; = col. pauh], (C. pauh), to sprout or bud. **puh-phāng--chhut-lâi**, to leak out, as a secret. **puh-ín**, to bud at the side. **puh-iūn**, to bud so as to make a prolongation of last year's shoot.

puh-phā, to get blistered (v. phā).

puh [R. pùi, to bubble or boil]. **puh kóng-á**, to bubble up, as bubbles from anything fermenting, or as water from crab's holes (v. kóng). **puh-teng** (T.), bubbling, as in fermentation or corruption.

puh (T.) **thô-puh-á** (= A. phú), a sort of small insect.

pùh (=phùh). **chián pùh-pùh**, very insipid.

pùh (cf. phók), sound, as of a man falling. **pùh--chit-ē**, id.

pui (cf. kui), the gable end of a house. **pui-thâu**, the sharp top of a gable. **liâm pui-thâu**, to make the gable head. **siu pui-thâu**, to build the gable end. **siu-pui**, id. **pui-toà**, the thick raised edges of the roof at the gable. **thùt-pui**, roof of an addition made with the ridge in the same line as the original one, but lower. **chhut-pui**, eaves made to project very much in front, as in large houses.

pui (C.) **tsū-pui**, = A. tsū-bui, much pleased with one's self, as at success.

pûi (R. hûi), fat (not polite when said to a man); corpulent; rich, as land; manure; strong and closely woven, as cloth.

pûi-chhân, rich rice-fields. **èng-pûi**, to manure. **lóh-pûi**, id. **hē-pûi**, id.

49

pûi-sán, fat and lean; fertile and barren, as land (v. sán). **pûi-péh**, fat and fair. **pûi-nńg**, fat and plump, as man or animal. **pûi-thún**, short and stout. **óe-pûi**, id. **pûi-lûi-lui**, very fat. **pûi lut-lut**, id. **pûi-phàng**, very fat (said in praise). **pûi-phiàng**, id. **pûi-phòng**, id. **pûi-phauh**, id., as child or young boy.

pûi-ti, a black medicinal legume; a fat pig-like fellow, said in scolding (v. ti). **pûi-tsō**, a sort of blackish soap; said also for the legume called pûi-ti.

chiáh-pûi, to eat so as to grow fat. **chiáh-pûi, thang-hē--lâng thâi-bah**, said of an utterly useless man who only eats and amuses himself, as if fatted for slaughter. **chiáh-bōe-pûi**, unable to get fat; when said of one's self, "I am so constantly anxious about many matters;" when said of or to another, implies that he is too covetous and unfair, but all he gets will not make him fat. **pûi kàu-bô-bák-chiu**, so fat as to have no eyes. **pûi kàu bô-khoà^n--kì^n chhiú-bák**, hand so fat that the knuckles disappear.

pùi (R. id.) **pùi-á**, small pimples; prickly heat. **hoat-pùi**, to have such pimples. **si^n-pùi**, id. **pùi-chhùi**, the head of a pimple. **pùi-á-chhùi**, id. **pùi-kat** (T.), pimples and eruptions on child's head. **hoat kàu chit-thâu chit-bīn pùi**, face and head all over prickly heat. **chhioh-pùi-á-thâng** (C.), a small caterpillar that makes the skin itch by crawling over it.

pùi [R. to bubble and boil, = col. puh, pūi]. **pùi--chhut-lâi**, to boil over. **pùi--khí-lâi**, id.

pūi [R. pùi, to boil]. **ám-pūi**, coagulated scum of rice-water (Cn. ám-phí). **mâi^n-pūi** (Cn.), scum of soft-boiled rice.

pūi [R. hùi or hūi, name of insect; cf. gūi, būi, phūi]. **chhiū-pūi**, a sort of stinking insect (T. jiō-phūi). **chióh-pūi** (C.), id. **ám-pūi** (Cn.), id. (s. scum).

pūi (R. hūi), to bark; to bark at. **ngáu^n-ngáu^n-pūi**, barking away. **háu^n-háu^n-pūi**, id. **khòng-khòng-pūi**, to bark very loud. **chhī-káu, pūi ka-kī**, to be requited with ingratitude.

pui^n (C.), = A. png, a surname.

pui^n (C.), = A. png, a large tree, the Liquidambar formosanus. **pui^n-leng**, its juice (v. leng). **pui^n-siû^n**, id. (v. siû^n). **chióh-pui^n**, a very hard wood, used for the teeth of a rice-cleaning mill.

pui^n (C.), [R. hong, wind]. **pui^n-sí-hē**, a sudden heavy fall of rain, as in a squall. **pui^n-sí-hong**, a sudden squall. **khí pui^n-sí**, a sudden squall rising.

pûi^n (Cn.), = A. pêng, a side.

pūi^n (Cn.), = A. péng, to turn. **phah-pūi^n**, to cheat or swindle.

pūi^n (C.), = A. pn̄g, rice boiled dry and entire. **pūi^n-lē**, = A. tsoá^n-lí, a rice-strainer.

puih (T.) **puih-chhùi**, to scold each other slightly.

pùih (R. poát, = col. poáh, phoáh), (C. péh, póeh; Cn. póeh), to draw out; to pull up; to stretch out lengthwise. **ôe-pùih**, a shoe-lifter. **pùih-ôe**, to put up the heels of shoes (that were worn slipshod with heels down), and so pull them on. **pùih-hoe**, to pull flowers out of the hair. **pùih tek-than**, to dredge for a sort of spout-fish. **pùih-to**, to draw a sword. **pùih-kiàm**, id. **khui-chí^n pùih-tsoâ^n**, to draw away a neighbour's custom by opening a new shop next door (lit. take away his spring by a new well).

pùih-tn̂g, to pull a thing out to its full length. **pùih tit-tit**, to pull out straight, as rope or cloth. **khùn kàu-pùih-tit-tit**, to lie in bed stretched out quite straight.

thoa-pùih, to urge a friend strongly, trying to get him to go along with us. **thoa-thoa pùih-pùih**, id. **bōe-kham--tit i thoa-pùih**, could not resist his urgency (and so went with him). **kiông-thoa kiông-pùih**, to use very strong pressure to get a person to go with us. **kiông-pùih**, id. **kiông-pùih--tsáu**, to draw a man out of danger and hurry away.

peh-pùih, very poor and miserable. **ke-sū peh-pùih**, very ill off for money. **pi^n-pùih--lâng**, to bring a man into great poverty and straits by throwing one's self on him for support, though it was very hard for him to get on before. **khit--i pi^n-pùih**, to be thus brought to the lowest poverty.

pun (R. hun), to divide; to distribute; to separate; to adopt, as a child. **sa^n-pun**, to divide among one another. **pun-phi^n**, to divide what is not enough for all, so that each gets some part. **pun-phɛ^n** (C.), id. **pun ke-hé**, to divide family possessions. **pun-ké**, to divide profits according to shares. **sa^n-chi^n, pun toā-hūn**, to wrangle for the lion's share (v. hūn). **pun bōe-tit-sī**, not enough for all. **pun-kui-lūi**, to assort.

ū-pun-tiu^n, generous, fond of making presents to others, as children. **pun-sim** (C.), just and fair in dealings. **chiàu-pun**, to divide equally (as gains), giving equal shares to all. **chhiu-hun, mî^n-jit pî^n-pun**, at autumnal equinox day and night are equal.

pun-chheh, to distribute books. **pun-toa^n**, to send out accounts or notices (v. toa^n). **pun-piá^n**, to distribute cakes, so as to make a confederacy or conspiracy. **pun-phoe**, to distribute letters, sometimes for similar purpose.

pun-chiáh, to beg, as a beggar; a beggar. **pun--chiáh**, to make arrangements to have meals separate from each other. **pun-khui-chiáh**, id.

pun-thiah, to separate, as partners. **pun-soà^n**, to be dispersed, as members of a family. **pun-khui**, to separate; to part; to go apart. **pun-lī**, id. **pun-lō͘**, to part company going different roads, as at a division of the road; to branch off, as roads.

pun (C.) **pun-ta^n**, = A. pin-ta^n, a pole for carrying loads on the shoulder.

pun (C.) **pun-n̂g**, = A. pin-n̂g, the areca nut, &c.

pûn (C.) **pûn-toā^n**, = pîn-toā^n, lazy.

pûn (R. hûn, pûn), to blow with the mouth. **pûn-hong**, id. **pûn-khùi**, to breathe heavily. **pûn-khì**, id. **pûn-phī^n**, to blow in an angry way through the nose. **thé-khùi pûn-hāi^n**, to sigh and groan bitterly. **pûn-hé**, to blow the fire or a match; to blow out a light. **pûn-hoa-hé**, to blow out a light. **pûn-sit-hé** (Cn. T.), id. **pûn-lê**, to blow on a shell, as man selling pork. **pûn-chhe**, to blow a sort of clarionet (v. chhe), (and so with other wind instruments). **pûn thn̂g-á-teng**, to blow bubbles of béh-lê-ko (v. teng, "bubbles").

pûn-bīn--ê, having a silver coating over base metal, as dollars.

pún [R. the root], origin; originally; naturally; capital of money; a volume; classifier of books; a memorial to the emperor. **toā-pún**, large capital; a large plant or book; large as a shop.

bòk-pún, woody or shrubby, as plant. **chhó-pún**, herbaceous, as plant. **pún-chhó**, the Chinese book of botany, or herbal.

pún-sū, talent. **hó-pún-léng**, talented; skilful. **láu-pún**, experienced.

kun-pún, origin. **goân-pún**, id.; originally. **pún-goân**, origin (v. goân). **ti-un pò-pún**, to be grateful to parents. **pún-jiên**, originally. **pún-lâi**, id. **pún-chiâ^{n}**, id. **pún-ū**, originally has, or there is. **pún-bô**, originally has not, or there is not. **pún-ài**, originally desire. **goá pún-tsai**, I know it already (so with many other verbs). **pún-sek**, original colour; unbleached. **pún kin-ná-jit**, this very day. **pún siōng-sî**, on all previous occasions; in past time regularly.

pún-téng, one's own proper duties; naturally (v. téng). **pún-hūn**, duty; proper business (v. hūn).

pún-sin, one's self; self; myself; yourself; himself, &c. **goá pún-sin**, I myself (&c.) **pún-sin-lâng**, one's self; the very man himself (or myself, &c.) **pún-lâng**, id. **pún sé-tsāi**, original place; native place or place of long residence. **pún-kok**, native country; my own country. **pún-tōe**, native place. **pún-tōe-lâng**, natives of the place. **pún-tōe-ōe**, vernacular language. **pún-tōe-hiu^{n} bōe-phang**, native articles are despised. **pún-hú**, the prefect of our department; said also by him of himself. **pún-koāi^{n}**, the hien mandarin of our district; said also by him of himself.

pún-thâu, master of female slave, especially said by herself.

chhiú-pún, a folded book of red paper for writing a petition to a mandarin; the petition itself. **jip chhiú-pún**, to send it in. **tì chhiú-pún**, id. **pài-pún**, to send up a memorial to the emperor. **chiū^{n}-pún**, id.; also, the previous volume of a book. **téng-pún**, the previous volume, or the first of two. **sòe-pún**, a small volume. **chit-pún-chheh**, one volume; one book of one volume.

kàm-pún, the square regularly formed characters, printed or written.

pún-chî^{n}, capital in business; member's ticket of the Triad society. **lāu-pún**, portion set apart for wife when she becomes a widow. **bô-pún**, without capital. **kè-pún**, cautious in trade; careful in the use of one's capital. **khah-siong-pún**, too expensive. **chioh-pún**, to borrow capital. **chiàh-pún**, to live on one's capital, instead of on gains. **sih-pún**, to sell at a loss. **khui-pún**, id. **lap-pún**, to lose money in trade. **bōe-kàu-pún**, not up to cost price. **chiàu-pún bōe**, to sell at prime cost. **che-sī goá chiàu-pún ê-kè**, this is just what I paid for it. **sió-pún to-lī**, small capital and great profits. **tsòe-pún**, to be used as capital. **chéng-pún**, to invest capital. **hē-pún**, id. **hē-tāng-pún**, to invest a great deal of money. **chhut-pún**, to lay out money; to invest capital. **chhut-pún hē-hoan**, to pay money in advance for a friend (v. hoan).

pùn (R. pún). **pùn-ki**, a hod or basket with handles (hī), for mortar, &c. (v. hī).

pùn (R. hùn), dung; manure. **pùn-sò**, dirt. **pùn-táu**, a scoop for dirt and sweepings, with a handle. **pùn-chhiá^{n}**, do., with no handle. **pùn-hia**, a bucket fastened on a pole for lading out fluid or half fluid manure. **pùn-kháu**, the anus. **pùn-te** (C.), an ashpit.

khioh-pùn, to gather manure. **èng-pùn**, to manure. **lóh-pùn**, id. **pàng-pùn**, to go to stool. **sio-pùn**, to burn weeds, grass, straw, &c., mixed with earth in alternate layers for manure. **sio kòe-nî^{n}-pùn** (C.), to burn small heaps of rubbish mixed with earth on the last night of the year.

pūn, broken by rocks or by the banks, as the flow of the tide, so as to make eddies. **tò-pūn**, id. **tò-pūn-lâu**, tide thus broken and eddying. **lâu pūn**, id. **hong tò-pūn**, the wind eddying in heavy gusts.

pūn (R. id.), awkward, clumsy, and slow, *e.g.* ready to fall or to strike against things when trying to go faster; unwieldy, as man with too many clothes, or as vessel too heavily laden; dull, as a sound. **pūn-chhêng**, awkward, clumsy, coarse, and ugly, as man or thing. **pūn-chhiâng**, id.; vulgar (v. chhiâng). **chhe-pūn**, clumsy; ill-formed; awkward-looking. **chhún-pūn**, vulgar; clownish; clumsy; quite wanting in propriety; coarse, as language. **kóng-ōe chhún-pūn**, to talk very coarsely and vulgarly. **im khah-pūn**, the sound is dull and indistinct, not sharp and clear. **pî^{n}-pî^{n}-lō poàh-sí pūn-ti-bú** (the clumsy fat pig falls and is killed on a level road), said of a man failing because he thought it was all right.

khah áu-pūn, the sail must be quite full, as in tacking.

pūn [R. the coarse part of the bamboo; used also for the former word]. **tek-pūn**, coarse bamboo hurdles.

pūn, the deck of a vessel. **pūn-bīn**, the deck. **pūn-téng**, on the deck. **pūn-kiáh**, the strong wooden knees nailed to the deck and to the sides to support the sides. **pūn-thiu**, the long strong horizontal timbers close by the hatches, that run from one end of a junk to the other. **tiong-pūn**, the lower or second deck. **jī-pūn**, id. **jī-iên-pūn**, id. **sa^{n}-iên-pūn**, the third deck. **sa^{n}-pūn**, id.

put [R. not; will not; = col. m̄]. **put-chì**, very —; extremely — (not so much used by the Chinese as some other phrases of same meaning). **put-chí-hó**, very good (&c.) **put-sī**, in the wrong (v. sī). **put-siong-kan**, setting a bad example to inferiors. **put-pêng**, indignant at injustice to another (v. pêng).

put-lūn, no matter which —. **put-koán**, id. **put-khu**, id. **put-jit**, some day soon, not fixing what day. **put-sî**, at any time; always (v. sî). **tang-sai, bû-sé-put**, willing to take anything (v. sé).

put-tān, not only —. **put-kò**, only (v. kò). **put-kè kî-sò**, innumerable. **bû-sé put-chì**, addicted to all sorts of wickedness (v. sé). **put-it**, of various sorts or opinions. **put-tông**, different (v. tông). **put-téng**, of different qualities of the same kind of article (v. téng). **put-tēng**, not yet fixed. **put-pit**, it is better not to —. **put-kip**, to be inferior to. **put-tì**, it will not have the (hurtful) effect —. **put-tē**, to fail in getting a degree. **put-tek put-tiòh-kóng**, cannot but speak, though unwilling. **put-ti-chiok**, insatiable (v. ti; v. chiok). **put-siòk**, superior to the common average of persons. **put-jîn**, cruel; unfeeling. **put-hàu**, unfilial; disobedient to parents. **put-siàu**, id. **put-hô**, at variance, as persons or evidence. **put-tiong**, unfaithful to employer or superior.

put [R. pat, a rake without teeth; a scraper]. **pê-put**, a sort of wooden shovel or hoe. **pê-put-á**, id. **kiáh pê-put, ka-kī kòng-hiáh**, to raise a matter that injures one's self.

put (R. pat ?), to scrape together, as corn, sand, &c. **put-lut**, id. **put-thô**, to scrape earth together. **put pùn-sò**, to scrape dirt together, as for manure. **thàn-chî^{n}, ná^{n} teh-put-kim**, to earn money, as if shovelling it up. **put-gûn**, said of making great gain.

pùt (R. hùt), (C. "hùt" in more literary phrases; "ang" in more colloquial), Buddha; a Buddhist idol; any image, even sometimes those that are not for worship. **pùt-á**, a small idol; a small image or figure. **pùt-lá**, id. **pùt-á-pò**, a storm about 4.4. **pùt-á-thâu**, a head without a body, used as a child's toy. **pùt-á-thô**, clay for making idols or images. **thô-pùt-á**, small clay figures used as toys by children. **ná^{n} thô-pùt-á**, idle and stupid, like a clay image. **pùt-bák**, having immovable eyes.

pùt-kong, an idol; a god. **sîn-pùt**, spirits and idols; objects of worship. **pùt-siōng**, an image or picture of an idol (properly Buddhist). **chit-sien-pùt**, a solid image. **chit-tiu^{n}-pùt**, a picture of an idol (or of idols) not yet pasted on rollers. **chit-pak-pùt**, do. pasted on rollers. **oàh-pùt**, a living Buddha; the Dalai Lama or one of the other living Buddhas. **tsng oàh-pùt**, to be a barber (+). **chhài-pùt**, idols to which no animal food is offered. **tang-sai-pùt**, said of the feuds of the votaries of different idols, as at Chin-chew city. **pùt-tsó**, Kwan-yin. **koan-im pùt-tsó**, id. **sek-hia pùt-tsó** (T.), Shakya-muni; Buddha. **tán pùt-tsó** (T.), to levy black-mail on road (v. tán).

tsng-pùt, to make idols (+). **chhāi-pùt**, to set up an idol. **chhiá^{n}-pùt**, to invite the spirit of an idol to enter the image or to come on a sorcerer; to invite an idol to move somewhere else. **pài-pùt**, to make obeisance to an idol. **hàu-pùt**, to make offerings to an idol. **hòk-sāi pùt**, to worship idols. **ngiâ^{n}-pùt**, to carry idols about in procession. **kng-pùt**, to carry an idol between two men. **mn̄g-pùt**, to consult an idol. **koan-pùt**, to call the spirit of an idol to a medium or to a branch for writing oracles.

siá pùt-jī, to trace characters by a branch held (by tâng-chí) before an idol. **khoà^{n} pùt-jī**, to examine these characters and interpret the oracle, as Tauist priests do. **pùt-iòh**, medicine prescribed by idols. **pùt-toā^{n}**, place screened off in a house for pictures of idols, in some rites (v. toā^{n}). **pùt-tiù^{n}**, curtains hung up before an idol's shrine. **tiòh pùt-thâu**, to have the turn for a year of cultivating a field and worshipping an idol held in common. **tsòe pùt-thâu**, id.

pùt [R. poat, a cymbal, = col. poàh]. **nâ^{n}-á-pùt**, = nâ^{n}-á-poát, the guava. **chhâ nâ^{n}-á-pùt**, a very hard medicinal fruit that grows on a thorny shrub.

pùt [R. intractable; a comet]. **liû-pùt thài-sòe**, the demon which causes eclipses by appearing naked, so that the luminary runs away ashamed. **thǹg kàu chit-sien ná^{n} liû-pùt--nih^{n}**, as naked as the eclipse demon (said in scolding a naked child).

PH.

pha (R. phau), (C. phoa), to throw out, especially with a circular motion; to cast anchor; to throw out a net. **pha-tià^{n}**, to anchor. **pha-bāng**, to cast a net. **pha-hî**, to catch fish by casting a net.

pha-hng, to lay waste; waste; desert.

pha lién-pó, to gamble in the manner called "lién-pó" (v. pó).

pha-lâi pha-khì, to go round and round in a circle, as a boy at play, or as a man on horseback. **koh--tsài pha--lâi**, to turn round and come back. **chit-jit pha-pha-tsáu**, to go about idly, as truant boy, or as idle fellow spending money on low amusements; to leave one's master's work for amusement or for one's own business. **sì-ûi pha chit-lin-tńg**, to make a circuit fully round a place. **chhia pha-lin-táu**, to make a somerset. **pha kí-lîn**, to throw one's body sidewise round like a wheel.

pha (R. phau). **lān-pha**, the scrotum. **toā-pha**, having a very large scrotum; hydrocele, or similar diseases of that part.

pha [R. pa, pha, a bunch, as of flowers], a bunch of fruit like grapes or lung-yen; classifier of large tails or queues (of men or animals), also of flames and lights. **toā-pha-bé**, a large tail, of animal (v. bé). **chit-pha thâu-tsang**, one large thick queue. **nn̄g-pha-hé**, two lamps burning; two lights. **pha-pha-tòh**, blazing up fiercely, as fire (v. tòh).

phà (= phā). **âng phà-phà**, very red.

phā — **phī-phā-háu**, sound of flames blazing fiercely when blown upon by wind. **phā-phā-háu**, noise of fire. **phā-phā-tòh**, to blaze up fiercely, as fire (v. tòh).

âng-phā-phā (= phà), very red, as fruit. **n̂g phā-phā**, very yellow, as fruit.

phā (R. phàu), a bubble. **tsúi-phā**, bubbles on water (s. blister).

phā [R. phāu, phàu, = col. pháuh], a blister. **tsúi-phā**, id. (s. bubble). **phòng-phā**, to rise in blisters. **puh-phā**, id. **thǹg kàu puh-phā**, scalded and blistered. **khí chit-phā**, a blister formed.

a-phièn-phā, a pellet of opium prepared in the flame, carried in the pocket, and often swallowed when there is no opportunity for smoking. **hun-phā**, id. **sio hun-phā**, to prepare such a pellet in the flame.

phā (same word?) **ū-phā**, prosperous, as man; prospering, growing rich, and powerful; beautiful, as things. **ké-ū-phā**, assuming airs of great consequence. **chit-niū^{n}, chit-ū-phā**, the more you yield the more he will insist on, as a spoiled child. **bô-phā**, without any influence or ability.

phà^{n} (cf. phò), hollow; porous; not solid; too soft; good for nothing; false. **tēng-phà^{n}**, solid and soft, &c. **khang-phà^{n}**, empty; hollow (lit. or fig.) **tē-lāi khang-phà^{n}**, empty; illiterate. **phà^{n}-phùh**, corpulent and flabby, seeming strong, but really of weak constitution; said also of things that seem large and good, but are hollow within. **toā-phà^{n}--ê**, large soft inferior potatoes.

phà^{n}-kó, empty stories. **kóng phà^{n}-kó**, to tell baseless or exaggerated stories for amusement. **kóng phà^{n}-tâm**, id.

phà^{n}-sok, a wood from which incense is made. **phà^{n}-chhâ**, soft or porous wood. **phà^{n}-chiòh**, porous stone. **phà^{n}-chhek**, empty rice chaff (v. chhek). **phà^{n}-chhih**, crabs that have almost no meat in them.

phà^{n} [R. to fear; be afraid of; cf. col. poeh]. **khū-phà^{n}**, to fear greatly. **ti-hoat phà^{n}-hoat**, they who know the law should obey it (v. hoat). **chin-kim put-phà^{n}-hé**, real gold fears not fire. **iú-hong, put-phà^{n}-lâu**, having the wind we need not fear the tide. **tiong-sîn put-phà^{n}-sí**, a faithful statesman fears not death. **jîn phà^{n}-ló; chè phà^{n}-thó**, men fear old age, debtors fear the demand for payment. **siù-tsâi phà^n sòe-khó**, Sew-tsai graduates fear their examinations.

phah (R. phok), to strike; to beat; to work in a substance; to make; to cause (used as an auxiliary); to have, as some diseases, &c.; to copulate (vulg.); to shoot; to invade; to attack; to take, as a city.

sa^n-phah, to fight with fists. **phah-mē^n**, to fight and scold. **phah-kûn**, to beat one's self, as men in the streets. **phín-phah**, threatening to beat, as an overbearing man. **phah kúi-ē**, how many strokes did he beat? **phah kúi-ê**, how many men did he beat? **phah-tùi**, two men fencing. **phah-tūi**, two troops at sham fight, as in drill. **phah-chhiú**, to fight for amusement, as actors and low characters. **phah-chhèng**, to shoot with a gun. **phah-bōe-tio̍h**, the ball cannot reach him.

phah ien-chhun, to set quails a fighting.

phah-su, to be overcome in boxing, or such contest. **phah-iâ^n**, to conquer. **phah-phiâ^n**, to beat a man who had first beaten us, as in beating or gambling (v. phiâ^n). **phah-pià^n**, to fight for life or death; to make a very dangerous venture (v. pià^n). **phah-poh**, id. **phah-kéh**, to act intentionally opposite to the wish of a superior or partner (v. kéh).

phah-sí, to strike dead; to kill. **phah-sí-lâng**, to kill a man. **phah-siong**, to wound. **phah-phoà**, to break. **phah-chih**, id. **phah-tn̄g**, to break, as a thread. **phah-tó**, to knock down, as a thing. **phah-poa̍h**, to make to fall, as a child (v. poa̍h). **phah-sńg**, to spoil; to waste (v. sńg). **phah-phái^n**, to spoil. **phah-soà^n**, to scatter. **phah-koá^n**, to drive away. **phah-tsáu--khì**, to drive away, as birds; dead. **phah-tsâm**, to prevent a plan or quarrel, &c., by speaking betimes against it. **phah-hoa**, to extinguish. **phah-sit** (Cn.), id. (v. sit).

phah ka-la̍uh, to let fall. **phah-lo̍h-sin**, to cause a miscarriage. **phah-thu̍t-sin**, id. (v. thu̍t). **phah-thu̍t**, to put a joint out of gear, as of machine, or of furniture. **phah-lut**, to let something slip out of place (v. lut). **phah sit-lo̍h**, to lose. **phah-m̄-kì^n**, id. **phah-bô**, to lose, or let a thing be spoiled or lost in our hands. **phah-bô--khì**, id. **phah-chhí^n**, to waken another unintentionally. **phah-chhi^n-kia^n**, to startle or scare. **phah-lâng bô-hong-sîn**, to put a man openly to shame by scolding him.

phah-khang, to open a way, as for a situation, or for making money out of a man (v. khang). **phah sa^n-thâu**, to open a communication, as between two rooms. **phah koa^n-si**, to litigate. **phah-chiò**, sailors taking their idol to a temple, and having rites there. **phah hì-phûn**, to act a sort of plays for the dead. **phah-ûn**, to work together, and divide profits about equally. **têng-thâu phah-khí**, do it all over again from the beginning (v. khí). **phah-thâu-tùi**, to sell a female slave to become the legitimate wife of her purchaser.

phah-sǹg, to calculate; to suppose (v. sǹg). **phah-chiet**, to take off discount. **phah bé-á**, to write down a sum in numerals (v. bé). **phah-kè**, to propose a price (as a third party) to the buyer and seller. **phah-phièn**, to deceive. **phah lê-á**, to talk or joke idly. **phah chhiu-hong**, to get some help (by asking) from a friend, as money or things, not expected to be repaid. **phah thong-thò**, to conspire against a man. **phah-tat**, to make a plan, as for building, or for an accusation (v. tat).

phah-hō, to make a mark. **phah-chhe**, to mark with a diagonal cross (thus ×). **phah chhiú-ìn**, to make the print of one's hand with ink (v. ìn). **phah-kó**, to write a rough draft (v. kó). **phah-phiò**, to make out a pawn-ticket.

phah-phe, to spread a bed or mat to sleep on. **phah kong-koán**, to make ready a lodging, as for a mandarin. **phah-thì^n**, to put in a support (v. thì^n). **phah-pē**, to fasten wood or bamboo on the sides of a junk for transport. **phah-thiâu**, to lay a plank, as for a gangway; to make a scaffolding for a house. **phah pe-thâu**, to make a new landing-place and mart. **phah chit-téng-kiō**, to make ready a sedan for a journey.

phah-liú, to make a knot, used as a button (v. liú). **phah-kat**, to make a knot (v. kat). **phah-khe**, to make a hoop (v. khe). **phah pó-thâu**, to make an axe. **phah-soh**, to make ropes. **phah-phâng**, to manufacture sails. **phah-chhio̍h**, to make mats. **phah-bāng**, to make a net. **phah tiò-á**, to make fish-hooks. **phah-to**, to make a knife. **phah chien-sí**, to make a large spoon.

phah-thih, to work in iron (v. thih). **phah-tîn**, to work in rattan. **phah-chio̍h**, to work in stone, quarrying or cutting. **phah-jī**, to cut words in stone. **phah-mī^n**, to make a sort of preparation of dough (v. mī^n). **phah-mí^n**, to beat cotton with a bow. **phah-chhi^n**, to work up the indigo plant in the vat, extracting the indigo. **phah-iâm**, to manufacture salt. **phah-lé**, to make a sort of briny sauce.

phah-m̂, to produce flower-buds.

phah-eh, to belch or hiccup. **phah-uh**, id. **phah-ka-chhiù^n**, to sneeze. **phah-chhìn**, to take a cold or ague. **phah-koâ^n phah-jiėt**, to have fever and ague. **si^n-chhng phah-lāu**, to have venereal sores, **phah hong-to̍k**, to have venereal or rheumatic sores.

phah-hé, to strike fire with a flint or match. **phah-hún**, to smear with face powder. **phah-chéng** (vulg.), to copulate, as animals. **phah-lân**, to take off fish scales. **phah chhim-khín**, to take soundings. **phah tsúi-pān**, id. **phah tsúi-tô**, id. with lead. **phah-tsúi**, to take in water for use, as vessel. **phah-iû** (T.), to buy oil.

phah-siâ^n, to take a city. **phah tē-ge̍k**, to rescue souls from the Buddhist hell. **phah-mn̂g**, to knock at a door. **phah-bô-mn̂g**, to knock, but not get in. **phah-chiáu**, to shoot birds. **phah-la̍h**, to hunt. **phah-hó**, to hunt tigers. **phah-phek**, to beat time with the "phek." **phah-lô**, to beat a gong. **phah-kó**, to beat a drum (v. kó).

khit-hong phah, to be driven out of course by a violent wind. **khit-lûi phah**, to be struck by lightning. **khit koài-hong phah**, to be taken with an incurable palsy on one side of the face. **phah--tio̍h i sim-koa^n-tóe**, to speak so as to touch his heart with the feeling of his wickedness.

ū-phoà-phah, to have some fault, as man or thing (v. phoà).

phah-tsǹg, a sort of drill worked by means of a hammer (v. tsǹg).

phài [R. to branch, as streams; a division of a clan; a sort], a division of a clan larger than "thiâu;" to allot. **tsong-phài**, a clan. **tso̍k-phài**, a division of a clan. **chi-phài** (R.), id. **tâng-phài**, belonging to the same great branch. **chhin-phài**, closely related, as ancestors and posterity of same surname within five generations. **phài-ē**, branch of clan; direct near posterity.

phài-phe, to anticipate; to conjecture beforehand (v. phe). **bô-phài-pān** (C.), unexpectedly.

sí-phài, fashionable form of dress. **sái-phài**, proud, overbearing, and lofty in bearing. sái phài-thâu, id. kek phài-thâu, to affect to be a man of importance; to talk or behave in a proud overbearing way. kek koa^n-phài, to affect the style or manner of mandarins or of their relations. kek ū-chî^n-phài, to affect the airs and appearance of a wealthy man when really not so. jī-phài, the style of hand of a good writer.

phài-io̍h, to prescribe medicine. phài-gia̍h, to make provision for a specified number (v. gia̍h). phài-poah, to appoint (men) to their several duties. hun-phài, id.; to allot. khe-phài, to allot and collect the shares of contributions which each is to pay, as to some governmental impost or local public fund. phài-iâm-siong, to compel a man to farm the salt tax. phài-kun-su, to levy contributions (nominally) for the army. phài-hù-hō͘, to levy imposts (squeezes or benevolences) from the wealthy. phài-chhái-mái^n, id. (v. mái^n).

phai^n (=phāi^n), sound of gongs.

phái^n, bad; spoiled; at variance, as persons; wicked; wickedness; sin. hó-phái^n, good and bad (v. hó). phái^n-lâng, a bad man. phái^n-kiá^n, a lascivious person; a robber or rowdy (v. kiá^n). phái^n kàu-jip kut-chhé, very very wicked. phái^n-sim, a wicked injurious heart; very unjust or cruel. phái^n-chhiú-jiáu^n, to pilfer. phái^n-chhi^n, a comet; a man who does great injury (v. chhi^n). i ná^n-teh-phái^n, he is getting on worse and worse. phah-phái^n, to spoil; to be spoiled; to die; dead, as a child. phái^n-thi^n, bad weather. thi^n beh-tsòe-phái^n, it is going to be bad weather. tsòe-phái^n, to behave wickedly. tsò-phái^n (C.), id. tsō-phái^n, to spoil by rough writing or very black erasure, as pen or document.

kap-i-phái^n, at variance with him.

phái^n-kóng, not suitable to talk about. put-chí phái^n-kóng-ōe, very difficult to talk over to our views. phái^n-kiâ^n, difficult to walk upon; not safe for travelling. phái^n-ēng, not suitable for use. phái^n-giâ, troublesome to carry, as a large table. phái^n-sè, unsuitable; awkward; inconvenient (v. sè). phái^n-sì (C.), id. phái^n-sîn-khì, feeling of awkwardness and shame, as at being rebuked by a superior, or having to speak against a relative, benefactor, or friend. phái^n-sêng-khì, id. phah-lâng phái^n-sêng-khì, to put a man openly to shame by finding fault with him, as a superior.

phái^n-tāi, wickedness; death or great calamity. tú--tio̍h phái^n-tāi, to have a death in one's family, &c. phái^n-ōe, bad language; ill-omened language. kóng i tsú-lâng ê-phái^n-ōe, to tell stories (true or false) of his master's bad conduct. phái^n-sí, violent or painful death; very wicked or unjust (v. sí). phái^n-pī^n, a very sudden and fatal disease. phái^n-kè, a very low price (said by seller).

phāi^n (=phai^n), sound of gongs. phāi^n-phāi^n-háu, sounding loud, as gongs.

phāi^n (C.), to carry on the back of the shoulder, as child or thing. phāi^n tah-liên, to carry a double bag hanging over the shoulder.

phak [R. hok, to overturn; to upset], to invert; to lie with the face down; to turn a cup, &c., with the mouth down. phak-lak, many things or persons inverted or on their faces. thâu-khak phak-phak, head bent down. hī-á phak-phak, ears standing out too much so as almost to cover the opening (said to be like a pig). phak-chhio̍, odds and evens; heads and tails (v. chhio̍). phak-chhiú, the hand with the palm downwards. phak-tsô, the raised row of inverted tiles between the furrows of a tiled roof. phak-lek-soà^n, sort of bead moulding. phak-io (T.), shoulders bent, as an old man or yamun man. phak-bō͘, the 40th radical. phak-sūn-têng, a small open portico on pillars at a door. phak-oá^n, to lay down a bowl inverted; an inverted bowl. phak-tiá^n, an inverted rice-boiler (v. tiá^n). kūi-phak, to kneel and prostrate one's self. phí-phak-à^n, bending forward with arms stretched out, as if about to fall.

thán-phak, laid with mouth down, as bowl or cup; lying on the face. péng-phak, to invert with mouth down; to turn on the face or belly. péng-thán-phak, id. péng ka-lán-phak, id. péng-phak-khùn, to sleep on one's face. péng-phak teh-khùn, id. phak-teh-khùn, to lean one's head on the hands while sitting, and so fall asleep. phak-teh-thia^n, to listen secretly (with head bent down), as at a door. phak-teh-pài, to kneel and bow very low. phak-tē-hó͘, a sodomite (lit. tiger on face).

phak [R. phok, simple and plain, =col. phoh]. phak-sò, simple in taste, as man; plain and simple; not gaudy, as dress. phak-sit, plain and simple in dress, manners, &c.; not fond of display or boisterous mirth. khiām-phak, economical, as person. chit-phak, quiet in taste, not fond of display.

hō͘-phak, a thick medicinal bark (v. hō͘).

pha̍k [R. pō, violent; to scorch; =col. pāu, pō͘, &c.], to sun; to dry in the sun. pha̍k-jit, id. pha̍k-ta, to dry in the sun. pha̍k-pa, to dry eatables in the sun (v. pa). pha̍k-koa^n, to dry fruit, &c., in the sun. pha̍k-iâm, to make salt by evaporation. jit pha̍k, the sun dries or scorches.

pha̍k (cf. ho̍k). mn̂g-pha̍k, the two upright pieces of wood, one on each leaf of folding-doors, in which the door-bolts are fastened. téng-pha̍k, the piece of wood nailed on the end of the lintel to receive the upper projection (mn̂g-lûn) of the axis of the door-leaf, which serves as a hinge. î^n-pha̍k, a small piece of wood nailed on a sloping beam to keep the rafter from sliding down.

phan [R. to pull]. gâu phan-kè, skilful at getting a good price for one's goods. goá beh ko-phan--lí, will you kindly come along with me, sir! (said to a man of some influence or ability, either wishing to show him attention, or wishing his assistance in going to speak to some one else). lí hō͘-goá ko-phan--cheh, id. chhiú phan tan-kùi (R.), to become a Tsin-sze (v. kùi). phan-heng-thâu (T.), the upper corner of the flap of a dress where it is buttoned.

phàn (R. id.) liú-phàn, the double cord sewed on the edge of a dress, ending either in the knot that serves as a button, or in the loop that serves for a button-hole. ôe-phàn, loops at sides of woman's or child's shoe for tying it on; also, the strip of cloth between the two ribs on the toe of a double-ribbed shoe.

phang (R. hong), sweet smell; fragrant; savoury. phang-chhàu, fragrant and stinking (v. chhàu). phang phut-phut, very fragrant. chheng-phang, gently and pleasantly fragrant, not too strong. phang-bī, sweet odour or flavour. phang-hiu^n, sweet incense (v. hiu^n). kā-phang, to eat sweet-flavoured things (v. kā).

bí-phang, a lozenge-shaped cake of rice and sugar. moâ^n-phang, a lozenge-shaped cake containing hemp-seed. moâ^n-phang-chhoa̍h, diagonal lattice-work. moâ^n-phang-hoān, lozenge-shaped, or diamond-shaped.

phang (R. hong), a bee; a wasp. **bit-phang**, a honey-bee. **n̂g-phang**, id. **n̂g-io-phang**, id. **n̂g-phang chhut-siū**, people in great crowds (lit. bees from nests). **thô-kàng-phang**, sort of bee that has its nest in the ground. **kak-phang**, a wasp. **hé-thâu-phang**, id. **o-tèng-phang**, a sort of wasp. **khit-phang tèng--tio̍h**, stung by a bee or wasp.

phang-bit, honey. **phang-la̍h**, bees'-wax. **phang-hê**, larva of bee or wasp. **phang-tū**, a bee-hive. **phang-siū**, nest of bee or wasp. **phang-siū-eng**, a large boil or carbuncle opening at several places. **phang-siū-pè**, carbuncle on back, sloughing at several places.

phâng (R. hông, phông), a sail. **tsûn-phâng**, id. **gē-phâng**, a long large boat plying up the Chang-chew river. **chit-phì^{n}-phâng**, on one tack.

phoà-phâng, a bit of a rainbow appearing only at the end. **chhut phoà-phâng, ₒtsúi lâu-lâng**, when only the end of a rainbow appears, people will be drowned.

phâng-bé-tiah, a sort of secret slang language.

phâng-bīn, the starboard or right-hand side of a junk. **phâng-kám**, a mat cover. **phâng-kóng**, small bamboo instrument for throwing water on the sail. **phâng-chhùi**, the rope fastening the end of the lower yard or boom to the mast. **phâng-kûn**, an extra sail below the main-sail. **phâng-liâu**, the small ropes which meet in the main sheet (v. liâu). **phâng-kè**, the frame for the sail to rest upon when taken down. **phâng-ta̍h**, the swinging support for the sail when partially down. **phâng-pè**, canvas.

phah-phâng, to manufacture a sail. **tiu^{n}-phâng**, to fit a new sail to the boat, putting on the ropes, &c. **chhia-phâng**, to hoist up the sail; to spread sail. **lo̍h-phâng**, to furl the sail. **heh-phâng**, to lower the sail, taking in little or much. **heh^{n}-phâng** (C.), id. **hâ-phâng**, to take in a reef. **kè-phâng**, to pass the sail to the other side of the vessel. **chīn-phâng sái**, to sail as near the wind as possible while keeping the sail full. **phiò-phâng**, to splash water on the sail, to keep it from spoiling by drying.

phâng (R. hông, hōng, = col. phóng), to carry on both hands, as a large plate, or as a tray—done to show respect, even with small things, like a cup of tea. **phâng-pó**, to put the die in its case ready for the gambling called "lién-pó," as the gambling-house keeper does.

pháng (R. hóng), to spin; finest white grass-cloth. **pháng-cheh**, to make thread of cotton or of flax. **pháng-chit**, to spin and weave. **pháng-chhia**, a spinning-wheel (v. chhia). **pháng-mî^{n}**, to spin cotton. **pháng-se**, to spin yarn. **pháng-soà^{n}**, to spin thread. **pháng-si**, to spin silk (v. si).

chēng-pháng, fine white grass-cloth. **phiò-pháng**, bleached do. **kang-sai pháng**, finest sort from Kiang-si. **pháng-tiû**, sort of thin satin.

phàng (R. phòng, = col. phiàng), fat; corpulent. **pûi-pháng**, id.

phāng [R. hông, to sew, = col. pāng], a chink; a crevice; a seam in timber; an opening for finding fault or taking advantage of. **khang-phāng**, cracks and crevices; openings for finding flaws, faults, or opportunities (v. khang). **bô-phāng thang-hiâm**, having nothing that can be at all found fault with. **gâu chhē-phāng**, fond of finding fault; good at finding a way to injure another or to make money. **thàn-phāng**, to use an opportunity for evil. **chhn̂g-phāng**, to look out for our own selfish ends. **puh-phāng--chhut-lâi**, to leak out, as a secret. **khoà^{n}-chhut phoà-phāng**, to look out a way so as to get at a secret. **koe-nn̄g ba̍t-ba̍t, to ū-phāng**, in the closest matter (lit. egg) there is some hole. **làng-phāng**, to leave a space, as in writing; to take advantage of an opportunity to get away secretly, *e.g.* to get out of a troublesome affair, or to cheat out of money. **làng-phāng kiâ^{n}-tāng**, to leave a place where there is danger, on some pretext, avoiding the appearance of fear. **sio̍ng-hō-phāng**, taking advantage of a break in the rain (v. sio̍ng). **lī-phāng**, to open into a chink.

chhiú-phāng, the interstices between the fingers. **kha-phāng**, the opening between the legs, or on the inside of the bent knee. **kha tsńg-thâu-á-phāng**, interstices between the toes. **chhùi-khí-phāng**, the interstices between the teeth. **khí-phāng**, id. **soa^{n}-phāng**, a cleft in the hills where a road or stream comes through.

phau, a sort of pumelo. **phin-phau**, a creeping plant with a fruit like a fig, used in medicine, and also making the jelly called ò-giô-tàng.

phau (R. id. = col. pha). **phau-lông** (R.), the scrotum.

phau [R. to throw, = col. pha]. **phau siù-kiû** (R.), to throw the embroidered ball, an ancient custom (v. kiû).

pháu (R. id.), to ride fast; to gallop; sometimes said of travelling fast. **pháu-bé**, to ride a horse fast; to gallop. **pháu-lō**, to travel very fast. **pháu-chiet**, to carry an express message to the emperor from a high mandarin.

pháu lâng-ê-chî^{n}, to swindle people of their money and run off.

phàu [R. cannon], crackers or squibs. **toā-phàu**, a cannon. **hō-phàu**, a signal gun. **tē-lûi hé-phàu**, mines in war. **thien-phàu**, a congreve rocket or shell (s. ulcer). **phàu-tâi**, a fort; a fortification. **phàu-táng**, do., especially low. **phàu-siú**, artillery-men. **phàu-tūi**, a company of artillery-men, especially using gingalls.

pàng-phàu, to set off crackers. **kó-phàu**, a drum-shaped frame full of crackers, used at weddings. **pàng kó-phàu**, to set them off. **liên-phàu**, a string of crackers. **phàu-siâ^{n}**, a very large set of fire-crackers on a pole (v. siâ^{n}).

phàu [R. an ulcer or other skin disease]. **thien-phàu**, a venereal ulcer (s. cannon).

phàu, to infuse in boiling water; to melt (as sugar) in hot water; to make (as arrow-root) by pouring hot water on it. **phàu-tê**, to infuse tea. **phàu-io̍h**, to infuse medicine. **phàu thn̂g-sng**, to melt sugar-candy. **phàu-chiú**, to treat with hot spirits, as some medicines.

phàu (R. pâu), a long warm robe, quilted or lined, or made with skin or fur. **tn̂g-phàu**, id. **phàu-koà**, a long warm robe and the shorter dress worn over it. **phàu-thò**, a long warm robe and the long dress worn over it. **mî^{n}-phàu**, a long quilted dress. **nî^{n}-phàu**, a long warm woollen dress. **phê-phàu**, long dress made with skins or fur. **iû^{n}-ko-phàu**, do., lined with sheep-skins. **bé-tôe-phàu**, warm robe made with cuffs like horse-hoofs. **bóng-phàu**, mandarin's robe embroidered with dragons.

phāu [R. to embrace, = col. phō]. **phāu-ióng--ê**, a child adopted from childhood. **phāu-thâu chhú-chhoàn** (r.), to cover one's head and run away very much ashamed. **phāu-liông-oân,** sort of pill brought from Canton. **phāu-hūn chhiong-thiⁿ,** to harbour deep resentment.

phāu [R. pō, violent; sudden; to strike with the hand, &c.; = col. pə, pə̀, pāu, &c.], to strike the head with the hand.

phauh, fat and plump, as a child. **phauh-phauh,** very plump and good-looking, as child or young boy. **pûi-phauh,** id. **phauh-piau,** id.; also said of man.

phauh [R. phok, extensive; learned]. **ké-lauh-phauh,** ancient; old-fashioned (v. kə́).

pháuh (R. id.), hail, hailstones. **lóh-pháuh,** to hail.

pháuh [R. phàu, phāu, a blister, = col. phā]. **jiét-pháuh,** eruption like small boils on the head in hot weather, esp. on children. **hoat jiét-pháuh,** to have them. **khí-pháuh,** id.

phe (R. phi), (C. phoe), an embryo; an unfinished article or model. **phe-bô,** a model or pattern. **ôe-phe,** shoes shaped but not yet finished. **ôe-tóe-phe,** shoe soles not yet sewed on. **ìn-phe,** bits of marble shaped for seals, but with no characters cut. **pán-phe,** an unfinished coffin. **láng chit-ê-phe,** to make a commencement of a matter.

tsoá-phe, pasteboard. **pè tsoá-phe,** to make pasteboard.

lâng-sn̂g-phe, thin slips of wood used for making a frame (lâng-sn̂g) for cooking by steam.

ti-phe, a pig not fully grown. **ti-phe-á,** id.

phàiⁿ-phe, ill-behaved in youth; giving signs of becoming a bad man. **phái̍ⁿ-kut-phe,** id. **m̄-sī thák-chheh ê-phe,** he is not and will not be a good scholar. **chhát-phe,** a bad boy growing into a thief. **khit-chiáh-phe,** a boy or lad looking like a beggar.

sí-sin-phe, reckless of one's life; daring to do very dangerous things. **hiong-sin-phe,** id. **sam-seng-phe,** ready for quarrels, &c. (v. seng).

phe (C. phoe; T. phö). **phài-phe,** to conjecture beforehand. **bô-phài-phe,** unexpectedly. **bô-phe,** id.

phe-sí, to risk one's life. **phe-miāⁿ,** id. **phe siⁿ-miāⁿ,** id. **phe-siⁿ-miāⁿ thàn,** to work extremely hard for money, as if for one's life. **phe-siⁿ-miāⁿ khùn,** to sleep very very long. **phe-siⁿ-miāⁿ thák,** to study extremely hard. **phe-siⁿ-māⁿ poáh,** to gamble very eagerly till all is lost.

phe (C.) **phe tsúi-phe,** = A. khó tsúi-phi, to throw stones along the water.

phe (C.), = A. phoe, a letter; an official answer. **pâi thâu-phe,** to write notes through a book at the top of the pages.

phe (C.), = A. phoe, to smooth wood with an adze.

phê (R. phî), (C. phôe; Cn. phô), skin; bark; peel; leather; fur. **phê-chháu,** furs used for dresses. **phê-ôe,** leather shoes.

péh-phê (white skin), Malwa opium. **thô-phê,** skin of opium ball (v. thô). **thô-phê** (C. phóeh), clods of surface soil, as in ploughed fields. **thô-phê-thâu,** id. **chhân-thô-phê,** id. **chhiah-phê,** a sort of hard wood.

chióh-phê, a large flat rock. **thiⁿ-tōe-phê,** you know all about heaven and earth! (v. thiⁿ). **chhàn-phê,** the inner leather sole of a shoe. **chheh-phê,** the cover of a book. **pau-phê,** the wrapper of goods or dollars (v. pau). **pién-sit-phê,** a thin raw cake for wrapping up minced meat. **bih-phê,** thin split bamboo made of the outer part of the bamboo. **tîn-phê,** the rind of rattan, the best part. **chhiū-phê,** bark; linen stuffs.

khé-phê, skin that peels off where a wound is healing (v. khé). **chhe-phê,** sort of small eruption, chronic, but worst in the hot season. **hong jiét-phê,** the wind hotter than usual, sign of bad weather.

phê-phê-á kóng, to allude to a matter without giving much explanation; to give only a hint. **kóng phê-phê,** id. **goā-phê,** external; in outward appearance. **cheng-sîn-phê, gōng-āⁿ,** appearing intelligent, but really stupid.

bân-phê, incorrigible; stupidly stubborn. **tsòe o-phê,** to be madly attached to a company of actors (lit. black like a pig).

bīn-phê, the skin of the face. **kāu-bīn-phê,** brazen-faced. **kāu-phê,** id. **bīn-phê khah-kāu siâⁿ-chhiûⁿ,** very brazen-faced (like a city wall). **póh-phê,** thin-skinned; very sensitive to pain, or crying readily when scolded. **bīn-phê khah-póh sìn-tsoá,** very bashful and modest (like letter-paper). **lâu bīn-phê,** to keep one's respectability. **sià lâng--ê bīn-phê,** to affront and bring disgrace upon. **kò-bīn-phê,** to take care of one's character.

phê-hu, skin and flesh (v. hu). **hó-phê-hu,** good condition of body, such that a wound heals easily. **hó phê-bah,** id. **bah-phê,** skin of pork. **phê-mòhⁿ,** the outer cuticle. **chit-têng-phê chit-têng-kut,** skin and bone.

pak-phê, to skin. **lì-phê,** id. **khau-phê,** to scrape off skin, as from potatoes, with knife at a right angle.

phé (C.) **chhùi-phé** (= A. phóe), the cheeks. **kha-phé,** the hips. **kha-chhuiⁿ-phé,** id.

phé (C.) **phé-siàng,** = A. phì-siùⁿ, to talk scandal, &c. **phé-siùⁿ,** id.

phè [R. phà, a veil], (C. phè), a cloth sometimes worn by women like a vail; to hold a little of anything in the corner of one's dress. **phè-á,** a sort of vail. **hoe-phè,** a striped or spotted cloth, used for folding clothes in, or for making up a bundle. **hoa-phè** (C.), id.; also worn on the head by young married women. **chhiú-phè,** sort of kerchief used by women. **chhiú-phè-á,** sort of handkerchief for tying up a bundle, used by men or women. **hien chhiú-phè** (C.), to raise the bride's vail, as the bridegroom does at marriage. **lô-phè,** a kerchief carried by lady in her hand. **âng-lô-phè,** a red kerchief, used as vail for bride at marriage. **tà-phè-á,** to wear a cloth on the head, as in Chang-chew and some other places married women do. **tà-phè-á tè-lâng-tsáu,** to follow a man, as bad woman with a cloth on her head. **phè-á-kun,** a cloth worn over the head, especially by bad women. **chhiáⁿ m̄-kiâⁿ, tà phè-á-kun lâi-jip,** refusing when politely asked, but afterwards running after him to ask to be accepted (fig. from improper characters).

phè--khí-lâi, to lift up things (or keep them from falling), by a cloth spread out, or by the corner of one's dress held up. **phè-mihⁿ,** id. **ēng saⁿ-á-ku phè,** to hold something in the corner of one's dress held up. **phè-thô,** to hold some earth in the corner of one's dress, in order to throw it on the coffin (v. thô).

phè āu-táu, to cut out a man, as from employment or a purchase (v. táu).

phè (same word?), (C. phè), to support the end of a beam, as a stone or piece of brick-work on the top of a mud wall. **îⁿ-phè,** a piece of stone (or bricks) laid on the top of a wall of pounded mud and cement, to support the end of a beam, and keep the wall from splitting; a cross-bar placed under a beam to support it. **phè í^{n}-á,** to support the end of a beam, as with a stone.

phè [R. phèe, to associate; to mate; a fellow], (C. phòe; Cn. phö), to use as a condiment, as with rice, potatoes, or liquor. **mih^{n}-phè** (Cn. mńgh-phö), whatever is eaten along with rice or potatoes. **phè-mih^{n},** to use any such condiment. **phè-pn̄g,** to be used as a condiment with rice. **phè-chiú,** to be eaten as a condiment along with liquor. **tê-phè,** things eaten along with tea. **chiáh-tsoâ, phè hó-huih** (eat serpents with tiger's blood), said of a very wicked and daring man.

phè (C. phɛ̀). **chhì-phè,** a thorn-bush (v. chhì).

phè (C.), = A. phòe. **moâ^{n}-phè,** hemp bark stripped off for making ropes.

phè (C. phòe; Cn. T. phö), a chip or broken bit of stone, pottery, wood, &c. **chhâ-phè,** chips of wood. **chióh-phè,** chips of stone. **oá^{n}-phè,** broken bits of bowls. **kng-phè,** broken bits of jars. **kha^{n}-phè,** id. **chhù-hiā-phè,** broken fragments of tiles, as in ruined houses. **hāu-phia^{n}-phè** (C. hiā-phia^{n}-phòe), id.

kek lí-phè, to think out the proper manner of managing an affair.

phɛ̀ (C.) **phī-phɛ̀-háu,** sound of abundant rain falling.

phē [R. phī, to cover; a coverlet; sign of the passive; = col. pī], (C. phōe; Cn. phö), a coverlet quilted with cotton, which supplies the place both of sheets and blankets, and generally of mattress too, being folded round the person. **phòng-phē,** cotton beaten and made into the shape of a coverlet, and put loosely into a cover, but not fastened with the usual crossed threads. **phē-toa^{n},** cotton cover or case for the coverlet. **phē-jio̍k,** coverlet and mattress. **phē-á jio̍k-á,** do. for dead body.

phē-iāng, a cloth used for carrying a child on the shoulders.

chhu-phē, to spread out the coverlet ready for use.

kah-phē, to cover one's self with it.

phē (C.), = A. phōe, a weed like darnel.

phɛ^{n} (C.), = A. phi^{n} (to divide or pay in small portions, &c.)

phɛ^{n} (C.), = phī^{n}, to make level, &c. (in some phrases).

phɛ̂^{n} (C.), = A. phî^{n}, to make level; to sweep away, as a torrent; to take a short cut, as across a field. **hō͘ lóh kàu phɛ̂^{n}-iû^{n},** rain falling till the whole plain is swimming.

soá^{n}-phɛ̂^{n}, to go about idly or uselessly, *e.g.* wasting time on a number of things that come to nothing, or behaving ill, stealing, and doing mischief, as a bad uncontrolled young fellow; to stray about, as cattle. **lām-sám-phɛ̂^{n},** id.

phɛ̂^{n} (C.), = A. phî^{n}, a surname.

phɛ̂^{n} (C.) **phɛ̂^{n}-ô͘,** = A. phî^{n}-ô͘, the Pescadore Islands.

phɛ̄^{n} (C.) **chhoán-phī^{n}-phɛ̄^{n},** panting very hard; to do a thing carelessly and ill.

phéh (R. boåt), (C. phóeh), foam; froth. **tsúi-phéh,** foam on water. **ám-phéh,** froth of boiling rice-water. **pêh-phéh-noā^{n},** white frothy saliva at the mouth.

phéh, to go about as a poor vagrant or idle rowdy, looking at plays and consorting with low characters. **sì-kòe-phéh,** id.

phéh (C. phóeh). **thô͘-phéh,** clods of earth. **chhân-thô͘-phéh,** id. **chhân-phéh,** id.

phek (R. id.) **phek-gio̍k** (R.), a sort of precious stone. **phek-thô,** a very large sort of peach. **phek-san-giâm,** a temple near Amoy (above Emngkang), where there is a rock that moves.

phek (R. id.) **hó-phek,** amber. **tsu-phek-sán,** a medicine made of pearls and amber.

phek (R. id.) **phek-le̍k,** loud rattling sound of thunder (v. le̍k).

phek [R. to strike; to tap; sort of castanets], an instrument made of bits of wood loosely tied together, used for beating time as an accompaniment to music. **phek-ūi,** the place for beating it in a tune. **hoā^{n}-phek,** the man in a band who beats it. **phah-phek,** to beat it, as an accompaniment to music. **tńg-liâu phah-phek,** to change the rate of a song and strike the "phek." **at-liâu-phek,** to act at proper time and by proper rules in doing anything. **at-liâu at-phek,** id. **àn-liâu-phek,** id.; also, according to the rules of time, &c., in a song.

phek — **phek-chhài,** long turnips cut down and salted so as to make a soft preparation used as a sauce.

phek (R. id.), the animal soul or principle of animal life in man (classifier "tiâu" or "tè"); said to be found for a few days after death in the form of small black things in the bed or ground where a man has died. **hûn-phek,** spirits and souls. **sam-hûn chhit-phek,** the three spirits and seven animal souls which a man has.

lo̍k-phek, very miserable. **chhi^{n}-chhám lo̍k-phek,** id.

phek [R. a sovereign; to rule]. **ōe-phek-siâ,** able to drive away demons, &c., as a charm.

phek (cf. phēng), to try which is the better or superior. **phek-khoà^{n},** to compare two things to see which is the larger, better, &c. **phek-kun,** to play at a game like marbles, as children. **phek bûn-chiu^{n},** to try which is best at writing essays.

pheng (R. id.), to cook in melted fat. **pheng-iû,** id. **gâu pheng-tiāu,** good at cooking.

pheng, to shape and sew together (skins) for a dress, especially with the outside of some other material. **pheng iû^{n}-ko,** to make a dress with sheep-skin in this way. **pheng sím-mih^{n}-bīn,** of what stuff is the outside of this (fur) dress to be made?

pheng [R. to fall, as a mountain, = col. pang]. **tsō-sit san-pheng,** by idleness and eating, business or wealth (lit. mountain) dwindles away. **hiet-pheng** (C. hiet-peng), flow of blood from female organs.

phêng [R. pêng, level; just; balances; = col. pî^{n}, piâ^{n}, &c.], = pêng, to weigh in balances, &c. (A. phêng, = pêng; C. only phêng), (v. pêng).

sù-phêng, plays in the Swatow dialect. **phah sù-phêng-ké,** music with four sorts of instruments at idolatrous rites.

phêng — **io-phêng,** = io-pêng, a pouch or purse worn at the side.

phêng [R. to discuss; to criticize]. **phêng-lūn,** to criticize (generally but not always unfavourably), as conduct or character. **phín-phêng** (R.), to criticize, as men or writings. **kong-phêng,** to discuss a matter together, as a number of persons, in order to end a quarrel. **phoe-phêng,** to criticize, as men or books.

50

phêng [R. name of bird]. **tāi-phêng-chiáu**, an enormous bird, painted on the sterns of junks and by the side of Kwan-yin.

phèng [R. to make an agreement by presents]. **phèng-kim**, money sent at betrothal by bridegroom's parents to the parents of the bride. **phèng-gî**, presents so sent. **phèng-lé**, money and presents so sent. **tēng-phèng**, to fix the agreement of betrothal for daughter. **phèng-chhin**, id. **phèng-tiā^n-tio̍h**, betrothal arranged.

phèng-chhiá^n, to invite a minister, secretary, or teacher to court by presents, as ancient kings did. **phèng-chhiá^n gâu-lâng**, to invite a wise man to take office in that way. **phèng gâu-lâng**, id. **sam-phèng ngó͘-phèng**, such repeated invitations. **sam-phèng ngó͘-phèng, i m̄-lâi, I have asked him over and over, but he won't come.**

phēng (cf. phek). **phēng-khoà^n**, to compare two things to see which is the larger or the better, &c. **pí-phēng**, id. **phēng lí--ê tsō-hoà**, I will try to help you, but with great doubts of success. **phēng lí--ê soe-ōng**, id. (v. ōng). **phēng-hiong**, to put on an appearance as if about to strike or fight, as in violent altercation, or as a beggar knocking the doors, &c. (v. hiong).

phi (R. id.), to spread out, as clothes. **phi-sa^n**, to spread out clothes, as to dry. **phi-chhek**, to spread out rice to dry. **phi-khui**, to spread out, as in the sun. **phi hong-thâu**, to hang up to dry in the wind, as clothes.

phi-hong, sort of cape worn by mandarin ladies. **phi-kien**, sort of shoulder ornament or epaulette worn by mandarin or Kujin. **phi-kah**, Manchoo soldiers (v. kah).

siang-chhiú phi-sien, both hands stretched out in the form of a cross (v. sien). **thán-phi-sin**, turning sidewise so as to get through a narrow passage.

hoâi^n-phi, an inscription written horizontally, as over a door. **í-phi**, a cloth cover for the back of a chair.

phi-í, a reclining chair that draws out.

phi (same word?) **tek-phi**, a flat bamboo frame for sleeping on in hot weather. **tek-phi-í**, a chair or couch with the seat made of bamboo. **mī^n-phi**, a frame for drying boiled vermicelli.

phi — **tsúi-phi**, small flat stones thrown by children to skim along the water; an insect that skims very rapidly along the surface of the water. **phi tsúi-phi** (C. phe tsúi-phe), to throw stones thus. **khó tsúi-phi**, id. **tsúi-phi-á** (C.), a small shallow boat for shallow sandy rivers.

phi [R. a sharp spear]. **chì^n-phi**, an arrow-head.

phi — **ko-phi**, coffee (imitation of the sound). **ko-phi-tê**, coffee, as a beverage.

phi (T.), to scrape or scratch up (sand), as fowls do. **phi-phién** (A.), (v. phién).

phi (T.) **phi-sng**, = A. phi^n-sng, arsenic.

phi (= phih). **ûi^n phi-phi** (C.), very yellow.

phî [R. skin, = col. phê]. **tîn-phî**, prepared orange-peel. **chheng-phê**, a medicine; thick pumelo skin or some such skin. **tē-kut-phî**, a cooling medicine (bark of root of ké-kí), said to affect the kidneys. **ngó͘-ka-phî** (= pî), a yellow liquor from Tien-tsin and the north. **ngó͘-ka-phî-chiú**, id.

sau-phî, to scold by speaking ironically or sarcastically.

hó͘ sú, liû-phî, when a tiger dies he leaves only his skin (fig. of man's reputation). **san-i-bēng pok-siòng, ngó͘-phî**, geomancy, medicine, and the various sorts of divination are known only superficially. **ngó͘-phî ê-tāi-chì**, the things included in these five classes. **ngó͘-phî ê-lâng**, men who practise any of these.

phî (cf. phí), mean; void of self-respect; disreputable in his way of doing business; regardless of his character; low and contemptible; *e.g.* refusing over and over to pay a debt, or living on others and refusing to spend a cash. **kap-lâng-phî**, acting towards others in a mean despicable way without sense of shame. **chin-phî**, very mean and despicable. **chin-chià^n phî**, id. **phî-lién**, having unblushing impudence and effrontery. **phî-lién-bīn**, id. **phî-bīn**, id. (v. bīn). **m̄-tam-su-iá^n phî**, despicably refusing to pay his gambling debts.

phî (R. id.) **phî-koān** (R.), wearied out; quite exhausted.

phí [R. mean, despicable]. **phí-lí**, mean and stingy. **phí-lí-kúi**, a low mean wretch (lit. demon). **siáu-phí-lién**, despicably mean in dealing about the smallest sums. **siáu-phí-gién**, id. **phí-lē** (R.), despicably mean, as conduct. **put-chí khó-phí** (R.), contemptible and despicable, as man.

jîn-tsâi phí-úi, contemptible in appearance, as a little ugly man (v. úi).

phí [R. a scab; a disease of the head], a scab; an incrustation; a thin lamina. **kien-phí**, to become covered with a scab; hard scab formed. **siu-phí**, id. **tì-phí**, id. **tsu-phí**, the scab of small-pox, used for inoculation. **siā-phí**, scabs falling off, as in small-pox. **làu-phí**, id. **lâm-phí**, to pour parched beans on the head of a person just recovering from small-pox (v. lâm).

he-phí, thin bits of plaster peeling off a wall (v. he). **jiō-tháng-phí**, incrustation on urine-jars. **tiá^n-phí**, incrustation on a rice-boiler from boiling rice or other things. **pn̄g-phí**, incrustation of rice on a rice-boiler for a few days. **ko-pa-phí**, do. on a large rice-boiler, as of a junk, for a long time. **ám-phí** (Cn.), scum of rice-water.

tâng-phí, percussion-caps. **seng-khu tn̄g-tâng-phí**, not having even one cash about one. **chî^n-phí**, very thin small bad cash. **chî^n-phí-á**, id. **chit--ê gâi-chî^n-phí to-bô**, have not even one bit of a bad cash. **lê-phí**, the white inner coating of shells like mother-of-pearl (used for ornaments). **lê-phí-tsu**, false pearls made from shells. **an lê-phí**, to inlay with this substance.

chit-phí-á, a very little bit. **chháu-phí**, a small sod of turf (v. chháu).

phí (cf. phi, to stretch). **phí-phak-à^n**, to stretch out one's arms, as to keep one's self from falling.

phì (R. id.) **phì-lūn**, a comparison; to make a supposition; for instance, like as —. **phì-jū**, id. **phì-siù^n**, to talk in a jesting way of another's looks, &c. (v. siù^n).

phī — **phī-phī-chhoán**, to pant hard. **phī-phā-háu**, loud sound of flame in wind (v. phā). **phī-phè-háu** (C.), sound of much rain falling.

phī [R. to cover; sign of passive; = col. pī, phē]. **jîn siēn, phī-jîn-khi: má siēn, phī-jîn-khî**, as a good horse is ridden, so a good kind man is cheated.

phī (R. phi). **phī-sng**, = phi^n-sng, arsenic.

phi^n (R. phien), classifier of essays and such short compositions.

phi^n [R. phien, on the side; partial; selfish; unfair], to cheat; to bully; to act in an overbearing

海上絲綢之路文獻集成　科技與文化編

way; to insult or scold a man who dares not retort; to overreach or get the better of, as in trade or in dividing money. **sa^n-phi^n**, id. **phi^n-khàm**, to overreach or defraud of small sums by overcharging (v. khàm). **niū^n-lâng-phi^n**, very good-tempered in bearing insult or scolding; very easy in money matters, letting others get good bargains out of us, &c. **hō--lâng khah-phi^n--khì**, to let the other get rather more than his due from us, or let him have the upper-hand in scolding, &c.

ū phi^n-thâu, to get the better of a man, as in a dispute or quarrel; to get things very cheap or get large wages; advantageous, as a trade giving good profits. **khah-phi^n-thâu**, getting rather more than one's share. **hō--i khah-phi^n-thâu**, to be somewhat overreached or beaten by him. **bô-phi^n-thâu**, not succeeding in a dispute, lawsuit, or quarrel; not managing to get a thing cheap, &c.

phi^n (C. phɛ^n). **pun-phi^n**, to divide equitably what is not sufficient for all, so that each has some share, though not much; to deal small and serve all. **phi^n-hêng**, to pay by instalments. **ûn-ná-phi^n**, id.

phî^n [R. pêng, level; even; just; = col. pî^n, piâ^n, phiâ^n, &c.], (C. phê^n), to make level, as a piece of ground; to cut away earth, as with spade or hoe, to make it even; to take off a layer from a stone. **phî^n kak-á**, to lay on the clap-boards or laths on the rafters, ready for the tiles. **phî^n-tèng**, to lay them on and nail them down. **phî^n-thô**, to level ground.

thó-phî^n, to collect a number of men to go and beat a man who had beaten us. **koh kap-i-phî^n**, to win back from him what he had gained from us in gambling.

phî^n (R. phêng), (C. phê^n), a surname. **phî^n-tsó**, a very old man of the Shang dynasty, probably called by Confucius "ló-phêng." **phî^n-tsó chiáh poeh-pah-hè**, phî^n-tsó lived 800 years: he is the representative of old age in the pictures called tsâi-tsú-siū.

phî^n (R. phêng), (C. phê^n). **phî^n-ô**, the Pescadore Islands.

phí^n (cf. phí, phiá^n). **chit-phí^n-á**, a small bit, somewhat roundish.

phì^n (R. phièn), a slice; a lamina; a thin plate; classifier of walls, partitions, fixed screens, clouds, padlocks, pieces of glass, and thin extended surfaces. **chit-phì^n-á**, a small flat bit. **âng-tâng-phì^n**, sheets of copper. **hiā-phì^n**, broken bits of tile. **hoā-phì^n** (Cn.), id. **hiā-phì^n-á-chhù**, house made by children of bits of broken tiles.

ôe-phì^n, the side pieces of the uppers of a Chinese shoe. **chit-phì^n-ôe**, one of the slips for the uppers of shoes. **béh-phì^n**, the halves of stocking-legs.

bô-phì^n-thâu, not having a wind such as can be used for sailing on the course, not even by tacking. **chit-phì^n-phâng**, sailing on one tack without shifting sail. **koh-oát chit-phì^n**, make one tack more. **tsāi-phì^n-sái**, to sail easily with wind on quarter with full sails. **khioh tsāi-phì^n**, to shift the sail to the position for so sailing. **sái ngī^n-phì^n**, to sail right on one tack with a strong wind; dogged and immovable in one's course (v. ngī^n).

chhiú-phì^n khah-ngī^n, determined to carry on the feud with no compromise; not afraid to injure people.

phì^n (same word?). **phiah-phì^n**, disposition; temper. **phiah-phì^n hó**, disposition good; forbearing. **phiah-phì^n phái^n**, temper bad.

phì^n (cf. phī^n, phih^n). **phì^n-phì^n-chhoán**, to pant hard.

phī^n (C.) **chhoán phī^n-phē^n**, panting hard; to do a thing very hurriedly or carelessly.

phī^n (Cn.) **phī^n-si-pûi^n**, = A. pī^n-si-pêng, the 120th radical, at the side.

phī^n (R. phi, = col. phī), (T. phi). **phī^n-sng**, arsenic. **phī^n-chhng** (P.), id. **soa^n phī^n-sng** (C.), a poisonous berry, on a shrub about a foot high. **soa^n phī^n-sng-á-chí** (C.), id.

phī^n — **kha-phī^n-liâm**, the shin (v. liâm).

phī^n (R. pit), the nose; to smell; the knob on the end of a carrying pole; the eye of a needle.

phī^n-hoe, to smell flowers. **phī^n-phang**, to smell odours. **ū phī^n-phang**, to get a scent of a matter. **m̄-sái-phī^n**, you need not hope for it. **hó-phī^n-sai**, good at smelling (said in joke). **gâu-phī^n-chē**, you are very knowing! **n̂g-sng-hiā gâu-phī^n-chē**, id. (lit. yellow ants). **n̂g-sng-hiā gâu-phī^n-tsoā**, id.

chiam-phī^n, the eye of a needle. **ôe-phī^n**, the rib or ribs at the point of a Chinese shoe (v. ôe). **chit-phī^n--ê**, shoe with only one rib on the toe. **toa^n-phī^n--ê**, id.

phī^n-bák-chhùi, the features in general. **phái^n-chhùi-phī^n**, foul-mouthed, in language. **phī^n-khang**, the nostrils. **phī^n-khang-kháu**, the apertures of the nostrils. **phī^n-khang-mn̂g**, the hair in the nostrils. **sái phī^n-khang-kńg**, to talk in a nasal displeased tone; to whine discontentedly. **sái phī^n-khang-im**, id. **phī^n-im**, a nasal sound. **phī^n-lok**, the hollow part of the nose. **phī^n-lak**, id. **phī^n-lak-kóng**, id. **phī^n-lok-kóng**, id. **phī^n-kóng**, id. **phī^n-to**, the ridge of the nose when high and sharp. **phī^n-niû^n**, the ridge of the nose. **phī^n-niû^n chih-chih**, nose too flat between the eyes. **phī^n-lêng**, the ridge of the nose. **si^n phī^n-lêng**, to have a polypus in the nose. **phī^n-io**, the bridge of the nose and the part of the ridge near it. **phī^n-io chih-chih**, nose naturally too flat between the eyes (said of women). **phī^n-oa^n**, raised bridge of nose, not usual among Chinese. **phī^n-thâu**, point of nose.

phī^n-tsúi, water or liquid mucus from nose. **phī^n-sái**, hardened mucus from nose. **kāu phī^n-thâm-noā^n**, having much mucus flowing (v. noā^n). **phī^n-hun**, snuff. **phī^n-hiu^n**, id.

lâu-phī^n, running of the nose. **lâu phī^n-tsúi**, id. **tsát-phī^n**, nose stuffed with cold in the head. **sat-phī^n**, id. **sngh-phī^n**, to snuff up the nose inwards (v. sngh). **chhngh-phī^n**, to sniffle, outwards (v. chhngh). **chhèng-phī^n**, to blow the nose. **sàn-phī^n** (Cn.), id. **pûn-phī^n**, to blow through one's nose, in anger. **lek-phī^n**, to wrinkle the nose, in displeasure. **ng-phī^n**, to hold the nose, as to avoid a bad smell. **chiù-phī^n**, nose eaten away with disease. **lap-phī^n**, having lost the nose by disease.

péh-phī^n, a sort of small wild quadruped.

phia^n — **ka-chiah-phia^n**, the part of the back between the shoulders. **phia^n-liau**, the middle part of an animal (as pig or sheep), as cut up for food, including the ribs; the whole animal is cut into three parts, of which this is the middle one. **phia^n-liâu-bah**, the flesh on the ribs of an animal. **phia^n-liâu-kut**, the ribs. **phia^n-ki-kut**, id.

thoa-phia^n, to drag itself along, as a wounded animal, esp. on one side. **phah kàu-hō--lí thoa-phia^n**, I will beat you till you can hardly move!

phia^n (cf. hia^n). **hāu-phia^n-phè**, broken bits of tiles, as among ruins. **hiā-phia^n-phòe** (C.), id.

phia^n [R. peng, a weapon; a warrior; = col. pia^n].

lûi-phia^n, a demon of thunder. thien-phia^n, a demon of heaven. tōe-phia^n, a demon of earth. sam-phia^n, these three demons. hoān--tio̍h sam-phia^n, to be killed by them. khit-phia^n phah--tio̍h, said of a man of violent temper getting suddenly angry. phien-phia^n-sîn, a certain very malicious demon. phin-phia^n-sîn, id. phin-phia^n-jit, a very unlucky day. phin-phia^n-sî, a very unlucky time. phien-phia^n-sî sái-tit-kè, pù bōe-thè, if these very unlucky days be passed without injury, your wealth will never fail.

phia^n — kông-phia^n-phia^n, in a tremendous hurry and flurry.

phia^n (C.), a sort of rain-coat, made of leaves, worn by farmers. moa^n-phia^n, = A. moa^n-phiâ^n, the 53d radical.

phia^n (Cn.), = seng-bō, a sort of flat-topped cap worn by idols and by actors. tì-phia^n, to wear it.

phia^n (Cn.), to throw at one, as a stone (cf. pia^n, to throw).

phiâ^n [R. pêng, a shed; a stage; an awning; = col. pî^n], one slope of a roof. chit-phiâ^n, id. moa^n-phiâ^n, an open shed with a roof of only one slope; the 53d radical (v. moa^n).

phiâ^n [R. pêng, phêng, level or gently sloping ground], a natural sloping bank of sea or river, or at base of hill. soa^n-phiâ^n, the sloping base of a hill. hái-phiâ^n, the shore left dry at low water. thô-phiâ^n, a muddy sea-beach, or broad muddy bank of river at low tide. chio̍h-thâu-phiâ^n, a beach full of stones. chio̍h-phiâ^n, a gently sloping large rock with little or no soil on it.

sam-phiâ^n, a village S.W. from Chang-chew where there is a very famous temple. sam-phiâ^n tsó-su, the idol worshipped there.

phiâ^n [R. pêng, level; even; just; = col. pî^n, piâ^n, phî^n, &c.], to win again after having lost, as in gambling. phah-phiâ^n, id., in fighting or gambling. phah chit-ê-phiâ^n, id. tò-phiâ^n, to win after losing in gambling. khit--i tò-phiâ^n, to be beaten by him in gambling after having first beat him; also fig. of striking. phiâ^n--tò-lâi, to win what had been lost in gambling; also (T.), said of other things in general. phiâ^n-tò-tn̂g, do.; also said of fighting. poa̍h-phiâ^n--khí-lâi, to win back what was lost in gambling. phiâ^n--khí-lâi, id.; also fig. of making great gains in trade after great losses. tsòe--chit-ē phiâ^n, to settle a long account with a man (by a thorough beating) who had often beaten, cheated, oppressed, or domineered over us.

phiá^n, a large thick slice or cut, as of meat or of a cake; a thick flattish piece. kui-phiá^n, a whole thick slice; over a considerable surface, as a skin disease. he-phiá^n, large thick pieces of plaster coming off a wall. chháu-phiá^n, a sod of turf; also straw beaten very small and made into round cakes (v. chháu).

phiá^n (P.) bâ-phiá^n, a harlot (said in scolding). bâ-phiá^n-chhì, a very thorny weed that catches the dress.

phiah [R. phek, on the side; partial; depraved], to go to the side; to get out of the way; to avoid by going out of the way. phiah--teh, id. phien-phiah, out of the way, lonely, as place (v. phien). oan-koe phiah-hāng, crooked and unfrequented streets and lanes. tô-phiah, to get out of the way and avoid. phiah-pī, to get away and conceal one's self for a short time. phiah hē-lâng-kè, to step aside to let some one pass. phiah-khi-tiàm, to get out of harm's way by hiding one's self.

phiah (R. phek), disposition; temper. sèng-phiah, id. phiah-sèng, id. phiah-phì^n, id. (v. phì^n).

phiah-chèng, any disease to which any one is specially constantly liable. phái^n-phiah, troublesome in temper, *e.g.* unwilling to pay debts; having a constitutional tendency to some disease, *e.g.* to have boils each summer. hó-phiah, good-tempered. ū khì-phiah, having a peculiar temper. chia̍h-phiah, temper very dogged, obstinate, and crotchety. ke̍h-phiah, obstinate; perverse in disposition. kiū^n-phiah, fond of crossing others' wishes. koāi-phiah, perverse. koài-phiah, of a strange temper. ku-koài-phiah, id. áu-phiah, obstinate. chip-phiah, id. ngī^n-phiah, id. sio̍h-phiah, superstitious.

phia̍h (R. phek), a brick. chhì^n-phia̍h, slightly fired bricks. se̍k-phia̍h, well-burned bricks. e-phia̍h, id. phia̍h-tn̄g, a brick broken across. phia̍h-pêng, a brick broken into two halves lengthwise. tsng phia̍h, floor-tiles and bricks.

khoe-phia̍h, small flat-bottomed river boat with a mast.

phia̍h — sí kui-phia̍h, dead in great numbers, as in an epidemic.

phia̍h, to crucify. phia̍h-chha̍t, to crucify a robber or pirate.

phia̍h, measles. chhut-phia̍h, to have measles.

phiak, to uncoil itself suddenly with a spring, as a snake. phiak--lo̍h-lâi, to fall down suddenly, as a lizard or centipede from the roof.

phia̍k (cf. pho̍k). phia̍k-phia̍k-chhéng, to palpitate. phia̍k-phia̍k-toā^n, id. phia̍k-phia̍k-thiàu, to leap up and down frantically, as a sorcerer. sim-koa^n phia̍k-phia̍k, heart beating fast with fear or anxiety.

phia̍k (cf. pia̍k), sound, as of a bamboo struck. phah-kàu phia̍k-phia̍k-háu, to beat, making the blows of the rod ring on the skin. phih-phih phia̍k-phia̍k, sound as of heavy drops of rain on the roof.

phia̍k — phia̍k-he, to dash lime on a wall.

phian, phián, phiàn, better phien, phién, phièn (*q.v.*)

phiang (cf. piang). phin-phin phiang-phiang, the sound of a vibrating string. phōng-phiang, the sound of beating cotton with a bow.

phiàng (cf. piàng, phiāng, phōng). phiàng-phiàng-háu, to roar loud, as waves.

phiàng (cf. phòng, phàng). pûi-phiàng, fat; corpulent. pûi-phiàng-phiàng, id.

phiàng (C.) ûi^n-phiàng-phiàng, very yellow.

phiāng [R. pāng? a club; cf. piāng]. phiāng-ké, a long thick bamboo tube with a skin tied over the one end, and the other open; beaten by quacks, beggars, &c.

phiāng-phiāng-háu, sound of it.

phiāng (esp. T.) phiāng-phiāng-háu (= A. phiàng), sound of waves.

phiat, phia̍t, better phiet, phie̍t (*q.v.*)

phiau [R. piau, a branch; a spear; a signal; beautiful; = col. pio]. phiau-thâu, a label with name or sign of maker, often wrapped round, or pasted on a thing bought; it often states the nature or good qualities, or gives directions for use. hong-phiau, id.

phiau [R. sort of chrysalis; preparation of cuttle-fish]. **hái-phiau-siau**, a medicine made from the cuttle-fish.

phiau [R. tossed on the waves]. **phiau-lâi phiau-khì**, tossed about at mercy of winds and waves, as disabled vessel. **phiau sa^n-sì-jit**, tossed on the sea for three or four days, as disabled vessel after a storm. **phiau-liû**, carried away by a flood, as houses or timber, &c. **hē-tsúi phiau-liû--khì**, id.

phiau [R. blown by the wind; easy in manner; sometimes interchanged with the previous word]. **phiau-ièt**, animated, intelligent, unconstrained, or self-confident in manner. **phiau-phiet**, id. (v. phiet).

phiâu (R. id.), to commit fornication with a harlot; whoredom. **phiâu-piáu**, to commit whoredom. **phiâu-kheh**, a whoremonger. **toā-phiâu-kheh**, a rich whoremonger. **phiâu tó ím**, whoredom, gambling, and drunkenness. **tsáp-ê phiâu, káu-ê liáu**, of ten whoremongers nine come to poverty.

phien [R. at the side; selfish; unfair; = col. phi^n]. **phien-pi^n**, at the side. **phien-káng**, smaller ports; side ports; uncommon dollars from the smaller South American states. **phien-tsó phien-iū**, going to one side or another of the road (v. iū).

phien-phiah, secluded; unfrequented; secret; out of the way, as a place. **phien-phiah-jī**, a character rarely used. **phien-phiah-ōe**, words or phrases seldom used, often intended to make the hearer consider the meaning carefully.

phien-pâng, a concubine or wife of second rank. **phien-keng**, imperial concubine. **chhú-phien**, to take a concubine.

phien-su, partial; unfair; unjust; prejudiced. **phien-thán**, partial and unfair. **phien-tsòe**, to do something that is improper. **phien-kiò**, to give an appellation somewhat lower than should be, *e.g.* calling father "án-chek." **phien-ài** (R.), partial in affection, as parents.

phien-phien-beh, to wish and desire obstinately, as dangerous or hurtful things; to wish all the more because refused (C. thien, in this paragraph). **phien-beh**, id. **phien-phien-á m̄**, doggedly determined to oppose or refuse what is proposed. **lí-beh, goá phien-á m̄**, you are willing, but I will not on any account consent to it.

phien, = phin (C. thien). **phien-phia^n-sîn**, a very wicked demon (v. phia^n).

phien [R. classifier of essays, &c., = col. phi^n]. **si-phien** (X.), the Book of Psalms.

phién (cf. phún), to scratch on the ground, as fowl with bill, feet, and feathers. **phién-thô**, do. in earth. **phién-soa**, do. in sand. **phién-khui**, to stir or move about, as rice to see its quality, or as a heap of grass, &c., searching for something lost. **phién-khui-khoà^n**, id., as rice. **toà--teh phi-phién**, said of a man managing property for its absent owner, and making rather too free with the money; or of a man in charge of a large house, and using it as he pleases. **iau-koe phién piah-kha** (hungry hen scratching at the foot of the wall), a poor man trying to find some way of getting money from another.

phièn (R. id., = col. phì^n), a thin slice or lamina; classifier of clouds or regions of country; a stretch of a number of level fields. **kui-phièn**, a whole slice or thin piece; a whole region. **chhiet-phièn**, to cut into slices. **lê-phièn**, a slice of a sort of dried shell-fish.

chit-phièn-chhân, a stretch of numerous level irrigated fields. **toā-phièn-thó**, an extensive region of country about level. **hit-chit-phièn**, that region of country.

phièn-toa^n, a visiting card, or plain card (v. toa^n). **miâ^n-phièn**, a visiting card. **sió-phièn**, a blank red card, ready to be written upon. **thô-âng-phièn**, a large slip of red paper, for writing a notice or placard.

peng-phièn, Baroos camphor; camphor in powder or small crystals. **hông-phièn-ko**, a sort of sweet cake. **hûn-phièn-ko**, id.

a-phièn, opium. **a-phièn-thô**, crude opium. **a-phièn-thô-phê**, envelope of an opium-ball. **a-phièn-ko**, opium boiled and prepared ready for smoking. **a-phièn-hun**, id. **a-phièn-phā**, a small pellet of opium (v. phā). **a-phièn-sái**, opium refuse, used for mixing up again with opium. **a-phièn-hun-chhe**, opium-pipe. **a-phièn-kóng**, id., said in joke. **a-phièn-kúi**, a miserable confirmed opium-smoker. **a-phièn-sien**, id. **a-phièn-giàn**, craving or horrors of opium, from not getting the usual dose. **a-phièn-kut**, emaciated condition from opium-smoking. **a-phièn-hun-bīn**, cadaverous face of confirmed smoker. **chiàh a-phièn**, to smoke opium. **tiâu a-phièn**, unable to break off opium-smoking, except by medicine. **a-phièn chiàh-tiâu**, id.

phièn (R. id.), to deceive. **phah-phièn**, id. **khi-phièn** (r.), id. **phièn--lâng siet--lâng**, to cheat or deceive people. **háng-phièn**, to threaten and deceive. **háng-phièn-sùt**, id. **koái-phièn**, to swindle; to kidnap by alluring away. **phièn-chhiá^n hāi-gō**, said of breaking a promise (lit. starving a guest). **phièn-kúi**, do you think you can thus deceive me? (as you could a ghost). **teh-phièn-kúi**, id. **kúi-á phièn kúi-ông**, said of an inferior trying to deceive his superior, but quite unable. **moâ^n-phièn**, to deceive. **moâ^n-thi^n phièn-tōe**, to deceive Heaven and Earth. **moâ^n-thi^n phièn-lâng**, to deceive Heaven and men. **moâ^n-pē phièn-bú**, to deceive parents. **bêng-moâ^n àm-phièn**, to deceive and cheat both secretly and openly.

phiet [R. lame; feet turned outwards]. **phiet-kha**, the feet naturally turned outwards. **kha phiet-khui**, the feet much turned outwards, as in walking. **kiâ^n-lō phiet-phiet**, walking with the feet much turned outwards. **phiet-phiet oat-oat**, walking with feet turned out, and swaying about in a slow self-important manner.

phiet (R. id., = col. phoat), a down-stroke slanting to the left. **bú--jī bô-chit-phiet**, the character "bú" (military) has no slanting down-stroke, meaning that military mandarins are generally illiterate.

nī^n-phiet-chhiu, mustaches. **lí-phiet-chhiu**, id. **n̄g-phiet chit-tuh**, mustaches and a beard (said in joke).

kap-i phiet-chhe, to be at variance or not on good terms with him.

phiet — **phiet--chit-ē**, to give a slap with the hand, as on a boy's skin, so as to make the blow ring loud.

phiet — **giet--lâng phiet--lâng**, to scold severely, violently, or contemptuously, so as to make one quite ashamed (v. giet).

phiet — **phiau-phiet**, having an animated or intelligent appearance; easy and unconstrained in manner, as man who has confidence in his own ability and knowledge of the matter.

phiet (T. phiet; C. poâ^n), an earthen plate; a

plateful. **chit-phiet-chhài**, a plateful of condiments. **sì-phiet, chit-oáⁿ-thng**, four plates and a bowl of soup, as usual in feasts.

phiét (T.), = A. phiet, a plate.

phiét (R. id.), to flap the wings. **phiét-sit**, id. **phiét-phiét**, sound of flying or of wings flapping. **phiét-phiét-háu**, id.

phih (C.), word used in vile scolding (to commit impurity), = kàn.

phih — **phih-phih phiák-phiák**, sound as of heavy drops of rain.

phih (C. phi). **ñg-phih-phih**, very yellow, as face.

phihⁿ (cf. phì; C. phiⁿ). **phihⁿ-phihⁿ-chhoán**, to pant hard.

phin (= phien). **phin-phiaⁿ-sîn**, a very malicious demon (v. phiaⁿ).

phin — **phin-phin phiang-phiang**, sound of a vibrating string.

phin [R. phin? cf. pêng, the apple]. **phin-phau**, a sort of creeper with a fruit like a fig (v. phau).

phin (C.) **phin-pho**, = A. phun-pho, in great poverty.

phîn (R. phêng). **phîn-phông**, sound of waves or of water violently moved (v. phông).

phîn, sloping, off the perpendicular; leaning to one side; to stagger. **phîn-phîn-phîn**, very much off the perpendicular; holding his head to the side in a proud overbearing way, as a young fellow. **oai phîn-phîn**, much off the perpendicular. **khi-phîn**, leaning to one side; having one shoulder higher than the other, or head to one side; leaning over, as wall; having one shoulder high, as mountain. **thán-phîn**, to turn one's self sidewise so as to get through a narrow passage or to pass another in a narrow lane. **thán-phîn-sin**, id. **phîn-lâi phîn-khì**, to stagger, as when drunk. **phîn--chit-ē**, to stagger, as from a blow.

phín, to make an agreement; to promise formally. **phín-bêng**, id. **goá kā-lí-phín**, I promise you.

phín, to boast. **phín-phóng**, id. **phín-béng**, to boast of power or influence; to be overbearing. **phín béng-lám**, id. **phín-gâu**, to boast of ability. **phín pún-sū**, id. **phín-phah**, to be very overbearing, tyrannical, and unjust; always threatening to beat people. **phín ū-kong-lô**, to boast of merit.

phín [R. sort; kind; rank], rank of mandarins. **phín-chit**, official rank. **phín-kip**, titular rank. **kék-phín**, the very highest mandarin rank. **it-phín**, of the first general rank. **chiàⁿ-it-phín**, of the very highest grade of rank. **chiông-it-phín**, of the lower division of the first rank. **sì-phín**, of the fourth rank (&c.) **it-phín-lâm**, very bright light purplish blue.

phín-hēng, conduct; behaviour. **jîn-phín**, id. **phín-sèng**, character and disposition, natural or acquired. **phín-keh** (r.), general form of body. **phín-phêng** (R.), to criticize, as men or writings.

phín-liāu, materials. **toā-phín-oáⁿ**, a large sort of bowl.

phín — **phín-siau**, a flute. **phín-á**, id. **phín-ná**, id. **phín-ná-mėhⁿ**, the bamboo tongue of a flute. **phín-koán**, a flute and three guitars (v. koán).

phiô (R. phiâu), a floating weed like duck-weed, eaten by ducks. **tsúi-phû-phiô**, id. **hō-phiô**, to gather duckweed with a strainer.

phiô [R. phiâu, a cup made of a gourd], a sort of ladle or large cup for lading out things. **iâ-phiô**, a split cocoa-nut used as a ladle. **hāu-phiô**, ladle made from the shell of the king-crab. **chhâ-phiô**, a wooden ladle. **thih-phiô**, an iron ladle.

phiò [R. to pierce; light; nimble], light, as baggage or things; light and nimble in walking; slim and light in body, as man; lightly-built or lightly-laden, as a boat. **phû-phiò**, not to be depended on, because too impulsive, incautious, or forgetful; *e.g.* promising or doing things without consideration. **phû-phiò ê-ōe**, words not to be depended on, *e.g.* such as the speaker will readily forget, spoken without consideration, or without examining whether true or false. **kun-ki phû-phiò**, horoscope bad, as of child that will be unhealthy or unlucky.

phiò (R. phiàu), to bleach. **phiò-péh**, id. **phiò-pè**, to bleach cotton cloth. **phiò-péh-pè**, id. **kè-phiò**, to be bleached. **phiò-pháng**, bleached grass-cloth. **phiò-lō**, to bleach by laying out in the dew at night. **phiò-hong phiò-lō**, bleached by the wind and dew.

phiò-phâng, to splash water on a bamboo sail so as to keep it in good order.

phiò (R. phiàu), a warrant; a summons; said also of a pawn-ticket and some similar tickets. **chhut-phiò**, to issue a warrant. **pâi-phiò**, a warrant. **tsu-toaⁿ pâi-phiò**, warrants in either form, either in red in mandarin's own hand, or in black with official stamp. **pùih phiò-bé**, said of hangers-on about yamuns, who go along with constables, pretending to be such.

tǹg-phiò, a pawn-ticket. **phah-phiò**, to make out a pawn-ticket. **sit-phiò**, to lose a pawn-ticket. **pò-sit-phiò**, to announce the loss of a pawn-ticket. **chhut bí-phiò**, to give a ticket for extra pay in lieu of rations. **chîⁿ-phiò**, a note for so many cash; a sort of bank-note. **kìⁿ-phiò niáⁿ-gûn**, to get money on presenting such a note, as for soldiers' pay. **chiū-phiò niáⁿ-gûn**, id.

phit (R. id.), an entire roll or piece of cloth; classifier of whole pieces of cloth. **chit-phit-pè**, one whole piece of cotton cloth. **pè-phit**, piece goods; cotton in entire pieces. **phit-thâu siuⁿ-chho**, these piece goods are too coarse. **bōe phit-thâu**, to sell only goods in entire pieces, as a shop. **phit-thâu-kau**, a wholesale hong that deals only in a number of pieces of piece goods at once.

phit [R. one of a pair; to unite; classifier for a single horse]. **phit-phòe**, to unite in a pair, as man and wife, or as two things that make a pair (v. phòe). **chit-phit-bé**, one horse. **toaⁿ-sin phit-bé**, a man who has no relations alive or near him.

phit (T.) **phit-lô**, = A. pit-lô, a sort of small bird.

phng (R. hoan), (C. phuiⁿ), an adze; to smooth with an adze.

phǹg — **phǹg-phǹg-háu**, sound of the feathers of an arrow as it leaves the bow.

phńgh, sound made by a snake (esp. cobra) when just going to dart on its prey. **phńgh-phńgh-háu**, id.; said also of a man acting in a very imperious overbearing way.

pho [R. a wave]. **pho-nñg**, waves. **pho-lōng** (R.), id. **pêng-tē, khí hong-pho**, to cause great trouble or distress by false accusation when all was quiet and right. **phun-pho**, travelling about to great distances for a livelihood. **phun-phun pho-pho**, id. **phin-pho** (C.), in great poverty and misery. **tsúi-pho-hûn**, wavy lines of several colours at the foot of the dress of some mandarins or of actors. **ūi tsúi-pho-hûn**, to draw lines representing waves on dress, or on other places.

lêng-pho, Ning-po.

pho-lô-bit, the jack-fruit, grown at the Straits, &c.

pho (P.), a shrub with a fruit like a rasp, also called toā-pún hé-m̄. **chhì-pho**, the small trailing rasp, = A. hé-m̄, or distinguished as sió-pún hé-m̄.

pho [R. a mound or bank]. **soa-pho**, a sandy beach (Cn. soa-pe).

pì^{n} pho-pho, level, as a level road, or as sea without waves. **toā-lō͘, pì^{n} pho-pho**, the main road is level (said of good behaviour). **chit-ē-loáh, pì^{n} pho-pho**, if he take it in hand it will be put straight at once, though it could not be done by another.

sit-lát-pho, Singapore.

phó [R. slightly; somewhat; = col. phé]. **phó-liok-á**, to a slight degree; to a small extent. **phó-phó-á**, id. **phó-phó-bat**, to know slightly. **phó-phó ōe-hiáu-tit**, to understand somewhat.

phò (cf. phà^{n}), soft, light, and well raised, as bread; soft, juicy, and very pleasant to eat, as sugar-cane; soft and edible, as the bones of some fish. **phò-phò**, id. **thô͘ phò-phò**, the soil is easily worked. **phò-chióh** (porous stone), pumice-stone. **bīn-pau phò**, the bread is light and well raised. **péh-phò-ké**, a sort of white well-raised cake.

phò [R. to break, = col. phoà]. **phò-hiet**, to injure the blood by diminishing its quantity, as some eatables are supposed to do.

phō (R. phāu), to embrace; to clasp in the arms; to carry in the arms, as a child. **sa^{n}-phō**, to embrace each other. **phō--ê**, a son adopted from childhood. **phō gín-ná**, to carry a child in the arms. **thau-phō gín-ná**, to kidnap a child. **phō kha-thâu-u**, to put the arms round one's own knees, as when sitting with legs much bent.

phō-ún, to keep to safe investments in business.

phō-kò, man who acts in a lawsuit as the representative of a solitary woman, or of an old man or Kujin, or other who cannot properly be beaten in court.

huih phō-sim, the blood coming to the heart so strongly as to cause disease or death. **phō-sim-khùi**, feeling of pain at heart, or of confusion of thought from great fear or anxiety (v. khùi). **phō-sim-pêng**, the 61st radical written at the side.

phō [R. pe, a class, as of words under one radical; a set, as of books, &c.], a set, as of volumes; a clump of bushes, or thick tuft of grass. **kui-phō**, a whole set, as of volumes of a book; in a large bunch or tuft, as grass, &c., from one root, or in one tuft. **chit-phō thâu-mn̂g**, a large tuft of hair, such as the Chinese wear. **chit-phō chhùi-chhiu**, beard and whiskers all very thick, making one mass. **chit-phō chháu-á**, a large bunch of grass or weeds growing. **chit-phō chheh**, a complete set of a book, having all the volumes.

phe (R. id.), to spread out level; to lay even, as tiles or pavement; to pave; to make, as a bridge; (bed and bedding). **phe-pì^{n}**, to lay quite level and even, as tiles, &c. **phe-siet**, to put in order, as furniture. **phe-mî^{n}**, to spread out cotton in order to make it into quilted articles; to quilt with cotton. **phe-joán**, to paste or glue on the feathers called "joán" on female head-dress. **phe gê-pâi**, to lay down dominoes, as in gambling.

phe-bīn, to put the best articles on the top (as of a basket of fruit), either to look well, or for deceit. **phe-bīn-than**, putting on the appearance of diligence or goodness when observed.

phe-pâi, to set things all in nice order; to treat with much respect, or pay attentions to, as by fine talk, flattery, presents, or doing services. **kā--lâng phe-pâi**, to treat people so. **gâu phe-pâi**, fond of paying great attentions to people, or even flattering and fawning on them.

phe-kài, mats and coverlet, bedding used in travelling. **phe-pang**, boards of which a tressel-bed is made. **phe-chî^{n}**, money paid for bed in an inn. **chhn̂g-phe**, bed and bedding. **tâng-phe**, using one bed; a bed-fellow. **phah-phe**, to make ready a bed, as for a guest or new-comer. **phah tōe-phe**, to spread mats, &c., on the ground for sleeping on.

phe-tsng, to lay a tiled floor. **phe-chióh**, to pave with stone. **phe-iú^{n}**, to put on the thin under-tiles of a roof. **phe-kiô**, to make a bridge.

phe [R. hu, bran; husk; refuse; = col. khe]. **béh-phe**, wheat bran. **thâu-phe**, scurf of the head.

phe [R. pe, a plain]. **hn̂g-phe**, dry fields on hilly ground in general.

phe — **chhùi phe**, appetite bad, as from slight illness, or bad taste in the mouth.

phe (better phê). **phe-sat**, a Buddhist idol (v. phê).

phê [R. hû, to lift up], to lift with both hands put below, as a table, or such heavy thing; to raise up, as a door difficult to open. **tàu-phê**, more than one raising a heavy thing with the hands. **phê-khoà^{n}**, to try the weight of a thing by raising it on both hands. **phê--khí-lâi**, to lift up a little, as a table or large press, or one leg of it; to raise a little, as a door that catches in opening. **phê-mn̂g**, to lift up a door thus in order to open it. **phê-toh**, to lift up or move a table by hands below it. **phê-siu^{n}**, to lift up (or move a short distance) a heavy box by hands below it. **phê-kha**, to lay hold of a man's leg in order to throw him down.

phê-thá^{n}, to flatter and fawn upon. **phê-sáng**, id. (v. sáng).

phê (R. id.) **phê-sat**, a Buddhist idol (v. sat). **phê-thê**, a Buddhisatwa; a certain class of Buddhist idols.

phê (T. pō). **phê-oá**, a small sort of crab (cf. kiā-pe).

phê [R. pê, the Acorus]. **phê-thoân**, a round cushion for kneeling on in worship. **chháu-phê-thoân**, one made of straw. **tsang-phê-thoân**, one made of palm fibre.

phé (R. phó). **phé-liok-á**, slightly (v. liok).

phé [R. a garden; a place for recreation]. **siā-phé** (R.), archery ground near the temple of the god of war.

phé [R. a list; a book of lessons]. **tsók-phé**, a genealogical table; a family register. **kî-phé**, a book of chess lessons. **ūi-phé**, a book of drawing lessons. **hoā-phé**, id. **khek-phé**, a song-book with tunes. **khîm-phé**, a book of lessons for the harp. **liām-phé**, to repeat the notes of a tune by name.

phé [R. universal; everywhere]. **phé-thi^{n}-ē**, all under heaven; all the world.

phé-tô, the sacred island Poo-too, near Chusan (v. tô).

phé-si, to make offerings to the dead, esp. in the 7th month. **phé-tō͘**, great Buddhist rites for the dead, usually for very great numbers at once. **chē phé-tō͘**, to perform these rites. **phé-tō͘-kong**, = tāi-sū-iâ, the head of the demons of these rites: some say a collective name for the whole of the ghosts then worshipped. **toā-phé**, the greater rites. **sió-phé**, the smaller rites. **gín-ná-phé**, rites for the dead, for which subscriptions are made or collected by young boys.

phè [R. a shop; altered from "phe," to spread out], a ward in a town; a measure of ten lí; on the great roads, esp. in Cn., a league of about three miles; in the country parts, esp. in C., often four miles or more.

tsóng-phè, a ship's cook.

phè-hē, a warehouse or large shop; a firm; the master of a store or warehouse; a merchant. **hâng-kau phè-hē**, shops and warehouses.

phè-hūn, a ward or small division of a town (esp. in Cn.), about the size of a "pó," generally smaller than a "kéng." **phè-chhiah** (Cn.), rowdies.

phè-tsām, a resting-place (generally with a shop or eating-house) at the end of a stage of ten lí. **koaⁿ-phè**, the mandarin league of about three miles on the great roads. **té-phè**, a short league, about that length. **tn̂g-phè**, a long league, about four miles or more, as on the country roads. **bîn-phè**, id. **peh-siⁿ-phè**, id. **soaⁿ-phè**, id. **kúi-phè**, how many tens of lí. **kúi-phè-lē**, id. **phè-jī**, twelve lí. **n̄ng-phè it**, twenty-one lí.

phè (T.) **sek-phè-si**, = A. sok-pò-si, an attendant of the idol Sêng-hông (v. si).

phē [R. a book for accounts, sales, copies, registers, &c.] **siàu-phē**, an account-book. **siàu-phē-gán**, the title pasted outside. **tsóng-phē**, a ledger. **liû-súi-phē**, a scroll-book for entering sales, &c., just as made (v. súi). **hè-phē**, a book (in large establishments) in which goods are entered when bought or sold. **chhng-kháu-phē**, a book (in a vessel) recording what is shipped and delivered. **tsûn-kì-phē**, a book into which accounts are copied for reference if needed. **chhau-phoe-phē**, a letter-book.

iên-phē, a subscription-list. **jī-phē**, a copy-book. **tùi-phē**, a book of antithetic words and sentences. **sǹg-poâⁿ-phē**, a book of arithmetic by the abacus. **hoe-phē**, a book of patterns for embroidery, painting, or such ornamental work. **miâⁿ chiūⁿ koaⁿ-phē**, one's name put on the mandarin's books, as a party in a case.

phē— **chià-phē**, a place where a sugar-mill is worked. **thn̂g-phē**, place where sugar is refined, sometimes also including a sugar-mill.

phö (T.), = A. phe (to conjecture beforehand). **saiⁿ-phö**, id.

phö (T. Cn.), = A. phê, skin.

phö (T.) **thê-phö**, clods of earth.

phö (T. Cn.), = A. phè, a chip.

phö (T. Cn.), = A. phē, a coverlet; also (T.), a cloth for strapping a child on the back. **phö-á** (T.), that cloth.

phoa (C.), = A. pha, to cast a net or anchor, &c.

phoà [R. phoat, to dash water, = col. phoah]. **phoà-noāⁿ**, shamelessly urgent, as beggar. **chhāi-phoà-noāⁿ**, id., or as child or poor relative (v. chhāi). **sái-phoà-noāⁿ** (T.), id.

phoà— **chhàu-jiō-phoà**, smell of urine on clothes, beds, &c.

phoà (R. phò), to break, to tear; (to spend); broken, tattered, having holes or rents. **phoà-phoà**, quite broken; falling into decay; broken down, as an uncared-for house. **phoà-sàm**, greatly decayed or worn out. **phoà-noāⁿ**, tattered and ragged, as dress (v. noāⁿ), (a. shamelessly urgent). **phoà-sńg**, broken down; dilapidated. **phoà-siùⁿ**, maimed or greatly deformed. **phoà-pīⁿ**, unwell; sick; a serious flaw. **phoà-pāi**, all squandered or lost; wasted away, as family property; ruined and bankrupt. **khit--i phoà-pāi**, the whole affair is ruined by him, *e.g.* by his unlucky horoscope, or by his letting out a secret or doing some very improper thing.

ū phoà-phah, to have some fault or blemish, or at least good ground for suspicion. **bô-chit-tiám-á phoà-phah**, nothing whatever that can be found fault with. **khoàⁿ-chhut phoà-phah**, to find out a secret fault. **phoà-tiàⁿ**, secret let out so that the affair is quite ruined. **phoà-khang**, id. **phoà-phāng**, id. **khoàⁿ-chhut phoà-phāng**, to find a way of getting at a secret.

khoàⁿ-phoà, to see through, as an affair (v. khoàⁿ). **chhut-phoà**, to become known, as a secret. **kóng-phoà**, to tell the particulars. **söh-phoà** (Cn.), id. **tiám-phoà**, to explain something hard to understand, as a difficult passage; to give warning about a man or plan supposed by the other to be safe, while really very dangerous. **phoà-àn**, distinguishing the truth of a case by minute examination (v. àn). **phoà-tôe**, to give the meaning of the text in an essay (v. tôe).

phoà-pit, to go to school for the first time. **phoà-thé**, to break a bit of the plaster of a house to be repaired; done on a lucky day, and the work left to be done when convenient.

phoà-tsâm, to speak beforehand against another's plan so as to prevent its accomplishment.

phoà-khui, to break open. **phoà-khui sim-koaⁿ kóng**, to speak out one's whole mind. **phoà-sim**, id. **goá phoà-sim kā-lí-kóng**, I tell you all my heart. **phoà-pak**, to rip open the belly; to tell one's whole mind.

phoà-táⁿ, to lose one's courage; very much terrified. **phoà-gêh**, very unfavourable horoscope because the month disagrees with the year (v. gêh). **phoà-ke**, to injure the fortune of the house, as bride having bad horoscope (v. ke). **phoà-tsâi**, to waste wealth (v. tsâi). **phoà-chîⁿ**, to spend money in great quantities; to waste or lose money. **phoà-chîⁿ iah-miāⁿ**, to lose money but get long life (v. iah). **phoà-hùi**, to waste, as property.

phoà-kaⁿ, to break open a prison. **phoà-siâⁿ**, to take a city. **phoà-hiáh**, to wound one's own forehead, as a beggar. **phoà-chhâ**, to split wood. **phoà-bih**, to split up slips of bamboo. **phoà-ô**, to gather oysters.

phoà-phāng, a bit of a rainbow seen only at the end. **phoà-saⁿ**, ragged clothes. **tsúi lâu phoà-pè** (water floats away the tattered cloth), said of a man careless of matters intrusted to him. **phoà-kó kiù-gêh** (a broken drum may save the moon), don't throw away a broken article, it can be of some use.

tsûn phoà, shipwreck. **phoà-chhéhⁿ**, broken and harsh, as voice. **thâu phoà, hī ùih**, head and ears cut and wounded.

phah-phoà, to break. **kòng-phoà**, to break by a blow. **kòng-lòng-phoà**, id. **siak-phoà**, to break by dashing on the ground. **piak-phoà**, break by cracking, as a pot, &c. &c.

kau-phoà, a tonal mark.

phoaⁿ [R. phoan, water in which rice has been washed, = col. phun], a surname.

phoaⁿ (phoâⁿ? R. hoân, a fence). **phoaⁿ-khè**, the treasury of the provincial treasurer.

phoâⁿ (C. Cn.), = A. poâⁿ, to climb over.

phoàⁿ (R. phoàn), to give sentence or decision, as in a civil case about disputed property or terms of agreement about managing it. **phoàⁿ-toàn**, to give sentence. **phoàⁿ-àn**, id. **sím-phoàⁿ** (r.), id. **kong-phoàⁿ**, to make public decision, esp. as arbiter. **phoàⁿ hē--i**, to decide that it belongs or be assigned to him. **phoàⁿ kui sím-mih-lâng**, to decide to which party the property disputed belongs, as arbiter or judge. **phoàⁿ tióh-pê--i**, decide that he is to make reparation. **phoàⁿ-háp, bô phoàⁿ-khui**, in a dispute between man and wife, it should be decided so as to avoid separating them.

phoàⁿ-koaⁿ, civil and military assistants of the idol Sêng-hông; also used at the Tang-gák. **bûn-phoàⁿ**, the civil one. **bú-phoàⁿ**, the military one. **phoàⁿ-koaⁿ kip-sài**, both the civil and military attendants.

phoàⁿ [R. hoàn, to sell], to buy out of a wholesale store at a cheap rate, as pedlars and small shop-keepers do. **phoàⁿ-mihⁿ-khi-bōe**, to buy things very cheap in order to sell them at a profit.

phoāⁿ (R. phoān), to keep company with; to walk along with. **pôe-phoāⁿ**, id., as sitting or drinking together. **saⁿ-phoāⁿ**, to keep company together. **tsòe-phoāⁿ**, to be a companion. **tâng-phoāⁿ**, a companion; an equal. **hó-ê-phoāⁿ**, a good and useful companion. **bô-phoāⁿ**, without a companion. **ū-phoāⁿ**, to have a companion or associate. **ū chîⁿ-phoāⁿ**, to have good cash put along with it, as a bad cash that could not otherwise have been used.

saⁿ-phoāⁿ kiâⁿ, to walk together, as any one. **phoāⁿ-kiâⁿ**, to convey a bride to her future home, as a company of six or a dozen young men do. **phoāⁿ-pâng**, an old matron accompanying the bride to her new home, to assist her in receiving visitors and various ceremonies. **phoāⁿ-chē** (C.), = tiàu-tsoá, to call on a family performing the rites for the dead, and make offerings with them.

phoāⁿ-pau, ornamental purses worn at the girdle (v. pau). **tiám báng-hun, phoāⁿ-táⁿ**, to keep up one's spirits by getting a companion (v. báng). **phoāⁿ-chhiú**, taking something in the hand, just that it may not be empty, but without any special purpose. **phoāⁿ-chhiú ê-mih**, something thus taken in the hand, as a fan or tobacco-pipe. **phoāⁿ-chhiú bóng-kiáh**, just take it in your hand, as a stick. **phoāⁿ-toâⁿ**, to arrange ornamental things so as to look well together, as on a table or as before a shrine; to do something just as it happens to be in our way (v. toâⁿ). **hó-hī-chhâu phoāⁿ phûn-kéng** (a small plant round the roots of a pot-flower), said of a man joining others, though he might well be dispensed with.

phoah [R. phoat, to dash water; active], to dash or splash water about; to come in large drops on one or into a place, as rain or splashed water. **phoah-jip**, to be dashed in, as rain or waves. **phoah-tâm**, to wet or moisten by water splashing in, &c. **phoah-tsúi**, to dash or splash water about. **tsúi phoah-lòh-tōe** (water spilt on the ground), the thing is done now (or gone wrong), and cannot be helped or altered; words once spoken or deeds once done cannot be taken back. **tsúi phoah-lòh-tōe, oh siu-khí** (or "lân siu-tit-khí"), id.

phoah-iâm, to throw up salt water into the salt-pans. **phoah-chhân**, to scatter manure (esp. liquid) over fields.

phoah [R. phoat, a knife for cutting grass]. **phoah-chháu** (Cn.), to smooth away grass, roots, and a little earth, from the borders of fields. **phoah chhân-hoāⁿ** (Cn.), id.

phoáh (cf. phoân). **phoân-phoáh**, to treat with polite and obsequious attentions.

phoáh [R. poát, to pull, = col. poáh, pùih], to stretch out cloth with the hands while roughly measuring or examining it.

phoáh-tháng (C.), = poáh-tháng, a bucket for drawing water. **chit-phoáh-tsúi** (C.), a bucketful of water from a well.

phoáh, to throw loosely over one's shoulders, as a long cloth (kha-kun) or scarf; to lay loosely over a railing or on the back of a chair, as clothes; to hang, as a long cushion, on the back of a chair. **phoáh-lok--teh**, to lay thus on a railing, &c., as clothes to dry. **âng-lîn phoáh-kah**, having a red scarf thrown over the shoulders and crossed on the breast, as a new-made graduate; said also of the two long pieces of red cloth used on the sedan at a marriage (given respectively by the bride and bridegroom), which are a perquisite of the go-between.

phoáh (cf. phoân). **phoáh-kha**, to cross the legs, either the one over the other, or over another man's. **kha saⁿ-phoáh**, one leg stretched out and laid over the other foot; or legs of two men crossed, *e.g.* lying on the ground. **saⁿ-phoáh**, crossed or interlaced, as legs crossed, or as arms on each other's shoulders. **saⁿ-phoáh-chhiú**, crossing each other's arms, as over shoulders. **saⁿ-phoáh-keng**, arms on each other's shoulders, counted a vulgar attitude. **saⁿ-phoáh-sià**, image of two idols represented as if wrestling with each other (T. saⁿ-poáh-kong).

phoân [R. poân, a plate; to calculate; to hold friendly intercourse; = col. poâⁿ; cf. phoáh], to fawn upon, as a man of wealth or influence. **phoân-phoáh**, to treat with polite, obsequious attention. **phoân-soân**, to associate intimately and constantly, as friends. **tāi-phoân siáu-phoân**, licentious jesting, dalliance or illicit intercourse with women or bad companions. **phoân tsa-bó**, to be too intimate with women, but not necessarily implying criminal intercourse. **phoân tsú-tē**, to make associates of wealthy, idle, fast young fellows, so as to get money, food, or amusement, at their expense. **phoân thâu-ke**, to fawn upon and flatter an employer or patron.

phoân-kó, the first man, he who shaped heaven and earth into their present form.

phoân-thúi, cross-legged, as when sitting. **thiáp-phoân**, id. **kha thiáp-phoân**, id. **phoân-thúi teh-chē**, to sit with the legs drawn up and crossed on the seat. **thiáp-phoân teh-chē**, id. (=kha thiáp-khoân). **phoân-thúi-í**, a large stool.

phoàn [R. a semicircular pool at the Confucian temple, &c.] **phoàn-kiong**, the whole inclosure of the Confucian temple grounds in a Foo city. **jip-phoàn**, to become a Sew-tsai graduate.

phoat [R. to dash or splash, as water; lively; = col. phoah]. **hoát-phoat**, active and lively, as person; easy, graceful, and flowing, as written characters.

phoat-chiēn, fond of scolding and quarrelling, as woman. **sāi-phoat**, violent and shameless in demanding, as beggar, &c. (v. sāi). **siet-phoat**, id.; quarrelling in an unwomanly way, as a woman. **sat-phoat**, id. **sat-phoat-hū**, a railing, scolding, odious woman. **sat-phoat ê tsa-bó**, id. **sat-phoat lī-hāi**, do., as woman.

51

phoat (R. phiet), = phiet, a down-stroke to the left. **chit-phoat,** one such stroke. **nn̄g-phoat-chhiu,** moustaches. **phoat-chhe,** to make a diagonal cross; at variance.

phoe [R. phe, the official written answer to petitions, &c.; to criticize; a written comment or gloss; a document like a lease], (C. phe), a letter; an epistle; to write the official answer on a petition or complaint, as the mandarin does; to write the answer to an inquiry by divination; the mandarin's written answer to a complaint, &c.; to write a note, comment, or addition to a deed. **phoe-gú** (C. phe-gí), the answer of the mandarin to a petition or complaint, posted up at the gate of the yamun. **phoe tsún,** favourable answer to the petition. **phoe m̄-tsún,** refusal of it. **phoe pok,** answer unfavourable, or finding fault. **bē-phoe** (C. bōe-phe), answer not yet issued. **phoe-tsn̄g,** to write the answer on a complaint. **phoe-àn,** id. **tsu-phoe,** an order from the emperor.

phoe-bêng, to write an additional clause or explanation on a deed. **phoe tī-khòe-bé,** id., at the end of the deed. **phoe-phêng,** to criticize, as man's character or conduct, or as books or essays.

tiēn-phoe, a document given by the tenant of house or land to the owner as an acknowledgment of his ownership and proof of conditions of lease. **tāiⁿ-phoe** (T.), id. **tūiⁿ-phoe** (Cn.), id.

khó toā-pang-phoe, to be first on the list of the new Sew-tsai graduates, so as to become a lím-seng at once.

phoe-sìn (r.), a letter. **phoe-sìn óng-lâi,** correspondence on both sides. **phoe-tsat,** a letter; models of letters. **phoe-kheh,** a man who collects letters (as abroad, or for going abroad), and carries them for a small charge. **phoe-lông,** an envelope. **phoe-tē** (r.), id. **chit-tiuⁿ-phoe,** one letter. **siá-phoe,** to write a letter. **hê-phoe** (C. hôe-phe), to answer a letter. **kià-phoe,** to send a letter. **hong-phoe,** to seal a letter. **thiah-phoe,** to open a letter. **khoàⁿ-phoe,** to read a letter silently. **koáⁿ-phoe,** to be very busy getting a letter ready for an opportunity. **tsáu-phoe,** to be a letter-carrier or courier (tsáu-phoe ê-lâng).

phoe (C.), = A. phe, to conjecture beforehand; to risk, as life. **pān-phoe,** to conjecture or expect beforehand (v. pān).

phoe (C.) **tsoá-phoe,** = A. tsoá-phe, pasteboard.

phoe (C.), = A. phe, an unfinished article. **sí-lâng-phoe,** a man so sick that he is just ready to die; a useless fellow who might as well die.

phoe [R. phi? phe?], (C. phe), to cut horizontally; to cut off a thin slice; to smooth away, as wood with an adze. **phoe tsòe-nn̄g-pêng,** to slice into two slices. **phoe-phoe tsóeh-tsóeh,** may you be sliced up and minced small!

phôe (C.), = A. phê, skin; bark.

phóe (C. phé; T. Cn. phúi). **chhùi-phóe,** the cheek. **sièn chhùi-phóe,** to slap on the cheek with the palm. **koat chhùi-phóe,** id. **phah chhùi-phóe,** to strike the cheek with the hand or a piece of wood.

kha-chhng-phóe, the hip. **chē chit-phóe,** to sit on one hip.

oai-phóe, having one side (or one cheek) projecting more than the other, either originally or from an accident; *e.g.* as an article originally made with the two sides different. **oai chit-phóe.** id. **khi-phóe,** id.

phòe (C.), = A. phùi, to spit.

phòe (C.), = A. phè, a chip.

phòe (C. phè; Cn. T. phùi). **moâⁿ-phòe,** hemp-bark stripped off ready to be torn up into shreds.

chit-phòe lô-hē, one leaf of the aloe. **lô-hē chit-phòe,** id.

phòe [R. to associate; to mate; a fellow], (also, C., = A. phè, to be eaten along with, as a condiment). **saⁿ-phòe,** to make a suitable pair; to fit well together, as two things; to be betrothed or become man and wife. **siong-phòe,** fitting or agreeing well together, as colours, or as a set of two tables, or as a couch and its foot-stool, &c. **sù-phòe,** duly proportioned; suitably mixed. **kha-chhiú sù-phòe,** limbs well-proportioned. **phòe kun-sîn,** to mix certain medicines in proper proportions. **phòe-kah tú-hó,** articles (as dress) agreeing well together, and suitable to one's station. **chiàu-phòe,** mixed in proper proportions. **chiàu-phòe-tah,** id.; also, agreeing or fitting well, as articles of furniture or of dress. **ngé-hêng phòe-tah,** the five elements duly mixed in the horoscope or constitution.

phòe-hióng, to share in receiving worship and offerings, as the tablet of an inferior spirit placed at the side of the chief tablet.

phòe-tsûn, to be sent (as goods or troops) by a vessel that is going at any rate, not belonging to nor chartered by the sender. **i phòe goá-ê-hè,** he sends his goods by my vessel. **phòe-hè-toaⁿ,** a bill of lading. **phòe tsúi-lāi,** to lend money at very high interest to persons trading abroad.

phòe-chhin, to settle a marriage contract. **phòe-hàp,** betrothed or joined in marriage. **goân-phòe,** the first legal wife married by a man. **phòe-tùi,** to be man and wife (v. tùi).

phit-phòe, joined in a pair by betrothal or marriage, or as two things set down to correspond and making a suitable pair; when said of *persons* it is only of betrothal or marriage. **bô-phit-phòe,** unequally paired, as man and wife of very different age.

hun-phòe (C.), to give in marriage, as one's daughter or secondary wife (from "hun," marriage).

hun-phòe (from "hun," to divide), to allot or apportion, as soldiers to stations, or as salt to shops. **phòe hō-i-kò,** to allot to him to take care of, *e.g.* horse to soldier. **phòe-iâm,** to require a person (esp. shop that makes salted condiments) or region to buy so much salt at a fixed price from a certain government store whether they wish it or not.

mihⁿ-phòe (C.), = A. mihⁿ-phè, anything eaten along with rice or potatoes (v. phè).

phōe (C.), = A. phē, a quilted coverlet. **thien-tē-phōe,** mattress and coverlet for a corpse.

phōe (R. pāi), (C. phē), a weed like darnel or bastard wheat.

phóeh (C.), = A. phéh, foam; froth.

phóeh (C.), = A. phéh, phê. **chhân-thâu-phóeh,** clods of earth. **chhân-thô-phóeh,** id. **chhân-phóeh,** id. **thô-phóeh,** id.

phoh (R. phok), refuse from distillation, infusion, or similar process. **tāu-sī-phoh,** salted and pickled pease, after soy has been made from them, broken down small. **tsau-phoh,** refuse from brewing or distillation. **iû-phoh,** the browned residue from a mass of fat fried down, counted good eating. **iòh-phoh,** solid refuse of medicine that has had an infusion taken from it. **tê-phoh,** used tea-leaves. **tê-sim-phoh,** id.

phoh [R. phok, bark; unwrought wood; plain and

海上絲綢之路文獻集成 科技與文化編

simple; = col. phak]. **chhe-phoh**, naturally rough, big, or coarse-looking (opp. chheng-siù). **phoh-sit**, simple, quiet, and plain in dress, &c.; not fond of display.

chià-phoh, sugar-cane from which all the juice has been pressed out (some give this phrase to the former word).

phóh — **phóh-á**, a sort of tree. **phóh-á-hióh**, leaves used as sand-paper.

phok (R. id., = col. phoh, phak). **phok-sit**, straightforward; honest; simple and plain in tastes and manners. **phok-sò**, quiet, simple, and plain, as dress, or as man not fond of gaudy things.

phok [R. extensive; learned; to play a game]. **phok-hák**, learned; erudite.

té-phok, gambling.

phok — **phok-á**, a tree with small green flowers in bunches.

phok (cf. phòng). **phok--chhut-lâi**, to project, as part of a wall. **phok--khí-lâi**, to rise in large blisters, as lime on a wall bulging out and ready to fall, or as ill-pasted paper. **phok-phok**, id. **phok-kóng**, small bubbles or blisters formed on wall or on pasted paper.

phok (R. id., = col. phak). **phok-siau**, = phak-siau, purgative salts; sulphate of soda.

phok — **phok-phok**, sound as of a wooden box struck. **phok-phok-háu**, id.

phók (cf. pók, pùh), sound as of a fruit falling from a tree, or of a lizard falling from the ceiling. **phók--chit-ē**, do.; or sound of a pop-gun. **phók-á**, a child's pop-gun for paper pellets.

phah-phók, to make a noise by clapping hands. **phah phók-phók**, id.

phók-phók-chhéng, to palpitate. **phók-phók-toāⁿ**, id. **phók-phók-thiàu**, id., &c. (v. thiàu). **phók-phók-tiô**, to dance with emotion, as with rage or delight.

phông [R. bông, dark, = col. hông]. **àm-phông**, = àm-hông, very dark, as room or lamp.

phông [R. hông, a flame; flaming]. **hé-iām phông-phông**, fire blazing brightly.

phông (cf. phiàng, phiāng). **phông--chit-ē**, sound, as of a stone falling into a well. **phîn-phông**, sound of waves, or of water splashing. **phîn-phông-háu**, sound of waves, &c. **phah phîn-phông**, to make a noise by beating water, as man learning to swim, or as child amusing itself.

phóng — **tîn-phóng**, a flat piece of rattan wicker-work, as for the flat part of a couch or bed. **tîn-phóng-í**, a rattan-bottomed chair.

phóng [R. hóng; cf. hōng, phâng], to take up in the two hands together, as water, meal, &c. **chit-phóng**, as much as the two hands put together can hold: Scotch, "gowpen." **moáⁿ-phóng**, id. **kàu-moáⁿ-phóng**, id.

phóng (cf. phōng, pōng, phòng). **im phóng-phóng**, water rising very high; full and overflowing.

eng phóng-phóng, dust flying in clouds. **tīⁿ phóng-phóng** (T.), very crowded, as people.

phóng — **phín-phóng**, to boast.

phòng — **phòng--tióh**, to meet with unexpectedly. **saⁿ-phòng--tióh**, suddenly meeting, as two men. **khit--i phòng--tióh**, to meet with him when it is very unpleasant, *e.g.* as a man against whom we are plotting, or as one's master when doing some bad thing. **phòng--tióh i**, to meet him unexpectedly, either according to or against one's will; to get scolded by him just because he was bad-tempered when we met him, without our fault. **phòng-teng**, to provoke our superior's displeasure by some act (v. teng, "a nail"). **khit-i-phòng**, id.

kap-i-phòng, to make a venture in trade along with him; to ask a favour from him with but small hope of getting it. **phòng-tsō-hoà**, to make a venture (v. hoà). **phòng lí--ê tsō-hoà**, I will try to help you, but doubt of success. **sam-kiok-phòng**, sort of gambling with cards.

phòng [R. id., = col. phàng, phiàng; cf. phok, hàng], convex; embossed; to swell out; puffed out; swollen, as a corpse; to make an overcharge. **phòng-thap**, convex and concave. **phòng--khì**, to project; to jut out. **tò-phòng--chhut-lâi**, to project beyond the line, as a house in a street, &c. **saⁿ phòng-phòng**, clothes hanging clumsily about one. **piáⁿ phòng-phòng**, cakes well raised.

pûi-phòng, = pûi-phàng, corpulent. **phòng-phòng-toā**, children growing rapidly without illness. **phòng-lin**, grown fat on milk, as baby.

phòng-phā, to become blistered. **phòng-kóng**, rising in blisters or bubbles, as ill-pasted paper, or as lime on wall. **phòng-hong**, belly swollen, not severe. **pak-tó phòng-phòng**, belly large, either naturally or from illness. **n̂g-chéng-phòng**, dropsical swelling.

phòng-sim, pieces of silver flat on one side, and round on the other, each about ten taels. **phòng-hún**, powder for the face, in round cakes or balls. **phòng-té**, an embossed panel. **phòng-phē**, a coverlet of loose beaten cotton (v. phē).

phòng-kè (C. phòng-kòe), lady's head-dress of peculiar form. **soe phòng-thâu**, to dress one's hair so.

phòng-kè, price charged more than the real price. **kóng phòng-kè**, to ask such a price, expecting to get it by deceit. **phòng joā-tsōe-chíⁿ**, how many cash overcharged? **khui phòng-siàu**, to put down intentionally a larger sum than the real sum. **khui-khi-phòng**, id. **phòng-siàu**, id. **khui phòng-toaⁿ**, id. **ke phòng-tāng**, to charge more than the real weight. **sim-koaⁿ phòng toā-bú-ê**, heart almost bursting with grief; greatly elated at good news, and expecting far more than the news justify; very covetous, asking far more than the proper price. **sim-koaⁿ phòng joā-toā**, covetously asking far too much.

phòng (cf. phōng, pōng). **iām phòng-phòng**, fire blazing up, as of wood.

phōng (= pōng). **phōng-song**, loose and bulky, as parcel or dress (v. song).

phōng — **phōng-phōng**, sound, as of a leather box when struck. **phōng-phōng-háu**, to sound so, or as sound of belly distended with wind when struck. **phōng-phiang**, sound of beating cotton with a bow.

phōng — **phōng-phōng-siⁿ**, breeding abundantly, as men or animals.

phōng [R. phông, dust flying]. **eng phōng-phōng**, dust flying in clouds. **phōng-phōng eng**, id. **ien phōng-phōng-chhèng**, steam rushing out in great quantities. **phōng-phōng hun**, smoke coming out in clouds. **hun phōng-phōng**, id.

hé-chih phōng-phōng-tóh, fire blazing up.

phu (cf. pu, hu), to blow with the mouth, so as to cool a thing, or to make fire blaze up.

phû (R. hû). **phû-iông-hoe,** the tree mallow.

phû (R. pô), (C. pô). **phû-tô,** the grape; the vine (v. tô).

phû (Cn.) **phû-lî,** = hô-lî, a fox.

phû (R. hû), to float; able to move or float freely, as a vessel that has just weighed anchor, or as something that formerly could not be moved; to appear on the skin, as veins, or as some diseases; in full relief, as carving; weak and weary, as eyes or legs; bad, as horoscope.

phû-phû, careless in manner of doing business; not to be depended on, as one who readily forgets his promises. **phû-phiò,** id. (v. phiò). **phû-phû iô-iô,** walking in a swaggering way. **phû--ê miâⁿ-siaⁿ,** empty frame. **khah-phû,** rather careless; not deep in the water, as a gentle stroke of the oar, &c. &c. **poàⁿ-lám-phû,** hanging up a matter without giving a definite answer or settlement. **óh poàⁿ-lám-phû,** to learn only half well.

phû-sū, an island. **phû-chióh,** a rock loose on the surface (opp. tiâm--ê). **khek-phû,** to cut characters in relief. **méhⁿ phû,** the pulse in such a state that it is felt at a touch. **chhiⁿ-kun phû,** veins appearing on the skin. **im-chek-hûn phû-chiūⁿ-bīn,** lines showing benevolence appearing on the face, omen of good luck. **chhut-tsu bē-phû** (C.), smallpox not able to form the pustules fully, very dangerous form.

thun-thô phû-tîm, understanding to say just as much as is suitable (v. tîm).

bák-chiu phû, eyes looking very wearied or drunk. **kha phû,** legs weak and unable to stand, as from sickness (esp. a convalescent), or from liquor. **kun-ki phû,** horoscope bad, as of a child fated to be unhealthy or unfortunate. **kun-ki phû-phiò,** id.

phû-chîⁿ, a round flat socket for a lamp wick, either floating or supported on a stand. **phû-thâng,** a buoy. **phû-iû,** floating in oil or melted fat, as in cooking.

pàng-phû, to put out a boat so far that it will not get aground at low tide. **kiāu hē-i-phû,** prize up with a lever till it starts and moves. **tiáⁿ-kám phû,** the lid of the rice boiler moving in boiling (said of a very heavy sort of usury), (v. tiáⁿ). **kha-chhng thê-phû,** to make a slight movement, as if rising from one's seat, as in welcoming some one coming in.

phû-ku, to live at a place for a short time. **phû-ki** (C.), id.

phû chit--ê báu-miâⁿ, to put a name on the books of a sub-office in a yamun for protection (v. báu).

phú (T. puh). **thô-phú,** a gray or dark-coloured wingless insect that crawls on the ground, breeding in damp places. **tô-phú,** id. **thô-phú-á,** id.

phú — **siⁿ-phú,** to become slightly mouldy. **chhiūⁿ-phú,** id. **chhàu-phú-bī,** musty taste.

phú (cf. bū). **bák-chiu phú-phú,** eyes not seeing clearly (not so bad as "hoe"), as from old age, illness, or liquor; or only half open, as when just half awake. **bák-chiu beh-phú beh-phú,** eyes getting dim, as of old man.

phú — **phú-sek,** grayish. **thiⁿ phú-kng,** dawn. **phú-á-kng,** id. **phú-phú kng,** id. **phah-phú-kng,** id. **thiⁿ phú-phú, á-bē kng,** the very earliest and faintest dawn.

phū, to boil up, as when beginning to boil over. **phū--chhut-lâi,** to boil over. **phū--khí-lâi,** to boil and bubble up, as boiling rice.

phū-phū-ien, steam coming out in large quantities (cf. phōng). **phū-phū eng,** dust or powdered lime flying all about.

phū, noise of birds flying away. **phū--khì-lah,** the birds are flown!

phū (cf. phuh). **phū-phū-chhoán,** to pant and gasp for breath.

phuh (cf. phū, bū), to puff out, as smoke; to spurt or blow out from the mouth, as water; to blow in by a tube (as a medicinal powder), as into the ear, nose, or throat. **phuh--jip-khì,** to blow in thus, as a medicine. **phuh-ióh-hún,** to blow in a medicinal powder in this way. **phuh soa-ióh,** to blow a powder (by a tube) into another's nostrils for cure of cholera or colic.

phuh hun-chhe, to puff out tobacco smoke from the mouth in short puffs. **phuh chhiⁿ-hun,** to puff out the smoke of raw tobacco. **phuh-hiet-kák,** to blow away (the smoke) without swallowing it.

khì kàu phuh-phuh-thè (T.), to pant and blow with rage.

phúh [R. pók, thin; weak; = col. póh, púh]. **chiáⁿ-phúh-phúh,** very insipid.

phúh — **phàⁿ-phúh,** appearing fat and strong, but really weak; apparently large, but hollow within. **hàm-phúh,** dropsical swelling.

siaⁿ phúh-phúh, sound dull, as of a bad dollar or of lead when struck.

phúh — **chit-phúh-sái,** a lump of excrement.

phúi (Cn. T.), = A. phóe (the cheek, the hip, &c.)

phùi (R. phì), passing of wind. **chhàu-phùi,** id. **pàng-phùi,** to pass wind. **pàng-káu-phùi** (lit. like a dog's), I am not afraid of your threats (vulg.)

phùi (C. phòe), to spit; to scold very violently and contemptuously. **phùi-thâm,** to spit up phlegm. **phùi-huih,** to spit blood (v. huih). **phùi-âng,** id. **phùi-noāⁿ,** to spit. **phùi péh-noāⁿ,** white saliva about the mouth, as about to die. **phùi i-ê-noāⁿ,** to spit while speaking ill of him, a very great insult. **noāⁿ phùi-kàu-bīn, ka-kī chhit,** if he spit on our face we wipe it off (said of overcoming by patience and good temper). **phùi-bīn** (scolding phrase), mean, niggardly, shameless fellow; quite regardless of character. **phùi-bīn-lâng,** a man who for a little gain will do any shameful thing or submit to any indignity, being utterly careless of his character. **kā--i phùi--khì,** scold him violently and drive him away. **hē-i-phùi,** to be scolded very violently by him (by a superior) so as to be quite put to shame. **kù-i-phùi, ū sím-mihⁿ iàu-kín,** let him spit (and scold), it is of no consequence.

phùi (Cn. T.), = A. phòe, bark (as of hemp) stripped off.

phūi (T.) **jiō-phūi,** = Cn. jiō-pūi, a sort of stinking insect.

phūi (T.) **ám-phūi,** = ám-pūi, coagulated scum of rice-water.

phuiⁿ (C.), = A. phng, an adze; to smooth with an adze. **thán-tó teh-phuiⁿ,** to smooth horizontally with an adze.

phùiⁿ (C.), to ebb, as tide. **tsúi phùiⁿ,** ebb-tide. **phùiⁿ-chhut tńg-jip,** ebb and flood.

phun [R. phùn, to run away]. **phun-pho,** travelling about in search of employment (v. pho).

phun (R. phoan, = col. phoaⁿ), water in which rice has been washed. **bí-phun,** id. **sóe-bí-phun,** id. **sng-phun,** id., become sour by standing. **phun-ám,**

rice-water mixed with the water in which rice was washed. **phun-tsô,** a trough for such swill for pigs to drink.

phûn — **khê-phûn,** at variance, as two persons.

phûn [R. poân, a plate or dish, = col. poâⁿ, phoân]. **pîⁿ-pò-phûn,** paying merely the expenses, or very little more, as trade, either regular trade or a venture.

phûn (R. id.), a basin; a stoneware pot for flowers. **bīn-phûn,** a basin of earthenware or metal. **tâng-bīn-phûn,** a brass basin. **hoe-phûn,** a fine earthenware pot for flowers. **chit-phûn-hoe,** one containing flowers or a flower. **phûn-kéng,** the arrangement of flowers and flower-pots so as to look well (v. kéng).

lîm-phûn, to be in labour, as woman.

sio hé-phûn, to burn large heaps of fuel on 1.15 for people to leap through. **thiàu-hé-phûn,** to leap through these fires. **hì-phûn,** sort of plays acted for the dead, with figures of pig and monkey. **phah hì-phûn,** to have them acted. **poaⁿ hì-phûn,** id.

hó-phûn-kháu, generally successful in gambling. **chiáh phah-phûn,** to smoke only a little opium; not yet inveterate.

phún (cf. phién, phùn), to throw about earth or sand, as fowls or children. **phún-thô,** id.

phún--tsáu, to struggle and burst away after having been caught. **phún-khui--khì,** id.

phah-phún, to waste or spoil things by careless use; to struggle to get off, as man or fish; to flap the wings (as fowl) to throw off water or dirt. **phah-phún-ēng,** to use lavishly, as money; to spend lavishly. **lām-sám phah-phún,** id.

sái-phún (Cn.), to behave in an overbearing manner.

phùn [R. to run]. **phùn--tsáu,** to run away and escape. **tsáu phùn-phùn,** to run very quickly.

phùn (T. phut). **sang phùn-phùn,** well-cooked and mealy, as potatoes, &c.

phùn (cf. phún). **hoa-phùn,** making one's self big and self-important, as by dress, words, or bearing. **kek hoa-phùn** (esp. Cn.), to put on such an appearance.

phùn [R. to snort or sneeze; to spurt water], (cf. phut, phū), to splash up or out; to sprinkle; to spatter. **phùn-chhut,** to spark out, as water or sparks. **phùn-hō͘,** wet with some drops of rain. **phùn-tióh-hō͘,** id. **phùn-tsúi,** to water or wet in small quantities or a few drops. **tsúi-phùn,** an instrument like the rose of a watering-can with holes in it. **phùn-tháng,** a bucket for watering, made with a long bamboo spout.

kâm-huih phùn-thiⁿ (to spit blood towards heaven), daring to tell great lies, esp. accusing falsely of great crimes.

phùn-tiám, to splash with water or dirt; to get slightly wet with rain blown in; to make a small present. **kap--i phùn-tiám,** to make him a small present. **phùn-kim-tiám,** to spot over with gilt spots, as in painting, or as ornamental paper. **phùn-hō͘-tiám,** to get spotted with rain.

phut, to cut with sword or knife; to prune, as branches. **phut--sí,** to kill by a sword-cut. **phut chhiū-ki,** to cut off branches. **chiàⁿ-chhák tò-phut,** stabbing and cutting in all directions, as in close conflict; said also of an unskilful workman spoiling and wasting his material. **lām-sám-phut,** to cut at random, as with sword or knife, &c.

phut — **phut-phut-thiàu,** to leap about, as for joy, or as a child; to leap, as a flea. **phut-phut-tiô,** to leap about, as in rage, or as child urgently asking something.

phut (cf. phún, phùn). **súi phut-phut,** gaudily dressed. **kàu-hiah-phut,** how gaudily dressed! **chhēng--khì chin-phut,** to dress very gaudily. **chin-phut,** very gaudy, as dress. **káⁿ-phut,** spending far too much money on gaudy dress.

phut (R. id.) **phang phut-phut,** very fragrant.

phut (T.) **sang phut-phut** (= A. phùn), well cooked and mealy.

S.

sa (R. sand, = col. soa), (C. sɛ). **bān-lí tiông-sa,** the Prata shoals. **ngó͘-tiâu-sa,** five dangerous sand-banks between Shanghai and Shantung. **chiūⁿ-sa,** to come to that part when sailing north. **lòh-sa,** to get south of these banks when coming south.

sa-tsûn, junks from Ningpo and Shanghai (of medium size), with numerous characters on each side of the bow.

sa (cf. sā), (C. soa). **sa-bui,** eyes almost closed (v. bui).

sa (cf. sau). **hah-sa,** opening into chinks with drought, as a tub.

sa — **sa-som,** a medicinal plant (v. som).

sa — **sa-jîn,** a white medicinal fruit like an almond (Amomum Xanthoides?).

sa [R. siau, saltpetre and such salts; also written "sa," one of the characters for "sand;" = col. se]. **jiâu-sa** (r.), sal-ammoniac.

sa (C. sɛ). **chhiú-sa,** the mountains seeming almost to inclose a grave, as with arms stretched out. **sa-chhiú,** id. **tsó-sa iū-sa,** do. on the left and right; that on the right ought to be the shorter. **hó-sa,** the one on the right hand. **liông-sa,** that on the left. **hó-sa kè-bīn,** the right-hand one turning round and coming in front of the grave (counted unlucky). **hó-sa kè-bīn, pek-hó siong-jîn,** this form of grave urges the tiger to injure the posterity. **hó-sa chhoàn-tông, tsú-sun siàu-liân-bông,** if so, descendants die young. **liông-sa chhoàn-tông, tsú-sun heng-ōng,** if the left arm project thus the descendants will prosper.

sa (cf. la), to scrape or sweep up with the hand (with little finger downwards), as small things from a table, or as clothes for fear of rain; to draw nearer the wind, as sail. **sa-liâu,** to draw the sail nearer the wind. **sa-chîⁿ,** to sweep up cash from the table with the hand; to borrow money from many sources. **sa-liáh,** to borrow money from many sources. **sì-kòe-sa,** id. **chiàⁿ-sa tò-sa,** id. **chia sa, hia sa,** id. **sa-lâi that-khì,** to scrape together and borrow money so as to pay another. **ân-sa** (T.), very hard up for money. **sa-oá,** to sweep things together with the hand, as small things on table; to bring together with the hand, as the reeds or twigs forming a brush that have been already tied together at the other end. **chhìn-chhái-sa**, to snatch things without liberty.

lām-sám-sa, to play blind-man's-buff; to run about, as an idle useless boy; to snatch things improperly. **àm-bong-sa**, to grope about.

sa thâu-mn̂g, to brush away the hair from the forehead with the hand. **bák-bâi-mn̂g sa-bô-khí**, you are acting very absurdly and only injuring yourself (v. bâi).

sa (R.—; A. chhek; C. sa). **bák-sa**, a wooden railing of which the ends of the rails do not project above the upper horizontal bar. **bák-sa-mn̂g**, a gate made thus with perpendicular bars. **bák-sa-chí**, rails of a railing. **sa-lân**, the railing outside a yamun gate (v. lân).

sa (R. id.), (C. sɛ). **âng-sa**, a large good fish with very small scales, almost as if no scales. **it ngé, jī âng-sa**, the best fish is the "ngé;" the next is the "âng-sa."

sá [R.—; Cn. sá; C. soá, to sprinkle; to scatter]. **siau-sá** (R.), open and cheerful in manner; taking things easily and cheerfully without care or anxiety (s. play). **sá-liù**, skilful. **sá-thoat**, easy, kindly, and sociable (opp. u-khu), liberal and pleasant to deal with in business.

sá [R.—; Cn. sá; C. soá, to play or amuse one's self; = col. soá]. **siau-sá**, to take a walk so as to help digestion (s. cheerful).

sá (Cn.), = A. siù, to embroider, as shoes or child's cap. **sá-soàn**, coloured thread for embroidery.

sà [R. sound as of hoarse voice; cf. sā, soā]. **sà-sà-kiò**, sound as of a mat when shaken. **sà-sà-háu**, id.

sā (= sà; cf. soā). **sā-sā-kiò**, rustling sound, as of a new dress, or of reeds or trees.

sā (cf. sa, soa). **bák-sā-sī**, dozing; half asleep.

sa^n (R. san), a coat, shirt, gown, jacket, or such dress for the upper part of the body; clothes; dress. **sa^n-khò**, coat and trowsers; one's dress. **sa^n-á-khò**, id. **sa^n-á-toà**, strings of dress of children or priests (v. toà). **sa^n-á-tsoe**, stuff enough for a coat or shirt. **sa^n-á-kè**, a clothes-horse.

joáh-sa^n, a summer coat. **tn̂g-sa^n**, a long robe or gown. **té-sa^n**, a short dress or coat. **phoà-sa^n**, ragged clothes. **tiu^n-lāu-sa^n**, clothes prepared beforehand for the burial of parents. **chit-thò-sa^n**, a set of coats, vests, &c., worn at once. **sì-su-sa^n** (C.), four sets of clothes, including trowsers.

chhēng-sa^n, to put on a coat or gown. **moa^n-sa^n**, to throw a coat over one's shoulders without putting the arms in the sleeves. **thǹg-sa^n**, to undress. **pak-sa^n**, to strip off clothes, as robber. **sóe-sa^n**, to wash clothes; a washerman or washerwoman. **siu-sa^n**, to take in clothes for washing; to lay away clothes, as after airing. **kùi-sa^n**, to hang up clothes. **thò-sa^n**, to mend by putting in a piece below (inside) and sewing down the edges.

sa^n [R. siong, mutual, = col. sio, which is more usual in C.], used before verbs and some adjectives to express mutual or reciprocal action, but used also in many cases when the action is not mutual. **sa^n-kap**, together. **sa^n-phah**, to fight by blows. **sa^n-thâi**, to fight, as in battle. **sa^n-bat**, acquainted (with person). **sa^n-tâng**, quite similar; just the same. **sa^n-chhin-chhiū^n**, similar; like.

sa^n-têng, to undersell; to offer a higher price in buying so as to cut out another (s. three). **sa^n-chhiá^n**, to invite, as friends to a feast. **sa^n-kèng**, to treat another politely. **sa^n-kià**, to intrust with a commission. **sa^n-sàng**, to make a present. **m̄-thang sa^n-kòe**, do not be offended at him (or at me). **m̄-sái sa^n-moā^n**, you need not try to deceive me.

sa^n (R. sam), three. **tsài-sa^n**, over and over again; frequently. **n̄ng-sa^n**, two or three; a few. **sa^n-n̄ng**, id. **sa^n-sì**, three or four. **sa^n ka-láuh, sì tiòh-poáh**, all going wrong. **tiu^n-sa^n bé-sì**, Mr. So-and-so. **tiu^n-sa^n bé-it**, id. **tiu^n-sa^n lí-sì**, any one; "Jones, Brown, and Robinson." **mih^n bōe-tiu^n-sa^n, lâi-chhē lí-sì thó-chí^n**, to sell things to one man and ask the price from another.

sa^n-pái, thrice. **sa^n-kè**, id. **sa^n-têng**, threefold, as cloth, &c. (s. mutual). **sa^n-pē**, three times as much. **sa^n-kak**, three-cornered; thirty cents. **sa^n-géh-tsoeh**, the 3.3 when the ancestors are worshipped; graves are often repaired then instead of at the chhi^n-miâ^n. **sa^n-kha-tu**, forming a triangle, as three things or places. **sa^n-kha-tiam**, id. **sa^n-kha-bé**, id.; also a three-legged stool used by carpenters. **sái sa^n-kha-liâu**, sailing with wind abeam; standing with one foot forward ready to box.

sâ^n [R. sêng, to receive, = col. sîn], to catch, as something thrown to one; to seize, as a weapon, so as to prevent striking self or other.

sá^n (C.), = A. sím, siá^n. **sá^n-mih^n**, what? which? **sá^n-sū**, on what account?

sà^n (cf. sah^n). **kim nà^n-sà^n**, glittering or shining, as a smooth bright surface. **kim sà^n-nà^n**, id. **ɵ sà^n-nà^n**, black, glossy, and shining, as finest varnish, &c.

sà^n (cf. sah^n, sàm). **hê nà^n-sà^n**, doing things in a negligent careless way.

sah (R. sek), (T. sah^n). **chháu-sah** (Cn.), sort of grass slippers without heels.

sáh, to cook by boiling (gen. entire) in water alone, as meat, eggs, or vegetables. **kè-sáh**, already boiled, as flax. **sio-sáh**, roast and boiled. **sáh-koe**, to boil a fowl. **sáh koe-n̄ng**, to boil a hen's egg. **sáh-bah**, to boil a piece of meat (pork) entire. **sáh péh-hê**, to boil shrimps.

sáh (mere reduplication; cf. séh). **péh-láh-sáh**, very white.

sah^n, to snap up or catch in the mouth, as a dog does a fly or something thrown to it; to snap up, as a tiger does a small animal; to catch from above with the hand, as a ball or fly (but from below is "sîn"); to have a strong propensity or desire towards something heard of or met with. **sah^n--teh**, id. **sah^n hō-sîn**, to snap up flies, as dog.

teh-sah^n, talking about a matter as if we knew all about it, when wholly or nearly ignorant, in order to draw out the facts from another, or to make an appearance of knowledge. **lām-sám sah^n**, id. **sah^n-lâi sah^n-khì**, id. **hō--i sah^n--khì**, to be taken in by such talk, so that he gets the information he wishes.

sah^n-hong, slightly out of sorts, supposed to be caused by a draught of wind. **sah^n-tiòh-hong**, id. **sah^n--tiòh**, feeling a sudden pain about the breast, as from striking on something, or from a strain by sudden over-exertion.

sah^n-khùi, very deeply affected at sudden good or bad news. **sah^n sim-khùi**, very strongly moved with desire for a thing, either good or bad (stronger than sah^n-sim). **sah^n-sim**, mind strongly affected by sudden news good or bad, or sudden expectations of great advantage, sometimes so as to become ill. **sahⁿ-sim--chit-ē**, id. **sahⁿ-sim lim**, to gulp down eagerly (a liquid) in great quantities. **chin sahⁿ-sim**, very eager, or deeply affected. **m̄-sái sahⁿ**, don't let your mind be set on the news or rumour you have heard.

sahⁿ (cf. sàⁿ). **hê nàⁿ-sahⁿ**, doing things in a careless negligent way. **hê sahⁿ-sahⁿ** (T.), id.

sahⁿ [R. sek? to rest]. **sahⁿ-chīⁿ**, sudden lull in the wind.

sahⁿ (T.) **chháu-sahⁿ** (= Cn. sah), straw or grass slippers without heels.

sai (R. su), a lion. **hong-sai**, image of a lion with an officer on its back, put on a roof to ward off evil influences. **hé-sai**, sort of fireworks shaped like a lion. **kim-sai**, a lion-shaped footstool, for some idols, and for chair of first-class mandarin. **tåh kim-sai**, to have such a footstool. **chiòh-sai**, a stone lion; a subdivision of the Chìn-kang district of Chin-chew. **chiòh-sai iåh-kiaⁿ-lâng-kò**, the most powerful men are afraid to be accused before a mandarin. **în-lē-sai**, a man who leads others, either simply on the road, or to bad places; said also of the staff or long pipe by which a blind man feels his way. **hó-phīⁿ-sai**, good at smelling, as food (said jocularly). **hiòng-thien-sai**, said of a man with his face to the sky. **iô-sai**, children shaking about their heads with a hand at each temple.

sai-iaⁿ, a lion's mane. **thâu-khak sai-sai**, head large and round, as man's.

hé-sai, tigers and lions (a. shell-fish). **hé-pà sai-chhiūⁿ**, tigers, leopards, lions, and elephants. **hê-sai-káu**, a shaggy short-legged dog. **lâm-sai-káu**, id.

sai (Cn.) **iûⁿ-kóng-sai**, = am-pê-chê, the cicada. **iûⁿ-pō-sai**, id.

sai — **hé-sai**, a sort of shell-fish like a small crab (a. lion).

sai (R. se). **sai-gû**, the rhinoceros. **sai-gû-phê**, its skin (medicinal). **sai-kak**, its horn.

sai (R. se), west. **sai-hng**, the west. **sai--sì**, id.

sai-iûⁿ, western nations; Europe; foreign cotton cloth (v. iûⁿ). **sai-lé**, the Russians (v. lé). **soaⁿ-sai**, Shan-si. **siám-sai**, Shen-si. **kang-sai**, Kiang-si. **kńg-sai**, Kwang-si. **kúiⁿ-sai** (C.), id.

tang-sai, east and west. **tang-sai lâm-pak**, east, west, south, and north. **tang-sai-oàⁿ**, the two assistant priests (Tauist or Buddhist) on each side of the head priest at any ceremony. **tang-sai-thah**, the two great pagodas of Chin-chew. **tang-sai bû-sé-put**, willing to take anything. **khoàⁿ-tang khoàⁿ-sai**, to look in every direction. **kóng-tang kóng-sai**, to talk about many things, or not to the purpose; to gossip, esp. about others' faults, often falsely. **gî-tang gî-sai**, very suspicious. **bak-tang bak-sai**, to soil all over; to dirty everything. **bong-tang bong-sai**, doing many bits of work; having no leisure. **niⁿ-tang niⁿ-sai**, taking up small quantities of many things, *e.g.* tasting them. **tóe-tang tóe-sai**, holding miscellaneous articles. **saⁿ-jit soá-tang, sì-jit soá-sai**, constantly changing one's dwelling; inconstant. **cheng-lâm, tsáu-pak, kiâⁿ-tang, khì-sai**, to travel in all quarters.

sai-lâm, south-west; a S.W. wind (v. lâm). **sai-pak**, north-west; a N.W. wind. **sai-pak-hō**, sudden storm of rain from N.W. **hoat-m̄-chiâⁿ sai-pak**, thunder in the north, and sky all black, but passing off without a storm. **sai-pak tsòe-liáu, liâm-piⁿ hê-lâm** (=. . . chiah hê-lâm), suddenly becoming friendly again after a fit of passion.

sai [R. su, a teacher], affix to the names of skilled workmen and master tradesmen; *e.g.* **iâu-sai**, &c. **bák-sai**, a carpenter. **thô-sai**, a mason (v. thô). **táu-sai**, a man who measures cargoes of pease or beans when they are loose (not in bags) in the hold of a vessel.

sai-hū, a skilled workman; a journeyman (v. hū). **sai-á**, an apprentice. **sai-kiáⁿ**, man whom one has taught a trade. **sai-tē**, a younger apprentice, said by the older ones. **sai-hiaⁿ**, an elder apprentice, said by younger one. **sai-hiaⁿ-tī**, workmen who have learned under the same master.

sai-kong, a Tauist priest. **sai-ko**, a Buddhist nun. **sai-pē**, Bud. priest who adopts a boy as his son. **sai-kiáⁿ**, adopted son of Bud. priest.

sai [R. su, = col. si]. **sai-khia**, private; secret; one's own.

sai (Cn.) **thek sai-sai**, very pretty.

sái [R. sú, to use; to cause; to send], to use; very much used in C. for A. ēng, to use; scarcely any of the phrases are used in Cn. except m̄-sái.

sái-ēng, to use; to spend. **chhe-sái**, to employ, use, or send (a person). **sái-sō**, to instigate secretly to injure another. **sái-so**, id. **sái-lōng**, id.

m̄-sái, no need; not wanted; no I thank you; need not —. **m̄-khó-sái**, it does not require much work to do it. **m̄-khó sái-kang**, id. **mihⁿ-sái**, why? (implying blame, or meaning "there is no need"). **sái-sái** (C.), no need; no I thank you. **nāⁿ-sái**, all that is needed is —. **sái-kiaⁿ-bô** (need not fear not to get it), plenty of it can be got. **sái-hoat--goá tāi-oā**, what ever can I do? (can do nothing). **ōe-sái--tit** (Cn. ōe-tsōe--tit, it will do; can be used. **bōe-sái--tit** (Cn. bōe-tsōe--tit), it will not do at all. **bô-lē-sái** (C.), useless. **bô-sū-sái** (C.), id.; won't do at all.

sái-chîⁿ, to spend money. **sái-gûn**, id. **khiap-sái**, stingy.

sái-lē, to bribe. **sái kè-bé**, to pass a bad article (v. kè). **sái iên-tâu**, to gamble with loaded dice. **sái thùi-pau**, to swindle by giving a bad article in place of a good one (v. thùi). **sái kièn-sek**, to over-reach by cunning. **sái sek-tsúi**, to bully or intimidate. **sái-sèng**, to get very angry, or put on an angry appearance, of set purpose. **sái-tiàⁿ**, to bully. **sái-phài**, having a proud or haughty bearing. **sái-phún** (Cn.), to behave in an overbearing way. **sái ōe-tū**, to shut a man's mouth by a sharp and unanswerable reply. **sái àm-tók**, to injure a man by secret plots. **sái àm-pē**, id. (v. pē). **sái àm-chìⁿ**, id. (v. chìⁿ). **hó-sái**, having much influence with mandarins or with their subordinates, so as to be useful in a dispute; also (esp. C.), current, that can be used, as money, &c. **sè-thâu hó-sái**, having such influence. **ke-sái--i tsáp-ê-chîⁿ gûn-tsúi**, to get ten cash more in exchange for a dollar, as in buying. **sái-hoat**, to use magic.

sái bák-bé, to glance sidewise in a displeased or discontented manner, or proudly, imperiously, or lasciviously. **khoàⁿ--lâng sái-bák-bé**, id. **sái âu-siaⁿ**, to sing with voice from the throat (v. siaⁿ). **sái phīⁿ-khang-kńg**, to make a nasal displeased sound (v. phīⁿ).

sái-chhiò, to use anything with the lower concave side turned up, as a cover or the palm (v. chhiò). **sái-lé**, to scull a junk. **sái-to**, to use a sword. **sái pîn-pâi**, to use a shield. **sái tsúi-bō**, to work a water-mill. **sái tsúi-chhia**, to work a wheel for raising water. **sái-lôe**, to plough. **sái-chhân**, to plough rice-fields. **sái-chhat**, to varnish (or paint). **sái-tsoá**, to burn idolatrous paper. **sio-kim sái-tsoá**, id. **bô-gû, sái-bé**, if you can't get a cow use a horse; make the best you can of it.

sái [R. sú, to ride a horse quick; to sail], to sail. **sái-tsûn**, id. **sái joā-tsōe-tsûn**, sail how far? **sái-hong**, to sail by using the wind. **chīn-hong sái**, to sail as near the wind as can be with the sail full. **chīn-phâng sái**, id. **sái oá-koāⁿ**, to sail with the sail close on the mast (v. koāⁿ). **sái nn̄g-ki-hiuⁿ**, to sail not longer than two incense-sticks burn.

sái (Cn.), to commit uncleanness with —, only used in vile scolding.

sái (R. sí), excrement; dung; some sorts of refuse. **kāu jī-sái**, tautological, and full of superfluous words, as a composition. **hé-sái**, snuffings; spots from a lamp wick. **thih-sái**, fragments of rust beaten from red-hot iron, &c. (v. thih). **so iên-sái**, a way of making bad dollars (v. iên). **a-phièn-sái**, refuse of opium worked up again. **hun-sái**, id.; tobacco soot in pipe. **sái-khak** (Cn.), refuse from beaten cotton (v. khak).

hī-sái, wax from the ears. **phīⁿ-sái**, hardened mucus in the nose. **tsńg-kah-sái**, dirt under finger-nails. **hê-sîn-sái**, darkish spots all over the face.

bák-sái, tears. **lâu bák-sái**, to weep. **bák-sái lâu, bák-sái tih**, weeping profusely. **bák-sái lâu-jip bô-lâu-chhut**, grief too deep for tears. **bák-sái chhîm-chhîm-lâu**, tears flowing abundantly. **bák-sái chhiâm-chhiâm-lâu**, id. **bák-sái sì-lâm-sūi**, tears flowing all over the face. **bák-sái-ko**, thickened matter in the eye.

pàng-sái, to have a motion. **tìⁿ-sái**, to try hard to have a motion. **chhoah-sái**, to have a very loose motion. **sái-hák**, a necessary. **sái-tháng**, a bucket for carrying dung. **sái-chiap**, very thin excrement, as in diarrhœa, esp. said of child's.

sái [R. su, to belch]. **khe sái-eh**, to hiccup, as child.

sái [R. sú, a historian; a censor], a surname. **sái-hāng**, a street in Amoy. **sái-hāng lē-thâu**, a jetty in Amoy.

sái [R. sat, to scatter, = col. siet, chhāi]. **sái-phoà-noāⁿ** (esp. T.), = chhāi-phoà-noāⁿ, shamelessly urgent, as beggar, &c.

sài [R. to excel, = col. sè]. **sài-kè** (R.), to excel, as in rivalry.

sài (R. sè). **kiáⁿ-sài**, a son-in-law. **sin-kiáⁿ-sài**, a bridegroom. **kiáⁿ-sài poàn-tsú**, a son-in-law is half a son. **bē-sài**, husband of younger sister. **sun-sài**, husband of niece or grand-daughter. **ang-sài** (r.), a husband. **hó-ang-sài**, a good husband.

sài [R. a boundary; a frontier; by change of tone from "sek," to stop up; = col. "that"]. **chhut-sài**, to go beyond the deserts on the north of China; said only of Chiau-kun, the princess who was married to a Hun.

sài [R. sù, a messenger; by change of tone from "sú," to send; to cause; = col. sái]. **chhe-sài**, a messenger. **iâm-toā-sài**, deputy of the salt commissioner (v. iâm). **tsòe-koaⁿ tsòe-sài**, to be high mandarins in general. **kong-sài tāi-sîn**, an ambassador, as a foreign ambassador. **kip-sài**, = bú-phoàⁿ, assistant of the idol Sêng-hông. **bé-sài-iâ**, figures holding horses at temple-doors. **hó-sài-iâ**, the deified tiger. **thiⁿ-sài** (X.), an angel.

sài — **kong-pô tsó-sài**, all deceased ancestors from father upwards. **kong-pô khah-siàⁿ tsó-sài**, immediate ancestors are the most powerful protectors. **thiⁿ-tōe sam-kài, kong-pô tsó-sài** (these are the most important objects of worship). **thiⁿ-téng**, &c., id.

sài [R. to pare off; to reduce or diminish; by change of tone from "sat," to kill]. **sài--khì**, to drop or go out, as a custom; to remit, as a duty, or regular rate, or contribution. **sài-bô--khì**, id. **sài-lài bô-lô--khì**, id. **sài-khah-chió**, to reduce the rate levied.

sāi [R. sū, business, to serve]. **hòk-sāi**, to serve, as a master or a god.

sāi [R. sū, brother's wives, esp. elder brother's wife]. **tâng-sāi**, the wives of two brothers.

sāi [R. sū, alike; like]. **sék-sāi**, familiar; intimate; well acquainted with (person); open and frank; easily getting familiar with strangers. **siòk-sāi** (C.), id. **sék-sāi-lâng**, acquaintances.

sāi [R. sat, to scatter; to throw about; to sow; = col. siet, chhāi, sái]. **sāi-phoat**, violent and overbearing, as woman who is too bold and forward, trusting to being a woman; or as a man threatening to kill himself, or do violence if we don't give him money. **sāi-phoà-noāⁿ** (Cn.), shamelessly and doggedly determined, as a beggar.

saiⁿ (T.), = A. seng, formerly; previously.

saiⁿ (T.), = A. san, to weed out; to prune or take away. **saiⁿ-nai--koá**, take away a little.

saiⁿ (T.) **saiⁿ-á**, = saⁿ-á, a coat.

sak — **tiàⁿ-sak**, the iron point of the fluke of a wooden anchor.

sak (Cn.) **sak-kháu**, = A. sek-kháu, to rinse the mouth.

sak (cf. siak, siàng); also (Cn.), = A. siak, to dash; to strike hard.

pàng-sak, to abandon, as a person whom we ought to serve or protect; to reject, as customs, tenets, or occupation. **khì-sak** (r.), id. **sià-sak**, to lay down, as a load too heavy to carry; to throw away things to lighten a vessel; to sell at a sacrifice; to throw up the management of an affair that is growing troublesome or dangerous. **siah-sak**, to scrape off and throw away, as skins of roots, &c.

piaⁿ-piaⁿ sak-sak, m̄-chêng m̄-goân (= siak), throwing things about in a pet or rage.

tàn-sak (Cn.), to throw away. **kōe-sak** (Cn.); to change, as bad habit. **sóe-sak** (T.), to wash and throw away the washings; to kill; to exterminate.

sak, to push with the hands. **oe-oe sak-sak**, to push through a crowd (v. oe). **sak-oá**, to push shut, as a door; to push close together, as anything. **sak hō--i**, to put off one's self on him, as a duty or responsibility.

sak-sau, to bully.

báng-sak (Cn.), = A. báng-sut, a mosquito flapper.

sam [R. three, = col. saⁿ]. **sam-kàu**, the three religions, Confucian, Tauist, and Buddhist. **sam-kong**, the three headships, of sovereign, husband, and father (v. kong, a rope). **sam-kong**, the three lights, sun, moon, and stars. **sam-tsâi**, the three powers, Heaven, earth, and man. **sam-seng**, the three sorts of offerings. **sam-kài-kong**, the three gods of the three worlds (v. kài). **sam-koan tāi-tè**, id. **sam-pó**, the Buddhist triad. **sam-chheng**, the Tauist triad. **sam-phiaⁿ**, three powerful spirits (v. phiaⁿ). **sam-tsòk**, relatives of self, of mother, and of wife (v.

tsók). **sam-hûn chhit-phek**, the three spirits and seven animal souls of a man. **sam-háp-thé**, mortar. **sam-chhit**, a medicine (v. chhit). **sam-sek-kî**, a three-coloured flag (v. sek).

sam-pán, a small boat; a female slave with large feet. **sam-pán-lâng**, boatman of a small boat. **sam-pán-iô**, self-important strut in one's manner.

sam-hú, an official who rules a recent subdivision of a Foo or department, *e.g.* the mandarin at Chióh-bé.

sam-put-gē-sî, occasionally (v. gē; v. sî).

sam — **khoàⁿ sam-sek**, to keep neutral till it appears which side is going to win, so as to join the winning side.

sam [R. san, a mountain, = col. soaⁿ]. **sam-siau**, name of a mountain spirit.

sam — **sam-pan-khiah**, the openings in the battlements of a wall (v. khiah). **sam-poan-khiah** (C.), id.

sam (R. id.), a sort of pine or fir, Cunninghamia. **sam-chhâ**, pine-wood, a good sort. **sam-liāu**, timber, as ready for use. **sam-ke**, useless poisonous mushrooms.

sâm — **lâ-sâm**, dirty, filthy (moral or physical); said also by seamen of a dirty channel. **lâ-sâm-siáh**, dirty; filthy. **â-sâm** (P.), id. **bak-lâ-sâm**, to soil; to defile. **phah-lâ-sâm**, id. **è-lâ-sâm**, to make a place dirty, as with water, or mud, or filth.

sám [R. to mix]. **lām-sám**, at random; disorderly; any way all the same; ill-behaved (v. lām).

sám (Cn. T. sáng), to sprinkle with the fingers, as salt or such powder; to put on, as some wood on the fire. **sám hé-hu**, to sprinkle ashes with the hand. **sám ióh-hún**, to sprinkle a medicinal powder, as on a sore. **sám kù-sut**, to sprinkle sawdust, as on the fire. **sám-hé**, to put small quantities of fuel on a fire.

sàm [R. sàn, to scatter, = col. soàⁿ]. **tn̂g-saⁿ sàm-kûn**, long gown and full skirt of Ming costume (v. kûn).

sàm [R. sam, loose; dishevelled; cf. sàⁿ, sahⁿ, sàn]. **sàm-sàm**, not neatly put up, as parcel; beginning to have a bad point, as Chinese pen. **hê-sàm**, ill-made; roughly finished, as article of furniture or dress. **phah-sàm**, to put in disorder, as tangled hair, &c. **poāⁿ-sàm**, id. **phoà-sàm**, fallen into great decay or disorder; much broken down and dirty, as room or house; so much worn as to be in shreds, as clothes or umbrella. **sàm-pê-saⁿ**, a dress with the hem opened out and broken, used in deepest mourning (v. pê). **sàm-mn̂g**, hair dishevelled or in disorder. **sàm-thâu**, id. **thâu-mn̂g sàm-sàm**, id.

sàm-tām, covered with luxuriant herbage or brushwood, as hill.

sàm — **àm-sàm**, dark and dirty, as cave, or as room long unswept; improper, as affair or conduct; also (P.), densely luxuriant, as wild vegetation. **àm-sàm-lē**, a depraved course of life. **àm-sàm ê sé-tsāi**, a secret place where crimes can be committed in the dark; a brothel or gambling den, &c.; a man's private parts.

sàm [R. to do thrice; by change of tone from "sam," three]. **sàm-su** (R.), to reflect carefully upon.

sām — **sām-sām**, dispirited, shabby, broken-down appearance. **kiâⁿ-lē sām-sām**, to walk along with a seedy, shabby, broken-down look, as man who has failed to get on in life.

san (R. id.), (T. saiⁿ; Cn. suiⁿ), to prune; to thin out; to reject and expunge, as words or sentences. **san--koah**, to prune off. **san-chheh**, to expunge useless words or sentences from a book.

san [R. song, funeral ceremonies, = col. sng]. **khok-san-tiōng**, mourning-staff carried by widower at funeral (v. tiōng).

san [R. seng, a star, = col. chhiⁿ]. **lân-san**, miscellaneous; remnants or remainders; in small quantities (v. lân).

san (T. C.), = A. sien, rust; scurf on the body.

san (Cn.) **hiā-san**, = A. hiā-sien, sort of small worm.

san (C.) **san-hô**, = A. sien-hô, coral.

san [R. a mountain, = col. soaⁿ]. **san-súi**, landscapes (v. súi). **bêng-san**, famous mountains. **san-iá**, wild and wicked, as villagers. **san-tin hái-bī**, delicacies of land and sea. **hā-san-hé**, a very tight vest with numerous buttons (v. hé).

kang-san sit, the empire lost (fig. of man losing all his possessions). **san-chhoan siā-chek**, mountains, rivers, and imperial altars (said of imperial dominion). **san i bēng, pok siōng**, geomancy, medicine, and prognostication (v. siōng). **bān-san tiâu-tùi**, the hills forming an amphitheatre, as behind a grave, counted auspicious.

san-tsa, = sien-tsa, a small red fruit like a crab-apple. **san-che** (C.), id. **hoâi-san**, a medicinal root (v. hoâi). **siông-san**, a medicinal root (Lysimachia ?), used for ague. **san-iâng**, a goat-skin; a goat. **san-iông**, id. **chhoan-san-kah**, = lâ-lí, the scaly ant-eater.

sán [R. to produce, = col. soáⁿ]. **thé-sán**, productions of the ground; crops, fruits, &c. **sán-giáp**, estate; patrimony. **ka-sán**, wealth or possessions (of man or family) of any sort. **kheng-ka tōng-sán**, to lose one's all, esp. by lawsuits or prodigality.

seng-sán, to bring forth young; to be delivered of a child. **bô-seng-sán**, barren, as woman. **siáu-sán**, to have an abortion. **sán-bûn** (R.), the female organs.

sán [R. a medicinal powder; by change of tone from "sàn," to scatter; = col. soáⁿ]. **seng-chi-sán**, a compound powder for sprinkling on festering sores. **tsu-phek-sán**, a medicine made of pearls and amber. **tan-ko oân-sán**, four forms of medicinal preparations. **tan-ko oân-sán, chin-sien lân-piēn**, all in confusion, so that even one of the genii could not put them in order. **ióh-sán** (C.), = A. ióh-soáⁿ, finely-powdered medicine. **thong-koan-sán** (C.), = A. thong-koan-soáⁿ (*q.v.*)

sán, lean; thin; meagre; poor; woven too wide and loose, as cloth; sterile, as land. **kêng-sán**, very poor. **pûi-sán**, fat and lean; fertile and sterile, &c. **m̄-pûi m̄-sán**, neither fat nor lean, due medium. **chiáh sán-chiú**, to drink liquor with little or no condiment. **sán-pè**, cotton cloth woven very thin, with the threads too far apart. **pè sán-sin**, the cloth is too loosely woven, and easily torn or worn out. **sán-chhân**, poor land. **sán-tōe**, a place where no money can be made. **sán sé-tsāi**, id.

siau-sán, very lean and thin. **kut-bah siau-sán**, id. **n̂g-sán**, yellow and wasting away. **sán-gièn**, lean and thin. **sán-thiu**, tall, thin, and slender, as man. **sán-sòe**, lean, small, and insignificant in appearance. **sán thih-thih**, very lean. **sán tiu-tiu**, id. **sán tiuh-tiuh**, id. **sán khih-khih**, id. **sán gih-gih**, id. **sán ngiáuhⁿ-ngiáuhⁿ**, id. **tit-tit sán--lòh-khì**, wasting away. **sán-kut lòh-hióh**, very lean. **chiáh--liáu sán**, having enough

52

to eat, but yet lean. **siūⁿ kàu-sán,** to grow lean through excessive thought and anxiety. **khì kàu-sán,** to grow lean with anger or discontent. **sán kàu chit-têng-phê piⁿ chit-têng-kut,** all skin and bone. **sán kàu-chhun chit-ki-kut,** wasted to a skeleton. **sán kàu-liáu,** id.

sán (Cn.). **chìⁿ-sán,** = A. chìⁿ-soán, long fried cakes.

sàn [R. to scatter; to disperse; = col. soàⁿ]. **sù-sàn,** dispersed in all directions, as people. **sàn-khì,** feeling of warmth and redness of face, caused by liquor, pepper, ginger, siri leaf, &c. **tông-tsú sàn,** pupil so enlarged that the eye is quite lost (v. tông). **sàn-ién,** prodigal; spending money recklessly; very poor, and so daring to commit any crime (cf. next word).

sàn — **sàn-sàn,** very poor and reckless; capable of doing all sorts of mischief (cf. previous word). **sàn-chhiah,** very poor and miserable, often daring to commit great crimes.

sàn-iá, rude, wild, and uncultivated (as man), and careless of one's life; but not so bad as "húi-lūi."

sàn (C.) **sàn-hiong,** = A. sòng-hiong, very poor.

sàn [R. sam, dishevelled, = col. sàm]. **sàn-pê,** = sàm-pê, ravelled edges of dress in deepest mourning.

sàn (Cn.) **sàn-phīⁿ,** = A. chhèng-phīⁿ, to blow the nose.

sang (R. song), loose; to loosen, as a rope or a girdle; well boiled and mealy, as roots. **tēng sang,** hard and soft, as boiled roots. **sang phùn-phùn,** well boiled and mealy. **sang phut-phut** (T.), id. **sang khoà-khoà** (T.), id. **ō-pêng sio-sang,** a bit of boiled taro warm and mealy.

khin-sang, in good health; comfortable. **ta-sang,** dry and comfortable, as when perspiration has been wiped off; well cooked and mealy, as potatoes. **kùt khah-sang,** dig and loosen the earth, as about the roots.

pàng-sang, to loosen, as a rope. **pàng-làng-sang,** become too easy and remiss, *e.g.* not collecting debts, or as mandarin not punishing evil-doers, or as teacher letting boys have their own way.

sang [R. song, a pair, = col. siang], (esp. Cn., but not C.), = siang, both of the pair. **sang-ké-kiàm,** double-bladed dagger. **sang-kha táh sang-tsûn** (feet on two boats), trying to keep well with both sides.

sâng (= siâng, siūng), alike; similar.

sáng (Cn. T.), to lift on the palms of the hands turned forward, as in putting wood on the fire; also (= A. sám), to put on the fire, as wood. **sáng-hé,** to put fuel on a fire. **sáng-chhâ,** to put wood on the fire. **chhâ, sáng khah-jip,** put the wood further in on the fire. **sáng--jip-khì,** id.

phê-sáng (A.), to flatter. **phê-kha sáng-chhiú,** id.

sáng (T.) **tà-láng-sáng,** = hê-nàⁿ-sahⁿ, acting negligently.

sàng (T.), = A. siùng. **sàng--lòh-khì,** to dash on the ground.

sàng [R. sòng, the Sung dynasty; a surname], a surname.

sàng (R. sòng), to present; to accompany some distance on taking leave; to hand over, as a criminal. **saⁿ-sàng,** to make a present. **sàng-lé,** to give a fee to a teacher or doctor; to give a congratulatory present. **sàng-tiāⁿ,** to give the earnest-money. **sàng-toh,** to present a fully prepared feast to a friend. **sàng chhâ-bí,** to send presents of wood and rice to the idol "ông-iâ," as other temples or private persons do. **sàng-chhái,** to present red cloth to a mandarin; to perform rites on burning "ông-iâ" (v. chhái). **sàng-kó,** to send in to a mandarin the rough draft of a document. **sàng jit-thâu-á,** to give to the bride's parents a paper (jit-thâu-á), telling what days are proposed for marriage, &c. **sàng-jit,** id. **sàng-pn̄g,** to take rice to a man in prison. **ū-lâng thang koāⁿ-sàng--má,** is there any one to take food to the prisoner. **hoân-lí sàng chit-ê-mihⁿ,** I will trouble you to convey this thing (to some man).

sàng-tiàⁿ, to carry out the anchor from a vessel by a small boat. **sàng hong-chhe,** to help a friend to give a start to a paper-kite. **sàng jī-tsoá,** to carry the ashes of burned paper (written or printed) to the sea, with ceremonies.

sàng-nîⁿ, to make presents, and perform ceremonies on last day of year. **sàng-nîⁿ sàng-tsoeh,** do., and at the terms and festivals. **sàng-tsoeh,** to make presents at the terms or festivals (*e.g.* 5.5, or 8.15.), *e.g.* scholars paying teachers.

sàng-sîn, to make offerings and burn paper on 12.24, when the spirits ascend to report to Heaven. **sàng-ang** (C.), id. **sàng-ông khí-sin,** to burn the image of "ông-iâ" (v. ông).

ngiâⁿ-sàng, to treat with much respect, going out to meet a man when he arrives, and also accompanying him so far when he leaves. **pôe-sàng,** to accompany a friend when he goes to see a visitor off. **sàng-i-khì,** to accompany him some distance when he leaves. **sàng-lâng-kheh,** to see visitors away politely. **sàng-hêng,** to see one off for journey or voyage. **sàng-sūn-hong,** to make presents, and see off on voyage. **sàng-hong,** id. **sàng-sīn,** to make presents for travelling expenses to a man about to leave (v. sīn). **sàng-kè,** to accompany a bride to her husband's house, as a matron does (v. kè). **sàng-chhin,** to accompany a sister who is a bride to husband's house. **āu-sàng,** elder brother of bride doing so.

sàng-tsòng, to accompany a funeral.

ah-sàng, to escort and guard. **kè-sàng,** to send under guard, as criminal to be tried.

bé-sàng, the mizzen-mast, in Chinese vessels placed at the side, near the stern.

sāng (Cn.), = A. siāng, of the same sort or kind.

sap (= siap, sat). **sap-bûn** (f.), soap (v. bûn).

sap [R. siap, drizzling rain, = col. seh]. **hē-á sap-sap,** drizzling rain. **ien-bū-sap,** very small drizzling mist.

sap [R. siet, fragments, = col. sut, seh]. **sap-sap,** very minute scraps. **chhùi-sap-sap,** broken down very small. **tê khah-sap,** the tea is too dusty, broken down too small.

sap — **soa-sap,** very slippery; unfair; unpleasant or troublesome to deal with in business. **soa-soa sap-sap,** id. **kāu-soa-sap,** full of sand and impurities, as edible sea-weed, &c.; very troublesome and unsafe to deal with, as man who is always planning to get money out of people. **sap-sóe,** said of dirt or scum on moss, &c.; very troublesome in money matters.

sap — **lap-sap,** dirty, as things or conduct.

sap — **se-sap,** dark and shrivelled, as face; decayed, as village or family (v. se). **siau-sap,** do., do.; shabby-looking. **hiuⁿ-lí siau-sap,** village very much decayed, and become poor. **soe-sap,** broken-down and seedy-looking, as man or place. **sí-sap** (C.), broken-down, seedy, and ill-looking.

sap — **hê-sap-sap**, in a disorderly state, as tangled hair, or as spattered table or dishes.

sat (R. sek). **bát-sat**, a bed-bug. **bák-sat**, id. **bák-sat chiáh-kheh**, said of one who gets more from his guests than he gives them. **bát-sat chhiò chhiū-gūi**, the bed-bug laughs at the tree-bug; pot calling the kettle black.

sat-bú, a louse. **sat-bú-nn̄g**, eggs of louse. **sat-pìn**, a small tooth-comb. **sat-bú siⁿ kàu-chiâⁿ-sūi**, to have lice in great numbers. **sat-bú náⁿ-moâⁿ--nihⁿ**, id.

thô-sat, a mud-fish.

sat — **gâu-liáh ōe-sat**, fond of pointing out small faults, and picking holes in what another says. **chin-gâu liáh kiáu-sat**, fond of finding fault with opponent's play (in gambling), whenever possible; said also in general of a man who tries to find fault whenever possible.

sat [R. sek, to stop up, = col. that]. **sat-phīⁿ** (C.), nose stuffed with cold. **phīⁿ-khang sat-sat** (C.), id.

sat (R. id.) **phô-sat**, a Buddhist idol; sometimes affixed to name of an idol.

sat [R. to scatter, = col. soah, seh, siet, sāi, chhāi, &c.] **sat-phoat**, = siet-phoat, fond of railing or quarrelling in an unwomanly way, as an impudent woman (v. phoat).

sat (= sap, siap). **sat-bûn** (f.), soap.

sat [R. to kill; to end; hurtful spiritual influence; = col. soah, soàⁿ]. **gō-sat**, to kill by mistake. **sat-liók** (r.), to slaughter. **sat-liók thài-tāng**, very great, or too great slaughter, as by warrior full of the rage of battle, or as mandarin executing vast multitudes. **sat-khì**, murderous rage in the heat of battle; warlike or terrible appearance of countenance naturally. **sat-khì thêng-thêng**, do. (both senses). **tài chit-tiám sat-khì**, to have a terrible look about the eyebrows, &c. (said of a child that will have a very inauspicious and unlucky influence on parents and relatives).

sat-chhiú, daring to act when the consequences may be dangerous; fond of fighting, as soldier; daring to give medicine that will kill or cure.

sat-jîn siông-bēng, reparation must be made for killing a man. **chioh-to sat-jîn** (kill man with borrowed knife), to make use of another to do an injury. **iông-i sat-jîn**, a quack kills people. **sat-jîn thài-to**, to slaughter multitudes of people. **m̄-sat-seng, m̄-hāi-bēng**, not killing any living thing. **sat-seng ê-lâng bô-bé**, a butcher will not have good fortune at the last, esp. no posterity. **hân-tan-chhe sat kiú-hu**, nine men betrothed or married to the wife of Hân-tan died in succession!

iòk-kan iòk-sat, full of murderous or quarrelsome desires; determined to be at feud. **kan kūn-sat**, to commit adultery endangers life.

pėh-sí-sat, face sallow and unhealthy looking.

sau — **sau-phí**, to speak ironically or sarcastically. **sau i-ê-phí**, to speak to him sarcastically, so as to make him ashamed. **sau lâng--ê thé-biēn**, to put a man to shame before others. **sak-sau**, to bully. **siak-sau**, id.

sau — **sau-oá**, to bring together, as the edges of a wound, by a plaster.

bô-tau-sau, not in harmony, as persons not drawing well together; not careful; not managing well. **bô-tau bô-sau**, id. **kóng-ōe bô-tau-sau**, speaking not to the point, or not so as to make our meaning plain.

sau [R. siau, a twig; the tiller of a helm]. **sau-kong**, a man who lives in a boat, esp. with his family. **sau-pô**, wife living in a boat with her husband.

sau — **hoàn-sau**, a dealer in children sold as slaves (v. hoàn).

sau (R. siau), a small round water insect that eats wood. **tsúi-sau**, id. **kim-hî-sau**, a water insect used for feeding gold-fish. **hê-sau**, to catch them.

sau-sau, worm-eaten and decayed, as the bottom of a boat.

sau [R. siau, to melt away]. **bōe-tsáu-sau--tit**, said of a man so strict that one dare not trifle at *his* work, or try to abstract any of *his* goods or money; said also of money intrusted to us which cannot be tampered with.

sau (cf. sa). **sau-sau**, not cohesive. **sau-hong**, opening into chinks, as wood. **hā-sau** (Cn. hah-sa), id.

sau — **hâm-sau**, sound of cracked crockery; slightly cracked, as crockery. **hâm-sau-hûi khah-bōe-phoà** (such crockery does not readily break), sickly-looking people live long. **hâm-sau-hûi khah-oh-phoà**, id.

sau (cf. sàu). **sau-siaⁿ**, hoarse; to lose the voice by much or loud speaking. **háng-sau**, to wrangle with a loud voice in an overbearing way. **háu-sau**, id.

sau (C.) **sɛⁿ khí-sau**, = A. khí-pau, to have a gum-boil.

sàu — **poàⁿ-sàu**, not in good condition, but not yet in rags, as a well-worn dress; not quite good, but not yet spoiled, as a pen that has lost its fine point, but can still be used. **chhēng-poàⁿ-sàu**, to wear clothes till they get too much worn.

sàu [R. a revenue or war boat; to patrol]. **sàu-tsûn**, a war junk used against pirates. **poàⁿ-siong-sàu**, a war junk that trades extensively. **khoài-sàu**, a customs boat; the officer of such a boat.

iâm-sàu, sort of excisemen for the salt revenue. **sàu-peng**, the lowest sort of tide-waiters (not said of foreign tide-waiters). **sàu-pē**, sort of salt-excisemen.

chhut-sàu, to go out against pirates. **sûn-sàu**, to go about looking for pirates, &c. **lòh-sàu**, to serve on board war-junks as marines.

sàu-kak, a trumpet. [Two characters with the radicals "mouth" and "boat" are interchanged for the other phrases, but only the character with "mouth" for this.]

sàu (R. sò), to sweep with a brush. **sàu-tè**, to sweep the ground. **sàu-lân**, to scrape off fish-scales. **sàu-tû**, to remove quite away, as bad things. **táⁿ-sàu**, to sweep. **chhéng-sàu**, to dust and sweep. **piàⁿ-sàu**, to clean out and sweep. **lòh-tōe sàu**, to stoop low and sweep away an adversary's legs in boxing.

bāng-sàu, a broom made of the "bāng" reed. **tek-sàu**, a bamboo broom. **tek-sàu-chiú**, id. **sàu-chiú**, a broom. **sàu-chiú-chhiⁿ**, a comet. **sàu-soe**, a coarse bamboo brush. **sàu-se-á** (C.), a small bamboo brush.

sàu (R. sò), to cough. **khâm-sàu**, to clear the throat. **hâm-héhⁿ ka-sàu**, severe coughing (v. ka). **sàu-kāⁿ-huih**, to cough and bring up blood. **khí-sàu**, to have a severe cough or fit of coughing. **teh-sàu**, in the act of coughing. **teh sàu**, to cure or relieve a cough. **tɛh sàu** (C.), id.

m̄-sī sia^n-sàu, angry unpleasant sound or tone of voice, as in beginning a quarrel. phái^n-sia^n-sàu, id. bô-sím-mih^n-hó sia^n-sàu, talking in an unpleasant, displeased, or angry tone.

sáuh — sáuh-sáuh-háu, noise made by shoes in walking. sáuh-sáuh-kiò, id.

sáuh^n — sáuh^n-sáuh^n-liām, to murmur; to grumble. sáuh^n-sáuh^n-háu, id.

sáuh^n — sáuh^n-sáuh^n, looking yellow or sallow and unwell. sáuh^n-sáuh^n-á-pī^n, a gradual or tedious disease, sometimes worse, sometimes better.

hō͘-á sáuh^n-sáuh^n, constant but not heavy rain.

se [R. west, = col. sai]. se-iû^n (r.), = sai-iû^n, Europe, &c. se-á, Germans, often including Dutchmen. se-lé͘, Russians (v. lé͘). hô-lân-se, France. hoat-lân-se, id. se-thien, the Buddhist heaven. chiū^n se-thien, to become a Buddha. se-ông-bú, the queen of the "Sien," residing at "iâu-tî." se-siu^n, books of stories of the Tang dynasty.

se-jī-thâu, the 146th radical, written at the top.

tong-se (R.), east and west. tong-se lâm-pok, east, west, south, and north. tong-se-siu^n, two side houses on the east and west of a large house. bûn tong, bú se, civil mandarins on the east (more honourable), and military ones on the west, at imperial audience.

se — tsńg-kah-se, the line that divides the quick from the rest of the nail.

se (R. sa), (C. sɛ), silk gauze; thin crape; cotton yarn. thai-táu-se, very fine gauze used for sieves. lô-táu-se, a still finer sort of gauze. jiàu^n-se, crape. ú-se, inferior camblets or bombazette. chiang-se, a very thin but stiff silk-stuff from Chang-chew. lîn-lô se-toān, silks, satins, &c.

mî^n-se, cotton yarn, esp. native, from Shanghai (v. mî^n). hoan-se, foreign yarn. bāng-se, old nets torn up for caulking (v. bāng).

se-iang, a frame on which yarn is wound to be ready for weaving. se-sim, cotton wicks for lamps. se-bō, a sort of Ming cap (v. bō). se-á-tsoá, very thin brittle sort of paper. se-soà^n, sort of cotton thread. khan se-soà^n, to cover a cotton coverlet with a network of thread. khan-se, id.

pháng-se, to spin cotton thread. chhia-se, to transfer it from the "thih-chhái" to the "ák-á." hē-se, to wind yarn into hanks (v. hē).

se [R. sa? siau? names of various drugs], (C. sɛ). tsu-se, cinnabar. pêng-se, borax. pâng-se, id.? a white drug used for melting gold or silver, and for medicine. sîn-se, a red mixture for the ceremony (khai-gán) of touching the eyes of idols and ancestral tablets.

sɛ — sɛ-lô (C.), a brass wash-basin.

se (R. sa), (C. sɛ). ka-se, the most expensive sort of gown (without sleeves) worn by Bud. priests. moa^n ka-se, to wear it.

se (R. sa, = col. soa), (C. sɛ). thoah-se, the sole. thɛh-sɛ (C.), id. hé͘-se, another sort.

se (Cn.), = A. soa, cholera, severe colic, &c.

se (C.) hê-se-á, a small black stinging insect.

se (C.), = A. soe, a comb; to comb.

se (C.), = Cn. söe (comb?). tek-se, a sort of large bamboo broom. sàu-se-á, a small bamboo broom.

se (C.), = A. soe, distant in relationship; wide apart.

se (C.), = A. soe (vegetables).

sê [R. sûi, to hang down, = col. sē], C. sôe; Cn. sō͘).

sê-sê, hanging down, as the head, or as the flap of a long dress or loose wide collar, or as loaded branch; flabby, as skin or flesh; dull and disinclined to fly, as a bird when weary or ill. sê--lòh-khì, hanging down, as a withering flower, flap of dress, &c. sê-kak, one corner out of proportion to the other parts. tàm-sê, hanging down, as from weariness, fear, or shame; drooping, as flower or leaves in drought. lâng sê-sê, wearied and spiritless.

hong sê, the wind fallen. hong khah-sê, id.

sê — si^n-sê, to grow thick folds of skin on the neck, as a very fat man. chiâh kàu-si^n-sê, to grow so fat. pûi kàu-si^n-sê, id.

ām-sê, a child's bib; the dewlap of a cow or horse. noā^n-sê (T. C.), a child's bib.

sê, the sound of tambourines. lô-ién-sê (T. chê), persons shaking instruments like tambourines in idolatrous processions.

sê [R sòe, a year of age, = col. hè]. chhī hāu-si^n, ién lāu-sê, bring up a son and he nourishes his old father. lāu-sê (T.), father.

sé (C.), = A. sé͘, which (in some phrases).

sé (C.), = A. sóe, to wash.

sé (C.), = A. sóe, millet.

sè [R. hè͘, goods, = col. hè]. tsáp-sè-á, small articles sold by pedlars. tsáp-sè-á-tiàm, a shop for miscellaneous smallwares. tsáp-sè-láng, a basket for odds and ends, rags, &c. iô tsáp-sè, to shake a bell while hawking smallwares.

sè, to strike with a stick.

sɛ̀ (C.), = A. siēn, tired.

sè [R. sài, to excel in rivalry], (Cn. sō͘), to try one's chance at dice against the throw (mē͘) which the other had first made.

sè-kè, to be superior in excellence; to excel. khah-sè-kè, id. sa^n-sè, each vying with the other in gaudy splendour, as in showy processions, or gaudy dress, or ornaments of houses, &c. tàu-sa^n-sè, id.

sè gō͘-kâu, to get one die 5, and the other two equal, as the second player. sè kúi-tiám, how many dots on your dice? jī-kâu sè-io-khang, siang-lâng thiòng, the 2 wins over the ace, and both are pleased (as the ace was *sure* to lose in any case).

sè [R. to swear; an oath], (C. sì). hoat-sè, to swear. lip-sè (r.), id. sè-goān (r.), to vow.

sè [R. small; minute, = col. sòe], (also C. = A. sòe, small]. siōng-sè, minutely (v. sè). sè-àn (R.), to consider carefully.

sè-sin, a medicine. sè-pē^n (C.), consumption.

sè [R. sat, to scatter, = col. seh, soah, sāi, siet, &c.] sè-lè tī-thê-kha, all littered, or the floor in disorder. è-sè, all in confusion, all in a litter, as floor covered with torn paper or with shavings. m̄-thang è-sè lāi-bīn, don't litter the house. è-sè tōe-hng, to ruin the morals of a region by bad example.

sè [R. power; form], (C. sì), authority; power; influence; prestige. hó-sè, suitable; convenient; expedient; proper; all right; powerful from having influence to back one (s. rent). hó-sè-thâu, id. (+). hó-sè-bīn, suitable; convenient, as something to be done (+). hó-sè-lâng, man of influence with mandarins or powerful persons. hó-sè siá, convenient for writing (&c.) phái^n-sè, unsuitable; inconvenient; improper to be done in the circumstances; inexpedient. phái-sè-bīn, id. (+). phái^n-sè-thâu, id. (+). sè-thâu, influence, as of powerful man; prestige.

厦英大辭典

thok sè-thâu, to use another's influence. **giâ sè-thâu**, to use the influence or power of one's self, or of another. **sè-bīn**, influence; prestige (+). **sè-kè**, id. **seng-sè**, power; influence. **put-chí ū-seng-sè**, having great power or influence. **koân-sè**, power; influence; authority. **ū sè-lėk**, to have influence and ability (v. lėk). **sè iām**, his influence is great, *e.g.* by associating with powerful persons.

tek-sè, to get prestige or influence, as by success. **oá-sè**, to depend on another's influence. **iú-sè, put-khó chīn-liōng**, when you have power, don't use it to the utmost. **háng-sè**, to pretend to power and influence in a bragging way. **siáp-sè**, to be a cringing mean hanger-on. **sè-lī ê-lâng**, a mean hanger-on on the rich or powerful.

sūn-sè, to take advantage of an opportunity. **sēng-sè**, id.; to act at once.

ū-kiȯk-sè, getting on better now, as business or lawsuit. **tīn-sè**, strength or force of a mass of troops in battle. **chhát-sè**, the power of the rebels or robbers.

sin-sè, power; influence; posture of body for some action. **hó-sin-sè**, having considerable power or influence. **toā-sin-sè**, id. **khiā--khì hó-sin-sè**, to stand in a suitable attitude, as for working or fighting. **tiuⁿ sin-sè**, to set one's self in a proper attitude. **khiā-bé-sè**, to stand with one foot out and arms ready for boxing. **chhiú-sè**, attitude, esp. of hands. **hó-chhiú-sè**, in position or attitude convenient for doing something. **pháiⁿ-chhiú-sè**, in an inconvenient attitude. **pí-sè**, to hold a weapon, as if about to strike. **tsat-sè**, to do anything with hands or feet very cautiously, *e.g.* taking up a very fragile or very heavy thing. **tsat chit-ê-sè**, id. **koan éng-sè**, to watch the proper state of the waves, as in rowing. **khí-hó chi-sè**, the position of riding a tiger (v. hó).

nńg-sè, thin and weak, as boarding or wicker-work. **khiau-sè khiau-sè**, having a crooked form, *e.g.* women's small shoes. **hêng-sè**, form or shape, esp. of hill in relation to good luck. **soaⁿ-sè**, form or appearance of mountain (v. soaⁿ). **khoàⁿ tōe-sè**, to examine the lie of the country, as for house, grave, campaign, or battle. **tiāu-sè**, style of tune or manner of singing it.

sè (R. id.), (C. sì), the world; a generation. **sè-tāi**, a generation. **hō-sè**, after generations. **chhit-sè-sun**, descendant of the seventh generation. **sè-hē**, a genealogical table. **sè-sip**, hereditary, as office or title. **sè-ka**, a family honourable for generations (v. ka).

sè-kan, the world. **sè-kài**, id. **tîn-sè** (R.), this dusty weary world. **loān-sè**, times of anarchy or rebellion. **tsoán-sè**, to be born again as a human being, in the course of transmigration, after suffering in hell or in inferior births (s. rent). **kín-kín tsoán-sè**, to get speedily out of punishment into human form again. **kàng-sè**, to come down to the world, as by incarnation. **kiù-sè**, to save the world (v. kiù). **khoàn-sè-bûn**, Buddhist tracts. **koan-sè-im pút-tsó**, Kwan-yin. **jîn seng u-sè, chhit-sip kó-lâi-hi**, from of old, few live to seventy.

sè-kéng, present circumstances of a place (v. kéng). **sè-chêng**, the ways of the world, esp. as to prevailing customs (v. chêng). **sè-sū**, customary ceremonies (gen. involving expenses), as in worship of ancestors or of idols, at births, deaths, marriages, &c., and in intercourse with friends. **put-am sè-sū**, does not understand the rules and customs of politeness and propriety. **èng-sè**, to have polite intercourse, as by visits, presents, or polite phrases and ceremonies.

sè [R. sòe, customs dues, rent, &c.], (C. sòe, T. Cn. sō), to rent; to take on rent; rent, as of house or land. **tsûn-sè**, freight; passage-money. **lō-thâu-sè**, wharfage dues. **chhù-sè**, house rent. **tiàm-sè**, rent of shop.

sè-chhù, to rent a house, as the tenant. **sè-bé**, to hire a horse for one's self. **sè chit-thàng**, to hire (as horse) for going and back. **chhut-sè**, advertised for lease. **tah chhut-sè**, to put up a ticket "to let." **piēn-chhù chhut-sè**, "house to let." **tsoán-sè**, to sublet (s. world). **siu-sè**, to receive or collect rents. **hó-sè**, easy to rent (s. power).

koan-sè, customs dues. **pò-sè-koán**, office of collector of customs, where junks report themselves. **sin-sè-koan**, the foreign custom-house (Chinese). **sè-bū-si**, foreign commissioner of customs in imperial service. **siu-sè-toaⁿ**, receipt for customs dues, esp. import. **iûⁿ-tsûn ē sè-toaⁿ**, import duty receipt (foreign), allowing to sell at Amoy, or to send into the interior. **lāu-sè**, to smuggle. **tsáu-lāu-sè**, id. **liáh lāu-sè**, to seize smugglers or smuggled goods.

sè-khòe (C. sòe-khè), a deed of sale stamped by the local mandarin. **sè-khòe-kėk**, office for stamping such deeds. **sè-khòe-chhe**, constables attached to it.

sē [R. to pass away; to die], (C. si). **sien-sē** (R.), to die.

sē (C. sōe), to flow out, as water trickling down. **sē--lȯh-khì**, id. **sē--chhut-lâi**, to come flowing out, as saliva or betel-nut juice from the mouth.

ñg-sē-tsúi, thin fluid from a wound or sore.

nńg sē-sē, soft and watery, as dough.

sē [R. sûi, to hang down, = col. sê], turned rather low or downwards, said of the lower support (ē-kim) of a helm. **lȯh-sē**, id.

sē-ku, having one flap too long, as Chinese coat. **chhùi-ē-táu sē-sē**, chin hanging down very much.

sē (same word?). **lâ-sē**, spiritless; having an exhausted look. **kóng-ōe lâ-sē**, to talk very slowly without emotion, and without giving any distinct indication of opinion.

ē-táu lâ-sē, chin naturally very long and hanging down. **pûi kàu lâ-sē**, so fat that the flesh hangs flabby.

sē (C. sè, sɛ̀), wearied; exhausted (r.)

sē— sē-káu, a wild animal like a small wolf; musk is said to be got from it.

sɛⁿ (C.), = A. siⁿ, to live; to be born; to beget, &c.

sɛⁿ (C.) **cheng-sɛⁿ**, = A. cheng-siⁿ, cattle, &c.

sɛⁿ (C.) **àn-nɛⁿ-sɛⁿ**, = A. àn-niⁿ-siⁿ, thus.

sɛ́ⁿ (C.), = A. séng, to use sparingly; a province. **kán-sɛ́ⁿ siá**, to write words in a contracted manner.

sɛ̀ⁿ (C.), = A. sìⁿ, a surname; a clan.

sɛ̄ⁿ (C.), = A. sīⁿ (life, &c.)

seh (R. soat), snow. **lȯh-seh**, to snow. **pėh seh-seh**, very white. **seh toā-tè**, snow in large flakes. **sng-seh**, frost and snow. **sng-lȯh seh-tàng**, very, very cold, as weather. **sng-koāⁿ seh-tàng**, very, very cold. **lȯh-sng-seh**, frosty and snowy weather.

seh-bō, a winter cap or hood with ears, worn by children. **seh-lâi**, white winter pear from Shantung. **hiuⁿ-seh** (esp. C.), = hiuⁿ-thiap, small incense bags in women's hair for scent.

seh [R. soat, a brush; to scrub; = col. chhòe]. **chhat-seh**, a large broad Chinese paint brush.

seh [R. sat, to scatter, = col. soah, siet, chhāi, sái, &c.] **seh-seh,** to scatter, as small seeds; to spread out, as potatoes to dry. **seh hé-hoe,** to let sparks fall, as from a match. **seh-leh chí-lāi-bīn,** littering this room (or house) with small things, as grain, &c.

seh [R. siet, small fragments (C. siak), = col. sut, sap], (C. sɛh). **iù-seh-seh,** broken down very small, as eatables.

khioh-seh, to gather up fragments; to glean.

seh [R. siap, drizzling rain, = col. sap], (C. sɛh). **hō͘-á seh-seh,** very small rain.

seh [R. soat, to speak; to talk; to discourse upon and explain; cf. sòe], (C. soeh), to explain a book to a scholar in colloquial (Cn. söh, but with a much wider meaning, = A. kóng, to speak).

kóe-seh (C. ké-soeh), to translate a book-phrase into colloquial. **seh-chheh,** to explain a book to a scholar in colloquial. **thiaⁿ-seh,** to listen to this explanation by the teacher. **bat-seh,** to understand the meaning of a book, and not merely the sound of the characters (but "bat-söh," Cn., = A. bɛt-kóng, have or has said). **é-káu-seh,** blundering translation, *e.g.* taking words out of their connection in senses used in other phrases, or taking a proper name as a common word, &c.

seh jîn-chêng, to ask a favour for another. **seh-siā** (P. soeh), to give thanks to a man, generally with a present. **seh to-siā,** id. **chiūⁿ-thiⁿ seh-kè,** to ask an exorbitant price. **kóng-thiⁿ, seh hông-tè,** to talk idly about strange things (lit. heaven and emperor). **thoân-miâⁿ seh-siaⁿ,** to spread a report about a man, gen. bad.

seh-pėh, to talk prose in a play (opp. metrical parts); to talk a secret dialect or slang. **lí teh-seh khá-ōe,** you are joking at people, trying to turn the laugh against them. **hō͘--lâng seh-chhiò,** to be a laughing-stock, as because of some disgraceful action. **phaiⁿ-siaⁿ-seh,** angry or proud tone and style of talk. **bô-siaⁿ bô-seh,** no sound or noise whatever. **khiok-seh,** it is said that — (introducing phrase to a story). **khiok-seh tông-tiāu lí-sè-bīn,** said when going to tell some jocular or absurd story.

seh (C.), = A. soeh, to fill up a crack; to get in among the teeth, as food.

sɛh (C.) **thih-sɛh,** a sort of tree with large pinnate glossy leaves.

sɛh (C.) **sɛh-phoà,** to dash in pieces, as a jar (cf. siak, sak).

sėh, to whirl; to turn round; to go round in a circle; to revolve, as planet; to go about idly, or for bad pleasures; a gambling instrument made of a horizontal arm swinging round on a perpendicular axis. **sėh-lėh,** to whirl about, &c. **lâi sėh-sėh,** often said in asking another to go with the speaker to bad houses.

tńg-sėh, to settle or arrange, as a dispute (+). **sėh bé-lê,** over and over put off paying money, or returning a loan, or attending to some business, to the last not put right.

chiàⁿ-sėh, to revolve in the usual direction, as hands of watch. **tò-sėh,** revolve in opposite direction. **tńg chit-sėh,** to take a short walk and come back again (+). **sėh chit-sėh,** id.; also to make one revolution, as something set to whirl round. **sėh chit-toā-kho͘ ûi,** to move in a large circle, as walking or flying. **sėh lin-long,** to run round, as children at play.

sėh thn̂g-á, to gamble for sweetmeats by the "sėh." **thn̂g-á-sėh,** the instrument for this sort of gambling. **kim-ku-sėh,** a toy made to revolve by small beetles.

sėh (Cn.), to throw a stone (cf. tsòh). **sėh chióh-thâu,** id.

sėh [R. sėk, a cloth used by children]. **ām-sėh** (C.), = ām-sê, a child's bib; also (P.), the pod of a leguminous shrub thus shaped.

sėh (mere reduplication; cf. sâh). **pėh-lėh-sėh,** very white.

sɛ̍h (C.) **sɛ̍h-liû,** = siāh-liû, the pomegranate.

sek (Cn. sak, siak). **sek-kháu,** to wash the mouth. **sek-kháu-thn̂g,** = sóe-kháu-thn̂g, a small confection used at marriages. **sek-kháu** (C.), id.

sek [R. a rope; to pull with a rope; to demand; = col. soh]. **lek-sek,** to extort money. **lėk-sek,** id.

sek [R. to arrive at; to suit; pleased]. **sim-sek,** taking the fancy; interesting or pleasant to look at. **sim-sek-hèng,** to take a fancy for something, or to do something (v. hèng). **sim-sek-hìn** (C.), id. **phah-lâng bô-sim-sek,** to treat or speak to a man, so that he is put to shame before others. **poàh sim-sek,** to play a game of chance for amusement, and not for money. **sim-sek-á,** games of chance or gambling; sometimes said of opium. **sek-chhù-á,** gambling, &c. (v. chhù). **sek-chhù,** taking the fancy; games, &c.

sek (R. id.), (C. sih). **sek-sut,** a small sort of cricket (v. sut).

sek [R. to press tightly in; to fill up crevices, &c.; = col. sat, that]. **tí-sek,** to be supplied or used, as an inferior person or thing in place of a good one, often temporarily, as no better can be got. **té-sek** (C.), id. **put-kò sī lâi tí-sek,** only used to fill the place of a better.

sek [R. siòk, ripe, = col. sėk], hard, as a branch (opp. chíⁿ); well boiled, as sugar or confections. **sek chíⁿ,** firm and soft (as above). **koe sòe, chí sek** (melon small, but seeds firm and good), said of a little man who looks boyish, but is older or has more in him than appears.

sek [R. to know], wise; intelligent; skilful. **kiàn-sek,** cleverness, wisdom, knowledge, and skill. **sek-kiàn,** id. **bô-kiàn-sek,** quite ignorant about matters. **sái kiàn-sek,** to overreach a man by superior cunning. **tì-sek** (C. tì-sit), wisdom. **hó-gán-sek,** clever at knowing by a glance. **hó-bák-sek,** good at recognizing after a long time or calculating at a glance. **bák-sek hó,** id. **té bák-sek,** to make a rough calculation by looking at things.

gâu-sǹg-sek, disobliging and refusing to do anything beyond what one must do; always making excuses and delaying to do what is asked. **khah-bat-sek,** understanding well how to act in any circumstances. **put-sek sî-sū,** quite ignorant of the force of circumstances, *e.g.* quarrelling with a powerful man.

sek-kut, precocious and intelligent, as young child. **sek-kúi,** too sharp and cunning (lit. demon), (said of a very sharp and crafty man). **ké-sek,** pretending to be very knowing. **poàⁿ-sek poàⁿ-gōng,** rather under average ability and intelligence. **sek-sek-hì poáh--lòh pîⁿ-kha,** a skilful actor may fall off the stage. **sek-sek-lâng, bóe che lāu-chiú-àng,** said of a wise man making a great mistake.

sek (R. id.), colour; complexion; lust; (sort, as of goods). **bêng-sek,** fame; reputation (v. bêng, "name").

hè-sek, sorts of goods. **tsáp-sek-lâng,** men from many different places, or acquainted with different sorts of business. **m̄-sī lâng-sek,** he is a bad man, always ready to injure others, and dangerous to have dealings with. **bô-siá^n sī lâng-sek**, he is not a very good character. **chhoân-chhòk lâng-sek**, to get ready all the persons, as for a trial (v. chhòk). **gín-ná-sek**, character or behaviour of boy or child. **m̄-sī gín-ná-sek**, mischievous; disobedient; bad or troublesome, as boy or child. **phái^n-gín-ná-sek**, id. **chit--ê gín-ná-sek**, such a boy! so ill-behaved! **m̄-sī kioh-sek**, unfit for his work or position (v. kioh). **hòk-sek**, dress; garments, either as worn or laid by (s. knee).

gân-sek, expression of countenance; appearance of face; complexion. **khì-sek**, complexion, as indicating constitution. **bīn-sek**, complexion, countenance, colour, or appearance of face, esp. as to health. **hó-bīn-sek**, appearance of health. **phái^n-bīn-sek**, sickly-looking. **tsoàt-sek** (R.), very beautiful, as woman.

lú-sek, female beauty; lust; lewdness. **lâm-sek**, sodomy. **lâm-sek**, blue colour. **sek-iòk**, lustful desires. **hò^n-sek**, lewd; lustful. **tham-sek**, id. **sek-hong**, a very bad venereal disease. **hoān sek-hong**, very painful and dangerous disease several days after the act. **hâm-sek-hong** (Cn.), id. **tsau-sek**, debilitated by lasciviousness. **chiú-sek**, liquor and lust. **chiú-sek chi-tê**, man given to them. **hò^n-chiú-sek**, fond of them. **tham-bê chiú-sek**, id.

sek-tsúi, colour. **sái sek-tsúi**, to bully; to talk of one's influence or power in a loud, overbearing, unjust, or threatening way. **sek-tì**, colour. **hó-sek-tèk**, having a good colour, as face, silk, &c. (v. tèk). **súi-sek**, beautiful colour. **iàm-sek** (R.), of splendidly bright colour; gaudy. **chhiò-sek**, light, as blue. **tìm-sek**, dark, as blue. **sí-sek**, dull-coloured. **chhái-sek**, vari-coloured. **kài^n-sek**, having several colours. **pún-sek**, natural colour; not bleached or dyed. **pún-sek sai-iû^n**, gray shirtings.

sek-téng, coloured button of mandarin. **sek-liāu**, materials for colours; dry paint, not yet mixed. **ìn-sek**, red ink used for stamping (v. ìn).

kài-sek, to put a colour on a ground of another colour. **chhài^n-sek**, to work in varied colours (v. chhài^n). **jiám-sek**, to put on some colour on a plain sketch or on a simple ground. **ní^n-sek**, to dye. **ní^n-sek-pò**, dyed shirtings. **chhut-sek**, to make the colour appear, as in painting, or by putting a dress of the same colour below a thin dress. **thè-sek**, to lose the colour. **tsáu-sek**, id. **sit-sek**, to lose colour, as the face. **bīn sit-sek**, id. **bīn lek-sek**, paleness, as from fear or shame. **hoán-sek**, to change colour, as meat turned bad by heat. **piàn-sek**, to change colour, as man or thing. **thi^n piàn-sek**, the weather seems changing, as to rain or wind. **thi^n-siōng piàn-sek**, id. **khoà^n thi^n-sek**, to observe the signs of the weather.

tsng-sek, to put on a false colour or gloss on goods; to put on any false appearance. **tsòe-sek**, to cause or make a colour; to put on a bad colour that will not hold. **tsòe-sek ê-ōe**, boastful talk; praising one's self or friends or belongings too much. **tang-bīn tsòe-sek**, first streaks of dawn appearing in the east.

ngó-sek, vari-coloured, esp. black, red, white, yellow, and blue. **ngó-sek-hûn**, bright-coloured clouds. **kài ngó-sek**, to paint in various colours. **ngó-sek-pò**, coloured shirtings. **ngó-sek-bīn**, a scoundrel or wicked violent fellow, esp. hangers-on about yamuns; in plays such characters are represented with face of various colours. **ngó-sek-lién**, id. **ngó-sek-kî**, flags of various colours, or one flag of five colours. **sam-sek-kî**, flag of three colours, esp. Dutch or (r.) French. **khoà^n sam-sek**, to watch which side is going to win, so as to take that side.

sek [R. ornaments; to adorn]. **siú-sek**, ornaments for woman's head. **chhiú-sek**, ornaments for the head. **iám-sek**, to conceal under a false appearance, *e.g.* poverty, bad designs, or wicked conduct.

sek [R. chhek (C. chhip), the knee]. **sek-khò**, short leggings worn by women (v. khò). **hòk-sek** (C. hòk-sip), ornaments worn on the knees (s. colour). **pák hòk-sek**, to wear them.

sek [R. a guitar with many strings]. **khîm-sek**, harps and guitars in general.

sek [R. chek, a sort of millet]. **sek-á**, small coarse sort of millet, esp. for feeding birds. **sóe-sek béh-tāu**, millet, wheat, barley, and pulse. **sóe-sek thô-tāu**, millet and ground-nuts. **ah-kha-sek**, a very small sort of grain, having a head like a duck's foot.

sek [R. siok, rice growing, or with the husk on, = col. chhek]. **eng-sek-hoe**, the poppy. **eng-sek-khak**, poppy pods.

sek [R. a house], (C. sit, chit). **sek-á**, small lodgings connected with temples. **tì-sek-ka**, married (said of a man). **tsāi-sek-lú**, a virgin.

sek [R. id., tin, = col. siah], (also Cn., = A. siah, tin, pewter). **sek-thn̄g**, the Buddhist key of hell (v. thn̄g).

sek [R. a pattern; a model; = col. sit], (C. sit, sek). **thé-sek**, a form or pattern to be followed, as for an essay, or marriage contract, or legal document. **keh-sek**, proper rule or pattern, as for a document (v. keh). **tsn̄g-sek**, paper form on which to write a petition or accusation. **thiap-sek**, forms for writing invitations, &c. **khoán-sek** (esp. T.), = khoán-sit, a pattern. **sí-sek** (C.), = A. sí-sit, fashionable.

sek [R. to loose; to set free]. **tiah-sek-tiâ^n**, to put in a petition in court withdrawing our name from an action in which our name has been unjustly involved. **tiah-sek**, id. **jip tiah-sek**, id.

sek-kia, Buddha; Shakya-muni. **sek-kia-hút**, id. **sek-khia**, id.; also, the custard-apple. **sek-kàu**, Buddhism; the Buddhist sect. **sek-ka**, the Buddhist sect.

sek (cf. sut). **bák-chiu sek-khok sek-khiak**, eyes glancing about rapidly.

sek [R. to rest; to cease; posterity; interest], (C. sit, sek). **an-sek-jit** (X.), the Sabbath. **àn-sek-hiu^n**, gum benzoin. **hô-sek-tiâ^n**, a joint petition put in by the two parties in a suit saying that they have now made up the quarrel. **jip hô-sek**, to enter such a petition.

tsú-sek, male children; phrase used in fortune-telling.

lī-sek, gain; profit in trade; interest of money. **pàng-lī-sek**, lend money on interest. **pún-chî^n lī-sek**, principal and interest; capital and profit. **seng-sek**, to lie at interest.

sek [R. harvest; to amass; avaricious]. **lîn-sek** (R.), miserly; stingy; niggardly.

sek [R. to love; to compassionate; = col. sioh]. **khó-sek** (C.), = A. khó-sioh, alas! how lamentable! (but in other phrases C. sioh, = A.).

sek (P.), = A. siok (uncle), and perhaps in some other words.

sek (T.) **sek-phò-si**, = A. sok-pò-si, an attendant of Sêng-hông.

sek (Cn.) **sek-kan-tsú**, = A. sù-kun-tsú, a medicinal plant.

sek [R. a stone, = col. chioh, siah]. **thiet-sek sim-tiông**, cruel and pitiless. **kut-sek**, a sort of medicine. **chiá-sek**, a medicine. **bông-sek**, a medicine. **kam-sek**, a medicinal stone reduced to powder by roasting. **giâ-sek-lun** (r.), a composition of which small ornamental bottles are made.

sek [R. evening, = col. siah]. **tiau-sek** (R.), morning and evening. **tiau bûn-tō, sek sú, khó--i**, having learned the doctrine in the morning, though one dies in the evening it will do.

sek [R. a mat; a feast; = col. siah, chhioh], (T. siah, sek), classifier of meals or feasts. **sàng-sek**, to present a cooked feast to a man. **soàⁿ-sek**, the breaking up of a feast. **hàn-sek**, a feast in Chinese style. **boán-hàn-sek**, feast in Manchoo and Chinese style. **kúi-sek**, how many meals? (T. siah). **chit-sek-toh**, one feast or meal. **chit-sek-chiú**, one drinking feast. **kièn-tāi-sek-biēn**, extensively acquainted with rich or influential men.

sek (T.) **hō-sek**, = A. hé-sit, food. **jit-sek**, = A. jit-sit, daily food.

sek (P.), = A. siok, cheap, common, customs, &c.

sek (P.), = A. siok (connected); and so with some other words.

sek (R. siok, = col. sek), (P. siok), ripe; fully cooked; well learned; well acquainted with a thing. **chhiⁿ-sek**, raw and cooked, green and ripe, &c. **poàⁿ-chhiⁿ-sek**, half-raw; very slightly acquainted with the matter.

sek-chhat, glossy varnish thoroughly prepared.

tsú-sek, to cook thoroughly. **kè-sek**, too much cooked; too ripe. **sek láu-láu**, very ripe or over ripe, as fruit. **ké-chí toā-sek**, ripe fruit abundant.

sek-hoan, a tribe of Formosan aborigines who have submitted to Chinese rule and learned Chinese; (lit. civilized foreigners).

sek-sāi, well acquainted with a man; intimate (v. sāi). **siong-sek**, id. **bīn-sek**, slightly acquainted with a man (just knowing his face). **lō sek**, knowing the road well. **soàn-hoat sek**, good at arithmetic. **sek làu-làu**, well acquainted with, as road or language. **ké-sek**, pretending to know all about a matter. **liām-sek**, to learn a lesson thoroughly. **sek-chhiú**, skilful with the hand; accustomed to do something. **sek-hâng**, skilful; experienced. **kìⁿ-koaⁿ sek-hâng**, experienced in lawsuits; not afraid to come into court. **sek-tiûⁿ**, experienced, as in gambling. **koàn-sek** (P.), = A. koàn-siok, well experienced.

seng [R. cattle; sacrificial animals; = col. cheng, siⁿ], (Cn. söng). **seng-lé**, offerings of flesh to the dead or the gods. **tsòe-seng-lé**, to make such offerings. **ngó-seng**, the five sorts of offerings. **sam-seng**, the three sorts of flesh-offerings; one may be eggs or maccaroni. **sam-seng-tsâi** (v. tsâi). **sam-seng-phe**, very bold and ready for a feud, either by fighting or by lawsuit and examination.

seng (R. id.), (Cn. söng). **gōe-seng**, a sister's son. **gōe-seng-lú**, sister's daughter. **gōe-seng-sun**, sister's grandson.

seng [R. sound; fame; = col. siaⁿ]. **seng-sè**, power; influence (v. sè). **jím-khì thun-seng**, to repress one's anger and voice, as before a superior (v. thun).

seng (R. id.), to ascend; to raise, as flag; to promote or rise in official rank; raise the back of the sedan so as to let the passenger step out easily. **seng--chiūⁿ-khì**, to ascend. **seng-koâiⁿ**, id. (as in rank?). **seng-kî**, to hoist a flag. **seng-khí**, to hoist, as flag. **seng-tn̂g**, to ascend the tribunal and take his seat, as judge. **seng-thien**, to ascend to heaven. **pek-jit seng-thien**, do. in daylight.

ko-seng, regularly promoted to high office. **seng-kip**, to rise in rank and office (v. kip). **seng-koaⁿ**, to rise in official rank. **seng-koaⁿ-tô**, a diagram with titles of offices, &c., used for a game.

seng-bâ, a medicine for causing perspiration and curing giddiness (Thalictrum? Sida?). **seng-moâⁿ**, id.

seng (R. sien), (T. saiⁿ; Cn. süiⁿ), formerly; previously; in advance; first. **thâu-seng**, at first; previously. **khí-seng**, id. **tng khí-seng**, id. **tāi-seng** (Cn. tō-süiⁿ), at first; before; beforehand. **tāi-seng-tsai**, to know beforehand. **i tāi-seng-goá lâi**, he came before I came. **i seng-goá lâi**, id. **i khah-tāi-seng-goá lâi**, id. **seng-lâi**, to come first. **seng hō--i**, give him beforehand. **seng-chioh**, to borrow in advance; to get payment in advance.

seng [R. a star, = col. chhiⁿ, san]. **liû-seng** (R.), a shooting-star. **liû-seng-thûi**, a ball fastened to a chain, used in ancient warfare. **sái liû-seng**, to use this weapon. **khoe-seng**, the god of the N. star and of literature (v. khoe). **pak-táu seng-kun**, = Hiên-thien Siōng-tè (v. táu). **tiông-siū-seng**, the star of longevity. **hok-seng chiàu-iāu**, may the auspicious star favour you (v. iāu). **bâ-bīn, boán thien-seng**, a pock-marked face may seem dotted with stars.

lâm-seng, a medicinal plant.

seng — **seng-seng**, a sort of ape.

seng [R. song, double; a pair; = siang, sang]. **seng-taⁿ-but**, a small, thin, white marine worm, sharp at each end.

seng (R. id.), (Cn. söng), a musical instrument like Pan's pipes, esp. used in Changchew.

seng [R. sin; misery, pain]. **seng-khó**, miserable in body; toiling in wretchedness.

seng [R. sin, the body]. **seng-khu**, = sin-khu, the body.

seng [R. siông, the fir-tree, = col. chêng, chhêng]. **tō-seng**, a sort of fir-tree. **seng-gô** (C.), id. **seng-gô-lûi** (C.), its cones (large).

seng (P.), = A. siong (in some words).

seng [R. alive; to produce; raw; = col. siⁿ, chhiⁿ], (Cn. söng), to produce; life; a respectable male character in a play.

seng-oân (R.), a Sew-tsai (v. oân). **lím-seng**, a literary rank between Sew-tsai and Kujin. **kàm-seng**, a purchased title nearly like Sew-tsai. **kòng-seng**, the rank next to Kujin (v. kòng). **ìm-seng**, a son of a high mandarin, who gets on by influence. **tông-seng**, a candidate for the Sew-tsai degree. **hak-seng**, a pupil; a scholar; a disciple. **bûn-seng** (R.), id. **bûn-seng**, a card used as indenture for apprentice; the conditions are not written on it, as they are always understood. **thien-tsú bûn-seng**, the highest three literary titles (chiōng-goân, póng-gán, and thàm-hoe), conferred once in three years by the emperor in person. **lé-seng**, master of ceremonies, esp. at sacrificial offerings. **i-seng**, a doctor (v. i). **boán-seng**, polite phrase for "I," said to one slightly our superior, or from politeness to an inferior.

seng-toàⁿ, male and female characters in a play (v. toàⁿ). **hì-seng**, male character, as of a man in respectable circumstances. **lāu-seng**, character of old man (+). **sió-seng**, character of young, polite, or learned man. **tsng-seng**, to act the part of a young

海上絲綢之路文獻集成 科技與文化編

gentleman. **tsng lāu-seng**, to act the part of an old man.

seng-bō, sort of cap used in plays.

lȯk-kha-seng, ground-nuts, Arachis, = thé-tāu. **seng-khe**, bean-cake made from them. **seng-iû**, oil made from them.

seng-tē, sort of medicine in its raw form (v. tē).

seng-lí, trade; mercantile business. **tsòe-seng-lí**, to trade; to do mercantile business. **seng-lí-hoat**, rules and customs of trade. **seng-lí-tiûⁿ**, arena or affairs of trade. **seng-lí-chhùi**, tricks of trade by saying what is not just true. **seng-hoȧt-kè**, means of livelihood.

seng-sek, to lie at interest.

seng-sán, to bear young (v. sán). **seng-iȯk**, to get a child (said of either parent). **hoà-seng**, to become living by transformation, as animals (v. hoà). **hôe-seng** (R.), to return to life. **khí-sú hôe-seng**, to raise the dead to life (said of curing a man almost dying). **chhiau-seng**, to get a soul out of hell so as to be born again into the world; to spare a life sentenced to death (v. chhiau). **thėh seng-keng**, to take the horoscope of an intended pair to see how they suit. **seng-tióng**, to grow up to full age. **seng-sêng**, naturally so; to assist out of poverty into prosperity (v. sêng). **thien-seng tsū-jiên**, naturally so; certainly so; of course. **ióng-seng-tn̂g**, a foundling hospital. **hòng-seng**, to save animals alive for Buddhist merit (v. hòng). **sat-seng**, to destroy life (v. sat). **pó-seng tāi-tè**, = tāi-tō-kong, the god of medicine. **sú-seng iú-bēng**, death and life are decreed by Heaven (v. bēng). **seng-sú iú-tēng**, id. **tiông-seng put-sú**, long life without death. **tiông-seng put-ló**, long life without growing old. **tiông-seng lȯk-ūi**, honorary tablet to a living mandarin. **seng-lō**, means of avoiding death. **iáu-ū chit-tiám seng-khì**, a little life still remains, as in man, animal, or plant that seemed dead.

it-seng, one's whole lifetime; all life long. **pêng-seng**, during one's whole past life; usually (in the past). **seng-pêng**, id.

bȯk-seng, having the element "wood" strong in one's constitution; large-boned, stiff, and rather ungainly in form. **hé-seng**, having the element "fire" or the hot principle strong in the constitution, with tendency to a red face and prominent veins.

seng-khì, to be angry (+). **seng-ì**, interesting; pleasant to look at. **toā-seng-ì**, very much pleased. **seng-sū**, to breed trouble, as a quarrel or feud naturally springing up. **seng-toan**, id. **bû-tiong seng-iú** (r.), to raise groundless reports. **chhiok-kéng seng-chêng**, some circumstance exciting musing or melancholy emotions. **lȯk kėk, pi seng**, grief comes at the height of joy (v. pi).

sêng [R. sîn, a spirit]. **pháiⁿ-sêng-khì**, feeling of awkwardness and shame, as at having to speak against a friend, or being reproved by a superior (v. pháiⁿ).

sêng [R. to assist; an assistant or deputy; = col. sîn]. **sêng-siòng**, a prime minister. **sêng-siùⁿ**, id. **tán-chih sêng-siùⁿ**, you have kept me waiting a long time (as if you were prime minister). **bûn-sêng bú-ùi** (R.), civil and military officers (written on doors). **hiēn-sêng** (R.), = hun-koāiⁿ, the civil mandarin of a subdivision of a hien. **koāiⁿ-sêng**, id.

sêng [R. to ride; to take advantage of; to multiply; = col. sēng]. **sêng-hoat**, multiplication. **kui-tû sêng-hoat**, multiplication and division (v. kui). **sêng chhit-pái**, multiply by seven.

sêng (R. id.) **sêng-sim**, truthful; faithful, as man. **sêng-sit** (r.), id. **sêng-kèng**, sincerely reverential, as man. **tâu-sêng**, to submit to the mandarins on condition of complete impunity.

sêng [R. a city, = col. siâⁿ]. **sêng-hông-iâ**, the guardian deity of a city (v. hông). **iú-hok ku sêng-kok**, prosperous men live in cities and suburbs. **hù-kùi ku sêng-kok**, id.

sêng — **sêng-hî**, a large coarse-tasted fish, without scales and with few bones, much like the liâm-hî.

sêng (P.) **sêng-ka**, = A. siông-ka, resin.

sêng [R. id., = col. sâⁿ, sîn], (C. sîn), to receive, as a thing. **sêng-siū**, to receive; to accept. **sêng-jīn**, to confess, as an action. **tam-sêng**, to stand security; to assume responsibility, as for man whom we recommend, or of matter which we manage. **thài-kong tiò-hî, goān-chiá sêng-kau** (when Thai-kung fished, only the willing fish took the hook), I tell you plainly without any concealment, choose as you please.

hōng-sêng, to treat with much attention, as a superior or a visitor; to talk very politely, as to visitors; to adulate or fawn upon. **èng-sêng**, to promise to grant a request. **moáⁿ-chhùi èng-sêng**, mouth full of fair promises. **boán-khé èng-sêng**, id.

sêng-chiap, to succeed to (v. chiap). **lėk-tāi siong-sêng**, handed down from generation to generation, as throne or title of nobility. **sè-tāi siong-sêng**, id. **sêng i--ê ki-giȧp**, to succeed to his property. **sêng-koán**, to succeed to and have control of. **sêng-hū koán-giȧp**, to succeed to one's father and have control of the property.

keng-sêng, a certain clerk or secretary in a yamun, who receives petitions and complaints, &c., and prepares the draft warrants for the mandarin's inspection. **chhe-sêng**, this official and the constables. **sêng-chhe**, id.

sêng [R. id., = col. chiâⁿ, chhiâⁿ, siâⁿ], to complete; to accomplish. **sêng-chiū**, to accomplish, as an affair (v. chiū). **sêng-sū**, to accomplish a matter. **sêng-sū tsāi-thien**, the issue of an affair is in the hands of Heaven (v. tsāi). **sêng-kong**, to carry an affair to a successful issue. **lōng-ká sêng-chin**, a joke becomes a sad reality (v. lōng). **sip-koàn sêng tsū-jiên**, habit becomes a second nature (v. tsū). **sêng-bêng**, to attain to fame (v. bêng). **pėk-siú sêng-ka**, from poverty become rich. **sêng-tsó**, to found a family, as ancestor (v. tsó). **sêng-hȯt**, to become a Buddha. **sêng-sien**, to become a genie; to die. **tsòe khèng-sêng**, to perform Tauist rites, as on the completion of a temple, &c.

seng-sêng (lit. bring into being and make perfect), naturally so; originally; to assist a man from poverty to great prosperity, as patron. **seng-sêng bûn-lí**, naturally good-looking, as man. **seng-sêng put-siȯk**, having a noble appearance; not common-looking. **tióng-sêng**, to grow up to full age. **sêng-teng**, to come to age of puberty (v. teng). **chiâⁿ-lâng sêng-khì**, to get set up in the world, as by marriage, by getting an office or situation or a good business. **tsok-sêng**, to assist in business (v. tsok). **khan-sêng**, to assist a man who is out of employment till he can get on well. **tsàn-sêng**, to assist in accomplishing something. **siu-sêng**, to gather in, as the harvest; to wind up, as a business, not because of failure. **siú-sêng**, to be careful, as of property; very careful and well-behaved.

sêng-hȯk, to put on deep mourning, either at first, or when resuming it for special rites. **sêng-chhin**,

53

to consummate the marriage relation by intercourse. **kun-tsú sêng jîn-chi-bí**, a good man assists others to goodness. **khut-tá^{n} sêng-chiau**, to beat violently and force to confess.

put-chí-sêng, very like, as a portrait.

ló-sêng, having the good sense and staid manner of an old man, though young (v. ló).

iú-sêng, likely to prove useful in the world, as an industrious boy will afterwards. **bû-sêng**, useless, as a lazy boy. **bû-sêng ê-tsú-tē**, an idle useless boy. **put-sêng**, not complete; cannot be accomplished; does not succeed, as affair. **pān put-sêng**, unable to put the matter straight. **put-sêng-jîn**, ill-behaved, as a vagabond or unsatisfactory character. **put-sêng-bu̍t**, id. **put-sêng-mih^{n}**, id.; also ill-formed or unfinished article. **put-sêng-tiàm**, a shop that can hardly be called a shop. **bû-khiau, put-sêng-sû** (C. sî), if you don't go about the bush, you cannot accomplish the matter.

sêng-gú, a recognized book-phrase that has become colloquial.

lí--ê chek-sêng, it is your affair; if it go wrong, the responsibility is on you. **i-ū chek-sêng tī--teh**, the responsibility is on him.

séng [R. to examine; sparing; a province], (C. sé^{n}), to diminish or lessen, as expense, labour, or trouble; a province; the provincial capital.

séng-chhat, to investigate; to examine into (v. chhat). (In this paragraph it remains "séng" in C.) **put-séng jîn-sū** (not recognizing things), very foolish; in a swoon; very ill. **séng-chhin** (R.), to go to visit parents.

tsa̍p-poeh-séng, the eighteen provinces of China. **bé-séng**, the last province, Fuh-kien. **kè-séng**, to go from one province to another. **séng-hūn**, a province. **séng-siâ^{n}**, the provincial capital. **chhut-séng**, to leave the provincial capital. **kè-gûn chiū^{n}-séng**, to transmit treasure to the provincial capital, as mandarins.

kán-séng, to abbreviate; to do hurriedly, or with brevity (v. kán). **khiām-séng**, to use sparingly; economical. **liám-séng**, id. **kiám-séng**, more sparing in expense. **kien-ta-séng**, dispense with altogether. **séng-ēng** (C. sé^{n}-iōng), to use less; to use sparingly or economically. **séng-siàu**, effecting a saving of money; cheaper. **khah-séng-siàu**, id. **séng-chî^{n}**, cheaper; requiring less money. **séng sé-hùi**, economical. **séng liáu-chî^{n}**, to save expense, *e.g.* something not needing to be done that would have cost money. **séng-sū**, to avoid trouble and quarrels in the management of a matter, *e.g.* by caution, or by being willing to lose or suffer a little for peace. **séng-kang**, to spare labour. **séng lé-la̍t**, less trouble; to lessen the labour. **séng--tit lēng-lê khí-tsàu**, said of not needing any more (lit. one cooking-place enough).

sèng (R. id., = col. sì^{n}), nature (of man or of things); natural character or disposition; temper, often bad temper. **sim-sèng**, nature of the heart, temper, disposition. **sèng-chêng**, nature and dispositions. **pún-sèng**, original nature or character. **goân-sèng put-kái**, original bad nature not reformed. **péng-sèng**, original natural character. **pín-sèng**, id. **phín-sèng**, character and disposition, natural or acquired. **phiah-sèng**, disposition; temper. **sèng-phiah**, id. **sèng-khì phái^{n}**, temper bad. **sèng-tē**, temper, esp. bad temper. **ū sèng-tē**, to have a bad temper. **ū-sèng ū-tē**, id. **phái^{n}-sèng-tē**, bad-tempered. **hó-sèng-tē**, good temper; good-tempered. **kāu-sèng-tē**, irascible; bad-tempered. **sèng-tē tio̍h-pàng-lo̍h**, should restrain temper. **sèng-tē pàng-khah-hē**, let temper down a little.

io̍h-sèng, nature of a particular drug, as to its character and effects (v. io̍h). **lūn-sèng**, tough, as some sorts of wood.

khí-sèng, to get angry. **hoat-sèng**, do., naturally from a real and sufficient cause (right or wrong). **sái-sèng**, to put on an angry manner; to get angry for no cause at all, or excessively angry for a slight cause. **gōng sái-sèng**, suddenly and foolishly get into a great rage, either at man or thing, *e.g.* breaking or throwing away a thing that does not please us. **théng-sèng**, self-willed and overbearing, proud and quick-tempered; self-confident and imperious, as young fellow. **hé-sèng**, of a quick fiery temper. **sò-sèng**, hasty tempered. **chháu-á-sèng**, irascible and quick-tempered, but soon over. **kín-sèng**, id. **ok-sèng**, very crabbed and bad-tempered, as child. **pà-sèng**, id. **bô-tēng-sèng**, very fickle and of unsettled purpose. **hū-jîn tsúi-sèng**, women are unstable in purpose (like water), and easily moved to incontinence.

sèng [R. to conquer]. **hè^{n}-sèng**, fond of overcoming, or showing one's own power; domineering; ambitious. **tek-sèng**, to get the victory. **tek-sèng-koà**, a jacket opening at the side, made with many foreign buttons. **phah tek-sèng-ké** (to come back in triumph from war with drums, &c.), fig. of a man who has had a great success, as in a lawsuit.

sèng (R. id.), sage and wise in the highest degree; inspired; holy; sacred; applied to things connected with the sages, or the emperor, or some great divinities. **sèng-siōng**, the emperor. **sèng-kun**, an emperor with the virtue of a sage (v. kun). **sèng-chí**, imperial will or decree. **sèng-un**, imperial favour. **sèng-siū**, emperor's birthday (v. siū). **sèng-jū**, the "sacred edict." **sèng-jī** (C.), id. **sèng-chhâi**, ground-rent levied by military mandarins.

keh sèng-ông, an idol of the surname Keh. **tân sèng-ông**, one of surname Tân. **hé-sèng-kong**, the tiger-god of gamblers. **sèng-tûi^{n}** (Cn.), the temple of Hiân-thien Siōng-tè.

hián-sèng, to manifest power to answer prayer, as an idol appearing visibly.

sèng-jîn, a great inspired sage. **sèng-jîn-kham**, a binnacle. **chin sèng-jîn**, quite a sage! said ironically of a bad character. **chì-sèng**, the greatest sage (Confucius); most holy. **à-sèng**, a sage of second rank, as Mencius and Gân-hôe (Yen-yen). **sèng-hiân**, sages and wise philosophers. **sèng-kàu**, the doctrine of the sages. **iâ-so͘ sèng-kàu**, the sacred doctrine (or church) of Jesus. **sèng-keng**, sacred books; Scriptures. **sèng-chheh**, id. **sèng-hōe** (X.), the church. **sèng-tô͘** (X.), saints; holy disciples. **sèng-sîn** (X.), the Holy Spirit. **sèng-chek-mih^{n}**, things that have some trace or memorial of ancient sages.

sèng [R. a surname, = col. sì^{n}]. **hok-sèng**, a surname of two characters, *e.g.* su-má. **tso̍k-sèng**, a clan; surname of clan. **tông-sèng**, of same surname. **tông-sèng put-tsong**, same surname, but not nearly related (v. tsong). **ī^{n}-sèng**, of different surnames. **tsa̍p-sèng**, having several surnames in same village. **ko͘-sèng**, the only one of the surname among people of other surname or surnames. **ko-sèng**, what is your surname, sir? **tāi-sèng**, a great and numerous clan. **tāi-sèng-hú**, id. (v. hú). **siáu-sèng**, a small clan. **tāi-siáu-sèng-hōe**, small clans combining to resist the larger. **bâi-bu̍t sèng-bêng**, to conceal name and surname. **oā^{n}-miâ^{n} kóe-sèng**, to change name and surname; to take an alias (v. miâ^{n}).

sēng [R. abundant; a surname; = col. siā^{n}], abundant; plentiful. **sēng soe**, prospering and declining (v. soe). **hong-sēng**, very abundant (v. hong). **chhiong-sēng**, id. **bē-sēng** (R.), luxuriant, as vegetation. **sēng-tek**, virtuous character (v. tek). **kan-hé sēng**, having a slightly feverish tendency (v. kan, "liver").

sēng [R. overplus, = col. sīn]. **liōng-sēng** (R. liōng-sēng), exceedingly abundant, as money, crops, &c. **chî^{n}-tsúi liōng-sēng**, having money in great abundance, as man or firm.

sēng, to spoil, as a child; to indulge too much, as an inferior, allowing him to do as he pleases. **théng-sēng**, id. **sēng-khi-la**, to indulge or spoil him till he has it all his own way. **sēng-hêng**, spoiled, as child; dogged and impudent, as beggar. **sēng-káu chiū^{n}-tsàu, sēng-kiá^{n} put-hàu**, a petted dog makes free with the cooking-place; a spoiled child is unfilial. **sēng-ti giâ-tsàu, sēng-kiá^{n} put-hàu**, a pig allowed its own way burrows under the fireplace; a spoiled child, &c. **sēng--i chiū^{n} táh-pang, soà-beh-chiū^{n} bîn-chhn̂g**, allow him on the step, and he will go on the bed.

sēng [R. sêng, to ride, to multiply, &c.], to take advantage of an opportunity. **sēng-sè**, id. **sēng-ki**, id. **sēng-soà**, take advantage of the opportunity of doing something to do something more.

si [R. to bestow], a surname; to strew or scatter, as saw-dust. **si-si**, to strew, as saw-dust. **si-li**, id. **si tī-thô-kha**, to strew on the floor, as sand or saw-dust.

si-chè (R.), to bestow, as charity. **si-un**, to bestow grace or favour. **si-siá** (R.), to bestow (v. siá).

si — **si-jiō**, to get an infant to pass water, as a nurse does.

si [R. su, secret; private; = col. sai]. **ke-si**, implements; instruments; furniture; weapons. **ke-si-thâu**, id. **pí ke-si**, to practise fencing or the use of weapons. **ién ke-si**, id.

si [R. su, a spiral shell-fish]. **lê-si-teng**, a screw-nail. **lê-si**, id. **lê-si** (C.), id. **lê-si-tsoān**, a screw-driver. **tèng lê-si-teng**, to put in a screw-nail.

si [R. su, to think]. **siu^{n}-si**, deeply enamoured of a particular person so as to be sick (v. siu^{n}, mutual), (s. shrub).

si [R. su, name of shrub]. **siu^{n}-si**, a shrub with long narrow leaves, yellow flowers, and seeds in a legume, Abrus precatorius. **siu^{n}-si-chhiū**, id. **siu^{n}-si-chhâ**, its wood.

si — **n̂g-si**, sort of wood, much used for oars. **n̂g-si-chhâ**, its wood.

si [R. sort of labiate plant like verbena]. **si-chháu**, a plant like verbena, used for divination. **siáp-si**, to divine by slips of this plant.

si [R. name of an herb]. **thò-si**, a medicinal creeper with fine tendrils, sometimes ornamental (dodder ?). **thò-si-piá^{n}**, its seeds made up into a sort of cake. **thò-si-chí**, id.

si [R. se, west, = col. sai]. **si-koe**, the water-melon. **si-koe oá toā-pêng**, people like the larger half of a melon (favour the winning side).

hā-tsoh tong-si, low mean fellow ! (said in scolding).

si (C.), = A. su (ought).

si (C.) **phài kun-si** (= A. su), to levy contributions for the army, &c.

si [R. su, a book; a document; to write; = col. tsu], (also C., = A. su, a book, &c.)

siū^{n}-si, the president of one of the supreme boards at the metropolis.

siū^{n}-si (C.), = A. su-keng, the Shoo-king, the historical classic.

si [R. name of a bird]. **pe̍h-lēng-si**, the white egret or paddy-bird. **pe̍h-lē-si** (R.), id.; some say different. **lē-si** (R.), id. **lē-si-pân**, sort of wine-jug with long thin neck. **lē-si-kha**, having very long thin shaky legs, as man or piece of furniture.

chhi^{n}-si-á, a small yellow bird (Zosterops?).

si (R. id.), an ode; poetry; a hymn or psalm. **si-keng**, the Book of Odes; the Shi-king. **mô͘^{n}-si** (C.), id. **si-phien** (X.), the Book of Psalms. **chit-chhiú-si**, one ode. **chit-siú-si**, id. **ngó͘-giên-si**, odes in lines of five words. **chhit-giên-si**, of seven words.

si-ūn, a rhyming dictionary. **si-ong** (R.), a poet. **si-chhai**, sort of gambling by lines of poetry. **chhiam-si**, colloquial verses on slips of paper, drawn by lot in temples. **thiah chhiam-si**, to tear off one of these slips of verse after drawing the lot. **poe-si** (T.), divination by lots and verses of poetry (v. poe). **báng-á-si**, verses about mosquitoes (v. báng).

liām-si, to repeat odes. **gîm-si**, to chant or sing odes. **tôe-si**, to compose and write poetry, as on an ornamental scroll. **tsòe-si**, to make poetry. **tho̍k-si chhien-siú, put-tsok tsū-iû**, after learning a thousand odes one can make them naturally.

si (R. id.), a corpse. **sin-si**, id. **si-siú**, id. **sí-si**, id., said in scorn or spite. **tsoân-si**, corpse of suicide or of man killed, but not mutilated. **tsúi-lâu-si**, a corpse floated by the tide. **lō-pông-si**, a corpse lying on the roadside. **kiong-si**, a corpse that catches and kills people (v. kiong).

si-chhin, the relatives of a man who is found dead. **si-tsú**, that relation who has authority to ask explanation of, or reparation for, the death.

giām-si, to hold an inquest on a corpse. **kiám-si**, do. after it is far decayed, *e.g.* only bones. **biét-si**, to destroy a corpse so as to evade inquiry. **î-si**, to move a corpse to another man's premises so as to involve him.

si-jī-thâu, the 44th radical.

bē-kêng, chhut kêng-si, when about to become poor, a man has mean ill-behaved sons.

si (R. id.), silk, esp. in thread; fine thin threads, fibres, or shreds; said also of gut or fine wire; a very small quantity. **si-si**, very slim and thin, as the strokes of characters.

chit-si-á, a very small quantity. **chit-si-si-á**, id. **bô-lî-si**, not in the very least (v. lî). **chit-si-hô to bōe-tsòe--tit**, it won't do at all.

ti-tu-si, cobwebs. **ti-lâ-si**, id. **pe-si**, flying motes in the air (*e.g.* strings of spiders' webs, &c.) which injure the eyes. **ièn-si**, long strings of raw birds'-nests. **kiu^{n}-si**, ginger made into thin shreds. **ō-hoāi^{n}-si**, strings of taro stalks, used in making (ké) cakes. **tōe-á-si**, fine fibres of flax. **thâng-si**, strong gut made from the "png-thâng" caterpillar. **tâng-si**, fine brass wire. **thiu tâng-si**, to make fine brass wire.

î^{n}-si, sycee silver.

chhi^{n}-si, a thin silk stuff. **poeh-si-á**, very thin slim glossy silk stuff, much used for pasting things for the worship of the dead. **pháng-si**, a very strong good silk stuff. **âng-pháng-si**, red do. **kam-lâi-si**, a fine linen stuff (cambric?). **si-pè**, stuff made of silk and cotton mixed, made at Changchew.

si-thâu, coarse refuse silk; it makes a very strong stuff. **si-soà^n**, silk thread. **si-mî^n**, cotton and silk mixed in a thick soft mass for absorbing ink (v. mî^n). **hê-si-kheh**, a silk merchant from Central China (v. hê).

sa^n-pah-lák-si, a very thin sort of paper; there used to be 360 sheets in one bundle. **sam-liók-si-tsoá**, id. **ìn-si-tsoá**, id.

liâu-si, a transparent or translucent substance made from boiled rice. **liâu-si-teng**, lantern fitted with it instead of glass.

thò-si, to spin silk from the mouth, as the silk-worm (s. herb). **ki^n-si**, to spin silk; to weave mischievous plots (v. ki^n). **thiu-si**, to unwind silk from the cocoon. **iang-si**, to wind silk on the reel.

pī^n-si-pêng, the 120th radical at the side (v. pêng).

chhi^n-tek-si, a very venomous serpent that has long feelers like threads. **sûi-si-liú**, the weeping-willow. **kim-si-chiáu**, a beautiful little yellow bird. **kim-si chiáu-á**, id. **kim-si n̂g-chhek-chiáu-á**, id.

SI [R. su, to take charge of; to manage or rule; an official; a subdivision of a district]. **kong-si**, a company; a firm.

tø-si, a military officer about rank of major; between iû-kek and siú-pī. **àn-chhat-si**, the provincial judge. **àn-si**, id. **àn-si-ìn**, his seal; the impression of it is good for keeping away demons. **pò-chèng-si**, the provincial treasurer (v. pò). **iú-si-koa^n**, mandarins with regular jurisdiction, *e.g.* over definite territory. **chiū^n-si-koa^n**, high mandarins. **chiū^n-si**, id. **ē-si**, inferior mandarins. **ē-si-koa^n**, id. **hun-si**, a small mandarin assisting the Hien (koāi^n) mandarin, or managing a small subdivision of a Hien. **sûn-si**, id., *e.g.* **hái-m̂g-si**, the small official who manages the Hái-m̂g subdivision of Hái-têng district.

phah-koa^n-si, to begin or carry on a lawsuit; to enter an accusation before a mandarin. **si-toa^n**, = âng-khòe, the stamped register appended to a deed. **si-pêng** (r.), the rate of weights authorized by the provincial treasurer.

im-si, a spirit that rules in the invisible world. **im-iông-si**, name of an idol (v. iông). **chè-si** (X.), a priest. **tsap-jī si-koa^n**, the twelve assistants of Sêng-hông-iâ. **sok-pò-si**, an attendant of Sêng-hông. **sek-phè-si** (T.), id. **sek-phè-si-iâ** (T.), id.

SÎ (R. id.), a Chinese hour = two hours; a season; a period; time (but not "leisure," which is "êng"); a short period of good or bad fortune, shorter than "ūn." **sî-sîn**, a Chinese double hour, as in asking what hour it is (s. decline). **sî-tsūn**, a short time (v. tsūn). **sî-hāu** (r.), time. **sî-siàu**, id. **sî-cheh** (C.), id. **sî-jit**, hours and days. **sî-jit tiòh pó-sioh**, take care of time. **sî-jit tui--lán** (C.), time is pursuing us. **sî-khek**, double hours and quarters of hours (v. khek). **poà^n-sî**, one hour's time. **sî-poà^n**, three hours. **chit-tùi-sî**, corresponding hour next day.

sî-ūn, the fortune (good or bad) of a man's circumstances (v. ūn). **si^n-sî jit-gèh**, the eight characters of one's nativity. **poà^n-sî**, to calculate the time as to good or bad luck. **khat-sî**, the day of birth disagreeing with the hour, making the horoscope bad. **sî hó**, the time is fortunate and lucky. **i-ê-sî**, his time of good or bad fortune. **sī i-ê-sî**, his time of good fortune.

sin-sî, the period "sin," from 3–5 P.M. **sin-sî-thâu**, the beginning of it, 3 o'clock. **sin-sî-chià^n**, middle of it, 4 o'clock. **sin-sî-tiong**, id. **sin-sî-bé**, end of it, 5 o'clock; (and so with the other hours).

sù-sî, the four seasons. **sî-lēng**, the rites to be performed and the proper words to be used at the four seasons.

sî-cheng, a clock (v. cheng). **sî-pió**, a watch. **sî-chiam**, hour-hand of watch or clock.

sî-tēng, a small sort of fish.

thi^n-sî, weather. **hong-sî**, a sudden squall. **pui^n-sî-hong** (C.), id. (v. pui^n). **tsúi-si**, the time of the tide (v. tsúi). **jit--sî**, day-time. **mî^n--sî**, night-time. **àm--sî**, in the evening or night.

tī-sî, when? what time? **kin-á-jit sī tī-sî**, which day of the month is this? **pài-it tī-sî**, which day of the month is Monday? **chit-gèh sī tī-sî**, which month is this? **sím-mih^n-sî**, when? what hour? **hán--tit tī-sî**, rarely met with. **sam--put-tī-sî**, occasionally. **sam--put-jî-sî**, id. **sam--put-gē-sî**, id.; from time to time. **put-sî**, at any time; over and over; frequently. **put-khu-sî**, at any time. **put-kî-sî** (C.), id. **ū-sî**, sometimes. **ták-sî**, always; regularly; constantly. **sî-sî**, id. **siông-sî**, id. **sî-siông**, id. **sò-sî**, id. **éng-sî**, always or constantly (in past time).

chit-sî, at this time. **chit-sî lâi-sè**, this life and that of the next birth in transmigration. **chhú-sî**, now. **hit-sî**, then; at that time. **hit-ta^n-sî**, just at that (past) time (v. ta^n). **tng-sî**, id. (v. tng). **tong-sî**, id. **chek-sî**, immediately; at once. **sûi-sî**, immediately; according to circumstances (v. sûi). **liâm-sî**, immediately (v. liâm). **tâng-sî**, at the same time. **óng-sî** (r.), in past time. **ān-sî**, to set a time. **àn-sî**, according to the time; at right time. **chiàu-sî**, id. **tsat-sî**, to make ready to do a thing just at the right time. **kip-sî**, coming just at the proper time when needed (v. kip). **kàu-sî**, when the time comes or came; the time has come. **sî kàu**, id. **sî-kàu sî-tng**, bear it when the time comes; "sufficient for the day," &c. **kàu-hit-sî, kiâ^n hit-ê**, act according to the circumstances. **kàu-hit-sî, kiáh hit-kî**, id.

kè-sî, past the proper time (v. kè). **sit-sî**, to be out of season, as thing: to be out of employment and in want. **thè-sî**, out of season; become poor from state of wealth. **kiâ^n-sî**, in good repute and good practice, as doctor.

sî-kiâ^n, much in vogue; much sought after; fashionable. **tè--lâng sî-kiâ^n**, to follow new fashions. **kek sî-kiâ^n**, to put on a high price just to make a fictitious reputation. **sî-kiâ^n-lâng**, a man of great influence, who is much sought after, esp. an upstart; a notorious bad woman. **sî-kiâ^n-lâng kóng sî-kiâ^n-ōe**, said in joke of a man talking new slang phrases. **sî-kiâ^n-chèng**, a prevalent epidemic. **sî-khì-chèng**, id.

sî-kè, current price. **sî-pêng**, current rate for counting dollar's weight (v. pêng). **sî-phài**, fashionable form of dress. **sî-khoán**, customary fashion or shape of things. **sî-chè**, fashionable form; fashionable. **sî-sit**, id. **sî-sek** (esp. T.), id. **sî-i**, a doctor who is popular and successful though not learned. **sî-ūi**, current paintings of modern artists.

bô-liáu-sî, for ever; no end to it. **bô-thêng-sî**, without delay or intermission. **bô-sî thêng**, id.

SÎ [R. a spoon; a key], a spoon. **toā-ki-sî**, a large spoon. **sî-á**, a small spoon. **tê-sî**, a tea-spoon. **thng-sî**, a soup-spoon. **thng-sî-tsam** (Cn.), a spoon-shaped hair-pin. **iôh-sî**, instrument like a spoon for mixing medicines. **pn̄g-sî**, a rice-spoon. **pn̄g-sî-kut**, the shoulder-blade. **pn̄g-sí-chhèng**, a snake like a cobra (v. chhèng).

só-sî, key for Chinese padlock. **put-lī-sî**, sort of key which must be in when the padlock shuts. **tsoān-sî**, a key working by turning in manner of foreign key.

he-sî, a large trowel for smoothing lime, having the handle on the back, as on a shield. **hiu^n-sî**, sort of spoon for pressing down the ashes of incense in the incense-vessel. **chien-sî**, a flat piece of iron used for turning food on a frying-pan, &c. **khiau-sî**, long spoon-shaped appendages of the Ming cap called "se-bō."

SÎ [R. sû], to decline; to refuse; to take leave of; to dismiss. **sî-lî**, id. **sa^n-sî**, to take leave. **pài-sî**, take leave ceremonially. **sî-sîn**, respectfully ask the spirits to go home. **sî-nî^n**, to take leave of the old year with offerings. **sî kong-pô**, to take leave of the ancestral tablets, as when going from home or when about to die. **sî-hêng**, to leave a card on being about to leave home (v. hêng, to go). **sî-hêng** (T. hâi^n), to decline and send back, as present (v. hêng, to give back). **sî-koa^n**, to resign office. **sî-niû^n**, to resign the position of a soldier. **the-sî**, to decline; to excuse one's self (often falsely) from doing something. **sî--lâng**, to decline a man's services; to dismiss from service; to give up situation.

SÎ — **sî-hî**, a sort of fish good for eating and rather expensive.

SÎ (C.), = A. **sû**, a sort of temple.

SÍ [R. thí, ashamed]. **poeh-sí**, feeling ashamed, either from modesty or having done some shameful thing. **poeh-sí ê tāi-chì**, a shameful affair. **bô-poeh-sí**, shameless; brazen-faced. **m̄-bat poeh-sí**, utterly shameless.

SÍ [R. to fear]. **ùi-sí**, faint-hearted; very much afraid to meddle with a matter.

SÍ [R. the beginning]. **sí-tsó**, very remote ancestor; original ancestor, as of a clan or family. **sí-tsó-má**, most remote ancestress. **sí-chiong** (R.), beginning and end (v. chiong). **chîn sí-ông**, the founder of the Tsin dynasty (v. chîn). **goân-sí thien-tsun**, the supreme deity of the Tauists.

SÍ [R. to relax; abrogated]. **hòe-sí** (r.), to cease, as a rite; to come to an end, as a course of action.

SÍ (C.), = A. sú (hot weather).

SÍ (C.), = A. sú (historian; censor?).

SÍ (R. sú), to die; death; used in many phrases to indicate intensity or doggedness. **sí--khì**, to faint away or fall into a comatose state, appearing to be dead though afterwards reviving, as sick man.

sí-sit, loss by death, as of relatives. **sí-chéh**, all dead; exterminated, as family (v. chéh). **sí-bô-lâng**, id. **sí kàu-bô-lâng-khàu**, may you die the last of all your people, with none to lament for you! **sí-kui-phiáh**, all in the region dead.

si^n-sí, alive and dead (v. si^n).

oàh-oàh khì--sí, to die of grief, lit. or fig. (v. oàh). **khì--sí**, to be dreadfully grieved and displeased (v. khì). **thâi--sí**, to kill by *cutting*. **thâi-sí**, to *kill* by cutting. **tsâm--sí**, to kill by stabbing. **hāi--sí**, to kill. **phah--sí**, id. **i-sí**, to kill instead of curing (v. i). **óng-sí**, to die by murder or suicide, or by injustice (v. óng). **koâ^n--sí**, to die of cold; very very cold. **poáh--sí**, to die of a fall. **thiàu-lóh-tsúi--sí**, to drown one's self. **chhia-lóh-tsúi--sí**, to drown by throwing into the water. **chhò-sí**, to die from neglect, carelessness, or mistake. **tiō--sí**, to shake or shiver exceedingly. **kêng kàu-sí**, extremely poor. **kì^n-chî^n sí**, greedily fond of money. **beh-sí**, about to die. **chiáh beh-sí**, eating very greedily (said in scolding). **chiáh beh-thòe-lâng-sí**, id.

kiâm sí-sí, very salt. **kia^n-sí-lâng**, very dirty (+). **lâ-sí-sâm**, id. **am-sí-tsam** (Cn.), id. **ke-sí-sng**, exceedingly unneighbourly and unfriendly.

oán-sí, to tie firmly; to tie a run knot. **pák-sí-soah**, id. (v. soah). **sí-kat**, a hard firm knot; a run knot. **kiet-sí-kè**, to fix a settled rate of wages or price (v. kè). **chip-sí-koat**, very obstinate (v. koat). **chip-sí-pán**, id.

péh-sí-sat, sallow and unhealthy looking.

thák-sí-chheh, to read books in the character without understanding the meaning. **chiáh sí-pn̄g**, to eat and live, but be of no use in the world (v. pn̄g). **sí-chî^n**, money locked up, *e.g.* in property that makes little or no returns. **chiáh sí-chî^n**, to live on one's capital or property so as to waste it away. **sí teng-teng**, unproductive, as trade. **sí-mn̂g ê seng-lí**, a small trade that makes no progress, as in a village. **sí-mn̂g chē-tiā^n**, having moderate but regular gains, as a quiet small trade or yamun without much business.

sí-bái, just about going out, as a light; inactive and useless. **sí-sek**, dull-coloured. **sí-sng**, dispirited (v. sng). **sí-sîn**, very dull and lifeless in manner. **sí-sim**, discouraged; having lost all hope and spirit; having given up all thought or desire about a thing, either because it is hopeless or because it is felt to be wrong. **khó-í sí-sim, m̄-sái-siū^n**, don't think any more of getting it. **sí-àn**, a legal case finally settled or ended. **sí-tsōe**, a capital crime. **sí-chhùi**, unable to answer, as from modesty or being unmistakably wrong. **m̄-sí-chhùi**, will not yield the argument, though manifestly beaten. **chhùi éng-m̄-sí**, id.

sí-lâng, a dead man (+). **sí-lâng beh-miā^n**, said of the unlooked-for recovery of what we thought quite lost. **ná^n sí-lâng-sek**, cadaverous appearance. **sí-lâng-tit**, very stiff and dogged, though the circumstances have quite changed (v. tit). **sí kúi-lâng**, how many of them have died? **sí-pē**, having lost one's father; said also in scolding a man who looks very dull and foolish (v. pē). **sí-hoān** (scolding), you condemned criminal! (v. hoān). **sí-hoan** (scolding), foreigner who deserves to be killed! **sí-káu**, dog that should be killed! a dead dog.

sí-tsúi, stagnant water. **sí-sin-phe**, reckless of one's life. **phe-sí**, id.; to risk one's life. **sí-lē**, conduct that brings ruin, death, or destruction on one's self. **chhē sí-lē**, to bring premature death on one's self by wickedness. **thó-sí**, id. **hē-sí-thûi**, to make a very violent attack (v. thûi). **chhut-sí-lát-phah**, to strike very violently, as in an assault.

chin-sí, really dead. **poà^n-sí**, half dead. **hó-sí**, an easy death without pain. **phái^n-sí**, a violent or painful death. **chin-phái^n-sí**, very wicked, so as to deserve a painful death. **joā-phái^n-sí**, id. **tsá-sí**, may you die soon! (v. tsá). **tsó sí, iū sí**, each alternative is death. **toā-khùn sió-sí** (deep sleep like death), said of a man sleeping too soundly. **toā-bîn sió-sí**, id.

SÌ [R. sè, the world; a generation; one lifetime], (also C., = A. sè, world; generation, &c.) **chhut-sì**, to be born. **chhut-sì toà--lâi**, congenital. **chhut-sì koe-á**, a very young chick. **kè-sì**, to die. **chit-**

sin chit-sì, all life-long. **chit-sì-lâng**, id. **poàⁿ-sì-lâng**, about forty years old.

chit-sì, this present life. **āu-sì**, a future life by transmigration. **chit-sì tsòe, āu-sì siu**, sins of this life punished in the next transmigration. **kim-sì tsòe, āu-sì 'siu**, id. **kim-sì tsòe, kim-sì siu**, sins of this life punished in this life. **chêng-sì**, our life in a former transmigration. **thák chêng-sì-chheh**, said of a pupil who knows his lessons at a glance (had read them in a former life!)

sì-chiūⁿ, in the world. **sì-chiūⁿ ê-lâng**, men now living.

Sì [R. to bestow, by change of tone from "si," id.] **pò-sì**, to give a largess, &c. (v. pò). **phó-sì**, to make offerings to the ghosts in the 7th moon. **siá-sì**, to give alms; to give freely, as to a beggar. **siá-ióh sì-tê**, to give away medicine and tea. **pē-bú bô-siá-sì, sàng-kiáⁿ khì tsng-hì**, the parents don't care for their boy, but hire him out to be an actor.

sì-tsú, a contributor to a temple, either for priests or nuns.

Sì — **sì-som**, a medicine like chhi-som.

Sì (C.), = A. sù (perhaps, the people, &c.)

Sì (C.), = A. sù. **hê-sîn-sì**, spots made by flies.

Sì (C.) **iau-chiaⁿ sì-sóe**, fond of gadding about, or talking, or acting improperly, as women.

Sì [R. si, to instruct; a proclamation]. **liên-hôe sì-chèng**, utterly disgraced for ever in sight of all, as a miserable wretch, or as a man who has done shameful act.

Sì (same word?) **hiēn-sì**, descendants of the rich or great bringing disgrace on their ancestors by crime or poverty (v. hiēn).

Sì [R. to examine; to try; = col. chhì]. **khó-sì**, an examination for degrees. **sió-sì**, the examination for the Sew-tsai degree. **hiong-sì**, examination for Kujin degree. **hōe-sì**, examination for Tsin-sze degree. **hōe-sì-tiūⁿ**, id. **tiēn-sì**, examination for Han-lin. **sì-chhó**, the essay that got the Sew-tsai degree, printed for private circulation among friends.

Sì (next word?). **khiap-sì**, ugly.

Sì [R. sè, power; form], (also C. = A. sè, power, influence, &c.) **koāiⁿ-sì**, accustomed (v. koāiⁿ). **hó-chhiú-sì**, all going on well, *e.g.* as in sickness or as teacher managing pupils well. **chhìn ū-khí-sì**, to have the turn of the steelyard, in weighing. **niūⁿ--khì khí-sì**, weigh it with a large steelyard giving full weight. **tióh-ū khí-sì**, there must be full weight.

ke-sì, state of a family, as to its prosperity and the behaviour of its members (v. ke).

hit-sì, that direction. **àn-hiùⁿ-sì** (T. C.), thus; that way. **àn-chiùⁿ-sì** (T. C.), thus; this way. **chiūⁿ-sì**, weather side of vessel. **téng-sì**, upper or northern regions. **téng-sì-hong**, a wind astern. **téng-sì-hú**, the more distant departments of Fuh-kien. **ē-sì**, the lower or more southern regions; the lee side of a vessel. **ē-sì-hú**, the departments near Amoy, *e.g.* Chang-chew and Chin-chew. **ē-sì-hong**, a wind ahead. **pak-sì**, northern; the north; (so with the other quarters). **tsoân-chiu-sì**, on the Chin-chew side. **lāi-sì-sū**, inner islands. **goā-sì-sū**, outer islands.

sì-bīn (C.), = A. sè-bīn, power, influence, &c. (s. four).

Sì (R. sù), four. **sì-chiàⁿ**, all square and right; correct and proper; not awry. **sì-thīn**, well proportioned (v. thīn). **sì-pang**, regular; well-formed (v. pang, square). **sì-thiāu**, the horoscope (v. thiāu). **sì-kak**, four-cornered; 40 cents (v. kak). **sì-liām-hè**, tied at right angles, as string (v. liām). **tsòe-sì-chiu**, cut into four pieces at right angles, as a cake. **peh-sì-liét**, opened wide and square, as door. **sì-bák bô-chhin**, having no relations (v. bák). **sì-kùi**, the four seasons. **sì-kha--ê**, four-footed (v. kha).

sì-ló, a small mandarin appointed by the district mandarin (Hien) to assist him. **sì-ló-tia**, id.

sì-kòe, in every direction (v. kòe). **sì-kè** (C.), id.; fields (v. kè). **sì-ûi**, in every direction; on every side. **sì-hng**, do.; the four quarters. **sì-bīn**, the four sides; on all sides; in all directions. **sì-soàⁿ**, scattered in all directions.

saⁿ-sì, three or four (v. saⁿ). **tsài-sam tsài-sì**, carefully over and over again. **sì-poeh, saⁿ-tsáp-jī**, "six and half-a-dozen;" will make no deduction; just the same price, though under a different name. **sì-sì, tsáp-lák; jī-poeh, iáh-sī tsáp-lák**, take it any way, it comes to the same.

Sī (R. id.), to be; is; are (as in affirming that it really is what is said or thought; or as the copula, but in general the copula is omitted; never in the sense of "to exist, to be present," which is "ū;" nor to hold an office, profession, or business, &c., which is "tsòe;" *e.g.* "sī i-seng," it is the doctor, not another man; "ū i-seng," there is a doctor; "tsòe i-seng," to be a doctor); right; to be correct; yes, in affirming reality or identity (but "yes" is translated by various words, according to the nature of the question, esp. ū, tióh, and beh).

nāⁿ-sī, if it be; only. **káⁿ-sī**, I rather think it is (v. káⁿ). **tsóng-sī**, yet after all it is (v. tsóng). **chiàⁿ-sī**, yes, truly it is so. **chek-sī**, that is —; then it is —. **chiū-sī** (at beginning of phrase), that is —; then it is —; then he is, &c.; (at end of phrase), such is the correct statement; and that will be all right. **léng-chêng, chiū-sī**, I accept your kind intention (but decline your gift), and it is all right; no, I thank you, sir!

sī-toā, a superior. **sī-sòe**, an inferior. **sī sím-mih"-lâng**, who is it? **sī-tiâng** (Cn.), id.; who? **sī-tsòe** —, he is (such and such an office, or profession, or business, &c.)

sī-hui, right and wrong, as of a dispute or in a legal case.

put-sī, in the wrong. **jīn put-sī**, to confess one's self in the wrong. **chē put-sī**, id. **hē put-sī**, to acknowledge a fault. **hē m̄-sī**, id. **heh m̄-sī**, indeed it is not. **m̄-sī**, it is not. **m̄-sī-ōe**, improper words. **m̄-sī siaⁿ-sàu**, angry sound of voice, as at beginning of quarrel. **m̄-sī-lâng**, a bad man, inhuman or vicious. **m̄-sī lâng-sek**, id. **m̄-sī-sit**, dangerous; unsafe (v. sit). **m̄-sī-sî**, out of season, as fruit. **m̄-sī-ióh**, injurious medicine. **m̄-sī só-tsāi**, an improper place. **tsō-hoà m̄-sī**, luck bad. **sī m̄-sī**, is it or is it not? is it not so? **sī á-m̄-sī**, is it or is it not? **kám-m̄-sī**, how can it be otherwise (surely it is). **kiám-m̄-sī**, id.

sǹg-bōe-sī, innumerable. **sǹg bōe-tit-sī**, id. **pun bōe-tit-sī**, not enough to divide among all.

tsū-sī, always making one's self in the right (v. tsū). **thâu tióh, bé sī**, good luck from first to last. **tsō-hoà sī**, luck good. **jī-ūn sī**, id. **miāⁿ-ūn sī**, id. **tng-sī-sî**, just in season, as fruit, &c. **o-sī** (Cn.), to praise in a flattering way.

hó-bī-sī, good-natured and easy; not finding fault (v. bī).

Sī — **ûn-á-sī**, slowly. **bān-chiah-sī**, id. **liâu-**

á-sī, do.; cautiously. **khah-khoa^{n}-sī**, more leisurely; not in a hurry. **bêh-sī**, slowly.

bêh-bêh-sī, very numerous. **bát-bát-sī**, id. **iáp-iáp-sī**, in great quantities or multitudes, *e.g.* robbers or ants.

sī — **khah-sī--leh**, walk quicker! get on! **kiâ^{n} khah-sī--leh**, id.

sī-soā, quick. **khah-sī-soā**, quicker!

sī [R. tsāi, to be in; in; = col. tī], sometimes said instead of "tī," when it is a mere connective, *e.g.* **khah-koâi^{n} sī-thi^{n}**, = khah-koâi^{n} tī-thi^{n}, higher than heaven.

sī [R. to instruct, = col. sì]. **kò-sī**, a proclamation. **kà-sī**, to teach. **chí-sī**, to instruct; to point out. **sī-chiòng**, to warn all by example of punishment (v. chiòng).

sī [R. to look at; to treat or view as]. **biáu-sī** (r.), to despise; to treat with scorn.

sûn-sī, to make inspection all round; to examine and inspect for another. **tsō-sī put-kiù**, to sit and look without assisting.

kūn-sī, near-sighted. **kūn-sī-bák**, id. **ké kūn-sī**, to wear spectacles, pretending to be near-sighted.

sī — **bák-sā-sī**, drowsy; to doze; half asleep (previous word?).

sī [R. to wait upon, as attendant]. **sûi-sī** (R.), to follow, as attendant. **hōng-sī** (R.), to serve.

sī-nńg, vice-president of one of the supreme boards.
sī-ōe, imperial guards of the highest rank (v. ōe).

sī-chiá-kong (C.), = A. sū-chiá-kong, a large harmless serpent, worshipped at Chang-chew.

sī (R. id.), a Buddhist temple or monastery. **sī-ī^{n}**, id. **soa^{n}-sī**, a mountain monastery. **hê-siû^{n}-sī**, Bud. monastery. **lî-kə-sī**, Bud. nunnery. **sai-kə-sī**, id.

lé-pài-sī, a mosque; the mosque at Chinchew is so called; sometimes said for a chapel, which is properly "lé-pài-tn̂g."

sī [R. a family; a surname; but when added to a *personal* name it indicates a female]. **khóng--sī**, the surname Khóng (and so with other surnames). **bān--sī niû^{n}-niû^{n}** (Cn.), a female idol of surname Bān (*q.v.*)

sī [R. salted vegetables and fruits, = col. sī^{n}, sī^{n}]. **tāu-sī**, = tāu-si^{n}, pickled and salted beans. **tāu-sī-pê**, black beans boiled, dried, and kept till mouldy, to be made into soy. **tāu-sī-phoh**, beans from which soy has been made, broken down small. **mī^{n}-sī** (Cn.), = A. tāu-chiù^{n}, sort of salted sauce.

sī — **sù-sī**, in an orderly state.

sī (C.), = A. sū. **thâu-sī**, a clue (same as previous word?).

sī (C.), = A. sū (regular order). **thâu-sī**, a preface.
sī (C.), = A. sù (sympathizing); some say sì.
sī (C.), = A. sū, an island.
sī (C.), = A. sū, acting as interim mandarin.
sī (C.), = A. sē. **sien-sī** (R.), to die.

sī^{n} [R. sien, bright; fresh; = col. chhi^{n}]. **kng-si^{n}**, smooth, as a surface; clean and smooth, as skin, or other surface.

sī^{n}, sort of cast-iron or pot-metal. **tiá^{n}-si^{n}**, pot-metal for making rice-boilers. **lôe-thâu-si^{n}**, metal for making the coulters of ploughs, finer than that for rice-boilers. **si^{n}-tsu**, bullets made of pot-metal.

khan-si^{n}, to melt iron or pot-metal by bellows and furnace; also (Cn.), to smelt iron-ore. **si^{n}-kńg** (Cn.), iron-ore. **khan si^{n}-kńg** (Cn.), to smelt iron-ore. **oe si^{n}-kńg** (Cn.), id.

sī^{n} [R. tsu, abundant vegetation; a mat; this; here], (C. id.) **chháu-si^{n}**, a coarse straw mat placed under a bed-mat, or used alone by the poor.

sī^{n} [su? this; tsu?], (C. sε^{n}). **àn-ni^{n}-si^{n}**, thus. **àn-si^{n}** (T.), id.

sī^{n} — **si^{n}-si^{n} soáih^{n}-soáih^{n}**, sound, as of a bamboo chair drawn along the floor.

sī^{n} [R. seng, sacrificial or domestic animals, = col. cheng], (C. sε^{n}). **thâu-si^{n}**, domestic animals. **cheng-si^{n}**, id. (v. cheng). **thek-si^{n}**, you brute!

sī^{n} [R. seng, to bring into being; to produce; to bring forth; to beget; to have, as disease; to grow, as mouldy or rust; alive; living; life; = col. chhi^{n}]. **si^{n}-kòe**, to have itch. **si^{n}-sién**, to have various eruptions, as ring-worm, &c. **si^{n}-sien**, to grow rusty. **si^{n}-lâng**, to suppurate. **si^{n}-phú**, to grow mouldy. **si^{n}-kə**, id. **si^{n}-tsúi**, to grow damp; to yield water.

si^{n}-chhut, to produce. **hoat-si^{n}**, id.; to bear fruit. **tng teh-toā-si^{n}**, just when the fruit is produced in greatest abundance. **si^{n}-thoà^{n}**, to breed abundantly. **si^{n}-thâng**, to breed worms. **si^{n}-nn̄g**, to produce eggs, as birds. **si^{n}-kiá^{n}**, to get a son, as parent (v. kiá^{n}). **bô-si^{n}**, barren, as female. **bōe-si^{n}**, id. **tsù-si^{n}**, to ordain the time of birth (v. tsù). **siang-si^{n}**, twins. **thau-si^{n}**, illegitimate. **thi^{n}-si^{n}**, made or produced by Heaven. **thi^{n}-si^{n} tōe-iú^{n}**, Heaven produces, and earth nourishes.

si^{n}-pē, our own real father. **si^{n}-lán ê-pē**, id. **si^{n}-bú**, one's real mother. **si^{n}-tn̂g**, the womb of mammalia (gen. animals, not human); the ovary of a bird. **chhui-si^{n}-ióh**, medicine to assist in parturition. **si^{n}-gêh**, natal month. **si^{n}-sî jit-gêh**, the eight natal characters. **si^{n}-jit**, birth-day. **bô-si^{n} bô-jit**, no birth-day. **chiáh si^{n}-jit**, to keep a birth-day. **thi^{n}-kong-si^{n}**, birth-day of Yuh-hwang Shangti. **tsáp-jī si^{n}-siù^{n}**, the twelve signs for the twelve years of the cycle (v. siù^{n}).

sien-si^{n}, a teacher; a doctor (v. sien). **sin-sε^{n}** (C.), id. **hāu-si^{n}**, a son (v. hāu).

si^{n}-chiâ^{n}, to be produced and grow up; naturally, not artificially; certainly. **si^{n}-tsòe**, naturally of such and such form, &c. **si^{n}-tsòe m̄-koâi^{n} m̄-kē**, of middle stature. **hó-si^{n}-tsòe**, well-formed and good-looking, as person. **hó-si^{n}-tiu^{n}**, id. **gām-si^{n}**, foolish. **ngé-toan-si^{n}**, short and stout, but well-formed (v. ngé).

si^{n}-hūn, unacquainted with person or place; shy (cf. chhi^{n}).

si^{n}-giên tsō-gú, to invent and circulate lies. **si^{n}-kha si^{n}-chhiú**, to tell a story mainly false. **si^{n}-ki si^{n}-hióh** (r.), id.

tsāi-si^{n}, while alive; in this life. **si^{n}-chêng**, id. **pàng-si^{n}**, to spare the life of an animal, and let it go, for superstitious object. **sî-si^{n}** (take leave of life), ceremony just before putting the body into the coffin; also said in scolding a man for eating too much. **si^{n}-lâng-bó**, wife of a man still alive. **moâ^{n} si^{n}-lâng-bák**, to put on a false appearance on a man's presence. **si^{n}-lō͘**, way of escape from death.

si^{n}-sí, alive or dead; life and death. **tâng-si^{n}-sí**, sharing with each other for life or death. **sa^{n}-kap si^{n}-sí**, id. **kì^{n}-si^{n}-sí**, to engage in determined feud or conflict. **kap--i si^{n}-sí**, id. **kap--i kì^{n}-si^{n}-sí**, id. **chhut-si^{n} jip-sí**, to exert one's self very much (lit. hazard life). **tô-si^{n} bô-tô-sí,** he has escaped to live, not to die (said of not giving up a fugitive). **bōe-tit-si^{n}, bōe-tit-sí,** unable either to live or die. **si^{n} bô-toà-lâi, sí bô-toà-khì,** did not bring with one at birth, and cannot carry away at death.

tāu-si^{n}, sprouted pease, edible. **kià-si^{n},** a sort of misletoe; a small marine animal. **png-kià-si^{n},** misletoe growing on the liquidambar-tree. **song-kià-si^{n},** a parasite on the mulberry, medicinal. **kià^{n}-si^{n},** = kià-si^{n}, an animal like a spider, that lives in some empty sea-shells. **kià^{n}-si^{n} chiàm kə-lê-á-khak,** said of an assistant servant supplanting the principal servant, or of a man getting unjust possession of another's property.

Sî^{n} [R. sí, salted vegetables, &c., = col. sî^{n}]. **sî^{n}-sî^{n}-sî^{n},** minced very small. **chhò-bah-sî^{n},** to mince meat. **thô-á-sî^{n},** peaches beaten small with salt. **chheng-kó-sî^{n},** preparation of olives (Chinese), with salt and sugar. **ka^{n}-ná^{n}-sî^{n},** preparation of pickled olives.

iâm-sî^{n}, a white incrustation that forms on walls or clothes that have been damp (esp. by salt water), or on salted fish, &c. **chhiū^{n} iâm-sî^{n},** to form this white incrustation.

Sì^{n} (R. sèng), (C. sɛ̀^{n}), a surname; a clan. **jī-sì^{n},** a surname. **jī-sì^{n}-teng,** a lamp with our surname on it. **tsòk-sì^{n},** a clan of same surname. **miâ^{n}-sì^{n},** name and surname (v. miâ^{n}). **chiáh i-ê-sì^{n},** to take his surname and worship his ancestors. **sì^{n}-Lí,** of the surname Lí (often said in speaking of a man, as we would say Mr. Lí).

peh-sì^{n}, the people, as opposed to rulers. **bān-peh-sì^{n},** all people.

Sì^{n} [R. sèng, nature], (C. sɛ̀^{n}). **sì^{n}-miā^{n},** life (v. miā^{n}). **sim-sì^{n},** disposition; nature. **kín-sim-sì^{n},** impulsive. **sim-sì^{n} tiòh-pàng-lòh,** don't be sorrowful; don't be angry.

kì-sì^{n}, memory (as a mental power). **hó-kì-sì^{n},** a good memory; having a good memory.

Sì^{n} (R. sièn), a fan; the leaf of a door or window. **toā-ki-sì^{n},** a large fan. **iėt-sì^{n},** to fan; to use a fan. **kiáh-sì^{n},** to carry a fan in the hand. **khê-sì^{n},** a fan, properly made from one leaf, but often applied to others. **khôe-sì^{n}** (C.), id. **se-sì^{n},** fan made of thin cloth, or gauze, or paper. **se-á-sì^{n},** id. **kìn-sì^{n},** fan made of paper and fine silk gauze pasted together. **sə-pèh-sì^{n},** a white fan, properly from Soo-chow. **hòh-sì^{n},** large fan carried before very high mandarins. **chiáng-sì^{n},** id. **pa-chiau-sì^{n},** a very large ancient form of fan used by the genii.

hang-lê-sì^{n}, a fan for blowing the fire. **chhia-sì^{n}** (C.), = A. chhia-iáp, the leaves of a chain-wheel for raising water.

thang-á-sì^{n}, the leaf of a window that opens like a door. **mn̂g-sì^{n},** the leaf of a door. **mn̂g-pang hē-sì^{n},** all the doors of a house. **chit-sì^{n}-mn̂g,** one door. **toa^{n}-sì^{n}-mn̂g,** a door that has only one leaf. **siang-sì^{n}-mn̂g,** folding-doors.

sì^{n}-bah, the paper of a fan. **sì^{n}-hiòh,** id. **toā-hiòh-sì^{n},** a large fan made of a leaf. **sì^{n}-bīn,** the paper of a fan. **sì^{n}-thâu,** one end of a fan. **sì^{n}-pì^{n},** handle of fan. **sì^{n}-gán,** joint of fan. **sì^{n}-kut,** ribs of fan. **sì^{n}-tē,** case for fan such as one wears.

Sì^{n} — **kah-sì^{n},** manner of building a house by first making a framework of wooden pillars, &c., supporting the roof and filling up the interstices with boarding, or with reeds and plaster, or with lath and plaster. **kah-sì^{n}-khì,** to build a house in this way. **khiā-sì^{n}-khí,** id.

Sī^{n} [R. sí, salted vegetables, = col. sî^{n}], to salt or pickle; to smart or be injured, as the eye, or an open wound with medicine. **put-chí-sī^{n},** making the flesh smart, as salt, or some drugs on an open wound. **sī^{n} bák-chiu,** to destroy the sight by a drug put in the eye. **sī^{n}-kôe,** to pickle fish or shell-fish. **sī^{n}-chhài,** to salt vegetables. **sī^{n} kiâm-chhài,** id., esp. the mustard-plant. **sī^{n}-kiâm,** to salt. **sī^{n} kiâm-bah,** to salt pork. **ìm-sī^{n},** dry salted pease, made by covering them up close. **tāu-sī^{n},** = tāu-sì, a preparation of beans. **mi^{n}-iâm sī^{n}-sim-koa^{n},** accept the matter as fixed, there is no hope of changing it. **chî^{n} chhòng-iâm sī^{n}--teh,** said of a miser keeping his money useless.

Sia [R. a small quantity]. **sia-jî-á,** a very little; a very small quantity.

Sia (R. id.), to buy on credit; said also of the seller. **sia-siàu,** to buy on credit. **sia-hè,** id. **sia-mih^{n},** id. **sia-chioh,** to buy on credit and borrow money (v. chioh). **sia-khiàm,** to be in debt for goods bought on credit (v. khiàm). **tham-sia kùi-bóe,** to buy on credit is expensive. **pàng-sia,** to sell on credit. **goá hè sia--lí,** I give you the goods on credit. **bô-sia, put-sêng-tiàm; sia-liáu, tiàm put-sêng,** without giving credit one can't do business, but yet giving credit is ruinous.

Siâ (R. û, siâ), (C. Cn. T.), fields on a hill-side with little water. **tê-siâ,** a tea plantation. **kui-siâ,** a whole plantation on a hill-side.

Siâ (R. id.), depraved; immoral; lascivious; false, as doctrine, or as a sect; evil spirits; magical. **siâ-kàu,** a false religion. **siâ-sút,** magic. **siâ-hoat,** id. **iau-siâ,** evil spirits. **iau-siâ kúi-koài,** id.; magical arts. **kúi-siâ,** id. **ōe phek-siâ,** able to drive away hurtful spiritual influences, as charms. **khu-siâ tiòk-ėk,** to drive away the evil influences that cause epidemics. **khu-siâ tiòk-kúi,** to expel evil demons.

siâ-chèng, depraved and correct (v. chèng). **kan-siâ,** intriguing for dishonest purposes, as to injure people or to get money out of them. **siâ-sim,** a depraved or licentious heart. **siâ-sū,** immoral or licentious actions. **siâ-tāi,** id.

pak-lāi ū siâ-hé, said of a man who is much fevered.

Siâ (R. id., = col. chhiâ, chhoâh), oblique; to take down, as mast. **siâ-ûi,** to lower a mast. **siâ-bûn-pò** (= chhiâ), strong twilled cloth. **khi-siâ** (C.), = A. khi-chhiâ, awry.

moa^{n}-siâ-á, a small house or shed built against a wall or large house. **siâ-moa^{n},** id.

Siâ [R. a serpent, = col. tsoâ]. **siâ-mâu^{n}-chhiu^{n},** sort of crooked spear. **siâ-chhông,** a medicinal plant (v. chhông). **têng-siâ,** a fabulous winged serpent.

Siâ (R. id.), a surname.

Siá [R. to relinquish; to give away]. **siá-liá,** to bestow much. **siá-si,** to bestow, as charity (v. si). **si-siá koan-bók,** to give away coffins in charity. **si-siá koa^{n}-chhâ,** id. **hí-siá,** to give joyfully, as alms. **hí-siá--lâng,** id. **hí-siá lâng-ê-iòh,** to give medicine gratuitously.

ōe-siá--tit, can be parted from (only said of persons or places). **bōe-siá--tit,** cannot bear to part. **koah-siá,** to forsake, as man and woman (said by women). **loân-loân put-siá,** to love so much as not to part, as man and wife. **siá-ì siá-ì**, idle and listless, as man who has some money and does not care to work, or as man who neglects to do what he promised though he remembers.

siá-sin, to exert one's self greatly. **siá-sin siá-miāⁿ**, id. **siá sìⁿ-miāⁿ**, to risk one's life. **siá-bēng, sit hô-tûn** (r.), throw away one's life for good eating.

siá (R. id.), to write (only the manual act of writing, not to compose). **siá-jī**, id. **siá-liá**, to write away; to write on. **ló-chhó-siá**, to scrawl. **siá-phoe**, to write a letter. **thiap-siá**, men engaged in yamuns (esp. military yamuns) to assist in writing documents.

sià [R. a cottage], polite phrase for "my" in speaking of junior relatives; affix to the names of men who have a senior relative a mandarin or kujin; in some places also applied to persons of the surname Tīⁿ, who are nearly related to the line of Tīⁿ Kok-sêng, *i.e.* Coxinga. **sià-chhin** (polite), my relatives. **sià-tē**, my younger brother. **sià-tit**, my nephew. **a-ko-sià**, son or grandson of mandarin. **iâ-sià**, younger relative of mandarin or kujin. **sià-jîn**, id. **tiong-su sià-jîn**, sort of secretaries of high rank and great influence in the supreme boards at Pekin. **thiòng-sià**, a young man who amuses himself instead of working or studying. **hok-chiu hia, tsoân-chiu sià, ē-mn̂g kim-téng**, at Fuhchau great numbers wear official boots; at Chinchew multitudes are styled "sià," being relatives of mandarins or kujin; at Amoy gilt buttons on cap are very common.

sià (same as previous word?) **saⁿ-phoáh-sià**, name of a pair of idols (v. phoáh).

sià (R. id.), to have diarrhœa; to have a loose motion. **sià-pak**, id. **làu-sià**, id. **siet-sià**, id. **tsúi-sià**, watery diarrhœa. **hoat-sià**, to have a very sudden loose motion. **chí-sià**, to stop diarrhœa, as medicine. **sià-ióh**, purgative medicine.

sià — **tek-sià**, a cooling medicine.

sià (R. id.), to forgive; to pardon. **sià-bién**, id. **sià-tsōe**, to pardon guilt. **sià-chiàu**, an imperial decree of pardon. **tāi-sià thien-hā**, general pardon through the empire. **thien-sià-jit**, a few days in each year (changeable) said to be specially lucky. **sià-bé**, paper horses burned in worship. **sià-koaⁿ**, paper image of mandarin, burned in rites for the dead. **khiā-hoan pàng-sià**, to set up streamers and burn paper images at rites for the dead.

sià (R. id., cf. col. siā), to lay down, as a load; to unlade; to unsaddle; to injure, as a man's good name. **sià bé-oaⁿ**, to unsaddle a horse. **sià-pē**, to loose the ropes which fasten wood or bamboos to the sides of a junk. **sià-tsāi**, to unlade a vessel. **sià-tàⁿ**, to lay down a load. **sià-hē--teh**, to lay down, as a load. **sià-jīm**, to hand over one's office fully to the successor. **sià-chhèng**, to fire off a gun merely to empty it. **sià poàⁿ-kah**, to take off one arm of coat or shirt, leaving one shoulder bare. **sià-hè**, to sell off goods very cheap. **sià-sak**, id., at a sacrifice, so as to get ready money quickly; to throw away things to lighten a vessel (v. sak).

sià--tióh, brought into disgrace, as by the bad conduct of some relative or connection. **tng-bīn sià--i**, to make a man ashamed by speaking to his face of his disgraceful conduct, &c. **sià lâng--ê miâⁿ-siaⁿ**, to injure a man's good fame. **sià tsó-kong ê bīn-phê**, to disgrace ancestors by bad conduct. **sià thé-biēn**, to cause our superior to lose good character or respect through our bad conduct. **sià i--ê thé-biēn**, id.; also, to injure a man's good name by circulating reports against him that have some considerable foundation.

siā — **kong-siā**, a sedan-bearer. **kong-siā-kha**, do., said in counting how many are required.

siā (R. id.), to shoot, as an arrow. **siā-chìⁿ**, to shoot an arrow.

siā-kan, a medicine made from the soaⁿ-koaⁿ-lân-hoe. **siā-kan-thâu**, id.

siā [R. the musk-deer]. **siā-hiuⁿ**, musk.

siā — **siā-kə-bí**, sago.

siā [R. sià, to lay down a load; to unlade]. **siā-sū**, to withdraw from an affair.

siā (R. id.), to thank; to pay, as vow or fee; to fade or fall, as flower or scab; a surname (C. chiā, the surname; siā in all other senses). **siā-phí**, scabs falling off. **hoe siā**, the flower fades.

siā-thiap, a letter of thanks. **siā-lé**, a small reward or fee given to a man who has managed some business for us, as arbiter or agent, &c. **siā joā-tsōe**, how much should be given as reward for such service?

siā-un, to give thanks for favour or grace. **siā-hō͘**, to give thanks for rain. **siā-sîn**, to give thanks to the spirits, as for answer to a vow. **siā-goān**, to pay a formal vow. **siā-thó**, to give thanks to Thó-tī-kong after a burial. **siā-toāⁿ**, to make thank-offerings at a temporary shrine (toâⁿ) just before taking it down. **siā-siúⁿ**, to give thanks for a present, as actors or mandarin's attendants. **siā-teng**, to give a play as thanks for friends lighting lamps near our house. **siā-pō͘**, to make a return-visit as thanks to a man who had called on parent's birth-day, or had come and worshipped our dead relative. **siā-pài**, to pay respects ceremonially to a man who had come to worship our deceased relative (v. pài).

pài-siā, to give ceremonial thanks, as to friend for presents, or on visit, or in worship. **to-siā**, many thanks! thank you! **kám-siā**, to thank; to feel grateful; thank you! **kám-siā jip-kut**, extremely grateful. **seh-siā**, to give thanks. **tap-siā**, to express thanks for a favour, as by returning or repaying it. **chiok-siā** (r.), to give thanks in a prayer, as to a god. **khàu-siā**, to give thanks by knocking head, as to a very high mandarin who is our immediate master; also, *said* politely, "I thank you very respectfully," to a man very much our superior, or for a very great service.

siā [R. a village; an association; the tutelary spirit of a place], a village. **hiuⁿ-siā**, a village. **siā-lí** (r.), id. **siā-thâu**, id. **sì-siā-thâu**, the four principal wards of Amoy, viz. Hok-san, Hū-chē, Hô-hōng, and Hoâi-tek. **chit-siā**, one village. **kui-siā**, the whole village. **tsng-siā** (F.), a village. **hòe-siā**, to destroy a village. **hōe-siā**, villages combining, as for attack or defence. **siā-tiúⁿ**, a village elder or head man. **siā-gòk**, a man who has by bad means got to be a leader in a village. **moáⁿ-siāⁿ chhē siā-hiaⁿ** (search for a fellow-villager in a whole city), no clue to find him or it.

kiet-siā, to form a literary society for writing essays. **siā-iú**, friends in one literary society. **siā heng-tē**, id.

siā-chek (R.), the place for imperial worship of the gods of land and grain (v. chek). **siā-toāⁿ** (T.), a permanent altar without any image outside the walls of Tung-an city.

siaⁿ (R. seng), sound; voice; noise; tone; denomination in arithmetic. **hong-siaⁿ**, a rumour; a report.

54

chit--ê sī hong-sia^n--ê, this is a mere rumour. **miâ^n-sia^n**, fame; reputation. **ū miâ^n-sia^n**, famous. **phái^n-miâ^n-sia^n**, bad reputation; of notorious character. **thoân-miâ^n seh-sia^n**, to spread a bad report about a man (v. thoân). **ū-sia^n bô-iá^n**, utterly false, as report (v. iá^n). **kià-sia^n**, to spread a report; to send word. **pàng-sia^n**, to warn that if he does so-and-so, we will punish, injure, or accuse him.

sia^n-im, a sound. **tsúi-sia^n**, sound of water, as of a stream, or as vessel sailing rapidly. **phái^n-sia^n-seh**, angry or proud tone of talk (v. seh). **phái^n-sia^n-thâu**, id. **m̄-sī sia^n-sàu**, displeased sound of voice, as in quarrelling (v. sàu). **sau-sia^n**, hoarse. **é-sia^n**, voice broken and indistinct (v. é). **hó-sia^n-tiāu**, well sung, as tune (v. tiāu). **sái âu-sia^n**, to sing loud and high, as from bottom of throat. **sit-sia^n**, to lose one's voice. **bô-sia^n**, no sound; have lost one's voice. **toā-sia^n**, loud sound; loud voice. **toā-sia^n kiò**, to call out loud. **toā-bú-sia^n**, very loud voice or sound. **chhut-sia^n**, to use the voice; to emit a sound. **khan-sia^n**, to draw out one's voice loud and long, as in singing or reciting essays. **khui-sia^n thák**, to read with a clear distinct voice. **m̄-thang tsòe-sia^n**, don't say a syllable; keep quiet. **thun-sia^n lún-khì**, to repress anger and keep in one's voice, as before a superior (v. thun). **ìn-sia^n**, to answer with the voice; to echo a word distinctly. **sia^n àng--lâi**, sound re-echoing, as in a cave.

piâ^n-sia^n, the tones called "Ping" (v. piâ^n). **pê^n-sia^n** (C.), id. **cheh-sia^n**, any tone except the Ping. **chiū^n-sia^n**, the Shang tone; the second tone. **khì-sia^n**, the Khu tones. **jip-sia^n**, the Juh or abrupt tones.

hun-sia^n, the denomination of "hun" or candareens. **niú^n-sia^n**, denomination of taels. **khơ-sia^n**, denomination of dollars. **chiet khơ-sia^n**, reduce to dollars. **chiet chî^n-sia^n**, reduce to copper cash, as from silver. **tè-sia^n**, counting the price by the number of articles (of fixed size), not by weight or size, *e.g.* in buying cakes. **sǹg kiā^n-sia^n**, to count by the number of units of things (v. kiā^n). **siá tāng-sia^n**, to write the weight of a dollar on a small bit of paper pasted on it. **phín hit--ê tāng-sia^n**, to agree beforehand that the dollars are to be counted at such and such a weight. **joā-tsōe tn̂g-sia^n**, what length is it, counted in rods (chang) of ten feet each? **sím-mih^n pān-sia^n**, what depth of water in fathoms?

Siâ^n (R. sêng), a city; a city wall; a walled town; a citadel; a fort; the pan of a gun; the circular wards of a lock on which the slits in a key work. **toa^n-siâ^n**, having only one such ward, as lock for key with only one slit. **siang-siâ^n**, having two such wards.

siâ^n-siú, the garrison of a Foo city; its commander. **siâ^n-tî**, wall and moat of city. **sit siâ^n-tî**, to lose a city, as mandarin who fails to hold a city in war. **siâ^n-ip** (r.), a Hien district. **siâ^n-chhiû^n**, city walls. **siâ^n-tó-chí**, battlements. **siâ^n-khang**, a hole in a city wall, esp. for cannon. **siâ^n-téng**, on the top of the wall. **siâ^n-bé-téng**, id. **siâ^n-kha**, at the foot of the wall; near the wall. **siâ^n-mn̂g**, a city gate. **siâ^n-lâu**, tower at city gate. **siâ^n-àng**, space inclosed by the two walls at a city gate. **àng-siâ^n**, the outer wall at city gate. **siâ^n-lāi**, within the city walls; the city proper; within the city. **siâ^n-goā**, the suburbs; outside the walls. **siâ^n-chhī**, city and suburbs. **siâ^n-chhī ê-lâng**, a man belonging to the city (including suburbs). **siâ^n-tê**, a passage-boat to or from a city.

koāi^n-siâ^n, a Hien city; chief city of a district. **hú-siâ^n**, a Foo city; chief city of a department. **séng-siâ^n**, provincial capital. **sé^n-siâ^n** (C.), id. **kia^n-siâ^n**, the metropolis. **kim-siâ^n**, id. **bān-lí-tn̂g-siâ^n**, the Great Wall. **bók-siâ^n**, a wooden fort for a review. **thô-siâ^n**, a fort or line of circumvallation, built of clay or unburnt brick.

phoà-siâ^n, to breach a fortified wall; to take a city. **kong-siâ^n**, to attack a city. **kong tâng-siâ^n**, to gamble with the lién-pó.

phàu-siâ^n, a set of crackers on the top of a pole. **kat phàu-siâ^n**, to fasten them up. **khó phàu-siâ^n**, to fire other crackers at them, trying to hit them and set them off.

tē-gėk-siâ^n, hell. **óng-sí-siâ^n**, the part of hell for those who have died violent deaths. **phah-siâ^n**, to perform rites to get souls out of hell; to take a city. **phah chhèng-siâ^n** (T.), to perform rites to deliver souls from the part of hell for those who die of gunshot wounds. **kê chhèng-siâ^n**, to make a paper representation of that place for these rites.

Siâ^n, to excite desire, as by showing something or by example; to try to catch by a bait; to allure or try to allure, as to evil. **sa^n-siâ^n**, id. **siâ^n-sîn** (to allure flies), to entice young men, as a gaudily ornamented bad woman. **chhàu-chho siâ^n-sîn**, do. (lit. strong-smelling fish alluring flies).

Siâ^n [R. sêng, to accomplish; to complete; = col. chiâ^n, chhiâ^n]. **kúi-siâ^n-gûn**, of what quality is the silver? **chiok-siâ^n-gûn**, pure silver. **chiok-siâ^n-kim**, pure gold. **káu-siâ^n-kim**, gold with one-tenth of alloy. **poeh-siâ^n-kim**, gold with one-fifth of alloy.

Siá^n [R. sím, exceedingly; which? = col. sím], (C. sá^n, siá^n). **siá^n-sū**, why? why ever —? (with more or less idea of finding fault). **ū siá^n-sū**, what is the matter? **tsòe-siá^n-sū**, what are you (or is he) doing? **i teh-siá^n-sū**, what is he at? **bô-siá^n-sū**, nothing special; nothing the matter; with no harm. **bô-siá^n bô-sū**, id. **bô-siá^n-tāi**, nothing the matter. **siá^n-hè** (C. hòe), what is the matter? **ū siá^n-pō**, what can now be done? **lí beh-siá^n-tsai**, how can you know? (v. beh, what?). **siá^n-tsai** (Cn.), no one can tell (who can know?). **bô-siá^n-tsai**, I don't know much about it. **bô-siá^n-hó**, not very good. **bô-siá^n-hong**, not much wind; scarcely any wind. **bô-siá^n-lâng**, scarcely any one (present).

bó-siá^n-lâng, Mr. So-and-so, for example; any one; such and such a man. **bó-siá^n-pút**, such and such an idol, for example.

siá^n-mih^n (C.), = A. sím-mih^n, what? what thing? **siá^n-mn̍gh^n** (Cn.), what thing?

Sià^n [R. sèng, holy; a sage], powerful and efficacious, as a god, a temple, a charm, a medicine, or an influential man. **lêng-sià^n**, efficacious and powerful, as a god. **ū-lêng-sià^n**, id. **bô-sià^n**, without efficacious power. **bōe-sià^n**, id. **sià^n-jiah**, manifestation of power to assist, as of a god. **sià^n-pút**, a powerful idol. **khah-sià^n sam-kài**, almost certainly efficacious (v. kài). **sìn-sià^n**, to believe in the power of some god. **chhē-sià^n** (Cn.), to call the spirits of the dead, as sorceress or female medium. **sià^n-má** (Cn.), a sorceress. **sià^n-chiá** (Cn.), id.

chhùi sià^n, his words come true, as guess of future. **sià^n-chhùi**, id.

Siā^n, a large sort of tray (carried like a basket on a pole between two men), for carrying marriage presents and offerings. **siā^n-á**, id. **chit-kìng-siā^n**, one such ceremonial tray.

siā^n-koà, the hatches of a vessel; the cover of the hold.

siā^{n}-nâ^{n}, a basket made with several horizontal divisions or compartments. **siā^{n}-nâ^{n}-tsân**, one of these separate compartments.

siā^{n}, a large brick-built receptacle for salt at a public salt-store. **chhek-siā^{n}**, a large boarded receptacle for unthrashed grain in a granary.

siā^{n} [R. sēng, abundant], a surname.

siah (R. siok), to pare; to pare away. **siu-siah**, to pare down smooth; to make slight erasures, as in book or document. **siah-khi-chiam**, pare the point sharp. **siah-pit**, to sharpen a lead pencil or quill pen. **siah-lân**, to scrape off fish scales. **siah-kut lòh-hèk**, very very lean.

siah — **phiah-siah**, lonely; unfrequented, as place (cf. siám).

siah (R. sek), (Cn. sek), tin; pewter. **siah-pôh**, tin-foil. **siah-khì**, pewter articles. **phah-siah**, to work in pewter. **kheng-siah**, to work tin, as at mines. **khêng-siah**, to collect and melt small fragments of tin or pewter. **phoà-tâng kū-siah**, old or broken brass or pewter articles. **phái^{n}-tâng kū-siah**, id.

siàh [R. sėk, a stone, = col. chiòh], marble; soap-stone. **siàh-chiòh**, id. **siàh-hún**, powdered marble or soap-stone, put on the skin for coolness. **siàh-ìn**, a seal made of soap-stone. **siàh-hī^{n}**, an ink-stone of marble or soap-stone.

siàh-tsoá, marbled paper.

siàh-liû, the pomegranate (v. liû).

siàh (C. chhiàh), a sort of small ladle. **thih-siàh**, an iron ladle. **bê-siàh**, a ladle for taking out soft rice. **thn̂g-siàh**, spoon for syrup. **iû-siàh**, bamboo instrument for measuring or lading out oil. **tsúi-siàh**, a hollow half-cylinder (gen. a bamboo joint) for baling out water.

siàh [R. sėk, the evening]. **chhit-siàh**, the evening of 7.7.

siàh [R. sėk, a mat; a feast; a meal; = col. chhiòh]. **iân-siàh**, a feast; a banquet. **chiú-siàh** (r.), id., with liquor. **chit-siàh**, one feast; one company of men eating at once. **tsòe-n̄ng-siàh**, eating in two successive companies.

siàh — **bàuh-siàh**, = bàuh-soah, to deride a man as utterly unable to effect his purpose.

siàh — **lâ-sâm-siàh**, dirty; filthy.

siàh — **n̂g-siàh** (T. n̂g-sit-á), a sort of fish.

siak (cf. siàng), (Cn. sak), to dash down. **siak--lòh-lâi**, to dash on the ground. **siak--tó**, to fall down. **siak-tiū**, to thrash rice in a tub. **siak-bėh**, to thrash wheat or barley in a tub. **siak-tháng**, the tub for thrashing grain. **siak-tháng-thui**, an instrument like a small ladder put in the tub for the heads of grain to be struck upon.

siak-sau, to bully. **siak-í siak-toh**, to strike chairs and table, in anger or pet. **pia^{n}-oá^{n} siak-tī**, to throw about bowls and chopsticks, in a rage. **siak-thâu sí-hē--i**, to kill one's self by striking the head on the ground in a rage.

siak-sin, to exert one's self very much; much exhausted or uncomfortable. **ká^{n} phah-siak**, very venturesome. **chin phah-siak**, having a vast deal of toil and trouble in managing an affair; very much pained and tossing about restlessly, as sick man.

siak — **kiàk-siak**, active and lively in manner.

siak [R. siok? lek? brilliant; shining, = col. siàk]. **kim siak-siak**, glittering; shining. **pėh siak-siak**, brilliantly white (cf. siám).

siak — **àm siak-siak**, very dark, as night.

siak (Cn.), **toā-m̄-siak-kōe**, very numerous, = toā-bú sì-kòe.

siak (Cn.) **siak-kháu**, = A. sek-kháu, to wash the mouth.

siàk (= siak). **kim siàk-siàk**, glittering; shining brightly.

siam, to peep. **thau-siam**, id. **toà-teh-siam**, peeping at something. **ná^{n}-siam ná^{n}-siam**, looking about stealthily.

iap-siam--khì, to take a thing stealthily and conceal it secretly.

siâm (R. id.) **siâm-sû**, a sort of toad supposed to be very poisonous.

siâm, to snatch suddenly, as a man's cap, or hand, or queue. **tùi-chhiú kā--i siâm--teh**, seize him by his hand, *e.g.* to keep him from striking. **hê-siū^{n} bô-tn̂g-thâu-mn̂g hē-lâng-siâm** (a Bud. priest has no long hair to catch), said of a very niggardly man.

siâm [R. sîm, to search; usual; a fathom], a fathom; to join the hands before one; to embrace in the arms. **siâm tiâu-tiâu**, to seize firmly in the arms. **kun-tsú-siâm**, embracing another in joke, as in wrestling, or for amusement.

siám (R. id.) **siám-sai**, Shen-si province. **siám-kam**, Shen-si and Kan-suh.

siám [R. to avoid; to flash; = col. sih, siah; cf. siak], to avoid; to get out of the way; to sprain. **siám--tiòh**, to sprain or hurt one's self by a sudden movement.

siám-pī, to avoid; to get out of the way. **siám-pi^{n}**, id., as by going to the side. **siám-khui**, to get out of the road, going to one side. **siám-oá**, id., as by going close to a wall, or to the shore, or to the side of the road. **siám kui-pêng**, all go to *one* side of the road to let another pass easily. **khah-siám**, get further out of the way, *e.g.* to let one pass more easily. **siám-bih**, to keep out of the way by hiding. **tô-siám**, to run away. **tsáu-siám**, do.; to avoid; to shirk work. **thau-siám**, to run away stealthily. **siám--kè-khì**, to creep stealthily past.

siám-kak, quiet and lonely, as a place.

kim siám-siám, glittering; shining, as something polished. **lāi siám-siám**, very sharp.

siám — **bàt siám-siám**, very dense, as a crowd, or as thick clusters, or as a densely peopled district (cf. siap).

siám — **toā-siám**, the blade of the helm (v. toā, "helm").

siàm (R. sìm), (cf. siàp), to ooze; to leak in, as water. **siàm-lāu**, id. **siàm-chhut**, to ooze out. **siàm-jiō**, to pass urine in small quantities and with difficulty.

siām [R. the growing brightness of the sun; Siam]. **siām-lô**, Siam; Siam and Laos.

siām [R. to supply; sufficient]. **ióng-siām**, money set apart for himself, as by a father (when giving their portions to his sons), for his own use in old age, or for his burial. **ióng-siām-gûn**, id.

'**sian**, **siân**, **sián**, **siàn**, **siān**; better sien, siên, sién, sièn, siēn (*q.v.*)

siang (R. song, = col. sang, sng), a pair; both the two. **chit-siang**, a pair. **kui-siang**, making a pair; a pair. **chiâ^{n}-siang**, id. **siang-siang tùi-tùi**, in pairs. **siang-si^{n}**, twins. **siang-si^{n}-mn̂g**, folding doors. **siang-chhe-lē**, branching roads (v.

chhe). **siang-hù**, two sets. **siang-chiú^{n}**, a two-oared boat. **siang-chhiú**, both hands. **chit-siang-chhiú**, a pair of hands. **siang-kha**, both legs or feet. **siang-lúi bák-chiu**, both eyes. **siang-lâng**, both the men. **siang-lâng tńg**, bride and bride-groom going to spend some days at house of bride's parents a few days after marriage.

siang-bīn, both sides; both surfaces. **siang-bīn-to kúi**, a wretch who excites and inflames a quarrel, by slandering each side to the other. **siang-pêng**, both sides. **siang-pêng-oá**, trying to keep neutral, and on good terms with both sides. **kè-siang-thâu**, said of a son who keeps up the worship of two families. **khiā siang-thâu-bé**, to pretend to be on good terms with each side, while assisting each with what he learns from the other. **koà siang-thâu-bé**, id. **chit-chhùi siang-thâu-chhut**, said of a man talking a great deal and very fast, quite enough for two mouths.

siang-liāu, strong double-distilled spirits (v. liāu). **siang-to-hōe** (C.), = sio-to-hōe, the Triad, or Small Knife Society.

siang (C.), A. siong, mutual.

siang (C.), = A. siong, to wound; to hurt; sometimes said of a place pained, though not by a wound.

siang (C.), = A. siong, a merchant.

siâng (cf. sâng, siāng), alike; exactly similar; of the same sort. **bô-siâng**, unlike; quite different. **bô-siâng-lō͘**, not going by the same road; he is quite a bad character, while I am good. **bô-siâng-khoán**, of very different character; a different sort. **siâng-khoán**, of the same sort or character. **siâng-khoán-sit**, id. **siâng-chit-iū^{n}**, id. **siâng-sim**, like-minded; congenial. **siâng-kau-kài**, having a common boundary; conterminous.

siâng (C.), = A. siông, usual; generally. **siâng-kòe**, usually. **siâng-nî^{n}**, each year (in the past); year by year.

siâng (C.), = A. siông, minutely.

siâng (C.), = A. siông (a good omen).

siâng (Cn.), = A. sím-mih^{n}-lâng, who? **siâng-sōh**, who says so? **siâng-bōh**, who would be willing?

siáng (C.), = A. sióng (to look at).

siáng (C.), = A. sióng (to think).

siàng (cf. siak), (Cn. sàng). **siàng--lòh-khì**, to dash violently on the ground. **siàng-poe-á**, to throw three cash on the ground after striking one's knee; a sort of gambling. **siàng-heng** (C.), to beat the breast with a stone, as beggars do.

siàng (C.), = A. siòng, appearance of face or person; (high mandarins; to look at). **phé-siàng**, = A. phì-siù^{n}, to talk of others' faults; to talk scandal.

siāng (cf. siâng), (Cn. sāng), quite alike; of same form, sort, or character. **bô-siāng**, quite different; **siāng-sim**, like-minded; congenial. **siāng-khoán**, of the same sort or kind. **siāng-iū^{n}**, id. **siāng-lūi**, of the same sort, as men or things. **siāng-hiu^{n}-siā**, belonging to the same village. **siāng-hiu^{n}-lí**, id. **siāng-khiā-lāi**, living in different parts of the same large house.

siāng [R. siōng, above; upon; = col. chiū^{n}, chhiū^{n}], one of the musical notes. **má-siāng**, immediately (v. má).

Also (C.), **siāng**, = A. siōng, first-class, &c.

siāng (C.), = A. siōng (still, yet, &c.)

siap (R. siap? sip?), rough, as surface; very stiff, as door or drawer; sleepy, as eyes: bad tasted; somewhat sourish or bitter. **siap-siap**, id. **chhe-siap**, rough and coarse, as surface.

bák siap, eyes sleepy. **bák-chiu siap**, id. **kha siap**, disinclined to walk.

sò-siap, shrivelled, as skin of old man, or of fruit too long kept; very scant of money.

pak-siap, feeling of emptiness and slight pain in stomach; very poor and wretched; uncomfortable troubled state of mind; too dry, as food unpleasant to eat, or causing uncomfortable feeling after eating. **pak-siap--lâng**, to dun for help, as poor relatives.

kiâm-siap, salt and sour; bad-tasted (s. niggardly). **chhùi siap**, bad appetite, as from slight illness, or bad taste in mouth.

siap (R. id.) **kiâm-siap**, niggardly (s. bad-tasted). **kiâm koà-siap**, niggardly.

siap [R. sek, to fill up a cavity; to bribe; = col. soeh, that, siám], to fill up a small crevice. **siap-bát**, filled up, as a crevice; well drawn up, as document without flaws; closed, so as to be quite safe, or so that no secret gets out; quiet and out of the way, as place. **siap-tiáp**, closely, tightly, or neatly tied or packed up; neatly arranged, so as to take up little room; having much in little bulk.

soeh-siap, to give some money, or make some promise, so as to get a man's secret influence or false witness, or to keep him from giving some information to the other side that would bear strongly against us. **siap āu-chhiú**, id., esp. to arbiter, that he may take our side, or to underlings of yamun. **siap lâng--ê sin-sè**, to take advantage of another's influence or success, so as to get some affair of ours set right, though without any direct help from him.

siap — **iap-siap**, retired, as a house; keeping to the side, or out of sight (v. iap).

siap — **siap-bûn**, = sap-bûn, soap (mere imitation of foreign sound).

siap — **ka-tia^{n}-siap**, bark of a shrub (mangrove?) used as a dye.

siap [R. drizzling rain; a moment; = col. sap; cf. tiap]. **thêng-thêng siap-á-kú**, always procrastinating and promising to do it very shortly.

siáp (cf. siàm), to ooze or leak in small quantities. **siáp--chhut-lâi**, to ooze or leak out.

siáp [R. to wade across; relating to], to bribe. **poát-siáp san-chhoan** (R.), to travel far over mountains and rivers.

kan-siáp, related to; concerned with; implicated (v. kan). **koan-siáp**, id. (v. koan). **ū kau-siáp**, to have very intimate relations in business or friendship, so as to have more or less liability for his failure, or to be involved in grave suspicion for his wickedness.

siáp-su, to act with partiality or unjust selfishness. **bōe-siáp--tit**, cannot be managed by bribery. **siáp-sè**, to flatter; to fawn; to be a parasite; to get a superior (or endeavour it) to use his influence for private ends. **chhu-sì siáp-sè**, to follow the fashion and fawn on the powerful.

siáp (same as previous word?), to swindle, wheedle, or cozen, as a sharper, &c. · **siáp lâng-ê-chî^{n}**, to swindle a man out of money. **siáp lâng--ê chî^{n}-gûn**, id.

siáp, to bewitch. **khit-kúi siáp--khì**, to be bewitched by demons. **sam-siau siáp--khì**, made mad by the demon called sam-siau, as man or animal.

siáp (R. id.) **siáp-si**, to divine by the plant called "si."

海上絲綢之路文獻集成 科技與文化編

厦英大辭典

siáp — **māi^n-siáp,** a very durable wood of a slightly reddish colour.

siáp (contracted from si-tsáp), forty. **siáp-it,** forty-one.

siat, siát; better siet, siėt (*q.v.*)

siau [R. night]. **goân-siau,** the feast of lanterns on evening of 1.15. **thong-siau-chek,** long red candles.

siau (R. id.) **siau-sit,** a small brush for inside of ear (s. melt, news).

siau (R. id.) **siau-kun,** cramp. **pak-tó siau-sṅg-thiàn,** severe griping pains in the belly.

siau (R. id.), various sorts of seminal flux, as gonorrhœa, spermatorrhœa, &c., which are much confounded by the Chinese. **hā-siau,** id. **hē-siau** (C.), id. **hā-siau-hong,** chronic do.; often said by Chinese when really due to other causes.

siau (R. id.) **siau-sá** (R.), open and cheerful in manner; taking things in an easy and pleased manner (s. walk about).

siau [R. to walk about]. **siau-sá,** a walk, as for amusement, or to help digestion (s. cheerful). **siau-iâu** (R.), to wander about for pleasure (v. iâu). **siau-khién,** to walk about for health or amusement (v. khién). **siau-hân** (R.), to go about at leisure.

siau [R. the high part of the sky, = col. sio]. **pe-jip hûn-siau,** to fly up into the clouds (said of a man terribly afraid).

siau [R. name of an insect]. **hái-phiau-siau,** medicine made from the powdered bone of the cuttle-fish.

siau [R. saltpetre and various kinds of salts; cf. col. sa, se], saltpetre. **siau-ióh,** gunpowder. **siau-hông,** saltpetre and sulphur. **siau-ko,** black plaster for blistering. **iâm-siau,** white incrustation on damp places. **chhiū^n iâm-siau,** this incrustation forming. **phok-siau,** purgative salts; sulphate of soda. **gê-siau,** a medicinal salt.

siau (same as previous word?). **chhó-siau,** a vegetable purgative medicine.

siau (Cn.) **siau-koe,** = A. am-koe, a long sort of pumpkin.

siau — **ēng to-pán siau,** to strike with the flat of the sword.

siau [R. name of a demon]. **sam-siau,** a demon that haunts hills. **sam-siau-kang,** male do. **sam-siau-bú,** female do.

siau (R. id.), sort of clarionet or flute. **tōng-siau,** a clarionet, held straight out. **phín-siau,** sort of flute, held obliquely. **pûn-siau,** to play the clarionet or flute.

pit-siau, the stem of a hair-pencil as distinguished from the hair.

siau [R. name of a bitter plant; lonely; desolate; a surname; = col. sio]. **siau-sap,** shabby-looking (s. melt, shrivelled).

siau [R. to melt, as in or into water, = col. siu], to exhaust or spend; to reduce or remove, as swellings or some diseases and evils; to digest; to have a motion; to sell well; to shrink, as wood.

siau-sán, very lean (v. sán). **siau-bah,** to grow lean. **bah siau, kut hiān,** so lean that the bones appear. **iù-siau,** slim and delicate in figure, as man; small and neat, as one's leg, or as a small pig. **siau-siau--khì,** grown quite lean. **siau liáu-liáu,** id.

siau-sap, shrivelled, as face; decayed, as village (v. sap), (s. previous word).

siau-hoà, to digest. **ōe-siau-láp,** able to digest. **chiáh-bōe-siau,** unable to digest. **chiáh-m̄-siau,** id. **siau-iû,** to help to digest fat. **siau-tháu,** to have a motion, or pass water; to remove, as calamities, or as anger (v. tháu).

siau-tsai kái-eh, to remove or ward off calamities (v. tsai). **siau-chhiû kái-ut,** to remove sadness. **siau-chhiû kái-būn** (r.), id. **siau-tsōe,** to remove guilt, esp. by Tauist priest at temple of Sêng-hông, or by sorceress. **siau chē-koà,** id. **siau-àn,** to wind up a legal case or let it drop. **kau-siau,** to cancel, as account, by writing "oân" and making a large circle over it. **chhat-siau,** id.; to blot out. **siau-tû,** to remove, as evils.

siau-tók, to remove some poisonous influence. **siau-thâm,** to cure phlegm. **siau-chéng,** to reduce a swelling. **siau-tiù^n,** to reduce a swelling of the belly. **siau-soà^n--khì,** quite removed; wasted away or exhausted (v. soà^n). **kau-âm m̄-siau-tsúi,** the pipe or drain does not let the water flow through. **tsúi bōe-siau,** the water will not run off. **tsúi siau--khì,** the water has been drained off.

siau-sih, gradually diminish or waste away, *e.g.* by evaporation or melting, or in business; difference or loss in trade between gross and net, somewhat like tare. **kāu-siau-sih,** having a great deal of waste, as watered meat, &c. **kāu-siau,** id.

khai-siau, to expend money. **tû khai-siau-goā,** net gains after deducting food and other expenses. **tû khui-siau-goā,** id.

siau-tiā^n, to keep the earnest-money as a forfeit when a bargain is broken off. **hō--i siau--khì,** forfeit it (earnest-money) to him.

siau-tsng, knowingly buy stolen goods. **ū siau-thâu,** saleable; having a ready sale or good run in the market. **ū-siau,** id. **bô-siau,** not having a good sale, or none. **oh-siau,** not well saleable. **siau goā-kok,** its sale is all in foreign parts.

bōe-siau-kiēn, unable to resist, though very unwilling to obey (v. kiēn).

siau-sit, news.

siâu [R. siâ, oblique, col. chhiâ]. **siâu-bûn-pè** (r.), = chhiâ-bûn-pè, twilled cotton.

siâu, semen (vulg.) **hau-siâu,** a great lie! (very vulgar, but probably originally an imitation of the mand. "háu-siàu," ridiculous; absurd).

siáu [R. siu, to be ashamed]. **siáu-lóe,** ashamed; shy (v. lóe). **siáu-jîn,** ashamed; bashful (s. small). **ùi-siáu-jîn,** ashamed to see any one because of having done wrong; afraid to do a shameful thing (*e.g.* shameful pleasures) for fear of the shame of possible discovery; modest, as boy or girl. **ōe siáu-jîn,** having a sense of shame. **hiâm siáu-jîn,** to object because ashamed, *e.g.* ashamed to meet some one. **siáu-jîn-chháu,** the sensitive plant.

siáu [R. small, = col. sió]. **biáu-siáu,** very small; to treat with indignity. **siáu-jî,** my little boy. **siáu-lú** (polite), my daughter. **siáu-bêng,** my personal name. **siáu-sū,** a small affair. **siáu-éng,** a small portrait; a miniature (v. éng). **siáu-tsong,** a small branch ancestral hall. **koan-hē put-siáu,** the consequences may be very serious. **siáu-kúi-bīn,** very ugly, as face; the iron case of a lock.

siáu-hân, a term on or about Jan. 5th. **siáu-sú,** term on or about July 7th. **siáu-sí** (C.), id. **siáu-soat,** term on or about Nov. 22d.

siáu-soat, novels. **siáu-sîn**, idle, and fond of gambling or such low pleasures.

siáu-jîn, a man of low mean ideas; a worthless fellow (s. ashamed). **siáu-jîn-thâu**, a bad man. **siáu-khì-kúi**, a low miserly wretch. **siáu-khì**, miserly; parsimonious; reckoning to the last cash, or strictly requiring the most minute particulars. **siáu-chhû**, id. **siáu-kio̍k**, mean; niggardly, as man; made too small, as a thing. **siáu-sé-kièn**, not having seen much of the world; of contracted ideas (v. kièn).

siáu-piēn, urine; to make water. **siáu-kái**, to make water. **siáu-sûi**, do., said only of children. **siáu-sán**, to have an abortion.

tāi-siáu (R.), large and small. **tāi-siáu-sèng-hōe**, small clans combining against the larger. **tāi-tông siáu-īⁿ**, nearly the same, but somewhat different. **tāi-keng siáu-koài**, in much consternation (v. keng). **liōng-tāi-siáu**, to use more or less, as one pleases or is able. **ōe-liōng-tāi-siáu--tit**, may be used more or less at pleasure, as superfluities; *e.g.* as condiments and nice eating, as opposed to rice and fire-wood for cooking, which must be had. **mêⁿ tāi-siáu**, elastic, as woollen socks. **lêng-tāi lêng-siáu**, elastic, as socks. **sam-jit tāi, ngó-jit siáu**, having greater and smaller feasts each third and fifth day.

siáu [R. few; small quantity; = col. chió]. **to-siáu** (R.), many or few; much or little. **to-siáu** (Cn.), id. (R.) **siáu-sé-kièn**, and also **koan-hē put-siáu** (s. small), might perhaps be placed under this word.

siáu, mad; crazy; idiotic. **siáu-siáu**, id.; jesting foolishly. **siáu-gōng**, fond of gambling, low joking, or foolish pleasures. **chiáh-chiú siáu**, intoxicated and behaving absurdly. **siáu-káu**, a mad dog. **teh-siáu**, acting madly. **teh-siáu-kông**, quite mad. **lí teh-siáu**, surely you are mad (said to a man behaving very absurdly). **tìⁿ-siáu**, feigning madness. **tìⁿ-tien tìⁿ-siáu**, id.

siáu [R. id.? cf. col. sió], excited with sexual feeling. **hiâu-siáu**, id., said only of a bad woman.

siàu [R. id., by change of tone from siáu, "few"]. **siàu-liên**, young (v. liên). **siàu-iâ**, a mandarin's son (by some placed under "filial").

siàu [R. like; like one's father; filial]. **put-siàu**, unfilial; disobedient to parents; ill-behaved. **put-siàu-kiáⁿ**, disobedient son. **hā-liû put-siàu**, ill-behaved fellows; vagabonds. **m̄-bat-siàu**, unfilial; bad son. **siàu-iâ**, mandarin's son (by some placed under "young").

siàu [R. to laugh, = col. chhiò]. **kièn-siàu**, to be ashamed; shame! **lí tio̍h-kiàn-siàu**, you should feel ashamed of yourself! shame on you! **hō͘--i kiàn-siàu**, to make him feel ashamed.

hâm-siàu-hoe, the Magnolia fuscata.

siàu [R. siù, elegant; accomplished]. **tsùn-siàu** (r.), good-looking, as person.

siàu [R. soàn, to calculate, = col. sǹg], an account; to count or calculate; also (P.), a deed of sale, mortgage, or lease.

giáh-siàu, number, as of articles. **siàu-giáh**, id. **sí-siàu**, time. **pòe-siàu** (C.), position in genealogical rank. **hó-kioh-siàu**, skilful, as workman or actor (v. kioh). **hó-ē-siàu** (C. hó-ē-sùiⁿ), plan good; it can be managed (v. ē). **kàu-liâu kàu-siàu**, just at proper time or in right quantity (v. liâu).

siàu-phō͘, an account-book. **siàu-bák**, an account. **siàu-hāng**, account of amount due. **siàu-tiâu**, accounts of sums due. **chiah-ê siàu-tiâu**, these unsettled accounts. **siàu-kûi**, a book-keeper. **siàu-kûi-toh**, a shop-counter. **siàu-kûi-pâng**, counting-room. **siàu-pâng**, id. **koán-siàu**, a book-keeper; a sort of steward who keeps the accounts.

siàu-liām, to think of with warm affection, as dear friend or relative; to meditate gratefully upon, as some kindness.

siàu-iáh, to count the pages of a book. **siàu-chîⁿ**, to count cash. **bô-siàu-pái**, not counting how often; a great many times. **siàu koe-lō͘-chio̍h** (counting the stones on the streets), walking about at leisure. **chhī pē-bú, siàu-tǹg**, in feeding his parents he counts (and grudges) every meal.

sǹg-siàu, to calculate. **sǹg-goá-ê-siàu**, count it to my account, I will bear the responsibility. **khah-séng-siàu**, effecting a saving in money; cheaper (v. séng).

khiàm-siàu, to owe an account. **tó-siàu**, not to pay a debt (v. tó). **sia-siàu**, to buy on credit. **it-hoat ū-siàu**, to buy more and more on credit without paying. **it-hoat kāu-siàu**, id. **pàng-siàu**, to sell on credit. **chhut-siàu**, to sell or lend on credit, esp. goods. **chhut-jip chit-poàⁿ-tiâu-siàu**, to do a very small business. **jip-siàu**, to have part-payment. **seng jip-siàu**, id. **ū lâi-óng-siàu**, to have an account current.

hoāⁿ-siàu, to have charge of the accounts. **kì-siàu**, to make an entry in an account. **chiūⁿ-siàu**, to enter an item, or be entered in account (v. chiūⁿ). **tak-siàu**, to note down an account (v. tak). **khai-siàu**, to note down disbursements. **khui phòng-siàu**, to put down more than was paid out. **phòng-siàu**, overcharge (intentional). **tiòng-siàu**, overcharge by mistake. **sit-siàu**, to fail to put down in account, by mistake, either at first or in copying. **thau-chiáh-siàu**, intentionally falsify account so as to embezzle employer's money. **tùi-siàu**, to compare accounts. **hē-siàu**, to compare accounts so as to settle them. **hōe-siàu**, id. **hok-siàu**, to go over an account a second time to see if there be any error. **liàh-siàu**, to examine an account roughly to see if it be correct. **lėk-siàu**, to copy out the items for each customer. **poāⁿ-siàu**, to transfer accounts from one book to another. **chhau-siàu**, to copy an account. **chhau-kè-siàu**, to copy an account into a new book.

kè-siàu, to pay by a bill; to make over a debt to a third party to collect. **kòe-siàu** (C.), id. **kè i-ê-siàu**, to transfer to his account, as by a bill, &c. **tùi-toaⁿ kè-siàu**, make over a debt by a bill. **chheng-kè-siàu**, to pay a bill drawn on us; to pay a debt to our creditor's creditor by his direction. **chheng-siàu**, to pay off a debt by full payment. **chheng-kí-siàu**, to pay up the last instalment (at due time) so as to make the payment complete. **i beh-kā--lí chheng-siàu**, he will settle accounts with you (fig.) **oân-siàu**, to settle an account by payment (sometimes a little being taken off). **kau-siàu** (r.), to make payment of account, entire or partial. **chhat-siàu**, to mark an account as settled. **chiet-siàu**, to take a composition for a debt. **kā--i tsún-siàu**, to take an article as payment of a debt (v. tsún). **tú-siàu**, to be given in part-payment, as money; or in payment in place of money, as goods, &c. **siu-siàu**, to receive payment for accounts; to collect debts. **thó-siàu**, to collect debts. **pek-siàu**, to dun for payment. **thoaⁿ-siàu**, to divide expenses among partners.

kiet-siàu, to sum and balance the whole account, as at end of month (v. kiet). **tsûn-siàu**, to compare the accounts and the cash in hand, to see what balance there is, as at end of day, or of several days; to sum up at foot of page.

siâu [R. to connect; to continue]. **siāu-heng**, Shau-hing-foo, in Chekiang province, from which a great proportion of mandarin's private secretaries come. **siāu-hin** (C.), id.

siāu (R. id., = col. siō), a surname. **siāu-bú**, Shau-woo-foo, on the border of Kiang-si, on the road from Fuh-chau.

siáuh (= siáuh^n), noise of a thing breaking.

siáuh^n (= siáuh), noise of a thing breaking.

sien (C. T. san), (dist. sién), rust; hardened dirt on skin. **o͘-sien**, grayish black, as dirty face, or dark-coloured dollar. **thih-sien**, iron-rust. **tâng-sien**, verdegris on the article (v. tâng). **si^n-sien**, to grow rusty. **seng-khu si^n-sien**, body covered with hardened dirt. **sien si^n ka-nn̂g-têng**, id. very much. **káu-koeh-sien**, hardened dirt on the body. **ka-chiah-sien**, hardened dirt down the middle of the back. **chhiú-sien**, do. on the hand, especially inside of wrist. **kha-sien**, do. on leg or foot.

sien (R. id., = col. chhi^n). **sin-sien**, fresh and new, as food or colour; original and fresh, as a literary composition. **kî-chhì sien-bêng**, flags all new and beautiful.

sien [R. san, a mountain, = col. soa^n]. **sien-tsa**, = san-tsa, a small red crab-apple from North China.

sien (R. san). **sien-hô** (C. san-hô), coral. **sien-lô-chhiū**, a coral-tree.

sien [R. soan, to proclaim; a surname]. **tâng-sien-lô**, = tâng-soan-lô, an incense vessel of finest polished brass.

sien [R. sin, the body, = col. seng], (C. sin), classifier of idols, ancestral tablets, &c. **siang-chhiú phi-sien**, arms stretched out, as in form of a cross. **bā-hio̍h phi-sien**, id. **chit-sien-pu̍t**, one (Bud.) idol. **chit-sien kong-pô**, one ancestral tablet. **thn̂g kàu-chit-sien ná^n liū-pu̍t--nih^n**, said in scolding a naked child.

sien (R. id.), a genie, elf, or fairy (Tauist), (said half in joke of men addicted to various vices). **sien-tan**, the elixir of immortality. **sien-soa^n**, = hông-lâi, the isles of the genii, in the distant east. **sien-tōng**, a cave where the genii are worshipped; a temple at it. **sien-ho̍h**, a fabulous stork, living several hundred years. **sien-thô**, a fabulous peach, used by the genii. **sien-pa-chiú^n**, a small sort of cactus; a small instrument for scratching the back. **sien-ka^n** (Cn.), a very large sort of orange.

sîn-sien, objects of idolatrous worship in general. **sîn-sien bōe-kiù bô-miā^n-lâng**, the gods cannot save an ill-fated man. **sien-tsé**, title of any one of the genii (s. former). **sien-kong**, id., especially as to dreams. **khùn sien-kong-bāng**, to sleep in temple of genii, in order to get auspicious dreams. **oân sien-bāng**, id. **ûn sien-bāng**, id. **sien-ong**, an aged genie. **lâm-kek sien-ong**, the genie of the S. pole. **hô sien-ko͘**, the one female among the eight Sien. **sien-lú**, id. **sien-tông**, a young servant of the genii in their spirit-world. **tēng-kong-sien**, name of a Buddhist idol (v. kong). **ngó͘-kok sien-tè** (T.), the god of agriculture. **pat-sien**, the eight genii (including one fairy). **pat-sien-kóng**, a bamboo case for some of a barber's instruments. **pat-sien-toh**, a table for eight persons. **sì-sien-toh**, a table for four persons (v. toh).

tsúi-sien-ông, five spirits of the waters, esp. one great water-spirit, said to be same as tāi-ú, = ú-tè. **tsúi-sien-keng**, his temple. **tsúi-sien-mn̂g**, the gangway of a vessel. **tsúi-sien-hoe**, the narcissus. **tsúi-sien-chí**, a medicine made of insects that live in ordure. **tsúi-sien-tsū** (T.), id.

tsòe-sien, to become a Sien, as some good men are supposed to do. **sêng-sien**, to become a Sien; to die. **kui-sien**, to die. **sien-sē** (R.), to die.

sien--kong, a beggar (said in allusion to Lí thok-koái^n, one of the genii). **khit-chia̍h-sien**, phrase used in scolding; you are like a beggar! **thit-thô-sien**, a man who has nothing to do but go about amusing himself. **chiú-sien**, a man fond of liquor; a tippler; a drunkard. **a-phièn-sien**, an inveterate opium-smoker. **poa̍h-kiáu-sien**, an inveterate gambler.

poàn-sien, half a genie (said of man who can foresee or guess the future). **san-i-bēng pok-siòng, chīn-bat sī poàn-sien**, to know fully medicine, geomancy, and divination is to be half a genie. **tan-ko oân-sán, chin-sien lân-piēn**, all in great confusion (lit. drugs). **siet-sien, poa^n kâu-chè-thien**, to make a plausible pretence.

sien— **hiā-sien** (Cn. hiā-san), long narrow harmless worms with numerous legs, like small centipedes.

sien— **sien-chháu** (T.), = A. sin-chháu, a plant from which a cooling jelly is made.

sien [R. before; former; previous; = col. seng], sometimes placed after a man's name, as contraction of sien-si^n, but not very respectful. **sien-hō͘**, before and afterwards. **sien-tāi**, former generations; former ages. **sien-ti** (to foreknow), a prophet (v. ti). **sien-hong**, a military officer sent on before a superior officer to make preparations for him. **sien-jîn**, ancestors; the ancients. **sien-ông**, the ancient kings, from whom the Confucian doctrines came. **sien-tè**, a deceased emperor. **sien-kùn**, id. **sien-tsó͘**, deceased paternal grandfather (v. tsó͘), (s. genie). **tsó͘-sien**, ancestors in general. **sien-hū**, deceased father. **lēng-sien-tsun** (polite), your deceased father. **sien-bú**, deceased mother.

sien-si^n (C. sin-sɛ^n), teacher; doctor. **tsòe-sien-si^n** (C. tsò-sin-sɛ^n), to be a teacher or doctor (C. Cn. gen. doctor). **chhiá^n sien-si^n**, to call a doctor; to engage a teacher. **piah-sien-si^n**, = ka-tsoa̍h, a cockroach. **hong-súi sien-si^n**, a geomancer. **gī-o̍h sien-si^n**, teacher of a free school. **kà-o̍h sien-si^n**, a school-master. **toh-thâu sien-si^n** (the teacher on the table), the Imperial Dictionary. **kúi-kok sien-si^n**, a famous diviner (v. kok, "a valley"). **sien-si^n-niû^n**, a teacher's wife. **sien-si^n-má**, teacher's mother. **sien-si^n-kong**, teacher's father.

kóng-kó͘-sien, a man who makes his living by reading or telling old histories or historical novels. **tsáu-koe-á-sien**, street fortune-tellers, quacks, &c. **khoà^n-miā^n-sien**, a fortune-teller. **hoa-kî-sien** (an American missionary): in some parts all missionaries were supposed to be Americans. **pài-sien** (C.), to have our name put on the books of an official in a yamun for protection (v. báu).

siên [R. iên, saliva]. **liông-siên-hiu^n**, = liông-iên-hiu^n, a sort of medicine.

siên [R. the cicada, = col. chê; cf. C. tê; Cn. tsûn]. **siên-á**, a small sort of cicada. **chhiu-siên-á**, id. **chhiū-siên**, a small sort of cicada, am-pô-chê. **siên-thòe**, shells of the cicada, medicinal.

siên [R. to sit in Bud. abstraction]. **tsō-siên**, to sit cross-legged in abstraction without eating, as Bud.

priests do. **chē-siên**, id. **tsō-siên--sí**, do., till he dies of starvation. **chē-siên ūn-khì**, to sit cross-legged and meditate in abstraction, insensible to the world. **siên-pông**, cell of Bud. priest.

siên-chhn̂g, a couch with arms or rests at each end for the elbows (v. chhn̂g).

bák-chiu khoeh-siên-siên, very drowsy.

sién [R. few; by change of tone from sien, "fresh"]. **tiâu-sién**, Corea.

sién [R. id. = col. chhoá^{n}], (dist. sien), scrofulous and similar eruptions; ringworm; dirty scurf. **káu-sién**, id. **ta-sién**, dry sort. **noā^{n}-sién**, moist scurf; ringworm, &c. **si^{n}-sién**, to have such skin disease. **îm-sién**, sort of secondary syphilis.

sién [R. sé, sién, to wash, = col. sóe]. **tê-sién** (r.), = tê-sóe, a stoneware plate for a tea-pot. **tê-sién** (C.), id.

siàn [R. to strike with a fan or with the hand], to slap with the palm. **siàn chhùi-phóe**, to slap the cheek. **siàn hī-á**, to slap the ears. **siàn-phah gín-ná**, to slap and strike a child.

siàn [R. thread, = col. soà^{n}]. **siàn-pê**, broad facings or hem of lady's dress.

siàn [R. to fan a flame; to incite to evil]. **siàn-hong**, to be blown violently by the wind, as door slammed by the wind, or as child getting a cold from a draught. **siàn--tó**, to blow upon and upset a thing. **iâu-giân siàn-hék** (R.), to delude and mislead by false rumours and calumnies. **siàn-iân-tâu**, a married woman enticing a young man or having lascivious intercourse with him (v. tâu).

siàn (P.), = A. sìn, to believe.

siān (R. id.) **péh-siān-thô**, chalk.

siān [R. prepared food]. **ū-keng-siān**, to get food as well as salary, often done for a school-teacher.

siān [R. sīn, the kidneys]. **siān-chí**, the testes. **toā-sòe-siān**, one of them inflamed and swollen; orchitis. **siān-eng**, an abscess in the scrotum.

siān (C. sīn). **siān-lâng**, a lizard (C. sīn-thâng).

siān [R. sīn, a spirit]. **gâu piàn-siān-thong** (T.), = A. gâu piàn-sīn-thong, good at adapting one's self to circumstances.

siān (R. id., = col. chhoā^{n}). **siān-hî**, the thin sort of eel. **siān-hî-kut**, work like that of a closely wrought watch-chain.

siān [R. id.; C. soān]. **him-siān**, to desire much; to long for.

siān [R. good]. **siān-liông**, good and well-behaved, as man. **siu-siān**, to reform and cultivate virtue. **hò^{n}-siān**, virtuous. **khoàn-siān**, to exhort to virtue. **hêng-siān**, to act virtuously. **jîn siān, phī-jîn-khi; má siān, phī-jîn-khî**, a good horse is ridden, as a good man is over-reached.

siān-chiong, an easy natural death, as by old age or by a disease that is not painful.

siān-ok, good and bad; virtuous and wicked; righteousness and sin. **siān-ok chiong iú-pò**, good and bad will be requited at the last. **siān iú siān-pò, ok iú ok-pò**, good and bad have their reward or punishment. **kái-ok chiông-siān**, to reform what is bad and follow what is good. **kái-kò chhien-siān**, to reform what is bad, and move over into virtuous conduct. **ték kî-siān jî-chiông--chi, kî put-siān jî-kái--chi**, choose the good and follow it, the bad and reform it.

siān (C. sè, in some phrases), weary; tired. **iâ-siān**, id. **siān-siān**, very slow and lazy. **hioh-siān**, to take a rest because weary. **lâu khah-siān**, the strength of the tide nearly spent. **lóh siān-hō**, long-continued moderately heavy rains.

siān-sùh, inoffensive and unwilling to cause trouble; quiet and meek (v. sùh). **siān-sút** (T.), id.

siān-lâng (P.), a person of very little influence or having no influence to back him (s. lizard).

siet [R. to leak out; to let out a secret]. **lāu-siet**, to let out, or become known, as a secret. **lāu-siet kun-ki**, to let out secrets of the army; also more general (v. ki). **lāu-siet ki-koan**, to let out secrets. **bōng-siet**, nocturnal emissions, as in dreams.

siet [R. purging; diarrhœa; the previous word is also used for this one]. **siet-sià**, constant purging diarrhœa.

siet [R. sat, to scatter, = col. soah, seh, &c.] **siet-nāi^{n}**, too forward, impudent, and urgent, as in a dispute or in pressing a request (said of an impudent woman, or of a beggar who will take no denial, perhaps even threatening to kill himself). **siet-phoat** = sat-phoat, quarrelling in an unwomanly way, as an impudent woman.

siet [R. impure; to profane; to insult or treat irreverently]. **siet-tók**, to blaspheme. **áp-siet**, to treat rudely or with contempt.

siet (cf. chhek, R. red, = col. chhiah). **siet-sin lō-thé**, naked. **siet-thái**, showing contempt by gross vulgarity, *e.g.* by taking off one's clothes or similar indecency in the presence of the person insulted; also, to scold and revile shamelessly, as a woman.

siet (R. id.), to set up, as a rule, plan, or custom; to appoint, as an official. **siet-lip**, to set up or appoint, as rule, custom, or official. **siet koa^{n}-hú**, to appoint mandarins. **siet-hoat**, to set up a rule; to put an affair in proper order; to put matters right. **siet-bōe-lóh**, unable to establish it, as a rule. **siet-kè**, to make a plan or plot. **siet àm-kè**, to make a secret plot or conspiracy.

siet-sú, on the supposition that —; supposing that —; if (only used in formal language; "nā^{n}" is more common, but even it is usually omitted).

phe-siet, to lay out, to arrange in order, as furniture, &c. **siet-iân**, to make a great feast.

siet, to deceive, either in joke or in earnest; to jeer at; to cheat; to take one in. **khau-siet**, to jeer at; to make game of. **giét-siet**, to jibe or twit ironically (almost insulting) about some mistake, or fault, or ugly look. **kóng-siet**, to talk ironically; to ridicule a man in a covert way. **kóng-ōe sa^{n}-siet**, id. **söh-siet** (Cn.), id. **tng-bīn siet**, to twit; to talk jeeringly or ironically; to deceive in jest. **siet--lâng**, to cheat or deceive people; to make game of, as by inuendos, ironical language, or half-false jokes. **phiàn--lâng siet--lâng**, to delude or deceive people. **siet--lâng-khi-sí**, to delude people to their destruction.

siét [R. the tongue, = col. chih]. **khé-siét ê-sū**, an affair that requires much disputing. **kāu-kháu-siét**, causing or requiring much wrangling or disputing, as an affair; raising constant disputes, as man. **kháu lêng, siét piān** (mouth clever and tongue ready), having always an answer ready and a way of escape from what seemed unanswerable; always ready to find an excuse or an answer. **koat-siét**, a tongue-scraper. **pek-siét-niáu^{n}** (esp. Cn.), a man who has always something to answer; also (R.) = pit-lêng, a bird that can learn to sing in many (lit. hundred) ways, and to mew like a cat.

sih (cf. sìh). **sih-sih sut-sut**, making secret signs by whispers, &c. (v. sut). **sìh-sìh sut-sut**, id.

sih — **sih-sih soā-soā**, sound of a sieve, or of rain (v. soā).

sih — **léng sih-sih**, very cold, as food, &c.

sih [R. sict, a surname; name of a plant and of an ancient state], a surname; the surname of Hiên-thien Siōng-tè.

sih [R. siám, to flash; to avoid; = col. siak], to flash; to twinkle; to glance brightly. **sih--chit-ē**, **sih--chit-ē**, glancing; twinkling. **sih-chhoah**, slightly twitching, as skin; glancing, as lightning (v. chhoah). **kng sih-sih**, exceedingly bright; glancing brilliantly. **ná^{n} teh-sih, ná^{n} teh-sih**, constantly flashing over and over again, as lightning or fire-flies.

sih-nà^{n}, lightning (supposed to be nothing more than a *flash*, while the destructive power is in "lûi," thunder). **lûi-tân sih-nà^{n}**, thunder and lightning. **sih-nà^{n} teh-nih^{n} teh-sih**, lightning glancing and flashing.

sih, to shake, as the hand, as in writing or when carrying some heavy thing. **chhiú sih**, the hand trembling or shaking, as when trying to write. **chhiú sih-sih-tsùn**, id.

sih (C.) **sih-sut**, = A. sek-sut, a small sort of cricket.

sih (= sì). **iau-chia^{n} sih-soeh** (C.), = iau-chia^{n} sì-sóe, said of women behaving improperly.

sih (cf. sìh). **sih-bùh sih-sut**, to whisper (v. sut).

sih [R. sit, to corrode or waste away gradually; to be eclipsed, as sun or moon], to diminish gradually; to lose in trade; to lose in bulk; to settle down, as made ground. **sih--lòh-khì**, to waste away, as a liquid drying up; to lose in bulk, as a book pressed in binding, &c. &c. **ná^{n}-sih**, constantly diminishing or growing fewer. **siau-sih**, to diminish or consume away by degrees; diminished, as article in net form, as compared with the gross (v. siau).

lòh-sih, to lose in trade. **sih tām-póh**, to lose a little on a transaction. **siu^{n}-sih**, that is too low a price; I can't afford to sell at that price. **sih chhìn-thâu**, to lose in retail trade by giving customers the turn of the scales. **sih-pún**, to lose in trade; I make no profit, but only loss, by selling at such a price. **sih-pún, tsâi-tsú; bô-sih-pún, kioh-hu**, if there be any loss or additional charge it should fall on the wealthy employer, and not on the poor working men. **ká^{n}-thàn ká^{n}-sih**, clever and daring; venturing much, so as either to gain much or lose heavily.

sih^{n} — **sih^{n}-sih^{n} soáih^{n}-soáih^{n}**, sound of boards creaking.

sim (R. id.), the heart; the stomach; the mind; the centre; the delicate leaves of a bud. **sim-lāi**, in one's heart. **sim-koa^{n}** (heart and liver), the heart, lit. or fig. (v. koa^{n}). **sim-thâu**, the heart (lit. or fig.) **sim-thâu m̄-tiā^{n}**, mind deranged. **sim-thâu thià^{n}**, pain about the pit of the stomach, or about the heart (v. thià^{n}). **sim-tn̂g**, heart and bowels; heart (v. tn̂g). **sim-pak-lâng**, a very intimate and confidential friend (v. pak). **sim-kau ê-lâng**, a very dear friend. **ti-sim ê-lâng**, id.

sim-sìn, mind and affections; heart and mind (v. sìn). **sim-sèng**, natural disposition; character of mind or heart; temper. **sim-sì^{n}**, id. (v. sì^{n}). **sim-tē**, disposition; character. **sim-tōe**, id. (v. tōe). **sim-chêng**, affections and desires (v. chêng). **ū-sim-chiâ^{n}**, to have heart for a thing. **bô-sim-chiâ^{n}**, to have no heart for it. **ū-sim-sùt**, skilful in planning (v. sùt). **ū-sim-sū**, cautious; 'cute; scheming (v. sū). **ū-sim-su**, good at inventing or contriving (v. su). **ū-sim-ki**, good at thinking; intelligent. **ū-sim-khiàu**, to be intelligent (v. khiàu). **ū-sim-hiong**, prudent and shrewd (v. hiong). **toā-sim-hiong**, set on great gains, as merchant or thief, &c. **hó-sim-hēng**, virtuous (v. hēng). **toā-sim-hēng**, avaricious; venturous. **sim-goān**, desire of one's heart. **sim-ì**, bent of mind; desires (v. ì). **sim-chì**, purpose of mind (v. chì).

sim-hoe khui, feeling pleased (v. khui). **sim-hé**, internal heat (slightly feverish), *e.g.* making the mouth dry or eyes somewhat red. **sim-hé tòh**, rage stirred up. **sim-khì-thià^{n}**, dyspepsia; pain near the heart or pit of stomach. **sah^{n} sim-khùi**, heart much set on a thing (v. sah^{n}).

sim-sek, interesting; taking the fancy; pleasant to look at (v. sek).

sim-teng, lanterns lighted in honour of the god "thi^{n}-kong."

tiong-sim, the middle (v. tiong). **chiú^{n}-sim**, the middle of the palm. **chhiú-sim**, id. **chhiū-sim**, the heart of a tree, or of wood. **ka-chiah-sim**, the middle of the back, along the spine. **thâu-khak-sim** (C.), the central point on the head from which the hair radiates.

pit-sim, the hair of a hair-pencil (v. pit). **bō-sim**, the metal centre on which a mill-stone turns (v. bō). **só-sim**, the interior part of a Chinese padlock. **chhoan-sim**, the pin that runs up the hole of a (foreign) key.

tê-sim, tea-leaves. **hoe-sim**, the centre of a flower. **liên-chiau-sim**, the inner leaves of the arum (medicinal). **liên-chí-sim**, the sprout in centre of water-lily seed.

kiap-sim, the two horizontal timbers at top and bottom of a wooden partition into which the upright boards fit.

chek-sim, a candle-wick. **mî^{n}-sim**, a cotton wick. **se-sim**, id. **teng-sim**, lamp-wick, made of the pith of a reed (s. reed).

phòng-sim, silver in round pieces flat on one side, each about ten taels.

tiám-sim, a small hasty meal at any hour (v. tiám). **khang-sim**, having an empty stomach.

kah-sim, the front part of a carcass (about one-third part), *e.g.* of a pig (v. kah).

kah-sim, just to one's mind. **tâng-sim**, with one heart. **siāng-sim**, do.; congenial. **chê-sim**, with one heart. **tsôe-sim**, id. **hàp-sim**, id.

sah^{n}-sim, heart suddenly and deeply affected, as at good or bad news (v. sah^{n}). **tōng-sim**, to affect the heart with strong desire (v. tōng). **chhun-sim tāng**, longing for gratification of sexual feeling. **jip-sim ê-ōe**, language that goes to the heart. **tah-sim**, loving each other very much, as relatives or dearest friends. **tek-sim**, to win one's affections or regard. **tek-sim-lâng**, a favourite; one whom we value much, and on whose opinion we constantly rely. **tek-sim ê-lâng**, id. **tek-bîn-sim**, to win people's hearts, as master or mandarin. **bóe jîn-sim**, craftily win the hearts of the people (v. jîn).

ū-sim, inclined to act; thinking upon, as a friend. **koan-sim**, counting important (v. koan). **lip-sim**, to determine firmly; with fixed purpose. **tsoan-sim**, attentive; with undivided energy. **liû-sim**, to give close attention; attentive (v. liû). **tsûn-sim**, applying

55

the heart with fixed purpose (v. tsûn). **kì-sim**, to remember carefully (v. kì). **sòe-sim**, careful; cautious; humble. **sió-sim**, careful; attentive; discreet (v. sió). **khó-sim**, extremely diligent, as in teaching or study. **lô-sim**, thinking deeply or anxious about some matter (v. lô). **jièt-sim**, earnest. **chīn-sim**, with all one's heart; to exert one's mind to the utmost. **moá"-sīm**, with one's whole heart. **sò-sim**, very anxious to get a thing or to accomplish a matter, often so much as to get troubled or excited about it.

bô-sim, disinclined to do something. **bô-kui-sim**, not with one's whole heart. **chhìn-sim**, having lost heart about a matter. **sí-sim**, having lost all hope or desire of a thing (v. sí). **hê-sim**, to change one's purpose. **hôe-sim**, id. **jī-sim**, double-minded; undecided in purpose (v. jī).

pàng-sim, to set one's own mind at ease. **hòng-sim**, free from anxiety. **khoan-sim**, mind easy and free from anxiety. **ún-sim**, free from fear or sorrow. **chheng-sim**, having abundance for all one requires, and free from causes of anxiety (v. chheng). **chēng-sim**, quiet staid temper.

sòng-sim, to lose all sense of virtue, and dare to do all that is wrong. **phái"-sim**, wicked. **khui-sim**, very unfair and unjust, *e.g.* not paying debts, or abandoning one's wife (v. khui). **hū-sim**, ungrateful. **hūn-sim**, heart full of hatred.

sit-sim, mad; idiotic.

sit-sim, true in heart; sincere. **pîn-sim**, fair in dealings. **pun-sim** (C.), just; fair; honest. **hó-sim**, kind; benevolent. **hó-sim hó-hēng**, good in heart and conduct (v. hēng). **hó-sim khit-lûi-phah** (a good man killed by lightning!), I have done nothing wrong and yet you scold me! **tsòe-hó-sim**, to do a benevolent action. **hoat-sim**, to show kindness.

liông-sim, conscience (v. liông).

chit-sim beh-sí, chit-sim beh-chiàh-bí, undetermined in purpose. **ū-sim phah-chiòh, chiòh chiâ"-chiam**, by fixed determination even a stone may be made a needle. **chhát-sim, hê-siū"-bīn**, having a priest's face but a robber's heart. **jîn-bīn, siù-sim**, having a human face but a beast's heart (v. siù). **huih phō-sim**, the blood pressing too strongly on the heart, causing disease or death. **siū" kàu-huih-kong-sim**, much perplexed or troubled, as with great press of business, or with distress or anxiety. **tsáu kàu-huih-kong-sim**, to run so fast as to be quite exhausted and almost fainting.

sim [R. a sort of reed]. **teng-sim**, lamp-wicks made from the pith of a reed. **teng-sim-chháu**, the reed or rush from which lamp-wicks are made (Scirpus capsularis?); also used for mats. **teng-sim-chhiòh**, good mats (imported) made from this reed. **chháu-sim**, the best sort of reeds for mats.

sim (T.), = A. som, ginseng-root. **jîn-sim**, id. (s. heart). **chién-sim**, to buy ginseng **chiàh-sim**, to take it medicinally.

sim [R. —; Cn. sim; C. som, luxuriant, as foliage]. **im-sim**, very dense and luxuriant, as the foliage of trees.

hiu"-sim (Cn.), a tree with pinnate leaves like the ash; its trunk is very often decayed.

sim [R. sin, the body, = col. seng]. **sim-pi"**, at one's side.

sim [R. sek, daughter-in-law]. **sim-pū**, a daughter-in-law (v. pū).

sîm [R. usual; to search; a fathom; = col. chhîm, jîm, siâm]. **sîm-siông** (R.), usual; common. **tsa-sîm** (R.), to search for.

sím (R. id.), to judge; to examine judicially. **sím-mn̄g**, to make judicial investigation. **sím-toàn**, to give sentence; to judge finally. **sím-phoà"** (r.), to give decision, esp. as in a civil case of disputed property or marriage. **sím-àn**, to try a case. **sím-sū**, id. **sím-sit**, to inquire judicially into the truth of a matter. **sím-siông**, very careful and minute (v. siông). **tùi-sím**, to examine the case with both parties present. **chhut-sím**, to come forward to the trial, as a party. **hok-sím**, to examine the case a second time in court. **tsài-sím**, id.

sím-si, the provincial judge.

sím (R. id.), a surname.

sím [R. sim, exceedingly; which? = col. siá"], (C. siá", sá"). **sím-mih"**, what? which? (somewhat), (v. mih"). **sím-mih"**, id.

sím (P.), = A. chím, wife of father's younger brother.

sìm, elastic; springy; to yield or vibrate, as an elastic thing. **sìm-sìm**, id. **nńg sìm-sìm**, weak and yielding, as the boards of a floor or of a bed. **sìm-khoà"**, to try the strength of a plank or of a floor by treading on it.

sīm — **sīm-sīm**, very quiet in manner; silently meditating; saying little or nothing, as man nonplussed or ashamed, and unable to think of any plan. **sīm-sīm-chē**, to sit quiet. **khiā-teh-sīm**, thinking quietly without acting or speaking. **tiā"-tiā" sīm**, not speaking or acting. **tiā"-tiā"-sīm chit-pe-kú**, sitting in a dreamy inactive state for a long time (lit. half a day); unable to answer or to think out any plan to get out of the difficulty.

sīm [R. exceedingly —]. **sīm-tsōe** (r.), very many. **sīm-chì kàu-àn"-ni"**, even so far as to this state of matters.

sím-mih", what? which? (better sím-mih"; v. mih").

sin [R. the body; one's lifetime; = col. seng, sim, sien], the body; one's self; a person; (also C., = A. sien, classifier of idols, &c.)

chit-sin, one individual. **it-sin** (r.), id. **toa"-sin**, a solitary person, as one who has no relatives, or having no one to help him. **ke-toa"-sin**, id. **toa"-sin phit-bé**, do., or having no one near him. **ke-sin**, id. **ke-toa" chit-sin**, id. **i--ê tē-jī-sin**, his alter ego, who, without formal authority, is able to act for him.

thòe-sin, a straw image made to avert disease or other evils (v. thòe). **hûn-sin**, a rude image made to represent the deceased in the rites of khiā-hà for some tens of days after death. **kè hûn-sin**, to make it.

sin-khu, the body. **ak nn̄g-sa" sin-khu**, thoroughly drenched several times after changing one's dress each time. **sin-ku** (r.), the body. **jiòk-sin**, id. **hèk-sin**, id. **sin-thé**, id. **hin-sin** (C.), id. **moá"-sin**, the whole body. **moá"-sin-keh**, id. **thong-sin**, id. **pièn-sin**, all over or all through one's body. **téng-poà"-sin**, the upper half of the body. **ē-poà"-sin**, lower half of body. **ōe-si" kiá"-sin, bōe-si" kiá"-sim**, parents can form the body, but not the heart of a son. **sin-tsù-pī"** (Cn.), a natural disease, not caused by demons. **sin-miā"**, constitution of body, as strong or weak (v. miā"). **kiā"-sin**, strong in body; having a good constitution; in good health. **tâng-sin thih-kut**, not afraid of cold or of a beating (lit. made of brass and iron). **kim-sin**, highly gilt, as idol. **lâng-sin bé-thâu**, having a human body and a horse's head. **sin-chhēng**, clothing (v. chhēng).

tai-sin, vulgar; clownish. **khiáu-sin**, pretty; nice-looking, as child or girl. **sì-kak-sin**, just and of unbending integrity. **khiā-sin**, erect, as an image made standing (v. khiā). **thêng-sin**, to hold one's self erect. **thán-phi-sin**, turning one's body sidewise, as in a narrow road (v. thán).

hó-sin-tsôe, well-formed in body. **sin-tsâi**, bodily appearance, as good or bad looking (v. tsâi). **sin-tiu^n**, id. (v. tiu^n). **sin-io**, the waist, in regard to its shape (v. io).

sin-pi^n, at one's side. **sin-chiū^n**, on one's body; on one's self. **beh-kàu goá-sin-chiū^n**, about to come on me, as calamity.

sin-hūn, size of body, *e.g.* in regard to the size of clothes required; rank or position in life, especially as to wealth. **sin-hūn khah-toā**, he is large of body. **hó-sin-hūn**, wealthy.

ū-koa^n-sin, to be a mandarin. **péh-sin-lâng**, one of the common people; having no official rank.

ta-sin, having a pretty good income; dry, as a thing (v. ta). **êng-sin**, well off, and not needing to work. **hiong-sin**, a man who has committed murder with his own hand (s. sash).

chhut-sin, to attain to office or high literary rank; to rise from poor circumstances to comfort or wealth; to act alone, or as chief in some difficult or dangerous work. **kho-kah chhut-sin**, to advance by merit in literary examinations. **it-póng chhut-sin**, a Kujin becoming a mandarin. **lī-sin**, to escape from danger; to get leisure (v. lī). **thoat-sin**, to escape (v. thoat). **siók-sin**, to redeem, as from slavery, or from a bad house. **bōe-sin**, to sell one's self for a slave. **sin-khòe-jī**, deed of sale of a slave girl. **sûi-sin teh-toà**, to carry always about with one (v. sûi). **tsai-ē lîm-sin**, calamities come upon him (v. lîm). **sa^n-oe-sin**, to jostle one another on the road, as two men having difficulty in passing in a narrow or crowded road. **chiū^n-sin**, to possess a man, as a spirit. **hū-sin**, id.; also (C. hū-sîn), to inhabit an idol, as the spirit of another may do. **siá-sin**, to exert one's self greatly. **sńg-sin**, to exert one's self very severely; quite worn out and exhausted. **siak-sin**, id. **siu-sin** (R.), to regulate one's conduct well. **thiu-sin thè-āu**, to withdraw for fear (v. thiu).

khí-sin, to begin. **bōe-khí-sin**, does not grow, as a sickly boy. **hoan-sin**, immediately; in a moment. **oát-tńg-sin**, immediately; to turn round to look back (v. tńg). **bōe-tit--thang tsoán-sim**, having no way to turn (v. tsoán).

kè-sin, dead; past and gone, as things or men. **kòe-sin** (C.), id.

sin-si, a corpse. **sin-kè**, he has died (said in announcing a death). **sin-āu**, after death; behind the back. **chek-ok biét-sin**, accumulated guilt bringing death by a heaven-sent punishment. **hoà-sin**, to die and become a Buddha (v. hoà).

chiong-sin, all one's life long. **chit-sin chit-sì**, id. **chit-sin chit-miā^n**, id. **sí-sin-phe**, reckless of one's life (v. phe). **kúi-nā-pah-sin bô-kàu-sí**, a hundred deaths would not be enough; though he had a hundred lives his death would be inevitable, as man in great danger, or in case of guilt so great as certainly to draw down the vengeance of heaven.

ū-sin, to be pregnant. **ū-sin-īn**, id. **toà-sin** (Cn.), id. **ka-láuh-sin**, to have a miscarriage. **lòh-sin**, id. **thùt-sin**, id. **phah-lòh-sin**, to cause miscarriage. **bú-sin**, body of woman about to have a child, or within a month after delivery (v. bú).

chhiū-sin, trunk of tree. **tùi-sin**, shaft of pestle for large rice-mortar. **tià^n-sin**, shank of anchor. **lêng-sin**, placed about half-way down the slope of a hill, as lucky site for grave or house (v. lêng, "spiritual"). **làm-sin**, the body of a dress hanging too loosely. **kín-sin-á**, a warm close-fitting jacket. **sán-sin**, thin and weak, as cloth woven too loose and easily torn.

pún-sin, one's self (v. pún). **chhin-sin**, id. **tsū-sin put-lêng pó**, unable to protect one's self (v. tsū).

sin-sè, power and influence; attitude of body for some purpose (v. sè). **chiàh i--ê thúi-sin-bah**, living on and wasting his own capital (lit. the flesh of his thigh).

āu-sin, afterwards; further back, as back premises. **lāi-sin**, inside a place; further in than another place. **goā-sin**, outside of a place; further out than another place. **kháu-sin**, id.

sin [R. fire-wood; fuel]. **sin-súi ê sé-hùi**, funds for wood, rice, and water, supplied to a deputy mandarin when he comes to a place; sometimes also said of a teacher. **sin-súi chiok**, these funds sufficient. **thiap i--ê sin-súi**, to pay these expenses for him.

sin [R. to do or say a second time], a cyclical character; the period from 3–5 P.M. **sin-sî**, 3–5 P.M. **jit-lòh-sin**, id., said to distinguish it from "sin-sî." **sin-bēng** (R.), to repeat a command; (X.) Deuteronomy.

sin [R. to stretch out; to straighten; = col. chhun], to redress, as a wrong. **sin-oan**, to redress or avenge a wrong. **iú-oan bû-sin**, having wrongs, but no one to redress or avenge them.

sin (R. id.), new. **sin-sien**, new and fresh. **sin-ien**, having the gloss still on, as cloth. **sin-bûn**, news (v. bûn). **sin-koa^n**, a new mandarin. **sin-tsòe**, newly made. **sin-lâi**, lately come. **sin-lâng**, a new comer (said in joke). **sin-hun**, a marriage. **sin-niû^n**, a bride (v. niû^n). **sin-kiá^n-sài**, the bridegroom. **sin-chia^n**, New-years day; the New-year time. **sin-nî^n**, the coming year (said only near the end of the old one).

chhòng-sin, to repair and renew as good as new (v. chhòng). **oā^n-sin**, to change an old thing for a new one. **chhēng-sin**, to wear new clothes. **ngiâ^n-sin khì-kū**, to forsake the old for the new, improperly.

sin [R. a sash, worn by gentry]. **hiong-sin**, gentry and graduates (s. body). **hiang-sin** (C.), id. **sin-khim**, graduates belonging to a place. **sin-sū**, graduates and retired mandarins; may also include local military mandarins if they belong to the place.

ìm-sin (C.), = A. ìm-seng, sons of high mandarins, who get degrees by influence.

sin (= chhin), (T. sien; C. chhûn). **sin-chháu**, a plant from which a cooling jelly is made. **sin-chháu-tàng**, coagulated jelly made from it.

sin [R. bitter; toilsome], a surname; a cyclical character. **sin-kim**, wages for labour. **sin-lô**, id. **sin-hô** (Cn.), id. **sin-khó**, miserable in body, *e.g.* in severe painful sickness, or toiling in hot sun.

sè-sin, a medicine.

sin (C.) **sin-sɛ^n**, = A. sien-si^n, a teacher; a doctor.

sîn [R. êng, a fly]. **hê-sîn**, a fly; a house-fly. **hê-sîn-hé**, a small round insect. **hê-sîn-sái**, darkish spots over the face. **ku-sîn**, small dark-coloured aphis. **gû-sîn**, a stinging fly that attacks cattle. **kim-sîn**, a large blue-bottle fly; said also of a man with fine clothes, but with no talent. **chhɛ^n-sîn** (C.), the blue-bottle fly. **tsúi-sîn** (C.), sort of fly found on water (s. spirit). **chêng kàu tn̂g-sîn-pe tn̂g-báng-háu**, so silent that not even a fly or mosquito is heard. **siâ^n-sîn**, said of women enticing lads (v. siâ^n).

sîn (R. id.), a constellation; one of the cyclical characters; the time from 7–9 a.m. **sin-sî**, 7–9 a.m. **jit-chhut-sîn**, id. **sî-sîn**, a particular Chinese (double) hour; only said in asking what hour it is (s. spirit).

chhi^n-sîn, stars and constellations.

jit-sîn, a day viewed as lucky or unlucky; name of day of month, as designated not by numbers but by two cyclical characters, in relation to the horoscope and one's fate or fortune. **hó-jit-sîn**, an auspicious day. **toā-jit-sîn**, a very auspicious day. **phái^n-jit-sîn**, an inauspicious day. **kī-sin**, anniversary of the death of an emperor or of very near relative of emperor.

sîn [R. a servant; a minister of state], said by Tauist priests in addressing Heaven. **jîn-sîn**, a minister of state. **tiâu-sîn**, id. **tāi-sîn**, a great minister of state. **khim-chhe tāi-sîn**, a high commissioner or ambassador. **kan-sîn**, a traitorous minister (v. kan). **poān-sîn**, a minister in rebellion against his sovereign. **tiong-sîn**, a loyal and faithful minister. **tiong-sîn put-sū jī-tsú, liét-lú put-kà jī-hu**, a loyal statesman will not serve two masters; a pure lady will not marry two husbands in succession. **tiong-sîn put-hû jī-tsú**, &c., do. does not assist two masters, &c. **tiong-sîn put-phà^n-sí**; **phà^n-sí, hui tiong-sîn**, a faithful minister does not fear death; if he fear death, he is not a faithful minister.

kun-sîn, sovereign and minister. **ū-kun-sîn**, to be properly mixed, as various medicines, some principal and others secondary. **phòe-kun-sîn**, to mix in proper relations, as some medicines considered to be related to each other.

sîn [R. sêng, to receive, = col. sâ^n], to catch in one's upturned hand, as a ball or small thing thrown, or as water in a vessel or in hand; also (C.), = A. sêng, to receive.

bōe-iōng-sîn--tit, not fit to be employed for the business, as man, *e.g.* man wanting in ability or in faithfulness. **sîn-bāng**, to take the fish out of the mud or shallow water inclosed by nets at low water. **sîn hō͘-tsúi**, to catch rain water, as in a vessel or in the upturned hand.

sîn [R. sêng, to assist; an assistant official or deputy]. **mn̂g-sîn hō͘-ūi**, the guardian gods of doors and thresholds. **mûi^n-sin hō͘-ì** (C.), id. **mn̂g-sîn** (T. Cn. mn̂g-liên), inscriptions on the leaves of doors. **tah mn̂g-sîn**, to paste these inscriptions on. **kê mn̂g-sîn**, id. **ūi mn̂g-sîn**, to paint the guardian divinities of doors, namely, Sîn-tô͘ and Ut-lúi.

sîn [R. id. = col. sêng], a spirit; spiritual; (intelligent); in many phrases it refers to the expression of the countenance or the general appearance of the person, as indicating one's character, purpose, or state.

sù-sîn, four great medicines mixed, ready to be infused, viz. hòk-lêng, hoâi^n-soa^n, khiàm-sit, liên-chí. **sù-sîn-hún**, these four mixed in state of powder. **sù-sîn-tê**, infusion or decoction of them. **hòk-sîn**, one form of the medicine "hòk-lêng" (v. hòk). **khiàm-sîn**, a medicine (v. khiàm) (+).

sîn-biāu, very good and efficacious, as a medicine. **sîn-khak**, a famous medicine made at Chin-chew. **sîn-i** (R.), a very skilful doctor. **sîn-tông** (R.), a wonderfully talented and precocious young scholar.

sîn-sîn, very dull and spiritless, either naturally so, or from grief or sickness, &c. **bô-sîn**, not observing or understanding what is said, as from grief or abstraction; abstracted; absent in mind (+). **lóng-bô-sîn**, utterly wanting in animation, &c. **mô^n-sîn** (C.), mad; you are mad, or talking nonsense (v. mô^n). **khah-khiàm-sîn**, naturally rather dull, unintelligent, and unexcitable in appearance or manner (v. khiàm). **sí-sîn**, very dull and spiritless in manner (opp. oàh-tāng). **sit-sîn**, utterly dispirited, depressed, exhausted, or stupified, as with grief, fear, sickness, &c. **ià kàu-beh-sit-sîn**, so much exhausted as to be unable to think or listen. **ià-sîn**, exhausted, spiritless, and feeling slightly unwell, as from exertion or sickness; sleepy appearance from great exhaustion. **tàm-sîn**, appearance of low spirits or of distress (v. tàm). **koān-sîn koān-sîn**, dull and wanting in animation, as from weariness or illness.

loān-sîn, confused and almost out of one's mind, as with sad news, grief, or anxiety. **gōng-sîn**, appearance of dull inactive stupidity; stupid-looking. **khám-sîn**, appearance of active stupidity; doing absurd and foolish things.

siáu-sîn, foolish amusements, esp. gambling; fond of low jests and vile low talk. **siáu-sin-á**, id. **lâi siáu-sîn**, come and gamble or play at somewhat bad amusements.

sńg-sîn, to hurt one's self by late hours, &c. (v. sńg). **hùi-sîn**, troublesome, as an affair; many thanks for your trouble! (v. hùi). **hoân-sîn**, thank you, sir, for your trouble. **hō͘--lí hoân-sîn**, id. **hoân lí-ê-sîn**, id. **lô-sîn** (R.), thank you, sir!

tsù-sîn, diligent and attentive; with fixed determination. **sim-koa^n tsù-sîn**, id. **tsù-sîn-khoà^n**, to gaze steadily; to look intently. **bák-chiu tsù-sîn**, id. **ūn-sîn**, to sit in silent contemplation, as Bud. priest.

gīn-sîn, feeling disgusted at him, &c. (v. gīn). **chhiò-sîn**, smiling, kindly appearance of countenance. **ū-khiàu-sîn**, healthy, pleasant, and intelligent looking, as child; interesting, as thing.

phoà tôe-sîn, to bring out in the essay the meaning and spirit of the theme or text in a very profound and complete way (v. tôe).

sîn-chhái, appearance of health or animation and intelligence (v. chhái). **gán-sin hó**, having a very intelligent appearance about the eyes. **hó-gán-sîn**, id. **bák-sîn oàh-tāng**, eyes full of fire, intelligence, and animation. **bák-sîn chhāi-chhāi**, looking firmly and intently. **toā-bīn-sîn**, brazen-faced, without modesty, as girl who is too forward among men, or who urges her parents to get her married; rarely said of men. **phái^n-sîn-khì**, ashamed or awkward state of feeling, *e.g.* having to speak against a friend (v. phái^n).

sim-sîn, heart and mind; mind, with thoughts, affections, feelings, &c. **bô-sim-sîn**, having no inclination to attend to a thing, no heart for it, *e.g.* from anxiety about something else, or from grief, &c. **sim-sîn put-chí-toā**, taking a great deal of thoughtful care and trouble, as some work. **sim-sîn kè-tō͘**, thinking too deeply, so as to injure one's health. **óng-hùi sim-sîn**, to spend mental labour fruitlessly (v. hùi).

sîn-chêng, appearance or manner of acting or speaking, as showing one's purpose; purpose or inclination as manifested in one's manner. **sin-ì** (r.), id. **ì-sîn**, id. **bô-ì-sîn**, quite dispirited, or afraid, or utterly ashamed, so as to have no resource left; *e.g.* when suddenly confounded so as to have no answer. **bô-ì bô-sîn**, id.

hong-sîn, expression of countenance; appearance of face, as to intelligence. **phah--lâng bô-hong-sîn**, to put a man to shame before others, as by treating him rudely, or speaking to him sharply.

hong-sîn-toān, an ancient book of stories about spirits; said of absurd stories, lies, and great fickleness (v. hong, "to seal").

goân-sîn, natural constitution, as strong or weak. **sún goân-sîn**, to injure one's health, as by bad food, or by late hours, &c. **goân-sîn tsāi-keng**, = cheng-sîn tsāi-keng, having one's wits about one; keeping one's presence of mind; active-minded.

cheng-sîn, animal spirits; animated; lively; skilful. **bô-cheng-sîn**, dull; listless; very wearied: insensible. **ū-cheng-sîn**, lively; active; intelligent. **khah-cheng-sîn**, somewhat revived, as from swoon or sickness. **cheng-sîn chhiong-chiok**, intelligent; skilful; active-minded. **cheng-sîn put-chiok**, dull, drowsy, or absent state, such as is usual in old age, and sometimes comes on in sickness. **chhiúⁿ cheng-sîn** (Cn. chhiú), to bring back health by Tauist magical rites. **cheng-sîn-hé**, lamp used in these rites. **cheng-sîn tsāi-keng**, having all one's wits about one. **cheng-sîn hun-loān**, much confused and almost out of one's mind, as from fear, anxiety, sickness, &c.

sîn-hûn, the human soul or spirit (v. hûn). **sîn-tsú**, an ancestral tablet. **sîn-chí** (C.), id. **sîn-jí** (C.), id. **ke-sîn-pâi**, a large ancestral tablet with several names on it. **lán ke-sîn-pâi**, said of a boy blocking up the doorway. **sîn-ūi**, a tablet or scroll with the name of an idol or sage, for his spirit to reside at.

chhē-sîn, = khan-bông, to call up the spirits of the dead. **chhiáⁿ-sîn**, to invite the spirits to come, as to some ceremony. **sì-sîn**, respectfully ask them to go home after a ceremony (s. hour). **sàng-sîn** (C. sàng-ang), to make offerings on 12.24, when the spirits of the idols go up to heaven. **chih-sîn** (C. chih-ang), to make offerings when they come down again. **thè-sîn**, the spirit leaving or having left an idol, so that it has no power. **hū-sîn** (C.), = A. hū-sin, the spirit of a dead man going to reside in an idol, either his own image or another's. **pn̄g-sîn tsok-hok**, to make offerings to an idol so as to have a good feast (v. hok).

sîn-bêng, objects of worship; supernatural beings in general. **sîn-pùt** (C. ang-hùt), id. **sîn-sien**, id. (v. sien). **sîn-siōng**, an image or picture of a god, &c. **sîn-chhiāng** (C.), id. **tāi-sîn tāi-tō**, a regularly canonized and extensively worshipped idol; also, fig. of a very influential man; also (C.), any very highly honoured and powerful idol. **tāi-sîn-tō** (Cn.), id. **sîn-soah**, spirits and demons (v. soah).

soah-sîn, a certain malicious and hurtful demon (v. soah). **liok-sîn**, six spirits specially propitiated at building a house (done by Tauist priests). **siâ-sîn**, depraved spirits; wicked spirits. **sèng-sîn** (X.), the Holy Spirit. **chèng-sîn**, any good spirit regularly canonized or extensively worshipped; also, = thó-tī-kong, the guardian god of graves. **hok-tek chèng-sîn**, = thó-tī-kong. **hok-sîn**, id. **thó-sîn**, id. **seng, ûi chèng-jîn; sú, ûi chèng-sîn**, very good in life and a good spirit after death. **chèng-sîn**, all the spirits. **chiòng-sîn** (C.), id. **bān-sîn-kong** (Cn.), collective title for all the male ghosts that have no posterity. **bān-sîn-má** (Cn.?), collective title for all the female ghosts that have no posterity.

chhó-bók-sîn, a new spirit or idol much worshipped by the people, but not canonized; said also of a man, a mere upstart.

thien-sîn, heavenly spirits sent by superior gods as messengers or deputies; angels. **thien-sîn hā-kàng**, the heavenly spirits are sent down (on 12.25) by Siōng-tè to take charge of the world while the spirits of the idols are absent on their annual visit to heaven; on this day people have to be very careful of their conduct. **kim-kah-sîn**, angelic messengers of Gio̍k-hông. **kim-kah sîn-jîn**, id. **kim-kah-sîn-jit**, auspicious days when these good angels are going their rounds and the demons are terrified. **chhiū-sîn**, spirit of a tree, worshipped. **hoe-sîn**, spirit of a large flower. **chíⁿ-sîn**, guardian spirit of a well. **tsúi-sîn**, guardian spirits of streams or waters; geomantic character of a grave (or of a house) in relation to water. **tsúi-sîn hó**, the site auspicious so far as water is concerned. **koà-sîn-hó**, the answer by tortoise-shell divination is favourable (v. koà). **thèh-sîn**, spirits of a dwelling (v. thèh). **the-sîn**, spirits that guard unborn infants. **thai-sîn**, id. (v. thai). **hé-sîn-iâ**, the god of fire. **ngiâⁿ hí-sîn**, procession of military mandarins in spring.

sîn-lông, Shin-nung (v. lông, "husbandman"). **sîn-tê**, name of certain rulers or princes of demons able to devour them. **sîn-tê ut-lúi**, two names often written on doors as protection against demons. **sîn-tê ut-lu̍t**, id.

sîn-thong, power of a spirit or idol, as manifested in mighty works (v. thong). **sîn-jiah** (r.), a miracle. **sîn-se**, a red mixture used for touching the eyes (khai-gán) of an idol. **sîn-tiùⁿ**, a pair of curtains hung before an idol's shrine. **tsòe-sîn-hok**, to make large offerings of food to idols (v. hok). **sîn-chiá** (Cn.), a sorceress or female medium who calls up the spirits of the dead.

kúi-sîn, ghosts and spirits; demons and superior spirits; spiritual beings in general; worse and better spirits, though not quite strictly so, for some "kúi" are considered good, and some "sîn" are bad. **sîn-kúi**, id. **hàu kúi-sîn**, to worship spiritual beings by offerings. **kèng kúi-sîn**, to reverence or worship spiritual beings. **kèng kúi-sîn, jî oān--chi** (R.), reverence the spirits, but don't have much to do with them. **gî-sîn gî-kúi**, very suspicious of others. **ke-sîn thong goā-kúi**, a person in the house (or in the firm) in league with enemies outside to injure or plunder. **iú-san, iú-súi; iú-sîn, iú-kúi**, as water always accompanies hills, so great and powerful spirits always have inferior spirits or demons as their attendants, *e.g.* in the temples. **sîn put-ti, kúi put-kak**, so secret that none of the spirits know it. **bô-sîn-kúi thang-lâi**, very quiet and retired, as a place; scarcely any one comes, or has come; no business doing. **bô-sîn-kúi kiâⁿ-kàu**, id.; no fear of anything being lost. **bô-sîn bô-kúi**, no one present at all. **bô--chit-ê sîn-kúi**, id.

bô--chit-ê sîn-iáⁿ, utterly false; not the least foundation for the report; not a single person present.

sìn [R. to inquire into; to interrogate officially]. **sìn-mn̄g**, to inquire into officially in court, as mandarin. **tùi-sìn**, to examine the parties face to face in court. **chit-sìn** (R.), id. **hok-sìn**, to examine or try a case a second time on another court-day. **chhut-sìn**, to come forward to the trial, as a party does. **èng-sìn**, to appear at trial for examination, as witnesses or others (not the principal parties) named in the documents, and therefore summoned. **èng-sìn ê-lâng**, such persons.

sìn [R. a military station]. **sìn-hông**, station of small military mandarin, who can also act in small lawsuits. **sìn-tōe,** id. **sìn-tē** (C.), id. **lī sìn-tē,** to be driven from one's home or dwelling so as to have no part in it (for any cause, right or wrong). **khiā-sìn,** to occupy a military or police station, as small mandarin. **tsoan-hông-sìn,** assistant of a "siú-pí," having authority over the whole "iâ^{n}." **sìn** is also used at the end of the names of the small military stations, *e.g.* **chhia-chhân-sìn,** near Chang-poo.

sìn [R. quick; the previous word is sometimes used for this]. **sìn-sok,** quick; swift; urgently quick.

sìn (R. id.), the soft place on the top of an infant's head where the sutures join. **sìn-á,** id. **sìn--á** (T.), id. **sìn-hō,** id. **sìn-hōe** (Cn.), id. **sìn-bûn,** id. **sìn-mn̂g,** id. **sìn-mûi^{n}** (C.), id. **sìn-mn̂g** (C. mə̂^{n}), the hair at that place. **lâu sìn-mn̂g,** to let the hair grow at that place. **sìn-tsang,** a little boy's queue. **sìn-bō,** a child's cap that leaves the crown of the head bare; it has a flap at the back tied round the neck. **nńg-sìn,** having the soft part of the head softer than it usually is, specially apt to be injured.

sìn (R. id.), (P. sìn, sièn), to believe; to believe on; faithful; trustworthy; fidelity; faith; (a letter; news). **sìn-chiȯh,** arsenic, = phī^{n}-sng.

poe-sìn, the divining blocks. **sìn-poe** (C.), id. **sìn-khàu** (Cn.), id.

phoe-sìn, a letter (v. phoe). **ka-sìn,** a letter from home or to one's family. **pò-sìn,** to give sad intelligence. **im-sìn,** news by letter, as of a relative. **bô-im-sìn,** no news at all from or about him, *e.g.* of a relative gone abroad. **bô-im bô-sìn,** id. **ū-im-sìn--bô,** are there any news from him? **sìn-tsoá,** a thin sort of paper. **bīn-phê khah-pȯh sìn-tsoá,** very bashful. **poà^{n}-sìn,** paper thinner than sìn-tsoá, but thicker than ìn-si-tsoá (+).

sìn-sit, true; trustworthy, as a statement, or as a friend. **sìn-tek,** the virtue of fidelity, truthfulness, trustworthiness, or faithfulness. **jîn-gī lé-tì-sìn,** the five cardinal virtues: kindness, justice, propriety, wisdom, and fidelity. **tiong-sìn,** faithful and trusty. **sit-sìn,** to break one's word; to betray one's trust. **ìn-sìn,** proof in form of seal or stamp; stamp (public or private) on a document giving it credibility or validity. **ū-sìn-kù,** to have good, sure, and certain proof. **ū-pîn-sìn,** to have sufficient proof. **ū sím-mih^{n} pîn-sìn,** what good evidence is there? **ōe-pîn-sìn--tit,** may be safely trusted, as man or affair; trustworthy. **ōe-sìn-pîn--tit,** id. **bōe-sìn-pîn--tit,** untrustworthy, as man or document. **m̄-sī sìn-pîn ê-lâng,** he is not a trustworthy man. **bô-sìn-pîn,** unsafe, as man who does not keep his word. **ū-sìn-pîn,** quite true and trustworthy, as man, or promise, or engagement. **kui-sìn-thi^{n},** steady good fine weather (v. kui). **sìn-tn̂g,** mode of getting much money for a small pledge that is to be certainly redeemed (v. tn̂g).

ū-sìn, to be trusty or faithful. **lí ū-sìn--mah,** do you believe it?

siong-sìn, to put trust in (a person); trusting each other. **siong-sìn-i,** to trust him. **siong-sìn siong-kèng,** trusting and respecting each other. **m̄-sìn,** not to believe; not to trust; does not or will not believe or trust. **chhim-sìn,** to believe firmly. **sìn-tauh-tauh,** trusting very firmly or implicitly. **poà^{n}-sìn poà^{n}-gî,** half believing half doubting (v. gî). **sìn-sià^{n},** to believe in the power of an idol or spirit. **sìn-tiōng,** to place great confidence on a man. **sìn-jīm,** to trust a man and intrust him entirely with some matter (not examining what he does). **sìn-jīn,** to stand security slightly and only verbally, as for a man whom we have recommended. **sìn-hȯk** (r.), to believe and submit. **sìn-khò** (r.), to believe and trust upon. **sìn-thàn** (X.), to believe and obey. **sìn-iâ-sə** (X.), to believe on Jesus. **sìn-keng** (X.), the creed.

sīn [R. sìn, to be cautious or circumspect about some risk]. **kín-sīn,** to be on one's guard against something; to take great care, as to avoid danger or not to do something; to be circumspect or wary.

sīn-tiōng, valuable and important, as things; very cautious (v. tiōng).

sīn (R. sēng), surplus; to be a remainder; to remain over, as things. **û-sīn,** surplus. **î-sīn** (C.), id. **ū-sīn,** there is a surplus or remainder. **bat kàu-ū-sīn,** to know very thoroughly, as a man's whole character. **bô-sīn,** no remainder or surplus. **sīn joā-tsōe,** how much is over? **sīn-gûn,** money that is over (lit. silver). **sīn-chî^{n},** id. (lit. copper cash). **sīn-mih^{n},** surplus articles. **lâng chhī-lâng, sīn chit-ki-kut,** though fed by men he is nothing but bones (v. chhī).

sīn (R. id., = col. siēn), the kidneys (human), considered to be connected with the element of water. **goā-sīn,** the testes. **sim-sīn,** heart and kidneys. **pó-sīn,** strengthening the kidneys and making the eyes bright. **sīn-súi chhiong-chiok,** in good vigorous health, as a strong lusty young man (about 20 or 30) who sleeps soundly (masculine principle vigorous?). **sīn-súi chiok,** id. **tsúi siók-sīn,** the element of water has relation to the kidneys in the theory of medicine, &c.

sīn [R. —, C. chīn; Cn. sīn, to make a present to a person going a journey]. **sīn-gî,** presents given to persons going a great distance, esp. Kujin going to examination at the capital. **sàng-sīn,** to give such presents, esp. to graduates going to examination. **sàng sīn-gî,** id. **sòng-sīn,** id.

sīn — **sīn-lâng** (C. T.), = A. siēn-lâng, a lizard. **sīn-tâng** (C.), id.

sio [R. siau, name of a plant; desolate], a surname. **sio ông-iâ,** a famous idol of surname Siau.

sio [R. siau, the high part of the sky]. **ûn-sio,** the city of Yun-siau, between Chang-poo and Chau-an.

sio [R. siong, mutual, = col. sa^{n}], mutually, used before verbs and some adjectives; sometimes it does not give any idea of mutual relation. **sa^{n}** is more said in A., T., and Cn., but **sio** more in C. **sio-soà,** successively. **sio-bat,** acquainted (with a person). **sio-kap,** together. **sio-chio,** to call or invite. **sio-chhōe** (C.), = A. sa^{n}-chhē, to search for, as for a person.

sio [R. siong, to injure, = col. siu^{n}, too much]. **sio-ti** (C.), too sharp and too exacting in buying and selling (s. burn).

sio [R. siau, to burn], warm; to burn; to roast. **sio-lio,** to burn away. **sio-lio--khì,** to burn quite away. **sio-hu,** to burn to ashes. **hé-sio-chhù,** a house on fire. **hé-sio--ah,** fire! fire! **sio-pùn,** to burn grass, straw, &c., mixed with earth, for manure. **sio hé-phûn,** to burn heaps of fuel on 1. 15 for people to leap through. **sio-hiu^{n},** to burn incense. **sio lêng-chhù,** to burn houses for the dead. **sio-kim,** to burn mock paper (yellow or white) in worship of gods or of the dead. **sio kim-gûn,** id. **sio-tsoá,** id. **sio-kim-pùt** (Cn.), to burn paper to an idol. **sio-kim-kúi** (Cn.), do. to ghosts or demons. **sio-sè,** to burn paper prayers. **sio-tiáp,** do., another sort.

sio-hé, a cook, as in a hong. **sio-hóe** (C.), id. **sio-sáh,** roast and boiled. **sio-bah,** roast meat, esp. pork. **sio-koe,** roast fowl; &c. **sio-ti,** a young pig roasted whole. **sio-koah,** a slice of roast pig (v. koah).

sio-hûi, to make pottery (v. hûi). **sio-he,** to burn lime. **thih sio-âng,** heat iron red-hot. **sio hé-lô,** to kindle a fire in a fire-place or stove. **sio piáⁿ-lô,** to warm an oven for baking. **sio-tsàu** (T.), to kindle the cooking-fire. **sio hun-phā,** to make a pellet of opium in the flame, preparing to smoke it.

chhēng-sio, to wear warm clothes. **chiáh-pá chhēng-sio,** having plenty to eat and to wear. **ku-sio,** to sit crouching in the sun or in some warm place. **ún-sio,** to cover up and keep warm, as embers or food. **un-sio-tsúi,** to warm water on the fire. **hiâⁿ-sio-tsúi,** id. **thn̄g-sio,** to warm over again. **tīm-sio,** to warm up in a "tīm-koàn" (v. tīm). **sio-thng,** warm water; warm soup. **thàn-sio chiáh,** to eat (food) while it is still hot.

kip-sio, a very thin broad-bottomed earthen kettle, for boiling or warming anything very quickly. **tê-kip-sio,** one for boiling water for tea. **chiú-kip-sio,** one for warming liquor.

sio-jiėt, hot and fevered, either much, as with fever, or slightly, as with prickly heat; much excited and indignant, as at having one's bad deeds openly spoken of, or at being violently scolded. **sio-joáh,** warm or hot, as weather. **sio-chīⁿ,** warm, as weather. **sio-lō,** pleasantly warm, as weather, clothes, or food. **sio hōng-hōng,** very hot, as body or weather. **sio kún-kún,** very hot, as food or water, or as stone or wood heated by the sun, &c. **sio hù-hù,** very hot. **lâ-lûn-sio,** lukewarm (v. lûn).

sio-chiú, strong spirits (of various strength); any intoxicating liquor warmed. **kāu-sio,** very strong spirits that can burn. **hé-sio-chiú,** strong spirits. **sio-to** (Cn.), id. **kau-liâng-sio,** sort of strong spirits, the best is from Shan-tung. **tsùt-bí-sio,** strong spirits made from glutinous rice.

siô [R. siông, usual; common; = col. siûⁿ], inferior in quality, as a composition. **siô-siô,** indolent; slow and lazy. **tsòe-sū siô,** to manage a matter in a very dilatory way. **iông-siô** (C.), = A. iûⁿ-siûⁿ, of moderate abilities, rather useless, as a man.

sió (= só). **sió-kńg,** = só-kńg, a sort of cuttle-fish.

sió (cf. siáu, lustful). **sió-kiáⁿ,** a sodomite; a vile lascivious man. **sió-ngá** (Cn.), id.

sió [R. song, a pair; = col. siang]. **sió-to-hōe** (C. siang-to-hōe), the Triad Society (v. to); by some supposed to be the next word, "small."

sió [R. siáu, small], small; young; neap; right hand (side). **sió-khoá,** small; unimportant; few, in quantity (v. khoá). **sió-kiȯk,** scant in measure, as dress. **sió-thêng,** in a short time (v. thêng). **sió-lō͘,** a small road; a path. **sió-tō͘,** the bladder, esp. of pig. **sió-lī,** dysentery.

sió-tàu, about 11 or 11.30 A.M. **sió-moáⁿ,** a term about May 21st or 22d. **sió-iông-chhun,** a season of warm weather in winter. **gėh sió,** the month has only 29 days. **sió-tsúi,** neap-tides. **tsúi sió,** the tide is neap. **tsúi teh-sió,** the tides are coming nearer neap-tide.

sió-bō, an unceremonial cap. **sió-kiō,** a sedan with only two bearers. **sió-sì,** examination for Sew-tsai degree.

sió-iūⁿ, rather mean in one's actions.

sió-táⁿ, cowardly; afraid. **sió-sim,** careful; cautious; attentive; discreet. **sió-sim hāu-lô,** very attentive, as servant (v. lô).

sió-pêng, the right-hand side, counted less honourable. **sió-pâiⁿ** (T.), id. **toā-sió,** left and right; large or small, as month. **pái-sió,** take a step to the right. **sió--khì,** turn to the right, said by chair-bearers.

sió-tī, younger brother. **sió-bē,** younger sister. **sió-māiⁿ** (C.), id. **sió-chím** (of a man), younger brother's wife; (of woman) wife of her husband's younger brother. **sió-sím** (P.), id. **sió-chek** (C. sè-chek), husband's younger brother. **sió-ko͘,** husband's younger sister.

sió-hé, private business on his own account by manager of firm, &c. (v. hé). **sió-kang,** an under-workman; a labourer (v. kang). **sió-toàⁿ,** character of young female in a play. **sió-seng,** character of young and polite man in play.

sió-béh, bearded wheat. **sió-chióng,** Souchong tea. **sió-hôe,** = phàⁿ-chhek-hiuⁿ.. **sió-khe,** a large market town between Chang-chew and Ping-ho.

siò (= siù), a sheath; a scabbard. **to-siò** (esp. T. P.), a scabbard. **koeh-siò-á** (T.), sheath for sort of knife for cutting shrubs, &c.

siō (= siū). **gûn-siō,** sort of strong box for carrying silver. **chit-siō-gûn,** one thousand taels.

siō [R. siāu, a surname and name of place], a surname.

sio͘ⁿ (P. C.), in all the tones, = A. siuⁿ.

sioh (R. sek), to love; to be sparing of. **thiàⁿ-sioh,** id. **ài-sioh,** id. **ài-sioh-gûn,** to be sparing of one's money. **pó-sioh,** to love and cherish; to take great care of. **kèng-sioh jī-tsoá,** to reverence written or printed paper.

khó-sioh (C. khó-sek), alas!

sioh thé-biēn, careful of one's reputation, esp. prestige and influence. **sioh liâm-thí,** fair and honourable (though against one's friends or interest), and unwilling to do dishonourable things (v. thí). **bô-sioh bīn-phê,** has no regard for his own character. **sioh pún-hūn,** to keep to the behaviour and manners becoming one's station; to keep one's place; to attend to one's duty. **m̄-sioh pún-hūn,** to do what is above our rank or station, as in words, actions, or manner.

sioh-hok, to restrain one's self from taking a full swing of pleasure or power (v. hok). **sioh khùi-lát,** to spare one's strength when one should exert himself. **bô-sioh i-ê-bah,** not afraid of being wounded or beaten severely. **sioh siⁿ-miāⁿ,** to be very careful of one's self (often over-careful), *e.g.* taking great care when slightly unwell, or afraid to sit in a draught, or afraid to meddle with a matter, or travel on a road where there is some danger. **sioh kong-im** (r.), to economize time.

sio̍h — **gio̍h-sio̍h,** to jest at; to ridicule (a person).

sio̍h [R. sio̍k, common; vulgar; customs; cheap]. **sio̍h-sio̍h,** unimportant; common-looking. **sio̍h-khièn,** superstitious. **sio̍h-phiah,** id.

sio̍h — **bô-sio̍h bô-sio̍h,** easy-minded; taking things very easy; not readily getting angry; ready to forget what is ordered.

sio̍h — **kha-sio̍h,** the soft bad-smelling moisture of the foot. **chhiú-sio̍h,** moisture or slight perspiration on the hand.

sio̍h (cf. siûⁿ, io̍h), to get soft and bad, or waste away, as cooked food kept too long. **sio̍h--khì,** id. **sio̍h-lio̍h--khì,** id. **siⁿ-sio̍h,** to grow soft and begin to spoil (not yet mouldy), as cakes, coagulated jelly,

&c. **chhàu-siòh,** rather bad-smelling, as fish going to get bad.

tsáp-gėh siòh, the tenth month warm with much south wind.

siok [R. father's younger brother, = col. chek]. **pau-siok,** father's younger brother. **lāu-siok--ê,** polite appellation used in speaking to an old man. **siok-tit,** a cousin of any degree; blood relations in general, though very distant.

siok [R. a sort of bean; general word for pulse]. **tō-liông-siok, bėk-sú-chek,** the six grains.

siok [R. to shrink in, to draw back]. **lîm-tīn thòe-siok,** to desert or run away in battle (said of a man drawing back in fear from a dangerous affair just when it comes to the point).

siok [R. respectful; retiring; = col. sok]. **kam-siok,** Kan-suh province. **siok-chēng** (R.), = sok-chēng, quiet.

siȯk (R. id.), one of the Three Kingdoms (sam-kok). **siȯk-chiu** (R.), the city Suh-chau-foo, in Sze-chuen province. **siȯk-gím,** fine flowered silk from Suh-chau in Sze-chuen.

siȯk [R. ripe; well cooked; intimate; = col. sėk, sek], (also C., = A. sėk, ripe, &c.) **sêng-siȯk,** to grow ripe, as growing grain or fruit. **koàn-siȯk** (P. koàn-sėk), experienced, so as to be able to do a thing; skilful from habit (s. belong). **siȯk-tē,** a medicine (v. tē).

siȯk [previous word? following word?]. **khò-siȯk,** very free and easy in dispensing with ceremony, gen. with intimate friend; sometimes too free and easy. **khè-siȯk** (Cn.), id. **thò-siȯk** (C.), id. (C. also khò-siȯk).

siȯk [R. usual; customs; cheap; vulgar; = col. siȯh], (P. sėk, siȯk), cheap; low-priced. **siȯk-siȯk-hiàu,** to sell off at a great sacrifice.

siȯk-ke, all persons except Buddhist celibates. **koh-siȯk-ke,** to cease being a Buddhist priest.

chhe-siȯk, vulgar in appearance or manner. **chhe-siȯk-mih^n^,** common, cheap, inferior articles of food. **put-siȯk,** superior to the common average of men. **seng-sêng put-siȯk,** having a noble appearance; much superior to that of most men. **iá-siȯk,** rude and uncultivated. **iông-hu siȯk-tsú,** a common rough-looking illiterate man.

siȯk-gú, a proverb; a phrase in common use; colloquial language. **siȯk-gí** (C.), id. **siȯk-gú-ōe,** colloquial language.

siȯk-chêng, usual customs, as of a place. **sè-siȯk** (P. si-sėk), customs of the world, esp. idolatrous and superstitious. **ok-siȯk,** bad customs. **hong-siȯk,** customs. **bîn-hong thé-siȯk,** ways and customs of place or people. **siong-hong pāi-siȯk,** to corrupt and ruin the manners and customs of a place, as a very bad man or custom does. **jip-hong sûi-siȯk, jip-káng sûi-oan,** do at Rome as Rome does. **chiông-siȯk,** to follow the customs. **khiok-ì chiông-siȯk,** to follow the customs of a place against one's own desire. **thoat-siȯk,** very different from the generality of men, *e.g.* not following the usual customs, or not fawning like others on a powerful man, or having a specially fine personal appearance.

siȯk (R. id.), to belong; to belong to. **siȯk-tī-goá,** belongs to me. **siȯk sím-mih^n^-lâng,** to whom does it belong?

pē-siȯk, inferior officials of the supreme boards at Pekin. **ka-siȯk,** wife and family. **koàn-siȯk,** id. (s. ripe). **hā-siȯk ê-lâng,** people of very low or mean station, as coolies, beggars, &c. **i--ê hā-siȯk,** persons under his (a mandarin's) special control, as his soldiers and subordinate officers. **siȯk-hā,** inferior officers, soldiers, &c., over whom a mandarin has great power of control.

tsōe-siȯk, a crime.

siȯk (R. id.), to ransom; to redeem; to make atonement or satisfaction for. **siȯk-tò-tn̂g,** to ransom; to redeem. **siȯk-hôe,** id. **chhú-siȯk,** id. **chhí-siȯk** (C.), id. **siȯk-sin,** to redeem a person, as from slavery, or from a bad house. **siȯk-tsōe,** to make atonement or satisfaction for guilt.

siȯk [R. continuous; connected in unbroken succession; = col. soà]. **siȯk-hiên,** a widower's second wife. **siȯk-toān,** a medicine (v. toān).

chiap-siȯk, in uninterrupted succession (v. chiap). **liȯk-siȯk,** in slow but steady succession; gradually till completed; in small quantities, but tolerably regular (as money or supplies of food), so as to avoid extreme want; in general, of moderate quality, not very good. **liȯk-siȯk beh-hó,** very nearly completed, as work. **liȯk-siȯk chiū-hó,** need not be very particular, *e.g.* write in an easy current hand without wearisome exactness. **liȯk-siȯk-kóng,** to tell in the general without the details. **liȯk-siȯk-á-tsòe,** to do work in a very gradual manner. **liȯk-siȯk-á-thàn,** earning little, but regularly. **liȯk-siȯk-á-kàu,** coming one by one (or so) till all arrive; not all at once. **sûn-siȯk,** regular in time and quantity; good of its kind, according to pattern; all well made and of equally good quality, or of the same shape or sort. **sûn-sûn siȯk-siȯk,** id.; also, constant and regular in friendship without quarrelling; regular and well-behaved, as a boy; constant and steady, as gains in trade. **bô-sûn-siȯk,** crotchety or of peculiar temper, as man fond of going contrary to others' wishes, or sometimes pleased, sometimes angry; not equal in quality, as a lot of articles which should be all alike. **sé-kiâ^n^ sûn-siȯk,** regular, steady, and reliable in conduct. **khang-khè tsòe-sûn-siȯk,** having work from day to day; never long out of work. **hō-tsúi sûn-siȯk,** rain in due season as needed, and just in suitable quantity. **iáu-kú sûn-siȯk,** all going on well in family and business. **jîn-sū sûn-siȯk,** all one's affairs (in family and business) prosperous, without any death or considerable loss or calamity.

siong (R. id., = col. sa^n^, sio), (C. siang), mutually; but not always mutual. **siong-hó,** well acquainted; friendly. **siong-chhú,** id. (v. chhú). **siong-sėk,** id. **siong-ài,** loving each other, esp. as man and wife. **siong-sìn,** to trust (v. sìn). **siong-kèng,** to treat with politeness or respect (v. kèng). **siong-phòe,** suiting well together, as furniture, &c. (v. phòe). **siong-sū,** extremely alike. **siong-hōe,** to meet together. **siong-thoân,** to hand down, as trade secrets (v. thoân). **sè-tāi siong-sêng,** received from ancestors (v. sêng). **iú-bû siong-thong,** to have things in common; to share together (v. thong). **lông-pōe siong-i,** two men supplying each other's deficiencies (v. pōe). **khiok-ì siong-chiông,** to follow another's will against one's own desires. **biēn-biēn siong-koan,** looking at each other, with no way to get out of the danger or difficulty.

tsū-siong bâu-tún, to contradict one's self.

bô-siong-kan, it is of no consequence; it does not concern (us), (v. kan).

siong (R. id., = col. siu^n^), (C. siang), to wound; to hurt; to injure; a wound. **siong-hāi,** to injure; to hurt. **bô-siong-gāi,** not injured or causing injury

(v. gūi). **ōe-siong-bēng**, deadly, as blow or poison. **siong-hong pāi-siòk**, to ruin the morals of a place. **khah-siong-pún**, costing too much money. **lô-bîn siong-tsâi** (R.), to oppress the people and waste their money. **tòng-siong**, to object to a house being built up because it would injure the Fung-shuy or good luck of another house or grave.

siong-hong, to have a cold. **siong-sú** (C. siang-sí), disease caused by the heat. **siong-hân**, having become ill from taking a cold or chill. **siong-sit**, hurt by over-eating, esp. child.

siong-tiōng (C. id.), severe, as wound or disease; heavy, as price; serious or dangerous, as affair.

chek-siong, seriously ill from several days' over-exertion. **lô-siong**, consumption. **lōe-siong**, deep internal sickness. **lōe-siong gōe-kám**, predisposition to illness developed by taking a cold.

phah-siong, to wound by a blow or cut. **tio̍h-siong**, wounded; to be wounded. **tio̍h-toā-siong**, to be severely wounded. **tāng-siong**, severely wounded. **tsng-siong**, to wound one's self, as for begging, or in order to accuse another falsely. **giām-siong**, to ex-examine a wound officially, as mandarin or coroner (v. giām). **to-siong**, wound by sword or knife. **chhèng-siong**, gun-shot wound. **siong-hûn**, a scar or mark of a blow or bruise.

siong-sim, sad; deeply grieved for something past. **siong-sim khé-thàng**, sorely grieved, as at death of near relative. **thòe-lí siong-sim**, deeply grieved for you. **ai-siong** (r.), sorrowful. **pi-siong**, sad. **siong-pi**, id. **khó-siong**, to be lamented; alas! **kièn-kéng siong-chêng**, feeling of compassion caused by the sight of the case.

siong [R. a merchant; to consult], (C. siang). **siong-liông**, to consult together.

siong-tsûn, a trading junk; a merchant vessel. **kau-siong**, to have mercantile intercourse. **kau-siong bóe-bōe**, id.

hâng-siong, a great wholesale merchant, of a firm that sends tribute. **toā-siong**, a wholesale merchant (s. wound). **toā-siong-kheh**, a travelling merchant who deals in large quantities. **sió-siong**, a smaller merchant. **kheh-siong**, a travelling merchant (doing considerable business) coming from or going to a great distance. **toā-kheh-siong**, merchant trading thus to great distance with large capital. **iâm-siong**, a salt contractor (v. iâm). **sū-lông kong-siong**, the four classes of men, literati, farmers, workmen, and traders.

siong [R. siông, the fir-tree, = col. chhêng, seng]. **tē-siong** (C.), = A. tē-seng, the evergreen fir. **siong-gê** (C.), id.

siông [R. the fir-tree, = col. chhêng, chêng, seng], (P. sêng). **siông-ka**, resin. **siông-hiong** (Cn.), id. **siông-ke**, a fungus that grows on roots of trees.

gê-siông, Woo-sung. **siông-kang**, Sung-kiang-foo. **siông-khe**, a sort of tea (v. khe).

tē-siông-á (C.), sort of small shrub.

siông [R. to examine minutely; to inform a superior; details or particulars; minutely], (C. siâng). **siông-sè**, minutely; circumstantially; with minute detail. **un-jiû siông-sè**, gentle and cautious. **siông-sè-tsai**, to understand fully and minutely. **siông-sè séng-chhat**, to examine minutely into a matter. **i--ê siông-sè**, its minute details. **chhim-ti kí-siông**, intimately acquainted with the matter, or with one's character and history.

chham-siông, to consult together; to deliberate carefully together. **sím-siông**, very careful and minute, as in managing a matter or investigating an affair (said either of an official or of a private person). **tio̍h khah-sím-siông**, should be more minute and careful.

thong-siông, to send information, as one mandarin to another. **siông-bûn**, an inferior mandarin sending a despatch to his superior, giving an account of a matter. **siông hē-chiū^n-si-tsai**, id. **beh-siông--i**, will send information to the superior officer.

siông [R. usual, = col. siû^n, siô, chhiûng], (C. siâng). usually. **siông-siông**, usually; generally. **siông-sî**, id. **pún-siông-sî**, id., only of past time. **sè-siông**, id., of past time. **sîm-siông** (R. id.) **pêng-siông**, common; usual; ordinary; mediocre. **pêng-siông ê-lâng**, an ordinary sort of man, not above the average. **hui-siông**, extraordinary; uncommon. **chiàu-siông**, in the usual manner. **siông-êng**, in constant use. **siông-siū^n**, always thinking about —. **khah-siông-kóng**, more commonly said.

hoán-siông, to change from friendship to enmity, or from virtue to vice. **hoán-siông ê-lâng**, a man who does so. **hoán-siông beh-sí**, changing from friendship to great enmity, or from good conduct to great wickedness (said in scolding), because people are supposed to change so when near death. **hoán-hok bû-siông**, fickle in regard to friendship or to promises; saying the very opposite at different times. **hoán-bīn bû-siông**, fickle; ungrateful; readily getting angry or changing from affection to unfriendliness for slight causes. **hoán-biēn bû-siông**, id.

ngé-siông, the five cardinal virtues, = jîn-gī lé-tì-sìn, kindness, justice, propriety, wisdom, and truthfulness. **sam-kong ngé-siông**, the three headships (sovereign, father, husband), and the five virtues. **kong-siông** (R.), id.

siông-san, a medicine (v. san).

siông [R. the lady or goddess of the moon], (C. siâng). **goa̍t-lí siông-ngô**, the beautiful lady in the moon; proverb for female beauty and elegance.

siông [R. to repay], (C. chhiâng). **sat-jîn siông-bēng**, he who kills a man must make due reparation, usually by money, sometimes life for life.

siông — **khí-siông**, the tartar of the teeth. **chhùi-khí-siông**, id.

lâu-siông, slovenly, as person or room.

siông (R. id.), (C. siâng). **siông-sūi**, a good omen; good luck. **kiet-siông jû-ì** (C. kit-siâng jî-ì), may you have all good fortune up to your desires! (an auspicious phrase).

sióng [R. to reward; a reward; to look at, = col. siú^n], (C. siáng). **sióng-goán** (R.), to look at, as a pleasant view. **goán-sióng** (R.), id. **sióng-goa̍t**, (R.), to gaze at the bright moon.

khò-sióng, to give a largess to soldiers after a victory (v. khò). **kám-sióng**, an erroneous phrase (not Chinese), said by beggars to foreigners when asking alms, probably in imitation of the Canton-English "cumshaw," a corruption of "kám-siā," thankful.

sióng [R. to think, = col. siū^n], (C. siáng). **ì-sióng put-kip**, unexpectedly. **liāu-sióng put-tò**, did not consider beforehand so far as that; had no idea the matter would go so far.

siòng [R. id., by change of tone from siong, "mutual;"—to look at; appearance; to lead or assist; prime ministers, = col. siù^n], (C. siàng), to look at; appearance of countenance or of body; a likeness; a sort of fortune-telling. **saⁿ-siòng**, to look or gaze at each other. **chiáh-pá saⁿ-siòng**, looking idly at each other after eating, having nothing to do. **tùi-siòng**, looking intently at each other. **tsu-tsu-siòng**, to gaze earnestly or intently at. **tu-tu-siòng**, id. **kim-kim-siòng**, id. **bák-chiu siòng**, eyes gazing at —. **bák-chiu teh-siòng**, id. **lâm-siū-keng ê tāi-chiòng, chit-sien chiáh, saⁿ-sien siòng**, of the great idols at the "lâm-siū" temple, only one gets anything to eat (as he is counted the most powerful), while the other three only look on.

siòng-ki-hōe, to watch for an opportunity. **siòng i-ê-phāng**, to watch for some fault or weak point about him, so as to attack him. **siòng-hō-phāng**, to watch for and take advantage of a break in the rain.

siòng-miāⁿ, to tell fortunes by looking at the appearance of the face, and at one's general manner both in acting and resting. **siòng-sū**, a man who tells fortunes by looking at one's appearance and manner. **san-i-bēng pok-siòng**, geomancy, medicine, and the various sorts of divination. **san-i-bēng pok-siòng, ngó-phí**, these are all subjects which are but superficially known. **san-i-bēng pok-siòng, chīn-bat sī poàn-sien**, he who knows them all is almost one of the genii.

siòng-māuⁿ, the appearance of the countenance. **piàn-siòng**, changed to be unfavourable and unfriendly. **hok-siòng**, fat good-looking appearance. **phái ⁿ-siòng**, covetous; greedy; niggardly; *e.g.* refusing to pay though having money. **ke-khùt-siòng**, said of man who will not associate with others. **chiēn-kut-siòng**, appearance of meanness, *e.g.* rich man wearing ragged clothes, or guest refusing good accommodation (v. chiēn). **thih-teng-siòng**, said of child that needs a beating (v. teng).

khioh-siòng, to paint a likeness from life. **ūi-siòng**, to paint likenesses, either large or small.

tsáiⁿ-siòng, a prime-minister (there are two or more). **sêng-siòng**, id. **siòng-iâ**, id. **siòng-kok**, id. **tsó-siòng**, Tartar prime-minister. **iū-siòng**, Chinese prime-minister. **jip-siòng**, to become a prime-minister. **pài-siòng**, id. **chiōng-goân pài-siòng**, the senior wrangler of the Imperial Academy becoming also prime-minister. **tī siòng-kha**, having almost reached the rank of prime-minister. **chiòng-siòng**, civil and military officials of the very highest rank.

siōng [R. an elephant; form; shape; = col. chhiūⁿ], (C. siāng, chhiāng), form or shape, as of man [some phrases of this and the following word are sometimes interchanged].

khì-siōng, appearance and manner of a man, as indicating his feelings, emotions, intentions, or purpose, or as giving omens of good or bad fortune in divination; appearance of sky, as signs of weather. **khoàⁿ i--ê khì-siōng**, observe his bearing, manner, and appearance, as to judge of his intentions.

thien-siōng, any constellation or phenomenon (meteorological, astronomical, or astrological) in the sky or heavens, often in reference to weather (s. above). **thiⁿ-siōng**, id. **koan thien-siōng**, to examine the heavenly bodies or atmospherical phenomena, either for the weather or for astrological or astronomical purposes. **thiⁿ-siōng piàn-sek**, weather gives signs of change to rain or wind. **kéng-siōng**, any meteor or phenomenon in the sky, *e.g.* in reference to wind or weather.

siōng [R. like; a likeness; a picture; an image; an idol; = col. chhiūⁿ], (C. chhiāng, perhaps sometimes siāng). **chhâ-siōng**, a wooden image. **pùt-siōng**, an image or picture of an idol (properly Buddhist). **sîn-siōng**, image or picture of a god or idol. **ngó-siōng** (R.), an image of an idol. **ngió-siōng** (Cn.), id.

hêng-siōng, form or shape of man [by some placed under the preceding word].

hip-siōng, to take a photograph.

sù-put-siōng, a fabulous monster of tremendous power, having head and body of the "kî-lîn," tail of the dragon, and feet of hó, pà, sai, chhiūⁿ, respectively.

siōng [R. to value; still; yet; to rule or control (used in some official titles); = col. siūⁿ], (C. siāng). **tùi-tû-goā siōng-khiàm**, balance due. **tùi-tû-goā siōng-tsāi**, balance in hand.

siōng-chhiáⁿ, notwithstanding; even; very rarely used alone, almost always followed by "hô-hòng," "hòng-kiam," or some such phrase, making the sense "even . . . how much more;" *e.g.* the mandarin issues a proclamation, even (siōng-chhiáⁿ) the ignorant people obey: how much more (hô-hòng) should the literati do so. **i-ê-kiáⁿ siōng-chhiáⁿ m̄-káⁿ; bòh-kioh lí-káⁿ**, even his own son does not dare, how then dare you! **siōng-chhiáⁿ bô-hoaⁿ-hí**, yet after all he is not pleased (very rarely thus used in the concluding clause without an apodosis).

siōng-kú, yet; notwithstanding; either a connective particle like "siōng-chhiáⁿ," or in the sense of time (s. above). **siōng-kú bē**, not yet, *e.g.* when waiting for one's turn. **siōng-kú tsá**, it is still early. **khùn kàu-jit-tàu, siōng-kú m̄-khí--lâi**, having slept till noon, yet will not rise.

siōng [R. above; to ascend; first-class; = col. chiūⁿ, chhiūⁿ, siūⁿ, siāng], (C. siāng). **siōng-téng**, first-class; best quality. **siōng-téng-siōng**, best of the first-class; superfine. **siōng-hó**, best. **siōng-tiong-hā**, first-class, medium, and inferior (v. hā). **siōng-kú**, at the very longest of time (s. yet). **siōng-kang**, best Congou. **ki-siōng-pék**, superfine white grass-cloth.

siōng-tè, God (v. tè). **sèng-siōng**, the emperor. **hông-siōng**, id. **siōng-jîn**, official superiors of a mandarin. **siōng-khòng**, to enter an accusation in a superior court, as an appeal against a lower. **tsó-siōng**, ancestors.

put-siōng-soàn, utterly useless, as man or thing (v. soàn). **má-siōng**, immediately; just about to — (v. má).

siōng-goân, the feast of lanterns on 1.15. **siōng-hái**, Shanghai. **hông-tsoân lē-siōng**, Hades.

siōng [R. to enter an accusation in court]. **siōng-kùn**, a man who instigates to lawsuits (v. kùn). **pau-lám sū-siōng**, to engage for a large sum of money to be responsible for the success of a lawsuit, taking the whole management of it on one's self; considered a great crime.

siōng [R. to recite]. **siōng-keng**, to recite prayers. **siōng-tsàn** (R.), to praise.

sip [R. sèk, a vault or recess in a sepulchre]. **sip-chhù**, a small shed in which a coffined corpse is put till a lucky site and day are found for burial.

sip (R. id.), damp; moist. **sip-khì**, dampness. **hong hân, sú sip**, the four causes of disease: wind, cold, heat, and damp. **sip-tâm**, moist; damp; gathering moisture. **sip-jūn**, very slightly moistened by damp, as ground or other things. **sip-lūn**, id.

khì-sip, to heal a disease caused by damp; to cure dampness, as of a floor, &c. **sò-sip**, to suck up damp, as sawdust does. **siu-sip**, to remove moisture or damp, as by burning some drug, or by scattering sand or saw-dust, &c.

sip [R. chhip, rain falling; cf. sap]. **hō͘-á sip-sip**, small gentle rain. **sip-sip-á-tsúi**, a small quantity of water, *e.g.* as in cooking.

sip [R. chhek, the knee; C. chhip]. **hók-sip** (C.), = A. hók-sek, ornaments for the knees.

sip [R. ten, = col. tsȧp]. **sip-hun-hó**, the very best; very good. **sip-ok**, all sorts of wickedness (v. ok). **ngó͘-sip-kî**, the days ending in 5 or 0, *e.g.* 5, 10, 15, &c. **sip--jī**, the character "ten;" the figure of a perpendicular cross. **sip-jī-kè**, a cross for crucifixion. **tèng sip-jī-kè**, to crucify. **phiȧh sip-jī-kè**, id. **sip-jī-koe**, place where streets cross at right angles. **sip-jī-ke** (C.), id. **sip-jī-lō͘**, place where roads or streets cross at right angles. **sip-jī-hò**, tied with strings or ropes crossed (v. hò).

me͘ⁿ sip-pat, a sort of gambling (v. pat).

sip [R. to gather with the hand; to pick up; the character is also used as an alternative form for "ten"]. **siu-sip**, to gather up, as things when preparing for a journey; to apprehend and give up to the authorities; to put in coffin and bury; to kill; to make away with, as a man (s. stone). **khioh-sip**, habitually careful and economical; gathering up and taking care of things so that nothing is wasted.

sip [R. sėk, a stone, = col. chiȯh, siȧh]. **siu-sip-tan**, sort of pill used for curing internal injuries caused by beating, vomiting of blood, &c. (said to be made from dried urine).

sip [R. to practise; practised; skilled]. **hȧk-sip**, to learn by study or by practice; to be practised or skilled at something. **un-sip**, to revise, as a lesson. **kàu-sip**, a drill-sergeant. **sip-khì**, the manners and customs of a place. **ē-mn̂g ê sip-khì**, the customs and ways of Amoy. **sip-koàn sêng tsū-jiên**, practice or habit becomes natural.

sip — **sip-sip-háu**, unpleasant sound of supping up things into the mouth with too much noise.

sip [R. to attack secretly and suddenly; hereditary; double], (C. sit). **sè-sip** (C. sì-sit), hereditary; to inherit an office or title. **sè-sip bóng-thè**, perpetually hereditary. **sè-sip iû-kek**, the military rank of "iû-kek," held for five generations by descendants of distinguished mandarins. **sè-sip siú-pī**, rank of "siú-pī," similarly held for several generations.

sip (C. sit). **tsâu-sip**, to make a collection of elegant phrases from many sources, either for legitimate use in improving one's style, or for bad use, as for literary piracy.

sit [R. sek, pattern], (also C. in some phrases, = A. sek). **hȧp-sit**, fit; becoming. **m̄-sī-sit**, state of matters very dangerous, *e.g.* going a road full of robbers; dangerous to deal with, as man not fit to be intrusted with money. **sî-sit**, fashionable form or shape. **khoán-sit**, form; model; pattern; sort; character.

sit (R. sek), to be extinguished, as fire, lamp, or candle (esp. Cn.; also used in A., but usually "hoa," which is the only word used in C.) **hé sit**, the fire has gone out. **pûn-sit-hé**, to blow out a light with the breath. **chhe-sit-hé**, to blow out a light, as the wind does of itself. **phah-sit**, to extinguish; to quench. **phah oh-tit-sit**, difficult to quench. **im-sit**, to extinguish by covering up.

sit [R. sek, to rest; to cease; posterity; interest; to toil; to labour], (C. sit, sek; and sometimes C. sit, = A. sek).

siau-sit, news (s. ear-brush). **siuⁿ-sit** (C.), id. **thiaⁿ siau-sit**, to hear news. **thong siau-sit**, to give news or information for any purpose, right or wrong.

iám-kî sit-kó, flags hid and drums silent, as in an ambush, or secret march or attack. **an-sit** (C.), = A. an-sek (v. sek).

lāi-sit (C.), = A. lī-sek, interest of money.

poàⁿ-jit-sit, half a day's work. **chit-kang poàⁿ-sit**, a very little labour. **chit-tiám-sit**, one-third of a day's work (v. tiám). **tsòe sím-mih-sit**, what work do you do? **lō͘-thâu-sit**, work of carrying loads at the landing-places or jetties. **gín-ná pān toā-lâng-sit**, a child doing a man's work. **tsoh-sit** (Cn.), to do any sort of work (s. harvest).

sit [R. sek, harvest; grain ready to be reaped]. **tsoh-sit**, to till the ground (s. work).

sit-tiûⁿ, cultivated fields.

sit — **siau-sit**, an ear-brush made with hair (s. news). **siau-sit-kóng**, a case for an ear-brush.

sit [R. sek, a house]. **sit-á** (C.), = A. sek-á, small lodgings at temples. **tsāi-sit-lí** (C.), = A. tsāi-sek-lú, a virgin.

sit [R. to lose; to fail; to mistake]. **sit-lȯh**, to lose. **sit-lȯh-kha**, to lose one's footing. **sit-kha lȯh-chhiú**, to do a thing in a blundering way, as manual or literary work; to mismanage a matter. **sit-chhiú**, to cause injury by a slip of the hand. **bé sit-tôe**, the horse stumbles. **sit-pit**, to make a slip in writing. **sit-siàu**, to fail to put down in an account by mistake. **sit-hé**, to set on fire accidentally (s. extinguish).

sit-chhò, a mistake; a fault. **sit-gō͘**, a mistake; to make a mistake. **kè-sit**, a fault; a sin. **kòe-sit** (C.), id. **sit-bê** (R.), to lose one's way. **bān bû-it-sit**, not one mistake or fault in a myriad; no mistakes. **giên to, pit-sit**, in much talk there is sure to be some fault (v. to).

sit-sìn, to break one's word; to betray one's trust. **sit-tek**, to lose one's virtue; to commit some great crime. **sit-chit**, to fail in duty. **sit kiám-tiám**, not to take sufficient care, as of things intrusted (v. kiám). **sit-lé**, to be unpolite; I beg your pardon for my want of politeness. **sit-gî**, to fail in the ceremony due to a superior. **sit-pôe**, excuse me; beg pardon (said on leaving company or on refusing to eat something offered). **sit--lâng**, intentionally treat a man unpolitely in order to show one's feelings.

sit-sim, mad; idiotic; insane. **sit-sîn**, utterly dispirited, depressed, exhausted, or stupified (v. sîn). **sit-táⁿ**, to lose courage. **sit-hèng**, dispirited; having lost heart (v. hèng). **sit-ì**, dejected, as about some important matter. **sit-chì**, in very low spirits; without resolution. **phah-sit lâng-ê-chì**, to make a man lose heart.

sit-sî, to be out of season or out of fashion; to have no employment or way of livelihood; (to miss the proper time or opportunity?). **sit-tsúi**, to have too little water, as plant or field. **sit-sek**, to lose colour, as face. **sit-bī**, turned in taste, as meat too long kept. **sit-tāng**, to lose weight. **sit-hong**, to lose prestige. **sit-ài**, to be less loved (as child) than a more favoured one. **sit-siu**, to have an inferior harvest. **sit-siaⁿ**, to lose voice. **iau-ki sit-tǹg**, hungry from want of a meal or meals. **sit-phiò**, to lose a pawn-ticket (v. phiò). **khah-sit-ah**, strike very gently with the oar held in the right hand (v. ah).

sit-tsú, the man whose property has been stolen.

sit-jit, eclipse of the sun. **sit-géh**, eclipse of the moon. **géh sit**, the moon is eclipsed.

sit-khì, to lose one's good luck, influence, prestige, or prosperity; to become weak in health; to grow poor or powerless from state of wealth or influence. **sit--khì**, to faint away; to swoon. **hūn-lūn sit-lit--khì**, id.

sí-sit, loss by death, as of relatives. **sún-sit**, to become fewer by death, as inhabitants of village or members of family. **sńg-sit**, to lose, as things spoiled or taken away. **súi^{n}-sit** (C.), id. **sit-teng**, to lose male children or young men. **sit-tùi**, to lose husband, or wife, or mate. **sit-sū**, to be wrecked, as vessel; to meet with disaster, as expedition or enterprise. **seng-lí lóng-sit** (C.), the trade quite gone down.

tit-sit, to gain or lose. **kià-tit, put-kià-sit**, people intrust things to be kept, not to be lost. **kià-tek, put-kià-sit**, id. **tek-sit**, to gain or lose. **m̄-kia^{n} tek-sit**, not afraid to make the venture. **tek-sit bô-kia^{n}**, id. **m̄-ài tek-sit--lâng**, very careful to avoid giving offence to any party by word or action, often keeping neutral.

sit [R. to eat; food; = col. chiáh]. **hó-chiáh-sit**, good living; good food. **ū-chiáh-sit**, to live on good food. **hé-sit** (T. hō͘-sek), provisions; food (said in rerelation to those who eat it, as to numbers or payment). **hé-sit-chî^{n}**, money paid for food. **kap-goán siāng-hé-sit**, taking his meals regularly with us. **hé-sit-tû**, a cupboard. **sit-tû**, id. **jit-sit** (T. jit-sek), daily food. **jit-sit lân-tē**, have difficulty in earning daily food. **ím-sit**, food and drink; eating and drinking. **ím-sit hó**, plenty of good things to eat and drink. **i-sit chhiong-chiok**, food and clothing sufficient. **pién-sit**, sort of tart made of minced meat wrapped up in a flour-cake. **pán-sit** (C.), id. **péng-sit** (T.), id. **pién-sit-phê**, thin cake of unbaked flour ready for wrapping up meat.

háp-sit, to take meals together. **lēng-ke kok-sit**, to make arrangements to have meals separate (v. lēng). **keh-sit**, a severe chronic disease in which one is unable to swallow food (cancer in stomach?). **siong-sit**, hurt by over-eating, esp. child. **sit-chek**, id. (v. chek). **tsō-sit san-pheng**, by idleness and eating a whole mountain (of money) is wasted. **siá-bēng, sit hô-tûn**, said of throwing away one's life for good eating.

sit-té (Cn.), = pak-té, the belly.

sit (R. ek), a wing; a fin. **chiáu-sit**, a bird's wing. **sit-ké**, a wing. **sit-ké-mn̂g**, wing feathers. **sit-ké-oan**, bends and windings, as of a crooked road. **koe-sit-ké-oan**, id. **sit-ké-bé ta-lī**, getting on well alone and not now needing help from parents, &c. **sit-ké-ē**, under the wings, *e.g.* as chickens. **sit-ē**, id.

hî-sit, fins, especially pectoral. **soa-sit**, shark's fins, edible. **n̂g-sit-á** (T.), a sort of small fish.

iap-sit, small houses, often mere sheds, built on to the side houses (hō͘-lêng) of a large Chinese house. **iap-sit-á**, id.

phah-sit, to flap the wings. **lāng-sit**, to shake the wings. **chhńg-sit**, to dress the wings with the bill. **thién-sit**, to spread the wings. **thí-sit**, id. **lêng-sit**, to clip the wings of a living bird. **bán-sit**, to pluck out the wing feathers. **chhoah-sit**, id.

sit (R. id.) **khiàm-sit**, a sort of medicinal plant (v. khiàm).

sit [R. to waste away gradually; to be eclipsed, = col. sih]. **sit-jit** (r.), = sit-jit, eclipse of sun. **sit-géh** (r.), = sit-géh, eclipse of moon.

sit — **ui-sit**, prospering very much through some lucky influence, as a house or grave that is very auspicious, or as a man who has good fortune; giving a good omen, or causing great prosperity. **bô-ui-sit**, having an unlucky influence, *e.g.* to assist at a stranger's funeral, or to help in arranging a widow's second marriage.

sit [R. true; full; solid; fruit], true; solid; closely packed or pressed; nett. **hu-sit**, hollow and solid; false and true. **hi-sit** (C.), id. **thàm-hu-sit**, to investigate whether it be true or false, as a report or state of an affair.

bák-sit, very much or numerous (only said of things, esp. a great deal for a little money). **bát-sit**, id. **tsát-sit**, tightly pressed in. **sit-tōe**, solid ground.

kiet-sit, neatly and tightly tied or made up, as a thing; real and certain, not empty pretence, as words or affair; also (R.), to produce fruit.

thiáp-sit, neatly put up; neatly laid in order; not taking up too much room, as *multum in parvo;* well-behaved. **kui-kú thiáp-sit**, well-behaved. **thiáp-kut-sit** (Cn. T.), well-behaved. **táh-kut-sit** (T.), id.; very proper and regular in behaviour; honest; quiet and not fond of display.

phoh-sit, simple, plain, and quiet in taste, as to dress, manner, &c.; not fond of display. **phak-sit**, id. **phok-sit**, honest, straightforward, and simple in tastes (v. phok). **tok-sit** (r.), simple-minded, honest, sincere.

chēng-sit, nett, in weight, quantity, &c. **sit-lāi**, interior size, as length of room or house within the walls. **sǹg-sit--ê**, counting nett, as gains, &c. **tû-sit**, nett, as weight, measure, &c.

chin-sit, true. **sìn-sit**, true in fact. **láu-sit**, honest, truthful, as man. **sêng-sit** (r.), id. **khak-sit**, worthy of trust, as man or facts. **chhiet-sit**, just as it should be, according to pattern or promise; thoroughly truthful, honest, and safe, as man or word. **sit-sim**, true in heart, sincere. **sit-ì**, id. **bô-sit**, without truth or reality; insincere. **sit-sit-bô**, certainly not. **sit-tsāi**, truly; really. **tek-sit**, truly. **chiàu-sit-kóng**, speak truly. **kî-sit**, in reality; the truth of the matter. **tiók-sit**, the facts or real circumstances of the matter. **chiák-sit** (C.), id. **sit-kù**, evidence good, true, and sufficient for the purpose. **sím-sit**, to examine judicially into the truth of a case, as mandarin. **tsa-sit**, to find out the truth by investigation. **khêng-sit**, id. **ū-jip-sit**, truthful, honest, or safe, as man or affair. **bô-jip-sit**, not to be trusted.

sit-jīm, office actually his own (not merely "sū," acting temporarily; nor mere titular or brevet rank). **sit-siū**, id.

sit — **māu^{n}-sit**, acting as an impostor (v. māu^{n}).

sit [R. —; A. sip; C. sit, to attack secretly; hereditary, &c]. **sì-sit** (C.), = A. sè-sip, hereditary.

sit (same as above?). **tsâu-sit** (C.), = A. tsâu-sip, copying the phrases of others, as for literary piracy or other purposes.

sit [R. id., mere imitation of the sound]. **sit-lát**, Singapore (v. låt).

siu (R. id.), to repair; to reform; to mend. **siu-lí**, to repair. **siu-chéng**, to repair; to mend; to put in order, tidy up, or make neat, as a place. **siu-pî^{n}**, to make level, as road. **siu-lō͘**, to repair a road. **siu-kiô**, to repair a bridge. **siu-thióng**, to repair graves in a burying-ground.

siu-siah, to pare down smooth; to alter slightly, as a document. **siu kha-lan**, to cure corns.

厦英大辭典

toā-siu, a very thorough repair, as of a boat once in three years.

siu-sim, to reform and regulate the heart. **siu-sin** (R.), to be correct in conduct. **siu-hēng,** to reform and cultivate morality (Buddhist phrase). **siu-liān,** to reform and cultivate morality and virtue (Tauist phrase). **liān-tan siu-tō,** to follow Tauist rules so as to become one of the Sien or immortals. **siu-siān,** to reform and cultivate virtue. **siu im-chek,** to practise meritorious works.

siu [R. dried meat; to repair; the previous word is often used instead of this].

sok-siu, a teacher's salary.

siu [R. chhiu, autumn]. **siu-sip-tan,** a sort of pill (v. sip, "stone").

siu [R. to be ashamed, = col. siáu]. **lāu-put-siu,** you old shameless wretch!

siu [R. siū, to receive]. **kim-sì tsòe, kim-sì siu,** actions recompensed in this life (v. sì).

siu [R. siau, to melt; to spend; to reduce or remove; to shrink].

siu-sip, to remove dampness, as by sand, sawdust, or other means (v. sip). **siu-tsúi,** to dry gradually, as damp article when aired. **siu-tòk,** to remove poison, as cockroach, &c.

siu-phí, scab formed on a wound. **siu-chhùi,** edges of wound closed. **siu-kien,** scab forming.

siu (R. id.), to take in, collect, or receive, as money, clothes, &c.; to lay away; to make a retreat; to coffin or bury; to take one's female slave to be concubine. **siu--khí-lâi,** said of a master taking his female slave to be his concubine. **siu--khì,** to lay away; to lay past. **siu-khǹg,** to lay past; to hide or conceal, as men or things. **siu-liu,** to take in, collect, receive, bury, &c. **siu-liû,** to receive and entertain in one's house, as a person, as guest or lodger. **siu-saⁿ,** to take in clothes, as for washing.

siu-tê, to buy up tea where it is grown.

siu-sip, to gather up and put away; to deliver over to the authorities, &c. (v. sip).

siu-kun (to withdraw the army), to make a retreat. **siu-peng,** id. **siu-tūi,** do., as troops after drill.

siu-soah, to wind up an affair all right. **siu-tiûⁿ,** id. **siu-sū,** to wind up and settle an affair for another, as an arbiter or a superior relative. **bōe-siu--tit,** cannot be recalled, as word once spoken. **tsúi phoah-lòh-tōe, lân siu-tit-khí,** the thing is done now and cannot be mended (v. phoah).

siu-sêng, to take in the harvest; to wind up a trading business (not from failure).

siu-tang, to take in or gather the harvest. **gē-kak ū-siu,** to have a good harvest. **kúi-hun-siu,** how many tenths of a fair average harvest? **sit-siu,** to have an inferior harvest. **nīⁿ-tang sit-siu,** id. **chhut-siu,** harvest much above the average. **nīⁿ-tang put-chí chhut-siu,** extremely good harvest. **hó-siu,** good harvest. **nīⁿ-tang hó-siu,** id. **nīⁿ-tang hó-siu, chiáu-á chiáh joā-tsōe,** when the harvest is good the birds eat a good deal; willing to give some money to help when getting good profits.

siu-liám, to coffin. **siu-liām** (C.), id. **siu-bâi,** to bury. **siu á-bē,** is he buried yet?

siu-kaⁿ, to put in prison. **siu-lòh-kaⁿ,** id. **siu-koán,** to put in the less uncomfortable prison (from "koán," a public office or prison).

siu-koán, to have the management, as of a property, or have the care of a thing for another (from "koán," to rule). **kau-lí siu-koán,** I give it over to your charge.

siu-chîⁿ, to collect money; to receive payments, as of subscriptions or debts. **siu-siàu,** to collect debts. **siu-tsoe,** to collect rent of land. **siu-sè,** to collect house-rent. **siu-iên,** to collect subscriptions. **siu chîⁿ-niûⁿ,** to collect land-tax. **siu-tiāⁿ,** to receive earnest-money. **goân-siu chhut-tsûn,** the balance in one's own books. **siu-toaⁿ,** a receipt, as for money or goods. **hō-siu** (f.), a receipt for customs; this and the following phrases are used in the foreign customs. **chhut-kháu hō-siu** (f.), export duty receipt. **jip-kháu hō-siu** (f.), import duty receipt. **poàⁿ-sè hō-siu** (f.), coast-trade duty receipt for half-duty paid.

khang-chhiú siu toaⁿ-to, said of doing business with almost no capital (v. to, "sword").

siu-sok, gradually tapering. **siu pui-thâu,** to build up the tapering gable-end.

siû (R. id.), to swim. **siû-tsúi,** id. **gâu-siû,** good at swimming.

siû [R. an enemy; to revenge; deep enmity]. **kiû-siû,** an enemy. **siû-jîn,** id. **chhim-siû,** very deep settled enmity. **kiet oan-siû,** to be at open feud (v. oan). **pò-siû,** to revenge one's self; to take vengeance. **kong-pò su-siû,** to take private revenge under guise of public justice.

siû [R. to imprison; a prisoner]. **siû-kìm** (R.), to imprison. **kaⁿ-siû,** a prisoner. **siû-hoān** (r.), id. **sin-siû,** a recent prisoner. **kū-siû,** a prisoner who has been several years in prison. **kū-siû chiáh sin-siû,** said of partners in trade living on each other. **sin-siû chiáh kū-siû,** id.

siû [R. to return thanks; to recompense; to invite a guest to drink]. **èng-siû,** to hold mutual intercourse by giving and receiving presents, or by ceremonious visits, &c.

siú (R. id., = col. chiú), to hold fast, as a duty; to observe, as a command or ceremony; to keep, as a city or fort. **siú-sêng,** careful of one's property; well-behaved. **siú-hoat,** to be of good behaviour; to keep the laws or proper rules. **siú-hūn,** to do one's duty (v. hūn). **siú-kí,** to restrain one's self from evil. **an-hūn siú-kí,** to keep to one's duty and restrain one's self from evil. **siú-kí an-hūn,** id.

chip-siú, to keep, as a command. **kè-siú,** to guard or watch carefully, as house or fields. **khàn-siú,** to watch over and take care of, *e.g.* as tē-pó over a ward. **tìn-siú,** to guard, as a high mandarin guards a city. **pé-siú,** to guard, as against attack, as soldiers.

siú-pī, a military officer between tu-si and chhien-tsóng, about lieutenant-major. **siâⁿ-siú,** the mandarin who commands the garrison of a Foo city; the garrison of it. **siú-siâⁿ,** to guard a city. **siú-peng,** soldiers who do garrison work.

siú [R. the head, = col. chhiú], classifier of songs, odes, or hymns. **póng-siú,** highest name on the list of new graduates of any degree. **kài-siú-thâu,** the head of the beggars. **bān-ok, îm ûi-siú,** adultery is the greatest of all crimes.

chhiòng-siú, to raise a question or begin a discussion, &c. **ùi-siú ùi-bí,** afraid to see a person or to meddle in a matter (lit. afraid of beginning and end).

si-siú, a corpse. **hō-siú,** sort of trumpet with curved end.

siú-sek, ornaments for the head. **siú-khip,** a head that has been cut off (said in speaking of the number beheaded). **siú-kip,** id. **tsám-siú,** to behead. **kam-**

tsám-siú, a small officer who sees that the beheading takes place. **siú-e**, a plant used as a medicine for making hair black. **tùn-siú pài** (R.), to bow the head in worship or reverence.

Siú [R. the hand; the arm; = col. chhiú]. **tsúi-siú**, a sailor. **hiong-siú**, a murderer. **to-pé-siú**, an executioner. **kùi-tsú-siú**, id. **phàu-siú**, artillery-men. **chhèng-siú**, id. **su-siú**, a writer in a mandarin's office.

siú-chiok (R.), hands and feet (v. chiok). **pêk-siú sêng-ka**, from poverty become rich. **hùt-siú-kam**, the fingered citron.

Siù [R. id., by change of tone from "siú," the head]. **chhut-siù**, to give information against a man, as informer or as king's-evidence.

Siù (R. chhiàu? siàu? = col. siò), a scabbard; a sheath for a knife. **to-siù**, id., for sword or knife.

Siù — **kiuh-siù-á**, a small poignard carried concealed for assassination. **kiàh kiuh-siù-á sa^{n}-tsân**, to be at mortal feud with each other.

Siù [R. a constellation; by change of tone from "siok," to rest; to lodge; a constellation]. **chhi^{n}-siù**, the stars and constellations. **jī--sip-pat-siù**, the twenty-eight great constellations, or zodiacal signs, used for the days of the cycle (not lunar) of twenty-eight days or four weeks; of these, pông, hu, báu, seng, always fall on our Sunday.

Siù (R. id.), a quadruped; a wild beast. **liòk-siù**, six animals specially propitiated (by Tauist priests) when building a house. **siù-lūi**, quadrupeds, esp. wild beasts. **iá-siù**, wild quadrupeds. **niáu^{n}-siù** (R.), birds and beasts. **khîm-siù**, birds and beasts. **pe-khîm tsáu-siù**, id. **hui-khîm tsó-siù**, id. **soa^{n}-khîm iá-siù**, wild birds and beasts. **soa^{n}-khîm iá-siù liòk-thiok**, birds and beasts wild and tame. **gû-bé khîm-siù**, you brute! (said in scolding). **i-koan khîm-siù**, a mandarin or graduate behaving like a brute, wickedly or very lasciviously. **jîn-biēn siù-sim**, man's face but brute's heart. **jîn-bin siù-sim**, id. **lông put-lông, siù put-siù**, very miserable and unfit for work.

siù-bīn, the flat front of a boat; sometimes it has a beast's face painted on it.

Siù [R. to embroider]. **chhiah-siù**, to embroider (v. chhiah). **siù-hoe**, to embroider. **siù kim-hoe**, to embroider in gold, as flowers, &c. **siù-teng-hoe**, embroidered flowers on the gauze frame of a lamp. **siù-kiû-teng**, a lamp made to roll along when lighted. **gím-siù**, embroidered silk (v. gím). **sù-khai-siù**, square pattern on dress of military mandarin.

siù-chiam, a needle for embroidery. **siù-chién**, small scissors, such as milliners use. **siù-soà^{n}**, thread for embroidery. **siù-pâng**, a shop for embroidery, &c.; a room in a house where the young girls of the family sew, and where the women have undisturbed privacy. **siù-pâng-lāi**, in that private room (said of a young girl). **toà--tī siù-pâng-tóe**, said of a married woman who keeps too much secluded.

Siù [R. id. by change of tone from "siú," to guard; also written with "siù," to hunt]. **sûn-siù** (R.), to make a tour of inspection through the empire, as the ancient emperors did. **tāi-thien sûn-siù**, to make inspection instead of Heaven, said of the idol ông-iâ.

Siù [R. elegant; accomplished; = col. siàu]. **iù-siù**, delicate (not coarse); elegant; refined; polite. **tsùn-siù**, good-looking, as person. **chheng-siù**, polite and refined in appearance; rather thin, elegant, and nice-looking. **siù-khì**, elegant; refined; finely formed; said of men or things. **siù-bē** (R.), luxuriant and graceful in form, as plant (v. be).

siù-tsâi, a graduate of the Sew-tsai degree, the first that is taken, somewhat like B.A., but more like passing civil service examination.

Siū [R. sleeves; cuffs]. **siū-kháu**, cuffs, as of a coat. **chhiú-siū**, mitts, without fingers, for men, worn on the wrist; warm under-sleeves about a foot long, that slip under the cuffs of a dress. **ńg-siū**, do., for women. **thong-siū**, hands put into the sleeves of the other hand. **chhiú thong-siū**, id., = nn̄g-chhiú thong-siū, = siang-chhiú thong-siū. **khong-siū** (C.), id.

Siū (R. id.), long life; longevity. **siū-goân**, id. **siū-goân tn̂g**, having great longevity. **bô-siá^{n}-siū-goân**, not at all long-lived. **hè-siū**, length of life. **tn̂g-hè-siū**, long life. **chiáh tn̂g-hè-siū**, to live long. **té-hè-siū**, short life. **kiám hè-siū**, to have one's life shortened by Heaven on account of wickedness. **thi^{n} hè-siū**, idolatrous rites for long life, at temple of Sêng-hông. **thiam hè-siū**, id. **thiam-siū**, may you have long life! (v. thiam). **iáu-siū**, very short life (v. iáu). **tiông-siū**, long life. **tiông-siū-hiu^{n}**, long sticks of incense, burned on birth-day. **tiông-siū-seng**, the star of longevity. **siū-sò**, the appointed length of one's life. **siū-sò kai-chīn**, the fated time of life having come to an end, one must die. **hù-kùi tsâi-tsú-siū**, rank, wealth, posterity, and longevity. **hok-lòk-siū**, good fortune, official rank, and longevity (v. hok).

sèng-siū, the emperor's birth-day. **sèng-siū-hì**, plays on that day. **bān-siū**, the emperor's birth-day. **bān-siū-keng**, the temple where the emperor's tablet is worshipped. **bān-siū-têng**, a temporary shrine where the emperor is worshipped on his birth-day. **bān-siū-pî^{n}**, temporary stage at yamun gate for plays on emperor's birth-day. **bān-siū-kek**, the marigold. **bān-siū-pû**, the papaya.

chiok-siū, to call or send cards or presents to a man on his birth-day, with good wishes for his long life. **hō-siū**, to give presents or pay for a play for a man on his birth-day. **pài-siū**, to make a congratulatory visit to a man on his birth-day. **loán-siū**, sons and daughters in-law visiting the father on the evening before his birth-day. **joán-siū** (C.), id. (?) **siū-ku**, large turtle-shaped cakes, used on birth-days.

tāi-siū, a full-length portrait or picture. **ūi tāi-siū**, to paint or draw a full-length portrait. **khioh tāi-siū**, id. from life.

siū-pán, a coffin made for one's self during life, as by one's own directions, or by children. **siū-i**, grave-clothes prepared beforehand for parents. **siū-hék**, grave prepared before death. **siū-tê**, a scroll picture with the character "siū" on it. **siū-kim**, idolatrous paper with the character "siū" on it. **ìn-siū-kim**, to print such paper.

siū-bî, a sort of tea (v. bî).

Siū [R. to give; to give over or transmit; = col. siū^{n}]. **siū-chheh**, to give out a lesson. **tėk-siū--ê**, appointed to an office to hold it as his own for three years; office of Tau-tai and upwards thus given only by the supreme board of office; but lower offices may be given by the governor-general. **sit-siū**, id.

thoân-siū, to hand down, as traditions or instructions.

Siū (R. id.), to receive; to accept; to endure, as punishment or calamity. **sêng-siū**, to accept; to receive. **sîn-siū** (C.), id. **hióng-siū**, to enjoy, as good fortune. **jím-siū**, to endure patiently (v. jím). **niá^{n}-siū** (r.), to receive.

siū-tsōe, to receive the punishment of guilt (v. tsōe). **siū-hāi**, to suffer injury done by another man. **siū-khó**, to suffer misery or calamity. **siū-tsai**, to meet with calamity (v. tsai). **siū-sí**, to suffer violent death. **siū-un**, to receive grace or favour. **siū-thai**, to become pregnant; to conceive.

siū — **siū-khì**, anger; to be angry; to be angry at —. **siū-khì siū-toah**, in a passion (v. toah). **siū-khì tiu^{n}-toah**, sulkily refusing or pretending dislike (v. toah). **siū-khì kàu iô-thâu poā^{n}-hī**, all shaking with violent rage.

siū (= siō). **gûn-siū**, a strong box for conveying silver.

siū [R. a cave or den in a mountain], a nest; a den; a kennel. **chiáu-siū**, a bird's nest. **koe-siū**, a hen's nest. **koe-bú-sū**, a low spur of a hill, with a somewhat flat top and a depression (like a nest) on it; name of a village in such a situation. **phang-siū**, a nest of bees or wasps (v. phang). **pėh-hiā-siū**, a nest of white ants. **káu-siū**, a dog's kennel. **niáu-chhú-siū**, a rat's nest.

chhát-siū, a den of robbers; a stronghold of rebels.

chiap āu-siū, said of a virgin marrying a widower.

siū [R. the cord or girdle by which a seal (esp. an official seal) is tied on the person]. **în-siū** (R.), official seals and girdle of mandarin.

siu^{n} (R. siong), a box; a trunk. **chhâ-siu^{n}**, a wooden box or trunk. **bih-siu^{n}**, bamboo box or trunk. **phê-siu^{n}**, leather do. **pí^{n}-siu^{n}**, a broad, flat, shallow box. **siu^{n}-láng**, boxes and wicker-work baskets. **chit-khia-siu^{n}**, one box or trunk. **chit-kha-siu^{n}** (Cn.), id. **thê-siu^{n}**, an opium-box; the wood of it is bad.

tû siu^{n}-khak, to take off so much for the weight of the box, as tare and tret.

hì-siu^{n}, a man who spends much money on plays and actors, esp. on one particular company, making friends with the actors, esp. with the young men who represent the female parts. **tsòe hì-siu^{n}**, to act so, sometimes with the idea of sodomy. **tsòe hit-pí^{n} ê-siu^{n}**, to doat upon that company of actors.

siu^{n} (Cn.) **han-tsû-siu^{n}**, a long potato-bed.

siu^{n} (C.) **siu^{n}-sit**, = A. siau-sit, news (v. sit).

siu^{n} [R. siong, the two houses at the side of a large Chinese house; suburbs]. **se-siu^{n}**, books of stories or dramas about the Tang dynasty.

siu^{n} [R. siong, mutual, = col. sa^{n}, sio]. **siu^{n}-si**, deeply enamoured of some special person (counted disgraceful), (s. shrub). **siu^{n}-si-pī^{n}**, sick and wasting away through ungratified passion for another.

siu^{n} (same word?). **siu^{n}-si**, a sort of shrub (v. si), (s. mutual).

siu^{n} (R. siong), to inlay; to sew on an ornamental border on a dress, leaving a small margin of the original stuff at the edge, just as in inlaying. **siu^{n}-kim**, to inlay with gold. **siu^{n}-gûn**, to inlay with silver. **siu^{n}-gėk**, to inlay with jade-stone. **siu^{n}-kí^{n}**, to sew on an ornamental border (of different colour) near the edge of a dress. **siu^{n}-ôe**, do. on shoes. **siu^{n}-kún**, to put on such an ornamental border either (kún) at the very edge or (siu^{n}) a little way in from the edge (s. too much).

siu^{n} [R. siong, to injure; to hurt], too —; too much — (only used in combination).

tióh-siu^{n}, wounded; to be wounded.

siu^{n}-tsōe, too many. **siu^{n}-kún**, too hot, as liquid (s. inlay). **siu^{n}-tāng**, too heavy. **siu^{n}-tsá**, too early (&c. &c.) **khah-siu^{n}**—, too —; too much — (only in combination).

siû^{n} — **iu^{n}-siû^{n}**, to treat with great kindness and care; to take in a man, boarding, lodging, and treating him kindly, till he is able to shift for himself; to take great care of a child, pleasing it and keeping it in good temper.

siû^{n}, watery matter from a wound; soft slimy dirt. **lâu-siû^{n}**, to suppurate soft slimy matter. **lâu lâng-siû^{n}**, id. **tn̂g-á-siû^{n}**, mucous discharge in dysentery. **thê-siû^{n}**, soft mud, as on sea-beach. **chiù^{n}-chiù^{n} siû^{n}-siû^{n}**, softened and spoiled by damp. **iû^{n}-iû^{n} siû^{n}-siû^{n}**, growing soft or sticky with damp, as sweetmeats, coagulated jellies, and such eatables (s. common).

bé-iáh-siû^{n}, the dust, &c., that comes off a moth or such insect when touched.

pui^{n}-siû^{n} (C.), the juice of the "png" tree, used for mixing with incense.

siû^{n} [R. siông, common; usual; = col. siô, chhiûng]. **pí^{n}-siû^{n}**, commonplace; just tolerable; not very good. **iû^{n}-siû^{n}** (C. iông-siô), rather dull, slow, and mediocre in ability; without animation or temper.

siú^{n} [R. sióng, to reward; to gaze at with admiration and delight], to reward; to bestow, as a reward; a reward.

siú^{n}-hoe, to admire flowers. **siú^{n}-géh**, to gaze at the bright moon. **siú^{n}-teng**, to go about looking at the lamps on the Feast of Lanterns.

siú^{n}-sù, to bestow (as a superior), esp. as a reward. **pò-siú^{n}** (r.), to reward. **khò-siú^{n}**, to give rewards to soldiers after a victory. **thó-siú^{n}**, to ask a gratuity in addition to wages, *e.g.* as chair-bearers. **siā-siú^{n}**, to give thanks for a present, as actors and mandarins' servants do. **siú^{n} téng-tài**, to reward by giving official rank (military) and button. **siú^{n}-chî^{n}**, to give money as a reward. **siú^{n}-gûn**, id., silver. **siú^{n} gûn-pâi**, to reward with a medal.

siú^{n}-lién, to grant a favour to a third party out of respect for the person who asks it for him.

siú^{n}-thiap, a placard or advertisement offering a reward for something lost. **siú^{n}-keh**, a notice offering a reward for capture of criminal. **siú^{n}-kip**, id. **chhut siú^{n}-kip**, to issue such a notice.

hó-hiù^{n}-siú^{n} (esp. T.), good position and direction of grave or house for good fortune (v. hiù^{n}).

siú^{n} [R. sióng, = col. siū^{n}, to think]. **su-siú^{n}** (R.), to consider; to meditate.

siú^{n} — **khoà^{n}--liáu bô-niú^{n}-siú^{n}**, it seems much smaller than was expected. **thèh--liáu bô-niú^{n}-siú^{n}**, taking it up it seems much smaller or lighter than was supposed. **tsú--liáu bô-niú^{n}-siú^{n}**, shrinking to very small bulk in cooking, as vegetables, or as watered meat. **chiáh--liáu bô-niú^{n}-siú^{n}**, not satisfying hunger at all, as cakes or sweetmeats.

siú^{n} [R. sióng, dried meat]. **koe-siú^{n}**, dried fowl. **ah-siú^{n}**, dried duck brought from the north. **hî-siú^{n}** (Cn. hû-siū^{n}), dried fish.

siù^{n} [R. to look at; appearance; to assist; prime ministers; by change of tone from "siong," mutual]. **sêng-siù^{n}**, prime minister (v. sêng). **siù^{n}-kang**, confidential assistant or secretary of mandarin; respectful appellation of Kújîn and others (v. kang).

iū^{n}-siù^{n}, form and appearance. **kū-siù^{n}**, faded in appearance, as old dress. **sin-siù^{n}**, having a new look.

chheng-khì-siùⁿ, clean; cleanly. **phái^n-khoàⁿ-siùⁿ**, ugly, as man or affair. **lát-siùⁿ**, active and energetic; diligent at work. **phoà-siùⁿ**, maimed or greatly deformed. **khiū^n-siùⁿ**, very careful of one's dress, so as rarely to need new dress. **khièn-siùⁿ**, very narrow, exacting, and minute about money matters; niggardly and mean.

phì-siùⁿ, to talk scandal; to speak ill of a man behind his back; to taunt a man for his looks or for his niggardly ways. **keng-thóe phì-siùⁿ**, id. **phé-siùⁿ** (C.), id.

Siùⁿ, the animals used as the signs for the characters of the cycle of twelve. **tsáp-jī-siùⁿ**, these twelve animals, used to indicate the year in which a man is born. **tsáp-jī siⁿ-siùⁿ**, id., viz.:—

tsú,	thiú^n,	în,	báu,	sîn,	chī,
chhú,	gû,	hó͘,	thò͘,	lêng,	tsoâ,
rat.	cow.	tiger.	rabbit.	dragon.	snake.

gō͘,	bī,	sin,	iú,	sut,	hāi,
bé,	iûⁿ,	kâu,	koe,	káu,	ti,
horse.	goat.	monkey.	fowl.	dog.	pig.

lí, siùⁿ sím-mih^n, what animal is the sign of your natal year? **goá siùⁿ-hó͘**, I was born in one of the years that contains the character "în." **siùⁿ-ti**, born in a year that contains the character "hāi."

Siūⁿ [R. siōng, to value; yet; to rule; used in some official titles]. **hê-siūⁿ**, a Buddhist priest. **hôe-siūⁿ** (C.), id. **hê-siūⁿ-ôe**, shoes of Bud. pr. made with a single peak and very sharp; shoes of same shape, but more ornamental, are worn by children to keep off demons. **hê-siūⁿ-saⁿ**, dress fastened by strings, not by buttons, worn by Bud. pr., and also by children for same reason. **hê-siūⁿ-bō**, cap of Bud. pr. made with a ridge in the middle; also worn by children to keep off demons. **hê-siūⁿ-pài**, almost kneeling, and so saluting with palms put together. **hê-siūⁿ-pâng**, room of Bud. pr. in temple. **hê-siūⁿ-kiáⁿ**, a young priest who is the adopted son of a priest. **hê-siūⁿ-thûi**, said in joke of the bare head of Bud. pr. **hê-siūⁿ-thâu kòng kaⁿ-náⁿ**, bare head of Bud. pr. beating olives (said in joke). **chhát-sim, hê-siūⁿ-bīn**, robber's heart under priest's face. **iá kàu náⁿ hê-siūⁿ**, as wicked as a Bud. pr. **hê-siūⁿ bô-tn̂g-thâu-mn̂g hē-lâng-siâm**, said of a very niggardly fellow. **kau hê-siūⁿ, tò tāng-á-bí**, they who consort with Bud. priests must empty their rice-vessel.

siūⁿ-si, president of one of the six supreme boards at Pekin. **siūⁿ-su**, id.

Siūⁿ [R. siōng, above; up; = col. chiūⁿ, chhiūⁿ]. **siūⁿ-su** (r.), the Shoo-king, usually called "su-keng." **siūⁿ-si** (C.), id.

siūⁿ-poe, the bits of bamboo roots used for divining before idols. **chit-hù siūⁿ-poe**, a pair of these divining blocks. **chit-siūⁿ-poe**, the favourable throw of these blocks, one convex side up and one flat side up. **poàh chit-siūⁿ-poe**, to get this favourable throw. **poàh chit-siūⁿ**, id. **saⁿ-siūⁿ-poe**, this favourable throw repeated three times in succession.

Siūⁿ (Cn.), salted fish. **hî-siūⁿ** (esp. Cn.), = A. hî-siúⁿ, id.

Siūⁿ [R. siū, to give]. **siūⁿ-chheh**, = siū-chheh, to give out a lesson. **kúi-siūⁿ-chheh**, how many lessons consecutively? (as in one day).

Siūⁿ (R. sióng, = col. siúⁿ), to think; to consider; to think about, sometimes with the idea of desire. **siông-siūⁿ**, always thinking about —. **bat-siūⁿ**, diligent at work and regular in behaviour, as boy or lad. **gâu siūⁿ-lē**, intelligent; skilful in managing affairs. **gâu-siūⁿ**, good at planning or scheming, often with idea of cunning. **kāu-siūⁿ**, id. **ōe-hiáu-siūⁿ**, good at thinking or planning. **chhì-siūⁿ**, to consider; to try to think out. **chhim-siūⁿ**, to think deeply. **tiāⁿ-tiāⁿ siūⁿ**, to meditate silently. **gōng-siūⁿ**, foolish purpose; thinking of what one cannot get or cannot be done. **goá gōng-siūⁿ**, I beg to suggest that —. **kan-ta siūⁿ**, to think but find no good plan. **m̄-sái-siūⁿ**, no use of thinking or planning to get or accomplish it. **siūⁿ-khoàⁿ**, to consider carefully. **siūⁿ-lâi siūⁿ-khì**, to think in every direction. **siūⁿ-chhut**, to think out a good idea or plan. **siūⁿ-m̄-chhut**, to think but not be able to find out. **siūⁿ-bōe-kàu**, unable to get at the result by thinking. **bô-siūⁿ--kàu**, did not consider so far as that. **lâng-siūⁿ sé-bô-kàu**, what one could not think of before. **siūⁿ kàu-lóng-bô-jī**, think, but find it impracticable (v. jī). **siūⁿ kàu-sán**, to grow lean with anxious thought. **siūⁿ kàu--beh phùi-huih** (or "thò͘-huih"), to be painfully anxious (lit. till going to spit blood). **sim-koaⁿ siūⁿ kàu-beh-lak**, thinking till one almost faints. **siūⁿ-phoà sim-koaⁿ**, thinking very deeply and painfully. **siūⁿ-sim siūⁿ-koaⁿ**, deeply cogitating a plan for improper, injurious, or selfish ends. **teh-siūⁿ-sim**, secretly coveting or planning something selfish or improper, *e.g.* cheating, stealing, supplanting another, &c.

siūⁿ-toāⁿ, lazy. **siūⁿ-hēng**, indolent; selfishly lazy (v. hēng). **siūⁿ té-lē**, thinking of suicide.

siūⁿ-lóh-kè (C.), to regret having lost an opportunity; to repent or regret having done something. **siūⁿ thè-hòe** (C.), to regret or repent of what is past, often what cannot now be put right (v. thè).

Sm (Cn.), = A. som, ginseng.

Sng [R. song, mourning; funeral]. **sng-hà**, mourning dress.

Sng (R. soan), (C. suiⁿ), sour; acid; grieved; to steep in sour water, as clothes. **chhàu-sng**, soured so as to be spoiled. **sng-khùi**, having a sour smell. **sng-bī**, id.; a sour smell. **sng kiuh-kiuh**, very sour. **eh-sng**, to belch up sour stuff (v. eh).

sng-ám, soured rice-water. **ám-sng**, id. **sng-phun**, water in which rice was washed become sour. **sng-chhè**, vinegar.

sng-saⁿ, to steep clothes in soured rice-water, after washing, to make them whiter.

lí-á-sng, a sour preparation of plums. **soāiⁿ-á-sng**, sort of preserve made of mangoes. **ông-lâi-sng**, sort of preserve made of pine-apples. **iûⁿ-tô-sng**, do. of carambola. **sng-m̄-á**, a sort of preserve. **sng-tsó-ko**, a sort of preserve.

kiâm-sng-chháu, the oxalis (v. kiâm).

sim sng, the mind sad; distressed. **sim-koaⁿ sng-sng**, id.

Sng — **chhòng-ōe khì-sng--i**, to speak to him indirectly, blaming his bad practices. **chhòng-ōe sng-sóe--i**, id.

Sng [next word? cf. preceding word]. **sng-sóe**, uncomfortable feeling, as when colded (v. sóe).

Sng (R. soan), (C. suiⁿ), aching pains; feeling of pain and weariness about the bones or in the limbs. **sng-thiàⁿ**, id. **io-kut sng-thiàⁿ**, loins aching. **kut-thâu sng-thiàⁿ**, bones aching. **sng chit-tn̂g**, half the body sore or aching, as with long sitting, or with rheumatism. **kha sng**, legs feeling sore, as after a long walk. **chhiú sng**, arm tired and sore, as after lifting a heavy weight. **kha-chhiú sng**, limbs weary and sore. **chhiú-sng-chî^{n}**, a gratuity for some small service.

sng-ńg (C. sui^{n}-núi^{n}), weary aching feeling (v. ńg). **ńg-sng-khok**, slow in doing business (v. ńg).

ñg-sng (C. ûi^{n}-sui^{n}), pale and thin; yellow and emaciated. **ñg-sng-hiā**, said of very small ants (v. hiā).

sng-sóe, feeling of pain in bones, as when wearied or colded [same as previous words ?].

sí-sng, dispirited from bad treatment, as a child, daughter-in-law, or slave-girl.

sng [R. soan, teeth sore], (C. sui^{n}). **chhùi-khí sng**, teeth feeling pained or set on edge, as by eating something sour.

sng [R. song, a widow; lonely]. **ke-sng**, selfish and disobliging; unneighbourly or unfriendly (v. ke).

sng — **thâu-mñg-sng** (T.), = chhong-jî^{n}, a plant with prickly seeds.

sng [R. song, the mulberry], a surname. **sng-tsâi**, mulberry fruit. **sng-tsâi-hio̍h**, mulberry leaves. **sng-á-hio̍h**, id. **sng-tsâi-chhiū**, the mulberry tree. **sng-á-chhiū**, id. **sng-chhiū**, id. **sng-m̂**, mulberry fruit. **sng-sûi** (C.), id.

sng [R. sun, a grandchild], (C. sui^{n}), a surname. **sng-chin-jîn**, name of an idol; a god of medicine.

sng [R. song, frost, congealed or frozen], hoar-frost. **sng-seh**, frost and snow (v. seh). **kiên-sng**, to freeze; to congeal. **lo̍h-sng**, hoar-frost forming.

sng-kàng, the term on or about Oct. 23d. **ngiâ^{n} sng-kàng**, procession of military mandarins at the time supposed to be the beginning of frost. **sng-kàng-hoe**, a shrub with flowers like double mallow or lavatera, which blossoms at that term.

phī^{n}-sng, arsenic (v. phī^{n}). **phī-sng**, id. (P. phī^{n}-chhng). **phi-sng** (T.), id. **ke-ná-sng**, sometimes said for quinine, in imitation of the sound.

thñg-sng, sugar-candy (v. thn̂g). **sng-tsúi**, fine syrup.

tàng-sng, having very contracted views (said in scolding or chiding). **lí chin-tàng-sng**, your ideas are very mean and contracted, *e.g.* supposing that I cannot do what I am quite able for.

sng (R. soan, = col. chhoa^{n}, chhoà^{n}), (C. sui^{n}), a small pin for holding anything in its place; a small bolt or pin, as for door or window; to put in a small pin or wedge, as into a crack, or in order to make something firm. **sng-mñg**, to fasten a door with a wedge or small pin.

thih-sng, a small iron pin or wedge for keeping something in its place. **chhâ-sng**, wooden wedge or pin. **tek-sng**, bamboo do. **kim-sng**, the wooden bolts that support the lower support (ē-kim) of a helm.

sng (C. sui^{n}). **chhia-sng**, an axle; an axle-tree. **chhia-lûn-sng**, id.

sñg (R. chēng ?), classifier of large cakes cooked by steaming. **chit-sñg-ké**, one large steamed cake. **toā-sñg**, a large cake. **ka-nñg-sñg**, the whole cake.

lâng-sñg, a frame or vessel in which cakes are cooked by steaming. **lâng-sñg-phe**, thin slips of wood for making it. **pa̍k lâng-sñg**, to make this sort of frame.

sńg (R. sún), (C. sńg, súi^{n}), to injure; to lay waste; to waste; ruined; greatly weakened by disease. **sńg-ńg**, to waste or spoil very much; to lay waste and plunder. **si-kòe sńg-ńg**, to lay waste or spoil everywhere. **put-chí-sńg**, much injured, as health; much exhausted by hard work; much worn and spoiled, as a thing in constant use. **gâu-sńg**, wasteful, fond of extravagance or of bad pleasures.

phah-sńg, to waste; to lose, as money, &c. **chin phah-sńg**, a very great loss, *e.g.* death of influential relative. **phoà-sńg**, dilapidated; tattered. **sńg-sit**, to lose, as things taken away, spoiled, or lost. **sńg-tñg**, to spoil, either accidentally or of set purpose; to dirty and spoil a place, as poultry or pigs.

sńg-teng, to lose male children, nephews, &c., as family; or male inhabitants, as village. **sńg-gán**, injurious to the eyes, as late writing or sewing, or as some sorts of food. **sńg-sîn**, to injure one's self by long night work, or by gambling, plays, &c., so as not to get proper sleep. **sńg-sîn, kah bô-bin**, id.; said also of an affair giving much trouble but no profit. **sńg-sin**, to exert one's self very much; ill or wounded severely. **sńg-khùi tio̍h-la̍t**, causing or requiring much toil or trouble. **chhut-thâu sńg-kak**, to hurt one's self by meddling in the affairs of others, or by taking responsibility for others. **sńg-chî^{n}**, to waste money. **sńg-mih^{n}**, to use things wastefully, or spoil them.

sńg (C. id.) **khièn-sńg** (not Cn.), superstitious observances (v. khièn).

sńg [R. sún, a tenon]. **toá^{n}-toá^{n} khang-sńg**, = toá^{n}-toá^{n} khang-sún, constantly plotting improper ways for getting money out of people.

tńg-sńg (T.), to set right an affair, or get gain in a business, that seemed almost hopeless.

sńg [R. sóng, comfortable]. **khin-sńg**, light and active, as man; light and easily carried, as thing.

sǹg (C. sùi^{n}), to tie very tight. **sǹg-ân**, id. **sǹg-kín**, id. **sǹg kàu-hiah-kín**, to tie so very tight. **sǹg kàu bô-khùi**, to tie till unable to breathe. **sǹg-oá**, to tie up very tight; to hug.

sǹg-io, narrower at the middle, as the shape of an hour-glass. **khah-sǹg**, id.

pak-tó siau-sǹg-thià^{n}, severe gripping pain in belly.

sǹg (Cn.), = A. soàn (garlic). **sǹg-ngá**, garlic. **sǹg-thâu**, roots of garlic.

kúi-sǹg, a wild plant like garlic.

sǹg [R. soàn, to calculate, = col. siàu], (C. sùi^{n}), to count; to calculate; to number. **tá^{n}-sǹg**, to suppose; to consider. **phah-sǹg**, id. **phah lí-ê-sǹg**, consider for yourself; make your own calculation. **ō-phah-tit-sǹg**, can be relied on, as a trusty man, or as a plan sure to succeed, *e.g.* a safe way of making money; said also of having some money or property that can be depended on without the uncertainty of work or trade. **chhien-sǹg bān-sǹg, m̄-tàh--tio̍h thi^{n} chit-sǹg**, all human calculations are not worth one purpose of Heaven.

chiàu-sǹg, justly; honestly.

sǹg-gia̍h, to count how many; to include in the amount, as an item (v. gia̍h). **chiū^{n}-sǹg**, to include in the calculation or amount (v. chiū^{n}). **bô-beh kap-i-sǹg tsāi-lāi**, will not count him to be of the same class with ourselves. **sǹg-tsòe** — (C. sùi^{n}-tsò —), to consider to be —, to count as —.

sǹg-jit, to count or calculate by days (not by months), as wages of labour, or as heavy usurious interest of money. **sǹg-tā^{n}-jit**, to make a mistake in calculating the day, or the number of days. **sǹg-khí**, to begin a calculation (as of wages) at such a date.

57

sǹg-miā^{n}, to tell fortunes by cabalistic calculations. **sǹg-miā**^{n} **sien-si**^{n}, a man who tells fortunes in this way.

sǹg-siàu, to calculate (v. siàu). **sǹg háp-kiōng**, to perform addition; adding up the total. **kè-sǹg joā-tsōe**, count up the sum total. **thâu-bé-sǹg**, counting first and last inclusive. **liên-tē sǹg**, counting the weight of the bag in the amount. **sǹg-bōe-sī**, innumerable (v. si). **hâm-kháu sǹg**, to calculate mentally. **hoâ-sǹg**, to calculate roughly (v. hoâ). **àn-sǹg**, to make a rough calculation, mentally or on the fingers. **kek-sǹg**, to calculate roughly (v. kek). **chhui-sǹg**, to calculate mentally. **bóe-bōe sǹg-hun**, in business calculate to a fraction.

sǹg-poâ^{n}, an abacus. **sǹg-poâ**^{n}**-chí**, balls of abacus. **kiáh sǹg-poâ**^{n}, to take the abacus and calculate. **phah sǹg-poâ**^{n}, id. **tāng sǹg-poâ**^{n}, id. **thak sǹg-poâ**^{n}, id. **thak-sǹg**, id. **sǹg-poâ**^{n} **thak kàu-bô-kì**^{n}, to be very minute in calculation by it. **sǹg-poâ**^{n}**-kì**^{n}, the rods or wires on which the balls of the abacus run.

sǹg-hēng, disobliging: intentionally lazy and unwilling to help beyond what is obligatory. **gâu-sǹg-sek**, id.

SNGH, to snuff up (cf. chhngh, to snuffle outwards). **sngh-phī**^{n}, to snuff up the nose. **sngh phī**^{n}**-hun**, to take snuff. **sngh soa-ióh**, to snuff up medicines taken like snuff.

SO (R. id.), to rub with the hand; to roll on the palm, as thread. **so-loáh**, to stroke smooth, as cat's back; to get round a man by pleasant talk; to get parties reconciled, &c. (v. loáh). **lām-sám so**, to feel about in the dark; to feel, as a thief, for something to pilfer. **bong so tī**^{n}, to touch and take improper liberties with, as with woman.

so-chhiú, to rub one's hands together; also said of coming back empty-handed when we expected to get money. **so chhiú-chiú**^{n}, id. **khang-chhiú so**, coming back empty-handed instead of getting the expected money.

so-kng, to rub smooth (s. next word). **so-iû**, to rub on oil or paint. **so-hún**, to put on face-powder, as on face or body. **so ióh-oân**, to roll pills. **so-î**^{n}, to roll anything into round balls. **so iên-sái**, to fill dollars with lead by means of quicksilver. **so-soà**^{n}, to twist a thread by rolling it on the palm. **so chì**^{n}**-kǹg**, twist thus the twine used for stringing cash.

SO [R. sɵ, to search, as by police]. **so kng-kng**, all taken away, as by robbers or by soldiers.

SO (cf. sô, sō). **àm-so-so**, very dark.

SO [R. to instigate; cf. sō]. (Cn. sɵ). **kiau-so**, to instigate to evil, esp. to quarrels; to sow discord. **so-sú** (C.), id. **poan--lâng so--lâng**, to tell lies or gross exaggerations so as to injure people.

SO [R. to agitate; to disturb]. **hong-so**, rambling about for amusement, often for bad pleasures.

SO — **lô-so**, troublesome; annoying with repeated and useless talk. **lô-lô so-so**, id. **lo-so**, id.

SO [reduplication of "po"]. **po-so**, to flatter; to cajole, as obsequious man. **po-lo-so**, id. **gâu po-so--lâng**, fond of flattering people.

SO (R. id.), a shuttle. **so-á**, id. **hî**^{n}**-so**, id. **so-á-chhi**^{n}, a southern constellation of four bright stars in diamond shape (Southern Cross?). **jit-goa̍t jû-so, kong-im sū-chièn**, days, months, and time are like a shuttle or an arrow.

kiô-so, the piers of a bridge, shaped like a shuttle. **bāng-so**, a large wooden bodkin for making nets.

bí-so-ké, small shuttle-shaped cakes inclosing stuffing. **thó chit--ê oá**^{n}**-ko bí-so**, I got nothing for my pains, *e.g.* trying to recover a bad debt.

SO (same word?). **káu-bú-so**, a very good plump shuttle-shaped fish with small scales; it is about a foot long. **so-á-hî**, a smaller sort, also good to eat. **soa-so**, a smaller sort with sharp head and no scales. **khé-so** (C.), id. **kim-so**, a sort of small fish.

SO [R. sɵ, sapan-wood]. **so-bák**, a sort of reddish wood; sapan-wood. **so-bák-ko**, a purple paint made from sapan-wood, used for colouring things, esp. for idolatrous purposes.

SÔ (cf. sóh), to creep; to crawl; to go walking about. **sô-lô**, to crawl or walk about here and there. **kan-ta sô**, to go about without any definite aim; to crawl about, as a snake, not hurting any one. **sì-kòe-sô**, to wander about, *e.g.* looking at things, &c.

SÔ (cf. so, sō). **ɵ-lô-sô**, very black. **ɵ-sô-sô**, id. **àm-sô-sô**, very dark.

SÓ (R. id.), a Chinese padlock which shuts itself by a spring (classifier phì^{n}); to lock such a padlock; to put long stone slabs across a road to keep it from being swept away by water. **só--lóh-khì**, lock it fast. **só-tiâu--teh**, locked fast. **só-mn̂g**, to lock a door (all by Chinese padlock). **só-âu**, to catch another's neck in fighting; to bite the neck and hold it fast, as a dog does. **khui-só**, to open a lock. **pàng-só**, to take off a man's chains. **phah-só**, to make padlocks.

só-sî, key of Chinese padlock. **só-khak**, outer frame or socket of Chinese padlock. **só-sim**, the other half of the padlock, which goes into the frame. **só-niû**^{n}, the straight pin of it, which goes through the staple. **só-kúi**, the spring which catches the tongue when put in. **só-chhi**, the spring and wards of it.

kun-tsú-só, a very small padlock. **gék-só-pâi**, a small flat imitation padlock, worn by child as amulet. **pek-ka-só**, a small silver padlock bought with money given by many families, worn by child as amulet.

SÓ (T.), = A. chhó [R. só, small; minute]. **só-chhùi**, = A. chhó-chhùi, troublesome to settle, as involved affair with many intricate details. **bōe-só-chhùi**, all quite plain and straight, so that no trouble need be feared from it. **kap--i só-chhùi**, to have a great deal of troublesome and unpleasant or angry discussion with him.

SÓ (R. sɵ́), elder brother's wife; it is appended to the personal name of the husband as an appellation of his wife, when we would use "hia^{n}" or "ko" for himself, *e.g.* **pan-só**, the wife of a man called "pan-ko" or "pan-hia^{n}."

hia^{n}**-só**, elder brother's wife. **ko-só** (Cn.), id. **á-só**, do. (said by husband's younger brother in addressing her). **goán-só**, my elder brother's wife. **jī-só**, wife of second oldest brother. **tsun-só** (polite), your elder brother's wife. **lēng-só** (polite), id.

SÓ (cf. sió). **só-kńg**, = sió-kńg, a sort of cuttle-fish.

SÒ [R. dry; parched; scorched], causing thirst or having a heating effect, as some eatables; to absorb water, &c., as dry land, or as a sponge. **sò-jièt**, having a heating effect, as fat food. **sò-pé**, having a heating and strengthening effect.

ta-sò, dry; crisp; too dry, having no softness or gentle moisture, as skin; dry and hard, as face; poor. **thi**^{n} **ta-sò**, weather very dry, as in north wind. **thi**^{n}**-khì ta-sò**, id. **chhùi ta-sò**, very thirsty. **koa-**

sò, dry and hard, as one's skin in north wind, or as skin of old man. **koa-koa sò-sò**, id. **seng-khu kơ-sò**, dry and having small slightly itchy eruptions, as skin; dry, as skin, either slightly feverish or naturally so.

bīn sò-sò, surface not glossy, as of cloth; face rough.

ân-sò, hard up for cash. **sò-siap**, shrivelled, as skin; scant of money (v. siap).

sò-sip, to suck up damp, as sawdust, &c. **sò-koā^n**, to absorb perspiration, as dress. **sò-tsúi**, to absorb water, as sponge or floor. **sán-chhân gâu sò-tsúi** (barren land absorbs much water), a lean man eating much, or gains swallowed up by creditors.

Sò [R. to go quickly; hasty; violent]. **sò-sèng**, quick-tempered; irascible. **sò-sut**, too hasty in habit of speaking or doing things (v. sut). **sò-sim**, much excited with desire to get something or to have something done very speedily. **sò-pō** (r.), violently rude; headstrong and violent in temper.

Sò [R. to sweep, =col. sàu]. **chè-sò**, to sweep the graves clean, repair them, and make offerings on the days called chhi^n-miâ^n and toā-koā^n.

pùn-sò, dirt; sweepings; manure or filth. **pê pùn-sò**, to rake up dirt. **sò-âm**, a sink. **sò-chî^n**, a cesspool for such dirty water, &c., as is not available for manure.

Sō (cf. so, sô). **àm-sō-sō**, very dark.

Sō [mere reduplication]. **hō-lō-sō**, to express assent without consideration. **hái^n-lō-sō**, to do work in a superficial way without energy or care. **hāi^n-ló-sō**, cry of men working a sculling-oar together; to assent to or follow whatever another says or does.

Sō — **sō-hong**, to drift slowly before the wind, as vessel that has taken in as much sail as is possible. **khan-lâi-sō**, to arrange the vessel so as to drift as slowly as possible.

Sō [R. so, to instigate; cf. sū], to cause dissensions by instigation, slanders, and such bad means. **sái-sō**, to instigate to evil, *e.g.* to quarrels or feuds. **sō--lâng**, to incite people to deep enmity and open feud, esp. when already quarrelling a little. **sō--lâng oan-ke**, id.

sō-káu sa^n-kā, to set dogs to fight; (said of stirring up or inflaming enmity and feuds).

Sơ [R. to come to life again]. **iâ-sơ**, Jesus. **iâ-sơ-kàu**, Protestant Christianity; the Protestant Church. **iâ-sơ sèng-kàu**, id. **iâ-sơ chèng-kàu**, id.

Sơ (R. id.), a surname. **sơ-chiu**, Soo-chow. **sơ-hâng**, Soo-chow and Hang-chow. **sơ--ê**, from Soo-chow, as goods. **sơ-pán**, printed at Soo-chow. **sơ-chien**, superfine paper from Soo-chow. **sơ-gėk**, fine white jade-stone. **sơ-tó**, embossed panelling, as on a door.

kang-sơ, Kiang-soo province, named from Kiang-ning-foo (Nankin) and Soo-chow.

sơ-io, stooping in gait (v. io).

chí-sơ, a sort of medicine.

Sơ [R. name of a plant?]. **báng-á-sơ**, a feathery shrub with white blossoms, used for making the "báng-hun," which is burned to keep away mosquitoes.

Sơ [R. to search, as police, =col. so]. **sơ-ka**, to search the house, as of a mandarin in confiscating his property; to confiscate. **sơ kng-kng**, everything stolen or taken away.

Sơ [R. distant; not related; =col. soe]. **chhi^n-sơ**, unacquainted with a matter; inexperienced; raw and unpolished, as a composition. **chhi^n sơ-sơ**, id. **jîn-tē lióng-sơ**, people and place both strange to us. **pōe-chhin n̂g-sơ**, to leave relatives and make up with strangers. **pōe-chhin hiòng-sơ**, id.

sơ-hut (R.), careless.

Sơ [R. sort of butter made in the north], crisp; easily crumbling, as eatables; toasted or parched at the fire till crisp; stiff, as well-starched dress.

sơ-iû, fried crisp with fat. **chien-khi-sơ**, fry till crisp. **chhá-khi-sơ**, parch over the fire till crisp.

sơ-piá^n, crisp short cakes. **kháu-sơ-piá^n**, sort of crisp cake made with sugar. **chhùi-kháu-sơ**, id. **khiö-sơ** (Cn.), id. **iû-sơ-piá^n**, sort of cake. **bé-tôe-sơ**, round hollow cakes with sugar inside, made at Tâng-oa^n, very good to eat. **bé-tê-sơ** (C.), id. **bah-kut-sơ**, a dish made of pulverized pig's bones, onions, &c.

bô-sơ (T.), said of a dress not starched stiff enough, or that has lost the starch.

Sơ — **sơ-khak-chîm**, a crab that is firm and full of meat.

Sơ (cf. siau). **sơ-sap**, dark and shrivelled, as face of poor, miserable, or sick man; much decayed, as house, village, or family.

Sơ — **khang sơ-sơ**, empty. **khang lơ-sơ**, id.

Sơ (Cn.), = A. so; in many words in the several tones.

Sớ (sơ? or some other tone?). **kháu--sớ** (Cn.), so and so; said to avoid naming a person or thing which both parties understand to be meant (v. kháu).

Sớ [R. that which; he who; a place], (C. usually "sé," but sometimes "sớ;" *e.g.* sớ-tsāi, sớ-hùi), the relative pronoun: he who, that which, they who, those which, &c.; it precedes the antecedent, and is placed quite differently from the other relative particles "ê" and "chiá;" in combination with verbs it forms a phrase like a verbal noun or gerund.

sớ-tsāi, a place. **bô-sớ bô-tsāi**, no place; having no place. **gū-sớ** (C. gī-sé), a lodging-place; lodgings. **keng-i-sớ**, room for visitors changing their dress when they call to worship the dead (v. keng). **hó-jîm-sớ**, a good situation for a mandarin making money (v. jîm).

sớ-í, therefore (v. í).

sớ-hùi, expenses: money for expenses (v. hùi).

sớ-kiâ^n, behaviour; conduct. **hó-sớ-kiâ^n**, easy and unconstrained in intercourse; not wishing to be treated with ceremony. **sớ-tsòe**, behaviour; conduct.

sớ-kóng, that which is said. **lí sớ-kóng**, what you say. **goá sớ-hō--i**, what I give him. **goá sớ-ū**, what I have. **i sớ-beh**, what he wishes, &c. &c.

bû-sớ put-ûi, addicted to all sorts of wickedness. **bû-sớ put-chì**, id. **bû-sớ put-tsāi** (R.), omnipresent. **bû-sớ put-ti** (R.), omniscient. **bû-sớ put-lêng** (R.), omnipotent. **tang-sai bû-sớ-put**, willing to take anything.

Sớ [R. sờ, to calculate; a number]. **sớ-pái**, constantly; over and over; every time.

Sờ [R. plain; not ornamented; simplicity; original colour; formerly; usually]. **sờ-sờ**, plain; not ornamented; plain-looking; not good-looking. **sờ-tiû**, plain silk; not flowered. **sờ-bō**, plain cap of black cotton with no red. **phok-sờ**, quiet, simple, and plain, as a dress; not gaudy; simple and quiet in taste and manners, as man not given to display or vanity. **phak-sờ**, id. **sờ-sim-lân**, a variety of the flower "lân-hoe," with plain-coloured centre.

sờ-tsu, string of beads used by Buddhist priest.

pêng-sờ, formerly; hitherto; habitually in time past. **sờ-sî**, id. **sờ-siông**, id.

Sờ [R. a formal statement, as to a superior; sort of written prayer; to explain, as a commentary; by change of tone from "sơ," distant, not related], a Tauist or Buddhist written prayer, having a list of names written on it; it is read aloud and burned, so that the persons named may be protected by the gods. **sờ-bûn** (R.), id. **thák-sờ**, to read such a prayer aloud before burning it. **liām-sờ**, id.

tsù-sờ, a commentary on a commentary.

Sờ [R. to inform; to make one's defence; to accuse], to make one's defence in court, done in writing. **kò-sờ**, to put in written defence or accusation in court (v. kò). **chhut-sờ**, to come forward and enter the written defence. **sờ-tiāⁿ**, the written plea in defence, entered in court; it is often virtually or really a counter accusation. **sờ-oan**, to make defence against unjust accusation.

sờ-sû, a paper burned before an idol (usually Sêng-hông-iâ), stating that we are guiltless of crime; this Tauist rite is performed when suffering from what is supposed to be the effect of some imprecation.

hun-sờ, to explain one's conduct or make statement or defence before a superior, *e.g.* before master, or influential person, or official.

Sờ [R. to calculate; number; an account; fated number; fate; destiny].

pō-sờ, a plan; a contrivance (v. pơ).

lé-sờ, ceremony; politeness. **chiàu-lé chiàu-sờ**, according to the rules of ceremony or politeness. **bô-lé bô-sờ**, utterly without good breeding; very unpolite.

kè-sờ, price.

iú-sờ, not very many. **sờ-chhù**, several times. **put-kè kì-sờ**, innumerable. **tsáp-sờ-ê**, a little over ten (of anything). **tsáp-sờ-nîⁿ**, rather more than ten years of time.

tāi-ka-sờ, family flourishing, as to wealth, rank, or influence (v. ka).

siu-sờ, fated number of one's years (v. siū). **kiap-sờ**, fated time of great calamity (v. kiap). **tāi-sờ lân-tô**, fated death cannot be avoided (v. tô). **thien-sờ**, fate, the decree of Heaven, as to great calamities. **tsoâ-siong hé-eh, thiⁿ-tōe-sờ**, calamities by serpents and tigers are decreed by nature. **sùt-sờ** (R.), all sorts of magical and superstitious ceremonies. **chhok jī-sờ**, to try one's fortune by drawing lots with words on them. **thiah jī-sờ**, to tell fortune by taking a word to pieces, and giving meanings to the several parts. **kóng-ké, thiah jī-sờ**, said of man lounging about and talking idly.

Sờ (previous word?). **bī-sờ**, taste; flavour (v. bī).

Sờ (Cn.), = A. sò, in some words.

Sô (Cn.), = A. sê, hanging down.

Sö (Cn.), = A. sè. **sö-lêng-tsûn**, trying to excel each other at the race of the dragon-boats. **sö-pê-lêng-tsûn**, id.

Soa (R. sa), sand; small gravel. **kim-soa**, sort of fine sand used as emery powder; gold-dust; sand containing gold. **gûn-soa**, fine white sand, from Quemoy. **hái-soa**, sea-sand. **soa-he**, mortar made with lime and sand. **he-soa**, lime and sand ready to be mixed. **thô-soa**, coarse sand mixed with clay, for building. **thô-bí-soa**, fine gravel. **bé-khí-soa**, common gravel. **soa-bú**, small gravel, like small pease. **soa-bú-liáp, khoeh iáh-ū-iû** (some oil can be pressed even from gravel), some money can be squeezed out of even the poorest man.

soa-lėk, green without gloss, as cloth.

soa-tāng, sand ballast. **soa-tē**, a sand-bag.

soa-soàⁿ, a sand-bank. **soa-ûn**, a small sand-bank. **soa-oaⁿ**, a sandy beach, fit to be used for landing. **soa-pho**, a sandy beach. **khoe-soa-pơ**, sandy bed of a stream. **soa-hn̂g**, a sandy field or plot of ground.

soa-lîm, having urinary calculus.

soa-kòe, itch in small scattered granulated groups.

soa-hê, shrimps from sandy beaches. **soa-lâ**, sort of shell-fish (v. lâ). **soa-chhêng**, sort of edible sea-slug. **soa-tsûi**, an inferior sort of crab. **soa-thn̂g**, sort of small fish. **soa-so**, another sort of fish.

Soa — **hoan-soa**, to roll about on the ground, as a horse.

Soa — **soa-sap**, slippery and troublesome to deal with in business, as man (v. sap).

Soa (C.), to let small things fall, as rice or crumbs from a table. **phah-ka-soa**, id. **soa-loa**, id. **soa-loa--khì**, to get lost by dropping from the table, as small things. **soa-hiet-kák**, to let small things fall (as from table) so that they are lost. **soa-iû**, to let drops fall from an oil-jug.

Soa (better "sa"). **soa-bui** (esp. C.), = sa-bui, eyes small and almost closed, as if overcome with sleep, &c.

Soa [R. sa; cf. col. se], the shark. **soa-hî**, id. **ơ-soa**, a large dark very dangerous shark. **liông-bûn-soa**, the most edible sort of shark. **gōng-á-soa**, a large man-eating shark. **hé-soa**, a large-headed dangerous shark. **káu-bú-soa**, another sort, with small head and long tail. **káu-soa**, id. **ke-kòe-soa** (C.), another sort (lit. cock's-comb shark).

soa-sit, shark's fins, edible.

thẹh-soa (C.), = thẹh-sɛ, = A. thoah-se, the sole.

Soa (R. sa), (Cn. se), cholera and violent colics. **làu-thờ-soa**, cholera. **tiòh-soa**, to have a sudden attack of severe colic, cholera, or cramp in the stomach. **liáh-soa**, to shampoo or pinch the arms and legs, in order to cure it. **leh-soa**, to pinch the neck for a slight colic or pain in stomach.

soa-iòh, medicine for colic or cholera, taken by the nostrils like snuff.

Soa [R. sa? name of a plant]. **sam-soa**, the port of Sam-sah, near Fuh-ning (hok-lêng), between Fuhchau and Wenchau.

Soa (P.) **soa-á**, a sort of tree; its wood is moderately tough.

Soá (R. sú), to remove to another place. **poaⁿ-soá**, id., either things, or as persons changing their residence. **chhien-soá** (r.), to migrate or change residence. **soá-khui**, to remove out of the way. **soá-ūi**, to move or remove to another place, as men or things. **poaⁿ-soá-ūi**, id., either dwelling or things. **chhiâu-soá-ūi**, to move things slightly, without much alteration of their position. **soá-tsai**, to transplant (v. tsai). **saⁿ-jit soá-tang, sì-jit soá-sai**, constantly changing one's dwelling.

soá-pō, to walk with short steps, as man with chain on feet, or with sore foot, or as a child. **soá-kha**, to change the position of one's feet, as for relief in long standing. **kim-ke soá-kha** (C.), the golden fowl changing its feet (said to be the cause of earthquakes).

Soá [R. — Cn. sá; C. soá, to play or amuse one's self; cf. sá]. **kiâⁿ-soá**, to take a walk for exercise or amusement. **lâi kiâⁿ-soá**, come away with me for amusement; often means, come and visit bad houses.

soá, a very tough sort of rock, extremely difficult to work. **soá-kak**, the hardest parts of it. **he-soá**, mortar made of lime mixed with this tough rock.

soá [R. sé, sö, to wash]. **soá-kháu** (C.), to wash the mouth.

soà [R. siok, continuous; connected in unbroken succession], to add a piece; (to succeed to); to do in addition; also (as adverb before some verbs). **sa^n-soà**, connected in unbroken order or succession. **sio-soà**, id. **liên-soà**, doing several things in succession without stopping.

soà beh —, also will —. **chiū^n toā-pang, soà beh-chiū^n bîn-chhn̂g** (getting on the step will also get on the bed), get an inch and take an ell. **soà-ū**, and also there are —.

soà-chiap, to succeed to (v. chiap).

soà khah-tn̂g, to make longer, as a rope, by tying on a piece, or as a queue by making the false queue longer. **soà-tsáng**, to add a false queue to one's own hair; the false queue.

sūn-soà, to take advantage of an opportunity so as to do something more; in view of the opportunity. **sēng-soà** (?), id. **sêng-soà**, to take the opportunity of something being done to do or get something else done.

soà-soà-kiâ^n, to walk on a long time without resting, *e.g.* several hours or a whole day.

soà (cf. soā). **hong soà-soà, tsúi toā-toā** (T.), his word cannot be relied upon (lit. wind loud, water large).

soā [R. sok, quick; rapid]. **sī-soā**, quick.

soā (cf. sà, sā). **soā-soā-háu**, noise, as of running water, or of stiff cloth, or of such stiff thing shaken, or of walking on a hard road, or of rats or robbers on roof. **soā-soā-kiò**, rustling sound, as of stiff dress, or of reeds or trees. **sih-sih soā-soā**, sound as of a sieve shaken, or of moderately heavy rain without wind.

soa^n (R. san), (T. soai^n, in some phrases), a mountain; a hill; an island; dry land or the shore as opposed to water; wild, as a plant.

soa^n-tang, Shan-tung province. **soa^n-sai**, Shan-si province. **tn̂g-soa^n**, China (v. tn̂g). **tâng-soa^n**, Tong-san (between Swatow and Amoy). **tang-soa^n**, the east hill or mountain; name of several hills and villages. **kim-soa^n**, gold-producing countries (v. kim).

soa^n-sū, land in general, either mainland or island (v. sū). **soa^n-sī** (C.), id. **ē-mn̂g-soa^n**, Amoy Island. **kim-mn̂g-soa^n**, Quemoy Island.

soa^n-téng, dry land; on land; on a hill (+). **soa^n-lō͘**, route by land. **soa^n-chhau**, drill or review on land. **soa^n-lāi**, interest for money lent on shore (v. lāi, "interest"), (+). **chē-soa^n--ê**, the owner or charterer of a vessel staying on shore. **chiàh-soa^n**, to gain bit by bit on the land, as vessel tacking. **khí-soa^n**, to go ashore. **chiū^n-soa^n**, to go ashore; to climb a hill; to go to the fields from a village. **lôe-chiū^n-soa^n**, to run aground (v. chiū^n). **chhiong-soa^n**, to run a vessel aground intentionally. **oá-soa^n**, to approach the shore, as vessel. **hàh^n-soa^n**, to hug the shore. **iû-soa^n**, to go about the country in procession with idol, &c. (v. iû).

soa^n-hái, land and sea; land and water. **iû-soa^n iû-hái**, to go about on sea and land, as the idol ông-iâ. **pau-soa^n pau-hái**, daring to take the responsibility of anything anywhere. **chiâ^n-soa^n chiâ^n-hái**, in vast quantities. **tui-soa^n chek-hái**, to gather things in vast quantities. **soa^n-téng hái-ē**, on land, or sea, or river (+). **î-soa^n tó-hái**, to move mountains and seas.

chhut-soa^n, to bury. **soa^n-sîn**, the guardian spirit of a mountain. **hoah soa^n-lêng**, to call the good influence of the mountain, as at burial (v. lêng). **hoah-soa^n**, id. **soa^n-bú**, the peak where the auspicious influence has its source. **thióng-soa^n**, a hill used as a common burying-ground. **soa^n-kúi** (lit. mountain ghost), a man who acts as agent for buying grave-sites.

soa^n-tô͘, a picture or plan of hills, either for looking at or for guiding to a grave-site. **soa^n-sè**, form or appearance of mountains. **soa^n-sì** (C.), id. **soa^n-sè put-chí-koâi^n**, mountains very high. **soa^n-mn̂g**, outer gate of hill temple. **āu-piah-soa^n ū-khò**, he has very powerful supporters (*e.g.* your adversary has). **āu-piah-soa^n kiā**, said of a man who has powerful influence to support or back him, or of a man in business who has so much property that his business does not much concern him. **î-soa^n**, to remove mountains (v. î), (+).

hoe-soa^n, a rockery. **hoe-tn̂g-soa^n** (Cn.), a place for gambling with the "hoe-hē."

soa^n-bīn, the surface of the ground, as let for cultivation, but other rights reserved. **khoà^n-soa^n**, to guard fields from robbery, as a powerful man does for payment.

soa^n-tiû^n, the country as opposed to cities and towns. **soa^n-tiû^n-lâng**, a man from the country; a clown; a rustic. **soa^n-lāi**, mountainous country (+). **soa^n-lāi-kâu, chiàh chhiū-chí** (monkey from the mountains, living on seeds of trees), said in joke of an uncultivated mountaineer. **soa^n-hāu** (vulg.), a clown. **soa^n-kan**, among the mountains. **soa^n-kha**, the foot of a mountain; at the foot of the mountain. **soa^n-ē**, just at the foot of the mountain. **chhim-soa^n**, far among the mountains. **soa^n-pi^n**, id. **soa^n-pi^n kok-lok-phāng**, id., and in deep valleys. **soa^n-phāng**, a cleft in the hills, as where a stream or road comes through. **soa^n-khang**, a cave or hollow in the hills (v. khang). **soa^n-lang**, a narrow valley (v. lang). **soa^n-khi^n**, a ravine. **soa^n-pe͘**, a grassy part of a hill, level or nearly so. **soa^n-tōe**, cultivated ground on a hill. **soa^n-khàm**, a precipitous bank, as on shore or at a stream. **soa^n-nâ^n**, a wood among the mountains.

soa^n-thâu, a hill, esp. a rounded hill. **soa^n-chiam**, a mountain peak. **soa^n-bé**, top of a mountain; end or extremity of the mountain. **soa^n-bé-liu**, top of hill. **soa^n-chit**, the very ridge of the hill. **soa^n-phiâ^n**, gently sloping base of hill. **soa^n-lūn**, long, low, flat hill (v. lūn). **soa^n-niā^n**, shoulder of hill. **soa^n-liōng** (C.), id. **soa^n-lēng** (C.), sloping shoulder of hill. **soa^n-niá^n**, a mountain path or pass; mountains in general (v. niá^n). **soa^n-io**, a path along a ledge half-way up a mountain. **poà^n-soa^n**, half-way up a mountain. **chit-tsō-soa^n**, a mass of mountains. **chit-ûn-soa^n, chit-ûn hiu^n-siā**, villages and mountain ridges alternately.

hoâi-soa^n, sort of medicine (v. hoâi). **soa^n-iòh**, id. **soa^n-iòh-tsû**, id. **soa^n-tê**, kind of wild plant (not any sort of tea). **soa^n-bé-chî**, sort of plant and drug. **soa^n-chhi^n**, sort of wild plant (v. chhi^n). **soa^n-koa^n-lân**, a wild sort of "koa^n-lân" flower; (so with many other plants, wild sorts, or plants like them).

soa^n-káu, a fox. **soa^n-bâ**, a wild-cat. **soa^n-thò͘**, a rabbit. **soa^n-loâh**, a large harmless serpent. **soa^n-khîm iá-siù**, wild birds and beasts (v. siù).

soá^n [R. sán, to produce; to bear; produce of land].

siu-tse chiàh-soá^n, to draw rents and live on the fruit of one's land.

soá^n-lāi, within one month after child-birth. **soá^n-pâng**, the mother's room during that month.

soá^n [R. sán, a medicinal powder; in disorder or confusion; scattered; by change of tone from "sàn," to scatter; cf. col. soà^n, sàm], (C. sometimes sán).

iòh-soá^n (C. iòh-sán), a medicinal powder usually taken in the nostrils like snuff. **pêng-an-soá^n**, a sort of powder taken thus. **thong-koan-soá^n** (C. thong-koan-sán), another sort. **siau-iâu-soá^n**, a sort used for giving a comfortable feeling. **keng-hong-soá^n**, medicine for keeping children from getting startled. **pat-pó-soá^n**, a medicinal powder compounded of eight drugs.

soá^n-iā, running about without control, as a spoiled child, or as cattle and other domestic animals when turned loose. **soá^n-iā-kúi**, wandering ghosts; said also in scolding a child that is not kept in order. **soá^n-lā**, to go about in all directions looking for employment, or getting odds and ends of work. **soá^n-phê^n** (C.), to wander about, as bad fellows, or as cattle (v. phê^n).

soá^n-iàh, assistant constables or police whose names are not on the books of the yamun, being merely engaged as assistants by the regular constables or police. **soá^n-chìn-sū**, those Tsin-sze graduates who have once tried for Han-lin and have failed; they can never try again.

soà^n [R. sat, deleterious influences, = col. soah]. **hong-soà^n**, a deleterious influence producing a sort of palsy, supposed to be caused by demons. **khit hong-soà^n phah**, to be made ill by it. **hoān--tiòh hong-soà^n**, id.

soà^n [R. sàn, a sort of net for fish; name of a river]. **soà^n-thâu**, Swatow.

soà^n — **soa-soà^n**, a sand-bank. **chiòh-soà^n**, a reef of rocks.

soà^n [R. sàn, an umbrella]. **hē-soà^n**, an umbrella. **kiàh hē-soà^n**, to carry an umbrella. **hē-soà^n-tsat**, a venomous serpent coloured like the handle of an umbrella.

niû^n-soà^n, a state umbrella carried before a mandarin or great idol. **sa^n-tsân niû^n-soà^n**, a state umbrella having three layers (only used by first-rank mandarins). **bān-jîn-soà^n**, an honorary umbrella presented by the people to a good mandarin when he leaves.

ò-soà^n, to twirl the state umbrella, as when idols meet each other (v. ò). **iám-soà^n**, to dip or lower the state umbrella, as when two mandarins pass each other (so as to hide each other, and thus avoid the need of making long salutations), or as when an idol passes another idol, or the temple of a greater idol.

soà^n (R. sàn), to scatter; to disperse; to pay out, as pay or wages to many persons; well mixed, as paste, starch, &c. **khah-soà^n**, much scattered; wanting in union, as villages not thoroughly organized; thoroughly well mixed, as paste that has no lumps. **iā soà^n-soà^n**, to scatter about, as sand or seeds, or as things strewed about without order. **sì-soà^n**, scattered in all directions; scattered, as meeting, family, company, &c. **phah-soà^n**, to separate (other persons); to dishevel. **phah-soà^n thâu-mn̂g**, to dishevel hair. **thiah-soà^n**, to separate forcibly or cruelly, as man and wife. **pun-soà^n**, to be scattered, as members of a family, &c. **hun-soà^n**, to disperse, distribute, or be wholly scattered all in different directions, as things or persons; *e.g.* relatives dispersed in search of a livelihood, or fleeing from rebellion, &c. **koá^n-soà^n**, to drive away and scatter.

soà^n-táu, to disband, as soldiers; to melt away, as army before the enemy; to send soldiers back to their respective stations when the work is done for which they were collected; to dissolve partnership, alliance, or friendship, as any sort of persons. **lē-ke soà^n-thèh**, family all scattered away and quite dispersed. **soà^n-tūi**, to disperse the ranks of soldiers, as at a review, or for a manœuvre. **soà^n-sėk**, guests separating after a feast. **soà^n-òh**, to dismiss the school at the end of the year. **soà^n-kau**, to break up, as a company of actors. **hi soà^n**, the market broken up.

siau-soà^n--khì, to waste quite away; exhausted, as funds; cured, as a swelling or some other diseases. **siau-soà^n bô--khì**, id.

soà^n chî^n-niû^n, to pay soldiers. **soà^n-niû^n**, id. **soà^n kang-chî^n**, to pay out wages to workmen.

chiu^n bô-soà^n, the starch is not well mixed, as when full of lumps. **noá^n bô-soà^n**, not equally worked into the dress, as starch.

soà^n (R. sièn), thread; fine cord; (wire); (vermicelli); a moulding, as on a door or window. **chiam-soà^n**, needle and thread (v. chiam).

in-soà^n, to wind thread. **kap-soà^n**, to twine thread from two or three strands of yarn. **khan-soà^n**, to mark a line with a cord.

bóe-soà^n, to give money in order to find stolen articles, or to get on the track of a thief, runaway, or criminal. **bóe-soà^n-soh**, do., so as to get on a man's track.

gûn-soà^n, silver wire. **thih-soà^n**, iron wire. **thih-soà^n-lô**, a stiff fine stuff for mosquito curtains. **tâng-soà^n**, brass or copper wire. **thiu tâng-soà^n**, to make it.

mī^n-soà^n, vermicelli (v. mī^n).

tiò-soà^n, a fishing-line. **chín-soà^n**, a line for making a straight line. **hún-soà^n**, a tailor's chalk-line. **hun-kim-soà^n**, a string with a cash at the end of it (used for geomancy). **hm̂-lâng-soà^n**, a thread sewed very loosely to keep the cloth in position for sewing and afterwards removed. **thâu-mn̂g-bé-soà^n**, the tassel at the end of a man's queue. **bú-soà^n**, the larger string in some stringed instruments. **tsú-soà^n**, the smaller strings in a stringed instrument. **hê-chhiu-á-soà^n**, a sort of very thin twine. **si-soà^n**, silk thread. **se-soà^n**, cotton thread (v. se). **siù-soà^n**, thread for embroidery. **sá-soà^n** (Cn.), id.

khí-soà^n, to have a sort of bead-moulding near the edge, *e.g.* as table or door-frame. **khí phû-soà^n**, id. **phak-lek-soà^n**, sort of bead-moulding used on furniture. **tèng-soà^n**, to nail on the moulding, as on frame of door or window.

soà^n-toān, a fine soft sort of satin. **soà^n-thán**, a sort of rug made of cotton. **soà^n-jiàu^n**, silk camblet.

soà^n — **sok-soà^n**, a sort of prepared incense. **soà^n-hiu^n**, a long incense-stick with no bamboo in it. **hiu^n-soà^n-lok**, a long paper-bag for holding incense-sticks.

soah [R. sat, to end; deleterious influences; = col. soà^n], to end; to finish; to make an end of; to let a matter drop or take end, as work, or quarrel, or play; and no more; to kill, as a fowl; to cause death by malign inauspicious influence, as a very bad horoscope or deadly spiritual influence (rarely said of a disease); sort of malign injurious demon.

tsòe-soah, to have finished. **tsai-soah**, to know when one has had enough; to know when to stop. **m̄-tsai-soah**, insatiable; going on when he should have stopped. **pàng-soah**, to have done with an affair; to let it drop. **pàng-i-soah,** to let the quarrel with him take end; to let him off. **m̄-pàng-i-soah,** won't let him off; will keep up the quarrel. **goá m̄-pàng-lí-soah,** I won't let you off; I will have it out of you. **siu-soah,** to wind up an affair suitably. **ah-soah,** to restrain a man, as from quarrelling. **hoah-soah,** to order an inferior to stop a quarrel. **hoā^{n}-soah** (T.), to try to get a quarrel settled, as neighbours or bystanders. **hoâ-soah** (Cn.), id.

soah-hoàh, to determine a matter or decide what course is to be taken, as the leader or head-man in any affair or business.

báuh-soah, to despise or deride a man as quite unable to accomplish his purpose (v. báuh).

soah-bé, the end; the very last. **soah-bé-kiá^{n},** youngest son (v. kiá^{n}). **soah-liáu,** all finished; all over and past. **kè-liáu-sî, soah-liáu-tāi,** the matter is long past, ended, and quite dead, so that it should not be raised again.

soah-pn̄g, to finish the ceremonies (khiā-hà) for the dead. **soah gê-m̄g,** to pay so much as to content the officials and underlings of a yamun in winding up a case by mutual agreement.

soah-chī^{n}, fine fair weather.

gō͘-lí-lō͘ soah, not more than five lí.

soah-múi^{n} (C.), well on in the afternoon (v. múi^{n}).

chhit-soah poeh-pāi, all going wrong or gone wrong, as affairs.

soah-koe, to kill a fowl. **soah-huih,** do., by cutting the neck.

chit-pī^{n} soah chit-lâng, men die of many different diseases.

sí-soah, desperate, as a case that cannot in any way be set right; dull and mechanical at study or work, unable to think for one's self, and only doing mechanically what is taught or ordered. **chip sí-soah,** to be very dogged. **pák-sí-soah,** to tie a run-knot.

soah-sîn, certain very malicious and hurtful demons. **sîn-soah,** spirits and injurious demons. **hiong-sîn ok-soah,** malicious and injurious spirits and demons. **hong-sîn ok-soah,** id. **chhit-soah ê-sîn,** certain hurtful demons (seven? four?). **soah-khì,** deadly influence from persons or things. **hong-soah,** deadly influence of wind on a house or grave. **koan-soah,** demons very dangerous to young infants, esp. at the times called "koan." **thó͘-soah,** demons that are apt to be very hurtful at the time of making a grave or beginning to build or repair a house. **chhit-tsáp-jī tē-soah,** the seventy-two evil spirits of the earth. **thien-kong tē-soah,** certain spirits of heaven and earth (v. kong). **soah khah-tāng,** the injurious spiritual influences very powerful. **toà-sam-soah,** fated to be injured by three such malicious demons. **poeh-jī toà-soah,** his horoscope will have injurious effects on his parents and other relatives. **hoān sam-soah,** to come under the baleful influence of three malicious demons. **hoān--tióh lō͘-soah,** injured in luck by having a long straight road pointed directly at it, as grave. **hoān-soah,** to come under baleful spiritual influence, as grave or house. **bōe-kham--tit siū-soah,** unable to resist such evil influences, as a grave.

soah--tióh, injuriously affected by baleful spiritual influence. **sa^{n}-soah,** to conflict so as to cause great injury, as the horoscopes of father and son, or of husband and wife. **ōe-soah i-ê-pē,** will have a deadly effect on his father, as the conflicting horoscope of his son. **soah--sí,** to cause a person's death by an injurious horoscope, or by the influence of the "soah-sîn," or by magic; said also of assassination. **soah-bó͘,** to have one's wife die by some such malign influence.

chè-soah, to ward off these baleful spiritual influences. **tìn-soah,** id.

soah [R. sat, to scatter, = col. seh, siet, &c.], to sprinkle or drop a little of, as salt, sugar, &c. **soah-iâm,** to sprinkle salt, as on food. **soah-iû,** to throw some small bits of fat on hot meat when cooking, so as to give it a good taste.

soah-kiâm, to put in a little of some salt condiment, *e.g.* soy. **soah-chhò͘,** to drop or pour on a little vinegar.

soàh — **kông soàh-soàh,** behaving foolishly and mad-like. **bâng soàh-soàh,** very much pressed with business, so as to have no leisure. **gê soàh-soàh,** mind much perplexed.

soai^{n} — **soai^{n}-á** (T.), = A. soa^{n}-á, a hill.

soâi^{n} (cf. sông), clownish, rude, and vulgar; utterly wanting in propriety.

soāi^{n} — **soāi^{n}-á,** a mango; a bubo. **bah-soāi^{n},** an inferior sort of mango. **soāi^{n}-á-sng,** sort of preserve made from mangoes. **soāi^{n}-á-hong,** sort of venereal disease connected with a bubo.

soàih^{n}, sound of things suddenly crushed or squeezed. **sih^{n}-sih^{n} soàih^{n}-soàih^{n},** creaking sound, as of boards or of a bamboo chair. **soàih^{n}-soàih^{n}-háu,** do., or of carrying a load on a bamboo pole, or of sedan carried.

soan [R. sour, = col. sng]. **hân-soan-khì,** overcautious manner of man, afraid to say yes or no, esp. from fear of expense; mean or niggardly. **hân-soan,** id. **hân-soan-kheh,** afraid to come forward or to meddle in a matter; very shy, *e.g.* afraid to meet influential people in company; too hard or mean in using money. **hân-soan-kheh; nih^{n}, kia^{n}-sí; pàng, kia^{n}-pe,** afraid either to meddle or to let alone; if he hold (the bird) tight, it may die; if loose, it may fly away.

soan (= chhoan). **soan-tîn,** to throw out suckers.

soan [R. chhoan, to press into a small opening, = col. chhng]. **soan phī^{n}-khang,** to affect the nostrils powerfully, as a strong smell, good or bad.

soan [R. name of a flower, said to be a sort of iris, = lók-chhong-hoe]. **soan-chhó,** an ornamental flowering-plant. **soan-chháu,** id.

soan [R. to proclaim; to publish; cf. col. sien], a surname. **soan-thoân** (R.), to proclaim or publish, as doctrine. **soan-pò͘** (R.), id.

tâng-soan-lô͘, a brass incense vessel; the best are made of the fine brass of the reign Soan-tek of the Ming dynasty. **soan-lô͘,** id. **thoàn soan-lô͘,** to warm and polish such a vessel till it is quite bright. **chiâ^{n} soan-tek--ê,** one really made of the fine brass of the reign Soan-tek.

soan (R. id.) **soan-hoa** (R.), great noise of talk and clamour (v. hoa).

soân [R. a boat, = col. tsûn]. **soân-bō,** a large felt cap. **soân-bō liàm-khang,** a felt cap with a hole in it (said of a story that is false). **kau-chiu-soân,** a large felt cap from Shantung.

soân [R. to go round; to twine; = col. hoan]. **chiu-soân,** to set right a dangerous or very troublesome quarrel or such affair for another, as arbiter. **kàn-soân,** to manage, or try to manage, a troublesome piece of business, either for self or other. **phoân-soân,** to have constant, intimate, friendly intercourse together.

soán (R. id.), to torture the fingers by pressure in

an instrument. **soán--khí-lâi**, id. **soán-chí**, the instrument used for torturing the fingers of women only. **pàng-soán**, to take off this torturing instrument.

soán (Cn. sán). **chì^n-soán**, sort of long cakes fried in fat.

soán [R. to choose]. **kéng-soán** (r.), to select. **chhiau-soán** (R.), to choose the best, as men or things. **thiau-soán**, to select after repeated trials, or very careful examination. **thiau-soán ê-mih^n**, very choice things. **thiau-soán ê-peng**, choice soldiers. **kham-tit-soán**, worthy of being chosen. **soán kiá^n-sài**, to choose a son-in-law. **soán hông-hō͘**, to choose an empress. **soán jin-tsâi**, to select able men for places of trust; to select a good-looking son-in-law. **soán bí-lú**, to select beautiful girls for the imperial harem. **soán-poàt**, to select one Sew-tsai once in twelve years from each Hien district (v. poàt).

soàn [R. to count, = col. sǹg, siàu]. **soàn-hoat**, arithmetic. **kui-tû soàn-hoat**, id. **kiú-kui soàn-hoat**, id. **soàn-hoat chhi^n**, not good at accounts. **soàn-hoat sek**, good at arithmetic.

put-siōng-soàn, utterly useless (as man or thing); not worth counting though present. **put-siōng-soàn ê-lâng**, an utterly useless man.

kui-lêng hok-soàn, may you live as long as the tortoise and the stork! **chhien-soàn bān-soàn, m̄-táh thi^n chit-soàn**, myriads of plans are not worth one purpose of Heaven.

soàn (R. id.), (Cn. sǹg). **soàn-á**, garlic. **soàn-thâu**, garlic roots. **soàn-jiông**, garlic pounded small. **soàn-á-péh**, garlic root and the white part of the stalk, cut down small.

soān [R. — Cn. siēn, C. soān]. **him-soān**, = him-siēn, to desire very much; to delight in.

soān — **soān-chióh**, the diamond. **hé-soān**, a first-class clear diamond, which reflects light with brilliant colours. **tsúi-soān**, an inferior diamond. **kim-gek-soān**, precious metals and jewels. **soān-pit**, a glazier's diamond.

soat [R. snow, = col. seh]. **tāi-soat**, the term on or about December 7th. **siáu-soat**, the term half a month sooner, about Nov. 22d. (s. speak). **soat-i**, sort of dress sometimes worn by mandarins (v. i).

soat-bûn (f.), soap.

soat [R. to speak, = col. seh, sòe]. **soat-chhiàu**, joking and jesting. **soat-chhiòng**, id. **tâm-giên soat-chhiòng**, to chat and jest. **tâm-kim soat-kó͘**, to talk idly about things in general (lit. modern and ancient). **tâm-thien soat-tē**, to talk idly about things that do not concern us. **chhú gán-chiên chi-sū; hô-pit tâm-thien soat-tē**, I speak only of the present affair; why should we talk of things that have no connection with the matter? **jîn, put-soat put-ti: kó͘, put-tá^n put-hiáng**, said of a man not acknowledging a favour done him.

siáu-soat, novels (s. snow).

hō͘-soat, to tell lies.

soat — **soát-soát-háu**, noise, as of filing.

soe (R. sə), (C. se), a comb; to comb. **kak-soe**, a comb made of horn. **chhâ-soe**, a wooden comb.

hī^n-soe, the reed of a loom (v. hī^n). **beh-soe**, an iron comb for taking the ear off wheat or barley.

soe-tsng, to comb and adorn the head, only of woman (v. tsng). **soe-thâu**, to comb the hair. **soe-thâu-kun**, a cloth thrown over the shoulder by woman at toilet. **soe phòng-thâu**, a peculiar way of dressing women's hair.

soe (C. se; Cn. söe). **sàu-soe**, a coarse bamboo brush. **kiū^n-soe** (T.), id. **tek-söe** (Cn.), id.

soe (R. sə; by some divided into two separate words), (C. se; Cn. söe), not nearly related; widely separate, as bars, rows, threads, &c.; at variance, as persons.

chhin-soe, nearly related and not nearly related; relatives and persons not related. **khah-soe chit-pi^n**, a little more distant in relationship. **khah-soe chit-ûn**, one degree more distant in relationship.

soe-làng, set wide apart; of loose texture (v. làng). **soe-soe pâng**, to sew very wide cross-stitches. **soe-chí-thang**, a window made with fixed bars (v. thang).

soe [R. sə, vegetables], (C. se). **chhài-soe**, vegetables. **kim-hî-soe**, weeds for gold or silver fish. **hé-soe**, sort of edible sea-weed fried in fat.

soe (R. id.), to lose good fortune; to be unprosperous; to fail in strength or luck; to grow poor or unfortunate; to fail, decline, or decay; also (vulg.), unable to have children, as man. **soe-bî**, to meet with reverses; to lose prosperity. **soe-lám**, sickly; very weak from a chronic disease, or as an old man; declining in health. **soe-jiók**, weak and infirm. **soe-póh**, scanty, as crop of fruit (v. póh). **soe-sap**, fallen into decay, as person or place; broken down and seedy-looking. **liōng-pōe-soe**, in great poverty; very weak and broken down in health. **soe kàu-lut-thâu-tsang**, matters come to a very ruinous and unfortunate state (lit. to lose one's queue).

soe-khì, all one does going wrong and failing; rapidly growing very poor; rapidly diminishing in numbers, as family or village. **khì soe**, constitution broken down, as by long illness or old age. **lâng-khì soe**, very few people there, as in place laid waste or rapidly declining. **lâng-khì khah-soe**, id.

chhek-soe, to meet with bad luck or bad omen. **phah kah-i-soe**, to say that a man's enterprise is sure to fail, so as to make a bad omen and cause it really to fail. **hiám-hiám soe**, had almost taken part in some case or matter which would have brought great calamity; had almost seen something that would have been a very bad omen.

sēng-soe, prosperity and adversity; success and failure. **sēng-soe iú-sî**, prosperity and adversity have their fated times. **heng-soe**, prosperity and adversity. **soe-ōng**, decaying and prospering (v. ōng).

sôe (C.), = A. sûi, to hang down, as something drooping; also (P.), = A. C. sûi, to hang down, in general.

sóe (R. sé, often erroneously read "sién"), (C. sé; Cn. söe), to wash. **sóe-lóe**, id. **sóe-tn̄g**, to wash and then rinse or wash again. **sóe-chheng**, to wash clean. **sóe chheng-khì**, id. **sóe-tû** (r.), to wash quite away. **sóe-ek**, to wash or bathe by throwing water over one's self. **ēng hông-hô ê-tsúi lâi-sóe, iáh-bōe chheng-khì**, cannot be washed clean even with the waters of the Yellow River; said of a bad name. **sóe-kháu** (C. sek), to wash the mouth (v. kháu). **sóe-kim**, to wash out gold from sand.

tê-sóe (C. tê-sién), an earthen plate for teapot and small cups; a small piece of cloth or netting put below tea-cups on salver.

sóe-tsûn, to clean a boat's bottom, by sweeping, rubbing, &c., or by burning. **tā^n-sóe**, id.

sóe gē-kak, to lay waste the crops of an enemy, as in a feud. **sóe bé-kha**, to wound a horse's legs severely, as in war. **sóe-sak** (T.), to exterminate utterly; to wash and throw away the water. **liáh-khi-sóe**, seize and behead him; esp. said by the Small Knife Society.

sóe-chē, to expiate guilt, by burning paper and making offerings. **sóe-hùt**, an idol carried about the shops, and getting some money at each. **sóe-lé** (X.), baptism. **kiâⁿ sóe-lé** (X.), to perform baptism. **niáⁿ sóe-lé** (X.), to be baptized.

chiuⁿ-sóe, to wash and starch; to speak very angrily; to insult by talk. **sng-sóe**, to steep clothes in sour water, and then wash them; also (T.), to speak to a man somewhat angrily, or to blame him indirectly for his bad practices (s. next two words).

sóe — **sng-sóe**, feeling of pain in bones, as when feverish or wearied; feeling out of sorts, as in cold damp rainy weather. **kut-thâu sng-sóe**, id. (s. preceding and following words).

sóe, to sorn upon. **sng-sóe** (?), id. (s. two preceding words). **sap-sóe**, dirt and scum left by the tide or floating, or in sea-moss and such eatables; getting money or things by cunning or importunity, and not giving back; to sorn on one, getting food or other things from him. **khoe-sóe**, to sorn on a man, getting things (esp. meals) out of him by constantly hanging about. **sóe--lâng**, to sorn on people. **sóe pn̄g-tn̂g**, to get a meal out of a man.

sóe (=soeh). **iau-chiaⁿ sì-sóe** (C.), a scolding phrase applied to women gadding about, and speaking or acting improperly.

sóe [R. sú; cf. col. sòe], (C. sé; Cn. sŏe), millet. **toā-sóe**, the common large millet. **hoan-sóe**, id. **lē-sóe**, id. **sóe-á**, small sort of millet. **káu-bé-sóe**, short millet with ears hanging down like a dog's tail. **ah-kha-sóe**, =ah-kha-sek, a small grain in heads like a fowl's foot. **sóe-sek béh-tāu**, millet, wheat or barley, and leguminous plants. **sóe-bâng**, a stalk of millet with emptied ears, used as a brush. **sóe-á-chí**, sort of cake made from millet.

sòe [R. a year, =col. hè, sè]. **sòe-kun**, the name of a year (=nîⁿ-kō), as denoted by the two cyclical characters, but so called only as used in divination. **sòe-khó**, the triennial examination of Sew-tsai graduates, for the degree of "lîm-seng," preparatory to trial for Kujin. **sòe-kòng**, title of a lîm-seng, who after twelve years has not been able to take the degree of "poàt-kòng."

liû-put-thài-sòe, the demon of eclipse.

bān-sòe (ten thousand years old), phrase used in praising the emperor. **bān-bān-sòe**, id. **bān-sòe-iâ**, the emperor. **chhien-sòe-iâ** (lit. thousand years), title of younger brother of emperor. **chhien-sòe**, id. **kiú-chhien-sòe** (lit. nine thousand years), the extraordinary title given to the notorious eunuch Gūi Tiong-hiân, in the end of the Ming dynasty.

sòe [R. id., by change of tone from "sut," to lead]. **tsú-sòe**, commander-in-chief (s. small). **chiòng-sòe**, first-class military mandarins, as general, admiral, and commander-in-chief. **sòe-jī-kî**, a flag with the word "sòe" on it; used by commander-in-chief and by some idols.

goân-sòe, commander-in-chief. **goân-sòe-iâ**, name of four idols, surnamed Khng, Tiō, Bé, and Un; also (Cn.), a deified dog. **khng goân-sòe**, a red-faced idol, attendant on Má-tsé-pô, or on Tāi-tō-kong. **tiō goân-sòe**, a black-faced one. **bé goân-sòe**, the white-faced one. **un goân-sòe**, the attendant idol mounted on a tiger. **tiong-tân goân-sòe**, a title of the idol "lô-chhia." **tiên goân-sòe**, title of the idol "siùⁿ-kang-tia."

sòe (R. sè), (C. sè; Cn. sŏe), small. **sòe-sòe tn̂g-tn̂g**, long and slender. **òeh-sòe**, small, as a place. **sòe-kiáⁿ**, a small boy; a child. **sòe-hàn**, a young person; small, as man. **sòe-chiah**, small, as animal; a small animal (so with other classifiers). **sòe-á-chiah**, a small animal.

sòe-tsoh, a spy.

sòe-jī, small characters.

sòe-jī, careful. **sòe-jī kiâⁿ**, walk carefully and slowly; polite phrase at parting. **m̄-thang sòe-jī**, **chiáh kàu-pá**, don't stint yourself; eat abundantly. **tsú-sòe**, careful (s. commander). **sōe-sūn** (Cn.), careful. **sòe-sim**, careful; humble. **sim-koaⁿ sòe**, contented with moderate gains, *e.g.* willing to take a low price, or not making dangerous ventures.

sòe-î, a concubine. **sòe-kīm**, wife of wife's younger brother. **sōe-kū** (Cn.), =kū-á, wife's younger brother. **sōe-chek** (An.), = A. sió-chek, husband's younger brother. **goán-sòe--ê**, my younger brother.

sī-sòe, an inferior.

toā-sòe, large and small; great and small; old and young. **bô-toā bô-sòe**, not paying proper respect to superior, esp. as disobedient boy. **bák-chiu toā-sòe-lúi**, partial. **pàng toā-sòe-bák**, to wink at faults. **toā-sòe-sim**, partiality, as in treating or paying agents, children, &c. **toā-sòe-siān**, orchitis in one of the testes.

sòe [R. sú, millet, =col. sóe]. **sòe-á-bí**, =sek-á, a small sort of grain.

sòe [R. id., by change of tone from "soat," to speak], to try to persuade or talk over a man.

sòe, to try to find, as something that has gone to the bottom of the sea. **sòe-tiàⁿ**, to fish up a lost anchor.

sòe (C.), = A. sè, rent; customs dues; to let or rent.

sōe (C.), = A. sē, to flow out.

sōe (C.) **sōe-hùn**, to scatter powdered manure on fields. **sōe-hūiⁿ**, id. on dry fields.

soeh [R. sek, to fill up, = col. siap, that], (C. seh), to fill up, as a crack or chink, by pressing something in; to press one's way through a crowd; to make steady, as a table, by putting some thin thing under one of the feet. **soeh hé-n̂g**, to creep stealthily along unobserved under the shadow of the lamp, as a thief.

òeh-soeh, very scant of room because of crowding. **òeh-òeh soeh-soeh**, id.

soeh-phāng, to press something into a chink or crevice. **soeh piah-khang**, do. into a chink in a partition wall. **soeh-khí**, to get in among the teeth, as meat.

soeh-siap, to give money in order to get assistance by influence, false witness, &c. (v. siap). **hē-soeh** (T.), to give a bribe to one person.

chióh-soeh, a sort of small green crab.

soeh (C.), = A. seh, to explain, as a book; also (P.), = A. kóng (in some phrases), to speak. **ké-soeh** (C.), = A. kóe-seh, to explain, as a book. **soeh to-siā** (P.), to give thanks.

soeh (C.) **iau-chiaⁿ sih-soeh** (=sóe), behaving improperly, as woman.

soh (C.), = A. suh, to suck.

soh [R. sek, a rope; a chain; to demand], a rope; a cord; a cable. **soh-á**, small rope; twine. **tsang-**

58

soh, rope made of palm fibre. **o͘-soh**, black ropes, used for binding criminals.

phah-soh, to make ropes. **ká-soh**, to twist ropes, in making them. **kiâⁿ-soh**, to walk on the tight rope, esp. as northern men. **tàh-soh**, id.

tàh-soh, ropes that suspend the sail (like a swing) when partially rolled up. **tiàⁿ-soh**, cable for anchor. **pē-soh**, rope that binds on quantities of wood on the side of a junk. **khe-lòh-soh**, porter's ropes (v. lòh). **lak-soh**, the string of a drill (v. lak). **chîn-soh**, a building-line or plummet. **chhia-soh**, endless band of spinning-wheel. **sai-kong hoat-soh**, magical cord used by Tauists. **kè-soh**, cord used for tying women's hair. **gû-liāu-soh**, rope for a cow (v. liāu). **bé-soh**, a halter for leading a horse. **khan-mn̂g-soh--ê**, man who leads men to bad houses.

soh-lē, ropes, in regard to number and direction. **tsòe-soh-lē**, to rig up a sail on a vessel. **kāu-soh-lē**, having many ropes in many directions; having a great many matters to manage. **soh-lē tsōe**, id. **kap-pán-tsûn kāu-soh-lē**, a foreign vessel has a great many ropes; said also of much business.

sòh — **chhiú-sòh**, flat armlets. **koà-sòh**, to wear flat armlets.

sòh (cf. sô). **sòh-lâi sòh-khì**, to walk back and forwards. **sòh chit-tsoā-lâi, sòh chit-tsoā-khì**, id. **sòh thit-thô**, to go about for amusement. **sì-kòe-sòh**, to go about idly. **chiah-pá sì-kòe-sòh**, to do nothing but eat and go about idly (said in scolding boys).

söh (Cn. T.), = A. seh, snow. **söh-sún** (Cn.), = A. tang-sún, winter shoots of bamboo.

söh (Cn.), = A. kóng, seh, to speak, &c. **söh-siet**, to twit; to talk half joke half earnest.

sok [R. quick, = col. suh, soā]. **sìn-sok**, rapid; rapidly; quickly. **hé-sok**, very quickly, as in executing another's orders. **sok-pò-si**, an idol attending on Sêng-hông (v. si).

sok [R. the first of the month]. **sok-bōng**, the 1st and 15th of a month.

sok [R. siok, respectful; retiring; quiet]. **sok-chēng**, quiet, without disturbance.

sok — **sok-soàⁿ**, a sort of prepared incense.

phàⁿ-sok-hiuⁿ, a fine sort of incense. **phàⁿ-sok**, the wood from which it is made. **sok-chhâ**, id.

sok [R. to bind; to restrain; a bundle], a small bag; a bundle, as of incense-sticks; a scabbard. **chhiú-sok**, gloves. **chhiú-n̂g-sok**, covers for the cuffs of a coat, for keeping them clean. **to-sok**, scabbard for sword or knife. **kiàm-sok**, scabbard for short sword. **hau-pau-sok**, a bit of stone or shell used as clasp for a sort of purse or pouch. **hun-pau-sok**, two such bits for clasp of tobacco-pouch.

chit-sok-hiuⁿ, a bundle of incense-sticks in a long paper-bag. **kui-sok-hiuⁿ**, id.

sok-kim, a teacher's salary. **sok-siu**, id.

sok-chhiú, to fold the arms on the breast, with hands in opposite sleeves or under the arms. **sok-chhiú bû-chhek**, arms folded on breast and having no way out of the danger or difficulty.

iok-sok, to restrain. **khu-sok**, to keep in very strict discipline, and restrain well, as sons, employés, &c. **sok-pák**, behaving well because of the presence of some one.

kiet-sok, neat and tidy, as person or thing; neatly put up, as parcel, basket, box, or book, made convenient for carrying; neatly put on, as dress neither too tight nor too loose. **sok-kiet**, id.; also said of house or room, small but neat and nice. **sok-hiet** (Cn.), small and neat, as house or room.

siu-sok, gradually tapering; gradually reduced, as the opening of a wound, or as expenditure. **khang-chhùi siu-sok**, the wound very nearly healed up. **taⁿ khah-siu-sok**, expenditure now less than before, as by strict economy; behaviour now improved, as of man formerly bad.

sök (Cn.), = A. sek (in one or two words only).

som (R. id.), (Cn. sm, söm; C. sim), ginseng, biche-de-mer, &c. **chién-som**, to buy ginseng. **chiàh-som**, to take ginseng medicinally.

hái-som, biche-de-mer. **o͘-som**, a black sort. **o͘-jiàu-som**, a large rough sort. **chhì-som**, a prickly sort.

jîn-som, ginseng (Panax). **iûⁿ-som**, foreign ginseng. **tóng-som**, a cheap sort, not a real Panax (sort of Convolvulus or Campanula?). **táng-som**, id. **tan-som**, a very cheap sort (Salvia?). **goân-som**, a very cheap inferior sort. **hiên-som**, id.

sa-som, a plant, the stalks of which are used as a cooling medicine; it grows on the mountains near Chang-chew. **soa-som**, a medicinal plant (Adenophora?). **soaⁿ-som**, a small mountain shrub used for making a cooling infusion. **soaⁿ-som-á**, id. **soaⁿ-som-tê** (C.), infusion of it.

song [R. the mulberry, = col. sng]. **song-kià-siⁿ**, a parasite of the mulberry (used medicinally).

song — **phōng-song**, bulky; taking up a great deal of room out of proportion to its weight, as parcel loosely tied or basket almost empty; clumsy and hanging loosely, as dress when many clothes are worn at once, or as pocket full of large things. **pōng-song**, id. **phōng-phōng song-song**, id.

song [R. frost, = col. sng]. **siū-chhīn hong-song**, much exposed to weather and cold, as travellers. **khī-song**, the bloom on dried persimmons (v. khī). **liók-goát-song**, a cooling medicine.

song [R. mourning; funereal, = col. sng]. **song-sū**, matters connected with funeral and mourning. **song-hí-sū**, births, deaths, marriages, and such ceremonies. **song-hòk**, deep mourning. **sam-liên-song**, mourning for twenty-seven months for parents. **ki-liên-song**, one year's mourning, as for uncle.

ku-song, to be in mourning for parents. **ki-song** (C.), id. **bāi-song**, to call and worship the corpse before burial, as friends do. **būn-song** (R.), id. **tiàu-song** (R.), to call and make offerings to the "hûn-sin."

song [R. a pair, = col. siang, sang, seng]. **song-chhin**, father and mother. **hok bû-song-chì**, good fortune does not come in pairs (v. hok).

song-á-chiòh, granite slabs of the usual size and shape. **song-á**, id.

sông (R. siông), (cf. chhêng, chhiâng, soâiⁿ), vulgar, clownish, ignorant, and stupid; quite without politeness. **sông-sông**, id. **sông-tai**, id.; stupid. **thó-sông**, vulgar, clownish, clumsy, and ignorant. **tai-sông-gōng**, vulgar, foolish, and clumsy. **sông-tâng**, id. (s. fir).

sông [R. siông, the fir-tree, = col. chhêng, seng]. **sông-ka**, = siông-ka, resin from fir-wood. **sông-tâng**, a sort of coarse soft fir-wood, apt to breed white ants, and is almost useless; it makes little smoke, and is used for distilling (s. stupid).

sóng (R. id.), comfortable; pleasant, as a place. **sóng-khoài**, comfortable. **sóng-lī**, pleasantly laid ent, arranged, or furnished, as house or garden; feeling comfortable, as after change of dress, &c. **m̄-sóng-lī**, feeling uncomfortable in body; dirty or disorderly, as house; not well settled, as affair that will probably soon be as bad as ever. **chheng-sóng**, at leisure; neat, clean, and pleasant, as place.

sóng-kháu, pleasing the palate.

sòng [R. to lose; by change of tone from "song," funereal]. **sòng-sit**, to lose. **sòng-sim**, having lost all sense of shame, ready for any wickedness. **sûi-thâu sòng-chì**, hanging the head and having lost all spirit. **sòng-tá^{n}**, to lose all courage. **sòng-tám**, id. **bûn-hong sòng-tám**, to lose all courage on hearing the news.

sòng, very poor. **sòng-hiong**, id. **chhiah-sòng**, id. **chhám-sòng**, wretchedly poor. **sòng-hiu̍h-hiu̍h**, extremely poor. **sòng-khiu̍h-khiu̍h**, id. **sòng-gih-gih**, id. **sòng-giēn-giēn** (esp. T.), id.

sòng-goá pún-téng, though poor, I hurt no one by it but myself.

sòng [R. to make a present; to accompany on leaving; = col. sàng]. **sòng-hêng**, to see a friend off on a journey. **sòng-sīn**, to present money, as to a graduate when he goes to the examinations. **sūn-hong siong-sòng**, may you have a good wind on your voyage.

sòng [R. name of a state and of a dynasty; a surname; = col. sàng]. **sòng-tiâu**, the Sung dynasty. **sòng-thé-jī**, the common square form of characters used in printing. **kiông-tông jio̍k-sòng**, the powerful Tang and weak Sung dynasties. **hong-tông bô-iá^{n}-sòng**, baseless stories of these ancient dynasties. **hau-tông, bô-iá^{n}-chiah-sòng**, id.

lū-sòng, Luzon; the Philippines. **lī-sòng** (C.), id. **toā-lū-sòng**, Spain. **sòng-kha**, Luzon; small sort of shrimp from it. **sòng-bí**, still smaller shrimps from it.

sōng — **sōng-sōng**, spiritless, having a dull apathetic appearance, as if not caring for anything. **kiâ^{n}-lē̤ sōng-sōng**, walking very slowly and quietly with short steps, without spirit, vigour, or vivacity. **lok-sōng**, appearance of being in very reduced circumstances; looking dispirited and broken-down, *e.g.* in countenance or dress, &c.

sőng (Cn.), = A. seng, to be born, &c.; so with several words in various tones.

su [R. ought], (C. si). **su-tio̍h**, ought to —. **hông-kiâu, su hā-má**, at a bridge one should dismount. **su-tiám hu̍t-chiên-teng**, should light candles before idols.

su [R. to need; to be in want of], (C. si). **kun-su**, forced contributions or squeezes, said to be for military purposes. **phài-kun-su**, to levy such contributions. **koan kun-su**, to subscribe or promise to pay so much of them. **kiáu kun-su**, to pay the amount.

su [R. beard, with whiskers and moustaches, = col. chhiu], (C. si). **liông-su-chháu**, a medicinal plant.

su [R. sū, to wait]. **su-hē̤** (Cn. sü-hīō), to wait for (v. hē̤). **su-hāu**, id.; also, to wait upon, as a servant.

su [R. to take charge of, as an office; an official; = col. si], (Cn. sü). **su-má**, a surname. **su-tē̤**, a surname. **su-bēng tsàu-kun**, the god of the fire-place.

su [R. this], (C. sü). **su-bûn**, polite; gentlemanly.

su [R. mutually; all; to help]. **kūi-su**, an assistant of the "hē̤-pâng," who collects the land-tax of a subdivision of a Hien district, *e.g.* of Amoy island or of Koàn-kháu.

su (C.) **hin-su**, the body. **hun-su**, id. **hin-su-tūi^{n}**, the trunk of the body. **ē-su**, = A. ē-sin, the lower part of the body. **ē-su ê in-chiû^{n}**, clothes of lower part of the body. **thàu-su tâm**, all wet through. **tsûi^{n}-su lóng-tâm**, id.

kui-su, an entire suit of clothes. **tsoân-su**, id. **sì-su-sa^{n}**, four suits of clothes.

háh-su (A.), fitting well, as dress. **ûi-su-kûn** (A.), an apron.

su [R. to think], (Cn. sü). **su-siú^{n}** (r.), to think; to consider. **sàm-su** (R.), to reflect deeply. **su-chhun** (R.), woman longing for sexual intercourse.

su-niû^{n}, to consult together (v. niû^{n}).

ū sim-su, very good at contriving or inventing. **kāu-sim-su**, too anxious about matters. **hó-sim-su**, skilful at inventions, as in making things or managing matters. **sió-khoá ê sim-su**, it was no trouble at all (said politely when praised for one's work, or when thanked for trouble taken for another). **sim-su kò-tē̤**, to think too deeply on any matter, so as to injure one's health. **sim-su kè-tē̤**, id.

ló-kong-su, a medicinal plant, tall and half shrubby, with lilac flowers.

su (R. id., = col. sai), (Cn. sü), secret; private; illicit; selfish. **phien-su**, partial; partiality. **su-hā**, private; one's own; secretly. **su-khia**, private; one's own. **su-kha** (Cn.), id. **thiet-biēn bû-su**, strictly impartial, as mandarin (lit. iron face). **thien-tē bû-su**, heaven and earth are impartial. **siáp-su**, to act by partiality or unjust selfishness.

kong-su, public and private; just and selfish. **poàn-kong-su**, half public, half private. **ká-kong hêng-su**, to advance private ends under pretence of the public good. **kong-pò su-siû**, to gratify private revenge under show of public justice.

su-giáp, personal private property. **su-iok**, a private or clandestine agreement.

su-thong, illicit sexual intercourse; to give traitorous information. **su-ha̍p** (R.), illicit sexual intercourse. **su-io̍k** (R.), evil desires or passions (v. io̍k).

su-iâm, smuggled salt. **liáh su-hè**, to seize smuggled goods.

su-chiàm, to take unjust possession of public property for one's self. **su-àm**, to appropriate secretly part of public funds. **iú-su-pè**, improperly using opportunities to get money without superior's knowledge, as in a commission or lawsuit.

tau-su, self-confident and somewhat proud (v. tau).

su [R. to pay taxes or tribute; to lose in a contest], to lose in a contest of any sort; to be inferior in some quality. **su--lóh-khì**, to lose heavily in gambling. **su-lu--khì**, all lost by gambling. **chhân-hn̂g bé-kiá^{n} su-lu--khì**, lands and family all gambled away.

khah-su, to be inferior in some quality. **bô-khah-su**, not at all inferior. **khah-su--i**, to be excelled by him. **khah-su tio̍h-khì**, as it cannot be helped, I must just go, though unwilling. **khah-su i beh-khì**, against my will, wish, or anxiety, he *would* go. **khah-su thâu-ke beh àn-ni^{n}**, though I know it is not the proper way, my master *will* have it so.

phah-su, to be overcome in boxing or fighting. **phah-su--lâng**, id. **thâi-su**, to be defeated in battle. **oan-su--i**, to be worsted in a quarrel with him. **poáh-su**, to lose in gambling. **poáh-su-kiáu**, id.

sa^{n}-su, one man maintaining that a thing is so, or that something will happen, while the other maintains the opposite. **kap--lâng sa^{n}-su**, to try which of the two is right; to wager. **lâi sa^{n}-su**, come and see which is right, *e.g.* turning up a dictionary to decide a dispute about a word. **bô-sa^{n}-su**, neither of the two is inferior to the other. **sa^{n}-su-chî^{n}**, to gamble for money.

su-iâ^{n}, to lose or win. **su-iâ^{n}-chî^{n}**, to play for money, by gambling or by trial of strength, &c. **tsòe-su-iâ^{n}**, to play at a game of chance. **poáh-su-iâ^{n}**, to gamble. **poáh bô-su-iâ^{n}**, to play a game of chance for amusement and not for money. **bô-su-iâ^{n}**, neither losing nor winning; a drawn game. **bô-kì^{n} su-iâ^{n}**, contest not yet decided. **tam su-iâ^{n}**, to bear honestly the responsibility of defeat, as by paying one's due, *e.g.* what is lost in gambling; to pay one's subscription faithfully; to bear properly some responsibility that falls on us to act liberally, as in entertaining guests on some special occasion. **m̄-tam su-iâ^{n}**, won't act up to the agreement; *e.g.* won't drink the liquor of his forfeit; won't pay gambling debts; won't bear his share of common expenses or furnish his share of labour for a common object. **m̄-tam su-iâ^{n} phí**, meanly refusing to pay his gambling debts or to bear his share of expenses, &c. **ún-iâ^{n} bô-su**, certain to win. **ká^{n}-iâ^{n} ká^{n}-su**, daring to make a great venture, as in gambling or trade.

SU [R. a teacher, = col. sai], (Cn. sü), affix to the literary name (not surname) of a teacher; affix to the name of a Buddhist priest in politely addressing him.

thài-su, prime minister. **thài-su-iâ**, id. **su-iâ**, a confidential adviser and secretary of a mandarin. **ló-su**, the principal or president of the college of the department or district, = hú-òh or koāi^{n}-òh, who is the head of the literati of that department or district (often two in one district); an official teacher of military exercises; the title is often sold as an empty title; (said politely of a learned instructor or preacher). **kun-su**, an officer on the staff of commander-in-chief, who plans battles, campaigns, &c. (s. need). **tsn̄g-su**, a pettifogging lawyer who lives by inciting legal cases and writing documents for them. **kàu-su** (T.), a teacher of boxing or gymnastics; but (R.), a religious teacher, minister, or missionary. **bók-su** (X.), a pastor, minister, or clergyman.

tê-su, a tea-taster.

hoat-su, polite title of Tauist priest. **su-hū**, polite title of Buddhist priest. **su-kong**, the adoptive father of the adoptive father of a young Buddhist priest. **tē-lí-su**, a geomancer. **ték-jit-su**, a man who chooses lucky days for others. **jit-su**, id.

thien-su, the Tauist high-priest of China, who can rule demons (said to officiate for the emperor once in ten years). **tiu^{n} thien-su**, id., as he is always of the surname Chang, = tiu^{n}.

tsó-su-kong, a black-faced idol. **chheng-súi tsó-su**, do., from the village of Chheng-súi in Tâng-oa^{n}. **sam-phiâ^{n} tsó-su**, do., from Sam-phêng beyond Chang-chew. **poát-mê tsó-su**, title of an idol brought from India.

tsúi-su, marines. **tsúi-su-koa^{n}**, a naval mandarin. **tsúi-su thê-tok**, an admiral. **lék-lō tsúi-su**, military and naval.

thien-tē, kun chhin su, in heaven and earth the most important persons are sovereigns, parents, and teachers. **thien-hā, kun chhin su**, do., in the whole world.

SU [R. a book; a writing; to write; = col. tsu], (C. si; Cn. sü).

chhó-su, running hand. **hêng-su**, less contracted form of current hand, between chhó-su and khái-su. **khái-su**, the written or printed character of the ordinary square form.

sù-su, the four books. **su-keng** (C. siū^{n}-si), the Shoo-king or historical classic. **siū^{n}-su**, id. (from "siū^{n}," above). **thong-su**, an almanac. **tsoân-su**, entire works; collected works. **khau-su**, document fixing the division of family property (v. khau). **bûn-su**, an official letter; a despatch. **tsáu-bûn-su**, to carry an official despatch, as courier. **bûn-su-koán**, a sort of post-office. **gê-sî-su**, sentences pasted up at 5.5. **su-tiên**, lands left by ancestors to support those descendants who become students or literati.

siū^{n}-su, president of one of the six supreme boards (+). **tiong-su sià-jîn**, secretaries of the supreme boards. **tiong-su-khe**, these secretaries. **su-pān**, a clerk or writer in a mandarin's office. **su-siú**, id. **tō-su**, writers in the Tautai's office (v. tō).

tāi-su, an amanuensis who writes a deed of sale, agreement, mortgage, lease, &c.; an official clerk in a yamun who copies out the accusations or petitions that are to be presented. **tāi-su-koán**, the office in a yamun where these documents are copied out.

tô-su, a seal, of a private person.

SÛ (R. id.), (C. sî; Cn. sû), an ancestral hall; temples for certain deceased worthies. **sû-tn̂g**, an ancestral temple. **bûn-kong-sû**, temple of the commentator Chu-hi or Tsu-bûn-kong. **tiong-liêt-sû**, temple of canonized mandarins who died for the state (v. liêt). **tiong-ióng-sû**, do., of military mandarins. **bêng-hoân-sû**, temple of the most distinguished deceased mandarins of the department or district. **hiong-hiên-sû**, temple of the canonized literati of the district. **ke-né^{n}-sû** (Cn.), sort of asylum for old men.

SÛ (Cn. sû). **siâm-sû**, a mythical three-legged venomous toad.

SÛ [R. sū, hereafter; to inherit; posterity], (Cn. sû). **hē-sû**, posterity. **āu-sû**, id. **hiō-sû** (Cn.), id. **chhut-sû**, transferred to another to be his son. **kè-sû**, to be adopted, as son. **thoân-sû**, to continue the line of posterity, either by having a son or by adoption. **tsoát-sû**, to have no posterity. **bô-sû**, id. **bô-sû-têng**, shrines for tablets of men who have no posterity. **bô-sû-tân**, id.

SÛ [R. leisurely, = col. chhî], (Cn. sû), a surname (A. sû, chhî; C. chhî).

SÛ [R. an expression; a phrase; an accusation; to request], (Cn. sû). **tâu-sû**, a written complaint given in to the tē-pó or bé-khoài, before beginning a regular lawsuit. **pàng tâu-sû**, to give in this document. **pau-lám sû-siōng**, to engage illegally to manage a lawsuit successfully (v. siōng). **bû-khiau, put-sêng-sû**, without some roundabout dealing the matter cannot be set right.

sè-sû, prayers asserting our innocence, burned before idols.

si-sû ko-hù, four sorts of poetical compositions.

ū-giên-sû, able to talk much and well, and to the point. **kàu-giên-sû**, too talkative. **bô-giên-sû**, not good at talking so as to commend one's case, only able to say a few words. **giên-sû khah-toán**, unable to state one's own case well.

ká-sû, false stories, *e.g.* blaming others or excusing one's self.

hu-sû ê-ōe, deceitful talk [or does this phrase belong to the following word?].

Sû [R. to refuse; to decline; to resign; an expression; = col. sî], (Cn. sû). **the-sû**, to decline meddling with a matter, by false excuses (v. the). **thok-sû** (R.), id.

kiông-sû, to maintain doggedly and plausibly that we are right when unquestionably wrong. **kiông-sû, toȧt chêng-lí**, id.

Sú [R. heat of weather], (C. sí; Cn. sû). **sú-khì**, scorching heat of summer. **hong-hân sú-sip**, the four causes of disease, wind, cold, heat, damp. **hân-sú-chiam**, a thermometer.

siong-sú (C. siang-sí), unwell through the heat. **tiòng-sú**, to have a sun-stroke, or severe illness from heat, sometimes got within the house. **pī-sú**, to avoid the heat by going into the country, or to the seaside.

tāi-sú, the term on or about July 23d. **siáu-sú**, term on or about July 7th. **chhú-sú** (C. chhí-sí), term on or about Aug. 23d.

Sú [R. a historian; chronicles; a surname; = col. sái]. **sú-kì**, annals or history of a kingdom.

gū-sú, a censor; one at Pekin for each province. **tién-sú**, a petty civil officer about the rank of a sûn-kiám.

Sú (= tsú). **lām-sú-kóng**, to talk falsely or improperly. **lām-sú** (C.), = lām-sám.

Sú [R. millet, = col. sóe], (C. sú, sí; Cn. sû). **tō liông siok, bék sú chek**, the six sorts of grain.

Sú [R. to cause; to send; to use; = col. sái], (Cn. sû). **siet-sú**, supposing that (v. siet). **sú-hùi**, money expended; expenses. **so-sú** (R.), to instigate to a quarrel, or to dangerous actions. **sū--i lóh--khì** (Cn.), to send him down, as the supreme God sends some spirit.

sú-kun-tsú, a sort of medicine.

Sú [R. death; to die; = col. sí], (Cn. sû). **sú-seng**, death and life (v. seng). **sú-bûn-koan**, the gate of hades. **kièn-sú jû-biên**, to look on death as sleep, as man bent on revenge, &c. **khùi-sú bû-tē** (R.), dreadfully ashamed.

Sú [R. —; C. chí; A. tsú? name of a large ruminant animal]. **sú-bí**, a sort of flapper carried by the genii (tail of the animal?).

Sù (C. sì). **hê-sîn pàng-sù**, flies making spots on things.

Sù [R. four, = col. sì], (Cn. sû). **sù-hong**, square (v. hong). **sù-phòe**, duly proportioned (v. phòe). **sù-chèng**, upright, as conduct (v. chèng). **sù-sàn**, dispersing in all directions, as people.

sù-su, the four books. **sù-si** (C.), id. **sù-sî**, the four seasons. **sù-kùi**, id. **sù-khùi** (C.), id. **sù-chi**, the limbs (v. chi). **sù-kun**, four principal medicines. **sù-bút**, four other medicines (v. bút). **sù-sîn**, four powerful medicines (v. sîn). **sù-hái**, the four seas. **sù-î**, the outside barbarians. **sù-hâng**, the four lictors who walk or stand before a mandarin. **sù-phêng**, plays in the Swatow dialect (v. phêng).

sù-jī-thâu, the 122d radical written at the top.

Sù [R. to arrange; four; large; reckless; profligate; used as an alternative form of the previous word], (Cn. sû).

sù-thīn, all arranged, as marriage; well proportioned (v. thīn).

hòng-sù, disrespectful in conduct. **hêng-hêng sù-chì**, perversely and resolutely wicked.

sù-bû--lâng, to insult people, and put them to shame by violent scolding (v. bû).

Sù [R. —; C. sì; Cn. sù; coarse silk; to mix; confused]. **sù-sù**, having the edges ravelled, as a dress. **jû-jû sù-sù**, all in disorder, as things or talk. **jû-sù-bāng**, confused dreams. **sù-pê**, ravelled edges of dress, in deepest mourning.

Sù [R. chhù, order]. **sù-sī**, in an orderly state.

Sù (Cn. sû), to bestow (said only of a very high superior). **siùⁿ-sù**, id. **un-sù**, gracious gift, as from emperor (v. un). **khim-sù**, bestowed by imperial favour, as degree. **sù chìn-sū**, to bestow the degree of Tsin-sze on the successful competitors.

Sù [R. multitude; nearly; a concubine], (C. sì; Cn. sû). **sù-bîn**, the people in general (v. bîn).

sù-ki (R.), almost; very nearly; probably.

sù-bú, father's secondary wife or concubine (said by son of principal wife). **sù-chhut**, born of a secondary wife or concubine. **sù--ê**, id. **sù-má**, grandmother who is a concubine or secondary wife. **sù-tsó-bú**, id.

Sù [R. to send; a messenger; = col. sài; by change of tone from "sú," to cause or send], (Cn. sû). **sù-chiá**, a messenger sent by a sovereign.

sù-kun-tsú, name of a medicine.

Sù [R. sò, plain; simplicity; original colour]. **sù-eng**, white jessamine.

Sù — **bák-chiu sù-sù**, eyes almost shut, as when very sleepy.

Sù [R. sympathizing; compassionate], (C. sì; Cn. sû). **sù-sim**, sympathizing; sympathetic; humane and kind. **khoan-sù**, to act leniently, as for small faults, or as allowing delay in paying debts. **jiâu-sù** (R.), to forgive, as a superior. **sù-tsōe**, pardon me, sir, for my want of politeness (said on making some slight breach of etiquette, or on receiving what we count too great attention or politeness from the other). **sù-tsōe sù-tsōe**, id.

Sù [R. to be anxious, = col. sū; by change of tone from "su," to think], (Cn. sû). **ì-sù**, meaning; intention; purpose; feeling of mind. **bô-ì-sù**, meaningless; spiritless; aimless. **bô-ì-bô-sù**, id.

Sū [R. sù, to be anxious; by change of tone from "su," to think], (Cn. sû). **ū-sim-sū**, careful; cautious; considerate; hard to cheat or get round. **toā-sim-sū**, too cunning; always deceitfully and selfishly planning for personal gain. **sim-sū toā**, id.

Sū [R. to make an offering in worship], (Cn. sû). **chè-sū**, to make a sacrifice or offering in worship; a sacrificial offering to the dead, or to a god. **sū hê-thó**, to make an offering to the spirit of the earth at a burial.

sū-giáp, property enjoyed in turn by relatives, as they take the turn of making the ancestral offerings (a business). **sū-tiên**, fields for that purpose.

Sū [R. hereafter; to inherit; posterity; = col. sû], (Cn. sû). **sū-hō**, afterwards.

Sū (R. id.), (C. sī; Cn. sû). **hái-sū**, an island, not large. **phû-sū**, id. **soaⁿ-sū**, land in general as opposed to sea, whether mainland or islands. **bô-soaⁿ bô-sū**, in the wide ocean far from any land. **khoàⁿ--liáu bô-soaⁿ-sū**, could see no land at all. **goā-sì-sū**, outer islands (v. sì). **kó-lōng-sū**, Kulangseu island. **koe-sū** (lit. hen island), Pagoda island, near Amoy.

Sū [R. order; a preface], (C. sī; Cn. sû), a preface; an inscription in small letters at the corner of a tablet.

thâu-sū, a preface (s. clue). **pâi-sū**, an inscription in small letters at the corner or side of a wooden tablet, *e.g.* telling who put it up, or the date. **chit-tè-sū**, one preface or small side inscription.

chhù-sū, order of arrangement; regular order. **chiàu-chhù-sū**, in regular order, as one after another.

SŪ [R. a clue], (C. sī; Cn. sü). **thâu-sū**, the clue of an affair (s. preface). **chhē thâu-sū**, to try to find the clue of an involved affair.

SŪ [R. sû, different]. **sū put-ti**, yet strange to say the effect (or fact) is that —; said of what comes to pass quite contrary to expectation.

SŪ [R. like; similar]. **siong-sū**, extremely like. **jī sū jîn-hêng**, a man's writing has a resemblance to his personal appearance. **chhe-tsú sū i-hók**, wife and children are like dress. **kong-im sū-chièn**, time is like an arrow (v. chièn).

SŪ (R. id.), (Cn. sü). **chhut-sū**, to become a mandarin.

SŪ [R. sī, to wait upon], (C. sī). **sū-chiá-kong**, a large sort of serpent which is worshipped.

SŪ (cf. sō). **sū-káu saⁿ-kā**, to set dogs a-fighting; to set men a-quarrelling.

SŪ — **sú-sū-háu**, to whizz, as a bullet or arrow; sound of boat moving rapidly through the water; said of a man hurrying away in great haste. **sū-sū-kiò**, to whizz, &c. **thiàⁿ kàu sū-sū-kiò**, to be in such pain as to draw in one's breath with a sibilant sound.

SŪ (R. id.), (C. sī; Cn. sü), a prefix to an official title showing that it is held only temporarily, as a man of sufficient rank appointed for the time by the governor-general. **sū--ê**, holding the office pro tempore; acting —. **sū-ê-koaⁿ**, id. **sū-lâi sū-khì**, moved back and forwards, as "acting" officials holding office temporarily.

SŪ (Cn.), = A. chī, a cyclical and horary character. **sū-sî**, = A. chī-sî, 9—11 A.M.

SŪ (R. id.), (Cn. sü), business; an affair; a matter; troublesome affairs, as lawsuits, quarrels, disputes, &c. **sū-chêng**, an affair; matters; circumstances. **sū-lí**, an affair or matter in relation to its cause or to the way of setting it right. **sū-kè**, matters to be attended to (v. kè). **sū-giáp** (R.), business; occupation; profession (s. sacrifice). **chit-toāⁿ-sū**, one affair or piece of business. **chit-tiûⁿ-sū**, one long and complicated affair from beginning to end. **chit-khan-sū**, one lawsuit, or considerable dispute, or quarrel.

siáⁿ-sū, why ever —? (v. siáⁿ). **bô-siáⁿ-sū**, nothing the matter. **bô-sū**, id. **ū-sū**, to have business (esp. troublesome affairs) to attend to; to be involved in some trouble.

pún-sū, talent; ability.

sūn-sū, matters falling out just as we wish or desire. **sit-sū**, to meet with disaster. **put-chè-sū**, it will not do, as a plan, entreaty, or counsel. **i-o chiông-sū**, to follow another's views blindly. **bô-sū-sái** (C.), it will not do.

tiong-sîn put-sū jī-tsú, a faithful statesman does not serve two masters.

sè-sū, customary rites of many sorts, usually involving expenses (v. sè). **hiong-kiet sî-sū**, lucky and unlucky times and matters. **put-sek sî-sū**, ignorant of the force of circumstances (v. sek). **kong-sū**, public business. **chhe-sū**, official duty on which one is sent. **hí-sū**, auspicious matters, esp. getting a son (v. hí). **hó-sū**, good or benevolent actions. **chhò-sū**, faults, esp. gambling and vicious indulgence. **êng-sū**, other people's matters (v. êng).

ke-sū, circumstances of a family, *e.g.* as to wealth or expenses. **hó-ke-sū**, wealthy. **ke-sū toā**, having a great many persons depending on him for food. **ke-sū chhim-chīn--khì**, family property all expended.

jîn-sū sūn-siók, affairs of business and family all going well, without sickness or calamity. **jîn-sū put-sūn**, one's trade going wrong, or sickness or death in the family. **ti-jîn-sū**, come to the years of discretion. **put-séng jîn-sū**, very foolish and stupid, as man; very ill, or in a swoon or faint. **chit--ê jîn-sū**, a small present given for services kindly done. **sàng-jîn-sū**, to make such a present.

to-sū, a busybody. **hèⁿ-sū**, id.; a meddler; a tattler (v. hèⁿ).

chhap-sū, to meddle in others' affairs (v. chhap). **pān-sū**, to manage an affair. **tsòe-sū**, to act in a matter; to begin a troublesome matter; to raise a quarrel or cause trouble. **tsò-sū** (C.), id. **tsòe-sū, tióh sòe-jī**, in doing any special business one should be careful. **chhòng-sū**, to raise a feud or dispute, often falsely (v. chhòng). **chhióng-sū**, to cause a feud or troubles. **lāu-sū**, to bring on troubles by improper conduct. **seng-sū**, to be the cause (naturally) of such troubles; a quarrel or dispute arising. **séng-sū**, to avoid causing trouble, *e.g.* by not insisting too strongly on our rights. **séⁿ-sū** (C.), id. **ūi-sū**, to be involved in a legal case so as to have to defend one's self in court.

thong-sū, an interpreter. **hoan thong-sū**, an interpreter for a foreign language. **tong-sū**, to have the chief management, as in a shop (v. tong). **táng-sū**, man who oversees some public work (v. táng). **koán-sū**, a sort of steward or head-servant. **tsóng-sū**, to have the general oversight or management of a number of matters. **kì-sū** (X.), the clerk of a meeting.

chip-sū, the insignia of office, &c., carried before a mandarin; also (X.), a deacon. **pâi chip-sū**, to set in order the insignia, &c., for the mandarin.

sū-tsú, one of the two principal parties in a lawsuit or feud. **sū-toan**, cause or origin of some very troublesome affair. **kāu sū-lē**, having a great deal of troublesome business; constantly having some disease, when cured of one just getting ill of another.

SŪ [R. a scholar; a literary man; the class of literati and government officials], (Cn. sü), one of the musical notes. **sū-lông kong-siong**, the four classes of men, literati, farmers, workmen, and traders. **sin-sū**, those persons in a place who are allowed to wear a button, as Sew-tsai graduates and upwards.

chìn-sū, a Tsin-sze or graduate of the highest rank, like D.C.L. or LL.D. **bú-chìn-sū**, a military graduate of the highest rank. **saⁿ-pah-lák chìn-sū**, 360 Tsin-sze graduates, said to have been put to death by a Ming emperor, and afterwards, as a reparation, canonized by the royal title of ông-iâ. **tiòng chìn-sū**, to become a Tsin-sze. **tāi-hák-sū**, four high literary chancellors (v. hák).

ké bêng-sū, putting on proud airs and scarcely looking at people, as if a distinguished scholar. **kek bêng-sū**, id. **koà bák-kiàⁿ, ké bêng-sū**, said in joke of a man wearing spectacles.

siòng-sū, a fortune-teller who tells fortunes by looking at a man's appearance and general manner. **tō-sū**, a Tauist priest. **kun-sū** (R.), soldiers and petty military officers.

tāi-sū, a title of the idol Kwan-yin. **koan-im**

tāi-sū, id. **tāi-sū-iâ**, the king of the ghosts and demons of the 7th month, much worshipped in that month; has a very hideous face, and has a small image of Kwan-yin on his head; said to be an incarnation of Kwan-yin; name also given collectively to all the tablets of a temple for those who have no posterity. **tāi-sū-peh**, id.

suh (R. sok), (P. soh), to suck; to draw out matter, as a poultice does. **suh-lin**, to suck milk. **suh chhân-lê**, to suck snails out of the shells. **suh lâng-huih**, to draw out matter and blood, as poultice.

suh [R. sok, quick, = col. soā]. **kín suh-suh**, very quick.

sủh — **sủh-sủh**, dull; without talent. **sủh-gièn**, very dull, low-spirited, and broken-down, as from poverty and want of work. **siēn-sủh** (T. siēn-sủt), quiet and indisposed to act, as from natural disposition or slight illness, or from fear, or discouragement, or remembrance of punishment; unwilling to make a quarrel, or even to retaliate when scolded, struck, or attacked; gentle and quiet in disposition; often said of a person formerly troublesome, but tamed by calamity or punishment; often said of a child.

sui (R. id.), although. **sui-jiên**, id. **sui-bóng**, id. **sui sī** —, although it is — (or are). **sui ū** —, although there is — (or are).

sui (R. id.) **iên-sui**, coriander. **iên-sui-chháu**, a small plant often grown round the roots of plants in flower-pots.

sui, the spout of a tea-pot, kettle, &c. **tê-koàn-sui**, spout of tea-pot. **hó-chhut-sui**, it pours out well. **ám-péng-sui-khang**, scupper-holes.

sui (R. id.) **tsang-sui**, a rain coat or cape, gen. made of the fibre of the "tsang" palm. **moaⁿ tsang-sui**, to put on such a rain-coat.

sui — **mn̂g-sui**, short hair round the root of the queue, meant to be afterwards braided into it; hair hanging down at side of woman's head. **mn̂g-sui-á**, id. **giah mn̂g-sui**, to part the hair on woman's forehead.

sûi (C.) **sng-sûi**, mulberry fruit.

sûi (R. id.), the Suy dynasty, A.D. 590-620, just before the Tang dynasty. **sûi-tiâu**, id.

sûi [R. to follow; according to; one by one; each], to follow; to obey; according to.

sûi-piēn, anyhow; just as may be convenient. **sûi-piēn-lâng**, any one.

sûi-ì, to follow one's own inclination; just as one likes; just as you please; often said when inviting another to eat. **sûi lâng--ê ì-goān**, to fulfil or act according to a man's wish (+). **hu-chhiòng hū-sûi**, husband and wife harmonious (v. chhiòng). **jip-káng sûi-oan, jip-hong sûi-siók**, in a channel follow the windings; in a place follow the customs. **sûi-tsúi jip**, to go in with the tide (+).

saⁿ-sûi, to keep company, as good friends, or as man and wife. **siong-sûi**, id. **sûi-pút**, to follow an idol in procession. **sûi-hiuⁿ**, to go in an incense procession. **sûi-jīm**, to accompany a mandarin to his seat of office, as wife and family, sometimes mother; but his father must not. **kun-sûi**, to follow, as a servant or attendant. **sûi-kè-kán**, female slave who goes with a bride at marriage (v. kè).

sûi-sî, immediately. **sûi-sî èng-pièn**, to act according to circumstances. **sûi-sî tńg**, to change one's plans according to circumstances.

sûi-āu chiū-kàu, I will arrive immediately.

sûi-kàu sûi-tng, must just bear it when it comes.

sûi-khì sûi-lâi, to go and come immediately. **sûi-tsûn khì, sûi-tsûn lâi**, to go and come by same vessel or same voyage. **sûi-tsúi khì, sûi-tsúi lâi**, to go and come by the first change of tide (+). **sûi-thàn sûi-chiáh**, to use money for food just as earned; to live from hand to mouth.

sûi-chhiú lâi-khì, come away with me at once (s. hang down). **sûi-chhiú siu--khí-lâi**, lay it away at once without delay. **sûi-chhiú théh--khì**, take it away in the hand at once, as a small thing; often with the idea, as you are going at anyrate. **kiáh chìt-ki-sìⁿ sûi-chhiú**, to take a fan in the hand, just to have something in one's hand. **sûi-chhiú-mih**ⁿ, some small thing (as a fan, pipe, or handkerchief), such as people usually carry with them.

sûi-sin teh-toà, to carry constantly with one, *e.g.* a pipe, or a long box used as a pillow. **hē-soàⁿ sûi-sin**, taking an umbrella along with one. **sûi-sin-pó**, some article counted very precious and always carried with one, *e.g.* some rare and valuable ornament, or the tools of a skilled workman, instruments of a surgeon, or books of a learned man; said of a man's talents for mental or manual work; also, of an opium pipe, or of a concubine taken with one in travelling.

sûi lâng--ê lėk-liōng, according to a man's ability (+).

sûi-lâng-chiáh, one by one eating separately. **sûi-lâng-lâi**, coming forward one by one. **sûi-kiaⁿ-théh**, take up each thing separately, one by one. **sûi-hāng**, each article separately, as in lifting things, or in discussing matters. **sûi-jī-kí**, point out word by word. **sûi-jī-thák**, read out word by word, as scholar, giving the full sound of each word separately.

sûi-tah (Cn.), at each place; at many places.

sûi (R. id., = col. sê, sē), (P. sôe, sûi), to hang down to allow to hang down. **sûi-lóh**, to hang down, as branch, &c.; to let down, as a door-screen. **sûi--lóh-khì**, let down, as door-screen. **pàng-sûi**, to let hang down, as arms at side. **chhiú pàng-sûi**, let your arms hang at your side. **chhiú sûi--lóh-khì**, id. **sûi-chhiú teh-khiā**, standing with the arms hanging straight down at one's side, as before a superior. **sûi-chhiú**, let down the sedan! (said to chair-bearers), (s. follow).

sûi-gû, the broad flat plate on the cover of a box, that falls down and lets through the staple for the padlock.

sûi-thâu sòng-chì (R.), hanging down one's head with a dispirited look. **sûi-si-liú**, the weeping-willow.

sì-lâm-sûi, thoroughly drenched, as ground, &c. **hō͘ sì-lâm-sûi**, rain overflowing all around. **bák-sái sì-lâm-sûi**, tears flowing profusely. **chiáh kàu sì-lâm-sûi**, eating so as to slobber one's self over, as child.

súi, pretty; beautiful; lovely. **súi giang-giang**, very pretty. **khah-súi pút-tsó**, more lovely than Kwan-yin.

koà-súi--ê, worn for mere ornament, not for any use. **ài-koà-súi**, fond of wearing ornaments, *e.g.* armlets, bracelets, trinkets, &c.

súi-chhong, how very pretty! (ironically for ugly). **lí iáh súi-chhong**, you are as bad as the man with whom you are finding fault. **lí súi-khoán**, id. (ironical).

súi [R. water, = col. tsúi]. **hó-chhùi-súi**, good at polite phrases and flattering talk. **ū-chhùi-súi**, id. **ēng chhùi-súi phièn--lâng**, to deceive people by fair speeches. **hó-kháu-súi**, good at talking people over, esp. with a little falsehood.

hong-súi, a grave; the good luck of a site, esp. for grave; the Fung-shuy. **chit-hiét hong-súi**, one grave. **khàm hong-súi**, to examine officially a disputed grave; this work of examination is counted unlucky for the mandarin, so that red things must be presented to him for good luck. **hong-súi sien-si^n**, a geomancer who looks out sites for graves, &c. **hong-súi khah-pek**, the hills rising too near the front of a grave. **hong-súi-thâu**, a family beginning to prosper very much, whose ancestors were not distinguished. **hong-súi-bé**, a family formerly prosperous and flourishing dwindling away or losing wealth and influence, its members without talent, and wasting what still remains. **hong-súi chhut-khì**, the good luck of a grave all gone.

hong-súi put-gû, great and sudden calamity, as by wind, water, robbers, fire, &c. (v. gû).

bān-súi tiâu-tang, tidal stream flowing always to the east (v. tiâu). **sù-súi lâi-tiâu**, water from all quarters seeming to meet in front of a grave.

san-súi, a landscape picture. **ūi san-súi**, to paint a landscape. **koan-san goán-súi**, to walk for amusement looking at scenery. **iú-san, piēn iú-súi**, where there are hills there must be water (said of things naturally joined in pairs). **iú-san, iú-súi; iú-sîn, iú-kúi**, as water accompanies hills, so the spirit of a great canonized man has inferior spirits as attendants.

liû-súi, a scroll-book in which sales, &c., are entered just as they are made, to be afterwards copied into the "jit-chheng." **liû-súi-phō͘**, id. **lo̍k-hoa liû-súi**, in great misery and poverty.

siáu-súi, urine. **bô-siáu-súi**, unable to pass urine. **lī-súi**, to be diuretic. **pó-pì lī-súi**, tonic and diuretic. **sīn-súi chhiong-chiok**, lusty, as young man (v. sīn).

sin-súi ê só-hùi, money for cooking, as for deputy mandarin (v. sin). **toān-súi-hó^n--sí**, to kill by want of food and water.

ú-súi, the term about Feb. 18th or 19th. **bók-pún súi-goân**, men should reverence the source of their being, (parents and ancestors), as trees have roots and streams sources.

súi-gûn, quicksilver. **súi-koan**, a spirit or god that rules the sea. **súi-gû**, a buffalo (v. gû). **ng súi-gû**, to play at blind-man's buff. **ng súi-hî**, id. **súi-koe** (C. ke), a large sort of frog.

SÚI — **pìn-súi**, the hair (of women) hanging down at the side of the head about the temples. **lâu pìn-súi**, to let that part of the hair grow.

SÚI — **jiáu^n-súi**, ornamental wood-work, like border and brackets, below the edge of a table (v. jiáu^n). **lėk-súi** (T.), id. **toh--ê tsáu-súi** (Cn.), id.

SŪI [R. to accord with; to accomplish or effect]. **sūi-ì**, the matter falling out just as we would desire. **chhèng-sim sūi-ì** (R.), just answering to our desire.

SŪI [R. to sleep, = col. chē]. **tók-sūi-chhn̂g**, a couch or bed made for one to sleep on. **toā-tók-sūi**, a bed of a rather larger size, that can hold two. **sió-tók-sūi**, the smallest sort, that can only hold one. **sam-keng put-sūi, hiet put-kui-keng**, if you pass the third watch without sleeping, the blood does not go in its right course.

SŪI [R. a good omen]. **siông-sūi**, a good omen. **siâng-sūi** (C.), id.

sūi-hiu^n, a shrub with beautiful white flowers.

sūi-tién, Sweden. **sūi-kok**, id. **sūi-sū**, Switzerland.

SŪI [R. a sort of disease]. **piȅn-sūi**, palsy. **poàn-sūi**, id.

SŪI (R. id.), an ear of corn; a bunch, as of grapes. **tiū-sūi**, a head or ear of rice. **bėh-sūi**, ear of wheat or barley (v. bėh).

kiet-sūi, the ear just formed fully, after the flower is past, and before the grain is hardened, which is "jip-liàp." **chhut-sūi**, the ear just appearing at first before flowering. **sat-bú si^n kàu chiâ^n-sūi**, having lice in great numbers.

SŪI [R. sū, a tree, = col. chhiū]. **gōng-á-soa chiú sien-hô-sūi**, great sharks guard the coral tree; said also figuratively. **san-hô-sūi** (C.), = A. sien-hô-chhiū, a tree of coral.

SUI^n (C.), = A. sun, sng, a surname.

SUI^n (C.), = A. sng, sour.

SUI^n (C.), = A. sng, soreness of the teeth.

SUI^n (C.), = A. sng, feeling of weariness and dull pain.

SUI^n (C.), = A. sng, a small pin or wedge.

SUI^n (C.), = A. sng, an axletree.

SŪI^n (Cn.), = A. seng, beforehand; formerly; in advance.

SŪI^n (Cn.), = A. san, to thin, weed out, or prune away.

SÚI^n (C.) **thô-súi^n**, = A. thô-sún, sort of edible marine worm.

SÚI^n (C.), in some phrases, = A. sún, to injure. **súi^n-sit**, to lose, as things stolen, taken away, or spoiled.

SÙI^n (C.), = A. sǹg, to calculate. **hó-ē-sùi^n**, = A. hó-ē-siàu, a good plan; easy to accomplish.

SÙI^n (C.), = A. sǹg, to tie very tight.

SUN (R. id., = col. sng), a grandson; a nephew; a surname (C. sui^n, only as a surname).

sun chin-jîn, a god of medicine.

ta-po͘-sun, a son. **si^n ta-po͘-sun**, to have a son born to one.

sun-á, a brother's son; any male relative of the same surname who is one degree further from the common ancestor. **chek-sun hia^n-tī**, male blood-relations of the same surname in general.

toā-sun, eldest son of eldest son. **lāi-sun**, son's son. **goā-sun**, daughter's son. **tit-sun**, son of brother's son. **goā-tit-sun**, son of brother's daughter, or of wife's brother's son. **piáu-tit-sun**, grandson of cousin of different surname (v. piáu). **gōe-seng-sun**, grandson of sister. **lú-sun**, grand-daughter. **tsa-bó-sun**, a grand-daughter; a prostitute (v. bó).

cheng-sun (R.), great-grandson. **ka^n-ná^n-sun**, id. **goân-sun** (R.), great-great-grandson. **ngó-tāi-sun**, id. **chhit-sè-sun**, descendant of the seventh generation.

sun-sài, husband of niece or of grand-daughter. **sun-sim-pū**, wife of nephew or of grandson.

kiá^n-sun, posterity. **kiá^n-kiá^n sun-sun**, posterity for some generations. **sí-kiá^n chéh-sun**, may all your posterity be cut off. **kiá^n-sun-tháng**, a tub used at accouchement. **tsú-sun-tháng**, do., only said when it is bought at marriage time. **tsoát-tsú biét-sun**, may all your posterity be cut off!

jî-sun, posterity (v. jî).

SÛN (R. id.), a decade, esp. of years; a period of varying length in the ceremonies for the dead. **kúi-sûn**, how many decades of years old? as old man (+).

sam-sûn, the throw of the dice when all three have

厦英大辭典

the same number. **tâu-á sam-sûn**, id. **sam-sûn-chiú**, drinking three times at beginning of feast.

sa^{n}-sûn, the third set of rites for the dead; done by a married daughter, or by the son-in-law, if the family be wealthy, with great expense and display. **kè-sa^{n}-sûn**, to have this third set of rites performed. **tsáp-it-sûn**, eleven rounds of these rites, often done for the wealthy. **lō͘-bé-sûn**, the concluding set of rites for the deceased. **tsòe-sûn**, to perform rites before the "hûn-sin" of the deceased, at intervals of fixed length (*e.g.* sometimes five days make one "sûn"); greater number according to age and wealth of deceased. **tsòe-kúi-sûn**, which of these successive rites is now being performed? **pâi kúi-sûn**, how many of these sets of rites are there in all? (+). **chhui joā-tsōe-sûn**, id.

gō͘-sûn-tsoeh (X.), Pentecost, the feast of the fiftieth day.

sûn (R. id.), to go about to inspect or examine what is doing, or the state of matters; to visit a second time a patient who has already been visited. **sûn chit-tsoā**, to go once and inspect for another; to go a second time and examine the patient, often done for one fee. **ū-sûn**, makes a second visit for one fee, *e.g.* when the fee is large. **bô-sûn**, does not visit a second time without an extra fee.

sûn-khoà^{n}, to go about and inspect. **sûn-tsa**, to inspect or investigate, as mandarin or official spy. **sûn-ki^{n}**, to patrol at night. **sûn-iā**, to make secret examination at night. **sûn-sàu**, to go about looking for pirates, &c. **sûn-sī**, to go round inspecting or overseeing, as any one. **sûn-siù** (R.), ancient imperial tour of inspection (v. siù). **chhut-sûn**, to go out on a round of inspection, anciently done by emperor, now by viceroy. **tāi-sûn**, to inspect for the emperor, as an officer was sent round under the Ming dynasty; or for Heaven, as some idols are said to do.

sûn-kiám, a small mandarin who assists the Hien mandarin (v. kiám). **sûn-si**, the lowest civil assistant mandarin. **sûn-pō͘**, a sort of aide-de-camp or assistant of a high mandarin. **sûn-pō͘-thia^{n}**, id. **bûn-sûn-pō͘**, civil do. **bú-sûn-pō͘**, military do. **sûn-hong**, sort of head policeman used by military mandarin for keeping a general watch over his district. **iâm-sûn-noâ^{n}**, sort of excisemen for salt revenue (v. iâm).

sûn-ài, a short wide-mouthed trumpet.

sûn [R. all around; to comply with]. **bô-sûn-chêng**, impartial, as mandarin or schoolmaster.

sûn [R. to comply with; to follow; to accord, = col. sūn]. **sûn-kui tō-kú**, following correct rules and customs; well-behaved.

sûn [R. bûn, wavy lines]. **bau-sûn**, to fold in or out, so as to make a hem or border; to make a sort of rim on a metal or stoneware vessel. **lek chit-sûn**, to make a fold, as in a dress or hat, either for ornament or in order to shorten it. **lek-sûn**, a fold, crease, or wrinkle, forming of itself, as in a dress worn too long, or as on the neck of a fat man, or wrist of fat child. **chhēng kàu lek-sûn**, to wear a dress till it is full of creases, &c., and needs to be washed. **pak-té lek-sûn**, the belly making folds, as in great hunger.

bák-sûn, the wrinkle at the edge of the upper eyelid. **bák-chiu-sûn**, id. **bák-chiu têng-sûn**, the upper eyelid having a wrinkle on it, counted good-looking. **bák-chiu bô-têng-sûn**, the upper eyelid coming straight down without any wrinkle.

sûn [R. name of a plant, and of a state], a surname.

sûn [R. yielding; docile; tamed; gentle]. **sûn-sûn**, gentle and kindly; mild in temper; genial in manner; obedient, submissive, and easily taught, as lad; quiet and easily managed, as horse. **sèng sûn-sûn**, good-tempered and gentle. **un-sûn**, gentle, meek, and good; mild, pleasant, and kind. **sûn-liông**, well-behaved, of good character; trustworthy, esp. in money matters [these last two phrases are also written with the second word below].

sûn [R. pure; genuine; honest]. **hong-siòk sûn-hō͘**, manners and customs very excellent (v. hō͘).

sûn [R. pure silk; pure; perfect; whole; sincere]. **sûn-tsoân**, perfect in character; blameless. **sûn-tsoân-hó**, extremely good, without a fault or flaw. **sûn-sûn**, quite rightly made or of proper quality, according to the pattern, said esp. of several articles all alike and like the pattern; always right and good, *e.g.* milk every day good and pure. **iáu-sûn**, id. **sûn-pān**, all the articles like each other and like the pattern. **kéng khah-sûn--ê**, to choose picked articles of the best quality. **sûn-phek bû-hâ** (R.), a perfect gem without a flaw, unblemished in character.

sûn-siòk, regular and good, as conduct; all good and equally good, as articles (v. siòk).

chiú sûn-sûn, the liquor is of moderate strength.

un-sûn, meek; gentle; good-tempered. **sûn-liông**, trustworthy [these two phrases interchanged with the second last word].

sûn [R. good, as wine; generous; good], mellow, as liquor; mellow and not too strong.

sún [R. to injure, = col. sńg], (C. sún, súi^{n}). **sún-hāi**, to be injurious, as food, &c. **sún-hoāi**, to damage; to spoil; to destroy. **sún-sit**, to become few by death, as family or village. **sún-teng**, to lose male children or relatives (v. teng). **sún goân-khì**, to injure one's constitution, as lust or excess. **sún-pî**, to disagree with the stomach. **sún im-chek**, to commit sins so as to draw down punishment from Heaven.

hu-sún, consumption. **sún-pī^{n}**, id. **lòh-sún**, to fall into consumption (s. tenon).

iú-sún bû-ek, useless and hurtful. **sún-jîn lī-kí**, to injure others for one's own benefit.

sún — **ka-lún-sún**, to shiver (v. ka).

sún (R. id.), young edible shoots of bamboo and some other plants. **sún-koa^{n}**, dried bamboo shoots. **sng-sún**, pickled bamboo shoots. **tek-sún**, edible bamboo shoots. **lék-tek-sún**, the softest sort. **tang-sún**, winter bamboo shoots, that have not come above ground. **chhun-sún**, spring do., coarser. **phái^{n}-tek chhut hó-sún**, said of a son better or better-looking than his father.

ka-pók-sún, edible shoots of a water plant. **ka-pèk-sún**, id. **ka-ték-sún**, id. **kha-péh-sún**, id. **ka-pèh-sún** (C.), id.

thô-sún (C. súi^{n}), a sort of edible marine worm. **thô-sún-tàng**, a gelatinous eatable made from it.

chiòh-sún, a solitary upright pillar-shaped rock (s. tenon).

chhi^{n} sún-sún, pale, as face in sickness or in sudden fear.

sún (R. id.), a tenon. **mn̂g-sún**, the pivot of a Chinese door. **chiòh-sún**, a stone tenon (s. shoots). **khang-sún**, mortice and tenon. **toá^{n}-toá^{n} khang-sún**, constantly plotting improper ways of getting money out of people.

chiap-sún, to fit tenon and mortice (v. chiap). **jip-sún**, id. **lòh-sún**, id.; also to agree well together (s. injure). **tàu-lòh-sún**, to fit tenon and mortice together. **lâu-sún,** joints become loose, as of furniture. **lak-sún,** id. **thè-sún,** mortice joint separating and giving way.

sún (T.) **sún-lak,** elegantly formed, as piece of furniture, or as person's limb or whole person.

sùn (Cn.) **sùn--tsóh-jit,** second day before yesterday.

sùn (R. id., = sūn), the ancient emperor Shun. **giâu-sùn,** Yaou and Shun, the patterns of imperial excellence (v. giâu).

sūn (= sùn), the emperor Shun.

sūn (sound probably changed from "tsûn," a boat). **phak-sūn-têng,** a shed or small portico put up before a door.

sūn [R. sûn, to comply with; to follow; to accord], to go over characters making them plainer, as by making thin lines thicker; to make red lines black, as children do in learning to write; to put colour into words engraved on stone, or brighten up old faded colour. **sūn-o͘,** to put black into words cut in stone. **sūn-âng,** do., red. **sūn-chhi^{n},** do., blue (&c.) **sūn bōng-pâi,** to put colour into the engraved words of a grave-stone, or brighten up the old. **sūn siōng-tāi-jîn,** to write in black on the red lines of a child's first copy-book, which begins "siōng-tāi-jîn."

sūn (Cn.) **sōe-sūn,** = sòe-jī, careful; cautious.

sūn (R. id.), to obey; obedient; favourable, as wind or tide. **sūn-sūn,** very obedient or favourable; also, salutation at parting. **hong sūn-sūn,** wind favourable. **sūn-hong,** a favourable wind. **sàng-sūn-hong,** to give a present to one going on a voyage. **sūn-hong siong-sòng,** may the voyage have propitious gales! **kiàh sūn-hong-kì,** to watch how the wind blows and trim one's conduct to suit. **sūn-lâu,** with favourable tide. **sūn-tsúi,** id. **sūn-tsúi hêng-chiu,** all going well.

sūn-sū, matters all going well according to our plans or desire; all well without any illness. **sūn-kéng,** id. **sūn-ūn,** in a happy, prosperous, fated period of life, without calamities; things going much as we wish. **bô-sūn-liù,** contrary to expectation and quite inconvenient (v. liù). **ún-sūn,** safe and tranquil, as weather, trade, &c. **hō͘-tsúi sūn-siòk,** rain regular and suitable (v. siòk). **hong tiâu, ú sūn** (R.), wind and rain in due season. **thien-khì put-sūn,** weather quite unseasonable, *e.g.* great cold in summer. **jîn-sū put-sūn,** affairs of the family in a sad state (v. sū).

sūn-lō͘, just in the road we are going. **sūn-piēn,** taking advantage of the opportunity to do something without extra trouble. **sūn-chhiú,** taking the opportunity to do something else of the same sort as what is being done. **sūn-sè** (C. sì), to take advantage of the opportunity. **sūn-soà,** do.; in consequence of the opportunity. **sūn-hà chhoā,** to marry just immediately after a parent's death.

sūn-géh, within a month before the time of child-birth.

kui-sūn, to make submission and return to obedience or allegiance. **sūn-hók,** id. **sūn-thàn** (r.), to obey. **sūn jîn-ì,** very compliant. **hàu-sūn,** obedient to parents. **hô-sūn,** harmonious and submissive, as husband and wife. **sūn-thien,** to obey Heaven (v. thien).

sut (R. id.), a cyclical and horary character. **sut-sî,** 7—9 P.M.

sut [R. to compassionate; to pity]. **un-sut** (r.), to compassionate or have mercy on, as ruler on people; to act kindly and considerately, as master towards servants or employés; to assist, as with money, &c. **chiu-sut** (R.), to help by gifts, as the poor. **thé-sut** (r.), to act compassionately; to have tender concern for, as ruler towards people in distress, or when they have some small fault; or as master towards servant.

sut, to beat, whip, or switch with a thin rod or switch; to dust by beating with a rod. **bùt-sut,** to beat with a thin rod. **sut tek-chhì,** to beat or switch with a thin bamboo.

báng-sut, a flapper for driving away mosquitoes; a sort of palm-tree.

sut [R. siet, small fragments, = col. seh, sap], fragments; small crumbs or bits. **sut-sut-á,** in small bits or fragments. **chhun chit-sut-á,** only a small fragment or remnant remains, as of cloth or anything.

kù-sut, saw-dust. **chhâ-sut,** small chips of wood. **piá^{n}-sut,** small crumbs of bread.

hāng-á hāng-sut, a very out-of-the-way corner of a lane.

sut (Cn.) **theh sut-sut,** having absolutely nothing left, all being stolen away, or being awfully poor.

sut [R. name of insect]. **sek-sut,** a small sort of cricket or beetle. **sih-sut** (C.), id. **kā sek-sut,** to set crickets to fight; sort of gambling. **khì-thia^{n}-sek-sut,** dead (lit. gone to hear the crickets).

sut [R. to lead; suddenly; hastily]. **sò-sut,** habitually hasty, apt to act or speak without deliberation, or not attending to the rules of politeness. **chhó-sut,** hasty, careless, negligent, or not particular in doing work. **sut-tit,** very outspoken, blunt, or hasty in speaking, without considering the consequences (but generally right in itself).

sut [R. sùn, to glance rapidly], to wink. **sut-bák,** id. **chit-bák-sut-á,** for a moment. **pí-chhiú sut-bák,** to beckon and wink. **bák-chiu sut-khok sut-khiet,** eyes glancing about rapidly.

sut [R. to make a whistling noise with the mouth; cf. sùt]. **sih-sih sut-sut,** whispering and making secret signs to one another. **sih-bùh sih-sut,** id.

sùt (R. sut), to inform by a sort of whistling or hissing sound, as a secret signal. **kho-sùt-á,** id. **ēng-chhùi sùt,** id. **sih-sih sùt-sùt,** making secret signs by whispers or such sounds. **sùt-sùt-háu,** said of man eagerly desiring to get something, the opportunity for which has come, but may soon be lost. **thià^{n} kàu sùt-sùt-háu,** to be in such pain or cold as to draw in one's breath with a sibilant sound.

sùt [R. to recite; to narrate]. **thoân-sùt** (R.), to deliver a message.

sùt (T.) **siēn-sùt,** = A. siēn-sùh, quiet, inoffensive, and indisposed to quarrel; exhausted and dull, &c.

sùt [R. a rule; an art; a plan; magical rites]. **ū sim-sùt,** skilful and wise in action, whatever circumstances may arise. **sim-sùt hó,** good and kind; fond of assisting and doing good to others. **sim-sùt phái^{n},** constantly scheming evil and injuring people. **sim-sùt bóng-khì,** not much to blame in his conduct. **sim-sùt put-toan,** constantly planning and carrying out schemes injurious to others.

siâ-sùt, magical or black arts. **iau-sùt,** id. **iau-hoat koài-sùt,** id. **hoat-sùt,** id. **i--ê hoat-sùt khah-koâi^{n},** his magic is more powerful. **sùt-sè** (R.), magical and superstitious rites in general.

sùt (same as previous word?). **háng-phiēn-sùt,** to intimidate, delude, and deceive. **láu-phiēn-sùt,** to deceive and defraud. **khit--lâng sùt--khì,** to be deceived or imposed upon.

sùt (mere reduplication). **kùt-lùt-sùt,** very slippery, as a muddy road. **tit-lùt-sùt,** very straight.

swa, swá, swà, swā, swaⁿ, swáⁿ, swàⁿ; better **soa,** soá, soà, soā, soaⁿ, soáⁿ, soàⁿ (*q.v.*)

swah, swáh, swaiⁿ, swâiⁿ, swāiⁿ, swáihⁿ; better **soah,** soáh, soaiⁿ, soâiⁿ, soāiⁿ, soáihⁿ (*q.v.*)

swan, swân, swán, swàn, swān; better **soan,** soân, soán, soàn, soān (*q.v.*)

swat, swát; better **soat,** soát (*q.v.*)

T.

t is often related to **l, n,** or **ch,** the one being in the colloquial and the other in the reading form, sometimes both colloquial.

ta [R. tông, the Tang dynasty; Chinese; = col. tn̂g]. **ta-po͘** (C. tsa-po͘), male (said only of men); a male person. **ta-po͘-kiáⁿ,** a son. **ta-po͘-sun,** id. (v. sun). **ta-po͘-lâng,** a male person; a husband (said in relation to his wife). **ta-po͘-hàn,** a male person (said in a scolding or vulgar way).

ta (same as previous word?). **ta-ke** (C. toā-kɛ), husband's mother (v. ke). **ta-koaⁿ,** husband's father. **ta-ke-koaⁿ,** husband's parents.

ta [R. chiau, to scorch or dry with fire, = col. tâ], dry; dried; (only).

ta-sò, dry and crisp (v. sò). **ta-pē,** too dry, as surface of skin or of eatables. **chhàu-ta,** scorched; singed. **sio chhàu-ta,** to singe; singed.

chhùi-ta, thirsty. **ta-sién,** dry scurf on the body.

ta-tēng, too dry and hard, as eatables; having enough to live on; giving a laconic answer and refusing to take a smaller sum (v. tēng). **ta-sin,** having a tolerable income, as from capital, property, or business; dry, as tobacco or other things, either properly dry or too dry. **ta-tiú,** now able to take care of itself, as young child not now needing to be tended. **ta-sang,** dry and comfortable, as after changing dress or wiping perspiration; dry and mealy, as potatoes.

ta-lī, quite dry, as house that has no damp; dry and comfortable, as after wiping sweat. **ta lī-lī,** perfectly dry, as a dried up river, or as things dried. **lāi-bīn ta-lī,** the house dry; not damp. **khah-ta-lī,** now getting on a little better, so as not to need to work so very hard or to dress so ill; *e.g.* from business improving, or from children beginning to earn something. **sit-ké-bé ta-lī,** now able to get on alone, and not needing help from parents or friends. **ta-lī ê-seng-lí,** a trade that lets our hands and feet be kept dry, *e.g.* dry goods business. **kha-ta chhiú-ta ê-seng-lí,** id.

lim-ta, to drink till quite empty (v. lim). **chiáh--i m̄-ta,** cannot make him submit or get the money out of him, as he is too powerful; I am not able to do the work he wishes, or not able to serve him satisfactorily. **thát-ta,** to drain off moisture till quite dry. **chhit-ta,** to wipe dry. **piàⁿ-ta,** to pour out till quite empty. **phák-ta,** to dry in the sun.

kien-ta, only; merely, = kan-ta.

kan-ta, only; merely; (to no purpose); not watered, as meat. **kan-ta, bô-koàn-tsúi,** in its natural state, as meat into which water has not been injected. **kan-ta chhá,** to fry without water or sauce, &c. **kan-ta lim,** to drink without eating. **kan-ta chiáh,** to eat a simple dish without condiments; to eat at another's charge without making any return; said also of an idle useless fellow. **kan-ta chiáh-pn̄g,** to eat rice alone, without any condiment. **kan-ta liáu,** all expended; quite used up. **kan-ta bô,** do.; none now, though there was before. **kan-ta kiâⁿ,** to have a walk for nothing. **kan-ta sô,** to ramble about without object. **kan-ta siūⁿ,** unable to think out a plan; fruitless thought. **kan-ta béng,** boasting or threatening without any real power. **kan-ta soah,** the matter quite ended without any advantage or reparation. **kan-ta ià,** wearied with doing nothing; ennui.

ta (same as previous word?), a large rock in water, either always above water or sometimes covered. **ta-á,** a smaller rock in water. **tsûn khoà-ta,** the boat is aground on shallows or on a rock. **khoà tī-ta-téng,** aground on a rock. **thâu-kun-ta,** the Cornwallis rock near Amoy. **ta** is thus used in the names of many rocks.

ta-mn̂g, green edible sea-weed growing on rocks. **ta-me͘ⁿ** (C.), id.

tâ [R. chiau, scorched or dried with fire, = col. ta]. **ko͘-tâ,** shrivelled, dried, and withered up, as wood, grass, or sick man. **ko͘-tâ--khì,** shrivelled or withered away. **khàu kàu nâ-âu tâ--khì,** loudly lamenting till the throat is dry.

o͘-tâ, dark appearance of face, as in bad health, or as of an opium-smoker. **bīn lóng-tâ,** face all become dark, as by sickness or opium-smoking.

sim-koaⁿ tâ--khì, deeply grieved and distressed. **sim tâ kàu-saⁿ-tah** (T.), very long and deeply distressed.

tâ (R. nāiⁿ). **bô-tâ-oâ,** having no resource; better bô-tā-oâ (v. oâ). **bô-tâ-tit-oâ,** id.

tá [R. náⁿ, that; there; what? which? = col. tó, tah].

tá-lòh, where? (v. lòh). **tá-lòh chit-ê,** which? **tá-ūi,** where? **beh tá-khì,** where are you going? **lí tá-khì,** id.

chit-tá (Cn.), = chit-tah, this place.

tà (T.) **tà-láng-sáng,** acting in a negligent manner.

tà (Cn. tàu, tà), to cover, as with clouds, mist, or a sort of veil; to cover with paws or hands, as tiger or man catching a man; to spread out its hands to a person, as child.

báng-tà, mosquito-curtains. **báng-tà-chhiu,** fringes of mosquito-curtains. **báng-tà-bí,** ornamental top of mosquito-curtains. **koe-tà,** a wicker-work basket or coop (with no bottom) for keeping fowls. **koan-tà,** a sort of pall for a coffin. **kiong-lú-tà,** a vari-coloured cape worn on some special occasions by rich young women. **chhim-chíⁿ-tà,** a framework of bamboo poles covering the central court of a house. **teng-hé-tà,** a shade or cover for a lamp to keep off wind. **teng-tà-hé,** lamps kept burning night and day beside a corpse covered with a tin or earthen cover. **hun-tà** (r.), cover for top of chimney.

hûn tà-bát-bát, sky all overcast with clouds. **tà-bū,** sky all obscured with mist. **tà-bông-bū,** id. **tà-bê,** id.

tà put-kièn-thien, to put up awnings in the street so that the sky is quite hid. **kap-goá tà-put-kièn-thien,** he will not let me see him, will not give me information or assistance, or puts off paying what is due, &c.

tà sek-khò, to put on trowsers, as women do.

tà-bīn, to cover or shade the face with a cloth or vail (not quite like our vails). **tà phè-á,** to wear such a cloth over the face (v. phè).

tà--lóh-khì, to fall down on one's face or on one's hands. **tsòe sì-kha-hé teh-tà,** to go on all fours (lit. tiger), as man climbing a steep hill, or as lame beggar crawling on ground.

tò-tà, to turn round and seize, as tiger pursued or man attacked.

lām-sám-tà, to get money out of people by frightening them. **tà-iá^n,** id., by meddling in a matter with which we have no concern. **tà chit-ê-iá^n,** id.

tà tī-bāng--nih^n, to be caught in a net, as a bird.

tā [R. nāi^n, a resource; how? = col. tā], (C. tāi). **bô-tā-oā,** having no resource (v. oā).

ta^n [R. tong, proper; ought; to bear; to manage; now; = col. tng, tṅg, tà^n], now; at present. **kàu-ta^n,** by this time; till now; till this time. **tsá--ta^n-sî** (better tsá-tà^n--sî), formerly. **hit-ta^n-sî,** at that time; just at that time. **jit-ta^n-sî,** in the daytime. **ū-ta^n-sî,** sometimes. **ū-ta^n-sî-á,** id.

ta^n (C.) **thâu-khak ta^n-ta^n,** holding one's head very erect. **thâu-khak khah-ta^n,** hold your head more erect, and do not bend forward so much.

ta^n (R. tam), to carry two loads on one pole over the shoulder, as one man does. **ta^n-tà^n,** id. **ta^n tāng-tà^n,** to carry a heavy load thus. **ta^n-kang,** men who carry loads in this way, or their labour. **ta^n-teh,** constantly carrying heavy burdens, as labourers. **ta^n-tsúi,** to carry two buckets of water on a pole. **ta^n-tsúi--ê,** a water-carrier. **lē-thâu ta^n-teng-sim, lē-bé ta^n-thih-thûi,** said of an affair growing much more difficult and serious.

ta^n chit-thâu, to carry one load only at the end of the pole (as one man).

pin-ta^n, a wooden or bamboo carrying-pole, used by one man on his shoulder. **pín-ta^n** (esp. T.), id. **pun-ta^n** (C.), id. **kiáh pin-ta^n,** to carry a carrying pole in the hand, with no load. **tek-ta^n,** a bamboo carrying-pole. **chhiam-ta^n,** carrying-pole with sharp ends (v. chhiam).

kiō-ta^n, the cross-bars which connect the ends of the poles of a sedan, and rest on the shoulders. **tià^n-ta^n,** the cross-bar of an anchor.

gû-ta^n, a yoke for a cow or ox, for ploughing. **gû-lê-ta^n** (C.), id.

seng-ta^n-but, a small edible marine worm, sharp at both ends.

tâ^n— **têng-tâ^n,** making a discrepancy or inaccuracy. **kóng-ōe têng-tâ^n,** to contradict one's self, either from forgetfulness, or from intention to deceive. **siá-jī têng-tâ^n,** to make a mistake in copying. **thia^n--liáu têng-tâ^n,** heard inaccurately. **sǹg-siàu têng-tâ^n,** to make a mistake in calculating, esp. by omitting or erroneously counting some item.

tâ^n, to clean the bottom of a boat or junk by burning, &c.; to heat a dose of opium on the point of a chhiám-á, in the flame of a lamp. **ēng-hé tâ^n,** to warm a small thing by moving it back and forwards over a flame. **tâ^n-sóe,** to clean a boat's bottom by burning, &c.

tâ^n (same as previous word?). **ài-tâ^n-hé** (T.), fond of flying into the flame of a lamp, as some insects.

tá^n [R. to strike], to make a rough calculation. **áu-tá^n,** to beat violently. **kong-tá^n,** to assail; to attack, as a city. **tá^n-chièn,** to do battle. **put-tá^n put-chiau,** without beating he won't confess (v. chiau). **sam tá^n-liáng** (C.), three men compelling two to do what they wish, as in money matters.

tá^n-sàu, to sweep. **tá^n-chhà,** to annoy, as by noise. **it-bóng tá^n-chīn** (to catch all at one cast of the net), to appropriate to one's self what others should share. **tá^n si-soà^n** (Cn.), = phah si-soà^n, to make silk cord, by twisting.

tá^n-tiàp, to heal. **tiet-tá^n i-seng,** a surgeon for falls, wounds, and such accidents only. **tiáp-tá^n i-seng,** id.

tá^n-pān, dress; style of dress, &c. (v. pān). **tá^n-chéng,** to adorn one's self. **tá^n-chien,** to rest and take a meal at a stage on the road, as mandarin (v. chien).

bô-tá^n-kín, good and pleasant to deal with (v. kín).

tá^n-sǹg, to calculate. **tá^n-tsāi,** to make a guess of a whole cargo, as in buying it. **tá^n joā-tsōe,** make a rough guess how many there are, or how much. **tá^n-thàm,** to make secret or quiet investigation or inquiries about a matter. **tá^n-thèng,** id.

tá^n (R. tám), gall; courage.

hîm-tá^n, the gall of the bear, medicinal. **lêng-tá^n-chháu,** a febrifuge medicinal plant (gentian?).

tá^n-thâu, courage. **ū-tá^n-thâu,** brave; courageous; bold. **ū-tá^n,** id. **bô-tá^n,** cowardly. **bô-tá^n-thâu,** id. **hó-tá^n-thâu,** brave; bold. **hó-tá^n,** id. **toā-tá^n,** id. **hó-toā-tá^n,** audacious. **sió-tá^n,** cowardly.

sit-tá^n, to lose courage. **lek-tá^n,** id. **phoà-tá^n,** to get terribly afraid. **sim kia^n, tá^n chièn,** very much terrified. **khiap-tá^n** (Cn.), cowardly (r.)

pàng-tá^n, to be very courageous. **hòng-tá^n,** quite without fear of consequences, often too foolhardy. **gōng-tá^n,** foolhardy. **gōng-gōng-tá^n,** id. **bòng-tá^n,** id.; making dangerous ventures. **tsòng-tá^n,** to stir up one's own courage; very bold, without fear. **tàu-tsòng-tá^n,** to stir up each other's courage, as to do some act together. **thiā^n-tá^n,** to make one's self less afraid, as by a companion, or by some other slight precaution which affects one's own feelings, but scarcely adds any real security. **tiám báng-hun, thiā^n-tá^n,** id. **tiám báng-á-hiu^n, thiā^n-tá^n,** id. **kāng-chhát chioh-tá^n** (borrowing courage from a robber), very bold and wicked.

tiòng-tá^n--sí, to die of great fear, grief, or joy (v. tiòng).

tà^n [R. tàm, by change of tone from "tam," to carry], a load such as one man carries; a pecul weight.

toā-tà^n, Tai-tan island, at mouth of Amoy harbour.

sió-tà^n, Siau-tan island.

chhut-tà^n, to go out to sea past Tai-tan island; to go about trading as a pedlar.

tó-tà^n, pedlar become bankrupt. **ta^n-tà^n,** to carry two loads on one pole (v. ta^n). **sià-tà^n,** to lay down the load. **tán-tà^n,** to wait with a carrying-pole, looking out for a job.

tāng-tà^n, a heavy load. **chit-tà^n pè-tē,** a pair of coarse grass-bags. **chheh-tà^n,** books and other luggage of a travelling literary man. **tê-tà^n,** tea-pot, &c., carried on a journey, as by a mandarin. **thì-thâu-tà^n,** the apparatus of a barber, carried on a pole on his shoulder.

tàⁿ-ūi, burden or capacity of a vessel, counted in peculs. **tsûn, joā-tsōe tàⁿ-ūi**, what is the burden of the vessel in peculs?

tàⁿ [R. tong, ought; bear; now; = col. taⁿ, tng]. **jit-tàⁿ--sî**, day-time. **mîⁿ-tàⁿ--sî**, night-time. **tsá-tàⁿ--sî**, formerly.

tsài--tàⁿ-sî (T.), in the morning.

tàⁿ [R. tàn, to speak to one another], (An.) **tàⁿ-ōe**, to talk. **gâu-tàⁿ-ōe**, oily-mouthed. **lām-sám-tàⁿ**, to talk at random, without regard to truth.

tāⁿ — **chhiò-tāⁿ**, having usually a cheerful pleased smiling look.

tāⁿ (Cn.), = A. chhò, to mistake. **bô-tāⁿ**, no mistake. **kì-tāⁿ**, to make a mistake in writing. **sōh-tāⁿ**, to make a mistake in speaking. **thiaⁿ-tāⁿ**, to make a mistake in hearing. **thiaⁿ--liáu tāⁿ-hī**, to mistake from hearing indistinctly. **kiâⁿ-tāⁿ**, to go a wrong road. **kiâⁿ-tāⁿ-lō**, id.

saⁿ-gō-tāⁿ (T.), to make an omission or mistake, as two persons each trusting to the other, &c. **saⁿ-tāⁿ-gō** (A.), id.

tāⁿ-bák (A.), to mistake in looking. **sǹg-tāⁿ-jit** (A.), to make a mistake in calculating the day, or the number of days.

tāⁿ — **tàn-tāⁿ** (Cn.), to throw away. **pàng-tàn-tāⁿ** (Cn.), id.

hìⁿ-tāⁿ (An.), to throw away.

tah [R. tap, to answer]. **tah-èng**, to promise verbally.

tah (R. tap), to strike gently with the palm; to touch; to pat; to rap; to set up or build, as tent, awning, or building; to buy oil or liquor; to embark; also (Cn.), to ask a man to do a favour, or take a message; to send goods.

tah-chhiú, to clap the hands, as with joy. **tah chhiú-chiúⁿ**, id. **tah-chhiú tah-kha**, to clap the hands and stamp the feet for delight. **tah ka-chiah**, to pat on the back. **tah-heng**, to strike one's breast with the open palm, as in promising to be security. **tûi-heng tah-liú**, to strike one's breast and the buttons with the palm (v. tûi). **tah-toh**, to strike the table with the hand, in anger. **tah-í tah-toh**, strike chairs and tables in anger.

tah-hoāⁿ, to steady one's self by laying the hand on something; to depend on another's care, as a widow (v. hoāⁿ). **tah-piah**, to lean on a wall (s. paste).

tah-thê, to touch the ground with hand or foot. **kha m̄-bat tah-thê**, feet never touching the ground, as a delicate person or one always using sedans. **siang-kha kūi-tah-tah**, kneeling humbly on both knees.

tah-niahⁿ, to be startled. **tah-hiahⁿ**, id. (v. hiahⁿ).

tah-bā, intimate with; likely to succeed (v. bā).

tah-than, to catch a few of the shell-fish called "than." **tah-chìⁿ**, to make the arrow ready to shoot (v. chìⁿ).

tàu-tah, active and diligent, esp. two men acting together harmoniously and actively; well put on, as dress neat and tidy, not in the way. **tsòe tāi-chì tàu-tah**, to do things in an active, neat, and proper manner. **an-tah**, to arrange, as an affair, or as troops (v. an). **tiau-tah**, neat and tidy, as dress, or as person in regard to dress. **táⁿ-pān tiau-tah**, dress neat and neatly put on.

pè-tah, to give small bribes, as to subordinates in yamun, to get their help in a case.

tah-iâⁿ, to encamp. **tah-pîⁿ**, to erect a theatrical stage. **tah pè-pîⁿ**, to put up an awning. **tah phû-kiô**, to make a floating bridge. **tah-liâu**, to put up a hut or rough shed. **tah chháu-chhù**, to put up a hut of straw, grass, &c. **tah-tsō**, to set up the wooden pillars and beams which make the framework of a Chinese house, before filling in the walls. **tah-pang**, to put up a board or boards for scaffolding, as for repairs. **tah phâng-kám**, to put up a bamboo mat as a covering.

tah chhìn-thâu, to give good weight (the turn of the scales) in selling. **tah-chiú**, to buy liquor. **tah-iû**, to buy oil; to lade out oil, as in one's own house (only this second meaning in Cn.)

tah-kau, a boat-hook.

tah-tsûn, to take passage in a boat, either alone or with others. **toaⁿ-tah**, to take a boat for a short passage alone. **tah-tē**, to take passage in a passage-boat. **tah-kheh**, a passenger. **kià-tah**, to send, as goods or letter. **tah-hō** (Cn.), = A. kià-hè, to send goods. **tah-phoe** (Cn.), to send a letter.

tah (Cn.), = tá. **hit-tah**, that place; there. **chit-tah**, this place; here. **ták-tah**, every place. **sûi-tah**, at each place; at many places. **nn̄g-tah**, two places. **m̄-tsai-tah**, not know the locality.

tah, an exclamation at the beginning of a sentence, calling attention to what one is going to say, like "now" or "well then."

tah (cf. tiap). **khah-tah-kú-á**, after a short time.

tah (R. tap). **tah-liên**, a double bag, slung over the shoulder.

tah [R. thiap, to paste on; to join or add to; to supply a deficiency; attached; close to], to paste up; to paste on. **tah-piah**, to paste on the wall. **tah ko-ióh**, to put on a medical plaster. **tah-tsoá**, to paste up paper. **tah kò-sī**, to put up a proclamation.

lám-tah-tah, to take in the arms and embrace, as in joke.

chiàu-phòe-tah, fitting well or mixed in due proportions (v. phòe).

tah-sim, loving each other very much, as relatives, or as very intimate confidential friends. **tah-sim ê-lâng**, a most intimate and confidential friend. **kap-i tah-sim**, to be on terms of most intimate friendship with him.

koaiⁿ-tah-tah, shut quite close, as door or window. **koaiⁿ-khì-tah**, shut it close! **koaiⁿ-bô-tah**, laid to, but still at a small angle, as folding-doors not quite shut and not ready to be bolted. **bô-tah**, id.

pó-pó tah-tah, to mend many places where there are flaws, cracks, &c., but not making a thorough repair. **chhèng-phīⁿ kê, ùn-noāⁿ tah**, put together with mucus and saliva, said in joke or censure of very slim work.

sim tâ kàu-saⁿ-tah (T.), long and deeply grieved and distressed in mind. **sim-koaⁿ beh saⁿ-tah** (T.), id. **pak-tó kap-ka-chiah saⁿ-tah**, belly cleaving to the back, as man in the last stage of leanness, just going to die.

tah — **kàu-tah-tóe**, to the utmost extreme, as of distress (v. tóe).

tåh (R. táp), to tread; to tread or trample on; to draw water by the tread-wheel. **thún-tåh**, to trample on. **thut-tåh** (r.), id. **tåh-khì-tsāi**, to plant one's foot firmly. **kha-pō tåh-khì-tsāi**, to stand firm and in proper position, as for some exercise; to feel one's footing carefully, as in a dark night; to examine carefully and make sure of the position, as before engaging in some dangerous enterprise. **táh kha-pē**, id. **táh-pē**, to walk slowly, as chair-bearers going up a hill. **táh-niá^n**, id. **táh-phoà**, to break by treading on. **táh-pí^n**, to flatten by treading on. **gē-táh--tióh**, to step on by mistake.

táh-kùt--khì, to stumble by treading on a slippery place. **táh-thùt**, to stumble with a sudden jerk, as on a stair (v. thùt). **táh-tien**, to stumble. **táh-hām**, to fall down from treading on bad footing, *e.g.* on undermined place, &c.; to fall into sudden calamity when all seemed safe. **táh-thām**, to step down unexpectedly; to lose money unexpectedly (v. thām). **táh-liu** (Cn.), to stumble. **táh-lui** (Cn.), to stumble and fall backwards.

táh-khoà^n, to measure distance by paces; to try the strength of a plank or floor by treading or stamping on it.

táh-tsúi, to draw water by treading a wheel. **táh-chhia**, id. **táh nn̄g-khu**, to draw water for two fields by treading. **táh-tùi**, to work a rice-mortar by treading (v. tùi). **táh-soh**, to walk on a tight rope. **táh-khiau**, to walk on stilts (v. khiau). **chēng-iû táh-hé**, certain idolatrous rites (v. chēng). **táh soa^n-lêng**, to look out for good grave-sites. **táh-chhi^n**, to ramble about the hills at the time of the "feast of tombs." **tì chit-ê-thi^n, táh chit-ê-tōe**, on the same earth and under one sky (v. tì). **chiáu-á sa^n-táh**, a bird treading another.

kiâ^n-táh, behaviour; conduct; manner of walking, as to elegance, health, vigour, &c.

chháu-táh, to cause much trouble or disturbance, as at a man's house, *e.g.* a man who is not wanted there constantly coming, or many persons coming purposely to cause trouble.

táh-chióh, a stone used for pressing and smoothing cloth; to tread it, as two men do in a see-saw way. **kha-táh**, a footstool, or anything put to serve as a footstool, as a sand-bag or block of wood, &c. **kha-táh-í**, a footstool. **táh-pang** (C. toā-pang), a long footstool along the side of a bed (v. pang). **táh-táu**, id. **bîn-chhn̂g táh-táu**, a bed and this footstool. **bé-táh-thèng**, stirrups. **bé-táh-tèng** (C.), id. **chiáu-táh**, a roost. **chiáu-táh-lâng**, a trap for birds. **chiáu-táh-chhì**, a medicinal thorny plant.

táh (same as previous word?), the support for a sail when lowered (hung like a swing). **phâng-táh**, id. **táh-soh**, the ropes by which it is suspended. **thâu-táh**, the fore support for a large sail. **bé-táh**, the aft one. **giâ-táh**, to put the support in position ready to receive the lowered sail.

táh [R. tì, to meet with; to be worth; value; = col. tát]. **m̄-táh**, not worth; not equal to. **m̄-táh--tióh**, nothing better than to —; the best way is to —; had better —.

táh--i chit-hūn, appoint one share to him. **táh chit-hūn khí--lâi**, set apart one share.

táh [R. tiàp, to pile up; to lay in order; = col. thàh]. **táh-kut-sit** (T.), = thiàp-kut-sit, well-behaved.

tai (R. id.) **tai-tai**, stupid, dull, and ignorant, as a clown. **tai-sin**, id. **sông-tai**, id.

tsu-tai, too strict in keeping to ancient ways, as a pedantic scholar.

tai — **kə-tai**, a sort of fish found in fresh water.

tai [R. thai, to carry a load between two; to lift]. **kə-tai-chí^n**, idolatrous paper marked to represent cash, cut by alternate longitudinal slits into long shreds, and tied at one end in two bundles of 40 or 50 each, the ends streaming away loose; they are left hanging when a play is to be renewed, but are burned when the play is ended.

tai — **tai-á**, a sort of grain like millet, used for feeding birds, &c. **tai-á-bí**, id. **káu-bú-tai**, a sort with ears like a dog's tail. **káu-bō-tai** (T.), id.

tâi (R. id.), a small stinging insect smaller than a flea, almost like dust. **koe-tâi**, a sort bred on fowls. **khng-tâi**, a sort that breeds in bran, making it useless. **bí-tâi**, a sort that breeds in rice.

chhiū^n-tâi, to produce this insect. **si^n-tâi, id. bí-chhek si^n-tâi**, rice growing full of it.

tâi (R. bâi), to bury. **tâi káu-soh**, to fasten the two ends of a rope in the bottom of the sea for tying boats to. **tâi tē-lûi**, to set a mine, as in war.

tâi (R. id.), a small square raised platform; the raised divan on which the seat of a judge is set.

tâi-oân, Formosa (v. oân). **sam-sien-tâi**, a sort of rice from Formosa.

hák-tâi, the literary examiner for the whole province. **thê-tâi**, a general or admiral. **tìn-tâi**, lieutenant-general or admiral. **hiáp-tâi**, an officer like a colonel (v. hiàp). **chè-tâi**, the governor-general. **bú-tâi**, lieutenant-governor of one province. **giét-tâi** (R.), the provincial judge, = àn-chhat-si. **tō-tâi**, the Taoutai or Tautai. **pat-tâi**, a mandarin who has eight bearers.

phàu-tâi, a battery. **kî-koa^n-tâi**, the square pedestal, about 2 feet high, for the flagstaff of a Tsin-sze or very high mandarin. **hì-tâi**, a permanent stage for plays, as before a temple. **hoe-tâi**, a stand of stone or brick work for flower-pots. **kià^n-tâi**, a stand for a mirror or picture. **chek-tâi**, a sort of large candlestick. **koan-jit-tâi**, the highest hill on Amoy Island.

lāu-tâi, to make a great noise with musical instruments just before a play.

ōe-tit--thang hā-tâi, able to settle a dispute peaceably and without too much loss of dignity, *e.g.* by arbiter arranging to split the difference.

tái [R. bad; wicked]. **ûi-hui tsok-tái**, to behave very wickedly (v. hui).

tái [R. tsái, sediment, dregs, &c.], (C. tsái). **che-tái**, sediment; dregs; a troublesome man. **kāu-che-tái**, full of dregs (said of things not clear and distinct, or of a man who is fond of borrowing or asking money, or who is dishonest). **che-che tái-tái**, id.

iû-tái, sediment of oil. **ióh-tái**, thick dregs of medicinal infusion; full of sediment. **huih-tái**, blood in small quantities, as on the skin. **jiō-ê-tái**, sediment in urine jars.

tái-bī, too strong-smelling, though somewhat pleasant. **tái-tái**, id.

tài [R. a sash; a belt; to take with one; to lead; connected; related; on account of; fated to a condition; = col. toà].

koan-tài (R.), cap and belt of a mandarin.

tài-liām, out of regard to a person. **tài-gî**, to harbour suspicion. **tài-iu-iông**, having a morose sulky look. **tài chit--ê hiâm ê ì-sù**, having some meaning of finding fault, as a phrase or a man's manner.

tài-chit, an inveterate, chronic, or incurable disease. **tài-pēng**, quite unwell while doing something (v. pēng). **tài chhi^n-n̂g**, face greenish yellow, as when very unwell.

tài chit-tiám sat-khì, fated to be very hurtful to its parents, as child (v. sat).

tài si-toa^n, including the expense of the official stamped certificate of the deed of sale. **si^n bô-tài-lâi**,

sí bô-tài-khì, not brought with us at birth, nor carried away with us at death.

koái-tài, to allure (a woman or child); to abscond. **tài-léng**, to have the command of soldiers and lead them.

tài — **hái-tài-chhài**, a long edible sea-weed like tangle.

tài — **pėk-tài**, a running of the female genitals. **pėh-tài**, id.

tài [R. to wear on the head; to be security for; a surname; = col. tì, tè].

tam-tài, to be security for a man; to be responsible for; to bear the responsibility.

téng-tài, a mandarin button. **ū téng-tài**, to have official rank. **siúⁿ téng-tài**, to bestow a button of military rank, as a reward (done by high military mandarins).

iûⁿ-tài-lâi (C. Cn.), a plant with very prickly seeds.

tāi [R. sū, business; an affair]. **tāi-chì**, business; an affair (v. chì). **hó-tāi**, good actions; a good and proper matter. **pháiⁿ-tāi**, wickedness, death, or great calamity. **bô-iáⁿ-tāi**, a groundless affair. **bô-siáⁿ-tāi**, not much wrong; nothing the matter. **bô-goá-ê-tāi**, it is no affair of mine.

bô-tī-tāi, it does not concern (you, &c.) **bô-tī-toā-tāi** (C.), it does not much concern (you, &c.)

tāi (= lāi). **beh--tāi**, whatever do you want? what is the matter? what now? what would you be at?

tāi [R. tē, order]. **tāi-seng**, at first (v. seng). **tāi-thâu**, at first; formerly.

tāi (R. id.) **chheng-tāi**, a kind of medicinal salt.

tāi [R. careless; impertinent; unpolite]. **tāi-bān**, to slight; to treat disrespectfully.

tāi [R. tō, a helm; a rudder; = col. toā]. **tāi-kong**, a steersman; the captain of a small boat having only a few men (sometimes said of the mate of a vessel); politely said to the boatman of a small boat; often applied to assistants in the foreign hongs. **siang-chiúⁿ-tāi**, the boatman of a two-oared boat. **kə-á-tāi**, boatman of a sculling cargo-boat. **iȧp-tāi**, the boatman whose name (not surname) is "iȧp."

tāi (R. id.) **tāi-pōe**, tortoise-shell (s. great). **tāi-pē**, id.

tāi — **kong-tāi**, a shell-fish like the "than," but smaller. **kong-tāi-oaⁿ**, a jetty on Kə-lōng-sū Island.

tāi (R. id.) **tāi-hî**, a sort of large fish.

tāi — **káu-bú-tāi** (T.), an animal like a large lizard, or like the "tə-tēng."

tāi (esp. C., but sometimes A.) **bô-tāi-oâ**, = bô-tā-oâ, having no resource (v. oâ).

tāi [R. great, = col. toā]. **tāi-siáu**, large and small (v. siáu). **tāi-hong**, generous; liberal (v. hong). **tāi-liōng**, magnanimous (v. liōng).

tāi-jîn, a high mandarin, as Tautai, Hiȧp, Consul, or upwards (s. instead). **tāi-kà** (polite), you, sir! **tāi-kè** (C.), id. **tāi-kan**, a traitorous statesman; a crafty intriguing man. **tāi-tiōng-hu**, a brave man (v. tiōng).

tāi-ke, all of you; all (persons). **tāi-peng**, a very large body of soldiers. **tāi-sèng**, a numerous clan.

tāi-liȯk, on the whole; in general; on an average; generally speaking; about —. **tāi-iok**, id. **tāi-ì**, id. **tāi-khài**, id.; said also in asking for leniency in punishment.

tāi-hȧk, the great learning; one of the four books. **tāi-siū**, a large picture of a man on a scroll. **tāi-sė lân-tô**, one cannot escape from fated death.

tāi-piān, to go to stool.

tāi-sú, the term on or about July 23d. **tāi-sí** (C.), id. **tāi-hân**, the term on or about Jan. 20th. **tāi-soat**, term on or about Dec. 7th.

tāi-chheng, the Manchoo dynasty. **tāi-eng-kok**, Britain. **tāi-bí-kok** (r.), the United States. **tāi-hoat-kok** (r.), France.

tāi-sū, title of Kwan-yin, or of ruler of ghosts (v. sū). **tāi-chiòng-iâ**, a hideous paper image used in the 7th month (v. chiòng, "all"). **tāi-chiòng-iâ** (C. chiàng), attendants of Tāi-tō-kong (v. chiòng, "military officer").

tāi-hông, rhubarb. **tāi-pōe**, a sort of tea (s. tortoise-shell).

sîn-thong kóng-tāi, miraculous power very great. **bōng-tsū-tsun-tāi**, self-conceited; vain; proud.

tāi-jī-á-pêng, the character "tāi" without the right-hand down stroke (used in forming some words).

tāi [R. a generation; in place of; instead of; = col. tē], a generation.

tāi-pān, an agent or temporary substitute authorized to act for us (v. pān). **tāi-su**, an amanuensis for important documents, often official (v. su). **tāi-pit**, an amanuensis, esp. private. **tāi-jîn**, an image of paper or bamboo, used in place of a man in rites to avert sickness or calamity from him (s. great).

tāi-chhut-chîⁿ, to pay money on another's account. **tāi-chhut**, id. **tāi-sûn**, to make inspection for the (Ming) emperor, or for Heaven.

kau-tāi, to commit to; to hand over.

sè-tāi, a generation. **sì-tāi** (C.), id. **sè-sè tāi-tāi**, from generation to generation. **lėk-tāi**, successive generations; also (X.), the books of Chronicles. **lėk-tāi siong-thoân**, handed down from generation to generation. **sien-tāi**, former generations. **chêng-tāi**, id. **tsûiⁿ-tāi** (Cn.), id. **hē-tāi**, posterity; future generations. **āu-tāi**, id. **hiō-tāi** (Cn.), id.

sam-tāi, three generations. **thiên sam-tāi** (R.), to write out a statement of one's pedigree for three generations, as before competing for a degree. **sam-tāi put-chheng**, having a blot on that pedigree. **khah-siàn sam-tāi**, said of a man whose sayings and plans are usually accomplished.

ngé-tāi-sun, a great-great-grandson. **it-jîn sam-tsú, liȯk-tāi chhien-teng**, if each man have three sons, in six generations it makes a thousand men.

tâiⁿ (T.), = A. hêng, to give back; to return a thing; to give.

táiⁿ, to cut off, as a leg or a branch, by many successive strokes; to prune away so; to hack at, as a branch or a limb. **táiⁿ-kha**, to cut off a leg. **táiⁿ kha-khū**, to cut off the foot at the ankle, as a robber's. **táiⁿ ka-chiah**, to cut and hack at a man's back, *e.g.* a burglar when caught.

táiⁿ [R. tái, bad, wicked]. **ûi-hui tsok-táiⁿ** (= tái), to act wickedly.

tàiⁿ (T.), = A tiàm, a shop.

tāiⁿ (T.), = A. tēng, hard.

tāiⁿ (T.), = A. tēng. **hē-tāiⁿ**, the threshold, &c.

tāiⁿ (T.), = A. tiēn (a tenant; to rent), in several phrases.

taihⁿ (T.), exclamation of surprise, *e.g.* at things falling.

tak — **tak-siàu**, to make a memorandum of an account, as on a slip of paper or small memorandum-book; to jot down an item. **chhiáⁿ-tak**, just jot it down, or take a memorandum of it, as of a sale or account.

tak [R. chhiok, to gore; to meet with; to oppose; to resist; to come suddenly against; = col. chhok, chhek], to gore; to indent; to crush, as an insect between the nails or the teeth; to cut gently with the end of a knife; to stumble; (to oppose violently); to sail very close to the wind; to lay to.

tak-tak, to make a number of gentle cuts with the end of a knife, as in mincing small. **tak sat-bú**, to kill a louse between the nails or teeth. **tak--chit-ē**, to give a sharp rapid bite, as when breaking open a melon seed or when biting the nails.

tak-khí, the teeth chattering, as with cold; to shut the teeth rapidly so as to break open something. **koâⁿ kàu-ōe-tak-khí**, so cold that the teeth chatter.

tak--tio̍h, to stumble or strike against unintentionally. **tsńg-kah tak--tio̍h**, to indent with the finger-nail; to hurt the finger-nail by coming against something. **tak-tio̍h-chio̍h**, to stumble or strike against a stone. **tak--tio̍h mê-thâng-chhì**, suddenly find one's self involved in a lawsuit with a very dangerous man (v. thâng). **beh-poa̍h beh-tak**, stumbling and ready to fall. **tak--tó**, to trip and stumble, as on a stone or step. **tio̍h-tak**, to stumble. **kha tio̍h-tak**, id. **bé, sì-kha, ū-sî tio̍h-tak**, a horse, though it has four legs, sometimes stumbles (strength, wealth, and influence are not always to be depended on).

hâm-bîn hâm-tak, just half wakened out of sleep, and hardly knowing what one is doing (said of a man doing things very carelessly or in ignorance of what should be done).

tak-bé, slightly blunted, as needle.

tú-tak, to oppose and carp at a master's orders, sometimes doing the thing ordered, or part of it. **tí-tak** (C.), = tú-tak, id. **tak-tìⁿ**, constantly causing trouble or long delays, as man or affair (v. tìⁿ). **put-chí tak-kha̍p**, matters always going wrong (v. kha̍p).

saⁿ-tak-chhùi, to have a slight altercation. **tak-kháu**, having some sour ill-tempered words, as at the beginning of a quarrel; not so strong as saⁿ-mē̤ⁿ. **kap--i tak-kháu**, to have a slight altercation or some unpleasant words with him.

tak-hong, to sail closer to the wind in order to sail slower. **tak chit-tè**, to lay to, or to anchor for a very short time. **tak-tiàⁿ**, to anchor for a very short time.

tńg-tak (T.), to manage to settle an affair, or to gain money, where others would fail.

ta̍k [R. tio̍k, to drive away; each], each. **ta̍k-ê**, each one (severally and disjunctively). **ta̍k--ê**, every-one. **ta̍k-lâng**, each man. **ta̍k-hāng**, each sort, &c. **ta̍k-pái**, every time.

ta̍k (C.) **ta̍k-kɛ**, = A. tāi-ke, all (said only of persons).

ta̍k [R. tso̍k, muddy; turbid; not clear]. **iû-ta̍k**, sediment of oil.

ta̍k [R. to̍k, only; solitary]. **ke̤-ta̍k**, unsociable and disobliging; selfishly refusing to give any assistance.

ta̍k [R. to̍k, poison; poisonous; = col. thāu], poisonous; very wicked and injurious, as man. **ta̍k-sim**, wicked malevolent heart. **ta̍k-chhiú**, violent injurious hands. **hē ta̍k-chhiú**, to lay violent hands on a man.

joa̍h-ta̍k, very hot and sultry.

phang-ta̍k (Cn.), the sting of a bee or wasp. **hang-ta̍k**, the poisonous spike of the skate fish.

ta̍k— **ta̍k-á**, a sort of fish. **ta̍k-á-kôe**, do. pickled. **ta̍k-á-phê**, sort of fish-skin (used for rubbing varnished articles to make them smooth).

ta̍k (R. to̍k). **nâⁿ-ta̍k**, harrows used for preparing wet fields for planting out young rice (s. carrot). **lâ-ta̍k**, id. **phah nâⁿ-ta̍k**, to harrow the wet rice-fields.

ta̍k [R. po̍k, name of a plant]. **nâⁿ-ta̍k**, = nâⁿ-po̍k, carrots (s. harrow). **lâ-ta̍k-chhài** (Cn.), id.

tam (same as next word?). **tam-chhiūⁿ**, to rest firmly on the wall, as a beam that has a good hold. **bô-tam-chhiūⁿ**, has no proper hold on the wall, as beam of which the end is decayed or worm-eaten.

tam [R. to carry or bear, esp. on a pole across the shoulder; to endure; to bear responsibility; = col. taⁿ, tàⁿ], to stand security. **tam-sêng**, to assume responsibility (v. sêng). **tam-jīn**, to be responsible for; to guarantee; to stand security. **tam-niá**ⁿ, id. **tam-tài**, id. **tam-pó** (r.), to stand security.

tam-tng, to bear, as office, honour, or responsibility.

m̄-tam su-iâⁿ, will not act honourably according to agreement, as in paying common expenses or gambling debts, or in drinking for a forfeit (v. su).

tam-hoân, to have a great many anxieties, as about numerous troublesome matters to be managed. **kāu tam-hoân, lâng kōe-lāu**, they who have many anxieties soon grow old.

tam [previous word? or following word?]. **tam-gē̤**, to injure another very seriously by disappointing just expectations, as by marrying and soon leaving (v. gē̤).

tam (R. id.?) **tam-koh**, to waste time. **tam-koh sî-tsūn**, id. **tam-koh sî-jit**, id. **tam-koh nîⁿ-tang**, to waste one's years. **tam-koh tāi-chì**, to procrastinate at some business or work, delaying the finishing of it.

tam (R. id.), to take up on the point of the finger, as a fine powder; to wet the very tip (as of one's finger) in a liquid; not so deep as "ùn." **tam-khoàⁿ**, to take up on the tip of the finger so as to try what an article is like, esp. tasting it. **tam-bāi** (Cn.), id.

tam [R. name of a man]. **ló-tam**, = ló-kun, Lau-tsze, the founder of Tauism.

tâm [R. to converse; to discuss; talk; a dialect]. **tâm-lūn**, to converse or discuss together. **saⁿ-kap tâm-tâm**, to talk together. **tâm-giên**, to chat. **tâm-kim soat-kó**, to talk idly about ancient and modern things (v. soat).

chhiàu-tâm, jests and jocular talk (v. chhiàu). **kóng phàⁿ-tâm**, to tell baseless stories for amusement.

hiang-tâm, a local dialect; local vernacular or colloquial; a patois. **hiong-tâm** (Cn.), id. **hiuⁿ-tâm** (Cn.), id.

tâm, damp; moist. **sip-tâm**, id. **thàu-tóe-tâm**, wet to the skin.

tâm kà-kà, very wet, as leaky house or boat or slushy road. **tâm káuh-kauh**, very damp or wet. **tâm chiuh-chiuh**, id. **tâm lok-lok**, very wet, as road. **tâm tėh-tėh**, id. **tâm chhih-chhih**, all damp, *e.g.* with dew.

ak-tâm, to drench; drenched. **bak-tam**, to soil by wetting. **phoah-tâm**, to wet by splashing water on. **jê-tâm**, to wet by rubbing, as in washing clothes. **ùn-tâm**, to wet by dipping into. **ù-tâm**, damaged (as goods) by leakage or by a great quantity of water. **tè-tâm**, damaged by damp soaking in gradually, or by lying beside some damp thing.

tâm [same as previous word?]. **tâm-chièn**, offerings of preserved fruits, &c., made to idols. **tâm-chièn-a̍p**, do., on a frame.

tâm (tām?). **tâm-á-iû**, tar; pitch (probably imitation of the word "tar").

tám [R. gall; courage; = col. táⁿ]. **hó-tám-lėk**, courageous. **ū-tám-tì**, wise, skilful, fearless and self-reliant (v. tì). **sòng-tám**, to lose courage (v. sòng). **tám-hân**, much afraid; very timorous.

tám-tám, timorous; afraid of consequences; nervous about a matter. **sim-lāi tám-tám**, id.

tiòng-tám, to be greatly affected by sudden good or bad news, causing a feeling like fainting or choking in the throat.

liông-tám, = lêng-táⁿ-chháu, a sort of cooling medicine (centaury? gentian? and some other bitter herbs).

tám — **tám-hoân**, refined sulphate of iron.

tám — **tám-hóng**, to take a thing, pretending that the owner has commissioned us to get it; to get money on the pretence that a third party has sent us to ask it.

tám (R. tām). **tám-hók**, mourning of simple black, worn for three or four months additional after the regular 27 months or nominal three years.

tàm (cf. tìm, thìm). **tàm-tàm**, hanging down, as head. **thâu-khak tàm-tàm**, hanging the head. **tàm-thâu**, to nod the head, as when giving security to a shopkeeper for a friend who is buying from him. **bák-chiu tàm--lóh-khì**, eyes looking down. **tàm-sê**, hanging down one's head, as from weariness, sleepiness, fear, or shame. **tàm-gām**, appearance of dullness and want of ability. **tàm-sîn**, dull appearance, as of a very old or sickly man, or as when in very low spirits.

tām [R. thiâm, quiet, = col. tiām]. **tām-tām-á kiâⁿ** (esp. Cn.), to walk slowly, as with a sore foot.

tām [R. fresh; tasteless; heartless; cold; light-coloured, not gaudy; dull or unsuccessful, as trade or affairs].

tām-tām, having but little or no emotion. **tām-tām bóng-kè**, to get along so-so, but no more, from day to day, barely able to make both ends meet. **tām-tām kè-jit**, id. **seng-lí tām-tām**, very little business doing, but not losing.

chheng-tām, in very poor circumstances. **ke-sū chheng-tām**, very poor, as a family. **chhám-tām**, very poor and unfortunate, affairs going wrong; distressed appearance of countenance when all is going wrong.

léng-tām, grown cold in affection; having greatly or wholly lost interest in a matter, feeling weary and heartless about it; feeling dreary and lonely, *e.g.* having no companion; cloudy and overcast, as sky when about to rain.

hàm-tām, swollen and flabby, as face, &c.

tām-tsong, neatly and plainly dressed, as a woman; not gaudy.

àm-tām, dull or indistinct, as a colour; not bright; gloomy or overcast, as sky or weather. **tām-n̂g**, yellowish, dull yellow. **tām-chí-sek**, dull purple (so with some other colours).

tām-póh, small in quantity; a little of a thing (v. póh).

tām-tek, a sort of bamboo, used as a febrifuge.

tām-súi, the port or district of Tamsuy in North Formosa; there is also a small place in the south of the same name. **hú-lók-tām**, Tai-wan-foo, Lók-káng, and Tamsuy.

tām (R. id.) **tām-hók**, = tám-hók, extra mourning for three or four months.

tām [R. name of a plant; Hibiscus?]. **ám-tām-hióh**, a sort of leaf used in adulterating tea.

tām (C.) **sàm-tām**, very much covered with grass or brushwood, as a mountain.

tan [R. only; solitary; a bill, ticket, card, account, &c.; = col. toaⁿ]. **tan-tan it-kò**, only one (man). **tan-tan chit-ê**, id. **tan-teng**, solitary, as only son (v. teng). **tan-sin phit-bé**, quite solitary, as man without relatives, or going somewhere all alone. **tan-hong tók-bī**, a medicine that is taken alone, not mixed with other drugs; said figuratively of one sort of goods, esp. of drugs. **hō put-tan-hêng**, calamities do not come singly (v. hok, good fortune).

tan-hông, red paper, such as is used for visiting cards (s. red).

tan — **ân-tan**, stretched very tight and stiff (v. ân).

tan — **hân-tan**, a man whose bride was betrothed in succession to nine men who all died before marriage. **hân-tan-chhe**, his bride (v. chhe).

tan [R. red; sincere; some powerful medicines]. **tan-sim** (R.), loyal to sovereign, as minister.

ūi tan-chheng, to paint in colours. **tan-tî**, the red level place at a palace door; the depressed level place for water in front of a grave (v. tî).

hông-tan, red-lead. **tan-hông**, a sort of ochre colour (s. card).

kim-tan, the Tauist elixir of immortality. **lêng-tan**, id. **sien-tan**, id. (+). **liān sien-tan**, to make it as the genii (sien) do. **liān-tan**, to use the elixir of immortality. **liān-tan siu-tō**, to practise Tauist rules so as to become a Sien. **siu-tan**, id. **tan-lô**, a place where the genii prepare that elixir.

ióh-tan, a very small sort of pill. **siu-sip-tan**, a sort of medicine (v. sip). **tan-ko oân-sán**, four sorts of medicines (v. ko). **tiám-tan**, to apply a powerful drug (powdered or fluid) to a sore or diseased place.

tan-kùi, a small red flower (v. kùi). **tan-som**, a very cheap sort of ginseng. **bó-tan**, the Chinese tree peony, Paeonia moutan. **bó-tan-hoe**, id. **sien-tan-hoe**, a bright scarlet flowering shrub (+). **kok-tan**, the red Amaryllis; some say a different flower.

tan — **chhut-tan**, to have a dangerous sort of fever with dark spots.

tan (Cn.), = A. teng, a nail.

tan [R. teng, to ascend; to note down; to record], (Cn. T.), to note down or make a memorandum of, as an account. **chhiáⁿ-tan**, just note it down.

tân [R. tîn, to arrange; to state; old; stale; an ancient state], a surname. **tân-lîm poàn-thien-hā**, the surnames Tân and Lîm make up half the world.

tân [R. têng, a shed], (also Cn. = A. têng, a shed for resting, as on a road).

bô-sū-tân, a shrine for ancestral tablets that have no posterity. **chêng-tân**, name of a village on the coast between Tìn-hái and Phû-lâm-kió.

tân [R. an altar, = col. toâⁿ]. **tiong-tân-iá**, = lô-chhia, a young idol. **tiong-tân goân-sòe**, id.

tân [R. to fillip; to play on a stringed instrument; to make a mark with a chalk-line, = col. toāⁿ, toāⁿ].

tân-ap, to restrain people from making disturbance or rebellion by a sufficient display of force.

tân [same as previous word?], to sound loudly. **lûi tân**, the thunder peals. **chhèng tân**, the gun makes a report. **lô tân**, the gong sounds. **ki-ki-tân**, sound of whistling, &c. (v. ki). **chhùi chiáp-chiáp-**

60

tân, very talkative. **kóng-ōe bōe-tân**, one's advice not valued.

tân-kéʳ (C.), = A. chéng-kéʳ, to beat gongs, &c., at beginning of a play.

tán [R. téng, a rank, class, or sort; like; to act in place of; to wait for], to wait for. **tng-tán**, to be watching for a man, *e.g.* so as to catch him or to injure him, or to be on our guard against him; to wait for an opportunity, or as a man out of employment waiting for a job. **tán-tàⁿ**, to wait with a carrying-pole to get some job. **tán-tsôe**, to wait till all have come. **khoā-khoā-tán**, to wait very long, generally unwillingly (v. khoā). **ihⁿ-ihⁿ-tán**, to wait anxiously, as for news, or for a person. **ōe-tán--tit**, can wait without much inconvenience. **kōe-kōe tán--tit**, can easily wait. **tán-chih**, to go out and wait to receive a man at an appointed place. **tán-chih sêng-siùⁿ** (waiting for the prime minister), said in joke of waiting very long for a man. **tán-chih tsáiⁿ-siòng**, id. **tán put-tséʳ**, to wait for Kwan-yin, as at an idolatrous procession; also (T.), to wait on the roadside, as robbers, to plunder or levy black-mail. **tán-mih̄ⁿ oh-kàu**, **tán-lâng kōe-lāu**, in waiting for things or men, the time seems very very long.

tán-thāi (Cn. T.), to wait for.

tàn [R. the morning; a female character in a play; = col. toàⁿ, hoàⁿ].

goân-tàn, New-year's morning. **it-tàn ʳ-hʳ**, if some day one should die (v. hʳ). **sam-tāi liáp-chek**, **it-tàn khèng-khong**, dissipate in one morning the accumulations of three generations.

tàn (Cn.) **tàn-sak**, to throw away. **tàn--khì**, id. **tàn-tāⁿ** (An.), id. **hìⁿ-tàn-tāⁿ** (An.), id.

tàn (Cn.), = A. tèng, to nail.

tān [R. only]. **m̄-tān**, not only. **m̄-tān-nāⁿ**, id. **put-tān** (r.), id. **tān goān àn-niⁿ** (r.), that is just what I desire. **tān tit--tióh bóng-kiâⁿ**, I go just because I cannot help it, though I would much rather not. **tān tit--tióh bóng-chhap**, I meddle with the matter only because I cannot possibly avoid it.

tān [R. to fear]. **sù-bû-khī-tān**, recklessly wicked without reverence or fear. **put-tān-hoân** (R.), willing to take any trouble (so as to get it done).

tang (R. tong), the east; eastern. **tang--si**, the east. **tang-hng**, id. **tang-bīn**, id. **tang-bīn tsòe-sek**, first dawn. **bān-súi tiâu-tang**, a distant eastern region where the current is always to the east (v. tiâu).

tang-sai, east and west (v. sai). **tang-lâm**, south-east (v. lâm). **tang-pak**, north-east.

khau-tang, to beat against an east or north-east wind, as in sailing towards Fuh-chau. **tsá tang, bô hó-lâng** (T.), an east wind in the morning will be very violent before evening.

tang-iûⁿ, Japan. **tang-tʳ**, Formosa. **kńg-tang**, Canton, Kwang-tung. **kúiⁿ-tang** (C.), id. **liâu-tang**, Liautung in Manchuria. **soaⁿ-tang**, Shantung province. **soaⁿ-tang-lâi**, pears from Shantung. **soaⁿ-tang-hún**, vermicelli from Shantung.

tang (R. tong), winter; harvest; also (esp. E.), a year.

tang-thiⁿ, winter. **chhun hē, chhiu tang**, spring, summer, autumn, and winter. **ah-tang**, to pass the season (esp. winter) in port.

tang-koe, a sort of pumpkin (v. koe). **tang-sún**, winter bamboo sprouts (v. sún).

jip-tang, the term at the beginning of winter, on or about Nov. 7th. **lip-tang**, id. **tang-chì**, the shortest day; the winter solstice, Dec. 21st or 22d; it is the great day for worshipping ancestors. **tang-tsoeh**, id. **tang-cheh** (C.), id. **tsòe-tang**, to keep this feast. **chè-tang**, to make the ancestral offerings at it. **chiáh-tang**, to partake of this ancestral feast.

pàng-tang, to give holidays or vacation at harvest time. **siu-tang**, to take in the harvest (v. siu). **nîⁿ-tang hó-siu**, harvest good. **hó-nîⁿ-tang**, good harvest. **pháiⁿ-nîⁿ-tang**, bad harvest. **tam-koh nîⁿ-tang**, to waste one's years. **tsáu-kè nîⁿ-tang**, to waste and lose a good opportunity. **nîⁿ-tang géh-tsoeh**, the various festivals of the year (v. tsoeh). **tang-bé**, end of harvest. **lák-géh-tang**, the first rice-harvest, about the sixth month. **tsá-tang**, id. **téng-tang**, id. **ún-tang**, the second rice-harvest, about the tenth month. **múiⁿ-tang** (C.), id. **tṅg-tang**, id., so called because it is a long time from it till the first harvest of the following year. **ē-tang**, id. (+).

tê-tang, the tea-harvest. **béh-tang**, wheat or barley harvest. **thô-tāu-tang**, the harvest of ground-nuts. **hái-tang** (Cn.), the take of fish, as in a year. **pháiⁿ-tsu-tang** (C. T.), a season when small-pox is very virulent.

chiâⁿ-poàⁿ-tang, about half a year. **téng-poàⁿ-tang**, first half of a year; first six months. **ē-poàⁿ-tang**, second half of a year; last six months. **ē-tang**, latter part of a year (+). **poàⁿ-tang han-tsû** (T.), potatoes planted after the first rice-crop has been reaped.

tang — **tang-hoa-hún**, a plant, and a medicinal preparation from it.

tang [R. tong, name of a plant]. **tang-e-chhài**, parsley. **tang-o-chhài**, id. **tang-o**, id. **tang-ö-chhài** (Cn.), id.

tang [R. tông, name of a tree]. **ka-tang-chhiū**, a sort of tree that grows large, but is of no special use. **ka-tang**, id. **phû-tang** (C.), another sort of tree.

tang [R. tong, name of a plant]. **bâng-tang**, a sort of reed much used for making stems for candles. **liáh bâng-tang tsòe-koáiⁿ** (to take a reed for a staff), to employ a man for a work for which he is quite unfit. **khiā bâng-tang-hng** (set up a memorial-arch of reeds), said of a widow who makes a false pretence of purity (used also in other figurative senses).

tang — **bāng-tang**, the tailor-bird. **bāng-tang-á**, id. **bāng-tang-á-chiáu**, id. **bāng-tang siⁿ giâ-nn̄g** (T.), tailor-bird laying goose-eggs (said of a man boasting of being able to do what is utterly beyond his power).

tang [R. tong, pendent stone ornaments; jingling sound]. **tin-tin tong-tong**, sound of tight string when struck.

tang (cf. tàng). **tang--tióh**, to hurt the foot by striking on a thing so that the place grows hard. **kha tang--tióh**, id.

tang (C.) **tang-ng**, = A. tiong-ng, midst; among (but in other phrases C. tiong, = A.)

tâng — **tâng-chièn-áp**, a set of fruits and sweet things presented to an idol.

tâng — **kha-tâng**, the lower leg (from knee to ankle). **kha-tâng-kut**, the bone of the lower leg; the shin-bone. **toā-kha-tâng**, elephantiasis. **hàm-kha-tâng**, id.

tâng [R. thiông, an insect, = col. thâng]. **sìn-tâng** (C.), = A. siēn-lâng, a lizard.

厦英大辭典

tâng [R. tông, together with; alike], alike; of same sort; having some share in the same thing. **saⁿ-tâng**, alike; of the same sort; the same in kind, quality, value, &c. **hô-tâng**, harmonious, as persons; agreeing, as evidence, or as articles with the pattern. **saⁿ-hô-tâng**, id. **kóng-ōe saⁿ-hô-tâng**, agreeing in what they say. **tùi-tâng**, agreeing perfectly, as evidence. **m̄-tùi-tâng**, disagreeing, as evidence. **bô-tâng**, dissimilar; unlike.

háp-tâng, an agreement as to the division of family property (usually made before the father's death); a copy is kept by each party. **khau-su háp-tâng**, id.

tâng-chit-iūⁿ, of the same sort; alike. **tâng-khoán**, id.

tâng-sim, of the same mind; unanimous. **tâng-sim chit-ì**, id. **tâng-sim hiáp-lėk**, with one mind and united strength.

tâng-phoāⁿ, a companion. **tâng-sāi**, wives of brothers. **tâng-mn̂g**, husbands of sisters. **tâng-mn̂g--ê**, id. **tâng-mûiⁿ** (C.), id.

tâng-sî, at the same time. **saⁿ-tâng-hè**, of the same age. **tâng-nîⁿ**, having graduated in the same year as Kujin or higher graduates. **tâng-oàⁿ**, having taken the degree of Sew-tsai in the same year. **tâng-pńg**, having become Kujin or Tsin-sze in the same year. **tâng-sìⁿ**, of same surname. **tâng-miâⁿ**, of same personal name. **tâng-hiuⁿ**, of same village. **tâng-hiėt**, having the same grave, &c. &c. **tâng-tō ê-lâng**, persons of same trade or profession. **tâng-toh ê-lâng**, persons who eat at the same table. **tâng-kiâⁿ jû-tâng-miāⁿ**, fellow-travellers or emigrants assisting each other in dangers of the way, and sticking together constantly afterwards. **tâng-ke-kiám**, sharing each other's fortunes. **tâng-siⁿ-sí**, do. till death. **tâng-ū tâng-bô**, fortunes strictly united, as of man and wife. **tâng-khó tâng-tiⁿ**, do.; sometimes said also of very close friends who assist each other with money. **ang-bó tâng-khó tâng-tiⁿ**, man and wife have their fortunes identical.

tâng-oaⁿ, the Hien city or district of Tung-an or Tung-ngan, in which district Amoy stands.

tâng (R. tông), copper; brass. **âng-tâng**, copper. **chhiⁿ-tâng**, brass. **nńg-tâng**, soft brass. **chhit-pó-tâng**, very fine brass. **pėh-tâng**, a white metal that looks like silver (said to be an alloy of copper with arsenic, &c.), much used for armlets and such ornaments; said also of zinc, nickel, &c.

tâng-si, very thin brass wire. **tâng-soàⁿ**, thicker brass or copper wire. **tâng-phí**, percussion-caps. **tâng-e**, a brass pot with a cover (said also of other metal). **tâng-kó**, a sort of rattle used by pedlars (v. kó), (s. boy, sorcerer). **tiò-tâng**, copper wire to which a hook is sometimes attached (s. tube). **phoà-tâng kū-siah**, old brass and pewter articles (v. siah).

tâng-kòng, a man who has got the degree of kòng-seng for money alone. **tâng-kòng**, a large brass cannon.

tâng-chîⁿ, good common cash. **tâng-gûn**, silver coin adulterated with brass. **tâng-pau**, brass dollar coated with silver. **pau-tâng**, id.

tâng-chhiⁿ, verdigris (v. chhiⁿ). **tâng-lėk**, id. (?). **tâng-hông**, id. **tâng-sien**, id., only on the article. **chhiūⁿ tâng-sien**, verdigris forming on a thing; to get covered with verdigris. **chhiūⁿ tâng-hông**, id. **seng-khu tn̄g-tâng-sien**, I have no cash on me. **hin-su tūiⁿ-tâng-chhɛⁿ** (C.), id.

kong tâng-siâⁿ, to gamble with the "lién-pó." **chiáh kiáu-tâng**, to live by gambling. **chiáh-tâng chiáh-thih**, to live by bold bad means (v. thih).

tâng-gê-tsô, falsely and doggedly refusing to admit a fault (v. tsô).

phah-tâng, to work in brass. **tèng-tâng**, to mend articles of brass or other metals; the men who do this work also mend broken glass, earthenware, &c.

tâng-soaⁿ, Tong-san town, island, or harbour, between Amoy and Swatow.

tâng [R. tông, a boy; a lad; a student]. **tâng-chí**, a sorcerer, medium, or fakeer, who professes to be under the afflatus of a spirit. **tâng-ki**, id. **tâng-sin** (C.), id. **chin-tâng**, a real spiritualist medium, or sorcerer. **ké-tâng**, a pretended one.

koan-tâng, to perform incantations to call the spirit to the medium, fakeer, or sorcerer. **koan-ki tiô-tâng**, to make incantations and get the afflatus for oracles. **tiô-tâng**, to leap about or gesticulate violently under the afflatus. **thiàu-tâng**, id. **chiūⁿ-tâng**, to take possession of the man, as the spirit does; to be possessed by the spirit. **liáh-tâng**, to become possessed. **thè-tâng**, to leave the medium or sorcerer, as the spirit does at the end of the rites. **thè-tâng-kó**, to draw back from an affair which we were taking in hand (v. thè).

tâng [R. tông, a tube; a cylinder or cylindrical vessel; cf. col. thâng].

tek-tâng, a cylindrical bamboo vessel or spout. **chîⁿ-tâng**, a bamboo till for receiving cash, as in a shop. **pit-tâng**, a cylindrical vessel for holding pens or pencils. **hiuⁿ-tâng**, cylindrical vessel for incense-sticks. **chhiam-tâng**, cylindrical vessel for holding divining-sticks (used as lots). **chiam-tâng**, small cylindrical vessel for needles. **tiò-tâng** (C.), bamboo floats for line with hooks (s. brass).

hō-tâng, a trumpet. **pûn toā-tâng**, to blow a very long straight sort of trumpet (used on joyful occasions).

ien-tâng, a chimney. **ien-tâng-khe**, tubular tiles for chimney.

hiā-tâng, = hiā-thâng, semi-cylindrical tiles for roofs, &c.

tâng (= tàng). **tâng-á**, = tàng-á, the small upright timbers between the two horizontal beams of a couple for the roof of a house.

tâng — **sông-tâng**, a sort of useless soft wood (v. sông).

tâng — **sông-tâng**, dull and foolish; clumsy, clownish, and ignorant, as a big useless fellow. **sông-tâng-khì**, id.

tâng [R. tiók, each, = col. ták]. **tâng-kòe** (C.), = A. ták-kè, every time, often, constantly.

táng [R. tóng, to rule; to store up; curiosities; to understand], a surname.

táng-sū, to have the oversight and management of some public work (*e.g.* of building a temple), as a man appointed by the subscribers; the head-man who has the charge of the volunteers in a subdivision of a ward; a sort of secretary in the Giók-pín Academy, who has charge of routine work, *e.g.* recording names, paying money for prizes, &c.

táng [R. tóng, confused or disturbed in mind, sometimes confounded with the former word]. **táng-hiahⁿ**, hurried and careless, so as to break or spoil things.

táng [R. tóng, a faction, cabal, club, or secret confederacy; to combine or club together improperly].

táng-som, = tóng-som, a cheap plant like ginseng (v. som).

táng [R. tsái, dregs, refuse, = col. tái]. **huih-táng**, clotted blood in a mass or large quantity.

táng — **phàu-táng**, a long fort or fortified wall.

táng [R. tə, a hole; an aqueduct; a waste-weir or sluice, = col. táu]. **táng-mûi^n** (C.), = Cn. táu-mn̂g, a sluice for water.

tàng [R. tòng, a pillar; a post; cf. tāng]. **tàng-á**, small upright timbers between the two horizontal beams of a couple for a roof.

hó-ke-tàng, having great wealth. **hó-ka-tàng**, id.

tàng (T.), = tè thang (lit. place to —). **bô-tàng-chhē**, = bô-tè thang-chhē, cannot be found by searching.

tàng [R. tòng, suitable; safe; firm; to pledge; by change of tone from "tong," ought, take responsibility or management, oppose, = col. tǹg, tng, &c.]

ún-tàng, safe; certainly (v. ún). **tàng-chin**, positively so; certainly it is so.

kau-tàng, an affair or business. **tng sím-mih^n hāng-tàng**, what office (subordinate) have you in the yamun?

péng-tàng (C.), troublesome, as boy too fond of playing and touching things. **gâu pái^n-tàng** (T.), fond of altering what had better have been left as it was, as a rolling stone who never settles long at anything, or as a troublesome meddlesome child.

tàng (R. tòng), coagulated substances; gelatinous preparations in the form of jellies; frozen; (extremely cold).

tàng-chí, chilblains; frost-bite (v. chí). **tàng-chih**, to make the tongue feel cold, as ice; to send a very strong and unpleasant sensation through the tongue, as some drugs. **tàng-lō**, to cool or bleach in the dew; to catch cold by exposure to the night dews. **tàng-khí**, teeth very cold from eating some cold thing; teeth chattering with cold. **koâ^n kàu tàng-khí**, so cold that the teeth chatter.

sng-koâ^n seh-tàng, extremely cold (v. seh).

tàng-sng, having very contracted ideas, as about another's power (v. sng).

kiên-tàng, to coagulate. **tsáu-tàng** (C.), coagulated jelly beginning to soften and get bad.

ám-tàng, coagulated rice-water. **bah-tàng**, jellied pork-soup. **gû-bah-tàng**, jellied beef-soup. **sin-chháu-tàng**, a coagulated preparation from the plant called sin-chháu. **chhin-chháu-tàng**, id. **ò-giô-tàng**, coagulated jelly from the ò-giô plant. **thê-sún-tàng**, jelly made from the animal called thê-sún (v. sún).

tàng — **tàng-bák**, to stare at one in an angry or displeased manner, showing the white of the eye very much. **kap-goá tàng-bák**, he stared angrily at me, turning the white of his eyes. **bák-thâu tàng-tàng**, eyes naturally showing much of the white, apt to suggest the idea of displeasure. **bák-chiu tàng-tàng**, id.

tàng (cf. tang), to make an indentation with the thumb-nail. **tàng--chih**, to pluck off with the nail, as a flower. **êng tsńg-kah tàng**, to imprint the nail, as in the flesh, &c.

tāng [R. tōng, to move]. **tín-tāng**, to move (v. tín). **oah-tāng**, moving about much or rapidly; active; lively; in constant motion. **bák-sin oah-tāng**, eyes full of fire and animation. **ngiáuh^n ngiáuh^n-tāng**, constantly moving; always at work.

khí-tāng--lí, I beg to trouble you to —; thank you, I have given you a great deal of trouble. **khí-tāng--lâng**, to ask people to do favours for us.

kiâ^n-tāng, to go to stool; to die. **tsā-hng kiâ^n-tāng**, he died last night. **làng-phāng kiâ^n-tāng**, to get out of the way when it is dangerous to remain, but using some opportunity or plausible excuse so as not to appear afraid. **liu-kiang kiâ^n-tāng**, to steal away quietly so as to avoid some duty or a danger which should be shared.

tsáu-tāng, to go to stool; to get priests or sorcerers to perform rites (burning paper, &c.) on occasion of a sudden dangerous illness or great calamity. **tsáu-tāng-á**, to go to stool.

tōe-tāng, an earthquake. **tē-tāng** (C.), id. **chhùi chiáh-tāng**, said of one who is constantly eating.

hoah-ōe-tāng, what he says usually obeyed. **seng-lí tsòe-bōe-tāng**, unable to get on in business, as from want of funds, &c. **sim lióh-lióh-á ū-tāng**, mind somewhat excited, as by fear, desire, &c. **chhun-sim tāng**, longing to get married, &c., as woman. **gî-sim tāng**, suspicions rising in the mind.

tāng sǹg-poâ^n, to use the abacus in calculation. **tāng ké-gák**, to use musical instruments for joyful music. **tāng lô-kó**, id. (superstitious). **tāng kan-ko**, to begin a feud or lawsuit (v. ko, spear). **tāng chhə-hoat**, to act violently, *e.g.* striking, &c. **hong-tāng-chióh**, a large rock near Amoy which is moved by the wind.

tāng-kang, to begin work at the very beginning of a piece of work. **tāng-thó**, to begin building or repairing a house without the proper rites, or at an inauspicious time, so as to cause pain to a woman with child, &c. **tāng--tióh**, to become ill in consequence, as pregnant woman.

tāng-chhiú, to begin fighting or quarrelling. **pí-kha tāng-chhiú**, to move about one's arms and legs in a boisterous or troublesome manner. **tāng-kha tāng-chhiú**, id. **kun-tsú tāng-khó, put-tāng-chhiú**, a respectable man uses his mouth, not his hands, as in quarrel, &c.

tāng (R. tiōng), heavy; important; heinous; serious or severe, as danger or calamity; large, as wages; strong, as words, or as horoscope; hot, as sun; bad-smelling, as breath of sick man; (ballast).

tāng ih^n-ih^n, very heavy. **tāng hoaih^n-hoaih^n**, id. **tāng-tìm**, id. **tāng-tì**, id. **kàu-tāng**, up to full weight. **kāu-tāng**, very fat and thick, as person; very thick and strong, as pottery or box, &c. **tîm-tāng**, very unwell; very severe, as sickness. **hāng-tāng**, heavy and cumbrous; severe, as sickness (v. hāng). **chhə-tāng**, rough and hard, as work requiring much strength; heavy and coarse, as a thing.

khin-tāng, light and heavy; important and unimportant; weight or importance, in general or in the abstract. **tāng-khin-thâu**, the two loads on a carrying-pole very unequal in weight.

sit-tāng, net weight. **mê^n-tāng**, gross weight. **bē-tû-tāng**, gross weight not yet reduced to net. **chhut-tāng**, rather more than the weight, *e.g.* 101 or 102 instead of 100. **chēng-tāng**, net weight. **chēng-tāng**, to adulterate with an inferior article so as to add to the weight. **cheng-tāng**, to make an article of fixed price somewhat larger when the price of the material falls (v. cheng).

sit-tāng, to lose weight; to be less than the weight stated; too light, as dollar. **thi^n-tāng**, to add more so as to make heavier. **ke-pòng-tāng**, to pretend that a thing is heavier, and charge it so. **ke-phòng-tāng**, id. **thīn-tāng**, to put something heavy in one of the loads on a carrying-pole to make them balance evenly. **tūi-tāng**, to divide into two parts of equal weight, as on balances (v. tūi). **thūi-tāng**, hanging down heavily, as weighted curtain, or as pocket with heavy things in it.

tìm-tāng, to feel the weight of a thing with the hand. **chhìn-tāng**, to weigh with a steelyard. **pêng-tāng**, to weigh with balances.

siá tāng-sia^n, to write a dollar's weight on a bit of paper pasted on it. **phín hit--ê tāng-sia^n**, to agree that the dollars are to be counted at such-and-such a weight (v. sia^n). **pó͘ gūn-tāng**, to make up the deficiency of a light dollar.

soa-tāng, sand-ballast. **teh soa-tāng**, to put in sand-ballast. **chio̍h-tāng**, stone-ballast. **té͘-tāng**, ballast; said also of very cheap and heavy goods which would not be worth taking for the freight, just taken almost as ballast. **teh té͘-tāng**, to take in ballast.

tāng-chhìn, a false steelyard which makes things much lighter than they really are. **tāng-tsāi**, a heavy load, as of vessel. **tāng-tà^n**, a heavy load carried on a pole.

tāng-n̂g, a rich deep yellow.

tāng-io̍h, very powerful and rather dangerous medicine. **tāng-siong**, severely wounded. **tāng-hêng**, severe punishment. **tāng-lāi**, usury. **pàng-tāng-lāi**, to take heavy usury. **pàng-tāng-chè**, id.

tāng-bîn, to sleep soundly (v. bîn).

tāng-pún, requiring a great deal of capital, as a business. **chia̍h tāng-hong**, to need a strong wind to sail well, as a junk that has much breadth of beam.

jit tāng, the sun very hot. **poeh-jī tāng**, horoscope very good, so as not to fear unlucky days, &c. **miā^n put-chí-tāng**, weight of his fate great, either good or bad. **kóng-ōe bōe-tāng**, our words not counted of weight; advice not followed. **ui-hêng chin-tāng**, manner very stern and dignified.

sé͘-hùi tāng, expenses heavy.

thâu-khak tāng, head feeling heavy and sick. **ba̍k-thâu tāng-tāng**, eyes feeling heavy, with a slight headache, as in a feverish cold.

tāng, a small earthen jar or pot. **tāng-á**, id. **kim-tāng**, an earthen jar for the bones of the dead. **àng-tāng**, larger and smaller earthen jars. **àng-àng tāng-tāng**, unwilling to do what one is asked or ordered; sulky ill-pleased look, as of child.

kau hê-siū^n, tò tāng-á-bí, he who keeps company with Buddhist priests must empty his rice-jar. **kau lî-kó͘, tò tāng-á-bí**, she who consorts with nuns must —, &c.

tap [R. to answer; to requite; = col. tah], to return a favour or kindness. **pò-tap**, id. **tap-siā**, to return a kindness; to repay with gratitude; to give thanks for a favour. **tap-lé**, to perform a polite ceremony (esp. a call or a gift) in return for the same previously done to us. **tap-pài**, to return a ceremonial call. **tap-tsoá**, giving presents in return for the rite called "sàng koan-thâu-tsoá."

ìn-tap (R.), to answer. **ìn-tap jû-liû**, fluent at answering. **tùi-tap** (r.), to answer. **tùi-tap jû-liû** (r.), fluent at answering. **tùi-tap jî-liû** (C.), id.

būn-tap (R.), question and answer; also (X.), a catechism.

put-tap put-chhit, all full of blunders, so as to be unsuitable for use, as a document.

tat [R. a proper name]. **tat-kí**, the notoriously wicked concubine of the tyrant Chow (tiū) of the Shang dynasty.

tat — **chhù-tat**, a plan of a house. **phah chhù-tat**, to draw a plan of a house. **phah-tat**, id.; also, to arrange for another the plan of an accusation, or the way of managing an affair. **ōe thòe-lí phah-tat, bōe thòe-lí chhut-la̍t**, willing to plan for you the manner of the accusation or defence, but unwilling to make exertions for you, esp. unwilling to appear at the trial, or to be any way involved.

tat (cf. tah). **tiau-tat**, = tiau-tah, neat and tidy, as dress well put on, and not hanging loosely; neatly dressed.

ta̍t [R. to pervade; to pass or see through; to advance or prosper; intelligent]. **thong-ta̍t**, to understand thoroughly. **chhit-thong pat-ta̍t**, quite clear of obstacles and safe for travelling, as a road (v. pat). **liān-ta̍t** (r.), understanding thoroughly; well experienced. **ta̍t-tō-lí**, reasonable and right, as an argument in a discussion, or as a plan proposed for settling a quarrel.

hoat-ta̍t, to prosper, as in wealth, or as sons getting office, &c. **hián-ta̍t** (R.), to become a mandarin, or very powerful, or illustrious. **kong-bêng hián-ta̍t** (R.), speedily rising to high literary honours.

ta̍t-mê^n tsé͘-su, name of an idol (v. mê^n). **ta̍t-mē^n**, id.

ta̍t [R. tī, to meet with; to be worth; to value; = col. ta̍h]. **ta̍t-çhî^n**, worth some money; costly; valuable. **m̄-ta̍t**, not worth. **m̄-ta̍t chiū^n kúi-ê-î^n**, not worth more than a few cash. **bē-ta̍t chiū^n kúi-ê-î^n**, id. **bóe-m̄-ta̍t**, to pay too much for a thing. **bóe-khi-ta̍t**, to buy at a good bargain. **kiâ^n-m̄-ta̍t**, to get no good (gen. injury) for one's trouble.

m̄-ta̍t--tio̍h, = m̄-ta̍h--tio̍h, the best way is to —.

ū-kang ta̍t--i, work worth the pay. **ū-kang ta̍t--lí ū-hu**, must have my wages for each day's work; doing work worthy of proper wages. **i bô-sím-mih^n thang-ta̍t--lí**, he is not worth the money you pay him. **i bô-sím-mih^n thang-ta̍t--tit**, id. **bô-hit--ê pún-sū thang-ta̍t--tio̍h-i**, I have not the ability for the work he has to be done.

tiōng-ta̍t, to be worth (so much); to be worthy of, as of the honour, &c. **put-chí tiōng-ta̍t**, worth a great deal, as man or thing. **ōe-tiōng-ta̍t--tit**, worthy to get it, as a thing or an honour. **ōe-tiōng-ta̍t--tit-i**, the kindness he shows is all justly due for kindness formerly shown to him. **bōe-tiōng-ta̍t--tit**, not worth or worthy of it. **tiōng-ta̍t joā-tsōe**, how much is it worth?

ta̍t [R. name of a plant]. **kok-ta̍t-pín**, coarse bamboo wicker-work, used for hurdles, partitions, &c. **kok-ta̍t**, id.

a-ta̍t-chí, a sort of confection brought from the Straits.

ta̍t [R. te̍k, a wind-instrument like a flute or pipe]. **ta̍t-á**, a sort of flageolet or flute. **ta̍t-lá**, id. **pûn ta̍t-lá**, to play it.

tau — **tī chí-tau** (esp. Cn. T.), here; in this place. **hí-tau** (esp. Cn.), there.

kūn-tau, near at hand; a place near. **tùi-hn̄g--tau kóng**, to give an indirect hint or allude to a subject, as to see how a man's mind lies towards a proposal.

nî^n-tau, the end of the year (v. nî^n).

goán-tau, my home or dwelling; our home. **goá-tau**, id. **lín-tau**, your home or dwelling. **i-tau**, his home or dwelling. **in-tau**, id.; their home.

goá-ū jîn-chêng tī i-tau, I have shown him such kindness that he is under obligation to show kindness to me.

khì in-tsó-tau (lit. gone to his ancestors), said jocularly of death; said also of things spoiled or broken.

pē-bú kha-tau, our parents' house; parental home (v. kha).

tau [R. to grasp; to correct], to haul close; to detain forcibly, as men or things, *e.g.* to get the payment of what is due, or to get ransom-money, whether rightly or wrongly. **tau-oá,** to haul close. **tau-liû,** to detain forcibly, as men or things.

tau-su, self-confident and very independent in spirit (rather too proud), *e.g.* refusing to accept help in managing a matter; refusing advice or instruction; quite indifferent whether or not his goods be bought or his services accepted.

tau — **bô-tau-sau,** not managing well (v. sau).

tau (= tāu). **niá"-tau,** = niá"-tāu, the collar of a dress.

tau — **ô-á-tau,** a preparation of oysters and potato-starch made into a paste. **ô-á-tau-mī",** id. **tau-mī",** id.

tâu — **nâ"-tâu,** the Pandanus or screw-pine.

tâu [R. tô, to throw; to leap in; to have recourse to; to give one's self up to; to agree; = col. tiô], to throw one's self into, as into water or fire; to join, as the army or a secret society; to make submission on promise of impunity and employment; to make a complaint to.

tâu-ki, to agree in opinion (v. ki). **i-khì siong-tâu,** id.

tâu-hioh, to stay at a place, as for a night. **tâu-hɛh"** (C.), id.

tâu-hé, to rush into the flame, as a moth; to throw one's self into a fire. **tâu-tsúi,** to throw one's self into the water. **tâu-tsúi--sí,** to drown one's self. **tâu-thai,** to enter into the womb, as a spirit becoming incarnate (v. thai).

tâu-hē, to vow and pray to. **tâu-kò thi"-tōe,** to lay one's wrongs before Heaven and earth. **tâu--lâng,** to make appeal or complaint to a man against a third party, esp. one over whom he has some authority or control. **tâu in-sī-toā,** complain to his superior. **tâu in-pē-bú,** complain to his parents. **tâu pó-tiú",** to make formal complaint to the tepo (tē-pó) of the ward. **tâu sien-si",** to make complaint to a teacher. **tâu kā-sien-si"-kóng,** id.

chē-tâu, to accept or bear responsibility; to become responsible, as for payment, or for the good conduct of another. **chhē-tâu** (C.), id. **m̄-chē-tâu,** will not be responsible, *e.g.* for goods after they are bought, or for another's conduct, or for his making payment, &c.

tâu-sû, a written complaint given in to the tē-pó (v. sû).

tâu-bûn, to give in a mandarin's despatch to another mandarin, as courier. **tâu bûn-su,** id.

tâu-hâng, to make submission on promise of impunity, or on good conditions, as of employment, honour, or reward. **tâu-sêng,** id. **tâu-tò,** to return to one's duty or allegiance, or to honest employment, on condition of impunity, as rebel, pirate, deserter, &c. **ka-kī tâu-tò,** to make this arrangement in person. **tâu-kun,** to enter the army; to enlist (one's self). **tâu hái-iû",** to become a pirate. **tâu siọ-to,** to join the Triad Society.

tâu — **iên-tâu,** a dandy; a coxcomb; a very nice-looking young fellow (s. dice). **si"-tsòe iên-tâu,** to be very well formed, healthy, and nice-looking, as a lad about twenty. **kek iên-tâu,** to dress finely, grow a large queue, &c., as a nice-looking young fellow wishing to draw the attention of other people's women. **sièn-iên-tâu,** said of a married woman enticing or having illicit intercourse with a young fellow.

tâu [R. tô, dice, = col. kâu], dice. **tâu-á,** id. **poàh tâu-á,** to gamble with dice. **iô tâu-á,** to shake the dice. **tâu-á-oá",** the bowl for rattling the dice. **tâu-á sam-sûn,** the three dice having each the same number of dots.

hoe-hē-tâu, sort of teetotum used in gambling. **hoa-hōe-tâu** (C.), id.

iên-tâu, dice loaded with lead for cheating (s. dandy). **sái iên-tâu,** to use loaded dice.

táu — **hièn-táu,** to boast falsely or in an exaggerated way; to affect to be powerful, influential, or liberal, *e.g.* sometimes giving liberally once or twice so as to make a reputation, but not really liberal. **hièn-táu ê-ōe,** big boastful talk. **i-ê-ōe khah-hièn-táu,** he talks in a very boastful, false, or exaggerated manner.

khiàng-táu, too sharp in business (v. khiàng).

táu [R. tə, a hole; an aqueduct; a sluice; = col. táng]. **táu-âm,** a sluice or place where the water flows out from inclosed plots at low water.

táu-mn̂g (Cn.), flood-gates; gate of a sluice (C. táng-mûi"). **táu-mn̂g-thâu** (Cn.), id.

táu [R. tó, to guard; a wall for guarding a place]. **soà"-táu,** to disband or disperse, as soldiers; to separate, as friends or partners (v. soà").

táu [R. tə, the belly, = col. tó]. **tsai-hoe oā"-táu,** superstitious rites for curing a woman's barrenness, or for enabling her to have male children when she had only daughters before; the woman swallows (without chewing) a small dough image of a naked male child in the presence of her husband, in the temple of Tsù-si" niû"-niû", along with many more rites.

táu [R. tó, the ornamented top of a pillar]. **koe-chih-táu,** sort of projecting brackets for supporting the beams of a roof. **táu-á,** id. (s. measure). **tiam-táu** (T.), id.

táu — **chhi"-táu-chiòh,** the ordinary green granite of Amoy.

táu [R. tó, to overturn; to fall; to invert], to move some of the cards back and forwards once or twice before dividing or dealing them, so as to prevent cheating; to shuffle, as cards. **táu-lâi táu-khì,** id.

táu [previous word? following word?] **chhia pha-lìn-táu,** to make a somerset. **phah-kun-táu,** id.

táu (R. tó), a dry measure somewhat like a peck; = 10 "chin;" one-tenth of a "chiòh." **táu-á,** the wooden measure used for measuring it. **chiú-táu-á,** a small measure for taking out spirituous liquor. **bí-táu,** a rice-measure containing one "táu." **chit-táu-bí,** one "táu" of cleaned rice. **chin-táu,** small and large dry-measures. **koa"-táu,** the measure used in the rice-shops. **chhó-jī-táu,** a measure about 1·2 of the above, used for uncleaned rice (chhò-bí) and for beans. **ú-hō-táu,** a still larger measure, about 1·3 or 1·4 of the common rice-measure, used in some sorts of business. **toā-táu,** id.

táu-thâu ū, very good measure. **táu-thâu chiok,** id.

táu-kài, a small stick used for levelling the grain in the measure. **táu-sai,** a man whose business is to measure cargoes of pease or beans loose in the holds of junks.

táu-chhìn (peck and steelyard), weights and measures. **táu-chhìn kong-pîⁿ**, weights and measures just. **táu-chhìn khek-pók**, do. unjust.

pn̄g-táu, a sort of bucket for holding boiled rice at meals. **nâⁿ-táu**, a basket with no handle (v. nâⁿ). **kim-táu**, a jar for holding the bones of the dead (v. kim). **bák-táu**, box holding ink and ink-line for carpenter's work.

pùn-táu, a scoop for dust and sweepings. **pùn-táu-í**, a bamboo arm-chair shaped like a dust-scoop. **pùn-táu bák-kiáh-cheh**, sort of heel-taps for women's shoes.

thai-táu, a sieve (v. thai). **khōng-táu**, sort of sieve used in a mill. **lô-táu**, sort of box-sieve in a mill, which shakes from side to side, finer than "thai-táu." **lô-táu-se**, fine gauze, such as is used for sieves.

hé-táu, a three-sided screen for a lamp, esp. used at plays. **táu-teng**, a rice-measure with a lamp in it, used in some idolatrous rites (v. teng). **kî-koaⁿ-táu**, a square box-shaped ornament near the top of a flag-staff. **bāng-táu**, id. **kiō-táu**, the space under the seat of a sedan, used for carrying things. **táh-táu**, a long footstool with three drawers, below the front of a bed (v. táh). **tsoán-táu**, a revolving-box for petitions. **tsoán-táu-tiâⁿ**, a petition entered for an extra fee on a day that is not one of the regular days at the yamun for receiving petitions.

ut-táu, a smoothing-iron. **pó-táu**, a gambling instrument for the lién-pó (v. pó). **hoe-táu-pû**, a sort of gourd. **chiⁿ-bō tì-toā-táu**, wearing an enormous felt cap.

hê-táu, a bucket for raising water for irrigation, swung on two ropes between two men; a man having a projecting chin.

ē-táu, the chin. **chhùi-ē-táu**, id. **ē-táu-chhiu**, the beard. **ē-táu chiam**, the chin sharp.

chhùi-táu, the mouth, said in relation to speaking or to appetite (v. chhùi).

kha-chhng-táu, the hips; the buttocks.

phè āu-táu, to cut out a man, *e.g.* in getting an employment or buying what he expected to secure for himself, esp. by speaking against him behind his back.

pù-táu, wealthy. **hó-ka-tsù-táu**, id. (v. tsù).

pak-táu, Ursa Major; the Great Bear; the Plough. **pak-táu-chhiⁿ**, id. **pak-táu seng-kun**, the god of that constellation, = Hiên-thien Siōng-tè. **pak-táu tsù-sí, lâm-táu tsù-siⁿ**, he decrees death, but the god of the southern constellation decrees life. **lâm-táu**, a southern constellation of six stars. **lâm-táu seng-kun**, its presiding divinity. **hē lâm-táu**, to worship him (as when sick) by holding up incense towards heaven. **khoe-seng that-táu**, the god of the North Star represented as kicking the Plough. **pài táu-bú**, to worship Ursa Major, done with seven lamps by a special sect, *e.g.* the clan in Amoy of the surname "Sun."

tàu (R. tò), together; to put together; to act together or assist; to contend; to tell lies; a measure of a bamboo sail from one joining to another, *i.e.* about two feet.

tàu-bîn-chhn̂g, to put together the parts of a bed. **tàu-lòh-sún**, to fit tenon and mortice together. **tàu-ôe**, to make shoes by putting together the several parts. **tàu-khì-hó**, put it well together, as the parts of an article of furniture. **tàu-bô-sūn**, not fitting well together, as the parts of an instrument or machine, &c. **tàu-bōe-tiâu**, the parts not keeping well together. **bô-tàu-thih**, not fitted with iron, *e.g.* at the point.

tàu-oáⁿ-giáh, to use inferior bowls to make up a set; said also of other things, and of men.

gâu-tàu, fond of telling lies or making random guesses, and giving them out as true. **lām-sám tàu**, id.; also, to put together ill, as the parts of a machine or piece of furniture. **tàu kàu ū-thâu ū-bé**, to tell a false story very plausibly, with all the parts well put together. **tàu kàu ka-n̂g**, id.

tàu-kha-chhiú, to assist one another. **tàu-saⁿ-pang**, id. **tàu-saⁿ-kāng**, id. **tàu-chhòng**, to assist one another in making or mending something. **tàu-hē**, to vow and pray together. **lâi-tàu-hí**, come to congratulate on a joyful occasion. **saⁿ-tàu-chhàu**, fortunately met by accident. **tàu tsòe-chit-tui**, to form one company (v. tui). **tàu-oang**, to join in one company or clique. **tàu-tīn**, to unite in one procession. **tàu-lāu-hì**, actors joining in one company (v. hì). **tàu sī kha-ké**, he is a good comrade, as for business or for drinking or other pleasures. **tàu-ké**, to be partners in business. **tàu-hé-kì**, id. **tàu-kau**, to take a share in trade in a large firm. **tàu-kēng**, to assist a man with a little money to keep him from ruin. **tàu-thâu tàu-bé**, to give some little help. **tàu-tsō-hoà**, to make a venture (v. hoà). **tàu lí--ê tsō-hoà**, I will try to assist you, but with great doubts of success.

tàu-tah, active and harmonious; just as we would have wished (v. tah).

saⁿ-tàu, to make trial which is superior; to make a contest in rivalry; to assist each other. **saⁿ-tàu-súi**, to try which can have the most beautiful dress. **tsng saⁿ-tàu**, id. **lâi-tàu**, come and try which of us is superior. **tàu-kháu**, wrangling; mutual scolding. **tàu-béng**, contending, as in threatening or in gymnastics (v. béng). **tàu-ok**, contending in angry overbearing disputing. **tàu-khoài**, trying which can be the quicker. **tàu-kín**, id. **tàu-khùi-lát**, to try which is the stronger. **tàu-kú**, to try which can do, or wait, or bear the longer. **chē tàu-kú**, to try which can sit the longer. **tīm tàu-kú**, two men waiting long, each wishing the other to do what one or other must do, *e.g.* till one leaves the field clear, or till one takes the first step in a quarrel which is unavoidable, but which each wishes the other to begin. **khoa-pù tàu-gâu** (r.), to boast emulously of wealth and wisdom. **tàu-hoat**, to contend in magic. **tàu-tsáu**, to try a race. **tàu-lêng-tsûn**, to race with the dragon-boats. **tàu-tiám**, a sort of gambling (v. tiám).

siâ put-tàu-chèng, the evil cannot compete with the good.

tiuⁿ-tàu, to put together the parts of a thing that was made in separate parts, *e.g.* of a machine or piece of furniture; also (T. Cn.), to put together in a well-proportioned manner, as the several articles of a suit of clothes (s. cover). **tiuⁿ-tàu kha-chhiú**, to get ready assistants for doing some piece of work; to make one's dress ready for work or fighting. **tiuⁿ-tàu khì-khū**, to put together the several parts of a machine.

tàu (Cn.), = A. tà, to cover or spread over (but not in all the phrases; some remain "tà").

tàu-bê (Cn.), thick mist.

tiuⁿ-tàu (A.), to lay a trap for a man, *e.g.* to try indirectly what his purpose is; to make trial of a man's honesty, as by leaving money in his way; to pretend not to wish a thing so as to get it cheaper (s. together) (cf. tiuⁿ-tauh). **gâu tiuⁿ-tàu--lâng** (A.), good at such modes of indirectly trying another's intention.

tàu — **jit tàu**, the middle of the day, 11—1. **tiong-tàu**, noon. **téng-tàu**, forenoon. **ē-tàu**, afternoon. **jit tàu-tàu**, fully past noon. **kè-tàu**, some time past mid-day. **jit-tàu-pn̄g**, dinner, when taken about mid-day. **chiàh jit-tàu**, to take the mid-day meal. **chiàh-tàu**, id. **sió-tàu-á**, about 11 A.M. or 11·30. **sió-tàu**, id. **koh chit-chhùn-á jit chiū-tàu**, in a few moments it will be mid-day.

tàu [R. tò, to arrive at; to reach; completed; = col. kàu]. **tàu-tí**, = tò-tí, in fine; but at last.

tàu [R. thiàu, to leap]. **tàu-kâu**, = thiàu-kâu, three dice used in gambling (v. kâu).

tàu — **khún-tàu-khún-tàu** (T.), fat, short, and corpulent.

tāu (R. tə), pease or beans; pulse. **sóe-sek be̍h-tāu**, millet, wheat, or barley, and pease or beans. **chèng-tāu**, to sow pease or beans by dropping them into their place. **phah-tāu**, to measure pease or beans loose in the hold of a junk, as the "táu-sai" does.

tāu-pêng, split pease. **tāu-khə**, bean-cake from North China, used as manure. **tāu-piáⁿ**, id. **tāu-āⁿ**, stuffing of cakes or pies, &c., made of pulse. **tāu-iû**, soy (v. iû). **tāu-chiùⁿ**, a thick salt sauce made from pulse. **tāu-sī**, salted beans (v. sī). **tāu-sīⁿ**, id. **tāu-chhiam**, sort of dough in long narrow strips. **tāu-tsó**, a confection made of sugar, flour, and pulse.

tāu-hoe, soft bean-curd not yet pressed or shaped. **tāu-chiuⁿ**, id. **tāu-hū**, bean-curd shaped, but not yet pressed. **tāu-hū-phê**, do. made into thin sheets for wrapping round eatables. **teh tāu-hū**, to shape the "tāu-hoe" into pieces of "tāu-hū." **tāu-koaⁿ**, bean-curd that has been pressed in a cloth. **tāu-jú**, do. cut into smaller squares and salted. **tāu-kiâm** (Cn.), id. **tāu-che**, refuse from manufacture of bean-curd. **tāu-thâu**, id.

tāu-chhài, sprouts of pease, used for food. **tāu-siⁿ**, id. **tāu-chhiⁿ**, id., but shorter. **tāu-tîn**, stalks of leguminous plants. **tāu-ngoeh**, whole pods of pease or beans, including the seeds; they are cooked and eaten whole. **tāu-khak**, husks of pease or beans. **le̍k-tāu-khak**, the thin pellicle (not husks) of the pea called "le̍k-tāu" (+). **tāu-mə̍hⁿ**, the thin pellicle of a pea or bean.

pa-tāu, the croton-oil bean. **pián-tāu**, a legume used as a medicine for diarrhœa (Lablab?). **pîⁿ-tāu**, id. **pə̂-kiuⁿ-tāu**, sort of pea infused to make a half medicinal drink. **koan-im-tāu** (Cn.), id. **chhiah-sió-tāu**, a bean used as a cooling medicine.

ho-lin-tāu, pease. **bah-tāu**, sort of pease, gen. sold in the pods. **le̍k-tāu**, small green pease (like the vetch) from North China (+). **le̍k-tāu-hún**, pease-meal. **le̍k-tāu-ko**, white short cakes having stuffing made of this pea.

chiam-tāu, a small round sort of bean. **bí-tāu**, a small dark bean, largely used for the stuffing of cakes. **to-tāu**, a bean with large knife-shaped fleshy pods. **a-kong-tāu**, a bean with long, thin, dark, reddish pods. **kong-áⁿ-tāu**, id. **liân-hoa-tāu**, a large and very coarse bean, much used for manure. **ə-tāu**, black beans. **chhiⁿ-jîn ə-tāu**, small black bean with green kernel. **chhài-tāu**, sort of bean with a very long pod. **bé-khí-tāu**, a sort of flat bean. **poàh bé-khí-tāu**, to play a game of chance with them, for mere amusement, not for money.

thə̂-tāu, = lôk-kha-seng, the Arachis, ground-nut, or pea-nut, from which oil is made. **thô-tāu** (Cn.), id.

tāu-hə́, a small winged beetle, found among dried pease or peans. **tāu-á-chiáu**, a bird that cries "ti-ti" about the time when pease and beans grow, = chek-lêng. **tāu-á-hî**, a small fish about half an inch long. **tāu-khə̀** (C.), = A. tə-khə̀, nutmeg.

tāu [R. tə, the neck, = col. tau] the fixed collar of a coat or dress. **niáⁿ-tāu**, id. **saⁿ-á-tāu** (r.), id.

tsūn-thâu ngiúⁿ-tāu, to shake about one's head and neck in an improper manner, as a boy showing that he does not care for what is said, or as an impudent ill-behaved girl. **náuⁿ-thâu tsūn-tāu** (r.), id.

tāu-lāng, the lower part of a pig's neck. **tāu-lāng-bah**, the meat of it, not considered good eating.

tāu — **kng-tāu**, the two long strong timbers which run the whole length of a boat or junk, forming the sides of the hatches.

tāu (R. tə), (Cn. tīō), a small clause; a subdivision of a clause. **kù-tāu**, clauses and sub-clauses. **hó-kù-tāu**, good style of composition. **m̄-chiâⁿ kù-tāu**, not a good style.

tāu [R. tō, a thief or robber]. **láu-khiâng-tāu** (lit. a skilful and powerful thief), said in scolding a man who is very unfair and exacting in money matters; said in imitation of mandarin. **chin-khiâng-tāu**, id.

tauh — **tih-tauh**, bad and dangerous to have dealings with, as man always cheating, intriguing, or committing bad conduct. **put-chí tih-tauh**, very bad and dangerous, as man. **kap--lâng tih-tauh**, to have illicit intercourse. **kap--i ū tih-tauh**, id.

tauh (cf. tà, tàu), to catch in a trap, or between two sticks; to fasten a latch or small bolt. **.tauh--tio̍h**, caught, as in a trap.

tauh-á, a small bolt, as for door or window. **mn̂g-tauh**, the latch of a door. **mn̂g-tauh-á**, id. **hə́-chih-tauh**, self-acting bolt of door or lock, to open which a key is needed. **niáu-chhú-tauh**, a rat-trap. **ki-tauh-á**, a trap, as for birds. **chiáu-tauh**, a trap for birds. **chiáu-á-tauh**, id.

chhèng-tauh, iron trigger holding the match of a match-lock. **tauh hé-lêng**, to light a match-lock.

tiuⁿ-tauh (cf. tàu), to lay a trap for a man, to see if he will steal or lie, or that he may show himself in his true colours.

tauh [R. tok, firm, strong, sincere]. **tēng-tauh**, strong; solid; strongly made, as piece of furniture; having a good deal of wealth. **tūiⁿ-tauh** (Cn.), id. **chhùi-khí tēng-tauh**, teeth very strong.

sìn tauh-tauh, believing very implicitly. **chhin tauh-tauh**, very intimate and friendly.

táuh (R. tâp), (C. tiàuh). **táuh-táuh**, constantly; incessantly. **táuh-táuh-lâi**, constantly coming. **táuh-táuh-kóng**, constantly speaking, &c.

táuh — **tih-tih táuh-táuh**, sound, as of rain pattering, or clock ticking, or shoes clattering. **tih-táuh tih-táuh**, id.

táuh--chit-ē, **táuh--chit-ē**, sound of clock ticking.

te [R. low]. **ko-te** (R.), high and low. **kiàn-ko-te**, determined to have out the quarrel, and see who is uppermost. **sè-chêng khàn-léng-loán, jîn-biēn tiók-ko-te**, said of following a man according to his wealth or rank, not according to merit or right.

te — **chien-te**, a cake fried with a little fat. **chîⁿ-te**, a cake fried swimming in melted fat. **be̍h-te**, a fried cake of meal, sugar, &c. **be̍h-te-ké**, id. **ô-te-chîⁿ**, oysters, rice, and pulse fried in fat.

te [R. tui? a heap?]. **pùn-te** (C.), an ash-pit.

厦英大辭典

tê (R. chhâ), (C. tê), tea; the Camellia; warm infusions of various plants.

tê-chhiû, the Camellia. **tê-tsâng**, a tea plant. **tê-á** (C.), the Camellia, from which oil is made. **tê-ku-á** (C.), a beetle found on the Camellia. **soaⁿ-tê**, a small wild flowering shrub (not tea).

jî-tê, cutch or catechu (v. jî).

iù-tê, fine tea, as in the leaf. **chhe-tê**, coarse tea. **lám-tê**, inferior tea. **khé-tê**, wild uncultivated tea. **soaⁿ-lē-tê**, the worst of tea, not pure.

lėk-tê, green tea. **chhun-tê**, Hyson tea, gathered in spring. **bú-î-tê**, Bohea tea. **kang-hu-tê**, Congou (v. kang). **sió-chióng-tê**, Souchong (v. chióng). **tāi-pōe-tê**, a good sort (v. pōe). **hoa-hiong-tê**, tea flavoured with flowers to conceal its inferior flavour.

io̍h-tê, a medicinal infusion. **tê-thng**, any warm infusion. **tê-bí-tê**, real tea; infusion of tea-leaves. **âng-bí-tê**, infusion of reddish rice. **koe-nn̄g-tê**, infusion or decoction of eggs and sugar. **thn̂g-sng-tê**, warm solution of sugar-candy. **o-thn̂g-tê**, warm solution of coarsest raw sugar. **gêng-géng-koaⁿ-tê**, infusion of dried dragon's-eye fruit. **sù-sîn-tê**, infusion of the four drugs called sù-sîn. **kiuⁿ-bú-tê**, infusion of ginger-root. **pê-kiuⁿ-tê**, infusion of the herb pê-kiuⁿ.

tê-hio̍h, tea-leaves, either fresh or prepared. **tê-sim**, prepared tea-leaves. **tê-bí**, id. **tê-ki**, tea-leaves mixed with the ends of twigs. **tê-boa̍h**, broken tea-leaves, cheaper than the entire. **tê-e̍h**, very small particles or dust of tea.

tê-phoh, used tea-leaves (v. phoh). **tê-lē**, used tea-leaves. **tê-lé** (C.), id. **tê-tóe**, the tea left in the cup after drinking. **tê-chhip**, incrustation on old tea-pots.

tê-iû, oil made from Camellia seeds. **tê-á-iû**, id. **tê-khe**, refuse from making Camellia oil.

tê-sek, tea colour. **tê-chîⁿ**, dark coloured rock-crystal, used for spectacles.

tê-su, a tea-taster. **tê-kheh**, a merchant who travels to buy tea at the plantations; a tea-man. **tê-tsú**, the owner of a tea plantation.

tê-chièn, a store for preparing and storing tea. **tê-tsàn** (C.), id. **tê-hâng**, a wholesale tea warehouse; also name of a port on the North river, between Phé-lâm and Chang-ping Hien. **tê-tiàm**, a retail shop for tea (leaves). **tê-koán**, a shop for selling tea to drink on the premises. **bōe-sio-tê--ê**, man who sells hot tea on the street from a large teapot.

tê-tang, tea-harvest. **tê-siâ**, a tea-plantation on a hill-side. **tê-soaⁿ**, a tea-producing region.

tê-phè, cakes or confections eaten with tea. **tê-liāu**, id. **tê-liāu-tiàm**, a confectioner's shop. **moâⁿ-tê** (C.), a diamond-shaped confection made with hemp-seed (v. moâⁿ).

tê-lé, a small present given on receiving a cup of tea, as to a Bud. priest at a temple, or when calling after a marriage. **teh tê-poâⁿ**, to give such a small present (+). **bóe-tê-chîⁿ**, a small reward given for some small service (v. bóe).

tê-poâⁿ, a salver for a tea-pot (+). **tê-sóe**, an earthen plate for tea-pot and cups, or a small cloth put on it. **tê-sién** (C.), small plate for tea-pot. **tê-tih**, small porcelain plate for tea-pot. **tê-tsûn**, a metal saucer. **tê-au**, a tea-cup. **tê-ê**, a covered bowl for infusing tea. **tê-tháng**, a wooden vessel for keeping tea warm. **tê-sim-koàn**, a jar for tea-leaves, used as a tea-caddy. **tê-koàn**, a tea-pot, esp. with a roundish body (v. koàn). **tê-pân**, a tea-pot, esp. tall and thin. **tê-e**, a small earthen tea-kettle (v. e). **tê-kó**, id., sometimes of other materials (v. kó). **tê-lô**, a small hand-stove for infusing tea. **tê-tsúi**, good water, suitable for infusing tea. **tê-tàⁿ**, tea-pot, &c., carried on a journey, as by a mandarin.

tsoaⁿ-tê, to boil water in order to infuse tea. **chhiong-tê**, to infuse tea. **phàu-tê**, id. **hip-tê**, to infuse tea in a covered cup. **phâng-tê**, to bring tea for guests. **chhiáⁿ-tê**, to offer tea to a person. **chia̍h-tê**, to drink tea. **phè-tê**, to eat along with tea. **thîn-tê**, to pour out tea. **pâi-tê**, to set out a feast with tea for the spirits of the ancestors in the ancestral hall, as from the 12th to the 15th of the first month. **sià-io̍h si-tê**, to give away medicine and tea.

chhái-tê, to gather tea-leaves. **siu-tê**, to buy up tea at the plantations. **pān-tê**, id. **pē-tê**, to dry tea-leaves; to fire tea.

tê [R. tôe, the heel; a hoof], (T. tô). **lé-tê**, the knob on which a sculling-oar works. **tn̂g-poeh chhâi, thâi chit-ki lé-tê** (to cut down a beam of 18 feet to make a pin for a scull), said of a workman wasting his materials very much. **tê** (C.), = A. tôe, a hoof.

tê — tê--teh (T.), = A. kê--teh, involved in delay by something that must be done before what we wish to do.

tê (C.), = A. tôe, to collect subscriptions, a theme or text, &c.

tê (P.) **am-pó-tê**, = A. am-pe-chê, the cicada.

té (R. toán), (Cn. tó), short. **té-chió**, not enough; deficient. **té-kheh**, id. (v. kheh).

té-kang, a person engaged for a short term of work. **té-miāⁿ**, short life; short-lived. **kiâⁿ té-lē**, to commit suicide. **siūⁿ té-lē**, to purpose suicide. **siūⁿ té-hēng**, to do work in a negligent or slipshod way—no matter how, if it just be done; or to neglect it entirely. **kiaⁿ-tāi-chì té-té**, to do things to get present advantage, without regard to the future or to what is right.

té-saⁿ, a short coat or jacket. **té-hiû**, a short wadded or warmly-lined coat or jacket.

tn̂g-té, long and short; length in general or in the abstract. **lū-tn̂g lū-té**, thinking very anxiously. **khoà-tn̂g lū-té**, id. **pí-tn̂g lūn-té**, to find fault with many things (v. lūn). **m̄-chhap-lí-tn̂g, m̄-chhap-lí-té**, I will not meddle with your matters at all; I will have no dealings with you. **lia̍h-tn̂g pó-té**, to make a surplus compensate for a deficiency. **tsóeh-tn̂g pó-té**, id. **saⁿ tn̂g, chhiú-n̄g té**, said of one not able to gratify his desires (lit. dress long but sleeves short).

té (C.), = A. tóe, bottom. **tī phe-té**, in the letter, as money inclosed.

té (C.), = A. tóe, to contain.

té (C.), = A. tóe, to oppose; also (in some phrases), = A. tí, *e.g.* **té-thóng**, = A. tí-thóng, and **té-sek**, = A. tí-sek, to be used in place of, as a makeshift.

tè [R. a god; an emperor]. **tè-ông**, emperors and kings. **chheng-ông chheng-tè**, said of being one's own master (v. chheng). **hông-tè**, the emperor (v. hông). **sien-tè**, a deceased emperor. **tè-to**, the metropolis. **tè-tiēn-khí**, built in the style of a palace (v. tiēn).

tè-kun, Kwanti; also Tāi-tō-kong (v. kun). **koan-tè**, Kwanti (v. koan). **tè-iâ** (T.), id. **ga̍k-tè**, the chief god of the Tang-ga̍k temple. **ngó-hién-tè**, five idols which are counted improper objects of worship (said to have some connection with rebellion). **ngó-tè**, id.

n̂g-tè, the ancient canonized emperor Hien-oân. **sîn-lông tāi-tè**, Shin-nung (v. lông). **ngó-kok tāi-tè**, the god of agriculture (v. kok). **sam-koan tāi-tè**, = Sam-kài-kong (v. koan). **pó-seng tāi-tè**, = tāi-tō-kong, god of medicine.

siōng-tè, God; the supreme god; a very great god. **gio̍k-hông siōng-tè**, Yuh-hwang Shang-ti, of the surname Tiuⁿ (Chang), born under the Hàn dynasty. **gio̍k-tè**, id. **hiân-thien siōng-tè**, the god of the north pole, of surname Sih, represented treading on a serpent and a tortoise. **siōng-tè-iâ**, id. **siōng-tè-kong**, id. **tsúi-tn̂g siōng-tè**, a title of Hiân-thien siōng-tè, as worshipped at a temple on Amoy harbour. **hia̍p-thien siōng-tè**, a title of Kwanti.

tè (C. tòe), to follow; to go after; to imitate, as a person's example; sometimes said of illicit connection.

kun-tè, to follow, as a servant (C. kin-tòe). **tīⁿ-tè**, to be in constant attendance and service, as sick-nurse or body-servant. **tè--liáu ōe-ià**, growing weary of constant attendance.

saⁿ-tè, mutually following; to follow each other; agreeing with one another's wishes or desires (s. piece). **n̄ng-kù saⁿ-tè**, two phrases closely connected like one phrase. **chîⁿ bô--beh tè--i**, money will not come to him.

tè-lâng-ê-khoán, to follow a man's example. **tè--lâng sî-kiâⁿ**, to follow new fashions. **tè-kiáⁿ kiò**, said of a woman addressing a relative by using the form of expression which her own son should properly use, as is often done. **tè-chhiú**, immediately thereafter. **tè-bé** (C. tòe-bóe), id. **khah-tè-bé**, afterwards; at a subsequent time; at a later time. **khah-tè-bé kúi-jit**, some days later. **tè-bé-goá-lâi**, coming after me. **tè-chhùi-bé**, to repeat a man's words, as after a teacher; or as in pretence of obeying; or for a direct insult.

tè-tsúi jip, to go in with the tide as it rises. **tè-jit-lo̍h**, may I die as the sun goes down if I am swearing falsely! **tè-hé-hoa**, may life go out as a lamp! (said as an oath to prove one's truthfulness).

tè-hì, to follow a company of actors, seeing them wherever they act, and having too much intercourse with them (v. hì). **tè tsa-bó**, to have illicit connection with a woman.

tè [R. khoài, a piece; a place; perhaps some of the phrases belong to "tē," the earth, a place], a place; a locality (in this sense sometimes enclitic); a bit; a piece; a small piece; a lump; classifier of lumps of stone, bits of ink, small bits of various materials, feasts, tables, chairs, bowls, animal souls (phek), colloquial songs (koa, khek), prefaces and small inscriptions (sū); also (Cn.), of houses.

tè-siaⁿ, counting price by number of single articles, *e.g.* of cakes. **poàⁿ-tè**, one half of any article of which "tè" is the classifier; a very small bit. **chit-tè-tsū**, one small cloth spread below a tea-pot.

ka-n̂ng-tè, a whole piece; entire; one lump or mass. **kiet ka-n̂ng-tè**, to coagulate or crystallize, &c., into one mass. **kiet tsòe-chit-tè**, id.

phâiⁿ-kut-tè, giving signs that he (a boy) will grow up an idle useless fellow.

hit-tè, that place. **kàu-hit-tè**, come to that state of matters. **kóng kàu-hit-tè, kiâⁿ kàu-hit-tè**, to act according to what we have said. **chí-tè**, this place. **pát-tè-khì**, gone elsewhere. **hioh-i-tè**, to stay at his house.

bô-tè thang-tsáu, having no place to escape to; having no way of escape. **bô-tè thang-hē**, no room to lay or stow any more; quite full, as a vessel, &c.; no place to lay it.

àm--tè, a dark place; Hades. **kng--tè**, a place where there is plenty of light. **chiūⁿ--tè**, an itchy place (v. chiūⁿ).

kàu-tè, to arrive at the place; arrived. **kàu-tè--lah**, now we have arrived! **tìn-tè**, to block up the place; to be in the way; to take up room uselessly; to cumber the ground.

tè [R. tē, the earth; ground; a place; = col. tōe]. **sàu-tè**, to sweep the floor [perhaps some phrases of the previous word belong here].

tè [R. —; C. chè; Cn. chek; narrow; to press; a quiver], (C. tè), to strain or filter with a coarse sieve, or through a "tsoáⁿ-lí." **tè-ta**, to strain or filter dry. **tè-khì-ta**, strain it quite dry. **tè-tsúi**, to strain off the water, as from rice. **tè-ám**, to strain rice-water from boiled rice.

tè (better "teh"), a prefix and enclitic affix to verbs (v. teh).

tè (R. id.) **tè-cheng**, sort of bells used by priests.

tè [R. tài, to wear on the head, = col. tì], (Cn. tō), a surname.

tè — o-tè-tè, very black.

tē [R. a dyke; an embankment], (T. tō), a piece of land reclaimed from the sea. **hái-tē**, id. **tē-hoāⁿ**, a sea-dyke.

tē [R. name of a tree]. **tông-tē-hoe**, a shrub with a red flower.

tē (C.), = A. tōe, flax.

tē [R. to transmit; to hand from one to another], (Cn. tōe). **phah-tē-kè**, to send a criminal to be dealt with by the mandarin of his native place. **thoân-tē** (C.), = A. thoân-tōe (*q.v.*)

tē [R. order; rank; = col. tāi, tōe], prefix for ordinal numbers.

chhù-tē, successive order. **téng-tē**, rank; station; quality of articles. **put-tē**, to fail in taking a literary degree. **sam-kip-tē**, the highest three of the new Han-lin graduates in each triennial examination, viz. chiōng-goân, póng-gán, and thàm-hoe.

tē-it, = tōe-it, the first (in this paragraph, A. tē, tōe; C. only tē; Cn. tōe). **kài-tē-it**, the very first or best (v. kài). **tē-it-hó**, the best. **tē-it-pháiⁿ**, the worst. **tē-jī**, the second. **tē-kúi**, which in order?

tē [R. tí, bottom, = col. tóe]. **bák-tē-bô**, to despise; to treat scornfully. **bák-tē khoàⁿ-bô**, id. **bák-tē chin-bô**, to despise or scorn very much. **bák-tē put-chí-bô**, id. **bák-tē-ū**, to hold (a man) in estimation. **bák-tē ū--i**, to think well of him. **bák-tē put-chí-ū**, to think very highly of.

tē (R. tāi), a generation; an age. **āu-tē**, future generations. **chit-tē kè-chit-tē**, from one generation to another. **tan-teng kè-tē**, only one son in each generation. **thàn-chîⁿ bô-kè-tē**, his wealth shall not descend to his sons, as of wicked man.

tiāu-tē, a dynasty (v. tiāu).

tē [R. a younger brother, = col. tī]. **pau-tē**, a younger brother by same father. **tē-hū**, = sió-chím, younger brother's wife. **heng-tē** (R.), elder and younger brothers. **kè-heng-tē**, a half-brother by either parent when the other parent is dead and the survivor re-married. **heng-tē jû siú-chiok, chhe-tsú sū i-ho̍k**, brothers are like hands and feet, wife and children like clothes.

tsú-tē, an ill-behaved son; also (R.), junior relatives

(v. tsú). **tē-tsú**, a worshipper or devotee of an idol (v. tsú). **tê-tē**, a young Bud. priest; sometimes said of Tauist. **sai-tē**, a younger apprentice or Bud. priest (said by the older ones). **khòe-tē**, a sodomite.

tē (R. tāi), a bag; a pocket; a pouch; to carry in a pocket; to stuff materials into a long bag, as in making a sausage or the preparation called "báng-hiuⁿ."

tē-á, a small bag. **lak-tē**, a small bag, esp. of cotton; a pocket in a dress. **lak-tē-á**, id. **té-tē**, = té-koāⁿ, a pouch worn on the belly (v. té). **pè-tē**, a sack; a large coarse bag used for carrying goods. **chit-khia pè-tē**, one sack. **chit-tàⁿ pè-tē**, a pair of sacks. **pè-tē-hì**, sort of puppet-shows. **chhī niáu-chhú, kā pè-tē**, to have an enemy in our own house. **pè-tē-chiáu**, = hái-lâm-gōng, a sea-bird with a large bag under its bill.

soa-tē, a sand-bag, as for extempore fortifications. **chîⁿ-tē**, a sort of purse. **chìⁿ-tē**, a quiver. **keng-tē**, a bag for holding a bow. **sìⁿ-tē**, a fan-case worn at the side. **chím-thâu-tē**, a cover for a pillow. **pit-tē**, a bag for holding Chinese pens, as for the examinations. **hiuⁿ-tē**, bags of incense worn round the neck for the sweet smell. **phoe-tē** (r.), an envelope, = phoe-lông. **chhu-tē**, a bag tied on the end of a pole for catching larvæ and such insects. **kiáⁿ-sun-tē**, the scrotum (said vulgarly or in coarse joke).

chit-tē-bí, = chit-pau-bí, one bag of rice, about 150 "kun" or Chinese pounds.

tē-chîⁿ, to carry cash in one's pocket. **tē-gûn lâi**, to bring silver in the pocket. **seng-khu tē-gûn**, having silver in one's pocket.

tē [R. the earth; ground; a place; = col. tōe, tī, tè], (in many of the phrases A. tē = tōe; Cn. tōe; but C. always tē); also (C.), = A. tōe, earth, &c.

thien-tē, heaven and earth (v. thien). **tē-gėk**, hell (v. gėk). **tē-giòk** (C.), id. **tē-gák** (C.), id. **tē-hú** (Cn.), Hades. **tē-tsông-ông**, a god who rules the world of spirits, associated with Giâm-lô-ông. **tē-soah**, the evil spirits of the earth (v. soah). **thé-tē-kong** (C.), = A. thé-tī-kong, the god of the ground.

tē-hng-koaⁿ, the mandarin of a region. **tē-hng** (C.), = A. tōe-hng, a region. **tē-hong** (r.), a region. **tē-hong-kúi**, a spirit supposed to preside over a region; a very tall man. **tē-pó**, = pó-tiúⁿ, the tepo or head man of a ward, appointed by the mandarin.

tē-tê, a map or chart. **tē-kiû**, a terrestrial globe; a sort of mark for archery (v. kiû).

tē-lí, geomancy; good or bad luck of graves; geography. **tē-lí-su**, a geomancer. **tē-lí sien-siⁿ**, id. **pāi tē-lí**, to injure the good luck of a grave-site, to injure the Fung-shuy. **kiâⁿ tē-lí**, to practise geomancy. **tiōng tē-lí**, to have great faith in Fung-shuy and geomancy. **thien-bûn tē-lí**, astronomy and geography; astrology and geomancy.

hok-tē, a good grave-site (v. hok).

koán-tē, school premises (v. koán). **tsō-tē hun-tsng**, to be a receiver of stolen goods. **khùi-sú bô-tē** (R.), terribly ashamed and confounded.

tē-pē, relative station, rank, or position (v. pē). **tē-ūi**, official station and rank (v. ūi).

tē-pán, a wooden floor. **tē-chien**, a carpet. **tē-lûi**, a mine for exploding in war (v. lûi).

sèng-tē, temper (v. sèng). **sim-tē**, = sim-tōe, character and disposition (v. tōe). **bīn-tē súi**, face pretty. **bīn-tē khiap-sì**, face ugly (v. bīn).

seng-tē, a sort of medicine in its raw form (Rehmannia? Digitalis?). **siòk-tē**, this drug in its prepared state, in a glutinous form, prepared by drying in the sun and mixing with honey. **kui kiong, chiok tē**, this drug with three others, making up the "sù-bùt." **tē-kut-phî**, sort of febrifuge medicine. **tē-jû**, a sort of medicine (v. jû). **tē-jî** (C.), a drug like a bit of a child's flesh (v. jî).

tɛⁿ (C.) **kha-āu-tɛⁿ**, = A. kha-āu-tiⁿ, the heel.

tɛⁿ (C.), to push. **tɛⁿ-khui**, to push separate, *e.g.* as the joints of furniture.

tɛ̂ⁿ (C.) **tháng-tɛ̂ⁿ**, = A. tháng-tîⁿ, a wooden instrument for knocking the hoops firmly on a barrel or bucket.

tɛ̂ⁿ (C.), = A. tîⁿ, to knock the hoops firmly on a barrel, &c.

tɛ̀ⁿ (C.), = A. tìⁿ, to make strong efforts; to pretend (cf. nìⁿ, nɛ̀ⁿ).

tɛ̄ⁿ (C.), = A. tīⁿ, the surname Ching.

tɛ̄ⁿ (C.) **tɛ̄ⁿ--sí**, = A. nihⁿ--sí, to strangle to death with the fingers.

teh (C. tɛh), to press down; to crush by a weight; to plant, as potatoes; (to pay a small instalment or percentage, or take off a small discount); to gamble in certain ways; to keep down certain symptoms by medicine; also, **tɛh** (C.), = A. tìg, to stamp, as a mark or seal.

taⁿ-teh, constantly carrying heavy burdens on a carrying-pole. **giâ-teh**, constantly carrying heavy loads with the arms. **teh-sí**, to crush to death by a great weight. **khit bái-kúi teh**, to have a very oppressive feeling in a sort of nightmare (v. bái). **chhia toā-soaⁿ lâi-teh--goá**, crushing me by false accusations of great crimes, or forcing me by overwhelming influence of powerful men. **teh té-tāng**, to ballast a vessel (v. tāng).

teh-chhiám, to lay down the keel of a vessel with the customary idolatrous rites. **teh han-tsû**, to plant potatoes. **teh-tsoá**, to lay idolatrous paper on graves, laying stones on it to keep it from blowing away, as in 3d month, &c. **teh bōng-tsoá**, id.

chheh-teh, a long piece of metal or heavy wood for keeping a book open.

teh khì, to keep down or cure a tendency to cough, or vomit, or some pains, as medicine. **teh sàu**, to cure or relieve a cough. **teh thâm**, id. **teh kiaⁿ**, to keep up one's spirits and keep down fear, as some cordial or medicine.

teh-tóe, to be at the bottom of a pile or heap; to be the last of a lot of goods (v. tóe).

teh pêng-tóe, to take off a very small discount on paying a large price in dollars (v. tóe). **teh tô-tóe**, to take off a very small discount (v. tô). **teh chit-chîⁿ**, to take off one mace of discount on 100 dollars. **teh-tiāⁿ**, to pay a small earnest, as at beginning of betrothal. **teh-toaⁿ**, to pay a small instalment of passage-money (v. toaⁿ). **teh-lâi teh-khì**, to pay only in part what we owe and then borrow more, or get more goods on credit from the same person. **teh-tōe-gûn**, money lent or advanced without interest, as on engaging a man or on taking a house, to be repaid if the man leave service or if the house be taken back. **teh-tōe**, to advance money thus, as when renting a house, like a combination of renting and mortgaging. **teh-tāiⁿ** (T.), to advance money on a field rented. **teh-tūiⁿ** (Cn.), id. **tɛh-tiēn** (C.), id. **teh-nâⁿ**, to send back something (*e.g.* balls of raw sugar) in the basket that brought a present. **teh tê-poâⁿ**, to give a small present on getting a cup of tea. **teh-phoe**, to be sent with a letter, as money, *e.g.* one dollar or so.

teh liân-pó, to gamble with the liân-pó. **teh hoe-hē** (C. tɛh hoa-hōe), to gamble with the hoe-hē. **teh phak-chhiò**, to gamble with cash, like odds and evens (v. chhiò). **teh sang-jī** (T.), = A. siang-chhiò, both cash evens. **teh-tit**, to play the game called "tit." **teh-iâⁿ teh-su**, to lay down stakes so as to win or lose.

teh tāu-hoe, to form soft bean-curd into large soft squares. **tɛh-ìn** (C.), = A. tǹg-ìn, to stamp with a seal or stamp. **tɛh-âng** (C.), = A. tǹg-âng, to stamp with red ink. **tɛh jī-hō** (C.), to stamp a shop-mark or trade-mark.

teh (R. tok), (Cn. töh), to peck, as a bird. **teh gē-kak**, to pick up grain, as bird. **teh chiáu-á-koà**, to prognosticate by a bird picking up one slip or lot out of several.

tɛh [R. chek, boards or mat of bed, = col. chioh]. **chhñg-tɛh** (C.), a wide-worked bamboo frame in bottom of bed, for supporting the mattress.

teh (cf. leh), an enclitic affix after some verbs. **giâ--teh**, carrying a large thing with the arms. **khê--teh**, involved, obstructed, entangled, &c. (v. khê). **kê--teh**, id. **hē-teh**, to lay down (v. hē). **kì--teh**, to write down.

tī--teh, present; at home (v. tī).

teh (cf. tih, tīh), (C. teh, lí), prefix to verbs, expressing the continuance or present doing of the action, somewhat like the present participle, or like an imperfect or present tense; sometimes also prefixed to adjectives, so as to express a present or continuous state.

teh-kóng, in the very act of speaking. **teh-kiaⁿ**, trembling (s. press). **teh-sàu**, in the act of coughing (s. press). **goá teh-siūⁿ**, I am considering. **teh-khùn**, sleeping. **teh-chhiò**, laughing.

teh-beh, about to — (sometimes written "tit-beh," or "tih-beh"), but better "tīh-beh."

tsat-teh-ēng, economical. **phak-teh-pài**, to kneel and bow very low.

teh sòng-hiong, in a state of deep poverty. **lí teh-gōng**, you are acting foolishly.

teh siáⁿ-sū, what *is* he about? what *are* you doing?

tèh [R. toát, to take away forcibly], (Cn. T. tōh; C. sometimes thèh), to snatch away, often what has been first snatched from another. **chhiúⁿ-tèh**, to snatch away. **tèh--lâng**, to snatch from a man, or get it out of his hands. **tèh-tò-tńg**, to snatch back, as from robbers. **khit--i tèh--khì**, to have something taken away by another when it was almost within our grasp, *e.g.* by his having superior influence to back him, or offering more money. **ēng-pē lâi-tèh**, to get a thing out of a man's hands by some cunning plan or roundabout contrivance.

tèh (C. tɛ́h), to ebb; ebb-tide. **tsúi tèh**, ebb-tide; beginning of ebb. **tsúi tɛ́h-ta** (C.), dead low-water.

thê-tèh, soft muddy sea-beach at low water. **hái-tèh**, id. **liâu-tèh**, to wade across the wet sea-beach with some water on it. **táh-tèh**, id.

tâm tèh-tèh, very wet, as roads.

tèh (C.) **èh-tèh**, = A. òeh-tòeh, narrow.

tɛ́h (C.) **nâⁿ-tɛ́h-á**, a sort of small shallow boat for shallow rivers.

tek (R. id.), virtue; moral conduct. **tek-hēng**, behaviour (v. hēng). **sēng-tek**, excellent and virtuous character. **sēng-tek ê-lâng**, a man of excellent character. **sit-tek**, to lose one's virtue; to commit some great crime.

sìn-tek, the virtue of truthfulness or trustworthiness. **jîn-tek**, the virtue of kindness, love, or benevolence. **un-tek**, great favour and kindness (v. un).

chìn-tek, to make progress in learning.

chek-tek, to accumulate merit (or rarely demerit). **ū-chek-tek**, to accumulate or have great virtue or merit. **hó-chek-tek**, very virtuous or meritorious (person). **bô-chek-tek**, without virtue. **pháiⁿ-chek-tek**, having much demerit.

lú-tek, female character or virtue. **lí-tek** (C.), id. **lú-tek chin-pháiⁿ**, her character is very bad.

kong-tek (lit. virtuous and meritorious acts), rites performed for the dead, to get them out of Hades, or get their condition there improved. **tsòe-kong-tek**, to get such rites performed for the dead. **kong-tek che-chhàm**, great Buddhist rites for the good of the dead. **kong-hun tō-tek**, great virtue and merit (v. tō).

chiú-tek, manner in which a man is affected by liquor. **hó-chiú-tek**, able to take much liquor without being seriously affected by it, or at the worst getting drunk quietly. **pháiⁿ-chiú-tek**, getting disorderly when in liquor.

hok-tek chèng-sîn, the god of the ground and of graves (v. hok). **thien-tek-hng**, an auspicious hill near the grave, where the geomancer stands apart at the time of burial calling aloud to the auspicious influence of the mountain. **lí khì-toà thien-tek-hng teh-sóng**, you are keeping aloof from the matter in which you should take part, so as to escape responsibility.

tek-hòe, the city and Hien of Teh-hwa (v. hòe). **soan-tek**, title of the reign of a Ming emperor, when very fine brass was made (v. soan).

tek [R. to obtain; to get; = col. tit]. **tek-sit**, to get or lose (v. sit).

tek-sim, to gain a person's affections (v. sim). **tek-thióng**, do., as concubine or eunuch (v. thióng). **tek-ì**, to get one's wish. **tek-koat**, to hit on the right plan; all right (v. koat). **tek-hoat**, id. **tek-kái** (esp. C.), joyful; delighted. **tek-sè**, to get prestige or influence, as by success. **tek-tiong**, moderate; taking the mean (v. tiong). **tek-tō**, highest class of Bud. priests (v. tō). **ōe-tek-lī**, profitable, as business transaction (v. lī). **tsá tek-tsú**, will have a son at an early age (a fortune-teller's phrase).

tek-tsōe, to offend; I beg your pardon (v. tsōe).

hô-tek-khé, why trouble yourself?

put-tek-í, have no alternative; could not help it. **put-tek put-tiòh-kóng**, cannot but speak, though unwilling. **put-tek khai-kiau**, cannot manage to set it right, as quarrel (v. kiau).

thiu háp-tek, to take off a percentage for brokerage. **háp-tek ê-chîⁿ**, brokerage.

tek [R. certain; distinct; sign of the genitive or possessive]. **tek-tek**, certainly. **tek-khak**, id. **tek-ū**, certainly there is (or there are). **tek-sī àn-niⁿ**, certainly it is so; what I say is really the fact.

tek-bô, certainly not. **tek-tek-bô**, id. **tek-khak-bô**, id.

tek (R. tiok), (C. tek, tiok), bamboo. **pan-tek**, bamboo with spotted stem. **chhì-tek**, thorny bamboo. **chiòh-tek**, a thin and very hard sort of bamboo, with short joints, good for tobacco-pipes. **lėk-tek**, a green sort of bamboo, with large leaves and soft stem. **lėk-tek-sún**, shoots of this sort, counted good. **bâ-jî-tek**, a fine spotted bamboo with long and indistinct joints. **moâⁿ-tek**, sort of bamboo with large leaves and long joints. **hó-tek**, good bamboo.

âng-tek, an ornamental plant (not a bamboo) with

one bunch of red leaves at the top, Dracoena ferrea. **tãm-tek**, a reed used as a febrifuge. **tek-á-chháu**, sort of stiff grass.

tek-chià, the common sugar-cane, not the sort sold for chewing. **tek-ē**, the taper-pointed taro. **chhiⁿ-tek-si**, a venomous serpent, said to have long feelers. **chhiⁿ-tek-pio**, id. **tek-lê**, a long tapering sort of shell-fish. **tek-than**, a sort of shell-fish (v. than).

tek-á-ki, bean-curd dried in thin sheets, and rolled into tubes for eating. **tiòh-chiáh tek-á-ki**, I will beat you with a bamboo if you don't be quiet (said to a child).

tek-hióh, a bamboo leaf. **tek-hióh-to**, a two-edged sword. **tek-háh**, small sheathing leaves at bamboo joints. **tek-bák**, a bamboo joint. **tek-tsat**, a bit of bamboo from one joint to another; a short bit of bamboo. **tek-á**, a thin bamboo shoot. **tek-chhì**, a long thin bamboo branch or thorn (v. chhì). **tek-pì** (C.), a small bamboo shoot at side of main stem. **tek-sún**, young short bamboo shoots, edible (v. sún). **tek-bí**, bamboo flower. **tek-méhⁿ**, the soft inside of the bamboo.

tek-nâⁿ, a bamboo grove. **tek-liâu**, a store where bamboo is sold.

tek-ko, a bamboo pole. **tek-taⁿ**, a split bamboo, used as a carrying-pole. **tek-ơ**, the movable bamboo beam of a well-sweep. **tek-bih**, slips of bamboo for wicker-work. **tek-teng**, a bamboo pin, used as a nail. **tek-sng**, a small bamboo pin, peg, or wedge. **tek-hû**, a small bamboo peg with a bit of red cloth tied on it, used as a charm. **tek-thāng**, a bamboo float. **tek-kóng**, a bit of bamboo, from a few inches to a few feet long. **tek-khiò**, a bamboo conduit for water, gen. split, but sometimes whole. **tek-kéng**, do., generally entire. **tek-pán**, bamboo boarding, as for threshold of door or sill of window. **tek-poe**, flat bamboo stick for beating (v. poe). **tek-chhéng**, bamboo scrubbing-brush. **tek-se** (C.), sort of large bamboo brush. **tek-söe** (Cn.), id. **tek-keng**, a bamboo bow.

tek-pâi, a bamboo raft. **tek-tsoá**, common paper, made from bamboo. **tek-kah**, an under-shirt or vest made with bits of bamboo. **tek-bé**, short bamboo benches (lit. horses) for laying boards upon to make a tressle-bed. **tek-í**, a bamboo chair or stool. **tek-phi**, a light flat bamboo frame for sleeping on in summer (v. phi). **tek-pūn**, coarse bamboo hurdle. **tek-tsáh**, coarse bamboo barrier, as at a gate, to keep out pigs. **tek-ûi**, a bamboo fence. **tek-chhú**, fire-work in shape of rat, jumps about when lighted.

tek [R. tėk, a reed]. **lô-tek**, a sort of large coarse reed.

tek [R. the principal wife]. **tek-chhe** (R.), the legal or principal wife. **tek-chhut--ê**, born of the principal wife, as a son. **tek--ê**, id. **tek-tsú** (R.), son of the principal wife.

tek-bú, father's principal wife (said in relation to the son of a secondary wife or concubine).

tek (P.) **thien-tek-kok**, = A. thien-tiok-kok, India.

tėk [R. a marsh; to irrigate; to soften; fertile; favour; kindness].

lūn-tėk (R.), well-watered. **jūn-tėk** (R.), id.; full of fresh blooming vigorous health and well off.

hó-sek-tėk, smooth, healthy, and well-coloured, as face showing good health; glossy and well-coloured, as flowers, jade-stone, silk, or satin. **ū-sek-tėk**, id. **bô-sek-tėk**, having a bad colour, as face of person in bad health, &c.

un-tėk (R.), favour; grace. **in-tėk** (C.), id. **kóng-tėk tsun-ông**, the honourable king of wide-extended favour, a title of the idol Keh Sèng-ông.

tėk-sià, a cooling medicine.

tėk [R. northern barbarians]. **î-tėk**, outside barbarians in general.

tėk (cf. tåk). **tėk-hî**, sort of fish that has three sharp points. **tėk-pô**, sort of fish the skin of which is used like sand-paper.

tėk [R. an enemy; a competitor; a rival; an equal; to rival, compete with, or oppose].

tùi-tėk, an enemy; to oppose. **tėk-kok**, a hostile kingdom. **tėk-peng**, enemy's soldiers. **tėk-jîn**, an enemy.

tí-tėk, to oppose.

bû-tėk, superior to all other persons or things; peerless; matchless; super-excellent; so powerful that no one can fight or overcome him. **khiā bû-tėk-pâi**, said of a quail or cock-chafer that beats all its antagonists; said also figuratively of a man (lit. erecting a tablet saying he is peerless).

tėk (P.), = A. tiòk (to drive away).

tėk (cf. pėk, pók). **ka-tėk-sún**, edible shoots of a certain water vegetable.

tėk [R. to choose; to select], (cf. C. tòh). **tėk-soán**, to select carefully, esp. a son-in-law or daughter-in-law. **tėk-jit-su**, a fortune-teller who chooses lucky days. **tėk-jit-koán**, stall or shop of such a man.

tėk [R. tí, to meet with; to be worth; to value; to manage; to rule; = col. táh, tát].

tėk-jit ê kong-tsô, special messengers of the gods for each day (v. tsô). **tėk-jit-sîn** (Cn.), special messengers of the gods who take turn day by day of watching over the world.

tėk-hû ê sù-chiá (C. tit-hû sù-chiá), special messengers between Tauist priests and the gods.

tėk [R. specially; of set purpose; alone]. **tėk-siū--ê**, specially appointed to an office as his own (v. siū). **tėk-téng**, second set of candidates (at the Giòk-pîn Academy) chosen for rewards or bursaries, gen. about ten in each set.

teng (R. id.), a male person, as in counting the number of sons or inhabitants; a cyclical character in the cycle of ten; a surname.

teng-hiuⁿ, cloves.

teng-jī-tú, a T-headed prop for a door.

teng-iu, to be in mourning for parent or grandparent (v. iu).

chè-teng, to sacrifice to Confucius in the first decades of the 2nd and 8th months, on those days which contain the character "teng."

jîn-teng, male persons (said in counting sons or descendants of a family, inhabitants of a village, or members of a clan). **jîn-teng hi-bî**, population small. **jîn-teng heng-ōng**, posterity numerous. **jîn-teng ióng-tsòng**, male relatives numerous and strong. **lâm-teng**, a male person. **kúi-teng**, how many men? **kơ-teng**, having no brother or son, or near male relative. **tan-teng**, solitary, as an only son; having no brother. **tan-teng kè-tē**, only one son in each generation.

tsòng-teng, a strong young man, *e.g.* from about 20 to 30 or 40 years of age. **iù-teng**, a lad, *e.g.* under 16 years of age; also (?), a man who wears a long dress and does not do manual work. **chhơ-teng**, a man who does hard rough manual work; a labourer or workman.

ka-teng, a boy or lad indentured for a long period as a servant, almost like a slave. **hn̂g-teng** (r.), a gardener.

chheng-teng, assistant of supercargo, who keeps the accounts, and keeps an account of goods shipped and unshipped. **chheng-teng-thâu**, id. **chhin-teng**, confidential attendants brought by a mandarin from his own home; also (C.), = A. chheng-teng, assistant of supercargo.

peng-teng, a soldier. **khó iû-teng**, to examine candidates for the position of a soldier (v. iû). **khó î-teng** (C.), id.

sêng-teng, to come to the age of puberty, as about 15 or 16 years old. **sip-liók sêng-teng**, in the 16th year one comes to the age of puberty.

chhut-teng, to have or get sons, grandsons, or male inhabitants. **sit-teng**, to lose male children or younger relatives; to lose male inhabitants, as village. **sún-teng**, id. (+). **sńg-teng**, id. **thiam-teng**, to have an addition or additions to the number of sons, or of male inhabitants of village (+). **it-jîn sam-tsú, liók-tāi chhien-teng**, if each man has three sons, it makes a thousand in six generations.

teng-tsâi-kùi, male posterity, wealth, and rank. **tsâi-teng-kùi**, id. **tsâi-teng-kùi saⁿ-jī-tsn̂g**, all these in full measure. **to-teng toàt-tsâi**, a numerous family keeps one poor. **thiam-teng chìn-tsâi**, to increase in family and in wealth (+). **sún-teng lâu-tsâi**, to lose sons and wealth (+). **phoà-tsâi sún-teng**, id.

teng [R. to witness; to raise, as troops; to collect, as taxes], (Cn. cheng; C. tin).

teng-hiòng, to collect or levy dues, taxes, or customs, &c., as mandarins. **teng chîⁿ-niûⁿ**, to collect or levy the land-tax. **khai-teng** (R.), to distribute the tax-papers for the land-tax or house-tax to the collectors on a lucky day.

teng (P.), = A. tiong, middle; and so perhaps in some other words.

teng (R. id.), to repeat a command; to remind of a former command. **teng--i**, remind him of the order. **koh-teng--i**, id. **teng-lêng**, to give minute and frequent instructions or injunctions (v. lêng).

teng [R. to ascend; to note down], (Cn. töng). **teng-kek**, to become emperor. **teng-ūi**, to come to the throne, as a king. **teng-sien**, to become a Sien or Tauist divinity.

teng-tiēn, to take his seat on the throne, as emperor at audience. **iú-lō͘**, **bók-teng-chiu** (R.), if there be a road don't go by boat. **teng-ko-jit**, a day (9.9) when literary men climb hills and fly kites so as to get high degrees.

teng-kho, to become a Kujin or Tsin-sze. **kho-kah liên-teng**, to become a Kujin and a Tsin-sze in rapid succession.

ngé-kok hong-teng, crops abundant.

teng-kì, to note down (v. kì).

teng — **teng-í**, a tall stool with steps like a ladder.

teng (R. id.), (Cn. tan), a nail; a pin (as of wood or bamboo) used as a nail. **tèng-teng**, to nail a nail (v. tèng).

tek-teng, a bamboo pin used as a nail. **tsoá-lién-teng**, paper twisted hard, and used for binding together the pages of a book; also dipped in oil and used as a light. **tâng-teng**, a copper nail. **thih-teng**, an iron nail. **lí sī thih-teng-siòng; saⁿ-jit bô-phah, chiū siⁿ-sien**, you are like an iron nail, rusting if three days not beaten (said to a bad child).

tsu-teng, a round-headed nail. **jiáuⁿ-súi-teng**, sort of small iron nails (v. jiáuⁿ). **lê-si-teng**, a screw-nail. **lê-si-teng** (C.), id. **saⁿ-kha-teng**, three-cornered spikes thrown in the way of robbers, &c.

khau-teng, projecting ends of bricks in a wall, so that the wall, if lengthened, can be firmly built together.

teng-lóeh, the head of a nail (v. lóeh). **teng-á-thûi**, a hammer (v. thûi). **teng-tháng**, a tub with sharp nails, used as a pitfall (v. tháng), (s. lamp).

sí-teng-teng, unprogressive, as trade.

phòng-teng, to provoke the displeasure of one's master or superior, as by doing something worse than he expected, or by deceiving him, and his finding it out unexpectedly. **khit--i phòng-teng**, id. **ōe-phòng-teng**, it will provoke his displeasure (*e.g.* if you do so).

teng — **teng-khī** (Cn.), a sort of persimmon (v. khī).

teng (R. id.), a small hard boil, as on the eyelid or such hard bony place. **siⁿ-teng**, to have such a hard painful boil. **hó-kháu-teng**, a boil between thumb and finger. **chhùi-kháu-teng**, a boil on the lip.

toā-teng-hông, a plant used for reducing inflammation.

teng (T.) **teng-níⁿ**, = C. to-níⁿ, = Cn. tiong-níⁿ, a sort of azalea.

teng (R. id.), a lamp; a lantern; (bubbles blown by or for children); also (T.), bubbles rising from fermentation or corruption.

chit-ki-teng, one lamp or lantern.

teng-hé, a lamp made of a small saucer on a stand, with wicks swimming in oil. **táu-teng-hé**, a rice-measure containing a lamp kept burning without going out for three days and nights in rites after marriage. **táu-teng**, id. **teng-hé-tà**, a cover or shade for a lamp to keep off the wind (v. tà). **teng-hé-tàu** (esp. Cn.), id. **teng-hé-khàm**, id. **teng-hé-hoe**, large spots in a burning wick, counted lucky (v. hoe). **tng teng-hé hoa**, may my life go out like this lamp if I swear falsely.

teng-pâi, a long lantern with inscriptions. **teng-chhai**, enigmas on transparent lanterns (v. chhai). **teng-ko**, a pole with a lamp at the end of it, superstitious (v. ko).

teng-kâu, a small bamboo frame for the cheapest lamps. **sio teng-kâu**, to burn these at the end of the year. **pàng-phàu, sio teng-kâu**, do. along with firing off crackers. **teng-khiā**, an upright stand for a saucer-lamp. **teng-hé-khiā**, id. **teng-tâi**, a large stand for a lamp. **teng-kiáh**, a pillar-shaped stand for a saucer-lamp.

teng-tsō, the part of a candle-lantern which supports the candle. **teng-khak**, frame of a lantern. **teng-tháng**, frame of a large lantern (s. nail). **teng-khè**, cylindrical frame of a lantern. **teng-bî**, the top of the frame of a lantern. **teng-koāⁿ**, the fixed handle over the top of a lantern. **teng-kiâⁿ**, id. **siù teng-hoe**, to embroider the frame of a lantern (v. hoe).

teng-sim, the wick of a lamp, made of the pith of a rush (v. sim). **lō͘-thâu, taⁿ teng-sim; lō͘-bé, taⁿ thih-thûi**, matter insignificant at first becoming very serious. **teng-thio**, a small instrument like a spoon, laid on the wick of a saucer-lamp.

kiⁿ-teng, a watchman's lantern; a lantern on a pillar at a watch-station. **lō͘-teng**, a lantern at the road-side, often put up (esp. in 7th month) for a vow. **chhiú-teng**, a lantern carried in the hand in walking;

厦英大辭典

a road-lamp. **toh-thâu-teng**, a lamp for use on the table. **tháng-teng**, very large gauze lanterns, hung at the doors of temples and of great persons. **kiong-teng**, lanterns like those of temples, used at marriages. **thien-teng**, lanterns hung up in honour of Thi^n-kong. **sim-teng**, id. **jī-sì^n-teng**, a lantern with one's surname on it. **sì^n-teng**, id. **sin-niû^n-teng**, ornamental lanterns for marriages. **tsáu-bé-teng**, a lantern that turns round when lighted. **póh-piá^n-teng**, a lantern that folds flat like a cake. **sì-kak-teng**, a square lantern. **tsu-kat-teng**, a fire-balloon. **khóng-bêng-teng**, id. **pàng tsúi-teng**, to set afloat burning lamps on the water for the ghosts of drowned persons.

moâ^n-teng, lanterns with coarse hempen cloth over them, in deepest mourning (v. moâ^n). **liû-lî-teng**, sort of lantern used in temples; a scabbed head. **po-lê-teng**, a glass lantern. **liāu-si-teng**, a lantern made with a thin transparent preparation of rice (v. si). **ô-kià^n-thang-teng**, lantern made with oyster-shells. **ô-kià^n-teng**, id.

kat-teng, to hang lanterns all along a street, as in idolatrous rites. **kat hoe-teng**, to make a great illumination with vast numbers of gaudily coloured lanterns. **tiám-teng**, to light a lamp. **tiám-teng kat-chhái**, to hang up great numbers of coloured lanterns and gaudy hangings. **tiu^n-teng kat-chhái**, id. **tiám-teng, ū-hūn: pun-ku, thiàu-khám**, I have done favours to you, but you neglect to return them. **iòk-kiû thien-siōng-hok, su-tiám hút-chiên-teng** (or "pút-chêng-teng"), if you wish to get Heaven's happiness, light lamps before Buddha. **siú^n-teng**, to look at the illuminations. **khoà^n-teng**, id. **ngiâ^n-teng**, to carry lanterns in procession, as in honour of ông-iâ. **siā-teng**, to give a play in return for friends lighting lanterns before our door.

kùi-teng, to hang up a lamp on a wall. **tiàu-teng**, to hang a lamp or lantern from the roof or from a beam. **bák-chiu tiàu-teng**, the upper eyelid puckered up at the middle. **kiáh-teng**, to carry a lamp or lantern in the hand. **kiáh-teng, m̄-tsai kha-ē àm**, telling others' faults, but not knowing our own.

jiên-teng-hút, name of a Buddha (v. jiên).

pûn thn̂g-á-teng, to blow bubbles with the thick syrup called béh-lê-ko. **pûn béh-lê-ko teng**, id. **puh-teng**, to bubble, as in fermentation, or when something is corrupting.

têng (R. id.), (Cn. tân), a small ornamental open shed or summer-house on four or more pillars; a small temple or shrine. **têng-á**, id.

bān-siū-têng, the emperor's temple. **bô-sû-têng**, a small shrine for the ancestral tablets of persons who have no posterity. **koan-im-têng**, temple of Kwan-yin. **kèng-jī-têng**, a small temple or shrine for collecting written or printed paper to be burned. **jī-tsoá-têng**, id. **khí tē-têng**, said of a literary man or head man of village collecting and embezzling money on pretence of building a temple.

hûn-têng, a sedan with a cover, but open at the sides, in which the ancestral tablet is carried at a funeral. **thài-tsú-têng**, a small paper shed in which the idol called "sóe-hút" is carried (v. thài). **pn̄g-têng**, a small paper shed for the figure that represents the spirit of the deceased, used in the ceremonies for persons recently deceased. **bók-ék-têng**, a miniature paper-room for a bath-room for the spirits in the rites of khiā-hà.

liâng-têng, an awning for coolness, as on top of house. **phak-sūn-têng**, a small open porch or shed on pillars at a door. **chih-koa^n-têng**, a resting-place with a large open shed on a great road, for the use of mandarins and other travellers. **ké-têng**, a shed for musicians playing in while a mandarin is eating; also, one with a drum in it, carried at idolatrous processions. **ién-bú-têng**, a grand-stand for mandarins at review-ground. **hàu-tsú-têng**, a stone shed, put up by imperial command, with inscription in honour of a son of great filial virtue.

têng [R. thêng, to ascend in the sky, as a bird, spirit, or kite], (C.), = C. thêng, to be at the zenith, as one of the heavenly bodies. **góeh têng** (C.), the moon at zenith. **chhit têng, peh tó** (C.), in the 7th month at the zenith, in the 8th somewhat inclined (said of the Pleiades at day-break).

têng [R. thêng; C. têng, a stage on a journey; a road; a measure; a surname; = col. thiâ^n].

chiên-têng, a graduate, civil or military. **ū chiên-têng**, to be a graduate; to have a graduate, as a village or clan.

lō͘-têng (T. C.), = A. lō͘-thêng, a journey. **khí-têng** (T.), to begin a journey.

têng [R. a court for audience]. **tiâu-têng**, the imperial court; sometimes said of the emperor himself.

têng [R. a court; a paved yard or open space before a door or within a house; = col. tiâ^n].

ka-têng ê-sū, private family matters. **ka-têng ê tāi-chì**, id. **ke-têng ê-sū**, id.

kong-têng (r.), the hall of judgment. **kong-têng ê só-tsāi**, a place where many influential persons (*e.g.* literati and head-men) are met together to discuss and settle some public matter.

têng [R. clear, as water; to grow clear, as by depositing sediment]. **têng-chheng**, to settle and become clear and transparent, as muddy water. **hông-hô sa^n-chheng-nî^n chit-pái têng-chheng**, the Yellow River grows clear once in 3000 years; said of something suddenly coming right after we had quite lost hope of it; or of something that after long continuing bad suddenly changes for the better, *e.g.* a bad debt recovered, or a very bad man for once doing a kind or good action, and then relapsing. **hông-hô têng-chheng**, id.

hái-têng, the city and district of Hái-têng-biēn, in Chang-chew department, between Amoy and Chang-chew.

têng (R. id.) **têng-siâ**, a fabulous winged red serpent (Tauist).

têng (R. thiên), (Cn. tōng), to transcribe a copy, especially a fair copy. **têng-chheng**, to write out a fair copy from a scroll (s. clear). **têng-chin**, id. **têng-chià^n**, id. **koh-têng chit-tiu^n**, take another copy. **têng-liók**, to transcribe an essay with red ink, as in examination for Kujin degree.

têng, to undersell; to cut out by offering more, or accepting less than another. **sa^n-têng**, id. (s. manifold). **kàng-kè lâi-têng--i**, to undersell him. **khit--i têng--khì**, to lose an article or a place by another secretly offering more or accepting less.

têng [R. tiōng, double; manifold; to repeat; by change of tone from "tiōng," heavy], (P. tiông), double; twofold; so many fold; classifier of folds, plies, layers, strata, ranges of hills, doors within doors, concentric walls, heavens; coats, &c., worn at once.

têng-pē, double. **têng-tsài**, a second time; over again. **têng-koh**, id. **têng-thâu**, id. **koh-têng**

chit-pái, once again. **têng-têng tia̍p-tia̍p**, piled on one another; crowded densely together (v. tia̍p). **têng-têng tha̍h-tha̍h**, id. (v. tha̍h).

têng-oā^n, to change over again, as after a previous change. **têng khí-chhù**, to rebuild a house. **têng-kám**, having a relapse. **têng-tâ^n**, making a discrepancy, as in an account, or as repeating a story over again, either by mere mistake or deceitfully (v. tâ^n).

têng-kù, stammering, esp. repeating clauses. **têng-chih**, stammering. **si^n têng-chih**, to have a diseased growth under the tongue. **ba̍k-chiu têng-sûn**, the upper eyelid having a slight wrinkle (v. sûn). **têng-keng**, the border at the neck of a dress, where it is made doubly strong (v. keng).

toa^n-têng, having only one thickness, as of cloth or paper, &c. **toa^n-têng-be̍h**, stockings made of only one thickness of cloth. **siang-têng**, made with two plies or thicknesses of material. **sa^n-têng**, of three plies or thicknesses (s. undersell). **sa^n-têng-siâ^n**, having three concentric walls, as city. **kúi-têng-sa^n**, how many coats (have you) on? **chit-têng-sa^n**, one coat out of several worn at once. **chit-têng-mn̂g**, one door or gate in a set of several in succession one within the other. **chit - têng - soa^n**, one of several ranges of mountains. **chit-têng-tsúi**, one of several transverse lines of water, as in a view. **chit-têng-mo̍h^n**, a layer of outer skin, as on the body, or of outer bark on a tree. **lí sim-koa^n chit-têng-mo̍h^n**, you are very dull of apprehension! **sán kàu chit-têng-phê pi^n chit-têng-kut**, skin and bone (v. pi^n).

téng [R. a rank; a class; to wait;=col. tán], (Cn. tńg), a rank, class, or sort; to act in place of, as in filling a vacancy.

téng-thòe, to act in place of; to fill the place of (v. thòe). **téng-thè** (C.), id. **‚téng i-ê-kheh**, to succeed to the place he left vacant.

téng-hō, sort, class, kind, of men or things. **téng-tē**, rank; station; quality. **téng-kip** (R.), a step of rank. **téng-khip** (R.), id.

pún-téng, one's own proper or prescribed duties; naturally; according to what is proper. **lí--ê pún-téng**, your own proper duties. **phái^n-goá-pún-téng**, I injure no one but myself (said in answer to some one finding fault with our conduct). **khai-goá-pún-téng**, I spend no one's money but my own, and no one else has any concern with it. **sòng-goá-pún-téng**, though I am poor it hurts no one else.

tâng-téng, of the same rank or class, as persons. **pî^n-téng**, of the same rank. **pêng-téng**, id. **put-téng**, of various sizes or qualities (said of articles of the same sort or kind). **put-téng-kè**, at various prices, as several articles larger and smaller, or better and worse, but of the same kind of things.

it-téng, first-class (v. it). **siōng-téng**, id. (v. siōng). **tiong-téng**, of medium quality; second-class. **hā-téng**, of third or inferior sort. **sa^n-téng**, id. **chhiau-téng**, the best ten competitors for prizes at the Gio̍k-pín examinations at Amoy. **tek-téng**, the second set of these competitors.

téng (R. id.), summit; top; above; on; upon; upper; previous; official button on a cap; classifier of hats, caps, sedans, &c.

téng-ē, upper and lower; above and below (v. ē).

oân-téng, to have one's head fully shaved, as Bud. priest or nun. **chhèng-téng**, head broken out in a sort of eruption (v. chhèng).

thâu-kun-téng, sort of extra top-sail in a junk. **ho̍h-téng**, a stork's crest (v. ho̍h).

thi^n-téng, in heaven; high heaven (v. thi^n). **soa^n-téng**, dry land; on land; on a hill (v. soa^n). **chhù-téng**, on the roof of a house (v. chhù). **lâu-téng**, an upper story; upstairs. **toh-téng**, on the table. **po-téng**, on the top of the bulwarks of a vessel. **thâu-khak-téng**, on the top of the head; crown of head. **koe-téng**, in the street; in the market.

chia̍h-pn̄g-téng, just after eating, *e.g.* speaking of the time for taking medicine.

téng-bé, boys on horseback in an idolatrous incense procession (v. bé).

téng-thâu, on the top; above. **téng-bīn**, above; on the top; on the top of. **bīn-téng**, on the top; upstairs. **thâu-bīn-téng--ê**, first-class, as things or men. **téng-siōng**, of the very best quality (v. siōng).

téng-chin, of first-rate excellence, as a thing; very strict, as master who will not let faults pass; very sharp in mercantile matters, as man who is always trying to make a very good bargain.

téng-sì-hong, a head-wind (v. sì).

téng-chhiú, previously done by another; title-deed of the seller, &c. (v. chhiú). **téng-pòe**, parents and their equals in genealogical rank. **téng-pe**, forenoon. **téng-tàu**, id. **téng-jit**, a former day, &c. **téng-chiu^n**, the chapter immediately preceding. **téng-pang**, on the former occasion.

téng-pɛ̂^{n} (C.), = A. chiū^n-piâ^n, the upper ping tone. **téng-khì** (C.), = A. chiū^n-khì. **téng-jip** (C.), = A. chiū^n-jip.

téng-tài, the official button on a mandarin's cap (v. tài). **sek-téng**, id. **téng-bō**, official cap. **téng-tsō**, the small round brass plate on the top of the cap, on which the official button rests. **tì téng-tsō**, to wear a cap with that brass plate, but no button, as a degraded mandarin, or as some literati or gentry. **tì-téng**, to wear a cap with official button. **ū téng-tì**, to have the rank that allows to wear such a button. **kià-téng**, to take away the official button for a time till the case can be thoroughly investigated; to suspend from rank.

âng-téng, the red button of first-rank mandarins; properly the translucent button of the first rank, but sometimes said of the second. **hoe-âng-téng**, opaque red coral button, second rank. **chhi^n-téng**, transparent light blue button, third rank. **chhi^n-liāng-téng**, id. **lâm-téng**, dark opaque blue button, fourth rank. **pe̍h-liāng-téng**, clear colourless crystal button, fifth rank. **pe̍h-chio̍h-téng**, opaque white button, sixth rank. **kim-téng**, gilt button, seventh to ninth ranks. **lêng-téng**, wearing a feather in cap, as special mark of honour (v. lêng). **gûn-téng**, white button (?) of a Sew-tsai graduate.

téng (R. id.), a small steelyard, used for weighing medicines, silver, &c.; to weigh with it. **téng-á**, a small steelyard. **toā-téng**, a somewhat larger sort, used for medicines, but smaller than a chhìn. **io̍h-téng**, steelyard for weighing medicines. **lî-téng**, steelyard for weighing fine medicines; also used for silver; generally marked so as to make a dollar equal to 7 chî^n 2 hun. **gûn-téng**, a small steelyard for weighing silver. **chhit-jī-téng**, steelyard that makes a dollar equal to 7 chî^n 2 hun, used in Changchew, and in all places round, except Amoy. **khè-tô-téng**, id. **chhit-lio̍k-téng**, steelyard that makes a dollar equal to 7 chî^n 6 hun. **hā-tô-téng**, id.

téng-gûn, to weigh silver with a small steelyard.

kah-téng, to test a steelyard by another, to see if it be correct.

téng-á-thûi, the weight of a small steelyard. **téng-á-koái^{n}**, its beam. **téng-á-poâ^{n}**, its scale. **téng-á-khak**, its case. **téng-á-áh**, id.

téng [R. a tripod; a sort of caldron; = col. tiá^{n}]. **téng-lô**, a narrow-mouthed three-legged vessel for burning incense. **téng-lô-thoàn**, a variety of the seal character, in which each word has three long legs like an incense vessel; supposed to keep away evil influences, and counted very good for graves.

téng (C.), = A. tién, to mortgage.

téng (T.) **téng-kong-á**, a very small sort of dragon-fly.

tèng [R. id.; by change of tone from "teng," a nail], (Cn. tàn), to nail; to sting, as a wasp; to sew or hem finely; to sew by sending the needle quite through, and then back again quite through; to sew on, as figures cut in cloth of another colour; to fasten the sheets of a book together slightly; to throw down, as a top; to throw down, as a cash or shell in gambling, so as to make another turn upside down.

tèng-teng, to nail with a nail. **tèng lô-si-teng**, to put in a screw-nail. **koa^{n}-chhâ tèng-teng, chiū kóe-pì^{n}**, he will never reform till his coffin is nailed up.

tèng-tiâu, to nail fast. **si^{n}-kun tèng-tiâu**, unwilling to rise up, as if rooted and nailed fast. **tèng-sí**, to nail firm; to nail to death, as by crucifixion. **tèng sip-jī-kè**, to crucify. **phī^{n}-tèng**, to lay on and nail firm, as the thin lath or boards on a roof.

tèng-tâng, to work in brass.

tèng iâng-kong (C.), to fix in the ground a peg with the words iâng-kong on it, as in making a grave (v. iâng).

khit-phang tèng, to be stung by a wasp or bee. **o-tèng-phang**, a sort of wasp.

tèng-chheh (Cn. tàn-tsü), to bind a book roughly by merely fastening the sheets together, as with pins of twisted paper.

tèng-sa^{n}, to sew a dress finely. **tèng kau-hûn**, to sew on figures cut in velvet (or some stuff different from the dress) in a hooked pattern. **kau-chiam tèng, bát-liú pâng**, very careful, as in examining or managing a matter, or as in the use of money.

tèng kan-lòk, to throw down a top to make it spin. **tèng ham-khak-chí^{n}**, to throw down a cockle-shell so as to make another one turn upside down, as boys do in a sort of gambling. **tèng âng-khī-tì**, to throw down the dried calyx of the persimmon in the same way.

tèng — **tèng-iâm**, to salt slightly.

tèng (C.) **bé-tàh-tèng**, = A. bé-tàh-thèng, a stirrup. **bé-tèng**, id. (v. thèng).

tèng [R. to criticize; to adjust; to settle; to edit]. **tèng-chhìn**, to mark the beam of a steelyard. **tèng chhìn-hoe**, id. **kong-tèng**, sort of large steelyard made specially correct, for wholesale trade; some say that it adds about 4 per cent, to the weight according to the usual "pah-sì-tô," so as to allow for the loss of weight in selling by retail.

tèng-bêng (R.), to settle the agreement for marriage of son or daughter.

tèng [R. tiòng, to hit the centre; to accomplish; exact; to be hit; by change of tone from "tiong," centre], (C. sometimes tiòng).

tèng-ì, to suit one's fancy or desire; agreeable to one's wish. **sa^{n}-tèng-ì**, fully agreeing and highly pleased with each other, as man and wife; rarely said of partners in business. **m̄-tèng-lâng-ì**, not according to one's desire; not to one's taste. **m̄-tèng-lâng-bák**, bad-looking, as a thing, or as an action. **m̄-tèng lâng-bák-chiu**, id. **m̄-tèng-lâng-thia^{n}**, speaking so that the other is not willing to hear. **sa^{n}-tèng-thia^{n}**, willingly listening to another, or to one another; about of one mind.

tēng — **tō-tēng**, a reptile like a snake with feet, supposed to be very poisonous. **tō-tēng kā, bóe koa^{n}-chhâ**, if the tō-tēng bite you, you must buy a coffin; but it is also said never to bite!

tēng [R. hān, a limit; a threshold; also written by a distinct word, hān or hiēn], (T. tāi^{n}; Cn. tūi^{n}).

hō-tēng, a threshold. **mn̂g-tēng**, id. **thang-á-tēng**, a window-sill. **chit-kha hō-tēng-lāi, chit-kha hō-tēng-goā**, unsettled in purpose.

tēng [R. to fix; to settle; steady; = col. tiā^{n}]. **it-tēng**, certainly; assuredly it is. **pit-tēng**, surely must be; surely must. **tēng-sī** (r.), certainly it is —. **put-tēng**, not yet fixed. **bô-tēng-kiàn**, unsettled in purpose. **bô-tēng-sèng**, fickle; changeable. **tēng-tòng**, safe and steady, as man. **tēng-tio̍k**, settled, as affair.

tiâm-tēng, strongly made, as furniture; firmly rooted, strong and healthy, as tree; having a good deal of secret wealth, as man. **ū-tiâm-tēng**, to have a good deal of concealed wealth.

seng-sú iú-tēng, life and death are determined, as by fate.

tēng-kui, to fix or settle a rule; to set up, as a new institution, *e.g.* a new tax, examination, or registration; to settle definitely, as situation for a man. **á-bē tēng-kui**, not yet fixed, as rule, &c. **tēng-hun**, to betroth. **tēng-chhin**, id. **tēng-phèng**, to settle the marriage contract, as for son or daughter. **tēng hng-hiù^{n}**, to settle the lucky direction, as for house or grave. **tēng hun-kim**, id.

tēng-tsōe, to condemn, as a judge. **tēng i-ê-tsōe**, to condemn him. **tēng sí-tsōe**, to condemn to death. **tēng sí-àn**, id. **tēng-àn**, to give judgment.

tēng [R. tiēn, fixed; settled; to make a libation], (Cn. tūi^{n}; T. tāi^{n}), hard; solid; firm; plump. **tēng-nńg**, hard or soft. **tēng-phà^{n}**, solid or not solid.

tēng-tauh, hard; solid; strongly made; having a good deal of money (v. tauh). **tēng khok-khok**, very hard and strong; so hard as to give a clear ringing sound when struck. **tēng kháuh-kháuh**, too hard, as eatables insufficiently cooked. **tēng hoaih^{n}-hoaih^{n}**, very hard, *e.g.* as cakes.

kien-tēng, hard; solid; firm; strongly made. **kin-tēng** (C.), id. **kiet-tēng**, id. **o-tēng**, having a rather thin and darkish face, as man neither fat nor lean.

ta-tēng, become too dry, hard, and unpleasant to eat, as eatables; having enough to live upon, though not wealthy; pretty well off; curt and laconic in manner, as workman or shopkeeper who will not even discuss the lowering of his terms, but will have nothing to say to us unless we take his terms, as he feels quite independent of us. **ke-hé ta-tēng**, wealthy. **ta-tēng ê seng-lí**, a very safe and steady trade, esp. in some article which no one else can make or produce, so that we can fix and keep our own price. **chhun chit-tè tēng-tēng**, pretty well off, though not wealthy.

thâu-khak tēng, robust and vigorous, as a child; supposed to be through the protecting care of the idols. **kiá^{n}-sun thâu-khak tēng**, may your posterity be strong and healthy, said as an auspicious wish to parents. **tēng-chîⁿ**, dollars adulterated by being filled with brass or copper.

ti [R. name of a plant]. **ti-bú**, sort of cooling medicine (v. bú). **ti-bé**, id.

ti — **ti-ti-háu**, sound of incessant chirping of birds.

ti (R. id.) **ti-tu**, a spider. **hoan-ti-tu**, an absurdly unreasonable man.

ti-tu-bāng, a spider's web, spread out round and entire. **ti-tu kiet-bóng**, ornamental network, esp. on top of mandarin's sedan. **ti-tu-si**, spiders' webs, esp. hanging loosely or in fine threads. **ti-lâ-si**, id. **ká ti-tu-si**, to take away spiders' webs, as with a stick. **kiⁿ ti-tu-si**, do.; also to weave spiders' webs. **ti-tu kiⁿ-si**, the spider weaves its web. **ti-tu khan-si**, id.

ti [R. to know; to feel; = col. tsai]. **thong-ti**, to inform; to notify. **ti-hōe**, to notify formally. **pín-ti** (R.), to inform a superior official by a document.

ti-hú, the prefect or governor of a Foo department. **ti-chiu**, the prefect of a Chow department. **ti-koāiⁿ**, the mandarin of a Hien district; the sub-prefect.

put-ti-chiok, insatiable (v. chiok). **sū put-ti**, yet strange to say, the fact or result is —. **put-ti put-tsōe**, without knowledge guilt is not reckoned. **ti kî-it, put-ti kî-jī**, knowing only very little of the matter. **kàu put-ti thien-tē**, so as to be quite unconscious, as in a very severe illness, or when drunk or very sleepy. **jîn put-soat put-ti**, a man's mind is not known unless he speak (v. soat).

ti-tsōe, to confess a fault or crime. **ti-kò pit-kái**, reform on learning one's fault.

ti-chêng, grateful. **ti i-ê-chêng**, to be grateful to him. **ti-un pò-pún**, to show gratefulness to parents (v. un).

ti-kí ê-lâng, a very intimate friend. **ti-sim ê-lâng**, id.

ti-im, to understand the meaning, to know what to do. **put-chí ti-lí**, knowing well and doing one's duty, as servant or employé. **sio-ti** (C.), over sharp and exacting, as in trade. **it-kú sêng-bêng, thien-hā ti**, on becoming a Kujin, the whole world knows.

sien-ti, to know beforehand; a prophet. **sien-ti-lâng**, a prophet. **bī-pok sien-ti**, I know before you tell me (lit. before divination).

ti [R. id., C. ti; Cn. tü], (Cn. tü: T. often tu, as also in the villages of Amoy island), a pig; a sow; a hog; the zodiacal sign corresponding to the character "hāi" in the cycle of 12. **siùⁿ-ti**, born in a year that has hāi as one of its characters.

tn̂g-ti, long-shaped. **chhiú-ti-á**, the fleshy part of the upper arm.

kiáu-ti, a man always gambling and constantly losing. **toā-ti-kheh**, a big foolish-looking fellow.

pûi-ti, a black legume, used as a cooling medicine (Acacia concinna?). **pûi-ti-chí**, its seeds. **n̄ng-chiah pûi-ti**, two of these pods, put in a bag on a bride's breast.

hô-ti, a porcupine. **hái-ti**, a porpoise. **hái-ti-á**, a sort of fish.

liù-ti, to catch a pig with a noose. **iam-ti**, to castrate pigs; a man whose trade is to do so. **thâi-ti ê-lâng**, a butcher who kills pigs.

ti-á-gê, a wholesale shop for selling live pigs. **ti-tsàu**, a place for killing pigs. **ti-tiam**, a block on which pork is laid out for sale. **ti-lak-soh**, a cord for leading a pig. **ti-tiâu**, a pig-sty (v. tiâu). **ti-tsô**, a pig's trough. **ti-tsáh**, a barrier for keeping in pigs. **ti-tsang**, hair on back of pig's neck.

ti-kang, a male pig, a hog. **ti-ko**, do., as used for covering (v. ko). **ti-kong**, a large male pig. **ti-phe**, a pig not full grown. **ti-á**, a small pig.

ti-bú, a sow that has had a litter (s. plant). **ti-bú-chhih**, sort of crab (v. chhih). **ti-bú-chhêng**, a sort of tree like a banyan. **ti-bú-chhài**, a sort of edible vegetable; often grown round the roots of pot flowers. **ti-bú-leng** (esp. C.), id. **âng-ti-bú** (C.), sort of snake, the bite of which only causes a slight pain, but is not dangerous. **chhin-chhiūⁿ ti-bú thoa-thê**, said of a fat, lazy, slovenly woman. **pîⁿ-pîⁿ-lē poáh--sí pūn-ti-bú**, a fat sow stumbles on a level road, and is killed by the fall.

tî (R. id.), a pond; a reservoir; a surname. **tî-á**, a small pond. **tî tn̂g**, large and small ponds. **hî-tî**, a fish-pond. **hòng-seng-tî**, a pond at a temple for keeping fish alive. **siâⁿ-tî**, city wall and moat (v. siâⁿ). **chhè-tî**, a necessary.

hīⁿ-tî, the cavity for water in a Chinese ink-stone.

huih-tî, the bloody pool in the Buddhist hell, for women who die in the first month after child-birth. **tî-thâu hu-jîn** (T.), the goddess of child-birth.

tî-ông-iâ, an idol of the surname Tî.

khui-tî, to make a pond. **kut-tî**, to dig a pond deeper than before. **chheng-tî**, to clean out a pond.

tî [R. level place at front of palace]. **tan-tî**, the red depressed area before the audience-hall of a palace; the depressed area just before the principal hall of the temple of Confucius or of Kwanti; the low flat piece of ground in front of a grave, where water runs off.

tî [R. thû, a hoe; to hoe or dig up; = col. tû]. **tî-thâu**, a hoe, used as a spade (s. pond). **tî-thâu-pìⁿ**, the handle of a hoe. **tî-thâu-chhùi pùn-ki-hī**, I am neither good at speaking nor at understanding difficult matters.

tî [R. slow; dilatory]. **iên-tî**, to procrastinate. **tî-oān**, id. **tî-gî** (R.), doubting and hesitating how to act, and therefore delaying.

khah-tî, past the time and thus useless; too late. **hoán-hóe khah-tî**, to repent too late. **hóe--chiá tî**, it will then be too late to change one's mind.

lêng-tî, to cause much trouble and annoyance (s. cut in pieces). **gâu lêng-tî--lâng**, constantly causing trouble and annoyance, as restless child, or as master who in many ways makes his employé's life miserable.

tî [R. to cut in small pieces]. **lêng-tî**, to kill a man by the slow torture of cutting him in pieces bit by bit (s. slow). **lêng-tî--sí**, id. **lêng-tî koah-bah**, id.

tî, = tîh, to wish for; to desire. **ài-tî-mihⁿ**, grasping; covetous.

tî [R. chhî, to hold with the hand; to grasp; to maintain; to assist]. **tiâu-tî**, on purpose; with fixed intention. **bô-tiâu-tî**, without previous intention; unpremeditated; unintentional, as an action.

tiuⁿ-tî, to be on one's guard; to take precautions against some one or some danger; intentionally. **bô-tiuⁿ-tî**, when off one's guard; unintentionally; most unexpectedly. **tioh-tiuⁿ-tî**, be on your guard! take care what you say or do. **tî-hông**, to be on one's guard; to take precautions.

kì-tî, memory; the mental power of memory. **hó-kì-tî**, having a good memory.

chhiâⁿ-tî, to bring up, as children, till they are married or can take care of themselves.

hû-tî (C.), = A. **hû-chhî**, to support, as a feeble person or child in walking.

tî (C.), = A. tû, to take away.

tí [R. to sustain; to oppose; to be worth; to be a substitute for; = col. tú, tóe], (C. tí, té).

tí-tng, to bear, as responsibility; to be able to oppose (v. tng). **māiⁿ--chiá tí-tong**, the seller bears the responsibility (v. tong).

tí-miāⁿ, to pay life for life. **chiong-mihⁿ tí-chîⁿ**, to compound for a debt by giving articles valued at so much. **chiong-mihⁿ tí-gûn**, do., for debt up to the value of silver coins. **tùi-tí**, to square up accounts (as by money, goods, or other accounts) so that all is settled.

tí-giāh, to act as substitute; to make up a loss, as a security does; to be taken in place of something lost or spoiled. **tí i-ê-giāh**, to act in place of another temporarily in some small matter; said also in scolding a man for laziness, as if only filling up another's place temporarily without heart in the matter. **tí-thóng** (C. té-thóng), to be used, as a worse thing, to fill the place of a better, as temporary substitute (v. thóng). **tí-sek** (C. té-sek), put in the place of a better, as inferior or useless person or thing (v. sek).

tí-tėk, to oppose; to withstand.

tí-tak (C.), = A. tú-tak, to oppose another's wishes; to object to or refuse to do a thing; to carp at a master's orders, &c.

tí [R. bottom, = col. tóe, tē]. **tí-lí** (r.), the original cause or beginning of a matter that has become involved, *e.g.* of a lawsuit or violent feud. **kóng kàu tí-lí**, to discuss thoroughly to the very bottom. **kàu-thiet-tí**, to the very bottom, as of a subject (v. thiet). **bô-tí-chí**, without limit; endless, as affair (v. chí). **m̄-tsai tí-hē**, to know nothing of the matter (v. hē).

tò-tí (R.), in fine; but after all —. **tàu-tí**, id.

chéng-tí-oa, an inexperienced fellow (lit. frog at bottom of well).

tì [R. wisdom]. **tì-sek**, wisdom. **tì-sit** (C.), id. **tì-hūi**, id. **jîn gī, lé tì sìn**, the five great virtues. **it-jîn tì, put-jû lióng-jîn gī**, one man's wisdom is not so good as two men's consultation. **tsâi-tì lióng-kiam**, having both natural ability and acquired wisdom or skill. **ū-tám-tì**, wise and courageous, calm and self-possessed, as in danger or alarm, or as in managing some difficult business; esp. said when found in a young person or in some one where they would not have been expected.

kè-tì, a plot; a skilful scheme. **hó-kè-tì**, an artful plan or skilful scheme for getting at something in a roundabout way. **siet-kè-tì**, to plot; to scheme secretly.

tì [R. to place; to set; to purchase; to acquire]. **tì hiuⁿ-oàⁿ-toh**, to set an incense table. **tì-lêng** to set up the "hûn-sin" and hangings, &c., ready for the rites of "kong-tek."

an-tì, to set in order, as furniture, or as room for a person; to furnish with a lodging, as guest. **an-tì--tit tú-hó**, all nicely arranged, as furniture, &c. **pè-tì**, to arrange nicely, as things. **an-pâi pè-tì**, to arrange in proper order, as furniture. **pè-tì siuⁿ-tsók**, too crowded with furniture, as room.

kiàn-tì, to acquire by purchase, as property. **tì-hè**, tó buy goods.

tì sek-ka, having got a wife (v. ka).

tì [R. tài, to wear on the head; a surname; = col. tè], to wear on the head, as a cap, hat, or mask; to carry on the head, as a load. **tì-bō**, to wear a hat or cap (v. bō). **tì-lóeh**, to wear a broad sun-hat. **tì-téng**, to wear an official button on the cap. **tì-kè**, to put on a sort of ornamental head-dress, as woman at marriage. **tì báng-kun**, to wear a sort of Ming head-dress, as actors. **ài-tì hé-thoàⁿ-láng**, fond of being much flattered and made of much consequence (lit. wear a charcoal basket).

tì-phí, to become covered with a scab.

ū-téng-tì, to have official rank.

thâu-khak tì-thiⁿ, kha táh-tōe, said of a man so poor as to have no house, and nothing but what is on his person. **tì chit-ê-thiⁿ, táh chit-ê-tōe**, living under the same heaven, and on the same earth. **kha táh lín-ê-tōe, thâu tì lín-ê-thiⁿ**, we are wholly supported by and dependent on you, and should obey you.

tì [R. to tend towards; to conduce or lead towards an effect; having a tendency or hazard]. **tì-kàu**, having the (hurtful) effect that —. **tì-kàu àn-niⁿ**, come to such a sad state. **í-tì-kàu**, having this result that — (very different from what was desired or expected). **ok-chek sé-tì**, resulting from accumulated guilt calling down Heaven's vengeance. **put-tì**, it will not have any injurious effect.

tì-miāⁿ ê sé-tsāi, a vital place. **tì-miāⁿ ê tāi-chì**, a matter of life and death. **ōe-tì-bēng**, mortal, as wound or disease. **tì-pīⁿ**, causing sickness; to grow unwell; to take a disease. **chèng tì-khi-chhim**, the disease deeply seated. **chèng tì-lâi-tāng**, id.

tì-gî, to distrust; to have suspicions. **tì-tiōng** (esp. C.), to value much; to count of importance.

bô-ì-tì, having no mind to it; without heart about it; working lazily or idly; feeling disheartened and unhappy, as when slighted or coldly received. **ū-ì-tì**, catching the fancy, or pleasing the taste, as a beautiful thing.

tì-ì, to apply the mind or heart. **tì-sim tì-ì**, id. **liû-sim tì-ì**, to apply one's mind earnestly and attentively. **tsoan-sim tì-ì**, with one's whole mind and heart. **tsoan-sim tì-chì**, id.

tiâu-tì, of set purpose.

tāng-tì, very heavy.

saⁿ-liên tì-toà, joined very closely together, as relations, or as things (v. toà).

kéng-tì, scenery; circumstances, state, or fortune, as of man or place.

tì [R. fine; elegant]. **piau-tì** (r.), pretty, only of persons. **cheng-tì**, minute, distinct, and beautiful, as workmanship; small and beautiful, as things.

sek-tì, colour.

tì [R. pi, to protect]. **tì-ìm**, to protect or assist, as by power or influence.

tì (R. tè), the calyx of a flower, esp. the solid part of the calyx where it joins the stalk, the receptacle of a flower; the thickened part of the calyx persistent on some fruits where they are attached to the stalk; the crown of the root, as of a turnip or radish. **hoe-tì**, the calyx of a flower. **khī-tì**, the persistent calyx of the persimmon, where it is attached to the stalk. **khī-tì-bō**, a skull-cap with a large button in the centre, worn by children. **âng-khī hó-chiāh, tsūi-lâng khī-tì** (or "tùi-tá-lóh khí-tì"), you are now prosperous, but forget who first helped you on.

kun-tì, the origin of an affair; the antecedents of a man. **tóe-tì**, the origin of an affair, &c. (v. tóe).

hī-tì, the small lobe which half covers the hole of the ear. **lê-tì**, the cover or lid of a spiral shell-fish. **sim-koaⁿ-tì**, the soft depression in the middle of the breast. **sim-koaⁿ tì-á-khut**, id.

tī [R. to govern; to rule well; to heal]. **tī-lí**, to govern. **chhú-tī** (R.), to decide the case of a criminal, as mandarin. **tī-tsōe**, to punish crime, as mandarin. **tī-hoat** (r.), manner of government. **put-lêng tī-ka, ien-lêng tī-kok**, unable to rule his household, how can he rule his kingdom? **tī-kúi**, to rule demons. **chiong-kûi tī-kúi**, said of a powerful man ruling others (v. kûi). **tī-siâ**, to rule evil spirits. **tī-iau**, id. **tī-iau**, to allay hunger (said in joke). **tsúi ōe-tī-hé** (water can rule fire), a quiet man will overcome a violent man in the end.

tī-pī^n, to heal disease. **i-tī**, id. **chit-hāng tī chit-hāng**, one component of the dose affects one special symptom or ailment. **tsoan-tī gán-khe**, exclusively attending to eye diseases, as oculist.

chhòng-tī, to harass or molest, not very severely; to make sport of. **thòng-tī** (Cn.), id.

tông-tī, the reign of Tung-chih. **tông-tī-kun**, the emperor Tung-chih, son of Hien-fung, whom he succeeded in 1862. **sūn-tī-kun**, the emperor Shun-chih, founder of the Manchoo dynasty.

tī (R. id.), piles. **goā-tī**, external piles. **lōe-tī**, internal piles. **tī-chhng**, piles at the anus. **chhoan-tiông-tī**, fistula.

tī (R. id., = col. khī, thī). **tī-koe**, = khī-koe, the pheasant.

tī [R. sī, to be, this, = col. chī]. **tī-sî**, when? (v. sî). **tī-chit-jit**, what day? **tī-chit-ê**, what person? what thing? **tī-tá-lòh**, where? **tī-tá-lòh chit-ê**, which? (v. lòh).

tī [R. tit, to meet with; to value; to manage or attend to; = col. tàt, tàh]. **bô-tī-tāi** (esp. C.), it does not concern you (v. tāi, business).

tī [R. tsāi, to be in; in], in; at; in reference to; with regard to; sometimes an untranslatable particle of relation, which is very often omitted.

tiām-tī, quiet and staid in manner.

tī--teh, present; at home; alive. **sa^n--kap tī--teh**, present with another. **bô-tī--teh**, not present; not at home; deceased. **tak-ūi tī--teh**, everywhere present. **i tī-teh-chē**, he is sitting inside or about the door doing nothing.

tī-chia, here. **tī-chí-tau**, id. **tī-chit-tá**, id. **tī-hia**, there. **tī-hí-tau**, id. **tī-hit-tá**, id. **tī-hái--nih^n**, in the sea. **tī-chhù-lāi**, in the house. **tī-chhù-téng**, on the roof. **kàu--tī hit-sî**, come to that time.

tsāi-tī-goá, as to what depends on me; in my power.

siòk-tī-goá, belongs to me. **hâng-hòk tī-i**, to make submission to him. **tek-tsōe tī-i**, to offend against him.

kia^n-sí tī-lâng, very very dirty.

khah-koâi^n tī-thi^n, = khah-koâi^n-thi^n, higher than heaven (in this and some such phrases, C. sometimes sī). In many of these last phrases, "ti" is usually omitted.

tī [R. tē, the earth, = col. tōe]; also (Cn.) = hn̂g, dry fields on ground that is not irrigated.

thó-tī-kong (C. thó-tē-kong), the god of the earth and of graves. **thó-tī**, id. **chhân-thâu ê thó-tī-kong**, his spirit supposed to reside in the fields; incense and paper are there burned to him. **thó-tī-pô**, the goddess of the earth, counted more gentle than thó-tī-kong. **thó-tī-má**, id. **thó-tī-kong bô-ūi-hō, hó m̄-ká^n kā-lâng**, without his warrant a tiger dares not devour a man; an inferior would not venture to act so unless sure that his chief approves of it; thieves could not manage it, unless a servant or employé were in league with them. **thó-tī-kong, thó-tī-pô; hō-lí-than, hō-lí-ô; kàu-sî, mih^n to-bô**, vowing oysters and razor-fish to the god and goddess of earth, but not paying the vow (said of asking a man's help and promising reward, but failing to give it). **thó-tī-kong thó-tī-pô**, id.

chhân-tī (Cn.), = chhân-hn̂g, fields in general, both wet and dry. **tī--ê** (Cn.), from a dry field, as potatoes. **tī--gê** (Cn.), id.

tī [R. id.; C. tī; Cn. tū], chopsticks. **tī-khia**, one chopstick. **gûn-tī**, silver or silver-tipped chopsticks. **gê-tī**, ivory chopsticks. **oá^n-tī**, bowls and chopsticks. **oá^n-tih-tī**, bowls, small plates for condiments, and chopsticks. **tī-lâng**, a cylindrical vessel for holding chopsticks. **kiáh-tī**, to use chopsticks.

hé-tī, two iron rods used (like chopsticks) as tongs; sometimes connected by a chain, just to keep either from being lost, but still handled like chopsticks. **hiu^n-tī**, sticks used (in the manner of chopsticks) for arranging incense on the incense vessel, instead of tongs.

tī [R. tē, a younger brother]. **sió-tī**, a younger brother. **iét-tī-á**, small queue at the side of a child's head.

hia^n-tī, elder and younger brothers; brothers in general (v. hia^n).

tī [R. small; young; tender], the eye of a potatoe, where the sprout comes out. **han-tsû-tī**, do., of a sweet potatoe.

tī — **sek-tī**, colour; better "sek-tī."

tī [R. kí, one's self, = col. kī]. **ka-tī** (C.), = A. ka-kī, one's self.

ti^n [R. cheng, the tendon Achilles], (C. tɛ^n). **kha-āu-ti^n**, the heel. **chhiú-āu-ti^n**, the elbow.

kak-ti^n, a shoe-horn.

ti^n — **tùn-ti^n**, to make objections or excuses, as man wishing to avoid doing what he is ordered.

ti^n (R. tiâm), sweet; good-tasted (said of any sort of good taste, sometimes even of a thing that tastes well because it is sufficiently salt).

kam-ti^n, sweet. **ti^n but-but**, very sweet. **bô-ti^n-thâu**, insipid; not good tasted.

ti^n-kiâm, chiáh bô-hiâm, willing to take whatever comes to hand (v. kiâm). **tâng-khó tâng-ti^n**, sharing each other's fortunes (v. tâng).

khah-ti^n-bit, sweeter than honey. **ti^n bit-bit**, very sweet. **ōe ti^n-bit-bit**, having very sweet words, as a flatterer, or as a polite man who means nothing by it, or as a deceiver. **chhùi khah-ti^n-bit**, id. **chhùi ti^n, chih kút**, mouth sweet and slippery; full of flattery and deceit. **thn̂g-ti^n bit-ti^n**, very friendly and sweet (like sugar and honey), often with idea of deceit. **kōe thn̂g-ti^n bit-ti^n**, id.

ɵ-ti^n, a tree with small berries (barely edible); the leaves are infused as a sort of tea for drinking. **ɵ-ti^n-chhiū**, id. **ɵ-ti^n-chí**, its berries.

chiú-ti^n (C.), fermented liquor not yet distilled, but ready for distillation.

tî^n (R. tiên), to twine; to entwine; to entangle; to wind, as thread, or as the queue; to procrastinate or cause trouble by involving matters.

tî^n-lâi tî^n-khì, causing much delay and annoyance. **î^n-tî^n**, involved; causing delay; troublesome (v. î^n). **kau-tî^n**, troublesome and involved. **tak-tî^n** (C. tak-tɛ̂^{n}), full of difficult and troublesome items, as an affair, esp. more and more difficulties turning up when all seemed straight; very troublesome to deal with, as man who constantly raises new difficulties, for mere opposition, or in order to get more money.

tî^{n}-poà^{n}, to entangle or embarrass, as an impediment, *e.g.* business or family that cannot be left. **tî^{n}-tî^{n} poà^{n}-poà^{n}**, all involved and entangled, as affair. **bó-kiá^{n} tî^{n}-poà^{n}**, family acting as an encumbrance; keeping from work or travel. **tî^{n}-kha poà^{n}-chhiú**, to be in the way, as ropes, furniture, &c.; to be a hindrance, encumbrance, or impediment; keeping from work, *e.g.* as family. **tî^{n}-kha tî^{n}-chhiú**, to be such an encumbrance or impediment.

tî^{n}-tè, to be in constant attendance, as body-servant or sick-nurse.

tî^{n} kè-á-lê, to wind one's queue into a knot at the back of the head. **tî^{n} kè-á-bé**, id. **tî^{n} thâu-tsang**, to wind one's queue round the head.

tî^{n}-kut-á-tsoâ, a sort of sore on the toe (v. tsoâ).

tî^{n} — **tsúi-tî^{n}** (esp. T.), = **e-thiu**, the thin bamboo by which the bucket of a well-sweep is suspended.

tî^{n} — **poâ^{n}-tî^{n} lē-hùi**, expenses of a journey. **poâ^{n}-tî^{n}**, id. (cf. chî^{n}).

tì^{n} (cf. nì^{n}), (C. tè^{n}), to feign; to make a pretence in one's appearance; (to make strong efforts).

tì^{n}-sí, to feign death. **tì^{n}-chhìn-chhiò**, to smile or laugh as if pleased, when really angry. **tì^{n}-bô-lát**, to feign want of strength. **tì^{n}-bô-khoà^{n}**, intentionally look away so as not to see. **tì^{n} m̄-bat--i**, to pretend not to know him. **tì^{n}-tien tì^{n}-siáu**, to feign madness. **tì^{n}-gōng**, to act intentionally as if foolish, so as to put people off their guard, *e.g.* allow one's self to be cheated. **tì^{n}-gōng, sái phái^{n}-chî^{n}**, to pass bad cash while pretending to be very simple. **tì^{n}-gōng, sái lám-gûn**, id., passing bad silver coins.

tì^{n}-lát, to strain or exert all one's strength, as for some heavy lift or great effort. **tì^{n}-sái**, to make strong efforts to have a motion of the bowels. **tì^{n}-jiō**, to try hard to pass water.

tì^{n} [R. tèng = têng, to look hard; to stare], (C. tè^{n}). **tì^{n}-bák**, to look hard with the eye, as in displeasure. **bák-chiu tì^{n}-toā-lúi**, do., with eyes widely distended. **bák-chiu tì^{n} toā-bóng-lúi**, id. **tì^{n}-toā-lúi**, id.

tī^{n} [R. tēng, a surname; an ancient state], (C. tē^{n}), a surname. **tī^{n} kok-sêng**, Coxinga, the king of Formosa at the beginning of the Manchoo dynasty.

tī^{n} (cf. tīh^{n}, nīh^{n}), (C. tē^{n}), to grasp tightly; to squeeze and strain through a cloth. **tī^{n}-ân**, to grasp tightly. **tī^{n}--sí**, to strangle with the hand. **tī^{n} kûn-thâu-bú**, to clench the fist. **tī^{n} kûn-thâu**, id. **bong so tī^{n}**, to touch too freely, as a woman, as indication of improper intentions. **bô-lâng ōe-tī^{n} goá-ê-chih**, no one can keep me from saying what I please.

tī^{n} (C. tē^{n}), to knock the hoops firmly on a barrel. **tī^{n}--lòh-khì**, id.

tī^{n} (C. tē^{n}). **tháng-tī^{n}**, a wooden chisel-shaped instrument, used for driving the hoops firmly on a barrel, tub, &c.

tī^{n}, to push against with the back; to prop up, as a door, with wood, &c., to keep it from opening. **tī^{n}-khui**, to push off, as a boat, by pushing with one's back. **tī^{n}-mn̂g**, to push a door with one's back, as to keep it from being opened.

sa^{n}-tī^{n} (T.), to stand back to back, as two houses, or as two men who agree to help each other against all others. **sa^{n}-tī^{n} kha-chhng**, id.

tī^{n}, full; well-filled; crowded; flood-tide. **tī^{n} moá^{n}-moá^{n}**, very full, as with liquid. **tī^{n} lâu-lâu**, full and overflowing, as liquid. **tī^{n} that-that**, very full; choke-full, as with goods, furniture, dirt, &c. **that-that-tī^{n}**, id.; crowded in great quantities. **tī^{n} phóng-phóng** (T.), crowded, as with people; choke-full, as with dirt; very fat, as face.

î^{n}-tī^{n}, very fat and plump, as fat man; very round and full, as large fine well-grown grain of rice.

tóe-tī^{n}, to fill quite full. **ûi kàu-tī^{n}**, to crowd round in great numbers, as spectators.

pá-tī^{n}, stuffed full; fat, plump, and healthy, as well-formed limb. **ke-hé pá-tī^{n}**, wealthy. **thàn--khi pá-tī^{n}**, to make a great deal of money; to become wealthy. **chiàh kàu pá-tī^{n}**, to gorge one's self quite full.

tsúi tī^{n}, flood-tide; beginning of flood-tide; quite full of water; water quite full, as in any place or thing. **tsúi tiām-tī^{n}**, tide quite full; slack-water at high tide; the very top of the tide.

tia [R. father]. **tia-tia**, papa! **á-tia**, id. **in-tia**, his father; their father. **in-tia-niû^{n}**, his father and mother.

peh-tia, father's elder brother; respectful title used to an old man.

ló-tia, a mandarin. **lāu-tia** (Cn. T.), id. **sì-ló-tia**, a small mandarin who assists a Hien mandarin. **sì-lāu-tia** (T. Cn.), id. **chhiòh-ló-tia**, said in derision of a petty military officer.

thài-tia, title used in speaking to the father of a Kujin or mandarin.

siù^{n}-kang-tia, = Tiên goân-sòe, the god of actors (v. kang). **pâi-thâu-tia**, an idol which is an attendant on Sêng-hông-iâ; he wears the conical hat of a lictor, and is specially worshipped by the underlings of yamuns; he is very helpful for finding lost articles. **ná^{n} pâi-thâu-tia**, said of a man who is in the way, obstructing road or work.

tia^{n} [R. teng, name of a tree]. **ka-tia^{n}**, mangrove, and some similar shrubs that grow in water. **hái-ka-tia^{n}**, a shrub that grows very abundantly below high-water mark. **ka-tia^{n}-phê**, mangrove bark, used for dyeing red; brought from the Straits. **ka-tia^{n}-siap**, id. **ka-tia^{n}-lê**, a sort of shell-fish.

tia^{n} (C.), = A. tien, to stumble. **tia^{n}--lòh-khì**, to fall down, as person. **tia^{n}-lòh-hái**, to fall into the sea. **tia^{n}-lòh-chí^{n}**, to fall into a well.

tiâ^{n} [R. têng, a legal petition or accusation; to present a petition; to make a statement], a written petition, accusation, or defence, sent in to a mandarin. **kò-tiâ^{n}**, a written accusation. **sè-tiâ^{n}**, a written defence or counter accusation. **kong-tiâ^{n}**, a public petition, accusation, or representation, by a public body or company, or by the inhabitants of a street or ward, &c. **âng-tiâ^{n}**, a petition or accusation on red paper, only used by the gentry or by strangers. **hô-sek-tiâ^{n}**, a joint petition by the parties, making up the quarrel (v. sek, "to rest"). **tiah-sek-tiâ^{n}**, to enter a petition withdrawing one's name from a case (v. sek, "to loose"). **tsoán-táu-tiâ^{n}**, a petition entered on a day that is not one of the regular days. **chhoàn-tiâ^{n}** (C.), id. **thoân-tiâ^{n}**, to enter such a petition.

jip-tiâ^{n}, to enter a petition, accusation, defence, or complaint. **chhui-tiâ^{n}**, to enter an additional complaint, petition, or accusation, urging haste in the case which has already been raised by the first petition, but not yet taken effect; such an additional petition. **pé-tiâ^{n}**, to enter such an additional petition. **thè-tiâ^{n}**, to withdraw a petition or accusation. **siu-tiâ^{n}**, to receive a petition, &c. **kūi-tiâ^n**, to present a petition to a mandarin by kneeling on the road.

kiáu-tiâ^n, to send in a report, statement, or petition to one's superior officer.

tiâ^n-bêng (r.), to state one's case distinctly in the document sent in to the mandarin.

tiâ^n-jī, to examine a pupil's writing, to see if the characters be well written.

tiâ^n [R. thêng, a road; a stage; a surname; = col. têng, thiâ^n]. **kang-tiâ^n**, a piece of literary work, or of fine work, not rough manual work.

tiâ^n (R. têng), a paved court, as at a house or temple; sometimes not paved. **goā-tiâ^n**, an outer court; a court-yard. **keng-tiâ^n**, a court or yard before a temple. **chioh-tiâ^n**, a court paved with stone. **bōng-tiâ^n**, a level place just in front of a grave.

iâm-tiâ^n, open salt-pans for making salt by evaporation. **ng-tiâ^n**, a plot of ground used as a seed-bed where young rice is raised to be planted out. **than-tiâ^n**, a place where the shell-fish called "than" are bred and caught.

tiá^n [R. téng, a tripod; a caldron], a broad round shallow vessel of iron or pot-metal (somewhat like a small segment of a globe), used as a rice-boiler and frying-pan. **hé-tiá^n**, a rice-boiler (v. hé). **hûi-tiá^n**, a large thin shallow earthen pot with a lid, used for cooking. **tâng-tiá^n**, a brass or copper boiler, as for opium. **kim-tiá^n**, a metal tripod (or such vessel) used for burning idolatrous paper. **jiét-tiá^n**, a heated frying-pan. **phak-tiá^n**, an inverted frying-pan; name often given to a dome-shaped hill.

tsù-tiá^n, to cast rice-boilers. **thuh-tiá^n**, to stir food while frying. **khau-tiá^n**, to scrape soot off a rice-boiler. **khoe-tiá^n**, id. **lóh iû-tiá^n**, to be thrown into a caldron of boiling oil or melted fat, an ancient punishment. **khah-khiap lóh-iû-tiá^n**, more miserable than that; said of being very much tormented.

tiàu-tiá^n (to hang up the rice-boiler), to have nothing to live upon. **thâu-lē tiàu-tiá^n**, id. **kā-lí tiàu-tiá^n**, I will destroy your means of living.

tiá^n-si^n, pot-metal. **tiá^n-chhòe**, sort of bamboo scrubbing-brush or scraper, for cleaning rice-boilers. **tiá^n-thûn**, soot scraped from rice-boilers. **tiá^n-phí**, an incrustation of rice in a rice-boiler. **chhàu-tiá^n-lo**, singed in a frying-pan or rice-boiler.

tiá^n-kám, the lid of a rice-boiler. **tiá^n-koà**, id. **tiá^n-kám-koà**, id. **tiá^n-kám phû**, the cover of the rice-boiler rising of itself when the rice boils. **pàng tiá^n-kám-phû**, to lend money (to gamblers) charging heavy interest three times each day, *i.e.* each time the rice boils. **chioh tiá^n-kám-phû**, to borrow on such exorbitant usury.

tià^n (R. tèng), an anchor. **chit-keng-tià^n**, one anchor. **chit-mn̂g-tià^n** (C. mûi^n), id. **sòe-mn̂g-tià^n**, a small anchor. **chhién-tià^n**, an anchor with only one fluke. **toā-tià^n**, the principal anchor. **hù-tià^n**, the second anchor, used in stormy weather. **sa^n-tià^n**, a third anchor. **bé-tià^n**, an anchor at the stern.

tià^n-soh, a cable for an anchor. **tià^n-lê**, a small rope for tying the anchor cable firmly. **tià^n-chhia**, the windlass for the anchor.

tià^n-sin, the shank of an anchor. **tià^n-ta^n**, the cross-bar or stock of an anchor. **tià^n-khí**, the fluke of an anchor. **tià^n-sak**, id.

pha-tià^n, to anchor. **phoa-tià^n** (C.), id. **tak-tià^n**, to anchor for a very short time. **tok-tià^n**, id. **kià-tià^n**, id., as when waiting for wind or tide. **sàng-tià^n**, to carry out the anchor by a small boat to some little distance. **soá-tià^n**, id. **thoa-tià^n**, to drag anchor. **khì-tià^n**, to lose the anchor. **sit-tià^n**, id. **tsām-tià^n**, to cut away the anchor. **tn̄g-tià^n**, the anchor cable snapped; to have one's resources cut off. **thâu-lē tn̄g-tià^n**, id. **kàu-chia, tn̄g-tià^n**, after this point will have no more to do with him.

khioh-tià^n, to raise the anchor; to weigh anchor. **khí-tià^n**, id. **chhia-phâng khí-tià^n**, to hoist the sail, and weigh anchor. **chhia-tià^n**, to raise the anchor by a windlass. **liú-tià^n**, do., by pulling the rope by hands only. **sòe-tià^n**, to fish for an anchor, or fish it up.

tang-tià^n (lit. East anchor), Chapel Island, outside the mouth of Amoy harbour. **lâm-tià^n**, False Chapel Island, a good deal further south. **pak-tià^n**, Dodd Island, near the east end of Quemoy; the Chinese say that Amoy island is a ship, having these three islands as its anchors.

tià^n — **phoà-tià^n**, a secret let out, so that the whole affair is ruined.

tià^n — **sái-tià^n**, to use inflated threatening language; to bully. **sái-sái tià^n-tià^n**, id.

tiā^n [R. tiēn, a sort of dye]. **chhi^n-tiā^n**, a sort of dye for blue, &c.

tiā^n [R. tēng, to fix; to settle; fixed; steady], steady; motionless; earnest-money.

pit-tiā^n, I think it certainly is —.

hān-tiā^n, to limit, as a fixed time for payment. **gí-tiā^n**, to give judgment.

tiā^n-tióh, fixed; settled; firm, as plan, purpose, or arrangement. **bô-tiā^n-tióh**, not yet fixed or determined, as plan, purpose, or settlement of affair; perhaps I will, perhaps not; unsteady, as person. **bô-tiā^n bô-tióh**, id.; very unsteady or unsettled, as person or purpose. **sim bô-tiā^n-tióh**, mind not steady; very fickle or slightly deranged. **sim-thâu m̄-tiā^n**, slightly deranged; out of one's mind. **tsú-ì bô-tiā^n**, fickle in purpose; purpose not fixed.

hoā^n-tiā^n, to keep one's mind at ease; not afraid. **sim-thâu hoā^n-tiā^n**, heart tranquil, or set determinedly to a thing. **sim-koa^n hoā^n-tiā^n**, id. **hoā^n-khi-tiā^n**, steady it, as by pressing on it with the hand.

pêng-tiā^n, at peace and quiet, as country formerly disturbed. **pî^n-tiā^n**, id. **bô-tek-tiā^n**, not behaving well, as an idle boy playing about; not correct in conduct, as woman whose behaviour raises suspicions about her character.

tiā^n-tsòe, made to order. **tiā^n-chhiah**, made to order, as shoes or stockings.

tiā^n-tiā^n un--teh, constantly and strongly set on low vices.

tsù-tiā^n, to fix by divine decree or fate. **thi^n tsù-tiā^n**, Heaven decrees; decreed by Heaven. **in-iên tsù-tiā^n**, marriages decreed by Heaven. **tsù á-bē-tiā^n**, not yet decreed by Heaven.

tiā^n-gûn, earnest-money. **tiā^n-chî^n**, id. **tsòe-tiā^n**, to be an earnest, as money. **sàng-tiā^n**, to give the earnest-money. **kau-tiā^n**, id. **teh-tiā^n**, to give a small sum at the first betrothal. **siu-tiā^n**, to receive or accept earnest-money, as in closing a bargain. **thòeh-tiā^n**, id. **chiáh-tiā^n**, to have a feast (both sides together) when the money and presents have all been given over, shortly before the marriage, but a good while after the betrothal. **chiáh toā-tiā^n**, do., when the gifts and feast are very great, as in the case of wealthy persons. **siau-tiā^n**, to appropriate the earnest-money as a fine when the other party does not fulfil the bargain. **tiā^n hō͘--i siau--khì**, to forfeit the earnest-money to him, by not fulfilling the agreement.

tiā^n [same as previous word? cf. tiām]. **tiā^n-tiā^n**, still; quiet; motionless; be quiet! also a sort of adverbial particle at the end of a sentence, having the sense of "only," or of "and that is all."

tiā^n-tiā^n-sīm, not speaking or doing anything (v. sīm).

sí-mn̂g chē-tiā^n, quiet, steady, and regular, with moderate gains, as a trade, or as a yamun where there is not much money to be made.

nā^n-tiā^n, = tiā^n-tiā^n, only, and that is all; said only at the end of a sentence. **hó͘ sa^n-kau, chit-pái tiā^n** (tigers pair only once), said of finding a man so deceitful or dangerous in some affair that one will never have anything to do with him again.

tiā^n (R. tēng), an ingot, as of gold or silver; the classifier is "chiah," or "khò."

kim-tiā^n, an ingot of gold, usually about 4 oz.; a bundle of idolatrous paper representing gold. **chí-kim-tiā^n**, a medicinal compound made in the shape of a gold ingot.

gûn-tiā^n, an ingot of silver, usually about 30 oz.; wooden pegs, shaped like ingots, used for fastening down a coffin-lid. **jip gûn-tiā^n**, to close a coffin-lid with these pegs. **gûn-tiā^n-khang**, holes in the coffin for these pegs. **gûn-tiā^n-hoān**, having the shape of a silver ingot or hour-glass.

tiah (R. tek), to pluck; to pick. **tiah-hoe**, to pluck a flower. **tiah ké-chí**, to pluck fruit. **tiah bīn-mn̂g**, to pluck out the hair of the face, one by one.

tiah-ìn, to take away the official seals from a dismissed mandarin.

toa^n-tiah, to choose one particular article or person out of many; to take up one particular matter out of many to discuss by itself, as in an involved affair; said also when the husband has no relatives (or almost none) for the bride to take care of or serve. **toa^n-toa^n tiah**, to choose one out of many. **tiah-hì**, to select a play to be acted. **tiah-chhut**, id. **tiah-miâ^n tiah-sì^n**, to speak of or to a person simply by his surname and name, without adding any polite designation. **tiah i-ê-miâ^n**, to call out his name, as in a crowd.

tiah-sek, to enter a petition withdrawing one's name from an action (v. sek).

thâu-bé tiah, moored stem and stern.

tiah-ngoeh, pincers; nippers. **tiah-ngeh** (T.), id. **tiah-ní^n** (T.), id. **tiah-á**, pincers, esp. small ones. **chhùi-chhiu tiah-á** (C.), small pincers for the beard.

chiú^n-tiah, the cross piece at the end of the handle of an oar.

phâng-bé-tiah, a sort of secret slang.

tiȧh (R. tėk), to buy grain, pease, or beans. **tiȧh-jip--khì**, id. **thiò-tiȧh**, to sell and buy do. **chhái-tiȧh**, to go or send and purchase grain or pulse from many places where it is produced. **chhiū^n-tiȧh**, to buy grain, &c., and store it up for a higher price. **tún-tiȧh**, id. **tiȧh-bí**, to buy rice. **tiȧh-bėh**, to buy wheat or barley. **tiȧh-tāu**, to buy pease or beans.

tiȧh — **poa^n-tiȧh**, to lengthen out a dispute or discussion, just saying the same thing over and over.

tiam, to indent by pressure; to hurt, as the foot on gravel; to smart, as the eye; to mend, as by work in which an awl is used.

tiam-hûn, to make an indentation; a mark made by indenting. **tiam-chhiú**, to have the hand indented, as by something sharp or heavy. **tiam-kha**, to indent the foot, as a small stone trod upon. **chē tiam--tiȯh**, to hurt one's self by sitting on something hard and uneven.

bȧk-chiu tiam, the eye smarting, as with something getting into it.

tiam-ôe, to mend the soles of shoes; to cobble. **tiam phê-ôe**, to mend leather shoes; said also in joke of a mosquito. **tiam sì-tè**, to mend the soles and heels of both shoes. **thâu-tiam**, to put on entire soles from toe to heel.

tiam, a block for cutting anything upon; an anvil.

chhâ-tiam, a wooden block for cutting things upon. **tsoá-tiam**, a block for cutting paper on; a thick packet of idolatrous paper for burning. **to-tiam**, a block for cutting meat or vegetables. **bah-tiam**, a block for cutting meat on. **ti-tiam**, a block used as a counter for exposing pork for sale.

chiú^n-tiam, an oar-pin (v. chiú^n). **lô͘-tiam**, the pivot or pin on which a sculling-oar works.

tiam-táu (T.), small upright supports in a roof.

sa^n-kha-tiam, in the form of a triangle, as three places or things.

thih-tiam, an anvil. **tiò-á-tiam**, an anvil for making fish-hooks.

tiâm [R. tîm, to sink, = col. thiām], to sink. **tiâm-lȯh-tsúi**, to sink in water. **tiâm--lȯh-khì**, id. **jih-tiâm**, to press down in water, as person or animal to be drowned; to press down in brine, as meat to be pickled.

tiâm-lāu, to leak seriously, as boat.

khek-tiâm, to cut into the block, in engraving, so as to print white on a black ground. **tiâm--ê**, firmly fixed in the ground, as a rock; cut in, as characters on a block.

tiâm-tēng, firmly rooted, as tree; strongly made, as furniture; having much wealth (v. tēng). **ū-tiâm-tóe**, having some considerable amount of money or property.

toā-tiâm (T.), = A. toā-tîm, exceedingly.

tiâm (C.) **tiâm-chēng**, = A. thiām-chēng, quiet in taste and habits.

tiám (R. id.), a dot; a speck; a small drop; a very small quantity; a dot written as a comma or stop; a dot used as one of the strokes in writing a character; to put a small drop on a place; to touch lightly with a medicine; to punctuate; to go over a list marking particular names or items with a dot; (to warn or give information); to light, as a lamp, or as incense; (to strike gently); an hour (foreign); one-third of a day's work; an instrument on which the watches are struck at a yamun, five strokes being given at each watch, except the first and last; one-fifth part of a watch, *i.e.* about twenty-four minutes.

hoe-tiám, spotted with small spots. **pan-tiám**, spotted; slightly pock-marked (v. pan). **kim-tiám**, bright spangles, often worked on the toes of shoes. **chit-tiám**, a dot, in writing characters. **sè kúi-tiám**, how many dots on your dice? as second players. **tàu-tiám**, a sort of gambling. **tàu kúi-tiám**, id.

chit-tiám-ơ, a speck of black. **chit-tiám-tsúi**, a small drop of water. **hō͘-tiám**, a small drop of rain. **lóng-bô-hō͘-tiám**, not a drop of rain. **tn̄g-tiám-hong**, not a breath of wind.

phùn-tiám, to splash with water, dirt, &c.; to make a small present (v. phùn).

chit-tiám-á, a slight degree of, as of some feeling,

emotion, or quality, especially on the good side. **khah-chiáⁿ tiám-á**, somewhat insipid. **chit-tiám-á khah-hó**, slightly better. **chit-tiám-á ê ì-sù**, a slight purpose or intention towards good. **tháu chit-tiám hūn-khì**, to give vent to one's anger. **poàn-tiám put-iû-jîn**, nothing is from man (but all from fate, "bēng," *q.v.*) **bô-poàⁿ-tiám-liōng**, passionate or overbearing. **ū chit-tiám-liōng**, kind and forbearing. **chit-tiám liông-sim**, with a good or conscientious feeling. **ū chit-tiám-sim**, to have a purpose or intention towards something good.

tiám-sim, lunch or any small light meal out of the regular series of meals, esp. of biscuits, cakes, cold food, &c. **chiáh tiám-sim**, to take lunch or any slight refreshment. **bōe-tiám--tit sim**, can't get a bite, as in great haste.

chhoàng-tiám, beautiful, as dress or persons.

tiám-tsúi, to take soundings with a bamboo pole. **tiám-pé**, to drive two or three nails into a coffin, as a graduate or mandarin does for a fee. **tiám i--ê huih-lē**, to strike him with the point of the finger in some part that causes great pain, weakness, or sickness. **tiám bé-tôe**, to shoe a horse.

tē-tiám, a comma or other stop in punctuation, marked by a single dot.

tiám-chheh, to punctuate books. **tiám-tsū** (Cn.), id. **tiám-kù**, to punctuate (v. kù). **tiám-hiét**, to point out the exact place and position for a grave, after the site has been chosen. **tiám-tan**, to apply a small quantity of medicine to a sore. **tiám-kì**, to put medicine on a mole, so as to cure it. **tiám-gán**, to touch the eyes of an idol with the consecrated paint called sìn-se. **tiám-tsú**, to consecrate an ancestral tablet by dotting it with red.

tiám-miâⁿ, to mark the names on a roll, *e.g.* those who are present or absent. **tiám-báu**, to mark the names on a roll, as of troops, or of subordinates in a yamun. **tiám-peng**, to mark the roll of soldiers. **tiám-hoān**, to mark the roll of prisoners.

tiám-jip hān-lîm, to choose into the Imperial Academy. **khim-tiám--ê**, appointed by imperial command, as mandarins.

kiám-tiám, to make a list or inventory; to examine circumstances carefully (v. kiám). **tiám-hè**, to take an inventory. **tiám khan-thâu**, to take a list of pledges in pawn-shop.

tiám-tīn, cautious; careful in managing matters. **tiám-tiám-kim**, careful in business; very knowing, so as to be hard to cheat.

chí-tiám, to give information or private advice. **tiám-phoà**, to give a hint to a man so that he may understand, esp. of some secret plot or unseen danger; to explain something difficult to understand, *e.g.* a difficult passage in a book. **tiám-hoà**, to instruct, as a spirit does in a dream, &c. **tiám-chhíⁿ**, to warn of a plot or secret danger, as a friend by a hint, or as a god by a dream. **tiám-tuh**, to warn by a hint, or by private information (v. tuh). **tiám-ki**, to give secret information, as by a hint or sign which others do not understand.

tiám-teng, to light a lamp (v. teng). **tiám-chek**, to light a candle. **tiám-liám**, to light many, as lamps or candles. **tiám-iû**, to light an oil lamp, as opposed to a candle. **goá kā-lí tiám-iû**, I will remember this against you (v. iû). **tiám-hiuⁿ**, to light a stick of incense.

chit-tiám-cheng, one o'clock. **nňg-tiám-cheng**, two o'clock, &c. **nňg-tiám-cheng kú**, two hours' time; two hours long. **nňg-tiám-kú** (r.), id. **kúi-tiám-cheng**, what o'clock?

chit-tiám-kang, one-third part of a day's work, as divided into three parts by breakfast and dinner. **chit-tiám-sit**, id. **chit-jit saⁿ-tiám**, one day's work is divided into three parts called "tiám." **khàng chit-tiám-kang**, to lose or intermit one third part of a day's work.

phah-tiám, to beat the watch at a yamun, three strokes at the first and last watch, five strokes at the others. **kòng-tiám**, id. **kòng-kúi-tiám**, how many strokes in beating the watch? **jī-kiⁿ saⁿ-tiám**, at the third division of the second watch. **jī-kiⁿ kúi-tiám**, at which division of the second watch? **it-kiⁿ, saⁿ-tiám khí; gē-kiⁿ, saⁿ-tiám chí**, the first and fifth watches have only three strokes.

tiám-hoàⁿ (Cn.), very lately; just lately.

tiám — **tiám-chhái**, = kiám-chhái, perhaps.

tiàm (R. id.), (Cn. tūiⁿ; T. tàiⁿ), a shop. **tiàm-thâu**, id. **chit-khám-tiàm**, one shop. **tiàm-hē**, a shopkeeper (s. stay). **tiàm-tiēn**, the tenant of a shop. **tiàm-kheh**, id. **tiàm-tsú**, the owner of a shop. **tiàm-tsú-lâng**, the keeper of an inn or eating-house. **tiàm-kháu**, the front of a shop at the door. **tiàm-thang-pang**, the movable boards of a shop-front. **phah-tiàm-bīn--ê**, a beggar who sings and knocks at each shop-door for a cash. **tiàm-hō**, name of shop or small firm. **tiàm tó**, bankrupt, as shop-keeper.

khui-tiàm, to open a shop; to keep a shop. **hioh-tiàm**, to stay a night or so at an inn. **tién-tiàm**, to mortgage a shop. **bô-sia, put-sêng-tiàm**, without giving credit a shop will not prosper (v. sia).

kheh-tiàm, an inn. **pňg-tiàm**, an eating-house (v. pňg). **pňg-tiàm-kong**, keeper of eating-house, especially if old. **bí-tiàm**, a shop for selling rice. **tňg-tiàm**, a pawn-shop. **pán-tiàm**, a coffin-shop. **pau-thâu-tiàm**, a shop for selling dried fruits, &c., which sells only entire bags of them. **thih-á-tiàm**, shop for old metal articles. **chîⁿ-tiàm**, a money-changer's shop. **chîⁿ-kūi-á-tiàm**, id. **chîⁿ-tiàm ê-lâng**, a money-changer. **chiú-tiàm**, a shop for spirits, &c.

tiàm — **tiàm-bī**, to dive, as for getting up something.

tiàm, to stay; to dwell; to harbour; to hide one's self. **tiàm-tī-hia**, lives there. **tiàm-ńg**, to stay in the shade.

tiàm-chhát, to harbour robbers or pirates. **tiàm-hó**, to have tigers usually living there.

tiàm-hong, to take shelter from the wind. **tiàm-hō**, to take shelter from the rain. **tiàm-bát-bát**, to hide very secretly so as to keep out of danger. **tsáu-khi-tiàm**, to escape and hide from danger. **phiah-khi-tiàm**, to keep out of harm, trouble, or danger, by keeping out of the way. **bih-khi-tiàm**, id. **kiu-thâu-tiàm**, to keep out of the way, so as to avoid responsibility. **kiu-kha-tiàm**, id.

tiām [R. to lay down; to sink into; to remunerate; to pay up; to place under; a cushion]; a cushion for a seat; to make up a deficiency, as in a subscription or as a balance in a friend's account; to plant, as seeds; to lay down, as stepping-stones; to pickle with dry salt.

tiām--khí-lâi, to raise higher by something put below, as the foot of a table.

í-tiām, a chair-cushion. **í-jiok-tiām**, a long cushion for seat and back of chair. **phê-tiām**, leather

厦英大辭典

cushion for seat. **pài-tiām**, cushion for kneeling upon at worship.

tiām hoe-chí, to plant flower seeds.

tiām-pé, to make up a deficiency, as in a subscription or in another man's accounts. **pê-tiām**, do., for a man for whom we stand security. **seng-tiām**, to lend some money to make up a deficiency. **tiām-chíⁿ**, to pay some cash to make up another's deficiency.

tiām-iâm, to pickle with a large quantity of salt.

tiām-pang, the boards forming the floor of a small boat. **tiām-hiâⁿ**, the timbers lying across a boat's keel, on which these boards rest. **tiām-ún**, the horizontal bead running round the outside of a boat about water-mark.

tiām (R. thiām), very quiet and staid in manner, while going on quietly with one's work, or even while taking active measures. **kek-tiām**, to put on the appearance of being very quiet, for some special purpose. **tiām-tiām**, still! be quiet! **tiām-chēng**, quiet; not fond of gaiety or amusements. **tiām-tī**, staid and quiet in manner. **tiām-tsâi**, staid quiet manner. **tiām-tiòk**, calm, thoughtful, and self-possessed (v. tiòk). **tiām-tsàt**, id.; cautious and self-possessed. **tiām-tiām-á kiâⁿ**, to walk along very leisurely.

tsúi tiām-tīⁿ, slack water at high-water. **tiām-hong**, no wind. **tiām-hoang chīⁿ-nn̄g** (T.), wind and waves still.

tiām (?), to eat single grains of rice, pulse, &c. (C. ?)

tian, tiân, tián, tiān; better **tien, tiên, tién, tiēn** (*q.v.*)

tiang — **tiang-tiang-háu**, sound of brass making a ringing sound.

tiang (C.), = A. tiong (R.), to open or spread out. **koāi-tiang**, = A. koāi-chiang, obstinate in dispute; determined to have one's own way.

tiâng (Cn.) **sī-tiâng**, = A. sím-mih̄ⁿ-lâng, what man? who?

tiâng (C.), = A. tiông (R.), long.

tiâng (C.), = A. tiông (R.), intestines; bowels.

tiáng (C.), = A. tióng (R.), old; long.

tiàng (C.), = A. tiòng, swollen. **tiàng-hong put-gí**, a very fatal disease (v. tiòng).

tiàng (C.), = A. tiòng (R.), flooded.

tiāng (C.), = A. tiōng (R.), a measure of ten feet. **tiāng-hu**, husband; &c. &c.

tiāng (C.), = A. tiōng, to intrust, &c.

tiāng (C.), = A. tiōng, an instrument for beating criminals, &c.; also (R.), a staff. **khok-song-tiāng**, = A. khok-san-tiōng, a staff carried by a widower at the funeral of his wife.

tiap — **tiap-á-kú**, for a moment; a very short time. **chit-tiap-á-kú**, id.

tiap-á-hn̄g, a short way off. **tiap-á-toā**, not very large. **khah-toā tiap-á**, a little larger (cf. tiám).

tiap [R. tiėt, to stumble]. **tiap-táⁿ i-seng**, a doctor for falls and wounds, = tiėt-táⁿ i-seng.

tiáp — **hit-tiáp**, then. **chit-tiáp**, now; immediately. **thàn-chit-tiáp**, to improve the present moment; this very moment.

tiáp [R. to pile up; to repeat; = col. tháh]. **têng-tiáp**, repeating over and over in writing; tautological. **têng-têng tiáp-tiáp**, piled up or crowded in large quantities, *e.g.* as crowded houses or graves; much repetition and tautology in writing. **tiáp-jī**, to repeat a word, as in poetry; to write two words in the space where there should be only one, as in a legal document with fixed spaces for the words.

siap-tiáp, closely packed together; well fitted together and neatly put up, so as to take up little room.

tiáp-tiáp-lâi (Cn.), coming over and over again (cf. táuh).

sì-gō-tiáp (Cn.), four or five times.

tiáp — **táⁿ-tiáp**, to mend; to treat medically; to heal or cure.

tiáp — **tô-tiáp**, to annoy; to tease; to give trouble, esp. as a troublesome child does to its parents or relations; to maltreat, as a woman does to a female slave; to annoy a man by constantly asking him to do small bits of work, or by asking him over and over to do what he is unwilling to do, till he at last does it (though unwilling) to get rid of the annoyance. **tô-tô tiáp-tiáp**, id.

tiáp [R. a butterfly, = col. iáh]. **hê-tiáp**, a hinge, hinges, of the foreign form; often erroneously written ho-tiáp. **kim-si hê-tiáp**, name of a beautiful flower like a butterfly.

tiáp [R. a tablet for writing upon; a certificate or diploma], a slip of yellow paper with a prayer on it, used by burning. **chit-tiuⁿ-tiáp**, one such paper prayer. **sio-tiáp**, to burn a paper prayer. **pàng-tiáp**, id. **tiáp-bûn**, a written prayer burned, as before Sêng-hông-iâ.

tō-tiáp, the certificate of a regularly appointed Buddhist priest.

tiát, better tiėt (*q.v.*)

tiau (R. id.), to carve, as figures. **tiau-tok**, to rule and keep in order, as relatives (v. tok). **tiau-tok**, to carve and polish, as a gem. **tiau-khek**, to carve, as wood (v. khek). **tiau-put**, to carve images. **tiau ang-á**, to carve toy figures. **hiú-bók put-khó-tiau**, rotten wood cannot be carved.

tiau-keng sai-hū, a man who manufactures bows (s. bend).

tiau-hoe, to dress flowering shrubs into various fanciful shapes. **tiau hoe-bák**, id. **tiau chhiū-bák**, to dwarf trees, and make them take curious shapes.

tiau, to bend, esp. downwards. **tiau--lòh-lâi**, to bend down, as a branch. **tiau--teh**, to hold down tightly, as a branch. **tiau-oai**, to tie so as to make crooked, as a tree. **tiau-keng**, to bend a strong bow (without an arrow), as for practice (s. carve). **tiau lêng-hê**, to hold a lobster on a tightly stretched string; to tie up a thief or prisoner so tight as to be very painful.

tiau (R. id.) **tiau-chhú**, a marten. **tiau-chhú-phê**, marten's fur. **tiau-phê**, id. **tiau-chhú-bō**, a cap made with marten's fur.

tiau (R. id.), to wither, as a plant almost dying. **tiau-thâu**, even the root dried up and withered, as of plant just about dead.

tiau [R. restless; perverse; outrageous; = col. thiau]. **tiau-bân**, = thiau-bân, obstinately disobedient to orders, or refusing to pay money due.

tiau — **pàng-tiau**, to threaten; to intimidate. **pàng-tiau pàng-tńg**, id.

tiau [R. morning; the character differs only by a tonal mark from "tiâu," a dynasty, to have audience]. **tiau-sėk** (R.), morning and evening (v. sėk). **ngó-tiau-chiò**, Tauist rites of "chiò" for five days. **sam-tiau-chiò**, do. for three days. **sam-tiau**, three days (said of the rites performed three days after the birth of a child). **tsòe-sam-tiau**, to give rice to friends who call at that time. **tsòe tsáp-it-tiau**, to do so at rites eleven days after the birth.

tiau — **tiau-tat**, neat and neatly put on, as dress. **tiau-tah**, id.

tiau [R. tiâu, to harmonize; to restore peace; to adjust; to regulate; to compound; a tune; =col. tiāu]. **tiau-hô**, mixed well together in proper proportions; harmonious (v. hô).

tiâu [R. to harmonize; to adjust, &c.; =col. tiau, tiāu]. **hong tiâu, ú sūn**, wind and rain suitable in season and quantity.

tiâu [R. liâu, a hut]. **bé-tiâu**, a stable. **gû-tiâu**, a cow-house; a cow-pen. **iûⁿ-tiâu**, a sheepfold. **ti-tiâu**, a pig-sty. **ti-tiâu-kong**, the guardian spirit of the pig-sty.

tiâu, firmly tied, glued, or fastened in any way; inveterate, as a bad habit; fast, as a colour. **tiâu-sim**, fixed in the mind. **àm-hō͘ tiâu-mîⁿ**, late rain lasts through the night. **tiâu a-phièn**, enslaved to opium, and unable to give it up. **tiâu-hun**, id. **chiáh-tiâu**, id.

khiā-tit-tiâu, to stand steadily; able to hold one's own. **tòng-tit-tiâu**, to oppose effectually.

tèng-tiâu, to nail firm. **kat-tiâu**, to tie firm, as a knot. **pák-tiâu**, tied firmly or bound fast, as a person or thing. **tsáh-tiâu**, to ward off effectively, as by shield or door. **kì-tiâu-tiâu**, to remember perfectly. **kò͘-tiâu-tiâu**, to guard or watch carefully and safely. **kô͘ tiâu-tiâu**, gummed or pasted firmly.

bōe-tiâu, not firmly fastened, tied, pasted, &c.; will not hold. **bōe-tiâu-bák**, not suitable for writing on; will not take on the ink, as paper that is oily, greasy, or too coarse. **kô͘-bōe-tiâu**, pasted so ill that it does not stick. **nîⁿ-bōe-tiâu**, the dye not fast. **tng-bōe-tiâu**, cannot bear it; it cannot be endured. **lún-bōe-tiâu**, unable to bear or forbear.

kun-ki tiâu-tsòng, said of a child having such a good horoscope that it will be healthy and prosperous.

tiâu — **tiâu-kò͘-ì**, on purpose. **tiâu-ì-kò͘**, id. **tiâu-tì**, id. **tiâu-tî**, id. (v. tì). **tiâu-kang**, deliberate; for the special purpose, as an act. **tiâu-chhoân--ê**, specially selected. **tiâu-kò͘**, to hire specially. **tiâu-chhiàⁿ**, id. **tiâu-lâi**, having come of set purpose for the special object. **tiâu-kang lâi**, id.

tiâu [R. a branch; a thin strip; anything long and slender; =col. liâu], an item; a particular; classifier of long narrow things, as roads, ropes, rivers, sweet-potatoes, sticks of ink; also of laws, negotiations, affairs, stipulations, accounts, lives, souls, breaths (khùi); also sometimes of masts; and (C. Cn.) of trowsers.

tiâu-kui, stipulations; regulations. **tiâu-khoán**, regulations, particulars, or articles of an agreement. **tiâu-kiāⁿ**, id. **tiâu-toāⁿ**, id. (v. toāⁿ).

tiâu-tit, adjusted; honest (v. tit).

tiâu-bák, an account; a list of articles. **siàu-tiâu**, accounts, as unpaid (v. siàu). **chit-tiâu-chîⁿ**, an item of cash in an account, to be paid to or collected from one person.

chit-tiâu-sū, one whole affair from beginning to end. **chêng-lí chit-tiâu, bô-nn̄g-tiâu**, there is only one correct statement and solution of the question, and on discussion it must be plain to all. **kúi-nā-tsáp-tiâu ká-lá tsòe-chit-tui**, many troublesome matters come on one at once.

bák-tiâu, a stick of ink. **gûn-tsu-tiâu**, a stick of red ink. **kim-tiâu**, a bar of gold, about ten ounces. **mîⁿ-tiâu**, long thin rolls of raw cotton (v. mîⁿ). **mīⁿ-tiâu**, thin narrow strips of dough (v. mīⁿ). **bí-hún-tiâu**, vermicelli made from rice-flour. **tîn-tiâu**, rattan sticks or fasces carried before a mandarin. **chiⁿ-tiâu**, a rug. **liú-tiâu-thang**, a window made with long thin slips of wood (v. liú). **hoat-tiâu**, a main-spring.

hiuⁿ-tiâu, long slips of yellow paper giving notice of incense processions; a long incense stick. **nn̄g-tiâu-hiuⁿ**, a fore-and-aft schooner.

hong-tiâu, long strips of red paper, pasted by authority of mandarin on shops, vessels, &c., *e.g.* when confiscated, or when taken temporary possession of for military purposes; also used for pasting up mandarin's luggage, or boxes of government treasure when transmitted; said also of strips used for sealing up boxes of treasure sent by hongs. **pang-tiâu**, long strips of paper on a house temporarily occupied by a mandarin, telling his style and titles; also (T. Cn.) = hong-tiâu. **kìm-tiâu**, public prohibitions on long strips of paper, issued by mandarins. **tsám-tiâu**, inscription stating the crime for which a man is put to death. **pò-tiâu**, document informing a man that he has got a degree or mandarin title.

chhiah tiâu-tiâu, quite naked.

chit-tiâu náⁿ han-tsû, a stupid-looking fellow (lit. like a potato!).

tiâu [R. id.; differing only by a tonal mark from "tiau," morning], a dynasty; to have an audience of a sovereign in the audience-hall.

tiâu-têng, the imperial audience-hall, where the council meets; the imperial court; said also of the emperor himself in his public character. **tiâu-sîn**, ministers of state. **tiâu-lāi-koaⁿ**, id. **tiâu-hók**, court dress worn by mandarins at audience. **tiâu-i** (r.), id. **tiâu-tsu**, a necklace worn at audience.

chē-tiâu, to hold an audience. **thè-tiâu**, to retire from the audience-hall, as the sovereign does. **kièn-tiâu**, to attend the daily audience at the palace. **jip-tiâu**, to enter the audience-hall, as mandarins. **chiūⁿ-tiâu**, id. **tiâu-kìⁿ**, to have an audience of the sovereign. **tiâu-pài**, id. **tiâu-kun**, id. **tiâu thien-tsú**, to have an audience of the emperor. **tiâu-kòng**, to present tribute in person.

tiâu-tē, a dynasty. **oāⁿ tiâu-tē**, to change the dynasty. **tiâu-tē-bé**, end of a dynasty; said of calamities and crimes abounding, as signs of change of dynasty. **kok-tiâu-bé**, id. **kok-tiâu**, the reigning dynasty. **chheng-tiâu**, the Manchoo dynasty. **bêng-tiâu**, the Ming dynasty. **goân-tiâu**, the Mongol or Yuen dynasty. **tông-tiâu**, the Tang dynasty, &c.

káu-tiâu, a part of a room screened off from the rest by white curtains or hangings, containing the "hûn-sin," for the ceremonies of "kong-tek." **kat káu-tiâu**, to put up these curtains.

tiâu-lâm (R.), facing the south, as a grave. **bān-san tiâu-tùi**, the mountains forming an amphitheatre behind a grave, as in a very good site. **sù-súi lâi-tiâu**, water from four quarters seeming to meet in front of a grave. **bān-súi tiâu-tang**, a place far to the east where the tide always flows towards the east, so that vessels can hardly come back: probably the stream of Japan. **lióng-kiok tiâu-thien**, fallen on one's back, with feet turned up towards the sky.

tiâu-sién (R.), Corea.

tiàu (R. id.), to summon; to cite a person. **tiàu-mn̄g**, to summon and examine. **tiàu-kiaⁿ--khì**, to summon to the capital. **tiàu-peng**, to summon soldiers from other stations. **tiàu-hoān**, to order up a criminal to be tried. **tiàu-toaⁿ**, a document issued by a mandarin telling actors what play to perform, or calling priests to assist at an eclipse, &c.

tiàu — **tiàu-ka**, to make a smooth surface with glue or size, as on cloth, to make it sell well; or on an old hat, to make it look good. **tiàu ka-tsúi**, id.

tiàu — **toan-tiàu**, to ask an exorbitant price or wages for what cannot be dispensed with (v. toan). **khiâu-tiàu**, id. **khiau-tiàu**, id.

tiàu [R. distant]. **tiàu-oán**, very distant, as places. **lō͘-tô͘ tiàu-oán**, road or journey very long.

tiàu (T.) **tiàu-kâu**, = A. thiàu-kâu, set of three dice in gambling (v. kâu).

tiàu [R. to hang; some divide it into two words; the one for hanging a man, and for idolatrous rites; the other for all the other phrases], to hang up or suspend, hanging freely (but "kùi" is to suspend on a wall); to make certain offerings to the dead, serving as a sort of condolence with, or compliment to the relatives.

koà-tiàu sim-koaⁿ, anxious and sad, as about an absent friend.

tiàu-lâm, to beat against the south wind in sailing south (v. lâm).

tiàu-kak, slanting, as a thing folded or drawn so (v. kak). **tiàu-oai**, hung up off the perpendicular. **tiàu-ku**, having one flap too much drawn up, as a dress. **tiàu-koh**, arm of dress too tight at the armpit.

bák-chiu chhâ-chhâ tiàu-tiàu, eyes fixed and staring upwards, as about to die. **bák-chiu tiàu-tiàu**, id.

tiàu-koe, large Shanghai fowls.

tiàu-àn, to call up the papers of a case appealed from a lower court.

chit-tiàu-chîⁿ (r.), a string of a thousand cash. **it-tiàu-chhién**, id. (said in imitation of mandarin).

tiàu-o͘, a well-sweep (v. o͘). **tiàu-o** (C.), id. **tiàu-tháng**, a hanging bucket, as for drawing water (v. tháng). **tiàu-kiô**, a draw-bridge. **tiàu-thui**, a hanging ladder, as of ropes, *e.g.* on a vessel. **tiàu-chhng**, a hammock. **tiàu-kiàⁿ**, a mirror suspended on a frame or wall. **tiàu-tsàng**, the perpendicular threads of a loom (v. tsàng). **tiàu-bah poàh-sí-niauⁿ**, hanging meat makes the cat fall and be killed (said of tantalizing people).

tò-tiàu, to turn upside down, as a book; tied with feet up and head down. **tò-thâu-tiàu**, id.; placed in the opposite direction to what is right.

toā-tiàu, the rudder-band, by which the rudder is raised or lowered. **àm-tiàu**, a rope attached to the middle of the rudder. **phâng-bé-tiàu**, one of the ropes that lies along the mast.

tiàu-chhiú, to let the hand swing freely, as in writing very large characters. **tiàu-tiáⁿ**, to have no means of livelihood (v. tiáⁿ). **tiàu-chhát**, to tie up a thief by the hands, so that his feet barely touch the ground. **tiàu-teng**, to hang a lamp, as from the roof. **si-soàⁿ tiàu tâng-cheng**, means very inadequate, or matters in a very dangerous state.

jih-tiàu, to hang one's self. **tiàu-ām**, id. **tiàu--sí**, id. **tiàu ka-lé** (lit. hang a puppet), id. (v. lé). **tiàu-kúi**, ghost of a man who had hung himself. **tiàu-kúi kiò--lí**, go and hang yourself! (as the ghost of a man who hung himself tries to tempt others to do the same). **náⁿ tiàu-kúi--nihⁿ**, said of a man with a long lank lean neck.

tiàu-tsoá, to make offerings to the "hûn-sin" of a dead man, as friends of the family do. **tiàu-song** (R.), id. **tsok-tiàu** (r.), id. **tiàu lán--ê pē-bú**, coming to worship our parents after death, as friends do. **hoân-tiàu**, to go and pay respects in person to friends who have come and worshipped our deceased parent.

liáu-tiàu, quite dead; quite dropped, as an affair on which no more action is taken.

tiāu (R. id.), an omen. **tiāu-thâu**, id. **chhái-tiāu**, id. (v. chhái). **khiàu-tiāu**, superstitious and magical arts. **khïò-tiāu** (Cn.), all sorts of superstitious rites, much more general than the Amoy phrase.

liáu-tiāu, an omen of the coming ruin of a family; said of lavish wasting of patrimonial wealth, or of property all spent in yamun expenses. **iâⁿ-kiáu su-kiáu-tiāu**, to win in gambling is the sure omen of losing. **kiet-hiong bī-lâi, sien iú-tiāu**, an omen appears before good or bad fortune.

tiāu — **tiāu--khì**, to become mute or insensible, as on suddenly hearing very bad news. **khó kàu tiāu--khì**, almost swooning or fainting at sad news. **khó kàu tiāu-tiāu**, id. **kiaⁿ kàu tiāu--khì**, do., through sudden fear. **soà-tiāu--khì**, immediately struck speechless and almost paralyzed on suddenly hearing bad news.

tiāu [R. liāu, materials; to manage]. **tsâi-tiāu**, ability; skill; talent.

tiāu [R. tiâu, to harmonize; to adjust; to restore peace; to compound; to regulate; and by change of tone "tiāu," a tune; = col. tiau], a tune, as for a song, hymn, or chant.

tiāu-chhú, to adjust a dispute or quarrel for another, as a sort of arbiter. **tiāu-chhí** (C.), id. **tiāu-thêng**, id.

tiāu-ióng, to take care of one's own health. **tiāu-iáng** (C.), id.

gâu pheng-tiāu, good at cooking.

tùi-tiāu, to exchange places, as persons. **tiāu-lâi tiāu-khì**, id. **tiāu-kè-lâi, tiāu-kè-khì**, id.

thiaⁿ--lâng tiāu-tō͘, willingly obey the rules, as of master or employer.

khek-tiāu, a song-tune. **koâiⁿ-tiāu**, tune on a high key. **chhiùⁿ-koâiⁿ-tiāu**, to sing on a high key; to ask an exorbitant price for a thing. **kē-tiāu**, a tune on a low key. **hoán-tiāu**, to give a peculiar mournful turn up at the end of a strain.

ū-tiāu, melodious, as music. **ū-liāu ū-tiāu**, sung well, as a song; good at singing. **bô-liāu bô-tiāu**, not melodious; out of tune. **hó-siaⁿ-tiāu**, well sung, as tune. **m̄-chiâⁿ siaⁿ-tiāu**, singing not well performed. **siaⁿ-tiāu bô-hiáp**, sung out of tune. **tiāu-sè**, the style of a tune. **tiāu-sì** (C.), id. **ū-tiāu-sè**, singing well; according to tune. **hó-tiāu-sè**, able to sing well; tune and voice suitable to each other. **bô-tiāu-sè**, not sung well; out of tune. **tiāu-sè khah-m̄-hó**, style of singing or reciting not at all good; also, in a bad state, as an affair that is all going wrong.

tiàuh (C.) **tiàuh-tiàuh**, = A. tàuh-tàuh, constantly; very frequently.

tien (R. id.), to stagger; to reel. **tien-lâi tien-khì**, to stagger about. **táh-tien**, to stumble.

tien-tó, to stumble and fall; said also of calamity. **tien-tien tó-tó**, constantly stumbling and falling; meeting with many calamities. **tien-lâi tó-khì**, to reel and stumble about, as drunk man. **chhit-tien poeh-tó**, constantly stumbling and falling; in constant trouble and calamity.

tien (R. id.; cf. col. thien). **tien-kông**, mad; madness. **hong-tien**, id. **tien-gōng**, idiotic; crazy. **tìⁿ-tien tìⁿ-gōng**, feigning to be mad or idiotic. **tìⁿ-tien tìⁿ-siáu**, id.

tiên [R. thiên, to fill up; to make up a deficiency; to pay; = col. thūn], to make up a deficiency or debt. **tiên-tùi**, to pay an account or debt by a bill, draft, &c., on a third party. **tiên-pé** (C. thiên-pé), to make up a deficiency or debt, as a third party.

tiên-pīⁿ, to fill up, as ground, by levelling it up.

tiên [R. to tread in a path; to go in an orbit]. **tiên-tē**, the course or orbit of one of the heavenly bodies. **kiâⁿ tiên-tē**, to move in the orbit.

tiên [R. an irrigated field; a surname; = col. chhân]. **tiên-thé**, lands in general. **su-tiên**, fields left by ancestors for keeping descendants at school, or for those who take a degree. **si-tiên** (C.), id. **sū-tiên**, fields left to supply the expense of offerings to ancestors. **cheng-chhe toát-tiên**, to take away forcibly a man's wife or fields (v. chhe).

sim-tiên (r.), disposition of heart.

tiên goân-sòe, = siùⁿ-kang-tia, the idol specially worshipped by actors.

tién [R. a classic; a canon; statutes or ordinances; to mortgage; to pawn; a dictionary; grace; favour], (C. tién, téng), to mortgage, but not quite the same as the British mortgage. **tién-khòe**, a deed of mortgage. **tién-jī**, id. **tién-tsú**, the mortgager. **chhut-tién**, to be in the market for mortgage, as house, &c. **chhut-tién ê-lâng**, the mortgager. **tién-chhut**, to mortgage. **tién--lâng**, to mortgage to some one. **hō-i-tién**, to mortgage to him. **kā-lâng-tién**, to take on mortgage. **tsoán-tién**, to re-mortgage. **tién bōe**, to mortgage or sell. **tién bóe**, to mortgage or buy.

hiòng-tién, a licensed pawn-shop. **toā-tién**, a large pawn-shop, which takes low interest. **sió-tién**, a low-class pawn-shop that takes heavy interest. **tién-tn̂g** (Cn.), a pawn-shop. **chí-tién hāu-siok**, to close a pawn-shop and wait to see if the pledges be redeemed.

un-tién, favour; grace (v. un). **in-tién** (C.), id.

tién-chheh, classical books. **chhut-keng jip-tién**, correct in style and composition.

jī-tién, a dictionary.

kò-tién, manner or style of the ancients, as to customs, ceremonies, or way of doing things; done according to ancient custom. **bat kò-tién**, well acquainted with ancient matters. **ín kò-tién**, to quote old books, or the customs or actions of the ancients, as authority or precedent. **chiàu-kó-tién**, according to the way of the ancients.

tién-sú, a very small civil mandarin (v. sú). **tién-lī**, a title acquired by men who have charge of civil cases in yamuns (v. lī).

tién [R. to open out; to exhibit; = col. thién]. **tién-khui**, to open out, as wings, or as a book. **phīⁿ-khang tién-tién**, nostrils naturally rather wide open.

tién-sit, to spread wings. **tién-tsang**, to set up the mane, as horse, or neck feathers, as cock. **lāu-bé tién-tsang**, the old horse erects his mane; said of an old man with youthful vigour and ability.

tién-ui, to put on a terrible appearance, as tiger or soldier. **tién sîn-thong**, to show one's supernatural power, as idol, or one's special skill, as workman. **tién pún-sū**, to boast of or display one's own skill or ability. **ka-kī tién i--ê khùi-lát**, he boasts of or displays his strength. **tién-pó** (C.), to boast or brag.

tiēn (R. id.), (Cn. tiēn, tūiⁿ), the imperial hall of audience; temple of some first-class gods which are allowed imperial honours. **kiong-tiēn**, imperial palace (residence) and audience-hall. **keng-tiēn**, id. **kim-loân-tiēn**, imperial audience-hall. **hông-tè-tiēn**, do.; also a temple at Amoy where the emperor's tablet is worshipped; formerly it contained an image of the emperor Kia-king, represented as a banished man for having got a child too soon after his father's death. **tè-tiēn-khí**, built in the style of an imperial palace, as the temples of some of the highest canonized gods.

chē-tiēn, to give an audience, as emperor. **teng-tiēn**, to take his seat on the imperial throne, at audience. **thè-tiēn**, to leave the audience-hall, as emperor (s. rent). **chiūⁿ-tiēn**, to go to the audience, as ministers of state.

tiēn-sì, examination for the Han-lin degree, presided over by the emperor.

bú-tong-tiēn, temple of Hiên-thien Siōng-tè.

tiēn [R. fixed; settled; to make a libation; = col. tēng]. **tiēn-chiú**, to make a libation of spirituous liquor. **koàn-tiēn** (R.), to make a libation.

tiēn [R. lightning, = col. nā]. **tiēn-bú**, the goddess of lightning. **lûi-kong tiēn-bú**, the god of thunder and goddess of lightning.

tiēn [R. to cultivate the land, esp. on rent], (Cn. in some senses tūiⁿ; T. tāiⁿ).

chhù-tiēn, the tenant of a house. **tiàm-tiēn**, tenant of shop. **tiēn-hō**, tenant of farm. **tiēn-phoe**, document given by the tenant to the landlord, serving as proof that he is only tenant.

tùi-tiēn, to introduce our tenant to the new proprietor to whom we have sold the property, or to our creditor to whom he is for the present to pay the rent so as to clear off a debt. **jīn-tiēn**, to go security for a man who rents a house or land, as a precaution against his taking unjust possession of it. **thè-tiēn**, to withdraw our security in such a case (s. audience-hall). **teh-tiēn** (esp. C. teh), to advance money (without interest) when renting fields, not repaid unless the fields are taken back. **teh-tiēn-gûn**, money thus advanced.

tiėt [R. to stumble]. **tso-tiėt**, to meet with great calamity.

tiėt-táⁿ i-seng, = tiàp-táⁿ i-seng, a surgeon for falls and wounds.

tih, to strike gently with the hand in play, as children do. **tih-lâi tih-khì**, striking one another gently in play, as children. **gâu-tih**, disposed to strike with the hand in play. **chhiú gâu-tih**, id.

chhîm tih chhāⁿ, sound as of several musical instruments (v. chhāⁿ).

tih — **tih-tuh**, talking differently at different times, in a deceitful or half-joking way (v. tuh).

tih — **tih-tauh**, of dangerous character or depraved behaviour (v. tauh).

tih (R. tek), a drop; to drop. **chit-tih-á**, a very small drop. **nāⁿ-âu tih-á**, the uvula.

tih-hō, to have rain dropping, as from the roof. **tih bák-sái**, to drop tears. **tih-tsúi**, water dropping; the eaves of a house; the place below the eaves on which the water drops.

tih (sometimes written "teh," but more accurately pronounced "tih"), (C. lí).

tih-beh, about to —.

tih [R. tí, the bottom, = col. tóe]. **phah--tiòh lâng sim-koaⁿ-tih**, to touch a man's heart or conscience by a remark about some evil he had done, though perhaps we may not have intended or not even known of it.

tih (cf. thih). **chhìn tih-tih**, very cold.

tih (cf. thih). **tih-tih-háu**, to stutter in speaking. **kóng-ōe tih-tih-háu**, id. **tih-tùh**, to stammer or falter in speaking, as a liar who has to invent new lies on the spot. **lí kóng-ōe tih-tùh**, you are evidently hesitating because you are telling lies. **tih-tùh-hm̂**, a toy that makes a humming noise. **tih-tùh-m̂**, id.

tih-táuh tih-táuh, sound of shoes clattering, or of rain dropping, or of clock ticking (v. táuh).

tih, a very small plate, like a small saucer, for holding condiments. **tih-á**, id. **chek-tih**, sort of small candlestick. **tê-tih**, small porcelain plate on which a teapot stands. **poâⁿ-tih**, large and small plates. **toā-poâⁿ sió-tih**, id. **óaⁿ-tih-tī**, bowls, small plates, and chopsticks. **au-á tháh tih-á** (cups on small plates), said of incest.

tih (cf. tì), (C. tihⁿ), to desire or wish for, as a person or thing. **beh-tih**, to have a desire to get. **ló-tia beh-tih--lâng**, the mandarin wishes the men immediately, as for a case. **bô-beh-tih**, does not care for it (or him) at all. **ài-tih**, to wish very much. **ài-tih-mihⁿ**, grasping. **ài-tih lâng-ê-mihⁿ**, id. **m̄-tih**, I don't wish it; to count of no use; not caring for.

tihⁿ (C.), = A. tih, to desire or wish for.

tihⁿ (= nihⁿ, tīⁿ). **tihⁿ--sí**, to strangle with the fingers.

tim (cf. thim), reserved in manner; not frank, open, or communicative; too cautious and knowing to be got round; planning deep and saying little; precocious and intelligent, as child of four or five. **im-tim**, crafty and designing; cunning and scheming. **tsòe-lâng-tim**, keeping one's counsel to one's self, as a deep schemer.

tîm [R. id., = col. tiâm, thiâm], to sink. **tîm-lîm**, id. **tîm--lòh-khì**, id. **tîm-lûn** (r.), to perish.

tîm-hiuⁿ, lign-aloes; garrow-wood. **tîm-hiuⁿ-sek**, colour of aloes.

béh tîm, the pulse in such a state that it is not felt till decidedly pressed.

tîm--khì (C. tiâm), to embezzle. **tîm--khì lâng-ê-mihⁿ**, to take or keep unjust possession of things borrowed or intrusted, refusing to return them, saying that they are lost or stolen. **tîm-lék**, to hide a thing belonging to another, and refuse to give it up.

tîm-tāng, severe; painful; very unwell. **toā-tîm** (T. toā-tiâm), exceedingly —.

chhim-tîm, very deep and profound; very cautious. **chhim-tîm kun-tsat**, very cautious and careful in doing business. **tîm-chiâm**, thoughtful and careful in considering before speaking or acting. **tîm-gîm**, to think silently, as in planning or composing.

poàⁿ-phû-tîm, barely floating, and almost submerged, as heavy wood. **thun-thò phû-tîm**, knowing how to say just enough and no more, or to hit the due medium between firmness and yielding, as in managing an affair (v. thò).

tìm, to throw, as a stone. **tìm chiòh-thâu**, to throw a stone; to stone.

tìm, strong and decided, as a colour; opposed to "chhiò." **tìm-sek**, id. **tìm-chhíⁿ**, a pretty deep decided blue colour, like good new blue cotton. **tìm-âng**, a decided red.

tìm — **tìm-khoàⁿ**, to try the weight by poising on the hand, either of one thing, or comparing the weight of two things. **chhiú tìm-khoàⁿ**, id. **tìm-tāng**, to try the weight by the hand.

tāng-tìm, very heavy. **khah-tāng-tìm**, extremely heavy.

tìm (cf. thìm, tàm). **tìm-thâu**, = thìm-thâu, to nod the head, as sign of being pleased or consenting.

tīm (R. id.), word used as the pronoun of the first person by the emperor alone; "I the emperor."

tīm — **tsúi-tīm**, a small bird found on rivers.

tīm (R. sim), to stew in a covered vessel placed in an outer vessel of boiling water. **tīm-koàn**, the inner vessel used for this sort of stewing. **tīm-sio**, to warm over again in this way, as food. **tīm-iòh**, to make a medicinal preparation in this way, either of the medicine alone, or mixed with food. **tīm-koe**, to stew a fowl in this way.

tīm — **tīm tàu-kú**, two men each waiting for the other to do what one or other must do, or to take the first step in a matter which each is afraid to begin. **beh-tīm kàu tī-sí**, why are you procrastinating so long?

tīm (cf. tiām). **tīm-tiòk** (Cn.), quiet in manner; not acting or speaking at random; externally well-regulated and staid, as conduct; calm and quiet in speaking.

tin [R. precious; cf. col. chin]. **tin-pó**, very valuable; precious (v. pó). **tin-tiōng**, to count precious; to value highly, as a servant or employé who is found very useful, or as a thing. **tin-tiōng ê-lâng**, a person highly respected or honoured.

san-tin hái-bī, the delicacies of land and sea.

tin — **tin-tong**, one cash odds and the other evens (v. tong).

tin [R. teng, a jingling sound, as of stones]. **tin-tin tang-tang**, sound of a vibrating string. **tin-tin tong-tong**, id.

tìn [R. cheng, evidence; proof; to verify; to collect, as taxes]. **chhim bô-tin**, to embezzle so much money as not to be able to give any plausible account of it. **khui bô-tin**, unable to account for all the money for which one is responsible, but not necessarily implying dishonesty. **khai-khong put-tin**, to embezzle employer's money, and spend it for one's own purposes, so as to be unable to give an account of the whole amount. **khai-khong bû-tin**, id. **khai-khong bô-tin**, id. **khai bô-tin**, id. **tsáp-saⁿ-bān khai-bô-tin**, said of embezzling to an enormous extent.

tin-hiàng (C.), = A. teng-hiòng, to levy taxes; and so in some other phrases, **tin** (C.), = A. teng.

tin (Cn.) **thien-tin**, = A. thien-tsin, the city of Tien-tsin.

tîn [R. to set in order; to arrange; to make a statement; old, as a thing; stale; name of an ancient state; a surname; = col. tân; and by change of tone, tīn, tsūn].

tîn-lé, to make ceremonial presents, as to mandarins or influential men. **tîn-bêng** (r.), to set forth a statement, as of our desires, requests, or good deeds.

tîn--khì, to grow musty by long keeping, *e.g.* as sugar or preserves. **tîn-phî**, prepared orange-peel.

kə-tîn, a fabulous animal like a winged dragon. **kau-tîn**, id. (s. entangle).

tîn [same as previous word?]. **tiám-tîn**, skilful and cautious; managing matters carefully and safely.

tîn [R. tiên, to entangle, = col. tīⁿ]. **kau-tîn**, phrase used by the chair-bearer who walks first, to warn the other of some obstruction in the way (s. arrange).

tîn [R. dust]. **tîn-ai** (R.), small dust flying about in the air. **tîn-sè** (R.), this toilsome world.

tîn (C. kin), to pour off water, as from sediment, or from something boiled or infused, or from lime or such medicinal powder that is being washed, or as clearer water from the more muddy. **kè-tîn**, to be thus treated, as medicine.

tîn (R. id.) **in-tîn**, a bitter medicinal plant used for eye diseases; Artemisia or wormwood?

tîn (R. têng), rattan; various sorts of creeping plants; long trailing stems of vines, potatoes, or creepers. **tîn-bú**, the crown of the root, as of the sweet-potato. **kun-tîn ōng**, having numerous living posterity.

tîn-phê, the outer rind of rattan, the best part of it for wicker-work. **tîn-nñg**, the inner part of the rind, not so good. **tîn-kùn**, a strong rattan stick (v. kùn). **tîn-tiâu**, thin rattan rods, scourges, or fasces (v. tiâu). **tîn-phóng**, rattan wicker-work (v. phóng). **tîn-té**, flat piece of rattan wicker-work, as for bottom of chair, or for a panel. **tîn-í**, a chair with rattan bottom. **tîn-chhñg**, a rattan couch or sofa. **tîn-gû** (T.), a small instrument attached to a kite, which makes a humming noise.

tîn-pâi, a rattan shield, the usual sort of Chinese shield.

phah-tîn, to make articles with rattan wicker-work. **chhng-tîn**, to make wicker-work with rattan.

soan-tîn, to throw out suckers or trailing shoots. **chhoan-tîn**, id. **khan-tîn**, id.

koe-tîn, trailing stems of melons, cucumbers, or pumpkins. **bán-koe chhiû-tîn**, to follow up a clue step by step, examining to the bottom of an affair, often in a roundabout way. **tāu-tîn**, long stalks of peas, &c. **in-in tāu-tîn, chit-toā-thoa**, said of a long involved story with no clue. **han-tsû-tîn**, stalks of sweet-potatoes.

tîn-ñg, gambouge.

khoe-tîn, a medicinal creeper with small leaves. **kau-tîn**, a medicine used to keep children from starting in sleep. **lō-tîn**, a sort of medicinal plant. **ka-to-tîn**, a large woody creeper that grows to the top of high trees. **chhiûⁿ-piah-tîn**, a small-leaved creeping shrub, of the fig tribe, that grows on old walls. **bô-thâu-tîn**, a stringy rootless parasite with edible berries. **bé-oaⁿ-tîn**, a plant; a sort of medicinal salve (v. oaⁿ). **koe-sái-tîn**, a bad-smelling medicinal creeper. **phoà-pè-tîn**, name of a plant. **siak-phoà-oáⁿ-tîn**, Strophanthus divergens.

tín [R. chin, to shake; to move; to deliver; to save]. **tín-tāng**, to move, as person or thing. **bô-tín-tāng**, no movement; quite motionless; no beginning of action in a matter. **bô-tín bô-tāng**, id.

tìn [R. to repress; to pacify; to keep in subjection; to guard; to protect; a mart; a trading place], to hold, as a city or military post; a military officer like a lieutenant-general or admiral.

tìn-tâi, the lieutenant-general or admiral (Chen-tai), the next in rank to a Thê-tok. **chiang-chiu-tìn**, the lieutenant-general commanding at Chang-chew. **thê-tìn**, general or admiral and his lieutenant.

tìn-tiōng, having a dignified manner (v. tiōng).

tìn-siú, to guard or occupy (a city) with troops, so as to keep in order, as a high mandarin does. **tìn-ap**, to keep the people quiet and in subjection, as a mandarin does. **tìn-soah**, to ward off the malign influences of the "soah-sîn."

tìn-moáⁿ, crowded, as a room, with things or persons. **tìn-bát-bát**, crowded very close.

tìn-tè, to be in the way; to be useless and obstructive; to occupy the place uselessly. **tìn-ūi**, id. **tìn toā-bú-ūi**, to take up a great deal of room. **tìn nñg-lâng ê-giâh**, to take up the place of two persons. **tìn-tàⁿ**, to take up much room in a load (for carrying on a pole on the shoulder), so as to cause inconvenience, as a bulky thing. **tìn-lō**, to obstruct the way, as some bulky thing, or as people in the way. **tìn-lō-thâu**, to obstruct the landing-place. **sí-káu tìn-lō-thâu**, a dead dog blocking the road, said in scolding. **tìn-kang**, to obstruct work, as visitors, or as talk, or many small matters.

tìn-kang-hú, Chin-kiang-foo. **tìn-hái**, Chin-hai, name of several cities—one near Ningpo, one near Swatow, one on the promontory south of the entrance to Amoy harbour. **tìn-lâm-koan**, a gateway between Amoy and Emungkang.

tīn (cf. A. thīn). **tīn-tīn** (T.), the two ends (as of a beam) equal in size, or very nearly so. **thâu-bé tīn** (T.), id.

tīn [R. id., by change of tone from "tìn," to set in order, &c.; cf. col. tsūn], a company of men, as in a procession; a troop; a body of soldiers; classifier of ranks, herds, gusts, showers, &c.

tīn-sè, the strength or force of a body of troops in battle. **tīn-hoat**, military manœuvres. **tīn-bông**, having died in the ranks.

hiuⁿ-tīn, an idolatrous incense procession. **chit-tīn-hiuⁿ**, id. **bô-jī-tīn**, words not in regular line, or not of equal size (v. jī). **bê-hûn-tīn**, said of enticing into vice, &c. (v. bê). **kiú-liông-tīn**, arrangement of army in battle in nine divisions. **bé-iàh-tīn**, arrangement with two long divisions in front.

chiâⁿ-tīn, to form into ranks, &c.; a whole troop or procession. **tsōe-tīn**, to make up a large company or procession. **tàu-tīn**, to unite in a procession (idolatrous). **kui-tīn**, to fall into the ranks. **chhut-tīn**, to go out in procession, or in rank and file, or to battle. **pâi-tīn**, to arrange in rows or ranks; to arrange soldiers in battle array. **pâi-peng pè-tīn**, to arrange soldiers in ranks. **pè-tīn**, id. **tok-tīn**, to carry the standard and have oversight of a body of soldiers. **lîm-tīn**, to come to close quarters, as two armies; to join battle; to come to the crisis of the case, as a matter going before mandarin or arbiters. **lîm-tīn thè-siok**, to draw back at the tug of war. **chièn-tīn**, to be engaged in battle, as armies. **piàⁿ-tīn**, battle raging fiercely. **iâⁿ chit-tīn**, to gain one victory. **su kúi-tīn**, how many battles has he lost? **pāi-tīn**, to be defeated; a defeated army. **siu-tīn** (r.), to draw off the troops. **siu-peng soàⁿ-tīn**, id. **soàⁿ-tīn**, to disperse the ranks, as of troops, or of idolatrous procession.

chhim-tīn, to venture into a position of considerable danger, *e.g.* making a risky venture in trade, or spending much more than is suitable to our income.

tiô [R. tiông, long, = col. tñg]. **tiô-thoà**, Chang-tai Hien (tiông-thài), in the department of Chang-chew. **tiô-lòh**, Chang-loh Hien, in the department of Fuh-chau.

tiô [R. tiâu, the tide]. **tiô-chiu**, Chau-chau-foo or Tie-chew, in the province of Canton, near Swatow. **tiô-chiu-ai**, plays in the Swatow dialect. **tiô-iûⁿ**, Chau-yang Hien, near Swatow.

tiô [R. tô, to throw; to have recourse to; to agree; = col. tâu], to leap; to jump; to frisk or dance about. **tiô-thiàu**, to leap about. **tiô-chhut**, to leap or start out, as from a pit. **tiô-kha-koe**, to hop and jump

海上絲綢之路文獻集成 科技與文化編

厦英大辭典

about. **tiô-tâng**, to leap or dance about in an excited or ecstatic state, as the "tâng-chí." **tò-tiô**, to rebound. **chhio-tiô**, active and lively, as child or animal. **chhiauh-chhiauh-tiô**, to dance about, as with rage, or as Tauist sorcerer (v. chhiauh). **chhiák-chhiák-tiô**, to palpitate; to jump up and down noisily or angrily. **phók-phók-tiô**, to dance with emotion, as with rage or delight.

tiô (Cn.), = A. *tê* (to throw; to agree).

tió (Cn.), = A. *tè* (R.), a rice-measure. **tió-bí sam-chiên**, a measure of rice for three cash, as in the golden age of Yaou and Shun.

tiò (R. tiàu), a hook; a fish-hook; to fish with hook; to angle; to stitch widely or baste; to sew very loosely, so as to keep in place for the closer sewing.

tiò-á, a small fish-hook. **thih-tiò**, an iron hook, as for fishing. **chit-mn̂g-tiò**, one hook. **kau-tiò**, a (good-sized) fishing-hook (+).

tiò-khí, the barb of a hook. **kau-tiò-khí**, id. **tiò-koaⁿ**, a fishing-rod. **tiò-soàⁿ**, fishing-line. **tiò-tsô**, a fishing-boat. **tiò-tâng**, copper wire by which a hook is sometimes attached. **tiò-tâng** (C.), bamboo floats for a line with hooks.

phah tiò-á, to make fish-hooks. **pàng-tiò**, to fish with a hook or hooks. **pàng-kau-tiò**, to set a line with hooks. **chhiû-tiò**, to haul or pull in a line with hooks so as to get the fish. **chiáh-tiò**, to bite the hook; to take the hook.

tiò-hî, to angle for fish; to fish with a hook. **tiò-hî-ong** (r.), an old fisherman. **tiò-péh-hî**, a sort of game; to play it.

tiò-tiâu, to stitch on loosely so as just to keep in place (opposed to "tèng," or "thīⁿ," which are much closer). **tiò-liâm**, id., or as button, or as figures cut in cloth of a different colour. **tiò-lí**, to put in a lining in a dress. **tiò bān-jī**, to embroider the character "bān," as on child's dress (v. bān).

tiò (Cn.), = A. *tè* (R.), to quarrel; to fight.

tiō [R. tiāu, an ancient state in Shan-si; a surname], a surname. **tiō goân-sòe**, a black-faced attendant idol in temples of Má-tsó and of Tāi-tō-kong.

tiō (R. tiāu). **tiō-á**, a small iron frying-pan or rice-boiler with a handle. **thih-tiō**, id.

tiō, to shake, as with cold, emotion, &c.; to tremble. **khéh-khéh-tiō**, to shiver with cold; to shake with fear. **géh-géh-tiō**, id. **hoā-hoā-tiō**, to move about in excitement, as a multitude excited with fear, or when preparing for a feud or battle. **tiō--sí**, to shake exceedingly, as with fear or cold. **oáh-oáh tiō--sí**, id. **chhò-tiō hī-khang**, to deafen a man's ears with noise.

péh-tiō-á, feeble stooping appearance of man in weak health, or of an old man.

tiō — **péh-tiō**, a white mark on the skin over a considerable surface (s. shake). **khí péh-tiō**, to get this white mark on the skin.

tiō (C.), to scold a man indirectly by making an appearance of scolding children or other by-standers.

tiō (Cn.), = A. *tē* (R.), leguminous plants; but "*tē*" is also said.

tiō (Cn.), = A. *tè*. **kù-tiō**, a comma or dot used in punctuation.

tiō [R. tiāu, an omen]. **khiò-tiō** (Cn.), = khiò-tiāu, superstitious and magical charms or incantations.

tieⁿ (C. P.), in the various tones, = A. tiuⁿ.

tioh (cf. tiuh), to pull; to pull out; to drag; to draw towards one's self. **tioh-ân**, to pull tight. **tioh--lòh-lâi**, to pull down towards one's self. **tioh-chhut**, to pull out; to express distinctly. **chhēng-ôe tioh-béh**, to wear shoes and stockings.

tioh hī-á, to pull the ears. **tioh chih-bé**, to lisp in speaking (v. chih). **tioh tsńg-thâu-á**, to pull the joints of the fingers, either one's self or by barber in shampooing. **tsńg-thâu-á tioh-tioh**, id.

tiuⁿ-tioh, to refuse sulkily to do something when asked, often with purpose of getting more money.

tioh [R. tiòk? cf. tiòh], to play, as at chess.

chhut-tioh, superior to others in excellence or in skill, as person or thing. **khah-chhut-tioh**, id. **koâiⁿ-tioh**, skilful at any sort of work or play.

ū-tóe-tioh, to have a safe foundation, as title-deeds; to have some property, as man; to have considerable knowledge or talent, as for teaching or for business; said of managing a matter well and putting all right, so as to make a lasting settlement. **i--ê tóe-tioh**, his original circumstances and history from the beginning.

tioh-kî, to play at chess.

tiòh [R. tiòk, right; according to; to effect], right; correct; ought; all right; to hit the mark; to get, as a disease, or as one's turn of work, duty, or rights; yes, in answer to the question, "Is it right?" or "Ought it?" affix to many verbs (often enclitic) expressing accomplishment or taking effect; prefix to some verbs and nouns expressing action.

tiòh-lát, to cause or require much strength or exertion, as a heavy lift or a matter very difficult to settle rightly. **sńg-khùi tiòh-lát**, to cause or require a great deal of toil and trouble, *e.g.* teaching wild boys or managing a very involved case. **bô-tiòh-lát**, not done with sufficient exertion; not producing the desired effect, as an ill-aimed blow, *e.g.* hammer not hitting the nail on the head.

tiòh-boâ, to labour; to work hard; to toil. **tiòh-kip**, in great haste and urgency. **tiòh-pīⁿ**, to have a disease; unwell. **tiòh-chhám**, to meet with calamity. **tiòh-hiā**, to be infested with white ants, as house. **tiòh-chhèng**, to be hit by a shot from a gun (v. chhèng).

tiòh-pan, to come to one's turn, as constables or police. **tiòh-kong**, one's turn come for attending to the common ancestral rites (v. kong). **tiòh-thâu**, to have (in one's turn) the care of the idolatrous rites of a family or ward. **tiòh-nîⁿ**, one's year come (in turn) for such a purpose.

tiòh-hoat, to hit on the right way of doing a thing. **tiòh-lō͘**, the right road; to hit on the right road; exactly fit for the use or purpose wished. **tiòh-ê-lō͘**, the right road.

ū-tiòh, to hit the mark; to succeed, as in taking an animal in a trap; to be successful, as at an examination. **siā ū-tiòh**, to hit the mark with the arrow. **lóng-tsóng tiòh**, all are right; it affects them all, as an accusation against one man which will cause serious trouble to many. **thâu tiòh, bé sī**, all right from beginning to end.

bōe-tiòh, not able to reach, *e.g.* man not tall enough, or rope too short; cannot hit the mark, as from some inherent defect or unfitness. **phah-bōe-tiòh**, to miss in shooting, &c. **bē-tit--thang tiòh--i** (C.), no one can catch or kill him, as a tiger.

bōe-tiòh-lán-tit, we cannot possibly get any of it (v. tit). **bô-thang-tiòh lán-tsāi**, we cannot get permission to carry any of it, as in our boat.

bô-tiòh, not obtaining the desired result, as at examination; not hitting the mark. **tit-bô-tiòh**, did not manage to get it. **khì-bô-tio̍h**, though he went, he failed to get it, *e.g.* too late.

m̄-tio̍h, wrong. **m̄-tio̍h-lō͘**, wrong road. **chhùi tio̍h, sim m̄-tio̍h**, speech fair, but heart bad.

eng-kai-tio̍h, ought to —. **su-tio̍h** (r.), id. **tio̍h-khì**, ought to go. **m̄ tio̍h-khì**, yet had better go (v. m̄).

tiāⁿ-tio̍h, fixed; settled (v. tiāⁿ).

toà--tio̍h, on account of; out of regard to (as a person). **ūi--tio̍h**, because of.

tit--tio̍h, to get (v. tit); in this paragraph the "tio̍h" is sometimes not enclitic, as when it becomes emphatic. **tú--tio̍h**, to meet with; to find by chance. **gū--tio̍h**, id. **chhē--tio̍h**, to find by searching. **jip--tio̍h**, to overtake. **jiok--tio̍h** (C.), id.

tiok [R. name of a country]. **thien-tiok-kok**, India.

tiok [R. bamboo, = col. tek], (also C., = A. tek). **jîn-biēn-tiok**, a fine sort of bamboo. **tiok-á-thâu**, the 118th radical, written at the top.

tio̍k [R. to drive away; each; = col. ta̍k]. **pek-tio̍k**, to drive away or expel, as a man. **kek-tio̍k**, do.; to drive away, as from a village, or society, or employment. **koáⁿ-tio̍k**, id. **khún-tio̍k** (R.), to expel; (X.) to persecute. **khu-siâ tio̍k-e̍k**, to drive away the evil influences that cause epidemic diseases (v. siâ).

tio̍k [R. right; according to; to effect; = col. tio̍h]. **tēng-tio̍k**, all settled and arranged, as an affair. **kui-tio̍k**, correctly settled, as an affair, or at least so well arranged that it is in the fair way of being suitably settled. **kun-tio̍k**, to get a party to come forward by imprisoning some one connected with him till he comes, as mandarins do.

tiām-tio̍k, quiet and self-possessed; not talking at random or acting rashly; not showing much emotion, even in press of business or in danger, but considering carefully. **tīm-tio̍k** (Cn.), id.

put-tio̍k, ill arranged, as business or affair; done it all wrong; ill-behaved and unsafe to deal with, as man. **bû-tio̍k**, unsafe, as man or affair, or as mode of sending something.

ū-tio̍k-lo̍k, well-behaved and truthful, as man whose honesty and integrity can be depended on; safe to deal with, as man of substance or of integrity; having a safe foundation, as affair; having good and definite proof, as title-deeds or such matters. **iú-tio̍k iú-lo̍k**, id. **pān--khì ū-tio̍k-lo̍k**, well settled and securely arranged, as affair. **kau--khì ū-tio̍k-lo̍k**, to hand over (as letter, money, &c.) to a safe man, who will certainly deliver it. **tsa ū-tio̍k-lo̍k**, on examination it is found that there is abundant evidence of its correctness and security. **bô-tio̍k-lo̍k**, not safe to deal with, as man; unsafe and unlikely to come to a good issue, as affair.

tio̍k-kip, in great haste, as on urgent business. **jîn-biēn, tio̍k ko-te**, valuing or following men according to their prosperity (v. te).

tio̍k-sit (C. chiak-sit), the real circumstances of the case.

tiong [R. middle; medium; mediocre; central; Chinese; cf. col. tiòng, tong], middle. **tiong-ng** (C. tang-ng), among; between. **thâu-khak tiong-ng**, the point on the head where the hair radiates. **tiong-kan**, between; among. **tiong-sim**, the middle; the very centre. **chhiú-tiong-sim**, the middle of the palm.

tiong-tiong, of medium quality, mediocre. **tiong-téng**, of medium quality. **tiong-pān**, id. **tiong-hō**, id. **siōng tiong hā**, superior, medium, and inferior. **tiong-kāu-tsoá**, sort of paper of medium thickness. **tiong-kēng-tsoá**, id.

kui-tiong, to be in the middle; a sort of medicine. **tùi-tiong**, just in the middle. **tek-kí-tiong**, to hit the happy mean. **tek-tiong**, moderate; usually neither specially good or bad; sometimes has the idea of the happy mean. **tek-tiong ê-kè**, a fair average price. **liáh tiong-hô**, to split the difference as in bargain or dispute. **liáh tiong-noâⁿ**, id.

tiong-iông, the happy mean; the due medium; the Chung-yung or Classic of the doctrine of the mean.

tiong-lâng, a middleman in making a bargain or agreement. **tiong-lâng-lé**, fee paid to middleman. **tiong-lâng-chîⁿ**, id. **tiong-lâng-gûn**, do., if in value of silver. **tiong-pó** (r.), a middleman who stands security; (X.) a mediator. **tsòe-tiong**, to act as middleman. **tsòe-tiong--ê**, id.

tiong-tsun, the principal priest in a ceremony (v. tsun). **tiong-su-khe**, sort of secretaries in supreme boards (v. su). **tiong-tân-iâ**, name of an idol (v. tân).

tiong-goân, the 15th day of the 7th month. **tiong-chhiu**, 8.15. (v. chhiu). **tiong-liên**, middle-aged. **tiong-tsáiⁿ**, the second finger (v. tsáiⁿ). **tiong-khí**, the front teeth. **tiong-keng**, the middle one of three houses or rooms. **tiong-káng**, the middle channel or mouth of river. **tiong-mn̂g**, the middle door or gate of a group of three, as in a wealthy man's house; esp. in a yamun. **tiong-àn**, a long narrow table (v. àn). **tiong-tn̂g**, the central hall of a house.

poàⁿ-tiong-tn̂g soah--khì, to fail half-way (v. poàⁿ). **tiong-heng**, to prosper after an unprosperous beginning, as a dynasty. **jit tiong-kiā**, sun at zenith (v. kiā).

chiông-tiong, from among them. **lōe-tiong**, in the matter; among them. **chhú-tiong ê tō-lí**, the principle or rationale of this matter. **goá--ê ì-tiong**, in my purpose. **thiⁿ-tiong**, in the sky, &c. &c.

jîn-tiong, the middle part of the upper lip. **jîn-tiong tn̂g**, do., long; supposed to indicate long life. **jîn-tiong té**, do., short; supposed to augur short life. **jîn-tiong-pe̍k**, incrustation of urine jars, used medicinally.

tiong-kok, China, the central kingdom. **tiong-hoa**, id.

tiong-chîⁿ, half a dollar. **tiong-gûn**, id. **chit-ê-tiong**, id.

kong-tiong ê-chîⁿ, Annamese cash, used at Amoy (v. kong).

sang-tiong, one odds and one evens, in tossing cash.

tiong — **tiong-nîⁿ** (Cn.), = C. to-nîⁿ, a sort of Azalea.

tiong [R. to open out; to stretch or lay out; to boast; a sheet, as of paper; classifier of sheets, letters, &c.; a surname; = col. tiuⁿ], (C. tiang). **khai-tiong**, said of opening a shop, as first opening of new shops, or after the New-year holidays. **khai-tiong tāi-kiet**, may great prosperity attend this shop. **khai-tiong tsùn-hoat**, id.

tiong [R. faithful; trusty; devoted; loyal; patriotic]. **tiong-hō͘**, faithful and honest; well-behaved and trustworthy. **tiong-hīō** (Cn.), id. **tiong-tit**, upright, trusty, and straightforward. **tiong-sìn**, faithful and trusty. **tiong-gī**, faithful and devoted, esp. as loyal mandarin (v. gī). **put-tiong**, unfaithful to duty; disloyal; treasonable. **poàⁿ-kan-tiong**, of very doubtful fidelity.

厦英大辭典

chīn-tiong, devoted to duty; diligent and faithful in discharge of duty. **chīn-tiong chīn-hàu**, faithful and filial to the utmost. **chīn-tiong, lân í chīn-hàu**, a mandarin who fulfils his duty to the sovereign can hardly fulfil his duty to his parents. **chīn-tiong pò-kok**, extremely loyal and grateful to the dynasty. **tiong-kun pò-kok**, loyal to sovereign and showing gratitude to the dynasty. **tiong-kun ài-kok**, id. **tiong-kun ài-bîn**, loyal to sovereign and loving the people.

tiong-sîn, a loyal and faithful statesman (v. sîn). **tiong-liét-sû**, temple to distinguished mandarins who have died for the state. **tiong-ióng-sû**, do., for such military mandarins.

tiông [R. to do over again, = col. têng; by change of tone from "tiōng," heavy]. **tiông-hok**, to say over and over tautologically, as in an essay. **tiông-iông-tsoeh**, the 9.9. **tiông-iông-jit**, id.

tiông [R. the bowels, = col. tn̂g, chhiâng], (C. tiâng). **tāi-tiông**, the great intestines. **siáu-tiông-tūi**, inguinal hernia. **tūi-tiông** (r.), id. **chhoan-tiông-tī**, fistula. **jūn-tiông**, to mollify the bowels, so as to remove costiveness, as some sorts of food or medicine. **lūn-tiông**, id.

thiet-sék sim-tiông, heart and bowels of iron and stone; cruel and pitiless.

tiông [R. long in time or space; to be superior in skill or excellence; = col. tn̂g], (C. tiâng). **tiông-toán** (R.), long and short (v. toán).

tiông-keng, the evening-star. **bān-lí tiông-sa**, the Prata shoals.

tiông-kiú, lasting very long. **biên-tiông** (R.), id. **tiông-siū**, long life (v. siū). **tiông-seng put-sú**, long life without death (v. seng).

chhun-tiông, to lay up surplus gains; to accumulate, as gains, esp. interest on money.

sé-tiông, that in which we surpass others; our special ability; the amount of gain made on a transaction; the balance of clear gain, as at end of month or year. **goá--ê tiông-kî**, that in which I am specially proficient above others (+). **kièn-tiông**, that in which one excels others, as skill, &c. **i--ê kièn-tiông**, that in which he specially excels. **lí sé-kièn-tiông**, that in which you are specially proficient. **lí sé-tiông-kî**, id. **ū-kièn-tiông**, to excel others in skill or excellence of some kind. **i-ū sím-mih^{n} kièn-tiông**, in what is he specially skilful or proficient? **bû-it kièn-tiông**, without any excellence to recommend one. **bû-it-tiông khó-chhú**, id.

tióng [R. to grow; to increase; greater; senior; a superior; = col. tiú^{n}, chiáng, tńg; by change of tone from "tiông," long], (C. tiáng). **seng-tióng**, to be born and brought up. **tióng-sêng**, to grow up to manhood.

liên-tióng, senior; elder. **tióng-pòe**, elder brothers and persons of same generation with our parents, or higher. **tióng-tsú**, the eldest son. **ka iōng tióng-tsú**, in a household the eldest son has the management. **bók-bû tsun-tióng**, contemptuously despising superiors.

tióng-kè, to rise in price, as an article that becomes dearer in the market; also, to charge a little above the usual price for one or more picked articles. **chî^{n}-kè khah-tióng**, the value of copper cash has risen (v. kè). **tióng phái^{n}-chî^{n}-tsúi**, to give extra cash (in changing silver) because of bad cash being mixed.

koan hûn-tióng, the god Kwanti.

tiòng [R. to overflow; to rise very high, as tide; an inundation; = col. tiù^{n}], (C. tiàng). **tsúi tiòng**, tide very high and overflowing. **tiòng-tsúi**, water rising very high, as in high tides or flood on river. **hái-tiòng**, remarkably high tides.

tiòng-siàu, to overcharge an account by mistake.

tiòng [R. dropsical swelling; said also of other similar swellings; = col. tiù^{n}], (C. tiàng), belly inflated and distended, as with overeating or indigestion. **ké-tiòng**, dropsy in the abdomen. **té-tiòng**, swelling of the belly from indigestion, &c.; also said (but inaccurately) of dropsy in the belly. **chiáh--khi té-tiòng**, you eat till your belly swells (said in scolding a glutton). **pak-té-tiòng**, a sort of swelling of the belly.

tiòng-hong put-gú, a sort of disease, very sudden and fatal.

tiòng-tám, feeling of great emotion, almost like choking sensation, as on receiving sudden exciting news, good or bad. **tiòng-tá^{n}**, id. **tiòng-tá^{n}--sí**, to die from sudden excessive grief, fear, or joy.

tiòng [R. vexed; disappointed], (C. tiàng). **tiòng-hūn** (R.), to hate exceedingly; to be deeply displeased at one's self, as for some fault or mistake.

tiòng [R. tòng, a post or pillar; = col. tàng]. **tiòng-liông**, important or useful, as man or thing.

tiòng [R. to hit the centre of the mark; to accomplish; to be taken with a disease or in a plot; by change of tone from "tiong," middle], to succeed in getting a Kujin or Tsin-sze degree. **chìn-tiòng**, to get degrees in general, literary or military, high or low. **tiòng kú-jîn**, to get the Kujin degree. **tiòng chià^{n}-pńg**, id. **tiòng hù-pńg**, to have one's name on the list of those whose merit is sufficient, but who do not get the degree because the legal number is made up.

kièn-tsòh kièn-tiòng, to hit the mark every time.

tiòng-iōng, skilful; useful, as man (v. iōng).

tiòng-kè, to be entrapped in a plot. **tiòng-sú**, to have a sun-stroke. **tiòng-tók**, to have taken poison accidentally; very dangerous, wicked, and injurious, as man. **tiòng tsoâ-ké**, to be bewitched so as to have dropsy (v. tsoâ). **tiòng-té-un-pī^{n}**, may you have dropsy and plague! (said by women in scolding).

tiōng [R. heavy; important; serious; severe; grave; to regard or count important; = col. tāng], to set the mind upon; to consider valuable and important. **m̄-thang-tiōng**, don't set your mind on —. **tiōng-chiáh**, to be very fond of eating. **tiōng hong-súi**, to count the Fung-shuy of great importance. **sien tiōng i-koan, hō tiōng-jîn**, value a man at first according to his dress, afterwards for his own character.

kèng-tiōng, to reverence; to respect. **tsun-tiōng**, to treat with respect; honourable or high in rank. **ka-kī pó-tiōng**, to take care of one's health. **tùi-tiōng**, to value much; to regard as important; to respect. **tì-tiōng** (C.), id. **tin-tiōng**, to value highly (v. tin). **sìn-tiōng**, to place great confidence on a man.

sīn-tiōng, valuable or important, as a thing that should be taken care of; very careful and exact in managing matters; very careful of one's health, e.g. dressing according to the weather. **sīn-tiōng ê-mih^{n}**, things of some value. **tìn-tiōng**, having a dignified manner, as man of age, rank, or wealth.

hō-tiōng, grave, sedate, sober, and decorous in manner; large and fat in one's figure. **hiō-tiōng** (Cn.), id. **sì-pang hō-tiōng**, fat and full-faced.

siong-tiōng, severe, as wound, illness, or calamity; great, as price, wages, or expenses; expensive.

tiōng-tát, to be worth so much; to deserve the honour (v. tàt). **tiōng-thèng**, dull of hearing. **giên tiōng**, one's words counted of weight, valued, or followed. **tiōng-àn**, a serious case in law. **tiōng-hoān**, a great criminal, *e.g.* a leader of rebels or pirates. **put-sek kheng-tiōng** (R.), not able to discriminate the important and the unimportant, &c.

tiōng [R. the second of three; second brother; second month of a season], commission or brokerage for selling goods. **pèng-tiōng**, commission or brokerage in general. **goā pèng, lāi tiōng**, commission (usually of 2 per cent.) taken both from buyer and seller by commission-agent. **tiōng-gûn**, brokerage or commission on goods sold for us, taken by the broker or commission-agent. **tiōng-chîⁿ**, id. **hâng-tiōng**, id. **thiu-tiōng**, to take off the commission for selling goods.

tiōng-nî, Confucius.

tē-tiōng, a sort of medicine.

tiōng [R. a measure of ten Chinese feet; used in the names of some relationships; = col. tiūⁿ, tn̄g], (C. tiāng). **it-tiōng-hông**, the hollyhock (lit. ten feet of red).

tiōng-hu, a husband. **tāi-tiōng-hu**, a brave man; a hero. **ùi-bó, tāi-tiōng-hu**, he who fears his wife is a hero indeed!

kok-tiōng, the emperor's father-in-law.

tiōng [R. a staff; a cudgel; = col. thn̄g], (C. tiāng). **khok-san-tiōng**, a long staff, half pasted over with white paper, carried by husband at funeral of his wife.

hêng-tiōng, the man in a yamun who has the office of beating criminals and persons under examination. **tn̄g-hêng-tiōng**, to have this office. **kiò hêng-tiōng**, to call that person to come, *e.g.* in order to beat a man.

tiōng [R. to rely upon; to trust in; to fight], (C. tiāng), to intrust with a commission or with the management of a matter. **thok-tiōng**, to intrust; to give a message to take or commission to perform, generally small or simple. **í-tiōng**, to intrust with the whole management of an affair, as man in whom we have full confidence (much stronger than thok-tiōng).

tit [R. tek, to obtain; to get; to acquire; may; can], to get (but rarely used alone; usually an auxiliary expressing ability, possibility, or accomplishment; very often enclitic after a verb, meaning that it may or can be done; enclitic also with some other shades of meaning).

tit-sit, to get or lose (v. sit). **tit-lâng-thiàⁿ**, readily taking people's affections. **bōe-tit i hoaⁿ-hí**, unable to please him, as man whom we try to flatter, or as a fretful child. **beh-tit lí--ê siau-sit**, I will procure for you the information you wish. **ài-tit**, to wish to —. **ài--tit**, id. **bōe-tit**, cannot —. **i bōe-tit-i--sí, i bōe-tit-i--sí**, two men at deadly feud, and about equally matched. **khiām-chhêng tit-sin**, take care of clothes, and they are as good as new. **ū-thang-tio̍h lán-tit**, there is a way for us to get a portion of it or the benefit of it. **bô-thang-tio̍h lán-tit**, we cannot get any share of it, because the parties who could have allowed it are unwilling. **bōe-tio̍h lán-tit**, we cannot possibly get it; no use making the attempt.

tit--tio̍h, to obtain; to get; to effect. **tit-tio̍h**, id. **ōe-tit--tio̍h**, able to get it. **bōe-tit--tio̍h**, unable to get it. **tit-bōe-tio̍h**, to try, but not get it. **bán-tit-tio̍h**, can be pulled, as fruit in our reach; to recover, as a debt, by getting it from a man who owed money to our debtor.

ōe-tit--thang, able to —; able to make arrangements to —. **ōe-tit--thang àn-niⁿ**, it can be so arranged; that way will do. **bōe-tit-thang-khì**, it will not do to go; cannot manage to go.

oh-tit-kóng, cannot well be told; difficult to tell or say. **oh-tit-thiaⁿ**, difficult to be heard; seldom heard (v. oh).

khiā-tit-tiâu, standing steadily; can hold one's own. **tsòe ōe-tit-lâi**, able to effect it. **tn̄g bōe-tit-khí**, feeling unworthy of so much kindness or honour (v. tn̄g).

ōe-phah-tit-sǹg, can think about it. **ōe-tsú-tit-ì**, can decide for himself (v. tsú). **bô-tā-tit-oā**, cannot help it. **bô-hoat--tit lâng tā-oā**, have no resource against the man.

bōe-phah--tit, exempt from being beaten in court, as graduate or old man. **bōe-kiâⁿ--tit**, ought not to be done; it won't do; cannot be travelled, as road. **ōe-sái--tit**, will do (lit. can be used). **ōe-tsòe--tit**, id. **ōe-tsòe-io̍h--tit**, fit to be used as medicine.

hán--tit, rarely (v. hán). **bo̍h--tit**, do not —! **bo̍h-tit-kóng**, don't speak!

it--tit, to recollect. **kì--tit**, id.; to remember. **bōe-kì--tit**, to forget.

kun-tit, yet after all the same (v. kun).

khah-tit, somewhat improved; a little better, as after severe sickness or trouble; rather better than others or other things, but still only tolerable or passable. **beh-khì, m̄-tit; m̄-khì, iáh m̄-tit**, hardly knowing whether to go or not, as either is very inconvenient. **beh-khì, m̄-tit: beh-tiàm--teh, m̄-tit**, id.; to go or stay, &c.

tit — **ùi-tit-lo̍h** (Cn.), = A. tùi-tá-lo̍h, by what route or road? **kàu-tit-lo̍h** (T.), = A. kàu-tá-lo̍h, up to what point?

tit (R. id.), a brother's son. **tit-á**, id. **tit-lá** (r.), id. **tit-lú**, brother's daughter. **lōe-tit**, son of wife's brother. **khim-tit**, son of wife's sister. **piáu-tit**, son of cousin of different surname (v. piáu). **tit-sun**, son of brother's son (v. sun). **sià-tit** (polite), my nephew. **chhin-tông-tit**, son of cousin (v. tông).

tsȯk-tit, a very distant (junior?) relative of the same surname. **siok-tit**, relatives of same surname. **tsú-tē-tit**, younger relatives. **tsú-tit**, sons, nephews, and such younger relatives as are under our control. **tiau-tok tsú-tit**, to keep younger relatives in proper order.

tit [R. insects torpid or in holes]. **kiⁿ-tit**, March 5th or 6th, when insects are supposed to come out. **kɛⁿ-tit** (C.), id. **lûi kòng-tit, pah-jī-jit**, when it thunders on that day, there will be 120 days of rain. **lûi phah-tit, pah-jī-jit**, id.

tit [R. tī, to meet with; to be worth; to manage; = col. tàt, táh, tėk]. **tit-tn̂g**, the official interpreter in a yamun who interprets verbally between mandarin and people. **tit-hû sù-chiá** (C.), = A. tėk-hû ê sù-chiá, certain spiritual messengers.

tit [R. tėk, specially; of set purpose]. **tit-chhiàⁿ**, to hire specially.

tit (R. id.), straight (lit. or fig.); honest; straightforward; blunt; simple and rather foolish; settled and arranged, as a dispute or quarrel; a sort of game of chance.

hoâiⁿ-tit, straight and across (v. hoâiⁿ). **tit-lu̍t-su̍t**, very straight.

thán-tit, lying straight along (not across), (v. thán). **tó tit-tit**, lying stretched out straight. **khiā-tit**, to stand up straight. **áu-tit**, to straighten by bending. **at-tit**, id. **thit-khi-tit**, make it straight (v. thit).

pî^{n}-tit, pretty straight and level, as road; tolerable, as state of affairs; of moderate talents or tolerably good character (neither very good nor very bad). **chèng-tit**, just, honest, upright. **chià^{n}-tit** (r.), straight, as a thing. **tiong-tit**, upright and straightforward; bold in saying what is right. **sut-tit**, very blunt and plain spoken (v. sut). **gōng-tit**, too blunt; simple and rough. **tsoat-tit**, I am a simple straightforward man. **ngī^{n}-tit**, blunt, straightforward, and honest; not afraid to speak his mind or do his duty, though at the risk of giving offence. **sí-ngī^{n}-tit**, excessively blunt, dogged, or outspoken; *e.g.* running into very great danger for a very small cause, or in order to obey orders to the most minute point. **sí-lâng-tit**, very stiff and dogged; keeping to one's own original plan when the circumstances have totally changed. **sí-tit-tit**, lying out straight, as in a faint or in death.

it-tit, straightforward; determined on a course. **tit-tit-khì**, to go straight forward. **tit-tit-kóng**, to speak boldly and bluntly. **tit-thàu-khì**, to go straight forward, as into a door (v. thàu). **thâu-lō͘ tit**, straightforward in dealings; keeping promises, and at proper times. **bô-tit-lō͘**, crotchety or peculiar in temper, so that it is hard to work with him. **put-tit**, unfair or dishonest, as man. **oh-tit**, difficult to set right, as affair. **bōe-tit**, cannot be put straight, as an affair. **ki^{n}-bōe-tit**, id.; said also of a man constantly borrowing. **tit, kah ná^{n} chhài-koe-chhiu**, as straight as cucumber tendrils! said ironically of man far from straightforward in dealings.

tiâu-tit, arranged and settled, as dispute; completed, as affair; honest and upright, as man. **pān tiâu-tit**, arranged and settled; to manage till all straight. **siá tiâu-tit**, written out well and completely. **bōe-tiâu-tit**, so ignorant of business, &c., that one cannot manage an affair rightly along with him; cannot be put right, as affair. **phái^{n}-kha bōe-tiâu-tit**, hard to get payment out of, as a bad customer.

tit-khùi, a long expiration, inspiration, or jet (v. khùi). **tit-âu**, monotony or broken sound of voice; a deep inspiration (v. âu).

pâi tit-kék, to set out a board for the gambling called "tit." **chiáh-tit**, to play a similar game, but only for amusement, not for gambling. **ūi-tit**, to draw the diagram used for this sort. **teh-tit**, to play one of these games. **kiâ^{n}-tit**, id.

tiu [R. to throw away]. **tiu-tsúi**, to throw into the water, as cargo. **hiet-tiu** (T.), to throw away. **pàng-hiet-tiu** (T.), id. **tòng-hiet-tiu** (T.), id. **tiu-hē** (Cn.), to throw down, as a thing we don't wish.

tiu — **kiēn-tiu**, good-tempered and nice looking, as child; active, fond of playing about pleasantly and not shy.

tiu [R. tiû, grain growing close; closely crowded]. **bát tiu-tiu**, very closely crowded or packed.

sán tiu-tiu, very lean.

âng tiu-tiu, very red.

tiû [R. grain growing close, = col. tiu]. **jîn-ien tiû-bit**, population numerous.

tiû (R. id.), silk stuffs; woven silk; silk goods. **tiû-toān**, silk and satin. **tiû-nńg**, soft silks. **ú-tiû**, thin glossy silk and cotton stuffs. **phàng-tiû**, a thin sort of satin. **mî^{n}-tiû**, a strong mixed silk and cotton stuff of nankeen colour, much used for trowsers. **iû-tiû**, a strong glossy stuff from Canton. **gím-tiû**, flowered silk. **hoe-tiû**, id. **sò͘-tiû**, plain silk stuff. **hún-tiû**, sort of white silk stuff. **kién-tiû**, a silk stuff of a yellowish white. **kán-tiû** (C.), id. **chhun-tiû**, a thin sort of silk. **lêng-tiû**, another thin sort.

tiû [R. embarrassed, undecided]. **tiû-tû**, to be in doubt; wavering; to wait in suspense; undecided in purpose.

tiû [R. a tally; to calculate], a tally; a bamboo tally about two feet long, used in counting bales. **pàng-tiû**, to give out the tally to the coolie. **kiáh-tiû**, to take and carry the tally, as coolie. **kau-tiû**, to give up the tally (along with the bale), as coolie. **siu-tiû**, to receive the tally from the coolie when he gives in the bale.

chiōng-goân-tiû, a game of chance played with dice and slips of ivory or bamboo like lots or tallies, having on them the titles of the literary degrees and ranks from Chiōng-goân downwards; also, these slips themselves.

tiû (Cn.) **kiam toā-tiû**, set at a small angle from one of the four cardinal points, as a house. **chē toā-tiû**, id. **kiam sió-tiû**, set at a larger angle from one of the cardinal points. **chē sió-tiû**, id.

tiû, to clean powdered articles by washing and pouring off the water. **kè-tiû**, to be thus washed. **tiû tsúi-hún**, to wash face-powder.

tiú — **ta-tiú**, now able to take care of itself, as child that does not now need to be constantly tended.

tiú — **pē-tiú-á**, the lark. **pe-tiú-á**, id.

tiù [R. daytime]. **tiù-iā** (R.), day and night.

tiù — **o͘-tiù-tiù**, very black.

tiù (Cn.), to stay regularly or live at a place (R. tsū ?). **tiù-ke**, to have one's family living at a place.

tiū [R. tiōng, a staff], to strike with a small stick.

tiū [R. tiông, long, = col. tn̂g]. **tiū-chhun-hoe**, sort of red flower (v. chhun).

tiū (R. id.) **ú-tiū** (R.), the universe. **í-tiū** (C.), id. (R.)

tiū (R. id.), the tyrant Chow, the last emperor of the Shang dynasty. **kiét-tiū**, the two notorious tyrants Kieh and Chow, of the Hia and Shang dynasties, whose crimes made them lose the throne and put an end to their dynasties by the decree of Heaven. **hā-kiét siong-tiū**, id.

tiū [R. rice full-grown], growing or full-grown rice. **tiū-sūi**, a head or ear of rice. **tiū-chháu**, rice-straw. **tiū-kó**, rice-stalks; straws of rice. **tiū-kó-thâu**, stubble of rice. **tiū-thâu**, id. **tiū-kó-tsáng**, id. **tiū-tháng**, a tub for thrashing rice. **tiū-khûn**, a heap or stack of cut rice. **tiū-pû** (C.), a heap of cut rice.

pò͘-tiū, to plant out young rice. **tiah-tiū**, to pluck off the ears of rice instead of cutting. **siak-tiū**, to thrash rice. **koah-tiū**, to cut the rice; reapers. **koah-tiū-kang**, reapers of the rice-crop. **koah i--ê tiū-á-bé**, to have an intrigue with a woman who already has an intrigue with another man, so drawing her away from him. **ōh i--ê tiū-á-bé** (T.), id.

tiu^{n} [R. tiong, to open out; to stretch or lay out in order; = col. chiang], to make a thing by putting together its parts; to make a pretence; the surname Chang; a sheet, as of paper, &c.; classifier of sheets of paper, letters, picture-sheets, beds, tables, chariots, mills, bows, harps, &c.

tiu^{n}-sa^{n} lí-sì, Mr. So-and-so; any one (v. sa^{n}). **tiu^{n} thien-su**, the Tauist high-priest of China. **tiu^{n} chin-jîn**, name of an idol. **tiu^{n} chin-kun**, id. **tiu^{n} thien-kun**, id.

sin-tiu^n, bodily appearance, as to one's general shape. **hó-sin-tiu^n**, well-formed in person. **hó-si^n-tiu^n**, good-looking.

chin-tiu^n, truly (v. chin).

tiu^n-tî, to be on one's guard; intentionally (v. tî). **tiu^n-hūn**, to distribute into equal portions, arranging them as on a table or other flat place. **ū-pun-tiu^n**, generous; liberal (said of children).

tsú-tiu^n, to determine of one's own will (v. tsú).

tiu^n-iū^n, to put on a false appearance. **tiu^n kàu-bô-iū^n**, very skilful in deception. **tiu^n kàu-hit-iū^n**, so very deceitful! **tiu^n kàu hit-ê-khoán**, id. **gâu-tiu^n**, skilful at deception. **tiu^n sím-mih^n**, for what purpose is he putting on that deceitful appearance? **tiu^n chit-ki-chhùi**, all mere talk without any power (v. chhùi). **tiu^n-khi-bih**, to keep out of the way, pretending not to be present when sought for.

tiu^n-toah, to refuse sulkily as a pretence in order to get more money, &c. (v. toah). **tiu^n-tioh**, id. **tiu^n-lâng**, to pretend not to wish what we really do wish, *e.g.* pretending not to wish a thing, so as to get it cheaper; or refusing to sell, so as to raise the price.

tiu^n-tauh, to lay a trap for a man so as to see what he really is, *e.g.* leaving money open to try his honesty. **tiu^n-tàu**, id.; to pretend not to wish a thing so as to get it cheaper (v. tàu, "to cover").

tiu^n-tàu, to put together, as parts of a machine, or as men for a work (v. tàu, "together").

tiu^n-keng, to string a bow. **tiu^n-mn̂g**, to make a door for a doorway. **tiu^n-phâng**, to fasten a new sail on a boat. **beh-tiu^n-phâng**, I wish a new sail for my boat (said to the sail-maker). **tiu^n-lôe**, to make a plough. **tiu^n-teng kat-chhái**, to hang up lanterns and hangings. **tiu^n oáh-kúi** (C.), to make ingenious contrivances with secret springs, wheels, &c. **tiu^n oàh-kúi** (C.), id.

tiu^n-lāu, to prepare grave-clothes, fittings, and ornaments for one's own burial, while still alive and perhaps quite well. **tiu^n-lāu-sa^n**, grave-clothes made ready beforehand. **tiu^n-lāu ê-mih^n**, coffin, grave-clothes, or such things made ready beforehand for burial.

tiu^n sin-sè, to put one's self in position with reference to another, *e.g.* preparing for fighting, or throwing a ball or shuttlecock; to put on some special false appearance, *e.g.* airs of importance, or a bland kind manner, &c.

chit-tiu^n-pút, one picture of an idol on paper not yet pasted. **nn̄g-tiu^n-phoe**, two letters.

tiû^n [R. tiông (C. chhiâng), an area; an arena; a place for market, examinations, gambling, or such crowded busy operations; = col. chhiâng], classifier of examinations for degrees, and of some sorts of busy or long-continued affairs.

soa^n-tiû^n, the country, as opposed to large towns. **chháu-tiû^n** (C.), grassy ground (v. chháu). **sit-tiû^n** (r.), cultivated fields. **iâm-tiû^n**, salt-pans (v. iâm). **tiám hiét-tiû^n**, to mark out the precise position for a grave on a site already chosen.

hi-tiû^n, a market-place. **hu-tiû^n**, id. **chièn-tiû^n**, a battle-field. **kà-tiû^n**, a review-ground. **kà-tiû^n-pe**, id. **hoat-tiû^n**, an execution-ground; the place where Tauist priests work magical ceremonies. **kóng-ké-tiû^n**, a place where stories are read or told for money. **kiáu-tiû^n**, a gambling place. **pó-tiû^n**, a place for gambling with the "lién-pó." **lién-pó-tiû^n**, id. **hoe-hē-tiû^n**, place for gambling with the "hoe-hē."

kang-tiû^n (C.), work.

khang-khè-tiû^n, a place where work, such as building, is being done. **seng-lí-tiû^n**, place or arena of trade; affairs of trade. **koa^n-tiû^n ê-lâng**, a man who has had much intercourse with mandarins.

khe-tiû^n, examinations for degrees. **kho-tiû^n** (C.), id. **thâu-tiû^n**, the first examination for the Kujin degree. **jī-tiû^n**, the second examination for it. **sa^n-tiû^n**, the third. **sa^n-tiû^n thàu**, having passed the three examinations for Kujin. **kú-jîn-tiû^n**, examinations for Kujin degree. **hōe-sì-tiû^n**, examinations for the Tsin-sze degree. **chìn-sū-tiû^n**, id.

tiû^n-nâ^n, sort of basket used by students going to the examinations.

siu-tiû^n, to close up an affair. **sėk-tiû^n**, thoroughly experienced, as in gambling. **koàn-tiû^n**, to be the best in a competition, as a literary essay, or as a horse or game-cock; said also of men racing, and sometimes of other competitions. **kài-tiû^n**, id. **hiá^n-tiû^n**, losing one's presence of mind; flurried, as at an examination or in transacting important business at a critical time. **lîm-tiû^n**, to enter the field of battle or place of examination. **jip-tiû^n**, to enter the literary examinations. **jip toā-tiû^n**, to enter the examination for Tsin-sze. **bat-chiū^n toā-tiû^n**, to have managed matters of considerable importance, or to have had intercourse with men of high rank. **bōe-chiū^n toā-tiû^n**, unfit to be used on important business, as man.

chit-tiû^n-sū, one whole affair or piece of business from beginning to end, with all the details involved in or connected with it. **chit-tiû^n tāi-chì**, id. **chit-tiû^n ê tāi-chì**, id. **chit-tiû^n ê hó-ì**, a benevolent action. **chit-tiû^n lāu-jiėt**, a great concourse of people, as at some festival, or amusement, or joyful ceremonies. **chit-tiû^n ê lāu-jiėt**, id. **chit-tiû^n chhiāng-chhiāng-kún**, a great number of people come together and making a great noise. **chit-tiû^n-ōe**, the whole talk or story about one subject from beginning to end. **chit-tiû^n lóng-sī lí-ê-ōe**, you have all the talk to yourself. **mē^n chit-tiû^n**, to burst into a fit of scolding or railing. **chit-tiû^n-ōe**, this talk about one matter. **chit-tiû^n-sū**, this one matter.

tiú^n [R. tióng, to grow; greater; senior; superior; = col. chiáng; by change of tone from "tiông," long]. **hâng-tiú^n**, the hired manager of a large hong. **hé-tiú^n**, the captain of a junk or ship; the sailing-master. **hóe-tiú^n** (C.), id. **hōe-tiú^n**, head man of a meeting or association. **hoat-tiú^n**, the chief of a company of four boys at an idolatrous procession.

pó-tiú^n, the tepo or head man of a ward. **liēn-tiú^n**, the head man of a subdivision of a ward (v. liēn). **kah-tiú^n**, the head man over ten families. **tūi-tiú^n**, officer in command of a small body of soldiers. **ėk-tiú^n**, an officer on the general's staff for consulting on plan of battle or campaign. **tsai-tiú^n**, an official who disburses the money prizes at the Giók-pîn academy.

tsók-tiú^n, the head of a clan. **pâng-tiú^n**, the head of a branch of a clan. **siā-tiú^n**, a village elder; a head man in a village. **ke-tiú^n**, a village elder; the head or manager of a large mercantile house; polite phrase in addressing an old man. **toā-ke-tiú^n**, the principal elder of a village or of a group of villages. **ke-tiú^n-hōe**, an assembly of village elders, as of a very large village or of a group of villages.

tiú^n-ló, (X.) an elder in the church; a presbyter. **tiú^n-ló-hōe**, (X.) a consistory or kirk-session.

tiú^n, a small gong in a wicker frame, used in some ceremonies. **tiú^n-tiú^n**, sound of striking such a small gong. **tiú^n-tiú^n-háu**, sound of small gongs; said also of a child or boy talking a great deal too much. **phah tiú^n-tiú^n**, to make a sound with a small gong, as some sorts of pedlars. **tsòe phah-tiú^n-tiú^n**, to be such a small pedlar (many of them buy stolen articles).

tiù^n (R. tiòng), a pair of curtains opening at the middle. **báng-tiù^n**, mosquito-curtains. **báng-tiù^n-kau**, hooks for keeping them open. **sîn-tiù^n**, a pair of curtains in front of an idol's shrine. **pút-tiù^n**, id. of Buddhist idol. **ang-tiù^n** (C.), id. **chiong-kun-tiù^n**, curtains hung on the tribunal of a high mandarin (civil or military) where he sits in judgment. **kiō-tiù^n**, curtains in front of mandarin's sedan.

tiù^n-chhiu, fringes of curtains. **tiù^n-bî**, embroidered or painted top of bed-curtains in front. **tiù^n-kau**, hooks for curtains. **tiù^n-chha**, pieces of cloth for fastening curtains to bed-posts (v. chha). **tiù^n-pâng** (r.), a tent.

tiù^n, to make a dress of two different sorts of stuff, outside and lining. **tiù^n-lí**, to make a dress with a lining; to put a lining into a dress. **tiù^n sím-mih^n-lí**, of what stuff will you make the lining?

tiù^n [R. tiòng, a swelling, esp. dropsical, and of the belly], feeling of overloaded stomach, or of indigestion. **siau-tiù^n**, to reduce a swelling or distention of the belly, &c.

tiù^n-hong, belly swollen, as with wind, *e.g.* after eating pease; very full of wind, as a sail. **tiù^n-khì**, feeling of repletion and overloaded stomach, or of indigestion. **tiù^n-lâng**, full of matter and about to burst, as boil or carbuncle. **tiù^n-tsúi**, swollen with damp or water-logged, as wood or leather; full of water, as a diseased swelling of the body. **tiù^n-jiō**, the bladder too much distended, as from difficulty of passing water or want of opportunity.

pá-tiù^n, having eaten too much (v. pá). **tiù^n ân-ân**, distended and tight, as belly with over-eating or with wind. **pak-tó tiù^n**, belly overloaded or swollen. **chiàh kàu pak-tó tiù^n-phoà**, to eat till ready to burst. **kóng-ōe, tiù^n-phoà lâng--ê pak-tó-tñg**, to talk in such an irritating way as to make the hearer burst with rage.

tiù^n-kui, having the crop very much distended, as fowl that has eaten voraciously, or that has been stuffed to make it weigh heavy. **tiù^n-kui--sí**, to die of being so stuffed. **kóng-ōe tiù^n-ām-kui**, so full of rage as to speak in a loud indistinct way, as if choking with rage. **kóng-ōe, tiù^n ām-kún-kui**, id. **chhi^n-kun tiù^n-ām**, the veins appearing swollen on the neck of man talking loud, long, and excitedly.

tiù^n-ti, pûi; tiù^n-káu, sán; tiù^n-lâng, chiâ^n hông-thán, by eating enormously a pig grows fat, a dog grows lean, and a man gets jaundice.

tiù^n [R. tiòng, to overflow], to swell high, as tide or flood; to raise, as a sunken or stranded vessel, by floating it with caissons or logs of wood, &c. **tiù^n-oá**, to raise and float ashore, as wreck, by such means.

tiù^n tiàu-e-bé, to help to raise the short heavy end of a well-sweep while another man is pulling down the long arm.

tiù^n (C.), to pull; only in some phrases (cf. tiuh, tioh).

tiū^n [R. tiōng, a measure of ten feet, = col. tñg], husband of aunt; also (Cn.), husband of elder sister.

tiū^n-lâng, wife's father. **tiū^n-m̄**, wife's mother. **tiū^n-lâng-chek**, younger brother of wife's father. **tiū^n-lâng-peh**, elder brother of wife's father.

toā-tiū^n, eldest brother of aunt, either of paternal or maternal aunt. **sòe-tiū^n**, husband of youngest aunt. **á-tiū^n**, aunt's husband! (said in addressing him). **î-tiū^n**, husband of maternal aunt, or of mother's cousin. **ko-tiū^n**, husband of paternal aunt. **tông-ko-tiū^n**, husband of father's cousin of same surname.

tâng-mñg-tiū^n, husband of wife's sister.

chí-tiū^n (Cn.), husband of elder sister. **goán-tiū^n** (Cn.), my elder sister's husband.

tiuh, to beat, as the pulse; to have a slight twitching feeling on the skin; (also, C. = tioh, to pull).

tiuh chih-bé, to lisp in speaking (v. chih). **tiuh-tôe**, to have a slight limp.

tiuh-tiuh (Cn.), to twitch one's clothes so as to throw off dust, &c.

tiùh — **sán tiùh-tiùh**, very lean.

tng [R. tong, to bear; to support; ought; then: at that time; = col. ta^n, tǹg, tàng, tong], to bear; to sustain, as an office or honour; to lie in wait for; to lay a trap for.

tng-tñg, in open court. **tng-bīn**, face to face. **tng-bīn kóng**, to speak face to face. **tng-bīn hó, tng-bīn liông-pōe**, from state of prosperity suddenly fallen into great distress.

tng-chhám, just now become very miserable. **teh-tng-heng**, in great repute, as idol. **tng hoat-chi^n**, just now making much money. **hé tng-hoat**, frantic with rage; sudden conflagration or inflammation (v. hoat). **tng i siá-jī**, just when he was writing. **jit tng-kiā**, sun just at zenith. **tng-ióng**, just about come to one's full strength; also, to be a militiaman or brave (v. ióng). **tng-hó**, just now prosperous.

tng hit-tiáp, just then; just at that time. **tng-sî**, just at the time (not said of future time). **tng-sî hó**, just now prosperous. **tng-hit-sî**, just at that time. **tng-sî-sî**, just in season, as fruit. **chià^n-tng-sî**, just at the proper time or season, as ripe fruit, or as young strong man about 17. **tng khí-thâu**, just at the beginning. **tng-chhoe**, id. (v. chhoe). **tng goân-chhe**, id. (v. goân). **tng goân-chhe** (C.), just at the beginning. **tng goân-chhe** (A.), to be a constable.

tng teng-hé hoa, may I die as this lamp goes out that is burning before me! (said by a man in swearing).

tng-tán, to watch for a man, as in order to catch or injure him, or to be on our guard against a thief or man going to injure us; to be watching for an opportunity, as man out of employment waiting for a job. **tng-tán hé-hoa**, taking the opportunity of the lamp going out.

tng-chhát, to lay wait for a thief. **tng-chiáu**, to lay a trap for a bird. **tng hé-bāng**, to set the net called "hé-bāng," and wait for the tide. **chhìn-bê tng iau-lâng**, cold rice will catch a hungry man. **chhìn-pūi^n tng iau-lâng** (C.), id. **phoà-ké tng khit-chiàh**, a bit of a cake attracts a beggar.

tam-tng, to sustain or be able to bear, as an office, responsibility, or honour. **tng chit-jīm**, to bear office. **tng-chhe**, to be employed as a messenger or servant by mandarins (v. chhe). **tng-peng**, to be a soldier. **sin-tng--ê**, raw recruits. **tng-nî^n**, one's year come (in turn) for some duty or office, *e.g.* for care of worship. **sî kàu, sî tng**, bear it when the time comes; *e.g.* you need not be anxious; or, I don't care now. **sûi kàu, sûi tng**, id.

tng-bōe-lâi, unable for such duties, or for such a business. **tng-bōe-tiâu**, cannot bear or undertake it; I feel unworthy of such honour or kindness. **tng-m̄-khí**, feeling unworthy of such kindness or condescension. **tng-bōe-khí**, unable to undertake such a difficult business or office; feeling unworthy of such kindness or politeness. **tng bōe-tit-khí**, id. **tng bōe-tit-tiâu**, unable to make head against the calamity, or to bear severe pain or sickness; unable for such important and difficult duties or office.

tí-tng, to bear, as responsibility; to bear the brunt of opposing, or the duty of resisting, *e.g.* of resisting a robber when guarding a house, or of keeping away people who come to stop a work. **bōe--chiá tí-tng**, the seller bears the responsibility, as of the deeds. **káⁿ tí-tng**, not afraid to bear the responsibility or to resist; willing to bear the expense, *e.g.* of entertaining guests whom some one must take in. **káⁿ kap--i tí-tng**, I am not afraid to resist or fight with him, or to go to law with him if he accuse me.

tn̂g [R. tông, the Tang dynasty], a surname. **tn̂g-lâng**, a Chinaman. **tn̂g-soaⁿ**, China, but usually not including Formosa. **tn̂g-ōe hoan-jī**, Chinese words written in foreign characters, *e.g.* in Roman type. **tn̂g-jī**, Chinese characters.

tn̂g [R. tông, an artificial pond or tank], a word much used in the names of villages, esp. of military stations and stages on great roads.

tî-tn̂g, ponds and tanks of various sorts, large and small, natural and artificial.

thê-tn̂g, the office at the provincial capital for transmitting imperial despatches, &c. (v. thê).

tn̂g (R. tiông), long; to have a balance in hand, especially of another's money committed to us for some special purpose.

tn̂g-té, long and short (v. té). **kú-tn̂g**, for a long time (v. kú).

tn̂g-kang, a person hired for a term of some length. **tn̂g-pái**, a junk that plies with goods once in several days. **tn̂g-niⁿ**, for the whole year, *e.g.* making agreement for labour for the whole year, or to buy goods or food for the whole year. **khah-ū tn̂g-mn̂g**, steady and safe, as trade or friendship (v. mn̂g, "gate"). **tn̂g-thâu-mn̂g**, the long-haired or Taiping rebels. **tn̂g-miāⁿ**, long-lived. **tn̂g-hè-siū**, longevity. **tn̂g-saⁿ**, a long gown, robe, or dress. **tn̂g-hiû**, a long warm dress.

bô-lē-tn̂g, utterly wanting in ability. **bô chit-lē-tn̂g**, id. **khah-ū lē-tn̂g**, has a good deal of ability, or more ability.

chhun-tn̂g, to stretch out long, as caterpillar, or as branches of tree gradually lengthening or encroaching; interest or gains accumulating. **chhun tn̂g-chhiú**, to be a beggar. **chhun-tn̂g kè-lâi**, to grow longer and gradually encroach or cover, as branches of tree. **ū-chhun-tn̂g**, interest or gains gradually accumulating.

sé-tn̂g--ê, the amount of gain on a transaction; the balance of clear gain, as at end of month or year. **ū-khah-tn̂g, chiah beh-khì**, will go if a good deal more (or a considerable sum) can be earned by it. **ū-tn̂g, chiah beh-khì**, id. **lí tò-tn̂g--goá saⁿ-pah-chîⁿ**, you have 300 cash of mine in your hands, as of balance on commission or change of a dollar. **hē--i tò-tn̂g--khì**, to have a balance of money lying in his hands. **goá hē--lí tò-tn̂g joā-tsōe**, what balance of my money have you still on hand? **goá hē--lí tn̂g--khì saⁿ-pah**, you have still 300 cash of mine in your hands. **goá saⁿ-pah hē--lí tn̂g--khì**, id. **tn̂g joā-tsōe-chîⁿ tī-lí-tau**, how many cash of mine have you still on hand? **tn̂g-lí joā-tsōe**, how much of your money is still in my hands as a balance? **tn̂g koá-chîⁿ**, there is a balance of a few cash over. **tn̂g-chîⁿ joā-tsōe**, what balance is over still to be returned?

tn̂g-chîⁿ (Cn.), = A. kə-tai-chîⁿ, idolatrous paper in long shreds in bundles (v. tai).

tn̂g [R. tiông, bowels, = col. chhiâng]. **tn̂g-á**, bowels; entrails. **toā-tn̂g**, the great entrails; the colon (s. hall). **toā-tn̂g koàn-tsùt-bí**, sort of rice-sausage. **toā-tn̂g jip tsùt-bí**, id. **tn̂g-thâu**, the anus. **thé tn̂g-thâu**, to have internal piles coming down. **thut tn̂g-thâu**, id. **lâu toā-tn̂g-thâu**, id. **siⁿ-tn̂g**, the womb of mammalia, but not said of women's; the ovary of a bird. **tē-tn̂g-am**, said of a literary man pretending to collect money for building a temple, and spending it on his own belly.

tn̂g-tē, the intestines; the inner part of a man (literal or figurative). **koah tn̂g-tē**, to hurt the bowels, as poison; to wound the heart, as severe grief. **koah tn̂g koah-tē**, id. **koah sim-tn̂g**, id. **koah-lâng sim-tn̂g**, to grieve one very much, *e.g.* the death of a son (+). **lėk-tn̂g lėk-tē**, very much exhausted by great labour of body or mind. **sim-pak tn̂g-tē**, heart, bowels, and intestines (lit. or fig.), (+). **hó sim-tn̂g**, kind-hearted; compassionate. **sim-tn̂g nn̂g**, very soft-hearted; easily prevailed upon to grant a request. **phāiⁿ-sim-tn̂g**, having a cruel or unfeeling heart. **phoà-pak thiu-tn̂g**, to cut open the belly and draw out the bowels, one of the punishments of the Buddhist hell. **phoà-pak liû-tn̂g**, id.

tn̂g (R. tông), a hall, as in a large house or public building; classifier of examinations in court.

tiong-tn̂g, the middle hall of a large house (s. part). **thiaⁿ-tn̂g**, the large central hall in a very large house. **tn̂g-tsàh**, the wooden partition (with doors in it) across the central hall of a large house. **tn̂g-tsâiⁿ-āu**, the back part of a central hall thus divided (it is smaller than the front part).

toā-tn̂g, a mandarin's hall of judgment (s. entrails). **toā-tn̂g-goā**, in the outer part of the yamun. **jī-tn̂g**, a second hall behind the public hall for more private examinations. **āu-tn̂g**, id. **kong-tn̂g**, a mandarin's hall of justice. **chì-kong-tn̂g**, the upper part of the hall for the examination of candidates for the Kujin degree, where the examiner sits. **chhoan-tn̂g**, the inner hall just behind the great hall of a yamun. **tng-tn̂g**, in open court. **chē-tn̂g**, to sit on the tribunal. **seng-tn̂g**, to enter the hall and take his seat on the tribunal. **chiūⁿ-tn̂g**, to appear before the tribunal. **thè-tn̂g**, to leave the tribunal, as mandarin when the business is over. **tn̂g-téng**, on the tribunal or judgment-seat; also, the upper part of the examination hall near the examiner. **thiau-tn̂g**, to call up a young and talented student near the examiner's seat.

tn̂g-keng, evidence given in court. **tn̂g-khàn**, the mandarin examining with the papers of which side the verbal evidence agrees. **tn̂g-jū**, a written order issued by the mandarin on the tribunal. **tn̂g-jī** (C.), id.

chiàⁿ-tn̂g, the principal mandarin of a place, as opposed to his assistants. **tsó-tn̂g**, the literary mandarin (ló-su) of a Foo or Hien district, or the chief one if there be two. **iū-tn̂g**, assistant literary mandarin of a district; sometimes said of other assistant mandarin. **tit-tn̂g**, interpreter between mandarin and people.

oh-tn̂g, a school-house. **sû-tn̂g**, an ancestral temple. **lé-pài-tn̂g**, a chapel or church. **chhài-tn̂g**, public hall of vegetarians. **iok-eng-tn̂g**, foundling hospital. **ióng-seng-tn̂g**, id. **bêng-lûn-tn̂g**, the great hall of a Confucian temple.

tn̂g [R. toān, a bit or piece, = col. toāⁿ], (C. tūiⁿ), a

厦英大辭典

piece of any long-shaped thing broken or cut in two, esp. about a half; one end of a long thing consisting of two distinct parts, though not sundered; *e.g.* the upper and lower parts of the trunk, or of a door in two very different forms above and below; (used in pedlar's slang to mean 50 cash).

tùi-tn̂g, at or by a half; taking a half; *e.g.* cutting or breaking across into about equal halves. **tsòe nn̄g-tn̂g**, making two pieces of it, *e.g.* of a stick or sugar-cane cut across. **tsām tsòe nn̄g-tn̂g**, cut it across into two pieces by one blow, as of a knife, chisel, or axe. **saⁿ-tn̂g**, three pieces of a long thing.

tiong-tn̂g, the middle part (s. hall). **poàⁿ-tiong-tn̂g soah--khì**, to fail half-way. **téng-tn̂g**, the upper end or part. **ē-tn̂g**, the lower half or part, *e.g.* lower part of the body, *i.e.* the belly and under. **sng chit-tn̂g**, half the body all sore, as with rheumatism or long sitting.

phiáh-tn̂g, a brick broken across about the middle, used for building. **tsúi-khò-tn̂g**, very short trowsers or drawers like bathing-drawers or caleçons. **khò-tn̂g** (Cn.), id.

tn̂g [same as previous word? or R. tông? a boy, a lad, = col. tâng].

lâng-tn̂g, a lad about 15 or 16, just changing from boy to lad; a hobbledehoy. **lâng-tn̂g-á**, id. **chiàⁿ-lâng-tn̂g**, to be a big boy or boyish lad.

tńg [R. toān, to cut; to sever; = col. tn̄g]. **tńg-tsâi**, to cut the navel-string of a new-born child. **koah-bah chit-tńg-thiàⁿ**, to get it over by one bitter pang (v. thiàⁿ).

tńg — **pàng-tiau pàng-tńg**, to intimidate; to threaten (cf. háng).

tńg [R. tiōng, to overflow; to rise high, as tide; sometimes read "tióng," = col. tiùⁿ], to rise, as the tide. **tsúi tńg**, tide rising; flood-tide; tide beginning to flow. **tsúi-tńg-koe**, a fowl crowing about midnight; not a bad omen.

tńg-thâu, the first of the flood-tide (s. turn).

tńg [R. tióng, to grow; to increase; senior; = col. tiúⁿ, chiáng; by change of tone from "tiông," long, = col. tn̂g]. **tńg toā-lâng**, to become an adult, or of marriageable age, as boy or girl. **tńg-pìⁿ**, id. **tńg-chhiâⁿ**, id. **tńg m̄-chiâⁿ-chhiâⁿ**, weak and sickly about that age. **tńg-m̄-chiâⁿ**, id. **tńg-m̄-khí**, weak about that age, as from want of good food or from disease, so as to be small and puny-looking all one's life. **beh-tńg**, just about to be of the age of puberty. **bē-tńg-kut**, not yet come to the age of puberty, as boy.

tńg — **tńg-liên-hoân**, to fire numerous guns in rapid succession, making a running fire.

tńg [R. tsoán, to turn; to transfer], (C. túiⁿ, in most of the phrases], to turn about; to return: to manage and arrange, as a dispute, as a third party does.

tńg-lâi tńg-khì, to turn back and forwards. **chiàⁿ-tńg**, to turn in the direction of the hands of a watch; opposed to "tò-tńg." **îⁿ-îⁿ-tńg**, to whirl about, as a top or wheel. **tńg-sėh**, to revolve, as a ball, or as a star; to arrange a quarrel, as an arbiter.

tńg hong-bīn, wind changing; to change from anger or displeasure to friendliness. **tńg lâm-hong**, to change to a south wind.

tńg-tsn̄g, Buddhist rites for the soul of a woman who has died in the first month after childbirth (v. tsn̄g).

tńg-chhù, bride going to make a short call at her parents' house, but not passing the night (usually four days after marriage). **siang-lâng-tńg**, both bride and bridegroom making this call.

oāⁿ-tńg-chhiú, to change hands, as in carrying a heavy thing; or as showing one hand after the other to doctor to feel the pulse; or to fortune-teller (+). **tńg-keng**, to change a load from one shoulder to the other, as coolie or chair-bearer. **tńg-liâu**, to change the rate of a song. **tńg khah-kín**, to change to a quicker rate. **bōe-tńg-siaⁿ**, unable to pronounce articulately, as in severe illness, or from singing too long.

tńg-âng, to put on ordinary dress when putting off mourning; to change to red colour, as fruit or face; to grow reddish and just ready to die, as rice-plants in drought. **tńg-hân**, to become suddenly cold and dangerously ill. **tńg khé-phê**, wound healed so far that the new skin is forming, and the old peeling off at the edges.

tńg-bák, to give a quick peculiar glance with the eye, as on seeing a man do something wrong, or when he is just going to do it, so as to prevent him. **bák-chiu tńg-lûn**, eyes turning round and showing the white, esp. as superior displeased at what an inferior is doing or just going to do. **bák-chiu bōe-tńg-lûn**, eyes immovable, as when about to die, or in a long steady angry stare.

chhiò kàu-bōe tńg-khùi, to laugh till quite out of breath.

tńg-sin, to turn one's self round. **bōe-tńg-sin**, unable to turn one's self; unable to set the matter right without loss of influence or reputation; having no place for reply or excuse, and so utterly ashamed. **bô tńg-sin ê sé-tsāi**, id. **oát-tńg-sin**, to turn one's self round so as to look back; immediately.

oát-tńg-thâu, to turn one's head round; to turn round. **chit-ē-khì, bô-tńg-thâu**, to go and not come back at all.

oát-lìn-tńg, to turn one's self round (v. lìn). **oát-tńg-lâi**, to turn one's self (or one's head) round, *e.g.* to look at or face a man; to turn a thing round to face us; to take a walk and come back. **thâu-khak oát-tńg-lâi**, to turn one's head round. **oát-tńg-chhiú**, to stretch out the hand backwards with the palm backwards; immediately. **oát-tńg-chhiú lâi-khiú--i**, turned his hand backwards and caught him (+).

oat-tńg-chhiú, chiū-sī, just turn off the road at that place and you are at it.

tò-tńg, to turn back or round. **oát-tò-tńg**, to turn back; to turn the wrong end, as of a book (+). **tò-tńg--khì**, to turn round and come backwards. **péng-tò-tńg**, to turn upside down or wrong side up; to invert. **chē-tò-tńg**, to take back an article which the purchaser returns. **théh-tò-tńg**, to take back (a thing). **thó tò-tńg**, to demand back, as property, especially what we have a right to claim and redeem.

tńg khah-hó-liōng, become less strict and exacting, esp. not minute about money matters. **hôe-sim tńg-ì**, to change one's mind towards good. **pháiⁿ tńg-chiâⁿ-hó**, to change from badness to goodness.

tńg chih-koan, to change one's line of argument merely to oppose what the other says, without regard to truth. **sûi-sî-tńg**, to accommodate one's self and one's plans to the change of circumstances. **bô-chhûn āu-tńg**, not making proper provision for the future.

tsai-tńg, willingly receiving advice, correction, or reproof, and making good use of it. **m̄-tsai-tńg**, unwilling to take advice or correction, or to accept the good offices of an arbiter; incorrigible. **phah-thâu,**

chiū-tsai tńg-bé, on hearing the beginning he understands how to bring it to a proper conclusion.

tńg-tó, to be in constant and profitable circulation, as money always invested to good purpose and rapidly making profit over and over. **gâu tńg-tó**, skilful at making rapid and large returns out of one's money. **tńg-tó--khì hó-sè**, money laid out so as to make large and rapid returns.

seng-lí tńg, one's trade improving. **seng-lí khah-tńg**, id. **seng-lí tsòe-m̄-tńg**, trade all gone wrong.

tńg-sńg (T.), to set right an affair that would have been hopeless in other hands, as a skilful or influential friend; to make a business profitable under great difficulties, *e.g.* with very little capital. **tńg-tak** (T.), id.; esp. of a business with very small capital; often has the idea of being rather too sharp. **chhit-oaiⁿ, poeh tńg-tak** (T.), constantly finding means of getting money out of people, either quite wrongly or considerably too much.

tńg-sū, to adjust and arrange a dispute or feud, as a mutual friend or mediator by his good offices. **tńg tāi-chì**, id. **tńg-bōe-chiâⁿ**, unable to arrange the quarrel properly. **tńg-bōe-lâi**, id. **tńg bōe-tit-lâi**, id. **bōe-tńg--tit**, the feud is too violent or the case too bad to be settled thus.

tǹg [R. tòng, suitable; safe; firm; to pledge or pawn; = col. tàng; by change of tone from "tong," to bear; ought; to take the responsible management of, = col. tng, taⁿ], to pawn; to put in pledge. **kā-lâng-tǹg**, to take on mortgage.

tsún-tǹg, a pledge between friends, not in a pawnshop. **sìn-tǹg**, to give a thing in pledge for its full value, or more than its value, at a pawnshop where the head or one of the assistants is an acquaintance; the ticket is marked "sìn-tǹg," and it is a point of honour that it is to be redeemed, or that it is not to be sold without warning.

tǹg-tiàm, a pawnshop. **tién-tǹg** (Cn.), id. **tǹg-phiò**, a pawn-ticket. **tǹg-thâu**, a thing pawned. **thó tǹg-thâu**, to redeem a pledge. **thó-tǹg** (Cn.), id.

lí kàn-tǹg (Cn. T.), why have you brought this evil on yourself so as to get no pity? **lí kàn-tǹg kàu-àn-niⁿ** (Cn. T.), id.

bóe hoe-tǹg (Cn.), = A. teh hoe-hē, a sort of gambling. **hoe-tǹg-soaⁿ** (Cn.), a place where this sort of gambling is carried on.

tǹg (= tn̄g). **ǹg-tǹg**, = ǹg-tǹg, obstinately self-willed, as young person.

tǹg (cf. thǹg, tūn, thǹg), (C. tùiⁿ), to warm slightly over a small stove. **tǹg-sio**, id.

tǹg [R. tùn, to bow the head to the ground; to adjust; a meal], (C. tùiⁿ), a meal; classifier of meals. **chit-tǹg-pn̄g**, one meal. **chit-tǹg-pn̄g-kú**, about half an hour, or nearly an hour. **sóe pn̄g-tǹg**, to get a meal out of a man by sorning on him. **sòng kàu-bô-chit-tǹg**, just starving with poverty. **chhī pē-bú, siàu-tǹg**, he counts every meal his parents get (v. chhī).

kiám-tǹg, to want a meal; to abstain from a meal, as from want of leisure. **kiám toā-tǹg**, to abstain from breakfast occasionally, as a superstitious observance, gen. on 1st and 15th of the month, often done by women. **iau-ki sit-tǹg**, hungry or starving from want of a meal or meals. **chiáh--liáu bô-chiàu-sî-tǹg**, eating at irregular hours.

mńg-tǹg (Cn.), supper. **ê-hng-tǹg**, id. **chiáh tsá-tǹg** (Cn.), to take breakfast.

tǹg [same as previous word?] (C. tùiⁿ, in some phrases; but in some others "tɛh" is used instead).

tǹg--lòh-khì, to set down heavily; to fall down heavily. **tǹg-poàh-chē**, to come down unexpectedly on the ground, when meaning to sit down on a chair where there is none. **tǹg-kha** (C. tsàm-kha), to stamp with the foot. **tǹg koáiⁿ-á**, to strike with a walking-stick straight down on the ground or floor, in sign of anger. **tǹg-í tǹg-toh**, to strike chair and table in anger.

tǹg sim-koaⁿ, to strike one's breast, as when terribly disappointed at losing a good opportunity, especially by one's own fault, or at finding good news to be false. **tǹg-heng**, to beat one's breast with the palm, in great displeasure or anger, esp. when determined to quarrel; also (C. tùiⁿ-heng), to beat one's breast with a large stone, as beggars do. **tǹg-heng phoà-hiáh**, to wound breast and forehead, as beggars do.

tǹg-ìn (C. tɛh-ìn), to stamp with a seal or stamp. **tǹg-jī**, to stamp characters, as on goods. **tǹg jī-hō** (C. tɛh), to stamp a shop-mark. **tǹg-âng** (C. tɛh-âng), to stamp with red ink. **tǹg-oân**, to receipt an account by stamping the word "oân."

tn̄g (= tǹg). **ǹg-tn̄g**, = ǹg-tǹg, idle, self-willed, proud, and obstinate, as child or young person who will not obey orders (cf. hòng-tōng?)

tn̄g [R. tōng? a tub for washing]; to rinse with water after washing; to wash a second time. **koh-tn̄g**, id. **sóe-tn̄g**, to wash and rinse or wash a second time. **ka-tn̄g** (C. kɛ-tn̄g), id. (s. sever).

tn̄g [R. tiōng, a measure of 10 feet, = col. tiūⁿ], a chang, or measure of 10 Chinese feet. **tn̄g-it**, 11 feet. **tn̄g-jī**, 12 feet. **tn̄g-jī-thûi**, a long club, 12 feet long. **tn̄g-saⁿ, liên gō͘-chhùn**, 13 feet 5 inches. **jī-tn̄g sì**, 24 feet. **nn̄g-tn̄g**, 20 feet.

niûⁿ-tn̄g, to measure how many chang. **niûⁿ kúi-tn̄g**, id.

tn̄g — **lō͘-tn̄g**, the road-way; a much-frequented road (s. sever). **toā-lō͘-tn̄g**, a much-frequented road. **hit--ê sī lō͘-tn̄g**, that is a place where people constantly walk. **tú-á tī lō͘-tn̄g**, just in the very road-way. **m̄-thang-hē tī lō͘-tn̄g**, don't lay it in the road or door-way, where people constantly walk. **m̄-thang-chē tī-lō͘-tn̄g**, don't sit in the road, &c.

tn̄g [R. toān, to sever; to cut or break asunder], (C. tūiⁿ), to cut asunder; to break in two; to sever; to cut off; to discontinue; to cease.

lō͘ tn̄g, not having any intercourse; not coming and going; having no means of livelihood (s. road-way). **thâu-lō͘ tn̄g**, having no means of livelihood. **tn̄g-lō͘**, to leave off going to a place, *e.g.* breaking off bad courses practised there, or having a quarrel or owing a debt there. **kap--i tn̄g-lō͘**, having no more intercourse with him.

that-tn̄g, to block up, as road. **that-tn̄g lâng-ê-lō͘**, to be an obstacle in a man's way (usually figurative). **keh-tn̄g**, to separate, as a wall or river, &c. **kàn-tn̄g**, to break a constant succession.

kat-tn̄g, to have no more intercourse; to break off intercourse. **koah-tn̄g**, to cut off or asunder with a knife, by drawing the knife along. **tsám-tn̄g**, to cut off or asunder with one blow of a sword, knife, or axe; to cut off, as friendship (v. tsám). **tsām-tn̄g**, to cut in two with a chisel. **liàm-bōe-tn̄g**, cannot well

海上絲綢之路文獻集成 科技與文化编

break off the connection, or cannot find it in one's heart to do so, *e.g.* when a near relative has done something very bad, or in the case of an illicit connection. **ka-tn̂g**, to cut asunder with scissors (s. rinse). **kā-tn̂g**, to bite asunder.

sńg-tn̂g, to spoil, as a thing (v. sńg). **phah-tn̂g**, to break; to spoil.

tn̂g-khùi, to expire (v. khùi). **tn̂g-lin**, to wean. **tn̂g-leng**, id. **tn̂g-kun** (C. tūiⁿ-kin), to cut up by the roots; to remove utterly, as a disease or bad habit or band of robbers. **tn̂g-chiúⁿ**, to have a line quite across one's palm (v. chiúⁿ). **phah-tn̂g-thâu**, to break off the head, as of a clay image. **tn̂g-tiàⁿ**, anchor cable broken (v. tiàⁿ). **tn̂g-soh**, to cut or break a rope.

tn̂g-tiám-hong, not the least breath of wind. **tn̂g-poàⁿ-tih**, not half a drop, *e.g.* of rain. **tn̂g-chiah-koe**, not even one fowl. **tn̂g-chiah-báng**, not a single mosquito. **seng-khu tn̂g-tâng-sien**, I have not a bit of a cash on me. **seng-khu tn̂g-tâng-phí**, id. **kàu-tn̂g-chhiⁿ**, till nothing green is left, *e.g.* in a great drought. **sí kàu-tn̂g-chit-ê**, all dead, and none left. **sio kàu tn̂g-keng**, to burn so as not to leave one house. **chēng kàu-tn̂g-sìn-pe tn̂g-báng-háu**, so still that not even a fly or mosquito is heard.

tn̂g [R. tōng, to strike; to dash or strike against; to meet with accidentally]. **tn̂g--tio̍h**, to meet with, as on the way; to come upon or against accidentally. **saⁿ-tn̂g**, to meet with another person accidentally. **saⁿ-tn̂g-thâu**, to meet another on the road accidentally when going in opposite directions. **tn̂g hì-koà**, to take an omen from the first play one meets (v. koà).

tú-tn̂g, casually meeting with; casually occurring. **tú-tn̂g ū**, fortunately have on hand. **tú-tn̂g bô**, happen not to have. **tú-tn̂g kàu**, chance to reach. **n̂g-tsn̂g m̄-tàh tú-tn̂g**, scheming is not so good as to get a fortunate opportunity. **sì-kòe-tô sì-kòe-tn̂g**, having to go about getting little jobs here or there, or begging, borrowing, and asking from friends.

tn̂g--tó, to overset by coming against. **chhiong-tn̂g**, to come against accidentally. **lām-sám tn̂g**, to run against carelessly on the road, as persons or things.

tn̂g-mn̂g, to push a door with the body, as man inside keeping it from being opened; or as pig trying to push open a door. **sái chhiú-āu-tiⁿ tò-tn̂g**, to strike backwards with the elbow.

tit-tn̂g, coming on too hastily; *e.g.* too quickly, so as to run against things; or showing want of politeness by not waiting till permitted. **hoâiⁿ-kiâⁿ tit-tn̂g**, going on boldly anywhere without fear.

to (R. id.), a knife; a sword; a large quantity of paper, somewhat like a ream. **chit-to-tsoá**, one bundle of paper folded all in one, from 25 sheets to 360 sheets, according to the thickness.

to-á, a knife; a small knife. **to-káⁿ** (An.), id. (s. son). **chit-ki-to**, one knife. **lāi-to**, a sharp sword or knife.

toaⁿ-to, a solitary swordsman, said of Kwan-ti (koan-tè) when he set out as a warrior. **khang-chhiú siu toaⁿ-to**, able to wrest a great sword from an enemy with unarmed hands; said of man able to carry on a large business with no capital or little.

sio-to (Cn.), strong spirits. **sio-to-chiú** (Cn.), id.

sió-to-hōe, the Triad Society; a rebellious society, often called "the Small Knife Society," from a mistaken translation; the new members enter the society under a yoke of two crossed swords. **siang-to-hōe** (C.), id. **sió-to**, id.; belonging to the Triad Society. **sió-to-hoán**, the rebellion of the Triads at Amoy.

that-á-to, the short sword commonly used by soldiers. **io-to**, a sword worn at the girdle. **pē io-to**, to wear it, as military mandarin. **kúi-thâu-to**, an executioner's sword with a demon's head on the handle. **pó-to**, a very valuable sword. **hāu-bé-to**, a bayonet.

chiam-bé-to, a sharp-pointed knife. **tsôe-thâu-to**, a knife with a broad square end. **tek-hio̍h-to**, a knife shaped like a bamboo leaf, worn in a sheath. **chhâ-to**, a large cleaver for splitting wood. **tsoá-to**, a blunt knife for cutting folded paper. **chhiàm-to**, a knife for engraving blocks for printing. **khek-to**, a knife for carving wood.

bīn-to, a small razor for the cheeks, or for the second shaving. **thì-thâu-to**, a razor for the head. **thih-thâu-to**, id. **hī-to**, a small knife for cleaning out the ear.

koan-to, a sort of halbert or crooked spear (v. koan). **toā-to**, do., as carried before some high mandarins. **khau-liâm-to**, sort of halbert.

ka-to, shears, scissors (v. ka). **chién-to**, knife fixed on a pivot, for cutting medicines, &c. **tsáh-to**, a knife on a pivot; a fixed knife used by coopers (v. tsáh). **khau-to**, a plane (v. khau). **oan-to**, sort of large convex plane, for smoothing the inside of buckets, &c. (v. oan).

hé-to, a steel for striking fire. **hiā-to**, a small thick trowel, used for laying bricks, and for breaking them. **piah-to**, a large sort of trowel, with a handle on the back, as on a shield.

chhah-to, to wear a sword or knife at the side; the 18th radical written at the side. **khiā-to**, the 18th radical written at the side. **tsah-to**, to carry a sword concealed about one's dress. **kiáh-to**, to take or carry in the hand a sword or knife. **puih-to**, to draw a sword. **boâ-to**, to sharpen a knife or sword.

phīⁿ-to, the ridge of the nose when it is high and sharp, as in a Roman or aquiline nose. **phīⁿ to-to**, ridge of nose very high and sharp. **kha-liâm-to**, the foot used as a hook for tripping up another. **chhiú-to**, the side of the hand (at the little finger) when held flat and straight. **ēng chhiú-to tsáⁿ**, to strike with the edge of the hand held so.

sai-to, sort of long narrow fish. **hái-ka-to**, sort of crab with two very long claws and the rest very short. **to-tāu**, sort of legume with long knife-shaped pods.

to-peng ê tsai-ē, calamities of war or rebellion. **to-chhiuⁿ ê tsai-ē**, id. **chhiuⁿ-to**, spears and swords (v. chhiuⁿ). **to-pé-siú**, executioners.

chhò-to, to make a mistake in using a knife; to make a mistake in anything. **hó-to-lē̍**, a good cut of meat. **hó-to-tè**, id. **it-to lióng-toān**, to settle at once and finally (v. toān). **kè-to-tsáh**, to be cut in two by a machine, a form of punishment.

siang-bīn-to kúi, a man who talks fair to each side, and slanders the other side to each, so as to stir up enmity.

to-bah, the blade of a sword or knife. **to-chhùi**, the edge of it. **to-chhùi-kháu**, id. **to-mīⁿ**, the sharp steel edge. **to-kǹg**, the steel point or edge. **to-pòe**, the back of knife or sword. **ēng to-pán phah**, to strike with the flat of a sword. **ēng to-pán siau**, id. **to-khoân**, the hilt, esp. round. **to-pìⁿ**, handle of sword or knife. **to-kheng**, the eye of a knife where the handle is inserted; the back of a knife. **to-thâu**, the point of a square-ended knife at the end of the edge. **to-bé**, the end of the edge of a square knife close to the handle. **to-āu** (T.), id.

to-siù, a scabbard. **to-siò**, id. **to-sok**, id. **to-kè**, a stand for swords and spears, as at gate of city or of yamun. **to-chióh**, a whetstone. **to-tiam**, a block on which vegetables (and other food) are cut.

to-siong, wound made by sword or knife. **to-hûn**, mark left by such a wound after it has healed.

to (Cn. tiong). **to-nîⁿ**, a small wild Azalea with a red edible fruit.

to [mere imitation of a foreign sound]. **to-lô-nîⁿ**, a sort of foreign woollen stuff.

to [cf. ta-po͘, male]. **to-ngá** (Cn.), a son (a knife). **to-káⁿ** (Cn. esp. An.), id.

to [R. many; much; = col. tsōe], (Cn. to͘). **chha-put-to**, just about the amount, or almost enough; about, in amount or quality; tolerable; it will just do (lit. difference not much). **giân to, pit-sit; lé to, pit-tsà**, in many words there will be some mistake; in much politeness there is cunning. **bēng-to͘ to-chhún**, my fate is very bad (v. bēng).

to-siā, thank you! **to-sū**, a meddling fellow; a busybody. **to-chi-chiet**, confused, as a business (v. chiet). **to-teng toát-tsâi**, a large family diminishes wealth.

ké-to-toā, you are making yourself very big, quite above what you ought.

to, = to͘ (Cn. to͘), a particle used at the beginning of a clause, generally with the idea that the fact is not what was expected; well; indeed; yet; still; probably it may, but I think —, &c.; it is pronounced very short and unaccented, almost like "tòh" or "toh" [generally supposed = R. to͘, all; altogether; metropolis].

to-bô, well, there is none of it; and there is none. **to-bô--lah**, id. **chhē to-bô**, on searching, after all could not find it. **to m̄-tsai**, indeed I do not know. **to m̄-hó**, it won't do at all. **lí to-m̄-thiaⁿ goá-ê-ōe**, you will not listen to me (though you ought). **chit-si-hô to bōe-tsòe--tit**, indeed it will not do at all. **goá to bōe-hiáu--tit**, I don't understand it.

to-hó, well, that will do; and so that will do. **to-tióh**, well, then, it is quite right; thus it is quite right. **ū-iáⁿ to-tióh**, indeed it is quite true. **to sī àn-niⁿ**, indeed it is so. **koe-nn̄g bát-bát, to ū-phāng**, though an egg is very close, yet it has pores; hard to keep a matter quite secret.

m̄ to —, well, it is; yet indeed; well after all; you had better; it is best to.

tô [R. to escape], to escape; to steal gradually in small quantities. **bô-thang-tô**, no way to escape. **tô-chhut**, to escape out of a place. **tô--chhut-lâi**, to steal things gradually little by little, as from the house where one stays, or the shop in which he is engaged. **ûn-á tô**, id.

tô-tsáu, to run away; to abscond; to escape. **tô-phiah**, to get temporarily out of the way of danger. **tô-khui--khì**, id.

tô-pī, to escape, get out of the way, or run off (right or wrong). **tô-siám**, id. **tô-thoat**, to run away, escape, or abscond. **thoat-tô**, id.

tô-chè, to abscond, so as to avoid paying a debt. **tô-hong**, to run into port or under shelter to avoid a storm. **tô-lān**, to flee from great calamity. **tāi-sò͘ lân-tô**, the fated period of death cannot be escaped. **kiap-sò͘ lân-tô**, the fated time of great calamity cannot be avoided.

tô sìⁿ-miāⁿ, to escape with one's life. **tô-miāⁿ**, id. **tô-sìⁿ**, **bô tô-sí**, he flees to get life, not death (said of saving the life of a fugitive).

tô-peng, a deserter or fugitive soldier.

tô [R. to͘, a measure; a rule; capacity; to measure; to pass the time].

tô-chiáh, to get only one's own food and some clothes for the work done for another, having nothing over for family or for laying up. **tô-chit-chhùi chiáh**, id. **tô-pá**, to get barely one's food for bits of work, esp. from relatives or acquaintances.

sì-kòe-tô, sì-kòe-tn̂g, to wander about living by small jobs, or by begging and asking from others [or is this the previous word?].

tô [R. to wash out; to stir about; to cleanse; = col. toā], to clean out, as a well or pond. **tô-chíⁿ**, to clean out a well. **tô-tî**, to clean out a pond. **tô thâm-á**, to clean out a deep pond used for irrigation. **soa tô--khí-lâi**, to take out sand, as from well or pond.

tô, vegetable tallow. **tô-á-chhiū**, the tree from which vegetable tallow is made. **tô-chhiū**, id.

tô-chek, candles made of vegetable tallow. **tô-tháng**, vessel containing the tallow in which the candles are dipped.

tô [R. tó, pendent branches; classifier of flowers], a bunch of fruit, such as dragon's-eye (gêng-géng), or lāi-chi. **chiâⁿ-pha chiâⁿ-tô**, in great quantities, *e.g.* very great gains.

tô — huih-tô, a large mass of soft clotted blood.

tô — tô-tiáp, to annoy; to tease, esp. in order to get one to do something (v. tiáp).

tô (R. id.) **phû-tô**, a grape-vine; grapes. **pô-tô** (C.), id. (+). **phû-tô-chhiū**, a vine. **phû-tô-tsâng**, id. **phû-tô-koaⁿ**, raisins. **phû-tô-chhiⁿ**, purplish blue. **soaⁿ-pô-tô** (C.), a sort of wild vine.

iûⁿ-tô, a curious angular fruit, the Carambola, sometimes called the Chinese gooseberry, but not in any way similar to a gooseberry. **iûⁿ-tô-sng**, a preserve made from it.

tô [R. the weight of a steelyard; it is not always written with the same character].

tsúi-tô, a sounding-lead. **tsúi-tô-soh**, a sounding-line. **phah tsúi-tô**, to take soundings with the lead. **pàng tsúi-tô**, id.

tô-oáⁿ, scales of balance. **tô-chí**, weights for scales. **tô-jíⁿ**, id. **niûⁿ-tô**, the weight for a large steelyard.

khàu tô-tóe, to take off a very small discount, by regular custom of trade, from the price paid for goods, gen. about one mace (chíⁿ) on a hundred dollars. **teh tô-tóe**, id.

khò͘-tô, the scale of weights making a dollar count 7 mace 2 candareens, the regular rate in other places than Amoy; said only of steelyards thus marked for weighing dollars, for balances are always counted at this rate; and when money is counted under the denomination of taels, it is always by this rate. **khò͘-tô-téng**, a small steelyard, marked so as to make a dollar 7 „ 2, exactly agreeing with the scale of the "khò͘-pêng." **hā-tô**, the rate of the Amoy steelyard weights, making one dollar weigh 7 „ 6; so that a given weight according to the "hā-tô" is 5 or 6 per cent. lighter than by the "khò͘-tô." **hē-tô** (C.), id. **hā-tô-téng**, small steelyards graduated according to the Amoy standard, making $1 = 7 chíⁿ 6 hun.

pah-sì-tô, the common medium-sized steelyard used at Amoy (its weight is said to be 7 kun). **pah-sì-tô**

chiàⁿ, steelyard correct according to Amoy weights. **chheng-sì-tô chiàⁿ**, do., said of the very large steelyards called "niūⁿ." **pah-lák-tô**, = mn̂g-kháu-chhìn, the Cantonese steelyard, making the "kun" two ounces heavier than the Amoy rate (the ounces also being proportionally heavier); used in Amoy by pedlars, while the "pah-sì-tô" is used in shops.

tô [R. to carry a burden, as a beast of burden; by some divided into two words], to carry a load on the back, as a mule or ass does.

lòk-tô, a camel.

lû-tô, mules or asses, as used for carrying burdens. **lî-tô** (C.), id.

tô sòe-kiáⁿ (T.), to carry a child on the back, as woman. **hō-goá teh-tô** (T.), you make me a mere drudge toiling continually. **teh-thoa teh-tô** (T.), constantly toiling and drudging.

úi-tô (Cn. úi-tô), an idol that guards the gate of a Buddhist temple; if his baton be pointed almost to the ground, then the temple receives travelling priests for some days; he and "úi-hô" are placed in front of Kwan-yin [by some this is placed under the following word]. **úi-tô-hùt**, id. **úi-tô-chhì**, a large upright cactus with a fine flower.

tô [R. steep and precipitous; a syllable much used in Buddhist phrases: some also place "úi-tô" under this word].

o-bî-tô-hùt, Amida Buddha, the Buddha most usually worshipped; often written as a charm, or recited as a prayer. **o-mî-tô-hùt** (Cn. ə-bî-tô-hùt), id. **o-mí-tô-hùt**, id. **bî-tô**, id.

phó-tô, the sacred island of Poo-too, in the Chu-san archipelago, near Ningpo. **phó-tô-soaⁿ**, id. **lâm-phó-tô**, name of the largest temple near Amoy.

bit-tô-cheng, litharge.

tô [R. the end of a sleeve], the part cut out of a square piece of cloth in making an ordinary Chinese coat; the large flap on the breast of a Chinese coat.

toā-tô, the large flap on the breast of a Chinese coat. **sīn chit--ê toā-tô**, enough of cloth is over (as of the cloth cut out) for making the large flap.

tô-thâu, the piece of cloth cut out in making a coat.

tó [R. to pray]. (Cn. tó). **kî-tó** (R.), to pray; to pray to.

tó [R. an island]. (Cn. tó). **hái-tó** (R.), an island. **hā-tó** (R.), Amoy Island. **lō-tó** (R.), id.

hông-lâi-tó, the dwelling of the Sien or Tauist genii.

tó [R. battlements; a target], (Cn. tó). **siâⁿ-tó-chí**, the battlements of a wall.

tó [R. ná, there; where? = col. tah, tá]. **tó-lòh**, = tá-lòh, where? (v. lòh).

beh-tó-khì, where are you going? **lí tó-khì**, id. **tùi-tó-ngá** (Cn.), from what place?

tó [R. id., = col. tò], to fall; to overturn; to lie down; fallen into ruins, or fallen flat on the ground; bankrupt or ruined; to lose one's case in court; extinct, as a branch of a family; (to kill, as animals).

tien-tó, to stumble and fall; calamity (v. tien). **poàh-tó**, to fall by stumbling (v. poàh). **poàh chit-tó**, id. **oái-chit-tó**, to twist or sprain the foot so as to fall. **ién-tó**, to throw down in wrestling. **chhia-tó**, to push over; to push and cause to fall. **sak-tó**, id. **péng-tó**, to turn upside down, as a thing. **pán-tó** (C.), id. **pûiⁿ-tó** (Cn.), id. **páiⁿ-tó** (T.), id. **áh-put-tó**, a toy figure with a round bottom, that cannot be overturned.

piēn-tó, to overcome in argument, so as to silence or shut up one's opponent. **piēn-tó--i**, to overcome him in argument. **khit--i piēn-tó**, to be overcome in argument, and silenced by him. **khit--i pok-tó**, id.

kà-ōe-tó, fully able to teach. **thàn--i bōe-tó**, his work is too heavy or too difficult for one's strength or ability. **chiáh--i bōe-tó**, id.

tńg-tó, money laid out so as to make large and rapid profits (v. tńg). **túiⁿ-tó** (C.), id.

thán-tó, lying down; laid down (v. thán). **tó thán-hoâiⁿ**, lying crosswise, *e.g.* across a bed. **tó thán-tit**, lying straight along. **tó tit-tit**, lying along at full length. **tó-teh-khùn**, lying down, resting, or asleep. **tó-tsāi-chhn̂g**, quite confined to bed. **tó-chhn̂g**, id.

tó lī-lī, fallen down flat, as house or wall; lying along the ground, as man; become quite bankrupt.

tó-tó khiā-khiā, lounging about idly, perhaps lying, perhaps standing.

tó-chhù, a ruined house. **tó-kiô**, a fallen and ruined bridge; sometimes the name of a village at an old ruined bridge. **tó-hoāi**, destroyed and ruined, as a house. **tó chit-khiah**, having a part broken down, as wall or bridge. **tó liáu-liáu**, all in ruins.

tó-thui, a fixed wooden stair with level steps, as distinguished from a mere ladder. **tó-io**, to throw one's head back and make the belly project (v. io). **tó-mîⁿ**, having the edge turned so as to be very blunt, as an ill-sharpened knife. **tó-ko**, the 62d radical.

siang-tó-tsúi, made with a ridge, as a roof of two slopes. **chit-tó-tsúi**, having only one slope, as the roof of a shed without a ridge. **poeh tó, káu pē** (T.), in the 8th month the Pleiades are somewhat down, in the 9th low down, at sunrise (v. pē).

tó-pâng, to overcast in sewing, folding in the rough edge of the cloth.

tó-pâng, the branch of the family become extinct. **tó-thiāu**, id., of a smaller branch.

tó-ūn, very bad luck; the fated season of one's death or great calamity. **tó-iông**, loss of virility.

tó-tiàm, bankrupt, as shopkeeper. **tiàm tó**, id. **hâng tó**, bankrupt, as merchant in large business. **tó-tàⁿ**, pedlar become bankrupt. **tó lâng-ê-siàu**, to fail to pay a debt, either as a bankrupt or refusing to pay. **hō--lâng tó-siàu**, to fail to recover a bad debt. **khit--lâng tó-siàu**, id. **siàu khit--lâng tó--khì**, id.

tó-tōe-kè, an extraordinarily low price, so low that it cannot be expected to fall lower. **tó-tōe-hè**, worthless or unsaleable goods which no one wishes to buy.

thâi-ti tó-iûⁿ, to have pigs and goats killed in great numbers, as for great feasts. **î-soaⁿ tó-hái**, to move mountains and seas, as by superhuman power.

tò [R. to arrive, = col. tàu, kàu], (Cn. tò, tò). **tò-jīm**, to arrive at one's seat of office, as new mandarin (v. jīm). **kî-lîn tò-chhú**, may the kî-lîn come here; written as an auspicious phrase; said also of a paper with these words on it. **hōng-hông tò-chhú**, may the phœnix come here (v. hōng).

tò-tí (R.), = tàu-tí, in fine; on the other hand; but at last; but after all.

tâu-tò, to give up one's wicked course of life, on condition of impunity and employment, as a rebel, pirate, or deserter (v. tâu). **put-tò**, not arrived, as a party in a legal case, or student at examination, or soldier at call of roll. **pín put-tò**, to report to the mandarin that the party does not appear. **pín-tò**, to report that the parties have arrived.

jit-chí bī-tò; m̄-sī thiⁿ-tōe bô-pò, the time (of recompense) has not yet come; it is not that Heaven and earth do not recompense.

tò [R. tó, to overturn; to invert; to fall; cf. col. tó͘], back again; (inverted); on the contrary; wrong side; left side; to pour out; classifier of voyages.

tò-tńg, to turn back or round (v. tńg). **tò-péng,** inverted (v. péng). **tò-thâu,** in opposite direction to the original or natural direction. **tò-thâu-thàn,** to lose instead of gaining in trade. **tò-thâu-tsai,** to fall head foremost. **tò-thâu-tiàu,** placed with wrong end up (v. tiàu). **tò-bīn,** reverse side; wrong side, of a thing that has two surfaces.

tò-pêng, on the left side; the wrong or reverse side, as of a mirror or such flat thick article. **tò-chhiú-pêng,** left side. **tò-chhiú,** left hand. **tò-kha,** left foot.

tò-khah-tsōe, but yet they are more than ever; more than before, though expected to have been fewer or less. **tò-khah-hó,** better than before, though expected to have been worse; &c. &c.

chiàⁿ-kóng tò-kóng, to say opposite things at different times (v. chiàⁿ). **kóng-ōe khì-khì tò-tò,** to talk so as to avoid giving a decided answer yes or no, sometimes appearing to say the one, sometimes the other. **khì-tò lióng-lân,** in a sad dilemma, equally bad to go on or to turn back.

chit-tò-tsûn, one whole voyage of a vessel, both going and returning.

tò--khì (C. túiⁿ--khì), to go back; to go home. **tò--lâi,** to come back; to come home. **tò--lâi-khì,** let us go home or turn back together. **tò-tsé͘,** to die; to be broken or spoiled so as to be quite useless, as a thing (lit. return to ancestors).

tò-thè, to move backwards without turning round; to become worse in work, &c. (v. thè). **tò-kiâⁿ,** to walk backwards. **tò-lun,** to push a boat straight backwards, as when aground. **tò-bé-lun,** id. **tò-chē,** id. **tò-thiàu,** to rebound. **tò-tiô,** id. **tò-toāⁿ,** id. **tò-séh,** to revolve in the direction opposite to that of the hands of a watch.

tò-tn̂g, to have in one's hands a balance of another's money (v. tn̂g). **tò-thoāⁿ,** to offer less than we had said we would give; to lose in skill or knowledge (v. thoâⁿ). **tò-thoaⁿ** (C.), id. **tò-poáh,** to make a counter charge, as a set off (v. poàh). **tò-pau,** to cut off and surround an enemy by a flank movement of one body of men. **tò-phiâⁿ,** to win after losing in gambling. **hók-tò,** to recover something that was lost or taken violently or unjustly, as a city or a thing (v. hók).

tò-chhut, to pour out. **tò-tsúi,** to pour out water. **tò-koá-tê,** pour out a little tea. **tò-thn̂g,** to pour sugar into a mould, as in making confections. **tò thn̂g-ké͘,** to make a large drum-shaped confection (used for marriages) by a mould. **tò-soa,** to pour out sand. **hō͘ chhia-teh-tò,** rain pouring in torrents. **bák-sái chhē-chhē-tò,** tears flowing abundantly. **kau hê-siūⁿ, tò tāng-á-bí,** they who consort with Bud. priests must empty their rice-jar (v. tāng).

tō [R. to tread; to walk]. **sûn-kui tō-kú,** following correct rules of conduct, esp. of well-behaved young person. **siú-kui tō-kū** (Cn.), id.

tō [R. a sort of rice], (Cn. tə). **tō liông siok, bék sú chek** (R.), the six grains.

tō [R. to lead; to guide; = col. chhoā, thoā]. **tō-lông,** to help out of great poverty or trouble; to help a man to get on in trade or business by patronizing him, as good customer, &c. (said politely by shopkeeper to customer).

tō [R. indolent], (Cn. tō, tə). **lán-tō,** lazy; indolent.

tō [R. to rob; a robber; = col. tāu]. **kan-îm té͘-tō,** lasciviousness, gambling, and robbery. **pîn-kiông khí tō-sim,** poverty gives rise to the desire to rob or steal. **kiông-tō** (r.), a robber; a highwayman (s. way).

tō [R. a way; a road; to speak; principles of reason or justice, rationale or method, &c.; = col. thâu], (Cn. tō, tə), doctrine; right principles of reason or of conduct; the Tau-tai or Intendant of Circuit; Tauist; the supreme regulative or ruling principle of the universe, according to the Tauists; also (X.) the Word or Logos.

khui-tō, to clear the road before a mandarin, by beating gongs, &c. **hoah-tō,** do., by shouting loud, as his attendants do. **chhoàⁿ-tō,** to cross the road in front of a mandarin, very improper.

bōng-tō, a large stone tablet at the road-side, having an inscription stating that the grave of some illustrious person is close at hand.

chhn̂g-tō, a broad board on front of bed, used for sitting on. **bîn-chhn̂g-tō,** id.

tông-tō, of the same trade, profession, or business (v. tông). **tâng-tō,** id. **tâng-tō ê-lâng,** man of same occupation. **óh i-tō,** to learn medicine.

tō-lí, doctrine; good doctrine; right principles; principle or rationale of a matter. **tát tō-lí,** reasonable and right, as an argument, or as a plan for settling a quarrel. **ū-tō-lí,** just and proper; reasonable and right. **tō-lí-lāi,** id. **bô-tō-lí,** unreasonable and wrong. **tō-lí-goā,** id. **kóng tō-lí,** to explain doctrine; to preach. **thoân tō-lí,** id.; to transmit doctrine (v. thoân).

tō-tek (R.), virtue. **kong-hun tō-tek,** great virtue and merit. **tō-tek-keng,** the original Tauist classic by Lau-tsze.

siu-tō, to cultivate virtue, esp. Tauist. **liēn-tan siu-tō,** to practise Tauist rules so as to become a Sien. **tek-tō ê hê-siūⁿ,** a Bud. priest who has attained to great merit.

kong-tō, just; equitable. **tsòe kong-tō-lâng,** to act as a sort of arbiter. **ka-kī kong-tō,** making one's self always right. **kong ka-kī-tō** (E.), id. **lú-sòng pa-lé, kong ka-kī-tō** (Cn.), as overbearing as a Spanish padre (v. lé).

hē-tō, very honest, fair, and safe to deal with.

bû-tō, unjust and oppressive, as a ruler. **pà-tō,** violent or oppressive, as man (v. pà). **kiông-tō beh,** doggedly determined on it (v. kiông), (s. rob). **tsó-tō,** false doctrine. **tsó-tō hėk-chiòng,** deceiving the multitude by false doctrine (said of Tauist sorcerers, &c.)

thien-tō, the method or manner of Heaven's justice (v. thien).

tāi-tō-kong, = Gê chin-jîn, = pó-seng tāi-tè, the god of medicine. **tāi-sîn tāi-tō,** a regularly canonized and widely-worshipped idol (said figuratively of a very powerful man), (v. sîn).

tō-kong, Tau-kwang, the title of the emperor (father of Hien-fung), in whose reign the first Chinese war and treaty were made.

tō-kàu, the Tauist sect or religion. **tō-ka,** the Tauist sect. **jû tō sek,** Confucianism, Tauism, and Buddhism. **tō-sū,** = sai-kong, a Tauist priest. **tō-ko,** a Tauist nun. **tō-toāⁿ,** the residence of a Tauist priest (v. toâⁿ). **iau-tō,** a crafty Tauist magician.

tō-iâ, the Tautai, or Intendant of Circuit, who rules several (usually three) departments. **tō-tâi** (r.), id. **piaⁿ-pī-tō,** a Tautai who has also the management of naval and military funds. **ē-mn̂g-tō**, the Tautai of Amoy. **heng-tsoân-éng-tō**, do. ruling Hing-hwa, Chin-chew, and Yung-chun. **chiang-chiu-tō**, the Chang-chew Tautai. **theng-chiang-liông-tō**, id. **tsan-tō**, the Tautai surnamed Tsan.

tō-chhe, constables or police belonging to the Tautai's yamun. **tō-su**, a writer in the Tautai's yamun. **pài tō-su**, to get one's name on their books for influence and protection. **bóe tō-su**, to buy the position of such a writer, either real or fictitious, for protection. **tō-báu**, to have one's name thus on the books of the Tautai's yamun, so that the constables of inferior mandarins dare not meddle him.

iâm-tō, the commissioner or superintendent of the salt-tax for a whole province. **iâm-hoat-tō**, id. **niû^n-tō**, the commissioner (at provincial capital) for paying the army. **kang-an niû^n-tō**, the commissioner who pays out the money for the troops in Kiang-nan, *i.e.* Kiang-soo and Ngan-hwei provinces.

to͘ (Cn.), = A. to; many; much.

to͘ [R. all; the metropolis], a region of country (a subdivision of a Hien) containing a considerable number of villages; these subdivisions are often (esp. Cn.) described by their numbers, *e.g.* jī-tsâp-sì to͘. **hōe-to͘** (Cn.), villages combining to prevent feuds or brigandage. **sam-to͘**, a part of the mainland near Amoy.

tè-to͘, the metropolis. **to͘-sêng-hông**, the tutelary god of the metropolis and of the empire (v. hông). **tang-to͘**, Formosa.

to͘-chhat-ī^n, the Censorate in the capital. **to͘-thóng**, the high Tartar military official just below a "chiong-kun;" Tartar lieutenant-general or major-general. **to͘-si**, a military officer between "iû-kek" and "siú-pī."

bān-poan, to͘ sī-bēng, all things are of fate (v. bēng).

to͘ (= to), a particle used at the beginning of a clause with somewhat of an adversative sense; yet; but indeed; indeed; well then, well (A. to͘, to; Cn. to͘); [this word is by many counted the same as the previous one].

to͘ sī àn-ni^n, indeed it is so. **lí to͘ m̄-thàn goá-ê-ōe**, you see you would not obey me or follow my advice.

tô͘ [R. to slaughter, as animals], a surname. **kìm-tô͘**, to forbid the slaughtering of animals, as in a long drought. **khui-tô͘**, to remove this prohibition, as after three days, or when rain comes.

tô͘ [R. tû, a kitchen; a slaughter-house]. **tô͘-chí**, a man who keeps a shop for supplying cooked food or entire cooked feasts, sending them to order.

tô͘ [R. a road]. **lō-tô͘** (r.), a road. **poàn-tô͘ jî-hòe**, to fail half-way. **chiét-tô͘ chhiú^n-kiap**, to plunder on the highway.

phái^n ūn-tô͘, season of fated calamity. **bēng-tô͘ phái^n** (r.), one's fate bad; my fate is bad. **bēng-tô͘ to-chhún**, my fate is very bad.

tô͘ [R. a map; a plan; to plan; to scheme; a seal]; a map or plan; a picture used as an illustration or sketch; to plan or scheme; to plot against.

tham-tô͘, to covet and scheme; to plot or intrigue for gain. **kiông-tô͘**, to plot so as to bring overwhelming influence to injure a man. **tô͘--lâng**, to plot secretly so as to supplant a man or to oust him from his property or situation, &c. **tô͘-bô͘**, to scheme, plot, or plan, gen. bad. **tô͘-bô͘ lâng-ê-giâp**, to plot to get a man's property.

tô͘-kì, an official seal; the man in a yamun (= tāi-su) who stamps it. **tô͘-kì-ìn**, the stamp of it on a document. **tô͘-su**, a seal or stamp. **tô͘-chiong**, id.

tē-tô͘, a map or plan of a place. **soa^n-tô͘**, a picture of hills, as for a view, or pointing out a grave-site. **hêng-tô͘**, a portrait taken for detective purposes. **ūi hêng-tô͘**, to draw such a portrait. **seng-koa^n-tô͘**, a diagram with names of offices and degrees, used in a game of chance. **siū-tô͘**, a scroll with a picture of some emblem of long life, or having the word "siū" written large, given on a birth-day. **chhun-gû-tô͘**, the common Chinese sheet-almanac.

jip pán-tô͘, to be received into the Chinese empire, as a region.

tô͘ [R. a disciple; to banish], to banish to a short distance, *e.g.* for three years beyond the limits of the Foo department. **liû-tô͘**, to banish or exile in general. **tsám-ká kun-liû-tô͘**, beheading, strangling, and three sorts of transportation or banishment (in order of severity). **gí-tô͘**, to condemn to banishment. **būn-tô͘** (R.), id.

bûn-tô͘ (R.), a disciple; a scholar. **lí--ê ko-tô͘** (polite), your scholar. **tô͘-tē**, a young Buddhist priest. **sù-tô͘** (X.), an apostle.

tô͘-lūi (r.), a sort or class of people. **hit-hō ê tô͘-lūi**, that sort of people. **chiú-sek chi-tô͘**, a man fond of drink and lust.

su-tô͘, a surname.

tô͘ [R. mud; miry; to daub; to plaster or besmear, = col. thô͘].

hô͘-tô͘, loose and careless in speech or behaviour; negligent in managing matters; ill-behaved so as to cause injury to others; equivocating or making a matter intentionally indistinct so as to deceive; dishonest. **hô͘-tô͘-kóng**, to talk at random without proof; to tell falsehoods; to speak indistinctly about a matter so as to delude, and yet able afterwards to deny having said so-and-so. **kóng-ōe hô͘-tô͘**, to deceive by indistinct or ambiguous language, or by concealment of the truth, or by false additions.

tô͘-hiu^n (C. Cn.), = A. thô͘-hiu^n, name of a plant.

tô͘ [R. to throw; to leap into; to have recourse to; to give one's self up to; to agree; = col. tâu, tiô]. **i-khì siong-tô͘**, agreeing in feelings; congenial in spirit. **giên-gú tô͘-ki**, to agree in expression of opinion (v. ki).

tô͘-ô͘, game of throwing sticks into a jar.

tô͘ [R. a bitter plant]. **tô͘-bî-hoe**, a flower like a small rose.

sîn-tô͘, name of a prince of demons who can devour refractory demons (v. sîn).

tô͘ (Cn.), = A. tô. **o͘-bî-tô͘-hút**, = A. o-bî-tô-hút, Amida Buddha.

tó͘ [R. kó͘, dropsy]. **tiōng-tó͘**, may you have dropsy! said in cursing (v. tiōng). **tó͘-tiōng**, swelling of belly (v. tiōng).

tó͘ [R. to͘, the belly, = col. táu]. **pak-tó͘**, the belly; the mind (v. pak). **sit-tó͘** (Cn.), the belly. **sái-tó͘** (Cn.), id.

tsûn-tó͘, the hold of a vessel. **tó͘-lāi**, in the hold of a vessel. **tó͘-tāng**, ballast (v. tāng).

chhiú-tó͘, the fleshy part of the lower arm. **kha-tó͘**, the calf of the leg. **kha-āu-tó͘**, id. **si^n tó͘-hí**, to have a long sore on the calf of the leg. **tó͘-eng**, an abscess on a fleshy part.

tó͘-koā^n, a broad pouch or sporran worn on the belly. **tó͘-tē**, id. **tó͘** (Cn)., id. **tó͘-á** (T.), id. **iám-tó͘** (Cn.), id. **iam tó͘-koā^n**, to put one's hand in this broad pouch, as for money (v. iam).

io-tó͘, a broad leather girdle with several pockets in it, girt round the waist.

tó͘, a flat or nearly flat piece of wood-work or wicker-work (or in metal, plaster, &c.) of a square, round, or other regular shape; a panel; classifier of panels, squares, framed or inclosed spaces, compartments of pictures or panelled work, &c. **chit-tó͘-jī**, one panel, square, or compartment containing words, as on an ornamental scroll or flat piece of work. **chit-tó͘-hoe**, one panel, or one compartment of a scroll, &c., containing carved or painted flowers.

pîn-tó͘, a wooden partition. **pang-tó͘**, a wooden or lath partition. **bî-tó͘-pang**, the panelling over a Chinese door. **jia-hong-tó͘**, the panelling at the back and ends of a bedstead.

kiàⁿ-tó͘, the wooden back of a mirror or framed picture. **tîn-tó͘**, a piece of rattan-work of square, round, or other regular shape, *e.g.* for seat or back of chair. **po-lê-tó͘**, a square of glass, as in window or door.

phòng-tó͘, an embossed panel. **so͘-tó͘**, id. (lit. like Soo-chow work). **thap-tó͘**, a concave or depressed panel. **thām-tó͘**, somewhat concave or worn into a hollow (v. thām).

tó͘ [R. tò͘, together; to contend; = col. tàu]. **saⁿ-tó͘**, disputing as to facts, &c., or flatly contradicting each other, each determined to have the last word. **nn̄g-ê saⁿ-tó͘**, each flatly contradicting the other. **kap-i-tó͘**, to have an altercation with him, saying the very opposite of his words. **tó͘-khì**, to have a violent altercation or wrangling, each giving the lie to the other, or saying he will do what the other forbids. **tó͘ i-ê-khì**, to get up his temper and refuse to give in or to accept advice, esp. as a young headstrong fellow. **tó͘-béng**, each trying to overcome the other, as by boasting, threatening, or fighting. **tó͘-ióng**, two persons boasting of superior strength or courage, or trying which is the stronger.

tó͘ — **tó͘ tsō-hoà**, to make a venture in trade.

tó͘ [R. to gamble, = col. kiáu]. **tó͘-phok** (r.), gambling. **tó͘ su-iâⁿ** (r.), to gamble for money. **phiâu tó͘ îm**, fornication, gambling, and drunkenness. **kan-îm tó͘-tō**, adultery, gambling, and robbery.

tó͘ [R. to look at]. **tó͘-báuh**, to make a rough calculation or average guess, as by looking at without measurement, *e.g.* of price, number, or quantity. **tó͘-bák**, id. **tó͘ bák-sek**, to calculate roughly at a glance.

tó͘ [R. tó, to overturn; backwards; left hand; = col. tò]. **tó͘-kháu**, the oar held in the left hand, and so on the port or right hand side of a small boat (v. kháu).

tó͘ [R. to guard; a wall for guarding a place; = col. táu]. **hông-tó͘**, to guard an important place by an extra garrison, as when war or rebellion is near. **hông-tó͘-peng**, soldiers or garrison guarding such a wall or important position.

tó͘ [R. a rice measure, = col. táu], (Cn. tió). **tó͘-bí sam-chiên**, one "táu" of rice cost three cash, as in the golden age of Yaou.

tó͘ (T.) **tó͘-bóng**, = A. ló͘-bóng, acting in a hurried or careless manner.

tó͘ (T.), = A. tó, tá. **beh-tó͘-khì**, where are you going?

tó͘ (Cn.), = A. tó. **hái-tó͘** (R.), an island.

tó͘ (Cn.), = A. tó (R.), to pray.

tó͘ (Cn.) **siâⁿ-tó͘-chí**, = A. siâⁿ-tó-chí, battlements.

tò͘ [R. together; to contend; = col. tàu, tó͘], (Cn. tiò). **hâi-tò͘**, to fight with deadly weapons. **tò͘-kháu**, wrangling loudly. **tò͘-khì**, slight altercation or wrangling, sometimes even with use of the hands, but very slightly. **tò͘-kan**, fighting for a woman, as lewd fellows.

tò͘ (R. id.), to envy; to be jealous, as a woman; not said of a man in sense of jealousy.

oàn-tò͘, envy; to envy. **chit-tò͘** (r.), id. **chék-tò͘** (C. Cn.), id. **ò͘ⁿ-tò͘**, to envy. **ò͘-tò͘**, id. **tò͘-khī**, envious.

sip-hū, kiú-tò͘, of ten women, nine dislike their husbands keeping concubines.

tò͘ [R. very black or dirty, *e.g.* as muddy water], to spread, as oil or grease, or as damp, or as ink on bibulous paper; to infect or spread from one to another, as a disease. **tò͘--tiòh**, infected; damaged by damp, &c., spreading. **tò͘-tò͘**, having a blotted look, as a dot or stroke with an ill-defined edge. **tò͘--kè-khì**, to spread through to the other side, as ink, &c. **tò͘-tâm**, damaged by damp or by water soaking in, as goods. **o͘-tò͘**, blotted or spattered with ink or dark-coloured dirt; blurred, as writing when the ink is too thin and spreads; having a dirty white, instead of a pure white, as meal or salt; having a dark colour, as dull red.

ài-tò͘-lâng, infectious. **ōe-tò͘-lâng**, id. (cf. to͘).

tò͘ (Cn.), = A. tò, to arrive, &c.

tō͘ [R. a rule; a measure; capacity; a degree of a circle or in geography; to measure; to pass the time; also by change of tone "tók;" cf. col. tô], a degree of a circle or in geography.

tō͘-liōng, generosity; kindness (v. liōng).

hoat-tō͘, a rule; a law; a method; a plan of procedure. **bô-hoat-tō͘**, without rule or order; disorderly. **chiàu-hoat-tō͘**, orderly; proper. **tiâu-tō͘** (r.), rules made by a superior (v. tiâu). **chè-tō͘**, regulations of a state or dynasty as to rites and ceremonies, forms of dress, &c. **chheng-tiâu ê chè-tō͘**, the rites, rules of dress, &c., of the Manchoo dynasty.

kè-tō͘, too much (s. ferry). **kòe-tō͘** (C.), id. **sim-su kè-tō͘**, thinking too deeply about a matter, to the injury of one's health. **sim-su kò-tō͘**, id. **lô-sim kò-tō͘**, having a very great deal of thought and anxiety in the management of a matter (v. lô).

tiên-tō͘, an orbit, as of one of the heavenly bodies (v. tiên).

phó͘-tō͘, ceremonies for the benefit of the multitude of ghosts (v. phó͘). **chhiau-tō͘**, to assist a soul to get deliverance from punishment, and to be born into this world again.

tō͘-tiáp, a certificate given to a Buddhist priest who has been ordained by the head priest of a great recognized monastery.

tō͘ chit-chhùi chiàh, to get only one's own food for one's work, leaving nothing over for family or for accumulation. **tō͘-pá**, id., especially from acquaintances. **jit-sit lân-tō͘**, having much difficulty to earn daily food.

tō͘ [R. thó͘, earth; land]. **kok-tō͘**, a kingdom. **kok-tō͘-bé**, said of great multitude of calamities or crimes, as portending the end of the dynasty.

tō͘-tāng (C.), = A. tōe-tāng, an earthquake.

tō͘-ún, an earth-worm. **tō͘-gín** (C.), id. **tō͘-bún** (Cn.), id. **o͘-tō͘-thâng**, we worms of the earth, said in addressing Heaven. **tō͘-kâu** (Cn. thô͘-kâu), an insect like a grasshopper without wings. **tō͘-phú**, sort

海上絲綢之路文獻集成　科技與文化編

of insect. **tē̤-peh** (T.), an insect that burrows in the ground. **tē̤-pit** (Cn.), id.

tē̤ [same as previous word? by some assigned to the following word]. **tē̤-tēng**, a sort of reptile, like a snake with feet (v. tūng). **tē̤-tiōng**, a sort of medicine (made from the Euonymus?).

tē̤ [R. a sort of tree; to shut out; to stop; to block the way], a surname.

tē̤-seng, a sort of fir-tree of general shape much like the spruce-fir, with dense dark foliage, almost like a cedar, and large cones. **tē̤-siong** (C.), id. **tē̤-seng-lûi**, its fir-cones.

tē̤-pi-iû, castor-oil.

tē̤-tsoān, to invent an unauthorized meaning for a phrase, or a false addition to one's commission, &c. (v. tsoān).

tē̤-koan, a sort of bird; a sort of flower (v. koan).

tē̤ [R. to cross a stream or channel; a passage-boat]. **tē̤-tsûn**, a passage-boat. **kheh-tē̤**, a passage-boat for passengers. **hè-tē̤**, a passage-boat for goods. **hoâi^n-tē̤**, a ferry-boat across a stream or narrow channel. **siâ^n-tē̤**, passage-boat to or from the Foo city, *e.g.* Chang-chew. **hi-tē̤**, passage-boat to or from a market. **thàu-tē̤**, a passage-boat that goes the whole way. **thàu-bé-tē̤**, a passage-boat that plies from Chióh-bé to Koa^n-jîm. **chióh-bé-tē̤**, the Chióh-bé passage-boat; and so with names of other places.

kè-tē̤, to cross the ferry (a. rule). **tah-tē̤**, to take passage in a passage-boat.

tē̤ [R. the belly; the paunch; = col. *tó*, *táu*], the paunch of an animal. **tē̤-lāi**, in the belly. **tē̤-lāi khang-hu**, feeling weak with hunger (v. hu). **tē̤-lāi khang-phà^n**, illiterate. **léh-tē̤**, to rip up the belly, as of a fish.

tn̂g-tē̤, bowels and belly; mind and feelings (v. tn̂g). **sió-tē̤**, the bladder of a quadruped, esp. of a pig.

tē̤-tsâi, the navel. **tē̤-iong**, a large boil on the belly. **tē̤-kûn**, a pouch tied on a bride's belly, containing about a dozen symbolical articles, when she goes to be married. **khí tē̤-têng**, said of a literary man absorbing for his own use money said to be collected for building a temple.

phái^n-tē̤-tháng, wicked in conduct (v. tháng).

lèk-tē̤, a girth for a horse; a rope passed from bow to helm along the bottom of a junk. **bé-lèk-tē̤**, a girth for a horse. **tē̤-toà**, id.

gû-tē̤, tripe, from the cow. **ti-tē̤**, tripe from the pig. **hî-tē̤**, edible part of entrails of fish. **chhe̤-hî iù-tē̤**, rough exterior, but considerable ability.

tē̤ [R. to gild]. **tē̤-kim**, to gild metal by means of melted gold, much thinner than "lèk-kim." **tē̤ kim-tsúi**, to gild in an extremely thin way, which very soon spoils; often a mere imitation of gold.

tē̤ (cf. tè̤). **khit--i tē̤--khì**, to catch a contagious disease from him, *e.g.* itch; to be led into bad courses by a bad companion. **tē̤ kàu-phái^n**, to lead into bad courses, as companion.

tē̤ [R. nutmeg, cardamom], (Cn. tiō; C. tāu). **tē̤-khè̤**, nutmeg (v. khè̤).

tē̤ — **tē̤-chè̤**, the birthday of a child just one year after birth (C. mê^n-chè̤).

tē̤, to consume away to ashes gradually without flame, as charcoal. **hé-thoà^n tē̤-lē̤--khì**, the charcoal gradually burning away to ashes.

tē̤ (R. id., = col. tāu), a very small clause of a sentence; a sub-clause. **kù-tē̤**, clauses and sub-clauses. **tē̤-tiám**, a comma.

tē̤ (C.) **tē̤-pân**, = A. tòk-pân, an earthen jar for sticking flowers in.

tē̤ [R. tsū, self; from]. **an-jiên tē̤-tsāi** (C.), = an-jiên tsū-tsāi, in ease, comfort, and quiet.

tē̤ (Cn.), = A. tō, doctrine; in some of the phrases.

tē̤ (Cn.) **sûn-kui tē̤-kū**, = A. sûn-kui tō-kú, correct in conduct.

tē̤ (Cn.), = A. tō, sort of grain.

tē̤ (Cn.) **lán-tē̤**, = lán-tō, lazy; indolent.

tĕ̤ (T.) **lé-tĕ̤**, = A. lé-tê, the knob on which a sculling oar works.

tḗ̤ (Cn.), = A. té, short.

tḕ̤ (Cn.), = A. tè, a surname.

tĕ̤ (T.), = A. tē. **hái-tĕ̤**, a flat plain on the sea-shore, reclaimed from the sea, or very rarely inundated. **tĕ̤-hoā^n**, the retaining wall of land reclaimed from the sea, or protected against it. **pang-tĕ̤**, the retaining wall burst and the land inundated.

tĕ̤ (Cn.), = A. tē, a pocket.

toâ [R. tô, to wash out; to stir about and cleanse], to stir about in water so as to clean. **toâ-bí**, to wash rice by stirring it in water, so as to remove sand and gravel. **toâ-soa**, id.

toâ (= tsoâ), to shake with a horizontal and almost circular motion, as a tray of grain. **toâ-chhek**, to shake uncleaned rice thus in a wicker tray, so as to clean it.

toá (Cn. and part of T.) **beh-toá-khû**, = A. beh-tá-khì, where are you going?

toà [R. tài, a belt, band, sash, or girdle; to take along with; united; related; on account of: in consideration of; fated to], a sash; a girdle; tape; ribbon; to lead or carry about; to be fated to some condition.

toà-tióh, on account of (a person or his kindness); out of regard to; out of consideration for. **toà--tióh**, id. **ū sa^n-toà-tióh**, willing to do a favour on account of some third party.

toà-gî, to harbour suspicion. **toà-pī^n**, while quite unwell; said of exerting one's self notwithstanding (v. pī^n).

toà-liān, to wear a chain, as prisoner. **toà-hà**, to be in mourning (v. hà). **toà-péh**, id. **toà-chhe̤**, to be in deepest mourning.

toà-kúi-thai, appearance as if pregnant, when it is merely a swelling of the stomach from some other cause. **toà-sin** (Cn.), to be pregnant. **toà-in** (Cn.), id. (v. în).

toà-chî^n, to carry cash; to have cash about one. **toà-chhiú**, to carry in the hand, taking away or bringing. **toà-chhiú--lâi**, to bring in the hand. **toà-chhiú--khì**, to take away in the hand. **soà-toà-chhiú**, to take in the hand when one is going at any rate.

toà-lâng-khì, to lead a man away. **toà ke-koàn**, to take one's family along with one. **toà pan-peng**, to lead soldiers to a place to relieve others, *e.g.* to the garrison of Formosa.

tsóng-toà, officer in command of a body of soldiers. **hiáp-toà**, his assistant.

sa^n-liên-toà, connected together, as relatives or connections; connected or adhering, as things, so that when you take up the one it draws the other with it. **sa^n-liên tì-toà**, joined closely, as relations, or as the parts of the body; really involved in an affair. **sa^n-liâm tì-toà**, id. **sa^n-liâm-toà**, id. **káu sa^n-toà**, dogs united in copulation.

toà kùi-jîn, fated to be of high rank; this and the whole paragraph are fortune-tellers' phrases. **poeh-jī toà-soah,** his horoscope will be very injurious to parents or relatives. **toà-siang-to lâi chhut-sì,** fated to have an unlucky influence on the life of relatives, as child. **toà ko-loân,** fated to be a widow (lit. solitary phœnix). **toà iáh-bó,** fated to be licentious. **toà thô-hoe,** fated to a vile course of life, as woman.

si-toà, a silk tape, ribbon, or sash. **kiàm-toà,** a ribbon or sash with the ends pointed. **toā-toà,** an ornamental sash. **io-toà,** a sash or girdle for fastening the clothes. **hâ io-toà,** to gird one's self with it. **sa^n-á-toà,** strings for the clothes of children, or of Bud. priests. **kat sa^n-á-toà,** to bring presents to children in the first month, supposed to make them grow taller. **khò-toà,** tape for tying on trowsers round the waist. **kûn-toà,** band for tying on woman's petticoat. **bō-á-toà,** string for cap. **bėh-toà,** garters. **ôe-toà,** shoe-ties. **kak-toà,** an ornamental girdle of Ming pattern, worn by mandarins' wives, also at marriages and in plays. **pe-toà,** the wavy ornament, like a sash, behind and above the head of some idols.

ui-toà, the umbilical cord; the navel-string.

pui-toà, the thick raised edges of a roof along the top of the gable-wall.

pâi-toà, a sort of long sword used in war.

toà [R. tsū], (Cn. tiù), to dwell; to inhabit; to stay in a place; to contain, as inhabitants.

toà koa^n-hú, to have a mandarin living there. **toà-hì,** to lodge a theatrical company in one's house, hiring them out for money.

toà tá-lóh, where do you live? **sa^n-kap-toà,** to live together. **lâu-i-toà,** detain him. **toà-hɛh^n** (C.), to stay, as a guest. **toà-chia tsòe-tsé,** means to live all his life and leave his posterity here (v. tsé).

toā (R. tō, = col. tāi), a helm; a rudder. **chit-mn̂g-toā,** one helm. **hoa^n-toā,** to hold the helm; to steer. **lāng-toā,** to pull up the helm higher, as in shallow water. **pài-toā,** to unship the helm and lay it along the deck. **khì-ûi, sit-toā,** to lose masts and helm.

toā-lêng, the tiller-rope. **toā-nî^n,** id. **toā-gê,** the tiller. **toā-thâu,** the shaft of the helm. **toā-hióh,** the blade of the helm. **toā-siám,** id. **toā-siám-pang,** id. **toā-tiàu,** the ropes that hold up the helm.

toā, to tow, as boat or raft. **toā-tò-tńg,** to tow back again. **toā-tsûn,** to tow a vessel. **toā-tsûn--ê,** man who engages sampans to tow a vessel out or in.

toā (R. tāi), great; large; grown up; very; left side; hot, as sun.

toā--ê, an elder brother; respectful address to another, esp. to one about our own rank and age. **goán-toā--ê,** my elder brother. **toā-chiah,** large; said of a vessel or of any animal of which "chiah" is the classifier. **toā-ki,** a large branch; large, as anything of which "ki" is the classifier. **toā-tsâng,** large; grown large, as plant or tree.

toā-hàn, a tall person; a large man; an adult or grown up man (v. hàn). **toā-lâng,** an adult; a married man; also (C.), a Kujin (v. lâng). **bōe-toā,** not growing well, as young person. **toā-hì,** colloquial play by adult actors. **toā-pan-hì,** play in mandarin by adult actors.

toā-sòe, large and small; old and young (v. sòe). **khoah-toā,** wide and broad; extended far and wide.

toā-tîm, exceedingly; very. **toā-lîm,** id. **toā-tiâm,** id. **toā-ē,** id. **toā-poà^n,** the greater half. **toā-hūn,** the larger share. **toā-bú sì-kòe,** everywhere; very common (v. kòe; v. bú). **tióh toā-siong,** to be wounded severely (+). **toā-pan-gî,** extremely cheap. **toā-pak,** the far north of China, esp. Shantung (+).

toā-lō͘, a great road; generous, charitable, or liberal in use of money. **toā-pān,** liberal; dignified and easy in manner; large-bodied (v. pān). **toā-liōng,** generous (v. liōng). **toā-chhiú-bīn,** free in the use of money.

toā-tá^n, bold; courageous. **toā-sim-sū,** too cunning and fond of gain. **toā-sim-hiong,** too fond of large gains (v. hiong). **kóng toā-ōe,** to talk boastfully, or as if not at all afraid. **ké-to-toā,** pretending to be of much importance; putting on airs quite above our position.

toā-pêng, the side of honour; the left-hand side; the larger half of a thing cut in two (v. pêng). **toā-pûi^n** (Cn.), id. (C. pûn; T. pâi^n). **pái-toā,** take a step to the left (said by chair-bearers). **toā--khì,** id.

toā-ūi, a seat or place of honour; a large place. **toā-bō,** a ceremonial cap. **toā-gėh,** a month in which much business is done, *e.g.* the 7th or the 12th. **toā-jit,** a very auspicious day (v. jit).

jit toā, the sun very hot. **gėh toā,** the month is one that has 30 days.

sī-toā, a superior. **sī-toā-lâng,** id. **i sī-toā,** he is the elder brother. **lāu-toā,** a village elder or head man. **toā-ló,** title of a mandarin of medium rank (v. ló). **toā-hú,** the chief mandarin of a Foo, as opposed to the "jī-hú." **toā-iâ,** subordinate officers in a yamun (v. iâ). **toā-tsóng,** the head of the police. **toā-koa^n,** a high mandarin.

toā-siong, a great wholesale merchant (v. siong), (+). **toā-sia^n,** a loud voice. **toā-pak,** having a large bore, as cannon (+). **toā-kɵ,** a large cargo-boat (+). **toā-ûi,** the mainmast. **toā-liâu,** the mainsheet (v. liâu). **toā-tn̂g,** the hall of judgment. **toā-tn̂g,** the large entrails. **toā-pó-bú,** the thumb; the big toe. **toā-kha,** having feet of the natural size (not bound), as woman.

toā-bėh, barley.

toā-bó, the legal wife. **toā-kiá^n,** the eldest son. **toā-hia^n,** eldest brother. **toā-chí,** elder sister. **toā-peh,** husband's elder brother. **toā-kū,** wife's elder brother. **toā-kīm,** wife of wife's elder brother, or of oldest maternal uncle. **toā-î,** wife's elder sister. **toā-kɵ,** father's eldest sister (+).

toā-pang, sort of long footstool at a bed, with three drawers in it.

toā — **toā-koa^n** (C.), = A. ta-koa^n, husband's father (s. great). **toā-kɛ** (C.), = A. ta-ke, husband's mother. **toā-kɛ-koa^n** (C.), husband's parents.

toa^n [R. toan, straight; correct; origin]. **in-toa^n,** cause, reason, or origin of action or affair. **in-toa^n khí-lí,** id.

toa^n — **n̄g-toa^n,** small embryo eggs in the ovary. **nūi^n-toa^n** (C.), id.

khɵ-toa^n (Cn. kiò-loa), to cackle when about to lay eggs. **koe-noā^n khɵ-toa^n,** the young fowl cackling when going to lay an egg.

toa^n [R. tan, name of a disease; cf. col. tsoâ^n]. **hé-nâ^n-toa^n** (T.), a small red eruption common on children.

toa^n [R. tan, only, single; a bill, ticket, &c.], a bill, an order, a cheque, a receipt, an account, an invoice, a list, a ticket, a card; singly, alone.

toa^n-toa^n, alone; singly; solitary. **kɵ-toa^n,** id. (v. kɵ). **toa^n-sin,** id. (v. sin). **toa^n-têng,** of one fold or thickness of material. **toa^n-iáp,** single, as a flower.

toa^n-sì^n-kiá^n, an only son. **toa^n-tiah**, to select one article or subject, &c., out of many (v. tiah).

phē-toa^n, a cover for a quilted coverlet. **phōe-toa^n** (C.), id.

phièn-toa^n, a visiting-card; a plain red card for one's name. **phièn-toa^n-tē**, a paper bag for holding visiting-cards. **pài-toa^n**, to send one's card instead of calling.

toa^n-á, a bill; a receipt; a ticket. **toa^n-thâu**, id. **toa^n-thâu-á**, notices (as to soldiers) to be ready at a particular day. **pîn-toa^n**, a certificate, receipt, or such document used as evidence; on the evidence of a document such as a receipt or certificate. **pín-toa^n**, a report given in to a superior, as by a police-officer or tē-pó. **si-toa^n**, a document issued by the provincial treasurer, affixed to a deed of sale or mortgage as proof of registration. **tsu-toa^n**, a document written in red ink by a mandarin, used as a warrant or summons.

siu-toa^n, a receipt for money or goods. **chioh-toa^n**, a receipt for money borrowed, with promise to pay. **hōe-toa^n**, a bill of exchange; an order for money on a place at some distance. **gûn-toa^n**, a money-order, bill, cheque, &c., especially for silver. **chî^n-toa^n**, do., especially for copper cash. **kî-toa^n**, a bill stating the time for payment. **tùi-toa^n**, a bill of exchange; a money-order, draft, or cheque, as on another place. **tùi-toa^n kè-siàu**, to pay by a bill. **tùi-toa^n niá^n-gûn**, to receive money in payment of a bill, cheque, draft, &c. **tùi-toa^n siu-gûn**, id.

chē-toa^n, to accept a bill. **jīn-toa^n**, to certify the goodness or security of a bill, as a third party. **m̄-jīn-toa^n**, to protest a bill. **goân-toa^n pok-hôe**, bill protested.

khui-toa^n, to write out an account. **pun-toa^n**, to send out accounts, as at terms or at end of year. **thoân-toa^n**, to distribute to all the members of a trading guild notices of the price fixed for an article; to send out notices to persons to be all ready on a particular day for some special purpose formerly agreed upon.

thiah-toa^n, to take out a ticket for passage in a vessel. **teh-toa^n**, to pay an earnest of the passage money, which is forfeited if he does not go.

liāu-toa^n, a list of materials to be used in some work, especially in building or repairing a house. **tsáp-mih^n-toa^n**, an inventory; a list or catalogue of various articles. **hè-toa^n**, in invoice, a bill of lading, &c. **hē-hè-toa^n**, a shipping order. **chhut-hè-toa^n**, an order to deliver goods from a vessel, issued by the hong. **phòe-hè-toa^n**, a bill of lading. **tsài-hè-toa^n**, a bill of lading. **tsûn-hè-toa^n**, inventory of goods still on hand.

chhut-tsúi-toa^n, a sort of bill of lading for goods to be sent from the port into the country, given by the hong, certifying that the duty has been paid on the goods, and allowing them to be put on board. **toa^n-tóe**, a certificate (like chhut-tsúi-toa^n) stating the quantity of goods on which duty has been paid, on the evidence of which they may be sent into the country within a fixed time.

chhut-kháu-toa^n, a port-clearance. **chhng-kháu-toa^n**, a ship's manifest (v. chhng). **âng-toa^n**, a permit allowing goods (for export) to be taken on board. **chhi^n-toa^n**, a permit allowing the landing or trans-shipping of imports. **pò-toa^n** a ship's manifest, or similar document (v. pò). **giām-toa^n**, certificate of the amount of goods found on board, given by customs officer.

hê-lê-toa^n, a ticket sold by the head of the beggars to a shop, forbidding beggars to enter it. **khit-chiáh-toa^n**, id. **mī^n-toa^n**, ticket for so many meals at an eating-house (v. mī^n). **kn̂g-toa^n**, ticket of admission to examinations (v. kn̂g). **hì-toa^n**, list of plays from which one is selected by lot. **poáh-toa^n**, to select one of these by lot before the idol that is to be honoured. **tiàu-toa^n**, an order issued by a mandarin to actors or priests (v. tiàu).

toâ^n [R. toân, globular; a lump; united; = col. thoân, thn̂g, nn̂g]. **toâ^n-î^n**, the denoûment of a play, when the parties recognize each other, and all comes right.

toâ^n — **hâm-toâ^n**, the place in a boat, just below the deck, in which the mast is fixed firmly.

toâ^n [R. tân, sandal-wood, = col. thiâ^n]. **toâ-hiu^n**, sandal-wood; incense made from it. **toâ^n-hiu^n-chhâ**, sandal-wood. **toâ^n-chhâ**, id.

toâ^n-oát-tsú (Cn.), the benefactor who gave the site or a large endowment for a temple, often worshipped in a shrine at the back of the temple (Sank. danapata).

toâ^n [R. tân, to fillip; to play an instrument with the nails; to repress, as disobedient persons; cf. col. toā^n], to play a stringed instrument with the finger. **toâ^n-khîm**, to play the harp or such instrument. **teh-toâ^n-chhiù^n**, playing on a stringed instrument and accompanying it with the voice. **tsū-chhiù^n tsū-toâ^n**, to manage one's business (commercial or legal) one's self, without employing any one to consult with, as teacher, shroff, &c., but not necessarily excluding subordinate assistants.

chheng-sim-toâ^n, amusing one's self idly; free from care and rather jolly, often with the idea of avoiding work or anxiety which he should share.

toâ^n (R. tân), an altar; a shrine; usually temporary. **pùt-toâ^n**, a place prepared in a house, by hanging up pictures of the gods, &c., for the rites of "khiā-hà" or of "tsòe-chiò." **hút-toâ^n** (C.), id. **sam-pó-toâ^n**, a temporary shrine for the Buddhist Triad. **thi^n-kong-toâ^n**, temporary shrine put up (usually across a street) for the worship of Giók-tè. **thi^n-tōe-toâ^n**, the altars of Heaven and Earth at the capital, where the emperor worships twice a year. **siā-chek-toâ^n**, imperial altar to gods of land and grain, where the emperor or high mandarin deputed by him sometimes worship. **siā-toâ^n** (T.), a permanent altar at Tâng-oa^n (v. siā), (+).

tō-toâ^n, a place where a Tauist priest lives. **sai-kong-toâ^n**, id. **tō-toâ^n tsāi-chhú**, a Tauist priest lives here (written up at his house).

hiên-toâ^n-kong, a title of the idol Tiō goân-sòe, attendant of Tāi-tō-kong.

kat-toâ^n, to set up a temporary shrine. **pâi-toâ^n**, to set up one richly ornamented. **thiah-toâ^n**, to take down the shrine when the rites are finished. **siā-toâ^n**, to make offerings and plays before the shrine just before taking it down.

phoā^n-toâ^n, to arrange ornaments so that they look well together, as on a table or shrine, though they are not needed; to buy something that might have been dispensed with; to do anything just because it happens to come readily, though it might about as well not have been done; to keep company with a person (either sitting or going somewhere), merely to fill up the time or for company's sake, but without any special purpose. **tàu-phoā^n-toâ^n**, several persons thus keeping company with each other.

toá^n — **toá^n-toá^n**, constantly over and over, when it would have been better not to do so. **toá^n-toá^n m̄-tióh**, always wrong. **toá^n-toá^n-lâi**, coming constantly and troublesomely. **tóaⁿ-tóaⁿ to-sū**, always causing trouble to people, as a busy-body. **tóaⁿ-tóaⁿ chhú-chiet**, always trying to get off too much discount in paying.

toàⁿ [R. tàn, morning; a female character in a play; =col. hoàⁿ], a female character in a play (all acted by male actors). **hì-toàⁿ**, id. **lāu-toàⁿ**, an aged female character in a play. **sió-toàⁿ**, a young female character. **khé-toàⁿ**, a tragic female character. **hoe-toàⁿ**, a young pretty female character, in cheerful or amusing scenes, esp. comic. **bú-toàⁿ**, character of a female warrior. **koh-toàⁿ**, girls, or boys in the character of girls, carried on an ornamented frame at idolatrous processions. **seng-toàⁿ**, male and female characters in a play, all done by men. **ang seng, bé toàⁿ**, husband and wife both young and good-looking.

tsng-toàⁿ, to act the part of a female character, as a man. **tsò-toàⁿ** (C.), id. **tsng-toàⁿ-thiap**, to act high and low female characters. **taⁿ-láng khah-jiét tsng-toàⁿ**, the bearers of the baggage more earnest about it than the actors (said of a servant or employé more ardent and earnest about a business than the master). **thiap-toàⁿ**, to assist in a female character, as actor who usually represents a man.

kin-toàⁿ, at present; now (said esp. in the language of plays, and in Cn.) **tsūi-tsai kàu-kin-toàⁿ**, who would have thought before that we should have been so miserable at this time? **ū-kin-toàⁿ, bô-bîn-hoàⁿ** (having a present but no future), absorbed in the present and reckless of the future, as man who wastes his money lavishly, or who gets his money by cheating, &c.

bîn-toàⁿ (Cn.), shortly afterwards.

toāⁿ [R. toān, a bit; a piece; classifier of affairs and pieces of work; =col. tn̄g]; a small section or paragraph in a book or essay, less than a chapter but longer than a verse; a small bit or piece of a thing; a block of houses, gen. several tens, making a subdivision of a ward or "pó;" a small company or division, as of volunteers. **thâu-toāⁿ**, the first paragraph or section, as in an essay; the first division of the "thoân-liēn" volunteers. **chit-pó, hun tsòe kúi-toāⁿ**, into how many sections is the ward (pó) divided?

chhiú-toāⁿ, skill in work, of any sort. **hó-chhiú-toāⁿ, chit-kún chiū-noāⁿ** (so skilful that at one boiling it is cooked tender), said of managing a matter quietly and successfully.

tiâu-toāⁿ, particulars, as in an agreement. **ū-tiâu-toāⁿ**, all properly arranged and settled. **ū-tiâu ū-toāⁿ**, id. **bô-tiâu-toāⁿ**, managed in a confused and unsatisfactory manner; to manage a matter in a confused way. **bô-tiâu bô-toāⁿ**, id. **it-tiâu it-toāⁿ kā-i-kóng**, tell him fully with all the particulars.

chit-toāⁿ-sū, one piece of business; one affair. **chit-toāⁿ ê-sū**, id. **chit-toāⁿ ê hó-ì**, a piece of good advice or of kind treatment.

toāⁿ (cf. toāⁿ), to fillip with the finger; to bound or leap, as a ball; to palpitate or throb; to explode, as a cracker. **tò-toāⁿ**, to rebound.

toāⁿ-chîn, to make the chalk-line or ink-line strike the wood (or other material) so as to make a straight line. **toāⁿ thâu-khak**, to fillip the head, as of a child. **toāⁿ gêng-géng-hút**, to play with the stones of the lung-yen fruit, like marbles. **khit-phàu toāⁿ-tiòh**, to be hit by an exploding cracker.

phók-phók-toāⁿ, to palpitate, as the heart; to throb painfully, as with headache or toothache. **phiák-phiák-toāⁿ**, id. **kóng kàu toāⁿ-phoà lâng-hī-khang**, to talk so much about a thing that one dislikes to hear of it any more.

toāⁿ-khui (C.), to burst, as a gun.

toāⁿ-chí, pellets shot from toy bows. **kim-toāⁿ-chí**, id.

ûiⁿ-toāⁿ (C.), a round yellowish fruit about the size of the gêng-géng, but with several seeds.

toāⁿ [R. tō? lán?], lazy. **toāⁿ-toāⁿ**, id. **pîn-toāⁿ**, id. **pûn-toāⁿ** (C.), id. **siūⁿ-toāⁿ**, id. **toāⁿ-kut**, a lazy fellow; lazy. **khah-toāⁿ sí-lâng**, lazier than a corpse. **pîn-toāⁿ i--ê kha-chhiú**, he is lazy at work.

toah [R. toat, to pluck; to seize and pull; cf. col. tiuh], to shun angrily and sullenly; to refuse sulkily; to give an angry shake of the arm (or of the body) in breaking off a discussion; to give a short sharp pull or twitch, *e.g.* to clothes after they have been washed, to make them dry, smooth, and even, or to make them hang well.

toah--tsáu, to break away from another who is urging us to wait with him, or who is gently holding our dress as an indication of his desire to keep us with him. **toah-khui**, to turn away from a man, as not worth wasting time on.

tiuⁿ-toah, to refuse sulkily to do what one is asked, or to answer when spoken to, though he has no real objection to the thing; especially putting on the appearance of unwillingness in order to get more money. **siū-khì tiuⁿ-toah**, id. **siū-khì siū-toah** (C.), = A. siū-khì siū-toàh, angry sulky behaviour.

toàh (C. toah). **siū-khì siū-toàh**, sulky angry behaviour. **siū-khì siū-toàh, piaⁿ-oáⁿ siak-tī**, throwing away bowls and chopsticks in a pet or rage.

toàh [R. tát, name of a plant]. **kún-toàh** (Cn.), = A. ka-boàh-chhài, a sort of vegetable. **kún-toàh-chhài** (Cn), id.

toan [R. straight; correct; decent; commencement; origin; a piece of business; = col. toaⁿ]. **toan-chiàⁿ**, correct in conduct. **toan-chiàⁿ ê-lâng**, a man of correct conduct. **ngé-koan toan-chiàⁿ**, the features of the face and the ears all well formed and regular, without any serious blemish. **toan-hong sì-chiàⁿ**, correct in conduct; well arranged; straight and even (v. hong). **toan-tsong**, correct in conduct, as woman. **toan-khái**, well written or printed, as characters of the form called "khái." **put-toan**, not correct in conduct, *e.g.* given to gambling, lust, drink, or any wickedness. **tsòe-put-toan**, to commit impurity. **sim-sút put-toan**, heart and actions very wicked and injurious.

īⁿ-toan, false doctrine.

sū-toan, the origin of a quarrel or troublesome affair. **ē-toan**, the cause of a calamity; a matter that may afterwards cause much trouble. **hō-toan** (C.), id. **seng-toan**, to give rise to a quarrel or to serious trouble.

toan-goàt (R.), the first month of the year. **toan-ngé**, the 5th day of the 5th month. **toan-ngé-tsoeh**, id.

toan, to demand a higher price or higher wages than proper, quite refusing to take the smaller and proper amount, as when one's labour, or an article which no one else has, is very urgently needed. **toan--tiòh**, id. **toan--lâng**, id. **toan-tiàu**, id., or to strike work, as a man in employment, just at the time his services are urgently needed, so as to compel the raising of his wages.

toân [R. globular; a lump; united;=col. toâⁿ, thoân, thn̂g, nn̂g]. **toân-toân-îⁿ**, unbroken, as a family (v. îⁿ).

chit-toân ê hó-ì (C.), a good piece of advice.

toân [R. to transmit; to hand down; to propagate; to deliver a message;=col. thoân; and by change of tone "toān," books of history], sometimes (esp. Cn.) said instead of "thoân," to transmit; to hand down, &c. (*q.v.*)

toán [R. short; shortcomings; faults; errors;=col. té]. **ngé-toán-siⁿ**, short and somewhat stout, but well-formed and well-set (v. ngé).

toán-hēng, wickedly and secretly injuring others. **kóng lâng-ê-toán**, to talk openly of a man's faults.

toán-kièn, going to kill one's self. **khì toán-kièn**, to commit suicide. **siūⁿ toán-kièn**, intending to commit suicide. **chhē toán-kièn**, id.

giên-sû khah-toán, unable to state one's own case well.

tiông-toán (R.), long and short; good and bad. **chiát-tiông pó-toán**, to make up for deficiency in one part by great abundance or super-excellence in another part. **chhien-jit tiông, it-jit toán**, said of a scholar who is generally able to write good essays, but makes serious mistakes at the examination (lit. one day out of a thousand).

toàn [R. to judge; to decide; to determine; certainly; cf. by change of tone, "toān," to cut]. **toàn-jiân**, decidedly; certainly. **toàn-toàn-m̄**, determinedly will not. **koat-toàn**, decidedly; determinedly; most certainly; decided, determined, or fixed in purpose. **ì-sù koat-toàn**, purpose fixed. **iu-jiû koáⁿ-toàn**, undecided in purpose; not strict enough in punishing faults.

tȯk-toàn, to decide or venture on one's own responsibility, as in speaking or acting. **ka-kī tȯk-toàn**, to do a thing of one's own will without consulting others. **káⁿ tȯk-toàn**, I feel perfectly sure; I have no hesitation in making the statement. **tȯk-toàn-bô**, I am absolutely certain that it is not so, or will not be.

toàn-iok, to fix an engagement; to make a definite agreement or arrangement. **toàn-ioh**, id. **saⁿ-toàn-ioh**, id. **toàn-kè**, to agree on a price, fixing it after discussion. **sien-toàn, hō put-oàn**, make a definite agreement at first, and then there is no room for bad feeling afterwards. **sien-toàn, hō put-hoān**, make the agreement and do not break it.

kong-toàn, to judge and decide justly or publicly, as mandarin or arbiter, or as several headmen or partners met together to settle a dispute. **phoàⁿ-toàn**, to give sentence. **sím-toàn**, to give judgment; to judge and decide; to give sentence. **sím-toàn put-bêng**, to judge unjustly. **toàn-lí, put-toàn-chhin**, to judge according to right principles, not according to relationship or influence.

toān [R. to cut; to sever; to cut off;=col. tn̄g; cf. by change of tone "toàn," to decide; to judge]. **kat-toān**, to break off intercourse or have no dealings with a person. **toān-tsoát** (R.), to have no intercourse or friendship with a person.

kài-chiú toān-ien, neither drink spirituous liquor nor smoke opium or tobacco. **toān-súi-hóⁿ--sí**, to put to death officially by starvation (lit. without water or fire).

hiuⁿ-ien put-toān, incense burns unceasingly, as in much-frequented temple. **put-toān bān--jī**, a continuous border made in the form of the character "bān."

siȯk-toān, a medicine made from a plant (Cirsium lanceolatum?).

toān [R. a bit; a piece; classifier of affairs;=col. toāⁿ, tn̄g]. **tāi-toān**, grave, sedate, or dignified in manner; having a self-possessed manly bearing; liberal and pleasant to deal with in business. **m̄-tāi-toān**, mean or contracted in views; too light and jocular in manner.

it-to lióng-toān, to settle and determine a matter at once and finally, after it has been long in suspense or under discussion; to cut off a bad course of life at once (lit. make two pieces by one blow of the knife).

toān (R. id.), satin. **ú-toān**, camblet, and similar strong alpaca or woollen stuffs. **kòng-toān**, satin. **soàⁿ-toān**, a fine soft sort of satin. **tiû-toān**, silk and satin. **lîn-lô se-toān**, fine materials for dresses; fine clothing.

toān-á, a small bit of satin, esp. for rubbing things smooth. **toān-kún**, a satin border on a dress.

toān [R. books of history; historical records, esp. with a moral bearing; by change of tone from "toân," to transmit]. **keng-toān**, classical books. **tsó-toān**, the commentary on the Chhun-chhiu (v. tsó). **hong-sîn-toān**, a book of ancient stories; fabulous; fickle (v. hong). **hok-im-toān** (X.), a Gospel.

toȧt [R. to take away forcibly; to plunder;=col. tėh]. **to-teng toȧt-tsâi**, a large family diminishes wealth. **cheng-thien toȧt-kok**, to aim at the throne, as insurgents. **cheng-chhe toȧt-tiên**, fighting to take away one's wife or lands (v. chhe).

kiông-sû toȧt chêng-lí, to maintain doggedly that we are right, though manifestly wrong.

tôe [R. id.; some read "tōe;" to exchange, barter, or sell;=col. tūi].

tôe-hè-ìn, a stamp put on goods when sold from a shop.

hoat-tôe, for sale, as goods.

tôe (R. tê), (C. tê; Cn. tôe), to write down, as one's name, or as a piece of poetry, or as an inscription on an ancestral tablet, &c.; to subscribe; a theme or text.

tôe-bȧk, a theme; a text. **tôe-thâu**, id. **chiong-hit--ê tsòe tôe-thâu**, to allege it as a justification or pretext, true or false. **liáh-hit--ê tsòe-tôe**, id. **chhut-tôe**, to give out a theme or text. **chiȧh-tôe**, fitting well to the text. **jip-tôe**, id. **phoà-tôe**, to give the meaning of the text in our own words in the first sentence of the essay. **phoà tôe-ì**, id. **phoà tôe-sîn**, to give the meaning of the text in a more deep and thorough manner.

tôe-iên, to subscribe money. **tôe-chîⁿ**, id., esp. copper cash. **tôe-gûn**, to subscribe silver. **koan-tôe** (C. kien-tê), to subscribe money. **kong-tôe**, subscribed for a public purpose, as money collected from many persons. **tôe khah-hó-khoàⁿ**, make a (larger) subscription that looks better.

tôe-tsàn, to write an inscription (on a scroll or picture) in praise of a man or of an idol, written at the foot of the picture or scroll. **tôe-si**, to compose and write poetry, as on a scroll or wall. **tôe-miâⁿ**, to write down one's name, as in an inscription; to write the name of a child, in choosing its name. **tôe miâⁿ-jī**, to write down one's name, *e.g.* as in an inscription. **kim-pńg tôe-miâⁿ**, to become a Tsin-sze, or such high graduate.

tôe [R. tê, the heel; the hoof], (C. tê; Cn. tôe), a hoof. **tsàm-tôe**, to stamp with the foot. **tiuh-tôe**, to limp very slightly. **ah-bú-tôe**, having a peculiar gait, shaking from side to side.

chhiú-tôe, the inner side of the wrist at the root of the palm; the carpus; the heel of the hand. **lí--ê chhiú-tôe**, your handwriting. **chhut chhiú-tôe**, to write a deed of sale with one's own hand, and stamp it with the impression of the hand or finger in ink. **tsām chhiú-tôe hē--i**, to stamp it so.

kha-tôe, a hoof. **kòng lí--ê kha-tôe**, I will strike your feet (said only to children running about too much). **ti-kha-tôe**, pig's feet, for cooking or cooked. **āu-tôe**, the hind-feet. **chêng-tôe**, the fore-feet. **khòng-tôe**, pig's feet stewed or boiled very soft. **gû-tôe**, a cow's hoof. **bé-tôe**, a horse's hoof. **bé-tôe-ńg**, sleeves of ceremonial dress, shaped like horse-hoofs. **bé-tôe-se**, sort of round sweet cake. **bé sit-tôe**, the horse stumbles.

káu-tôe-hoe, a plant with a large sweet white flower.

tóe (R. tí, = col. tē), (C. té; Cn. tŏe), bottom; base; foundation; original state, condition, or constitution.

ē-tóe (C. ɛ-té), bottom; below. **tóe-ē**, below; down below.

ū-tóe, to have a solid foundation, as a statement or affair, or as man's reputation, &c.; to have a bottom; right at bottom, &c. **bô-tóe**, bottomless; baseless; unfounded; not having a safe foundation, as a deed; no bottom, as in sounding. **béng bô-tóe**, braggardly; overbearing, but without any real power.

tóe-tì, origin of an affair; antecedents, past history, or original circumstances of a man. **ū-tóe-tì**, having a safe foundation, as title-deeds; having some good antecedents, as man, *e.g.* having respectable ancestors, or himself having genius, talents, wealth, or good name. **ū-tóe-tioh**, id.; having talents or property (v. tioh). **ū-tóe-chioh**, having a good foundation, as to health, wealth, &c. (v. chioh). **ū-tóe ū-koà**, fully and correctly drawn up, as document; all properly arranged and settled, as a matter.

khí-tóe, first origin; originally; to make the beginning, as of a family or of a custom.

kun-tóe (C. kin-té), original commencement or root of a matter; original circumstances or condition of a man, often with the idea of something wrong. **ū-kun-tóe**, to have property, wealth, or influence, &c. **bô-kun bô-tóe**, nothing known of his antecedents, at least nothing satisfactory. **iah lâng--ê kun-tóe**, to rake up and talk openly of some old story about a man's wickedness, or something about which he is ashamed. **mn̄g kàu-kun-tóe**, to inquire to the very root of the matter. **mn̄g bē-kàu kun-tóe**, having inquired but superficially into the matter, or not having got to the bottom of it; not understanding it fully, nor knowing how much is true.

kàu-tóe, to the very bottom. **tó kàu-tah-tóe**, utterly gone wrong and ruined, as affair. **chhám kàu-tah-tóe**, miserable to the utmost extreme. **su kàu-tah-tóe**, to lose terribly, as in gambling or fighting. **kàu-thàu-tóe**, to the very bottom, as in investigating a matter; or as a heap of goods, saying that the whole quantity is the same as those on the surface. **kóng thàu-tóe**, to tell all the circumstances. **thàu-tóe-tâm**, thoroughly drenched; wet to the skin.

hu-tóe, naturally of a weak constitution.

ū-tiâm-tóe, to have a good deal of money or property. **ū hó-giáh-tóe**, come of a wealthy family; originally rich. **ū-chheh-tóe**, having originally a good education. **ū kú-jîn-tóe**, having the rank of Kujin before being appointed to the office.

chē-tóe, to settle, as sediment.

teh-tóe, at the bottom of a pile; the last of a lot of things. **teh-tóe-hè**, worthless goods. **teh pêng-tóe**, to take off a small discount (about ¼ per cent.) when a large quantity of goods is paid for in silver (v. teh).

hè-tóe (C. hòe-té), the remainder of a lot of goods. **chhng-tóe**, the remnant of a cargo, in bottom of hold. **tê-tóe**, the tea left in a cup after drinking. **hun-tóe**, opium refuse; it is worked up again for use. **lê-tóe**, sort of dollars, of somewhat inferior silver (v. lê).

tsûn-tóe, to preserve a copy or record, as of a document (v. tsûn).

tsûn-tóe, the bottom of a vessel. **o-tóe**, a boat or small junk with a black bottom. **péh-tóe**, a boat with a white bottom, like a small "khan-hong." **thùi-tóe**, to repair a vessel's bottom.

kha-tóe, the sole of the foot. **ôe-tóe** (C. ê-té), the sole of a shoe. **tsoá-tóe-ôe**, shoes with paper soles. **béh-tóe** (C. bóeh-té), the thick quilted sole of a Chinese stocking. **láp-tóe**, having thick stiff quilted soles, as Chinese stockings.

lap-tóe, having lost the bottom, as an old bucket.

khò-tóe, the seat of trowsers.

sim-tóe, one's inmost heart. **phah--tióh i sim-koa^{n}-tóe**, to say something that touches his sin or fault, so that he cannot but feel it. **phah--tióh i sim-tóe**, id.

toa^{n}-tóe, a sort of certificate of goods having paid duty, used for sending them into the country (v. toa^{n}).

hái-tóe, the bottom of the sea; at the bottom of the sea. **thô-tóe**, below the surface of the ground. **chí^{n}-tóe**, the bottom of a well; at the bottom of a well. **nâ^{n}-tóe**, in the bottom of the basket; the bottom of the basket. **ki-tóe**, a foundation.

tóe [R. tí, to resist; to oppose; to sustain; = col. tú], (C. té), to oppose; to resist. **tóe--lâng**, to resist people. **ká^{n}-tóe**, not afraid to scold at him, or to fight him, when attacked in the same manner. **kap-lâng tóe-chhiú**, to strike back when struck; to pay back violent abuse, scolding, or discussion in the same manner.

tóe (R. thú?), (C. té), to fill in, as a liquid, or as boiled rice; to contain, as a dish. **tóe-tī^{n}**, to fill quite full, as a dish. **tóe-pn̄g** (C. té-pūi^{n}), to fill full of boiled rice, as a bowl or such dish; to contain rice, as a bowl.

tòe (C.), = A. tè, to follow. **tòe-bóe**, = A. tè-bé, to follow after. **kin-tòe**, = A. kun-tè, to follow, as attendant.

tōe [R. tē, order; rank], (Cn. tŏe; C. tē; A. tē, tōe), = tē, prefix to ordinal numbers. **tōe-it**, first. **tōe-jī**, second. **tōe-kúi**, which? (in order), answered by an ordinal number.

tōe (R. thú), (C. tē; Cn. tŏe), a sort of flax. **tōe-pò**, fine grass-cloth. **báng-tiù^{n}-tōe**, coarse flaxen stuff for mosquito-curtains.

tsai-tōe, to plant flax. **cheh-tōe**, to pick out flax fibres, making them into thread.

tōe-á, flax ready to be made into thread; flaxen cloth worn in mourning. **tōe-á-soà^{n}**, thread made from flax; linen thread. **tōe-á-si**, fine fibres of flax, used as thread, or to be joined together to make string or twine. **tōe-á-hók**, mourning dress for near relatives. **tōe-á-sa^{n}**, id. **chhēng tōe-á**, to be in deep mourning.

tōe [R. tē, to hand from one to another; to transmit], (C. tē; Cn. tŏe). **thoân-tōe** (R.), to hand along through several hands, each handing to the other, as a letter transmitted from courier to courier, or as an essay handed up to the examiner.

phah-tōe-kè, = phah-tē-kè, to send a criminal to be dealt with by the mandarin of his native place.

tōe (R. tē), (C. tē; Cn. tőe), the earth. **thi^{n}-tōe**, heaven and earth; nature (v. thi^{n}). **tōe-ē**, the earth below (v. thi^{n}); below the earth. **kiú-tsoân tōe-ē**, the invisible world.

tōe-bīn, the surface of the ground. **tōe-bīn-chiū^{n}**, upon the earth. **tōe-mêh^{n}**, veins or strata in the ground. **tōe-khì**, influence of the ground, as on disease or in geomancy. **chiōng-goân-tōe**, a place for a grave that would produce a "chiōng-goân" graduate. **im-tōe put-jû sim-tōe**, a good heart is better than a good site for a grave.

tōe-hng, a place; a region. **tōe-hng-koa^{n}**, the mandarin who has special charge of a place, *e.g.* as the Hai-fang (hái-hông) has of Amoy. **sìn-tōe**, a military station. **tōe-tsø**, land-tax (v. tsø). **pún-tōe**, native place (v. pún). **tōe-thâu sek**, well acquainted with the place. **tōe-thâu chhi^{n}**, not acquainted with the place. **tōe-kài**, a boundary of country, territory, or property. **tōe-thé**, a region; a place. **thé-tōe**, id.

tōe-pē, rank, station, or relative position (v. pē). **tōe-ūi**, grade of station or rank (v. ūi). **kièn-siàu kàu bô-tōe**, put to shame before the world, as one who does a disgraceful act.

tòng-tōe, living long in a place, as a permanent inhabitant. **chē-tōe hun-tsng**, to be a receiver of stolen goods. **tó-tōe-kè**, an extraordinarily low price. **teh-tōe-gûn**, money advanced when a house is rented, and not asked back till about to leave (v. teh).

tōe-ki, a foundation. **tōe-hām**, a pitfall. **tōe-chhìn**, sort of strong lever for raising great weights. **tōe-kiû**, a terrestrial globe (v. kiû).

tōe-tāng (C. tø-tāng), an earthquake. **tōe-gû**, the cow that causes earthquakes (v. gû).

tōe-phia^{n}, one of the spirits called "sam-phia^{n}." **tōe-kong**, the Earth, viewed as a god. **tōe-kong-si^{n}**, his birth-day, on 1.10. **tőe-má** (Cn.), the Earth, as a goddess. **thi^{n}-kong tőe-má** (Cn.), Heaven and Earth, as god and goddess, or the god and goddess of Heaven and Earth.

sit-tōe, solid firm ground, not recently filled in or hollow. **khàng-tōe**, open vacant ground without buildings. **chhù-tōe**, a site where an old house had formerly stood. **hn̂g-tōe**, land used for dry fields. **chhân-tōe**, land used for irrigated fields. **ngī^{n}-tōe**, hard soil. **chiòh-tōe**, rocky ground, not good for a grave-site, nor for cultivation, *e.g.* little soil on a large rock, or ground full of rocks. **tsng-tōe**, a tiled floor or court. **thô-tōe**, an unpaved earthen floor; the natural surface of the ground.

tóeh [mere reduplication]. **óeh-tóeh** (C. éh-téh), narrow; very narrow.

toh (R. tok), a table; a feast. **bōng-toh**, the flat plain stone in front of the upright stone of a grave, used as a table for offerings. **lêng-toh**, a table placed before the place for the spirit in the rites performed soon after death.

kong-tsō-toh, the table used as a mandarin's tribunal. **gûn-toh-á-tāi^{n}** (T.), a money-changer's shop.

àn-toh, a long, narrow, high table (v. àn). **oà^{n}-toh**, id. (v. oà^{n}). **hoâi^{n}-thâu-toh**, a table at the side of the room. **kî-liông-toh**, a long table, narrower than oà^{n}-toh (v. kî). **sì-sien-toh**, a small square table, size for four men to sit at. **la̍k-sien-toh**, a somewhat larger size, suitable for six men. **pat-sien-toh**, a large square table, as for eight men. **ge̍h-toh**, a round table. **siên-chhn̂g-toh**, table with raised rim on three sides. **se-hē-toh**, a table that comes off the legs, which fold up. **lē-si-toh**, id. **í^{n}-oai^{n}-toh**, a folding-table. **kí-toh**, a very small table for tea; a tea-poy. **siá-jī-toh** (f.), a table made with a desk.

toh-pêng, one-half of a double table. **toh-kūi**, a table with drawers, cupboard, &c., in it (v. kūi).

toh-bīn, the top of a table; the board of a table, as distinguished from the legs; presents of eatables made to bridegroom. **toh-kheng**, frame of top of table. **toh-kha**, legs of table; at the foot of the table. **toh-koai^{n}**, cross-bars or rounds connecting the legs of table. **toh-kî^{n}**, rim or border of table. **toh-ûi**, curtain in front of table between the legs (v. ûi). **toh-kun** (f.), a table-cloth.

toh-téng, on the table. **toh-thâu-teng**, a lamp for use on a table. **toh-thâu sien-si^{n}**, the teacher on the table (said of a dictionary).

iên-toh, a feast. **boán-hàn-toh**, a feast in Manchoo and Chinese style. **chit-sék-toh**, one meal or feast. **chit-tè-toh**, one table (the article of furniture). **chit-chiah-toh** (C.), id. **tâng-toh ê-lâng**, persons who eat at the same table. **ha̍p-toh**, the feast of the bride with her female friends.

chē-toh, to sit at table. **chhiá^{n}-toh**, to invite to a feast. **sàng-toh**, to present a whole prepared entertainment to another. **hoa̍t hì-toh**, to make a man give a play and a feast, as a forfeit. **pān-toh**, a man who keeps a shop for preparing feasts, = tø-chí. **pâi-toh**, to lay the table; a table-boy. **chiū^{n}-toh**, to be placed on the table, as things for a feast. **nâ^{n}-á-poa̍t bōe-chiū^{n}-toh--tit**, guavas cannot be put on the table to present to guests or divinities (said of a slave or such person of low condition being unfit to see a distinguished guest).

toh [R. tok, lofty; erect; eminent], a surname.

tòh [R. tiok, to kindle], to flame; to blaze up; to take fire; to kindle (neuter); but in Yun-siau and Chau-an it is a bad word used in vile scolding, so that "oàh" is used there for "blaze" or "kindle."

hé tòh, the fire blazes up or kindles. **sim-hé tòh**, rage or passion excited. **khoài-tòh-hé**, easy to set on fire. **kōe-tòh-hé**, id. **ná^{n}-tòh ná^{n}-iām**, blazing more and more fiercely. **iām phông-phông pha-pha-tòh** (= phā-phā-tòh), id.

jit chit-sit chit-tòh, alternate cloud and sunshine.

tòh [R. tiok, right; correct; to cause; accomplished; = col. tiòh]. **m̄-tòh-khì**, = m̄-tiòh-khì, you had better go; we had better go.

tòh [R. tek, to choose], (C.), to separate the good and bad, as of vegetables. **kán-tòh**, to choose out; to select. **tòh-chhut-lâi**, to choose out, as the good. **tòh--khí-lâi**, id. **tòh-chhang**, to clean onions before cooking them, rejecting the useless parts. **tòh-chhang tòh-chhài**, to clean away the refuse of vegetables before using them. **tòh chhang-chhài**, id. (all these phrases are only C.)

tőh (Cn.), = A. teh, to peck.

tőh [R. toat, to take away forcibly, = col. téh], (Cn. T.), = A. téh, to snatch away; also (T.), = A. kè-ki, to make a new plant by tying earth round a branch, so that it roots itself, and is cut off.

tok [R. firm; strong; sincere; = col. tauh]. **tok-**

sit (r.), sincere and truthful; honest and simple-minded. **tok-sìn** (R.), very faithful.

tun-tok (r.), correct in conduct (v. tun), (s. rule).

tok (cf. tak). **tok-tiàⁿ**, = tak-tiàⁿ, to anchor for a short time, as when waiting for good wind or tide. **tok chit-tiáp-á-kú**, id.

tok (cf. tuh). **phīⁿ tok-tok**, the point of the nose turned down and pointed.

tok— **kiâm tok-tok**, very salt.

tok (T.) **tok-ka-tsŏ**, = A. tuh-ka-chē, to nod in sleep or doze.

tok [R. to strike; to beat], to beat so as to bruise; to pound with a stone; to hurt by knocking against something. **tok-phoà**, to strike so as to break, as a shell or thin piece of earthenware; to wound, as one's head, by striking it against something.

tok-hiàh, to wound one's forehead, as beggars do to excite pity. **tok koe-nñg**, to strike an egg on something so as to break the shell. **tok-jí-á**, to make bits of tile round by beating them, as for children's play (v. jí).

tok (R. id.), to carve, polish, or work, as a gem. **tok-ìn**, to cut a seal, as on a valuable stone. **tok-gėk**, to work jade-stone. **giòk put-tok, put-sêng-khì**, if jade be not wrought it does not become a useful article.

tiau-tok, to carve and work, as a gem (s. oversee).

tok (R. khok? cruel; excessive), (Cn. khok), to drive too hard a bargain; to make people buy too dear or sell too cheap. **tok--lâng pan-gî**, to make people sell to us too cheap. **khit--i tok-kùi**, to be made to pay too dear to him. **khit--i tok--khì**, to be made to sell too cheap or buy too dear from him.

tok-kiáu, several men combining to cheat in gambling. **tok lâng-ê-kiáu**, id.

tok (R. id.), to oversee. **tok-kang**, to oversee work or workmen. **tok sai-hū**, to oversee workmen. **tok-khí**, to oversee the building of a house. **tok-tsō**, to oversee the building of a boat or junk. **tok-tīn**, to have the oversight of a body of soldiers, as standard-bearer. **tok-tūi**, do. of small body of soldiers. **tok-lēng**, the boy who carries the largest flag of the 13 in an idolatrous procession.

tsóng-tok, governor-general or viceroy. **tok-bú**, governor-general and lieutenant-governor. **thê-tok**, general or admiral (v. thê).

kam-tok (r.), to oversee; also (X.), a bishop.

chek-tok, to reprove or correct, regulate, and guide in the right way. **tok-chek**, id. **tun-tok** (r.), to teach and train carefully (v. tun), (s. firm). **kàu-tok**, to instruct and keep in good order, as dependants or younger relatives. **hó-kàu-tok**, skilful at keeping inferiors in good order; easily kept in order, as boy. **tiau-tok**, to keep in good behaviour, as junior relatives (s. carve). **tiau-tok tsú-tit**, to keep junior relatives in good order.

ki-tok (X.), Christ.

tók [R. a great standard or banner]. **pó-tók-kî**, a large flag with a dragon on it, used by commander-in-chief or such high official. **chè-tók**, to make offerings to that flag, as general on going to war.

tók [R. dirty; muddy; to defile; to desecrate; to annoy]. **siet-tók**, to blaspheme or insult with great contumely, as a god or superior.

mēⁿ-tók--lí, I beg to trouble you, sir! I have given you too much trouble.

tók [R. to measure; by change of tone from "tø," a measure; a rule; to measure]. **bōe-chhek-tók--tit**, cannot be searched to the bottom, as a mystery or secret, or as the heart and its purposes (s. tablet). **put-khó chhek-tók**, id. (the phrase is only used in these negative forms).

chhúi-tók (R.), to draw an inference from premises or evidence. **chhún-tók** (R.), to examine into the thoughts and purposes, as of another, or of one's own heart.

tók [R. a tablet for writing on; a document; a letter]. **chhek-tók**, a book of forms for writing letters (s. measure).

àn-tók-iâ, a prime-minister in the Hàn dynasty named Siau Ho, worshipped by the subordinates in mandarin's offices.

tók (C. tø). **tók-pân**, a sort of earthen vessel for holding flowers, which are stuck in it.

tók-pân, a sort of bright-green beetle.

tók (R. id., = col. tåk). **tók-tók**, only; solely. **tók-tók chit-ê**, only one. **tók-tók-goá tiāⁿ-tiāⁿ**, only I myself. **tan-hong tók-bī**, a drug which is taken alone, not combined with other medicines.

kø-tók (r.), solitary, as a person having no relatives. **koan-koáⁿ kø-tók**, the four sorts of solitary persons, viz. old bachelors, widows, orphans, and those who have no relatives. **kø-mñg tók-chhī**, the only house that has a special article.

tók-toàn, to assert or decide on one's own responsibility (v. toàn). **tók-sūi-chhñg**, a bed or couch suitable for one person (v. sūi). **tók-siⁿ ê-kiáⁿ** (r.), an only son.

tók-hoát, a medicinal root.

tók (R. id., = col. tåk, thàu), poison; poisonous; miasma; malarious; noxious humour or morbific influence even in one's own body. **tók-iòh**, poisonous drugs. **tók-khì**, poisonous influence; malarious infections or morbific poison. **hah--tiòh tók-khì**, to be injured by malaria or infection. **hoat jiėt-tók**, boils or eruptions (as on children) in hot weather. **hong-tók**, sores arising from chronic rheumatism or from venereal causes. **phah hong-tók**, such sores breaking out. **piēn-tók**, sort of diseased swelling near the groin (v. piēn).

ngó-tók, five sorts of food considered bad for men of weak constitution.

kóe-tók, to cure boils or eruptions which are supposed to have been caused by eating something deleterious. **kái-tók**, id. **siau-tók**, id. **siu-tók**, to remove poisonous matter by eating it up, as the cockroach is supposed to do.

pàng-tók, to administer poison secretly, as by poisoning wells, &c. **hē-tók**, id. **hók-tók**, to take poison (v. hók). **tók--sí** (r.), to kill by poison. **tiòng-tók**, to have taken poison accidentally; very dangerous or injurious, as a plot or conspiracy against a man.

im-thim-tók, malicious and crafty; plotting mischief; dissembling deeply for the purpose of injuring. **im-tim-tók** (r.), id. **im-thim tèng-tók** (C.), id.

sái tók-pē, to use secret plots or schemes so as to inflict severe injury on a man. **sái àm-tók**, id. **chhāi àm-tók**, id.

tók-chhiú, acting so as to injure another very seriously, as by actual violence, or by heavy accusations before mandarin. **hē tók-chhiú**, to deal murderous blows; to attack a man with intent to murder; to enter a very terrible accusation in court against a man. **tók-chhùi**, scolding with very foul words or terrible curses. **siet tók-chhùi**, to scold or curse thus. **siet chit--ê tók-chhùi**, id.

海上絲綢之路文獻集成 科技與文化編

tók-thâng, a venomous or poisonous reptile. **tók-tsoâ**, a venomous serpent. **khah-tók sí-tsoâ**, more poisonous than a dead serpent (said of a thing or of a man; applied to a man, it means that his curses or maledictions generally come true).

khok-tók, very cruel to an inferior, esp. to female slave. **khé-tók**, to treat harshly and severely, as woman does to female slave, &c. **khé-tók chêng-lâng-kiáⁿ**, to maltreat or oppress a stepson.

ok-tók, wicked and cruel. **hêng-gék ok-tók**, extremely wicked, cruel, and oppressive. **ok-sim tók-hēng**, wicked, cruel, and injurious heart and conduct. **chhàu-sim tók-hēng**, id. **tsòe-ok tsòe-tók**, to act very wickedly and injuriously. **tsòe-ok tsòe-tók, khiâ-bé khók-khók; hó-sim hó-hēng, bô-saⁿ thang-chhēng**, the wicked and oppressive ride jollily on horses; the well-behaved have no clothes.

tom (R. id., = col. tôm), (C.), sound of a stone in water. **tom-tom-kiò**, sound of water pouring long and loud into water.

tôm (R. tom), sound of a stone in deep water.

tong [R. to bear; to sustain; to be equal to; to oppose; to have the responsible management; ought; proper; now; at present; = col. tng, taⁿ; and by change of tone, tòng, tǹg, tàng].

tong-kim, now; at present. **tong-jit**, just on that day (in past time). **tong-sî**, just then (past). **pí-tong-sî**, id. **tong-sî ióng**, just come to one's full strength, as about 18 or 20. **liâm-tong-sî**, suddenly.

tong-tông, openly and publicly (v. tông).

tong-tong-háu, constantly talking on when he ought to stop (s. sound of water). **tong-tong-chiáh**, constantly eating instead of stopping as he ought.

ân tong-tong, very firm, as a knot. **chiáh kàu-pá-tong-tong**, I have eaten quite enough.

tong-sū, to have the chief management, as in a shop. **teh tong-sū**, id. **tsòe tong-sū**, to be the person who has the management. **tong-koân**, having for the time the power or authority, as manager of a firm; having considerable influence or power just then.

tong-thâu, to refuse to sell in order to raise the price, as when few of the article are in market.

tong-bōe-tiâu, unable to endure it; intolerable. **bōe-tong--tit** (r.), do.; cannot endure so much honour or politeness. **ōe-tong--tit**, able to pay up, as subscription; able to carry, as load; able to bear the state of matters, *e.g.* cold, state of feud, &c. **tsū-tsok tsū-tong**, doing so, must bear the consequences. **kám-tsok kám-tong**, id. **sék kám-tong**, "this stone can bear the bad luck," written on a stone in the wall of a house in an unlucky situation. **it-jîn kám-sú, bān-hu bók-tong**, if one man be not afraid to die, a myriad will not venture to meddle with him, *e.g.* a man who is desirous to cause trouble. **bóe--chiá put-bêng, bōe--chiá tí-tong**, if anything in the sale be not clear, the seller bears the responsibility.

tong-kui, sort of medicine (v. kui).

bú-tong-tiēn, the temple of Hiên-thien Siōng-tè (v. bú).

tong [R. water; sound of water]. **tong-tong-háu**, the sound of water rushing rapidly in a gutter or small channel (s. bear; now).

tong [R. pendent stone-ornaments; jingling stones; = col. tang]. **teng-teng tong-tong**, sound of a bell. **tin-tin tong-tong**, sound of a vibrating string.

tong [R. tiong, middle; centre]. **tin-tong**, one odds and one evens. **khui-tin-tong**, to take the hand off the coins, showing them one odds and one evens.

tong [R. winter, = col. tang]. **thien-bûn-tong**, a medicinal plant (Melanthium? Asparagia?).

bék-bûn-tong, another medicinal plant (Ophiopogon? Scorzonera?).

tong [R. east, = col. tang]. **tong-se** (R.), east and west (v. se). **hā-tsoh tong-si**, you low mean fellow! (said in scolding).

tong-ka, the man who owns a school-house, and engages the teacher for the children, whether they be his own children or of others; the patron of a school. **tong-kɛ** (C.), id. **tong-kun**, id. **hiên-tong** (R.), the gentleman who has engaged you as teacher. **kùi-tong** (R.), id.

tsok-tong, to be host or patron; to act as host, *e.g.* for visitors from a distance; to be the person whose turn it is to provide the repast for the meeting of a literary society; to be the man who provides the funds (and the place) for a school.

tông [R. a boy; a lad; a student; = col. tâng]. **tông-seng**, a student or candidate who competes for the degree of Sew-tsai. **bú-tông**, a candidate for the degree of military Sew-tsai. **bûn-tông**, candidate for that literary degree. **ló-tông**, an old candidate. **iù-tông**, a young candidate. **sîn-tông** (R.), a wonderfully talented and precocious young scholar, *e.g.* able to write examination essays when nine or ten years old.

bók-tông (r.), a boy who tends cattle. **sien-tông**, boys supposed to wait on the genii, &c. (sien), in their residence (s. pupil). **tông-tsú** (R.), a boy or young lad, about ten years old (s. pupil).

ki-tông, = tâng-chí, a Tauist conjuror, medium, fakeer, or devotee.

tông [R. united; together; alike; = col. tâng]. **hô-tông**, agreeing together, as persons, or as evidence; of one mind; of the same sort or form, *e.g.* agreeing with the pattern. **kap--i hô-tông**, agreeing with him; of the same mind. **thong-tông**, all alike, as men or things. **thong-tông sī àn-niⁿ**, all are just alike or of the same sort; all are of the same opinion or purpose. **thong-tông ûi-hui**, to work wickedness together.

kong-tông, publicly; all being together; in the presence of all the parties interested. **kong-tông gī-lūn hâng-chêng**, to meet publicly to discuss and fix the current market price.

tāi-tông siáu-īⁿ, nearly the same, but slightly different (v. īⁿ). **tāi put-tông**, exceedingly different. **put-tông** (R.), quite different.

tông-bê, to plan or plot together, generally more or less bad, either in the object or the manner of the planning. **lûi tông** (thunder the same), plagiarism in an examination essay.

tông-pau hiaⁿ-tī, brothers by same father or mother (v. pau). **tông-sèng**, of same surname (v. sèng). **tông-tsong**, of same division of a clan (v. tsong). **tông-chhong**, fellow-students (v. chhong). **tông-póng**, having taken the Kujin degree at the same time. **tông-liâu** (R.), fellow-magistrates or officers. **tông-tō**, of the same trade, business, or profession. **tông-tō-tiong**, id. **put-tông-tō**, of different business or profession; also, he and I are very different characters, he being low, unfair, and bad, while I am honest and correct.

tông [R. the Dryandra and some similar trees, = col. thâng]. **gê-tông**, a tree with large leaves (Dryandra? Eleococcus?). **ngêⁿ-tông**, id.

tông [R. name of various sorts of trees, = col. tang]. **kam-tông** (R.), = ka-tang, a large tree of very little use. **tông-tē**, a sort of shrub (v. tē).

hái-tông, a low tree with large brilliant red flowers (Begonia? Cydonia?)

tông [R. the Tang dynasty, Chinese, = col. tn̂g]. **tông-tiâu**, the Tang dynasty. **hong-tông**, fabulous. **hong-tông bô-iá**ⁿ, id. **hong-tông, bô-iá**ⁿ**-sòng**, fabulous or mythical stories of the Tang and Sung dynasties (v. sòng).

tông [R. to stretch out; sudden; impertinent]. **tông-tu̍t** (r.), sudden and unexpected; too forward; rather impertinent.

tông [R. a sort of flag]. **tông-hoan**, long narrow idolatrous flags or streamers, sword-shaped at the point.

tông [R. name of an insect]. **tông-lông** (R.), = chháu-kâu, an insect somewhat like a large grasshopper. **tông-bông** (Cn. col.), id.

tông [R. the pupil of the eye]. **tông-tsú**, the pupil of the eye (s. boy). **bo̍k-tông-tsú**, id. **tông-tsú sàn**, the eyesight irrecoverably lost by enlargement of pupil. **tông-tsú sàn-tāi**, id.

bo̍k-tông, quite blind, said in scolding (s. boy).

tông [R. a hall, especially the large central hall of a house or public building; the hall of judgment; used in the titles of many officials; illustrious; cousins, &c., more or less distant, of same surname; = col. tn̂g].

thien-tông, heaven (v. thien).

io̍k-eng-tong, a foundling hospital.

boán-tông-hông, a large hanging chandelier for a great many lamps.

tong-tông, openly and publicly in presence of many persons, *e.g.* when discussing or settling some matter.

bīn-chêng-tông, the spot right opposite a grave, towards which it looks. **chhoàn-tông**, to come circling round from behind the grave till fully opposite the front, as hills sometimes do (v. sa).

lēng-tông (polite), your mother.

chhin-tông, cousins of the same surname. **chhin-á-tông**, id. **chhin-tông hia**ⁿ**-tī**, male cousins of same surname. **chhin-tông-peh**, father's senior cousin of the same surname. **chhin-tông-tit**, son of male cousin of same surname.

tông--ê, cousin of same surname; sometimes used rather more widely (but in all these phrases always of same surname, being in the male line). **goán-tông--ê**, my cousin. **tông-hia**ⁿ**-tī**, male cousins, *i.e.* sons of father's brothers. **tông-chí-bē**, female cousins, *i.e.* daughters of father's brothers. **tông-hia**ⁿ, senior male cousin. **tông-sió-tī**, junior male cousin. **tông-toā-chí**, elder female cousin. **tông-sió-bē**, junior female cousin. **tông-ko͘**, father's female cousin, more or less distant. **tông-peh**, senior cousin of father. **tông-chek**, junior cousin of father (all in the male line only).

chiông-tông, second cousins, &c., of same surname, by male line, one or more degrees more distant than "chhin-tông." **chêng-tông** (C.), id. **chiông-tông hia**ⁿ**-tī**, male second cousins, &c. **chiông-tông-tit**, son of male second cousin. **chiông-tông-peh**, father's senior second cousin, &c. **chiông-tông-chek**, son of grandfather's cousin, being younger than our father (all in the male line only).

tông-tông lâm-tsú-hàn, you big lazy fellow! (said in scolding a man for begging or fawning and sorning on others instead of supporting himself).

tóng (R. id., = col. táng), a faction, club, or cabal; a secret or seditious confederacy; a company or party of accomplices or associates for some bad purpose; a gang, as of robbers; to club together, gather in a company or make a cabal, as for some bad purpose.

tóng-lūi, a set of associates or confederates for some improper purpose. **chha̍t-tóng**, a gang or company of thieves or robbers. **ok-tóng**, a wicked injurious clique or confederacy. **kan-tóng**, conspirators who form a traitorous confederacy or conspiracy. **phoà-hia-tóng**, set of broken-down literati who prey on the people by means of the influence they have at the yamuns. **kāng-oang-tóng**, of the same bad company, clique, or confederacy. **kui-oang kui-tóng**, forming such a coterie or company for improper purposes. **ū-oang-tóng**, to have a set of associates, conspirators, or members of such a company, who assist each other through thick and thin. **ū-oang ū-tóng**, id.

kiet-tóng, to form a clique, confederation, or party for a bad purpose. **hōe-tóng**, id. **tóng-chiòng**, to collect a crowd or mob for some bad purpose. **tóng-lâng**, id.

tóng-som, an inferior sort of ginseng, not a real ginseng (v. som).

tóng [R. disturbed or confused in mind, = col. táng]. **bóng-tóng**, careless; reckless (v. bóng).

tóng [R. to rule; to understand; to store up; curiosities; = col. táng]. **put-tóng** (R.), I do not understand the language (said in imitation of mandarin).

kó-tóng, curiosities, esp. old curiosities. **kó-tóng-tiàm**, an old curiosity-shop. **pâi kó-tóng**, to set out curiosities and ornaments, as on a table.

tòng [R. firm; suitable; safe; to pledge; by change of tone from "tong," to bear; to oppose; to take responsibility; = col. tǹg, tàng, tng, &c.], to hinder; to forbid procedure, *e.g.* a sale or a building, esp. by making a claim on the property, or alleging some injury to our own; to stop a leak roughly; the difference made (as on a sail) by the turn of one spoke of the windlass.

thò-tòng, safe, as man who may be depended on, and who is quite safe to deal with; or as affair that may be depended on as quite secure. **tēng-tòng**, safe to deal with; steady and reliable, as man.

tòng-kéng, the guardian idol of a place.

tòng-tōe, an inhabitant; one who lives a good long time at a place (opposed to phû-ku or chhah-ku).

tòng--teh, stop! halt! (said when a procession is to halt).

tsó-tòng, to hinder; to obstruct, as a person; to forbid procedure. **tsú-tòng** (P. in some places), id. **tòng-siong**, to object to the building of a house, because of injury to the good luck (hong-súi) of a neighbouring house, temple, or grave. **tòng-tsū**, effectually hinder or stay procedure. **tòng-bōe-tsū**, unable to hinder; cannot be prevented; to try to hinder, but fail in the attempt. **tòng-bōe-chè**, id. **tòng-bōe-gē**, cannot manage to hinder it. **tòng-bōe-tiâu**, cannot bear it; unendurable; intolerable. **tòng-tit-tiâu**, to hinder effectually; effectually prevented.

koh-chhia chit-tòng, turn the windlass (used as capstan) one spoke more in hoisting (enlarging) the sail. **koh chhia chit-tòng-phâng**, id. **n̄ng-tòng-phâng**, so much of the sail as is let out by two successive bars of the windlass.

tòng [R. a pillar or post, = col. tàng, tiòng]. **ke--ê tòng-liông** (r.), the mainstay of a family. **put-chí tòng-liông**, of very great use, as man; very important, as matters or things.

tòng [R. tông, name of a river and of a town]. **tsú-tòng tè-kun,** a title of the god Bûn-chhiong or Wen-chang (v. kun).

tòng — **tòng-gōng,** having a dull or foolish-looking manner (v. gōng).

tòng — **tòng-hiet-tiu** (R.), to throw away.

tōng [R. a cave; profound; thoroughly], a cave or grotto; used in the names of temples at caves or grottoes. **tōng-hiėt** (r.), a cave or grotto. **soaⁿ-tōng,** a mountain-cave. **chiòh-tōng,** a rocky cave; a chamber among great rocks. **keng-biō am-īⁿ, soaⁿ-giâm tōng-sī,** various sorts of idolatrous temples, monasteries, nunneries, &c. **sien-tōng,** temple of the genii.

kó-lōng tōng-thien, the highest rock on Kulang-seu or Kó-lōng-sū.

hoà-sin-tōng, a cave or old broken-down grave, where a beggar lies down to die. **khí hoà-sin-tōng,** said contemptuously of a beggar's death.

lū tōng-pin (C. lī), the name of Sien-tsó, one of the eight Sien, who is specially worshipped by barbers.

tōng-siau, a sort of clarionet. **tōng-koán,** a clarionet and three sorts of guitar, all used together (v. koán).

tōng [R. vast; to squander; dissipated]. **hòng-tōng,** dissipated; disorderly or reckless in behaviour; regardless of restraint or of any one's advice or opinion. **lōng-tōng,** id. **lōng-tōng-tsú,** a dissolute young fellow.

kheng-ka tōng-sán, to lose all one's property, esp. by luxury and extravagance, or by ruinous law-suits.

hō-hō tōng-tōng (R.), very majestic, as Heaven or God.

tōng [R. tiōng, a measure of ten feet, = col. tn̄g, tiūⁿ]. **it-tōng-hông,** = it-tiōng-hông, the hollyhock (lit. ten feet long of red flowers].

tōng [R. to move, = col. tāng]. **tōng-chēng,** to raise a matter; to start a subject. **hêng-tōng kú-chí,** behaviour. **kú-tōng,** id. **hó-kú-tōng,** well-behaved.

tōng-sim, to excite desires, esp. for lustful pleasure; also for wealth, rank, or fame. **tōng jîn-sim,** id., esp. as money does. **tsâi tōng-jîn-sim,** money excites desire.

kám-tōng, to influence the heart with emotion or influence, as a spirit, or as doctrine or kindness. **hàu kám-tōng-thien,** filial piety moves the heart of Heaven.

lāu-tōng, to be in commotion or turmoil. **nāuⁿ-tōng,** id. **iâu-tōng,** agitated, as the people (v. iâu). **tōng-iâu,** id. **lô-tōng,** I will trouble you, sir, to —; I have given you a great deal of trouble.

goân-hong put-tōng, the original cover or wrapper unopened.

kan-hé tōng, slight redness of eyes and sleeplessness, esp. caused by too much anxiety. **hiet-khì ūn-tōng,** the vital energy, or principle, or animal spirits moving about through the body, so as to make the circuit of all parts of the body in 24 hours, as is supposed to take place in a healthy person; (not at all the idea of circulation of blood); it is counted dangerous to be struck at the place where the vital energy is at any particular hour of day or night. **khì ūn-tōng,** the animal spirits moving thus.

tōng [R. to strike; to dash or strike against; to meet accidentally; = col. tn̄g]. **tōng--tiòh,** to run against or come into collision with. **lâm-sám tōng,** to run carelessly against, as persons or things. **chhiong-tōng,** to come upon suddenly and violently, as a flood. **saⁿ-tōng,** to come into collision. **sio-tōng,** to commit impurity together (said in vile scolding).

sái-chhiú-khiau tò-tōng, to strike backwards with the bent elbow.

tōng (Cn.), = A. teng, to ascend, &c.

tōng (Cn.), = A. têng, to transcribe, &c.

tóng (Cn.), = A. téng, a sort; to wait, &c.

ts — Words beginning with **ts** are placed under a separate initial after the end of **th**.

tu, a small heap, as of earth, lime, &c. **ka-n̄g-tu,** a whole (small) heap. **chit-tu-á-thô,** a small heap of earth. **toā-tu-thô,** a large heap of earth.

tu (R. id.) **ti-tu,** a spider (v. ti).

tu [R. to, all; altogether]. **kun-tu,** yet after all; all the same (v. kun). **kin-tu** (C.), id.

tu [R. tsù, intently, = col. tsu]. **tu-tu-siòng,** to gaze at intently; to stare at.

tu — **hu-tu,** sound of a horn or trumpet. **hu-tu hu-tu,** id.

tu (cf. lu, tū), to push away; to thrust away; to resist, esp. by passive resistance, preventing the opponent from advancing or carrying out his purpose; to oppose or resist, as by pressing against; to push a boat with a pole. **tu--teh,** held fast, so that he cannot move, or can do no harm, *e.g.* as a dog fastened with a sort of bamboo instrument; or as a prisoner fastened with a bamboo below his chin, so that he cannot move, in order to torture him and extort money. **kā--i tu--teh,** to hold him fast, so that he cannot get away. **kā--i tu-hē** (C.), id. **tu--khì,** to push away, as with the end of a stick. **tu-khui,** to thrust away or to the side.

tùi-tu, to oppose with so much effect as at least to keep back the opponent for some time, and to show a considerable probability of ultimate success. **kap-i-tu,** to oppose or resist him. **khí-peng kap-i-tu,** to raise troops to oppose him.

tu-lâu, to move against the stream of a river, or of the tide; tide or stream contrary. **tu-hong,** to go against the wind; a head-wind. **tu-chhàt,** to resist or keep off robbers or rebels. **tu se-ló** (to resist the Russians), a very difficult and dangerous affair (v. ló).

tu chhiú-bé, making trial of strength by pushing against each other's hands. **tu-tsâi,** to make trial of strength by pushing a pole placed against each other's body near the navel.

ûi-tu, the wooden support in front of a mast. **káu-tu,** an instrument made of bamboo and rope, for holding a dog tight, as when leading it.

saⁿ-kha-tu, placed in a triangular form, as three things, persons, or places (v. saⁿ).

tu (K.), = A. ti, a pig; said also in some other parts of Tn̂g-oaⁿ, esp. in the villages of Amoy island.

tü (T. Cn.), = A. ti, a pig. **hì-tü** (T.), = A. hì-siuⁿ, a man who is specially fond of a particular company of young actors.

tû [R. to remove; to exclude; to expel], (C. tî; Cn. tû), to subtract; to deduct; with the exception of, without counting —.

siau-tû, to remove or dispel, as evils or calamities. **sàu-tû,** to remove away entirely, as bad persons or things. **tû--chhut-khì,** to remove or drive away, as a wicked fellow who cannot be allowed to stay any more at a place. **tû-lû--khì** (r.), id.

tû-lêng, to end the ceremonies of "hàu-pn̄g," some

time after a man's death, by burning all the fittings and articles used in the rites.

kui-tû sêng-hoat, multiplication and division (v. kui). **khàu-tû**, to deduct, as from wages or payments. **chhit-khàu poeh-tû**, to run up a heavy list of deductions and countercharges, making out that there is very little, if anything, to be paid. **khit--i chhit-khàu-poeh-tû bô--khì**, to have the whole account swallowed up by such countercharges, so as to get nothing. **tû-sit**, net weight or measure. **ōe-sṅg, bōe-tû**; **thó-bí, oāⁿ han-tsû**, said of a man being very stupid in dealings, as potatoes are much less valuable than rice (C. bat-sùiⁿ, m̄-bat-tî; thiò-bí, bé han-chî).

· **tùi-tû**, balancing an account; subtraction. **tùi-tû-goā**, the balance stands — (on whichever side). **tùi-tû-lâi-goā**, id. **tùi-tû-goā siong-khiàm**, balance due. **tùi-tû-goā siōng-tsāi**, balance in hand. **tû-khai-siau-goā**, net gain after deducting food and all other expenses. **tû-chhut í-goā**, with this exception. **tû-i í-goā**, excepting him. **tû bé-lâng í-goā**, with the exception of Mr. So-and-so. **tû-sí í-goā**, with the exception of death alone. **tû-hui tióh-kiâⁿ àn-niⁿ**, the only practicable or possible way is to take this course. **tû-hui tióh-àn-niⁿ, chiah tú-hó**, no other way will suit, if you wish to have it all right.

tû — **gû-tû**, rough in manner, and obstinately thinking himself very knowing, and so doggedly refusing to take advice, though really wanting in intelligence, and ignorant of what should be done. **gû-tû-ok**, overbearing, threatening, coarse, and dogged in manner, as if he would strike people, while at the same time stupid, esp. as a lad about fifteen or eighteen (cf. thû, tsû).

tû [R. thû, to dig; to hoe; a hoe; = col. tî], (C. tî; A. tî, tû; Cn. tû). **tû-thâu**, a hoe; said especially in the villages on Amoy island, while "tî-thau" is said in the town of Amoy.

tû (R. id.) **tiû-tû**, to be in doubt and suspense; perplexed and undecided.

tû [R. a kitchen; a slaughter-house; = col. tê]. **tû-pâng**, a mandarin's cook; a mandarin's kitchen.

tû, a cupboard; a press for holding things; a wardrobe; a set of shelves, &c.; a sort of cage or trap. **tû-á**, a small press, cupboard, &c. **tek-tû-á**, a bamboo table with a small press in it. **saⁿ-á-tû**, a wardrobe or press for clothes. **chheh-tû**, a set of book-shelves, with or without doors. **piah-tû**, a cupboard or set of shelves in a wall. **oáⁿ-tû**, a cupboard or press for crockery. **chhài-tû**, a cupboard for provisions. **hé-sit-tû**, id. **sit-tû**, id.

lók-tû, a cage in which important criminals are sent to be tried or executed. **khiā-tû**, an upright cage in which criminals are made to stand with only the head out; to stand in this cage till dead.

niauⁿ-tû, a cage for a cat. **niáuⁿ-chhú-tû**, a cage for white mice which work a treadmill. **phang-tû**, a bee-house. **bé-tû**, a horse-box. **chíⁿ-á-tû**, a pigeon-house; a dove-cot. **kap-tû**, id. **lán-tsún kap-tû**, like a dove-cot; said of a very small house.

hé-tû, a trap for tigers. **ka-tsáu-tû**, a sort of trap for catching fleas.

tû--teh, confined in a cage, as a wild beast; confined so that he cannot escape, as a man, esp. as a prisoner in a clan feud.

tú [R. tí, to oppose; to resist; to sustain; to be a substitute; to be equal in worth; to come against; to meet with; cf. col. tóe, tu, tū], to meet with; (just now; just the size or quantity; just the thing); to be given in payment in place of something else; to deduct or keep off so much from a payment, as for debt, or on account of a fault.

tú--lâng, to shut a man's mouth by something that he cannot answer, esp. what he himself has done or said. **chhòng-ōe tú--i**, to stop his mouth by something he had said or done.

tú-tak, to carp at a master's orders.

pīⁿ-tú-theng, neither party able to overcome the other. **ngīⁿ tú-ngīⁿ**, each party refusing to make any abatement of claims. **beh kap--i tú-tsúi**, determined to be at feud with him.

tùi-tú, to balance accounts, so that neither owes anything, *e.g.* by debts or items done on the other side, or by articles valued at so much. **kiàh pn̄g-sî, tú-niauⁿ** (to keep off the cat with the spoon), id. **hō-lí-tú**, I will allow you to take off part of my wages, price, &c. **tú kang-chîⁿ**, to deduct so much from wages, *e.g.* to make up for a debt. **tú saⁿ-khơ**, to deduct three dollars, as from wages. **tú-siàu**, to be paid towards the liquidation of a debt, as part payment in money, or as work or goods accepted in lieu of money. **chiong-chit--ê hō--lí tú-siàu**, I give you this article in place of money, in payment of my debt. **chiàh-mih̄ⁿ tú-siàu**, to eat without paying, as payment of debt due us by the man who supplies the food.

tú-giàh (C.), = A. tí-giàh, to make up the want of a person, as a substitute.

tú--tióh, to meet with. **tú-gū**, do.; to happen (v. gū). **tú-gī** (C.), id. **tú-tn̄g**, do.; to meet with casually (v. tn̄g). **saⁿ-tú-thâu**, to meet with each other coming different ways. **saⁿ-tú**, id. **saⁿ-tú-chhùi**, two persons conversing in a low voice with heads very close together, *e.g.* concerting some united secret action.

tú tsō-hoà, to make a venture (v. hoà). **tú lí--ê tsō-hoà**, I will try to help you, but have much doubt of success.

tú-chhái, perhaps. **chhàu-tú-khám**, unexpectedly.

tú-tú, just now; just a moment ago (always of past time, or of what is now as the result of the past, but never of the future). **tú-tú ū**, it happens that just now there is or are, or I have, &c. **tú-tú hit-tiáp**, just at that very moment. **jit tú-tú-tàu**, just at noon. **tú-tú-hó**, just right; just as it should be; just at the proper time, or in proper quantity or manner. **tú-hó**, id. **tú-á**, just now; just immediately before; just this moment (all of the past, never of the future). **tú-á-chiah**, id. **tú--chiah**, id.

tú [R. tsú; to prop; a prop; cf. col. tū], to prop; to prop up; to support by a prop. **tú-piah**, to prop up a partition (v. piah). **tú-mn̂g**, to put a bar, prop, or piece of furniture against a door, so as to keep it shut; to be as high as a door, as boxes, books, &c., piled up beside it. **thâu-khak tú-mn̂g**, head as high as the door. **tú-thiⁿ**, so great as to reach up to heaven.

tú (same as previous word?), a prop. **mn̂g-tú**, a long thick bar for preventing a door being opened, set end-on against the door. **teng-jī-tú**, a T-headed bar for such purpose. **kong-jī-tú**, a support shaped like the letter H, *e.g.* between the beams of a floor where a stair or ladder is placed. **jîn-jī-tú**, the horizontal beam (tie-beam) of a couple for a gable roof. **piah-tú**, a support for a weak or falling partition.

tú-thûi, a short pole used for resting a carrying-pole upon when the porter halts for a little.

tù [R. to manifest; to make public; to set forth; to

narrate; to write books; by change of tone from "tiök," to accomplish; correct], (C. tì).

tù-hiēn (r.), to manifest.

tù-chheh, to compose books, especially useful books.

tù [R. tsù, to fix the mind upon, = col. tsu, tu], a stake in gambling; money laid down in gambling. **kə-tù**, a single large stake. **sió-tù**, a small stake. **poåh sió-tù**, to play for a small stake. **toā-tù**, a large stake. **poåh toā-tù**, to play for a large stake. **toā-tù-poåh**, id. **beh-thàn toā-tù**, determined to have great gains, as in trade. **beh-thàn toā-tù-chîⁿ**, id.

chhut-tù, to lay down a stake on one's own game. **png-tù**, to lay a stake or wager on another in gambling. **png lí-ê-tù**, I lay my stake beside yours, to share your fortune in the game. **png thâu-tù**, to lay one's stake on the first of the two laid down. **png jī-tù**, to lay one's stake on the second.

chiåh-tù, to win the stakes. **goá-chiåh lí-ê-tù**, I win, getting your stake. **chiåh-i saⁿ-tù-thâu**, to be so much superior to another as to be able to beat him out of all question, so as utterly to despise his attempts.

lí thèng goá-ê-tù, you pay the stakes to me.

chē-tù, to accept the responsibility for another in any matter.

phah-piàⁿ-tù, to risk all at once, as on one throw in gambling, or in one venture in trade, or in a quarrel where loss is ruin.

tù [R. tsū, to rest; to sojourn; to reside or be stationed]. **tù-teh-thó**, to wait demanding payment, insisting on having it before going away, as a creditor, or as a mandarin or his subordinates.

tū [cf. tu, tú, tsū; these groups of phrases under "tū" should perhaps be all under one word, or should be differently arranged], to keep shut or open, as a door, by placing something against it. **tū-mn̂g**, to keep a door shut or open by a chair, or bar, or prop, &c.

tū (cf. tú), to stop a man's mouth, as by a sharp or sarcastic reply. **tū--lâng**, to stop a man's mouth, especially by quoting what he himself had said or done.

lí-kóng chit-ê-ōe beh-lâi tū--sí-goá, you say this merely to make me unable to answer, and so to trouble me and get the better of me, not in fair argument.

ōe-tū, giving a sharp, gruff, or unpleasant reply, so that the other is quite taken aback. **sái-ōe-tū**, id. **kóng-ōe ōe-tū**, id. **oā-tū** (C.), id.

àu-tū-tū, morose; sulky (v. pū).

lū-tū (C.), = A. lū-kū, gruff in reply.

tū (same as one of previous words?) **tū-khùi**, breathing very difficult, as in asthma, or as when near death. **khì ài-tū**, id. **khùi beh-tū--khì**, id.

khùi beh-tū--sí, having very great difficulty in breathing, as in asthma, or some severe disease of the throat.

tū (same as previous word? or following word?) **tū--sí**, to get drowned, as by falling into water; to drown a man or animal by holding down in the water.

tū [R. tsù? to soak]. **tū-tsúi**, to soak in water for a short time, *e.g.* for a quarter of an hour or so.

khit-tsúi tū--sí, to be drowned.

liåh hí-tsúi--nihⁿ tū, take and hold down in the water, as man or thing; *e.g.* in order to frighten a man or to make him very uncomfortable for a little.

tū-kiâm, to salt or pickle by plunging in brine.

tū (T.), = A. tī, chopsticks.

tū (Cn.), = A. tī, chopsticks.

tū (K.) **tū--teh**, = A. tī--teh, present.

tuh (cf. tùh). **tih-tuh**, speaking in a deceitful way, *e.g.* saying things quite different or seriously varied at different times, or so that it is not clear whether it is in joke or earnest; over-sharp in money matters; unsafe to deal with. **kóng-ōe tih-tuh**, to talk in an unsettled, varying, slippery way, as in order to deceive.

tuh — **tiám-tuh**, to give a hint what to do, or to warn of danger (often secretly or privately), as by a sign or wink or hint not generally understood. **thau-tiám-tuh**, to warn secretly or give a secret hint, as by signal or word or other sound.

tuh (cf. thuh, thok, tùh), to feel the ground, as with a staff or stick; to strike or thrust downwards with a stick.

tuh koáiⁿ-á, to feel one's way with a stick. **tuh-tōe**, to feel the ground, as with a stick. **tuh thê-kha**, id.

tuh, to nod the head, as when drowsy. **tuh-bîn**, to nod in sleep; to be drowsy; to dose. **tuh-ka-chē** (T. tok-ka-tsö), id. **tuh-ka-tsōe** (C.), id.

tuh-ku, nodding; head bent down, as in sleep or drowsiness, or as in sickness or old age. **chē kàu tuh-ku**, to sit vacantly and wearily, having nothing to do.

thâu-khak tuh-tuh, keeping the head bent down, as man much depressed in spirits or ashamed; or as man walking in a very sedate or thoughtful way; or when looking down to avoid the appearance of looking at people; or from usual habit, &c.

tuh (cf. tok). **thâu chiam, phīⁿ tuh**, face long and nose sharp.

tuh — **n̂g-phiet chit-tuh**, beard and mustaches (said in joke).

tuh — **ə tuh-tuh**, very black.

tùh (cf. tsùh), to strike hard with the point of the finger; to strike with the point of a stick in the direct line of the stick, as in making a hole; to pierce or thrust through.

tùh-phoà, to pierce and burst open, as a boil or blister, &c., with a needle; said also of making a man's baseless pretentions collapse, *e.g.* a man who pretended that he had powerful influence to back him. **tùh--tióh lâng--ê hùi-bú**, to speak openly of something that makes a man greatly ashamed, *e.g.* a flaw in his pedigree, or some secret shameful crime.

tùh — **tih-tùh**, to stammer and falter in speaking, as when telling lies (v. tih).

tùh [R. tek, to choose; cf. C. tóh]. **kéng-chiaⁿ tùh-phiaⁿ**, to choose the best of the meat (said of a man difficult to please, always choosing the best of everything). **kái ⁿ-chiaⁿ tùh-phiaⁿ** (T.), id. **kúiⁿ-chiaⁿ tùh-pûi** (Cn.), id.

tui [R. a heap; to pile up], a heap; a large quantity or company; a police-station.

tui-thâu, a police-station. **khùn-tui**, to pass the night at a police-station, as the soldiers stationed there in turn.

thê-tui, a heap of earth and rubbish gradually formed. **bān-jîn-tui**, common burying-ground, where multitudes of the common people bury.

chit-tui, one heap; one company or lot. **chit-toā-tui** (r.), a large quantity or lot; a multitude of men, &c. **tsòe chit-tui**, to meet together; to come together; to become one heap. **lúi-lúi tsòe-chit-tui**, to gather into a heap. **tsòe-tui**, to begin to cohabit, as betrothed persons without the regular ceremonies. **tāi-ke tsòe-tui**, all met together. **tàu-tsòe-tui**, to gather into one heap, or all close together, as a number of things. **chí** **tàu-tsòe-tui**, to collect money together for some special purpose, from various quarters and in various ways.

tui-chek, to gather together in great abundance (v. chek). **báuh-tui**, to bargain for in the lump, without measuring.

lûi-tui, wearisome and troublesome, as man not straightforward in discussing a matter or dispute, *e.g.* unfairly perverting the facts or making unnecessary difficulties; troublesome and difficult to set right, as an involved affair; confused, disordered, and dirty, as an untidy room, or as a heap of various things. **lui-tui**, id. **lûi-lûi tui-tui**, extremely so. **lâng lûi-tui**, he is very troublesome to discuss or deal with, because he intentionally perverts the facts, &c. **pān-sū lûi-tui**, to manage a matter carelessly, *e.g.* leaving many flaws.

tui [R. to pursue; to chase; to overtake and catch; to trace back; to reflect upon], to pursue; to chase; to make official search for stolen things.

tui-koáⁿ, to chase. **tui-kàu** (r.), to overtake. **tui-tióh**, id. **tui kàu-tsáu-bô-lō͘**, to pursue till there is no way of escape.

kiù-tui, to take vigorous action to recover stolen articles, as mandarin does by arresting parties or sending constables to the place. **pí-tui**, to beat a man till he gives back or recovers the stolen property, as mandarin does to a thief or to the "bé-khoài." **tui-hêng**, to send and apprehend a criminal so as to recover the stolen property for the owners. **tui-thó** (r.), to demand back a thing very urgently.

tui-liām (R.), to think on kindness or good deeds done to us in time long past.

tûi (R. id.), to strike with a mallet over and over; to beat as metal in making foil; to beat as iron, making it malleable; to thump with the fist; to shampoo the body by beating with the hand, esp. the upper part of the body; to beat, as grain.

tûi-píⁿ, to beat flat with a mallet, &c. **tûi-kim**, to beat gold into foil. **tûi-pè͘**, to beat cloth with a mallet. **tûi-saⁿ**, to beat clothes in washing them. **tûi-thê͘**, to beat clay in working it up for mortar.

tûi-heng, to beat one's breast with the fist, as in grief or displeasure, esp. grief for one's own folly, as on failing to use a good opportunity, or as when a calamity has been brought on by one's own fault or mistake. **tûi-heng tah-liú**, to beat the breast with the palm so as to make the buttons shake, as in anger, or as in asseverating that what we say is true.

tûi-io, to shampoo the loins. **tûi-kûn liáh-lêng** (Cn.), to shampoo, as for illness.

túi (T.), to pull out or pull up, *e.g.* to pull pins out of a woman's hair.

tùi [R. kùi, honourable; noble; to honour; to count important]. **tùi-tiōng** (C. tī-tiōng), to value; to count important; to respect, as a person.

tùi (R. id.), a pair; an antithesis; opposite to; agreeing with; to correspond to; to answer; from; towards; by, as by a road; to, as in speaking to; to transfer money by a bill or draft to another place.

chit-tùi, a pair; an antithesis. **siang-siang tùi-tùi**, in pairs.

saⁿ-tùi, just right opposite; exactly agreeing, &c. **mn̂g-hō͘ saⁿ-tùi**, belong to families of equal rank or station, or of equal relationship. **sì-bák saⁿ-tùi**, said of two persons looking helplessly at each other unable to avert calamity (v. bák).

tùi-tâng, alike; exactly agreeing, as evidence (v. tâng). **tùi-chîn**, made according to the proper and prescribed pattern or rule; to be successful, as a request. **tùi-lō͘**, pleasing to a person; suitable (v. lō͘), (+).

bô-tùi, not making a proper pair or antithesis; not placed properly opposite. **chì-tsun bô-tùi**, most honourable without compare. **bô-tùi-kéng** (Cn.), unsuitable; not pleasing. **bōe-tùi**, it does not agree; does not suit; it is not right or correct.

tùi-tiong, just in the middle. **tùi-tn̂g**, at or by the half, *e.g.* breaking in two (v. tn̂g). **tùi-poàⁿ**, at the middle; by the half; half-way. **tùi-poàⁿ-pun**, to give away one half; to divide (as gains) in equal halves. **tùi-poàⁿ-thàn**, to gain cent. per cent. **tùi-o͘**, just hitting the mark.

chit-tùi-sî, same hour on next day. **tùi-nîⁿ**, exactly one year after; same day in next year; esp. said of making offerings to the dead exactly one year after death. **tsòe-tùi-nîⁿ**, to perform these rites or have them performed. **tùi-nîⁿ-hà**, mourning for one year, as for grandfather (v. hà). **bô-tùi-kî**, not yet due, as a bill.

tùi-oāⁿ, to barter; to exchange. **tùi-tiāu**, to exchange places, as persons (v. tiāu).

tùi-toaⁿ, a bill of exchange or money order (v. toaⁿ). **tùi-kè**, to pay by a draft or bill, &c., or by an account on the other side. **tùi-gûn**, to transfer money by a bill or draft, as to another place, or for payment through a third party. **tùi-chîⁿ**, id. **tùi-tso͘**, to pay a debt by assigning rents to creditor till it is paid up. **tiên-tùi**, to pay a debt by a bill or draft on another.

tùi-siàu, to compare accounts. **tùi-tû**, to balance an account (v. tû). **tùi-tú**, to settle an account or debt by articles valued at so much, or by debts on the other side. **tùi-tí**, id. (v. tí).

tùi-lō͘, by road (+). **tùi-tsûn**, by boat. **tùi-mn̂g**, by the door or gate (+). **tùi-chit-tiâu** (Cn. ùi-chit-tiâu), by this road or route. **tùi-chia khì**, go by this way or place. **tùi-chia**, id.

tùi-āu, from behind. **tùi-tá-lóh**, from what place? towards what place?

tùi-i-thó, to demand it from him.

tùi-i-kóng, speak to him. **lí kap--i tùi-kóng**, speak to him yourself without any intermediate party or middleman. **tùi-thâu-kóng**, the two parties making a bargain or settling an affair for themselves without any arbiter or such medium. **tùi-káng**, id. **tùi-tap**, to answer; to reply, as in speaking. **èng-tùi jû-liû** (R.), answering fluently. **tùi-chhèk**, two parties discussing a matter in order to settle it. **tùi-chek**, to discuss a dispute, as the parties before a mandarin or arbiter. **tùi-chit** (R.), id. **tùi-chí**, to make statements face to face, as the two parties. **tùi-chèng**, to examine and compare the evidence on both sides. **tùi-sîn**, to judge a case with both parties present. **tùi-sím**, id.

tùi-chhin, to settle a marriage contract for one's daughter. **tùi-tiēn**, to introduce our old tenant to the man to whom he is now to pay the rent (v. tiēn).

tùi-hoán, on the other hand; on the contrary; opposite; contrary. **tùi-péng** (r.), id. **tùi-kéh**, in direct opposition to one's wishes or plans.

tùi-ték, an enemy; to oppose, as an enemy. **m̄-sī i--ē tùi-ték**, he cannot contend with him. **tùi--lâng bōe-kè**, cannot venture to attempt it because quite unable to overcome the opponent or opponents. **béng-hó bōe-tùi--tit kûn-thâu tsōe**, a fierce tiger cannot stand a great many blows. **béng-hó bōe-tùi--tit kâu-kûn**, do., or a crowd of monkeys.

tùi-chhiú, an enemy; fighting hand to hand; a fellow-labourer; a fellow-worker; a partner in trade, &c. **m̄-sī i--ê tùi-chhiú**, he is no match for him. **m̄-sī i--ê tùi-chhùi**, he is no match for him with his tongue (v. chhùi). **tùi-kha poáh**, two men gambling together.

tùi-thâu, an enemy or opponent; from the head or beginning (s. mortar and pestle). **tùi-thâu chhin-ke**, persons previously connected by affinity whose children are married to each other. **tùi-thâu gō͘**, a misunderstanding on both sides. **tùi-thâu ū-tsú**, there are two other parties on whom the responsibility rests (v. tsú). **tùi-thâu oan-ke-tsú**, the very person with whom we are at feud. **tùi-thâu ū-khò**, each side has powerful backers. **tùi-thâu ū sè-kò͘**, id. **m̄-sī i--ê tùi-thâu**, he is unable to oppose him; is no match for him. **tùi-thâu kàu-bé**, from beginning to end.

tùi-bīn, just opposite in position; face to face. **tùi-siòng**, looking intently at each other. **tùi-hiòng**, right opposite, as house or grave-site. **tùi-chiò**, to be right opposite, as wall or house (v. chiò). **tùi-mn̂g**, doors just facing each other (+). **tùi-chhiong**, right opposite, so as to affect the fortune of a house or grave. **lâm-pak tùi-chhiong**, south and north right opposite, as in regard to a house. **poeh-jī tùi-chhiong**, one's horoscope coming in collision with that of some near relative. **ngó͘-kúi tùi-chhiong**, having an irrepressible feud. **kap--i ngó͘-kúi tùi-chhiong**, at most violent feud with him. **bān-san tiâu-tùi**, the hills making an amphitheatre half round the grave.

tùi-khim, a jacket or coat made so as to open right up the middle of the breast.

ū-thâu-tùi, to be husband and wife. **tsòe thâu-tùi**, id. **phah thâu-tùi**, to sell a female slave to become another man's legal wife. **phòe thâu-tùi**, a female slave becoming another man's legal wife, done by a regular deed of sale. **phòe-tùi**, to be man and wife. **sit-tùi**, to lose one's mate or consort (said of men or animals). **bô-tùi pát-ê**, does not pair with another after death of its mate (said of the "gān" or wild goose).

liên-tùi, ornamental scrolls with antithetic sentences. **chit-tùi-liên**, a pair of them. **mn̂g-tùi**, pair of antithetic scrolls pasted at the sides of a door. **tùi-lūi**, a book of antithetic words and phrases, learned by children. **tùi-phō͘**, a copy-book of antitheses. **chhit-jī-tùi**, antithetic sentences of seven words. **poeh-jī-tùi**, do. of eight words. **liām-tùi**, to repeat antithetic sentences or phrases. **pài-tùi**, to worship Confucius or Khoe-seng by means of antithetic sentences.

tùi (R. id.), a large stone mortar (with a heavy stone pestle) for hulling rice, by pounding, usually worked by the foot. **tùi-khū**, id. **tùi-thâu**, the stone end of the pestle for such a mortar (s. opposite). **chiòh-tùi-thâu**, id. **tùi-sin**, the shaft or handle of the pestle.

bí-tùi, a large stone mortar with a heavy pestle, for hulling rice by pounding. **chhiú-tùi**, such a mortar worked by the hand. **kha-tùi**, do. worked by the foot. **tsúi-tùi**, do. worked by water-power.

cheng-tùi, to work a mortar for hulling rice by pounding, usually done with the foot. **lap-tùi**, to tread the pestle in thus pounding rice. **táh-tùi**, id. **táh-tùi-lâng**, a sort of trap for catching birds or beasts. **káu-táh-tùi**, a machine driven by a sort of treadmill worked by a dog; a self-acting steelyard for separating light from heavy cash; the working beam of a steam-engine.

tùi (cf. tūi, to hang down). **hī-á toā-tùi**, ears very large (v. hī).

siáu-tiông-tùi, inguinal hernia. **tùi-tiông**, id.

tūi [R. tōe; some read "tōe;" to exchange; to barter]. **tūi-gûn**, to get silver in dollars, either for copper cash, for sycee silver, or for gold ingots. **kim tūi-gûn**, to get silver in exchange for gold. **tūi-kim**, to get gold in exchange for silver. **tūi kim-tiâu**, to buy a small bar of gold for silver.

tūi [R. swelling of legs]. **tūi-khì**, legs swollen by disease.

tūi [R. id., = col. lūi], to let down by a rope; to descend by a rope. **tūi-lòh**, id. **tūi--lòh-lâi**, to get lowered to us by a rope (s. hang down).

chhien-kun-tūi, = lâm-kong, the rope that lies close by the side of the mast; also, a medicinal plant.

tūi [R. to fall down; to hang down heavily; cf. col. thūi, tùi; perhaps should be divided into two words], a pendant, as of a coronet or crown. **iên-tūi**, a lead weight or sinker, as for a sounding lead, or for a net, or for driving a clock, &c. **thô-tūi**, earthenware weights for nets. **bāng-tūi**, small weights for sinking nets. **hī-tūi**, ear-rings. **bák-kiàⁿ-tūi**, weights for keeping spectacles on, hanging over the ears. **hô͘-lô͘-tūi**, gourd-shaped weight of a pendulum.

tūi--lòh-lâi, to hang down heavily, as branch loaded with fruit almost bent to the ground, or as a flagstaff gradually falling by its own weight (s. let down by rope). **tūi-chîn**, to let the plummet hang down.

tūi-cheng, spermatorrhœa.

hòe-tūi, dilapidated; in a ruinous condition; fallen into decay. **hùi-tūi** (C.), id.

tūi-tāng, to divide, as by balances, into parts of equal weight; to make a thing hang straight down by weights, *e.g.* mosquito-curtains. **kap-gûn tūi-tāng**, worth its weight in silver. **tūi pîⁿ-tāng**, to balance so as to make equal in weight. **tūi-pîⁿ**, id. **tūi hô͘-i-pîⁿ**, id. **kap-kim tūi-tūi** (tūi-tāng?), worth its weight in gold.

tūi (R. id.), a troop or company of soldiers, usually about 50, sometimes about 100. **tūi-ngó͘**, ranks of soldiers; rank and file (v. ngó͘).

chhèng-tūi, a company of musketeers or riflemen. **phàu-tūi**, a company of artillery, *e.g.* with gingalls. **keng-chìⁿ-tūi**, the company of archers, from whom military mandarins are usually chosen. **bé-tūi** (C. bé-tūi), a company or troop of cavalry. **bé-tūi** (C. bóe-tūi; Cn. bō͘-tūi), the last company or troop.

tūi-tiúⁿ, the officer commanding a body of troops, larger or smaller. **tūi-koaⁿ**, a very small officer commanding 20 or more men. **toà-tūi-koaⁿ**, id. **tok-tūi-koaⁿ**, id. **tok-tūi**, to command such a small company. **chhoā-tūi--ê**, a standard-bearer for a small company or troop.

tsàn-tūi, to stand in ranks, as on receiving a high mandarin. **pâi-tūi**, to form the ranks. **thiam-tūi**, to add more troops or companies of soldiers. **kiâⁿ-tūi**, to march slowly and in regular order, as troops. **phah-tūi**, two troops or companies engaged in mock battle, as in review. **hun-tūi**, to divide a large mass of soldiers into small troops. **pun-tūi**, id. **soàⁿ-tūi**, to disperse the ranks. **khe-tūi**, to sound a signal with the trumpet to call the troops close together for any purpose. **siu-tūi**, to withdraw the troops, as after drill, or in good order after battle.

ngiâⁿ-tũi (P.), = C. ngiâⁿ-gẽ, a sort of idolatrous procession (v. gẽ).

tũiⁿ (C.), = tn̄g, a piece; a bit.

tũiⁿ (Cn.), = T. tāiⁿ, to give.

túiⁿ (C.), = A. tńg, to turn; to settle or arrange a dispute, as a third party. **túiⁿ--khì**, = A. tò--khì, to go back. **túiⁿ--lâi**, = A. tò--lâi, to come back. **túiⁿ-chhiò**, to turn round and laugh, or smile and be pleased again, after being angry. **oát-túiⁿ-chhiú**, to change hands, as in carrying a heavy load, or in showing one's hands to a fortune-teller.

tùiⁿ (C.), = A. tǹg, to warm over a small stove.

tùiⁿ (C.), = A. tǹg, a meal.

tùiⁿ (C.) **tùiⁿ-heng**, = A. tǹg-heng, to beat one's breast with a stone, as beggars do.

tũiⁿ (Cn.), = A. tiàm, a shop. **tũiⁿ-kha**, id. **tũiⁿ--n̂gh**, = A. tiàm--nih, in the shop. **tũiⁿ-tsú**, a shopkeeper.

tũiⁿ (C.), = A. tn̄g, thn̄g, a part of a limb when part of it is lost. **hin-su-tũiⁿ**, a trunk having head, hands, and feet cut off (said in scolding). **kha-tũiⁿ**, a part of a leg, when part has been cut off or devoured. **chhiú-tũiⁿ**, an arm or part of an arm when cut off, or left by wild beast, &c.

chhiū-tũiⁿ, = A. chhiū-thn̄g, a stump of a tree, either in the ground or cut down.

tũiⁿ (C.), = A. tn̄g, to cut separate; to sever; to separate.

tũiⁿ (Cn.), = A. tiēn, a temple of a first-class deity; only used in some few phrases, *e.g.* **sèng-tũiⁿ**, the temple of Hiēn-thien Siōng-tè in Anhai.

tũiⁿ (Cn.), = A. tēng, hard.

tũiⁿ (Cn.), = A. tēng, threshold. **bīn-tũiⁿ**, the threshold.

tũiⁿ (Cn.), = A. tiēn (R.), to cultivate the ground; to rent; only used in some of the phrases. **tũiⁿ-hō͘**, the tenant of a farm.

jīn-tũiⁿ, to go security for tenant (v. tiēn).

tũiⁿ (Cn.), = A. tē. **tũiⁿ-it**, the first.

tun [R. tūn, blunt; dull; stupid], blunt; not sharp. **chhùi tun**, slow of speech; not fluent. **chhùi-chih tun**, id. **bák-chiu tun**, not good at recognizing a thing or person seen before. **tun-to chhut lāi-chhiú**, a blunt knife brings out the skill of the workman.

tun [R. unsuccessful.] **tun-chien** (R.), very unlucky and unfortunate, as man.

tun [R. a heap; a mound; a low pillar]. **tun-á**, a small round hill.

ien-tun, low chimneys on hills, &c., used as beacon signals, also at the mandarin stations on great roads.

kim-tun n̂g, one of the great branches of the surname Hwang (n̂g), so large that they sometimes say their surname is "kim."

tun [R. great; full; liberal; to consider important; to impel to do].

tun-pé, to practise shooting at a mark very close at hand. **tun chháu-pé**, id., at a mark made of straw or reeds.

phok-sit tun-hō͘ (R.), honest and simple in tastes. **lâng-khoán tun-tok**, his conduct and behaviour is very good (from "tok," firm; steady). **put-chí tun-tok** (r.), very correct, proper, and diligent in managing a matter, esp. good at teaching. **ka-kī tun-tok**, to train one's self; developing one's good qualities, and restraining evil tendencies. **tun-tok** (R.), to teach and train gradually and carefully, as a teacher does (from "tok," to rule or govern). **tun-tok hák-seng**, to train one's pupils with care. **tun-tok tsú-tit**, to train one's junior relatives well, and keep them in good order.

tûn [R. a young pig; cf. col. thûn]. **hô-tûn** (R.), a porpoise. **siá-bēng, sit hô-tûn**, said of throwing away one's life for good eating.

tûn (cf. thún). **tûn-táh** (Cn.), to tread or trample on. **lām-sám tûn** (Cn.), to tread carelessly upon.

tûn (R. id.), the lips. **ē-tûn**, the lower lip. **téng-tûn**, the upper lip. **chhùi-tûn**, the lips. **chhùi-tûn-phê**, id. **poāⁿ chhùi-tûn-phê**, to have a long wordy dispute. **ien-chi tiám chhùi-tûn**, to stain the lips with rouge. **chhùi-tûn khiàu-khiàu**, lips protruded (v. khiàu). **chhùi-tûn ngiauh-ngiauh**, id. **chhùi-tûn bau-bau**, lips naturally turned a little inwards.

bau-tûn, to turn in the lips, as children; to plate with metal, turning it in over the edges, *e.g.* pewter on a stone tea-pot. **thè-tûn**, the ground in front of a grave projecting on a somewhat lower level, counted auspicious, so that when not naturally so it is often built up in that form. **kâm-tûn**, to take the lips between the teeth, slightly biting them, as a child does.

tûn-im, labial sounds. **chhí pėk, tûn hông**, teeth white and lips red, counted very good-looking. **tûn hông, chhí pėk**, id.

hī-á-tûn, the earlap.

kāu-tûn, a fish with thick lips, somewhat like the "ka-làh."

tún [R. a shield; a buckler]. **mâuⁿ-tún**, to contradict one's self. **bâu-tún**, id. **ka-kī mâuⁿ-tún**, id.

chháu-tún, a round cushion for kneeling on. **gím-tún**, a round cushion of flowered silk, used at court.

tún (a flat cylindrical stone), to fasten a criminal to a large round stone by a locked chain. **tún-hoān**, a criminal chained to such a stone. **tún-chhát**, to chain a thief to a round stone, as by order of mandarin; a thief thus fastened, or who has been so chained.

chióh-tún, a short cylindrical stone with a hole in the middle for fastening a criminal to it; or without a hole, for sitting on as a seat.

bō-á-tún, a mill-stone. **chit-tún-bō**, a pair of mill-stones. **téng-tún**, the upper mill-stone. **ē-tún**, the lower mill-stone.

tún (T.) **bú-tún**, = A. bú-thún, short and stout.

tún [R. a receptacle for grain; to store up grain], to store up in large quantities. **tún-tiáh**, to buy and store up grain, pulse, potatoes, &c., for a better price. **tún-tháh**, to store up in great abundance. **tún-lún tháh-láh**, id. **tún-thiap**, id. **tún-hè**, to store up goods in large quantities, waiting for a better price. **tún chhâ-chháu**, to store up wood and grass, &c., for fuel.

tùn [R. to bow the head to the ground; to adjust; a meal; = col. tǹg]. **tùn-siú pài**, to bow the head to the ground in reverence or worship.

chéng-tùn, to arrange in good order. **an-tùn**, to put in order, as a room, arranging its furniture, &c.; to put an affair into a somewhat better state; though far from settled, yet in a way of getting settled, or at least keeping it from getting worse, *e.g.* keeping from fighting or lawsuits; to make arrangements for sustaining one's family when going from home.

tùn [R. to shake; to move; to rub or feel with the

厦英大辭典

hand], to pull hard, as cloth or yarn, in order to stretch it, as with one end fastened, or between two persons; to shake or pull one's own clothes, so as to make them hang even, or to shake off dust. **tùn-se**, to pull yarn in order to make it straight. **tùn-chhiú**, to shake hands, as Europeans do.

tùn-tiⁿ, to make excuses or objections, as man told to do something. **tùn--tsáu**, to break away and run off, as man or animal. **gâu-tùn**, constantly making movements that show unwillingness, as cow when ploughing, or as horse when led or ridden.

tùn (mere imitation of the foreign sound), a ton of measurement of a foreign ship.

tūn [R. confused; disorderly; chaotic]. **hūn-tūn**, chaos. **hūn-tūn ê-sî**, the period of chaos. **hūn-tūn chhe-khai**, when chaos began to give place to order. **hūn-hūn tūn-tūn**, good and bad confusedly mixed; unconnected and confused, as talking without any clear meaning; in confused crowds, as men, so that we cannot count them, or pick out a man among them. **pān--liáu hūn-tūn**, arranged in a very inaccurate or slipshod way, as a matter; without clearness, precision, or correctness. **kap--i hūn-tūn**, to put in an article of little or no use among others given to a man, just to make up the required number.

tūn [R. blunt; dull; stupid; = col. tun], dull in intellect; stupid. **bān-tūn**, stupidly slow and dull, as at learning, or at work, or at going a message. **kha-chhiú bān-tūn**, limbs very slow at moving, as old man, or as man naturally so.

tūn (cf. thn̄g, tn̄g), to stew or boil slowly over a slow fire, as over embers without flame. **ûn-ûn-á-tūn**, id. **tūn-khi-noāⁿ**, boil or stew very slowly till it is tender.

tūn [R. tūn, tûn, to collect together in large quantities; to station troops], to station for a long time, as soldiers, esp. a military colony.

tūn-chek, to store up gradually, and accumulate large quantities of some article, without selling any of it, in hope of higher price.

tūn-tsat, to encamp, as an army. **tūn-peng**, to station a large body of soldiers for a long time at an important place, so long that they settle down and cultivate the land there. **tūn-hoan**, to station half-civilized aborigines on the borders of the savage territory in Formosa; aborigines so stationed.

tut — **khó tut-tut**, very thick, as paste or mud; very crowded, as animals. **kāu tut-tut**, very thick, as liquid.

pûi tut-tut (T.), = A. pûi lut-lut, very fat, as man or animal.

tút — **ko-tút-biên**, a warm glossy foreign woollen stuff.

tút, to give the final polish, as to brass, pewter, or gilding, esp. with a woollen cloth, fine brush, or bit of ivory.

tùt [R. sudden; precipitate; inconsiderate; insolent]. **tút-jiên**, suddenly.

tùt [R. to rush against suddenly; also written with the previous word]. **tông-tút**, too forward; rather impudent or impertinent; too free and easy, as in asking a favour from a stranger; sudden and unexpected, as events coming in a way we would not have thought of. **chin tông-tút**, extremely so.

pông-tút, occurring suddenly and unexpectedly.

twâ, twá, twà, twā; better toâ, toá, toà, toā (*q.v.*)

twaⁿ, twâⁿ, twáⁿ, twàⁿ, twāⁿ; better toaⁿ, toâⁿ, toáⁿ, toàⁿ, toāⁿ (*q.v.*)

twah, twàh; better toah, toàh (*q.v.*)

twan, twân, twán, twàn, twān; better toan, toân, toán, toàn, toān (*q.v.*)

twát, better toát (*q.v.*)

TH.

tha [R. he; she; him; her; another], (C. thaⁿ). **tsū-kí put-lêng pó, ien-lêng pó tha-jîn**, unable to protect himself, how can he protect others?

thà (cf. thok, thuh), to poke, stir, or push about with a long pole; to raise a subject to a man by giving him information of which he had no idea before. **thà-là**, to poke away, or stir about with a pole, as in removing cobwebs, or poking an animal out of a nest or hole. **thà-thà**, id. **thà-là--chhut-lâi**, to poke out from a hole, as an animal; to drag to the light things that were formerly secret, or known to few, esp. the bad conduct of others. **thà--lòh-lâi**, to take down from a height with a pole. **thà--lòh-khì**, to push down with a pole, as in a pit or pool. **thà--chhut-lâi**, to take out, as dirt out of a hole, or out of a bottle, by stirring it with a stick.

thà-khui, to push away, or push things separate with a pole. **thà-oá**, to draw things near us, or near each other, as with a stick or pole. **thà-hàp**, to draw things together with a pole. **thà e-kun**, to remove the bride's vail, as the bridegroom does at the marriage.

thà hē-i-tsai, to let him know about it for the first time.

thaⁿ (C.), = A. tha (R.), he; another.

thâⁿ (Cn.), [R. tiông, over again; double; twofold, &c.; = col. têng]. **thâⁿ-bêng**, to explain again more clearly. **thâⁿ bêng-pék**, id. **koh-thâⁿ**, id.; to tell over again.

tháⁿ (C. théⁿ), to carry on the palm of the hand [but in C. tháⁿ is to push away with the palm turned forwards with the fingers downwards]. (cf. thuh.)

tháⁿ-koâiⁿ, to raise up high on the palm. **tháⁿ-koâiⁿ khi-phah**, raise up (the gun) high and shoot! **tháⁿ--lòh-khì**, to lift or carry down gently on the palm. **ēng-chhiú tháⁿ--khì**, to carry away gently on the palm.

tháⁿ--khì, to fend off with the palms turned outwards, as a man going to strike. **tùi-sim-tsô tháⁿ--khì**, to fend off a man thus from one's breast.

tháⁿ chit--ê tāi-chì hē-i-thiaⁿ, tell this whole matter to him fully and thoroughly from beginning to end. **tháⁿ-chhut chit-ê-sū**, id.

phê-tháⁿ, to flatter and fawn upon a superior or an influential man, as an inferior does.

tháⁿ [R. thán, level; even]. **pîⁿ-tháⁿ**, level, as a road.

khín-tháⁿ, shallow, as learning, or as a dish; simple and easy.

thá (T.) **tháⁿ-hoâiⁿ**, = A. thán-hoâiⁿ, crosswise; across.

thāⁿ [R. sek, ornaments; to adorn]. **tsng-thāⁿ**, to adorn or ornament, as women; beautifully adorned; toilette; to talk in a false boastful way of one's self. **tsng-hoe thāⁿ-hún**, to dress herself up with much ornament, as woman.

thah [R. thek, to kick, = col. that]. **thiàu-thah**, = thiàu-that, very playful, as child.

thah (R. thap), a pagoda. **pó-thah**, a Buddhist pagoda. **saⁿ-tsàn-thah**, a three-storied pagoda. **chhit-tsàn-thah**, a seven-storied pagoda. **tsō-thah**, to build a pagoda (v. tsō).

hiuⁿ-thah, a spiral roll of incense, which burns for several days. **kim-thah**, = kim-tháh, paper pasted in hollow squares, burned in idolatrous worship.

kim-thah, a city and country near Siam (Rangoon and Burmah?). **sam-thah-kî**, the flag of Hamburg.

thah [R. tiàp, to pile up; to repeat; = col. tháh]. **chhâ-thah**, a square or hexagonal pile of timber, made by laying the pieces crosswise tier above tier. **kih chhâ-thah**, to pile up such a pile of wood.

tháh [R. tiàp, to pile up; to repeat; = col. thiàp, thah], to pile things one above another; to build up a house one story higher; a pile, as of books, &c.; laid or put on in addition; to excel others.

tháh-làh, to pile things on one another, esp. in a confused manner. **saⁿ-tháh**, laid on each other, as books, timber, &c. **tún-tháh**, to store away things in large quantities. **têng-têng tháh-tháh**, piled or crowded together, *e.g.* as graves in a public burying-ground. **têng-tháh-khiàm**, to get deeper and deeper in debt to the same man (v. khiàm).

liên-tháh, in rapid succession. **saⁿ-liên-tháh**, id. **liên-tháh-lâi**, coming in rapid succession.

tháh-lâu, to build a story higher. **tháh tī téng-bīn**, placed on the top of another thing. **koh-tháh chit-piàn**, to put on another coat, as of varnish. **ke-tháh chit-niáⁿ**, put on an additional article of dress, *e.g.* additional coat or vest. **tháh kah-á**, to put on a vest, as over a coat. **tháh bé-koà**, to put on a jacket, as over a coat.

tháh-thâu, laid on the top of a pile, *e.g.* a specially good fruit topping a pile of fruit, or something red for good luck. **khit--i tháh-thâu**, to be excelled by him; said of the man who was himself previously at the top. **khah-tháh-thâu--i**, to excel him or it; said of persons or things. **bô-lâng ōe-tháh-thâu--i**, none is able to excel him. **bô-khah-tháh-thâu**, there is none better or more excellent.

ài-tháh--lâng, wishing to excel or be ahead of others, as in a subscription or other good work. **khah-tháh--lâng**, to excel others in such things.

chhin tháh-chhin, to marry into a family with which there is already a connection by marriage. **au-á tháh tih-á** (cups on small plates), said of incest.

kim-tháh, = kim-thah, paper pasted in hollow squares, and burned in the worship of the gods.

chit-tháh-chheh, a pile of books. **chheh chit-tháh**, id. **tsoá chit-tháh**, a pile of paper. **chiâⁿ-tui chiâⁿ-tháh**, in great heaps and piles; in great quantities.

thai (R. su), a sieve; to sift with a sieve. **thai-táu**, a fine sieve. **thai-táu-kiâⁿ**, the rim of a sieve. **thai-táu-se**, fine gauze for sieves.

bí-thai, a rice-sieve, through which the broken rice falls, while the chaff is also shaken to one side. **mīⁿ-thai**, a sieve for drying boiled maccaroni or vermicelli.

thai-lâi thai-khì, to select the very best (things or men) by a series of successive selections. **kè-thai**, to be sifted; to be chosen out very carefully. **thai mīⁿ-hún**, to sift wheaten flour. **thai chhùi-bí khí--lâi**, to sift out the broken rice. **lô-bí thai-chhek**, to sift or riddle cleaned and uncleaned rice.

thâu-thai--ê, the largest and best sort of the dried lung-yen or dragon's-eye fruit. **jī-thai--ê**, the second-rate sort of it.

thai [R. to carry, to lift up, = col. khai, tai, thê]. **thai-kú**, to assist a man, especially by giving him custom. **thai-kí** (C.), id.

thai-chhiang, a gun carried and worked by two men.

thai [R. id. = col. the], the embryo or fetus in the womb. **hit-thai**, on that occasion of child-birth. **thai-ui**, the placenta or after-birth. **pau-thai**, the caul.

thai-sîn, the guardian spirit of unborn infants. **hoān--tióh thai-sîn**, to displease that spirit, *e.g.* by moving the bed or furniture of the room of a pregnant woman, or doing in that room various sorts of work which are counted unlucky.

an-thai, Tauist rites for removing the pains of a pregnant woman. **siū-thai**, to become pregnant; to conceive. **hoâi-thai**, to be pregnant. **toà-kúi-thai**, unreal appearance of pregnancy, caused by wind or dropsy or some other cause. **tâu-thai**, to enter into the embryotic state, as a spirit becoming incarnate. **tâu-thai chhut-sì**, to become incarnate, as a god or spirit. **chhut-bú-thai**, newly born, as infant.

thai-chioh, to borrow money on the security of a house, land, ship, &c. **thai-jī**, a deed giving the security of a ship, house, &c., for a loan. **thai-chioh-jī**, id. **chiong-tsûn ûi-thai**, to make the vessel the security, as in a bottomry bond.

thai (same as previous word?). **hong-thai**, a typhoon. **hong-thai-hō͘**, violent squalls of rain in a typhoon. **tsòe hong-thai**, there is a typhoon; to have a typhoon.

tsòe-thai, there is a typhoon; to have a typhoon. **ū-thai**, there is a typhoon brewing. **làk-gėh chit-lûi, chí káu-thai**, thunder in the 6th month keeps away many (nine) typhoons. **chhit-gėh chit-lûi, káu-thai lâi**, thunder in the 7th month brings typhoons.

hé-thai, exceedingly sultry weather.

thâi [R. sat; to cut; to kill; and by change of tone "sài," to cut off; to reduce; = col. thài], to cut; to wound by cutting; to behead; to kill; esp. by cutting; to fight or do battle.

saⁿ-thâi, to fight or do battle. **toā-thâi**, a great battle. **kap-i-thâi**, to fight with him. **thâi-iâⁿ**, to conquer in battle. **thâi-su**, to be defeated in battle. **thâi-pāi**, id.

thâi--lâi, to come along fighting, as army. **thâi-lâi**, to cut, kill, or fight much. **thâi-lâi thâi-khì**, to fight with each other, as armies in battle, or as men in single combat. **tit-tit-thâi**, slaughtering right on. **lām-sám thâi**, to cut, wound, and kill right and left without distinction; to kill promiscuously.

thâi-thâu, to behead. **thâi-lâng**, to kill a man, to wound a man, by cutting. **thâi-sí-lâng**, to kill a man, esp. by cutting. **thâi-lâng pê-miāⁿ**, to pay damages or make reparation for killing a man. **jip-**

chē, **bô-thâi-lâng**, not to hurt an enemy who comes into our house.

thâi-ti, to slaughter a pig; a butcher who kills pigs. **thâi-gû**, to slaughter a cow. **thâi-ti tó-iû^n**, to have pigs and goats slaughtered, as for great feasts. **chiáh-pûi, thang hē--lâng thâi-bah** (growing fat just to be slaughtered), said in scolding an utterly useless man.

thâi chit-ē, to give one cut with a blow of a sword or knife. **thâi--tsòe nn̄g-tn̂g**, to cut across into two pieces, as a stick. **thâi--tsòe nn̄g-pêng**, to cleave in two, longitudinally. **tit-tit-chhâ thâi kàu-khiau** (to hack a straight bit of wood so as to make it crooked), to mismanage and ruin an affair that would have gone well.

thái [R. chím, how? what? = col. tsái^n, thài; or perhaps same as the following word].

beh-thái, = beh-thài, how can —? how ever —? **beh-thái-ōe**, how can — ever?

thái [R. khí, how?]. **thái-thó**, how — ever —? (v. thó).

thái, exclamation to frighten and drive away animals, as dogs or cats.

thái [R. nāi^n, leprosy]. **thái-ko**, leprosy. **thái-ko-iâ^n**, a place where lepers live; a lazar-house. **thái-ko chiū^n-bīn**, having lost all modesty and sense of shame. **thái-ko thái chiū^n-bīn**, id.

thái-ko-chhêng, a sort of tree.

thái [R. thé, the body, = col. thóe]. **siet-thái**, shameless vulgarity done to show that he has utter contempt for us, *e.g.* exposing his person indecently, or doing indecent acts in our presence; or as a woman scolding with vile language.

thài (R. id.), very great; exceedingly; too great; too much. **thài-kò**, overmuch; beyond what is proper or needful; far too much; excessively. **thài-toā**, too large. **thài-sòe**, too small. **thài-tsá**, too early. **thài-oà^n**, too late.

thài-iông, the sun (v. iông). **thài-im** (R.), the moon (v. im). **thài-kek**, the original principle of the universe. **thài-siōng ló-kun**, title of Lau-tsze as deified. **liû-pùt thài-sòe**, name of an unlucky star; the demon of eclipse. **thài-pêng**, great peace and prosperity; Taipings (v. pêng).

thài-hō, empress dowager (v. hō). **thài-tsú**, the heir apparent; also = lô-chhia, name of an idol. **toā-thài-tsú**, the eldest son of the emperor. **thài-tsú-têng**, a small shed of bamboo and paper in which little boys carry about the "sóe-hút" idol round the shops, getting a few cash from each (said also in joke or inuendo of the small salver and lamp used in opium-smoking). **phâng thài-tsú-têng--ê**, the boys who carry it about, the worst and vilest boys; counted worse than beggars (said in scolding a boy as most vile). **thài-tsú thài-pó**, the guardian of the heir apparent.

thài-pó, guardian of heir apparent. **thài-su**, prime minister (v. su). **thài-hù**, a title of high rank at court (v. hù). **thài-kàm**, an imperial eunuch (v. kàm). **thài-iâ**, title of very small civil mandarins (v. iâ). **thài-thài**, wife of the prefect of a Foo department, or of a Hai-fang, or of a Kujin. **chià^n-thài**, principal wife of do. **jī-thài**, secondary wife of do. **lāu-thài-thài**, mother of mandarin or Kujin. **láu-thài** (r.?), id. **thài-lāu**, father of mandarin or graduate. **thài-má**, mother of do.

thài-kong, name of an ancient worthy; also (Cn.), great grandfather.

thài-hô-koe, a very small sort of fowl like a bantam.

thài [R. great and prosperous; sometimes interchanged with the preceding word]. **kok-thài bîn-an**, the kingdom flourishing and the people enjoying tranquillity.

thài-san, a famous mountain in Shan-tung.

thài (= thái). **beh-thài**, = beh-thái, how?

thài [R. sài, to reduce; to diminish; to dispense with; by change of tone from "sat," to cut or kill, = col. thâi], to have done with; will have no more of it! be done with it! **thài--khì**, id. **bô, chiū-thài**, if there be none, then just let there be none.

thài [R. figure, gait, habit, or manner of a man]. **thé-thài** (r.), a man's external manner and bearing. **hó-thé-thài**, having a very good-looking appearance, as to gait and manner.

thāi [R. to wait; to treat]. **khoán-thāi**, to treat; to treat well, esp. to treat a guest kindly, giving him refreshments, &c.; to entertain. **hó-khoán-thāi**, to treat kindly; to entertain well. **phái^n-khoán-thāi**, to treat ill or unkindly. **khek-kí thāi-jîn**, to stint or deny one's self in order to treat others well. **khut-kí thāi-jîn**, id.

ióng-jī thāi-ló, to bring up children expecting them to treat their aged parents well (v. jī).

tán-thāi (Cn.), to wait; to wait for. **thāi-ká^n** (An.), just a very short time ago.

thak [R. thek, to cut flesh from bones; to scrape off; to pick out; cf. col. thuh?], to pick, as the teeth; to pick things out of crevices, &c.; to press into crevices, as oakum or saw-dust.

thak-thak, to mend slightly, as a dress, &c. **pó-thak**, to take out bad parts and put in new, as in a wall, or vessel, or dress; when done to a dress it implies that the edges are carefully smoothed, so that the patch is invisible or nearly so.

thak-khí, to pick the teeth. **thak chhùi-khí**, id.

sat-pìn-thak, a cleaner for cleaning a small-tooth comb (literally a comb for lice).

thak-thek, to reprove and scold a man for faults with much minuteness or in an exacting manner. **thóe-thak**, to joke and jeer at a man's defects of bodily form or at his faults in conduct, either behind his back, or said to another as if he were supposed not to hear it. **thé-thak** (C.), id.

thak (cf. thok, thuh?), to move the balls of an abacus. **thak sǹg-poâ^n**, to calculate by the abacus (v. sǹg). **thak-siàu**, id. **thak-khoà^n**, make trial of the calculation by the abacus.

thák (R. thòk), to read aloud; to study books. **thák-chheh** (to read books aloud), to study books; to be a student (v. chheh). **thák-tsu** (Cn.), id. **thák-keng**, to read classical books aloud; to study classical books. **thák sa^n-piàn**, to read aloud three times over. **thák-pó**, to read up what was not read at the proper time. **kì^n-thák kì^n-bat**, whatever he reads he remembers. **khûn-thák**, to study diligently. **khó-thák**, to study with much toil, difficulty, exhaustion, or pain, *e.g.* so as almost to make one's self ill, or as a poor student undergoing great hardships. **chiàu-jī thák-jī**, to keep to the simple sense of the document, just as it is written, *e.g.* in a written agreement.

thák-siàu, to read an account aloud, so as to let others who are interested hear it. **thák-sò**, to read a prayer aloud before burning it.

tham (R. id.), to covet; covetous; greedy; grasping. **tham-sim**, id. **am-tham**, foolishly greedy. **tham-têˆ**, to covet and plot or intrigue to get. **tham-loân**, to hanker after or doat upon improper things. **tham-bê**, ensnared by vicious desire (v. bê).

tham-chiȧh, gluttonous; small-pox very thick on the body. **tham-chiȧh-lâng liên-oáⁿ iȧh-chī**, a glutton licks even the bowl. **tham-chhông**, extremely gluttonous (said in scolding). **tham-tsâi**, covetous; avaricious; to be avaricious. **tham-lī** (r.), id. **tham-chíⁿ**, id. **tham-bîn**, sleeping very sound; very difficult to waken. **tham-sek**, lewd; lustful.

tham-joȧh, wearing a great many clothes even in hot weather. **hō--i khah-tham-joȧh**, make him wear plenty of clothes though it be hot; said to be good for a child. **tham-joȧh, bô-tham-koâⁿ**, should wear plenty of clothes to guard against cold, even though it be rather warm.

tham-sia kùi-bóe, to buy on credit is expensive. **tham-koaⁿ ù-lī**, avaricious mandarins. **tham--jī pîn-jī-khak**, the character "covetous" has its form very like that of "poor."

thâm (R. id.), a deep pond; a pond for irrigation. **thâm-á**, id. **thâm-khut**, large and small ponds of water (v. khut). **toā-thâm**, a deep pool in a river, as at rapids, or at a waterfall (s. wine-jar).

thâm — **thâm-hoe**, a large flower, somewhat like a lily, much grown at temples; Crinum.

thâm (R. id.), a sort of spirit-jar. **chiú-thâm**, id. **toā-thâm**, a large one (s. pool). **sòe-thâm**, a smaller one.

chit-thâm-chiú, a jar of spirituous liquor.

thâm [R. tâm, thâm], phlegm; mucus from the throat. **thâm-noāⁿ**, mucus and phlegm (v. noāⁿ). **thâm-koàn**, a spittoon.

thâm-hé, tendency towards cancerous swelling of throat.

thâm-loān, crazy; idiotic (v. loān). **hong-thâm pè-sim**, to have an attack of dull quiet madness; said in scolding, You are crazy!

khí-thâm, gurgling in throat, as of man about to die. **khák-thâm**, to cough up phlegm, or try to bring it up. **khak-thâm**, id. **phùi-thâm**, to spit out phlegm. **kāu-thâm**, to have much phlegm.

khì-thâm, to remove phlegm. **siau-thâm**, id. **teh-thâm**, to cure or relieve the tendency to have phlegm, as medicine.

thâm [R. clouds spreading themselves]. **gōh ûi-thâm** (Cn.), the moon has a halo.

thám (C. khám). **thám-mέⁿ** (r.), speedily; very quickly.

thàm [R. tham, thàm, to feel about for; to search for; to explore; to sound; to investigate; to make inquiries; to visit], to visit; to make a call; to take soundings. **thàm-hoe**, the third literary Tsin-sze.

saⁿ-thàm, to visit; to make a call. **thàm-kheh**, to pay visits, as a new graduate or mandarin. **thàm-pâng**, the younger brother or nephew of a bride taking presents to her a day or two after the marriage. **saⁿ-jit thàm-pâng**, do. on the third day. **saⁿ-jit kū-iâ thàm-pâng**, id.

thàm-khoàⁿ, to investigate, as for information, *e.g.* to find a man's purpose, or to test the goodness of a dollar, or the quality of goods. **thàm-thiaⁿ**, to make inquiries about something, usually somewhat secretly. **táⁿ-thàm**, to make investigation. **thàm-hu-sit**, to investigate whether the matter be true or false. **thàm-kun-chêng**, to make secret inquiry into the state of the army, as for the enemy. **thàm-kha-lō͘**, to look secretly in the daytime, so as to know how to come at night to steal.

thàm-tsú-bé, a spy. **tsòe-chhȧt-thàm**, to be a thief's spy.

thàm-tsúi, to take soundings. **thàm joā-tsōe-tsúi**, id. **thàm chhim-khín**, to try the depth, as of a well; to investigate how a matter stands.

thàm-thâu, to thrust one's head forward, so as to see or hear something.

thām (cf. thap). **thām-tέ**, somewhat concave, as a hand-net, or as bottom of chair long used, &c.; either so made intentionally, or become so by long use.

thām-tsúi, to step suddenly into water.

táh-thām, to step unexpectedly down a step, or into a hole, or into water. **kha táh-thām**, id. **seng-lí táh-thām**, to lose in trade suddenly and unexpectedly, *e.g.* by an unlucky venture. **seng-lí táh-thām-thām**, id.

chhim-thām, to spend all one's reserved funds, and get deeply in debt. **thām-ēng**, to use more than our income. **thām-thūi--lâng**, to be deep in debt to people.

than (R. chheng), a long narrow bivalve shell-fish; the razor-fish. **se-kha-than**, a large sort. **tek-than**, a smaller sort.

piⁿ tek-than, to catch the "tek-than" by dredging. **tah-than**, to catch the "than" shell-fish in small quantities.

than-tiâⁿ, a place where these shell-fish are bred and caught. **than-khak**, the shell of the razor-fish. **than-kha-chí**, upright rails of a railing almost divided in two by long longitudinal slits.

ngiauh-than, quite dead (said of a man). **than--khì**, id.

hiau-than, much warped, as wood; faithless; disappointing trust (v. hiau). **phe-bīn-than**, putting on the appearance of goodness or diligence when observed (lit. good shell-fish laid on the top). **phe-bīn-than, chìm-tsúi-ô**, shell-fish laid so as to show the best on the top, and oysters well soaked in water; said of the tricks of trade.

thân [R. tâm, to talk; to converse]. **lân-thân**, plays in the Swatow dialect.

thán [R. name of a disease]. **hông-thán**, jaundice, in children, or a disease of children, caused by overeating, which makes them yellow and sickly. **n̂g-thán**, id. **tiȯh n̂g-thán**, to have this disease. **n̂g-sng-thán**, sallow and jaundiced, as child or young lad.

thán (R. thám), a small carpet; a rug; a coverlet, generally woollen. **thán-á**, id. **thán-ná**, id. **soàⁿ-thán**, a rug, &c., made of cotton. **mn̂g-thán**, a hairy woollen rug. **jiông-thán**, a velvet or fine hairy rug or coverlet. **tē-thán**, a large carpet. **tōe-thán** (Cn.), id.

thán — **lán-thán**, idle; indisposed to take trouble.

thán [R. to bare the arm; to disclose; unfair]. **phien-thán**, unfair through partiality.

thán (T. thán, tháⁿ).

thán-píⁿ, turned so as to strike with the flat side, as a sword; on or with the flat side. **thán-phi-sin**, turning sidewise, as to get through a narrow passage, or to pass another on a narrow road. **thán-phîn**, id. (v. phîn). **thán-hoâiⁿ**, transverse; horizontal; crosswise (v. hoâiⁿ). **thán-khi**, lying over; slanting (v.

khi). **thán-chhu**, sloping; laid down sloping or inclined. **thán-chhoáh**, diagonal, as lattice-work (v. chhoáh).

thán-khiā, perpendicular.

thán-pīⁿ, lying level, as on the ground. **thán-tó**, do., having formerly been upright. **péng thán-tó**, to turn a thing upside down; to turn on the back. **tó thán-tit**, to lie down, as on a bed; lying straight along the length of it, not across; fallen or lying straight along. **thán-tit**, laid or lying straight along.

thán-chhiò, lying with face upwards; inverted, or turned upside down with the concave side up. **thán-phak**, turned with face down; inverted so as to have the face or concave side down (v. phak). **péng-thán-khap**, to invert so (v. khap).

thán — **ân-thán** (C.), drawn very tight, as rope or cloth, or as a parcel tightly tied; firm and plump, as the flesh of a person in good and vigorous health.

thàn [R. to sigh, =col. thò; cf. C. thàn]. **chin thàn-khì** (C.), (R.), really it is very hard to manage; indeed it is hardly worth the labour.

thàn, to drive away, as animals; but not so quick as "koáⁿ." **thàn-ti**, to drive away pigs. **thàn-iûⁿ**, to drive away goats. **thàn-gû**, to drive cows or oxen.

thàn [R. thin, to follow; to walk after; to take advantage of an opportunity], to follow, as an example or command; to obey or act according to; to take advantage of an occasion or opportunity; at the time of, especially while yet —; to earn; to gain; to make money.

thàn-bēng-lēng, to obey a command. **thàn-tō-lí**, to follow a doctrine. **thàn-hoat-tō**, to obey a rule, regulation, or law. **m̄-thàn**, to refuse to obey.

thàn lâng--ê sé-kiáⁿ, to follow a man's example. **thàn lâng-ê-iūⁿ**, id. **saⁿ-thàn-iūⁿ**, id.

saⁿ-thàn saⁿ-hán, to follow the example of others (v. hán).

thàn-chhùi, to accept an offer just as it is made, *e.g.* giving the price asked, or accepting the price or conditions offered; to get a thing just as we expressed a wish for it, or find matters just as we guessed. **thàn goá-ê-chhùi thák**, read word by word after me. **thàn goá--ê chhùi-bé**, id. **thàn i-ê-chhùi**, to follow implicitly what he says.

thàn goá--ê ì-goān, just as I would wish, as events.

thàn-chhiú, everything going on just as we should like, in an affair; to take the opportunity of one's self or another doing something, to do or get done something similar.

thàn-phāng, to use an opportunity for evil, or for injuring another. **thàn-ki-hōe**, to take advantage of an opportunity. **thàn-sè-bīn**, to take advantage of favourable circumstances.

thàn-êng, to take advantage of the opportunity when one has leisure. **thàn-âiⁿ** (T.), id. **thàn-ûiⁿ** (Cn.), id. **thàn-pīⁿ**, taking the opportunity when the sea is smooth. **thàn-sio chiáh**, to eat (or drink) while it is still warm. **thàn-siàu-liên**, while yet young. **thàn-bē-lāu**, diligently using our time before old age comes on. **thàn-bē** —, to take the opportunity before —. **thàn-bô-hō**, to take the opportunity when there is no rain. **thàn-chhut-jit**, to take the opportunity of fine sunny weather.

thàn-tsá, as soon as possible. **thàn-kín**, acting quickly or promptly. **thàn-chit-tiáp**, at the present moment. **thàn-chi-tsöeh** (Cn.), id.

thó-thàn, to earn money, as by trade or business. **tsoán-thàn**, to earn money. **thàn-chîⁿ**, id. **thàn-thiu-hun**, to get a commission on agency or brokerage, &c.

thàn-chhēng, to earn enough for clothing, as well as for food. **thàn-chhī-bó-kiáⁿ**, to earn enough to feed one's family. **thàn-i bōe-tó**, his work is too heavy, or too difficult for me. **thàn-i khah-chió-chîⁿ**, to take a smaller profit out of him. **phe-sìⁿ-miāⁿ-thàn**, to work very very hard to earn money.

thàn-chiáh, to earn one's food. **thàn-chiáh lâng**, a man who lives just on what he earns; a man who earns just enough for support. **sûi-thàn sûi-chiáh**, to live from hand to mouth. **thàn bô-thang-chiáh**, unable to make enough to live upon. **thàn chit-ê-chhùi chiáh**, to earn just enough for one's own food, but having nothing to spare for any one else.

ún-thàn, safe, good, and profitable investment. **ōe-thàn**, profitable, as work or investment. **kāu-thàn**, getting a very high profit; making money rapidly. **toā-thàn-chîⁿ**, making a great deal of money.

bô-thàn, no profit; too small a profit, *e.g.* one-ninth. **tò-thâu-thàn**, to lose in trade instead of gaining.

háp-thàn, making cent. per cent. **háp-thàn ê seng-lí**, trade that makes cent. per cent. **tùi-poàⁿ-thàn**, to make cent. per cent. **saⁿ-hūn thàn-chit-hūn**, to make fifty per cent. **ka-it-thàn**, to gain ten per cent. on the capital. **ka-jī-thàn**, to gain twenty per cent., &c.

thang [R. thong, to go through; to pervade; to succeed; successful; prosperous], may be done; may be; may; you may; it is allowable; sometimes used as a mere auxiliary almost like the English "to" of the infinitive.

m̄-thang, you must not; must not; don't do that. **thang m̄-thang**, may I or may I not? is it allowable? may it be done? **thang á-m̄-thang**, id.

i bô-thang, he would not give his consent. **goá bô-thang**, I was not willing to allow it.

bô-thang-hó, not at all good. **bô-thang-chiáh**, having nothing to eat. **bô-thang-hō--lí**, have nothing to give you. **bô-mihⁿ thang-hō--lí**, id. **bô-ōe thang-kóng**, having nothing to say; unable to say anything, *e.g.* in answer to a charge or argument.

ū thang-hō--lâng, to have enough to give to others. **ōe-tit--thang** —, able to —; it can be — (v. tit).

kng-thang, thoroughly understanding a matter; bright, as a well-lighted house. **thang-kng**, id.; also, too loose in texture, as cloth between the threads of which light can be seen (cf. lāng-thang, from "thang," a window).

khah khui-thang, feeling now more easy in mind. **sim khui-thang**, the heart glad and comfortable after grief or anxiety, *e.g.* on some one coming and comforting, or on getting good news, or on return of prosperity. **sim-koaⁿ khui-thang**, id.

thang [R. lông, a basket, =col. lâng, láng], (C. lang). **hé-thang** (C. hóe-lang), a small portable charcoal stove in a small basket, held under the clothes to warm one's self. **chioh hé-thang**, to warm one's self with such a stove.

thang (R. chhong), a window. **thang-á**, id. **thang-á-kheng**, window-frame. **thang-á-chí**, perpendicular bars in a window, for keeping out thieves. **thang-á-bâi**, lintel of window. **thang-á-têng**, window-sill. **thang-á-mn̂g**, a window closing with hinges like a door. **thang-á-sìⁿ**, a window-shutter hinged like a door-leaf. **thang-á-iám**, a window-shutter hanging from hinges on the top, supported when open by a stick. **thang-á-thìⁿ**, a stick for supporting a thang-á-iám when open. **thang-á-thoah**, a sliding window-shutter.

gêh-thang, a circular window. **îⁿ-thang**, id. **liú-tiâu-thang**, a window made with long narrow slips of wood close together. **chiôh-thang**, a window with a stone frame and stone or iron upright bars. **se-thang**, a window made with thin gauze. **soe-thang**, a window made with fixed bars of tile or brick-work. **soe-chí-thang**, id.

hoe-thang-chí, ornamental trellis-tiles.

ô-kiàⁿ-thang, a window made with very thin oyster-shells. **ô-kiàⁿ-thang-teng**, a lantern made with thin oyster-shells.

thiⁿ-thang, a fixed light in a roof, made of thin oyster-shells or of thick glass, *e.g.* bottle glass. **thiⁿ-thang-hiā**, tiles made with glass or oyster-shell fixed in them, for this use. **thiⁿ-thang-pín**, a cover for a sky-light, generally made with oyster-shells, but sometimes of other materials, sometimes quite opaque.

tiàm-thang-pang, the movable boards of a shop-window.

phah-thang, to make a window. **that-thang**, to close up a window permanently, as by building it up or boarding it over.

thoah-thang, having a sort of squint, from the iris being on one side.

lāng-thang, having holes in it, as gauze; loose in texture, as inferior cloth; having open spaces, as a railing. **kek-lāng-thang**, to make work so as to leave spaces, as in a trellis, &c.; made with empty spaces in them, as some cakes (cf. thang-kng, from "thang," may, to go through).

thâng [R. thiông, an insect; a reptile; = col. lâng], an insect, especially a long creeping insect, as a worm, caterpillar, or maggot. **thâng-thoā**, insects, worms, caterpillars, &c. **thâng hiā**, caterpillars, ants, and such insects. **siⁿ-thâng**, to breed worms or maggots.

chiēn-thâng, said of a very playful and troublesome child. **e-tē-thâng**, said by men of themselves in addressing Heaven. **pîn-toāⁿ-thâng**, a very lazy fellow. **pîn-á-thâng** (Cn.), id.

tôk-thâng, a poisonous reptile. **būn-thâng**, worms in the belly. **chiù-thâng**, worms that perforate wood, bamboo, &c., supposed also to cause the decay of teeth. **hoe-thâng**, insects that breed in flowers and feed on them. **chhài-thâng**, green caterpillars found on vegetables. **png-thâng**, large green caterpillars found on the "png" tree.

thâng-si, gut made from the entrails of the caterpillar of the "png" tree.

mn̂g-káu-á-thâng, a sort of hairy caterpillar. **káu-á-thâng**, id. **mêⁿ-káu-á-thâng** (C.), id. **siⁿ-mn̂g-thâng**, sort of hairy caterpillar, esp. found on fir-trees. **siⁿ-mêⁿ-thâng**, id.; also (Cn.), = mêⁿ-thâng-chhì.

mêⁿ-thâng-chhì, a hairy and prickly worm about two inches long, found in the sea; it wounds the hands in catching fish, and hurts the mouth when eating fish or shrimps. **mn̂g-thâng-chhì**, id. **tak--tiòh mêⁿ-thâng-chhì**, to find one's self unexpectedly engaged in a quarrel with a very powerful and dangerous man, esp. with an "ông-ngē," or litigious literary man.

thâng-io (Cn.), name of a sort of bird.

thâng [R. tông, a tube; a cylinder; = col. tâng]. **hiā-thâng**, semi-cylindrical tiles for roofs. **hoā-thâng** (Cn.), id.

thâng [R. tông, name of a tree, Dryandra, &c.]. **thâng-chí**, a tree with large leaves and large whitish flowers (Elaeococca?); also its seeds, from which oil is made. **thâng-iû**, oil made from it; much used for paint. **thâng-chí-iû**, id. **thâng-iû-he**, this oil mixed with lime, much used for caulking and cementing.

thâng [R. tông, a boy; a lad; a surname; = col. tâng], a surname.

thâng — **thâng-thn̄g** (C.), a stick carried by a son at a funeral.

tháng (R. thóng), a cask; a barrel; a tub; a bucket; a pail.

hia-tháng, the leg of a boot. **bêh-tháng**, the leg of a stocking. **bóeh-tháng** (C.), id.

kau-tháng-á, a bucket with a semi-circular handle over the top. **kau-tháng**, id. **toā-tháng**, a large tub, &c. **tháng-á**, a tub, barrel, bucket, &c., esp. if not large.

kha-tháng, a foot-pail; a tub. **chiôh-kha-tháng**, a stone tub. **kha-tháng-lāi**, a very confined district (said in speaking of a man who has never been far from home, or who considers a short journey from home to be a great distance). **bīn-tháng**, a basin for washing, usually made of wood. **bīn-tháng-kè**, a wash-stand.

tsúi-tháng, a bucket for carrying water. **poàh-tháng**, a bucket for drawing water from a well (v. poàh). **phoàh-tháng** (C.), id. **hè-tháng**, a bucket for raising water swung on a rope between two men. **e-tháng**, the bucket of a well-sweep. **phùn-tháng**, a bucket for watering with (v. phùn). **tiàu-tháng**, a hanging bucket, as for drawing water. **kim-tiàu-tháng**, said of a man who is unwilling to help when asked, or even unwilling to work for payment; said to have been originally applied to a noted fortune-teller who spoke to no one, but let down a bucket as his means of communication.

chhe-tháng, a bucket for carrying manure. **sái-tháng**, id. **jiō-tháng**, a bucket for urine, often set in a room for use. **bé-tháng**, a close stool for use in a house.

siak-tháng, a tub for threshing rice (v. siak). **tiū-tháng**, id. **tô-tháng**, a vessel containing tallow for dipping candles. **ti-tháng**, a tub for scalding pigs in.

tê-tháng, a wooden vessel in which a tea-pot is put to keep it warm. **chhe-tháng**, a large wooden vessel for cooking rice by steam. **gô-chiú-tháng**, a Chinese still, made like an alembic. **gô-tháng**, id.

kiáⁿ-sun-tháng, sort of tub used at an accouchement. **io-tháng**, id. **tsú-sun-tháng**, id., so called at the time of marriage, when it is usually provided. **chē io-tháng**, to use it, as woman at time of confinement.

chhèng-tháng, a small barrel for carrying powder for guns. **chhèng-iôh-tháng**, id.

teng-tháng, the frame of a very large lantern. **teng-tháng**, a large tub with nails fixed in it, covered up like a pit-fall, so that enemies or thieves fall into it and are wounded. **tháng-teng**, a very large sort of lamp.

tháng-poàⁿ, a tray.

khiā-tháng, to stand in an upright cage, with only the head out, till starved to death.

khe-tháng, to put on the hoops on a bucket, tub, &c.; (must not be said in T. where it has a bad meaning). **phah-tháng** (T.), to make a bucket or tub. **tsòe-tháng** (T.), id.

tháng-khe, a hoop for a barrel, bucket, or tub, gen. bamboo, sometimes of iron. **tháng-chhiûⁿ**, staves of tub, bucket, or barrel. **tháng-koà**, cover of bucket. **tháng-koā^n**, handle of bucket, across the top. **tháng-kiàh**, perpendicular handle of bucket rising straight from the side. **tháng-pì^n**, id. **tháng-khì^n**, instrument for knocking the hoops on a bucket, tub, &c. **tháng-khiâm** (C.), id. **tháng-tī^n**, a wooden instrument, shaped like a chisel, for this purpose. **tháng-tɛ̂^{n}** (C.), id.

pak-tɵ́-tháng toā, belly very large, as of corpulent man. **hó-bīn-kháng**, **phái^n-tɵ̄-tháng**, having a pleased friendly look, but cherishing wicked injurious purposes. **ná^n thih-tháng** (like an iron barrel), said of a strongly fortified place, or of a strongly built house secure from robbers.

thàng [R. thòng, pain; to feel pain; grieved; distressed; miserable; to feel for; to love].

thià^n-thàng, to love.

thàng-thià^n, to feel pain; to be pained. **khɵ́-thàng**, in deep sorrow and distress; painful and miserable. **siong-sim khɵ́-thàng**, in very great and deep sorrow, *e.g.* for death of near relative.

lún-thàng, to be much afraid of going to a place, *e.g.* going to be examined by a mandarin, or as boy going to be scolded by the teacher, or as man afraid to go to a place in the dark.

thàng [R. thong? to go through; to pass through; to communicate with; = col. thang], classifier of journeys, voyages, &c.

sa^n-thàng, having a passage right through; communicating by a door or road. **bô-thàng**, no thoroughfare; no communication through. **thàng--jip-khì**, to lead right in, or right through, as a road or passage. **thàng-siâ^n**, leading to the city, as a road or street.

thàng-kè, to be made quite through, as a hole; to pierce or pass quite through. **tsâu kàu thàng-kè**, to stab quite through, the point coming out on the other side. **kiâ^n kàu thàng-thàng**, to walk all about, *e.g.* through a whole region of country, or all through a house to the very innermost parts.

bô-thàng-bé (C. bóe), broken off in the middle without being brought to a proper result or completion, as any sort of matter. **bōe-thàng-bé**, not fit to be carried on to the end, as something that from its very nature cannot be carried through to a proper end, *e.g.* an improper connection.

chit-thàng-bé (C. bɛ́), a ride on horseback for one complete round going and coming, as at examinations, or for amusement. **pháu-bé chit-thàng**, to ride a horse one round, going and coming. **pháu chit-thàng**, id. **sè chit-thàng**, to hire a horse for one complete round or journey.

thàng-sim-thià^n, sending pangs to the heart, *e.g.* as a very painful boil. **thàng-sim-léng**, delightfully cool and refreshing, as cold water. **koâ^n kàu thàng-sim-koa^n**, bitterly cold (lit. so as to pierce to the heart). **thià^n kàu-thàng-sim-koa^n**, extremely painful, as a boil, &c.

thāng (cf. lāng). **hê-thāng** (C. hɛ̂-lāng), a sort of wicker-work trap for catching fresh-water shrimps.

thāng, a float or buoy, as for an anchor or for a net; or for marking a channel, rock, bank, &c. &c. **phû-thāng**, id. **tek-thāng**, a bamboo float, usually made of one joint, or not much more. **bāng-bé-thāng**, floats for fishing-nets, esp. for marking the limits of the net.

thāng [R. lōng, to brandish; to instigate; to incite; = col. lāng].

thiu-thāng, to teach how to do the work, as a raw servant or apprentice.

thap (R. id., = col. lap, nah^n), concave; an indentation, depression, or cavity; to sink or settle so as to make a depression or cavity; to fall in, as a roof; to mend by putting in a good piece (as of wood) in place of a decayed piece, somewhat like inlaying; to have illicit intercourse.

sa^n-thap, fitting into each other, as mortice and tenon (+). **sa^n-thap-ka**, to cut cloth to advantage, by arranging the pieces to be cut out so as to fit into each other, and lose as little of the stuff as possible. **thap-lâi thap-khì**, to arrange things well in packing, so as to fit well into each other, and take up as little room as possible; to cut cloth carefully so that there is no waste, as by arranging the patterns to fit well, and leave little or no unused material; or as in making a new article out of the good parts of old clothes.

pɵ́-thap, to mend, as a dress, by changing the cloth.

phòng-thap, convex and concave; embossed and depressed; cut in relief, and cut into the material.

thap-thap lap-lap, fallen in, sunken, subsided, or depressed, as ground; not level because parts are sunken. **thap--lòh-lâi**, to sink down making hollows, as an old roof. **thap--lòh-khì**, do., as old roof or floor, &c.; to fall or stumble at a hole, or cavity, or sunken place. **thap-chit-khang**, to subside, making a hole, as ground.

thap-tɵ́, a concave or depressed panel. **thap-jī**, characters cut into the material, *e.g.* cut into the block for printing, so as to print white on a black ground. **thap-bák**, sunken eyes; having deep-set or sunken eyes. **bák-chiu thap-thap**, id. **thap-bák-kɵ**, sort of fish with sunken eyes (v. kɵ).

thap-thâu-chhia, to fall down head-foremost. **thap-thâu-ké**, small round cakes made of starch, having a hollow on the upper side.

thap-bėh, to put on stockings as well as shoes. **thap khɵ̀-kha**, to put the ends of the legs of the trowsers into the stockings.

thap-kha, to interlace the legs, as in wrestling. **sa^n-thap-kha**, legs alternating, as of men sitting close together opposite each other (+). **sa^n-thap-kha teh-kiâ^n**, to walk close on the heels of another man. **kiâ^n-lɵ̄ sa^n-thap-kha**, walking along with very short steps, neither foot going beyond the other, or not much beyond it, as old or sick man. **thap-kha kiâ^n**, to walk with very slow short steps, as old, lame, or sick man. **thap-pɵ̄ kiâ^n**, to measure the ground by the lengths of our foot.

thap--tiòh tsa-bɵ́, to have illicit intercourse with a woman.

thap [R. id.? a bed; a couch; cf. col. that]. **pit-thap**, the cover for the point of a hair-pencil.

that (= thap). **pit-that**, = pit-thap, the cover for the point of a hair-pencil.

that [R. sek, to press tightly in; to fill up crevices; = col. sat, soeh, siap], to stop up, as a hole or channel; to stuff or fill up, as a crevice or opening; to supply, as a deficiency, especially if only temporarily, partially, or inadequately; to obstruct or block up, as a road. **that-hē**, id. **that-tn̄g**, to stop up, as a road (v. tn̄g). **that-lɵ̄**, to block up or stop up a road. **that-mn̂g**, to build up a door. **that-thang**, to build up a window. **that-lāu**, to stop a leak; to caulk. **that-bát**, to stop up close (v. bát). **tī^n that-that**, choke-full or crowded, as things (v. tī^n).

pɵ́-that, to fill up cracks, chinks, or leaks, as in a

roof, boat, or floor; to make up a deficiency, *e.g.* of money entrusted to us, of which we cannot give a full account, or of a debt that we cannot fully pay.

that hī-khang, to stop one's ears, as when determined not to hear. **that-chhùi** (to shut up another's mouth), to put to silence; shut up now! be silent! **that chhùi-khang**, to give some eatable to a child to keep it quiet; to give a sop or douceur to keep a man quiet who could give us trouble.

that-giàh, to act as another's substitute (temporarily), especially when not quite so good; to be given as payment for a debt or security, &c., as some article given in place of money, or part payment in money, or by a bill, &c.; to supply a vacancy or deficiency, esp. by a temporary or inadequate arrangement. **that-chè**, to pay a debt, as for another. **sa-lâi that-khì**, to borrow from one (or more) in order to pay another, or to scrape up various sums from various sources for such purpose. **that-lâi that-khì**, to make up a deficiency in one place or time by super-abundance in another.

kan-that, a cork or stopper for a bottle. **hī-that**, the flaps of a mourning cap covering the ears, indicating that the mourner should have no ear for anything but his grief. **siⁿ hī-that**, to have a growth stopping up the ear.

that [R. thek, to kick, = col. thah], to kick with the toes, or sometimes backwards with the heel; but not with the sole of the foot, which is "lap." **tò-that**, to kick backwards with the heel. **that-tó**, to kick over. **khí-kha that**, to lift the foot and kick. **sái pe-that**, to make a sudden flying kick in boxing. **lâm kûn, pak that**, Southerners box, Northern men kick. **that-kiû**, to kick a ball.

thiàu-that, restless, as a child always moving about, climbing, running, &c.

tsau-that, to ill-use, maltreat, or insult; to spend recklessly, or use wastefully, as money or things; to throw away recklessly, as one's own life. **chiau-that** (esp. T.), id. **tsau-that mihⁿ**, to use things recklessly or wastefully, *e.g.* from not taking proper care.

that— **that-á-ôe**, sort of shoes worn by soldiers.

that [R. to strike; to beat; to castigate]. **that-á-to**, short sword used by soldiers (v. to).

thát, to drain off, or pour off a liquid from the more or less solid part (which is kept back), *e.g.* through a small hole, or between a cup and its cover. **thát-ta**, to pour off thus till quite dry. **thát-ám**, to drain off rice-water from boiled rice. **thát-thng**, to pour off soup or juice from meat.

thau (R. thə), secretly; stealthily; to steal. **thau-bân** (C.), secretly; clandestinely. **khit-chhát thau--khì**, to be stolen by a thief. **khit-chhát thau--ê**, the man whose property has been stolen.

thau-siⁿ, illegitimate, as child.

thau-tsáu, to run away clandestinely. **thau-lâi àm-khì**, to come and go clandestinely. **thau-phah**, to beat or strike secretly, especially severely.

thau-siam, to look at surreptitiously. **thau-khoàⁿ**, id. **thau-thiaⁿ**, to listen secretly; to overhear. **thau-mn̄g**, to ask secretly. **thau-chhau**, to copy secretly and surreptitiously, as a document.

thau-thùi, to take away a good article secretly, replacing it with a bad one. **thau-tsông**, to conceal and hide, as stolen or contraband goods, or as a criminal. **thau-chiáh**, to eat clandestinely; to steal and eat at once.

thau-thóeh, to steal, as a small thing. **thau-théh**, id. **thau-thöeh** (T. Cn.), id. **thau-thóeh--lâng**, to steal from a man. **thau-liáh**, to kidnap, as a man; to steal, as a fowl. **thau-phō**, to steal, as a child, carrying it in one's arms. **thau-khan**, to steal, as a cow or horse. **thau-hiahⁿ**, to steal, as clothes. **thau-giâ**, to steal or take away secretly, as a chair, or such heavy thing carried with both arms; (and so with other modes of carrying). **thau-miⁿ-bí**, to steal a small quantity of rice, taken up in the fingers. **thau-lāu**, to steal small things, or to steal a small quantity of something out of a large quantity (v. lāu). **thau-niⁿ thau-liàm, chit-sì-lâng kheh-khiàm**, they who steal are always in poverty and want. **thau-chhiáⁿ**, to steal, as an idol or ancestral tablet.

thâu [R. tō, way, road, reason, &c.] **thâu-lō͘**, employment, business, situation (v. lō͘).

m̄-tsai-thâu, beg your pardon, sir! (lit. I did not know), said on coming against a man or treading on his toes accidentally, &c.

thâu [R. thiok, domestic animals, = col. thek, chhiūⁿ].

thâu-siⁿ, domestic animals.

thâu (R. thô), the head; a head; top; source; beginning; first; chief; principal; end, especially lower end, but sometimes the point; root, stump, or crown of the root of some plants; the core of a boil; a promontory, and so used in the names of many places; either of the two loads on the ends of a carrying-pole, or of the things in the two scales of a balance; suffix to many substantives, especially of round or roundish things, but also of things of other shape, sometimes even of documents, qualities, places, directions, and ideas; in some phrases indicates the rubbish or refuse of the substantive to which it is affixed.

thâu-bé, beginning and end; first and last (v. bé). **thâu-bóe** (C.), id.

khí-thâu, the beginning; at first. **tāi-thâu**, at first. **thâu-seng**, id. **thâu-saiⁿ** (T.), id. **goân-thâu**, beginning; fountainhead. **thâu-sū**, the clue to a matter. **thâu-sī** (C.), id.

thâu-khí, prospering in business; having influence with powerful men (v. khí).

thâu-chêng, in front. **thâu-tsâiⁿ** (T.), id. **tsòe-thâu-chêng**, to be first; to go first; to walk first. **tsòe-thâu**, id., to be head. **chìⁿ-tsòe-thâu**, to strive or try hard to be first. **thâu-ûi**, the foremast. **thâu-chhip**, the bowsprit.

thâu-chit-ê, the first. **thâu-chit-jit**, the first day. **thâu-jit**, id. **thâu-chit-pái**, the first time. **thâu-chit-chiuⁿ**, first chapter, &c. **thâu-it-téng--ê**, man of great influence; first-class, as thing (v. it). **thâu-bīn-téng lâng**, man of great influence or importance. **thâu-miâⁿ**, first name on a list. **thâu-hō**, first quality or sort; first signal or mark. **thâu-chiūⁿ--ê**, first-born child of man. **thâu-tsūn**, first-born of beast (v. tsūn). **thâu-chiam**, he who gets the first place in carrying an idol. **thâu-tsām**, first stage in a journey. **thâu-pang**, first fleet or company, &c. **thâu-tīn**, first troop or company. **thâu-mn̂g**, first door in a series (+). **thâu-mûiⁿ** (C.), id. **chiàh thâu-chheng**, to smoke opium refuse made up once again.

iòh-thâu, the first infusion of medicine. **chiú-thâu**, liquor distilled in the first distillation. **lin-thâu**, the beginning of giving milk (+). **ké-chí-thâu**, the first fruit of the season (said of the "pî-pê" or loquat). **géh-thâu**, the beginning of the month. **chiaⁿ-géh chiaⁿ-thâu**, the first half of the first month. **nī^{n}-thâu,** the beginning of the year. **chhun-thâu,** beginning of spring.

kang-thâu, the beginning of a work (+). **ōe-thâu,** the beginning of a conversation or discussion (v. ōe). **lâu-thâu,** the first of the tide (v. lâu). **khó-thâu-bê,** rice boiled soft and adhesive, almost like paste.

kang-thâu, the upper end of an inlet (v. kang), (+). **pi-thâu,** the part of the embankment at a dam or weir. **lō͘-thâu,** a landing-place or jetty (v. lō͘; v. bé, "end"). **bé-thâu,** a busy port (v. bé), (+). **hāng-thâu,** the spaces at the corners of the central house in a large Chinese house.

thâu-lâng, a head-man. **thâu-ke,** the master of a house or shop (v. ke). **thâu-chhiú,** a head workman; the head of several workmen. **thâu-náu^{n},** a headman of any sort (v. náu^{n}). **thâu-bák,** a headman: the leader or officer of a small troop. **seng thâu-bák,** to be made head of about twenty soldiers, not counted a mandarin. **thâu-tsàng,** the leading man in a place or in an affair; the clue of an affair (v. tsàng).

tsáng-thâu, to have the chief management of a matter, &c. (v. tsáng), (+). **tsóng-kun-thâu,** point from which many roads diverge, &c. (v. kun, "root"). **tio̍h-thâu,** one's turn come to take charge, as of idolatrous rites common to several or many persons (+). **tio̍h pu̍t-thâu,** to have the use (in one's turn) of a field common to several persons, burdened with the duty of performing certain rites to an idol. **chhut-thâu,** to undertake responsibility, esp. in a case when *one* must first take action so that others will follow or join him.

koa^{n}-thâu, mandarin's confidential assistant in his yamun (+). **mn̂g-thâu,** mandarin's private secretary. **pan-thâu,** head of the police in a yamun. **kài-siú-thâu,** the head or superintendent of the beggars. **hu-thâu,** headman of coolies carrying sedans, &c. (v. hu). **sai-hū-thâu,** a master tradesman. **kheh-thâu,** a coolie-broker; a man who levies dues on passengers (v. kheh). **chha̍t-thâu,** head of a band of robbers or pirates. **kiáu-thâu,** keeper of gambling-house. **hē-thâu,** man who gets up a subscription for mutual help. **hōe-thâu** (C.), id. **hōe-thâu,** head of a society, especially of the Triads (v. hōe). **kàu-thâu** (head of the religion), phrase sometimes used for chaplain or missionary, but not a suitable phrase. **kài-thâu,** head of a community of Bud. priests. **chhài-thâu,** headman of a vegetarian society (+).

hé-thâu, a cook. **hóe-thâu** (C.), id. **a-thâu,** a female slave. **chhng-lâng-thâu,** you clownish fellow! you rustic! (said in scolding).

kiau-thâu, proud. **siáu-jîn-thâu,** extremely cunning and wicked. **hat-thâu,** to scold or reprove violently. **tong-thâu,** refusing to sell in hope of a better price.

háng-thâu, boastful and bragging in manner. **phái^{n}-sia^{n}-thâu,** angry or proud tone of talk. **kek phài-thâu,** to put on the airs of an influential man though really insignificant (v. phài). **sè-thâu,** power, influence, prestige (v. sè). **sì-thâu** (C.), id. **ū khùi-thâu,** to have power or influence, or the appearance of it (v. khùi). **la̍t-thâu,** strength. **tá^{n}-thâu,** courage. **khah-phī^{n}-thâu,** getting rather more than one's share (v. phī^{n}). **bô-phī^{n}-thâu,** not having a wind that can be used for the course.

chiet-thâu, discount (v. chiet). **ū-siau-thâu,** saleable (v. siau). **táu-thâu ū,** very good measure, as of grain, &c. (v. táu). **ū-chhio̍h-thâu,** to have a little more than the strict measure, as of cloth. **sih-chhìn-thâu,** to lose in trade by giving customers a little over-weight (v. chhìn). **hun-thâu,** a small commission, as for taking a customer to a shop. **thiu-thâu,** a small commission or percentage; to take off such a percentage.

ū-hèng-thâu, having a very strong desire for something. **ū-hìn-thâu** (C.), id. **bô-hêng-thâu,** having no nice clothes to wear. **bô-tī^{n}-thâu,** insipid; tasteless. **kim-thâu,** the gloss on a new article, as on new cloth, or as fresh varnish on furniture. **ien-thâu,** do., esp. on cloth. **pe̍h-thâu-khòe,** a deed of sale having no official stamp (+). **ū hún-thâu,** well adorned, as woman (v. hún).

khan-thâu, an article pawned (v. khan). **tiāu-thâu,** an omen. **chhái-thâu,** id. **chèng-thâu,** a disease. **chìn-thâu** (C.), id.

pō͘-thâu, a port or trading town (v. pō͘). **tui-thâu,** a station of police or of soldiers. **tiàm-thâu,** a shop. **tūi^{n}-thâu** (Cn.), id. **hâng-thâu,** a hong, said esp. of one to which goods are sent (v. hâng). **tōe-thâu se̍k,** well acquainted with the place (v. tōe). **siā-thâu,** a village (v. siā). **chhân-thâu-má,** title of spirits of a shrine having no posterity (v. chhân).

hng-thâu, a medical prescription. **tôe-thâu,** a theme or text. **jī-thâu-á,** a small note or letter. **toa^{n}-thâu,** a ticket, bill, receipt, &c. **phiau-thâu,** a bit of paper having on it the shop-mark or name of the firm, and some notice of the article, pasted on or wrapped round the thing sold.

thê-thâu, rubbish, esp. of earth, stones, broken bricks, &c. **he-thâu,** refuse of lime, esp. coarse lumps separated by riddling out. **be̍h-thâu,** large lumps of wheat or barley riddled out from flour or meal. **chhek-thâu,** light empty refuse rice. **tāu-thâu,** husks and refuse of beans, &c. **han-tsû-thâu,** refuse of grated sweet-potatoes after making starch. **si-thâu,** coarse refuse silk, it makes a very strong stuff. **chhiû^{n}-thâu,** top of wall; ruins of wall (v. chhiû^{n}).

chio̍h-thâu, a stone, esp. a roundish piece or lump of stone. **chhâ-thâu,** a lump of wood; a bit or block of wood, esp. somewhat roundish. **tsng-á-thâu,** a broken bit of tile (v. tsng). **bín-thâu,** sort of round cakes (v. bín). **kun-thâu,** the thick muscular parts of the body. **gûn-thâu,** silver money (v. gûn), (+). **chî^{n}-thâu,** money; a sort of fish (v. chî^{n}).

í-thâu, a stool. **oá^{n}-thâu,** a large bowl. **chím-thâu,** a pillow (v. chím). **kám-thâu,** a woman's mourning head-dress (v. kám). **tô-thâu,** the bit of cloth cut out in making a Chinese coat. **kat-thâu,** a knot. **pau-thâu,** a bagful of goods such as are sold in bagfuls. **toā-thâu,** the stock or shank of a helm. **pó-thâu,** an axe. **tī-thâu,** a hoe. **tû-thâu,** id. **lôe-thâu,** a plough. **hō-thâu,** a trumpet; a blow-horn. **soa^{n}-thâu,** a hill. **tùi-thâu,** a sort of stone pestle (v. tùi), (+).

ō͘-thâu, a root of taro. **chhài-thâu,** roots of long turnips shaped like radishes (+). **chhang-thâu,** onion roots; onions. **soàn-thâu,** garlic. **sǹg-thâu** (Cn.), id.

sim-thâu, the heart; the mind; the pit of the stomach (v. sim). **sim-koa^{n}-thâu,** id. (v. koa^{n}). **chhùi-thâu,** the mouth, figuratively (v. chhùi). **chih-thâu,** the root of the tongue; the tongue, in some phrases (v. chih). **lin-thâu,** teats (v. lin), (+). **leng-thâu,** id. **keng-thâu,** the shoulder (v. keng, T. kai^{n}; Cn. kūi^{n}). **kûn-thâu,** the fist; boxing (v. kûn), (+). **tsńg-thâu-á,** the fingers; the toes (v. tsńg). **tsái^{n}-thâu** (T.), id. **tsūi^{n}-thâu** (Cn.), id. **kha-thâu-u,** the knee. **bé-pà-thâu,** the small of the back.

chhiú-thâu, power of a person. **i--ê chhiú-thâu**, his power or authority. **gū--tio̍h i--ê chhiú-thâu**, to fall into his power so that he has the opportunity of injuring us. **chhiú-thâu ū-chîⁿ**, he has under his control the money of another man, *e.g.* money of relatives, or rent of house which he manages for others.

jit-thâu, the sun; a day. **jit-thâu-té, mîⁿ-thâu-tn̂g**, day short and night long. **àm--thâu**, the dark night; the night time. **tsá--thâu**, in the morning.

pē-thâu bú-kut, scolding by means of vile epithets applied to a man's parents (v. pē).

soàⁿ-thâu, Swatow. **koe-lâng-thâu**, Kelung in Formosa. **pe̍h-chio̍h-thâu**, the White Fort at mouth of Amoy harbour. **pe̍h-soa-thâu** (the white sand point), a point at the entrance of the Anhai Creek, and so with the names of many heads and capes.

koaⁿ-thâu, the stubble of the seed called "koaⁿ" (+). **tiū-kó-thâu**, stubble. **bô-thâu-tîn**, a sort of creeper (v. tîn). **chhiū-thâu**, the stump of a tree, or part where the stem and root meet (v. chhiū). **chhùi-chhiu-thâu**, stumps of beard. **tsáng-thâu**, root of woman's queue (+).

phīⁿ-thâu, the tip of the nose. **ôe-thâu**, the toe of a shoe. **chìⁿ-thâu**, an arrow-head. **to-thâu**, the corner of a square knife (tsôe-thâu-to) at the sharp side of the square point. **hun-chhe-thâu**, the bowl of a pipe.

ba̍k-thâu, the inner corner of the eye. **ba̍k-bâi-thâu**, the space between the eyebrows. **tn̂g-thâu**, the anus (v. tn̂g).

kûn-thâu, the waistband of a petticoat (+). **khò-thâu**, the top or waistband of trowsers (v. khò). **kiō-thâu**, the knob on the top of a sedan. **toh-thâu-teng**, a lamp for use on a table. **tsûn-thâu**, the bow or prow of a vessel (v. tsûn).

sai-thâu, lions' heads, images for keeping away bad luck. **bé-thâu**, a horse's head; having a horse's head (+). **ti-thâu**, a pig's head (much used in offerings). **gû-thâu**, a cow's head; having a cow's head (v. gû). **káu-thâu chhú-hī** (monkey's head and rat's ears), said of a very ugly man.

hoan-thâu, Spanish dollars (+). **kng-thâu**, having one's head bare; no cap on. **chhàu-thâu**, head all covered with scabs or eruptions. **gûn-thâu**, a silver-head (+). **pe̍h-thâu**, growing white and ripe, as a boil. **âng-thâu**, having a red head, esp. a junk having red bows. **chhiⁿ-thâu**, having green bows, as junk. **píⁿ-thâu**, having a flat end (v. píⁿ). **chiam-thâu**, sharp-pointed. **tsôe-thâu-to**, a square knife having a broad square end instead of a point.

āu-thâu, behind (v. āu); the hinder one of two loads carried on the ends of one pole on the shoulder (+). **chêng-thâu**, the front one of two such loads (v. chêng). **tāng-khin-thâu**, the two loads on a carrying-pole very unequal in weight. **chit-thâu**, one of the two loads on a carrying-pole. **áu chit-thâu**, to carry only one load at the end of a pole instead of the usual two.

lāi-thâu, inside; also (C.), my wife. **goā-thâu**, outside. **téng-thâu**, above. **ē-thâu**, below. **pak-thâu**, the north (of China).

piⁿ--thâu, at the side (v. piⁿ). **tò-thâu**, turned in the opposite or wrong direction (v. tò). **chiàⁿ-thâu**, the right end; in the right direction; at first; also (T.), at beginning (v. chiàⁿ). **hē--khi tio̍h-thâu**, lay it in the proper direction or position. **m̄-tio̍h-thâu**, the wrong end (+). **hoâiⁿ-thâu-toh**, a table placed at the side of a room. **tùi-thâu**, opposite; face to face; an enemy; a match for (v. tùi), (+).

thap-thâu-chhia, to fall head foremost. **khùn hong-thâu**, to sleep in a place on which the wind blows (v. hong).

ke̍k-thâu, exceedingly; to the utmost. **chīn-thâu**, id. **têng-thâu**, over again another time (v. têng).

kè-thâu, too much. **khah-tha̍h-thâu--i**, to be superior to him in excellence (v. tha̍h). **thê-thâu**, making characters project one or more places above the others, as very honourable names. **ōe-tit jip-thâu**, able to get a favourable beginning, as in an affair. **khoàⁿ-thâu**, to protect voyagers, as a powerful pirate to whom they pay yearly black-mail; to protect, as a powerful patron does to a gambling-house; to watch, as a sentinel set by bad men to give them notice of danger (v. khoàⁿ). **hoan-thâu**, to turn one's head round; immediately, as in regard to coming back (v. hoan), (+). **chhiūⁿ-thâu**, certain rites performed before marriage (v. chhiūⁿ). **thâi-thâu**, to behead. **thì-thâu**, to shave (v. thì). **kháp-thâu**, to knock one's head on the ground in worship or reverence.

thâu-tùi, man and wife (v. tùi). **thè-thâu-hun**, marriage after a previous betrothal had been broken by death. **bó-thâu-chhin**, wife's relations. **āu-thâu** (Cn.), wife's own relations (said in reference to herself; sometimes also said of the original relatives of a step-son), (+).

pún-thâu, the master of a female slave. **hiaⁿ-thâu**, paramour of a bad woman.

thâu-chhùi, number of persons in a family (v. chhùi). **hó-thâu-chhùi**, making profitable voyages, as vessel. **chit-chhùi siang-thâu chhut**, a man talking quite enough for two (v. siang).

thâu-khak, the head. **thâu-á**, id. **thâu-khak-oáⁿ**, a skull. **thâu-khak-chhé**, brains. **thâu-bīn**, head and face (v. bīn). **thâu-hia̍h**, the forehead. **thâu-mn̂g**, the hair of the head (+). **thâu-mô͘ⁿ** (C.), id. **thâu-tsang**, the queue (v. tsang). **thâu-phe**, the scurf of the head. **thâu-lâu-á**, pimples on the head. **thâu-khoe**, a cap made of coarse yellow hempen cloth, worn by sons at funeral. **thâu-pò**, a cloth worn by men on the head, like a turban. **thâu-kun**, do. worn by women.

tháu, to untie; to disentangle; to open out, as a knot. **tháu-khui**, id. **siau-tháu**, to remove, as calamities or anger; to have a motion or pass water (said in making inquiries about a sick man; said also of the lower animals). **ū-siau-tháu**, marketable, as goods.

tháu-kat, to untie a knot. **tháu-kó**, to open out the strands of a rope or cord. **bōe-tháu-kó**, the matter cannot be set right because the parties (or one party) stand too stiffly on their supposed rights. **i kóng, khah-ōe tháu-kó**, if it be he who conducts the discussion it will be more easily (or somewhat easily) put right, as he will yield a little.

ū tháu-thoah, knowing well when to be firm and when to yield a little.

tháu-khiò, to remove the injurious effects of incantations (done by counter Tauist rites). **tháu-chē**, to perform rites for removing guilt, as Tauist priests do.

kóng tháu-khì, to relieve one's mind or one's feelings by telling one's wrongs to another. **tháu chit-tiám hūn-khì**, to relieve angry feelings long pent up, as by telling it or by getting vengeance (v. hūn).

tháu [R. thò? through; to pass through; = col. thàu; or same as preceding word?].

tsúi ōe-tháu, the water flows away freely, as in a pipe or drain. **tsúi bōe-tháu**, the water will not run off, as when a pipe or drain is choked. **kau-âm tháu-tsúi**, the drain lets off the water freely. **kau-âm bōe-tháu**, the drain is choked.

miâⁿ-siaⁿ chin-tháu (= thàu), his fame is spread far and wide. **jī-hō chin-tháu**, the name of the shop or firm is very famous.

thàu [R. thè, through; to pass through; cf. col. tháu, thiàu], thorough; right through; passing right through; to communicate, as by a road or door; to lead to, as a road; to give secret or minute information; to mix, as a liquid; boisterous or violent, as wind, rain, waves, current, &c.; wide-spread, as man's fame; classifier of journeys, voyages, heavy showers, &c.

saⁿ-thàu, having a passage through; making a direct communication. **phah saⁿ-thàu**, to make a direct communication, *e.g.* between two rooms, by making a new door-way. **bô-thàu**, no way through. **thàu-kè**, to pass right through, as a liquid, or as in boring a hole or piercing. **thàu-piah-long**, to have one's feet fastened in a wall, as a captive.

thong-thàu, quick of apprehension; intelligent. **thàu-thiet**, comprehending thoroughly. **bat thàu-thàu**, to know thoroughly. **tsai kàu-thàu**, id. **miâⁿ-siaⁿ chin-thàu**, his fame is very wide-spread.

kóng thàu-ki, to tell with all the particulars (v. ki). **kóng thàu-tóe**, id. (v. tóe). **kóng-ōe thàu-thàu**, to speak very distinctly.

tsáu-thàu, to ask counsel of idols, sorcerers, witches, fortune-tellers, &c., especially on behalf of a sick man; to convey secret and clandestine information; to inform upon. **tsáu-thàu siau-sit**, to convey secret information, as a traitor. **thàu-hong**, to give secret or stealthy information.

thàu-á, a man who reveals secrets in a traitorous manner.

thàu--jip-khì, leading right in and through, as a road. **thàu-siâⁿ**, leading to the city, as a road. **thàu pak-kiaⁿ**, leading to Pekin.

tit-thàu-beh, determined to have it (or to do so), no matter what others wish, or without regard to risk, sometimes even when we have no right, or without regard to the rights of others. **tit-thàu-kiû**, to beg very urgently, taking no denial. **tit-thàu-chièn**, to recommend very urgently, as for an employment or situation. **tit-thàu-jip**, to go straight in, as into a door. **tit-thàu-khì**, to go right forward, as to a place. **tit-thàu-khí**, to go on rising, as in price. **kè-chîⁿ tit-thàu-khí**, the price is rising higher and higher. **tùi-chia tit-thàu-khí**, to go straight up from this point, as a road or path.

thàu-tsá, early in the morning.

thàu-mîⁿ, through the night (v. mîⁿ). **thàu-hō-lâi**, to come through the rain.

chit-thàu-hō, an abundant fall of rain, such as to soak the ground thoroughly and leave a good deal on the surface. **chiâⁿ-thàu-hō**, id. **poàⁿ-thàu-hō**, a moderate fall of rain, not so much as to soak the ground well. **poàⁿ-thàu**, id. **nn̄g-saⁿ-thàu**, great floods of rain over and over again.

chìm-khi-thàu, soak it quite thoroughly. **ak kàu saⁿ-thàu-thàu**, wet to the skin. **khièn-khi-thàu**, stir it (*e.g.* paste) till it is well mixed and of uniform consistence.

hong thàu, the wind is boisterous or violent. **hong thàu-ki-ki**, wind boisterous and howling. **hong thàu-kiāng-kiāng**, id. **hong-éng thàu**, wind and waves boisterous. **lâu thàu**, the tide or current is very strong.

saⁿ-tiûⁿ thàu, to have passed the three examinations for the Kujin degree. **chiàh--i saⁿ-tù-thàu**, superior to him beyond all comparison (v. tù).

thàu-hien, to make an entirely new roof. **thàu-tiam**, to put on a whole new sole on a shoe. **thàu-tō**, a passage-boat that goes the whole way (v. tō). **thàu-chháu**, made of entire lengths of reeds or grass, not of short pieces joined, as a good mat. **thàu-lêng** (T.), the whole backbone of a pig.

thàu-tsúi, to pour in water into another liquid; to mix water. **thàu-khah-pòh**, to dilute. **thàu-khah-chiáⁿ**, to dilute so as to make it more insipid, less salt, or less sweet.

hun-chhe-thàu, a long wire for cleaning a tobacco-pipe. **a-phièn-thàu**, a cleaner for an opium-pipe.

thàu (C.), = A. thé. **thàu-khùi**, to sigh. **thàu-khùi hīⁿ-hāiⁿ**, sighing bitterly.

thāu — **thāu-khì**, very much involved and troublesome to set right, as affair. **náⁿ-thāu-khì**, getting more and more involved and difficult to set right.

thāu [same as previous word?]. **thāu-khì**, harbouring a feeling of resentment or displeasure.

chiàh-thāu, to harbour bitter revengeful feeling against a man, determined to make him suffer for the injury he has caused us, *e.g.* by having him accused before a mandarin, or causing him to meet with some great calamity, not for the purpose of getting gain or recovering debts or losses, but just to gratify spite.

thāu [R. tòk, poison, = col. tàk], to poison. **thāu--lâng**, to poison people. **ōe-thāu--lâng**, poisonous. **thāu-sí-lâng**, to kill a man by poison. **thāu bin-thâng**, to kill internal worms by drugs. **thāu-hí**, to poison or drug fish so as to catch them. **thāu niáu-chhú**, to set poison for rats. **thāu-káu**, to set poison for a dog.

tháuh [R. tàp, constantly, = col. tàuh], (C. tiàuh). **tháuh-tháuh-lâi**, constantly coming. **tháuh-tháuh-kóng**, repeating over and over in a wearisome way.

the [R. thèng, to prop up; to support; to extend; to pole a boat; = col. thìⁿ, theng], (C. thɛⁿ, to pole a boat, but "the" in other senses), to recline or lean on a couch or chair; to lean against; to push along with a pole, as a boat.

the-tsûn, to push a boat with a pole; to pole a boat. **the-ko**, id.

the kau-í, to lean back in a chair. **poàⁿ-the**, to recline. **poàⁿ-the-tó**, id.

káu-í-the, the back of a chair.

the [R. chhui, thui, to calculate; to investigate], (Cn. thö), to excuse one's self; to decline to meddle with a matter on some pretext; to refuse with excuses and polite words that sound well, but generally more or less false. **the-khui**, id. **the-sí**, id. **the-sû**, id. **the-sû iá-kè**, id. **the sū-kè**, id. **the-sû thok-kè**, id. **the-thok**, id., often including the idea of putting it off on some one else. **saⁿ-the**, to shift a piece of work on each other, neither willing to do it himself. **saⁿ-oe-the**, id.

the-òh, to play truant from school. **the-pīⁿ**, to refuse or decline on pretence of sickness. **the-bô**, to say falsely that we have not the thing asked for, or did not do the thing found fault with. **the bô-tī--teh**, to say "not at home," when really at home. **the hō-kúi** (to put it off on the ghosts), to deny what is evidently brought home to us, *e.g.* to deny stealing what no one else *could* have stolen.

the (R. thai), the embryo or fœtus in the womb. **pau-the**, the caul. **the-sin**, = thai-sin, guardian spirit of unborn child (v. thai). **the-m̂ng**, the hair on an infant before it is shaven, which is done one month after birth. **koà-the-m̂ng**, still having the hair it had while unborn, as in the first month.

thâu-the, first-born of mother, either human or of lower animals. **āu-the**, the next time she has a child. **la̍k-chhit-the**, six or seven successive births of children.

ū-the, to be pregnant. **chē-the**, id. **hoan-the**, the unborn infant moving just before birth. **thu̍t-the**, to cause (or have?) an abortion. **ka-la̍uh-the**, to have a miscarriage. **làu-the**, to have a miscarriage (said only of beasts).

the--nih^{n} toà--lâi, congenital, dating from the embryotic state. **tī-hí the--nih^{n}**, id., in the embryotic state.

bō-the, the inner framework of a cap, made first. **the-á-bō**, a cap with a hole in the centre, worn by new-born infants.

the (C.), = A. thoe, a hair-pin.

thê [R. to lift in the hand; to take up; to carry; to bring forward; to bring into notice; occurs in the names of several offices and of some idols].

thê-khí, to raise a question for discussion; to introduce a subject of conversation. **thê-àn**, to call up a case from an inferior court. **thê-hông**, to take precautions against some danger. **thê-poa̍t**, to assist a man to get employment (v. poa̍t). **thê-hê**, id., as by some money, or by giving work or helping to a situation. **kha-chhng thê-phû**, to rise slightly from one's seat, *e.g.* making a slight sign of respectful recognition to a man coming in, or in order to let something be taken from below us.

thê-tok, a general or admiral. **thê-tâi**, id. **tsúi-su thê-tok**, an admiral. **tsúi-thê** (r.), id. **lio̍k-lō͘ thê-tok**, a general. **lio̍k-thê** (r.), id. **kiú-bûn thê-tok**, the military governor of the metropolis. **thê-tìn**, general and lieutenant-general; admiral and commodore.

thê-tok ha̍k-chèng (R.), = ha̍k-tâi, the chief literary examiner of a province. **thê-ha̍k-tō**, title of a Tautai who is at the same time literary examiner of his territory, as in Formosa.

thê-t̂ng, an office at the metropolis or at the provincial capital for forwarding important despatches and for giving notice of the promotion of mandarins.

tsún-thê hu̍t-bú, name of an Indian goddess with eighteen hands, Maritchi, worshipped both by Buddhists and Tauists. **phê-thê**, Buddhi -, syllables entering into the titles of various Buddhist divinities, especially of Buddhi-satwa, contracted to "phê-sat."

thê [R. thai, to carry; to lift up; = col. tai, khai]. **thê-thâu**, to place characters one or more places above the highest words of the other columns in the page, as is done to names of high honour. **toa^{n}-thê**, placed one place higher than the tops of the other columns of words. **siang-thê**, placed two places higher, still more honourable.

thê (C. thôe; Cn. thō͘), a boil, especially a somewhat small boil. **thê-á**, id. **si^{n} thê-á**, to have such boils. **kòe-thê**, large spots of itch (v. kòe).

thé [R. body; substance; form; respectability; prestige; = col. thóe, thái]; also (C.), = A. thóe, in some phrases.

sin-thé, the body. **chhek-sin lō͘-thé**, naked (v. lō͘). **sù-thé** (r.), the four limbs.

hêng-thé, external form. **thé-thóng**, external manner, appearance, or character (v. thóng). **thé-thài**, external manner or bearing (v. thài). **thé-sek**, pattern, as for essay or document (v. sek). **jī-thé**, shape of a word, as written or printed. **sòng-thé-jī**, characters of the common square form. **sū-thé** (r.), the state, nature, or character of an affair, esp. in regard to the way of setting it right. **tsa-bó-thé**, a feminine look.

thé-hō, name given from personal appearance, as a sort of nickname. **thé-hō-mia^{n}**, id. **thé-thak** (C.), to jest at people's personal appearance. **keng-thé** (C.), to talk scandal about people.

bô-lé bô-thé, without politeness.

thé-biēn, respectability; prestige (v. biēn). **bô-thé**, without respectability, &c. **sit-thé**, to lose respectability, influence, or prestige. **thiên-thé**, affecting too much style, or lying about idly (v. thiên). **thien-thé**, id. **koa^{n}-thé**, proprieties of dress, manner, &c., for a mandarin. **kok-thé**, the dignity of the kingdom. **sit-kok-thé**, to lose its dignity or prestige, as a kingdom, by defeat or disgrace. **tsòng-kok-thé**, to increase the dignity and honour of the state, as a good and great mandarin.

it-thé, alike; having similar character or privileges. **tāi-ke it-thé**, all alike. **it-thé khoán-thāi**, to treat alike and impartially. **sam-ūi it-thé** (X.), the Trinity in Unity.

thé-thiap, to sympathize with; to make allowance for another's circumstances, or adapt one's feelings to his with kind consideration. **sa^{n}-thé-thiap-sim**, sympathizing heart. **thé-sut** (r.), to compassionate; to act with tender consideration towards (v. sut).

thé-hōe, to consider carefully the meaning of a saying or the state of a man's mind, feelings, and purpose till we quite understand it, so as to shape our own conduct.

thè [R. to change, to substitute, to abolish, instead of, in place of, = col. thòe, thùi].

sè-sip bóng-thè, hereditary, as rank.

thè (R. thòe, thùi), (Cn. thō͘), to retire; to recede, to draw back; to ebb; to lose or diminish, as colour, auspicious influence, prosperity, fever, &c.

thè--khì, to retire; to draw back, &c.; to remove one dish from the table when another is brought. **thiu-thè**, to draw back, as army, in good order (v. thiu). **thè-pi^{n}**, to step aside, as to let a mandarin pass. **lí thè-pi^{n}--khì**, you get out of the way! (said in scolding an inferior). **thè-pī**, to keep at a respectful distance from a superior. **thè-khui**, to step aside. **thè-khui niū^{n}--i**, to get out of the way to avoid disputing with him at present. **thè-āu**, to walk backwards.

tò-thè, to walk backwards without turning round from a place to which we had advanced, *e.g.* on opening a door and seeing some one in undress; to retreat, as an army drawing back in good order from a position found to be unsuitable or unsafe: to become worse than before, as in some work, art, or study. **tò-thè-kiâ^{n}**, to walk backwards without turning round. **tò-thè-pō͘**, to step backwards, as to avoid something.

ū-thè-pō͘, to have means or resources ready for an emergency, *e.g.* a new plan ready to use if the first fail. **thè-chit-pō͘**, to make no discussion or dispute with him at present.

chìn-thè, to advance or retire (v. chìn). **kōo-heng kōe-thè**, rapidly prospering and as rapidly declining. **kē-hin kē-thè** (C.), id.

tsúi thè, the flood recedes; the tide ebbs, especially when it was a specially high tide. **chiú thè--lah**, he has become sober after a debauch. **thè-hé**, to diminish feverishness or inflammation. **thè-jiėt**, to remove fever or severe inflammation, as medicine. **jiėt thè**, the fever has abated. **hong-súi thè-khì**, the good luck of the grave is gone. **thè-sîn**, the spirit leaving an idol, or having left it, so that it becomes utterly powerless. **thè-tâng**, the spirit leaving the magician or sorcerer (tâng-chí) when the ecstasy or afflatus is over. **thè-tâng-kớ**, to draw back from an affair which we were taking in hand. **phah thè-tâng-kớ**, id. **thè-chí^{n}**, to become less profitable than before, as a shop, mill, &c. **thè-sî**, to pass out of season, as a fruit; to lose one's wealth or influence. **thè-sek**, to fade or lose colour, as cloth. **thè-ka**, to open, as a joint where the glue has given way. **thè-sún**, to open out, as a mortice joint.

hō͘-thè, descendants who are a disgrace to their ancestors.

thè-ūi, to abdicate. **sî-koa^{n} thè-chit**, to retire from office. **thè-tiâ^{n}**, to withdraw a complaint or accusation from the court. **thè-tiēn** (T. tāi^{n}; Cn. tūi^{n}), to withdraw one's security from a tenant. **thè-tiēn**, to leave the audience-hall, as the emperor does. **thè-tiâu**, to end the audience by retiring, as emperor. **thè-tn̂g**, to dissolve the court by leaving the tribunal, as mandarin. **thè-hun**, to break a betrothal (v. hun). **thè-chhin** (C.), id.

thè-hêng, to send back, as goods that we do not buy. **thè-chhut**, to retire, as from a company. **hó-thè**, having a good and easy way to get out of the matter. **lîm-tīn thè-siok** (C.), = A. lîm-tīn thòe-siok, to shrink from danger or from important business when it comes to the point.

thè-hòe (C.), to regret or repent of what has been done, often of what cannot now be changed. **siū^{n}-thè-hòe** (C.), id. **thè-hóe** (C.), id.

thè — **khì kàu phuh-phuh-thè** (T.), to pant and blow with rage.

thē [R. lūi, lazy, indolent, sickly], (C. thōe). **thē-thē**, dull and wanting in animation, as a man.

thē (C. thɛ̄), the sea-blubber, jelly-fish, or medusa. **thē-lin**, the part in the centre from which the arms and feelers radiate (edible). **thē-poâ^{n}**, the meat from the large body of the medusa, white or slightly coloured. **thē-kha**, the brownish red part of the medusa, arms, feelers, &c., used as a cooling food.

léng-tsúi thǹg-thē, to talk ironically or sarcastically. **thē kè-hê tsòe-bák**, the medusa hires a shrimp as an eye (said of an ignorant or idle man trusting to another's knowledge or skill in managing a matter, and so being often imposed upon).

thɛ^{n} (C.), = A. the, to push with a pole, as a boat.

thɛ̂^{n} (C.), = A. thî^{n}. **thɛ̂^{n}-bák**, eyes dazzled.

thɛ́^{n} (C.), = A. thá^{n}, to hold up on the palm of the hand. **thɛ́^{n}-bē-tiâu**, cannot bear it up on the palm. **thɛ́^{n}-koân**, = A. thá^{n}-koâi^{n}, to hold up high on the palm.

thɛ̂^{n} (C.), = A. thiâ^{n} (R. thêng), a surname.

thɛ̀^{n} (C.), = A. thì^{n}, to prop up. **thɛ̀^{n}-chhiú**, to support the hand or arm on something, because without such support we could not hold it up.

theh [R. thek, naked; to take off clothes; perhaps this word should be divided into two words], (C. thɛh).

thǹg-pak-theh, naked; almost naked. **thùi^{n}-thɛh-thɛh** (C.), id. **thǹg-theh** (Cn. T.), id. **thǹg-theh-theh** (T.), id.

khang-chhiú pėh-theh, empty-handed; bringing no presents. **khang-chhiú thɛh-chhiú** (C.), empty-handed.

chhiú^{n} theh-theh, to plunder everything; all plundered and taken away. **liáu theh-theh** (Cn.), all spent, as money. **tsáu theh-theh** (Cn.), all run away. **chiáh kàu theh-theh** (Cn.), entirely eaten up.

sōe ōe-theh (Cn.), it can be washed quite clean.

theh sut-sut (Cn.), nothing left at all, *e.g.* all plundered, or terribly poor. **theh liu-liu** (Cn.), all taken away; naked.

pak-tó-lāi theh-theh-kúi, exceedingly suspicious of everyone and everything. **chit-sin theh-theh-pó**, your whole body is surely very precious! (said to a man who will not do us the least favour, or who is very angry if we happen to touch him when speaking to him).

theh — **pėh theh-theh**, very very white, as face, or as any white things. **si^{n}-tsòe pėh-theh**, naturally having a face of fair beautiful complexion, or skin of whole body fair.

thɛh (C.) **thɛh-soa**, = A. thoah-se, the skate-fish. **thɛh-sɛ**, id.

thėh [R. thėk, a dwelling; a residence], (C. thɛ̍h), the inclosed yard of a house, as in front. **thėh-mn̂g**, the outer-gate of the courtyard at the front of a house.

ké-chí-thėh, an inclosed orchard near a house. **chhài-thėh** (Cn.), a yard where vegetables are grown.

chhù-thėh, houses in general. **chhân-hn̂g chhù-thėh**, lands and houses. **kè-chhù kè-thėh**, passing about idly from house to house, as a busybody. **lō͘-ke soà^{n}-thėh**, family scattered to the winds. **ín-kúi jip-thėh**, to lead demons to enter the courtyard or house, fig. of wicked persons.

thėh-sîn, the spirits that belong to the house itself, not to the family. **hàu-thėh-sîn**, to worship these spirits by offerings, done without images. **hàu-thėh-bú**, to worship the goddess of the courtyard.

an-thėh, to perform rites at the building of a new house so as to secure its good fortune.

thėh, = thōeh (C. thɛ̍h; A. thöeh, thėh; Cn. thōeh), to take up with the hand; to carry or take in the hand, as a small thing. **thėh-lėh**, to take up various small things. **thėh-tò-tńg**, to demand back; to bring back, as a small thing.

thau-thėh, to steal a small thing, such as can be easily taken in the hand. **thėh kè-ki--khì**, passed from the hand of one to another and so on, so that it cannot be traced, as a stolen article.

thėh-chiet, to accept a composition for payment. **thėh-jit**, to go and get a lucky day from a fortuneteller.

thek [R. to cut flesh from bones; to pick out; = col. thak]. **thek-kut**, to take out the bones, as out of a fowl, leaving it entire to be cooked whole.

thek [R. thiok, domestic animals, = col. thâu, chhiū^{n}]. **thek-si^{n}**, you brute! you beast!

thek [R. to reprove; to scold violently; to drive away], (P. thiok). **thek-mē^{n}**, to reprove and scold (an inferior) very violently. **thak-thek**, to scold and reprove for faults, going minutely into the details. **kài-thek**, to reprimand severely, sometimes also giving a slap, not for pain, but for the disgrace of it; esp. said of literary mandarin doing so to graduates; said also of teacher to pupils, or senior relative to junior relations.

thek [R. a commission or special order from the emperor or from God, sometimes interchanged with the following word], (C. thit).

thek-hong, to appoint by imperial decree to posthumous title and honour. **thek-lēng**, Tauist charms on yellow paper.

khò-thek, a yellow roll with the imperial decree conferring an honorary title of rank on a relation of a high mandarin. **ìn-thek**, a yellow roll that is fastened to an idol's seal, as if containing the commission given by Heaven to the idol.

thek [R. to order; to command; sometimes interchanged with the preceding word, sometimes with the following], to order to perform a duty, as a high mandarin orders a lower mandarin, or as a mandarin orders his constables.

thek-chhe, to order out constables on duty. **thek-koāi^{n}**, to order the Hien mandarin to manage some matter, as the Tautai does. **thek-thia^{n}**, to order a Ting mandarin (*e.g.* the Hai-fang), to do it. **thek-hú**, to order a prefect to do so.

thek [R. id. (C. thit), to adorn; to ornament]; also (Cn.), = A. súi, pretty, beautiful.

chéng-thek (C. chéng-thit), to adorn or set in nice order, as one's person or house.

thek sai-sai (Cn.), very pretty or beautiful, as a person.

thek (Cn. T.) **lí thek-koái**, = A. lí thok-koái^{n}, one of the eight Sien or genii.

thek (esp. C.) **thek-kák**, = A. khioh-kák, a worthless fellow; a ne'er-do-well; a thing that is quite useless, as a broken article.

theng [R. thèng, to prop up; to support, &c.; = col. thi^{n}, the]. **pi^{n}-tú-theng**, neither party able to overcome the other, as in a drawn game or even contest of any sort.

theng [R. name of a city and department]. **theng-chiu**, Ting-chow city or prefecture (department), on the borders of Kiang-si province (the Hakka dialect is spoken there). **theng-chiu-hú**, id.; or the prefect of Ting-chow. **theng-chiang-liông-tō**, the Chang-chew Tautai, who rules Ting-chow, Chang-chew, and Lung-yen.

thêng [R. to ascend; to mount], to ascend in the sky, as bird or paper kite. **thêng--khí-lâi**, id. **thêng-koâi^{n}**, id. **thêng-khong**, to mount up high in the sky. **thêng-hûn**, to mount on the clouds, as spirits, genii, &c. **thêng-hûn khí--khì**, id. **thêng-hûn kà-bū**, to mount on the clouds and mist, as spirits, &c. **hong-chhe thêng**, the paper kite ascends.

sat-khì thêng-thêng, full of deadly rage, as in battle; naturally of bold and terrible appearance (v. sat).

góeh thêng (C.), = C. góeh têng, the moon at zenith.

thêng (R. id.), (Cn. thêng, thiâ^{n}), to cease; to pause; to stop or delay (neuter); to hold one's self erect.

sió-thêng, in a short time; by-and-by; wait a little. **sió-thêng-á**, in a very short time; in a few moments. **khah-thêng-á**, after a short time. **koh-chit-thêng**, after a short time; almost immediately. **thêng chit-khek**, wait a very short time. **thêng-chit-jit chiū-khì**, wait one day and then go. **thêng-thêng tiap-á-kú**, always procrastinating and promising to do it immediately. **thêng-thêng siap-á-kú**, id. **bô-thêng**, without stopping; without pause or intermission. **bô-thêng-sî**, id. **bô-sî-thêng**, id. **bô-thêng-khek**, very speedily; without delaying a moment.

thêng-kang, to suspend working. **thêng-kha**, to stop in walking; to halt. **thêng-chhiú**, to stop in working or writing. **thêng-khùi**, to stop to take breath; to pause a little. **thêng-pit**, to pause in writing. **thêng-pn̄g**, to intermit for a few days the rites for the dead. **thêng-koan**, to keep a coffin unburied, waiting till an auspicious site or day be found. **pió-á thêng**, the watch stopped.

thêng-sin, to hold one's self erect, esp. standing. **thêng--khí-lâi**, to raise one's self as erect as possible while still kneeling. **chē-khi-thêng**, sit straight up. **khiā-khi-thêng**, stand straight up. **tò-khiā-thêng** (C.), to stand on one's hands.

thêng [R. têng, to adjust or settle an affair]. **tiâu-thêng**, to settle an affair, as a sort of arbiter.

thêng [R. a road; a stage; a measure; a surname; = col. têng, thiâ^{n}].

thêng-tsú, an ancient commentator.

khí-thêng, to commence a journey. **lō-thêng** (r.), a stage on a road; a journey (C. T. lō-têng). **joā-tsōe lō-thêng**, how long is the journey? **chit-thêng kè-chit-thêng**, making a number of journeys or calls over and over, *e.g.* in dunning for a debt, or asking a man over and over for what he has promised to give.

théng (R. id.), a lorcha; a junk with sharp bow and stern. **théng-á**, id. **kńg-tang-théng**, a Cantonese lorcha. **khoài-théng**, a swift-sailing mandarin lorcha. **hoe-théng**, a Cantonese "flower-boat," or floating brothel.

théng [R. confident in one's powers; to act in an impulsive manner; precipitate; = col. chhéng].

théng-sèng, self-willed and overbearing, as young person. **théng-kiông**, to act in an overbearing manner, trusting in his strength, power, or influence. **théng-koâi^{n}**, to be proud and insolent, as a female slave beloved of her master acting insolently towards her mistress.

théng i-ê-lát, to stir up and exert his strength.

théng [R. to pull up; to draw out; to relax a little], to spoil, as a child; to indulge or favour too much, as a servant or employé. **théng-sēng**, to indulge and spoil, as a child; to let an inferior have too much of his own way. **théng-sēng-khi-koâi^{n}**, indulging and spoiling him till self-will is become habitual. **théng-khi-koâi^{n}**, id. **m̄-thang-théng**, must not spoil him by letting him have his own way.

thèng [R. tèng, a stirrup], (C. tèng). **bé-táh-thèng**, a stirrup. **thèng-kun**, the straps on which the stirrup hangs. **thoa-thèng**, to be dragged along by the horse, with foot in stirrup, when fallen from horseback.

thèng— **lí-thèng goá-ê-tù**, you pay the stakes to me, in gambling.

thèng [R. to listen, to hear; to wait; to let him have his way; = col. thia^{n}], to let a man have his way.

thèng-hāu, to wait.

tá^{n}-thèng, to try to get information. **tiōng-thèng**, very dull of hearing.

thèng--lâng, to let a man have his own way. **thèng lâng--ê sé-ài**, id. **thèng-tsú-ì**, do just as you please. **thèng-kiâ^{n}**, do it if you like. **thèng-khi-kiâ^{n}**, id. **thèng-khoà^{n}**, you may look if you like. **thèng-chiáh**, you may eat if you please. **thèng-**

海上絲綢之路文獻集成 科技與文化编

lâi, he may come if he pleases. **thèng-chhōng**, may wear it if you like (&c.) **thèng-koán--i**, you may rule or punish him just as you please. **giên thèng, kè chiông**, his words and counsel are followed. **thèng-thien iû-bēng**, to submit to Heaven's decree of fate.

thèng-chho, messengers used in a mandarin's yamun (v. chhe).

thi [R. to stick; to adhere; adhesive], to catch with bird-lime. **eng-ka thi**, id. **thi am-pô-chê**, to catch cicadas with bird-lime.

mī^n-thi, glutinous raw paste made from wheaten meal.

liâm **thi-thi**, adhering very firmly, *e.g.* cemented with bird-lime.

lô-lô **thi-thi**, involved, as an affair difficult to set right; confused and involved, as talking, esp. when it comes to nothing. **lô thi-thi**, id. **lô-lî-thi**, involved and hard to set right, as affair; very troublesome and unpleasant to deal with, as a man who is not straightforward, *e.g.* objecting, turning about, and drawing back when all seemed about settled. **kóng-ōe lô-lî-thi**, to talk a great deal all involved and indistinct, the more that is said making it no plainer, but only darker and darker.

thi [R. thèng, to prop up; to support; to pole a boat; = col. the], to pole a boat.

thi (T.), = A. thí, to open out, as a fan or an umbrella.

thî (R. thê), to crow, as a cock; to sob.

thî-khàu, to bewail with sobs and cries (v. khàu). **thî-háu**, to sob bitterly; to sob and cry, as a child. **toā-kiá^n thî, sòe-kiá^n háu**, children large and small sobbing and crying. **hih^n-hih^n-thî**, to sob and cry. **huih^n-huih^n-thî**, to sob bitterly. **kháuh-kháuh-thî**, do.

koe thî, the cock crows. **koe-thî**, cock-crowing. **koe-thî jī-lóh**, the second cock-crowing. **koe-thî kúi-lóh**, which of the three crowings? **koe-bú thî**, the hen crows, said to be a very bad omen; said also of a wife ruling her husband.

thî (R. thai), moss and such plants. **si^n-thî**, to grow moss; to get covered with moss. **hé-thî**, sort of edible sea-weed. **chhi^n-thî**, green moss that grows on damp walls and floors, &c. **chhiū^n chhi^n-thî**, to grow moss, as damp places. **phī^n-khang-kháu chhiū^n chhi^n-thî**, nostrils all filthy (said of a dirty child).

thî [R. thû, a hoe; to hoe or dig up; = col. tî, tû]. **thî-thoá^n** (C.), to hoe up or dig up weeds, grass, &c., on hills or fields, *e.g.* for fuel. **thî-hûi^n** (C.), to hoe up weeds in dry fields.

thí [R. ashamed; modest; = col. sí]. **ū liâm-thí**, to have a strong sense of honour or self-respect, so as not to do what is dishonourable. **kè-liâm-thí**, to take good care of one's reputation and good name for correct conduct, avoiding what would hurt our character. **bô-kè liâm-thí**, having no respect for one's own reputation; doing wicked things without any shame. **bô-liâm-thí**, id. **bô-sioh liâm-thí**, id. **sioh liâm-thí**, acting justly and honourably though against one's own interest or feelings, or in opposition to relatives or friends, avoiding what is unfair or dishonourable, and thus keeping unblemished our reputation for fairness and honour.

thí-chhiò, to laugh at so as to make ashamed.

thí (cf. thién), (T. thi), to open out, as wings or umbrella, or as tangled cords or plaited queue. **thí-khui**, id. **thí-khoà^n**, to open out (as umbrella, &c.), so as to look at or try it.

thí-sit, to spread the wings. **thí hō-soà^n**, to open out an umbrella. **thí-sì^n**, to open out a fan.

thí (cf. thiah). **thí-phoà** (C.), = A. thiah-phoà, to tear to pieces, as a sedan or as clothes.

thí (C.), = A. thú, a surname.

thì [R. thè, = col. thih], to shave. **chià^n-thì**, to shave in the direction of the hair. **tò-thì**, to shave against the direction of the hair.

thì-thâu, to shave the head; to perform shaving, or get shaved. **thì-thâu-to**, a razor. **thì-thâu-tà^n**, the barber's implements, &c., carried on a pole on the shoulder. **thì-thâu ê-lâng**, a barber. **thì-thâu sai-hū**, id. **thì-thâu-chhiū^n**, a mandarin's barber.

thì-chhùi-chhiu, to shave the beard.

thì-bīn, to scrape smooth, as the surface of an idol; scraping off the old paint and gilding before repainting and regilding.

thì — **thô-thì**, a sort of fish, somewhat like the "bé-ka."

thī [R. tī, = col. khī]. **thī-koe**, a pheasant. **thī-koe-bé**, a pheasant's tail. **chhah thī-koe-bé**, to wear pheasants' tail-feathers in the head, as in the Ming dynasty, now done in plays.

thi^n (R. thiam), to add more; to add to; to increase the amount. **ke-thi^n**, id. **thi^n khah-ke**, id. **khah-thi^n**, adding yet more. **thi^n ke-kiám**, to add more or less. **thi^n-tāng**, to make heavier; to add more weight. **thi^n tām-pòh**, to add a little; to give or put in a little more in addition. **thi^n-thâu thiap-bé**, to give a man a little help merely to eke out his own endeavours. **thi^n-thâu thi^n-bé**, to add some lies to a story fundamentally true. **thi^n-kha thi^n-chhiú**, to add lies to a story founded on fact.

thi^n-pn̄g, to fill the dish with boiled rice. **thi^n-chháu**, to give more fodder. **thi^n-tsúi**, to give more water, *e.g.* to bird in cage. **thi^n-iû**, to put more oil into the lamp. **thi^n teng-sim**, to put in a wick.

thó-thi^n, to ask for more than was promised, or than is due. **thàn-thi^n**, to earn more. **pó-thi^n**, to add some so as to make up a deficiency. **bóe-thi^n**, to buy more. **thák-thi^n**, to read (aloud) more; to study more or longer lesson.

thi^n (R. thien), Heaven; the heavens; the sky; weather; a season; the supreme power or principle of the universe; the divine power; God, often with a pantheistic idea: applied in some phrases to things related to the emperor, as he is considered the vicegerent of Heaven.

thi^n-tōe, Heaven and Earth; heaven and earth; nature; the universe: sometimes means the supreme being in a pantheistic and dualistic sense. **kèng-thi^n-tōe**, to worship Heaven and Earth. **siā thi^n-tōe**, to give thanks to Heaven and Earth, as for some favour. **thi^n-tōe bô-pò**, Heaven and Earth allowing wickedness to go unpunished (v. pò). **liông-sim sió-thi^n-tōe**, conscience is a miniature of Heaven and Earth, in regard to the principles of justice. **tsoâ-siong hé-eh, thi^n-tōe-sè**, calamities by serpents and tigers are decreed by Heaven and Earth. **thi^n-tōe-bé** (end of heaven and earth), said of extraordinary calamities or unexampled crimes, as portending the end of the dynasty. **kóng thi^n-tōe-phê**, to talk about very strange and out-of-the-way things, absurd stories, or pure inventions; to tell incredible tales, possibly may be true, but such as the hearer cannot take in. **m̄-tsai thi^n-tōe**, observing or perceiving nothing, as man drunk or very sleepy, or in a state of unconsciousness; or as young child that can do nothing for itself, depending entirely on its parents. **m̄-tsai-thi^n m̄-tsai-tōe**, id.

bô-thi^n bô-tōe, contrary to Heaven and Earth (said of very wicked conduct). **moâ^n-thi^n phièn-tōe**, to deceive Heaven and Earth. **mē^n-thi^n oàn-tōe**, to repine and find fault with Heaven and Earth. **hɵ-thi^n hɵ-tōe**, to tell great lies, as in accusing people falsely. **thi^n--tsai tōe--tsai**, Heaven and Earth know it to be true. **thi^n-tsai tōe-kì^n**, do., as in calling Heaven and Earth to witness. **thi^n-téng tōe-ē**, heaven above and earth below; the universe (+). **thi^n ɵ, tōe àm**, heaven and earth dark; very dark weather; great distress and calamity (+). **thi^n hoán, tōe loān**, heaven and earth in disorder (said of very great calamities). **thi^n chheng-chheng, tōe lêng-lêng**, the influences of nature all propitious, a Tauist phrase. **tī chit-ê-thi^n, tàh chit-ê-tōe**, living on the same earth, and under the same heaven. **chiū^n-thi^n seh-kè, lòh-tōe hoân-chhiên** (chiên?), to ask an enormous price, but accept a very small one.

thi^n-kong, the god of heaven, sometimes heaven personified, sometimes the supreme god; often confounded with Giók-hông. **thi^n-kong-si^n**, his birthday. **thi^n-kong-toâ^n**, temporary shrine for his worship. **thi^n-kong-lɵ̂**, an incense-vessel for the worship of Heaven.

thi^n-má (Cn.), the goddess of heaven. **thi^n-má-si^n** (Cn.), her birth-day.

thi^n-lí, = thien-lí, the principles of Heaven's justice, esp. in reference to vengeance. **ū thi^n-lí**, according to the principles of Heaven's justice, esp. said of Heaven's vengeance on criminals. **tiòh-ū thi^n-lí**, you should speak the truth; you should act fairly and justly. **háp-thi^n-lí**, right; proper; according to the laws of Heaven. **chiàu-thi^n-lí**, id. **thi^n-lí thi^n-lí**, Nemesis! what a just Heaven-sent judgment on wicked men! **thi^n-lí kūn**, the vengeance of Heaven speedily overtaking crime. **bô-thi^n-lí**, said of wicked, violent, oppressive conduct carried on with a high hand, *e.g.* tyranny or plundering.

thi^n-ì, Heaven's decree or purpose. **tsai thi^n-ì**, to have an instinctive knowledge of coming weather, as some animals (+). **thi^n tsù-tiā^n**, Heaven decrees it. **chhien-sǹg bān-sǹg, m̄-tàh--tiòh thi^n chit-sǹg**, innumerable calculations and purposes are not worth one purpose of Heaven. **oàn-thi^n chhoeh-miā^n**, to repine and murmur at Heaven and fate. **thi^n bô-bàk**, Heaven has no eyes (said when great criminals are quite unpunished, and prosper all the more by their crimes). **thi^n ū-bàk**, Heaven's eye sees (as when calamity suddenly overtakes wicked men). **khoà^n-thi^n chiàh-pn̄g**, to live on honest gains (+). **thi^n tī thâu-khak-téng**, Heaven is above my head; I am speaking all true; Heaven sees and will punish me if I speak falsely (said as a sort of oath). **gėk-thi^n**, to offend against Heaven. **ū-thi^n bô-jit-thâu ê-ōe**, falsely saying that people commit incest, &c.

thi^n-ūi, the imperial throne. **pià^n thi^n-ūi**, to rebel and aim at the imperial throne, as insurgents. **phah thi^n-ūi**, id. **chē-thi^n**, to be emperor.

thi^n-ē, under heaven; all under heaven; the empire. **thi^n-kha-ē**, all under heaven. **thong-thi^n-ē**, id. **moá^n-thi^n-ē**, id. **thi^n-ē thài-pêng**, all under heaven at peace and in prosperity.

thi^n-téng, above the sky; in the sky; in heaven; heaven above (+). **poà^n-thi^n**, up in the air; up in the sky. **thi^n-tiong-ng**, in the sky; in the air.

hē-thi^n, summer. **tang-thi^n**, winter. **chhun-thi^n**, spring. **chhiu-thi^n**, autumn. **hó-thi^n-nî^n**, a year of abundance (v. nî^n). **sī lán-ê-thi^n**, it is just the weather for us; it is our opportunity or time of good fortune and prosperity. **sī i-ê-thi^n**, it is his season of good fortune.

hó-thi^n, fine weather; fair weather. **phái^n-thi^n**, bad weather. **koâ^n-thi^n**, cold weather. **joàh-thi^n**, hot weather. **chiâ^n-thi^n**, fair weather after rain. **m̄-chiâ^n-thi^n**, very changeable uncertain weather, scarcely either rain or fair. **kui-sin-thi^n**, settled weather (v. kui). **âng-thi^n chhiah-jit-thâu**, clear, hot, cloudless sky. **liû-bîn-á-thi^n**, pleasant warm weather in winter, such as vagrants like.

thi^n-sî, season; weather. **thi^n-khì**, weather. **khoà^n-thi^n-sek**, to watch the signs of the weather (+). **kì^n-thi^n-keh**, the sky clear and cloudless (+). **thi^n-siōng**, any atmospheric or celestial phenomenon (v. siōng). **thi^n-hûn**, the clouds of the sky; the clouds of heaven. **thi^n-lē**, dew (v. lɵ). **thi^n-lē** (X.), the way to heaven. **thi^n-kng**, dawn; early daylight (v. kng). **thi^n thiah-hàh**, dawn breaking. **thi^n ɵ-im**, dark cloudy sky (v. ɵ). **thi^n khí hē-ì**, appearance as about to rain (+).

kì^n-thi^n, open to the sky; a small open back-court, smaller than a "chhim-chí^n," and behind it (+). **bô-kì^n-thi^n**, very dark; not having a look of the open sky, which is counted bad for the luck of idols or ancestral tablets, as these should always have a clear view of the open heaven. **chiū^n-thi^n**, to ascend to heaven. **chhiong-thi^n**, to mount up to heaven, as vapour, &c. (v. chhiong). **tú-thi^n**, so high as to reach to heaven, as mountain.

thi^n-chí^n, a skylight window. **thi^n-thang**, a fixed light in a roof (v. thang). **thi^n-chhioh**, a quadrant or sextant. **ná^n thi^n-thiāu**, said of a very tall man (v. thiāu, "pillar").

thi^n-pi^n hái-kak, the most distant regions (v. pi^n). **sai-thi^n** (r.), the Buddhist heaven (better "se-thien"). **kiâ^n-lē, oá piah-pi^n; tsòe-sū, khah-toā-thi^n**, appearing very modest and retiring, yet daring to do improper things that cause very serious troubles.

thí^n [R. têng? thêng? to gaze or stare intently], (C. thê^n). **thí^n-bák**, to dazzle the eyes, as sun or lamp too bright or too near. **thí^n-jit**, eyes somewhat dazzled by gazing at the sun. **thí^n-péh**, eyes dazzled by looking at a bright, white, sunny wall, &c.

thì^n [R. thèng, to prop up; to support; to extend; to pole a boat; = col. theng, the], (C. thè^n), to prop up so as to keep from falling or closing, as with a prop, or with the hand pressing strongly; a prop.

thì^n--khí-lâi, to prop up or support by pushing upwards, *e.g.* as a hanging shutter. **thì^n--khí-khì**, id. **thì^n-koāi^n** (C. thè^n-koān), to raise slightly higher by a prop, as a hanging shutter or trap-door, or as a cover or pot-lid; to prop up and keep from falling, as branch of tree. **thì^n-bōe-tiâu**, unable to sustain the weight, as a prop, or as one's hand when all our strength cannot keep a thing from falling.

thì^n-ām, to stretch out the neck looking upwards, as a beast.

thang-á-thì^n, a stick for holding up a window-shutter that hangs by hinges on the top alone. **phah-thì^n**, to put in a support to keep anything from falling; to put supports under the arms in the proper attitude, as for drawing the bow.

phái^n-āu-thì^n, bad descendants.

thī^n (R. tiet), to run a seam; to sew wide and loose before the finer and firmer sewing, such as "pâng" or "chhiám."

pó-thī^n, mending and sewing.

thia^n [R. thèng, to listen; to hear; to let a man have his way], to listen; to listen to; to take advice; to obey.

m̄-thia^n, will not listen; will not take advice; will not obey. **bô-beh-thia^n**, id. **thia^n goá-ê-chhùi**, follow my advice or instructions. **sa^n-tèng-thia^n**, willingly listening to another (v. tèng).

thia^n--ki^n, to hear (lit. perceive by listening). **thia^n-m̄-ki^n**, not able to hear; quite unable to hear, as from indistinctness or from distance. **thia^n-bōe-ki^n**, id. **thia^n-m̄-chhut**, to hear slightly, but not able to make it out. **thia^n-bô**, to listen, but find that there is nothing to be heard, or that nothing is heard. **thia^n bô-bêng**, not able fully to make it out or understand it. **thia^n bô-hiên**, to hear indistinctly, as what is spoken too low or not clearly. **thia^n bōe-hiáu--tit**, to hear, but be unable to make out the meaning. **thia^n-chhò**, to make a mistake in hearing. **thia^n-tā^n** (esp. Cn.), id. **thia^n bô-chin**, id. (v. chin). **thia^n-lóh-hī**, to hear so as to understand clearly and remember well.

hó-thia^n, pleasant to hear, as pleasant sound, or as good news, &c. **phái^n-thia^n**, unpleasant to hear. **oh-thia^n**, difficult to get accurate information, as from variety of reports or other causes; difficult to understand when heard.

thàm-thia^n, to make secret inquiries. **thau-thia^n**, to listen secretly. **phak-teh-thia^n**, to listen secretly, as with head bent down close to a door. **thia^n-hī thia^n-piah**, to listen secretly, as an eavesdropper.

ài-thia^n, to wish to hear; to like to listen. **kóng hō͘-i-thia^n**, tell him; speak that he may hear. **goá-kóng lí-thia^n**, I tell you that you may listen or hear.

thia^n-hiu^n, to burn a stick of incense before an idol at night, throw it into water which is stirred about, and when it stops go in the direction pointed to by the burned end, and listen for the first word heard, taking it as an omen.

thia^n, classifier of Chinese halyards. **chit-thia^n-lit**, one large rope that hauls up a Chinese sail to the wind like halyards.

thia^n [R. theng, a hall, sitting-room, or parlour; an assistant mandarin; a Ting district or recent subdivision of a prefecture], the central hall of a house, where the idols are placed, and where visitors are received; classifier for mandarins in general; affix to titles of assistant mandarins and mandarins of Ting districts.

toā-thia^n, the large central hall of a house; a mandarin of considerable rank who manages matters for a superior mandarin of very high rank; often said of the "chham-hú." **thê-tok ê toā-thia^n**, the "chham-hú," as at Amoy. **tsóng-tok ê toā-thia^n**, a high official at the vice-regal capital who transacts business in place of the viceroy. **i--ê toā-thia^n**, said in joke, or half in joke, of a man whom some one intrusts with the management of his affairs. **toā-thia^n-iâ**, = tiong-kun-hú, an idol placed at the corner of some large temples (esp. of ông-iâ, pó-seng tāi-tè, and má-tsó) as a medium between worshippers and the great divinity of the temple, and also to be used by that great divinity for giving commands to spirit-soldiers.

pē-thia^n, a small mandarin who assists the prefect of a Foo or the district-mandarin of a Hien. **hái-hông-thia^n**, the Hai-fang, *e.g.* at Amoy; also, his office. **siú-pī-thia^n**, the military officer called a Show-pei, one step below a Tə-si. **tsoan-hông-thia^n**, = tsoan-sin, assistant of a "siú-pī." **chiên-thia^n**, assistant military mandarin of vanguard. **tiong-thia^n**, do. of centre; (&c.) **lí-tsûn-thia^n** (f.), harbour-master.

chit-thia^n-koa^n, one mandarin, *e.g.* said when indicating that in some affair or place there is only one mandarin taking the management. **sa^n-thia^n-koa^n**, three mandarins, *e.g.* when speaking of their all living in one town, or going together somewhere to manage some matter jointly.

thia^n-tn̂g, the central hall of a very large house. **thia^n-bīn**, the central hall of a house. **thia^n-pîn**, central transverse partition in the chief hall of a large house, dividing the hall into a front part and a back part. **thia^n-kháu-pîn**, a partition across the very front of the central hall, which is far more usually open to the court. **thia^n-pi^n-pâng**, rooms at the side of the central hall. **thia^n-āu-pâng**, rooms behind it.

koa^n-thia^n, a waiting-room or sitting-room in a temple; a waiting-room in a high mandarin's yamun (*e.g.* of general or admiral) for his subordinate mandarins meeting with each other, or consulting together, or for visitors waiting in before they are taken to the reception-room; cabin for first-class passengers in a junk, where also Má-tsó-pô is worshipped. **hoe-thia^n**, reception-room in a yamun for private interviews with the mandarin. **pan-thia^n**, sitting-room for mandarin's attendants. **kong-pan-thia^n**, sitting-room in yamun where the constables, police, &c., sit together; it usually contains an image of Thó-tī-kong. **kong-thia^n**, the common central hall in a large house, used jointly by several families that have also separate private rooms. **khui-chhùi-thia^n**, the central hall of a house when it has no partition across the front, but is quite open to the court. **kheh-thia^n**, hall where guests are received; a parlour or drawing-room. **hō͘-chhù-thia^n**, the central halls of the side houses which stand crosswise at the ends of the principal house. **tang-sai-thia^n** (east and west rooms), two good large sitting-rooms facing each other on the sides of the court before the principal house.

chhut-thia^n, to come out of her chamber to the central or public hall on the third day after marriage (as the bride does) to worship the idols and ancestral tablets, and to be introduced to her husband's relations. **chiū^n-thia^n**, id. **chiū^n toā-thia^n**, id. **chhiá^n chhut-thia^n**, to invite the bride to come out thus (done by a little girl).

thiâ^n [R. thêng, a road; a stage; = col. têng], (C. thê^n), a surname.

thiâ^n [R. tân, sandal-wood; = col. toâ^n]. **thiâ^n-hiu^n-sek**, light grayish purple, almost like buff, but with a little more red. **thiâ^n-hiu^n-kién**, a silk stuff of a light purplish gray, brought from Shanghai, &c.

thiâ^n (Cn.), = thêng, to delay; to wait.

thiàⁿ, to be pained; to ache painfully; to love; to be sparing of; to spare; to use sparingly and carefully, as money. **thiàⁿ kàu-jip-kut**, to love very warmly and affectionately, as father and son, or as husband and wife; to have very severe pain.

thiàⁿ-thàng, to love. **thiàⁿ-sioh**, id.; to use sparingly. **sa^n-thiàⁿ**, mutual love or affection; to love one another. **thiàⁿ-lâng**, to love others.

chî^n tióh-thiàⁿ, should take good care of money. **àm-lē ká^n-kiâ^n, chî^n-gûn bô-thiàⁿ**, lavishing money on licentious pleasures.

koah-bah chit-tńg-thiàⁿ (to cut one's flesh and have it all over by one great pang), said of expelling or disowning a bad son or near relative, or of paying a large sum so as to be cured at once, or to get rid once for all of a man who is constantly asking for money.

thàng-thiàⁿ, to be pained; painful sensations; pain. **ài-thiàⁿ**, constantly or frequently painful; constantly causing pain, as disease or sore. **tsai-thiàⁿ**, to feel pain. **ōe-thiàⁿ**, painful; pained; feeling pain. **bōe-thiàⁿ**, not painful. **lún-thiàⁿ**, to bear pain patiently (v. lún).

siⁿ-thiàⁿ, to have painful sores, severe boils, abscesses, &c.

pīⁿ-thiàⁿ, disease and pain; severe sickness. **bô-pīⁿ bô-thiàⁿ**, no sickness or pain. **hong-thiàⁿ**, rheumatic pains. **thiu-thiàⁿ**, severe shooting pains; lancinating pains. **tsòe-tsūn thiàⁿ**, spasms; sudden severe pains. **sng-thiàⁿ**, dull painful aching (v. sng). **thâu-khak-thiàⁿ**, headache. **pak-tó thiàⁿ**, pain in the bowels. **sim-koaⁿ thiàⁿ**, severe pain about the heart or the pit of the stomach. **sim-koaⁿ-thâu thiàⁿ**, id. **sim-khì-thiàⁿ**, id. **chhùi-khí-thiàⁿ**, toothache. **khí-thiàⁿ**, id. **khí-thiàⁿ tsai khí-thiàⁿ-lâng**, one who has or has had toothache sympathizes with another who has it.

thiāⁿ — **thiāⁿ-bêng**, to tell a thing over again to see that it be clearly understood. **koh-thiāⁿ kúi-kù**, repeat in a few sentences, as instructions.

thiāⁿ, to take a little food or medicine so as to make one's self feel somewhat more comfortable. **thiāⁿ--chit-ē**, to take a little strengthening medicine, or opium, or liquor. **sió-khoá-thiāⁿ**, to eat a little, as a lunch or such light meal, when there is not time for a regular meal; to take some strengthening medicine; to take opium pills (or such like) to stave off the craving.

thiāⁿ-táⁿ, to take some slight means of keeping up our spirits (v. táⁿ).

thiah [R. chhek; C. chhek, thek], to tear; to separate or dissolve, as a connection; to tear open; to tear in pieces; to pick, as oakum.

khui-thiah, to explain distinctly, as the meaning of a phrase or saying, or of a doctrine. **thiah-bêng**, to explain one's meaning clearly, as in speaking more fully of what was merely alluded to.

phah-thiah, to divide the several details, as of an involved or difficult business, so that they may be taken up separately either by several men or successively by one man; to arrange for the due settlement of an affair in its several items, *e.g.* the gradual liquidation of a debt; to appoint to their several duties, as men in our employment; to send out, as members of a family or employés, to make a living, instead of crowding idly together.

hun-thiah, to separate, as in trade or in regard to meals; to discriminate or explain, as in discussing. **pun-thiah**, to part or separate, as partners or associates.

thiah-kó, to dissolve partnership. **thiah hé-kì**, id. **thiah-chiáh**, to arrange to have meals separate, as persons who formerly messed together. **thiah-soàⁿ**, to tear asunder, as man and wife.

thiah-lih, to tear, as cloth or dress. **thiah-phoà**, to break or destroy by tearing; to tear or pull in pieces. **thiah chhùi-chhùi**, to tear to fragments. **thiah-khui**, to tear or break open, as a letter or small box. **kha thiah-khui**, legs somewhat separated.

thiah-phoe, to open a letter. **thiah-chhù**, to pull down a house. **thiah-tsang**, to pick asunder palm fibre, as for making ropes.

thiah jī-sò, to tell fortunes by analyzing written characters (v. sò).

thiah-toaⁿ, to take out a ticket, as for one's passage. **thiah-ióh** (T.), to buy medicines according to prescription.

thiⁿ thiah-háh, morning dawn breaking (v. háh).

thiam [R. to add; to increase; = col. thiⁿ]. **ka-thiam** (r.), to add, as more money or wages.

thiam-teng, to have an increase in the number of sons or of male inhabitants (v. teng). **thiam-tūi**, to add more troops of soldiers. **thiam-siū**, may you have your allotted term of life lengthened by Heaven! (polite phrase used on birth-day). **kā-lí thiam-siū**, id. **thiam-hok thiam-siū**, may your good fortune be increased and your life lengthened! (especially said on birth-day). **thiam hè-siū**, superstitious rites for long life, performed at the temple of Sêng-hông-iâ. **gím-siōng thiam-hoa**, said of adding to what is already very good, as wealth or literary talent (lit. flowers on flowered silk).

thiâm [R. very quiet, tranquil, and staid in manner, = col. tiām], (C. tiâm). **thiâm-chēng**, quiet in tastes and habits, not fond of company, gaiety, excitement, or display; esp. said of women. **hong thiâm, lōng chēng**, wind and waves quiet.

thiám [R. to flatter; to fawn upon]. **thiám-mīⁿ** (R.), to flatter. **thiám-bī** (R.), id.

thiám — **thiám-chhái**, = kiám-chhái, khiám-chhái, perhaps.

thiám, very severe, as a disease, or as a beating; very thoroughly done, as cooking of meat. **chin-thiám**, id. **pīⁿ thiám**, the disease is very severe. **phah put-chí-thiám**, to beat very severely. **tsú-khi-thiám**, cook it very thoroughly, as in boiling.

thiám (cf. khiám, kín). **thiám-mé̤ⁿ** (r.), = kím-mé̤ⁿ, quickly.

thiām [R. tîm, to sink; = col. tiām], to submerge by throwing into water, esp. in order to drown; to get deeper and deeper in debt. **thiām-hái**, may you be drowned! **liáh--khi thiām-hái**, to seize and drown. **thiām-lóh-hái**, to throw into the sea, as a stone, or as goods of an enemy, that he may lose them; or as man (or animal) in order to drown him. **thiām-lóh-chíⁿ**, to throw into a well, as a child, or as another's goods.

thiām — **thiām-chiú**, a very good sort of spirit; glutinous rice boiled very dry has been soaked in it so as to make it very strengthening. **péh-thiām-chiú**, id. **péh-thiām**, id. **tsùt-bí-thiām**, id.

thian, thiân, thián; better **thien**, thiên, thién (*q.v.*)

thiàng (C.), = A. thiòng (R.), pleasure, &c.; in C. the phrases have a bad meaning.

thiap (cf. siap, siam, siám ?) **iap-thiap**, keeping out of view, as some sore, or something of which we are ashamed. **lóng-bô-iap-thiap**, without the least sense of shame or decency, as a man doing wicked things openly, or exposing his person immodestly, &c. **khah-iap-thiap**, hiding out of view, as what is dirty or offends against decency; very quiet, frightened, and shrinking in manner, as an inferior ought to appear before a superior.

thiap [R. to join or add to; to supply a deficiency; attached; close to; to paste on; = col. tah], to supply a

海上絲綢之路文獻集成　科技與文化編

deficiency; to make a small payment in addition to what was formerly paid, or for some damage or want.

thé-thiap, to sympathize (v. thé).

pang-thiap, to give regular monetary assistance, as to a widow or sick person who is our relative, or who has special claims on us. **png-thiap**, id. **thi^n-thâu thiap-bé**, to give a little help where it is urgently needed, no more than is just sufficient to tide over difficulties.

· **chiàu-thiap**, paying a small proportion according to rule or custom, *e.g.* the mortgager bearing some portion of expense of repairs; paying a small present, as to a messenger, according to usual custom and rate.

thiap-tsúi, to pay a small premium, as for silver of superior purity, *e.g.* sycee silver as compared with the average silver of dollars; to pay a percentage to a silversmith for the silver lost in working; the small premium or percentage thus paid. **bûn-gûn ê thiap-tsúi**, premium on sycee silver. **thiap pêng-tsúi**, to pay a small premium (about 3 or 4 mace on 100 dollars) on dues paid into custom-house or yamun. **thiap gûn-tsúi**, to pay a small premium or percentage when the silver we gave was inferior in quality or deficient in weight. **thiap gûn-hun**, do. for light weight, or for different rate at which dollars are calculated at different places. **thiap-kè-ān ê-gûn**, demurrage (v. ān).

thiap-siá, men employed to assist the "su-pan" to write documents in yamuns, esp. in military yamuns. **thiap-thiāu**, an additional pillar or pilaster put on close to a wall (v. thiāu).

hiu^n-thiap, incense bags fastened in women's hair, for the scent only.

thiap (= thiet). **thò-thiap**, = thò-thiet, not standing much on ceremony or forms of polite salutation; coming straight to the point without circumlocution, as in making a bargain (v. thò).

thiap [R. chhiap, a concubine], a low female character in a play, done by men. **tsāg-thiap**, to represent the character of a female slave, or low-class female in a play. **tsng toà^n-thiap**, to represent female characters in general in plays; all done by men and boys.

thiap [R. cards; written scrolls; placards; petitions; copy-lines, &c.], a visiting-card; a letter of invitation, &c.; a petition; a dose of medicine.

chit-thiap-iòh, one dose of medicine.

thiap-sek, forms used for preparing invitations, &c. **thiap-àh**, a case for invitation cards, or for cards on which some polite phrase is written. **pài-thiap-àh**, id. **thiap-lông**, envelope for card. **thiap-thò**, case or envelope for cards.

hoat-thiap, copy-lines of ancient characters. **òh hoat-thiap**, to copy such characters. **lîm-thiap**, id. **thiap-jī**, characters written in the style of these copy-books. **ū thiap-ì**, to be written in that style, as a word. **ū thiap-khì**, id.

thiap-á, a placard that violently attacks a man, truly or falsely. **khiet-thiap**, id. **siù^n-thiap**, a hand-bill posted up as an advertisement, offering a reward, as for something lost. **lē-thâu-thiap**, a hand-bill, placard, or notice posted up on a wall.

pín-thiap, a formal petition. **lé-thiap**, a document sent along with presents (as at birthday or at betrothal), stating what presents are sent; in a case of regular betrothal it is sent before the "hun-tsu;" in the case of a "sim-pū-á" it is only a few days before the marriage. **hun-tsu lé-thiap**, the marriage contract and this ceremonial card. **bûn-seng-thiap**, a card which serves as the indenture of an apprentice.

pài-thiap, a visiting card or card of invitation. **miâ^n-thiap**, our card with words written on it, saying that we call and pay our respects. **sî-thiap**, a card declining an invitation. **siā-thiap**, a card or letter of thanks. **âng-thiap**, a red card. **thô-âng-thiap**, id. **pėh-thiap**, a white card, used in mourning.

pàng-thiap, to distribute cards of invitation; to distribute cards announcing his degree, as a new graduate does. **oā^n-thiap**, to exchange cards, with name and nativity, in token of very close friendship. **oā^n-thiap hia^n-tī**, men who have formed a bond or covenant of very close friendship by thus exchanging cards. **chip-thiap--ê**, the man in a yamun who has charge of the cards of the mandarin and of visitors. **hê-thiap**, to send a ceremonial card or other "thiap" in answer to one sent by the other party; esp. said of the answer which settles betrothal. **kū-thiap**, to write a ceremonial card. **kī-thiap** (C.), id. **kū-thiap**, an old ceremonial card.

thiáp [R. tiàp, to pile up; to repeat; = col. thàh], to pile; to lay in successive layers; (a pile). **thiáp--khí-lâi**, to pile up, as in successive layers. **thiáp-liáp--khì**, id. **thiáp-hó**, fully piled up. **thiáp-chiâ^n-tui**, to pile up a heap.

tún-thiáp, to store up in heaps, or in large quantities.

thiáp-khoân, to lay in coils one above another, as ropes (v. khoân). **kha thiáp-khoân**, cross-legged. **kha thiáp-phoân**, id. (v. phoân).

thiáp-sit, neatly put up; well-behaved (v. sit).

thiat, better **thiet**, *q.v.*

thiau [R. to carry on a pole; to raise up gently, as with a pin; to stir up or loosen, as with the point of a stick; to sew or embroider; to stir up or instigate; to select; a spoon; = col. thio, thiô, thiáu].

thiau-hu, a carrier of baggage or burdens. **kien-thiau pòe-hū**, to carry loads on shoulder and back, as pedlars, &c.

thiau-soán, to choose out carefully (v. soán). **toā-thiau**, the great choosing of graduates for various offices (esp. of Kujin graduates), once in twelve years, by the emperor.

thiau-lāng, airy, as a room; having plenty of space between, as houses, trees, &c.; elegant and graceful, as limbs, or as walking (v. lāng).

thiau-kiong (C.), = A. thng-sī, a small spoon for soup.

thiau [R. chhiau; C. thiau; to excel; to raise]. **thiau-tñg**, to call a very young and talented scholar near his own seat, as the examiner sometimes does.

thiau-thoat (r.), = chhiau-thoat, easy-minded; not anxious about danger or troubles.

thiau [R. weak, young, and tender; light and frivolous]. **kheng-thiau**, light and frivolous in manner, esp. as young man; apt to be rather neglectful and too easy-minded about matters intrusted to him; opposed to "hə-tiōng." **kheng-kheng thiau-thiau**, id.

thiau [R. tiau, restless; perverse; outrageous]. **thiau-lân**, to cause trouble and annoyance intentionally in many ways (v. lân). **thiau-bân**, = tiau-bân, obstinately troublesome and disobedient, *e.g.* very lazy about doing what is ordered, or constantly putting off the payment of what is due.

thiâu [R. tiâu, a branch; a thin strip; anything long and slender, = col. liâu]. **chit-bé kng-thiâu-thiâu**, extremely poor; having on no clothes at all.

70

thiâu — thiâu-á, a pimple on the face.

thiâu (R. id.) **thiâu-á-hî**, a sort of mud-fish. **thiâu-hî**, id.

hoe-thiâu, a longer sort of mud-fish.

sì-kha-thiâu (F.), a sort of large lizard which lives in hedges.

thiáu [R. thiau, to carry on a pole; to select, &c.; = col. thio, thiô; sometimes in C. also read "thiáu"], to choose, as persons; also said of things. **kè-thiáu**, choice already made; having been selected. **thiáu iû-teng**, to select some men as soldiers elect (out of a number of candidates) ready to fill up any vacancies that may occur. **thiáu hān-lîm**, to choose a Tsin-sze graduate and make him a Hanlin.

thiáu (Cn.). **soat-thiáu**, vile jesting at each other (cf. A. soat-chhiàu).

thiàu (R. id.), to leap; to jump; to overleap; to pass over. **tò-thiàu**, to rebound. **tiô-thiàu**, to leap about. **thiàu-bú**, to dance and gesticulate. **thiàu-kha-koe**, to hop. **thiàu-tsáu**, to jump, as frog, &c.; to give a leap in order to escape, as man.

thiàu-thah, very playful and restless, as child. **thiàu-that**, id. **thiàu-iák** (C.), lively and in good health and spirits, as child. **oàh thiàu-thiàu**, active, as fish. **kiâⁿ-lê̤ thiàu-thiàu**, to walk (naturally) with a very springy elastic step. **thiàu-kúi**, restless imp! said to a troublesome child; a troublesome unruly boy. **thiàu-hàn**, a troublesome unruly boy, fond of trifling and noisy play. **thiàu-hān** (T.), id. **giét-tsú thiàu-hàn**, a wild, idle, ill-behaved boy.

thiàu-tâng, to have the afflatus for giving an oracle. **thiàu-kâu**, a set of three dice, used in gambling (v. kâu).

chhiák-chhiák-thiàu, to jump and frisk about incessantly. **phiák-phiák-thiàu**, to jump about frantically, as sorcerer. **phut-phut-thiàu**, to jump about, as in delight; to jump about, as a flea. **pók-pók-thiàu**, to jump about, as a flea. **phók-phók-thiàu**, to palpitate, as with fear; to dance with rage; to dance with delight or desire, as child; to leap, as a flea. **khì kàu-phók-phók-thiàu**, dancing with rage.

thiàu-iáh, to pass over one leaf of a book, as in reading, &c. **thiàu-khám**, to pass by a shop, as in distributing things. **thiàu-keng**, to pass one house in a row, *e.g.* one house left unburned in a fire. **thiàu-chiuⁿ**, to pass one chapter without reading it; (&c.) **thiàu-kip seng**, to be promoted two or more grades of rank at once.

thiàu [R. thò, to pass through; thorough; to communicate, as a road; = col. thàu], a plank or flat stone used as a bridge or gangway; stepping-stones in a stream. **thiàu-pang**, a plank used as a bridge or gangway (+). **ū-thiàu**, there is such a bridge of plank or single stone, &c.

phah-thiàu, to lay a gangway or plank, &c., so used; to make a scaffolding, as for building or repairing a house. **tah thiàu-pang**, to make such a scaffolding.

thiāu (Cn.). **khé-thiāu**, a plant like a dock with red flowers.

thiāu (R. tsū), a pillar; a column; a post; a division of a clan, smaller than "phài" or "pâng."

sì-thiāu, a man's horoscope (lit. four columns), consisting of four pairs of characters; said even though written in one column. **i--ê sì-thiāu hó**, his horoscope is good. **poeh-jī pâi sì-thiāu**, to arrange the eight words of the horoscope in four columns.

tó-thiāu, the branch of a family become extinct. **béng-pâng lám-thiāu**, a weak branch of a powerful family.

thiāu-poāⁿ, a large square slab of stone sunk in the ground, as foundation for pillar. **thiāu-ē chióh**, stone pedestal of a pillar. **thiāu-tsu**, the round part of the stone pedestal of a pillar. **thiāu-pêng**, a pilaster; a half pillar. **thiap-thiāu**, an additional pillar or pilaster set close to a wall as an additional support, esp. to receive the boards of a partition. **e-thiāu**, the fixed post of a well-sweep. **chhù-thiāu**, the pillar of a house. **am-thiāu**, pillar of a temple. **lêng-thiāu**, pillars having dragons carved on them. **chhâ-thiāu**, a wooden pillar. **chióh-thiāu**, a stone pillar.

thih-teng tèng-toā-thiāu, the affair is settled finally and conclusively. **náⁿ thiⁿ-thiāu**, said of a very tall strong man. **bōe-tsún-îⁿ**, **bōe-tsún-thiāu**, said of person or materials not suitable for our purpose (v. tsún).

thien [R. phien, at the side; selfish: unfair; = col. phiⁿ]. **thien-thien-á m̄**, doggedly refuses; doggedly will not. **thien-á m̄**, id.

thien [R. tien, crazy; mad]. **thien-thien thóh-thóh**, talking or behaving in an absurd and extravagant way, as if mad or drunk (v. thóh).

thien (esp. T.) **thien-thé**, = thiên-thé, fond of idleness, finery, and nice things (v. thiên).

thien [R. heaven; a day; nature; natural; used in some Buddhist phrases for the Indian deva; = col. thiⁿ], heaven; the heavens; the sky; nature; the supreme principle in nature; God (often in a somewhat pantheistic sense); divine; imperial, in some phrases, as the emperor is considered the vicegerent of Heaven.

thien-tē, heaven and earth; the universe; nature; the two end pieces of a coffin, "thien" being the larger one, at the head; sometimes said of the upper and lower boards of a coffin. **thien tē jîn**, heaven, earth, and man, the three powers of nature. **thien-tē hêng-tsai**, Heaven and earth send calamities. **thien-tē, kun chhin su**, in the whole of nature the chief persons are the sovereign, parents, and teacher. **thien-tē-phōe** (C.), small mattresses above and below a dead body.

thien-bûn tē-lí, astronomy and geography; astrology and geomancy (+). **thien-kong tē-soah**, the good and bad spirits of heaven and earth (v. kong). **thien-lô tē-bóng**, Heaven and earth are like a net to catch the wicked. **tâm-thien soat-tē**, to talk about things in general. **hoan-thien hok-tē**, to act in a very disorderly or rebellious way (v. hok), (+).

giâu-thien sùn-jit, the days of Yaou and Shun, the golden age (v. jit). **thien-thien tsùi**, drunk every day.

thien-tông, heaven, the place of celestial happiness. **thien-têng**, id. **chiàh thien-tông**, to get one's living by improper means; said esp. of the hangers-on about yamuns, who meddle in lawsuits or squeeze money out of people by threats of accusing them, *e.g.* for gambling, selling beef, keeping bad houses, &c. **seng-thien**, to ascend to heaven (v. seng). **se-thien**, the Buddhist heaven (v. se). **thien-bûn khai**, heaven's gate open on 6.6 (v. bûn).

kóng sam-sip-sam thien, to tell incredible stories, gen. baseless; esp. putting off payment of debt by false stories about abundance of money expected soon. **kóng sam-thien-goā ê tāi-chì**, to tell quite incredible stories.

thien-siōng, an atmospheric or celestial phenomenon

海上絲綢之路文獻集成 科技與文化編

(v. siōng). **thien-bûn**, astronomy (+). **khim-thien-kàm**, the chief astronomer at the metropolis. **tà-put-kièn-thien**, to put awnings all over a street (v. tà). **thien-lô-pán**, a ceiling (v. pán). **bān-thien**, the open framework on the top of a bedstead (v. bān).

thien-chhi^{n}, dull purple colour. **thien-lâm-sek**, dark brownish purple.

thien-hā, all under heaven; the Chinese empire. **thien-hā thong**, an instrument for picking locks. **thien-kok** (X.), the kingdom of heaven.

thien-tsú, the Lord of heaven, the Roman Catholic name for God (+). **thien-chí** (C.), id. **thien-tsú-kàu**, the Roman Catholic Church; Romanism. **thien-tsú-tông**, a Roman Catholic cathedral, church, or chapel.

thien-tsú, the Son of Heaven, the Chinese emperor (+). **thien-tsū** (Cn.), id. **thien-tsú hoān-tsōe, ú sù-bîn tông**, if the emperor contract guilt he is the same as the people. **giâm-lô thien-tsú**, = Giâm-lô-ông, the judge of the dead.

thien-un, imperial favour (v. un). **cheng-thien toát-kok**, to aim at the throne, as insurgents.

thien-su, the Tauist high-priest of China; he lives in Kiang-si province (v. su).

thien-sîn, the spirits sent from heaven (v. sîn). **thien-koan**, a spirit supposed to rule the sky (v. koan). **thien-phia^{n}**, one of the three spirits called "sam-phia^{n}" (v. phia^{n}). **tiu^{n} thien-kun**, an idol of the surname Chang (v. tiu^{n}). **thien-hē niû^{n}-niû^{n}**, the goddess Má-tsó-pô. **thien-hïō niû^{n}-niû^{n}** (Cn.), id. **thien-hui** (Cn.), id. **thien-siōng sèng-bú**, id.; this last phrase is also applied by Roman Catholics to the Virgin Mary. **goân-sí thien-tsun**, Tauist title of the supreme God. **thien-teng**, lanterns lighted in honour of the god Thi^{n}-kong. **thien-peng**, the soldiers of the gods.

chè-thien, to worship Heaven by offerings (v. chè). **sūn-thien**, to obey Heaven. **sūn-thien-hú**, Shun-t'ien-foo, the city and department of Pekin. **sūn-thien--chiá tsûn, gék-thien--chiá bông**, they who obey Heaven are preserved; they who disobey perish. **gék-thien**, to offend against Heaven.

thien-bēng, the will or decree of Heaven, esp. in regard to kingdoms (v. bēng). **thien-sò**, the decrees of Heaven or fate as to calamities. **lāu-siet thien-ki**, to let out Heaven's secrets (v. ki). **thien-ūn**, the date of a year expressed in cyclical characters, as used for superstitious purposes. **thien-tsai hêng-hō**, calamities sent by Heaven. **thien-hó**, a tiger sent by Heaven, esp. said if it kill a man without devouring him. **sú-seng iú-bēng, hù-kùi tsāi-thien**, life, death, wealth, and honour are under the decree of Heaven. **bô-sū tsāi-jîn, sêng-sū tsāi-thien**, man purposes, but Heaven accomplishes. **jîn-lék pó thien-kong**, man's labour improving on Nature's work (v. kong, "work").

thien-jiên, naturally; of course; certainly. **thien-seng tsū-jiên**, id. **thien-jiên m̄-hoa^{n}-hí**, certainly he will not be pleased. **thien-tsu**, good literary talents. **thien-lûn**, the three natural relationships (v. lûn).

ū thien-liông, conscientious in dealings (v. liông, "good").

thien-lí, the laws or principles of Heaven's justice as to right and wrong, esp. as to punishment. **thien-lí thien-lí**, what a judgment! the Nemesis has come! **thien-lí liông-sim**, conscience, esp. said as a sort of adjuration; I speak quite true (v. liông). **chiàu-thien-lí**, acting justly and rightly towards others. **tsûn-thien-lí**, id. **thien-lí chiau-chiau**, Heaven's justice is manifested, as in calamities coming on the wicked. **thien-lí kūn**, id. **thien-lí kūn, m̄-thang lām-sám**, Heaven's justice is at hand; must not act wickedly.

thien-tō, the manner of Heaven's justice, as in the punishment of wicked men. **thien-tō pò-èng**, calamity sent by Heaven on evil-doers. **thien-tō chiau-chiau**, id.

thien-phàu, a congreve rocket; a venereal ulcer. **hong-thien-kek**, a sort of halbert.

hoan-thien (T.), to come in by the roof, as thieves (+).

liâu-thien, to abscond with something; to abscond, as employé who owes money or has money in his hands; to run away, as a thief, esp. by roof of house. **khit--i liâu-thien**, to have money or some small thing carried off by him. **liâu-thien liâu-thien**, very easy-minded. **liâu-liâu thien-thien**, id.

thiên (cf. T. thien) —. **thiên-thé**, fond of idleness, ease, and lazy amusements; very slow at work, or refusing a job because of preferring to lie about doing nothing; fond of wearing fine things, and dainty about one's food, as a spoiled child or idle young fellow; fond of luxurious idleness, having everything done for him by servants; affecting too much style; said also of a beggar who has got as much as he wants, and is now making himself at ease and jolly. **siu^{n}-thiên-thé**, extremely fond of idleness, lazy luxury, &c. **tó--teh thiên-thé**, lying about idly doing nothing.

thiên [R. to transcribe a fair copy, = col. têng]. **thiên sam-tāi** (R.), to write out one's pedigree for three generations before being admitted to the literary examinations. **thiên lí-lék**, to write an account of one's origin and honours, as a mandarin on being promoted to higher office (v. lék).

thiên [R. thiên, tiên, to fill up; to make up a deficiency; = col. thūn, tiên].

thiên-pó (esp. C.), to make up a deficiency, as in a subscription.

thién [R. tién, to open out; to exhibit; cf. col. thí], to spread or open out, as umbrella or wings. **thién-khui**, do., as wings, book, or fan.

thiet [R. to take away; to send away; to remove, as a subordinate who is unsuitable or not required, or as things not now wanted]. **thiet--khì**, to take away, as dishes after a feast; to abolish, as a custom, rite, or tax; to dismiss, as soldiers to their own stations, as after a review or campaign. **thiet-ióng**, to disband volunteers or militia. **thiet-hôe**, to disband, as militia, &c. **thiet-lêng**, to remove and burn the "hûn-sin" (which represents the deceased) and the other fittings used in the rites performed for a man recently deceased, as is done when the rites are ended.

thiet-iên, to remove the dishes and remnants of a feast [this phrase is also written with the next word].

thiet [R. thiet; C. thiet, tiét, to pervade; to penetrate; thorough; to remove; cf. col. tah]; (in the sense of "remove," interchanged with the previous word).

thàu-thiet, understanding a matter very thoroughly; very intelligent. **thong-thiet**, intelligent; acute; having a thorough understanding. **it-lí thong, pek-lí thiet**, to comprehend the whole on understanding the principle of one part.

kàu-thiet-tí, = kàu-tah-tóe, to the very bottom; to

the utmost; quite thoroughly. **kóng kàu thiet-tí,** to discuss thoroughly. **khoàⁿ kàu thiet-tí,** to see to the bottom of an affair or of a man. **pān kàu thiet-tí,** to examine into and punish a crime with full vigour of law; to investigate a charge officially and thoroughly till the wrong is made plain, and reproved or punished. **sòng kàu-thiet-tí,** exceedingly poor. **chhám kàu-thiet-tí,** extremely miserable.

thiet (= thiap), (C. thoat).

thò-thiet, = thò-thiap, dispensing with much ceremony or circumlocution (v. thò). **thiet-thò,** id.

thiet [R. iron, = col. thih]. **thiet-sek sim-tiông,** pitiless; with heart of iron and stone. **thiet-biēn bû-su,** strictly impartial, as mandarin. **thiet-pán put-ék,** certainly and unchangeably so; determined to keep to one's purpose. **thiet-pán put-í,** id.

thih (esp. Cn.), = thì, to shave. **thih-thâu,** = thì-thâu, to shave the head (v. thì).

thih (R. thiet), iron. **chhiⁿ-thih,** unwrought iron; cast-iron. **kǹg-thih,** steel. **bé-kháu-thih,** tin-plate. **bûn-gûn piⁿ-tsòe bé-kháu-thih,** a good thing changed to bad or useless.

chhī-thih, to temper iron in water. **chhū-thih** (C.), id. **phah-thih,** to work in iron, as a smith. **phah-thih sai-hū,** a blacksmith.

thih-sái, fragments beaten from red-hot iron by hammering, as in a forge; a heavy sort of stone, probably some sort of iron-ore. **koàn-thih-sái,** made to swallow a sort of heavy stones, as fowl, in order to weigh heavier in selling. **thih-sái-hé** (T.), curiously shaped lumps of iron-ore, or such heavy stones or iron-cinders. **thih-hún,** iron-filings or rust, used as medicine. **thih-koáⁿ** (C.), iron-ore.

thih-khe, an iron hoop. **thih-soàⁿ,** iron wire (v. soàⁿ). **thih-thûi,** an iron hammer. **thih-teng,** an iron nail. **thih-tiam,** an anvil. **thih-lô,** a smith's forge. **thih-á-tiàm,** a shop for old metal articles. **thih-pán,** iron made into sheets or plates, as material. **thih-pán-sek,** dark iron-gray.

thih-bé, a musical instrument made of bits of glass hung by strings so as to jingle. **thih-chhiū,** a sort of palm (Caryota).

thih-lâng, a man who can stand much fatigue and hunger and all sorts of weather; a daring dangerous man, fond of fighting, not afraid of mandarin's or of Heaven's justice. **thih-kut-á-siⁿ,** short and strongly set, as man. **tâng-sin thih-kut,** not afraid of cold or being struck or beaten; said also in scolding, you must be very bold indeed to venture here. **chiàh-thih chiàh-tâng,** to live by bold, bad, wicked means. **chiàh-tâng chiàh-thih,** id. **thih kòng-thih** (iron beat iron), diamond cut diamond; about equal in power, cunning, or 'cuteness. **thûi kòng-thih,** id. **thih-khí,** doggedly refusing to admit one's fault, and telling manifest lies about it (v. khí). **tsám-teng tsòeh-thih,** resolute and determined, listening to no advice or entreaty to the contrary. **sim náⁿ-thih-phah,** cruel and pitiless, like wrought-iron.

náⁿ thih-tháng, as strong as an iron bucket, said of a strongly-built house secure against robbers, or of a strong fort or city.

thih [R. tī, slow, dilatory]. **thoa-thih,** going on very slowly, as a piece of work; to make wearisome delays while all the time doing something; much involved and slow to get right, as an affair; tedious and lingering, as a disease. **gâu-thoa-thih,** always making slow work of it.

thih — **thih-thih,** extremely weak and quite prostrated with severe illness. **pīⁿ kàu thih-thih,** id. **pīⁿ-khi-thih,** id. **thih-thih--khì,** to pass away in death quite gently and without pain.

thih (cf. gih, khih). **sán-thih-thih,** extremely lean.

thih (cf. tih). **chhin-thih-thih,** very cold, as things.

thih (cf. tih, ngih, khih). **thih-thih-kiò,** to stammer or stutter. **thih-thih-kóng,** to stammer (naturally). **thih--ê,** a stutterer or stammerer. **thih-thih-háu,** to stammer or stutter (naturally); also (said in scolding), talking on very fast, or very fond of talking.

thim (cf. tim). **im-thim,** crafty and designing; keeping one's plans secret for some bad purpose. **im-thim-tòk,** crafty and malicious; plotting mischief and dissembling deeply.

thím, to strike gently and lightly with the fist on the upper part of the head, more gently than "phāu" or "pāu." **thím thâu-khak,** id.

thìm (cf. tìm, tàm), to nod; to pitch, as a vessel dipping her bows in the waves. **thìm-thâu,** to nod the head, as when much pleased, or in giving permission. **thâu bô-thìm,** not to nod the head.

thìm-éng, to dip into the waves, as a boat when pitching.

thīm (An.), = A. thiām, to throw into the sea or into the water. **thīm-hái,** id.

thîn [R. chim? to pour out gently; careful], to pour out gently in small quantity from a spout, as tea, liquor, &c. **lim-thîn,** drinking and pouring, as intoxicating liquor (v. lim).

thîn-tê, to pour out tea. **thîn-chiú,** to pour a small quantity of spirituous liquor. **thîn-iû,** to pour oil.

thīn (T. thîn, tîn), to make of equal weight, as the two loads on the end of a pole; equal or nearly equal in size at both ends, as a beam; to arrange the betrothal, as of one's daughter. **m̄-thīn,** not corresponding well, *e.g.* as fine and tattered clothes worn at once.

saⁿ-thīn, so similar as to make a good pair, as things; agreeing well together, as the several articles of a suit of clothes; betrothed; engaged to be married. **m̄-saⁿ-thīn,** not corresponding well, as good and bad clothes worn at once. **chhin-chiâⁿ saⁿ-thīn,** betrothed; fixed to be married, as two persons. **ke-piáu saⁿ-thīn,** marriage between persons already related by affinity (but never of same surname). **kap hit--ê saⁿ-thīn,** very like, as two things that make a good pair; betrothed to that person.

thīn bó-lâng, betrothed to so-and-so. **thīn-i,** to betroth or engage her (*e.g.* one's daughter) to him. **saⁿ-ún-thīn,** to arrange the betrothal of son or daughter. **thīn-tiāⁿ-tiòh,** fully settled, as betrothal.

sù-thīn, well arranged, as several things that agree well together; well proportioned, as one's face, or as the component parts of a thing; all arranged very suitably, as a marriage. **sì-thīn,** id.

ìn-thīn, suiting each other exactly in form, as things or persons; making an exact pair, as things set opposite; well proportioned, as features of face, esp. of woman: said also of other things, *e.g.* of the projecting houses on each side of the central house, well proportioned to it and equal to each other. **saⁿ-ìn-thīn,** id., especially making a good pair, as things of same size and shape; or suiting well together, as the several articles of a suit of clothes. **thâu-bé saⁿ-in-thīn**, the two ends well proportioned, *e.g.* of a good stick of timber.

thīn-pîⁿ, to make the beam of a balance level by equal weights; to make the loads at the two ends of a pole equal in weight. **thīn kàu-pîⁿ**, id. **thīn-tāng**, to make the loads at the two ends of a pole equal or about equal. **thīn-thâu**, id.

thio [R. thiau, to carry on a pole; to raise up gently, as with a pin; to stir or open up; to stir up or instigate; to select; to sew or embroider; a spoon; = col. thiáu, thiô], to lift or turn up gently, as with a needle or pin or point of finger; to embroider finely; the up-stroke in writing Chinese characters.

thio--chhut-lâi, to pick out, as with a pin or needle, *e.g.* a thorn or splinter from one's flesh. **thio--khí-lâi**, raise it up a little, as with point of finger or needle, &c.

teng-thio, a small implement like a spoon for trimming the wick of a lamp. **thio-hé**, to raise up the lamp-wick a little. **thio teng-hé**, id.

thio-bêng, to write a supplementary agreement on a document, *e.g.* about money advanced on a lease.

thio-hoe, to embroider finely. **thio-hoe chhiah-siù**, to embroider in general.

poan-thio, to raise up evil reports against a man so as to set people at variance.

chit-thio, an up-stroke in the writing of the Chinese character.

thio-chhiú, the 64th radical (the hand), as written at the side; so called because one of the strokes is tilted up. **thio-tsâi**, id., so called because similar to the character "tsâi," ability. **thio-tsâi-pêng**, id. **thio-thé**, the 32d radical, as written at the side. **thio-jiȯk-pêng**, the 130th radical, as written at the side.

thio [R. thô, the head, = col. thâu]. **chhut-thio**, to project, as bricks or tiles from a wall, or as ends of stones in a wall left as small steps.

thiô [R. thiau, to carry on a pole; to select; = col. thio, thiáu]. **chhin-thiô**, to select in person. **chhin-thiô--ê**, chosen by one's self, as persons or things; selected and bought by one's self, as things; obtained by merit in examination and not by influence or money, as a degree. **chhin-chhiú thiô--ê**, chosen or bought by one's self; made by one's own hands, as cakes, sweetmeats, &c.

thiô [R. tô, to throw; to leap into; = col. tâu, tiô], (T.), = A. tiô, to hop; to bounce; to spring up. **thiô-kha-khō**, to hop. **thiô-kha-chhėk**, id.

thiô-kha-koe (A.), to hop.

thiô [R. thô, the head, = col. thâu], (Cn.), = A. thô, thâu, but only in a few phrases.

chhut-thïô, = A. chhut-thio, to project, as in a building.

ū-hêng-thïô, = A. ū-hêng-thâu, having good-looking clothes to wear. **chit-hù hêng-thïô**, whole dress good-looking. **ū-hêng-thiô, hó-hêng-tsió** (r.), having nice dress, it is pleasant to walk about.

thiò (R. thiàu), to sell grain, pulse, or potatoes. **thiò-bí**, to sell rice. **thiò-tiȧh**, to sell and buy grain, &c. **thiò-chhut tiȧh-jip**, id. **tsòe bí-thiò**, to open or keep a rice-shop where rice in husk (chhek), bought from many places, is separated from the husk and sold in the form of cleaned rice, "bí."

thiò, = phiò. **thiò-pėh**, = phiò-pėh, to bleach.

thioⁿ (C.), = A. thiuⁿ, in the several tones.

thiok [R. domestic animals, = col. thek, chhiūⁿ, thâu]. **liók-thiok**, the six domestic animals. **soaⁿ-khîm. iá-siù liók-thiok**, beasts and birds, wild and tame.

giėt-thiok, you vile mischievous brute! (said in scolding a boy or girl for something extremely bad, esp. impurity).

thiok (R. id.) **chek-thiok**, to accumulate gradually. **thiok-chek** (r.), id.

thiok (C. esp. P.), = A. thek, to scold, &c.

thiông [R. a reptile; an insect; = col. thâng, lâng]. **chhu-thiông**, small worms that breed in sour or rotting things; also, sort of worms in the bowels, smaller than "būn-thâng."

thiông [R. tiông, the bowels, = col. tn̂g, chhiâng]. **liông-thiông** (T.), a sort of soft marine animal.

thióng [R. a grave; a tomb]. **thióng-soaⁿ**, a burying-ground, usually on hills. **thióng-tōe**, id. **gī-thióng**, a public burying ground. **ké-thióng**, an ancient burying-ground. **siu-thióng**, to repair the graves in a burying-ground.

thióng [R. grace; kindness; favour; affection; to show special love and favour, as to a concubine]. **un-thióng** (R.), very special imperial favour and affection, esp. towards members of the harem.

thióng-ài (R.), to be immoderately fond of, as of a concubine. **khì-chhe thióng-chhiap**, to divorce one's wife and advance a concubine to her place, which is a serious crime.

tek-thióng, to get into a man's special favour or affections (by partiality or favouritism), as a concubine or eunuch, or low servant, so that the favourite's advice and desires are followed, instead of what is right. **tek-thióng ê-lâng**, a low favourite who has got a man's affections.

thiòng [R. thòng, pain; grieved; distressed; miserable; to feel for; to love; = col. thàng]. **thiòng-hūn**, to hate exceedingly; to detest or regret bitterly.

thiòng-ím, drinking a great deal of intoxicating liquor (v. ím), (this phrase is by some placed under the following word).

thiòng [R. joyous; joy; to delight; pleasure], (C. thiàng, which often has a bad meaning).

thiòng-lȯk, pleasure; to be merry; delighted; generally has rather a bad meaning, or is capable of it. **lȯk-thiòng**, fond of low and bad pleasures; leading an idle or fast life. **lí teh lȯk-thiòng**, you are treating this as a joke or as a small matter, while it is really of very great consequence.

thiòng-khoài, pleased and happy, as in some amusement with friends, or at some success, *e.g.* getting an affair to come straight without trouble. **thiòng-sià**, a young man or lad who amuses himself instead of working or studying diligently.

tâng-gûn bóe tsoá-hia, siang-lâng thiòng, to buy paper boots with brass dollars pleases both parties, each supposing he has cheated the other.

thiòng-ím (see previous word).

thit, to sport with in a lascivious way; to commit lasciviousness with.

thit-thô (C. chhit-thô), to play; to amuse one's self; to take amusement; to take a pleasure excursion; to make sport with; often used in a bad sense, to have illicit intercourse with. **poȧh thit-thô**, to play a game of chance for amusement, without money or very little. **chiȧh thit-thô**, to eat sweetmeats and such dainties instead of solid food. **chiȧh--liáu thit-thô**, to do nothing but eat and amuse one's self. **thit-thô hiân-koán**, to amuse one's self with musical instruments. **thit-thô tsa-bé**, to commit fornication. **hó-thit-thô**, pleasant for amusement, as a place or road; pleasant to play at, or to amuse one's self with. **sió-lō hó-thit-thô**, the small road is good for amusement (said in the rites of "khan-bông" in coaxing the spirits of the dead to come up).

thit-thô-kha, a young fellow fond of low, licentious, and vicious pleasures. **thit-thô-sien**, a man who has nothing to do but to amuse himself. **thit-thô-lâng**, a man fond of low or licentious pleasures; a prostitute. **thit-thô ê-chiáu**, fancy birds, as singing birds, &c.

thit i-ê-thô, to amuse one's self along with another who stands all the expenses.

thit tsa-bé, to commit fornication. **thit-piáu**, id. **poàh chiàh thit**, gambling, opium-smoking, and lewdness. **chiàh poàh thit**, id.

thit (C.) **chéng-thit**, = A. chéng-thek, to adorn; to ornament.

thit (C.), = A. thek, by imperial command, &c.

thit, to make straight; to straighten. **thit-khi-tit**, make it straight, as a thing, or as an affair. **thit-bōe-tit**, cannot be made straight, as a crooked thing; the dispute, quarrel, or affair cannot be made straight or set right. **ún-ku thit-bōe-tit** (a hunchback can't be straightened), a matter far wrong at first cannot be put straight; a natural disposition crooked and crabbed cannot be eradicated; his affairs are never straight.

thiu — **ki-ki-thiu**, to cry, as a ghost, or as a child constantly crying for things.

thiu (R. id., = col. chhiu), to draw out, as a lot, as an arrow, as wire or silk; to take off a percentage or commission; a syphon; to draw off by a syphon. **thiu-chhut**, to pull out, as a long thing from among others; to select or extract.

thiu-liām, to take a passage from a book at random for the scholar to recite. **thiu-peng**, to take a certain proportion of soldiers for some special purpose.

thiu-chhiam, to draw out divining lots. **thiu-khau**, to draw lots.

thiu-thâu, to take a small percentage; brokerage. **thiu-hun**, to take off a percentage for commission; commission for transacting some business; much more than "thiu-thâu." **thàn-thiu-hun**, to earn money for commission or agency. **thiu tiōng-gûn**, to take off commission or brokerage for selling goods.

jī-pat thiu, taking a commission of 20 per cent. **thiu káu-poeh**, to take off 2 per cent. commission. **thiu khòng-ngō**, to take 5 per cent. **tsáp-hūn thiu chit-hūn**, to take 10 per cent. **it-kiú thiu**, id.

thiu-hiòng, to collect duties or customs.

thiu-sin tò--khì, to betake one's self home, as in fear. **thiu-sin tsáu--tò-khì**, id. **thiu-sin thè-āu**, to draw back, as through fear. **thiu-tò-tńg**, to retreat in good order, as army. **thiu-thè**, id.; also to draw back from what one had promised to do, on finding it inconvenient or dangerous. **gâu-thiu-thè**, fond of drawing back from promises. **thiu-thiu thè-thè**, in the habit of drawing back and not fulfilling promises.

thiu tâng-soàⁿ, to make brass or copper wire. **thiu tâng-si**, to make very thin do. **thiu-si**, to unwind silk from cocoons.

thiu-thāng, to teach a new servant or apprentice how to do his work. **thiu ka-lé**, to move puppets by pulling the strings. **oàn-kúi thiu chih-kun**, said of a man who formerly concealed his guilt making confession before a mandarin, or letting out the truth by his transparent lies (lit. the avenging ghost pulls his tongue).

thiu-thiàⁿ, sharp shooting pains.

thiu-tsáng, to pull out hairs from a bunch of hair to make a false queue. **phoà-pak thiu-tn̂g**, to rip up the belly and pull out the bowels, a punishment in the Buddhist hell.

sán thiu-thiu, very thin, tall, and slender, as a man.

tsúi-thiu, a pump for water. **o-thiu**, a long thin bamboo suspending the bucket of a well-sweep. **chiú-thiu**, a syphon for spirituous liquor.

thiu-chiú, to draw off spirituous liquor by a syphon.

khan-thiu, a broad edging or border about an inch broad, made by sewing a separate piece of cloth on a dress. **khan-thiu-liâu**, the strip of cloth thus sewed on. **pūn-thiu**, the two long strong timbers of the deck, at the sides of the hatches, which run the whole length of the junk from stem to stern.

thiú [R. the second double hour, 1–3 A.M.; one of the cyclical characters, answering to the ox as its symbol; persons born in a year that has this character are dull or foolish; = col. thiúⁿ], the clown in a play; he wears an ornamental dress. **thiú-kioh**, id. **tsng-thiú**, to act the part of the clown.

thiúⁿ (R. thiú), a cyclical and horary character; the second in the cycle of 12. **thiúⁿ-sî**, 1–3 A.M.

thng (R. thong), soup; broth; gravy; also (esp. Cn. but also A.) warm water. **thng-sî**, a soup-spoon. **thng-tsoâⁿ**, a warm spring.

thng-thâu, various medicinal infusions or decoctions. **ū-thng-thâu**, to be mixed properly, as medicines. **bô-thng-thâu**, mixed improperly, as medicines selected by lot before an idol.

iòh-thng, a medicinal decoction or infusion. **tê-thng**, any warm infusion (or decoction?). **ám-thng**, thin rice gruel. **lé-thng**, sort of brine used as sauce. **sù-kó-thng**, infusion of four sorts of dried fruit. **ké-thng**, soup containing slices of baked flour. **chhài-thng**, vegetable soup. **gû-bah-thng**, beef soup; beef-tea. **sio-thng**, warm soup; warm water. **kún-thng**, boiling soup; boiling water.

kûn-thng, to make a decoction; to boil into soup. **un-thng** (esp. Cn., but also A.), to warm water.

thn̂g (R. tông; C. thông), sugar. **o-thn̂g**, raw sugar; coarse brown sugar. **péh-thn̂g**, white sugar. **kak-thn̂g**, loaf sugar. **chhiah-soa-thn̂g**, sugar having the appearance of yellowish sand; brought from Formosa and other places.

peng-thn̂g, sugar-candy. **thn̂g-sng**, id. **kiuⁿ-bú-thn̂g**, a small solid squarish confection made of sugar and ginger, somewhat like toffee. **jūn-thn̂g**, sugar worked up into a tough tenacious confection. **bêng-thn̂g**, a confection of sugar made very clear, usually with hemp-seed on the top. **thn̂g-liâu**, sweetmeats. **thn̂g-ké-á**, sweetmeats. **bit-chièn thn̂g-kó**, sweetmeats used in idolatrous offerings. **thn̂g-ké**, a sort of large drum-shaped cake of sugar, used at marriages. **poeh-kak-thn̂g**, an eight-cornered confection used at marriages. **sóe-kháu-thn̂g**, a large cake of sugar used at marriages. **sek-kháu-thn̂g**, id.

thn̂g-á, small sweet confections. **thn̂g-á-séh**, an instrument for gambling for confections. **séh thn̂g-á**, to gamble for confections with the "séh." **pūn thn̂g-á-teng**, to blow bubbles like soap-bubbles with syrup (v. teng).

thn̂g-tsúi, molasses; treacle. **thn̂g-chheng**, sugar and water.

thn̂g-lāu, a conical vessel for refining sugar. **thn̂g-siàh**, a sort of spoon for syrup. **thn̂g-chhiám**, a pointed hollow bamboo for taking samples out of sugar baskets (v. chhiám). **thn̂g-hâng**, a sugar warehouse. **thn̂g-phē̍**, premises where sugar is refined; sometimes also including a sugar-mill.

lāu-thn̂g, to refine sugar. **oân-thn̂g**, to make raw sugar into balls. **tò-thn̂g**, to pour sugar into a mould to make confections (v. tò).

káu-láng-thn̂g, tsáp-it thâu-ke (eleven owners of nine baskets of sugar), so many men have a share that nothing can be done, as each will have his own way.

thn̂g [R. toân, a globular mass; a lump, &c.;=col. thoân, toâ^n, n̂g], (C. thûi^n).

ka-n̂g-thn̂g, a whole lump, as of clay. **chit-thn̂g-soà^n**, a ball of thread.

thǹg (C. thùi^n), to buy a thing from a friend, or from some one who happens to have it and lets us get it as a favour, not from a shop or trader; to exchange loads, or get another to carry a load or sedan in our place, as coolies do. **thǹg-lâng-ta^n**, to get another to carry the load instead of us.

goá kā-lí-thǹg, I should much like to buy it from you (more polite than "bóe"), said to a friend or some one we meet who has something we wish to buy, but not in the way of regular business.

thǹg (R. thùn), (C. thùi^n), to take off, as clothes, &c.; to shed, as hair or tusks; to take off the hinges, as a door. **thǹg-thǹg lut-lut**, taking off one's own clothes.

thǹg-bō, to take off one's hat or cap. **thǹg-sa^n**, to take off one's coat. **thǹg sa^n-á-khò**, to take off all one's clothes. **thǹg-khò**, to take off one's trowsers. **thǹg-khò-lān**, not wearing trowsers, as man; naked below the waist so as to leave one's private parts exposed. **thǹg-pak-theh**, naked, or nearly naked (v. theh). **thǹg kng-kng** (C. thùi^n-kui^n-kui^n), to strip stark naked.

thǹg-chiah-kha, barefooted. **thǹg-chhiah-kha** (r. or Cn.?), id. **thǹg-béh**, to take off stockings. **thǹg-ôe**, to take off shoes. **goá kā-lí-thǹg chháu-ôe**, I will give you a feast in honour of your safe return from your journey.

thǹg-mn̂g (C. thùi^n-mûi^n), to take a door off its hinges.

thǹg-mn̂g (C. thùi^n-mê^n), to shed hair or feathers (naturally), as bird or dog, &c. **thǹg-gê**, to shed its tusks, as elephant.

thǹg [R. thong, soup; hot water;=col. thng], to scald; to treat with hot water. **thǹg--tiòh**, scalded. **kún-tsúi thǹg--tiòh**, scalded by boiling water.

thǹg-khí, teeth sore from something hot in the mouth.

léng-tsúi thǹg-thē (scald a jelly-fish with cold water), to talk ironically or sarcastically of a man's faults.

thǹg — **thǹg-á** (C.), a sort of triangular hand-net.

thn̄g (C. thūi^n), to warm over again, to warm up again, as food (cf. tǹg). **thn̄g-sio**, id.

thn̄g, to glaze, as pottery; the glazing on pottery.

thn̄g-kng, to glaze, as pottery. **kè-thn̄g**, to be glazed. **ū kè-thn̄g**, it is glazed.

lâm-thn̄g, to pour on the glazing material; to glaze. **bô-thn̄g**, unglazed, as pottery. **ū-thn̄g**, glazed. **koà-thn̄g**, id.

thn̄g [R. tiōng, a staff; a cudgel]. **hà-thn̄g**, sticks adorned with fringed paper, carried by sons at funeral: for father, made of bamboo; for mother, made of the "khó-lēng" tree. **thâng-thn̄g** (C.), a stick carried by a son at funeral.

sek-thn̄g, the Buddhist key of Hades, used by Bud. priests to frighten demons (it is shaped like a leaf, made of brass with wooden handle). **sek-thn̄g-chiam**, a hair-pin of similar shape worn by elderly females. **chhah sek-thn̄g-chiam**, to wear this sort of hair-pin.

thn̄g — **soa-thn̄g**, a small sort of fish (v. soa).

thn̄g (C. thūi^n). **mn̂g-thn̄g** (C. mûi^n-thūi^n), a long thick bar (esp. perpendicular) for barring a Chinese door.

thn̄g [R. toān? a bit; a piece;=col. toā^n, tn̄g; or should perhaps be divided into two words?], (C. thn̄g, thūi^n, tūi^n).

chhiū-thn̄g (C. chhiū-tūi^n), the stem, trunk, or stump of a tree.

chhiú-thn̄g, the arm from elbow to wrist when the hand has been lost, as by a wound or disease or frost-bite. **kha-thn̄g**, the lower part of the leg, from knee to about the ankle, said when the foot is gone, as by disease, shot, or frost; only a leg or a bit of a leg, as when the rest has been devoured by a tiger or lost in battle. **sīn chit-ki kha-thn̄g**, only a stump of a leg or a bit of a leg remaining (as above).

tho (cf. lo, lu), to peck and suck or gobble up, as a duck. **ah teh-tho**, the duck feeling in the mud with its bill. **ah-bú-chhùi bóng-tho**, the duck just feeling about for something, said of making a request or attempt without much expectation of success, but may as well try it.

tho [R. to rise and swell, as waters; to pass bounds], (Cn. thə). **tsōe-ok tho-thien** (r.), iniquity swollen up heaven-high.

thô — **koe-thô**, a chicken not above the weight of one Chinese pound.

thô — **thit-thô**, to play; to amuse one's self; to make sport with; to have illicit intercourse with (v. thit). **chhit-thô** (C.), id.

thô (Cn.) **thô-tāu**, = A. thô-tāu, ground-nuts (Arachis).

thô [R. tô, steep; precipitous; a syllable much used in Buddhist phrases].

bān-thô-hoe, a sort of Datura with large white trumpet-shaped flowers, it is poisonous and powerfully narcotic, and said to cause madness. **lí chiàh bān-thô-hoe**, surely you are mad! said to a man behaving very absurdly or forgetfully.

thô [R. a peach tree or fruit]. **thô-á**, a peach. **thô-á-chhiū**, a peach-tree. **thô-á-sī^n**, salted peaches. **thô-á-pêng**, peaches split up, dried, and preserved. **thô-á-tsang** (C.), a small queue on the side of a child's head.

ti^n-thô, the common peach. **khó-thô**, the bitter peach. **hut-thô**, the walnut. **eng-thô**, a very large fruit (not a real peach) growing on a small tree (Cerasus pseudo-cerasus?). **chhit-chhùn-thô**, a peach that grows on a tree only seven inches high. **phek-thô**, a very large and fine sort of peach. **sien-thô**, a fabulous peach that bears fruit only once in 3000 years, the fruit of which causes immortality.

mī^n-thô, imitation peaches made of sweetened flour, used in the worship of idols.

thô-jîn, kernels of the bitter peach, used medicinally.

thô-hû, charms made of peach-leaves or branches.

thô-ki, a peach-branch, used much for divination; it has great power over spirits; it is not proper to strike any one with a peach-branch, as it may influence the soul so as to cause madness.

thô-âng, peach colour; colour of peach-blossoms; a bright red. **thô-âng-tsoá**, bright red paper, such as is used for cards. **thô-âng-thiap**, a red calling-card.

thô-hoe-bīn (face like peach-blossom), said of a young woman whose face looks as if fond of licentious pleasure. **thô-hoe-siáu**, inclination to lasciviousness in women, said to be strongest about the time when the peach blossoms. **toà-thô-hoe**, fated to lead a licentious life, as woman, said by fortune-tellers.

thó [R. khó, may or can be]. **thái-thó**, however —? how — ever —? **beh-thái-thó**, id. **thái-thó thang**, how can — ever —? how dare —? **thái-thó ōe àn-niⁿ**, how can it be so?

thó (R. id.), to demand back; to demand payment; to ask for a thing; to challenge; to bring upon one's self, as calamity or hatred; to earn, as money, or make a living; to fish; to raise water, &c.

thó-siàu, to collect debts. **thó-chè**, id. **thó-chîⁿ**, to collect money due. **chiáh-bah, sim hoaⁿ-hí; thó-chîⁿ, bīn iu-iu**, very happy while eating the meat, but looking very sad when payment is asked for. **thó-chiet**, to collect a percentage on a bad debt (v. chiet). **thó-bô**, to demand or demand back, but get nothing. **thó-bô-chîⁿ**, unable to get back any money. **tui-thó** (r.), to demand back very urgently. **thó-tò-tńg**, to demand back again, as money or things lent, or as property mortgaged or leased. **tù-teh-thó**, insisting on payment, and refusing to go till it be paid. **kā-lâng-thó**, to demand or ask urgently from a man. **pek-thó**, to demand payment urgently; to dun for payment. **chhui-thó**, id., but not quite so strong as "pek." **bô-thang-thó**, no way of getting repayment. **kêng sí tsáu, bô-thang-thó**, from the very poor, the dead, and the runaway, no payment can be got. **bô-tè thang-thó**, there is no place where it can be got. **thó-miāⁿ**, to demand the death of the murderer, as the ghost of a murdered man does.

thó jîn-chêng, to ask for a favour or kindness for another, as a man who has some influence or some claim on the person asked. **thó-siúⁿ**, to ask for a reward in addition to the regular wages or pay. **thó-thiⁿ**, to ask for more. **thó-hūn**, to ask for a situation or for permission to join in some business, work, service, or employment. **thó kià-kha**, to ask to be allowed to stay and work for board and lodging, but no pay.

thó-kha khit-lō͘ kiâⁿ, to have had all the walking in vain. **bô-chhái-kang, thó kha-kiâⁿ**, id.

thó-thàn, to earn money. **thó-chiáh**, to seek for food, as a beggar, or as a wild beast, or as a hungry ghost. **thó-chhâu**, to gather grass or shrubs for fuel. **chhut-jit, thó hō͘-lâi-niû** (C.), in fine weather prepare food for rainy weather.

thó-bí, to take rice out of the jar, as for cooking. **ōe-sǹg bōe-tû; thó-bí, oāⁿ han-tsû**, said of a very foolish man (as rice is much superior to sweet-potatoes).

thó-hái, to fish, as in the sea. **thó sió-hái**, to catch marine animals at low tide. **thó-hî**, to fish. **thó-tsan**, to fish with a hand-net lifted up by the hand.

thó-tsúi, to draw water.

thó-chièn, to challenge to battle. **thó-phīⁿ**, to collect several men and go and beat a man who had beaten us.

thó-sí, to draw death on one's self by one's own conduct. **tsū-tsok-giét thó-sí**, to draw death on one's self by great wickedness.

thó-lâng, to demand back a man who had been sold or seized or imprisoned, or who has died or been lost while under the other's care, &c. **thó-lâng khì kā-i-kóng**, to ask some person to go and tell him.

thó tsa-bó͘, to go after lewd women. **thó khè-hiaⁿ**, to seek a paramour, as a bad woman. **thó ta-po͘**, id. **sì-kòe thó--lâng**, going about, as a bad woman, enticing men to lewdness.

thò (Cn.), = C. thō. **thò-thò**, gently sloping, as a road.

thò [R. id.; C. thó; safe, secure]. **thò-tòng**, safe, as an affair, or as a man safe to deal with (v. tòng). **chèng-thò**, safe and honest; trusty and truthful, as man who keeps his word; safe and correct, as an affair that we may safely engage in.

thò [R. to envelop or inclose; an envelope, wrapper, or outer dress; a loop, as of a rope or river; a snare or plot; of general use or application], a loose outer dress, esp. for keeping the inner dress clean; a cover, as for a pillow; a set, as of songs, or of outer and inner dress; classifier of tricks in boxing, of songs and song-tunes; to rehearse or practise, as one's part in a play, or as evidence to be given; to mend by putting a piece inside and sewing or pasting the edges, as a torn dress, or as a leaf of a book mended by pasting paper inside the double leaf.

chit-thò, a set of two or more articles of dress worn at once on the upper part of the body, *e.g.* coats, vests, gowns, &c. **chit-thò-saⁿ**, id. **kui-thò**, the whole set of such articles of dress worn at once on the upper part of the body.

kûn-thò, the arts or tricks of boxing. **kúi-nā-thò kûn**, several tricks in boxing.

khek-thò, a tune for a set of songs (+). **chit-thò-khek**, a set of two or three songs, so much as is usually sung at a stretch. **chít-thò-tsáiⁿ**, id.

thò-khek, to practise songs along with others and with instruments, to see if all be in tune. **thò-hì**, to rehearse a play. **thò kha-pō͘**, to practise steps, as actor, soldier, or sedan-bearer. **thò-keng**, to rehearse evidence in preparing for a trial. **thò kháu-keng**, id. **thò-piēn**, rehearsed all ready.

thò-thâu-ōe, polite and customary forms of expression used on meeting and conversing with people, esp. in beginning a conversation or when going to ask a favour. **thò-thâu-gú**, id. **thò-gú**, id.; also regular customary phrases used in letters, &c.

piēn-thò-ōe, regular conventional phrases used in certain circumstances. **piēn-thò-tāi**, easy simple matters which any one can do. **piēn-thò ê tāi-chì**, id.

kàu-hiah-khek-thò, you are far too polite to me, said by guest or visitor to host (+). **put-chí khek-thò**, using a great deal of ceremony in intercourse with visitors or guests. **ū-khek-thò**, using much ceremony with guests.

thò-thiap, dispensing with ceremony and circumlocution, as a visitor, or as in doing business; not standing too much on ceremony; free and easy, esp. as visitors or guests. **thò-thiet**, id. **thiap-thò** (r.), id. (+). **thò-siòk** (C.), very free and easy; without much ceremony. **thoat-thò** (C.), id.

khoàn-thò, a snare. **thò-bē**, to conspire secretly to mislead or injure another.

phah thong-thò, to make a plot or conspiracy

厦英大辭典

against a man. **saⁿ-thong-thò**, id. **thong-thò-tāi** (?), small customary observances, sometimes superstitious. **thong-thò ê-ōe** (?), polite phrases used when people meet.

thò pháiⁿ-lâng, to engage a bold bad man to assist in some wickedness, *e.g.* robbery, false lawsuits, &c. **thò-chhut pháiⁿ-lâng**, id.

thò--chhut-lâi, to mend by putting a piece inside. **thò-saⁿ**, to mend clothes by putting the piece inside and sewing down the edges. **thò-ôe**, to mend the uppers of shoes in this way.

goā-thò, an outer dress, esp. worn as a cover. **ńg-thò**, an outer sleeve worn as a cover to the sleeve or to the cuff. **niáⁿ-thò**, a sort of cape worn round the neck and fastened below the arms; it is so called because it covers the collar of the dress. **hiû-thò**, a dress worn over a warm wadded dress. **iûⁿ-ko-thò**, an outer dress worn over a sheepskin dress. **phàu thò**, a long warm robe and the outer dress worn over it. **chím-thâu-thò**, a pillow-case without ends. **chheh-thò**, a case or cover for holding several volumes of a book. **thiap-thò**, sort of case or envelope for cards (+).

joáh-lóeh-thò, the bamboo or rattan wicker-work in the inside of a summer cap which makes it fit firmly on the head.

thō (C.), = Cn. thò. **thō-thō**, sloping gently, as a road.

thơ (Cn.) **thơ-thien**, = A. tho-thien, swelling up to heaven, as guilt.

thô͘ [R. the head, = col. thâu]. **kú-thô͘ sam-chhek, iú sîn-bêng**, lift up your head three feet, and the spirits and gods are there, so beware of acting wickedly.

thô͘ [R. name of a river; the 12th month], a surname.

thô͘ [R. tô͘, mud; miry; to daub; cf. R. thó͘; cf. col. tô͘], earth; mud; clay; soil; mortar; opium; having a dull surface, as a gem.

thô͘-thô͘, having a dull bad surface, as a gem of inferior quality.

chhàu-thô͘, having an unpleasant earthy taste, as water or tea. **chhèng thô͘-khì**, affected by the cold damp air of the ground (v. chhèng). **thô͘-kauh** (T.), very thick mist.

thô͘-lâng, a sort of hand-mill for cleaning rice, separating it from the husk (v. lâng).

thô͘-sai, a mason; a builder. **thô͘-kang**, a mason; a bricklayer. **thô͘-tsúi-chhiūⁿ**, id. **thô͘-tsúi sai-hū**, a builder; a mason. **thô͘-bák-sai**, masons and carpenters.

thô͘-soa, sand and clay mixed for building (v. soa). **he-thô͘**, mortar made of lime and clay.

thô͘-thâu, rubbish; clods of earth. **báuh thô͘-thâu**, to make an estimate for removing rubbish. **thô͘-thn̂g**, a lump or clod of earth. **chhân-thô͘**, the soil of rice-fields. **hoan chhân-thô͘**, to work the rice-fields (v. hoan). **hái-thô͘**, sea-mud. **keh-thô͘**, the hard subsoil just below the mould. **thô͘-bê**, mud. **thô͘-siûⁿ**, soft slushy mud. **noāⁿ-thô͘**, soft mud; said of a soft submissive temper (v. noāⁿ). **thô͘-hún**, dust.

oáⁿ-thô͘, clay for making bowls and such pottery. **hún-thô͘**, yellow clay used for colouring cards, &c. **pùt-á-thô͘**, white tenacious clay used for making idols. **chhiah-jîn-thô͘**, reddish clay, used for mortar. **péh-siēn-thô͘**, chalk. **péh-thó͘-thô͘**, id.

péh-hiā-thô͘, the covered galleries made by white ants. **oan-iuⁿ-thô͘**, the nests of the insect called "oan-iuⁿ." **tsàu-sim-thô͘**, clay from the inside of an old fireplace, used medicinally.

thô͘-kat, unburned bricks (v. kat). **thô͘-tūi**, earthenware weights for nets. **thô͘-jíⁿ**, small, flat, rounded bits of tile for children's play. **thô͘-pùt-á**, small earthenware figures used as toys.

thô͘-thoàⁿ, coals.

thô͘-pô-éng, great waves at the mouth of a river; the bore (v. pô).

thô͘-kha, the floor; an earthen or tiled floor; the surface of the ground, said in relation to sitting, kneeling, lying, &c., on it. **kūi thô͘-kha**, to kneel on the ground. **tó tī thô͘-kha**, lying on the ground. **thô͘-phê**, clods of surface-soil (v. phê), (+). **thô͘-bīn**, the surface-soil. **thô͘-keh**, the reddish subsoil (v. keh). **thô͘-tōe**, an earthen floor; the natural surface of the ground. **thô͘-tóe**, down in the ground; below the surface of the ground, *e.g.* under the earthen floor.

thô͘-téh, soft muddy beach at low-tide. **thô͘-phiâⁿ**, a mud-bank on the sea-shore.

phè-thô͘, to hold some earth in the flap of one's long dress in order to shake it on the coffin when it has been laid in the grave. **thoa-thô͘**, to drag along in the mud (v. thoa). **kùt-thô͘**, to dig the ground. **chhiau-thô͘**, to mix mortar. **chiū i-thô͘, tsoh i-chhiūⁿ**, make the articles according to the money he allows.

a-phièn-thô͘, opium; crude opium (v. phièn). **ơ-hun-thô͘**, id. **hun-thô͘**, id. **âng-thô͘**, an inferior sort of opium; Turkey opium. **pún-tōe-thô͘**, Chinese opium. **thô͘-bah**, the good opium in a ball of opium. **thô͘-phê**, the skin of opium-balls, made up of leaves, &c.; some opium of inferior quality is got by boiling it down (+). **thô͘-ko**, crude opium, as it is taken from the ball. **thô͘-siuⁿ**, an empty opium-box. **thô͘-kėk**, a local board for collecting the opium revenue.

thô͘-sat, the mud-fish. **thô͘-sún**, sort of edible worm found in the sea (v. sún). **thô͘-kiu**, id. **thô͘-lêng**, a sort of eel (v. lêng). **thô͘-thoh**, sort of fish (v. thoh). **thô͘-poe** (T.), a long-shaped shell-fish (v. poe). **thô͘-kúi** (T.), = kàn-á, a small shell-fish (v. kúi).

thô͘-ún (Cn. tô͘-ún), the earth-worm. **thô͘-gín** (C.), id. **thô͘-phú**, = tô͘-phú, a sort of insect. **thô͘-kâu** (Cn.), = A. tô͘-kâu, a sort of insect (the mole-cricket ?)

thô͘-tāu (Cn. thô-tāu), = lòk-kha-seng, the earth-nut, Arachis. **thô͘-hiuⁿ**, = hiong-hū, a medicinal plant.

thó͘ [R. earth; ground; land; region; local; cf. col. tô͘, thô͘], the element of earth; local; rude or unpolished in manner.

thó͘-tī-kong, = hok-sîn, the god or spirit of the earth and of graves (v. tī). **thó͘-tē-kong** (C.), id. **thó͘-sîn**, id. **hō͘-thó͘**, id. **hīo-thó͘** (Cn.), id. **hông-thien hō͘-thó͘**, Imperial Heaven and Empress Earth. **sū hō͘-thó͘**, to make offerings to Thó͘-tī-kong at a burial. **siā-thó͘**, to give thanks to him on the completion of the burial. **khí-thó͘**, to begin the work of making a grave, or to begin the funeral procession. **an-thó͘**, to set down the coffin for burial; to perform rites to cure a woman or child suffering from the consequences of "tāng-thó͘." **hoah-thó͘**, to perform rites before building, making, or repairing a house or grave. **phoà-thó͘**, to begin repairing a house by breaking the plaster on a lucky day, and placing a bit of yellow paper on the spot, so that the work may go on any day. **tāng-thó͘**, to begin building or repairing a house on an unlucky day or without proper rites, so as to cause pains to a pregnant woman or to a new-born child within the first month. **hoān--tióh thó͘-sîn**, to have sudden and severe pain in the abdomen, as a pregnant woman,

71

because some article in her bed-room has been moved, or because of the repairing of the house being begun on an unlucky day. **thé-soah,** hurtful demons that cause injury when a house or grave is begun to be built, made, or repaired on an unlucky day

thé-tōe, a region; a place; a locality. **thé-tē** (C.), id. **tōe-thé,** id. **tiên-thé,** lands in general. **pì^n-iû^n khòng-thé,** an extensive plain. **toā-phiên-thé,** id. **āu-kài-thé,** the vacant ground behind a large house within the retaining wall.

thé-sán, the productions of the ground; the fruits of the earth.

tsúi-thé, the climate of a place. **phái^n-tsúi-thé,** unhealthy, as a place. **put-hók tsúi-thé,** not agreeing with the climate; climate not suiting. **chiáh m̄-tióh tsúi-thé,** injured by the climate.

pî-thé, the state of the stomach and appetite (v. pî).

thé-im, colloquial dialect, vernacular or patois. **thé-húi,** local robbers, ruffians, banditti, or rebels; not part of any great rebellion. **bîn-hong thé-siók,** usual customs of a place, including the customary superstitious observances. **hong-thé jîn-chêng,** customs of a place and character of the people. **thé-ki^n-pò,** coarse cotton cloth spun and woven in the locality. **thé-hoan,** local or native foreigners, *i.e.* aborigines in Chinese territory, *e.g.* in Formosa. **thé-hoan-ah,** common sort of duck.

thé-hók, China root (v. hók). **thé-nî^n,** a local and inferior sort of the medicine called "nî". **thé-sam-chhit,** = chhiu^n-to-ióh, a sort of Sempervivum, or house-leek.

thé-si^n-kiá^n, a man born abroad of Chinese father and foreign mother, *e.g.* of Malay mother at Singapore. **thé-sɛ^n-á** (C.), id.; also said in scolding. **thé-si^n-khoán,** having a peculiar look, different from ordinary Chinamen; like such a person.

sam-háp-thé, mortar made of lime, clay, and sand. **péh-thé-thê,** white chalk. **thé-siā^n,** a fort, outer wall, or line of circumvallation, made of unburned bricks or clay. **thé-lâu,** a very large house of several stories built very strong like a fort, generally round or square, surrounding a courtyard.

kui-thé, to die. **iám-thé,** to cover up with earth. **thé-kong,** men who dig the grave, put the body in the coffin, and bury it (+).

thé-thé, very clownish. **chin-thé,** id. **thé-kong,** vulgar; clownish; unpolished and unlettered (+). **hoan-kong-thé,** rude, vulgar, ill-bred, and unpolite; very ignorant of what should be done in a matter, but yet acting and giving orders as if he knew it all, so that it is almost impossible to manage an affair properly along with him. **chhit-thé poeh-thé,** very vulgar or clownish. **thé-sông,** vulgar; clownish. **thé-lē,** id. **thé-khì,** id. **thé-pù,** rich, but ignorant and rude.

thé-bîn, the rabble; clownish. **thé sai-hū,** an ignorant clumsy workman. **thé-siā,** a village that has no good literary men.

thé-siū^n, I venture to think.

thé-hō, a colloquial name of person or place, when it is not merely a colloquial variation of the reading sound, but totally different from the polite or literary name.

kim bók súi, hé^n thé, the five elements, metal, wood, water, fire, and earth.

thio-thé, the 32d radical as written at the side. **chhiâ-thé,** id.

thé (C. thàu). **thé-khùi,** to sigh. **thé-khùi pûn-hāi^n,** to sigh and groan bitterly.

thé (cf. thóng, thè), to protrude (also, esp. C., = thóng, exceeding, and somewhat more).

thé-eh, to belch.

thé-chih, to protrude the tongue (v. chih). **thé-í^n,** to begin to bud. **thé-lûi,** blind with the ball of the eye protruding enormously.

khah-thé (esp. C.), = khah-thóng-thâu, and a little more, said at the end of the clause. **chit-pah khah-thé,** rather more than a hundred. **chit-pɛh thé** (C.), = A. chit-pah thóng, rather more than a hundred. **chit-pɛh thé-thâu** (C.), id.

thè (R. id.), a rabbit. **soa^n-thè,** id. **thè-á-teng,** a rabbit-shaped lantern. **thè-á-bé** (rabbits' tails), said in joke of rods fringed with cut paper, carried by mourners at funeral. **thè-á-chháu,** a plant with a milky juice, much used for feeding rabbits.

siù^n thè, born in one of the years of which the rabbit is the sign, that is a year which has the word "báu" in its cyclical name.

thè [R. name of a plant]. **thè-si,** a medicinal plant (v. si), (s. vomit).

thè [R. id.; cf. col. thé], to vomit; to disgorge; to speak out, as the whole truth. **thè-chhut,** id. **thè--chhut-lâi,** id. **thè-lè,** to vomit in considerable quantity, or over and over; to make a thoroughly full statement of the whole facts. **thè-lè--chhut-lâi,** id.

áu-thè, to vomit. **làu-thè,** purging and vomiting; cholera. **ài-thè,** having a tendency to vomit from some special cause: sick and squeamish.

thè-huih, to vomit or bring up blood; to spit blood. **thè-si,** to spin silk from the mouth, as silkworm (s. plant).

thè-chhut chin-chêng, to tell out the exact truth; to say just what one thinks, or the very facts of the case.

ū thun-thè, knowing just what and when to say, or not to say, as from policy or politeness. **ōe-hiáu thun-thè,** id. **kóng-ōe ū-thun-thè,** to speak with caution, *e.g.* in a dispute, saying just so much as circumstances make suitable and no more; to take care not to wound another's feelings, as by alluding to unpleasant circumstances. **kóng-ōe bô-thun-thè,** to talk on thoughtlessly without considering whether what we say damages matters, or without considering that we are hurting people's feelings, *e.g.* using a proverb about a step-mother (āu-bú) when one is present. **thun-thè phû-tîm,** understanding well to say just enough and no more, as in managing a matter, knowing when to be firm and when to yield; adapting one's self to the circumstances, esp. as to power or want of power, and avoiding any expression that would tend to prevent success. **poà^n-thun poà^n-thè,** telling only half one's mind. **poàn-thun poàn-thè,** id.

thè-bák, prominent eyes. **bák-chiu thè-thè,** the eyes prominent.

thè [R. sù, to bestow; to give], (Cn.), = A. hē, to give; to cause; sign of the passive in many phrases. **thè-i-phah,** to be struck by him.

thö (Cn.), = A. the, to decline.

thô (Cn.), = A. thê, small pimples.

thö (Cn.), in some phrases = thöe, = A. thòe, in place of; instead of.

thö (Cn.), = A. thè, to recede; to retire.

thoa (R. tho, = col. thoah), to drag; to pull; to draw along; to procrastinate; to be chronic, as disease; to be in constant sickness or pain.

thoa-thoa, dull and heavy looking in manner, as a child (opp. léng-lī), or as a woman.

thoa-kang, to procrastinate intentionally. **gâu-thoa**, fond of procrastinating; always putting off. **thoa-khiàm**, delaying too long to pay a debt. **thoa-bé**, to procrastinate. **thoa-bé-chhì^{n}**, a comet. **thoa-thih**, making slow work of it; very tedious (v. thih).

ná^{n}-thoa, ná^{n} siong-tiōng, getting worse and worse, as a sick person. **ûn-á-thoa**, getting gradually worse, as illness; growing gradually more wicked.

thoa-boâ, to toil; to labour very hard. **thoa-sin boâ-miā^{n}**, to exert one's strength very much, *e.g.* to the danger of health. **thoa-sin thoa-miā^{n}**, id. **thoa-miā^{n}**, to hazard one's health by toiling very hard at some special work, when quite unfit for such hard work. **thoa-miā^{n} khì pān-sū**, to manage a difficult affair at the risk of one's health or life from over exertion. **thoa-pī^{n} tsòe-kang**, to work when quite too unwell for it (v. pī^{n}).

thoa-lūi, to involve another man, as in debt or some dangerous affair. **thoa-thūi**, involving in trouble, or causing impediments, as family (v. thūi). **khan-thoa**, to accuse falsely of some fault or crime. **sa^{n}-khan sa^{n}-thoa**, to draw along each other by the hands. **in-in tāu-tīn chit-toā-thoa**, said of a long and intricate story with no clue.

thoa-pùih, to urge strongly to go along with us, as a friend (v. pùih).

thoa-keng, to draw a bow for exercise, as if the arrow were in it.

thoa-tsúi, to damp by drawing gently along the surface of water, as gold-leaf or very thin paper. **thoa-thê**, to drag along in the mud, as the end of one's queue, or as part of a dress which one is carrying. **pak-tó thoa-thê**, belly dragging along on the ground, as fat pig.

thoa-phia^{n}, to drag itself along painfully, esp. on one side, as a wounded animal (v. phia^{n}).

thoa-tit, to pull straight, as a coverlet, or as one's clothes. **thoa-pí^{n}**, to pull straight and even, as a coverlet. **thoa-poáh**, to overset by pulling, as a child. **thoa-poáh--lòh-khì**, id. **thoa--tó**, to overset by pulling, as things. **thoa-ka-láuh**, to make a thing fall down by pulling.

thoa-moâ^{n}, to wear coarse ropes made of raw hemp bark tied round the waist at funeral (v. moâ^{n}). **thoa tek-poe**, to carry bamboo staves or fasces before a mandarin.

thoa-thèng, to be dragged along with the foot entangled in the stirrup. **thoa-tèng** (C.), id. **thoa-tià^{n}**, to drag anchor. **thoa-tsûn**, to pull along a small boat, as one man or two. **thoa-chhia**, to draw a carriage or cart. **thoa-pê**, to harrow.

thoa-chioh (C.), the low horizontal piece of wood in a plough, the end of which bears the ploughshare.

pit-bé thoa--tiòh, some dirt got on the point of the pen so that it makes a blot in writing.

káu thoa, may dogs drag and tear you! **káu-kā khì-thoa**, may dogs worry and drag you! **khit-kúi thoa--khì**, to be dragged away by demons or ghosts.

thoa-ôe, to walk with the heels of our shoes turned down. **thoa-ê** (C.), id.

chhién-thoa, slippers made without heels. **ê-thoa** (C.), id.

toā-thoa, a large sedan-chair holding several persons, carried by three or four bearers. **thoa-tóe-kiō**, a sedan made so as to let the feet rest inside, or on a sliding bottom.

oan-iu^{n} thoa ka-tsoáh, said of a child carrying a burden quite beyond its strength. **chháu-soh thoa án-kong, chháu-soh thoa án-pē**, unfilial conduct towards one's father causes unfilial conduct by one's son.

thoa, a down-stroke sloping down from left to right. **chit-thoa**, id.

pit thoa--khì, to draw the pen along so as to make a down-stroke towards the right. **thoa siu^{n}-tn̂g**, to make this sort of stroke too long.

thoà [R. thài, great and prosperous]. **tiô-thoà**, Tiông-thài or Chang-tai Hien, one of the Hien districts of Chang-chew.

thoā [R. thài, to wash; to rinse clean], to rinse; to wash a second time. **sóe-thoā**, to wash and rinse. **ûn-á-thoā**, to rinse gradually. **thoā--liáu koh-thoā**, to rinse again after rinsing. **thoā-sa^{n}**, to rinse clothes. **thoā-bí**, to rinse rice a second time.

thoā [R. tō, to lead; to guide; = col. chhoā; cf. col. toā?], to learn bit by bit by looking on, or with slight hints, without any regular instruction, as persons hanging on about a school when others are being taught, or by looking on, and perhaps helping a little at some work, *e.g.* as cook's assistant. **ûn-á-thoā**, to learn gradually in such a way. **thoā kàu-ōe**, to pick up knowledge or skill gradually in that way till able to do the thing. **kap hák-seng thoā**, to learn gradually from the scholars, as person hanging on about the school, or as younger child taught by an older scholar somewhat as a monitor. **thoā tsú-chiáh**, to learn cooking without regular instruction, as another servant looking on, or as cook's assistant.

hō-i-thoā, to learn from him by example, good or bad. **khit-i-thoā**, id. **hō-i-thoā kàu-ōe**, to learn gradually from him till quite able. **hō-i-thoā kàu-phái^{n}**, gradually imitate his wickedness till quite bad.

ín-thoā, to lead another to follow and imitate us, or to go to some place with us, either good or bad, but usually bad. **khit--i ín-thoā**, to be led into bad courses by him.

thoā--lâng tsòe-phái^{n}, to lead others into evil by example and companionship. **ná^{n}-thoā ná^{n}-phái^{n}**, following him deeper and deeper in wickedness.

thoā [R. tsāi, a reptile without feet; a fabulous animal; sometimes read "tī"].

thâng-thoā, insects and reptiles of all sorts.

thoa^{n} [R. than, rapids], rapids in a river. **chiū^{n}-thoa^{n}**, to ascend the rapids. **lòh-thoa^{n}**, to descend the rapids.

hái-thoa^{n} (r.), soft muddy place left by the tide at low water.

thoa^{n} [R. than, to spread out, as for sale; to share or divide, as dividends or instalments; a sort of gambling], to divide into equal or proportionate parts, as expenses.

ûn-á-thoa^{n}, to pay a debt gradually by instalments. **thoa^{n}-hêng**, to pay a percentage, *e.g.* as in general average. **thoa^{n}-chió--khì**, to pay only a percentage, as a bankrupt, &c.

tò-thoa^{n} (C.), = A. tò-thoâ^{n}, to pay less than was promised.

thoa^{n}-siàu, to allocate the expenses in equal proportions among partners. **thoa^{n}-chî^{n}**, to take up so much money from each, *e.g.* for some festival or celebration. **thoa^{n}-tsúi**, to have to pay a percentage for jettison by general average. **chiàu-thoa^{n}**, to divide expenses according to the stake or share that each has.

kong-thoa^n, to divide expenses proportionally and justly. **pî^n-pî^n-thoa^n**, to allocate the very same amount of expenses to each.

mi^n-thoa^n, a sort of gambling (esp. by Cantonese), in which the cash are laid in several groups. **pâi-thoa^n**, to set out this sort of gambling.

thoâ^n, to offer less than the offer that had previously been made and accepted, or less wages than the man had been usually receiving; to give less than we had promised. **thoâ^n--i**, to offer him such a smaller sum. **thoâ^n i-ê-chî^n**, id. **thoâ^n--i khah-chió**, to offer him less than we had offered and he had accepted. **thoâ^n--lí pah-poeh**, I now offer you 180 (*e.g.* cash), being less than the wages you had before.

tò-thoâ^n (C. tò-thoa^n), to lose more or less of one's skill or knowledge; to go back instead of making progress in learning or ability; to offer less than the offer that had been made and accepted.

thoâ^n — **hâm-thoâ^n**, = hâm-toâ^n, the place where the foot of the mast is fixed.

thoá^n, to uproot or cut away about the roots with a hoe, as small plants. **thû-thoá^n**, to hoe up or cut up, as weeds, grass, &c., on the hills or fields. **thoá^n hiet-kák**, to cut up, or cut away with a hoe, and throw away, as weeds.

thoá^n-pî^n, to level slightly and smooth down the surface of a piece of ground, filling up slight depressions with its own earth.

thoá^n-chháu, to cut up or hoe up grass and small shrubs, as in gathering them for fuel. **thoá^n chháu-á**, id. **thoá^n chháu-kun**, to hoe or cut up grass, &c., by the roots, as for fuel. **thoá^n chháu-phiá^n**, to tear up turf for fuel.

thoà^n [R. thàn, charcoal; coal]. **hé-thoà^n**, charcoal. **hé-thoà^n-bê**, broken down charcoal. **thoà^n-bê**, id. **hé-thoà^n-láng**, a charcoal-basket. **ài-tì hé-thoà^n-láng**, said of a man fond of being flattered and made of importance. **sio hé-thoà^n**, to make charcoal.

tēng-thoà^n, good hard charcoal, such as is bought in the shops. **phà^n-thoà^n**, very soft charcoal, not bought from the shops (sometimes bought from distillers), but simply half-burned wood from a fireplace, extinguished by covering up, and kept for use.

thô-thoà^n, coals. **thô-thoà^n-bê**, broken down coals or cinders. **mûi^n-thoà^n** (R.), coals. **bôe-thoà^n** (r.), id. **lâm-thoà^n**, coals from the south, *e.g.* Swatow, &c.

thoà^n [R. thoat, to escape; to get free; = col. thoah]. **thoà^n-ké**, the strands of a rope or of a plaited queue opening out of themselves.

thoà^n, to spread, as ink on paper, or as a sore or cutaneous disease on the body. **thoà^n-thoà^n**, spreading thus, or gradually shading into each other, as colours that have no marked line of separation. **tit-tit-thoà^n**, to spread more and more (as above). **thoà^n--khì**, to spread, as ink on bad paper, or as when pasting paper, or as ink that was rubbed down the day before. **thoà^n-lâi thoà^n-khì**, to spread more and more on the body, as a cutaneous disease or a sore.

thoà^n-khui, to blot, as ink of itself, or as pencil writing further than was intended. **jī thoà^n-kha**, the stroke made longer than was intended in writing a word. **thoà^n-kha**, id.; said also of spots or stripes on an animal when the colours gradually shade away into each other.

thoà^n khah-ōng, to spread still more, as a cutaneous disease on the body; to spread and grow very luxuriantly, as grass or shrubs; to increase greatly, as population.

si^n-thoà^n, to spread, multiply, and increase, as a family or race. **thoà^n-nn̄g**, to spawn or produce eggs in great abundance, as fish or insects.

pêh-thoà^n, diphtheria.

thoah (R. that), an otter. **hái-thoah**, id. **tsúi-thoah**, id.

thoah-niá^n, a collar for the neck made of otter's skin.

thoah (C. theh). **thoah-se**, the sole. **thoah-se-hí**, id.

thoah — **cheh-thoah** (r.), = tsau-that, to waste, abuse, or use lavishly.

tsöh-thoah (Cn.), to waste or spend lavishly; to abuse in using, as money or things. **tsöh-thoah-mn̍gh** (Cn.), to waste things. **tsöh-thoah-kang** (Cn.), to spend labour or time wastefully.

thoah — **siū boâ-thoah**, to pass through much experience of the world, especially hard experience, by being thrown on one's own resources. **keng-kè boâ-thoah**, id. **kham--tit boâ-thoah**, able to rough it and bear toil, as a strong man; strong and fit to stand rough usage, as cloth, or as an implement or article of furniture, &c.

thoah, to wash, as rice, by rubbing it between the hands with little water. **thoah-bí**, to rub rice between the hands with a little water, so as to clean it (this is the first washing of rice; the second is "thoā"). **thoah--liáu tiòh-thoā**, after washing the rice by rubbing it should be rinsed.

thoah ko-á-hún (T.), to rub with the hands rice flour mixed with sugar, for making a sort of cakes. **thoah-ko-á** (T.), those cakes.

thoah [R. thoat, to escape; to get free; = col. thoà^n; perhaps some phrases belong to the following word]. **ū-tháu-thoah**, knowing when to be firm and when to yield, *e.g.* splitting the difference of price. **bô-tháu-thoah**, unyielding and obstinate; doggedly keeping to what one has said at first.

ōe-thoah--tit, the difficulty can be avoided, or the matter can be shelved, *e.g.* can avoid paying the money, or doing the unpleasant or inconvenient thing asked. **thoah-tit-kè**, able to get out of the difficulty; to pass the time of ague without the usual ague fit; to avoid or get safely through a danger, difficulty, serious trouble, or severe sickness that had seemed hopeless.

thoah [R. tho, to drag or draw along; to procrastinate: = col. thoa; cf. also the preceding and following words].

thoah--kè-khì, to put off, as a payment when it falls due. **chit-jit thoah-kè chit-jit**, to put off day after day, as payment of money due, or as something that we ought to do; day after day getting no better, as sickness. **bóng-thoah bóng-kè**, getting on with difficulty, as a poor man barely able to make his way; or as a sick man who does not call a doctor, but just bears his sickness as well as he can.

kap-i-thoah, to make difficulties or delays so as to avoid doing or paying what he asks, esp. by false excuses. **khit-i-thoah**, to fail in the attempt to collect expenses, or to recover a debt from him at the due time.

thoah [same as previous word?], a drawer; to draw along, as a drawer or sliding door or window.

thoah-thang, sort of squinting (v. thang).

thoah-khui, to pull open, as a drawer. **kha**

thoah-khui, to open one's legs wider. **kha thoah-khui teh-khiā**, standing with one foot out from the other. **toh-kha thoah-khui**, pull out the movable leg of a table. **kha thoah-khah-khui**, open your legs wider.

thoah--chhut-lâi, to draw out, as a drawer, or as the sliding lid of a box. **tò-thoah--chhut-lâi**, to open a drawer from the inside, as a secret drawer.

thoah-lin, the knob or round handle of a drawer. **thoah-leng**, id.

mn̂g-thoah, a sliding door. **thang-á-thoah**, a window shutter that is drawn along horizontally.

àm-thoah, a secret drawer. **toh-thoah**, a drawer in a table. **toh-kūi-thoah**, a drawer in a sort of small table. **tû-thoah**, a drawer in a clothes-press or standing cupboard. **bîn-chhn̂g-thoah**, a drawer in a bed.

thoân [R. toân, to transmit; to hand down; to propagate; to deliver a message; = col. chhoân; and by change of tone, "toān," historical records], to transmit: to hand down, as doctrine by teaching or by preaching; to summon, as a man who is not apprehended like the common people, *e.g.* a graduate or the head man of a town; (Cn. sometimes "toân").

siong-thoân, to transmit one to another, as trade secrets or ancestral wisdom. **siong-thoân--ê**, handed down from former generations, as medical art or as trade secrets. **sè-tāi siong-thoân**, id. **lék-tāi siong-thoân**, handed down from generation to generation. **saⁿ-thoân**, to transmit one to another, as news or as customs, &c.

liû-thoân, to hand down, as a tradition or custom, from age to age; tradition or old custom. **ûi-thoân** (R.), tradition handed down from ancestors. **tsó-thoân**, handed down from ancestors, as a property or as a trade secret. **pì-thoân**, secrets handed down from one generation to another, as in some arts, manufactures, &c.

thoân-sû, to continue the line of male posterity. **thoân-chéng**, to have descendants; to leave male posterity. **thoân-ūi**, to transmit the throne to the successor.

thoân-ōe, to translate language verbally, as interpreter before a mandarin. **thoân-keng** (C. chhoân-kiong), an interpreter in a yamun.

thoân-lēng, to deliver or make known a military order given by his superior officer, as a smaller officer or soldier. **thoân-sùt** (R.), to deliver a message. **thoân-lô**, to give information by beating a gong.

thoân-toaⁿ, to send out notices, as to members of an association (v. toaⁿ). **hông-gān thoân-su**, the bird called "hông-gān" can carry letters afar. **thoân-tiâⁿ**, to enter a complaint at a yamun on a day which is not one of the usual days. **thoân-tōe** (R.), to hand along through several hands, as letter or essay (v. tōe).

thoân hē-lâng-tsai, to make known to people, as news, regulations, &c. **chit-chhùi thoân-chit-chhih**, to spread from mouth to mouth, as a report. **thoân miâⁿ-siaⁿ**, to spread abroad, as a man's good reputation. **thoân-miâⁿ seh-siaⁿ**, to make a man's bad reputation widely known. **thoân-bûn--lâi** (r.), learned only from others.

thoân-kàu, to teach, propagate, transmit, or proclaim doctrine committed to us. **thoân kàu —**, to transmit to —. **thoân tō-lí**, to transmit, proclaim, teach, or preach doctrine. **thoân-tō**, id.; also (X.), a preacher. **thoân-pò** (R.), to proclaim or spread abroad, as doctrine.

thoân [R. toân, a globular mass; a lump; globular; united; harmonious; to surround; to inclose; = col. toâⁿ, thn̂g, nn̂g].

thoân-thoân-îⁿ, = toân-toân-îⁿ, unbroken, as a family none of whom has died. **thoân-oân** (R.), id. (v. oân).

phô-thoân, a sort of round cushion for kneeling on (v. phô). **pat-thoân**, a circular flowered pattern often worked on silk. **pat-thoân-khe**, id. **pat-thoân-khe ê bé-koà**, a jacket made of flowered silk with this pattern.

thoân-thoân ûi-tsū, surrounding in a circle, as a crowd, or as police or besiegers (v. ûi).

thoân-liên, a method of organizing the people of the several districts of a town, so as to guard against disturbances (v. liên).

thoàn [R. to work by melting or heating in the fire, to practise, experienced], to purify in the fire, as gold; to prepare by gradual heating in the fire, as medicine. **kè-thoàn**, to be purified in the fire, as gold; not said of silver, which is "kheng." **thoàn-liēn** (r.), to try or purify with fire, as gold. **kè-thoàn-liēn**, to be thoroughly experienced in a matter.

thoàn soan-lô, to polish an incense vessel of fine brass by heating it and rubbing very bright.

thoàn (R. toān). **thoàn-jī**, the seal character, generally used on seals, also much used in ornamental inscriptions cut on stone and in title-pages of books. **téng-lô-thoàn**, a form of the seal character in which each word has three long legs like a tripod (v. téng). **chin chhó, thoàn lē**, four usual forms of Chinese characters.

hiong-ien thoàn-chhut pêng-an jī, the smoke of incense forming the shape of the words "pêng-an" (peace and quiet), a good omen.

thoat (R. id., = col. thoah). **thoat-lī**, to escape: to escape from; to get off. **thoat lī-lī**, to escape thoroughly; to escape far away. **thoat-lī-khi-hn̄g**, id. **thoat-bōe-lī**, unable to get off. **thoat-sin-lī**, to get out of the way, so as to avoid imminent danger. **thoat-sin**, to escape; to get off or get free. **thoat-sin-tsáu**, id. **thoat-tsáu**, to escape or run away, either rightly or wrongly. **tsáu-thoat**, to escape and get safe off. **thoat-tô**, to run away; to abscond. **tô-thoat**, id.

hoat-thoat, to sell off speedily at a sacrifice, as when selling off stock, or as some contraband article; to escape secretly; to help another to escape. **khit--i hoat-thoat**, to have your man escape from you, whom you thought you were sure of catching and holding.

mėhⁿ thoat, the pulse gone, as of a dying man.

thoat-siók, different from other people (v. siók).

thoat-hoân, not to be absorbed in the world's affairs; to die, as a Bud. priest. **thoat-hoà**, easy-minded, not anxious about adverse circumstances; cheerful in temper, not particular about ceremony. **sá-thoat**, having a kindly, friendly, sociable manner; pleasant to have business dealings with; pleasant as an acquaintance. **thiau-thoat** (R.), easy-minded, not anxious about danger or trouble. **chhiau-thoat**, easy and unconstrained in manner; not particular about ceremony; not anxious or troubled about affairs; also (R.) to rescue souls from the Buddhist hell, so that they are again born into the world.

thoat-thò (C.), = A. thiet-thò, dispensing with ceremony, circumlocution, &c.; free and easy in intercourse.

thoe [R. tho, to draw; to drag; to procrastinate; = col. thoa, thoah].

oe-thoe kè-jit, to do almost no work while drawing full wages.

thoe (R. chhai), (C. the: Cn. thöe), a hair-pin shaped somewhat like a spoon, used by women. **thâu-thoe**, id. **kim-thoe**, a gold or gilt hair-pin. **gėk-thoe** (C. giök-the), a hair-pin made of jade-stone.

thöe (Cn.), = khau, to plane. **thöe-to** = khau-to, a plane.

thôe (C.), = A. thē. **thôe-á**, small boils.

thóe [R. thé, body; form; manner; appearance; = col. thái], (C. thé).

tsa-bó-thóe, a feminine manner in a man. **bú-hêng-thóe**, id. **lâm-jîn lú-thóe**, a man with a feminine look and manner. **lâm-jîn lú-thóe; m̄-sí, gō lín niû^n-lóe** (or "in niû^n-lóe"), poor feminine looking fellow, though you don't die you disappoint your mother's hopes (or "he disappoints his," &c.)

thóe-thak, to joke and jeer at a man's faults or defects (v. thak). **keng-thóe**, to give a nickname from a man's personal appearance; to jeer at a man, or talk sarcastically about his looks; to talk scandal about a man's conduct, generally behind his back. **keng-thóe phì-siù^n** (C. keng-thé phé-siè^n), to talk ill of a man behind his back, about his conduct or his personal appearance, esp. about his niggardly ways.

thòe [R. thè, to change; to put in the place of; to substitute; to abolish; instead of; for; in place of; = col. thùi], (C. thè; Cn. thöe, sometimes thö), in place of; instead of; for; to take the place of; to be substitute for.

téng-thòe, to be in place of; taking the place of. **téng-thòe i-ê-kheh**, to fill the vacancy left by him.

thòe-oā^n, to change for another person, as in doing work or taking duty (v. oā^n). **thòe-pê**, to make up a deficiency for another. **thòe-i-pê**, to make up the deficiency for him. **thòe-lâng siók-tsōe**, to make satisfaction or atonement for another's guilt. **thòe-lâng-sí**, to die for a man.

thòe--i khó-lîn, to have compassion on him; to pity him.

sa^n-pái-thòe, to do work or keep watch by turns, while the others rest; to relieve guard by turns, &c.

thòe-sin, a paper image of a man, having his name and nativity written on it, used as a substitute for the man in certain rites, *e.g.* in Tauist rites for keeping away disease and calamity, or in black arts for causing evil.

kiò kau-thòe, the ghost of a drowned man or suicide causing a man to be drowned, or tempting a man to kill himself, so that the ghost may get back again to life, which it cannot do till some one thus takes its place. **liàh kau-thòe**, to succeed in causing a man's death by suicide or drowning, as such a ghost. **tsúi-kúi kiò-kau-thòe**, the ghost of a drowned man doing so, esp. after three years.

thòe [R. thòe, thùi, to retire; to recede; = col. thè].

tsoā-thòe, the cast-off skin of a serpent, used medicinally. **siên-thòe**, the shell of the cicada (am-pò-chê, R. siên), used medicinally.

tsai chìn-thòe, understanding what to do and what not to do in special circumstances (v. chìn). **thòe-pī**, = thè-pī, to keep at a respectful distance (v. pī). **thòe-pi^n pī--i**, to get out of the way so as to avoid him, *e.g.* a mandarin. **lîm-tīn thòe-siok**, to draw back when it comes to be dangerous (v. siok).

thōe [R. lūi, lazy; indolent; sickly]. **thōe-thōe** (C.), = A. thē-thē, dull of apprehension; foolish-looking; wanting in animation, as man.

thóeh (C. thêh: A. thêh, thóeh; Cn. thöeh), to take up with one hand, as a small thing, at least not a large thing. **thóeh--khí-lâi**, to lift up, as a small thing. **thóeh--khì**, to take away in one hand, as a small thing. **thóeh--lâi**, to bring in one hand, as a small thing.

thau-thóeh, to steal, as a small thing that can be taken in the hand (for the phrases used for stealing other things, v. thau).

thóeh-tiā^n, to accept earnest-money.

ôe-thóeh, a small bit of cloth at the heel of a shoe for pulling it on, as on the shoes of women, children, and soldiers. **kak-thöeh** (Cn.), a horn shoe-lifter.

thóeh (Cn. köeh).

keng-thâu thóeh-thóeh, the shoulders lean and high, as naturally so, or from opium-smoking, &c. **kek thóeh-keng**, to shrug the shoulders.

thoh (cf. thuh).

thê-thoh, a fish like the "bé-ka," but somewhat larger, brought salted from the north.

thóh — **chiú-thóh**, a sort of jar with a stroop for spirituous liquor. **chiú-thóh-á**, a smaller sort.

thóh (cf. thúh).

thien-thóh, acting in an absurd way, such as feigning madness or pretending to be drunk, as bad fellows in low company. **thien-thien thóh-thóh**, talking, walking, or acting in wild, extravagant, absurd, or swaggering way, as if drunk or feigning it; telling incredible yarns or talking absurdly like a drunk man. **thien-thóh ê-ōe**, such absurd and ridiculous talk. **kóng thien-thóh**, to talk in that absurd extravagant way.

thóh-thóh (C.), = A. thúh-thúh, foolish; stupid. **gōng-thóh** (C.), id.

thok [R. thò, to envelop; a cover or wrapper; to mend; to rehearse; = col. thuh], (T. thuh).

thok kéng-á-hì, to make a sort of play or show somewhat like a magic-lantern.

thok phôe-ang (C.), another sort.

thok — **thok-pit-á**, a sort of small bird kept by children.

thok (cf. thuh, tuh).

thok koái^n-á, to lean on a staff or feel the way with it.

thok [R. a bag, = col. lok, lak].

thok báng-á-hun, to press into long bags the stuff used for burning to drive away mosquitoes, done by pushing it in with a stick.

thok (cf. thuh, thà, tuh, túh), to pick, as the teeth; to pick out of a hole, as what stops it up; to make a hole or wound, as with the point of a sharp knife.

thok-khí, to pick the teeth. **thok chhùi-khí**, id. **chhèng-thok**, a ramrod. **khí-thok**, a tooth-pick. **phah-khí-thok**, to irritate a man intentionally; to stir up his bile.

thok-tiá^n (C.), = A. thuh-tiá^n, to stir up the food frying in a frying-pan.

thok [same as previous word? cf. thuh].

thâu-thok, = thâu-thuh, a sort of two-pronged ornament for a woman's head.

thok [R. to commission; to intrust; to depend or trust on; to make excuses for declining], to commission; to intrust with, as a message or a piece of business. **thok-tiōng**, id. **iong-thok**, id. **chiok-thok**, id.

pài-thok, to ask courteously to do a commission, as a friend. **hù-thok**, to intrust to a man's care, as things, or money, or child. **thok-ke**, to intrust one's own son to a guardian to take care of and educate him when he becomes an orphan. **tsoán-thok**, to intrust to another a message or business that was intrusted to us. **gō-thok**, to have one's confidence misplaced; to put mistaken confidence in a man. **thok-lâng-khì**, to intrust or engage a man to go to give a message or execute some commission for us. **thok-kià pān-hè**, to commission a man to buy and bring goods for us from a considerable distance.

thok jîn-chêng, to ask a man to ask a favour for us from a third party. **thok sè-thâu**, to engage a man's influence for managing an affair. **thok-hok**, I enjoy good fortune through your favour, a polite phrase said esp. in answer to "how do you do?"

hē-sîn thok-pùt, to pray and vow to the spirits and Bud. idols.

thok-bāng, to give instruction by a dream, as the spirit of an idol or of an ancestor. **thok-lán-bāng**, to give us instruction by a dream. **thok i-ê-bāng**, to give him instruction by a dream.

thok sū-kè, to make false excuses for not doing what we are asked or told to do; to assign false reasons or pretexts for our desire to do something or to go somewhere. **the-sū thok-kè**, id. **the-thok**, to decline taking or executing a commission, and put it off on another, esp. by a false excuse (v. the).

thȯk [R. to read aloud; to study; = col. thȧk]. **kò-gán put-tsài-thȯk**, able to repeat after reading once. **chhong-chiên khùn-khé-thȯk**, to study very diligently at the window (v. chhong).

thong [R. thóng, the whole; to rule; the chief].

thong-kiōng, in total.

thong [R. soup; hot water; = col. thng, thn̂g], the ancient emperor Tang or T'ang, the founder of the Shang dynasty. **thong hoát-kiét**, Tang conquered Kieh.

thong [R. tông, the sound of a drum]. **thong-ké**, a sort of drum suspended from the neck. **sam-thong-ké**, a band of music that plays at the meal-time of a high mandarin; also used at some special rites by the people. **toā-sam-thong**, id.

thong (R. id.), the sound of drumming. **thong-thong**, id. **thong-thong-thong**, id.

thong [R. tong, water; sound of water; or R. tsong, sound of water]. **thong-thong-háu**, the sound of water.

thong [R. name of a plant; also written with the following character].

thong-chhó, a plant that grows in Formosa, from the pith of which rice-paper and artificial flowers are made, Aralia papyrifera; also, a cooling diuretic medicine (Clematis?). **bȯk-thong**, a similar diuretic medicinal plant (Clematis?).

thong [R. to go through; to perceive clearly; to communicate with, as road or person; to have dealings with, esp. underhand or improper; successful, current, to pervade, the whole, complete; = col. thang, thàng], all through, pervious, ingenious; all right, as a plan; the whole of —; all over —; a great beam of a roof. **thong**, that is good, very good! as a plan. **thong--lah**, id. **m̄-thong**, not suitable, as a plan. **sim m̄-thong**, much perplexed and unable to think out a proper plan. **bô-thong**, not suitable, as a plan; very dull and unintelligent, as a man who can hardly be made to understand a matter. **bōe-thong** (r.), not passable, as a road. **kà--liáu lóng-bōe-thong**, cannot understand though taught long. **kà--liáu ōe-thong**, will become intelligent if taught sufficiently.

thong-khì, causing a thorough draught, as by opening a door or making a good flue; comfortable feeling of body, *e.g.* after getting a good sneeze, or as by the use of medicines taken like snuff.

thong-koan, to remove a feeling of discomfort (*e.g.* dyspeptic or bilious feeling) by the use of a medicine taken like snuff. **thong-koan-soá^n**, a medicine taken like snuff. **thong-koan-sán**, id.

thong-koan iá-bē-kè, not having yet read so much as to be able to compose essays or to read books which he has not seen before. **kè-thong-koan**, to have got the length of being able to compose essays and to read any ordinary book easily. **thong-koan kè-liáu**, id.

thong-thàu, intelligent; quick of apprehension. **thong-tát** (r.), to understand thoroughly. **thong-thiet**, intelligent and acute; understanding thoroughly (v. thiet).

cheng-thong, skilful at some special sort of work or affair. **lêng-thong**, very acute and discerning; skilful and wise. **ū-pièn-thong**, ready and able to accommodate one's plans and actions to the circumstances; versatile (+).

sîn-thong, the power of a spirit, idol, or other supernatural being, as shown in wonderful changes and miracles. **sîn-thong kóng-tāi**, the power of the spirit (or idol, &c.) is very great. **sîn-thong kóng-toā**, id. **tién sîn-thong**, to manifest great supernatural power; said also of a man showing his special ability in some one particular, *e.g.* his special superiority in some business, art, or handicraft. **gâu pièn-sîn-thong**, versatile; good at adapting one's self (rightly or wrongly), and one's plans, words, or actions to the circumstances. **gâu pièn-siēn-thong** (T.), id. (+).

heng-thong (R.), to be prosperous.

thong-thi^n-ē, all under heaven; the whole empire (v. thi^n). **thong-kok**, the whole kingdom. **thong-koe**, the whole street. **thong-ke** (C.), id. **thong-ke**, the whole family or household. **thong-kɛ** (C.), id. **thong-sin**, the whole body. **thong-si-kòe**, everywhere; all around.

thong-poā^n, all of the same sort; all alike, as goods; but also used generally. **thong-poā^n sī àn-ni^n**, all are alike or of the same sort. **thong-thong sī àn-ni^n**, it is constantly so; all of them are so. **thong-tông**, all alike or unitedly (v. tông).

thong-hêng, universally prevalent or current; the same in all places; used, or can be used everywhere. **thong-ēng**, such as can be used everywhere for common use by several parties, interchangeable. **bōe-thong-ēng--tit**, such as can be used only in particular places. **thong-chheng**, general title or polite way of addressing people, *e.g.* chek, peh, toā-ló, &c.

thien-hā thong, an instrument for picking locks.

thong-sū, an interpreter (v. sū). **thong-su**, an almanac. **thong-si** (C.), id.

thong-ti, to inform; to give information. **thong-siông**, to send a despatch to a superior mandarin, as an inferior mandarin does. **thong siau-sit**, to give information of any sort. **thong--chit-ē**, to give a secret hint or a piece of secret information. **thong-hong**, to give secret information; having a draught of air or wind through it; well aired, as a house. **thong koan-chiet**, to have underhand dealings with officials. **thong-koa^n**

to have a personal interview with a mandarin. **thong-chhàt**, to have communication or connection with rebels or robbers. **thong-óng**, to be on intimate terms with, often with bad or questionable characters; passable, as a road (v. óng). **kau-thong**, to have intercourse with, as with improper characters, or for improper purpose.

chhoàn-thong, to conspire with enemies against one's employer or associate. **phah-thong-thò**, to plot or intrigue together against a man, &c. (v. thò). **thong-bê**, to make a plot or conspiracy together (v. bê).

su-thong, to have illicit, traitorous, or lascivious intercourse together. **thong-kan**, to have lascivious intercourse.

siong-thong (r.), having direct communication, as two rooms or houses by a door or short passage. **iú-bû siong-thong**, to have things in common or assist one another with each other's possessions. **tsûn-chiah siong-thong**, vessels constantly going back and forwards.

thong-hē-kūi, a counter at the door of a shop. **thong-lē-kūi**, id. **thong-siū**, putting each hand into the sleeve of the other.

thong-niûⁿ, the great beams on which the rafters rest for a flat roof or floor; the great horizontal beam which connects the ends of the sloping beams of a couple for a gable-roof. **toā-thong**, id. **jîn-jī-thong**, the tie-beam connecting the ends of the beams of a couple for gable-roof. **chhiâ-thong**, the sloping beams of a couple for a gable-roof. **hoâiⁿ-thong**, id.

thông (T.), sound of a stone in deep water (cf. col. tom, tôm).

thóng [R. the whole; to rule; the chief; = col. thong].

thóng-hat, to govern; to rule; to have authority over a region, as a mandarin.

it-thóng, the whole, as of a ruler's dominions. **tāi-chheng it-thóng**, the Chinese empire, as governed by the Manchoo or Ta-tsing dynasty.

tɵ-thóng, the Tartar lieutenant-general or major-general at the provincial capital; the next in rank to the Chiong-kun or Tartar general.

thóng — **tí-thóng**, to be used as a substitute for another person or thing, generally only temporarily, or as a worse used instead of a better from the pressure of circumstances; *e.g.* as a worse man put clandestinely in the place of a better; or as a man put in to make up the number though unfit for the work; or as a piece of work that may perhaps just be allowed to pass though quite inferior; or as an article taken in payment of a debt though not really worth so much; or as part payment counted as a full discharge. **té-thóng** (C.), to use temporarily as a substitute though not so good. **chhòng-ōe lâi tí-thóng**, to make excuses or objections either quite false or greatly exaggerated. **chhòng chit-ê-sū kap--i tí-thóng**, to make a false charge to set off against a charge made against us.

thóng [same as previous word?]. **thé-thóng**, bodily appearance, deportment, or general character; general form or state of an affair; the special customs, old usages, or superstitions followed on particular occasions, *e.g.* on boy going to school, &c. **i--ê thé-thóng**, his general character, manner, or deportment. **hit--ê thé-thóng sī tsáiⁿ-iūⁿ**, what is the general state of that matter?

tsòe thé-thóng, to work at a piece of work just for the appearance, but really doing almost nothing, *e.g.* just to get the wages or to avoid blame.

thóng (cf. thé), to protrude, used as an affix to numbers, meaning "somewhat more than —."

thóng-chhut, to protrude; to project.

thóng-thâu, to put out the head; to project, as a mast seen far off, or as a house higher than others, or built on higher ground; or as characters written rather higher than the rest so as to look out of line and ugly; or as the end of a stroke in writing projecting beyond the others so as to look ill. **khah-thóng-thâu**, projecting beyond others, as high house or character out of line.

nn̄g-pah thóng-thâu, rather more than 200, *e.g.* one or two more. **nn̄g-pah thóng**, id. **saⁿ-tsàp-thóng**, one or two more than 30.

tsát thóng-thóng, packed very full and tight; overloaded, as stomach (v. tsát).

thòng [R. pain; grieved; distress; miserable; to feel for; to love; = col. thiàng, thiòng].

thòng-hūn, to hate exceedingly; to abhor; to hate and loathe, either as one's own wickedness or another man's. **thòng-hīn** (C.), id. **thòng-sim hūn**, to hate with all one's heart, as one's personal enemies.

thòng (Cn.) **thòng-tī**, = A. chhòng-tī, to annoy; to maltreat.

thōng, to pile up in a pile, as books, coins, bowls, plates, &c.; a pile of such things.

thōng-chheh, to lay books in a pile, one above another.

chit-thōng-chheh, a pile of books. **chit-thōng-chîⁿ**, a pile of copper cash. **chit-thōng-gûn**, a pile of dollars laid one above another.

thû (cf. tû, tsû), (Cn. T. thū).

u-thû (Cn. T. ū-thū), ignorant, thick-headed, and foolish, as in study or business; so dull of apprehension and so doggedly fond of his own way that he cannot be made to learn the right way to act, and so spoils matters. **u-u thû-thû**, id.

gû-thû, = gû-tû, stupidly dogged and coarse in manner (v. tû).

thû [R. to dig; to hoe; a hoe; = col. tî, tû], (C. thî; Cn. T. thū), to hoe, as ground.

thû-thoáⁿ, to cut up, as weeds from the fields, or grass and small plants for fuel from the hills, with the hoe. **thû-chháu**, to hoe up weeds, grass, or small plants in this way.

thú [R. chhú, a pestle; a sort of stick or baton for beating things]. **hâng-mô-thú**, a baton for conquering demons, carried by the idol úi-tô.

thú [R. tsú, a bag for clothes; to stuff clothes with cotton; a surname], (C. thí; Cn. thū), a surname.

thuh (cf. thoh).

thô-thuh, = thô-thoh, a good sort of fish, somewhat like the "bé-ka," said to come from Formosa.

thuh [R. thò, to envelop; a cover or wrapper; to mend, as clothes or paper; to rehearse; = col. thok], to mend, as a dress, by putting in a piece below, so that the old remains; to paste on a single thickness of paper, as for the purpose of strengthening a weak place or to mend a tear, or to make a beginning for pasting more thick and strong.

thuh chit-têng, to mend a dress by putting in a piece below (without cutting away the old), and sewing down the edges, so that the new piece does not appear.

thuh tī-piah--nihⁿ, to paste an additional thickness of paper on a smaller piece of paper which it is desired to strengthen, and then paste the edges of the new piece on a wall so as to stretch the whole smooth.

thuh éng-á (T.), = A. thok kéng-á-hì, to make a sort of play or show with a lantern. **thuh phō-kâu** (T.), another sort of play or show (lit. with the leather monkey).

thuh [R. thok, to carry on the palm; to bear up; to prop up, as with a support or prop, or with the hand; to lift up and hold up high to shew it, as on the hand or on a pole.

thuh--khí-lâi, to support by a prop, *e.g.* to support an awning by a stick or bamboo.

thuh-koâiⁿ, to hold up high, as on the hand or on a pole, *e.g.* a tiger's body, or the head of a slain enemy. **thuh hē-lâng-khoàⁿ**, to lift up high to exhibit it. **hê-siūⁿ thuh-poah**, a Buddhist priest supporting a tambourine or cymbal on a bamboo pole resting on his head or palm, &c.

thuh koáiⁿ-á, to lean upon a staff. **thuh chhiú-bé**, to try each other's strength by pressing against one another's palms. **thuh-chhiú**, to lean on the hand, as the head; to support with the hand. **chhiú thuh--leh**, support or ward off with the hand. **chhiú thuh-thâu-khak**, the head bent to the side, and the upper part of the head resting on the hand. **thuh chhùi-ē-táu**, to support the chin on the hand.

thuh [same as previous word? cf. col. tuh], to feel the way with a stick.

thuh (cf. tuh), to give secret information of a man's faults, esp. to his employer or superior.

tng-bīn thuh--i, to tell a man's faults openly to his face before others.

thuh lâng--ê thâu-lō, to tell a man's faults so as to make him lose his situation.

thuh (cf. thok, tùh, thak), to make a hole larger, as with the point of a knife in carving wood; to smooth away anything rough from a surface with the point of a knife, &c.; to pick, as the teeth; to loosen or dig up dirt, as with a hoe.

thuh-khí, to pick the teeth. **thuh thê-kha**, to loosen and remove dirt on the floor.

thuh-tiáⁿ, to stir up things frying in a frying-pan.

thuh-á, a sort of straight hoe or spade. **chhèng-thuh**, a ramrod.

thuh (= thok, same as previous word?).

thâu-thuh, = thâu-thok, a two-pronged ornament for a woman's head. **kō-thuh** (Cn.), = A. kè-á, the hair ornament worn by women.

thúh (C. thóh).

thúh-thúh, naturally stupid-looking and wanting in animation; very dull, quiet, and reserved in manner, not seeming to understand or take any interest in what we say. **thúh-thúh ná hàu-lâm**, looking as dull and spiritless as a man in deepest mourning for his parents.

gōng thúh-thúh, wanting in ability.

thui (R. the), a ladder.

lâu-thui, a ladder. **lâu-thui-chí**, the steps of a ladder. **ōe-lòh lâu-thui**, there is a way open to set the matter straight without too much sacrifice of one's dignity.

tó-thui, a fixed wooden stair with broad flat steps, as distinguished from a mere ladder.

to-thui, a ladder of swords. **chiūⁿ to-thui**, to climb a ladder of swords, as Tauist sorcerers. **tek-thui**, a bamboo-ladder. **soh-á-thui**, a rope-ladder. **tiàu-thui**, a hanging-ladder, as at a hatchway or gang-way. **hûn-thui**, scaling-ladders. **giâ-kang-thui**, a ladder made of one longitudinal piece of timber only, with the steps nailed across it and projecting on each side (like the feet of a centipede). **siak-tháng-thui**, a small instrument just like a ladder, inside the tub used for threshing grain, on which the heads of the grain are struck in that mode of threshing.

náⁿ thiⁿ-thui--nihⁿ, like a ladder to the sky, said of something extremely high. **náⁿ teh-peh thiⁿ-thui**, like climbing a ladder to the sky (said of some extremely difficult matter).

thui [R. chhui, thui, to push away; to push from one; to decline; to shirk responsibility; to make excuses; to resign; to calculate; to infer; = col. the: perhaps should be divided into two words], to rub with a long and gentle movement, as for the removal of pain or disease, either simply with the hand, or with some medicinal preparation, or as in shampooing; to rub plaster smooth with a smooth stone; to varnish a second time so as to make smooth; to get a separate account opened for us at the land-tax office under a new name (hō-thâu-miâ), instead of being classed along with others under one name.

thui-kuih, to rub with long and gentle, and with short and hard rubs, as in shampooing.

thui-úi (C.), (R.), = A. chhui-úi, to excuse one's self, esp. by an excuse more or less false.

thûi (R. sûi), the weight of a steelyard. **téng-á-thûi**, the weight of a small steelyard. **chhìn-thûi**, the weight of an ordinary moderate-sized steelyard. **niūⁿ-thûi**, the weight of a large steelyard.

liû-seng-thûi, a sort of weapon used in ancient warfare (v. seng).

thûi [R. a metallic hammer]. **thih-thûi**, an iron hammer. **thih-thûi boâ chiâⁿ-chiam**, said of a poor man overcoming great difficulties and getting rich. **lō-thâu, taⁿ teng-sim; lō-bé, taⁿ thih-thûi**, appearing easy at first, but very difficult at last, as a heavy burden on a long road, or as an affair that becomes troublesome and dangerous.

teng-á-thûi, a hammer for small nails.

thûi [R. a pestle; a wooden mallet, club, or thick stick], a pestle; a stick for beating a drum or gong, &c.; a strong, thick, wooden stick for beating with; a long club; a strong, round, wooden lever.

chióh-thûi, a stone pestle. **lûi-thûi**, a pestle for a mortar. **náⁿ lûi-thûi**, as bare as a pestle, said of the shaven head of a Bud. priest (+). **khū-á-thûi**, a sort of pestle for a mortar. **cheng-khū-thûi**, a pestle for a large rice-mortar worked by the hand.

géng-thûi, a sort of pestle for a hand-mortar; a roller for dough. **phah chit-thûi** (C.), to roll out the dough once into a flat cake, as in preparing for making maccaroni.

chhâ-thûi, a wooden pestle, beetle, or heavy stick for beating things. **in-chiūⁿ-thûi**, a beetle for beating clothes in washing. **lōng-thûi**, a thick stick for beating indigo in the vat. **he-thûi**, a stick for mixing mortar. **khút-thûi**, a stick for stirring paste.

ké-thûi, a drum-stick. **lô-thûi**, a stick for beating a gong. **lô-á-thûi**, do. for small gong. **cheng-thûi**, stick for striking a bell or a bossed gong. **khók-thûi**, stick for beating the "khók" used by watchmen like a rattle. **pók-piang-thûi**, the stick used for beating the string of the bow used in beating cotton.

tú-thûi, a pole for supporting a man's burden while he takes a rest. **khǹg-á-thûi**, a short, round, thick carrying-pole.

kim-kòng-thûi (T. kim-koe-bōng), a sort of mace

72

carried before mandarins, Kujin graduates, and some idols; also, an ancient instrument of war.

bák-thûi, a very large, round, thick stick of China ink.

kha-bák-thûi, a short, round, thick, heavy stick for beating the ankles in punishment or in examination in court.

chê-bî-thûi, a strong heavy club about a man's height (lit. level with eyebrows). **chhit-chhioh-thûi**, a sort of club or heavy pole, seven feet long, for use in war or for keeping off robbers. **tn̄g-jī-thûi**, a club or strong pole, twelve feet long.

óh-thûi, to learn the exercise with the long pole or club. **kà-thûi**, to teach it. **thûi-á sai-hū**, a man who teaches it. **hē sí-thûi**, to strike very violent or murderous blows, as with a club or with the hand; to attack violently by plots, or intrigues, or by accusation in court.

kong-kùn-thûi, a man far too sharp to be swindled or imposed upon, often with the meaning that he cheats others. **hê-siū^{n}-thûi**, said in joke of a Bud. priest in allusion to his shaven head (+).

thûi (cf. thut, thút), having the point become blunted by use, as a fine brush or hair-pencil. **thûi-thûi**, id.

thúi (R. id.), the thigh. **kha-thúi**, id. **téng-thúi**, id. **ē-thúi**, the lower leg. **toā-thúi**, the thick fleshy part of the thigh. **thúi-lûn**, the thigh-joint. **thúi-thâu**, the buttocks; the hips. **thúi-thâu-bah**, the flesh at the buttocks. **thúi-thâu-lông**, a large boil at that place.

lok-thúi, thigh full of deep sores (v. lok). **phoân-thúi**, sitting with the legs drawn up under the body (v. phoân).

chiáh i--ê thúi-sin-bah, wasting his capital by living upon it.

khò-thúi, leggings (v. khò).

chêng-thúi, the fore-quarter or fore-leg of an animal, as cut up; *e.g.* a shoulder of mutton. **āu-thúi**, the hind-quarter or hind-leg of an animal, as cut up. **ien-thúi**, a bacon ham. **hé-thúi**, id. **gû-á-thúi**, a leg of veal. **sì-thúi**, the four quarters of an animal, as of pig, sheep, goat, cow, or fowl, when cut up. **lòh tsòe sì-thúi**, cut up into the four quarters, as quadruped. **tsām tsòe sì-thúi**, do., as a fowl.

thùi [R. thè, to change; to put in place of; to substitute; to abolish; instead of; in place of; = col. thòe], to change, as its feathers or leaves; to repair by putting in an entirely new piece at the old joining; to substitute one thing for another, especially clandestinely put a worse in place of a better.

thùi-mn̂g, to moult and get new feathers, as a bird. **thùi-mê^{n}** (C.), id. **thùi-hióh**, to change the leaves, as a tree or shrub.

pó-thùi, to repair by taking out the whole of a bad piece by the original seam or joining, and put in an entirely new piece. **thùi-tóe**, to renew a vessel's bottom. **thùi-ńg**, to put in a new sleeve.

thùi-oā^{n}, to cheat by substituting a worse thing for a better that had been promised; to give an uglier or worse girl as bride instead of the better one who was agreed on; to take the place of a student, and write for him at the examinations; to put in a new piece by the old seam, so that no patching is seen, and it is about as good as new, *e.g.* a new leg on a table, or a whole new piece in a dress.

sa^{n}-thùi, to change deceitfully and fraudulently, as person or thing. **thau-thùi**, secretly put a bad article or person in place of a good one. **khit--lâng thau-thùi**, to be cheated thus. **khit--lâng thùi--khì**, id. **phái^{n} thùi-hó**, bad fraudulently put in place of good. **sái thùi-pau**, to swindle by giving a bad or worse article in place of the good one that was agreed on, *e.g.* worse than the sample; to show a false bridegroom or bride much better or better-looking than the one who afterwards is really married.

thūi [R. tūi, to fall down; to hang down heavily], to hang down heavily, as a pocket with a weight in it. **thūi-thūi**, hanging heavily, as a weighted pocket or bag, &c.

thūi-tāng, heavily weighted and hanging down, as a pocket; to fasten a weight on a curtain so that it may hang down evenly.

lūi-thūi, causing obstruction or impediment, as a heavy weight about one's dress, or as family or business keeping one from going far from home [or does this phrase belong to the next word?].

thūi [R. lūi, to involve in trouble or responsibility].
thoa-thūi, causing impediment, as troublesome business or numerous family. **khit--i thoa-thūi**, to be involved in trouble by him, *e.g.* by a relative or by a man for whom we have stood security.

thām-thūi, to be very awkward and embarrassing, as an ill-arranged or bulky load inconvenient to carry; cumbrous and embarrassing, *e.g.* having pockets full of bulky or heavy things; to be deeply involved, as by owing debts to many persons, or by having to fulfil obligations for persons for whom we have stood security. **khit--i thām-thūi**, to have a debt owed us by him which he cannot pay, so that we are much inconvenienced. **sì-kòe thām-thūi--lâng**, to be deep in debt to a number of persons. **bó-kiá^{n} thām-thūi**, getting deeper and deeper in debt from unavoidable expense of wife and family.

thûi^{n} [R. thôan, to transmit; to hand down; to propagate], (C.), to hand down from generation to generation (only said in some few phrases).

thûi^{n} (C.), = A. thn̂g, a roundish lump, as of earth. **chit-thûi^{n}-thô**, a lump or clod of earth.

thùi^{n} (C.), = A. thǹg, to take off, as clothes, or as hair, &c.

thùi^{n} (C.), = A. thǹg, to exchange, as loads; to buy (as a favour) from a friend or neighbour.

thūi^{n} (C.), = A. thn̄g, to warm up again, as food.

thūi^{n} (C.) **mûi^{n}-thūi^{n}**, = A. mn̂g-thn̄g, a great bar right across a door, either upright or transverse.

thūi^{n} (C.), = tūi^{n}, thn̄g, said of a portion of a leg, arm, &c. (only used in some phrases: in others "tūi^{n}" and "thn̄g" are used).

thun (R. id.), to swallow; to swallow up, as another's property; a nest of pottery or frying-pans, that fit into each other.

ka-nn̄g-thun, a whole nest (usually five) of smaller and larger articles of the same shape, so that all the smaller lie inside the largest, as some kinds of pottery, and as frying-pans or rice-boilers. **chit-thun**, one such nest of larger and smaller articles one within another.

ka-nn̄g-thun, to swallow whole. **pa-lun-thun**, to bolt one's food. **kóng-ōe pa-lun-thun**, to talk in a very indefinite indistinct manner. **thun--lòh-khì**, to swallow down. **thun-lòh-âu**, id. **thun-bōe-lòh**, unable to swallow; unpleasant to swallow; unable to defraud a man as we intended. **thun bōe-lòh-âu**, id.

thun-chiah, to devour. **hiau-thun**, to swallow up another's money or property wrongfully.

thun-noāⁿ, to swallow one's spittle (v. noāⁿ) **thun-kim**, to swallow gold leaf, as a means of suicide. **thun-kim--sí**, id.

thun-lún, to bear patiently. **thun-siaⁿ lún-khì**, to repress one's feelings, anger, and voice, as in the presence of a high superior or of a powerful enemy. **lún-khì thun-siaⁿ**, id. **lún-khùi thun-siaⁿ**, id. **jím-khì thun-seng**, id.

ū-thun-thò͘, understanding well how much to say and what not to say (v. thò͘).

thun (R. id.), a tree with large shining pinnate leaves, used medicinally for indigestion; said to live several thousand years (Cedrela Sinensis?) **thun-chhiū**, id. **thun-kun**, its root, used medicinally. **thun-gê**, its buds, edible.

thun (R. id.?)

un-thun, very dirty; filthy. **un-thun-kúi**, you filthy imp or wretch! said in scolding.

thûn [R. thun, black].

ien-thûn, soot. **thûn-ai** (C.), id. **tiáⁿ-thûn**, the soot that gathers on a frying-pan or rice-boiler. **chhéng-thûn**, to sweep the dirt from the beams, roof, idols, &c., in the 12th moon.

thûn — **thûn-thûn**, having a dull or indistinct colour; having lost the gloss, or having never had it.

thûn — **thûn-bú**, a barren woman.

thûn [R. tûn, a young pig]. **ti-thûn-á**, a half-grown pig. **káu-thûn-á**, a half-grown dog. **gû-thûn-á**, a young cow. **niáu-chhú-thûn**, a half-grown rat.

thûn-á (T.), a half-grown or young quadruped in general.

gín-á-thûn, a boy just about reaching manhood, about 14 or 15 (cf. lâng-tńg).

thún (T. tún).

bú-thún, short and stout. **bú-thún bú-thún**, id. **pûi-thún**, id.

thún [R. chhún, stupid]. **gû-thún**, = gû-chhún, stupid; foolish.

thún [R. chién, to tread, = col. thut], (Cn. thún, tûn), to tread or trample on. **thún-táh**, id. **lām-sám thún**, to tread or trample carelessly.

thùn — **ùn-thùn**, stupid; dull of comprehension; confused in mind; stupid at business.

thūn [R. tiên, thiên, to fill up; to make up a deficiency; to pay], to fill up, as with earth, mud, sand, rubbish, &c.

thūn-thô͘, to fill up with earth. **thūn--lóh-khì**, to empty into a pit or hole, as earth. **thūn-pîⁿ**, to fill up ground till it is level. **thūn-tōe**, to fill up ground with earth, rubbish, &c.; ground that has been thus filled up; made ground. **thūn-hoāⁿ**, to enlarge a dyke or sea-wall, making it higher or thicker. **thūn-chíⁿ**, to fill up a well.

tit-tit-thūn, to be constantly losing money in a business (lit. to be constantly filling up with earth). **tit-tit thūn--lóh-khì**, id.

thut (R.), to degrade from office; to lose an office, as mandarin (cf. col. lut).

thut — **saⁿ-thut-lō͘**, to miss one another by going different roads.

thut [R. chién, to tread, = col. thún]. **thut-táh** (r.), = thún-táh, to trample on.

thut, to rub hard with the hand, as in washing out a stain, or washing off ingrained dirt, or rubbing between the thumb and fingers, *e.g.* rubbing off a skin or pellicle; to rub with the foot, as one foot rubbing the other in washing, or as when washing a tub full of potatoes with the feet. **thut-lut**, id., either with hand or foot. **thut-thut**, id. **ēng-chhiú thut**, to rub hard with the hand, as in washing out indurated dirt; to rub between finger and thumb, as in taking the skin off ground-nuts. **thut-kha**, to rub the feet together, as in washing the feet, &c. **kha thut-thut**, id.

thut-kha thut-chhiú, to struggle violently with hands and feet, as child unwilling to be carried.

thut [R. to lose the hair, bald, = col. thu̍t, lut.]

thut-mn̂g, having lost the hair of his head. **thâu-khak thut-thut**, head bald.

thut-lû (lit. bald ass), said in scolding a shaven Bud. priest.

thu̍t [R. thut, to lose the hair, bald, = col. lut: cf. col. thûi].

pit thu̍t-bé, the point of the hair-pencil has become blunt, as by use. **pit-bé thu̍t-thu̍t**, id.

thu̍t (to be dislocated or put out of gear, to have a miscarriage, &c.)

thu̍t--khì, to get dislocated, as a limb; to slip out of the hands, as a thing not firmly held, or as an animal tied too loosely. **thu̍t--chhut-khì**, to get dislocated; to get out of joint, as joint of machine or of furniture. **thu̍t--chhut-lâi**, to get out of gear, as a machine; to have a miscarriage. **thu̍t--tsáu**, to slip out of its place, get out of joint or out of gear, as wheel or machine; to let slip out of our hand, as animal held too loosely; to let a pen or instrument in the hand slip out of place, so as to do harm unintentionally.

phah-thu̍t, to put out of gear or out of its socket by accident; to make a joint in furniture or in a machine start from its place. **chī-chūi phah-thu̍t**, who put it out of gear or out of joint?

táh-thu̍t, to make a false step so as to give one's self a shake or a twist, as by missing a step on a ladder or stair, or as in stepping down on a hill or uneven road to a lower level. **kha táh-thu̍t**, id.

thu̍t-lûn, to dislocate, as a limb. **thu̍t tn̂g-thâu**, internal piles protruding. **thu̍t-sin**, to have a miscarriage. **thu̍t-the**, to cause abortion or to have a miscarriage.

thu̍t (same as previous word?)

thu̍t-kui, having the ridge of the roof in the same line with that of a larger house, but on a lower level; said also of eaves carried out at a lower level with an angular connection at the change of level, a very common arrangement for the broad eaves of temples.

thu̍t-pui, built at the end of a house, in the same line, but with the ridge of the roof lower. **thu̍t-puiⁿ** (C.), id.

thu̍t-lí, the lining of a dress too full, so that it shows outside at the edges.

thwa, **thwà**, **thwā**; better, thoa, thoà, thoā, *q.v.*

thwaⁿ, **thwâⁿ**, **thwáⁿ**, **thwàⁿ**; better, thoaⁿ, thoâⁿ, thoáⁿ, thoàⁿ, *q.v.*

thwah, better thoah, *q.v.*

thwân, **thwàn**; better, thoân, thoàn, *q.v.*

thwat, better thoat, *q.v.*

TS.

Ts is by many written **ch**; but the two sounds are quite distinct. The sound of the **s** however in **ts** must not be made too strong.

In the lower series of tones, the sound sometimes changes to Dz, especially in Tung-an (Tâng-oa^{n}) and Chin-chew.

tsa — **tsa-bó͘**, a woman (v. bó͘).

tsa (C.), = A. ta. **tsa-po͘**, = A. ta-po͘, a man (a male).

tsa [R. dregs]. **a-tsa**, dirty; filthy (lit. or fig.); taking or borrowing things and not returning them.

tsa (R. id.), (C. chɛ). **sien-tsa**, a small red crab-apple from the north, used as a preserve, and also in medicine. **san-tsa**, id.

tsa [R. to investigate], (C. chɛ, chhɛ), a surname. **tsa-mn̄g**, to investigate officially. **tsa-chhat**, do., as messengers of mandarin. **tsa-khoà^{n}**, to investigate, as any one. **tsa-khàm**, to make careful investigation, as mandarin or head-man of place or head of a house. **tsa-giām**, do., as mandarin. **tsa-kiám**, to examine a list or inventory, to see if all be there. **khe-tsa**, to investigate officially and minutely. **sûn-tsa**, to go about the country making investigation, as mandarin. **tsa-sit**, to get at the truth by investigation. **tsa ū-tio̍k-lo̍k**, examine and find full evidence.

tsá [R. tsó], early; ancient; former; when said about the time of day or night, it refers to day-light, not to the time measured by hours. **tsá-tsá**, id., very early. **tsá-oà^{n}**, early and late. **tsá-àm**, morning and evening. **bô-tsá bô-àm**, at any or all hours. **tsá-àm ōe-lâi**, he may be here at any time. **tsá-mńg ōe-lâi**, id. **tsá-mńg**, early or late; morning or evening; before long. **tsá-múi^{n}** (C.), id.

tsá--thâu, very early in the morning. **tsá-khí**, early in the morning. **tsá-khí-thâu**, very early in the morning. **tsá-khí-pn̄g**, breakfast. **chia̍h tsá-khí**, to take breakfast. **chia̍h tsá-tsai**, to abstain from animal food at breakfast. **chheng-tsá**, early in the morning. **tsá-tsúi**, the morning tide. **gâu-tsá**, early up! in very good time. **pàng-tsá**, very early in the morning. **thàu-tsá**, id.

thàn-tsá, as early or soon as possible. **iáu-tsá**, still early; plenty of time yet; before the time. **tsá-chiâ^{n}**, soon accomplished. **tsá-koâ^{n}**, the winter is early. **tsá-joa̍h**, summer early. **tsá-sí**, may you die soon! **tsá-sí tsá-hó**, the sooner you die the better! **tsá-kiá^{n}**, a child of very young parents. **tsá tek-tsú**, will have a son at an early age (said by fortune-tellers). **tsá-tang**, the early or summer crop of rice, about 5th or 6th moon. **tsá-bí**, rice of the summer crop. **tsá-iû**, id., esp. from Formosa.

tsāi-tsá, long ago. **kó͘-tsá**, ancient; anciently. **tsá-chêng**, formerly, as some years ago. **tsá-chiân**, id. **tsá-bō͘** (C.), id. **tsá-jit**, formerly; on some former day. **tsá-nî^{n}**, in a former year. **tsá-hui^{n}** (C.), yesterday.

tsá-liâm-ngá (Cn.), a very short time ago. **tsá--kan** (Cn.), long ago; early in the morning.

tsà (R. id.), (C. chè), deceitful; feigning. **kan-tsà**, deceitful; intriguing; treacherous. **káu-tsà**, id. **tsà-gûi**, very deceitful. **tsà-hâng**, to make feigned submission, as rebels. **lé to, jîn pit-tsà**, a man too polite is sure to be a hypocrite. **bâi-bêng tsà-sú**, to conceal one's name and pretend to be dead. **bâi-bêng tsà-sí**, id.

tsā (R. tso̍k). **tsā-jit**, yesterday. **tsā-bō͘-jit**, id. **tsā-bō͘ tsá-khí**, yesterday morning. **tsā--ê tsá-khí**, id. **tsā-bō͘-tsài** (T.), id. **tsā-hng**, yesterday evening. **tsā-mî^{n}**, last night. **tsā-ē-po͘**, yesterday afternoon. **tsā-jit-tàu**, yesterday at noon.

tsâ^{n}, to put out one's arms, so as to prevent a man from falling, or striking, or escaping; to put out a light, as a sudden gust of wind. **tsâ^{n}--khí**, do.; to make a diversion in a conversation, as to prevent a dispute between two others.

tsá^{n} [R. tsám, to cut off], to cut off straight and even; to strike with the edge of the hand; also (T.), to cut corn before it is ripe, as for one's own use. **tsá^{n}-sa^{n}**, to cut off the end of a coat or dress. **tsá^{n} chhiú-ńg**, to cut a sleeve shorter. **tsá^{n}-piah**, to cut a square hole in plaster of wall, in order to plaster it anew.

ēng chhiú-to tsá^{n}, to strike with the edge of the hand. **tsá^{n}--chit-ē**, id. **tsá^{n} poà^{n}-io**, to strike at the waist.

poà^{n}-tsá^{n}, a sword about two feet long, with blade and handle about equal length. **lô-hàn-tsá^{n}**, a dress having the upper and lower parts of different stuffs.

tsá^{n} [R. chéng, to set in order]. **tsôe-tsá^{n}**, = tsôe-chéng, neat and even; all in right order, as furniture, teeth, &c.

tsà^{n}, to dry in the sun for a short time. **tsà^{n}-jit**, id.

tsā^{n}, to scoop out or scoop up, as water, meal, &c. **tsā^{n}--khí-lâi**, id. **tsā^{n}-tsúi**, to scoop up water, in larger quantity than "iú^{n}." **hoâi^{n}-tsā^{n}**, to get great gains suddenly.

tsah, to place things about one's person under one's dress, gen. about waist or lower part of dress; (but in the breast is "kûi"); to pull up, as sleeves or trowsers; to tuck up, as curtains; to assist in lifting, holding, or carrying a sedan.

tsah-to, to carry a sword, concealing it under one's dress. **tsah-mih^{n}**, to carry things under one's dress. **thau-tsah**, to conceal things furtively about one's dress. **tsah-kiō**, to steady the poles of a (mandarin's) sedan, as his attendants do; to help to lift the sedan, &c.

pih-tsah, to prepare sleeves of dress and legs of trowsers for a journey or work. **tsah-tsah pih-pih**, id. **tsah-khò͘**, to pull up trowsers by pulling up the waist above the cord that girds one. **tsah khò͘-thâu**, id.

kûi-kûi tsah-tsah, to carry some things (or child) in bosom, and other things placed in other parts of dress; to carry in one's dress in general. **bô-chhái lāu-bú kûi-kûi tsah-tsah**, not worth your mother's toil in nursing you.

tsa̍h, a portcullis; a hurdle or such thing used as a barrier; to fasten the feet in sort of stocks. **tsúi-tsa̍h**, flood-gates; a sluice. **tsúi-tsa̍h-mn̂g**, the gate of it. **ti-tsa̍h**, a low barrier at mouth of pig-sty. **tek-tsa̍h**, a low bamboo barrier (as at a gate, or on a road) to keep cattle, &c., from straying. **tn̂g-tsa̍h**, the wooden transverse partition across the central hall of a large house. **mn̂g-tsáh**, a low barrier in a door, to keep domestic animals from straying. **mn̂g-tsáh-á**, a small half door, as a wicket in a shop. **poàⁿ-tsáh-mn̂g**, id. **siâⁿ-mn̂g-tsáh**, a portcullis.

tsáh-í, a folding chair with leather bottom.

liáh khi-tsáh--teh, seize and put his feet through holes in a wall, or in a sort of stocks, till ransomed.

tsáh (R. chiet, = col. tsòeh), to cut or chop down small; to screen off; to screen; to hinder; to help, as in a lawsuit. **tsáh-tn̂g**, to cut down small, as medicinal plants. **tsáh-chháu**, to chop straw small, as in order to mix with lime, &c. **chháu-tsáh**, a machine for chopping straw. **io̍h-tsáh**, a machine for chopping medicines small. **tsáh-to**, a knife on a pivot for chopping medicines; also, a fixed knife on a block having its edge up, on which coopers smooth the staves of barrels, &c., in making them.

tsáh-tiâu, to ward off effectually, as by door, shield, &c. &c. **tsáh-hong**, to screen from the wind. **tsáh lâu-tsúi**, to put a net across a stream or tidal channel. **tsáh-lō͘**, to obstruct the way, as robbers, or as troops. **tsáh lâng--ê thâu-lō͘**, to get the start of a man, so as to get the place he was trying for. **tsáh lâng--ê ōe-thâu**, to interrupt or stop a man who is talking.

jia-tsáh, to screen from view, &c. **âⁿ-tsáh**, to screen (a party in a quarrel) from danger. **noâⁿ-tsáh**, to hinder by stretching out one's arms, as in separating combatants.

tsáh-ké, to separate the divisions of an essay.

tsáh, to cook (as a fowl) in a large quantity of melted fat, almost swimming in it, but not so much as "chìⁿ."

tsai (R. id.), to transplant; to plant out; young plants for transplanting; also said of some animals. **poâⁿ-tsai**, to transplant. **tsai ké-chí**, to plant out fruit-trees. **tsai-chèng**, to sow or transplant; to plant in general. **tsai-pôe**, to tend, as plants or children; to bring up and train. **chit-jit soá-tsai, saⁿ-jit khiā-n̂g**, a man does not at once get settled well in a new situation.

tsai-hoe oāⁿ-táu, superstitious rites for the cure of barrenness in a woman (v. táu).

hî-tsai, young fish put in a pond to breed. **koe-tsai**, little chickens kept for breeding. **chià-tsai**, young sugar-cane plants. **chhài-tsai**, young plants of vegetables. **hoe-tsai**, young flowering plants, as from a nursery.

tsai [R. che, to push over].

tò-thâu-tsai, falling head foremost; said also of things. **tò-tsai--lo̍h-khì**, id. **thap-thâu-tsài**, id.

tsai (R. id.), calamity; troubles; afflictions. **tsai-ē**, id. **tsai-eh**, id. **tsai-iong**, id. **tsai-hō** (R.), id. **tsai-hāi**, id. **tsai-lān**, id. **tsai-ē lîm-sin**, calamity come upon (him). **siau-tsai kóe-eh**, to ward off calamities. **siau-tsai kái-eh**, id.

tsúi-tsai, calamities by means of water. **tsúi-tsai hóe-eh** (C.), calamities by water or fire. **thien-tsai**, Heaven-sent calamities. **thien-tsai hêng-hō**, Heaven's judgments coming in the form of sore calamities. **thien-tē hêng-tsai**, id. **siū-tsai**, to meet with calamity. **lêng-hó kau-chièn, ku-pih siū-tsai**, when the strong go to war with each other weak neighbours suffer.

tsai (R. ti), (C. tsaiⁿ), to know, as a fact; to feel; to have a sensation. **tsai--kiò**, to know. **tsai--kioh**, id. **goá tsai-tsai**, I know it very well. **thiⁿ--chai, tōe--tsai**, Heaven and earth know it is true. **lí--tsai, goá--tsai**, you and I know it.

tsai-iáⁿ, to understand it well; skilful (v. iáⁿ). **tsai-soah**, to know when to stop, when one has enough (v. soah). **tsai-iau**, to feel hungry. **tsai-khó**, to feel calamity; to feel miserable. **tsai-thiàⁿ**, to feel pain. **khí-thiàⁿ, tsai khí-thiàⁿ-lâng**, a man with toothache can sympathize with another who has it.

m̄-tsai, not to know; don't know; not having anything to do with the matter. **m̄-tsai-thâu**, I beg your pardon; I did it unintentionally. **m̄-tsai thiⁿ-tōe**, not able to perceive anything, as in unconsciousness (v. thiⁿ). **m̄-tsai-chhíⁿ**, very soundly asleep. **lâng m̄-tsai**, to be insensible, as from a fall or illness; also, men do not know. **m̄-tsai-tńg**, will take no advice, and will not reform (v. tńg).

tsai [R. to fast more or less; = col. che]. **chiáh-tsá-tsai**, to abstain from animal food at breakfast only. **chiáh-tn̂g-tsai**, a long course of vegetarianism. **tsai-niûⁿ**, vegetables and condiments used by Buddhist priests and vegetarians.

hoà-tsai, to beg for food, as Buddhist priests. **ū-tsai-cheng**, to have the rule of entertaining travelling certified priests, as certain endowed monasteries do. **tsai-tiúⁿ**, an official who has charge of paying the rewards at the "Gio̍k-pín" examinations at Amoy. **tsai-kài bo̍k-io̍k**, to fast and perform ceremonial ablutions.

tsâi — **sng-tsâi**, a mulberry (v. sng).

tsâi [R. materials, = col. chhâi]. **lâng-tsâi**, bodily appearance. **chiâⁿ-lâng-tsâi**, a fine-looking man. **jîn-tsâi**, personal appearance, mien, carriage, and air. **jîn-tsâi chhut-chiòng**, tall and very good looking. **hó-jîn-tsâi**, id. **bô-jîn-tsâi**, producing no talented men, as a place; far from good-looking, as a man. **m̄-chiâⁿ jîn-tsâi**, ugly in appearance, as a man. **jîn-tsâi phí-úi**, small and ugly looking (v. úi). **soán jîn-tsâi**, to choose men of good ability, or good looking, for situations, or as son-in-law. **kéng kiáⁿ-sài-tsâi**, to choose a man of good ability or good-looking for a son-in-law. **bô-koaⁿ-tsâi**, wanting the dignified manner suitable for a mandarin. **m̄-chiâⁿ-tsâi**, ugly or out of proportion, as man or thing. **sin-tsâi súi**, graceful and beautiful, as young person. **hó-sin-tsâi**, id. **m̄-chiâⁿ sam-seng-tsâi** (lit. not fit to be used as a sacrificial offering), he is not fit to be employed on an important matter. **thê-poe m̄-sī sam-seng-tsâi** (T.), said of a man of very small ability.

io̍h-tsâi, raw materials of medicines.

tsâi-chit, natural ability (v. chit); this last phrase is sometimes assigned to the next word.

tsâi (R. id.) **tsâi-tiāu**, talent; ability. **tsâi-chêng**, id. **hó-tsâi-chêng**, having good abilities. **tsâi-lêng**, power. **hó-tsâi**, good talents. **lāi-tsâi**, well acquainted with the classics, and having intellectual ability. **goā-tsâi**, skill in talking, and politeness, and managing matters, or in poetry, &c. **kháu-tsâi**, eloquence.

tiām-tsâi, staid quiet manner. **chiét-tsâi**, clever and skilful. **tsâi-tsú**, a man of ability (a. wealth). **hù-kùi tsâi-tsú-siū**, wealth, honour, talent, posterity, and long life; the five blessings.

sam-tsâi, the three powers, heaven, earth, and man. **siù-tsâi**, the lowest grade of graduates, a Sew-tsae or B.A. **lê-tsâi**, a male slave, usually bought or hired for a limited time; an abusive epithet. **pák lê-tsâi**, to hire or buy, as a slave for one's self.

thio-tsâi, the 64th radical as written at the side (v. thio). **kiah-tsâi**, id.

tsâi (R. id.), wealth. **chî^n-tsâi**, id. **tsâi-lī**, id. (v. lī). **tsâi-pėk**, id. **tsâi-pó**, treasures of all sorts. **chin-tsu tsâi-pó**, pearls and other precious things. **kim-gûn tsâi-pó**, gold, silver, and other precious things.

ka-tsâi, household wealth. **hoâi^n-tsâi**, gains got by good luck or very suddenly, generally by somewhat improper means. **hoat-tsâi**, to grow rich. **chìn-tsâi**, id. **phoà-tsâi**, to waste one's wealth. **phoà-tsâi sún-teng**, to waste wealth and lose sons, &c. (v. teng). **tsâi-sè-lėk**, wealth, influence, and ability (v. lėk). **chiau-tsâi-ông**, the god of wealth.

tsâi-hù, an account-keeper on shipboard. **tsâi-tsú**, a man of wealth (s. talents). **tsâi-khì**, success in making money. **hó-tsâi-khì**, do., said in good wishes. **sa^n-pn̄g tsâi-khì**, to join capital in trade. **liên-tsâi hé-kì**, joint-stock partnership, as in a business firm.

bē-tsâi hāi-bēng, to plot for wealth at the expense of life (v. bēng). **tsâi tōng-jîn-sim**, money excites desire. **jîn bû kan-khó-kè, lân-tek sè-kan-tsâi**, no gains without pains.

tsâi— **tsâi-hông** (C.), = A. chhâi-hông, a tailor.

tsâi [R. chê]. **tē-tsâi**, the navel. **pak-tsâi**, id. **tē-tsâi-toà**, the navel cord. **tn̍g-tsâi**, to cut it on birth of infant. **tu-tsâi**, to try each other's strength by pushing against one another by a wooden bar placed against the body of each near the navel.

cheng-tsâi, the hollow of the boss of a gong.

tsái— **bȧk-tsái** (C.), = bȧk-sái, tears.

tsái (C.), = A. tái, dregs, *e.g.* **che-tsái**; **iû-tsái**, = A. che-tái, iû-tái, &c.

tsái, several words, as tsú-tsái, tsái-siòng, &c., sometimes written "tsái," are better "tsái^n" (*q.v.*)

tsài (R. id.), again; over again. **koh-tsài**, id. **tsài-koh**, id. **têng-tsài** (r.), id. **tsài-sa^n**, several times. **tsài-sam tsài-sì**, carefully several times over and over. **kò-gán put-tsài**, able to repeat after reading once. **kò-gán put-tsài-thȯk**, id. **tsài-kóng**, to say again. **tsài-sím**, to examine the parties again in court. **tsài-kiû**, to pray again.

tsài (R. id.), to support; to bear up; to carry or transport, as a vessel or carriage, &c. **tsài-hè**, to transport goods. **tsài-chî^n tsài-hè**, to carry a very valuable and gainful cargo, as opium, &c. **chih-tsài-bōe-tiâu**, to have a load too heavy to be carried; said also of a man in weak health.

kì-tsài, written down.

tsài— **bîn-ná-tsài**, to-morrow. **mɛh^n--tsài** (C.), in the morning; this morning. **tsā-bē-tsài** (T.), yesterday morning. **tsài--tà^n-sî** (T.), in the morning.

kū-nî^n peh-tsài (T.), long past and out of date, as an affair.

tsài (R. tsai), an enclitic particle. **kai--tsài**, happily; by good luck; fortunately. **put-chí kai--tsài**, how very fortunate!

tsāi [R. to be in; in; = col. tī], steady, as a chair, or anything set down firmly. **tsāi-tsāi**, steady and firm, as a thing, or as the mind; in one's right mind, having command of one's self, without fear, &c. **bô-tsāi**, not steady, as a chair or stepping-stone, &c. **khiā-tsāi**, to stand firmly and steadily. **khiā-m̄-tsāi**, to stand unsteadily. **hē-m̄-tsāi**, to set or lay down unsteadily. **ké-khi-tsāi**, make it steady by putting something underneath. **táh-khi-tsāi**, plant the foot firmly (v. tȧh).

tsāi-ngé, calm and collected; self-possessed, as before a superior, or as in danger. **hāi-tsāi**, firm and steady in character; calm and collected in manner, not afraid in danger; said also of a man who is *too* stiff, *e.g.* not rising when a visitor enters (s. animal). **tsū-tsāi**, steady; self-possessed; without fear; in right mind. **tsū-tsū tsāi-tsāi**, id. **an-jiên tsū-tsāi**, comfortable in mind and safe and not afraid. **an-jiên tē-tsāi** (C.), id.

sit-tsāi, truly. **chīn-tsāi**, exceedingly —. **hiēn-tsāi**, present; now; here present (v. hiēn).

put-tsāi, no matter. **chhut-tsāi-lí**, just do as you please, gen. with the idea I warn you you had better not. **kù-tsāi-lí**, id. **peng-koân tsāi-chhiú**, having authority from others (as company or relatives) to manage a common matter as we please. **pîn-tsāi-goá**, just as I may please (v. pîn). **bē-sū tsāi-jîn, sêng-sū tsāi-thien**, man purposes but Heaven accomplishes (v. thien).

tó-tsāi-chhn̂g, bed-ridden. **tsāi-àn**, the case pending. **tsāi-iâ^n**, to be on duty in yamun of naval mandarin, not on board. **tsāi-sek-lú**, a virgin. **tsāi-lāi**, included; inclusive (v. lāi). **tsāi-goā**, not included. **kûn-thâu, ko-ko tsāi-siōng**, though very skilful there are others still more so, said originally of boxing. **tsāi-si^n**, in this life. **tsāi-tsá**, long ago. **tsāi-giȧh**, having a regular engagement, as man employed in a hong for a long term (opp. "kià-kha"). **tsāi-tōe-lâng**, persons belonging to the place or very long resident in it. **chhiâng-tsāi**, constantly present at a place. **tsāi-phì^n-sái**, to sail with wind on quarter and sails full (v. phì^n). **tsāi-tsúi** (C.), of course, said in answering (v. tsúi).

só-tsāi, a place. **bô-só bô-tsāi**, no place. **bû só put-tsāi**, everywhere present. **tùi-tû-goā siōng-tsāi**, balance in hand. **mn̂g-lâu sui-phoà, ki^n-kó goân-tsāi** (though the gate-tower is ruined the watch-drum remains), said of a man who has become poor, but must still pay ceremonial expenses.

tsāi, cargo; a cargo. **tāng-tsāi**, a heavy cargo; heavily laden, as ship. **toā-tsāi**, id. **boán-tsāi**, a full cargo; full load (v. boán).

tsāi-chî^n, money for freight; freight. **tsāi-gûn**, id. **lám-tsāi-jī**, a bill of lading, as in foreign vessels. **khàu-tsāi**, to deduct from freight, *e.g.* to pay for damage. **khàu i-ê-tsāi**, id.

tá^n-tsāi, to make a rough estimate of whole cargo, as in buying it. **hē-tsāi**, to put cargo on board. **khioh-tsāi**, to be taking in cargo, as vessel. **sià-tsāi**, to unload, as ship. **pau-tsāi**, to charge in the lump for a large lot of goods carried. **ìn-tsāi**, to collect goods for a vessel, or ship cargo for others, as a third party (v. ìn). **ún-tsāi** (T.), to accept a freight, as ship's officer or shipping agent. **oá-tsāi**, to intrust goods (as to hong or commission-agent) to be shipped. **hē--lâng oá-tsāi**, to receive goods to be shipped, as hong.

tsāi [R. tsāi, tí, a reptile; a fabulous animal; = col. thoā]. **hāi-tsāi**, a fierce fabulous animal like a lion or "lion-unicorn," said to be very faithful and very good at killing traitors; it is embroidered on the breast of high military mandarins (s. steady, in). **hāi-tsāi-pó**, the breast ornament of a high military mandarin.

tsai^n (C.), = A. tsai, to know.

tsâi^n (cf. tsâh). **tn̂g-tsâi^n-āu**, the back half of the central hall of a house (v. tn̂g).

tsâi^n (T.), = A. chêng, front; before.

tsái^n (R. id.) **tsú-tsái^n**, to rule; a ruler. **tsái^n-**

siòng, prime-minister. **ip-tsái^n** (R.), the mandarin of a Hien or district.

tsái^n — **liām-tsái^n**, to practise songs. **chit-thò-tsái^n**, a set of two or three songs.

tsái^n [R. chím, = col. thái; cf. sím], (C. tsoá^n; Cn. tsüi^n). **tsái^n-iū^n**, how? **tsái^n-á-iū^n**, id. **àn-tsái^n-iū^n**, id. **bô-àn-tsái^n-iū^n**, nothing special; did not do anything, esp. wrong. **bô-tsái^n-á-iū^n**, id. **bô-kàu tsái^n-iū^n-phái^n**, not very bad; not much to blame or find fault with. **bô-su kàu tsái^n-iū^n**, to lose in the contest, but not suffer or lose much.

beh-tsái^n, how? **beh-tsái^n-ōe**, how can (you) ever! **tsái^n-thang** —, how can —?

tsái^n [R. chí, a finger, = col. tsńg].

chhiú-tsái^n, a sort of thimble; also (r.), the fingers. **kha-tsái^n**, the toes. **tsáp-it-tsái^n**, a man with an extra finger or thumb. **kí-tsái^n**, the fore-finger. **jī-tsái^n**, id. **tiong-tsái^n**, the middle finger. **kí tiong-tsái^n**, to point with the middle finger, counted a very vile obscene action, as representing the male. **bû-bêng-tsái^n**, the ring-finger. **bé-jī-tsái^n**, id. **láu-á-tsái^n**, id., said in joke. **bé-tsái^n**, the little finger. **bé-tsái^n-á**, id. **tsái^n-thâu-á** (T.), = A. tsńg-thâu-á, a finger.

chiam-tsái^n, a thimble. **tâng-tsái^n**, a brass do. **thih-tsái^n**, iron do. **phê-tsái^n**, leather do. **pè-tsái^n**, a thimble of metal with cloth outside.

tsài^n (T.), = A. chèng. **ka-tsài^n**, sort of mat of grass or straw.

tsak — **tsak-tsak**, crowded. **tsak--teh**, id. **ak-tsak**, inconveniently crowded and disorderly, as a lumber-room (s. annoy).

tsak, to annoy; to vex; to trouble. **tsak-tsō**, id. **tsak-tsô**, id., I will trouble you, sir! **ak-tsak**, sad, anxious, or uncomfortable in mind (s. crowded). **bòh--tit tsak--goá**, don't trouble me. **sim-koa^n tsak-tsak**, heart grieved and anxious.

tsák (C. tsáuh).

tiòh-ka-tsák, slight obstruction by something in the throat or nose; removed by coughing, swallowing saliva, or blowing the nose. **tò-ka-tsák**, id.

tsák (r.?), = chhák, to pierce.

tsák [R. tsók, a clan; a family]. **m̄-sī i--ê chéng-tsák**, not his own son, said in disparagement of an adopted son or of wife's unfaithfulness. **hó-chéng-tsák**, said of a good or good-looking son.

tsam (R. id.) **am-tsam**, dirty, unclean, filthy, of body or mind. **am-sí-tsam**, very filthy.

tsam, to eat or suck up by a proboscis, as bees, flies, or ants do. **phang tsam-hoe**, the bees feed on the flowers.

tsam [R. a hair-pin, = col. chiam]. **tsam-hoe**, to put flowers in cap or hair, especially tinsel flowers in cap of new graduate. **tsam-koà**, to invest a new-made graduate (Sew-tsae) with sash and gilt or tinsel flowers (v. koà). **tsam** (Cn.), = A. chiam, a hair-pin. **kim-tsam** (Cn.), = A. kim-tsam, sort of flower. **kō͘-tsam** (T.), a hair-pin. **thng-sí-tsam** (T.), one shaped like a spoon.

tsam (Cn.), = A. chiam, a needle. **kan-tsam**, mariner's compass, &c.

tsâm (R. chhâm). **tsâm-gâm**, firm; strongly made, as table, &c.

tsâm — **phoà-tsâm**, to disconcert and defeat a plan by speaking against it. **phoà-chhùi-tsâm**, id. **phoà-chhùi phoà-tsâm**, id. **phah-tsâm**, id., or to prevent a quarrel by seasonable words.

tsám [R. to behead; to cut, = col. tsá^n, tsām]. **tsám-tn̄g**, to cut asunder with one blow, as of knife, axe, or sword; to forsake and have done with. **kap i tsám-tn̄g**, to have no more to do with him. **tsám-chháu tn̄g-kun**, in cutting up weeds remove the root, said of exterminating an enemy's family; also of cutting off all intercourse with a man, or of breaking off a bad habit. **tsám-bōe-tn̄g**, cut not quite asunder; to try to get free from some engagement, &c., but not able.

ū-tsám-tsóeh, acting with rapidity, wisdom, and decision (v. tsóeh).

tsám-tiâu, inscription telling the crime for which a man is put to death. **tsám ká, kun-liû-tô͘**, beheading, strangling, and three sorts of banishment. **tsám-siú**, to behead. **kam-tsám**, to preside at and witness an execution. **kam-tsám-koa^n**, the presiding mandarin at an execution. **kam-tsám-siú**, a lower official for the same. **sien-tsám hō͘-tsàu**, first behead and afterwards report to emperor.

tsám — **tsám-bé-to** (C.), a crooked sword about two feet long. **khau-liâm tsám-bé** (C.), id.?

tsám — **tsám-jiên**, very —.

tsàm (R. id.) **tsàm-làm**, to dip (as foot) in water.

tsàm, to stamp with the foot. **tsàm-kha**, id. **tsàm-khoà^n**, to try the strength (as of plank or floor) by stamping on it. **tsàm--chih**, to break by stamping on. **tsàm-tôe**, to stamp with the foot. **tsàm-tōe**, to stamp on the ground. **tsàm--chit-ē**, to give one stamp with the foot.

tsām — **lām-lām tsām-tsām**, mixed in confusion (v. lām). **tsām-tsòh**, not uniform, as things; mind anxious and confused (v. tsòh).

tsām (R. id.), a stage on a journey; a resting-place on a road at end of a stage; a division of a subject in oral teaching. **lō͘-tsām**, a stage on a road where there is a rest. **phè-tsām**, a resting-place at the end of a stage of ten lí. **iàh-tsām**, a stage where couriers, horses, &c., are kept. **an iàh-tsām**, to have relays of horses or couriers ready at regular short stages (gen. about ten miles) for important despatches. **khah-tn̂g-tsām**, a long piece of road with no resting-place on it. **koá^n-tsām**, to travel in haste by long stages. **thòg-tsām**, to exchange with another man for part of the journey, as porters and chair-bearers do. **chit-tsām kè-chit-tsām**, one stage after another.

tsām, to push with a pole so as to turn the boat's head round more or less.

tsām (R. tsám). **tsām-thâu**, to behead. **tsām chhiú-tôe hō͘--i**, to make a mark on a document with hand or finger inked. **tsām péh-koe**, to behead a white cock before an idol (esp. Sêng-hông), and burn a written prayer (tiáp) asking the god to kill the offerer if he be guilty.

tsām (R. id.), to chop; to stamp with a stamp; to stamp, as dollars; a chisel or stamp. **tsām--chih**, to break, as by a blow of a chisel. **tsām-tn̄g**, to cut asunder, as by a chisel. **tsām tsòe-tn̂g**, to cut into two parts, as a long thing into two short ones, by such a blow. **tsām-pêng**, to cut (as by chisel) longitudinally into two long narrow pieces. **tsām-tsoá**, to cut the edges of paper even by a blow. **tsām-chheh**, to cut the edges of a book even. **tsām-tià^n**, to cut away the anchor. **tsām-lòe**, to make or sharpen a file.

ná" chióh--nih" tsām-jī, unalterable like letters cut in the rock. **tsām-jī**, to stamp words, as on metal.

ū, tsoè-hó͘ tsām, when he has money he is voracious like a tiger (v. **hó͘**).

gûn-tsām, a stamp for marking dollars. **chióh-tsām**, a stone-chisel. **tsng-tsām**, a cold-chisel for splitting off bits of tiles. **tsoá-tsām**, a knife for cutting large sheets of paper into smaller sheets. **tsoá-chí"-tsām**, a stamp for making the round scalloped holes in idolatrous paper that represent cash. **kim-chí"-tsām**, a stamp for cutting the long wavy lines on idol-paper representing gold. **pû-tsām**, to beat up and renew the wedges for splitting stone.

khám-tsām, a rule. **chiaù-khám-tsām**, according to rule; properly. **bô-khám bô-tsām**, disorderly; not managing well. **kàu hit--ê khám-tsām**, when it comes to that time or state of matters.

tsan (R. cheng), a surname; mand. Tseng.

tsan (R. cheng), a small net that is lifted out of the water to catch the fish; it is usually stretched square on a bamboo frame fastened by a hinge on the bow of a boat or to a sort of windlass on shore; to use this sort of net.

khan-tsan, to draw a net by one man on shore and one man in a boat. **khan tsan-á**, id. **kiáh-tsan**, to raise up a net on bow of boat by walking up the ladder attached, so as to lower the ladder and lift the net. **thó-tsan**, to catch fish by this sort of net. **tsan-hî**, id. **tsan--ê**, fish caught by this sort of net, counted better than those inclosed in large nets (bāng).

tsan — **tsan-á-tsûn**, small boats about the size of a passage-boat, either for trade or for fishing.

tsan — **tsan-tsûn**, a junk of about one to three thousand peculs (tà"), with high sharp stern. **phû-lâm-kiô tsan**, such junks belonging to Phû-lâm-kiô, south of Amoy. **tsan-tsô**, a large boat or small junk (larger than a "khan-hong"), such as ply to the Pescadores, &c. **lâm-tsan**, small junks from the south, esp. Tâng-soa" (Tong-san) or Swatow.

toā-kán-tsan, a sort of war-junk. **sió-kán-tsan**, smaller sort of war-junk.

tsan — **āu-tsan-khí**, the back-teeth; the molars. **āu-piah-tsan**, id. **thâu-tsan-khí**, the front-teeth.

tsan (R. cheng). **kha-āu-tsan**, the heel.

tsân (R. chêng, = col. tsàn), a tier or layer, as of a basket made of several layers; classifier of plans or methods of action; a division of a statement or discourse on doctrine or business affairs. **nā"-tsân**, a horizontal division of a basket. **sam-tsân-bah**, pork having fat and lean in alternate layers. **sa"-sì-tsân ê-hoat-tō͘**, several plans or methods, either successive or contemporaneous. **chit-tsân tō-lí**, one head or division of a discourse on doctrine.

tsân, to stab. **tsân-sí**, to stab to death.

tsân (R. id., = col. chhân). **tsân-jím**, cruel.

tsân (C.), = A. chêng, before. **tsân-ē**, formerly.

tsàn (R. chêng, = col. tsân), one story of a house; one step of a flight of steps or of a ladder. **áu-tsàn**, to make folds or flounces, as on skirt of foreign gown. **kiā-á-tsàn**, steps of a stone stair. **sa"-tsàn-lâu**, third story; a building of three stories. **chhit-tsàn-thah**, a seven-storied pagoda.

tsàn (R. id.), an inscription on a scroll or on a map. **tôe-tsàn**, to write an inscription on a scroll in praise of a person or of an idol. **chheng-tsàn** (R.), to praise.

tsàn (C.), = A. chèng. **ka-tsàn**, a sort of grass-mat.

tsàn (R. id.) **tsàn-sêng**, to assist in accomplishing a purpose, *e.g.* by recommending to favour.

tsàn — **tsàn-khiā**, to stand in order, as people before a mandarin. **tsàn-tūi**, to stand in ranks to receive a high mandarin on his arrival. **tsàn-pan**, to stand in order, as the attendants of a mandarin at a trial, &c.

tsàn (R. chièn). **tsàn-keng**, a storehouse or go-down. **tsàn** (C.), = A. chièn, in several phrases.

tsān (R. tsàn), to help; to aid. **sa"-tsān**, do. **tàu-sa"-tsān**, id. **pang-tsān** (r.), id., chiefly said by foreigners and those who have intercourse with them. **tsān i-āu-chhiú**, give him some assistance (v. **āu**). **tsān-kûn**, to assist in beating a man. **tsān-kang**, to help with labour. **tsān-chí"**, to help with money. **chiu-tsān** (T.), id.

tsang (R. tsong), a low scraggy palm, Chamoerops; its fibrous bark used for making ropes, mats, &c.; brown colour like this stuff. **tsang-chhiū**, that palm. **tsang-sek**, brown colour. **tsang-háh**, sheathing leaves at its joints. **tsang-sui**, rain-coat made of it. **tsang-chèng**, mat made of it. **tsang-kiáh**, wooden clogs fastened with a strip of palm-fibre (v. **kiáh**). **tsang-hu**, small shreds and dust of it when broken down small, used for strewing on floor. **thiah-tsang**, to pick palm-fibre, as for making ropes, &c. **lì-tsang**, id.

tsang (R. tsong), a queue; a tail worn on the head. **ku-tsang**, a woman's queue. **sìn-tsang**, tail on child's forehead. **kak-tsang**, a pair of tails on sides of child's head. **kè-á-tsang**, one do. on side of child's head. **thô-á-tsang** (C.), do. **thâu-tsang**, the queue. **thâu-tsang-bé**, silk end of it. **thâu-tsang-bé-soà"**, the threads used for this. **thâu-tsang-kè**, artificial hair ornament fastened on woman's head. **pī" thâu-tsang**, to plait the tail; to wear a tail. **lâu thâu-tsang**, to grow a tail.

tsang (R. tsong), a mane. **ti-tsang**, hair on back of pig's neck. **bé-tsang**, a horse's mane. **lāu-bé tién-tsang**, said of an old man with youthful vigour.

tsang, to lay hold of, as a man's queue, &c. **tsang--khí-lâi**, to pull out or up, *e.g.* to pull a man out of the water by his queue.

tsang — **chhiah-tsang-hî**, a sort of fish.

tsang (R. tsong). **tsûn-tsang**, a number of junks at anchor together. **pàng-chhut tsûn-tsang**, to let one junk out of the crowd of junks, as one ready to sail.

tsâng, to dash water on person or thing; to sweep away (soil), as a torrent. **tsâng-tsúi**, to dash water on. **tsâng-ėk**, to bathe by dashing water over one's self.

tsâng (R. chhông), a bush; classifier of trees, shrubs, and plants. **chhiū-tsâng**, a tree. **chit-tsâng-chhiū**, one tree. **toā-tsâng**, large, as a plant; to grow large, as a plant. **toā-tsâng-chhiū**, a large tree.

tsáng [R. tsóng, all]. **bong-bô-tsáng**, to search in vain for a clue. **liáh-bô-tsáng**, id. **bô-tè thang-liáh-tsáng**, no way of finding a clue to the affair.

tsáng-kun-thâu, the most important particular in an affair on which the rest depend; the chief manager of a matter. **tsáng-thâu**, to have the chief management (s. tail). **i teh-tsáng-thâu**, he has the chief management.

gē-tsáng-thâu, the divisions of the hair at the root

of the queue; the root or head of anything; the most important point in an affair.

tsáng, an artificial queue or tail. **chhài-tsáng**, the leafy tops of radishes, turnips, &c., when the root is cut off. **chhài-tsáng-á-bé**, id. **tiū-kó-tsáng**, rice-stubble.

tsáng-thâu, the root of a woman's queue (s. all). **soà-tsáng**, to join the false tail to the real one. **thiu-tsáng**, to draw out hairs in order to make an artificial tail.

tsàng, the perpendicular threads or cords in a loom.

thâu-tsàng, a leading man in a place, or in the management of a matter; often not formally appointed, but others follow his lead; the clue or beginning of an affair.

hī^{n} tsàng, the reed of a loom and the perpendicular cords. **hī^{n}-soe khàu-tsàng**, id. **tiàu-tsàng**, the perpendicular cords in a loom which work up and down. **khàu-tsàng**, id. **bē-lòh hī^{n}-se khàu-tsàng** (C.), said of a man putting troublesome obstacles in our way, or of persons not getting on well together.

tsàng (R. tsòng), a confection made of rice, &c., put up in bamboo-leaves. **bah-tsàng**, that confection made of rice and pork. **ki^{n}-tsàng**, do. made with alkali. **pák-tsàng**, to tie it up in the bamboo-leaf. **tsàng-hiòh**, bamboo-leaves for this purpose.

tsap (Cn.), = A. chiap, juice.

tsáp (= chiáp). **tsáp-tsáp-kóng**, to talk incessantly.

tsáp — **tsáp-tsáp-háu**, to smack the lips in sign of displeasure at one's self for a mistake, or of slight displeasure at another, often towards a superior.

tsáp (R. id.; some read "sip"), mixed; confused. **chham-tsáp**, id. (v. chham). **chhap-tsáp**, id. **láp-láp tsáp-tsáp** (C.), id. **hūn-tsáp**, confusedly mixed, esp. of persons. **lâm-lú hūn-tsáp**, men and women meeting together without distinction.

pak-tsáp, having various colours mixed indistinctly; skilful at many things. **tsáp-tsô**, puzzled with many cares. **tsáp-liām**, to talk incessantly or incoherently; to talk in delirium; said in scolding.

tsáp-méh^{n}, feeling anxious, out of sorts, or uncomfortable about many affairs (v. méh^{n}). **tsáp-méh^{n}-hiòh**, various leaves used for adulterating tea. **tsáp-bók-hiòh**, id. **thâu tsáp-méh^{n}-hiòh**, to adulterate tea with them.

tsáp-sek-lâng, men of many different places or trades. **tsáp-mih^{n}**, miscellaneous articles. **tsáp-mih^{n}-toa^{n}**, a catalogue or inventory, &c. **tsáp-hè**, a mixed assortment of goods. **tsáp-hè-toa^{n}**, a list or inventory of goods. **tsáp-sè**, miscellaneous articles, as for sale (v. sè). **tsáp-chhâ**, miscellaneous, small, or odd pieces of various sorts of wood; furniture made by piecing together small pieces of various sorts of wood. **tsáp-chhâ-á-tiàm**, shop for wood and wooden utensils. **tsáp-tsok**, miscellaneous literary compositions. **tsáp-gím**, a bowl of mixed meats (v. gím). **tsáp-chhe-pâng**, a room in a yamun where the constables (chhe) stay. **tsáp-sèng**, containing people of several surnames, as a village. **tsáp-sè^{n}** (C.), id. **tsáp-chhùi ê-seng-lí**, a miscellaneous small business.

tsáp-chéng (vulg.), a bastard (v. chéng).

miā^{n} khah-tsáp, one's fate too heavy (beyond the due mean), so as to have a great many troublesome matters to manage.

tsò-tsáp, = sûn-kiám, the very lowest civil mandarin; rather a depreciating phrase. **tsò-tsáp-koa^{n}**, id. **tsò-tsáp gê-mn̂g**, his yamun.

tsáp (R. sip), ten. **tsáp-hūn** (ten parts), complete; exceedingly (v. hūn). **tsáp-jī-hūn**, quite complete; very best. **tsáp-jī-á**, a small book full of the most absurd stories, and idolatrous and superstitious instructions. **toā-tsáp-jī**, a larger book of same sort. **tsáp-chiok**, complete; sufficient. **tsáp-tsn̂g**, complete.

it-gē it-tsáp, 5, 10, 15, and so on. **tsáp-jī**, twelve. **jī-tsáp**, twenty. **it-jī-tsáp-ê**, between ten and twenty; about ten or twenty. **tsáp-sè**, a little over ten. **tsáp-goā**, a good deal over ten; often about twenty. **it-tsáp-goā**, id. **tsáp-goā-goā**, a long way above ten. **chhut-tsáp**, the days of the moon from 11th to about 14th.

tsat — **tsat-iâ^{n}**, to encamp. **tūn-tsat**, id. **an-iâ^{n} tsat-chē**, id.

tsat (R. chiet, = col. tsoeh), a piece between two joints; a verse; to make due and fit arrangement; classifier of affairs. **chit-tsat-á**, a little bit. **chit-tsat tāi-chì**, just one single matter or affair. **chit-tsat ê-tāi-chì**, this matter. **chit-tsat-sū**, id.

jîn-sim tsat-tsat-ko, the human heart is always ambitiously aiming higher and higher after each advancement.

kun-tsat (C. kin-tsat), very careful or cautious; prepared before for whatever may come. **ū-kun-tsat** (r.), id. **chhim-tîm kun-tsat**, very cautious and wide awake.

tsún-tsat, using in a careful, moderate, or temperate manner, as money, or as food or drink; carefully regulating one's strength, as when walking on a difficult road, or working at delicate work. **ū-tsún-tsat**, id. **bô-tsún-tsat**, using in a careless, reckless, or immoderate manner.

tsat-hoáh, to use a moderate average amount, as of food or of strength. **tsat-sî**, to make one's arrangements to do a thing at the time fixed. **tsat-sî tsat-tsūn**, id. **tsat-sè**, to regulate one's strength, position of hands or feet, and movements very carefully, as in doing any piece of work. **tsat kha-pē**, to take much care of one's steps, as on a difficult road. **tsat kàu tú-hó**, to regulate or arrange it just properly. **tsat--khi m̄-hó-sè**, not well arranged (as above).

kut-tsat, a bone from one joint to the next. **chhiú-tsat**, the parts of the arm between the several joints, esp. the lower arm. **téng-tsat**, the arm from elbow to shoulder. **chhiú ē-tsat**, the arm from elbow to wrist. **kha ē-tsat**, the lower leg. **tsat-tsu**, a whitlow; an abscess or painful boil at a joint.

ngāu-tsat, water-lily roots sliced and prepared with honey. **tek-tsat**, a bamboo joint; a short bit of bamboo.

hē-soà^{n}-tsat, a very venomous serpent with markings like the handle of a Chinese umbrella. **káu-tsat-chhèng**, a gingall or swivel gun with nine knobs that look like joints. **káu-tsat-á**, a low shrub with a corymb of numerous berries.

tsat, to wrap (straw or cloth) very tightly round and round. **tsat-chháu**, to wrap up carefully with straw, as furniture to be sent a distance. **tsat-pè**, to bandage tightly with cloth, as a cut finger or sore leg.

tsat (R. id.) **phoe-tsat**, a letter; a chit (derived from this word); a book of models for letters. **pē-tsat**, a short decree of a supreme board.

73

tsȧt (R. chěk). **bȧk-tsȧt**, the cuttle-fish (v. bȧk). **bȧt-tsȧt**, id.

tsȧt [R. chěk, a thief]. **bȧk-tsȧt-chháu**, a plant used as sand-paper; also medicinal; Equisetum hyemale?

tsȧt (R. chěk), closely packed, filled, or pressed in; obstructed; tight. **m̄-thang-tsȧt**, don't make it tight; leave it loose. **cheng khah-tsȧt**, work it up till it becomes stiffer, as mortar. **tsȧt-sit**, tightly pressed in. **pá-tsȧt**, closely packed; quite full; said of a wealthy man.

tsȧt-pak, solid, as an image, &c. (opp. khang-khak); stupid. **tē-lāi tsȧt-tsȧt**, unable to think out the proper course. **sim tsȧt**, heart sad; mind confused. **sim-koaⁿ tsȧt-tsȧt**, unable to think what to do or say.

tsȧt-thóng-thóng, packed quite tight or full, as things or persons. **sim tsȧt-thóng-thóng**, anxious and troubled about many troublesome or dangerous matters. **pak-tó tsȧt-thóng-thóng**, feeling of dyspepsia or indigestion, as from an overloaded stomach.

âu tsȧt, a choking feeling, as about to weep. **tsȧt-phīⁿ**, nose stuffed, as with a cold.

tsȧt [R. chěk, quiet]. **tiām-tsȧt**, cautious and self-possessed.

tsau (R. tso), (T. chiau; Cn. tsöh). **tsau-that** (Cn. tsöh-thoah), to insult; to maltreat; to spend wastefully, as food; to throw away, as one's own life (v. that).

tsau — **au-tsau**, ugly, as face; dirty, filthy, as face or clothes. **au-au tsau-tsau**, id.

tsau — **chhâ-tsau**, a fire-brand partly burned.

tsau — **loān-tsau-tsau**, very much perplexed or confused in mind, as by troublesome or painful matters, or by a multiplicity of business. **tsau-loān**, id. **būn-tsau-tsau**, much grieved (cf. chiau, chiâu, chhiau).

tsau, debilitated; broken in constitution; worn out. **lāu-tsau**, worn out and useless; quite spoiled, as an old shoe or article of dress. **tsau-láu**, id.

tsau-bîn, worn out by want of sleep from any cause. **tsau-hun**, constitution broken down by opium. **tsau-chiú**, do. by liquor. **tsau-sek**, do. by lasciviousness. **tsau-tsa-bó**, id.

tsau (R. tso), dregs; refuse. **tsau-phoh**, the refuse or dregs from brewing or distillation. **chhè-tsau**, dregs of vinegar. **tsu̍t-bí-tsau**, glutinous rice fermented and salted, as it remains after making liquor. **péh-tsau**, a white condiment, much used with fish. **âng-tsau**, a red salt condiment, like thick sauce, made of rice and leaven, brought from Fuh-chau. **tsau-bah**, pork cooked with it; and so of other meats. **tsau-hî**, to preserve fish in this condiment. **chiú-tsau**, refuse of rice after making liquor.

tsâu (Cn.), = A. chiâu, complete. **sio kàu tsâu-tsâu**, burned away to nothing.

tsâu (C.), = A. chiâu. **tsâu-sim peh-pak**, = A. chiâu-sim peh-pak, grieved in mind; very sad.

tsâu, to exterminate. **tsâu-biėt**, do.

tsâu — **tsâu-sip**, to make extracts from others' compositions, as for literary piracy, or for other purposes.

tsâu (R. id.) **tsâu-hiėt**, a den, as of wild beasts or bad men.

tsáu (C.), = A. jiáuⁿ. **toh ê tsáu-súi**, = A. jiáuⁿ-súi, the ornamental carved work between the legs of a table.

tsáu (= chháu). **hô-lî-tsáu**, foxes' fur.

tsáu (C.) **tsáu-á**, a daughter. **tsáu-á-kiáⁿ**, id. **tsáu-kiáⁿ**, id.

tsáu (R. tsó). **ka-tsáu**, a flea. **ka-tsáu-báng**, a small water insect. **ka-tsáu-tû**, a flea-trap. **ka-tsáu tsòe-sū, lūi sat-bú**, the flea does the mischief, and involves the louse; the real culprit escapes, while a man not guilty, or slightly so, bears the penalty.

tsáu (R. tsó), to run; to cause to run; to escape; to differ; (to die); sometimes enclitic, sometimes with the meaning to move slightly, to run away.

tsáu-chhiú, hastily; without much care; in haste, *e.g.* selling off perishable eatables very quickly. **khah-tsáu-chhiú**, do it more rapidly, without taking such pains, as there is no need of so much care. **tsáu-tsáu**, rapidly, *e.g.* sewing very loosely with very wide stitches. **put-chí-tsáu**, sailing very fast, as a vessel.

tsáu-bé, to make a horse go fast (v. bé). **tsáu-bé-ūn**, the 162d radical. **tsáu-ûi-chhiûⁿ**, an inclosing wall.

tsáu-thâu, to ask counsel of idols, sorcerers, &c.; to give secret information (v. thâu).

tsáu-tāng, to go to stool (v. tāng); also said of some idolatrous rites. **tsáu-pak**, to have diarrhœa.

phah-tsáu--khì, to die (as child); to drive away, as birds. **tsáu--khì**, to die, as child. **tsáu-khì-tiàm**, id. (lit. run away and hide).

tsáu-hō, to take shelter from rain. **tsáu-chhȧt**, to flee from robbers. **tsáu-hiòng**, to smuggle. **tsáu-chè**, to abscond without paying debts. **bōe-tsáu-sau--tit**, dares not make free, as with money or work (v. sau). **tsáu-hoān**, an escaped criminal.

tsáu-sek, to lose the colour. **tsáu-tàng** (C.), coagulated jelly beginning to soften and get bad. **tsáu-im**, variation in sound. **tsáu-khiuⁿ**, difference of dialect; to vary, as a word in another dialect. **tsáu-pān**, different from pattern or sample, as in a fraud. **tsáu-tsoȧh**, to differ. **tsáu-cheng**, id.

tsáu-tsúi, a courier who carries letters and small parcels; to draw off water, as a drain or gutter. **tsáu-tsúi ê-lâng**, a courier. **tsáu-bûn-su--ê**, a government courier. **tsáu-phoe**, to carry letters, as a courier. **tsáu-chhiàng**, to go about, as street singers (v. chhiàng).

tsáu-khui, stand off. **tsáu-pī**, to get out of the way, as to escape an enemy or calamity. **tsáu-siám**, to escape; to avoid; to keep out of the way; secretly neglect one's duty. **tsáu-thoat**, to escape (v. thoat). **tô-tsáu**, to escape; to flee away; to abscond. **tùn--tsáu**, to break away and run, as man or animal. **phùn--tsáu**, to run away and escape. **tsáu-phùn-phùn**, to run fast. **toā-pō-tsáu**, to run quickly with long strides. **tsáu-lī**, to succeed in running away. **toah--tsáu**, to break away from another who is urging us to stay, often in disgust or in a pet (v. toah). **kùn--tsáu**, to escape by struggling violently; to burst away. **khit--i tsáu--khì**, to have our man escape from our grasp. **thu̍t--tsáu**, to slip out of place, as an instrument in the hand, or as a machine getting out of gear. **lun--tsáu**, to move a little so as to avoid being seen or caught. **tsáu-lȯh-hái**, to escape by sea. **saⁿ-chhoā-tsáu**, to escape, abscond, or elope together. **pāi-tsáu**, to be defeated and routed. **hó-kiâⁿ-tsáu**, in good state for travelling, as a road, or as one's dress. **cheng-lâm tsáu-pak, kiâⁿ-tang khì-sai**, to travel in all directions.

tsàu (R. tsò), to memorialize or report to the throne; a memorial to the throne. **tsàu hông-tè**, to send in a memorial to the emperor. **chiet-tsàu**, id. **mōⁿ-**

海上絲綢之路文獻集成　科技與文化編

tsàu, to memorialize the throne improperly. **pó-tsàu**, to recommend to the emperor for employment, or for remission of punishment; the memorialist is considered a security for his good conduct. **tsún-tsàu**, to grant the prayer of the memorial, as emperor does.

tsàu-chiuⁿ, a report or memorial to the throne. **tsàu-pńg**, id. **tsàu-pán**, a long tablet of jade or ivory held by high officials on having an audience, in former dynasties, not now used; it is held in the hand by some idols.

tsàu (R. tsò), a fireplace; a cooking stove or furnace (a slaughter-house). **tsàu-á**, a small portable furnace for cooking. **tiáⁿ-tsàu**, rice-boiler and cooking-place. **chiâⁿ-tsàu-hé**, fuel enough for kindling the fire once. **tsàu-kha**, a kitchen. **tsàu-pîⁿ**, cook's galley in vessel. **tsàu-khang**, the mouth of a cooking furnace. **tsàu-sim-thô**, clay from old cooking-places, used as medicine. **tsàu-hiàh**, the flat part of a built cooking-place round the circular hole where the rice-boiler is placed. **tsàu-hiàh-thâu**, id. **sin-sim-pū sóe-tsàu-hiàh**, the new daughter-in-law washes the corners of the cooking-place; a new broom sweeps clean. **sēng-káu chiūⁿ-tsàu**, a dog allowed too much liberty gets up on the cooking-place (v. sēng).

tsàu-koe, a small speckled cricket.

kháu-tsàu, a family using one set of cooking implements; a household; said in speaking of the number of households in a village or town. **tâng-kháu-tsàu**, of the same household.

tsàu-kun-kong, the god of the fireplace; he reports to Heaven about all the actions of the family. **tsàu-kun**, id. **tsàu-sîn**, id. **su-bēng tsàu-kun**, id.

ti-tsàu, a slaughter-house for pigs. **gû-tsàu**, a slaughter-house for cows.

tsāu (R. id.), to pay the balance; to give the change due on a purchase.

tsāu-chhē, to search carefully.

tsāu-chîⁿ, to pay the balance of cash; the balance due. **tsāu-chîⁿ kè-lâi**, to pay the balance, as in cash when a dollar had been given. **tsāu chîⁿ-bé**, to pay the change or balance due. **tsāu bêng-pėk**, pay the balance in full. **saⁿ-tsāu**, to settle the balance. **saⁿ-chiam-tsāu**, to settle a small balance over on a payment.

tsauh [R. chėk, chip; quiet]. **chēng-tsauh**, still, lonely, and dreary, as a place. **chēng-tsauh-tsauh**, id. **khah-chēng-tsauh**, more quiet; be quiet!

tsáuh (C.), = A. tsȧk. **tióh-ka-tsáuh**, something small in the throat causing a cough.

tsáuh (= chiàuh). **tsáuh-tsáuh-kóng**, to talk incessantly; what a long story! **tsáuh-tsáuh-lâi**, always coming again and again.

tsió (Cn.), = A. tsáu (in some few book phrases), to walk. **hó-hêng-tsió**, pleasant to walk about, as in fine dress (v. thiô).

tsng (R. tsong), a surname.

tsng (R. tsong). **chîⁿ-tsng**, a private bank.

tsng (R. tsong). **hiuⁿ-tsng** (r.), a village. **liēn-tsng** (Cn.), to combine together, as the head-men of a group of villages (under the sanction of the mandarins), as for putting down feuds and plundering, or preventing rebellion. **liēn-tsng-kėk** (Cn.), this sort of association.

tsng-siā (F.), a village. **chit-tsng-chhân**, a lot of contiguous fields (belonging to one man or family). **chhân-tsng** (esp. T. F.), a lot of contiguous fields (gen. with the houses all in the same piece of ground) belonging to one family or person. **bó-lâng ê chhân-tsng** (T. F.), such a man's estate, with lands and houses. **chhun-tsng** (F.), a village. **kui-tsng** (F.), a whole village.

tsng (R. tsong), stolen property; plunder. **chhȧt-tsng**, id. **pun-tsng**, to divide stolen goods, as thieves or robbers. **chē-tōe hun-tsng**, to be a receiver of stolen goods. **siau-tsng**, to buy stolen goods knowingly. **tui-tsng**, to recover stolen property, as mandarin. **pí-tsng**, to beat till the stolen property is given up. **kiáu-tsng**, to give up the stolen property, or its equivalent, to the mandarin. **liȧh-kan chiūⁿ-chhn̂g; liȧh-chhȧt chiūⁿ-tsng**, the proof of adultery is seizure in the act; the proof of robbery is the stolen property.

tsng (R. tsong), (perhaps two characters in this group), to adorn; to feign; to act a part in a play or procession; to pack up; pattern of goods.

tsng-sek, to put on a false, counterfeit, or feigned appearance, on self or on goods. **tsng-tsòe**, id. **pháiⁿ-lâng tsng-tsòe hó-lâng**, a bad man putting on a false appearance of goodness. **tsng-bô tsòe-iūⁿ**, to make a false pretence. **tsng chit-kù-ōe**, to tell a specious falsehood. **tsng-siong**, to wound one's self intentionally, as a beggar; or as in order to make up false evidence, or involve another man.

tsng-pùt, to make idols (v. pùt). **tsng-koh**, a platform with young girls (or boys in that character) on it, carried in idolatrous processions. **tsng kè-sū**, dressing in the character of ancient personages, as in such processions. **tsng-lâng**, to dress in character (gen. boys about 12) either ludicrous or ancient, as in spring or at incense processions. **khoàⁿ-tsng-lâng**, to go and look at these spectacles. **tsng-seng**, to take the character of a young man in a play (v. seng). **tsng-toàⁿ**, do., of young woman, done by lads (v. toàⁿ). **tsng-thiap**, do., of female slave, &c. (v. thiap). **tsng-thiú**, do., of sort of clown. **tsng-chiāⁿ**, take part of an actor with painted face. **tsng-sîn chiâⁿ-sîn; tsng-kúi chiâⁿ-kúi**, what's worth doing at all is worth doing well (lit. whether it be a spirit or a demon).

tsng-thāⁿ, to adorn one's self (as woman); to talk boastfully and falsely of one's self. **chiūⁿ-tsng**, to adorn the person (as beautiful young woman), (s. plunder). **soe-tsng**, to adorn hair and head, as woman. **soe-tsng-lâu**, an ornamental upper story for the women of a family. **ah-bú tsng-kim, iȧh-sī pîⁿ-chhùi**, said of a richly dressed person with an ugly face (like a flat-billed duck decked in gold plumage).

tsng-liâm, marriage outfit of dress, ornaments, and furniture (sometimes also lands or houses) given by parents to daughter at marriage, as a sort of dowry. **kè-tsng**, bride's marriage outfit. **kiám-tsng**, box that holds the bride's shoes, foot-bandages, trowsers, &c. **kiám-tsng-siuⁿ**, id.

tsng-thâu, pattern of goods. **chhiūⁿ-tsng**, to buy goods and lay them up, waiting for a rise in price. **pān iûⁿ-tsng**, to deal in goods to be sent over the ocean. **chit-tsng-hè**, a sort of goods, according to a special pattern.

tsng-hun, to pack tobacco: to put opium in the pipe. **tsng-tê**, to pack tea (&c.) **goân-tsng-hè**, goods in the original state as made, not dressed up to look better than they are, nor flavoured to conceal their own flavour.

tsng (R. tsoan), (C. tsuiⁿ), a strong thick tile; (a

small fine brick). **tsng-phiah-hiā**, tiles and bricks of all sorts.

gān-chí-tsng, a small fine brick for fine or ornamental work. **sì-kak-tsng**, large strong square tiles for floors, or for roofs fit to be walked on. **tsng-tsām**, a cold chisel for splitting off bits of tiles. **tsng-á-thâu**, a broken bit of tile for using where a whole tile is too large. **tsng-á-hu**, powder of tiles or bricks. **tsng-á-sek**, colour of tiles, dull red.

sio-tsng, to make tiles in the kiln. **phe-tsng**, to lay a tiled floor or flat roof. **tsng-pî^n**, a flat roof or verandah laid with tiles. **tsng-tōe**, tiled floor or court. **tsng-tiâ^n**, tiled court. **tsng-thia^n**, central hall of house paved with tiles. **tsng-mn̂g**, a door faced with strong tiles, as a security against robbers.

tsn̂g [R. tsoân, entire; complete; = col. chiâu], (C. tsûi^n), entirely. **chiâu-tsn̂g**, complete. **tsâu-tsn̂g** (Cn.), id. **tsn̂g-jiên**, entirely. **tsn̂g-jiên-ōe**, quite able. **sa^n-jī-tsn̂g**, all the three things in full, said at the end of several enumerations of three things (v. jī).

kng-tsn̂g, smooth and even, as clothes; surface smooth and unbroken, as of wall or ceiling.

tsn̂g-beh, wishing to have all or the whole. **tsn̂g-goān**, entirely willing. **tsn̂g-bāng**, to place all one's hope (as on some person).

tsn̂g [R. chiông, to follow], from; since; only said of time. **tsn̂g-sòe-hàn**, from youth or childhood.

tsńg [R. chí, a finger], (T. tsái^n, Cn. tsúi^n, C. chéng). **tsńg-thâu-á**, a finger; a toe. **chhiú tsńg-thâu-á**, a finger. **kha-tsńg-thâu-á**, a toe. **tsńg-thâu-á-bak**, joints of fingers; the knuckles in the middle of the fingers. **tsńg-thâu-bú**, the thumb. **kha-tsńg-thâu-bú**, the big toe; the great toe.

tsńg-kah, a finger-nail. **tsńg-kah-hoe**, the henna plant (Lawsonia inermis) cultivated for its sweet-scented flowers; said to be good for diseases of the nails; sometimes said of the balsam. **soa^n-tsńg-kah-hoe**, a wild plant (Symplocos?) with flowers somewhat like the henna. **tsńg-kah-se**, the line dividing the quick from the rest of the nail. **tsńg-kah-jiông**, the quick of the nail (v. jiông).

tsǹg (R. tsoàn), (C. tsùi^n), a drill, awl, or such boring instrument. **tsǹg-á**, an awl; a gimlet; a bodkin, &c. **toā-tsǹg**, a large drill or auger. **kim-kong-tsǹg**, one made of good steel. **lak-tsǹg**, a drill worked by a bow and string. **ín-tsǹg**, an awl used for making a hole for the needle. **phah-tsǹg**, a sort of drill that is first hammered in, and then turned round by the hand, not by a bow; to use this sort of drill. **pí^n-tsǹg**, an instrument, like a broad dagger, used by robbers for making holes in walls, and as a weapon.

tsǹg [R. tsoàn, same as previous word? or, koàn, to pass through? or more than one word], (C. tsùi^n), to bore a hole; to make one's way; to rush on. **tsǹg-khang**, to bore or make a hole, as insect or instrument. **tsǹg-hī**, to bore the ears for ear-rings.

tsǹg--kè-khì, to make away and escape. **tsǹg-tsáu**, id. **tá-lóh tsǹg--chhut-lâi**, out of what hole have you crept? said in scolding children or bad useless fellows. **hō--i tùi-thē-kha beh-tsǹg--lóh-khì**, to make him so ashamed that he is ready to sink into the earth.

ǹg-tsǹg, good at watching for opportunities of making money; artful in planning and scheming. **gâu-ǹg-tsǹg**, id. **ǹg-tsǹg m̄-táh tú-tn̄g**, artful scheming is not so good as just to receive what falls to our lot.

tsn̄g [R. tsōng, form; a formal accusation], a written complaint given in to a mandarin. **jip-tsn̄g**, to give in such a complaint. **kò-tsn̄g**, id. **siá-tsn̄g**, to write out the copy given in; the official (= tāi-su) who so writes it from the copy prepared by the party. **siu-tsn̄g**, to receive the complaint, as the underlings of yamun. **phoe-tsn̄g**, to write the answer on it (v. phoe).

kiet-tsn̄g, a document which the parties sign, stating that the case is finally settled. **niá^n-tsn̄g**, a paper of security, *e.g.* given when a man is bailed out. **gū-tsn̄g**, an accusation before the supreme court of review at the capital. **kò-gū-tsn̄g**, to enter such an accusation or appeal. **tsn̄g-su**, a literary man who gives himself to the writing of legal complaints. **tsn̄g-sek**, paper with crossed lines for writing such complaints. **tsn̄g-tsoá**, id. **tsn̄g-sek-tsoá**, id.

tsn̄g (R. tsōng). **tńg-tsn̄g**, Buddhist rites for saving from the blood pool (huih-tî) the soul of a woman who has died within one month after child-birth; done by turning round and round a paper frame (prayer-mill), and then burning it. **khan-tńg-tsn̄g**, to turn this prayer-mill. **khan-tsn̄g**, id.

tsn̄g [R. tsoán, to turn?]. **kńg-tsn̄g**, eddy of water, as at a rock, or of wind.

tsn̄g [R. tsoān, to eat or drink], (C. tsūi^n), to suck very slightly, only with the lips, so as barely to taste, as the teat, or as the point of a Chinese pen. **tsn̄g-lin**, to have the teat just in the mouth, without sucking much, as when sick or fully satisfied. **pa-lun tsn̄g-chih**, to lick one's lips. **tsn̄g pit-á-bé**, to be a pettifogging lawyer. **tsn̄g-pit-bé**, id.

tsn̄g [R. tsōng, entrails]. **sió-tsn̄g**, the small viscera of lower animals.

tsn̄g [R. tsān or tsoān], (C. tsūi^n), the place on the head from which the hair radiates; sometimes it is double.

tso [R. to meet with; an occasion; = col. tsoa]. **chit-tso**, this time. **āu-tso**, next time; another occasion. **tso-gū**, opportunity, fortune, as good or bad (v. gū). **tso-hong**, to meet with wind, as a ship. **tso-un**, to be taken with great calamity (v. un). **tso-chien**, to meet with very bad fortune. **tso-tiėt**, id. **tso-lān**, to meet with calamity. **tso-kiap**, to meet with great calamity, as plunder or slaughter.

tso-koa^n-hû, to be at law; to have a lawsuit.

tso, feeling of dull pain in stomach, as hunger or indigestion. **sim-koa^n-thâu tso**, id. **tso-loān**, id. **chiáh--liáu tso-loān**, feeling uncomfortable after eating, with tendency to vomit. **chiau-tso** (R.), sorely grieved so as to feel quite ill.

tsô (R. id.), a trough; applied to various long trough-shaped instruments or cavities, *e.g.* of gutter, jawbone, &c.; to put cash in an instrument for counting them.

chí^n-tsô, an instrument with trough-shaped cavities for counting cash, used in shops. **tsô-chí^n**, to put cash in this instrument so that they are formed into rows ready to be counted and strung.

géng-tsô, a long trough-shaped mortar worked by a wheel, used by apothecaries. **hī^n-tsô** (C.), cavity for water in a large ink-stone. **niau^n-tsô**, the cavity in which the foot of the mast rests. **pán-tsô**, a sort of breech-loading gingall.

phun-tsô, a trough for the water that has washed rice, and other slops, for pigs. **ti-tsô**, a pig's trough. **bē-chiū^n-tsô**, not yet set to eat at the trough, said of

厦英大辭典

a sucking pig. **bé-tsô**, a horse's eating-trough or manger. **khit-chiáh sí tī-bé-tsô--nih**ⁿ, said (in joke) of a sudden change from poverty to prosperity.

tsúi-tsô, a gutter (built) on the roof of a house. **chhù-tsô**, id. **chhiò-tsô**, the long furrows of a tiled roof. **phak-tsô**, the long ridges of reversed tiles on roof alternate with these furrows. **hiā-tsô**, these furrows or ridges of the tiles of a roof (either of them).

gê-tsô, the lower jawbone. **gê-tsô-kut**, id. **gê-tsô-khí**, the canine teeth. **gê-tsô-chhi**, the part of the cheek about the roots of the molar teeth. **gê-tsô-chhi toā**, that part of the cheek large and projecting. **gê-tsô-thâu**, the back part of the lower jaw. **gê-tsô-thâu ngīⁿ**, jaws firmly clenched, as when about to die. **thih-khí, bân-gê-tsô**, obstinately refusing to admit a fault or error, and doggedly telling lies about it. **tâng-gê-tsô**, id. **tâng-gê-tsô, thih-chhùi-khí**, id.

tsô-thâu-bah, the meat of a hog's neck near the head.

tsô [R. tsō, black; lictors]. **tsô-pêng**, the right-hand side of a yamun as you enter, so called because the underlings called "tsō-lē" stay on that side. **tsô-khoài-koán**, the rooms occupied by the underlings on each side close to the entrance-gate of the yamun.

tsô (R. id.), to annoy by noise. **tsô--lâng**, id. **tsak-tsô**, to vex; to annoy. **tsô-tsak**, id. **tsô-tsak hī-khang**, to stun the ears by noise. **hī-khang tsô**, a ringing in the ears. **tsáp-tsô**, perplexed and troubled, as by many sorts or pieces of business.

tsô [R. a sort of junk or boat]. **tiò-tsô**, a fishing-boat. **bāng-tsô**, a boat for fishing by nets. **bí-tsô**, a boat carrying rice. **tsô-á-tsûn**, a boat of that sort. **hiā-tsô**, a boat carrying tiles (s. gutter). **hoā-tsô** (Cn. T.), id. **tsan-tsô**, a small junk, such as usually go to the Pescadores. **hoàn-tsô**, a medium-sized junk, about 800 or 1000 peculs.

tsô [R. a sort of officer], a surname. **tsô-chhò**, an ancient mandarin infamous for intrigue. **kan-hiông náⁿ tsô-chhò--nihⁿ**, as treacherous as Tsô-chhò.

ték-jit ê kong-tsô, messengers of Yuh-hwang Shangti (giòk-hông) for each special day, just as mandarins have their constables (chhe) assigned to each day.

sim-koaⁿ-tsô, the place where the breast and stomach meet. **sim-koaⁿ-tsô teh-thiàⁿ**, pain at that part. **heng-tsô teh-thiàⁿ**, id. **tùi-sim-tsô tháⁿ--khì**, to fend off a blow from our breast with our palm turned outwards.

tsó [R. the left side], a surname. **tsó-iū**, right and left; more or less (v. iū). **tsó-pêng** (r.), left side. **tsó-iāⁿ**, the left wing of an army, one-fifth of the whole; the officer commanding it.

tsó-tō, false doctrine, said of Tauists (v. tō).

tsó-tn̂g, the literary mandarin of a city (= ló-su), who is head of the literati there. **tsó-siòng**, Tartar prime-minister.

tsó-toān, an ancient commentary on the Spring and Winter classic (chhun-chhiu), written by Tsó khiu-bêng.

tsó (R. id.), the jujube fruit or Chinese date, not a real date; round date-shaped confections. **tsó-á**, jujube fruit. **âng-tsó**, dried do. **tsó-koaⁿ**, id. **ɵ-tsó**, a large sort, dried. **kim-tsó**, the jujube fruit; also, a sort of lime, esp. preserved in sugar. **chhùn-kim-tsó**, a date-shaped confection made of rice-flour and sugar. **tāu-tsó**, a confection made of rice-flour, sugar, and legumes. **moâⁿ-tsó**, do. of rice and hemp-seed. **chìⁿ-tsó**, balls of rice-paste with stuffing of minced-meat, &c., fried in melted fat.

sng-tsó-ko, a preserve made from another sort of fruit (Rhamnus ?).

tsó [R. to walk or run, = col. tsáu]. **hui-khîm tsó-siù** (R.), birds that fly and beasts that walk.

tsò (= tsō). **chiâu-tsò**, grieved and pained at heart.

tsò [R. to assist]. **tsò-tsáp** (r.), a very small mandarin, like sûn-kiám (v. tsáp). **hû-tsò** (r.), to assist, as a mandarin assists the sovereign.

tsò (C.), = A. tsòe, to be; to do; to act; (to be carefully distinguished from tsō, to make). **boeh-tsò-nīⁿ**, what *can* I do, as in this extremity. **tsò-sin-sɛⁿ**, = A. tsòe-sien-siⁿ, to be a doctor.

tsō [R. tsô, a boat]. **koaⁿ-tsō**, a sort of barge or house-boat, used by mandarins, esp. revenue officers.

tsō [R. to sit, = col. chē]. **tsō-hiòng**, the direction of a house or grave as to good luck (v. hiòng). **tsō-tē hun-tsng**, to be a receiver of stolen goods. **tsō-sī put-kiù**, to sit and look on without helping. **tsō-sit san-pheng**, sitting idle and eating soon brings a man to ruin (like a falling mountain).

tsō (P.), = C. P. chhē, = A. chē, to take the responsibility, as in money matters.

tsō (R. id.), a seat of dignity; a pedestal or socket; a set of figures joined in one group; classifier of mountains, towers, standing screens, wardrobes, cupboards, blocks of houses, &c.

pùt-tsō, an idol's throne. **pat-tsō**, a sedan with eight bearers, used only by mandarins of the first rank red button. **kong-tsō**, a mandarin's tribunal. **kong-tsō-toh**, the table of his tribunal. **kong-tsō-ūi**, the seat of the tribunal (v. ūi).

tsō-tsú, a high mandarin whom a lower mandarin takes as his patron.

chē-tsō, to sit performing the Buddhist rites (phó-tɵ) for the souls of the dead in the 7th moon. **chiūⁿ-tsō**, to begin these rites, as the priest does.

tah-tsō, to set up the wooden pillars and beams of a Chinese house before the walls are built. **thong-tsō**, the cross-beams of a boat. **lôe-āu-tsō**, the cross-stick at the back of a plough. **āu-tsō-bah**, meat of the hind-quarter. **teng-tsō**, the part of a lantern that supports the socket. **téng-tsō**, the small round brass plate on which a mandarin-button rests (v. téng). **hoe-kan-tsō**, the pedestal of a flower-glass or small flower-jar. **lut-tsō**, to get out of the socket.

chit-tsō-chhù, a block of houses. **chit-tsō-soaⁿ**, a mass of mountains. **chit-tsō ang-á**, a set of figures for sale.

tsō [R. tō, a road]. **thang-á-tsō**, the sill of a window.

tsō (cf. tsò, tsô). **tsak-tsō**, to trouble; to annoy; I give you much trouble. **chiâu-tsō**, grieved and vexed in mind.

tsō [R. black]. **tsō-tsō**, to make quite black, as in thoroughly obliterating a wrongly written word. **tsō-lō**, id. **tsō-pháiⁿ**, to disfigure a writing by black blots or erasures; to spoil a pen by writing too thick.

tsō-lē, the attendants of a mandarin who punish and torture people; they wear a black dress. **tsō-pan**, id.

tsō-hoân, sulphate of iron; copperas. **chiáh-tsō**, to be dyed with sulphate of iron.

pûi-tsō, a sort of black soap (v. pûi). **tsō-chhì**, a thorny medicinal plant (Acacia ?).

tsō [R. tsū, to dwell]. **tsō-chí**, place of residence, as written on a document or envelope (v. chí).

tsō (R. id.), to make; to build. **tsō-hoà**, to create; to create and transform; fortune or luck, good or bad (v. hoà). **chhòng-tsō** (r.), to create. **tsō-tsûn**, to build a boat or junk. **tok-tsō**, to oversee the building of a boat. **phe-kiô tsō-lē**, to make bridges and roads. **tsō chhâ-kiô, tap bú-un: sat kan-hu, pò hū-siû**, he made a wooden bridge to recompense his mother (to help her to go on an intrigue), but he killed the adulterer (after his mother's death) to revenge his father's quarrel. **tsō-thah**, to build a pagoda. **tsō-thah, tiòh-tsō thàng-bé** (or, **kàu-bé**), in doing any good or proper work you should finish what you begin. **tsō-chheh**, to take a list of names. **tsō ke-kah**, to make a census.

ū-tsō-ì, to have a settled purpose to do something, esp. to have a secret fixed purpose to do it as soon as the opportunity occurs, and to seek an opportunity, and not now doing it only because of some obstacle. **ū-chhûn tsō-ì**, id. **m̄-sī tsō-ì**, it is not of set purpose. **tsō-sí-koat**, obstinate. **thong-bê tsō-kè**, to make a plot or conspiracy together. **tsō-hoán**, to rebel. **si^{n}-giên tsō-gú**, to raise trouble by false reports or exaggerations. **tsō kàu ū-ki ū-hiòh**, to invent falsehoods so complete in all the details as to look quite true. **tsō kàu ū-kha ū-chhiú**, id.

tse (Cn.), = A. tso, in some words in the several tones.

tse (R. id,), a surname.

tse (R. id.), rent; to rent. **chhân-tse**, rent of fields. **chhù-tse**, house-rent. **chhut-tse**, to offer publicly or advertise for lease. **siu-tse**, to collect rent. **tùi-tse**, to pay a debt by assigning temporarily certain rents to the creditor. **tse-koán**, to rent a lodging, as students come for the examinations.

tē-tse, land-tax paid to government for the ground on which houses are built, &c., as in Amoy. **tōe-tse**, id. **tē-tse-hū**, receipt for it. **tē-tse-chhoàn**, id. **tē-tse-khe**, office of receiver of the Amoy land-tax.

seng-oân-tse, property left by will that the rents may be enjoyed by such descendants as become graduates. **tse-koá^{n}**, a sort of factor who collects rents for a wealthy proprietor.

tsô (Cn.), = A. tsô, in some cases.

tsó (Cn.), = A. tsó, left.

tsó [R. tsó, to run or walk], (Cn. tsió). **hêng-tsó**, gait, mien, and manner. **hó hêng-tsó**, stately mien; good or graceful gait and appearance or demeanour. **phái^{n}-hêng-tsó**, gait and mien not good-looking.

tsó [R. id., = col. tsoā]. **chiù-tsó** (R.), to make imprecations.

tsó (R. id.), an ancestor; great-grandfather; ancestral; title of many idols.

tsó-bú, paternal grandmother (v. bú). **goā-tsó**, maternal great-grandfather. **ka-tsó** (polite), my grandfather. **ka-tsó-bú** (polite), my grandmother. **khai-ki-tsó**, original founder of a family. **sí-tsó**, original ancestor, as of a tribe or race. **ko-tsó**, great-great-grandfather. **tsó-tsó**, id. **cheng-tsó**, great-grandfather (v. cheng). **sien-tsó**, deceased paternal grandfather (lit. former). **sien-tsó-bú**, deceased paternal grandmother. **kúi-kok sien-tsó**, an ancient diviner (now worshipped).

tsó-sien, deceased ancestors. **kong-pô tsó-sài**, id. (v. sài). **tsó-siōng**, distant ancestors. **tsó-chiū^{n}**, id. **tsó-kong**, distant male ancestors. **chek-kong-tsó**, younger brother of paternal great-grandfather. **peh-kong-tsó**, elder brother of do. **tsó-tsong**, ancestors in general. **hián-tsó êng-tsong**, to reflect glory on ancestors. **sià-tsó jiók-tsong**, to bring disgrace on the name of ancestors by wicked deeds.

tsó-ke, ancestral home; native place; often said of Europe or America, esp. in speaking of articles being brought from those parts. **tsó--chhù**, ancestral temple. **tsó-bōng**, ancestral graves. **tsó-hûn**, id. **tsó-tōe**, ancestral lands. **tsó-giáp**, ancestral property. **tsó-thoân**, handed down from ancestors, as property, or as trade secrets or medical knowledge.

tò-tsó, to die; to be spoiled or broken, as a thing; to be dead. **khì-chhē in-tsó**, he is dead. **khì in-tsó-tau**, id.

pōe-tsó, to transgress and abandon ancestral customs. **chè-tsó**, to make offerings to ancestors. **pài-tsó**, to go to worship ancestors, as graduates on getting their degree. **chiáh-tsó**, to eat the memorial-feast in the ancestral temple. **sêng-tsó**, to found a family, becoming their ancestor. **toà-chia sêng-tsó**, means to live here all his life, and leave his posterity here after him. **toà-chia tsòe-tsó**, id.

tsó-pô (T.), female ancestors.

má-tsó, the goddess of the sea and sailors, and queen of heaven, of surname Lim (= thien-siōng sèng-bú), born under Sòng-Thài-tsó of the Sung dynasty, in Bî-chiu, near Hing-hwa (heng-hoà), of father named Goān. **má-tsó-pô**, id. **tsó-pô-biō**, her temple. **má-tsó-biō**, id. **má-tsó-keng**, id. **má-tsó-pô-hî**, the large white fish called also péh-gô. **má-tsó-pò**, a storm about the time of her birth-day.

sien-tsó, title of any of the eight "sien" or genii. **pùt-tsó**, the Buddhist Supreme (v. pùt). **tsó-su-kong**, a black-faced idol (v. su). **ang-kong-tsó**, an idol in general. **thó-tī-kong-tsó**, the god of the ground. **ngó-tsó**, five Buddhist priests of the Ming dynasty, worshipped by rebels, esp. by the Triad or Small-knife Society.

tsó (R. id.) **tsó-tòng**, to prohibit; to hinder. **tsó-chí**, to hinder; to obstruct. **noā^{n}-tsó**, to hinder or prevent, as something just going to be done. **tsó-keh**, to obstruct.

tsō [R. to assist]. **sa^{n}-tsō**, to assist; to help. **tàu-sa^{n}-tsō**, id. **pang-tsō**, id. **hû-tsō**, to assist with funds. **chiu-tsō**, id. **tsu-tsō** (r.), id. **tsū-tsō** (Cn.), id. **pó-tsō**, to make up a deficiency. **tsō-chiàn**, to help in battle. **kiap-hù tsō-pîn**, to plunder the rich and assist the poor, as robbers and pirates say.

tsō (Cn.), = A. tsō, to make, in many phrases.

tsō (Cn.), = A. tsō, to sit, in some phrases.

tsō (Cn. T.), = A. chē, to sit.

tsō (T.), = A. chē. **tok-ka-tsō**, = A. tuh-ka-chē, drowsy.

tsō (Cn. T.), = A. tsōe, guilt.

tsō (T.), a column of words in a page, = tsoā.

tsoa [R. tso, to meet; an occasion]. **kè-tsoa**, the opportunity past for ever; too late, and no possibility of setting it right now, as coming too late to get a thing, or as a disease gone too far for cure.

tsoa, to draw out one, as a lot or a card, out of several. **tsoa-chhiam**, to draw lots, as for office; to get (as office) by lot. **tsoa pâi-á**, to draw cards.

tsoâ (R. siâ), a snake; a serpent; a sort of skin disease. **tsoâ-chhiu**, the forked tongue of a serpent.

tsoâ-thôe, the cast-off skin of a serpent, used in medicine. **tsoâ-khak**, id.

moâⁿ-tsoâ, coarse yellow hempen stuff like ropes, tied round the head in deepest mourning. **tsoâ thé-chih**, the self-acting bolt of a lock (v. chih).

pe-tsoâ, an eruption in lines on the skin; ring-worm. **siⁿ-tsoâ**, to have a sort of suppurating swelling at the finger-joints. **tîⁿ-kut-á-tsoâ**, a sort of ulcer or sore on the toe. **tîⁿ-io-tsoâ**, an eruption that goes half round the body. **tîⁿ-sin-tsoâ**, do. going round the body; if quite round it is supposed to be fatal.

tâng-tsoâ thih-káu, the brazen snake and iron dog in Hades. **tiòng-tsoâ-ké**, to be bewitched so as suddenly to have dropsy and die quickly, and after death become the slave of the wizard; done by a demon of serpent nature in the form of a man speaking to you; if you answer, the charm at once takes effect; a good antidote is a centipede in a box, as the snake is afraid of the centipede. **chhī-tsoâ-ké**, to keep these elvish serpents, especially in inns. **sí-tsoâ**, a dead serpent. **tòk-tsoâ**, a venomous serpent (v. tòk). **chhī-tsoâ, kā koe-bú** (feed a serpent to eat our hens), to have a hidden enemy in our own household.

káu-bú-tsoâ, a sort of large lizard. **n̂g-âm-tsoâ**, yellow-necked serpent. **chháu-hoe-tsoâ**, a variegated harmless kind. **gím-tsoâ**, a large variegated serpent; drums are made of its skin. **tsúi-tsoâ**, a water-snake. **nêⁿ-tsoâ** (C.), a very poisonous sort of serpent.

tsoâ (contracted from "chī-tsūi-á"). **tsoâ-á**, who? **tsoâ-kóng**, who ever said so? (said in surprise, or showing that we don't believe it).

tsoâ (= toâ), to shake about horizontally with a somewhat circular motion, as a tray of grain. **tsoâ-tsoâ tsòe-chit-tui**, to shake the tray horizontally so as to bring the grain into a heap.

tsoá [R. chiá, elder sister]. **goán-tsoá--ê**, my elder sister's husband.

tsoá (R. chí), paper. **chit-tiuⁿ-tsoá**, a sheet of paper. **jī-tsoá**, written or printed paper (v. jī). **tsoá-hê**, the worm that eats paper. **tsoá-tóe**, the remains of a lot of paper; shoes having paper soles. **tsoá-pōe**, the wrong side of the paper. **tsoá-kha-chhng**, id., (somewhat vulgar). **tsoá-phe**, a sort of pasteboard.

tsoá-tiam, a block on which paper is cut and smoothed; a quantity of paper in one block burned at once in worship. **tsoá-tsām**, a knife for cutting smooth large quantities of paper (v. tsām). **tsoá-to**, a blunt knife for cutting folded paper; a paper-knife. **tsoá-hu**, ashes of paper (v. hu). **tsoá-mn̂g**, paper broken down very small. **tsoá-mīⁿ**, id.; but (C.) the ashes at the end of a half-burned match (v. mīⁿ). **tsoá-kun**, thin strips of paper for making matches or for mixing with lime. **tsoá-lién**, long slips of paper rolled up and dipped in oil, as matches (v. lién). **tsoá-lok**, paper-bags used in shops. **chit-to-tsoá**, one bundle of paper having the sheets all folded within each other. **chit-khún-tsoá**, several of these tied in one large bundle.

pè-tsoá, to paste paper, *e.g.* on a wall. **tsòe-tsoá sai-hū**, a paper-maker. **kê-tsoá**, to make idolatrous paper. **sio-tsoá**, to burn paper in worship. **sái-tsoá**, id. **tiàu-tsoá**, to go to the house where a friend has recently died, and join in the worship of the dead. **sàng koan-thâu-tsoá**, to make presents of the paper called "koan-thâu-tsoá" for the coffin. **tap-tsoá**, to make small presents in return for these rites. **teh-tsoá**, to put paper on the tombs in spring. **pàng-tsoá**, to scatter paper as the coffin is carried along. **hē-tsoá**, to make imprecations or incantations while burning paper, done by old hags (v. hē).

tsoá-chîⁿ, mock money burned in idolatrous rites. **kim-tsoá**, yellow do. in imitation of gold. **kim-gûn-tsoá**, do. standing for gold and silver. **chheh-á-tsoá**, many sorts mixed (acc. to book called chheh-á) for curing disease. **teng-tsō-tsoá**, paper made into a shape like a lantern base, and burned in the rites called "chiò," in worship of Thiⁿ-kong. **khai-gán-tsoá**, yellow paper with pictures of horses and chariots, burned by sorcerers (tâng-chí) to hasten the arrival of the spirit to possess him.

pe̍h-tek-á-tsoá, common white paper made from bamboo. **mīⁿ-tsoá**, soft strong flexible paper (v. mīⁿ). **ko-lê-tsoá**, strong paper from Corea. **khī-á-tsoá**, paper treated with the juice of green persimmons, so as to be stronger; used for umbrellas. **sìn-tsoá**, common paper for letters, &c. (v. sìn). **hoân-tsoá**, paper sized with alum. **kak-tsoá**, a sort of paper that does not readily tear. **ké-á-tsoá**, thin coarse sort used for making idolatrous paper. **sam-liòk-si tsoá**, a very thin paper used for children tracing characters in school. **chien-tsoá**, a fine glossy paper (v. chien). **kēng-tsoá**, sort of drawing-paper (v. kēng). **lô-bûn-tsoá**, writing-paper with water-lines. **siàh-tsoá**, marbled paper. **tsn̄g-tsoá**, paper with crossed lines for legal documents.

sin-bûn-tsoá, a newspaper (a foreign phrase). **miâⁿ-jī chiūⁿ-tsoá**, to have had one's name set down in a formal document. **tâng-gûn bóe tsoá-hia, siang-lâng thiòng**, to buy paper boots with brass dollars, and each party is highly delighted at cheating the other.

tsoā [R. tsé, to make imprecations]. **chiù-tsoā**, to swear. **kóe-tsoā**, to remove the binding power of an oath by ceremonies, esp. by using a rice-sieve, and wiping one's mouth with idolatrous paper. **chiù-toā-tsoā**, to swear a great oath. **chiù-tāng-tsoā**, id. **chiù sí-chéh-tsoā**, to imprecate death on self and whole posterity if what is sworn be false. **chiù-sí-tsoā** (r.), to imprecate death on one's self if it be false. **kí-thiⁿ chiù-tsoā**, to swear by Heaven. **lām-sám chiù-tsoā**, to swear falsely.

tsoā, a line; a row; a column of characters; classifier of journeys, voyages, roads.

gâu-phīⁿ-tsoā, you are very knowing (v. phīⁿ). **kà lóng-bōe chiūⁿ-tsoā**, though taught he cannot learn to do it right. **chiâⁿ-tsoā**, making or becoming a line, row, road, &c.

he-tsoā, a line of caulking, &c. **áu-tsoā**, a line made by folding paper. **se-tsoā**, the lines of the threads in cotton-cloth. **pè-tsoā**, the lines of the cloth, as in embroidery. **bô-chit-tsoā thang piⁿ-phê**, not having a thread to stretch on his skin; nothing to wear. **pè chit-tsoā-chhân**, to plant out a row of rice.

kiâⁿ-tsoā, to walk back and forwards, as after a meal. **kiâⁿ-chit-tsoā**, to take a walk or journey, voyage, &c. **kiâⁿ-té-tsoā**, to go a short voyage or journey. **chit-tsoā-tsûn**, one voyage of a ship. **āu-tsoā**, the next time, as of boat sailing, &c. **n̄ng-tsoā-hoâiⁿ, chit-tsoā-koâiⁿ**, making one voyage to the north of China and two to Formosa in each year, as junks often do. **chit-tsoā-khì, chit-tsoā-lâi**, constantly coming and going, back and forwards.

tsoaⁿ [R. chien, to fry], to boil water. **tsoaⁿ-tê**, to boil water in order to be used for infusing tea.

tsoâ^{n} (R. tsoân), a stream at the fountain-head; the water issuing from a spring or fountain. **tsúi-tsoâ^{n}**, id. **tsoâ^{n}-tsúi**, spring-water.

oàh-tsoâ^{n}, a flowing fountain. **sí-tsoâ^{n}**, a pond not fed from a spring or stream. **thng-tsoâ^{n}**, a hot spring. **ngī^{n}-tsoâ^{n}**, a strong perennial spring. **soa^{n}-tsoâ^{n}**, a mountain spring, seldom or never dry. **chiòh-tsoâ^{n}**, a spring among rocks. **khui-chí^{n} púih-tsoâ^{n}** (to draw away the water of a neighbour's spring by the well we dig), to injure a neighbour's prosperity by opening an opposition establishment close at hand.

tsoâ^{n} — **hé-nâ^{n}-tsoâ^{n}**, a sort of erùption on children (cf. toa^{n}).

tsoâ^{n} — **hóe-nâ^{n}-tsoâ^{n}** (C.), a fire or conflagration bursting out through want of care.

tsoâ^{n} [R. tsân, to injure; broken food], slops from eating. **chhùi-tsoâ^{n}**, the dirt that remains on things used in eating, as ôn plates, bowls, chopsticks, &c. **niau^{n}-tsoâ^{n}**, a cat's slops; filth made by a cat in eating. **bak-niau^{n}-tsoâ^{n}**, having the marks of a cat's teeth on it, or such filth. **bak-káu-tsoâ^{n}**, do. of a dog.

tsoá^{n} (C.), = A. tsái^{n}. **tsoá^{n}-iû^{n}**, = A. tsái^{n}-iû^{n}, how? **tsoá^{n}-nī^{n}-iû^{n}**, id. **tsoá^{n}-kóng**, what do you say? **àn-tsoá^{n}**, how can that be?

tsoá^{n} — **tsoá^{n}-lî**, a wicker-work (bamboo) strainer for lading out rice. **tsoá^{n}-nî^{n}**, id.

tsoá^{n} (R. tsán), a small cup; classifier of lamps and of edible birds' nests. **chiú-tsoá^{n}**, a small wine-cup. **pô-lê-tsoá^{n}**, a wine-glass. **gėk-tsoá^{n}**, a cup made of jade.

teng-hé-tsoá^{n}, a small saucer used for a lamp. **hiáng-tsoá^{n}**, a small gong used by priests; a sort of musical instrument (v. hiáng). **ièn-tsoá^{n}**, bits of raw "bird-nest" shaped like a small cup or spoon.

tsoà^{n} [R. chien, to fry], to fry down fat from a lump of fat or fat meat. **tsoà^{n}-iû**, do. (to be carefully distinguished from tsoa^{n}).

tsoā^{n} (R. chiēn), to spout out in a jet. **tsoā^{n}-chhut**, id. **huih tsoā^{n}--lâng**, blood spouting out on by-standers. **tsoā^{n}-huih**, to spout out blood, as a severe wound. **tsoā^{n}-jiō**, to make water in a large stream. **chhun koâ^{n}, hō ná^{n}-tsoā^{n}**, when it is cold in spring there is heavy rain.

tsoā^{n} (R. chiēn), cheap, because the supply is abundant. **kùi-tsoā^{n}**, dear and cheap. **noā^{n}-tsoā^{n}**, very cheap and abundant. **i--ê chí^{n}-gûn noā^{n}-tsoā^{n}**, he is too free in spending money. **kam-noā^{n}, m̄-kam tsoā^{n}**, will let it rot rather than sell it cheap or give it away.

tsoah (Cn.) **tsoah-ngá**, a small bamboo frame put in the bottom of a rice boiler when cooking, to keep the food from being singed; also used when cooking by steaming. **chhö-tsoah**, id.

tsoah (Cn.), = A. chiah, this, thus, &c.

tsoah, to shake back and forwards, as man or boat, &c.; to spill by shaking; to tremble; to be in an excited state, as people at rumours of rebellion, &c. **tsoah--chhut-lâi**, to get spilled, as water by shaking. **phah-tsoah**, to shake so as to spill.

le kàu phah-tsoah (T.), far too merry and jolly.

iô-tsoah, in an excited state, as the people at reports of approaching calamity, rebellion, &c.

tsoȧh — **chién-tsoȧh**, the worm that eats books. **ka-tsoȧh**, a cockroach. **hái-ka-tsoȧh**, an insect (like a slater) found in boats. **ka-tsoȧh-sit** (lit. wings), a sort of acacia with pinnate leaves; also (C.), a water-plant with thin oblong leaves that float on the surface. **ka-tsoȧh-hièn**, bad smell from cockroaches. **chhàu-ka-tsoȧh-hièn**, id.

chhù-tsoȧh, a sort of middleman or house agent, who helps in buying or renting houses (not polite). **soa^{n}-ka-tsoȧh** (Cn.), a man who looks out grave sites to sell; also (C.), a sort of insect.

tsoȧh, to differ, esp. for the worse; to sprain severely, much worse than "ut--tiȯh." **tsoȧh--tiȯh**, to be sprained. **tsoȧh-kun**, a very bad sprain.

khah-tsoȧh, rather different; not quite so good. **tsoȧh hn̄g**, the difference is great. **tsoȧh tsōe**, id. **tsoȧh-pān**, to differ from the pattern. **tsoȧh-bī**, slightly tainted, as meat. **seng-lí lóng-tsoȧh**, trade has become very dull and small. **cheng-tsoȧh**, to differ (v. cheng). **tsáu-tsoȧh**, to differ; to be put out of order, *e.g.* as something evenly arranged, as a neat pile of books. **chit-ē-loȧh, chiū tsáu-tsoȧh** (prov.), don't touch it, or you will injure it (v. loȧh). **hun-kim-á-tsoȧh**, very slight divergence, as from the pattern, or very slight want of regularity in a piece of work, *e.g.* the rays of a fan not being quite even when shut.

tsoȧh (C.), = A. chhoȧh, diagonal.

tsoāi, to twist or wrench backwards and forwards. **tsoāi-lâi tsoāi-khì**, id.; to twist one's self from side to side; said also of toes or other things so twisted. **tsoāi-chih**, to break by twisting back and forward, as a nail. **tsoāi-tn̄g**, id. **oai-oai tsoāi-tsoāi**, all twisted and awry; not even. **chhit-oai poeh-tsoāi**, all wrong together.

tsoan — **tsoan-hông**, a petty military officer (v. hông).

tsoan (R. id.) **tsoan-tsoan**, exclusively; undividedly. **tsoan-it**, mind set exclusively on one thing. **sim tsoan-it**, id. **tsoan-sim**, id. **tsoan-sim ti-chì**, id. **tsoan-ì**, id. **tsoan-ì-kè**, id.; of set purpose. **tsoan-bū** (R.), to attend with one's whole heart. **tsoan-liēn**, to be specially skilful at one kind or department of work. **tsoan-tī gán-khe**, exclusively treats eye diseases.

tsū-tsoan, to take on one's self; to act without due authority. **tsoan-koân**, to have or take the sole management, either of our own affairs, or of what is committed to us, or by unjust assumption or usurpation.

tsoân [R. a spring or fountain, = col. tsoâ^{n}]. **tsoân-chiu**, Chin-chew. **chiang-tsoân**, Chang-chew and Chin-chew (v. chiang).

kiú-tsoân tōe-ē, the invisible world; Hades. **hông-tsoân lō-siōng** (R.), id. **hông-tsoân**, id. **hông-tsoân lō-chiū^{n}**, id.

sėk-tsoân, a fountain among rocks. **sèng-tsoân**, a sacred fountain.

tsoân [R. complete, = col. tsn̂g, chiâu]. **tsoân-jiân**, entirely. **sûn-tsoân**, perfect, as in character (v. sûn). **oân-tsoân**, complete; to complete. **oân-bêng tsoân-chiet**, good reputation preserved till death (v. chiet). **hok-lók-siū tsoân**, good fortune, rank, and longevity all complete. **tiong-hàu lióng-tsoân**, fidelity and filial piety both perfect (esp. of a mandarin).

pó-tsoân, to keep in safety (v. pó). **chiu-tsoân**, to arrange a dispute or agreement all right for another. **kiû-tsoân chek-pī**, to insist on having everything quite perfect, without the least error.

tsoân-si, an unmutilated corpse, as when strangled

厦英大辭典

or otherwise killed, but not beheaded, and having the limbs all entire. **tsoân-sin**, the whole body (alive). **tsoân-su** (C.), an entire suit of clothes. **tsoân-su**, an entire set of volumes; complete works of an author. **tsoân-si** (C.), id. **lâu-tsoân-hoat**, to let all the hair of the head grow, as women. **tsoân-ke**, whole household. **tsoân-iet**, salted scorpions, used in medicine.

tsoân-báuh, to contract for in a lump. **tsoân-léng**, I accept the whole (of a present).

tsoán [R. to turn; to transfer; = col. tńg]. **ūn-tsoán**, to revolve in orbit, as moon, &c. **thiⁿ teh-ūn-tsoán**, heaven revolving round the earth. **tsoán-táu-tiâⁿ**, a complaint entered on an unusual day at the yamun (v. táu).

tsoán-gán, a short time after; said only of things past.

tsoán-pièn, able to adapt one's plans, language, or conduct to suit changed circumstances; versatile. **hoan-tsoán**, id. **ū-hoan-tsoán**, id. **bô-tè thang-khì hoan-tsoán**, having no way to get money, &c.; quite at a stand. **bōe-tit--thang tsoán-sin**, having no room to turn in, as in a narrow road; quite at a stand in managing a matter. **tsoán-oan**, to put another face on a matter (gen. somewhat false), so as to get a quarrel settled for a man (v. oan). **oán-tsoán**, adapting one's words, &c., very nicely to the occasion, with delicate tact; going round about to reach an end. **oán-tsoán-khǹg**, to exhort in a specially kind and winning way, often somewhat round about. **oán-tsoán-kiû**, to beseech in a delicate, winning, and insinuating way.

tsoán-sè (C. sì), to be transmigrated again into human form, after punishment (v. sè). **tsoán-sè** (C. sòe), to sublet. **tsoán-tién**, to remortgage. **tsoán-kau**, to hand over to another a thing first committed to us. **tsoán-thok**, to hand over to a third party, as a thing, message, or commission, first intrusted to us.

tsoán, to earn or gain, as money or food. **tsoán-thàn**, id. **tsoán-chiáh**, to get one's living by any means, work or begging. **tsoán-chîⁿ**, to get money by work or begging. **hiau-hēng tsoán**, to get a living by bad means. **kiông-tsoán**, to demand money (as a beggar) importunately and improperly. **hó-tsoán**, good for getting money at, as a house where beggars are liberally treated.

tsoán [R. chién, to cut]. **tsoán-jiông**, the mule pink or sweet william, &c.

tsoán [R. chhoàn, to cook]. **chien-tsoán**, to fry and then boil. **chien-tsoán-á**, id.

tsoàn (R. chhoàn), (T. and also A. chhoàn), to supplant another in employment. **tsoàn-thâu-lō͘**, id. **khit--i tsoàn--khì**, to be so supplanted. **khit--i tsoàn-bô--khì**, id. **tsoàn-bô-khì**, to fail in the attempt to supplant.

tsoān (R. id.) **tsū-tsoān**, to pretend to have knowledge or authority, *e.g.* to pretend to have got a message to deliver, or a commission to execute; to invent false additions to what we were authorized to say; to invent wrong meanings, or wrong characters for words, to conceal our ignorance; to invent new and unclassical phrases.

tsoān [R. id.; cf. tsūn], to turn or twist, as a key, or as the neck; a foreign lock; to lock a foreign lock; to wind up, as a watch.

gâu lién-tsoān, skilful at screwing money out of people, by hook or by crook, as by swindling, by intimidation, &c.

tsoān-chih, to twist off. **tsoān pio-á**, to wind up a watch. **tsoān-mn̂g**, to lock a door with foreign lock. **tsoān-khui**, to unlock a lock of foreign style.

tsoān-sî, the key of a foreign lock. **pio-á-tsoān**, a watch-key. **chiú-tsoān**, a cork-screw. **lê-si-tsoān**, a screw-driver. **thoah-tsoān**, the lock of a drawer. **kap-bān-tsoān**, lock of a strong chest, as for money. **mn̂g-tsoān**, a door-lock. **tèng-tsoān**, to put on a lock on a door (all of foreign style, while the Chinese form is a padlock, called "só").

tsoat (R. id.) **chhi-tsoat**, stupid. **gû-tsoat**, stupid, said of one's self. **ù-tsoat**, very dull of apprehension (v. ù). **tsoat-tit** (I am) a simple straightforward man. **tsoat-lōe** (R.), my wife. **lōng-kháu sêng-tsoat**, trying to act cleverly, but really very stupidly. **lōng-kháu hoán-tsoat**, id.

tsoat — **tsoat--chhut-lâi**, to break out, as grain from a bag that bursts open.

tsoát [R. to destroy; to cut off; to the utmost, sign of superlative; = col. chéh].

tsoát-kau, to break off intimacy. **tsoát-chêng**, quite alienated in feeling. **kat-tsoát**, determined to have no more intercourse. **koat-tsoát**, id. **tsoát-tn̄g**, to break off, as a habit, an acquaintanceship, &c. **toān-tsoát** (R.), having broken off all intercourse or friendship.

biét-tsoát (r.), to exterminate. **tsoát-tsú biét-sun**, may all your posterity be cut off! **tsoát-sû**, without male posterity.

tsoát-bāng, to lose hope; to despair.

kū-tsoát, to reject; to cast off. **khì-tsoát**, id. **khì tsoát**, has expired. **khùi tsoát**, id.

tsoát-biāu (r.), very excellent. **tsoát-khó-ò͘ⁿ** (r.), very hateful. **tsoát-sek** (R.), very beautiful, of a woman.

tsoe (C. che), dough. **ńg-tsoe**, soft dough. **tēng-tsoe**, stiff dough. **mīⁿ-tsoe**, wet dough from wheaten flour. **ké-tsoe** (C. kóe-che), dough for soft steamed cakes. **piáⁿ-tsoe**, dough prepared for making cakes or biscuits. **liàm piáⁿ-tsoe**, to break off enough of dough for each cake.

tsoe (C. che).

phái"-kut-tsoe (made of bad stuff), said in scolding a boy who behaves ill and seems likely to turn out a bad man. **hó-gín-á-tsoe**, well-behaved boy giving promise of being a good man.

hó-sin-tsoe, body well formed.

saⁿ-á-tsoe, material enough for making one coat.

tsoe — **bák-kiáh-tsoe**, an implement like a wooden clog (bák-kiáh) with a strap of palm-fibre across it, held in the hand by poor cripples who crawl on the ground.

tsôe — **hó-sin-tsôe**, well formed in body, neither too fat nor too lean.

tsôe [R. chê, in good order; even], (C. chê; Cn. tsôe), in some phrases interchanged with "chê."

tsôe-tsôe, regular; all equally; all together; all evenly; blunted, as the point of a hair-pencil. **siá tsôe-tsôe**, write evenly. **bô-tsôe**, uneven; unequal; irregular, as a number of things that were expected to be even or equal.

tsôe-thâu-to, a knife made with a square end, as those used in kitchens.

chéng-tsôe, to adjust in order. **tsôe-chéng**, in good and regular order, as furniture, clothes, teeth, &c. **tsôe-tsáⁿ**, id. **pâi-khi-tsôe**, arrange neatly and evenly. **pí-khi-tsôe**, put them together and see that they are all the same length, &c. **chhèk-tsôe**, to shake (as pencils or lots) so as to make them all even. all arrived; to arrange a matter so as to please all; **hiàh-kha tsôe**, the line dividing the hair from the bare part of the forehead nearly even and level across the brow, counted good-looking in women. **siang-kha khiā-tsôe**, standing with feet even, as in making a respectful bow.

tsôe-chip, to assemble in large or full numbers. **kiò-khi-tsôe**, call all the persons together, as for some special purpose. **chhoân-tsôe**, to make all ready for some purpose, as men or things. **chhú-tsôe** (C. chhí-chê), fully assembled, *e.g.* for a procession. **chit-tsôe-lâi**, id. **tán-tsôe**, to wait till all have come. **hōe-tsôe**, to assemble for some common action. **hē-tsôe**, id. **tāi-ke tsôe-kàu**, all have arrived. **tsôe-pī**, all complete in number, as a number of things. **tsáp-chèng tsôe-khí**, attacked by a complication of diseases at once. **ngé-lē̤ tsôe-hoat**, calamities come at once from all quarters. **bān-lē̤-chìⁿ tsôe-hoat**, id.

tsôe-siaⁿ, with united voice. **tsôe-sim**, with one heart. **tsôe-kiáu**, to unite capital to set up a gambling-house. **tsôe-lién-pó**, to join capital to set up a place where gambling is done by the "lién-pó" (*q.v.*) **tsôe-pó**, id.

tsóe — **tsóe--lâng**, to treat a man curtly and slightingly, so as to show displeasure and make him ashamed, esp. in an indirect manner, as by some roundabout allusion, or by saying something to another. **náⁿ-tsóe--lâng**, as if you wish to slight people, said (*e.g.*) as to refusing a present.

tsòe (R. tsò), (C. tsò; Cn. tsòe), to make; to act; to do; to be, especially with the idea of doing; to perform, as rites; to keep, as feast or birth-day; counterfeit, "made up;" to make a betrothal or be betrothed (as the word is so much used about marriage, great care must be taken in its use on other matters).

siⁿ-tsòe, to be naturally; naturally so (v. siⁿ). **tsòe-chiâⁿ**, to complete (v. chiâⁿ). **tsòe-kè**, to have done it; to have done it before. **kā-lâng-tsòe**, to make a thing for a man. **tiāⁿ-tsoè**, made to order. **piēn-tsòe**, ready-made. **chiàu-tsòe**, doing one's work diligently and well. **ōe-tsòe--tit**, it will do; can or may be done. **bōe-tsòe--tit**, will not do; may not be done. **tsòe bōe-tit-lâi**, unable to effect it. **lí ka-kī tsòe-tit-lâi**, you have brought this trouble on yourself. **àm-tsöe-chìⁿ** (Cn.), secretly.

tsòe-lâng, behaviour (v. lâng). **tsòe-chêng**, to do a favour (v. chêng, "feelings"). **tsòe-chêng** (T. tsâiⁿ; Cn. tsûiⁿ), walk first (v. chêng, "front"). **tsòe-thâu**, to be first; to be head (v. thâu). **tsòe-kang**, to do work. **tsòe-khang**, to conspire together to injure or deceive a man. **tsòe-gōe**, to make small things just to pass the time. **tsòe-si**, to make odes or hymns. **tsòe-seng-lí**, to trade. **tsòe-bák**, to be a carpenter; to do carpenter's work. **tsòe-bāng**, to dream. **tsòe-lī**, to have dysentery. **tsòe-kùi**, wanton joking or gestures, as men and women. **tsòe-sū**, to act, esp. to begin a troublesome affair. **sū sī-i tsòe**, it was he who raised the trouble. **tsòe-pó**, to put the die (of the gambling called "lién-pó") in its shell ready for the gambling.

tsòe-lí-kóng, speak on just as you like: don't be afraid, but speak out; say on. **tsòe-lí-thák**, read it out aloud if you wish; read it and let us hear. **tsòe-i-khì**, went away of his own accord. **i tsòe-i, goá tsòe-goá**, he and I are quite separate. **bīn tsòe-bīn, kha tsòe-kha**, legs and top (of a sort of table) able to be taken separate.

tsòe-tiāⁿ, to be a pledge or earnest; to be used or given as an earnest. **tsòe seng-lé**, to be used as a ceremonial offering.

tsòe-hong, to be windy; there is wind. **tsòe-hong lòh-hō̤**, to have wind and rain. **tsòe-tang-lâm**, a violent south-east storm rising. **tang-bīn tsòe-sek**, first light of dawn in the east. **tsòe-phâiⁿ-thìⁿ**, it is stormy. **thìⁿ beh-tsòe-phâiⁿ**, the weather is going to be bad. **thìⁿ tsòe-o̤**, sky all dark and cloudy, as if going to rain.

tsòe-tīn, to go in a large company. **tsòe-phoāⁿ**, to go as a companion. **tsòe-pû**, to come together (v. pû). **tsòe chit-tui**, to meet or collect together (v. tui). **tsòe-tùi**, to be a pair; to be antithetical. **tsòe-kheh**, to go for a few days to visit her own relations, as a wife; to get married, as a virgin.

tsòe-sien-siⁿ, to be a doctor. **tsòe-tiong--ê**, to act as middle-man. **tsòe-nìⁿ--ê**, a dyer. **tsòe-pùt**, to become a Buddha. **tsòe-kúi**, to be a ghost or demon; to cause trouble secretly. **tsòe hê-siūⁿ**, to have Buddhist priests performing rites for the dead in one's house; to be a Buddhist priest.

tsòe-chiaⁿ, to keep the new-year. **tsòe-tang**, to keep the winter festival (ancestral). **tsòe-kī**, to keep the anniversary of a death with ceremonies. **tsòe-tùi-nìⁿ**, to perform these rites on the first anniversary, *i.e.* just one year after the death. **tsòe-sûn**, to make offerings at set intervals to the dead (represented by the "hûn-sin") soon after death (v. sûn). **tsòe pah-jit**, to have these rites for a hundred days. **tsòe-siⁿ-jit**, to keep a birth-day (v. siⁿ). **tsòe-chiò**, to perform the Tauist rites called "chiò."

tsng-tsòe, to counterfeit (v. tsng). **tsòe-tsoh**, counterfeit, as goods. **tsòe-sek**, to make a colour, esp. a false colour (v. sek). **tsòe-chhiú**, counterfeit work. **tsòe-hè**, to make old goods look new for purpose of deceit. **tsòe-àn**, to make a false accusation in court. **teh-tsòe-àn**, telling lies.

tsòe-sim-pū, to get a daughter-in-law; to betroth a girl to one's son; to be a daughter-in-law. **tsòe i--ê sim-pū**, to be his daughter-in-law. **tsòe-bó**, to make arrangements (betrothal, &c.) for getting a wife for one's self. **kā--i tsòe-bó**, to make arrangements for getting a wife for him, *e.g.* for one's son or nephew. **tsòe chit-ê-bó hō̤--i**, id. **hō̤--i tsòe-bó**, to give one's daughter (or niece, &c.) to him to be his bride. **tsòe-chhin**, to settle a marriage contract; to have affinity with each other, as the parents of the couple. **tsòe chhin-ke**, to fix a marriage alliance between each other's children. **tsòe chhin-chiâⁿ**, to marry a wife or get one's son or nephew married; to espouse or betroth, as self or son, &c., said either about bride or bridegroom. **tsòe-tiāⁿ-tiòh**, the engagement of betrothal made. **tsòe--lâng**, to betroth one's daughter (or niece, &c.) to a man. **tsòe-tsòe hō̤--lâng**, to give away one's daughter (or any girl under our control) to a man to be his wife, esp. without much care in choosing the son-in-law. **m̄-káⁿ khì-tsòe**, dares not take her for bride, &c. **tsòe-lâi tsòe-khì**, two or more marriage connections formed between two families. **tsòe tá-lòh-lâng**, of what place is the person to whom betrothed. **lí--ê tsa-bó-kiáⁿ tsòe sím-mih-lâng**, to what man is your daughter betrothed. **i-ê-kiáⁿ tsòe lí--ê tsa-bó-kiáⁿ**, his son is betrothed to your daughter.

tsòe [R. an excrescence, = col. cheh]. **chìn-tsòe**,

marrying and going to live in the house of the bride's father for a longer or shorter time (gen. short), but retaining one's own surname and having full power over one's own household, thus differing from the manner of marriage called "chio." **jip-tsòe** (R.), id.

tsòe-á (C.), = A. cheh-á, a wart.

tsōe (R. id. = col. chō), (Cn. tsö), guilt, liability to the punishment of crime.

tsōe-siók, a crime. **tsōe-kò** (R.), id. **tsōe-giét**, great wickedness. **tsōe-ok** (r.), great guilt or crime (v. ok). **khin-tsōe**, slight guilt. **tāng-tsōe**, great guilt. **sí-tsōe**, guilt deserving death. **chhut-tsōe**, to be banished or transported.

tsōe-àn, a criminal case. **tsōe-hoān**, a criminal. **tsōe-jîn**, a man with whom fault is found; also (r.), a criminal against the laws of man or of heaven. **goá-sī i--ê tsōe-jîn**, he looks on me as utterly opposed to him.

hoān-tsōe, to incur guilt; to commit a crime. **tek-tsōe**, to offend; to incur blame or displeasure; I beg your pardon. **tek-lán-tsōe**, to offend us. **tek-lâng-ê-tsōe**, to offend people. **sù-tsōe** (polite), pardon me, sir, for my want of politeness, &c. **hėk-tsōe u-thien** (R.), to incur guilt against Heaven. **jīn-tsōe**, to confess guilt or fault. **hók-tsōe** (R.), id. **ti-tsōe**, id. **tī-tsōe**, to punish guilt, as magistrate. **pān-tsōe**, id. **chhú-tsōe** (R.), id. (v. chhú, "to manage"). **chhú-tsōe** (R.), to contract guilt (v. chhú, "to take"). **tēng-tsōe**, to condemn, as a judge. **būn-tsōe** (r.), id. **chek-tsōe**, to lay the blame upon; to charge the fault upon, *e.g.* for managing a matter ill or spoiling something. **put-ti, put-tsōe**, in case of ignorance, guilt is not reckoned or counted. **sià-tsōe**, to forgive guilt. **siau-tsōe**, to remove guilt by rites (as Tauist priest or sorceress), esp. at the tutelary temple. **siók-tsōe**, to atone for guilt. **siū-tsōe**, to bear the punishment. **péh-á thau-chiáh; o-á siū-tsōe**, the white dog stealthily eats meat and the black one suffers for it (or o-á &c., péh-á &c.) **thòe-lâng chē-tsōe**, to bear the responsibility of another's guilt. **thòe-lâng chiáh-tsōe**, id.

tsōe (R. to), (C. chē; Cn. tsöe), many; much. **tsōe-tsōe**, id. **tsōe-chió**, many and few; much or little; how many? (v. chió). **hiah-tsōe**, so many (v. hiah). **joā-tsōe**, how many? (v. joā).

chhùi tsōe, talkative. **tsōe-ōe**, talking much when he should be quiet.

tsōe (C.) = A. chē. **tuh-ka-tsōe**, drowsy and nodding.

tsoeh [R. chiet, a joint; a term; = col. tsat], (C. cheh; Cn. tsöeh), a term of the year; a festival. **tsoeh-khùi**, the twenty-four terms of the solar year. **tsòe-tsoeh**, to keep a festival-day. **tsoeh-gî**, presents given to teachers at terms. **nî^{n}-tsoeh**, the terms and festivals of the year. **bô-nî^{n} bô-tsoeh**, not keeping the heathen yearly terms and festivals. **sàng-nî^{n}-tsoeh**, to make presents at the terms (v. sàng). **nî^{n}-tang géh-tsoeh**, all the terms, festivals, and anniversaries of a year, at which rites are regularly performed and expenses incurred. **kong-pô si-kī, nî^{n}-tang géh-tsoeh**, do., both public and private.

sa^{n}-jit-tsoeh, the 3.3. **gō-jit-tsoeh**, the dragon-boat festival, 5.5. **tiōng-iông-tsoeh**, the 9.9.

thàn-chí-tsöeh (Cn.), take advantage of the present opportunity.

ū-chî^{n}, jit-jit tsoeh; bô-chî^{n}, tsoeh-tsoeh khang, a man who has money has a festival every day of the year; to a man without money every festival is an empty name. **tsoeh-chêng bô-êng; tsoeh-āu chiū-pān**, can attend to the business only when the festival is over.

tsóeh [R. chiét, to cut off, to obstruct, = col. tsáh], (Cn. tsöeh; C. chéh, chhiet, in different phrases), to slice vertically. **tsóeh-hun**, to slice down tobacco. **tsóeh tsòe-sì-chiu**, to cut into four quarters, as a cake. **phoe-phoe tsóeh-tsóeh**, may you be sliced up and minced small!

ū-tsám-tsóeh, able to decide with wisdom and promptitude and act with rapidity. **tsám-teng tsóeh-thih** (lit. cutting nails and iron), decided and determined, so as to listen to nothing to the contrary.

tsoh (R. tiok), to build, as a wall or dyke. **tsoh-chhiū^{n}**, to build a wall. **tsoh-tsàu**, to build a fire-place, as in kitchen. **tsoh-pi**, to build a weir or dam on a river. **tsoh-tsúi**, to bank up or dam up a water-course so as to turn it into the fields.

tsoh [R. tsok, to do; to make], to work the fields. **tsoh-hn̂g**, to cultivate dry fields. **tsoh-chhân**, to cultivate irrigated fields. **chèng-tsoh**, to do agricultural work in general; to farm. **tsoh-sit**, to do agricultural work; also (Cn.), to do any kind of work.

tsoh-siū, to build a nest. **tsoh-bit**, to make honey, as bee. **tsòe kap-tsoh**, to be a carpenter who makes furniture, an upholsterer, or cabinet-maker. **kap-tsoh-tiàm**, a furniture shop.

gē-tsoh, a coroner. **sòe-tsoh**, a spy. **hā-tsoh**, mean and low in character, position, or actions (v. hā). **tsòe-tsoh**, counterfeit.

hoat-tsoh, to come to light, as a secret; to come to pass, as a plot; to break out on the body, as a disease, often one that has been long kept hid; to begin to grow tall and big, as a boy just changing into a man. **ke-ūn hoat-tsoh**, the family now becoming prosperous.

kóng tsáp-tsoh gē-gōh (T.), to talk intentionally in an involved and indistinct way (v. gêh).

tsóh [R. tsók, yesterday, but the colloquial for "yesterday" is only "tsā" *q.v.*]

tsóh--jit, the day before yesterday. **tsóh-jit-mî^{n}**, the night before last. **lóh--tsóh-jit**, the second day before yesterday. **sūn--tsóh-jit** (Cn.), id.

tsóh (R. tėk), to throw, as a stone; to shoot, as an arrow. **tsóh-hiet-kák**, to throw away. **tsóh--khì**, id. **tsóh--lâi**, throw it to me. **tsóh-khi-chià^{n}**, throw straight. **tsóh-chiū^{n}--khì**, to throw upwards. **tsóh-chì^{n}**, to shoot an arrow. **tsóh-chióh-thâu**, to throw a stone.

tsóh-sí-lâng, to kill a man by a stone or an arrow. **tsóh chit-khang**, to make a wound or indentation, as by a stone thrown. **tsóh chit-lâu**, to make a swelling by throwing a stone.

bák-chiu tsóh-chiáu, the skin of the eye drawn up at the corner, giving a squinting look.

tsóh — **tsām-tsóh**, unequal in size, shape, or goodness, as things that should be all uniform; feeling anxious and uncomfortable about a number of troublesome matters. **tsáp-tsóh**, confused and involved, as an affair; anxious and uncomfortable about many affairs.

tsöh (Cn.), = A. cheh, to dry with a gentle touch of a cloth or of the finger.

tsöh — **tsöh-thoah** (Cn.), = A. tsau-that, to abuse or use lavishly (v. thoah).

tsöh (Cn.), = A. chéh, to exterminate.

tsok [R. to make; to do; to act; = col. tsoh]. **tsok-lók**, to manifest delight by gestures or appearance. **pn̄g-sîn tsok-hok**, to have a good feast on the occasion of worshipping an idol. **tsok-ui tsok-hok**, to behave proudly and insolently, as a mandarin or a powerful and prosperous man (v. ui). **tsok-gák**, to play music. **tsok-ip**, to make a ceremonial bow. **tsok-tiong**, to act as middle-man. **tsok-tong**, to act as host (v. tong, "east").

tsok-sêng, to assist in business, as by money or by good name. **tsok-chhái**, to make a present to a man with expression of good wishes for his prosperity. **tsok-tiàu**, to make offerings at the ceremonies for a deceased friend, sort of condolence.

tsáp-tsok, miscellaneous literary compositions, not including essays. **tsū-tsok tsū-tong**, he who does it must himself bear the responsibility. **kám-tsok kám-tong**, id.

tsok-giét, to act very wickedly. **ûi-hui tsok-tái**, id. **tsok-hoat**, to practise black arts. **tsok-pè**, to molest, as a demon causing disease; to hinder an affair secretly and maliciously. **tsok-koài**, to molest people, as a demon; to act in an idle ill-behaved way, as a fast and disorderly youth; to injure a man by secret plots or opposition. **tsok-lōng**, to annoy or possess, as a demon; to play tricks on, to befool, as a man. **tsok-tsōng**, to molest or afflict, as a demon; to injure by black arts or intrigues.

tsók — **pè-tì siu^{n}-tsók**, too crowded with furniture, as a room.

tsók (R. id.), a tribe or clan, esp. of same surname; kindred. **tsong-tsók**, id. **thong-tsók**, the whole kindred. **tsók-tiong**, among persons of the same kindred. **pún-tsók**, of our relatives or clan. **tsók-sì^{n}**, a clan of one surname. **tsók-sèng**, id. **tsók-phài**, a great division of a clan.

tsók-chhin, a very distant relative of the same surname. **tsók-tit**, id. (junior?). **kiông-tsók**, a powerful clan. **tsók-tiú^{n}**, the head of a clan. **khai-tsók**, to found a family or clan. **tsók-phó**, a genealogical table.

kiú-tsók, the nine relations, from great great-grandfather to great great-grandson. **sam-tsók**, our own relatives, with those of wife and mother. **chhiau sam-tsók**, to exterminate all the relatives of a man, of his wife, and of his mother. **biét-tsók**, to exterminate a whole family.

tsúi-tsók, the fishy tribes.

tsom (C.), = A. tsam, a hair-pin.

tsom (C.), = A. chim (moral maxims). **tsom-gân**, = A. chim-giên, id.

tsong — **kui-tsong**, the whole quantity of goods of a particular sort in a hong. **kui-tsong kui-ih**, in whole quantities; wholesale. **kui-tsong ê-seng-lí**, a wholesale business. **kui-tsong bóe**, to buy the whole of the goods of one sort that are in the hong. **kui-tsong bōe**, to sell the whole lot, as above.

tsong — **chhok-tsong**, taking what comes to hand without selection; whatever we may chance upon, as the first man we may meet, or first thing we find. **chhok-tsong thoèh-hō--i**, give him at random, as money, &c. **chhok-tsong mñg--i**, ask him whatever comes up in our mind; ask him to read or repeat a passage "ad aperturam."

tsong (R. id.), a clan. **tsong-tsók**, id. **tāi-tsong kū-tsók**, a great and numerous clan. **siáu-tsong**, a small ancestral hall of one branch (of a large family that has a common ancestral hall), that counts only a few generations back. **tsong-phài**, a clan. **tsó-tsong**, ancestors (v. tsó).

tsong--ê, having the same surname though not nearly related. **tông-tsong--ê**, of the same clan. **tông-sèng, put-tông-tsong**, of the same surname but of different clan. **tông-sèng put-tsong**, id.

tsong (R. id.) **chèng-tsong**, correct in conduct. **toan-tsong**, do., especially of women.

tsong [R. to adorn; to feign; to pack or store up (perhaps two words); = col. tsng].

tsong-jiám, to put colour on a white ground, or on a black and white sketch (v. jiám). **iām-tsong**, splendidly dressed, as woman. **tām-tsong**, simply and plainly but neatly adorned, as woman.

tsong-khiang (C.), making a false show and pretence (v. khiang).

kun-tsong, military stores. **kun-tsong-kék**, an arsenal.

tsong [R. footmarks; traces]. **tsong-chek**, traces. **bā bô-tsong-chek**, to search but find no trace. **lâi bô-tsong, khì bô-chek**, going and coming without leaving any trace; very sudden or secret in movements, so that no one knows; *e.g.* as a thief. **lâi bô-tsong, khì bô-jiah** (or **bô-iá^{n}**), id. **lâi bû-tsong, khì bû-éng**, id.

ōe sī-hong; jī sī-tsong, spoken words are wind, but written words leave a mark; sometimes translated "words when written are also deceitful," from "tsong," to adorn; to feign.

tsông (R. id.) **tsun-tsông** (R.), to reverence; to adore; to worship.

tsông (R. id.), to hide, as person or thing. **tsông-lông**, id. **thau-tsông**, to conceal and hide, as stolen goods or smuggled articles, or as a criminal. **ún-tsông**, to hide and keep secret, as a thing picked up, or as stolen goods. **àm-tsông**, to hide or secrete, as a thing or person. **bâi-tsông** (R.), id.

tē-tsông-ông, a god supposed to rule the spirit world.

tsông, to spring or leap up; to rear; to rush rapidly. **tsông--tsáu**, to escape and run away. **tsáu-tsông**, to work hard and hurry about constantly in haste without resting. **tsông-lâi tsông-khì**, to leap and frisk about; to work in great haste; moving about rapidly back and forwards. **tsông-lâi tsông-khì, tsông-bô-lō**, trying all ways but not finding any successful. **tsông-bô-lō**, id. **tsông-jip tsông-chhut**, rushing out and in, as in great bustle. **tsông--chhut-khì**, to rush out. **tsông--jip-khì**, to rush in. **tsông--khí-lâi**, to rear, as a horse.

tsóng (R. id.), all; prefix, with a meaning nearly like "yet after all;" affix to the name of a military officer of the rank "tsóng-iâ," *e.g.* "bák-tsóng," the "chhien-tsóng" named "bák."

lóng-tsóng, all. **lóng-lóng tsóng-tsóng**, id. **tsóng-láng**, to sum up in a rough general way. **tsóng-sǹg**, to reckon up the total amount. **tsóng-phō**, a ledger. **tsóng-phò**, a ship's cook. **tsóng-kiet**, a general balance, as at end of year, or at closing an account or a business (v. kiet). **tsóng-miâ^{n}**, a general term or name. **tsóng-hō**, id. **tsóng-hō-miâ^{n}**, id.

tsóng-lí, to rule; to manage, as an official appointed for some special duty. **tsóng-koán**, to have general oversight over a number of persons employed. **tsóng-koá^{n}**, a sort of boatswain (not now used) in the old large Amoy junks. **tsóng-sū**, to have the general management and oversight of many matters. **tsòe tsóng-kun-thâu**, to have the chief management of a matter.

tsóng-thâu, head-man of the police, messengers, or constables in a yamun. **chhe-tsóng**, id. **toā-tsóng**, a still more powerful head of these police. **tsóng-pó**, a head-man of the villages round Amoy (v. pó).

tsóng-tok, governor-general; viceroy. **tsóng-peng**, a general officer in army or navy. **tsóng-toā**, an officer temporarily appointed to the command of a force. **tsóng-iâ**, commander of a thousand soldiers (on paper). **chhien-tsóng**, id. **pé-tsóng**, a captain supposed to command a hundred soldiers. **peh-tsóng** (C.), id. **pé-tsóng** (C.), id. **pah-tsóng** (Cn.), id., only of cavalry. **bé-pah-tsóng** (Cn.), id. of cavalry. **toā-tsóng-chhâi**, examiner for the Tsin-sze (chìn-sū) degree.

tsóng-sī, yet after all; nevertheless it is —. **tsóng m̄-sī-i**, it would appear (though there was room for doubt) that it was not he. **m̄ tsóng-tióh-khì**, well, as there is no help for it, must just go. **m̄ tsóng--tióh àn-niⁿ**, well, as there is no other way, it must just be done so. **tsóng káⁿ m̄-sī**, probably it is not, but with two or three to ten that it may be so. **tsóng bô-lâng chhin-chhiūⁿ lí-ê-khoán**, there is no one in all the world so bad as you! **tsóng-bô**, though antecedently improbable, yet now it seems probable that —, *e.g.* **tsóng-bô sī-i thau-thóeh**, though one would not have suspected him, yet it would seem that he is the thief, as there is apparently no other explanation possible.

tsòng (R. id.), to bury. **bâi-tsòng**, id. **tâi-tsòng**, id. **tsòng-bōng** (r.), id. **an-tsòng**, to bury in proper way with due ceremonies. **chìn-tsòng**, to place the coffin in the grave. **chhut-tsòng**, to carry out and bury. **sàng-tsòng**, to attend a funeral. **chiàm-tsòng**, to take unjust possession of a grave for burial. **háp-tsòng**, to bury together at once. **hū-tsòng**, to bury side by side with a relative previously buried. **tsòng-kim**, to bury a jar with old bones. **tsòng-koan**, to bury a body in coffin, opp. to burying old bones. **în tsòng, báu hoat**, in a few hours after the burial the propitious influence begins.

tsòng [R. tiòng, to hit the mark]. **put-tsòng-iōng** (C.), = A. put-tiòng-iōng, or put-chiòng-iōng, dull and useless, as a man.

tsòng [R. strong, as a young man]. **tsòng-teng**, a strong young man, from about twenty to forty. **bîn-tsòng**, lictors of civil mandarins, who use rattan whips. **bîn-tsòng-thâu**, a head-man over several of them.

tsòng-kiēn, strong and robust, as man. **kien-tsòng**, firmly made, as furniture; strong, as a city, &c. **ióng-tsòng**, vigorous and strong, as a grown-up man. **sim tsòng**, firm-hearted. **kun-ki tiâu-tsòng**, having so good a horoscope (as child), that it will grow strong and be fortunate.

tsòng-táⁿ, to stir up one's courage; very bold (v. táⁿ). **tsòng kok-thé**, to increase the power or dignity of the state, as a wise or powerful mandarin. **tsòng-iông ê-ióh**, medicine taken by men for venereal purposes.

tsòng — **tāi-tsòng-iâ** (C.), a paper image worshipped in the seventh moon.

tsōng — **bōng-tsōng**, careless; clumsy; clownish; unmannerly; awkward; uncouth. **bōng-tsōng-hàn**, a clownish awkward fellow.

tsōng [R. form, = col. tsn̄g, chiōng]. **hêng-tsōng**, form; shape. **kî-hêng koài-tsōng**, a strange appearance. **m̄-chiâⁿ-tsōng**, ill-shaped; ugly **chit-tsōng, náⁿ kaⁿ-siû**, very dirty and disorderly in dress and hair, like a prisoner. **lí hó-tsōng**, you are just as bad (as he with whom you find fault). **tìⁿ chit-ê-tsōng**, put on an appearance for a pretext. **tiuⁿ chit-ê-tsōng**, id.

tsōng chit-kù-ōe, to pretend that a man said something which he did not say. **khioh chit-kù-ōe lâi-tsōng--i**, to pretend that one man said a thing that was not said by him, but by another. **chháu-tsōng** (esp. C.) to pretend that a thing or affair exists which does not exist. **chháu-lōng-tsōng**, id.

tsōng-goân, = chiōng-goân, the highest of the new Hanlin members at one time (v. goân).

tsōng — **tsok-tsōng**, to possess or to injure in any way, as an evil spirit; to injure by some black art, or by some secret intrigue or trick, as man.

tsōng [R. id., by change of tone from "tsông," to hide or lay up]. **sam-tsōng**, a Buddhist priest of the Tang dynasty, who invented the rite called "tńg-tsn̄g" for women who die within the first month. **tông-sam-tsōng**, id.

tsōng (R. id. = col. tsn̄g). **ngé-tsōng**, the five great internal organs, heart, liver, lungs, stomach (and kidneys? or bladder?). **ngé-tsōng liòk-hú**, all the great internal organs and intestines.

tsöng, or **chöng** (Cn.), = A. cheng, in some tones and words.

tsöng — **lē-tsöng** (Cn.), = lə-chêng, an expression of surprise and displeasure at a man spoiling something by his folly or awkwardness.

tsu (R. id.) **gûn-tsu**, vermilion; red ink. **tsu-se**, cinnabar. **thê-tsu**, an inferior red paint.

tsu [R. red], a surname. **tsu-bûn-kong**, the commentator Choo-he or Chu-hi, worshipped in temples of Ting districts, or divisions of Hiens, where there is no temple of Confucius. **tsu-tsú**, id. **tsu-hu-tsú**, id.

tsu-âng, bright red colour. **tsu-lí**, a sort of small plum or cherry. **tsu-lí** (R.), red shoes of very high mandarins. **tsu-toaⁿ**, an order written in red ink by the mandarin's own hand, used as a warrant. **chhut-tsu-jū**, to issue such a document. **tsu-phoe**, an order from the emperor, through the prime minister, &c. **tsu-kn̄g**, an essay that has got the Kujin degree.

tsu-i-kong, an assistant of the idol Bûn-chhiong, wearing a red dress. **khoe-seng tsu-i**, the two assistants of Bûn-chhiong.

tsu [R. to assist; money; talents; to rely], (Cn. tsü).

tsu-tsē, to assist with money or gifts. **tsu-chià**, to rely upon (v. chià). **kang-tsu**, wages; pay. **chiú-tsu**, a small gratuity for carrying a letter or parcel. **chiú-tsu-chîⁿ**, id.

thien-tsu, good literary talents. **tsu-chit**, literary talents, as good or bad.

tsu [R. wealth], (Cn. tsü). **ka-tsu**, wealth, as of a household. **ka-tsu pah-bān**, extremely wealthy. **ka-tsu chhiong-chiok**, id.

tsu [R. appearance of person], (Cn. tsü). **hong-tsu**, complexion; appearance of face, as to health or sickness. **hong-tsu hó**, looking very well, as in good health.

tsu (Cn. tsü). **tsu-niûⁿ**, a woman (v. niûⁿ).

tsu [R. juicy; pleasant taste], (Cn. tsü). **tsu-bī**, taste, flavour, as of food. **tsu-bui**, pleased with one's self, as for good fortune (v. bui). **tsu-im**, allaying feverishness, and cooling to the system. **tsu-im-pó**, food or medicine that has this effect, as frogs, tortoise, &c. **tsu-im ê-mih**ⁿ, id. **tē-lāi teh-tsu-im**, chuckling inwardly over some success, or over the misfortunes that come upon an enemy, esp. when not done by us.

tsu (R. id.), a pearl; a bead; applied to various round things.

chin-tsu, a pearl. **phàⁿ-tsu**, an artificial pearl. **lê-phí-tsu**, false pearl made of the shells of shell-fish. **pāng-khak-tsu**, false pearl made of mother-of-pearl. **tsáu-bé khoàⁿ-chin-tsu**, in such haste as to miss seeing important things. **pó-tsu**, a wonderfully precious pearl. **tsu-pó**, pearls and other very precious things. **giâ-kang-tsu**, a pearl supposed to be produced by the centipede, and to emit light at night. **iā-bêng-tsu**, id.

tsu-phek-sán, a medicine made of pearls and amber. **tsu-lê**, a sort of shell-fish. **koe-bú-tsu**, a small wild pea, bright scarlet with a red spot. **íⁿ-tsu**, a sort of tea. **tsu-chi**, gunpowder tea. **chhang-tsu**, onions cut down for eating. **chhì-tsu-chhì** (Cn.), = C. hāu-á-chhì, a low trailing shrub with shining leaves and black berries.

hī-tsu, the lower lobe of the ear. **tsu-teng**, round-headed nails. **thiāu-tsu** (T. tsui), a round pedestal or base of a pillar. **chióh-tsu**, id., esp. a round stone socket for a movable wooden pillar, as for an awning.

siⁿ-tsu, a sort of shot for guns. **siⁿ-tsu**, a small white speck forming in the eye. **bák-chiu siⁿ-tsu**, id. **bák-chiu khí-tsu**, id.

gán-tiong bû-tsu, said of a man who does not well understand men or things. **iú-gán bû-tsu**, id. **jiók-gán bû-tsu**, id. **siók-gán bû-tsu**, id.

tsu-koaⁿ, an ornamental head-dress worn by the ladies of very high mandarins. **tsu-liû**, the fringe of pendants hanging down from that sort of head-dress, or from a crown. **tiâu-tsu**, a court necklace of beads, worn by mandarins. **hiuⁿ-tsu**, scented beads, used by any one simply for the scent. **sò-tsu**, Buddhist prayer-beads.

tsu — **chhut-tsu**, to have small-pox. **chhut-tsu bē-phû** (C.), small-pox that does not fully form the pustules, suppressed small-pox, very dangerous. **chiàⁿ-tsu**, real small-pox. **tsúi-tsu**, chicken-pox.

chèng-tsu, to inoculate; said also for vaccination. **tsu-phí**, the scab of small-pox. **tsu-chéng**, the scab, as used for inoculation. **hó-tsu-ûn**, a season when small-pox is of a mild type. **pháiⁿ-tsu-ûn**, a season when it is very virulent and deadly. **pháiⁿ-tsu-tang** (C. T.), id.

tsu-niûⁿ-má, the goddess who protects children from small-pox. **tsu-pô**, id. **tsu-kong-pô**, the god and goddess of do. **tsu-kong-má**, id. **tsu-kong tsu-má**, id.

tsu [R. a deep ulcer, carbuncle, &c.], (C. chhi). **tsat-tsu**, a whitlow. **chím-tsu**, a large boil or carbuncle on the back of the neck. **âm-kún-tsu**, a carbuncle on the neck. **iong-tsu**, a large sloughing carbuncle. **iong-tsu hoat-pòe**, a large sloughing carbuncle on the back.

tsu [R. all, a particle of various meaning]. **tsu-hê**, feudal lords and princes. **tsu-kat**, a famous ancient warrior (v. kat).

tsu [R. su, a book; but col. "chheh" is from a different word], (Cn. tsû, stands both for "tsu" and "chheh").

tsu-chheh, books. **keng-tsu**, classical books. **ēng-tsu-kù**, to quote a book phrase. **tsu-láng**, a book basket.

tsu-tai, over-cautious and too fond of ancient customs, as literary men.

hun-tsu, a marriage contract. **lī-tsu**, a written divorce. **chiàn-tsu**, a challenge (v. chiàn). **bûn-tsu**, an official letter.

tsu-īⁿ, a college. **tsu-pâng**, a school-room; a school-house. **tsu-pâng siùⁿ-kang**, a sort of clerk or writer in a yamun for preparing documents. **tsu-pâng-báu**, having one's name on the books of a civil mandarin's office, not for work, but only for protection. **tsû-pān** (Cn.), = A. su-pān, a mandarin's clerk or secretary.

tsu (R. id.) **tsu-tsu**, constantly; diligently. **tsu-tsu-lâi**, always coming. **tsu-tsu àn-niⁿ-siⁿ**, always so.

tsu (R. id.) **tsu-jû**, a fruit used as a heating medicine (Xanthoxylum piperitum?). **ngê-tsu**, id. **gê-tsu-jû**, id.

tsu [R. a small ancient coin]. **ngé-tsu-chîⁿ**, an ancient coin with the words "ngé-tsu" on it, used as a charm.

tsu [R. tsù, intently, = col. tu]. **tsu-tsu-siòng**, to gaze intently.

tsû, a sound made in calling poultry.

tsû (R. id.), (Cn. tsû). **tsû-pi**, tender affection, as of parents or superiors. **tsû-sim**, kind affectionate heart, as of parents, &c. **jîn-tsû**, warm affection, as of parent or superior. **ka-tsû** (R.), my mother.

tsû-nñg, a wood; a medicine (v. nñg). **soaⁿ-tsû-ke**, a medicinal plant (v. ke).

tsû (R. id.), (C. chî, Cn. tsû). **chiuⁿ-tsû**, a sort of toad.

tsû (cf. thû, tû).

tsû-tsû, doggedly set on something. **tsû-tsû-beh**, doggedly determined to have or to do something. **siūⁿ kàu-tsû--khì**, to think about a thing till obstinately set on it.

u-tsû, over-anxious about everything, so as to have a dull unpleased look and a somewhat troublesome temper (v. u).

tsû (R. name of many edible or medicinal roots, esp. tuberous]. (C. chî; Cn. tsû).

hoan-tsû, sweet-potatoes. **han-tsû**, id. **an-tsû**, id. **han-tsû-hún**, potato-flour. **han-tsû-thâu**, the refuse from making potato-flour. **han-tsû-thñg**, confection of potato and sugar. **han-tsû-khe**, sweet-potatoes sliced and dried. **han-tsû-chhiam**, do. cut into long narrow strips and dried. **han-tsû-lêng**, long potato-beds. **han-tsû-kau**, the long hollows between the potato-beds.

chhèng han-tsû, to boil potatoes till dry, with the skins on. **teh-han-tsû**, to plant potatoes. **ngiauh han-tsû**, to dig up potatoes. **iáh-han-tsû**, id. **é-han-tsû**, do., not very many. **lôe-han-tsû**, to take up a whole field of them with the hoe. **teh-kóng sím-mih han-tsû**, whatever are you talking about? **chit-tiâu han-tsû**, one potato. **chit-tiâu náⁿ-han-tsû**, a very stupid-looking fellow (like a potato). **ōe-sñg, bōe-tû; thó-bí, oāⁿ han-tsû**, said of a man being very stupid (v. tû).

hô-lân-tsû, the potato (not the sweet). **hñg-tsû**, sweet-potatoes grown on dry fields. **toā-tsû**, the yam. **chhân-tsû**, id.

soaⁿ-ióh-tsû, a medicinal root like hoâiⁿ-soaⁿ

(Dioscorea sativa?). **soaⁿ-tsû**, id. **chióh-tsû**, a medicinal root.

tsú [R. to bear; to undertake; Cn. tsü]. **tsú-sòe**, to be careful; to take care (s. lord).

tsú (cf. sú). **loān-tsú**, recklessly; at random; in a disorderly or irregular manner. **loān-tsú-lâi**, to come in a disorderly manner. **loān-tsú thóeh-mihⁿ**, to take things improperly. **loān-tsú-bong**, to grope about, as in the dark; to touch improperly, *e.g.* parts of another person's body.

tsú — **tsú-tòng** (in some parts of P.), = tsé-tòng, to hinder.

tsú [R. tsú, purple]. **tsú-bî-chhiⁿ** (Cn.), = A. chí-bî-chhiⁿ, name of a star (v. bî).

tsú (R. id.), (C. chí; Cn. tsü), to cook by boiling; to prepare (as some things) by boiling; when said of meat it is not with water alone (sàh), but along with other things, so as to make at the same time some soup or sauce, &c.

tsú-chiáh, to cook food in general. **tsú-chiáh--ê**, a cook; a wife. **goán hit--ê tsú-chiáh--ê**, my wife. **tsú-pn̄g** (C. chí-pūiⁿ), to cook rice. **tsú-noāⁿ**, to boil quite soft. **tsú-thiám**, id. **tsú-sèk**, to cook thoroughly.

tsú-chhat, to boil varnish in preparing it. **tsú a-phièn**, to boil opium in preparing the extract for smoking.

tsú [R. a sort of tree]. **tsú-tòng tè-kun**, another name of Bûn-chhiong (v. kun).

tsú [R. a son; seed; a horary and cyclical character; midnight; a viscount; used in forming the titles of many philosophers; also sometimes has almost no meaning, merely forming nouns], (Cn. tsü).

tsú-chiok, a viscount. **tsú**, id. **kok-tsú-kàm**, the ancient university of Pekin, which sells the degree of "kàm-seng." **kong-tsú**, son of a governor-general or high mandarin; also (polite), your son (s. lord). **thien-tsú**, the emperor (v. thien), (s. lord). **hông-tsú** (R.), son of the emperor. **thài-tsú**, the heir-apparent (v. thài).

kun-tsú, a good man; a superior man. **kú-tsú** (R.), a Kujin graduate. **thàm-tsú-bé**, a spy. **lâm-tsú-hàn**, a male person, esp. grown up (v. hàn). **kūi-tsú-siú**, an executioner. **iông-hu sio̍k-tsú**, a rough common-looking illiterate man. **tsâi-tsú**, a learned man (s. lord).

hu-tsú, a title of great philosophers or sages. **khóng-hu-tsú**, Confucius. **bēng-tsú**, Mencius. **tsú-lō͘**, Tsze-loo, the disciple of Confucius, &c.

tông-tsú, the pupil of the eye (v. tông).

tsú-soàⁿ, the thinner strings of a stringed instrument.

tsú-sî, 11 P.M. to 1 A.M.; an hour before and after midnight. **tsú-sî-chiàⁿ**, midnight. **tsú-ngó͘**, midnight and mid-day; the pole-star (v. ngó͘).

hū-tsú, father and son. **chhe-tsú** (R.), wife and sons (v. chhe). **jîn-tsú**, a son of a man (v. jîn). **tsú-sun-tháng**, a tub for accouchement (v. sun). **goá--ê tsú-bîn**, my people (as it were my children), said by mandarins. **hù-kùi tsâi-tsú-siū**, the five blessings. **tsá-tek-tsú**, will get a son at an early age (said by diviners). **tek-tsú**, son of the principal wife. **kiáⁿ-sài poàn-tsú**, a son-in-law is half a son. **gī-tsú**, an adopted son (not bought). **kè-tsú**, son of wife by former husband (v. kè). **tióng-tsú**, eldest son (v. tióng).

tsú-tē (lit. sons and younger brothers), an ill-behaved or prodigal son; also (R.), younger relatives in general. **tsú-tē-lâng**, a fast young fellow of a rich family, fond of expense and amusement. **tsòe tsú-tē**, to be such a lavish spendthrift. **bû-sêng ê tsú-tē**, an idle, useless, ill-behaved son. **tsú-tē-bé**, descendants wasting away all the property of ancestors in foolish pleasures. **lông-kun tsú-tē**, a rich and handsome young fellow (v. lông). **koan-ka tsú-tē**, young relatives of mandarins, as sons, grandsons, and nephews. **gō͘ lâng--ê tsú-tē**, to waste the time of youth by inefficient teaching, as a useless teacher. **tsú-tē-tit**, younger relatives. **tsú-tit**, id. (v. tit).

tē-tsú, votaries of an idol. **ang hién, tē-tsú liáu-chhién**, when the idol is powerful the worshippers spend money.

giét-tsú, a bad wicked boy (v. giét). **lōng-tōng-tsú**, an ill-behaved, prodigal, licentious son. **liù-tsú-kiáⁿ**, a wicked lad, esp. about 15–20. **piáu-tsú-kiáⁿ**, you whoreson! (scolding).

sù-kun-tsú, a medicinal seed. **chi-tsú**, a medicine, &c. &c. **pek-tsú-liên**, the tall blue lily with a head of numerous flowers (Agapanthus). **tsúi-sien-tsú** (T.), = A. tsúi-sien-chí, a medicine.

tsú (R. id.), (C. chí, in some phrases, esp. some transferred book phrases), a lord or master; (proprietor, patron, &c.; to rule; to determine).

tsú-sòe, a general; a commander-in-chief (s. careful). **tsú-chè**, to preside at sacrificial offerings. **tsú-hun**, the superiors of bride and bridegroom who arrange the marriage. **tsú-kó**, to attend to the drawing up of drafts, of despatches, and official papers. **tsú-lēng**, a man who commits a crime, not with his own hand, but by using another man as his instrument.

tsú-kong, master, as of a slave; a patron whom his dependants obey. **tsú-pók** (R.), master and slave. **tsú-bú**, mistress of a (female) slave. **tsú-lâng**, master, as of a slave; the host at a feast or of an inn; a patient, or father, &c., of patient, who invites the doctor for self or son, &c. **tsú-lâng-ke**, an innkeeper; a patient, or father of patient, &c. **tiàm-tsú-lâng**, innkeeper. **hó tsú-lâng-thâu**, pleasant to serve, as master kind and pleasant to those in his employment.

tsú-kheh, a regular customer or dealer with us, buyer or seller. **hó-tsú-kheh**, pleasant to deal with in business, as customer or dealer. **tsú-kò͘**, a customer of a shop (v. kò͘). **ún-tsú**, a safe customer to allow credit to.

tsú-tsáiⁿ, a supreme lord or ruler; to govern or rule. **tsú-chhí**, to have the management of an affair. **tsú-chhâi**, to determine a matter definitely and authoritatively, as man who has the management in his hands. **tsú-tiuⁿ**, id., to determine of one's sole will. **chit-lâng tsú-tiuⁿ, m̄-tát n̄ng-lâng su-niûⁿ**, the counsel of two is better than the sole will of one. **tsú-ì**, to act or to determine a matter as we please; a settled purpose or intention. **ka-kī tsú-ì**, free to act as we please. **thèng-tsú-ì**, just act as you please; follow your own views or desires. **tsú-ì bô-tiāⁿ**, purpose not settled; irresolute. **bô-tsú-ì**, id. **ōe-tsú-tit-ì**, having power to act as we think best, and so settle the matter; can act according to his own views.

kong-tsú, a king's daughter (s. son). **kàu-tsú**, the founder of a religion. **tsō-tsú**, a high mandarin who acts as patron of a lower mandarin or graduate. **un-tsú**, a great benefactor. **ún-tsú**, a safe customer. **sì-tsú**, a man who contributes to the building or support of a Buddhist temple, or of priests or nuns. **si-tsú**, the near relative of a man who has died in suspicious circumstances (*e.g.* on the street at another's door);

he has the right of demanding explanation or reparation for the death. **sit-tsú**, the man whose things have been stolen or plundered. **lê-tsú**, the man whose turn it is to take charge of the idolatrous ceremonies of a ward. **tsâi-tsú**, a wealthy man (s. son). **chè-tsú**, a creditor (v. chè). **gûn-tsú**, the buyer, mortgagee, or tenant of property who pays out the money. **oāⁿ-tsú**, to change owner, as house or land. **kè-tsú**, id. **kòe-tsú** (C.), id. **giáp-tsú**, proprietor of land or house. **chhù-tsú**, owner of a house. **tién-tsú**, the mortgager. **tsûn-tsú**, owner or charterer of a vessel; supercargo, as his representative or of the charterer; the captain of a vessel may be so called if there be no supercargo, &c., on board, and he have full control of the vessel. **pán-tsú**, owner or supercargo of a junk. **hè-tsú**, owner of goods, as in shop or ship. **kui-tsú bóe**, to buy all the goods belonging to one owner, as in commission-agent's hong. **sū-tsú**, either of the two principal parties in a lawsuit, &c. **láng-tsú**, a man who hires out actors. **hì-tsú**, id. **koāiⁿ-tsú**, chief mandarin of a Hien district. **iâⁿ-tsú**, the commanding officer of an "iâⁿ" or fifth part of an army.

kéng-tsú, the guardian idol of a ward or region (v. kéng).

thien-tsú, name for God used by the Church of Rome, therefore called "thien-tsú-kàu" (v. thien), (s. son), [C. thien-chí, and so in all the phrases of this paragraph]. **bók-tsú**, ancestral tablets. **sîn-tsú**, id. **hoán-tsú**, bring back the tablet in procession from the grave. **chìn-tsú**, to introduce the new tablet into the ancestral hall. **tiám-tsú**, to consecrate the tablet by dotting it at several places with a red mixture, just after the coffin is laid in the grave but before it is covered up; before this is done, the relatives call the spirit to leave the coffin and come to the tablet; if possible a graduate or mandarin is hired to dot the tablet.

goá ū-tsú, I have a man who takes the whole responsibility off me; *e.g.* said to a man who rightly applies to us first, while we refer him to the responsible party. **oan ū-ke, tùi ū-tsú**, the quarrel concerns the two parties only, and no one else. **tùi-thâu ū-tsú**, each of the parties has a man to bear the responsibility, *e.g.* each having a document from a relative in a case of disputed sale; or, I can refer to two parties who were in possession in succession before me, as of a disputed property or stolen article. **oan-ke tùi-thâu ū-tsú**, the quarrel concerns only the parties; *e.g.* said in dissuading from meddling, or in explaining that others need not be involved. **tùi-thâu oan-ke-tsú**, the very person with whom one is at feud.

tsù (R. id.), a commentary; to make a commentary; to decree or ordain, as Heaven. **tsù-sè**, a commentary on a commentary. **tsù-chheh**, to write comments or notes on a book. **tsù-kái**, to explain by writing notes on it, as a book or document. **tsù-bêng**, id.

tsù-tiāⁿ, to ordain, as Heaven or fate (v. tiāⁿ). **tsù-sí**, to decree the fated time of death. **tsù-siⁿ**, ordain time of birth. **tsù-siⁿ niûⁿ-niûⁿ**, the goddess of childbirth. **tsù-siⁿ tsù-sí**, to ordain the times of birth and death. **bē-tsù-siⁿ seng tsù-sí**, our death is ordained before our birth is. **lâm-táu tsù-siⁿ; pak-táu tsù-sí**, the gods of the south and north constellation decree birth and death respectively.

tsù (Cn.) **sin-tsù-pīⁿ**, a natural disease, as opposed to one caused by demons.

tsù [R. to set the mind, &c., upon]. **tsù-bák**, with fixed gaze. **tsù-ì**, very attentive or diligent; very desirous; mind always thinking of and set upon. **tsù-sim tsù-koaⁿ**, id. **tsù-sîn**, id. (v. sîn).

tsù (R. id.), to cast, as metal. **tsù-chíⁿ**, to cast cash, as Chinese do. **tsù-tiáⁿ**, to cast rice-boilers.

tsù (R. id.) **chìm-tsù**, to soak through; drenched with rain; very constant rains. **chìm-tsù-hō**, very constant soaking rains.

tsù (C. chì). **ka-tsù**, a small coarse straw bag used by beggars, and also for holding things. **ka-tsù-pau**, the coarse straw matting of which these bags are made. **ka-tsù-táu**, such a bag specially large and strong, used by beggars. **hó ka-tsù-táu** (r.), wealthy.

tsū [R. self; from; naturally]; (Cn. tsū). **tsū-tsá**, from of old; formerly. **tsū-sí chì-chiong**, from first to last.

tsū-jiên, naturally. **thien-seng tsū-jiên**, naturally; certainly so. **tsū-jiên jî-jiên** (r.), self-existent. **sip-koàn, sêng tsū-jiên**, habit becomes a second nature. **bién-kióng, sêng tsū-jiên**, at first doing it with much difficulty, but afterwards it comes quite naturally. **put-kièn tsū-bêng**, of course it is so (there is no need of seeing it); beyond all question. **ok-jîn, tsū-iú ok-jîn mô**, oppressors are certainly oppressed in their turn.

tsū-kí (r.), one's self. **tsū-chìn**, to commit suicide. **tsū-tsāi**, steady, as mind or thing; calm mind without distraction (v. tsāi). **tsū-jû**, quite well again; perfectly recovered (v. jû). **tsū-chiok**, self-sufficient and somewhat proud. **tsū-tsoan**, taking upon one's self without authority. **tsū-chheng**, self-styled; to boast or praise one's self. **tsū-khoa**, to boast. **tsū-ko**, proud. **tsū-toā**, proud and boastful. **bōng-tsū tsun-tāi**, proud; vain or self-conceited. **tsū-sī**, always making one's self in the right. **ka-kī tsū-sī**, id. **tsū-khiam**, using humble phrases; acting in a humble manner; at least apparently so. **tsū-tsok-giét**, to bring evil on one's self by one's own wickedness. **tsū-tsok tsū-tong**, he who does it on his own responsibility must himself bear it. **tsū-pō tsū-khì**, to injure one's self by one's own fault; esp. to throw away invaluable opportunities and reject his own good fortune; *e.g.* a boy who will not study, or a man who will not take a good situation. **tsū-siong bâu-tún**, to contradict one's self. **put-kìm, jî tsū-kìm**, to restrain one's self without a formal prohibition. **tsū-pēng put-lêng-i**, cannot cure himself. **tsū-sin put-lêng-pó: ien-lêng-pó tha-jîn**, unable to protect himself, how can he protect others? **chiú put-tsùi-jîn, jîn tsū-tsùi; hoa put-bê-jîn, jîn tsū-bê**, it is not liquor and women that intoxicate and seduce men, they do it themselves.

hek-pék tsū-hun, right and wrong (black and white) manifest themselves at the last. **tsū-lâi-hé** (R.), lucifer matches.

tsū — chi-chí tsū-tsū, making a whispering noise. **chī-bú chī-tsū**, id.

tsū [R. to stop; to withstand; to dwell; to cease]. **thoân-thoân ûi-tsū**, to stand round in great numbers (v. ûi). **tòng-tsū**, to hinder effectively. **tòng-bōe-tsū**, to try to hinder but fail in the attempt.

tsū (R. id.), (C. chī, Cn. tsū). **tsū-chip**, to assemble; to meet together. **tsū-hōe**, id.

tsū — kang-iâu-tsū, the preserved flesh of a marine animal.

tsū [R. jū, a written or printed word, = col. jī], (Cn. tsū). **tsū-miâⁿ**, the name by which a man is called among his friends; often assumed at marriage, = jū-miâⁿ.

厦英大辭典

tsū [R. tsō, to make]. **tsū-hòɛ** (C.), = A. tsō-hoà, fortune or luck.

tsū, a cloth spread to keep from soiling, or under a teapot, &c.; to spread a cloth under a teapot or vase. **tsū tê-koàn,** to be spread under a teapot, as the cloth on the salver. **tih-á tsū tê-au,** saucers placed under the tea-cups, as foreigners do. **chit-tè-tsū,** a cloth spread below teapot, &c.

bėh-tsū, a cloth worn inside the stocking. **thê-kha-tsū,** a door-mat. **í-tsū,** a very thin cushion of leather or cloth thrown over the back and seat of a chair; a thicker cushion (tiām) is often laid upon it. **bé-oaⁿ-tsū,** a piece of leather put on a horse's back below the saddle. **jiō-tsū,** a cloth put under babies at night.

tsuh (cf. tuh). **chih-tsuh,** mischievous, said of children.

tsuh, to squirt, as from a small leak or from a syringe. **tsuh--chhut-lâi,** to trickle out as from a small leak. **tsúi-tsuh,** a syringe.

tsu̍h (= tu̍h), to make a hole by striking with the point of a stick.

tsui (R. id.) **ka-tsui,** the turtle-dove. **ka-tsui-bȧk,** a staple. **ka-tsui-lê,** a small spiral shell-fish. **ka-tsui bô-gī,** the turtle-dove has no gratefulness (different from chíⁿ-á, the pigeon), for though long fed by a man, it does not come back, and a pair often quarrel.

tsui [R. tsu, a pearl]. **thih-tsui,** an iron boss put on a door for striking the ring that is used as a knocker. **tâng-tsui,** a brass boss for same purpose.

thiāu-tsui (T.), = thiāu-tsu, a round stone base for a pillar. **chióh-tsui** (T.), id.

tsui (P.), a sort of oak. **tsui-chhiū,** id. **tsui-á-chí,** its acorn.

tsui-chí (Cn.), a fruit about the size of a large fig, with hard smooth black shell, used as a tobacco pouch.

tsui, convex, as grain in a measure, or as a swollen boil. **tsui--khí-lâi,** to lip óver, as water in cup just ready to overflow; heaped up in the middle higher than the edge, as rice or other dry articles in a measure. **tīⁿ kàu tsui-tsui,** full and heaped up, as in a measure. **tsui-tsui moáⁿ-moáⁿ,** id. **chit-liȧp tsui-tsui,** a boil much swollen.

kớ-tsui, plump and pleasant-looking, as a child. **kớ-kớ-tsui,** pretending to know what he does not know, or to be able to do what he cannot, *e.g.* to manage a difficult matter.

tsui — **oáⁿ-ke-tsui** (C.), the broken bottom of a bowl. **oáⁿ-kim-kơ-tsui** (C.), id.

tsui (R. id.) **bé-tsui,** the fleshy part of a bird's tail. **koe-bé-tsui,** do., of a fowl. **ah-bé-tsui,** do., of a duck. **bé-tsui-kut,** the coccyx bone.

tsûi — **soa-tsûi,** an inferior kind of crab.

tsûi, to cut off by cutting all round, as sugar-cane, or as the neck or a limb; to cut off with a knife, not by one cut but in a sawing manner. **tsûi kam-chià,** to cut sugar-cane in bits.

tsúi (R. súi), water; a surname; (tide); (a season or brief opportunity); a small discount or percentage.

chit-tsúi, at this time; in a very short time (afterwards). **chit-tsúi-á,** a short and passing time when anything is just in season, *e.g.* fruit; said also of time of youth or of prosperity, especially of a short season gone for ever. **kàu-tsúi,** just in season and best condition, as fish or fruit; said also of a young person just come to marriageable age. **thâu-tsúi,** first-born, of an animal. **thâu-tsúi-chhun,** tea of the first crop. **chit-nîⁿ, siⁿ kúi-tsúi,** how often has the animal young in one year. **khí-tsúi,** to become desirous of the male, as female cattle when grown old enough for it.

pò-tsúi, to give information of a criminal's hiding-place, so that he may be caught.

tsāi-tsúi (C.), of course (= tsū-jiên), said in answering a question; what need of your asking or my telling such an evident thing? **tsāi-tsúi--ê** (C.), id.

tsúi-sî, the time of tide. **hù-tsúi-sî,** to be in time for the tide. **koáⁿ tsúi-sî,** hastening to be in time for the tide. **míⁿ-tsúi,** tide in the night. **tsúi-pān,** state of tide; depth of water, &c. (v. pān). **sūn-tsúi hêng-chiu,** I wish you a good voyage. **bô-lâu-tsúi,** tide not suitable (v. lâu). **tsúi hoan-thâu,** tide just beginning to flow. **tsúi tīⁿ,** flood-tide. **tsúi tn̂g,** id. **tsúi hiàⁿ,** tide just beginning to ebb. **tsúi lek,** id., just beginning to leave a mark. **tsúi lek-hûn,** id. **tsúi khó,** ebb-tide. **tsúi tėh** (C.), id. **tsúi-phùiⁿ** (C.), id. **tsúi-bé,** down the stream, as from where one is washing or drinking.

sek-tsúi, colour. **sái sek-tsúi,** to bully (v. sek). **chhéng pang-tsúi,** to act or talk in a proud bragging way.

tsúi-thớ, climate of a place (v. thớ). **tsúi-âng,** light red. **tsúi-tsu,** chicken-pox. **tsúi-ka,** solid glue. **tsúi-chiú,** weak liquor. **tsúi-soān,** an inferior diamond. **tsúi-chiⁿ,** rock-crystal. **tsúi-gûn,** quicksilver. **tsúi-hún,** paint for the face in round bales. **tsúi-hun,** tobacco mixed with arsenic, smoked through water. **tsúi-lāi,** very heavy interest on money lent on security of vessel or goods going to sea. **tsúi-lō͘,** way by water. **tsúi-siú,** a sailor. **tsúi-su,** marines (v. su). **tsúi-chhau,** a naval review. **tsúi-bū,** affairs about vessels and navigation (v. bū). **tsúi-kha,** a water-carrier. **taⁿ-tsúi,** id.; to carry water in buckets on a pole. **tsáu-tsúi,** a carrier of letters and small articles, sometimes also a pedlar. **tsúi-kheh,** id. **thô͘-tsúi-chhiūⁿ,** a mason; a builder. **pėh-tsúi-á** (C.), a fisherman living in a boat. **pėh-tsúi-pô** (C.), a boatwoman; a fisherwoman living in a boat.

tsúi-tsoâⁿ, a spring of water. **tsúi-kéng,** an aqueduct or conduit for water. **tsúi-khiò,** a bamboo spout or tube. **tsúi-phùn,** the rose of a watering-can. **tsúi-chin,** a dipper; a small bucket with straight handle. **tsúi-chhiu,** spray. **tsúi-hoe,** id. **tsúi-phėh,** foam. **tsúi-khì,** damp vapour; damp. **tsúi-iáⁿ,** reflected image in water.

tsúi-phi, a small shallow boat. **tsúi-tô,** a sounding line; sounding lead. **tsúi-lêng,** a fire-engine. **tsúi-thiu,** a water-pump. **tsúi-chhia,** a chain water-wheel for irrigation (v. chhia). **tsúi-tsáh,** a flood-gate. **tsúi-tháng,** a water bucket. **tsúi-tīⁿ** (T.), a thin bamboo suspending the bucket of a well-sweep. **tsúi-bō,** a water-wheel. **tsúi-tùi,** a machine for beating rice clean, worked by water.

kúi-kúi tsúi-tsúi, very deceitful and ready to stir up strife. **kúi-tsúi,** id. **hū-jîn tsúi-sèng,** woman's nature is like water, prone to evil courses.

tsúi-kúi, the ghost of a drowned man. **tsúi-chiò,** rites to appease the ghost of a drowned man. **tsúi-sîn,** spirits that preside over streams or waters; also, the relation of a grave to water, as good or bad. **tsúi-sien-ông,** a water-god (v. sien).

thiap-tsúi, to pay a small premium, as on silver (v. thiap). **tō͘ kim-tsúi,** to gild thinly with imitation gold. **lâm gûn-tsúi,** to pour melted silver over other metals; to plate with silver. **gûn-tsúi,** a small premium (about twenty cash on a dollar) allowed when a sum specified in cash is paid in dollars; a small percentage allowed to the buyer when he changes a dollar for a small payment, and takes the balance in cash. **chiáh gûn-tsúi**, to lose this percentage, as the seller does. **kā-i-chiáh tsáp-ê-chîⁿ ê gûn-tsúi**, to give him ten cash more in exchange for a dollar, as shopkeeper does. **ke-sái--i tsáp-ê-chîⁿ gûn-tsúi**, to get ten more cash out of him for his dollar, as customer does. **sái joā-tsōe gûn-tsúi**, how much premium for silver over cash? **khàu gûn-tsúi**, to take off a small percentage, as in paying soldiers, &c.; also, to pay a rather smaller quantity when paying in silver, if silver of a better quality be given than was bargained for, *e.g.* when sycee is paid instead of dollars. **chîⁿ-tsúi**, cash or money in regard to quantity. **chîⁿ-tsúi liōng-sēng**, money abundant. **phái̍ⁿ-chîⁿ-tsúi**, a small percentage on account of bad cash allowed to be mixed. **tióng phái̍ⁿ-chîⁿ-tsúi**, to give more cash in change because bad cash are mixed. **chiet phái̍ⁿ-chîⁿ-tsúi**, to take off a small discount when all the cash are good, because it was allowable to have mixed some bad ones. **thàn phái̍ⁿ-chîⁿ-tsúi**, to get this small premium when a dollar is given and a balance of cash received. **chiáh phái̍ⁿ-chîⁿ-tsúi**, to give this small discount, as the shopkeeper who is paid in silver, and loses the difference between good and bad cash.

beh kap--i tú-tsúi, determined to be at feud with him.

kè-tsúi, to cross the water; on the other side of the strait or inlet; to let water in, as shoes; to be washed slightly, as clothes; small roofs built at the two front corners of a large central house, connecting it with the side houses (hō͘--chhù), so that one can cross over without getting wet. **kòe-tsúi** (C.), do., do.; also, = A. léng-lông, the covered roads on each side of the central court of a house. **tih-tsúi**, the eaves of a house, or the space covered by them. **siang-tó-tsúi**, a roof made with a ridge (v. tó).

chhī-tsúi, to temper metal in water. **gàn-tsúi**, id. **chhiau-tsúi**, to mix in water, as lime or any powder. **thàu-tsúi**, to dilute with water. **jip-tsúi**, to leak. **chiáh-tsúi**, to drink water; to draw so much water, as a vessel. **lap-tsúi**, to step into water unintentionally.

koàn-tsúi, to pour water into a dead animal so as to water the meat (v. koàn). **kūi-tsúi**, dropsical swelling of limbs. **pá-tsúi**, well filled up, as fruit or grain large and good. **kâm-tsúi**, to be swollen with damp, as wood. **siⁿ-tsúi**, to grow moist.

thó-tsúi, to draw water, as from well or river, &c. **táh-tsúi**, to tread a chain water-wheel. **iúⁿ-tsúi**, to lade out water, as with a cup or dipper. **hō͘-tsúi**, to raise water by a bucket swung between two men. **chhiūⁿ-tsúi**, to raise water in any way. **phah-tsúi**, to take in fresh water for use in a vessel. **phah-tsúi-tô**, to take soundings with the lead. **tiám-tsúi**, to take the depth with a bamboo pole. **tiu-tsúi**, to throw things overboard, to lighten the vessel. **thoaⁿ-tsúi**, to pay a percentage or average on account of jettison. **chiūⁿ-tsúi**, to discharge goods from a vessel. **chhut-tsúi**, to put goods on board; to repolish a gem that has a dim surface. **chhut-tsúi-toaⁿ**, a document certifying that the goods have paid duty, and giving permission to put them on board. **kek-tsúi**, to dam up water. **pàng-tsúi**, to open a way for water to escape. **siu-tsúi**, to expel damp, as by drying.

huih-tsúi, thin watery blood. **n̂g-sē-tsúi**, thin matter from a wound or sore. **sí-tsúi**, stagnant water. **kak-tsúi**, very fine clear syrup from white loaf sugar. **bit-tsúi**, honey syrup. **thn̂g-tsúi**, molasses. **sng-tsúi**, a sort of molasses, finer and clearer. **tê-tsúi**, good water fit for making tea.

tsúi — **ka-tsúi-á** (T.), a fish like the cuttle-fish, but without any bone.

tsùi [R. tsù, with set purpose]. **tsùi-sim**, very much desiring a thing.

tsùi (R. id.), drunk; intoxicated, as with liquor or opium. **tsùi a-phièn**, intoxicated with opium. **tsùi-hun**, do., or sick with tobacco. **tsùi-hàn**, a drunkard. **tsùi-ì**, nearly drunk. **tsùi-ong-í**, a sort of lounging chair.

tsùi-gán, eyes having a soft swimming look (naturally), as if half drunk; people with such eyes are supposed to have special tendencies to lasciviousness.

tsùi-chiú, drunk; bad-tasted, as pine-apple. **put-tsùi-chiú**, able to drink much without getting drunk. **chiú-tsùi**, drunk. **chiáh-chiú-tsùi**, to get drunk. **thien-thien tsùi**, daily drunk. **tsùi-bông-bông**, dead drunk. **tsùi-bong-bong**, id. **toā-tsùi**, id. **tsùi-maⁿ-maⁿ**, very drunk. **tsùi-ham-ham** (C.), very drunk. **tsùi kàu-m̄-tsai thiⁿ-tōe**, dead drunk.

bô-chiáh, kan-ta tsùi (lit. drunk without drinking), said of a man making unpleasant jokes, or talking in a foolish manner, or telling manifest falsehoods. **chiú put-tsùi-jîn, jîn tsū-tsùi**, it is men who intoxicate themselves; it is not the liquor that does it.

tsūi (R. sûi). **chī-tsūi**, who? **chī-tsūi-á**, id. **tsūi-tsai**, unexpectedly; who would ever have thought it!

tsūi (R. id.) **chiâu-tsūi** (r.), pale and wan with grief and melancholy; miserable and mournful looking.

tsuiⁿ (C.), = A. tsng, a thick tile.

tsûiⁿ (C.), = A. tsn̂g, complete.

tsûiⁿ (Cn.), = A. chêng, before. **tsûiⁿ-lâng-káⁿ**, = A. chêng-lâng-kiáⁿ, a step-son.

tsúiⁿ (Cn.), = A. tsńg, tsáiⁿ (C. chéng). **tsúiⁿ-thâu-ngá**, fingers.

tsúiⁿ (Cn.), = A. tsáiⁿ. **tsúiⁿ-iūⁿ**, how?

tsùiⁿ (C.), = A. tsǹg, an awl.

tsùiⁿ (C.), = A. tsǹg, to bore; to rush on or make one's way, &c. (perhaps two words).

tsúiⁿ (Cn.), = A. chèng. **ka-tsúiⁿ**, a sort of grass mat.

tsūiⁿ (C.), = A. tsn̄g, to suck with the lips.

tsūiⁿ (C.), = A. tsn̄g, an eddy.

tsūiⁿ (C.), = A. tsn̄g, the centre from which the hair radiates.

tsun [R. high in rank; to honour], to set up as the principal person in a matter. **tsun-pi**, high and low in rank (v. pi). **tsun-kùi**, high in rank; honourable. **tsun-kèng**, to honour; to reverence. **tsun-tiōng**, honourable; noble; to pay regard to; to treat with respect. **tsun--i**, unitedly appoint him as the head man or manager in a joint affair. **chhui-tsun**, to put a man in the chief place of honour or power in a company met together. **saⁿ-tsun**, each urging the other to take the most honourable place, as in sitting or walking. **teh tsun-ūi**, do., as to a seat. **tsun-chhûn**, to inform a superior or a friend of what we mean to do.

tsun-chheng, to give a title rather more honourable than is strictly due. **bú-lōng tsun-tióng**, to treat a superior with insult, *e.g.* by practical jokes, &c. **bók-**

bû tsun-tióng, to treat superiors with disrespect or contempt. **bōng-tsū-tsun-toā**, self-conceited. **bōng-tsū-tsun-tāi**, id.

lēng-tsun (polite), your father. **lēng-sien-tsun**, your deceased father. **tsun-hu-jîn** (very polite), your wife. **hú-tsun** (R.), the chief mandarin of a Foo (a department).

tiong-tsun, the principal priest (Tauist or Buddhist) in a ceremony; in a procession he walks last. **goân-sí thien-tsun**, the supreme god of the Tauists.

tsun, to shiver and shake, as with cold.

tsun [R. to obey]. **tsun-thàn** (R.), id. **tsun i-ê-lēng** (r.), to respect and obey his commands.

tsûn [R. siên, a cicada, = col. chê]. **am-kóng-tsûn** (C.), = am-pê-chê, the cicada. **àm-kóng-tsûn** (Cn.), id.

tsûn [R. chiên, before; = col. chêng]. **tsûn--nîⁿ**, the year before last. **lóh-tsûn--nîⁿ**, the second year before last; three years ago.

tsûn [R. soân; C. (R.) chhoân], a ship; a boat; a junk; a vessel. **tsûn-chiah**, boats and vessels in general. **chit-chiah-tsûn**, one boat or vessel. **tsûn-á**, a boat.

bèh-tsûn, the quilted part of a stocking's foot, not including the sole. **tê-tsûn**, metal saucer for a teacup. **bát-tsát-tsûn**, the bone of the cuttle-fish.

ông-tsûn, a model of a junk made for the worship of "ông-iâ" (v. ông). **tsoá-tsûn**, paper boats for idolatrous worship. **lêng-tsûn**, a dragon-boat (v. lêng).

tē-tsûn, a passage-boat. **siong-tsûn**, a trading junk. **kah-tsûn**, a boat engaged to wait on a ship. **chhién-tsûn**, a very flat boat for shallow streams. **chièn-tsûn**, a war vessel. **sàu-tsûn**, a mandarin junk, for war or customs. **chhe-tsûn**, id. **tn̂g-tsûn**, a Chinese junk. **kap-pán-tsûn**, a foreign-built vessel. **hé-hun-tsûn**, a steamer. **hé-ien-tsûn** (r.), id.

pak-tsûn, a junk trading to the north of China; said also in joke of pirates. **iûⁿ-tsûn**, junk trading to foreign parts. **hú-tsûn**, junk trading to Tai-wan-foo. **sa-tsûn**, junks from Ningpo, &c., with many characters on each side of the bow. **téng-kau-tsûn**, junks from Chin-chew, Chimmo, An-hai, &c. **ē-kau-tsûn**, junks belonging to about Amoy or Tâng-oaⁿ (Tung-an). **lâm-tsûn**, junks from Chang-poo (Chiuⁿ-phê) and further south. **lâm-á-tsûn**, id.

hîn-tsûn, sea-sick. **ut-tsûn**, feeling bilious or uncomfortable from being long in a boat without exercise. **chit-tò-tsûn**, one voyage of a vessel. **chit-oaⁿ-tsûn**, a distance such as junks usually make in one tide in one day. **chit-kiⁿ-tsûn**, a distance such as would be sailed in about three hours on an average; about eleven miles. **sái joā-tsōe-tsûn**, how far has the vessel sailed?

pák-tsûn, to charter a vessel. **chéng-tsûn**, to fit out a vessel for sea with fittings, provisions, cargo, &c. **sái-tsûn**, to sail a vessel. **kiâⁿ-tsûn**, to be employed in a vessel in any capacity. **chē-tsûn**, to go by boat or ship. **chhut-tsûn**, to set off by ship to a distant place. **chiūⁿ-tsûn**, to embark. **lóh-tsûn**, id. **khí-tsûn**, to disembark. **tah-tsûn**, to go as passenger in a boat or vessel. **kè-tsûn**, to hire a boat for a considerable time. **khui-tsûn**, to set sail. **khau-tsûn**, to tack. **làu-tsûn**, to run before the wind. **toā-tsûn**, to tow a vessel, as by a number of small boats, or by a tug. **thoa-tsûn**, to draw along a small boat, as one or two men on foot. **phòe-tsûn**, to be sent by a vessel that is going at any rate, as goods, or as soldiers.

tsûn-tsú, the owner or charterer of a vessel; a supercargo or representative put on board by him, who has control over the movements of the vessel; the captain of a vessel, if he have full control and charge of the vessel from the owner or charterer. **tsûn-hē**, the owner or part owner of a junk, in whose name the ship's papers are made out; junks in regard to their number. **kúi--ê tsûn-hē**, how many vessels? **tsûn-hō**, the name of a vessel. **tsûn-chhng**, the hold. **tsûn-ù**, a dock. **tsûn-tóe**, bottom of a vessel (s. lay up). **tsûn-thâu**, the bow. **pàng tsûn-thâu**, to lend money to a man going by ship (on heavy interest), to be repaid when he returns. **siang-kha tah-siang-tsûn**, to try to keep neutral between two courses or parties. **chiūⁿ-lâng-tsûn, ài lâng-tsûn-tsáu**, men wish the ship to sail well in which they sail (prov.)

tsûn (R. id.), to lay up for use; to remain over; to examine how much money is on hand after the day's sales and payments (cf. chhûn).

tsûn-ì, applying one's mind or heart with fixed determination. **ū-tsûn-ì**, id. **tsûn-sim**, id. **tsûn-sim tióh-hó**, should keep the purposes of the heart right. **tsûn-sim kan-hiau-hiám**, secretly plotting villainy.

liû-tsûn, to keep in reserve. **tsûn-lok--teh**, to reserve and lay up for use. **tsûn-khǹg--teh**, id. **tsûn-àn**, to lay up the papers of a case, as for future examination. **tsûn-tóe**, to keep a record or copy for future reference if needful (s. boat). **tsûn chit-ê-tóe**, id. **tsûn-chheh-tóe**, do. in a book for the purpose.

tsûn-siàu, to examine what is the balance in hand at the end of the day's sales, or as after a few days, or at the foot of the page. **goân siu chhut tsûn**, balance in hand in one's books. **tsûn-kì-phē**, a book with entries of moneys paid out, &c., kept for future reference. **tsûn-hè-toaⁿ**, an inventory of goods still on hand.

sūn-thien--chiá tsûn, they who obey Heaven are preserved (v. thien).

tsûn (R. id.) **chhái-tsûn**, the leather guard on a spindle that keeps the thread from fouling on the endless band.

tsún (R. id.), to permit; to give a favourable answer to a petition. **ún-tsún**, id. **m̄-tsún**, will not permit. **phoe tsún**, the mandarin's answer favourable. **phoe m̄-tsún**, mandarin's answer unfavourable. **tsún-tsàu**, to grant the prayer of a memorial, as the emperor does.

tsún-pī, prepared beforehand; all prepared and ready.

tsún (R. id.), to be like; just like; to be equal to, fit for, or used as a substitute or pledge for; to be correct (as watch) or true (as statement). **tsún-tsún**, quite correct, as watch or statement; just suited, as one thing to another, *e.g.* as punishment to crime. **kóng-ōe put-chí-tsún**, acting according to promise. **tsún-á** (C.), like; alike.

ū, tsún-bô, though having it, yet all the same as if not having it. **bô, tsún-tsòe-ū**, though not having it (or though it is not), I will yet let it be counted as if it were there (or as if I had it). **kā--i tsún-siàu**, to accept it from him (an article or a composition) as payment of a debt, or so much part payment. **chit-ê hē--lí tsún-siàu**, I will give you this as or towards payment; sometimes only part payment counted as payment in full. **chhìn-bah lâi tsún-siàu**, to give meat (as butcher) so as gradually to pay off a debt due.

keng-thâu tsún-lē͘, hē͘-lâng-kiâⁿ, their shoulders are like a road for men to walk on.

tsún-chîn, a rule or pattern, esp. fig. (v. chîn). **tsún-tn̂g**, a pledge between friends.

pîn-tsún, a written document as proof of authority to do something; a certificate, receipt, voucher, &c. **ū-pîn-tsún**, having good and sufficient proof, as affair or person; always truthfully keeping his word; his word quite to be depended on.

bōe-tsún-îⁿ, bōe-tsún-thiāu, too large for a beam, but too small for a pillar; said of material quite good in itself, but not suitable for our purpose; said also of a man who is useless or unsuitable. **bōe-tsún--tit îⁿ, bōe-tsún--tit thiāu**, id.

tsún-thê hùt-bú, the goddess with eighteen hands (v. thê).

tsún [R. to adjust; to regulate]. **tsún-tsat**, to use in duly limited proportion, as money, food, &c. (v. tsat). **bô-tsat-tsún** (Cn.), = bô tsún-tsat, not using in proper moderation.

tsùn [R. precipitous]. **hiám-tsùn** (R.), very precipitous. **koâiⁿ-soaⁿ tsùn-niáⁿ**, lofty mountains and steep passes.

tsùn (R. id.) **tsúi-tsùn**, an artificial watercourse or canal for irrigation, larger than "kau." **tsùn-kau**, do., large and small. **chit-piⁿ sī-kau, chit-piⁿ sī-tsùn** (on each side there is a ditch), to act either way would be unsuitable, as offending some friend. **tsùn-á-kîⁿ**, at the side of the irrigation canal.

tsùn [R. handsome]. **chhong-tsùn**, handsome and beautiful, as person; good-looking; sometimes in irony, very ugly! **tsùn-siù**, good-looking, as man. **tsùn-siàu** (r.), id.

tsùn [R. a fine horse]. **pat-tsùn-má**, the eight splendid horses of Chiu-Bȯk-ông, often represented in pictures. **khai-tiong tsùn-hoat**, may this new shop speedily amass wealth.

tsùn [R. chièn, to fight; to tremble]. **chhiú tsùn**, the hand trembles. **chhiú sih-sih-tsùn**, id.

tsùn-ké, an ornament in woman's head-dress that is made to shake by spiral wires.

géh-géh-tsùn, to shake or shiver, as from fear, cold, or old age. **khéh-khéh-tsùn**, id. **khiáuh-khiáuh-tsùn**, id. **ngiáuh-ngiáuh-tsùn**, id. **gih-gih-tsùn**, id.

tsūn (R. tsoān), to twist; to wring, often so as to hurt. **tsūn-saⁿ**, to wring clothes. **tsūn--sí**, to kill by wringing the neck, as a fowl.

koāi-tsūn, perversely disobedient; intentionally disobliging; fond of acting contrary to others' wishes (v. koāi). **tsūn-thâu ngiúⁿ-tāu**, to twist and shake about one's head and neck in a disobedient or light manner. **náuⁿ-thâu tsūn-âm** (C.), id.

kùn-tsūn, to struggle to get off from a man who holds us; to make all sorts of excuses so as to avoid paying money for some common expense; (wriggling out of it). **kap--lán kùn-tsūn**, struggling hard to break away from us. **kún-lún-tsūn**, to writhe, as in pain; to wriggle about, as a snake or worm; very much entangled (as cord) and difficult to open out; twisted and involved, as tendrils or ropes; knotty and twisted, as roots of trees. **kún-lún tsūn-tsūn**, to writhe or wriggle, &c.

tò-tsūn--chhut-lâi, to bring up again (food or insect, &c.) from the crop and eject it, as a fowl does.

tsūn [R. tîn, a troop; a squall], classifier of gusts, showers, &c.

chit-tsūn, now; at this time. **sî-tsūn**, time; a short period of time. **liâm-sî liâm-tsūn**, immediately.

thâu-tsūn, first-born of beasts, esp. of pigs; first squall or gust of wind.

hong-tsūn, convulsions in a child. **tsòe-tsūn-thiàⁿ**, spasms. **koâⁿ-jiét-tsūn**, periodic attack of fever and ague.

hong-tsūn, a squall. **chit-tsūn**, one squall or gust. **hō͘-tsūn**, a shower. **chit-tsūn-hō͘**, one shower. **chit-tsūn-jit, chit-tsūn-hō͘**, alternate sunshine and rain. **chit-tsūn chit-tsūn**, one gust of wind, or squall, or shower after another; one convulsion (disease) after another.

tsut [R. a soldier]. **chhiong iu lē tsut**, four of the lowest classes of persons—courtezans, play-actors, lictors, and other low underlings of yamuns. **bû-bêng siáu-tsut**, a very low-conditioned or worthless fellow. **gû-thâu liók-tsut**, clownish fellow (said in scolding).

tsut-á, playing cards with the word "tsut" (common soldier) on them.

tsut— **àm-tsut-tsut**, very dark; quite dark; without any light.

tsut— **ut-tsut**, deeply grieved and vexed; feeling of disgust and discomfort (v. ut).

tsùt, to wipe up (as one spot of wet or soft dirt) rapidly and roughly with one motion of the hand. **tsùt--chit-ē**, id. **tsùt-ta**, to wipe dry (as with a brush or cloth) by one motion of the hand. **lâm-sám-tsùt**, to wipe or brush too roughly or heavily, so as to injure a thing, *e.g.* spoil the point of a pen. **tsùt-pháiⁿ**, to spoil, as a pen, by drawing it too roughly. **tsùt-lùt-pháiⁿ**, id.

tsùt pòh-piáⁿ, to make thin cakes on a frying-pan.

tsùt— **khó-tsùt-tsùt**, very thick, as boiled rice; very numerous, as animals or men.

tsùt (R. tsùt, sùt). **tsùt-bí**, glutinous rice. **tsùt--ê**, id. **toā-tsùt**, a large sort of it. **tsùt-á**, small sort of it. **toā-khak-tsùt**, a very large sort. **chhiah-khak-tsùt**, the best sort (= kim-pau-gûn), counted very nourishing.

tsùt-bí-thiâm, spirits in which glutinous rice has been soaked. **tsùt-bí-sio**, liquor distilled from glutinous rice. **tsùt-bí-tsu**, false pearls made of it. **tsùt-bí-ku**, turtle-shaped cakes made of it. **tsùt-bí-kô͘**, paste made of it.

tsùt [R. a medicinal plant.]

chiau-tsùt, a medicinal plant, prepared by treating with fire. **péh-tsùt**, a white sort. **chhong-tsùt**, a purgative medicine; also used for burning to remove damp.

TS'H.

This initial is sometimes heard before **a, ng, o, o͘, ö, u, ü** (especially in T. and Cn.), and more frequently the sound is somewhere between Ts'h and Chh. I have not been able to find any settled rule for these cases, and have therefore used everywhere the spelling **Chh** (*q.v.*)

厦英大辭典

U.

Including ü.

u often becomes **i** in Changchew. When it becomes **i** in Changchew, it becomes **ü** in Chin-chew; but this latter change often takes place when the **u** remains in Changchew.

U (R. id.?), a small pit, depression, or puddle. **oáⁿ-u,** the cavity in the bottom of a bowl on which it rests.

lap-u, = lap-o, concave, as a hole or depression, esp. when it has become so by deterioration; lower than the surrounding ground, as a piece of ground; situated too low, as a house or village. **bih-u,** to hide in a hole, as in order to shoot or catch men.

U — **bák-u,** the socket of the eye. **chhim-bák-u,** having deep-set eyes.

U — **kha-thâu-u,** the knee. **kim kha-thâu-u** (lit. having a golden knee), said of a high mandarin who never or rarely kneels; said also of a man of independent spirit who tries to keep clear of yamun business so that he may not need to kneel, and who also avoids those ceremonies (*e.g.* to the deceased relatives of friends) that require kneeling. **chhut-kiaⁿ, kim kha-thâu-u,** except at the metropolis, does not need to kneel to anyone at interviews, as a Tau-tai or official of similar or higher rank.

U [R. ku, to dwell; to reside]. **sì-kòe-u,** = sì-kòe-ku, go about, as a vagrant with no settled dwelling whom no one will keep long.

U — **pûn āuⁿ-u,** to blow a sort of trumpet with a curved mouth.

U (= col. uh, eh). **phah u-á** (C.), = A. phah-eh, to hiccup.

U [R. u, ù, dirty; filthy; vile; depraved; to defile], (C.) **tham-koaⁿ u-lī** (R.), = A. tham-koaⁿ ù-lī, avaricious and venal mandarins.

U [R. distant; wide of the mark; mistaken; bent; distorted; depraved; = col. ù], (T. Cn. ü). **u-khu,** having a very peculiar temper; unsociable or troublesome to have dealings with; very cautious, over-anxious, or suspicious and afraid of taking action, or sticking doggedly to one plan without making allowance for change of circumstances.

u-tsû, over-anxious about everything, often so far as to be bad-tempered; having a displeased or anxious appearance. **u-tsû-tsû,** id.

u-thû, so dogged and dull of apprehension as to be apt to spoil matters (v. thû).

U [R. a preposition of very varied meaning; at; in; to; in relation to], (C. i; Cn. ü). **hék-tsōe u-thien,** to offend against Heaven. **jîn seng u-sè** (r.), of men born in the world (v. sè).

chì-u (r.), with regard to. **chì-u bó-lâng,** as regards Mr. So-and-so. **chì-u ōe-hó ōe-phâiⁿ,** as to whether the consequences may be good or bad.

Û (R. id.), (C. î; Cn. ü), a preposition much like the preceding, and sometimes interchanged with it.

Û [R. myself; I; a surname], (C. î; Cn. ü), a surname; there is also another surname of the very same sound and tone, but with a different character.

Û [R. a chariot; to sustain or carry; the earth], (C. î; Cn. ü).

kham-û-sien (R.), a geomancer.

Û [R. the remainder; surplus; superabundant], (C. î; Cn. ü).

kî-û, surplus; remainder; that which remains over; they who remain over. **kî-û--ê,** id. **û-sīn,** the surplus, remainder, or remnant. **iú-û,** there is a remainder or surplus.

lâu chit--ê û-tōe hō͘--lâng, to leave a man some measure of respectability before others, *e.g.* by refraining from reproving him to the utmost. **lâu û-tōe,** id. **bô-lâu û-tōe** (leaving him with no ground to stand on), leaving him without any room for self-respect or respect from others, as by scolding or reproving him to the utmost before those who used to respect or look up to him. **bô-lâu û-tē,** id. **kàu bô-û-tē,** so as to leave him no room for respect, &c.

Ú [R. the sides of a roof; to shelter or cover; heaven], (C. í). **ú-tiū** (R.), the universe.

Ú [R. with; to give; = col. hō͘], (C. í; Cn. ü). **jîn bû-it-bu̍t ú-thien** (R.), man has nothing to give to Heaven. **ú sù-bîn tông** (R.), just the same as the common people.

Ú (R. id.), (C. í). **tāi-ú,** the great Yu; the emperor Yu, founder of the Shang dynasty, who immediately succeeded Yaou and Shun. **ú-tè,** id.

ú-hō-táu, a large sort of dry measure (táu), about 1.4 of the usual "táu."

Ú [R. rain, = col. hō͘], (C. í). **kam-ú** (R.), seasonable rain after drought. **ú-kéng,** the appearance of the sky when rain is falling, as represented in a picture.

ú-súi, a day on or about February 18th or 19th. **kok-ú,** a day on or about April 20th.

ú-jī-thâu, the 173d radical, written at the top of the character.

hong-ú-chiam, a barometer. **hong, chêng, ú, lō͘,** wind, fair weather, rain, and dew. **hong tiâu, ú sūn,** wind and rain in due proportions.

Ú [R. wings; feathers], (C. — R. í; but in colloquial **ú,** as the colloquial is a mere imitation of the foreign sound), woollen stuffs, such as camlets, merinos, alpacas, &c., said in imitation of the word "wool;" the various phrases have a good deal of indefiniteness in meaning.

nîⁿ-ú, broadcloths, tweeds, and woollen stuffs in general (v. nîⁿ). **hoe-ú,** flowered camlets and such woollen stuffs.

ú-mô͘ⁿ, good strong camlets, and such strong alpaca or woollen stuffs. **ú-toān,** id., or nearly the same.

ú-se, thinner alpacas, bombazettes, merinos, and such thin woollen stuffs.

ú-lîn, thin glossy stuff (mixed wool and cotton?), sometimes flowered, sometimes plain, such as bombazettes, lastings, &c. **ú-tiû,** id., or similar sorts of stuffs; all these phrases are rather indefinite.

Ù [R. u, distant; mistaken; distorted], (T. ü).

ù-tsoat, very dull of apprehension, foolish, and useless. **ù-tsoat put-thong,** id.

Ù [R. satiated; loathing: = col. ùi].

ù-chhùi, feeling surfeited so as to loathe food.

Ù [R. u, ù, dirty; filthy; depraved; to defile], (C. ù, u, ì, in different senses).

ù-òe, dirty; filthy; soiled; to soil. **ù-bī**, a rotten smell, as of something corrupting.

tham-koaⁿ ù-lī (C. u), avaricious and corrupt mandarins.

ù-tâm, damaged by damp or by water, as goods; injured by getting wet, as the end of a stick of ink. **ù-tióh-tsúi**, wetted accidentally by falling or dipping into water, or as goods by a leak. **ù-tsúi**, id. **ù-tióh-kak**, the corner got wet, as of a bale.

ù, to singe; to burn with a hot iron; to warm by coming near something hot.

saⁿ-ù, to sit or lie close together to keep each other warm. **ù-sio**, to warm by putting near the fire or close to a hot tea-pot or large dish of hot rice; to sit or lie close together so as to keep warm in cold weather.

ù--tióh, scorched or singed by fire or by a hot iron. **ù-tióh-hé**, slightly singed or burned, as dress, hair, or skin.

ù-hûn, to make lines with a red-hot iron. **thih sio âng-âng khì-ù**, make the iron red-hot and burn with it, as in making a hole or mark. **ēng-hiuⁿ ù-lâng-bah**, to put a bit of burning incense on a man's skin, *e.g.* to make him start. **ù hō-i-tóh**, to touch with a bit of smouldering tinder or paper, &c., and make it take fire by blowing on it.

ù (R. ò), = ò, a dock. **tsûn-ù**, id. **ù-lāi**, within the dock.

oaⁿ-ù, a good safe anchorage or harbour.

ū (R. iú), to have; there is; there are; yes, in answer to such questions as "Have you?" "Is there?" "Are there any?" sometimes also used somewhat like an auxiliary of past time.

ū-bô, to have or not to have; there is or there is not; is there or is there not? have you or have you not? **ū--bô**, is there any? have you any? is there? have you? **tâng-ū tâng-bô**, fully share each other's fortune, as man and wife. **ū-miâⁿ bô-sit**, having the name but no reality. **ū, tsún-bô**, having it, but much as if not having it (v. tsún). **ū, kóng-bô**, to have, but deny having; to say there is not when there is. **bô, kóng-kàu-ū**, to tell lies till the false appears quite true. **chiáh, bô; phah-mēⁿ, ū**, almost nothing to eat, but plenty of scolding and beating. **ū-hûn bô-iáⁿ ê-ōe**, false deceitful words. **ū-thiⁿ bô-jit-thâu ê-ōe**, falsely accusing of incest and such crimes in reproachful language. **ū-chhut bô-jip**, having expenses but no income (v. jip).

nāⁿ-ū, there is only; there are only; I have no more than —; if there be. **nāⁿ-ū chiah-ê**, there are only these; we have no more than these. **chi-ū**, there is only; there are only. **iáu-ū**, there is still more; there are still; there is more yet; to have more. **iá-ū**, id. **kú-ū**, yet there is still; yet there is; yet there are.

thó-ū, to succeed in getting by asking for. **kiû-kàu-ū**, to ask or pray for till we get it.

ū-sî, sometimes. **ū-kan--á** (P.), id. **ū-lâng**, there are men; there is some one. **ū-lâng-kóng**, some men say. **ū-lâng-chiáh**, some people eat it. **ū-ê**, there are some of them that —. **ū-ê —, ū-ê —**, some —, some —. **ū--ê**, they who have it; they who possess. **ū-thang-hō--lâng**, there is some that can be given.

ū-iáⁿ, it is true; quite true! **ū-tō-lí**, reasonable and right. **ū-gī**, grateful (v. gī). **ū-lé**, polite. **ū-lát**, strong. **ū pún-sū**, skilful; wise. **ū-pīⁿ**, unwell.

ū-hūn, to have a share. **ū-giàh**, rich. **ū-chîⁿ**, id. **ū-hè**, aged. **ū-sin**, to be pregnant.

ū-chhun, to have a surplus or remainder. **ū-sīn**, id. **ū-tióh**, to hit the mark; to be successful (v. tióh). **ū tiāⁿ-tióh**, it is quite fixed. **goá ū-kóng**, now I have said it. **ū sio-kim, ū pó-pì**, if you burn paper (in worship) you will certainly get protection (from the gods).

û [R. a large elephant; easy; amused; idle], (C. î; Cn. ü). **iû-û put-koat**, undecided in purpose.

ū [R. to make ready, to prepare, beforehand; sometimes interchanged with the preceding word].

ū-pī, ready and prepared beforehand.

uh (cf. u, eh). **phah-uh** (C.), = A. phah-eh, to hiccup; to belch.

ui (R. id.), majestic appearance, such as to inspire fear or awe; stern and terrible dignity.

ui-hong, majestic, dignified, dreadful, or awe-inspiring appearance. **ui-hong lím-lím**, id. **ké ui-hong**, to put on such an appearance falsely. **tsok ui-hong**, to put on a dignified or majestic appearance, so as to make people afraid (+).

ui-hêng, stern awe-inspiring manner (v. hêng). **ui-lêng**, mighty power and majesty, as of an idol (v. lêng). **ui-gî** (R.), grand and magnificent appearance, such as to cause reverence.

ui-giâm, stern and severe; majestic and dreadful.

tién-ui, to put on a fierce appearance, as tiger about to spring, or as warrior in battle. **tsok-ui**, to put on a majestic or terrible appearance so as to frighten people. **tsok-ui tsok-hok**, to behave haughtily and insolently, as an official, or as a man in prosperity and power. **hoah hé-ui**, the loud shouting of the attendants of a mandarin as he takes his seat on the tribunal. **kâu pñg-hó-ui** (monkey borrowing tiger's majesty), attendants or servants of mandarin making themselves very big through their master's power. **iâu-bú iông-ui**, a grand military officer showing his dignity; said also of a man making himself appear of great importance, either real or pretended.

ui (same as previous word?).

ui-sit, very prosperous, auspicious, or lucky (v. sit).

ui [R. oat, to scrape a hole; to bore; = col. iah, uih], (C. oɛ), to bore. **ui--chih**, to break by boring. **ui têng-keng**, to cut out the round hole for the neck of a dress.

ui-khang, to bore a hole. **ui-khang iah-piah**, to break through a wall, as in order to steal or rob. **ui hī-khang**, to pick the ears (v. hī).

ui [R. i, clothes; a robe; a dress], the placenta of the womb. **thai-ui** (R.), id. **gín-ná-ui**, id. **ui-toà**, the navel-string. **ui bōe-lóh**, the placenta not coming away after birth, a very dangerous symptom.

sàng koàⁿ-ui, to make a present of clothes for winter wear, only said in a song. **ui-kè** (C.), a stand for hanging clothes on in a bride's outfit.

ui (C.), = A. i, to heal; to cure; only said in phrases originally and purely colloquial, but book phrases that have come into common use remain "i."

ûi (R. id.) **ûi-kéh**, to oppose authority; to disobey. **ûi-pōe** (R.), id. **ûi-bēng** (R.), to disobey legal authoritative commands (s. leave).

ûi-kìm, to break a prohibition.

ûi (R. id.), to surround; to inclose; to besiege. **ûi-lûi**, to surround thoroughly.

sì-ûi, all round; on all sides. **chiu-ûi** (r.), all round about.

chit-ûi, as large in circumference as the two hands can grasp with the fingers just meeting.

ûi-khe, to make a circle; to have a halo (v. khe).

ûi-teh-khoàⁿ, all round about looking at something.

ûi kàu-tīⁿ, surrounding in a great crowd. thoân-thoân ûi-tsū, surrounding in a dense crowd, as some object that attracts attention; forming a close circle round, as army round a city or other army, or as police round a house in order to arrest a man. ûi-lô͘ (surrounding the fire-place), a meal taken together by all the members of a family on the last day of the year.

ûi-khùn, to surround and besiege; to beleaguer or surround, as a city or an army. ûi--teh, besieged, as a city; blockaded, as a port. ûi-siā, to surround a village, as in a feud.

kóe-ûi, to compel the raising of a siege, as the relieving army does; to deliver a man from trouble or danger by exhorting or frightening his enemy. kái-ûi, id.

ûi-kî, to play the sort of chess called "o-pêh-jí."

ûi-sin-kûn, an apron. ûi-su-kûn, id.

tek-ûi, a bamboo fence, as round a house, yard, &c. chhiûⁿ-ûi, a wall on the edge of a terrace, the ground being usually about two or three feet higher than that below. ûi-chhiûⁿ, an inclosing wall. tsáu-ûi-chhiûⁿ, id.

ûi-pîn, a standing screen, either folding or on a fixed stand, as at a door or before a bed.

ûi [R. a curtain; a cloth-screen]. chhn̂g-ûi, the curtain below a bed. kiō-ûi, the curtain or screen before one's legs in a sedan.

toh-ûi, a curtain hanging from a table to the floor in front between the legs. chhâ-toh-ûi, wooden screen-work in front of a table between the legs down to the floor.

ûi [R. to leave behind; to bequeath; to omit or lose involuntarily or unintentionally]. ûi-lāu (R.), to omit an item, as from an account. bōng-ûi, involuntary emissions of semen, as in sleep.

ûi-bēng (R.), last will and testament of any one (s. disobey). ûi-chiàu, last will and testament of the emperor. ûi-giáp, property left by parents or ancestors. tsó͘-kong ê ûi-giáp, ancestral inheritance. ûi-thoân (R.), tradition handed down from ancestors. ûi-hiù bān-liên, to leave a bad reputation to unnumbered years.

ûi [R. certain doors of palace or harem; examination hall]. chhiu-ûi (R.), the examination for the Kujin degree. chhun-ûi (R.), the examination for the Tsin-sze degree.

ûi [R. to be; to do; to act]. ûi-kì, sort of mark for recognition or memorial of parted friends (v. kì).

ûi-chí, to be the limit (v. chí). ûi jîn-tsú, to act as a son (v. jîn).

chiong-tsûn ûi-thai, to make a vessel security for a bond. chí-lòk ûi-má (to point at a stag as a horse), said of accusing a man falsely. hoā-hó͘ put-sêng, hoán ûi-káu, trying to paint a tiger makes it a dog, said of a most contemptible failure (v. hoán).

lân-ûi, to maltreat; to treat oppressively, *e.g.* by compelling to do more work or to pay more money than proper. ûi-hui, to act wickedly (v. hui). hui-ûi, id. bû-só͘ put-ûi, committing all sorts of wickedness.

ū-lêng-ûi, to have ability or power to effect a result; able to accomplish a thing. lí khah-ū lêng-ûi, you are more powerful and more able to do it. lí khah-lêng-ûi, id. bô-lêng-ûi, to be very powerless; to have too little power to effect anything of importance, *e.g.* as an old frail man, or a man with no influence, or an army too weak for the duty. bû-lêng-ûi, id.

ûi (R. id.), a mast. tsûn-ûi, id. ûi-tu, the support for the mast in front of it. ûi-bé, the top of a mast.

toā-ûi, the largest mast of a vessel. tiong-ûi, the mainmast (middle mast) of a three-masted vessel. thâu-ûi, the foremast. bé-ûi, the mizzenmast of a ship; but in a junk it is called "bé-sàng."

chit-ki-ûi, one mast. chit-tiâu-ûi (r.), id. saⁿ-ki-ûi, a full-rigged ship. nn̄g-ki-ûi, a brig. nn̄g-ki-poàⁿ-ûi, = nn̄g-ki-poàⁿ, a barque. ki-poàⁿ-ûi, a two-masted schooner; but a three-masted schooner is "ki-poàⁿ-poàⁿ."

khiā-ûi, to set up a mast. siâ-ûi, to take down a mast. chiap-ûi, to fit together the parts of a foreign mast. póng-ûi, to put on an additional piece of wood on a mast by iron hoops (v. póng). chiūⁿ-ûi, to climb a mast. peh-ûi, id. khì-ûi sit-toā, to lose mast and helm.

ûi (C.), = A. î (R.), only.

úi [R. bent, as under a burden; to sustain, as an office; to delegate or depute; crooked or involved; to reject; the last; really], to depute an inferior official with full powers, as commissioner or deputy, to examine into and settle an affair.

úi-oân, a deputy or commissioner sent or deputed by a superior mandarin with power to examine into or manage some affair, or for some special temporary purpose. úi-goân, id. úi-pâi, credentials of a mandarin appointed to a post, or of deputy or delegated official. úi-i-khì, to send or commission him as deputy. úi hái-hông khì-pān, to appoint the Hai-fang as deputy to manage the matter, as the Tau-tai often does. úi hō͘ hái-hông khì-pān, id.

goā-úi, a petty officer in the army, somewhat like a sergeant-major, just below the "pé-tsóng," and just above the "giàh-goā."

úi-khiok, involved, as an affair; using much cunning and planning in a matter (v. khiok). kóng-ōe khah-úi-oán (r.), to talk in a gentle winning way (v. oán).

phí-úi, having a contemptible or undignified look, as a small and ugly man. jîn-tsâi phí-úi, personal appearance small, mean-looking, and ugly, as of a man.

úi [R. to make excuses; to evade; to put off on another]. chhui-úi (r.), to make excuses or pretences for not doing a thing; to lay the blame or duty on another, generally with the idea of more or less falsehood. thui-úi (C.), id. (r.)

úi [R. a reed]. lô͘-úi (R.), a sort of reed. lô͘-úi-sè, the tax paid to government by the men who cut reeds (on river banks) for making mats, as in Northern and Central China.

úi [R. — C. úi; Cn. ûi, soft or prepared leather; the 178th radical; a surname], a surname.

úi-hō͘, name of an idol (v. hō͘). úi-tô, name of another idol (v. tô).

ùi [R. to console; to comfort]. an-ùi, to console; to soothe; to condole with; to comfort, as by kind conversation.

ùi [R. to press smooth; to make tranquil; military officers].

mn̂g-sîn hō͘-ùi (C. mûiⁿ-sîn hō͘-ì), mandarins of doors and officers of thresholds, words written on the leaves of outside folding-doors as a defence against demons; sometimes instead of the words there are the pictures of a civil and military mandarin respectively on the two door-leaves; sometimes the words written are "sîn-tô͘ ut-lúi," or "sîn-tô͘ ut-lut," the names of powerful spirits able to terrify demons. **bûn-sêng bú-ùi** (civil mandarin and military officer), words sometimes written thus.

ùi [R. ù, satiated; loathing]. **ùi-chhùi**, feeling very full or surfeited, so as to have a dislike to food. **chiàh kàu ùi-chhùi**, to eat till one feels a loathing at food.

ùi [R. tùi, a pair; opposite to; towards; from; by a road], (Cn.), = A. tùi, by a place; by a route or way. **ùi-chit-tiâu**, by this road or route. **ùi-chit-tá**, taking the route by this place; this way. **ùi-tit-lóh**, by what place or way? **ùi-i-kiû**, ask it from him.

ùi (R. id.), to fear; to dread; (to venerate); to be timid. **ùi-ùi**, timid; afraid to meddle in some matter, to engage in some work, or to go somewhere, *e.g.* in the dark. **m̄-ùi**, don't be afraid! there is no cause for anxiety, it is all safe.

kèng-ùi, to venerate; to reverence; to adore.

kia^n-ùi, lest. **khióng-ùi**, lest; for fear that; very much afraid (v. khióng).

ùi-kia^n, shy and easily frightened, as child. **ùi-sí**, much afraid; faint-hearted. **ùi-khū** (R.), to fear greatly.

ùi-siáu-lóe, shy; very bashful. **ùi-siáu-jîn**, very bashful or ashamed (v. siáu). **ùi-kì^n-lâng**, shy and bashful, as from natural disposition, from modesty, or illness, or being ashamed of having done something shameful. **bô-ùi-lâng**, without proper modesty, as a woman who talks too freely with men, or as a boy who makes too free with his seniors or elder relations.

ùi-hoân, unwilling to undertake a troublesome work or duty. **ùi-boâ**, unwilling to exert one's self; unwilling to meet with trouble or inconvenience. **ùi-kiâ^n**, afraid of the trouble of walking. **ùi-sū**, taking great care to avoid raising quarrels or disputes; afraid to meddle with a matter for fear of the consequences.

ùi-siú ùi-bí, timid and fearful, *e.g.* unwilling to see a person for fear of getting somehow involved by him in some troublesome or dangerous affair (lit. afraid of beginning and end).

ùi-ngiau^n, easily tickled (v. ngiau^n). **ùi-lâng-chhiu**, afraid of having his cheek tickled, as child. **ùi-bó**, afraid of his wife, as man who dares not do anything without consulting her (v. bó).

ùi chhàu-chho, not liking to taste strong-smelling fish.

ùi-léng, to have an aguish chill; to be afraid of eating things counted too cooling (léng); also (C.), ague. **ùi-hong**, feeling colded and chilled in a draught of air; afraid of exposing one's self to a draught of air. **ùi-koâ^n**, shivering, chilled, or shaking with cold or with ague; afraid of cold; fond of wearing a great many clothes. **khah-bōe ùi-koâ^n**, wears few clothes even when it is cold. **khah-bô ùi-koâ^n**, not now so much afraid of cold, *e.g.* having now recovered from bad health.

ùi-joàh, afraid of heat, *e.g.* afraid of going out or working hard in hot weather, liking to wear very few clothes in warm weather, or taking them off before other people do. **khah-bōe ùi-joàh**, can bear heavy clothes in hot weather; easily bears exposure to the sun or hard work in hot weather.

ūi [R. the stomach].

pī-ūi, the stomach and the pancreas; the stomach in relation to appetite. **khui pī-ūi**, to whet the appetite. **pī-ūi m̄-khui**, having no appetite at all.

ūi-khì hân, having a tendency to vomit sour watery stuff. **ūi-khì lēng**, id. **ūi-khì phái^n**, appetite bad. **ūi-khì hó** (r.), having a good appetite.

ūi [R. because of; on account of; to side or take part with; to help; by change of tone from "ûi," to be; to act], to take the side of; to take part with, as in a lawsuit, feud, or violent quarrel; to side with.

in-ūi, for; because of; on account of.

ūi--tióh, for the sake of; on account of; for; because of; to be involved in. **ūi-tióh-sū**, to get involved in a lawsuit or such dangerous affair. **ūi--tióh jîn-bēng**, involved in payment for a man's death.

ūi-sū, to be involved in some very dangerous matter; *e.g.* in a lawsuit so that one must defend himself in court, or in responsibility for a death (jîn-bēng).

ūi-bêng ūi-lī, for the sake of fame or of wealth (v. lī).

ūi--lâng, to take a man's side in a quarrel, dispute, or lawsuit; to side with or assist in such a matter. **sa^n-ūi**, mutually supporting or assisting one another, as in feuds, quarrels, or lawsuits. **khah-ūi-goá**, he rather sides with me. **lí ūi-i, bô-ūi-goá**, you are quite on his side and not at all for me.

ūi [R. hoā, to paint; to draw; a picture; = col. oā], (C. ōe, P. oāi, ōɛ), to draw or paint, as face, picture, map, &c.; to make a mark, as in signing.

ūi-hō, to make one's mark as signature; this is the really important and valid part of the signature. **chhiam-miâ^n ūi-hō**, to put down the name and make the mark completing the signature. **ūi-chio**, to sign a confession that our sentence (of death) is just and that we ought to die.

ūi-hûn, to draw a line, as with ink or paint. **ūi-e chhat-péh**, to scrawl about, as on walls, &c.; said also of a child's dirty face.

ūi-bīn, to paint one's own face; to have one's own face painted, as an actor, or as for an idolatrous procession. **ūi-bâi**, to paint the eyebrows of women. **ūi-ôe**, to paint on shoes the lines to be embroidered.

ūi-tô, to draw a map or plan. **ūi-tit**, to draw the diagram used as a board for the game of "tit." **ūi-siōng**, to draw or paint a likeness or portrait of any sort. **ūi tāi-siū**, to draw or paint a full-length portrait on a scroll. **ūi ang-á**, to draw pictures of persons, as of men or idols. **ūi jîn-bùt**, to draw pictures of persons; if anything else be in the picture the persons must be the principal object. **ūi-pùt**, to draw a picture of an idol (Buddhist). **ūi pùt-siōng**, id. **ūi san-súi**, to draw or paint landscapes. **ūi hoe-chiáu**, to paint or draw birds or flowers, without human figures.

chhái-ūi, to paint in various colours. **chhái^n-ūi**, id. **ūi tan-chheng**, to paint in colours (lit. red and blue). **ūi bák-tsúi**, to paint with ink in black and white (+). **chí-bék-ūi**, to paint by dipping the nail in ink (v. bék).

jī-ūi, scrolls with characters and scrolls with pictures. **bák-tsúi-ūi**, pictures in black and white, done with ink (+). **sî-ūi**, pictures by moderns. **kó-ūi**, pictures by painters of former days. **bêng-ka-ūi**, pictures by famous painters.

ūi-kiâ^n, a framed picture. **ūi-phó**, a book of drawing lessons. **ūi-kang**, the work of painting, as regards wages or amount of work; painters of ornamental work, as engaged for hire.

ūi (R. id.), a place; a seat, as at table; space or room; rank; a throne, the seat of a spirit; classifier of persons of some consideration or position.

ūi-á (r.), a place. **chit--ê ūi-á**, this place.

chit-ūi, here; this place. **hit-ūi**, that place; there. **tá-ūi**, where? **pát-ūi**, another place; elsewhere. **kóng tùi-pát-ūi--khì**, to talk about something quite different from the matter in hand.

tsai-ūi, to know the place. **goā-ūi ê-lâng**, person who comes from a very distant place.

bô-ūi, there is no vacant room. **bô-ūi-chhù**, no place, *e.g.* no place to live in.

toā-ūi, a principal or chief seat; a seat of honour, as at a feast; a large place. **sòe-ūi**, an inferior seat; a small place. **hiâm sòe-ūi**, to find fault with a place because it is too small. **téng-ūi**, an upper seat. **ē-ūi**, a lower seat.

pē-ūi, a vital place on the body, where a blow is fatal (from "pē," a division or class).

pē-ūi, rank (from "pē," a pace of two steps). **kàu sím-mihⁿ pē-ūi**, what rank has he reached? **koaⁿ-ūi**, official rank.

tē-ūi, grade of official rank, &c. **tōe-ūi**, id. **sím-mihⁿ tē-ūi**, what rank? (*e.g.* has he reached). **toā-tē-ūi**, high mandarin or literary rank, *e.g.* a Kujin. **pa̍t-jit ōe toā-tē-ūi**, he will come to high rank some day, said of a promising boy. **ū tē-ūi**, to have some rank or position; to have a very good situation or great wealth. **hē--i khah-ū tē-ūi**, leave him some measure of respect (bīn), as by refraining from scolding or reproving to the utmost. **lâu chit--ê tē-ūi hē--i**, id. **hē--i bô-tē-ūi**, to scold him to the utmost, so that no room for respect is left. **hē--i bô-tē-ūi thang-khiā**, id.

tàⁿ-ūi, the burden or capacity of a vessel counted in peculs. **káu-ūi**, the space occupied by a row of boats tied to one rope (káu-soh). **phek-ūi**, the place in a song for striking the "phek."

tìn-ūi, to occupy room uselessly; to obstruct the way (v. tìn).

kui-ūi, to come back to their proper places, as workmen after a short respite, or as scholars after play-time. **kui-ūi chē**, to go and sit down in their proper places, as scholars. **kui pún-ūi**, to return to his or their original position; esp. said of a spirit that had been incarnate returning to his original station; sometimes said of other things, *e.g.* of troops. **oāⁿ-ūi**, to change places, as men or things (v. oāⁿ). **soá-ūi**, to move to another place (v. soá). **chhiên-ūi**, each politely refusing to sit in the more honourable place and pressing the other to sit. **teh tsun-ūi**, id.

an-ūi, to consecrate the place for an idol or ancestral tablet and enthrone it with ceremonies in its shrine or place; to invite a very highly honoured guest (*e.g.* a mandarin or a new son-in-law) to take his seat at table with very special ceremonies on some special occasions; done by placing a wine-cup and a pair of chopsticks opposite the seat he is to occupy, and making very formal bows to him, &c. **an-ūi tāi-kiet** (an auspicious inscription put on the shrine of a new idol), may this newly consecrated seat have great good fortune.

sîn-ūi, the seat, throne, or abode of the spirit of an idol or sage, sometimes a tablet, sometimes a scroll only. **lêng-ūi**, the place (often a paper house) where the "hûn-sin" is placed in the rites for the dead, and where the spirit of the dead person is supposed to stay (v. lêng).

lo̍k-ūi, a tablet put up in honour of a living mandarin; it signifies a wish for his long life and prosperity. **tiông-seng lo̍k-ūi**, id. **lo̍k-ūi-pâi**, id. **chhāi lo̍k-ūi**, to set up such a tablet.

kong-tsō-ūi, the mandarin's seat on the tribunal or judgment-seat (+).

thiⁿ-ūi, the imperial throne (v. thiⁿ). **ông-ūi**, a royal throne. **pó-ūi**, id. **tsō-ūi** (r.), a throne.

teng-ūi, to come to the throne. **chiap-ūi**, to succeed to the throne. **chhoàn-ūi**, to usurp the throne.

thoân-ūi, to transmit the throne to one's successor **thè-ūi**, to abdicate.

niūⁿ-ūi, to abdicate in favour of another; to give place politely to another; to yield the place voluntarily to another. **chē-ūi**, to sit on the throne; to reign; to be a sovereign; to take their seats, as arbiters, or as guests at a feast.

khí-ūi, to rise, or rise slightly from one's seat, as a mark of respect to visitors or guests when they enter; to rise and leave the table when one has eaten enough at end of a meal.

kúi-ūi, how many persons? **liėt-ūi**, a polite phrase used in addressing several persons (v. liėt). **sam-ūi it-thé** (X.), three persons and one substance or essence; the Trinity in unity.

uiⁿ (C.), = A. ng, to cover with the hand. **uiⁿ pak-té**, to hold one's belly, as in great pain.

ûiⁿ (C.), = A. n̂g, yellow, a surname. **ûiⁿ phi-phi**, very yellow. **ûiⁿ phiàng-phiàng**, id.

ûiⁿ (C.) **lê-ûiⁿ**, = A. lôe-n̂g, the bent body of a plough.

ûiⁿ (C.), = A. n̂g (sulphur).

ûiⁿ (Cn.), = A. êng, leisure.

úiⁿ (C.) **úiⁿ-á**, = A. ńg-á, a small sort of basket.

úiⁿ (C.), = A. ńg. **káu-úiⁿ**, = A. káu-ńg, a sort of pawn-shop.

úiⁿ (C.), = A. ńg, a sleeve.

úiⁿ (C.), = A. ńg, to take under the arm.

úiⁿ (C.), = A. ńg, a surname (R. goán).

ūiⁿ (Cn.), = A. oá, to lean upon; to be near; only said in some phrases.

ūiⁿ (C.), = A. n̄g. **ba̍k-chiu ūiⁿ**, eyes dim, as when wearied with looking long.

uih [R. oat, to scrape a hole; to bore; a cleaner for a pipe; = col. ui, iah], to bore or make a hole; to pick out, as from a hole or chink; to take up on the finger, as paste; to scoop out, as the eye.

uih-khang, to make a hole, as in a wall. **uih-pé**, to alter a writing by cutting out a word or more, and pasting in the correction.

uih ba̍k-chiu, to scoop out the eyes. **uih ba̍t-sat**, to pick out bugs from chinks. **uih-kē**, to take up a small quantity of paste, as on the point of the finger, or on a small slip of bamboo, *e.g.* for pasting up a letter.

uih-á, a pipe-cleaner; a picker for a pipe; also (T.), = A. lién-á, an instrument for twirling the pellet of opium in the flame.

uih ham-khak-chíⁿ, = kuih ham-khak-chíⁿ (C. oeh), a game played by children, making the shells of the "ham" turn over by pressing them with the finger nail. **uih koe-ko**, to play that game with shells. **uih koe-ko, phah chháu-lô**, a sort of song or chorus shouted by children in a kind of noisy game.

u̍ih [R. ėk, to draw a line; to mark by a line; to devise; a line], to draw a line; a short horizontal line; a short line; a stroke, as in writing Chinese characters.

chit-u̍ih, one short horizontal stroke; a short stroke; one stroke in addition to the radical making up the character. **chit-khiā chit-u̍ih**, one perpendicular and one horizontal stroke (v. khiā). **kúi-u̍ih**, how many strokes in addition to the radical has the character? **saⁿ-u̍ih**, it has three strokes besides the radical.

chheng-soàn bān-soàn, m̄-ta̍h thiⁿ chit-u̍ih (or "chhien-soàn," &c.), all human plans are not equal to one line (*i.e.* purpose) of Heaven.

76

ùih [R. ėk, to engrave; to carve; to scratch; to cut open].

ùih-hûn, to scratch or score a line, esp. with the nail, or with a knife, or with a bit of brick or tile. **ùih po-lê**, to scratch a line on glass with a diamond, as in order to break it off.

thâu phoà, hī ùih, wounded about head and ears, as by an accident, or by being beaten or struck.

taⁿ ùih--lah, now then it is quite ruined or spoiled, as a thing, or as an affair gone entirely wrong; now it is all up. **taⁿ--chiah ùih--lah**, id.

un [R. oan, to oppress]. **un-khut**, to treat unjustly on the basis of a false charge; to accuse falsely, either to a private person or magistrate. **un-ut** (r.), id.

un [R. warm; temperate; mild and gentle; to revise, as a lesson], genially warm and temperate, as climate; to warm or heat up; a surname.

un-chiu, Wan-chow or Wen-chow-foo, between Fuhchau and Ningpo. **un-thai-chiu**, Wen-chow-foo and Tai-chow-foo, both in Chekiang province.

un goân-sòe, an idol of surname Un, represented riding on a tiger, as attendant on *Má-tsó* or Tāi-tō-kong.

un-sip, to revise thoroughly, as a lesson.

un-hô, mild and gentle, as temper; genial and mild, as weather. **chhun-khì un-hô**, spring weather mild and genial.

un-jiû, mild and gentle (v. jiû). **un-sûn**, good, meek, and gentle; kind, mild, and good-tempered.

un-tsúi, to warm water. **un sio-tsúi**, id. **un-chiú**, to warm spirituous liquor. **un-thng** (Cn.), to warm up warm water.

ùn [R. pestilence; a very severe epidemic or infectious disease. **ùn-ėk**, a pestilence, plague, or severe epidemic (v. ėk). **ùn-iȧh** (C.), id. **ùn-hėk** (Cn.), id.

tso-ùn, to be afflicted with pestilence, insurrection, conflagrations, or such great disasters. **siū-tso-ùn**, id. **tiȯh-ùn**, to have a severe epidemic or pestilence, as in a place. **tiòng-té ùn-pīⁿ**, may you have dropsy and pestilence (said by women in scolding).

ùn — **ùn-ài**, the mumps (s. favour). **siⁿ ùn-ài**, to have the mumps.

ûn — **ûn-lun-khûn**, coiled up, as a snake, dog, or cat (v. khûn).

ūn, to sit, lounge, or lie down, so as to soil or crease one's clothes; to throw down in a confused disorderly way, as clothes or ropes; to go about spending one's time in the haunts of low vile pleasures. **lām-sám ūn**, id. **sì-kòe-ūn**, to sit or lie down here and there, so as to soil, crumple, or spoil one's dress; to go about in a lazy and disorderly way, spending one's time in improper places. **tȧk-jit ūn--hia**, day after day frequenting those bad places.

ūn-ūn--teh, thrown about in a confused disorderly way, as clothes or ropes; soiled or spoiled by sitting or lying down, as clothes on the person; going about low haunts and bad places. **ūn-lun--teh**, id. **tiāⁿ-tiāⁿ ūn--teh**, madly set for a long time on gambling, or such bad courses.

ūn-pháiⁿ, to crush, break, or spoil by sitting or lying down on. **ūn-jiâu**, to crumple, as one's dress, by sitting on it. **ūn--chih**, to break by sitting or lying upon.

ūn tī-kiáu--nihⁿ, constantly mad upon gambling, as for days and weeks, or for a longer time, so that he will not give it up. **ūn tī tsa-bó--nih**ⁿ, madly set on a bad woman for a long long time.

ûn [same as the previous word?]. **ûn-thun**, dirty; filthy (v. thun).

ún [R. grieved; anxious], (C. in; Cn. ün). **ún-khûn** (C. in-khîn), courteous, kind, and attentive to visitors or guests.

ûn [R. name of a fish]. **ûn-hî**, sort of small fish with a sharp head. **chiam-chhùi-ûn**, id.

un (R. id.), (C. in; Cn. ün), favour; grace; unmerited kindness. (Special care must be taken in C. to say "in," and not "un," which suggests the meaning of epidemic or calamity.)

un-tién, favour; grace. **un-hūi**, id. **un-tek**, id. **i ū un-tek tī goán-tau**, he deserves favour or kindness from me in return for what he has done for me. **un-chêng**, kindness; favour; grace; kind disposition. **hó-un-chêng**, kind and affable. **pò-tap un-chêng**, to requite favour. **i ū un-chêng tī goá-tau**, I owe him gratitude and favour, or kindness for favours given to me or my relatives or friends. **un-tėk** (R.), favour; kindness. **un-thióng** (R.), special imperial favour and affection, esp. to members of harem.

thien-un, imperial favour; also (R.), the favour of Heaven. **hông-un**, imperial favour. **toā-un**, great favour or grace.

un-ài, to love greatly, as man and woman (s. mumps). **un-sut** (r.), to compassionate; to act kindly and considerately (v. sut). **un-sù**, a gracious gift, as from a sovereign; to bestow royal favour, as sovereign does. **bāng-lí khah-un-sù**, please show me this kindness (said in a half joking, half polite way). **un-khe**, an additional special examination for degrees, granted by imperial favour. **un-kòng**, the degree of "kòng-seng" given on some special occasion, *e.g.* on the birth of an heir to the throne.

un-jîn, a benefactor. **goá--ê un-jîn**, my benefactor. **tap-siā un-kong**, to give thanks to a powerful spirit for his aid. **un-kúi**, the spirit of a man who was under great obligations to us, requiting us by giving assistance at the examination for the Kujin degree.

khai-un, to pardon a fault or crime; to forgive a debt in whole or in part. **si-un**, to bestow grace or favour. **ka-un**, to bestow a high favour, or forgive a great fault.

siū-un, to receive kindness, grace, or favour. **siū-un put-pò**, to be ungrateful for kindness received. **bông-un pōe-gī**, ungrateful; to be ungrateful. **bông-un** (r.), id. **ke-un**, to be ungrateful (v. ke). **kám-un**, grateful or thankful for favour. **siā-un**, to give thanks for favour or grace. **pò-un**, to requite favour or kindness (+). **pò-tap chhim-un**, to requite very great kindness. **ti-un pò-pún**, to requite the kindness of our parents.

un chhièn, kindness or favour small. **un sòe** (C. in sè), id. **un kāu**, favour or grace very great. **un koāiⁿ** (C. in koān), id. **un chhim**, id. **un toā**, id.

ûn [R. hûn, clouds]. **ûn-sio**, the city of Yun-siau, a Ting district or subdivision of Chang-chew, near Tong-san, on the road from Chang-poo to Swatow.

ûn [R. oān, slow, =col. bān]. **ûn-ûn**, gradually; slowly; cautiously (s. walk about). **ûn-á-sī**, id. **ûn-ûn-á**, id. **ûn-ûn-á-kóng**, to tell bit by bit. **ûn-ûn-á-kā**, to nibble gradually.

ûn-á-kiâⁿ, walk slowly; good-bye, said to the person going away. **ûn-á liên-hôe**, may you be always miserable, and unable either to get deliverance or to die!

ûn--chit-pē, take one step more slowly, said by chair-bearers; also said in general, just wait a little.

ûn, a small sandbank; also (C.), a small dam, weir, &c., in a stream, either partly or wholly across it.
soa-ûn, a small sandbank.

ûn [R. oân, round; to interpret, as dreams; = col. î^n].
ûn-bāng, to go to a temple in order to dream there for an augury. **ûn sien-bāng**, to go to dream at the temple of the eight genii.

ûn [R. lûn, a wheel; a joint].
chhun-ûn (T. chhun-lûn), to stretch one's limbs, as when tired or slightly unwell.

ûn [R. sûn, to go about to inspect], (Cn. ûn), to walk about, as for exercise or amusement, or when looking at a place; to take a stroll; to go about idly or indulging in depraved pleasures. **ûn-ûn**, id. (s. gradually). **ûn-lâi ûn-khì**, to stroll about walking back and forwards. **lâi--khì ûn-ûn**, come and take a stroll. **sì-kòe-ûn**, to stroll about in many directions or places.

ûn [R. equal; even; alike], one of the successive rows of rafters or beams between two great beams; one of the rows of tiles, &c.
chiàu-ûn, in regular order or succession, as taking turns in work or a game.
chiâu-ûn, in good and sufficient measure, and in constant regular succession, as rain, or as work, *e.g.* as the regular steady gains of ordinary work or trade. **kang-hu chiâu-ûn**, employment constant and regular for a long time. **hē-tsúi chiâu-ûn**, rains regular and sufficient.
phái^n-tsu-ûn, a season when small-pox is specially virulent and fatal.
phah-ûn, to do work together and divide the profits about equally. **phah thong-ûn**, id. **khien-chhé-ûn--khì**, taking things at an average, as good and bad mixed. **chhé-ûn**, id.
chit-ûn soa^n, chit-ûn hiu^n-siā, ranges of mountains and groups of villages alternating in succession. **kúi-ûn chheh**, how many piles or rows of books? **chit-ûn î^n**, one row of rafters or small beams between two great beams.
jī-ûn, sets of characters used by relations for the several generations, so that the genealogical rank of any one is at once known by his name. **tâng-jī-ûn**, of the same generation, equally distant from the common ancestor. **siāng-jī-ûn**, id. **toā chit-jī-ûn**, one generation nearer the common ancestor. **toā-chit-ûn**, id. **khah-toā-ûn**, higher in genealogical rank. **toā-ûn ê-lâng**, a man higher in the genealogical tree. **ē-ûn**, one generation lower in genealogical position. **sòe-chit-ûn**, one generation further from the common ancestor. **sè-chit-ûn** (C.), id. **khah-soe chit-ûn**, one degree more distant in relationship.

ún [R. id., = col. ín], (Cn. ûn), to promise; to consent; to give permission; to accede to or grant a request. **iông-ún**, to allow of; to bear with; to permit; to tolerate. **êng-ún** (P.), id. **èng-ún** (r.), to promise. **sa^n-ún-thīn**, to arrange the betrothal, as of son or daughter.
ún-tsún, to grant; to permit. **ún chit-siū^n poe**, to grant a favourable answer by the divining sticks (one concave, the other convex), or by cash before the ancestral tablets.
ún-hō͘ (T.), = A. ín-hè, to promise goods to a customer. **ún-kheh** (T.), to engage to carry a passenger. **ún-tsāi** (T.), to make an agreement to carry goods; to accept a freight, as an officer of the vessel, or as the Hong that manages the sending of goods.

ún [R. ín, to lead]. **ún-tsúi-chio**, = **ín-tsúi-chio**, a medicinal plant.

ún [R. ín, an earthworm], (C. gín, kín; Cn. bún). **thô-ún**, a worm; an earthworm. **tô-ún**, id. **kâu-ún** (L.), id.

ún — **ún-ku**, hunchbacked; a hunchback (v. ku), (s. hide).

ún, a bead, as running round the outside of a boat. **tiām-ún**, a horizontal bead round a boat about water-mark, above or below, as it is lightly or heavily laden. **phû-ún**, a bead round a boat quite above the water, often of a different colour.

ún [R. boán, late, = col. mńg].
ún-tang, the second rice-harvest, about the 10th month. **ún-kùi**, id. **ún-bí**, the rice of the second harvest.

ún (R. id.), safe; certain to succeed, as a plan; secure, as an investment; sure to —. **m̄-ún**, insecure. **bô-ún**, id.
an-ún, safe and tranquil. **ún-ún**, very safe or secure. **ún-sim**, mind devoid of fear or anxiety. **ún-sūn**, safe, as a trade or business without risks; safe and quiet, as good weather for sailing.
ún-tàng, safe; secure; sure to —; certainly will —. **ún-tàng ōe-hó**, certainly it can be put right, or can be completed.
ún-thàn, the investment or business is safe, sure to give a profit. **ún-iâ^n bô-su**, certain to win. **ún-chiàh ún-khùn**, you may eat and sleep in security; there will be no danger; I will manage it all right for you.
ún-tsú, a safe customer; a man to whom we may safely lend money or give goods on credit. **phō-ún**, to confine one's self to safe investments.

ún [R. to hide; to conceal; to cover up; private; not in office], (C. sometimes ín; Cn. sometimes ûn), to cover up, as with thick stuffs, in order to keep warm; to ripen by covering up in a jar, as persimmons and some other fruits; to cover, as a hen covers her chickens (C. ún).
ún-sio, to cover up and keep warm, as embers, or as food; to sit or lie close together so as to keep warm. **ún koe-á**, to keep chickens warm, as under the wings. **ún tī bí-kng--nih^n**, to ripen by covering up in a rice-jar, as plantains pulled unripe (C. ún).
ún-tsông, to hide away, as treasure-trove, or as stolen goods. **ún-lék**, to hide or keep secret, as an affair, thing, or person. **ún-moā^n** (r.), to deceive by concealing (C. ín, ún). **ún tī sim-lāi**, to keep in one's own heart, as one's sorrows. **ún-sin-hoat**, the magical art of becoming invisible.
ún-ku (C. ín-ki), to dwell in seclusion, as a retired statesman (v. ku, "to dwell"), (s. humpbacked).
ún-gú, a phrase with a hidden meaning (v. gú). **ún-hong**, a very dangerous kind of venereal disease.

ùn (R. id.), to dip the end of a thing in a liquid; to wallow. **ùn-tâm**, to dip in so as to damp.
ùn-noā^n, to wet with saliva, as by putting to the lips, or with the tongue.
ùn-bák, to dip in ink, as the pen. **ùn-tsúi**, to dip in water. **ùn-iâm**, to dip in salt. **ùn-kiâm**, to dip in some salted condiment. **ùn-ti^n**, to dip in some sweet preparation. **ùn-thn̂g**, to dip in sugar.

ùn (cf. ut).
ùn-būn, grieved; vexed; feeling dull and weary, as with ennui in bad weather when having nothing to do.

ùn [R. hùn, stupid or incapable at business]. **ùn-**

thùn, stupid at managing business; dull of understanding (v. thùn).

ùn, an inclosed pool for catching fish, overflowed when the tide is full. **ùn-hoāⁿ**, the embankment of such a pool, made of mud. **phoà-ùn**, to break that embankment and let out the water, so as to catch the fish.

ūn, to lean or rub upon so as to dirty one's clothes, &c.

ūn--tio̍h, to rub or press upon unintentionally so as to soil one's clothes (as by rubbing on paint), or so as to break or spoil something. **ūn-phāiⁿ**, to break or spoil a thing by coming against it. **ūn--chih**, to break by coming against. **ūn--tó**, to overset by one's clothes catching on something when passing.

ūn (R. id.), rhyme; rhythm; timbre or quality of tone, as of a musical instrument. **si-ūn**, a rhyming dictionary. **bé-ūn**, the last rhyme in a poem, *i.e.* that in the last line (s. revolve).

im-ūn, rhythm; cadence; timbre or quality of tone, as of voice or instrument. **im-ūn tiau-hô**, harmonizing well, as voice and instrument; music harmonious. **im-ūn bô-hia̍p**, the tune in singing or reciting not well executed as to melody, or not harmonious. **im-ūn thiaⁿ-khi-hn̂g**, voice clear and loud (as in singing or chanting), so that it is heard far off.

ah-ūn, to agree in rhyme; to rhyme well, as a line of poetry, according to Chinese rules. **ha̍h-ūn**, to rhyme correctly, as two words; to accord or agree in sound or harmony, as voice or instrument. **ōe-lo̍h-ūn**, fit to make a rhyme. **bōe-lo̍h-ūn**, does not make a proper rhyme.

oá-ūn, to rhyme; to sing near the tune; to guess a word from the context, &c.; to guess from slight knowledge, so as not to be far from the mark (s. revolve). **oá-ūn lâi-kóng**, to speak as if confident of the fact, though it is really only a shrewd guess. **oá-ūn lâi-ioh**, to guess from appearances and such circumstantial evidence.

ūn [R. to revolve; to go round in a circuit or orbit; to transport; a revolution; the course of nature or of fate; = col. In], a period of good or bad fortune, esp. of five years; to echo; to transport goods or provisions in large quantities; to spread, as a sore growing large; to break out, as new boils near an old one.

ūn-niūⁿ, to transport provisions, as for the army (v. niūⁿ). **ūn-hè**, to transport goods of one or few sorts (esp. grain) in large quantities for long periods. **ūn-koan**, to bring home a corpse in a coffin from a distant place. **ūn-hô** (R.), the Grand Canal.

iâm-ūn, a large sea-going salt-junk (v. iâm).

siaⁿ ūn--lâi, the sound re-echoes or echoes back.

lâm-hong-ūn, the clouds moving with the south wind.

ū âu-ūn, pleasant taste and mellow feeling left in the mouth after drinking good tea. **khah-bô âu-ūn**, mouth not having that pleasant feeling, as after inferior tea.

hiet-khì ūn-tōng, the vital principle or animal spirits making the complete round of the body in one day (v. tōng). **chē-siên ūn-khì**, to sit cross-legged absorbed in meditation or abstraction, insensible to the world's affairs, without eating or speaking, as Bud. priest. **ūn-sîn**, to sit thus in silent abstraction. **lí ūn-sîn**, good-bye, sir! said to a Bud. priest when one leaves his temple (lit. you may now return to your abstraction).

ūn-lâng, to suppurate in a new place, as old boil spreading, or as new boils breaking out near the original boil.

tsáu-bé-ūn, the 162d radical, written half inclosing the other part of the character; it is the radical of this word "ūn."

ūn-tsoán (r.), to revolve in an orbit, as a planet (v. tsoán).

thien-ūn, the cyclical date of the year in reference to matters connected with the gods and with superstitions. **ke-ūn**, period of good or bad luck for a family. **lâng-ê-ūn**, a man's luck, good or bad, for a period of several years. **kho-ūn**, fated time for success in getting a degree. **lāu-ūn**, the last years of an old man's life. **bé-ūn**, the concluding years of a man's life (s. rhyme). **sí-ūn**, period of life in which death comes. **tó-ūn**, period when death, or some very great calamity, or bad fortune comes. **eh-ūn**, a calamitous season of life.

bô-ūn, very unlucky, as man. **m̄-sī-ūn**, a very unlucky period of life. **hó-ūn**, period of good fortune. **phāiⁿ-ūn**, fated season of bad fortune, not so long as "phāiⁿ-miāⁿ-ūn." **phāiⁿ-ūn-tê**, id. **ūn phāiⁿ**, one's fortune unlucky for a considerable length of time.

sūn-ūn, in a happy-fated period; matters all going on well. **chhut-ūn**, to escape from a period of bad luck into one of good fortune. **pó-ūn**, to mend a man's fate by special rites and ceremonies.

oá-ūn khoàⁿ-miāⁿ, to say that a man will have good fortune when he is already plainly prosperous (s. rhyme).

jī-ūn, one's fortune, as good or bad, esp. in relation to one's horoscope. **bô-jī-ūn**, unfortunate, as man whose affairs are always going wrong. **hó-jī-ūn**, good fortune; fortunate. **sī jī-ūn**, id. **m̄-sī jī-ūn**, bad fortune; all going wrong.

khì-ūn, fortune, good or bad, as of person, place, or kingdom, esp. for a considerable time. **ūn-khì**, id. (+). **ūn-khì ōng**, in great prosperity; self and family all well and prosperous, esp. making a great deal of money.

miāⁿ-ūn, character of a man's fated condition as to life and good or bad fortune for the greater part of one's life, for half one's life, or more. **miāⁿ-ūn sī**, fortune extremely good for a long period, longer than "hó-ūn," but not so long as "hó-miāⁿ." **hó-miāⁿ-ūn**, id. **miāⁿ-ūn m̄-sī**, fortune extremely bad for a very long period. **phāiⁿ-miāⁿ-ūn**, id.

sî-ūn, time or state of a man's fated good or bad fortune, sometimes quite short. **i--ê sî-ūn**, his fated condition or circumstances as to good or bad fortune at the time. **sī i--ê sî-ūn**, it is his time of good fortune.

sî-ūn-miāⁿ, specially good or bad fortune, as of a man, "sî" being the shortest, "miāⁿ" for the whole life, and "ūn" properly for several years. **sî-ūn-bēng** (r.), id. **sī-ūn-miāⁿ saⁿ-jī**, fortune, as extremely good or extremely bad. **sî-ūn-miāⁿ saⁿ-jī-tsn̂g**, id.

ut [R.—; C. ut; Cn. ùi], to smooth with an iron; to iron, as clothes. **ut-saⁿ**, to iron clothes. **ut-táu**, a smoothing-iron for clothes.

ut [R. fragrant herbs used in offerings; vexed unpleasant feelings; cf. col. ùn], uncomfortable feeling, as when too hot, or bilious, or dyspeptic, or grieved, disquieted, or anxious.

ut-kim-hiuⁿ, a fragrant plant used in medicine (golden turmeric?). **ut-kim-hiong-chiú**, sort of fragrant spirituous liquor of pleasant taste.

ut-lúi, title of a man of the Tang dynasty now worshipped as a spirit who keeps away demons. **sîn-tê**

海上絲綢之路文獻集成 科技與文化編

ut-lúi, the names of two powerful spirits, terrible to demons, which are often written on doors as a protection. **sîn-tê ut-lu̍t,** id.

ut-hé, feeling uncomfortable and unwell, as from biliousness or slight feverishness. **ut-tsûn,** feeling uncomfortable from being long in a vessel. **ut-tsut,** feeling uncomfortable, vexed, grieved, or disgusted at some matter. **ut-tsut-joa̍h,** sultry weather, such as brings on a typhoon unless it be followed by heavy rains. **ut-joa̍h,** sultry and oppressive, as weather. **ut-ek,** vexed, grieved, sad, and uncomfortable in mind. **ut-būn,** id. **iu-ut** (R.), sad and disquieted.

kái-ut, to cure the uncomfortable feeling, as of biliousness or dyspepsia.

ut-áuⁿ, pronouncing indistinctly, as from a fault in the palate or tongue (v. áuⁿ).

ut [R. khut, to bend; to treat very unjustly], to bend without breaking; to sprain, esp. by giving the ankle a slight twist; to accuse falsely; to treat unjustly, as by false accusation or by neglecting talent. **ut-lut,** to bend, &c. **ut-teh-chē,** to sit crouching or bent.

ut--tio̍h (C. ó--tio̍h), to sprain slightly, as ankle or wrist, not so bad as "tsoa̍h." **ut--khì,** id. **kha ut--tio̍h,** foot sprained.

ut-chím, neck stiff and sore from sleeping in a bad position.

áu-ut, to insist falsely and violently that a man owes money or has done something wrong, so as to treat him unjustly and oppressively. **un-ut,** = oan-khut, to injure or oppress by accusing falsely of crime. **gâu-ut--lâng,** fond of maligning or falsely accusing people so as to injure them. **khit-i-ut,** to be thus falsely accused by him. **ut--sí lâng--ê tsâi-tiāu,** to cause another's talents to be passed over and not rewarded or properly appreciated, *e.g.* by spreading calumnies against him, or by preventing his getting an opportunity of showing his powers, or as an examiner not giving a degree to a deserving candidate.

u̍t (cf. a̍ihⁿ, e̍h).

ihⁿ-u̍t, discontented, distressed, or disgusted at the state of matters, *e.g.* at some misfortune that has come on us, or at an inconvenient dilemma; grumbling, as at an order which we must obey, but feel unwilling. **ih-u̍t,** id. **ihⁿ-ihⁿ u̍t-u̍t,** id.; also said of the indistinct manner of speaking of a man who is afraid to speak out, *e.g.* when ashamed to speak, or as when asking a favour, or when dissatisfied and grumbling.

u̍t [R. a sort of bird, = lu̍t].

u̍t-pāng siong-chhî, gû-jîn tek-lī, when the bird and the oyster seize each other the fisherman gets profit, said of the yamun people getting gain out of lawsuits.

W.

wa, wâ, wá, wà, wā; better **oa,** oâ, oá, oà, oā (*q.v.*)

waⁿ, wâⁿ, wáⁿ, wàⁿ, wāⁿ; better **oaⁿ,** oâⁿ, oáⁿ, oàⁿ, oāⁿ (*q.v.*)

wa̍h, better **oa̍h** (*q.v.*)

wai, wái, wāi, waiⁿ, wāiⁿ, wa̍ihⁿ; better **oai,** oái, oāi, oaiⁿ, oāiⁿ, oa̍ihⁿ (*q.v.*)

wa̍k, better **oa̍k** (*q.v.*)

wan, wân, wán, wàn, wān; better **oan,** oân, oán, oàn, oān (*q.v.*)

wang, better **oang** (*q.v.*)

wat, wa̍t; better **oat,** oa̍t (*q.v.*)

APPENDIX.

I.

VARIATIONS OF SPELLING IN OTHER BOOKS ON THE LANGUAGE OF AMOY.

SPELLING OF MEDHURST'S DICTIONARY.

The spelling used in the *Dictionary of the Hok-kien Dialect*, by the Rev. Dr. Medhurst, differs very widely from that used in this book. It is founded on the principle of imitating the English sounds of vowels, and is therefore extremely confused, besides being somewhat too much influenced by the Chinese tables of initials and finals, a subject into which I cannot enter here.

The initials, when consonants, are for the most part the same as mine, except the following:—

gn is used instead of **ng**.

ch is used both for **ch** and **ts**.

The aspirated consonants are indicated not merely by **h**, but by a small comma inserted between the **h** and the other consonant.

u^{m} is used instead of **m**, a syllable that really contains no vowel.

w is usually used instead of **o** at the beginning of a diphthong; **woey** instead of **oe**; **woo** or **wu** instead of **u**; and **wui** instead of **ui**.

y is used as an initial instead of **i** at the beginning of a diphthong; **yë** instead of **i** in some diphthongs; **yew** instead of **iu**; **yi** instead of **i** before **m**, **n**, **p**, and **t**; also **yung** instead of **iong**.

The greatest changes occur in the finals. A final means in Chinese nomenclature the whole of a word excepting the initial consonant or consonants, or even the whole word if there be no initial consonant.

The following list will enable the student to understand Medhurst's spelling of these finals. The first is Medhurst's spelling, the second is its equivalent as used in this Dictionary.

ae - - - -	**ai**	**ëuk** - - - -	**iok**
ai^{ng} - - - -	**ε**^{n}	**ew** - - - -	**iu**
aou - - - -	**au**	**ey** - - - -	**e**
ay - - - -	**ε**	^{n}**o** - - - -	**ɵ**^{n}
e - - - -	**i**	**oe** - - - -	**ɵ**
e^{ng} - - - -	**ng**	**öey** - - - -	**oe**
ëa - - - -	**ia**	**öey**, when preceded by **m**,	**oε**
ëang - - -	**iang**	**oo** - - - -	**u**
ëaou - - -	**iau**	**u**^{m} - - - -	**m**
ee^{ng} - - -	**i**^{n}	**wa** - - - -	**oa**
eeh - - - -	**ih**	**wae** - - - -	**oai**
ëem - - -	**iam**	**wan** - - -	**oan**
ëen - - - -	**ien**	**wang** - - -	**oang**
ëep - - - -	**iap**	**wu** - - - -	**u**
ëet - - - -	**iet**	**wui**^{ng} - - -	**ui**^{n}
ëo - - - -	**io**	**wun** - - -	**un**
ëo^{ng} - - - -	**iɵ**^{n}	**wuy** - - -	**ui**
ëung - - -	**iong**		

I have not thought it necessary to swell the list by inserting syllables ending in **h**, **k**, **p**, or **t**, which are regularly formed from vowels or diphthongs of which the equivalents are given above. Nor have I noticed the short mark placed by Medhurst above some vowels, as this is sufficiently indicated by these four final letters, **h**, **k**, **p**, **t**.

Medhurst writes the nasal sometimes ^{n}, sometimes ^{ng}, and places it sometimes in the middle of a word, sometimes at the beginning or the end. I always place it at the end, as it qualifies the whole vowel part of the word; and I always write it ^{n}.

In other respects Medhurst's spelling agrees with mine, or, if there be other variations, they must be very few.

But it must be remembered that Medhurst's dictionary is not of the Amoy form of the language, it is of the Changchew dialect, and, indeed, strictly of that variety of the Changchew dialect which is spoken at Chang-poo or Chiu^{n}-phɵ́, so that the difference in the words is partly a difference of spelling and partly of dialect, such as is indicated in this Dictionary by C. or P.

VARIETIES OF SPELLING USED IN SOME OTHER BOOKS.

The books issued by the mission-press of the American Reformed Church differ but slightly in orthography from this Dictionary. Instead of **ɵ** they use **o·**. **ch** is used both for **ch** and **ts**. The finals **ien** and **iet**, are spelled **ian** and **iat**. The nasal ^{n} is not appended to words beginning with **m**, **n**, or **ng**, because all such words are *understood* to be nasal. Hyphens are used to a much less extent than in this Dictionary (which indeed may be said of all other publications), and only in some of their publications is there any attempt to indicate the penultimate accent; in their later issues it is indicated by a small dot on a level with the top of the letters, *e.g.* **jit·sî**, = jit--sì.

The *Manual of the Amoy Dialect*, published by the late Rev. E. Doty of the same mission, differs from mine in the same points, and in the following. The aspirate is indicated by an inverted comma. He writes the finals **eng**, **ek**, as **ieng**, **iek**. He does not use hyphens at all. In his book, and those which follow (as also in Medhurst), there is no attempt to indicate the penultimate accent; and so enclitic words are often written as if in the "chiū^{n}-jip" tone, *e.g.* **sih**, **mah**, &c.

In the *Manual of the Amoy Colloquial*, by the Rev. John Macgowan **o·** is used instead of **ɵ**; **ch** both for **ch** and **ts**; and in order to avoid the necessity of making types with a perpendicular accent, the "ē-jip" tone is written with an acute accent instead of a perpendicular accent, so that it is distinguished from the "chiū^{n}-sia^{n}" tone by the finals, **h, k, p, t.**

The books reprinted or edited by Dr. Maxwell of the Formosa Mission use **o·** instead of **ɵ**; spell the finals **ian, iat**, where I have **ien, iet**, and make but a limited use of hyphens.

Other books that have been published in the Amoy vernacular are quite out of print, and so rare that it is not necessary to allude to the variations of spelling in them.

II.

SOME VARIATIONS OF THE TONES IN THE DIALECTS OF CHANG-CHEW, CHIN-CHEW, AND TUNG-AN.

The description of the tones given in the Introduction applies strictly to the form of the language spoken in Amoy itself and the immediate neighbourhood. In the various dialects closely allied to the pure Amoy dialect there are slight variations of tone, many of them too minute to be described, and only to be caught by the ear. In general no attention need be paid to them unless one live in the region where the particular dialect is spoken. Some of the more noteworthy variations are described below.

1. CHANG-CHEW.

The **chiū^{n}-piâ^{n}** or upper first tone, called in Chang-chew the **téng-pê^{n}**, is not quite level, but has a very slight upward movement; this upward movement is generally so slight as to be scarcely noticed except by a very practised ear, but in some phrases it is quite marked.

The **ē-piâ^{n}** or lower first, called there the **ē-pê^{n}**, is more drawn out than in Amoy. The description of the Amoy tone still applies to it, but there is a sort of drawl in the pronunciation, and the rise of the voice at the end is often not so decided as at Amoy, so that occasionally it might almost be mistaken for the "**ē-khì.**"

The two **khì** tones (the upper and lower third) seem to be not so sharply distinguished as in Amoy, at least I have sometimes found it difficult to say whether a word pronounced alone belonged to the "**chiū^{n}-khì**" or to the "**ē-khì**;" but, strange to say, whenever the word loses the accent by being the first word of a group of two in which the second has the accent, then the distinction becomes quite clear, according to the rules for the tones of unaccented words given in part of the Introduction on "Tones in Combination."

The **ē-jip** or lower fourth tone is the one on which the greatest change takes place. It may be described as almost exactly the "**ē-piâ^{n}**" tone cut short at the end, that is to say, the voice first falls very low and then ends in a sharp abrupt upward jerk, somewhat like the English "*What?*" pronounced not as a mere interrogation, but with a strongly marked tone of great surprise and astonishment. Occasionally this tone is so pronounced that it is not easily distinguished from the "**ē-piâ^{n}**."

2. CHIN-CHEW.

The dialect of Chin-chew is usually spoken with greater rapidity than that of Amoy, several words being often run almost into one; and as it has also a more guttural sound, it is sometimes rather difficult to follow. It will be seen that some of the changes in the tones are connected with this tendency to a hurried pronunciation.

The **chiū^{n}-piâ^{n}** begins much as the Amoy tone, but instead of remaining level has a very slight downward slope; but this downward motion has not the least resemblance to the rapid falling swing of the "**chiū^{n}-sia^{n}**:" it is still pronounced with the calmness and quiet regularity of the Amoy tone. It bears a considerable resemblance to the usual inflection given to the same tone (the first tone or Shang ping) in the Mandarin.

The **ē-piâ^{n}**, while retaining the general shape of the Amoy intonation (first downwards and then upwards), is pronounced on a higher key and with more rapidity or abruptness, and the rising at the end is very marked.

The **chiū^{n}-sia^{n}** or second tone, which in Amoy is not divided (and not even attempted to be divided) into an upper and a lower tone, is said by the literary men of Chin-chew to be divided into the upper second or **chiū^{n}-chiū^{n}**, and the lower second or **ē-chiū^{n}**; but I have not been able to observe any difference, nor have I marked any special divergence from the usual Amoy intonation of the "**chiū^{n}-sia^{n}**," except that in some parts of the Chin-chew region it approaches somewhat to that peculiarity of the Tung-an dialect which is described below.

The two **khì** or **khù** tones (the upper and lower third) are changed in a very striking manner: they are both pronounced with a rapid or abrupt ending, much like that of the "**chiū^{n}-jip**," but on a lower key. The two "**khì**" tones thus altered are rather apt to be confounded with each other; but just as in the Chang-chew dialect, whenever a word belonging to the "**chiū^{n}-khì**" tone stands first in a group of two, while the second word has the principal accent, then at once this tone becomes clearly distinguished from the "**ē-khì**," according to the rules given in the Introduction on "Tones in Combination."

3. TUNG-AN.

The dialect of Tung-an, Tung-ngan, or **Tâng-oa^{n}**, is for the most part intermediate between that of Chin-chew and the dialect of Amoy in the more strict or limited sense. Its tones are usually much the same as those of Amoy, while in those parts of the district of Tung-an which lie towards Chin-chew there is a tendency towards some of the tonal peculiarities of the Chin-chew dialect.

The **chiū^{n}-sia^{n}** or second tone, and the **chiū^{n}-jip** or upper fourth tone, are almost or quite undistinguishable from each other.

The **ē-piâ^{n}** or lower first, and the **ē-khì** or lower third, when they lose the accent by standing first in a group of two words while the second has the principal accent, become quite undistinguishable from each other, each being pronounced low and level; but the "**ē-piâ^{n}**" when alone, and when accented, has much the same intonation as in Amoy.

厦英大辭典

III.

EXTENT OF THE AMOY VERNACULAR, AND ITS SUB-DIVISION INTO DIALECTS.

The vernacular of Amoy has attracted special attention, because Amoy was one of the five ports opened to foreign trade by the treaty of Nankin, and because its language differs very widely from the languages spoken at the other ports opened by that treaty, so widely different indeed as to be mutually unintelligible. Since the date of that treaty several ports in the island of Formosa, where the same dialect is spoken, have also been opened to trade; but the name of *Amoy* was applied to this dialect or vernacular long before these ports were opened, and would have been so doubtless though they had all been opened at once, because of its superior importance as a place of trade and intercourse.

Before the port of Amoy was opened to foreign trade the dialect of Amoy, in its more limited sense, had not attracted attention. The name then given to this form of the Chinese language was the "Hok-kien dialect," the title used in Medhurst's quarto dictionary, and the special form of the language exhibited in that dictionary is the dialect of Chang-poo or Chiuⁿ-phó, a district or county in the department or prefecture of Chang-chew.

Amoy stands in the department or prefecture of Chin-chew, but the dialect spoken at the city of Chin-chew differs from that of the town of Amoy almost as much as that of Chang-chew does. We have thus the three great varieties of the Amoy (A.), the Chang-chew (C.), and the Chin-chew (Cn.), which, with smaller variations, may be said to form one language spoken in five departments of the province of Hok-kièn or Fuh-kien, namely, three Foo departments, Chang-chew (Chiang-chiu-hú), Chin-chew or Tseuen-chow (Tsoân-chiu-hú), and Formosa or Tai-wan (Tâi-oân-hú), and in two Chow departments, Yung-chun (Eńg-chhun-chiu) and Lung-yen (Liông-gâm-chiu or Lêng-nâⁿ); but in some parts of these Chow departments other dialects of Chinese are also spoken.

1. CHANG-CHEW, &c.

The most marked peculiarities of the Chang-chew dialect (in addition to the tonal changes noted in No. II.) are these—

e into **oe** in many words, and *vice versa* **oe** into **e** in about as many, a singular pair of opposed changes for which I have not been able to find any simple rule.

ng into **uiⁿ**, when the final in the reading form is **n**; also in a few words from the reading final **-ong**, when it corresponds to the Mandarin **-wang**.

iong into **iang** in those words which also appear in the colloquial form **iuⁿ**, corresponding to the Mandarin **yang**; but those words which correspond to the colloquial **ng** and to the Mandarin **ang**, do not become **iang**, but remain **iong**.

iok into **iak** in many words, but far from being a general rule.

u into **i**, and **un** into **in**, in many cases; but occasionally **in** changes to **un**.

iⁿ into **ɛⁿ** when the reading final is **eng**; but when the reading final is **ien** or **iam**, the col. remains **iⁿ**.

a into **ɛ** in those words which have also a colloquial form in **e**.

e into **ɛ** in colloquial words from the reading form **a**.

eh into **ɛh**, in most or all words formed from the reading final **ek**, and also in some other words.

eng into **an** in many colloquial words from the reading form **ien**.

iuⁿ into **ioⁿ**.

oe into **oa** in words from the reading form **oa**.

iet into **oat** in many words.

ek into **it** in some words.

muiⁿ into **moɛⁿ** in some words.

The dialect of Chang-poo (P.) or Chiuⁿ-phó is merely a variation of the Chang-chew dialect. The chief points of difference are (1) **oai** or **oɛ** instead of **oa** in those words where the Amoy has **oe**. (2) **iong** in many words for the Amoy **eng**, and in like manner **iok** for **ek**; but conversely **eng** often for **iong**, and **ek** for **iok**. These changes also take place in some other parts of Chang-chew prefecture. (3) **eng** often remains the same as the Amoy form where the Chang-chew has **an**. But the dialect of Chang-poo varies considerably at the two ends of that long District or county.

In *Ping-ho* district (Pêng-hô) the dialect is in the main like the rest of Chang-chew with some of the peculiarities of Chang-poo. But on the western border of the Ping-ho district the Hakka dialect is spoken.

Tiô-thoâ or Chang-tai is said to have some remarkable peculiarities, due partly to its position on the borders of Chin-chew prefecture, and perhaps still more to the fact that in former times it was a part of that prefecture.

Chau-an (Chiàu-an) is said to approach in dialect to the language of Swatow (see No. IV.), but I have not had opportunities of observing.

Hái-têng and *Lâm-chēng* speak very nearly the dialect of Chang-chew city and of *Liông-khe*, the district in which that city stands, but in the parts of Hái-têng near Amoy the influence of the strictly Amoy dialect is very decidedly felt.

The Chow department of *Lung-yen* or *Lêng-nâⁿ* uses to a large extent the dialect of Chang-chew, but in parts of it the Hakka is spoken.

2. CHIN-CHEW, TUNG-AN, &c.

The dialect of Chin-chew city (Cn.) and of the district of Chin-kang in which it stands, is also spoken with but slight variations in the adjoining Hien districts of Nan-an or Lâm-oaⁿ (L.), Hūi-an or Hūi-oaⁿ (H.), and Ankoi or An-khoe (An. or Ank.) Some variations of the dialects of these districts are noted in the Dictionary; and it may be observed that a considerable part of Lâm-oaⁿ, bordering on Tung-an, partakes of many of its peculiarities.

The principal variations of the Chin-chew dialect are as follows:—

u into **ŭ**; this takes place almost invariably when in Chang-chew **i** takes the place of the Amoy **u**; it also occurs in many words, especially in the syllable **su**, where the Chang-chew retains **u**.

un into **ŭn** almost or quite invariably where the Chang-chew changes to **in**, and also in some other words.

eng into **ti**^{n} when it comes from the reading termination **ien** or **iam**; this occurs in all cases where the Chang-chew has **an** for the Amoy **eng**, and in some also where the Chang-chew agrees with the Amoy sound.

eng into **öng** in some words.

e into **ö** almost invariably where the Chang-chew changes to **oe**; so also **eh** into **öh**.

oe into **öe** almost invariably when the Chang-chew changes to **e**; so also **oeh** into **öeh**.

o into **ɵ** generally in those words which have **au** in Mandarin.

ɵ or **au** into **ïo** in many words where the reading **ɵ** corresponds to the colloquial **au**. In **ïo** the accent is on **ï**, not on the **o**.

ch, **ts**, or **j**, sometimes into **dz**, or a sound near it (only in the lower series of tones).

j is often pronounced very thick so as to change to **l**, or very nearly so.

Another remarkable feature of the Chin-chew dialect is the large number of totally different words (not merely differently pronounced) that are used, *e.g.* **söh** for **kóng**, to speak; **thɵ̀** and **khit** for **hɵ̄**, to give, or sign of passive; **bōe-tsōe--tit** instead of **bōe-sái--tit**, &c.

Tung-an (T.) or Tâng-oa^{n}, though on the one hand it is the district in which Amoy stands, and on the other hand it is a district of the department or prefecture of Chin-chew, has yet a very marked variety of dialect for itself. It is said to have originally belonged to the prefecture of Chang-chew, which may perhaps partly explain its peculiarities. In many points it is more or less similar to the Chin-chew, from which the following are the chief variations:—(1) **ai**^{n} instead of the Chin-chew **ti**^{n}, especially when that takes the place of the Amoy **eng**; (2) **oai**^{n} in some cases instead of the Amoy **oa**^{n}; and in several other particulars it is intermediate between the Chin-chew and the pure Amoy.

Kwan-kow or Koàn-kháu (K. or Kk.) is a part of Tung-an district, near the island of Amoy. Among its special peculiarities are the frequent use of **io** instead of **ɵ**, and the extensive use of **u** for **i**. These peculiarities are said to be shared by the dialect of Tiô-thoà, referred to above under Chang-chew. But the use of **u** for **i** in some words is also found in many other parts of Tung-an and even in the villages on Amoy island.

The Chow department of *Yung-chun* or *Eñg-chhun* has in most parts nearly the same form of dialect as Chin-chew. The district of *Tāi-tiên* or Toā-chhân, in that department, is said to have a dialect widely different, but I have not had an opportunity of examining it.

3. COLONIZATION AND EMIGRATION.

Formosa has been colonized within about 200 years mainly by emigrants from Amoy, Chang-chew, and Chin-chew. The several parts of the island are usually found to be specially inhabited by emigrants from the several parts of the mainland, but in Formosa the various forms of the dialects mentioned above are a good deal mixed up.

Singapore and the various Straits Settlements, *Batavia* and other parts of the Dutch possessions, are crowded with emigrants, especially from the Chang-chew prefecture; *Manila* and other parts of the Philippines have great numbers from Chin-chew, and emigrants are largely scattered in like manner in Siam, Burmah, the Malay Peninsula, Cochin China, Saigon, &c. In many of these places there is also a great mixture of emigrants from Swatow. The Chinese in California and Australia are chiefly from other parts of China, but yet in Australia at least there is a considerable proportion of emigrants from the Amoy region.

In such fields of colonization and emigration there is a certain tendency to mix up the minor varieties of the sub-dialects; and at Singapore, Batavia, &c., a good many Malay words are often used in combination with the Chinese phrases.

In Formosa large tribes of the Aborigines have learned the Amoy vernacular or some of its dialects.

IV.

RELATION TO OTHER LANGUAGES.

Of the other languages of China the most nearly related to ours is the vernacular of *Chau-chau-foo* or *Tie-chiu*, in the province of Canton or Kwang-tung, on the borders of the province of Fuh-kien. The only treaty-port in that region of country is *Swatow*, so that the language is often called the "Swatow dialect." The ancestors of those people emigrated many centuries ago from the province of Fuh-kien, and to this day they are distinguished from the other inhabitants of the Canton province by the appellation "Hok-ló," that is the persons from Hok-kièn or Fuh-kien. That dialect of Swatow or Tie-chiu differs from the Amoy much as Dutch differs from German, or as Portuguese from Spanish, so that those who understand one or other of the dialects well can make out the greater part of what is said in the other. A large proportion of the changes which take place in passing from the Amoy to the Swatow are also found more or less in the various local dialects of the Amoy illustrated in this book, such as the Chang-chew, the Chin-chew, &c.

The island of *Hai-nan* (Hái-lâm), also in the Canton province, differs much more than the Swatow, but still is more nearly related to the Amoy and Swatow than to any of the other languages of China. But the centre of that island, just as is the case in Formosa, is inhabited by aboriginal races totally different from the Chinese, and having languages of a quite different stock.

Fuh-chau-foo, the capital of Fuh-kien province, is the chief seat of another "dialect," which is largely spoken in the centre and north of the province; it has many points of resemblance to the Amoy, but is quite unintelligible to the Amoy Chinese with the exception of an occasional word or phrase.

Hing-hwa-foo (Heng-hoà), which lies between Fuh-chau and Chin-chew, has a "dialect" or language of its own, though it contains only two counties or Hien districts; it is said to be unintelligible both at Fuh-chau and at Amoy, but I have not been able to examine it.

To the other languages of China the Amoy vernacular is less closely related. Yet they all evidently spring from one common stock. That common stock is *not* the modern Mandarin dialect, but the ancient form of the Chinese language as spoken about 3000 years ago. The so-called "Mandarin," far from being the original form, is usually more changed than any of the other languages or dialects of China.

The clue to the ancient form of the Chinese language was discovered by the Rev. Joseph Edkins of the London Missionary Society, now stationed at Pekin; he has given copious explanations on the subject in his *Grammar of the Mandarin Dialect*, and in his *China's Place in Philology*.

Among the sources from which the ancient form of Chinese has been thus recovered, a prominent place is held by the Amoy dialect, especially because its final consonants very generally retain the ancient form.

It is in the *ancient* form of the Chinese language that the relation of Chinese to the other languages of the world becomes most distinct, as is shown in *China's Place in Philology* above referred to, so that for this purpose the study of the Amoy vernacular is of considerable importance.

V.

ENCLITICS.

The mark used in this Dictionary for an enclitic word is a double hyphen placed before it. The enclitics may be roughly divided into the following classes, which do not lay claim to any scientific precision or exhaustive minuteness:—

Final particles used at the end of a sentence, or sometimes at the end of a verb, adjective, or substantive, *e.g.* **ah, á, lah, leh, loh, gioh** or **giȯh, kioh, ioh, hêⁿ, hehⁿ, nihⁿ, chiah, cheh, tsài.**

Some are interrogative, *e.g.* **má** or **mah, nihⁿ, lāi, tāi.**

Most of these words enumerated above are never used except as enclitics, so that it is sometimes very difficult to determine the proper spelling, or the reading form to which the colloquial corresponds.

Certain *adverbs* and *adjectives*, and some particles, which are also used as accented words, *e.g.* **ê, nihⁿ, tsāi, hia, keng, koáⁿ** or **koá.** Some of these are usually enclitic, others but rarely.

Negative words placed at the end of a sentence to give an interrogative sense, *e.g.* **bô, m̄, bōe, bē.** These words are much more commonly used in other positions where they are not enclitic.

Substantives which are generally used as ordinary words in other positions, but which are occasionally enclitic, *e.g.* **sî**, time; **sì**, a clan or surname; **sì**, world; **sì**, power or direction; **kan, bīn, jī, iūⁿ, lâng, nîⁿ, jit, gėh, ko, kong, hō, chhù, tè, thâu.**

Some such substantives and adjectives are very extensively used as enclitics in the names of places, especially **thâu, chhù, piⁿ, tau, ē,** and **lāi.**

Pronouns, when not emphatic, *e.g.* **goá, goán, lán, lí, lín, i, in.** In some cases such unemphatic and enclitic pronouns are used indefinitely, as is the case very generally with **lâng** quoted among the substantives.

Verbs in common use as ordinary words, but which are also sometimes enclitic, *e.g.* **kìⁿ, lâi, khì, tsáu, chiūⁿ, liáu, sí, kàu, tn̄g, phoà, poáh, khoàⁿ, tó, chih, chiáh, siā, tsai.** Sometimes in such cases the verb, as used after another verb, may be either enclitic or not according as the one or the other is meant to be emphatic; *e.g.* **thâi--sí**, to kill by *cutting;* **thâi-sí**, to cut so as to *kill.*

Some of the verbs enumerated above come to be almost like auxiliaries when enclitic, but this is specially the case with the enclitics **tiȯh, tit,** and **teh.** Of these the last **teh** has not been definitely identified with any word in the reading form, and it is very doubtful whether it is the same as the verbal prefix **teh** of the same sound. In many of the phrases with **tiȯh**, that word may be pronounced either as an enclitic or not, *e.g.* **chhē--tiȯh**, or **chhē-tiȯh**, with but little if any difference of meaning.

Double enclitics are chiefly found among the verbs, *e.g.* **lȯh-lâi, lȯh-khì, khí-lâi, khí-khì, kè-lâi, kè-khì, tò-khì, lâi-khì, m̄-khì, chhut-lâi.** All these are found following a verb which takes the primary accent, *e.g.* **puih--khí-lâi, phah--m̄-khì, tò--lâi-khì**; where the principal accent is on the first word, the second is quite unaccented, and a slight secondary accent usually falls on the third word; but sometimes the third word also is quite unaccented, while on the other hand it sometimes recovers more or less of its own original tone.

Double enclitics are very rare except in the case of verbs, but examples of other parts of speech are found in **sien-siⁿ** and **chit-ē**; but the latter is often contracted to **cheh.**

It is of great importance to attend carefully to these various enclitics, both in order to speak idiomatically and correctly, and because numerous phrases have a totally different meaning according as the last word is accented or enclitic; *e.g.* **koaⁿ--lâng** and **koaⁿ-lâng; āu--jit** and **āu-jit; pun--chiáh** and **pun-chiáh; thè--khì** and **thè-khì; bô--khì** and **bô-khì; taⁿ--lâi** and **taⁿ-lâi; tsòe--lâng** and **tsòe-lâng,** &c.

VI.

Several other appendices entered into my plan, and the materials have been collected in considerable abundance, but time does not allow of their being arranged and extended at present for publication. But in the Companion, Key, or Sequel to this Dictionary, which I shall endeavour to publish ere long, there may be expected, besides the Chinese characters for the words, such tables as the following:—

A table of phrases in pairs, where the second word of each pair is identical in sound and tone, while the first words agree in sound and differ only in tone; *e.g.* **khí-thâm** and **khì-thâm**; **hûi-khì** and **hùi-khì**; **ké-ì** and **kè-ì**, id. Sometimes there are three, four, or even five phrases thus connected in sound, *e.g.* **kàu-bé**, **káu-bé**, and **kâu-bé**.

Table of remarkable changes in the initials of the words.

Table of remarkable changes in the finals of words.

Phrases where decided difference of sense is caused by change of accent or by a slight pause.

Table of words which are found *at least in three* forms—the literary and *two* or more purely colloquial forms—of such words I have already collected several hundred.

Remarkable changes of tones.

THE END.

GLASGOW: W. G. BLACKIE AND CO., PRINTERS, VILLAFIELD.

国家出版基金项目
NATIONAL PUBLICATION FOUNDATION

海上絲綢之路文獻集成

總主編 陳支平 陳春聲

科技與文化編 88

主編 王揚宗 葉農

海峽出版發行集團
THE STRAITS PUBLISHING & DISTRIBUTING GROUP
福建人民出版社

本册目次

厦荷大辭典［一］

（*Chineesch-Hollandsch woordenboek van het Emoi dialekt*）

〔荷〕佛蘭根（J. J. C. Francken） 赫萊斯（C. F. M. de Grijs）編

《厦荷大辭典》，荷蘭佛蘭根、赫萊斯編。佛蘭根（J. J. C. Francken），荷蘭漢學家。一八五七年赴閩南地區專事厦門白話之研究，一八六三年逝世，遺稿於一八八二年出版。赫萊斯（C. F. M. de Grijs），荷蘭漢學家。一八五七年隨佛蘭根來華，從事文言文之研究，曾整理佛蘭根遺稿。此書係閩南語辭典，收録厦門話白話用語，保留諸多十九世紀閩南語詞彙。全書以厦門話羅馬字母順序編排，先列漢字，其下羅列含該字之詞語、單句，亦注音釋義。凡有異讀者，先注厦門音，再注他音。據一八八二年巴達維亞版影印。

厦荷大辭典

CHINEESCH-HOLLANDSCH

WOORDENBOEK

VAN HET

EMOI DIALEKT

DOOR

J. J. C. FRANCKEN EN C. F. M. DE GRIJS

UITGEGEVEN DOOR HET

BATAVIAASCH GENOOTSCHAP VAN KUNSTEN EN WETENSCHAPPEN.

BATAVIA
LANDSDRUKKERIJ
1882.

VOORBERICHT.

Toen schrijver dezes in 1856 uit Batavia naar China gezonden werd om chineesch te leeren, besloot hij zich met der woon te vestigen te Emoi, daar de meeste Chineezen op Java uit Emoi en omstreken afkomstig zijn. Al dadelijk deed zich de behoefte aan een chineesch woordenboek van de Emoi-taal gevoelen. De Heeren J. J. C. **Francken** en G. **Schlegel**, die een paar jaar later naar China kwamen met hetzelfde doel, besloten evenzoo het te Emoi gesproken chineesch te beoefenen, en stieten op denzelfden hinderpaal, namelijk het gemis van een Emoi-chineesch woordenboek.

Om hierin te voorzien werd door elk der aanstaande tolken, een woordenboek op touw gezet, dat meer en meer in omvang toenam maar slechts langzaam vorderde, daar elke uitdrukking, elk woord, uit den mond van Chineezen moest worden opgeteekend; behalve toch een woordenlijstje van den Amerikaanschen zendeling E. **Doty**, en een Chineesch woordenboekje 十五音 de *Sip ngō im* door **Medhurst** vertaald, was er nog niets over het Emoisch uitgegeven.

De tolken op Java aangesteld, hadden de gelegenheid om hun woordenboek gaandeweg uit te breiden en te herzien; vooral **Francken** gaf zich hiervoor veel moeite, zoodat zijn werk wel het eerst in aanmerking mocht komen voor publicatie.

Francken was te bescheiden en te verstandig, om zich te haasten zijn werk wereldkundig te maken; hij wist te goed hoe onvolledig het nog was, en hoeveel jaren van ondervinding, studie en kritiek er noodig zijn, eer men een volledig woordenboek tot stand brengt. Hij werkte dus voort, terwijl hij als tolk te Soerabaja op velerlei wijze in contact kwam met Chineezen van allerlei slag. Helaas, nog slechts korten tijd werkzaam, werd hij door eene hevige ziekte ten grave gesleept; daar lag zijn werk, dat zulk een schoon geheel zou vormen, nog onvoltooid.

Het Bataviaasch Genootschap besloot op advies van zijn bestuurslid Doctor G. **Schlegel**, om het werk van **Francken** uit te geven onder redactie van eerstgenoemde.

De eerste vellen waren pas afgedrukt, toen Dr. **Schlegel** naar Europa vertrok en ik werd uitgenoodigd door het Bataviaasch Genootschap, bij monde van den President Mr. **den Kinderen**, om mij met de verdere uitgave te belasten. Deze vereerende uitnoodiging aanvaardde ik als een heiligen plicht aan de nagedachtenis van mijn vriend **Francken**: wel was ik overtuigd dat het werk niet op die volkomenheid kon bogen, welke **Francken** er aan gegeven zou hebben, ware hij blijven leven, maar door zijn werk was toch een rijke bron van kennis toegankelijk voor allen, die de Chineesche taal willen leeren spreken.

Van het recht om tusschen het werk van FRANCKEN het mijne in te lasschen, heb ik maar spaarzaam gebruik gemaakt, alleen dan heb er ik uitdrukkingen bijgevoegd als zulks volstrekt noodig was, terwijl ik maar weinig heb behoeven weg te laten of te veranderen.

Sedert dit werk voor de helft is afgedrukt, is er een Chineesch-Engelsch Emoi-woordenboek van C. DOUGLAS verschenen, dat in uitgebreidheid het Chineesch-Hollandsch Emoi-woordenboek overtreft.

Het woordenboek is ter Landsdrukkerij te Batavia gedrukt, de drukproeven werden mij te Samarang toegezonden; een ieder die weet hoeveel moeielijkheden de correctie op zulk een afstand ondervindt, zal het mij niet te zwaar aanrekenen, dat de correctie te wenschen overlaat.

C. F. M. DE GRIJS.

Samarang, December 1881.

INLEIDING.

Tout autre écrivain peut aspirer à l'éloge, la seule chose que le lexicographe puisse espérer, c'est d'échapper à la critique et encore cette récompense toute négative ne lui est elle que rarément accordée.

Un dictateur littéraire revue, d. d. m. 14 *Fevr.* 1880.

BENAMING. Het Chineesch-Hollandsch Woordenboek van het Emoi-dialekt bevat het Chineesch zooals het gesproken wordt in Emoi; de benaming dialekt is minder juist, beter ware het te spreken van de Emoi-taal.

Van deze taal bestaanverschillende dialekten of varianten, zooals:

Tsiang-tsiu	dialekt.	Eng tshun	dialekt.
Tsin-tsiu	„	Tai-wan	„
Tang-oa̱	„	Hui̱ oa̱	„
Emoi	„	Lam oa̰	„
Tsiu pho̱	„	Tsang tsa̩i	„
An khe	„		

GELUID. 音 Het geluid, dat eenig lichaam geeft wanneer het met een ander in aanraking komt, heet *Im* 音 Het klinken van metaal, steen, hout, het ruischen en klotsen van het water, het knetteren van het vuur, enz. zijn geluiden. Op het gebied der spraak noemt de Chinees ook elk eenvoudig (éénlettergreepig) woord, een geluid 音: *Kim soa, ertsberg,* zijn alzoo twee geluiden, die het denkbeeld van *ertsgebergte* uitdrukken. De Chinees verstaat dus onder 音 hetzelfde, wat wij in onze taal, éénlettergreepige wortelwoorden noemen.

SCHRIFT. 音 is de hoorbare uitdrukking van een begrip, dat wij in ons letterschrift, zichtbaar met letters uitdrukken. Het Chineesch heeft tot zichtbare voorstelling een beeldschrift gekozen, dat het begrip, in den beginne zuiver zinnebeeldig, door teekens aanduidde zonder het overeenstemmende woord, de mondelinge uitdrukking van het begrip, zichtbaar uit te drukken; d. i.: het Chineesche schrift was in den beginne zuiver beeldschrift; dit beeldschrift ontwikkelde zich later tot een geluidschrift.

Het schriftteeken heet 字 *Dzī,* de uitspraak of het hoorbare woord 音 *Im.*

UITSPRAAK. Om nu de uitspraak van een woord uit te drukken, is elk geluid in twee deelen gesplitst, te weten: de ingang en de uitgang van het geluid.

Ons woord *Berg* wordt in het Chineesch uitgedrukt door het karakter 山, dat duidelijk beeldschrift is; de uitspraak van dat woord 山 wordt uitgedrukt met behulp van twee algemeen bekende woorden 師 en 姦 *sje* en *kan*, de ingang van het eerste woord is *sj*; de uitgang van het tweede woord is *an*; de ingang nu van het eerste woord vereenigd met den uitgang van het tweede woord, vormen te zamen het woord *sjan*, dat de uitspraak is van het karakter 山 *berg*.

De ingangen der woorden zijn de medeklinkers waarmede de woorden aanvangen, in het Emoisch dertien in getal, te weten:

B Dz G H K L M N Ng P S T Ts

De uitgangen zijn vocalen, hetzij alleen of in verbinding met anderen of wel met consonanten, in de Emoi-taal 58 in getal, te weten:

a ah ai aih ak am an ang ao aoh ap at.

e eh eng engh em emh; deze *e* wisselt af met de geheel toonlooze E.

i ia iah iang iao iaoh iep iet iem ien ih ik im in ing io ioh iok iong ip it iu iuh.

o oa oah oai oan oat oe oeh oh ok ong en *ō;* deze *ō* stelt voor de *o* zooals in *kopje, stot.*

u ui uih un ung ut.

Wij teekenen hierbij aan, dat elke letter afzonderlijk wordt uitgesproken, dus *lien* wordt uitgesproken *li-en.*

Deze ingangen en uitgangen kunnen in vereeniging, slechts een beperkt aantal eenlettergrepige woorden vormen, lang niet voldoende voor de omgangstaal, maar het beperkte aantal éénlettergrepige woorden, wordt aanzienlijk vermeerderd door het gebruik van den *neusklank*, de *aspiratie* en de *tonen.*

NEUSKLANK. Wanneer de vocaal met een neusklank moet worden uitgesproken, wordt dit in het woordenboek door een ~ onder de vocaal aangewezen, zoo wordt de klank *Ka* veranderd in *Ka̰*.

ASPIRATIE. De medeklinkers *k p t ts* worden somtijds met een zeer sterke aspiratie uitgesproken, dit is in het woordenboek aangetoond, door een *h* of door een ‘ achter den medeklinker te voegen; zoo wordt *Ka* veranderd in *K‘a*, en *Ka̰* veranderd in *K‘a̰*.

TONEN. De wijziging der stem waarmede een geluid wordt uitgesproken en voorgedragen heet toon, in het Chineesch 聲 *Sia̰*.

De toon is eene muzikale eigenschap waardoor de spraak het gezang nadert.

Onze westersche talen kunnen toonloos gelezen worden, en blijven toch verstaanbaar; in het Chineesch heeft elk woord een bepaalden toon, waarop het moet voorgedragen worden zal het verstaanbaar zijn; wilden de Chineezen den woordtoon afschaffen of aan willekeur blootgeven, dan zouden vader en zoon elkander niet meer kunnen verstaan en er eene spraakverwarring plaats grijpen als tijdens den Babelschen torenbouw.

In 't Chineesch is de toon een integreerend bestanddeel van elk woord en geeft aan het gesprek het karakter van gezang. Terecht zegt Prémare in zijne Notitia linquae sinicae:

„Meri soni sunt litterarum quasi corpus; accentus autem sunt ipsis loco animae."

Er zijn vier tonen of toonwijzigingen 四聲 *Si sia̰*.

1. De effen gelijke toon 平聲 *Piá̰ sia.* Deze ligt in de toonlijn waarin men spreekt; de stem mag bij dezen toon noch rijzen noch dalen. De woorden met gelijken toon zijn *lang.*

2. De hooge toon 上聲 *Tsiū siā*. Deze is hoog, scherp, beslissend. Het woord wordt eenige tonen hooger ingezet, en de stem zinkt op het einde tot den normaaltoon. In het woord *beklagen* heeft *kla* den hoogen toon.

3. De verdwijnende, heengaande toon 去聲 *k'ì siā*. Het woord wordt met een getemperde stem ingezet op den normaaltoon, en de stem daalt aan het einde wegstervende.

4. De ingaande, afgesneden toon 入聲 *dzìp siā* Deze is gekenmerkt doordat het woord nauwlijks aangegeven, plotseling wordt afgebroken en als in de keel blijft steken. Deze toon is dus *kort*. De woorden in dien toon, eindigen in de taal van Emoi op *p k t* of *h*.

Deze vier tonen, die alle Chineesche talen en dialekten gemeen hebben, worden in de taal van Emoi nog in twee onderdeelen gesplitst, te weten:

De hooge gelijke toon	上平	*tsiū piâ*.	De hooge heengaande toon	上去	*tsiū k'ì*.
„ lage „ „	下平	*ē piâ*.	„ lage „ „	下去	*ē k'ì*.
„ hooge hooge „	上上	*tsiū tsiū*.	„ hooge ingaande „	上入	*tsiū dzìp*.
„ lage „ „	下上	*ē tsiū*.	„ lage „ „	下入	*ē dzìp*.

De twee gelijke tonen onderscheiden zich doordat de lagere gelijke toon wordt aangevangen met een octaaf onder den normaaltoon en dan stijgt tot dien toon.

De twee hooge tonen zijn in naam verschillend, maar inderdaad 't zelfde.

De twee heengaande tonen zijn van elkander onderscheiden, doordat de lage heengaande toon aanvangt beneden den normaaltoon en lang en effen blijft.

De twee ingaande tonen zijn van de andere tonen onderscheiden doordat de woorden op een medeklinker eindigen; zij zijn van elkander onderscheiden, doordat de lage ingaande toon iets lager wordt ingezet dan de hooge ingaande toon.

C. DOUGLAS geeft in zijn *Chinese English Dictionary of the vernacular or spoken language of Amoy*, het volgende resumé der 8 tonen:

Afgebroken en kort. Alle woorden eindigende op *h k p t*.		*tsiū dzìp* langzaam rijzende en dan snel dalende	*toh*.
		ē dzìp afgebroken rijzende	*tòh*.
Niet afgebroken. Geen woord eindigt op *h k p t*.	Gelijke of even muzikale noten.	*Tsiū piâ* hoog en gelijk	*to*.
		ē k'ì laag en gelijk	*tō*.
	Enkele buiging.	*Tsiū k'ì* laag, langzaam naar beneden gaande	*tò*.
	Dubbele buiging.	*ē piâ* langzaam omgebogen eerst dalende en dan rijzende als in verbazing of ondervraging	*tô*.
		tsiū siā een weinig naar boven en dan snel naar beneden als de toon van een streng bevel	*tó*.

De tonen zijn in ons woordenboek aangegeven als volgt:

Hooge gelijke toon zonder teeken		*To*.	Hooge heengaande toon	\	*Tò*.
Lage „ „	∧	*Tô*.	Lage „ „	—	*Tō*.
Hooge „	/	*Tó*.	Hooge ingaande „ zonder teeken.		
			Lage „ „	|	*Tòh*.

De tonen zooals zij hierboven beschreven zijn, gelden voor elk woord afzonderlijk, worden de woorden in combinatie gebruikt dan ondergaan de tonen wijzigingen, die soms in ware toonveranderingen overgaan, zoo heeft bv. het woord *láng* mensch, den lagen gelijken toon, maar dikwijls verandert die in den lagen ingaanden toon en wordt dus als zoodanig uitgesproken, bv. in de uitdrukking *I ǐng soa ũa láng*, dat uitgesproken wordt als of er stond *I ing soa ũa làngh*; hetzelfde heeft dikwijls plaats met het woord *laî* komen.

Behalve deze toonverandering heeft men nog te letten op den *klemtoon*, waarvoor geene steekhoudende regels te geven zijn; dit valt vooral op in sommige woorden, die als vaste samenstellingen telkens voorkomen en als ware *veellettergrepige* woorden te beschouwen zijn, bv. de uitdrukking *ts'a put to* ongeveer, *óng laî* omgang, enz.; zelfs zijn er enkele gevallen waarin de klemtoon de beteekenis van eenige uitdrukking wijzigt, bv. *hong ts'e* met den klemtoon op *hong* beteekent *de wind blaast*, maar met den klemtoon op *ts'e* beteekent het *een vlieger*; al deze wijzigingen en bijzonderheden met teekens aan te geven is steeds onvoldoende gebleken en zijn daarom weggelaten; hij die goed Chineesch wil leeren spreken, kan dit onmogelijk uit boeken leeren, maar alleen uit den mond van een Chineeschen leermeester.

C. D. G.

CHINEESCH-HOLLANDSCH
WOORDENBOEK

VAN HET

EMOI-DIALECT.

ALPHABETISCH GERANGSCHIKT.

A

鵶 Kraai met witten nek.
A *o̲ a*, 烏 |, kraai, (*Corvus pectoralis.*)

a ts'ing, | 青. kraaijenblaauw. (zwart met blaauwen glans.)

a p'ièn, | 片, opium, (geprep.)

a p'ièn ko, | 片 膏. geprepareerde opiumkoek.

a p'ièn t'o̲, | 片 塗. opium, (ongeprepareerd.

a p'ièn kan / *a p'ièn king* } | 片 間. opiumkit.

a p'ièn kui, | | 鬼. opiumschuiver.

a p'ièn gièn, | 片 癮, verslaafd aan, ondermijnd door, opium.

a p'ièn lī, | 片 痢, diarrhœa door opium rooken veroorzaakt.

a p'ièn sien, | 片 仙, *lett.* opiumgeest. *d. i.* zoodanig door opium ondermijnd, dat men er weldra van sterven zal.

•亞 *a pan*, | 班, Topsgast.
A

丫 *a t'aò*, | 頭, meid, slavin.
A

阿 Voorvoegsel voor iemands naam; *b. v.* *A-hai*, *A-gū̲*, enz.
A

a ko, 阿 哥, oorspr. slechts tegen den tweeden en verdere keizerlijke prinsen gezegd; thans eerenaam voor kinderen van mandarijnen.

ts'īng kah nā̲ ko sià ni̲h, of *ts'īng ko tsùn a ko sià ni̲h*, prachtig, kostbaar, gekleed gaan.

a ki, 阿 鬾, scheldnaam voor Europeanen.

a guī, | 魏, Asa-fœtida.

a ka, | 膠, Soort harsgom.

a hia̲, | 兄, tegen een' broeder gezegd.

A

腌 A *a tsa*, | 渣, *a a. tsa tsa*, slikkerig, morsig; onheusche behandeling.

壓 A *a put tó*, tuimelaar.

啞 A *a iên*, | 鉛, zink.
i-i a-a, ook *o-o*, galmen, schreeuwen, zingen, als bij het roeijen.
a pan, zonder reden beknorren.

仔 À Sluitwoord, verkleinwoord; vormer van adverbia.
gû á, 牛 |, kalf.
k'in k'in á, 輕輕 |, ligtelijk, even.
bān bān á, 縵縵 |, langzaam. (bijw.)
t'àn á pá, 趁 | 飽, de kost verdienen.
á ū, of *iá ū*, | 有, of 也有, er zijn er nog; is er nog?
á hó of *iaó hó*, | 好, 也好, ook goed, nog goed, het kan er door.

噯 À *à pà*, | 豹, wild, van paarden: ondeugend, van kinderen.
bī sū à à, 味數 | |, onbepaalde, onzuivere smaak.
sia à à, 聲 | |, onbepaald geluid.

À Aan de borst of onder de armen. *Kui-á*, *kui kui á á*. bij zich steken en onder de armen nemen, zoo als eene bedelares kleêren, enz., voor haar kind.
nāng (*nō*) *p'ì siang á*, twee schijven bij- of op-elkander nemen, (als van brood).

俯 À Vooroverbuigen. À *io*, eene buiging maken; *à lòh k'ì k'oà*, zich vooroverbuigen om te kijken; *à hī k'ang pi kóng*, 俯耳空邊講, aan het oor zeggen.
à t'suì, | 嘴, den mond naar iets toebuigen, als beesten naar hun voedsel.

À *à tsiáh*, alles alleen opeten; alles voor zich zelven houden; onmeêdeelzaam zijn, (van kinderen.)

AH

à ìk, tot zich halen, beschermen (als kuikens of kinderen.)
à i tsit hūn, iemand in zijn deel te gemoet komen.
à tsáh, beschermen, bedekken, (als eene moeder haar kind tegen den vader die het slaan wil.)
à tit i tiaô, goed beschermen, (als eene hen hare kuikens tegen roofvogels, of een sterkere een' zwakkeren.)

Ā *ā* . . . *ā* . . . òf . . . òf.
ā sī. òf . . . òf.

餡 Ā Spijs in gebak.
taū ā, 豆 |, boonenspijs, (in koekjes.)
p'oà kaù ná taū ā nih, stuk als boonenspijs, (zoo als vergane kleêren.)
sa ē kā, bē kì ā / *„ ē „ boē „ „* } drie happen gedaan, en nog niet aan de vulling zijn, *d. i.* nog geen derde gedeelte van het werk gedaan hebben.

Ah

鴨 Ah Eend; *tsui ah*, 水 |, wilde eend.
ah bú toe / *„ bó tê* } | 母蹄, eenden pooten: *d. i.* scheeve voeten.
ah hing, tred in een eendenei: *ah hing-á*, jonge eenden.
ah tsai, jonge eenden.
ah lik, | 緑, eendengroen met bronzen glans.
ah hing sia, geluid als van pas uitgekomen eendjes, *d. i.* schor, heesch.
tsiáh ah, 食 |, eenden eten; in verzekerde bewaring gezet worden.
ah sai sik, | 屎色, eene kleur als eendemest, *d. i.* leelijk, dof.

押 Ah Onderteekenen, invullen, begeleiden. als overziener meêgaan, escorteren: noodzaken, dwingen, iets doen plaats hebben; doen passen op (als een rijm.
ts'iem ah, 簽 |, invullen (als den datum, enz, op proclamatien)

ah dzit tsi, 丨 日 指, den datum invullen.
ah hoe ah / *ah hoa ah* } 丨 花 丨, onderteekenen.
ah sàng, 丨 送, begeleiden, escortéren.
ah hè / *ah hoè* } 丨 貨, goederen begeleiden.
ah tsûn, 丨 船, met een schip meêgaan, (b. v. als supercarga.)
ah hoān, 丨 犯, misdadigers escortèren.
ah laī, 丨 內, in reserve meênemen, hebben, (als ankers, enz., op een schip.)
ah tsiṳ̄ / *ah tsiṳ̄* } 押 槳, de geleidende riem, *d. i.* de achterste, die tevens als roeder dient.
ah koán, 丨 舘, in verzekerde bewaring zetten.
ah lah, *ah láh*, 丨 掠, dwingen, tot iets noodzaken.
ah souh, 丨 息, doen ophouden, te gengaan
ah hòng, 丨 放, op vrije voeten doen stellen.
ah ts'ien, 丨 遷, met geweld doen verhuizen (door de overheden in overbevolkte plaatsen gedaan.)
ah t'aô ts'iṳ̂, *īm tsiṳ̂ dziā* / » » *t'siṳ̂* » » *dziâ* } 丨 頭 槍 不 成 惹, stoot men iemand aan het hoofd, dan kan hij zijne buiging niet maken.
ah un, 丨 韻, doen rijmen, rijmen.
ah tiā · loh k'i ts'iṳ̂ / » » » *ts'iṳ̂* } 丨 調 落 去 唱, op éène wijs zingen.
ah tang, 丨 冬, overwinteren, (van schepen.)
ah kṳng, 丨 扛, scheeps-timmerman.

盒 Áh　Doos, doosje, trommel. In *Tsiang-tsiu* ook *áp* uitgesproken.

hè sit áh / *hoè* » » } 伙 食 丨, eetenstro mel.
tiém sim áh, 點 心 丨, dito.
kiṳ̀ áh, 鏡 丨, toiletdoos, (met spiegel).
soe tsṳng áh / *se* » » } 梳 粧 丨, dito (van (vrouwen.)
tsáp ts'ùi áh, 雜 碎 丨, doos voor allerlei kleine benoodigdheden.
paì t'iep áh, 拜 帖 丨, doosje voor visitekaartjes.
áh gî, 丨 儀, huwelijksgeld in eene doos overgebragt.
tèng tu (*ti*) *ē áh*, langwerpig, ovaal doosje.

押 (!) Áh　Gelijkmaken, in eene regte lijn brengen.

áh ts'ioh, 丨 尺, lange maatstok om groote oppervlakten te meten, of om voorwerpen in eene regte lijn te brengen.
áh to, 丨 刀, groote troffel.
īng (*iōng*) *tik ko áh lòh k'ì*, 用 竹 篙 押 落 去, met een' bamboestok neêrhouden (als rijp graan tegen den wind.)

Ai

哀　Oh!
Ai　*ai siong* (*siang*), 丨 傷, treuren.
Ai　*ai k'ok*, 丨 哭, bedroefd weenen.
ai paī, 丨 敗, in het ongeluk zijn
ai ts'ám, 丨 慘, bedroefd.
pi ai, 悲 丨, medelijden hebben, inwendig bedroefd zijn.
kú ai / *kí* » } 舉 丨, beginnen te beweenen, weenen over een lijk.
ai oàn, 丨 怨, bedroefd en tevens kwaad zijn op.
ai paī, slechten moed op het slagen

van iets geven; ongelukkig voorteeken zijn.

ai ai kiò, | | 叫, kermen.

ai kiû, | 求, meėwarig smeeken.

bī ai ai, onbepaald, sterk, scherp van lucht of geur.

ki tioh kuī á t'aô tsiū ai, 見着櫃仔頭就 |, de punt van een' koffer ziende, gaan weenen (zoo als de hoofdrouwer bij het aankomen van de lijkkist) *d. i* zonder eerst te onderscheiden of waar goed of slecht is, terstond over den prijs gaan spreken.

kuī lòh k'ì ai, 跪落去 |, nederknielen en weenen, (bij begrafenis plegtigheden.)

sia im ai oàn, 聲音 | 怨, meėwarige geluid-klanken, (als van een gezang over eene verguisde bijzit, enz.

ko ai tsú. 孤 | 子, weeskind.

ai ėh (*o*), | 嗝, boos, toornig zijn.

愛 Aì Houden van, gaarne .....; beminnen, verlangen, wenschen, willen; de gewoonte hebben om..., neiging gevoelen om ......

aì t'it t'ô, veel van uitgaan houden.

aì beh / *ai boeh* } | 要, wenschen, verlangen om ....

aì boē kì tit / » *bē* » » } | 忘記得, geneigd zijn om te vergeten; veelal, steeds, vergeten; vergeetachtig

aì t'ò, | 吐, neiging gevoelen om te braken, misselijk.

aì k'ùn, | 睡, veel van slapen houden, slaperig.

un aì koah boē lī / *in* » » *bē* » } 恩 | 割不離, zoo beminnen dat men niet van elkander te scheiden (*lett.* snijden) is.

lîng aì, 令 |, eerenaam voor dochter; uwe dochter.

aì kè làng / *aì koè làng* } | 過儂, zich wel eens, of gewoonlijk, aan anderen mededeelen (van eene besmettelijke ziekte.)

隘 Aì Pas, engte.

aì mîng / » *mui* } | 門, straatpoorten.

aì k'aó, | 口, voorname posten, grenspas.

koan aì, 關 |, grenspost, pas.

aì á / *o á* } 胡茄, kleine soort hoboë.

hī á si un aì, 耳仔生瘟 |, een gezwel of zweeren in het oor hebben.

in aì siang ping se, 瘟 | 相册生, moogt ge aan beide kanten oorgezwellen krijgen.

t'it t'ô dzī sa ke, *in aì siang ping se*, sjouwt ge tot de 2e of 3e wacht, zoo moogt ge aan beide kanten oorgezwellen krijgen.

aì iâ, uitroep van verwondering, He!

Ak

沃 Ak Bevochtigen, nat maken, begieten.

ak hoe / » *hoa* } | 花, bloemen begieten.

ak tâm, | 濕, bevochtigen.

ak hé / » *hoé* } | 火, een' brand begieten, blusschen.

ak hō, | 雨, door regen nat geworden.

ak aû, | 喉, de keel bevochtigen, nat maken.

ak pui, | 肥, door mest bevochtigen, bemesten.

偓 Ak *ak tsak*, | 促, gedrongen, benauwd; onfrisch (als op een' heeten dag.)

扼 Ak *mîng ak* / *mui ak* } 門 |, overdekte deur; deurportaal.

toā ming ak ê lâng / » *mui̤* » » » } 大門丨的人, een aanzienlijk man.

Am

庵 Klooster, tempel.

Am *li (ni̤) ko̤ am,* 尼姑丨, nonnenklooster.

am biō, 丨廟, kloosters en tempels, tempels in het algemeen.

hê siṳ̈ am / *hô siō am* } 和尙丨, mannen klooster.

闇 *am k'âm,* 丨憨, dom, idiotisch.

Am *am am k'âm k'âm,* dito

am k'âm gōng, 丨憨戇, dito.

am k'âm gōng, k'ah k'iep tsiáh p.ah t'it, idiotisch te zijn is erger dan (aan) drank, spel of hoererij (verslaafd te zijn.)

腌 *am tsam, am-am tsam-tsam,* vuil.

Am

栖 *koe am,* 雞丨, kippenmand (zonder bodem.

Am *am po̤ tsí, (am kong tsùn,)* sprinkhaan.

Âm *âm t'ng,* 飯湯, rijstwater.

âm tsiṳ / *âm tsio̤* } 丨漿, stijfsel, (van rijstwater gemaakt.)

âm seng, of *âm sui̤,* stijfsel!

bák bai ming bô tsiṳ âm / » » *mô* » *tsio̤* » } de wenkbraauw-haren niet gestijfd hebben, (zoodat ze voor de oogen hangen) *d. i.* niet zien tegen wien men spreekt.

湆 *âm âm,* 丨丨, zacht, slap.

Âm *âm mui̤ ê taī tsi* / » *moē̤* » *sü* } 闇昧的事, duistere zaken, bedekte termen, als voor overspel.

暗 Duister, donker, onduidelijk; bedekt,

Àm geheim, heimelijk; onverlicht, dom;

àm àm, 丨丨, duister, donker.

àm bok bok, 丨漠漠, pikdonker.

géh àm mi̤ / *goéh àm me̤* } 月丨夜, donkere nacht.

o̤ àm mi̤ / » » *me̤* } 黑丨夜, dito.

o̤ hûn sit àm, 黑雲深夜, donkere, buijige nacht.

bō̤ àm, 冒丨, laat in den avond.

àm k'ùn, 丨睡, laat gaan slapen.

àm àm hong, 丨丨摹, in donker rondtasten.

hông hun àm, 黃昏時, tusschen licht en donker, avondschemering.

àm kong tsiaú, 丨鵂鶹, kleine uil.

àm àm tsut tsut, onduidelijk, onbegrijpelijk: duister (van eene zaak.)

àm tsī̤, àm tsoè tsī̤ / » *tsē̤,* » *tò tsē̤* } heimelijk: in het geheim; stilletjes.

àm sàm ê só̤ tsai, eene geheime, bedekte, plaats.

àm sàm ê tai tsi, heimelijke, slechte dingen.

àm sàm pī (pē̤), venerische ziekten.

àm pī, inwendige ziekte.

kiâ àm lō̤, 行丨路, heimelijke, slechte, dingen doen.

sai àm pō̤, 行陰行, iemand heimelijk benadeelen, (als door vergiftiging.)

kng (kui̤) tsiáh tsit poà, àm tsiáh tsit poà, 明食一半丨食一半, één deel nemen wat hem toekomt en een ander deel wederregtelijk nemen.

àm tsī̤ hē ih, iemand iets bedekt beloven, in de hand stoppen (om iets van hem gedaan te krijgen.)

àm hóng, 丨訪, in het geheim gaan onderzoeken (van mandarijnen).

kng iâ àm su / *kui̤* » » » } den schijn aannemen iets om der wille van de zaak te doen, maar heimelijk op zijn eigen voordeel bedacht zijn.

àm hō, | 號, geheim teeken, wachtwoord.

àm bé, | 碼, geheime koopmanstaal.

àm k'àm, 掩蓋, bedekt houden, vóórliegen.

kap làng àm hàp, 與人 | 合, geheime sympathie; met iemand overeenstemmen.

àm iok, | 約, heimelijk overeenkomen.

àm kùi, | 機, geheime sluiting; veer.

àm sung, geheime pin-knip, (aan eene sluiting.)

àm tsioh, | 石, bedekte, blinde, klip.

sim kog o àm é lâng, 心肝黑 | 的人, een duister, onverlicht mensch.

t'ó hin bák àm, of *o àm hin*, 頭眩眼音。黑 | 眩, duizelig, door afmatting of honger.

àm tèh, de duistere plaats, de onderwereld.

haò àm tèh, 祀陰間, aan de geesten der onderwereld offeren (in de 7de maand.)

àm tèh teh kiò lih, de onderwereld roept, of roepe u: *d. i.* op het punt zijn te sterven: als scheldwoord: moogt ge spoedig sterven!

àm t ī t'ai, | 私殺, een sluipmoord begaan.

àm tsī t'o, | 竊聽, heimelijk beluisteren

àm tsī k'oò, | 竊省, afloeren.

àm bong sa, | 摸, betasten.

àm dzip kim hè, 暗入禁貨 smokkelen.

àm lō, | 路, slechte handelingen.

溝 Am — *àm k'ang*, | 孔, waterloop, goot.

àm k'ang ku, iemand die nooit de wereld om geweest is. (*lett*, eene goot-tor.)

kao àm, 陰溝, watergoot.

tsui àm, 水溝, dito.

sò àm, kolk, overdekte goot voor vuilnis.

Am — *am kún*, 頷頸, nek.

àm sé, 頷垂, breede kraag; kossem van koeijen.

àm sé kun, 頷垂巾, een slabbetje dat kinderen aankrijgen.

o a péh ām, kiáh to lai tsām, de kraai heeft een' witten nek, neem een mes en snijd hem af.

tiaò ām, zich ophangen.

am sing, 茂盛, digtbegroeid.

ts'iu nà am, digtbegroeid, van een bosch.

An

安 An — Rust, rustig, tot rust brengen, rust genieten, stil, vrede, vreedzaam; berusten in, tevreden zijn met; plaatsen, zich nederzetten; bevestigen aan; aanbrengen (als verguldsel).

ping an, 平 |, rustig, vreedzaam.

an dzién, | 然, rustig.

an sim, | 心, rustig van harte.

an ún, | 穩, veilig.

an bin, | 民, het volk tot rust brengen, geruststellen.

an uì (ui), | 慰, troosten, condoleren.

an ki (ke) | 更, de rust-wacht *d. i.* de eerste (van 7—9 's avonds).

an sim lòk giép, | 心樂業, zich rustig, gestadig, aan zijn vak houden.

an t'éh, | 宅, rust en vrede aan een huis geven; inwijden.

厦荷大辭典

an t'êh sin, | 宅 神 . aan de huisgoden offeren.
tsiè (tsù) ping an tsiò, offeranden voor rust en vrede doen.
k'ah oē (ē) an tit, 更 能 | 得, meer rust kunnen hebben, genieten, (na ziekte of oproer).
an iù, | 養, voeden, in het leven houden (als visch enz.)
an hūn, | 分, in zijn' stand berusten; zich aan zijn' pligt houden.
an uī, | 位, plaats nemen, plaats doen nemen, (als gasten.)
nēng ping an toā ts'ing, 兩 册 | 大 砲, aan beide kanten een kanon plaatsen.
an pai, | 排, in orde brengen — op zijne plaats zetten.
an tùn, | 頓, in orde, in gereedheid brengen; regeling, schikking maken voor; nederzetten, plaatsen.
an sin, | 身, zich neerzetten, met der woon vestigen.
ts'ing an, 請 |, *lett.* naar iemands rust of gezondheid vragen, *d. i.* de complimenten doen.
ts'ing an tsīng, 請 | 靜, goede nachtrust wenschen.
būn an, 問 |, naar een's zieken gezondheid vragen.
an t'ô, | 土, in de aarde ter ruste leggen, begraven.
an tsòng, | 葬, dito.
an iâ, | 營, kamperen, zich legeren; een kamp opslaan.
an tsē (tsē), | 寨, dito.
an kim, | 金, vergulden, verguld.
an hû, | 符, amuletten aan iets bevestigen of plakken.
an lâm, | 南, Annam, Cochinchina.
an k'oe tê }
an k'e tê } | 溪 茶, Ankoi thee.
an tsoá, (*Tsiang tsiu*), hoe!
an tsè iū, hoe!
an sik hiu, | 息 香, Benzuin.

阿 Án
án (ing) tsik, 阿 叔, oom.
án (ing) koa, | 官, vader! } door
án (ing) nê, | 母, moeder! } kinderen geroepen.
án (ing) tsé, 阿 姐, betiteling van een anderman's slavin.
án gū (ê-gū), streelen; tegen de wang tikken (zooals een kind).
án tsiù si (án tsiù se), *án hiù si*, aldus, alzoo.
án ni si, *án ne se*, ook *án tsit se*, aldus, zoo.

按 Àn
Doen stilhouden (als troepen), daarlaten, volgens; langs; onderzoeken; als pand geven.
àn ping put tōng, | 兵 不 動, zijne troepen doen halt houden, *d. i.* zich niet met iets willen inlaten.
àn hē teh, | 下, zoo lang daarlaten, onaangeroerd laten (in een gesprek.)
àn hoat, *àn lút*, | 法, | 律, volgens de wet.
àn dzit sing, | 日 算, volgens (bij) den dag berekenen.
àn giáh hing ìh, | 額 還 之, elk volgens zijn deel teruggeven.
àn tò loh, 向 何, waarlangs? in welke rigting?
àn hit ê lō, | 此 路, langs dien weg.
àn lō lai, | 路 來, over land komen.
àn ts'at si, | 察 司, provinciale regter.
àn k'oà, onderzoeken, beproeven, ruw berekenen.
àn mih, goed als onderpand geven.

AN

àn tsiah iṳ̄ } *àn tsoá iō̤* } 丨如何, hoe!

案 Àn Regtzaken; geregtelijk verhooren.

àn kiā̤, 丨件, regtzaken.

àn tsing, 丨情, omstandigheden; gesteldheid eener regtzaak.

àn iû, 丨由, omstandigheden eener regtzaak.

bīng àn, 命丨, criminele zaak.

tò àn, 倒丨, eene regtzaak verliezen.

hò àn, 好丨, eene goede regtzaak (waarbij voor advokaten veel te verdienen is); goede kans, goed geluk.

àn tók kong, 丨督公, god der regtzaken, *Themis*.

sim àn, 審丨, *mêng* (*muī*) *àn*, 問丨, regterlijk ondervragen, verhooren.

kiet àn, 結丨, uitspraak, gedaan over eene regtszaak; vonnis.

hoan àn, 翻丨, eene regtszaak op nieuw verhooren, onderzoeken.

àn toh, 丨棹, lange werk, of schrijftafel.

緊 Àn Stijf, strak, stijf aangehaald; dringend;

ts'ui àn, 推丨, stijftrekken.

àn àn tong tong, 丨丨密久, stijfaangehaald.

pák àn, 結丨, stijfbinden.

koai (*koa*) *àn*, 閉丨, stijf digtdoen.

ts iú t'aô àn, of *tsi t' ô àn*, 手頭窮, in moeijelijke geldelijke omstandigheden zijn.

ts'ui àn lai, sterk aandringen (op betalingen, enz.)

sia seh àn, sterk aandringend: met aandrang, nadruk, spreken.

限 Àn Den tijd bepalen om . . . . .

ān siaò, 丨賬, tijd voor eene betaling vaststellen.

ANG

tiép ān bò pin, 叠丨無凴, steeds een tijd vaststellen, maar het nooit nakomen.

Ang

Ang *ang i*, 女巫, waarzegster.

ang i ts'ùi, 女巫口, waarzegstermond, *d. i.* ongeloofwaardig in hetgeen men zegt.

ang á t'aô, 瞳子頭, pupil van het oog. Hoofd eener pop.

翁 Ang Man, echtgenoot.

ang saì, 翁婿, man, (echtgenoot.)

ang bó̤, 翁妻 } *ang pô*, 翁婆 } man en vrouw.

ang tsiá á, (*Ts.-ts.*) 翁姐仔, man en vrouw.

ang, 翁, familienaam.

ang kong, 翁公, afgodsbeelden.

kè ang tsiáh ang, 嫁夫食夫, zoodra (eene vrouw) getrouwd is, komt zij ten koste van haren man.

hò ang hò t'il t'ò, 艮夫艮足娛, bij een goeden man is men gelukkig.

p'ai ang put dzû bô, 惡夫不如無, beter is het geen man, dan een slechten man te hebben.

ang kiá̤, 翁子, man en kinderen.

尫 Ang *ang á*, 丨仔, poppetjes, beeldjes; prenten; (*Tsiang-tsiu* afgoden.

汪 Ang Familienaam.

枉 Áng *áng táng*, 枉晃, onbezonnen, niet naar de omstandigheden weten te handelen.

甕 Àng Pot met kleinen mond en dikken buik.

tsui àng, 水丨, waterkan, martevaan.

kang á ang tāng, 缸仔｜礶, wijd-, en naauw-mondige potten.

kòng p'oà ts'ọ̀ àng, 摃破醋｜, de azijnpot stuk slaan, *d. i.* zijne jaloezij over eene vrouw ten eenen male doen uitkomen.

àng t'aô, ｜頭 kop van de pot, *d. i.* gunsteling, favoriet, (door vrouwen van mannen gebruikt).

àng kóng, ｜廣, gevuld, opgestopt; veel geld verdienend.

sị àng, 生｜, een buikgezwel hebben.

齆 Àng *àng p'ī*, ｜鼻, eene belemmering, verstopping in den neus.

kóng oē (*oā*) *àng-àng*, 講話｜｜, door den neus praten.

siâ̤ àng, 城｜, geschutspoorten eener vesting; ruimte tusschen de poorten eener stad; zijdeurtje in eene vestingmuur.

àng siâ̤, ｜城, ruimte tusschen de twee stads-, of vesting-poorten.

siâ̤ mîng (*muî̤*) *àng*, 城門｜, dito.

siâ̤ àng laī ê tièm, 城｜內的店, de winkels binnen de buitenste stadsmuur.

紅 Âng Rood; rood van schaamte; rood als een bewijs; rood als het toppunt van hitte en voorspoed.

âng sik, ｜色, roodkleurig, rood.

âng tâng, ｜銅, rood koper.

âng hiā, ｜蟻, roode mier.

âng ó, ｜襖, rood bruidskleed.

âng sa, ｜鯊. roode visch?

âng kak ts'ì, ｜角翅, vliegende visch.

âng k'ī, ｜柿, persimmon, (soort roode mispel).

âng pai, ｜牌, uitklaringsbiljet, pas.

âng mîng lâng / » *mô* « }｜毛人, een Engelschman.

bīn lóng boē âng, / » » *bē* » }面總未｜, volstrekt niet kleuren, schaamteloos.

âng pao, ｜包, rood pakje, het visitegeld aan doktoren en priesters gegeven.

sàng hoe âng / » *hoa* » }花送｜, bloemen en in rood papier gewikkelde geschenken geven, *d. i.* handgeld, godspenning, of belooning geven.

âng lîn p'oáh kah / » » » *kan* }｜鏻單肩, roode sjerpen over iemands vest doen, *d. i.* beloonen.

koà âng, 掛｜, roode stoffen over (den draagstoel) hangen *d. i.* door geschenken beloonen.

sio kaò âng âng âng, 燒至｜｜｜, rood gloeijend verhit.

âng p'ā p'ā, of *âng hê hê* / » » » » *hê̤ hê̤* }｜熠熠, vuurrood.

âng t'ị ts'iah dzit t'aô, ｜天赤日頭, roode lucht en vuurroode zon, *d. i.* brandend heet.

âng ko ts'iah ts'ih, rood als krabben, *d. i.* verbrand door de zon.

âng iēm, ｜豔, schitterend rood, wellustig rood (als in de kamers van rijke maintenés, enz).

hiēn si dzī hō âng âng âng, 現時字號｜｜｜, thans is zijne firma allerroodst, *d. i.* in vollen bloei.

bīn sik tsit tsūn péh tsit tsūn âng, 面色一時白一時｜, bij vlagen bleek en rood in het gezigt uitzien (van vrees of pijn).

âng t'aô ts'át, ｜頭賊, rood-hoofdige rebellen, de *T'aì-ping*-rebellen, die in den beginne roode hoofddoeken droegen.

2

àng ts'iū îm / *» ts'io̤ »* } 丨 樹 梅, roode boschframbozen.

àng kûn, 丨 裙, vrouwen-rok.

àng sai iṳ̂, 丨 西 洋, roode shirtings.

洪 Àng Familienaam.

A o

甌 Ao Kom, kop, kopje.

tê ao, 茶 丨, theekopje.

po lê ao, 玻 璃 丨, glazen kop, bierglas.

tsiú ao, 酒 丨, wijnkopje.

k'àm ao, 蓋 丨, kopje met dekseltje er op.

漚 Ao Door water laten doortrekken, in het water laten staan; op een' hoop bij elkander gooijen.

sa̤ á ao tsui kè mi̤ / *» » » » koè mê̤* } 衫 仔 丨 水 過 夜, kleêren eene nacht in het water laten staan.

ao laî kaoh k'ì, door elkander gooijen en laten verstikken, verrotten.

sa̤ á lām sám ao, 衫 仔 雜 踏 丨, kleeren slordig bij elkander frommelen.

ao tsao, 丨 糟, vuil, gefrommeld.

ao ao tsao tsao, 丨 丨 糟 糟, verdrietig, neerslagtig.

tsoè nn̄g tù ao lóh k'ìh / *» » » aó » »* } 做 兩 注 丨 落 去, twee inzetten bij elkander doen; bij den gewonnen inzet, nog eenen nieuwen voegen.

歐 Ao Familienaam.

ao iông / *» iâng* } 丨 陽, familienaam.

拗 Aó Vouwen, om vouwen, kreukelen; buigen, ombuigen; koppig, halsstarrig; in strijd met alle regt of waarheid.

aó laó, 丨 丨, kreukelen.

tuì aó, 對 丨, gelijkelijk omvouwen, *d. i.* winst zamen deelen.

aó pô̤, 綻 旁, zoomen, een' zoom leggen tegen.

aó kak, 丨 角, eene vouw of oor in een boek slaan.

aó dsiaò, 丨 縐, gekreukeld, gerimpeld.

aó oan, krombuigen.

aó k'iao, 丨 曲, ombuigen, krombuigen.

aó ts'iú bé / *» » boé* } 丨 手 尾, elkanders armen trachten te buigen (een spel).

aó aó lóh k'ìh, 丨 丨 落 去, neêrgeslagen (als graan door regen en wind).

aó tit, 丨 直, regtbuigen.

aó lâng ê ts'in t'aô, / *ut » » » »* } 丨 人 之 稱 頭, iemands weegschaal ombuigen, *d. i.* door eene valsche weegschaal minder uitwegen dan er is.

tsit pah kun aó sīn kaó tsáp gō̤ / *» peh kin ut » » » »* } 一 百 斤 丨 剩 九 十 五, met eene valsche schaal uit 100 pond slechts 95 wegen.

aó hān, 丨 悍, koppig, halsstarrig, onhandelbaar.

aó tsip, tsip aó, 丨 執, 執 丨, zich onveranderlijk aan zijn idée houden; onbuigzaam.

aó ut lânh, 丨 惱, iemand valsch betichten.

aó k'ut, 枉 屈, do.

kiông aó i dzīn / *kiâng » » »* } 强 丨 伊 認, met geweld iemand valsch doen bekennen.

aó hoai̤ } *» hoa̤* } ┃ 橫, in de knoei brengen, vrees aanjagen.

siang aó, 雙 ┃, dubbel gevouwen.

毆 Slaan; *aó tá*, ┃ 打, slaan.

Aó *sio aó*, 相 ┃, vechten.

嘔 Braken, uitspuwen.

Aó *aó hông*, ┃ 紅, bloedspuwen.

aó huih } *» hoeh* } ┃ 血, do.

aó t'ò, ┃ 吐, braken; *ao lah*, do.

aó sim hiet, ┃ 心 血, het bloed uit het hart spuwen, (gezegd van iets dat veel moeite kost).

Aó̤ *nt aó̤*, lispelen, te korte tong hebben.

臭 Niet versch, bedorven, stinkend, verrot.

Aò *aò k'ih*, verrot, bedorven.

aò ts'aò, ┃ 臭, stinkend, bedorven.

sim kik aò ts'aò, 心 極 ┃ 臭, zeer bedorven van harte.

aò lók lók, door ouderdom verrot, (als eijeren, vleesch).

aó bī, ┃ 味, verrotte lucht, stinkend.

aò laò laò, stinkend, verrot.

aò hiù ê bī, 臭 之 味, stinkend; verstikte lucht.

aò kaò ts'aò, ┃ 至 臭, bedorven en stinkend, (van iemands naam).

aò lông, verrot, bedorven, slecht, (van handelingen).

mia̤ sia̤ aò lông lông, zijn goede naam is bedorven.

aò piaó, ┃ 嫖, stinkende hoer (scheldwoord).

懊 Boos, grommig, knorrig, norsch.

Aò *aò laó, aò naó̤*, ┃ 惱, grommig, knorrig.

aò t'aô ê bīn, ┃ 頭 之 面, er knorrig uitzien.

aò aò ts'aò ts'aò, ┃ ┃ 愁 愁, grommig, norsch.

aò aò pū pū, boos stilzwijgen; pruilen.

喉 De keel, strot; de mond (van een kolk, enz).

Aô *na̤ aô*, 咽 ┃, keel, strot.

kaó sia̤ k'it tsiáh aô, 狗 聲 乞 食 ┃, stem als een hond en strot als een bedelaar, *d. i.* leelijke, gemeene stem.

pàng tit aô, 放 直 ┃, in de keel gooijen, inzwelgen.

aô tī, ┃ 塡, tot aan de keel vol (van droefheid); op het punt zijn te weenen.

aô ūn, ┃ 韻, geurig van thee (wanneer de geur weêr in de keel opkomt).

si̤ aô hông } *se̤ » »* } 生 ┃ 癀, een keel-gezwel hebben.

ien aô ê só̤ tsaī, 咽 ┃ 的 所 在, de strot, de voornaamste plaats- de sleutel- tot een rijk.

Aô *aô kiò*, 喊 叫, gillen.

toā sia̤ iá aô, 大 聲 野 呼, hard roepen, schreeuwen; eene stem in de woestijn.

後 *aō boé* } *» bé* } ┃ 尾, achteraan, het laatste.

Aō *aō bó* } *» bú* } ┃ 母, stiefmoeder.

aō pē̤ } *» pē* } ┃ 父, stiefvader.

aō dzit, ┃ 日, overmorgen.

aō lai, ┃ 來, naderhand, later.

aō sin, ┃ 身, later, hierna.

aō si, ┃ 時, later, hierna.

aō kè̤ } *» kè* } ┃ 次, een anderen tijd.

aō kè, 再 嫁, ten tweeden male huwen.

aō niō, 丨 娘, stiefmoeder.

aō iā, 丨 營 }
aō kūn, 丨 軍 } achterhoede.

aō ts'iú, 丨 手, verzorger, (zoo als een vader in zijnen zoon kan hebben).

aō tsan k'í, 長 齒, maaltand.

tīng aō lō, 斷 丨 逕, allen verderen omgang afbreken.

toān aō lō, 斷 丨 路, de terugkeer afsnijden, versperren, beletten.

aō bú tók, 丨 毋 酷, slecht (stiefmoederlijk).

dzit aō, 日 丨, naderhand, later.

hó aō tsìn, 好 丨 進, een goede zoon.

p'ai aō tsìn, 歹 丨 進, een slechte zoon.

aō kaì t'ō, 丨 界 土, achterplaats.

t'è aō, 退 丨, achteruitgaan, achteruittreden.

aō bīn, 丨 面, van achteren, de achter kant, verkeerde kant.

ah aō, 押 丨, een transport goederen achterna geleiden.

tsing ts'iú t'éh tsī, aō ts'iú liaó, 前 手 取 錢 丨 手 了, zoo gewonnen, zoo geronnen.

aō mîng }
» mui } 丨 門, achterdeur.

bò ts'ùn aō, 無 慮 丨, niet voor den volgenden dag, voor de toekomst, zorgen.

bò laô aō pō, 不 留 餘 地, niet aan de toekomst denken; iemand op eens zoo bedriegen, dat men nimmer meer door hem begunstigd zal worden.

tè aō }
toè » } 隨 丨, achteraan, achterna.

aō t'aô, 丨 頭, achteraan.

tsing aō }
tsân » } 前 丨, van voren en achteren.

aō bé mîng }
« boé mui } 丨 尾 門, achterdeur.

aō hoe hîng }
» hoa hui } 丨 花 園, achtertuin.

aō ang, 丨 夫, tweede man.

aō k'a soah tsaī, 丨 脚 踏 在, den achtervoet vast neer zetten, *d. i.* secuur handelen.

aō taī, 丨 代, latere geslachten, nakomelingen.

Ap

壓 Ap *k'i toā ap soè*, 欺 大 丨 小, grooten bedriegen en minderen verdrukken.

īng sè ap lâng }
īng sì » » } 以 勢 丨 人, op zijne eigene of een ander man's magt steunende, menschen verdrukken.

bīn tsing siu ko ap }
« tsân sio » » } van voren te veel overgapen (als eene zeer groote deur die tegen over eene kleine staat).

tìn ap, bezet houden, gestationeerd zijn te.

t'àn ap, do. bewaken.

狎 Ap *ap siet*, vrij, familiaar behandelen.

kap i teh liók ap, iemand plagen die iets gedaan heeft, wat men hem had afgeraden, en wat nu ook slecht is uitgevallen.

hi á ap tsui, de visschen smekken het water op.

At

遏 At *at tsí*, 丨 止, tegenhouden, stoppen.

at huih }
» hoeh } 丨 血, het bloed stoppen.

at tsih, 丨 折, stuk breken (als een stok.)

at tīng } | 斷, doorbreken, in tweeën
» tuī }
breken.

at lóh, | 下, ten onder houden, temperen.

at lóh t'aò, | 下 首, het hoofd buigen, bukken, bedaarder worden.

at hoe ki } | 花 枝, een' bloemtak afplukken.
» hoa » }

at sìng } | 筭, op de vingers tellen.
» suì }

bò at sìng } 不 | 筭, niet berekenen, bedenken (als de onkosten die nog van iets afmoeten).
» » suì }

at tse giáh beh hō̤ ìh } zoo berekenen dat men elk (zijner schuldeischers) een deel kan betalen.
» » » boeh « » }

at liaò, 按 僚, de maat slaan.

at tsíng t'aò á } | 手 指, de vingers doen knappen.
» tsíng » » }

Ba

麻 *bà hong*, | 瘋, melaatschheid.
Bà *bà pì*, | 痺, slapen (van den voet).

bà ióh, | 藥, geneesmiddel tegen melaatschheid; pijndoovend geneesmiddel.

bà bīn, | 面, mottig, pokdalig.

boē bà bīn, 不 | 面, zich niet schamen, schaamteloos.

ts'en bà bà, 凉 | |, kil, verklimd, stijf van koude.

猫 Lichtekooi, hoer.
Bà *là ts'iong* } | 娼, lichtekooi.
» ts'iang }

p'ai bà, 歹 |, do.

pi aó tsú bà, 嫖 子 |, do. (scheldwoord).

貓 Wilde kat.
Bà *soa bà*, 山 |, do.

bà dzi gán, | 兒 眼, katterige, dodderige oogen door dronkenschap.

蝥 *pan bà*, 班 |, spaansche vlieg.
Bà *bà li*, scheepshut (maleisch *balé*).
kap i bà lī, intiem met iemand zijn.

覓 Zoeken naar, uitzien naar.
Bā *bā t'aò lō̤*, | 生 路, naar eene kostwinning, betrekking uitzien.

bā ts'ù, | 厝, naar een huis uitkijken, zoeken.

碼 Eene el, (van het Engelsche *yard*).
Bā

密 *bā bā*, digt, geheim.
Bā *bā sún*, 浹 筍, met zwaluwstaarten bevestigen.
bā lī, goed overeenstemen.
bā li soai, tamelijk, het kan er nog door.

霧 Verstikt.
Bā *ts'iū bā* } 汚 跡, verstikt (van kleeren).
ts'iō̤ » }

bā hióh } 鵜 鷹, wouw. (Milvus Govinda).
laī » }

bā hióh bā koe á } 鵜 鷹 掠 鷄 子, de wouw steelt de kuikens weg.
laī hióh boáh ke á }

bā bā, 峇 峇, op Java of in den Archipel geboren Chinees, *liplap*.

Bah

肉 Vleesch (varkens vleesch).
Bah *gû bah*, 牛 |, rundvleesch.

iū bah } 羊 |, schapenvleesch.
iō̤ » }

ti bah, 猪 |, varkensvleesch.

tsiā bah, 赤 |, mager vleesch.

bah hú sé. | 脯 絲, fijn gesplitst gedroogd vleesch.

bah pó, | 脯, gedroogd vleesch.

bah koā. | 乾, do.

si bah, 死 |, dood (ongevoelig) vleesch.

ts'ò bah tsiù / » » *tsiō* } 剉 | 醬, vleesch fijnhakken.

ts'ò bah si. 剉 | 泥, do.

bah oân. | 膾, een bal gehakt.

tsiâ bah piá, 成 | 餅, verpletterd, tot mors gewreven worden door eene omvallende muur, enz.

tsiáh hi tsiáh bah iā tióh ts'ài sa / » » » » » » » *sio* / *kah* / » } 食 魚 食 | 也 着 菜 相 甲, bij het eten van visch en vleesch moet men ook groenten gebruiken, *d. i.* somtijds iets minder goeds te hebben, doet het goede beter uitkomen.

lâng bah ts'iah ts'iah boē oē tsiáh tit / » » *tsiā tsiā bē ē* » » 人 | 赤 赤 不 能 食 得, men kan het hem toch niet van zijn lijf afsnijden.

koah bah ts'ī hó, 割 | 飼 虎, vleesch hakken om er een tijger mede te voeden, *d. i.* anderen begunstigen en daardoor juist zich zelven benadeelen.

tsì bah, 箭 |, punt van eene pijl.

t'iā bah bah, 愛 | |, vurig beminnen.

sam tsân bah, 三 層 |, ribvleesch.

liém tó bah, 臉 肚 |, vleesch bij den buik.

aō t'ui bah, 後 腿 |, achterpoot.

tsing t'ui bah, 前 腿 |, voorpoot.

kièn tsi bah. 見 子 |, vleesch van de kuit.

pa tsiak tsit bah, 脊 |, vleesch bij de ruggestreng.

bah sún. | 笋, vleesch aan fijne draden gesneden.

bah tàng. | 湅, vleesch gelei.

Bai

之 Bai — *bai á,* of *tsi bai,* 之 仔。之 |, vulva, (lage uitdrukking).

歹 Baí — Slecht.

bai kang hu. | 工 夫, slecht werk.

si bai, 死 |, stil, niet levendig (van personen).

lâng k'oà li bai, 人 看 你 |, men ziet u voor nietig of slecht aan.

ts'in ts'iū bai kiu / » *ts'iō* » » } 相 似 | 鬼, als een onduidelijke, snel voorbijgaande geest of spook (van iemand dien men eens klaps ziet, en die zoo weder weg is).

goá tsa hing k'it bai kui teh, 我 昨 夜 被 | 鬼 塡, ik heb gisteren avond de nachtmerrie gehad.

Baí — Duister, onduidelijk zigtbaar, veraf; flaauwtjes (als vuur).

hé bai bai / *hoé* » » } 火 眇 眇, het vuur is op het punt van uitte gaan.

眉 Bai — De wenkbraauwen; *van daar:* eene smalle strook.

bák bai, 目 |, de wenkbraauwen.

nī bai / *oū* » } 畫 |, de wenkbraauwen verwen.

bák bai t'aò p'ah tsoè tsit kat / » » » » *tsò* » » } 目 | 頭 打 做 一 結, een' knoop tusschen de wenkbraauwen hebben, *d. i.* er droefgeestig, somber uitzien.

it dzī bai, 一 字 |, doorloopende

wenkbraauwen, *lett.* wenkbraauwen als het karakter *it*, (zoo als de wandelende Jood van *Sue*.

liú hióh bai, 柳葉丨. fraaije, (*lett.* wilgenbladen) wenkbraauwen (van vrouwen).

koan kong bai, *koan tè iâ bai*, 關公丨。關帝爺丨. wenkbraauwen als de oorlogs-god, *d. i.* schuins opgaande.

oàn kong bai / *koan » »* } 袁公丨. rijstvogel.

peh bák bai / *péh » »* } 白目丨, mees.

tsit bai á, 一丨仔. eene smalle strook.

géh bai á / *goèh » »* } 月丨仔. smalle strook van de maan.

楣 Bai *mîng bai tíng*, / *mui̤ » »* } 門丨頂. bovendrempel, bovenst dwarshout van een deurkozijn.

埋 Bai Wegstoppen, door iets bedekken, bebegraven.

bai hók. 丨伏, zich verschuilen, in hinderlaag liggen.

bai bút, 丨沒. verdonkeremanen, uit den weg ruimen.

bai tsòng, 丨葬. begraven.

siu bai, 受丨. kisten en begraven.

覔 Bai (mai̤) Beloeren; zoeken, kijken naar; met belangstelling komen bezoeken, informeren naar, (als naar een zieke).

sì kè bai̤ bai̤ / *» » mai̤ mai̤* } 四方丨丨. overal zoeken, kijken naar.

siaò king bai̤ mîng p'ûng / *» » mai̤ mui̤ »* } 算間丨門縫, de huizen tellen en door de deurreten loeren, (als policiedienaars 's avonds, om te zien of er in huizen gedobbeld wordt).

ts'ì bai̤ / *» mai̤* } 試丨, beproeven.

sa bai̤ / *sio mai̤* } 相丨. elkander komen bezoeken, naar elkanders gezondheid komen informeren

bai̤ song, 丨喪. bij een sterfgeval bezoeken, gaan condoleren.

bai̤ pī̤, bai̤ tsìng / *» pē̤ » tsìn* } 丨病, 丨症, visites bij zieken afleggen (van doktoren.

bai̤ méh, 丨脈. de pols voelen.

kià bai̤, 寄丨. opdragen naar iemands gezondheid te informeren.

Bak

汚 Bak Bezoedelen, vuilmaken; zich bezoedelen, vuilmaken aan.

bak bak, 丨丨. besmeren.

bak t'ô, 丨塗, bespatten, vuilmaken.

bak tióh / *« tioh* } 丨着, bezoedelen, vuilmaken door . . .

bak tâm, 丨濕. nat maken.

bak kia lâng / *bak la sâm* } vuil maken.

bak tsuí, 丨水. zich nat maken.

bak a p'ièn, 丨牙片, zich schuldig maken aan het gebruik van opium.

bak t'ô̤ bak dziō, 汚泥汚溺, op den grond liggend weilen, zich vuil maken (van kinderen).

bak bak tak tak, alles vuilmakend, als inkt, kleverige, stoffen, enz. overal heengemorst.

墨 Bák Inkt.

bák tsuí, 丨水, vloeibare inkt, (Chin. en Europ); schoensmeer.

bák taó, 丨斗. inktdoos.

bák taó tsîn, 丨斗繩, inktlijn.

bák tiaô, 丨條, eene pijp Chin. inkt.

bák koàn, 丨鑵, inktkoker.

bák tsui nī / » » *oū* ｜水劃, ongekleurde teekening, zwarte prent met Oost-Ind. inkt. geteekend.

bák ti, zwart geschreven, zonder dunne trekken.

木 Bák
Boom; hout, van hout gemaakt, houten.

ts'iū bák, 樹｜, boomen in het algemeen.

bák sai hū, ｜司阜 / *bák kang*, ｜工 } timmerman.

bák liaū, ｜料, hout, timmerhout.

bák sa, ｜栅, palisade, paalwerk.

bák hiu, ｜香, putchuk.

bák kiáh, ｜屐, klompen, regenschoenen.

bák kiáh tseh / » » *tseh* ｜屐卽, hak van een' vrouwenschoen.

tsoè sió bák, 做小｜, het fijne timmermanswerk doen.

bák sat, ｜虱, houtluis, luis.

目 Bák•
Oogen; de oogen, mazen van een net; het oog, *d. i.* het hoofd, de aanvoerder, leider van iets; uitgroeisel, uitstekend gedeelte.

bák tsiu, ｜睭, oog.

bāng á bák, 網仔｜, mazen van een net.

bák tsiu p'é / » » *p'oè* ｜睭皮, de oogleden.

bák tsiu o àm, ｜睭烏暗, zijne oogen zijn donker, *d. i.* hij is dood.

p'ī bák ts'ùi, 鼻｜嘴, neus, oogen en mond, *d. i.* voorkomen, gelaat.

ts'ùi kap bák teh sa tsī / » » » » *sio tsè* 嘴與｜着相戰, (uw) mond en (mijne) oogen zijn in twist, *d. i.* hoe kunt gij mij tegenspreken wat ik voor mijne eigene oogen gezien heb.

bák tú bák, ｜對｜, oogen voor oogen, voor beider oogen, *d. i.* in beider tegenwoordigheid (ontvreemden, weggoochelen, enz).

bè bák, 迷｜, de oogen misleiden, verblinden, oogbedrog (als na een droom).

t'ī ū bák, 天有｜, de hemel heeft oogen, *d. i.* berstraft het kwade.

bák sin oáh, ｜神活, levendig uit de oogen kijken.

bák k'ang, ｜孔, oogholte.

bák tsiah mêng / » » *mô* ｜睫毛, oogharen.

bák bai, ｜眉, wenkbraauwen.

bák kiā, ｜鏡, bril.

laò bák sai, 流｜渣, weenen.

laò sai ko, ｜渣膏, zucht (in de oogen).

bák iû, ｜油, tranen (van het lagchen.)

tâm bák ki, 淚｜, druipoogen.

laò bák iū, ｜洒涕, traanoogen, (door lange blootstelling der oogen aan wind of vuur)

bák nih kú, 瞬息久, in een oogenblik.

ts'iah bák, 妬｜, verleidelijk voor het oog, in het oog vallend.

bô bīn bô bák, 無面無｜, geene oogen in zijn hoofd hebben, *d. i.* niet zien tegen wien men spreekt, of dat die persoon nu geen tijd heeft.

hó bák sik, 好｜識, goed van gezigt.

p'ai-, of *bô-bák sik*, 無｜識, slecht van gezigt.

sai k'iā bák, 用竪｜, iemand met strakstaande oogen, *d. i.* norsch aanzien.

tit bák, 直 丨, regt voor zich uitziende, zonder te zien wat er om zich heen gebeurt.
t'oa bák bé } *» » boé* } 拖 丨 尾, veel beduidende ooglonkjes geven.
īm bat bák, 不 識 丨, zijne menschen niet onderscheiden.
kè bák } *koè »* } 過 丨, onder de oogen gehad, of bezigtigd hebben.
bák laī ū ih, 丨 中 有 他, goed over iemand denken.
bák teh bô, 丨 地 無。看 輕, minachten.
bák sáh sī, *bák ka tsē*, 丨 瞌 睡, 丨 磕 睡, dutten, sluimeren.
bák kim, 丨 今, nu, op het oogenblik.
bák ē } *» ē* } 丨 下, tegenwoordig.
t'aô bák, 頭 丨, aanvoerder, leider
toê bák, } *tê »* } 題 丨, onderwerp, tekst voor een opstel.
bák nih, 轉 瞬, knipoogen.
tsoā bák, 泉 丨, wel-opening, bron.
bák bai mîng bô tsiu̲ ám } *» » mô̤ » tsio̤ »* } 丨 眉 毛 不 漿 粒, de haren der wenkbraauwen niet gestijfd hebben, (zoodat ze voor de oogen hangen), *d. i.* niet zien tegen wien men spreekt.
bák tsiaó, 丨 鳥, belhamel.
ts'iú bák, 手 丨, knoken van de hand.
tsiū bák, 樹 丨, boomknoest.
t'sâ bák, 柴 丨, afgehakte boomknoesten.
k'a bák, 脚 丨, beenknokels.
tik bák, 竹 丨, bamboeknoesten.
bák tsiu dzîn, 丨 睭 仁, pupil, oogbal.

ts'oáh bák } *t'oah t'ang* } 斜 丨, scheelzien.
bák t'iá, 丨 痛, zeere oogen.

密 Solide, vast in elkander.
Bák *ū bák sit*, 有 丨 實, solide, niet slinken of geslonken, zeer veel.
bô bák sit, 不 丨 實, slinken.

Ban

挘 of 摘 Uittrekken, aftrekken, plukken.
Bán *bán hoe* } *» hou* } 丨 花, bloemen plukken.
bán k'i, 丨 齒, kiezen trekken.
bán mîng } *» mô̤* } 丨 毛, veêren uittrekken.
kiông kiông bán láng } *kiâng kiâng » »* } iemand met geweld plukken, *d. i.* uitvlugtsels zoeken om hem minder te betalen.
bán koe ts'iù tin } *» koa t'in »* } zie onder *ts'iù*.

挽 Trekken.
Bán *bán tńg*, 丨 轉, omtrekken, terugtrekken, (als zijn paard).
īng soh á bán k'ih laih } *iōng » » » » »* } 用 索 仔 丨 去 來, met een touw ophijschen.
tuì soh á bán tsiū k'ih } *» » » » tsō̤ »* } 由 索 仔 丨 上 去, tegen een touw opklimmen.
bán bīn, 挽 面, het gezigt (van vrouwen) scheren; met een koord en meel glad vijlen.
k'a tsiah bán mi, eene koude rilling over den rug krijgen, (van vrees).
gâo bán láng, gaauw driftig worden, korzelheid (van vrouwen).
bán hoê, 丨 回, teruggeven.
bán ts'aó, 丨 草, planten zoeken, botaniseren.

3

bán ting } | 轉, omtrekken, terug-
» *tńg*
trekken.

頑 *bàn p'è* } | 皮, hardhoofdig, on-
Bàn » *p'oè*
begrijpelijk; hardgevoelig.

aó bàn, 刁 | } stijfhoofdig.
tiao bàn, *t'iao bàn*
koppig.

tiá bàn bàn, 釜 | |, de pan is dik-gebodemd.

siq bân bân, 聲 | |, dof van geluid.

綏 *bàn bàn*, langen tijd vereischen, lang-
Bàn zaam gaan, (als het genezen eener ziekte).

bàn k'áng, | 固, stevig, sterk, lang-durend.

幔 Bedekken, behangen met.
Bàn *bàn tsoá* } | 紙, met papier be-
Moâ *moâ* »
hangen, beplakken.

goā bīn bàn tsit ting pò } 外 面
» » *moâ* » » «
| 一重布, van buiten met een' doek bedekken.

閩 De oude naam voor de Prov *Fokien*.
Bàn *bàn oát*, | 粵, Fokien en Canton.

bàn hai koan, | 海 關, chef der douane in Fokien-plaatsen.

bàn dzin, | 人, de zuidelijke Chinezen.

萬 Tiendnizend; veel, alle; uiterst, toch,
Bān vooral. Familienaam.

bān bān, | |, honderd millioen.

pah bān làng } 百 | 人, een mil-
peh » »
lioen menschen.

pah bān ê làng } 百 | 的 人,
peh » » »
een millioenair.

ts'ing ts'ing bān bān } 千 千 | |,
ts'an ts'an » »
bij duizenden en tien duizenden, *d. i.* in groote hoeveelheid.

tsiâ bān lâng, 成 | 人, ongeveer ten bedrage van 10,000 menschen.

bān it, | 一, tienduizend tegen één, *d. i.* de mogelijkheid bestaat toch dat . . . .

bān hūn tsi it, | 分 之 一, do. het kan toch gebeuren dat . . .

bān bû it sit, | 無 一 失, van 10,000 zal er niet een verkeerd zijn, *d. i.* sekuur, veilig.

bān siū kik, | 壽 菊, goudsbloem.

tsoè bān siū } 做 | 壽, het is de
tsò » »
verjaardag des Keizers.

bān soè iâ, | 歲 爺, de Keizer

bān kun ê tsú soè, | 軍 的 主 司, hoofd-aanvoerder van alle troepen *d. i.* hoofdzaak of persoon waarom alles draait.

bàn kin bân t'ô, | 巾 | 土, blijvende — zekere bezitting.

bān li ting siâ } | 里 長 城,
» » *ting* »
de groote Chinesche muur.

bān dzī hiu áh } | 字 香 匣,
» » *hio* »
reukwerkbak waarin het reukwerk in met elkander corresponderende rijen gestrooid wordt.

ts'ien giên bān gú } 千 言 | 語,
» *gân* » *gi*
met vele woorden, (zeggen, vermanen, enz).

bān dzin soà, | 人 傘, eere-zonnescherm door het volk aan een' goeden mandarijn gegeven.

kap bān } 夾 |, geldkist.
» *pān*

bān sū, | 事, alle zaken, in alle zaken.

bān bōng, | 望, toch vooral, of vurig, hoopen dat . . .

ts'ien bān tioh, 千 | 着, toch vooral moet . . . .

慢 Langzaam; zachtjes aan.
Bān *bān bān*, 丨丨, langzaam.
k'a ts'iú bān tūn, 脚手丨鈍, langzaam in zijne handelingen.
bān ts ak, *bān ts'iá* 丨且, langzaam aan, wacht eens even.
bān tsiah sī, 丨且時, do.; aanstonds,
sī kim bān tiā tiā, » » » *nā tiā* 是今丨定定, binnen korten tijd, binnen weinige dagen.
bān pi hong, 丨瘅瘋, eene soort kinder-ziekte.
taī bān, 怠丨, met minachting behandelen.
tsiáh bān t'ô hoe tsuí » » » *hoa* » 食卐桃花水, van de Datura gegeten hebben, *d. i.* krankzinnig zijn.

瓣 De hokjes, afdeelingen, in oranjes, meloenen, enz.
Bān *tsit bān kam* » *liēm* » 一丨柑, een stukje, afdeeling van eene oranje.
soàn bān » *liēm* 蒜丨, afdeeling in knoflook.
kik bān » *liēm* 格丨, opgevuld, gezwollen; (van de afdeelingen in meloenen, oranjes, enz).

Bang

濛 *hō̤ á bang bang*, 微雨丨丨, stofregen.
Bang *hō̤ goàn ts'e bang k'ih* » » *t'se̤* » » 被原差丨去, door politie dienaars gevat, gevangen worden.
iù bang bang, 幼丨丨, zeer fijn, (als meel, stof, enz).

蚊 Muskiet.
Báng *báng tà*, *báng tiā*, 丨帳, muskieten gordijn.
báng tà king, 丨帳弓, toeslaand muskieten gordijn.
báng hun, *báng hiū* » *á* « » *á hiō̤* 丨烟, 丨香 muskieten verdrijvend reukwerk.
k'ih báng á k'a l'ing tioh » » » » *liòng* » 被丨子脚踜着, door een muskieten poot getrapt zijn, (zegt men tot een kleinzeerig mensch).
bák tsiu ts'ú báng ts'ú báng, 視眇, bijziende.
pì̤ bô báng, 變無路, geen uitweg meer hebben.
báng t'àng, 丨虫, muskieten.
báng ts'uì, 丨嘴, muskieten beet.
báng hia, 丨揖, muskieten net, (waarin men ze vangt).
báng sut, 丨鞭, soort zweep of staart waarmede men muskieten afslaat; muskieten waaijer.
báng á sia, 丨仔聲, muskieten geluid, *d. i.* een fijn stemmetje.
tsiaó á tìng báng á tō̤ 鳥仔腸
ke á tìng tseh á tō̤ 鷄仔腸
丨仔肚
雀仔肚 vogel-ingewanden en muskieten-buik, *d. i.* klein van eten
tsiaó á tìng báng á liōng, 鳥仔腸丨仔量, zeer onverdraagzaam, oninschikkelijk.

忙 Verward, niet weten wat te doen, verlegen.
Bâng *bâng bâng*, 丨丨, besluiteloos.
ts'iú bâng k'a loān, 手丨脚亂, met de handen in het haar zitten.

bàng loān, 丨 亂, verward.

kóng oē bàng bàng / » *oā* » » } 講 話 丨 丨, onzamenhangend spreken, (als in dronkenschap).

bàng tiù / » *tiò* } 丨 埸, verlegen zijn in 't publiek, (manchetten koorts).

bàng bàng, 茫 丨, onduidelijk, (voor het gezigt).

芒 Bàng *bàng ts'aó*, 丨 草, mossen.

tsik bàng, 燭 丨, kaarsenpit.

pák tsik bàng, 縛 燭 丨, kaarsenpitten binden of maken. Gekheid met vrouwen maken.

網 Bāng Net, vischnet; met een net vangen; mazen, stoppen.

bāng á bák, 丨 仔 目, mazen van een net.

ts'iah bāng, 打 丨, netten knoopen.

bāng hi, 丨 魚, met een net visschen; in netten gevangen visch, (die minder versch is).

bāng t'ih soà, 丨 鐵 線, met ijzerdraad omwinden.

sa p'oà ìng soà bāng / » » *iōng* » » } 衣 被 用 線 丨, kapotte kleêren met garen stoppen of mazen.

dzip i è bāng, 入 伊 的 丨, in iemands net komen, *d. i.* door hem bedrogen worden.

bāng á tē, 丨 仔 袋, geknoopt zakje.

夢 Bāng Droom, droomen.

bin bāng, 眠 丨, droomen.

bāng kì, 丨 見, droomen van . . .

bāng kì tsit è bāng, 丨 見 一 個 丨, een' droom gehad hebben.

oán bāng, 完 丨, droomen uitleggen.

dzú sù lák bāng / *dzi si bāng* } 亂 丨, zwaar of verward droomen.

k'ùn bāng, 𥊍 丨, in een' tempel slapen om in zijn' droom de bedoeling van de godheid te vernemen.

ts'oā dziō tāng, 帶 尿 丨, droom waarbij men in bed watert, (zoo als kinderen).

望 Bāng Uitzien naar, hopen.

liaò bāng, 瞭 丨, uitkijken naar.

ìng bāng 企 丨 / *kì bāng* 冀 丨 } hopen.

t'iā sia bāng iá, 聽 聲 丨 影, naar iemands geluid luisteren en naar zijne schaduw uitzien, *d. i.* vurig naar iemand uitzien.

bô bāng, 無 丨, zonder vooruitzigt of hoop zijn.

bāng tang á, winterkoningje, snijdervogeltje, enz.

bāng ka láh, 孟 加 拉, Bengalen.

Bao

Bao *bao lóh k'i*, kromgetrokken naar beneden.

bao pi, / *ba» ki* } aan de kanten kromgetrokken, omgevouwen.

卯 Baó *baó si*, 卯 時, van 's morgens 5—7 uur.

tiém baó, 點 丨, inspectie houden over de menschen in een mandarijn-bureau; hunne namen afroepen; appel houden.

ìng baó, 應 丨, antwoord geven bij het afroepen van zijn' naam.

t'i kng baó, / » *kni* » } 天 明 丨 's morgens vroeg.

mih maoh / » *maóh* } zonder tanden, (als de mond van een oud mensch).

in of *ing baó*, 應 ｜, voldoen aan het vereischte, (zoo als een schuldenaar).
k'it i baó ts'it k'ih, door hem ingesloten, verdonkeremaand worden.

矛 Baó *ka kī baó tún* / » » *maŏ* » } 自 相 ｜ 盾, zich zelven tegen spreken.
baò baò / *maŏ maŏ* } onzeker (van eene zaak).
oē baò tit / *ē maŏ* » } 能 謀 得, het kan ruw weg berekend, of afbetaald worden; (als geld van kennissen waarvan men den interest wel later met hen vinden zal).
baò lai baò k'i / *maŏ* » *maŏ* » } ｜ 來 ｜ 去, eene loopende rekening met elkander hebben (dan eens geldschieten, dan eens te vorderen hebben).

Baō *baō baō tsoè tsit ē* / » » *tsò* » *ē* } 昌 ｜ 作 一 次, goeden en slechten door elkander mengen.
baō soah bò t'ang boé, ｜ 算 不 可 買, zich overtuigd houden dat iemand iets niet koopen kan.
baō ki, ｜ 旁, om den rand geslagen, (als de omslag van een boek).
baō mī, vermicellie (met specerijen, bouillon enz.) mengen.

Baoh

Baóh *baoh* of *maŏh*, 包 買, geheel en al opkoopen, aannemen.
baoh kang, 包 工, een werk aannemen.
baoh ka ning tui / » » *nuī* » } de geheele massa bij elkander rekenen.
baoh tsoè tsit ē / » *tsò* » *ē* } ｜ 做 一 個, alles bij elkander rekenen, pachten.
baoh soah, ｜ 算, iemands toekomst voorspellen, voorzeggen.

baóh ké tsi / » *koé* » } ｜ 菓 子, de vruchten van eene plaats opkoopen.
hó p'ai tsoàn baóh, 好 歹 全 ｜, goed en slecht gelijk opkoopen.

Bat

識 Bat Kennen.
sa bat / *sio* » } 相 ｜, elkander kennen.
bat, 曾, aanduider van den verleden tijd.
bat k'oà ki, 曾 看 見, gezien hebben, ooggetuige geweest zijn.
bat sū, 知 事, kennis van zaken hebben.
bat lâng k'ah hó bat gûn (*gin*), ｜ 人 較 好 ｜ 銀, zijne menschen te kunnen onderscheiden is beter dan goed en slecht geld van elkander te kennen.
bē bat / *boē* » } 未 曾, . . nog niet (*b. v.* gedaan hebben).
bat tsit pai, 曾 一 次, eens was het . . , gebeurde het dat . . .
bat dzī, ｜ 字, letters of karakters kennen; kunnen lezen.
bat lō, ｜ 路, den weg weten.
bat lé, ｜ 禮, de beleefdheid kennen, beleefd zijn.

密 Bát Geheim, digt, sluitend.
bát bát, ｜ ｜, do.
bát tsiét, 稠 ｜, digt, ingesloten, ommuurd.
siep bát, do.; weggestopt.
i king siu bát, 已 經 收 ｜, reeds gekist, (van een lijk).
bát bát sī, dikop, overal opgehoopt zijn, (als mieren in een huis).
bát tsát, 墨 魚, inktvisch.

bát tsát k'ak } 墨魚殼, schaal
 » » *tsùn* }
van een' inktvisch.

bát tsát tsó, 墨魚鮓, gezoute inktvisch.

Be

尾 Bé Boé Staart, van daar g tal-letter voor visschen, slangen, enz. Het eind, achterste gedeelte, laatste; uiteinde, afloop van eene zaak.

tsit bé hi } 一 | 魚, een pees visch.
 » *boé* » }

bô t'aô bô bé, 無頭無 |, zonder kop of staart.

t'aô bé tiah, 頭 | 斷, kop en staart van iets afzonderen en alleen het beste er van nemen.

bé sàng, of *bé aū sàng*, | 送, | 後送, bezaanszeil.

bé ui, | 桅, bezaansmast.

bé tsai } | 指, de pink.
 » *tsai* }

bé dzī tsai, 無名指, derde vinger.

bé liu, einde, uiteinde; achteraan, ten laatste.

lō bé, 路 |, ten laatste.

bé sin, | 身, aan het einde.

bé laô ting, | 樓頂, de kajuit.

bé aū, | 後, van achteren, achteraan, ten laatste.

bé bīn, | 面, van achteren, later.

kaò bé bīn, 至 | 面, ten laatste.

tsù t'aô kaò bé, 自頭至 |, van begin tot eind

hong t'aô pò bé, 風頭暴 |, (in tijd van) harde wind.

hó bé king, *hó bé sao*, 老境美, 好 | 梢, gelukkige oude dag.

bé kiók, | 局, afloop van eene zaak.

tìng k'a tsiū iep bé } 頓足即
 tuì » » » *boé* }
歛尾, stampt men op den grond dan loopt hij druipstaartend weg, *d. i.* bang.

馬 Pé Bé Paard; fig., wat men als paard gebruikt.

bé á, | 仔, veulen.

bé bé } | 尾, paardenstaart.
bé boé }

bé si, of *bé bé si*; *bé mîng* } | 絲,
bé si, of *bé boé si*; *bé mô* }
| 尾絲, | 毛, paardenhaar.

bé oa, | 鞍, zadel.

bé p'it, | 匹, paarden.

bé kang, 牡 |, hengst.

bé bú } 牝 |, merrie die reeds ge-
lé bò }
veuld heeft.

bé bú á, | 母仔, jonge merrie.

iem bé, 閹 |, ruin.

bé tiaô, | 廐, paardenstal.

bé hu, | 夫 }
bé t'aô, | 頭 } , paardenknecht, stalknecht.

bé tsang, | 鬃, paardenmanen.

bé kā kiu } | 銜韁, bit.
bé » *kiu* }

bé t'aô lông, | 頭籠, hoofdstel.

bé táh t'ìng } | 踏鐙, stijgbeugels.
bé » *ìng* }

bé tsô, | 槽, paardenruif.

bé toé t'ih, | 蹄鐵, hoefijzer.

bé pi, | 鞭, zweep, karwats.

bé ping, | 兵, cavallerist, cavallerie.

bé soh, *bé pì*, | 轡, teugels.

loh bé, 下 |, voor, of bij, iemands aankomst.

bé lō, | 路, paardenweg, rijweg.

ts'ien li bé, 千里｜, koerier.

teng ts'ien li lé, 當千里｜, koerier zijn.

tsoè lâng ê bé tsi, 爲人｜子, looper voor iemand zijn.

bé k'aó t'ih, ｜口鐵, ijzerblik.

bé k'i ts'aó, ｜菌草, Spinazie?

kà bé tsi, 佳｜趾, de schroef waarmede men eene vioolsnaar spant.

bé ts'ing, ｜銃, ruiterpistool.

bé koà, ｜褂, schondermantel.

bé k'oài, ｜快, politiedienaren.

t'io bé k'i / *koē bē* » } 結｜菌, met punten afzetten (als een zakdoek).

bé i, ｜椅, werkbank, schaafbank, schraag.

sa k'a bé, 三脚｜, schraag, drijvertje voor eene nachtpit.

bé pò, ｜布, doek gedurende de menses gebruikt; stondendoek.

bé t'âng, ｜桶, strontpot.

bé koh, ｜兒, koelie in een bordeel.

loān bé bé, 亂｜｜, zeer verward, (van eene volkrijke stad).

碼 Bé Bē — De cursijve, verkorte cijfers. De Pacht.

bé tsi, ｜子, de verkorte cijfers.

p'ah bé tsi, 打｜子, cursijve cijfers schrijven.

ts'ò toā bé, 錯大｜, zich vergissen in het hoofdgetal, bij cursijfcijfers, (als duizend voor 10,000 zetten).

a p'ièn bé á, kiaó bé á, tèng tièm bé á, 鴉片｜仔。博｜仔。當店｜仔, pacht op opium, dobbelhuizen en pandjeshuizen.

houh bé á, 唱｜仔, openbaar verpachten.

kiò bé á, 叫｜仔, de belanghebbende firmas voor eene verpachting bij elkander roepen.

pák bé á, 瞨｜仔, eene pacht pachten.

kè bé á / *koè » »* } 過｜仔, eene pacht overdoen of overgeven.

tsioh bé, 石｜, plaats aan de *Tsiang-tsiu* rivier.

瑪 Bé Boé — *bé lò* / *boé »* } 瑪瑙, kornoelje, agaat.

螞 Bé — *bé iáh*, ｜蝶, vlinder, kapel.

鰢 Bé — *bé ka hi*, makreel.

Beh

欲 Beh Boeh — Verlangen, zullen, willen; moeten.

aì beh, 愛｜, willen....

beh t'ai oē / *boeh » ē* } 何以, hoe dan toch?

beh tsiáh kin, kòng p'oà oá, ｜食快打破碗, door gaauw te willen eten de kom breken, *d. i.* door te veel overhaasting eene zaak bederven.

teh beh, op het punt van te..; zullen.

beh hō pát lâng ts'òng, ｜與別人造, als men het een ander zou laten doen, dan....

迷 Bê — Misleiden, verleiden; verdwalen.

bê hik, ｜惑, verleiden, misleiden.

bê lō, ｜路, van den weg afdwalen, verdwalen.

bê k'i, ｜去, verdwijnen.

bê hûn hiu / *» » hio* } ｜魂香, bedwelmend reukwerk, (door dieven gebruikt.)

bê bák, 丨目, oogbedrog.

tit tit bê lòh k'ih, 直直丨落去, zich meer en meer door iets laten verleiden of medeslepen.

糜 Bè Moai Boeboer.

bè pīng / *moai pui* } 丨飯, boeboer en rijst.

ám bè, 淡丨, slappe boeboer.

t'ô bè tsiu / » *moai tsio* } 土丨欒, slik, modder.

妹 Bē Moē Moai *s ó bē*, 小丨. jongere zuster.

bē saì / *moē hu* } 丨夫, man van zijne jongere zuster.

tsi bē, 姊丨, zusters.

hiŋ tī tsi bē, 兄弟姊丨, broeders en zusters.

未 Bē Boē Nog niet.

iáo bē / » *boē* } 尙丨, nog niet.

bē tsing, of *bē tsīng bē*, 丨曾, nog niet.

bē ū, *bē bāt*, *bē bat ū*, 丨有, 丨曾, 丨曾有, niet ge . . . hebben, nog niet voorgekomen zijn dat . . .

Beh

麥 Béh Bẹ́h Tarwe.

béh hu, of *hun*, 丨灰 of 粉, tarwemeel.

toā béh, 大丨, gerst.

sió béh, 小丨, tarwe.

béh lê ko / » *lẹ* » } 丨芽飴, suikergoed.

béh lê ko ts'iú, 丨芽飴手, kleverige hand.

p'ah béh, *siak béh*, 打丨, tarwe dorschen.

béh ts'aó / *bẹ́h kó ts'aò* } 丨草, gerststengel.

koah béh, 割丨, tarwe maaijen.

hoŋ hi kaò béh sik, 歡喜到丨熟, zoo verheugd als of de tarwe rijp was, *d. i.* zeer verheugd.

襪 Béh Boéh Sokken, kousen (genaaide).

béh tìng / » *tuì* } sokken.

béh t'áng, kuit van de kous.

ts'ing oè tiò béh, / » *ê* » *boéh* } 穿鞋穿丨, schoenen en kousen dragen.

oê béh bō, 鞋丨帽, schoenen, kousen en hoed, *d. i.* kleêren.

Bi

密 Bi *bi dzìp laìh*, 密入來, heimelijk binnensluipen.

bi bih, 丨埋, zich verschuilen.

bi lai siém k'ì, 丨來閃去, voor elkander wegschuilen en uit den weg gaan.

bi tsing bi aō / » *tsàn* » » } 丨前丨後, van voren en van achteren toesluipen, (als om iets af te luisteren).

米 Bí Gepelde, ongekookte rijst. Familienaam.

tiáh bí, 糴丨, rijst koopen.

t'iò bí, 糶丨, rijst verkoopen.

bí k'ng, 丨糠, de huid van gestampte rijst, kaf.

bí ts'eng, 丨倉, graan-pakhuis.

bí hún, 丨粉乾, vermicellie.

bí laū, 丨漏, zeefmolen.

ū tsit bí liép toā, 有一丨粒大, zoo groot als een rijstkorrel.

ts'uì bí, 碎丨, gebroken rijst.

ts'ò bí, 糙 ｜, nog niet gezuiverde gepelde rijst.

pėh bí / *pḛh* » } 白 ｜, witte, gezuiverde rijst.

o̱ bí, 黑 ｜, zwarte rijst; naam voor opium.

tsút bí, 糯 ｜, kleverige (moskovisch) rijst.

níng bí / *nuį* » } 軟 ｜, zachte rijst.

ťīng bí / *ngḛ̄* » } 硬 ｜, harde rijst.

bí ts'oè / » *ts'è* } 米 碎, rijst-meel.

hê bí / *hḛ̂* » } 蝦 ｜, gedroogde garnalen.

già lan bí, 呀 噸 ｜, cochenille.

sòng bí, 宋 ｜, gedroogde garnalen van *Manilla*.

bí niû / » *niô̱* } ｜ 糧, levensmiddelen, fourage.

bí ts'ik, ｜ 粟, rijst.

bí p'un, rijstwater (waarmede varkens gevoed worden); spoeling.

bí dzin, ｜ 人, eene fraaije vrouw.

尾 Bí Zie Bé.

uì siú uì bí / *uį* » *uį* » } 畏 首 畏 ｜, van voren en achteren beven (zoo als vrouwen die zelden uitgaan); besluiteloos zijn; iets niet durven beginnen.

微 Bi

bi bi á ts'iò, ｜ ｜ 笑, glimlagchen.

bi bi á k'oà̱ kì̱, ｜ ｜ 見, even flaauw zien.

bi biaó, ｜ 杳, onzeker, niet bepaald, gegist.

bi biaō, ｜ 妙, fijn, klein.

ts'im bi ún ò / » » *in* » } 深 ｜ 奥 妙, fijn (als een mikroskopisch voorwerp).

bi bi á tsuì, ｜ ｜ 醉, een weinig beschonken, aangewit.

hong bi bi á, 風 ｜ ｜, een weinig wind, een koeltje.

ts'îng bi, bâng tà bi, 床 ｜。蚊 帳 ｜, tweede dwarslatten aan de bedstijlen.

ts'iū bi hoe, 薔 ｜ 花, roos.

hoe bi tsiaó, 花 ｜ 鳥, garrula sinensis.

泳 Bī Onder water gaan, duiken.

bī tsuí, ｜ 水, onder water duiken.

tiêm bī, 沉 ｜, do.

ts'in t'uî bī, 稱 錘 ｜, als een gewigt onder water gaan; zinken als een baksteen.

tit tit bī lóh k'ìh, 直 直 ｜ 落 去, hoe langer hoe meer onderduiken, *d. i.*: zich meer en meer aan iets overgeven.

bī ts'i, zich verslikken, geen adem halen.

謎 Bī Raadsel.

tsoè tsit ê bī hō̱ lâng bī / *tsò* » » » » » *ioh* } 造 一 ｜ 與 人 ｜, iemand een raadsel te raden geven.

味 Bī Geur, smaak, reuk; de smaken worden verdeeld in bijtend, zuur, zout, bitter en zoet; van daar: voor verschillende voortbrengselen of spijzen. De smaak of geur in eene uitdrukking.

tsu bī, 滋 ｜, smaak.

k'ì bī, 氣 ｜, smaak, geur van iets. Aard, karakter.

bī sò̱, ｜ 數, smaak, lucht.

ts'aù bī, 臭 ｜, stinkend.

ts'ut bī, 出 ｜, zijn' geur verliezen. Trekken, te trekken staan, aftrekken, (als kruiden).

sit bī, 失 ｜, van zijne smaak of geur verliezen.

4

hai bī, 海丨, zee-voortbrengselen, (als visschen enz).

soa bī, 山丨, wild (gevogelte, enz).

sam ts'oan ngó bī / *» ts'an » »* } 三餐五丨, dagelijks drie maaltijden met allerlei spijzen, (van rijken gezegd).

ū ì bī, 有意丨, vol beteekenis, uitdrukking.

it bī tsoè . . . / *» » tsò* } 一丨作, niets anders doen dan . . . ; voor eene eenige smaak doen, *d. i.* uitsluitend doen.

iá bī, 野丨, vreemde, wonderlijke smaak. Wild, (als hazen).

未 Bī — *bī si*, 丨時, van 1—3 uur des middags.

bī pit, 丨必, nog niet zeker, niet bepaald.

bī pit dzién, 丨必然, nog onzeker.

kè k'ì bī lai é sū, 過去丨來之事, verledene en toekomstige zaken.

Bih

匿 Bih — Schuilen, zich verschuilen; bukken.

bih k'ì, 丨去, zich verbergen.

bih teh, 伏的, bukken, zich verschuilen, verstoppen.

bih hé ing dzip laih / *seh hoé ing » »* } in de schaduw schuilende binnensluipen (als dieven).

bih ts'ih, heensluipen (vreezen iemand te zien).

bih hō, 丨雨, voor den regen schuilen.

bih ing, 就蔭, in de schaduw schuilen.

bih ts'uì, 丨口, pruilen, den mond tot schreijen zetten.

liem k'a bih ts'iú, 踮足丨手, op zijne teenen loopen.

bih sa ts'ē / *bih tièm ts'oē* } 躲相尋, wegkruipertje of verstoppertje spelen.

kē bih bih, 下丨丨, zoo laag dat men er voor bukken moet.

bih hing, 丨行, zich terug trekken, (als eene kip voor den haan, of als zij eijeren moet leggen); ook van preutsche meisjes gezegd.

篾 Bih — Gespleten bamboes.

bih ts'ióh, 竹簟, van gespleten bamboe gevlochten mat.

bih k'o, 丨箍, gespleten bamboezen hoepel (van eene ton).

bih ni / *mui li* } 丨簾, 門簾, bamboezen deurscherm.

bih nâ, 丨籃, bamboezen mand, korf.

bi pán, 丨板, breede stukken gespleten bamboe; bamboe-latten.

p'oà tik bih, 破竹丨, bamboe splijten.

bih ki á, 丨枝仔, een stokje gespleten bamboe.

Bik

默 Bik — Uit het hoofd opschrijven.

bik ts'eh / *» ts'eh* } 丨書, zijne les opschrijven (uit het hoofd).

hó kuì bik, 貴丨美, Uw schrift, (beleefde term).

kuì bik ts'oàng, 貴丨麗, Uw schrift is fraai.

bûn bik é lâng, 文丨的人, fatsoenlijk, litterarisch man.

Bit

蜜 Bit *bit t'ing*, 丨糖, honig.
bit p'ang, 丨蜂. honigbij.
bit tô tsing, 丨陀僧, zilverglid, litharge, (medecijn).
bit pô, 丨房, honigkoek, (die van de honigraat gesneden wordt).
bit koàn, 丨礶, honigpot.

蝙 Bit *bit pô*, 丨融, vleermuis.
bit iā ih, of *bit su ih*, een regtsgeding tegen iemand winnen of verliezen, (te *Singapore* en *Java* gebruikt).

密 Bit *bit bit*, 丨丨, geheim (van eene zaak).
ts'in bit, 親丨, intiem.
ki bit, 機丨, geheim.
tsin bit, 縝丨, solide, volledig (als beleefdheid of voorzorgen).

Biao

藐 Biaó *biaó sī*, 丨視, minachtend neerzien op.
biaó ih, 丨他, iemand minachten.
k'i biaó, 欺丨, minachtend behandelen.

渺 Biaó *bông bông biaó biaó*, 茫匕丨匕, in het niet verzinken, als een gestorvene; ook een ver zeegezigt.

杪 Biaó Seconde. Uiterste top van een' boom.
biaó tsiem, 丨針, secondewijzer.

妙 Biaō Goed, uitmuntend, fraai, intiem.
tsoát biaō, 絶丨, uiterst fraai; zeer intieme vrienden zijn.
k'iaò biaō, 竅丨, fraai, kunstig.
biaō biaō biaō, zeer goed.
bi biaō, 美丨, fraai, fijn.

廟 Biaō *tsong biaō* } *tsó* „ } 宗丨, 祖丨, voorouderlijke tempel.

Bien

免 Vermijden; het behoeft niet.
Bién *bién tit*, 丨得, het buiten iets doen; om te vermijden dat ....
bién lē, 丨勵, anderen aanzetten, aansporen, aanmoedigen.
bién kióng, 勉强, zich moeite geven om, zich inspannen.
sià bién, 赦丨, vergeven.
lân bién, 難丨, moeijelijk tegen te gaan.

冕 Bién *bién liû*, 丨旒, kroon van een vorst.
hien bién, 軒丨, prachtig, luisterrijk.

愍 Bién *bién kī*, 丨忌, geboortedag van een' overledene.

面 Biēn *t'é biēn*, 體丨, fatsoen, fatsoenlijk.
lién biēn, 臉丨, fatsoen.
kò of sioh lién biēn, voor zijn fatsoen zorgen.
toā hong biēn, 大方丨, roijaal.
it biēn tsi kao, 一丨之交, slechts zelden met elkander omgang gehad hebben, niet zeer intiem zijn.
biēn biēn sī hút } *bīn bīn* „ „ } 丨丨是佛, van alle kanten zijn het goden, *d. i.*: met geen van beide partijen wil ik onaangenaamheden hebben.
it biēn ... it biēn .... 一丨。一丨, aan de eene zijde ... aan de andere zijde ...

聯 Bién *bién lóh*, 丨絡, zich vereenigen, aan elkander sluiten; eenparig handelen.

綿 Biėn *biėn iòng* / *" iò* } 丨羊, schaap.

Biet

滅 Biét *biét bò*, 丨無, verwoesten, vernietigen.

biét liét k'ih, geheel en al verwoest.

biét si, 丨屍, een lijk verstoppen.

biét lùn ė taī tsì, 丨倫的事, zaken die de familiebetrekkingen vernietigen (als overspel, enz).

tsaò biét, 剿丨, uitroeijen (als roovers).

Bin

刡 Bín Borstel, -borstelen.

sa á bin, 衣丨, kleèren-borstel.

oė bin / *ė "* } 鞋丨, schoen-borstel.

k'i bin, 齒丨, tanden-borstel.

t'aò mîng bin / *" mò "* } 頭毛丨, haar-borstel.

敏 Bín *bin tsiét*, 丨捷, vlug, kundig, knap.

憫 Bín *lin bin*, 憐丨, medelijden hebben met.

眠 Bin *bin ts'ing*, 丨床, bed.

bin tsìng t'aò, 丨床頭, hoofdeinde.

bin ts'ing bé, 丨床尾, voet-einde.

bin bin, 丨丨, sluimeren.

bin bāng, 睡夢, droomen, droom.

tāng bin, 重丨, vast slapen.

k'ing bin, 頃丨, ligt slapen.

an bin, 安眠, rustig slapen.

kiaò làng ė bin, 攪其丨, iemand in zijn' slaap storen; wakker maken.

sit bin, 失丨, niet uitgeslapen zijn.

k'ùn lòh bin, 寢入丨, ingeslapen zijn.

tsiok bin, 足眼, genoeg geslapen hebben, uitgeslapen

pá bin, 飽丨. do.

tsit tiep á kù bin, 轉眼丨, een oogenblik insluimeren.

bin nih k'oà, 丨中見, in zijne sluimering zien.

明 Bin *bin á tsaì*, 明早, morgen.

bin á ē hing / *" " ē hui* } 丨晚, morgen avond.

民 Bin *liû bin*, 流丨, verbannen; leegloopers, rondzwervers.

bān bin, 萬丨, het volk.

tsú bin, 子丨, het volk, de kinderen (van den vorst).

bin hu, 丨夫, lastdragers (bij een leger).

gû bin / *gi "* } 愚丨, het domme volk; de lagere volksklasse.

dziaò loān bin, 擾亂丨, het volk in tijd van oproer.

Bin *soa sè bin bin*, de berg is langzaam afglooijend.

面 Bīn Het gelaat, aangezigt; fatsoen; een vlak, de platte kant of zijde van iets; numerale voor vlaggen, gongs, muren, spiegels.

bīn maō, 丨貌, gelaat, voorkomen.

bīn sik, 丨色, gelaatskleur.

pì bīn, 變丨, van gelaat veranderen, stuursch kijken.

bīn bò, 丨模, gelaatsvorm.

bīn tē, 丨地, gelaat, voorkomen, (platte uitdr.).

tsáp dzī bīn á, 十二丨仔, dobbelbord.

ts'ut t'aô lō bīn, 出頭露丨, voor den dag durven komen, niet bedeesd, (van vrouwen).

bīn sik bīn sik, 丨熟丨熟, iemands gelaat meer kennen; hem gezien hebben, (maar niet weten te huis te brengen).

tsi so īm bat bīn / *ts'e t'aô » » »* 青頭不識丨, iemand vreemd zijn en niet kennen.

iaô bē ū t'aô bīn, 未有頭丨, nog niet gevormd, gefatsoeneerd zijn, (als een pas begonnen beeldhouwwerk).

bīn hûn, 面紋, gelaatstrekken.

bô bīn bák, 無丨目, onbeschaamd, onbeschoft.

t'aô bīn tíng ê láng, 頭丨頂人, een fatsoenlijk mensch.

peh p'oà bīn, 擘破丨, zich het gelaat open rijten, *d. i*, alle schaamte verloren hebben.

ts'iû bīn, 愁丨, er neerslagtig, bedrukt, uitzien.

koé t'aô oā bīn / *ké » » »* 改頭換丨, geheel en al veranderd (als een huis); ook iemand die van arm rijk is geworden, enz.

toā t'aô toā bīn ê láng, 大頭大丨之人, iemand die zoo gerespecteerd had kunnen worden! (hoe jammer is het dat hij nu . .)

moā bīn ts'un hong, 滿丨春風, er vrolijk, in zijn schik, uitzien.

o bīn ts'át, 黑丨賊, *lett.* dief met zwart gemaakt gelaat, *d. i.* goederen waarvan men de goede en slechte soorten niet gereedelijk kan onderscheiden.

bô soé bīn / *» sé »* 不洗丨, zijn gelaat niet wasschen, *d. i.* zijn fatsoen te grabben gooijen.

lak bīn, 落丨, zich of een ander schande aandoen.

bô hó bīn sa k'oà / *» » » sio »* 不好丨相看, elkander niet met een goed gelaat aankijken, *d. i.* niet op goeden voet met elkander zijn.

bīn kun / *» kin* 丨巾, handdoek.

bīn kià, 丨鏡, spiegel.

bīn p'ûn, 丨盆, waschkom.

bīn t'ang kè, 丨桶架, waschtafel.

bīn tsing / *» tsân* 丨前, vòòr.

p'ai bīn ts'iû, p'ai bīn k'áng / *bai » siû, bai » »* 惡丨像, 惡丨孔, er slecht, boosaardig, uitzien.

toā bīn sin, toā bīn k'áng, 大丨神, 大丨孔, onbeschaamd, niet bedeesd, (van vrouwen).

tsià bīn, 正丨, en face; de regte kant van stoffen.

poà bīn, 半丨, ter zijde gezien, en profil.

tíng bīn, 頂丨, boven. van boven.

sì bīn, 四丨, van, of aan, alle kanten.

hong bīn, 風丨, kant van waar de wind komt.

p'o, of pai, bīn tsing k'iā, 鋪(排)丨前事, de mooije kant voorhangen.

p'o, of pai, oā bīn, 鋪(排)椀丨, het beste boven op leggen; de beste zijde voorhangen.

k'ah ū bīn, 更有丨, meer kans hebben (om het te winnen); zekerder, sekuurder (van waren).

bīn àng, | 紅, blozen.

bīn pì, | 變, het voorhoofd fronzen, zuur kijken.

aō bīn, 背 |, achterkant, verkeerde kant van papier, enz.

bīn lik sik, | 忸 色, ontstellen, van gelaatskleur veranderen.

k'àm t'aò k'àm bīn, 勘 頭 勘 |, het hoofd en gelaat bedekt hebben, *d. i.*, dom (schaamteloos).

蝱 Bīn *bīn t'àng*, | 虫, wormen, (in het ligchaam).

麵 Bīn *bīn pao*, | 包, brood.

Bing

猛 Bing Dapper, sterk, moedig.

hiông bing, 雄 |, do.

iông bing, 勇 |, sterk, ferm.

bing làng, | 人, anderen gewelddadig, overmoedig, behandelen.

bing tsiông / » *tsiàng* } | 將, dappere aanvoerder.

bing làng, | 人, een woeste kerel.

bing hó boē tuì tit kaò kùn / » » *bē sùi tit kùn t'aò tsē* } | 虎無對得猴羣, een sterke tijger kan den troep apen niet fronteren, *d. i.* hoewel sterk zijnde, voor de overmagt moeten zwichten.

bing siù, | 獸, verslindende beesten.

明 Bing Helder, klaar, duidelijk, begrijpelijk.

bing bing, | |, duidelijk.

bing pik, | 白, duidelijk; afgedaan, uitgemaakt.

bing tì, | 智, wijs, wijsheid.

bing kak ting, | 角 燈, doorschijnende, hoornen lantaarn.

ts'ing bing, 清 |, feest der gravenreiniging, (in de 3e maand).

盟 Bing Door een' eed zich tot iets verbinden, zweeren.

bing hia tī, | 兄 弟, broederschap zweeren.

bing tsù / » *tsi* } | 主, hoofd van een eedgenootschap.

kiet bing, 結 |, broederschap aangaan.

名 Bing Naam, goed ter naam, beroemd.

taī bing, 大 |, (welk is) uw (*lett.* groote) naam?

bing ka / » *ke* } | 家, beroemde familie of geslacht.

bing sin, | 臣, beroemd minister.

hó bing bōng, 令 聞, goed ter faam, beroemd.

bing kong, | 光, beroemd, gerenommeerd.

sí tit ū bing bòk, 死 得 有 | 目, een roemvollen dood sterven.

鳴 Bing *bing kim*, | 金, op de gong slaan, met de gong soldaten commanderen.

銘 Bing *bō tsì bing*, 墓 志 |, levensbeschrijving die met den overledenen begraven wordt.

k'ik bing, 刻 |, iemands levensbeschrijving drukken.

令 Bīng *bīng līng*, | 命, bevelen.

niá bīng, 領 |, bevel ontvangen om.

hōng bīng, 奉 |, een keizerlijk bevel ontvangen.

tsin bīng, 眞 |, eerste keizer eener dynastie.

k'im bīng, 欽 |, Keizerlijk bevel.

gik bīng, 逆 |, zich tegen een bevel verzetten.

孟 Familienaam.
Bīng *bīng tsú*, | 子, Mencius, de beroemde Chinesche philosoof (geb. 371, gest. 288 voor Chr).

Bio

描 Natrekken, (schrift) doortrekken.
Biô *biô dzī*, | 字, karakters natrekken.
biô hoe / » *hoa* } | 花, bloemen natrekken.

浮 *biô biô*, | |, rank op het water,
Biô (van een schip).

廟 Tempel.
Biō *king biō* / *am* » } 宮 |, do.
tsó̤ biō, 祖 |, voorvaderlijke tempel.
kūn biō k'i sîn, 近 | 欺 神, digt bij den tempel behandelt men de geesten met minachting, *d. i.* door steeds met hooge personen omtegaan, verliest men het gezag voor hen uit het oog.
sing hông biō, 城 隍 |, plaatselijke tempel voor den beschermgod der plaats.
hé sin biō / *hoé* » » } 火 神 |, tempel van den god tegen brand.
biō kong, | 公, tempelbewaarder, koster.
lóh biō sio hio̤, 落 | 燒 香, in den tempel wierookstokjes gaan branden.

Bo

無 Niet, neen.
Bô *lóng bô*, 都 |, volstrekt niet.
bô ún, | 穩 } onveilig.
bô ún tang, | 穩 當 } onveilig.
bô t'ò tang, | 妥 當 } onveilig.
bô bī, | 味, smakeloos.
bô lát, | 力, zwak.
bô háp gi, 不 合 宜, onbetamelijk.
bô háp lé, | 合 禮, onfatsoenlijk.
bô háp hoat tō̤ / « *tsiaù* » » } | 合 法 度, onwettig.
bô kong tō, 不 公 道, onregtvaardig,
bô sik / *boē* » } 不 熟, onrijp.
bô lō̤ īng / » » *iōng* } | 用, nutteloos.
bô lī ik, | 利 益, onvoordeelig.
bô kaù giáh, | 够 額, niet genoeg.
bô tá̤, | 胆, lafhartig, lafhartigheid.
bô sóng k'oaì, | 爽 快, onwel, niet gezond.
bô laó sit, | 老 實, bedriegelijk, onopregt.
bô iá̤, 虛 誕, onwaar.
bô tiā̤ tióh, | 定 着, onzeker.
bô kaì hān, | 界 限, grenzenloos.
bô soah bé / » » *boé* } | 終, eindeloos.
bô sìn, | 信, ongeloof.
bô kú, | 久, binnen kort, weldra.
bô ts'ut sia, | 出 聲, stom, niet kunnen spreken (van verbazing, enz).
bô tsoē, | 罪, onschuldig.
bô moá̤ ì, 不 滿 意, onvoldoende, onvolledig.
bô kè pó / *bû kè̤* » } | 價 寶, duur, kostbaar.
bô tsiaù tsêng / » » *tsuî* } 不 全, onvolledig, defect.
bô t'oa k'ièm, | 拖 欠, naauwgezet in het betalen.
bô koh tsoè / » » *tsò* } | 再 做, niet meer doen; laten staan.

bô hē lóh } *» hē »* } ǀ 着 落, onopregt, niet te vertrouwen.

bô sioh k'ùi lát, 不 惜 氣 力, zich niet inspannen.

bô tsip it, ǀ 執 一, niet vast besloten hebben om . . . .; niet stijfhoofdig zijn.

bák tsiu bô ih } *bák teh » »* } 眼 孔 ǀ 他, iemand minachten.

bô lò lò k'ì, ǀ 盡 沒, geheel en al te niet gegaan.

p'ah bô, 打 ǀ, vernietigen, wegdoen.

bô giáh, ǀ 額, klein van gehalte zijn, niet uitzetten; niet veel geld hebben; arm zijn.

bô ì bô sù, ǀ 意 ǀ 思, zonder hoop of vooruitzigt zijn.

bô sim t'ang . . . . . ǀ 心 可, niet gestemd zijn om . . . , geen lust hebben om . . .

ū bô lai kóng, 有 ǀ 來 講, kom mij zeggen of het er is of niet.

bô m̄ beh, ǀ 不 要, niet niet willen, *d. i.* stellig willen.

bô m̄ ì aì, ǀ 不 意 愛, iedereen wenscht er van.

帽 Hoed.

Bō *dzoáh bō*, 凉 ǀ, zomer-hoed.

tiaô bō, 朝 ǀ, audientie-hoed.

ts'aó bō, 草 ǀ, stroo-hoed.

bō ig, ǀ 纓, franje aan een hoed.

âng bō, 紅 ǀ, roode muts van mandarijn-bedienden.

toā bō, 大 ǀ, groote hoed.

sió bō, 小 ǀ, kleine hoed.

磨 Tot meel malen.

Bō *bō á*, ǀ 仔, molensteen.

tsióh bō, 石 ǀ, do.

bō hún sai hū, ǀ 粉 師 阜, meelmaler.

oe bō } *e bō* } 推 ǀ, molen.

gû bō, 牛 ǀ, molen waar eene koe in loopt.

sai gû bō, 用 牛 ǀ, do.

tsui bō, 水 ǀ, molen wiens rad door een stroom water in beweging wordt gebragt.

tsoè bō á sim } *tsò » » »* } 造 ǀ 仔 心, het middelste gedeelte van den molen zijn, *d. i.* door beide partijen aangevallen worden, (tusschen stam en schors).

Bọ

妻 Vrouw, echtgenoot.

Bọ́ *tsa bọ́*, ǀ 婦, vrouwelijk mensch, vrouw.

toā bọ́, 嫡 ǀ, wettige vrouw.

ts'oā bọ́, 娶 ǀ, huwen (eene vrouw).

bọ́ t'aô ts'in, 妻 家 親, vrouws familie.

bô bọ́ m̄ sai ts'oeh, poà kun sì niú / *» » » ts'eh, » kin » nió* / *ka kī ngoeh* } *» lī ngẹh* } 無 ǀ 不 必 切 半 斤 四 兩 自 已 齧, heeft men geene vrouw, dan kan men niet in zijne verwachting te leur gesteld worden, en zijn half pond en vier ons (vleesch) kan men alleen oppikken.

ts'oā hó bọ́ kiā hó tsó } *» » « kiō » »* } 娶 好 ǀ 賽 好 祖, eene goede vrouw is nog beter dan goede voorouders.

bọ́ lộ, ǀ 奴, slaaf van zijne vrouw; onder de plak zitten.

bọ́ kiá, ǀ 子, vrouw en kinderen.

畝 *kui bọ́ ê ts'ân*, 幾 ǀ 之 田, eenige akkers rijstveld.

Bọ́

某 Deze of gene . . . persoon, plaats, enz.
Bó̤ bó̤ ê, 某個, zeker iemand.
bó̤ lâng
» wûh lâng } 丨人, do. Deze of gene.
bó̤ dzit, 丨日, op dien en dien dag.
牡 bó̤ tan hoa, 丨丹花, de Pionia
Bó̤ mutan.
厶 oat bó̤, 乙丨, de kromme trek in de
Bó̤ Chinesche karakters.
oat bó̤ á, hoekige draai van eene straat.
謀 List, streek, plan; een plan maken,
Bó̤ beramen.
kè bó̤ 計丨, list, streek.
tô̤ bó̤, 圖丨, eene list of streek op iets bedenken.
tâng bó̤, 同丨, gemeenschappelijk raadplegen, beramen.
bó̤ tsai hāi bīng, 丨財害命, plannen op iemands geld en zijn leven maken.
模 Vorm, gietvorm.
Bó̤ p'e bó̤
p'oe » } 形丨. vorm, ruwe omtrek, schets van iets.
ts'in l'siū hit bó̤ nih k'ì ìn k'ìh laih, 相似此丨予去印去來, als in denzelfden vorm afgedrukt; sprekend op elkander gelijkend.
tsit bó̤, 一丨, een hoop, (als kcemest).
p'ông kaò tsiâ bó̤, 凸至成丨, tot een' bult opgezwollen, (als een luizen-beet).
霧 tà bó̤, (tà bū, tà bōng), 罩丨, mist,
Bó̤ mistig weêr.
慕 Uitzien naar, verlangen naar.
Bō̤ bō̤ bing, 丨名, (slechts) naar den naam van iets verlangen, (als van geleerd te zijn).
gióng bō̤
giáng » } 仰丨, verlangend uitzien naar.
冒 bō̤ bing, 丨名, zich aanmatigen, den
Bō̤ schijn aannemen; den uiterlijken vorm van iets aannemen.
暮 Donker, laat in den avond.
Bō̤ bō̤ àm, 丨暗, laat in den avond.
bō̤ iā, 丨夜, in den nacht.
墓 In het distrikt Tâng-oa hetzelfde als het
Bō̤ Emoische bōng, graf. Komt in Emoi voor in:
bō̤ am
bōng » } 丨庵, huisje bij een graf, en bō̤ tsì bing (zie bing.)
摸 bō̤ pit, 丨筆, het penseel op den
Bō̤ inktsteen afstrijken, uitrollen.
募 tsio bō̤ ping ting, 招丨兵丁,
Bō̤ soldaten werven.

Boa

末 boa boa
Boa boáh boáh } 丨丨, zanderig, korrelig in den mond, (van eten).
磨 Slijpen.
Boâ boâ kng
» kui } 丨光, polijsten, gladboenen.
boâ tsióh, 丨石, slijpsteen.
tióh boâ, 勞丨, werken; lastig, veel werk vereischend.
tióh boâ lìh, 勞丨你, ik heb u veel last aangedaan; dank u voor uwe moeite.
t'oa boâ, 搽丨, werken.
boâ kiâ, 丨鏡, (stalen) spiegels slijpen.
boâ kiâ eh, 丨鏡者, spiegelslijper, schaarslijper.
boâ bák, 丨墨, Chin. inkt wrijven.
siū boâ, 受丨, last of werk te verduren hebben.

Boah

抹 Inwrijven met.
Boah boah he
» hoe } 丨灰, bepleisteren, bekalken.

boah hún, 丨粉, met meel inwrijven (zooals de vrouwen haar gelaat).

boah ióh, 丨藥, met zalf of geneesmiddelen wrijven.

p'óng sai boah bīn, 捧屎丨面, zijn gelaat met mest besmeren *d. i.* zich zelven schande aandoen, zijne eigene schande vertellen.

kā i boah ts'ùi tsik ē, 與他丨嘴唇下, iemand den mond bestrijken, *d. i.* door geld iemands stilzwijgen koopen.

tah boah á tiā tiā / » » » *niā* » } 搭丨仔而矣, slechts besmeren. Oppervlakkig, voor de leus, doen.

ts'ùi tùn p'ê sa tah boah tiā tiā / » » *p'oê sio* » » *niā* » 嘴唇皮搭丨而矣, slechts voor de uiterlijke beleefheid doen (als iemand inviteren, die met de persoon is, die men eigenlijk inviteren wil).

boah piah, 丨壁, eene muur bekalken.

tsit boah á tiā tiā, 一丨仔而矣, een streekje; klein, weinig.

末 Boáh — *ióh boáh*, 藥丨, poeder.

hé t'oà boáh / *hoé* » » } 火炭丨, houtskoolpoeder.

gíng boáh / *gán* » } 研丨, tot poeder wrijven.

sio hu gíng boáh / » » *gán* » } 燒灰研丨, tot asch verbranden en tot poeder wrijven, (als uit wraak).

ka boáh ts'ài / *kaō* » » } 茄丨菜, soort kool.

iù boáh boáh, 幼丨丨, fijn, korrelig, als poeder.

Boáh — *suí kaò boáh*, 美到丨, zoo fraai dat het iemand betoovert, *d. i.* wegslepend fraai.

Boan

滿 Boán — *boán t'ien kong*, 丨天光, hanglamp met armen.

boán tông hông, 丨堂煌, glazen hanglamp met armen.

boán tsiu lâng, 丨州人, Mandschoerier.

晚 Boán — *boán sing*, 丨生, een later geborene, jongere, met minder ondervinding; als beleefdheids formule: Ik.

Boat

末 Boát — *boát tsiòng* / » *tsiàng* } 丨將, Ik; als nederige term door een' ondergeschikten jegens zijne meerderen gebruikt.

bi boát, 微丨, weinig voordeelgevend.

li boát, 厘丨, do.

kok boát, 國丨, einde van een rijk of dynastie.

boát bé kiá, 丨尾子, een onheilbrengend kind.

Boe

Boe — *boe boe bih bih*, ter zijde gaan, wegsluipen.

買 Boé Bé — Koopen; door zijne handelingen of hoedanigheden krijgen, zich verschaffen, winnen.

boé k'eh, 丨客, kooper, kalant.

boé boē ê lâng / *bé bē* » » } 丨賣之人, koopman (een die koopt en verkoopt).

boé pūn, 丨辦, compradoor, hofmeester (op een schip).

boé tê / » *tê* } 丨茶, geschenk, of vergoeding geven.

boé lâng ê sim, 丨人心, de genegenbeid van anderen winnen, of zich verschaffen.

boé hiēn tsi̱; hiēn boé, 丨現錢;現丨, à contant koopen.

boé ki siaò, 丨期數, op crediet koopen.

hiēn boé, hiēn boē }
» bé, » bē 現丨, 現賣, à contant koopen en verkoopen.

tā̱ boé, bô tā̱ boē }
ts'o bé, bô ts'o bē 悞丨, 不悞賣, men koopt wel goederen te duur in, maar het gebeurt (zelden) dat de verkooper zich in den prijs vergist.

boé lâng t'aô, 販人頭, koelie-kooper: menschen-ronselaar.

boé of *tsɛng ts'át hè* }
bé » hoè 丨(贓)賊貨, gestolen goederen opkoopen.

boé soā̱ of *boé soā̱ soh*, 丨線引, door omkooping iets te weten, of iemand te vatten, krijgen.

pao hong boé boē, 包封丨賣, negotieren zonder monster te zien.

boé goá hó, 丨我好, mijne genegenheid voor zich koopen, winnen.

tsoè boé boē }
tsò bé bē 做丨賣, handeldrijvend.

tâng tsi̱ bé tsoá hia, 銅錢丨紙靴, met (valsch) kopergeld papieren schoenen koopen, *d. i.* elkander beet hebben.

媒 Boè *tsiaó boè*, 鳥丨, lokvogel in eene knip.

kiaó boè, 賭丨, *lett.* dobbel-lokker, *d. i.* iemand die anderen tot dobbelen lokt.

霉 Boè *mi̱h tsìm kaò boè k'ìh*, 物浸至丨去, iets door en door weeken.

未 Boē Bē Niet; geen nood; niet kunnen.

boē toā, 不會大, dwergachtig.

oē boē }
ē bē 能否, kan het, of kan het niet?

boē tsoè tit, 做不得, onmogelijk, niet te doen.

boē kì tit, 忘記, vergeten.

boē i tit, 醫不得, ongeneeselijk.

boē saí tit, 用不得, niet te gebruiken; dat gaat niet, dat kan niet.

boē lún tit, 忍不得, ongeduldig,

賣 Boē Bē Verkoopen.

boē hî ê lâng, 丨魚的人, vischverkooper.

boē tsik ê lâng, 丨燭的人, kaarsenverkooper.

boē pō̱ ê lâng, 丨布的人, katoenverkooper.

boē tê sim ê lâng, 丨茶心的人, theeverkooper.

boē tiû toān ê lâng, 丨細緞的人, zijdehandelaar.

boē tsiú ê lâng, 丨酒的人, wijnverkooper.

boē ts'eh ê lâng }
» ts'e̱h » » 丨書的人, boekverkooper.

boē hō̱, 丨付, verraden.

piēn boē, 便丨, gemaakt verkoopen.

pièn boē, 變丨, tot geld maken, verkoopen.

boē gûn, boē tsi̱ }
bē gin bē » 丨銀, 丨錢, do.

tsin tsu boē kaò tsiā̱ niao̱ ts'ú sai
» » bē » » » ts'í »
珍珠丨到成鳥鼠屎, zoolang iets te koop houden (wachten met te verkoopen), tot dat het bedorven is: (*lett.* paarlen te koop houden, tot dat zij in muizedrek zijn veranderd.

sí pih boē kaò sa̱ tsáp dzī, 死鼈丨到三十二, eene doode schildpad tegen 32 cash (per ons) willen verkoopen; *lett.* veel geld voor slechte waar willen hebben.

boē tsáp sè, 賣雜貨, garen en band enz., verkoopen; diversen verkoopen.

boē goá, ｜於我, aan mij verkoopen.

Boh, Bok

勿 Bóh *bóh tit*, ｜得, doe het niet; het mag niet.

kah i bóh tit, 與他｜得, (ik) bemoei er mij niet meė, laat het zijn gang maar gaan.

咯 Bók *bók bók haó*, 咯咯然, slobberen (van varkens).

漠 Bók *p'ah bit bók*, 打沒｜, waterbellen blazen.

木 Bók *bók koa*, ｜瓜, papaija.

Bók *bók dzi̱*, ｜耳, fungus, (eetbare).

ts'ó bók sin, 草｜神, *lett*, planten boom-god; bekrompen (van idée); met weinig in zijn schik.

bók k'aò, ｜戽, groote theepot.

sió bók, 小｜, kleine lijkkist, waar beenderen in gedaan worden.

koan bók, 棺｜, lijkkist.

bók hi of gû, ｜魚, houten visch, waarop nachtwachten en Boedhistische priesters de uren slaan.

莫 Bók *bók hui*, ｜非, is het niet? . . .

牧 Bók *bók tông*, ｜童, herdersknaap.

Bók *bók su*, ｜師, herder, (naam door de zendelingen aangenomen).

目 Bók *bók liók*, ｜緑, index op een boek.

寞 Bók *àm bók bók*, 暗｜｜, donker, duister.

Bong

摸 Aanraken, voelen, tasten, betasten.

Bong *àm àm bong*, 暗暗｜, in donker rondtasten.

ts'un tsʻiú bong sim koa, 伸手撫心, zijne hand op het hart leggen, het zichzelven eens afvragen.

bong tai̅ tsi / *sū* } ｜事, eene zaak aanroeren, beginnen.

bong k'ang, ｜孔, een gat (manier) op iets zoeken.

ts'i̱ mi̱ eh kō̱ bong / *ts'e̱ mė̱ » » »* } 盲眼者靠｜, de blinde gaat op zijn gevoel af, *d. i.* slechts naar het uitwendige van iets kunnen oordeelen.

ìng bōng beh ts'un tsiú bong tioh t'i̱ 向望要伸手｜着天, hopen zijne hand uitstekende, den hemel te zullen voelen, *d. i.* zeer hooge verwachtingen hebben.

Bong *bong bong kiò*, bombammen (als eene groote klok).

莽 Verward, slordig, nalatig.

Bóng *bóng tóng*, ｜儱 / *» ts'óng.* ｜傖 }, zorgeloos, nalatig.

ló̱ bóng, 魯｜, zorgeloos, nalatig.

Bóng Toch maar (aansporend), zoo maar; het gaat nog, het kan er nog door, tamelijk, middelmatig; niet vast gezegd.

bóng kiâ, 姑行, toch maar loopen.

bóng kong, ｜講, zoo maar zeggen, uit scherts zeggen.

bóng ts'ī, ｜養, toch maar opvoeden, (van meisjes gezegd).

bóng t'ouh, ｜且, het er toch zoo lang meė doen.

bóng k'ó, 稍可, het kan er nog door; middelmatig.

bóng bī sī, 姑如是, het is niet

stellig; laat het nu maar zoo; zoo maar voor de leus.

bóng kiâ kiâ, 姑緩行, eene wandeling doen.

bóng kè / *» koè*} 聊過, nog door (zijn dag) komen; te eten hebben, maar meer ook niet.

bóng bóng tsiū sī, 聊聊就是, middelmatig, zoo zoo, het heeft niets over.

bóng beh / *» boeh*} 適要, het is nog niet gezegd dat ....

蟒 Groote slang, boa (?)

Bóng *bóng tsoâ*, ｜蛇, do.

bóng p'aò, ｜袍, mandarijnkleed met boas geborduurd.

bóng kûn, *bóng ó*, ｜裙, ｜襖, do. Geborduurde bruidsrok van mandarijn dochters.

toā bóng ê, 大莽一塊, een groot voorwerp.

toā bóng sì koè, 大都有四處, overal, alom.

網 *tsū taò lô bóng*, 自投羅｜,

Bóng zich zelven in het net werpen, *d. i.* zich zelven rampen of moeijelijkheden berokkenen. In het net loopen.

妄 *sim koa bòng bòng*, 心肝｜｜, gezwol-

Bòng len, groot van verwachtingen zijn.

亡 *biét bông*, 滅｜, vernietigen.

Bông *bông bīng*, ｜命, de overledene.

bông hûn, ｜魂, de zielen der afgestorvenen.

siaò liên bông, 少年｜, vroegtijdige dood.

忙 *ts'ong ts'ong bông bông*, 怱匕｜匕,

Pông in drukte, overhaast.

hông hông bông bông, 慌匕忙匕, verward.

茫 *bông bông biaó biaó* (of *iáo iáo*). ｜｜

Bông 渺匕, (of 窈匕), verwarde duisternis, chaos; verdwijnen (als de ziel na den dood).

t'aô hîn bông bông, 頭眩茫匕, duizelig zijn.

忘 Vergeten, zich niet herinneren.

Bông *bông un poē gī* / *» in » »*} ｜恩背義, ondankbaar voor weldaden zijn.

bông kì, ｜記, vergeten.

蒙 Duister, beneveld; dank verschuldigd zijn.

Bông *bông bū*, ｜霧, duister, niet duidelijk.

bông lông ê lâng, ｜朧的人, een dodderige kerel.

to bông lí, 多｜爾, ik ben u veel dank verschuldigd dank u zeer.

bông lí ê in tsing, ｜你的恩情, dank voor uwe gunsten.

墓 Graf.

Bōng *kó bōng*, 古塚, een oud graf.

bōng pi, ｜碑, grafzuil.

bōng pai, ｜牌, grafsteen.

bōng tsoá, 冥紙, graven-papier.

ts'iū (of *tsiū*) *bōng*, 上塚, aan de graven offeren.

teh (of *hièn*) *bōng tsoá*, 獻冥紙, papier op de graven offeren.

tsó bōng, 祖墳, een voorouderlijk graf.

bōng toh, ｜棹, graftafel; vierkante verhevenheid in het midden van een graf.

bōng tiâ, ｜埕, geplaveide vloer van een graf.

bōng ts'iú, ｜拱, de beide boogvormige armen, aan weerskanten van een chineesch graf.

bōng k'ong, ｜壙, grafkuil.

bōng mo͘g, | 沙, grafheuvel achter het graf.

bōng tsì bing, | 志 銘, tablet waarop de levensloop van den overledene uitgesneden staat en die met hem in het graf gedaan wordt.

boē bōng ts'iū, 賣 | 樹, een boom bij een graf verkoopen (die het graf beschermende, zeer geëerd worden); *d. i.* voor een oogenblikkelijk klein voordeel, zich een groot toekomstig nadeel berokkenen.

望 Bōng *hó bing bōng*, 好 名 |, goed ter faam staan.

sok bōng, 朔 |, de eerste en de 15de der maand.

Bōng *bōng tsōng*, *bōng bōng tsōng tsōng*, zorgeloos, nalatig.

夢 Bōng *bōng ui*, *bōng siet*, | 遺, | 洩, nachtelijke pollutics.

Bú

母 Bú Bó Moeder; vrouwelijk; wijfje, (bij dieren); dat wat voorbrengt, wat iets anders doet ontstaan.

laō bú, 老 母 } moeder.
bú ts'in, 母 親 }

pē bú } 父 |, vader en moeder.
pē̤ » }

bú kiá, | 子, moeder en kind.

ling bú, 乳 |, natte min.

bú i, | 姨, tante van moeders zijde.

bú kū, | 舅, oom van moederszijde.

bú kū á, | 小 舅, de jongere oom van Mdsz.

bú toā kū, | 大 舅, de oudere dito.

bú kīm, | 妗, tante (vrouw van uw oom van moeders zijde).

k'ioh kiá bú } 推 生 婆, vroedvrouw.
» tsiá » }

aō bú, 後 |, stiefmoeder.

io kiá bú, 養 娘, kindermeid.

bú àh, | 阿, kindermeid, drooge min.

toā ti bú, 大 猪 |, eene groote zeug; een groote stommerik.

sat bú, 虱 |, luis.

sat bú tsiâ suī, 虱 母 成 穗, luizen zoo dicht als korenaren.

kang bú tuì, 公 | 對, een paar; mannetje en wijfje.

bú gûn } | 銀, kapitaal.
bó gin }

bú tsī, | 錢, kapitaal, geleend geld.

bú laī, | 利, kapitaal en interest.

sing (of *se̤*) *bú*, 生 |, eigen moeder.

iáng bú, 養 |, voedstermoeder.

dzī bú, 字 |, de 214 klassenhoofden, sleutels; ook de Europ. letters.

kûn t'aô bú, 拳 頭 |, de vuist.

tsih (of *te̤*) *kûn t'aô bú*, 捻 拳 頭 |; de vuisten ballen.

kà bú, 酵 |, gist.

ts'ò bú, 醋 |, schimmel op azijn (?) die men later weer bij het azijn maken gebruikt.

hé bú } 火 |, stuk brandend hout of kool waarmede men de kagchel aanmaakt.
hué » }

侮 Bú Minachten; den gek steken met.

bú bān, | 慢, veronachtzamen, minachten.

武 Bú Militair, integenoverstelling van civiel; ongeletterd. Krijgskunst.

bú koa, | 官, militaire mandarijn.

bûn bú, 文 |, civiel en militair.

bûn bú tsoân tsai, 文 | 全 才, zoo wel grondige litterarische als militaire talenten bezitten.

k'ó bú, 考 |, een militair examen doen.

óh bú, 學 |, de krijgskunst bestuderen.

bú gē { | 藝, krijgskunst.
» *gē*

bú hu, | 夫, een ongeletterde, onbeschaafde kerel.

bú èh bô tsit p'iet, | 下無一擎, militaire mandarijnen zijn niets waard, *lett.* het karakter *bú* heeft den trek ノ niet. *

撫 Bú *bú ióng*, | 養, opvoeden, opbrengen.

bú ī, *bú tai*, | 院, | 台, gouverneur eener provincie.

鵡 Bú *ing bú*, 鸚 |, papegaai.

舞 Bú Dansen; zwaaijen met, schermen; hanteren; beredderen.

t'iaò bú, 跳 |, dansen.

bú kièm, | 劍, een zwaard zwaaijen, schermen.

bú toā ki koan to ê lâng, | 大支關刀的人, iemand die een groot zwaard zwaait, *d. i.* die voor groote zaken geschikt is.

bú lōng, | 弄, zwaaijen met; naar verkiezing handelen met (als met het penseel).

bú tsit hāng toā tai tsì, | 一件大事, eene groote zaak doen, beredderen.

Bú *toā bú ê*, 大 | 的, een groote (van een voorwerp).

toā bú lâng, 大 | 人, een groot persoon.

* *Nota.* Het karakter ter regterzijde van het karakter *bú* is 戈 (een speer), zonder den dwarsstreep ノ. S.

toā bú sì koè } 大 | 四處,
» *bōng* » *kè* }
overal, alom.

bú t'ún bú t'ún, | 春 | 春, in elkander gedrukt, klein van persoon.

嗎 Bû *bû lâ iû*, | 嘮由, Maleijer. Ook spottender wijze geschreven, 無來由, die geene herkomst heeft, *d. i.* een wilde, barbaar.

無 Bû *bû lé*, 無禮, onbeleefd.

bû tsing, | 情, ongevoelig, ondankbaar.

it bû só iú, 一 | 所有, niets bezitten, dood arm zijn.

gán ti bû dzin, 眼底 | 人, zich zelven boven alle anderen verheven achten.

bû hoat bû t'ien, | 法 | 天, om God noch gebod geven.

務 Bū Zaak, aangelegenheden; het moet.

sū bū, 事 |, zaken.

put ám sè bū, 不諳世 |, niets van de wereldsche zaken afweten.

bū iaò, | 要, het moet, stellig.

bū pit, | 必, het moet, behoort.

tsng kong bū, 當公 |, algemeene aangelegenheden regelen (zoo als overheden doen).

Bū Uit den mond proesten, als water.

bū tsui, 噴水, met water uit den mond besprenkelen.

誣 Bū Valsch betichten, aanklagen.

bū kò, | 告, valsch aanklagen.

bū loā, | 賴, valsch betichten.

lām sám bū ih, 濫滲 | 伊, iemand zonder grond valsch betichten.

霧 Bū Digt bewolkte lucht.

bōng bū, 濛 |, duister.

taò bū } 罩 ｜, mistig.
tà » }

kaō bū, 厚 ｜, dikke mist.

bū bū ｜ 𠃊, duister, dof.

巫 Bū Familienaam.

Bun

莞 Bun *bun bun á tsʻiò*, ｜ 然 笑, glimlagchen.

刎 Bún *O kang tsū bún*, 烏 江 自 ｜, zich te *O-kang* den nek afsnijden, *d. i.* iets doen waarvan men later zeer berouw zal hebben.

bún kìng kau, ｜ 頸 交, zulke goede vrienden zijn dat men den hals voor elkander zou laten.

吻 Bún *boah bún á tsʻiò*, 抹 ｜ 仔 笑, glimlagchen.

bún lùn, ｜ 喻, oppervlakkig.

文 Bûn Streepen in hout, enz.; de letteren, letterkunde; litterarisch, civiel, beleefd, fatsoenlijk.

tsʻâ bûn, 柴 ｜, streepen in hout, hout-aderen.

bûn hoat, ｜ 法, woordvoeging, syntaxis.

bûn bɪk ê lâng, ｜ 墨 的 人, een geletterd, fatsoenlijk man.

bûn ngá (ngé), ｜ 雅, verfijnd, beschaafd, beleefd.

su bûn ê lâng, 斯 ｜ 的 人, een beschaafd mensch.

su bûn ngá ì, 斯 ｜ 雅 意, fatsoenlijk en verstandig.

hun bûn, 分 ｜, een weinigje.

sin kʻu tīng hun bûn } 身 中 絶 分 ｜, doodarm zijn.
hin su tuī » » }

bûn koa, ｜ 官, civiel mandarijn.

bûn bú koa, ｜ 武 官, civiele en militaire mandarijnen.

bûn tsiu, ｜ 章, litterarisch opstel.

bûn lí, ｜ 理, beleefd, beleefdheid, beschaafd.

bûn lí ke, ｜ 理 家, eene fatsoenlijke familie.

bûn su, ｜ 書, brieven van mandarijnen aan elkaar, officiële brieven.

bûn su koán, ｜ 書 館, postkantoor.

紋 Bûn *bûn gin* (of *gûn*), ｜ 銀, ongemunt zilver, sycee.

bûn tiā, ｜ 錠, schuitjes-zilver, sycee

門 Bûn *bûn sing*, ｜ 生, leerling.

bûn sing tʻiep, ｜ 生 帖, verzoekschrift om als iemands leerling aangenomen te worden.

bûn bûn ú lō, 門 𠃊 有 路, voor alles is eene vaste manier; *lett.* voor elke deur is een weg.

聞 Bûn Hooren, berigt krijgen van.

sin bûn, 新 ｜, nieuws.

sin bûn tsoá, 新 ｜ 紙, nieuwspapier, courant.

饅 Bûn *bûn tʻaô*, ｜ 頭, soort gebak, tulband; (bij offeranden aan overledenen gebruikt).

蚊 Būn *būn tʻâng* } ｜ 虫, lijfwormen.
bīn » }

悶 Būn *iu būn*, 憂 ｜, bedroefd.

ut būn, 鬱 ｜, niet in zijn schik of op zijn gemak zijn.

sim kog būn būn, 心 中 ｜ ｜, inwendig bedroefd zijn, als na eene scheiding van vrienden, enz. Niet op zijn gemak zijn.

sim koa tsao būn, 心中燥｜, inwendig erg bedroefd; gefolterd.
būn būn tso tso, ｜｜燥匕, do.
tsiáh tsiú koé būn } 飲酒改｜,
» » ké » }
wijn verdrijft het verdriet.

悶 Būn *hák būn*, 學悶, litterarische kennis.
sa tōng būn } 相動｜, elkander
sio » » }
aanspreken.
būn liû ts'iong tô, ｜流充徒, tot verbanning veroordeelen.
būn tsiâ si tsoē, ｜成死罪, tot de straffe des doods veroordeelen.
būn an, ｜安, naar iemands gezondheid vragen; de groeten doen.

Būn *būn pīng* } ｜飯, rijst zóó koken, dat
būn puī }
het water uitgedampt is als de rijst gaar is.

笨 Būn *hô lô būn* } 葫蘆｜, ganzenbord.
» » pūn }

Bút

抈 Bút Zweepen; slaan met een voorwerp.
bút làng, sut làng, ｜人; 朴人, iemand slaan met een slap voorwerp.
bóh tit lūm sám bút, 勿得濫滲｜, sla niet zoo in het wilde.

沒 Bút *bút ióh*, ｜藥, mirre.
put bút, 不沒, niet ordinair, ongewoon (van personen).
bai bút k'ìh, 埋｜去, verstoppen, doen verdwijnen.

物 Bút *būn bút*, 萬｜, alle dingen.
dzîn bút, 人｜, menschen en dingen; knappe kundige menschen.
dzîn tsing bút li, 人情｜理, gesteldheid der menschen en geaardheid der dingen.
bút bī, ｜味, kracht gevende, versterkende levensmiddelen, als vleesch, visch, enz.
iú bút iú tsik, 有｜有則, is er zulk een voorwerp, dan is er ook eene manier om het te maken.
bút kiā, ｜件, voorwerpen.

Dze

撚 Dzê Dzoê Wrijven, (als bij het wasschen van goed); uitwrijven in het water.
dzê bák tsiu, ｜目, de oogen wrijven.
dzê pò, ｜布, een' doek uitwasschen, uitwrijven.
dzê sa, ｜衫, een kleed uitwasschen.
dzê sìh, ｜死, dood wrijven (als eene mier met den vinger).

Dzi

兒 Dzi Kind, klein kind, kindje.
toā kán soè dzi } 大婢小姨,
» » sè » }
vele vrouwelijke bedienden (hebben).
dzi sun boán gán, 兒孫滿眼, vele kinderen en kindskinderen hebben.
pó dzi, 鴇｜, hoerenwaardin.
pó dzi á, ondeugende duivel, (van kinderen gezegd).
kiá dzi, 子｜, kinderen.
dzi hì, ｜戲, kinder-komedie, kinderspel, kleinigheid.
siaó dzi k'e } 小｜科, geneesheer
» » k'o }
van kinderziekten.
hai dzi tê, 孩兒茶, Terra Japonica.

而 Dzi *dzi ts'iá*, ｜且, daarenboven.

字 Dzī Schriftteeken, geschreven woord, karakter, letter, teeken; geschrift, schriftelijk bewijs.

6

siá dzī, 寫 〡, schrijven.

dzī liaô á, 〡 條 仔, strookje beschreven papier, biljet.

dzī t én, 〡 典, woordenboek.

dzī hō, 〡 號, merk, teeken.

dzī tsoá, 〡 紙, beschreven papier.

dzī uih (of *ouh*), *dzī im*, *dzī ì*, 〡 畫, 〡 音, 〡 意, de trekken, de klank en de beteekenis van een karakter.

dzī bú } *dzī bō* } 〡 部, klassenhoofd, een van de 214 sleutels. Europesche letters.

dzī tīn, 〡 陣, eene rij letters.

dzī keh } *dzī keh* } 〡 格, gelinieerd transparent.

tò tiaò bô tsut dzī, 倒 懸 無 一 〡, al hangt men hem het onderste boven op, er komt geen karakter uit, *d. i*: een ongeletterde.

sip dzī hò, 十 〡 互, kruisband.

sip dzī koe, *sip dzī tō t'aô* } *sip dzī ke*, } 十 〡 街, 十 〡 路 頭, kruisstraat.

sip dzī kè } *sip dzī kè* } 十 〡 架, kruis.

dzī sì } *dzī sè* } 〡 姓, familienaam.

miâ dzī, 名 〡, persoonsnaam.

ū dzī (*ū*) *bák*, 有 〡 墨, een schriftelijk bewijs van iets hebben.

dzī iū } *dzī iō* } 〡 樣, soort, aard, vorm van geschrift.

ū hoe dzī, 有 花 〡, voorspoed genieten.

dzī ūn sī, 命 運 是, bij geluk, door geluk.

dzī bák sìng poâ } *dzī bák sǹ poâ* } 〡 墨 算 盤, koopmanskennis, bezittend.

tsoè dzī } *tsò dzī* } 做 〡, een geschrift, papier, opmaken.

lâng sìn dzī, *gû sìn p'ī*, 人 信 〡, 牛 信 鼻, menschen gelooven aan (zijn te houden aan) schriftelijke bewijzen, en koeijen aan den neus.

it dzī tát ts'an kim, 一 〡 値 千 金 één karakter is duizend goudstukken waard.

ū dzī bē bô tsī, 有 〡 賣 無 錢, met al zijne litterarische kennis nog niets verdienen.

餌 **Dzī** Lokaas, aas.

hî dzī, 魚 〡, vischaas, aanslag, vischdeeg.

tsiáh tioh dzī, 食 着 〡, van het lokaas geproefd hebben.

pàng dzī, 放 〡, lokaas uitgooijen.

二 **Dzī** Twee; wordt, uitgezonderd wanneer het als telwoord staat, alleen gebruikt wanneer het getal *twee* achter een ander getal moet gevoegd worden.

dzī tsáp, 〡 十, twintig.

tsáp dzī, 十 〡, twaalf.

dzī géh } *dzī goéh* } 〡 月, de tweede maand.

paì dzī, *lé paì dzī*, 拜 〡, 禮 拜 〡, Dingsdag.

dzī mêng } *dzī muî* } 〡 門, de tweede, binnenste deur van een gebouw.

dzī hun ts'in, 〡 婚 親, weduwe die hertrouwt.

dzī pat t'iu hun, 〡 八 抽 分, in 2 en 8 verdeelen, iemand 20% (van winst, enz.) geven.

dzī ts'iú, 〡 手, tweede hand, helper, assistent.

dzī kaó mî } *dzih kaó mê* } 廿 九 夜, oudejaarsavond; de 29e nacht (Passer malam).

dzī ki, of *dzī ke*, 丨 更, de tweede wacht, van 9—11 uur 's avonds.

膩 Vet.

Dzī *iû dzī*, 油 丨, vet; zacht, glad, als de haren van eene kat.

soè (*sè*) *dzī*, 細 丨, voorzigtig.

自 *dzī tiaò*, 丨 縊, zich ophangen, zelfmoord begaan.

Dzī

Dzia

遮 Overschaduwen, bedekken.

Dzia Tsia *dzia tiòh*, 丨 着, overdekken, bedekken.

dzia iém, 丨 掩, bedekken met.

dzia tsáh, 丨 截, tusschen beide komen, (*b. v.* tusschen twee vechtende menschen).

dzia pè, 丨 蔽, verborgen houden; maken dat men iets niet te zien of te weten krijgt.

dzia hō, 丨 雨, den regen afweren, (als eene paraplui).

dzia tiòh hé t'aô / » » *hoé* » } 丨 着 火 頭, iemand in het licht staan, (van lamp-, of zon-licht).

dzia keh, 丨 隔, afweren (als pijlen).

dzia iû, *siém*, of *ni tsi*, 丨 簷, luifel vóór een' winkel.

dzia sin pai, 護 身 盾, schild om zich te dekken; rugsteun.

惹 *dziá sū*, 丨 事, aanhitsen tot.

Dziá *dziá lâng hoân ló*, 丨 人 煩 惱, iemand grieven.

dziá siū k'ì, 丨 惱, beleedigen, belgen.

dziá ts'ut taī tsì / » » *sū* } 丨 出 事, iets opmaken wat niet bestaat; standjes zoeken.

dzin dziá, of *dzin dzin dziá dziá*, 人 丨, zachtzinnig, lief, (als kinderen).

dziá ē / » *kō* } 惹 禍, zich rampspoed op den hals halen.

dziá sat t'aô tsiū pè / » » » *tsiō pè* } 丨 虱 頭 上 爬, zich onnoodig moeijelijkheden op den hals halen; *lett.* de luizen ophitsen U te krabben.

揖 Eene buiging maken.

Dziā *ts'iò dziā*, 作 丨, eene Chin. buiging maken.

ts'iò dziā kiem pè k'a / *ts'iò dziá* » *pè* » } 作 丨 兼 抓 脚, in éene moeite door doen.

ip dziā (of *dziá*), 下 揖, eene buiging maken.

Dziah

跡 Spoor, kring door een nat voorwerp achtergelaten.

Dziah Tsiah *dziah dziah*, 丨 丨 vlak; gevlekt (van verschillende kleur).

k'a dziah, 足 丨, voetspoor.

tè lâng è k'a dziah / *toè* » » » » } 踐 人 之 丨, in iemands voetstappen treden.

kó dziah, 古 蹟, oud overblijfsel.

bô iá bô dziah, 無 影 無 丨, er is schaduw noch spoor van; het is onwaar.

bô k'a dziah kui, 無 足 丨 鬼, een duivel zonder voetstappen; iemand dien men niet hoort aankomen.

huih dziah / *hoeh* » } 血 丨, sporen van bloed, (bij slagten of baren).

hit è só tsaī sī i è huih dziah / » » » » » » *hoeh* » } 此 處 是 伊 的 血 丨, dit is zijne geboorteplaats.

Dziao

爪 Klaauw, nagels, (van beesten).

Dziáo *hó̤ ts'ut dziáo*, 虎 出 丨, de tijger steekt zijne nagels uit, (als om iets te grijpen).

p'ai̤ ts'iú dziáo, 歹 手 丨, ontfutselaar.

gà dziáo / *gè̤ »* } 牙 丨, helpers (in eene slechte zaak).

dziáo suí, 雌 虎, uitgewerkte hoeken, lofwerk, (aan tafels, enz.).

dziáo á, 丨 啞, Java.

擾 *dziáo loān*, 丨 亂, verwarring.

Dziáo *hoān dziáo*, 繁 丨, verward, moeijelijk uit te maken, (van zaken).

kiaó dziáo, 攪 丨, verwarren, ingewikkeld maken, lastig vallen.

lô dziáo, 勞 丨, lastig vallen.

dzù dzù dziáo dziáo / *dzi dzi » »* } 紛 紛 丨 丨, verward door elkander.

遶 *dziáo king*, 丨 境, alom gaan en het Dziáo verkeerde veranderen.

鐃 *kòng dziáo á*, 打 丨 仔, op de Dziáo cymbaal, groote gong, slaan.

縐 *dziaò se* / *» se̤* } 丨 紗, krip, floers.
Dziaò

soà̤ dziaò, 丨 綫, gestreepte zijde.

dziaò se tō̤ / *» se̤ »* } 丨 紗 肚, nooit genoeg kunnen eten.

抓 Klaauwen, krabben.

Dziaò *tsit bīn toá toá dziaò*, 一 面 多 Dziaò̤ 瘢 痕, vol krabbels in het gelaat.

niaò̤ niaò̤ dziaò dziaò; *pan pan niaò̤ niaò̤*, 痳 痳 瘢 瘢, pokdalig en vol krabbels of lidteekens.

dziaò hûn, 丨 痕, krabbels; voren door de hark gemaakt; plooijen.

ts'iú dziaò tióh bīn, 手 丨 着 面, zijn gelaat stuk krabben.

縐 Slap, slodderig, gekreukeld, gerimDziaò peld.

t'aô iu bīn dziaô, 頭 憂 面 丨, bedroefd, knorrig van uiterlijk.

sa̤ á tsē kaò dziaô dziaô dziaô, 衫 仔 坐 至 丨 丨 丨, zijne kleeren vol kreukels hebben van het zitten.

磽 *dziaô sa* / *» soa* } 丨 沙, ammoniac-zout.
Dziaô

饒 Kwijtschelden, vergeven. Familienaam.

Dziaô *dziaô dzū*, 丨 裕, genoeg, overvloed hebben.

dziaô mia̤, 丨 命, iemands leven sparen.

Dziem

染 *dziém tioh*, 丨 着, besmet worden Dziém (door eene ziekte).

sì koè dziém lâng / *» kè » »* } 四 處 丨 人, besmetten.

dziém tioh si k'ì, 丨 着 時 氣, door eene heerschende ziekte aangetast worden.

dziém sik, 丨 色, kleuren aan iets aanbrengen; verwen, (als het haar).

Dzien

然 *ngó̤ dzièn*, 偶 丨, bij toeval, toevallig.
Dzièn

pún dzièn, 本 丨, oorspronkelijk.

tsū dzièn, 自 丨, van zelf, natuurlijk, zeker.

sui dzièn, 雖 丨, alhoewel.

i dzièn, 依 丨, nog steeds.

kó dzièn, 果 丨, inderdaad.

kì dzièn, 既 丨, alreeds.

t'ien dzièn, 天 ｜, van natuur, natuurlijk.

koat dzièn, 决 ｜ }
toàn dzièn, 斷 ｜ }, vast voorgenomen zijnde om te . . . .

dzièn hō̱, ｜ 後, later, daarna.

an dzièn, 安 ｜, rustig, op zijn gemak.

蹍 *k'a dzièn tiok*, 脚 ｜ 着, met den
Dzièn voet in iets trappen.

Dziet

熱 Heet, vurig, (als een paard).

Dziét *dziét sim*, ｜ 心, willig, verlangend.

laō dziét, 鬧 ｜, woelig, tierig, druk bezocht.

dziét pī̱ }
» pē̱ } 瘧 病, voortdurende koorts.

koà dziét pī̱ }
» » pē̱ } 寒 ｜ 病, intermittérende koorts.

dziét tsìng, ｜ 症, heete koorts.

dziét sià, ｜ 瀉, diarrhoea.

dziét kong, ｜ 狂, ijlen (razen).

hoat dziét, 發 ｜, gloeijen, na eene koù gevat te hebben.

sio dziét, 燥 ｜, in vuur geraken, (bij het spel, enz.).

p'ah t'ih eh sūn dziét, 打 鐵 的 乘 ｜, men moet het ijzer smeden terwijl het gloeit.

t'àn dziét }
t'án » } 乘 ｜, terwijl het nog heet is; van het oogenblik gebruik maken dat iemand willens is iets te doen.

dziét toē of *tè*, ｜ 蹄, vurige looper, (van paarden).

koē dziét koē t'è }
k'oaì » k'oaì » } 易 ｜ 易 退, waar men gemakkelijk meê ingenomen is, krijgt men ook gemakkelijk tegenzin in.

dziét iû, 熬 油, vet braden.

bô iû kan ta dziét, 無 油 空 ｜, geen vet hebben en het vruchteloos willen braden, *d. i.* iets willen koopen, maar het geld er niet voor hebben.

dziét tiá̱, ｜ 鼎, de pan heet maken; heete pan.

ts'in dziét, 親 ｜, zeer intiem met elkander.

toē k'ì dziét }
lē » » } 地 氣 ｜, heete aarddampen.

sip dziét, 濕 ｜, vochtige, klamme, warmte.

Dzih

遏 Drukken, neerdrukken, onderdrukken,
Dzih sterk duwen.

dzih pī̱, ｜ 匾, platdrukken.

dzih tsát, 按 實, stijf indrukken, induwen.

kiông kiông dzih, 强 强 ｜, met geweld drukken, onderdrukken.

dzih soah, ｜ 止, doen ophouden, (een gevecht, enz.).

dzih sit hé }
» hoa hoé } ｜ 息 火, het vuur uitdrukken, zijn' toorn onderdrukken.

àm ing àm dzih, 私 囑 私 託, heimelijk afkoopen.

dzih mêng }
» muî̱ } 推 門, sterk tegen eene deur aan duwen.

廿 In zamenstellingen, zamentrekking van
Dzih *dzī tsáp*, 二 十, twintig.

dzih it, ｜ 一, een-en-twintig.

dzih tsàp t'aò, (eig. *tsáp t'aò*), 二 十 頭, omstreeks den twintigsten der maand.

Dzik

遏 Dzik *dzik ts'ut laih*, 丨出來. uit-knijpen (zie *Tsik.*)

Dzim

忍 Dzím *dzim siū*, 丨受, ondergaan, doorstaan, geduldén.

put dzim, 不丨, niet kunnen zien dat, niet dulden dat.

dzím naī, 丨耐, geduldig, verdragen, dulden.

tsân dzim, 殘丨, wreed.

dzím sim, 丨心, wreedaardig.

dzím k'uì t'un sia, 丨氣吞聲, zijn' toorn inhouden en geen woord tegenspreken.

探 Dzim *ing ts'iu dzim ts'ut lai* / *iōng » » » »* } 以手丨出來. met de handen iets uit een gat halen. (Zie verder onder *Tsim*).

任 Geschikt zijn voor.

Dzīm *dzīm ì*, 丨意, naar verkiezing.

dzīm sing, 丨性, zijn eigen zin volgen.

ts'ut t'aô dzīm taī tsì, 出頭丨事, iets ondernemen.

tsit dzīm, 職丨, ambtspligten.

tò dzīm, 到丨, zijn ambt aanvaarden.

lī dzīm, 離丨, zijn ambt neêrleggen.

dzīm lô dzīm oàn, 丨勞丨怨, ondank tot loon krijgen.

dzīm īng, 丨用, in zijne dienst hebben.

oē sìn dzīm t.t / *ē » » »* } 可信丨的, te vertrouwen, te gelooven.

dzīm moā, of *moā dzīm*, 丨滿, of 滿丨, zijn' ambtstijd uitgediend hebben.

tsiep dzīm, 接任, een ambt over-nemen.

kai dzīm, 改丨, op eene andere plaats een ambt aanvaarden.

sui dzīm, 隨丨, een' mandarijn volgen naar de plaats waar hij is aangesteld.

tsiū dzīm / *tsiō »* } 上丨, zijn ambt aanvaarden.

dzīm sò / *» sé* } 丨所, ambtsplaats.

hō dzīm, 賀丨, een' mandarijn komen verwelkomen.

hiēn dzīm, 現丨, in actieve dienst zijnde.

Dzin

仁 Kern van eene vrucht.

Dzin *nīng dzin* / *nuī »* } 卵丨, door van een ei.

hīng dzin, 杏丨, amandelen.

moā dzin, 蔴丨, hennepzaad.

bák tsiu dzin, 眼珠丨, oogbal.

péh dzin / *péh »* } 眼青 (白丨), wit (van het oog).

o dzin, 丨睛, (烏丨), zwart (van het oog).

ts'ùi k'ì dzin, 齒䶗, tandvleesch.

dzin tik, 仁德 / *dzin aì*, 丨愛 }, menschlievendheid.

put dzin, 不丨, onmenschlievend.

ts'iah t'ō dzin, 赤土涔, schoone aarde.

tsì dzin dzin dzin, 錢丨丨丨, zuiver, gaaf, (van duiten).

人 Mensch.

Dzin *kú dzin* / *kí »* } 舉丨, *lett.:* verkozen persoon; titel van de gepromoveerden aan eene academie.

hién dzin, 賢 人, een wijsgeer.
sìng dzin, 聖 ｜, een heilige, wijze.
ū dzin tsing, 有 人 情, welwillend.
dzin som, 人 參, ginseng, Panax quinquefolia.
tông tsú dzin, 瞳 子 ｜, pupil van het oog.
dzin sim oh tsai, ｜ 心 難 知, 's menschen hart is moeijelijk te kennen, te doorgronden.
dzin ting, ｜ 丁, spruiten van een geslacht.
dzin biēn siù sim, ｜ 面 獸 心, een gezigt als een mensch, een hart als een beest.
siaó dzin, 小 ｜, gemeene man.
tí hā dzin / *tè hē* » } 底 下 ｜, bedienden, dienstboden.
kuì dzin, 貴 ｜, braaf, welwillend, mensch.
bí dzin, 美 ｜, fraaije vrouw.
hū dzin lâng, 婦 人 郎; 女 人, vrouw, vrouwelijke persoon.
taī dzin, 大 ｜, Excellentie (ook uit beleefdheid tegen iemand gezegd.)

認 Bekennen, herkennen.
Dzīn *dzīn tit*, ｜ 得, herkennen.
put dzīn, 不 ｜, ontkennen.
pó dzīn, 保 ｜, borgstaan voor.
pó dzīn lâng, 保 ｜ 人, borg.
tam dzīn, 擔 ｜, er voor in staan.
dzīn ts'in, ｜ 親, uitvinden dat men nog in de familie van elkåar is.
dzīn tsoē, ｜ 罪, eene misdaad bekennen.
dzīn tsing, ｜ 贓, zijn gestolen goed herkennen.
dzīn īm tiòh, ｜ 不 是, excuus vragen (zijne schuld bekennen).
dzin tsin, ｜ 眞, in werkelijkheid datgene zijn wat het moet voorstellen.
tsiáh dzīn, 食 ｜, zich iets aantrekken; zich als eigenaar van iets opwerpen.
gō dzīn, 悞 ｜, verkeerdelijk voor het zijne aanzien.
dzīn t'sò ｜ 錯, zijn ongelijk bekennen; verkeerdelijk houden voor.
mō dzīn, 冒 ｜, valschelijk voor het zijne uitgeven, doen doorgaan.
boē dzīn tit goàh (*goá*), / *bē* » » » } 不 ｜ 得 我, hij herkende mij niet.
kì dzīn, 記 ｜, kenteeken, merk.
dzīn p'iò bô dzīn lâng, ｜ 票 不 ｜ 人, men erkent het lombard-briefje en niet de persoon.

Dzio

尿 Urine.
Dziō *ts'ing dziō*, 淸 ｜, urine.
pàng dziō, 放 ｜, urineren.
ts'oā dziō, 泄 ｜, in zijn bed wateren.
ts'oā dziō bāng, 泄 ｜ 夢, in zijn' droom wateren.
dziō p'è / » *p'ē* { ｜ 帕, blaas.
dziō ō, *dziō kang*, 溺 壺, ｜ 缸, waterpot.
dziō tai, ｜ 滓, bezinksel van urine.
kik dziō, 激 溺, opstopping van urine.
lún dziō, 忍 溺, zijn water ophouden.

sièm dziō, 遣 丨, wateren van benaauwdheid.

ts'aò dziō p'oà, 臭 丨 氣, pislucht.

Dzioh

弱 Dzióh *pī tit dzióh* / *pē » »* } 病 得 丨, magteloos door ziekte.

pī kaò dzióh dzióh dzióh, 病 到 丨 丨 丨, magteloos door ziekte.

p'ah tit dzióh, 打 到 丨, magteloos geslagen.

dzióh sin, 丨 身, afgemat, vermoeid.

dzióh dzióh dzioh, slap, gekreukeld.

Dziok

弱 Zwak.

Dziók / Dziák *kiông dziók* / *kiâng dziák* } 强 丨, magtig en zwak.

kiông pâng kiông pâng, 强 房 丨 房, de magtige en de zwakke partij in een clan.

loán dziók, 軟 丨, zwak, zachtzinnig.

搙 Kneeden, (deeg of aarde); modderig.

Dziók *dziók mī hún*, 丨 麵 粉, meel, deeg, kneeden.

t'ìng tsiah k'a sì koè dziók. 脱 跡 脚 四 處 踳, op bloote voeten overal doorbaggeren, doorloopen.

koe lō dziók dziók, 街 路 溽 匕, modderig, smerig, van een' weg.

肉 Vleesch.

Dziók *kut dziók*, 骨 丨, been en vleesch, *d. i.* volle broeders.

dziók gán, 丨 眼, vleeschoogen, (tegen iemand die oneerbiedigljk geen onderscheid tusschen ouderen en jongeren maakt).

dziók kuì, 丨 桂, cassia, kaneel.

dziók kuì tsí, 丨 桂 子, cassiaknoppen.

辱 Schande aandoen.

Dziók *sià tsó dziók kong*, 舍 祖 丨 宗, zijne voorouders schande aandoen.

siū dziók, 受 丨, verdrukt schande aangedaan worden.

虐 Verdrukken, tyranniseren.

Dziók / Dziák *pō dziók*, 暴 丨, verdrukken; onderdrukken.

褥 Matras; kussen.

Dziók *dziók á*, 丨 仔, matras.

tíng p'ē ē dziók / *» p'oē ē »* } 頂 被 下 丨, van boven een deken en van onderen eene matras, (van bemiddelde menschen gezegd).

Dzióng

嚷 Dzióng / Dziáng Luidruchtig, leven, geraas, leven maken, hard schreeuwen.

dzióng naō, 丨 鬧, kijven.

dzióng ts'át, 呼 賊, schreeuwen dat er dieven zijn.

dzù dzù dzióng dzióng / *dzi dzi dziáng dziáng* } 紛 匕 攘 匕, verward door elkander.

dzù dzióng ê bāng, 紛 丨 的 夢, verwarde, benaauwde droom.

絨 Dzióng Floszijde, fluweel; in fijne draden aan elkanderhangende floszijde; versleten.

tsit p'a dzióng, 一 繼 丨, een kwast van floszijde.

haí dzióng, 海 丨, spons.

tsién dzióng, 剪 丨, fluweel.

dzióng dzióng, 丨 丨, versleten; tot pap gekookt.

茸 *lòk dziòng*, 鹿 〡, hertshoorn.

Dziòng *tsíng kah dziòng* / *tsíng » »* } 指 甲 〡, vleesch onder de nagels.

dzip dziòng, 入 〡, in het vleesch gegroeid, (van nagels).

Dzip

追 Vervolgen, nazitten, achternagaan.

Dzip Dzik *dzip ts'át*, 〡 賊, dieven achternazitten.

dzip tioh, 〡 着, inhalen, vatten.

koá p'oe k'ì dzip, 赶 信 去 〡, met een' brief achterhalen; achternazenden.

sa dzip tsaó, 相 〡 走, om het hardst loopen, wedrennen. Met het front naar dezelfde kant gerigt, (als twee deurvleugels die beide naar de zelfde kant open slaan).

dzip dzip liáh liáh, 〡 〡 捉 捉, achterhalen en vatten.

dzip hè, 〡 貨, snel goederen opkoopen, (als wanneer de prijs zal stijgen).

dzip tsing dzip aō, 〡 前 〡 後, van voren en achteren nazitten.

入 Ingaan, binnengaan.

Dzip *ts'ah dzip*, 插 〡, insteken; zich in eene gemeente vestigen, aan de bewoners aansluiten.

dzip ê gûn / *» » gîn* } 〡 之 銀, inkomsten.

t'aò dzip, 透 〡, doordringen in.

dzip tiû / *» tiô* } 〡 場, een examen ondergaan.

dzip koa, 〡 官, verbeurd verklaren.

dzip tiâ, 〡 呈, eene klagt indienen.

dzip k'aó hè / *» » hoè* } 〡 口 貨, invoer.

dzip k'aó hiòng / *» » hiàng* } 〡 口 餉, inkomende regten.

dzip káng, 〡 港, de rivier (haven) binnengaan.

dzip ts'ù, 〡 厝, een huis betrekken, binnengaan.

dzip pín, 〡 稟 / *dzip tsīng*, 〡 狀 } eene aanklagt, of rekwest indienen.

dzip laī, 納 息 (〡 利), nog voor een zekeren tijd interest bijbetalen; zooals in een pandjeshuis, wanneer de tijd van aflossing verstreken is.

t'sut dzip, 出 〡, uitgaven en inkomsten.

dzip ts'iú, 〡 手, in handen; ontvangen hebben.

tsi dzip gûn, gûn dzip tsi / *» » gîn, gîn » »* } 錢 換 銀, 銀 換 錢, koper- voor zilver-geld, zilver- voor koper-geld inruilen.

dzip gê / *» gê* } 〡 衙, mandarijnen bij een regtsgeding omkoopen.

dzip k'ang iā sī si, ts'ut k'ang iā sī si, 〡 穴 亦 死, 出 穴 亦 死, geene uitkomst in den nood hebben.

ts'ng soa dzip tsioh / *ts'ui » » »* } 穿 山 〡 石, hij kruipt in bergen en gaat in steenen, *d. i.* voor geene moeijelijkheden terugdeinzen.

gò dzip, 轉 〡, naar zich toedraaijen.

dzip hoē, 〡 會, in eene societeit opgenomen worden.

dzip mêng / *» mui* } 〡 門, de deur binnenkomen, ingaan.

dzip sim, 〡 心, tot in het hart doordringen, (als haat).

dzip ì, 〡 意, naar iemands zin zijn.

7

dzip tsí, | 子, eene kogel inladen, (in een geweer).
só dzip, 所 |, inkomsten.
dzip hān lim, | 翰 林, in het collegie der *Han-lin* (Academie van wetenschappen te Peking) opgenomen worden.

Dzit

日 Dzít De zon.
sit dzít, 蝕 |, zons-verduistering.
dzit nih, | 處, in de zon.
dzit sih, | 時, dag, des daags.
dzit t'aò, | 頭, de zonschijf.
dzit t'aò tong kiā, | 頭 當 豎, de zon is juist op haar hoogste punt, *d. i.* in den bloei van zijn leven.
dzit lóh se song ē lâng, | 落 西 山 的 人, iemand even als de zon die achter de westelijke heuvels ondergaat, *d. i.* iemand die niet lang meer te leven heeft.
dzit sit, | 食, dagelijksch voedsel.
ts'ing t'ien pik dzit, 淸 天 白 |, op klaarlichten dag.
dzit dzit, 日 日 } dagelijks.
ták dzit, 各 | }
dzit taò, | 午, middag, twaalf uur.
p'ák dzit, 曝 |, in de zon droogen.
dzit ts'ut, | 出, zonsopgang.
dzit lóh, | 落, zonsondergang.
dzit ts'ing, | 淸, journaal, (van kooplieden).
kin ná dzit, 今 |, heden.
tsā dzit, 昨 |, gisteren.
tsóh dzit, 前 二 |, eergisteren.
tsing dzit / *tsûn* » } 前 |, vroeger, eertijds.
ing dzit / *àn* » } 閑 |, vacantiedag.
si dzit, 生 |, geboortedag.
hó dzit tsi, 吉 | 子, gelukkige dag.
ts'ē dzit / *ts'oē* » } 擇 |, een' gelukkigen dag uitkiezen.
dzit poà po, | 半 晡, achtermiddag.
teng t'aò péh dzit / *tṇ* » *péh* » } 當 頭 白 |, op klaarlichten dag.
dzit àm, | 暮, na zonsondergang.
dzit tsi, | 子, bepaalde dag, datum.
dzit ki, | 期, bepaald verloop van dagen, termijn.
aō dzit, 後 二 |, overmorgen.
to aō dzit, 後 三 |, over-overmorgen.
kaó nà dzit, 九 閃 |, korte dagen in de 9de maand.
ū dzit, 有 |, de een of andere dag.
t'aò dzit taò, 透 | 午, op het midden van den dag.
dzit oà taò, | 晩 午 } tegen den middag.
dzit sió taò, | 小 午 }

Dziu

揉 Dziû K'iû Frommelen, kreukelen.
dziû dziû / *k'iû k'iû* } | | do.
dziû dziû tsoè tsit pé / *k'iû k'iû tsò* » *pé* } | | 做 一 把, in een' bal bij elkander frommelen (als papier).

柔 Dziû Toegeven, inschikkelijk zijn; toegevend, inschikkelijk, zachtzinnig.

un dziû, 温 丨, inschikkelijk, toegevend.

dziû tsit pō, 丨 一 步, een weinigje toegeven.

dziû ih, 丨 伊, inschikkelijk, toegevend jegens iemand zijn.

dziû dziok / » *dziák* } 丨 弱, zachtzinnig, toegevend.

īng dziû hoat / *iōng* » » } 用 丨 法, op eene zachtzinnige manier, (als door middel van een hefboom).

dziû sūn, 丨 順, toegeven, inschikken.

kong dziû siong tsè, 剛 丨 相 濟, het harde en zachte geven elkander toe.

鰇 Dziû *dziû hi*, 丨 魚, inktvisch.

磠 Dziû *dziû ing* / *niû ni* } 丨 磺, zwavel.

拭 Afwrijven, dweilen.

Dziù *dziù toh*, 丨 棹, de tafel met water afnemen.

dziù t'ō k'a, 丨 塗 脚, de vloer dweilen.

dziù ts'ng, 丨 筅, dweilstok, dweil.

dziù sin k'u, 丨 身 體, het ligchaam afwrijven, afdroogen.

Dzoa

若 Dzoā Loā *dzoā toā*, 丨 大, hoe groot?

dzoā tsoē / » *tsē* } 幾 多, hoeveel?

dzoā pù, 厥 富, hoe rijk? zeer rijk.

dzoā kú, 許 久, hoe lang? zeer lang.

Dzoah

暑 Hitte, heet, warmte.

Dzoáh *dzoáh pò*, 夏 布, graslinnen.

dzoáh sa, 夏 衫, zomerjas.

dzoáh t'i, 夏 天, zomers.

dzoáh loéh / » *léh* } 暑 笠, windhoed.

dzit put tsí dzoáh, 日 極 熱, eene heete zon.

dzoáh ták t'i, 酷 暑 天, brandend heet, (van het weder).

dzoáh toē / » *tē* } 熱 地, warme plaatsen, heete streeken.

koā dzoáh sa, 寒 熱 衫, winter- en zomer-kleèren.

Dzu

乳 Melk.

Dzú Dzí *dzú bú* / *dzí bó* } 丨 母, natte min.

dzú ti á, 丨 豕 仔, speenvarkentje.

dzú hiu / *dzi hio* } 丨 香, wierook, olibanum.

愈 Dzú Dzí *dzú ... dzú ...* hoe meer.., des te...

dzú dzú / *dzí dzí* } 丨 丨, steeds, gedurig.

絮 Dzû Dzî *dzû dzû*, 丨 丨, verward (van haren of garen).

dzû dzû t'sáng ts'áng, 丨 丨 怱 怱, dito.

dzû dzû dziáo dziáo, 丨 丨 擾 ヒ, verward door elkander.

dzû dzû sàm sàm, 丨 丨 毿 ヒ, in de war, verward, (als het haar).

dzû liēm, liēm dzû, 譫 語, ijlen, (gedurende eene ziekte).

dzû sù lák bāng, 亂 夢, verward, zwaar droomen.

dzû loān, 風 癲, verward (van geest).

如 Dzû Dzî *put dzû ...* / » *dzi* } 不 丨, staat niet gelijk met...; beter is het....

儒 Dzû — *dzû lai*, 如 來, Tathâgatha.
dzû kaò, 丨 教, Confucianisme.

俞 Dzû Dzi — Familienaam.

Dzun

韌 Dzūn Lūn — Taai, rekbaar, elastiek.
k'iù dzūn / » *lūn* } 趍 丨, elastiek; terughoudend, gierig (van personen).
dzūn pi pi, 丨 卑 卑, zeer taai.
dzūn pò pò, 丨 捬 匕, zeer taai, (als vleesch).
p'è dzūn / *p'oè lūn* } 皮 丨, taai van vel.
p'è dzūn dzūn dzūn / *p'oè* » » » } 皮 丨 丨 丨, ongezeggelijk (van menschen).

E

鍋 E Oe — Ketel, pot om iets te kooken, of te warmen.
e á, 丨 仔, aarden pot.
tè e / *tẹ oe* } 茶 丨, theeketel.
loán e, 煖 丨, tafelkomfoor.
pù e á / » *oe* » } 煾 丨 仔, in een pot koken, (van iemand die alleen is, en er geen fornuis op nahoudt).

倭 E Oe — *e hoan*, 丨 番, Japanezen.
ok kà ná e nìh, 惡 如 丨 子, boosaardig, slecht, als een Japanees.
e lè, / *e k'è* } 丨 犁, knijzen, knijzig (van een kind).

痿 E — *tsu e lòh k'ìh*, 痘 丨 落 去, de maselen slaan naar binnen.

嬰 E Ẹ — *ẹ á*, 丨 兒, kind, kindje.
iù ẹ, 幼 丨, do.

瘂 É É — Doofstom.
sia é é / » *ẹ́ ẹ́* } 聲 丨 丨, do.
é káp káp, 丨 哈 哈, geen mond meer open doen.

翳 È — *k'i è* / » *ì* } 生 丨, een wit vlies over het oog hebben (oogziekte).
bák tsiu k'i è, 目 賙 起 丨, do.

穢 È — *k'it lâng è tioh*, 被 人 丨 着, door iemand beschaamd gemaakt worden; een mal figuur slaan.
è kaò tsìt sì koè / *oè* » » » *kè* } 丨 至 一 四 處, overal heen morsen.

裔 È — *hō è*, 後 丨, afstammelingen, nakomelingen.

的 É — Adjectief partikel.
sìng é, 算 丨, bij het stuk tellen.

個 È — Numeraal partikel voor menschen en dingen in het algemeen.

下 Ē Ē — Beneden, onder; het onderste, laatste van iets, volgend; doen neerkomen, (van daar): slag.
ē toé / *ē té* } 丨 面, beneden.
ē t'ui, 丨 腿, onderdij, het been.
ē k'a lâng, *k'a ē è lâng*, 足 丨 人, onderhoorigen, bedienden.
ē ts'iú lâng, *ts'iú ē è lâng*, 手 丨 之 人, do.
ē taò, *ē pọ*, 丨 午, 丨 日, namiddag.
ē taò tèng, 丨 午 餐, middagmaal.
ē hng / » *huị* } 丨 晚, avond.
kin ē hng, 今 丨 晚, heden avond.
ē pai, 丨 次, eene andere, volgende keer.
ē dzit, 丨 日, volgende dagen.

ting ē dzit, 頂 〡 日, vorige of volgende dag, omstreeks dien dag.

tsit ē k'i, 一 〡 去, op eens weggaan.

tsoè tsit ē } *tsò » ē* } 做 一 下, op eens.

hó ē siaò, 好 〡 計, knap, bij de hand.

hó ē, 可 幸, geluk, gelukkig dat...

p'ai ē, 不 便, ongelukkig dat...

p'ah i tsáp ē, 打 伊 十 〡, geef hem tien slagen.

ìng ē } *hiàng »* } 向 〡, nederwaarts.

ē tsàn, 〡 層, benedenste verdieping.

ē tsat, 〡 節, onderste gedeelte van den arm.

禍 Ē Hō Ramp, rampspoed; onaangenaamheid.

tsai ē } *» hō* } 災 〡, rampspoed.

ē ts'i } *» ts'e* } 〡 星, vonk, aanleiding tot, oorsprong van onaangenaamheden.

ē kun } *hō kin* } 〡 根, aanleiding tot onaangenaamheden.

Eh

者 Eh Substantief partikel.

厄 Eh *eh ūn*, 〡 運, ramspoed.

tsai eh, 災 〡, rampen.

t'oah kè tsit ê eh } *» koè » » eh* } 脫 過 一 個 〡, aan een gevaar, ramp ontkomen.

呵 Eh Hé daar!

噎 Eh *p'ah in eh*, 打 咽 〡, een dubbele boer laten.

tsiáh kaò p'ah eh, 食 至 打 〡, eten tot men er bij boert, *d. i.* overvloedig eten.

t'ǵ eh, 放 〡, hikken.

p'ah eh, 打 噎, een boer laten.

p'ah k'o sai eh } *p'ah uh á* } de hik hebben.

eh sıng } *ik sui* } 〡 酸, het zuur hebben; beschamend, schandelijk.

檜 Éh Oéh *k'ıng éh* } *» oéh* } 糠 〡, stof van kaf, zemelen.

斁 Éh *kaō éh*, 不 快, onwel, onfrisch; verdrietig, lastig van humeur.

éh sin } *oéh »* } 〡 神, in slecht humeur of stemming zijn.

pak tó laī éh éh éh, 腹 肚 內 〡 〡 〡, inwendig onwel, niet opgeruimd.

k'oà kì tsiū éh goàh, 看 見 就 〡 我, het hindert mij als ik het zie.

Em

姆 Ém Vrouw van zijn ouderen oom van vaders zijde.

ts'i ím } *ts'e »* } 親 〡, moeder zijner behuwddochter of zuster.

tiū ím } *tiō »* } 岳 母, behuwd-moeder.

tsim ím, 嬸 〡, vrouw van zijne ooms van vaders zijde.

peh ím } *peh »* } 伯 〡, tante (vrouw van vaders ouderen broeder).

ím á, 阿 媽, vrouwtje, (zoo als men tegen eene oude vrouw zegt, wier naam men niet kent),

kang eh ím eh, 公 者, 〡 者, mannetje en wijfje.

梅 Ém *ím á*, 〡 仔, gele pruim.

ts'iū ím } *ts'io »* } 樹 〡, arbutus.

âng ts'iū ím, 紅 樹 〡, paarsche pruim.

péh bit ts'iū ím, 白 密 樹 |, witte pruim.

葩 Ém *hoe ím* / *hoa »* } 花 |, bloemknop.

p'ah ím, 結 |, knopzetten.

tiah ím, liém ím, 摘 |, 採 |, de knoppen dunnen.

枚 Ém *tih tuh ím*, 叮 噹 |, glazen bolletje met steel, waarop men door blazen geluid maakt.

唔 Em Niet, on-

ĭm t'ang, | 可, het mag niet.

ĭm sī, | 是, het is niet zoo.

ĭm tióh, | 着, niet juist, niet zoo.

ĭm sūn, | 順, ongehoorzaam.

ĭm t'ùn, | 遵, niet opvolgen.

ĭm sai, | 用, niet behoeven, het is niet noodig.

ĭm bat, | 識, niet kennen, onwetend.

ĭm hó, | 好, niet goed.

ĭm tsìng king, | 正 經, onzedelijk, zedeloos.

ĭm sik, | 熟, ongaar, onrijp.

ĭm tih, | 要, weigeren, van de hand wijzen.

ĭm sìn, | 信, niet gelooven, wantrouwen.

goá beh i ĭm, 我 要 他 |, ik wil, maar hij niet.

pī tióh tsiáh ióh, ĭm tsiah oē hó, 病 着 食 藥 | 食 能 好, bij ziekte moet men medecijnen gebruiken, want hoe kan zij anders beter worden?

ĭm t'àn tsit tiép iaó bē oà tsiā tióh k'ì, | 從 此 次 未 晚 就 當 去, nu het nog niet te laat is, moet gij gaan.

ĭm dzīn, | 認, niet erkennen, verzaken.

ĭm tsē, | 坐, een wissel protesteren.

Em *hó ĭm*, 蓬 藨, framboos, (Rubus thunbergii).

Eng

秧 Eng Pas ontsproten graanplant, graanscheut.

pò eng, 佈 |, graanscheuten poten.

iā eng, 播 |, graanscheuten zaaijen.

eng p'ak sí liáo liáo, | 曝 死 了 了, de jonge scheuten zijn geheel door de zon verbrand.

央 Eng *tiong eng*, | 中, midden, midden in.

掩 Eng Ui Bedekken, verbergen, weghouden, niet laten zien, stoppen, digtstoppen.

eng teh, | 住, de hand voor het gelaat houden.

eng ts'ùi, | 口, den mond digt stoppen.

eng iep, | 匿, heimelijk weghouden.

eng p'ī, | 鼻, den neus digt houden.

eng tsáh, | 截, bedekken, verbergen voor.

eng k'ang, 彌 縫, een gat stoppen. (eene schuld betalen).

bak tsiu tsìng dzièn kā lâng eng k'ì / *» » tsui » » » ui »*

目 睭 全 然 與 人 | 去, iemands oogen geheel en al bedekken, hem ontwetend van iets laten.

hō lâng eng teh séh / *» » ui tit séh* } 被 人 | 得 轉, door iemand om den tuin geleid worden.

eng ts'ì mi kang / *ui t'se mé* } 裝 瞽 爲 戲, blindemannetje spelen.

eng sui gû, | 水 牛 戲, do.

厦荷大辭典

ing si hi, | 死魚戲, do.

ing k'o koe, | 鷄伏雞, verstoppertje spelen.

àm ing àm dzih / » *ui* » » } 私囑私託, heimelijk afkoopen.

k'ang ing boē bát, 空|不會密, een gat niet digt kunnen houden, stoppen; *d. i.* schuld, die men met toevertrouwd geld gemaakt heeft, niet kunnen dekken.

ing ing iep iep t'éh hō lâng, | | 匿匿取與人, heimelijk weg stoppen en aan iemand geven, (zoo als bedienden hun meesters goed aan menschen buiten 's huis).

影 Schaduw, lommer.
Éng

bih íng, 伏 |, in den schaduw schuilen.

hioh íng / *heh* » } 兡 |, in den schaduw uitrusten.

siém íng, 躲 |, in den schaduw gaan.

im íng, 陰 |, schuilen.

dzip lâng íng / *dzik* » » } 逐人 |, iemands schaduw volgen, iemand naloopen, (als bedelaars).

挾 Onder den arm houden.
Éng
Ui

íng tsit pao sa á / *ui* » » » » } |一包衫仔, een pakje kleeren onder den arm dragen.

íng kah koéh / *ui* » *néh* } 响胛 |, tegen de borst en onder den arm houden; zich met iets volladen.

袖 Mouw.
Éng
Ui

ts'iú íng, 手 |, mouw.

hiù íng, 裘袂, mouw van een jas.

阮 Familienaam.
Éng

阿 *íng kong*, | 公, grootvader.
Éng

íng pē, | 父, vader.

íng hia, | 兄, oudere broeder.

Éng *kaó íng á* / » *ui* » } 校携仔, kleine lombard, waar men 4% voor 4 maanden betaalt.

向 Gerigt naar, gekeerd naar; het hart
Èng gerigt hebben naar, *d. i.* hopen.
Ui

ìng pak, | 北, naar het Noorden gekeerd, op het Noorden uitziende.

ìng būng, | 望, hopen.

sim sa ìng, 心相 |, sympathiseren.

ìng aū tìng / » » *pai* } | 後次, op eene volgende keer, op de toekomst, hopen.

ū ìng, 有 |, iets hebben om op te hopen.

bô ìng, 無 |, niets hebben om op te hopen.

ìng tsiū, | 上, opwaarts.

ìng tíng bīn, | 頂面, opwaarts.

ìng ē / » *ē* } | 下, nederwaarts.

ìng ē toé / » *ē tè* } | 下面, do.

ìng tsing / *hiàng tsiên* } | 前, voorwaarts.

ìng aū, | 後, achterwaarts.

嚮 *ìng tìng ê lâng* / » *tīng* » » } |侗的人, een
Èng onhandelbaar, ongezeggelijk mensch.

黃 Geel. Als keizerlijke kleur, keizer-
Eng lijke afkomst aanduidend; familie-
Ui naam.

ìng sik, | 色, gele kleur, geel.

ìng nìng nìng k'ih / *ui nui nui* » } | 濃濃去, geheel geel geworden.

ìng ìng sìng sìng / *ui ui sui sui* } | | 酸酸, geel, mager, afgevallen.

ìng âng ts'i péh o / *ui* » *ts'e péh* » } |紅青白烏,

geel, rood, blaauw, wit en zwart.

ts'i̤ ing ts'i̤ ing / *ts'e̤ ui̤ ts'e̤ ui̤* } 青 | 青 |, geel met blaauwe tint, (van het gelaat).

ing gâm gâm, | 金 金, goudgeel.

tiu ing, 籐 |, guttegom.

kiṳ ing / *kio̤ ui̤* } 薑 |, kurkuma.

ing tsing, *hàm ing*, | 瘇, 膖 |, geelzucht.

aó ing, 拗 |, verlept, verfletst (als afgeplukte bloemen, groenten).

ing péng / *ui̤ péng* } | 榜, gele, *d.i.* keizerlijke, proclamatie.

tsióh ing, 石 |, soort vernis, (atal).

ing sai iṳ̀ / *ui̤ » iò̤* } | 西 洋, gele shirtings.

dziû ing, / *niô̤ ui̤* } 硫 |, zwavel.

橫 Êng

王 Êng *làng ing*, of *ông*, 人 |, hoofd, belhamel van een troep menschen.

昏 Eng *bák tsiu īng īng* / *» » uī̤ uī̤* } 目 賙 | 匕, beneveld, verduisterd, (van de oogen).

Uī̤ *bák tsiu o̤ īng*, 目 賙 烏 |, dof, beneveld, van de oogen, (als wanneer men lang in de zon gezien heeft); verblind.

Gai

呆 Gai *gai gai*, | 匕, dom; gedwongen, vreemdklinkend, als een gezegde.

gai làng, | 人, een dom mensch; foutvinden in.

ts'i gai, 癡 |, dom.

gai tsi̤, | 錢, slechte munt.

tsit koai kah tsit gai, 一 乖 配 一 |, een schrandere behoort bij een dommen (*b. v.* man en vrouw).

ts'iú gai gai gai, 手 | | |, verkleumde handen.

t'i̤ ē bû gai toā, 天 下 無 | 大, op aarde maakt men er geen aanmerking op dat iets te groot is

捱 Gaî *k'ò gai*, 苦 |, arm, behoeftig.

厓 Gaî *giêm gai*, 嚴 |, zeer gestreng.

礙 Gaī *gaī bák*, | 目, het oog kwetsen.

siong gaī / *siang »* } 傷 |, kwetsen, zich snijden.

gaī tioh, | 着, in moeijelijkheden brengen, in verlegenheid brengen.

k'oà gaī, 挂 |, terughouden.

hṳ̄ làng k'oà gaī, 被 人 挂 |, door iemand teruggehouden, met iemand opgescheept, zijn.

gaī gióh, | 虐, raar, onlekker, hinderlijk zijn.

bô siong gaī, 不 相 |, elkander niet in den weg, niet hinderlijk zijn,

bô gaī tioh, 不 | 着, niet beschadigd, benadeeld zijn, door.

kūn gai, 干 |, in verlegenheid brengen, een hinder in den weg zijn.

tūn gaī, 但 | . . . maar wat eene hindernis is, wat het lastig maakt, is dat . . . . .

Gak

樂 Muzijk.

Gák *tsok gák*, 作 |, muzijk maken.

gák sing, | 生, muziekant.

dzip gák, 入 |, op muzijk brengen.

gák p'ó̤, | 譜, muzijkboek.

gák k'i, | 器, muzijk-instrument.

kó̤ gák, 鼓 |, muzijk, (blaas- en ketel- instrumenten.)

岳 Behuwdvader.
Gák *līng gák hū*, 令 | 父, Uw behuwdvader.
līng gák bú (*bó*), 令 | 母, Uwe behuwdmoeder.
tang gák biō, 東 | 廟, tempel aan den regter der onderwereld gewijd.

Gam

巖 *tsâm gâm*, 巉 |, stevig, sterk,
Gâm (oorsp. hoog en solide).
戇 *gām gām*, dom.
Gām *gām lâng*, een domme kerel.
gām gām t'ùh t'ùh, dom.

Gan

眼 *gán tsiên*. | 前, onlangs, kortelings.
Gán *hó gán lìk*, 好 | 力, goed, fijn van gezigt.
hó gán kaì, 美 | 界, fraai uitzigt.
gán sîn, | 神, het leven in het oog.
bi lai gán k'ì, 眉 來 | 去 (眉 傳 情), de taal der oogen spreken (van vrouwen).
gán kià, | 鏡, bril.
sì gán, 扇 |, pin van een waaijer, spil.
ka to gán, 交 刀 |, pin van eene schaar.
kong gán, 光 | (工 雅), schrander, moeijelijk te bedriegen.
gán tsiaó, | 鳥, de belhamel, de voorste van een troep menschen.
gán tông k'oà kì, | 同 看 見, gelijkelijk gezien hebben, gezamelijk.
gán k'óng toā, | 孔 大, groote oogkassen hebben, *d. i.* weinig geld, of lagere personen, gering schatten.

淬 *gàn tsuí*, | 水, in het water bekoelen.
Gàn *gàn kèng*, | 鋼, staal bekoelen; ijzer blusschende tot staal maken.
gàn tsì, | 錢, den offerwijn op het papieren offergeld schenken.
koâ kaò gàn lâng, 寒 到 | 人, zoo koud als of men gelijk gloeijend ijzer in koud water gebluscht werd.
líng kaò gàn k'í, 冷 到 | 齒, zoo koel dat de tanden er van ijzen.
put tsì gàn ts'iú, 不 至 | 手, zeer koud in de hand, (als een stuk ijs).

凝* Koud, verkleumd van koude.
Gàn *ts'iú gàn gàn gàn*, 手 | | |, verkleumde hand.

顏 Familienaam.
Gân *gân sik*, | 色, uiterlijk, gezigt.
gân iông, | 容, uiterlijk, voorkomen.

鴈 Wilde gans.
Gān *haí gān*, 海 |, zee-gans.
gān tsí tsng, | 子 磚, kleine baksteenen.
gān pai dzī, | 排 字, de wilde ganzen vormen vliegende een karakter.
paì gān, 拜 |, voor de ganzen buigen; (door bruid en bruidegom als belofte van huwelijkstrouw gedaan).

Gao

賢 Verstandig, knap, knap in . . . .
Gaô *gaô lâng*, | 人, een knap mensch.
gaô t'ià, 善 愛, zeer genegen, zeer vurig beminnen.
gaô sioh, 善 惜, zeer genegen.

---

* Zie verder onder *giên*.

8

gaò p'ièn, 善 騙, knap in het bedriegen, bedriegend.

gaò siū k'ì, 善 怒, driftig, ligtgeraakt.

gaò tsoè làng } 善 為 人, een goed-
« *tsō* » }
hartig mensch zijn.

gaò p'aó gaò tsaó, 善 跑 善 走, vlug draven en rennen, *d. i.* dan hier dan daar heen reizen, heentrekken.

Gap

呷 *hi gap tsui*, 魚 | 水, de visch
Gap smekt water in.

Ge

牙 Kies, maaltand, tand; ivoor, ivoren;
Gè middelaar bij iets.
Gḙ *gé tsò t'aò*, | 曹 頭, de kaken.

tàng gê tsò t'ih ts'ui k'i, 銅 | 曹 鉄 嘴 齒, koperen kaken en ijzeren tanden, *d. i.* harnekkig volhouden.

ts'oàn gè, 穿 |, uitgroeijende tand.

gè tsò ts'i, | 曹 鰓, kaak, kieuwen (van visch).

già kang gè, 蜈 蚣 |, tanden (bek) van een duizendpoot.

hòng sik gè taò, 黃 色 | 斗, diep geel (achteraan den nek van vechtkrekels) en een bek als eene graanmaat, *d. i.* voor geen ander behoeven onder te doen, in bloeijenden toestand, (gew. ironisch gezegd).

toū gè, 舵 |, roerpin.

gè to, | 刀, ivoren vouwbeen.

gè tī, | 箸, ivoren eetstokjes.

ts'iā gè } 象 |, olifantstanden, ivoor.
ts'iō » }

gè pai, | 牌, dominosteenen; ook toetsen eener piano.

p'o gè pai, 鋪 | 牌, domino spelen.

tsoè gè, 做 |, middelaar in een koop zijn.

gè làng, | 人, gildemeester.

gè pó, | 保, dienstboden-bestelster.

ts'à gè è làng, 柴 | 的 人, houthandelaar.

tsò ti á gè, 做 猪 仔 |, commissionair in varkens zijn.

禡 *bé gè* } 尾 |, laatste onthaal aan
Gè *boé* » }
zijne bedienden gegeven (op den 16den dag der 12 maand).

芽 Spruit.
Gè *béh gè* } 麥 |, tarwe spruiten, (voor
Gḙ *béh gḙ* }
medicijnen gebruikt.

puh gè } 出 |, spruiten schieten, uit-
» *gḙ* }
spruiten.

gè tè, | 茶, slechte thee, van jonge bladeren gemaakt.

倪 Familienaam.
Gè

衙 Mandarijnbureau.
Gè *gè ming* } | 門, do.
Gḙ *gḙ mui* }

gè iáh, | 役, bedienden in do.

gè luī, | 內, in het mandarijnbureau.

p'ang pò gè, 蜂 報 |, de bijen vliegen in zwermen uit.

bán tih gè, 蚊 值 |, de muskieten vliegen uit, (tegen den avond).

naō gḙ, 鬧 |, gonzend uitvliegen, (als bijen of muskieten).

Gè *gè gè*, verward, niet weten wat te doen.

li tih gḙ mah, 爾 慌 忙 否, zijt ge gek?

Gè *gè làng*, 拂 人, iemand kwellen; zich door anderen gehaat maken.

藝 Gē Kennis, kunde in een vak; vak, ambacht, beroep, werk.

ki gē, ts'iú gē, 技 |, 手 |, ambacht, beroep.

bô kang gē, 無 聊 奈, geen werk hebben.

it gē sui sin, 一 | 隨 身, iemands ambacht volgt hem overal.

gē tsing dzin pin, | 精 人 貧, een knap werkman is dikwijls arm.

sip gē kiú put sing, 十 | 九 不 成, twaalf ambachten en dertien ongelukken.

ngiâ ang tsng bé gē, 迎 翁 装 馬 |, bij processien, voorstellingen uit de oudheid te paard geven.

ū ts'ut tsi̤ bô kng gē, 有 出 錢 無 扛 |, geld uitgeven maar er geen optogt voor hebben, *d. i.* nutteloos zijn geld uitgeven.

pé̤ gē, 棚 |, stellaadjes waarop verkleedde kinderen bij processien worden rondgedragen.

giâ kang gē, 蜈 蚣 |, voorstelling van een duizendpoot waarop kinderen gedragen worden.

t'ih ki gē, 鉄 幾 |, stellaadje waarop kinderen op zeer hooge ijzeren staken zitten.

tsò t'é gē, 做 體 |, den schijn aannemen iets uittevoeren.

迓 Gē *ū gē,* 有 |, bijval vinden.

bô gē } *» gē̤* } 無 |, beschaamd staan, met beschaamde kaken terugkomen.

Gē *gē gē gē* } *gē̤ gē̤ gē̤* } juist passend in, juist treffend, getroffen.

p'a tiâ gē } *» » gē̤* } het anker houdt.

Gē *ïng bé ló gē gē* } *iong bé̤ » gē̤ gē̤* } 用 瑪 瑙 | |, met een agaten poetser poetsen, (als zilver om het te doen blinken).

Geh

月 Géh Goéh Maan, maand.

sit géh, 蝕 |, maansverduistering.

tsit géh dzit, 一 |, ééne maand.

tsiâ géh } *tsia̤ »* } 正 |, de eerste maand, (nieuwjaar).

géh géh, | |, maandelijks.

ták géh, 逐 |, do.

géh king, | 經, de menses.

géh niû } *» niô̤* } | 娘, de moeder Maan.

géh niû ui k'o̤ } *goéh ui̤* } | 暈, een krans om de maan.

géh ki̤, | 見, roos.

géh kuì, | 桂, maandroos.

géh k'im, | 琴, maanvormige guitaar.

géh toh, | 棹, ronde tafel.

lák géh lák, 六 | 六, 6de maand, 6de dag.

sa̤ géh tsoeh } *» goéh tseh* } 三 | 節, 3de maand, 3de dag.

go̤ géh tsoeh } *» goéh tseh* } 五 | 節, 5de maand, 5de dag.

goéh kiong, | 宮, paleis der maangodin.

géh kng mi̤ } *goéh kui̤ mé̤* } | 夜, maan-schijn nacht.

siú géh } *siô̤ goéh* } 賞 |, naar de maan kijken.

géh i̤, | 圓, volle maan.

géh poà̤, | 半, helft van de maand.

géh bai, | 眉, smalle strook van de maan.

géh toā / *goéh* » } 丨大, eene volle maand van 30 dagen.

géh soè, (of *siói*), 丨小, kleine maand van 29 dagen.

lūn géh, 閏丨, schrikkelmaand.

géh tsi̱, *géh gûn* / *goéh* » *goéh gin* } 丨錢, 丨銀, maandgeld.

sūn géh, 彌丨, voldragtig.

géh laī, 産丨中, de eerste maand na de bevalling.

géh laī pâng, 産房, kraamkamer.

géh laī lâng, 丨内人, kraamvrouw, (gedurende de eerste maand na hare bevalling).

ts'in ts'ik gō̱ géh, 親戚五丨, aangetrouwde familiebetrekking voor wie men 5 maanden moet rouw dragen.

géh péh si soà / *goéh pe̱h* » » } 丨白絲線, maanwit zijdegaren, (met eene blaauwe tint).

moá̱ géh, 滿丨, eene volle maand na de bevalling.

géh bé / *goéh boé* } 丨尾, einde der maand.

géh kong kong, 丨公公, de maan; Maangod; (door kinderen gezegd).

Gi

擬* Gi — *tīng gi*, 定丨, veroordeelen, uitspraak doen.

gi tiā̱ tioh, 丨定着, do.

gi tsoē, 丨罪, do.

gi gī, 丨議, raadplegen over.

su gi, *àm gi*, 私丨, 暗丨, heimelijk raadplegen.

gi tō̱, 丨徒, tot verbanning veroordeelen.

gi tsám, 丨斬, tot onthoofding veroordeelen.

語 Gí — *bóh tit gi lai gi k'i*, 勿得丨來丨去, gekscheert of stoeit niet zoo met elkander.

gi gi gē gē, 丨丨吃乜, stoeijen, gekheid maken.

疑 Gi — Twijfelen, aarzelen; achterdocht, vermoeden hebben.

gi ngai̱, 丨惑, twijfelen, achterdocht hebben.

giaû gi, 撓丨, do.

gi sim tāng, 丨心重, achterdochtig, kwaaddenkend.

bô gi gō̱, 不丨誤, geen vermoeden op iets hebben, niet gedacht hebben dat . . . . . onverwachts.

ti gi, 遲丨, aarzelend dralen.

gi sing koaì, 丨生怪, achterdocht doet vreemde (denkbeelden) ontstaan.

to gi ê lâng, 多丨的人, een zeer achterdochtig mensch.

gi kui gi koaì gi tsaó tuì ts'át k'ìh,

丨鬼丨怪丨走對賊去,

eerst spoken verdenken en van daar achterdocht op dieven krijgen, (van iemand die 's nachts geruis hoort).

ts'i̱ gi, 生丨, twijfelachtig, ongerust worden, enz. (als in een groot onbewoond huis).

gi tsiah bóh tiāng, *tiāng tsiah bóh gi*,

丨就勿重重就勿丨,

twijfelt men aan iemands soliditeit, dan moet men hem niets opdragen; draagt men hem iets op, dan moet men niet aan hem twijfelen.

儀 Gi — Regels, vormen waaraan men zich voor zijn stand of fatsoen te houden heeft, welvoegelijkheid, decorum.

* Zie verder onder *gú*.

sit gi, 失 ｜, tegen de welvoegelijkheid handelen.

ui gi, 威 ｜, waardigheid, decorum.

koa gi, 官 ｜, het decorum van een magistraat.

lé gi, 禮 ｜, dat waaraan men volgens de beleefdheid gehouden is: geschenken.

tsoeh gi, 節 ｜, geschenken bij jaarfeesten (aan meesters, enz.)

tsì gi, 贄 ｜, geschenken bij een bezoek aan hoogeren.

宜 Gi Betamelijk, billijk, met de omstandigheden overeenkomen.

háp gi, 合 宜, betamelijk.

pān gi, 便 ｜, goedkoop.

in si tsè gi / » » *tsì* » } 因 時 制 ｜, zich naar den tijd, de omstandigheden, regelen.

siang gi, 相 ｜, betamelijk, overeenkomend.

義 Gī Betamelijk, billijk, billijkheid; gevoel van pligt en billijkheid; ten behoeve van het algemeene welzijn, (als vrijwilligers, armscholen, enz.) publiek; aangenomen (als kinderen).

put gī, 不 ｜, onbetamelijk, onbillijk.

so en k'ing tsai tiōng gī, 疎(輕)財重 ｜, schatten min-, en billijkheid hoog-achten.

bōng un poē gī / » *in* » » } 忘 恩 背 ｜, snood ondankbaar voor ontvangene weldaden.

ko un hū gī / » *in* » » } 辜 恩 負 ｜, do.

ū tsing ū gī, 有 情 有 ｜, gevoel voor erkentelijkheid en betamelijkheid hebben.

ū dzin gī ê lâng, 有 仁 ｜ 的 人, iemand die gevoel van billijkheid bezit.

dzin gī tsî, 仁 ｜ 錢, weldadigheids geld.

tsing gī, 情 ｜, gevoel van billijkheid, menschlievendheid.

gī iòng, ｜ 勇, vrijwilligers

gī ping, ｜ 兵, do.

gī óh, ｜ 學, publieke, kostelooze, school.

gī ts'eng, ｜ 倉, publiek weldadigheids graan-pakhuis, (waaruit de overheden in tijd van gebrek graan aan het volk verdeelen.

tiong gī, 忠 ｜, opregt, getrouw, eerlijk.

gī t'iông, ｜ 塚, publieke armenbegraafplaats.

gī tsú, ｜ 子, aangenomen zoon.

gī hū, ｜ 父, aangenomen pleegvader.

kiet gī tsoè hia tī / » » *tsò* » » } 結 ｜ 爲 兄 弟, zich als elkanders broeders aannemen, broederschap zweren.

誼 Gī *sè gī* / *sì* » } 世 ｜, van oudsher goede vrienden geweest.

議 Gī Spreken over, handelen over, bespreken, bepraten, beraadslagen; na beraadslaging tot een besluit komen, bepalen.

gī lūn, ｜ 論, spreken, handelen over, bespreken.

gī hô, ｜ 和, over de vrede onderhandelen.

gī hoē, ｜ 會, in eene vergadering bespreken.

gī tiā, ｜ 定, tot eene uitspraak over eene misdaad komen.

kong gī, 公 ｜, in het publiek gezamenlijk bespreken, bepalen.

嘻 Gī *gī gī ts'iò*, ｜ ｜ 笑, glimlagchen, goechelen (van genoegen).

Gia

抬 Già — Dragen, op de schouders dragen (zonder juk).

già hè / *» hoè* } | 貨, goederen dragen.

già kang, | 傭, lastdrager.

già kè / *» kẹ* } 荷枷, de cangue dragen.

già t'i̤ lai k'àm làng, 舁天來蓋人, iemand met den hemel bedekken, *d. i.* iets zwaars ten laste leggen.

già sin sè / *» » sì* } 舁身勢, een stevigen steun in iemand hebben.

t'ao già mìng si̤, taò ī̀m tiòh ping, / *» » mui̤ » » » »* 偷 | 門扇下不着邊, heimelijk iemands deurvleugel wegdragen en ze aan de verkeerde kant inzetten, *d, i.* door eene fout zijne bedriegerij laten uitkomen.

già lān ī̀m tsai tìng king / *» » » » tui̤ kan* } | 羼不知轉肩, niet naar de omstandigheden weten te handelen, niet weten te geven en te nemen, (lage uitdrukking).

già of *,già hiṳ* / *ngià̤ ang* of *hio̤* } | 香, | 翁, eene processie houden.

ui̤ sui̤ già toā pè è kam tsià, 黃瘆舁大把的甘蔗, geelzucht hebben en een groote bos suikerriet willen dragen, *d.i.* boven zijne krachten willen handelen.

già i, | 椅, een stoel dragen.

鵝 Già Gò — Gans.

Già — *la già*, groote spin.

蜈 Già — *già kang*, | 蚣, duizendpoot.

呀 Già — *già lan bi*, | 蘭米, gedroogde cochenille.

Gà — *già lan sik*, | 蘭色, cochenille-kleurig.

Giah

挖 Giah — *giah k'ui*, | 開, openpulken.

giah mìng / *» mui̤* } | 門, eene deur uittillen.

giah ts'oṳ, giah ts'ì, 挑刺, een splinter uithalen.

giah soa kin, | 沙筋, iemand die eene beroerte heeft aderlaten.

giah sìng poà̤ / *» sui̤ »* } | 算盤, op het rekenbord rekenen.

額 Giáh — *kaò giáh*, 够 |, genoeg.

to giáh, 多 |, goedkoop, veel voor weinig geld.

hó giáh, ū giáh, 好 |, 有 |, rijk.

ū giáh siaò, 多 | 數, er is genoeg om ieder zijn deel te geven.

giáh goā, | 外, fourier.

sit giáh, k'oat giáh, 失 |, 鈌 |, te kort zijn in hoeveelheid.

tsiok giáh, 足 |. genoeg, voldoende.

giáh siaò, | 數, bepaald aantal, hoeveelheid.

sìng làng giáh tiā tiā / *sui̤ » » niā tiā* } 數人 | 而矣, nietswaardig mensch, slechts voor een mensch tellen.

làng giáh, 人數, hoeveelheid menschen, personeel.

k'ièm làng giáh, 鈌人 |, personee te kort (noodig hebben).

kè giáh / *koè »* } 過 |, toegift boven de bepaalde hoeveelheid.

ts'ut giáh, 出 |, do.

hūn giáh, 分 丨, respectievelijk deel.
hūn tsîng giáh, 分 前 丨, do.
tsaī giáh, 在 丨, voltallig.

Giak

謔 *giák lâng*, 丨 人, iemand voor den
Giák gek houden, het tegenovergestelde
Giét van iemands wezenlijke toestand zeggen.
Giak *gô giák giák haô* / *» giét giét »* } de ganzen gaggelen, kakelen.

Giang

鈴 *giang á*, 丨 子, schel, tafelschel.
Giang *giang á tsu*, 丨 仔 珠, klepel in eene bel.
giang hō i tsai, 丨 與 伊 知, iets even aanroeren, iemand een weinig met iets bekend maken.
ts'iù hè siū lai giang giang / *» hoê siō » » »* } 倩 和 尙 來 丨 丨, een Boeddhistische priester roepen om bij het luiden van zijn bel eene plaats te zuiveren, enz.
gin gin giang giang, rinkelen, tinkelen (als schelletjes).
Giàng *giàng kà k'iàng*, 敢 且 果, boosaardig, hardnekkig.
giàng tsa bó, 潑 婦, eene boosaardige vrouw.
giang bé, 駻 馬, een wild paard, (scheldw.)
仰 *giàng k'i*, 丨 齒, vooruitstekende
Giàng tanden.
tsióh t'aô giàng giàng, 石 鏻 匕, vooruitstekende rotsen.
ts'uì k'i giàng giàng, 嘴 齒 丨 丨, uitstekende tanden.
ts'uì ts'iu giàng giàng / *» » ts'àng ts'àng* } 嘴 鬚 丨 丨, opstaande snor.

Giem

儼 *giém dzièn*, 丨 然, veel gelijkende op;
Giém even als.
嚴 Gestreng. Familienaam.
Giém *giêm giêm*, 丨 丨, gestreng.
giêm ân, 丨 緊, do.
giêm kin, 丨 謹, do.
ui giêm, 威 丨, gestreng uitzien.
giêm hing, 丨 刑, gestreng behandelen (niet vergeven).
giêm gai, 丨 厓, zeer streng.
giêm līng, 丨 命, streng bevel.
giêm kìm, 丨 禁, streng verbieden, tegengaan.
giêm hát, 丨 劾, anderen niet genoeg geven, overdreven zuinig.
giêm lô ông, 閻 羅 王, god in de onderwereld, (Yamaradja).
oáh giêm lô, 活 閻 羅, een gestrenge mandarijn, (*lett.* een levende Yamaradja).
giêm koŋ hú ts'ut kaō ts'át, 丨 官 府 出 厚 賊, een gestrenge mandarijn veroorzaakt (door zijn gebrek aan zachtzinnigheid) vele dieven.
giêm kà sī, 丨 教 示, strenge opvoeding geven.
巖 *soŋ giêm*, 山 丨, bergtempel.
Giêm
驗 Schouwen, nazien, onderzoeken, visi-
Giēm teren; probatum, op de proef goed bevonden (als medicijnen), de verwachte uitwerking hebben; uitkomen, (als eene voorspelling).
giēm k'oà, 丨 看, nazien, onderzoeken.
siòng giēm / *siàng »* } 相 丨, schouwing houden.

tsa giēm / *tse* » } 查 |, onderzoeken, visiteren.

giēm si, | 屍, lijkschouwing houden.

giēm siong / » *siang* } | 傷, iemands wonden onderzoeken.

giēm pī / » *pē* } | 病, eene ziekte schouwen, (als van soldaten).

giēm hè / » *hoè* } | 貨, goederen nazien, visiteren.

giēm tsùn, | 船, een schip visiteren.

poà giēm, *poà bò giēm*, 半 | 半 不 |, ten halve visiteren; slechts ten halve de gewachte uitwerking hebben.

tsing giēm / *tsui* » } 全 |, volkomen de verwachte uitwerking hebben.

ìng giēm, 應 |, zeker genezend, probatum; uitkomen.

boē giēm, *ĭm giēm* / *bē* » } 未 |, 唔 |, geene goede uitwerking hebben, (van medicijnen).

haō giēm, 效 |, vervuld worden, uitkomen (als eene voorspelling).

king giēm kui nā làng hó, 經 | 幾 個 人 好, het heeft reeds bij verscheidene lieden goede uitwerking gehad, (van medicijnen).

Gien

頑 **Gién** Brutaal, stijfhoofdig.

gién t'aô, | 頭, brutaal, de belhamel.

gién tsiaó. | 鳥, belhamel.

癮 **Gièn** Sterk verlangen naar, verslaafd aan.

gièn tsî, | 錢, vurig naar geld verlangen.

gièn kaò laò noā, | 到 流 涎, van verlangen watertanden.

gièn ts'īng, | 穿, zich gaarne fraai willen aankleeden.

kan gièn, *kan ta gièn*, *k'ang gièn*, 乾 |, 乾 焦 |, 空 |, vruchteloos naar iets verlangen.

kè gièn, 過 | / *koé gièn*, 改 | } zijne sterke lust naar iets bevredigd hebben.

gièn tsiú, | 酒, verslaafd aan wijn.

gièn a p'ièn, | 鴉 片 / *a p'ièn gièn*, 鴉 片 | } verslaafd aan opium.

gièn kiaó, | 賭, aan dobbelspel verslaafd.

gièn boeh k'oà, | 要 看, sterk verlangen iets te zien.

瘦 **Gièn** Mager, dun.

sán gièn, 消 |, mager, ingevallen.

gièn sien, | 仙, mager als een geraamte, (door opium).

iao koà gièn, 飢 寒 |, hongerig, koud en mager.

言 **Gièn** **Gàn**

sing gièn tsō gú / *se gàn* » *gí* } 生 | 造 語, leugens verzinnen.

to gièn ê làng, 多 | 之 人, een veelpraatsch.

put gièn siong, 不 | 相, men behoeft dat er niet bij te zeggen, (iedereen weet dat).

gièn gú t'ong / *gàn gí* » } | 語 通, van te voren met iemand raadplegen wat te zeggen.

唁 **Gièn** **Gin** **Giēn**

bák tsiu gièn gièn, 目 睭 | |, groote oogen opzetten.

giēn giēn nah, in uiterste armoede zijn.

song giēn giēn, do.

súh giēn, stomp, dof (van aard).

súh giēn ti ko kaò, do.
tsiáh súh giēn, van onbetamelijke inkomsten leven, (als bedienden in bordeelen).

Giep

業 Giép Bezigheid, beroep; eigendom, bezitting; aanduider van den verleden tijd.
ke giép, 家 |, bezigheid, broodwinning; bezitting.
lô giép, 勞 |, met werk overladen, druk bezet.
giép tsú } | 主. eigenaar.
» *tsi* }
bô ts'ân t'ó kon giép, 無田貰官 |. zelf geen land bezittende, het van de overheden ter leen vragen.
tso giép, 租 |. eene bezitting die men verhuurt.
kong giép, 公 |. algemeen eigendom.
su giép, 私 |. privaat eigendom.
sū giép, 事 |, bezigheden, zaken.
king king giép giép ê lâng, 兢兢 || 的人. een ijverig man.
tsiáh giép, 食 |, van zijne bezittingen, interest, leven.
koán giép, 管 |, zijne bezittingen beheeren.
giép i king, | 已經, alreeds ge...

㥦 Giép Moeijelijk, zorgvol; hevig, sterk.
giép miā, 命 蹇, een zorgvol leven.
giép tsè } | 債. ongelukkig lot.
» *tsè* }
tsoè lâng put tsi giép, 做人不止 |, een zwaar, rusteloos, leven hebben.
tsûn siū hong giép, 船受風 |, het schip kreeg een hevigen wind.
hong siu giép, 風太 |, de wind is te hevig.

Giet

蝎 Giet *giét lá*, | 子, scorpioen.

齧 Giet *giet tsit k'ang*, | 一 空. een gat inbijten, (als insekten).
sik sut giet giet háó, 蟋蟀 || 吼. de krekel piept.

孽 Giét Orspr. kind van eene bijzit, onwettig; van daar: ondeugend, slecht, zedeloos, wonderlijk, wonderbaarlijk (in slechten zin); de gevolgen van slechte, onbehoorlijke handelingen.
giét tsú kiá, | 子孩, ondeugende, zedelooze kinderen.
giét ê gín á, 狡 猾 兒. een ondeugend, zedeloos kind.
tsok giét, 作 |, slecht, zedeloos, zijn.
giét ê taī tsì, 邪 事, onbehoorlijke dingen.
giét bút, | 物. ondeugend, slecht, wezen of ding.
giét oē, 䜊 語, zedelooze gezegden.
iao giét, 妖 |, wonderlijke (dingen).
giét siet, | 設, wonderbaarlijke instellingen.
giét tiaō, | 兆, wonderlijk, slecht, voorteeken.
giét sin, | 神, in slecht humeur.
oan giét, 寃 |, gedurige twist.
kiet oan giét, 結 寃 |. reden tot gedurigen twist.
tsū tsok giét, 自 作 |, rampen, kwalen, die men zich zelven op den hals haalt.

Giét *giét kièn*, 踢 毽, een vederbal met de handen voortslaan.

9

Gih

屹 *hân gih gih*, 寒｜｜, bibberend (als van koude); kleingeestig, bekrompen.
Gih
Gíh *ts'iah gih gih* / *» gih gih* } 赤｜｜, naakt arm.

sòng gih gih / *» gih gih* } 貧｜｜, dood arm.

lí bóh tit hân gih ê iū, 你勿得寒｜的樣, stel U niet zoo kil (bekrompen) aan.

Gíh *gih tsióh*, 疊石, steenen opstapelen, (van steenen gebouwen).

gih ts'â lóh k'ì sio / *kih » » » »* } ｜柴落去燒, hout kruiselings opstapelen om te verbranden.

Gik

逆
Gik Zich verzetten tegen, handelen tegenstrijdig met ....; oproer maken, afvallig worden; tegen, als stroom of wind.

gik t'ien só hing / *» » sé »* } ｜天所行, zich verzetten tegen de handelingen des hemels, onnatuurlijke dingen doen.

gik tsí, ｜旨, tegen het keizerlijk bevel aan handelen.

hing gik, 橫｜, onbezonnen, ruw, te werk gaan.

ngó̤ gik, 忤｜, weêrbarstig, ongehoorzaam.

poē gik, 背｜, oproer maken, afvallen.

gik laô, ｜流, tegen stroom.

gik hong, ｜風, tegenwind.

tò gik ts'ut laih, 倒｜出來, terugkomen, (als spijzen wanneer men zich verslikt).

gik tsú, ｜子, weêrbarstige, slechte zoon.

玉 Edele steen.
Gik
Giók *gik tsióh* / *giók »* } ｜石, do.

kim ki gik hióh, 金枝｜葉, een aller fatsoenlijkst mensch, *lett.* gouden takken, en edelsteenen bladeren.

獄 Gevangenis.
Gik
Gák *ka gik* / *» gák* } 監｜, do.

tē gik / *» gák* } 地｜, hel.

Gim

擬 Het er voor houden, iets voorzien, voorspellen.
Gim
Gí *gim gī* / *gí gī* } ｜議, bedenken, het er voor houden.

gim tsit ê taī tsì / *gí » » » »* } ｜一事, iets voorspellen.

kā i gim teh / *» » gí »* } 與他｜的, iemands toekomst voorspellen.

gim i k'oà tseh / *gí » » »* } ｜伊看節, iemand polsen, peilen.

錦 Gebloemde zijde, gebloemd, fraai, weelderig, tot verfraaijing aangebragt, als vleitaal.
Gim
Kim *gim tiû* / *kim »* } ｜綢, gebloemde pongee.

gim lòng, ｜囊, zijden enveloppe, (waarin geheime dépèches verzonden worden).

gim p'ē / *kim p'oē* } ｜被, gebloemde, geborduurde deken.

gim siù kang san, ｜繡江山, een bloeijend rijk.

ū hoe ū gim / *» hoa » kim* } 有花有｜, fraai smaakvol.

gim k'ik, 南曲, liefelijke muzijk.

hoa gim tē / *» kim »* } 花｜地, wereldsche, verkwistende, plaats.

p'ah ts'ùi gim, 打 碎 |, over koetjes en kalfjes praten.

koe gim ts'ùi } 花 | 觜, fraai,
hoa kim »
maar ongemeend, spreken.

sip gim tó, 什 | 斗, fancy-teekening, (als nabootsing van oude versleten boeken).

pièn tē gim, 遍 地 茵, mos; berekening op den grond, of een stuk papier, opgemaakt.

gim ló, | 饒 of 漢 席, mengsel van vleesch, visch, enz.; (kimlo).

gim tsoâ, | 蛇, groote slang.

tsit gim é hoe } 一 | 的 花, een
» *kim* » *hoa*
takje bloemen. (van een bloemtros).

tsit gim kè tsit gim } 一 | 過 一 |,
» *kim koè* » *kim*
het eene bloemblad na het andere.

ki gim p'oē tà ke lam, 已 | 被 罩 雞 籠, een geborduurde deken over eene kippenmand doen *d. i.* eene vlag op een modderschuit.

吟 Zingen, (van menschen en vogels).
Gim *gim si*, | 詩, een vers zingen.

tim gim, 沉 |, overdenken, neuriën.

gim gô, | 哦, neuriën.

li teh gim goàh, 爾 乃 嘲 我, gij plaagt mij.

tsit ki ts'ùi gaô gim, 一 枝 觜 賢 |, knap vertellen. spreken.

gim ǐng, | 詠, neuriën, zingen.

矜 *gim á*, | 仔, trapje.
Gim *gim k'i*, | 墘, steenen trappen vóór een huis.

kē gim } 下 |, een laag trapje.
kē »

拎 Vasthouden, grijpen.
Gīm *gīm hè* } | 貨, goederen nemen.
Kīm *kīm hoè*

gīm tiā, | 定, handgeld (bij een koop) ontvangen.

gīm k'ang k'è } | 空 契, werk
» » *k'oè*
halen, (als naaisters).

sa gīm ts'iú, 相 | 手, het onderling eens zijn.

ts'iú laī gīm mih, 手 內 | 物, iets in de hand houden, hebben.

Gin

嬰 *gin á*, | 子 kind.
Gin *tsa po gin á*, 男 孩, jongetje.

tsa bó gin á, 女 孩, meisje.

ū gin á p'iah, 有 | 兒 癖, kinderachtig.

狺* *gin lâng* } | 人, stuursch, kwaad,
Gin *kim* »
kijken.

bák tsiu gin lâng } 目 賙 | 人,
» » *kim* »
iemand stuursch aankijken.

齗 Plagen, iemand tegenstaan, (als een
Gin mensch, eten, enz).

lāng gīn, 弄 |, sarren, plagen.

gīn goá sin, 拂 我 意, het staat mij tegen.

gin sin, | 神, tegen iemands zin aandoen.

lāng gīn é oē } 弄 | 之 語,
» » » *oā*
plagerij.

gīn lâng, | 人, iemand onaangenaam aandoen.

lâng gīn, 人 |, iemand treiteren, boos maken.

gīn tióh lâng, | 着 人, iemand boos maken.

gīn lân tsiaó, | 羼 鳥, voor den

* Zie verder *gún*.

duivel! uit kwaadaardigheid, (lage uitdrukking).

gīn tse k'ì, | 此 氣, tegenstaan, belgen.

研 Fijn wrijven.
Ging *gîng boáh*, | 末, do.
Gán *īng ts'iú gîng gîng*, 用 手 | |, wrij-
Kán ven, (zoo als men een gezwel doet).

gîng tsióh, 礎 石, wrijfsteen om goed glad te krijgen.

gîng pò, | 布, goed met een glanssteen glad wrijven na dat het geverwd is.

hō li boē gîng tit » » *bē gán* » } 彼你不能 | 得, ik laat mij niet door u beet nemen.

gîng tsô, | 槽, vijzel waarin apothekers kruiden fijn wrijven.

Gîng *gîng tsio*, 芽 蕉, pisang.

gîng gîng / *lîng kán* } 龍 眼, drakenoog, (zekere vrucht), Dimocarpus longan.

迎 *gîng tik*, | 敵, te gemoet gaan,
Gîng om te strijden.

gîng tsiep, | 接, zijne gasten te gemoet gaan.

hông gîng lâng, 逢 | 人, iemand vleijen; ontvangen.

凝 Stollen, stremmen.
Gîng *huih gîng teh* / *hoeh gîng* » } 血 | 的, het bloed stolt.

ping gîng, 冰 |, het ijs is gestremd.

迎 *ts'in gīng*, 親 |, zijne nieuwe vrouw
Gīng aan haar huis gaan afhalen.

Gio

吻 *teh giò*, | 笑, met de lippen zijne
Gió bedoeling te kennen geven (zoo als vrouwen doen).

li beh giò goá mah / » *boeh* » » » } 你 要 | 我 乎, komt ge mij toelagchen, *d. i.* ge zijt immers niet tegen mij opgewassen.

蚧 Mossel; vulva.
Giò *to ts'ùi giò giò*, 刀 口 鈍 匕, bot, van een mes.

giò eh, 同 名 者, zeggen naamgenooten van en tegen elkander.

tsiaó ts'ùi pì tsiâ giò ts'ùi, 鳥 嘴 變 做 | 嘴, een vogelbek zoo plat maken als een mossel, *d. i.* zijn vroeger grootspreken hebben moeten laten varen.

橈 *kah giò*, 校 |, de riemen spannen, met
Giò elkander vergelijken, (als bij een wedren met booten).

boē oē kah giò, / *bē ē* » » } 不 能 校 |, niet met elkander kunnen overeenstemmen.

giò poe / » *pe* } | 標, pagaai, korte roeispaan.

茭 *lō giō* / *lō kiō* } 鹵 |, sjalotten.
Giō *giō lâng kaò bô t'é biēn*, | 人 至 無 體 面, van iemand iets zeggen waarvan hij liever niets wilde hooren.

Gioh

謔 *gioh ih*, | 伊, iemand uitlagchen.
Gióh *gioh lâng*, | 人, iemand sarren.

gaī gióh, 礙 |, vreemd, onlekker, onwel.

Giok

虐 *pō giók* / » *giák* } 暴 |, verdrukken, onder-
Giók drukken.
Giák

瘧 *giók tsik* / *giák tsit* } | 疾, koorts.
Giók
Giák

Giong

仰 Gióng / Giàng — *gióng bō̲* / *giáng* » } | 慕, verlangend uitzien naar.

kiú gióng, 久 |, lang heb ik naar u uitgezien, gezegd tot iemand dien men voor het eerst ziet.

gióng koāⁿ / *giáng koāⁿ* } | 縣, den Districts-chef (hiēn) met iets belasten.

giáng tsi ting, (verbasterd tot *niáⁿ ts'i ting*), | 止 亭, naam van eene beroemde koepel te *Tsiang-tsiu*, door den beroemden 朱 文 公 opgerigt.

Go

鵝 Gans.

Gô — *gô nuī ting*, | 卵 燈, lantaarn in den vorm van een ganzen-ei.

t'ien gô, 天 |, wilde gans, waarvan veeren aan pijlen gemaakt worden.

鵞 Gô — *gô soaⁿ*, | 山, een van verlichte papieren lantaarns gevormde berg.

熬 Distilleren, brouwen.

Gô — *gô tsiú*, | 酒, wijn distilleren.

摮 Ronddraaijen, omwinden.

Gô — *gô lai gô k'ì*, | 來 | 去, over-en-weer draaijen, overal heen zwerven.

lin lin gô, 紊 匕 |, omwinden.

p'ah kim ku gô, 打 金 龜 |, goudtorren laten rondvliegen.

gô sit, 旋 息, uitdraaijen (als eene lamp).

gô tsit lìn, | 一 轉, ééns ronddraaijen.

餓 Hongerig, hongerlijden.

Gō — *gō kuí*, | 鬼, hongerige duivel.

gō sih, | 死, doodhongeren.

gō lō sih, | 匕 死, van honger sterven.

gō tsiâⁿ lâng pó̲, | 成 人 殍, uitgehongerd als een geraamte.

傲 Gō̲ — *kiao gō̲*, 驕 |, trotsch.

ông ngō̲ gō̲, advokaat van kwade zaken.

吳 Gô̲ — Familienaam.

蜈 Gô̲ — *gô̲ k'i*, | 蜞, bloedzuiger.

gô̲ k'i ting, | 蜞 釘, spijkers aan beide uitersten puntig.

梧 Gô̲ — *gô̲ tông ts'iū*, | 桐 樹, dryandria cordifolia.

五 Vijf.

Gō̲ — *gō̲ ki̲* / » *ke̲* } | 更, de vijfde wacht, van 3—5 uur 's morgens.

gō̲ kak, | 穀, granen (in het algemeen), graangewas.

gō̲ dzit tsoeh / » » *tseh* } | 日 節, de vijfde dag der vijfde maand.

it gō̲ it tsáp, 一 | 一 十, geheel en al, tot in de kleinste bijzonderheden.

gō̲ tsáp, | 十, vijftig.

gō̲ p'âng tsûn, | 篷 船, houtboot met vijf zeilen.

ts'in ts'ik gō̲ géh, zie onder *géh*.

午 Middag, van 11 uur VM tot 1 uur NM.

Gō̲ — *gō̲ si*, | 時, do.

tsiàⁿ gō̲, 正 |, 12 uur 's middags.

仵 Gō̲ — *gō̲ tsoh*, | 作, lijkschouwer.

誤 Gō̲ — Misleiden; zich vergissen, verkeerdelijk; teleurstellen, in den war, in verlegenheid, brengen; verzuimen.

ts'ò gō̲, 錯 |, zich vergissen; eene fout begaan.

gō̲ sin, | 身, zich zelven misleiden, schaden.

sit go̤, 失悞, zich vergissen.

ts'ok go̤, 錯 |, do.

go̤ t'ia̤, | 聽, verkeerdelijk hooren.

go̤ k'oa̤, | 看, verkeerdelijk aanzien, (voor het zijne, of voor echt houden, terwijl het van een ander, of nagemaakt is).

sa̤ go̤ } *sio* » } 相 |, elkander in de war brengen, misverstaan.

tam go̤, 耽 |, in de verlegenheid brengen, door iemand te lang op iets te laten wachten; teleurstellen.

k'eh lâng go̤ k'ih } *k'ih* » » « } 被人|去, door iemand in verlegenheid gebragt worden.

bô go̤, 無 |, niet teleurstellen, niet te vergeefs laten wachten.

go̤ bó go̤ kiá, | 妻 | 子, vrouw en kinderen teleurstellen, (door een vroegtijdigen dood).

go̤ liaó kang hu, | 了工夫, zijn werk verzuimen, laten liggen.

悟 Go̤ Duidelijk inzien, tot inzigt komen; voorzien.

liaó go̤, 了 |, tot inzigt komen, uit den droom geraken.

hiáo go̤, 曉 |, do.

síng go̤, 醒 |, tot bewustzijn, inzigt, komen.

go̤ ts'ut hit ê taī tsì, | 出此事, iets inzien, op het denkbeeld van iets komen.

bô gi go̤, 不疑 |, onvoorziens, onverwachts.

Goa

我 Goá Ik; op het einde van een zin, of na een ww. ook *goàh* uitgesproken.

goá kā kī } *» kī ti* } | 本身, ik zelf.

lí tsò lí, goá tsò goá, 你作你 | 作 |, gaat gij uw gang, ik zal den mijnen gaan.

阿 Goà Uitroep van verwondering.

外 Goā

goā bīn, | 面, buiten.

hi goā, 此 |, daar buiten.

lîng goā, 另 |, behalve dat . . . nog . . .

goā sun, | 孫, dochter's zoon.

goā tsa bo̤ sun, | 孫女, dochter's dochter.

goā kong, | 公, grootvader van moederszijde.

goā tsó̤, | 祖, overgrootvader van moederszijde.

goā má, | 媽, grootmoeder van moederszijde.

goā ke } *» ke̤* } | 家, familie van vrouwszijde.

goā ke ts'in } *» ke̤ »* } | 家親, vrouwsfamilie.

goā p'ê } *» p'oê* } | 皮, uitwendig (schoon of beleefd).

goā ui, | 委, sergeant.

goā t'ò, | 套, overkleed.

goā k'ì | 氣, uitwendig opgesierd.

goā t'aô, | 頭, buiten's (lands of huis).

goā kok, | 國, buitenlandsch rijk.

goā hák, | 學, uitwendig, minder degelijke, geleerdheid.

goā tsai, | 才, uitwendige talenten, beleefheid, enz.

goā koa̤, | 官, buiten- (*d. i.* niet in Peking residerende) mandarijn.

kaò goā ê lâng, 教 | 之人, niet tot dezelfde leer behoorende menschen.

koà goā ê lâng, 化 | 之 人, zich tegen het wettig bestuur verzettenden; die buiten de grenzen der beschaving zijn.

ts'ut goā, 出 |, buiten's lands gaan.

tsiáh oā laī seh oā goā, 食 碗 内 說 碗 |, iemands brood eten en hem achter den rug belasteren.

tû ts'ú í goā / *ti „ „ „* } 除 此 以 |, alles wat daar buiten gelegen is, met uitzondering van dezen . . . .

tû í goā / *ti „ „* } 除 以 |, do.; die er buiten gerekend.

goā hâng, | 行, niet tot zijn vak behoorende zaken.

tsiáh goā lō bí, 食 | 路 米, rijst der buitenwegen eten, *d. i.* verbannen worden.

goā iû, | 洋, overzeesche plaatsen.

goā káng, | 港, buitenreede.

goā kang lâng, | 江 人, tot eene Noordelijke provincie behoorenden.

ū ts'ut dzip laī goā ê lâng, 有 出 入 内 | 之 人, iemand die veel gereisd heeft.

goā ts'in laī ts'ik, | 親 内 戚, aangetrouwde en eigen familie.

poà laī poà goā, 半 内 半 |, half in, half buiten, *d. i.* middelmatig.

tsit k'a laī, tsit k'a goā, 一 脚 内 一 脚 |, een voet binnen een voet buiten, *d. i.* aarzelen, in beraad staan.

tuì tû laī goā / *„ ti „ „* } 對 除 内 |, met alles er af gerekend, afgetrokken, (nog zoo veel schuldig blijven).

goā k'e sien si / *„ k'o sin se* } | 科 先 生, chirurgijn.

Goan

阮 Goán Gún — Wij, (niet gij).

玩 Goán — *kó goán*, 古 |, antiquiteiten, rariteiten.

goán k'ì, | 器, do.

原 Goân — Oorsprong, bron (eener rivier); afkomst, oorspronkelijk, oorspronkelijke toestand, oorzaak, omstandigheden; te voren, het eerst.

tsuí goân, 水 |, bron, oorsprong.

hoat goân, 發 |, zijn oorsprong nemen, ontspringen.

goân tsip / *„ tsik* } | 籍, geboorteplaats.

pún goân, goân pún, 本 |, | 本, oorspronkelijk.

goân tsaī, | 在, do.

goân toé / *„ té* } | 底, do.

goân laî, | 來, do.; nog even als te voren, niet anders dan . . . .

insiaò goân, 依 |, volgens het oorspronkelijke, evenals te voren.

iû goân, 猶 |, do.

goân tsiên ê oē / *„ tsân „ oā* } | 前 之 話, te voren uitgesproken gezegden.

goân t'aô, | 頭, oorsprong, oorspronkelijk.

kun goân / *kin „* } | 根, do.

goân iû, | 由, oorzaak, omstandigheden.

goân ts'e / *„ ts'e* } | 差, politiedienaar, buiten de bureaux.

goân kè, | 價, oorspronkelijke prijs.

goân kū, | 舊, volgens den oorspronkelijken, ouden, toestand.

goân kò, 丨告, de aanklager.

goân pī, 丨被, aanklager en aangeklaagde.

goân àn, 丨案, de oorspronkelijke aanklagt, regtszaak.

goân hong gùn / » » *gin* } 丨封銀, rolletje geld dat nog steeds het oude zegel heeft.

goân hong put tōng, 丨封不動, nog onaangeroerd, steeds verzegeld, (van voorwerpen of van eene maagd).

goân mịh, 丨物, de oorspronkelijke, eigenste, voorwerpen.

goân làng, 丨人, de eigenste persoon.

goân p'ìng, 丨聘, eerste vrouw. Voorafgaande huwelijkgeschenken.

goân tsing, 丨情, verschoonen, niet kwalijk nemen.

sa goân tsing / *sio* » » } 相丨情, zich in elkanders positie verplaatsen, en daardoor elkander iets niet kwalijk nemen.

goân liōng / » *liāng* } 丨諒, vergeven, niet kwalijk nemen.

元 Goân Begin, eerste; de eerste, het hoofd.

goân tàn dzit, 丨旦日, nieuwjaarsdag.

goân siao, 丨宵, lantaarnfeest, 15de avond der 1ste maand.

siōng goân / *siāng* » } 上丨, do.

kaì goân, *hoē goân*, *tsiong goân*, 解丨, 會丨, 狀丨, hoogste graad van *Kú-dzin*, *Tsìn-sū* en *Hān-lim*.

tiong goân, 中丨, 15de der 7de maand.

願 Goān Wenschen, verlangen, wensch; bewilligen, in iets toestemmen; gelofte voor het verkrijgen van zijn wensch.

sim goān, 心丨, verlangen, wensch.

tsing goān, 情丨, do.

ì goān, 意丨, do.; wenschen.

kam goān, 甘丨, bewilligen, goed vinden.

put goān, 不丨, niet bewilligen.

goān pê, *goān hing* / » *poê*, » » } 丨陪, 丨還 toestemmen, beloven, om iets te vergoeden, terug te geven.

tsiok goān, 祝丨, biddende zijn verlangen aan de goden te kennen geven.

tsiok goá e goān, 足我之丨 ik heb mijn wensch.

goān hoát, 丨罰, aannemen een boete te betalen.

goān ts'ih ts'ih, 丨切切, zeer gewillig, het hoofd neerhangend, als een ter dood veroordeelde.

goān si, 丨死, gewillig sterven.

hoat goān, 發丨, eene gelofte doen beloven.

hē goān, 祈丨, do. aan de goden

siā goān, 謝丨, eene gedane gelofte nakomen.

hing goān / *hoân* » / *hân* » } 還丨, do.

k'ang goān, 虛丨, een ijdele wensch

koé goān / *ké* » } 改丨, eene gedane gelofte veranderen; ze vervullen, maar er een draai aan geven.

Goe

外 Goē *goē sing*, 丨甥, zuster's zoon.

goē sing lú, 丨甥女, zusters dochter.

bū goē, 務丨, zijn werk van uitwendige zaken maken.

藝 Goē — *bô goē* } 無 ｜, niets te doen hebben, *» gē* } zich vervelen.

tsoè goē, 做 ｜, iets voor tijdpassering doen.

Gok

鱷 Gók — *gók hî*, ｜ 魚, krokodil.

愕 Gók — *ts'ok gók*, 錯 ｜, eensklaps ontstellen.

gók dzièn, ｜ 然, do.

鶚 Gók — *gók tsiaó*, ｜ 鳥, de eerste, de belhamel.

làng gók, 人 ｜, de belhamel van een troep menschen.

gók t'aô, ｜ 頭, belhamel.

gán gók, 眼 ｜, do.

•

Gong

昂 Gông Gâng — *gông gông*, ｜ 匕, trotsch, blufferig; onverschrokken, onbeducht.

gông gông tik ì, ｜ ｜ 得 意, do., vol eigendunk.

gông ngiáh, 竦 狂, verward, niet weten hoe of wat te doen.

tsì k'ì gông gông, 志 氣 ｜ 匕, niet willen bekennen dat men voor een ander onderdoet.

戇 Dom.

Gōng — *gōng gōng*, ｜ 匕, do.

gù gōng } 愚 ｜, do.
gi » }

gōng bīn, ｜ 面, do.

gōng tit, ｜ 直, dom, maar opregt.

gōng tuh tuh, ｜ 篤 匕, dom, halsstarrig.

hai lâm gōng, 海 南 ｜, booby, Sula piscatrix.

gōng gōng á, ｜ ｜ 貪, dom en hebzuchtig.

poà tien gōng, 半 癲 ｜, dom, half krankzinnig.

am k'ám gōng 奄 坎 ｜ } , zeer dom, idioot.
k'ong » » 空 « » }

gōng sin, ｜ 神, stil (van aard), verstompt (van geest).

gōng saì, ｜ 屎, dom stuk stront, (scheldwoord).

poáh gōng kiaó, 打 ｜ 賭, dom weg dobbelen, van geen uitscheiden weten.

gōng t'aô gōng bīn, ｜ 頭 ｜ 面, er dom uitzien.

tîng soa gōng, 唐 山 ｜, zeggen uitlandige Chinezen van een nieuw aangekomene die wildvreemd is.

gōng ku, ｜ 龜, domme schildpad, dommerik.

gōng kui, ｜ 鬼, stomme duivel.

gōng hì ka laóh pî, ｜ 戲 交 落 棚, de domme komediant valt van het tooneel af, *d. i.* eene vergissing maken in iets wat men dagelijks doet.

Gu

語 Gú Gí — *siók gú*, 俗 ｜, spreekwoord.

sîng gú, 承 ｜, spreuk.

gièn gú t'ong, 言 ｜ 通, van te voren met iemand raadplegen wat te zeggen, enz.

lūn gú, 論 ｜, de gesprekken van Confucius.

ìn gú } 隱 ｜, geheime kromtaal, dieventaal.
ìn gí }

牛 Rundbeest.

Gû — *iem gû káng*, 閹 ｜ 犺, os.

10

ts'io gû káng, 牡 | 犺, stier.

gû káng, | 犺, do.

ts'iah gû, 赤 |, koe.

gû bú, | 母, do.

gû kiá, | 子, kalf.

suí gû, 水 |, karbouw.

sai gû, 犀 |, rhinoceros.

gû bah, | 肉, rundvleesch.

gû bah koa, | 肉 乾, gedroogd rundvleesch, rookvleesch.

gû kak, | 角, koehorens.

gû kun / *» kin*, | 筋, rundpees, zenuwen.

gû lin / *» ling*, | 乳, melk.

gû lin iû, | 乳 油, boter.

gû lin piá, | 乳 餅, kaas.

gû ka, | 膠, lijm.

gû p'ê / *» p'oê*, | 皮, koehuiden.

gû niâ, | 頸, bult van eene koe.

gû iû tsik, | 油 燭, talkkaars.

gû ta, | 擔, koejuk.

gû tiaô, | 椆, koestal.

pûn gû kak kóng, 吹 | 角 管, op een koehoorn blazen, zoo als de Tao-priesters.

soa gû, 山 |, koebeest (dom als eene koe).

gû t'aô bé bīn / *» » bê »*, | 頭 馬 面, leelijk en slecht.

gû tsaò, | 灶, slagthuis.

gû t'aô liok tsut ê lâng, | 頭 六 卒 的 人, een beest van een kerel.

gû k'it, 牛 杙, koepaal.

gû liaō, | 綜, koehalster.

k'oeh gû bō / *k'eh » »*, 挾 | 磨, een rijstmolen waarvoor eene koe loopt.

gû pi, | 虱, koeluis.

gû sai ku, | 屎 龜, mesttor.

gû tsai si ĩm tsai tsaó, | 知 死 不 知 走, eene koe weet dat men haar zal slagten, maar heeft het begrip niet om weg te loopen; zegt men tot iemand wiens leven in gevaar is en die niet tracht te ontvlugten.

gû ki á / *» ke »*, | 羹 仔, fijn gehakte afval van geslagte runderen.

gû k'a lōng / *» » long*, | 脚 孔, gaten door koeijen in een slikkerigen weg getrapt.

mī gû, 麵 |, groote koeketer, iemand die veel van meelspijs houdt.

愚 Gû Gi

gû gōng / *gi gōng*, | 戇, dom.

gû tit, | 直, dom, maar opregt.

gû bin, | 民, het domme volk.

遇 Gū Gī

Tegenkomen, ontmoeten; gebeuren, voorvallen, te beurt vallen

sio gū, 相 |, elkander ontmoeten.

gū tioh, | 着, iets tegenkomen, ondervinden; gebeuren, voorvallen.

gū tioh hó ts'i / *gī » » ts'e*, | 得 吉 星, voorspoed genieten.

king gū, 竟 |, gebeuren, te beurt vallen.

tsò gū, 遭 |, do.

寓 Gū Gī

Tijdelijk verblijf, woning; tijdelijk gebruiken; van daar figuurlijk: bezigen.

gū sá / *gī sé*, | 所, verblijfplaats, woning.

kuì gū sá / *» gī sé*, 貴 | 所, (waar is) uwe geëerde woonplaats?

pē gū só } 敝 丨 所, mijne woon-
pī » sé }
plaats.
k'eh gū } 客 丨, herberg.
k'eh gī }
gū i, 丨 意, zinnebeeldig (zeggen of schrijven).

御 Keizerlijk, alles wat tot den keizer behoort.
Gū
Gī *gū sù*, 丨 史, keizerlijke censor.
gū lim kun, 丨 臨 軍, keizerlijke garde, lijfwacht.
gū oân, 丨 園, keizerlijke tuinen.
gū kà ts'in tsing, 丨 駕 親 征, de keizerlijke wagen trekt zelf ten strijde, *d. i.* zelf iets gaan doen.
Gū *kūng i gū tsèh*, hem streelen, aanhalen, (kinderen).

唔 *an gū* } 嬰 丨, praten als kinderen
Gū *e gū* } doen; ook van domme geletterden gezegd.

Gui

危 In gevaar zijn.
Gui *gui hiém*, 丨 險, gevaarlijk.
lim gui, 臨 丨, in het gevaar zijn.
gui kip, 丨 急, dringend, gevaarlijk.
pī kaò gui gui gui } 病 至 丨 丨 丨,
pē » » » » }
zeer gevaarlijk ziek.

巍 *gui gui*, 丨 丨, grootsch.
Gui

魏 Familienaam.
Guī *a guī*, 阿 丨, asa foetida.
Guī *ts'iū guī*, boomluis.

僞 *tsō guī*, 造 丨, namaken (vervalschen.
Guī *tsà guī* } 詐 丨, bedriegelijk, valsch.
tsè guī }

GUN

Gun

阮 Ik, wij (niet gij).
Gún *gún siang lâng* } 丨 兩 人, wij
» nō » }
beiden, (man en vrouw).
gún ko toa, 丨 孤 單, ik alleen.
gún tao, 丨 厝, in ons huis, bij ons.

銀 Zilver, geld.
Gûn *sui gûn*, 水 丨, kwikzilver.
Gîn *gûn tsu*, 丨 硃, vermiljoen, vermilj. inkt.
gûn hi, 丨 魚, zilver visch.
bûn gûn, 紋 丨, ongemunt geld.
gûn toa, 丨 單, wissel, bankbiljet voor zilveren spetie.
hiòng gûn } 餉 丨, belasting; ook
hiàng gîn }
soldaten soldij.
kià gûn, 寄 丨, geld remitteren.
bó gûn } 母 丨, kapitaal.
bó gîn }
laī gûn, 利 丨, interest.
gûn kuī, 丨 櫃, geldlade.
hiēn gûn, 現 丨, contant geld.
p'ah gûn sai hū } 打 丨 師 阜,
» gîn » » }
zilversmid.
gûn ts'iū } 丨 匠, do.
gîn ts'iō }
p'ah gûn tièm, 打 丨 店, zilversmidswinkel.
gûn tsui, 丨 水, percentage.
tiōng gûn, 忠 丨, makelaarsloon.
tiong gûn, 中 丨, halve dollars.
gûn hàn, 丨 漢, melkweg.
hōng gûn, 俸 丨, tractement van mandarijnen.
lē gûn } 例 丨, vastgestelde gelde-
lī gîn }
lijke opbrengst; tariefloon, leges.

gùn tsi̤ (of *tsi̤ gùn*) *tièm*, 錢 | 舖, wisselhuis.

gùn kik } | 局, schatkamer.
gin kiek

gùn kao t'ih uih } | 鉤 鐵 畫, degelijk, mannelijk handschrift.
gin » » oáh

gùn tsoá, | 紙, zilverpapier.

gùn k'ì, | 器, zilverwerk.

gùn sìn, | 信, brief met geldswaarde er in.

tsiok tāng gùn, 足 重 |, zuiver geld.

tàng gùn, 銅 |, met koper vermengd zilver.

hoe gùn } 花 |, gestempeld geld.
hoa gin

háp á gùn, 合 子 |, valsch geld, in tweèn gevijld, uitgehold, en wèer bij elkander gevoegd.

pao á gùn, 包 仔 |, valsch geld.

gùn tiā̤, | 錠, staafzilver.

gùn k'òng, | 礦, zilvermijn.

gùn ts'iṳ̄ hòng } | 象 黃, het zilver slaat uit, (met zwavel uitslag).
gin ts'iō̤ »

lō̤ toé gùn } 爐 底 |, zilverzwart dat op den bodem van de pan overblijft.
» té gin

loè pi̤ gùn } 濾 邊 |, gekartelde munt.
lē » gin

gùn tiā̤ sún, | 錠 筍, houten pen, wig in den vorm van eene zilverstaaf, zwaluwstaart.

kièm tsui gùn, 鹹 水 |, *lett.* zoutwater zilver; uit zee opgevischt zilver.

ts'uì gùn, 碎 |, stukjes zilver (als geld gebruikt); den mond vol geld hebben, over niets dan geld spreken.

gùn k'ò, | 鋯, schuitje zilver.

p'oe gùn } 信 |, geld in een brief.
p'e gin

tsuō gùn bé } 找 | 尾, het te kort komende geld geven.
» gin boé

Ha

嘘 Beademen, door adem vochtig maken.

Ha *ha sio*, | 燒, warm ademen (als een verstijfd penseel).

呵 *hi hi ha ha*, | 匕 呵 匕, hard op overlezen.

Ha *ha ha toā ts'iò*, | 匕 大 笑, schateren van lagchen.

嗄 Een groote mond opzetten tegen, toejouwen.

Ha *teng bīn ha làng*, 當 面 | 人, iemand in het gezigt toejouwen.

toā siā tsiū ha làng, 大 聲 就 | 人, iemand hard toeschreeuwen, (om te komen).

kā ha lak, 敢 | 落, aandurven, voor zijne rekening nemen.

ha lak i boē tó } | 落 伊 無 倒, op zich nemen, maar niet kunnen volvoeren.
» » » bē »

Ha *ha li sah*, het kan er nog eenigzins door, middelmatig.

孝 *hà sa̤*, | 服, rouwkleederen.

Hà *k'iā hà*, 堅 |, in de rouw zijn (van een huis).

seng hà, 喪 |, rouw.

tāng hà, 重 |, zware rouw, rouw.

k'in hà, 輕 |, ligte rouw.

toà hà, 帶 |, in den rouw zijn.

t'èng hà } 脫 |, uit de rouw gaan.
t'ui̤ »

hà t'ēng, 哭 杖, rouwstok, die de oudste zoon achter het lijk van zijn' vader draagt.

hà bō, 喪 帽, rouwhoed.

hà moá, 服 闕, de rouw is gedaan.

搳[1] Hà — Bij elkander binden; ombinden, omdoen (als een das), zich omgorden met.

hà ts'aò, 草 丨, gras bij elkander binden.

hà kùn / *hàh* » } 丨 裙, een rok aandoen.

hà io / *hàh* » } 丨 腰, om zijn middel binden, zich omgorden met.

hà ke si, 丨 器 械, wapens (in een gordel, (bij zich steken).

kim hoa lóng, 金 花 朗, gouden band om hoed of mouwen.

瑕 Hà, Hê̤ — Berst in edelsteenen.

hạ̀ ts'ù, 丨 疵, beschadiging, berst in edele steenen.

ū hà hùn, 有 丨 痕, gebarsten.

hà giok, 丨 玉, gebarsten edelsteen.

哄 Hạ̀ — Toejouwen; men zegt, dit wanneer men iemand niet goed verstaan heeft: wat zegt ge?

bóh tit hạ̀ goàh / » » *hạh* » } 勿 得 丨 我, jouw mij niet toe.

hō̤ li boē hạ̀ tit / » » *bē hạh* » } 彼你不能丨得, gij kunt er mij niet om toejouwen.

toā lâng hạ̀ gin á / » » *hạh kin á* } 大人丨囝仔, ouderen jouwen kinderen toe.

li tih hạ̀ tsuī á / » » *hạh* » » } 你 直 丨 誰 仔. wien jouwt ge toe?

hạ̀ ts'aò seng / *hạh* » *suī* } 丨 臭 酸, door digt bij het vuur gestaan te hebben zuur worden, (als melk).

hạ̀ lai hạ̀ k'ì / *hạh* » *hạh* » } 丨 來 丨 去, elkander toegrommen (van honden en menschen).

---

[1] Zie verder onder *hê*.

下 Hā, Hē̤ — *hā tsoh*, 丨 作, laag, gemeen.

hā tsiēn, 丨 賤, onaanzienlijk, laag, verachtelijk.

hā ting, 丨 等, ondergeschikte.

hā liû, 丨 流, lage volksklasse.

hā siók é lâng, 丨 屬 之 人, onderhoorige menschen.

siōng tiong hā / *siāng* » *hē̤* } 上 中 丨, bovenste, middelste en laagste (soort).

hā san hó̤, 丨 山 虎, strak, om het lijf spannend onderbuis.

ū hā 有 丨, ontlasting hebben.

lé hā u dzîn pit iú só̤ kiû / » *hē̤ i* » » » *sé* » } 禮 丨 於 人 必 有 所 求, is men zoo beleefd, dan heeft men ook zeker om iets te verzoeken.

hā tseng, 丨 庄, lage kwaliteit goederen.

hā tô / *hē̤* » } 丨 宅, Emoi geldschaal, vier *hun* ligter dan de *k'ò̤-tô*.

毫 Hā — *hā là* / *hā lah* } 丨 氌, fijne wollen stof (veel voor regenmantels gebruikt).

暇 Hā — *hân hā ē si* / *ân hē̤* » » } 閑 丨 之 時, in vrijen, ledigen tijd.

嘩 Hā — *hā sa* / *ha sao* } springen, barsten (als een natte emmer die in de felle zon gezet wordt).

狺 Hā̤ — Grommen als een hond.

kaó hā̤, 犬 丨, de hond gromt.

跨 Hạ̄ — *hā̤ kè k'ì* / » *koè* » } 丨 過 去, over iemands hoofd stappen.

Hai

腸 Hai — *pak tó̤ toā hai hai*, 腹 肚 大 丨 丨, een gezwollen buik.

ts'im hai hai, 深淵匕, zeer diep.

hai siōng, ｜相, groot.

k'ah hai, 更｜, grooter.

嗥 Hai *hai hai t'san*, (of *kiò*), ｜｜吽, kreunen, kermen.

hai hai haó, ｜｜吼, janken.

hai boē soah } *bē* » } ｜不能息, zonder ophouden kreunen, janken.

海 Hai Zee.

hai hoā, ｜岸, zeestrand.

hai ki, ｜墘, do.

hai oan, ｜灣, baai.

hai sū, ｜嶼, eiland.

hai koan, ｜關, bureau van in- en uit-gaande regten.

hai iū } » *iō* } ｜洋, zeeroover.

hai ts'át, ｜賊, do.

hai liōng } » *liāng* } ｜量, royaal.

hai ti á, ｜猪仔, zeezwijn, bruinvisch.

hai lâm gōng, ｜南戇, Booby, Sula piscatrix.

hai som, ｜參, biche-de-mer.

hai ts'ài, ｜菜, agar-agar.

hai bī, ｜味, zeevisch.

lòh hai, 下｜, naar zee gaan, (als visschers).

hai bīn t'àn tsiáh, ｜面謀食, zijn brood op zee verdienen.

ts'ut hai, 出｜, in zee steken; Supercarga voor het aankoopen van lading; ook de kapitein zelve wanneer hij daarmede belast is.

hai mîng } » *mui* } ｜門, haven, zeeplaats.

t'ó hai, 漁於｜, vischvangst op zee doen.

táh (of *liaò*) *hai téh*, 涉｜汐, door zee naar land waden.

hai k'aó, ｜口, zeegat.

goā hai, 外｜, open zee.

hai ang, ｜魟, walvisch.

hai koe bú } » *ke bó* } ｜雞母, supercarga, commissionair voor schepen.

hai kak, ｜角, uitstekende punt land in zee.

hai ta } » *toa* } ｜礁, strand dat bij afnemend water droog loopt.

hai hong, ｜風, zeewind.

hai hê siū } » *hoê siō* } ｜和尚, zeeduivel.

hai ling ông } » *liông* » } ｜龍王, zeegod, Neptunus.

hai dziông, ｜絨, spons.

Hai *tsò lâng hai hai*, oppervlakkig zijn, er over heen loopen.

嚡 Haì Helaas!

駭 Hai *hai lâng*, ｜人, iemand afschrik voor zich inboezemen; kort af, onbeleefd, antwoorden.

諧 Haî *hô hai*, 和｜, harmonieren (van man en vrouw.

骸 Hai *hai koàn*, ｜罐, beenderen-urn.

kut hai, 骨｜, beenderen van een lijk.

si hai, 尸｜, lijk.

孩 Hai *hai dzi á*, ｜兒仔, kindertjes, speelpoppetjes.

iù hai, 幼｜, kindertjes.

害 Haī Benadeelen, schaden.

haī lâng, ｜人, iemand benadeelen.

siong haī } » *siang* » } 傷｜, wonden, benadeelen.

lī haī, 利 ｜, gevaarlijk, schadelijk, geducht.

sún haī, 損 ｜, benadeelen, beschadigen.

hé bô hūm haī, 佢無陷｜, dat kan geen kwaad, dat komt er niet op aan.

bô haī, 謀 ｜, beramen om iemand te benadeelen.

àm haī, 暗 ｜, heimelijk benadeelen.

haī dzin tsik haī ki, ｜人卽｜己, benadeelt men anderen dan benadeelt men zich zelven.

haī tiòh hit ê mih, ｜着此物, iets schaden, benadeelen, (zoo als een brand boomen, enz., doet).

haī sìh, ｜死, door vergif of het zwaard om het leven brengen.

haī lâng sòng, ｜人貧, iemand arm maken, tot ellende brengen, (zoo als opium doet).

bô iaò haī ê só tsaī, 無要｜的所在, eene plaats van niet veel belang.

械 Haī *haī tò*, ｜鬪, met wapens vechten.

亥 Haī *haī si*, ｜時, 9—11 uur 's avonds.

獬 Haī *haī tsaī*, ｜哉, onbeschroomd, onverschrokken.

鞋 Haī Zuchten, hijgen.

Haih

駭 Haih Uitroep van vrees voor iets.

Hah

哈 Hah *hah hī*, ｜嘘, geeuwen, gapen.

呵 Hah *hah hah ts'iò*, ｜｜笑, schateren van lagchen.

翕 Hah Door iets aangedaan worden, vatten (als koude); zich warmen bij iets.

hah tioh hong, ｜着風, koude vatten.

hah nńg / *» nuī* ｜軟, zacht warmen, (als lijm boven warm water).

lâng k'ì hah lâng, 人氣｜人, de adem der menschen maakte het benaauwd, (als in eene komedie).

hah sio, 烘 煖, zich bij een warm voorwerp warmen.

hah sio k'uì, 燕｜氣, do.

hah dzit k'uì, ｜日氣, zich in de stralen der zon warmen.

hah i tse sin sè / *» » » » sì* ｜伊此身勢, *lett.* zich bij de magt van een ander warmen, *d. i.* doen voorkomen als behoorde men tot een geducht persoon of koningrijk, om zich gezag te geven.

hah tse k'uì, ｜此氣, do. zich bij den damp van iets warmen.

合 Háh Háp Overeenstemen, passen bij; passen (als kleêren, harmonieren met.

háh ì, ｜意, met zijne bedoeling overeenkomend.

háh īng, háh lō īng / *háp iōng, hap » iōng* ｜用, geschikt voor dat waarvoor men het gebruiken wil.

háh k'oán / *háp of áh »* ｜欵, overeenstemmen met dat waarvoor het bedoeld was.

háh sin / *áh »* ｜身, passen, goed aan het lijf staan (van kleêren).

háh ts'īng / *áh »* ｜穿, passen, goedstaan, (van kleeren).

háh pān, ｜班, do.

háh k'a / *áh »* 貼 脚, passen, (van schoenen).

HAK

īm háh bák / *» áh »* 不 | 目, niet met het oog harmonieren.

háh pi / *áh »* | 脾, naar iemands smaak zijn, (van een penseel).

háh tsui t'ó / *áh » «* | 水 土, zich naar het klimaat kunnen schikken.

bé háh goá k'iâ / *bē áh » »* 馬 | 我 騎, dat paard rijdt naar mijn zin.

sy háh / *sio áh* 相 睦, harmonieren.

tsit lâng háh tsit lâng / *» » áh » »* 一 人 | 一 人, de eene mensch hoort bij den ander, (b. v. gezegd van eene leelijke vrouw die nog een man krijgt).

nīng lâng boē háh tit / *nō̤ » bē áh »* 二 人 不 能 | 得, zij kunnen niet met elkander overweg.

䈄 Háh — Het blad dat om bamboesknoopen zit.

tik háh, 竹 籜, do. bamboeschede.

kah háh, | 籜, do.

sún háh, 笋 |, bamboespruiten.

喝 Háh — *gaó hâng háh* / *» » áh* 善 哄 |, zeer overdrijven, bluffen.

Hak

買 Hak — *hak ts'ân*, | 田, een land koopen.

hak giép, | 業, bezittingen koopen.

hak ts'īng, hak sin ts'īng, | 穿, | 身 穿, kleeding koopen, aanschaffen.

kā i hak k'ìh, 與 他 | 去, zich aanschaffen, koopen.

hak hō̤ ìh, | 與 他, koopen en aan iemand geven, voor iemand iets aanschaffen.

學 Hák — Leeren, aanleeren; wetenschappelijke kennis; leer, leerschool.

HAM

hák sip, | 習, leeren, aanleeren.

hák sing, | 生, leerling.

hák būn, | 聞, litterarische kennis.

p'ok hák, paó hák, 博 |, 飽 |, geleerd, knap,

hák tai, hák ī, | 臺, | 憲, examinator.

hák sū i, | 士 椅, groote leuningstoel.

tai hák, 大 |, leerschool voor groote menschen; eerste der klassieke boeken.

siaó hák, 小 |, leerschool voor kinderen.

kà siaó hák, 教 小 |, een kinderschool hebben.

礐 Hák — Drooge gemetselde put om verf, mest, enz., in te doen.

sai hák, 屎 |, mestput, geheim gemak.

k'ù hák, 踞 |, op het geheim gemak gaan.

tsit tsióh hák, 一 石 |, een onderaardsche kuil of kamer (voor geld, enz.)

斛 Hák — *hák pán*, | 板; planken waartusschen men een aarden muur stampt.

kui nō̤ tsióh hák ė ts'ik, 幾 多 石 | 的 粟, verscheidene schepels rijst.

hák koat, | 抉, klopper om aarde vast te slaan.

Ham

憨 Ham — Dom, lomp.

ham būn, | 慢, do.

酣 Ham — vrolijk van wijn, aangewit.

ham t'iòng, | 暢, do.

tsiú ham, 酒 ｜, de hoogte hebben van wijn.

tsiáh kaò tsuì ham ham, 食到醉｜匕, zich bedrinken.

Ham Ooglid.

ting ham, *ē ham*, 頂瞼, 下瞼, bovenste en onderste ooglid.

gû bák ham, 牛目銜, oogkleppen van eene koe.

si bák ham / *se* „ „ } 生目疳, een strontje op het oog hebben.

bák tsiu ham ham, 目珠蚶匕, gezwollen oogen, door weenen of slapen.

蚶 Schelpen, kammossel.

Ham *ham á tsi*, *ham k'ah*, ｜仔錢, ｜壳, mosselschaal.

撼 Tot gruis stampen.

Hám *hám p'oà*, ｜破, stuk stampen, stuk kraken.

hám ts'uì, ｜碎, do.

kè tsi kap i hám hám, 價錢與他｜｜, met iemand over den prijs dingen.

hám pì, ｜扁, plat slaan (als vleesch).

噉 Eten.

Hám *gaô hám*, 善｜, gaauw, veel, eten.

hám tsoè tsit ts'uì, ｜做一嘴, in een stuk op eten.

hám i boē tó, ｜伊不能倒, niet kunnen opeten, niet tegen iets opgewassen zijn.

肣 Opgezwollen.

Hâm *hâm hâm*, ｜匕, do.

hâm ts'iú hâm k'a, ｜手｜脚, opgezwollen armen en beenen.

tsò lâng hâm hâm, 作人｜匕, onbezonnen.

hâm hâm tām tām, ｜匕淡匕, opgezwollen (ziekelijke toestand).

hâm tām, *hâm tsing*, ｜淡, ｜腫, uitwendig dik, (maar inwendig zwak).

hâm tiù / „ *tiò* } 浮脹, gezwollen, (van den buik), waterzuchtig.

hâm ûng / „ *ûi* } ｜黄, waterzuchtig gezwollen en geel van uiterlijk.

hâm koò boē ts'ing k'ò tit / „ „ *bē bûng tà* „ } ｜至穿袴不得, blufferig, grootsprekend.

hâm kià, 凸鏡, vergootglas, bolle lens.

hâm koā koā, ｜誇匕, vergrootend over iets spreken, overdrijven.

hâm siên, ｜癬, do.

含 In den mond houden; bevatten, omvatten; in zich houden, inhouden, verdragen.

Hâm *hâm t'ò*, ｜吐, in den mond houden en uitspuwen, *d. i.* zwijgen en spreken op zijn' tijd.

hâm tsu put t'ò, ｜珠不吐, eene parel in den mond houden, *d. i.* zijne gedachte niet zeggen.

hâm hô, *hâm hâm hô hô*, ｜糊, ｜｜糊匕, binnen 'smonds prevelen, mompelen, onduidelijk spreken.

pao hâm, 包｜, bevatten, omvatten, in zich sluiten.

hâm tsaī laī, ｜在內, omvatten, insluiten.

hâm ts'iaò hoe / „ „ *hoa* } ｜笑花, magnolia.

hâm dzim, ｜忍, verdragen, dulden.

hâm hūn, ｜恨, zijn toorn, gramschap, inhouden.

hâm oàn, ｜怨, do.

HAM

函 Hâm — Inhouden, bevatten.
p'oe hâm / *p'e* » } 書 ｜, enveloppe.

涵 Hâm — *hâm iông* / » *iáng* } ｜ 勇, verdraagzaam.

銜 Hâm — Mandarijn-graad, rang; groef.
koa hâm, 官 ｜, mandarijngraad.
tsit hâm, 職 ｜, do.
k'ang hâm, 空 ｜, oningevulde mandarijn aanstelling; mandarijn in naam.
toā k'ang hâm, 大 空 ｜, van groote familie.
sún hâm, 筍 ｜, groef voor eene wig.
tsoè pien hâm, 做 邊 ｜, eene groef in hout maken.

啣 Hâm — *toā ts'aó hâm*, 大 草 ｜, groot van eten zijn.
ì á hâm t'ô, 燕 仔 ｜ 塗, de zwaluw pikt aarde op, (om haar nest te maken).

陷 Hām — Instorten, invallen, storten in; vallen, ingenomen worden (van eene stad); kuil om anderen in te laten vallen.
hām lòh k'ìh, ｜ 落 去, instorten.
pún tsî hām lòh k'ìh, 本 錢 ｜ 落 去, instorten, intéren, van een kapitaal.
sing lí tsit sî hām lòh k'ìh, 生 理 一 時 ｜ 落 去, de handelszaak stortte in eens in.
hām haī, ｜ 害, in nadeel, verderf, storten.
hām tsoē, ｜ 罪, zich, of anderen, in eene misdaad storten.
loē hām, 內 ｜, (uitwendig gezond schijnend) inwendig eene wegterende ziekte hebben.
siâ hām, 城 ｜, de stad, vesting, is gevallen, ingenomen.
hām tīn, ｜ 陣, ingesloten, omsingeld worden. (zoo als in een gevecht).
t'ô hām, 塗 ｜, kuil.
hām k'ī / » *k'ē* } ｜ 坑, do. als hinderlaag.
tē hām, 地 ｜, overdekte kuil, do.
hām ts'àm, ｜ 塹, bedorven, defect.
hām ts'àm pī / » » *pē* } ｜ 塹 病, venerische ziekten.
hām he, ｜ 礐, dof geluid van een gebarsten voorwerp, gebarsten.
hām sao, ｜ 瑣, gebarsten.

旱 Hām / Hān — *hām poát* / *hān* » } ｜ 魃, regengod.

兼 Hām — *hām tsit ê*, ｜ 此 個, benevens dit.

酣 Hām — *hām bîn*, ｜ 眠, hardop droomen, dodderig, nog half slaperig.

咸 Hām — *hām tsaī laī*, ｜ 在 內, bevatten, inbegrijpen.

HAN

Han

番 Han — *han tsû* / *hoan tsi* } ｜ 薯, obie, zoete aardappel.

罕 Hán — *hán tit*, ｜ 得, zelden, zeldzaam.
hán iú, ｜ 有, zeldzaam voorkomend.
hi hán, 希 ｜, zeldzaam, weinig voorhanden, eenig.

鬨 Hán — *hán hoā*, ｜ 嘩, hard schreeuwen, ruzie hebben, levenmaken.
hán lai hán k'ì, ｜ 來 ｜ 去, over en weer schreeuwen, (zoo als in een gevecht).
hán pan / *hoàn* » } ｜ 班, luid schreeuwen.

door de bedienden van een mandarijn gedaan, wanneer deze op zijn regters-stoel gaat zitten.

漢 Hàn Naam eener dynastie; van daar: een zoon van Hàn *d. i.* een Chinees; man, mensch, kerel, zoowel in goeden als slechten zin.

hàn tiaô, 丨朝, de Hàn dynastie; van 202 v. C. tot 220 n. C.

hàn gɪk } *» giók* } 丨玉, edele steenen uit den tijd der Hàn dynastie.

boán hàn, 滿丨, Manschoeren en Chinezen.

boán hàn siáh } *» » sik* } 滿丨席, groot feestmaal.

lô hàn k'a, 羅丨脚, menschen die niets te doen hebben, en door hunne sterkte aan de kost komen.

hó hàn, 好丨, ferme, dappere, ook gezette kerel.

toā hàn, 大丨, groot mensch.

hàn tsiàng, 丨將, do.

soè hàn } *sè »* } 小丨, nog niet volwassen mensch, jongen, kind.

lâm tsú hàn, 男子丨, een man, kerel.

lám hàn, 弱丨, zwak persoon.

bɪng hàn, 猛丨, ferme kerel.

t'iet hàn, 鐵丨, ijzeren Hein *d. i.* die zich onwrikbaar aan de waarheid houdt.

tsuì hàn, 醉丨, dronkaard.

poáh kiaó hàn, 賭博丨, dobbelaar.

k'o̲ lóh hàn, 箍落丨, lage kerels, koelies.

iá hàn, 野丨, onbeleefd, onbeschoft mensch.

ts'ɪng hàn, 村丨, boerenkinkel.

t'o̲ hàn, 土丨, do.

t'so̲ siók hàn, 粗俗丨, iemand van ruwe manieren.

寒 Hân* Koud; arm, bekrompen; nederige term voor *mijn*.

siong hân } *siang »* } 傷丨, eene koû vatten.

hân gih gih } *» gih gih* } 丨屹乜, bekrompen, kleingeestig.

tám hân, 胆丨, ontstellen, verschrikken.

hân soan, 丨酸, kleingeestig, teruggetrokken.

hân dzû } *» dzi* } 丨儒, arme geleerde.

pîn hân, 貧丨, arm.

hân siâ, 丨舍, mijn huis.

hân ka } *» ke̲* } 丨家. do.

sàng hân i, 送丨衣, (in de 9de maand) winterkleêren aan de geesten cadeau geven.

hân k'iōng, 丨窮, arm-(als scheldw.).

韓 Hân Familienaam.

閑 Hân Rust, ledige tijd; in toom houden.

an hân tsū tsaī, 安丨自在, zijne tegenwoordigheid van geest behouden.

hân hā ê si } *ân hē » »* } 丨暇之時, in vrijen, ledigen tijd.

ts'ing hân, 清丨, niets te doen hebben.

銜 Hân *hông hân*, 防丨, beteugelen, onder contrôle zetten.

īng soh á hân laìh, 以索丨來, met een touw los bij elkander binden.

* Zie verder *hing*.

限 Hān Ān — Bepalen, afperken, vaststellen, bepaalde tijd of ruimte, termijn.

hān ki, 丨 期, een' tijd vaststellen.

hān si hān k'ik, 丨 時 丨 刻, uur en minuut bepalen.

iú hān, 有 丨, beperkt, te bepalen, niet zeer veel.

bô hān toā, 無 丨 大, onbeperkt, in groote hoeveelheid.

bô hān liōng / » » *liāng* 無 丨 量, onbeperkt, in groote uitgestrektheid.

taī hān, 大 丨, groote grensplaats, *d. i.* levenseinde.

kè hān / *kòe* » 過 丨, den vastgestelden tijd, of plaats overschrijden.

k'oan hān, 寬 丨, den termijn rekken, verschuiven, uitstel geven.

hān tiā, 丨 定, beperkt, bekrompen, (in zijne denkbeelden).

閬 Hān — *mîng hān* / *mui* » 門 丨, deurdrempel.

旱 Hān — Droogte, langdurige droogte.

k'òng hān, 亢 丨, lange droogte.

hān poát, 丨 魃, God van lange droogte.

hān poát ts'ùi, 丨 魃 觜, steeds ongeluk verkondigend.

tuì hān lō lai, 對 丨 路 來, over land komen.

汗 Hān — Zweet.

hān kun / *hān kin* 丨 巾, zweetdoek, zakdoek.

翰 Hān — *hān lim*, 丨 林, keizerlijke academie te Peking; lid dezer acad.

Hang

烘 Hang — Roosten, (boven het vuur).

hang lô 丨 爐, fornuis, komfoor.

hang hé / » *hoé* 丨 火, zich bij het vuur warmen, koesteren.

hang ta, 丨 乾, bij het vuur droogen.

hang sio, 丨 燒, warm maken, opwarmen boven het vuur.

hang bin pao, 丨 麵 包, brood roosteren.

魴 Hang — *hang hi*, 丨 魚, (soort brasem), rog.

哄 Háng — Vrees aanjagen, bevreesd maken, bedreigen, bedriegen, bedotten.

háng i kia, 丨 伊 驚, iemand schrik aanjagen.

háng hoah, 丨 喝, hard schreeuwen.

háng p'ièn, 丨 騙, onnoodig vrees aanjagen.

háng hip, 丨 嚇, vrees aanjagen, overbluffen.

háng sao, 丨 嘯, iemand wegschreeuwen.

háng lâng, 丨 人, iemand bedreigen, vrees aanjagen.

sai háng t'aô, 用 丨 頭, bedreigingen gebruiken.

háng p'ièn sút, 丨 騙 術, bedriegen, misleiden en paaijen (zoo als men kinderen doet).

瘋 Hàng — *hàng hàng*, 丨 丨, opgezwollen.

hàng p'ê / » *p'oê* 丨 皮, opgezwollen, van de huid.

hàng tsing, 丨 腫, do.

hàng hah, 丨 喝, bluffen, blufferig.

kóng tiòh, bīn tsiū hàng k'ih laih. 講 着 面 就 丨 起 來, zoodra er over gesproken werd, zwol zijn gelaat op, *d. i.* werd hij boos.

行 Hâng — Rij; handelshuis, magazijn, verrigting, loop van zaken.

pai hâng, 排 丨, op eene rij, volgens de rij.

hâng ngó, 丨 伍, in rij en gelid.

hâng hō, 丨 號, naam van een koopmanshuis, firma.

hâng kao, 丨 郊, handelshuis.

hâng k'aò, 丨 口, do.

hâng tièm, 丨 店, do.; winkel.

k'ui hâng tsē tièm, 開 丨 坐 店, handelaar, winkelier zijn.

sam hâng, 杉 丨, houtmagazijn.

hâng siong } *» siang* } 丨 商, handelaar, koopman.

hâng ke } *» ke* } 丨 家, do.

oá hâng, 倚 丨, zich aan een handelshuis consigneren; ook in een hoerenhuis komen, (van ligte kooijen).

tsûn t'aò hâng, 船 頭 丨, handelshuis waaraan een schip geconsigneerd is.

hâng hè } *» hoè* } 丨 貨, magazijn goederen. ligt en digt, onsterk, goed.

hâng tsing, 丨 情, marktprijs.

dzī hâng, 字 丨, rij-karakters.

hâng tó, 丨 倒, bankroet, faillissement.

hâng tó bô t'ang hing, 丨 倒 不 可 還, insolvent, te kort schietend totaal, frauduleus bankroet.

li tsng sìm mih hâng tàng } *» » sám á » »* } 你 當 甚 麼 丨 當, voor welke zaken zijt gij? wat neemt gij waar?

tsaī hâng, 在 丨, kennis van zaken hebben.

sik hâng, 識 丨, do.

goā hâng, 外 丨, uitwendige beleefdheden.

縫 *hâng sa*, 丨 衫, kleêren doorrijgen,
Hàng (om ze sterk te maken).

降 Zich onderwerpen, overgeven.

Hâng *hâng hok*, 丨 服, do.

tsà hâng } *tsè »* } 詐 丨, in schijn zich onderwerpen.

杭 *hâng tsiu*, 丨 州, Hangchow.
Hâng

巷 Steeg, laan.

Hāng *hāng ts'im kaó ok*, 丨 深 狗 惡, hij zich te huis zijnde, veel vermogen, *lett.*: in diepe steegen zijn de honden kwaadaardig.

hāng á, 丨 仔, steegje.

kut t'aò hāng, 禿 頭 丨, doodloopende steeg.

bōng ling hāng, 摸 乳 丨, naauw steegje,* *lett.*, "Borsten-voel steegje."

bô tuè hāng } *» té »* } 無 底 丨, steegje zonder eind.

hāng t'aò mìng } *» » mui* } 丨 頭 門, achterdeurtje dat in eene steeg uitkomt.

ts'ú hāng bû lō k'oà tsoè pak káng hi t'iaò, 此 丨 無 路 看 作 北 港 魚 跳, zegt men van iemand die karakters gedurig verwart, *lett.*: de karakters *ts'ú hāng bû lō* ziet hij aan voor de karakters *pak káng hi t'iaò*, (die veel op elkander lijken).

hāng t'aò hāng bé, 丨 頭 丨 尾, hoek van een steegje.

項 Soort. Familienaam.

Hāng *tsáp hāng*, 什 丨, allerlei soorten van.....

---

* Naam van een zeer naauw en donker steegje in Emoi, waar men de handen moet uitsteken om niet tegen elkander aan te loopen, en daardoor dikwijls de vrouwen die men ontmoet aan de borsten grijpt. (*Schl.*)

ū hē hāng / » *hē* » } 有下丨, geregeld, niet verward, handelen.

bô hē hāng / » *hē* » } 無下丨, niet geregeld, verward, handelen.

tsi (of *gûn*) *hāng* / « (*gin*) » } 錢(銀)丨, geldzaken.

k'ièm hāng, 欠丨, schuldzaken.

hāng tāng, 丨重, zeer zwaar.

hu huì toā hāng tsi, 虛費大丨錢, veel geld verkwisten, verteren.

hit è hāng hāng, 此的丨丨, dat dinges, geweet wel wat, (manier om iets geheim te zeggen).

Hao

囂 Hao *hao k'ì*, 丨氣, liegen, leugenachtig.

hao siaò, 丨唐, leugen, (scheldw.).

hao lák, 丨謊, onopregt, leugenachtig.

hao hao hoah hoah, 丨ㄝ喝ㄝ, toeschreeuwen.

hao hao hat hat, 丨ㄝ喝ㄝ, hard wegschreeuwen.

hao p'ig p'è, panscherven, *zie: Haō p'ig p'è*.

瘊 Hao *t'ai ko bīn hao hao*, 癩膏面丨ㄝ, gevlekt als het gezigt van een melaatsche.

啼 Haó Schreijen.

t'i haó, 啼號, do.

t'i t'i haó haó, 丨ㄝ哭ㄝ, weenen, (als eene vrouw).

吼 Haó Schreeuwen.

haó kiò, 嗚叫, hard schreeuwen, schreijen.

mg mg haó, 哞ㄝ叫, bulken, als eene koe.

hémh hémh haó, 嘶嘶叫, hinneken.

haó kaò lih k'ui, 丨到裂開, in één gil doorschreeuwen.

t'si haó péh leh, 忽然大丨, op eens hard beginnen te schreijen.

tsi (of *gûn*) *haó* / « (*gin*) » } 錢(銀)丨, het geld loopt op zijn eind.

hao t'ià, 丨痛, schreeuwen van pijn, (schertsend ook wel als scheldw. gezegd).

haó hi, 丨豨, schreijen, dreinen, (lage volkst.).

gû sig bé haó, 牛聲馬丨, hard spreken, zwetsen.

haó tó bān lí tèng siâ, 丨到萬里長城, de Chinesche muur omverhuilen, *d. i.* hard schreijen.

haó loā lâng, 丨賴人, iemand willen noodzaken iets terug te nemen, wanneer men het zelf gebroken of bedorven heeft.

kē haó tō bô bák sai, 假哭都無目淚, veinzen te huilen, maar geene tranen voor den dag krijgen.

孝 Haò Ouderliefde, onderlievend; van daar vóór betrekkingen van een overledene geplaatst.

ū haò, 有丨, ouderlievend.

haò kìng, 丨敬, ouderliefde.

haò kìng, haò sūn, 丨敬, 丨順, eerbiedig aanbieden, geven, (van minderen aan meerderen).

haò hīng, 丨行, ouderlievende handelingen.

haò tsú, 丨子, ouderlievende zoon.

haò lâm, 丨男, de zoons of naaste mannelijke verwanten van een overledene; thans ook gezegd tegen iemand die veel leven maakt.

haò lâm haò tak, 丨 男 丨 篤, er bedrukt, knorrig uitzien.

haò hū, 婦 丨, behuwddochter van een overledene.

haò lú } 丨 女, dochters van een
» *lí* } overledene.

haò sun, 丨 孫, kleinkinderen van een overledene.

祀 Offeren aan, als offer brengen.
Haò *haò pút* } 丨 佛, aan een afgod
» *hút* } offeren.

haò sîn, *haò kuí*, 丨 神, 丨 鬼, aan de geesten offeren.

haò tsó kong, 丨 祖 公, aan zijne voorouders offeren.

haò sing lé, 丨 牲 醴, dieren offeren.

haò ts'aì king, 丨 菜 莖, plantaardige stoffen offeren.

tsit dzit haò sa tuì, 一 日 丨 三 頓, dagelijks drie eetmalen offeren, (gedurende 100 dagen na den dood zijner ouders).

荷 *haò pao*, 丨 包, beugeltasch.
Haò

寒 *haò liaò bân p'ê* } 丨 了 性 鈍,
Haò *aò* » » *p'oê* }
Aò hardgevoelig worden, niet meer om slaag geven.

候 Wachten, wachten op, als een bediende
Haō wachten bij zijn heer, bedienen; zijne opwachting maken, bezoeken; tijd.

t'ing haō, 等 丨, wachten.

haō lâng ê siao sit, 丨 人 的 消 息, op berigt van iemand wachten.

haō kè } 丨 價, wachten (met te ver-
» *kè* } koopen) tot dat de marktprijs bekend wordt.

haō pó koa, 丨 補 官, beambten die op eene openstaande plaats wachten, candidaat mandarijn, ambtenaar ter beschikking.

sū haō, 伺 丨, wachten (zoo als een bediende), bedienen.

paì haō, 拜 丨, bezoek brengen.

tsiaò sî haō, 照 時 丨, volgens geregelden tijd, op gezetten tijd.

haò put tsi kú, 停 不 止 久, lang aanh ouden, (zooals een dokter een zieke).

haò poà ts'i sik, 丨 半 青 熟, half gaar laten smeulen, eene wond niet fiks behandelen, enz).

haō k'iap khì, 丨 壞 去, iets langzaam doen tot dat het bedorven is; (deze drie laatsten ook wel *haò* uitgesproken).

劾 Zich moeite geven, inspannen.
Haō *haō lik*, 丨 力, zijne krachten inspannen.

haō lô, 丨 勞, een bevel, last, vervullen.

haō iōng, 丨 用, korporaal.

效 Goede uitwerking hebben, uitkomen.
Haō *haō giēm*, 丨 驗, goede uitwerking hebben, (zooals eene medecijn); uitkomen, (zooals eene voorspelling).

ìng haō, 應 丨, do.

ū kong haō, 有 功 丨, do. (van medecijnen).

鱟 De koningskrab, Limulus longispina.
Haō *haō kóng*, 丨 管, pooten van die krab.

haō k'ak á, 丨 殼 仔, kleine waterschepper van hare schaal gemaakt.

haō hia, 丨 杓, groote dito.

haō hiáh, 丨 額, vooruitstekend voorhoofd.

haō peh ts'eh / » *peh ts'eh* | 伯册, jalouziën.

tsui haō, 水 |, watertor.

tsit nguoh haō, 一耦 |, een paar koningskrabben; een overspelig paar.

liáh haō, 掠 |, eensklaps overvallen, (zooals dieven of een overspelig paar).

tit tioh (of *liáh tioh*) *hó haō*, 得着好 |, eene goede, gelukkige kans hebben.

soa haō, 山 |, dommerik.

haō k'a haō ts'ìu, | 脚 | 手, niets goed doen.

haō p'ia p'è, | 甓片, panscherven.

ts'in ts'iū gin á k'i haō p'ia ts'ù / » *ts'iō kin* » » » *p'ing* » 親像囝仔起 | 片厝, als kinderen die een huisje van panscherven opbouwen, *d. i.* wat men zoo even bepaald heeft, weêr verbreken.

後 Haō Later, nakomend.

haō si / » *se* | 生, zoon.

haō á, | 仔, do.

haō si á / » *se* » | 生仔, een jongmensch, jongeling.

Haoh

强 Haóh *haóh tsui*, | 水, hard, niet gaar kunnen worden, (van aardappelen, enz).

haóh haóh, | 匕, hard, ongaar, (zooals aardappelen).

ō haóh haóh, 芋 | |, krakerij, harde terongs.

Hap

哈 Hap Happen, (zooals visch naar kroost doet): overzwelgen, van daar: overdrijven.

hap tsui, 呷水, naar water smekken, (van visch).

hap hong, | 風, den wind doen uit- en ingaan, (zooals bij een blaasbalk, harmonica, enz.).

翕 Hap *tsi hō i hap k'ih*, 錢與他 | 起, zijn geld hebben laten overhappen, *d. i.* te veel voor iets betaald hebben.

gaò hap, 𠢕 |, sterk overdrijven.

hap sien, *hap k'eh*, | 仙, | 客, overdrijver.

kóng hap oē / » » *oā* 講 | 說, overdrijvend spreken.

夾 Hap Kraken, (zoo als pitten), kraker.

hap hō i pí, | 與他 匾, plat kraken, drukken, (zooals een noot).

hap p'oà, | 破, stukkraken.

hap ka ná, | 橄欖, olijven kraken.

hit t'ô hap, 核桃 |, nootenkraker.

合 Háp Op elkander doen sluiten, sluiten, vereenigen, toedoen, als een boek of parapluie; op elkander slaan, overeenstemmen, overeenkomen, passen bij; betamen; numerale voor twee bij elkander hoorende voorwerpen, als dolken; een paar.

háp gi, | 宜, overeenstemmende met billijkheid, billijk, betamelijk.

háp hoat, | 法, wettig.

háp ì, | 意, overeenkomen.

háp iok, | 約, do.

háp lâng ì, | 人意, naar iemand zin zijn.

háp sit, | 式, gepast, geschikt.

háp īng / » *iōng* | 用, geschikt (voor het beoogde doel).

k'ao su háp tâng / » *si* » » 閣書 | 同,

testament en afschriften daarvan met een gemeenschappelijk zegel bestempeld.

tâng sim háp ì, 同心｜意, van gelijk hart en overeenstemmenden zin, *d. i.* harmonierend.

háp hé } ｜夥, compagnieschap aan-
» hoé } gaan.

háp sim, ｜心, sympathiseren.

poà k'ui poà háp, 半開半｜, half geopend en half digt, nog onzeker, (van eene zaak).

p'oà háp bô p'oà k'ui, 判｜無判開, men velt een oordeel om ze bij elkander te houden, niet om ze te scheiden, (bij personen, die uit den echt willen scheiden).

iā háp, 夜｜, magnolia.

háp á gûn } ｜仔銀, valsch geld,
» « gîn } dat in tweeën gevijld, uitgehold en weêr te zamen gevoegd wordt.

háp tsióng } ｜掌, de handen tegen
» tsiáng } elkander sluiten en buigen, (van priesters); overeenkomen, op elkander slaan.

háp tsióng bō } ｜掌帽, hooge
» tsiáng » } muts van Boeddha-priesters, mijter.

háp hun, ｜婚, in het huwelijk treden, den eersten huwelijksdag hebben.

háp tiù } ｜帳, het gordijn over een
» tiō } bruidsbed doen.

háp toh, ｜棹, huwelijksmaal waarop bruid en bruidegom te zamen eten.

háp si, ｜時, voor den tijd passen.

háp tsik liû, put háp tsik k'ì, ｜則留不｜則去, stemt men overeen dan blijve men, stemt men niet overeen dan ga men weg.

put háp, 不｜, het betaamt niet dat . .

háp kai, ｜該, betamen, behooren.

háp ing, ｜應, do.

háp tsi t'àn, háp t'àn, ｜錢賺, ｜賺, 100% verdienen.

t'àn nn̄g háp, 賺兩｜, 200% verdienen.

Hat

轄 Hat *koán hat*, 管｜, besturen, beheeren.

t'ê hat, 提｜, do.

t'óng hat, 統｜, als hoofd te zeggen hebben over, besturen.

hat tiaô, ｜槖, geldriem om het lijf gedragen.

hat tiaô, ｜條, veer, (van horologiën, springmatrassen, enz.).

喝 Hat Hard schreeuwen.

hat ts'ai, ｜采, toejuichen, applaudisseren.

hat ih, ｜伊, iemand toejouwen.

hao hao hat hat } 囂匕｜匕,
ho̤ ho̤ » » } hard wegschreeuwen.

hat ts'iù, ｜嚏, niezen.

sa̤ hat, 相｜, tegen elkander schreeuwen, redetwisten.

īng oē hat ih } 用話｜伊,
iōng oā » » } wetende dat iemand iets niet koopen kan, het hem onder de waarde aanbieden.

乏 Hát *hát hát*, ｜匕, een weinig, krap, bekrompen, bijna niet meer.

hat tsui, ｜水, eene bepaalde hoeveelheid water mogen gebruiken op rantsoen.

tsi t'aô k'ah hát, 錢頭缺｜, krap in geld zitten.

ân hát, 緊｜, do.

12

hát hát teh īng / » » *tih iōng* } 丨匕直用, afgepast gebruiken.

k'ò hát, 涔丨, weinig te eten hebben, (en daardoor niet kunnen groeijen).

核 Hát — *k'an hát*, 牽丨, klier-opzetting in de liezen.

He

灰 He Hoe — Kalk.

he hún, 丨粉, kalk.

boah he, 抹丨, kalken.

oà he, 發丨, kalk aanmaken.

he pao, 丨包, pakje kalk, gebruikt om iemand de oogen te verblinden.

siak he pao, 撒丨包, een kalkpakje werpen.

he si, 丨匙, troffel.

tsoá he, tsoá kun he / » *hoe*, » *kin hoe* } 紙丨, 紙根丨, met papier aangemaakte kalk, (die niet afgeeft).

tsióh he, 石丨, steenkalk.

k'ak á he, 殼仔丨, kalk van oesterschelpen.

he tsui, 丨水, kalkwater.

ts'ing he tsui, 筅丨水, witten.

t'âng iû he, 桐油丨, kalefaterkalk.

bāng se he / » *se* » } 網紗丨, kalk en versleten netten, waarmede Chin. schepen gekalefaterd worden.

he tsi, 丨糬, voeg-kalk.

boah he tsi, 塞丨糬, met kalk voegen.

he hùn, he lō, he tsoū, 丨痕, 丨路, 丨導, kalkvoegen tusschen de steenen.

he soá, 丨磠, zandkalk, kalk me verweerde steen.

he iô, 丨窰, kalkbranderij.

he liaô, 丨寮, kalkhuis.

he t'aô, 丨頭, uitschot van kalk (onverbrand).

laô hióh he, 蔞葉丨, fijne kalk waarmede siri bestreken wordt, siri kalk.

ts'aó p'iá he, 草肼丨, cement.

sim hoe liaòh, 心丨了, niet mee aan iets denken.

瘕 He — *he ku*, 丨痀, aamborstig.

he ku saò, 丨痀嗽, heesch als ee aamborstige.

He — *bak tsiu he he*, kleine, half geopen de oogen.

瑕 He — *hām he* / » *he* } 陷丨, gebarsten (geen he der geluid gevend), ziekelijk.

伙 Hé Hoé — *hé sit*, 丨食, voedsel, eten.

hé sit áh, 丨食盒, etenstromme

hé sit nâ, 丨食籃, etenskorf.

hé tiá, 丨鼎, personen die gezame lijk eten.

夥 Hé Hoé — Ook voor het laatste gebruikt. Co pagnon, assistent, compagniescha personen die deel van iets uitmake als van een rooverkomplot.

hé tiû / *hoé tiû* } 丨長, navigateur.

toā hé, 大丨, eerste stuurman.

dzī hé, 二丨, tweede do.

sa hé, 三丨, derde do.

hé kì, 丨計, compagnon, personen een handelshuis, (ook soms die gee compagnons zijn).

liên tsai ê hé kì, 連財的丨計 een aandeelhebbende compagnon.

háp hé, 合 〡, kompagnieschap aangaan,

t'iah hé, 撤 〡, eene vennootschap ontbinden.

tsit hé ê ts'át, 一 〡 的 賊, een komplot dieven.

soà hé, 散 〡, uit elkander gaan, (van eene rooverbende).

tsit ke hé ê làng / *» ke hoé » »* } 一 家 〡 的 人, de huisgenoten.

tōa ke hé / *» ke hoé* } 大 家 〡, van groote bezittingen, rijk.

pān kong hé á, 辨 公 〡 仔, botje bij botje doen, (van spelende kinderen).

火 He Hoé **Vuur.**

hé t'si / *hoé ts'e* } 〡 星, vonken.

hé hu, 〡 灰, asch.

hé hu sik, 〡 灰 色, grijs.

k'í hé, 起 〡, vuur aanleggen.

hé tóh, 〡 然, het vuur gaat aan; in vuur, woede, onsteken.

hé ōng, 〡 旺, vlammen.

hé iēm, 〡 燄, do.

tiém hé, 點 〡, licht opsteken.

hé hoa, 〡 熄, het vuur gaat uit.

hé t'oà, 〡 炭, houtskool.

hé t'oà àng, 〡 炭 甕, doofpot.

hé lô, 〡 爐, kagchel, haard.

hé sio ah, 〡 燒 呵, brand! brand!

hé tsióh, 〡 石, vuursteen.

hé tsì, 〡 箭, vuurpijl.

hé koàn, 〡 鑵, vuurpot.

hé to, 〡 刀, vuurslag.

hé k'î, 〡 鉗, tang.

hé tī, 〡 箸, do.

peh hé / *peh hoé* } 白 〡, kleine vuurpijlen.

hé iem, 〡 鏟, aschschop.

hé kńg (kui), 〡 管, blaaspijp.

hé hiū, 〡 艾, tonder.

hé hiū k'oeh / *hoé » k'eh* } 〡 艾 筴, tonderdoos.

hé kim t'si / *hoé » ts'e* } 〡 金 星, vuurvlieg.

hé hun tsûn / *hoé lûn »* } 〡 烟 (輪) 船, stoomboot.

hé hun kik sí 〡 烟 激 死, doodsmoren, (door rook).

hé ióh, 〡 藥, buskruid.

hé ióh kóng, 〡 藥 管, kruidhoorn.

hé ióh kik / *» » kiok* } 〡 藥 局, kruidmagazijn.

sim hé, 心 〡, inwendig vuur.

tsit p'a hé, 一 抛 〡, eene vlam.

hé sîn iâ, 〡 神 爺, vuur-god.

tē lui hé p'aò, 地 擂 〡 砲, loopgraaf, kruidmijnen.

hé nū tsoà / *» » tsih* 〡 濫 饌, 〡 濫 舌, door vuur aangetast worden.

hé sai, 〡 屎, afgebrande lampenpit.

sio hé eh, 厨 子, kok.

ióh hé, 慾 〡, wellustig gevoel.

tōng hé, 動 〡, opwekkend (van eten).

hé gán kim tsing, 〡 眼 金 睛, helder ziende, (in eene zaak); goed inziende.

hé tsing, 〡 種, vlammetje (om het vuur aan te maken).

hé t'ai, 〡 炱, heete orkaan, (zonder regen).

hé tsih, 丨 舌, vuurtong; uiteinde eener vlam.

ting hé, 燈 丨, lamplicht.

hé hoe, 丨 花, vonk.

hé iù, 丨 油, lampolie.

t'ai làng pàng hé, 殺人放丨, moorden en brandstichten.

t'iaò hé p'ùn, 跳丨盆, door den vuurstapel springen.

kè hé, 過丨, door het vuur gaan; over het vuur houden, als kleeren.

kè hé hang, 經丨烘, over het vuur droogen.

hē hé k'i } *hē hoé k'e* } 下丨坑, in de vuurkolk, in het verderf, zijn.

hé ling } *hoé liòng* } 丨龍, lont.

hé ling hé bé } *hoé liòng hoé bé* } 丨龍丨馬, spoedig, onmiddelijk.

hé ling pao, 丨龍包, patroontasch.

hé iēm soa, 丨燄山, vuurspuwende berg.

hé tsi, 丨井, heete bron; brandput.

hé haō, 丨候, aanduiding van het vuur; naar de kleur van de vlam, weet men wanneer hetgeen men stookt goed is.

bò hé k'i, 無丨氣, bedaard, volstrekt niet driftig zijn.

hé koe } *hoé ke* } 丨鷄, haan van een geweer.

hé koe } *hoé ke* } 丨雞, kalkoen.

hé ts'ú, 丨鼠, eekhoorntje.

hé hāng, 丨烘, aloë.

hé sìng, 丨性, driftig, haastig.

hé taó, 丨斗, strijkijzer; ijzeren bakje waarin men geolied hout brandt om voor te lichten.

hé ts'at, 丨漆, lak.

hé ts'ièm, 丨籤, soort van constabelstok.

Hé 貨 Hè Hoè

Dit; als dat zoo is.....

Lading, koopwaar.

hè toa, 丨單, reçu.

hè pān, 丨辦, monster, staaltje.

ts'o hè, 粗丨, grove waar.

iù hè, 幼丨, fijne, kostbare, brekende waar.

aò hè, 臭丨, stinkende waar.

hè ts'aó, 丨物, de soort, kwaliteit.

hè sik, 丨色, do.

k'i hè, 起丨, lossen.

ts'ut hè, 出丨, laden.

hè k'eh } *hoè k'eh* } 丨客, koopman.

tsáp hè tièm, 什丨店, kom- en-eisch winkel.

hè kè } *hoè kè* } 丨價, prijs van de waar.

ts'ut mìng ēm dzīn hè } *» mui » » hoè* } 出門唔認丨, als goederen een maal zijn huis uit zijn, ze niet meer als de zijnen willen terugnemen.

hiòng hè } *hiàng hoè* } 餉丨, aan belasting onderhevige goederen.

hè k'a, 丨脚, uitschot van goederen, waar het goede reeds is "uit" gezocht.

hè t'aô, hè bé, 丨頭, 丨尾, het neusje en staartje van goederen.

hè bīn, 丨面, bovenste (uitgezochte) goederen.

iù hè } *iù hoè* } 洋丨, buitenlandsche goederen.

hè tsú, 丨主, eigenaar van goederen.

hè tō, 丨渡, goederen veerschuit, pakschuit.

boē hè t'aô siak hè bé } *bē hoè » sak hoè boé* } 賣丨頭

厦荷大辭典

揀 ｜ 尾, heeft men het neusje van de waar verkocht, dan verkoopt men het staartje (uitschot) à tout prix.

hè tsin kè sit, ｜ 眞 價 實, de waar is goed en de prijs is de ware, *d. i.* goede waar en vaste prijs.

hó hè siu laī tù, 好 ｜ 收 內 厨, beste waar bergt men in de binnenkast.

bé ts'át hè, 買 賊 ｜, gestolen goederen opkoopen.

歲 Hè Hoè Jaar, (van ouderdom).

ni hè, 年 紀, leeftijd.

hè siū, 年 壽, do.

li ū kui hè, 你 有 幾 ｜, hoe oud zijt gij?

ū hè, 高 壽, bejaard, op jaren.

t'iem hè siū, 添 ｜ 壽, levensjaren verlengen.

脆 He Hoè *hè hè ē mih*, ｜ ヒ 之 物, onsterk, gemakkelijk te breken goed.

蝦 Hè Hẹ Garnaal.

ling hè } *liông hẹ* } 龍 ｜, kreeft.

hè bi, ｜ 米, gedroogde garnalen.

hè bí in, ｜ 米 腰, een middel als eene gedroogde garnaal, *d. i.* gebogen uit eerbied of door ouderdom.

hè bé tsìng } *hẹ boé tsụi* } ｜ 尾 鑽, boor met twee zijhaken.

tiao ling hè } *» liông hẹ* } 釣 龍 ｜, krombinden, (zoo als men kreeften, of ook gevatte roovers doet).

hi hè tsui tsut, 魚 ｜ 水 族, vischjes en water insekten, *d. i.* onbelangrijke, nietswaardige, menschen of dingen.

p'ang hè, 蜂 ｜, bij in de chrysalide, (eene Chin. delicatesse).

tsit bé àng hè hè, 一 尾 紅 ｜ ヒ vuurrood als een garnaal.

霞 Hè Hẹ *ts'ut àng hè*, 出 紅 ｜, er zijn roode streepen door de lucht.

kin á ts'ut sì àng hè, 囝 仔 出 世 紅 ｜, vuurrood als pas geboren kinderen.

回 Hè Hoè Teruggaan, terugkeeren, terugbrengen, teruggeven; ook eene andere taal vertolken, vertalen.

hè t'aô kiō, ｜ 頭 轎, een teruggaande draagstoel.

hè hok, ｜ 復, antwoord terugbrengen.

hè p'oè } *hoè p'e* } ｜ 信, een schriftelijk antwoord terugbrengen.

hè pò, ｜ 報, antwoord komen brengen op . . . .

hè sim tíng ì } *hoè » tuị »* } ｜ 心 轉 意, van gedachte veranderen; bedaren.

hè tāng, ｜ 重, de zwaarte (emballage, enz.) aftrekken.

hè tsit poạ, ｜ 一 半, de helft teruggeven, (zooals bij reeds gekochte goederen).

hoat hè, 發 ｜, terugzenden, (goederen die niet bevallen).

hè k'ì hing ìh } *hoè » hân »* } ｜ 去 還 伊, terug gaan geven, (zooals rondventers de onverkochte waren aan hunne bazen).

hè paì, hè t'àm, ｜ 拜, ｜ 探, eene visite, een bezoek, terugbrengen.

hè lé, ｜ 禮, eene beleefdheid beantwoorden.

hè ts'iú, ｜ 手, een klap teruggeven.

hè oā, 傳 話, vertolken, vertalen.

hè īm tioh, ｜ 不 着, verkeerd vertolken, vertalen.

hè p'àng, | 篷, zeil inkorten.

hè tsit tsàn, | 一 層, één rif inleggen.

下 Hè Hoè — Neèrzakken, dalen, verminderen (zooals in prijs), gaan liggen (zooals wind).

hè lòh k'ì h, | 落 去, neèrzakken, neèrkomen.

kè tsi k'ah hè / *kè » » hoè* } 價 錢 更 |, de prijs is wat gedaald.

hong k'ah hè, 風 稍 降, de wind is wat bedaard.

sio k'ah hè, 燒 稍 |, de warmte is verminderd, gedaald.

和 Hè Hoè — Accompagneren, (in muzijk).

hè siū / *hoè siū* } | 尙, Boeddha-priester, (die niet huwen mag).

hè siū loè lō, | 尙 濾 路,
hoè siū sè ke, | 尙 灑 街, zooals een priester die de straat reinigt, (door gedurig hetzelfde te prevelen); gezegd van menschen die uit toorn of gewoonte bij zich zelve op straat spreken.

hè siū sì bó, ī̄m ká k'aò, | 尙 死 婦 不 敢 哭, sterft de vrouw van een priester, dan durft hij niet te weenen, *d. i.*: is iets wat men voor anderen niet weten wil ongelukkig uitgekomen, dan mag men zijne droefheid niet uiten.

hè siū t'aò kòng tioh ka ná, | 尙 頭 擊 着 橄 欖, een olijf die tegen het hoofd van een priester aankomt, (wegens het gladde van zijn kaalgeschoren hoofd zal de olijf er afvallen); bet.: een voorwerp op eene gevaarlijke plaats zetten.

hè siū tsiáh sì tsú, | 尙 食 施 主, zooals een priester die van zijne donateurs leeft, *d. i.*, zonder iets te doen, aan de kost komen.

夏 Hē Hē — Zomer.

hē t'i, | 天, do.

dzip hē, 入 |, den zomer ingaan.

kao hē, 交 |, overgang tot den zomer.

hē tsì, | 至, zomersolstitium.

ts'un hē pò, 春 | 婆, rondventster.

下 Hē Hē — Neerleggen, neerzetten; doen neerzakken, indoen, inwerpen; leggen, als een strik of val, van daar: eene bedekte of verraderlijke manier, streek, gebruiken.

hē lòh, | 落, nederzetten.

hē tsiâ tui, | 成 堆, ophoopen.

tìng hē tsit è uī, 楝 | 此 的 位, leg het hier neer!

ū hē lòh, 有 | 落, vertrouwd, te vertrouwen, sekuur; in orde, geregeld, (niet verward).

bò hē lòh, 無 着 落, onvertrouwd, onbepaald, onopregt, ongeregeld.

hiet hē, 放 |, neèrleggen, laten rusten, (van eene zaak).

pàng hē kiá, 放 | 子, een kind neerleggen, ter ruste leggen.

hē dzī, | 餌, lokaas uitwerpen.

hē bāng, | 網, een net uitzetten.

hē tiò, | 釣, de vischhaak in (het water) doen.

hē tsìng, | 種, zaad inleggen, zaaijen.

hē hè, | 貨, goederen in (een schip) laden.

hē lòh ka to ts'ioh, | 落 交 刀 尺, de schaar en de maatstok ter hand nemen om een kleed te knippen, *d. i.* eene zaak afpassen en dan gaan doen.

ī̄m ká hē loh ka to ts'ioh, 不 敢

丨落交刀尺, eene zaak niet durven beginnen.
hē ts'iú, 丨手, de hand aan iets leggen, iets beginnen.
hē pit, 丨筆, de pen op het papier zetten.
hē àm pō, 丨暗步, eene geheime streek gebruiken, onverwachts aanvallen, enz.).
hē tók pō, 丨毒步, eene vergiftige, *d. i.* hoogst schadelijke, streek doen.
hē tók ts'iú, 丨毒手, iemand verraderlijk dooden.
hē tók (of) *tók ióh*, 丨毒, 毒藥, iemand vergiftigen.
pàng hē, 放丨, de les eindigen, vrij-afgeven, (van meesters).
hē kiá, 置其子, zijn kind ter ruste leggen.

許 Hē Hē̤ Beloven, eene belofte doen; eene gelofte doen, bidden, offeren aan.
hē lâng ê tsî, 丨人的錢, iemand geld beloven.
toā hē sió koé / » *hē̤* » *ké*, 大許小解, mooije beloften doen, maar er weinig van nakomen.
àm hē, 暗丨, achtershands geven of beloven, om iets gedaan te krijgen.
hē pút / » *hút*, 丨佛, eene gelofte doen, aan een afgod bidden.
hē sîn t'ok pút / *hē̤* » » *hút*, 丨神托佛, van de goden afbidden, smeeken.
hē t'i hē toē / *hē̤* » *hē̤ tē*, 祈天祈地, aan den hemel en de aarde bidden.
hē ih, 丨伊, dringend smeeken.
hē mîng k'aó / *hē̤ mûi* », 戶祝, aan de deurgoden offeren.
ts'ing hē bān hē / *ts'an hē̤* » *hē̤*, 千罪萬罪, zijne schuld bekennen, duizend maal excuus vragen.
sa hē / *sio hē̤*, 相丨, elkander zijn ongelijk bekennen, excuus vragen, zich verklaren.
hē m̄ tióh, 丨不着, zijn ongelijk, schuld, bekennen.

係 Hē Betrekking hebben op, in verbinding staan met.
kap goá bô kan hē, 與我無干丨, het heeft met mij niets te maken.

會 Hē Hoē Societeit, vereeniging.
hoe hē, 花丨, dobbel-speel-vereeniging.
iô hē, 搖丨, in eene dobbel-vereeniging gooijen, om te bepalen wie het eerst zijn' inleg zal terug hebben.
tsio hē, 招丨, leden voor eene vereeniging verzamelen, werven.

Heh

Heh Uitroep van verwondering.
heh beh tsai á iū / » *boeh tsoá iō̤*, 丨要如何, hoe moet dat dan toch!

嚇 Heh *i beh p'ah goáh goá heh ih* / » *boeh* » » » *he̤h* », 伊要打我我丨伊, hij wilde (bedreigde) mij (te) slaan, en ik gaf er hem de permissie toe.

赫 Heh *hōng heh*, 謊丨, onbezonnen, verward.

Hem

媒 Hîm Bûn *hîm lâng*, 丨人, middelaar, koppelaar, (bij een huwelijk.)
hîm lâng kong, 丨人公, middelaar, (fatsoenlijk).
hîm lâng pô, 丨人婆, middelaarster, (verachtelijke).

葏 *hîm koa*, ｜乾, bies.
Hîm

嘷 *hīm hīm kiò*, ｜匕 吽, brullen, van
Hīm een tijger.

Hemh

Hemh Met iets slaan.

hemh tó, 擊 倒, met iets omver-slaan.

hemh tioh tsit k'ang, 擊 着 一 孔, een gat in iets slaan.

hemh p'oà sū, 擊 破 事, eene zaak bederven.

hemh p'oà oa̱ tsiù tsoā, 擊 破 碗 發 誓, een kopje stuk gooijende zweren.

Hemh Ja, zoo!

piah hemh, meikever.

hemh kòh, sufferige, stille, kerel.

Hémh *tsit ê ts'uì hémh hémh*, niet zeggen, geen mond open doen.

hémh hémh bò béh kóng, met gesloten mond, niet willen zeggen.

hémh hémh tsiáh sa oa̱ p'oa̱, Jantje domoor vreet drie en een halve kom (rijst) op.

Heng

方 Plaats; voorschrift, recept.

Heng *tē heng*, 地 ｜, plaats.

Hong *tē heng koa*, 地 ｜ 官, plaatselijke overheden.

heng hiò, ｜ 向, dat waarheen eene plaats gekeerd is, *d. i.* de ligging, het uitzigt.

ióh heng, 藥 ｜, receptje.

tan heng tók bī, 單 ｜ 獨 味, in zichzelven voldoende geneesmiddel.

pì heng, 秘 ｜, geheim, weinig bekend, recept.

坊 Eerepoort (voor uitstekend deugdzame
Heng personen opgerigt).

tsióh heng, 石 ｜, steenen eerepoort.

ts'à heng, 柴 ｜, houten eerepoort.

k'iā heng, 竪 ｜, eene eerepoort oprigten.

haò tsú heng, 孝 子 ｜, eerepoort voor een' ouderlievenden zoon.

荒 Onbebouwd, woest, verlaten; gebrek,
Heng hongersnood.

Hui̱ *p'a heng*, 抛 ｜, onbebouwd liggend (land).

heng hoè, heng heng hoè hoè, ｜ 廢 ｜ ｜ 廢 匕, woest, onbebouwd, verwoest, verlaten.

ts'aò ts'i̱ heng, 臭 生 ｜, stinkend en verwoest; verlaten, (zooals eene plaats waar moordtooneelen hebben plaats gehad).

ts'i̱ heng, 生 ｜, huiverig (zooals een groot leeg huis).

ki heng, 饑 ｜ hongersnood.

Heng Brommen, gonzen.

heng heng kiò, gonzen van muskieten.

ts'uì laī teh heng, 口 中 吟 哦, neuriën, binnen 'smonds prevelen.

晚 Avond, nacht.

Heng *ē heng*, 下 ｜, do.

Hui̱ *tsà heng*, 昨 ｜, gisteren avond.

Heng *tuì tíng bīn heng k'i laih*, 從 上 描 起 來, van boven afscheppen.

Héng Wijze om toestemmend te antwoorden.

園 Tuin.

Hîng *ké tsi hîng* / Hui̱ *koé » hui̱* } 菓 子 ｜, vruchtentuin.

ts'aì hîng, 菜 ｜, groententuin.

hoe hîng, 花 丨, bloemtuin.

ts'ân hîng, 田 丨, velden.

iû hîng, 油 丨, olie-werkplaats.

kò hîng eh, 顧 丨 的, tuinman.

遠 Verafgelegen, ver.

Hîng *dzoā hîng*, 何 丨, hoe ver?

Huī *hîng lō*, 丨 路, lange weg.

hîng lo lo, zeer ver.

tsoáh hîng hîng hîng, 差 丨丨丨, het verschilt veel.

hîng hîng lai eh, 丨 匕 來 的, van veraf gekomen.

ts'it hîng poeh hîng / » *huī peh huī* } 七 丨 八 丨, zeer ver afgelegen.

k'oà tit hîng, 看 得 丨, ver uitzien, (zooals van een hoog huis); van ver doorzigt, (van personen).

Hengh

Hîngh Ja, zoo, ik versta u.

Hîngh *hîngh hîngh*, 𪖈 聲, den neus ophalen.

Hi

希 Weinig, zeldzaam.

Hi[1] *hi hán*, 丨 罕, zeldzaam voorkomen.

hi hán kiá, 丨 罕 子, eenigst kind.

hi bi ê kiá, 丨 微 的 子, do.

hi bi, 丨 微, weinig, in geen bloeijenden toestand.

稀 Wijd uit elkander, niet zamenhangend, dun.

Hi *pò hi hi* 布 丨 匕, dun, doorzigtbaar, van stoffen.

bē tsú liaó hi hi, 糜 煮 了 丨 匕, de boeboert was na het koken niet zamenhangend.

嘻 *hi hi haó ts'iò, hi hi ts'iò*, 丨 匕 吼 笑, 丨 匕 笑, goechelen, gigchelen.

Hi *hi hi hoū hoū*, 丨 丨 諱 匕, geruisch als van een naderenden wind.

tsoè làng hi hi hoū hoū / *tsò* » » » » } 做 人 丨 匕 諱 匕, een aardig mensch, die niet ligt geraakt is.

禧 *hō sin hi*, 賀 新 丨, nieuw geluk wenschen, (op het nieuwjaar).

Hi

熙 *k'ong hi*, 康 丨, (keizer) K'anghi, (A. D. 1662—1723).

Hi

彼 *hi tao*, 丨 處, daar, aldaar.

Hí *hi tsit làng*, 此 一 人, die man daar.

hi goā, 此 外, buiten gelegen, buiten.

tsi taī hí taī, 此 事 彼 事, dan dit, dan dat hebben.

喜 *hong hi*, 歡 丨, verheugd.

Hí *pò hi*, 報 丨, eene verheugende tijding brengen.

ū hi sū, 有 丨 事, zwanger.

hi ts'iok, 丨 雀, ekster.

hō hi, taò hi, kiong hí, 賀 丨, 投 丨, 恭 丨, gelukwenschen.

肺 De longen.

Hì *hì kíng* / » *kuī* } 丨 管, slokdarm.

hì hú ê oē, / » » » *oā* } 丨 腑 的 話, woorden uit het diepst van zijn hart.

sa tsai hì hú / *sio* » » » } 相 知 丨 腑, elkander door en door kennen.

戲 *há hì* / *hoà* » } 呵 丨, geeuwen, gapen.

Hì

[1] Zie verder onder *hu*.

戲 Hì

hì lāng, 丨 弄, scherts.

k'ì k'oà hì, 去 看 丨, naar de comedie gaan.

pog hì, 演 丨, comedie spelen.

tseng hì, 裝 丨, do.

hì tai, 丨 臺 } theater.
hì pi } 丨 棚
» pê }

pò tē hì, 布 袋 丨, poppenkast.

hì tià } 丨 埸, comedie-gebouw.
» tiō }

toā hì, 大 丨 子 班, comedie door volwassen menschen gespeeld.

hì á, 小 丨 子 班, comedie door kinderen gespeeld.

iá hì, 影 丨, Chin. schim.

dzi hì, 兒 丨, kinderspel.

hì tog, 丨 單, lijst van comediestukken, affiche.

tiém hì, 點 丨, een comediestuk aanwijzen.

tiah hì, 摘 丨, een comediestuk aanwijzen, uitpikken.

hì ts'oàn, 丨 闖, aan comedie verslaafd.

hì toà, 丨 旦, mannelijke actrice.

ka lé hì, 傀 儡 丨, marionnettenspel.

hì pâng, 丨 房, kleedkamer van een tooneel.

hì pān, 丨 班, comedianten-troep.

hì bûn, 丨 文, comedie-stuk.

pog kaò hì, 演 猿 丨, een' aap kunsten laten maken.

tsoè pá hì } 作 把 丨, goochelen.
tsò » » }

hì hiok hì hiok } 丨 謔, comieke gezegden op een tooneel.
» hiak » hiak }

hì p'ûn, 丨 盆, comedie waarin allerlei geesten voorkomen.

hì hì hiaoh hiaoh, 丨 匕 謔 匕, veel van gekheid houden, (van vrouwen)

hì ts'ut, 丨 出, tooneelstuk; acte van een tooneelstuk.

hì hì hiá hiá, onvoorzigtig, onbesuisd

hì hì hoán hoán, do.

bò beh k'oà láng è hì } 不 要 看 人 的 丨, iemands komedie niet
» boeh » » » » }
willen zien, *d. i.* niet door iemand willen begunstigd worden, hem geen dank willen schuldig zijn.

bē bat hì hai } 未 𠀾 些 兒
boē » » » }
er is nog niets van aan, het is e nog ver van af.

Hì

hì k'ì, 抛 起, schommelen.

hì lai hì k'ì, 抛 來 丨 去, heen en weer schommelen.

hì ts'iu ts'ien, 抛 鞦 韆, schommel, wip.

hì ts'ien ts'iu, 打 韆 鞦, in een schommel wippen, schommelen.

k'a hì ts'iú hì, 脚 抛 手 抛, met handen en voeten waggelen, zwaaijen

lā lì hì } 搖 擺, heen en weer
» lò » }
schommelen, (van een hangend voorwerp).

hì t'ô, 丢 土, aarde (in mandjes) opgooijen.

hì hiā, 丢 瓦, pannen opgooijen (zooals metselaars).

hì tsiū k'ì, 丢 上 去, opgooijen.

hì lòh laih, 丢 落 來, neergooije (van boven).

sì koè hì } 四 處 丢, overal heen
» kè » }
gooijen.

kap i hì, met iemand in twist zijn procederen.

魚 Visch.
Hi *hi koa*, ｜乾, gedroogde visch.
hi pó, ｜脯, do.
hi sit, ｜翅, de vinnen.
hi tsú, ｜子, kuit van visch.
hi ts'ì, ｜鰓, de kieuwen, (bij visschen).
hi lân, ｜鱗, schubben.
hi tō, ｜肚, vischbuikjes.
hi kut, ｜骨, graten.
kim hi, 金｜, goudvisch.
gûn hi / *gin* » } 銀｜, zilvervisch.
bé ka hi / *bé ka* » } 鰢鮫｜, makreel.
soa hi, 鯊｜, haai.
gók hi, 鱷｜, krokodil.
ts'iu hi / *ts'io* » } 鯧｜, bot.
k'ing hi, 鯨｜, walvisch.
ngó hi, 鰎｜, baardvisch.
tsit ts'ùi pīng tsit bé hi kaò / » » *puī* » *boé* » » } 一口飯一尾｜到, voor alles wat men meer doet, ook meer geld moeten hebben.
hi ka, ｜膠, vischlijm.
hi hâng, ｜行, vischmagazijn, stapelplaats.
hi á ts'ī, ｜仔市, vischmarkt.
hi kè á, ｜架仔, visch-stalletje.
Hi Hé! (uitroep als men van iets terugschrikt).
耳 *hī á*, ｜仔, oor.
Hī *hī k'ang*, ｜孔, oorholte.
hī k'ang kui, ｜孔竅, binnenste van het oor.
hī kao, ｜鈎, oorringen.
hī kiô, ｜膜, trommelvlies.

hī á tûn, ｜仔唇, oorlel.
hò hī k'ang, ｜好孔, fijn van gehoor.
hī sai, ｜渣, oorvuil.
hī k'oân, ｜環, oorring.
hī tuī, ｜旒, oorbel.
hī lō lō, ｜膠匕, tuiten in het oor.
kiáh t'aô kiáh hī, 起頭起｜, regts en links om zich heen kijken.
sa hī á, 三｜仔, drie-oorige, (naam van een aard-mandje).
tsèng hī / *tsnì* » } 攢｜, de oorlel doorsteken, voor oorbellen.
tâm hī, ｜濃臭, druipende ooren.
ū hī bô ts'ùi, 有｜無口, bedaard luisteren, maar zijn' mond niet in het gesprek steken.
hī k'ang k'in, ｜輕, ligtgeloovig.
hī k'ang tāng, ｜重聽, hardhoorig.
kaò t'aô ts'ú hī / » » *ts'í* » } 猿頭鼠｜, er leelijk uitzien van gelaat.
bòk dzī hī, 木｜子, kleine ooren, *lett.* champignon ooren.
ts'aò hī lâng, 臭｜聾, doof.
bô hī t'ang k'ī, 無｜可鉗, geen oor hebben om aan beet te pakken, geen vat op iemand hebben.
pùn ki kīn tú koa ū hī, 糞箕僅適攜有｜, bij aardmandjes neemt hij zulke die een oor hebben, *d. i.* men kiest datgene waar men het meeste nut van kan hebben.
硯 Inktsteen.
Hī *hī áh*, ｜盒, inktsteendoos.
hī ti, ｜池, waterbakje op den inktsteen.
hī poâ, ｜盤, bladje waarop men den inktsteen plaatst.

laó k'i hī } *» k'e »* } 老坑 ┃, fijne soort inktsteen.

t'ȯ hī, 土 ┃, kleien inktsteen.

tsióh hī, 石 ┃, grove inktsteen.

tiao hī, 雕 ┃, een' inktsteen vormen, fatsoeneren.

hī ti tsui m̄ tsai kik si loā tsē lâng, ┃池水唔知激死若干人, hoe vele menschen heeft de inkt, (*lett.* het inktwater) niet ten val gebragt?

pit kap hī ing bô k'áp, 筆與┃永無磕, het penseel kan het nimmer tegen een' inktsteen uithouden, *d. i.* een zwakkere kan zich niet met een' sterkeren meten.

Hia

彼 Hia Aldaar.

hia taī ke, ┃大家, al die daar.

罟 Hia Spits uitloopend netje om insekten in te vangen.

hia báng á, ┃蚊仔, muskieten in een netje vangen.

báng hia, 蚊┃, netje om muskieten in te vangen.

靴 Hia Laarzen.

hia p'aò bō, ┃袍帽, feestgewaad.

hia t'áng, ┃筒, kappen van de laarzen.

p'ê hia } *p'oê hia* } 皮┃, leêren laarzen.

iû hia, 油┃, vetlaarzen.

ting hia, 釘┃, laarzen met spijkers.

lú hia } *lí »* } 女┃, dames-laarsjes.

tsièn hia, 戰┃, strijdlaarsen.

i t'aô hia, 圓頭┃, laarzen met ronde punten, (van militaire overheden).

tsê t'aô hia, 劑頭┃, laarzen met vierkante punten, (van civiele overheden).

嚇 Hia *toā sia hia lâng*, 大聲┃人, iemand hard wegjouwen.

Hia *īng ts'iú hia ih* } *iong » ha »* } 用手┃他, met de hand bedreigen vóór dat het nog tot vechten komt.

檥 Hia *haō hia*, 鱟┃, schepper van den koningskrab gemaakt.

pù hia, 匏┃, schepper van den kalabas gemaakt.

īng tsuí hia hia tsuí, 用水┃┃水, met een waterschepper water scheppen.

兄 Hia Oudere broeder.

hia tī, ┃第, broeders.

ing hia, 阮┃ } *toā hia*, 大┃ } oudere broeder.

hia ko, ┃哥, oudere broeder.

hia só, ┃嫂, oudere broeder's vrouw.

hia bē } *» moaī* } ┃妹, oudere broeder en jongere zuster.

k'eh hia, 客┃, overspeler.

馨 Hia *bī sȯ hia hia*, 氣味┃匕, prikkelend heet van smaak.

hia hia loáh loáh, ┃匕辣匕, sterkriekend; ieders aandacht trekken, als iemand die van eene verre reis terugkomt.

hia si, ┃時, in trek zijn.

響 Hiá *hiá tia*, ┃塲, het boven alle anderen winnen.

鄉 Hiá *hiá péh* } *» péh* } ┃白, plotseling licht in duister, (zooals het lichten van water).

hiá sit, ┃翼, de vlerken opslaan van schrik, (bij vogels).

hiá ts'iú, ┃手, eensklaps schok-

ken van de hand, (zooals bij schieten).
hiā bák, | 目, in de oogen schitteren, (zooals zonlicht).

向 Overhellen naar.
Hiā *hiā sin*, | 身, achterover vallen.
tò hiā, 到 |, do.
hiā k'ui, | 開, van elkander los gaan, uitelkander gaan, zich van iets afscheiden, onttrekken aan.
hiā ts'ut, hiā dzip, | 出, | 入, overhellen, inhellen (bij eene muur).

蹻 Hiā *hiā ts'iú hiā kiok* / » » » *k'a* } | 手 | 脚, met handen en voeten in beweging zijn, (onder het spreken).

燃 *hiā hé*, | 火, het vuur opstoken.
Hiā *hiā tsui*, | 水, het water opstoken.
hiā t'sâ, | 柴, hout verstoken, opstoken.
ū hiā, bò hiā, 有 |, 無 |, lang of kort branden, (als goede of slechte kolen).
hiā hé / » *hoé* } 火 |, in het vuur werpen, het vuur met iets opstoken, iets verbranden.

Hiā *kiā hiā*, 驚 惶, ontstellen, schrikken.

瓦 Dakpannen.
Hiā *hiā iò*, | 窰, pannenbakkerij.
hiā hoe / » *hoa* } | 花, dakpanbloemen, bestaande uit tegen elkander geplaatste dakpannen, die het dieven moeijelijk maken ongehoord op daken te loopen.
ts'ù hiā p'è / » » *p'oè* } 厝 | 片, panscherven.
hiā to, | 刀, troffel (van metselaars).
hiā t'âng, hiā sien, | 虫, | 䖮, duizendpoot, tusschen de dakpannen gevonden.
tsng p'iáh hiā / *tsui* » » } 磚 壁 |, steenen en pannen.

蟻 *kaó hiā*, 螻 |, mieren.
Hiā *péh hiā*, 白 |, witte mieren.
pe hia, 飛 |, vliegende mieren.
hong hiā, 風 |, verweerd door wind en mieren.
ts'iⁿ hiā / *ts'iⁿ* » } 生 |, mieren aantrekkend.
ìng sng hiā / *ni sni hiā* } 黄 |, kleine, geele, mieren.
o hiā, 黑 |, zwarte mieren.
kaó hiā tìng, 螻 | 釘, prikkeling als of men door mieren gestoken werd.
hiā lō, | 路, mierenweg.
kaó hiā òng, 螻 | 王, mierenkoning.
hiā siū, | 巢, mierennest.
hiā t'ō, | 土, aarde van een mierennest.

艾 *hé hiā* / *hoé* « } 火 |, zwam, tondel.
Hiā *hiā mi*, | 棉, fijne tondel, zwam.
hé hiā k'at, 火 | 戛 / *hoé* » *pao*, 火 | 包 }, tondelzakje.

Hiah

彼 *hiah ē*, | 個, die, dat.
Hiah

許 Zoo, zoozeer . . . .
Hiah *hiah tsoē* / » *tsē* } | 多, zooveel.
hiah tsió, | 少, zoo weinig.
hiah kù, | 久, zoo lang.
kaò hiah gōng, 到 | 戇, zoo dom! zoo dom als dat!

捧 Op den arm dragen.
Hiah *hiah sa*, | 衣, do.; klaarleggen, uitleggen, nemen.
hiah ts'â, 執 柴, hout bij elkander vatten.

hiah p'ē hiah ts'ióh } 執被執蓆, zijn deken en slaapmat met zich
« *p'oē* » » } dragen, (zooals iemand die eene wacht gaat betrekken).

額 *t'aô hiáh*, 頭 丨, voorhoofd.
Hiáh *hiáh tsing* } 丨 前, do.
» *tsàn* }
hiáh kak, 丨 角, uithoeken van het voorhoofd.
k'àm hiáh, 蓋 丨, vooruitstekend voorhoofd.
k'ok hiáh, 鵠 丨, vooruitstekend voorhoofd.
hiáh k'a, 下 丨, voorhoofd-vleugels.
liù hiáh } 脫 丨, kale, onbehaarde voorhoofd-vleugels.
t'ut » }
p'oà hiáh, 破 丨, bedreigen zich het voorhoofd te kwetsen, wanneer men hen niets geeft, (zooals bedelaars doen).
tsaò hiáh, 灶 丨, steenen van een oven.
k'ap hiáh, 磕 丨, met het voorhoofd tegen iets aanstooten, (van droefheid of woede).

嚇 Eensklaps beven, ontstellen.
Hiáh *tah hiáh*, 搭 丨, eensklaps ontstellen, schrikken.
hiáh sit, 丨 翼, de vleugels opslaan; ontstellen.
k'ùn liáo hiáh hiáh, 眠了丨丨, niet rustig slapen, spoedig wakker schrikken.

Hiang.

馨 *hiang hiang*, 丨 匕, sterk in den neus
Hiang dringend, van lucht.
bī hiang hiang, 味 丨 匕, sterk van lucht.
iù hiang, 油 丨, vetkoekjes, (door Mahomedanen op de sterfdagen hunner betrekkingen aan de familie rondgedeeld).

響 Weêrgalmen, sterk van geluid.
Hiáng *hiáng liāng*, 丨 喨, sterk van geluid, (zooals eene gong).
siang siá hiáng, 相言諾, van weêrszijden goedvinden.
in ih siang siá hiáng, 應伊相言諾, stellig goedvinden, vast belooven.
hiáng lô, 丨 鑼, schelle gong.
hiáng tàng, 丨 銅, schelklinkend koper, (voor gongs gebruikt).
hiáng bé, 丨 馬, onverschrokken roovers, wier paarden schelletjes dragen.

Hiao

枵 Omkrullen, kromtrekken, oprollen.
Hiao *hiao hióh*, 丨 葉, omkrullen, kromgetrokken, (zooals hout of eene balk door den wind).
hiao k'í, 丨 起, opgekruld.
hiao t'an, 丨 坦, kromtrekken, kromgetrokken.
hiao t'an k'ak, 丨 坦 殼, kromgetrokken.
ts'ióh ka i hiao laih, 蓆與他丨來, eene mat oprollen.
tuì ē toé hiao k'í laih, 自下氐丨起來, van onderen ophalen, (zooals de onderste waar uit eene kist).

儌 Zoeken, trachten te verkrijgen.
Hiao *hiao hiém*, 丨 險, eig. op gevaarlijke wijze trachten te krijgen, van daar:

een ander bedriegen, onhartelijk behandelen.

hiao hīng, | 倖, onverdiend, bij geluk (krijgen); zorgeloos, onhartelijk.

kōng hiao, 防 |, onzeker, onveilig, onuitgemaakt.

僥 Hiao Valsch, geveinsd, onhartelijk, ondankbaar, bedriegelijk behandelen; ook voor het voorgaande gebruikt.

hiao p'ièn, | 騙, bedriegen, iets geleends niet teruggeven.

hiao t'un, | 呑, *lett.* valschelijk inslikken, *d. i.* niet terug betalen.

hiao lâng ê tsî, | 人之錢, iemand in geld bedriegen.

hiao lâng, | 人, bij iemand in schuld blijven, niet afbetalen.

hiao sim ê lâng, | 心之人, een onhartelijk mensch.

hiao hûn, | 痕, ondankbaar, onhartelijk van uiterlijk.

put tsí hiao, 不止 |, zeer onhartelijk.

hiao tsing pók gī ê lâng, | 精薄義的人, een ondankbaar mensch.

hoán hiao, 反覆, wispelturig, zijne belofte intrekken.

驍 Hiao *hiao ióng*, | 勇, dapper.

曉 Hiaó Verstaan, begrijpen.

hiaó tit, | 得, do.

ū hun hiaó, 有分 |, te vertrouwen, geloofwaardig.

bô hun hiaó, 無分 |, niet te ververtrouwen, ongeloofwaardig.

hiaó lí ê lâng, | 理之人, een mensch die rede verstaat.

hiaó gō, | 悞, van scherp inzigt zijn.

t'ong hiaó, 通 |, grondig, door en door verstaan.

hiaó dzū peh sì, | 諭百姓, aan het volk te kennen geven, mededeelen, bevelen.

Hiaò *hiaò hiaò k'ìh*, 輕然賣去, à tout prix verkoopen.

hiaò tòh, 僥倒, de prijs van iets bederven, door laag te verkoopen; een ander mans zaak doen springen.

嬓 Hiaô Geil, wellustig.

hiaô siaó, | 瑣, do.

hiaô hoe, | 花, geile vrouw, (scheldwoord).

hiaô lak lak, geil, wellustig, (van vrouwen).

tsáp poeh hiaô eh, 十八 | 的, (eene vrouw) die in alle hare handelingen wellust aanduidt.

Hiaoh

Hiaoh *hiaoh k'ak*, 殻脫, bladderen, afschilferen.

hiaoh ts'at, *ts'at hiaoh*, 脫漆, 漆脫, bladderen van verw.

hiaoh k'ìh laìh, 脫起來, bladderen.

hiaoh p'ê, 脫皮, losgaan, van den omslag of leder.

謔 Hiaoh *kóng oē hiaoh lâng*, 講話 | 人, in zijn spreken iemand met een steek onder water belagchelijk maken.

hì hiaoh, *hì hì hiaoh hiaoh*, 戲 |, gekheid maken met iemand.

Hiem

Hiem *ts'aò hiem hiem*, erg stinken.

險 Hiém Gevaar, gevaarlijk, gewaagd; in groot gevaar verkeerend, van daar: bijna, nagenoeg, het scheelde niet weinig of...

hiém haī, | 害, gevaarlijk, gewaagd.

gui hiém, 危 |, do.

kè hiém / *koè* » } 過 |, het gevaar door zijn.

lim hiém put hiém, 臨 | 不 |, op het oogenblik van gevaar, geen gevaar hebben, *d. i.* gered geworden.

hing hiém hiao hīng, 行 | 徼 倖, gevaarlijk, dingen op goed geluk af doen; gevaarlijk, niet te vertrouwen.

hiém kè, | 計, gevaarlijke list.

ts'i hiém, 試 |, het gevaar beproeven, gevaarlijke dingen doen.

lūng hiém, 弄 |, met het gevaar spelen, zich er te veel aan bloot stellen.

hiao hiém, 徼 |, anderen door zijne handelingen in gevaar brengend.

kan hiém, 奸 |, do.; arglistig.

hiém aì, | 隘, gevaarlijke, moeijelijk te nemen, pas of plaats.

hong p'o tsui hiém, 風 波 水 |, gevaren van wind en golven.

kiâ hiém lō, 行 | 路, gevaarlijke dingen doen.

hiém hiém sí, | 匕 死, bijna gestorven.

hiém tsit hiém, | 一 |, het scheelde weinig of . . . .

hiém sia dzi, | 些 兒, het scheelde geen haartje of . . . .

hiém hiém k'ièm tsit tiém, | 匕 欠 一 點, het scheelde zeer wenig of . .

hiém tsit tiém á, | 一 點 仔, dito.

hiém hiém tó, | 匕 倒, bijna vallen.

喊 Hièm — Hard schreeuwen.

hoah hièm, 喝 |, do.

hièm ts'át, | 賊, schreeuwen dat er dieven zijn.

hièm lâng, | 人, iemand hard toeschreeuwen.

kiò hièm, 叫 |, hard schreeuwen (om hulp, of als men onregtvaardig behandeld wordt).

hièm oan, 叫 冤, bij de mandarijnen komen berigten dat er twist is.

嫌 Hièm — Laken, afkeuren, aanmerking maken op, laakbaar, achterdocht wekkend, verdacht.

hièm gi, | 疑, laakbaar.

hièp hièm, 挾 |, met iemand in onmin zijn, steeds tegen iemand ingenomen zijn.

pī hièm, 避 |, maken dat er niets op U te zeggen valt, het laakbare vermijden.

hoān hièm, 犯 |, zich laakbaar gedragen.

k'i hièm, 棄 |, verstooten (iemand).

hièm koa hièm kiēn, | 肝 | 腎, *lett.* op de lever en de spiermaag aanmerking maken, *d. i.* op alles aanmerking maken.

hièm tang hièm sai, | 東 | 西, do.

Hien

掀 Hien — *hien k'ui*, | 開, openen, (zooals eene doos), ontblooten, ontdekken.

hien koà, | 蓋, een deksel opligten.

hien mîng lî / » *mui* » } | 門 簾, een scherm opligten.

hien sa, | 衣, zijn kleed opligten.

軒 Hien — *hien bièn*, | 冕, prachtig, luisterrijk.

tsu hien, 書 |, studeer-plaats.

su hien, 私 ｜, stil studeervertrek.

hien hat, ｜ 豁, ruim, luchtig, (van eene plaats).

só tsaī hien gòng, 所 在 ｜ 昂, dito.

tièm bīn siang ping hien, 店 面 雙 邊 ｜, een dubbel-open front aan een winkel hebben.

顯 Hién Helder, licht, luisterrijk, roemvol, beroemd; duidelijk, klaarblijkelijk; duidelijk maken; luister geven aan, beroemd maken; ruim, luchtig, openlijk.

hién bing, ｜ 明, ten toon spreiden.

hién dzièn, ｜ 然, klaarblijkelijk, duidelijk.

hién k'ó, 考 ｜, roemvol door een examen komen.

ing hién, 榮 ｜, luisterrijk.

hién tsó ing tsong, ｜ 祖 榮 宗, zijne voorouders eer aan doen, (zooals iemand die tot hooge posten klimt).

hién tát è si, ｜ 達 的 時, ten tijde dat hij algemeen bekend, beroemd, was.

koa ts'i teng hién, 官 星 當 ｜, op het roemvolste tijdstip van zijne officiële betrekking zijn.

hién ing, ｜ 應, zigtbaar.

hién tién ts'ién, ｜ 典 淺, duidelijk, met aanhalingen van classieke schrijvers, en gemakkelijk te begrijpen, (de vereischten van een litt. opstel).

hién iòng, ｜ 陽, ruim, luchtig; algemeen bekend, besproken; in het oogvallend, (zooals een hoog gebouw); openlijk, (zooals dieven.)

Hién Waggelen, schommelen.

iô iô hién hién, 搖 匕 攊 匕, schommelen, (zooals een schip).

koā koā hién, sterk heen en weer schommelen.

Hién *hién è lâng*, (*Ts-ts.*) menschen als die, zulke, deze menschen.

獻 Hièn Aanbieden, als eene offerande aan de goden, of van minderen aan meerderen: offeren; aanbieden, geven, in handen stellen van; voor den dag doen komen, aan het licht brengen, laten zien; opengaan als bloemen; hoog van zich opgeven.

tsè hièn, hièn tsè, 祭 ｜, ｜ 祭, eene offerande doen.

hièn put, ｜ 佛, aan een afgod offeren.

hièn tsoá, hièn tsoá tsi, ｜ 紙 錢, papiergeld op de graven offeren.

hièn hō, ｜ 與, aanbieden, (van minderen aan meerderen).

hièn ts'iú, ｜ 醜, (ik zal u mijn) leelijk (schrift) aanbieden, (beleefdheids formule).

hièn siâ, ｜ 城, eene vesting overgeven.

hièn k'ang siâ, ｜ 空 城, eene leège stad achterlaten, zijn huis leèg achter laten.

hièn só tsaī hō ih, ｜所 在 與 他, eene plaats overgeven, in handen stellen van ....

kòng hièn, 貢 ｜, schatting opbrengen.

hièn lóh kong, ｜ 落 公, ten algemeenen nutte geven.

hièn sió sim, ｜ 小 心, overmate gedienstig.

hièn tsing hō ih, ｜ 情 與 他, iemand eene gunst bewijzen.

hièn kè, hièn ts'ik, ｜ 計 ｜ 策, een plan, krijgslist, voorhouden, voorleggen.

hièn ts'ut, ｜ 出, laten zien, voor den dag komen.

14

hièn kꞓng, | 光, in het openbaar, openlijk.
hièn kong, | 功, bewijzen van verdiensten geven.
hièn ts'iú toū, | 手 單, eene proef, bewijs van zijne kunde geven.
toū hièn ts'iú, 大 出 手, royaal, niet karig.
hièn pėh, | 白, voor den dag, aan het licht, brengen.
hièn pún siòng, | 本 相, den aap uit de mouw doen komen.
hièn hing, 披 胸, de borst ontblooten.
ká kap lâng hièn hing, 敢 與 人 披 胸, voor zijne verantwoording durven nemen.
hièn kiō, | 轎, draagstoel die aan alle kanten kan opengezet worden.
hièn k'ui, | 開, opengaan, (zooals bloemen), opensplijten.
gaù hièn t'aû, 善 | 頭, hoog van zich opgeven.
hien k'ang, | 空, do.
gaù toū hièn siò hièn, 善 大 | 小 |, do.
ts'it hièn poeh hièn, 七 | 八 |, op allerlei manieren hoog van zich opgeven.

憲 Hièn *hièn si gê mêng*, | 司 衙 門, provinciaal geregtshof.

Hièn Vlok haren aan het achterste gedeelte van eenden — tevens het meest stinkende der veêren, van daar: stinkend.
ah hièn, 鴨 尻 毛, zulke eendenveêren tot oorpeuters gebruikt.
ts'aù hièn, hièn kī, 臊 臭, stinkend (zooals onreine beesten).
ū tse hièn, 有 些 |, er is een luchtje aan.

賢 Hiên Wijs, verstandig, knap.
hiên lâng, | 人, wijze, wijsgeer.
put hiên, 不 |, niet verstandig, (beleefde berisping tot eene vrouw).
hiên hoē, | 貨, knap, (van eene huisvrouw).
hiong hiên, 鄉 |, een dorpswijze.

絃 Hiên Snaar; strijkinstrument.
k'im hiên, 琴 |, snaren van eene luit.
hiên koán, | 管, strijk-en-blaas-instrumenten.
kong á hiên, 北 三 |, driesnarige viool.
sam hiên, 三 |, driesnar. guitaar.
dzī hiên, 二 |, tweesnar. viool.
hiên soȧ, | 線, snaar.
king hiên, 弓 |, snaar, pees van een boog.
hiên king, | 弓, strijkstok van eene viool.
siók hiên, 續 |, eene snaar aanspannen, *d. i.* een tweede huwelijk aangaan.
siōng hiên / *siūng* » } 上 |, toenemende maan.
hā hiên / *hē* » } 下 |, afnemende maan.

懸 Hiên Ophangen aan; zich ongerust maken over; onafgedaan, onuitgemaakt.
hiên liông / » *liâng* } | 梁, zich ophangen.
sim kon hiên hiên, 心 肝 | 匕, niet op zijn gemak, ongerust over iets zijn.
hiên hē teh, | 下 的, eene zaak onafgedaan laten liggen.
taī tsì hien teh, 事 | 直, do.
sim hiên hiên, 心 | |, gedurig denken aan.

hiēn bōng, | 望, hopen op.

現 Hiēn Zigtbaar, aan het licht komen, duidelijk; tegenwoordig, voorhanden, gereed, contant.

ts'ut hiēn, 出 |, aan het licht komen.

hiēn ts'ut, | 出, aan het licht brengen.

kui ts'ut hiēn, 鬼 出 |, het spook vertoont zich.

hiēn pò hiēn kì, | 報 | 見, duidelijke, zigtbare bestraffing, (des hemels).

hiēn kì, | 見, zigtbaar, nog in het leven plaats hebbend.

hiēn tsaī, *hiēn si*, *hiēn kim*, | 在, | 時, | 今, thans, nu.

lō hiēn, *ts'ién hiēn*, 露 |, 淺 |, in het oog vallend.

hiēn ū, ... | 有, duidelijk is het ...

ū hiēn, 有 |, klaar, bij de hand, contant, hebben.

ū hiēn bòh, 有 | 否, is het U duidelijk?

hiēn gûn } *,, gîn* } | 銀, contant geld.

hiēn boé } *,, bé* } | 買, à contant geld koopen.

hiēn hiēn piēn piēn, | | 便 便, gereed, klaar, bij de hand.

hiēn kah piēn, | 又 便, do.

hiēn hing, | 還, gereedelijk, onmiddelijk teruggeven.

tsit ts'ing sia ēm tát sì pah hiēn, 一 千 賒 不 當 四 百 |, duizend op crediet is niet zoo goed als vier honderd contant.

hiēn tsī hiēn tsui bô sia bô k'iēm, | 錢 | 水 無 賒 無 欠, contant geld en bijkomende onkosten zonder krediet of schuld, *d. i.* geheel contant afbetaald.

hiēn p'in, | 聘, duidelijk bepalen, overeenkomen.

hiēn dzīm, | 任, in actieve dienst zijn.

k'oà lâng bô hiēn, 看 人 無 |, op iemand zien als of hij er niet was, *d. i.* gering achten.

hiēn lâng, | 人, de zichtbare man, *d. i.* in persoon, de man zelve.

hiēn sì, | 試, schaamtevol, schaamte veroorzakend.

限 Hiēn Bepaalde grens, begrensd, beperkt.

ū hiēn, 有 |, beperkt, niet buitengewoon veel.

Hiep

刼 Hiep *hiep lân ê mih*, | 人 的 物, iemands goed met geweld nemen of houden.

kiông kiông hiep lâng, 强 强 | 人, met geweld ontnemen, afstelen.

Hiép Schudden, losschudden.

hiép k'uìh, | 開, losschudden, lostrekken.

hiép t'ih ting, | 鐵 釘, een spijker losschudden.

hiép i boē tín tāng, | 之 不 能 振 動, er is geen verwikken of verwegen aan, niemand is tegen hem bestand.

協 Hiép Harmonieren, doen overeenstemmen; vereenigd, helpen, assistéren.

hô hiép, 和 |, harmonieren.

hiép ūn, | 韻, de eindklanken op elkander doen slaan, rijmen.

kiep hiép, 洽 |, stevig, stijf in elkander (gepakt).

hiép lik, | 力, met vereenigde krachten.

hiép sim, | 心, één van zin.

hiép pān, | 辦, helpen, assistéren; leden van een collegie, enz.

挾 Hiép Onder den arm houden, van daar: op iets steunen, als bedreiging of voorwendsel aannemen; in zich voeden, (als haat).

hiép sè / » *sì* | 勢, op zijne magt steunen, (en daardoor onbillijk handelen).

hiép hiêm, | 嫌, in onmin met iemand zijn, iemand iets misgunnen.

hiép tsè / » *tsì* | 制, door bedreigingen verhinderen of dwingen.

hiép oàn, | 怨, haat in zich voeden.

脅 Hiép *hiép kut*, | 骨, de ribben.

Hiet

血 Hiet *hiet tsièn*, | 戰, bloedig gevecht.

hiet tsìng, | 症, bloedspuwing.

sit hiet, 失 |, bloed verliezen.

hiet k'ì, | 氣, geestdrift.

hiet hàn, | 漢, iemand wiens woorden als een evangelie zijn.

hiet sìng è lâng, | 性 的 人, iemand waar geestkracht in zit.

Hiet *hiet kák, hiet kák k'ì, hiet k'ìh*, 丢 去, wegwerpen.

hiet sak, 丢 推, weggooijen.

hiet kiû, 擲 毬, met ballen gooijen, (in de hoogte).

hiet to, 擲 刀, met messen gooijen.

hiet kè k'ì, 抛 過 去, overgooijen op, (zooals een vuurpot op een schip).

hiet k'ut à, 抛 掘 仔, kuiltje gooijen, (kinderspel).

hiet hē, 放 下, laten liggen, rusten, (van eene zaak).

穴 Hiét *tsit hiét*, een gat, hol.

tsaò hiét, 巢 |, roovershol, schuilnest.

hó hiét, 虎 |, tijgershol.

tiém hiét, 點 |, de plaats voor een gat aanwijzen, (zooals gravenmeesters doen).

Hik

嚇 Hik *hik p'ièn* / *heh* » | 騙, bedriegen, foppen.

赫 Hik *kui hièn hik*, 鬼 顯 |, waar, zigtbaar, van een geest.

Hik *hik sin*, | 身, lijk, ligchaam na den dood.

hik sin bē ts'in, | 身 未 凈, zijn ligchaam is nog niet koud, hij is nog niet lang dood.

惑 Hik *sièn hik*, 謟 |, verleiden, ompraten, (zooals oproermakers de domme menigte doen).

bê hik, 迷 | misleiden, verleiden.

hik lâng, | 人, menschen misleiden.

檄 Hik *hik bûn*, | 文, proclamatie, aanmaning, (zooals de vijand aan belegerden zendt).

Hik *hoai hik*, iemand onregtvaardig, onbillijk, behandelen.

或 Hetzij ...., of .....

Hik *hik tsiá*, | 者, welligt, misschien.

Him

Him Overschreeuwen.

him hoah, him hoah him hoah, hard schreeuwen.

him lai hoah k'i, 喝來喝去, tegen elkander opschreeuwen.

toā him, 大喝, hard uitvallen, hard overschreeuwen.

toā him sai gaī tsi, 大喝用呆錢, iemand overschreeuwend slecht geld uitgeven, *d. i.* onregtvaardig handelend, iemand op hoogen toon willen beduiden dat het zeer billijk is.

歆 Him *him soān*, ｜羨, iets van iemand roemen, (met verlangen het zelf ook te bezitten, zoals rijkdom, kinderen, enz.); prijzen.

熊 Him Beer.

him tsiū / *„ tsiō* } ｜掌, beerenklaauwen, (eene Chin. delicatesse).

tsia him poáh sai, 車喝跋獅, als een beer en een leeuw duikelen, *d. i.* overal opklauteren en stoeijen, (van jongens).

lâng him, 人｜, soort baviaan.

ti ko him, 猪哥｜, baviaan, veel op een varken gelijkende.

噤 Hīm *ts'ùi hīm hīm*, 口｜｜, geen mond open doen.

Hin

興' Hin Bloeijend, voorspoed, (veel voor winkelnamen gebruikt).

goân hin, 源｜, (winkelnaam).

Hin' *hin sin*, 形身, ligchaam.

悻 Hin *hin hin*, ook *hing hing*, ｜匕, haastig, hals-over-kop.

眩 Hin Duizelig, duizeligheid.

t'aô k'ak hin, 頭殼｜, duizelig, hoofdpijn.

hin tsûn, 暈船, zeeziek, (zonder braking).

' Alléén in het Tsiang-tsiu dialect gespr.

o àm hin, 烏暗｜, duizelig worden.

t'aô hin bák àm, 頭｜目暗, duizelig door afmatting of honger.

t'aô hin bōng bōng, 頭｜茫匕, duizelig zijn.

iû hin, 恙｜, vallende ziekte.

hin gōng, ｜戇, duizelig, dommelig.

hin tioh, ｜着, verlangend zijn naar.

hin kiō, ｜轎, duizelig worden in een draagstoel.

hin soa, ｜山, land duizeling krijgen, (zooals iemand die na langen tijd, op een schip geweest te zijn, aan land komt).

Hing

胸 Hing *hing k'ám*, ｜膛, borst.

hing k'áh, ｜脇, borstblad.

hing k'ám kut, ｜膛骨, borstbeen.

koe hing / *ke „* } 雞｜, kippenborst.

hing keh, ｜膈, maagholte.

k'ùn hing, 裍｜, borst van beesten.

tèng hing / *tui „* } 搥｜, zich op de borst slaan.

hing tsing, ｜前, voor de borst, de borst.

k'i kaò tui hing, 氣到搥｜, zoo toornig dat men zich op de borst slaat.

hing k'ám kut poh, ｜膛骨薄, een dun borstbeen, *d. i.* niet veel op zich durven nemen.

t'ing hing koah bán king, 蕩｜幷挽肩, met de borst vooruit en de schouders opgetrokken, (zooals een manke).

興 Hing *tng hing ê si*, 當｜的時, op het tijdstip van bloei, voorspoed.

hing ōng, | 旺, voorspoedig, voorspoed genieten.

hing ping, | 兵, soldaten werven.

hing k'i, | 起, er boven op komen, (in zijn stand).

hing soe, | 衰, voorspoed en tegenspoed.

悻 Hing *k'i hing hing tò lai ling ling*, 去 | | 回 來 冷 冷, vol vuur, verheugd over iets, weggaan, en koel terugkomen.

興 Hìng Verlangend zijn naar .... om ....

hìng hìng, | 匕, verlangend naar iets zijn, begeerte voor iets gevoelen.

kao hìng, 高 |, hevig verlangend zijn naar.

sit hìng, 失 |, zijn vroeger verlangen naar iets verloren hebben.

hìng t'aô, | 頭, begin, opwelling van begeerte.

m hìng, 唔 |, iets niet gaarne doen.

k'i hìng, 起 |, het verlangen rijst op, welt op.

paï hìng, 敗 |, eene begeerte naar iets bederven, wegnemen.

sing hìng, 勝 |, gebruik maken van het oogenblik dat men iets verlangt.

hìng tsiú, | 酒, verlangend zijn naar wijn.

tsiú hìng, 酒 |, het verlangen naar wijn.

saò hìng, *sò hìng*, 掃 |, alle verlangen naar iets wegnemen, (zooals eene bedroevende tijding doet).

si hìng, 詩 |, lust, neiging, om verzen te maken, (zoo als Chin hebben, wanneer zij op eene fraaije plaats komen; dichtervuur.

刑 Hing Straf, straffen.

hing hoát, | 罰, straf, straffen.

hing pō, | 部, ministerie van justitie.

hing pàng, | 房, departement van justitie in een mandarijn-bureau.

hing bing su iâ, | 名 師 爺, officier van justitie.

néng hing, *tāng hing*, 嫩 |, 重 |, zachte, of zware straf.

k'ok hing, 酷 |, allergestrengst straffen.

hing k'ū } | 具, strafwerktuig.
" *kī* }

hing tiōng } | 仗, straf-uitvoerder.
" *tiāng* }

形 Hing Vorm, gedaante, voorkomen, uiterlijk, manieren.

hing tsōng, | 狀, voorkomen.

hing t'é, | 體, vorm, uiterlijk voorkomen.

bīn hing, 面 |, voorkomen, gelaat.

hing siōng } | 像, voorkomen.
" *ts'iāng* }

soa hing, 山 |, vorm, gedaante, van een berg.

ki hing koài tsōng, 奇 | 怪 狀, er wonderlijk, vreemd, uitzien.

hing sè, | 勢, voorkomen (van dingen).

hing iông, | 容, voorkomen, gelaat.

m tsiâ làng hing, 不 成 人 |, niet het voorkomen van een mensch hebben, *d. i.* niet als een mensch handelen.

ui ing hing tô, 畫 影 | 圖, iemands signalement schetsen en aan grensplaatsen aanplakken.

tsa bó hing hai, 女 | 骸, vrouwelijk voorkomen, verwijfd.

nĕng hing nĕng kaī, 嫩 丨 嫩 骸, zacht, verwijfd, voorkomen.

koe nēng hing
ke nuī » } 鷄 卵 丨, hanetred, (in een ei.

bih hing, 匿 丨, kruipen, (als een grolsche kat).

ah hing, 鴨 丨, waard, (mannelijke eend).

行 Hing Loopen, gaan, reizen; doen, handelen.

hó hing tsó, 美 丨 走, een fraaijen gang hebben.

hing li, 丨 李, reisbagage.

hing koán, 丨 館, reis herberg, (gebouw waar men tijdelijk vertoeven kan).

bi hing, 微 丨, heimelijk de rondte doen, (zooals mandarijnen).

hing tōng kú tsi, 丨 動 舉 止, handel en wandel.

kong hing, 公 丨, in het openbaar doen, openlijk.

hing hiong, 丨 兇, een moord begaan.

hing kióng, 丨 强, geweld gebruiken.

hing sut, 丨 述, levensbeschrijving.

橫 Hing Dwars, overdwars; niet volgens den regten, betamelijken weg; onbetamelijk, onredelijk, tegen regt en billijkheid in.

hing hing, 丨 匕, onredelijk, onregtvaardig.

hing ok, 丨 惡, onbeschaamd, boosaardig, slecht.

hing gik, 丨 逆, do.

ts'iōng hing
ts'iàng » } 縱 丨, onverschrokken, teugelloos, in boosheid.

hing hiong, 丨 兇, woest, wreed.

hing hing sù tsì, 丨 行 肆 至, slecht, onbetamelijk, handelen.

還 Hing Teruggeven, terugbetalen, betalen.

hing tsè
» *tsè* } 丨 責, schuld betalen.

hing ki siàu, 丨 期 數, do.

t'am sia ui hing, 貪 賒 畏 丨, gaarne crediet krijgen, maar niet gaarne betalen.

行 Hīng Gedrag, levenswandel, handelingen; denken, diep denken, berekenen.

tik hīng, 德 丨, deugd, handelingen, gedrag.

p'in hīng, 品 丨, handelingen, levensgedrag.

lóng sim kaú hīng, 狼 心 狗 丨, slecht van handelingen.

siu sim siu hīng, 修 心 修 丨, zijn hart en handelingen verbeteren.

ho of p'ai sim hīng, 好 (歹) 心 丨, goed, of slecht, van harte.

toā sim hing, 大 心 丨, voor groote zaken geschikt.

ū hīng ê lâng, 有 丨 的 人, een verstandig, diepdenkend, mensch.

kaū hīng, 厚 丨, diep denken.

sńg hīng, 算 丨, met berekening doen, niet meer doen dan men volgens de letter verpligt is, (b. v. zooals werklieden).

siū hīng
siō » } 想 丨, do.

k'it hing teh kaù boē toā hàn
» » *teh* » *bē* » » } 吃 丨 直 至 不 大 漢, door zijn vele denken niet groot kunnen worden.

杏 Hīng Amandel.

hīng dzin, 丨 仁, amandel.

hīng hoe
» *hoa* } 丨 花, amandel bloesem.

莧 Hīng *hīng ts'ai*, 丨 菜, soort spinazie.

幸 Geluk, bij geluk.
Hīng *hīng tit*, 丨得, bij geluk, gelukkig dat .....
put hīng, 不丨, ongelukkig.
bān hīng, 萬丨, zeer gelukkig.
ing hīng, 榮丨, vereerd, (door iemands bezoek).

倖 *hiao hīng*, 僥丨, op goed geluk
Hīng rekenen.
Hīng Ten geschenke geven, cadeau doen.
Hān *hīng piá*, 送餅, koekjes cadeau doen.

Hioh

遏 Rust houden, pauseren, uitrusten; roesten, zitten op, (zooals vogels).
Hioh
Heh *hioh k'ùn*, 𩀨息, ter ruste liggen.
hioh hō, 丨雨, voor den regen schuilen.
hioh taò, 午憩, middagschoft houden.
hioh kang, 放工, uitrusten van het werk.
tsiaó hioh siū, 鳥棲巢, de vogel zit op zijn nest.
an hioh, 安息, uitrusten.
hioh ts'oán, 丨喘, uithijgen.
hioh k'eh tièm, 宿客店, in een logement logeren, vertoeven.
taò hioh, 投丨, zijn intrek nemen te ...
hioh mi / » *mê* } 丨夜, overnachten.
kiâ lóng bò hioh, 行總無丨, loopen zonder uit te rusten.
hioh dzoáh, 丨熱, voor de warmte gaan uitrusten, slapen.
hioh nâ hioh tà, 丨籃丨擔, met zijn mand of mars uitrusten.
ū ts'iū piēn ū tsiaó hioh, 有樹便有鳥棲, waar boomen zijn, zijn ook vogels die er in roesten, *d. i.* waar eene gelegenheid bestaat, zijn ook menschen die er gebruik van maken.

葉 Boomblad.
Hióh *ts'iū hióh*, 樹丨, do.
toā hióh, 大丨, groot blad. (paraplui).
hoe hióh / *hoa* » } 花丨, bloemblad.
tê hióh, 茶丨, theebladen.
tik hióh, 竹丨, bamboesbladen.
sì hióh, 扇丨, waaijerblad.
laó hióh, 蔞丨, siriblad.
hun hióh, 烟丨, tabaksbladen.
tsàng hióh, 粽丨, bamboesblad waarin de *tsàng* gebonden worden.
péh hióh liēn, 白丨蓮, witte lotus.
kóng kaò ū ki ū hióh, 講到有枝有丨, zoo spreken dat er takken en bladen aan zijn, *d. i.* knap leugens opmaken, (een boom opzetten).
tsit ki tsiâ tsit hióh ê lâng, 一枝成一丨的人, iemand als een takje met een blad, *d. i.* een net, keurig mensch.
Hióh *bā* (of *laī*) *hióh*, wouw, (Milvus govinda).

Hiong

兇 Wreed, slecht, boosaardig; woest, onbesuisd; snel, in allerijl.
Hiong *hiong ok*, 丨惡, slecht, boosaardig.
hiong bing, 丨猛, wreed, woest.
hiong hoān, 丨犯, moordenaar.
hiong sin, 丨身, do.
hiong sin p'e, 丨身坯, vorm voor

een moordenaar, (tegen slechte menschen gezegd).

t'ing hiong, 挺 〡, woest voor den dag komen, als een vechter met een zwaard.

hing hiong, 行 〡, do. Woest, wild, handelen, als een roover.

hiong kòng, 〡 狂, onbesuisd te werk gaande.

hiong hiong kong, 〡 匕 講, onbesuisd zeggen, zoo maar wegpraten zonder er bij te denken.

hiong hiong, 〡 匕, spoedig, snel, in der ijl.

hiong tsiong, 〡 衝, eensklaps, op het eerste gezigt, in allerijl, onbesuisd.

hiong hiong tsi ng tsiong, 〡 匕 衝 匕, do.

凶 Ongelukkig, rouwaanbrengend.
Hiong *hiong sū*, 〡 事, ongelukkige dingen, sterfgevallen.

hiong soah, 〡 煞, geest van ongeluk, doodplaag.

hiong tsòng, 〡 葬, begraven binnen zeven of tien dagen na het overlijden.

hiong tai, 〡 理, do.

鄉 Dorp, gemeente.
Hiong
Hiang *hiong iòng*, 〡 勇, landweer, schutterij.

hiong sì, 〡 試, examinatie voor *kù-dzin*.

hiong ts'in, 〡 親, dorps-genoot.

hiong siu, 〡 收, in de dorpen belasting gaan op halen.

hiong sin, 〡 紳, de notabelen van een dorp.

享 Genieten, jouisseren van .....
Hióng
Hiáng *hióng hok*, 〡 福, geluk genieten.

hióng lók, 〡 樂, vreugde genieten, smaken.

p'oè hióng, 配 〡, iemand in eene offerande adsisteren.

響 *ing hióng*, 影 〡, schijn van iets, zonder dat de zekerheid nog bestaat.
Hióng
Hiáng *hióng ìng*, 〡 應, weêrgalmen, weêrklank vinden, (zooals de stem des oproers in de naburige streken).

晌 *poà hióng*, 半 〡, een poosje, eene wijl.
Hióng

餉 *hiòng gûn* } *hiàng gîn* } 〡 銀, in- en uitgaande regten, belasting, geld voor de soldaten.
Hiòng
Hiàng

ts'ut k'aò hiòng, 出 口 〡, uitgaande regten.

dzip k'aò hiòng, 入 口 〡, inkomende regten.

hiòng hāng, 〡 項, belasting.

hiòng sè } *hiàng soè* } 〡 稅, do.

p'ah hiòng, 打 〡, belasting opleggen.

ting hiòng, 徵 〡, belasting opleggen, heffen.

láp hiòng, 納 〡, belasting betalen.

ts'ut hiòng, 出 〡, soldij uitbetalen.

niá hiòng, 領 〡, soldij ontvangen.

tsaò hiòng, 偷 〡, smokkelen.

hiòng lē } *» lī* } 〡 例, vaste belasting, vaste regten.

liáh hiòng, 掠 〡, smokkelwaar vatten.

hiòng tìng, 〡 當, gepatenteerd pandjeshuis.

hiòng koán, 〡 關, belastings kantoor.

kun hiòng, *ping hiòng*, 軍, 兵 〡, fourage, soldij voor het leger.

向 Familienaam.
Hiòng
Hiàng *sa hiòng* } *sio hiàng* } 相 〡, tegen elkander zitten.

sim sa hiòng / *„ sio hiàng* } 心相丨, sympathiseren.

hiòng lai, 丨來, van vroeger tot nu, te voren, vroeger

sim koa tsoan hiòng tī .... 心肝專丨於 ...., uitsluitend verlangen naar ......

tsē hiòng, 坐丨, ligging, uitzigt, van een huis.

hiòng iòng, 丨陽, licht, verlicht, (van een huis), licht uitzigt.

i hiòng, 意丨, rigting van zijne begeerte, meening.

sim hiòng, 心丨, begeerte.

hiòng pak, 丨北, naar het Noorden uitzien, (van een huis).

hiong t'ien sai poáh to, 丨天西跋倒, achterover omvallen.

it hiòng lóng bò k'oà kìh, 一丨總無看見, van al dien tijd af niet gezien hebben.

hiòng tsièn, 丨前, vooruitgaan, de leider van iets zijn.

雄 Hiòng *hiòng tsòng*, 丨壯, sterk, robust.

hiòng lang, 丨猛, do.

ing hiòng hò hàn, 英丨好漢, dappere, moedige kerel.

ts'u hiòng gán / *ts'i „ „* } 雌丨眼, schuinstaande oogen, het eéne oog lang gerekt, het andere rond.

bē kì ts'u hiòng, 未見雌丨, nog niet weten aan welke kant de overwinning valt.

荒 Hiông *hiòng hiòng*, 丨匕, verwoed, leelijk er uit zien.

hiòng kai kài, 丨介匕, onbesuisd, teugelloos.

siū hiòng, 甚丨, zeer woest, opvliegend.

kan hiòng, 奸丨, onopregt.

hiau hiòng, 僥丨, do.

t'ai hiòng, 太丨, al te onbesuisd, al te erg.

熊 Hiòng Familienaam.

Hip

壓 Hip Met iets toedekken, zoo dat er geen lucht in of uit kan komen; onder iets vangen (als insekten); smoren, smorend, benaauwd; onderdrukken, verdrukken, voor overmagt of een grooten mond doen zwichten.

hip ts'ut bī, 丨出味, toedekken, om te laten trekken.

hip au, 葢鐘, kopje met deksel.

tò hip, 覆丨, een uitgehold voorwerp over iets omkeeren; met de holle hand bedekken.

p'ē laī hip si kià / *p'oē „ „ „ „* } 被內丨死囝, onder de dekens zijn kind dood smoren, *d. i.* zich een verdriet berokkenen waarover men zich tegen anderen niet durft te beklagen.

toā lin hip sè kià, 大乳丨小兒, onder groote borsten een klein kind smoren, *d. i.* iemand door zijne magt, of gezag intimidéren.

hip hoa, 丨化, uitsmoren, uitdooven, (vuur).

hip koā, 丨汗, uitzweeten, door iets over het ligchaam te doen.

hip hip, 丨匕, benaauwd, bedompt.

hip dziét, 丨熱, benaauwd heet, (zoo als in een klein vertrek).

hip dziét ē pī
" " " pē } 激熱之病, ziekte door benaauwde warmte veroorzaakt.

hip kah bô k'ùi, ｜到無氣, zoo verdrukken dat men geen adem halen, zich niet verdedigen, kan.

ìng sì hip lâng, 以勢｜人, iemand door zijne magt verdrukken, doen zwichten.

hó hip, 虎｜, overbluffen, overschreeuwen, overdonderen.

hip tsiòng, ｜衆, zenuwachtig, (door de tegenwoordigheid van vele menschen).

磁 Hip *hip tsióh*, ｜石, magneet.

hip tsioh tsiáh ngē bô tsiáh nńg, ｜石食硬不食軟, magneet haalt harde en niet zachte voorwerpen aan, *d. i.* bij voorkeur met een ongemakkelijk persoon te doen hebben.

歙 Hip Toedekken, digtdoen, om er de lucht niet uit te laten.

㪧 Hip Insekten vangen door een voorwerp op hen te werpen.

Hit

彼 Hit *hit ē*, ｜個, die, dat.

hit tau, ｜處, aldaar, ginds.

hit uī, ｜位, do.

hit só tsuī, ｜所在, do.

hit nih, ｜爾, do

hit tsit dzit, ｜一日, dien dag..

㩐 Hit *hit lai hit k'ì*, 丢來丢去, heen en weer schommelen.

kap i hit, 與他｜, met iemand in onmin zijn, twist hebben.

lō nì hit, 露爾｜, schommelen, waggelen, (zooals iets dat niet stevig staat).

āng soh hit k'ìh, 用索｜去, met een touw slinger, weg slingeren.

Hiu

休 Hiu *hiu tì*, ｜致, voor goed ontslagen, afgezet.

hiu tsu
" si } ｜書, acte van echtscheiding.

hiu hiu tsoè i k'ì, ｜匕做伊去, weggaan zonder verder iets van zich te laten hooren.

bô beh pàng i kan hiu, 無要放伊干｜, eene zaak zoo maar niet willen laten afloopen, het er niet bij laten zitten.

幽 Hiu *ts'ing hiu*, 清｜, zindelijk en rustig, (van eene plaats).

咻 Hiu *hoah hiu*, 喝｜, schreeuwen, (als teeken).

hiu lâng, ｜人, iemand met *hiu* toeroepen.

鄉 Hiu *hiu lí*, ｜里, dorp.

Hio *hiu ts'ng*,
hio ts'ui } ｜村, do.

Hiang *hiu siā*, ｜社, do.

hiu ē, ｜下, do.

lóh hiu, 下｜, naar een dorp gaan, een dorp binnen trekken, in een gevecht.)

hiu kan ē lâng, ｜間之人, een dorps mensch.

hoè hiu
huì " } 廢｜, een dorp verwoesten.

tâng hiu, 同｜, van hetzelfde dorp.

liên hiu, kun hiu, 連｜, 近｜, aangrenzend, naburig, dorp.

sì ngó hiu, 四五｜, (menschen van) de dorpen in de rondte.

香 Hiu̱ Hio̱ Reukwerk, reukstokje, vuurstokje.

ki lâm hiu̱, 奇楠丨, reukhout.

k'ui hiu̱, 開丨, een nieuw dorp stichten; een verbond, loge oprigten, (van het Hemel en Aarde verbond gezegd).

hiu̱ ts'â, 丨柴, sandelhout.

hiu̱ ts'ú, 丨鼠, muskusrat.

hiu̱ ko̱, 丨菰, gedroogde champignons.

hiu̱ i̱, 丨橼, groote ronde citroenen.

kiáh hiu̱, 舉丨, een offerstokje in de hand nemen om te offeren.

hiu̱ ts'ìng, 丨槍, schoten bij eene processie gedaan.

ngiâ hiu̱, 迎丨, eene processie vormen.

hiu̱ liaō, 丨料, stukje reukwerk.

bê hûn hiu̱, 迷魂丨, bedwelmend reukwerk.

hiu̱ lô̱, 丨爐, reukwerk-komfoor.

hiu̱ tâng, 丨筒, reukwerk-koker.

ts'ìng hiu̱, 薰丨, reukwerk tusschen kleèren, enz., leggen.

hiu̱ t'ng, 丨湯, reukwater, (waarmede men zich wascht).

hiu̱ tīn, 丨陣, de achtereenvolgende rijen eener processie.

tim hiu̱, 沉丨, aloë.

àn sik hiu̱, 安息丨, Benzuin.

toâ hiu̱, 壇丨, reukwerk van sandelhout.

ū tsiáh ū kiâ k'ì, ū sio hiu̱ ū pó pì, 有食有行氣,有焚丨有保庇, eet men, dan heeft men er de uitwerking van; brandt men reukwerk, dan wordt men beschermd.

hiu̱ hê / *hio̱ hoê* } 丨火, reukwerk-asch, als amulet bij zich gedragen.

hiu̱ iû, 丨油, welriekende olie.

hiu̱ oân, hiu̱ i̱, 丨圓, welriekende bal, soort reukzeep.

hiu̱ tìng, 丨凳, stoel, zetel, met reukwerk, (bij processien gedragen).

hiu̱ kong, 丨扛, reukwerk-dragers, (bejaarde menschen die met reukwerk in de hand achter eene processie komen).

hiu̱ tē, 丨袋, reukwerk-zakje, (om den hals gedragen).

tse mṇh nā hiu̱ liaō kùi kùi k'ì k'ì, 此物若丨料貴匕氣匕 die dingen zijn peperduur, (lett. duur als reukwerk).

ki hiu̱, 消瘦(枝丨), mager (als een reukstokje.).

hiu̱ hiu̱, 丨匕, zeer mager.

ki hiu̱ sán soè, 枝丨瘦衰, mager en klein.

朽 Hiú *hiú noā*, 丨爛, bedorven, verrot, zooals kleèren die te lang in het water hebben gestaan.

hiú hoāī, 丨壞, vermolmd, verrot, (van hout).

noā hiú hiú, 爛丨匕, zacht; op het punt van te bederven.

ts'aò hiú, 臭丨, aangestoken, op een punt verrot; zooals vruchten, aardappelen).

䥢 Hiú̱ Hard klinken, als een afgaande pijl.

hiú̱ tâng, hiáng tâng, 丨銅, helklinkend koper.

灑 Hiù *hiù tsui*, 丨水, water sprenkelen, (met de hand of een kwast).

hiù lù, 洒丨, sprenkelen.

hū i hiù tioh, 彼他｜着, door iets bespet, besprenkeld zijn.
hiù tsioh t'aô á, ｜石頭仔, met steenen slingeren.

Hiù *koâ hiù hiù*, 寒凍匕, rillen van koude.

向 Hiù *hiù ping* / *hiò* » ｝｜邊, daar, aan die kant.
àn hiù si / » *hiò se* ｝如此, aldus.
hong hiù, 方｜, of *tsē hiù*, 坐｜, ligging van eene plaats.

裘 Hiû Gewatteerde jas.
p'ê hiû / *p'oê* » ｝皮｜, jas van schapenvacht.
mî hiû, 綿｜, gewatteerde jas.
kiep hiû / *koeh hiû* ｝夾｜, ongewatteerde jas.
tsiáh pē pīng ts'īng bú hiû / » *pē puī* » *bo* » ｝吃父飯穿毋｜, door zijne ouders onderhouden worden, onbezorgd leven.
tông hiû, 長｜, lange jas.

Hiuh

Hiuh *hong hiuh hiuh kiò* of *hao*, 風嘶匕然, de wind loeit.

Ho

Ho Heet eten opslobberen.
dzit t'aô ho ho ho, de zon is brandend.
ho dzit, door eene heete zon beschenen worden.

好 Hó Goed; als bijw. goed te.... gemakkelijk te....
hó sè / » *sì* ｝｜勢, geschikt, goed.
hó hàn, ｜漢, welgezet, vet, een dappere, ferme kerel.
hó boē / » *bē* ｝｜賣, goed te verkoopen, gevraagd.
hó tá, ｜胆, dapper.
hó k'oà, ｜看, fraai om te zien.
hó tiaō t'aô, ｜兆頭, goed voorteeken.
hó giáh, ｜額, rijk.
siong hó, 相｜, goede vrienden zijn.
hó kì ti / » » *sè* ｝｜記性, goed van geheugen.
kóng hó oē / » » *oā* ｝說善言, mooije praatjes hebben.
hó t'ia, 可聽, welluidend.
hó sim, 善心, menschlievend, goedhartig.
hó ì, 美意, met goede bedoeling.
hó k'a hó ts'iú, 手足善全, gezond van lijf en leden.
hó pò, 善報, goede belooning voor goede daden.
hó sū, 美事, goede dingen, heugchelijke dingen.
hó tsiáh, 甘食, lekker.
hó sim k'ih lui p'ah sih, 善心被雷打死, ondank tot loon krijgen.
kóng hó ts'ui, / *hó ts'ui kóng*, ｝善婉覻, zachtzinnig, bedaard tot iemand spreken, vermanen.
hó hó lâng, ｜｜人, een goed mensch; gezond en wel.
tsoè hó lâng, 做｜人, den goeden man uithangen, *d. i.* al is het zelfs noodzakelijk toch niet met iemand in onmin willen komen.
hó sim ē lâng, ｜心的人, ie-

mand die over alles vlugtig heen loopt.

hô ts'ùi taô, | 觜 斗, van alles, goed en slecht, eten.

hô lí tsit làng, 幸 的 有 你, gelukkig dat gij er waart, zoo dat ... het komt alleen door uwe goedheid dat ....

hô tsit ê, 幸 的 此 ..., wat het nog goed maakt is ..., gelukkig nog dat ....

詼 Hô Goed zoo, ik keur het goed.

和 Hô Eendragt, eendragtig, harmonie, harmonieren, overeenstemmen, overeenkomen; verbond van vriendschap, traktaat, een traktaat sluiten; bij elkander passen, bij elkander doen passen; van daar: stemmen, als eene viool; mengen, als medecijnen.

hô hó, | 好, harmonieren.

ka hô bān sū sing, 家 | 萬 事 成, met harmonie in een huis komt alles tot stand.

hô sūn, | 順, eendragtig, (van eene familie).

hô k'ì, | 氣, geest van eendragt.

hô ping, | 平, in harmonie.

tiong hô, 中 |, regtvaardig, billijk.

hô háp, | 合, overeenkomen om.

hô iok / *iak* | 約, eene overeenkomst, contract, traktaat, sluiten.

káng hô, 講 |, over eene verzoening, tractaat, onderhandelen.

ts'ù hô, 處 |, eene zaak bijleggen.

hô poâ, | 盤, met het rekenbord overeenkomen, hetzelfde tot uitkomst krijgen; koopwaren juist op een tijd aanbrengen dat ze goed te verkoopen zijn.

hô hô, | |, bij elkander passen, (van voorw.)

tsit ê boē hô tit hit ê mih, 此 物 不 能 | 彼 物, dit past daar niet bij.

hô soà, hô hièn, 調 線, 調 絃, snaren stemmen.

hô ioh, 調 藥, medicijnen mengen.

河 Hô Rivier.

t'ien hô, gûn hô, hô hàn, hô k'oe, 天 |, 銀 |, | 漢, | 溪, melkweg.

laī hô, 內 |, binnenwater.

壕 Hô *hô kau*, | 溝, gracht.

何 Hô Wat, hoe, waarom. Familienaam.

hô tíng, | 等, wat voor een soort van .... ?

hô tíng ê hó, | 等 的 好, onvergelijkelijk goed.

hô k'ó, | 苦, waarom zich daarover zoo moeijelijk te maken!

hô hòng, | 況, hoe veel te meer.

bû naī hô, 無 奈 |, onvermijdelijk, er is geen hulp voor.

荷 Hô *hô liên*, | 蓮, lotusbloem.

hô lan, | 囒, Holland.

hô lan tsû, | 囒 薯, aardappelen.

hô lan taō, | 囒 豆, doperwten.

豪 Hô Knap, niet bekrompen van ideé; voor groote zaken geschikt.

hô kiét, | 傑, knap, uitstekend man.

hô sóng, | 爽, royaal, niet karig om verfraaijingen, enz., te maken.

hô ti, | 猪, egel.

tai ke hò hìng, 衆 家 ｜, allen verlangen er zeer naar.

毫 Haartje; een weinig.

Hô *hun hò*, 分 ｜, een weinigje.

si hò, 絲 ｜, do.

號 *hō p'aò*, ｜ 炮, verkennings-schot, saluutschoten.

Hō *tsiok hō* / *tsiak »* } 渾 ｜, bijnaam, (goede of kwade).

àm hō, 暗 ｜, geheim teeken.

tsoè àm hō / *tsò » »* } 作 暗 ｜, een geheim teeken geven.

ki hō, 旗 ｜, vlag.

tièm hō, 店 ｜, naam van een winkel.

ki hō, 記 ｜, merk, teeken.

hō t'aô, ｜ 頭, trompet.

hō līng, ｜ 命, bevelen

hō p'o̱, ｜ 薄, koopmansboek.

dzī hō, 字 ｜, merk, teeken, naam.

li hō siá mih mià, 爾 表 何 名, wat is de naam van Uwe firma.

hō mià, ｜ 名, onderscheidingsnaam.

ts'ut hō, 發 ｜, een teeken geven.

ts'ut hō, 出 ｜, buiten models-.

pàng hé hō / *» hoé »* } 發 火 ｜, een vuurteeken geven.

t'o̱ hō, 土 ｜, bijnaam.

nī hō / *oū »* } 畫 ｜, zijn teeken zetten onder, onderteekenen.

tsoè hō, 做 ｜, een merk op iets zetten.

t'é hō, 體 ｜, benaming van een voorwerp.

t'é hō làng, 體 ｜ 人, iemand een bijnaam geven.

hō tsoè, ｜ 做, heeten, noemen,

gûn hō / *giu »* } 銀 ｜, persoon die de belasting-gelden int.

pien hō, 編 ｜, een onderscheidingsnaam of teeken geven.

kuì hō, 貴 ｜, Uw geeërde winkelnaam.

pē hō, 庳 ｜, mijn winkelnaam.

koà hō, 卦 ｜, zijn naam teekenen, (voor men op audientie gaat.)

賀 Familienaam.

Hō *hō hi*, ｜ 喜, gelukwenschen, feliciteren.

hō lé, ｜ 禮, met geschenken komen gelukwenschen.

hō siū, ｜ 壽, iemand op zijn verjaardag gelukwenschen.

hō ni, ｜ 年, nieuwjaar wenschen.

i o hù hō, 咿 呵 赴 ｜, met de groote troep meêspreken, (zonder de zaak te voren te onderzoeken).

呼 *ho̱ k'ip*, ｜ 吸, ademhalen.

'Ho̱ *ho̱ hoàn*, ｜ 叫, roepen, bij zich roepen.

ho̱ hoah, ｜ 喝, vrees aanjagen.

tsio ho̱, 招 ｜, toeroepen, aanhalen, (kinderen).

ho̱ iok, ｜ 約, duidelijk, luid, overeenkomen.

it ho̱ pik lòk, 一 ｜ 百 諾, roept gij eens, dan antwoorden honderd, *d. i.* door zijn geldelijk vermogen, al zijne wenschen kunnen krijgen.

tsièn ho̱ hō̱ iòng, 前 ｜ 後 擁, van voren uitschreeuwen en van achteren antwoorden, (zooals bij het gevolg van een mandarijn.

嘑 Liegen.

Ho̱ *ho̱ t'i̱ ho̱ toē*, ｜ 天 ｜ 地, vreeselijk liegen, vergrooten.

ho hoah ê sing li, 虛喚的生理, windhandel.

kè tsi tsiaò ho, 價錢照丨, de prijs is al (naar dat men er op biedt.

k'ang (of *kan*) *ho bān dzī gō*, 空丨萬字誤, sterk bluffen.

o o ts'ut tsaī li ho, 嗚乙出在你丨, gij kunt vertellen, wijs maken, wat gij wilt.

虎 Tijger.

Hó *hó lòng*, 丨狠, boosaardig.

hó t'aò kam, 丨頭柑, bittere oranje.

hó lók, 丨鹿, onopregt, leugenachtig.

hó tsiòng / » *tsiàng*, 丨將, dappere aanvoerder.

hó hip, 丨嚇, overschreeuwen.

hó sin hó, 蝴蠅丨, springspin.

ū tsoè hó hām, bò tsoè hó t'ì ūm / » *tsò* » *ūm* » *tsò* » *t'ę tsām* 有作丨鹹無作丨伏塹, heeft hij het (*d. i.* geld) dan is hij als een tijger die hongerig is; heeft hij het niet, dan zit hij (te kijken) zooals een tijger op zijne hurken.

hó lòng pà piu, 丨狠豹彪, als een tijger, wolf, luipaard en tijgerkat *d. i.* een slecht mensch.

hó t'aò tsáh, 丨頭閘, werktuig om misdadigers door midden te hakken.

hó t'aò pai, 丨頭牌, bord met een tijgerkop bovenaan, door mandarijnen gebruikt.

hó t'aò ièn ām, 丨頭燕頷, een hoofd als een tijger en een nek als eene zwaluw, *d, i.* een sterk, korthalzig, mensch.

kap hó ióh, 治丨藥, tijger-vergift mengen, *d. i.* met de schrijvers uit een mandarijn bureau onderling bepraten om zeker persoon valschelijk aan te klagen.

kāng hó tsioh tá, 向丨借膽, buitengewoon veel durven, *lett.* De gal van een' tijger leenen.

t'ong siā hó, 通城丨, de grootste bandieten van eene plaats.

hó pan kaó, 丨班犬, een tijgergevlekte hond.

hó bō, hó á oé, 丨帽, 丨子鞋, muts en schoenen met een tijgerkop.

dzim hó tsih, 探丨舌, een tijger tong uithalen, *d. i.* uiterst moeijelijk te doen.

hó hi bīn, 丨魚面, er leelijk uitzien.

hó ui, 丨威, tijgerwaardigheid, indrukwekkendheid, ontzag.

hó dziaó hoe, 丨爪花, tijgerklaauw, (naam eener bloem).

hó lâng, 丨人, iemand overbluffen.

hā san hó, 下山丨, strak, om het lijf spannend buis.

hó p'ê kao í, 丨皮交椅, stoel, zetel, met een tijgervel bedekt.

sa hó, 相丨, elkander bedriegen.

hó īm, 蓬藥, framboos, (Rubus thunbergii).

hó t'i, 丨艙, gedroogde, eetbare, algen. (enteromorpha).

琥 *hó p'ik*, 丨珀, amber.

Hó

戽 Uitscheppen (water).

Hò *hò tsui*, 丨水, water uitscheppen, met water gooijen.

hò taó, 丨斗, waterschepper; uitstekende kin.

hò tsui sa ak / » » *sio* » 搁水相沃, elkander nat gooijen; over en weer geschenken geven.

厦荷大辭典

họ̀ k'a, 反踏, met de achterpooten slaan, (zooals paarden).

họ̀ ts'iú, 揮手, met de hand wegwenken.

họ̀ họ̀ kiò, 深匕喚, dringend roepen.

họ̀ họ̀ pai, 叠匕拜, verscheidene buigingen achter elkander doen, als of men water hoosde.

họ̀ k'ut á sui ak
» » » sio » } | 窟水相沃, elkander met het water uit eene plas nat gooijen, *d. i.* een onbeduidend gevecht.

họ̀ lai họ̀ k'i, | 來 | 去, ongeregeld, onregelmatig, handelen.

họ̀ kè lai họ̀ kè k'i, | 過來 | 過去, over en weer opkleenen, als touw op een stok.

gê tsò koā koā (of *k'aō k'aō*) *họ̀*, 牙槽呱匕 |, klappertanden.

họ̀ kiah, onvoorzigtig, niet vast in zijne handelingen.

互 Họ̀ *p'ah sip dzī họ̀*, 打十字 |, een kruisband leggen over.

好 Họ̀ *họ̀ sū siōng*, 好事像, nieuwsgierig.

Họ̀ *họ̀ sik*, | 色, veel van de vrouwen houden.

họ̀ ko, | 高, eerzuchtig.

họ̀ po, | 褒, veel van loftuitingen houden, gaarne geprezen worden.

k'ok họ̀, 酷 |, vurig verlangen, wenschen.

葫 Hộ *hộ lộ*, | 蘆, kalabas, pompoen, flesch.

hộ lộ pû, | 蘆匏, do.

hộ lộ tui, | 蘆墮, de gewigten aan eene klok.

hộ lộ būn
» » pūn } Zie onder het woord Būn.

蝴 Hộ *hộ tiêp*, | 蝶, oorspr. vlinder; (in de volkst.) scharnier.

hộ sin, | 蠅, vlieg.

hộ sin hộ, | 蠅虎, *lett.* vliegentijger, springspin.

kim hộ sin, 金 | 蠅, paardevlieg.

hộ sin sai, | 蠅屎, sproeten.

胡 Hộ *hộ tsio*, | 椒, peper.

糊 Hộ Oorspr. stijfsel, kleverig; van daar: verward in elkander, niet duidelijk, niet afgedaan, zonder regel, onbesuisd; leugenachtig.

hộ tộ, | 塗, verward, (zooals zaken), onbesuisd, zonder regel.

hộ tộ kóng, | 塗講, verward spreken, wouwelen.

hộ li hộ tộ, | 里 | 塗, onbesuisd, onvoorzigtig.

hộ hūn, | 混, verward, onduidelijk.

hộ ts'e ts'e (of *ts'eh ts'eh*)
» ts'e ts'e } | 差差, verward door elkander.

hộ kiah, onvoorzigtig, onbesuisd.

hâm hộ 含 |, onduidelijk mompelen; ter halver wege doen.

hộ soat, | 說, leugenachtig spreken, beleefde term voor liegen.

hộ liù p'iù, | 溜漂, onopregt; eene zaak niet duidelijk uitmaken.

hộ hàm, | 泛, onopregt, niet te geloven.

鬍 Hộ Baard; verward in elkander, als haar van een baard.

hộ ts'iu, | 鬚, baard.

hộ eh put dzin, niau eh kan sin, | 者不仁 癡者奸臣,

16

gebaarden zijn onmenschlievend, pokdaligen valsch.

hô sai kaò, 丨 鬍 狗, langharige hond.

hô hô sàm sàm, 丨 匕 毿 匕, in de war, slordig, verward door elkander.

hô hô sap sap, 丨 匕 霅 匕, dof, vuil.

湖 Hô Een meer. (Komt alleen met deze boeken-uitspraak voor).

hô si, 丨 絲, ruwe zijde.

hô si k'eh, 丨 絲 客, koopman in ruwe zijde.

狐 Hô *hô li*, 丨 狸, vos.

hé sio hô li, 赤 丨 狸, bruine vos.

壺 Hô *iā hô*, 夜 丨, nachtpot, waterpot.

撈 Hô Scheppen, uitscheppen, opscheppen, afschuimen.

hô pēng / » *puī* } 丨 飯, rijst opscheppen.

hô p'iô, 丨 薸, kroost scheppen.

侯 Hô *hô tsiok*, 丨 爵, markies.

Hô *hô á*, 然 耶, ah! is het zoo!

Hô

雨 Hō Regen.

lóh hō, 落 丨, het regent.

hō tàm tsui ta, 丨 濕 水 乾, door regen en alle weêr moeten.

hō tsui, 丨 水, regenwater.

hō á meng meng / » » *mo mo* } 細 丨 霏 匕, fijne motregen.

hō meng á, hō hoe á, 丨 霏 仔, 丨 花 仔, do.

hō soà, 丨 傘 paraplui.

hō soà t'aô, 丨 傘 頭, punt van eene paraplui.

hō soà kut, 丨 傘 骨, baleinen eener paraplui.

hō soà toā kut, 丨 傘 大 骨, paraplui-stok.

ts'iong kông hō, ts'i tsin hō, 愴 惶 丨, 青 貞 丨, plotselinge regenbui.

hō ts'iu, 丨 鬚, fijne regendroppels, regenspetten.

hong t'ai hō, 暴 風 丨, storm en regen.

dzia hō, 遮 丨, tegen den regen beschermen.

hō i, 丨 意, regenachtig, naar regen staande.

k'it hō, 乞 丨, om regen bidden.

sin hō, 承 丨, regen opvangen.

siò hō tsiép loh, 細 丨 轍 下, weinig, maar gestadig vallende regen. *d. i.* niet veel te gelijk, maar gestadig door verdienen.

p'oah hō, 潑 丨, door inkomende regen nat worden.

tsìm hō, 浸 丨, door regen doortrokken.

àm hō tiaò mi / » » » *mé* } 晚 丨 連 夜, avond-regen duurt de nacht door.

hō tsui tsiep ìng, 丨 水 接 應, de regen valt geregeld; na bepaald tijds verloop.

tsit liép hō tìm sih tsit é làng, 一 粒 丨 投 死 一 的 人, elke droppel regent een mensch dood, *d. i.* hevige regen.

護 Hō Beschermen, bewaken; veilig; helpen.

pó hō, 保 丨, beschermen.

hō sin é mih, 丨 身 之 物, beschermings-, verdedigings-wapen.

hō sàng, ｜送, geleide doen.

hō ts'ù, ｜厝, zijgebouwen, bijgebouwen.

t'án hō, 袒｜, iemand partijdig helpen.

hō hong ìn, ｜封印, stempel waarop 護封, "veilig verzegeld", staat.

hō kap ting, ｜合釘, spijker met een kop.

戶 Hō Deur; huis, huisgezin; persoon, met betrekking tot zijn beroep.

mêng hō / *muî* » } 門｜, deuren (in het algemeen).

k'ui mêng k'ui hō / » *muî* » » } 開門開｜, de deuren open doen.

hō tīng / » *tūn* } ｜閾, drempel.

p'ò hō, 鋪｜, winkels.

tsûn hō, 船｜, schepen.

ke ke hō hō, 家匕｜匕, elk huis, huisgezin.

hō k'ao ts'eh, ｜口册, buurt-register.

hō pō, ｜部, ministerie van inkomsten.

tiên hō, 佃｜, landbouwers van een heer.

láh hō, 獵｜, jager.

後 Hō Na, later, achter, achternakomend.

pān hō sū, 辦｜事, de dingen gereed maken na (iemands leven), *d. i.* de lijkkist en lijkkleêren.

hō sin ê lâng, ｜身之人, nakomelingen.

hō ê / » *î* } ｜裔, verre afstammeling.

hō sū, ｜嗣, afstammelingen, erfgenamen.

poè hō oē / » » *oū* } 背｜話, woorden achter iemands rug gezegd.

厚 Hō Dik; veel, zeer.

hō lé, ｜禮, zeer beleefd.

ù hō bōng, 有｜望, van veel verwachting, veel belovend.

tiong hō kó ì, 忠｜古意, solie-de en opregt.

后 Hō Keizerin, koningin.

hông hō, 皇｜, keizerin.

hō t'ó, ｜土, aardgoden.

su hō t'ó, 事｜土, aan de aardgoden offeren, (bij begrafenissen gedaan).

Hō *se hō* / » *iang* } 紗梣, haspel.

hō se, haspelen.

與 Hō Geven; maken dat . . . , laten . . . . ; zich laten . . . . ; van daar: aanduider van den lijdenden vorm.

koah tsî hō ìh, 刮錢｜伊, iemand wat geld geven.

hō lâng k'oà, ｜人看, aan anderen laten zien.

hō lâng p'ah, ｜人打, geslagen worden.

hō lâng ts'ok gok, 令人錯愕, anderen verwonderen.

hō lâng kièn koè / » » » *koà* } 使人見怪, iemand ongenoegen veroorzaaken.

hō i tit, ｜之直, regtmaken.

hō i sú huì, 給伊使費, schade vergoeden.

hō i hâng hók, 使之降服, onderwerpen.

Hō *hō hō hō*, goed zoo.!

海上絲綢之路文獻集成 科技與文化編

Hoa*

花 Hoa Bloem, bloemrijk, fraai; in wellust of overdaad gebruiken, verkwisten.
hoa giên k'aó gú } *» gân k'á gí* } 丨言巧語, fraaije maar niet gemeende woorden.
hoa koe liú hāng, 丨街柳巷, hoerenstraat, (*lett.* "bloemstraten en wilge-lanen).
ien hoa ê lâng, 烟丨之人, ligtekooijen, (fats. term).
hoa hùi, 丨費 verteren, verkwisten.
hoa tsoē tsoē tsī, 丨多多錢, veel geld verkwisten.
hu hoa, 虛丨, opgeschikt, kwistig.

譁 Hoa Geruisch, leven.
soan hoa, 宣丨, leven maken, rusie hebben.

熄 Hoa Uit, uitgedoofd.
p'ah hoa, 樸丨, uitdooven, bluschen.
pùn hoa, *gò hoa*. 噴丨, 鏊丨, uitblazen, uitdraaijen, zooals een lamp.)
sim hé hoa, 心火丨, zijn hartevuur is uit, *d. i.* zijne toorn is bedaard.

Hoá Hoà *hoá hoá*, oppervlakkig, onduidelijk.

化 Hoà Van gedaante veranderen, in iets anders overgaan, veranderen; door lessen of voorbeeld veranderen, verbeteren, civiliseren, civilisatie.
pièn hoà, 變丨, veranderen, overgaan in.
kám hoà, 感丨, door vermaning verbeteren.
kaò hoà, 教丨, door onderwijs verbeteren.
hoà goā ê lâng, 丨外之人, menschen buiten de beschaving, of die zich niet aan het bestaand bestuur houden, zooals de Miao-tzse en inboorlingen van Formosa.
kiû hoà, 求丨, om verandering in zijn lot smeeken, aalmoezen vragen.
hoà ièn, 丨緣, aalmoezen ophalen, (van priesters).
hoà tsoè tsúi, 丨做水, in water veranderen, overgaan, (zooals ijs).
hoà hé } *» hoe* } 丨火, in vuur veranderen, door vuur verteerd.
siau hoà, 消丨, verteren, (van spijzen).
hit ê lâng k'ah hoà, 此人更丨, die man is niet haatdragend.
hoà sin, 丨神, veranderlijk, vergeetachtig, van aard.
sió sū hoà bô sū, 小事丨無事, kleine geschillen in niets doen uitloopen.
hoà king. 丨境, sche tsen, niet meenen.
hoà sing, 丨生, door gedaante-verandering geboren, (zooals kapellen).
hûn hoà, 渾丨, ongemerkt, onzigtbaar in iets overgaan, (zooals eene reparatie waarvan men de aanhechtingsplaats niet ondekken kan).
tsō hoà, 造丨, geluk, lot.
tsō hoà sī, 造丨是, geluk, gelukkig dat....
tsō hoà m̄ sī, 造丨不是, bij ongeluk, ongelukkig dat....
bô tsō hoà sī, 無造丨是, do.
p'ông tsō hoà, 逢造丨, bij geluk. van het goed geluk afhangen.
tú tsō hoà, 賭造丨, do.

華 Hoà *gèh hoà* } *goèh »* } 月丨, gekleurde krans om de maan.

Hoà *hoà i soah*, 慰息, zachtzinnig twistende personen scheiden.

* Zie verder onder *hoe*.

hoà kèh k'ìh, (eene beleediging) zachtzinnig op een ander schuiven.

hoà sìng, | 筫. ongeveer berekenen, eene ruwe berekening maken.

譁 Schreeuwen, jolen, levenmaken.

Hoā *hoā hoā kún*, | | 吼. schreeuwen, levenmaken.

hoā hoā haó, | | 號. loeijen, (zooals een bergstroom).

hân hoā, 閧 |. schreeuwen, levenmaken.

hi hi hoā hoā, 嘻匕譁匕, geruisch maken, als een komende windvlaag.

tsoè lâng hi hi hoā hoā, 爲人嬉匕譁匕. een aardig mensch zijn die niet ligt geraakt wordt.

hoā tseh liem pi bô k'ìh, | 節卽時無去, even geruisch maken en in een oogenblik weg zijn, (als wind), van daar: ineens op zijn, (als bezittingen).

畫 *hoā kong*, | 工. schilder.

Hoā *hoā ts'iū* } | 匠. do.
Oā » *ts'iṳ̄* }

歡 *hoṉ hi*, | 喜. vreugde, blijde, in zijn
Hoṉ schik zijn met.

hoṉ t'aô hi bīn, | 頭喜面, er verheugd uitzien.

恍 *hoṉ́ hoṉ́*, | 匕. onduidelijk zigtbaar,
Hoṉ́ als gering beschouwen.

hoṉ́ hoṉ́ tsiū sī, | 匕就是. oppervlakkig slechts, door de vingers zien.

hoṉ́ tseh boē kì tit, | 節不能記得, door iets gering te achten het vergeten.

hoṉ́ tseh tsiū kè, | 節就過, in een ommezien is het om, (van tijd).

keng hoṉ́ keng hoṉ́, 光 | 光 |, flaauwe lichtschemering, (zooals bij het aanbreken van den dag).

Hoṉ̀ *bin hoṉ̀*, 明且. naderhand, later.

bin hoṉ̀ sing li t'àn tsi, 明且生理賺錢. wanneer ik later met koophandel geld verdiend zal hebben.

鼾 Snorken.

Hoṉ̀ * *ts'ī ts'ī hoṉ̀*, 睡 | 然. do.

kṉ̀ kṉ̀ hoṉ̀, snorken.

按 De hand leggen aan, in handen hebben,
Hoṉ̄ behandelen, het beheer over iets hebben; zich vasthouden aan, steunen op.

hoṉ̄ toā, | 舵. aan het roer zijn, een schip sturen.

hoṉ̄ tsìng, | 症. eene ziekte behandelen.

hoṉ̄ àn, | 案. eene regtszaak in handen hebben, bepleiten.

hoṉ̄ ke, | 家. het huishouden besturen.

hoṉ̄ siaò ē lâng, | 數的人, boekhouder.

sim koṉ hoṉ̄ tiṉ̄, 心肝 | 定, zijne tegenwoordigheid van geest behouden, inwendig rustig blijven.

hoṉ̄ tiṉ̄, | 錠. het roer in handen hebben, aan het hoofd eener zaak zijn.

hoṉ̄ t'aô hoṉ̄ bé, | 頭 | 尾. geheel en al in handen hebben.

hoṉ̄ t'aô ts'iú, | 頭手. de eerste plaats, hoogste post, in eene zaak hebben.

hoṉ̄ sing li hoṉ̄ boē tiaò, | 生理 | 不能當. eene handelszaak beheeren, maar het niet kunnen uithouden.

hoṉ̄ tiá, | 鼎. het toezigt over de pan, het koken, hebben, (van koks).

hoṉ̄ lô, | 爐. voor den oven te zorgen hebben, (zooals koks en bakkers).

---

* Zie verder onder *hoai*.

oá hoā, 倚 ｜, steunen op.

tah hoā, 踏 ｜, steun, houvast om tegen op te klimmen.

ū tah hoā, 有 踏 ｜, iets hebben om zich aan vasttehouden, iemand hebben waar men heen kan gaan, (zooals reizigers).

bô tah bô hoā, 無 踏 無 ｜, niemand hebben om zich op te verlaten, (zooals in een proces); niets hebben om iets op te zetten, (zooals in een leeg huis).

hoā tá, ｜ 胆, zijnen moed steun geven, (zooals een wapen dat men bij zich neemt).

釬 Hoā Soldéren.

hoā ioh, ｜ 藥, soldeersel.

hoā tiaō, ｜ 定, vast solderen.

kap hoā ê ts'ùi, 合 ｜ 的 觜, plaats waar iets gesoldeerd is.

岸 Hoā Dijk; de kant van het water, wal, land.

tē hoā, 地 ｜, dijk tegen overstroomingen.

ts'ân hoā, 田 ｜, paadjes tusschen de rijstvelden, tevens als dam dienende.

oá hoā, 倚 ｜, aan land liggen, van een schip.

tsiū hoā, 上 ｜, aan land, aan wal, gaan.

齦 Hoā *k'í hoā*, 齒 ｜, tandkant, *d. i.* tandvleesch.

Hoah

喝 Hoah *hoah hoah*, ｜ 匕, hard en vertoornd spreken.

toā hoah, 大 ｜, schreeuwen.

hoah hièm, ｜ 喊, do.

hoah soah, ｜ 息, scheiden, tusschen beiden komen, als bij vechtende personen.

hoah kûn, 猜 拳, elkander laten raden, hoeveel vingers men opsteekt, het Italiaansche Morra-spel.

hoah bé á / *» bē »* } ｜ 碼 子, openbaar verpachten. (Java-Chineesch).

tsū kē hoah koai, 自 下 ｜ 上, bij opslag verkoopen of verpachten.

tsū koai hoah kē, 自 上 ｜ 下, bij afslag verkoopen of verpachten.

tit tit hoah k'ih laih, 價 登 匕 哄 起, meer en meer in prijs stijgen.

hoah ts'át, 喊 賊, schreeuwen dat er dieven zijn.

hoah lát, ｜ 力, schreeuwen om meer kracht te kunnen zetten.

hoah siā tsiū kaò, 發 聲 就 到, in een oogenblik is men er digt bij.

hoah lō, 喊 路, schreeuwen om menschen uit den weg te doen gaan.

hō hoah, 呼 ｜, hard toeschreeuwen; aan het hoofd staan van.

hoah him hoah hó, ｜ 熊 ｜ 虎, hard schreeuwen.

hoah ui hoah liáh, ｜ 圍 ｜ 掠, schreeuwen om (dieven) te omsingelen en te vatten.

ū hoah soah, 有 ｜ 息, de magt hebben om iets te doen ophouden.

tsoè taī tsì kō hoah, 做 事 孤 ｜, hard over iets spreken; maar er zelf niets aan meê doen.

hùn hoah, 訓 ｜, overschreeuwen, overbluffen.

hāng hoah, 哄 ｜, door hard schreeuwen vrees willen aanjagen.

Hoah *hoah to*, 抹 刀, een mes aanzetten. (slijpen).

跨 Hoáh Stap, schrede, voetstap; stappen nemen.

toā hoáh, toā hoáh pō, 大 ｜, 大

| 步, groote stappen.

toā hoáh kiâ, 大 | 行, groote stappen nemen.

sa pō tsoè nn̄g hoáh, 三 步 做 二 |, drie stappen in tweeën nemen, *d. i.* groote stappen nemen.

kui hoáh têng, 幾 | 長, hoeveel voetstappen is het lang?

hoáh kèh k'ìh / » *koè* », | 過 去, overheen stappen.

hoáh kè / » *koè*, | 過, overstappen, (zooals een drempel).

Hoai

Hoai Oai *mîng hoai hoai haó*, 門 門 匕 吼, de deur kraakt.

懷 Hoai In den boezem dragen, steeds denken aan; boezem, schoot, het hart.

hoai t'ai, | 胎, zwanger.

hoai īn, | 孕, do.

k'ai hoai, 開 |, het hart opruimen, droefheid verzetten.

koà hoai tsai sim, 挂 | 在 心, steeds denken aan, zich ongerust maken.

Hoai *ē hoai*, 下 頦, onderkin.

lak ē hoai, 落 下 頦, uitzakken van de onderkin, (gezegd van iemand die veel praat of lacht).

槐 Hoai *hoai hoe*, | 花, soort cassia-bloemen, (tot het verwen van kleêren gebezigd).

橫 Hoai Hoâ Dwars, overdwars, dwars overgaan; dwars in handelingen, onredelijk, onbillijk.

t'án hoai, 坦 |, dwars, overdwars.

hoai koai, | 棒, dwarslatten, sporten.

hoai tit, | 直, overdwars en overlangs, *d. i.* in het vierkant.

hoai bīn, | 面, dwars gezigt, *d. i.* boosaardig van uiterlijk.

hoai hûn, | 紋, dwarsloopende streepen.

hoai koe á, | 街 子, dwarsstraatje, zijstraatje.

hoai ts'â giâ dzip tsaò, | 柴 扲 入 竈, met alle geweld iets onmogelijks willen doen.

hoai si, | 生, bevalling waarbij het kind zich dwars vertoont.

hoai hi lō nìh, | 在 路 上, dwars over den weg liggen.

hoai kèh k'ìh, | 過 去, dwars oversteken, (zooals over een weg).

kiâ hoai iû, 行 | 洋, dwars overzee steken, (zooals van Emoi naar Formosa).

hoai ts'oâ / *hoâ* », | 閂, dwarshout; dwars, onbillijk, in zijne handelingen.

sai hoai ts'oâ (of *tsi*), 用 衡 閂 een dwarshout onder iets plaatsen; dwars doorgaan.

hoai kiâ tit tn̄g, | 行 直 撞, onbesuisd handelen.

hoai hik, | 逆, onbetamelijk (handelend).

hoai bah bīn, | 臉 面, do.

hoai pik pik, | 愎 匕, zeer onredelijk, dwarszinnig.

hoai hoai kéh kéh / » » *kéh kéh*, | 匕 逆 匕, dwars over elkander, verward.

hoai pà pà, | 霸 匕, onbillijk, onredelijk, in handelingen.

hoai piàng piàng, | 柄 匕, do.

荍 Hoai̤ Hoâ̤ *ō̤ hoai̤*, 芋 ｜, taro-stengel (van de Arum Aquaticum), als voedsel gebruikt.

壞 Hoaī *sún hoaī*, 損 ｜, vervallen.

paī hoaī, 敗 ｜, do.

tsiù hoaī, 蛀 ｜, doorvreten van insekten.

hoaī sū, ｜ 事, eene zaak bederven.

hoaī liaó, ｜ 了, bedorven, in duigen (van eene zaak).

Hoan

番 Hoan Keer, maal; vreemdeling, vreemd, buitenlandsch.

kui nō̤ hoan, 幾 個 ｜, verscheidene malen.

sam hoan ngō̤ hok, 三 ｜ 五 覆, herhaalde malen overzien.

hoan lâng, ｜ 人, vreemdeling.

hoan á, ｜ 仔, do. (eenigzins verachting aanduidend).

hoan t'aô gûn / » » *gîn* } ｜ 頭 銀, Spaansche dollar.

hoan gûn / » *gîn* } ｜ 銀, vreemd geld.

hoan k'eh / » *k'e̤h* } ｜ 客, vreemdeling, iemand die lang uitlandig geweest is en gew. rijk terug komt.

hoan moa̤, ｜ 縵, regenmantel.

t'ong hoan, 通 ｜, met de vreemdelingen gemeene zaak maken.

ts'i̤ hoan, 生 ｜, ruwe vreemdelingen, zooals de inboorlingen van Formosa.

sik hoan, 熟 ｜, half ruwe, (*lett.* gare) vreemdelingen, die verkeer met China hebben.

hoan béh suī / » *be̤h* » } ｜ 麥 穗, Indischkoren.

hoan kiu̥, ｜ 蒟, Spaansche peper.

hoan tsû / » *tsî* } ｜ 薯, aardappel.

hoan tsû hún, ｜ 薯 粉, aardappelmeel.

hoan soé / » *sé* } ｜ 黍, bezemkoren.

hoan soé bàng, ｜ 黍 芒, do.

hoan koah, ｜ 葛, knollen.

hoan ts'i̤ / » *tse̤* } ｜ 菁, indigo.

hê hoan, 和 ｜, gijzelaar zijn.

kiâ̤ hoan, *hoàn hoan*, 行 ｜ 販 ｜, buitenlands handel gaan drijven.

hoan á si̤ / » » *se̤* } ｜ 仔 生, uit een vreemdeling geboren, (scheldw.).

hoan á tit, ｜ 仔 直, dom, gemakkelijk te bedriegen, als een vreemdeling.

kap hoan á teh k'iáng tsiâ̤ dzī, 與 ｜ 人 說 話 官 字, even als of men met een vreemdeling mandarijnsch sprak, *d. i.* iemand niet verstaan.

hoan á t'ai ka láh / » » » » *le̤h* } ｜ 仔 刣 鮫 鱲, als een vreemdeling die een kalahvisch opensnijdt, *d. i.* niet weten hoe eene zaak aan te vatten.

hoan pa li kiao, onbegrijpelijk, onduidelijk.

翻 Hoan Heen en weer vliegen, fladderen, heen en weer gaan; omwoelen, omkeeren, teruggaan, terugkeeren; terug doen komen (uit de maag), herkaauwen; herdoen, op nieuw doen, vernieuwen.

hoan pak, ｜ 駁, bedenkingen maken tegen.

hoan hong, ｜ 風, fladderen, (zooals vlinders).

hoan lai hoan k'i, 轉 來 轉 去, op en neer woelen.

bé hoan kiao, 馬 | 沙, rollen van paarden.

hoan ts'ɛng, | 艙, het ruim omwoelen, onderste boven halen, (om iets te zoeken).

hoan sin, | 身, zich over en weer draaijen, zich omdraaijen.

hoan sin á, | 身 仔, in een ommezien.

gaō hoan ts'ia, 善 | 車, knap waren omzetten.

tien hoan tò hok, 顛 | 倒 覆, in de war, door elkander, alles onderste boven.

hoan t'ien hok tē, | 天 覆 地, do. de gewaarwoording van een' beschonkene.

hoan si̤, | 生, *lett.* weer leven krijgen, als suiker popjes die gaan smelten.

hoan t'aô lai, | 頭 來, terugkomen (naar eene plaats waar men niet te huis hoort).

hoan hûn laìh, | 魂 來, weder bijkomen (uit eene flaauwte of schijndood).

hoan uī, | 胃, herkaauwen.

hoan kui, | 歸, do.. (van apen).

hoan ts'aó, | 草, gras herkaauwen (van koeijen en paarden).

hoan àn, | 案, eene regtszaak op nieuw laten onderzoeken; eene regtszaak geheel en al omkeeren.

hoan k'òng, | 控, op nieuw aanklagen; van iets in cassatie komen.

ting t'aô hoan, 重 頭 |, van voren af aan weder (natellen, enz.).

hoan pán, | 板, vernieuwde drukplanken, druk.

hoan k'ik, | 刻, op nieuw uitgesneden; nieuwe oplage.

hoan kaì, | 蓋, een dak repareren, vernieuwen.

翻 Hoan Vertalen, vertolken.

hoan ik, | 繹, do.

hoan ik koa̤, | 繹 官, vertaler, tolk.

hoan ik m̄ tióh, | 譯 唔 着, verkeerde vertaling.

幡 Hoan Vaandel, als voor afgodsbeelden gehangen.

tông hoan, 童 |, vaandels voor afgodsbeelden gehangen of gedragen.

ín lō̤ hoan, 引 路 |, vaandels waarmede kinderen bij eene begrafenis vooruitgaan.

紛 Hoan Verward, onduidelijk.

hoan hoan, | 匕, verward, onverstaanbaar, (zooals een kind).

hoan t'áng, | 捅, onbegrijpelijk, moeijelijk iets aan het verstand te brengen (van pers.).

hoan t'ì t'ai, | 憶 嚎, verward, onduidelijk, onbegrijpelijk.

吩 Hoan *hoan hù*, | 附, gelasten, bevelen.

反 Hoán Terugkeeren, terugbrengen; omkeeren, omgekeerd, integendeel; het tegendeel doen, veranderen; oproer maken, oproer.

hoán tsú, | 主, de tablet van een' overledene van de begrafenis naar huis terugbrengen.

hoán tíng, | 轉, integendeel, omgekeerd.

hoán bīn bû tsing, | 面 無 精, ondankbaar kwade vrienden met iemand worden.

hoán kóng, *tò hoán kóng*, | 講, 到 | 講, het omgekeerde, tegendeel, zeggen van wat men neemt.

liem pi̤ kóng liem pi̤ hoán, 即 時

講卽時 |, zóó iets zeggen en onmiddelijk daarna het tegendeel zeggen.

hoán bīn, | 面, boos worden.

hoán hing, | 行, zijne handelingen veranderen (van goed tot kwaad).

hoán siòng, | 相, van levenswandel veranderen.

hoán king, | 供, zijne getuigenis veranderen.

hoán pièn, | 變, veranderen.

hoán koà, | 卦, van idée, plan, veranderen.

hoán bī, | 味, van smaak veranderen.

hoán sik, | 色, verkleuren.

hoán ts'i, | 濕, vochtig worden.

hoán hok, | 覆, ongestadig, wispelturig.

i hoán i hok ê lâng, 移 | 移覆之人, een wispelturig mensch.

hoán pak, 翻腹, braken.

hoán hiao, | 僥, zijne belofte niet nakomen.

hoán ti, | 池, ommekeer, verwarring in een vijver door plotselingen regen na sterken zonneschijn, zoodat de visschen sterven.

hoán loān, | 亂, oproer maken.

hoán poān, | 叛, rebelleren.

tsō hoán, 造 |, oproer maken.

bô hoán taī gik, 謀 | 大逆, oproer, afval, beramen.

hoán poē, | 背, afvallen (van zijn rijk).

hai hoán, 海 |, zeebeving.

pog hai hoán, 譜海 |, de zeebeving spelen. *d. i.* ruzie hebben.

hoán kg, | 監, oproer in de gevangenis maken.

hoán ke lā t'éh, | 家撈體, ruzie in huis hebben.

恢 Hoán　*hoán hoé*, | 悔, berouwen, bejammeren.

販 Hoàn　*hoàn á*, | 仔, rondventer.

hoàn sao, 牙婆, kinderen-verkoopster.

gû hoàn, 牛 |, koekoopers.

hoàn gû, | 牛, koeijen koopen.

laó hoàn, 撓 |, knappe, doorkneede rondventer.

p'og hoàn, 拚 |, in het klein verkoopen om te laten rondventen.

hoàn sik bóh hoàn ts'i, | 熱莫 | 生, men drijve handel in iets waarvan men verstand heeft, en niet in iets waarvan men niets afweet.

泛 Hoàn　*hoàn hoàn*, | 匕, onbepaald (spreken), oppervlakkig (handelen), enz.

hoàn lūn, | 論, algemeene redenering.

喚 Hoàn　*ho hoàn*, 呼 |, roepen, zeggen.

煩 Hoàn　Lastig vallen; lastig makend, als vele zaken tegelijk; vermoeijen met ..... folteren; bedroefd.

to hoàn, 多 |, iemand lastig vallen, (beleefde term).

lô hoàn, 勞 |, do.

sū t'aì hoàn, 事太 |, te veel zaken tegelijk aan het hoofd.

hoàn dziáo, | 擾, lastig, moeijelijk uit maken.

hoàn sin, | 神, zijn geest vermoeijen met.

hoàn lô, | 惱, bedroefd, droefheid.

hoàn sim, | 心, zich door droefheid aftobben.

hoân sim peh pak, 丨心白縛, door droefheid gefolterd.

礬 Hoân Aluin, met aluin bedekken.

ts'i hoân, 生丨, witte aluin.

peh hoân, 白丨, do.

bing hoân, 明丨, heldere aluin.

t'ô hoân, *soa hoân*, 土丨, 山丨, ruwe aluin.

tsō hoân, 皂丨, koperrood.

tám hoân, 膽丨, blaauwe vitriool.

hoân tsoá, 丨紙, dik met aluin doortrokken papier.

hoân bīn, 丨面, eene dunne aluinlaag over iets leggen; overtrekken, (als kussens).

īng hoân hoân, 用丨丨, met aluin aluinen, (om iets voor bederf te bewaren).

還 Hoân Terugkomen, terugkeeren, teruggeven, betalen.

hoân siok, 丨俗, in de wereld terugkeeren (van een Buddha priester).

koh tsaì hoân hûn, 再丨魂, weder bijkomen (uit eene flaauwte).

sūn hoân, 順丨, geleidelijk terugkomen, van de opeenvolging in de natuur.

hoân goān, 償願, eene gelofte vervullen, afdoen.

ts'ing hoân, 清丨, geheel afbetalen.

kau hoân, 交丨, teruggeven (een huis, voorwerp, enz.)

環 Hoân *liên hoân pó*, 連丨保, onderling voor elkander borg staan, instaan.

犯 Hoān *hoān tsoē*, 丨罪, misdadig, eene misdaad begaan.

hoān lâng, 丨人, misdadiger.

hoān hoat, 丨法, de wet overtreden.

hoân kìm, 丨禁, de bepalingen overtreden.

hoān tióh lâng ē kang, 丨人之工, iemand belet aandoen.

hoân tióh, 丨着, in den weg loopen van . . . . ., zich verzetten tegen.

hoān hiêm, 丨嫌, zich laakkaar gedragen.

ka hoān, 監丨, gevangenen.

siû hoān, 囚丨, zware gevangenen.

liû hoān, 流丨, bannelingen.

sí hoān, 死丨, ter dood veroordeelden.

hoān huì, 丨諱, dingen zeggen die men moest verzwijgen; den naam van zijn vader uitspreken.

hiong hoān, 凶丨, slechte booswicht.

bô sa hoān tsoā, 不相丨閂, elkander niet in den weg staan, ieder zijn eigen weg gaan.

hoān tik hoān sit, 丨得丨失, niet zeker zijn of men het houden zal of niet, enz.

hoān giaô, 丨蕘, achterdogt wekken, niet in den haak schijnen.

kè hoān, 過丨, gevangenen, misdadigers, transporteren.

ts'iok hoān tióh, 觸丨着, zich vergrijpen tegen, zondigen tegen.

Hoān *hoān sū*, 凡事, in alle zaken, in het algemeen.

hoān mih, 丨物, elk voorwerp.

hoān kan, 丨間, de werld.

lí hoān lí, goá hoān goá, 你丨你, 我丨我, gij betreft u zelven, ik betref mij zelven; wij hebben met elkander niets te maken.

i hoān i, i hoān i, 伊丨伊, 伊丨伊, het zijn verschillende personen.

范 Hoān Familienaam.
hó hoān, 好 丨, goed fatsoen, goed model.

患 Hoān *hō̤ hoān*, 後 丨, latere ellende, verdriet.

梵 Hoān *hoān gú*, 丨 語, de Boeddhistische taal, (het sanscrit).

Hoat

發 Hoat Voor den dag, te voorschijn, komen, ontspruiten, uitkomen, als tanden, uitbreken, als puisten; voor den dag, te voorschijn, brengen, doen uitkomen; in het werk stellen, laten zien; geven, zenden aan, uitbetalen; verdienen.
hoat ts'ut, 丨 出, voor den dag komen.
hoat hiēn, 丨 現, aan het licht brengen, komen.
hoat kak, 丨 角, aan den dag komen, bekend worden; hoornen krijgen.
hoat gê, hoat k'i, 丨 牙, 丨 齒, tanden krijgen.
hoat tok, 丨 毒, uitslag hebben.
hoat liép á, 丨 瘡 仔, steenpuisten hebben.
hoat lui, 丨 雷, opsteken van donder, donderen.
hoat kò̤, 丨 酵, gisten.
hoat sim, 丨 心, uit weldadig oogmerk doen.
hoat dziét, 丨 熱, heete koorts krijgen.
hī á hoat hong / » » » *hōng*, 耳 子 丨 風, de ooren gloeijen.
hoat tát, 丨 達, in voorspoed geraken.
hoat tsik, 丨 蹟, er boven opkomen.
hoat tien, *hoat siáo*, *hoat kòng*. 丨 癲, krankzinnig, dol.
hoat ping, 丨 兵, soldaten te voorschijn brengen, d. i. doen optrekken.
hoat tsoh, 丨 作, in werking gaan, uitwerking doen.
kū i toā hoat lát, 教 伊 帶 丨 力, zich zeer moeijelijk om iets, of iemand maken.
hoat boē, 丨 賣, te koop.
hoat hing ih, 丨 還 伊, aan iemand teruggeven.
hoat hê, 丨 還, terugzenden (zoo als slechte waar).
hoat lóh, 丨 落, bekend maken, aanlageren.
hoat kao, 丨 交, uitleveren aan.
hoat hiòng / » *hiàng* 丨 餉, soldij uitbetalen.
hoat hu kè / » » *kè̤* 丨 傭 價, draagloon betalen.
hoat tsai, 丨 財, rijk worden.
hoat tsi̤, 丨 錢, geld maken, verdienen.

法 Hoat Wet, regel, bepaling, manier om iets te doen, reglement, voorschriften (van priesters.)
lút hoat, 律 丨 / *hoat lút*, 丨 律 wet.
tsīn hoat pūn. 盡 丨 處 治, volgens de strengste term der wet straffen.
kok hoat, ông hoat, 國 丨, 王 丨, rijkswetten.
ti hoat p'à̤ hoat, 知 丨 怕 丨, kent men de wet dan vreest men ze.
siú hoat, 守 丨, zich aan de wet houden.
bû hoat bû t'ien, 無 丨 無 天, om God noch gebod geven.

bô hoat bô hoat, 無 | 無 |, ongemanierd.

lip hoat, 立 |, wetten, manieren, op iets vaststellen.

siet hoat, 設 |, manieren, plannen maken.

hoat tō, | 度, manier, regel.

hoat t'iep, | 帖, schrijfvoorbeeld.

ka hoat, 家 |, regels in een huishouden.

hong hoat, 方 |, manier om iets te doen.

put hoat, 不 |, onwettig, tegen de wet strijdend, (als overspel).

soat hoat, 說 |, de reglementen, regels, voorlezen, (van priesters).

hoat koa, | 官, opzigter over de regels in een Taoistisch klooster.

hoat su, | 師, Taoist. priesters die reglementen instellen.

hoat soh, | 索, touw met een houten slangenkop, (gebruikt om geesten uit te drijven).

hoat lik, | 力, uitwerking van zekere manieren.

hoat sút, | 術, regels, manieren, (van Boedh. en Taoist).

siâ hoat, 邪 |, heterodoxe manieren, zwarte kunst.

奈 Hoat Bestand zijn tegen, opgewassen, zijn tegen, aan kunnen.

bô hoat tit, 無 | 他, niet bestand, opgewassen tegen.

bô hoat ih, bô i hoat, 無 | 他, 無 | 何, niet tegen iemand opgewassen, niets aan iemand kunnen doen.

tsiáh i bô hoat, 食之無 |, niet kunnen opeten, eene zaak niet aankunnen, er niet in slagen zich onregtvaardig iemands geld toe te eigenen.

ta bô hoat ih, 擔 無 | 伊, niet kunnen dragen.

乏 Hoát Bedriegen, valsch, nagemaakt.

hoát tìng tièm, | 當 店, een pandjeshuis bedriegen, (door slecht geld).

sì koè teh hoát lâng, 四 街 直 | 人, overal menschen bedriegen (met waar of geld).

hoát hè, | 貨, nagemaakt, valsch geld.

罰 Hoát Straffen, bestraffen, eene straf doen ondergaan; van daar ook: temmen; beboeten, eene boete opleggen.

hìng hoát, 刑 |, bestraffen, straf.

hoát ts'i bé, | 生 馬, een paard temmen, dresseren.

hoát tsî, hoát gûn, | 錢, | 銀, geldelijke boete opleggen.

hoát hōng, | 俸, doen boeten, door inhouding van (een mandarijns tractement).

hoát lâng ê toh, | 人 之 棹, iemand voor een feestmaal beboeten, (wegens eene beleediging of ongelijk).

hoát hì tsiú, | 戲 酒, met comedie en wijn beboeten.

hoát ting ts'ai, | 燈 彩, met eene illuminatie beboeten.

活 Hoát Levend, levendig.

sing hoát kè / *» » kè* } 生 | 計, plannen bedenken om aan de kost te komen.

hoát p'oat, | 潑, levendig, (van aard).

hoát hoát hoát, | 匕 匕, zeer fijn gewreven.

伐 Hoát *tsing hoát*, 征 |, bestrijden, ten strijde trekken tegen.

hoát lòh, | 落, regelen, in orde brengen.

Hoe *

花 **Hoe** **Hoa** Bloem; gebloemd, veelkleurig, fraai, voorspoedig, gebloemd; *d. i.* wellustig, met ligtekooijen betrekking hebbende; van fijne, dunne, naar bloemen gelijkende dingen, als sneeuwvlokken, houtkrullen; gespikkeld; van daar: niet helder voor de oogen, onduidelijk.

hoe hing, 丨園, bloemtuin.

mi̱ hoe, 棉丨, watte, katoen.

hoe k'a, *hoe p'ûn*, 丨缸, 丨盆, bloempot.

hoe sim, 丨心, bloemhart, fig. vulva.

hoe im, 丨蓓, bloemknop.

kim hoe, 金丨, goudpapieren bloemen.

kim hoe àng, 金丨紅, soort slechte opium.

ts'ò hoe, 蒲草丨, rijstpapierbloemen.

hoe sik mi̱h, 丨色物, dingen die even als eene bloem spoedig verkleuren.

hoe ts'aó mi̱h, 丨草物, dingen die gemakkelijk bederven.

hoe ting, 丨燈, gebloemde papieren lantaarn.

kat hoe ting, 結丨燈, met gebloemde lantaarns illumineren.

hoe hoe, 丨丨, veelkleurig; duister, moeijelijk uit te maken, van zaken.

hoe tiém, 丨點, gespikkeld, spikkels.

hoe iép, 丨片, bloemblad.

hoe hióh, 丨葉, kelkbladen.

hoe tì, 丨蒂, vruchtbodem.

hoe ki, 丨枝, bloemsteel.

tsi hoe pò̱, 紫丨布, gebloemd katoen.

sàng hoe àng, 送丨紅, handgeld geven, (voor een werk aan dienstboden, enz.).

tsit pé hoe, *tsit ts'ok hoe*, 一把丨, 一簇丨, een bloemruiker.

tsoá hoe, 紙丨, papieren bloemen.

hoe ah, 丨押, handteekening.

hoe kòng, 丨貢, gebloemd satijn.

hoe t'ang tsí, 丨牕子, gebloemd, uitgesneden, traliewerk.

hoe hoe lik lik, 丨丨綠匕, fraai, (hoofdz. uitwendig).

hoe hiet, 丨勢, opgesierd.

hoe gûn, 丨銀, gemerkt geld, dollars.

dziòng hoe, 絨丨, vloszijden bloemen.

hoe liém bīn, 丨臉面, schaamteloos.

ū hoe dzī, 有丨字, voorspoed genieten.

hoe k'a, 丨脚, gevlekte pooten; gedurig uitzijn, wegloopen, van slechte handelingen zijn.

hoe tsè / *hoa tsè̱* } 丨債, schuld aan hoeren.

hoe king, 丨間, hoerenhuis.

hoe t'ing, 丨艇, bloemboot, soort bordeel.

tsiáh hoe tsiú, 食丨酒, met lichtekooijen feest houden.

k'ao to hoe, 敲(鉋)刀丨, schaafkrullen.

tsui hoe, 水丨, waterspetten.

seh hoe, 雪丨, sneeuwvlok.

dzit hoe á, 日丨仔, een weinig zon.

lāng koai á hoe, 弄拐子丨, met een stok draaijen, kunsten er meê maken.

* Zie verder onder *he*.

lāng ts'iú hoe, 弄手 ｜, trararietjes met de hand maken.
taû á hoe, 骰子 ｜, blokjes, ruitjes, als dobbelsteenen.
t ing á hoe, 甎子 ｜, groote blokken, ruiten.
bák tsin hoe, 目賙 ｜, slecht van gezigt.

悔* Berouw hebben, spijt hebben van;
Hoé kwaad op zich zelven zijn.
Hoè *hoán hoé*, 反 ｜. berouw hebben.
ts'àm hoé, 懺 ｜, berouw toonen, boete doen (voor een afgod).
hoé gō, ｜ 悞, tot berouw over, inzigt van, zijne verkeerdheid komen.
tui hoé, 追 ｜, berouw over vroegere zaken gevoelen.
hoé hun, ｜ 婚*, spijt gevoelen over een aanstaand huwelijk, van een huwelijk afzien.
hoé ts'in, ｜ 親, do.
oàn hoé ka kī, 怨 ｜ 自已, kwaad op zich zelven zijn.

Hoé Een teeken met de oogen geven; een wenk geven.
hoé bák, 動目, met de oogen toewenken.
tuì i hoé bák tseh, 對伊動目睫, iemand een oogwenk geven.
bák gin bák hoé, 目狺目動, achter den rug vertoornd nakijken.
hoé hoé ták ták, nijdig met de oogen toewenken.

Hoé *hoé lō*, 路賄, omkooping.

廢 *hong hoè*, 荒 ｜, eig. woest, onbe-
Hoè bouwd; zijn pligt verzuimen.
Huì *hing hing hoè hoè*, 荒匕 ｜ 匕, onbebouwd.

* Zie verder onder *hé*.

hoè bò k'ìh, ｜ 沒去, vernietigd, verdwenen.
hoè hak kak k'ì, ｜ 丟去, verwerpen (eene gewoonte.)

化 *hoè ièn*, ｜ 緣, de vaste inschrijving
Hoè komen ophalen.
Hoà

晦 *aó hoè*, 拗 ｜, duister, onbegrijpelijk,
Hoè (zooals een zin).

回 Terugkeeren, terugzenden; beantwoor-
Hoê den; van idée veranderen; afdeeling van een verhaal.
óng hoê, 往還, heen en terug.
liên hoê, 連 ｜, steeds teruggezonden, niet als vrouw aangenomen worden, (scheldw. tegen vrouwen).
hoê lé, ｜ 禮, eene beleefheid beantwoorden, terugbewijzen.
hoê sim tsoán ì, *tsoán sim hoê ì* } *» » tui » tui » » »* } ｜ 心轉意, van plan veranderen.
hoê hoê kaù, ｜ ｜ 教, Mahomedanisme.
hoê pī, ｜ 避, uit den weg gaan, zich verwijderen.

茴 *sió hoê*, *siaó hoê*, 小 ｜, anijs.
Hoê
toā (of taī) hoê, 大 ｜, steranijs.

Hoê *hoê lâng*, iemand uit gekheid iets afnemen.
hoê soé lâng ê pīng tîng, overal een maal eten zien opteloopen.

踩 Met den voet over iets schrappen, af-
Hoê schrappen.
k'a hoê hoê, 脚 ｜ ｜, de voeten afschrappen.
hoê sìh } *dzoê »* } ｜ 死, doodschrappen (zooals insekten).
hoê tioh kia lâng, ｜ 着汚穢, zich aan iets vuil maken.

會 Hoē Vereenigen, vergaderen, bijeenkomen; vergadering, vereeniging, societeit, verbond ter beraadslaging van gemeenschappelijke belangen; in vereeniging met anderen gemeenschappelijk doen; ontmoeten, ontmoeting, *d. i.* gelegenheid; gaan ontmoeten, *d. i.* een bezoek afleggen bij ...; bekend maken; begrijpen, de bedoeling vatten.

tsū hoē, 聚 |, vergaderen, bijeenkomen.

hoē koán, | 舘, vergaderhuis, voor pers. van andere provinciën.

sing hoē é sò tsaī, 省 | 的 所 在, plaats waar menschen van de geheele provincie bijeenkomen, (in de provinciale hoofdst.).

t'ien tē hoē, 天 地 |, hemel- en-aarde verbond.

kiet hoē, *tsoè hoē*, 結 |、做 |, een verbond vormen.

biēn hoē, 面 |, in elkanders gezigt, mondeling, bepalen (zooals de prijs).

hoē siaò, | 數, in elkanders tegenwoordigheid, eene rekening opmaken.

hoē tog, | 單, een wissel op een' derden geven; credietbrief.

hoē sim, | 審, (met nog andere overheden) gezamenlijk verhooren.

li hoē, 理 |, iemand volgens billijkheid over iets spreken.

hoē goân, | 元, hoogste der Hanlim.

hoē sì, | 試, examinatieplaats voor Hanlims.

hoē lò, | 擄, met een menigte gaan vatten.

goá hoē tioh li tsit pai, 我 | 着 你 一 次, ik heb u eens ontmoet.

bē bat hoē bīn, *bē bat siong hoē*, 未 嘗 | 面, 未 嘗 相 |, elkander te voren nooit ontmoet, gezien, hebben.

hoē k'eh, | 客, gasten ontvangen; vrienden visite brengen.

paì hoē, 拜 |, een bezoek afleggen bij.

hoē ts'in, | 親, familiebetrekkingen voor het eerst gaan bezoeken.

ti hoē, 知 |, alom bekendmaken.

hoē tsoé, *hē tsoé*, | 齊, alom bekend maken (zooals het plan voor oproer).

hoē iâ, 營 |, aan den kommandant van eene leger-afdeeling bekendmaken.

hoē ì, 意 |, iemands bedoeling vatten.

t'é hoē, 提 |, de bedoeling, beteekenis vatten.

boē hoē tit, 無 | 得, niet te berekenen, ontelbaar.

蟹 Hoē Soort krab.

tsiù hoē, 咒 |, do.

kim tsi hoē, 金 錢 |, goudkrab.

k'a ts'iú nâ hoē nih, 脚 手 如 |, handen en voeten als een krab hebben, *d. i.* langzaam in zijne manier van doen zijn.

Hok

覆 Hok Herhalen, nogmaals, over, overdoen; overbrengen, oververtellen, beantwoorden; omkeeren.

hè hok / *hoè* 》 回 |, beantwoorden; antwoord brengen over....

hok sút, | 述, oververtellen, mededeelen.

hok p'oe, | 信, een' brief beantwoorden.

hok tsí, | 旨, berigt, uitslag van iets aan den keizer brengen.

hok siaò, | 數, overrekenen.

hok tsèh, nazien, overdoen, overrekenen.
sam hoan ngó hok. 三番五｜, herhaalde malen overzien,
kā i hok tsit ting, 加伊｜一重, er nog eene laag overdoen.
hoan hok, *hoan hoan hok hok*, 反｜, 反乜｜乜, wispelturig.

福 Geluk.
Hok *hok k'ì*, ｜氣, do.
pók hok, 薄｜, ongeluk, ongelukkig.
ho lāū hok, 好老｜, gelukkige oude dag.
sioh hok, 惜｜, zorg dragen voor zijn geluk.
tsiet hok, 折｜, zijn geluk vergooijen.
hok oân bah, ｜圓肉, gedroogde ging-ging.
hok kièn, ｜建, Fokkien.
hok tsiu, ｜州, Fuchow.
hok sam, ｜杉, Fuchowhout.
hok tsiu siâ, ｜州城, de stad Fuchow (die voor de rijks hoofdstad wil doorgaan, *d. i. kè kia* hetgeen ook beteekend veinzen bang te zijn.

蝠 *piên hok*, 蝙｜, vleermuis.
Hok

霍 Familienaam.
Hok

宓 Familienaam.
Hok

複 Dubbel.
Hok *hok sìng*, ｜姓, dubbele familienaam.

腹 *hok loān ê pi̤*, cholera.
Hok

服 Dienen; zich onderwerpen, zijne minderheid bekennen, toegeven; kleêren, kleeding, rouwkleêren, rouw; innemen als medicijnen.
Hók *hók saī*, ｜事, dienen, (zooals zijne ouders of vorst).
m̄ sa̤ hók, 不相｜, niet toegeven.
sa̤ hâng hók, 相降｜, toegeven.
hâng hók, 降｜zich onderwerpen.
paì hók, 拜｜, buigende bekennen dat men voor iemand onder doet: beleefdheids term; ik maak U mijn compliment.
put hók, 不｜, zich niet onderwerpen.
i hók, 衣｜, kleêren, (in het algemeen).
kong hók, 公｜, uniform, staatsiekleed.
kiet hók } 吉｜, kleeding bij plegtige gelegenheid.
kit „
sò hók, 素｜, gewone kleeding.
hà hók, 喪｜, rouwkleed.
ki liên hók, 期年｜, éénjarige rouw.
sam liên hók, 三年｜, driejarige rouw.
k'oat hók, 缺｜, uit den rouw gaan.
hók tok, ｜毒, vergift innemen, zich vergiftigen.
hō i hók ioh, 與他｜藥, iemand (die men b. v. gekwetst heeft) geld geven, om geneesmiddelen in te nemen.

伏 Neêrleggen; verschuilen, in hinderlaag leggen.
Hók *bai hók*, 埋｜, zich verschuilen, in derlaag liggen.
hók ping, ｜兵, soldaten in hinderlaag leggen.

18

hók àn toé, 丨案底, voorloopige aangifte, aanklagte doen, om de zaak later onderzocht te hebben.

hók lō, 丨路, zich op den weg verborgen houden, verschuilen.

復 Andermaal, terugnemen, terugkrijgen.

Hók *k'ih hók*, 克丨, heroveren, terugnemen, terugkrijgen.

hoe hók, 恢丨, do.

hók tò tíng / » » *tuí* } 丨回, terugkrijgen (wat men verloren had), zijne woorden inhalen.

袱 *pao hók*, 包丨. reis valies.

Hók *hók sik* / » *tsip* } 丨膝, kousen-knieband.

鶴 Kraanvogel.

Hók *hók tíng*. 丨頂, kuif van een kraanvogel.

hók sì, 丨扇, waaijer van kraanvogel vèeren.

Hong

風 Wind, (de oorzaak van verscheidene ziekten), lucht; hoorbaar naar onzigtbaar, *d. i.* gerucht; gewoonten, faam, gesteldheid, manieren.

Hong *toā hong*, 大丨, sterke wind, storm.

hong t'ai, 丨颱, orkaan, typhoon.

koan hong ki, 觀丨旗, windwijzer.

hong ki, 丨旗, windvlaag.

t'ong hong, 通丨, wind door strooming, togt.

tsē hong t'aò, 坐通丨, op de togt zitten.

hong hiā, 丨蟻, (verweerd door) wind en mieren.

ping hong, 屏丨, houten windscherm.

siao hong, 消丨, splijten, bersten, (zooals hout door droogte).

kám tioh hong, 感着丨, eene koude vatten.

hong t'se / » *ts'e* } 丨箏, vlieger.

hong tse bé, 丨箏尾. staart van een vlieger.

hong suí, 丨水, gunstige of ongunstige ligging voor een graf, de kennis daarvan.

sūn hong, 順丨, gunstige wind.

gik hong, 逆丨, tegenwind.

soè hong / *sè* » } 細丨, flaauwe koelte

kông hong, 狂丨. rukwind. storm.

tíng lé hong, 捲螺丨. dwarlwind.

bô hong, 無丨, windstilte.

hong tsīng, 丨靜, do.

kaai hong, 怪丨, zonderlinge wind.

hong k'ím, 丨琴, orgel.

hong tù, 丨厨, vliegenkast.

hong kuī, 丨櫃, blaasbalk.

hong kó, 丨鼓, kafmolen.

ts'ut hong, 出丨, lucht doorlaten.

laō hong, 漏丨, uitlekken.

hong pòng, 丨謗, gerucht gew. onwaar.

hong siŋ pòng iŋ, 丨聲謗影, onwaar.

t'iŋ hong é oē, 聞丨之音, van hooren zeggen hebben.

hong siŋ, 丨聲, zich snel verspreidend als het geluid van den wind.

k'it hong soŋ p'ak, eene beroerte krijgen.

tsaò hong, 走 丨, over en weer berigt komen brengen.

t'ia hong, 聽 丨, eene zaak zien uit te hooren; op de loerstaan.

k'iā hong, 覷 丨, op de uitkijk, op de wacht staan, (zooals dieven).

k'oà hong, 看 丨, do.

hong liû, 丨 流, veel van vermaak houdend, vrolijk, weelderig.

hong so, 丨 騷, veel van uitgaan houden.

hong siòk, 丨 俗, zeden en gewoonten, gebruik.

hong k'ì, 丨 氣, gesteldheid, gewoonte, mode.

t'àm ke hong, 探 家 丨, naar de faam van eene familie vragen (vóór tot een huwelijk te besluiten).

hong ūn, 丨 韻, manieren van iemands omgang.

hong lô, hang lô, 丨 爐, 烘 爐, komfoor.

hong lô sì, 丨 爐 扇, waaijer om een kamfoor aan te waaijeren.

方 Hong Kant, hemelstreek, vierkant, manier om iets te doen; passerd, geschikt.

sù hong, 四 丨, in het vierkant, vierkant.

oai hong, 歪 丨, scheef, niet vierkant.

hong koat, 丨 丈, manier, wijze.

toā hong biēn, 大 丨 面, royaal.

tsaī lâng è hong biēn, 隨 人 豐 丨儉, het hangt af van volgens iemands stand.

tsoè lâng hong piēn, 爲 人 丨 便, bereidwillig, hulpvaardig zijn.

hing hong piēn, 行 丨 便, naar zijn vermogen handelen (geven, enz.).

hong tiōng, 丨 丈, gastenvertrek in een Boedh. klooster.

封 Hong Aanstellen, verhoogen in ambt, digtzegelen, verzegelen, digtdoen, zegel; nummer: voor brieven, een verzegeld pakje inhoudende 50 dollars.

hong k'ò, 丨 誥, eere ambt, (aan de ouders van een hoogen mandarijn) geven.

hong p'oe, 丨 信, een brief verzegelen, toelakken.

hong bát bát, 丨 密 丨, digtzegelen.

hong p'oe ka, 丨 信 膠, zegellak.

hong tiaò, hong siu, 丨 條, 丨 箱, een kist verzegelen.

hong p'è, 丨 皮, plaats waar een brief, is digt gemaakt.

tsit hong è gûn, 一 丨 銀, een pakje met 50 dollars.

ka hong, 加 丨, een dubbel zegel op doen.

lō hong, 露 丨, een open, niet digtgemaakt briefje.

t'ao k'i hong, 私 起 丨, heimelijk een zegel openbreken.

tsit hong è p'oe, 一 丨 信, een brief.

hong k'aó, hong mng, 丨 口, 丨 門, zundgat.

hong sin, 丨 神, *lett.* de geesten ambten geven; *d. i.* onwaarheid, verdichtsels vertellen.

hong sin toān è lâng, 丨 神 傳 人, een ongestadig, wispelturig mensch.

hong ts'ien, 丨 遷, naar eene andere plaats verhoogen.

荒 Hong Verward, overhaast, onbesuisd.

hong bông, 丨 慌, in allerijl, ontsteld,

in de war, niet wetende wat te doen.

sim hong, 心 丨, met zijn geest bij iets anders zijn; verward, geagiteerd van geest.

sim kong hong hong kòng, onbesuisd, onvoorzigtig.

hong hoè } 丨 忙, verwaarloozen; ver-
» *huì* }
vervallen, in verval.

hong kòng hoè sū, 丨 狂 廢 事, zijne bezigheden laten loopen, verwaarloozen.

瘋 Melaatschheid; krankzinnig.

Hong *bâ hong*, 痲 丨, melaatschheid

hong ko, 丨 膏, trekpleister.

hong tien, 丨 癲, gek, idiotisch.

t'aô hong koàn gán, 頭 丨 貫 眼, hevige hoofdpijn zoodat de oogen er van zeer doen.

丰 Hong *hó hong tsu*, 美 丨 姿, van eene fraaije gelaatskleur.

峯 Hong *tsiem hong*, 尖 丨, puntig, (zooals een berg, een penseel, enz.).

做 Namaken, nadoen.

Hóng *hóng lâng ē pit tsit*, 丨 募 人 筆 跡, iemands hand namaken.

hóng iū } 丨 樣, namaken, volgens
» *iē* }
een model maken.

tám hóng } 膽 丨, valschelijk voor
tá » }
het zijne willen laten doorgaan.

髣 Hóng *hóng hut*, 丨 髴, onduidelijk (zien of hooren), ter loops.

hóng hut t'iā, 丨 惚 聽, onduidelijk, onnaauwkeurig hooren.

訪 Onderzoeken, navorschen.

Hóng *hóng ts'at*, 丨 察, onderzoeken, (zooals beambten),

àm hóng, 暗 丨, in het geheim onderzoeken.

况 Gesteldheid.

Hóng *king hóng*, 景 丨, gesteldheid, toestand, omstandigheden (van personen).

放 Laten gaan, loslaten, vrijlaten, zijn
Hòng vrijen gang, teugel laten.

hòng sù, 丨 肆, losbandig, zich niet aan den regel houden.

hòng tōng } 丨 蕩, onbesuisd, bui-
» *lōng* }
tensporig.

hòng kò, 丨 告, de gelegenheid openstellen om aanklagten in te leveren.

ah hòng, 押 丨, iemand op vrije voeten doen zetten.

hòng tá, 丨 膽, moedig aan ...., lett zijn moed loslatend.

hòng sim, 丨 心, zich geruststellen, niet bezorgd over iets maken.

hòng ts'iòng, 丨 縱. losbandig.

sim kon hòng hòng, 心 肝 丨 丨, grootsche ideés hebben.

况 *hô hòng*, 何 丨, hoeveel te meer.

Hòng *hòng kiem*, 丨 兼, daarenboven nog.

hòng ts'iá, 丨 且, do.

皇 Keizer, keizerlijk.

Hông *hông tè*, 丨 帝, de keizer.

hông siōng } 丨 上, do.
» *siāng* }

hông hō, 丨 后, de keizerin.

hông t'aì hō, 丨 大 后, keizerin moeder.

ts'in hông ts'in tè, 親 丨 親 帝, de eerste persoon op een plaats zijn, eigen meester zijn.

hông ts'in kok ts'ih, 丨 親 國 戚, leden van de keizerlijke familie.

hông kiong 丨 宮, keizerlijke paleis.

hông hû, 丨甫, eene dubbele familienaam.

黃 Hông Geel.

ts'iū hông, 起丨, geelgeworden als metalen die op vochtige plaats liggen.

t'ō hông, 土丨, gele kleur uitwerpen, (kleurstoffen in water).

hông hô, 丨河, de gele rivier, *d. i.* Hoang-ho.

hông hun àm, 丨昏時, tusschen licht en donker, avondschemering.

giû hông } *ngû*, } 牛丨, bezoar van runderen.

癀 Hông Geelzucht; opzwellen en gloeijen van eene wond, ontsteken, ontsteking, inflamatie.

hông t'án, 丨丹, geelzucht.

hoat hông, 發丨, ontsteken, onsteking: zich vertoornen, zich niet meer kunnen inhouden.

t'è hông siao tsing, 退丨消腫, de ontsteking wegnemen, (van medicijnen).

惶 Hông *sing hông sing k'iong*, 誠丨誠恐, wezenlijk opregt bevreesd, (iemand te beleedigen). met alle mogelijke voorkomenheid behandeld.

hông k'iong, 丨恐, vreezen dat ...., uit vrees dat ....

紅 Hông Rood; fraai.

aô hông, 嘔丨, rood, bloedspuwen.

hông gân pók bīng, 丨顏薄命, roode gelaten, (*d. i.* fraaije vrouwen hebben gewoonlijk) ongelukkig lot.

tsīng put tsi hông, 穿不止丨, zich opgesierd, kwistig aankleeden.

hông sik gê taù, 丨色牙斗, sterk, (van krekels ook van menschen.

liêm lâng è hông, iemand rood wegnemen, *d. i.* het eenigste ontnemen wat hem nog tot fats. man maakte.

防 Hông Maatregelen. voorzorgen nemen tegen, bewaken, afweren.

hông hân, 丨閑, voorzorgen nemen, tegen; beteugelen.

hông tó, 丨堵, de grenzen bewaken.

koan hông, 關丨, waken voor, bewaken.

t'ê hông, 提丨. voorzorgs maatregelen tegen.

ti hông, 知丨, op zijne hoede zijn.

hái hông, 海丨, tweede fú op zeeplaatsen.

妨 Hông Hindernis, in den weg zijn, hinderen.

hông gaī, 丨碍, hindernis.

put hông } *bû* } 不丨, het hindert niet, komt er niet op aan.

hông tioh li è kang. 丨着你的工, hinder U in uw werk, doe U belet aan.

逢 Hông Tegenkomen, ontmoeten, aantreffen.

hông gin lâng, 丨迎人, iemand ontvangen, 2e vleijen.

ts'o siong hông, 初相丨, elkander voor het eerst aantreffen.

慌 Hông *hông hông bông hông*, 丨匕忙匕, verward, overhaast, in drukte.

鴻 Hông Wilde gans.

hông gān t'oân su, 丨鴈傳書, de wilde ganzen brengen brieven over.

縫 Hông Naaijen.

ts'ai hông, *ts'ai hông eh*, 裁丨, 裁丨者, kleêrmaker.

奉 Hōng Van een hoogeren ontvangen; eerbiedigljk geven aan, aanbieden.

hōng tsi, | 旨, keizerlijk bevel ontvangen, op keizerl. bevel.

tah hōng tsi, 打 | 旨, op een stuk hout slaan door Boeddha priesters gedaan om de omstaande priesters te doen ophouden met bidden.

hōng sin, | 申, vleijen, gedienstig zijn, 2e aanraden iets te doen.

hōng hing kò sū, | 行 故 事, voor de leus, schijn doen.

hōng sàng, | 送, cadeau geven.

hōng hoân, | 還, teruggeven, (beleefheidsterm).

hòng kong sū, | 公 事, dingen ten behoeve van het publiek gedaan.

俸 Hōng — Salaris, traktement van beambten.

hōng lók, | 祿, traktement.

hōng gûn, | 銀, do.

hōng liêm, *hong sin iōng liem*, salaris en emolumenten.

鳳 Hōng — De mannelijke phoenix.

iem koe t'àn hōng pe, 閹 鷄 從 | 飛, een kapoen die als de phoenix wil vliegen, *d. i.* menschen boven zijn stand willen navolgen.

hōng koa / *„ koan* } | 髻. bruidshoed (met twee phoenixen).

訌 Hōng — Onder elkander afspreken.

hōng tsêng làng, | 粧 人, afspreken om eene maskerade te houden.

骸 Hōng — *hōng kim* / *kim táo* } | 礶, beenderenurn.

烘 Hōng — *sio hōng hōng*, 燒 | ㄔ, warm tot stoomens toe.

hoat hōng, 發 |, op eens gaan gloeijen.

Hu

虛 Hu Hi — Ledig; geene degelijkheid bevattende hol, nominaal, nederig; onwaar.

k'ang hu, 空 |, ledig, (zonder geld, hongerig).

hu hoa, 華 |, ijdel, verkwistend.

hu hùi, | 費, onnuttig verteren, verkwisten.

hu hu hoàn hoàn, | ㄔ 泛 ㄔ, wispelturig.

hu sit, | 實, het holle en degelijke, *d. i.* de ware toestand van iets.

hu hu sit sit, | | 實 ㄔ, ofschoon hol, toch waarheid bevattend.

hu lám, | 弱, zwak, niet sterk, zwak in een vak.

hu dzī, | 字, partikels.

hu tsi, | 錢; geld of winst waar de onkosten nog afmoeten.

hu sim, | 心, bescheiden, nederig.

k'iem hu, 謙 |, nederig.

hu ·û, | 詞, holle, onware gezegden.

墟 Hu Hi — Markt, marktplaats, dorp waar opzekere dagen markt gehouden wordt, marktvlek.

hu ts'ī, | 市, vaste markt.

hù hu, 赴 |, zich naar de markt, spoeden, naar de markt gaan.

sī hu ē dzit, 是 | 的 日, het is markt dag.

夫 Hu — Man; echtgenoot; drager, lastdrager; knecht; vrouw.

taī t'iōng hu, 大 丈 |, volwassen man.

tiōng hu, 丈 |, man en echtgenoot.

hu ts'oe / *„ ts'e* } | 妻, man en vrouw.

muī hu, 妹 |, zwager, (jongere zuster's man).

k'ong hu tsu, 孔 | 子, Confucius.

kang hu, 工 |, werk, veel werk vereischend.

kiō hu, 轎 |, draagstoeldrager.

bé hu, 馬 |, paardenknecht.

ts'ia hu, 車 |, koetsier.

k'a hu, 脚 |, lastdragers, koelies.

kang hu t'aô, 工 | 頭, koeliehoofdman.

p'aì hu, 派 |, eene lijst voor lastdragers opgeven, bestellen.

hu dzin, | 人, mevrouw, (tegen mandarijn vrouwen) eere term voor vrouw.

灰 Hu — Asch; fijn als asch, vermolmd.

hé hu, 火 |, asch.

tsoá hu, 紙 |, papier-asch

tsi lô̤ hu, , asch van goud- en zilverpapier.

béh hu, 麥 |, tarwemeel.

hu hu, | 匕, vermolmd, verteerd (van boomen, papier, enz.).

hun hu, 烟 |, tabak of sigarenasch.

膚 Hu — Huid, vel; zacht vleesch onder de huid.

p'ê hu, 皮 |, vel, huid.

hún hu ts'uì kut, 粉 | 碎 骨, verbrijzeld zijn.

bô ū ki hu, 無 肌 |, vleesch noch vel hebben, *d. i.* zeer zwak.

Hu *hu hu tseh*, streelen, aanhalen, (zooals men kinderen doet.

府 Hú — Departement.

hun hú, 分 |, tweede officier van een *fu*.

koa̤ hu, 官 |, ambtenaar in 't algemeen.

kuì hú, 貴 |, Uw (geëerd) departement.

hú siōng, | 上, huis, (beleefdh.)

hú laī, | 內, in Uw huis, (beleefheidsterm).

hú kò̤, | 庫, gouvernements schatkist.

t'ong hing kok hú tsiū koaī, door elke *hú tsiu* en *hiēn* bekendmaken.

腐 Hú — *hi hú ê oē* / *» » ê oā* } 肺 | 之 言, woorden uit het diepst van zijn hart.

sa̤ tsai hì hú / *sio » » »* } 相 知 肺 |, elkander door en door kennen.

脯 Hú — *bah hú*, 肉 |, gedroogd vleesch.

許 Hú — *hú to*, | 多, zoo vele, zeer veel.

ing hú, 應 |, goedkeuren, toestemmen.

富 Hù — Rijk.

hù kuì, | 貴, rijk en aanzienlijk.

hù hō̤, | 戶, rijke families.

hù dzū / *» dzī* } | 裕, rijkdom en overvloed.

hù tsiok, | 足, rijk en genoeg overvloedig.

赴 Hù — Gaan naar: zich spoeden naar; komen te, bij tijds komen of klaar zijn.

hù hu / *» hi* } | 墟, zich naar de marktplaats spoeden.

ēm hù, 不 |, niet bij tijds, te laat.

hù hù, | |, nog ruimschoots bij tijd.

oē hù tit lí īng, 可 | 你 用, het zal bij tijds klaar zijn als gij het gebruiken moet.

ēm hù tsiáh, 不 | 食, niet bij tijds gereed zijn om het te eten.

hù si, hù k'ik, | 時, | 刻, tegen den bepaalden tijd klaar zijn.

boē hù ts'iú, 不 | 手, niet klaar, gereed, bij de hand zijn.

bô hù ĭng, 不 | 用, niet voldoende zijn voor het gebruik.

bô hù goá ĭng, 不 | 我 用, niet gereed zijn op den tijd dat ik het gebruiken moet.

副 Hù Helpen, assistent, hulp, onder, vice; duplikaat; een stel als van een servies.

hù pêng kòng, | 榜 貢, hoogste graad van *siù tsai*.

hù tsiòng } *„ tsiàng* } | 將, vice generaal, onder bevelhebber; adjudant van een bevelhebber.

hù ts'iú, | 手, assistent.

tsit hù tsit tsiàⁿ, 一 | 一 正, een in reserve en een die steeds gebruikt wordt.

kui hù, 全 |, kompleet stel.

tsit hù hù eh, 一 | |, een over kompleet voorwerp.

siong hù, 相 |, tot een zelfde stel behoorend.

tsit hù, 一 |, een stel van servies, enz.

taò hù, 湊 |, een stel volledig maken.

付 Hù Geven aan, in handen stellen van iemand.

hù t'ok, | 託, belasten met, opdragen.

kao hù, 交 |, toevertrouwen aan.

咐 Hù *hun* (of *hoan*) *hù*, 吩 |, gelasten.

負 Hù *tsū hù*, 自 |, zich aanmatigen.

訃 Hù *pun hù im*, 分 | 音, dood communicaties rondzenden.

賦 Hù *si hù*, 詩 |, versmaat.

Hù *hong hù hù kio* (of *haò*), 風 嘶 然, de wind loeit.

扶 Hû Helpen, bijstaan; onder de armen ophouden; ondersteunen; met beide handen tillen.

hû tsō, | 助, helpen.

hû ts'i } *„ si* } | 持, ondersteunen, helpen, bijstaan.

hû hû ts'ah ts'ah, | | 挿 |, ondersteunen als een oud mensch onder de armen.

hû k'i laìh, | 起 來, opillen.

hû loh laìh, | 下 來, aftillen.

符 Hû Sluiten op, slaan op, overeenstemmen met; amulet, geschreven behoedmiddel tegen gevaren of geesten.

hû hap, | 合, overeenstemmen, op elkander slaan.

hû tâng, | 同, overeenstemmend, eensluidend.

siong hû, 相 |, overeenstemmen.

put hû, 不 |, niet overeenkomen, niet uitkomen (als eene berekening).

sⁿ kak hû, 三 角 |, driekante amulet.

hō sin hû, 護 身 |, ligchaam beschermende amulet.

uī hû tiaō koan tsiòng, 畫 | 召 官 將, tooverteekens schrijven om de geesten duivels te roepen (zooals Taoist. priesters doen; *d. i.* alle personen bij elkander roepen die bij iets noodig zijn.

附 Hū Digtbij, nabij; toenaderen, instemmen.

hū kūn } *„ kīn* } 近 |, digtbij, in de buurt.

hū hō, | 和, instemmen, gelijkgeven (of het zoo is of niet).

負 Hū Op den rug dragen; den rug keeren naar; van daar, niet vergelden, ondankbaar zijn.

k'i hū, 欺 |, verdrukken.

ko hū, 辜 |, ondankbaar zijn jegens.

k'ui hū, iemand onkosten laten maken en hem ondank tot loon geven.

父 Hū Vader.

ka hū, 家 |, mijn vader.

sien hū, 先 |, mijn overledene vader.

hū ts'in, | 親, vader, (beleefheids-term).

婦 Hū Vrouw; getrouwde vrouw.

hū dzin lâng, | 人, vrouw.

p'oat hū, 嫖 |, boosaardige slechte vrouw, (fats: term).

hu hū, 夫 |, man en vrouw.

駙 Hū *hū má*, | 馬, echtgenoot eener keizerlijke prinses.

腐 Hū *tāo hū*, 荳 |, boonenwrong.

咎 Hū *tùi hū*, 歸 |, iemand verwijten; de schuld geven als eene zaak niet goed is uitgevallen.

傅 Hū *sai hū*, 師 |, werkman, baas.

Hū hū kùn, verward door elkander spreken, joelen.

Pùn hū tu tu, op de trompet blazen.

Hui

非 Hui Niet goed, slecht; niet zoo, niet.

ui hui tsok tai, 爲 | 作 歹, slecht handelen.

hui ui, ui hui, | 爲, 爲 |, het kwade doen.

kòng lâng ē sī hui, veel op iemand aan te merken hebben.

k'ó sī sin hui, 口 是 心 |, met de mond zoo, maar met het hart niet zoo, *d. i.* anders spreken dan men het meent.

hui ts'in hui ts'ik, | 親 | 戚, geene familie betrekking van iemand zijn.

hui tông siaó k'ó, | 同 小 可, het is niet gemakkelijk; van geene geringe gevolgen.

hui siông / » *siâng* } | 常, niet alledaagsch, buitengewoon.

飛 Hui Vliegen, wegvliegen, vliegend, snel.

hui liêm tsaó piah, uit de goten vliegen en tegen de muren klouteren, (van vlugge dieven).

hûn hui p'ik sàn, 魂 | 魄 散, doodsverschrikt zijn.

hui pò, | 報, vliegend, *d. i.* snel gaan bekendmaken.

妃 Hui Keizerlijke bijzitten. *kiong hui*, do.

灰 Hui *hui ts'ú* / » *ts'í* } | 鼠, rat van wiens vel bont en penseelen gemaakt worden.

揮 Hui *tsi hui*, 指 |, Man-tsiu majoor.

熏 Hui *īng hé hun hui eh*, 用 火 煙 | 的, door rook berookt, (zooals hout of porcelein.)

Hui *kè tsuì hui* / *koè* » » } afgieten, doen bezinken en het fijne bovendrijvende gebruiken.

匪 Huí slecht, onwettig; schurken, bandieten.

huí luī, | 類, slechte soort menschen, schurken.

t'ó huí, 土 |, plaatselijke bandieten.

毀 Huí Vernielen, verwoesten; vervallen, stuk. lasteren.

huí hoāi, | 壞, bedorven, vervallen.

huí biét, | 滅, stuken vernietigd.

huí pòng, | 謗, lasteren, belasteren.

sio huí, 燒 |, verbrand, door brand vernield.

翡 Huí *huí ts'uì tsiaó*, | 翠 鳥, ijsvogel.

19

huî ts'uì gik, | 翠 玉, chrysopras.

費 Huì Verbruiken, gebruiken, onkosten maken, verkwisten, verspillen, opmaken, onkosten, uitgaven.

huì tsi, | 錢, geld verbruiken, verkwisten.

huì ing, | 用, verbruiken.

hoa huì, 花 |, verkwisten.

p'oà huì, 破 |, uitgeven, verliezen.

huì si, | 時, tijd verspillen.

huì k'ì, | 氣, lastig, moeijelijk.

huì kang hu, | 工 夫, tijd aan een werk verspillen.

huì sim, | 心, zijn geest afmatten.

huì sin, | 神, zich veel moeite geven, dank U, (beleefdheidsterm).

huì lát, | 力, zijne krachten verspillen.

k'ai huì, 開 |, onkosten maken, uitgaven doen.

huì k'ao siét, veel woorden aan iets verspellen.

huì ke hé, | 家 貨, zijne bezittingen opmaken.

só huì, 所 |, onkosten, uitgaven.

huì liáo liáo, | 了 匕, geheel en al te niet, (zooals bezittingen.)

hû huì / *hi* „ } 虛 |, onkosten.

lō huì, 路 |, reisgeld.

poâ huì, 盤 |. do.

tsûn huì, 船 |, onkosten voor een schip; passagegeld.

tsáp huì, 什 |, verschillende uitgaven.

siū huì, 受 |, gij hebt veel onkosten voor mij gemaakt, (beleefdheidsterm.)

緯 Huì Inslag van een weefsel.

ki huì, 經 |, schering en inslag.

諱 Huì Verbergen, bedekt houden; melk naam dien alleen ouders tegen hunne kinderen gebruiken, maar die anderen niet zeggen kunnen.

iém huì, verbergen, bedekken.

pī huì, het gebruik van zijn vaders naam vermijden.

hoān huì, zich schuldig maken aan het gebruik van iemands melknaam, iemand in tegenwoordigheid van minderen beleedigen.

huì miâ, | 名, naam dien men van zijne ouders krijgt.

惠 Huì Gunst, weldaad.

bô huì tsi huì, 無 費 之 |, weldaad, gunst, die den gever geen geld kost.

un huì / *in* „ } 恩 | weldaad.

瓷 Hui *hui k'ì*, | 器, aardewerk.

hui sai hū, | 師 阜, pottenbakker.

sio hui, 燒 |, aardewerk bakken.

hui iô, 磁 |, aardewerk bakkerij.

hui sio ê sim koa, | 燒 的 心 肝, hardvochtig.

肥 Huì *hui hō*, | 厚, dik en vet.

Huih

血 Huih Hoeh Bloed.

huih kun, 助 |, aderen.

huih si, | 絲, bloeddraden.

t'ò huih, 吐 |, bloedspuwen, ook lastig verward, (van eene zaak).

huih tsui, | 水, vloeijend bloed, bloedwater.

huih kéng, | 脅, slagaderen.

p'ùi huih, 噴 |, slijm en bloed opgeven.

huih kong sim, | 攻 心, opstopping van bloed bij het hart.

kik huih, 積 〡, opstopping van bloed.

tsí huih, 止 〡, het bloed stoppen.

huih tsì, 〡 箭, bloedstraal.

huih liû, 〡 瘤, bloedgezwel.

ts'inh huih, 刺 〡, steken, slagten, (koeijen, enz.).

koah huih, 割 〡, snijden, slagten, (kippen, enz.).

tíng huih sik } *tuī hueh* » } 無 〡 色, bleek *bô huih sik* } worden.

hē huih, 下 〡, bloed ontlasten.

páng huih, 放 〡, bloed aftappen met lating.

huih lō, 〡 路, de weg dien het bloed volgt.

huih lim, 〡 淋, bloed urine.

si huih, 死 〡, dood stilstaand bloed.

at huih, 遏 〡, de bloeds omloop, afbinden.

p'ah huih p'ùn, voorstellingen uit de hel geven.

huih tm } *» táng* } zwarte stukken bloed.

ts'iŋ huih tô, stolten van bloed.

huih dziah, 〡 跡, sporen van bloed.

Hun

分 Hun Deelen, verdeelen, scheiden, onderscheid maken tusschen, onderscheiden, uit een zetten; gelijkelijk verdeelen van daar dag en nachts evening; een deel, een tiende, een weinigje; candareen het honderste deel van een tael; assistent; onder.

hun piēn, 〡 辨, onderscheiden.

hun piét, 〡 別, scheiden van elkander afgaan.

hun luī, 〡 類, sorteren.

hun p'oè 〡 配, over elk verdeelen.

kun hun, } *kin* » } 均 〡, gelijkelijk verdeelen.

hun t'iah, verdeelen (zooals eene som geld)

hun tsâng, in meerdere boomen of planten verdeelen (zooals eene te vol staande bloempot).

hun p'aì, 〡 派, afzenden.

hun bing, 〡 明, duidelijk uit een zetten; duidelijk, klaar.

put hun hik pik, 不 〡 黑 白, geen onderscheid maken tusschen kwaad en goed.

hun p'oà, 〡 判, uit een zetten en uitspraak doen.

hun sò, uit een zetten, weêrleggen.

hun hē, weêrleggen, iets tegen zeggen; tegen spreken, redetwisten.

bô hùn bô hē, 無 〡 無 下, zonder naar reden te vragen, naar geen reden luisteren.

hun kai, uit elkander zetten, verklaren.

ts'un hun, 春 〡, lente's dag en nacht evening.

ts'iu hun, 秋 〡, herft's dag en nacht evening.

ū hun ts'ùn, 有 〡 寸, regelmatig, afgemeten.

tsáp hun, 十 〡, 10 deelen, zeer.

tsáp hun hó, 十 〡 好, zeer goed.

kaò hun, tot rijpheid gekomen, (van vruchten).

hun hô, 〡 毫, een weinigje.

hun bùn, 〡 文, do.

hun li si, 〡 厘 絲, een haartje, een weinigje.

hun koai } *» koān* } 〡 縣, assistent magistraat van een *hien*.

hun hú, | 府, assistent magistraat van een *hu*.

hun tsiu, | 州, assistent magistraat van een *tsiu*.

烟 Hun Rook; tabak, sigaren, opium.

hé hun, 火 |, rook.

tīng hé hun, 斷 火 |, geen pot meer koken, dood arm, niets te eten hebben.

tsng ts'ut hun, 當 炎 |, op het top punt van bloeien verdienste zijn.

ts'ut hun, 出 |, rooken (van een kagchelen).

kaō hun, *sì hun*, rooktabak.

hun sai, | 屎, tabaksasch.

hun hu, | 灰, tabak of sigarenasch.

tsui hun, 水 |, watertabak.

tsui hun ts'e, 水 | 吹, waterpijp.

hun ts'e / » *ts'oe* } | 吹, pijp.

hun ts'e t'âo, | 吹 頭, pijpenkop.

hun ts'e t'ong, | 吹 筒, pijpen doorsteker.

hun ts'e iah, pijpenwroeter.

tsit poah hun, een dot tabak.

p'ī hun, 鼻 |, snuif.

hun pao, | 袍, tabakszak.

hun tē, | 袋, tabakzak, sigarenkoker.

t'oe hun, tabak raspen kerven.

tsiah p'ī hun, 食 鼻 |, snuiver.

o hun, 烏 |, zwarte tabak, *d. i.* opium.

tsao hun, *tài hun*, verslaafd aan opium.

hun poā k'a kong kè, bij de opium pijp den koop bepraten.

kaō hun tièm, 厚 | 店, tabakswinkel.

熏 Hun Rooken, berooken.

hé lô hun / *hoé* » » } 火 爐 |, het fornuis rookt.

bak tsiu hō hun hun tioh, 目 子 被 | 所 熏, rook in de oogen krijgen.

hun báng, | 蚊, muskieten uit (een vertrek) rooken.

昏 Hun Zonsondergang, avondschemering, duister.

hun kun, een duistere, de domme vorst.

hun niō, suf, (door ouderdom).

婚 Hun Huwelijk, huwen.

hun in, | 姻, huwelijk.

tsú hun, over een huwelijk beschikken, het huwelijk vaststellen, bepalen.

hun tsu / » *si* } 書 |, huwelijks contract.

háp hun, 合 |, door het huwelijk vereenigd worden.

tsiú hun toh, 主 | 棹, bruiloftsmaal.

sin hun, 新 |, pas getrouwd.

紛 Hun Verward door elkander, vele zaken tegelijk.

hun hun, | 匕, do.

hun hun loān loān, | 匕 亂 匕, in verwarden toestand.

hun sim, | 心, door bezigheden overstelpt.

吩 Hun *hun hù*, | 咐, gelasten.

粉 Hún Meel, ook als blanketsel gebruikt; fijn als meel; witten, verfraaijen, opsieren.

bi hún, 米 |, rijstemeel.

tang hún, 冬 |, meel van groene erwten.

hún tsiu̱, ｜粹, stijfsel.

bīn hún, 面｜, blanketsel.

tsui hún, meel water, (om te blanketten).

boah hún, 傳｜, zich blanketten.

ū hún t'aô, 有｜頭, fraai, (gew. van vrouwen).

bô hún t'aô, 無｜頭, leelijk, (gew. van vrouwen).

ts'iū̱ hún, met een meellaag bedekt (zooals vruchten).

hún ts'uì, ts'uì hún hún, ｜碎, 碎｜｜, aan schilfers, tot gruis,

bah hún hún, 肉｜｜, fijn van vleesch, vel.

hún piah, ｜壁, een muur witten, kalken; een gewitte muur.

hún sik, ｜飾, verfraaijen, opsieren, mooijer doen voorkomen dan iets inderdaad is.

bô hún tit, 無｜的, moeijelijk te bedotten.

憤 Hun — Inwendig sterk door iets gedreven.

hoat hún, 發｜, zich inspannen, met ijver aanvatten.

hún k'ì, 敢｜, hevige toorn.

悻 Hun — *hún hún*, haastig in ijl.

楥 Hùn I — Schoenleest, op de leest zetten.

oê hùn, 鞋｜, schoenleest.

hùn oê, ｜鞵, schoenen op eene leest slaan.

奮 Hùn — Voor den dag doen komen, uitstrekken, uitspreiden.

hùn ióng, ｜勇, zijne sterkte voor den dag doen komen, dapper, moedig.

hùn tsì, zijn zin op iets zetten, lust in iets krijgen.

hùn k'ah toā, vergrooten, uitbreiden, (zooals een wijk).

hùn lâng, zweren, etteren.

訓 Hùn — Onderwijzen, leeren.

kaò hùn, 教｜, onderwijzen, onderrigten.

hùn tō, ｜導, inspekteur van onderwijs.

釁 Hùn Hìn — Geschil, twist.

hùn iû, ｜尢, reden, oorzaak van twist.

k'í hùn, 起｜, reden, aanleiding tot twist geven of zijn.

雲 Hûn — Wolken, bewolkt; drijven als wolken.

o̱ hûn sit àm, 黑｜深夜, donkere bewolkte nacht.

bô hun iá̱ / *» » (tsiah)* } 無｜影, onwaar.

hûn hō̱, ｜雨, overdrijvende regen.

ngó̱ ts'ai, (of *sik*) *hûn*, 五彩, (色), gekleurde wolken.

hûn iû, ｜遊, overal rondtrekken, (zooals priesters).

痕 Hûn — Rimpel, plooi, vouw; likteeken, kras. streep.

tsin t'aò hûn, 枕頭｜, rimpels strepen op het gelaat door het hoofdkussen veroorzaakt.

tsih hûn, plooi, plooijen.

hûn sam, ｜衫, Europ. overhemd.

tsuí hûn, 水｜, spoor dat een schip achterlaat, kielwater.

hiau hûn, 微｜, ondankbare trekken in het gelaat.

tsuí p'o hûn, 水波｜, gemarmerd, (geverwd).

kuih hûn / *koeh »* } 劃｜, met krassen gekrast.

墳 Hûn — Graf,

hùn bōng, | 墓, graf.

tsó hùn, 祖 |, voorvaderlijk graf.

魂 Hûn De geest die het leven in den mensch uitmaakt, ziel.

sin hùn, ling hùn, 神 |, 靈 |, ziel.

hùn put hū t'é, | 不附體, de ziel bleef hem niet in het ligchaam, *d. i.* doods verschrikt.

sam hùn ts'it pik, 三 | 七魄, drie zielen en zeven dierlijke geesten, die men aan den mensch toeschrijft.

hoân hùn, 返 |, tot het leven terugkomen, bijkomen (uit eene flaauwte)

in hùn, 引 |, de ziel van een afgestorvene terugroepen.

iû hùn, 游 |, rondzwervende dwalende zielen.

hùn sin, | 身, ziel ligchaam, papieren afbeeldsel van een overledene.

hùn ting, | 亭, zielen kastje, waarin de tablet van een overledene bij de begrafenis gedragen wordt.)

焚 Hûn *sio hûn bé*, 燒 | 馬, papier met paarden enz: beteekend aan de geesten verbranden (één dag vóór het uitgeleiden en inhalen der geesten).

渾 Hûn *hùn tsiâ*, | 成, onmerkbaar in elkander overgaand, zoo gemaakt of gerepareerd dat men de aanhechtingsplaats niet zien kan.

分 Hūn Deel, aandeel, respectivelijk deel; pligt, stand; in iets deelen.

sa hūn tsit, sa hūn nñg, 三 | 一, 三 | 兩, één derde, twee-derde.

hūn tsit hūn, | 一 |, voor één deel in iets deelen, één deel in iets hebben.

hūn goā, | 外, buitengewoon, (duur enz).

tsiaò hūn k'ui, (of *pun*). 照 | 開, | | 分, zijn deel in winst en verlies nemen.

hùn giáh, hùn tsing giáh, | 額, | 前額, respectivelijk deel.

tsiaò kui hūn, 按幾 |, in hoevele deelen, aandeelen?

pún hūn, 本 |, pligt.

hūn lai è tai tsì, | 內之大事, zaken die tot zijn pligt behooren, pligtzaken,

hūn ē / » *ē* } | 下, tot zijn pligt behoorende; onderstaande.

an hūn siú ki, 安 | 守己, zich tot zijn pligt, stand, bepalen.

tsit hūn, 職 |, pligt, betrekking.

sin hūn, 身 |, stand, fatsoen.

toā sin hūn, 大身 |, van hooge stand.

bing hùn, 名 |, pligten van de betrekking tot elkander.

oát hūn, 越 |, zijn pligt, stand te buitengaan.

kè hūn / *koè* » } 過 |, zijn overschrijden.

恨 Hūn Hīn Haat, wrok, haten, ontevreden zijn over.

oàn hūn, 怨 |, haat, haten.

oàn sin hūn miā, 怨身 | 命, ontevreden zijn met zijn lot.

iém hūn, 陰 |, inwendig wrok, spijt over iets hebben.

kì hūn tsai sim, 記 | 在心, wrok; haat in zich hebben, gegriefd zijn over.

hiép hūn, 挾 |, haat in zich hebben, wrok hebben jegens.

tsit pak è hūn k'ì, 滿腹 | 氣 opstopping van haat.

t'òng hūn, 痛 丨, ingekankerd-uiterst haten.
k'ó hūn, 可 丨, hatelijk, te haten verachtelijk.
k'ioh hūn, verschillende redenen tot wrok op zamelen.

混 Hūn In een chaos, verward, door elkander, onduidelijk, onbepaald; verwarring brengen in (zooals in land grenzen), valschelijk verruilen.
hūn tsáp, 丨 雜, verward door elkander, gemengd.
hūn loān, 丨 亂, door elkander warren.
hūn hūn, 丨 丨, door elkander (gebruiken), verward onduidelijk.
hūn tù, hūn hūn tù tù, 丨 塗, 丨 混 丨 塗, onduidelijk, verward, onbepaald.
hùn tsiàng tsiàng, 丨 障 七, niet duidelijk onderscheiden-verward.
hūn tūn, hūn hūn tūn tūn, verward, onduidelijk.
k'it lâng hūn k'ìh, door iemand bedrogen worden (iets slechts voor het goede in de plaats vinden).

暈 Hūn Hūn *hūn k'ìh*, 丨 去, flaauw vallen.
si hūn / *se* » } vreemd, onbekend, (met pers. of plaats), schuw.

Hut

忽 Hut Eene fijne draad zijde; oppervlakkig, onnaauwkeurig; eensklaps, onverwachts.
hut hô li hut, de geringste kleinigheden, fijnste bijzonderheden.
hut lióк / » *liák* } 丨 畧, oppervlakkig.
hóng hut, 恍 丨, onnaauwkeurig, oppervlakkig, eensklaps, plotseling.
hut dzién, 丨 然, eensklaps.

拂 Hut Oorspr, wegvegen; zich verzetten tegen.
hut lâng è i sù, 丨 人 意 緖, zich tegen de algemeene opinie verzetten.
i sù, hut hut, tsoē i ts'ut mêng, knorrig de deur uitgaan.

核 Hút Pit eener vrucht.
hut t'ô, 丨 桃, walnoot.
lān hút, 外 腎, de ballen, (testiculi).
tsiù hút, (vruchten) met kleine pitten.
hút hút, 丨 七, vol kluiten, kl nters.
sim t'aò tsit hút, eene opstopp ng van boosheid, of droefheid hebben.
t'ô á hút k'ik tsiû kaô, 丨 桃 刻 成 猴, een perzikpit tot een aap uitsnijden *d. i.* geverseerd, meester in zijn vak zijn.

佛 Hút *hút siú kam*, 丨 手 柑, Boeddha hand citroen (gekonfij).
hút kaò, 丨 教, Boeddhisme.
liām hút, 念 丨, den naam van Boeddha herhaaldelijk uitspreken.
soé hút / *sé* » } 洗 丨, *lett.* een Boeddha beeld wasschen (waarvoor ieder een geld bijdraagt); iemand die kletsnat van regen is.
hōng hút, 奉 丨, aan Boeddha offeren.
hút gûn, 丨 銀, Fransch geld, *d. i.* dollars.

I

衣 I Kleederen, kleeding.
i hók, 丨 服, kleeren.
i tsiû / *i tsiô* } 丨 袖, do.
ho i tsiû kè / » » » *kè* } goed kleeden.
piēn i, 便 丨, civiele kleeding.

i koan, | 冠, kleeding, kleeder dracht..
ts'ìng i koan, 整 | 冠, uniform aan doen.
i siu, | 箱, bagage.
pò i sui hūn, katoenen kleeren volgens zijn stand.
t'ai i, 胎 |, baarvlies.

依 I Steunen op, vertrouwen, zich verlaten, op, volgens; toegeven.
i oá, | 靠, vertrouwen, zich verlaten op.
bò i bò oá, 無 | 無 靠, geen steun hebben, alleen staan in de werld.
i i, | 倚, steunen, zich verlaten op.
i dziên, | 然, nog steeds, als te voren.
i si hàng tsing, | 市 行 淸, volgens den marktprijs.
i làng, iemand toegeven, zijn zin geven.

醫 I Genezen, heelen; geneesheer.
i pī / *» pē* } eene ziekte genezen.
i tsing, | 淸, do.
i sing | 生, geneesheer, doktor.
i koán, i sing koán, | 館, | 生 館, hospitaal.
bing i, 名 |, beroemde geneesheer.
si i, gelukkige (maar niet knappe) geneesheer, kwakzalver.
t'aì i, 太 |, keizerlijke geneesheer.

伊 I Hij, zij.
i ka kī, | 家 己, hij of zij zelf.
i i o o, neuriën, zingen.

以 Í Zich bedienen van, gebruikmaken van, het middel om, met, door; kenmerkt het voorafgaande als een punt van uitgang.
i lé sy koán t'aī, | 禮 相 款 待, elkander met beleefdheid behandelen ontvangen.
só i, 所 |, daarom, daardoor.
i kip, | 及, benevens.
i piēn, | 便, om zoodoende..., om daarna.....
k'ong hi i lai, 康 熙 | 來, van af Kang-hi.
.... *i goā*, | 外, buiten, behalve...
bē hoán i tsiên, 未 反 | 從, voor het oproer.
tsáp dzī tiém i aō, 十 二 點 | 後, na twaalf uur.
sy p'in i hā, 三 兵 | 下, beneden onder den derden rang (van mandarijn)
dzī tsáp hé i siōng, 二 十 歲 | 上, boven de twintig jaar.

倚 Í Steunen op, zich verlaten op.
i i, i naī, steunen zich verlaten op.

椅 Ì Stoel, bank.
kao i, 校 |, stoel.
i t'aò, | 頭, tabouret.
tin i, 藤 |, rottingstoel.
tik i, 竹 |, bamboesstoel.
i liaò, bank.
i tiêm, stoelkussen.
i koai / *» koa* } arm leuning eener stoel.
i kiō, | 棹, tafelstoel, (voor kinderen).
i toh bin tsing, | 棹 眠 床, meubelen in het algemeen.

已 Í Alreeds.
i king, | 經, alreeds.

put tik i, 不 得 丨, het kon niet anders of..., onvermijdelijk.

意 丨 Bedoeling, meening, idèe, voornemen, dunk, gedachten, gezindheid; opinie; beteekenis.

hó i, *p'ai i*, 好 丨, 歹 丨, goede, slechte bedoeling.

tíng i, *tsoán i*, van idée veranderen.

sa sim nēng i / » » *nō̤* » } 三 心 二 丨, drie harten en twee meeningen, *d. i.* tot geen besluit kunnen komen.

taī ke i k'i, 大 家 丨 氣, de meening, opinie van allen.

i k'i sa háp, 丨 氣 三 合, overeenstemmen.

háp i. 合 丨, do.

ting i, 定 丨, met zijn idée overeenstemmen, naar zijn zin zijn.

bô i, 無 丨, zonder voordacht.

bô i bô i, 無 丨 無 丨, zonder plannen, teleurgesteld.

tsip i, 執 丨, zich aan zijn idée vasthouden, vastbesloten.

i kièn, bedoeling, inzigt.

koat i, 決 丨, vastbesloten zijn.

i goē, *i goā*, 丨 外, 丨 外, onverwacht.

kò̤ i, 固 丨, voorbedachtelijk, met moedwil.

put i, 不 丨, onverwachts.

iú i p'uh i bû i, voorbedachtelijk iemand iets doen, waarop hij niet bedacht is.

dzīm i, 任 丨, naar zijn eigen dunk handelen.

bô ū i bī, 無 有 丨 味, geene fijne beteekenis hebben.

hoē i, 會 丨, de beteekenis, bedoeling vatten.

i sù, 丨 思, beteekenis, bedoeling, opinie, meening.

lé i put kai, 理 丨 不 該, volgens de beleefdheid behoort dat niet.

i ài, 丨 愛, houden van, verlangen, wenschen.

king i, *k'ièn i*, 敬 丨, 虔 丨, eerbiedig.

穢 丨 *i tsì*, 丨 臭, vuil, smerig.

姨 丨 Vrouws zuster, zwagerin; tante, moeders zuster.

toā i, 大 丨, vrouws oudere zuster.

i á, 丨 仔, vrouws jongere zuster.

bú i, 毋 丨, moeders zuster, tante.

i tiū, 丨 舅, oom, man van moeder's zuster.

i piaó hia tī, neven, zoons van moeder's zuster.

soè i / *sè* » } 小 妾, bijzit.

丨 *ang i*, 女 巫, waarzegster, tooverheks.

彝 丨 *bú i tê*, 武 丨 茶, Bohea thee.

夷 丨 *sù i*, 四 丨, oorsp. de vier barbaarsche volken om China, van daar, aan vier kanten, de vier windstreken.

移 丨 Overplanten, verplaatsen, verzetten; veranderen, verhuizen; overzenden als eene dépèche.

i soá, 丨 徙, verzetten, verplaatsen.

i lai i k'i, 丨 來 丨 去, heen en weer verplaatsen.

i k'ih, verplaatsen, verzetten.

i hoán i hok ê lâng, een wispelturig mensch.

ts'ien i, 遷 丨, uit den weg ruimen, een einde maken aan.

i tsioh, 丨 借, leenen van.

i ik, 丨 易, veranderen.

boē i ik tit, 莫 丨 易, onveranderlijk.

i i út út, aarzelen.

pog i, 搬 丨, verhuizen.

koé i, 改 丨, verhuizen, (naar eene andere plaats).

i bûn, 丨 文, eene dépèche toezenden, (naar een ander district).

嚶 丨 *i i oai oai*, 咿 丨 嚶 丨, kraken, (zooals een rad), geluid van een viool.

i oai toh, kleptafel.

蜓 丨 *ts'ân i* / » *e* } 蜻 丨, libellula, waterjuffer.

liem ts'ân i, 拈 蜻 丨, een libellula, beetpakken; 2e kind dat kort gebonden bosjes haar heeft.

嬰 丨 *i á*, 丨 兒, kind, dreumes.

iù i, do.

蕙 丨 Bloem knop.

hoe i / *hoa* » } 花 丨, bloemknop.

puh i 萌 丨 / *hoat* » 發 丨 / *t'ó* » } ontspruiten, ontkiemen.

bē kui hoe bē puh i, 未 開 花 未 萌 丨, nog geen bloemen hebben of spruiten geschoten hebben, *d. i.* nog zeer jong zijn.

燕 丨 *i á*, 丨 子, zwaluw.

i bé / » *boé* } 丨 尾, zwaluw staart.

圓 丨 Rond, afgerond, rond in handelingen; zonder hoeken, gaaf, afgedaan.

i i, 丨 匕, rond.

i lìn lìn / » *lièn lièn* } zuiverrond.

i kō lō sō, / *i lō kō*, / *i ts'ia ts'ia*. } zuiverrond.

i kō kō bô tìng hō, rondrollen en geen stempel dragen (als geld) *d. i.* iemand die alleen in de wereld is, een van wien men geene zekerheid heeft.

t'i toē i tin lin ts'oan gō si tog sin, hemel en aarde zijn rond; bij voorkeur hongeren, alleenstaande menschen dood; alleenstaande, ongehuwde menschen gaat het gewoonlijk slecht.

géh i, 月 丨, de maan is rond, vol.

tsoè lâng i, rond in zijn handelingen zijn.

pān tit i, eene zaak rond, goed afdoen.

pān sū k'o boē tit i, eene zaak niet af kunnen maken.

so i ti pī, rondrollen en in een knijpen *d. i.* naar verkiezing met iets kunnen handelen; een zaak schikken.

p'ah t'it p'oà siu tit i, 打 得 破 收 得 丨, eene zaak eerst bederven maar ook weer goed maken.

i lâng oē pi pi lâng oē i, 丨 人 能 平 平 人 能 丨, ronde menschen kunnen plat en platte menschen kunnen rond worden, *d. i.* rijken kunnen arm en armen kunnen rijk worden.

丸 丨 Balletje, pil.

tun t'ih i, 吞 鐵 丨, een ijzeren pil slikken, *d. i.* iets eten waar men niet van houdt.

kap pâng i, 合 房 丨, huwelijkspil, bij huwelijksceremonie gegeten.

i á t'eng, 丨 仔 湯, balletjes soep.

i á teng soe ōng iù, 丨 仔 湯 衰 旺 鴦, bij balletjes soep kan men ongelukkig en gelukkig opscheppen, *d. i.* de prijs van allen is dezelfde, maar er loopen mindere soorten onder.

ióh i, 藥 |, pil.

tang tseh i } 冬 至 |, meel-
„ tseh „ }
balletjes op het wintersolstitium gegeten.

poà ni i, 半 年 |, halfjaar's ballen.

櫞 *hiu i* } 香 |, groote ronde citroen.
hio „ }

| 楹 Balk, dakbalk.

| *i á* do.

Ê *dzi ki i beh sing tsoè tiong tsit*, de tweede balk wil de nokbalk worden *d. i.* hooger gezag willen aannemen zooals eene bijzit na den dood der wettige vrouw.

延 *i ti*, verward, ingewikkeld, blijven hangen.

| *i i ti ti*, do.

tsoè i ti, diarrhoea, hebben (bedekte term).

院 Openbaar gebouw, collegie, gesticht, klooster.

| *kòng ī*, 貢 |, provinciaal examinatie-gebouw.

hān lim ī, 翰 林 |, collegie voor Han-lim.

hàk ī, examinator.

tsu ī } 書 |, collegie.
si „ }

iòng tsè ī } 養 祭 |, weldadig-
iáng „ „ }
heids gesticht.

ko nó ī, 姑 老 |, oude mannen en vrouwenhuis.

sī ī, 寺 |, klooster.

li ko ī, 尼 姑 |, nonnenklooster.

hê siū ī, 和 尙 |, mannenklooster.

易 Gemakkelijk.

| *iòng ī*, 容 |, gemakkelijk.

異 Verschillend, vreemd, zeldzaam.

| *ki ī*, 奇 |, zeldzaam.

Ia

埃 *ing ia*, 蒙 |, stof, vuil.
Ia

野 Wildernis, woestenij, onbebouwd, woest,
Iá wild; ongemanierd, onbeschoft, ruw, slecht, hebzuchtig, inhalig.

k'òng iá, 曠 |, wildernis, woestijn.

soa iá, 山 |, do.

kao iá, 郊 |, onbebouwde plaats, wildernis.

iá goā ê lâng, | 外 之 人, menschen in de wildernis, onbekende binnenlanden.

iá siù, | 獸, wilde beesten.

iá bī, | 味, wild in het algemeen; vreemde, wonderlijke lucht.

iá ts'iah, onbeschoft; korzelig, (door warmte of van aard).

iá hàn, , ruwe kerel.

iá ts'àt, | 賊, *lett.* ruwe, onverschrokken dief, *d. i.* onbeschofte kerel.

san iá, ongemanierd, ruw.

iá siók, | 俗, ruwe manieren.

iá tà, onbezonnen op zich nemen.

iá sim, | 心, slecht van harte onopregt, inhalig.

也 Nog, behalve dat nog.

Iá *iá ū*, | 有, ook nog, nog is er.

Iā *iá eh tī tó lóh*, waar zijn de overige, anderen?

哇 Uit de mond doen komen (als eten).

Iá *iá ts'ut iá dzip*, | 出 | 入, eten
Ê dan uit de mond doen komen en dan weer inhalen (zooals kinderen doen).

ts'ùi laī iá ts'ut laih, 嘴 內 | 出 來, het uit zijn mond aan anderen geven (zooals vogels aan hare jongen).

疲 Ià Vermoeid, afgemat, lusteloos, iets moede zijn onwel.

sin k'u ià, 身 軀 丨, onwel.

boē ià, 未 丨, onvermoeid.

ià lai, lusteloos, vermoeid.

k'oṅ kaò ià, tot moede wordens vervelens toe, gezien hebben.

ià sin, 倦 神, lusteloos.

sing ià lak lak teh t'ing haū ih, reeds tot vermoeijens toe op iets gewacht hebben.

ià lak lak, iets moede zijn, volstrekt geen zin meer in iets hebben.

k'oaì ià, 快 丨, spoedig de lust voor iets verliezen.

耶 Ià *ià so*, 丨 穌, Jesus.

椰 Ià Kokosnoot, klappernoot.

ià l.ng, ià tsui, 丨 將, 丨 水, kokos melk.

ià bah, 丨 肉 kokosvleesch.

ià k'ak, 丨 殼, kokosbast.

ià ts'oè, 丨 刷, boender van kokos bast.

ià oṅ, 丨 椀, kom van een kokoschel.

ià iù, 丨 油, kokosolie.

爺 Ià Vader; eere titel aan beambten en aanzienlijke lieden gegeven.

lô ià, 老 丨, titel voor mandarijnen.

siaò ià, 小 丨, titel voor mandarijn zonen.

á ià, vader, (door of tegen mandarijn kinderen van hun vader gezegd).

ko ià, 姑 丨, schoonzoon van een mandarijn.

toā ià, 大 丨, titel voor hooge mandarijn bedienden.

o kui kè tsoè toā ià, 烏 龜 假 大 丨, de boerenbaas doet zich als een *toā-ià* voor (schertsend gezegd van iemand die zich deftiger dan te voren kleedt).

ông ià, 王 丨, keizerlijke prinsen.

ông ià kong, 王 丨 公, naam van een afgod.

呀 Ià *à ià*, uitrap van verwondering of verrassing.

撒 Iā Strooijen, rondstrooijen, verspreiden.

iā tsing, 丨 種, zaaijen.

iā soà, 丨 散, strooijen.

ìng soa iā làng, iemand met zand begooijen.

soà iā, 散 丨, zich overal rondstrooijen, verspreiden (zooals bloemzaad).

p'ah soà iā, overal verspreiden, strooijen; overal heen slenteren (zooals slavinnen).

iā tsi, 丨 錢, geld (te grabbelen) gooijen.

tsi gùn mì teh iā, zijn geld weggooijen, verspillen.

夜 Iā Nacht.

dzit iā, 日 丨, dag en nacht.

iā ts'im, diep in den nacht.

bō iā, 暮 丨, gebruik makende van den nacht . . . . , in den nacht.

liên sing iā, den nacht door (reizen, enz.).

ts'a iā / *ts'e »* } 查 丨, de nachtelijke rond te doen.

iā háp, 丨 合, Magnolia.

kìm hoān iā, 禁 犯 丨, verbieden dat men des nachts over straat ga.

iā ts'e, 丨 叉, naam van een leelijken duivel, (voor leelijke vrouw gebruikt).

也 Iā Nog, verder, ook, zelfs.

iā ū, 丨 有, er is nog, ook heeft men, ook zijn er.

iā bô, 丨無有, er is niet meer, overigens niet.
tsīn toā iā bô, zeer groot en er is geen (grooter).

纓 Ia̱ Franje aan een hoed.
bō ia̱, 帽丨, do.
bé ia̱ / *bé̱ »* } 馬丨, kwast, franje voor de borst van een paard hangende.
âng ia̱ bō, 紅丨帽, hoed met roode franje (zoo als mandarijn bedienden hebben).

涕 Ia̱ *laò bak ia̱*, 眼洒丨, tranen, traanoogen door lange blootstelling aan wind of vuur.

漾 Ia̱ *hi kún ia*, 魚滾丨, de visch borrel, spartelt in het water.
tsui ia, 水丨, beweging, kring, voren in het water (zoo als van de riemspanen).

影 Iá̱ Schaduw, schim; de schaduw van waarheid; schemering; schitteren, flikkeren; als een schim vluchtig zien.
tsoá iá̱, iá̱ hì, 紙丨, 丨戯, Chinesche schim.
dzip lâng iá̱ / *dzik » »* } 逐人丨, iemands schaduw na loopen (zoo als bedelaars).
o̱ gû toā iá̱, 烏牛大丨, een zwarte koe geeft eene groote schaduw *d. i.* iemand die grooter, rijker schijnt dan hij is.
uì iá̱, 畏丨, voor de schaduw vreezen, *d. i.* beschroomd bedeesd.
ū iá̱, ū iá̱ dziah / *» » tsiah* } het is waar, inderdaad.
bô iá̱, bô iá̱ dziah, niet waar.
tsai iá̱. 知丨, zijne zaken verstaan, door en door kennen.
o̱ iá̱, 烏丨, donkere schaduw.
o̱ iá̱ tā̱, in schemer bedriegen.
iá̱ àm, 晚丨, duister, donker, schemer.
iá̱ péh, morgen schemering.
liáh iá̱, 掠丨, *lett.* naar de schaduw grijpen gissen, niet stellig weten.
bô (of *ū*) *hûn bô iá̱*, 無痕無丨 onwaar, er is niets van aan.
iá̱ keng / *» kui̱* } 丨光, flikkeren, schitteren, (zoo als spiegelglas).
ts'ut lai teh iá̱ lâng, iemand slechts een schim van zich laten zien (zoo als schoone vrouwen).
ts'ut lai iá̱ tseh, een vlugtig overzigt van iets nemen, (zoo als van een feest).

贏 Iâ̱ Overwinnen, het winnen op van; overtreffen.
t'ai iâ̱, 殺丨, de overwinning betalen.
iâ̱ tsi̱, 丨錢, geld winnen (in het spelen).
iâ̱ kiaò, winnen met dobbelen.
su iâ̱, 輸丨, verlies en winst (bij het spelen); wedden.
taò su iâ̱, wedden.
bô su iâ̱, niet beslist wie de bovenhand heeft, gelijkstaand.
su iâ̱ tsit iū̱ bīn / *» » » iō̱ »* } 輸丨一様面, bij verlies of winst een zelfde gelaat behouden.
tam su iâ̱, tegen winst of verlies kennen.
ki̱ su iâ̱, 見輸丨, zien wie het verliezen en wie winnen zal. beslissende uitslag van verlies of winst, overwinning of nederlaag.
dzit pún ê ts'at k'ì k'a iâ̱ tiong kok eh, 日本的漆器丨中國, Japansch verlakt overtreft het Chinesche.

營 Iâ̱ Kamp, legerkamp, kampement, legerafdeeling; buurt waar gewoonlijk een laag soort menschen bij elkander wonen.
iâ̱ tsē / *» tsē̱* } 丨寨, legerkamp, legerplaats.
kun iâ̱, 軍丨, do.

iâ̤ ping, | 兵, soldaten uit het kamp-leger.
an iâ̤, kamperen.
siu iâ̤, het kamp opbreken.
nō iâ̤, 後 |, achterhoede.
tsò iâ̤, 左 |, linkervleugel.
tiong iâ̤. 中 |, centrum van het leger.
ngó iâ̤, 五 |, de vijf leger afdeeling, het leger.
teng iâ̤ ngó, in het leger dienen, soldaat zijn.
toā iâ̤, 大 |, hoofdkamp (waar in de opperbevelhebber woont).
iâ̤ kui, | 規, regels in het leger kamp.
hoán iâ̤, 反 |, rusie een standje hebben.
iâ̤ poâ̤, | 盤, legerkamp, kampement.
k'it tsiáh iâ̤, 乞 食 |, bedelaarsbuurt.
lóh iâ̤, in de (bedelaars) buurt wonen.
t'ai ko iâ̤, 痳 瘋 |, melaatschen huis.

颺
Iā̤

In beweging geraken als door wind; stuiven; wegwaaijen, wegslaan (zooals vliegen).
iā̤ hong, | 風, in den wind waaijen.
iā̤ iā̤ pe / *» » poe* } | 飛, opstuiven, (zooals asch).
tsit ê iā̤ put tsi toā, een groote kring (op het water als wanneer men er iets ingeworpen heeft).
iā̤ báng, | 蚊 muskieten wegwaaijeren, wegslaan.
pī k'ò ĕm ài iā̤ hó̤ sin, zoo ziek dat men zelfs geen lust heeft de vliegen weg te slaan.
sa̤ á ku iā̤ tseh p'ah p'oà, met de slippen van zijn kleed tegen iets aanslingeren zoodat het breekt.

Iah

挖
Iah
Ó̤

Omwroeten, omwoelen, opbreken, op-breken; krabben, afkrabben.
iah t'ó̤, | 土, de grond omwoelen.
iah mêng, | 門, een deur opbreken.
iah piah, | 墊, een muur omwoelen, opbreken.
hoan tsû iah, 番 薯 |, aardappelsteker.
hun ts'e iah, 烟 吹 , pijpenwroeter.
iah tsiū, | 槳, pagaaijen.
sa̤ iah sa̤ ts'iah, elkanders slechte handelingen aan het licht brengen.
iah k'âng, | 爬, afkrabben en pulken, zeuren, zaniken, alles er uit flappen (zooals over iemands slechte daden.

Iah

tsiṳ̄ iah iah / *tsiō̤ » »* } jeuken.

益
Iah

Voordeel, voordeel aanbrengen.
tsin iah, voordeel aanbrengend (van pers).
t'ao si̤ iah tsú lâng, huisdieren brengen hun meester voordeel aan.

帙
Iáh

Blad van een boek.
ts'eh iáh / *ts'eh »* } 書 |, blad van een boek.
iáh ts'eh, | 書, de bladen van een boek omslaan.

役
Iáh

Bedienden in een mandarijnbureau, politiedienaar.
gê iáh / *gê̤ »* } 衙 |, policiedienaar in een bureau.
koán iáh, bedienden in een bureau.
ts'e iáh / *ts'e̤ »* } 差 |, politiedienaar.

蜴
Iáh

Tor, motje,
iáh á, Maria tor, motje.

toā tsui iáh, 大 水 | } vliegende
péh tsui iáh, 白 水 | } mier.
péh hiā iáh, 白 蟻 | }

tióh iáh, 鼻 |, kankers in de neus, weggevreten (neus).

蝶 Iah *bé iáh* / *boé* » } 螞 |, vlinder, kapel.

易 Iáh *iáh king*, | 經, boek der verandering, diagrammen.
ka iáh, veel gezocht, gevraagd, (van waren) gewild.
ka iáh lī ts·ī, do.

Iáh *ts'iah iáh*, zich onfrisch gevoelen door stof warmte, enz.); niet in zijn schik.

悅 Iah *iù iù iáh iáh*, deftig, fraai, voorspoed aanduidend.

驛 Poststation, pleisten plaats.
Iáh *iáh tsām*, 驛 站, poststation.
p'aì hu iáh, gereedheid maken voor lastdragers en pleister plaatsen.
iáh bé, | 馬, paarden aan eene pleis ter plaats, postpaard.
ts'in ts'iū iáh bé, 像 似 | 馬, als een postpaard, (van slechte vrouwen die met een ieder omgang hebben).

Iang *

Iang *iang se* / » *se* } haspelen.
se iang, haspel.

Iang Opd agen, belasten met.
iang lāng, iemand iets opdragen te doen.
sa t'ok sa iang, elkander iets opdragen.

揚 Iāng *iāng k'i*, van opschik houdend.

負 Op den rug dragen, (zooals kinderen).
Iāng *iāng kiá*, *iāng gin á*, een kind op den rug dragen.

* Zie verder onder *iong*.

iāng kè k'oe, | 過 溪, iemand over een beek dragen.
iāng kun / » *kin* } | 巾, buidel lap waarin men een kind draagt.
p'ē iāng, 被 |, vierkante lap met banden om kinderen op den rug te dragen.
ka tsiah iāng sa oá, 背 脊 | 相 倚, met de ruggen tegen elkander staan, *d. i.* elkander bijstaan.

Iao

餓 Honger; hongerig, honger hebben, uitgehongerd.
Iao *pak tó iao*, 腹 |, honger hebben.
ū iao, 有 |, do.
iao koā gō, honger en koude lijdend.
iao kui, | 鬼, hongerige duivel, veelvraat.
iao lö, *iao lö kui*, hongerig, heb zuchtig veel vraat.
tī iao, 治 |, honger stillen.
iao ki sit tèng, uitgehongerd en een maal verliezen, misloopen.
iao hng, | 荒, hongersnood; hongerig.
iao sa sa / » *sà sà* } zoo zeer honger hebben dat men het eerste het beste eet.
iao sah sah, hongerig, zeer verlangen naar iets.
ts'aò ts'i iao, plotselinge honger.
ts'ī iao / *ts'ì* » } , plotseling honger.
iao kaò pak tó ngh ka tsiah, zoo uitgehongerd dat de buik tegen de rug aankomt.
iao kè ki / » *koè* » } over zijn honger zijn, de honger niet meer gevoelen.
iao loān, dol van den honger.

妖 Uiterst zeldzaam voorkomen, monster-
Iao achtig; vreemd, wonderbaarlijk (in

slechten zin) ongeluk voorspellend; onbegrijpelijk, bovennatuurlijk, tooverachtig, magisch.

iao tsi } | 精, magisch, magische
» *tsia* } gedaante verwisseling (zoals van beesten in tooverwezens).

iao kouì, | 怪, magisch, tooverwerk.

tī iao, 治 |, den boozen geest uitdrijven.

iao giét, | 孽, wonderbaarlijk en onheil voorspellend, (zooals eene hen die kraait).

iao gièn, | 言, geestentaal, *d. i.* niet te vertrouwen taal, gerucht

iao sút, | 術, magische kunsten, manieren.

iao hout, | 法, do.

tsō iao, 造 |, wonderbaarlijke dingen, verzinnen, opmaken.

tiòh iao, betooverd, door een tooverslag getroffen (zooals iets dat eensklaps verloren is.

iao t'iaó. | 佻, fraai en dartel, niet vast in hare deugd staande (van fraaije vrouwen).

嬈 Iao *iao kiao*, | 嬌, fraai, lief, (van vrouwen).

尙 *iaó kú*, toch nog.

Iaó *iaó ū*, | 有 toch nog.,

iaó bē } | 未, nog niet.
» *boē* }

iaó bē boē } | 未 賣, nog onver-
» *boē bē* } kocht.

iaó k'ièm, | 欠, nog te kort komend.

iaó eh, , de overigen.

夭 Iaó *iaò siū*, | 壽, vroegstondige dood,

要 Iaò Noodig hebben, moeten; noodig, noodzakelijk, van belang, gewigtig, voornaam, dringend.

iaò īng, | 用, noodig hebben, noodzakelijk moeten gebruiken.

iaò boé, | 買, moeten koopen.

iaò tsiàh sī kim put iaò tsiah sī t'ó, voor wie het noodig heeft is iets als goud, voor wie het niet noodig als aarde.

iaò sī iaò sí, | 生 | 死, moet gewilt ge-leven of sterven door roovers gezegd, uw geld of uw leven.

iaò kín, | 緊, van belang, noodzakelijk dringend.

kín iaò, 今 |, dringend, noodzakelijk.

kip iaò, do.

koan iaò, van groot gewigt, voornaam.

kan iaò, do.

ts'iet iaò, 節 |, van uiterst van belang, noodzakelijk.

kán iaò, 簡 |, het voornaamste bevattend, beknopt.

iaò hoān, | 犯, voorname gevangenen.

iaò sìn, | 信, gewigtige brief.

謠 Iaò Een gerucht verspreiden, rondvertellen.

iaò gien } | 言, gerucht, praatje.
» *gân* }

iaò gièn huì pòng, geruchten en lastertaal.

sì koè iaò, overal rondvertellen.

tsit ē iaò ták lâng tsai, naauwelijks was het verspreid of ieder een wist het.

tsiao iaò, alom bekend, veel besproken.

搖 Iaò In beweging brengen.

iaò tōng. | 動, in beroering brengen (zooals het volk), agiteren.

姚 Iaò Familienaam.

耀 Iaō *iaō bú iòng ui*, | 武 容 威, de luister van zijne overwinning tentoonspreiden.

Iem

閹 Iem Ontmannen, lubben, besneden.

iem bùt, ｜物, ontmannen.

iem bé / » *bé̤* } ｜馬, gesneden hengst-ruin.

iem koe / » *ke* } ｜雞, kappen.

iem ti eh, ｜猪, varkens lubber.

ts'ṳ̄ iem koe lâ, veretterd, verrot, (zooals een wond).

poà iem iû, 半｜, manwijf.

鐽 Iem *hè iem*, 火｜, aschschop.

拑 Iem Met een pincet aanpakken.

ùn á iem iem kaò liaó, zoo lang (van geld) af genomen hebben tot dat er niets meer overblijft.

iem ts'ut lâih, iets met de hand uit een gat halen.

厭 Iem *bû iem*, 無｜, nimmer tevreden.

ka iem, *ka iem koà*, koude rilling over het lijf.

掩 Iém Verbergen, niet laten zien; bedekken, beschermen, toedoen, aanzetten, (zooals een deur).

dzia iém, 遮｜, verbergen, verborgen houden.

iém huì, ｜諱, do.

iém ki sit kó̤, ｜旗息鼓, met verborgen vaandels en stille trom, *d. i.* in groote stilte op trekken.

iém soà, ｜傘, een groot scherm, (parasol) zoo lang voor twee mandarijnen houden tot dat zij bij elkander zijn.

it hoat iém, *it hoat lâng tsai*, hoe meer hij het verheelde des te meer kwam men het te weten.

iém sim kià, ｜心鏡, metalen borstplaat, (vroeger door soldaten gedragen).

tó koà iém, 肚｜, schaamte lap, (door naakte koelies gedragen).

iém hong, ｜風, tegen den wind beschut.

iém àn, ｜案, eene regtszaak door geld of eene andere aanklagt dekken.

iém hé hu, ｜火灰, met asch bedekken, inrakelen, (zooals vuur).

iém pui, ｜肥, met mest bedekken, bemesten.

iém iòng, ｜映, in elkander terugkaatsend, (zooals van twee spiegels ook van bergen).

iém mîng / » *muî* } ｜門, de deur aanzetten.

mîng poà iém, / *muî* « » } 門半｜, de deur half aanzetten.

poà iém mîng, 半｜門, half aanstaande deur, *d. i.* geheime ligtekooi.

飲 Iém *iém hūn* / » *hīn* } ｜恨, haat in zich koesteren.

厭 Iém *iém tsiēn*, ｜賤, niet kunnen lijden, niet houden van.

饜 Iém *iém ts'uì*, ｜口, iets moede, tot verwelens toe gegeten hebben.

鹽 Iêm Zout.

ts'i iêm / *ts'e̤* » } 青｜, ruw zout.

sik iêm, 熟｜, fijn zout.

iêm lò̤, ｜鹵, pekel, vocht dat uit het zout druipt.

iêm koán, ｜舘, zoutbureau.

p'ak iêm, 曬｜, zoutdroogen.

iêm tiâ, ｜田, zoutbeddingen.

su iêm, 私｜, gesmokkeld zout.

iêm tiû / » *tiô* } ｜埕, plein waar het zout op gedroogd wordt.

21

iém koàn, 丨 罐, zoutvaatje.

mi iém sē sim koŋ / *me » sī » »* } 搣 丨 洗 心 肝, *lett.* zijn hart inzouten, niet meer aan iets denken, iets opgegeven hebben.

ts'uì iém iém, 碎 丨 匕, tot gruis gebroken.

iém tui, 丨 堆, zouthoop.

koŋ iém, 官 丨, 's rijkszout, (waarvan belasting betaald is).

iém ūn saì, 丨 運 使, superintendent over het zout.

ka sa iém sī teh, met 30 pCt. meer zout gepekeld, *d. i.* uiterst zout, ook een gierigaard die geen gebruik van zijn geld durft te maken.

炎 Iēm Vlammen, hard branden.

hé iēm / *hoé »* 火 丨, het vuur vlamt.

ts'u iēm hū dziét, 趨 丨 赴 熱, zich aansluiten, omgaan met, rijke en aanzienlijke menschen.

dzit t'aò teng iēm, 日 頭 正 丨, de zon op haren hoogsten stand.

艷 Iēm *iēm tsong*, 丨 粧, opgesmukte kleeding van vrouwen.

sè iēm, 世 丨, van voorouders her van hooge familie.

hoe k'ui teng iēm, 花 開 方 丨, de bloemen zijn in volle bloei.

àng iēm, 紅 丨, fraai rood, als het ameublement in een huis.

iēm sik, 丨 色, fraai van kleur, (gew. rood).

Ien

煙 烟 Ien Rook, damp, mist, stoom.

hé ien / *hoe »* } 火 丨, roet, aanslag van vuur.

o ien, 烏 丨, do. (dunnelaag).

ien t'ùn, 丨 窻, roet.

ts'ut ien, 出 丨, rook door laten, lek zijn.

ien tun, 丨 墩, vuurseinen bij wacht stations geplaatst.

hiŋ ien, 香 丨, damp van reukwerk.

ien hé, 丨 火, vuurwerk

ien tàng, 丨 筒, schoorsteen.

ien t'ui, 丨 腿, ham, (gerookte).

ien ts'iàng, 丨 腸, gerookte saucijs. saucijs de Bologne.

ien bū, 丨 霧, mist, damp.

lòng ien sàn bū, 狼 丨 成 霧, als mist uit elkander, geheel en al uiteen.

tsui ien, 水 丨, stoom.

ien tsiàng è k'ì, moerassige dampen.

bé iáh ū ien, 螞 蝶 有 丨, die kapel heeft (gevaarlijke) stof [op de vlerken].

bát tsát ien, 目 鰂 丨, het zwarte in een inktvisch.

soŋ ien, 山 丨, onbeschaafd, boersch.

ien hoe ts'uì / *» hoa »* } fraai, verleidelijk in zijn spreken.

鮮 Ien Glans op nieuwe stoffen.

ien taò, 丨 骰, glans op nieuwe stoffen.

sin ien, 新 丨, glans van nieuwheid.

king ien, , glanzend, glad.

胭 Ien *ien tsi*, 丨 脂, rood blanketsel, rouge.

咽 Ien *ien aò*, 丨 喉, de strot.

ien aò è sò tsaī / *» » » » sé «* } 丨 喉 之 處, de sleutel tot een wijk.

姻 Verwantschap van vrouws zijde.
Ien *ien ts'un*, aangehuwde verwanten.
ien ka koàn tē, 丨家眷弟, do.

淵 Eene diepte, afgrond, golf.
Ien *ts'a k'i t'ien ien*, } 差去天丨,
ts'ę » » » }
er is hemels breed verschil in (*lett.* als van den hemel en een afgrond).
ien goân, 丨源, de bron, oorsprong van een diep water van daar, oorsprong, afkomst (zooals van eene uitvinding of kennis).

鴳 *ien ts'un*, 丨鶉, kwartel.
Ien

偃 *sa ièn* } 相丨, stoeijen.
siò » }
Ien *ièn tó*, 丨倒, omverstoeijen; omverzeulen, omverleggen (van een zwaar voorwerp).
ièn i boē tó, 丨他不倒, niet kunnen omzeulen, *d. i.* niet tegen iets opwassen zijn, niet aan kunnen.
ièn k'i ièn tó, 丨起丨倒, op en neer zeulen, helpen op te rijzen en te gaan liggen, (zooals een zieke).
kap ì ièn, 共伊丨, met iemand twist aanvangen, niet toegeven.

演 Exerceren; spelen als comedie.
Ien *ts'ao ién*, 操丨, exerceeren.
ién tin pai, 丨籐牌, met de schilden exerceeren.
ién bú gē, 丨武藝, militaire exercitie houden.
ién bú ting, 丨武亭, gebouw van waar een officier de exercitie ziet.
toā ts'oa ién, 大抄丨, groote exercitie, parade.
toā ts'ia ién, groote parade *d. i.* feest houden.
ién hì, 丨戲, comedie spelen.

燕 Zwaluw; eetbare vogelnestjes.
Ien *ièn o*, 丨窩, eetbare vogelnestjes.
kòng ièn, 貢丨, vogelnestjes aan den keizer opgebragt.
ièn tsoá, 丨盞, het geheele vogelnest.
mǫ̂ ièn, 毛丨, nog behaarde vogelnestjes.
ièn si, *ièn tiaô*, 丨絲, 丨條, gezuiverde, uitgezochte draden van een vogelnestje.
ts'aì ièn, 菜丨, van groenten nagemaakte vogelnestjes.
ièn ts'uì, 丨碎, het uitschot van vogelnestjes.

宴 Feestmaal.
Ièn *siet ièn*, 設丨, een feestmaal aanrigten.
sù ièn, 賜丨, een feestmaal schenken, (van den keizer gezegd).
hù ièn, 赴丨, naar een feestmaal gaan, (van ministers).
im ièn, 飲丨, drinkpartij van den vorst aan zijne ministers.
Ièn *ièn k'ì*, 小器, met weinig te vreden, in zijn schik.

鉛 Lood, looden.
Ièn *ièn hún*, 丨粉, loodwit.
hik ièn, 黑丨, lood.
pèh ièn, 白丨, tin.
ièn tan, 丨丹, menie.
ièn tiaô, 丨條, staven, stukken lood.
ièn tsi, 丨子, kogel.
ièn sai, 丨屎, vuil op gesmolten lood.
siu ièn, 廂丨, met lood beleggen, afzetten.
ièn t'áng, 丨桶, looden theekist.

ièn koàn, | 礶, looden theebusje.

ièn taò, | 骰, met lood vervalschte dobbelsteenen.

aì sièn ièn taò, 愛扇|骰, gaarne geheime omgang met jongelingen hebben (van bejaarde vrouw gezegd.)

ièn t'aò á kut, |骰仔骨, jongelieden die zich steeds bij de dames bemind willen maken.

捐 Ièn Gift, contributie.

toé ièn tê » } 題|, eene inteekeningslijst opmaken, contribuéren.

ièn tsi̱, | 錢, geld aan priesters of tempels gegeven.

kao ièn, 交|, zijne contributie betalen.

ièn p'ō, | 薄, register waarin de vaste contributie staat opgeteekend.

緣 Ièn Voorbeschikte betrekking, genegenheid tusschen personen, overeenstemming van gemoed, sympathie; oorzaak, reden waarom.

ièn hūn, | 分, voorbeschikte betrekking, (tusschen man en vrouw of vrienden).

ū ièn, 有|, sympathie voor elkander hebben.

ū làng ièn, 有人|, innemend van aard.

bô làng ièn, 無人|, niet innemend, onmogelijk om mede te sympathiseren.

in ièn, 因|, oorzaak reden.

in ūi sim mi̱h ièn kò̱, 因爲何故, om welke reden, waarom?

hoè ièn, 化|, geld ophalen (van priesters gezegd).

ièn tsìt tsoàh / » » *tsoā* } met een rand beleggen (zooals een kleed).

沿 Ièn Volgen, volgende, langs; laag.

ièn lō̱, *ièn tsìt lō̱*, | 路, | 一路, den geheelen weg langs.

ièn tsām lai, | 暫來, van pleister-plaats tot pleister-plaats gekomen.

ièn hai, | 海, langs zee.

ièn koe ièn hāng, | 街 | 巷, langs alle straten en steegjes.

nīng ièn / *nō̱* » } 二|, twee lagen.

sa̱ ièn ê ts'ìng, 三|銃, drie dekken geschut.

延 Ièn Verlengen, uitstellen, vertragen, dralen, langzaam.

ièn ts'ièn, | 遷, dralen, uitstellen.

ièn oān, | 緩, dralen, vertragen.

ièn ti, | 遲, uitstellen, vertragen.

oe ièn, 挨|, langzaam, dralend.

筵 Ièn Feest, feestmaal.

ièn siàh / » *sik* } | 席, feestmaal.

tsiú ièn tiong, 酒|中, aan den wijn feestdisch.

芫 Iên *ièn sui*, | 荽, korianderzaad.

緣 Iēn *iēn làn kan*, | 欄杆, de rand van een kleed borduren.

Iep

奄 Iep Weghouden, achter den rughouden, niet laten zien.

ẖng iep / *ni̱* » } 遮|, heimelijk weghouden.

iep mi̱h, | 物, iets achter de rughouden om het niet te laten zien.

iep t'iep, weghouden.

iep siep, 丨 濫, weghouden, achterhouden.

t'ao iep, 偷 丨, heimelijk achter den rug houden.

iep bé / *» boé* } 丨 尾, druipstaartend.

iep bé kaó, 丨 尾 狗, als een drupstaarten hond, druipstaartend

iep aō ts'iú, 丨 後 手, iemand achterstand geven.

ts'iú bô pák iep aō, 手 無 縛 丨 後, Uwe handen zijn niet op Uw rug gebonden *d. i.* het is geen schanddaad.

laī kù tsit tè iep á, 內 一 箇 丨, een reepje voering aan de binnen slip van een jas.

葉 Iép Familienaam.

hoe iép / *hoa »* } 花 丨, bloemblad.

tsuí ts'ia iép, 水 車 丨, de bladen, plankjes van een waterrad.

iép iép sī, 丨 匕 是, in groote menigte, veel.

ts'eh iép kim, 册 丨 金, best goudblad dat oorspr. tusschen de bladen van boeken ingelegd werd om zoo doorgesmokkeld te worden.

iet

閲 Iet *iet lik* / *oát »* } 丨 歷, ondervinding.

謁 Iet *iet sing*, 丨 聖 een heilige, wijze, bezoeken aanbidden (zooals bedevaart-gangers doen).

iet tsó, 丨 祖, zijn voorvaders komen bezoeken (van afgodsbeelden die in processie naar den tempel van hun stam afgod geleid worden.

煬 Iét Waaijen, wuiven, aanwaaien.

iét sì, 丨 扇, zich waaijeren.

iét hong, 丨 風, do. wapperen, (zooals een vlag).

iét k'ui, 丨 開, uitwaaijen, (van een vlag).

iét ki, 丨 旗, met vlaggen wuiven, seinen.

iét hé, 丨 火, het vuur aanwaaijen.

iét bé, 丨 尾, kwispelstaarten.

iét ts'iú, 丨 手, met de hand tot zich wenken.

īng ts'iú iét lâng, 用 手 丨 人, iemand met de hand toe wuiven.

p'âng iét kè bīn, 帆 丨 過 面, het zeil omwerpen.

tíng iét, 重 丨, oververven, (zooals verkleurde stoffen.)

悅 Iét *hí iét*, 喜 丨, verheugd in zijn schik.

p'iao iét, *p'iao p'iao iét iét*, kwispelen, in zijn schik, opgeruimd, zijn.

Ih

臆 Íh De pens, darmen, trijp van beesten.

iû ih, 羊 丨, schapenpens, trijp.

gû tō laī tsoe tsoé ih, 牛 肚 內 多 丨, de darmen van een koe.

tsoè tsit ih / *tsò » e* } 做 一 丨, (door natheid) aan elkander plakken (zooals de bladen van een boek).

p'ang ih, 蜂 丨, bijencellen.

laī bīn tsit tíng ih tióh t'iah k'ì laîh, 內 面 一 重 丨 抽 起 來, het binnenste vel moet men er aftrekken, (zooals bij nooten.)

Ih *péh ih*, Chinesche zeep.

Íh *t'iu kì ih tseh*, een snik, beklemde gil hooren, als van iemand die iets tegen het lijf of een steek krijgt.

Ih *ih ih oaih oaih*, verdraaid spreken.
ih ih iuh iuh, aarzelend.

Ik

溢 Ik Overloopen, (zooals een put), overgeven, opgeven (uit de maag); klotsen als water.
ik ts'ut laih, ｜出來, overloopen, overgeven, uitklotsen.
ik tsui, ｜水, water uit de maag opgeven.
hai tsui ik lai ik k'i, 海水｜來｜去, evenals het water der zee heen en weer klotsen, stroomen, van geld dat nu inkomt en zoo weer uitgaat.

益 Ik Vermeerderen; voordeel, winst; voordeelig.
li ik, 利｜, voordeel.
iu ik, 有｜, do.
bu ik, 無｜, omvoordeelig; nutteloos.
iu sún bò ik, 有損無｜, nadeel, schade en geen voordeel aanbrengen.
ik iu, ｜友, een voordeel aanbrengende vriend.

抑 Ik Verdrukken, verdrukt, bedrukt.
ik lik, ｜扐, verdrukken, kwellen, dwingen.
ut ik, 鬱｜, onwel; bedrukt.

億 Ik *tsit ik*, 一｜ honderd-duizend.

憶 Ik Herdenken.
tui ik tsiong tsièn è tai tsi, 追｜從前事, verledene zaken herdenken.

浴 Ik Wasschen, baden.
soé ik, 洗｜, zich baden.
tsàng ik, 淋｜, do.
ik pâng, ｜房, badkamer, badhuis.
ik ti, ｜池, badkom, badplaats.

易 Ik Veranderen.
king ik, 經｜, veranderen.
boé i ik, 不移｜, niet te veranderen.
kai ik, 改｜, veranderen.
ik tiaò, ｜朝, van dynastie veranderen.

譯 Ik *hoan ik*, 繙｜, vertalen, vertolken.

疫 Ik Pest, verpestend, besmettelijk.
un ik, 瘟｜, pest, besmettende ziekte.
ik k'i, ｜氣, verpestende dampen.

繹 Ik on.
lók ik put tsoát, 絡｜不絶, onafgebroken, aan een trein voort.

液 Ik *tsin ik*, 津｜, inwendige vloeistoffen als slijm, speeksel.

翼 Ik Vleugel, vlerk.
ú ik, 羽｜, vlerken, *d. i.* handlangers, helpers.

Im

陰 Im Het vrouwelijk, ondergeschikt principe in de natuur; schaduw, beschaduwd, luchtig, koel; geheim, verborgen; de onderwereld.
im iông } ｜陽, het vrouwelijk en het mannelijk principe.
im poe, ｜靠, de beide orakel blokjes op den platten kant vallend.
tsit è im p'oè tsit è iông, 一｜配壹陽, een instaande hoort bij een uitspringende (van zegel karakters).

im tsìng, | 症, gezwel uit de beenderen voortkomende.

kong im sìn sok, 光 | 迅 速, tijd gaat snel voorbij.

im ling, | 冷, luchtig, koel.

o im koâ, 烏 | 寒, koud, kil (van het water.

im but, *im hō*, *im bùn*, | 物, | 貨, | 文, vrouwelijk geslachts deel.

im tsik, | 隲, geheime weldaad.

im tòk, *im im t'im t'im*, *im t'im tòk*, | 毒, | 匕 沉 匕, | 沉 毒, verborgen, heimelijk slecht.

im kan, | 間, plaats der afgestorvenen, onderwereld.

kui im, 歸 |, naar de onderwereld gaan, sterven.

im hùn, | 魂, geesten in de onderwereld, zielen der afgestorvenen.

淹 Im Rijzen, zwellen, van eene rivier, overstroomen.

tsui im kaù ām, 水 | 及 暗 項, het water is tot aan de nek gerezen, *d. i.* in uiterste nood.

im tsui, *im toā tsui*, | 水, | 大 水, overstroomd worden.

k'it tsui im sìh, 被 水 | 死, door het water omkomen, verdrinken.

k'it i im tioh, 被 伊 | 着, door iets overstroomd worden; door overvoerde markt niet veel verdienen.

音 Im Geluid, klank; noot in muzijk, tijding, berigt.

siaⁿ im, 聲 |, geluid, klank.

im ūn, | 韻, eind klank.

sit im, 失 |, zijn geluid verloren hebben, geen geluid kunnen geven.

tsiàⁿ im hì, 正 | 戲, comedie waarin men mandarijnsch spreekt.

pat im, 八 |, de acht nooten.

im sìn, | 信, brief, berigt.

bô im bô sìn, 無 | 無 信, geen tijding of brieven hebben.

ka im } *ke* » } 佳 |, goede tijding van iemand.

飲 Ím *im tsiú*, | 酒, wijn drinken.

im sit, | 食, eten en drinken.

im ièn, | 宴, op eene feestmaal zijn.

蔭 Ìm Beschaduwen, overschaduwen, beschermen, onder zijne bescherming nemen, helpen; eene erfelijke waardigheid.

tì ìm, 致 |, beschaduwen, beschermen.

ìm éng, | 影, beschaduwen.

ìm kan, *ìm ta*, | 乾, in de schaduw gedroogd.

ìm taū gê, | 豆 芽, boonen toedekken om ze te laten spruiten.

ìm si, | 尸, een uitgedroogd lijk.

ìm kaù pêh pêh pêh, | 至 白 匕, blank door geringe blootstelling aan de lucht.

siū ìm, 受 |, beschermd, ontzien worden, niet veel in de open lucht komen.

siū ìm kiáⁿ, 受 | 子, een kind dat nooit veel te zorgen heeft gehad.

hong ts'e ìm tsú, 封 妻 | 子, zijne vrouw in aanzien doen stijgen en zijne waardigheid op zijne kinderen doen neerdalen.

tì ìm, 庇 |, door erfenis gekregen (adel of geld).

hok ìm, 福 |, bescherming van de fortuin, geluk.

un ìm / *in* » } 恩 丨, een gunst bewijzen, begunstigen.
ìm làng, 丨 人, iemand helpen, het werk voor hem doen, enz.
ìm kọ́, 丨 股, iemand kosteloos een aandeel in iets geven.
ìm hun, 丨 分, een deel in iets geven.

掩 Ìm Toedekken; uitdooven (zoals vuur).
ìm hé / » *hoé* } 丨 火, vuur uitdooven.
ìm hé t'oǹ / » *hoé* » } 丨 火 炭, do.

淫 Îm Wellustig overspelig, overspel, overspel bedrijven met
kan im, 姦 丨, overspel.
im ts'ú / » *ts'i* } 丨 鼠, wit konijn, (ook van wellustige vrouwen gezegd).
hò im, 好 丨, wellustig.
im hū, 丨 婦, wellustige vrouw.
im loān, 丨 亂, door wellust in verwarden toestand (zooals een huisgezin.
im làng ê bó kiá, 丨 人 妻 子, overspel met ander mans vrouw en dochters bedrijven.

In

因 In Oorzaak, aanleiding, reden; om, wegens, ter oorzaak van.
in iû, 丨 由, oorzaak, reden.
in toa, 丨 單, aanleiding oorzaak.
in toa k'i lí, 丨 單 起 理, de oorzaak waaruit iets ontstaan is.
t'ó bô in toa, 討 無 丨 單, eene reden zoeken om zich met iets in te laten.
bô in bô toa, 無 丨 無 單, zonder reden, oorzaak.
ū tsit ê in, 有 一 丨, er is eene reden, aanleiding voor.
goá kap i bô in, 我 與 他 無 丨, ik heb geen reden, voorwendsel om mij met hem intelaten.
in iên, 丨 緣, reden om.
in uī, 丨 爲, wegens, omdat, daar.
in uī hit ê iên kò, 丨 爲 緣 故, om die reden, daarom.
in hô, 丨 何, waarom?

纏 In Omwinden, kluwen, kloen.
in soh à, 丨 索 仔, touw opkloenen.
in soà, 丨 線, garen kluwen.
in tsoè tsit kiû, 丨 做 一 裘, tot een kloen opwinden.
tsit in, 一 丨, een kloen.
koai á làm sám in, 拐 仔 亂 丨, met een stok in de rondte slingeren.

伊 In Zij, zijlieden.

引 Ín Leiden, geleiden, introduceren; lokken, tot zich halen, aantrekken verleiden; wat tot geleider dient als het staartje aan een sisser, kruitgeleider, enz.; aanhalen als een gezegde, aanleiding; inleiding tot een boek.
in ts'oā, 丨 導, leiden.
in lō, 丨 路, den weg leiden.
in tsìn, 丨 進, geleiden, medenemen, introduceren.
in kièn, 丨 見, op eene audentie introduceren.
oān in, introduceren.
in iú, 丨 誘, verlokken, verleiden.
tsio in / *tsiao* » } 招 丨, lokken.
in hé, 丨 火, vuur halen van, aansteken (pijpen).

in hé ê mih, ｜火之物, vuur aanhalende, brandbare stoffen.
sa in sa tsoā (of *t'oā*), elkander mede slepen.
bô tsiem put in soā, 無針不｜線, zonder naald kan men de draad er niet door krijgen, *d. i.* zonder middelaar-spion kan de zaak niet slagen.
in sim, ｜心, vuurgeleider aan een sisser.
in k'ang, ｜空, het zundgat, schoorsteengaatje (aan een geweer). 2e iemand eene goede gelegenheid aan de hand geven.
boē kè in, 不過｜, niet afgaan, (van vuurwerk); niet gelukken.
ióh in, 藥｜, toedrank, datgene waarmede men een geneesmiddel inneemt
in kó, ｜古, de oudheid aanhalen.
in tsing, ｜證, als bewijs aanhalen.
in k'í, ｜起, aanleiding om tot zijn gesprek te komen; aanhalen. aanheffen, inzetten (zooals een lied).
k'í k'ik in, aanleiding tot iets geven (gew. tot twist).
tsit tè sió in, 一節小｜, eene korte inleiding (van een boek.)

許 **În** Beloven, toezeggen, toestemmen.
in lâng, ｜人, aan iemand beloven.
in ts'ò, ｜剉, bij vergissing toestaan, beloven (als waren tegen een te lagen prijs.
in boē, ｜賣, toestemmen, beloven te verkoopen.

印 **Ìn** Zegel, stempel, merk, afdruksel; zegelen, stempelen, drukken, afdrukken.
koā ìn, 官｜, mandarijn zegel, ambtszegel.
ìn siū, ｜綬, ambtszegels.
miā ìn, 名｜, naam zegel.
dzī hō ìn, 字號｜, zegel met den naam van een handelshuis.
hong ìn, 封｜, de zegels wegsluiten, (door beambten, 10 dagen voor nieuwjaar).
k'ai ìn, 開｜, de zegels ontsluiten, (20 dagen na nieuwjaar).
k'àm ìn, *têng ìn* ⎫ 蓋｜, een ze-
tuì „ ⎭ gel zetten, zegelen, stempelen.
ìn ts'eh, 册｜, boeken drukken.
k'ik ìn, 刻｜, een stempel uitsnijden, graveren.
k'ik lóh ìn pán, 刻落｜板, reeds in druk platen uitgesneden *d. i.* onveranderlijk.
ìn á tsióh, ｜仔石, druksteenen.
ìn sik, ｜色, roode zegel inkt.
ìn ka, zegellak.
ìn sìn, ｜信, zegel op eenen brief zetten, brief.
hé ìn, 火｜, ingebrand merk.
koà ìn, 掛｜, de zegels voor iets hebben, met de magt over iets belast.
si tor ìn koè, certificaat van een stuk, officieël bewijs van eigendom.
ìn tsit ê dziah, ｜一個跡, een afgedrukt spoor van pooten, enz.
ìn dziah ìn dziah, ｜跡｜跡, vol vlekken, niet gelijk van kleur.
tsit k'ang ìn tsit dziah, 一空｜一跡, met het eene gat het andere stoppen.
ìn lâng ê k'a dziah, ｜人足跡, iemands spoor volgen, hem op de hielen volgen.
goā bīn ìn kiā lâng dzip laih, vuil van buiten binnen brengen, (zooals aan de voeten).

22

ING

ts'in ts'iū hit bō nih k'ì ìn k'ih laih, 似佯的｜起來, als in de zelfde vorm afgedrukt, sprekend ot elkander gelijkend.

應 Antwoorden.

In *ìn tap*, ｜答, antwoorden.

ìn sia, ｜聲, antwoord geven, (van uit de verte) weergalmen.

ìn hó, ｜好, goed, antwoorden, toestemmen, goedkeuren.

gaô ìn oā, 賢｜話, knap antwoorden, excuses hebben.

ìn ts'uì ìn tsih, ｜嘴｜舌, op alles toestemmend antwoorden, een ja broêr zijn.

sa ìn t'în, bij elkander passen, overeenstemmen.

寅 *in si*, ｜時, van 3—5 uurs morgens.

In *koe pò in* } *ko » »* } 雞報｜, de haan kondigt de dageraad aan.

tóng in è koā, 仝｜官, gelijkstaande mandarijnen.

響 Echoën, bulderen als geschut.

In *īn lâng è hī k'ang*, ｜耳, iemands ooren verdooven.

toē īn k'i laih, 地｜起來, de grond dreunt.

孕 *sin īn*, 身｜, zwanger.

In *hoai īn*, 懷｜, do.

Ing

鷹 Arend, valk.

Ing *ing á bák*, ｜仔目, arendsoogen.

kap ing 鴿｜, valk.

鸚 Papegaai,

Ing *ing bú*, ｜鵡, papagaai.

ing ko, ｜哥, do.

ing ko p'ī, ｜哥鼻, papegaaineus, kromme neus.

ing ko ts'uì, ｜哥嘴, krom als een papegaaibek.

ing ko kè } *» » kē* } ｜哥架, papegaaihanger; galg.

嬰 *iok ing tòng*, 育｜堂, vondelingshuis.

Ing

應 Behooren, betamen.

Ing *ing kai*, ｜該, behooren, betamen, passen.

ing tong, ｜當, het behoort, moet.

英 Fraai, uitstekend; edelmoedig, mannelijk, degelijk.

Ing *ing hoa t'aì lō*, ｜華太露, zijne kunde te veel tentoonspreiden.

ing hiòng, ｜雄, een held, edelmoedig, degelijk mensch,

tsing ing, 鍾｜, degelijk, mannelijk,

ing kiet lī, ｜吉利, Engeland, Engelsch.

Íng Stof, vuil; stuiven.

ing in, stof, vuil.

tsit p'ah tsit ing, slaat men er op dan stuift het op.

ing tioh he hūn, door kalk bestoven, (op of in iets).

永 Altijddurend, eeuwig, steeds, gewoonlijk.

Ing *ing ing*, ｜匕, eeuwig, in der eeuwigheid.

ing oán, ｜遠, do.

ing bô, ｜無, nimmer.

ing si, *ing siông si*, ｜時, ｜常時, steeds, gewoonlijk.

ing dzit, ｜日, gewoonlijk.

ing nî, ｜年, steeds elk jaar.

ing ī̂m, ing bô beh, 丨 不 要, nimmer willen.

k'oan ing tsî, 寬 丨 錢, algemeene benaming voor Japansch geld.

穎 Ing *ing gi*, 丨 悟, spoedig vatten, begrijpen.

浪 Ing Golf, golfslag, deining.

hong ing, 風 丨, wind en golfslag.

tu hong ing, 征 風 丨, wind en deining weêrstand, *d. i.* voor de moeijelijkheden moeten opdraaijen.

ing hoe } 丨 花, de spetten van een
» *hoa* } golf.

ing toā, 丨 大, zware deining, golfslag.

tsoè ing, 作 丨, er is eene zware deining; een gedrang vormen.

lòh ing k'i } 落 丨 坑, in de diepte
» » *k'e* } van een golf neêr gaan.

影 Ing Schaduw, schim; portret.

ing hióng } 丨 響, als eene schim,
» *hiáng* } snel voorbijgaan, flaauw (zien enz.).

ing bīn, 丨 面, portret.

siaó ing, 小 丨, do.

hap ing kià, 合 丨 鏡, photographisch toestel.

k'ioh ing, k'ioh siaó ing, k'ioh ing bīn, 摹 丨 面, een portret nemen.

應 Ìng Antwoorden, beantwoorden, vergelden; aan de verwachting voldoen, uitkomen, de verwachte uitwerking hebben; in overeenstemming, verband met.

ìng sing, 丨 成, toestemmen, beloven.

pò ìng, 報 丨, vergelden.

ìng siû, 丨 酬, elkander, wederkeerig verzoeken, omganghebben met.

it ho it ìng, 一 呼 一 丨, een geroep beantwoorden, er op te hulp komen.

hióng ìng, 響 丨, weêrgalmen, weêrklank vinden.

ìng tsiep, 丨 接, ontvangen (vrienden), conversatie houden met.

ìng giēm, 丨 驗, aan de verwachting beantwoorden, uitkomen.

ū ìng haū, 有 丨 候, goede uitwerking hebben (zooals medicijnen), (van afgoden).

ū ìng, 有 丨, krachtdadig.

ling ìng, 靈 丨, zigtbare uitwerking vergelding bezittend (van afgoden).

sui ki ìng pièn, 隨 幾 丨 變, naar de omstandigheden handelen.

kiû ìng, 求 丨, te hulp komen.

tsiep ìng, 接 丨, als hulptroep zijn, helpen, (in een gevecht).

tsiaò ìng, 照 丨, een oogje houden op, bijstaan.

ìng si ìng dzit, 丨 時 丨 日, op den bepaalden tijd en dag.

kám ìng, 感 丨, bewogen, hulp verleenen, vergelden.

壅 Ìng *ìng pui*, 丨 肥, bemesten, met mest bedekken.

ìng ts'ân, 丨 田, een rijst veld bemesten.

蕹 Ìng *ìng ts'aì*, 丨 菜, eene watergroente.

ìng ts'aì hô, 丨 菜 河, vijver, poel voor die groente.

榮 Ing Luister, luisterrijk, eer, roem, roemvol,

hién ing, ing hién, 顯 丨, luisterrijk, roemvol.

ing hīng, 丨 幸, vereerd zijn (door iemands bezoek); met zich zelven tevreden, ingenomen.

ing ing, 丨影, met zich zelven ingenomen.
hong ing ē bōng, 封丨之墓, praalgraf op keizerlijk bevel gemaakt.
koan taì ing sin, 冠帶丨身, de mandarijngraad slechts als eere titel hebben.
la ing, 勝丨, verkwistend zijn, (in overvloed).
ing keng, 丨光, luister, roemvol.

營 Zwoegen, onvermoeid,
Ing *ing ui*, 丨爲, vlijtig, ijverig doen.
king ing, 經丨, onvermoeid werkzaam.

閒 Ledige, vrije tijd, ledigheid, niets anders te doen hebbende, uit verveling, onbeduidend.
Ing
An
ū ing, 有丨, tijd hebben.
bò ing, *bò ing kang*, 無丨, 無丨工, geen tijd hebben.
ing ing kè dzit, 丨匕過日, zijn dag in ledigheid door brengen,
ing sin, 丨身, op zijn gemak.
kóng ing oē, 說丨話, keuvelen, overkoetjes en kalfjes spreken.
ing ts'uì, 丨嘴, niet anders te vertellen hebbende, uit verveling.
ts'ing ing, 清丨, onbezorgd, een gemakkelijk leven leiden.
ing king / *àn kan* } 丨間, verblijf waar mannen in hun ledigen tijd bij elkander komen.
ing taī / *ân sū* } 丨事, onbeduidende zaken.
koán ing taī, 管丨代, nieuwsgierig.
ing làng. 丨人, ledigloopers, nieuwsgierigen die niets met eene zaak te maken hebben.

用 Gebruiken, zich bedienen van, met nut dat men van iets heeft; onkosten, uitgaven.
Ing
lōng
boē ing tit, 無丨的, niet te gebruiken.
ū lō īng, 有路丨, van nut zijn.
īng làng, 丨人, menschen gebruiken, in zijn dienst hebben.
ing līng līng k'ì / *iōn liōng liōng* } 丨匕匕去, geheel en al op gebruikt.
īng to t'ai làng, 丨刀殺人, iemand met een zwaard dooden.
īng kang, 丨功, met inspanning, zorg, doen.
īng sim, *īng sim īng kan*, 心心丨肝, met inspanning, zorgvuldig.
k'ai īng, 開丨, onkosten, uitgaven.
huì īng, 廢丨, do.
tsáp īng, 什丨, verschillende uitgaven
dzit īng, 日丨, dagelijksche uitgaven, behoeften.

Io

腰 De lendenen, middel, de zij; het midden van iets.
Io
ts'un io, 伸丨, zich de lendenen uitrekken.
siang ts'iú ts'ah io, 双手插丨, met de handen in de zij.
io to, 丨刀, zwaard.
io tsiah kut, 丨者骨, lendebeen.
io tsí, 丨子, de nieren, (van varkens).
io tsáh, 丨截, werktuig om iemand door midden te hakken; ontlijven.

ŋ̇ io, 灣 |, de lendenen buigen, eene buiging maken.

sìm io, 沁 |, slap, elastiek in het midden, (zooals paarden en lange voorwerpen).

soŋ̇ io, 山 |, de helft van den berg.

幺 De één, aas op dobbel en dominosteenen.

Io *io k'ang*, | 空, do.

siang io, 双 |, dubbele één (op dominosteenen).

tsit ki io, 一 支 |, een steun-pilaar in eene familie.

io dzī sŋ̇, | 二 三, aas, twee en drie, (in welk geval men met dobbelen verliest).

poàh siang io, 賭 双 |, twee azen gooijen.

Io Liefderijk, verplegen, opvoeden.

io kiŋ̇, een kind verplegen.

hó io ts'ī, gemakkelijk optevoeden, gezond opgroeijen.

io ling, met melk voeden (zooals eene min doet).

io sioh, liefkozen, liefderijk verplegen.

sŋ̇ io sŋ̇ sioh, elkander liefderijk behandelen, (tegen kinderen gezegd).

邀 *sŋ̇ io* / *sio* » } 相 |, te zamen gaan, elkander afhalen.

Io

Iô *kà iô iô*, verward, in verwarring, van eene plaats.

tàm iô iô, kletsnat.

iô tsìh k'a kut, de beenen stuk slaan.

iô tsuí / *iŋ̇* » } | 水, waterscheppen.

搖 Schudden, inbeweging brengen, wrikken, waggelen, schommelen.

Iô *iô t'aô*, | 頭, (afkeurend) het hoofd schudden.

iô t'aô poŋ̇ hī, | 頭 擛 耳, (afk.) het hoofd en ooren schudden.

iô taô paî bé / » » » *boé* } | 頭 排 尾, met kop en staart schudden, zwierig loopen.

iô bé, | 尾, kwispelstaarten.

iô k'a hŋ̇ ts'iú, met voeten en handen in beweging zijn.

iô k'a ts'ẽng hoe, | 脚 穿 花, in zijn loopen met het achterste waggelen.

iô lâng bô tsai, | 人 無 財, een man die zwierig loopt maar geen geld heeft.

iô tsing, | 鐘, de bel luiden, schellen.

iô ts'iú, | 手, met de hand afwijzen.

iô nŋ̇, | 籃, wieg.

iô tsî ts'iū, | 錢 樹, aan den geld boom schudden, *d. i.* veel geld met iets maken, gew. lichtekooien.

iô kim hô lô, | 金 胡 蘆, den gouden pompoen schudden, *d. i.* do.

iô hē, | 會, dobbelen wie het eerst de gezamenlijke inleg van verscheidene personen zal hebben, (wie het gewonnen heeft werpt niet meer maar betaalt telkenmale zijnen oorspronkelijken inzet tot dat ieder op zijn beurt gewonnen heeft).

iô lô, | 櫓, de wrikker, wrikken.

iô tsûn, | 船, een schuit wrikken.

iô kó, | 鼓, rammeltrom, (kleine trom met twee slingerende knoopen, door rond-venters gebruikt).

p'ù p'ù iô iô, 浮 乜 | 乜, drijvend en waggelend, *d. i.* onzeker, onveilig, onbepaald.

窰 Oven, keet, bakkerij voor aardewerk.

Iô *hé iô* / *hóe* » } 灰 |, kalkoven.

hui iô, *oâ iô*, 磁 |, 碗 |, bakkerij van aardewerk.

hiā iô, 瓦 |, dakpannen bakkerij, ook van een klein benaauwd huis gezegd.

sio tsit iô ê hui, 燒一｜磁, een oven aardewerk afgebrand, afgewerkt hebben.

ioh

億 Raden, gissen.
Ioh *hō̤ lâng ioh*, 與人｜, iemand te raden geven.
ioh m̄ ts'ut, ｜不出, niet kunnen raden; niet hebben kunnen raden, niet gedacht hebben dat . . . . .
ioh tāng, ｜重, het gewigt gissen, op de gis af.
ioh tui / » *tu* ｜堆, raden hoeveel er zijn, bij den hoop berekenen.
ioh hūn, ｜份, bij den hoop berekenen, verkoopen, enz.

蚼 *ts'i ioh* / *ts'e* « 青｜, kleine groene kikvorsch
Ioh
Ioh *ioh ioh*, slap.

藥 Medicijn, geneesmiddel, kruid.
Ióh *tsiáh ióh*, 食｜, medicijnen gebruiken, innemen.
ióh tiàm. ｜店, apotheek.
ióh ko, ｜膏, zalf, pleister.
kô̤ ióh, 糊｜, pleister, een pleister opleggen.
ióh tsuí, ｜水, drankje.
ióh í, *ióh oân*, ｜圓, pillen.
ióh hún, *ióh boáh*, *ióh soá*, ｜粉, 末, ｜線, poedertje.
ts'i ts'aó ioh / *ts'e* » » 青草｜, uitwendige medicijn.
pó̤ ioh, 補｜, versterkende medicijnen..
ióh tse, ｜查, bezinksel van medicijnen.

ióh t'iep, ｜帖, pakje medicijnen.
ióh tû, ｜厨, medicijnkas.
ióh tsai hâng, ｜栽行, medicijn magazijn.
ióh to̤, *ióh hng*, ｜單, ｜方, receptje.
k'ui ióh to̤, 開｜單, een recept geven.
p'aì ióh, 派｜, medicijnen voor schrijven.
tsè ióh, *hô ióh*, 製｜, 和｜, medicijnen klaarmaken, mengen.
kap ióh, *t'iah ióh*, *tsién ióh*, 合｜, 採｜剪｜, medicijnen halen, koopen.
ióh sìng, ｜性, medicijn kracht.
oā ióh, 換｜, medicijnen ververschen.
tók ióh, ｜毒, vergift.
hé ióh, 火｜, kruit, schietkruit.
ts'ìng ióh, 銃｜, do.
hé ióh kóng, 火｜筒, kruithoorn.

鑰 Op slot doen.
Ióh *ióh mèng*, ｜門, een deur op slot doen.
ióh kap bān, ｜甲辦, een geldkist op slot doen.
ióh k'ih laìh, ｜起來, opslot doen.

Iok

約 Binden, beteugelen; instelling, bepaling; zich verbinden, beloven, overeenkomen, bepalen; overeenkomst, contract, afspraak; bondig, in het algemeen, ongeveer; buurt, dorp dat zich onder een hoofd of raad schikt.
Iok *iok sok*, ｜束, in toom houden, beteugelen, bepalingen, instelling.

su iok, 私 丨, private overeenkomsten, instellingen.

iok lâng, 丨 人, met iemand overeenkomen, beloven,

goā ū iok tsit ê lâng, 我 有 丨 一 人, ik heb met iemand afgesproken.

háp iok, 合 丨, overeenkomen, overeenkomst.

hô iok, 和 丨, een vredes traktaat sluiten, traktaat.

sìn iok, 信 丨, eene overeenkomst nakomen.

lip iok, 立 丨, overeenkomen, een verbond sluiten.

sit iok, 失 丨, de overeenkomst, het traktaat schenden.

tsiaù iok, 照 丨, volgens overeenkomst, afspraak.

toàn iok, 短 丨, overeenkomen.

iok dzī, *iok tog*, 丨 字, 丨 單, schriftelijke overeenkomst contract.

iok dzit, 丨 日, een dag bepalen.

iok kaù kiâ kaù / » *kaù* » *kaù* } 丨 到 行 到, zijn afspraak, belofte volbragt hebben·

iok iok, 丨 乜, ongeveer, niet veel verschillend.

tāi iok, 大 丨, ongeveer, in het algemeen.

iok liok / *iok liák* } 丨 畧, do.

iok liōng / » *liāng* } 丨 量, do.

kán iok, 簡 丨, beknopt, in het algemeen.

iok iok tseh, alles bij elkander genomen, (zijn idée over iets geven).

iok tsiā, 丨 正, hoofd, oude van een dorp.

hiong iók, 鄉 丨, dorpsraad, dorpsraadhuis.

慾 Iók *iók hé* / » *hoé* } 丨 火, wellust.

sik iók, 色 丨, wellust, wulpschheid.

su iók, 私 丨, begeerte verlangen,

iók kut, 丨 骨, iemand die wellustig van aard is.

育 Iók *iók ing tông*, 丨 嬰 堂, vondelingshuis.

ióng iók, 養 丨, opvoeden, opbrengen.

kiok iók, 掬 丨, do.

浴 Iók *bók iók*, 沐 丨, zich wasschen en zuiveren, (voor dat men eene offerande gaat doen.)

Iong

央 Iong / Iang *iong t'ok* / *iang* » } 丨 託, verzoeken te doen opdragen, belasten met.

tiong iong / » *iang* } 中 丨, midden, midden in.

癰 Iong *iong tsu* / » *t'si* } 丨 疽, een zweer, puist op den rug.

hì iong / » *ing* } 肺 丨, long ontsteking.

殃 Iong *tsai iong*, 災 丨, rampen.

雍 Iong *iong ts'ìng*, 丨 正, 3de keizer van de *Ts'ing* dynastie.

勇 Ióng Sterk, stevig.

ióng tsòng, 丨 壯, krachtig.

ióng bing, 丨 猛, dapper.

hiong ióng / *hiang* » } 鄉 丨, schutterij.

ióng kám, 丨 敢, dapper, moedig, resoluut.

hò ióng, 好 丨, houden van vechten.

ióng kiā, 丨 健, gezond, sterk, stevig.

gī ióng, 義 ｜, vrijwilligers.

hùn ióng, 奮 ｜, al zijne krachten inspannen.

tsòng ióng, 壯 ｜, vrijwilliger, schutter.

kī ióng, 技 ｜, zware voorwerpen, steenen enz. bij militaire oefening gebruikt.

養 lóng làng *ióng liêm* } ｜ 廉, emolumenten boven zijn mandarijn salaris. *iáng* »

ióng tsú, ｜ 子, pleegkind, aangenomen kind.

bú ióng, 撫 ｜, opvoeden, verplegen,

p'aō ióng, 抱 ｜, opvoeden een gekocht kind.

tiaō ióng, 調 ｜, zich ontzien, voor zich zorgen, (na eene ziekte).

pó ióng, 保 ｜, zich ontzien, (na eene ziekte).

pó ióng, 補 ｜, versterkende dingen gebruiken, zich ontzien, (na ziekte).

ióng siēm, ｜ 老, kapitaal dat men voor zijn eigen en zijn vrouw's oudendag houdt, (terwijl men aan de kinderen hunne erfportie uitbetaald).

poē ióng, verzorgen en opvoeden, (zooals kinderen).

擁 lòng *ióng tsiòng*, ｜ 衆, oploop van menschen.

iòng sīng, ｜ 盛, in groote hoeveelheid komen (zooals menschen of koopwaren).

容 Iòng Dulden, gedoogen, verdragen, verdraagzaam, toegevend; uiterlijk, voorkomen, gelaat.

iòng ún, ｜ 隱, dulden, verdragen. laten blijven,

iòng dzím, ｜ 忍, verdragen, dulden.

boē iòng tit, 不 ｜ 的, niet te verdragen.

t'ien put iòng, te put tsaì, 天 不 ｜ 地 不 載, de hemel dulde mij niet onder zich en de aarde drage mij niet, (bij eeden gezegd).

k'oan iòng, 寬 ｜, toegevendheid, inschikkelijkheid, gebruiken.

ts'iong iòng, 充 ｜, langzaam, niet overhaast.

iòng ts'iòng, ｜ 從, dulden, laten blijven.

hâm iòng, 含 ｜, dulden, lijden.

iòng ī, ｜ 易, gemakkelijk, (te doen).

iòng maō, ｜ 貌, voorkomen gelaat.

iu iòng bīn, 憂 ｜ 面, bedroefd uiterlijk.

hing iòng, 形 ｜, voorkomen uiterlijk, manieren.

hí iòng, 喜 ｜, vrolijk uiterlijk.

gàn iòng, 顏 ｜, voorkomen, gelaat.

陽 lòng làng Het mannelijk principe in de natuur; licht, helder.

iòng bút, ｜ 物, mannelijk geslachtsdeel.

tó iòng, 倒 ｜, impotent.

hoán iòng. hoê iòng, 反 ｜, 回 ｜, bijkomen uit schijndood.

hiòng iòng, 向 ｜, naar het licht gekeerd, licht, helder.

揚 làng *hién iòng*, 顯 ｜, in het oog vallend, (zooals een hoog gebouw), openlijk (stelen enz).

楊 lòng *iòng liú*, ｜ 柳, wilgenboom.

iòng muî } ｜ 梅, bubo. » *moê*

庸 lòng Het midden houden, middelmatig, ordinair; ongemanierd.

tiong iòng, 中 ｜, het ware midden, (tweede der klassieke boeken).

iòng iòng siòng siòng, ｜ 匕 常 匕, middelmatig, ordinair.

iông i sat dzin, 丨醫殺人, een middelmatig onkundige doktor vermoord zijne patienten.

iông siók ê lâng, 丨俗之人, een zeer ordinair ongemanierd mensch.

iông hu siók tsú, 丨夫俗子, onopgevoede kerel.

用* Gebruiken.

Iōng *tsiet iōng*, 節丨, zuinig.

huì iōng. 費丨, onkosten, uitgaven.

tiòng iōng, 中丨, geschikt voor het gebruik.

tiōng iōng ih, 重丨他, iemand voor alles gebruiken.

iōng sim, 丨心, met zijn hart er bij, zorgvuldig.

Ip

邑 *siâ ip*, 城丨, stad.

Ip *to ip*, 都丨, (groote) stad.

sio ip, 小丨, kleine stad.

ai ip, 鄙丨, » »

揖 *ip dziā* } *» dziá* } 丨下, eene buiging maken.

Ip *tsok ip*, 作丨, do.

It

一 Één; eerste; één onverdeeld, bepaald,

It zeker; elk; geheel, tot een geheel bij elkander, tegelijk.

it si kan, 丨時間, in een oogenblik.

bān it, 萬丨, 10,000 tegen één *i. d.* de mogelijkheid bestaat dat . . . . , het mogt eens.

it hiēn... it piēn, ... 丨現丨便, eensdeels kontant geld andersdeels gereede goederen, *d. i.* kontant handel drijven.

it tsik . . . it tsik, do. in de eerste plaats . . . in de andere.

tsáp it, 十丨, elf.

toē it, 第丨, de eerste; uiterst . . ., zeer.

ts'oe it, 初丨, de eerste (der maand).

paì it, 拜丨, Maandag.

it hoat, 丨發, eensklaps, op eens.

it p'in, 丨品, van den eersten mandarijn rang.

tsoan it, 專丨, uitsluitend.

it sim, 丨心, do.

tsip it, 執丨, zich aan één ding houden.

it t'óng, 丨統, één geheel uitmakend, geheel en al.

kui it, 歸丨, tot een geheel bij elkander, geheel en al.

tiók it, 逐丨, elk een.

it lō, 丨路, den geheelen weg langs.

it it, 丨匕, elk, stuk voor stuk; stellig, zeker.

it it dzī dzī, 丨匕二匕, stuk voor stuk, van A tot Z.

it ì, 丨意, vastberaamd, stellig.

it tiā, 丨定, bepaald, zeker.

it tīng put i, 丨定不移, een maal vastgesteld is het onverandelijk.

put it, 不丨, niet bepaald, onzeker.

it ts'è, 丨切, in eens, alles, alle, altegader, alle tegelijk.

憶 Voor den geest terugroepen, herdenken,

It zich herinneren; verlangen naar, den voorkeur geven aan.

* Zie verder onder *īng*

23

it tióh, ｜着, zich herinneren, herdenken.

it tióh, ｜着, verlangen naar, houden van.

boē it tit, 不｜的, zich niet herinneren.

Iu

憂 Iu Bedroefd, treurig, niet opgeruimd, knorrig; droefheid, rouw over den dood van ouders.

iu būn, ｜悶, bedroefd.

t'aô iu bīn iu, 頭｜面｜, bedroefd uiterlijk, knorrig.

bīn (of *bák t'aô*) *iu iu tsoè tsi' pé*, 目頭｜匕作一把, knorrig de wenkbraauwen, tot elkander fronsen.

iu sim, ｜心, inwendig bedroefd.

iu ut, ｜鬱, bedroefd, neerslagtig.

iu ts'iû, ｜愁, bedroefd.

iu iu t'iạ̀, ｜匕痛, zamentrekkende pijn, (zooals in de buik).

ting pē iu (of *bú*) / » *hū* « *bó* } 丁父｜, rouw over vader of moeder.

ting iu lī dzīm, 丁｜離任, wegens den rouw over zijne ouders, zijn ambt neêrleggen.

iu k'o̤, ｜苦, verdriet.

優 Iu *ts'iong iu lē tsú*, 倡｜隷卒, hoeren, comedianten, mandarijn koeiies en lagere bedienden, (de vier verachtelijkste klassen in China).

iu dziû koạ́ toàn, ｜柔寡斷, besluiteloos.

有 Iú *iú ts'ù* / » *ts'ì* } ｜趣, aangenaam.

iú tsing, ｜情, menschlievend.

iú sún, ｜損, nadeelig, schadelijk.

iú ik, ｜益, voordeelig.

iú lé, ｜禮, beleefd.

it bû só iú, 一無所｜, niets is er over.

酉 Iú *iú si*, ｜時, van 5—7 uur 's namiddags.

友 Iú *ping iú*, 朋｜, vriend.

hó iú, 好｜, goede vriend.

sún iú, 損｜, een vriend waar men niet veel aan heeft.

ts'ong iú, 牕｜, een vriend met wien men gezamenlijk gestudeerd heeft, academievriend.

誘 Iú *koai iú lâng*, 拐｜人, menschen misleiden, (zooals koelie-wervers doen).

in iú, 引｜, lokken, uitlokken.

iú p'ièn, ｜騙, misleiden, bedriegen.

幼 Iù Fijn, niet grof.

iù iù; ｜匕, do. kruimels.

iù meh meh, jeugdig, jong, (van bladeren, kinderen, enz.)

iù tóng, ｜童, jonge candidaat.

iù sap sap, fijn tot gruis.

iù boàh boàh, ｜末末, fijn tot gruis.

iù p'ê / » *p'oê* } ｜皮, fijn van vel.

iù siù, ｜秀, teer, fijn van gestel.

iù liép mi̤h, ｜粒物, breekbare, fijne waar.

iù e̤, ｜兒, klein kind.

tsiông (of *tsīng*) *iù ê si*, 冲｜之時, van zijne jeugd af aan.

iù soè, ｜歲, klein, fijn.

iù tsí, fijn, subtiel, zaak.

iù níng, ｜軟, fijn, zacht, (ook van karakter).

pò iù á, 布 | 仔, snippers van stof.

tsoá iù, 紙 |, papiersnippers.

iù lō, | 路, fijn, (van handenarbeid).

lâm hū ló iù, 男 婦 老 |, mannen, vrouwen, grijsaards en kinderen.

koa iù, 粗 |, oud grof en jong fijn, (van vruchten).

油 Iû Olie, vet; verfolie, verf, geolied; met olie inwrijven, oliën.

hé iû, 火 |, lampolie.

ts'ài iû, 菜 |, saladeolie.

moâ iû, 麻 |, hennepolie.

iû tà. | 担, olietonnen, (die olieverkoopers dragen).

iû kóng, | 筩, bamboe-oliekoker.

iû laū, | 漏, olietrechter.

hiang iû, 香 |, welriekende olie.

k'oeh iû, 壓 |, olieperseu.

iû ts'ia, | 車, oliepers, olieperserij.

iû k'o, | 箍, Chinesche zeep, (uit theewrong bereid).

iû ts'at, | 漆, olieverw; met olie verwen.

t'âng iû, 窓 |, verwolie.

iû dzī, | 膩, vet, overvloed.

tsáh iû, 炙 |, in het vet steken, door vet halen.

iû lâ, | 膀, vet, dik,

p'û iû, 浮 |, bovendrijvend vet.

iû p'éh p'éh / *» p'oéh p'oéh* } | 沫 沫, vet, magtig (van eten).

iû pò, | 布, geolied goed.

iû sa, | 衫, oliejas.

iû tsì oê, | 精 鞋, vilten geoliede schoenen.

iû kaó, | 狡, vet, vuil van het hoofd of de nek.

tsīng iû, 清 |, met olie zuiveren, de kwade geesten uitjagen.

iû iáh, | 驛, vet van gelaat, fraai.

iû ták, iû tai, | 毒 | 屎, bezinksel, droesem van olie.

so iû. 蘇 |, met olie inwrijven.

iû tsûn, | 船, een schip oliën, teren.

遊 Iû Reizen, rondreizen, rondtrekken; een uitstapje nemen, een pleiziertochtje maken.

iû hai, | 海, op zee reizen.

tsiu iû, 周 |, overal rondreizen.

sì koè iû, 四 方, overal rondtrekken.

iû óh ê lâng, | 學 的 人, rondreizende geleerden.

iû si, | 絲, de fijne spiraal in een horologie.

iû kik, | 擊, luitenant-kolonel.

iû sui hó hân, | 手 好 閒, van ledigloopen houden.

iû tsûn, | 船, schuitje varen.

iû siû, iû gōán, | 賞 | 玩, een pleiziertochtje te water maken.

iû k'oe, | 溪, een tochtje op de rivier maken.

游 Iû Familienaam.

尤 Iû Familienaam.

由 Iû Dat waaruit iets ontstaan is, reden, oorzaak; van uit, langs.

hùn iù } *hìn* » } 釁尢, reden, oorzaak tot twist.

in iù, 因 ｜, reden waarom.

kun iù } *kin* » } 根 ｜, oorsprong, oorzaak.

tuì ē mêng iù toā tā ts'ut iū, 在厦門｜大担出洋. van *Emoi* langs *Taitan* in zee gaan.

猶 Iû *iù goân*. ｜原, even als te voren, nog steeds.

又 Ook, nog.

Iū *iū koh*, ｜更, ook nog.

右 Regtsch.

Iū *iū ping*, ｜邊, regterkant.

iū kun, ｜軍, regtervleugel (van een leger).

iū iâ, ｜營, do.

iū ts'iú, ｜手, regterhand.

tsó iū, 左｜, omstander, gevolg (pers). *d. i.* omstreek, omendebij.

tsó iū lîn, 左｜隣, de buren.

lîn iū, 隣｜, do.

佑 Iū *pì iū*, 庇｜, beschermen.

賄 Iū *siū iū*, 受｜, zich laten omkoopen.

柚 Iū *iū á*, ｜仔, pompelmoes.

Iū (*mī á*), *bun tàn iū*, 文旦｜, do. van *bûntan*, (beste soort).

bit iū, 蜜｜, zoete pompelmoes.

iū p'ê bīn, ｜皮面, gerimpeld gelaat.

鴦 Iu̍ *oan iu̍*, ｜鴦, mandarijn-eend (mannetje en wijfje).

tsit tuì ná oan iu̍, 一對若｜鴦, een paar als mandarijn-eenden (van een fraai gehuwd paar gezegd).

oan iu̍ t'oa ka tsóah, ｜鴦牽茄蠘, (als) een wesp, die een kakkerlak voorttrekt; van een kind, dat een zwaar voorwerp wil verzeulen.

舀 Uitscheppen, uithoozen.

Iû *iu̍ tsuí*, ｜水, water uitscheppen.

Iô̤ *iu̍ tsoá*, ｜紙, papier uit de pap halen, waarin het gestaan heeft.

iu̍ tsik, ｜燭, kaarsen maken

養 Voeden, opvoeden, grootbrengen.

Iú *iu̍ ts'ī*, ｜育, voeden, opbrengen, verzorgen.

Iô̤ *iu̍ kiá*, ｜子, een kind opbrengen, pleegkind.

iu̍ eh } *iáng* » } ｜的, pleegkind.

an iu̍ } *iáng an* } ｜安, voeden, in het leven houden, (zooals visschen).

īng tsuí iu̍ hoe } *īong* » *iáng* » } 用水｜花, bloemen water geven.

iu̍ bah, ｜肉, nieuw vleesch aanzetten.

poe iu̍, ｜培, opvoeden, verzorgen.

ti laī bô tsuí, boē iu̍ tit hi, 池内無水難｜魚, er is geen water in de vijver om de visschen in het leven te houden, *d. i.* na den dood van zijn zoon kan men zijne schoondochter niet noodzaken bij zich in huis te blijven.

㼽 Met platte pannen beleggen, (onder de dakpannen).

Iu̍ Iô̤

羊 Schaap, geit, bok.

Iû *iu̍ ko*, ｜羔, schaap.

Iô̤ *iu̍ ko bīn hoán ts'oan*, ｜羔面反穿, een schapenvacht omgekeerd aantrekken aan de eene zijde is het glad aan de andere behaard *d. i.* eensklaps van goed, boos worden.

iû mîng, 丨 毛, schapenvacht.

iû mîng tsut tī iû sin siōng } 丨
» mô̤ » » » » siāng }

毛 出 在 丨 身 上, schapenwol komt uit het ligchaam van het schaap voort, *d. i.* zelf te betalen hebben voor iets wat ter zijner eere gedaan wordt.

iû bah, 丨 肉, schapen-, geiten-vleesch.

iû bah pao tiû si k'aó, 丨 肉 包 漲 死 狗, een doode hond met een bal bokken-vleesch, *d. i.* dom weg iets verliezen.

iû ko bí tsiú, 丨 肉 米 酒, bokken-vleesch en beste wijn.

soa iû, 山 丨, geit.

iû tiaô, 丨 欄, schapenstal.

kô̤ iû eh, *ts'ī iû eh*, 牧 丨, schaapherder.

iû hin, 丨 眩, stuip, vallende ziekte.

poà iem iû, 半 奄 丨, manwijf.

tai ti tó iû, 殺 猪 屠 丨, varkens en geiten slagten, (zooals bij groote offeranden).

iû bé, 丨 尾, bokken-staart, (van eene korte hoofdstaart gezegd).

iû á bák, 丨 仔 目, met de oogen geopend slapen.

iû hī, 丨 耳, loopende ooren.

洋 iû iô — Oceaan, zee; overzeesch- buitenlandsch- vreemd, Europeesch.

goā iû, 外 丨, buitenzee, buitenland.

iû tsûn, 丨 船, jonk voor buitenlandschen handel.

ts'ut iû, 出 丨, in zee steken.

sai iû, 西 丨, Portugal; Europa, Europeesch.

tang iû, 東 丨, ooster oceaan; Japan, Japansch.

iû bīn, 丨 面, de zeevlakte, zee.

hai iû, 海 丨, zeeroover.

hai iû bīn, 海 丨 面, gelaat als een zeeroovers.

tîng iû tó sū, 長 丨 賬 嶼, lange zee en groote eilanden, *d. i.* het is verder af dan het schijnt.

iû hè, 丨 貨, overzeesche, buitenlandsche waren.

hoàn iû, 販 丨, in buitenl. Eurp. waren handelen.

iû kao, *iû káng*, 丨 郊, 丨 行, handelshuis in Europ. waren.

iû âng, 丨 紅, carmijn.

塲 Iû — Uitgestrekte ruimte, vlakte.

k'ui tsit ê iû, 開 一 仔 丨, eropent zich eene groote vlakte.

Iô — *bin hó̤ lók iû*, 猛 虎 落 丨, *d. i.* als een sterke tijger die in de vlakte neerkomt.

pi iû k'òng t'ô̤, 平 丨 曠 土, effen vlakte en uitgestrekt terrein.

楊 Iû Iô — Familienaam.

iû tô, 丨 䔩, carambola, bliembing.

鎔 Iû Iô — Smelten, versmelten.

iû gûn, 丨 銀, zilver smelten.

iû tâng, 丨 銅, kopergeld smelten, *d. i.* zijne bezittingen opmaken.

iû t'îng, 丨 糖, suiker smelten.

iû liaó liaó, 丨 了 匕, geheel en al versmolten of op gemaakt (van bezittingen).

Iû Iô — *iû iû siû siû* } *iô » siô »* } vuil, smerig; langzaam, dralend; dom, stomp.

簷 Iû — *dzia iû*, 遮 丨, luifel.

樣 Voorbeeld, patroon, model; manierwijze, schijn, vorm; voorkomen.
Iū
Iō *tsaò iū*, 依 |, het model volgen.

oh iū, 效 |. nadoen, navolgen, nastreven.

sin iū, 新 |, nieuw model.

tsit iū, 一 |, van éénc en dezelfde soort gelijk.

iū siū, 相 |, voorkomen, vorm.

tsai á iū / *tsoá s »* } 如 何 |, hoe?

koh iū, 異 |, verschillend; zonderling, vreemd, raar.

ts'at iū, 賊 |, voorkomen als van een dief.

toā bò toā iū, 大 模 大 |, zich deftig aanstellen.

puh iū 吐 |, knop zetten, (blad of bloemknop).

hoat iū, knoppen schieten. krijgen.

ǐm tióh iū, 不 着 |, niet passend voor zijn staat, (zooals kleeding).

k'oà iū, 看 |, iets afkijken, model naar iets nemen.

sa k'oà iū, 相 看 |, een voorbeeld in elkander nemen.

ū iu t'àn iū, 有 | 趁 |, een reeds bestaand voorbeeld navolgen,

ǐm tsiā iū, 不 成 |, niet aan anderen gelijk, (door armoede), 2e niet als het model worden, 3e niet goed staan, (kleeren enz).

ki iū, 奇 |, verschillend, vreemd.

tiu iū, 張 |, den schijn van iets aannemen.

ka oè iū, 鉸 鞋 |, het patroon voor schoenen knippen. (door den aanstaanden bruidegom aan de bruid gegeven die volgens dit model schoenen voor zijne familie borduurt).

hó iu, 好 |, goed model, goede vorm.

oát sin iū, 越 新 |, een nieuw model maken, nieuwe mode invoeren.

tsoè iū, 作 |, den schijn vorm van iets aannemen, voor den schijn doen.

ū tsit è lâng iū, 有 一 箇 人 |, het voorkomen van een mensch hebben, er als een mensch uit zien (en toch zoo slecht handelen).

Ka

鉸 Knippen.
Ka *ka to, ka tsién*, | 刀, | 剪, schaar.

ka to ping, | 刀 平, een been van een schaar, (steeds ongeluk aanbrengend.

ka sa, | 衫, kleêren knippen.

ka tsién tsoè, | 刀 剪 作, knippen en maken, (kleêren).

ka tsing kah phò lâng p'a, | 整 甲 扶 羼 胞, vleijen, gatlikken.

ka tīng / *» tuī* } 斷 |, afknippen.

背 *ka tsiah*, | 背, de rug.
Ka *ka tsiah kut*, | 背 骨, ruggegraat.

ka tsiah aō, | 背 後, achter iemands rug.

ka tsiah aō mē hông tè, | 後 罵 皇 帝, den keizer achter zijn rug uitschelden, *d. i.* iemand achter zijn rug belasteren.

ka tsiah aō ts'ah toā ia koan lâng tsoh ts'át, | 後 插 大 英 管 人 作 賊, een breek ijzer op den rug dragen en met den menigte meê roepen *houdt den dief*, *d. i.* in een ander een gebrek afkeuren, waaraan men zelf mank gaat.

狡 *ka tsaó*, | 早, vloo.

Ka *ka tsaó tsoè sū luī sat bú* / » *tsò* » » » » *bó* } | 早 作 事 累 蝨 母, een onschuldige betichten van iets, dat men zelf gedaan heeft.

鴣 *ka līng*, | 伶, spreeuw.

Ka *ka tsui*, | 鵻, duif.

ka tsui bák, | 鵻 目, een kram.

ka līng boē siu tsih, | 伶 未 收 舌, als een spreeuw wiens tong nog niet geschikt gemaakt is om te spreken, van iemand die zeer onduidelijk spreekt.

ka līng tsièm k'eh tsiaó siū, | 伶 占 客 鳥 巢, als een spreeuw die het nest van een ekster inneemt *d. i.* zich niet geweld eene woning ten koste van anderen bezorgen.

蟉 *ka tsoáh*, | 蠘, kakkerlak.

Ka *ka tsoáh taī*, | 蠘 屎, geneesmiddel voor tandpijn bij kleine kinderen.

ka tsoáh liáh tsoè t'ih ting, | 蠘 誤 作 鐵 釘, een kakkerlak voor een spijker houden, *d. i.* iets niet goed gezien hebben.

膠 Lijm, gom, hars; lijmen, vastplakken.

Ka *ts'iū ka*, 樹 |, bomhars, gom.

tsuí ka, 水 |, gom.

siông ka, 松 |, hars.

hi piō ka, 魚 |, vischlijm.

liêm ka, 黏 |, lijmen, met gom vastlijmen,

軥 *ka lak*, | 軚, katrol, blokken op een
Ka schip.

茭 *kā tsing*, | 正, strooijen matras.

Ka *ka tsú, ka tsú pao*, | 注, | 注 包, bedelzak.

ka liáh, | 掠, groote van bamboes, gevlochtene horde.

ka tia p'ê / » » *p'oê* } | 程 皮, rhizophoren bast.

ka tià p'ê ùn hai tsui / » » » » *tsun* } | 程 皮 蘊 海 水, rhizophoren bast in het zeewater doopen.

咬 *ka la pa*, | 嚁 吧, Batavia.

Ka *ka la pa ùn lō lai*, | 嚁 吧 從 路 來, overland van Batavia gekomen, zegt men van een hoogst zeldzaam, moeijelijk te krijgen ding.

Ka *ka laóh*, vallen, afvallen.

p'ah ka laóh, laten vallen.

ka laóh sin, | 落 身, eene miskraam hebben.

Ka *ka nêng* / » *mui* } volledig, in zijn geheel, volslagen.

ka nêng tè, in zijn geheel, een geheel stuk.

ka nêng hāng teh, volledig thans omgekeerd gebruikt voor iets wat volstrekt niet volledig is.

ka nêng nà, een geheele mand, een mand vol.

ka nêng k'ang, een volslagen, geheel gat.

袈 *ka se* / » *se* } | 裟, overjas van een Boed-
Ka dha priester.

交 *ka tiā* / *ko* » } | 定, bestellen, besteld

Ka *ka iáh*, | 易, veel gekocht, gewild.

佳 *ka im*, | 音, goede tijding, brief.

Ka *ka bùn ts'ioh*, | 紋 蓆, Malakka mat.

傀 *ka lé*, | 儡, marionetten, poppen.

Ka *ka lé hì*, | 儡 戲, poppenspel.

tiaò ka lé, 弔 | 儡, marionetten ophangen, *d. i.* zich ophangen.

ka lé bé / » » *bé̱* | 儡 馬, paard uit de poppenkast, *d. i.* weinig voor onderhoud kosten en van veel nut.

家 Ka Ke̱ Huis, huisgezin, familie.

ka siok, | 屬, huisgenooten.

ú ka ê làng, 有 | 之 人, iemand van fatsoenlijken huize.

siaó ka ê làng, 小 | 之 人, een bekrompen mensch.

ka tsu, ka tsai, | 資, | 財, familiebezittingen.

ka hoat, | 法, manieren, regels van een huis.

ka tông, | 僮, huisjongens.

lâm ka, lú ka, 男 |, 女 |, de familie van den bruidegom en de bruid.

kok ka, 國 |, het rijk.

tong ka, 東 |, heer, baas, (zooals door meesters gebruikt van hen die hen geëngageerd hebben).

ka hong, | 風, de faam van eene familie.

taī ka, 大 |, van groote familie, faam.

sè ka / *sī* » 世 |, van beroemde voorouders.

加 Ka Bijdoen, vermeerderen, verhoogen; vermeerdering boven het kapitaal dat is percenten.

ka pē / *ke̱ poē* | 倍, verdubbelen.

ka liaō, | 料, de hoeveelheid vermeerderen.

ka kip, | 級, in mandarijngraad doenstijgen.

ka sing, | 陞, verhoogen, (in rang of prijs).

ka kiém, | 歉, meer of minder, min of meer.

ka it, | 一, 10 pCt.

ka dzī t'àn, | 二 鑽, 20 pCt. verdienen.

ka lí lò, ka lí lò ha̱i, | 里 勞 未 里 勞 稀 ○, het is er nog ver van af, in lang nog niet.

ka iêm, ka iem koa̱, | 淹 | 寒, van koude rillen, koude rilling.

tióh ka tsák, 着 | 擢, zich verslikken.

Ka *ka kī* / » *tī* zelf, eigen; alleen.

goa ka ki, ik zelf, ik alleen.

ka ki tsit làng, alléén, zonder iemand anders.

茄 Kah *ka pók mi̱* / » *poà* » | 薄 綿, katoen, kapok.

ka liò / » *lio* | ○, geroep aanhouden.

監 Ka̱ Gevangenis.

ka̱ gik / » *giók* | 獄, do.

koa̱i ka̱ / *koa̱* » 禁 |, in de gevangenis opsluiten.

siu ka̱, 收 |, do.

ka̱ kìm, | 禁, opsluiten, gevangen zetten.

ka̱ hoān, | 犯, gevangenen.

k'oà̱ of *kó̱ ka̱ ê làng*, 管 | 之 人, gevangenbewaarder.

tsaó ka̱, 逃 |, uit de gevangenis vlugten.

kià ka̱, 寄 |, tijdelijk (zoolang) in de gevangenis opsluiten.

ka̱ siû, | 囚, hongerige duivel, gegevangene.

kiep ka, 刼 |, de gevangenis open breken (en de gevangenen er uit halen).

橄 Ka *ka ná*, | 欖, olijf.

ka méng, | 莓, vergiftige plant.

絞 Ká Omwinden, draaijen, slaan (als touw) wringen, worgen.

ká ts'ia, | 車, draaispil.

ká soh á, | 索仔, touwslaan, lijndraaijen.

ká ká tsoè tsit tui, | ヒ 作 一 堆, in elkander verdraaid, (zooals een ankerketting); tegelijk, bij elkander komen, van vele bezigheden).

ká sih, | 死, doodwurgen.

tsiu ká tai, 上 | 臺, schavot beklimmen.

ká ân, | 緊, stijf aanwringen.

kiao ká t'ià, 繳 | 痛, zamentrekkende pijn (in de ingewanden).

īng oē tò ká lâng, 用話倒 | 人, iemands woorden verdraaijen.

kún ká, 混 |, stoeijen; veel met zijn geld werken, zijn kapitaal omzetten.

假 Ká Ké Valsch, nagemaakt, geveinsd; veinzen, voorgeven; tot voorwendsel nemen, verondersteld dat . . ., voor het geval dat.

ká mō dzī hō, | 冒字號, valschelijk iemands merk aannemen.

ká tsing ká ì, | 情 | 意, veinzen het goed met iemand te meenen, geveinsd.

lōng ká sing tsin, 弄 | 成真, van gekheid op meenens uitdraaijen.

ká tsià, | 藉, valschelijk uitgeven voor, voorgeven, tot voorwendsel nemen.

ká sù ē oē, | 詞, voorwendsel,

ká sú, | 使, verondersteld dat . . . . ingeval dat

ká dzû, | 如, do.

Ká *laī ká bù*, *bù ká laī*, kapitaal met interest op interest.

敢 Ká Durven,

ká tsoh / *» tsò* } | 作, wagen.

m̄ ká, 不 |, niet durven,

m̄ ká m̄ ká, 不 | 不 |, ik zal het nooit meer doen.

lí ká m̄ká ká m̄ká, 汝 | 否, heb nu nog eens het hart om het te doen, (gezegd als men een kind slaat).

tsīn ká ē lâng, 真 | 的人, iemand die alles durft te doen.

ká tng, | 當, op zich durven nemen.

ká si sí, *ká si ká si* / *» se » » se » »* } | 生 死, niet om zijn leven geven.

ká piò, | 說, het er durven uitgooijen, zich niet schamen iets onbetamelijks te zeggen.

ká kóng oē, | 說話, niet bevreesd om rond voor zijne meening uit te komen

ká ts'ut t'aô, | 出頭, het eerst de hand aan iets durven leggen.

ká tsiáh ká ts'īng, | 食 | 衣, zoodra men geld heeft, het aan eten en kleeden opmaken.

kiò m̄ ká, 叫不 |, roepen dat men het niet meer zal doen.

ká tsiū t'ék lai tsiáh, | 就取來食, als gij durft eet het dan onmiddelijk, *d. i.* men moet niet lang wachten om een koop te sluiten.

或 Willigt.
Kà̤ *heh kà̤*, 若 |, welligt, zou dat zoo zijn?
kà̤ ū iá̤, | 有 之, welligt, de mogelijkheid bestaat dat het waar is.

教 Les geven in; onderwijzen, leeren.
Kà *kà sī*, | 示, onderwijzen, onderwijzing.
kà òh, | 學, onderwijzen op eene school.
kà òh sian si̤, | 讀 先 生, schoolmeester.
kà kiá̤, | 子, zijne kinderen onderwijzen, opvoeding geven.
kà koh, | 藝, repetitie voor eene processie houden.
kà ĩm tsiṳ̄ tsoā, | 不 上 路, niettegenstaande alle onderwijzing toch niet op de lijn blijven, (als koeijen voor een ploeg) *d. i.* na alle onderwijzing toch niet beter worden.
kà pe, | 飛, leeren vliegen, (zooals een vogel hare jongen doet).

價 Prijs.
Kà *put dzī kà*, 不 二 |, geen twee
Kè prijzen, *d. i.* vaste prijs.

較 Vergelijken, van daar twist hebben
Kà over.
kà kè, | 價, over den prijs twisten.
kà ts'in, | 秤, over de weegschaal twisten, eig. vergelijken.
kà tiù / » *tiò̤* } | 場, exercitieplein; executieplein.

駕 Keizerlijke wagen, van daar beleefde-
Kà lijk voor gij, UED.
kuì kà, / *tsun kà*, } 貴 |, *lett.* de geeerde wagen, *d. i.* gij, UED.
k'ut kà, 屈 |, zich wel willen vernederen.

Kà Dun, waterig, nat.
kà kà, do.
kà lok lok, nat (zooals meel waar te veel water bij gedaan is.
tāī tsì kà lok lok, de zaken zijn in verwarden toestand.

酵 Gist.
Kà̤ *kà̤ bú* / » *bo* } | 母, do.
lóh kà̤, 下 |, gist in doen.
hoat kà̤, 發 |, gisten.
teng hoat kà̤ ê si, 當 發 | 之 時, ten tijde dat men op het toppunt van voorspoed is.
tsiú kà̤, 酒 |, wijngist, (bij wijn maken gebruikt).

咬 Bijten, knarsen, tusschen de tanden
Kā houden.
kā teng / » *tṳ̄* } | 斷, doorbijten.
kā ts'ùi, | 嘴, wrang (van vruchten).
kā k'i kun, | 齒 根, op de tanden knarsen.
kā gê ts'iet tsi, | 牙 切 齒, tanden-knarsen, (van woede).
kā tsih sìh, | 舌 死, zich den tong doorbijten en dood bloeijen.
lōng kaó sa̤ kā, 弄 狗 相 |, honden ophitsen elkander te bijten, *d. i.* menschen tegen elkander ophitsen.
niaú ts'i kā, 鳥 鼠 |, bijten als een rat, *d. i.* kleine diefstal begaan.
sa̤ kā bé, 相 | 尾, elkander in de staart bijten (van visschen vangt men er één dan volgen er meer), *d. i.* achter elkander aankomen.
kā kin kin, kā tiaò tiaò, | 緊 匕 | 條 匕, bijten zonder los te laten; vast bepalen, (zooals vaste prijs.)

dzit kā kā kā, 日 | | 乜, de zon brandend heet.

bé kā kin, 馬 | 薑, paardebit.

kā ts'aò bah, | 臭 肉, het kwaadvleesch uitzuigen, (van zalf).

sa kā bák, 相 | 目, elkander met de oogen toespreken, (tegen vrouwen).

kā lai kā k'ì, | 來 | 去, heen en weer met zich tusschen de tanden dragen, (door arme menschen gezegd van iets wat zij steeds met zich gevoerd en nu verloren hebben.

向 Kà Van, tot; voor . . . om der wille van.

kā i t'ó, | 伊 討, van iemand terugvragen.

kā i kóng, | 伊 說, tot hem zeggen.

kā lâng boé, | 人 買, voor iemand koopen.

kā i k'oà tseh, | 伊 看 這, bekijk het eens.

帶 Kà Met zich slepen, meênemen; tusschen voegen.

kà t'ô, | 泥, aarde meênemen (zooals een uitgetrokken plant).

kóng oē kà noā, 說 話 | 沫, onduidelijk spreken.

kà ī sim pi, | 伊 身 邊, met zich meêslepen, aan zijne zijde houden (zooals kinderen).

kà kà koéh koéh, | 乜 計 乜, zich met iets volstoppen, volladen.

gaò kà, 善 |, behendig ontfutselen.

kà tsit kù oē / *» » » oā*, | 一 句 話, een gezegde invoegen.

kà king, | 肩, stutten, helpen.

lâm hong k'à sai, 南 風 | 西, zuiden wind die wat naar het westen overhelt.

Kā *kā kā hoā*, snorken.

脚 K'a De voet, het been, poot; benedenste gedeelte, voet, poot van dingen; voor personen in zoover zij een deel van iets uitmaken; numerale voor doozen, trommels en voor één voorwerp van een paar.

k'a liêm, | 臁, de scheen.

k'a poā, | 盤, wreef.

k'a tsing t'aô á, | 踵 頭 仔, teenen (van de voet).

k'a dzī tsai, | 二 指, de tweede teen.

k'a táh, | 踏, voeten-bankje.

toā k'a, 大 |, groote ongebonden voeten.

pák k'a, 縛 |, de voeten binden, gebonden voeten.

k'a péh / *» péh*, | 帛, voet-zwachtel, (van vrouwen).

k'a kè / *» kê*, | 枷, voetblok.

tióh k'a tak, 着 | 觸, struikelen.

toā k'a tâng, elephantiasis aan de voet.

t'ìng tsiah k'a / *t'ùì » »*, 裸 跡 |, blootvoets.

k'a ts'iù, | 手, voeten en handen; helpers, bedienden.

k'a bō ts'iù ìn, | 摹 手 印, afdruk van voet en hand (bij gewigtige onderteekeningen gedaan.

liêm k'a tè ts'iù / *» » toè »*, 隨 | 轉 手, na even zijne hielen geligt te hebben.

k'a ts'iù bān tūn, | 手 慢 鈍, langzaam in zijne manier van doen.

k'a ts'iù p'oà siù, | 手 破 相, gebrekkig van lijf en leden.

ka kī k'a ts'iù oē tāng, 自 已 |

手能動, zelf kunnen handelen, geen hulp van anderen noodig hebben.

k'a t'aò ts'iú bé, 丨頭手尾, ondertusschen, van den minsten vrijen tijd gebruik maken om . . .

tsiem k'a iù ts'iú è lâng, 尖丨幼手的人, een verfijnd, een fatsoenlijk mensch.

ts'o̱ k'a toā toè / » » » *tè* } 粗丨大蹄, grof, onfatsoenlijk.

tsiū lâng k'a ē sí, 在人丨下死, aan iemands leiband loopen.

tîng k'a kut, 長丨骨, met de neus in de pot vallen.

k'iā k'a, 伽丨, op de beenen staan; op de wacht, uitkijk staan, (van dieven).

k'a pō̱, 丨步, voetstap; manier van loopen.

toá toá k'a sit / » *kaō* » » }, eene massa kleine onaangenaamheden.

tsoè nēng k'a tiṳ ti / *tsò̱ nō̱* » *tio̱* » } 作兩丨提防. voor beide gevallen voorzorgen nemen.

sa̱ k'a tiò nēng k'a t'iaò, 三丨踃二丨跳, huppelen, springen.

sa̱ k'a ts'ut nēng k'a dzip, 三丨出二丨入, onverwachts komen en weer weggaan.

boâ k'a p'ê, 磨丨皮, zich afloopen, veel loopen.

kià k'a, 寄丨, zich tijdelijk ergens ophouden.

lō̱ k'a, 爐丨, niet vast op de pooten staan, van plan zijn om weg te gaan, (zooals bedienden).

k'a dziah, 丨跡, voetspoor, spoor.

p'ai̱ of hó k'a dziah uī, 善惡丨跡位, onheil of geluk aanbrenger.

toh k'a, 棹丨, poot van de tafel.

t'aò mêng k'a, 頭毛丨, grens waar het hoofdhaar ophoudt.

pìn k'a, 屏丨, grens van het haar bij de slapen.

ts'iū k'a, 樹丨, aan de voet van een boom.

soa̱ k'a, 山丨, voet van een berg.

tsaò k'a, 灶丨, keuken.

kiaó k'a, 賭博丨, dobbelaar.

tuì k'a kiaó, 對丨賭, met tweeën dobbelen.

sa̱ k'a kiaó, 三丨賭, met drie personen dobbelen.

sì k'a siaò, 四丨賑, hij kan voor een gerekend worden (zooals werklieden.

hó k'a kó̱, 好丨股, ervaren, knap in een vak.

ēm sī k'a kó̱, 不是丨股, niet ervaren in een vak zijn.

tī k'a, 猪丨, eetstokjes.

tsit k'a ē tī k'a, 一丨猪丨, één eetstokje.

k'a ts'eng / » *ts'ui̱* } 丨穿, achterste, aars; achterkant, verkeerde kant, (van papieren).

k'a ts'eng aō, 丨穿後, achter iemands rug.

tîng k'a ts'eng, 長丨穿, lang bij iemand blijven zitten; plakken.

釭 K'a̱ Aarden pot; (een voet lang).

hoe k'a̱ / *hoa* » } 花丨, bloempot.

k'a̱ p'è / » *p'oè* } 丨片, panscherf.

hō̱ lâng tsoè k'a̱ p'è, 爲人作

丨片, voor een ander eene twist opnemen.

p'oà k'a p'è / » » *p'oè* } 破丨碎, potscherf.

pīng k'a, 飯丨, rijstpot.

toā k'a soè poah, 大丨細盤, groote potten en kleine borden, (van een feestmaal gezegd.

巧 Vernuftig.

K'á *ki k'á*, 奇丨, wonderlijk vreemd.

k'á koài, 丨怪, zonderling, vreemd.

kah hiah k'á, 何其丨, Zou er zoo iets wonderlijks bestaan, verwonderlijk!

k'á bī, 丨味, wonderlijke, vreemde smaak.

k'á oē / » *oā* } 丨語, vreemde woorden.

k'á kiā, 丨話, zegt men tot iemand dien men ziet op eene plaats waar bij hoogstzelden komt; *lett.* wonderlijk, zeldzaam gaan.

k'á iū, 丨樣, vreemd zonderling.

koai k'á, 乖丨, lief en schrander. (van kinderen).

扣 Slaan, kloppen op.

K'à *k'à mñg*, 丨門, aan de deur kloppen.

k'à k'ók á, 丨鐸仔, den klap slaan, (zooals nachtwachten of waarzeggers).

kap lâng k'à k'ók, 與人丨柝, met iemand over koetjes en kalfjes spreken).

k'à hun sai, 丨烟屎, het vuil. de asch van een pijp of cigaar slaan.

k'à t'ô, 丨泥, aarde afslaan, steenen bikken.

pō tséng t'aô á k'à dzia kong, 餔指頭仔丨遮風, de nagels bijten en tegen den bedderand slaan. *d, i.* een benaauwden dood-sterven.

k'à tsih k'a kut, 丨折脚骨, de beenen stuk slaan.

k'à ke hé, al zijne bezittingen tot het geringste toe, *lett.* bij elkander geklopt.

k'à là tsoè tsit tui, alles tot het laatste toe bij elkander brengen.

tsīn k'à hō ìh, iemand alles geven.

king k'à, alles bij elkander geklopt, tot het laatste toe.

K'ạ In elkander grijpen, in verband staan met.

k'ạ tioh, in verband staan met..., een weinig in iets betrokkens.

tióng kao k'ạ, aan beide einden in elkander grijpend, *d. i.* onbepaald, zoowel toestemmend als niet kunnen zijn.

kao k'ạ, met elkander in betrekking zijn, nog iets afterekenen hebben met....

kap lâng ū kao k'ạ. do.

k'ạ tàng ou im, wat *Tàng-ou*, klanken in zijn spreken hebben.

bák tsiu ki k'ạ bák sai, nog wat zucht in de oogen hebben.

p'ùi t'àm ū k'ạ tūm poh huih, er is wat bloed onder zijne slijm.

Kah

教 Bevelen, gelasten, laten.

Kah *kah i lai*, 丨伊來, iemand gelasten te komen; laat hij komen.

ts'e kah ìh, 差丨伊, iemand uitzenden en bevelen, in zijn dienst hebben.

kah tiā tioh, 丨定着, de geregelde bezorging van waren gelasten.

tiaò kah i lai, 弔丨伊來, iemand opzettelijk laten komen; bestellen.

kah tsûn, 丨船, kleine booten bij een schip aannemen; huren.

海上絲綢之路文獻集成 科技與文化編

甲 Kah Hard uitwendig omkleedsel als koolbladen, nagels; harnas; de eerste der 10 stammen, het hoofd over iets; buurt van huizen.

kah háh, 丨 葉, buitenste omkleedsel van bamboes.

tsíng kah, 丼 丨, nagels van de vingers.

ka tsíng kah ē lâng, 鉸 丼 丨 的 人, een nagel knipper, *d. i.* vleier

tsui kah, 水 丨, dunne nagels.

tsióh kah, 石 丨, dikke nagels.

tsièn kah, 戰 丨, strijd harnas.

k'oe kah, 匼 丨, helm en harnas.

kah tsí, 丨 子, de zestig deelige cyclus.

tsiáh kaò tsit kah tsí, 食 到 一 丨 子, zestig jaar oud zijn.

o kah, 阿 丨, waterschout, waterpolitie.

kah tiŋ, 丨 長, hoofd eener buurt.

ke kah pai, 假 丨 牌, buurt register.

tsō ke kah, 造 庚 丨, buurt volkstelling houden.

kah háh lóh tsui, sui ting t'iah, ligt men den bamboesschors in het water, dan kan men huid voor huid er aftrekken, *d. i.* eene zaak stuk voor stuk behandelen.

夾 Kah Onder de arm houden; tusschen voegen, mengen met; juk of raam waarin men gras draagt.

kah ko, 丨 戈, ra's van een schip.

pì á koh kah tik, 邊 再 丨 竹, aan de kanten nog bamboes bevestigen (om iets sterker te maken).

kah si̤, 丨 扇, versterken, stutten, (zooals een deur of muur).

kàn kah, *kuì kah*, tusschen voegen, afwisselen, (zooals spijzen).

ts'àn kah, 燦 丨, afwisselen, (zooals kleuren).

sa̤ am kah, 相 庵 丨, door elkander mengen, (zooals goeden en kwaden).

hó kah p'ai̤, 好 丨 呆, goeden en slechten.

kah p'ai̤ tsi̤, 丨 呆 錢, slechte duiten er ondersteken.

tà kah, 担 丨, bamboezen of houten juk voor gras.

īng tin kah, 用 籐 丨, met rotting omwinden (zooals kisten).

koâ kah hong toā, 寒 丨 風 大, koud en daarbij nog harde wind.

蓋 Kah Bedekken,

kah p'ē / » *p'oē* 丨 被, met een deken toedekken.

k'an p'ē tú á kah k'a, 牽 被 丨 脚, zijne voeten nog juist met den deken kunnen dekken, *d. i.* juist genoeg hebben maar niets meer.

合 Kah Overeenstemmen, overeenkomen, passen, geschikt zijn voor.

kah ì, 丨 意, met zijn idée overeenstemmend.

kah īng, *kah lō̤ īng*, 丨 用, 丨 路 用, geschikt voor het gebruik.

kah k'a, 丨 脚, aan de voet passen (van schoenen).

kah ts'iú, 丨 手, naar zijne hand zijn, (van penseelen).

裌 Kah *kah á*, 丨 仔, vest.

kah á koè bèh / » » *kè boèh* 丨 仔 改 袜, van een vest in een kous veranderen, *d. i.* in staat of stand dalen.

kah á puih kaò bò ts'iú ѐng, bé koà / » » *péh* » » » *ui̤ bō̤* » *puih kaò bò laī ku* / *tióh » » » ki* | 仔拔到無手袖馬掛拔到無內裾, zoo lang aan eene vest trekken dat er geen mouwen aan zijn, en aan een mantel tot dat er geen slippen aan zijn, *d. i*, iemand ongemeend beleefd behandelen.

在 Kah Afhangen van , . . .
kah sú tsaī īng, | 所在用, het hangt af van de plaats waar het gebruikt wordt.
kah lâng tsoè / *» » tsò* | 人作, het hangt af van den persoon die het doet.

較 Kah Vergelijken.
kah niû, | 量, de weegschalen vergelijken.
kah pièn tiû, zich met alle anderen meten.
kah hiah . . . , . zoo . . . , . zoozeer . . . ,
kah hiah p'ai, | 惡, zoo slecht!
nā kah, 那 |, wanneer het zoo ver komt dat . . . , ingeval.

更 K'ah Meer . . . . aanduider van den vergrootenden trap; overhellende tot, wat, wel wat, tamelijk, voor het grootste gedeelte.
k'ah tsoē, | 多, meer.
k'ah tsió, | 少, minder.
k'ah té, | 短, korter, wel wat te kort.
k'ah siū toā, | 過大, te groot.
k'ah iâ, | 勝, overwinnen. overtreffen.
koh k'ah . . . , 又 |, nog meer . . .
kìng k'ah hó, | 好, nog beter.
k'ah sī po lê tsoè, | 是玻璃作的, voor het grootste gedeelte van glas gemaakt.
k'ah sī . . . , tsit ping, | 是此邊, het helt meer over tot . . . .
k'ah k'i, | 去, wat weggaan, wat verder gaan.
k'ah kóng iā boē tsoè tit, | 說亦不是, al spreekt men er nog zooveel over het kan toch niet gebeuren.
k'ah p'ai, iā sī li ê kiá, | 惡亦是汝子, hoe slecht hij ook wezen moge hij is toch Uw kind.

籭 K'ah Vischkorf.
k'ah á, do.
k'ah á ts'i, | 仔差, de uitstekende eindjes bamboes in een vischkorf.

閤 K'áh Aanzetten als een deur; aankomen, aandrijven, tegen blijven hangen, vastblijven aan, aandoen.
k'áh mìng / *» mui* | 門, de deur aanzetten.
k'áh piah, | 壁, tegen de muur aankomen, aanwaaijen.
k'áh oá, | 倚, aankomen tegen.
tsûn k'áh hoā, 船 | 岸, het schip kwam tegen den wal, strand.
sa k'áh, 相 |, tegen elkander aankomen, aandrijven.
k'áh tsoè tsit pù, | 作一匏, in een hoop op elkander drijven, (zooals vuil aan het zeestrand).
tang hong k'áh pak, 東風 | 北, oostelijke wind met een streek Noord.
k'it hong k'áh kè k'ìh / *(» » áh koè »)* 被風 | 過去, door den wind overdrijven, (zooals regen).
sì koè k'áh, 四處 |, overal tegen aan drijven; overal wat blijven hangen, (van pers.)

k'áh tang k'áh sai, 丨東丨西, overal aandoen, niet regt-uitgaan.

gaò k'ǫ k'áh, 萶粆丨, overal blijft wat aan de maat en den strijk-stok hangen.

īm k'ǫ k'áh lâng, 不粆丨人, niets meer met anderen uitstaande hebben (zooals geld).

Kai

搴 Kai — *kai tsaì*, gelukkig, bijgeluk!

該 Kai — Behooren, betamen, passen; schuldig zijn.

kai dziên, 丨然, behoorlijk. (daar het zoo behoort).

ing kai, 應丨, moeten, behooren,

háp kai, 合丨, behooren.

kai tióh, 丨着, het moet, behoort.

put kai, 不丨, het behoort niet, men mag niet.

kai si, 丨死, hij moet dood gaan, (zooals een vogel dien men bij vergissing gedood heeft).

tuì tû laī goā siōng kai tsáp k'ǫ, 對除來外向丨十元, met aftrekking van alles blijft er nog tien dollars schuld over.

kai ts'in ê lâng, 丨親之人, degenen die door afkomst zijne familiebetrekkingen zijn; familiebetrekkingen.

偕 Kai — *kai koat*, 丨訣, omsluiten, in zich bevatten, (zooals de beteekenis van een woord).

解 Kaí — Ontwarren, uiteenzetten; verklaren.

k'ai kaí, 開丨, ontwarren, ophelderen.

kaí uì, 丨圍, uiteenzetten, ontwarren.

t'oè lâng pai kaí, 代人排丨, eene zaak voor iemand ontwarren.

hun kaí, 丨紛, uit elkander zetten, verklaren.

kaí kiù, 丨救, te hulp komen, redden (zooals van de doodstraf).

kièn kaí, 見丨, tot duidelijk inzigt komen.

kaí tiaū, 丨召, van ambtelijke stand plaats veranderen.

siaò kaí, taī kaí, 小丨, 大丨, een kleine en groote boodschap doen, (beleefde term).

kaí p'i, de holte tusschen binnendij en buik, de liezen.

kaí dzīm, 丨任, zijn ambt neerleggen.

改 Kaí — Veranderen, verbeteren.

kaí tǫ, 丨途, van beroep veranderen.

kaí pièn, 丨變, veranderen, (zooals van beroep).

kaí kò, 丨過, eene overtreding, gebrek verbeteren.

Kaì — *kaì lâng, kaì ts'aí lâng*, 慢丨彩人, plagen, treiteren.

戒 Kaì — Waarschuwen tegen, verbieden, verbod, gebod, regel; zich onthouden van, ontzien voor.

tsai kaì, 齋丨, vasten en boete doen.

p'ǫ kaì, p'oà kaì, 鋪丨, 破丨, de geboden breken, tegen de regels zondigen.

kaì tsiú, 丨酒, zich onthouden van wijn.

kaì sik, 丨色, zich onthouden van allen slechten omgang met vrouwen.

誡 Kaì — Vermanen, verbieden.

king kaì, 丨警, vermanen, schrik inboezemen.

kaì t'ik, | 飭, vermanen, beknorren.

介 Kaì — *kaì ì*, | 意, zich ongerust maken over, folteren met.

ko kaì, | 孤, excentriek, zonderling, niets met anderen te maken willen hebben.

tsoè lâng kaì kaì, 作 人 | 匕, een zonderling mensch zijn.

芥 Kaì — *kaì loáh*, | 辣. mostaard.

界 Kaì — Afscheiding, grens, grensscheiding.

kao kaì, 交 |, aanrakende grenzen.

king kaì, 境 |, grens.

ts'ân kaì, 田 |, grenzen van een rijst veld.

toē kaì / *tē* » } 地 |. grenzen van een rijk.

kaì tsí, | 址. grenspaal, grenssteen. (van velden).

sè kaì, 世 |, de wereld.

sam kaì, 三 |, de drie grenzen, *d. i.* hemel, aarde en de mensch.

kè kaì, 過 |, zijne grenzen of magt overschrijden.

sin k'i kaì, 新 去 |, van den grond af nieuw opbouwen.

ts'im kaì, 侵 |. inbreuk op iemands grenzen maken,

gán kaì, 眼 |, uitzigt, vergezigt.

kaì hān / » *ān* } | 限, grens, uiterste grens, perk.

蓋 Kaì — Bedekken; overtreffen, aller, uiterst.

kám kaì, 𩟔 |, welwillend beschermen.

kaì toé, | 底, grondverwen.

kaì sik, | 色, oververwen.

kaì t'aô, | 頭, het bruidshaar opmaken.

kaì sè / » *sì* } | 世, boven de wereld uitstekende, buitengewoon.

kaì tó tsit sì koè, | 倒 四 方, alles overtreffen.

kaì toē it, | 第 一, allen overtreffende.

kaì it hó, | 一 好, uiterst goed.

kaì p'ai, | 惡, aller slechtst.

kaì tsoē, | 多, aller meest.

kaì pù, | 富, de rijkste.

kaì ē mîng tsoē, | 厦 門 第 一 多, het meeste van geheel Emoi.

hiòng kaì kaì, 凶 | 匕, zeer onverschrokken, ruw.

解 Kaì — *kaì goân*, | 元, hoogste der *ku-dzin*.

槪 Kaì — Afstrijken, als eene maat, strijkstok.

kaì pi pi / » » *pē* } | 乎 匕, gelijk afstrijken.

taó kaì, 斗 |, strijkstok.

kaì ts'ioh, | 尺, plak, liniaal, (waarmede Chinesche meesters hunne leerlingen slaan.

間 Kai, Kàn — *kai ts'ah*, | 插, tusschen in zetten, met andere kleuren afzetten.

kai lai kai kì, | 來 | 去, afgewisseld, (zooals kleuren).

kai dzit, | 日, nu en dan.

開 K'ai — Openen, openzetten; uiteenzetten, uitleggen; een begin maken met, beginnen, aanvangen; uitgeven, uitbetalen, betalen, uitgaven; ontslaan; doen ophouden.

sin k'ai tiong, 新 | 張, een nieuwe winkel opzetten.

hó of p'ai k'ai k'aó, 好 | 口 不 好 | 口, een gelukkig of ongelukkig ding zeggen.

k'ai gán, k'ai kong, | 眼, | 光, de oogen openen, *d. i.* door offeranden een nieuw afgodsbeeld bezielen.

k'ai liét, | 列, uiteenzetten, duidelijk opmaken.

tuì i k'ai kai, 對伊|解, iemand iets uitleggen.

k'ai bing, | 明, duidelijk uiteenzetten.

sim kog īm k'ai kai, 心肝不|改, inwendig niet bepaald hoe in iets te handelen.

k'ai hoai, | 懷, inwendig verheugd.

k'ai ki tsó, | 基祖, stamvaders.

k'ai k'ūn, | 困, land ontginnen.

k'ai hók, | 復, weer in betrekking komen.

k'ai song, | 喪, den rouw beginnen, in den rouw gaan.

k'ai kang, | 工, een werk beginnen aan het werkgaan.

k'ai tsī, | 錢, geld uitgeven, uitbetalen.

k'ai sin lò só huì, | 辛金所費, salaris en onkosten uitbetalen.

k'ai bù ting k'ìh, | 無徵去, het is aan verschillende dingen opgegaan.

k'ai huì, k'ai īng, | 費, | 用, uitgaven, onkosten.

k'ai siaò, | 賬, eene specifieke rekening opmaken.

k'ai kú, 抬舉 (*t'ai kú*) iemand er boven op helpen.

k'ai hoat, | 發, uitgeven, beschikking maken over.

k'ai siao, | 消, opmaken, opgebruiken, uitschrappen, (zooals kwade schuld),

k'ai laō ping, | 老兵, oude soldaten ontslaan.

k'ai kik, | 激, uit den dienst ontslaan, (militairen).

li k'ai sim mīh lō k'ìh, 爾|什麼路起, waaraan hebt gij het uitgegeven.

楷 K'ai — *k'ai dzī, k'ai si*, | 字, | 書, gewone, (niet cursief) karakters.

siaó k'ai, 小 |, klein fijn schrift.

toan toan k'ai k'ai, 端 匕 | 匕, regt, niet scheef, (van zittende personen of karakters).

k'ai k'ai, | 匕, onverschrokken, brutaal.

覬 K'ai — *k'ai dzù lâng*, | 戲人, iemand plagen.

概 K'aì — *k'aì dziên*, | 然, onbeschaaid, onverschrokken.

k'ì k'aì, 氣 |, voorkomen gew. goed (van personen), voorkomen, handelwijze,

taī k'aì, 大 |, in het algemeen, oppervlakkig,

it k'aì, 一 |, allen,

慨 K'aì — *k'óng k'aì*, 慷 |, gul, royaal.

kám k'aì, 感 |, getroffen, bewogen door.

Kaī — *k'ām k'aī*, plagen treiteren,

k'aī haó, geluid van gongs.

Kak

角 Kak — Hoorn, hoornen; hoek, kant, uitstekend gedeelte; nummer voor brieven.

lòk kak, 鹿 |, de horens, het gewei van een hert.

kak toà, | 帶, hoornen gordel, (als een hoepel om het lijf gedragen.)

gû kak kóng, 牛 | 管, koehoorn waarop toovenaars blazen),

kak ts'ia tièm, | 奢 店, hoorn- en ivoorwinkel.

sì kak, 四 |, vierhoekig, vierkant; regtschapen.

sa kak bák, 三 | 目, driehoekige oogen, *d. i.* vertoornd uitzien.

poeh kak, 八 |, achthoekig; steranijs.

kak t'ṅg, | 糖, kandij-suiker.

kak tsuí, | 水, kandij-siroop.

tiaò kak, 弔 |, langwerpig vierkant.

kóng oē sa tsiem lák kak, 說 話 三 占 六 |, driepuntig en zeshoekig in zijn spreken, *d. i.* gevaarlijk.

tsoè làng ke kak, 作 人 過 |, steeds moeijelijkheden met anderen zoeken.

kik kak, 激 |, de hoekjes, vol-stoppen; volledig, overvloedig, (van keus).

piah kak, 壁 |, hoek van een muur, (zoowel binnen als buiten).

oat kak, | 軋, een hoek omslaan.

kik kui kak, 激 歸 |, zich in een hoek, op een hoop verzamelen.

kak mèng, | 門, zijdeur, (van een mandarijn bureau).

siém kak, 躲 |, ter zijde gaan.

kak t'aô, | 頭, hoek, kant, buurt.

k'iā ū kak t'aô, 竖 有 | 頭, veel te zeggen hebben in zijn buurt.

ko tsit kak, 再 一 |, in welken hoek, welke kant?

tsit kak, hit kak, 此 | 彼 |, deze, die kant.

tsit kak bûn su, 一 | 文 書, een officiële brief,

tsit kat gûn, 一 | 銀, een dubbeltje, tien cents.

桷 Kak Dakspar, lat.

kak á, | 仔, do.

kak á ki, | 仔 枝, lat, latje.

雄 Kak Mannetje, (bij kippen enz).

koe kak, | 雞, haan.

覺 Kak Begrijpen; merken, bemerken.

put kak, 不 |, eensklaps, onverwachts.

put ti put kak, 不 知 不 |, ongemerkt.

sit kak ts'at, 失 | 察, verzuimen, te onderzoeken.

穀 Kak *gō kak*, | 五, granen, (in het algemeen).

Kák Gooijen, werpen, weggooijen.

hiet kák, weggooijen.

hiet kák k'ì, do.

kák hiet tiu } do.
» » *keh* }

k'ioh kák } nietswaardig, waard om
t'ik » } weg te gooijen.

sì koè kák, overal heen gooijen.

ṅg tsióh t'aô sa kák, elkander met steenen gooijen.

殼 K'ak Het omhulsel, bast, buitenste gedeelte. dop, (van granen), schaal pantser, huid, vel, schelp, (van dieren).

t'aô k'ak, 頭 |, het hoofd.

t'aô k'ak oá, 頭 | 碗, hoofdschedel.

koe nn̄g k'ak, 雞 蛋 |, eijerschaal, dop.

k'ang k'ak, 空 |, hol.

k'ang k'ak tsú tē, 空 | 子 弟, jongelieden die den schijn willen aannemen tot voorname familie te behooren.

tièm k'ak, 店 |, *lett.* winkelbast, *d. i.* winkel zonder kapitaal.

pòh k'ak á, 薄 | 仔, slechte gemeene lijkkist.

k'ing k'ak, 輕 |, het geraamte van iets, (van voorwerpen waaraan men pas begonnen is).

tsit ē k'ing k'ak tiā tiā, 一 箇 輕 而 已, niets dan het geraamte, *d. i.* slechts den uiterlijken schijn van rijkdom enz.

lē á k'ak á, 螺 仔 | 仔, hoorntjes en schelpen.

pāng k'ak, 蚌 |, paarlemoer.

k'ak á hé / » » *hoe* } | 仔 灰, kalk van oesterschelpen.

iâ k'ak, 椰 |, kokosnootschil.

ku k'ak, 龜 |, schilpad pantser.

haū k'ak á, 鮫 |, pantser van den koningskrab, (als water-schepper gebruikt).

hiaoh k'ak, 脫 |, bladderen, (zooals verw.) vervellen.

k'i k'ak, 起 |. loslaten van de huid.

tsiáh pui tsiū tìng k'ak, 食 肥 就 脫 |, vet gegeten zijn huid, vel, afwerpen, *d. i.* invoorspoed zijne vroegere ellende vergeten.

確 Stellig, zeker, waar.
K'ak

tik k'ak, 得 |, stellig zeker.

k'ak sit, *k'ak tsin*, | 實. | 眞, zeker, stellig.

k'ak sī . . . . | 是, stellig is het . . . .

k'ak sìn, | 信, ware tijding.

麴 *.péh* of *àng k'ak* / *pēh* » » } 白 | 紅 |, witte en roode wijngist.
K'ak

K'ák Rochelen.

kák t'âm, slijm uitrochelen.

k'ák ts'ut lai, uitrochelen, uitspuwen.

k'ák huih, *k'ák hóng*, bloed uitrochelen.

Kam

甘 Zoet, aangenaam van smaak; gewillig, goedwillig, gewillig doen, instemmen, toestemmen.
Kam

kam tī, | 甜, zoet.

kam ts'ó, | 草, zoethout.

k'am ts'ó ko, | 草 膏, drop.

kam tsià, | 蔗, suikerriet.

kam tsià hām p'oh t'un, | 蔗 含 皮 吞, suikerriet met vezels en al inslikken, *d. i.* laag inhalig.

kam tsià kām háh pō, | 蔗 含 葉 餔, suikerriet met bast en al kaauwen.

kam kút kam kút, | 滑 | 滑, geleidelijk, zacht in de keel gaande.

kam goān, | 願, instemmen, toestemmen, gewillig.

kam sim, | 心, gewillig, vrijwillig.

ēm kam, 不 |, niet inwilligen, niet toestemmen.

kam noā ēm kam tsoā, | 爛 不 | 賤, liever laten bederven dan goed koop te verkoopen.

kam kiet dzī, | 結 字, schriftelijke verklaring dat men genoegen neemt in eene regterlijke uitspraak.

kam siok, 丨 肅, N. W. provincie van China.

柑 Kam Sinas-appel, oranjes.
kam á, 丨 仔, oranjes.
kam á bit, 丨 仔 蜜, zwart roode lijm op betelbladeren gesmeerd.
hút siú kam, 佛 手 丨, de Buddha band citroen, (sterkriekend en geconfijt.)

疳 Kam *kam tsik*, 丨 積, opstopping door te veel eten, (van kinderen.).
kam ts'ɛng, 丨 瘡, venerische zweren.

監 Kam Overzien, een oogje houden op, controléren.
kam tsám koa, 丨 斬 官, mandarijn die bij eene executie tegenwoordig is.
kam lai kam k'ì, 丨 來 丨 去, elkander wederkeerig controléren.

感 Kám Bewegen door invloed uitoefenen op, roeren, aanzetten tot; bewogen, getroffen door; bevangen worden door.
kám tōng, 丨 動, roeren, bewegen (zooals iemands hart), vermanen aanzetten tot.
kám ìng, 丨 應, bewogen door (gebeden), en er gehoor aan geven (van God gezegd).
kám ìng p'ien, 丨 應 篇, boek over belooning en straffen.
kám hoà, 丨 化, tot verandering bewegen, beteren, zich beteren.
kám siā, 丨 謝, erkentelijk, dank betuigen, bedanken.
kám un / *in* 丨 恩, dankbaar.
kám kaì, 丨 戒, welwillend beschermen.
kám kik, 丨 激, getroffen, geroerd door.
kám k'aì, 丨 慨, geroerd door, door een voorbeeld tot andere inzigten komen.
kám mō, 丨 冒, een koude vatten.
kám hàn, *kám lìng*, 丨 寒, 丨 冷, door koude bevangen, koude vatten.
kám tiòh hong, 丨 着 風, koude vatten.

敢 Kám Durven.
k'i kám, 豈 丨, hoe zou ik (Uwe beleefdheid) durven (aannemen), ik voel mij zeer vereerd.
iòng kám, 勇 丨, sterk en dapper.
kám kah, 丨 甲, eene zaak aan durven.
kám tsok; *kám tong*, 丨 作 丨 當, iets op zich durven nemen.

蓋 Kám Bedekken, dekken.
ing t'ô kám, 用 土 丨, met aarde bedekken.
moā kám t'aò, 幔 丨 頭, hennepen hoofddeksel door vrouwen bij een begrafenis gedragen.

筴 Kám *oê kám á*, 鞋 丨 仔, naaidoosjes waarin de vrouwen patronen en borduurgereedschap voor schoenen hebben.
kám ô, 丨 壺, rijstmand.
p'àng kám, 篷 丨, scherm, schut tegen de zon.

監 Kàm *kàm ts'al gū sú*, 丨 察 御 史, keizerlijke critici (die aanmerking op het bestuur mogen maken), censor.
kàm láp, 丨 納, eene offerande aannemen, (van geesten).
kàm sing, 丨 生, aspirant candidaat.
kàm tsiò, 丨 詔, bewijs dat men candidaat voor een graad is.
t'aì kàm, 太 丨, keizerlijke gesnedene.

鑑 Kàm *kong kàm*, 綱 丨, 's rijks geschiedenis.

含 In den mond houden.

Kâm *ts‘uì kàm kàm*, 嘴鍼匕, geen mond open doen.

ts‘uì kàm kap, 嘴 |, do.

kàm ts‘uì laī hō̤ i iṳ̂, | 嘴內乎伊溶, in de mond laten smelten, (zooals een ulevel).

kàm huih bū, (of *p‘ùn*) *t‘ī*, | 血噴天, bloed naar den hemel spuwen. *d. i.* iemand zonder eenige reden belasteren.

kim kâm, 金 |, ulevel, suikerbal.

龕 Nis, kastje, waar een afgodsbeeld of de

K‘am tabletten van voorouders in geplaatst zijn: examinatiecel.

pút k‘am, 佛 |, afgods kastje.

kong pô k‘am, 公婆 |, voorouders kastje.

sìng dzîn k‘am, 聖人 |, offerkastje voor de wijzen, heiligen, (op schepen).

k‘am hāng, | 港, cellengang in de examinatie plaats.

k‘am kun, | 軍, soldaten die in den cellengang wacht houden.

piah k‘am, 壁 |, nisje, kasje in de muur.

堪 Verdragen, dulden; bestand zijn tegen;

K‘am waard zijn.

oē k‘am tit, 能 | 的, kunnen verdragen.

boē k‘am tit, 不 | 的, niet kunnen verdragen; niet bestand zijn tegen, niet kunnen inhouden; niet waard zijn.

put k‘am, 不 |, niet kunnen verdragen, niet waard zijn.

k‘am boē tiaò; | 未來, niet kunnen verdragen, uithouden.

坎 Insnijden keep, kerf, holte; lijn, streep;

K‘ám numerale voor winkels.

k‘ik k‘ám, kik k‘ám, 刻 |, inkepen, insnijdingen maken.

kap i k‘ik k‘ám, 與伊刻 |, iemand niets toegeven, met iemand niet goed overweg kennen.

ū k‘ám tsūm, 有 | 斬, geregeld, ordelijk.

hing k‘ám, 胸 |, de borstholte, borst.

uìh k‘ám } *oáh* „ } 畫 |, lijnen trekken.

tsit k‘ám tièm, 一 | 店, éene winkel.

keh k‘ám tièm } *ke̤h* „ „ } 隔 | 店, aangrenzende winkel.

k‘ám k‘ó, | 考, onvoorspoedig, ongelukkig.

K‘ám *ts‘aò k‘ám*, toevallig,

憨 Dom, idiotisch.

K‘ám *kong k‘ám*, 悾 |, do.

k‘ám k‘ì, | 氣, do.

k‘ám sîn, | 神, do.

k‘ám gōng, | 戇, do.

am k‘ám, 暗 |, do.

am k‘ám siṳ̄, 暗 | 想, domme, idiotische gedachten.

砍 Hakken, neêrvellen.

K‘ám *k‘ám ts‘â*, | 柴, hout hakken.

k‘ám lám k‘ìh, | 匕去, geheel en al weghakken, neêrvellen.

K‘ám *k‘ám ts‘ē̤*, bekkens.

k‘ám ts‘ē̤ kó̤, bekkens en trom, bij begrafenissen gebruikelijk.

蓋 Dekken toedekken, bedekken; bedekt

K‘àm houden, verbergen, verborgen houden.

k‘àm ts‘aó, | 草, met stroo dekken.

k‘àm koà, | 掛, een deksel doen op.

k'àm ao, 丨 甌, kopje met deksel.

k'àm kun, 丨 巾, met een doek-tent bedekken.

k'àm ìn, 丨 印, een zegel, stempel zetten.

k'àm t'aò k'àm bīn, 丨 頭 丨 面, het hoofd en gelaat bedekken, (van schaamte), hebzuchtigen dom.

k'àm hiáh, 丨 額, het voorhoofd bedekken, (zooals haren); vooruitstekend voorhoofd.

hiáh k'àm, 額 丨, klep aan een pet.

bō á tì k'àm k'àm, 帽 仔 戴 丨 匕, de muts in de oogen hebben.

k'àm k'àm ê lâng, 丨 匕 的 人, een dom, suf mensch.

k'àm bát bát, 丨 密 匕, digt toedekken, verborgen houden.

dzia k'àm, 遮 丨, bedekken, niet bekend maken.

àm k'àm, 丨 暗, geheim houden.

moâ k'àm, 瞞 丨, bedriegelijk, verborgen houden, (zooals een te kort van geld).

勘 K'àm Vergelijken, onderzoeken, nazien, navorschen, opnemen.

tùi k'àm, 對 丨, wederzijds vergelijken.

kaò k'àm, 丨 較, onderzoeken, nazien.

k'àm giēm, 丨 驗, visiteren, onderzoeken.

tsa k'àm, 查 丨, onderzoeken.

k'ó k'àm, 考 丨, do. nazien, raadplegen.

kiù k'àm, 究 丨, grondig onderzoeken.

k'àm háp, 丨 合, nazien of de duplikaten op elkander sluiten.

k'àm toē / » *lē* } 丨 地 eene plaats, stuk gronds opnemen.

táh k'àm, 踏 丨, eene plaats opnemen, opmeten.

嵌 Kuil, afgrond tusschen twee bergen.

K'àm *poáh lóh k'àm*, 墜 落 丨, in den kuil vallen; achter uitgaan in handel.

咳 K'ām *k'ām saò*, 丨 嗽, hoesten.

砛 K'ām *sa k'ām*, 相 丨, tegen elkander aanstooten.

k'ām p'oà, 磕 破, stuk stooten.

k'ām oá, 丨 倚, tegen elkander aanstooten, (zooals schepen, deuren enz).

k'ām lai k'ām k'ì, 丨 來 丨 去, door elkander gerekend geslagen door elkander bonzen, (zooals goederen in een schip).

siōng siōng teh k'ām lâng, 常 匕 去 丨 人, anderen steeds plagen, treiteren.

k'ām k'ām, 丨 匕, in elkander gedrukt, (zooals oude menschen).

Kan

奸 Kan Slecht, onopregt, listig. bedriegelijk.

kan tsà / » *tsè* } 丨 詐, valsch, bedriegelijk.

kan hiông, 丨 雄, schurkachtig.

kan k'iaó, 丨 鬼, listig, do.

kan sin, 丨 臣, onopregt, (*lett.* een oneerlijk ambtenaar).

kan kui, 丨 詭, do.

poà tiong kan, 半 忠 丨 的 人, slechts half te vertrouwen persoon.

kan hiao hiém, 丨 僥 險, bedriegelijk, gevaarlijk, (van personen.).

kan tóng, 丨 黨, een slecht komplot.

姦 Overspel, overspelig.

Kan *kan im*, 丨 淫, overspel, overspelig.

ke kan, 雞 |, sodomie.

kan hu, | 夫, overspeler.

kan hū, | 婦, overspeelster.

kan tsiâ, | 成, zaken van overspel, overspel.

干 Kan Schild, wapens; inverband staan met, betrekking hebben op, aangaan; gevolgen hebben; betrekken in; zondigen tegen; de stam van boomen.

tōng k'i kan ko, 動起 | 戈, twist, vijandschap beginnen.

kan siép, | 涉, in verband staan met, aangaan.

kap goá bô kan siép, 與我無 | 涉, het gaat mij niet aan.

kan hē, | 係, betrekking hebben op, van gevolgen zijn.

bô kan kè / » » *koè* } 無 | 計, niet aangaan.

kan tsìng / » *tsìn* } | 證, getuigen; getuigenis.

bô siong kan / » *siang* » } 無 傷 |, niet aangaan; dat doet er niets toe, komt er niet opgaan.

put siong kan ê làng, 不相 | 的人, iemand van niet veel belang.

kan naī, | 礙, een beletsel is het dat...., eene daarmede in verband staande reden, daar, dewijl.

kan hoān, | 犯, tegen iets zondigen, overtreden.

t'ien kan, 天 |, hemelsche stammen, de 10 deelige cyclus.

kan lók, | 轆, taatstol, tol.

p'ah kan lók, 打 | 轆, taatstollen.

tìng kan lók, 釘 | 轆, op elkanders tol lenzen, gooijen.

矸 Kan Flesch,

kan á, | 仔, fleschje.

po lê kan, 玻 璃 |, glazen flesch.

sìng kan / *suì* » } 筫 |, bij de flesch berekenen.

hoe kan / *hoa* » } 花 |, bloemvaas.

kan t'at, | 塞, stop, kurk van eene flesch; kleine jongen.

艱 Kan Moeijelijk, lastig.

kan lân, | 難, moeijelijk.

kan k'ó, kan kan k'ó k'ó, | 苦, moeijelijk, lastig, moeijelijke omstandigheden, ellende.

kan kè, kan kè ts'ông / » *lân* » *lân* » } | 計, | 計 創, moeijelijk te doen.

杆 Kan Rond, omheining.

lân kan, 欄 |, omheining; borduursel, rand om kleeren, heg.

乾 Kan Droog.

ìm kan, | 蔭, in den schaduw gedroogd.

kan niû, | 糧, droog proviand.

kan ki / » *ke* } | 庚, het kompas.

kan ta, | 礁, alleen, op zich zelven; om niet.

kan ta sàng làng, | 礁 送 人, 已, voor niet geven, cadeau doen.

kan ta kóng tiū tiū, | 礁 說 而 zoo maar zeggen zonder het te kunnen vervullen.

kan ts'â kūn dziét hé / » » *kīn* » *hoé* } | 柴 近 烈 火, als droog hout bij het heete vuur, *d. i.* in sterke verzoeking.

kan laū, | 漏, afschilfering van de huid, soort schurft.

間* In, tusschen.

Kan *tiong kan*, 中 |, midden in, tusschen, onder.

簡† Verkorten, verkort, beknopt, compact, bondig; familienaam.

Kán *kán tsiét*, | 捷, beknopt, compact, (van woorden of dingen).

kán iaò, | 要, beknopt, tot het voornaamste teruggebragt.

kán síng, | 省, verkort.

kán síng siá, | 省 寫, verkort schrijven.

kán liok / » *liák* } | 畧, verkort, beknopt; oppervlakkig.

kán iok, | 約, verkort, beknopt.

kán piēn, | 便, handig, geschikt, praktisch.

kán piēn è si, | 便 之 時, te geschikter tijd.

kó kán, 苟 |, onvoorzigtig, onnaauwkeurig.

敢 *kán t'ang án ni* / *kám* » » » } | 可 如 此,

Kán kan of mag dat wel zoo?

揀** *kán soán*, | 選, zorgvuldig uitzoeken, uitkiezen.

Kán

妲 Slavin, vrouwelijke bediende.

Kán *tsa bó kán*, 女 |, do.

niû kán, | 娘, meesteres en slavin.

侃 *k'án k'án tsoè i kóng*, | 七 作 伊

K'án 說, royaal, rondeweg, onbedeesd spreken.

---

* Zie verder onder *king*.

† Zie verder onder *king*.

** Zie verder onder *k'ing*.

幹 Kennis, bekwaamheid, talenten; doen,

Kàn beredderen.

ū ling kàn, 有 能 |, talenten kennis van zaken hebben.

ū tsai kàn, 有 才 |, do.

bô lō kàn, 無 路 |, onbekwaam, onkundig.

kàn toā sit, | 大 識, voor groote zaken geschikt zijn.

kàn bô sit, | 無 識, voor niets geschikt zijn.

kàn hàm sit, | 喊 識, gewaagde, gevaarlijke dingen doen.

ká kàn, 敢 |, durven doen.

kàn pān, | 辦, behandelen, beredderen.

kàn soān, | 旋, beredderen, beheeren, (eene zaak).

kàn si si, | 生 死, doodelijke twist hebben.

間 *bô kàn tīng* / » » *toān* } 無 | 斷, zonder tusschenpoozen.

Kàn

kàn tsit dzit, | 一 日, een dag tusschenbeide, om den anderen dag.

kàn kièn, | 見, bij tusschenpoozen, niet altijd voorkomende.

hoán kàn kè, 反 | 計, list om personen die goede vrienden zijn elkander te doen wantrouwen.

澗 Bergstroom.

Kàn *toā kàn ts'iong sió kàn*, 大 | 冲 小 |, groote bergstroomen storten zich in kleineren.

⿰虫間 *kàn á koè*, | 仔 鮭, gezoute mosselen.

Kàn

Kàn Lage term voor; coitus uitoefenen.

sg kàn, do.

kàn lim laū bú / » » *miô lé* } laag scheldwoord in

26

de lage volkstaal, zelf als uitroep van verwondering, vreugd, enz. gebruikt.

ts'ò kàn lák kiaō làng, iemand gemeen uitschelden.

牽 K'an Trekken, voorttrekken, voortslepen, in iets betrekken, medeslepen; lokken. bijde hand-leiden, voorthelpen; rekken.

k'àn bán, 丨 挽, voorttrekken, (zooals beesten).

tú tú k'an p'ē kah k'a, 抵 匕 丨 被 覆 脚, de deken juist over de voeten kunnen trekken, *d. i.* maar juist genoeg hebben om te leven.

k'an hong kuī, 丨 風 櫃, de blaasbalk trekken.

k'an kù / » *kì* } 丨 鋸, zagen (met twee personen).

k'an soà, 丨 線, met garen of touw uitloopen.

k'an tsin, 丨 繩, een lijn trekken, (met een koord).

k'an p'âng, 丨 篷, het zeil in handen hebben.

k'an hong á, 丨 風 仔, overdekte boot met zeil.

k'an tsiū t'aò, 丨 頭 上, naar lij wenden.

k'an t'oa, k'an liên, 丨 拖, 丨 連, medeslepen, in eene zaak betrekken.

sa k'an ts'iú, 丨 相 手, elkander bij de hand leiden.

k'an ts'iú, 丨 手, eene vrouw huwen, (uitlandig).

k'an hoan pô, 番 丨 婆, eene vreemde vrouw huwen, (minachtend gezegd).

k'an k'ioh, 丨 曲, voorthelpen, er boven op helpen.

k'an t'oéh, 丨 ○, de behulpzame hand bieden.

sa k'an sa t'oa, 相 丨 相 拖, elkander meênemen, als naar een feest elkander in een zaak meêslepen.

k'an k'a, 丨 脚, medespelers lokken, aantrekken (in speelhuizen.

k'an kiò, 丨 叫, de behulpzame hand bieden.

k'an sing, 丨 成, helpen zijn doel te bereiken, er boven ophelpen.

ùn á k'an. 温 仔 丨, langzaam rekken (zooals met provisie, handel, enz.)

k'an sai hong, 丨 西 風, rouwfeest 100 dagen na den dood: hierbij zijn priesters tegenwoordig.

縴 K'an *k'an t'iu*, 丨 襯, eene stootkant streep, voering tegen een kleed leggen.

件 K'an Verpande goederen.

k'an t'aò, 丨 頭, verpande goederen.

tìng k'an t'aò, 當 丨 頭, goederen verpanden.

t'ó k'an t'aò, 討 丨 頭, panden loskoopen.

p'ah k'an, 打 丨, panden wier lostijd reeds verstreken is verkoopen.

tiém k'an, 點 丨, den reeds verloopen tijd van panden onderzoeken.

tsit k'an taī tsì, 一 丨 大 志, éene zaak één ding.

牽 K'an *k'an kun*, 丨 根, spieren, wortels, vertakkingen uitzenden.

k'an hát, 丨 核, opzwelling door weêrpijn veroorzaakt.

k'an soà, 丨 線, met een lijn, streep afzetten.

看 K'àn *k'àn kò*, 丨 顧, verzorgen, zorgen voor.

k'àn p'ò, 丨 破, doorzien, (zooals eene zaak).

讞 *k'àn gū* / *» gí* } | 語, uitspraak van een vonnis.
K'àn
k'àn sī, | 是, vastgesteld, vastbepaald.

kang

工 Werk, arbeid; werkman, arbeider; dagwerk, eene schoft bij arbeidslieden; werkloon, loon; ledige tijd, tijd voor iets.
Kang

kang hu, | 夫, werk, arbeid.

put tsi kang hu, 不只|夫, veel werk, tijd vereischend.

kang hu tê, | 夫茶, Congou thee.

kang hu p'ī, | 夫病, langdurige ziekte.

soah kang, 歇 |, een werk afbreken.

tang kang, 動 |, een werk beginnen.

t'oa kang, 拖 |, een werk rekken.

t'ing kang, 停 |, een werk staken.

siu kang, 收 |, een werk eindigen.

kang goē / *» gē* } | 藝, beroep, ambacht.

bô kang gē, 無 | 藝, geen werk hebben.

lâng kang, 人 |, koelie.

têng kang, 當 |, vaste arbeider.

toā kang, 大 |, werkbaas.

bák kang, 木 |, timmerman.

t'ô̤ kang, 土 |, metselaar.

sió kang, 小 |, assistent, opperman.

kang tsī, | 錢, werkloon.

kang liāu, | 料, werkloon en bouwstoffen.

tsá kang, *oà* (of *ē toà*) *kang*, *ē po̤ kang*
» » » ē » » ē » »

早 | 晏 | 下午 |, ochtend, middag en namiddagschoft.

ū kang, *bô kang*, 有 |, 無 |, tijd of geen tijd hebben (om iets te maken).

tiau kang, 雕 |, opzettelijk, exprès.

tsiàu k'í kang, 照起 |, volgens den regel.

bô k'í kang, 無照起 |, zonder regel.

kang tsing, | 情, werk, arbeid, moeite aan iets.

kang pō̤, | 部, ministerie van openbare werken, (te Peking).

kang pâng, | 房, departement van openbare werken, (in een mandarijnbureau.

kang kò̤, | 顧, belooning voor zijne moeite.

江 Rivier. Familienaam.
Kang

kang tsuí, | 水, rivierwater.

kang hoā, | 岸, rivieroever.

kiâ (of *tsaú*) *kang ô̤* / *» » » hô̤* } 行 | 湖, over rivieren en meeren, *d. i.* door het land reizen als waarzeggers.

kang ô̤ ê lâng, | 湖之人, rondreizende lieden, kwakzalvers, waarzeggers, enz.

kang ô̤ oē, | 湖話, algemeen erkende waarheden, holle taal.

kóng oē k'ak kang ô̤, 說話 | 較湖, oppervlakkig, in het algemeen spreken.

kang san. | 山, grondgebied, rijk, land.

kièn tì kang san, 建置 | 山, een rijk vormen; bezittingen verwerven.

goā kang lâng, 外 | 人, Chinezen

van eene andere meer noordelijke provincie.

hik liòng kang, 黑 龍 丨, de Amoor, (vroeger verbanningsplaats).

kang pī bē tsui, 丨邊 賣 水, aan den rivierkant water verkoopen, *d. i.* goederen voeren naar eene plaats waar in overvloed voorkomen.

公 Kang Mannetje van dieren.

kang bú, 丨母, mannetje en wijfje.

kang bú tuì, 丨母 對, een paar.

bē kì kang bú, 未 見 丨母, nog niet weten wie de overhand heeft.

bé kang, 馬 丨, hengst.

蚣 Kang *già kang*, 蜈 丨, duizendpoot.

港 Káng Riviermond, inham der zee, (haven).

káng k'aó, 丨口, monding eener rivier, haven.

káng mìng, 丨門, ingang tot eene haven.

káng lō, 丨路, weg naar eene haven.

ts'oā káng eh, 導 丨的, loods.

k'ūt t'aô káng, 窟 頭 丨, haven waar men niet verder landwaarts kan ingaan.

káng sim, 丨心, midden eener haven.

k'ui ts'uì káng, 開 嘴 丨, open haven.

kè káng á, 過 丨仔, eene rivier oversteken.

tsaī káng ē dzit tsi, 在 丨日 旨, ligdagen.

kim káng, 禁 丨, verboden haven, (waar uitvoer van zekere artikelen verboden is.)

k'ui káng, 開 丨, eene haven openstellen.

tsit káng mìng ē hè, 丨門 的 貨, eene stapel goederen.

ē mìng káng, 厦 門 丨, het inkomen der Emoi haven.

犺 Káng Mannetje (bij beesten koeijen en schap).

gû káng, 牛 丨, stier.

iû káng / *iô* » } 羊 丨, ram.

講 Káng Spreken, bespreken, onderhandelen over; onderzoeken, uitleggen.

káng kiù, 丨究, onderzoeken, bestudéren.

káng kè, 丨價, over den prijs onderhandelen, negotiéren.

káng hô, 丨和, over vrede onderhandelen.

k'ui káng, 開 丨, uitleggen, verklaren.

káng (tông) tìng, 丨堂, preêkstoel.

淍 Káng Stroom, straal.

tsit káng tsui, 一 丨水, een stroom water.

kui káng, 歸 丨, in een straal.

toā káng hong, hong toā káng, 大 丨風, sterke windstroom.

Kàng Geheel, gansch.

káng dzit, 丨日, den ganschen dag.

káng géh, káng nî, 丨月, 丨年, een geheele maand, jaar.

káng ts'ing káng bān, 丨千 丨萬, bij duizenden en tienduizenden.

降 Kàng Neerkomen, neerdalen; dalen, verminderen, afnemen, afslaan.

t'ien sin kàng hā / » » » *hē* } 天 神 丨下, de hemelgeesten komen néer op aarde, (12de maand 25sten dag).

kàng tsin kiu, | 真香, reukwerk van sandelhout waarop de geesten neêrdalen.

sing kàng, 霜 |, dat gedeelte van het jaar waarin de ijzel begint neer te komen, het eind van de 9de maand.

ngià sing kàng, 迎 | 降, de geesten des winters inhalen, (door mandarijnen in de 9de maand gedaan).

kàng kip, | 級, in rang dalen.

kàng ting, | 等, een graad verminderen (van mand:)

kàng k'i, | 氣, afnemen, bekoelen, (van drift of warmte).

kàng kè, | 價, afslaan in prijs.

洚 Kàng *kaó kàng hong*, 九 | 風, buitengewoon harde wind (zooals in de 9de maand.)

kaó kàng tsui, 九 | 水, buitengewoon hoog water.

k'i kaó kàng, 起九 |, buitengewoon hoog rijzen van het water.

訌 Plagen.

Kāng *ìm t'ang kāng ih*, 不可 | 伊, plaag hem niet, kom er niet aan.

共 Kāng *kāng tsit lâng*, | 一人, dezelfde man.

kāng tsit liaó koe, | 一條街, dezelfde straat.

kāng tsit laī bīn kiā, | 一內面住, te zamen inwonen.

taò sa kāng / » *sio* » } 湊相 |, elkander gemeenschappelijk gaan helpen.

向 Van.

Kāng *kāng lâng t'éh*, | 人取, van iemand afnemen.

kāng ì boé tām póh, | 伊買淡薄, een weinigje er van koopen.

孔 K'ang Holte, gat, een gat voor iets, gelegenheid.

bák k'ang, 眼 |, oogholte.

p'ī k'ang, 鼻 |, neusgaten.

hī k'ang, 耳 |. oorholte.

tit tióng hó k'ang, 得着好 |, eene goede gelegenheid vinden.

àm k'ang ku, 庵 | 龜, iemand die nooit buiten 's huis komt.

k'ang k'aó ok, | 口惡, iemand die veel durft te zeggen zoolang hij in zijn eigen huis is.

toā k'ang lâng. 大 | 人, iemand die zich gaarne groot voordoet.

toá toá k'ang sèng / » *kaō* » *siaò* } | 笱甚多, nog met kleinigheden veel verdienen.

k'ang lō tsoē, | 路多, veel gelegenheid voor zich hebben om . . . openstaande gelegenheid om . .,

k'ui k'ang, 開 |, eene gelegenheid voor iets zoeken, (om geld te verdienen, enz.)

t'at k'ang, 塞 |. een gat stoppen, (met geleend geld eene schuld betalen).

tsiong tsit k'ang t'at hit k'ang, 將一塞一 |, het eene gat maken om het andere te stoppen.

k'ang ts'ui, | 嘴, opening van een gat.

tsiù k'ang, 咒 |, met gaten doorvreten, (hout, kleê en, enz.)

àm k'ang, 庵 |, heimelijk gat, geheime weg.

niaú ts'ù k'ang ui kaò tsiâ oân kong mêng, 老鼠 | 挖到成𩋆門, een ratten gat zoo uit hollen dat het een boog-deur wordt, *d. i.* van eene kleine zaak tot eene groote worden.

aō k'ang k'it lâng ui k'i, 後 | 被

人挖去, heimelijk achter zijn rug benadeeld worden.

lap k‘ang, 溿 |, invallen, inzakken, (zooals aarde boven een gat), verminderen, verliezen van kapitaal.

ū k‘ang, 有 |, eene goede gelegenheid voor iets bebben, geld hebben.

boē kè k‘ang, 未過 |, eene moeijelijkheid niet te boven kunnen komen.

kiu k‘ang kì tièm, 求 | 去潛, zich in zijn gat terugtrekken, niet met anderen omgaan.

p‘oà k‘ang, 破 |, aan het licht komen, uitlekken.

k‘ang t‘aò toā, | 頭大, een sterken steun in iemand hebben.

kaò k‘ang t‘àng tsui k‘ut, 猴 | 通水窟, de apenkuil correspondeert met de plas, *d. i.* door de eene persoon in kennis met eene andere komen.

bák k‘ang oéh, 目 | 狹, jaloersch.

toā bák k‘ang k‘o̱, 大目 | 環, iemand die datgene nog voor gering houdt wat anderen voor groot aanzien.

hiaò k‘ang, 嬲 |, wellustig, geil.

bô bīn k‘ang t‘ang kì̱ làng, 無面 | 可見人, beschaamd zijn om zich aan anderen te vertoonon.

空 Ledig.

K‘ang *k‘ang k‘ang*. | 匕, do.

k‘ang k‘ak, | 壳, hol, ledig.

k‘ang sim, | 心, nuchter, (nog niet gegeten hebben).

k‘ang k‘iah, | 隙, gat, reet.

k‘ang ts‘iù, | 手, met leège handen, zonder iets te bezitten.

k‘ang sin, | 身, leèg, zonder iets te bezitten.

k‘ang k‘ak tsú tē, | 廓子弟, arm, maar fatsoenlijk gekleed.

k‘ang p‘āng, | 縫, fout in iemand.

t‘àng hit ē k‘ang p‘āng, 乘其閒隙, van die gelegenheid gebruik maken om . . . , ondertusschen.

ts‘ē k‘ang }
ts‘oē „ } 求 |, naar eene zwakke plaats zoeken, iets zoeken om aanmerking op te maken.

k‘ang ts‘uì pō̱ tsih, | 嘴嚼舌, mooie beloften doen maar ze niet vervullen.

tsiú k‘ang pâng, 守 | 房, zonder man zijn (van eene vrouw).

k‘ang p‘ò̱, | 冇, hol, leeg, veel drukte maar geen voordeel geven.

k‘ang hu, | 虛, leeg, hol, zonder beteekenis.

k‘ang hu dzī, | 虛字, partikel.

k‘ang làng, | 人, niets bij zich hebbend, zooals men daar staat.

k‘ang tsùn, | 船, leeg schip, (zonder lading.)

k‘ang k‘ak ts‘oán, | 壳喝, uiterlijk rijk voorkomen zonder het te zijn.

k‘ang lok lok, k‘ang kok kok, | 碌匕 | 哭匕, totaal leeg, hol.

k‘ang ts‘ù, | 厝, leeg-staand huis.

k‘ang siaò, | 賬, holle rekening van welks betaling men niet zeker is.

k‘ang tièm ts‘ut sè, | 店出稅, een leège winkel te huur.

k‘a tseng k‘ang k‘ang, 脚穿 | |, met de billen achter uitsteken, (zooals bij bukken).

toā k‘ang gâng ē làng, 大衙的人, een man van gewicht.

抓 Krabben, afkrabben, peuteren aan.
K'àng *k'àng p'oà p'ê*, | 破 皮, de huid stuk krabben.
k'àng p'ī sai, | 鼻 屎, in de neus pulken.
k'àng k'a ts'eng tsaó, | 脚 穿 走, zich het achterste krabben en wegloopen.
iah k'àng, , afkrabben; openrijten, ophalen; (zooals vroegere verkeerdheden).
pê ts'eng k'àng ts'ioh, 抗 床 | 席, een benauwden dood sterven.
ùn á k'àng, 温 仔 |, langzamerhand afkrabben, bij kleine hoeveelheden betaald krijgen.
k'àng ts'eh p'ūng, | 册 縫, de hoekjes en gaatjes van een boek doorsnuffelen, *d. i.* zorgvuldig nazien.

炕 匟 Gastenbank met een laag tafeltje in
K'àng het midden; bed dat van onderen verwarmd wordt.
k'àng ts'êng, | 床, gastenbank.
tsē k'àng, 坐 |, op de gastenbank zitten.
k'ùn k'àng, 睡 |, slaapplaats die verwarmd wordt.
k'àng ki, | 几, het tafeltje dat op de gastenbank staat.

曠 Wijd, uitgestrekt, onbebouwd.
K'àng *k'àng toē*, | 地, leêge ombebouwde grond.
k'àng po, | 鋪, ruime vlakte.

間 Plaats laten voor, openlaten.
K'àng *k'àng péh* / *péh* | 白, plaats voor een karakter openlaten.
k'àng tsit dzit, | 一 日, één dag tusschen beiden.

Kao

交 In verband staan of brengen met, te
Kao doen hebben met; in contract, aanraking komen met; geven, overhandigen, overbrengen op, opdragen, omgang hebben met, omgang.
kao koan, | 關, handel drijven met.
kao siong, | 商, do.
la kao, 勝 |, bedriegelijk handelen met (steeds schuld zien te ontduiken).
kao oā, | 换, inruilen.
kao tsièn, | 戰, strijden, gevecht.
kao tsiep, | 接, omgang hebben met.
kao kiet, | 結, do.
kao lap, | 納, overgeven, overdoen, (eene zaak).
kao poâ, | 盤, do. (een ambt.)
kao hō ih, | 與 他, aan iemand overhandigen, geven.
kao ki lièn, | 枝 連, verward in elkander, (van een zaak).
kao in, | 婚, huwen, (buitenslands), (maleisch kawin).
sū kao ts'ap, 相 | 雜, met elkander te maken hebben, omgaan.
kao koā, | 官, met mandarijnen omgaan.
kao poê, | 培, omgang met.
lām kao, 濫 |, met goeden en slechten omgaan.
kao tī, | 纏, ophouden, inwikkelen, een beletsel zijn om iets anders te doen.
sū kao tī, 相 | 纏, elkander ophouden.
sū kao, 相 |, den coïtus uitoefenen, (van dieren).
kao kaì, | 界, aanrakende grenzen.

gaò kao tah, 善 | 搭, goed slag hebben om kennis aan te knoopen.

kao k'à, | 加, nog iets bij zich slepen, dubbelzinnig.

kao hù, | 付, op een ander overdragen, opdragen.

kao tài, | 帶, do.

kao t'ok, | 託, opdragen.

kao tài dzī, | 代 字, geschreven volmacht, akte van volmacht.

kao ts'iù, | 手, omgang hebben, te maken hebben met.

k'óng kao, 廣 |, uitgebreide kennissen.

kao tsiem tìng, | 針 釘, stikken, naaijen; veel moeite aan iets besteden.

kao ts'un, kao hē, kao ts'iu, kao tang
» » » *hē* » » » »
| 春, | 夏, | 秋, | 冬, overgang tot de lente, zomer, herfst, winter.

kao í, | 椅, stoel.

鉤 Kao IJzeren haak, haken, vasthaken, met een haak ophalen

t'ih kao, 鉄 |, ijzeren haak.

tah kao, 搭 |, haak om aan te klampen (zooals een schuithaak).

tiò kao, | 釣, visch-haak.

tò kao k'ì / » » *ts'ì* } 到 | 刺, weêrhaak.

kao tiaò, | 弔, vasthaken, vastzetten, (zooals een deur met een haakje).

kao p'oà, | 破, een haakje aan een karakter zetten om zijn toon aanteduiden.

sa kao p'oà, 相 | 破, door elkander doen mengen,

kao hī, | 耳, de ooren uitpeuteren; oorlepeltje.

kao siao, | 消, doorhalen, (eene rekening).

kao tàng, | 當, bezigheid.

溝 Kao Gracht.

kao á, | 仔, gracht.

hò kao, 河 |, gracht, kanaal.

郊 Kao Wildernis.

kao iá, | 野, wildernis.

hàng kao, 行 |, handelshuis.

九 Kaò Negen.

tsáp kaò, 十 |, negentien.

kaò tsáp, | 十, negentig.

kaò hun á, | 分 仔, achtste dollar.

kaò poeh kao / *peh* » » } | 八 郊, handelshuis waar men 2 pCt. commissiegeld rekent eig. voor 98—100 moet terugg ven.

iû kaò poeh, 洋 | 八, agenthuis op de buitenlanden.

ts'it kaò lák sa tuì i kóng, 七 | 六 相 對 說, iemand alles van iets vertellen.

kaò niû gû p'ê tsoè tsit si pak / » » » *p'oê tsò* » a » } | 領 牛 皮 作 一 時 縛, negen koehuiden in ééns afvillen, *d. i.* iemand voor verschillende overtredingen in ééns doorhalen.

kaò tsàn laò t'ui tsoè tsit tsán loh
» » » » *tsò* » » »
| 層 樓 梯 作 一 層 落, van een trap van negen treden in eens afspringen.

狗 Kaó Hond.

láh kaó, 獵 |, jagthond, fig. iemand die voor een ander de kastanjes uit het vuur haalt.

siaó kaó, 瘋 〡, dolle hond.

kaó t'ou, 〡 拖, mogen de honden u wegslepen, (scheldwoord.

kaó k'ang, 〡 空, hondengat, (in een muur).

kaó siū, 〡 袖, hondenhok.

kaó tóng, 〡 黨, een troep honden.

kaó tú, 〡 柢, holle bamboes met een doorloopend touw, (aan den nek van valsche honden gedaan).

kaó tiaó, 〡 欄, hondenhok; hut waarin de naaste betrekkingen van een overledene wonen, tijdens den rouwtijd,

kaó soh, 〡 索, honden touw; gemeenschappelijk touw waaraan verscheidene booten worden vast gebonden.

ti kaó tsing si, 猪 〡 鐘 生, als varkens, honden en huisdieren, *d. i.* onmenschelijk, ondankbaar.

si kaó noā ti, 死 〡 爛 猪, als een doode hond en een verrot varken, *d. i.* iemand die men niet van zich af kan krijgen, als bedelaars.

kaó bah siòng } 〡 肉 相, evenals
» » *siàng* }
honden, *d. i.* rijken vleijen.

p'ai kaó, 惡 〡, een schurk.

p'ai kaó lâng, 歹 〡 人, een slecht mensch

kaó siņ k'it tsiáh aó, 〡 聲 乞 食 喉, een geluid als een hond en een strot als een bedelaar.

kā kaó m̄ haó, 咬 〡 不 吠, een bijtende hond schreeuwt niet.

soā kaó, 山 〡, vos.

kaó sat, 〡 虱, hondenluis.

ts'aò kaó lin } 臭 〡 獻, stinkende
» » *hièn* }
honden lucht.

螻 *kaó hiā*, 〡 蟻, mier.
Kaó

kaó hiā keng t'âng } 〡 蟻 扛 虫,
» » *già kang* }
als mieren die een worm, (duizend poot), wegdragen, *d. i.* hoogeren door vleijerijen voor zich trachten in te nemen.

kaó hiā paì t'i toē } 〡 蟻 拜 天 地,
» » » » *tē* }
als een mier die aan hemel en aarde wil offeren, *d. i.* een laag mensch die met een aanzienlijk mensch wil omgaan.

kaó hiā siū tsoè tsui, 〡 蟻 游 過 水, overstrooming in een mierennest, het gat loopt vol, Chin. *kik-k'ang*, bet. zich hooger willen voordoen dan men is.

kaó sin, 〡 蠅, springvlieg.

垢 (滓) Vuil, bezinksel,
Kaó

iû kaó, 油 〡, vuil (van het hoofd).

kaó koeh sien } 〡 隔 仙, vuil op
» *keh* » }
het ligchaam.

tsui kaó, 水 〡, bezinksel, algen in water.

狡 Onopregt, bedriegelijk.
Kaó

kaó koè, 〡 獪, slecht, bedriegelijk.

kaó tsà } 〡 詐, valsch, onopregt
» *tsè* }

口 *é kaó* } 啞 〡, doofstom.
Kaó *é* » }

到. 至 Komen te, aankomen, bereiken; tot, tot aan.
Kaò

kaò tè, lai kaò tè, 〡 處, 來 處, op de plaats der bestemming aankomen.

sì tè to kaò, 四 處 都 〡, overal geweest zijn, komen.

kaò ts'ù, 〡 厝, te huis aankomen.

kaò tao, 〡 彼 處, op de plaats aankomen.

p'ah sìng bô kaò, 打 箕 無 |, niet zoover gedacht hebben als.

kaò si, | 時, de tijd is daar, het is tijd.

kaò pui, | 肥, zijne uiterste vetheid bereikt hebben, (van beesten).

beh kaò t'aò 將 盡 |, het loopt op zijn eind.

kaò ts'iù, | 手, in handen; ontvangen hebben.

kaò kik, | 極, ten uiterste.

ū kaò hè, 有 | 貨, er zijn goederen aangekomen.

kaò p'oe, | 批, er zijn brieven aangekomen.

够 Kaò — Genoeg voldoende, genoegzaam, overvloedig; grondig, volledig.

kaò giáh, | 額, genoeg.

bô kaò īng, 不 | 用, niet genoegzaam.

bô kaò géh, 不 | 月, vroegtijdig, (van geboorte).

kaò kang, | 工, volledig afgewerkt; overvloedig, overbodig in beleefdheid.

kaò lé, | 禮, overtollig in beleefdheden.

kaò pún, | 本, gelijk spelen, (in handel).

kaò ts'ìn, | 秤, overvloedig gewigt.

kaò hé, | 火, reeds lang genoeg op het vuur geweest.

kaò liēn, | 鍊, door en door geoefend, ervaren.

校 Kaò — Vergelijken, onderzoeken; nazien; twisten, disputéren.

pi kaò, 比 |, onderling, vergelijken.

k'ó kaò, 考 |, examineren.

kaò k'àm, | 勘, onderzoeken, raadplegen, nazien.

ké kaò, 計 |, disputéren, twisten over.

tsing kaò, 爭 |, twisten, een standje schoppen.

kaò laū, | 鬧, do. (in zijn huis).

教 Kaò — Onderwijzen, leeren; leer, sekte.

kaò hùn, | 訓, onderwijzen, onderrigten.

kaò sip, | 習, onderwijzen, drillen, driller van rekruten.

kaò tok, | 篤, onderwijzen en een oogje houden op.

sam kaò, 三 |, de drie sekten: *dzû kaò, tō kaò, sik kaò*, 儒 |, 道 |, 釋 |. Confucianisme, Taöisme, Boedhisme.

siâ kaò, 邪 |, valsche leer.

t'ien tsú kaò, 天 子 |, Catholicisme.

iâ so̤ kaò, 耶 蘇 |, Protestantisme.

kaò tsú, | 主, stichter eener sekte.

t'oân kaò, 傳 |, eene leer verspreiden; verkondigen.

kaò ko̤a, | 官, opzigter over het onderwijs.

窖 Kaò — *iû tsit kaò*, 油 一 |, een pot olie, (van verschillend gewigt).

猴 Kaò — Aap; overspeler.

kaò tōng, | 洞, apenhol.

kaò kui, | 歸, strot van een aap.

to̤ kaò, 肚 |, mol.

kaò tan kaò tan / *» ting » ting* } | 丁 | 丁, steeds mager en klein blijven.

si̤ tsoè kaò kaò kaò, 生 作 | |

丨, mager en klein, als een aap, (van menschen).

tsoè kaò pū loē, 作丨舞弄, gekheid met iemand maken.

kaò k'a kaò ts'iú, kaò k'a hì á ts'iú, 脚丨手丨脚戲仔手, steeds met handen en voeten in beweging zijn.

pog p'ê kaò } 作皮丨, Chinesche
» *p'oê* » }
schim vertoonen.

pog kaò hì, 作丨戲, apen comedie spelen.

liáh kaò, 擒丨, een overspeler vatten.

kim si kaò, 金絲丨, gouden en zijden aap, *d. i.* rijke kalant, (in winkels en bordeelen.

tsióh kaò, 石丨, steenen aap, *d. i.* iemand die niet gemakkelijk van zijn geld afstapt.

kaò kā tīng soh } 丨咬斷索,
» » *tuī* » }
de aap bijt zijn touw door.

kaò si ts'êh lò p'oà, 丨死鑼破, zijn aap is dood en zijn gong kapot, *d. i.* in ellendige omstandigheden zijn.

kaò t'aô ts'ú hī } 丨頭鼠耳,
» » *ts'i* » }
een hoofd als een aap en ooren als een rat, *d. i.* leelijk.

kaò tì hiáng tsog, de aap zet de kleine gong op, *d. i.* een dom mensch die zich met iets moeijelijks belast.

(*kaò kā kaò*), 丨咬丨, de eene aap bijt den andere, van twee overspelers die over eene vrouw twist hebben.

(*kaò p'ō ts'ó*), 丨抱棗, als een aap die den dadel omgrijpt, van misdadigers die met een dwarshout onder de armen opgehangen worden.

(*kaò sui sè gaô tsiō ts'iū*), 丨自小善抓樹, al is een aap klein hij klimt behendig in een boom, *d. i.* kunde kent geen ouderdom.

(*kaò pêh tsiō ki kog boé*), 丨扒上旗竿尾, als een aap die op het uiterste eind van den vlaggestok geklommen is, *d. i.* op het toppunt van zijne grootheid zijn.

侯 Kaò Familienaam.

鉤 Kaò *k'it lâng kaò k'ìh*, 被人丨去, gevat worden.

厚 Kaō Dik; zwaar, (zooals tabak), sterk van thee en wijnen; veel, overvloedig, zeer.

kaō laō of *laó*, 丨乇, dik.

kaō póh, 丨薄, dikte.

kaō liaō, 丨料, dikke materialen, stof.

kaō hoàn tsoá, 丨礬紙, dik geäluind papier.

kaō p'ê, 丨皮, dik van schil; onbeschaamd.

kaō hun, 丨烟, zware tabak.

kaō bah, 丨肉, met veel vleesch, (van vruchten).

kaō bīn p'ê, 丨面皮, onbeschaamd.

kaō p'iah, 丨躲, ligtgeraakt.

kaō k'oê } 丨魁, do.
» *k'ê* }

kaō k'e hai, 丨魁骸, veel omslag bij iets maken, (zooals comedianten).

kaō hō tsui, 丨雨水, overvloedige regen.

kaō lé, 丨禮, overvloedige, groote beleefdheid.

kaō sú huì, 丨所費, vele onkosten.

kaō siaò, 丨賬, vele rekeningen, (in tevorderen).

kaō tsi, 丨錢, voor veel geld.

kaō báng, | 蚊, veel muskieten, vol van muskieten.

kaō pún, | 本, groot kapitaal.

kaō k'ièn sèng, | 黎 , zeer bijgeloovig.

鉋 K'ao Schaaf, schaven, afschaven, afschrappen.

k'ao ts'à, | 柴, hout schaven.

k'ao to, | 刀, schaaf.

k'ao á, | 仔, kleine schaaf.

k'ao to hoe, | 刀 花, schaafkrullen, schaafsel.

k'ao hun, | 烟, tabak kerven.

k'ao kèng, | 光, gelijk, glad schaven, schrappen.

k'ao tiá, | 鼎, het roet van een pan afschrapen.

k'ao tsih, | 舌, de tong afschrapen.

k'ao ts'aó, | 草, onkruid wieden.

k'ao p'ê, | 皮, de schil afschaven, schillen.

k'ao k'at làng, | 倚 人, iemand schaven, hem in geld bedriegen.

k'ao siet láng, | 舌 人, iemand zijdelings benadeelen of bespotten.

敲 K'ao Met een stok slaan tegen; naar zich toetrekken, omwenden, wenden met een schip.

k'ao tsing, | 鐘, tegen de klok aanslaan, de klok luiden.

gaò k'ao tiaò làng, 善 | 弔 人, met iemand heen en weer slingeren, *d. i.* wetende dat hij iets hebben moet het hem niet gereedelijk geven.

k'ao hong, *k'ao tsûn*, | 風, | 船, een schip wenden.

k'ao tse lai k'ao tse k'ì. | 來 | 去, heen en weer zeilen (van een schip), overal naar iemand zoeken.

k'oa tsit é lai k'ao tsit é k'ì, | 一 次 來 | 一 次 去, zoowel bij het ontvangen als bij het uitgeven van geld naar zich toerekenen.

鉤 K'ao *k'ao liêm*, | 鐮, speer met een weerhaak.

鬮 K'ao Een lot uittrekken, loten; een lot.

liem k'ao, 拈 |, een lot uittrekken, loten.

lin k'ao, do.

k'ao hun, | 份, uittrekken, loten voor zijn deel.

k'ao su / » *si* } | 書, testament.

tsit k'ao soà, 一 | 線, eene kluwen garen.

口 K'aó Mond; het gat, mond, ingang van iets; mond als numeraal voor menschen, putten, monden.

k'aó k'ì, | 氣, lucht uit de mond; aard van een gesprek

k'aó niû, | 糧, fourage, soldij.

k'aó king, | 供, mondelinge getuigenis.

toā k'aó hàm, 大 | 含, groot van eten.

sió k'aó, 小 |, klein van eten.

k'aó hō, | 號, wachtwoord.

haí k'aó, 海 |, zeegat.

káng k'aó, 空 |, riviermond.

hāng á k'aó tsióh sai, 巷 | 石 獅, als een steenen leeuw aan de ingang van eein steeg, *d. i.* iemanp die veel op zch durft te nemen.

tiàm k'aó, 店 |, deur van een winkel.

k'aó t'aò gú, | 頭 語, stopwoorden: woorden die men gebruikt bij den aanvang van een zin en die bij verschillende personen en verschillende plaatsen afwisselen.

ming k'aó, 門 丨, gat van de deur.

dzip k'aó, ts'ut k'aó, 入 丨, 出 丨, een haven inkomen, uitgaan.

k'aó lē gûn, 丨 禮 銀, haven en belasting geld.

ts'uì k'aó oē, 嘴 丨 話, woord dat iemand op de lippen ligt, (en dat hij zonder voordacht zegt).

tsoē tsoē k'aó siét, 多 多 丨 舌, veel woorden, veel spreken kostend, (zooals eene verwarde zaak).

dzin k'aó, 人 丨, inwoners, bewoners.

k'aó tsaò, 丨 灶, huisgezin, personen die gezamenlijk eten.

tsit k'aó tsí, 一 丨 井, éène put.

tsit k'aó laó hióh, 一 丨 荖 葉, een mondvol, pruimpje siri.

巧 Vernuftig, knap, listig, geslepen.

K'aó *kan k'aó*, 港 丨, listig, geslepen.

k'aó piēn, 辯 丨, vernuftig.

k'aó ling siet piēn, 丨 能 舌 辯, knap, behendig spreken.

k'aó kè pik ts'ut, 丨 計 百 出, listige plannen kwamen er bij honderden bij hem uit.

ts'aò k'aó, 臭 丨, juist, gelukkig, bij geluk.

扣 Aftrekken, disconteren, afhouden; gesp,

K'aò knoopsgat; toeknoopen; een strik, lus.

k'aò tsi, 丨 錢, geld aftrekken, disconteren.

k'aò tû, 丨 除, aftrekken.

k'aò tô toé } 丨 宅 底, do.
» ping té }

k'aò sit, 丨 實, na alle onkosten er afgerekend.

k'aò sin lô, 丨 辛 勞, van iemands loon aftrekken, inhouden.

k'aò k'ìh lai, 丨 起 來, aftrekken.

liú k'aó, 鈕 丨, knoopsgat.

k'aò liú á, 丨 鈕 仔, toeknoopen.

laò k'aò, een strik leggen aan, in een strik vangen, (beesten en menschen).

oáh k'aò, 活 丨, loopende strik, lus.

p'ah oáh k'aò, 打 活 丨, nog een slag om zijn arm houden, in de veronderstellende wijs spreken.

p'ah si k'aò, 打 死 丨, regtuitspreken, zonder een slag om zijn arm te houden.

叩 Het hoofd ter aarde buigen.

K'aò *k'aò t'aô*, 丨 頭, het hoofd ter aarde slaan.

k'aò siā, 丨 謝, buigen, bedanken.

哭 Schreijen, weenen, beweenen.

K'aò *t'i k'aò*, 啼 丨, schreien.

k'aò ts'ám, k'aò ts'an, 丨 餐, zich erg beklagen.

k'aò ko pô, 丨 姑 婆, eene oudtante beweenen, ook van iemand die hard schreeuwt.

梏 Boei, boeien.

K'aò *k'a k'aò ts'iú k'aò*, 脚 丨 手 丨, handen en voeten boeien of geboeid.

kè k'aò, 假 丨, over eene moeijelijkheid komen (zooals door geld te leenen.)

Kaoh

漚 Tot verrotting, gisting doen overgaan,

Kaoh rotten.

kaoh ts'i á, 丨 青 仔, indigo met kalk water doen gisten.

kaoh hák, 丨 礐, in een mestput doen gisten.

kaoh t'ô kaoh pùn, 丨 泥 丨 糞, tot aarde en vuil verrotten,

hè kaoh kaoh kaoh, 貨 | | |, de waar is verstikt, bedorven.

餃 Kaoh Rol, deeg met gekookte spijs er in; rollen.

tsit kaoh, 一 |, een spijs broodje.

kaoh pin ning, | 梹 榔, siri aan pakjes rollen.

kaoh lai kaoh k'i, | 來 | 去, over den grond rollen, (zooals vechtende personen).

tsioh kaoh tioh k'a, 石 | 着 脚, de steen rolt op zijn voet.

k'it ing kaoh k'ih, 被 浪 | 去, door de deining omgeslagen worden.

sim mih lâng tá kaoh ih, wie heeft voor zijne begrafenis gezorgd!

㗭 Kaóh Borrelen, als kokend water.

kaóh kaóh liêm, 絮 | 語, onophoudelijk bij zich zelven mompelen.

kaóh kaóh kóng, | 匕 話, zonder ophouden, herhaaldelijk zeggen.

kaóh kaóh kiò, | 匕 吽, binnens monds, mompelen.

e á kaóh sai / *(oe » tsú »)* | 仔 煮 屎, do. (scheldterm.)

磕 K'aoh *k'aoh laóh*. | 落, geluid van een vallend voorwerp.

K'aóh *k'aóh k'aóh tsùn*, | 匕 戰, beven, rillen.

k'aóh k'aóh tiō, | 匕 趙, do.

kiá k'aóh k'aóh, 驚 | 匕, beven van vrees.

níng k'aóh k'aoh, 軟 | 匕, zeer zacht.

k'i k'i k'aóh k'aóh, 欺 | 匕 匕, rammelen, ritselen (zooals voorwerpen), gedurig op elkander zwetsen; nutteloos; niet volledig; oncompleet (van dingen.)

k'aóh tseh tsū tsih, | 着 多 折, stoot het dan breekt het, (als fijn glas),

kiá kaò k'aóh k'i, 驚 到 | 齒, klappertanden van vrees.

K'aoh *k'aòh k'aóh*, zonder ophouden.

k'aòh k'aòh lai, onophoudelijk, gedurig komen.

Kap

合 Kap Vereenigen; met, benevens.

kap kó, | 股, gezamenlijk aandeelnemen in.

kap iok, 約 |, eene overeenkomst aangaan.

kap pâng, | 房, juist gehuwd zijn.

kap pâng î, | 房 圓, meelballen door het bruidspaar gegeten.

kap soà, | 線, garen in elkander spinnen.

kap ts'eh | 册, een boek binden, inbinden.

kap ioh, | 藥, medicijnen mengen, medicijnen koopen.

kap ts'ùi, | 嘴, naad, aanhechtingsplaats.

kap tsē, kap tsoū, 縫 處, doorloopende naad.

sa kap, 相 |, gezamelijk.

kap lâng kóng, | 人 說, met of tot iemand spreken, zeggen.

ìm kap lìh, 不 | 汝, ik wil niet meer met U (spelen).

Kap *bô kap kiá*, 無 | 子, geene kinderen te verzorgen hebben.

夾 Kap *kap būn* / *» pūn* | 辦, geldkist.

蛤 Kikvorsch, pad.
Kap *ts'ân kap á*, 田 | 仔, do.
ts'iū kap á, 樹 | 仔, boom kikvorsch.
kap á giò á, | 仔 蚧 仔. mosselen.

鴿 Duif.
Kap *kap á*, | 仔, duif.
ts'in ts'iū pàng kap, 却 似 放 |, even als een duif op te laten, *d. i.* onzeker, onveilig.
kap ling, | 鴿, belletje rond den nek van duiven gebonden.
kap ing, | 鶯, valk.

舺 *kap pán tsûn*, | 板 船, schip met
Kap ra's.
Káp *káp káp*, gebonden van eten, niet te droog en niet te nat.
lô káp káp, gebonden, (als water en meel).
k'ó káp káp, gebonden, (als rijst).
káp tsiáh, snelle werking van het eene voorwerp op het andere.
k'a ts'iù káp tsiáh. gaauw, vlug, actief van bedienden, (zoomals bij het aankomen van waren).

闔 Oorspr. dubbele deur, familie; digt-
K'ap doen, digtvallen, met den binnensten of hollen kant naar beneden neervallen; de achter zijde van Chinesche munten waarop de Mandschu karakters staan, munt.
k'ap hú pîng an mah, | 府 平 安 麽. is Uwe familie welvarende! (bel. term).
k'ap lòh lai, | 落 來, neervallen, naar beneden omslaan.
píng k'ap, t'án k'ap, píng t'án k'ap, 翻 |, 亶 |, 亶 翻 |, voorover.
lién k'ap ts'iò, 轉 | 笑, munt en kruis werpen.
tsit k'ap tsit ts'iò. 一 | 一 笑, één munt één kruis, *d. i.* half ja, half neen zeggen.
tsit k'ui tsit k'ap, 一 開 一 |, één open één digt *d. i.* do.

恰 Juist, treffend.
K'ap *k'ap ts'iet*, | 切, juist treffend, juist op den kop.
k'ap ts'in ts'iū. | 似, sprekend gelijkend.

哈 *ióh hún īng ts'iù k'ap lòh k'ì*, 藥
K'ap 粉 用 手 | 落 去, een poedertje in het hol van de hand in de mond gooijen.

磕 *k'áp tioh*, | 着, tegen aanstooten.
K'áp *k'áp t'aô*, | 頭, het hoofd ter aarde buigen.
kòng kaò k'áp k'ì, 言 之 | 齒, klappertanden van vrees.
kiṅ kaò k'áp k'ì, 驚 至 | 齒, do.
sa k'áp, 相 |. tegen elkander aanaanstooten.
k'áp tioh hit ê lâng, | 着 此 個 人. dien man beleedigen, kwetsen, (in zijn spreken of handelingen).
taū hū kap tsiòh-bô k'áp, 豆 腐 與 石 無 |, boonenwrong kan niet tegen een steen stooten, *d. i.* een zwakkere kan zich niet met een sterkeren meten.
k'áp t'aô sih, | 頭 死, zich met het hoofd tegen iets doodslaan, zich met iets niet kunnen vereenigen.
íng íng tuì k'áp, 常 | 對 |, gedurig met elkander in de war zitten.
goá bô k'ì k'áp tioh, 我 無 去 | 着, ik heb er niet aangeraakt, ik heb er niets meê te maken.

kiû k'áp, 求 |, zonder ophouden smeeken.

kap i k'áp, 蛤 伊 |, iemand dringend om iets smeeken.

tak tak k'áp k'áp, tegen iemand aanstooten, iemand willen verhinderen.

láp láp k'áp k'áp, *lett.* overal tegen aanstooten. *d. i.* dan hier dan daar in handel drijven.

Kat

結 Kat Binden, knoopen; knoop. strik. bepalen.

kat tiaò, | 緊, vastbinden.

kat k'ì kin of ùn, | 至 緊, stijfbinden, aanhalen.

p'ah kat, 作 |, een knoop leggen.

kat ts'ai, | 彩, guirlandes uithangen.

kat sṳ́ á toà, | 衫 仔 帶, (kinderen), een fooitje geven.

oáh kat, | 活, strik.

p'ah oat kat, 打 活 , een strik leggen.

ts'é kat, 這 |, do.

si kat, 死 |, dubbele knoop.

kat si, | 死, in den war geknoopt; vastbepalen.

kat si kè, | 死 價, vasten prijs bepalen.

kat t'aò, | 頭, plaats van aanknooping, knoop.

t'aò kat, 改 |, een knoop losmaken.

toá toá kat t'aò, 多 匕 | 頭, niets dan knoopen, *d. i.* moeijelijk te ontwarren, uittemaken.

taī tsì p'ah tsoè tsit kat, 代 至 打 作 一 |, verscheidene zaken komen verward bij elkander.

kat teh hō̤ lìh, | 以 與 汝, afgebonden zal ik het U geven, (zooals een rits duiten), *d. i.* ik zal het U stellig geven.

tse i̤ p'ah siep poeh kat, 一 文 四 十 八 |, op een duit 48 knoopen leggen, *d. i.* zeer gierig.

siṳ kat kik, 過 | 極, al te inhalig gierig.

sṳ á ku kat sṳ liêm, 衫 裾 | 作 夥, met de slippen van zijne kleeren aan elkander gebonden, *d. i.* van elkander afhankelijk..

bák t'aò p'ah tsoè tsit kat, 目 頭 打 作 一 |, er bedroefd uitzien.

kat tiā, | 定, vastbepalen, overeenkomen.

dziét kat, 熱 |, warmte puistjes.

葛 Kat Familienaam.

ū koa kat, 有 瓜 |, betrekking van iemand zijn; nog zaken met iemand aftehandelen hebben.

割 Kat *kat kù* / *» kì* } | 鋸, met geweld bezetten innemen.

墼 Kat *t'ô̤ kat*, 泥 |, ongebakken, in de zon gedroogde, steenen.

桔 K'at Scheppen, opscheppen.

k'at k'ìh lai, | 起 來, opscheppen.

k'at tsui, | 水, waterscheppen.

kām bē k'ṳ toé iā k'at k'ìh, 在 止 底 也 | 去, zelfs den bodem van de boeboerpan uitscheppen *d. i.* niets voor anderen overlaten.

戛 K'at Slaan.

k'at hé, k'iet hé. | 火, vuurslaan.

hé to k‘at of *k‘iet*, 火刀|, vuurslag met toebehooren.

剋 K‘at — *k‘at k‘ó*, |苦, smart leed doorstaan, het zich getroosten.

boē k‘at tit, 未|的, niet te verdragen.

boē k‘at tit k‘ó, 未|得苦, niet langer kunnen verdragen, uitstaan.

k‘ao k‘at lâng 磽|人, iemand in kleinigheden bedriegen.

級 K‘at — *tsit k‘at tsit k‘at* / » *k‘e̤* » » } 一|一|, vol insnedingen.

K‘at — *k‘oà k‘at*, 掛|. binderpaal.

Ke

家* Ke — Huis, woning, huisgezin, familie; huishouden, huiselijk, familie (zaken); personen, lieden.

ke laī, |內, binnen's-huis, huishouden.

k‘iū ke, 居|, wonen.

ke kah, *tsō ke kah*, 甲造|甲, huistelling, volkstelling houden.

ke kah pai, |甲牌, buurtregister.

ke tiŋ̄, |長, hoofd van een dorp of van een handelhuis.

ke si, |私, wapens, gereedschap.

ke koè / » *kè* } |計, do.

ke si tsáp mih, |私什物, huisraad.

ke hé / » *hoe* } |伙, bezittingen.

ke hé t‘aô á, |伙頭仔, meubelen, huisraad.

ū ke hé, 有|伙, bemiddeld.

p‘oà ke p‘oà hé, 破|破伙, zijne bezittingen verliezen.

p‘oà ke kiá, 破|子, een zoon die een huisgezin ruineert.

hoa̱ ke, *koán ke*, 掌|, 管|, een huishouden besturen.

koán ke pò, 管|婆, huishoudster.

ke koàn, |眷, huisgenooten.

sió ke koàn, 小|眷, bijzitten.

k‘iēm ke, 欠|, zuinig in het huishouden zijn.

toā ke sū, 大|事, een huishouden dat veel geld kost.

toā ke k‘aó tsaò, 大|口灶, een groot huishouden.

tsó̱ ke, 祖|, voorouderlijke woonplaats, geboorteplaats.

pún ke, 本|, van denzelfden familienaam.

ke giép, |業, bezittingen.

ke sū, |事, huiselijke zaken.

ts‘in ke, 親|, aangehuwde familie.

oan ke, 寃|, twist, twist hebben.

ts‘ut ke, 出|, Boeddha priester worden.

siók ke, 俗|, de menschen in de wereld, (door Boeddhistische priesters zoo genoemd.)

k‘aò ke k‘aó, 哭|口, den baas des huizes *d. i.* zijn man beweenen, (bij zijn overlijden).

ta ke / *toā* » } 大|, mansmoeder.

ke koa̱, |官, man's moeder en vader.

tai ke, 大|, allen, gezamenlijk.

laū lâng ke, 老人|, oude lieden.

siaò lièn ke, 少年|, jongelieden.

加 Ke — *ke oē* / *ke̱ oā* } |話, redetwisten, kijven.

* Zie verder onder *koo*.

加 Ke Ke Bijdoen, vermeerderen, bijvoegen; verhoogen, meer.

ke t'i, 丨添, vermeerderen.

ke kip, 丨級, in rang verhoogen.

ke kang, 丨工, meer werk aan iets besteden; overbodig werk.

ke tsit pē / » *poē* } 丨一倍, nog eens zooveel.

m sai ke pai, 不使丨次, het is niet meer dan ééns noodig.

ke kiém, 丨歉, meer of minder.

ke tsió, 丨少, do.

ke kiém hó, 丨歉好, meer of min, (zooals het uitkomt) alles is goed.

ke ke è, 丨乜箇, verscheidenen.

ke ke iû kaō kaō soàn, 丨乜油厚乜蒜, meer vet en veel uijen, *d. i.* meer geld geven maar dan ook iets goeds hebben.

雞 Ke *ke kan*, 丨姦, sodomie.

假* Ké Valsch, geveinsd, nagemaakt; den schijn aannemen van, veinzen.

piēn tsin ké, 辯真丨, onderzoeken wat echt en wat nagemaakt is.

ké tsoè / « *tsò* } 丨造, den schijn aannemen van, veinzen.

ké ì, 丨意, geveinsd, niet gemeend.

kè iá (of *iá*), 丨影, schijn aannemen van, geveinsd.

ké lì / » *lè* } 丨○, doen als of .... den schijn nemen als of

ké tsin tiu, 丨真張, do.

ké tsīn tsing, 丨盡情, veinzen het goed te meenen,

---

* Zie verder onder *koe*.

ké k'iēn, veinzen te grijnen, (zooals groote kinderen), iets veinzen, willen doen voorkomen.

ké kut, 丨滑, eigenzinnig, veel van zich zelven denken.

ké k'ik ts'iù boē oē lóh aô, 丨曲唱未落喉, niet gemeende taal kan men niet vlot uiten.

架 Ké Koé Iets onder een voorwerp zetten om het hooger te maken, schragen.

ké kouì / *koé koàn* } 丨高, iets hooger maken, als eene lamp door er iets onder te zetten.

giâ i ké k'a, 夯椅丨脚, een stoel nemen om op te staan.

ké k'a, 丨脚, zich verheffen, (door geld, enz.)

ké k'a ts'iú, 丨脚手, zich wieken bijzetten, tijdelijke hulp van anderen nemen.

ké oá, 丨碗, den bodem van een kom met iets bedekken, ophoogen, (om het geen men er in wil doen meer te doen voorkomen.)

菓 Ké Koé Vrucht.

ké tsí, 丨子, vrucht.

ké tsí hing, 丨子園, vruchtentuin.

kan ké tièm, 乾丨店, kruideniers winkel.

粿 Kè Koè *ké p'in*, 品丨, koek in het algemeen.

sa tè ké bô t'ang tióh kaò sì àh. 三箇丨無可着到四仔, waar drie koeken zijn kan men de vierde niet krijgen, *d. i.* van waar die reeds koopers heeft, kan men niets krijgen.

過 Kè Koè Overschrijden, te bovengaan, aanduider van den comparativus; te zeer, te veel, te buitengaan, overtreden, overtreding, fout; voorbijgaan, voorbij, verleden, aanduider van den verledenen tijd, overlijden, sterven; overgaan, oversteken, over; overgaan op, overdoen aan, overbrengen op, oververtellen, enz.; doorbrengen, slijten, passéren, voorbijgaan, *d. i.* niet blijven hangen aan, geen onaangenaam gevoel of wroeging achterlaten.

kè t'aô 丨 頭, overschrijden, te bovengaan; alte...; aan een ander overgaan (als pacht).

k'ah kè t'aô, 愈 丨 頭, zijn doel voorbijgaand, alte zeer...

kè hān, kè ān, 丨 限, den grens overschrijden.

kè ki, 丨 期, den bepaalden tijd overschrijden.

kè hūn, 丨 份, zijn rang te bovengaan.

kè tō, 丨 度, buiten zijn baan treden (zooals sterren).

tsit ki toā kè tsit ki, 一 枝 大 丨 一 枝, hoe langer hoe grooter, (zooals van boomen in eene rij.)

kè hé, 丨 火, over het vuur houden, roosteren; te veel vuur, aangebrand,

kè sit, 丨 失, fout, kleine overtreding.

king kè, 丨 經, voorbijgaan, bijgewoond hebben.

kè sin, 丨 身, voorbijgaan; sterven, gestorven.

kè liaó, 丨 了, reeds voorbij.

kè bīn, 丨 面, voorbijgaan.

kè bák, 丨 目, voor zijne oogen, (zien).

ki kè liaó, 見 丨 了, reeds gezien hebben.

kè k'ùi, 丨 氣, den geest geven.

kè óng, 丨 往, sterven.

kè sì, 丨 世, do.

kè lō, 丨 路, den weg overgaan, langs den weg.

kè tsuí lâng, 丨 水 人, menschen van de overzijde der (Emoi) rivier.

kè ts'u kè t'éh, 丨 厝 丨 宅, van het eene huis naar het andere gaan, zooals om te babbelen,

tsit dzit kè tsit dzit, 一 日 丨 一 日, van den eenen dag op den andere

kè dzit, 丨 日, den volgenden dag; een dag doorkomen, doorbrengen.

kè ts'ùi kè tsih, 丨 嘴 丨 舌, van den een aan den ander oververtellen.

kè ts'iú, 丨 手, in de hand geven, in eene andere hand laten overgaan.

ēm t'ang kè ts'iú, 不 可 丨 手, geef het niet uit uw hand, draag het niet aan een ander op.

kè k'a kè ts'iú, 丨 脚 丨 手, van den een aan den ander overgeven, door vele handen laten gaan.

kè liaó ts'iú, 丨 了 手, in zijne handen ontvangen hebben.

kè mêng, 丨 門, huwen, (van een vrouw).

kè si lâng k'aó, 丨 仙 人 口, uit de mond van een levend mensch hebben, van iemand leeren die de zaak of taal verstaat.

kè k'aò (of *k'iaò*) *tai* / » » *sū* 丨 竅 事, nu eenmaal zoo aangenomen gebruiken.

hit ê pī oē kè lâng, 此 病 能 丨 人, die ziekte is besmettelijk.

kè siaò, 丨 賬, eene schuld op een derde overdragen.

tùi kè 對 丨, aan een derden persoon afbetalen; onderling vergelijken.

kè ki, 丨 枝, enten, (als boomen.)

kè tsit mi̱, 丨一夜, een nacht door brengen, overnachten.

sìn i ïm kè, 信他不丨, iemand niet gelooven.

kè sim, 丨心, geene wroeging in het gemoed achterlaten.

kè sim tāi / » » *sū* } 丨心事, iets om later geene wroeging te hebben, (b.v. alles voor een zieke beproeven).

liông sim tuì lâng ïm kè, 良丨心對人不丨, men kan het niet over zijn geweten verkrijgen.

ké ì, 丨意, naar zijn zin, in zijnschik.

tsit kè, 一丨, éène keer, één maal.

嫁 Kè Kè̱ Een man trouwen, huwen; uithuwelijken.

kè ang, 丨翁, een man trouwen,

kè ts'oā, 丨娶, huwen (in het algemeen).

ts'ut kè, 出丨, uitgehuwelijkt zijn.

sàng kè, 送丨, eene bruid begeleiden (van de koppelaarster).

kè koe tè koe pe kè kaó tè kaó tsaó / *kè̱ ké toe ke poe* » » *toè* » » 丨雞隨雞飛丨犬隨犬走, die aan een haan getrouwd is volgt hem in zijn vliegen, aan een hond getrouwd dan volgt men hem in zijn loopen, *d. i.* de vrouw neemt den stand van haren man aan.

kè tseng, 丨粧, huwelijks-uitzet, bruidschat.

aō kè, 後丨, hertrouwen, (van eene vrouw).

sui bú kè / » *bó* « } 隨某丨, zijne moeder in haar tweede huwelijk volgen.

冠 Kè *koe kè* / » *koè* } 雞丨, hanenkam.

koe kè hoe / » » *hoa* } 雞丨花, de hanenkam, (bloem).

髻 Kè Koè Bruidsmuts, bruidskapsel; kapsel van vrouwen.

ts'iu̱ t'aô tì kè, 縛頭戴丨, het hoofdhaar opmaken en de bruidsmuts opzetten.

kè lō̱, 丨路, naad in het haar eener vrouw.

oàn pó kè, 灣宝丨, hoofdkapsel van vrouwen.

kè soh, 丨索, ingevlochten koord in het haar eener bruid.

繼 Kè Stief.

kè tsú, 丨子, stiefzoon.

kè lú, 丨女, stiefdochter.

kè hing tē, 丨兄弟, stiefbroeders.

kè toā tsì, 丨大姊. stiefzuster.

kè hū, 丨父, stiefvader.

kè bú, 丨母, stiefmoeder.

計 Kè Bij elkander rekenen, tellen; plannen, beramen; plan, list, streek.

kè sìng, 丨算, bij elkander rekenen, optellen.

kè kiōng, 丨共, gezamenlijk, totaal bedrag.

kè bō̱, 丨謀, een plan beramen; plan.

kè ts'ik, 丨策, plan.

kè tì, 丨智, plan, list.

tók kè, 毒丨, gevaarlijke, venijnige streek, list.

àm kè, 暗丨, geheime list, streek.

tiòng kè, 中丨, in een list vallen.

i kè tsiū kè, 依丨就丨, iemand in zijn eigen list vangen.

kè kaò, 丨較, disputeren, redetwisten.

kip kè, 急 丨, vlug handelend.

價 Kè Kẹ̀ Prijs, waarde.

kè tsi, 丨 錢, prijs,

goân kè, 原 丨, oorspronkelijke prijs.

kè sọ̀, 丨 數, bedrag, de prijs.

si kè, 時 丨, marktprijs

kóng kè, *liēm kè*, 言 丨, den prijs zeggen.

tsoè kè, *p'ah kè*, 作 丨, 打 丨, den prijs instellen.

tó toē kè / *si ti á* „ } 死 猪 仔 丨, buitengewoon lage prijs.

tiaò kè, 條 丨, den prijs doen stijgen, (door niet te verkoopen).

put dzī kè, 不 二 丨, vaste prijs.

put ting kè, 不 等 丨, geen vaste prijs.

lóh kè, 落 丨, afslaan.

解 Kè *kè sàng*, 丨 送, geleiden, escorteren, (zooals goederen).

kè ts'e / „ *ts'ẹ* } 丨 差, een goederen geleider.

架 Kè Kẹ̀ Rek, stander, kapstok, stomme knecht; stalletje.

sa á kè, 衣 丨, kapstok.

ing ko kè, 鸚 哥 丨, papegaaijen banger ook galg.

pit kè, 筆 丨, penseelen stander.

seng ts'ọ́ kè, 酸 醋 丨, olie en azijn stel.

ts'aì kè á, 菜 丨 仔, groenten stalletje.

hi kè á, 魚 丨 仔, vischstalletje.

pai kè á, 排 丨 仔, op een stalletje uitstallen.

枷 Kè Kẹ̀ Schandbord waarmede misdadigers om den hals te pronk staan, cangue, halsblok.

giâ ke, het schandbord dragen.

giâ bọ̄ kè, met zijne vrouw opgescheept zitten.

siang lien kè, 双 連 丨, dubbele cangue, (voor 2 pers).

kè hoān, 丨 犯, tot de cangue veroordeelden.

p'ah kè, 打 丨, do.

t'ṅg kè, 脫 丨, het schandbord afdoen.

kè hō; 丨 號, de soort van een cangue; de inscriptie op de cangue.

ū tsít lāng è taī tsì kè teh, 有 一 件 事 丨 的, er zit mij iets dwars in den weg, in de maag.

t'ṅg tsit è kè, 脫 一 箇 丨, van eene last, moeielijkheid, verlost zijn.

低 Kē Kẹ̄ Laag, laag in prijs.

kè tsi kē / *kè* „ *kẹ̄* } 價 錢 丨, laag van prijs.

koâi kè / *koân kẹ̄* } 高 丨, hoog of laag, van plaats en prijs.

kē gûn / „ *gin* } 丨 銀, slecht zilvergeld.

tsui ts'ē ts'ē laò lóh kē / *o ts'ẹ̄ ts'ẹ̄* „ „ „ } 水 淤 匕 流 落 丨, het water ruischt naar de laagste plaats, *d. i.* de straf komt, meestal op den laagsten neer.

kē hè, 丨 貨, mindere waar, lager in soort.

kē tseng, 丨 粧, lagere waren, (in soort).

kē siâ gûn, 丨 錫 銀, geld van laag gehalte.

koâi kē king. 高 丨 肩, scheef van schouders, mank.

t'iâ koâi bò t iâ kē, gehoorgeven aan wat het voordeeligste, niet aan wat minder is.

kē k'a kaó boh siū koui teh tîng ê bah
» » » boeh siō koàn » » « »
丨脚狗不思高棹上肉, de hond op korte pooten wil denken om het vleesch op eene hooge tafel te krijgen, te verlangen naar iets dat men niet verkrijgen kan.

哽 Ké Kẹ́ — *kẹ́ sih*, 丨死, verslikken.
Zich verslikken (halverwege de keel blijven zitten).
kẹ́ tióh, 骾着, in de keel blijven steken.
kẹ́ tioh nâ aô, 丨在咽喉, in de keel blijven steken.
kẹ́ tioh hî kut, 丨着魚骨, een graat in de keel krijgen.

科 K'e — *k'e tsi*, 丨錢, geld ophalen, bijeen halen.
k'e p'aì, 丨派, naar elks vermogen opleggen (zooals belasting), verdeelen over.
goā k'e, 外丨, uitwendige geneeskunst, chirurgie.
laī k'e, 内丨, inwendige geneeskunst, medicijnen.
pâng k'e, 房丨, (de zes) departementen in een mandarijn-bureau.

稽 K'e Ke — Onderzoeken, navorschen, nazien, nagaan.
k'e k'ó, 丨考, onderzoeken, navorschen.
k'e tsa, 丨查, do.
k'e ts'at, 丨察, nazien, onderzoeken
k'e k'àm, 丨勘, do.
bô k'e k'ó, 無丨考, niet nategaan, niet te bepalen, (van getal).
bû k'e e oē, 無丨之言, woorden waarop men niet aan kan.

窖 K'e — *k'e á*, 丨仔, kleien smeltkroes.

葵 K'e — *k'e sì*, 丨扇, ronde bladwaaier.

詼 K'e — *k'e hai*, 丨諧, oorspr. gekheid maken, (in de volkstaal) maniėr van gaan of doen.
kaū k'e hai, 丨多諧, veel omslag bij iets maken (als comedianten).
kiâ k'e, 行丨, maniėr van loopen, (van tooneelspelers).

啟 K'é — *su k'é* / *si »* } 書丨, mandarijnschrijver, schriftelijk mandarijnwerk.
tsing k'é t'ì aū k'é toē, 前丨天後丨地, van voren het aan den hemel en van achteren aan de aarde zeggen, (als eene ontvangene gunst).

睨 K'é — *ti ko ìm áh p'oā gō niû k'é ting*,
猪哥姆伴五娘丨燈, de oudevrouw leelijk als een beer, (mannelijk varken) vergezelt *gō niû*, (eene beroemde schoonheid) om het lantaarnfeest te zien, *d. i.* een leelijk mensch die een fraaijen en prachtig gekleeden vergezelt.

架 K'è — *k'è pit*, 丨筆, een penseel op een drager leggen.
k'è k'a, 丨脚, zijne voeten door iets schragen, op iets doen rusten.
k'a k'è, 脚丨, voetbankje.
k'è sa, 丨衫, kleėren ophangen.
taô k'è, 投契, goed overeenstemmen, (van pers.)

跛 K'è k'oè — *k'è k'a*, 丨足, lam, mank.

欹 K'è K'oè ẹ — *k'è ts'iú*, 丨手, een stijve arm.
sa k'è / *sio k'ẹ̀* } 相逆, niet harmonieren, in disharmonie zijn met.
tùi k'è, 對丨, dito.
k'è k'ang, 丨空, in het gat blijven

bokken, (zooals een schroef), niet geleidelijk gaan (van eene zaak), niet harmonieren (van personen).

k'ê tioh, 礙着, blijv en hangen in .., in zijn val opgehouden worden door

taī tsì k'ê teh, 大志礙的, die zaak is hangende, nog niet afgedaan.

Keh

隔 Keh Kęh — Schot beschot, tusschenwand; splitsen, afschieten (als een vertrek in tweeën;) door een tusschenwand gescheiden, aangrenzend; gescheiden, met één tusschen beiden.

keh tsoè nn̄g keh, 丨作二丨, in tweeën afschieten.

keh tn̄g, 丨斷, do.

king keh } *kan kęh* } 間丨, apartementen, vertrekken.

keh piah, 丨壁, aangrenzend.

keh piah pàng, 丨壁房, aangrenzende kamer.

keh piah ê lâng, 丨壁之人, de buren.

keh piah pùn tìng hé, 丨壁分燈火, zijn buurmans licht uitblazen, *d. i.* zich bemoeijen met zaken die hem niet aangaan.

keh piah tiòng tsìn sū iû t'aô puih kaò tn̄g 丨壁中進士羊頭拔到斷, daar zijn buurman *Tsin-sū* is geworden (van vreugde) zijn geit zoo trekken dat de kop er af is, *d. i.* tot zijn eigen nadeel zich overeen anders voordeel verheugen.

keh hiu, 丨鄉, aangrenzend dorp.

keh tsit king } *» » kan* } 丨一間, een huis tusschen beide.

keh nî, 丨年, een jaar tusschen beide.

keh dzit, 丨日, een dag tusschen beide.

keh hia pê tsiū } *» » pò tsiò* } 丨靴抓癢, met een laars tusschenbeiden zich krabben, *d. i.* niet op den kop raken.

(*keh soa ïm tsai kiá t'i*), 丨山不知子啼, is men door een berg gescheiden dan weet men niet dat zijn kind weent, *d. i.* verwijderde vrienden weten elkanders rampen niet.

挌 Keh Kęh — Afweren, pareren.

keh tsū, 丨住, do.

格 Keh — Regel, vaste vorm; lijn.

kek sik } *» sit* } 丨式, vaste vorm, regel, model.

keh kiòk, 合丨合局, manier om iets te doen; voorkomen, gesteldheid.

dzī keh, 字丨, schrijftransparent.

p'áh keh, 畫丨, linieeren.

keh ts'ioh, 丨尺, liniaal.

骼 Keh Kęh — Beenderssysteem, geraamte.

kut keh, 骨丨, do. gestalte.

toā keh tsing, 大丨種, van groot ras.

toā keh koe, 大丨雞, kippen van een groot ras.

膈 Keh — *lòh ē keh*, 落下丨, in de ondermaag komen.

keh sit, 丨食, het gegetene weer overgeven.

郭 Keh Koeh — Familienaam.

keh á hî, 丨仔魚, knorhaan.

逆 Kèh — Zich verzetten tegen, niet gehoorzamen; weêrspannig, tegenstrijdig met, in den weg liggen, niet overweg kunnen met.

ni kéh, | 違, zich verzetten tegen, overtreden.

keh bīng līng, | 命 令, zich tegen een bevel verzetten, het niet gehoorzamen.

kéh tsih hī k'ang kui of *ming nig* | 截耳孔毛, onuitstaanbaar om aan te hooren.

hoai hoai kèh kéh, 橫 乜 | |, onbesuisd weêrbarstig.

kéh kun, | 筋, wederspannig.

kéh ts'iú bé / » » *boe* | 尾 手, in den weg zijn.

kéh k'a bé, | 脚 尾, do. van geen nut.

sa kéh, tuì keh, 相 |, 對 |, met elkander overhoop liggen.

p'ah kéh, 打 |, met elkander overhoop liggen. (en daarom scheiden.)

kéh lai kéh k'ì, | 來 | 去, niet overweg kunnen met elkander; dwars over elkander liggen.

kéh p'iah, | 僻, weêrspannig, eigenzinnig,

kéh i tse p'iah, | 伊 齊 僻, iemands zwakke zijde, hoofdfout, aanvoeren.

kéh tioh i é kun, | 着 伊 肋, do.

kéh tòh, | 倒, omstruikelen.

koe kéh kéh kaó / *ke kéh kéh* » | 假 格 乜 叫, kakelen, in angst schreeuwen, van kippen.

客* K'eh K'eh Gast, bezoeker, kennis, vriend; kalant, handelaar in, koopman; passagier.

lâng k'eh, 人 |, gast, bezoeker.

k'eh lâng, k'eh á, | 人, Hakka-Chinees (van de Cant. uitspraak *hák*).

* Zie verder onder *k'oeh*.

k'eh á oē, | 仔 話, Hakka dialect.

(*k'eh á pun iêm*), | 匕 分 鹽, als Hakkas die zout uitdeelen, *d. i.* verward door elkander schreeuwen.

k'eh t'ia, | 廳, receptie kamer.

tsoè k'eh, 作 |, te gast zijn, gehuwd zijn, (van vrouwen).

sin k'eh, 新 |, nieuwe gast, nieuw aangekomene.

tsú k'eh, 主 |, vaste kalant.

hó k'eh, 好 |, goede kalant.

tsui k'eh, 水 |, reizende koopman.

goā k'eh, 外 |, buitenlandsche, vreemde gast.

tsiep k'eh, 接 |, gasten ontvangen.

hoē k'eh, 會 |, kennissen, vrienden bezoeken.

si k'eh, 辭 |, bezoeker afwijzen.

k'eh mîng tsoē, | 門 多, vele kennissen of kalanten hebben.

hó k'eh tsîng, 好 | 情, gastvrij.

k'eh pâng, | 房, logeerkamer.

k'eh tièm, k'eh koán, | 店, | 舘, logement, herberg.

k'eh koa, | 官, logés, (zoo door den logementhouder genoemd).

hè k'eh, 貨 |, handelaar; supercargo.

tah k'eh, 搭 |, passagier, (op een schip).

k'eh t'aô, | 頭, hoofd van passagiers (thans ook) koelie-ronselaar.

bô tsi k'eh, 無 錢 |, iemand die geen geld heeft.

k'eh tsiaó, | 鳥, ekster.

(*k'eh tsiaó tsièm ki t'aô*,) | 鳥 占

枝頭, als een ekster die het puntje van één tak inneemt. *d. i.* zonder regt de hoogste plaats innemen.

k'eh tsiaó pò ēm tiòh hi / *k'e̤h „ „ „ „ „* } | 鳥報不着喜, de ekster verkondigt onware vreugde, *d. i.* iets mededeelen dat later blijkt niet waar te zijn.

契 K'eh — *k'eh hia*, | 兄, overspeler, hoerenlooper.

缺 K'eh, K'oeh — Ontbreken, weinig hebben van .... gebrek hebben aan; eene openstaande post, vacatuur.

k'iam k'eh, 欠 |, ontbreken.

k'eh ing tsi, | 用錢, gebrek aan geld hebben.

k'eh kiá, | 子, weinig kinderen hebben.

k'eh k'eh k'eh, | | |, weinig voorhanden.

tsió k'eh, 少 |, weinig gebrek aan, veel voorhanden; weinige vacatures.

ts'ut k'eh, 出 |, eene vacatuur veroorzaken

haū k'eh, 候 |, op eene openvallende plaats wachten.

pó k'eh, 補 |, eene vacatuur aanvullen.

t'at k'eh, 撻 |, eene opengevallen, plaats aanvullen, (van soldaten of bedienden.)

k'eh tsit k'eh ē koa, | 一 | 的官, er is eene mandarijnpost opengevallen..

K'eh, K'ū — *lui k'eh k'eh tâng* / (*„ k'ū k'ū „*) } de donder ratelt.

K'eh, K'oah — *k'eh k'eh tiō* / (*k'oah k'oah „*) } rillen, bibberen, (van koude of vrees).

搁 K'éh — *k'éh sih*, | 死, verstikken, wurgen.

戰 K'éh — *k'éh k'éh tiō*, | | 兢匕, beven van koude of vrees.

kiá k'éh k'éh, 驚 | 匕, do.

k'éh k'éh tsùn, (of *ts'oah*), 凜 | 慄, van koude of vrees rillen.

tsuì ē taó k'éh k'éh hō, 嘴下斗 | | 呼, van koude klappertanden.

嗄 K'e̤h — *k'e̤h k'e̤h háo*, | 匕吼, dof geluid van slecht geld.

loh k'e̤h, 落 |, gedurig hoesten.

k'e̤h ts'ut lai, | 出來, de strot digt knijpen zoodat men iets niet inslikken kan.

Keng

光 Keng, Kuī — Licht, helder; helder van geest, glad, nakt, niet bezittend.

t'i keng, 天 |, dageraad, bij het aanbreken van den dag.

géh keng mi, 月 | 夜, maneschijn nacht.

keng ts'iū, | 昌, helder, ruim, (van een plaats.)

t'i keng ts'iū, 天 | 昌, de hemel klaart op.

t'ang keng, 窗 |, doorzigtig, transparent.

keng t'ang, | 窗, van helder doorzigt.

bák tsiu ēm keng, 目周不 |, niet helder uit zijne oogen kijken. *d. i.* zijne menschen niet onderscheiden.

keng kià ē lâng, | 鏡的人, een man van helder doorzigt.

hâng tsing keng 行情 |, de markt door en door kennen.

keng si, | 生, glad en frisch (zooals nieuwe voorwerpen.)

keng kút, | 滑, glad.

kè keng, 括 〡, gladmaken.

siu keng, 收 〡, glad, gelijkmaken.

keng pi gùn, 〡 邊 銀, geld met gladden rand.

tsit bīn keng keng tsit bīn si mêng, 一 面 〡 一 面 生 毛, aan den eenen kant glad aan den anderen kant behaard, *d. i.* eensklaps van goed kwaad worden.

lìn keng t'aò, 溜 〡 頭, blootshoofd.

t'èng keng keng, lìn keng keng, 脫 〡 〡 溜 〡 〡, gansch naakt.

keng k'ō k'ō, 〡 浩 匕, niets bezittend.

ts'iah k'oát k'oát keng k'ō k'ō, 赤 鉠 匕 〡 浩 匕, bar. dor. niets bezittend.

ïng k'ì keng keng, 用 去 〡 匕, geheel opgebruiken.

扛 Met twee personen dragen.

Keng *keng kang*, 〡 工, draagkoelie.

keng kiō, 〡 轎, een draagstoel dragen.

tuì keng, 對 , te zamen dragen; elkander in iets helpen.

缸 Pot met wijden mond.

Keng *tsui keng*, 水 〡, steenen watervat.

dziō keng, 尿 〡, pispot.

捲 Oprollen; draaijen, dwarlen, spiraalvormig.

Kéng

Kuį *kéng ts'ah*, 〡 聯, eene teekening oprollen.

kéng ts'ióh, 〡 蓆, een mat oprollen.

kéng lê, 〡 螺, slak, alikruik.

kéng lê hong, 〡 螺 風, dwarlwind.

tsui kéng lê, 水 〡 螺, het water vormt een draaikolk.

kéng néng tsēng, 〡 輪 轉, draaijend van een hoos of draaikolk.

ling kéng tsui, 龍 〡 水, de draken trekken het water op, waterhoos, figuurlijk van een groot huishouden waar veel verbruikt wordt.

kéng nèng nèng leh tsit sok á, 〡 匕 匕 者 一 束 仔, in een pakje bij elkander gerold.

筒 Holle buis, pijp, koker; rijstmaat, (20ste van *taò*).

Kéng

Kui *k'ì kéng*, 氣 〡, lucht, longpijp.

nâ aò kéng, 咽 喉 〡, slokdarm.

huih kéng, 血 〡, bloedader.

mêng kéng, 毛 〡, porien van het ligchaam.

ts'àng mêng kéng, 葱 毛 〡, kippenvel krijgen.

ts'ang kéng, 葱 〡, holle buis of pijp.

ts'aò bak si kéng, 臭 肉 生 〡, in kwaad vleesch vormen zich gaten.

hé kéng, 火 〡, blaaspijp.

sai p'ī k'ang kéng, 使 鼻 空 〡, door den neuskoker antwoorden.

pùn p'ī k'ang kéng, 從 鼻 空 〡, door de neus blazen als koeijen, snorken.

kéng k'im i, 〡 琴 椅, sofa.

bi kéng, 米 〡, rijstmaat.

廣 *kéng tang*, 〡 東, Canton.

Kéng *kéng tang bák kiàⁿ tsaī lâng kah bák*, 〡 東 目 鏡 在 人 合 目, of een Canton bril naar iemands oogen

Kuį is hangt van den persoon af.

kéng tang tê e, 〡 東 茶 鍋, als een Canton theepot waarin het water spoedig raast (*ts'ang*), *d. i.* iemand die zich steeds beklaagt.

鋼 Staal.

Kéng *gùn kéng*, 潤 〡, gloeijend ijzer blusschend tot staal maken.

kìng tsui, | 水, de glans op staal.

nē kìng, 勁 |, hard staal.

to bō kìng, 刀 無 |, het mes is niet scherp.

ts'è kìng, 初 |, bros staal.

槓 Kist, koffer; stokken aan een draagstoel.
Kìng

gûn kìng, 銀 |, kisten met geld.

lâng kìng, 籠 |, manden en kisten, bagage.

siu kìng, 箱 |, kisten en koffers.

kiō kìng, 轎 |, stokken van een draagstoel.

絭 *oū kìng tsî*, 換 | 錢, een nieuw koord met eene medaille of zakje met
kìng offerasch om den hals doen, (als op den 7den dag 7de maand).
Kuì

貫 Een rist van 1000 duiten; aan een rist doen, aanrijgen, doorrijgen; doorsteken.
Kìng
Kuì

tsî kìng, 錢 |, een rist cash.

nēng kìng tsî, 二 | 錢, twee risten duiten 2000.

kìng tsî, | 錢, duiten aanrijgen, aanristen.

kìng sa liên, | 相 連, aan elkander rijgen.

gû kìng p'ī, 牛 | 鼻, een koe een ring door den neus doen, iemand onschadelijk maken.

kìng hī, | 耳, de ooren doorsteken, (voor oorbellen).

kìng t'aò kèh k'ì, | 透 過 去, door en door steken (als met een mes).

Kìng *kìng bîn*, half wakker half droomende schreeuwen.

糠 *bí k'eng*, 米 |, rijstkaf.
K'eng

ts'o k'eng, 糟 |, kaf,

beh k'eng, 麥 |, zemelen.

k'eng tai, | 臺, kaf insekt, niets beduidend wezen.

k'eng èh
„ oéh } | 幼, kafstof.

k'eng k'eng k'eng, | | |, zeer fijn, subtiel, (zoowals kleine water insekten.)

圈 Als zeer goed aanteekenen.
K'eng *k'eng k'o*, 環 |, do.

p'ah liû k'eng, 打 鈕 |, krullen voor goedkeuring trekken.

勸 Vermanen, verbieden; aanraden, aanzetten.
K'èng
K'uì

k'èng lâng, | 人, iemand vermanen aanraden.

k'èng sè tsiū ê lâng, | 世 上 的 人, de menschen op de wereld vermanen, een afschrikkend voorbeeld geven.

k'ó k'èng, 苦 |, dringend vermanen.

sa k'èng sa k'èng, 相 | 相 |, elkander vermanen, troosten.

k'èng hô, | 和, tot eendragt vermanen, verzoenen.

k'èng tsiú, | 酒, aanzetten om meer wijn te drinken.

藏 Bergen, opbergen, wegbergen; verbergen, wegstoppen, geheim houden.
K'èng

k'èng tsî, | 錢, geld opbergen.

siu k'èng, 收 |, opbergen.

k'èng koan kiū, | 棺 柩, een lijkkist nog eenigen tijd boven aarde laten staan.

boē k'èng tit, 難 | 的, niet te bewaren (zooals vruchten); niet kunnen inhouden.

k'èng ts'át, | 賊, dieven verbergen, huisvesten.

k'ìng bát, 丨 密, verstoppen, geheim houden.

k'ìng pō, 丨 步, een geheim verborgen houden.

壙 Gat voor een graf.
K'ìng *tai siang k'ìng*, 埋 双 丨, in een dubbel graf begraven, (twee lijken).

tsoè làng k'ìng k'ìng k'ìng, stijfhoofdig trotsch zijn.

Ki

枝* Tak, twijg; numerale, voor lange dunne
Ki voorwerpen.

ts'iū ki, 樹 丨, boomtak.

tsiep ki, 接 丨, op een tak overenten.

ts'aó ki, 草 丨, grashalmpje.

ki hiu } 丨 香, als een offerstokje *d. i.* mager.
» hio }

ki ki ki, 丨 丨 丨, zeer klein, subtiel.

機 Datgene dat iets in beweging brengt,
Ki beweegoorzaak, drijfveer, machinerie; omstandigheden, gelegenheid.

ki koan, 丨 關, doorzigt in eene zaak.

ki koan kièn sik } 丨 關 見 識, schrander.
» » » sit }

ki pâng, 丨 房, machine kamer, werkplaats, (zooals in weverijen).

ki bit, 丨 密, geheim.

ki hoē, 丨 會, gelegenheid.

hó ki hoē, 好 丨 會, goede gelegenheid.

t'àn ki hoē, 順 丨 會, van de gelegenheid gebruik maken.

kièn ki dzi tsok, 見 丨 而 作, de omstandigheden afziende daar naar handelen.

幾 *ki ki...* 丨 匕, op het punt zijn van....
Ki het scheelt niet veel of .....

iaó sù ki, 要 事 丨, kan er nog door middelmatig.

基 Fondament, grondvest, het begin, de
Ki oorsprong, grond waarop later voortgebouwd wordt.

toē ki } 地 丨, fondamenten.
tē » }

p'ah toē ki, 下 地 丨, de platte grond voor iets maken.

ts'iû ki, 牆 丨, fondament voor een muur.

ki giép, 丨 業, bezittingen, eigendommen.

k'ai ki, 開 丨, den grondslag tot iets leggen.

ting ki, 定 丨, den troon aanvaarden.

譏 *ki ts'ì*, 丨 刺, bespotten, uitlagen.
Ki

箕 Wan, zeef; mandje om aarde enz. in
Ki te dragen; de kringvormige strepen op den binnenkant der vingers.

poà ki, 簸 丨, wan.

pùn ki, 糞 丨, aarde mandje.

pùn ki ts'iù, 糞 丨 嘴, dom weg heen spreken.

饑 Honger, hongersnood.
Ki *ki hng*, 丨 荒, hongersnood.

ki bin, 丨 民, volk dat door hongersnood lijdt.

肌 *bô ki hu*, 無 丨 膚, geen spieren
Ki of vleesch hebben, (van een uitgeteerden zieke).

朞 Een vol jaar.
Ki *ki liên hók*, 丨 年 服, éénjarige rouw.

嘰 *pik ki* } 嗶 丨, long ells.
Ki *pit »* }

* Zie verder onder *ku*.

Ki *âng ki ki*, vuurrood.

乩 *ki tông*, *tâng ki*, ｜童, tooveraar.
Ki

Ki *sig ki ki*, schel van geluid.
ki ki kū kū, tjilpen.
ki ki kiaoh k'aoh, zwetsen.
ki ki haó, sissen, piepen.
a ki. term voor vreemdelingen.

指* Duiden op, aanduiden, aanwijzen.
Ki *ki ki toh tóh*, ｜匕盤匕, op iemand wijzen en hem uitschelden.
ki tsai } ｜指, wijsvinger.
» *tsai* }
(*ki tang koa k'áp tióh hô lô*.) ｜冬瓜碍着胡盧, op den wintermeloen wijzende tegen een pompoen aanstooten, *d. i.* tegenover iemand die een zeker gebrek heeft datzelfde gebrek in een andere laken.

已 Zelf, zich zelf,
Ki *tsū ki*, 自｜, zelf.
siú ki, 守｜, zijn pligt betrachten.

紀 *king ki*. 經｜, beroep, bezigheid.
Ki *ni ki*, 年｜, leeftijd, ouderdom.
tsit ki ni. 一｜年, een tijdsverloop van twaalfjaar.

几 Smal tafeltje.
Ki *tê ki*, 茶｜, tafeltje om thee enz. op te zetten, een knaap.
ki toh, ｜棹, hoog langwerpig tafeltje.
ki siōng ki, ｜上｜, het eene tafeltje op het andere, *d. i.* bediende van een bediende zijn.

記 Opschrijven, opteekenen; herdenken,
Ki onthouden, nadenken, zich herinneren souvenir; merk, teeken.
pún t'aô kì liên maō, 從頭｜年貌, iemands leeftijd en signalement opgeven.
kì tsaì, ｜載, opteekenen.
kì lòh k'ì, ｜落去, opschrijven.
kì siàu, ｜賬, do. opteekenen, (eene post).)
ting kì, 重｜, dubbeld opschrijven.
dzit kì, 日｜, dagelijksche opteekening, dagboek.
kì liēm, ｜念, herdenken.
kì sim, ｜心, steeds denken aan.
kì sim kì koa, *kì sim kì ti*. ｜心｜肝｜心｜致, steeds onthouden.
kì tit, ｜得, onthouden, zich herinneren.
boē kì tit. 不｜得, vergeten.
kì ti, ｜致. geheugen.
hó kì sì } 好｜性, goed van geheugen.
» » *sè* }
piaó kì, 表｜, souvenir, bewijs, om elkander later te herkennen.
kì hō, ｜號, merk. teeken, signaal.
kì dzīn. ｜認, merk, bewijsteeken.

痣 Sproet, wrat.
Ki *o kì*, 烏｜, zwarte sproeten.
kì ts'iu, ｜鬚, haar op een wrat.
tsu se kì, 硃砂｜, roode sproeten.
hô sin sai kì, 狐蠅屎｜, eene menigte zwarte stipjes op het gelaat.

既 Reeds, alreeds.
Ki *kì dziên*, ｜然, reeds.
kì sī. ｜是, daar het reeds .... is, waarom den nog ....?

計 *hé kì*, 夥｜, bediende of compagnon
Ki in eene zaak.

---

* Zie verder onder *kú*.

旗* Vlag, vaandel.
Ki
ki hióh, vlaggen.
ki ts'i } ｜幟, vaandels.
» *ts'i* }
ki tì, ｜帶, wimpel.
ki hō, ｜號, seinvlag, onderscheidings vlag.
ts'ai ki, ki ts'ai, 彩｜,｜彩, vaandel, standaard.
ki ē làng, ｜人, de Mandschu soldaten.
pat ki, 八｜, de acht vaandels van het Mandschu leger.
k'iā ki, 竪｜, een vlag opzetten, planten, (van mandarijnen ook van oproerlingen).
ki koa, ｜杆, vlaggestok.
ki koa k'oeh } ｜杆合, palen of
» » *néh* }
steenen waartusschen een vlaggestok staat.
ki koa taò, ｜杆斗, vierkante bank boven aan een vlaggestok.
ki koa hó tè ling, ｜杆虎隨龍, de tijger beneden aan de vlaggestok wil den draak aan den top volgen *d. i.* op iemands zak loopen.

棋 Schaakspel.
Ki
ki poâ, ｜盤, schaakbord.
bu ki, 武｜, schaakspel.
ts'iū ki, 象｜, olifantspel.
bùn ki, 文｜, soort damspel.
ki dzí of *tsí*, ｜子, schaakstuk, (360).
ui ki, 圍｜, schaak of dam spelen.
ki kik } ｜局, een opgezet schaak-
» *kiók* }
spel.
tióh ki, 釣｜, een schaakstuk winnen.
sat ki, 殺｜, iemand een spel schaak of dam doen verliezen.
k'im ki su hoā, 琴｜書畫, muziek, schaakspel, letterkunde en schilderkunst.

椅 *ki làm hiu*, ｜楠香, reukhout
Ki

奇 Vreemd, verwonderlijk, wonderbaarlijk, buitengewoon, zeldzaam.
Ki
ki k'á, ｜巧, wonderlijk, vreemd, zich verwonderen.
ki koài, ｜怪, verwonderlijk, vreemd, buitengewoon.
ts'ut ki, 出｜, wonderbaarlijk, buitengewoon
kièn ki, 見｜, zeldzaam, vreemd.
ki siòng, ｜相, wonderlijk voorkomen.
ki hing koài tsōng, ｜形怪狀, wonderbaarlijk voorkomen, handelwijze.
ki siâ, ｜蛇, slang als geneesmiddel gebruikt.

其 *ki û* } ｜餘, daarbuiten, overigens.
» *î* }
Ki

期 Vaste tijd, termijn.
Ki
hān ki siaò, 限｜賬, een termijn voor betaling bepalen.
tsiū (of *tíng*) *ki*, *ē ki*, 上｜下｜, eerste en laatste termijn van betaling.
boé ki siaò, 買｜賬, tegen een vasten betaaltermijn koopen.
kè ki, 過｜, over den termijn.

祈 Smeeken, bidden.
Ki
ki tó, ｜禱, bidden.
ki kiû, ｜求, om hulp bidden.

* Zie verder onder *kû*.

蜞 Kî *kî lîn*, | 麟, fabelachtig beest dat bij de geboorte en den dood van Confucius zou gezien zijn. (de beschrijving komt veel met den giraffe overeen.

Kî *kî bú kî kiúh*, (of *kiaoh*,) kakelen, levenmaken, (zooals kinderen),

忌 Kī *kī sîn*, | 辰, dag waarop alle openbare vermakelijkheden wegens den dood des keizers verboden worden, sterfdag (van iemand) deze wordt jaarlijks herdacht.

tsoè kī / *tsò* » } 做 |, offeren aan zijne voorouders, (op den sterfdag).

tsiṅ kī, 正 |, sterfdag van een overledene.

bién kī, 愍 |, geboortedag van een overledene.

技 Kī *kī gé*, | 藝, ambacht, beroep.

妓 Kī *ts'iong kī*, 娼 |, hoer, ligtekooi.

己 Kī *ka kī*, 自 |, zelve.

欺 K'i Bedriegen, misleiden; met minachting behandelen, verdrukken.

k'i p'ièn, *k'i moâ*, | 騙, | 瞞, bedriegen.

sa k'i, 相 |, elkander bedriegen.

k'i kun, | 君, zijn vorst bedriegen.

k'i hū, | 父, verdrukken.

k'i bú (of *báng*), / » *báng* } | 負, verdrukken, kwellen.

k'i hū ka tsoáh boē tsiáh bí / s » « » *bē* » » } | 負 蟉蠘不食米, minachtend denken dat een kakkerlak geen ongekookte rijst kan eten, *d. i.* gering over iemand denken.

崎 K'i *k'i k'u*, *k'i k'i k'u k'u*, | 嶇 匕, steil.

攲 K'i Schuins, schuinsstaand, schuinshouden, overhellen.

ts'iâ k'i / *siâ* » } 斜 |, schuinshouden,

k'i ts'iâ, | 斜, schuinsstaand.

k'i tsit ping, | 一 平, naar eenen kant overhellen.

t'án k'i, *t'án k'i sin*, | 身, schuinsch, overhellend; schuinshouden, overhellen.

k'i tsim, | 枕, schuins op het hoofdkussen liggen.

k'i k'iao, *k'iao k'i*, | 翹, 匕 |, met omwegen, niet regtuit (van prs).

起 K'í Opstaan, rijzen, stijgen; aansteken, ophouden, omhooghouden; ligten, opligten; oprigten, bouwen; doen opkomen; doen ontstaan; in beweging, op de been brengen; beginnen, een aanvang maken met; achter ww. beteekent het: er in slagen, voltooijen; maal, keer, numerale voor zaken en bij elkander hoorende personen.

k'i sin, | 身, opstaan; vertrekken, (op reis); beginnen.

k'i sin tsoè, | 身 造, beginnen te doen.

t'aô k'i sin, 頭 | 身, zoo juist, daareven,

peh k'i, 爬 |, opstaan.

k'i kè, | 價, in prijs stijgen, opslaan,

kè tsi k'i loh, 價 錢 | 落, op en afslag.

k'i bé, | 馬, te paard stijgen; bij iemands vertrek.

k'i tiâ, | 錠, het anker ligten.

k'i hè, | 貨, goederen lossen.

p'ai k'i tó, 歹 | 倒, lastig te hanteren (van voorw.)

k'i hé, | 火, vuur aansteken.

k'i hé lô, | 火爐, de kagchel aanmaken.

k'i p'ê, | 皮, de huid of schil afnemen.

t'aô kiáh ı̄m k'i, 頭舉不 |, het hoofd niet omhoog houden, *d. i.* moedeloos zijn.

k'i ts'ù, | 厝, een huis bouwen.

k'i ts'iú, | 手, een begin maken met, beginnen.

k'i t'aô, | 頭, het begin; in den beginne.

k'i t'aô soah bé, | 頭煞尾, begin en eind.

k'i tì, | 致, in den beginne, grondslag; de reden waarvan iets zoover gekomen is.

k'i ki, | 基, do.

k'i toé, | 底, oorspronkelijk, aanvankelijk.

tsiaò k'i kang, 照 | 工, volgens den regel.

k'i ping bé, | 兵馬, een leger op de been brengen.

k'i làng sa p'ah, | 人相打, menschen bij een brengen om te vechten.

k'i ke si, | 家私, wapens ter hand nemen, (zooals vijandige dorpen.)

k'i lô tāng siā, | 鑼動社, door het slaan op de gong, een dorp op de been brengen.

k'i hók, | 服, weer in betrekking komen, (na den rouw).

k'i gī, | 義, op het idèe komen voor . . . het plan voor iets maken.

k'i oai làng, *k'i k'iau làng*, | 冤人, iemand onder eenig voorwendsel kwellen, beüchten.

k'i kièn, | 見, beweegredeu, oorzaak.

k'i ts'ong ts'i, | 閂刺, aanleiding tot twist geven.

k'i ē ts'i, twist en daardoor rampen veroorzaken.

boē boē k'i, 賣未 |, niet kunnen koopen, (niet genoeg geld er voor hebben.)

tsoè tit k'i, 作直 |, kunnen doen volvoeren.

tsoè ı̄m k'i, 作不 |, niet kunnen volvoeren, niet goed opgaan.

pān tit k'i, *pān ı̄m k'i*, 辦的 |, 辦不 |, kunnen, niet kunnen regelen.

k'i tāng, | 動, lastig vallen, (meer bel. term.)

tsit k'i taī tsì, 一 | 大至, eene zaak.

toā k'i àn, 大 | 案, gewigtige regtszaak.

sa k'i, 三 |, driemaal.

tsit k'i è làng, 一 | 的人, bij elkander hoorende, of gelijktijdige menschen.

tsoè k'i hó, 作 | 好, goed doen, gew. als *k'i* gehoord.

齒 K'i Tand, kies; tand van een rad.

ts'uì k'i, 嘴 |, tanden, gebit.

tiong k'i, 中 |, voorste tanden.

k'i kun, | 根, wortel van een tand.

k'i hoā, tandvleesch.

ling k'i, 乳 |, melktand.

aō tsan k'i, 後層 |, maaltand.

k'i bin, | 抿, tandenborstel.

k'i t'ok, | 托, tandenstoker.

bán k'í, 拔 ｜, tanden trekken.

t'uì k'í, 脫 ｜, tanden wisselen.

tsiù k'í, 咒 ｜, holle kies.

ang pô k'í, 翁 婆 ｜, *lett.* man en vrouw tanden, *d. i.* de twee voorste tanden (waarvoor vrouwen veel zorg dragen).

kā k'í kun, 咬 ｜ 根, knarsetanden.

ting k'í, 頂 ｜, achter elkander gegroeide tanden.

poâ bé k'í, 盤 馬 ｜, met puntjes, (*lett.* paarden tanden), afzetten, veel werk aan iets besteden.

t'ih k'í, 鉄 ｜, met ijzeren tanden, *d. i* halstarrig.

ts'ia lún k'í, 車 輪 ｜, tanden van een rad.

去 K'ì Gaan, weggaan, uitgaan; achter een werkwoord beteekent: weg, op als *t'éh k'ìh*, wegnemen, *tsiák liáh k'ìh*, geheel en al opgegeten, in dit geval wordt het toonloos, en als *k'ìh* uitgesproken.

lai k'ì, 來 ｜, komen en gaan; zullen gaan; laat ons gaan.

it tit k'ì, 一 直 ｜, regtuit, regt door gaan.

sui k'ì sui lai, 隨 ｜ 隨 來, zoo zeggen en zoo terugkomen.

oē tit k'ì, 能 得 ｜, kunnen gaan; het kan er door, tamelijk.

bóng k'ì, 罔 ｜, het kan er nog door, zoo zoo.

lai k'ì siaò, 來 ｜ 賬, berekening van inkomsten en uitgaven.

kóng oē k'ì tò, 說 話 ｜ 到, het eene oogenblik zus, het andere zoo spreken.

k'it k'ì tò tò, ｜ 七 到 到, zeer veranderlijk (in zijn spreken).

k'ì tò hiém, ｜ 到 險, nog veel gevaarlijker.

k'ì tò haī, ｜ 到 害, integendeel, nog schadelijker.

kóng lai kóng k'ì, 說 來 說 ｜, over en weer spreken.

kiâ lai kiâ k'ì, 行 來 行 ｜, over en weer loopen.

氣 K'ì Damp, lucht, atmospheer; het leven gevend bezielend beginsel; adem; karakter, aard; levensvuur, drift; woede, toorn, vertoornen, vertoornd; gesteldheid, toestand.

k'ì bī, ｜ 味, lucht, geur; aard, karakter.

t'i̱ k'ì, 天 ｜, weersgesteldheid.

k'ì kńg, ｜ 管, lucht, longpijp.

tsaú k'ì, *siet k'ì*, 走 ｜, 洩 ｜, de kracht of geur verliezen.

bô k'ì mêh, 無 ｜ 脉, eene zwakke pols hebben.

k'aó k'ì, 口 ｜, lucht uit de mond; aard van een gesprek.

tsì k'ì, 志 ｜, energie.

ū tsì k'ì ê lâng, 有 志 ｜ 的 人, iemand die eergevoel, naijver bezit.

ū k'ì tsiet, 有 ｜ 節, gevoel van eer hebben.

k'ì ūn, ｜ 運, lot, noodlot,

k'ì siòng, ｜ 相, uiterlijk voorkomen.

k'ì k'aì, ｜ 概, do.

k'ì sò, ｜ 數, vooruitzigt, voorkomen van den toekomst.

k'ì sè, ｜ 勢, algemeen voorkomen, toestand.

ū tsai k'ì, 有 財 ｜, gelukkig in financiele zaken.

huì k'ì, 廢 ｜, lastig te doen.

k'ì sik, ｜ 色, gelaatskleur.

K'I

siū k'ì, 受 |, vertoornd, vertoornd worden.

k'ì si làng, | 死 人, iemand zeer vertoornd maken.

lō k'ì, 魯 |, toorn.

dzim k'ì, *lún k'ì*, 忍 |, zijne toorn inhouden.

tsiáh k'ì, 食 |, vuur voor iets opvatten, moet alle geweld willen doorzetten.

ū hé k'ì, 有 火 |, vurig, opvliegend.

忌 K'ì Een afschrik hebben van . . . niet mogen lijden.

tò k'ì, 妬 |, jaloersch.

k'ì sin, | 辰, de sterfdag van iemand die reeds overleden is.

棄 K'ì Verwerpen, verstooten, wegwerpen; verachten.

k'ì hièm, | 嫌, verstooten; versmaden, verachten.

k'ì dzin, | 人, verachtelijk, niets waardig mensch.

tsū pō tsū k'ì, 自 暴 自 |, zich vergooijen.

k'ì sak, | 去, verstooten, (als eene slechte vrouw).

k'ì ts'e t'iòng ts'iep, | 妻 寵 妾, zijne vrouw verstooten en zijne bijzit tot gunsteling maken.

k'ì sè, | 世, gestorven, dood.

器 K'ì Werktuig, gereedschap.

k'ì kū / » *kī* } | 具, gereedschappen, huisraad.

ke k'ì, 家 |, meubelen, huisraad.

k'ì hai, | 械, wapens.

siaó k'ì, 小 |, kleingeestig, bekrompen, met weinig tevreden.

put sing k'ì è làng, 不 成 | 的 人, iemand die voor niets tegebruiken is, waarvan niets teregt zal komen.

K'I

蜞 K'i *gō k'i*, 蜈 |, bloedzuiger.

gō k'i pó, 蜈 | 補, als een ledige bloedzuiger, *d. i.* iemand met geweld uitzuigen.

gō k'i kā kap, 蜈 | 咬 蛤, als een bloedzuiger die een kikvorsch beet heeft, bijt, *d. i.* niet loslaten (zooals vechtende kinderen.)

騎 K'i *k'i má*, | 馬, anker van een horologie,

k'i hō tsi sè làng hā, | 虎 之 勢 難 下, positie van iemand die op een tijger rijdt en er moeijelijk af kan, *d. i.* in netelige zaken zijn waar aan men zich niet onttrekken kan.

sī k'i, 生 |, een sterk zaamgetrokken likteeken op het hoofd hebben.

tsit liëp k'i, 一 粒 |, een op getrokken likteeken.

柿 K'ī *áng k'ī*, 紅 |, persimmon.

k'ī á tsiep, | 汁, persimmom sap, gebruikt om parapluien enz. te verwen.

tsìn k'ī, 浸 |, in kalk gelegde persimmom.

忌 K'ī Een tegenzin hebben, (tegen eten).

k'ī k'ik, | 尅, niet houden van ..., niet kunnen verdragen.

sī k'ī / *sio* » } 相 |, niet van elkander houden, elkander niet kunnen verdragen.

ùi k'ī / *ùi* » } 畏 |, niet houden van ...,

kìm k'ī, 禁 |, zich onthouden van ..., verboden (als om besm. zieken te bezoeken.

si si k'ī . . . , 死 乜 |, een doodelijke afkeer hebben van . . .

sù bù k'ī tán è làng, 肆 無 | 憚

之人, iemand die volstrekt niet, verlegen, bevreesd is.

更 Ki̱ Kẹ Wacht van twee uren, zij beginnen 's avonds om 7 en eindigen 's morgens om 5 uur.

au ki̱, dzī ki̱, 按｜, 二｜, de eerste en de tweede wacht

ki̱ liaò, ｜寮, wachttoren.

ki̱ hu, ｜夫, nachtwaker.

tsiú ki̱, 支｜, de wacht houden.

ts'ī ki̱, 差｜, do.

sûn ki̱, 巡｜, wachtloopen.

sit ki̱, 失｜, niet op wacht zijn, zijn wacht verzuimen.

ki̱ k'ók, ｜梏, klap van den nachtwacht.

ki̱ ting, ｜燈, wachtlamp.

ki̱ lô, ｜鑼, wachtgong.

ki̱ ts'im, ｜深, diep in den nacht.

ki̱ hiu̱, ｜香, vuurstokje dat juist in een wacht opbrandt.

kuí ki̱ tsûn, 幾｜船, hoeveel wachten aan boord? *i. d.* hoe lange zeereis?

ki̱ ki̱ ts'ị }
» » ts'ẹ } ｜匕醒, bij elke wacht wakker, *d. i.* glad, op zijne hoede zijnde.

經 Ki̱ Weven, spinnen, (zooals een web).

ki̱ pò, ｜布, doek weven.

kap i ki̱, kap i p'áng, 同伊｜同伊紡, met iemand weven en spinnen, *d. i.* onafgebroken rusie hebben.

ki̱ si, ｜絲, een web spinnen.

kap i ki̱ si, 同伊｜絲, iemand eindelooze moeijelijkheden maken.

lô ki̱, 落｜, het kompas,

Ki̱ *kaó sa̱ ki̱*, 狗相｜, paren, spelen van honden.

鹼 Potasch, soda, loog.

Ki̱ *ki̱ tsuí*, ｜水, loogwater.

ki̱ hu, ｜灰, loogasch.

ki̱ iû, ｜油, vet dat uit potasch druipt?

teh ki̱, 壓｜, met water, loog uit asch doen druipelen.

ki̱ soa, ｜沙, bezinksel, poeder van loog.

tsiáh ki̱, 赤｜, potasch eten, *d. i.* het bitter te verantwoorden hebben.

ts'aò ki̱, 臭｜, bittere smaak (zooals aan iets dat te dikwijls opgewarmd is.

枷 Ki̱ Kẹ Vlegel.

lièn ki̱, 連｜, do.

見 Kì̱ Zien; achter ww. bet. het; gewaar worden; bezoeken, eene visite afleggen bij; ontmoeten; beduidt ook, elk, alle.

ǐm ki̱, 不｜, niet te zien krijgen, niet te vinden zijn.

p'ah ǐm ki̱, 失不｜, verliezen.

ts'uì ki̱ bák ki̱, 嘴｜目｜, voor zijne eigen oogen gezien hebben.

k'oà ki̱, (*ki̱h*) 看｜, zien.

p'ih ki̱, 臭｜, ruiken.

t'ia̱ ki̱, 聽｜, hooren.

bô dzit t'ang sa̱ ki̱, 無日可相｜, elkander nimmer meer kunnen terugzien.

sa̱ ki̱ bīn, 相｜面, elkander zien, ontmoeten.

ki̱ tioh, ｜着, ontmoeten.

paì ki̱, 拜｜, een bezoek brengen.

pín kì, 憑 ｜, een bezoek brengen, lagere aan hoogere.

tiaô kì, 朝 ｜, op audientie bij den keizer gaan.

tiaò kì, 召 ｜, ter audientie roepen.

kì tsin, ｜ 眞, inderdaad, in wezenlijkheid.

kì tsìng, ｜ 証, aan den dag komen, uitkomen (zooals een ziekte).

boē kì, tsìng tìt 未可 ｜ 証的, het daglicht niet kunnen zien (van eene zaak).

bē kì su iâ, 未 ｜ 輸 赢, nog niet weten aan welken kant de overwinning is.

kì kui, ｜ 鬼, eene onwaarheid zeggen.

kì lâng hó, ｜ 人 好, met ieder een goed zijn.

kì tsî sí. ｜ 錢 死, op het zien van geld sterven, *d. i.* geldwolf.

kì tsoè kì hó, ｜ 造 ｜ 好, al wat hij doet doet hij goed.

kì mīng kì bô, ｜ 問 ｜ 無, op alles wat men vraagt, neen antwoorden.

kì t'ia kìh kì kóng, ｜ 聽 ｜ 說, alles wat men gehoord heeft zeggen.

kap lâng kì si si, 與 人 ｜ 生 死, met iemand op leven of dood vechten of twisten.

桁 Kì Dwarsbalken van een dak; de staafjes van een rekenboek.

dzī tsáp kì ê sìng poâ, 二 十 ｜ 的 箕 盤, een rekenbord met twintig staafjes.

dzī kì i sing tsoè tiong tsit, 二 ｜ 楹 作 中 職, de tweede balk klimt op tot nokbalk, van een bijzit die na den dood der wettige vrouw de baas wordt.

kè kì, 加 ｜, op eene volgende afdeeling overbrengen.

k'ong tsit kì, 空 一 ｜, een afdeeling tusschen open laten, (zooals bij aanduiden van 108 enz.).

kià kì, 寄 ｜, zoolang op het eene staafje laten staan om het later op een ander over te brengen.

墘 Kì Rand van een tafel, kopje enz.

kì kì, ｜ 匕, op den rand, op het randje.

hai kì, 海 ｜, zeestrand.

moá kì, 滿 ｜, boorde vol.

k'ong kim kì, 鑲 金 ｜, goud randje, (zooals aan koppen).

lîm kì, 臨 ｜, op het uiterste randje.

tī hí tsui kì nìh, 在 水 ｜ 的, op den rand van het water zijn, *d. i.* dringende nood, in moeijelijke omstandigheden.

ts'ù kì, 厝 簷, rand van een dak.

baó kì, 卯 ｜, om den rand geslagen, (zooals de omslag van een boek.)

攀 K'ì Vastgrijpen, vasthouden, beethouden; zich vastklimmen aan, opklouteren.

k'ì lâng ê king t'aô, ｜ 人 肩 頭, iemand bij de schouder vast grijpen.

k'ì sa á ku / *„ „ „ ki* ｜ 衫 仔 裾, aan de panden van zijn kleed vasthouden.

k'ì lâng k'eh ｜ 人 客, gasten vasthouden, niet willen laten weg gaan.

k'ì k'ip, ｜ 扱, zich vasthouden aan zekerheid op iemand.

bô k'ì bô toà, 無 ｜ 無 帶, niets hebben om zich aan vast te houden, (zooals aan iemand die geene relaties heeft).

gaô k'ì ke, 善 ｜ 價, knap het huis houden besturen.

k'i k'i puih puih, | 匕 拔 匕, vasthouden en trekken, (zooals iemand dien men niet willen laten weggaan.

k'i ts'iú, | 手, bij de hand beet houden; lastig als kinderen.

ts'iú k'i, 手 |, lastig, grijnend, (zooals kinderen die steeds gedragen willen worden).

k'i ts'iū peh piáh, | 墻 扒 壁, tegen muren op klouteren.

k'i ts'ū tin, | 樹 籐, slingerplanten tegen een boom.

k'i piah tin, | 壁 籐, klimmers tegen een muur.

k'i bô tsui p'éh } *„ „ „ p'oéh* } | 無 水 沫, zelfs geen schuim om zich aan vast te houden, in uiterste nood zonder de minste hulp.

鉗 Tang, knijptang.
K'i

k'i á, | 仔, do.

hé k'i, 火 |, vuurtang.

ïng gô k'i ting lai k'i tiuô, 用 吳 釘 來 | 住, met klamp spijkertjes of krammen vast krammen.

梏 *k'â k'i* } *„ k'aô* } 脚 |, voetboeijen.
K'i

Kia

寄 Toevertrouwen aan de zorg van, in
Kia handen stellen van, opdragen aan; verzenden, overbrengen overmaken, tijdelijk wonen of doen wonen te....

kià hè | 貨, goederen consi.neren, verzenden,

kià t'ok, | 托, opdragen, belast met.

kià tik put kià sit, | 得 不 | 失, men draagt iemand iets op opdat het teregtkome en niet dat het verloren ga.

kià hù, 付, opdragen.

kià tsiáh kià toā, | 食 | 住, door een ander opgebragt worden' (van behoeftige kinderen).

kià bai, | 閩, een ander een bezoek voor zich laten afleggen.

kià oē, | 話, mondelings overbrengen.

kià gûn, | 銀, geld overmaken.

kià p'oe, | 批, een brief verzenden.

kià tah, | 搭, overzenden, (geld waren enz).

kià tiā, | 錠, het anker voor den boeg laten hangen.

kià siā k'i kū lâng kong, | 聲 去 與 人 說, iemand doen te weten komen.

kià hē teh, | 住 的, zoolang deponéren.

kià si, | 生, parasiet.

kià k'a. | 足, tijdelijk er gaan wonen.

kià ka, | 監, zoo lang in de gevangenis opsluiten.

崎 Steil.
Kiā *kiā á*, | 仔, trapjes, trappen.

kiā á tsân, | 仔 層, trapjes.

kiā kâh ná piah nih, 的 似 壁 的, zoo steil als een muur

aō piah soa kiā, 後 壁 山 |, de achter bergen zijn steil. *d. i.* hij heeft vermogende menschen om op te steunen.

tsiū kiā, lóh kiā, 上 |, 下 |, trapjes op en afgaan.

sa tsàp lák kiā, 三 十 六 |, de 36 trapjes, (naam van een straat in Emoi).

奇 K'ia Oneven; een stuk van een paar; nummer voor kisten, koffers, manden, ringen.

k'ia géh, *k'ia dzit*, 丨月, 丨日, oneven maand, dag. (1ste 3de enz.)

tī k'ia, of (*k,a*), 箸丨, eetstokjes.

k'ia k'a, *tog k'ia*, 丨脚, een enkel stuk van een paar.

tsit k'ia oé, 一丨鞋, éene schoen.

siang k'ia, 雙丨, een paar, beiden, *b. v.* eetstokjes enz.

tsit k'ia láng, 一丨籠, een mand.

tsit k'ia ts'iú tsi, 一丨手指, een vinger ring.

sik k'a hút, *sik k'ia*, 釋迦佛, Boeddha.

騎 K'ià Rijden op, berijden.

k'ià bé / » *bé* 丨馬, paardrijden.

k'ià pò bé ê tsa bó, 丨報馬的女人, een boosaardige vrouw, vrouw die de broek aan heeft.

k'ià láng ê bé, 丨人的馬, op een ander mans paard rijden, *d. i.* met een ander mans geld handel drijven.

k'ià láng ê tsi, 丨人的錢, met een ander mans geld handelen.

k'ià bé long / » *bé* » 跨住, zitten als of men te paard zat.

t'án hoai sin k'ià kè k'ih / » *hoai* » » *koè* » 側身丨過, elkander dwars inzeilen.

k'ià láng ê tè, 丨人的地, beslag op iemands waren leggen; zich door iemands goederen securiteit geven.

tsing si sq k'ià, 前生相丨, de beesten paren, dekken.

竪 K'iā Opzetten, oprigten, regt op zitten; regt opstaan, opstaan, staan; post eener deur.. stijl.

k'iā ni, 丨桅, een mast opzetten.

k'iā ki, 丨旗, een vlag oprigten,

k'iā sam tó, 丨三斗, een houten tusschenschot opzetten.

k'iā pai, 丨牌, een bord voor zijn winkel opzetten.

k'iā tit, 丨直, regt opstaand.

t'án k'iā, 從丨, regtop.

k'iā sin, 丨身, op de voeten, regtop staande, (van een afgodsbeeld).

k'iā k'i sin, 丨起身, opstaan.

sīng kaò k'iā k'i lai, 先到丨起來, zoo vrij gelaten dat hij u tegen het lijf opstaat, (van honden); door te veel toegevenheid het respect uit het oog verliezen.

k'iā pan, 丨班, in twee gelederen staan, (aan beide kanten van een mandarijn.

k'iā k'a hioh siēn, 丨脚遏病, staande uitrusten.

k'iā ts'ī, 丨市, uit nieuwsgierigheid overal blijven staan kijken.

k'iā t'ing, 丨騰, staan wachten.

k'iā k'a, *k'iā hong*, 丨脚, 丨風, op den uitkijk, wacht staan, (zooals dieven).

k'iā pe hi, *k'iā ts'àn*, *i*, 丨爬的, op de handen loopen.

k'iā liên, 丨輦, moeijelijkheden maken.

k'iā t'ui, 丨梯, ladder.

mêng k'iā, 門丨, deurpost.

k'iā t'iaō, 丨柱, regt opstaande pilaren, pilaren opzetten.

tsioh mêng k'iā, 石門丨, steenen deurstijl

k'iā kông, 丨槓, regt opstaande deurstaken.

伽 K'iā *k'iā lâm iâ*, | 藍 爺, plaatselijke Boeddhistische god.

居 K'iā Wonen, bewonen, zijn in.

k'iā ke } | 家, wonen.
» ke̱ }

k'iā k'i | 起, do.

k'iā ts'ù, | 厝, een huis bewonen.

k'iā géh, | 月, een maand verblijven te

k'iā soa̱ ê lâng, | 山 的 人, bergbewoner.

k'iā tsu pâng, | 書 房, een school bewonen, houden.

k'ṳi hà, k'iā seng hà, | 喪 孝, in den rouw zijn.

K'iā *k'iā k'a* (of *kó̱*) *lai boé*, gezamenlijk in vereeniging met anderen koopen.
k'iā hé sit, zijn eigen huishoudon hebben.

k'iā ts'ò̱, azijnmaken.

驚 Kia̱ Vreezen, bang zijn, verschrikken, bevreesd zijn voor.

kia̱ kiá̱, | 慌, ontstellen, schrikken.

k'ia̱ k'i̱h, | 的, vreezen dat . . . , uit vrees dat.

kiā uì } | 畏, vreezen dat . . . , uit
» uì̱ }
vrees dat, . . . , op dat niet.

kia̱ si, | 死, doodelijk verschrikt, bevreesd.

tioh kia̱, 着 |, schrikken.

kia̱ t'ià, | 痛, kleinzeerig,

kia̱ sim, | 心, omzigtig, voorzigtig.

ts'i̱ kia̱, 生 |, schrikken, schuw zijn.

p'ah ts'i̱ kia̱, 打 生 |, aan het schrikken maken.

kia̱ p'oà tá̱, | 破 胆, voor zijn leven den schrik van iets hebben.

kia̱ sin kia̱ mia̱, | 身 | 命, doodsbeangst

京 Kia̱ Hoofdstad van het rijk.

kia̱ sia̱, | 城, hoofdstad, Peking.

pak kia̱, lâm kia̱, 北 |, 南 |, Peking, Nanking.

kia̱ pò, | 報, Peking courant, staatscourant.

kia̱ ts'ao, | 抄, afgeschreven, do.

tsiū̱ kia̱, 上 |, naar de residentie (Peking) gaan.

kia̱ koa̱, | 官, Peking manderijnen.

Kia̱ *kia̱ lâng*, vuil, smerig.

kia̱ si lâng, do.

kia̱ si tī lâng, do.

子 Kiá̱ Kind, zoon.

si̱ kiá̱ } 生 |, baren, een kind ter
se » }
wereld brengen.

tsa bó̱ kiá̱, 女 |, dochter.

kiá̱ saì, | 婿, schoonzoon, bruidegom.

pē kiá̱, 父 |, vader en kind.

kiá̱ sun, | 孫, nakomelingen.

iū̱ kiá̱ } 養 |, een gekocht kind op-
iō̱ « }
voeden.

piaó kiá̱, 鴇 兒 |, hoerenkind.

tsáp tsing kiá̱, 什 種 |, do.

gaî kiá̱, gōng kiá̱, 呆 |, 戇 |, dom kind, dom mensch, stommerik.

kiaó pi̱ kiá̱, 賭 博 |, dobbelaar, (minachtend.)

kiá̱ dzi, | 兒, kinderen.

k'oè kiá̱, 缺 |, aangenomen kind.

鏡 Kià̱ Spiegel; lens, kijken; van helder doorzigt.

bīn kià̱, 面 |, spiegel.

bák kiâ, 目 〡, bril.

gán kiâ, 眼 〡, do.

hién bi kiâ, 顯 微 〡, mikroskoop.

p'òng kiâ, 凸 〡, do.

kiâ àh, 〡 盒, toilet-doos.

tsiò kiâ, 照 〡, in den spiegel kijken.

kiâ kè, 〡 架, toilet-spiegel.

kiâ tai, 〡 臺, do.

kiâ siu / » *sio* } 〡 箱, toilettafel met laden.

kiâ pin, 〡 屏, lijst van een schilderij.

hī kiâ, 耳 竅 〡, trommelvlies.

keng kiâ ê lâng, 明 〡 之 人, een man van helder doorzigt.

hè sik kiâ, 霞 色 〡, door en door kennis van waren hebben.

hàm kiâ, 凸 〡, bolle, vergrootende lens.

tiaò kiâ, 召 〡, bijhalende lens, kijkers.

kūn sī kiâ / *kīn* » » } 近 視 〡, bril voor bijzienden.

kiâ tú kiâ, 〡 廚 〡, als twee spiegels tegenover elkander, *d. i.* elkanders inzigten door en door zien, kennen.

kiâ kiâ, 〡 〡, door en door kennen.

pik hoa kiâ, 百 花 〡, veelhoekige spiegel.

行 Kiâ Loopen, gaan, begaan; een gang, troep menschen; gangbaar, gezocht; doen, handelen, handelwijze; werken als medicijnen, gisten als bier, in werking zijn; doen gaan, zenden, rondzenden.

kiâ lō, 〡 路, loopen, gaan.

kiâ k'ui, 〡 開, uit den weg gaan.

kiâ lâm tsaó pak, 〡 南 走 北, van Zuid naar Noord trekken, reizen.

kiâ ts'a lō, 〡 差 路, den verkeerden, slechten weg opgaan.

kiâ ī̆m tió lō, 〡 不 着 路, een verkeerden weg opgaan, verdwalen.

kiâ tīn, 〡 陣, marcheren van soldaten.

kiâ soa, 〡 山, naar eene goede plaats voor graven uitzien.

kiâ tsûn, 〡 船, varen, op een schip dienen, een schip besturen.

sa p'oā kiâ, 相 伴 〡, te zamen gaan, elkander vergezellen.

k'ang kiâ, 空 〡, gaan zonder iets meê te nemen, voor niets gegaan zijn.

bô ts'ai k'a k'it lō kiâ, 無 采 一 路 〡 到 脚 酸, voor niet gegaan zijn.

boē kiâ tit, 未 〡 的, niet te begaan, het gaat niet.

kiâ té lō, 〡 短 路, een eind van zijn leven maken.

tâng kiâ ê lâng, 仝 〡 的, reis genooten.

tsit kiâ ū loā tsoē lâng, 一 〡 有 若 干 人, hoe vele menschen waren er bij die reis.

si kiâ, kiâ si, 時 〡, 〡 時, algemeen gezocht, gewild.

kiâ k'a pō, 〡 脚 步, de passen leeren, (als tooneelspeler); handelen, niet werkeloos zijn.

p'aí só kiâ, 歹 所 〡, slechte handelingen.

kiâ pō, 〡 步, zetten doen, (bij het schaakspel); marcheren, (als rekruten).

kiâ ki, 丨 棋, schaakspelen.

kiâ táh, 丨 踏, handelingen, handelen, omgang.

hó kiâ táh, 好 丨 踏, fraai van gang; goed te begaan (zooals een weg).

kiâ soá, 丨 徙, uitspanning nemen.

kiâ gi, 丨 儀, handelwijze.

kiâ lé, 丨 禮, groeten, salueeren.

kiâ pâng, 丨 房, coïtus uitoefenen.

kiâ sim mi̤h hâng tsing, 丨 什 麽 行 情, wat is de markt prijs?

ióh k'ì teh kiâ, 藥 氣 旣 丨, de medicijnen werken.

kiâ k'ì, 丨 氣, werken (van medicijn.)

kiâ laī, 丨 利, op interest uitzetten.

kiâ king, 丨 經, de menses hebben.

kiâ p'oe sin, 丨 批 信, een brief zenden.

kiâ bûn, 丨 文, dépêches rondzenden.

kiâ toā, kiâ p'ièn, kiâ dzī, 丨 單, 片, 丨 字, eene circulaire rondzenden.

規 Kiâ — *nâ kiâ*. 籃 丨, rand van een mand.

健 Kiā — Sterk.

tsng kiā } *tong* » } 當 丨, in de kracht zijns levens.

kiā tsâng, 丨 欉, een stevige boom, *d. i.* stevige ferme kerel.

ióng kiā, 勇 丨, sterk, stevig.

sin kiā, 身 丨, do.

kà bú put tsi kiā, 酵 毋 不 只 丨, de gist is zeer sterk.

ts'ò kiā, 醋 丨, de azijn is sterk, straf.

件 Kiā — Nummer voor zaken.

ták kiā, 逐 丨, alles, elk ding.

kiā kiā, 丨 乜, alle dingen, zeer sterk.

sū kiā, 事 丨, zaken.

àn kiā, 案 丨, regtszaken.

iù liép kiā, 細 軟 丨, fijne, breekbare waar.

mi̤h kiā, 物 丨, voorwerpen.

K'ia — *k'ia póh*, zwak, niet sterk.

kiah

挑 Kiah Giah — Uittrekken, (zooals een splinter).

kiah ts'oa, 丨 刺, een splinter uittrekken.

k'a aū kiah, 脚 後 丨, uitstekend gedeelte aan den enkel.

舉 Kiáh — Omhoogsteken, omhooghouden, opheffen; in de hand houden, handteeren van lange dunne voorwerpen, dragen.

kiáh koai, 丨 高, omhooghouden.

kiáh t'aô, 丨 頭, het hoofd opheffen.

kiáh bák, 丨 目, de oogen opslaan.

kiáh t'aô kiáh hī, 丨 頭 丨 耳, overal onbeschaamd rondkijken.

kiáh t'aô ts'ù, 丨 頭 厝, klein zijgebouw.

kiáh ting, 丨 燈, een lantaarn dragen inzonderheid van de kinderen die bij een huwelijks processie in draagstoelen vooruit gaan.

t'oè i kiáh ki, 代 伊 丨 旗, voor iemand de vlag opsteken, *d. i.* de twist beginnen.

kiáh sim mih ki, 丨 什 麽 旗, welke vlag ophoudende *d. i.* op welke manier, met welke list.

31

kiáh ki, | 軋, een gespleten wilgen tak met twee personen los in de handen houden, en uit de karakters die een genius die tak in het zand doet schrijven, zijne toekomst opmaken.

kiáh piáh, | 筆, het penseel in de hand houden, handteeren.

kiáh to, | 刀, een zwaard in de hand houden.

kiáh tsiem tsi, | 針 指, de naald handteeren.

kiáh ts'iú p'ì, | 手 勢, met gebalde vuist voor elkander staan.

Kiáh Opwippen, opspingen.

king t'aô kiáh kiáh, 肩 頭 | ヒ, hoogopstaande schouders.

tsing sin kiao kiáh, 精 神 橋 |, helder van geest.

屐 Klomp, regenschoen; hak, van een schoen.

Kiáh *ts'à kiáh*, *bák kiáh*, 柴 |, 木 |, klompen.

bák kiáh tseh } 木 | 仄, hak van
» » *tseh* } eene vrouwenschoen.

oê aū kiáh, 鞋 後 |, hak van een schoen.

業 Ambacht, beroep. Zie *giép* en *giáh*.

Kiáh *tsáp kiáh t'àn bô t'ang tsiáh*, 什 討 無 食, met tien ambachten nog de kost niet verdienen, twaalf ambachten en dertien ongelukken.

鈌 Een gat uit.

K'iah *k'ang k'iah*, 空 |, hoekjes en gaatjes.

p'oà k'iah, 破 |, een spleet reet in iets maken.

soa kiah, 山 |, rots spleet.

ts'ân kiah, 田 |, gat, spleet in den voren van een rijstveld, (om het water te laten uitloopen.

t'at k'iah, | 塞, een rijstveldgat digt maken; voor niets anders dengen dan om een gat te stoppen. (scheldterm).

tsit k'ang tsit k'iah, 一 空 一 |, alle hoekjes en gaatjes, alles tot in de kleinste bijzonderheden.

p'ī k'ang p'ī k'iah, 鼻 空 鼻 |, in alle gaten en reeten snuffelen, doorsnuffelen.

t'at tē k'iah, 塞 地 |, (alleen goed zijn om), de gaten van den grond te stoppen, *d. i.* een nietswaardig mensch zijn.

tsit k'ang tú tsit k'iah, 一 空 抵 一 |, met het eene gat het andere gat stoppen, *d. i.* juist met zijne inkomsten zijne uitgaven bestrijken.

Kiang

鐵 Kiang *toā oá kiang*, 大 碗 |, een groote kom, kop.

强 Kiāng *kiāng sìng*, | 性, slecht, boosaardig van karakter.

sìng tò kiāng, 性 |, do.

kiāng ts'ùi, | 嘴, halsstarrig in zijn spreken.

鏗 K'iang *k'iang k'iang haô* (of *tâng*), | 鏘. ritselen rammelen, het geluid van geld.

k'in k'in k'iang k'iang, 丁 ヒ | ヒ, rammelen, (zooals glazenlamp door de wind).

k'iáng liang tsit ē, | 鏘 一 下. een gekletter, (zooals van een vallend voor-werp.

k'i k'iang, 起 |, reden tot twist maken waarze niet bestaat.

tsong k'iang, 粧 |, een vreemd dialect nadoen; veel beleefdheids vormen gebruiken,

K'iáng *tuì i k'iáng*, 對 伊 |, tot iemand zeggen, zijn gevoelen uitspreken.

海上絲綢之路文獻集成 科技與文化編

僵 k'iàng lé, | 馬, een sterk wild paard,
K'iàng d. i. boosaardig man
tsa bó k'iàng, 潑 婦 |, een boosaardige vrouw.
k'iàng t'aô, | 頭, boosaardig van vrouwen.
k'iàng k'iàng, | 匕, robust; sterk, stevig.
ióng k'iàng k'iàng, | 勇 匕, sterk, stevig, kras, (van voorwerpen of ondelieden.)

Kiao

驕 kiao ngō } | 傲, hoovaardig, trotsch.
» gō
Kiao kiao t'aô, | 頭, do.
kiao ing, | 榮, van groote inbeelding.
kiao pit paī, | 必 敗, hoogmoed komt voor den val.
tsoè i kiao k'ìh, 佐 伊 | 去, boos, beleedigd weggaan.
hoan kiao. 翻 |, rollen, (van paarden.)

挑 kiao so, | , aanzetten, ophitsen.
Kiao

撟 kiao kiáh, | 匕, stevig, fiksch.
Kiao

嬌 Fraai.
Kiao iao kiaó bi lú, 妖 | 美 女, eene fraaije vrouw.
sik tsui kiao kiao kiao, 色 水 | | |, fraaije levendige kleur.

Kiao kiao á, | 仔, wellustige teekeningen.

攪 Door elkander doen, mengen.
Kiao sa kiao, kiao sa ts'am, 相 |, | 相 參, door elkander mengen.
koan pa li kiao, 翻 敺 理 |, verward ongeregeld.

kiao kú | 絞, kramp in de buik.

攪 Mengen, vermengen; verwarren; lastig
Kiaó vallen, storen.
kiaó tsiú, | 酒, in wijn mengen, met wijn mengen.
kiaó mī, | 麵, deeg aanmaken.
kiaó ts'á, | 抄, in de war brengen. lastig vallen, storen.
kiaó dziaó, | 擾, do.
kiaó loān. | 亂, verwarren.
kiaó lā, | 搨, lastig vallen.
kiaó lâng è bīn, | 人 的 眠, iemand in zijn slaap storen.

賭 Spelen, dobbelen; dobbelspel, spel.
Kiaó poáh kiaó, | 博, dobbelen, spelen.
kiaó king, kiaó tiû } | 間, | 塲,
kan » tio }
speelhuis, dobbelhuis.
poáh kiaó hàn, | 博 漢, dobbelaar.
kiaó kui, | 鬼, do.
kiaó k'a, | 脚, dobbelaar.
tuì k'a kiaó, 對 脚 |, met tweeën dobbelen.
sa k'a kiaó, 三 脚 |, met drieën dobbelen.
kiaó kùn, | 棍, knappe ervaren dobbelaar.
poáh gōng (of gūm) kiaó, 敆 戇 |, dom weg blijven doordobbelen.
kiaó sat, | 虱, fout, bedriegerij bij het spel.
poáh kiaó tsi k'ièm sa nī, 敆 | 錢 欠 三 年, dobbelgeld kan men drie jaar schuldig blijven.
pàng kiaó tsè, 放 | 債, dobbelgeld leenen.

KIAO

kòng kiao, 誑 丨, een onkundige in het spel bedriegen.

tok lâng ê kiaó, 琢 人 的 丨, iemand in het spel bedriegend.

hoat kiaó hòng, 發 丨 癀, razernij bij het spel krijgen.

sù tsìng kiaó, 四 正 丨, eerlijk dobbelen.

ū lō̤ ê kiaó, 有 路 的 丨, dobbelspel met bedriegerij.

kiaó pi̤ kiá, 丨 邊 子, arme dobbellaars.

liáh kiaó, 拿 丨, dobbelaars vatten.

pai á kiao, 牌 仔 丨, kaartspel.

taô á kiaó, 骰 仔 丨, spel met dobbelsteenen.

kiaó hong kùn t'aò pòng, 丨 風 羣 頭 謗, dobbellaars leugens en boksers overdrijving, *d. i.* overdreven gerucht.

繳 Uitleveren, teruggeven.

Kiaó *kiaó hing ìh*, 丨 還, aan iemand teruggeven, uitleveren.

āo ku kiaó k'ìh lai, 後 裾 丨 起 來, de achterslip opligten.

謝 Bedanken.

Kiaó *kiaó lìh*, 丨 汝, ik dank U.

kóng kiaó, 說 丨, dankzeggen, bedanken.

矯 *kiaó tsing*, 丨 情, omwillig, steeds

Kiaó het tegen overgestelde van anderen willen.

裱 *kiaó pè tièm*, 丨 褙 店, behangers

Kiaó winkel.

kiaó kiaó kiò, 丨 乜 叫, joelen, zwetsen.

kiaó hán, 丨 捍, zwetsen.

橇 Opwippen, optillen met een hefboom.

Kiaō *kiaō k'ìh lai*, 丨 起 來, opwippen.

kak kiaō, opwippen (zooals steenblokken.)

kiaō tsióh t'aò, 丨 石 頭, steenen opwippen.

ts'â kiaō 柴 丨, houten hefboom.

tuì kiaō, 對 丨, elkander dwarsboomen.

kiaō ts'uì k'ì, 丨 嘴 齒, de tanden met geweld openbreken.

kiaō lìng tíng, kiaō kè lai, 丨 反 轉, 丨 過 來, met veel kracht inspanning omwenden.

ts'oh hàn kiaō lâng, 噪 空 丨 人, iemand gemeen uitschelden.

K'IAO

曲 Krom, gebogen, krombuigen.

K'iao *oan k'iao*, 灣 丨, krom, verward.

k'iao ku, 丨 龜, krom van rug; kromgetrokken, door winden, enz.

k'iao píng / » *pán* } 丨 屏, geheel en al krom trekken, (zooals door de zon.)

aó k'iao, 丨 拗, krombuigen.

ut k'iao, 鬱 丨, krom doen trekken, (zooals bamboes door hitte verwarmd.)

sa̤ tsat k'iao, 三 節 丨, in drie bogten gekromd.

k'iao k'i, 丨 拘, alles ten slechte verdraaijend.

k'i kiao lâng, 拘 丨 人, iemand iets ten laste leggen waaraan hij slechts gedeeltelijk schuld heeft.

k'iao pī lâng, (of *k'iaó*), 丨 變 人, onverdiend ten laste leggen, iemand moeielijkheden maken.

k'iao tsiū k'i, 丨 就 欹, komt er een kink in den kabel dan is het geheel en al mis.

蹺 *tàh k'iao*, 踏 丨, stelten loopen.

K'iao *k'iao ka*, 丨 脚, de beenen kruisen.

竅 Gat, opening; doorzigt, scherpzinnig-
K'iaò heid vernuft, vernuftig, kunstig.

sim koa ts'it k'iaò, 心 肝 七 〡, de zeven openingen in het hart, schrander, van goed doorzigt en overleg.

tit tioh tsit ê k'iaò, 得 着 一 〡, een gat, middel, op iets vinden.

it k'iaò put t'ong, 一 〡 不 通, zonder het minste overleg of doorzigt.

t'ong k'iaò, 通 〡, van goed doorzigt.

bô p'oa k'iaò, 無 半 〡, zonder het minste doorzigt.

ki k'iaò, 机 〡, vernuftig, scherpzinnig.

ū k'iaò, ù k'iaò; 有 〡, vernuftig,

k'iaò biaō, 〡 妙, fraai, kunstig.

sin k'iaò, 神 〡, vernuftig, kunstig.

翹 Opwippen, opsteken omkantelen.
K'iaò *ts'ìn kaò k'iaò k'iaò k'iaò*, 秤 到 〡 匕 匕, zoo wegen dat de schaal geheel en al overhangt.

k'iaò t'aô, 〡 頭, het hoofd opsteken, zich met zaken in laten, (van vrouwen).

k'iaò pán, 〡 板, een opwippende plank, do.

k'ōng k'a k'iaò, 孔 脚 〡, achterovervallen, kantelen, (zooals met een stoel).

k'iaō ts'ùi, 〡 嘴, opstaande mond, (bijnaam).

tsûn táh k'iaò poáh lóh tsúi, 船 踏 〡 跌 落 水, op een boot stappen en door het omkantelen in het water vallen.

si k'iaò k'iaò, 死 〡 匕, dood.

tó k'iaò k'iaò, 倒 〡 匕, zoo lang als men is op den grond vallen, liggen.

[illegible] *k'iaò lâng*; 〡 人, iemand kwellen,
K'iaò lastig maken, (van kinderen).

k'iaò k'ó, 〡 苦, iemand verdriet, last geven.

k'iaò k'ó lâng, 〡 苦 人, het iemand lastig maken, kwellen.

k'iaò k'ò lâng, 〡 强 人, iemand treiteren.

k'iaò i tang k'iaò i sai, 〡 伊 東 〡 伊 西, zonder ophouden kwellen, drijven; moeielijkheden maken.

k'iaò pī (of tī) lâng, 〡 騙 人, iemands woorden verdraaijen.

k'iaò tiaò lâng, zie *k'iao*.

Kiaoh

矯 *kiaoh k'í*, 〡 起, opstaan.
Kiaoh *haū bé kiaoh*, 鮫 尾 〡, opwippen als de staart van een konings krab, *d. i.* met een lang voorwerp dat men onder den arm heeft lieden achter ons stooten.

kiaoh k'í kiaoh tó, 〡 起 〡 倒, oprijzen en weer gaan liggen, (van zieken.)

kiaoh bōē tit t'ang k'í, 〡 未 得 起, niet op kunnen staan, zich niet knnnen oprigten, opwerken, (ook van een vervallen handelszaak.

Kiaóh *ki ki kiaóh kiaóh*, zwetsen.

Kiaóh Geluid van vallende voorwerpen.

撟 *kiaóh kiaóh kiò*, 〡 匕 叫, kloppen
Kiaòh tegen een deur enz.

Kiaoh *t'aô k'ak toa kaò oē kiaoh*, op het hoofd tikken dat het klinkt.

t'aô k'ak hō i toa kaò oē kiaoh, hij heeft securiteit noodig.

kiaoh kiaoh haó, tikken, tokkelen kloppen.

kŏng kiaoh, losstaande, schommelen, waggelen, tikken.

tsit k'ŏng tsit kiaoh, niet harmonieus, niet eendragtig.

Kiep

劫 Kiep Plunderen, rooven, uitplunderen, bestelen.

ts'iŭ kiep, 搶 ｜, plunderen, uitrooven.

kiŏng kiep / *kiăng* » 强 ｜, geweldddadig stelen.

p'ah kiep, 打 ｜, plunderen, rooven.

kiep ts'át, ｜ 賊, struikroover.

kiep lăng, ｜ 人, iemand uitplunderen.

soŭ kiep, op verschillende plaatsen plunderen.

kiep koan, ｜ 棺, graven bestelen.

kiep iă, (of *tsē*) ｜ 營, eene legerplaats uitplunderen.

toū kiep sŏ, 大 ｜ 數, groot raadsbesluit des hemels.

峽 Kiep Bergengte, pas.

kè kiep, 過 ｜, door een pas komen, een gevaar, moeielijkheid overkomen.

boē kè kiep, 未 過 ｜, eene moeielijkheid niet kunnen overkomen.

tsit kiep p'ah kè tsit kiep, 一 ｜ 打 過 一 ｜, van de eene moeielijkheid door de andere komen.

夾 Kiep Tusschen twee voorwerpen drukken; dubbeld, gevoerd.

kiep kŭn, ｜ 棍, strafwerktuig waarin de handen en voeten van misdadigers zamen gedrukt worden.

kiep tsàp, ｜ 雜, verward, gemengd, (zooals een gesprek.)

kiep hiŭ, ｜ 裘, gevoerde (niet gewatteerde) jas.

kiep k'ŏ, ｜ 褲, gevoerde broek,

sī toa eh á sī kiep eh? 是 單 的 也 是 ｜ 的, is het een enkele of een gevoerde?

浹 Kiep *kiep sim*, ｜ 心, aan het hart liggend, geliefkoosd.

kiep hiep, ｜ 洽, compact op elkander.

壞 K'iep Bedorven, versleten

p'ah k'iep, 打 ｜, bederven, stukmaken.

bák tsiu k'iep lah, 目 周 ｜ 的, slecht van gezigt.

k'iep liaoh, ｜ 了, bedorven, induigen, (van eene zaak.)

k'iep ì, ｜ 意, slechte bedoeling.

ĩm bat hó k'iep, 不 識 好 ｜, geen onderscheid tusschen goeden en slechten kunnen maken.

k'iep sì, 醜 ｜, leelijk.

k'iep hì, ｜ 戲, slechte nietswaardige comedie.

k'iep saí, ｜ 使, onhulpvaardig, ongedienstig, onmeêdeelzaam, een zelvig zijn, (van kinderen.)

挾 K'iep Bedreigen met.

sa k'iep, 相 ｜, elkander wederzijds bedreigen iets wat men noodig heeft niet te geven.

k'iep i ē kè tsī, ｜ 伊 的 價 錢, iemand in den prijs dwingen als wetende dat hij iets noodig heeft.

bóh tit sa k'iep, 莫 相 ｜, dwingt elkander niet, laat elkander hierin vrij.

Kiet

結 Kiet Knoop, knoopen; binden, vereenigen, aanknoopen, aangaan, zich vereenigen tot, zich vormen tot, zetten, (zooals vruchten, roofjes.) stremmen (van vocht); te zamenvatten, vaststellen, afmaken.

kiet liû, ┃ 紐, knoop op de muts.

kiet liên, ┃ 連, vereenigen, in verband brengen of staan.

kiet sok, ┃ 束, stijf om het lijf.

kiet sit, ┃ 實, vast stevig in elkander.

kiet siā, ┃ 社, een hulpbond vormen

kiet tóng, 黨 ┃, een komplot vormen.

kiet iok, 約 ┃, overeenkomen.

kiet hoat, ┃ 髮, eerste huwelijk.

kiet ts'in, ┃ 親, een huwelijk aangaan.

kiet kao, ┃ 交, omgaan met.

kao ping kiet iú, 交朋┃友, vriendschap aanknoopen.

kiet láp, ┃ 納, omgang hebben met.

kiet paì (of gī) hia tī, ┃ 拜兄弟, broederschap aanknoopen, zweeren.

kiet oán, ┃ 怨, haat aanknoopen.

kiet oan, ┃ 冤, vijandschap, twist aanknoopen.

kiet kó, ┃ 果, eig. vrucht zetten; uiteinde, een einde maken aan, (zooals aan iemands leven.

kiet ping, ┃ 冰, tot ijs stremmen, bevriezen.

kiet p'i, ┃ 痞, roofjes zetten.

kiet hè, ┃ 貨, de geheele hoeveelheid koopwaren koopen.

kiet siàu, ┃ 賬, balans opmaken.

kiet àn, ┃ 案, eene regtszaak beslissen.

kiet tsn̄g, ┃ 狀, een regtsgeding afmaken.

liaó kiet, 了 ┃, afgedaan.

kiet kiok, ┃ 局, afgedaan, afloop eener zaak.

kū kiet, *kū kam kiet*, 具┃, 具甘┃, zich aan iemands uitspraak onderwerpen.

pó kiet, 保 ┃, borg, bewijs dat er verder geene moeielijkheden zullen zijn.

ts'ut kiet, 出 ┃, schriftelijke verklaring geven.

kán kiet, 簡 ┃, compact, kleine hoeveelheid.

桔 Kiet Kit *kiet á*, ┃ 仔, limoentjes.

吉 Kiet Geluk aanbrengend, gelukkig.

kiet dzit, ┃ 日, gelukkige dag.

kiet tiaō, ┃ 朝, goed voorteeken.

kiet tsòng, ┃ 葬, begravenis drie of meer dagen na den dood.

pì kiet, 閉 ┃, verstopping, geene ontlasting hebben.

潔 Kiet Zuiver, eerbaar.

tsing kiet è hū dzin lâng, 清┃的婦人, eene eerbare vrouw.

kiet kiet kiet, ┃匕┃, zeer goed, stevig, (van voorwerpen.)

竭 *kan kiét*, 乾 丨, arm, behoeftig, (van
Kiét eene plaats).

soa kiét hai kiét, 山 丨 海 丨, arm aan land- en zeevoortbrengselen.

kiét lik, 丨 力, zijne krachten op iets uitputten, als zijne krachten aan iets besteden.

傑 *hò kiét*, 豪 丨, held, een royaal, gul,
Kiet degelijk menschen.

kọ kiét, 古 丨, aardig, snoeperig.

訐 *ñ k'iét*, 狡 丨, niet te vertrouwen,
K'ièt met draaierijen omgaande.

k'iet dziën it sin, 丨 了 然 一 身, alleen één, één alleen.

k'ièt hé, 夏 火, vuurslaan.

Kièt *sa k'iét* } 相 丨, elkander niets toe-
sio » } geven, dwarsboomen.

tùi k'iét, 對 丨, do.

kap i si k'iét, 與 伊 死 丨, eeuwig met iemand in onmin zijn, dwarsboomen.

p'ê k'ièt k'ièt k'ièt, strak, gespannen vel.

k'ièt k'ièt k'ièt, hard en schraal (van land, vruchten, enz.)

Kiem

兼 Met, benevens.
Kiem *hòng kiem*, 况 丨, daarenboven, toch.

hó kiem p'ai, 好 丨 歹, goed en kwaad.

kiem koán, 丨 管, te gelijkertijd nog waarnemen.

kiem li, kiem pān, 丨 理, 丨 辦, te gelijkertijd waarnemen.

boē kiem tit, 未 丨 的, niet te gelijkertijd kunnen waarnemen, doen.

tsit ê lâng kiem nēng hāng taī tsì, 一 人 丨 兩 件 事, een man neemt twee zaken tegelijk wordt.

it kiem lióng kò, 一 丨 兩 故, voor twee doeleinden tegelijk dienen.

減 Verminderen, afnemen van schrijven.
Kiém *kiém pit*, 丨 筆, verkort.

kiém kè } 丨 價, de prijs verminderen.
» *kè* }

kiém sing, 丨 省, verminderen in uitgaven, zuiniger worden.

kiém tsió, 丨 少, verminderen.

kiém īng } 用 丨, zuinig gebruiken.
» *iōng* }

ke kiém } 加 丨, veel of weinig.
ko » }

kiém hing, 丨 刑, eene straf verminderen

kiém tsit pọa, 丨 一 半, met de helft verminderen, de helft er van afnemen.

kiém sin koàh, 丨 收 的, een weinig op afrekening aannemen.

kiém kóng, 丨 說, in het kort vertellen, weinig van iets zeggen.

或 *kiém ts'ai*, 丨 者, welligt òf , , , òf
Kiém *kiém ū*, 丨 有, is dat toch wel zoo!

kiém bô, 丨 無, is of was het immers niet?

檢 *kiém tiém*, 丨 點, nazien, natellen.
Kiém *sûn kiém*, 巡 丨, schout.

kiém tseng siu, 丨 粧 箱, bruidsnaaidoos.

kiém giēm, 丨 驗, onderzoeken, nazien.

劍 Dolk.
Kièm *kièm toà*, 丨 帶, bandje, lint met uitloopende spitse punt.

kè kièm mi̱ } *koè » mẹ̄* } 過丨銑, uiterst scherp, scherp van doorzigt.

kièm tu kièm, 丨抵丨, beiden even ervaren zijn, aan elkander gewaagd zijn.

kièm kik, 丨戟, glad, moeielijk te bedriegen.

kièm kik ē lâng, 丨尅之人, iemand die niets over zijn kant laat gaan.

bák tsiu put tsi kièm, 目不只丨, scherp van gezigt.

kè kièm mêng, 過丨門, scherp van doorzigt; ook zeer scherp.

kièm ts'iu, 丨鋒, puntige palen voor eene omheining of hek.

kièm tsiem, 丨簪, zwaard vormige haarnaald, (tegen bekooring van booze geesten.)

siang kó̱ kièm, 双股丨, dubbele dolk die elk slechts een halve steekplaat heeft en beiden in één schede gaan.

kièm sok, 丨束, zwaardschede.

鹹 Zout.

Kiêm *kiêm tok tok*, 丨獨乚, uiterst zout.

kiêm tsui, 丨水, zoutwater.

kiêm hi tièm, 丨魚店, zoute visch-winkel.

kiêm siep, 丨澁, zout en wrang; gierig.

kiêm k'i, 丨氣, zout, salpeter-dampen.

kiêm kè, 丨價, hooge prijs, peperduur.

kè tsi̱ kiêm, 價錢丨, do.

kiêm tsuí tsi̱, 丨水錢, geld door zeevaren verdiend.

kiêm seng ti̱ } *» sui̱ »* } 丨酸甜, konfituren.

kiêm bah, 丨肉, gezoute vleesch.

kiêm nn̄g, 丨蛋, gezoute eijeren.

kiêm tsiá, 丨沒, gezoute en ongezoute waren.

kiêm koè tsiá ts'aì, 丨畦沒菜, gezoute waren en versche groenten, dagelijksche behoeften.

kiêm siep lūn, 丨澁潤, gierig, vasthoudend aan geld.

kiêm tī ts'eng, 丨痔瘡, *lett.* zoute aambeijen, *d. i.* gierig.

tsi̱ kiêm, 錢丨, niet van zijn geld afkunnen.

kiêm tsui k'oah lâng tsiàh, 丨水渴人飲, dorstigen drinken zoutwater *d. i.* gedwongen zijn niet zoo in zijn voordeel te handelen als men wel zou willen doen.

ti kiêm tsiá bò hièn, 甜丨沒無嫌, alles eten wat slechts voor de hand komt, b. v. alles goed of slecht koopen.

謙 *k'iem sùn*, 丨遜, nederig.

K'iem *k'iem sūn* } *» sùn* } 丨順, do.

k'iem ku } *» hi* } 丨虛, nederig, bescheiden.

k'iem k'iem k'iem, zeer nederig.

tsū k'iem, 自丨, zich vernederen, (in beleefdheid vorme).

kò k'iem, 告丨 nederig spreken.

m sai kò k'iem, 不用過丨, wees niet al te nederig.

boē k'iem tit } *bē » »* } 不丨得, zoo overtuigd zijn van zijne kunde dat men complimenten bijna niet met nederige termen kan beantwoorden.

k'iem dziōng, 丨讓, nederig, (bel. term).

k'iem hu siep sè, | 盧涉世, nederig en met alle menschen zacht omgaan, gedienstig, hulpvaardig.

歉 *i sù k'iém k'iém*, 意 | 然, inwen-
K'iém dig verlegen niet op zijn gemak, (zooals een jongere die op een hooge plaats zit).

欠 Gebrek hebben aan, niet hebben, mis-
K'ièm sen, ontbreken; noodig hebben; schuldig zijn.

k'ièm īng, | 用, noodig hebben, gebrek hebben aan.

k'ièm k'eh, k'eh k'ièm, | 缺. do.

k'ièm bé, | 馬, geen paard, *d. i.* geen geld hebben.

k'ièm tsi, | 錢, geld schuldig zijn; geld gebrek hebben.

k'ièm kang hu, | 工夫, niet genoeg afgewerkt; geen werk hebben.

tsáp hāng k'ièm tsáp it hāng, 十項 | 十一項, van de tien ontbreken er elf, er ontbreekt nog veel aan.

k'ièm tsiú, | 酒, geen wijn (in huis) hebben.

k'ièm tsè, | 債, schuld hebben, schuldig zijn.

k'ièm tsè ėh, | 債的, schuldenaar

im k'ièm tsè, 不 | 債, geen schuld (van een vroeger leven) aan iemand hebben, gezegd van iemand die kwistig met een anders geld is.

k'iem toa. | 單, schuldbekentenis.

kòng k'ièm, 抗 |, zijne schuld maar niet afdoen.

t'oa k'ièm, 拖 |, een schuld rekken.

k'ièm tsi taī òng, | 錢大王, koning der schuldenaars, de groote schuldenaar.

koà k'ièm, | 掛, schuldig zijn.

芡 *k'ièm sit*, | 實, naam eener medicijn.
K'ièm.

拑 *kū i k'ièm teh*, 爲伊 | 的,
K'ièm in beslag nemen, als securiteit houden.

k'ièm k'aò, | 口, geen mond open doen.

儉 *k'iēm k'iēm*, Zuinig,
K'iēm *k'iēm ke* / *» ke* } | 家, zuinig huishouden, zuinige huishoudster.

k'ûn k'iēm / *k'in »* } 勤 |, vlijtig en zuinig,

k'iēm ts'ui, | 嘴, het uit zijn mond sparen.

gaō k'iēm, 善 |, zuinig.

k'iēm sing / *» sé* } | 省, zuinig.

tsiet k'iēm, 節 |, zuinig.

k'iēm p'ak. (*è lâng*) / *» p'ok* } | 樸, zuinig en eenvoudig.

k'iēm tīng neh tō, | 腸 ○ 肚, het uit zijn mond sparen, (om het aan zijne kinderen of anderen te geven).

k'iēm tsiáh k'iēm īng, | 食 | 用, zuinig zijn in eten en behoeften.

k'iû k'iēm, 球 |, zuinig, inhoudend, bang zijn om uitgaven te doen.

Kien

堅 Sterk, stevig, duurzaam; vastbesloten,
Kien standvastig, beraden.

kien kò, | 固, stevig, duurzaam.

kien tsòng, | 壯, sterk, duurzaam,

kien tīng, | 有, hard, stevig, standvastig.

kien kien kien, | | |, goed, fraai, (van voorwerpen of vrouwen).

kien sim, | 心. vastbesloten.

bô kien sim, 無 | 心, besluiteloos, onbepaald (van karakter.)

kien ì, kien tsip, | 意, | 執, vastbesloten.

sim kien ì tsiet, kien sim tsiet ì, 心 | 意 切 | 心 切 意, vast voorgenomen.

慳 Kien *kien lîn*, | 吝, gierig.

凝 Kien Bevriezen, stremmen, stollen; verdroogen verdroogd.

kien ping, kien tàng, | 氷, | 凍, bevriezen.

kien hong, | 風, door den wind gestold.

kien koa, | 乾, verdroogen, verdroogd.

kien pó, | 補, verdroogen, indroogen.

kien k'ih k'ih, | 柿 欺, ingedroogd, arm.

kien ta, | 礁, enkel, zuiver, onvermengd; alleen, slechts.

肩 De schouder,

Kien *kien t'iao poè hū é láng*, | 挑 背 負 之 人, lastdragers, rondventers.

繭 Popje, cocon.

Kién *t'âng kién*, 虫 |, insekten pop.

Kán *ts'âm kién*, 蠶 |, cocon van den zijdeworm.

pì kién, 變 |, pop worden.

t'iu si pak kién, 抽 絲 剝 |, de zijde afwinden en de cocon open maken. *d. i.* stuk voor stuk verklaren.

蹇 Ongelukkig.

Kién *miā ūn kién*, 命 運 |, ongelukkig lot.

見 Kièn Zien; ter audiëntie komen bij den keizer; inzigt, doorzigt, verstand.

kièn sik / » *sit* } | 識, kennis, doorzigt, verstand.

ts'ién kièn, 淺 |, gering doorzigt.

kièn ts'ién pièn lién, | 錢 變 臉, op het zien van geld van gelaatskleur veranderen.

kièn king sing tsing, | 景 生 情, op het gezigt van iets eene droevige herinnering krijgen.

kièn biēn sing tsing, | 面 生 情, op het zien van iemand gunstiger worden.

tiaò kièn, 朝 |, ter audiëntie roepen.

ìn kièn, 引 |, introduceren; voorstellen (aan den keizer.)

kièn tsìng, | 証, ooggetuige, getuige.

kièn siaò, | 笑, zich schamen, schaamte veroorzakend.

kièn koaì, | 怪, kwalijk nemen.

tah put kièn t'ien, 搭 不 | 天, vlaggen, tenten over de straten spannen.

tsì kièn, 質 |, geldelijk cadeau bij het engageren van onderwijzers, visitegeld aan dokters.

k'ó kièn . . . , 可 |, hieruit blijkt dat . . . .

kièn boé kièn hó, | 買 | 好, alles wat hij koopt is goed.

建 Oprigten, daarstellen, vestigen.

Kièn *kièn tì*, | 置, daarstellen, oprigten.

kièn kong lip giép, | 功 立 業, zijn naam, roem vestigen.

hok kièn, 福 |, Fokkiën.

鞬 Kièn Pluimbal, vederbal.

giét kièn, 踢 ｜, met de handen een vederbal slaan.

t'at kièn, 㧚 ｜, met de voeten een vederbal schoppen.

凝 Bevriezen, stollen.

Kiên *kiên ping*, ｜ 冰. bevriezen.

kiên tàng, ｜ 凍. do.

kiên liên k'ìh, 皆 ｜ 凍, geheel en al bevrozen, stollen, hard worden.

kiên bīn, ｜ 面. aan het oppervlak stollen.

kiên tsit ting p'éh, ｜ 一 重 皮, er is een vlies overgestremd, (als over melk).

窮 *put tsi kiên*, 不 只 ｜, geen geld
Kiên hebben, zeer arm zijn.

健 Stevig, sterk, gezond; stijfhoofdig.

Kiēn *k'ong kiēn*, 康 ｜, stevig, gezond.

ióng kiēn, 勇 ｜, stevig, sterk.

tsòng kiēn, 壯 ｜. do.

kiēn tin, ｜ 紬, klein maar stevig.

kiēn koai, 乖 ｜, stijfhoofdig, voor geen ander willen onder doen.

kiēn hàn, ｜ 漢, een stijfhoofdige kerel.

腱 Spiermaag.

Kiēn *koe kiēn*, ｜ 鷄, spiermaag van een
Kīn kip.

ah kiēn, 鴨 ｜, eenden spiermaag.

túh tióh kiēn, 抵 着 ｜, de spiermaag raken, *d. i.* den spijker zoo juist op den kop slaan dat men niets meer in te brengen heeft.

kap goá boē siao kiēn, 與 我 無 消 ｜, hij kan zich niet tegen mij verzetten, ik heb magt over hem.

k'oà íng kong tsiáh koe kiēn koē koē máh! 看 王 公 食 雞 ｜ 快 七 的? gij ziet grootvader een spiermaag eten (en denkt dat het zeer gemakkelijk is, he? *d. i.* een moeielijke zaak voor gemakkelijk houden omdat de persoon die ze ten uitvoer brengt het door en door verstaat.

牽 Voortrekken, medeslepen, in eene zaak
K'ien betrekken; gesp, lip van een slot.

k'ien liên, ｜ 連, medeslepen, betrekken in, verklappen.

k'ien ts'é, ｜ 策, do.

k'u k'ien } 拘 ｜, zich steeds aan
k'i „ } het oude houdend, bekrompen van geest.

k'ien kióng } ｜ 强, gedwongen, ge-
„ *kiáng* } forceerd (spreken).

k'ien lai k'ien k'ì, k'ien ùn k'ìh, ｜ 來 ｜ 去, door elkander geslagen gerekend.

k'ien á, ｜ 仔. gesp.

liú á k'ien, 鈕 仔 ｜, oog achter aan een knoop.

mìng k'ien, 門 ｜, ring. knoop van een deur.

K'ién *siaó k'ién*, 小 犬, mijn zoon (nederig term).

繾 *k'ién k'oán*, ｜ 綣, gastvrij, vol, be-
K'ièn leefdheden.

遣 *ts'e k'ién*. 差 ｜, zenden (iemand.)
K'ièn *ts'ui k'ién*, 推 ｜, op het punt van nood (als) tot redding gezonden komen.

譴 *t'i k'ièn tsik*, 天 ｜ 責, de hemel
K'ièn zendt zijne straffen; straf des hemels.

𡃤 *k'i k'ièn t'aò*, 起 ｜ 頭, reden tot
K'ièn twist opvatten.

kap i k'ièn, 仝 伊 丨, met iemand in onmin, twist zijn.

k'ièn sìng, bijgeloof.

煎 *k'ièn iû*, 丨 油, met vetbraden.
K'ièn *k'ièn siù* / *» siō* } veel van iets eten, veelvraat.

健 *iòng k'ièn k'ièn*, 勇 丨 丨, sterk, kras,
K'ièn (van oude menschen.)

虔 *k'ièn ì* 丨 意, eerbiedig.
K'ièn *k'ièn sim*, 丨 心, do.

k'ièn sìng, 丨 誠, opregt eerbiedig.

k'ièn kìng, 丨 敬, do.

K'ièn *gin á put tsi k'ièn*, zeer lastig zijn grijnen van een kind.

kè k'ièn, doen als of men wil gaan grijnen; (van kinderen.)

K'ih

缺 Een stuk af.
K'ih *k'ih kak*, 丨 角, een hoek afgebroken.

k'ih ts'uì, 丨 嘴, een gespleten lip, hazenlip.

p'ah k'ih, 打 丨, gebroken, een stuk uit.

k'ih k'ih lih lih, 丨 匕 裂 匕, met stukjes er uit en gebarsten.

laô sao k'ih hī, 含 沙 丨 耳, gebarsten en zonder oortje.

k'ih ku, 丨 器, insnijding, split van een kleed.

K'ih *kiu k'ih k'ih*, doods verschrikt zijn, zoodat men staat te rillen.

lùn k'ih k'ih, do.

瘦 *sán k'ik k'ih*, 丨 峭 匕. zeer mager.
K'ih *k'ih k'ih k'ih*, zeer arm.

tsit p'i á bah k'ih k'ih, 一 片 肉 丨 縮 丨, een plat dun stukje vleesch.

bah sui si k'ih lòh k'ih, 肉 隨 時 消 丨, zijn vleesch slonk onmiddelijk, (zooals verlies van veel bloed).

koâ k'i' k'ih, 寒 甚, verkleumd van koude.

Kik

激 Water in zijn loop tegengaan; opstop-
Kik pen, eene opstopping, overmaat doen ontstaan van woede, inspanning van krachten, sterk dringen, aanzetten, tot het uiterste brengen.

kik sui bû liû, 丨 水 無 流, het water in zijn loop stoppen, *d. i.* zijne onderdanen tot het uiterste brengen.

kik pièn, 丨 變, tot het uiterste en daardoor tot oproer of twist brengen.

sa kik, 相 丨, elkander aanzetten, sarren, uitdagen.

kik k'ì, 丨 氣, in toorn doen ontsteken.

k'ik lâng gīn, 丨 人 恨, sarren.

kik sing, 丨 成, door sterke aansporing tot iets maken.

kik hō i pui, 丨 與 他 肥, vetmesten.

kik sih, 丨 死, verdrinken.

kik p'òng, 丨 脹, zich opblazen, (als kikvorschen).

kik lát, 丨 力, zijne krachten verzamelen, inspannen.

kik p'éh, 丨 泡, schuinen, trotsch.

kik oē á dzin (*kih ts'uì k'i p'ūng*) 丨 嘴 齒 縫, iemands woorden, fijntjes uitpluizen; befitten.

kik ka, 丨 脚, aan de voeten knellen.

kik sai tsig tsù } ｜屎蟾蜍,
» » *tsig tsi* }
een aan verstopping lijdende kikvorsch, *d. i.* iets willen zeggen maar het er niet kunnen uitbrengen.

革 Kik Ontslaan, afzetten; verstooten.
kik tsit. ｜職, van zijn post ontslaan.
k'ai kik, 開｜, ontslaan (van militairen.)
kik k'ih, kik sak, ｜去, ｜揀, van zich afstooten,
kik liòk. ｜逐, verdrijven, wegjagen, (zools schadelijke lieden.)

烝 Kik *kik tsiù*, ｜酒, wijnbrouwen.

格 Kik Onderzoeken, grondig berekenen.
kik sim sū, ｜心事, nauwkeurig nagaan, onderzoeken.
gaò kik sing, 善｜算, knap berekenen.
gaò kik sù liòk ē lâng, 善｜四六的人, iemand die knap berekend, van helder doorzigt.
kik kaò tú á hó, ｜到恰好, zoo berekenen dat het juist voldoende is.
kih lóng ī̄m ts'ut, ｜不出, volstrekt niet op iets kunnen komen.
kik sù liòk, ｜四六, de uiterste prijs die men geven kan.

假 Kik Zich voor doen als, den schijn aannemen van.
kik tiēm, ｜靜, den schijn van bezadigdheid aannemen.
kik p'aì, ｜派, zich als iemand van eene andere plaats voordoen.
kik k'uì t'aô, ｜氣頭, zich als aanzienlijk voordoen.

kik lo sing, ｜老成, zich den schijn van oud geven
kit kut, ｜骨, weerbarstig, stijfhoofdig.
kik k'ô, ｜魁, trotsch.
kik k'ang, ｜空, zich hooger willen voordoen, dan men is, (lage volkstaal.)

隔 Kik Afschieten, een schot zetten tusschen.
kik nēng keh } ｜二格, in tweeën afschieten.
» *nō keh* }
kap i kik k'ám, 仝他｜坎, met iemand overhoop liggen.

戟 Kik Speer met drie punten.
kièm kik ē lâng, 劍｜的人, iemand die niets over zijn kant laat gaan.

菊 Kik *kik hoe* } ｜花, de Chineesche Aster.
(*kiok hoa*) }
kik hoa sim, ｜花心, hart als een aster, (zooals wortelen en oude groenten).

擊 Kik *kong kik*, 攻｜, bestrijden, aanvallen, bestormen.

極 Kik Top, toppunt; uiterste, ten uiterste, zeer, pool.
pak kik, lâm kik, 北｜, 南｜, Noorden Zuidpool.
kaò kik, 到｜, tèn top, ten uiterste.
dzip kik, 入｜, ten uiterste.
kik tsik pièn, ｜則變, na het toppunt komt verandering,
tsing kik, 情｜, zich tot het uiterste gebragt zien.
kik mîng, ｜門, op zijn uiterst, od zijn hoogst.
kik t'aô, ｜頭, tot het eind, zoo ver als men kan.
kik kak, ｜角, ten top, ten uiterste.

kik t'aô pō, ｜頭步, uiterste, laatste middel.

kik hó, ｜好, zeer goed.

siu kak kik 想到｜, al te inhalig, gierig.

局 Kik Kiók Magazijn, groote werkplaats; numerale voor spellen schaak.

hé ióh kik, 火藥｜, kruidmagazijn, kruidmolen.

kong kik, 公｜, pubiek magazijn.

gûn kik, 錢｜, geld magazijn.

tsî kik, 銀｜, munt.

kun tsong kik, 軍總｜, magazijn voor het leger.

pai ki kik, 排棋｜, een schaakspel opzetten, ook groote vertooning maken.

ts'ik kik, 測｜, kleingeestig, niet inschikkelijk, (zooals bij betaling.)

刻 K'ik Snijden, uitsnijden, graveeren; een kwartier, oogenblik.

k'ik dzī, 字｜, karakters uitsnijden.

k'ik hoe sai hū, ｜花司父, beeldhouwer.

k'ik k'ám, ｜坎, inkepen, inkerven.

tiao k'ik, 雕｜, uitsnijden, houwen.

k'ik ts'iú, ｜手, manier om te, of kunde in het graveeren.

hoan k'ik, 翻｜, oversnijden, (zooals verouderde drukplaten).

k'ik lóh in pán, ｜在印板, op drukplaten uitgesneden, onveranderlijk.

k'ik póh, 薄｜, verdrukken, slecht behandelen.

k'ik pak, ｜剝, knevelarij plegen, afpersen.

si k'ik, 時｜, uur en kwartier.

si k'ik boē lī lit, 時｜未能離, geen oogenblik kunnen verlaten.

k'ik tsiem, 針｜, uurwijzer.

lip k'ik, 立｜, onmiddelijk, terstond.

tsit k'ik, 一｜, do.

尅 K'ik *sū k'ik*, 相｜, niet harmonieeren.

siong k'ik, 相｜, met elkander in strijd, (zooals water en vuur.)

kap i ū k'ik, 仝他有｜, met iemand in onmin zijn.

k'ik k'ui, ｜虧, schade, verlies, lijden of doen lijden.

克 K'ik Overmeesteren, veroveren.

k'ik hók, ｜服, heroveren.

k'ih k'ûn k'ik k'iēm, ｜勤｜儉, vlijtig en spaarzaam.

k'ik kí t'aī dzin, ｜己待人, zichzelven te kort doen om er anderen mede te dienen.

曲 K'ih Lied.

ts'iù k'ik, 唱｜, zingen.

k'i k'ik in, 起｜引, een lied aanheffen; aanleiding tot twist geven.

k'ik koán, ｜舘, zangschool.

gim k'ik pī, 錦｜棚, stellaadje waarop gezongen wordt.

Kim

金 Kim Goud; familienaam; helder.

kim kó, ｜鼓, gongs en trommen.

kim soa, 沙｜, stofgoud.

sok kim, 束｜, traktement (van meesters).

kim póh, ｜薄, goudblad.

kim á, | 仔, goud.

kim kim, | |, helder.

kim kʼoe / *» koa* } | 瓜, pompoen.

kim hi, | 魚, goudvisch.

kim gûn tsoá, | 銀 紙, verguld papier dat bij offeren verbrand wordt.

kim gûn hoe, | 銀 花, kamper foelie.

kim hoe / *» hoa* } | 花, goudpapieren bloemen.

kiò kim, 叫 |, door het slaan op de gong elkander toeseinen.

bák tsiu kim, 眸 子 |, heldere oogen.

bák tsiu kim kim é si, wanneer zijne oogen nog helder zijn, *d. i.* nog tegenwoordig of in leven is.

an kim, 貼 |, vergulden.

pao kim, 包 |, dik vergulden.

lik kim, 煑 |, in het vuur vergulden.

kim tsʻat, | 察, verlakt.

tiém tiém kim, 點 匕 |, alles in de uiterste puntjes, volmaakste toestand.

kim siu laò tʻiah, | 收 樓 折, iets toch doen niettegenstaande men reeds vergoeding gehad heeft om het niet te doen.

kim giên, | 言, kostbare gezegden.

tsʻien kim, 千 |, dochter, (beleefdheidsterm.)

kim siâ, | 城, de keizerlijke residentie plaats.

kim si kaô, | 絲 猴, kinderen van rijke familie.

kim gûn tièm, | 紙 舖, goud en ziverpapier winkel.

kim soà, | 線, gouddraad.

kim liên, | 蓮, voeten van vrouwen, (eeretitel).

kim pò gik, | 報 玉, veel winst gevend,

tʻun kim si, 吞 | 而 死, door goud in te slikken zich van het leven berooven.

tsiok kim, 足 |, zuiver goud.

kút kim, 現 |, goud graven, veel geld verdienen.

kim sih sih, | 爍 匕, flikkeren van lichtglans.

kim tún á, | 盾 仔, gouden souverein

kim loân tiēn, | 鑾 殿, keizerlijke audiëntiezaal.

pʻah kim ku gô, 打 | 以 遨, in de rondte gaan, draaijen.

tsin kim put pʻò hó, 真 | 不 怕 火, zuiver goud vrees het vuur niet.

kim tsi lók, | 錢 鹿, gevlekt hert

tō kim, 鍍 |, verguldsel opleggen vergulden.

kim iû, | 油, goudverf.

kim tiém, | 點, (op een kleed geborduurde), gouden stipjes.

kim tsʻong, | 葱, gouden kwast.

kim tāng, *kim taó*, | 甕, beenderen urn.

今 Kim — Thans, tegenwoordig.

hiēn kim, 現 |, op het oogenblik

tong kim, 當 |, do.

bák kim, 目 |, do. op het oogenblik

kim dzit, | 日, heden.

Kim — *kim* (*gín*) *lâng*, iemand foppen, uit gekheid zeggen, niet meenen,

禁 Verbieden.

Kìm *kìm tsí*, | 止, do.

kìm tsí, | 子, gevangenenbewaarder.

kìm tsó, | 阻, verhinderen.

kìm kṇ, | 監, in de gevangenis zetten.

kìm k'uì, | 息, zijn adem inhouden.

kṇ kìm, 監 |, opsluiten, gevangen zetten.

k'u kìm / *k'i* » } 拘 |, vatten en gevangen zetten.

ts'ut kìm, 出 |, een verbod uitvaardigen.

k'ui kìm, 開 |, een verbod opheffen.

kìm tiaò, | 條, artikelen van een verbod.

kong kìm, 公 |, met algemeen goedkeuren verbieden; onderling overeenkomst van de bewoners eener plaats om 't een of andere te verbieden.

hoān kìm ê mịh, 犯 | 的 物, contrabande.

giêm kìm, 嚴 |, streng verbieden.

kìm k'ī / » *kī* } | 忌, zich onthouden van ...

kìm k'aó lī, | 口 痢, diarrhoea zonder te kunnen eten.

kìm káng, | 港, verboden om uitgevoerd te worden.

siu kìm, 收 |, vatten en gevangen zetten.

kìm hè, | 貨, contrabande.

kìm ts'ù, | 厝, een huis voor anderen verbieden, niet voor ieder een openstellen.

kìm iok, | 約, artikelen van verbod.

kìm tē ê só tsaī, | 地 之 所, verboden plaatsen, (als de keizerlijke stad), plaatsen waar de politie werkzaam is, (zooals in steden).

kìm ts'ūi, | 嘴, zich ontzeggen eenige dingen te eten, (zooals zieken).

妗 Tante, vrouw van zijn ouderen oom van

Kīm moeders zijde.

kīm pô ts'uì, | 婆 嘴, mond als van eene oude tante, *d. i.* fraai maar onopregt in zijn spreken.

bú kīm / *bó* » } | 母, tante (van moederskant).

toā kīm, 大 |, tante, (vrouw van moeder's ouderen broeder).

soè kīm, 小 |, zuster, (vrouw van zijne vrouw's broeder).

拎 *kīm gīng*, | 執, opnemen.

Kīm *kīm toà*, | 帶, eene securiteit, onderpand in iets hebben.

kīm tiā, | 定, handgeld (bij het sluiten van een koop) ontvangen.

欽 *k'im ts'e*, | 差, keizerlijk gezant.

K'im *k'im bīng*, | 命, keizerlijk bevel.

k'im ts'ī, | 持, omzigtig.

k'im t'ien kàm, | 天 監, keizerlijke astronoom.

k'im hoān, | 犯, keizerlijke misdadigers, (die opbevel des keizers opgevat of door hem geregt worden).

k'im kìng, | 敬, zeer eerbiedigen, hoogachten.

k'im àn, | 案, aanklagt bij den keizer.

襟 *tuì k'im ê sa*, 對 | 衣, van voren

K'im in het midden opengaand kleed.

k'im hiā tī, | 兄 弟, zwagers door huweijk met zusters uit een huis.

tâng k'im, 仝 |, do.

禽 Vogels.

K'im *k'im siù*, | 獸, vogels en viervoetige dieren.

k'im hing, | 胸, borst van beesten.

擒 Grijpen, vatten, gevangen nemen.
K'im *k'im liáh*, | 掠, vatten, gevangen nemen.
k'im ts'át k'im ts'át siú, | 賊 | 賊 首, bij het vatten van roovers moet men het roovers hoofd vatten.
ts'i̱ k'im pèh k'ìh, 青 | 白 | 去, plotseling onverwachts gegrepen worden, ook van een plotselingen dood.

琴 Luit met zeven snaren.
K'im *toâ k'im*, 彈 |, de luit spelen.
k'im soà, (of *hièn*), | 線 | 絃, snaren eener luit,
géh k'im, 月 |, ronde guitaar.
hô k'im, 和 |, eene luit stemmen.
k'im īm, | 音, naklank eener luit.
hong k'im, 風 |, orgel.

Kin

今* *kin ná dzit*, | 日, heden.
kin mi̱ / » *mé̱* } | 夜, van nacht.

緊 Snel, gaauw, spoedig; dringend, noodzakelijk; vast aan, strak, stijf.
Kin *koâ kin*, 趕 |, haasten, spoedig.
kin kin, | 匕, gaauw snel,
kin mi̱ / » *mé̱* } | 醒, spoedig, haastig.
kin sìng, sim sìng kin, kin sim sìng, (of *si̱*), | 性, 心 性 |, | 心 性, driftig, haastig van aard.
pàng kin 縫 |, snel, gaauw.

kin tsiép k'oàì, | 接 快, gaauw. snel.
kin t'in tsiep lim, | 充 接 飲, zoo inschenken en zoo weer uitdrinken; haastig handelen.
kin kiâ bò hó pō, | 行 無 好 步, gaauw gaat niet zeker.
bò kin bò bōn, (of *k'oa̱*), 無 | 無 緩, niet weten naar de omstandigheden langzaam en gaauw te handelen.
kin kiu̱ / » *kiu̱* } | 羌, haastig, niet dralend.
bò tá kin, 無 打 |, hulpvaardig, gedienstig.
kin kap, | 蛤, gaauw in elkander zetten, (als kleèren), gaauw en goed afdoen (als een zaak).
kin sim, | 心, gaauw afgaan, (van een lontgeweer.
kin iaò, | 要, dringend, noodzakelijk, voornaam.
iaò kin, 要 |, noodzakelijk, voornaamste, van belang.
bò iaò kin, 無 要 |, het komt er niet op aan.
kin kip, | 急, dringend noodzakelijk.
ts'ūi kin, pik kin, 推 |, 迫 |, haasten, aandringen, (als op betaling.)
àn kin, 安 |, stijfaangehaald,
pák kin kin, 縛 安 |, stijfbinden.
kin sin á, | 身 仔, strak om het lijfsluitend kleed.

謹 Vlijtig, zorgvuldig.
Kin *kin sīn*, | 慎, zorgvuldigd, omzigtig.
k'ùn kin / *k'in* » } | 勤, naarstig, vlijtig.

耿 Familienaam.
Kin

* Zie verder onder *kim*.

絹 Kìn — *kìn á*, ｜ 子, kanefas, soort van taf.

僅 Kin — *kīn kīn*, ｜ 匕, alleen slechts
kīn kièn, ｜ 見, voor het eerst zien' (een voorwerp.)

輕 K'in — Ligt, ligt, gering achten; ligt, gemakkelijk.
k'in tāng. ｜ 重, gewigt.
tsai lâng è k'in tāng, 知 人 ｜ 重, iemands toestand kennen.
k'in sin, ｜ 身, ligt, (zooals een vaartuig), soortelijk ligt; zich ook met lage zaken ophouden.
k'oà k'in, 看 ｜, gering achten minachten.
k'in sang, ｜ 鬆, frisch (zooals na een bad.)
k'in tsûn, ｜ 船, ligt geladen schip.
k'in sia soè seh, ｜ 聲 細 說, omzigtig spreken.
k'in k'oaì, ｜ 快, werkzaam, hulpvaardig; handig, (zoools een klein boek).
k'in séng, ｜ 省, gemakkelijk te doen, handig.
k'in k'ó, k'in k'in k'ó k'ó, ｜ 考、｜ 匕 考 匕, ligt, gemakkelijk.
sai k'in ts'în, 使 ｜ 槿, een ligte, (valsche) schaal gebruiken.
tāng t'aô k'in, 重 頭 ｜, ongelijk zwaar aan de beide uiteinden.
k'in k'a ts'eng, ｜ 脚 穿, voor iedereen opstaan, nederig.
kut t'aô k'in, 骨 頭 ｜, laag, zwak, (van aard).
ts'uì t'aô k'in, 嘴 頭 ｜, ligt, zacht in den mond, (oorspr. van beesten ook van kooplieden die niet veel over vragen).
toē ling k'in, 地 龍 ｜, stil in de natuur, (zooals 's nachts).
hī k'ang k'in, 耳 空 ｜, ligtgeloovig.
k'a pō k'in, 脚 步 ｜, zacht in zijn loopen.
k'in k'a liem ts'iu. ｜ 脚 斂 ｜, omzigtig, voorzigtig.
pī liaó k'ah k'in, 病 了 ｜, zijne ziekte is ligter, minder.
k'in k'in á, ｜ 匕 仔. ligtelijk, zachtjes, een weinig, even.
k'in k'in kòng kòng, rammelen, tegen elkander aanstooten, (van voorw.)

淺 K'in — Ondiep.
k'in k'in, ｜ ｜, do.
k'in keh. ｜ 格, dunne laag, (zooals korst van bergen voor dat men aangoede aarde komt.)
k'in t'á. ｜ 挺, gemakkelijk te kennen, niet diep.
tsai lâng è ts'im k'in, 知 人 深 ｜, iemands toestand door en door kennen.
k'in póh, ｜ 薄, ondiep en dun.
k'in tsuí, ｜ 水, ondiep water.
k'in tsìng, ｜ 凈, ligte ziekte.
k'in pah téng, ｜ 腹 腸, niet veel kunnen in houden, verzwijgen.
k'in lâng boē k'èng pō, ｜ 人 莫 藏 步, ondiepe menschen, *d. i.* zonder doorzigt, kunnen hunne plannen niet voor zich houden.
k'in ts'iû póh piah, ｜ 墻 薄 壁, ondiepe (*d. i.* lage) wallen en dunne muren (een plaats waar men ligt afgeluisterd kan worden).

肯 K'in — *k'in īm k'in*, ｜ 不 ｜, stemt ge toe of niet?

King

經 King Schering van een weefsel; standaard, klassieke boeken, gebeden boek; de menses; gaan door, voorbijgaan; verleden; handelen, doen.

king hui, 丨緯, schering en inslag.

king tsu } 丨書, klassieke boeken.
» *si* }

ts'ut king dzip tién, 出丨入典, in klassieke boeken voorkomende, in de klassieken doorkneed.

king tsè, 丨濟, kennis om een rijk te besturen.

king koán, 丨權, onverandelijk, onverandelijk.

siōng king, liēm king, 誦丨, 念丨, gebeden opzeggen.

king ts'àm, 丨讖, brevier, boete gebeden (van Boeddh.)

géh king, king tsui, king ki, 月丨, 丨水, 丨期, de menses.

kiâ king, 行丨, de menses hebben.

king kè, 丨過, voorbijgaan; bijgewoond hebben.

king ts'iú, 丨手, door iemands handen gaan.

king kè i è ts'iú, 丨過伊之手, het is door zijne handen gegaan.

king it sū tióng it tì, 丨一事長一智, na elke zaak wordt men een stap wijzer.

king giēm, 丨驗, uitkomen, goede werking hebben.

king lik, 丨歷, ondervinding hebben van.

i king, 已丨, reeds.

king kì, 丨見, zeker, voorwaar, (als of men het reeds zag.)

king kí, 丨紀, beroep, broodwinning.

king ing, 丨營, bedrijvig. onvermoeid werkzaam.

king lik, of *king lik t'ia*, 丨曆 房, hoofdklerk in een mandarijn bureau.

弓 King Kiong Boog, handboog.

king tsì ping, 丨箭兵, boogschutters bij het leger.

king hiên, 丨弦, pees van een boog.

lō king, 路丨, kruisboog.

kiáng king, 响丨, rottingen gonsboog die men bij vliegers op laat.

tiao king á, 雕丨仔, als een boog ombuigen, krombuigen.

bán taò (of *tà*) *king*, 蚊罩丨, toeslaand muskieten scherm.

宮 King Kiong Tempel.

king biō, 丨廟, tempel.

king kong, 丨公, deurwachter, oppasser in een tempel.

間 King Kan Numer. voor huizen, kamers.

king á, 丨仔, hut.

sa king pâng, 三丨房, drie kamers.

供 King Kiong Getuigenis afleggen.

k'ao king, 口丨, mondelinge getuigenis.

tèng king, 當丨, getuigenis voor den regter afgelegd.

hoán king, 反丨, zijne getuigenis veranderen, verdraaijen.

驚 King Vreezen, vrees aanjagen.

king tōng, 丨動, vrees aanjagen; beleefd lastig vallen.

king t'ien tōng tē, 丨天動地, de geheele wereld met vrees en verbazing bevangen.

taī king siaó koaì, 大｜小怪, schrik aanjagend en wonderlijk.

king sim, ｜心, gejaagd, onrustig, (zooals vreezende te laat te komen).

king hong, ｜風, een stuip krijgen. (van kinderen); gebarsten (als porselein.)

更 Veranderen.

King *king ik*, ｜易, veranderen.

king oā, ｜換, do.

king tiong, ｜重, zich uitbreiden, (zooals eene handels zaak.)

king i tsoá, ｜衣紙, kleeren omruilens papier, papier met kleeren beteekend en voor de overledenen verbrand.

king i só, ｜衣所, vertrek waarin de hoofdrouwdrager bezoeken ontvangt.

肩 *king t'aô*, ｜頭, de schouders.

King

Kan

梗 Stengel van graan of bloemen; numer

King voor ankers.

tsit king hoe / » « *hoa* } 桼｜花, een takje bloemen van een bloem tros.

撐 Afduwen, afsteken, afstooten.

King *king k'ui*, ｜開, afsteken, van elkander afsteken, zich onttrekken aan.

king lìng. ｜另, afstooten en zich vooruitstooten, (zooals kikvorschen), *d. i.* zich vooruit zien te stooten in de wereld.

庚 *kuì king to siaó*, 貴｜多少,

King hoe oud zijt gij! (bel. term.)

兢 *king king giép giép ê lâng*, ｜｜業

King 匕的人, een ijverig werkzaam man.

king t'oé / « *t'é* } ｜體, een toepasselijken bij naam geven.

景 Uitzigt, ligging, (van eene plaats);

King voorkomen, toestand, gesteldheid, omstandigheden.

kong king, 光｜, uitzigt; landschap, toestand, uitzigt in de toekomst.

king tì, ｜致, do.

hó kong king, 好光｜, fraai uitzigt; goed uitzigt in de toekomst.

hó king, 好｜, fraai uitzigt, fraaije natuur.

king hóng, ｜況, toestand, omstandigheden, (van pers.)

king sik, ｜色, toestand, (van pers.)

sè king, 世｜, toestand der eeuw.

k'ó king, 苦｜, ellendige toestand.

ts'ok (of *ts'iok*) *king*, 觸｜, van de omstandigheden, het toeval afhangend.

siat king, 設｜, invoeren, nieuw instellen; foppen.

境 Grens, grenspaal, einde.

King *king laī*, ｜內, binnen de grenzen.

king kaì, ｜界, grens.

king tsú, ｜主, grensheer, dorpsgod.

dziaó king, 繞｜, de rondte in de gemeente doen, (van een afgod die rond gedragen wordt.

king gū, ｜遇, overkomen, wedervaren, voorvallen, ontmoetingen in het leven.

bé king / *boé* » } 每｜, laatste levensjaren.

lók king, 樂｜, gelukkige oude dag.

警 Vrees aanjagen, vermanen.

King *king kaì*, ｜戒, vermanen.

king sing, ｜省, vermanende tot inzigt brengen.

揀 Kiezen, uitkiezen; uitzoeken.

King *king tsiáh king ts'ing*, ｜食｜

穿, keurig op voedsel en kleeding zijn.

king kiá sài, | 婿, zich een schoonzoon kiezen.

king làng kóng, | 人 說, zijn man uitkiezen om iets te zeggen.

king sú tsaī, | 所 在, de plaats kiezen, van de plaats afhangen, (zooals de vraag naar zekere waren.)

龔 King Kióng Familienaam.

繭 King Kán Rimpel, plooi, vouw.

k'ioh king, 積 |, met plooijen gerimpeld.

bīn p'ê k'ioh king, 面 皮 曲 |, rimpels op het gelaat.

liep king, 攝 |, met plooijen, rimpels.

pah king (of *kién*) *kûn*, 百 | 裙, fijn geplooide vrouwen rok.

敬 Kìng Eeren, eerbiedigen; aanbidden, offeren.

kìng tiōng, | 重, eerbiedigen, hoogachten.

kìng ùi, | 畏, eerbiedig vreezen.

kìng dzī t'ák tsoè ùi dzī / » » » *tsò ùi* » } | 字 讀 作 畏 字, het karakter eerbiedigen lezen als vreezen, *d. i.* iemands eerbied voor vrees houden.

kìng lìng, | 領, met eerbied, hoogachting aannemen, (invitatie schenke.)

kìng kín, | 謹, eerbiedigen en zorgvuldig nakomen (een bevel).

kìng ts'ik siā bô kìng toā hia, | 粟 棫 無 | 大 兄, de rijstvaten en niet den ouderen broeder eeren, *d. i.* iemand alleen om zijn geld eeren.

kìng ì, | 意, eerbiedig.

kìng tsiú, | 酒, elkander toedrinken.

kìng paì, | 拜. aanbidden.

kìng toh, | 棹, een tafel met spijzen offeren.

hièn kìng, 獻 |, offeranden aanbieden.

kìng oá, | 碗, kopjes met offeranden.

ts'aì kìng, 菜 |, plantaardige offeranden.

竟 Kìng Ten uiterste, volstrekt; nog meer . . .

goá kìng ǐm tsai, 我 | 不 知, ik weet het volstrekt niet.

kìng k'ah hó, | 好, nog beter.

kìng ǐm saí kóng, | 不 使 說, daar behoeft men nog veel minder over te spreken.

kìng dziên bô kia, | 然 無 驚, nog veel minder vreezen.

徑 Kìng Weg; handelwijze.

lō kìng, 路 |, weg; broodwinning.

hing kìng, 行 |, handeling, levenswandel.

窮 King Kióng Arm.

ke king, 家 |, arm van familie.

king ts'ùn t'ih, | 寸 鐵. dood arm.

king laū sán, | 老 瘦, arm, ouder mager.

king kuí, | 鬼, arme duivel,

bē king ts'ut king si / *boē* » » » » } 未 | 出 | 尸, voor dat men nog arm is zich als een arme aanstellen.

king hàn, | 漢, arm mensch.

king k'ó, | 苦, arm en ellendig.

king kuí bô hoat tit kip kè tā oà, | 鬼 莫 發 急 計 何,

de duivel van armoede is tegen geen vlijt bestand, *d. i.* door vlijt overwint men armoede.

king si tsaó, 丨死走, arm, dood of gevlugt, (gevallen waarin men zijn geld niet terug kan krijgen.

king si si, 丨死乜, lijkarm, doodarm.

king k'ih k'ih, 丨鉄乜, zeer arm.

king ts'ù bò king lō, 丨厝無丨路, al is men arm in huis, buiten of heeft men toch geld noodig.

king kui pé aō mîng, 丨鬼把後門, zeer inhalig; eigenbelangzuchtig.

king lâng bò pù ts'in, 丨人無富親, arme lui hebben geen rijke verwanten.

輔 Kîng Tegen aanzetten, stutten met.

toā soè kîng, } 大小相丨, grooten
» *sè* »
en kleinen die elkander stutten.

sa kîng, 相丨, elkander stutten, ondersteunen, helpen.

kîng oá, 丨倚, tegen iets aanzetten, stutten met.

boè kā kîng tit, 莫相丨的, niet op te houden, niet te helpen (van personen.

toā tsiòh soè tsiòh kîng, 大石小石丨, een groote steen moet door kleinen gestut worden, *d. i.* hoe groot men ook zij men heeft altijd helpers noodig.

k'a ts'eng kîng sa oá, 脚穿丨相倚, elkander rugsteunen, (zooals bij een koop of eene valsche beschuldiging.)

kîng lai kîng k'ì, 丨來丨去, elkander stuttende, door elkander.

梗 Kîng *kîng tsoá*, 丨紙, wit teekenpapier.

輕 K'ing Ligt, geringachten; ligtzinnig, onbezadigd.

k'ing tsiēn, 丨賤, minachten.

k'ing sin, 丨身, zich niet ontzien, zich tot alles leenen.

k'ing sìn, 丨信, ligtgeloovig.

k'ing pók, 丨薄, weinig beduidend, onbezadigd.

k'ing k'ì, 棄丨, verstooten.

k'ing hò sò sut } 丨毫掃率,
» *hû* » »
oppervlakkig, onbesuisd.

k'ing hō sò sut ê lâng, 丨毫掃率的人, een ongestadig mensch.

k'ing t'iao ê lâng, 丨起的人, een ligtzinnig, onbezadigd mensch.

筐 K'ing Open mandje.

k'ing á, 丨仔, do.

tseh k'ing, 坐丨, spinmand, (waarin vrouwen de afgehaalde draden doen.)

銎 K'ing Oog voor de steel van een houweel enz.

pò t'aô k'ing, 斧頭丨, oog van houweel.

to k'ing, 刀丨, rug van een mes.

規 K'ing Vierkant raam, lijst, rand om iets.

nâ k'ing, 籃丨, rand van een mand.

goā k'ing, 外丨, buitenste rand.

k'ing k'ak, 丨殼, de romp, ruwe omtrek van iets, (ook van zaken.)

卿 K'ing Edelman, adelstand.

kong k'ing, 公丨, adelstand.

sam kong kiú k'ing, 三公九丨, hooge adel.

傾 K'ing Omkeeren, in iets uitkeeren; smelten, zuiveren, (van metalen.)

k'ing ka tōng sán, 丨家蕩產, al zijne bezittingen opmaken.

k'ing k'à (of *k'ing*,) 丨 扣, alles bij elkander zoeken.

k'ing pún tsi (of *k'ing*) 丨 本 錄, zijn kapitaal bij een garen.

k'ing kok è ping, 丨 國 之 兵, alle over zijnde strijdbare mannen in het rijk uitkeeren, oproepen.

k'ing tsien, 丨 煎, (metalen) smelten, zuiveren.

k'ing gûn, 丨 銀, zilver smelten, zuiveren.

肯 Willen, zullen.

K'ing *tiòng k'ing*, 中 丨, juist, juist geraakt; de spijker juist op den kop staan.

頃 *k'ing k'ik kan*, 丨 刻 間, in een
K'ing oogenblik.

k'ing k'ik á, 丨 刻 仔, do.

磬 Steenen thans ook metalenplaat, (waar-
K'ing op personen slaan.

k'ing tsi, 丨 錢, zilveren medaille, plaat in de vorm van de *k'ing* door kinderen om de hals gedragen.

慶 *k'ing hō*, 丨 賀, gelukwenschen.

Kìng *tsoè k'ing sing* / *tsò » »* } 作 丨 成, feliciteren met de voltooijing van iets.

K'ing *k'ing ling ling*, in het geheel, alles bij elkander . . . . .

k'ing gûn / *» gin* } zilver zuiveren; al zijn geld bij elkander halen.

k'ing siaò, al zijne rekeningen opmaken.

k'ing pún tsi, zijn kapitaal bij elkander brengen.

k'ing k'à, bij elkander schrapen, bij elkander brengen, (overblijvend geld, goed enz.)

k'īng (of *k'ing*) *oá lai*, bij elkander zenden rekenen.

虹 Regenboog.

K'īng *ts'ut k'īng*, 出 丨, er staat een regenboog aan den hemel.

k'īng dziō, 丨 尿, weinige regendroppels die vallen als er een regenboog staat.

桱 *k'īng ts'iū*, 丨 樹, talkboom.

K'īng *k'īng iû*, 丨 油, talk.

k'īng tô, olie van de talkboom.

Kio

叫 Roepen, ontbieden, halen; schreeuwen;
Kiò noemen, heeten.

kiò lai, 丨 來, om iemand roepen.

kiò tsí / *» tsé* } 丨 醒, wakker maken, to[t] inzien brengen.

kiò mêng / *» muî* } 丨 門, roepen om de poor[t] of deur te openen.

ai ai kiò, 哀 匕 丨, janken.

kiò kim, 丨 金, door het slaan op d[e] gong elkander toeseinen.

kiò sim mih miâ, 丨 何 名, hoe hee[t] het?

kiò koe / *» ke* } 丨 街, langs de straat be[...] delen.

haó kiò, 吼 丨, hard schreeuwen schreijen.

kiò kiù lâng, 丨 救 人, omhulp roe[...] pen.

ts'ut tù hō lâng kiò, 出 抵 與 人 丨, iemands iets in den we[g] leggen om met hem aan den gang t[e] geraken.

kiò k'ó, 丨 苦, het uitschreeuwen va[n] de pijn.

kiò kog ts'è / *» » ts'iè* } 丨 官 摧, het uit[-] schreeuwen wanneer men gestraf[t] wordt.

kiò t'i kiò toē / *» » » tē* } 丨 天 丨 地, heme[l] en aarde tot zijn hulp aanroepen i[n] nood.

p'ien kiò, 偏 呼, iemand bij een anderen naam dan zijn eigelijken noemen.

kiò tsûn, | 船, om een schuit roepen.

kiò tsoè } | 做, noemen, heeten.
» tsò }

miâ kiò, 名 |, heeten, genoemd worden.

kiò kuí kiò koaì, | 鬼 | 怪, hard schreeuwen, roepen.

tsit kiò tsit ìn, 一 | 一 應, zóó roepen zóó antwoorden; elkander over en weer uitschelden.

kiò kao t'oè, | 交 替, iemand tot aflossing roepen, gezegd van iemands geest drie jaren na dat hij verdronken enz. is.

kiò kiō, | 轎, een draagstoel roepen, bestellen.

t'aò kiò bé ìn, | 未 應, onmiddelijk antwoorden als men geroepen wordt.

kiò lé long, | 嚟 嚨, op vendutie verkoopen.

kiò bing, | 明, duidelijk bespreken, zeggen.

kiò k'í, | 起, van iets spreken, iets ophalen afspreken.

kiò t'i t'i ēm t'ia, kiò toē toē ēm ìn, | 天 七 不 聽 | 地 七 不 應, geen hulp kunnen krijgen, (zooals bij een schipbreuk.

soa ting bô hó kiò, soa ē bô hó ìn, 山 頂 無 好 | 山 下 無 好 應, wordt er op den berg slecht geroepen dan wordt er aan den voet van den berg ook slecht geantwoord, *d. i.* die uitscheldt moet ook verwachten terug gescholden te worden.

橋 Brug.
Kiô

tiaò kiô, 弔 |, ophaalbrug.

ún ku kiô, 曲 |, ronde bolle brug, boogbrug.

tsioh kiô kè } 做 | 過, een brug-
» « koè }
leenen om over te gaan, *d. i.* hulp leenen.

siu kiô tsō lō, 修 | 造 路, bruggen repareren en wegen maken.

ts'â kiô, 柴 |, houten brug.

p'û kiô, 浮 |, drijvende schipbrug.

kiô pán, | 板, planken of steenen van een brug.

kiô k'a, | 脚, bruggenhoofd onder de brug.

kiô sin, | 神, beschermgeesten van een brug.

蕎 De solanum melongena.
Kiô

kiô béh, | 麥, boekweit.

轎 Draagstoel.
Kiō

tsē kiō, 坐 |, in een draagstoel zitten.

kiō hū, | 夫, stoeldrager.

hoe kiō } 花 |, bruidsstoel.
hoa » }

sin niû kiō } 新 娘 |, do.
» niô » }

ts'ai kiō, 彩 |, do.

kiō pan, | 班, stoeldragers.

sì kiō, 四 |, stoel van vier dragers.

kiō taó, | 斗, zitplaats in een draagstoel.

kiō li, | 簾, scherm van een draagstoel.

kiō tsáh, | 閘, voetscherm van een draagstoel.

kiō koà, | 蓋, bovenste gedeelte van een draagstoel.

kiō t'ang, ｜窗, rampjes van een draagstoel.

kiō king, *kiō tièm*, ｜間, ｜店, winkel waar men draagstoelen verhuurt.

kiō kìng, ｜杠, draaghouten aan een draagstoel.

bé kiō, *tsoē tsoē tsoē*, 馬｜多匕, velen te paard en in draagstoelen.

kiō k'a, ｜脚, stoeldragers.

kiō ē, ｜夫, do.

kiō pán, ｜板, handleuning in den draagstoel.

怪 K'iò *hē tsoá tsoè k'iò* / *hē « tsò »* } 作｜, bidden om allerlei wonderlijkedingen.

koé k'iò, 過｜, eene door anderen gedane gelofte voor iemands verderf door toovenaars enz. verijdelen, uitwisschen.

tik k'iò 竹｜, bamboozen waterleiding.

k'iò tsui, ｜水, waterleiden.

Kioh

脚 Kioh Numer. voor komedianten.

ki kioh, 奇｜, vorm, uiterlijk.

iù kioh, 幼｜, fijn zachtzinnig mensch.

tsit kioh hì, 一｜戲, één tooneelspeler.

ts'o kioh, 粗｜, ruwe grove kerel.

hu kioh, 夫｜, lastdragers,

kang kioh, 工｜, do.

kioh siaò, ｜數, aantal lastdragers.

hó kioh siaò, 好｜數, knap in zijn vak, uitstekende boven anderen.

kioh á, ｜仔, lijkkistdragers.

tsoè kioh e lâng, 作｜的人, koelies.

pih ts'iú lák kioh, 比手動｜, zijne mouwen en broek opstroopen.

pān kioh siaò, 辦｜數, zijn aantal bedienden, lastdragers in gereedheid brengen.

koe kioh / *ke »* } 雞｜, een schelpdier in den vorm van een schildpadspoot.

tsit kioh, 一｜, die kerel (met soort minachting).

ts'it kioh hì pò bān ping, 七｜戲呼萬兵, in eene comedie van zeven acteurs tien-duizend soldaten opgeven, *d. i.* met weinig middelen veel doen of willen doen.

kóng kioh (of *kiò*), 言｜, spreken van . . . , zeggen dat . . . . wat ik zeggen wil, enz.

拾 K'ioh *k'ioh lioh*, ｜匕, verzamelen.

k'iong k'ioh, 强｜, oprapen, bij een garen.

k'ioh seh / *» seh* } ｜屑, nalezen, (als op een veld).

k'ioh ts'ik, ｜粟, do.

k'ioh béh / *» béh* } ｜麥, do.

k'ioh k'í lai, ｜起, oprapen.

k'ioh k'í, ｜齒, tanden uitnemen, uittrekken,

k'an k'ioh, 牽｜, uit den nood helpen.

k'ioh t'oâ k'ioh bé, ｜頭｜尾, het weinig overgeschotene, afval bij elkander garen.

k'ioh tióh mih, ｜着物, oprapen, (van den grond).

k'ioh káh, ｜擲, waard om weg gegooid te worden, niets waardig.

k'ioh sip, ｜ 什, niets weg gooijen, zuinig.

k'ioh k'a tsiū kiâ, ｜ 足 即 行, onmiddelijk gaan, niet talmen.

k'ioh siaò, ｜ 數, de verschillende posten opzoeken en bij elkander schrijven.

k'ioh k'ioh k'i hó, ｜ 乜 至 好, goed geregeld bij elkander zoeken.

k'ioh bi, ｜ 米, rijst oppikken.

k'ioh tsi, ｜ 錢, geld bij elkander brengen, ophalen.

k'ioh siaó iāg ｜ 小 影, een portrait nemen.

boē k'ioh tit, 未 ｜ 的, niet kunnen aanleeren, overnemen.

k'ioh tioh sì miā, ｜ 着 性 命, er zijn hagje uithalen, uit een gevaar zijn.

k'ioh ts'â ·gin á, ｜ 柴 孖 仔, jongen die de gevallen stukken hout opraapt, krullen jongen.

lân san k'ioh kui hāng, 零 刪 ｜ 歸 項, in kleine hoeveelheden bij elkander brengen.

k'ioh kut, ｜ 骨, doods beenderen opgraven, (om in een urn te doen).

k'ioh koan, ｜ 棺, een lijkkist opgraven.

k'ioh king, ｜ 景, gerimpeld geplooid.

育 K'ioh *k'ioh kiá*, ｜ 子, een kind helpen baren.

k'ioh tsiá, ｜ 婆, vroedvrouw.

k'ioh kiá bú / *» tsiá bó* } ｜ 婦 女, do.

Kiok

鞠 Kiok *ts'iu kiok kiong*, 手 ｜ 躬, met de handen in elkander en voorover gebogen, uit eerbied of luiheid.

趣 Kiòk *ū kiòk*, 有 ｜, schrander, rijzig, fraai, aan het oog voldoen.

bô kióh, 無 ｜, zich vervelen, vervelend.

局 Kiók *dzip kiók*, 入 ｜, aan de conclusie, beslissing komen.

kiók ts'iok, ｜ 促, naauw, bekrompen.

k'iok p'ièn, ｜ 騙, met een streek bedriegen.

kiet kiók, 結 ｜ / *bé kiók* / *boè »* } 尾 ｜ / *liaò kiók* 了 ｜ } afloop, ontknooping, einde van een zaak.

ki kiók, 機 ｜, voorkomen, toestand der zaken.

pò kiók, 布 ｜, uitmaken, doen.

pai kè kiók, 排 計 ｜, een middel, een weg op iets vinden.

tong kiók, 當 ｜, in de zaak betrokken.

kiók goā è lâng, ｜ 外 之 人, menschen die niets met de zaak te maken hebben.

却 K'iok *k'iok sī*, ｜ 是, toch, inderdaad is het . . .

K'iak *k'iok iā*, ｜ 也, toch ook . . . , toch eigenlijk ook.

k'iok lâng è ì sū, ｜ 人 之 意, zich tegen iemands bedoeling zetten, iemands bedoeling kwetsen.

曲 K'iok *ui k'iok*, 委 ｜, ingewikkelde, lastige (zaak).

tsing lí k'iok, 情 理 ｜, niet goed van beginselen.

k'ut k'ut k'iok k'iok, 屈 匕 ｜ 匕, krom, niet gelijk.

oan oan k'iok k'iok, 灣 匕 ｜ 匕, krom, slingervormig.

k'iok tsiòng, 丨 從, gedwongen, opvolgen, gehoorzamen.

Kiong

恭 Eerbiedigen, eerbiediglijk.
Kiong *kiong king*, 丨 敬, eerbiedigen, eerbiediglijk.
kiong hí, 丨 喜, gelukwenschen, ik feliciteer u!
kiong kiù, 丨 救, eerbiedig smeeken, verzoeken.
ts'ut kiong, 出 丨, afgaan, stoelgang hebben.

供 Geven, aanbieden.
Kiong *kiong kip*, 丨 給, geven schenken.
kiong hōng, 丨 奉, aanbieden, (zooals geschenken).

宮 Verblijf; keizerlijk paleis.
Kiong *kòng kiong*, *kiong tiēn*, 公 丨, 皇 丨, keizerlijk paleis.
kiong laī, 丨 內, in het keizerlijk paleis.
kiong lú, 丨 女, vrouwelijke bedienden in het paleis.
tsú kiong, 子 丨, baarmoeder.

拱 *kiong ts'iú*, 丨 手, buigen, (de handen schudden als de Chineezen), de handen in de mouwen bij elkander houden.
Kióng

强 Dwingen, noodzaken.
Kióng *bién kióng*, 勉 丨, zich inspannen om, dwingen noodzaken.
kióng piēn, 丨 辯, balstarrig, volhouden.
k'ièn kióng, 牽 丨, geforceerd, gedwongen, (spreken).
sa kióng, 相 丨, elkander aanzetten, forceren.

强 Geweld, geweld gebruiken, gewelddadig, sterk.
Kiòng
kiàng *kiòng kiòng*, 丨 匕, met alle geweld.
kiòng tō, 丨 盜, met geweld, rooven.
kiòng kan, 丨 姦, verkrachten.
hing kiòng, 行 丨, alle geweld gebruiken om . . . . .
kiòng dziòk, 丨 弱, sterkte en zwakte.
kiòng pak, 丨 剝, gewelddadig bestelen.
kiòng pà, 丨 霸, gewelddadig in bezit nemen.
tò kiòng, 鬥 丨, met geweld willen doordrijven.

窮 Tot het uiterste gaan, uitputten, tot het
Kiòng uiterste gebragt, uitgeput, het toppunt bereiken, arm, tot ellende gebragt.
kiòng kong kik k'aó, 丨 工 極 巧, het toppunt van volmaaktheid bereikt hebben, (van handwerk.)
bù kiòng tsīn, 無 丨 盡, grenzeloos.
kiòng kik, 丨 極, uiterste, toppunt van, (armoede enz.)
san kiòng sui tsīn, 山 丨 水 盡, uiterst ver; tot het uiterste toe.
bút kiòng tsik pièn, 物 丨 卽 變, na het toppunt, de crisis, komt verandering.
kiòng k'ò bòk tui, 丨 寇 莫 追, tot het uiterste gebragte struikroovers vervolge men niet verder *d. i.* iemand die zijne straf reeds heeft, kwelle men niet meer.
pin kiòng, 貧 丨, arm, behoeftig.
kiòng k'ó, 丨 苦, arm en ellendig.
kò kiòng, 固 丨, in zijne armoede nog zijn pligt betrachten.

共 *kè kiōng*, 計 丨, bij elkander tellen,
kiōng gerekend.

kiōng sìng / » *suì̤* } | 寘, do.

háp kiōng, 合 |, do.

kiōng kè, | 計, bij elkander gerekend.

t'ong kiōng, 通 |, alles bij elkander.

t'óng kiōng, 統 |, do.

tsóng kiōng, 總 |, in het geheel, do.

kong kiōng, 公 |, gemeenschappelijk.

kiōng tsóng, | 總, gezamenlijk bij elkander.

kiōng gûn, | 銀, al het geld bij elkander geteld.

kiōng sū, | 事, gezamenlijk doen handelen.

恐 K'ióng *k'ióng uì* / » *nì* } | 畏, uit vrees dat, op dat niet.

k'ióng p'à̤, | 怕, do.

tān k'ióng . . . 但 |, ... alleen vrees ik dat . . . .

hông k'ióng, 惶 |, vrees, bevreesd zijn dat . . . .

sing hông sing k'ióng, 誠 惶 誠 |, inderdaad bevreesd, (*b. v.* om onbeleefd te zijn).

Kip

急 Kip Dringend, uiterst noodzakelijk; haastig. haasten, aanzetten, aandringen op; dringende nood.

kip kip, | 乜, dringend, spoedig,

kip iaò, | 要, dringend, noodzakelijk.

kín kip, 緊 |, do.

kò kip, 告 |, tot haast aansporen, dringend aanzetten.

kip kè, | 計, onvermoeid, snel handelen.

lim kip, 監 |, op het dringende, gevaarlijke oogenblik.

kiù kip, 救 |, in het oogenblik van nood te hulp komen.

tióh kip, 着 |, ongeduldig zijn naar.

tsing kip, 情 |, haastig, geagiteerd.

kip sìng, | 性, haastig van gestel.

gui kip, 危 |, gevaarlijk.

kip pik, | 廹, sterk aandringen op, (betaling, enz.)

kip ts'iok, | 促, sterk aandringen op.

級 Kip Mandarijn graad rang; afgehakt hoofd.

p'ín kip. 品 |, graad, rang.

ke kip, 加 |, een graad hooger zijn.

ka kip, 加 |, een graad verhoogd worden.

kàng kip, 降 |, een graad dalen.

siú kip, 首 |, afgehakt hoofd.

Kip *kip sio*, | 燒, theeketel.

給 Kip Geven, schenken, ter handstellen.

kiong kip, 供 |, geven, schenken.

kip lō̤ huì, | 路 費, reisgeld geven.

kip pin, | 憑, een bewijs geven.

kip bûn su, | 文 書, eene dépêche overhandigen.

及 Kip *put kip*, 不 |, te laat, niet gelijk komen aan.

hù put kip, 赴 不 |, te laat komen.

kip si, 時, juist op den tijd komen dat men het noodig heeft, op den juisten tijd komende.

kip kaò, . . . | 至, . . . tot aan . . .

í kip, 己 |, met, benevens.

kip sin, | 身, op zijn persoon nederkomen, (als een onheil.)

笈 *pêh kip*, 白 |, plant tot stijfsel gebezigd, een zeer vergtftige plant.
Kíp

K'ip *k'ip k'ip*, | 匕, kort, van een handsvat, enz.

k'a k'ip tiauh, 脚 | 着, met de pooten zich vast klemmen aan, (zooals vogel aan de takken.)

kip tiaò tiaò, | 着 匕, zich vast houden aan, (eene zaak of een voorwerp.)

k'i̱ kip, 牽 |, iets om zich aan vast te houden; securiteit.

bô k'i̱ bô kip, 無 牽 無 |, geen houvast aan iets hebben, geene zekerheid op iemand hebben.

K'it

乞 Bedelen, vragen om, smeeken om.

K'it *k'it tsiáh*, | 食, bedelaar.

k'it tsi̱, | 錢, om geld bedelen.

kiû k'it, 求 |, bedelen.

k'it kiá̱, | 子, een kind koopen.

k'it hō̱, | 雨, om regen bidden.

k'it bô tit t'ang tióh, | 未 得 着, om iets vragen maar het niet kunnen krijgen.

k'it tsiáh k'it, | 食 |, bedelaar van bedelaars, iemand iets willen afbedelen wat hij zelf gekregen heeft.

k'it tsiáh iá̱, | 食 營, bedelaarsbuurt.

k'it tsiáh t'aô, | 食 頭, hoofd der bedelaars, bedelaars gilden meester.

k'it tsiá̱h bāng toā ts'ù, | 食 望 大 厝, de bedelaar hoopt op een groothuis, *d. i.* van een magtigen om hulp uitzien.

k'it tsiáh kut, | 食 骨, lage manieren hebben.

k'it tsiáh mē̱ kaó, kaô nē̱ k'it tsiáh, 食 罵 猴 匕 罵 | 食, de bedelaar en de aap schelden elkander uit.

k'it tsiáh pô boē siū tit hong ts'ien » » » *hō̱* » » » », | 食 婆 未 受 皇 誥, eene bedelares kan niet tot eere posten verhoogd worden, *d. i.* gemeene lieden kunnen niet in aanzien stijgen.

k'it tsiáh sin hông tè ts'ùi, | 食 身 皇 帝 口, ligchaam als een bedelaar en mond als een keizer, *d. i.* een arme lekker bek.

k'it tsiáh pô kiá̱ beh t'àn lâng tsiáh hûn p'ièn ko koe, | 食 婆 子 要 從 人 食 紅 片 糕 粿, het bedelaars kind wil even als anderen, koekkippen, (eene kinderlekkernij) eten, *d. i.* naar iets verlangen dat buiten zijn staat is.

k'it tsiáh hiêm p'oà ké, | 食 嫌 破 粿, de bedelaar maakt aanmerking op stukkende koek *d. i* aanmerking maken op iets dat men ontvangen heeft.

k'it tsiáh si tī bé tsô, | 食 死 在 馬 槽, de bedelaar sterft in den paardentrog, een uitgehongerde die zich dood eet.

(*k'it tsiáh sûn koé hióh*,) | 食 巡 街 遏, als een bedelaar die de bladeren waar koek in geweest is opraapt, *d. i.* iemand die niet het minste kan zien verkwisten.

(*k'it tsiáh k'ioh tioh siah koat á lâ k'i tit kiáh*,) | 食 拾 着 錫 連 枴 仔 忘 記 携 去, de bedelaar raapt tin op, (nemende dat het zilver is) en vergeet zijn stok meê te nemen.

祾 Aanduider van den lijdenden vorm ook waar wij het niet uitdrukken.
K'it

k'it làng p'ah, | 人打, geslagen worden.

k'it làng p'ièn, | 人騙, bedrogen worden.

k'it i koâ k'ih, | 伊寒着, door koude bevangen worden, koude vatten.

k'it i kút tó, | 伊滑倒, uitglijden.

k'it i tsai lòh lai, | 伊栽落來, voorover naar beneden vallen.

k'it i tiòh k'a tak, | 伊着脚旦, struikelen.

K'it *p'i k'it ih*, er iemand gemakkelijk laten afkomen, (als schuldigen.)

杙 Spaak, pin

K'it *tìng k'it*, 定 |, een spaak inslaan.

gû k'it, 牛 |, koe spaak, (pin waaraan de koe vaststaat).

kang hu k'it, 工夫 |, steeds werkzaam blijven, zonder baas te worden.

k'i k'it, 牽 |, houvast, securiteit voor iemand.

bô k'i bô k'it, 無牽無 |, niets hebben om zich aan vast te houden, geene securiteit voor iemand hebben.

gaô p'ah k'it, 賢打 |, knap spaken inslaan, *d. i.* knap grondslagen voor iets leggen.

Kiu

縮 Intrekken, terugtrekken, zich terug-
Kiu trekken; inkrimpen, krimpen, (als goed); zich terugtrekken in, (als een muis in zijn gat.)

kiu dzíp k'ang, | 入孔, zich in zijn hol, gat terugtrekken.

kiu dzíp siâ, | 入城, in de stad terugtrekken (als soldaten..)

kiu kiu noëh noëh, | 匕畏匕, met zich zelven verlegen, terugtrokken bedeesd.

kiu k'ì tièm, | 去潛, zich terugtrekken, en verschuilen, (als een rat), sterven.

kiu ts'iú, | 手, zijn hand in (zijn mouw) halen.

ts'un tseh kiu tseh, 伸的 | 的, uitsteken en weder terugtrekken, zoo toe treden en dan weder terugtrekken.

kiu k'ah té, | 短, inkrimpen, (als nieuw goed in water.)

kiu lin k'ih, | | 去, inkrimpen, zich terugtrekken, wegkrimpen, niet voor den dag komen, niet voor den geest komen.

九 Negen.

Kiú *kiú liù*, | 流, de negen (lagere) standen, zooals alle soorten van geestelijken, nonnen, toovenaars.

kiú liòng poâ, | 龍盤, confituren bak met negen afdeelingen.

久 *kiú piét*, | 別, voor langen tijd af-
Kiú scheid nemen.

kiú gióng / *giáng* | 仰, lang heb ik naar U uitgezien, (beleefdheidsterm.)

tiōng kiú, 重 |, lang van duur.

kiú oán, | 遠, lang, (van duur tijd.)

ts'iah kiú kiú, 赤 | |, moedernaakt.

救 Helpen, te hulp komen, redden.

Kiù *kiù kip*, | 急, in het dringende oogenblik helpen.

kiù ìng, | 應, te hulp komen.

kiù ping, | 兵, hulp troepen.

kiù ah! | 仔, help!

kiù sè, | 世, het menschdom helpen, redden, (door medicijnen enz.)

kiù k'ó kiù lān, | 苦 | 難, in ellende en rampen helpen, (van Boeddha.)

koé kiù, 改 |, redden, (als een tegen gift of hulptroepen).

kiù kiông. | 窮, in nood helpen.

kiù t'àng kiù t'oā īm kiù nīng k'a lâng, 虫|拖不可|二脚人, insekten helpe men maar geene menschen, (daar deze te ondankbaar zijn.)

kiù hé, | 火, bij een brand te hulp komen.

kiù pún, | 本, zijn (verloren) kapitaal redden, terug winnen.

kiù miā mīng, | 命毛, haren voor levensredding (door 如來 aan 孫悟空 geven) *d. i.* hulp in nood.

究 Kiù Onderzoeken, navorschen, bestuderen, nagaan.

káng kiù, 講 |, onderzoeken, navorschen.

kiù k'àm, | 勘, grondig onderzoeken.

kun kiù / » *kin* } 根 |, op het spoor nagaan, (als dieven wanneer men weet waar het gestolene is.)

kiù sim, | 心, met een onderzoekenden zin, *d. i.* grondig onderzoeken.

kiù kìng, | 更, ten laatste.

縮 Kiù Intrekken, zamentrekken, terugspringen als een elastieken bal.

kiù k'ìh; | 起, intrekken, terugspringen.

k'a ts'iú kiù liù lat, 脚手|匕去, handen en voeten intrekken, (door kramp.)

p'é tò kiù k'ìh lai, 皮都|起來, het vel krimpt in om.

p'ē kun kiù kiù kiù. 鼻根|匕, de neus sterk zamentrekken, *d. i.* niet van zijn geld afkunnen.

kiù soā dziaù, | 線繡, chenille of fluweel

求 Kiû Zoeken naar; vragen, verzoeken, smeeken, bidden.

kiû ts'ē, | 尋, naar iets zoeken. (zooals naar geneesplanten.)

kiû ts'in, | 親, ten huwelijk vragen.

kiû tsing, | 情, vergiffenis, inschikkelijheid vragen.

kiû t'ok, | 託, verzoeken op zich te nemen, opdragen.

kiû iòh, | 藥, om medicijn vragen.

kiû ki put kiû dzin, |己不|人, men zoeke hulp bij zich zelve en niet bij anderen.

boē kiû tit, 莫|的, niet te verkrijgen.

kiû k'it, | 乞, bedelen.

kiû hoè / » *hoà* } | 貨, bedelen, *lett.* omverandering in zijn lot smeeken, (van priesters.)

k'ó kiû, 叩 |, erbarmelijk smeeken.

ai kiû, 愛 |, meewarig, smeeken.

kiû hō, | 雨, om regen bidden.

k'ún kiû, 懇 |, dringend smeeken.

kiû hē, | 會, met een belofte aan de goden afsmeeken.

kiû sin t'ok pút, | 神託佛, de geesten en Boeddha bidden.

kiû t'i kiû toē, | 天 | 地, aan hemel en aarde smeeken, bidden.

毬 Kiû Bal, bol, tros, (als druiven), kloen.

p'ah kiû, 打 |, met ballen spelen, kegelen, biljarten.

lōng (of *lāng*) *kiû*, 跟 |, kegelen.

t'at kiû, 踢 |, de bal schoppen.

tē kiû, 地 ｜, aardbol, aardglobe.

dzû dzû tsoè tsit kiû, 圓 匕 作 一 ｜, in een bal door elkander verwaard.

pak lak tsoè tsit kiû, 縛 匕 作 一 ｜, op eens bij elkander komen, (van vele zaken.)

舊 Kiū *kò kiū*, 故 ｜, van ouden tijd, van vroeger.

i kiū, 依 ｜, even als te voren.

niû sin k'ì kiū, 夯 新 去 ｜, het nieuwe aannemen en het oude verwerpen.

柩 Kiū *k'ìng kiū*, 殯 ｜, een lijk kisten en nog eenigen tijd boven aarde laten staan.

舅 kiū *ts'e kiū*, 妻 ｜, zwagers, (vrouws broeders.)

薑 Kiu̱ Gember.

kiu̱ bú, ｜ 母. do.

Kiu̱) *hoan kiu̱*, 番 ｜, lombok, spaansche peper.

bing kiu̱, 明 ｜, galanga wortel, beste gember.

ti̱ kiu̱, 甜 ｜, gekonfijte gember.

tsui kiu̱, *tsi̱ kiu̱*, 水 ｜, 幼 ｜, watergember, jonge gember, (waarvan gemberbier gemaakt wordt.)

kiu̱ ing, ｜ 黃, kurkuma.

siang ts'iú nñg p'ì̱ kiu̱, 双 手 二 紕 ｜, beide handen als twee schijven gember, *d. i.* zonder iets te bezitten.

pô kiu̱ tê, 蒲 ｜ 茶, thee van eene wilde plant.

麞 Kiu̱ *kiu̱ á*, ｜ 子, soort hoornloos hert.

韁 Kiu̱ *bé kā kiu̱*, 馬 咬 ｜, bit van een paard.

Kiu̱ *k'iu̱ k'i̱*, al zijne krachten onvermoeid op iets inspannen.

ts'iah kiu̱ á, krekel.

强 Overtreffen, beter zijn dan.

Kiu̱ *kiu̱ kè* }
Kio̱ *kio̱ koè* } ｜ 過, overtreffen, beter zijn dan.

p'ai̱ p'ai̱ kiu̱ kè bô, 歹 匕 ｜ 過 無, hoe slecht het ook is, het is toch beter dan niets.

彊 Met geweld, hardnekkig, koppig.

Kiu̱ *kiu̱ peh nì̱* }
kio̱ peh nè̱ } ｜ 抓, zich zelven dwingen, zijne laatste krachten inspannen.

kiu̱ ts'ùi, *ts'ùi kiu̱*, ｜ 嘴, koppig in zijn spreken.

kih kiu̱ ê lâng, een koppig mensch, die altijd het tegenovergestelde van anderen wil.

kiu̱ kut, ｜ 骨, zich tegen eene ziekte verzetten, er niet aan toegeven.

kiu̱ kiu̱, ｜ 匕, hard, nog niet goed rijp of gaar.

鳩 K'iu *k'iu tsip*, ｜ 集, bij elkander brengen, brengen, op halen (zooals geld).

k'iu tsoè tsit ē, ｜ 作 一 箇, bijeenbrengen.

扭 K'iú Grijpen, vatten, beetpakken; trekken, voorttrekken, sleuren.

k'iú liáh, *k'iú k'iú liáh liáh*; ｜ 掠 ｜ 匕 掠 匕, vatten, beetpakken.

hō̱ i k'iú k'ìl, 與 伊 ｜ 去, gevat worden.

sa̱ k'iú, 相 ｜, elkander sleuren. worstelen.

k'iú lai k'iú k'ì, ｜ 來 ｜ 去, elkander trekken, sleuren, (zoo als bij vechten).

k'iú hing á, ｜ 胸 仔, bij de borst

van zijn kleed pakken, (voor schuld).
k'iú lák, | 把, voortrekken en beet houden (zooals dieven.)
k'iú tn̄g, | 斷, stuktrekken.
k'iú koah pún tsi̤, | 些 本 錢, zijn kapitaal wat bij elkander garen.
kiú tàm pòh, | 淡 泊, een weinig opsparen.

K'iù *k'iù tùn*, hazelip.

縐 Gekruld.
K'iù *k'iù k'iù*, do.
k'iù kak, | 角, omgekruld, (zooals de bladeren van een boek.
k'iù k'iù liù liù, 縮 | 蠕 ㄝ, gekruld.
k'iù kun, | 筋, kramp.
k'a k'iù ts'iú k'iù, 脚 | 手 |, kromgetrokken, verkleumde handen en voeten.
k'iù k'iù tsoè tsit tui / « » *tsò* » » } | | 作 一 堆, bij elkander brengen,
k'iù kèng, | 鋼, ombuigen, (als een mes wanneer men er een te hard voorwerp meė snijden wil.
k'iù ki̤, | 墘, omgetrokken aan den rand, (als een boek).

K'iù Inhoudend van geld, gierig.
k'iù k'iēm, karig, vasthouden aan geld.

球 K'iù *liù k'iù*, 琉 |, *Liù-k'iù* archipel.

柔 Taai.
K'iū *k'iū k'iū dzūn dzūn*, | | 潤 ㄝ, taai.
k'iū kàh dzūn, | 且 潤, taai, elastiek.
k'iū teh teh, | 短 ㄝ, zeer taai.
néng k'iū k'iū, 軟 | ㄝ, zacht en taai.
tsing k'iū k'iū k'iū, zeer gastvrij, onvermoeid in pligtplegingen.

腔 K'iṳ / K'io̤ Plaatselijke wijze van uitspraak der woorden en klanken, tongval.
k'iṳ k'aó, | 口, eigenaardigheid in een dialect, dialect.
hiṳ ē k'iṳ / *hiṳ́ ē k'io̤* } 鄉 下 |, dorpsaccent.
kóng oē k'iṳ k'iṳ, 說 話 | |, een vreemd accent in zijn spreken hebben.
k'aó k'iṳ, 口 |, plaatselijk accent.
tâng oa̤ k'iṳ, 同 安 |, het *Tâng-oa̤* dialect.

K'iṳ̄ *oē k'iṳ̄ ts'uì* / *ē k'iō̤ ts'uì* } 能 節 食, zich ontzien in zijn eten, niet te veel eten.

Kiuh

Kiuh *lūn kiuh kiuh*, zeer taai.
laō kiuh kiuh, ingekrompen van onderdom.
kiuh liuh tsit tè á, tot een klein stuk inkrimpen.
ing to kū i kiuh sih, met een mes doodsteken.

Kiúh *kiúh kiúh t'iu*, een akelig, een krijschend geluid uitstooten.
ki ki kiúh kiúh, piepen mompelen.

K'iúh *k'iúh k'iúh k'iúh*, zeer kort, (om aan beet te pakken).
k'iúh tsit tè á tsi̤, heimelijk wat geld opsparen, (zooals eene huismoeder).
lé k'iúh k'iúh, zeer kort.

Ko

高 Ko Hoog, verheven, uitstekend.
ko sing, | 陞, in mandarijn graad stijgen.

tsū ko ê lâng, 自 | 的 人, iemand die zich boven alle anderen verheven rekent.

hò ko ê lâng, 好 | 的 人, een eerzuchtig mensch.

ko kièn, | 見, van uitstekend helder doorzigt.

ko kuì, | 貴 zeer duur,

ko ts'ioh, | 尺, lange maatstok.

ko lê ts'aì. | 麗 菜, kool.

Oudere broeder, soort eere titel, mannetje bij beesten.

toā ko, 大 |, oudere broeder, eere naam in het algemeen.

a ko kiá, 亞 | 子, keizerlijke prinsen, ook tegen hooge mandarijns zonen gebruikt.

ko só, | 嫂, zwagerin, (vrouw van zijn ouderen broeder.)

ti ko, 猪 |, mannelijk varken, beer.

bé ko, 馬 |, hengst.

Boom voor een schuit.

tik ko, 竹 |, bamboezen schuitenboom.

tsûn ko, | 船, schuitenboom.

t'e ko, 把 |, boomen.

tik ko sui tsat sò, 竹 | 隨 節 扒, langs een bamboezen stok van geleding tot geleding kruipen *d. i.* in volgorde afdoen.

koaī ko, 怪 |, vreemd, zonderling, anders dan gewoonlijk.

tōng kan ko, tōng k'i kan ko, 動 干 | 動 起 干 |, strijden, vechten, twisten.

Vet, zalf, pleister, alles wat een pappige massa vormt, gelei; dik, pappig.

pak tō laī ū ko, 腹 內 有 |, vet in de buik hebben *d. i.* verzadigd.

ko liông ê tsú tē, | 粱 的 子 弟, zonen van rijken huize.

ko ioh, siao ko, | 藥, 消 |, pleister.

tiaò ko, hong ko, 弔 |, 風 |, trekpleister.

bák sai ko, 目 屎 |, vuil, zucht in het oog.

bák ko, 目 |, verdroogde inkt

koe ko, 雞 |, hanen strontje. *lett.* kippenstront vulg. een strontje op 't oog.

ts'ih kó, 蠘 |, vleesch in krabben.

ké tsí ko. 瓜 子 |, vruchten gelei.

ko ko ko, | | |, vet, pappig.

lô lò ko ko, vuil en pappig.

糕 Ko Gerezen, luchtige koek.

koe nn̄g ko, 雞 蛋 |, colombijntjes.

ko koé, | 粿, niet afwillen van iets, (dat toch niet veel waarde heeft.)

羔 Ko *iû ko*, 羊 |, schaap, schapenvacht, pels.

ko to (of *tút*) *biên*, | 突 綿, merinos, alpaca.

哥 Ko *ing ko*, 鸚 |, papegaai.

t'ai ko, melaatsch, melaatschheid.

Ko *ko p'i*, | 丕, koffij.

ko p'i tsí, | 丕 子, koffijboonen.

果 Kó *kó dzièn*, | 然, inderdaad.

kó tsin, | 真, do.

ts'ing (of *ts'ién*) *kó si*, 青 | 豉, gezouten olijven.

kiet kô si miā } 結 | , een einde aan
» « *sè* » }
iemands leven maken.

in kò, 因 |, oorzaak en uitwerking aanleiding en de vrucht daarvan, (Boeddh.)

稿 *p'oe kó*, 批 |, klad van een brief.
Ko *p'ah kó*, 打 |, een schets, klad van iets maken.

kó kong, | 工, kladschrijver bij een mandarijn.

ts'ó ko, 草 |, een klad, schets.

k'i kó, 起 |, een klad, schets maken.

béh ko ts'aó, 麥 | 草, graanstoppel,

告 Aanklagen, aanklagte inleveren tegen;
Kò bekendmaken; bij hoogeren vragen.

kò tsēng, | 狀, aanklagen.

kò sò, | 訴, aanklagen en verdedigen.

kò koa, | 官, bij de overheden aanklagen.

bū kò, 誣 |, valsch aanklagen.

goân kò, *pī kò*, 原 |, 被 |, aanklager, aangeklaagde.

hòng kò, 放 |, gelegenheid openstellen om aanklagten in te leveren, (op de dagen met 3, 6 en 9.)

kò sī, | 示, proclamatie.

kò péh, | 白, bekéndmaking, advertentie.

kò kè } | 假, om verlof vragen.
» *kò* }

kò pī, | 病, wegens ziekte om verlof vragen.

kò lō, | 老, wegens ouderdom om zijn ontslag vragen

過 Overschrijden, overtreden, overtreding.
Kò *kò tō*, | 渡, den baan, regel, overschrijden, buiten den regel.

tsoē kò, 罪 |, overtreding, fout.

Kò Roeijen.

kò tsiú } | 槳, roeijen.
» *tsiō* }

kò tsùn á, | 船 仔, een boot roeijen.

箇 *kò kò*, | 乚, elk een.
Kò Kò

箬 *ti kò*, 猪 |, varkens mand.
Kò *kò ti*, | 猪, een varken in een mand dragen.

kò kò k'ì, | | 去, wegstelen.

kò tse ke hé k'ih, | 齊 家 伙 去, veel bezittingen medenemen, (bij het huwelijk).

oai kò, *oai li kò*, 歪 |, scheef worden, uitzakken.

oai oai kò kò, 歪 乚 | 乚 do.

擓 *kò hong*, | 風, scheef op den wind
Kò zweven, (van vogels ook van pijlen.)

Kō *kō tsit lìn*, ééns rondrollen.

kō k'ì kō lai, weg rollen en terug komen rollen.

kō t'ng, in de suiker rollen, roeren, door de suiker halen.

i lo kō, zuiverrond.

k'ók k'ók kō, neer rollen. (zooals een steen van een berg.)

kō kaò toā, rollen tot het groot is, (van het moederloos kind.)

科 *ting k'o*, 登 |, *Kú-dzin* en *Tsin-*
K'o *sū* worden.

siaó ting k'o, 小 登 |, beleefde term voor trouwen.

k'o tiû, | 場, examinatieplaats.

pâng k'o, 房 |, de zes departementen in een mandarijnbureau.

k'o taò dzī, | 斗 字, het oude oorspronkelijke Chin. figurenschrift.

熬 K'o *k'o ts'ài*, | 菜, groenten goed laten koken.

可 K'ó Kunnen, te . . . , *lijk* als aanduider van het gerundium.

k'ó i, | 以, het kan, het kan er door.

k'ó lin, | 憐, te bejammeren.

goá k'ó lin ih, 我 | 憐 伊, ik heb medelijden met hem.

k'ó ò, | 惡, te haten, hatelijk.

k'ó kièn, k'ó ti, | 見, | 知, hieruit kan men zien, weten dat . . . , klaarblijkelijk.

考 K'ó Onderzoeken, nazien, examinéren, examen afnemen, examen doen, ondergaan.

k'ó sì, k'ó kaò, | 試, | 校 examen, een examen ondergaan.

k'e k'ó, ts'â k'ó (k'e), 稽 |, 查 |, onderzoeken, navorschen.

k'ó k'àm, | 勘, onderzoeken, nazien.

k'ó giēm, | 驗, onderzoeken, inspecteren.

k'ó ts'ing, k'ó pé, | 鎗 | 把, prijsschieten.

k'ó bé pō tsì, | 馬 步 箭, te paard en te voet pijl schijfschieten.

k'ó pi, | 棚, examinatieplaats.

ts'ut k'ó, 出 |, examen gaan doen.

k'ó koa, | 官, examen doen om beambte te worden.

k'ó tó, | 倒, overtreffen.

dzīm k'ó put tó, 任 | 不 倒, onovertreffelijk in een vak.

K'ó Droog, pappig.

k'ó tsút tsút, pappig; op elkander gepakt, gedrongen.

苦 K'ó *k'ó oā*, | 旱, droogte.

坷 K'ó *k'ám k'ó*, 坎 |, niet geleidelijk, steeds moeijelijkeden ontmoeten.

靠 K'ò Leunen, aanvallen tegen; steunen, zich verlaten op.

k'ò toh, | 棹, op de tafel leunen.

k'ò tsim, | 枕, leunkussen.

k'ò pán, 板 |, arm leuning voor aan een draagstoel.

k'ò tioh ts'ién, | 着 淺, aan eene ondiepte vastraken.

oá k'ò, 倚 |, steunen, zich verlaten op.

tsing k'ò tioh, 船 | 着, geheel toevertrouwen aan.

k'ò sè k'it sè gō, | 勢 被 勢 誤, op iemands magt steunen en juist daardoor teleurgesteld worden.

k'ò i è tsi, | 伊 的 財, op zijn geld steunen.

k'ò t'i k'ò toē, | 天 | 地, zich op hemel en aarde verlaten.

k'ò tioh i è sè, | 着 伊 的 勢, op zijne magt steunen.

k'iao k'ò, 蹺 |, van de behoefte waarin iemand verkeert, profitéren om hem beettenemen.

k'ò i t'aò bák tsiaó, | 伊 頭 目 鳥, zich op den belhamel verlaten, aan den sterksten aansluiten.

k'ò k'ò siók siók, | ヒ 熟 ヒ, door langen omgang doen als of men bij iemand te huis was.

k'ò gai, | 崖, oorspr. door op iets te leunen in zijn groei verhinderd worden als meloenen; door schraal voedsel niet groot worden; zeer arm.

k'ò hát, | 乏, do.

誥 K'ò — *k'ò hong*, 丨封, tot eere ambten verheffen.

課 K'ò — *kòk k'ò*, 國丨, 's rijks inkomsten.

顆 K'ò — *tsit k'ò in*, 一丨印, één stempel zegel,
tsit k'ò oân pò, 一丨灣宝, een baar.
kim gûn k'ò, 金銀丨, goud en zilver inbaren.

犒 K'ò — Belooning geven, onthalen.
k'ò kun, 丨軍, een zegevierend leger onthalen.
k'ò lō, 丨勞, do.

傲 K'ò — *kik k'ò*, 裝丨, trotsch.
k'ò k'ò k'ò, zeer trotsch.
k'ò lai k'ò k'ì, 丨来丨去, waggelen in zijn loopen, trotsch.

光 K'ō Kuị — *kng k'ō k'ō*, niets bezittend.

枯 Ko̱ — *ko̱ tà*, 丨礁, verdrogen, verdorven.

鴣 Ko̱ — *tsiá ko̱*, 鷓丨, patrijs.
ko̱ ìn tsiaó / *ni̱ e* 丨黃鳥, groote uil.

舡 Ko̱ — Ladingboot, wrikboot.
ko̱ á, *ko̱ à tsûn*, 丨仔, 丨仔船, wrikboot.
toā ko̱, 大丨, groote ladingboot.

辜 Ko̱ — Overtreding schuld.
bû ko̱ siū k'ut, 無丨受屈, onschuldig verdrukt, valschbetigt worden.
ko̱ hū, 丨負, met ondank beloonen.
ko̱ un hū gī, 丨恩負義, ondankbaar voor weldaden.

姑 Ko̱ — Tante, van vaderszijde; beleefde term voor vrouwen. Tijdelijk, zoo lang.
ko̱ pô, 丨婆, oud-tante.
ko̱ tiū̱, 丨丈, oom, (man van vaders-zuster.)
ko̱ niû̱, 丨娘, jonge jufvrouw.
ko̱ i kū kīm, 丨姨舅妗, tante, (van vader en moeders zijde) ooms, (van moeders) en tantes, (moeders broers vrouw.)
ko̱ piaó hia̱ tī, 丨表兄弟, neven, (vader's zuster's zoon.)
li ko̱ / *ni̱ „* 尼丨, Boeddh. non, 師丨 *sai-ko̱*, (bel. term).
tō ko̱, 道丨, Taoistische non.
ko̱ ts'iá, 丨且, zoolang maar..., toch maar
ko̱ put tsiong, 丨不將, door nood gedwongen,
toā ko̱, 大丨, tante, (vaders oudere zuster.
sió ko̱, 小丨, zuster, (mans jongere zuster.)

Ko̱ — *ko̱ pi̱*, 丨杯, mast, (bij mast klimmen.)
ts'iu̱ ko̱, de prijzen bij het mastklimmen wegnemen.
tsiáh ná ts'ù ko̱, gulzig eten.

菰 Ko̱ — Champignon, paddestoel, schimmel.
hiu̱ ko̱, 香丨, gedroogde champignon.
mô ko̱, 毛丨, harige champignon.
hiu̱ ko̱ tì, 香丨底, begin van de hoofdvlecht.
si̱ ko̱, 生丨, beschimmelen.
si̱ ko̱ ts'iū̱ p'ū, 生丨帯霧, beschimmel en muf, ook tegen iemand gezegd dien men in lang niet gezien heeft.

孤 Ko̱ — Vaderloos, wees; enkel, alleen, alleen staand, verlaten.

ko tsú, ko dzi, ｜子，｜兒，vaderloos kind, halve wees.

ko ai tsú, ｜哀子，wees.

ko nó (of *lò*) *è lang*, ｜老的人，kinderlooze, oude lieden.

ko koá, ｜寡，weezen en weduwen.

ko lâng, ｜人，een enkel mensch.

ko toa, ｜單，enkel, alleen, alleen staand.

ko dzī sì, ｜字姓，kleine familie.

ko kai, ko ták, ko kút, ko seng, ｜介，｜厇，｜孀，｜獨，alleenstaand, niet met anderen te doen willen hebben.

kō si seng è lâng, ｜死喪的人，een excentriek mensch.

ko hûn, ｜魂，verlaten zielen, (aan wien niemand offert.)

ko mìng tók ts'ī, ｜門獨市，monopolie.

ko tsióng lân bing, ｜掌難鳴，een enkele palm van de hand kan geen geluid geven, *i. d.* waar twee kijven hebben beide schuld.

古 Kó Oud, oudheid; zonderling, vreemd,

kó tsá, ｜早，in de oudheid.

kó tóng, ｜董，rariteit, oudheden.

kó tsik, (of *dziah*) ｜蹟，overblijfsels, sporen der oudheid.

kóng kó, 說｜，van de oudheid verhalen.

kó ts'eh, ｜册，boeken over de oudheid.

kó hū, ｜白，oud, van ouds.

kó laoh p'aoh, geverseerd in de oudheid, oudheidkundig.

kó goán, ｜玩，antiquiteiten.

lā kó koan, iets uit de oudheid ophalen.

kó tì, ｜致，ouderwetsch.

kó hong, ｜風，van den ouden stempel.

ko p'ak, ｜朴，eenvoudig.

í king tsoè kó dzin, 已經作｜人，reeds tot de oudheid behooren *i. d.* gestorven.

kó koai, kó kó koai koai, ｜匕怪匕，zonderling, vreemd,

kó kiét, ｜傑，aardig, mooi.

oé kó, 矮｜，dwergachtig.

kó ts'iū t'aò, ｜樹頭，knoest van een ouden boom *d. i.* oud mensch, ook dwerg.

kó tsui, ｜雛，als een groot mensch, (van kinderen), koddig, aardig.

kó ì, ｜意，opregt, zonder streken.

估 Kò Waarderen, schatten; op vendutie verkoopen.

kò kè, ｜價，waarderen, schatten.

kò siaò, kò tú siaò, ｜賬，｜抵賬，schuld met goederen afdoen.

kò ts'ù t'éh, ｜厝宅，huizen op vendutie verkoopen.

kil lâng kò kò k'ìh, 被人｜匕去，verkocht worden, (voor schuld).

股 Kó Oorsp. heup; been, knok; draad van garen, streng van touw enz.; rabat, strook lands; deel, aandeel in eene zaak.

ts'iú kó, 手｜，het arm been, de arm.

sit kó t'aó, 翼｜頭，bovenste van het vleugelbeen.

lák kó kap eh. 六｜蛤的，een zes strenger, (van touw).

p'ì tsoè sa kọ, 紩作三|, in drie strengen vlechten.

háp kọ sing li, 合|生理, compagnieschap, vennootschap.

kọ t'aò, |頭, hoofd van aandeelhouders.

taò kọ, k'iā kọ, 湊|, 竪|, aan deel nemen.

nī kọ, néng kọ, 勁|, 軟|, grootste en kleinere aandeelen.

t'iah kọ, 折|, compagnieschap ontbinden.

hó k'a kọ, 好脚|, ervaren, knap in een vak.

鼓 Kọ́ Trom, trommel; ook van voorwerpen die door hunne buikvormige holle gedaante op een trommel gelijken.

p'ah k'ọ́, 擊|, op de trommel slaan, trommelen.

sam t'ong kọ, 三通|, drie roffels.

kim kọ, 金|, gongs en trommels.

kiét toā ki p'ah toā kọ 執大旗打大|, eene groote vlag ophouden en op eene groote trommel slaan, *d. i*, onbeschaamd voor iets uitkomen.

luī kọ, 擂|, roffelen.

kọ gák, |樂, trommels en muziek, muziek.

kọ ts'e, |吹, trommels en hobois, muziek.

iem ki sit kọ, 掩欺息|, in stille doen,

hó lò hó kọ, 好鑼好|, zich lief voordoende.

kọ p'aò, |炮, sissers in eene papieren trom gedaan en bij het inkomen van de bruid afgestoken.

tsing kọ, 鐘|beginnen iets te doen

tè kọ, 茶|, thee-ketel.

hong kọ. 風|, wanmolen.

kọ ts'ik, |粟, rijst wannen.

蠱 Kọ́ *kọ tiòng* } *» tiàng* } |漲, gezwollen buik, trommel zucht.

苟 Kọ́ Indien, ingeval dat . . ; onvoorzigtig, oppervlakkig.

kọ sú. |使, ingeval dat . . . , verondersteld dat . . . .

kọ kán, |簡, oppervlakkig, onvoorzichtig.

kọ ts'iá, |且, zoo lang maar, tijdelijk.

栒 Kō *kọ ki*, |杞, soort mispel, (als medicijn gebruikt.

顧 Kọ̀ Een wakend oog houden op, zorgen, zorgdragen voor, oppassen.

tsiaò kọ, |照, zorgdragen voor.

kọ ts'ù, |厝, op het huis passen.

kọ mng eh, |門的, deurwachter.

kọ iū eh, |羊的, schaapherder.

bò kọ miā sia, 不|名聲, niet voor zijn goeden naam zorgen.

kọ sì miā, |性命, voor zijn leven zorgdragen.

koán kọ, 管|, zorgen voor, de zorg het bestuur hebben over.

kàn (of *k'oà*) *kọ*, 看|, verzorgen onder zijne bescherming hebben.

siú kọ, 守|, bewaken, passen op.

boē kọ tit tsiáh, 未|得食, zich geen tijd gunnen om te eten.

hoa hí kaò boē kọ tit, 歡喜至未|得, uiterst verheugd.

僱 Kọ̀ Huren.

kọ ts'iā, 顧|, huren, afhuren.

kò kang, 丨工, werklieden huren,

kò kiō, kò tsûn, 丨轎, 丨船, een draagstoel, eene schuit huren.

故 Kò Oud; gestorven; oorzaak, reden, waarom.

kò kū, 丨舊, oud, (als vrienden).

kò iú, 丨友, oude, ook overleden vriend.

kò i tièm, 丨衣店, oude kleeren winkel.

sin kò, 身丨, gestorven, overleden.

tsi tsai sè kò, 錢財世丨, geld en magt.

iên kò, 緣丨, rede, oorzaak.

kò lâng oàn, 丨人怨, zich gehaat maken.

kò lâng mē, 丨人罵, maken dat men uitgescholden wordt.

固 Kò Stevig, sterk, duurzaam; moedwillig.

kien kò, 堅丨, stevig, duurzaam.

kò ì, tiaó kò ì, 丨意, 調丨意, moedwillig, met opzet.

kò tsip, 丨執, halsstarrig.

錮 Kò *kìm kò*, 禁丨, uitsluiten: de mogelijkheid benemen eene misdaad uittewisschen.

糊 Kò Stijfsel, stijfselachtig, pappig; plakken, beplakken.

moā tsi kò, tsut bí kò, stijfsel van eene zachte rijst.

hún tsiu kò, 粉漿丨, meelstijfsel.

ts'ing p'ī kò ūn noā boah, 用鼻丨用沫抹, niet soliede gemaakt.

noā kò kò, 爛丨匕, zacht, pappig.

ts'ùi kò kò, 碎丨匕, stukkend, tot gruis.

kò ioh, 丨藥, pleister, zalf.

kò tsoá, 丨紙, met papier beplakken, bamboezen geraamte van beesten enz.)

kò lò lò tī hi siaò nih, 丨蘆匕在此賬的, in zijn crediet boek gesmeerd, *d. i.* zijn kapitaal is over intevorderen schulden verdeeld.

懷 Kò *p'ō tī hi kò nih*, 抱在丨中, in de schoot dragen, houden, (zooals een kind.)

强 Kò Aanraden.

kò tsiâ, 丨成, aanraden.

kò tsiâ lâng boé, 丨成人要, iemand aanpraten iets te koopen.

sì koè kò lâng, 四處丨人, ieder een naloopen om zijne goederen te verkoopen.

怙 Kō Toevertrouwen aan, zich verlaten op.

boe kō tit / *bē* „ „ } 靠不得, zich niet kunnen verlaten op.

boē tsún kō tit, 未準丨的, do.

kō pát lâng, 丨他人, aan anderen toevertrouwen, zich op anderen verlaten.

liáh toā kō, 掠大丨, denken dat iemand zal doen wat hem toevertrouwd is, (*b. v.* de huis deur te sluiten) maar zich daarin vergissen.

t'ē kō hē tsoè bák, 蛇丨蝦作目, de zeekwal verlaat zich op de garnaal als zijne oogen.

箍 K'o Hoep, hoepel, band, kring, krans, bundel, bos, kuipen, bijeenvatten

t'áng k'o, 桶丨, hoepel om een kuip.

toā t'áng k'o, 大桶丨, steunpilaar eener familie.

k'o t'áng, 丨桶, een ton kuipen.

t'ih k'o, 鉄丨, ijzeren hoepel, band.

36

ts'â k'o̤, 柴 丨, takkebos.

bō á k'o̤, 帽 仔 丨, hoofdband, (door kinderen gedra·en).

géh niû ui k'o̤, 月 娘 圍 丨, er is een krans om de maan.

p'ah k'o̤, 打 丨, een net omsingelen en de visch opjagen,

o̤ kah toā k'o̤, 烏 兼 大 丨, donker en groot van gestalte.

toā bú k'o̤ 大 拇 丨, groot in omvang.

toā tĕng k'o̤, 大 腸 丨, builing, (van rijst en suiker).

bák k'o̤ âng, 目 丨 紅, roode oogkasten, (op het punt van te weenen)

k'o̤ tsoè tsit tui, 丨 作 一 團, bij elkander vatten, verband in iets bre gen.

k'o̤ loh, *k'o̤ loh hàn*, 丨 落, 丨 落 漢, sjouwerlieden, (vernederende term.)

k'o̤ lòh soh, 丨 落 索, een rottingen ring met touwen er aan.

呼 K'o̤ *tê k'o̤*, 茶 丨, Chineesche theezeep.

iû k'o̤ boáh, 油 丨 末, Chineesch zeeppoeder.

taō k'o̤, 豆 丨, lijnkoeken.

呼 K'o̤ Roepen, (als men kippen doet.)

k'o̤ koe, *ke* 丨 雞, kippen roepen.

k'o̤ ti, 丨 猪, varkens roepen.

k'o̤ toa, 丨 單, kakelen, (van kippen als zij een ei leggen.)

k'o̤ hong, 丨 風, om wind fluiten.

k'o̤ pi á, 丨 卑 仔, fluiten, (van den mond.)

k'o̤ uh á, *p'ah k'o̤ sai eh*, 丨 刄 匕, 打 苦 屎 噎, de hik hebben.

員 K'o̤ Dollar.

nñg k'o̤ poà, 二 丨 半, twee en een-halve dollar.

苦 K'ó Bitter, (van smaak); leed, verdriet, ellende, zwart; leed hebben over; lastig, het zich lastig maken; bitterlijk, dringend.

k'ó koe, 丨 瓜, bittere komkommers.

k'ó tsiú, 丨 酒, bittere wijn, bitter.

ts'uì k'ó k'ó, 嘴 丨 匕, bitter in den mond, *d. i.* geen eetlust hebben.

kan k'ó, 艱 丨, leed, ellende; lastig, moeielijk.

k'ó t'àng, 丨 痛, bedroefd, hartzeer hebben

k'ó ts'ó, 丨 楚, leed hebben, in ellende zijn.

siū k'ó, 受 丨, leed, ellende hebben.

k'ó king, 丨 境, ellendige toestand.

k'ó ts'oeh, 丨 啜, uiterste ellende.

sin k'ó, 辛 丨, ellende, smart.

k'ik k'ó, *k'at k'ó*, 極 丨, 渴 丨, smart, leed doorstaan, verdragen.

boē k'at tit k'ó. 未 渴 的 丨, ondoorstaanbaar, onverdragelijk.

k'ó bê tsî, 丨 無 錢, het bejammeren dat men geen geld heeft.

k'ó kiá, 丨 子, (den dood van) zijn kind betreuren.

k'ó sim, 丨 心, zich veel moeite, last voor iets geven.

hô k'ó, *hô pit k'ó*, 何 丨, 何 得 丨, waarom het zich zoo lastig daarover te maken.

k'ó kaò kien tâ k'ih, 丨 至 堅 乾 去, uitdroogen, vermageren van verdriet.

k'ó kiû, *k'ó k'ó kiû kiû*, 丨 求, bitter, dringend smeeken.

k'ǒ k'ìng, | 勸, dringend vermanen.

k'ǒ tók, | 毒, stiefmoederlijk behandelen.

口 Mond, mondelings.
K'ǒ *k'ǒ t'oân*, | 傳, mondelingsche overlevering.

k'ǒ siū, | 受, mondelings overleveren.

k'ǒ giet, | 孽, scherp, beleedigend in zijn spreken.

it k'ǒ tông im, 一 | 同 音, allen als uit één' mond zeggen.

koan ū liông k'ǒ, 官 有 兩 |, in het karakter *koan*, mandarijn, zijn twee monden, *d. i.* overheden kunnen partijdig zijn.

許 Familienaam.
k'ǒ

甚 *boē k'ǒ oē*, 未 | 話, niet te best
K'ǒ kunnen.

boē k'ǒ hiaò tit, 未 | 曉 的, niet te best verstaan.

褲 Broek.
K'ò *k'ò t'uí*, | 褪, broekspijpen.

tsuí k'ò, tsuí k'ò ting / » – » » *tuì* } 水 袴, zwembroek

k'ò t'aò ts'a, | 頭 乂, het boven stuk of band van een broek.

k'ò t'uí k'ò, 跨 腿 |, doorloopende broek, waarvan pijpen en het bovenste gedeelte aan één zijn.

k'ò k'a, | 脚, pijpen van een broek.

k'ui k'a k'ò, 開 底 袴, broek zonder bodem, (voor kinderen).

ts'īng bô toé k'ò, 穿 無 底 |, een broek zonder bodem aantrekken, *d. i.* in een put vallen.

k'ui toé k'ò, 開 底 |, broek met loopende spleet, (zooals kinderen dragen.

k'ò t'aô, | 頭, bovenste gedeelte, band van eene broek.

tiū ts'aó k'ò, 稻 草 |, opperhuid, bast van graanstoppels.

liù k'ò, 溜 |, uitrafelen.

sa k'ò, 衫 |. kleeren in het algemeen.

kaô sa kaô k'ò, 猴 衫 猴 |, apenjas en broek, *d. i.* hanssop.

庫 *k'ò pâng*, | 房, schatkamer.
K'ò *k'ò lī*, | 吏, thesaurier.

k'ò gûn / *gîn* } | 銀, geld uit de schatkist.

ts'ɛng k'ò, 倉 |, graanpakhuizen en schatkamers.

kok k'ò, 國 |, 's rijks schatkamer.

k'ò ts'î, | 錢, geld uit de schatkamer in de onderwereld aan zielen vòòr hunne rust op aarde gegeven.

kiaó k'ò tsî, 還 | 錢, het uit de schatkamer der onder wereld ontvangen geld na den dood teruggeven.

ts'im k'ò hāng, 侵 | 項, geld uit de schatkamer stelen, (van mandarijnen.)

寇 *tsaó k'ò*, 草 |, struikroover.
K'ò *tō (of taū) k'ò*, 泥 豆 |, nootmuskaat.

塗 *k'ô lâng*, | 人, iemand valsch be-
K'ô tichten.

k'ô k'áh, | 倚, overal lang blijven hangen, aan de maat en de strijkstok hangen.

k'ô k'áh lâng, | 倚 人, iemand bedriegelijk aansmeeren.

k'ô aô, | 喉, in de keel blijven hangen, (zooals castorolie.)

k'ô siaò lòh k'ìh, | 賬 落 去, in

zijn koopmans boek versnipperd zijn, (van zijn kapitaal.)

pún tsi̱ k'ọ k'ò hí siaò ni̱h, 本 錢 | 乚 在 賬, zijn kapitaal aan verschillende crediet posten in zijn boek hebben.

Koa

Koa* Voos, (zooals radijs komkommers, enz.)

koa ni̱, voos en hard.

koa toa, 瓜 鬆, broos, grof, ruw.

bin p'ê koa la̱h, 面 皮 | 了, gerimpeld van vel.

koa kat, | 葛, betrekking, omgang hebben met.

p'ò koa, | 瓜, ontmaagden.

跨 Koa Aandoen, (eene plaats.)

koa tang koa sai, | 東 | 西, overal aandoen.

koa louh, | 留, do.

koa k'a, | 脚, do.

koa lai koa k'ì, | 來 | 去, niet regtuit gaan, overal aandoen.

歌 Koa Lied.

ts'iu̱ koa } *ts'iọ̄ »* } 唱 |, zingen.

柯 Koa Familienaam.

稍 Koá Eenigzins.

koá ê, | 箇, weinigen, eenigen.

i e laō pē koá ê tsi̱ hō̱ ih, i ta̱ ïng liaó liaó, 伊 父 | 錢 與 伊 用 他 了 乚, het weinige geld dat zijn vader hem gegeven heeft, heeft hij geheel en al opgebruikt.

koá tsi̱, 幾 個 錢, eenig geld, een weinig geld.

koá mi̱h, | 物, het eene of andere ding.

koá lâng, | 人, eenige menschen.

掛 Koà Ophangen, tegen iets aanhangen, tegen, op iets doen leunen; omhangen, dragen, bezwaren, bezwaard zijn, (als met schulden), bezwaren, ten laste leggen, bezwaard zijn over, ter harte nemen, gedenken, zich ongerust, angstig maken.

koà ting, | 燈, een lamp ophangen.

koà bák kiạ̀, | 目 鏡, een bril opzetten, dragen.

koà i ê bák kiạ̀, | 伊 的 目 鏡, door een ander mans hulp doen,

koà pai, | 牌, een publicatiebord ophangen.

koà liēn, | 鍊, ketenen dragen.

koà ts'iú lòng, | 手 囊, handschoenen dragen.

koà hō, | 號, een schip aangeven, (als aangekomen.)

koà k'ièm, | 欠, schuldig zijn.

koà lâng ê tsi̱, | 人 的 錢, geld aan iemand schuldig zijn; met hypotheek bezwaard zijn.

koà siaò, | 賬, schuld uitstaande hebben.

koà sim, koà liēm, | 心, | 念, ter harte nemen, gedenken, zich angstig maken.

koà ì, | 意, zich ongerust maken over.

koà tiaò, | 弔, zeer denken aan, verlangen aan.

koà luī, | 累, meeslepen, opgescheept zitten met.

---

* Zie verder onder *koe*.

koà loā, 丨 賴, betichten, ten laste leggen.

koà gāi, 丨 礙, in den weg zijn, een hinderpaal zijn.

koà gi, 丨 疑, twijfelen.

掛 Diagrammen.

Koà *pat koà*, 八 丨, de 8 diagrammen.

pok koà, *poáh koà*, 卜 丨, 跋 丨, waarzeggen door middel der diagrammen.

蓋 Deksel.

Koà *tiá kám koà*, 釜 敢 丨, de deksel van een pot.

ts'ù koà, 厝 丨, dak

褂 Wijde overjas.

Koà *té koà*, *tĭng koà*. 短 丨 長 丨, korte en lange overjas.

p'aò koà, 袍 丨, feestkleed.

bé koà, 馬 丨, korte rijjas.

hō i koà, 號 衣 丨, uniformjas waarop het merk der soldaten staat.

pó koà, 補 丨, uniformjas op den rug en de borst met een geborduurde lap vogels voor civiele; viervoetige dieren voor militaire mandarijnen.

ting koà, *ē koà*, 頂 丨 下 丨, boven- en onderjas.

ts'īng ĭng bé koà, 着 黄 馬 丨, een geele korte jas aan hebben als keizerlijke prinsen; in het huis van een verwante meer dan een ander te zeggen hebben.

t'aì pîng koà, 太 平 丨, korte overjas met strakspannende mouwen.

kun ki koà, 軍 機 丨, kortmouwige overjas aan den kant digtgeknoopt.

芥 *koà ts'aì*, 丨 菜, mostaardplant.

Koà *koà ts'aì pak laî kah*, 丨 菜 剝 內 甲, bij de mostaard plant plukt men de binnenste bladen af, *d. i.* tot armoede vervallen, houdt men zoolang mogelijk uitwendig zijn ouden stand op.

過 *tsē koà* } *tsoè* » } 罪 丨, overtreding; ver-
Koà keerdelijk, misdrijvig, ten onregte.

誇 *tsū k'oa*, 自 丨, bluffen, grootspre-
K'oa ken.

k'oa k'aó, 丨 口, grootspreken.

gaû k'oa ê lâng, 善 丨 之 人, een sterke bluffer, pocher..

掛 Verwisseld met *koà*.

K'oà *k'oà oa*, 丨 鞍, het zadel afleggen.

Koà *k'oà liēm*, *k'oà ì*, *k'oà sim*, 丨 念, 丨 意, 丨 心, gedachtig zijn, steeds onthouden, zich ongerust maken over.

k'oà gāi, 丨 碍, hinderpaal, in den weg zijn.

k'oà k'at, 丨 渴, een hinderpaal ontmoeten.

跨 Leggen tegen of op.

K'oà *k'oà k'a*, 丨 脚, de beenen op iets leggen.

bô k'è bô k'oà, 無 果 無 丨, er is niets om onder iets te zetten of iets op te leggen, (als in een leeg huis.)

koà hit ê uī, 丨 在 那 處, leg het daar tegen of op.

涔 Blijven vastzitten op, op droog blijven.

K'oà *k'oà ta*, 丨 礁, op droog zitten, (van een schuit.)

koà ts'ién, 丨 淺, op eene ondiepte blijven vastzitten.

譁 *k'oā k'oā haó*, 丨 匕 吼, ruischen.

K'oā *k'oā k'oā kún*, 丨 匕 滾, op borrelen, (als kokend water.)

k'ōng k'oā, 控 〡, geluid van een voorwerp dat valt.

K'oā *k'oā k'oā tāng*, zeer sterk in beweging zijn.

官 Mandarijn.

Koa *koa hâm*, 〡 銜, mandarijngraad.

koa hú, 〡 府, mandarijn

dzip koa, 入 〡, verbeurd verklaard worden.

ū koa sin ē lâng, 有 〡 身 之 人, een officieël persoon.

koa t'ia, 〡 舵, de achtersteven, (bij een schip.)

dzú koa, 主 〡, mijn heer *dzú*; eere naam door vrouwen aan mannen gegeven.

koa lō, 〡 路, groote weg.

t'am koa, 貪 〡, inhalig mandarijn.

koa ka ē tsú tē / » *ke* « » », 〡 官 家 子 弟, mandarijn kinderen.

koa ke / » *ke*, 〡 家, mandarijn.

koá oân, 〡 員, mandarijnen.

koa oē / » *oā*, 〡 話, mandarijn-dialect.

kun koa / *kin* », 跟 〡, mandarijn bedienden.

pīng koa k'ùi, 倚 〡 勢, op de magt van een mandarijn steunen.

koan koa, 捐 〡, een mandarijn-ambt koopen.

kaó koa tsáp tsit, 九 〡 十 職, een laag mandarijn postje.

koa t'aô. 〡 頭, hoofd der mandarijn bedienden.

p'ah koa si / *p'oā* » «, 打 〡 司, eene aanklagt inleveren.

si koa t'è tsit, 辭 〡 退 職, zijn ambt neerleggen.

ts'ut koa, 出 〡, iemand in een handelshuis die alle zaken regelt welke betrekking op mandarijnen hebben,

kiò koa ts'è, 叫 〡 催, om vergiffenis onder de bastonnade smeeken.

gaò kiò koa ts'è, 善 叫 〡 催, pijn, enz. erger doen voorkomen dan het is.

tai koa hù, 帶 〡 府, regtszaken, aanklagten hebben.

koa hú mîng hō ē só hui, 〡 府 門 戶 的 所 費, de onkosten aan de mandarijnen, (als bij regtsgeding.)

hoān tiòh koa si, 犯 着 〡 司, zich eene aanklagte op den hals balen.

tęng koa toàn, 當 〡 斷, voor de overheden uitmaken.

菓 Koa *ké tsí koa*, / *koé* » », 子 乾 〡, gedroogde vruchten.

kien koa nī k'ak, 堅 〡 劲 殼, droog en hard; dood arm.

杆 Koa *koa bâng*, 〡 芒, lange grashalm met witte pluim, alang-alang.

ki koa, 旗 〡, vlaggestok.

tiò koa, 釣 〡, hengelstok.

koa tsin piah, 〡 蓁 壁, muur van bekalkt riet.

肝 Lever.

Koa *sim koa kiá*, 心 〡 子, geliefdkind, hartje.

sim koa, 心 〡, het hart.

棺 Koa *koa ts'â*, 〡 材, kist, lijkkist.

koa tsiaó, 〡 鳥, Upupo epops.

趕 Koá Uitdrijven, weg jagen, vervolgen, achter-nazitten, achtervolg, haasten, aanzetten, in allerijl doen; verdrijven, vervolgen.

koá kin, 〡 緊, snel.

tui koá, 追 ｜, achternazitten, vervolgen.
koá tioh, ｜ 着, inhalen.
koá i kin, ｜ 伊 緊, iemand haasten.
koá i k'ì, ｜ 逐 去, wegdoen, ontslaan.
koá k'ì, ｜ 去, uitdrijven,
koá k'ì, ｜ 去, achternagaan, achtervolgen.
koá noà k'ì, 盡 逐 去, geheel en al uitgedreven.
koá ts'ī, ｜ 市, zich naar de markt haasten.
koá k'uì, ｜ 氣, de lucht voortpersen.
teng koà tsui, 當 ｜ 水, op het toppunt van groei, levenskracht zijn, (van personen heesters, vruchten enz.)

推 Koá
koá kang, ｜ 工, tot harder werken aanzetten.
koá siaò, ｜ 賬, iemand dringend om betaling manen.
koá hong koá hién, ｜ 風 ｜ 險, gaauw bij de wind en het gevaar zijn, in allerijl, (gaan doen.)
koá tióh, ｜ 驅 逐, wegdrijven, wegjagen.
koá koá k'ì, 盡 ｜, geheel en al wegdrijven.
koá koá k'ì, 盡 ｜ 去, van zich afgooijen.
p'ah koá, 打 ｜, wegjagen, niet bij zich willen houden.
koá kin kak, ｜ 緊 角, naar één kant drijven, (als visch, schepen enz,)
koá lō̤, ｜ 路, zich haasten (in minder tijd doen afloopen dan gewoonlijk.)
koá tsām, ｜ 站, haasten om nog op eene pleisterplaats aan te komen.
koá p'oe, ｜ 批, in allerijl een brief zenden.
sa̤ koá k'a, 相 ｜ 脚, even groot van voet zijn, (als schoenen).
koá sè, ｜ 勢, van den toestand waarin iets verkeert, gebruik maken, (als van een rennend paard om over een slootte springen.)

寡 Koá
tsiú koá. 守 ｜, weduwe.
koá hū, ｜ 婦, weduwe.
tsiú si̤ koá / *» se̤ »* 守 生 ｜, weduwe van een levenden man, *d. i.* eene vrouw wier man op eene andere plaats woont.

管 Koá
tsong koá, 總 ｜, bootsman, hoofd der matrozen. enz.

寒 Koà
Koude, koud.
koà t'i, ｜ 天, 's winter.
koà dziét pī̤ / *» » pē̤* ｜ 熱 病, koorts.
koà ts'in, ｜ 冷, koud, koel.
o̤ koà, 陰 ｜, koude, natte koude.
o̤ im koà, 烏 陰 ｜, do.
k'i koà t'aò, 初 ｜ 生, de koude begint.
koà seng seh tàng, ｜ 霜 雪 凍, uiterst koud.
iaò koà, 饑 ｜, hongerig en koud.
koà kaò k'áp k'i, ｜ 至 戰 齒, zou koud dat men klappertandt.
ts'i̤ ts'in koà, 生 冷 ｜, plotselinge koude.
k'it i koà k'ìh, 被 伊 ｜ 去, eene koude vatten.
koà sa̤, ｜ 衫, winter kleederen.

汗 Koā
Zweet.
laò koā, 流 ｜, zweeten.
hoat koā, 發 ｜, aan het zweeten gaan uitbreken van zweet.

KOA

hip koā, 急 ｜, uitzweeten, (onder dekens.)

koā tsu, ｜ 珠, zweetdroppel.

ts'it koā, 拭 ｜, zweet afwisschen.

koā seng, tsaò koā seng, 酸, 臭 ｜ 酸, zweetlucht

kia kaò laò ts'in koā, 驚 至 流 冷 ｜, zoo vreezen dat het koud zweet u uitbreekt

ming king ts'ut koā è tsi, 毛 管 出 ｜ 之 錢, hard verdiend geld.

攜 Koā — Aan de hand dragen, opnemen; dragen; hengsel; rist.

koā nâ, ｜ 籃, een mand aan de hand dragen.

nâ koā, 籃 ｜, hengsel van een mand.

koā tsi, ｜ 錢, een rist duiten opnemen.

tsit koā tsi, 一 ｜ 錢, een rist duiten.

koā liēn, ｜ 鍊, ketenen dragen.

bō á koà koā, 帽 仔 掛 ｜, een storm band aan de muts hebben.

tsiâ t'oa tsiâ koā, 成 拖 成 ｜, aan bundels en risten, *d. i.* veel.

koā king, ｜ 貫, een geheiligde medaille dragen.

dzit goat t'á ts'it tsi koā, 日 月 担 七 星 ｜, zon en maan om hoog houden en het zevengesternte aan de handdragen, *d. i.* de beide handen vol met waren en aan de vingers nog een rist duiten hebben hangen.

koā kè bé, ｜ 家 尾, iemand op zijn paard overligten; iemand den loef afsteken.

bô oá bô koā, 無 倚 無 ｜, niets om op te leunen of aan vast te pakken, *d. i.* geene zekerheid op iemand hebben.

K'OA

寬 K'oa — *k'oa k'oa*, ｜ 匕, langzaam.

bô kin bô k'oa, bô k'oa bô kin, 無 緊 無 ｜, 無 ｜ 無 緊, niet weten wanneer gaauw en wanneer langzaam te handelen.

hù lí k'oa kin, 赴 爾 ｜ 緊, gereed hebben voor het geval dat gij het langzaam of gaauw noodig hebt.

看 K'oa — Kijken, zien, beschouwen.

k'oà kì, ｜ 見, zien.

kim kim k'oà, 注 覗 ｜, aanstaren.

tit tit k'oà, 直 匕 ｜, staren op.

k'oà ts'eh / » *ts'eh* ｜ 書, een boek door zien, lezen.

k'oà bing, ｜ 明, begrijpen.

k'oà k'in, ｜ 輕, minachten.

k'oà bô iaò kin, ｜ 不 要 緊, gering achten.

k'oà tsiū bák, ｜ 上 眼, goed van anderen denken.

k'oà miā sien si / » » *sin se* ｜ 命 先 生, waarzegger.

k'oà k'in hoat tō, ｜ 玩 法, de wetten vertreden.

tsiaò goà k'oà lai, 據 我 ｜ 來, naar zijn inzigt, oordeel.

k'oà kūn bô k'oà hēng / » *kīn* » » *huī* ｜ 近 不 遠, alleen aan het tegenwoordige denken.

k'oà p'oà, ｜ 破, uitvinden, te weten komen, merken dat . . . , de zaak goed inzien.

k'oà īm p'oà, ｜ 不 破, niet goed inzien,

tsi k'oà, 試 ｜, proeven,

t'ig k'oà, 聽 丨, afhooren, luisteren naar . . . .

tsoè k'oà / *tsò* » } 作 試, beproeven hoe iets gaat ?

siá k'oà, 寫 丨, proberen, (een pen of penseel.)

k'oà hûng ê lâng, 丨 園 的 人, tuinman.

k'oà gûn, 丨 銀, geld nakijken.

k'oà tsih, 丨 舌, de tong bekijken.

k'oà lâng īm k'i / *k'oà lâng īm tsiū bák* / » » *tsiō* } 丨 人 不 上, 丨 人 不 上 眼. anderen minachten.

bô k'oà bák, 無 丨 目, niet uit zijne oogen kijken.

k'oà k'oà, 丨 丨, alom rondzien, rondkijken; nog eens uitzien om zijne waren te verkoopen, enz.

k'oà bák, 丨 目, uitkijken, kijken.

k'oà sè bīn / » *sì* » } 丨 勢 面, de omstandigheden in aanmerking nemen.

k'oà t'aô, 丨 頭, op uitkijkstaan, als op een schip.

ts'i k'oà, 試 丨, beproeven.

k'oà kō, 丨 顧, zorgen voor.

k'oà iū / » *iō* } 丨 樣, afzien.

k'oà t'i tsiáh pēng / » » » *puī* } 丨 天 食 飯, al wat men heeft is eene zegening van den hemel.

k'oà soa ê lâng, 丨 山 的 人, bergwachter, gravenzoeker.

k'oà lâng soah iû, 丨 人 下 油, zijne menschen zien en daarnaar handelen,

tsaī lâng k'oà, 在 人 丨, het hangt van den persoon af hoe het te zien; zooals men het wil opvatten.

k'oà kè pinh / » *koè* » } 丨 透 壁, iets door en door zien.

sa k'oà, 相 丨, naar elkander kijken, (om iets te beginnen.)

k'oà t'i k'oà toē, 丨 天 丨 地, naar hemel en aarde (voor hulp) uitzien.

tsiēm k'oà, 占 丨, zoo lang inzien, (om te zien of iemand zich beteren zal.)

k'oà tièm k'aó, 丨 店 口, op den winkel passen.

k'oà sò tsaī, 丨 所 在, het hangt af van de plaats.

k'oà lai, 丨 來, ondervinding heeft geleerd dat . . .

曠 Breed, wijd.

K'oà *k'oà lòng lòng*, 丨 寬, zeer wijd.

ts'iú t'aô k'oà, 手 頭 丨, mild, royaal.

k'oà k'oà, 丨 丨, losstaand in iets, te wijd.

k'oà tsoh, 丨 做, ruim, voordeelig om te bebouwen,

Koah

割 Snijden, afsnijden; maaijen; zich aan
Koah iets onttrekken, scheiden.

koah k'ui, 丨 開, opensnijden.

koah tīng, 丨 斷, afsnijden, doorsnijden; zich aan iets onttrekken.

koah tīng ts'iú, 丨 斷 手, de hand afzetten.

kō tsui koah k'i, 被 水 丨 去, door het water afgespoeld, (als land.)

koah tiū, 丨 稻, koren maaijen.

koah bak ts'ī hō, 丨 肉 飼 虎, zijn eigen vleesch afsnijden om een

37

tijger te voeden, *d. i.* zich zelven benadeelen.

koah t'aô tsang, | 頭 鬆, de hoofdstaart afsnijden, (aan overspelers gedaan.)

koah huih, | 血, snijden, slagten, (kippen enz.)

koah aô, | 喉, zich onthalzen.

koah ting koah tō, | 腸 | 肚, zich inwendig met iets folteren.

koah tiaò, ts'ùn ts'ùn koah, | 弔 寸 匕 |, do.

tâng tsi koah, 銅 錢 |, aan kleine stukken doodsnijden.

ïm kiā lâng koah tsih, 不 怕 人 | 舌, zijne meening zeggen zonder voor de gevolgen te vreezen.

koah siá, | 舍, afhakken en weggooijen; niet meer met iemand omgaan.

boē koah siá tit, 難 | 舍, niet van iets of iemand afkunnen, niet kunnen scheiden.

sing li koah hō pát lâng, 生 理 | 與 別 人, zijne handelszaak aan een ander overdoen.

koah siaò, 悄 |, eene schuld afmaken, verreffenen.

koah bah tsit téng t'ià } | 肉 一 次 痛, zijn vleesch afsnijden doet
» » » *tui* »

maar ééns pijn, *d. i.* het is beter schuld in ééns aftebetalen.

葛 Koah Eene eetbare klimplant; Dioscorea japonica, waarvan men ook een soort linnen maakt.

koah hún, | 粉, meel van de Diosc.

kan koah, 干 |, gedroogde Diosc, (tot meel of verkoelende drank gebruikt.

koah sa, | 衫, graslinnen jas.

koah pò, | 布, soort graslinnen.

kao koah, 爪 |, in betrekking staa met.

結 Koah Eene troep, bij elkander hoorende liede

tsit koah ê lâng, 一 | 的 人 een troep menschen.

siāng koah ê lâng, 全 | 的 人 lieden die tot dezelfde troep h hooren, (zooals reizigers.)

oang koah ê lâng, 黨 | 的 人 soort van menschen, (in slechten zin

kui oang kui koah, 全 黨 全 | tot hetzelfde komplot behoorende.

Koah Daarenboven nog; en tevens.

toā koah k'oah. 大 兼 闊, groot e daarbij nog breed, ruim·

ū koah, 有 |, nog een weini voorhanden.

koah hiu, } 請 香, processie houde
» *hio*

闊 K'oah Wijd, breed.

k'oan k'oah, 寬 |, ruim, (van ee huis.)

k'oah ts'ui, | 嘴, houweel

k'oah toā, | 大, groot, ruim.

tō liōng k'oah, 度 量 |, verdraa zaam.

lō kiā k'oah, 路 行 |, hoe lang hoe meer iemands genegenheid wi nen.

kao poê k'oah, 交 培 |, met ve menschen omgaan, uitgestrekte co versatie hebben.

tsoè lâng k'oah, 做 人 |, een bree mensch zijn, *d. i.* met iedereen goed vrienden.

渴 K'oah *ts'uì koah*, 口 |, dorstig.

Koai

乖 Koai Ongezeggelijk, stijfhoofdig, tam, getemd, mak, gedwee, gehoorzaam, zachtzinnig.

kiēn koai, 見 |, stijfhoofdig.

koai k'á ɛ̤. | 巧, ondeugende, onverbiedelijke duivel, (tegen jonge lieden).

koai tiong, koai tsiang, | 張, | 將, stijfhoofdig, steeds het tegenovergestelde van anderen willen.

kà boē koai, 教不 |, ontembaar, (van kinderen en beesten.)

kō̤ lâng kà koai, 與人教 |, door iemand getemd zijn, (een geduchte les gehad hebben.)

koai k'á, | 巧, schrander, zoet, gehoorzaam.

koai laī, | 利, zachtzinnig, lief.

koai ioh ioh, zeer gedwee, gehoorzaam.

拐 Koaí Bedriegen, ontstelen, opligten, schaken (menschen).

koaí k'ì, | 去, een kind opligten, stelen.

koaí p'ièn, | 騙, bedriegen.

koaí lai koaí k'ì, | 來 | 去, over en weer beide partijen bedriegen.

koaí lâng, | 人, menschen opligten. (wegstelen.)

tsit ki ts'uì gaô koaí, 一枝手善 |, knap zijn om menschen tot iets overtehalen.

koaí taì, | 帶, schaken, (een meisje).

koaí kùn, | 棍, schaker.

kan koaí, 姦 |, onteeren en schaken.

koaí pô, | 婆, gemeen wijf, schaakster, enz.

koaí ts'uì, | 嘴, gevaarlijk, bedriegelijk in zijn spreken.

koaí tioh k'a, | 着脚, zijn voet verstuiken.

怪 Koaì Vreemd. zonderling, wonderlijk, wonderbaarlijk; zich verwonderen over, kwalijk nemen.

ki koaì, 奇 |, wonderbaarlijk, vreemd.

koaì sū, | 事, wonderlijke dingen.

koaì koaì, | |, zonderling.

koaì ì, (of ī), | 意, verschillend, vreemd.

k'á koaì, 巧 |, vreemd, zonderling.

ku koaì, 君 |, do.

koaì sút, | 術, wonderlijke handgrepen, streken.

ts'it tè koaì, soort legkaart uit 7 stukjes bestaande.

kuí koaì, 鬼 |, onopregt.

koaì bút, | 物, ondeugend, slecht ding.

kó koaì, kó kó koaì koaì, 古匕怪匕, van het hedendaagsche verschillende, zonderling.

ts'aī koaì, 栽 |, een wonderlijk voorwerp ergens plaatsen, (om menschen bang te maken).

tsok koaì, 作 |, door een boozen geest bezield; onwel zijn.

koaì p'iah, | 僻, altijd het tegenovergestelde van anderen willen,

siaó só kiēn to só koaì, 小所見多所 |, hoe minder men gezien heeft, over des te meer verwondert men zich.

kièn koaì, 見 |, kwalijk nemen.

bók koaì, 莫 |, neem het niet kwalijk.

bók koaì lâng kóng, 莫 | 人說,

men kan het niet kwalijk nemen dat de menschen dit zeggen.

乖 Koaī Slecht, hardnekkig, wederstrevig; wringen, gewrongen, verdraaien, verdraaid, niet overeenstemmen met, niet in den haak.

koaī p'iah, 丨 僻, stijfhoofdig, wederstrevig.

koaī tioh, 丨 着, gewrongen, verdraaid.

koaī tioh k'a, 丨 着 脚, de voet verdraaijen, verzwikken.

sa koaī k'a, 相 丨 脚, beentje draaijen.

koaī tioh i ê p'iah, 丨 着 伊 之 僻, iemands hoofdneiging, hoofdgebrek aanranden.

koaī tsūn, 丨 陣, verdraaid; zich onwel gevoelen; tegenspartelingen maken.

koaī ko, 丨 膏, do. niet met iemands constitutie overeenkomen, (als spijzen).

sa koaī, 相 丨, in den war zitten, niet volkomen in den haak.

ū sa koaī, 有 相 丨, in elkander verdraaid zitten, beide gelijk hebben en toch verschillen.

koaī kó, 丨 股, verdraaide, gewrongen streng (van touw); met iemand niet harmonieren.

koaī lién, 丨 輦, een afgodsstoel verdraaijen, *d. i.* vroegere vriendschap verbreken.

koaī tsi k'ì hō ìh, 丨 錢 去 與 他, door verkeerd rekenen te veel betalen.

koaī tsih, (*tsih*) 丨 折, stuk wringen, stuk draaijen.

快 K'oài Opgeruimd, vrolijk, gezond; snel, gaauw.

t'òng k'oài / *t'iàng* » } 暢 丨, opgeruimd, vrolijk.

sóng k'oài, 爽 丨, gezond.

k'oài dzin k'oài gú, 丨 人 丨 語 een rondborstig mensch spreekt rond uit.

ts'uì k'oài sim bô tók, 嘴 丨 心 無 毒, het juist zeggen zoovals men het meent.

k'oài piēn, 丨 便, gemakkelijk, handig; bereidwillig.

k'in k'oài, 輕 丨, bereidwillig, hulpvaardig.

k'oài k'ì k'oài lai, 丨 去 丨 來 gaauw gaan en gaauw terugkomen.

k'oài saò, 丨 艡, snelle kruisboot.

kin tsiép koài, 緊 接 丨, zeer vlug snel.

k'oài ts'e, 丨 差, courier.

bé k'oài / *bé* » } 馬 丨, politiedienaar.

關 Koai Koa Digt doen, sluiten, opsluiten.

koai ming / » *mui* } 丨 門, de deur digt doen

koai ka, 監 禁, in de gevangenis opsluiten.

koai noai noai k'ì / » *noa noa* » } geheel en al sluiten, stevig sluiten.

koai tsiōng, 丨 賬. opsluiten, op school doen wegens zijne lastigheid, (van een klein kind).

koai tièm, 丨 店, zijne winkel sluiten (als 's avonds).

tièm koai k'ì lai, 店 丨 起 來, zijne winkel-zaak sluiten.

liáh k'ì koai, 拿 去 丨, in hechtenis opsluiten, (van beesten.)

Koai Sporten, (van een stoel, enz.)

toh koai. dwarshouten tusschen de pooten van eene tafel.

laō t'ui koai, pooten van een ladder, leuning van een trap.

i koai, stoelsport.

枴 Koai *koai á*, | 仔, wandelstok.

ts'ìn koai, 桯 |, arm van een schaal.

Koai *sīn tsit ki koai*, 身如一枝 |, zeer mager, dood arm.

莖 Koai *ts'aì koai*, 菜 |, stengel, stronk van grassen, enz.

梗 Koai Kaal, als een boomstam zonder takken.

Koai *Paí k'oai*, verschillend van vroeger, slechter geworden.

慣 Koai *koaì sì*, | 性, gewoon zijn aan.

koaì làh, | 了, do.

k'oùˬ īm koaì, 着不 |, niet gegewoon zijn te zien, vreemd staan op te zien.

sìng koaì, 性 |, teugelloos aan iets laten gewennen, (als kinderen aan drift.)

高 Koai Hoog; hoog van prijs, hoog in rang en bekwaamheid.

k'ah koai, 愈 |, hooger, hooger, grooter zijn dan.

koai kà ná t'ì nih, | 到如天, hemelhoog.

ts'iú kiáh koai, 手檯 |, met ontferming neerzien op, zich ontfermen over iemand, vergeven.

koai ts'iú, | 手, hoog in kennis, (van geneesheeren.)

koai tiém, | 點, hoog in stand, aanzien.

koai dzī, | 字, hoog staan aangeschreven. (door kennis of stand.)

sim koq koai koai, 心肝 | ⺊, inwendig bedroefd zijn, (door eene herinnering enz.)

koai kim, | 金, goud van hoog gehalte.

koai tsεnq è hè, | 粧之貨, goederen van beste kwaliteit.

biēn koai kè, 念 | 價, een hoogen prijs opdreunen, overvragen.

koai kē tú hó, | 下抵好, de hoogte en laagte is juist goed.

koai k'a i, | 脚椅, stoel met hooge pooten.

tsiū koai, 墻 |, eene hoogte opgaan, omhoog gaan

縣 Koaī Koān District.

hú koaī, 府 |, *fú* en *hiēn*, een departement en een district.

koaī hūn, | 分, uitgestrektheid van een *hiēn*,.

ti koaī, 知 |, eerste „*hien*", mandarijn.

koaī sinq / » *siā* } | 丞, *hiēn*, ondermandarijn van een *hiēn*.

hun koaī, 分 |, dito.

koaī tìng, | 堂, bureau van een *hiēn*.

oai oai koaī koaī, door voorwendsels geld van een rijkere familie betrekking zien te krijgen.

Koan

關 Koan Grenspost; tolhuis, kantoor van in- en- uitgaande-regten; in verband staan met, betrekking hebben op; de gevolgen.

koan aì, | 隘, grenspost.

koan sè, | 稅, impost, regten.

koan k'aū, | 口, tolhuis.

hai koan, 海 |, ontvanger der in- en- uitgaande regten, hoppo.

lō̤ koan, 路 |, programma eener optogt.

koan hông, | 防, waken voor.

koan tè iâ, | 帝 爺, oorspr. god van den oorlog; thans door kooplieden aangebeden.

koan hē, | 下, te maken hebben met, betrokken zijn in; de gevolgen.

koan siép, | 涉, te maken hebben met, aangaan.

kaon iaò, | 要, van belang, waaraan veel gelegen is.

ū koan kin iaò, 有 | 緊 | 要, van belang.

siang koan ióng ì, 相 | 用 意, tweeledig op te vatten.

koan sim, | 心, oplettend, zorgvuldig.

kè t'ong koan, 過 通 |, de grenspassen door zijn, *d. i.* grondig verstaan

koan to, | 刀, breed zwaard met een insnijding.

k'ui koan, 開 |, belastingkantoor openen, oprigten.

觀
Koan
Bekijken, oplettend bezien, zien, kijken.

koan k'oà, | 看, naauwkeurig bekijken.

koan tsing kò aō, | 前 顧 後, voor en achter zich kijken.

sa koan kò, 相 | 顧, op elkander passen, elkander beschermen.

pông koan ê lâng, 旁 | 之 人, bijstanders, ooggetuigen.

koan im, *koan im tai sū*, | 音. | 音 大 士, de godin *koan-im*, der genade.

官
Koan
Overheidspersoon, beambte, mandarijn.

koan koan siong iū, | 七 相 佑, overheden beschermen elkander.

koan tsing pók dzù suí / » » » *dzi tsi* } | 情 薄 如 紙, genegenheid van overheden is dun als water of papier.

koan put lī ìn, *hoàn put lī ts'ìn*, | 不 離 印 販 不 離, de mandarijn mag zijne zegels niet verlaten noch de rondventer zijne weegschaal, *d. i.* ieder houde zich aan zijne pligt.

棺
Koan
De binnenste van twee lijkkisten, lijkkist.

koan bók, | 木, lijkkist.

koan tà, | 罩, lijkbaar met een kleed er over.

ū koan, | 運, een lijk in de lijkkist naar zijne geboorteplaats voeren.

k'ìng koan, 藏 |, een lijkkist opbergen, (niet terstond begraven.)

捐
Koan
Voor geld inschrijven, een ambt koopen.

koan toè, | 題, voor geld inschrijven.

k'ai koan, 開 |, eene rijksinschrijving openstellen.

koan láp, | 納, aan het rijk opbrengen.

koan láp koa tsit, | 納 官 職, een ambt koopen.

koan koa, | 官, eene mandarijn post koopen.

冠
Koan
Muts, hoed.

i koan, 衣 |, kleederdragt, kleederen.

鰥
Koan
Weduwnaar, oud ongehuwd man.

koan koá ko tók, | 寡 孤 獨, ongehuwde mannen, weduwen, weezen en kinderlooze lieden.

管
Koán
Kleine fluit, blaasinstrumenten, muziek; overzien, besturen, beheeren; zich bemoeijen, inlaten met.

hiên koán, 絃 ｜, strijk en blaas instrumenten,
lâm koán, pak koán, 南 ｜, 北 ｜, Zuider en Noorder muziek.
háh koán, 葭 ｜, harmonieren (van muziek of personen.)
koán uī, ｜ 位, muzieknooten.
ts'iū bô kab koán, 唱 無 到 ｜, niet in den toon of maat zingen.
sì koán tsing, 四 ｜ 全, volledig kwartet, (om bij te zingen); een volop voorziene tafel.

管 Koán *koán lí*, ｜ 理, overzien, beheeren.
koán kò, ｜ 顧, beheeren, besturen,
tsiáng koán, 掌 ｜, overzien, beheeren.
king koán, 經 ｜, beheer, departement; besturen.
koán tuī koa, ｜ 隊 ｜, aanvoerder van een troep soldaten.
koán kuī, ｜ 櫃, boek- kashouder.
koán siab, ｜ 賬, boekhouden, boekhouder,
koán ke, ｜ 家, het huis besturen, maître d'hôtel.
koán pan, ｜ 班, hoofd-direkteur van een troep, (bedienden, tooneelspelers, enz.)
siu koán, 收 ｜, onder zijne berusting en beheer hebben.
bô lâng koán, 無 人 ｜, niemand controleert hem of het.
īm koán ih, 不 ｜ 伊, laat u daar niet meè in, laat dat loopen.
put koán sim mih lâng, 不 ｜ 甚 麼 人, onverschillig wie ook?
koán sū, ｜ 事, huishouder, maître d'hòtel.
koán hú, ｜ 府, hoogere onder soldaten, soldaat.

舘 Gevangenis.
Koàn *koán á*, ｜ 仔, do.
bè k'oaì koán, 馬 快 ｜, dienders kamers.
kò koán, k'oà koán, 顧 ｜, 看 ｜, gevangenbewaarder.
ah koán, 押 ｜, opsluiten, arrest geven.

館 Koán Herberg, logement; openbaar gebouw, vergaderplaats; kantoor, school; ligte gevangenis.
k'eh koán, 客 ｜, herberg.
kong koán, 公 ｜, mandarijn of publiek gebouw.
hoē koán, 會 ｜, vergaderzaal.
tê koán, 茶 ｜, theehuis.
iêm koán, 鹽 ｜, zoutdépôt.
koán hu, ｜ 夫, kok.
koán hu tiàm, ｜ 夫 店, restauratie.
koán tsàn, ｜ 棧, kok.
i koán, 醫 ｜, hospitaal.
k'ik koán, 曲 ｜, zangschool.
hiòng koán, 餉 ｜, tolhuisje.
hì koán, 戲 ｜, gemeenschappelijke woning van tooneelspelers.
pan koán, 辦 ｜, woning van mandarijn bediendan.

捲 Rollen, oprollen.
Koán *koán su*, ｜ 書, gedeeltelijk opgerold boek, (tegen muren gestukadoord.)
koán tsien, ｜ 饘, oblie.

鑵 Kan, pot.
Koàn *tsui koán*, 水 ｜, waterkan.
t'ng koàn, 糖 ｜, suikerpot.
tê koàn, 茶 ｜, theepot.

灌 Koàn Zich ontlasten, instroomen van water; ingieten, met geweld doen drinken; plengen.

tsui koàn lòh lai, 水 丨 下 來, het water komt neêr stroomen.

koàn tsui, 丨 水, water inschenken, met water vervalschen.

koàn ièn, 丨 鉛, met lood volgieten, (valsch geld).

koàn kuī, 丨 潰, langs lekken, (als water van het plafond langs de muur.)

koàn ioh, 丨 藥, medicijnen met geweld ingeven.

koàn tsiù, 丨 酒, met geweld wijn ingeven.

koàn kaò tsuì, 丨 至 醉, zoolang ingeven dat iemand beschonken is.

koàn toē, 丨 地, (wijn) op den grond plengen.)

鑵 Koàn *koàn k'aò*, 丨 口, markplaats onder *Tsiang-tsiu.*

貫 Koàn Een rist van duizend duiten, aanrijgen zamenhang, verband.

bān koàn ê ka tsu / » » » *ke* » } 萬 丨 家 貲, enorm rijk.

koân ts'oàn, 丨 串, zamenhang, verband.

bô koàn ts'oàn, 無 丨 串, zonder zamenhang.

koàn t'ong, 丨 通, zamenhangend, logisch.

慣 Koàn Zich gewennen aan; gewoon aan.

koàn siók, *koàn sip*, 丨 熟, 丨 習, zich gewennen, gewoon aan.

sip koàn sing tsū dziên, 習 丨 成 自 然, heeft men zich aan iets gewend dan gaat het van zelf.

koàn liēn, 丨 鍊, zijn hoofdzaak maken van.

眷 Koàn Familie, huisgezin, huisgenooten.

ke koàn, 家 丨, huisgenooten.

siò ke koàn, 小 家 丨, bijzitten.

tsū koàn, 住 丨, een huishouden hebben.

冠 Koàn *koàn tiû*, 丨 埸, boven alle overigen uitmunten, (van persoon en dingen.)

權 Koân Magt, invloed; magt hebben over; omstandigheden; tijdelijk, zoolang.

koân pìng, 丨 柄, magt.

koân sè / » *sì* } 丨 勢, do.

ping koân, 兵 丨, militaire magt.

lōng koân, 弄 丨, van zijne magt misbruik maken.

t'ing koân, 挺 丨, zijne magt vergrooten

t'iông koân, 寵 丨, invloed van een gunsteling, bijzit.

bô koân, 無 丨, geen magt hebben over.

tsiáng koân, 掌 丨, de magt in handen hebben.

ts'ièm koân, 僭 丨, in magt toenemen.

koân pièn, 丨 變, naar de omstandigheden wijzigen.

hing koân, 行 丨, naar de omstandigheden handelen.

tsiēm koân, 漸 丨, tijdelijk.

tsiông koân, 從 丨, tijdelijk, zoolang.

倦 Koān *k'ùn koān*, 困 丨, slaperig, vermoeid.

寬 K'oan Uitgestrekt, ruim, wijd; langmoedig, inschikkelijk; uitstel geven, verlengen

k'oan k'oan, 丨 匕, ruim uitgestrekt.

k'oan k'oan līng ling, 丨 匕 令 匕, ruim (van tijd) uitstel geven, uitstellen.

k'oan k'oah, ｜闊, ruim, (van plaats).

k'oan hông, ｜弘. ruim, lankmoedig.

k'oan sim, ｜心, bedaard, op zijn gemak, zich geruststellen.

k'oan iông, ｜容, lankmoedig behandelen, den tijd verlengen.

k'oan ān, ｜限, den termijn verlengen.

k'oan oān, ｜緩, uitstel geven.

sìng tē k'oan, 性地｜, lankmoedig, inschikkelijk.

ts'iá k'oan tsit pō, 且｜一步, wees wat inschikkelijk.

pàng k'ah k'oan tseh, 放較｜這. wat inschikken.

ts'â k'oan, 柴｜, lange houten stok.

欵 K'oán Behandelen, ontvangen; vorm, manier, soort.

k'oán t'āi, ｜待, behandelen, onthalen.

p'ai k'oán t'āi, 歹｜待, slecht behandelen.

k'oán pá, ｜飽, zooveel mogen eten als men wil, (in eene restauratie.)

k'oán sit, ｜式, vorm, manier, wijze.

bô k'oán sit, 無｜式, dat is geen manier, onbetamelijk.

ū k'oán, 有｜, fraai.

so k'oán, 蘇｜, Suchow mode.

koán k'iaù, ｜竅, vorm, inrichting, (als van machines.)

ták k'oán, 逐｜, allerlei soorten, vormen.

bô lâng k'oán, 無人｜, niet als een mensch, onmensch.

pièn k'oán, 便｜, van manieren veranderen, gew. verbeteren.

lòh k'oán, 落｜, iemands betiteling opschrijven, (als op brieven.)

tiaô k'oán, 條｜, artikels, bepalingen.

k'ioh k'oán, 鞠｜, verschillende kleine overtredingen bij elkander vatten (en daarvoor vergoeding vragen.)

綣 K'oán *k'ién k'oán*, 繾｜, hartelijk, gastvrij.

檢 K'oán Nakijken, nazien, onderzoeken, sortéren.

k'oán mih, ｜物, goederen nakijken.

k'oán k'oán, *k'oán k'oà*, ｜匕, ｜看, nazien, nakijken, nazellen.

k'oán hing lí, ｜行李, zijne bagage nakijken.

k'oán k'oán siaò siaò, ｜匕算匕, onderzoeken, nakijken.

kè k'oán, 加｜, door iemands handen gegaan, door iemands nagezien zijn.

k'oán tà lóh niū, ｜担落｜, vrachten sortéren en op de weegschaal zetten.

勸 K'oàn *k'oàn sè bûn* / *k'oàn sì bûn*, ｜世文, morele boeken, traktaatjes.

k'oàn tsiú, ｜酒, iemand aanzetten nog wat wijn te nemen.

sa k'oán bién, 相｜勉, elkander vermanen en aanzetten.

圈 K'oàn *k'oàn soh*, ｜索, een touw oprollen, opslaan.

k'oàn k'í lai, ｜起來, een kring door iets halen, (als door een verkeerd karakter.)

tsit k'oân, 一｜, cirkel,

t'ih k'oân, 鐵｜, ijzeren ring.

環 K'oân *ts'iú k'oân*, 手｜, armband.

hī k'oân, 耳｜, oorring.

k'a k'oân, 脚｜, ring om het been gedragen.

gik k'oân, 玉 |, armband van nefriet. of jade.

k'oân tsit k'oân, | 一 圈, een cirkel trekken, de rondte om iets doen.

pak k'oân t'ò, 打 | 套, een cirkel vormige lus of strik leggen, iemand beet willen nemen.

sì pi k'oân ts'aó, 四 邊 | 草. aan alle kanten met gras omringen. bedekken, (als een zouthoop.)

kiú lién k'oân, 九 連 |, negen vereenigde ringen, (die door een kunstgreep ontward kunnen worden.)

Koat

決 Koat Beslissen, besluiten, vaststellen; bepaald, vastbesloten, stellig, onthoofden.

koat toàn, | 斷, beslissen, besluiten.

koat toàn beh, | 斷 要, vastbesloten, stellig, willen.

koat ì, | 意, vastbesloten.

koat dzién, | 然, stellig, zeker.

koat hoān, | 犯, misdadigers onthoofden.

訣 Koat Afscheidnemen op zijn sterfbed, streek, kunstgreep, manier, geheim.

tik koat, 得 |, eene goede manier, middel, op iets vinden.

pì koat, 秘 |, geheim, (als van eene uitvinding.)

kang ô koat, 江 湖 |, kwakzalvers streken.

koat piét, | 別, afscheid nemen op zijn sterfbed.

摑 Koat Slaan, een klap geven; kloppen.

koat ts'uì p'oé, | 嘴 䏲, in het gezigt slaan.

koat hī á, | 耳 仔, om de ooren slaan.

koat he hún, | 灰 粉, kalk op iets vastkloppen.

hák koat, 學 |, klopper om aarde kalk enz. platte slaan.

péh koat koat, 白 | 匕, sneeuwwit, (als een met meel beslagen gezigt.)

kō i boē koat tit, 與 伊 未 | 的, onderdoen voor.

īng k'a ùn tsuí koat ih, 用 脚 染 水 | 伊, iemand met een natte voet slaan, *d. i.* volstrekt niet bang voor hem zijn.

刮 Koat Afschrapen.

koat siét, | 舌, tongschraper.

括 Koat Bevatten, behelzen.

pao koat, 包 |, omvatten, bevatten.

缺 K'oat *k'oat giáh*, | 額, van het bepaalde aantal missen, niet meer compleet zijn.

闕 Koat *k'oat hē teh*, | 下 的, ter zijde leggen, (als iets wat men nog niet kan uitmaken.)

闋 K'oat *k'oat hók*, | 服, uit den rouw gaan.

Koe

雞 Koe Ke Hoen, haan, kip.

koe kak, ts'io koe, 雄 |, haan.

koe bú, | 母, hen.

koe á, | 仔, kuiken.

koe noā, | 妹, hen die nog geene eijeren gelegd heeft.

koe nn̄g, | 蛋, ei van eene kip

koe t'ò á, | 桃 仔, groote kuikens.

iem koe, 奄 |, kapoen.

koe hing haō hiáh ēm si iáh tsoè k'it tsiáh. | 胸 餃 額 不 死 也

作乞食, zoo iemand, met een kippenborst en een voorhoofd als een konings krab, niet sterft, dan wordt hij toch bedelaar.

koe bák, 丨肉, eksteroog; oogziekte waardoor men's avonds niet zien kan, slaperig.

koe bîn, 丨眠, losslapen.

hé koe, 火丨, kalkoen; haan van een geweer.

koe kū, 丨距, hanespoor.

koe kè, 丨冠, hanekam.

t'i koe, 雉丨, fasant.

koe tiaô, 丨欄, kippenhok.

koe tà, 丨罩, mand waaronder men kippen doet.

koe niaô kûn / *» k'a »* } 丨爪裩, borst in den vorm van een kippepoot.

iem koe kiâ, 奄丨行, op de handen loopen.

hô k'a koe, 鬍脚丨, kippen met beveerde pooten.

p'ah koe, 鬪丨, hanengevecht houden.

ts'ân koe, 田丨, reiger.

koe tai, 丨臺, kleine zwarte muskiet; met zich zelven verlegen, beschaamd.

koe liu, 丨溜, terug krabbelen, terugtrekken.

suí koe, 水丨, kikvorsch.

suí koe teh, 水丨的, als een kikvorsch, niet veel bezittende.

街 Koe / Ke — Straat, marktplein, markt.

koe lō, 丨路, straat.

sip dzī koe, 十字丨, kruisstraat.

k'oà koe; sûn koe; ts'â koe, 看丨, 巡丨, 查丨, de straat bewaken, straat wachter, politiedienaar.

koe ts'ī, 丨市, marktplaats.

tsiū koe, 上丨, naar de markt gaan,

koe kû, 丨衢, mark, straat.

oan koe p'iah hūng, 灣丨僻丨, achterafplaats.

ts'ut koe k'ih, 出丨去, op straat uitgaan.

kiò koe, 叫丨, langs de straat bedelen.

tsaó koe á, 走丨仔, rondtrekkende kwakzalvers.

瓜 Koe / Koa — Meloen, komkommer.

ts'ì koe, 刺丨, komkommer.

tang koe, 冬丨, wintermeloen.

si koe; 施丨, watermeloen.

k'ō kóa, 苦丨, bittere komkommer.

kim koe, 金丨, goud meloen

ts'aì koe. 菜丨, komkommer.

p'aị koe kaō tsí p'aị lâng kaō giên gi, 歹丨多子歹人多言語, slechte meloenen hebben veel pitten, slechte menschen praten veel.

koe sik piēn lut tì / *(koa sik tì lôk)* } 丨熟傑黜, is de meloen rijp dan valt ze van haar stengel, *d. i.* als de tijd daar is, gaat eene zaak van zelf.

koe soè tsí sik, 丨細子熟, de meloen is klein maar de pitten zijn rijp, *d. i.* klein maar knap.

改 Koé / Ké — Veranderen, verbeteren.

koé oā, 丨換, veranderen.

koé pì, 丨變, veranderen, verbeteren.

koé ts'iâ, 丨成, veranderen, goedmaken.

koé t'aò oñ bīn, | 頭 換 面, geheel en al veranderen.
koé dzī, | 字, een karakter veranderen, verbeteren.
koé tak á, | 達 仔, een weinig aan iets veranderen.
koé tak, | 達, plagen.
koé dzit, | 日, den dag veranderen, een anderen dag bepalen.
koé kè, | 計, hertrouwen, (van eene vrouw).

解 Koé Ké Ontwarren, uiteenzetten, uitleggen, verklaren; doen verdwijnen, de slechte gevolgen wegnemen, krachteloos zijn.
koé seh, | 說, verklaren, uitleggen.
koé bing, | 明, duidelijk maken, uitleggen.
koé p'oà, | 破, uitleggen, de gevolgen voorhouden en daardoor een twist bijleggen.
koe tsiú, | 酒, dronkenschap doen overgaan. (als thee of vruchten doen,) zijne gewoonte van dronkenschap opgeven.)

疥 Koè Puistje, zweertje.
koè á, | 仔, puistjes,
soa koè, 沙 |. drooge puistjes,
noñ koè, 爛 |, vocht uitlatende puistjes.
âng k'a koè, 紅 脚 |, roode gevaarlijke puistjes.

怪 Koè Koà Zich verwonderen over, kwalijk nemen.
boē koè tit . . . , 勿 | 的, hoe is het dan te verwonderen dat . . . .
boē oē koè tit lâng kóng, 勿 | 的 人 說, men kan het niet kwalijk nemen dat dit gezegd wordt.

劊 Koè Kui *koè tsú siú*, | 子 手, beul.

獪 Koè *kaó koè*. 狡 |, slecht, bedriegelijk.

處 *sì koe* / *sì kè* } 四 |, overal, alom.
Koè *toā sì koè*, 大 四 |, alom, in overvloed, voorhanden.

鮭 Koè Kè Ingelegde, gezoute visch.
hê koê / *hê kè* } 蝦 |, gezoute garnalen.
ts'aò noñ koè, 臭 涎 |, stinkend uit de mond.
sī koè, 豉 |, inzouten, gezouten, inmaken.
koè tsiep, | 湊, pekel van gezoute visch.
koe âng, | 甕. pot waarin gezoute visch is.
tsiù koè koè, 醬 | 匕, modderig morsig.

摩 Koè *ts'uì koè koè*, 碎 | 匕, aan schilfers gebroken.

易 Koē *koē koē*, | 匕, gemakkelijk.
tsoè lâng bē koē, 做 人 未 |, het is niet gemakkelijk zijne pligten als mensch te vervullen; een voorbeeldig mensch zijn; niet gemakkelijk te evenaren.

溪 K'oe Bergstroom, beek.
k'oe po, | 埔, kant langs een stroom.
k'oe laô t'aò, | 流 透, de stroom in de rivier is sterk.
k'oe pi tsûn lō pi ts'ù, 邊 船 路 邊 |, als booten langs de rivier en huizen, langs den weg; voor ieder een toegankelijk als bordeelen.
k'oe tsûn, | 船, platboomde rivierbooten.

敲 K'oe K'e Afkrabben, afschrapen, afschrijven.
k'oe soè / *k'e sè* } | 洗, bij kleine hoeveelheden van iets afnemen, afbrokkelen.

k'oe tioh, | 着, schrijnen tegen, afschrijnen.

k'oe siah, | 錫, afschrijnen en afschrapen, *d. i.* in kleinigheden bedriegen.

sa k'oe, 相 |, tegen elkander aanschrijnen.

oe k'oe, 挨 |, dralen.

盔 K'oe Helm.

t'ih k'oe, 鉄 |, ijzeren helm.

k'oe kah, | 甲, helm en harnas.

moâ k'oe, 麻 |, hennepen helm, *d. i.* muts door hoofdrouwers gedragen.

魁 K'oe *k'oe sing*, *k'oe sing kong*, | 星, | 星 公, de Noordster, god der geleerden.

k'oe sing lóh tsui, | 星 落 水, 味 筆, *k'oe sing* gaat in het water (om naar een penseel te duiken, *bī pit*), *bī pit*, beteekent ook niet stellig, nog onzeker.

恢 K'oe *k'oe hók*, | 復, eene plaats heroveren.

k'oe t'oâ k'oe bé, | 頭 | 尾, het hoofd, en voeteneind van een doodkist.

契 K'oè Overeenkomst, contract, akte, bewijs van eigendom; aannemen als verwante, aangenomen, eenigzins gelijkkomende met ons peet.

tsiò k'oè, 借 |, leencontract.

ts'ân k'oè, *ts'ù k'oè*, 田 |, 厝 |, bewijs van eigendom van een land en huis.

sè k'oè, 稅 |, een bewijs, akte van eigendom, van het belasting kantoor halen.

k'oè kì, *k'oè kì* | 記, bewijs van eigendom.

kap lâng k'oè lai k'oè k'ì, 與 人 來 | 去, elkander over en weer aannemen als broeders en zusters, enz.

k'oè pē, *k'oè bú*, *k'oè kiá*, *k'oè pē*, *k'oè bó*, *k'oè kiá*, | 父, | 母, | 子, een soort van peetoom peettante, petekind.

嚙 Knagen.

K'oè K'è *k'oè tsit k'ang*; | 一 空, een gat in iets knagen.

k'oè tsing kah, | 甲 指, op de nagels knabbelen.

K'oè Lang, hoog, rijzig.

ts'aó k'oè k'oè k'oè, 草 | | |, het gras is zeer rijzig, lang.

t'aô mìng k'oè k'oè k'oè, 頭 毛 | | |, zeer lang van haar.

Koeh

鍥 *koeh á*, | 仔, sikkel.

Koeh *taō koeh*, 豆 |, bast, schil van boonen.

Koéh Onder den arm of tusschen de beenen drukken.

kâ koéh, 扶 |, onder den arm nemen, helpen, ondersteunen.

tsing lâng koéh i tsit lâng, 衆 人 | 伊 一 人, allen hebben er hem uitgedrongen, uitgewerkt als een cantonneesche bediende uit een Fokkien winkel.

K'oéh Smalle tusschenruimte tusschen twee huizen.

ts ù k'oéh, 厝 |, een klein huis tusschen twee grooten.

k'oéh lai k'oéh k'ì, | 來 | 去, over en weer elkander dringen.

k'oéh tsiū tsut lai, | 漿 出 來, perst men dan komt het er uit, ook gezegd van geld dat men met moeite uit iemand krijgt.

合 De oogen sluiten.

K'oeh *k'oeh bák*, 丨眼, de oogen sluiten.

bák tsiu k'oeh, 目周丨, de oogen gesloten hebben, *d. i.* na zijn dood.

bák tsiu poà k'ui k'oéh, 目周半開丨, de oogen half open en digt hebben, doen als of men iets niets zag, door de vingers zien.

㝔 Tegen elkander aandringen, aanschuiven; naauw, gedrongen.

K'oeh *sa k'oeh, sa oe sa k'oeh* / *sio k'eh » » »* 相丨, 相挨相丨, tegen elkander aandringen, dringen.

k'oeh sio, 丨暖, tegen elkander aanschuiven voor de warmte

k'oeh k'ah oá k'ìh, 丨較倚去, digter aanschuiven.

bóng k'oeh, 罔丨, het zoolang maar met iets doen.

sán iû sa k'oeh, 瘦羊相丨, als magere geiten die elkander verdringen, *d. i*, vele arme lieden die op een hoop wonen.

k'oeh ts'oéh (of *toéh*) *ìh*, 丨最, tegen iemand aandringen, weg dringen.

k'oeh k'oeh k'oeh, 丨匕匕, naauw, gedrongen.

oe oe k'oek k'oeh, 狹匕丨匕, do.

榨 Uitpersen; kraken, fijn drukken, fijn-

K'oeh kneeden.

Tsà *k'oeh iû*, 丨油, olie persen.

K'eh *k'oeh tsià*, 丨蔗, suiker persen.

k'oeh ts'ia, 丨車, pers (olie of suiker.)

k'oeh p'oà, 丨破; stuk drukken, kraken..

Koh

復 Andermaal, nogmaals, wederom, nog.

Koh *koh tsaì, tsaì koh*, 丨再, nogmaals, wederom.

koh kóng, 丨說, nogmaals zeggen, herhalen.

koh hing, 丨行, teruggeven,

koh k'ah hó, 丨較好, nog beter.

異 *koh iū*, 各丨, verschillend.

Koh

胳 Armholte, oksel.

Koh *koh ē k'ang* / *» ē »* 丨下空, armholte.

koh ē, / *» ē* 丨下, oksel, (van een kleed.)

tiaò koh, 朝丨, strak onder de armen.

siang ts'iú ts'ah koh, 双手插丨, met de handen in de zij staan.

si koh soeh, 生雪丨, een gezwel onder den arm hebben.

閣 Stokken, stellaadjes, waarop verkleede

Koh meisjes worden rondgedragen.

koh pi, 丨秤, do.

koh toà, 丨旦, meisjes die daar opgedragen worden.

tsng koh, 庄丨, zich verkleeden om daarop rondgedragen te worden.

擱 Neèrleggen.

Koh *tam koh*, 擔丨, opgehouden worden, lang in de pen blijven, lang aanhouden.

laò koh, 溜丨, opgehouden worden, langer blijven dan men gedacht had.

Kok

國 Kok Land, rijk, koningrijk.
kok ka / *» ke* } 丨家, do.
tiong kok, 中丨, China.
kok kun, 丨君, vorst van een rijk.
pún kok, 本丨, mijn geboorteland.
kok hō, 丨號, regerings naam.
pang kok, 邦丨, rijk, land.
kok dzī bīn, 丨字面, vierkant gezigt.
kok tiaô ts'o, 丨朝初, begin eener dynastie
kok dzī k'ak, 丨字殼, vierkant geraamte, (van een karakter, een gebroken voorwerp enz.)

逐 Kok *kok ê*, 丨箇, elk een.
kok iū, 丨漾, allerlei, allerhande.

各 Kok *kok lâng*, 丨人, elk mensch, ieder een.
kok kok, 丨國, elk een; elk rijk.

穀 Kok *nó kok tièm*, 五丨店, graanwinkel, zaadwinkel.
nó kok put ts'a hun, 五丨不差分, (de prijs van het) graan verschilt (op de verschillen plaatsen) niet veel.
tsit koh hông ki iong dzi t'aī ló, 積丨防饑養兒待老, graan stapelt men op tegen hongersnood en kinderen voedt men op voor zijn ouderdom.

谷 Kok *san kok*, 山丨, valei.

廓 Kok *koan kok i k'im*, 棺丨衣襟, binnenste en buitenste lijkkist en lijkkleederen.

咯 Kók *p'ah kók ke* / *» » ke* } 打丨更, kakelen, (van kippen.)
tsit ê kók tsiū t'un lóh k'ih, 一丨下就吞落, in een slik inslikken (zonder te kaauwen.)

梏 K'ok *k'ok hiah*, 丨額, vooruitstekend voorhoofd.
t'aô k'ak k'ok k'ok, 頭殼丨丨, do.

柝 K'ok *ki k'ok* / *ke »* } 更丨, klepper waarop men de wacht slaat.
k'ok tsú tē, 丨子弟, kinderen van fatsoenlijke huizen bedriegen.
kap i k'ok, 與伊丨, iemnnd een standje schoppen.

酷 K'ok *k'ok tók*, 丨毒, stiefmoederlijk behandelen.
k'ok hing, 丨刑, overdreven straffen, mishandelen, overdreven winst op iets willen hebben.
k'ok dziét, 丨熱, ondragelijk heet, (van het weder.)

擴 K'ok *k'ok ts'iong k'ah toā*, 丨充, uitbreiden, (als handel.)

柝 K'ók *p'ah k'ók*, 擊丨, klepper, de wacht slaan; over koetjes en kalfjes spreken.
kòng k'ók, 摃丨, do.
ki k'ók, 起丨, klepper.
k'i k'i k'ók k'ók, geluid van overelkander rollende steenklompen, op den grond, enz.
k'ók t'aô, 丨頭, met het hoofd tegen iets aanstooten.
lók k'ók bé, lók k'ók ê lâng, 落丨馬落丨的人, een teugelloos mensch

k'ók dzí, | 字, knikkers die kinderen bij het bikkelen gebruiken.

ts'uì k'í noā k'ók k'ók tò, 嘴 齒 涎 | 到, watertanden.

Kong

公 Kong Publiek, openbaar, van of voor het algemeen, gemeenschappelijk, gezamelijk, billijk, regtvaardig, grootvader, achter mannelijke verwanten heeft het de kracht van ons oud; hertog; eeretitel in het algemeen; Patna opium.

teng kong sū, 當 | 事, publieke zaken beredderen.

ká kong hing sū, 假 | 行 私, den schijn aannemen van voor het publiek te handelen en inderdaad zijne private belangen behartigen.

kong hók, | 服, uniform.

kong tsìng, | 正, publiek, van het algemeen.

kóng si, | 司, compagnie, vereeniging. In Nederlandsch-Indië den gewonen titel voor Chinesche officieren.

kong si sing lí, | 司 生 理, compagnieschap.

kong hoē, | 會, gemeenschappelijke vereeniging, maatschappij.

kong gûn, | 銀, gemeenschappelijk geld.

kong ke, | 家, gezamelijk, te zamen.

kong hing, | 行, in het openbaar, openlijk.

kong tông k'oà kì, | 堂 看 的, allen gelijkelijk gezien hebben.

kong bùn tiong hó siu hīng, | 門 中 好 修 行, in een mandarijnbureau kan men goede handelingen doen.

kong ts'in, | 親, scheidsregter, middelaar.

kong kiōng, | 共, gemeenschappelijk.

kong kui, | 規, algemeen bekend, (als iemand die van eene verre reis terugkeert.)

kong kó, | 估, openlijk, iets openlijk schatten.

kong saì, | 使, plenipotentiaris, 's rijk gezant.

kong tō, *kong pî*
» » » *pîng* } | 道, | 平, regtvaardig, billijk.

t'ien kong tē tō, 天 | 地 道. zeer regtvaardig.

kong tìng niû, | 等 㮡, zuiver geijkte weegschaal.

kong má, | 媽, grootouders, voorouders.

kong pô, | 婆, voorouders.

pē kiá kong sun, 父 子 | 孫, vader kind, grootvader en klein kind.

goā kong, 外 |, aangehuwde grootvader.

tsik kong, 叔 |, jongere oud-oom.

peh kong, 伯 |, oudere oud-oom.

t'i kong, 天 |, god.

t'ó tī kong, 土 地 |, aardgod.

kong tsú, | 子, prinses.

taī kong, 代 |, schipper.

ing kong, 黃 |, Mijnheer Éng.

光 Kong Licht, helder, klaar, helder van verstand; kaal.

kong ts'aí, | 彩, helder, fraai.

kong gán, | 眼, knap, intelligent.

tsing kong, 精 |, buitengewoon ervaren, kundig.

kong kùn, | 棍, schurk, opligter. zwendelaar.

kong taī, | 代, kleine solen.

工 Werkman; werk, arbeid.

Kong *kong pō*, | 部, ministerie van openbare werken.

kong k'ió, | 巧, kunstig, fraai.

hoū kong, 化 |, schilder.

t'ó kong, 土 |, doodgraver, onbeschoft mensch.

kong siū, | 謝, stoeldrager.

sa dzī kong, sù dzī kong, 三 字 |, 四 字 |, Carolus III en IV dollars.

功 Verdiensten, daad die belooning verdient; gewenschte uitwerking van
Kong medicijnen.

kong lō, | 勞, verdiensten.

mō kong, 毛 |, zich valschelijk de verdiensten van iets toeschrijven.

tsoè kong tik, 最 | 德, uitvaart, lijkdienst, houden.

kong haū, | 效, goede uitwerking, (van medicijnen.)

攻 Aanvallen, bestormen.

Kong *kong tá*, | 打, bestrijden aanvallen.

kong kik, | 擊, aanvallen, bestormen.

kong pià è ióh, | 變 的 葯, beslissend geneesmiddel.

綱 *kong kàm*, | 監, geschiedenis.
Kong

講 Zeggen, spreken, vertellen, verhalen.

Kóng *kóng oē*, | 話, spreken.

kóng kioh . . . , | 掬, zeggen dat . . . , spreken over . . . . , wat ik zeggen wou . . .

kóng péh ts'át, | 白 賊, liegen.

kóng tsing, | 情, toegevendheid, vergiffenis voor iemand vragen.

goá kóng li t'ia, 我 | 汝 聽, hoor eens, ik zal het U zeggen.

kóng lóng lóng k'ì, | 朗 匕 去, geheel en al vertellen.

kā li kóng hòh, 與 汝 | 了, heb ik het U niet gezegd?

kóng koē kiā oh } | 快 行 難,
» *k'oài* » »
makkelijker gezegd dan gedaan.

kóng k'i, | 起, spreken van, iets op halen.

kóng lai kóng k'ì, | 來 | 去, over en weer spreken.

kóng p'oà, | 破, verklappen.

kóng p'oà m̄ tát tsī i, | 破 不 值 一 文 錢, is het verklapt dan is het geen duit meer waard.

kóng oē bò koai aū mêng, | 話 無 關 後 |, over iets spreken en de achterdeur niet sluiten.

kóng t'ong, kong t'ò, | 通, | 套, van te voren raadplegen wat te zeggen.

p'ai oē kiém kóng koah, 歹 話 歉 |, onaangename dingen moet men zoo weinig mogelijk zeggen.

kóng kè } | 價, over den prijs dingen.
» *kè*

bò kóng kè } 無 | 價, niet dingen,
» » *ké*
niet overvragen.

kóng t'i kóng toē, kóng ts'it kóng poeh, | 天 | 地, | 七 | 八, over koetjes en kalfjes spreken.

kóng k'ì kóng tò, | 起 公 道, dan zus dan zóó spreken.

boē kóng tit, 難 | 的, ik kan het U zoo niet zeggen, het is maar beter daarover te zwijgen.

ēm hó kóng, 不好|, moeielijk te zeggen, spreek er me niet van!

kóng tióh tsìu ēm kā̤ ìn, |着就不敢應, den spijker op den kop treffen.

筒 Buis, koker.

Kóng *tik kóng*, 竹|, bamboezen koker.

p'ī lok (of *lak*) *kóng*, 品仔|, neus-koker.

toā kóng, 大|, groot, (van een penseel.)

tsim kóng, 蟳|, krabbetangen.

puh kóng á, 發|呵, opborrelen.

p'òng kóng, 脹|, opzwellen.

廣 *kóng* (of *k'óng*) *kao*, |交, uitgebreide

Kóng kennissen, relaties.

攻 Slaan, stompen, beuken, stampen.

Kòng *kòng p'oà*, |破, stukslaan.

tsing kòng p'ah, 掙|打, stompen, beuken en slaan.

kióng kòng, 强|, met geweld beuken.

kòng kó̤, |鼓, op de trommel slaan.

kòng t'ng, |糖, suiker instampen, (van schepen die op Formosa suiker innemen.)

貢 Schatting opbrengen; schatting.

Kòng *kòng ièn*, |燕, schatting in vogelnestjes opbrengen.

pān kòng, 辦|, de schatting gereed maken.

tsìn kòng, 進|, schatting opbrengen.

hoe kòng; 花|, gebloemd satijn.

kòng toān, |緞, effen satijn.

kòng ī, |院, prov. examinatie plaats om *kú-dzin* te worden.

kòng sing, |生, geletterden iets hooger dan *siù tsai*.

銃 Kanon, stuk geschut.

Kòng *ling kòng* / *liòng* » } 龍|, groot kanon.

tâng kòng, 銅|, koperen stuk geschut.

toā kòng ts'ing, 大|銃, groot kanon.

誑 Bedriegen, beetnemen.

Kòng *kòng kiaó*, |賭博, in het dobbelen bedriegen.

kòng tsú tē, |子弟, aanzienlijke kinderen afzetten.

kòng p'ièn, |騙, bedriegen.

ēm t'ang hō̤ i kòng k'ì, 不可被他|去, laat u niet bedotten, beetnemen.

kòng kòng dzióng, |匕嚷, hard leven maken.

狂 Gek, krankzinnig, dol, razende; onbe-

Kòng suisd, woest.

tien kòng, 顛|, krankzinnig, gek.

kòng sìng, |性, do.

bâng kòng, 夢|, do.

ts'ī kòng ē lâng, 生|的人, een razende, krankzinnig.

hoat kòng, 發|, krankzinnig zijn.

dziét kòng, 熱|, razende, ijlende.

liēm kòng, 念|, razend ijlen, (in eene ziekte.)

kòng hong, |風, storm.

hong kòng, 風|, onbesuisd.

ts'iong kòng, 猖|, do.

kòng sī soā (of *soah*), *kòng soah souh*,

｜是沙，｜沙⺊，zeer on-onbesuisd.

kòng p'ig p'ig, ｜兵⺊, do.

檔 **Kòng** *ming kòng* } *mui* » } 門｜, dwarsbout op eene deur.

kòng ming, ｜門, een bout op de deur doen.

Kōng *liēm kōng*, vervloeking over iemand uitspreken, van de priesters in Siam gezegd,

kōng kōng lìn, rollen.

kōng kōng tíng } heen en weer draaijen,
kōng kōng gô } heen en weer gaan.

康 **K'ōng** *k'ong kiēn*, ｜健, sterk, gezond, stevig, fiksch van een grijsaard.

k'ong hi tsi, ｜熙錢, K'ang-hi cash, (groote.)

空 **K'ong** *k'ong k'ong*, ｜⺊, hol, ledig; te groot en te wijd voor iemand, (als een kleed).

k'ong k'ong haó, ｜⺊吼, hol klinkend.

ping k'ong, 平｜, onverwachts, plotseling, zonder reden.

poàn k'ong tiong, 半｜中, hoog in de lucht.

悾 **K'ong** *k'ong k'ám*, ｜坎, dom.

k'ong sin, ｜神, dom, suf.

k'ong k'ong ê lâng, ｜⺊的人, iemand die de wereldsche zaken onverschillig behandeld.

圜 **K'ong** *tsit k'ong*, 一｜, afgezet randje.

k'ong kim ki, ｜金墘, met een goud randje afzetten.

k'ong kam tsià, ｜柑蔗, suikerriet rondom afsnijden.

孔 **K'óng** Opening, gat; familienaam.

ts'it k'óng liû hiet, 七｜流血, uit de zeven openingen (van het hoofd) bloeden.

gán k'óng toā, 眼｜大, groote ooghollen hebben, *d. i.* moeijelijk te voldoen.

k'óng hong hing, ｜方兄, de oude jongen met het vierkante gat, *d. i.* de duit, geld.

k'óng ts'iok }
» *ts'ioh* } ｜雀, paauw.

k'óng ts'iok bé, ｜雀尾, paauwenstaart.

k'óng hu tsú, ｜夫子, Confucius.

k'óng tsú kong īm ká siu lâng keh mi
» » » » » » » *keh mê*
ê t'iep, ｜子公不敢收人隔夜的帖, Confucius durfde geene invitatie voor den volgenden dag aantenemen, *d. i.* men rekene niet op den dag van morgen.

慷 **K'óng** *k'óng k'aì*, ｜慨, gul, royaal.

鞏 **K'óng** *bàn k'óng*, 蠻｜, stevig, sterk.

廣 **K'óng** Uitgestrekt, breed.

k'óng kao, ｜交, uitgestrekte relaties.

taī bing k'óng tsiòng, 大明｜衆, in het openbaar, openlijk.

抗 **K'òng** Zich verzetten tegen, weigeren.

k'òng kū }
» *kī* } ｜拒, tegenhouden; zich verzetten tegen.

k'òng lâng ê hè, ｜人之貨, iemands goederen (als securiteit) inbeslag nemen.

k'òng tso, ｜租, weigeren belasting op te brengen.

k'òng sè, ｜稅, weigeren den huur te betalen.

k'òng k'ièm, *k'òng siaò*, 丨欠，丨賬，zijne schuld niet willen afdoen.

炕 *k'òng hān*. 丨旱，lange droogte.
K'òng

空 Lodig; leegte tusschen getallen, gelijk onze nul.
K'òng

tsit pah k'òng dzī, 一百丨二，102.

tsit ts'ing tog k'òng dzī, 一千吊二十，een duizend een enkele nul twee. 1020.

tsit ts'ing siang k'òng dzī, 一千双丨二，een duizend dubbele nul twee. 1002.

it siang k'òng dzī, 一双丨二，1002 of 10020.

控 Aanklagte brengen, aanklagen.
K'òng *k'òng kò*, 丨告，aanklagen.

k'òng koa, 丨官，bij de overheden aanklagen.

siōng k'òng, 相丨，bij hooge authoriteiten aanklagen.

oát k'òng, 越丨，regtstreeks bij hooge authoriten aanklagen.

hoan k'òng, 翻丨，appelleren, in cassatie komen.

壙 Gat voor een graf, grafkuil; kuil, mijn; wildernis.
K'òng

bōng k'òng, 墓丨，grafkuil.

k'ui k'òng, 開丨，een graf delven.

siang k'òng, 双丨，dubbeld graf.

siah k'òng, 錫丨，tinmijn,

kim k'òng, 金丨，goudmijn.

k'òng iá, 丨野，wildernis, woestijn.

曠 Ledig, hol, ruim.
K'òng *lòng lòng k'òng k'òng*, 浪匕丨丨，groot en hol, (als van een leeg huis.)

lòng k'òng toā, 浪丨大，te groot, te wijd, (van kleeren, schoenen.)

K'òng *k'òng ts'aì*, 丨菜，groenten door en door koken.

k'òng e, 丨碨，groote kookketel.

慷 *k'òng sóng ê lâng*. 丨爽之人，een onbekrompen mensch, (in handelingen.)
K'òng

空 *k'ōng k'ōng hièn*, 丨匕顯，waggelen.
K'ōng

k'ōng k'ōng kiâ, 丨匕行，domweg doorloopend.

k'ōng k'a k'iaò, 丨脚蹺，achterovervallen, (als wanneer men op een stoel zit te wippen)

k'īng k'ōng k'oā, 輕丨掛，geluid van een voorwerp dat naar beneden rolt.

k'ōng k'iaòk, 丨蹻，losstaande schommelen, tikken, kloppen.

tsit k'ōng tsit k'iaòh, 一丨一蹻，niet harmonieus, niet eendragtig.

k'īn k'īn k'ōng k'ōng, 輕匕丨匕，rommelen, (van geluid,)

k'ōng k'ōng k'ì k'ōng k'ōng lai, 丨匕去丨匕來，zonder ophouden heen en weer gaan, (van personen.)

k'ōng p'oà, 丨破，stuk stooten.

k'ōng tioh, 丨着，stooten tegen.

tsoè k'ōng 做丨丨
ioh tsià k'ōng 約蔗丨丨，stukjes hout enz. van verschillende lengte nemen en later uittrekken om te zien wiens stuk het naast bij de lengte van een zeker stuk suikerriet komt.

Ku

龜 Schilpad; ook wegens dekschilden voor torren gebruik.
Ku

ku k'ak, 丨 殼, schildpadpantser.

kim ku, 金 丨, goudtor.

hê ku, 蝦 丨, vuurwerk in den vorm eener schildpad.

ts'iū ku sin, 發 丨 蜖, boomluizen, hebben.

hoe ku á, 火 丨 仔, Mariator.

tsiù ku á, 咒 丨 仔, graan insekt.

âng mī ku, *âng ku á ké*, 紅 麵 丨, 紅 丨 仔 粿, roode koek als een schildpad.

tsui ku, 水 丨, watertor.

ku t'aô, 丨 頭, schildpadskop; fats. term voor roede hoofd.

tsoè lâng ná ku nī, 做 人 如 丨, als een schildpad zijn, *d. i.* hoe langer hoe meer terugtrekken.

ku k'a ts'un ts'ut lai, 丨 脚 伸 出 來 了, de schildpadpooten komen voor den dag; de aap komt uit de mouw.

ku t'aô to sī ku k'ak bah, 丨 頭 多 是 丨 脚 肉, de schildpadskop behoort toch ook tot het vleesch van de schildpad.

ku peh p'iah (« *peh* ») 丨 扒 壁, als een schildpad die tegen een muur opkruipt, *d. i.* moeijelijk te doen.

ku ts'oā pih loh lâm, 丨 導 鱉 去 落 濫, de schildpad sleept de zeeschildpad in de modder, *d. i.* elkander tot slechte handelingen leiden.

(*ku tsò ku peh piah haō tsó haō t'ó tsiáh*,) 丨 做 丨 扒 壁 鮫 做 鮫 討 食, laat de schildpad tegen de muur klouteren en de koningskrab naar eten zoeken, *d. i.* ieder zijn eigen gang gaan.

居 Ku Ki Wonen, bewonen; woning.

ku k'iā, 丨 住, wonen.

ku k'ù, 同 丨, met iemand zamenwonen.

ún ku ê lâng (*ún ki*) 隱 丨 之 人, een geletterde die geen post bekleedt.

ku ke ê lâng, 丨 家 之 人, iemand die stil leeft (geen handel doet).

ku san ê lâng, 丨 山 之 人, bergbewoner.

i ku, 移 丨, verhuizen.

su ku, 私 丨, privaat vertrek.

boē ku tit, 未 丨 的, niet lang bij zich kunnen houden, (als geluk.)

ku to, 丨 多, voor het grootste gedeelte.

裾 Ku Ki Slip, pand aan een kleed.

aū ku, 後 丨, de achter slippen.

sa á ku kat sa liêm (« « *ki* « *sio* ») 衫 仔 丨 甲 相 粘, met de slippen aan elkander gebonden, *d. i.* van elkander afhankelijk.

背 Ku *k'iao ku*, 駝 丨, kromme rug, kromgetrokken, (door wind enz.)

lun ku, *lam ku*, 踚 丨, 龜 丨, kromme rug.

ún ku, 戚 施, gebogcheld.

he ku, 蝦 丨, aamborstig.

tuh ku, 琢 丨, sufferig, dodderig, stomp.

奇 Ku *ku koài*, 丨 怪, verwonderlijk, vreemd; zich verwonderen.

久 Kù Lang van tijd, langdurig, langgeleden.

bô loā kù, 無 許 丨, niet zeer lang, in korten tijd.

bô loā kù ê lâng, 無 長 丨 之 人, iemand die niet lang meer te leven heeft.

nī ku géh ts'im, 年 | 月 深, lang, lang van duur.

kú tîng, | 長, van langen duur, voor langen tijd.

kú oā, | 旱, lange droogte.

kú hō, | 雨, langdurige regen.

kú siaò, | 賬 langgemaakte schuld.

却 Toch, maar, toch eigelijk,

Kú *aì boé īm kú bô*, 愛 買 | 無, willen koopen maar niet voorhanden zijn.

īm kú, 不 |, toch, maar.

kú tiòh, . . . | 着, toch, stellig moet het . . . .

tsûn i king piēn īm kú bô hó hong, 船 已 經 便 | 無 好 風, het schip is gereed maar wat de moeijelijkheid maakt is dat er geen goede wind is.

舉 Omhoogheffen; aanbevelen, recommandeeren; aanhalen, opheffen, er boven op helpen.
Kú
Kí

kú tsièn, | 薦, recommandeeren, aanbevelen.

kú dzin, | 人, tweede litt. graad.

t'ai kú, 太 |, er boven op helpen,

kú tsit hāng tsai pát hāng, | 一 件 知 他 件, haalt men een ding als voorbeeld aan dan kent men alle andere gevallen.

矩 *kui kú*, 規 |, manieren, gewoonte,
Kú gebruiken; afgedaan.
Kí *sui kui to kui* 循 規 蹈 |, volgens de ware manieren handelen.

韮 *kú ts'āi*, | 菜, sjalotten.
Kú *iaò kú*, toch, nog.

鋸 Zaag; zagen.
Kù *kù á*. | 仔, zaag.

ts'iú kù, 手 |, handzaag.

t'ih soā kù, 鐵 線 |, drilzaag, drilboor.

kù á k'i, | 仔 齒, tanden eener zaag.

kù á k'ing, | 仔 筐, zaagraam.

kù tīng, | 斷, doorzagen.

liaò kù, 遼 |. zagen.

k'an kù, 牽 |, zagen, (met twee personen.)

kun kù, 筋 |, *lett.* met een pees zagen, *d. i.* kleingeestig bekrompen.

kù sut, | 戌, zaagsel.

kè tsī ts'ut tsaī i kù, 價 錢 任 伊 |, de prijs is zooals hij dat wil.

據 Vasthouden; nemen, bezitnemen van; iets om zich aan vast te houden, zich op te verlaten; als bewijs, grond nemende, volgens, naar.
Kù
Kì

kat kù, 割 |, met geweld nemen, (van plaatsen.)

tsièm kù, 佔 |, in bezit nemen, overweldigen.

pin kù, 彈 |, bewijs.

tsìng kù } 証 |, bewijs.
(*tsìn*) »

ū tsìng ū kù, 有 証 有 |, de bewijzen zijn daar.

toā kù, 單 |, schriftelijk bewijs.

kù sit, | 實, naar waarheid.

kù i kóng, | 伊 講, volgens wat hij zegt; hij kan zeggen wat hij wil.

kù lâng ì aì, | 人 意 愛, al naar men het verlangt, zooals men wil.

句 Kù Zin, volzin.

tsit kù oē, 一 丨 話, een gezegde, zin.

m̄ tsiâ kù, 不 成 丨, geen zin vormen, geven.

siâ siâ kù kù, 聲 匕 丨 匕, bij elk geluid en elken zin, *d. i.* gedurig van hetzelfde oude spreken.

灸 Kù Zonder vlam aansteken, doen aanglimmen, aangloeijen, branden als een wond.

kù hé, 丨 火, doen aangloeijen.

kù hun, 丨 烟, zijn pijp aanhouden aantrekken.

kù toā poáh hun, 丨 大 撥 丨, aan een groote dot tabak rooken, trekken.

tsit ki hiu siang t'aô kù, 一 枝 香 双 頭 丨, een vuurstokje aan beide einden aangloeijen.

īng hiâ mi kù, 用 艾 絨 丨, met den bijvoet, artemisia, uitbranden.

柜 Kù Ki、 *kù tsoáh* } *ki* » } 丨 紙, afstooten, niet willen te maken hebben met.

pàng kù tsaī, 放 丨 在 伊, zijn gang laten gaan, aan zich zelven overlaten, (als een masteloos schip.)

kù tsaī i, 丨 在 伊, al naar hij wil.

kù lí beh, 丨 汝 要, zooals gij verkiest.

衢 Kù *koe kù* } *ke ki* } 街 丨, marktplaats.

t'ong kù, 通 丨, over de geheele markt.

舊 Kū Oud (van dingen), verleden, vroeger, te voren.

poà sin kū, 半 新 丨, half versleten halfafgedragen.

kū liaū, 丨 料, oude materialen.

kū lóh (liaò), 丨 了, reeds gedragen, halfversleten.

k'ì kū giâ sin, 去 丨 夯 新, het oude voor het nieuwe wegdoen.

kū siù, 丨 相, oud voorkomen.

kū lâng, 丨 人, oude kennis.

kò kū è ping iú, 做 丨 的 朋 友, een oude vriend.

kū nî, 丨 年, verleden jaar.

kū sî, 丨 時, vroeger, te voren.

tsiaò kū, 照 丨, evenals te voren.

kū dzīm è koa, 丨 任 的 官, een vroegere beambte.

kū siaò, 丨 賬, schuld van het vorige jaar.

kū hui, 丨 磁, oud porselein.

kū k'ih, 丨 齒, oud worden; verouderd, (van voorwerp:)

舅 Kū Zwager, vrouwsbroeder; oom van moederszijde.

toā kū, *kū á*, 大 丨, 丨 仔, zwager, (vrouws oudere en jongere broeder).

bó kū, 丨 妻, zwager.

kū iâ, 丨 爺, jongere broeder van de bruid.

ts'e kū, 妻 丨, zwager.

bú kū, 母 丨, oom, (moeder's oudere broeder.)

soè kū, 小 丨, oom, (jongere.)

dzī kū, 二 丨, oom, (tweede broeder)

kū kong, 丨 公, oud oom.

gōng ku, 戇 丨, jou domme gans (in scherts gezegd.)

俱 Kū Kī Alle.

kū kok tsê tsing, 丨 各 齊 全, allen volledig.

拒 Kū Kī Tegengaan, tegenhouden.

k'òng kū, 抗 丨, tegenhouden.

kū (of *kù*) *tsoát*, 丨絕, van zich afstooten, verwerpen.

lū kū, 呂 丨, kortaf, bits.

具 Kū — Gereed, klaarmaken; gereedschap, voorwerpen.

k'ì kū, 器 丨, voorwerpen, gereedschap.

kū kiet, *kū kam kiet*, 丨結, 丨甘禁, verklaring ten behoeve van iemand afgelegd ook onderwerping aan iemands uitspraak.

拘 K'u K'i — Beetpakken, vatten, in hechtenis nemen; bedwingen, in toom houden; zich houden aan.

k'u kìm, 丨禁, vatten en opsluiten.

liáh k'ì k'u, 擒去丨, in hechtenis nemen.

k'u pák, 丨縛, vatten en binden; aan bundels.

k'u k'u pák pák, 丨匕縛匕, stijf als in nieuwe kleêren; zeer in toom gehouden.

k'u k'ien, 丨牽, zich stijfhoofdig, onverandelijk aan het oude houden.

k'u sok, 丨束, in toom houden, onder contrôle houden.

put k'u, 不丨, onverschillig.

put k'u tsui, 不丨水, zich niet aan eene bepaalde hoeveelheid water houden (bij het koken van medicijn).

bô k'u, 無丨, zich niet houden aan . . .

k'u lé, 丨禮, zich aan de beleefdheid houden, op beleefdheid staan.

k'u hoat, 丨法, zich streng aan eene zekere manier houden.

u k'u ê lâng, 有丨的人, een man van etikette.

k'u tsip, 丨執, bekrompen, zich streng aan iets houden.

k'u siú, 丨守, zich met niets anders afgeven dan (zijne vak, enz.)

坵 K'u — Een stuk lands, tuin, enz.

sa k'u ts'ân, 三丨田, drie velden.

keh ku, 過丨, aangrenzend stuk land.

soa bô tsit k'u hai bô tsit tu, 山無一丨海無一堆, niets bezitten.

邱 K'u — Familienaam.

軀 K'u — *sin k'u*, 身丨, het ligchaam.

驅 K'u K'i — *k'u tiók*, 丨的, verdrijven, uitdrijven.

蹲 K'ù — Bukken.

k'ù teh, 丨去, do.

k'ù lóh k'ì, 丨落下, op de hurken zitten.

sa kap k'ù / *sio* „ „ } 相丨住, zamen nederhurken.

k'ù hák; 丨廁, eene groote boodschap doen.

k'ù king kak, 丨宮角, aan de hoek van een tempel neêr zitten, (als bedelaars).

k'ù k'a, 丨脚, inzakken, (als een zwaar voorwerp op dunnen voet.)

臼 K'ū — Mortier, vijzel.

k'ū á, 丨仔, vijzel.

tsing k'ū, 舂丨, groot rijst mortier.

tsióh tsing k'ū, 石舂丨, steenen mortier.

tsióh k'ū, 石丨, steenen waschbekken.

tuì k'ū, 碓丨, mortier.

k'ū t'ui, 丨鎚, stamper.

ts'iú k'ū, 手 |, holte binnen den elleboog.

t'út k'ū, 秃 |, uit het lid gaan, verstuiken.

mîng hō k'ū, 門 後 |, gat waarin een deur spildraait.

眶 K'ū *bák tsiu k'ū*, 目 周 |, oogholte, oogkas.

柩 K'ū *tsit k'ū koa ts'â*, 一 | 棺 柴, eene doodkist.

K'ū *lui k'ū k'ū tân*, de donder rolt.

Kui

歸 Kui Terugkeeren tot; zich concentréren. vereenigen op, zich schikken bij, verlaten op, uitloopen in; bij elkander voegen, vereenigen; behooren tot.

kui hók, | 服, zich weer onderwerpen,

kui sūn, | 順, tot gehoorzaamheid terugkeeren.

kui kiū, | 咎, de schuld wijten aan, verwijten.

kui mîng oá kak, | 門 换 桷, *lett.* zich op eene deur concentreren en in een hoek zijn, *d. i.* zich tot een enkele persoon of plaats bepalen, (als handel.)

kui oá, | 倚, digter bijkomen, naderen; zijn deel bijleggen.

kui kiet, | 結, ten laatste neêr komen, uitdraaijen op.

kui kak, | 角, in eene hoek vereenigen.

ū kui tiòk, 有 | 着, geregeld.

bû sò kui, 無 所 |, niets hebben om zich op te verlaten, (van oude lieden of zieken.)

kui k'ì, | 去, de geheele ruimte innemend, in zijn geheel.

KUI

kui it, | 一, in eens, geheel en al, alles bij elkaar.

kong kui sìn, 風 | 信, de wind waait geregeld in éénen kant.

dzī kui it tû, 二 | 一 除, door 21 deelen.

規 Kui Kompas; vaste regel, gewoonte, usance; raam, getouw, weefgetouw, pers; persen.

kui kú, | 矩, vaste regel, manieren, usance, afgedaan.

kui lē / » *lī* } | 例, reglement, vastgesteld.

kui kui kú kú, | 匕 矩 匕, geregeld in handelingen.

lō kui, | 陋, gids, (boekje) voor reizigers.

dzit kui, gėh kui, 日 |, 月 |, zonnewijzer, maanwijzer.

siù kui, 綉 |, borduurraam.

ts'ia kui, 車 |, draaibank.

tsit kui, pò kui, 織 |, | 布, weefgetouw.

hoe kui, 花 |, plantenpers.

ts'eh kui kui ts'eh, 册 | 匕 册, in eene boekenpers, boeken persen.

全 Kui De geheele hoeveelheid van, een geheel uitmakend, geheel, gansch, kompleet, volledig.

kui tsong ê hè, | 庄 之 貨, de geheele partij goederen.

kui hāng, | 項, de verschillende sommen tot één, bij elkander.

kui sim, | 心, met geheel zijn hart, uitsluitend.

kui dzit, | 日, de gansche dag.

kui hù, | 付, het geheele komplete stel.

40

kui ts'ìng, | 床, aan een rist, zamenhangend, (als een gesprek).

kui liép, | 粒, met kluiten, aan klonters.

胃 Voormaag, krop.

Kui *koe kui*, 雞 |, kippenkrop.

kaò kui, 猴 |, wangzak van apen.

hoan kui, 翻 |, herkaauwen, (van apen.)

ké kui, 格 |, in de krop of maag blijven zitten.

tiù tsui kui, 漲 水 |, een blaar trekken.

閨 Deur van de binnenvertrekken in een

Kui huis, vrouwenvertrekken.

ts'ut kui, 出 |, vrouwenvertrek uitgaan, *d. i.* huwen.

ts'im kui lú, 春 | 女, een meisje dat zelden uitkomt, eene maagd.

龜 Schildpad.

Kuí *o kui*, 烏 |, hoorndrager, hoerenwaard.

鬼 Geest van een afgestorvene, schim,

Kuí spook; duivel, duivelsch, bedriegelijk, listig; wat verborgen, onbegrijpelijk is als een spook *b. v.* geheime sluiting, veer.

kia kui, 驚 |, bang zijn voor spoken.

ts'it géh poà kui, 七 月 半 |, veelvraat.

tiaò kui, 縊 |, zich ophangen.

kui á beh p'ièn kui ìng (of *ông*), | 仔 要 騙 | 王, als een duiveltje die den koning der duivels wil bedriegen.

tsui kui, 水 |, watergeest.

kuí tsui, | 水, vol streken, bedriegelijk, onopregt.

kuí t'aô kuí naó, | 頭 | 腦, heimelijk fluisterend spreken.

kuí kɛng kui, | 扛 |, twee bedriegers tegen over elkander.

tsit k'ò laī t'eh t'eh kuí, 一 褲 內 太 匕 |, zijn broek vol duivels hebben *d. i.* steeds wantrouwen.

tsiú kui, kiaó kui, 酒 | 賭 |, wijndrinker, dobbelaar.

gōng kui, 戇 |, domme duivel, dommerik.

kuí hé, | 火, dwaallichtjes.

ná kui tsi, 那 | 精, glad, knap.

kì kui, 鐩 |, onwaarheid zeggen.

tsoè kui, 做 |, bedriegen, foppen; de raddraaijer van iets zijn.

sik kui, gaar, glad.

kui koaì, | 怪, vreemd, wonderbaarlijk; bedriegelijk, schelmachtig.

kui pō, | 步, listige streek.

kui kap bé habh, (of *haó*), | 仝 馬 吼, zich inlaten met iets dat hem niet aangaat.

mìng kuí, 門 |, geheime sluiting, veêr aan een deur.

oáh kuí, 倚 |, springveêr,

àm kui, 暗 |, geheime sluiting, veêr.

hī k'ang kui, 耳 空 |, trommelvlies.

kóng kui oē, 說 話 |, duivelstaal spreken *d. i.* liegen.

ke sin t'ong goā kui, 家 神 通 外 |, de huisgeesten, huisgenooten doen gemeene zaak met de buitenduivels, *d. i.* dieven, enz.

kui kui suī suī, | 匕 遂 匕, geheim, dieventaal spreken.

鈎 Kuí Eenige, verscheidene, vele; hoeveel?

kuí ê, | 介, verscheidene; hoevele?

kuí nn̄g lâng, | 人, verscheidenen, velen.

bô kuí dzit, 無 | 日, niet vele dagen, weldra, in korten tijd.

kuí tiém tsing, | 點 鐘, hoe laat?

貴 Kuì Aanzienlijk, geeerd, beroemd, bel. term voor Uw; duur, kostbaar.

hù kuì, 富 |, rijk en aanzienlijk.

tsun kuì, 尊 |, hoog in aanzien.

kuì k'ì, | 器, voornaam, aanzienlijk,

kuì dzin, | 人, geeërd, braaf, welwillend mensch.

kuì kok, | 國, Uw rijk land.

ts'ut kuì, 出 |, beroemde menschen opleveren, (van eene plaats.)

kuì kè, | 價, duur in prijs.

ko kuì, 高 |, zeer duur.

kuì gim / » *kim* } | 金, uiterst duur.

季 Kuì Jaargetijde; oogst.

sì kuì, 四 |, de vier jaargetijden.

nn̄g kuì, 二 |, twee oogsten.

sī kuì ê si, 是 | 之 時, tentijde van den oogst.

tsoeh kuì, 節 |, de 21 halfmaandelijksche feestdagen.

tsá kuì, míng kuì, 早 |, 晚 |, vroege en late oogst.

掛 Kuì Koà Hangen tegen, ophangen.

kuì ting, | 燈, een lamp ophangen.

kuì tī hi á bé nn̄h, | 在 耳 仔 尾, aan het eind van het oor hangen, van weinig belang.

鈎 Kui Koè *kuì tiòh*, | 着, zich ophalen aan.

kuì lih, | 裂, do.

桂 Kuì De cassiaboom.

dziók kuì, 肉 |, cassia.

kuì hoe, | 花, olea fragrans.

gėh kuì, 月 |, maandroos.

Kuī *ū kuì ū kuì*, innemend door schoonheid.

tsoè kuì, gekheid maken; (met zijne vrouw.)

懷 Kuî *kuî kiá*, | 子, een kind tusschen zijn kleeren houden.

kuî k'ìng, | 藏, wegstoppen, bij zich stoppen.

t'ao kuî 私 |, wegnemen en bij zich stoppen.

kuî kuî tsah tsah, | ヒ 截 ヒ, zijn ligchaam volbeladen hebben.

hē tī hi kuî nn̄h, 放 在 | 裡, in de borst stoppen, als een doek tusschen de kleeren.

葵 Kuî *hiòng dzit kuî* / *hiàng* » » } 向 日 |, zonnebloem.

pô kuî si, 蒲 | 扇, waaijers van palmbladen.

櫃 Kuī Kist, kast, bank, tafel met laden.

t'ih kuī, 鉄 |, ijzeren geldkist.

kuī pâng, | 房, geldkamer.

laī kuī, goā kuī, 內 |, | 外, binnen geldkist voor groote en buiten geldkist in den winkel voor kleine sommen.

ts'ik kuī, 粟 |, graankist.

siaò kuī, 賬 |, boekhouder.

tsiáng kuī, 掌 |, kashouder.

gûn kuī, 銀 |, kassier.

koán kuī, 管 |, do.

ts'èng kuī, 床 |, geldkist onder een bed.

liên kuī, 連 |, toonbank vóór in den winkel.

t'oah kuī, 獺 |, ladenkast.

tok kuī, 棹 |, tafel met laden.

laó hióh kuī, 荖 葉 |, sirikist, stalletje.

hong kuī, 風 |, blaasbalk.

跪 Knielen.

Kuī *kuī paì*, | 拜, knielende buigen.

kuī k'áp, *kuī kuī k'áp k'áp*, | 磕, knielen en het hoofd ter aarde slaan, dringend smeeken.

p'ah poà kuī, 做 半 |, op éénc knie knielen.

kuī liīn, | 鍊, op ketens knielen, (voor straf).

孕 *toà kuī*, 帶 |, drachtig, bevrucht zijn,
Kuī (van beesten.)

kuī tsui, | 水, opgezwollen, opzwellen.

開 Openen, open.

K'ui *tsoān k'ui*, | 鑽, met een sleutel open draaijen.

giah k'ui, 撽 |, met een ding open breken.

k'ui ts'oà, | 閂, openen door de bout van een deur afteligten.

ts'oà k'ui, 閂 |, do.

hien k'ui, 掀 |, open doen, (als een kist).

pek k'ui
peh » } 擘 |, met geweld openen, vaneenscheuren.

t'iah k'ui, 拆 |, openbreken, (als een brief.)

k'ui só, | 鎖, een Chineesch slot opensteken.

hiép k'ui, 挾 |, losschudden.

kiaū k'ui, 拔 |, openbreken.

p'i k'ui, 挖 |, ontvouwen.

k'ui hoe
» *hoa* } | 花, bloeijen.

k'ui pi, | 脾, de eetlust scherpen.

k'ui i è sim, | 彼 之 心, iemand uit den droom helpen.

k'ui tièm làng, | 店 人, winkelier.

k'ui ióh tièm, | 藥 店, apotheker.

k'ui p'àng, | 帆, het zeil ophijschen.

k'ui tsûn, | 船, het anker ligten.

k'ui toą, | 單, een rekening opmaken.

k'ui king
» *kiong* } | 弓, een boog spannen.

k'ui ts'iú, | 手, beginnen met.

k'ui ts'ân, | 田, land ontginnen.

k'ui soą, | 山, een berg ontginnen.

k'ui hâng, | 行, een handelshuis opzetten.

k'ui ts'uì káng, | 口 港, onveilige, aan den wind blootgestelde, onbeschermde haven.

k'ui p'oà, | 破, uitleggen, (eene zaak).

k'ui ts'ī, | 市, de eerste kalant van iemand zijn, hem het eerste handgeld in zijne pas geopende affaire gegeven hebben.

k'ui sią, | 聲, luid, hardop.

k'ui pō kià, | 步 行, groote stappen nemen, gaauwloopen.

k'ui ts'uì lā hī, | 口 脫 耳, open, niet beschut, niet beschermd van eene plaats; ook gebroken (van een voorwerp), niet meer te repareren.

k'ui siaò, | 數, eene rekening opmaken.

tsiaò k'ui, 照 |, ieder's te betalen deel aan iets, berekenen; gelijkelijk, de een niet meer dan de ander.

sim hoe k'ui, 心花 |, verheugd.

tsit k'ui tsit ts'iò, 一 | 一 笑, gedeeltelijk geopend gedeeltelijk diep; nog onzeker, onuitgemaakt.

tai tsì k'ui ts'iò, 大志 | 笑, onzeker als een dubbeltje op zijn kant, (van zaken).

k'ui tsi̤, | 錢, geld betalen, bijleggen.

k'ui pao, | 包, ontmaagden.

sin k'ui káng, 新 | 港, nieuw geopende, voor handel opengestelde haven.

k'ui k'ang hō lâng tsiáh tsui, | 空與人食水, door een streek, aanklagten, iemand aan anderen zijn geld doen verliezen.

k'ui tsi̤ puih tsoâ̤, | 井拔泉, een peot graven en een ander mans waterader daar door wegnemen; iemands klandisie wegnemen.

k'ui k'ing, | 筐, uit elkander gevallen, stukkend, niet harmonieren.

t'e k'ui, 推 |, afwijzen, weigeren, zich niet met iets willen bemoeijen.

t'i̤ sik k'ah k'ui, 天色稍 |, de hemel, lucht, klaart op.

k'ui ts'ùi háp ts'ùi, | 口合口, de mond open, of digt doende . . . . d. i. steeds spreken over.

k'ui tsia̤, *k'ui ts'un*, | 正, | 春, begin van het nieuwe jaar, van de lente.

k'ui toā mîng p'ah toa kó̤, | 大門打大鼓, openlijk voor iets uitkomen.

tsit lâng k'ui kui é tsi̤, 一人 | 幾箇錢, iedereen betaalt wat geld.

虧 K'ui *k'ui sim*, | 心, boosaardig, onbarmhartig.

siū k'ui, 受 | } geruïneerd zijn door.
kik k'ui. 尅 | }

詭 *k'ui tsà* } | 詐, listig bedriegend.
» *tsè* }

K'uí *k'ui kè*, | 計, listige plannen, list.

k'ui k'iet, | 黠, bedriegelijk, listig.

氣 K'ùi *bô k'ùi*, 無 |, gebrek aan adem, gestorven.

t'o̤ k'ùi, 嘆 |, zuchten, adembalen.

ts'oán k'ùi, 喘 |, ademhalen, hijgen.

tìng k'ùi | 轉, de adem lang inhouding, lett. doen terug komen, als trompetters.

tīng k'ùi } | 斷, den geest geven.
t'ui » }

kóng ts'ut k'ùi, 說出 |, zijn hart een weinig lucht geven, (aan iemand).

kik k'ùi, 激 |, trotsch zijn.

k'ùi t'aô, | 頭, voorsmaak, voorgeur.

t'oó k'ùi, 透 |, zijn hart lucht geven.

p'ō sim k'ùi, 抱心 |, aan den grond als vastgenageld staan.

kìm k'ùi, 禁 |, zijn adem inhouden.

ts'ut k'ùi, 出 |, van zijn geur verliezen, (als open staande thee).

ū k'ang k'ùi, 有空 |, langzamerhand overal kennissen gemaakt hebben.

bô k'ang k'ùi, 無空 |, geene goede

gelegenheid hebben om geld te maken.

ts'aò hièn k'uì, 臭 獻 ｜, een onaangename lucht van zich afgevend.

k'uì t'aô p'ang, ｜ 頭 香, geurige voorsmaak, (van thee.)

dzím sí k'uì, 忍 死 ｜, zich doodelijk inhouden, alles verdragen.

tsiep ēm tióh k'uì, 接 不 着 ｜, niet achtereenvolgens invallen van de wind als bij fluit blazen, *d. i.* niet onmiddelijk daar zijn als er gebrek aan is, (van levensmiddelen, enz.)

k'uì lát, ｜ 力, kracht inspanning.

愧 K'uì — *iú k'uì*, 有 ｜, zich schamen.

Kuih

抹 Kuih — Wrijven, schrijnen, krabben, schrapen, strijken, bestrijken, afstrijken.

kuih p'oà p'ê / *koeh „ „* } ｜ 破 皮, de huid stuk krabben, stuk schrijnen.

kuih he tsi, ｜ 灰 薯, met cement bestrijken.

kuih hí t'aò mîng nih, ｜ 在 頭 毛 的, aan het haar afstrijken.

īng tsíng t'aò á kuih iû, 用 手 指 ｜ 油, olie met de vingers opstrijken.

kuih o soa, ｜ 黑 沙, iemand die eene koliek heeft zoolang krabben dat het bloed naar boven komt, (met duiten of scherven gedaan.)

goá bô t'àn lí tse i t'ang kuih o soa, 我 無 賛 爾 一 文 去 ｜ 黑 沙, ik verdien niets op U, (vertoord gezegd.)

kuih tsī, ｜ 拭, door eten in den mond te strijken, te schuiven, voeden, (als kinderen.)

kuih kaò toā, ｜ 至 大, opbrengen, groot brengen, (zonder moedermelk).

Kun

巾 Kun Kin — Doek.

bīn kun, 面 ｜, handdoek.

ts'iú kun, 手 ｜, zakdoek.

tsiáh kun, 食 ｜, servet.

toh kun, 棹 ｜, tafellaken.

k'a kun, 脚 ｜, voorschoot, schortje, (als werklieden dragen.)

hūn kun, ｜ 汗, zweetdoek, zakdoek.

軍 Kun — Het leger; soldaten.

sam kun, 三 ｜, het leger.

kun tsong, ｜ 裝, legerfourage.

ts'iong kun, 將 ｜, naar het leger op de grenzen verbannen.

kun su / *„ si* } ｜ 需, legerfourage.

kun su gùn / *„ si gin* } ｜ 需 錢, geld voor het leger.

kun su, ｜ 師, raadgever in het leger.

kun līng, ｜ 令, krijgsbevel.

kun k'ì, ｜ 器, wapens.

ts'ut kun, 出 ｜, ten strijde trekken.

kám sú kun, 監 子 ｜, soldaten die voor den dood vreezen.

kun iâ, ｜ 營, legerkamp.

斤 Kun Kin — Het Chineesche pond van 16 oncen, kattie=0.6 Ned. pond.

sìng kun niú, 算 ｜ 兩, bij het gewigt berekenen.

ts'ien kun ts'ìn, 千 ｜ 桯, hefboom.

sa kun dzī, 三 | 二, 3 katties en 2 oncen.

君 Vorst, de edele.

Kun *dzin kun*, 人 |, vorst.

kun tsú, | 子, de edele.

根 Wortels van een boom; wortel, oorsprong, aanleiding.

Kun

Kin *ts'iū kun* / » *kin* } 樹 |, wortels van een boom.

si kun tìng tiaò, 生 | 訂 在, inwortelen, onafscheidelijk op iets.

lī kun lī hút, 離 | 離 核, van den wortel en de pit af zijn, *d. i.* niets met elkander te maken hebben.

kun pún, 本 |, oorsprong, aanleiding.

kun iû, | 由, aanleidende oorzaak.

kun goân, | 源, oorsprong, oorspronkelijk.

kun toé, | 底, oorsprong, afstamming, afkomst.

kun kiù, | 究, grondig onderzoeken.

筋 Pees, zenuw, spier; taai als een pees.

Kun *pàng k'a kun*, 放 脚 |, de hielpees af

Kin snijden.

siao kun, 消 |, kramp (tijdelijke.)

k'iù kun, 縮 |, kramp.

kun koai, 逆 |, kleingeestig, bekrompen, lastig, ongedurig.

kun kun kù kù, | 匕 據 匕, koppig, niet gewillig.

kun dzūn, *kun kun dzūn dzūn*, | 潤 | 匕 潤 匕, taai, elastiek.

跟 Volgen als een mindere zijn meerdere.

Kun *kun sui*, | 隨, volgen.

kun koa ê lâng, | 官 之 人, gevolg van mandarijnen.

kun pan, | 班, volgers, bedienden.

kun tè / » (*toè*) } | 從, volgen.

kun kiù, | 究, op het spoor, op de hielen nagaan, onderzoeken.

均 Gelijk, gelijkmatig

Kun *īm kun pi*, 不 | 平, niet gelijkelijk, niet regtvaardig.

kun hun, | 分, gelijkmatig verdeelen.

gaō kun ûn ê lâng, 善 | 分 之 人, iemand die tot in het geringste toe gelijk met anderen wil opdeelen.

滾 Koken; spartelen, slaan, stoeijen, rollen; verdraaijen, leven maken.

Kún *kún tsui*, | 水, kokend water.

kún ts'iâng ts'iâng, | 沸 匕, borrelend koken.

kún t'sng, | 湯, kokend water.

kún tē lui, | 地 雷, belegerings mijnen onder eene vesting.

p'ah kún, 打 |, stoeijen; slaan, spartelen, (als visch in water.)

kún lìng, | 絞, worstelen, zich kronkelen, (om los te komen.)

kún p'iò, | 漂, met alle geld biljetten tegelijk om betaling komen (een run op de bank.)

ká kún, 絞 |, stoeijen.

kún ká, | 絞, do. veel met zijn geld werken, zijn kapitaal omzetten.

kún tsūn, *kún lún tsūn*, | 陣, | 淪 陣, verdraaijen, verdraaid, (als een touw.)

hoā hoā kún, 陣 匕 |, hard leven maken.

諢 Gekscheren, schertsen.
Kún *gaò kún*, 善 |, gekscheren.

kún ts'iò, | 笑, gekheid, gekscheren, den gek steken mot.

ēm sī gaò kún, 不是戲 |, het is geen gekheid, men moet er niet zoo ligtelijk meê omgaan of overdenken.

aì kún, 愛 |, van schertsen houden.

緄 Beleggen, afzetten met band galon, enz.
Kún *sin kún*, 箱 |, beleggen, afzetten.

kún liaò, | 條, belegsel, galon.

kún ing k'aó, | 袖口, de mouws gaten beleggen, afzetten.

kún siù pi, | 綉邊, met een geborduurden rand afzetten.

kún ting king, | 項鎚, een afgezette, belegde hals aan vrouwen kleeren.

棍 Knuppel.
Kùn *lók kùn* / *ts'â* » } 木 |, houten lange staaf.

kong kùn, 光 |, bedrieger, schurk, spitsboef, zwendelaar.

kùn t'ui, | 肩, schurk spitsboef.

lau kùn, 老 |, doortrapte schurk.

kùn t'áng, | 桶, do.

ts'oàng kùn, 村 |, do. iemand die anderen steeds kwelt.

kiaó kùn, 賭 |, groote dobbelaar.

倔 *kùn kiū*, | 强, zich tegen iets ver-
Kùn zetten, tegenspartelen.

kùn tó tsaó, | 到走, ontsnappen, wegkruipen, (als een slang.)

拳 *kùn t'aò*, | 頭, vuist.
Kùn *p'ah kùn*, 打 |, met de vuist slaan, boksen.

liáh kùn, 較 |, boksen.

k'ang kùn p'ah hó, 空 | 搏虎, zonder steun van anderen iets moeijelijks gaan doen.

kiâ kùn, 行 |, boksen,

p'ah kùn boē kó ioh, 打 | 賣糊藥, zich wonden toebrengen en pleister (voor wonden) verkoopen.

kùn t'aò bù nih kaò ts'ut tsiep / » » *bó nèh* » » » } | 頭拇握至出汁, de vuist zoo knijpen dat er sap uitkomt, *d. i.* het iemand benauwd maken.

kùn t'aò bó bē tsing dzip piah, | 頭拇要入撞壁, een vuist kan men niet in de muur slaan, *d. i.* met beleefdheid krijgt men meer gedaan dan met geweld.

羣. Numerale, voor kudden schapen en vlug-
Kùn ten vogels, enz.

lâng kùn kaó tóng, 人 | 狗黨, soort zoekt soort.

oe kùn t'àn tīn, 挨 | 湊陣, met de groote menigte meêgaan.

Kùn Door en door koken.

kùn bah, vleesch door en door koken.

kùn noā noā, tot pap koken.

裙 Vrouwen rok.
Kùn *iù su kùn* / » *sū* » } 油司 |, rok, (door vrouwen en koks gedragen.)

近 Digt, digtbij, nabij gelegen, naburig.
Kûn kortelings, onlangs, nader bijkomen,
Kīn naderen.

tsiū kūn, 就 |, digtbij, naderen.

kūn tau, | 處, digtbij, niet veraf.

hū kūn, kūn hù, (of *hū*) 附 |, | 附, digtbij.

kūn lai, kūn sî, kūn dzìt, | 來, | 時, | 日, kortelings, onlangs.

lim kūn, 臨 〡, nabijkomen, digtbij zijn.
tsaī kūn, 在 〡, nabij, digtbij.
kūn sī, 〡 視, bijziende.
hn̄g iá kūn, 遠 乎 〡 乎, is het veraf of digtbij, is het nog veraf?
kūn hiu̯, 〡 鄉, naburig dorp.
kūn soa̯, 〡 山, digtbij het gebergte.
ts'in kūn, 親 〡, naderen, zich aansluiten aan.
kūn oá, 〡 倚, naderen.
kūn hó lâng, 〡 好 人, zich aan goedlieden aansluiten.
pik kūn / « *kīn* } 廹 〡, digt naderen, op de hielen zitten.
put kūn dzîn, 不 〡 人, niet te naderen zijn, (door stank of slechtheid).
kūn biō k'i sîn, 〡 廟 欺 神, hoe digter bij den tempel des te meer verguist men de geesten, *d. i.* dikwerf iemand te zien verminder het respect voor hem.

羣 Kûn — Hoop, menigte, kudde.
tsit kûn ê lâng, 一 〡 的 人, een troep menschen.
oē lang t'àn kûn, 矮 人 隨 〡, met de groote hoop meêgaan.
tsit kûn iu̯, 一 〡 羊, een kudde schapen.

刋 K'un Siu — Scheren, afvijlen, afschrapen, uitschrappen.
k'un ts'iu, *k'un ts'uì ts'iu*, 〡 鬚, 〡 嘴 鬚, de baard scheren.
k'un mn̂g, 〡 毛, de haren afschrappen, (als van een geslacht varken.)
k'un tia̯ / (*k'ao* ») } 〡 鼎, een pan afschrappen.
k'un p'ê / (*k'ao poê*) } 〡 皮, schillen.
īng laī to k'un k'ih lai, 用 利 刀 〡 起 來, met een scherp mes uitschrappen, (als een foutief karakter).

昆 K'un — Oudere broeder.
k'un tiong kuì uī, 〡 仲 幾 位, hoe vele broeders hebt gij?

崑 K'un — *k'un lûn soa̯*, 〡 崙 山, hoogste berg in het NW. van China.

坤 K'un — De aarde.
kièn tì tsit ê k'ièn k'un, 健 置 一 箇 乾 〡, *lett.* ergens een hemel en aarde daarstellen, *d. i.* bezittingen en familie krijgen.

K'un — *k'un k'iang*, lied dat zeer zacht, met begeleiding van de fluit, gezongen wordt.
ts'iu̯ k'un, eene zachte melodie zingen.

窘 K'ún — Lastig, benaauwd maken.
k'ún pik, 〡 廹, lastig maken; inbenarde omstandigheden.
k'ún tiôk, 〡 逐, vervolgen, niet verdraagzaam zijn.

墾 K'ún — Land ontginnen.
k'ai k'ún, 開 〡, ontginnen.

懇 K'ún — Dringend, smeeken.
k'ún kiû, 〡 求, dringend smeeken.

綑 K'ún — Omwinden, binden, vast aanhalen, bundel.
k'ún ân lai, 〡 緊 來, vast aanhalen.
k'ún pák, 〡 縛, stijfrollen en binden.
k'ún hîng lí, 〡 行 李, bagage bijelkander binden.
k'ún á soh, 〡 仔 索, bindtouw.
tsit k'ún, 一 〡, een bundel.

41

tsit k'ùn ê koŋ ts'â, 一 | 的 棺 廓, een omwonden doodkist.

gaò k'ùn làng, 善 | 人, iemand de voet dwars zetten, veel eischen voor iets wat hij bepaald noodig heeft.

困 K'ùn Uitgeput, vermoeid, gekneld door, in ellendige omstandigheden; insluiten, omsingelen.

k'ùn koàn, | 倦, uitgeput, vermoeid.

hioh k'ùn, 遏 |, van zijn vermoeijenis uitrusten.

k'ùn hoát, | 乏, in ellendige toestand, (van personen.)

k'ùn k'ó, | 苦, door smart genepen.

k'ùn kiòng, | 窮, door armoede gekneld.

k'ùn séng, van iemands dringende omstandigheid misbruik maken.

ui k'ùn, 圍 |, omringen en insluiten.

k'ùn siâ, | 城, eene stad omsingelen, belegeren.

siū k'ùn, 受 |, belegerd worden

k'ùn sì, | 死, uithongeren, (door belegering.)

睡 K'ùn Slapen; beslapen..

k'ùn boē loh bin, | 不 安 眠, niet kunnen inslapen.

k'ùn pá bin, | 飽 眠, uitgeslapen zijn.

k'ùn k'ì, | 起, na zijn slaap opstaan,

k'ùn ts'ī ts'ī, | 昏 七, slapen als een roos.

k'ùn sin, | 神, de slaapgeest.

ū k'ùn sin, 有 | 神, slaperig.

k'ùn tsī, | 靜, in diepe rust.

k'ùn ts'èng, | 床, bed.

k'ùn kui, | 鬼, slaapkop.

k'ùn sa, | 衫, slaapjas, kabaja.

k'ùn bō, | 帽, slaapmuts.

k'ùn oê, | 鞋, nachtschoenen, (door vrouwen gebruikt.)

k'ùn pàng, | 房, slaapkamer.

k'ùn bāng, | 夢, in een tempel slapen om in zijn droom de wil van een afgod te vernemen.

勤 K'ûn *k'ûn k'ûn*, | 匕, vlijtig.

K'în *k'ûn k'iēm*, | 儉, zuinig.

k'ûn sim, | 心, do.

k'ûn kin, | 緊, naarstig, vlijtig en omzigtig.

un k'ûn, 慇 |, volbeleefdheden, gastvrij.

K'ùn *ùn lùn k'ùn*, 混 綸 |, zich kronkelen als een slang.

k'ùn k'ùn, 混 | 匕, zich kronkelen, kruipen.

k'ùn kim soà, | 金 線, kransjes, borduren van gouddraad.

k'ùn tsit séh, | 一 圈, ééns rondgaan.

k'ùn soh á, | 索 仔, touw opslaan, oprollen.

芹 K'ûn *k'ûn ts'aì*, | 菜, selderij.

稛 K'ùn *ts'aò k'ùn*, 草 |, hooiberg.

Kut

骨 Kut Been, knook, graat, van been, visch-been, ivoor gemaakt; wat op een been gelijkt als de stokjes van een waaijer; vorm, gestalte, geaardheid.

ts'iú kut, 手 |, het armbeen, de arm.

kut lō, | 路, beendersysteem.

hi kut, 魚 〡, graat, vischbeen, balein.
kut t'aô, 〡 頭, beenderen, knoken.
k'ioh kut t'aô, 拾 〡 頭, doods-beenderen bij elkander rapen, (om in een urn te doen.)
kut tsat, 〡 節, beengeleding.
kut lûn, 〡 輪, beengewricht.
kut ts'é, 〡 髓, beenmerg.
oàn hūn dzip kut ts'é, 怨 恨 入 〡 髓, doodelijk haten.
k'a tâng kut, 脚 筒 〡, kuitbeen.
io kut, 腰 〡, lendenbeen.
kut tsu / *» ts'i* } 〡 疽, been versterf.
ka nîng kut si, 全 〡 生 成, geheel van been, *d. i.* zeer sterk van nature.
kut sui ki pai, 〡 隨 支 排, vel over been.
t'ih kut á si, 鉄 〡 仔 生, mager maar sterk.
kóng oē ū kut, 說 話 有 〡, streken onder zijn spreken hebben.
sì kut, 扇 〡, waaijer-stokje, been.
hō soà kut, 雨 傘 〡, paraplubalein.
kut dziók, 〡 肉, vleeschelijke verwanten.
gê kut, 牙 〡, ivoor.
kut tsiem á, 〡 籖 仔, beenen, ivoren haarspeld.
ki kut, 枝 〡, vorm, gestalte.
hó ki kut, 好 枝 〡, van fraaijen vorm, (van vrouwen.)
hó kut keh / *» » keh* } 好 〡 格, goed van uiterlijk, gedaante.
kut tè, 〡 底, vorm, gestalte.

kik kut, *ké kut*, 格 〡, 假 〡, weêrbarstig, altijd in de contramine.
kut p'iah, 〡 癖, geaardheid, gesteldheid.
sik kut, gaar, glad, moeielijk te bedriegen.

滑 Glibberig, glad.
Kút *kút kút*, 〡 匕, do.
keng kút / *kui »* } 光 〡, fijn.
kút tó, 〡 倒, omverglijden, uitglijden.
kút lút sút, 〡 律 術, glibberig, glad.
kút liù liù, 〡 溜 匕, glad, gesmeerd met olie enz.
kút aô, 〡 喉, de keel smeeren, gladmaken.
kút liúh siúh, 〡 鈕 匕, zeer glad.
kút liù, 〡 溜, glad, glibberig en afhellend.
kút tiáh, 〡 澤, glad.
ts'ui kút, *ts'ui kút kút*, 嘴 〡, 嘴 〡 匕, rad ter tong, er iets uitgooijen voor dat men er aan denkt.
lō kiâ kaò kút, 路 行 到 〡, een weg glad geloopen hebben *d. i.* dikwijls begaan hebben.
bong kaò kút, 捫 至 〡, zeer dikwerf gehanteerd hebben.
ts'iú kút p'ah p'oà, 手 〡 打 破, door een gladde vette hand iets breken.
kút tsit tó, 〡 一 倒, uitglijden.

掘 Uitgraven.
Kút *kút t'ô*, 〡 塗, aarde graven.
kút si, 〡 死, doodhakken, er onder hakken, (als een plant.)
kút kim, 〡 金, goud graven ook fig. veel geld verdienen.

K'UT

屈 K'ut — Krom, buigen, knielen, zich vernederen, verlagen; ingeven, inschikken, toegeven; onregt aandoen, valsch betichten.

k'ut ts'ioh, | 尺, haak, winkelhaak.

k'ut k'ut k'iok k'iok, | 匕 曲 匕, krom, niet gelijk.

k'ut sèng, | 算, *lett.* de vingers krombuigende, op de vingers tellen.

k'ut k'a, | 脚, de knie buigen.

k'ut k'a sạ tsiū, | 脚 相 就, elkander toegeven, zich naar elkanschikken.

k'ut kà / *» kẹ* } | 下, zich wel willen vernederen om.

k'ut lâng, | 人, iemand valsch betichten; onregt aan doen, er onderhouden.

óng k'ut, 枉 |, valsch betichten; het is moeite verspild dat . . . .

oan k'ut, 冤 |, valsch beschuldigen.

siū k'ut, 受 |, valsch beticht; verdrukt worden.

k'ut tá sing tsiao, | 打 成 招, door slaan tot eene bekentenis brengen.

k'ut sin, | 伸, zich zelven verlagen, vernederen.

窟 K'ut — Kuil, holte; plas, nummer: voor vijvers.

t'ộ k'ut, 塗 |, aardkuil.

lap k'ut, 踏 |, in een kuil vallen.

lóh k'ut, 落 |, do. in iemands strik vallen.

hiet k'ut á, 投 | 仔, petje of kuiltje gooijen.

tsiú k'ut, 酒 |, kuiltjes in de wangen, (bij het lagchen.)

tsui k'ut, 水 |, plas.

k'ut á, | 仔, do.

t'âm k'ut, 潭 |, diepe plas.

tsit k'ut ti. — | 池, één vijver.

禿 K'út — *k'út k'út*, | 匕, stomp, (als een penseel waar de puntharen van uitgevallen zijn.)

keng keng k'út k'út / *kui kui » »* } 光 匕 | 匕, glad en kaal, (zonder iets om het aan op te pakken.)

ko k'út, 孤 |, alleenstaand, (met anderen niet te maken willen hebben.)

k'út t'ui, | 鎚, *lett.* stompe hamer; stomp als de punt van een penseel, enz.

k'út t'aô hāng. | 頭 巷. steegje zonder eind, doodloopend steegje.

k'út t'aô káng, | 頭 港, doodloopende rivier, haven.

k'út bé, | 馬, stomp uiteinde.

tsoè lâng k'út ts'ing, 做 人 | 锖, teruggetrokken, een eenzelvig, zonderling mensch zijn.

LA

La

濫 La — *la sâm*, *la sâm li lō*, | 森, | 森 厘 撈, vuil, smerig.

la la tsa tsa, | | 渣 匕, do.

la kao, | 郊. bedriegelijk handeldrijven, betaling steeds willen ontduiken.

li li la la, 厘 匕 | 匕, spreken als jonge kinderen; overal wegens schuld in den war zitten.

娜 La — Vrolijk, kittig, (van meisjes), levendig.

la ing. | 鬧, door overvloed en voorspoed bedorven en weelderig geworden.

Le — *la giâ*, groote spin.

拉 La — Trekken.

la ts'é, | 洗, overal geld leenen.

la tsioh, | 借, do.

la tàó, | 斗, laten loopen, opgeven.

la lò hit / *lò »* } | 櫓 搖, slingeren, (als een poenka.)

攪 Lā — Roeren, rondroeren, aan iets roeren, zoeken, uitzien naar; lastig vallen.

lā lā tī hí t'sng nih, | 匕 落 湯 door de soep geroerd.

lā tsit è oē t'aô, | 一 箇 話 頭, iets aanroeren, beginnen over iets te spreken.

tsit lā tsit ts'aò, 愈 | 愈 臭, zoodra roert men er niet aan of het stinkt, *d. i.* het is maar beter over die zaak niet te spreken.

lā k'í t'aô, | 起 頭, eene zaak beginnen, aanvangen.

lā tsî k'ang, | 錢 孔, naar een gat zoeken om geld te leenen.

lā k'ang, | 孔, naar eene goede gelegenheid zoeken.

lā t'aô lō, | 頭 路, naar eene broodwinning uitzien.

lā lî hî. | 厘 拽, waggelend; onzeker, weifelachtig.

lā ke si, | 家 需, met wapen schermen.

kap i lā k'oà, 與 伊 | 看, met iemand schermen, hem peilen, uithooren.

k'ì lā ts'ut lai, 被 | 出 來, iets uithalen, eene goede gelegenheid vinden.

ts'á lā, 抄 |, lastig vallen.

ts'á ke lā t'éh, 抄 家 | 債, ruzie in huis hebben.

kiaò lā, 叫 |, last aandoen, lastig vallen.

Lah

了 Lah — Part: voor het verledene, eind partikel.

k'ì lah, 去 |, hij is reeds gegaan.

hó lah, 好 |, goed zoo, goed.

lai lah, 來 |, kom; ook, reeds gekomen.

蠟 Láh — Was, met was.

péh láh, 白 |, witte was.

p'ang láh, 蜂 |, gele was.

láh sik, | 色, waskleurig, goud-geel.

láh tsik, | 燭, waskaars.

ts'aì láh, 菜 |, witte was.

kaì láh, 盖 |, met was besmeren, glanzen.

pai láh, 培 |, met was boenen, polijsten.

sik tsui láh láh láh, 色 水 | | |, glanzende waskleur, (als op sinaas appels.)

pàng láh hé, 放 | 火, vuurpijlen afsteken.

gin á tioh láh, 小 兒 着 |, de spruw hebben, bij pas geboren kinderen.

獵 Láh — Jagen, jagt

p'ah láh, 田 |, jagen.

láh kaó, | 狗, jagthond.

láh hō, | 戶, jager, (van beroep.)

臘 Láh — *láh mui*. | 門, Chimonanthus fragrans.

曆 Láh — *láh dzit*, | 日, almanak.

爉 Láh — *láh bah*, | 肉, gedroogd, geroosterd vleesch.

Lai

懶 Lai — *ià lai*, 厭 ｜, vermoeid, moede.

laī tsì lì lai, 迫 至 娌 ｜, de zaak is verward.

來 Lai — Komen.

lai k'ì, ｜ 去, gaan.

t'éh lai, 取 ｜, brengen.

óng lai, 往 ｜, omgaan met.

lai óng, ｜ 往, do.

lai lik, ｜ 歷, afkomst, (van per.)

k'í lai, 起 ｜, opstaan, ontstaan.

aō lai, 後 ｜, later, daarna, toekomstig.

tsiong lai / *tsiang* „ } 將 ｜, toekomstig, later.

lai k'ì siaò, ｜ 去 賬, loopende rekening.

tsīn boē lai tit / „ *boē* „ „ } 真 莫 ｜ 的, allerslechts, volstrekt niet zeo.

oē tit lai / *ē* „ „ } 能 的 ｜, kunnen, niet kunnen komen, mogelijk of onmogelijk zijn . . . niet kunnen.
boē tit lai / *bē* „ „ } 未 的 ｜

siá tit lai, 寫 的 ｜, kunnen schrijven.

lai kaò, . . ., ｜ 到, gekomen tot aan . . .

hong lai hō, 風 ｜ 雨, het waait en regent.

lai ts'ing k'ì bing, ｜ 清 去 明, openlijk in zijn komen en gaan zijn, geregeld in zijne handelingen zijn.

iú lai iú óng, iú óng iú lai. 有 ｜ 有 往, 有 往 有 ｜, elkander wederkeerig ontvangen; geschenken geven.

hiòng lai, 凶 ｜, van oudsher.

tsū kó si í lai, 自 古 時 以 ｜, van de oudheid af tot nu toe.

sin lai eh, 新 ｜ 的, de, nieuw gekomene, de nieuweling, (van slavinnen of bedienden.

梨 Lai — *lai á*, ｜ 仔, peer.

òng lai, 王 ｜, ananas.

內 Laī — Binnen, binnen in, in, inwendig; het binnenste van een huis, vrouwen verblijf; huisgezin, huisgenooten, tot de familie behoorend, tegenoverstelling van aangetrouwd.

laī bīn, ｜ 面, binnen, in, inwendig.

laī hai, ｜ 海, binnen zee.

ū pak laī, 有 腹 ｜, degelijke kennis bezitten.

laī tsai, ｜ 才, degelijke kennis.

laī goā kng, ｜ 外 光, buiten en buiten glad, *d. i.* beiden tevreden gesteld.

laī k'e sien si, ｜ 家 先 生, geneesheer, (niet chirurgijn.)

laī koa, ｜ 官, binnen mandarijnen, *d. i.* in Peking residerende.

laī liêm ê koa, ｜ 簾 之 官, lid van den geheimen raad.

tuī lai liêm kóng, 對 ｜ 簾 說, beginnen met tegen de vrouwelijke personen in een huis over iets te spreken.

bô laī goā, 無 ｜ 外, zonder afscheiding tusschen huis en gastenkamer.

laī goā hâng, ｜ 外 行, binnen en buitenlansche marktprijs.

laī t'aô, ｜ 頭, huishouden.

ke laī, ts'ù laī, 家 ｜, 厝 ｜, in huis, het huishouden ook huisvrouw.

siang tsit laī ê lâng, 同 一 ｜ 的 人, menschen uit hetzelfde huis.

laī bô ts'ut goā bô dzip, | 無出外無入, met de buitenwereld geen omgang hebben.

laī p'ah ts'ut, | 打出, gemeene zaak met de buitenwereld hebben.

lai sin, | 身, wat binnen is, het binnenste, middelste.

sai laī lō, 使 | 路, de menschen in een huis omkoopen.

laī lō ê hè, | 路之貨, goederen uit het binnenland.

laī soa, | 山 gebergte in het binnenland.

soa laī, 山 |, in het gebergte.

sa dzit laī, 三日 |, binnen drie dagen.

laī ts'in goā ts'ik, | 親外戚, naaste en verwijderde verwanten.

laī sun, | 孫, kleinzoon van zoonszijde.

lán laī ê lâng, 咱 | 之人, iemand uit ons huis.

利 Laī Scherp, snijdend, scherp (van gezicht en gehoor), lief, vernuftig; interest.

tsiem laī, 尖 |, puntig en scherp.

laī to ts'iet taō hū, | 刀切豆腐, met een scherp mes boonen wrong snijden, *d. i.* regtvaardig beslissen.

ts'uì put tsí laī, 嘴不只 |, scherp in zijn spreken.

hī k'ang laī, | 耳朶, scherp, fijn van gehoor.

bák tsiu laī, 目 |, scherp van gezigt.

lîng laī, 冷 |, koel en ontlasting bevorderend.

p'aì laī, 派 |, boosaardig, slecht (van vrouwen.)

laī tsi, *laī gûn*, | 錢, | 銀, interest.

pit bé laī, 筆尾 |, scherp, gevaarlijk in zijn schrijven.

pàng laī, 放 |, op interest zetten.

pàng tsui laī, 放水 |. geld op interest geven aan kooplieden die over zee gaan.

kiâ laī, 行 |, op interest hebben, zetten.

si laī, 生 |, interest geven, op interest staan.

lîng laī, 靈 |, schrander, vernuftig.

koai laī, 乖 |, vernuftig, schrander, lief.

Lak

落 Lak Vallen, afvallen, niet houden aan; dalen in prijs of aanzien, afslaan, afzakken als k'eeren; uitvallen, uitlaten, overslaan.

hoe lak, 花 |, de bloemen vallen af.

lak ts'ut lai, | 出來, uitvallen.

lak hiet kák, | 去擲, uitvallen, (als uit eene zak), onder weg verliezen.

lak hióh, | 葉, de bladen vallen af.

lak tsi, *lak kè*, | 錢, | 價, in prijs afslaan.

lak sè, | 勢, in huur afslaan.

lak i ê t'é biēn, | 伊體面, iemands fatsoen te grabbelen gooien.

lak bīn, | 面, iemand schande aandoen.

lak tiém, 點 |, in aanzien dalen.

lak lak leh leh, | 七樆七, verlept, (als bloemen), slordig (in kleeren.)

lak tsui, | 水, in het water zetten, staan (als kleeren.)

lak dzī, | 字, een karakter uitlaten, overslaan.

lak siaò, | 賬, eene post uitlaten, vergeten.

tsî gûn lak lak haó, 錢銀 | 乜吼, het geld danst hem in de zak.

ná kiâ k'ù ná lak, 愈行褲愈 |, al loopende zakte zijn broek af.

lak p'i, | 痞, afvallen van roofjes.

橐 Lak　Zak; boren,

lak á, lak tē, | 仔 | 袋, zak in de jas.

lak k'ang, | 空, een gat inboren.

lak tsìng, | 鑽, boor, dril; boren.

īng lak tsìng lai lak, 用 | 鑽來 |, met een drilboor boren.

轆 Lak　*ka lak*, 茄 |, katrol.

sing ka lak, 升茄 |, een katrol ophijschen.

ka lak soh, 茄 | 索, katrol touw.

ià lak lak, 野 | 乜, zeer vermoeid.

六 Lák　Zes.

tsáp lák, 十 |, zestien.

lák géh t'i, | 月天, (heete) weersgesteldheid van de zesde maand.

lák ê lák ê lóng sî tsai, | 箇 | 箇俱相知, elkanders toestand, vermogen door en door kennen.

lák géh koah ts'ai ká ū sim }
» *goeh* » » *kê* » » } | 月葛菜甲有心, een mosterdplant in de zesde maand veinst een hart te hebben, d. i. geveinsd.

掠 Lák　Grijpen, pakken, beetpakken.

lák tioh t'aô tsang, | 着頭鬆, iemand bij den hoofdstaart vatten.

k'iú k'iú lák lák, 挪乜 | 乜, met geweld van alle kanten beetpakken.

lák p'oàh, | 破, grijpen en breken

lák tioh hé koàn }
» » *hoé* » } | 着火礶, een vuurpot, bom, aanpakken, d. i. een gewaagd ding doen.

lák lai lák k'ì, | 來 | 去, gedurig beetpakken, verzetten.

lák lâng ê hè, | 人的貨, iemands goederen in beslag nemen.

lák sai lák dziō, | 屎 | 尿, stront en pis aanpakken, (als een moeder van haar kind doet.)

dzû lák lák, lák dzû dzû, 亂 | 乜, | 亂乜, verward door elkander.

諾 Lák　Er uitgooijen, zeggen.

lūm sám lák, 亂 |, verward zeggen, alles door elkander er uitgooijen.

ts'it lák poeh lák, 七 | 八 |, do.

siaó siaó lák lák, 悄乜 | 乜, snakig, grappig, kodig, (zich niet zoo strak aan beleefdheid houden.)

hao lák lák, 呼 | |, liegen, leugenachtig.

Lak　*lák lák ts'oah*, | 乜動, ontstellen.

sim koa lák tsit èh, eensklaps ontstellen.

Lam

籃 Lam　*koe lam* }
ke » } 雞 |, mand waaronder men kippen doet.

lam koe / *» ke* } | 雞, kippen onder een mand doen.

goā bīn koh lam tsit niāh (of *niá*), 外面再 | 一領, nog een (jas) overdoen.

喃 Lam *sng lam*, 酸 |, zuur, wrang van smaak en slijm aanzettend als carambolas.

lam làng, | 人, iemands iets lekkers of aangenaams voorhouden wat hij moeielijk krijgen kan.

弱 Lám Zwak, krachteloos, niet sterk; onsterk, niet veel te beteekenen hebben.

lám hàn, | 漢, zwak mensch.

hū lam, 虛 |, zwak.

soe lam, 細 |, zwak, in gezondheid afnemend.

ts'ù lám, 厝 |, het huis is onsterk.

hè lám, 貨 |, de waar is onsterk,

lám làng īm ká tsng pó tiú, | 人不敢當保長, een zwakke moet geen buurtmeester worden, *d. i.* men doe niets boven zijne krachten.

lám kioh siaò, | 捔笑, een zwakke, (in een vak.)

lám lám noā noā, | 匕爛匕, langzaam dralen.

lám hì koh gaò t'ou pi, | 戲兼善拖枰, eene akelige komedietroep die de voorstelling nog rekt, *d. i.* iets slecht en langzaam doen.

(*lám kaó tìn lō t'aó*,) | 狗鎮路頭, als een zwakke hond die den weg bezet.

(*lám lám hì iā ū tsit kioh si kiá*,) | 匕戲也有一介好, als is een komedietroep nog zoo zwak er is toch wel één gewilde akteur bij, *d. i.* er is toch wel één goede onder de menigte.

攬 Lám Omarmen, om het lijf pakken, omvatten.

lám io, | 腰, om het middel pakken.

kun tsú lám, 君抵 |, elkander gelijkelijk om het lijf pakken.

niū li lám ē io, 讓汝 | 下腰, ik sta u toe mij om het middel te pakken, *d. i.* ik wel u de beste kans laten.

pao lám, 包 |, opkoopen, pachten.

tsóng lám, 總 |, omvatten, op zich nemen.

lám tsaī dzī, | 佴字, cognossement.

爛 Làm Modderkuil.

làm ts'ân, | 田. modderig veld.

pui làm làm, 肥 | , modderig van vet, (als een veld.)

làm làm, làm tsui, | , | 水, door of in het water op en neêrhalen.

南 Làm Zuid, zuidelijk.

làm sìh, | 勢, het zuiden.

kiâ làm tsaó pak, 行 | 走北, overal heen reizen.

tsí làm tsiem, 指 | 針, kompasnaald.

an làm, 安 |, Annam, Cochin-china.

làm kia, | 京. Nanking.

làm hong, | 風. Zuidewind.

楠 Làm *làm á ts'â*, | 仔柴, soort cederhout.

ki làm, 奇 |, reukhout van Siam aangebragt.

42

檻 Lâm
Gescheurd.
lâm lui, lâm lâm lui lui } 〡 壘 , 〡 匕
» *li* *li li*
鼺 匕 , gescheurd.

淋 Lâm
Met eene vloeistof overdekken, overgieten.
tsui tuì t'aó k'ak lâm lòh k'ì, 水 對 頭 壳 〡 落 去 , water over het hoofd gieten.
lâm bīn, lâm p'ê, 〡 面 , 〡 皮 , verglazen.
lâm tsik, 〡 燭 , kaarsen in het vet doopen.
lâm gùn bīn, 〡 銀 面 , verzilveren.
lâm si tsui, 〡 生 水 , met gesmolten metaal overgieten.
lâm sui gùn, 〡 水 銀 , met kwikzilver overgieten.
lâm p'i, 〡 痞 , afvallen van pokroofjes.
lâm si, 〡 錆 , verglazen, (metalen).

藍 Lâm
Blaauw.
k'iā lâm iâ, 伽 〡 爺 , plaatsgod der Boeddhisten.
lâm sik, 〡 色 , blaauw.
lâm ling, 〡 陵 , blaauwe kraaijenveêr.
lâm ting, 〡 亭 , blaauwe mandarijn knoop.
lâm ki, 〡 旗 , blaauwe vlag (der Manschus).

男 Lâm
Man, mannelijk; baron.
lâm hu lō iù, 〡 婦 老 幼 , mannen en vrouwen, oud en jong.
lâm dzi, 〡 兒 , jongelingen.
lâm tsú hàn, 〡 子 漢 , jongen, zoon.
lâm tsú ta po hàn, 〡 子 渣 蒲 漢 , man, jongen.
haò lâm, 孝 〡 , mannelijke hoofdrouwer, ook gezegd van iemand die geraas maakt.
haò lâm bīn, 孝 〡 面 , een dom droevig uiterlijk.
lâm dzin lú t'oé } 〡 人 女 體 ,
» » *li t'é* }
een verwijfd man.
lâm ka, 〡 家 , familie van den aanstaanden bruidegom.
lâm tsiok, 〡 爵 , baron.

濫 Lām
Overvloeijen, de palen te buiten gaande, buitensporig, teugelloos, onbetamelijk; kwistig, verkwistend; door elkander doen, mengen.
lām sám, 〡 滲 , onbetamelijk, onheusch, in het wild, onbehouden, kwistig.
lām sám kiâ, 〡 滲 行 , buitensporig handelen.
lām sám kóng, 〡 滲 說 , onbehouden, onwaar spreken.
lām īng, 〡 用 , kwistig gebruiken.
īng k'ì t'aì lām, 用 去 太 〡 , do.
lām kao, 〡 交 , met slechten omgaan.
sa lām, 相 〡 , met elkander mengen.
lām lām tsoè tsit ē, 〡 匕 做 一 堆 , door elkander mengen.
lām ham, 〡 蚶 , door elkander doen, mengen.
lām teh īng, 〡 底 用 , door elkander gebruiken, (als elkanders geld.)
lām tīn, 〡 陣 , verward in de gelederen, (als in een gevecht), van geen ophouden weten, (in slecht handelingen.)
ū lām, bô lām, 有 〡 , 無 〡 , in- en zonder gezelschap.

艦 Lām
tsièn lām, 戰 〡 , groot oorlogschip.

淋 *sì lām sui.* 四 | 垂, van alle kan-
Lâm ten afdruipen, als regen van een paraplu; tranen uit de oogen.

Lan

繭 Eelt.
Lan *k'a lan*, 脚 |, eksteroog.
si lan } *se* » } 生 |, vereelten.
kiet lan, 結 |, do.
siu k'a lan, 收 脚 |, eksteroogen, afsnijden.
tuì pi á lan k'i lai, 對 邊 | 起 來, van de kanten aftrekken, als nieuwe takken van een boomstam.

囒 *già lan*, 呀 | 色, cochenille, kleur.
Lan *hò lan*, 荷 |, Holland.

咱 *lán tsiah ê lâng*, | 一 切 人,
Lán wij, zooals wij daar zijn.
lán ê lâng, | 之 人, iemand uit ons huis.
lán ê, | 兮, de onze.
lán tao, | 家, in ons huis, bij ons huis.
lán ê koh, (of *kò*), | 兮 告, stopwoord, gelijkkomend aan ons, wat ik zeggen wou .....

懶 *lán tō*, (of *tō*). | 惰, lui.
Lán *lán t'án*, | 坦, lui.
ià lán, 厭 |, lui, geen trek in iets hebben.

零 Overschietend, overblijvend, maar niet
Lán genoeg om een geheel uit te maken, kleinigheden; achter getallen beteekent het; en nog ...., over de ....
lán san, | 星, overblijvend, klein overschot
lán san pò, | 星 布, overschietende stof.
lán san leh ts'ùi, | 星 兮 嘴, kleine hoeveelheden.
lán tsî pó siaò, | 錢 報 賬, verschillende kleine geld sommen en schuld vorderingen.
sì tsáp lán, 四 十 |, veertig en meer, over de veertig.

剆 *lán pi á ê hiòh*, | 邊 仔 兮 葉.
Lán de kant, of bladeren afsnijden, (zie *lan.*)

鱗 Schubbe.
Lân *hi lân*, 魚 |, visschschub.
hi lân ts'é, 魚 | 疊, op elkander leggen, (als schubben), *b. v.* dakpannen.)
hi lân tiép tsòng, 魚 | 疊 葬, als schubben op elkander begraven, (van eene publieke begraafplaats.
lut lân, 黜 |, de schubben afgooijen, verliezen.
p'ah lân, 去 |, de schubben afschrappen.

欄 *lân kan*, | 干, omheining, balus-
Lân trade.
siu lân kan, 廂 | 干, een rand, oplegsel, op een kleed, nanijen.

蘭 *lân hoe* } *» hoa* } | 花, Orchideæ.
Lân

難 Moeielijk, lastig.
Lân *kan lân*, 艱 |, moeielijk, lastig.
lân ê sū, | 兮 事, eene moeielijke zaak.
ui lân, 畏 |, moeielijk te doen.
t'iao lân, 挑 |, het iemand lastig maken, ongehoorzaam, oneerbiedelijk, (van kinderen.)

làn koaì, | 怪, men kan er zich moeielijk, niet over verwonderen dat ...., het is zeer natuurlijk dat.

屦 Penis, mannelijk schaamdeel.

Lān *lān p'a*, | 包, balzak.

toā lān p'a, 大 | 包, elephantiasis.

lān hút, | 核, de teelballen.

lān tsiaó, | 鳥, lage term voor teeldeel, als scheldwoord gebruikt.

lān tsiaó bīn, | 鳥 面, scheldw.

t'ing k'o̱ lān, 脫 褲 |, geen broek aantrekken, met ontbloot schaamdeel, (van kinderen.)

lān sin, *gōng lān*, *tuh lān*, | 神, 戇 |, 柢 |, scheldtermen met de bet. van dom.

難 Moeielijkheden, tegenspoed, wederwaardigheden, rampen.

Lān *tsai lān*, 災 |, rampen, wederwaardigheden.

tsò lān, 遭 |, wederwaardigheden ontmoeten.

lók lān, 落 |, in tegenspoed geraken.

taī lān, 大 |, groote algemeene ramp.

lān bin, | 民, een door rampen geteisterd volk.

tī hi lān nı̱h, 在 此 | 中 人, in ellende verkeeren.

pī lān, *tò lān*, 悲 | 逃, rampen ontvluchten.

kiù k'o̱ kiù lān, 救 苦 救 |, in ellende en tegenspoed helpen.

爛 *ts'àn lān*, 燦 |, helder flikkerend.

Lān

Lang

嚨 *tuì pı̱ á lang k'ih lai*, van den kant

Lang afsnijden, (als zij takken van een boom.)

lang soaı̱ á, | 檨 仔, manga's afplukken.

pa lang, opklaring van het weder.

k'ı̱ lang, 坑 |, holte of spleet van twee over elkander hellende rotsen of bergen.

ts'ı̱ lang lang, 青 | |, helder groen, (als zeewater.)

ts'im lang lang, 深 | , helder door diepte, (als zeewater.)

o̱ lang lang, 烏 | , donkerzwart, pikzwart.

籠 Groote mand; de ruwe omtrek van iets

Láng maken; omvatten, bij elkander doen.

sa̱ á láng, 衫 |, kleêrmand.

tin láng, 籐 |, rottingen mand.

siu̱ láng, 箱 |, koffers en manden, bagage.

hì láng, 戲 |, kisten voor komedianten kleêren.

láng tà̱, | 擔, mandenvracht, (de twee manden die rondventers dragen.)

láng k'o̱, | 褲, wijde schippers broek.

lang ts'o̱ p'e, | 粗 醅, eene ruw model maken, (kleeren in elkander rijgen.)

tsóng láng, 總 |, het ruw begin van iets maken.

lâng tsoè tsit tui, | 做 一 堆, bij elkander in een bundel doen.

朗 *bing láng*, 明 |, klaar en duidelijk.

Láng *âng láng*, 紅 |, onverlicht, niet

naar de omstandigheden weten te handelen.

空 Eene opening tusschen beiden laten of
Làng hebben.

làng k'ang, 離 丨, een gat, plaats open laten.

làng dzī, 丨 字, eene plaats voor een karakter openlaten.

p'ā làng làng, 冇 丨丨, met ruimten, niet stevig ingestopt.

k'ui làng làng, 開 丨 匕, wagewijd open.

sa t'àng làng, *sa làng t'àng*, *sā làng t'aó*, 相 通 丨, 相 丨 通, 相 丨 透, in elkander loopen, met elkander corresponderen, (als kamers.)

làng nēng dzit, 丨 二 日, twee dagen tusschen beiden latend, (*b. v.* een derdendaagsche koorts.)

làng p'āng, 丨 縫, van het minste oogenblik gebruik maken.

人 Mensch, man.
Làng *ta po làng*, 渣 埔 丨, een man.

tsa bo làng, 渣 某 丨, eene vrouw.

làng làng, 丨 匕, iedereen.

làng k'eh, 丨 客, gast, bezoeker.

tsú làng, 主 丨, gastheer.

tsiā làng, 成 丨, mensch, man zijn.

tsoè làng, 做 丨, mensch zijn, als mensch handelen.

gaò tsoè làng, 善 做 丨, een goed mensch zijn, zijne pligten als mensch goed vervullen.

bat làng kiū bat gùn, 識 丨 較 好 識 銀, menschenkennis is beter dan geldkennis.

làng kang, 丨 空, koelie.

làng sik, 丨 色, soort van mensch.

pát làng, 他 丨, een ander.

làng i, 丨 伊, hij, deze man.

籠 Mand, ben, kooi.
Làng *tsiaó làng*, 鳥 丨, vogelkooi.

táh tsì làng, 已 入 丨, vogelknip.

làng sìng, 丨 床, houten kookmand, ben, (die met het te kooken goed in het water gedompeld wordt.

膿 Etter.
Làng *làng huih*, 丨 血, etter en bloed.

tsú làng, *tiū làng* / „ „ *tiō* „ } 丨 注, 漲 丨, zweeren.

ts'ut làng, 出 丨, etteren.

hùn làng, 訓 丨, zweeren.

聾 *ts'aò hī làng*, 臭 耳 丨, doof.
Làng

礱 *t'ō làng*, 土 丨, pelmolen.

弄 *làng gīn*, 丨 恨, sarren, boosmaken.
Làng

攏 *īng to làng dzip k'ì*, 用 刀 丨
Làng 入 去, met een zwaard doorboren.

弄 Spelen, stoeijen, schertsen, gekscheren,
Lāng gering denken over, spelen met; beweging, kunsten maken met; uitkloppen; uitschudden; aanraken, even doen.

lāng kaó, 丨 狗, met honden stoeijen.

hì lāng, 戲 丨, schertsen met, gekscheren.

lāng sin niū, 丨 新 娘, de bruid plagen, (gedurende de bruidsdagen veroorloofd.)

lāng gīn, 丨 恨, plagen, sarren.

lāng hiém, 丨 險, met het gevaar spelen.

ts'uì lāng ts'uì, 嘴 丨 嘴, uit gekheid over iets spreken, (en met ernst eindigen.)

ts'uo meh lāng koe bú, 草蜢丨雞母, als een sprinkhaan die den gek steekt met (de kippen onder) een kippenmand, *d. i.* gewaagd spel spelen.

bong lāng ts'uì kóng, 罔丨嘴廣, zoo maar uit gekheid voor aardigheid zeggen.

lāng tse t'aô, 丨齊頭, een begin met iets maken.

lāng dzit hoe á, 丨日華仔, even doorkomen van de zon.

pì kaô lāng, 變猴丨, goochelen.

lāng hong, 丨風, de wind door iets laten spelen, in den wind hangen; de lucht bij iets laten komen.

lāng sai, 丨獅, kunstenmaken.

lāng ts'iú hoe, 丨手華, trararietjes, maken.

lāng tsi̱ kó̱, 丨鑼鼓, op de tamboerijn slaan.

lāng sìt, 丨翅, de vlerken uitschudden, klappen.

玲 Lāng *lāng t'ang*, 丨窓, door en door uitgehold, (als beeldhouwwerk.)

lāng k'a, 丨脚, van onderen los, (als steenen of boomen.)

pàng lāng sang, 放丨鬆, speling laten, loslaten, uitstel geven.

Lao

要 Lao *lao i kong*, 丨他說, door een streek iets uit iemand lokken.

ing oē lao ih / *iōng oā „ „* } 用話丨伊, met woorden iets uit iemand lokken.

sa̱ lao, 相丨, elkander willen uithooren.

hō̱ lí boē lao tit, 後汝䨦丨, ik laat mij niet door u uithooren.

老 Laó Oud, oud in, ervaren, geverseerd in een vak.

laó taò, 丨到, geverseerd in, degelijk.

laó pún, 丨本, ervaren, door kneed.

laó sit, 丨實, eerlijk, opregt.

laó liēn, 丨鍊, van lange ondervinding, ervaren.

laó tsaī hâng, 丨在行, ervaren, door kneed in.

laó ts'ah, 丨差, do.

拐 Laó Ontvreemden, op eene slinksche manier ontnemen, zakrollen.

laó á, 丨仔, zakkenroller, gaauwdief.

toā laó kùn, 大丨棍, een door trapte schurk.

laó kè ts'iú, 丨過手, met een streek in handen krijgen.

荖 Laò *laó hioh*, 丨葉, siri.

laó hióh tsí, 丨葉子, betelnoot.

pō̱ laó hióh, 哺丨葉; sirikaauwen.

aó laó, 甌丨, kreukelen.

惱 Laò Naó̱ *aò laó*, 臭丨, gromrig, knorrig, boos.

laó pao, 丨包, rouwmuts.

maô laó pao, 麻丨包, hennepen rouwmuts, (zware rouw).

橈 Laó *laó boē lìn téng*, 丨未還轉, niet kunnen veranderen (als een accent in zijn spreken.)

laó tioh kun, 丨着筋, een spier verrekken.

hióh i king laó laó, 葉已|經, de bladeren zijn reeds verdord.

溜 Laò Vloeijen, stroomen, uitvloeijen.

laò tsûn, |船, voor den wind gaan.

laò k'ang tsûn. |空船, met een leeg schip terugkeeren.

laò k'ang kiō, |空轎, met een leegen draagstoel teruggaan.

laò siâ. |瀉, diarrhee.

t'ò laò, 吐|, braking en diarrhee hebben.

laò t'ò tsìng, |吐症, diarrhee en braking.

laò tō soa. |肚沙, diarrhee en koliek.

laò hong, |風, lucht doorlatend, lek.

laò iû, |油, uittrekken, uitkooken van vet.

laò kaò ts'it hú lák tsap sa koāi, |至七府六十三縣, uit de 7 departement en 63 districten gedreven worden (van *Kok-sìng* die ze eerst veroverd had maar later weer verloor), *d. i.* een zeer groot verlies lijden; ook erge diarrhee hebben.

laò tsaó, |葉, uit een troep loopen.

脫 Laò Zich ontdoen, losmakén van; uit elkander vallen, afvallen.

laò hióh, |走, de bladen vallen af, uit.

laò sún, |筍, uit elkander gaan van zwaluw staarten; in duigen, bedorven (van eene zaak.)

lao ts'iā, |牆, uit een gevallen, in duigen, (van een ton.)

laò t'áng, |桶, uit een gevallen emmer; in duigen van eene zaak.

laò ts'o p'e, |粗皮, de ruwe oneffenheid van iets afschaven.

laò ts'éh, laò tseh, |仄, uitgevallen, slordig in kleeding.

laò p'i, |痞, afvallen van pokroofjes.

sì laò soà, 四|散, uit elkander vallen van voorwerpen, uit elkander gaan, (als een huisgezin.)

laò ti, |拔, uitgezakte, neergetrapte hielen, (van eene schoen.)

soh á laò tsoè nn̄g tiaô, 索仔|做二條, een touw in tweeën splitsen.

撩 Laò Lokken, in een strik vangen.

laò i kong, |伊說, iemand door de mand laten vallen.

laò i dzip siâ, |伊入城, met een streek in de vesting lokken.

laò k'aò, |扣, in een strik vangen.

hō i laò k'ìh, 被他|去, in iemands strik gevangen worden.

laò kaò tsiáh koe ko / ke, |猴食雞糕, een aap misleiden om van hanemest te eten, *d. i.* iemand tot iets leiden dat hem later berouwen zal.

laò hi dzip bāng. |魚入網, visch in het nek lokken, *d. i.* door fraaie praatjes misleiden.

留 Laò Laten blijven, bij zich houden, niet laten weggaan, ophouden.

laò lâng k'eh, |人客, gasten bij zich houden.

laò dzīm, |任, een goeden beambte niet laten weggaan.

laò kē teh, |在的, overlaten, laten liggen.

laò ts'iu, |鬚, een baard laten staan.

laò laò, |戀, ophouden.

laò koh, |連, ophouden, vertragen.

laô soā, | 傘, iemands paraplu achter houden en hem niet willen laten weggaan.

瘤 Laô Gezwel, buil, wen.

kòng tióh tsit laô, 損着一|, een buil stooten.

ām kún sī laô, 項下生|, een gezwel in den nek hebben.

hong laô, 風|, buil, opzwelling.

流 Laô Stroomen, vloeijen, voortdrijven; de stroom.

laô koā, |汗, zweeten, zweet.

laô bák saí, |眼淚, weenen.

laô p'ī laô huih, |鼻|血, uit de neus bloeden.

laô p'ī tsuí, |鼻水, een snot neus hebben.

laô k'í noā, |齒涎, watertanden.

hō tsuí laô k'ì, 被水|去, door het water weggespoeld worden.

pàng sí gín á laô, 做死子仔|, zich op den rug laten drijven (bij het zwemmen.)

toā laô tsuí, 大|水, springtij.

sūn laô, gik laô, 順|, |逆, met stroom, tegen stroom.

tò pūn laô, 到洄|, tegen strijdige stroom, (als aan de kanten eener haven.

tsaī laô, laô tsaī, 再|,|再, de stroom kentert.

laô siông, laô laô siông siông, |常|七常匕, vuil, slordig.

laô tsī, |薯, uitzakken, (als deeg of wangen.)

樓 Laô Hoog gebouw, toren; zoldering, boven verdieping.

mîng laô, 門|, toren boven een poort.

kī loâ, 更|, wachttoren.

siā laô, 城|, stadstoren, (boven de poorten.)

tsiū koāi laô, 上高|, op een hooge verdieping, toren, gaan.

tsiú laô, 酒|, wijnhuis.

laô t'ui, |梯, ladder, trap.

laô t'ui tsí, |梯徑, sporten van een ladder.

laô tíng, 頂|, boven, op de boven verdieping.

laô pán, |板, zolderplank.

poā laô, 半|, halve (niet geheel doorloopende) verdieping.

劉 Laô Familienaam.

老 Laō Oud (van jaren); eeretitel, voor oudere lieden.

laō lâng ke, |人家, oudelieden.

laō toā, |大, oud, (van pers.)

laō pē, laō bú, |父, |母, vader, moeder.

hó laō hok, 好|福, gelukkige oude dag.

laō k'ong kiēn, |康健, oud maar kras.

laō lâng tsiā soè kiá, |人成小子, oude menschen worden als kleine kinderen.

laō pô, |婆, oude dienstmaagd.

laō lâng ts'iu ts'iū hong tsiên tsik, |人如風前燭, een oud mensch is als een kaars voor den wind.

laō pō tiā, |步定, oudelieden handelen bezadigd.

laō tòng gōng / *» tàm »*, } |當戇, suf door ouderdom.

laō tuh ku, 丨 戚 施, krom, suf door ouderdom.

laō hì, 丨 戲, komedie door volwassen lieden gespeeld.

laō tien tó, 丨 顛 倒, suf door ouderdom.

ts'it laō poeh tuh, 七 丨 八 䟫, de meeste oudelieden strompelen in het loopen.

t'aì laō, 太 丨, eerenaam voor iemand wiens zoon beambte is.

sì laō tia, 小 丨 爹, zeer lage beambte.

漏 Laō Druipen, uitdruipen, doordruppelen; van daar voor dingen als water-zand uurwerk, vergiettest, schuimspaan, filtreertoestel, lekken, een lek; uitlekken, uitkomen; ontduiken als belasting.

bák laō, 目 丨, druipende oogen.

tâng laō, 銅 丨, wateruurwerk.

soa laō, 沙 丨, zandlooper.

laō á, 丨 仔, vergiettest.

t'ih laō, *laō siáh*, 鐵 丨, 錫 丨, schuimspaan.

tsui laō, 水 丨, leksteen, filtreertoestel.

tsiú laō, 酒 丨, wijntrechter.

tê laō, 茶 丨, roostertje binnen aan de tuit van een trekpot.

bí laō, 米 丨, wanmolen.

p'ah laō, 打 丨, lekspringen.

hō laō, 雨 丨, regenlek.

siêm laō, 洩 丨, doorzijpelen van een lek.

laō ts'ut, 丨 出, uitlekken.

laō siet, 丨 洩, do.

laō hong, 丨 風, do.

t'ao laō, 丨 透, heimelijk van iets ofstelen.

lao sè, 丨 稅, belasting ontduiken, smokkelen.

閙 Laō Getier, drukte, luidruchtige bedrijvigheid als op eene markplaats; geraas, leven maken, scholden.

laō dziét, 丨 熱, gejoel, getier, bedrijvig, drukte, (als bij een feest.)

ts'aó laō, 抄 丨, levenmaken.

laō hō lâng tsai, 丨 與 人 知, door leven te maken iets uitbrengen.

laō tai, 丨 臺, door het slaan op den trom toeschouwers bij het tooneel brengen.

laō t'ig, 丨 廳, met muziek in den zaal feesthouden (bij offerande gew. 3 dagen.)

laō pâng, 丨 房, leven, gekheid maken in de bruidskamer.

kap i laō, 與 他 丨, met iemand twisten, een standje schoppen.

豆 Laô *laō haō* / *taō kò* } 丨 哮, notenmuskaat.

kan laō, afschilferen van de huid, soort schurft.

Laoh

落 Laóh *ka laóh*, 遺 丨, afvallen, op den grond vallen.

soà laóh lauh, 丨 綫 遺, overal verspreid.

lauh laóh lóng, 丨 匕 說, achter elkander aframmelen.

Lap

湺 Lap Inzakken, intrappen, vallen, stappen in; in een strik doen vallen; eene inzakking, gat maken in (als in geld.)

lap k'ang, 丨 空, in een gat stoppen;

een gat in iemands geld doen ontstaan.

táh lap, 踏 丨, intrappen, (door op iets te staan.)

táh tsít lap, 踏 一 丨, een gat in trappen (op eene plaats waar geld begraven is) *d. i.* een onverwacht voordeel behalen.

lap lâng ê tsî, 丨 人 之 財, een gat in iemands geld maken.

k'a lām sám lap, 脚 亂 丨, overal in trappen, (als in donker.)

tsít t'ò kō ê lap tsoè tsít ê, 一 套 五 个 丨 做 一 个. een stel van vijf tot één in elkander zetten.

lap lâi lap k'ì, 丨 來 丨 去, het éene gat maken om het andere te stoppen.

lap k'ut, 丨 屈, tot een kuil inzakken.

p'ī lap lòh k'ì, 鼻 丨 落 去, zijn neus is ingevallen, weggevreten.

lap toé, 丨 底, de bodem is er uitgevallen.

tsoè sū lâi lap lâng, 做 事 來 丨 人, iets doen om iemand in een strik te vangen.

hō lâng lap k'ì, 被 人 丨 去, in iemands strik vallen.

lap (of *t'ap*) *tioh hit ê tsa bō*, 丨 着 一 个 女 人, overspel met eene vrouw begaan.

lap tioh t'ái ko hia, 丨 着 癩 疾 靴, in de laars van een melaatsche stappen *d. i.* onwetend zich in moeielijkheden brengen.

袮 Lap *béh lap*, 襪 丨, overkous.

遝 Lap *lap sap*, 丨 㳂, vuil, smerig, liederlijk.

lap sap pī, 丨 㳂 病, venerische ziekte.

ts'ap la, 雜 丨, door elkander schudden, (als kaarten.)

lap tseh lap tseh } 丨 仄, slordig, (van vrouwen.)
» tseh » tseh }

納 Láp Ontvangen, aannemen; opbrengen, betalen.

tsiep láp, 接 丨, ontvangen.

kàm láp, 鑒 丨, (eene offerande), aannemen.

láp hiòng } 丨 餉, belasting, regten betalen.
» hiàng }

láp sè tsî, 丨 稅 錢, huur betalen.

oân láp, 完 丨, opbrengen, betalen.

láp bé á, 丨 碼 仔, de pacht opbrengen, afbetalen.

láp lai, 丨 利, interest betalen.

sî sî teh láp lai, 常 匕 丨 利, gedurig kleine onkosten aan iets hebben.

láp láp tsáh, 丨 匕 食, alles alleen opeten.

láp oê toé, 丨 鞋 底, schoenzolen inzetten, aannaaijen.

láp tsít lui hoe, 丨 一 蕊 花, een bloem inborduren.

Láp *láp láp k'áp k'áp*, 丨 匕 閤 匕 in alles ongelukkig zijn.

攋 Láp *tsáp láp*, 雜 丨, allerlei verward door elkander.

láp láp tsáp tsáp, 丨 匕 雜 匕, gemengd, niet van eene soort.

kà láp láp, 爛 丨 匕, zeer gebonden (als stijfsel.)

Lat

力 Kracht; sterkte.

Lát *ū lát*. 有 ｜, sterk.

k'uì lát, 氣 ｜, sterkte, kracht.

toā lát, 大 ｜, machtig.

tióh lát, 着 ｜, zich ten uiterste inspannen op; voornaam, van belang.

bô lát, 無 ｜, zwak.

bô lát t'ang boé, 無 ｜ 可 買, niet in staat, bijvermogen zijn, iets te koopen.

lō̤ lát, 努 ｜, ik dank u.

tsioh lát, 借 ｜, volgends de overhellende richting kracht aanwenden.

tsiáh lát, 食 ｜, veel te dragen hebben, (als iets waar een zwaar voorwerp op ligt) met kracht aankomen, kracht zetten.

kut lát, 骨 ｜, kracht inspannen, vlijtig zijn.

tit lát, 直 ｜, veel te dragen hebben. meer diensten dan anderen bewijzen, (als kinderen of bedienden.)

ling bú lát, 乳 毋 ｜, jeudige kracht, (die spoedig vermoeid wordt.)

sai gōng lát, 用 戇 ｜, domme kracht aanwenden.

tioh lát bô hó k'oà, 着 ｜ 無 好 看, na veel inspanning nog weinig vergoeding voor zijne moeite vinden.

tsīn lát, 盡 ｜, zijne uiterste krachten inspannen.

pì lát, kik lát, 蔽 ｜ 激 ｜, zijne krachten verzamelen, inspannen.

ts'ut lát, 出 , kracht aanwenden, zich inspannen.

t'o̤ k'uì tióh lát, 吐 氣 着 ｜, zijne drift en kracht op iets verspillen, (als op een onwillige kind.)

lát koán boē kaò, ｜ 管 未 到, de krachten zijn niet toereikende.

栗 *lát tsí*, ｜ 子, kastanje.

Lát *lát ts'iū*, ｜ 樹, kastanjeboom.

si̤ lí lát, 生 理 ｜, klieren in den nek krijgen, (door venerische ziekte).

Le

ts'uì á le le le }
» » le̤ le̤ le̤ } praatziek, snapachtig (van vrouwen).

la le, do.

hiaô le le, zeer wellustig, (van vrouwen.)

禮* *lé sò̤*, ｜ 欸, welgemaniedheid, beleefdheid.

Lé *lé pō̤*, ｜ 部, departement voor de ritus.

lé lō̤, ｜ 路, beleefdheid, welvoegelijkheid.

kiâ lé, 行 ｜, groeten, zijn compliment maken.

ū lé, 有 ｜, beleefd.

hó (of ū) lé maō̤, 好 ｜ 貌, wel op gevoed.

sit lé, 失 ｜, onbeleefd, bel. term, ik gedraag mij onbeleefd, ik vraag u excuus voor mijn onbeleefdheid.

lé bút, ｜ 物, geschenken.

tap lé, 答 ｜, eene beleefdheid beantwoorden.

bô lé bô t'é (of sò), 無 ｜ 無 體, onbeleefd,

---

* Zie verder onder *loé*.

sàng lé, 送 ｜, geschenken geven.

soé lé, 洗 ｜, doopen, doop.

kat lé, 割 ｜, besnijdenis.

lé paì, ｜ 拜, godsdienstoefening houden; week.

lé hū lâng, ｜ 下 人, iemand met beleefdheid behandelen.

sing lé, 牲 ｜, offeranden, (vleesch en wijn.)

lé sing, ｜ 牲, ceremoniemeester.

lé t'iep, ｜ 帖, huwelijks kaart (door beide familiën aan elkander gezonden.)

lé t'é, ｜ 體, beleefdheids vereischten.

lé gî, ｜ 儀, beleefdheid; geschenken.

lé lé k'ut k'ut, ｜ 匕 滑 匕, uit schelden.

Lè *kap i lè*, met hem vechten, twisten.

kui t'ong oá lè lòh lai, de geheele hoop kopjes viel om.

璃 Lê *po lê*, 玻 ｜, glas.

e lê } 矮 ｜, knijzen, drijnen, (als
» *k'ê* } kinderen.)

螺 Lê *pùn lê*, 吹 ｜, op de hoorn blazen.

tik lê, 竹 ｜, bamboezen hoorn.

lê k'ak, ｜ 殼, schelpen.

tsân lê, 田 ｜, veldslak.

kè á lê, 髻 仔 ｜, de staart om het hoofd geworden.

seh lê, 旋 ｜, rondgaand, dwarlend.

kèng lê } 捲 ｜, dwarlend.
kui » }

ts'iú kui è lê, 手 幾 箇 ｜, hoeveel lijnen, kringen hebt gij op uwe vingers.

𠯈 Lè *lé long*, ｜ 曨, vendutie.

hō lâng lè long k'ìh, 被 人 ｜ 曨 去, openbaar verkocht worden voor schuld.

例 Lē Lī Wet, gebruik.

lût lē, 律 ｜, wet.

kui lē, 規 ｜, gebruikelijke manier.

it lē, 一 ｜, zelfde gebruiken, gewoonten.

bô ū tsit é lē, 無 此 ｜, dat is de gewoonte niet, dat is niet gebruikelijk.

tsiaò lē, 照 ｜, volgens de wet.

sin lē, 新 ｜, nieuwe wetsinstelling.

tiaô lē, 條 ｜, wetsbepaling.

ui lē, 違 ｜, tegen de wet zondigen.

su lē, 私 ｜, private bepalingen, wet, bepaling op zijn eigen houtje.

t'é lē, 體 ｜, voorkomen, toestand, (van eene plaats.)

iú lē bok tû bû lē bók siet } 有 莫 除 無 莫 設, waar die
» *lī* » *lī* » » » » }
gewoonten bestaan vernietige men ze niet, waar ze niet bestaan stelle men ze niet in.

tīng lē, 定 ｜, vaste gewoonte, manier, gebruik.

siók lē, 俗 ｜, plaatselijke gewoonte, gebruik.

隸 Lē *tsō lē*, 皂 ｜, volgers van mandarijnen, (met hooge zwarte mutsen op.)

勵 Lē *bién lē*, 勉 ｜, aansporen, aanmoedigen.

Leh

拈 Leh Knijpen, grijpen, beetpakken, tusschen twee vingers pakken.

leh ām kún / *» á »* } ｜項管, de keel plukken (bij buikpijn.)

leh t'aô tsang, ｜頭鬆, bij de hoofdstaart pakken.

leh soa, ｜沙, de keel rood trekken, (bij buikpijn.)

tuì tíng bīn leh k'ì lâi, 對上面｜起來, van boven afnemen, (als van een hoop waren.)

leh tó tsaó, ｜倒走, afnemen en weg loopen; (als een dief langs de straat.)

呢 Leh — Aanduider van den verledenen tijd.

列 Léh — Sneden, (over het ligchaam), sneden toebrengen.

Léh *ká t'at ká léh*, 敢殺敢｜, niet bang zijn voor moorden en neêrhouwen.

léh k'ui k'oa̍, ｜開看, opensnijden om te zien.

pit tsit léh, 畢一｜, splijten.

léh léh haó, ｜匕吼, kletteren van donder, gedurig met hetzelfde uitschelden.

Li

厘 Li — *li li á*, ｜匕也, een weinigje.

bák tsiu li li lut lut, 目州｜｜黜匕, onrustig om zich heen zien.

爾 Lí — Gij.

lí hia̍ goá tī, ｜兄我弟, gij oudere ik jongere broeder, *d. i.* ik erken U als mijn meerdere.

lí tsoè lí hōng heh goá tsoè goá tiā tióh / *» tsò » » » » tsò » » »* 做｜奉的我做我聽的, gij voor U zelven moogt ontstellen ik voor mij ben rustig, *d. i.* ik ben er volstrekt niet bevreesd voor.

里 Lí — Dorp, gehucht; de Chinesche mijl 578.5 Ned. el.

hia̍ lí, 鄉｜, dorp, gehucht.

siā lí, 社｜, dorp.

lí tiú, 長｜, dorpsoude.

gō lí ting, 五｜亭, rustplaats om de 5 li's.

ts'ien lí bé, 千｜馬, courier, renbode

理 Lí — Besturen, beheeren, regelen, schikken; rede, wat volgens het gezond verstand, billijk, behoorlijk is.

pān lí, 辦｜, regelen, schikken, doen.

lí ke, 家｜, een huishouden besturen.

put lí ih, 不｜伊, zich niet met iemand in laten.

tsi lí, 書｜, beredderen, op zich nemen.

tō lí, 道｜, rede, op het gezond verstand gegronde beginselen.

bû lí, 無｜, in het ongelijk zijn, onregt hebben; onregt aan doen.

ū tsing lí, 有情｜, gegrond zijn, gelijk hebben, (als in eene redenering.)

bûn lí, 文｜, beleefd. verfijnd.

tsiaò lí lō, 照｜路, volgens de behoorlijke manier.

ti lí, 知｜, au fond, toch eigenlijk.

lí hoē, ｜會, met iemand volgens regt en billijkheid over iets spreken, *tuì li*, 對 〡, tegen over elkander bepleiten.

裡 Lí De binnenkant, voering van een kleed.

sa̤ á li, 衫 仔 〡, do.

oê li, 鞋 〡, voering van een schoen.

lóng tsong li bīn kui ê i̤, 籠 總 〡 面 幾 個 錢, hoe veel is het bedrag van de voering en de buiten stof?

鯉 Lí *li hî*, 〡 魚, karper.

李 Lí Pruim, toebereidselen voor eene reis maken; familienaam.

li á, 〡 仔, pruim.

hîng li, 行 〡, bagage.

Tiṳ sa̤ li sì, 張 三 〡 四, *Tiṳ* de derde of *Li* de vierde, *i. d.* deze of gene, (gew. met minachting gezegd.)

毎 Lí *li li*, 〡 匕, steeds gedurig.

li ū, 〡 有, dat is gewoonlijk zoo.

li sī, 〡 是, steeds toestemmen, goedkeuren.

la sám li lô, vuil, smerig.

履 Lí *li li̍k*, 〡 歴, levensloop verschillende betrekkingen die iemand bekleed heeft.

ts'iong li li̍k, 唱 〡 歴, iemands levensloop uitroepen (als bij eene audientie.)

僞 Lì *lì k'iet*, 〡 黠, ondoorgrondbaar, niet te vertrouwen, met draaijerijen omgaande bedriegelijk, (van pers.)

裂 Lì Scheuren, (als kleeren), afscheuren.

lì p'oà bīn, 〡 破 面, het gezigt stuk scheuren, *d. i.* onbeschaamd voor iets uitkomen.

lì tsoá, 〡 紙, papier verscheuren.

lā li hi̤, 勝 〡 搖, heen en weer schommelen.

厘 Li Duizendste deel van een tael; een weinig.

li tîng, 戥 〡, fijne weegschaal, (voor medicijn of goud.)

t'àn tsit ê li tsí, 攢 一 个 〡 止, niet meer dan een-duizendste verdienen.

li li á, 〡 匕 仔, een weinigje.

li si á, 〡 絲 仔, een haartje, weinigje.

li boa̍t, 〡 末, weinig voordeel gevend.

hun li, 分 〡, een weinigje.

tsīn bô li, 真 無 〡, geen haartje goed of waar.

俚 Lî *p'i li*, 痞 〡, laag gemeen.

狸 Lî *hô li*, 狐 〡, vos.

簾 Lî Van bamboes gemaakte deurscherm, gordijn.

mn̂g li, 門 〡, deurscherm.

pò li, 布 〡, katoenen deurscherm.

li̍h li, 篾 〡, bamb. deurscherm.

kiō li, 轎 〡, scherm, gordijn in een draagstoel.

籬 Lî Heining, bamb. omheining.

li pa, 〡 巴, heining, (om grond of huis.

tik li, 竹 〡, bamb. heining, (om een huis.)

li pīng piah piah pīng li, 傍 壁 傍 〡, de heining steunt tegen den muur en de muur tegen de heining *d. i.* ep elkander steunen.

li p'oà kaó lâi tsóng, 〡 破 狗 來 走, is de heining stuk dan komen de honden er door stooten, *d. i.* geraakt men in verval dan komen allen op u neder.

離 Scheiden, afgaan van.

Li *li bó*, | 妻, zijne vrouw van zich afwijzen, scheiden.

li tsu } *» si* } | 書, akte van echtscheiding.

尼 Li Nî *li ko*, | 姑, Boeddha non, (zij mogen niet huwen.)

li ko sa, | 姑 衫, bedelaars kleed, deken.

li ko p'ō kiá, | 姑 抱 子, als eene non die haar kind draagt, *d. i.* vreezen dat anderen iets zullen zien.

li kō tsoè moá géh, | 姑 做 滿 月, als eene non die haren kerkgang doet (een maand na de bevalling gaan de Chineesche vrouwen offeren).

漓 Li *hō lim li*, 雨 淋 |, een hevige regenbui.

利 Lī Scherp; voordeel, winst, voordeelig, bevoordeelen; interest.

lī haī, | 害, gevaarlijk, schadelijk.

lī piēn, | 便, handig, geriefelijk.

lī ik, 益 |, voordeel, voordeelig, bevoordeelen.

lī lō, | 路, gelegenheid om voordeel te doen.

kièn lī maī lī, 見 | 賣 |, zoodra verkoopen als er wat op te verdienen is.

lī k'aó, | 口, lekker voor den mond (als versche waar).

ka iáh lī ts'ī, 加 額 | 市, voordeelig te verkoopen, gewild.

sè lī, 勢 |, rijken hoogachten, vleien.

lī put hun sam, | 不 分 三, winst moet men niet in drieën verdeelen (elk deel wordt te gering.)

lī ki sun dzin, | 已 損 人, zich zelven ten nadeele van anderen bevoordeelen.

lī sik } *» sit* } | 息, interest, voordeel van geld.

痢 Lī Diarrhee, dysenterie.

sió lī, 小 |, diarrhee.

tsoè lī, 做 | diarrhee hebben.

lī tsik } *» tsit* } | 疾, diarrhee, dysenterie.

a p'ièn lī, 亞 片 |, diarrhee door opium rooken veroorzaakt.

ts'iah lī, 赤 |, roode loop.

俐 Lī *līng lī*, 伶 |, schrander, knap; fraai, (van vrouwen.)

離 Lī Afgaan, afzijn van, verlaten, scheiden, verwijderd zijn van.

lī k'ui, | 開, afgaan van, verlaten, verwijderd zijn van.

lī piét, | 別, scheiden, elkander verlaten.

lī sin, lī k'a, | 身, | 脚, verlaten.

boē lī tit sin, (of *k'a*), 未 | 身 脚, niet kunnen verlaten, niet aan zich zelven kunnen overlaten.

lī k'ui ts'át lò loā tīng, | 開 賊 不 甚 遠, niet ver van de roovers, rebellen af.

t'è lī, 體 |, wijken, uit den weg gaan.

liaó lī, 了 |, afgedaan en iemand niet meer aangenaam.

lī dzīm, | 任, zijn ambt verlaten, neêrleggen.

siém īm lī, 躲 不 |, niet ontkomen aan.

吏 Lī — *lī pō*, 丨部, Ministerie van civiele zaken.

lī pàng, 丨房, afdeeling voor civiele zaken, in elk bureau.

Lih

lih lai, bedorven, verward, (van eene zaak.)

裂 Lih — Splijten, scheuren, (als kleederen,)

lih k'ui, 丨開, gescheurd.

lih lah, 丨了, bedorven, (van eene zaak.)

p'oà lih, 破丨, (gebroken en) stuk gespleten.

lih p'āng, 縫丨, gespleten (met groote reet.)

lih hùn, 丨痕, gespleten (met kleine reet.)

t'aô p'oà hī lih, 頭破耳丨, zwaar aan het hoofd gekwetst.

ts'iò lih lih, 笑丨匕, een wijden mond zetten van het lagchen.

k'ui lih lih, 開丨匕, gescheurd, gespleten.

lih ki, 丨墘, aan den rand splijten.

Lik

勒 Lik — Onderdrukken, verdrukken, dwingen.

boē k'am tit i lik, 未堪得伊丨, iemands verdrukking niet kunnen uithouden.

lik k'ah tsió, 丨再少. met geweld dwingen iets voor minder te geven.

扼 Lik — Beetpakken, terughouden, zijn gang niet laten gaan.

lik sè } 丨勢, terug deinzen, minder
» *sì* } durven.

lik tá, 丨胆, zijne moed tegenhouden, niet overmoedig te werk gaan.

bô lik sik, 無丨色, niet ontstellen.

lik loh k'ì, 丨落去, bezwijken, neêrzinken, (door ziekte of verbazing,)

攊 Lik — Bij elkander trekken, zamentrekken.

lik p'ī, 丨鼻, de neus optrekken.

lik hùn, 丨痕, geplooid.

lik sùn, *lik kng*, 丨巡, 丨稿, gerimpeld.

力 Lík — Kracht, sterkte, krachtinspanning, vermogen; met krachtinspanning doen.

ts'ut lik, 出丨, zich inspannen, moeite geven, verdienstelijk maken.

tsīn lik, 盡丨, met alle kracht inspanning vermogen.

lik liōng } 丨量, vermogen, (kracht
» *liāng* } en van gemoed.)

sè lik, 勢丨, magt.

ū kong lik tī kok nih, 有功丨在國, zich verdienstelijk jegens zijn rijk gemaakt hebben.

lik lō, 丨路, een weg in zeer korten tijd afleggen.

搦 Lik — *lik tsièn*, 丨戰, tot het gevecht uitdagen.

勒 Lik — Teugel, toom; beteugelen, inhouden, afpersen; wringen; knijpen, opstroopen.

lik kiu, 羌丨, teugel toom.

lik bé, 丨馬, zijn paard inhouden.

lik hoê bé, 丨貨馬, zijn paard omwenden.

lik tō, 丨肚, buikriem; touw aan het roer.

lik sik, 丨色, afpersen, afzetten.

lik huih, | 血, bloed uitpersen, uitknijpen.

lik ām kún, | 項 滾, zich de keel knijpen.

lik ts'iú ńg, | 手 袖, de mouwen opstroopen.

Lik *lik kim*, | 金, in het vuur vergulden.

歷 Lik Doorgaan, beleven, ondervinden; ondervinding; achtereenvolgend als geslachten.

king lik, 經 |, doorgegaan zijn, ondervinding hebben van.

lai lik, 來 |, levensloop.

lik lai, | 來, van vroeger af.

iet lik } *oát* » } 越 |, ondervinding.

lik liēn, | 鍊, gedurige oefening, ondervinding.

lik giēm, | 驗, proef ondervindelijk goed, (als medicijnen.)

lik taī, | 帶, de achtereenvolgende geslachten, elke generatie.

lik ni̤, | 年, elk jaar.

綠 Lik Groen.

lik sik, | 色, groen.

tâng lik, 銅 |, kopergoen.

hai hún lik, 海 粉 |, zeegroen, lichtgroen.

lik taō, | 豆, groene erwten.

hoe hoe lik lik, 哮 匕 | 匕, fraai, opgesierd.

溺 Lík Verdrinken, zich verdrinken in; fig. in ondeugd of liefde.

tim lik, 沉 |, diep in zijn verderf loopen.

tim lik lâng è mi̤h, 沉 | 人 之 物, iemands goederen verdrinken, *d. i.* verdonkeremanen.

lik aì, | 愛, vurig beminnen.

匿 Lík Verbergen, verborgen houden.

ún lík, *tsóng lik*, 穩 |, | 總, verbergen, huisvesten, (slechte lieden).

lik song, | 喪, den dood zijner ouders verborgen houden, (om zijn ambt te behouden of examinatie te passeren.)

列 Lík *lik siaò*, | 賬, posten gespecificeerd opteekenen.

lik lik tī hi tsóng p'ō̤ ti̤h, | 匕 在 此 總 簿 的, in het grootboek opteekenen.

Lip

立 Líp Regtop staan; oprigten, instellen, opmaken, vaststellen, bepalen; inzetten, (der jaargetijden.)

lip sin, | 身, zelfstandig mensch zijn.

tsū lip, 自 |, do. zijn eigen meester.

lip sit, | 式, stevig, standvastig.

siet lip, 設 |, oprigten.

lip iok, | 約, een contract, traktaat maken, overeenkomen.

lip dzī, | 字, een geschrift opmaken, opstellen.

lip ì, | 意, zijne meening vaststellen, vast plan maken.

lip tsì, | 志, zijn voornemen vaststellen.

lip sim, | 心, besloten zijn om, met voordacht.

lip i tsoè hông tè, | 伊 做 皇 帝, tot keizer aanstellen.

lip k'ik, *lip tsik*, | 刻, | 即, onmiddelijk, oogenblikkelijk.

lip hē, | 夏, den zomer inzetten, in gaan.

44

Liah

折 Afgebroken, afgescheurd, (van hout.)
Liah *liah k'ak*, | 殼, afgescheurd gespleten, (als boomen.)
liah p'é, | 皮, de huid, schil afhalen.
ts'iū ki liah lóh lai, 樹枝 | 落來, een tak aftrekken
liah ts'i, | 莿, volsplinters zijn, splinters uitsteken, (als hout.)
liah tsit kàk; | 一角, een hoek afgebroken.

拿 Vatten, beetpakken, grijpen; vangen,
Liáh vinden.
liáh tsoè, | 做, grijpende maken tot, *d. i.* houden voor.
liáh hi, | 魚, visschen vangen.
tsaó sa liáh, 走相 |, krijgertje spelen.
ts'i k'im oáh liáh, 生擒活 |, onvoorziens gebeuren, doen.
liáh iá, | 影, de schaduw grijpen, *d. i.* naar iets gissen.
liàh tsoè bô iá, | 做無影, voor onwaar houden.
liáh bák, | 墨, het hoofd van iets omkoopen.
liáh kûn, | 拳, boksen.
p'ah hó liáh ts'át, 打虎 | 賊, als tijgers jagen en dieven vangen, onvermoeid, rusteloos zoeken.
liáh tâng, | 銅, een toovenaar verhinderen zich slagen toetebrengen.
liáh sat, | 蝨, luizen vangen; de zwarigheden van te voren uitduiden en uit den weg ruimen.
liáh tióh li é sim sū, | 着汝的心事, ik heb Uwe meening gevat, ik zie Uwe bedoeling in.
liáh toā kō, | 大垢, zich wederkeerig in elkanders gedachten vergissen.
liáh m̄ tióh pān, | 不着辦, naar een verkeerd model maken.
liáh lō, | 路, eene manier, (door omkooping) vinden.
liáh laō, | 漏, een lek uitvinden.
liáh kiá saì k'oà tsoè ping, | 子婿看做兵, zijn schoonzoon voor een soldaat aanzien, *d. i.* aanzienlijke knappe lieden voor laag en dom houden.

辮 Vlechten.
Liáh *liáh t'aô tsang*, | 頭鬃, de hoofdstaart vlechten.
liáh tsiaó á bák, | 鳥仔目, met openingen vlechten, (als de zitting van rottingstoelen.)

搦 Knijpen, (de gewrichten.)
Liáh *liáh ling*, | 沙, pietjetten, masseren.
liáh sou, | 涼, iemand bij een koliek knijpen.
Liáh *liáh liàng*, gekscheren.
ka liáh, groote bamboezen horde.

掠 Met de hand bespannen, uitspannen.
Liáh *tsit liáh tèng*, 一 | 長, een span lang.
liáh tit, | 直, regt uitspannen; onbewimpeld.

Liang

涼* *liâng ling*, | 冷, koel maken, verkoelen.
Liâng *liâng liâng*, | 匕, koel, luchtig.

---

* Zie verder onder *liông*.

liáh liàng, gekscheren.

亭 *liāng liāng*, | 七, doorzigtig dun.

Liāng *kɛng liāng* } 光 |, doorzigtig, dun.
kui „ } (als porselein, glas.)

peh liāng } 白 |, witte doorzigtige
pèh „ } mandarijn knop.

liāng pi, *liāng ting*, | 棚, | 亭, open tent of torentje voor koelte.

Liao

縮 Krampachtig.

Liao *k'a ts'iú liao*, 手 足 |, magteloos, de vrees door de ledematen hebben.

pàng liao k'i, 放 | 去, loslaten, zoo lang laten liggen, (van eene zaak.)

了 Ten einde brengen, tot een besluit

Liaó komen, duidelijk inzien; afgedaan, geeindigd, aanduider van het verledene; verliezen, opmaken.

liaó kiók, | 局, ten einde gebragt, afloop.

bô liaó kiók, 無 | 局, eindeloos.

liaó kiat, | 結, afloop.

liaó tsiét, | 捷, spoedig afdoende, (in handelingen).

bô liaó si, 無 | 時, (zoo doende) komt er geen eind aan, zonder eind, steeds.

oē liaó boē tsīn ē tai tsì, 能 | 未 盡 分 的 事, eene eindelooze zaak.

liaó t'iet, | 徹, helder voor den geest hebben, inzien.

liaó dziên, *liaó kai*, | 然, | 改, tot de overtuiging, inzigt komen.

liaó gō, | 悟, tot bewustzijn, inzicht (van zijne verkeerdheid) komen.

LIAO

liaó lâh, | 的, daar loopt het mis, daar hebt ge het!

liaó put tik, | 不 得, daar blijft het niet bij; eindeloos, buitengewoon, zeer.

liaó sū, | 事, een eind aan eene zaak brengen.

liaó lī, | 離, afgedaan, iemand niet meer aangaan.

tsiáh liaó, 食 |, gedaan hebben met eten.

kè liaó si soah liaó taī, 過 | 時 煞 | 事, is die tijd voorbij dan is die zaak ook afgedaan, *d. i.* haal geen oude dingen op.

liaó tióh gûn, | 着 銀, geld bij iets verliezen.

liaó tsi, | 錢, geld verliezen, onkosten hebben aan.

ts'iú laī liaó ē tsi, 手 內 | 的 錢, geld dat men aan verschillende dingen verloren heeft.

liaó kɛng kɛng, | 光 七, geheel en al verliezen.

bô liaó liaó, 無 | |, volstrekt niet.

liaó ke kiá, | 家 子, een slechte zoon die zijne familie te gronde brengt.

liaó tiaō, | 兆, voorteeken van rampen, (als een slechte zoon.)

siang t'aô liaó, 双 頭 |, aan beide kanten verliezen.

寮 Strooḥut, wachthuisje.

Liaô *liaô á*, | 仔, hut, wachthuisje in een veld.

ki liaô, 庚 |, wachthuisje.

ts'aó liaô, 草 |, stroohut.

tsiú liaô, 守 |, bij een wachthuisje waken.

繚 *liaô á soh*, | 仔索, de touwen
Liaô aan een Chinesche zeil.

liáh sa k'a liaô, 掠三脚 |, naar de omstandigheden uitzien.

僚 *tòng liaô ê koa*, 仝 | 之官, ge-
Liaô lijkstaande ambtenaren.

聊 *bô liaô*, 無 |, niets te doen hebben,
Liaô uit verveling, voor tijd verdrijf doen.

bô liaô nai, 無 | 賴, niets te doen.

料 *bô liaô siaò*, 無 | 賬, weinig too-
Liaô nend.

遼 *liaô tang*, | 東, *Liaô-tang* in Korea
Liaô of Moukden.

Liaô *liaô kù*, zagen met 2 personen.

liaô tsoá, papier afscheuren.

調 *at liaô*, *tién liaô*, 遏 |, 點 |, de
Liaô maat slaan.

bô liaô tiaō, 無 | 調, uit de maat spelen.

ah liaô, 押 |, volgens eene melodie zingen.

涉 Doorwaden, overgaan.
Liaô *liaô tsuí*, | 水, door het water waden.

liaô ts'ân hoā, | 田岸, voorzigtig over een rijstveldpad loopen.

條 *í liaô*, 椅 |, bank.
Liaô *tsióh liaô*, 石 |, steenen plaat.

聊 *liaô liaô á*, | 匕仔, langzamer-
Liaô hand, van lieverlede.

liaô á sī, | 仔是, langzaam aan.

料 Denken, oordeelen, schatten, het er
Liaō voorhouden; regelen, besturen; benoodigheden voor iets, materialen, de stof waarvan iets gemaakt is.

liaō sū, | 事, eene zaak overpeinzen, overdenken.

put ts'ut goa só liaō, 不出我所 |, het is uitgekomen zoo als ik gedacht heb.

liaō sióng, *liaō sió*, *liaō sèng*, | 想, | 賞, | 筭, meenen, het er voorhouden, vooronderstellen.

liaō souh, | 煞, voorzien hoe iets zal afloopen.

liaō lí, | 理, regelen, besturen, in orde brengen.

ts'ai liaō, 裁 |, materialen, benoodigheden.

bák liaō, *sam liaō*, 木 |, 杉 |, timmerhout.

k'ò liaō, 苦 |, goed voor een broek, broekenstof.

sik liaō, 色 |, stukjes verf.

tê liaō, 茶 |, confituren bij de thee.

tso liaō, 佐 |, specerijen.

péh liaō eh, 白 | 的, van wit koper gemaakt, (als valsch geld.)

k'í ts'ù p'aì poà liaō, 起厝派半 |, bij het bouwen van een huis berekent men slechts de helft der bouwstoffen, *d. i.* meer onkosten hebben dan men voorzien had.

liaō k'ì, | 器, van rijst of glas nagemaakte edelsteenen.

廖 Familienaam.
Liaō

繚 Rondbinden; touw waaraan men de
Liaō Chineesche weegschaal houdt.

īng soh á liaō, 用索仔 |, met touw ombinden.

ts'ìn liaō, 桯 |, touw van een weegschaal.

Liem

拈 Met de vingers uithalen, uittrekken.
Liem

liem hiu̥, | 香, een reukstokje uithalen, (om te offeren.)

liem k'ao, | 鬮, loten, trekken.

liem ts'ân i̥, | 蜻 蜓, eene libellula pakken, kinderen met korte hoofdstaartje.

liem hó̤ ts'iu, | 虎 鬚, de tijgersbaard uittrekken, *d. i.* bepalen hoeveel elk aan een gemeenschappelijk maaltijd zal betalen, de bovenste uiteinden van eenige elkander in één punt snijdende lijnen worden genommerd en bedekt, ieder kiest een lijn aan de onderzijde het daarmede corresponderende cijfer duidt zijn inleg aan.

liem king tah tsì̥, | 弓 踏 箭, den boog trekken en den pijl aanleggend, *d. i.* onverwijld doen.

斂 Liem *liem liem*, | ㄴ, voorzigtig op de teenen loopen.

liem k'a kiḁ̂, | 脚 行, op de teenen loopen.

liem k'a bih (of *soh*) *ts'iú*, | 脚 ㄴ 手, voorzigtig op de teenen loopen.

liem liem táh tioh kaó sai tsiem, | ㄴ 踏 着 狗 屎 尖, voorzigtig loopende in een hondendrol trappen, *d. i.* met alle zijne voorzigtigheid er toch in loopen.

liem k'a tè ts'iú / *» toè » »* | 脚 隨 手, op de teenen loopend en met de handen volgend, *d. i.* onverwijld.

liem liem àh, | | 仔, op het nippertje, kantje af.

liem liem á kaù, | | 足, maar juist genoeg, nog juist, bijna, . . .

斂 Liém *liém sing* / *» sé* | 省, minder gebruiken dan vroeger, zuiniger worden.

liém sok, | 束, ingehouden, ingetogen, minder geld gebruiken,

siu liém, 收 |, verminderen in uitgaven, zuiniger worden.

k'ik liém lâng, 尅 | 人, een weinig van iemands regtmatig deel afhouden.

lièm tsió, | 少, van alles een weinig afnemen, een weinig van iets afnemen.

lièm tó̤, | 斗, de zijden, de lenden, (bij dieren.)

摘 Lièm Uitplukken, (als veèren), knijpen.

lièm koe, | 花, een bloem afplukken, aftrekken.

lièm lan, | 蘭, eelt aftrekken.

lièm soa, | 沙, zich de keel plukken bij buikpijn.

lièm tn̄g / *» tu̥ī* | 斷, zich niet meer met iets bezig houden, er niet meer aan denken.

lièm si sim, | 死 心, iets voor goed opgeven, niet meer aan iets te denken.

lièm liaó liaó, | 了 ㄴ, gedurig een weinig van iets afnemen tot dat er niets meer overblijft.

粘 Liêm Vastplakken aan; vastlijmen, kleverig; vastzijn, vasthouden aan.

liêm âng, | 紅, een rood papier op iets plakken, (als op geschenken.)

liêm tioh t'i, | 着 黐, met vogellijm lijmen, vangen.

liêm lô, | 澇, klevig, dik.

liêm t'i t'i, | 黐 ㄴ, zeer kleverig, zijne kennissen steeds in moeijelijkheden brengen.

liêm liêm siû̥ siû̥, | ㄴ 湘 ㄴ, kleverig.

lô liêm noḁ̄, 澇 | 涎, slijmerig speeksel, (door lang spreken veroorzaak.)

tsit ts'uì lô liem noḁ̄, 一 嘴 澇

| 涎, zonder tusschen poozen spreken, babbelen.

sa liêm tit toà, 相 | 滯 帶, met elkander in betrekking staan.

bô sa liêm tih toà, 無 相 | 滯 帶, niet met elkander te maken hebben, onzamenhangen.

lô liêm hiu, 滂 | 香, harsachtige lijm, (om potten digt te maken.)

ts'iú liêm, 手 |, zich met de hand stijf aan iets vasthouden.

k'a ts'iú liêm tsiép, 脚 手 | 緊, handig vlug, (met de handen en ter been).

si (of pák) sa liêm, 生 相 |, aan elkander gegroeid of gebonden, steeds de hulp van een tweede behoeven.

廉 Liêm Onbedorven, eerlijk, zedig, modest.

ts'ing liêm ê koa, 清 | 之 官, een eerlijk ambtenaar.

liêm t'i, | 耻, zedig, modest.

bô liêm t'i, 無 | 恥, onbeschaamd.

put liêm ê ts'uì, 不 | 的 口, alles zeggen wat hem voor den mond komt; alles eten wat hem voorgezet wordt.

ióng liêm ê gûn, 養 | 之 銀, geld om eerlijkheid te bewaren, *d. i.* emolumenten.

hōng liêm, 俸 |, traktement en emolumenten.

奩 Liêm *tseng liêm*, 粧 |, huwelijks uitzet, bruidschat.

臁 Liêm *k'a liêm*, 脚 |, scheenbeen.

鐮 Liêm *k'ao liêm*, 鈎 |, soort sikkel.

簾 Liêm Deurscherm, fig. vrouwenvertrek, vrouwen.

tuì laī liêm k'i, 對 內 | 去, van het vrouwenvertrek uitgaan, *d. i.* beginnen met de vrouw des huizes over iets te spreken.

Liêm *liēm k'a tè ts'iú* / *» » toè »*, | 脚 低 手, op de teenen loopen en met de handen volgen, onverwijld.

liêm pi, liēm si, liêm pi si, | 邊, | 時 | 邊 時, terstond, onmiddelijk.

念 Liēm Denken over, aan, herdenken gedachtig zijn; opzeggen prevelen, (als gebeden uitspreken; uit het hoofd opzeggen.

k'oà liēm (of koà), | 掛, steeds denken aan; zich ongerust maken.

siaò liēm, 賬 |, herdenken, steeds denken aan.

kì liēm, 記 |, steeds denken aan.

liēm tsing, | 情, steeds dankbaarheid voor iemand gevoelen.

sīm sīm liēm liēm, 心 匕 | 匕, steeds aan iets denken.

liēm king, 經 |, gebeden opzeggen opdreunen.

liēm hút, 佛 |, Boeddha aanroepen.

liēm kòng, liēm ts'iù, | 咒, | 詛 vervloeking over iemand uitspreken (van de priesters in Siam gezegd.)

liēm dzù, dzù liēm, tsáp liēm, liēm kòng, | 紛, 紛 |, 雜 |, verward spreken, ijlen, (in een ziekte.

sám liēm, liēm o liēm péh, 滲 |, 黑 | 白, verward, krankzinnig spreken.

naḡh naḡh liēm, 樂 匕 |, binnensmonds prevelen, mompelen.

liēm ts'eh, | 册, zijn les uit het hoofd opzeggen.

oát liēm, 越 |, uit het hoofd opzeggen.

捻 *tsit liēm*, 一 |, een handvol.
Liēm *liēm kûn t'aô bû*, | 羣 頭 毋, de vuist ballen.

殮 *liēm tsó*, | 祖, een lijk omzwachtelen.
Liēm

鐮 Hokjes in een klokhuis.
Liēm

Lien

撚 *k'ing lien kui* } 捲 |, omkrullen, kromtrekken.
Lien

姸 *hoe lien ts'ùi*, 花 | 嘴, mooie maar
Lien ongemeende taal.

嗹 *lōng lien liú ê lâng*, 弄 | 柳 之
Lien 人, een leeglooper, iemand die niets voor de kost doet.

撚 In de hand rollen, rollen; draaijen, in-
Lién draaijen; met een streek krijgen.

tsoá lién, 紙 |, gerolde fidibus.

lién tsoān, | 攢, een schroef indraaijen, met een streek iemand laten betalen.

lién hī, | 耳, de ooren schoonpeuteren.

lién p'ī k'ang, | 鼻 孔, in de neus kittelen.

lién soà, | 線, garen, draad, draaijen.

poàh lién pó, 賭 | 寶, op een draaibord spelen, oorspr, zette men in op de plaats waar men dacht dat het karakter *pó* zou komen.

lién pó king, | 寶 間, speelhuis.

lién p'ak ts'iò, | 朴 笑, een duit doen draaijen en zien of ze kruis of munt zal vatten.

lién ting tong, | 丁 冬, twee duiten do.

lién lâng ê tsî, | 人 之 財, iemand geld afzetten.

gaô lién k'ang, 善 | 孔, knap zijn in het vinden van een oorzaak om iemand te laten betalen.

lién tsìng, | 鑽, indraaijen, inboren.

lién dzip kòng, | 入 壙, (een dood kist,) over rollen in het graf neer laten.

輦 Oorspr. voertuig door menschen voort-
Lién getrokken; draagkoets waarin afgodsbeelden gedragen worden.

lién kiō, | 轎, draagkoets voor afgodsbeelden.

ts'ia lién, 車 |, groote do.

lién tsî, | 錢, rollen onder een wagen; steekplaat ter bescherming van de hand bij een zwaard.

koaī lién koe } 乖 |, zonderling, raar, niet frisch, niet wel.

pō lién lai, 步 | 來, te voet komen, komen loopen.

臉 Wang; gezigt, gelaat; fatsoen, goede
Lién naam.

pièn lién, 變 |, van gelaat veranderen *d. i.* vertoornd worden.

k'iū lién, 發 |, eensklaps opstuiven.

lién biēn, | 面, fatsoen, goede naam

kò (of *sioh*) *lién biēn*, 顧 | 面, voor zijn reputatie zorgen.

put kò lién, 不 顧 |, niet om zijn fatsoen geven.

sit lién, 失 |, zijn fatsoen te krabbelen gooijen, een mal figuur slaan.

siu lién, 羞 |, do.

滾 Omrollen.
Lièn *lièn piah tsî*, | 壁 錢, met geld gooijen, wie het digtste bij de muur gooit.

lin lièn kiù, 球 流 連, met ballen rollen, kegelen.

連 Vereenigen, verbinden, bij elkander
Lien voegen, op elkander volgen, achtereen, achtereenvolgens; aan een, medeslepen, betrekken in, benevens, zelfs.

su lièn, 双 |, vereenigen, vereenigd, aan elkander.

lièn soà, su lièn lì toà, | 續, 相 | 滯 帶, aan elkander verbonden, zamenhangen.

su lièn soà, 相 | 續, achtereenvolgens.

lièn tsaî, | 財, geld meêbrengen, (als compagnons in eene zaak.)

lièn lì ts'iū, | 理 樹, in elkander gegroeide boomen.

lièn hiu, | 鄉, aangrenzend dorp.

lièn hoàn ts'ìng, | 環 銃, achtereenvolgend aangehouden geweervuur.

lièn miṇ, | 名, handteekeningen onder elkander zetten.

kao ki lièn, 交 枝 |. ingewikkeld.

lièn kị, | 格, vlegel.

lièn luī, | 類, betrekken, medeslepen in.

lièn p'aò, | 炮, rist sissers.

k'an lièn tioh, 牽 | 着, in eene zaak medeslepen, betrekken.

lièn kuī, | 櫃, toonbank; (voor in den winkel.)

t'oa saí lièn, 拖 屎 |, eene zaak onafgedaan, er een staart aanlaten.

lièn lièn, | |, achtereenvolgens gedurig.

lièn dzit è hō, | 日 下 雨, een geheelen dag of twee dagen aan elkander regen.

lièn pīng iā bò t'ang tsiáh, | 飯 也 無 可 食, hij heeft zelfs geen rijst om te eten.

年 Jaar, ouderdom.
Lièn *lièn kì*, | 紀, ouderdom.

siaò lièn, 少 |, jong.

lièn hù lik kiòng, | 富 力 强, nog vele jaren te leven hebben en krachtig zijn, (tegen jongelieden gezegd.)

蓮 De Lotus, waterlelie.
Lièn *lièn hoe*, | 花, waterlelie.

lièn hoe paî, | 花 牌, cylinder van een horlogie.

kim lièn, 金 |, gouden lelies, *d. i.* kleine vrouwenvoeten.

lièn pọ, | 房, zaaddoos van der Lotus.

lièn su / » *si* } | 鬚, meeldraden.

lièn naō, | 藕, Lotus wortel.

lièn tsiao kiet kó, | 蕉 桔 果, de Lotus, pisang, lemoenen en vruchten (als geschenken bij huwelijk geven.)

鰱 *lièn hî*, | 魚, groote karper.
Lièn

聯 *mìng lièn*, 門 |, opschriften op den
Lièn posten.

lièn tuì, | 對, tegenover elkander hangende spreuken.

lièn pièn, | 匾, afhangende geschriften en opschriften, (boven de deur.)

tah lièn, 搭 |, groote beurs, die men bij het ophalen van geld over de schouders hangt.

零 *pah lièn sa*, 百 | 三, honderd en
Lièn drie.

鍊 Smeden; grondig beoefenen.
Liēn *liēn t'ih*, | 鐵, ijzersmeden.

t'oàn lièn, koàn lièn, 煆 丨, 眷 丨, grondig beoefenen,

鏈 Liēn Keten, ketting; ketenen.

kim liēn, 金 丨, gouden keten.

gûn liēn á, 銀 丨 仔, zilveren kettingje.

īng t'ih liēn liēn, 用 鉄 丨 乚, aan een ijzeren ketting vast ketenen.

tó koā liēn, 斗 掛 丨, ketting waaraan de Chin. hun beurs dragen.

koā liēn, 掛 丨, ketenendragen, kettingganger zijn.

煉 Liēn Metalen zuiveren; op de proef stellen.

liēn tan, 丨 丹, de pil van onsterfelijkheid maken, (van Taoisten.)

liēn sien, 丨 仙, over koetjes en kalfjes spreken.

ts'ì liēn, 試 丨, op de proef stellen, beproeven.

練 Liēn Zich oefenen in, beoefenen; exerceeren, drillen.

lik liēn, laó liēn, 歷 丨, 老 丨, herhaalde, langdurige oefening, ondervinding.

ts'ao liēn, 抄 丨, exerceeren, drillen.

king liēn, 經 丨, ondervinding hebben van, beoefend hebben

kaò liēn, 教 丨, voldoende, grondige, beoefening, ondervinding in iets.

ts'ao kûn liēn k'ik, 抄 拳 丨 曲, boksen en zingen (moet men) beoefenen, onderhouden.

Liep

聶 Liep Familienaam.

攝 Liep *liep king,* 丨 景, vereenigen, bij elkander brengen, rimpelen, (als het gelaat van een oud mensch.)

liēp lí, 理 丨, tegelijkertijd, tijdelijk waarnemen.

mō liep pát lâng ê dzī hō, 慕 丨 他 人 之 字 號, valschelijk iemands merk aannemen.

粒 Liėp Numer. voor zaadkorrels, knoopen, kogels, enz.

toā liėp, 大 丨, dik van ligchaam, dapper.

toā liėp bing, 大 丨 猛, groot en sterk.

liėp tsik, 丨 積, opsparen, sprokkelen,

k'ioh liėp, 抽 丨, klein, kiddig van gestalte,

bí liėp liėp, 米 丨 乚, korrelig, drooggekookt, van rijst.

kap i liėp, 與 伊 丨, goede vrienden met hem zijn.

liėp liėp kan sin k'ó, 丨 乚 艱 辛 苦, met veel moeite en opoffering opgespaard hebben,

bí liėp, 米 丨, rijstkorrel.

hoat liėp á, 發 丨 仔, puistjes hebben.

捏 Liėp *liėp ts'iú siòh,* 丨 手 油, met zweeterige handen hanteren.

liėp t'ô, 丨 土, aarde bij elkander pakken, kneden.

īng ts'iú liėp, 用 手 丨, in de hand kneden, vormen, (als porselein.)

Liet

列 Liét Uit elkander zetten, rangschikken, rij als soldaten of huizen.

pâi liét, 排 丨, uit elkander zetten, rangschikken; klaar zetten.

45

k'ai liét liét, 開 ｜ 匕, wagenwijd open.

liét toa̤, ｜ 單, eene rekening opmaken.

k'ai liét, 開 ｜, gespecificeerd opteekenen, (als op eene rekening.)

liét uī, ｜ 位, gij mijne heeren, gij lieden, (bel. uitdr.)

tsiā liét, 且 ｜, de geheele rij.

siang ping liét, 相 平 ｜, aan beide kanten in eene rij, (als winkels in eene straat.)

烈 Liét — Brandend heet; vurig, opvliegend; ten toppunt, in hoogsten bloei; kuisch.

liét liét haó, ｜ 匕 吼, een krassend geluid geven als het scheuren van goed, wind, enz.

sìng liét, liét sìng, 性 ｜, ｜ 性, opvliegend van aard, vurig.

sìng tè liét liét, 性 地 ｜ 匕, do.

sè t'aô liét liét liét, sè bin tńg liét, 梳 頭 ｜ ｜ ｜, 洗 面 轉 ｜, op het toppunt van magt, aanzien zijn.

liét lú, ｜ 女, eene kuische vrouw.

tsiet liét, 節 ｜, kuisch. eerbaar.

Lim

飲 Lim — Drinken.

lim tsiú, ｜ 酒, wijndrinken.

sán lim, wijn drinken zonder er iets bij te hebben.

lim t'iù kìng p'ah, ｜ 篩 摃 打, orgie houden.

lim tseh tsip tseh, ｜ 試 少 許, even van iets proeven, niet veel van drinken.

lim tioh, ｜ 着, er tegen aangeloopen zijn.

臨 Lím — *lím kī*, ｜ 墘, digt bij de kan, op het randje.

lím k'ièn lím k'ièn, op het randje af.

幾 Lím — *lím lím*, ｜ 匕, juist.

lím lím kaù ìng / " " " iōng ｜ 匕 足 用, juist genoeg, het heeft niet over.

k'ah lím, 無 ｜, minder.

Lìm — *lìm tsit k'ik*, ｜ 一 刻, wacht eventjes.

廩 Lím — Bezoldigde *siù tsai*, ｜ 生, *lím sing*.

凜 Lím — *ui hong lím lím*, 威 風 ｜ 匕, een deftige grootsche houding.

lím lím tsit k'ik, ｜ 匕 一 刻, zoo pas.

臨 Lîm — *lîm tsiong*, ｜ 終, op zijn uiterste liggend.

lîm p'ûn, ｜ 盆, in barensnood zijn.

lîm si, ｜ 時, als het oogenblik daar is.

lîm sin, ｜ 身, op zijn persoon komen, zijn persoon treffen.

林 Lîm — Familienaam.

hān lîm, 翰 ｜, hoogste litt. graad.

淋 Lîm — *soa lîm*, 沙 ｜, graveel.

kik lîm, 激 ｜, steen in de blaas.

tsioh lîm, 石 ｜, do.

huih lîm / hoeh " 血 ｜, bloed urine.

hō lîm li, 雨 ｜ 漓, hevige stortregen,

霖 Lîm — *ts'iu lîm*, 秋 ｜, hevige herfstregen.

kam lîm, 甘 ｜, weldadige regen.

盈 Lîm — (*tsui*) *lîm lîm*, (水) ｜ 匕, boordevol

Lin

奶 Melk, borst, (van een vrouw.)
Lin *gû lin*, 牛 丨, koemelk.
Ling *gû lin iû*, 牛 乳 油, boter.
gû lin piá, 牛 丨 餅, kaas.
lin koàn, 丨 礶, melkkan.
tīng lin / *tuī ling* } 斷 丨, van de melk afnemen, spenen.
mîng lin / *muî ling* } 門 丨, knop van een deur.
p'ong lin, 腫 丨, dik door de moedermelk, (als jonge kinderen.)
lin t'aô, 丨 頭, tepel van de borst.
si lin hó / *se ling* » } 生 乳 虎, zwerende borst.
lin iong / *ling iong* } 丨 癰, do.
lin ts'ang īm t'aó, 丨 葱 不 透, verstopping in den tepel.
pao á lin, 包 仔 丨, ronde kleine borst.
pò tē lin, 布 袋 丨, hangende borst.
suh lin / *soh* » } 吸 丨, aan de borst zuigen.
lin sún, (of *tsūn*), 丨 瘨, volheid van de borst.
Lin *lin long kó*, 丨 瓏 鼓, rammelaar, (zoo als de rondventers gebruiken.)
圓 *lin lin gô*, 丨 匕 遨, rondslingeren.
Lin *lin lin tíng*, 丨 匕 轉, do.
lin lin, 丨 , zuiverrond.
lin lin sêh, 丨 匕 走, ronddraaijen, (als een rad).
sêh lin lin, 走 丨 匕, ronddraaijen, rondgaan.
lin lin long long, geluid van kanonschoten.

爾 Gij lieden,
Lín *lin taī ke*, 丨 大 衆, gij allen.
滾 Rollen als een bal.
Lìn *kō kō lìn*, 猴 匕 丨, iets rond laten rollen.
seh tsit lìn, 轉 一 丨, ééns rond gaan, ronddraaijen.
tsit lìn téng, 一 丨 轉, een keer rond.
lìn kiû, 丨 球, ballen rollen, kegelen,
toa sin ts'ut lai lìn, 大 身 出 來 丨, alleen alle zorgen, moeielijkheden hebben,
lìn kaù tsit sì koè, 丨 到 一 世 界, overal heenzwerven.
憐 Medelijden hebben met, bejammeren.
Lin *lin bin*, 丨 憫, medelijden hebben met.
k'it ai kiù lin, 乞 哀 求 丨, ontferming en medelijdend afsmeeken.
goá lin ìh, 我 丨 憫 伊, ik heb medelijden met hem.
k'ó lin, 可 丨, het is te betreuren; medelijden hebben met.
lin sut ìh, 丨 恤 伊, medelijdend behandelen.
tông pīng siong lin, 同 病 相 丨, die aan dezelfde ziekte lijden hebben medelijden met elkander, *d. i.* die in dezelfde benarde omstandigheden verkeeren kennen elkanders leed.
鄰 Naburig, aangrenzend; buren.
Lin *lin iū*, *ts'ù pī lin iū*, 丨 右, 厝 邊 丨 右, de buren.
p'ò lin, 舖 丨, de buren, (oorspr, alleen van winkels gezegd.)
麟 Wijfje, van het kameelpaald, (giraffe.)
Lin *ki lin*, 麒 丨, mannetje en wijfje.

p'a ki lin, 撈 麒 ｜, op de handen dwars overbuitelen.

綾 Damast.
Lin *hoe lin*, 花 ｜, gebloemd damast.

pèh lin, 白 ｜. wit damast.

p'oá âng lin, 掛 紅 ｜. een stuk rood damast overwerpen. (over de draagstoel van bruid en bruidegom.)

吝 *kien lin*, 慳 ｜. gierig.
Līn *p'i lin*, 鄙 ｜. do.

Ling

奶 Melk.
Ling *ling k'i*, ｜ 齒. melktanden.

乳 Uijer, borst.
Ling *làt ling*, 律 ｜. melken.

ling bú } ｜ 母. zoogster min.
» bó

ts'iu ling, 樹 ｜. boomsap.

iâ ling, 椰 ｜. kokosmelk.

ming ling } 門 ｜. knop van de deur.
muî »

io ling, 搖 ｜. op een kind passen en het de borst geven.

nâ aò tsing ling á, 咽 喉 腫 ｜ 仔, lelletje in de keel.

寬 *ling k'i*, ｜ 去. afnemend, minder.
Ling dikwijls.

pàng ling ling, 放 ｜ 匕. slap laten hangen, loslaten, speling aan eene zaak laten.

tsit ē ling ku nū dzit, 一 下 ｜ 幾 多 日. laat men iets ééns loopen dan gaan er verscheidene dagen meė om.

ling ling ling, ｜ ｜ ｜. zeer dralend, langzaam in zijne handelingen.

冷 Koel, frisch.
Líng *lìng tsui*, ｜ 水, koud water.

liâng lìng. 涼 ｜. koelmaken.

pùn lìng, 噴 ｜, koel blazen.

lìng tâm, ｜ 淡, koud, koeltjes, ontvangen, behandelen, bedaard (van een plaats), flaauw in handel.

ts'in lìng, 凊 ｜, koel, frisch.

lìng ts'iò, ｜ 笑, minachtend lachen

sim koa lìng, 心 肝 ｜, koud voor iets zijn, niet meer aan iets denken

lìng tsing, ｜ 靜, eene vrouw niet kunnen bevruchten.

lìng to sat dzin, ｜ 刀 殺 人 koelbloedig iemand benadeelen.

lìng tsui t'èng t'ē, ｜ 水 脫 鮀 door bedaard te blijven iemand nog driftiger maken.

lìng gē làng, ｜ 拂 人. iemand koel weg sarren. (door spreken.)

lìng tîm làng, ｜ 朕 人, bedaard weg iemand sarren, (b. v. door iets niet gaauw te willen doen.)

伶 *lìng lî*, ｜ 俐. schrander.
Ling

領 *lìng tsing*, ｜ 情, voor lief aannemen
Ling *sing lìng* } 誠 ｜. ontvangen, aannemen.
sin »

lìng kaò, ｜ 教, iemands onderwijzing, vermaning aannemen.

t'òng lìng, 統 ｜. aanvoeren, het opperbevel hebben over, (soldaten.)

跉 Schoppen met de voet.
Lìng *lìng tó*, ｜ 倒. omschoppen.
Liàng *lìng k'ui ih*, 推 開. iemand v...

zich afstooten, niets met hem te maken willen hebben.

lîng k'a, ｜ 脚, met de voeten schoppen.

k'a lîng ts'iú lîng, 脚 ｜ 手 ｜, met handen en voeten spartelen als jonge kinderen.

óah lîng lîng, 活 ｜ 匕, springlevend.

kún lîng, 滾 ｜, zich kronkelen en spartelen (als een gevatten slang.)

king lîng, 揀 ｜, actief, knap, van alles partij weten te trekken.

龍 Draak.
Ling

ling hê, ｜ 蝦, kreeft.

ling kao ling hông kao hông, ｜ 交 ｜ 鳳 交 鳳, draken gaan met draken, feniksen met feniksen om, *d. i.* een ieder heeft zijn kring.

sì bé ling hê tiah, 四 尾 ｜ 蝦, de vier uitsteeksels (pooten) van een kreeft uittrekken, *d. i.* alle mogelijke zwarigheden uit den weg ruimen.

ling ho̤ ki, ｜ 虎 旗, draken en tijger vlag, blaauw of rood.)

ling tsûn, ｜ 船, booten die bij het drakenfeest gebruikt worden.

ling tsûn kut, ｜ 船 骨, ruggegraat.

tsui ling, 水 ｜, brandspuit.

hé ling, 火 ｜, lont.

hé ling hé bé, 火 ｜ 火 馬, als een vuurdraak en vuurpaard, zeer snel.

oáh kà ná ling nih, 活 到 如 ｜, spring levend.

ling pô̤, ｜ 袍, overkleed met draken geborduurd.

ling hiét, ｜ 穴, *lett.* drakengat, gat voor een graf.

ling hó̤ sio taù ku pih siū tsoē }
hông » siang tò̤ » » » tsai } ｜

虎 相 鬪 龜 鱉 受 罪, vechten de draak en de tijger dan krijgen de schildpadden er de straf voor, *d. i.* hebben grooten twist dan lijden de kleineren er onder.

hai ling òng, 海 ｜ 王, zeedraak, Neptunus.

toē ling tin tāng, 地 ｜ 展 動, de aarddraak beweegt zich, (bij eene aardbeving.)

ling king tsui, ｜ 絞 水, de draak trekt het water op, bij een waterhoos.

靈 Geest, geestelijk; ziel, overblijvende
Ling geest van afgestorvenen; met boven natuurlijke kracht bezield als een afgod; schrander, helder van verstand.

ling hûn, ｜ 魂, de ziel.

ling ts'ù, ｜ 厝, geesten huis, (van papier ter eere van overledenen verbrand.)

tû ling, 除 ｜, de rouw toebereidselen verbranden.

k'iā ling, 竪 ｜, in den rouw zijn, (van een huis.)

ling ùi, ｜ 位, zetel, tablet van een overleden persoon.

sim ling, 神 ｜, heldere denkvermogens.

ling t'ong, ｜ 通, scherpzinnig, knap, helder van geest.

ling kám, ｜ 感, krachtdadig, de gebeden verhoorend, (van afgoden.)

ling ìng, ｜ 應, do.

能 Kunnen, het vermogen bezitten om:
Ling verstandelijke vermogens, verstand, verstandig.

tsai ling, 材 ｜, verstand.

ling gièn } | 言, welbespraakt, goed
« *gàn* } ter spraak.

ling kàn, | 諫, knap.

ling oàn, | 完, knappe lagere mandarijn.

翎 **Ling** Veer; paauwen of kraaijen veer, (op mandarijn mutsen gedragen.)

tsi̱ ling, 箭 |, de veeren van een pijl.

hoe ling, 花 |, veelkleurige paauwen veer.

toa̱ gán ling, 單 眼 |, paauwenveer met één oog.

o̱ 'a ling, 烏 鴉 |, kraaijenveer.

làm ling, 藍 |, blauwe kraaijenveer.

伶 **Ling** *ling laī*, | 利, knap, schrander.

ling lī, | 俐, do. ook zindelijk, (van vrouwen).

淩 **Ling** Verdrukken, wreed behandelen.

ling dziók, | 辱, verdrukken.

ling ti, | 遲, langzaam doodmartelen.

凌 **Ling** Familienaan.

寧 **Ling** *ling k'o̱*, . . . | 口, beter is het om . . . .

勒 **Ling** *ling bé*, | 馬, een paard inhouden.

滰 **Ling** *kè ling*, 過 |, door een doek of papier filtreren.

稜 **Ling** *ts'iù ling*, 酒 |, kranen aan een wijnvat.

棱 **Ling** *sì ling*, 楧 |, vier rabatten, (lands.)

銘 **Ling** *ling tsing*, 旌 |, strook rood doek waarop met gele karakters den naam, betrekking, enz. van eene overledene gewerkt is.

寬 **Līng** Los, niet vast, verloopen, (van een schroef.)

k'ah n'ng līng 較 弛 |, zachter, slapper.

pàng līng, 放 |, loslaten.

līng ling, | |, do.

k'oan līng, 寬 |, los, niet te sterk, uitstel voor iets geven.

liōng līng, 亮 |, meer dan noodig is.

令 **Līng** *ling tsun*, | 尊, mijn heer Uw vader.

līng sien tsun, | 先 尊, wijlen do.

ling tòng, | 堂, Uwe moeder, (eeren.)

līng sien tòng, | 先 堂, wijlen do.

ling tsìng, | 正, Uwe vrouw.

līng sien tsìng, | 先 正, wijlen Uwe vrouw.

līng lòng, | 郎, Uw zoon.

līng ki, | 旗, bevelsvlag.

līng tsi̱, | 箭, pijl aan gewigtige dépêches gehecht.

t'oàn līng, 傳 |, een bevel bekend maken.

bīng līng, 命 |, bevelen.

hō līng, 號 |, bevel, commando door seinen of trompetten gegeven.

另 **Līng** *līng goā*, | 外, behalve dat nog . . . . buitengewoon . . . . , al te . . . . .

līng goā hē, | 外 放, afzonderlijk, apart leggen.

līng dzit, | 日, op een anderen dag.

kui līng, 全 |, een striem vormen. (als door een slag.)

翎 **Līng** *pėh ling si*, 白 | 鷺, reiger.

k'eh bàng á k'a līng tioh, 被 蚊 子 脚 | 着, door een muskieten poot getrapt worden; zegt men tot een kleinzeerig mensch.

ka ling, 膠 ｜, ekster.

Lio

剖 Horizontaal doorsnijden.

Liö *k'iu k'iu á liö k'i lai*, 輕 揺 起, voorzigtig bij elkander schrappen, afscheppen.

liö iû, ｜ 油, het vet van boven afscheppen.

liö p'ē, ｜ 皮, de schil afsnijden, schillen.

liö tsit ē bīn, ｜ 一 个 面, den bovenkant afsnijden.

Liok

六 Zes.

Liók *liók t'iok*, ｜ 畜, de zes huisdieren.

liók bû ts'it tsoát ē lâng, ｜ 無 七 絶 之 人, iemand die alleen op aarde staat, (sterk scheldw.)

liók pō, ｜ 部, de zes ministeriën.

p'ah siang liók, 打 雙 ｜, dubbele zes opzetten, (in het domino spel.)

liók p'ûh tsoân baóh, ｜ 色 全 收, gooit men met alle zes de dobbelsteenen hetzelfde dan wint men alles.

liók tsik, ｜ 賊, *oorspr.* de zes roovers, ooren, oogen, neus, tong, hart en begeerten die volgens de Boeddh. den mensch verderven, van daar van iemand gezegd, iemand die zich aan allerlei kwaad schuldig maakt.

陸 Land in tegenoverstelling van water; familienaam.

Liók *liók lō ping*, ｜ 路 燈, landtroepen.

liók tsièn, ｜ 戰, veldslag.

liók siók, ｜ 續, achtereen, achtereenvolgens.

畧 Verkort, beknopt, in het algemeen, oppervlakkig, ongeveer.

Liók
Liák *kán liók*, 降 ｜, beknopt,

taī liók, 大 ｜, in het algemeen, ongeveer.

iok liók, 約 ｜, do.

p'ó liók, 頗 ｜, do.

liók liók, ｜ 七, oppervlakkig.

iông iông liók liók ē lâng, 庸 七 ｜ 七 之 人, een oppervlakkig, middelmatig mensch.

liók siók, ｜ 續, ongeveer.

錄 Afschrift, uittreksel maken.

Liók *liók k'i lai goá k'oà*, ｜ 起 來 我 看, maak er voor mij een afschrift uittreksel van (als uit een koopmans boek.)

bók liók, 目 ｜, index.

pò liók, ｜ 報, nieuwsblad waarin de afloop van examina, enz. wordt opgegeven.

boē liók, 賣 ｜, afschriften van proclamaties, enz., rondventen.

Liong

兩 *it kú liông tik* / *it ki liáng* 一 舉 ｜ 得, dit heeft een dubbeld voordeel.

Lióng *lióng ping*, ｜ 邊, aan beide kanten.

lióng pien ē lâng, ｜ 邊 之 人, de menschen aan beide kanten.

lióng piēn, ｜ 便, beide partijen hebben hun zin.

lióng hú sióng, ｜ 抵 双, met elkander gelijk te zijn; niets van elkander te vorderen hebben.

lióng tsō, ｜造, beide pleitende partijen.

Liòng *liòng t'in*, ｜暢, verheugd, vrolijk, wulpsch.

量 *siong liòng* / *siang liâng* } 商｜, beraadslagen.

Liòng *mịh kūng lâng liòng k'ih*, 物向人｜去, half uit gekheid iemands goed wegnemend.

良 *liòng sim*, ｜心, een goed hart, ook

Liòng voor het geweten gebruikt.

tsiaò t'ien li liòng sim, 照天理｜心, volgens regt en billijkheid.

bò liòng sim, 無｜心, geen menschelijk gevoel hebben.

liòng bin, ｜民, goed volk, gehoorzame onderdanen.

sim liòng, 心｜, gedwee, gehoorzaam.

liòng sim hoat hiān, ｜心發現, zijn goed hart kwam voor den dag.

liòng ka lú tsú, ｜家女子, eene dochter van gegoede familie.

liòng si kiet dzit, ｜時吉日, gelukkige tijd, dag.

龍 *kiú liòng poâ*, 九｜盤, confituren-

Liông bak met negen afdeelingen; sambalbak.

狼 *liòng poē*, ｜狽, in verval ellende,

Liông (eig. twee soorten van wolven die niet zonder elkander kunnen loopen.

諒 Denken, het er voor houden.

Liōng *sióng liōng*, 商｜, het er voorhouden

Liāng dat....

liōng bò an ni, ｜無如此, ik geloof dat het niet zoo is.

liōng pit, ... ｜必, het er stellig voorhouden dat.

liōng tsing, ｜情, niet kwalijk nemen, vergeven.

t'é liōng, 體｜, vergeven, verontschuldigen.

讓 Toegevendheid gebruiken, geven.

Liōng. *liōng ìh* / *(niō)* „ } ｜伊, wees wat toegevend voor hem.

ts'iá liōng tsit pō, 且｜一步, eilieve geef wat toe.

隆 *liōng sīng*, ｜盛, overvloedig, meer

Liōng den genoeg.

量 Afmeten, bepaling; verdragen, verdraag-

Liōng zaamheid.

liōng k'ah ke, ｜較多, meer afmeten, meer nemen, dan men denkt noodig te hebben.

liōng liōng liōng, ｜｜｜, zeer ruim, meer dan genoeg.

tsat liōng, 相｜, afmeten, bepalen. (naar zijn capaciteit.)

tō liōng, 度｜, aard, verdraagzaamheid.

hó liōng, 好｜, verdraagzaam.

bò liōng, 無｜, onverdraagzaam.

ū toā liōng, 有大｜, grootmoedig.

ū liōng, 有｜, verdraagzaam; over hebben, meer dan genoeg.

tsiú liōng, 酒｜, capaciteit voor wijn.

ts'ién liōng, 淺｜, weinig kunnen verdragen, bekrompen.

hái liōng, 海｜, veel kunnen verdragen (als wijn); langmoedig.

liōng tìng bò liōn té, ｜長無｜短, men mag wel te lang maar niet te kort meten.

Liu

抽 Liu　Trekken, uittrekken; uithalen, afnemen van; ontsnappen.

liu k'ao, ｜鬮, een lot trekken, loten.

t'ao liu k'ì, 偷｜去, ontfutselen.

liu ts'iu ê lâng, ｜楸之人, bedriegers, schurken.

liu ts'iu tsiàh bák tsiu, ｜楸眘目周, naar de omstandigheden handelen.

liu k'a kiâ tāng, ｜脚行動, zich uit de voeten maken, (als voor schuldeischers).

liu k'ì, ｜去, ontsnappen.

liu liu k'ì, ｜匕去, regt doorgaan, (zonder terug te komen.)

ts'ing k'ì liu liu, 清去｜匕, zeer schoon, zindelijk.

榴 Liu　*liu lien*, ｜連, doerian.

bé liu, 尾｜, eind, uiteinde, achteraan.

tè bé liu, 隨尾｜, achteraan volgen.

liu bé, ｜尾, op zijn eind loopen, in verval geraken.

liu k'ì, ｜去, langzamerhand verminderen.

kiu kiu liu liu, 救匕｜匕, nederig, bedeesd; beschroomd.

k'iù k'iù liu liu, 虯匕｜匕, krimpen, krimtrekken.

Liu　*ts'aò kaó liu*, hondenlucht.

鈕 Liú　Knoop; familienaam, toeknoopen.

liú á, ｜仔, knoop.

liú k'aò, ｜扣, knoopsgat.

liú p'àn, ｜攀, knoopslus.

liú sa, ｜衫, zijn jas toeknoopen.

扭 Liú　Beetpakken, vasthouden; trekken aanhalen.

liú lak, ｜扐, met geweld vasthouden, (om tot betaling te dwingen, enz.)

k'iú k'iú liú liú, 楸匕｜匕, van alle kanten beetpakken.

liú oá lai, ｜倚來, naar zich toetrekken.

liú oá hoā, ｜倚岸, naar den wal toetrekken, (als een vaartuig.)

liú ân, liú kin, ｜緊、｜緊, stijf-aanhalen.

綹 Liú　*tsit liú mī soà*, 一｜麵線, een knot vermicelli.

tsién liú, 剪｜, zakkenrollen.

k'it i liú k'ì, 被其｜去, ontstolen worden.

柳 Liú　Wilg; familienaam.

liú ts'iū, ｜樹, wilgenboom.

liú hiòh bai, ｜葉眉, lange dunne wenkbraauwen.

liú tiaò t'ang, ｜條窻, raam met dunne vensterboutjes.

hoa liú bòk, 花｜木, rozenhout.

脫 Liù　Afdoen, uitdoen, uittrekken, uittrafelen, uitvallen, afschaven.

liù bō, ｜帽, zijn muts afschuiven.

liù keng t'aò, ｜光｜頭, blootshoofds.

liù keng keng, ｜光匕, naakt.

liù k'ò, 褲｜, uittrafelen, zijn broek, uittrekken.

liù k'í lai, ｜起來, opschorten, (als een broek.)

liù p'ê, ｜皮, het vel afschaven.

46

liù mîng, | 毛, uitvallen van de hoofdharen.

liù hiáh, | 額, uitvallen van de schedelharen.

溜 Liù *lóh liù*, 落 |, in een draaikolk komen, van schepen.

liù tó tsaó, | 逃 走, eensklaps wegvloeien, ontsnappen.

套 Liù Strik, valstrik, strikken leggen, verstrikken, bedriegen, beetnemen.

liù k'o̱, | 箍, strik, valstrik.

p'ah oáh liù, 打 活 |. eene loopende strik leggen.

lóh liù, 落 |, in iemands strik vallen.

saí tò liù, 用 倒 |, een loopende strik leggen; iemand achterom bedriegen.

k'it i liù k'i, 被 其 | 去, in iemands strik gevangen worden.

sì koè liù lâng, 四 處 | 人, anderen op allerlei manieren beetnemen.

liù niaó ts'ú, | 鳥 鼠, ratten verstrikken.

kiaó liù, 賭 |. doorkneede dobbelaar.

liù á po̱, | 仔 步, list, streek.

流 Liû Vloeijen, stroomen; doorgaan, doorreizen, omzwerven; verspreiden; verbanden, eene soort, klasse, stand.

p'iao liû, 飄 |, voortdrijven, (als een roerloos schip) overal omzwerven.

liû lóh, liû lok, | 落, rondzwerven.

lûn liû, 輪 |, om de beurt doen.

liû kè kui no̱ sing, | 過 幾 省, verscheidene provinciën doorgezworven hebben.

liû t'ong, | 通, overal doorgaan, gangbaar zijn.

liû t'oân, | 傳, alom mededeelen.

liû tô̱, | 徒, verbannen.

mīng liû, 問 |, tot verbanning veroordeelen.

liû hoān, | 犯, bannelingen.

liû bin, | 民, leegloopers.

hā liû, 下 |, lage volksklasse.

liû kaì, | 界, bedelaar.

put dzip liû ê lâng, 不 入 | 之 人, iemand die niet tot dien stand, graad kan gerekend worden.

liû ts'e, | 差, *oorspr*, transporteur van bannelingen; steeds uitloopen, zelden te huis zijn.

it liû sui, 一 | 水, geheel en al van dezelfde kwaliteit.

sam kaò kiú liû, 三 教 九 |, de drie sekten en negen lage standen, (waarzegger, enz.)

留 Liû Laten blijven, niet willen laten weggaan als een gast; doen overblijven, overhouden; in den geest houden, met het hart bij iets zijn.

tao liû, 挽 |. laten blijven, terughouden.

liû tsûn, | 存, overlaten (als spijzen).

liû ì, liû sin, | 意, | 神, steeds gedachtig zijn.

liû sim, | 心, met het hart bij iets, voorzigtig.

榴 Liû *siā liû* / *séh* » { 石 |, granaatappel.

瘤 Liû Gezwel, uitwas, wen.

si̱ liû, 生 |, een gezwel, wen hebben.

am kun si̱ liû, 項 上 生 |, een gezwel in den nek hebben; met iemand opgescheept zitten.

bah liû, 內 |, vleesch uitwas.

抽 *kuih liù*, 血 ｜, bloedgezwel.
Liù Afwinden, losmaken.

liù soà, ｜ 線, garen afwinden.

liù k'a, ｜ 脚, gebonden voeten losmaken (en als grooten laten groeijen).

p'oà pak liù tìng, 破 腹 ｜ 腸, de buik openen en de ingewanden er uithalen.

Liū *liū bé* / *liū* » } paarden rondmennen.

liū ké / » *koé* } (oud) brood overbakken.

kok tsaì liū, overbakken.

Lo

羅 *lo so*, ｜ 唆, verward, moeielijk uit
Lo temaken.

kóng oē lo lo kiò, 說 話 ｜ ｜ 叫, onduidelijk gaauw spreken.

lo li t'i, ｜ 厘 絺, in draden aan elkander hangend, verward, niet uittemaken.

ts'aò tiá lo / » » *lo* } 臭 鼎 ｜ } aangebrand.
ts'aò hé lo / » *kaé lo* } 臭 火 ｜ }

癆 *tióh lo*, 着 ｜, schurft hebben, (van
Lo honden.)

老 Oud, (van jaren); eerwaardig, als eere
Ló titel gebruikt.

ló liên, ｜ 年, oud van jaren, oudedag.

ló dziók ping, ｜ 弱 兵, oude zwakke soldaten.

poà ló laō, 半 ｜ 人, van gevorderden leeftijd.

ló sing, ｜ 成, opregt.

ló iâ, toā ló iâ, ｜ 爺, 大 ｜ 爺, titel voor overheden, WelEdele, WelEdelGestr. Heer!

ló tia, ｜ 爹, algemeen benaming voor overheden.

taī ló, 大 ｜, hooge literarische mandarijn.

ló su, ｜ 師, meester, onderwijzer.

籮 *ka ló*, 茄 ｜, ondiep bamboezen
Ló mandje.

臘 *tsiu ló*, 漿 ｜, kamfer.
Ló

惱 *hoân ló*, 煩 ｜, bedroefd zijn, betreuren.
Ló

瑙 *bé ló*, 瑪 ｜, de agaat.
Ló

腦 *t'aô ló* / » *naó* } 頭 ｜, hersenen.
Ló
Naó

美 *o ló*, 讃 ｜, prijzen.
Ló

潦 *ló ló ts'ó ts'ó*, ｜ 匕 草 匕, on-
Ló nauwkeurig, zorgeloos.

ló ts'ó siá, ｜ 草 寫, onnauwkeurig, krabbelen, schrijven.

魯 *ló dziók*, ｜ 肉, vleeschuitwas aan het
Ló oog.

gim ló, 錦 ｜, geregt van kippen, varkens, visch, groenten, enz.

豈 Groot, lang, (van menschen.)
Lò *lò lâng*, ｜ 人, lang mensch.

lò kuí, ｜ 鬼, lange lummel.

lò ko, ｜ 篙, lang.

lò siák siák, ｜ 削 匕, zeer lang (van persoon.)

sán lò, 瘦 ｜, mager en lang.

lò k'a, ｜ 脚, langbeenig.

lò k'oā k'oā, ｜ 誇 匕, zeer lang, (van een stok.)

Lò *lò aū dzit*, ｜ 後 日, over overmorgen.

lò tsóh dzit, | 昨 日, 3 dagen geleden.

勞 Werken, zich inspannen, zich afwerLô ken; moeite geven, lastig vallen.

lô sim lô lik, | 心 | 力, zijn geest en krachten inspannen.

lô lók, | 碌, zich afwerken, afslooven.

sin lô, 辛 |, tractement (van bedienden.)

oáh oáh lô si, 活 七 | 死, zich doodwerken.

lô hoân, | 煩, lastig vallen.

lô dziaó, | 擾, do.

lô tōng, | 動, het iemand lastig maken.

kong lô, 功 |, verdienstelijke daden, verdiensten.

癆 *lô tsìng*, | 症, tering.
Lô

Lô *lô bi*, | 米, rijst wannen.

bi lô, 米 |, rijst wan.

lô t'aô, fijne wan, zeef.

羅 Wijdgeweven zijde; familienaam.
Lô *dzoán* (of *loán*) *lô*, 軟 |, fijne zijde.

lô hàn ts'iá koan im, | 漢 請 觀 音, de *Lô hàn*, (18 beroemde leerlingen van Boeddha invitéren *Koanim*, *d. i.* in een groot huishouden weinig gasten vragen.

lô hàn k'a, | 漢 脚, leegloopers die op onbehoorlijke wijze aan de kost komen.

鑼 De gong, tong-tong.
Lô *p'ah lô*, 打 |, op de gong slaan.

lô kó tièm, | 鼓 店, winkel van muziek instrumenten.

k'ui lô ts'ē, 打 | 壽, onder het gong slaan (naar verloren kinderen). zoeken, omroepen.

hó lô hó kó, 好 | 好 鼓, zich lief voor doen.

p'ah toā lô, 打 大 |, onbeschaamd, publiek voor iets nitkomen.

騾 Muilezel.
Lô

濁 Troebel; klevig.
Lô *lô tai tai*, | 駘 匕, zeer troebel.

lô liêm noā, | 粘 涎, kleverig speeksel.

lô lô ko ko, | 匕 膏 匕, vuil en papperig.

bák tsiu lô lô, 目 周 | |, niet helder van oogen, (als van oudelieden.)

囉 Verward, lastig.
Lô *lô so*, | 唆, verward.

lô so k'eh, | 唆 客, lastige klant.

lô tsô, | 嘈, tot vermoeijenis toe lastig vallen.

hī k'ang lô lô, 耳 孔 | 匕, gonzen in het oor.

boē k'am tit i lô, 不 堪 得 他 |, ik kon zijn gedurig lastig vallen, vragen niet weerstaan (en gaf daarom toe.)

邏 *siēm lô*. 暹 |, Siam.
Lô *lô p'i*, | 丕, roepi.

ka li lô, 茄 里 |, het scheelt nog veel, het is er nog veel van af.

牢 Vastpakken, vastzetten.
Lô *kā i lô k'i lai*, 將 伊 | 起 來, vastbinden, vastzetten, opsluiten.

櫓 De achterste riem, wrikker van een
Lō boot.

iô lō, 搖 |, wrikken.

siang ki lō̤, 双 枝 ｜, twee wrikkers achter aan een boot.

tsiṅ kah lō̤, 槳·兼 ｜, met riemen en wrikker, *d. i.* snel.

勞 *lō̤ lát*, ｜ 力, dank voor uwe moeite.

Lō̤ *lō̤ lāng*, ｜ 人, iemand lastig maken, (als kinderen.)

鹵 Zouten, ruw, onbesuisd.

Ló̤ *lō̤ bah*, ｜ 肉, vleesch zouten, kruiden.

lō̤ t'ng, ｜ 湯, soep kruiden.

lō̤ mī, ｜ 麵, deeg kneden en kruiden.

lō̤ bóng, ｜ 莽, onbesuisd.

魯 Familienaam.

Ló̤ *lō̤ pan kong*, ｜ 班 公, god der timmerlieden.

lō̤ tsiú, ｜ 酒, goede zachte wijn.

怒 *lō̤ k'ì*, ｜ 氣, zich zeer kwaad maken.

Lō̤

嘍 *lâm sám lō̤*, 濫 滲 ｜, verward spreken, prevelen.

Ló̤ *o lō̤ péh lō̤*, 烏 ｜ 白 ｜, do.

ts'it lō̤ poéh lō̤, 七 ｜ 八 ｜, do.

老 *lō̤ ki*, ｜ 己, Cantonhoer, (van het

Ló̤ Cant. *lò keù*.

爐 Haard, stookplaats, fornuis, kamfoor

Lô̤ oven, smeltoven, gieterij, stoof.

hé lô̤, 火 ｜, haard, kachel.

p'ah hé lô̤, 打 火 ｜, den haard aanmaken.

piá lô̤, 餅 ｜, oven.

k'í lô̤, 起 ｜, uit den oven halen.

hang lô̤, 烘 ｜, komfoor, bewegelijk steenen fornuis.

ui lô̤, 圍 ｜, zich om den huiselijken haard scharen, (op het einde des jaars.)

lô̤ tsú, ｜ 主, hoofd van de reukwerkpot, (persoon wiens beurt het is voor de gemeensch. offeranden, enz. te zorgen.)

hiu lô̤, 香 ｜, reukwerkpot.

tiá lô̤, 鼎 ｜, pannengieterij.

t'ih lô̤, *siah lô̤*, 鉄 ｜, 錫 ｜, ijzersmelterij, tinsmelterij.

tíng lô̤, 鼎 ｜, reukwerkpot op pooten.

lô̤ toé, ｜ 底, bezinksel van metalen.

k'a lô̤, 脚 ｜, stoof.

ts'iú lô̤, 手 ｜, handstoof.

鸕 De aalscholver, kormoraan.

Lô̤ *lô̤ tsi*, ｜ 鷀, de kormoraan.

lô̤ tsi k'o̤ ām, ｜ 鷀 梱 項, als een kormoraan een ring om de nek hebben (om hem te beletten visschen in te slikken) *d. i.* niet geheel zijn eigen meester zijn.

lô̤ tsi boē tsai boé aū ts'aù, ｜ 鷀 未 知 尾 後 臭, de kormoraan weet niet dat hij van achteren stinkt, *d. i.* zijne gebreken niet inzien.

蘆 Bies.

Lô̤ *lô̤ tik*, ｜ 竹, hoog bies.

lô̤ hē } ｜ 衛, aloë en het aloë sap,
» oē }
waarmede vrouwen het haar inwrijven.

lô̤ hō iû, ｜ 衛 油, dito.

盧 Familienaam.

Lô̤

瓠 *hô̤ lô̤*, 葫 ｜, kalabas.

Lô̤ *lô̤ lô̤ lô̤*, ｜ ｜ ｜, opgezet, opgezwollen, dik, (van kinderen of honden.)

奴 slaaf, lijfeigene.

Lô̤ *lô̤ tsai*, ｜ 才, slaaf, een scheldwoord.

lô̤ pók, ｜ 僕, slaaf.

bé lô̤, 馬 ｜, paardenjongen.

hō lō̤ hoàn pī, 呼 | 喚 婢, slaven en slavinnen te roepen hebben, (van rijken gezegd.)

tsiú tsī lō̤, 守 錢 |, slaaf van zijn geld.

膠 Lō̤ *hī lō̤*, 耳 |, in het oor tuiten.

勞 Lō̤ *k'ò lō̤ sam kun*, 犒 | 三 軍, een leger onthalen (na eene overwinning.)

Lo *ming lō̤* } *mui* » }, dwarshout op een deur.

lō̤ ming } » *mui* } | 門, een dwarshout op de deur doen.

撈 Lō̤ *tsuí toé k'ì lō̤ k'ì lai*, 水 底 去 | 起 來, van den bodem des waters gaan opvisschen.

路 Lō̤ Weg, straat, weg om een doel te bereiken, manier; doeleinde, nut, handelingen, beroep.

kiâ lō̤, 行 |, gaan, loopen.

ts'ut lō̤, 出 |, op reis gaan.

lō̤ huì, | 費, reisgeld.

lō̤ t'aô, | 頭, begin eener straat, landingplaats.

lō̤ bé, | 尾, eind van een weg, ten laatste.

lō̤ ting, | 燈, straat lantaarns.

lō̤ tsām, | 塹, pleisterplaats.

lō̤ tīng, drukbezochte plaats.

lō̤ tà, | 担, wegdragers, sjouwerlieden.

k'ui lō̤ ts'ing, 開 | 銃, ochtend schot.

tīng lō̤, 斷 |, de omgang met iemand afbreken.

kiâ té lō̤, 行 短 |, zich van het leven berooven.

k'ui lō̤, 開 |, een weg maken, banen.

k'ai lō̤ sien hong, 開 | 先 鋒, de voorste zijn, vooropgaan.

toā lō̤, 大 |, de groote weg.

toā lō̤ ê lâng, 大 | 的 人, een groot moedig, degelijk mensch.

m̄ toā lō̤, 不 大 |, bedeesd, nederig.

ngō lō̤ ê lâng, 五 | 之 人, menschen van allerlei plaatsen.

lō̤ tô, | 途, weg.

lō̤ pi, | 碑, wegpaal, wegwijzer.

lō̤ koan, | 關, programma eener optogt.

lō̤ in, | 引, paspoort.

lō̤ king, | 徑, handelingen, beroep.

t'aô lō̤, 頭 |, broodwinning.

sím mih lō̤ īng, 麽 | 用, welk nut heeft het? waartoe dient het!

bô lō̤ īng, 無 | 用, van geen nut.

tsáp lō̤ īng, 什 | 用, van velerlei nut.

ū lō̤ īng, (of *ik*) 有 | 用, van nut voordeelig.

bô lō̤ kàn (of *sai*) 無 | 間, niet te gebruiken, van geen nut.

hó lō̤, 好 |, goede manier om iets te doen.

siū lō̤, 想 |, manier op iets bedenken.

hó pit lō̤, 好 筆 |, goed schrijven, een goede stijl hebben.

hó ts iú lō̤ 好 手 |, iets goed verstaan.

hó p'aí to lō̤, 好 歹 刀 |, goed, slecht te snijden.

露 Lō̤ Dauw; laten zien, vertoonen, voor den dag, aan het licht komen, aan den dag brengen, uitkomen, bekend worden: waggelen, los, niet stevig staan.

lō̤ tsui, | 水, dauw.

tsiáh lō̤, tàng lō̤, 食 |, 凍 |, bedauwd worden,

p'iò lō̤, 漂 丨, in den dauw bleeken.
k'iā t'ī lō̤, 豎 天 丨. onder den blooten hemel wonen.
lō̤ ts'ut lai, 丨 出 來, aan den dag komen. uitkomen.
lō̤ kun, 丨 根, met de wortels bloot komen.
lō̤ t'aò lō̤ bīn, 丨 頭 丨 面, zich steeds vertoonen, (van vrouwen.)
lō̤ hiēn, 丨 現, in het oog vallend.
hoat lō̤, 活 丨, aan den dag komen.
lō̤ ts'ut má kiok / » » *bé tê* } 丨 出 馬 脚, de aap komt uit de mouw.
paī lō̤, 敗 丨, aan den dag komen.
lō̤ k'a, 丨 脚, los op de pooten, (als een tafel.
lō̤ lō̤ hién, 丨 丨 顯, schommelen, (als een schip.)
lō̤ lī hit, 丨 裡 挾, schommelen, heen en weer slingeren.

鷺 Lō̤ — *lō̤ si*, 丨 鷥, reiger.

螺 Lō̤ — *lō̤ si*, 丨 絲, schroef.
lō̤ si ting, 丨 絲 燈, schroef.
lō̤ si tsoān, 丨 絲 鑽, kurkentrekker.

怒 Lō̤ Nō̤ — *lō̤ k'ì* 丨 氣, toorn, vertoornd.
ts'iok lō̤, 觸 丨, iemand toornig maken.

樂 Lō̤ — Houden van.
goá bô lō̤, 我 無 丨, ik houd er niet van.

鹵 Lō̤ — *hî lō̤*, 魚 丨, overblijvende pekel van gezoute visch.
tè lō̤, 短 丨, sterk afgetrokken thee.
lō̤ giō / » *kiō* } 丨 蕎, sjalotten.

賂 Lo — *sai lō̤ pò lō̤*, 使 丨 布 丨, omkoopen.

Loa

Loa — *īng ts'iú loa lai*, met de hand naar zich toehalen, toeschuiven, (als kaarten.)
taī tsì oē loa tit, over die zaak kan men vlugtig heen loopen.

爛 Loá — *loá ts'oá*, 丨 懶, oppervlakkig, (doen) niet grondig..

Loà — Waterval, rapid.
tsiṳ̄ loà / *tsiṳ̄* » } tegen den stroom, waterval opgaan.
lóh loà, de waterval afgaan.
tsûn k'an tsiṳ̄ loà, een schuit tegen een waterval optrekken.

藍 Loà. — *bí loà*, 米 丨, rijstzeef.

連 — *liû loà*, 流 丨, terughouden, niet gaarne afstaan.

賴 — Familienaam.

Loā — *oá loā*, 倚 丨, steunen op, zich verlaten op.
loā lâng, 累 人, verklappen als medeschuldige.
bû loā, 誣 丨, valsch betichten.
koà loā, 掛 丨, do.

暈 Loā — *tsit loā*, 一 丨, een bobbeltje als de beet van muskieten, enz.

幾 Loā — *loā tsoē* / » *tsē* } 丨 多, hoeveel?
loā kú, 丨 久, hoelang? hoe lang wel niet?
bē ū loā kú / *boē* « » » } 未 丨 久, nog niet lang geleden, onlangs.
loā tsá, 丨 早, hoe vroeg! hoe vroeg wel niet?

Loah

捋 Loah *loah kèh k'ì*, | 過去, aframmelend, over iets heenloopen.

tsit dzit loah kè tsit dzit } 一日 | 過一日, van den eenen dag op den anderen verschuiven.
» » *t'oah kòè* » »

loah tseh tsiū kè k'ì, | 些就過去, aframmelen.

loah hō i pī (of *kèng*,) | 與伊平, gelijk, glad wrijven.

捋 Loáh Wrijven, strijken over, met goede woorden verzoenen, prijzen, ophemelen; kammen, kam.

p'ah loáh, 打 |, slaan en wrijven, (als iemand die eene flaauwte heeft.)

so loáh, 挲 |, verzoenen.

loáh k'ui, | 開, uit elkander wrijven of kammen.

loáh ts'uì ts'iu, | 嘴鬚, de snor strijken.

ts'iu loáh, ts'uì ts'iu loáh, 鬚 |, 嘴鬚 |, snorkammetje.

loáh t'aò mìng, | 頭毛, het haarkammen.

loáh á, | 仔, fijne haarkam.

bé á loáh tioh tsiū k'iaò, 尾仔 | 着就蹺, strijkt men (een kat) over de staart dan staat deze op, *d. i.* gaarne geprezen worden.

aì lâng loáh, 愛人 |, gaarne geprezen worden.

kap i tsit ē loáh nīng ē loáh, 與伊一下 | 二下 |, iemand op hemelen, (en zoo, iets van hem gedaan krijgen.)

辣 Loáh Sterk, scherp, bijtend, heet als mostaard.

kaì loáh, 芥 |, mostaard.

hiⁿ hiⁿ loáh loáh, 馨匕 | |, sterkriekend; ieders aandacht trekken.

put tsí hiⁿ loáh hit ê lâng, 不只馨 | 此人, sterk naar iemand verlangen.

Loan

軟 Loán *loán dzióh* } | 弱, zacht, zwak, (van karakter.)
» *dziák*

nìng loán, 煖 |, zacht en fijn, (van zijde.)

ĭng ts'iú loán loán, 用手 | |, met de hand wrijven, (als een buil blaar enz.)

煖 Loán *loán koh*, | 閣, zomerhuis, waarin men 's winters stookt.

loán e, | 煨, tafelkomfoor.

loán lō, | 爐, tafelkomfoor, met eene vuurplaats.

t'ī k'ì k'ah un loán, 天氣稍温 |, de weergesteldheid is milder.

Loán *piaó loán*, 表 |, hoerenbediende; scheldwoord.

戀 Loân *loân loân put siá*, | 匕不舍, van iemand niet kunnen scheiden.

t'am loân, 貪 |, sterk verlangen naar.

sim koⁿ loân loân, 心肝 | |, iets niet van zich kunnen afgooijen, steeds aan iets denken.

鸞 Loân *ko loân miā*, 孤 | 命, weduwe staat.

loân hōng, | 鳳, de feniks.

鑾 Loân *kim loân tiēn*, 金 | 殿, audientiezaal des keizers.

亂 Verward,
Loān *kiaó loān*, 攪 〡, verwarren.
dziaó loān, 擾 〡, verwarring, rumoer.
loān lûn, 〡 倫, bloedschande.
hūn loān, 混 〡, verwarren.
tsok loān, 作 〡, oproer maken.
loān tsú, 〡 自, zonder grond, onbehoorlijk.
loān tsú lai, 〡 自 行, onbehouden te werk gaan.
loān hun hun, 〡 紛 匕, verward door elkander, ongeregeld.
loān lat, 〡 來, onbesuisd, ongepast handelen.
loān sim, 〡 心, niet weten wat te doen.
loān giên } 〡 言, verwarde taal.
» gân }
loān sè } 〡 世, oproerige tijd, verwarde tijd, (van een rijk enz.)
» sì }
pī loān, 避 〡, een oproer ontvlugten.
tsaó loān, 走 〡. do.
loān ts'eh ts'eh (*loān ts'a ts'a*) 〡 册 匕 }
loān ts'ah ts'ah 〡 穙 匕 } verward, in wanorde (van het rijk eene plaats enz.)
loān bé bé 〡 迷 匕 }

Loe

毋 *niû loé* } 〡 娘, moeder.
Loé *niû lé* }

咒 *loé mē*, 〡 罵, spotten met, schimpen op.
Loé *loé lâng*, 〡 人, iemands vervloeking afvragen.
loé liēm, 〡 念, verwenschen, vervloeken.

恥 *siaó loé*, 〡 羞, beschaamd zijn, zich
Loé schamen.

餒 *loé tsì*, 〡 志. neerslachtig, neergedrukt
Loé zijn.

鑢 Vijlen, raspen.
Loè *loè á*, 〡 仔, vijl.
kù loè } 鉅 〡, do.
kì lē }
loè piah, 〡 壁, tegen een muur aanschrijnen.
loè tsiū } 〡 癢, wegens jeuking tegen iets aanschrijnen.
» tsiō }
loè tioh tsit k'ang. 〡 着 一 孔, een gat krijgen door langs iets heen te schrijnen.
loè kng, 〡 光, glad vijlen.
páng loè. 板 〡, vijl.

犂 Ploegen.
Loê *loê t'aô*, 〡 頭, ploegschaar.
Lê *loê pì* } 〡 柄. ploegstaart.
» pè }
loê ts'ân, 〡 田, een veld ploegen.
t'oa loê, 拖 〡, een ploeg voorttrekken (als de koe.)
loê t'aô tì tiá, 〡 頭 載 鼎, zich met kracht voor een vriend inspannen.
loê tióh tsióh. 〡 着 石, op een rots loopen, (van schepen.)
loê liên, 〡 輦, hard met een afgodsstoel voortrennen.
it tit loê k'ì, 一 直 〡 去. regtstreeks doorrennen, (ondanks regen of duisternis.)

內 *loē koh*, 〡 閣, hooge raad, kabinet.
Loē *loē poān*, 〡 叛, met de belegeraars mededoen.
loē ìng, 〡 應. do.
tsoat loē, 拙 〡, mijne vrouw, (nederige term.)
loē tit, 〡 姪, neef, (zoon van vrouws broeders.)

振 Loē *loē loē ts'ut lai*, ｜｜出來, uittrekken, uithalen, (als ingewanden.) *ting á tō loē tsut lai hō li k'oà*, 腸仔肚｜出來與汝看, Ik leg mijn hart openlijk voor U bloot, (en nog gelooft gij mij niet.)

Loch

笠 Loéh *tik kah loéh* / » » *léh* } 竹𥰡｜, bamboezen hoed.

dzit tì loéh / » *ui k'o* } 日戴｜, krans om den zon (als teeken van regen.)

tik loéh, 竹｜, bamboezenhoed.

ts'aó loéh, 草｜, stroohoed.

loéh á, ｜仔, bamboezenhoed.

ting á loéh, 釘頭｜, kop van een spijker.

Loh

落 Loh Na ww. gewoonlijk toonloos neêr . . . af . . . neerkomen, vallen als regen, bladeren; neêrgaan, naar beneden gaan, afgaan; dalen, vallen van prijs; doen zakken, neerlaten in, indoen neernemen, afnemen van; neerzetten, onderzetten als eene handteekening; nederkomen van, neêrgaan naar; doen overgaan als een slot, op slot enz. doen; neêrgaan in, zich schikken, onderwerpen aan; afdeeling van een huis die één afzonderlijk dak heeft.

lóh hō, lóh seh, ｜雨, ｜雪, het regent, sneeuwt.

lóh hióh, ｜葉, de bladeren vallen af. zijne bladeren afgooijen.

lóh k'ì, lóh lai, ｜去, ｜來, naar beneden gaan, komen.

lóh bé, ｜馬, van het paard afstijgen, een feestmaal aanrigten bij iemands terugkomst.

boē lóh tai, 未｜臺, niet van het tooneel afkunnen; zich niet aan iets kunnen onttrekken.

lóh toé, ｜底, naar den bodem gaan zijne talenten niet aan den dag kunnen brengen.

lóh kè, ｜價, dalen in prijs.

k'í lóh kè, 起｜價, rijzen en dalen van prijs.

lóh hè, 貨｜, goederen inladen.

lóh tsûn, ｜船, aan boord doen.

dzit lóh, 日｜, de zon gaat onder.

lóh bin, ｜眠, inslapen.

lóh ki, ｜旗, een vlag neerhalen.

lóh pâng, ｜帆, zeil innemen, reven

lóh sa hūn tsit, ｜三分七, één rif leggen.

lóh niū lóh ping, ｜樑, ｜枰, op de weegschaal zetten.

lóh tsuí, ｜水, aan boord doen, inladen, in het water doen vallen.

hē lóh, 下｜, neerzetten.

ū hē loh, 有着｜, te vertrouwen. waarop men zich verlaten kan.

lóh ts'iú, ｜手, een begin maken met.

loh miâ, ｜名, zijne handteekening onder iets zetten.

lóh tsit dzī, ｜一字, een karakter uitlaten, overslaan.

lóh soh, ｜索, touw om lasten op te ligten.

p'ah boē oē lóh k'ì, 打未能｜去, het niet voor zich kunnen verkrijgen om te slaan.

sin lóh soa, 新｜山, pas, versch van het gebergte, binnenland komen.

lóh lâm, ｜南, naar het zuiden gaan.

lóh t'aô ê tsûn, ｜頭棚船, een (van het N.) neerkomend schip.

lòh siâ, | 城, naar de stad gaan.

tsiû tsiû lòh lòh, 上 𠃋 | |, heen en weer, op en neer gaan.

lòh i ê ts'ùi, | 伊 的 嘴, uitkomen zooals hij gezegd had.

lòh só, | 鎖, op de knip zijn, (van een deur.)

lòh iòh, | 鑰, op slot zijn.

lòh k'aù, | 扣, op de gesp, digt gegespt zijn; geschikt zijn (als eene twist.)

lòh sún, | 損, in de gleuf, groef zijn.

lòh sìng, | 性, zijn karakter buigen, zich laten temmen.

lòh ke kaù, | 家 教, zich naar de gewoonten van een huis schikken.

koe t'î sâ lòh, 雞 啼 三 |, de haan heeft driemaal gekraaid, de dag zal spoedig aanbrekend.

nōng lòh ê ts'ù, 二 | 之 厝, een huis met twee daken.

睦 Overeenstemmen; harmonieren.

Lòh *taī ke īm lòh*, 大 家 不 |, niet met elkander harmonieren.

Lok

置 Nederliggen, liggen op.

Lok *lok tī*, | 落, do.

lok hē, | 下, neêrleggen.

橐 *hiû soâ lok*, 香 線 |, zakje, peperLok huis voor reukstokjes.

tsoà lok, 紙 |, peperhuis.

p'ī lok kóng, 鼻 | 磺, de neuskoker.

hō soâ lok, 雨 傘 |, foudraal voor eene paraplui.

Lok *tsoè sū lai lok làng*, 做 事 來 | 人, iets doen om iemand in den strik te krijgen, beursch, (van vruchten,) voos.

lok k'ok, | 哭, slobberen, als te wijde schoenen.

k'oâ lok lok, 寬 | 𠃋, zeer te wijd.

kè lok lok, 架 | 𠃋, verward (als een staart).

lok lok, | |, zacht, rijp, (als van een zweer.)

tâm lok lok, 濕 | |, modderig, nat.

lok tsân, | 田, modderig, nat veld.

lok tsiúh tsiúh, | 兕 𠃋, modderig, nat, (als een weg of verrotte vruchten.)

lok ts'ih, | 蠘, zachte, rottende krab, handel die aan het kwijnen is.

落 *lok sōng*, | 霜, neêrgedrukt door geLok brek, te wijde kleeren aan hebben uitarmoede.

lok tsaī ki tiông, | 在 其 中, iets nu eenmaal gedaan hebben, begonnen zijn (en het niet kunnen veranderen.)

鹿 Hert.

Lók *lók hú*, | 脯, gedroogd hertevleesch.

lók kun, | 肋, hertepeezen.

lók dziông, | 茸, hertshoorn.

lók á toê, | 仔 蹄, vlug ter been, snelloopend.

dzip lók / *dzik »* } 逐 |, een hert nazetten, overal zoeken, op winst uit zijn.

hó lók, 虎 |, bedriegelijk, niet te vertrouwen.

ông lók, 王 |, do.

ông lók ts'ùi, 王 | 嘴, ongeloofwaardig.

lók tû, | 厨, houten kooi, (voor gevangenen.)

tsóh si lók, 射死 |, als of men op een dood hert schoot, *d. i.* een niets waardig mensch die zich alles laat gezeggen.

lók tsiáh tióh hé hu, | 食着火灰, als een hert dat asch eet, *d. i.* zich veel last berokkenen.

lók hú t'ua ts'ut k'ì ts'aó ê t'ua dzip lai. | 脯拖出去草鞋拖入來, gedroogd hertenvleesch uitdragen en strooschoenen inbrengen: van bedienden die hun meester bestelen.

lók t'ong king, | 通間, huis waarin bedelaars enz. leven.

硦 Lók Onvermoeid werken, werkzaam.

lò lók, 勞 |, onvermoeid werkzaam.

lók k'ók, | 哭, buitensporig, ongebonden, teugelloos.

lók k'ók bé (of *lâng*), | 哭馬, een teugelloos mensch.

絡 Lók *lóng lók*, 囊 |, vangen (als onder een net,) iemand beetnemen.

祿 Lók *lok ūi*, | 位, tablet die nog bij iemands leven voor hem opgerigt wordt.

hōng lok, | 俸, traktement van ambtenaren.

落 Lók Neêrvallen; vallen in.

lók k'ong, | 空, te niet gaan, verdwijnen, verliezen.

ū tióh lók ê lâng, 有着 | 之人, iemand die te vertrouwen is.

lók k'a sing, | 花生, aardnoot.

lók hoa liû sui, | 花流水, als afgevallen bloemen die door het water worden weggedreven, *d. i.* vervallen, te gronde gaan (van bezittingen).

駱 Lók Kameel; familienaam.

lók tô, | 駝, kameel; gew. echter muilezel.

烙 Lók Inbranden.

lók ìn, | 印, een brandend stempel zetten in (als aan schepen).

lók hō, | 號, ingebrand merk.

樂 Lók Vreugde, vrolijk, genoegelijk.

t'iòng lók, 暢 |, vrolijk, in zijn schik.

lók t'iòng, | 暢, gekheid maken, plagen.

lók king, | 境, aangenaam, genoegelijke toestand.

kan lók, 干 |, tol, drijftol.

Long

挊 Long *lut long*, 脫 |, verruilen, een goed ding voor een kwaad.

long pang, | 梆, onder de massa door smokkelen, in een schip smokkelen zonder er vracht van te betalen.

sì koè long, 四處 |, overal insteken.

lòng loh k'ì, | 落去, naar beneden insteken.

lê long, 嚟 |, vendutie.

long long haó, | 匕吼, schellen. (als bellen om den nek van een paard.)

lin lin long long, 連匕 | |, schellen rammelen (als een bel.)

攏 Lóng Alleen, geheel en al.

lóng tsóng, | 總, allen.

lóng t'òng, | 統, alleen, geheel en al.

long bô, | 無, volstrekt niet.

lóng kiōng, | 共, alles bij elkander, in het geheel.

lóng sìng } | 算, alles bij elkander
» suì }
gerekend.

lóng tsoè tsit ē, | 做 一 個, alles bij elkander.

朗 Long *tsiú lóng*, 酒 |, wijnhuis.

籠 Lóng *lóng lók*, | 絡, vangen onder een net zoodat het gevangene voorwerp er niet meer uit kan.

Lóng *oéh lóng á hiû*, 狹 | 仔 裘, naauw sluitende korte jas.

ts'iú lóng, 手 |, overmouw.

撞 Lòng *lòng p'oà sū*, | 打 破 事, eene zaak bederven.

lòng kè t'aô, | 過 頭, de plaats voorbij rennen, door al te sterk verlangen eene zaak bederven, te veel voor iets betalen.

放 Lòng *lòng toā ts'ìng* | 大 炮, een kanon afsteken

寬 Lòng *lòng k'òng*, | 曠, ruim, (van een gebouw.)

k'oà lòng lòng, 寬 | |, zeer wijd.

狼 Eene soort wolf.

Lóng *ts'ai lóng*, 豺 |, wolf.

lóng poē, | 狽, in verval.

hai lóng, 海 |, otter, (van het Noorden.)

lóng sim kaó hīng, | 心 狗 行, wreed.

lóng poē siong i } | 狽 相 依,
» » siang » }
als de *lóng* en de *poē* (twee mytische dieren) op elkander steunen.

農 Landbouwen, landbouwer.

Lóng *sū lóng kong siong*, 士 | 工 商, geletterden, landbouwers, werklieden en kooplieden.

濃 Dik, vet, (als olie of inkt), sterk van

Lóng lucht.

lóng ien sàn bū, | 烟 散 霧, als een dikke nevel en verspeide mist, *d. i.* vervallen, geruineerd.

bī put tsi lóng, 味 不 止 |, sterk, van lucht.

bák tsui lóng, 墨 水 |, de inkt is dik.

郎 *līng lông*, 令 |, Uw zoon, (bel. term.)

Lông *lông kun tsú tē*, | 君 子 弟, fatsoenlijke jongelieden.

廊 Gaanderij aan beide kanten van een ge-

Lông bouw.

lióng lông, 兩 |, de beide gaanderijen in een groot gebouw.

籠 Een omkleedsel, enveloppe; in iets doen.

Lông *ts'iú lông*, 手 |, handschoen.

p'oe lông, 批 |, brief enveloppe.

lông p'oe, | 批, een brief in de enveloppe doen.

lông t'aô, | 頭, hoofdstel.

ting lông, 燈 |, lampballon.

īng mih lông k'ì lai, 用 物 | 起 來, in iets schuiven, doen.

lông k'ì lai k'ing, | 起 來 收, opbergen, niet meer gebruiken.

浪 Golf, golfslag, de baren; ongestadig,

Lōng onbesuisd.

p'o lōng, 波 |, de golven.

hong lōng, 風 |, wind en golven.

lōng tōng, 蕩 |, onbesuisd.

lōng tōng kiá, | 蕩 子, een vagabond.

弄 Spelen, gekheid maken met, zwaaijen

Lōng met; ophitsen, aanzetten.

b lōng, *tsok lōng*, , 舜 |, 作 |, beetnemen, foppen.

lōng kiû, | 毬, kegelen.

lōng koân, | 權, misbruik van zijne magt maken.

pan bûn lōng hû, 班 門 | 斧, aan de deur van *Pan*, (god der timmerlieden) met de bijl manoeuvreren *d i.* zijne kennis tegenover knapperen willen toonen.

lōng k'ang, | 空, een gat, manier op iets vinden.

lōng lâng, *lōng sóng lâng*, | 人, | 唆 人, personen tegen elkander aanzetten.

lōng kui, | 鬼, ophitsen, aanzetten.

lōng ts'ut sū, | 出 事, tot twist aanzetten.

lōng kaó sa kā, | 狗 相 咬, do.

pai lōng, 排 |, ophitsen.

檔 Lōng *long ming*, | 門, een boom op de deur doen.

ming lōng, 門 |, deurstut-boom.

熉 Lōng *hé lōng*, 火 |, zonnetje, ronddraaijende bamboes bij vuurwerk.

Lu

溜 Lu *lu lòh lai*, | 下 來, neerzakken, neerglijden, afglijden.

lu lu lòh k'ì, | | 落 去, do.

穿 Lu *tit lu*, 直 |, regtstreeks binnendringen onaangediend binnengekomen.

lu lai, | 來, uitsteken, voor iemand zetten zonder iets te zeggen, naar iemand toeschuiven.

lu lai lu k'ì, | 來 | 去, over en weer schuiven.

lu dzip k'ì, | 入 去, inschuiven.

sì koè lu, 四 處 |, overal zorgeloos neerzetten, zich overal indringen, (bij menschen.)

Lu *lu lik*, bij kleinigheden opbieder (bij een koop.)

女 Lú *lú dzi* (*li* ») | 兒, meisjes, dochter.

ts'ù lú (*tsì* ») | | 處, ongehuwd meisje.

kui lú, 閨 |, do.

kè lú (» *li*) 繼 |, stiefdochter.

tit lú, 姪 |, broeder's dochter.

lú saì (» *sè*) | 婿, schoonzoon.

goē sing lú, 外 甥 |, zuster's dochte

li kang, | 工, vrouwelijke han werken.

lú tiōng hu (» *tiūng* ») | 丈 夫, eene mann lijke vrouw, vrouw die de broek aa heeft.

lú pī, | 婢, slavin, vrouwelijke b diende.

lâm lú, 男 |, mannen en vrouwen

屢 Lú *lú lú*, | 乜, steeds, gedurig.

lú ts'ù, | 次, steeds, gedurig.

鑢 Lù Boenen, poetsen, wrijven.

lù á, | 仔, vijltje.

kng lù (*kui* ») | 光, gladboenen.

lù sièn, | 銑, de roest van iets f wrijven.

lù p'oà p'ê, | 破 皮, de huid stu wrijven, stuk schrijnen.

lù hún, | 粉, tot poeder, meel wrijve (als aardappelen.)

驢 Lû Ezel.

toā lō lû (*tâng o* ») 大 路 | | 同 安 | |, ezel van de grooten weg, iemand die niet verd gaat als hij niet gegeten heeft.

t'ut lû, 禿 |, scheldnaam voor Boe dha priesters.

慮 Lū *kò lū* (*» li*) 過 ｜, onbenoodigd bezorgd zijn.
iu lū, 憂 ｜, bedroefd zijn.

呂 Familienaam.
Lū *lū sòng*, ｜ 宋, Spanje, Manilla.
Lī *lū sien tsò*, ｜ 仙 祖, god der barbiers.

侮 Lū *lū kū*, ｜ 詛, kortaf, afsnauwen, (van aard.)

Lū *lū toh á*, ｜ 索 仔, een touw uitlaten, latenschieten.
koh lū k'i, 再 ｜ 去, wat latenschieten.
pàng ts'ìng lù, 放 銃 ｜, geheel en al uitlaten, laten schieten, als het touw van een vlieger of harpoen.

Lui

壘 Lui *lui tui*, ｜ 堆, verward, (vertellen of handelen.)

推 Lui *lui lóh lai*, ｜ 下, afglijden, afrollen, als aarde of ronde op elkander gestapelde voorwerpen.

鐳 Benaming van een kwart dollar.
Lui *tsit lui*, — ｜, een kwart dollar.

蕊 Numer. voor bloemen.
Luí *hoe luí*, 花 ｜, bloemen.
hâm luí, 含 ｜, op het punt zijn te ontluiken, (van bloemen.)
bí luí, 米 ｜, gekookte rijst voor dat ze nog aan het uitzetten gaat.

壘 Luí *īng tsióh luí k'i lai*, 用 石 ｜ 起 來, van graniet maken, (als de voet van een muur.)
luí k'i lai, ｜ 起 來, een steenen omheining maken.
luí luí tuī tuī, ｜ ｜ 堆 七, volgeladen, met bagage, met vruchten (aan een boom), ook van vele kinderen.
luí tāng, ｜ 重, beider gewigt vergelijken.
tuì luí, 對 ｜, beider zwaarte vergelijken.

樓 Luí *lâm lâm luí luí*, 襤 七 ｜ ｜, verscheurd, (van kleeren.)

屢 Luí *luí luí ū*, ｜ ｜ 有, steeds gedurig komt dit voor.
luí ts'ù, ｜ 次, verscheidene malen, steeds.

彙 Luì *luì ts'uì ê hè*, ｜ 碎 之 貨, diverse artikelen.
hó luì p'ai, 好 ｜ 歹, voor goeden slechten in de plaats stellen.
k'it i luì t'ìn k'i, 被 其 ｜ 脫 去, voor goede, toevertrouwde dingen slechte dingen in de plaats vinden.
luì mìng, *t'uì mìng*, ｜ 毛, ruijen, verharen.

雷 De donder; familienaam.
Luî *t'i luî*, 天 ｜, de donder.
luî kong, 公 ｜, de dondergod.
luî kong kòng si hiā á, ｜ 公 打 死 螻 蟻, als de dondergod die een mier dood slaat, van een hooger in rang die een lager in rang duchtig straft.
luî kong kòng si kiaó ông, ｜ 公 打 死 賭 王, de dondergod slaat den koning der dobbelaars dood, *d. i.* ten eene male ongelukkig worden.
luî tàn, ｜ 鳴, het dondert.
k'i luî, *hoat luî*, 起 ｜, 發 ｜, er pakt zich donder zamen; door den bliksem getroffen worden.
luî ts'è, ｜ 迅, de donder knettert.
hō luî p'ah sí, 被 ｜ 打 死, door den donder (bliksem) gedood worden.

lui tân ts'ih ts'oah, | 鳴 迅 疾, donderen en bliksemen: zeer vertoornd zijn.

tē lui, 地 |, met kruid gevulde loopgraaf; bromtol.

lui tòng, | 同, aan elkander gelijk als donder, (*b. v.* van nageschreven opstellen.)

擂 Fijn wrijven, fijn stampen.

Lui *lui boáh*, | 盆, tot poeder wrijven, stampen.

lui poeh, | 砵, vijzel.

lui k'ū, | 臼, do.

lui t'ui, | 鎚, stamper.

lui hu gíng boáh / » » *gán* » } | 灰 研 末, tot asch en poeder wrijven, *d. i.* op alle mogelijke manieren afpersen.

lui tsui tsiáh lòh k'ì, | 水 食 落 去, iemand in water wrijven en opdrinken, *d. i*, hem duchtig willen straffen.

sì koè lui, 四 處 |, overal tegen aan schrijnen.

bák tsiu kọ họ lâng lui ts'ùt lai, 目 周 股 被 人 | 出 來, het oog door iemand uitgeslagen worden.

ts'ing peh lui, 松 柏 |. eikel van een pijnboom.

Luì

類 Soort, klasse.

Luī *it luī*, 一 |, gelijksoortig, gelijk.

siāng (of *tâng*) *luī*, 同 |, do.

pun luī, 分 |, sorteeren.

kui luī, 歸 |, de verschillende soorten bij elkander.

ts'ē kui luī, 册 歸 |, de soorten bij elkander zoeken.

huí luī, 匪 |, slechte lieden.

彙 *dzī luī*, 字 |, verkort woordenboek.

Luī

擂 Slaan op, of tegen.

Luī *luī kọ́*, | 鼓, op de trom slaan, roffelen.

luī mîng, | 門, hard op de deur slaan.

淚 Afdruipen, (oorsp. als tranen.)

Luī *tsik luī*, 燭 | de kaars druipt.

tsìk luī, 積 |, afdruipsel eener kaars.

累 Betrekken in.

Luī *lièn luī*, 連 |, betrekken, medeslepen.

t'oa luī, 拖 |, do.

luī bọ́ kiá, | 妻 子, zijne vrouw en kinderen in iets meeslepen.

k'ui luī, 虧 |, verlies bij iets lijden.

luī t'uī, | 拖, medeslepen, tot last zijn, zwaar.

縋 Neerlaten, laten zakken.

Luī *luī lòh k'ì*, | 落 去, neerlaten.

陞 Ophijschen.

Luī *luī ki*, | 旗, een vlag ophijschen.

luī ting, | 燈, een lamp ophijschen.

Lun

縮 Intrekken, kromtrekken,

Lun *lun t'aô*, | 頭, het hoofd, de kop intrekken.

lun t'aô k'ì k'oạ̀, | 頭 去 看, het hoofd slechts een weinig uitstekende bekijken.

kiu kiu lun lun, 退 匕 | 匕, bedeesd, ingetogen, teruggetrokken.

lun ku, | 龜, kromme rug.

tsoè sū kiu tseh lun tseh, 做事|一伸一, in handelingen zoo toetreden, en dan weer terugtrekken.

Lun *la lun á, la lun á sio*, leukwarm.

碾 Rolsteen, rollen.

Lún *tsióh lún*, 石|, rolsteen.

lún tsióh, |石, groote molensteen.

īng tsióh lún lún, 用石||, met een rolsteen rollen.

忍 Geduldig verdragen; inhouden als toorn,
Lún ophouden als water.

t'un lún, 吞|, verdragen.

lún k'i, lún k'uì, |氣, |愧, zijn toorn inhouden.

lún dziō, |尿, zijn water ophouden.

lún ts'uì, |嘴, minder eten.

凜 Rillen, beven van koude of schrik,
Lún ontstellen, schrikken, terugdeinzen.

ka lún sún, 絞|損, rillen, (van koude.)

lún kaò bô bah, |至無肉, doodsbeangst zijn.

lún neh, |攝, schrikken ontstellen.

lún sè, |勢, terugdeinzen, ontstellen.

lún ts'iú, |手, de hand terugtrekken, op het oogenblik dat men iets wil doen.

lún tá, |胆, zijn moed inhouden, niet overhaast handelen.

Lùn *gaò lùn*, rekken, dralen, verschuiven.

tsit dzit lùn kè tsit dzit (» » » *koè* » ») } van den eenen dag op den anderen verschuiven, uitstellen.

kap i bóng lùn, voor iemand maar wat inschikken.

lùn tseh ts'ùn tseh, niet in eens doen, bij tusschenpoozen.

潤 *sip lùn lùn*, 濕||, zeer vochtig.

Lùn *tâm lùn lùn*, 淡||, zeer nat.

輪 Wiel, rad, rol, (onder stoelen), rond-
Lûn loopende rand; rondgaan, ronddraaijen, volgens de beurt gaan.

ts'ia lûn, 車|, wagenrad, wiel.

tsuí lûn, 水|, waterrad, (door water in beweging gebracht.)

hé lûn tsûn, 火|船, stoomboot.

tńg lûn, 轉|, ronddraaijen, (als een wiel.

bák tsiu tńg lûn, 目轉|, de oogen verdraaijen.

lûn hoê, |迴, zielsverhuizing.

lûn liû, |流, om de beurt doen.

lûn liû tióh dzit, |流着日, de beurtdag.

tsiaò lûn, 照|, volgens de beurt.

tsè sū ê kao lûn, 祭祀閹|, beurtelingsche bestuur over gemeenschappelijke offeranden.

lûn kaò goá, |到我, de beurt is aan mij.

sim mih lâng lûn k'i, 何人|起, wie heeft het eerst de beurt?

圇 *bûn lûn kóng kè k'i*, 囫|說
Lûn 過去, onduidelijk over iets heen spreken.

䯟 Gewricht, lid.

Lûn *kut lûn*, 骨|, gewricht der beenderen.

t'ut lûn, 黜|, uit het lid gaan, verstuiken.

倫 *ngó lûn*, 五|, de vijf familiebetrek-
Lûn kingen.

48

論 Lūn　Spreken, redeneren over; volgens.
gī lūn, 議 ｜. redeneren, spreken over.
piēn lūn, 辯 ｜. do.
put lūn sim mih taī tsì, 不 ｜ 什 麼 事. onverschillig wat ook.
put lūn kang, 不 ｜ 工, zonder nog te spreken van het werk dat het be steld is.
lūn nį put lūn géh, ｜ 年 不 ｜ 月, er is daarbij van jaren en niet van maanden spraak, (*b. v.* studeren.)
lūn tsing lì. ｜ 情 理. volgens bel-lijkheid.

崙 Lūn　*kè hit ê lūn tsiū kaò*. 過 此 便 到, is men dien bergketen over dan is men er.

閏 Lūn　Schrikkelmaand, die het jaar tot 13 maanden maakt.
lūn géh, ｜ 月, schrikkelmaand.
lūn nį, ｜ 年, schrikkeljaar.

潤 Lūn　Bevochtigen. vochtig.
lūn aô. ｜ 喉. de keel bevochtigen.
sip lūn. 濕 ｜. vochtig. klam.
lūn láh ｜ 了, zachtzinnig.

嫩 Lūn　Slap, zacht, taai, elastiek.
tâm lūn (» *dzūn*) 沉 ｜. nat en zacht.
lūn lūn ts'i ts'i. ｜ ｜ 徐 匕. taai, zacht pappig.

Lut

脫 Lut　Loslaten van, losgaan, zich losmaken van. afvallen, uitvallen, afgaan. (als vuil), verliezen als een ambt; afzetten, degraderen.
lut ts'ut lai, ｜ 出 來. uitvallen. afvallen.
lut sút, ｜ 出, van iets afvallen, (als een rond glad voorwerp.)
lut ts'ui k'i, ｜ 嘴 齒. uitvallen van de tanden.
lūt tì, ｜ 蒂. van den stengel loslaten, (als rijpe vruchten.)
koe sik tì lut, 瓜 熟 蒂 ｜. zijn de meloenen rijp dan laat de stengel los. is de tijd daar dan gaat de zaak van zelve.
lut mòh, het vlies, de schil, afpellen. (als bij nooten.)
t'aô lō lut. 頭 路 ｜. zijne broodwinning verliezen.
t'aô lō lut tsō. 頭 路 ｜ 座. do.
lut tsō, ｜ 座, van zijn voetstuk afvallen.
oē lut long tit, naar verkiezing met iets kunnen handelen.
lut ling, ｜ 乳, van de borst afzijn.
boē tik pang k'ui kù lut. 不 得 梆 開 鉅 ｜. de plank niet kunnen openzagen noch de zaag er uithalen, *d. i.* genoodzaakt zijn eene lastige zaak voortezetten.
boē lut t'i, 未 ｜ 磃, niet van de vogellijm los kunnen komen, *d. i.* zich niet aan eene zaak kunnen onttrekken.
koa lut, 官 ｜. zijn mandarijn ambt verliezen.
tō tai lut loh lai tsoè toā hú 道 臺 ｜ 落 來 做 大 府, van *Toa tai* tot *Hú* verlaagd worden.
lut lì, ｜ 吏. van een ambt ontzet.

詎 Lut　Bedriegen, beetnemen, listig ontnemen.
lut p'iên, 騙 ｜. bedriegen.
k'it lâng lut k'ì, 被 人 ｜ 出, bedrogen, beetgenomen worden.

lut á. | 仔, bedrieger, schurk.

lut á pō, | 仔 步, schurken streek.

lut lâng ē mih, | 人 之 物. iemands goed ontfutselen.

律 *lút hoat*. | 法, wet.
Lút *lut lē*. | 例, wet.

tsiaò lút pān, 照 | 來 辦, volgens de wet straffen.

it lút. 一 |. gelijk.

kui lút. 歸 |. gelijk, gelijkelijk.

捋 *lút ling*, | 乳, melken.
Lút *lut béh suī*. | 麥 穗, korenhalmen afstroopen.

īng láh lút soà. 用 臘 | 線. garen over was strijken.

袓 Opstroopen.
Lút *lút ts'iú íng* (» » *ńg*) | 手 袖. de mouwen opstroopen.

Ma

酗 *ma ma*. | 匕. beschonken.
Ma *ma tsuì*. | 醉. do.

tsuì ma ma. 醉 | |. zeer do.

ma tsiú, | 酒. steeds beschonken.

ma ma haò, | 匕 吼. bulken van koeijen.

㧕 Maar, namelijk.
Má *má ū*. | 有, maar het is er immers.

má bô. | 無. » » » » niet.

i ai boé tsit ē uī má bô, 他 愛 採 此 處 | 無, hij wilde het koopen maar het was hier niet voorhanden.

媽 Grootmoeder van moederszijde.
Má *laō má á*, 老 | 仔, oude vrouw, oud moedertje.

Má *goā má*, 外 |, grootmoeder van moederszijde.

laī má, 內 |, grootmoeder van vaderszijde.

kong má, 公 |. grootvader en grootmoeder.

má tsó pô, | 祖 婆. godin der zeevarenden.

má tsó pô hî. | 祖 婆 魚. witte dolfijn.

馬 *má siāng*. | 上, in allerijl.
Má *ts'ien lí má*, 千 里 |. courier, brievenlooper.

亦 Toch ook, immers.
Mā *mā sī*. | 是, toch immers is het.

罵 *mā lâng*. | 人, iemand uitschelden.
Mā

Mah

麼 Eind vraag partikel, of niet?
Mah *sī mah*. 什 |. is het zoo niet?

ū mah, 有 |. is het er of niet?

hó mah, 好 |. is het goed? zijt gij welvarende?

Mai

Mai *bīn mai*, gelaat, gezigt, (lage uitdr.)

買 *mai tsiòk*. | 囑, omkoopen.
Mai *k'oà mai ū i*, 看 | 有 伊, (waarsch verdraaid mandarijnsch,) iemand geringachten.

Mao

毛 Moȯ *maȯ pīng*, 丨病, iets verkeerd, defect.

茅 Maȯ *maȯ ts'aȯ*, 丨草, lang stroo.

tsoè làng maȯ sin maȯ sin, 做人丨神丨神, slordig, nalatig, vergeetachtig zijn.

oè maȯ tit, 可丨的, men kan er vlugtig over heen loopen.

漠 Maȯ *maȯ maȯ*, 丨匕, onzeker, door elkander.

tsīng maȯ lah, 真丨了, zeer door de war, verward (als eene rekening.

矛 Maȯ *maȯ tún*, 丨盾, tegenstrijdig met.

鍪 Maȯ Een chacot, met veeren pluim.

tì maȯ, 戴丨, een chacot, steek opzetten.

貌 Maō *bīn maō*, 面丨, gelaat.

p'in maō, 品丨, voorkomen, uiterlijk.

giók maō tsu tûn, 玉丨朱唇, een fraai gelaat, (van vrouwen.)

tsai maō song tsoân, 才丨雙全, zoowel knap als fraai van uiterlijk.

siòng maō (*siáng* ») 相丨, gelaat voorkomen.

ū lé maō, 有禮丨, vriendelijk beleefd.

maō mī, *maō maō tsoè tsit tui* } zie *baō*.

Me

速 Mé *t'ám mé* (*t'iém* ») 至丨, haasten, haastig, onmiddelijk.

mé ts'ì, 丨醒, iets gaauw merken.

kin mé, 緊丨, onmiddelijk.

罵 Mē Uitlachen, uitschelden.

sa mē, 相丨, elkander uitschelden.

loé mē (*lé* ») 丨詈, bespotten, uitschelden.

tsiù mē, 咒丨, schelden.

t'ik mē, 斥丨, bekijven, uitschelden.

k'a ts'eng aū mē, 背後丨, achter iemands rug kwaad van hem spreken.

sa mē hūn bò oē, 相丨恨不能, elkander uitscheldende bang zijn geene woorden laag genoeg te hebben.

Meh

蜢 Meh *ts'aò meh*, 草丨, sprinkhaan.

怵 Méh *sim koa méh tsìt é*, 心肝丨然, eensklaps ontstellen.

哶 Mèh *iû méh méh haó*, 羊丨匕吼, blaten van schapen of geiten.

脉 Méh De pols,

k'ì méh, 氣丨, levenskracht.

huih méh, 血丨, de aderen.

bong méh, 按丨, de pols voelen.

bò méh, 無丨, geen pols hebben; niet meer slaan van de pols.

méh kó, 丨股, slagaderen.

toē méh (*tē* ») 地丨, aderen in de aarde.

Meng

芒 Meng Mui *meng meng á*, 丨丨仔, fijn, fijntjes.

iù meng meng, 幼丨匕, zeer fijn.

soa meng, 山丨, fijn gras op de bergen.

koah meng, 割丨, gras snijden eig. de uiteinden, toppen, van grassen.

濛 Meng *hō meng meng*, 雨丨匕, stofregen.

晚 **Laat.**
Míng *míng tsing*, | 種, laat zaaisel.
Muị *tsá míng*, 早 |, weldra: eerlang: morgen en avond: vroeg en laat.

bē míng (*boé muị*) 未 |, nog niet te laat.

k'ah míng. 甚 |, later.

míng po̱, | 晡, na den middag.

dzit míng, 日 |, laat in den dag.

míng kiá, | 子, kind dat men nog op gevorderden leeftijd krijgt.

門 Deur; numer voor kanonnen, geweren,
Míng enz.
Muị *míng hō̱*, | 戶, deuren (in het algemeen.)

toā sì míng, 單 扇 |, enkele deur.

sang sì míng (*siang » »*) 雙 扇 |, dubbele deur.

k'áh míng. 掩 |, de deur aanzetten.

míng sì, | 扇, deurvleugels.

míng k'iā, | 柱, posten van de deur.

míng bai, | 楣, boven drempel.

míng k'ing. | 規, deurkozijn.

k'à míng, 扣 |, aan de deur kloppen.

gê míng (*gî »*) 衙 |, mandarijn bureau.

míng k'ien, | 牽, knop van een deur, (met eene ring er aan.)

míng ling (*liu*), | 鈕, knop van een deur.

míng tuì, | 對, opschriften op de huisdeurvleugels geplakt.

k'ah toā míng, grootendeels.

tsui míng, 水 |, sluisdeuren.

míng ak, | 楄, overhelling, afdak boven een deur.

míng ting, | 丁, deurwaker, deur oppasser.

míng tsiū (*» tsiō̱*) | 上, do.

tâng míng, 仝 |, dochters uit hetzelfde huis gehuwd hebben.

tsit míng tiā, 一 | 錠, één anker.

míng t'aô, | 頭, mandarijn's geheim schrijver.

míng hong. 風 |, faam van een huis, (goede of kwade.)

tsīng míng ê kè, 盡 | 之 價, uiterste prijs die men geven kan.

kui míng oá kak, 歸 | 倚 角, geheel en al opgeborgen zijn, geconcentreerd zijn, (als handels monopolie).

míng lō̱, | 路, ingang of uitgang, deur met corresponderenden weg.

bô míng t'ang dzip, 無 | 可 入, geen deur hebben om integaan, *d. i.* geene gelegenheid hebben met iemand in betrekking te komen.

káng míng, 港 |, inkomen tot een haven, haven.

bē dzip míng ang tsiū si, 未 入 | 翁 就 死, voor dat zij gehuwd was stierf haar (aanstaande) man.

koaị míng ts'ut, 閉 | 出, uit eene affaire gaan zonder iets mede te nemen.

kóng oē bô koaị aō míng, 說 話 無 關 後 |, sprekende de achterdeur niet sluiten, *d. i.* onvoorzigtig spreken zonder zeker te zijn niet afgeluisterd te kunnen worden.

míng k'aó, | 口, gat van de deur.

tsui sien míng, 水 仙 |, gangboord.

pàng tsáp míng ts'ìng. 放 十 銃 |, tien geweerschoten lossen.

tsit ki siang mìng, 一枝雙|的, een dubbelloopsch (geweer).

悶 Mîng *mìng kui*, |機, geheime sluiting aan een deur.

毛 Haar, vederen.

Mîng *mìng kìng ts'ut koā ê tsî*, |曾出汗之錢, hard verdiend geld.

t'aû mìng, 頭|, hoofdhaar.

iû mìng (*iô mô*) 羊|, schapenvacht.

bīn si mìng, 面生|, haar op het gelaat hebben als een beest, (scheld,)

mìng sui, 綏|, haarkrans, die bijgenoegzame lengte bij den hoofdstaart wordt ingevlochten.

k'ó mìng, 苦|, haren over het ligchaam.

mìng ts'aó, |草, beestenvachten, (om aan te doen, kleederen van beesten vachten gemaakt.

àng mìng làng, 紅|人, roodharige menschen, (Eurp. Eng.)

問 Vragen, vragen naar.

Mīng (Muī) *ts'à mīng*, 查|, vragen naar, ondervragen.

mīng liû, |流, tot verbanning veroordeelen.

mīng k'oà, |看, gaan vragen naar iets.

kià mīng, 寄|, een ander opdragen iets te vragen.

tsioh mīng, 借|, zou ik U mogen vragen of . . . .

sa tsioh mīng, 相借|, elkander aanspreken.

mīng an, |案, in eene regtszaak ondervragen.

sim mīng, 審|, geregtelijk ondervragen.

sè mīng, 細|, zorgvuldig ondervragen.

mīng tsiâ si tsoē, |成死罪, ter dood veroordeelen.

mīng lō, |路, naar den weg vragen.

mīng ioh, |藥, om medicijnen vragen.

Mi

捻 Mi Me Opnemen, opgrijpen met de geheele hand.

mi soa, |沙, zand opnemen.

mi iêm si sim koā, |鹽或心肝 niet meer aan iets denken, iets opgegeven hebben.

mi tsit mi hō i, |一|與他, iemand een vingergreep van iets geven.

mi t'oa, 攤|, met de vingers verschillende hoopjes van iets afnemen.

mi mi tsoè tsit pé, ||做一把, tot een bundel bij elkander nemen (als penseelen enz.)

Mi *k'a mi ts'iú mi*, 脚|手|, handen en voeten zamengetrokken van koude enz.

k'a tsiah bâng mi, 背後挽|, eene koude rilling over den rug krijgen, (van vrees.)

夜 Mi Nacht, late avond.

tsó mi, 昨|, gisternacht of avond.

mi sih, |間, 's nachts.

kin mi, 今|, heden nacht.

poà mi, 半|, middernacht.

mi ts'im, |深, diep in den nacht.

tsē mi, 坐|, 's nachts op blijven zitten.

sa ki mi poà (*» e mê »*) 三更|半, diep in den nacht.

kui mi, 仝|, den geheelen nacht.

t'aò mi̤, 頭 |. gedurende den nacht, des nachts.

棉 Mi̤ Katoen, watten, wol, gewatteerd.

mi̤ hoe, | 花, katoen.

mi̤ á, | 仔, watten.

mi̤ se (» *se̤*) | 紗, katoen garen.

mi̤ hoe ts'iū, | 花 樹, katoenboom.

p'ah mi̤, 打 |, watten kammen.

綿 Mi̤ *mi̤ hiù*, | 裘, gewatteerde jas.

mi̤ p'ē (» *p'oē*) 被 |. gewatteerde deken.

dzip mi̤, 入 |, watteren.

si mi̤, 絲 |, zijden watten.

p'áng mi̤. 紡 |, watten spinnen.

mi̤ pò̤, | 布. wollige stof.

toā mi̤. 彈 |. watten kammen.

mi̤ king (» *kiong*) | 弓, boog die men gebruikt bij het wol of watten kammen.

tsi hoe mi̤ (» *hoa* ») 紫 | 花. bruine wol of watten.

訛 Mi̤ Uiterst scherp.

bò mi̤ bò kak, 無 | 無 角, niet afgerond noch met duidelijke hoeken.

kè mi̤ kè kak, 過 | 過 角, fijn afronden en de hoeken aanbrengen, de fijne puntjes aanbrengen, door de naauwe gevaarlijke hoekjes komen, (als een schip.)

to mi̤ mi̤ mi̤, 刀 | 匕, het mes is zeer scherp.

tó mi̤, 倒 |. omkrullen van het lemmer van een mes.

盲 Mi̤ *ts'i̤ mi̤*, 目 |. blind.

tsiah mi̤, 赤 |. kippig, bijziende.

bák tsiah mi̤, 目 赤 |. do. 's avonds niet kunnen zien.

慌 Mi̤ *mi̤ tsi̤*, | 爭, onverschrokken, door tastend, (in handel enz.)

mi̤ mi̤, | 匕, met alle geweld tocht;

mi̤ mi̤ mi̤, | | |, onverschrokken, (steeds terugkomen.)

mi̤ t'iòng, | 虫, ontembaar, onweerstaanbaar in zijne begeerte voor iets.

明 Mi̤ *mi̤ ni̤*, | 年, het volgend jaar.

麵 Mī *mī hún*, | 粉, meel.

iù ná mī nih, 幼 如 | 粉, fijn als meel.

mī piá, | 餅, soort beschuit, scheepsbeschuit.

mī pao, | 包, brood.

mī soà, | 線, vermicellie van tarwe.

mī soà oē (» » *oā*) | 線 話, langdradige taal.

mī t'ui, | 鎚, deegroller, deegbraker.

p'ah mī, 打 |, deegrollen.

ts'iao mī, 調 |, deegkneden.

kiaò mī, 攪 |, deeg aanmaken.

noá mī. 揉 |, deegkneden.

mī sit, | 食, gebak, meelspijs.

ts'i̤ mī (*ts'e̤* ») 生 |, ongebakken deeg.

mī tse (» *tso*) | 糟, deeg.

mī gû, | 牛, groote kockjes eter. iemand die veel van meelspijs eet.

tsat mī, 漆 |, soort stopverf.

mī tsià, | 炙, 'uitschot, meelgruis.

Mih

麽 Mih Hoe toch?

mih taī (*sá sū*) 何 事, wat? wat is er?

mịh hāng tsoè tsit t'àng, | 項 做, allerlei dingen gedaan hebben.

bọ́ mịh làng, 某 | 人. zekeriemand, deze of gene.

mịh miậ mị sì̤, | 名 | 姓, welke naam en familienaam?

mịh làng kóng, | 人 說, wie heeft het gezegd.

sim mịh làng, 甚 | 人, wie?

sim mịh, 怎 |, wat?

Mịb *mịh baó*, | 卯, zoo maar inslikken, (van eten of geld.)

物 Mịh Voorwerp, ding.

mịh p'è (» *p'oé*) | 配, bijgerechten.

mịh kiạ̄, | 件, dingen in het algemeen, voorwerpen.

mịh á mịh, 麼 仔 |, allerlei dingen.

p'aị mịh, 歹 |, slecht ding, slecht wezen.

mịh tsiáh, | 食, eetwaren.

Mia

名 Miậ Naam.

tâng miậ (*kāng* ») 同 |. van denzelfden naam.

piaó miậ, 表 |. den naam geven van.

ts'iem miậ, 簽 |, handteekening.

ts'ut miậ, 出 |, algemeen bekend, beroemd; zich aan het hoofd van iets stellen.

miậ siạ̄, | 聲, beroemdheid.

ū miậ siạ̄, 有 | 聲, beroemd.

huì miậ, 諱 |, melknaam.

dzú miậ (*dzí* ») 乳 |, do.

tsū miậ, 字 |, geletterde naam.

t'aō dzit miậ, 第 一 |, de eerste.

miậ sì̤, | 姓. naam en familienaam.

hō miậ, 號 |, onderkenningsnaam.

miậ dzī, | 字, persoons naam.

miậ kiò..., | 叫...., heeten, genoemd worden.

t'oân miậ seh siạ̄ (» » *soeh* ») 傳 | 說 聲, overal bekend.

bô miậ t'iep, 無 | 帖, anonieme brief.

miậ dzī t'aó, | 字 透, beroemd. alom bekend.

koé miậ oā sì̤ (*ké* » » *sè̤*) 改 | 換 姓. van naam en familienaam veranderen.

miậ p'ièn, | 片, naam, visitekaartje.

ū miậ bô sit, 有 | 無 實. den naam maar niet de daad hebben, slechts in naam zoo zijn.

ū miậ hiáh ê làng, 有 | 聲 之 人, een bekend beroemd mensch.

ts'ang miậ, 聰 |, knap, beroemd.

樒 Miậ *ts'à miậ*, 木 |, harstlaag in boomen.

ts'ing peh miậ, 松 柏 |. gomlaag in pijnboom.

明 Miậ *ts'ì miậ* (*tsing bing*) 清 |. gravenfeest.

命 Miā̤ Leven, lot.

sì̤ miā, 性 |, leven.

k'oā miā. 看 |, waarzeggen.

siòng miā, 相 |, do.

k'oā miā sien sị (» » *sin sẹ*) 看 | 先 生, waarzegger.

miā tsu, | 書, waarzeggersboek.

t'oa miā, 拖 |, met ziekte onder de leden, iets doen.

海上絲綢之路文獻集成　科技與文化編

siu tioh miā, 相 着 |, denk aan uw (ongelukkig) noodlot.

p'e miā } 拚 |, zijn leven blootstellen.
(*p'oe* ») }

hó miā, 好 |, gelukkig noodlot.

p'ai miā, 歹 |, ongelukkig

miā ūn, | 運, lot, noodlot.

giėp miā, 業 |, hard noodlot, hard leven.

poà tiaô miā, 半 條 |, slechts half in leven zijn, (door zware ziekte of ellende.)

ts'ut sin miā, 出 身 |, zich uiterst inspannen, overspannen.

Mo

毛[*] Familienaam.
Mô

mô hoē } | 蟹, rivierkreeft.
(» *hē*) }

mô ièn, | 燕, behaarde vogelnestjes.

mô t'âng ts'ì, | 虫 莿, fijne steekels over het lijf van visschen, ook gezegd van menschen waar men liever niet mee moet omgaan.

mô ko, | 菰, champignon, agaricus.

mô taī siaó bėh } | 大 小 襪, gebreide sokken.
(» » » *boėh*) }

kap lâng mô taī, iemand bedriegen, in moeijelijkheden wikkelen.

魔 *mô kui*, | 鬼, duivel.
Mô
Mô

冒 *mō hiém*, | 險, gevaar, kans loopen om, trotseren het gevaar.
Mō
Mō

mō hiém tsoè } | 險 做, gevaar loopen om.
(» » *tsoh*) }

mō miā, | 名, valschelijke iemands naam aannemen.

kà mō } 假 |, valschelijk uitgeven voor.
(*kė* ») }

kám mō, 感 |, een gevatte koude.

mō dzīn, | 認, valschelijk voor het zijne verklaren.

耄 Suf, (van oude menschen.)
Mō

ló mō, 老 |, do.

hun mō, 昏 |, suf, (door ouderdom.)

Moh

瘼 *moh moh*, 消 |, mager, ingevallen.
Moh

moh tiaô tiaô, zich tegen iets vasthechten, vastklampen, (als een vleermuis of nat papier tegen een muur.)

moh loh k'ì, plat worden, slinken, (als een blaas of zak waar men den wind uitlaat.)

膜 Vlies onmiddelijk onder de huid gelegen.
Móh

tik móh, 竹 |, bamboezen vlies, bij sommige fluiten gebezigd.

ts'ang móh, 葱 |, vlies van uijen; op fluiten geplakt.

koe nn̄g móh } 雞 蛋 |, eivlies.
(» *nuī* ») }

p'in á móh, 笛 仔 |, bamboezen vlies over een fluit.

sa móh móh, 衫 | |, dun gekleed.

sán móh móh, 瘦 | |, mager.

tsit ting móh túh p'oà, 一 重 | 抵 破, als een vlies door te steken, *d. i.* gemakkelijk.

Moa

袚 *moa sa*, | 衣, zich een kleed omgooijen, (los.)
Moa

moa tsang sui, | 棕 蓑, zich een regenmantel omgooijen.

49

[*] Zie verder onder *mng*.

肩 Moa̤ *sa̤ moa̤*, 駢 〡, de armen om elkanders schouders slaan.

槾 *toā moā*, 大 〡, lang overkleed.

Moa̤ *bōng moa̤*, 墓 〡, grafheuvel, langs een graf.

moa̤ soa̤, 〡 山, grafheuvel achter een graf.

滿 Moá̤ Vol, nummer voor hazardspelen.

moá̤ k'aò ē péh ts'at, 〡 口 說 謊, niets anders dan leugens vertellen.

pá moá̤, 充 〡, vol, verzadigd.

moá̤ tsiok sim ì, 〡 足 心 意, zijne begeerte voldoen.

bò moá̤ ì, 不 〡 意, onvoldoende.

moá̤ ki̤, 〡 墘, boordevol.

moá̤ géh (» *goéh*) 〡 月, een volle maand, 彌 月, volle dracht eener zwangere vrouw.

moá̤ sin, 〡 身, het geheele ligchaam.

moá̤ t'i̤ ē (» » *ē̤*) 〡 天 下, over de geheele wereld.

moá̤ sì koè (» » *kè*) 〡 四 處, overal.

moá̤ t'i̤ ts'i̤ (» » *ts'e̤*) 〡 天 星, heldere sterren hemel.

liên tsiong géh moá̤ (» » *goéh* ») 年 終 月 〡, einde van het jaar.

moá̤ soa̤, 〡 山, over het geheele gebergte, het gebergte vol.

moá̤ tiô̤, 〡 塲, de geheele troep, al de personen.

moá̤ bī̤n, 〡 面, het geheele gelaat.

k'ièm lâng tsè bē moá̤, 欠 人 債 未 〡, zijne schuld (van vorige levens) nog niet geheel afbetaald hebben (gezegd als een arm mensch gedurig om geld komt vragen.)

ān moá̤, 限 〡, de tijd van betaling huur enz. is daar, verstreken.

kè ì king moá̤ poâ̤, 價 已 經 〡 盤, de prijs is reeds zoo laag als maar kan.

nñg moá̤ ē kiaó, 二 〡 之 賭, twee dobbelspelen.

麻 · Moâ̤ Hennep.

moâ̤ sa̤, 〡 衣, hennepen kleed, begrafenis kleed.

蔴 Moâ̤ *moâ̤ laò pao*, 〡 荖 包, rouwmuts, (zware rouw.)

moâ̤ tsî, 〡 仁, hennep zaad.

moâ̤ iû, 〡 油, hennepolie.

moâ̤ dziông, 〡 絨, dweil, zwabber.

moâ̤ kûn, 〡 裙, hennepen doek, (bij grooten rouw gedragen.)

kā i t'ìng tsit niá̤ moâ̤ sa̤ lai ts'ìng, 爲 伊 脫 一 領 〡 衫 來 着, onwetend zich een ander mans last op de hals halen.

moâ̤ kut, 〡 骨, de stengels van hennep tot fidebussen bereid.

moâ̤ soh, 〡 索, henneptouw.

moâ̤ tsî, koekjes van fijne rijst met hennep er in, (ook voor vulva gebruikt.)

瞞 Moâ̤ Bedriegen.

moâ̤ p'ièn, 〡 騙, bedriegen.

k'i moâ̤, 欺 〡, bedriegen.

moâ̤ si̤ lâng bák (» *se̤* » ») 〡 生 人 目, publieke bedriegerij, iemand voor zijn oogen bedriegen.

moâ̤ koa̤ p'ièn kui, 〡 官 諞 鬼, in een regterlijk onderzoek, leugens vertellen.

厦荷大辭典

moâ ang p'iên sài, ┃ 翁 騙 婿, haren man bedriegen.

鰻 Moâ *moâ hi*, ┃ 魚, soort aal.

Mui

梅 Mui *iông mui* (*iâng boê*) 楊 ┃, bubo.

mui hoe, ┃ 花, perzikbloem.

媒 Mui *koa mui* (» *boê*) 官 ┃, vrouwelijke gevangenis oppasster.

煤 Mui *mui t'oà*, ┃ 炭, steenkolen.

hé t'oà mui, 火 炭 ┃, gruis van houtskoolen.

妹 Muī *muī hu*, ┃ 夫, zwager, (jongere zuster's man.)

Na

愈 Ná *ná tsoē ná hó* (» *tsē* ») ┃ 多 ┃ 好, hoe meer hoe liever.

ná .... ná .... ┃ .... ┃ ...., hoe meer .... des te ....

ná tsoē, ┃ 多, hoe langer hoe meer.

ná koâ, 漸 寒, hoe langer hoe kouder.

ná dzoàh, ┃ 熱, hoe langer hoe warmer.

若 Ná *ná ts'in ts'iū* (» « *ts'iū*) ┃ 相 似, na genoeg, als, evenals.

緩 Nâ *nâ kiâ*, ┃ 行, ga langzaam vooruit.

nâ kiâ nâ kóng, ┃ 行 ┃ 說, loopen en spreken.

拿 Ná *só ná*, 鎖 ┃, vatten en boeijen.

ná má tsing, ┃ 媽 僧, Lama priester.

橄 Nâ *ka nâ*, ┃ 欖, olijf.

電 Nâ *sih nâ*, 閃 ┃, bliksem.

nâ kng, ┃ 光, glinsteren, flikkeren.

kng nâ nâ, 光 ┃ ┃, helder, glimsterend.

kng kàu nâ bīn, 光 到 ┃ 面, zoo helder dat het een beeld terugkaatst.

nâ tsch tsiū k'ì, ┃ 一 便 去, zich een oogenblik vertoonen en weer weggaan.

嚨 Nâ *nâ aô*, ┃ 喉, strot.

nâ aô kut, ┃ 喉 骨, adams appel

籃 Nâ Mand, ben.

nâ kiā, ┃ 規, geraamte van iemand.

siū nâ, 盛 ┃, groote etenskorf.

nâ k'ing, ┃ 筐, hengselmand, ook rand om een mand.

sit nâ, 食 ┃, etenskorf.

kao nâ, 鉤 ┃, hangmand.

ts'ài nâ, 菜 ┃, groenten en alles wat bij de rijst gebruikt wordt.

nâ á poát, ┃ 仔 拔, guava.

林 Nâ *ts'iū nâ*, 樹 ┃, bosch.

tik nâ, 竹 ┃, bamboes bosch.

nâ pô, ┃ 蒲, boschje.

soa nâ, 山 ┃, bergbosch.

巖 Nâ *ling nâ*, 龍 ┃, district in *Fokiën*. waarvan daan thee en papier komt.

藍 Nâ Familienaam.

鐃 Nâ *hé nâ tsoâ*, 火 ┃ 泉, plotseling, bij toeval vuur vatten.

Nâ *nâ poáh*, ┃ 鈸, met bekkens gooijen, (als Boeddha priesters doen.)

但 Nā *m̄ nā*, 不 ┃, niet alleen ...., niet zoo weinig als .... meer dan ....

nā̠ sī an ni̠, | 是如此, en niets anders.

ı̄m nā̠ tsáp è tsi̠, 不 | 十文錢, niet zoo (weinig) als tien duiten *d. i* meer dan dat.

ı̄m nā̠ kaó tiém, 不 | 九點, later dan negen uur.

Nā̠ *nā̠ tioh hé* (» » *hoé*) } verschroeid worden, door vuur).

nā̠ o̠ ien, door rook of roet aangeslagen.

若 Als, wanneer, ingeval dat.

Nā̠ *tàn nā̠*, 但 |, slechts.

nā̠ tiā̠, 而已, slechts en anders niet.

nā̠ án ni̠, | 如此, als het zoo is.

nā̠ bô, | 無, tenzij.

Nah

凹 Concave.

Na̠h *na̠h p'ī̠*, | 鼻, ingebogen neus.

tsit na̠h tsit na̠h, 一 | 又一 |, vol bulten, deuken.

na̠h lo̍h k'ì, | 落去, inbuigen, met deuken worden.

k'í ts'in mo̠h na̠h, 起縱膜 |, roode hond hebben.

Nga

雅 *ngá̠ ngá̠*, | 乜, zeer beleefd.

Ngá̠ *hong ngá̠*, 風 |, beleefd, fatsoenlijk.

ı̄m ngá̠, 不 |, niet beleefd, niet lief.

bûn ngá̠, 文 |, deftig, beleofd.

ngá̠ tì, | 致, do. fatsoenlijk, fraai.

ngá̠ ì, | 意, beleefde bedoeling.

Ngai

齩 Kaauwen, knagen op.

Ngai̠ *ngai̠ tioh*, | 着, tegen iets aanschrijnen, aanstooten.

碍 *gi ngai̠*, 疑 |, twijfelen in twijfel. Ngai̠ trekken, vermoeden opvatten.

Nai

荔 *naī̠ tsi*, | 枝, *lai tsi*, vrucht, Dimocarpus litchi; Naī̠ *o̠ hióh*, 烏葉, *kùi lim*, 桂林, *tsiong goân hòng*, 黃狀元, *iā̠ tsing*, 野種, namen van *naī̠ tsi*.

naī̠ tsi ko̠a, | 枝乾, gedroogde *lai tsi*.

柰 *bû naī̠*, 無 |. er was niets aan te Naī̠ doen of......

bû naī̠ hô, 無 | 何, onvermijdelijk.

sat naī̠, 撒 |, slecht, boosaardig van vrouwen.

Nao

腦 *t'aô naó̠*, 頭 |, de hersenen, het Naó̠ hoofd, baas van iets.

aō naó̠, 拗 |, het achterhoofd.

hî naó̠, 魚 |, vischhersenen.

tsūn t'aô naó̠ taō, 伸頭 |, het hoofd in allerlei bochten wringen. (als bij zingen.)

惱 *hoat naó̠*, 發 |. vertoornd worden. Naó̠ *naó̠ hūn*, | 恨, vertoornd worden en haten.

aò naǵ, 懊 ｜, knorrig, niet opgeruimd zijn.

閙 Naō̤ *naō̤ tōng*, ｜ 動. verward geraas, leven maken.

dziṳng naō̤ (*dziáng* „) } 嚷 ｜, kijven.

Naoh

收 Naoh *naoh naoh kóng*, ｜ 匕 說, zwetsen, aframmelen.

naoh tse lai naoh tse k'ì, ｜ 一 來 ｜ 一 去, verward door elkander opzeggen; *lett*. dan van hier dan van daar kaauwen.

甲 Naoh *noah tsit ts'uì*, ｜ 一 嘴, een mondvol kaauwen, (van beesten.)

hō̤ kaó naoh tioh, 被 狗 ｜ 着, den honden te kaauwen, te eten geven.

Naóh *soǹ naóh naóh*, 散 ｜ 匕, overal verward verspreid.

nị nạ naóh naóh, van alles bij elkander geraapt, niet veel bijzonders.

Ngao

Ngaò *ngaò ioh*, ｜ 藥, medicijnen hard laten koken.

ngaō̤ mị (of *bin*), ｜ 夜, laat naar bed gaan, (als dobbelaars, enz.)

ngaò tsiú ｜ 酒, steeds wijn drinken.

ngaò sik, ｜ 色, zich steeds aan de vrouwen overgeven.

Ngaò *liok ngaò hoat tōng*, 六 ｜ 發 動, de zes diagrammen (die bij eene waarzegging gebruikt worden,) geraken in beroering, *d. i.* van alle kanten op eens uitbreken, (van eene ziekte of oproer.)

藕 Ngaō̤ *hên ngaō̤*, 蓮 ｜, Lotuswortel.

ngaō̤ hún, ｜ 粉, zetmeel van Lotuswortel.

ngaō̤ tsat, ｜ 節. geledingen in den Lotuswortel.

ts'è ngaō̤ ngaō̤, 䔖 ｜ ｜, broos.

樂 Ngaō̤ *ngaō̤ ngaō̤ liām*, ｜ 匕 念, overmompelen, prevelen.

goá sō̤ ngaō̤, 我 所 ｜, datgene waarnaar ik sterk verlang.

k'ok ngaō̤, 酷 ｜, sterk verlangen naar.

唧 Ngaóh *ngaóh ngaóh haò*, ｜ ｜ 吼. grommen, mompelen.

甲 Ngaoh *tsit ngaoh haō̤*, 一 ｜ 鮫, een paar koningskrabben.

Ngeh

Ngeh *bô lâm bô ngẹh*, niet veel werk van zijne pligt maken.

鑷 Oppakken, oppikken.

Ngẹh *īng tī ngẹh ts'aì*, 用 箸 菜 ｜, met de eetstokjes groenten oppikken.

ngẹh á, ｜ 仔, pincette, tangetje.

goá hō̤ lí boē ngẹh tit, 我 與 汝 未 ｜ 的. Ik laat mij door U niet oppikken, *d. i.* beetnemen.

夾 Knijpen, (tusschen knijpers.)

Ngéh *tsim kóng ngéh*, 蟳 鑛 ｜, krabbetangen.

sán tsim sa ngéh, 瘦 蟳 相 ｜, magere krabben knijpen elkander, *d. i.* arme menschen die elkander tot last zijn.

ts'iu ngéh tioh mīng p'ūng, 手 ｜ 在

門 縫, met de hand tusschen de deur blijven zitten.

nĕng làng ngĕ̤h i tsit làng. 二 人 ｜ 伊 一 人, met hun tweeën knijpen zij hem alleen, *d. i.* kwellen.

Neng

穿 *k'u nĕng dzĭp lai* (» *mui̤* » ») } 脚 ｜ 入 來, zijn voet in iets steken.
Mĕng *nĕng kè k'i* (» *koè* ») } ｜ 過 去, door iets kruipen, insteken (als een draad in de naald.)

laī bīn sì koè nĕng, 內 面 四 處 ｜, binnen's huis overal heen loopen.

tuì tsit k'ang nĕng ts'ut lai hō̤ goàh, 對 一 空 ｜ 出 來 與 我, steek het mij door dit gat toe.

軟 Zacht, elastiek.
Nĕng *nĕng tsiā̤.* ｜ 弱, zwak, tenger.
Nui̤ *nĕng dziók* (*mui̤ dziák*) } ｜ 弱, zacht, week.

nĕng sĕng t'iā̤. ｜ 酸 痛, zeer, pijnlijk,

nĕng nĕng dzūn dzūn. ｜ ｜ 膩 匕, zacht, elastiek.

iù nĕng, 幼 ｜, fijn en zacht.

nĕng k'a, ｜ 脚, zwak ter been.

k'a sĕng ts'iú nĕng (» *sui̤* » ») } 脚 酸 手 ｜, zwak aan armen en beenen.

nĕng sim. ｜ 心, teergevoelig, teerhartig.

nĕng ts'uì. ｜ 嘴, zachtzinnig.

nĕng ki. ｜ 枝, teeder twijgje.

nĕng nĕng sìm sìm, nĕng sim. ｜ 匕 滲 匕, slap, zwabberend als een lange dunne plant

nĕng nĕng siò siò, ｜ 匕 搖 匕 zacht en slap.

nĕng á, ｜ 仔, een zwak mensch. (di ligt te bedriegen is.)

nĕng tsú tē, ｜ 子 弟, zachtzinnig fats. jongelieden, (gemakkelijk te be driegen.)

nĕng gîn, ｜ 銀, geld waar nog eenig onkosten afmoet.

nĕng lūn, ｜ 潤, zacht, meêgevend (van stof.)

toūn nĕng, 緞 ｜, zijden-zachte stoffen

tsit sin k'u ts'ìng kaò nĕng kaoh kaoh 一 身 穿 至 ｜ 咯 匕, niet anders dan zachte *d. i.* zijden stoffe aan hebben.

nĕng t'e, ｜ 胎, zacht, souple mode (als van hoeden.)

kè tsi̤ k'ah nĕng, 價 錢 稍 ｜, d prijs is wat zachter, lager.

nĕng ts'iú, ｜ 手, zwakke, bevend hand, (als om te dooden.)

攢 *nĕng k'ì,* ｜ 去, doorkruipen.
Nĕng *nĕng k'ang.* ｜ 隙, door een gat krui-
Nui̤ pen.
nĕng kè (*nui̤ koè*) ｜ 過, doorkruipen.

nĕn tsi̤ k'ang, ｜ 錢 孔, door he gat van een chineeschen cent, hee kruipen, *d. i.* geldzuchtig.

kui nĕng, 鬼 ｜, als een geest over inkruipen, *d. i.* overal de goede gaatjes gelegenheden kennen, (voor handel enz.)

sì koè nĕng t'aò t'aò, 四 處 ｜ 透 匕, in alle hoekjes en gaatjes ge weest zijn.

nĕng p'ūng, van een gunstig oogenblik gebruik maken.

郞 *sī nĕng,* 侍 ｜, vice-president van een
Nĕng departement.

挪 *pin nîng*, 檳 〡, siri.
Nîng

膩 Vruchtvleesch.
Nîng *dzī nîng*, 〡 膿, de laag vet tusschen vel en vleesch.

卵 Ei.
Nîng Nuī *koe nîng* (*ke muī*) } 雞 〡, ei van eene kip.

nîng ts'ing, 〡 清, eiwit.

nîng dzîn, 〡 仁, dooier van het ei.

nîng k'ak, 〡 殼, eijerschaal.

si nîng (*sī* ») } 生 〡, eijeren leggen.

pū nîng, 毻 〡, op eijeren broeijen.

pàng nîng, 放 〡, eijeren schieten als visch.

nîng péh (» *péh*) } 〡 白, wit van een ei.

nîng moh, 毛 〡, eivlies.

p'ah nîng, 鬥 〡, hom schieten op de kuit.

ts'oah nîng, 妺 〡, kuit schieten.

laò nîng, 溜 〡, een ei zonder schaal voortbrengen.

ts'iú aō nîng, 手 後 〡, elleboog knokkel.

k'a aō nîng, 脚 後 〡, de kiel.

tsióh nîng. 石 〡, ronde steenen.

二 Twee.
Nîng *nîng ē*, 兩 箇, beiden, twee.

浪 *p'o nîng*. 渡 〡, de golven.
Nîng

Ni

拈 Met de vingers oppakken, (als snuif.)
Nị *nị liām*, 〡 捻, van alles wat afnemen proeven.

nị nị sị sị, 〡 七 針 七, van alles weinig eten.

乳 De borsten.
Nị *nị bú*, *ling bú*, 〡 母, natte min.

染 Indoopen, verwen.
Nị *nị kang*, 〡 缸, verfkuip.

nị pâng, 〡 房, ververij.

k'iū nị, 豎 〡, er eene ververij op na houden.

péh péh pì nị kaò o, 白 匕 布 〡 到 烏, zoo sterk een onschuldige van iets betichten dat het den schijn van waar krijgt.

nị pì sai hū, 〡 布 師 阜, lakenverver.

nị sik, 〡 色, verven, geverfd, (van stoffen).

企 Oplichten.
Nì Nè *nì k'a bé* (» » *boé*) 〡 脚 尾, de hielen oplichten, op de teenen gaan staan.

nì koaị, 〡 仰, zich op de teenen verheffen.

kiū peh nì, 强 〡, zich met geweld tot iets inspannen.

年 Jaar.
Nị *kè nị* (*koè* ») } 過 〡, het jaar overblijven te . . .

nị nị, 〡 〡, jaarlijks.

ták nị, 各 〡, do.

nị t'aò, 〡 頭, begin van het jaar.

nị bé (» *boé*) } 〡 杪, eind van het jaar.

nị hè (» *hoè*) } 〡 歲, leeftijd.

nị kí, 〡 紀, do.

tsing nị (*tsân* ») } 前 〡, vroegere jaren.

ing nị, 常 〡, elk jaar, jaarlijks.

tsùn ni̠, 存 丨, voor verleden jaar.

kū ni̠, 舊 丨, verleden jaar.

mę̂ ni̠, 明 丨, aanstaande jaar.

ni̠ hō, 丨 號. regeringsnaam.

pah ni̠ hè aō, 百 丨 後, na den dood (van U of mij.)

ni̠ tang géh tsoeh (» » *goéh tseh*) } 丨 冬 月 節, feesten door het jaar.

toū ni̠ toū tsoeh (» » » *tseh*) } 大 丨 大 節, algemeene feestdag in het jaar.

paì ni̠, 拜 丨. nieuwjaar wenschen.

sàng ni̠, 送 丨, nieuwjaars geschenken geven.

ni̠ taō, 丨 脚, eind van het jaar.

ni̠ pi̠, 丨 邊. do.

sin ni̠, 新 丨. nieuwjaar.

ni̠ laī, 丨 內, op het eind van het jaar.

hó ni̠ tsoeh, 好 丨 節, gunstige of vrolijke jaarfeesten.

tìng ni̠ ts'aì, 長 丨 菜, groenten op het oudejaar klaar gezet en op nieuwjaar weggenomen.

kè ni̠ pēng (» » *puī*) } 過 丨 飯, rijst die men op het eind van het jaar neerzet, (eten de muizen er van, dan is de aanstaande oogst onvoorspoedig, zoo niet voordeelig.)

ni̠ tang hó siu, 丨 冬 好 收, goede voordeelige oogst.

ni̠ tang hó siu tsiaó tsiah tsiáh bô loū tsoē, 丨 冬 好 收 鳥 隻 食 無 幾 多, van zooveel overvloed mist men een weinigje niet.

連 Familienaam.

Ni̠h *ìng ni̠* (*ui̠ ni̠*) 黃 丨, gentiaan.

披 Uithangen on te droogen.

Ni̠ Nẹ *ni̠ bāng*, 丨 網, een net uitspannen, uithangen.

ni̠ sa̠, 丨 衫, kleeren uithangen.

簷 Ni̠ *ni̠ tsi̠*, 丨 前, uitstekend gedeelte van een dak, waar langs het water afloopt.

哖 Wollen goed, flenel.

Ni̠ *tsui ni̠*, 水 丨, flenel.

sió ni̠, 小 丨, fijn laken.

勁 Hard, stijf.

Nī̠ Nẹ̄ *ìng nī̠ hoat* (*iōng nẹ̄* ») 用 丨 法, gewelddadig.

nī̠ tsiā̠, 丨 健, stijf, (van voorwerpen.

nī̠ piàng piàng, 丨 棒 匕, hard.

kóng nī̠ oē, 說 丨 話, harde taal spreken.

nī̠ k'í, 齒 丨, *lett.* harde tanden, *d. i.* iets niet willen opgeven.

sai nī̠ tsi̠, 使 丨 爭, met geweld indrijven.

nī̠ lát, 丨 力, stevige kracht.

nī sìng, 丨 性. onverdraagzaam.

ts'iú t'aô nī̠, 手 頭 丨, koelbloedig. hardvochtig, (als een geneesheer.)

poà̠ nī̠ níng, 半 丨 軟, hard en zachtzinnig zijn waar het behoort.

sim koa̠ nī̠ è làng, 心 肝 丨 之 人, een hardvochtig mensch.

ts'uì iaó kú teh nī̠, 嘴 尚 敢 說 丨, nog steeds halsstarrig in zijn spreken blijven, niet willen toegeven.

Nih

瞬 Knipoogen; krampachtig optrekken.

Ni̠h *bák ni̠h*, 轉 丨, de oogen knippen.

bák ni̠h kú, 轉 丨 間, in een oogen blik.

nịh bák, | 目, met de oogen knippen, wenken.

分 Nịh
Hulpwoord van plaats.

sọ̄g nịh, 山 |, op de bergen.

tsuí nịh, 水 |, in het water.

hit nịh, 彼 |, op die plaats.

dzít nịh, 日 |, in den zon.

bîn nịh, 眠 |, in zijn slaap.

tsít bák nịh, 一 刻 |, een oogwenk, oogenblik.

k'oạ̀ kaò bák tsiu ī̤m tsai nịh, 看至眼不識 |, sterk op iets staren.

kā i nịh bák, 與他擺眼, iemand heimelijk, (afkeurend) toewenken.

hé kim ts'i nịh tseh nịh tseh, 火金星 | 的 | 的, de vuurvlieg knipgat, flikkert.

lún nịh, 凛 |, ontstellen, schrikken.

nịh pak tọ́, | 腹肚, zamentrekken van de ingewanden, (als wanneer men gaat braken.)

拉 Nịh Nẹh
Knijpen, (als een sigaar), kraken (als een noot.)

nịh sí, | 死, doodknijpen, wurgen.

àm nịh, 暗 |, heimelijk, stilletjes een duw geven, (om iemand voor iets te waarschuwen.)

nịh kịg sí ê lâng, | 驚死的人, een besluiteloos, bekrompen mensch.

nịh tsiep, | 汁, sap uitknijpen.

nịh lâng, | 膿, etter uitknijpen.

nịh sí lâng ê kaò, | 死人之猴, iemands aap doodknijpen, *d. i.* iemand eene gelegenheid om geld te verdienen, afsnijden.

īng ts'iú nịh eh, 用手 | 的, met de hand gekneed, gefatsoeneerd, (zonder vorm te gebruiken.)

nịh lūn p'a pọ̄ ê lâng, | 孱包步之人, iemand die er slechts één middel op na houdt om zijn verlies te herstellen, een lafaard.

Nia

領 Niạ́
Das, numer. voor kleederen, matten, karpetten, medenemen.

niạ́ kun (» *kin*) | 巾, das.

niạ́ siū, | 受, aannemen, gebruik maken van, zich belasten met, op zich nemen.

pó niạ́, 保 |, waarborgen, borgstaan voor.

niạ́ tsēng, | 狀, bewijs van borgtocht.

tam niạ́, 擔 |, er voor instaan dat.

niạ́ ping, | 兵, soldaten medevoeren, aanvoeren.

niạ́ hiòng (» *hiùng*) | 餉, soldij voor de soldaten brengen.

niạ́ sin lò, | 辛勞, loon verdienen, ontvangen.

nńg niạ́ (*nuị* ») 軟 |, zachte halsboord.

nī niạ́ (*nẹ̄* ») 勁 |, stijve halsboord.

ôan niạ́, 圓 |, ronde halsboord.

niạ́ t'ò, | 套, soort bretels die aan de halsboord vast zijn en onder de armen doorloopen.

niạ́ tsị, | 錢, geld ontvangen, halen,

niạ́ ke hé, | 家伙, zijne bezittingen, erfenis ontvangen.

t'óng niạ́, 統 |, het hoofd van iets zijn.

嶺 *soŋ niạ́*, 山 ｜, rug, bergrug.
Niạ́ *kè niạ́*, 過 ｜, eene berghelling overgaan.
niạ́ t'aò kaò niạ́ k'a, ｜ 頭 到 ｜ 脚, van den top tot aan den voet van de berghelling.
poŋ̀ soŋ kè niạ́, 踰 山 過 ｜, over bergen en hellingen verhuizen, *d. i.* ver.

𩬳 *k'a tsiah niạ̄*, 背 脊 ｜, bult op den
Niạ̄ rug.
gù niạ̄, 牛 ｜, bult van eene koe.
k'i niạ̄, 起 ｜, een bult, verheven streep hebben, (als wegen voor het afloopen van regen.)

Ngia

迎 *ngiạ̀ tsih*, ｜ 接, zijne gasten aan de
Ngiạ̀ deur ontvangen.
ngiạ̀ ts'iạ́, ｜ 請, iemand verzoeken.
ngiạ̀ hiŋ (» *ang*) ｜ 香, processie houden.

𪧘 *gòng ngiah*, 狂 ｜, vreemd staan op
Ngiàh te kijken, niet op zijn gemak zijn, (als op een vreemde plaats.)
sang sang ngiàh ngiàh, 鹵 ㄝ ｜ ㄝ, opkruipen, niet vast in elkander liggen.
ngiáh ngiáh bò bák sít, ｜ ㄝ 無 餘 額, niet stevig ingeduwd, (als van watten.)

Niao

猫 Kat.
Niao̤ *siaó niao̤*, 㹱 ｜, krolsche kat.
soŋ niao̤, 山 ｜, wilde kat.
sŋ k'a niao̤, 三 脚 ｜, komfoor enz. op drie pooten.
niao̤ bú, niao̤ kang, ｜ 母, ｜ 公 kat, kater.
t'ih niao̤, 鐵 ｜, ratteklem.

痲 Pokdalig, mottig,
Niao̤ *bīn niao̤*, 面 ｜, mottig.
niao̤ niao̤ niaò̤ niaò̤, ｜ ㄝ 𦀉 ㄝ zeer mottig.
niao̤ pà pà, ｜ 豹 ㄝ, leelijk doo[r] mottigheid.

老 *niaó̤ ts'ú* (» *ts'i*) ｜ 鼠, rot, rat.
Niaó̤ *niaó̤ ts'ú á* (» *ts'i* ») ｜ 鼠 子, muis.
niao̤ ts'ú dzip (» *ts'i* ») ｜ 鼠 追, voetzoekers.
niaó̤ ts'ú taoh, ｜ ㄝ 搭, ratteval.

鳥 *niaó̤ tsiang*, ｜ 鎗, geweer.
Niaó̤ *niaó̤ ts'ìng*, ｜ 銃, do.
niaó̤ suí, ｜ , uitstekend eind, (als aan kapstokken, enz.)

Ngiao

𤸷 Kittelen.
Ngiao̤ *ngiao̤ ngiao̤*, ｜ ｜, kittelen (als in de keel).
uì ngiao̤ (*uì̤* ») 畏 ｜, niet tegen kittelen kunnen.
ngiao̤ sik sut, ｜ 蟋 蟀, krekels uit hunne gaten peuteren.
ngiao̤ p'ī̤ k'ang, ｜ 鼻 孔, in de neus kittelen.
ngiao̤ tseh tsiṳ̄ kiu k'ì, 一 ｜ 便 縮, kittelt men er aan dan trekt het in (als een schilpadskop.) hoe meer men er hem over spreekt des te meer trekt hij zich terug.
ngiao̤ tsiṳ̄, ｜ 縮, aan eene jeuking

kittelen, *d. i.* niet genoeg inspanning voor iets gebruiken.

Ngiaò *ngiaŋ ngiaŋ puī* (*ngaŋ ngaŋ* ») , keffen (als een hond,) ook van menschen gezegd.

Ngiaoh

蹻 Bewegen, opspringen stuiptrekken.
Ngiaoh

ngiaoh t'an, | 蟶, dood zijn.

ngiaoh hê, | 蝦, dood zijn.

ngiaoh á, | 仔, wervel.

ngiaoh ts'ùi, | 嘴, met den mond toewenken, (den mond vooruitstekend).

ngiaoh k'í lai, | 起 來, opspringen, (als een tuimelaar), er weer boven op komen, (in handel, ziekte, planten, enz.)

撟 *ngiaóh ngiaóh tāng*, | ヒ 動, trillen.
Ngiaoh *tsoâ bé ngiaóh*, 蛇 尾 |, de staart van den slang trilt.

boē ngiaóh / *bē* » } | 未, niet meer kunnen roeren, dood zijn.

Niu

兩 Tael, once.
Niú

kun niú / (*kin* ») } 斤 |, pond en once, gewicht.

ū kun niú / (» *kin* ») } 有 斤 |, pond en once hebben, *d. i.* verschil hebben van gewichtig en niet.

bô niú siú (» » *sio*) 無 | 賞, niet lang kunnen duren, niet lang goed blijven. (van waren.)

siaò kun tsáp lák niú, 算 斤 十 六 |, het pond tegen zestien oncen rekenen, *d. i.* al het slechte in iemands levensloop ophalen en verwijten.

kuí niú gûn, 幾 | 銀, hoeveel oncen taels zilver?

sìng niú siŋ, 算 | 聲, bij taels berekend.

娘 Jongejuffrouw, dame; vrouw, mevrouw; moeder.
Niû
(Niô) *ko niû*, 姑 |, jonge juffrouw, dame.

sin niû, 新 |, bruid.

tsu niû lâng, 妹 | 人, vrouwen.

niû kán, 婢 |, meesteres en slavin.

sien si niû, 先 生 |, mevrouw.

niû loé, | 母, moeder.

niû pē, | 父, (oorspr. ouders thans hoofdzakelijk) vader.

aū niû, 後 |, stiefmoeder.

géh niû, 月 |, de maand.

sim koŋ niû t'iŋ, 心 肝 | 痛, inwendige droefheid, smart.

梁 Balk, dwaarsbalk; familienaam.
Niû *hoaî niû*, 橫 |, dwarsbalk.
Niô *tiong tsit niû*, 中 脊 |, nokbalk.

tsiū niû, 上 |, den nokbalk opbrengen.

p'ī niû, 鼻 |, neusbeen, neushelling.

凉 *niû soà*, | 傘, groote parasol, voor
Niû mandarijnen uitgedragen.

量 Meten, de maat nemen; beraadslagen.
Niû *niû bí*, | 米, rijst meten.

niû pò, | 布, stoffen meten.

niû pān, | 辦, de maat nemen.

niû k'oà, | 看, meten hoeveel er is?

su niû, 思 |, beraadslagen.

糧 Levensmiddelen, voedsel, provisie; rantsoen van soldaten, soldij, belasting.
Niû

bí niŭ, 米 |, levensmiddelen.

ūn niŭ, 運 |, leeftocht, fourage vervoeren.

niŭ ts'aó, | 草, leeftocht en paardenvoer, leeftocht.

niŭ ts'ia, | 車, fouragewagen.

niŭ tō, | 道, opzigter over de belasting voor het leger.

tsiáh tsi niŭ, 食 錢 |, soldij genieten, *d. i.* soldaat zijn.

láp niŭ, 納 |, belasting opbrengen.

t'ó tsi niŭ, 討 錢 |, belastingen heffen.

niŭ ts'e, | 差, ophaler der belastingen.

niŭ pàng, | 房, dépot van belasting.

oàn niŭ, 完 |, belasting afbetalen.

蠶 Niŭ Ts'ân　Zijdeworm.

niŭ á, 仔 |, zijdeworm.

niŭ á sin, | 神, god der zijde wormen, (aan wien vrouwen op het einde des jaars offeren.)

niŭ á hióh, | 葉, zijdeworm bladen, moerbezien bladen.

ts'in tsiŭ niŭ tsiáh hióh, 似 | 食 葉, evenals zijdewormen die bladen eten, *d. i.* in een bodemlooze put vallen als voedsel in een groot gezin.

量 Niū Niō　Wegen; balans, weegschaal.

niū tāng, 衡 重, wegen.

niū kao, | 鉤, haak van een schaal.

niū t'ui, | 錘, gewichten van een balans.

ts'ien kun niū, 千 斤 |, groote weegschaal.

lóh niū 上 |, *tsiū niū* |, op de weegschaal zetten.

kiáh niū, 執 |, aan de weegschaal staan (vaste post in een winkel.)

讓 Niū　Inschikken, inschikkelijkheid gebruiken, toegeven, afstaan.

sa niū, 相 |, voor elkander inschikken, voorkomend zijn.

niū tsit pō, | 一 步, een weinig toegeven, inschikken.

niū ts'iú, | 手, toegevend, inschikkelijk.

niū i, | 伊, iemand toegeven, inschikkelijkheid voor iemand gebruiken.

niū ui, | 位, afstand van den troon doen.

Ngo

五 Ngó　*ngó king*, | 行, de vijf elementen.

ngó tsāng, | 臟, ingewanden.

ngó sik pò, | 色 布, gekleurde shirtings.

ngó sik bīn, | 色 面, boosaardig uiterlijk.

ngó lō siao, | 路 消, naar overal heen gevoerd, verkocht worden.

ngó hong tsáp ts'ú è làng, | 方 十 處 之 人, menschen van allerlei plaatsen.

ngó iŭ, | 營, de vijf kampen van het leger.

魣 Ngo　*ngo hi*, | 魚, baardvisch?

伍 Ngó　Familienaam.

hàng ngó, 行 |, luisterrijk, oorspr. de gelederen.

tuī ngó, 隊 |, gelederen.

tsāi ngo̤, 在 ｜, *lett.* in de gelederen zijn, *d. i.* stevig omwrikbaar.

put tak ngo̤, 不 答 ｜, niet betamelijk, onbehoorlijk.

dzip ngò̤, 入 ｜, in de gelederen gaan, soldaat worden of zijn.

偶 Ngo̤ *ngo̤ dzièn*, ｜ 然, toevallig.

ngo̤ gù (» *gī*) ｜ 遇, toevallig ontmoeten.

忤 Ngo̤ *ngò̤ gik*, ｜ 逆, zich verzetten tegen (zijne ouders.)

我 Ngo̤ *bô dzi ngo̤*, 無 汝 ｜, geen onderscheid maken tusschen U en mij, *d. i.* niet partijdig, onrechtvaardig.

午 Ngo̤ *tiong ngo̤*, 中 ｜, juist 12 uur 's middags.

tsú ngo̤ tsiem, 子 ｜ 針, kompasnaald, kompas.

tsú gno̤ tsiem kiáh tsiā̤ tsiā̤, 子 ｜ 針 執 正 匕, de kompasnaald staat recht, *d. i.* eerlijk, billijk handelen.

ngo̤ bùn laī, ｜ 門 内, binnen de deur juist tegenover het zuiden, (van de keizerlijke audientiezaal.)

蜈 ngò̤ *ngò̤ k'i*, ｜ 蜞, bloedzuiger,

梧 ngō̤ *ngō̤ tòng*, ｜ 桐, Dryandria cordifolia.

ngò̤ *òng ngō̤*, 枉 ｜, valsche advokaat, aanzetter tot valsche aanklagten.

傲 gō̤ *kiao ngō̤*, 驕 ｜, trotsch.

Noa

Rollen als deeg.

oá *noā̤ mī*, ｜ 麵, deegkneden.

noā̤ ts'oá, ｜ 怠, dralen, langzaam, (handelen.)

p'ah noā̤, 打 ｜, hanteren, versjouwen, verzeulen, (als koffers) en veel te lijden hebben, heen en weer geslingerd worden.

noā̤ ts'aì ｜ 菜, groenten kneden, wrijven, (vóór ze in te maken.)

sā̤ kap poā̤ noā̤, 相 與 搬 ｜, met elkander wederkeerig omgang hebben.

爛 Noā̤ *noā̤ soa*, ｜ 沙, in het zand rollend, (als beesten.)

tó teh noā̤, 倒 地 ｜, op den grond liggend en uit kwaadaardigheid rollen.

tuì kan k'o̤ noā̤ ts'ut lai, 對 辛 苦 ｜ 出 來, uit ellende gerold zijn. *d. i.* uit ellende er boven op gekomen zijn.

tó tī i sin k'u teh noā̤, 倒 在 身 上 ｜, tegen iemands ligchaam aan liggen rollen, *d. i.* alles op zijne verantwoording doen, op hem laten aankomen.

攔 Noā̤ Hinderen, beletten.

noā̤ tsáh, ｜ 截, hinderen in, tegenhouden.

noā̤ lō, ｜ 路, den weg onveilig maken.

noā̤ tsó̤, 阻 ｜, tegenhouden.

sū noā̤ hō i soah k'ì, 事 ｜ 乎 伊 止, een twist verhinderen, voorkomen.

poā̤ lō̤ k'ì noā̤ i, 半 路 去 ｜ 伊, halver-wege iemand gaan tegenhouden.

欄 Noā̤ *tsí noā̤*. 井 ｜, omheining om een put.

bé noā̤, 馬 ｜, omheining, bocht voorpaarden.

lòh noā̤, 落 ｜, zachtzinniger, handelbaarder worden.

爛 Verrot, zacht, beurs.

Noā̤ *ts'aò noā̤*, 臭 |, verrot, stinkend.

p'ah noā̤, 打 |, nat en zacht worden.

noā̤ tsoā̤, | 賤, goedkoop.

tsú noā̤ (*tsí* ») } 煮 |, tot pap kooken.

sìng tē noā̤ noā̤, 性質優柔, dralend van aard, zonder voortgang.

noā̤ sìng, | 性, do.

si kaó noā̤ ti, 死狗|猪, op den grond liggen en maar niet willen opstaan.

kam noā̤ īm kam tsoā̤, 甘|不甘賤, goed liever zien bederven dan het goedkoop te verkoopen.

k'i hū noā̤ t'ô̤ bô ts'ì, 欺負|泥無莿. verdrukken, (meenende dat.) zachte aarde geene stekels heeft, *d. i.* dat de zwakkere partij hem geen leed kan doen.

涎 *p'ùi noā̤* (*p'oè* ») } 噴 |, spuwen.

Noā̤ *lám noā̤*, 攬 |, slordig (van vrouwen.)

noā̤ ts'iu, | 湫, speeksel spatten.

k'ô̤ noā̤, 苦 |, ochtendspeeksel.

Ngoeh

鑷 *ngoeh á*, | 子, pincet.

Ngoeh Oppikken.
Nge̤h

hō̤ li boē ngoeh tit, 與汝未|的, Ik laat het mij door U niet ontstelen.

莢 *taō ngoeh*, 斗 |, dop van peulvruchten.
Ngoe̤h

夾ˊ Onder den arm dragen.

Ngoé̤h *ngoé̤h k'a*, | 足, knellen (aan den voet.

k'it i ngoéh tioh, 被伊|着, door iets gekneld worden, in de knel van iets zitten.

tsìng lâng ngoé̤h i tsit lâng, 衆人|伊一人, allen komen op hem alleen neér.

縮 *kiu kiu ngoé̤h ngoé̤h*, 畏ヒ||, verlegen.
Ngoé̤h

O

窩 Gat, grot, nest,

O *soa̤ o*, 山 |, berggrot.

ièn o, 燕 |, eetbare vogelnestjes,

呵 Geluid van zingen of schreeuwen.

O *o o ts'iù*. | | 唱, zingen.

i i o o, 吚 | |, geluid van zingende of hardop lezende kinderen.

i o hū hō, 吚|附和, met de groote hoop meespreken.

o o kiò, | 叫, geschreeuw van rondventers.

hoah iû o, 唱優 |, uitroepen voor mandarijnen,

o lièn k'oân, | 連環, rammelaar (belletjes in een doek gebonden.)

o si o neh, | 詩 | 雅, sterk verlangen, wenschen.

萵 *tang o ts'aì*, 冬|菜 peterselie.
O

謳 *o ló*, | 美, prijzen.
O

熬 *o hi*, | 魚, visch braden, bakken.

O *o bah*, | 肉, vleesch bakken.

襖 *áng ó*, 紅 |, bruidskleed, (rood.)

Ó *ó á*, | 子 do.

bóng ó, 莽 |, bruidskleederen, (van mandarijn dochters.)

ó á kûn, | 仔 裙, bruidskleed en rok.

pút ó, 佛 |, kleeren van afgoden.

Ó *ó ó*, uitroep.

澳 *ò kah*, | 甲, waterpolitie dienaar.

Ò *ò ming* (» *mu͘i*) } | 門, Macao.

tsûn ò, 船 |, scheepsdok.

噢 *ìn ò*, 應 |, toestemmen.

Ò

奥 *ts'im ò*, 深 |, moeielijk te begrijpen. (als een leerstelsel.)

Ò *ò biaō*, | 妙, diep en schoon.

愛 *ò giò* (*aì giók*) } | 玉, vijg.

Ò

蠔 Oesters.

Ô *ô k'ak*, | 殼, oesterschelp.

ô kiá k'ak, | 鏡 殼, oesterschelpen in de plaats van glas gebruikt.

ô k'ak (of *kiá*) *ting*, | 殼 燈, oesterschelpen lamp.

p'oà ô, 破 |, oesters openateken.

ô koê (» *kê*) } | 畦, gezoute oesters.

ô koa, | 干, gedroogde oesters.

ô tu, | 猪, oesterbanken.

ô tiâ, | 庭, oesterbanken, oesterplaat.

ô ke ts'ip, | 高 膝, aanzettende oesters.

ts'iū ô ko ts'ip (*tsiō* » » ») } 上 | 高 膝, met oesters begroeien, (als een schip).

ô á lìn, | 仔 轔, met aardappelmeel gestoofde oesters.

ô á bé, | 仔 粥, oesterboeboer rijst met oesters.

ô ling, | 乳, zeeanemone.

p'ī laò ô, 鼻 流 |, een snotneus hebben.

烏 Zwart

O *o sik*, | 色, do.

o bák bák, 黑 | 匕, zwart als inkt.

o bák, | 木, mahoniehout.

o bák ts'iū, | 本 樹, mahonieboom.

o taō, | 荳, zwarte boonen.

o im t'i, | 陰 天, regenachtig weêr.

o àm, | 暗, donker.

o àm mi, | 暗 夜, donkere nacht.

o bīn (*mé*) *lâng*, | 面 人, maleier. neger.

bák tsiu o àm, 眼 | 暗, donkere zwarte oogen, *d i.* dood

o a, | 鴉, kraai.

o ts'i (» *ts'e*) } | 青, bont en blaauw.

p'ah o ts'i (» » *ts'e*) } 打 | 青, bont en blaauw slaan.

o ts'i kik huih (» *ts'e* » ») } | 青 積 血, bloedblaar.

o kim ts'at, | 金 漆, verlaksel.

t'ui o kim (of *keng*) (*t'è* » » *kui*) } 替 | 金, verlakken.

o kim, | 金, glimmend zwart, er voorspoedig uitzien.

o ts'ùi gû, | 嘴 牛, iemand die anderen steeds uitscheldt.

o hùn sì àm (» » *péh* ») } | 昏 四 暗, duister worden als voor de oogen van iemand die eene flaauwte krijgt; ook bij een bewolkte lucht.

o âng pit, | 紅 筆, de zwarte en de roode penseelen, (in bureau's gebruikt.).

uī o ts'at péh (» » » *péh*) } 畫 | 漆 白, slecht knoeijerig geschreven, met allerlei kleuren aangekleed.

o kui, | 龜, hoerenbaas, hoorndrager.

am kún bák o, 項上漆|, een zwarte nek hebben, *d. i.* hoorndrager zijn.

o lik lik, |綠七, bont en blaauw.

t'i o tsit ping, 天|一平, de hemel wordt gedeeltelijk zwart, van eene wraakroepende misdaad gezegd.

o àng péh tah, |紅白跡, zorgeloos, niet zorgvuldig doen.

o pa lī sō, |擺里掃, zeer zwart.

o kui, |鬼, moor: klerk bediende, koelie, (in een zaak.)

o ìng sán, |黃瘦, afgevallen, mager.

o mg mg, |嫣七, pikdonker.

o lik bah, |綠肉, zwartachtig (kippen) vleesch.

o lo lo k'ì, geheel en al zwart geworden.

bīn o kui kui, 面|鬼七, zwart als een duivel, (van iemands gelaat.)

o sò sò, |糊七, pikzwart.

o ien, |烟, roet.

tióh o soa, 着|沙, een beroerte, koliek krijgen.

濛 O *o o pin i ho*, ||彌伊謊, hij kan zeggen dat er in is wat hij wil zoo lang men het niet gezien heeft kan men het niet gelooven.

黑 O *o hī moi*, |耳鰻, aal paling, rotting zweep, (om misdadigers te slaan.)

挖 Ó Optillen met een hefboom.

o k'í, |起, do.

ó t'ó, |泥, de aarde omwoelen.

ó k'ang, |孔, een gat inwroeten.

o piàh, |壁, een muur omwoelen, ondermijnen.

侵 Ó Bedriegen, in het spel.

ó lâng é tsî (of *siaò*), |人之錢, iemand met geld of met zijne rekening bedriegen.

惡 Ó *ò tò*, |妬, jaloersch zijn op, verafschuwen.

òan ò, 怨|, haten.

bān dzîn ò, 萬人|, door ieder eer gehaat.

k'ó tsi siaò ò, 真七可|, hatelijk, verachtelijk (schelw.)

湖 Ô Meer.

kiâ kang ô, 行江|, reizende waarzeggers.

k'ui tsit ê toā ô, 開一大|, een groot meer gevormd hebben.

壺 Ô *kim hî ô*, 金魚|, groote steenen pot om goudvisschen in te houden.

tiò ô, 投|, in den bak gooijen. een stok doen ombuitelen en in een bak mikken.

t'eng ô, 湯|, soepterrine.

dziō ô, 尿|, waterpot.

kám ô, 簸|, rijstmand.

胡 Ô Familienaam.

勸 Ô *ô hong*, |風, naar de wind wenden.

ô tsoán, |轉, tegenroeijen.

tò ô, 倒|, terugroeijen.

ô dzip lai, 入|來, naar zich toe strijken, (als rijst in een mand).

盂 Ô *ô ô*, 盂|, holstaande, uitgehold.

sa ô, 相|, elkander helpen.

搖 Ô *ô nâ*, |床, wieg.

iô ô nâ, |搖籃, wiegen.

Taro.

pin ning ō, 檳榔 |, siri taro, (groot en los)

ō hoai (» *hoā*) | 杆, schors van taro.

tik ō 竹 |, bamboes taro (lang met geledingen).

ō kiá ō sun, | 子 | 孫, de uitsprutsels aan taro.

tsuí ō hioh, 水 | 葉, groote bladen van de taro.

ō nīng, 蛋 |, kleine ronde taro.

Oa

Leunen tegen, aanleggen, aanzetten tegen, steunen op, zich verlaten op, afgaan op, vertrouwen op, toevertrouwen aan. consignéren aan, naderen; toenaderen digtbij, langs.

oá piah, | 壁, tegen den muur aan.

oá piah ts'ìng k'ò, | 壁穿袴, tegen een muur aan leunende zijn broek aantrekken, *d. i.* hulp van anderen noodig hebben.

oá k'ò, | 賴, zich verlaten op, vertrouwen op, steunen op.

i oá, oá loā, 依 |, | 賴, do.

oá hoā, | 岸, steunen op.

oá hoā k'ì, | 岸去, langs den kant gaan.

oá sè, | 勢, op eens anders macht steunen.

oá ōng k'oà miā, | 旺看命, afgaande op iemands voorspoed zijn lot voorspellen.

oá tsûn, | 船, een schip consignéren.

oá hè, | 貨, goederen consigneren.

kūn oá, 近 |, naderen, dicht bij komen.

hit tsiah tsûn oá sim mih hâng, 此船 | 何行, aan welk handelhuis is dat schip geconsigneerd?

oá tao, | 挽, dichtbij.

oá ni, | 年, tegen het nieuwjaar aan.

oá soṉ, | 山, langs den wal.

boē oá, 未 |, tot geene toenadering kunnen komen.

oá i hé sit, | 伊伙食, zich bij iemand in de kost besteden.

oá ì, | 意, toenaderen in meening, niet veel verschillend.

蜞 Oá *p'ō oá*, 蟛 |, kleine krab.

發 *oà he* (» *hoe*) | 灰, kalk aanmaken.

Oà *oà pui*, | 肥, mest aanmaken.

oà ts'i, | 青, indigo aanmaken om tot gisting te doen overgaan.

kap i oà, 與伊 |, met iemand aanvangen, als het sluiten van een koop.

oà taō iû, oà taō tsiù, | 豆油, | 豆醬, soja tot gisten zetten.

何 Oâ
bô ta tit oâ 無奈 |
bô ta oâ 無奈之 |
bô la oâ 無如 |
bô hoat ta oâ 無奈他 |
} onvermijdelijk.

垵 *oṉ ù*, | 澳, schuilhaven.

Oṉ *koa oṉ*, 掛 |, in eene schuilhaven binnenloopen.

k'ui ts'ui oṉ, 開嘴 |, onbeschermde haven.

siu oṉ, 收 |, in eene haven binnen komen.

鞍 *bé oṉ*, 馬 |, zadel.

Oṉ *pē oṉ* (*poē* ») 背 |, zadelen.

sià oṉ, 卸 |, het zadel afnemen.

oa̤ ts'àn, | 𩟲, paarden dekje onder het zadel.

安 Oa̤ *tâng oa̤*, 同 |, Plaatsnaam.

碗 Oá̤ Kom.

oá̤ poa̤, | 盤, kopjes en blaadjes.

oá̤ bō, | 帽, kapje mutsje.

pīng oá̤ (*pui̤* ») 飯 |, rijstkom, broodwinning.

t'ien ping oá̤, 天 秤 |, schalen van eene balans.

hai oá̤, 海 |, zeer groote kom.

oá̤ p'iet tī tū, | 盤 碟 箸, bordengoed, enz.

oá̤ ioh, | 藥, verwstof om porselein te kleuren.

oá̤ gih p'è (» *p'oè* ,,) } | 石 片, scherven van kopjes.

t'aô k'ak oá̤ ts'é (» » » *ts'oé*) } 頭 壳 | 髓, hersens uit de hersenpan.

t'i toē hé oá̤ (» *ē hoé* ») } 天 下 火 |, van alles afweten, overal geweest zijn.

tsit è ná oá̤ koh nih, 一 介 如 | 糕 的, er dom uitzien, suf.

oá̤ kim ko̤ | 金 孤, de voet van een kom.

oá̤ iò, | 窰, kommenbakkerij.

k'a t'aô oá̤, 脚 頭 |, kniebeen.

tsit tè oá̤ k'àm tsit è péh tsát, 一 介 | 盖 一 介 謊, de kom bedekt een leugen, *d. i.* leugenachtig.

kap i sa̤ oá̤ poa̤, 與 他 相 | 拌, met iemand leven (als met eene bijzit.)

p'àng i è pīng oá, 棒 伊 飯 |, iemands rijstkommen voordienen, *d. i.* voor het huishouden zorgen, (als eene vrouw).

tsiáh oá̤ laī seh oá̤ goā, 食 | 內 說 | 外, de kost bij iemand verdienen en buitenaf af kwaad van hem spreken.

oá̤ lò, | 鑼, kleine gong.

晏 Oà̤ Laat.

siṳ oà̤ (*sio* ») 過 |, te laat.

oà̤ tsui, | 水, laat hoogwater.

tsá kāng oà̤, 早 共 |, vroeg of laat, de een of andere tijd.

案 Oà̤ *hiṳ oà̤* (*hio* ») } 香 |, tafel met aangestoken offerstokjes er op.

kong oà̤, 公 |, rechterstafel.

oà̤ toh, | 棹, langwerpige tafel.

換 Oā̤ Verwisselen.

oā̤ tsui, | 水, water verwisselen.

koé oā̤ (*ké* ») } 改 |, veranderen.

oā̤ uī, | 位, verplaatsen, verzetten.

tuì oā̤, 對 |, inruilen tegen,

oā̤ tsi̤ gùn (» » *gin*) } | 錢 銀, geldwisselen.

oā̤ lai oā̤ k'ì, | 來 | 去, ruilen.

oā̤ k'ì, | 齒, tanden wisselen.

oā̤ sa̤, | 衫, van kleederen verwisselen.

t'oè oā̤ (*t'è* ») } 退 |, verruilen, omwisselen als met kleêren.)

oā̤ pang, | 班, van garnizoen omwisselen.

oā̤ iṳ (» *io̤*) } | 樣, van vorm veranderen.

t'ui oā̤ (*t'è* ») 退 |, verruilen, verwisselen. ruijen.

oā̤ kut t'aô, | 骨 頭, een ander mensch worden, (door verandering van leven, handel of stand.)

oā t'aô bīn, | 頭 面, vernieuwen, opknappen.

oā kè ka, | 過 脚, aan een anderen voet aantrekken, (van schoenen.)

koé t'aô oā bīn, 改 頭 | 面, geheel en al veranderen, (als een huis).

旱 Droogte.

Oā *t'i tsoè oā* (» *tsò* ») 天 做 |, de hemel kondigt droogte aan, er komt geen regen.

k'ó oā, 苦 |, droogte.

toā oā, 大 |, groote droogte.

幹 *hun oā*, 分 |, zich in vertakkingen

Oā verdeelen (van planten.)

Oh

難 Moeielijk.

Oh *oh tit*, | 的, moeielijk.

oh tit ts'òng, | 的 爲, moeielijk te doen.

oh kiā, | 行, moeielijk te begaan.

kiā lō oh oh, 行 路 | |, moeielijk langzaam loopen.

oh kóng, | 說, moeielijk te zeggen.

oh kè dzit, | 過 日, moeielijk door zijn dag komen, (door gebrek of disharmonie.)

學 Aanleeren, nadoen, leeren, school.

Oh *kong óh*, 公 |, publieke school.

gī óh, 御 |, publieke (kostelooze) school.

óh tîng, | 堂, school.

su óh, 私 |, private school.

gaò óh oē ê lâng, 善 | 話 之 人, iemand die altijd iets oververtelt.

k'ui óh, 開 |, eene nieuwe leercursus beginnen (na nieuwjaar).

dzip óh, 入 |, in school gaan.

lóh óh, 落 |, naar school gaan.

kà óh, 教 |, les geven.

soā óh, 散 |, vacantie geven, (op het einde des jaars.)

t'e óh, 走 |, uit school spijpelen.

óh ts'ùi óh tsih, | 嘴 | 舌, alles oververtellen.

óh koā, | 官, hooge geleerden in elk district.

k'ong tsú óh, 孔 子 |, tempel voor Confucius.

óh kui, | 規, schoolreglementen.

óh koai, | 乖, leeren om stil te zijn, (als jonge kinderen die op school zijn maar nog niets leeren).

óh taò, 斗 |, oppasser in een school.

sa kà sa óh, 相 教 相 |, elkander ondervragen en van elkander leeren.

óh sai á, | 司 仔, in de leer zijn.

Ok

惡 *ok lâng*, | 人, iemand kwellen.

Ok *ok lâng*, slecht mensch.

ok siok, | 俗, van slechte zeden.

ok tók, | 毒, slecht (van harte.)

ok k'iák k'iák, | 桀 驁, kwaadaardig.

ok sip, | 習, slechte gewoonten.

sip ok, 習 |, het slechte aanleeren.

ok kùn, | 棍, schurk.

tsik ok tsik tók } (tsò » t ò ») } 積 | 積 毒, slecht (opstapeling van boosheid.)
hing ok, 行 |, boosaardig handelen.
ok sim, | 心, boosaardig, slecht van harte.

Oah

活 Oáh Levend, levendig, in leven; niet aan één toestand gebonden, beweegbaar, bewegelijk loopend.
k'oa̤ oáh, 看 |, 開 |, gezond, opgeruimd, onbezorgd.
oáh lō̤, | 路, kostwinning.
oáh oáh bé pák tī hi si ts'iū } (» » bé̤ » » » ts'iū) } | | 馬 專 縛 在 死 樹, een levend paard aan een dooden post binnen, (d. i. een knap mensch buiten gelegenheid stellen met zijne kundigheden voordeel te doen.)
oáh t'iab t'iah oáh lîng lîng } (» » » » liòng liòng) } | 超 匕 | 跳 匕, springlevend.
oáh tāng, | 動, levendig (van aard), naar omstandigheden weten te handelen.
bák tsiu oáh tāng, 眼 | 動, levendige oogen.
oáh pút, | 佛, levende Boeddha, d. i. algemeen bemind mensch.
uī kaó oáh k'ì lat, 畫 至 | 起 来, schilderen als of het levend was.
oē si̤ oáh tit, 能 生 | 的, het leven kunnen behouden; vervoerbaar, te transporteren,
sim koa̤ oáh, 心 肝 |, inwendig levend, geprikkeld worden.
oáh tsui, | 水, levend, d. i. loopend water.
oáh tsoa̤, | 泉, levende, loopende bron, (van een kapitaal.)
oáh k'oa̤, | 看, rekbaar, (als eene beteekenis.)
oáh mîng, | 門, loopende deur d. i. winst.
oáh king, | 景, beweegbare poppen.
oáh pán, | 板 bewegelijke tijpen.
oáh kuí, | 鬼, springslot, springvèer.
oáh kat, | 結, loopende knoop d. i. strik.
oáh tsi̤, | 錢, levend geld, geen dood kapitaal.

Oai

歪 Oai Scheef.
oai ts'ia } (» siâ) } | 斜, scheef.
oai ts'oáh | 斜, scheef zijn.
oai tsoáh, | 斜, do. verschillen.
oai p'oé } (» p'é) } | 配, schuins, niet gelijk.
oai pi̤, | 旁, scheef, niet in het midden.
oai tsoāī, scheef zitten, als kleêren.
oai kò, oai li kò, | 箬, | 里 箬, do. uitzakken.
oai hong, | 風, scheef getrokken (als de mond.)
oai tsit ping, | 一 旁, scheef naar een kant overhellend.
oai k'a, | 脚, scheeve voeten.
oai ts'uì, | 嘴, scheeve mond.
oai p'i̤, | 肯, scheef.
oai p'in, | 僻, scheef waggelen.

oai p'ī, 丨 鼻, scheve neus.

oé kiâ liaó oai, 鞋 行 了 丨, schoenen scheef loopen.

ts'ai oai ts'ai tsoaī lâng, 採 丨 採 斜 人, iemand onbillijk behandelen, steeds op iemand neêr komen.

Oai Strijken, (als op een viool.)

oai kóng á hièn, op de viool strijken.

i i oai oai, gekraak van een deur of wagen.

oai lâng, iemand bedriegen in den nek zien, bedriegen, folheeren.

k'i oai lâng, iemand iets ten laste leggen waaraan hij slechts gedeeltelijk schuld heeft.

oai tsioh, op allerlei manieren van iemand trachten geld te leenen.

oai koat lâng, iemand kwellen, valsch betichten belasteren.

蹶 Oai *k'a oai tioh*, 足 丨 着, de voet verzwikken.

īng koai á ka i oai loh k'i, 用 枴 仔 與 伊 丨 落 去, iemand met een stok tegen de beenen slaan.

Oaī *koa oai lâng*, iemand verdrukken, bedriegen.

sin k'u tūm poh ū koai oaī, een weinig ongesteld, onwelzijn.

Oaih

Oaih *oaih tseh oaih tseh*, voortstrompelen (als met een verzwikten voet.)

ih oaih ê lâng, iemand die altijd streken moet gebruiken, niet oprecht handelt

Oak

啞 Oak *oák oák*, 丨 丨, kwaken.

gaò oák, 賢 丨, *lett.* goedkwaken, *d. i.* goed ter spraak zijn.

tsui oák oák haó, 水 丨 丨 吼 } kabbelen van water.

i i oák oák 咿 匕 丨 丨 }

kap i oàk, 合 他 丨, voordoen het goed met hem te meenen, iemand plagen.

Oan

冤 Oan Verdrukken, onrechtvaardig behandelen, grieven, beleedigen, vijandschap, twist.

oan óng, 丨 枉, verdrukken, valsch betichten.

oan kut, 丨 屈, do.

sò oan, 訴 丨, zijne grieven blootleggen.

oan siû, 丨 讎, vijandschap, wrok.

oan ke, 丨 家, twist, ruzie.

oan ke lō oéh, 丨 家 路 狹, bij twist is de weg smal, *d. i.* heeft men steeds gelegenheid op nieuw te beginnen.

oan liaó oan, 丨 了 丨, gedurig twist hebben.

oan óng bīn, 丨 枉 面, een onoprecht gelaat.

sin oan, 伸 丨, zijne grieven hersteld krijgen.

kiet oan, 孽 丨, twist maken.

oan giét, 丨 結, straf, plaag des hemels, gedurige twist.

oan lóng boē soah, 丨 久 不 息, eindeloos twist hebben.

si si oan. 死 丨, doodelijke twist.

oan hûn, oan kui, 丨 魂, 丨 鬼, de om wraak roepende ziel, geest van een vermoord persoon.

Om iets dwingen van kinderen,
oan beh hit è mih, ｜要此物, dwingen om iets te hebben.
oan mih tsiáh, ｜物食, om eten dwingen.

灣 Oan
Baai, zee inham.
hai oan, 海｜, baai, golf.

彎 Oan
Krom, gebogen, bocht; gekronkeld, geslingerd, in een bocht rondgaan.
oan k'iao, ｜曲, krom.
oan oan k'iok k'iok, ｜｜曲乜, krom, gekronkeld.
oan oat, ｜軋, krom.
ts'iú oan, 手｜, bocht van den arm.
oan tsit lìn t'àng, ｜一遍, ééns de rondte omgaan.
oan lai ts'e làng, ｜來尋人, iemand met een kleinen omweg, in éene moeite komen opzoeken.
oan koe p'iah hāng, ｜街僻巷, afgelegene buurt.
tng oan, 轉｜, omdraaijen, een hoek omgaan.
tsoán oan, 轉｜, (eene twist) schikken.
oan ām (» *hām*) ｜項, verward ingewikkeld.

鴛 Oan
oan iu (» *io*) ｜鴦, mandarijneend.

蜾 Oan
oan iu, ｜鴦, wesp, sphex.
oan iu kū ka tsoáh, ｜鴦牽茄截, als een wesp die aan een kakkerlak bijt: van kinderen die zware lasten dragen.

遠 Oán
ing oán, 永｜, eeuwig.
kiú oán, 久｜, steeds, eeuwig.
oán kūn (» *kīn*) ｜近, perspectief.
oán taī è làng, ｜代之人, menschen van verre, (veel vroegere) generatien.
tiaù oán, 懸｜, ver, verafgelegen, uitgestrekt, uit het bereik.

宛 Oán
oán dziên, ｜然, sprekend als of . . . volkomen als.
oán tsoán, ｜轉, overdraaijen op anderen, (als eene zaak,) draaijend spreken.
gaô oán tsoán, 善｜轉, knap zijwegen of uitwegen bedenken.
ni oán, 腕｜, niet rechtuit spreken.
ts'iú oán, 手｜, handbuiging.

苑 Oán
gū oán, 御｜, keizerlijke tuinen.

怨 Oàn
oàn hūn (» *hīn*) ｜恨, haten.
oàn tò, ｜妬, jaloersch zijn op, benijden.
oàn miā, ｜命, ontevreden zijn met zijn lot.
pò oàn, 報｜, wraak nemen.
sa oàn, 相｜, elkander haten.
bai oàn, 埋｜, haat in zich voeden.
oàn ò, ｜惡, haten.
oàn ts'oeh (» *ts'eh*) ｜慼, haten.
kiet oàn, 結｜, onderling haat aanknoopen.
kò làng oàn, 故人｜, zich gehaat maken, gehaat zijn.
tì oàn, 致｜, tot haat geraken.
k'àng bák tsiu ts'é oàn, 抓目睭

髓 ｜, zoo haten dat men iemand het oogmerg, wel zou willen uithalen.
ts'ut oân sig, 出｜聲, hatend spreken.

完 Oân Eindigen, voleindigen, afmaken; volledig, in zijn geheel; volledig maken.
oân kang, ｜工, een werk afmaken, voleindigen.
oân tiû, ｜場, afmaken, (als een huis.)
oân tsoân, ｜全, kompleet in zijn geheel.
ts'at oân, 擦｜, uitschrappen, door halen (eene betaalde rekening.)
oân siaò, ｜數, eene rekening afmaken, afrekenen.
oân láp, ｜納, opbrengen, afbetalen, (belasting.)
oân oē, ｜話, iemands woorden volledig maken.

元 Oân *tsit tiā oân pó*, 一錠｜寶, een kobang.

圓 Oân Rond, boogvormig, rond, (van inborst); volledig, volledig maken, uitleggen (als droomen.)
oân kong, ｜拱, boog van een brug.
oân kong mîng, ｜拱門, boogvormige deur.
tsoè lâng oân, 做人｜, een rond mensch zijn, niet van twist houden.
kok oân, 福｜, gedroogde gîng-gíng.
oân tîng, Boeddh. non worden.
tsit ke koh t'oân oân, 一家復團｜, het huisgezin is weer voltallig, kompleet.
oân bāng, ｜夢, droom uitleggen.

丸 Oân Balletje, pil.
ioh oân, 藥｜, pil.

t'îng oân, 糖｜, suikerballen.

員 Oân Mandarijn, officier.
koa oân, 官｜, mandarijnen.
ui oân, 委｜, lage officieren.
oân goē, ｜外, eeretitel aan een rijk man gegeven.

灣 Oân *tai oân*, 台｜, Formosa.
tai oân hú, 台｜府, de stad Formosa.

袁 Oân Familienaam.

轅 Oân *oân bûn*, ｜門, ingang tot een mandarijnbureau.

緩 Oān Uitstel geven.
tî oān, 遲｜, uitstellen (tijd.)
oān oān, ｜｜, langzaam.
tsiép tsiép oān, 連匕｜, telkens uitstellen.
k'oan oān, 寬｜, uitstel geven.
oān dzit, ｜日, dagen uitstel geven.
nīng dzit oān (*nō̤ » »*) 二日｜, twee dagen over zijn tijd.
oān k'uì, ｜氣, *lett*, dralen, langzaam gaan van den adem, niet geregeld, geleidelijk met iets kunnen voortgaan.

援 Oān *oān ín*, ｜引, introduceren personen aan elkander.

Oang

黨 Oang *oang koah*, ｜結, soort (van menschen) in slechte beteekenis.
kui oang kui koah, 全｜全結, tot hetzelfde komplot behoorende.
kāng oang ê lâng (*tâng » » »*) 同類之人,

gelijksoortige, gelijkstaande menschen.

kap i oang put tsi kú, 合 他 | 甚 久, lang met iemand omgang, connectie gehad hebben.

Oat

轉 **Oat** Omdraaijen, omkeeren, omslaan; met hoeken, gekronkeld, niet recht uit.

oat kak, | 角, een hoek omslaan.

tíng oat, | 翻, draai hoek, (van een straat); bijleggen (een twist).

oat hāng, | 巷, eene uit de buurt gelegene plaats.

oat pát uī k'ì, | 他 位 去, eenen anderen kant inslaan, omslaan.

oat dzìp, oat ts'ut, 屈 入 | 出, inbuigen, uitbuigen,

oat oan, | 彎, kronkelen, (als een weg).

taī tsì tsīn oan oat, 事 其 | 彎, die zaak is uiterst gekronkeld, ingewikkeld.

k'ì koh oat lai, 去 復 | 來, gaan en weer terugkomen.

tsáp poeh oat, 十 八 |, vol kronkelingen, vol streken, niet regtuit.

i i oat oat, 依 匕 | |, kronkelend, niet rechtuit, (van een weg sprekend enz.)

oat oat tsoat tsoat, | 匕 撮 匕, do.

oat soân, | 旋, schikken, bijleggen, een twist.

挖 **Oat** Graven, opgraven, oplichten.

oat lâng ê tsi̤, | 人 之 錢, iemand in geld bedriegen.

乹 **Oat** *tsit oat*, 一 |, een haakvormige penseeltrek.

oat k'ì lai, een merk bij iets zetten, zoo goed als uitschrappen.

越 **Oát** Overspringen, overschrijden, te boven gaan, overtreden; meer.

oát hūn, | 分, zijn rang te boven gaan.

oat hūn kóng oē, | 分 說 話, ongepast spreken.

oát k'òng, | 控, rechtstreeks bij hoogere autoriteiten aanklagen.

oát hoat, | 法, de wet overtreden.

oát dzú .... oát dzú, ... | 愈 ... | 愈 .... hoe meer ... des te ...

轉 **Oát** Omdraaijen, omwenden, omkeeren, veranderen.

oát t'aô, | 頭, het hoofd omdraaijen.

oát kè k'ì k'oà, | 過 去 看, zich omdraaijen om te zien.

oát lai oát k'ì, | 來 | 去, zich over en weer omdraaijen, (als in bed.)

oát tíng lai, | 翻 來, omdraaijen,

oát tíng sin, | 翻 身, zich omdraaijen.

oát lin tíng, | 一 轉, omdraaijen, in een omnezien.

oát p'âng, | 篷, het zeil omwenden, omgooijen.

oát hong bīn, | 風 面, de wind draait: naar de wind draaijen. fig. over een anderen boeg zeilen.

oat sin iū, | 新 樣, een nieuw model maken, nieuwe mode invoeren.

oát hiòng, | 向, de richting, het uitzicht veranderen.

boē i oát tit, 未 移 | 的, onveranderlijk.

Oe

挨 **Oe** Duwen, dringen, stooten, strijkelings langs gaan, langs schuiven; wrijven me-len; strijken als op eene viool; verschuiven, uitstellen talmen, dralen.

oe k'oeh, ｜擁, duwen, dringen.

sa oe, 相｜, strijkelings langs elkander gaan.

sa oe sa sak, 相｜相推, elkander duwen.

oe lai sak k'i, ｜來推去, het eene gat met het andere stoppen.

oe kûn t'àn tīn, ｜羣湊陣, met de groote menigte meêdoen, meêgaan.

sa oe k'oe, 相｜摩, elkander willen laten weggaan.

oe bō, ｜磨, den molen wrijven, *d. i.* malen.

oe lâng, ｜礱, molen.

oe ts'ik ｜粟, rijst pellen.

oe k'oe, ｜躕, dralen.

oe iên, ｜延, verschuiven, talmen, dralen.

tsit dzit oe kè tsit dzit, 一日｜過一日, van den eenen dag op den anderen verschuiven.

hō oe kè bīn, 雨｜過面, de regen drijft over.

矮 Oé É

oé eh, ｜匕, dwerg, kleine; (bijnaam.)

oé lâng, ｜人, dwerg, klein mensch; ook voor de japaneezen gebruikt.

oé oé, ｜｜, klein, dwergachtig.

oé sòe (*é sè*) ｜細, klein van ligchaam, jong.

oé lâng ū hîng, ｜人有行, kleine menschen zijn van scherp doorzicht.

oé kó, ｜鼓, klein en in elkander gedrukt, dwergachtig.

oé k'a, ｜脚, korte voet, (als kippen) laag bij den grond (van planten.)

īm sī oé iā īm sī sòe, 不是｜亦不是細, hij is niet kort of klein (tegen volwassen persoon gezegd die met jongen twisten.)

oé lâng ni k'a bé (*é* » *nê* » *boé*) ｜人企足尾, dwergen staan op de toonen. spreekwoord.

拿* Oè T'éh

(Met de hand) nemen.

oè tsî, ｜錢, geld nemen, ontvangen.

穢 Oè

ù oè, 汚｜, vuil, smerig.

oè pò, ｜布, stondenlap.

oè giên oè gú, ｜言｜語, liederlijke, lage gezegden.

鞋 Oé É

Schoen.

tsoè oé sai hū, 做｜師阜, schoenmaker.

tiêm oé sai hū; 補｜師阜, schoenlapper.

oé toà, ｜帶, schoenveter.

oé puih (» *péh*) ｜拔, schoenhoorn.

oé bin, ｜刡, schoenborstel.

oé hùn, ｜楦, leest (van een schoen.)

oé toé (» *té*) ｜底, zool van de schoen.

ts'iah oé, ｜訂, schoenen maken, (van vrouwen.)

t'oa oé, 拕｜, sloffen.

ts'aó oé, 草｜, sandalen.

king oé, 京｜, kleine vrouwenschoen.

ts'â oé, 柴｜, houten schoenen, klompen.

ts'iah oé tú tioh goá é k'a, 做｜抵着我之脚, Ik vind juist

---

* Zie verder onder *é*.

een schoen die mij past, *d. i.* Ik vind juist wat ik noodig heb.

諾 Oe — Uitroep, dat men het roepen van iemand gehoord heeft.

oė dzip lai, | 入 來, in groote menigte binnendringen.

oē lâng, | 人, iemands attentie op iets anders brengen, (*b. v.* om twist te voorkomen.)

話 Oe, Oā — Taal, woorden.

kóng oē, 說 |, spreken.

hė oē (*hoė oā*) } 傳 |, vertalen.

ke oē (*ke oē*) } 角 口, redetwisten.

ing oē (*ân oā*) } 閒 |, keuveltaal, praat over koetjes en kalfjes.

kaō oē, *tsoē oē*, 多 言, veel praat, onnoodige taal.

oē t'oā oē (» » *oā*) } | 以 引, uit het eene discours tot het andere komen.

koā oē, 官 |, mandarijn dialect.

si kiā oē, 時 行 |, algemeen gebruikt gezegde.

óh oē, 學 |, iemands woorden overbrengen, overklappen.

tsoè oē á (*tsò* » ») } 做 |, iemand indirect berispen, schelden.

toā oē, 大 |, grootspraak.

kóng toā oē, 講 大 |, groot spreken.

oē ì, | 意, bedoeling van woorden.

ts'uì tsing oē (*k'aó t'aô oā*) } 嘴 前 |, aanvangs woord, stopwoord.

kóng bô oē, 講 無 |, onzin, onwaarheid spreken.

kóng īm tsiā oē, 講 不 成 |, niet harmonierend met elkandor spreken.

能 Oē, E — Kunnen, in staat zijn om.

oē k'oā tit, | 看 得, zichtbaar.

oē sí, | 死, sterfelijk.

oē t'àn, | 賛, voordeelig.

oē t'àn tsi, | 得 利, voordeelig.

oē t'iā tit, | 愛 的, beminnelijk.

oē tsoè tit, | 做 的, , dat gaat, dat kan.

oē kiā tit, | 行 的, te doen, mogelijk.

siá oē lai, *siá oē tit lai*, 寫 | 來, kunnen schrijven.

ts'iú taô oē, 手 頭 |, zelf kunnen doen, geen hulp van anderen noodig hebben.

衛 Oē — *sī oē*. 侍 |, keizerlijk lijfofficieren.

Oeh

狹 Oéh, Eh — Naauw, smal.

oéh oéh, | 隘, do.

oéh toéh, | 窄, do.

oéh oéh soeh soeh, | 匕 窄 匕, naauw, waarin men zich of iets niet bewegen kan.

oé íng sū (» *ní* ») } | 袖 衫, een kleed met naauwe mouwen.

oéh oéh k'oeh k'oeh, | 匕 激 |, naauw, bekrompen.

bák k'ang oéh, 眼 孔 |, kleine oogen, *d. i.* wangunstig,

oéh tō tng, *tō tng oéh*, *tō liōng oéh*. 肚 腸 |, 肚 量 |, onverdraagzaam.

lō oéh, 路 |, zich hoe langer hoe minder bemind maken.

lō nú kiā nú oéh, 路 愈 行 |, do.

tn oéh lah, 今 | 了, het is leelijk gesteld met.

ts'i i t'aô oēh, 手 頭 |, bekrompen in geld zitten, niet veel geld in handen krijgen.

mn̂g lō͘ oéh, 門 路 |, zich hoe langer hoe minder vrienden maken.

óan ke lō͘ oeh, 寃 家 路 |, in twist zijnde, malkaar juist in een nauwe straat ontmoeten, *d. i.* goede gelegenheid hebben met iemand in twist te komen.

Ong

往 Ong Gaan, weggaan, verleden, te voren, vroeger.

óng lai, | 來, omgaan met; gaan en komen.

lai óng, 來 |, do.

kè óng, 過 |, gestorven.

óng hoê, | 還, heen en terug.

óng óng, | |, steeds.

pi óng siông kah tāng, 比 | 常 更 重, erger dan te voren, (van eene ziekte.)

i óng, 已 |, te voren, verledene.

óng si, | 時, te voren, vroeger.

óng dzit, | 日, vroeger.

óng ni, | 年, verleden jaar.

枉 Óng Met geweld, onrechtvaardig behandelen, verdrukken; vruchteloos, noodeloos.

oan óng, 寃 |, valschelijk betichten, medeslepen.

óng k'ut, | 屈, valsch, betichten; het was vruchteloos dat . . . .

óng k'ut li, | 屈 爾, het is zonder vrucht voor U geweest dat . , .

óng huì sim ki, | 費 心 計, het is vruchteloos zich den geest daarvoor zoo aftetobben.

óng si siâ, | 死 城, plaats in de onderwereld waar de zielen heen gaan van allen die geen natuurlijken dood sterven.

óng k'ut i tsiah toā hàn, | 屈 伊 若 大, hij is toch zoo 'n groote kerel niettegenstaande hij zoo groot is (toch kan hij niet.)

Òng *òng kóng*, groot, kolossaal (van winst, enz.)

王 Ông Vorst, koning, prins; hoofd bij roovers enz. familienaam.

kok ông, 國 |, vorst van een rijk.

tsit ki ông, 一 支 |, een koningheer, (in het kaartspel.)

ông kiong, ông hú, | 宮, | 府, paleis.

ts'in ông, 親 |, prinsen uit het keizerlijke huis.

ông put kìⁿ ông, | 不 見 |, de eene koning kan den anderen niet zien, *d. i.* niet in elkanders gezelschap willen zijn.

tsū ts'ing sam tsê ông, 自 稱 三 齊 |, zich zelven verheffen, op hemelen.

p'ang ông, 蜂 |. bijenkoning.

kaô hiā ông, 螻 蟻 |, mieren koning.

ts'át ông, 賊 |, roover, rebellenhoofd.

gín á ông, 小 兎 |, belhamel onder kinderen.

ông iâ, | 爺, god die gezegd wordt alles te onderzoeken wat op aarde geschiedt.

ông lai, ǀ 梨, ananas.

ông tsûn, ǀ 船, houten of papieren schuiten ter eere van *ông iâ* verbrand.

ngiâ ông, 夯 ǀ, processie ter eere van *ông iâ* houden.

ông līng, ǀ 令, de keizerlijke volmacht aan een hoogen ambtenaar om te beschikken over leven en dood.

ông gō, ǀ 做, advokaat. (slechte beteekenis.)

ông lôk ts'ùi, ǀ 鹿 ǀ, leugenachtig, niet te gelooven, (als kwakzalvers.)

ông má k'ah hièn ông kong, ǀ 媽 較 顯 ǀ 公, de vrouw van *ông iâ* is luisterrijker dan hijzelf; van eene vrouw die de baas over haar man is.

旺 Ong — Voordeelig, voorspeedig.

hing ōng (*hin* ») 興 ǀ, voorspoed genieten, bloeijen.

ōng lê, ǀ 螺, schelpvisch.

hé ōng (*hoé* ») 火 ǀ, vlammen.

ông k'ì ǀ 去, toestand van vooruitgang.

ōng sīng, 盛 ǀ, overvloedig.

p'ông soe ōng, 賭 衰 ǀ, van het toeval afhangend.

oá ōng k'oà miā, 倚 ǀ 看 命, naar het uiterlijke bevoordeelen.

ông tsâng, ǀ 欉, voordeelig staande, gezonde plant.

tsai ōng, 財 ǀ, bloeijend in bezittingen, rijk.

sing lí ông, 生 理 ǀ, bloeijend van handel.

ōng ts'iú ǀ 手, gelukkig in het spel.

ōng tiaô, ǀ 椆, voorspoedige stal, waarvan de beesten sterk voorttelen.

Pa

巴 Pa — Opgedroogde korst, koek, schijf, gedroogd, ingedroogd.

kien pa, 堅 ǀ, verdroogen, verkoeken.

bīn p'é pa (» *p'oe* ») 面 皮 ǀ, met een korst over het gezicht, strak.

king pa, 經 ǀ, uitspannen om te droogen (als visch.)

ah pa, 鴨 ǀ. gedroogde eenden.

hi pa, 魚 ǀ, gedroogde visch.

p'ak pa, 暴 ǀ, droogen.

si lâng pa, 死 人 ǀ, geraamte.

tsiâ lâng pa, 成 人 ǀ. mager als een geraamte.

pa tsiàh, ǀ 脊, rug.

Pa — *pa kiet*, ǀ 結. voorkomend gedienstig zijn.

pa kiet t'aô ke, ǀ 結 頭 家, de mooie, brave bij den baas uithangen.

tsoè sū pa kiet, 做 事 ǀ 結, schrander zijn.

pa loē (» *lē*) ǀ 弄, spelen met iets, knutselen.

芭 Pa — Pisang.

Pa — *pā tsiao hiòh*, ǀ 蕉 葉, pisangblad.

pa taō, ǀ 豆, croton tiglium.

pa taō tsoè pin nng tsiàh, ǀ 豆 做 檳 榔 食, croton als siri eten. *d. i.* erg ontlasting hebben.

sien pa tsiû, 仙 ǀ 掌, cactus.

疤 Pa — *miao pa pa*, 毛 ǀ 匕, zeer mottig.

笆 Pa — *li pa*, 籬 ǀ, bamboezen omheining.

吧 Pa *pa lâng*, 丨人, iemand uitschelden, (oorspr. mandarijnsch)

pa tun tsīng tsih, 丨唇吮舌, op de lip zuigen en met de tong smekken.

pa lun t'un, 丨崙呑, inslikken zonder te kaauwen.

哺 Pa *pa lang*, 丨明, opklaren (van het weder na regen.)

把 Pá In de hand nemen, beethouden, duidt even als *tsiong* het volgende woord in den accusatief aan.

pá pìng, 丨柄, de regeling van iets in handen hebben, beredderen.

tsoè sū ū pá pìng, 做事有丨柄, regel; een uitgangspunt in zijne handelingen hebben.

pá ts'i, 丨徐, regelen.

bō soè dzī pá hit ê tāi tsì p'ah p'ai, 莫畏縮丨事毀壞, door onvoorzichtigheid eene zaak bederven.

飽 Pá Genoeg eten, verzadigd, vol.

tsiáh pá, 食丨, genoeg eten; gegeten hebben.

pá eh, 丨呃, oprisping van verzadiging.

pá pui lui, *pá pui tī* (of *tīng* / » » » » » *lāng*) } 丨肥壘, 丨肥滿, verzadigd, dik gegeten.

pá tī, 丨滿, vol.

pá pá pá, 丨丨丨, meer dan genoeg, overvloedig.

oē kiò pá pá, 能呌丨匕, «*pá pá*» kunnen roepen (als van kleine kinderen als zij eten willen.)

pá bák, 丨目, het oog vol van iets hebben, zeer dikwijls gezien.

pá ts'i, 丨持, ervaren, volleerd in een vak.

tsoè pá hì, 做丨戲, kunsten maken.

t'àn á pá, 乘佝丨, juist genoeg voor zijn levensonderhoud verdienen.

kò ts'uì pá tī tī, 顧嘴丨已耳, niet meer dan de kost verdienen.

pá moā, 丨滿, vol.

覇 Pà Wild, woest.

pà sìng, 丨性, halstarrig.

pà tsiàm, 丨占, overweldigen.

à pà, 亞丨, ondeugend, (van kinderen) wild (van paarden.)

pà k'í lai, 丨起來, steigeren.

pà hoat, 丨活, strenge maatregel.

sì koè pà / (» *kè* ») } 四處丨, overal rondzoeken.

tsū pà it hong, 自丨一方, zelfstandig zijn, geen hulp van anderen noodig hebben.

○ Pà *pà t'aì*, 丨頭, kracht in de hand.

bé pà t'aô, 馬丨頭, het achtereind van den paardenrug of van een rug in 't algemeen.

pà ts'iú, 丨手, een stokje waarmede men de hand vastheid voor het boogschieten geeft.

豹 Pà Luipaard.

hó pà, 虎丨, tijgers en luipaard.

laō hiöh pà, 荖葉丨, groote siriekaauwer.

抛 P'a Uitwerpen, werpen; ankeren vallen, buitelen.

p'a bāng, 丨網, een net uitwerpen.

p'a tiā, 丨錠, ankeren.

p'a tsûn, 丨船, een schip ankeren.

p'a hō teh, 丨住的, uitwerpen en

laten liggen (als een net), overeen komen en daardoor gebonden.

p‘a tioh hit ê lâng, | 着 彼 人, iemand in zijn net vangen, (als vrouwen.)

p‘a lóh bé, | 下 馬, van het paard afvallen.

p‘a lîn taó, p‘a ki lîn, | 麒 麟, buitelen, omduikelen.

胞 *lān p‘a*, | 粦, balzak.

P‘a *toā lān p‘a*, 大 粦 |, gezwollen zak, elefantiasis.

gû lān p‘a, 牛 [illegible] |, koeblaas.

葩 Een tros (als druiven.)

P‘a *tsit p‘a hoe*, 一 | 花, een bundel bloemen, ruiker.

tsiâ p‘a tsiâ tô, 成 | 成 桃, aan trossen en risten (van vruchten.)

toā p‘a hé, 大 | 火, groote vlam.

冇 Poreus, hol.

P‘à *p‘à sam á*, | 衫, onsterk hout.

p‘à ts‘â, | 柴, zacht hout.

p‘à p‘à, | |, hol (van woorden) zacht (van voorwerpen.)

toā p‘à tsîm, 大 | 蟳, een groote holle krab; een dik maar zwak mensch, iemand die den schijn van rijk heeft zonder het te zijn.

p‘à soà, | 線, los borduurgaren.

p‘à sim, | 心, inwendig zacht (als vruchten.)

k‘ang p‘à, 空 |. uitwendig fraai maar inwendig hol.

p‘à làng, | 曠, niet stevig ingestopt.

p‘à ts‘ik hiu, | 粟 香, anijs.

p‘à tsik, | 粟, holle rijsthalmen.

p‘à siaò, | 賬, holle rekening, (die men niet betaald kan krijgen.)

p‘à p‘ih, | 仄, hol en daardoor dof van geluid.

p‘à kóng p‘à kóng, | 廣 | 匕, hol, niet solide.

怕 Vreezen.

P‘à *k‘ióng p‘à*, 恐 |, bevreesd zijn voor, vreezen.

k‘ū p‘à (*k‘ī* „) | 懼, do.

put p‘à, 不 |, vrees niet, wees niet bevreesd.

胞 Blaar, blaartje.

P‘ā *hé p‘ā*, 火 |, brandbaar.

tsuí p‘ā, 水 |, water-blaar, waterbel.

puh p‘ā, k‘ì p‘ā, p‘òng p‘ā, | 出, 起 |, 發 |, een blaar trekken, vormen.

tsiâ p‘ā, 成 |, do.

烘 Ontploffen, wegbranden.

P‘ā *p‘i p‘i p ā p‘ā*, 披 匕 | 匕, in eens wegbranden, (als papier) vervliegen, (als rijkdom.)

p‘ā tsèh tsiū bò k‘ì, | 一 次 就 無 了, in een oogenblik is het verdwenen (als voorspoed.)

彩 *ū p‘ā*, 有 光 |, voorspoed, bloeijend, P‘ā (als handel); van scherp doorzicht, helder verstand.

li tsīn bô p‘ā, 汝 眞 無 光 |, gij zijt volstrekt tot niets te gebruiken.

Pai

次 Maal, keer, reize.

Paí *tsit paì*, 一 |, éénmaal.

tsit paì, 此 |, deze keer, ditmaal.

pai pai, ták pai, | 匕, 逐 |. steeds telkens reize.

tsoē pai, 多 |, dikwerf.

aō pai, 後 |, later, een volgende keer.

ing pai, 常 |, steeds te voren.

ts'iṳ̄ tîng pai, ts'iṳ̄ té pai, 倩 長 |, 倩 短 |, voor langen, korten tijd huren, aannemen.

跛 Mank.

ʾai *pai k'a,* | 脚, mank.

擺 Inbeweging zetten, schudden, zwaaijen,
ʾai slingeren, aanzetten, met een streek bedriegen.

iö pai, 搖 |, zwaaijen, schudden.

pai ts'ioh, | 尺, slinger, (aan een klok.)

tsûn iö pai, 船 搖 |, het schip schommelt, stampt

pai k'oai, | 欵, van gesteldheid veranderen.

pai lōng, | 弄, aanzetten, ophitsen.

pai hǫ́, | 虎, iemand die behendig bedriegt of twist stookt.

k'it lâng pai k'ì, 被 人 | 去, door iemand bedrogen of aangehitst worden.

拜 Eene buiging maken, beleefdelijk groeten,
ʾài gelukwenschen, feliciteren met; bezoeken; eene visite afleggen; aanbidden, offeren aan; beleefdelijk verzoeken om; voorovervallen.

pài tiām, | , kussen om op te knielen.

pài haō, pài kì, 候, | 見, een bezoek afleggen bij.

pài t'àm, | 探, bezoeken.

kìng pài, 敬 |, eerbiedigen.

pài t'iep, 接 |. visite kaartjes.

kiet pài hiaⁿ tī, 結 | 兄 弟, broederschap sluiten.

pài hók, | 服, zijne minderheid bekennen.

pài sai hū, | 司 阜, een baas om onderricht verzoeken (met geschenken vergezeld) eene goede les gehad hebben.

pài nî, | 年, nieuwjaar wenschen.

pài si̍ jit, | 生 日, met zijn geboortedag feliciteren.

pài sî, | 辭, groeten en weggaan, eene zaak aan een ander overlaten.

pài siā, | 謝, bedanken, dankbetuigen.

pài siā t'iⁿ, | 謝 天, een dankbuiging maken, (op het eind van een tooneel stuk door den singende *Toā* gedaan), *d. i.* die zaak is gelukkig ten einde.

siā pài, 謝 |, bedanken voor de laatste eer eenen overledene bewezen; thans ook, hard schreeuwen.

lé pài, 禮 |, godsdienstoefening houden.

tsit lé pài, 一 禮 |. eene week.

pài put, | 佛, aan een afgod offeren.

pài tsó, | 祖, aan zijne voorouders offeren.

pài pé, | 把, vóór het mikpunt neêr vallen, (van een pijl).

pài pé hiaⁿ tī, | 把 兄 弟, broederschap zweeren.

pai lòh lai, | 落 來, voorovervallen, (van een staand voorwerp.)

pài toā, | 帶, het roer dwars leggen, (op ondiepe plaatsen.)

kap lâng pài, 與 人 |, iemand plagen.

排 Pai Uit elkander zetten, in orde stellen, rangschikken, tentoonspreiden, uitstallen; rang, rij; elk.

pai k'ui, 丨開, uit elkander zetten.

pai kai, 丨解, uiteenzetten, ontwarren.

pai pi, 丨比, in orde brengen.

pai tīn, 丨陣, in strijdorde stellen.

pai toh, 丨桌, tafel dekken.

pai liét. pai siet, 丨列, 丨設, rangschikken.

pai pan, 丨班, zich in een rij zetten, (als het gevolg van een mandarijn).

pai t'oa, 丨攤, over verschillende personen verdeelen.

pai tsi, *pai ts'iang*, 丨只, 丨昌, zwierig, opgesierd.

pai tièm bīn, 丨店面, voor een winkel uitstallen.

p'o pai, 鋪丨, voordeelig plaatsen, het weinige voordeelig doen uitkomen.

p'o pai oā, 鋪丨話, beleefde ophemelende taal.

pai hâng, 丨行, volgens den rang rij (van broeders).

toā pai hâng, 大丨行, de groote rij (broeders en zusters.)

ts'ui pai, 推丨, juist goed, ter regter tijd komen.

tsit pai pit, 一丨筆, een bundel, (10) penseelen.

pai ê, *pai lâng*, 丨个, 丨人, elk, iedereen.

pai hāng, 丨項, alles.

pai pō lâng, 丨布人, met een streek iemand tegenwerken.

牌 Pai Schild; steenen of houten bord, plaat met een opschrift, uithangbord; geschrift, certificaat, bewijs, papieren; medaille; speelkaarten, dominosteenen.

tîn pai, 籐丨, rottingen schild.)

tsiao (of *tsio*) *pai*, 招丨, uithangbord.

tn̂g k'a pai, 長脚丨, houten bord op langen voet, (waarop de betrekking van een overheid staat.)

hé pai, 火丨, plankje met het karakter *vuur* er op, bij gewichtige dépèches gevoegd.

pèh pai, 白丨, doodsbekendmaking (aan de deur geplaatst.)

âng pai, 紅丨, haven uitklaring.

tsûn pai, 船丨, scheepsbrief.

gûn pai, 銀丨, zilveren madaille.

pai á, *tsoá pai*, 丨仔, 紙丨, speelkaarten.

poáh pai á, 賭丨仔, kaartspelen.

pai á kiaó, 丨仔場, kaartspel,

p'o gê pai, 鋪牙丨, dominospelen

簰 Pai Een vlot.

tik pai, *sam pai*, 竹丨, 杉丨, bamboezen, houten vlot.

敗 Paī Vervallen, te gronde gaan, te gronde rigten, ruinéren; ondergaan, verval; verslagen worden, nederlaag lijden, onvoordeelig, onvoorspoedig; bedorven, uitgelekt van zaken.

paī hoaī, 丨壞, vervallen.

paī kok, 丨國, het rijk ondermijnen.

paī tiaô, 丨朝, eene dynastie te gronde richten, uitsterven van eene stal.

paī ke, 丨家, zijn huisgezin ruinéren.

beh paī lah, 將丨了, zijn val na bij zijn.

paī bîng sit tsiet, 丨名失節, zijn naam en eer verliezen.

kai paī, 該 ｜, te volkomen, bij iets moeten verliezen.

paī tiaū, 兆 ｜, voorteeken van verval, nederlaag, enz.

ai paī, 愛 ｜, slechte kans op het slagen van iets geven, ongelukkig voorteeken zijn.

t'ai paī, 太 ｜, verslagen worden.

paī tīn, paī ping, ｜陣, ｜兵, nederlaag lijden.

toā paī, 大 ｜. groote nederlaag.

paī ts'ī, 市 ｜. niet gewild, niet te verkoopen.

bö paī haī, 無 ｜ 害, onschadelijk zijn.

paī lō, ｜露, aan den dag komen.

paī pán, ｜板, uitgelekt.

派 P'aì Vertakkingen uitzenden als eene rivier; familietak; verdeelen over, ieder zijne plaats aanwijzen, afzenden, aanstellen; manieren, voorkomen.

hun p'aì, 分 ｜. verdeelen over, uitzenden.

siāng p'aì ê lâng (*kāng* » » ») 同 ｜ 之 人, menschen van dezelfde stamouders.

tsià p'aì, 正 ｜, de oorspronkelijke afstammelingen.

p'aì poah, ｜撥, aanstellen, ieder zijne plaats aanwijzen.

p'aì hù hō, ｜富戶, over de rijke familien verdeelen, (de betaling van rijks schuld.)

p'aì ts'ai mai, ｜菜碗, de levering van iets over het volk verdeelen.

p'aì giáh, ｜額, over het geheele aantal verdeelen.

k'e p'aì, 溪 ｜, verdeelen over.

tsiâⁿ p'aì, poàⁿ p'aì, 全 ｜, 半 ｜, geheel en ten halve op iemand verdeelen.

p'aì tsī, ｜錢, de betaling van geld over eenigen verdeelen.

p'aì iòh, ｜藥, een receptje schrijven.

p'aì p'e (» *p'oe*) ｜批, bedacht zijn op, het er voor houden dat . . .

bö p'aì p'e, 無 ｜ 批, niet bedacht op.

p'aì k'im ts'e, ｜欽差, een keizerlijke gezant afzenden.

koⁿ p'aì, 官 ｜, mandarijn manieren

kik koⁿ p'aì, 假 ｜ 官, zich als een mandarijn voordoen.

sai p'aì, 使 ｜, den bram uithangen, veel vertooning maken.

kiⁿ p'aì, 京 ｜, Peking manieren.

ū p'aì t'aô, 有 ｜ 頭, onbedeesd, niet verlegen, vrijmoedig.

潑 P'aì *p'aì laī ê tsa bo*, ｜賴婦人, een onbeschaamd robust vrouwspersoon.

歹 P'aị Slecht, als bijw. moeijelijk te . . . . slechte.

p'aị sū, ｜事, slechte handelingen.

p'aị taī, ｜事, do.

p'aị ts'iù dziāo, ｜手爪, ontfutselen, steeds wegstelen.

p'aị tiaū t'aô, ｜兆頭, een slecht voorteeken.

p'aị liēm t'aô, ｜念頭, slechte gedachten.

p'aị sè (» *sì*) ｜勢, onbetamelijk, moeielijk, slecht te doen.

p'aị k'ìh, ｜了, overleden, gestorven.

p'a siòng, ｜像, laag van karakter, gulzig in het eten.

p'aị naị k'ìh, ｜乃了, geheel en al bedorven.

p'ai kiá lâng, | 子 仔, een slecht mensch.

p'ai kaó, | 狗, een slecht mensch.

p'ai t'âng ts'ì, | 虫 莿, uiterst slecht (van pers.)

p'ai pak, | 腹, rommeling in de buik.

tsoè p'ai lâng, 弄 | 人, de kat de bel ontvangen.

p'ai sim, | 心, slecht van harte.

p'ai ts'ùi mē lâng, | 嘴 詈 人, iemand gemeen uitschelden.

p'ai sin k'ì, | 神 氣, niet goed staande, moeielijk, slecht te doen.

p'ai p'ê hu, | 皮 膚, slecht, moeielijk van genezen.

p'ai kè, | 價, slechte, geringe prijs.

p'ai siā saò, | 聲 嗽, vertoornd antwoorden.

kap i p'ai, 與 伊 |, met iemand geen goede vrienden zijn.

p'ai toé, | 底, een slechte grond hebben, *d. i.* den naam van slecht hebben.

hó am p'ai, 好 兼 |, goeden en slechten, (van waren of personen.)

p'ai k'oà siā, | 看 相, leelijk om te zien, niet mooi staan.

Pah

百 Honderd.

Pah *tsit pah*, 一 |, honderd.

Peh *pah poā*, | 般, honderde (allerlei) soorten van ....

pah iū lâng (» *iō* ») | 樣 人, honderderlei soorten van menschen.

pah bān, | 萬, een millioen.

tsit iū bi ts'ī pah iū lâng, 一 樣 米 飼 | 樣 人, eene soort rijst voedt honderd soorten menschen.

tsoè pah dzit, 做 | 日, de honderddagige rouw houden. (gedurende welken tijd men niet huwen kan.)

pah king kûn, | 經 裙, vrouwenrok met vele plooijen.

打 Slaan, vechten, slaan op ; schieten, maken,

P'ah daarstellen ; in eenen zekeren toestand brengen, vóór werkwoorden duidt het de werking aan ; bewerken (metalen enz); getroffen worden door, vatten als koude: uiten, laten als een boer : opslaan (als water), zich verschaffen, koopen; paren (bij beesten) ; spelen met.

p'ah si (of *sìh*), | 死, doodslaan.

p'ah lâng kiò kiù lâng, | 人 叫 救 人, iemand slaande nog om hulp roepen, nooit met zijn voordeel tevreden zijn.

p'ah o ts'i, | 烏 青, bont en blaauw slaan.

p'ah mē, | 罵, slaan en schelden.

p'ah hé, | 火, 樸 火, vuurslaan, brandblusschen.

p'ah sit hé k'ì, | 息 火 氣, iemands toorn bedaren.

sī p'ah, 相 |, vechten.

p'ah tsiaó, | 鳥, vogels schieten, jagen.

p'ah lah, | 獵, jagen.

p'ah pe tsiaó, | 飛 鳥, een vogel in de vlugt schieten, overspel op de geschikste plaatsen doen.

k'it lâng p'ah, 被 人 |, geslagen worden.

p'ah m̄ tiòh, | 不 着, mislaan, misraken.

p'ah kûn, | 拳, met de vuist slaan.

p'ah koe, | 鷄, hanengevecht.

p'ah hoa, 撲 熄, blusschen, uitdooven.

p'ah p'oà, | 破. breken.

p'ah hò liàh ts àt tiòh ts'in hia tī, | 虎 擒 賊 須 親 兄 弟, op tijger en dievenjacht heeft men volle broeders noodig en voor gewichtige zaken moet men te vertrouwen menschen hebben.

p'ah ts'â lâng, | 柴 人, met een houten pop vechten als boksers die zich met mechanieke poppen oefenen, *d. i.* het zwaar te verantwoorden hebben.

p'ah siong, | 傷, kwetsen.

p'ah soh, | 索, touwslaan.

p'ah p'âng, | 篷, zeilmaken.

p'ah lô, | 鑼. op de gong slaan.

p'ah ts'ui kó, | 嘴 鼓, op de mondtrommel slaan. *d. i.* zonder ophouden slaan.

hé to p'ah, 火 刀 |, vuurslag.

p'ah ts'iú, | 手, vechters, soldaten op een tooneel.

p'ah tsing, | 精, den coïtus uitoefenen (van dieren)

p'ah tó, | 倒, omverwerpen.

p'ah ts'ui ts'ui, | 碎 匕. aan schilfers breken.

p'ah p'ai, | 歹. bederven.

p'ah la sâm, | 汚, vuil maken.

p'ah keh, | 格, linieeren.

p'ah sip dzī hō, | 十 字 互, een kruisband omdoen.

p'ah kat, | 結, een knoop leggen.

p'ah kim sai hū, | 金 師 阜, goudsmid.

p'ah gûn sai hū) (» *gin* » ») | 銀 師 阜, zilversmid.

p'ah t'ih sai hū, | 鐵 師 阜, ijzersmid.

p'ah tâng sai hū, | 銅 師 阜, koperslager.

p'ah siah sai hū, | 錫 師 阜, tinnegieter.

p'ah soh sai hū, | 索 師 阜, touwslager.

p'ah tsióh sai hū, | 石 師 阜, steenhouwer.

p'ah k'ui, 劈 開, in tweeën hakken.

p'ah p'oah kè bō, | 破 計 謀, iemands plannen verijdelen.

p'ah t'ih lâng to; | 鉄 人 刀, mes van een ijzersmid, *d. i.* steeds twist willen hebben.

p'ah dzī hō, | 字 號, een merk zetten op.

p'ah tsit tiu dzī, | 一 張 字, een papier, geschrift opmaken.

p'ah lóh toé, | 落 底, tot een wet regel maken.

p'ah p'e, | 批, een model van iets maken.

p'ah hiòng, | 餉, belasting opleggen.

p'ah sìng, | 算, denken, bedenken, het er voorhouden.

p'ah sìng, | 虛 費, verspillen, verkwisten, het is zonde dat....!

p'ah kiep, | 刼, plunderen.

p'ah t'ò, | 討, intrigeeren.

p'ah sìng sî, | 失 時, zijn tijd verspillen.

p'ah ts'ien ts'iu, | 韆 鞦, wippen als kinderen.

p'ah sit lóh, *p'ah bò k'ì*, *p'ah ūm kì*, | 失 落, | 沒 去, | 不 見, verliezen.

p'ah pò, | 報, bekend maken.

p'ah koa si, | 官 司, procedeeren, aanklagen.

p'ah eh, | 噎, een boer laten, oprispen.

p'ah k'o sai eh, | 鼓 噎 呃, oprispen, booren, de hik hebben.

p'ah k'a ts'iù, | 嚏 噴, niezen.

p'ah k'a, | 脚, met de voeten tegen elkander aanslaan.

p'ah koā, 傷 寒, koude vatten.

p'ah ts'in, p'ah ling, | 凉, | 冷, een tocht vatten.

p'ah p'oh, onzeker, van het geluk af hangend.

p'ah pai, | 牌, een kaart opspelen.

p'ah kiù, | 毬, kegelen, biljarten.

p'ah tsui, | 水, water innemen, (van een schip)

p'ah p'ièn, | 騙, bedriegen.

p'ah kiō lai, | 轎 來, een draagstoel laten komen.

p'ah iù, | 油, olie koopen.

p'ah k'an t'aô, | 牽 頭, verpande goederen verkoopen.

p'ah hing, | 雄, treden, (als een haan.)

p'ah hing ih, | 還 伊, het slechte terug zenden.

p'ah mi tsiong, | 棉 精, gewatteerde deken maken, dekens watteeren.

p'ah p'aì i tsit k'o, | 派 伊 一 員, iemand voor één dollar aan iets laten betalen.

Pak

剝 **Pak** Afstroopen, af halen, villen; uittrekken; met geweld ontnemen, uitplunderen.

pak p'é, | 皮, villen.

t'ing pak t'eh, | 脫 衣, naakt.

pak kut, | 骨, de beenderen uit iets halen.

pak siet, | 洩, villen en afschrapen, *d. i.* ondermijnen, verzwakken.

pak siep, | 澁, hard in de maag liggend, wrang.

pak boē lut t'i, | 未 脫 褫, niet van eene zaak afkunnen.

pak sa á k'o, | 衫 褲, van zijn kleêren ontdoen, berooven.

pak sa á k'i ting, | 衫 去 典, zijne kleêren verpanden.

ts'iū pak, 刼 |, uitplunderen.

pak dzī kut, | 字 骨, een karakter ontleden, de beteekenis verder uitstrekken.

北 **Pak** Noord, het Noorden, de Noord.

pak sì, | 勢, het Noorden, Noordelijk.

pak hong, | 風, do. N. wind.

pak kiṇ, | 京, Peking.

sai pak hō, 西 | 雨, NW. regen. regenbui.

toā pak bé, 大 | 馬, groot Noordsch paard; groote vrouw.

toā pak, 大 |, de groote Noord *Tien-tsin*, *Peking* enz.

tsiū sió pak, 上 小 |, naar de kleine Noord, (Shanghai, Hangchow) gaan.

pak koán, | 管, Noorder muziek.

pak t'aô è lâng, | 頭 之 人, menschen van het Noorden.

pak tsûn kaò, | 船 到, de scheper van de Noord komen aan.

pak pi, | 邊, Noordelijk.

pak hong t'i, | 風 天, Noordenwind. weder.

駁 **Weêrleggen.**

Pak *pak bô taī tsì*, | 無 事, door weêr-legging twist voorkomen.

腹 De buik, (zetel der kennis) de inge-wanden, binnenste.

Pak

pak tǫ͘, | 肚, de buik.

pak tǫ͘ t'iǹ, | 肚 病, buikpijn.

pak laī, | 內, wat in de buik is, de ingewanden, (van beesten.)

ū pak laī, 有 | 內, knap, verstan-dig.

peh pak, 扒 |, inwendig bedroefd.

p'oà pak ê oē, 破 | 之 言, taal uit het binnenste zijns harten, open hartig.

sim pak ê lâng, 心 | 之 人, ge-liefkoosd persoon, favoriet.

tsát pak, 飽 |, massief, niet hol.

pak ping, ping pak, | 反, 反 |, het gegetene overgeven.

hoán pak, 反 |, do.

tsaú pak, 走 |, diarrhoea hebben.

幅 Een strook papier; num. voor teekening

Pak kaarten, enz. een strook, baan goed.

tsit pak toā siū, 一 | 大 壽, een levensgroot portret.

gǫ͘ pak pò tsoè, 五 | 布 做, van vijf banen stof gemaakt.

贌 Bevrachten.

Pák *pao pák*, 包 |, pachten.

pák tsûn, | 船, een schip bevrachter.

pák si, | 死, vast aannemen.

pák tiāⁿ tióh, | 定 着, vast aan-nemen, pachten.

pák boē, | 賣, het recht van verkoop voor iets pachten.

pá bé á, | 傌 仔, de pacht nemen, pachten.

縛 Binden;, numer. voor pakjes als sigaren.

Pák *pák tsoè tui* (» *tsò* »), | 做 堆, aan pakjes binden.

pák k'a pák ts'iú, | 脚 | 手, zijn eigen meester niet zijn, *lett*, aan handen en voeten binden.

k'ún pák, 綑 |, knevelen, binden.

pák sin, | 身, strak om het lijf sluitend.

pák k'a, | 脚, gebonden, kleine voe-ten.

pák ki kut, | 枝 骨, *lett.* het raam, de ruwe omtrek bij elkander binden als papierplakkers, *d. i* het begin, de grondslag voor iets maken.

pák pák pák, | 匕 匕, strak om het lijf spannend.

tsit pák oáⁿ, 一 | 碗, een bundel kopjes (10 stuks.)

伏 Voorover liggen of vallen.

P'ak *p'ak lak*, | 落, voorover.

p'ak teh, | 的, vooroverliggen.

p'ak teh k'oàⁿ, | 覗, voorover kijken.

樸 Eenvoudig, onopgesierd.

P'ak *p'ak sit*, | 實, eenvoudig.

p'ak sò͘, | 素, eenvoudig, onopge-sierd.

kó͘ p'ak ê lâng, 古 | 之 人, een ouderwets eenvoudig mensch.

仆 Voorover, met den buitenkant naar bin-

P'ak nen gekeerd, onderste boven, de holle kant naar binnen.

ping p'ak, 反 |, op de buik, voor-over liggen.

p'ih p'ak ā, 披 | 映, voorover-vallen.

hī á p'ak p'ak, 耳戢丨匕, met hangende ooren, druipstaartend.

p'ak ts'iú, 丨手, de holle kant van de hand op iets leggen.

tsit p'ak ts'iú toā, 一丨手大, zoo groot als een hand bedekken kan.

tò p'ak, 倒丨, onderste boven.

hē t'áng p'ak, 下田丨, onderste boven leggen.

sī p'ak k'ui tsʻiò, 相丨開笑, nog als een stuivertje op zijn kant, onzeker.

覆 Omkeeren op, (als aarde op een graf.)
P'ak *p'ak t'ō*, 丨泥, met aarde toedekken.

p'ak soā, 丨山, (drie dagen na de begravenis), op een graf gaan offeren.

hō̤ lí haī kaò tsit p'ak poeh tsʻiò, 被汝害至七顛八倒, Ik ben door U op allerlei manieren benadeeld.

曝 In de zon droogen.
P'ák *p'ák dzit*, 丨日, do.

p'ák iêm ê lâng, 丨鹽之人, zoutfabriekant.

p'ák si, 丨死, verdroogen, (als planten door eene sterke zon.)

p'ák koā, 丨乾, droogen, (als vleesch).

kut t'aô p'ák lō̤, 骨頭丨露, niet begraven worden.

p'ák dzit ok, 丨日惡, door de zon verbrand, (als landwerkers).

kóng hē teh ts'e kong p'ák dzit, 說下的吹風丨日, in zijn spreken iets in de wind en in de zon te droogen hangen, *d. i.* over iets spreken dat nog ver in de toekomst is.

朴 *mîng p'ák* (*muī p'aóh*) 門丨, bovendrempel, bo-
P'ák venkozijn van een deur.

Pan

班 Troep bij elkander behoorende lieden al
Pan komedianten, dienstdoende soldaten garnizoen bedienden; ook elk van het afzonderlijk; dienstbeurt.

hì pan, 戲丨, komedianten troep.

kiō pan, 轎丨, stoeldragers.

kun pan, 隨丨, gevolg, bedienden (van overheden.)

oā pan, 換丨, van garnizoen verwisselen.

pan ping, 丨兵, garnizoenssoldaten.

ts'e pan, 吹丨, horenblazer, tamboer

a pan, 亞丨, topgast.

tsiū pan, 上丨, zijn dienstbeurt waarnemen.

lóh pan, 落丨, de dienstbeurt neer leggen.

頒 Ronddeelen, verspreiden.
Pan *pan hing t'ien hā*, 丨行天下 door het geheele rijk verdeelen, (al een bevel).

斑 Veelkleurig, gevlekt, gespikkeld, pok
Pan dalig, mottig.

pan sik, 丨色, veelkleurig.

sī (of *ts'iū*) *pan*, 生丨, gevlekt, gespikkeld.

ts'iū o pan, 生烏丨, zwarte weer vlekken krijgen.

pan tik, 丨竹, gevlekte bamboes.

pan kaó, 丨犬, gevlekte hond.

hó pan sik, 虎丨色花, als een tijger gevlekt.

ts'ut pan, 出瘢, koorts met uitslag hebben, roodvonk.

pan bâ li, ｜貓 厘, Spaansche vlieg.
pan èh, ｜鞋, pokdalige.
bīn pan pan, 面｜｜, pokdalig, mottig.

便 Pan Goedkoop, voordeelig.
pan gî, ｜宜, goedkoop.
kap i kóng oē bô pan gî, 同伊說話無宜, men heeft er meer nadeel dan voordeel bij, om met hem te spreken.
k'ah pan, 較｜, goedkooper.

攀 Pan Trekken, duwen, rekken.
pan lai pan k'i, ｜來｜去, heen en weer trekken, (als een jas.)
pan k'iṅ, ｜直, uitrekken, uitduwen, (als een stoel.)
pan kaò kì tsiah beh boē, ｜到價方要賣, niet eer willen verkoopen voordat men op zijn prijs is.
pan ts'iú bé, ｜手杪, de sterkte der armen tegen elkander meten; zich met elkander meten.
pan tsí, 戒指, duimring van boogschutters.

板 Pán Plank, deel, lat, doodkist, platen van hout of metaal, drukplaat, drukplank, tijpen, bamboezen lat om misdadigers te slaan; castagnetten waarmede men de maat aangeeft, maat.
ts'â pán, 柴｜, plank
tē pán, 地｜, vloerplank.
pán í, ｜椅, houten bank.
t'ih pán, 鐵｜, ijzeren band.
tâng pán, 銅｜, koperplaat.
sam pán, 杉, sampan, boot.
koṇ ts'â pán, 棺材｜, planken van een doodkist.
póh pán á, 薄｜仔, dunne gemeene doodkist.
ts'oan pán, 川｜, doodkist van *Sù-ts'oan* hout.
k'ui pán tièm, 開｜店, een doodkistwinkel opzetten.
k'ò ts'iú pán, 靠手｜, lat in een draagstoel waarop de handen rusten.
pán pî, ｜枰, plat dak op een huis.
pán loē, ｜鑢, vijl
pán lâ iû, ｜膀油, de reuzels van een dier.
ìn pán, 印｜, drukplaten.
oàh pán, 活｜, bewegelijke tijpen.
si pán si pán, 死 死｜, niet weten te veranderen.
pán pán, pán pih pán pih, ｜匕, klein en breed (van pers.)
kó pán, 古, onderwets.
tsip kó pán, 執古｜, zich aan het oude houdend.
toā pán, sió pán, 大｜, 小｜, groote en kleine straf bamboes.
pán uī, ｜位, de maat, (in muziek).
bô pán, 無, uit de maat.
bān pán, kín pán, tiép pán, 緩｜, 緊｜, 疊｜, andante, allegro, presto.
pán tsú, ｜主, directeur eener komedie.
t'ien hô pán, 天河｜, zoldering.

舨 Pán *kap pán, kap pán tsûn*, 舺｜船, schip met ra's.

瓶 Pàn *tsiú pàn*, 酒｜, wijnkan.
iû pàn, 油｜, oliekan.
hoe pàn, 花｜, bloemenvaas, (met ooren.)

koū pân, 持 , de wijnkan ronddienen.

tók pân, 獨 |, lange vaas.

kó pân, 古 |, vaas uit de oudheid.

辦 **Pān** Besturen, beheeren, inhanden hebben, waarnemen, regelen, gereed maken, in orde brengen, beredderen; koopen, aankoopen; monster, proef, model.

pān lí, | 理, beheeren, regelen.

oē pān tit lai, 能 得 | 來, kunnen ten uitvoer brengen.

koán pān, 管 |, beheeren.

kàn pān, 揀 |, beredderen.

pān tsoē, | 罪, eene straf uitspreken.

pān hit é lâng, | 彼 之 人, vonnis over iemand uitspreken.

taī pān, 代 |, voor een ander regelen, waarnemen; zaakwaarnemer, supercargo.

ke pān, *kiem pān*, 加 |, 歉 |, er bij waarnemen.

hiép pān, 協 |, ministerie raden; gezamelijk regelen.

boé pān, 買 |, compradoor, hofmeester.

pān sū, | 事, eene zaak regelen.

pān p'e, | 式, het er voorhouden.

pān toh, *pān ièn*, | 棹, | 筵, een gastmaal aanrichten.

pī pān, 備 |, in orde, gereed maken.

pān lé lō, | 理 路, geschenken gereed maken.

ū ts'ûn pān, 有 存 |, toebereidselen, klarigheid maken.

pāng k'ang, | 孔, een gat op iets vinden.

pān k'oā tseh, | 看 的, eens beproeven, probeeren.

pān tê, *ts'aí pān tê*, | 茶, 採 | 茶, thee opkoopen.

pān hè, | 貨, goederen aankoopen.

hè pān, 貨 |, monster.

pān t'aô, | 頭, monster, proef.

k'oā pān, 看 |, een monster, proef model nazien.

ts'ūt pān toā, 出 | 大, buiten model groot

kaò pān hó, 至 | 好, juist als het model.

tsiā pān bô ts'ò, | 且 無 錯 juist, zoo is het.

bô pān, 無 |, niet zeker, niet stellig

pī pān, 備 |, de maat nemen.

lâng pān, 人 |, soort van mensch.

toā toā pān pān, 大 乜 | |, nie verlegen.

m̄ toā pān, 不 大 |, bedeesd, verlegen.

pān taī tsū, | 事, eene zaak in orde brengen.

pān tit m̄ hó, | 得 不 好, slecht ten uitvoer brengen.

p'ah tsui pān, 打 水 |, het water peilen.

扮 **Pān** *tá pān*, 打 |, zich opschikken, toilet maken, zich verkleeden.

扳 **P'an** Verklappen.

sā p'an, 相 |, elkander betichten.

p'an puih, | 拔, do.

ko p'an lâng 高 | 人, met hooge in aanraking komen.

襻 **P'àn** Lus, (aanschoenen, kleêren in.)

liú á p'àn, 鈕 仔 |, knooplus.

bô liú bô p'àn, 無 鈕 無 |, zonder knoopen of lussen. (van versleten kleêren).

盼 P'àn p'àn bōng, ｜望, verlangend uitzien naar.

Pang

枋 Pang Plank, deel.
tsûn pang, 船｜, dekplanken, deelen voor een schip.
sam á pang, 杉仔｜, houten deelen.
tiām pang, 墊｜, dekplanken, (vloerplanken in een vaartuig.)
tièm pang, 店｜, winkelblinden.
pín pang, 屏｜, houten schot.
tsiöh pang, 石｜, granietbladen.
t'iaò pang, 柱｜, scheepsplank.

幇 Pang Bijstaan, helpen.
pang tsūn, pang tsō, ｜助, helpen.
sio pang, 相｜, elkander helpen.
pang ts'iú, ｜手, een handje helpen, helper.
taò pang, 湊｜, helpen.
pang ìh tàm pòh, ｜伊沒薄, help hem wat.
pang t'iep, ｜貼, iemand in zijne uitgaven tegemoetkomen.
īng iöh pang hē teh, 用藥｜住, een pleister opleggen.

邦 Pang Land, rijk.
pang kok, ｜國, het rijk.
goā pang, 外｜, buitenland.

崩 Pang Nederstorten, instorten, (als een berg.) inzakken, neerzakken.
soa pang toē lih, 山｜地裂, de bergen stortten neder en de aarde spleet.
tsuí pang soa, 水｜山, als een door regen ingestorten berg, te niet.
pang hoaī, ｜壞, ingestort, uitgezakt, (van heuvels enz.)
king t'aò beh pang k'ì, 肩頭要｜匕去, mijne schouders zullen (door den zwaren last) inzakken.
pang lāng k'ì, 皆｜下, geheel en al, overal naar beneden storten, van bergen.

帮 Pang Eene bij elkander reizende troep van menschen of schepen, caravaan; eene reis van schepen.
taò pang kiâ lō, 湊｜行路, in caravaan reizen.
lòng pang, 囊｜, heimelijk met een schip meêsluipen.
ták géh dzít ū nn̄g pang e hé hun tsûn, 逐月有二｜火船, maandelijks zijn er twee stoomboot gelegenheden.
hok kièn pang, 福建｜, de Fokkièn buurt.
tsit pang é hè k'ah p'aì, 此｜之貨太歹, deze bezending, faktuur goederen is slechter.
pang pang k'ì, ｜｜去, bij elk convooi gaan.

放 Pàng Van zich afgooijen, wegwerpen; laten staan, opgeven; laten, laten gaan, loslaten, laten loopen, op vrije voeten stellen, den vrijen gang geven aan; uitwerpen, neêrleggen, uitzetten als geld op interest, afgeven; zich ontlasten van; doen afgaan als een geweer, afsteken oplaten.
pàng hiet kák, ｜棄, wegwerpen.
pàng soah, ｜丟, laten staan. opgeven.
pàng ts'iú, ｜手, laten loopen, loslaten.

pàng ling, | 寬 . loslaten.

pàng līng, 寬 | . loslaten hangen, (als een touw.)

pàng sang, | 鬆 , loslaten, (als een strak touw,) laten loopen.

pàng, sī, | 生 . in het leven laten, (van dieren).

pàng pe, | 飛 , laten uitvliegen.

pàng hā, | 暇 . de school laten uitgaan.

pang kè | 假 . vacantie geven.

pàng sim, | 心 , zich geruststellen.

pàng si sim, | 死 心 , iets opgeven, niet meer aan iets denken.

sim sì pàng lóh, 心 性 | 落 . zich niet moeielijk om iets maken.

pàng tá, | 胆 , moedig aan.

pàng k'a, | 脚 . groote stappen nemen.

pàng tiao, | 嚇 , bedreigen, bang maken.

pàng siā. | 聲 , bedreigen, zijn voornemen bedreigend te kennen geven.

pàng dzī, | 餌 , aas uitgooijen.

pàng tók, | 毒 . vergif inwerpen, iemand foppen.

pàng tsing tsí, | 種 子 , zaad van andere plaatsen overbrengen en zaaijen.

sī pàng p'oā, 相 | 伴 . elkander helpen, wederkeerig voor elkander werken.

pàng koan, | 棺 , de lijkkist inhalen.

pàng àm, | 湇 , een groot kolk schieten.

pàng tsá, | 早 , 's morgens vroeg.

pàng laī, | 利 , op interest uitzetten.

pàng tsè, | 債 , do.

pàng dzit lá tsī. | 日 仔 錢, tegen zwaren woeker uitleenen.

pàng p'ièn toā, | 片 單 . zijn visitekaartje afgeven.

pàng t'iep, | 帖 . kaartjes, invitatie afgeven.

pàng dziō, | 尿 . wateren.

pàng sai, | 屎 . kakken.

pàng p'uì, | 屁 . een wind laten.

pàng p'uì oē, | 屁 話 , nonsens, onwaarheden vertellen.

pàng àng, | 紅 . de roode loop hebben.

pàng ts'ing, | 銃 . een geweer afschieten.

páng ien hé, | 烟 火 . vuurwerk afsteken.

pàng hé, | 火 . in brandsteken.

pàng hé hō, | 火 號 , een vuursein geven.

pàng hong ts'e. | 風 箏 . een vlieger oplaten.

pàng tsè é lâng, | 債 之 人, geldschieter.

pàng siaò, | 數 , crediet op crediet geven: door een groot handelaar gegeven crediet.

pàng iû, | 羊 , de schapen uitlaten uit hun stal.

pàng pe, | 飛 . laten uitvlieger.

pàng k'oeh, 合 | 睫 . de oogen sluiten.

房 **Pàng** Kamer, vertrek; gebouw, pakhuis; departement in een bureau; afdeeling in eene familie, familietak, verwantschap.

pàng king, | 間 , kamers.

kò pàng, 庫 | . schatkamer.

kuī pàng, 櫃 | . geldkamer.

àm pàng, 暗 | . donkere kamer.

tsū pâng, 書 ｜, school.

tù pâng, 厨 ｜, bordenkamer.

tiaò pâng, 朝 ｜, wachtkamer voor de keizerlijke audientie.

pàng koa̱, ｜ 官, de civiele mandarijnen die bij eene examinatie assisteren.

tsiēn pâng, *tsièn pàng*, *tsàn pàng*, 棧 ｜, pakhuis.

kap pâng, 合 ｜, het huwelijks leven leiden.

kiâ pâng, 行 ｜, de bijslaap uitoefenen.

pàng k'e (» *k'o*) ｜ 科, de zaken behoorende tot de verschillende departementen in een mandarijn bureau.

pàng t'aò, *pàng hūn*, ｜ 頭, ｜ 份, familietak.

ts'in pâng, *soe pâng*, 親 ｜, 疎 ｜, naverwanten, verre verwanten.

pàng ts'in, ｜ 親, familieverwanten.

pàng tiú̱, ｜ 長, hoofd eener familietak.

kè pâng, 繼 ｜, als kind aangenomen worden.

siaò pang, 賬 ｜, rekenbureau, (rekenkamer.

縫 Naaijen, rijgen.

Pàng *pàng sa̱*, ｜ 衫, kleeren naaijen, in elkander rijgen.

kau tsiem pâng, 交 針 ｜, stikken.

馬 Familienaam.
Pàng

蚌 Groote schelpen.

Pāng *pāng k'ak*, ｜ 殼, moederpaarl, paarlmoer.

pāng tsu, ｜ 珠, paarl.

pāng bah, ｜ 肉, vleesch in een schelp.

棒 Lange stok.

Pāng *kiáh t'ui kiáh pāng*, 執 鎚 執 ｜, met korte en lange stokken gewapend zijn.

pāng t'ui p'ah kó̱, ｜ 鎚 打 鼓, aan een dooven man's deur kloppen.

蜂 Bij.

P'ang *p'ang siū*, ｜ 岤, bijen nest.

p'ang tû, ｜ 厨, bijenkorf.

bit p'ang, 蜜 ｜, honigbij.

p'ang bit, ｜ 蜜, honig.

p'ang pâng, ｜ 房, honigraat.

p'ang ts'ì tìng tiòh, ｜ 刺 釘 着, door een bij gestoken worden.

soa̱ p'ang, 山 ｜, wesp.

soá p'ang, 散 ｜, verspreide bijen, ook van iemand die overal rondzwerft.

ts'in ts'u̱i ìng p'ang ts'ut siū, 似 黃 ｜ 出 岫, als wespen die uit hun nest vliegen, (van eene plaats die uitloopt om iets te zien.)

p'ang láh, ｜ 蝋, was.

p'ang ông (» *ông*) ｜ 王, koning der bijen.

p'ang hó̱, ｜ 虎, doodshoofd vlinder.

p'ang ih, ｜ 液, honigraat, bijencel.

p'ang ts'ì, ｜ 刺, angel van eene bij.

p'ang hê (» *hê̱*) ｜ 蝦, bijen pop.

p'ang pô̱, ｜ 蒲, honigraat.

o̱ p'ang, 烏 ｜, hommel.

hó̱ t'aò p'ang, 虎 頭 ｜, do.

ìng p'ang (*u̱i* ») ｜ 黃, geele bij, (wijfje).

p'ang pò gê, ｜ 鬧 衙, de bijen vliegen in zwermen uit.

kak p'ang, 桷 ｜, groote wesp.

p'ang siū ing, | 岫 癬, negenoog.

香 Welriekend.

P'ang *p'ang ts'ìng ts'ìng*, | 清 匕, zeer welriekend.

p'ang hiu, | 香, reukwerk.

p'ang tsui, | 水, reukwater.

p'ang iû, | 油, welriekende olie.

miâ siâ p'ang, 名 聲 |, goede faam, beroemd.

p'ang ts'aó, | 草, welriekende planten.

p'ang hoe (» *hoa*) | 花, welriekende bloem.

soah p'ang, 撒 |, iets geurigs door mengen.

ts'ìng p'ang, 清 |, reukstof, geurigs tusschen, in iets doen, (als in thee, tusschen kleeren, enz.)

bi p'ang, 米 |, geroosté moskwische rijst.

k'ièn p'ang, 熬 |, geur aan iets mededeelen, (als uien in brandend vet).

紡 Spinnen.

P'áng *p'áng mi*, | 綿, wol spinnen

p'áng tseh (» *tseh*) | 績, spinnen en weven.

p'áng se (of *soà*), (» *sè*) | 線, sajet, garen, spinnen.

p'áng ts'ia, | 車, spinnewiel.

p'áng ts'ia lùn, | 車 輪, het spinnewiel draaijen.

bò p'áng bò tseh, 無 | 無 績, spinnen noch weven, (van vrouwen die niets uitvoeren.)

kap i p'áng, 與 伊 |, eene onafgebroken ruzie met iemand hebben.

胖 Vet, dik, gezet.

P'àng

p'àng p'àng p'àng, | | |, do.

pui p'àng, | 肥, gezet, dik.

篷 Zeil.

P'âng *p'ah p'âng*, 朴 |, zeilen maken,

toā p'âng, 大 |, grootzeil.

t'aô p'âng, 頭 |, fokkezeil.

p'âng pò, | 布, zeildoek.

p'âng king (» *kiong*) | 弓, matten over een schuit.

p'âng kám, | 簽, scherm, schut voor den zon.

ts'ia p'âng, 起 |, zeilzetten, zeil ophijschen.

loh p'âng, 落 |, zeil strijken.

hè p'âng (*hoè* ») | 回, zeil minderen, inkorten.

gō p'âng tsûn, 五 | 船, schuit met vijf matten schutten.

t'oa p'âng, 梳 |, 1° met het zeil door het water sleepen; 2° (een vlerk langs zich heen sleepen, (van kippen, enz.)

p'âng ui soh lō, | 拖 索 路, zeilen, masten en stag.

捧 In beide handen dragen, aanbrengen,

P'âng aandragen, ronddienen, overgeven aan, (als eene affaire.)

p'âng tê (» *tê*) | 茶, thee ronddienen.

p'ang bē tioh, | 未 着, bij het aanbieden van iets, te kort schieten.

行 *tsit p'âng tsì*, 一 | 箭, een bun-

P'âng del pijlen, (van 5 stuks.)

p'âng sing li lai tsoè, | 生 理 來 做, zijne handels zaken aan iemand opdragen.

p'âng tò, | 宅, verzegeld pakje geld waar ieder zijn stempel opzet.

P'àng *p'àng bé tiah* } ｜尾摘, kromtaal.
(» *boé* ») }

隙 Spleet, (in den muur), reet, gat, uitweg,
P'ăng uitvlucht.

t'at p'ăng, 塞 ｜, een gat, tusschenruimte opstoppen.

ū p'ăng, 有 ｜, een uitvlucht, uitweg hebben.

ts'ē (ts'oē) p'ăng, 尋 ｜, een uitweg voorwendsel zoeken.

mêng p'ăng } 門 ｜, reet in de deur.
(*muĭ* ») }

k'ang p'ăng, 壙 ｜, reet, spleet.

lih p'ăng, 裂 ｜, reet, spleet.

li p'ăng, 離 ｜, spijten, gespleten.

pit p'ăng, 畢 ｜, gespleten, gereten; uitgelekt van een zaak.

siòng p'ăng, 相 ｜ } naar eene
(*siàng*) *k'oì p'ăng*, 看 ｜ } goede gelegenheid, uitkijken.

lăng p'ăng kiĭ tăng, 離 ｜ 行 動. een gat zoeken om aan iets te ontkomen.

p'ī p'ăng, 片 ｜, rondsnuffelen, onderzoeken.

ū p'ăng t'ang dzip, 有 ｜ 可 入, er is een punt om hem op aan te vallen, te weêrleggen.

Pao

包 Omwinden, insluiten, inzakken, indoen,
Pao bevatten, omvatten; op zich nemen, er voor instaan, aannemen, pachten; omsluiten, omsingelen; baal, bundel, pakje.

pao t'aò pò, ｜頭布, de hoofddoek omwinden, omdoen.

pao p'è, ｜ 蔽, doekjes om iets winden.

pao p'ê, ｜ 皮, de omslag waarin iets is.

pao t'aò, ｜ 頭, emballage.

pao hong, ｜ 封, insluiten, (als een brief een pakje.)

pao hong boé boē, ｜ 封 買 賣, op goed vertrouwen handeldrijven.

ts'oá boē pao tit hé, 紙 不 得 ｜ 火, in papier kan men geen vuur pakken, *d. i.* die zaak kan niet geheim blijven.

ts'aó pao kim, 草 ｜ 金, goud in stroo gepakt, *d. i.* uitwendig zijne rijkdom niet toonen.

pao hàm, ｜ 涵, bevatten, inzich sluiten, omvatten.

pao koat, ｜ 訣, in zich bevatten, omvatten.

pao ī, ｜ 餃, spijs bevatten, (van gebak.)

pao koán, ｜ 管, op zich nemen, er voor instaan.

pao niá, ｜ 領, do.

pao soā, pao hai, ｜ 山, ｜ 海, alles in den omtrek pachten.

pao pák, ｜ 贌, pachten.

pao lám, ｜ 攬, voor zijne verantwoording nemen.

pao i, ｜ 醫, zich abonneren bij een doktor.

pao á bīn, ｜ 仔 面, rond, opgezwollen gelaat.

pao á gûn, ｜ 仔 銀, vervalscht geld.

bīn pao, mī pao, 麵 ｜, 麥 ｜, brood.

t'ui pao } 脫 ｜, heimelijk in de plaats
(*t'oat* ») } stellen van.

pao oā lai hè, ｜ 換 來 回, als

het niet goed bevonden wordt kom het dan verruilen.

nñg ping pao lai, 兩 邊 | 來, van beide kanten insluiten, (als dieven.)

pao lao hao, | 瘤 哮, zaamgetrokken, gerimpeld, (van gelaat.)

hò pao, 荷 |, beurs.

pao hók, | 袱, bagage, reistasch.

hun pao, 烟 |, tabakszak.

hé ling hé pao, 火 龍 火 |, lont en kruidzak.

pao pó, | 保, assureren, verzekeren.

pao boē pao boē (» *bé* » *bē*) | 買 | 賣, monopoliseren.

胞 Van dezelfde mooder, volle broeders.

Pao *pao tē,* | 弟, volle broeders.

tòng pao hiā tī, 同 | 兄 弟, do.

pao peh (» *peh*) | 伯, oudere oom van vaders zijde.

pao tsik, | 叔, jongere oom van vaders zijde.

胞 *toā p'ao lâng,* 大 | 囊, elefantiasis, opzwelling.

P'ao *pêh p'ao p'ao,* 白 | 匕, blank en opgezwollen.

雹 *p'ìi p'ao,* | 落, groote hagelsteenen.

P'ao

跑 Rennen.

P'aó *p'aó lâng ē mih,* | 人 之 物, iemands goed inpalmen, wegnemen en niet teruggeven.

p'aó kaò bé á tit, | 至 尾 仔 直, zoo hard rennen dat de staart recht uitstaat.

p'aó bé (» *bé*) | 馬, in galop rijden, galopperen.

p'aó ts'aò, | 走, wegloopen, (voorschulden), met iets wegloopen.

p'aó lō, | 路, hard loopen, rennen.

p'aó t'iaò, | 跳, rennen en hossen.

p'aó lâng ē tsī, | 人 之 錢, met iemands geld wegloopen

p'aò tsit t'àng, | 一 遍, een rit doen; overal geweest zijn, (op eene plaats.)

炮 Kanon; vuurwerk, voetzoeker, sisers.

P'aò *pàng p'aò,* 放 |, een kanon afschieten.

p'aò ts'ia, | 車, kanonwagen.

p'aò kè, | 架, affuit.

p'aò tai, p'aò siā, | 臺, | 城, fort, batterij,

toā p'aò, 大 |, kanon.

p'aò siú, | 手, kanonnier.

p'aò kè (» *kè*) | 架, kanonwagen.

hō p'aò, 號 |, seinschot.

sing p'aò, 升 |, saluutschoten (van mandarijnen.)

tsoh p'aò siā, 做 | 城, een lange rist vuurwerk aan een bamboe hangende ontstokend door er brandende voetzoekers tegen aan te gooijen.

p'aò á, | 仔, voetzoekers.

liên p'aò, 連 |, rist voetzoekers.

疱 *iông mui t'ien p'aò,* 楊 梅 天 |, bubos en sjankers.

P'aò

袍 Lang overkleed.

P'aò *p'aò koà,* | 掛, feestgewaad.

bông p'aò, 綢 |, lange kleeren met draken geborduurd

p'aò t'ò, | 套, drakenjas met overkleed.

泡 Opschenken, zetten, (als thee), mengen.

P'aò *p'aò kún tsui,* | 滾 水, kokend water opschenken.

p'aò tê, | 茶, thee opschenken, zetten.

p'aò tsiú, | 酒, wijn opschenken. met wijn aanmengen, (als medecijn.)

p'aò laì tsoè tsit ē, | 做 一 下, door elkander mengen.)

p'aò k'ó, | 考, gezamelijk exerceren, (van infanterie met cavallerie.)

抛 P'aū *p'aū t'aò ts'ú ts'oàn*, | 頭 鼠 竄, zoo hard mogelijk vluchten.)

p'aū iông ⎫
(» iûng) ⎭ | 養, opvoeden, (een gekocht kind.)

ka ki p'aū hū, 自 己 | 負, zich aanmatigen, veel op zich laten voorstaan.

p'aū hūn | 恨 ⎫
p'aū oàn | 怨 ⎭ toon. haat in zich voeden.

P'aoh

'aoh *paoh gê*, | 芽. uitspringende tanden.

laò paoh, 老 |, uit elkander gevallen, bedorven: in duigen.

taī tsì paoh lah, 大 事 | 仔. de zaak is bedorven.

aóh *pi pi paóh paóh*, knetteren (als zout in het vuur.)

脬 'aoh *p'aoh laoh*, | 然. opgeblazen, (als halfjarige kinderen.)

péh péh p aoh p'aoh
(péh péh » ») 白 匕 | 匕, blank en opgeblazen.

p'aoh ling, | 乳. opgezwollen door de moedermelk.

p'aoh sai sai, | 獅 匕, zeer opgezwollen, dik, (van kinderen.)

ké tsi p aoh p'aoh, 果 子 | 匕, opgezwollen van vruchten.

雹 Hagel.

P'aóh *loh p'aóh*, 下 |. het hagelt.

Pat

八 Pat *pat kioh*, | 脚. platluizen.

pat koà, | 掛. de acht diagrammen.

pat dzī kiâ, | 字 行, de voeten schuins wegzetten als het karakter acht.

pat dzī k'ai, | 字 開. open gaan als het karakter acht, (van deuren.)

pat sien kóng, | 箭 簧. koker waarin een barbier zijne acht instrumenten heeft.

pat dzī soe, | 字 梳, over elkander liggende scheiding in het haar.

pat ki ê lâng, | 旗 之 人, menschen van de acht vlaggen *d. i.* Mandschusoldaten.

別 Pát *pát ê*, | 個, een ander.

pát uī, | 處, ergens anders.

pát sò tsaī, | 所 在, do.

pát hāng, | 件, iets anders.

Pe

飛 Vliegen.

Pe *pe koai*, | 高. omhoog vliegen.

tsaó kaò ts'in ts'iū pe
(poe koán » » ») 走 到 似 |, wegloopen als of men vloog.

pe hî, | 魚, vliegende visch.

p'ah pe tsiaó, 打 | 鳥. een vliegende vogel schieten, *d. i.* overal rond gaan om te zien waar wat te verdienen valt.

ts'ah sit iī boē oē pe (» » » *bē* » *poe*) 插 羽 亦 | 不 去, al geeft men hem vleugels, hij zou toch niet kunnen weg vliegen, *d. i.* hij kan niet ontvluchten.

pe soa tsaó tsioh (*hui se tsó sik*) | 沙 走 石, het zand vliegt voort en steenen worden voortgedreven; van een hevige wind.

pe si, | 絲. vliegende spindraden, herfstdraden.

tsuì pe pe, 嘴 | 七, verward spreken.

saí pe t'al, 使 | 撻, knap kunnen springen.

hī k'ang pe pe, 耳 孔 | 匕, gegons in het oor.

pe pīng, | 飯, rijst naar binnen schuiven.

tsi pe tsaó, 錢 | 走. het geld vloog weg, van geld dat men zeker dacht te maken en tocht verloren gaat.

把 **Pé** De hand leggen aan, in de hand nemen, beet pakken, vasthouden; oppassen, bewaken, verdedigen; bundel, numer voor schoen, takkebossen, enz.

pé siú, | 守, bewaken.

pé tsóng, | 總, luitenant.

pé mîng ê lâng, | 門 人, deurwachter.

pé tsi, | 錢, geld eischen onder bedreiging iets uittebrengen.

pé tsi kìng t'aô, | 錢 貫 頭. op het geld passen.

pé koan, | 關, eene voorname plaats bewaken, verdedigen.

pé pien, | 邊, eene grensplaats bewaken.

pé tsoá, | 盞, een glaswijn (aan de bruid) geven, (voor zij haar huis verlaat.)

sa pé hē, 相 | 宿, eene zaak onderling schikken.

pé tiaô tiaô, | 柴 匕, tegenhouden.

ts'à pé, 柴 |, houtbundel.

hé pé, 火 |, fakkel, toorts.

mîng pé (*mui* ») | 門, op de deur passen, (dat niemand er in kome).

巴 **Pé** Mikpunt, doel, schijf.

p'ak pé, kó pé, 考 |, schijfschieten.

ts'ìng pé, 銃 |, schietschijf.

tsì pé, 箭 |, mikpunt voor boogschutters.

撥 **Pé** Afweren, van zich afhouden, uit een duwen.

pé ts'iú, | 手, met de hand afweren.

pé ts'ē, | 尋, doorzoeken.

siang ts'iú pé k'ui, 双 手 | 開, met beide handen uit een duwen, (als kreupelhout.)

裱 **Pè** (**Pcè**) Tegen elkander plakken, opplakken.

pè tsoá, | 紙, met papier beplakken, behangen.

pè pì pang, | 布 挷, vodden op elkander plakken, (voor schoenzoolen, enz.)

pè ts'ak, | 軸, eene teekening opplakken.

pè poh, | 箔, goud of zilver papier opplakken.

sì koè pè, 四 處 |. overal aanplakken, *d. i.* rond bazuinen.

pè pa, 巴 |, verkoeken.

敝 **Pè** (**Pī**) Verkeerd, slecht, gebrek.

tsok pè (» *pī*) 作 |, slecht in iets handelen, enz.

厦荷大辭典

pè pīng, | 病, iets defects, verkeerds aan.

蔽 Pè (Pi) Verbergen, bedekken.

dzia pè, 遮 |, bedekken, niet doen uitkomen.

pao pè, 包 |, doekjes omwinden.

pè k'ì, | 去, zwaar te verteren.

埧 Pè (Poè) Waterdijk.

tsok pè, 做 |, een dijk opwerpen.

背 Pè Rug, rugleuning.

kao i pè, 交 椅 |, leuning van een stoel.

si pè, 生 |, gezwel op den rug.

爬 Pè Pè Krabben, kruipen, klouteren, roeijen, pagaijen.

pè tsiū, 搔 癢, eene jeuking krabben.

li teh pè tsiu nèh, 汝 乃 爬 | 的, het is als of gij eene jeuking krabt, *d. i.* gebruikt de vereischte kracht niet.

pè k'àng, | 控, krabben, uitkrabbelen.

t'ǫ nih pè, 土 處 |, op den grond kruipen, (als kinderen.)

pè ts'iû peh piah, | 墻 | 壁, overal opklouteren.

pè k'i lai, | 起 來, opkruipen.

oē pè boē tsaó èh to k'ì, 能 | 不 能 走 者 盡 去, die kunnen kruipen maar nog niet kunnen loopen gaan er heen, (als naar een feest.)

pè tsiū, | 癢, roeijen, pagaijen.

pè ling tsûn, | 龍 船, drakenbooten roeijen.

pè dzip lai, | 入 來, instrijken, inhalen, inhalig.

耙 Pè Hark, harken, bij elkander halen, baggeren.

ts'â pè, 柴 |, houten hark.

pè ts'â, | 柴, hout bij elkander harken.

pè pùn sò, 掃 糞 垢, vodden, vuilnis rapen.

pè noā t'ó, 扒 泥 土, baggeren.

賠 Pè Vergoeden, schadeloosstellen, teruggeven, bijleggen, bijpassen.

pè pǫ́, | 補, vergoeden, schadeloosstellen.

pè t'at, | 塞, het te kort komende bijpassen.

pe miā, | 命, een moord met den dood bekoopen.

ū kong bò siù p'ah p'oà tioh pè, 有 功 無 賞 打 破 就 |, maakt men zich verdienstelijk dan wordt men niet beloond, breekt men het dan moet men het vergoeden, *d. i.* niets dan schade bij iets kunnen lijden

pè siaó loé, | 禮, zijne schande over iets afkoopen.

tsit è pè tsáp è, 一 个 | 什 个, voor één krijgt men tien terug, (bij dobbelen.)

敝 Pē Pī Beschadigd, defect, gebrek, fout; nederige term voor, mijne.

pē pīng, | 病, fout, gebrek, hapering.

pē sià, | 舍, mijn huis.

pē kok, | 國, mijn rijk.

父 Pē Vader.

laō pē } 老 |, vader.
(» *pē*)

k'oè pē, 契 |, pleegvader.

aō pē, 後 |, stiefvader.

55

pē bú, ｜ 母, ouders.

mē̤ làng pē t'aô bú kut, 罵 人 ｜ 頭 母 骨, iemands ouders uitschelden.

niû pē (*niŷ* ») } 娘 ｜, moeder en vader.

犂 Pē — Egge, eggen.

pē ts'ân (*pō̤* ») ｜ 田, het land eggen.

焙 Pē, Poē — Roosten, roosteren, branden.

pē tê, ｜ 茶, thee roosten.

taī pē, 大 ｜, naam eener ordinaire thee.

pē ts'ân, ｜ 田, een rijstveld doen indroogen.

倍 Pē — Vermeerderen, maal.

tsit pē k'ah toā, 一 ｜ 較 大, nog eens zoo groot.

ting pē, 重 ｜, dubbel zoo (groot enz).

負 Pē — Op den rug dragen.

pē gin á (*poē* » ») ｜ 兒 子, een kind op den rug dragen.

pē bé, 抹 馬, een paard zadelen.

坯 P'e, P'oe — Vorm; klad, ruwe schets, omtrek.

bô á p'e, 帽 仔 ｜, hoedevorm, hoedebol.

p'e bô, ｜ 模, ruwe schets.

p'ah ts'o̤ p'e, 打 粗 ｜, een ruwe schets, klad maken.

k'it tsiáh p'e, 乞 食 ｜, vorm voor: uitorlijk van een bedelaar, (scheld.)

si sin p'e, 死 身 ｜, veel kans hebben nog eens doodgeslagen te worden, (scheld.)

tsoá p'e, 紙 ｜, bordpapier.

ti p'e, 猪 ｜, bigge.

拚 P'e — Geringachten, niet geven om.

p'e sí, ｜ 死, den dood niet vreezen.

p'e tsit sin sí, ｜ 一 身 死, zijn leven voor iemand geringachten.

p'e sí ts'ut lát, 致 死 竭 力, zich uiterst inspannen

p'e miā tsaó, ｜ 命 走, in den wilde vluchten.

料 P'e — Denken dat . . . , het er voorhouden, veronderstellen dat.

p'aì p'e, pūn p'e (» *poe* » ») 派 ｜, 板 ｜, het er voorhouden, veronderstellen.

p'e kiò, ｜ 送, denken, veronderstellen dat . . . .

bô p'e, 無 ｜, het er niet voorhouden dat . . . . .

帕 P'è — Doek, sluijer, hoofdsluijer; bundel, zak; in een doek of bundel doen, vangen, overvallen.

hoe p'è, 花 ｜, gebloemde doek, (over kinderen gedaan.)

ts'iú p'è, 手 ｜, groote gebloemde doek.

ta p'è á, 盖 ｜ 仔, een hoofdsluijer aandoen.

sa̤ á p'è, 衫 仔 ｜, zak of bundel van zijn kleed gemaakt.

dziō p'è, 尿 ｜, waterblaas.

p'è hoe, ｜ 花, bloemen in den schoot doen.

tuì ē bīn p'è k'í lai, 從 下 ｜ 起 來, van onderen op binden, (als zeere borsten.

p'è i aō taó, ｜ 伊 後 斗, van een anderen kant overvallen, (als dieven), achter zijn rug een voordeel ontnemen.

p'è kut t'aô, ｜ 骨 頭, Ik zal Uwe beenderen in een doek doen.

配 Vereenigen, bij iets gebruiken, bijspijzen.

P'è *mi̤h p'è*, 食 |, bijspijzen.

P'oè *mi̤h p'è hó̤*, 物 | 虎, iemand die veel van de bijspijzen eet.

tsiú p'è, 酒 |, gerechten bij den wijn.

tê p'è, 茶 |, gerechten bij de thee.

p'è tê, | 茶, bij de thee gebruiken.

tsit tiaô si̤ miá̤ ká̤ p'è ih
» » » » » p'oè » 一條性命仝伊匹 |, voor iemands leven durven boeten.

[illegible] Scherf, schilfer.

'è *hiā p'è*
» p'oè 瓦 |, panscherven.

p'oà k'n̤g p'è, 破甕 |, potscherf.

tsióh p'è, 石 |, schilfers, brokjes steen.

[illegible] *ts'à p'è*, 柴 |, schilfers, splinters van 'è hout.

[illegible] *ts'ì â p'è*
» » p'e̤̍ 莿棘 |, doornboschje.

è *tsì p'è á*, 刺 | 仔, doornstruiken.

[illegible] Huid, vel, schil, bast, korst; leder, le-
ê deren; omhulsel, uitwendig; opper-
oê vlakkig.

gû p'ê, 牛 |, koehuiden.

p'ê ts'aó, | 草, huiden, bont.

iù p'ê, 幼 |, fijn van vel, kleinzeerig

poh p'ê, 薄 |, kleinzeerig.

bân p'ê, 頑 |, hardgevoelig, koppig.

kaō p'ê, 厚 |, onbeschaamd.

bô bīn p'ê, 無面 |, beschaamd staan.

hó p'ê bah, 美 | 肉, goed van genezen.

p'ê hu, | 膚, afschilfers van een huid.

ts'â p'ê, 柴 |, bast van hout.

tsit tsiah gû pak siang ni̤ṅ p'ê, 一隻牛剝双領 |, van éene koe twee huiden afvillen, *d. i.* alleen voor twee te betalen hebben.

tiem p'ê oe, 砧 | 鞋, schoenlappen.

p'ê tiēm, | 褥, leeren kussen.

p'ê siu̍, 廂 |, leeren koffers.

ts'o̤ p'ê, 粗 |, ruwe huid.

ts'o̤ p'ê ngī k'ak, 粗 | 勁売, ruw van manieren.

pak p'ê pak kut, 剝 | 剝骨, zich van alles ontblooten, (om dobbelgeld te hebben.)

goā p'ê, 外 |, het omhulsel uitwendige, uiterlijke, (beleefdheid enz.)

tsit tîng p'ê pi̤ tsit tîng kut, 一重 | 遮一重骨, vel over been.

p'ê īm toà kut, | 不帶骨, zijn vel zit niet aan zijne beenderen, *d. i.* niet gaarne inspannen.

p'ê p'ê á kóng, | 匕而說, oppervlakkig, vluchtig over iets spreken.

p'ai̤ p'ê bah, 歹 | 肉, slecht van genezen.

p'ê p'ê, | 膜, oppervlakkig.

toā p'i̤ṅ p'ê, 大 | 片, onverschrokken.

p'ê tiaô, | 條, lederen band, riem band enz.

被 Gewatteerde deken.

P'ē *p'ē to̤a*, | 單, deken (ongewatteerde.)

P'oē *mi̤ p'ē*, 綿 |, gewatteerde deken.

siù p'ē, 綉 |, geborduurde deken.

li ko̤ p'ē, 尼姑 |, bedelaars deken.

ts'iu p'ē, 秋 |, herfst, dunne deken.

kah p'ē, 遮 |, zich met een deken toedekken.

hàp p'ē, 壓 ｜, dubbelde deken.

p'òng p'ē, 發 ｜, holstaande, zachte gewatteerde deken.

襬 P'ē *p'ē iāng* (*kiāng po*) ｜ 褓, buidel waarin men een kind op den rug draagt.

Peh

爬 Peh Peh Opklouteren, opklimmen, beklimmen.

peh tsiā siā, ｜ 上 城, eene vesting beklimmen.

peh laô t'ui, ｜ 樓 梯, de trap op gaan.

peh koai peh kē, ｜ 高 ｜ 下, overal bijklimmen.

peh ui, 桅, in de mast klimmen

bóng peh bóng kè, 且 ｜ 且 過, het toch maar met iets zien te doen.

ts'iah peh peh, 赤 ｜ 匕, boosaardig (van vrouwen).

立 Peh *peh k'i sin*, ｜ 起 身, opstaan, oprijzen.

peh k'i lai, ｜ 起 來, zich oprichten, (als in bed.)

百 Peh *peh sì*, ｜ 姓, het volk.

擘 Peh Openbreken, doen splijten, openrijten.

peh k'ui, ｜ 開, openbreken.

tuì peh, 對 ｜, in tweeën splijten, met een tweede deelen.

peh tsoè nṅg ping, ｜ 做 二 平, in tweeën breken.

peh p'oà bīn, ｜ 破 面, zijn gelaat stukrijten, alle schaamte verloren hebben.

peh īm k'ui bīn, 變 不 出 臉, beschaamd zijn, (over zijn vervallen toestand.)

peh p'oà sim koa, ｜ 破 心 肝, zijn binnenste stukrijten, met inspanning denken.

伯 Peh Vaders oudere broeder, oom.

peh kong, ｜ 公, oud oom.

tsing tòng peh, 從 堂 ｜, oud ooms kind, twee, drie graden verwijderd.

peh tsik hiā tī, ｜ 叔 兄 弟, ooms en broeders.

peh pak, ｜ 腹, inwendig gefolterd.

peh mih, ｜ 物, iets openbreken, als vruchten.

柏 Peh Peh *ts'iû peh*, 松 ｜, pijnboom.

peh pì, ｜ 柄, zich zeer voor iets inspannen.

pì peh, 扁 ｜, strakhalen en trekken. geld afhalen, (als behoeftige betrekking.)

白 Péh Pèh Wit, (rouwkleur); helder, licht, klaar; duidelijk; bekendmaking, advertentie, bloot, enkel zonder iets anders, eenvoudig, zonder voordeel, vruchteloos, voor niet; platte volkstaal, kromtaal, bargoensch, de tekst van een lied, enz.

péh sik, ｜ 色, wit.

péh ts'ài, ｜ 菜, kool.

péh seh seh, ｜ 如 雪, sneeuwwit.

péh bàng bàng, ｜ 范 匕, wit als van eene gelijkelijk vespreide mist.

péh sai iū, ｜ 西 洋, witte shirtings.

péh hiā, ｜ 蟻, witte mier.

péh tō k'ò (» *taō* ») ｜ 荳 蔻, cardamon.

péh bit ts'iū ìm, ｜ 蜜 楊 梅, witte pruim.

péh taō, 豆 ｜, witte boonen.

péh tàng, ｜ 銅, wit koper.

péh tio, ｜ 蜩, sproetig,

PEH

péh léh léh k'i, ｜皆變, geheel en al wit geworden.

t'aô péh, 頭｜, witte hoofddoek, (bij rouw.)

péh tsiaò, ｜照, witte aankondiging, (van des keizers dood).

péh lîng si, ｜鷺鷥, reiger.

p'iò péh, 漂｜, bleeken.

péh p'ê, ｜皮, Malva opium.

péh bīn á, ｜面仔, *Fuchow* hoer.

nīng péh, 蛋｜, eiwit.

bák tsiú píng péh, 目反白｜, het wit der oogen verdraait zich (door toorn of angst.)

péh tsuí pô, ｜水婆, bootvrouw.

bák péh tsít t'ǵ, 目｜舌吐, de oogen worden wit en de tong steekt uit, *d. i.* benaauwd zijn.

k'àng péh, 空｜, eene plaats (voor een karakter) open laten.

péh ts'át, 說謊, leugen, leugenachtig.

kong péh ts'át, 說謊話, liegen.

ts'uì péh, 口｜, lekkerbekkig.

péh hî, ｜魚, lintmakreel.

p'ah péh, 猷｜, duidelijk, klaar.

hièn péh, 現｜, aan het licht brengen.

tang hng t'iah péh, 東方發｜, het wordt licht in het oosten, het wordt dag.

t'aò péh dzit, *tng t'aô* (of *tg*) *péh dzit*, 當｜日, 長當｜日, op helderlichten dag.

péh sin, *péh p'e*, ｜身｜坯, eenvoudig, nog onopgemaakt, (als meubelen.)

péh sin ê lâng, ｜身之人, iemand van het volk.

P'EH

k'ang ts'iú péh t'eh, 空手｜取, zonder iets mee te brengen.

ts'ut dzī péh, 出字｜, eene advertentie aanplakken.

kò péh, 告｜, advertentie, publicatie.

péh p'h tióh boâ, ｜匕觔勞, vruchteloos werken.

péh péh tsiáh, ｜｜食, zonder voordeel eten.

péh péh sàng lâng, ｜｜送人, om niet geven.

péh oē, ｜話, volkstaal.

siá péh dzī, 寫｜字, in volkskarakters opschrijven.

seh péh, 說｜, sprekende niet zingende zeggen, (in eene komedie.)

k'ik p'éh, 曲｜, de tekst, woorden van een lied.

ts'át péh, 賊仔｜, dieventaal.

hoàn á péh, 販仔｜, bargoensch van rondventers.

péh dzī, ｜字, karakter opschrijven.

péh péh, ｜匕, voor niets, kosteloos.

péh mîng, ｜毛, grijsharig.

ts'am péh, 斑｜, met witte haren gemengd; van hoofd en baard.

沫 Schuim, (van water, wijn enz.)

P'éh *tsui p'éh*, 水｜, schuim.

P'oéh *hai p'éh*, 海｜, zeeschuim.

p'ah p'éh, 打｜, schuimen; tot schuimer toe klotsen.

kiet p'éh, 結｜, do.

k'i p'éh, 起｜, do.

péh p'éh noā (*pę̄h* » ») } 白｜涎, schuimend speeksel.

ké p'éh, kik p'éh, 假 ｜, 激 ｜, den schijn van groot aannemen, trotsch zijn.

sì koè p'éh (» *kè p'oèh*) 四處 ｜, overal den grooten heer gaan uithangen.

aì p'éh, 好 ｜, veel van opschik houden.

k'i̱ tsui p'éh, 攀水 ｜, zich aan schuim vasthouden, *d. i.* nog niet stevig in eene zaak gevestigd zijn.

iû p'éh p'éh, 油 ｜ 匕, vet zoodat schuim er op drijft.

P'éh *t'ô̱ p'éh*, natte klonters aarde.

ping tsàn t'ô̱ p'éh ê lâng, omwerkers van aard: kluiten, *d. i.* landwerkers.

Peng

楓 Pɛng Pui̱ *pɛng ts'iu*, ｜ 樹, palmboom, ahornboom, sycamoor.

幫 Pɛng Er bij leggen, (als geld) versterken (als een zwak stuk hout.)

pɛng hō̱ i k'oah, ｜ 伊闊, een ander stuk aanbrengen om het breeder te maken.

pang (of *pɛng*) *t'iep*, ｜ 貼, in de onkosten tegemoet komen.

sa̱ pɛng (*sio* ») 相 ｜, op elkander steunen.

方 Pɛng Pui̱ Familienaam.

榜 Pɛ́ng *ts'ut pɛ́ng*, 出 ｜, eene aankondiging, uitvaardigen, (bij examinatien, offerande, enz.)

pɛ́ng bûn, ｜ 文, keizerlijke proclamatie.

ing pɛ́ng (*ui̱*) *pɛ́ng* 黃 ｜, do.

P'ɛ̀ng *p'ɛ̀ng p'ɛ̀ng kiò*, ｜ 匕 叫, sissen als een slang, boosaardig (van menschen.)

飯 Pɛ̄ng Gekookte rijst, voedsel.

tsiáh pɛ̄ng, 食 ｜, eten.

pɛ̄ng tɛ̂ng (» *tui̱*) ｜ 時, maal, eetmaal.

pɛ̄ng sî, ｜ 匙, rijstlepel.

pɛ̄ng tiàm, ｜ 店, restauratie, (gemeene soort van)

pɛ̄ng liép, ｜ 粒, korrel gekookte rijst.

tsiú pɛ̄ng, 酒 ｜, rijst voor het maken van wijn.

tsú pɛ̄ng, 煮 ｜, eten koken.

pɛ̄ng k'a̱ toā ê, ｜ 斗大个, de rijstpot is groot, *d. i.* het is een groot huisgezin.

pɛ̄ng sîn hông tè toā, ｜ 神皇帝大, de rijstgeest is zoo hoog als de keizer, *d. i.* onder het eten behoeft men voor niets uittescheiden.

pɛ̄ng si ts'ìng, ｜ 飢縱, opstaan als een rijstlepel, naam van een slang met platte kop.

pɛ̄ng siáh, ｜ 席, eettafel.

ts'á lı ê pɛ̄ng siáh, 攪汝 ｜ 席, Ik stoor U in Uw eten, (bel. term.)

pɛ̄ng oá̱ p'ah p'oà, ｜ 碗打破, zijn rijst kom is gebroken, *d. i.* hij heeft zijne broodwinning verloren.

傍 Pɛ̄ng Steunen op.

sa oá pɛ̄ng, 相倚 ｜, tijdelijk met elkander, (als man en vrouw) leven.

pɛ̄ng se (» *sì*) ｜ 勢, op zijn macht steunen.

pɛ̄ng lâng k'iā k'ì, ｜ 人竪乞, iemand in de onkosten van woning tegemoet komen.

pɛ̄ng sio k'uì, ｜ 熱氣, steunen op dichter zetten bij de warmte (als een bed bij de haard.)

pɛ̄ng tsoè kuì, ｜ 節季, tegen het inkomen van een nieuw jaargetij.

hópɛ̄ng p'ai̱, 好 ｜ 歹, goed en kwaad door elkander, (als winst en verlies.)

Pi

卑 Pi *k'iem pi*, 謙 |, nederig.

pi u kó tsiēn, laag, onbeschaamd in handelingen, (als vlieger enz.)

pi tsiēn, | 賤, van lagen stand.

tsun pi, 尊 |, aanzienlijk en onaanzienlijk.

悲 Pi *siong pi* (*siang* ») 傷 |, zeer bedroefd, door droefheid gekweld.

tsû pi, 慈 |, medelijden.

箄 Pi *pi á*, | 子, fluitjė.

tâng pi á, 銅 | 仔, mondorgel (Eurp.)

pùn pi á, 吹 | 仔, op een fluitje blazen.

碑 Pi *tsióh pi pai*, 石 | 碑, steenen opstaande plaat.

ts'ìn pi pi, 冷 | 匕, koud, kil.

畀 Pi *gû pi*, 牛 |, koeluis, gierig.

比 Pi Vergelijken, in vergelijking van.., gelijkstellen; de partijen; afmeten, mikken, eene positie nemen, aanleggen; slaan, de bastonade geven.

pí pīng (of *pīng*), | 例, vergelijken.

pí kaò, | 較, onderling vergelijken.

i pí goá k'ah toā, 伊 | 我 較 大, hij is grooter dan ik.

pí pān, | 辦, de maat nemen.

pí iū, | 樣, vergelijken bij iets.

pí dzū, | 喩, vergelijking, bijvoorbeeld.

boē pí tit, 未 可 |, niet te vergelijken met.

tsiong sim pí sim, 將 心 | 心, een anders hart bij het zijne vergelijken.

k'óng pí, 孔 |, bewijs.

put pí ts'în ts'iū, 不 | 相 似, niet te vergelijken bij, niet even als

dzī pí kam goān, 二 | 甘 愿, beide partijen stemmen er in toe.

pí ts'ùi tsoéh bah (» » *ts'iet* ») | 嘴 切 肉, het vleesch naar iemands mond afsnijden, *d. i.* maar juist genoeg koopen.

pí k'ì ts'ien ts'ien, zuiver aanleggen.

pí pō, | 步, aanleggen, mikken; zich in positie stellen.

pí bú, | 武, schermen.

pí sè, | 勢, zich in positie stellen.

pí ts'e, | 差, een bode tuchtigen.

pí tiu, 追 |, slaan, de bastonade geven, (om tot bekentenis te brengen.)

抵 Pí *pí tsiú*, | 掌, gesticuleeren.

pí k'a tūng ts'iú, 起 脚 動 手, gebaren maken als wilde men vechten.

痺 Pì Doof, verstijfd, slapend.

k'a pì, 脚 |, do.

bà pì, 痳 |, slapen, (van het been.)

pì lak, | 力, zijne kracht inhouden.

閉 Pì *pì kiet*, | 結, hardlijvigheid, zeer harde ontlasting.

庇 Pì *pì iū*, | 佑, beschermen.

pó pì, 保 |, do.

秘 Pì *pì koat*, | 訣, geheim, (eener uitvinding.)

pì hng, | 方, geheim, weinig bekend recept.

pì pún, | 本, geheim manuscript, (van medicijnen, enz.)

脾 De maag.
Pi *pi uī*, | 胃, maag, spijsvertering.
k'ui pi, 開 |, de eetlust opwekken.
hah pi, 合 |, naar iemands smaak zijn.
p'ai p'i k'ì (*bai pi ki*) } 歹 | 氣, van slecht humeur aard.
dzip pi, 入 |, eetlust geven.
sióh pi, 小 |, middelmatig, ordinair, niet zoo buitengewoon.

排 *tsit pi ging tsio* (« » *ge* ») } 一 | 芽 蕉, een strook (± 10) pisang.
Pi *tsit pi hi nīng* (s » » *tsi*) } 一 | 魚 卵, een strook vischeijeren.
tsoè pi tsi, 做 | 子, eene zekere waarde aan elk geven, (als aan fiches bij het kaartspelen.)
tsit pi è taī tsì, 一 | 大 事, deze: de onderhoorige zaak.

琵 *pi pé*, | 琶, guitaar.
Pi

枇 *pi pé*, | 杷, mispel.
Pi *pi pé kè tsi t'âm*, | 杷 菓 子 頭, de mispel is het proefje (de eerste) der vruchten.

備 *tsê* (of *tsoè*) *pī*, 齊 |, in zijn geheel volkomen.
Pī *pī pān*, | 辦, in orde brengen.
ū pī, 預 |, gereedgemaakt.
pī pān piēn, | 辦 便, gereedgemaakt.
tsún pī, 准 |, in gereedheid brengen, vooriets zich op zijne hoede stellen.
bú pī, 武 |, militaire toebereidselen

避 Ontwijken.
Pī *tò pī*, 逃 |, ontwijken, ontvluchten.
siém pī, 躲 |, ontwijken.
pī sú (» *si*) } | 暑, de warmte ontvluchten.
pī lān, | 難, rampen ontvluchten.

婢 *lú pī*, 女 |, slavin, vrouwelijke bediende.
Pī

鞭 Zweep, karwats; zweepslag.
Pi *bé pi*, 馬 |, karwats, zweep.
ts'ui pi, 催 |, met de zweep aanzetten.
t'ih pi, 鐵 |, ijzeren knuppel.
p'ah lâng nîng pah è pi, 撻 人 兩 百 |, iemand twee honderd zweepslagen geven.

扳 Trekken, strak aanhalen, spannen, strak spannen, overspannen, overtrekken.
Pi *pi peh*, | 扒, gelijktrekken, (als een tafelkleed.)
Pe *pi p'é*, | 皮, het vel uitspannen.
pi pi puih puih, | 匕 拔 匕, met geweld trekken.
pi puih k'ì, | 拔 去, over velen verdeeld worden.
pi bīn p'é, | 面 皮, een huid over het gelaat trekken, *d. i.* met iets van een ander pronken.
pi t'é biēn, 體 面, voor zijn fatsoen doen.
kâp lâng oē pi tit, 與 人 能 | 的, voor anderen niet onderdoen.
pi ts'iú bé, | 手 尾, de kracht der armen tegen elkander meten.
pi tsoá, | 紙, met papier strak bespannen.
pi kó, | 鼓, een trommel met leer overspannen.

pi pi pi, 丨丨丨, strak spannend, (van kleêren.)

邊 Zij, zijde, kant, rand.

Pi *pi á*, 丨仔, kant, aan den kant, ter zijde.

siém pi, 躲 丨, op zij gaan.

tsaó pi á k'ì, 走丨仔去, do.

k'iā pi á k'ì, 豎丨仔去, op zij gaan staan.

sin pi, 身 丨, aan zijn zijde, bij zich.

t'i pi hai kak, 天丨海角, zeer ver.

oai pi, 歪 丨, scheef, zijdelings overhellend.

p'ah ts ùi pi, 打 嘴 丨, op de wangen staan.

ts'ù pi t'aô bé, 厝丨頭尾, de buren.

siù pi, 綉 丨, geborduurde rand.

oá pi, 倚 丨, langs den kant.

pông pi k'oǹ è lâng, 旁丨看的人, bijstanders, toeschouwers.

sì pi, 四 丨, alle kanten.

pi ki, 丨墘, de rand.

ni pi, 年 丨, einde des jaars; rand. zelfkant van flenel.

lō pi hoe, 路丨花, bloem aan den wegkant, *d. i.* publieke vrouw.

Pi *liem pi si*, 一丨時, onmiddelijk, eensklaps.

goá liem pi lai, 我一丨來, Ik zal onmiddelijk komen.

扁 Platdrukken, plat.

Pi *pi pi*, 丨乜, plat gedrukt, plat.

teh pi, 壓 丨, platdrukken.

tē á pi pi, 袋仔丨乜, plattezak, *d. i.* geen geld hebben.

pi ts'ùi 丨嘴 / *ts'ùi pi pi* 嘴丨乜 } zijn mond digt houden en niet meer open doen, met de mond vol tanden staan.

pi bīn, 丨面, plat oppervlak.

so i lī pi, 挼員握丨, ronddraaijen en platdrukken, eene twist behendig kunnen bijleggen, geven en nemen.

變 Veranderen, vervormen, in iets anders

Pì overgaan, worden tot....; ontfutselen. afzetten.

koé pì, 改 丨, veranderen, verbeteren.

pì iū, 丨様, veranderen.

pì huih, 丨血, in bloed overgaan.

pì hing hai, 丨形骸, van vorm veranderen.

ts'it pì poeh pì, ts'it tsáp dzī pì, 七丨八丨, 七十二丨, gedurig veranderen.

pì p'ai, 丨惡, slecht worden.

pì bīn, 丨面, van gelaatskleur veranderen, booszien.

pì m̄ ts'ut bīn, 丨不出臉, beschaamd zijn.

pì kaô lāng, 丨猴弄, goochelen.

pì ku pì koai, 丨龜丨怪, van het een op het andere veranderen.

ping pì (*pán* ») } 板 丨, naar de omstandigheden veranderen.

tíng pì, 轉 丨, over de kinderjaren komen.

pì siòng, 丨相, van gesteldheid veranderen.

pì pō, 丨步, de manier op iets veranderen.

k'it i pi bàng k'ì, 被伊丨蚊去, *lett.* door iemand in muskiet veranderd, *d. i.* ontsteld zijn.

pi lâng ê tsî, 丨人之錢. iemand geld afzetten.

pi tsiáh pi ts'īng, 丨食丨穿, op de een of andere manier aan eten en kleeding zien te komen.

pi kuí pi koài, 丨鬼丨怪, zich in alle wonderlijke dingen verkleeden.

柄 Pi Pè Datgene waarbij men iets aanvat, handvatsel, hecht, steel; onderwerp van een gesprek.

to pi, 刀丨. hecht van een mes.

loē pi, 耒丨, ploegstaart.

oē pi, 話丨, onderwerp van een gesprek.

tsoè ts'iò pi, 做笑丨, tot onderwerp van lachen maken.

hō lâng tsoè ts'iò pi, 與人做話丨, zich belachelijk maken.

p'ah tsih kó pi, 打折古丨, een gesprek over vroegeren tijd afbreken. (door zijne komst.)

平 Pi Gelijk, effen, vlak; vreedzaam, gelijkelijk, gelijkmatig, regtvaardig: gewoon; ordinair.

pi pi, 丨匕, gelijk.

pi bīn, 丨面, gelijk oppervlak.

pi tāng, 丨重, evenwicht, balans.

pi ni k'ì, 丨匕去, geheel en al vlak, gelijk maken.

t'i pi toē īm pi, 天丨地不丨, alleen op aarde heeft men onderscheid van standen.

pi kè, 丨價, tegen gelijken prijs.

pi tú kè, 丨抵價, tegen elkander gelijk maken.

pi p'o p'o, 丨波匕, gelijk van oppervlak, gelijk, (zonder uitstekende personen.)

toē pi, 地丨, het waterpas.

pi toē, 丨地, vlakke grond.

pi tiā, 丨定, vrede, vreedzaam, effen.

pi tsiā tsiā, 丨正匕, gelijk, niet uitstekend, ordinair.

pi siō lâng, 丨常人, een ordinair mensch.

pi siō, 丨常, gewoon, ordinair.

pi pun, 丨分, gelijkelijk verdeelen.

pi iû k'òng t'ô, 丨洋壙土, uitgestrekte vlakte, landerijen.

kong pi, 公丨, regtvaardig, billijk, onpartijdig.

pi pi lō poáh sí pūn ti bú, 丨匕路跌死腯猪母, zelfs op een effen weg kan eene lompe zeug dood vallen, *d. i.* gemakkelijke zaken kunnen door dommen bedorven worden.

pi tsiā, 丨正, regtvaardig, billijk, middelmatig

pì tsiâ pi toē, 變成丨地, in eene gelijke vlakte veranderd zijn.

棚 Pi Stellage, stelling, steiger, tooneel, tent, mat.

hì pi, 戲丨, tooneel.

pi tíng ū hoh lâng, pi ē iā ū hoh lâng, 丨上有此人丨下亦有此人, zoo als men het op het tooneel vertoont gebeurt het ook in het dagelijksch leven.

ts'ien ts'iu pi, 千鞦丨, stellage van een schommel.

k'ó pi, 考丨, examinatieplaats.

taō pi, 豆丨, boonenstaken.

tsng pi, 粧丨, steenen vlak op een dak.

pán pī, 板 |, dekvlak met een koepeltje.

pò pī, 布 |, tent.

néng pī, 軟 |, hangmat.

病 Ziekte.
Pī
Pē

pī goân, | 源, oorzaak eener ziekte.

ū pī, 有 |, ziek.

pī t'iâ, | 痛, ziekte, ongesteldheid.

pī kun (» *kin*) | 根, oorsprong eener ziekte.

pī hó, | 好, van eene ziekte herstellen.

pò pī, 報 |, verlof vragen wegens ziekte.

dziét pī, 熱 |, doorgaande koorts.

koâ dziét pī, 寒 熱 |, tusschenpoozende koorts.

p'oà pī, 破 |, foutief, defect; ziek. ziekelijk.

ū pī pún, 有 | 本, eene ziekte kunnen doorstaan, tegen een knak kennen.

t'oa pī, 拖 |, zich tegen eene ziekte verzetten, niettegenstaande zijne ziekte nog werken.

pī tsìng / *pē tsìn* | 症, ziekte, aard eener ziekte.

pī tsai ts'ing, | 在 床, van ziekte in bed liggen.

pī kiá, | 子, ziekte door zwangerschap.

sún pī, 損 |, toring.

tsáp tsìng pī, 什 症 |, allerlei soort van ziekte.

tì pī, 致 |, ziekte berokkenen.

kò pī lâng, 顧 | 人, een zieke verzorgen.

sū haū pī lâng, 伺 候 | 人, do.

hām ts'âm pī, 艸 參 |, venerische ziekte.

àm sàm pī, 陷 塹 |, do.

lap sap pī, 遝 汚 |, do.

tioh pī, 着 |, ziek worden.

pī géh, | 月, ziekte door zwangerschap.

pī tsè, | 債, *lett.* ziekteschuld, straf des hemels om ziek zijn.

pī tsoâ kè ts'ân hoā, | 蛇 過 田 岸, langzaam gaan, met horten en stooten bij elkander krijgen, (als een opstel.)

編 Vlechten.
Pī

pī sa kó, | 三 服, in drieën vlechten.

pī á soà, | 仔 線, gevlochten koord.

p'ah pī á, 打 | 仔, vlechten.

pī t'aô tsang, | 頭 鬃, de hoofdstaart vlechten.

pī bih k'o, | 篾 環, een rotting hoepel vlechten.

k'iau pī lâng, 騙 | 人, iemands goed niet teruggeven, voorgevende *b. v.* dat het gestolen is.

披 Planten, gras uit elkander leggen.
P'i

p'i ts'aò, | 草, do.

p'i k'ui, | 開, openvouwen, openspreiden.

p'i sa, | 衫, kleederen uithangen.

poh poh á p'i, 薄 匕 仔 |, dunnetjes over iets heen strijken.

p'i p'ák, | 曝, uithangen om te droogen.

p'i sit, | 翼, de vleugel uitspannen.

P'i *p'i tsui p'i* (» » *p'e*) | 水 |, keilen.

p'i kọ ioh, | 膏 藥, zalf uitstrijken.

hò p'i t'ièn, (of *p'ien*) 好 | 展, uitgestrekt, ruim, (van eene plaats.)

p'i kien, | 肩, uitstekende gedeelte aan de schouders van een mandarijn kleed, (bijwijze van onze epauletten.)

p'i p'i pòk pòk, | 匕 拍 匕, flodderen in het water als kinderen of eenden.

丕 P'i *tik p'i*, 竹 |, platte bamboezen plank.

篇 P'i Numer. voor stukken beschreven papier. enz.

tsit p'i bùn tsiu (» » » *tsiọ*) 一 | 文 章, een literarisch opstel.

攤 P'i *p'i hing*, | 還, bij termijnen betalen.

p'i kiem, | 欠, bij kleine termijnen afbetalen.

p'i t'og, , in kleine hoeveelheden verdeelen.

侵 P'i Bedriegen, oneerlijk deelen.

sa p'i, 相 |, elkander bedriegen, niet gelijk staan, niet evenredig zijn.

u p'i, 有 |, er voordeel bij hebben goedkoop uitkomen.

u p'i t'aò, 有 | 頭, voordeel bij iets hebben door in groote hoeveelheid te koopen.

k'ah ū p'i t'aò, 較 有 | 頭, bij iets winnen, voordeel hebben van het geen een ander meer dan gij gedaan heeft.

u pi k'àm, 有 | 弊, van eene gezamenlijk te verdeelen winst eerst voor zich zelven afhouden.

痞 P'i *kien p'i*, 堅 |, een roofje zetten.

kiet p'i, 結 |, do.

tàng p'i, 銅 |, percussiedopje.

liù p'i (*liò* ») 落 |, afvallen van een roofje.

tsu p'i, 痘 |, vaccinatiestof.

tsit p'i á bah k'ih k'ih, 一 | 仔 肉 薄 匕, een dun stukje vleesch.

tsit p i á toā, 一 | 仔 大, klein.

tiá p'i, 鼎 |, afschrapsel, (aanbrandsel) van de pan, korstjes uit de pan.

譬 P'í *p'i dzū*, | 諭, vergelijking.

餅 P'i *ts'aó p'i* (» *p'iá*) 草 |, graszode

鄙 P'i Verachten.

p'i pòk, | 薄, do. minachten.

p'i lō, | 陋, leelijk.

p'i li, | 薄, inhalig, gierig, (om een duit twisten.)

p'i tsiēn, | 賤, verachten, verachtelijk, laag.

厚 P'i *p'i bīn*, | 顏, front d'airain, onbeschaamd.

p'i p'i p'i, | | |, do.

p'i liēn, | 臉, do.

p'i sai bīn, | 屎 面, onbeschaamd. zonder schaamte gevoel.

ti p'i (*tè* ») 假 |, doen als of men iets niet wist, een front d'airain aannemen.

脾 P'i *p'ai p'i k'i*, 歹 | 氣 slecht onaangenaam karakter.

片 P'i Numer. voor muren, wolken en uitgestrekte dunne dingen, planken, pannen.

tsit p'i sò, 一 | 鎖, een slot.

tsit p'i p'àng tsiū kaò, 一 | 帆 就 到, in korten tijd met goede wind er komen.

sì p'i pán á, 四｜板仔, (woning van) vier planken, *d. i.* doodkist.

tsit p'i ê oē, 一｜之話, een geheel gesprek.

tsit p'i ê tsân hing, 一　之田園, eene rij, strook velden.

tsit p'i po lê, 一｜玻璃, een plaat glas.

kóng kah tsit p'i p'áng tit, 說起一｜帆話, in eens achtereen afspreken.

○ P'i *p'i k'ih ih*, ｜去伊 / *p'i sì ih*, ｜死伊 / *p'i sih ih*, — zoo maar ongestraft laten, er iemand gemakkelijk laten afkomen.

bô p'i pát lâng, 無｜他人, gij laat geen ander (vreemde) ongestraft tegen iemand gezegd die zijn bloedverwant iets betaald wil zetten.

柄 P'i *kiáh ts'iú p'i*, 執手｜, met gebalde vuist voor elkander staan.

dzip mîng p'i p'i p'i, 入門｜｜｜, in huis komende kwaadaardig blijven staan.

平 P'i *t'ó p'i* 討｜, betaald zetten.

p'ah p'i tú ke (» » » *koè*) 打｜抵過, met het te hooge het te lage dempen, tegen elkander gelijk maken, vereffenen.

p'i tú kè (» » *koè*) ｜抵過, do.

p'i pi, ｜匕, gelijk maken (van den grond.)

kiaó su siū p'i, 賭輸思　, verliest men bij het dobbelen dan wil men (zijn verlies) weer gelijk spelen.

p'i pún, ｜本, zijn kapitaal weer gelijk maken, (als eene winst na een verlies.)

彭 P'i Familienaam.

p'i tsó, ｜祖, man uit de oudheid die 800 jaar oud werd; Chin. Methusalem.

攤 P'i *p'i hing*, ｜還, gedeeltelijk teruggeven.

p'i tsit poà, ｜一半, de helft teruggeven.

澎 P'i *p'i ô*, ｜湖, de Piscadores.

鼻 P'i Neus, reuk; ruiken.

p'i k'ang, ｜孔, neusgaten.

p'i tsui, ｜水, snot.

ts'ìng p'i, 哼｜, de neus snuiten.

p'ah p'i, 結｜, een sterke lus op iets naaijen.

si p'i ling (*se* » *liông*) 生｜龍, een neuspoliep hebben.

si p'i t'at, 生｜塞, do.

p'i sai, ｜屎, neusvuil.

laô p'i, 流｜, een snotneus hebben.

sngh p'i (*soh* ») 吸｜, de neus ophalen.

ts'ngh p'i (*ts'ih* ») 縱｜, de neus uitsnuiten.

sat p'i, 塞｜, verstopte neus.

tsát p'i, 嗐｜, do.

tsiù pi, 臭｜, weggevreten neus.

ing ko p'i, 鸚哥｜, papegaaijen neus.

laô p'i huih, *p'i laô huih*, 流｜血, uit de neus bloeden.

p'i k'ang hong, 孔風, adem uit de neus komende.

p'i hun, ｜烟, snuif.

lik p'i (*niau* ») 吮｜, de neus optrekker.

pûn p'i, 吹｜, door de neus blazen.

p'i lak (of *lok*) *kóng*, ｜孔廣, de neuskoker.

海上絲綢之路文獻集成　科技與文化编

PIA

kóng tioh p'ī lok kóng, 打｜着凹孔, zich de neus stooten, *d. i.* zich zelven schade berokken.

koà t'ih p'ī, 掛鉄｜, rond uit durven spreken, voor zijne meening uitkomen.

p'ī laò ēm tsai ts'ing, 流不知縱, zijne druipende neus niet weten te snuiten *d. i.* onverschillig zijn.

ēm hó p'ī kā i kā k'ì lai, 不好｜幷咬起來, jammer dat ik zijn neus niet kon afbijten, (gezegd van iemand dien men zeer haat).

嗅 P'ī *p'ī kì*. ｜見, ruiken.

p'ī bī. ｜味, ruiken.

hó p'ī sai, 善｜, fijn, scherp van reuk.

P'ī *tsai tse p'ī p'āng*. ｜知其情, een luchtje van iets hebben.

gaò p'ī tsē (*» » tsoā*) 善｜陣, fijn van lucht als honden.

p'ī ts'aò. ｜臭, stinkend van lucht.

p'ī p'ang. ｜香, welriekend van lucht.

p'ī p'āng. 縫, het luchtje van iets hebben.

kaò p'ī tsē (*» » tsoā*) 狗｜陣, de hond snuffelt rond.

砒 P'ī *p'ī sang*. ｜相, rot e..kruit.

Pia

兵 Pia *pia pō*, ｜部, departement van oorlog.

pia pāng, (of *k'e*) ｜房科, militair departement, (in mandarijn bureau's.)

丟 Pia *pia k'ì*. ｜去, gooijen, weggooijen.

pia ou siak tih. ｜碟擇碗, de kopjes en schoteltjes stukgooijen.

PIA

lām sám pia, 亂｜, overal rondgooij..

pia hiet kák k'ì, ｜棄去, weggooij..

īng oē pia ih, 用話｜伊, iema.. een gezegde naar het hoofd gooije..

餅 Piá Koek.

taò piá, 豆｜, boonen koekjes, .. koeker.

gû lin piá, 牛乳｜, kaas.

piá lō, ｜爐, oven.

piá iù, ｜末, koekkruimels.

piá sut. ｜幼, do.

bah piá, ｜肉, vleeschkoek.

ná bah piá, 似肉｜, leelijk (v.. vrouwen,)

poh piá, 薄｜, dunne koekjes, (op h.. eind des jaars gegeten,) soort pann.. koek (waar vleesch ingerold wordt.)

lé piá, 禮｜, geschenk koekjes, (b.. huwelijk gegeven.)

tiong ts'iu piá, 中秋｜, middel.. herfstkoeken, (eene spijs van suike.. en varkensvleesch.)

餅 Piá Lang, (een) (kalk, mes enz.), schijfje.

ts'aò p'iá, 草｜, tras, graszode.

ts'aò p'iá he, 草｜灰, tras.

傾 Pià *pià dzip*, ｜入, omkeerende gooijen in (als een vuurpot van het eene schip in het andere.)

pià tsui. ｜水, water uitgooijen.

pià si si. 决生死, op leven of dood vechten.

pià su iā, 决勝敗, de overwinning of nederlaag.

ts'iù tiong sim pià hé, 手掌中｜火, het geld niet koud laten worden in zijne handen.

ts'át piā ts'át, 賊 | 賊, roovers die tegen elkander vechten.

hō teh piā, 雨 | 直, de regen gutst neer.

piā k'ang k'ang, | 空 匕, leegmaken.

piā niā ts'ut k'ì, | 清 出 去, uitdragen, à tout prix verkocht.

siòk siòh piā, 賤 匕 |, à tout prix verkoopen.

piā hè toé (of *be*) / (» *hoè té hoé*) | 貨 底, uitverkoopen.

piā pún, | 本, à tout prix verkoopen om zijn kapitaal terug te krijgen.

ká piā, 敢 |, het er uit duwen, gooijen, zich niet schamen iets onbetamelijks te zeggen.

tsiang tsoân piā, 漳 泉 |, bloedig vechten tusschen *Tsiang-tsiu* en *Tsoân-tsiu* clans (niet zelden op *Formosa*.)

p'ah piā pō, 打 | 步, uiterste toevlucht middel.

piā saò, | 掃, schoon vegen, den boel opredderen en schoon vegen.

sin kū kaò piā, 新 舊 交 |, het nieuwe met het oude vermengen.

piā tsoè tsit kok, | 做 一 國, tot één rijk maken, (van verscheidene rijken.)

piā tsoè tsit tui / (» *tsò* ») » | 做 一 團, bij elkander doen.

piā k'a lō, | 脚 路, iets uit den weg nemen.

piā pâng t'aô, | 房 頭, van den eenen familietak in den anderen overgaan, (als geluk, voorspoed.)

piā pùn sò, | 糞 掃, vuilnis uitgooien, weggooien.

piā kè / (*poā koè*) | 過, overschenken, (om koel te maken).

piā hè, | 貨, goederen overladen, als van het eene schip in het andere.

抄 Piā *piā dzī*, | 字, een geschrift afschrijven, naschrijven.

piā k'í lai, | 起 來, een afschrift, teekening enz. van iets nemen.

平 Piā *piā siā*, | 聲, de gelijke toon.

ē piā, tsiū (of *tíng*) *piā*, 下 |, 上 |, de lage en hooge gelijke toon.

piā tseh, | 仄, de gelijke en de niet gelijke toonen.

bô piā tseh, 無 |, zonder regel.

兵 P'iā *t'ien p'iā dzít*, 天 | 日, dag die ongelukkig is door de »hemel soldaten"

k'it p'iā p'ah tiòh, 被 | 打 着, door den duivel getroffen, van een onbesuisd mensch gezegd.

kòng p'iā p'iā, 狂 | 匕, onbesuisd.

p'in p'iā, 眩 |, windhoos, onbesuisd aankomen (als beschonken lieden.)

○ P'ia *p'ia liaò kut*, | 骿 骨, de ribben.

oai p'iā, 歪 |, scheef.

siao p'iā, 消 |, kromtrekken, scheeftrekken, (als een boek door wind.)

Pia *haū p'ia p'ē*, 鮫 | 批, panscherven.

坪 P'iā *hai p'iā*, | 海, strand.

soā p'iā, 山 |, berghelling, (met velden bedekt.)

tó kui p'iā, 棹 櫃 |, bij massa omleggen (als graan), omvallen, vallen, (als getroffen soldaten), failleren.

t'aì p'iā mùng / (» *ping mui*) 太 | 門, deur die als scherm dient.

tsoè lâng p'iā p'iā p'iā, 做 人 | | |, onverschrokken, robust zijn.

p'iŋ pún, | 本. gelijkspelen (in spel of handel.)

koh kap li p'iŋ. 再與伊 |, nog eens met U beproeven mijn verlies terugtewinnen, revenge nemen.

Piah

壁 Piah Muur, scheidsmuur, tusschenmuur.

keh piah, 隔 |. aangrenzend vertrek.

keh piah ê lâng. 隔 | 之人, de buren.

tâng ts'iŋ t'ih piah, 銅墻鐵 |, koperen buiten, en ijzeren binnenmuren, een sterk huis.

hui liem tsaó piah, 飛簷走 |, op de daken vliegen en tegen den muren opklimmen. (van behendige dier.)

ui k'ang iah piah (*oe* » *ó* ») 挖空鑽 |, een gat boren en den muur omwroeten.

k'ui piah lŏ. 開 | 路. de fondamenten voor een muur hakken.

keh piah ū hī. 隔 | 有耳, de tusschenmuren hebben ooren.

kap piah kóng oē, 與 | 說話, als tegen den muur spreken.

oá piah sô. 倚 | 行, langs den muur kruipen.

hún piah, 粉 |, gewitte muur.

he piah, 灰 |, gekalkte muur.

tsióh piah. 石 |, steenen, granieten muur, steile rotskant.

k'ah kiā piah, 較峻 |, steiler dan een muur, zeer steil.

bih piah kui. 藏 | 鬼, spook dat zich tegen den muur verschuilt. van iemand die ongemerkt binnen sluipt.

aō piah, 後 |, van achteren.

piah kɛmh. | 打, meikever; dom suf.

piah kɛmh gû sai ku. | 打牛屎車, als een mesttor die tegen de muur aanvliegt, d, i door zijn dom heid in niets slagen.

piah pi pún sò, | 邊糞掃, a een bezem aan den muur, d. i. e zeer alledaagsch mensch.

僻 P'iah Zijdelings, op zij gaan, ontwijken. schu len, zich verschuilen; verscholen, a gelegen.

p'ien p'iah. 偏 |, verafgelegen, ze den voorkomend, (als een woord).

lŏ p'iah, 路 |, een weinig bezoch begane weg.

p'iah k'i tièm. | 去 匿. ter zij gaan.

oan koe p'iah hāng. 倚街 | 巷 afgelegen buurt.

p'iah hŏ. | 雨, voor den regen schu len.

p'iah hé iŋ (*seh hoé* ») | 火影, zich in de schaduw verschuilen. (van dieven.)

癖 P'iah Gesteldheid, aard, eigenschap, hoof neiging.

p'iah sìng. | 性, aard, hoofdneigin

p'iah pì, | 片, slechte neiging hoofdfout.

p'aip'iah, 歹 |, gebrek hoofdfout.

tsiú p'iah, 酒 |. hoofdneiging dronkenschap.

kut p'iah. 骨 |, eigenschap, hoof neiging, (gew. slecht.)

kaō p'iah ê lâng, 多 | 之人 een lichtgeraakt mensch.

gaó k'ioh p'iah, 善拾 |. stee kleine onbeleefheden onthouden.

koai p'iah, 怪 |, wonderlijk. stee het tegenovergestelde van andere willen.

甓 Briksteen.
P'iáh ts'i p'iáh } 生 |, half gebakken steen.
ts'e̱ » }
sik p'iáh, 熟 |, geheel gebakken steen.
sio p'iáh sai hū. 燒 | 師 阜, steenbakker,

闢 p'iáh lâng, | 人, kruisigen.
P'iáh p'iah p'iah tsoè tsil tui, uitspannen, (als huiden.)

痲 ts'ut p'iáh, 出 |, roodvonk, mazelen.
P'iáh

Piak

爆 Springen als een lampeglas.
Piak piak k'ui. | 開, do.
piak k'o, | 箍, springen van een hoepel.
tiá piak p'oà, 釜 | 破, de pan springt
piak p'oà t'áng, | 破 桶, stukspringen van een kuip; uitlekken van eene zaak.
tai tsì i king piak, 事 已 經 |, die zaak is reeds gesprongen, uitgelekt.
Piak piak kó, | 鼓, kleine schelle trom.

卟 piák piáh kiò, | 匕 叫, knetteren als vuur.
Piák piák piák tàn, | 匕 響, klappen (van een zweep.)

撲 p'iák k'ì, | 去, vast gooijen tegen.
P'iák p'iák tī hì piah nih, | 至 此 壁 今, tegen den muur aan gooijen.

Pih

繳 Omslaan, opslaan.
Pih pih ts'iú ìng, | 手 袖, de mouwen opslaan,
pih k'o̱ k'a, | 褲 脚, zijn broek opstroopen.
pih tsah, | 插, strak om het lijf.

鱉 Schildpad.
Pih pih k'ak, | 殼, schildpadpantser.
tsiú pih, 酒 |, de wijn schildpad, (gezegd in het binnenste van verslaafde wijndrinkers te zijn.)
dziō pih, 尿 |, waterpot.
t'ìng haū kaò pih si nīng } 等 候 至 | 生 卵, uiterst lang wachten.
(» » » » si mui̱ }

別 kok pih, 各 |, van alles kennis hebben.
Pih over alles meêpraten.
kó pih, 古 |, veel kennis van de oudheid hebben.
p'ih p'ak à, | 拔 映, voorovervallen.
P'ih p'ih p'ih, | |, ingedeukt, niet bol.

Pik

煏 Roosteren, bakken.
Pik pik hé } | 火, boven het vuur roosten.
(» hoe) }
pik pa, | 巴, roosten.

伯 pik tsiok } | 爵, graaf.
Pik (» tsiak) }

迫 k'ún pik, 窘 |, vervolgen.
Pik pik tsè, | 債, op betaling van schuld aandringen.
pik t'ó, | 討, om iets manen.
pih siaò. | 数, tot betaling manen.
pī pik, 被 |, gemaand worden.
pik ts'iet. | 切, gejaagd, geagiteerd.
kip pik, 急 |, dringend, haastig.
gui pik, 危 |, gevaarlijk, dringend.

PIK

kiöng pik (*kiàng* ») | 强, met geweld aandringend op.

pik kūn (» *kīn*) 逼近, dicht naderen.

pik pièn, | 變, noodzaken, er toe genoodzaakt worden om opstand te maken door zware belastingen enz.

pik àn, *pik kin*, | 緊, aandringen (op de betaling van schuld.)

pik ni, | 年, naar het einde van het jaar loopend.

sù bīn ts'iòng pik (» » *ts'iàng* ») 四面 |, zonder uitkomst in ellende zijn.

ts'ui pik, 催 |, aandringen (op betaling) aanzetten, haasten.

pik si, | 死, bij iemand zoodanig (op betaling aandringen dat hij zich van het leven berooft).

tui pik, 追 |, vervolgen, achternazetten.

kin pik, 緊 |, haastig, aandringen op.

pik ts'in, 親 |, er op aandringen dat een huwelijk voltrokken worde.

嗶 Pik — *pik ki*, | 吱, bombazijn.

百 Pik — *it dzin t'oân hu pik dzin t'oân sit*, 一人傳虛 | 人傳實, als één het vertelt dan is het niet waar maar als vele het vertellen is het waar.

pik ka sìng (» *ke* ») | 家姓, de verschillende families.

白 Pik — *bing pik*, 明 |, duidelijk, afgedaan.

pō (of *pō*) *pik*, 暴 |, aan den dag komen, uitkomen.

pik taì, | 滯, de witte vloed.

pik dzit ts'ing t'ien, | 日清天, op klaarlichten dag.

pò pik, 報 |, zich verklaren, zijne onschuld aan den dag brengen.

pók pik, do.

ts'ing pik, 淸 |, helder, zuiver (v. harte.)

pik tīng, | 碇, zeer wit beroemd porselein.

pik siú sing ka, | 首伐家, zijn huisgezin van de voet af er boven op brengen, rijkmaken.

闢 P'ik — Overloten, overgooijen.

kap i p'ik, 與他 |, met hem vergelijken, overdoen om te zien wie winner is.

魄 P'ik — *hûn p'ik*, 魂 |, de ziel en de geest.

ts'i ts'ám lók p'ik, 悽慘落 |, door ellende mismoedig.

璧 P'ik — *hó p'ik*, 琥 |, amber.

p'ik sik, 色 |, amberkleur.

拍 P'ik — Castagnetten.

p'ah p'ik, 他 |, castagnetten spelen.

PIT

Pit

筆 Pit — Penseel, pen, stift; schrift, handschrift, stijl, penseelstreek, numer. voor sommen gelds, posten enz.

tsui pit, 水 |, waterpenseel.

tâng pit, 銅 |, Europeesche pen.

iân pit, 鉛 |, potlood.

gô mîng pit, 鵝毛 |, ganzenpen.

tsit ki pit, 一枝 |, een penseel.

tsit pit, 一 |, een penseelstreek.

pit ts'iu, | 鬚, haren van een penseel; krul aan een trek.

lóh pit, 落 |, de pen op het papier zetten.

k'i pit, 起 |, de pen opnemen.

pit t'at } ｜塞, penseelen dopje.
(» *t'ap*) }

p'oà pit, 破 ｜, voor het eerst leeren schrijven.

pit kè soa, ｜架山, bergen als een penseelenlegger, (twee kleinere met een groote in het midden.)

pit kóng, ｜管, penseelhouder.

pit tsik, ｜跡, handschrift.

pit hoat, ｜法, stijl.

pit ì, 意 ｜, eigenlijke beteekenis.

pit lik, ｜力, stijl.

toàn pit, 斷 ｜, conclusie; eind besluit, (in eene geschrift.)

tsiáh pit bé, 食 ｜ 尾, van het penseeleind leven, (van advokaten in kwade zaken.)

tit kaò ná pit nih, 直如 ｜ 分, regt als een penseel, klaar, duidelijk.

taì pit, 代 ｜, voor een ander schrijven.

pit tsu, ｜資, loon voor publieke schrijvers.

tsit pit tsi, 一 ｜ 錢, eene som geld.

tsit pit siaò, 一 ｜ 數, eene post rekening.

Stellig, zeker, bepaald; het moet.

bī pit, 未 ｜, niet stellig, niet zeker.

pit tiā, *pit tīng*, *pit dziēn*, ｜定, ｜然, stellig, zeker.

pit tióh, ｜當, het moet.

Splijten; bersten, springen; uitkomen, aan het licht komen.

pit k'ui, ｜開, splijten.

pit sùn, *pit hùn*, ｜痕, ｜瑕, gebersten,

pit lèh, *pit sao*, ｜鬆, ｜隙, gespleten, gebersten.

pit p'āng ｜隙, opensplijten; uitkomen., (van eene zaak.)

sio kaò pit pit, 燒至 ｜ 匕, vorhit tot bersten toe.

pit tsùn, ｜㨃, splijten, bersten, (als rijpe vruchten); uitlekken, aan het licht komen.

ts'iú pit, 手 ｜, de handen springen, (van koude.)

Pit *t'ok pit á*, krukvogel, soort musch.
pit lò, de klaauwier.

帛
Pit *tsai pit*, 財 ｜, rijkdommen, schatten, bezittingen.

闢
Pit *k'ai pit í lai*, 開 ｜ 以來, van de oudheid af.

匹
P'it Numer. voor paarden.
p'it p'oè, ｜配, passen aan, bij elkander komen, passen, juist goed.

bé p'it, 馬 ｜, paarden.

tsit p'it bé, 一 ｜ 馬, één paard.

toa sin p'it bé, 大身 ｜ 馬, alleen zijn vrijgezel zijn.

p'it tik, ｜敵, tegen elkander opgewasschen, (als rijken.)

p'it p'oè tiā tióh, ｜配定着, ondertrouwd zijn aan . . ., uitgehuwelijkt zijn aan.

疋
P'it Numer. voor geheele stukken goed.
sìng p'it sìng tīng } 筭 ｜ 筭丈,
(*suì* » *suì* ») }
bij de ellemaat berekenen.

pò p'it, 布 ｜, stuk goederen.

p'it t'aò kao, (of *tiàm*) ｜頭郊, manufactuurwinkel.

Piang

○ Piang *p ah pah piang*, 打 朴 丨, het geluid van watte kammen.

àn piang piang, 緊 丨 匕, strak als een snaar.

冰 Piang *ts'in* (of *ling*) *piang piang*, 冷 丨 匕, zeer koel, koud.

nī piang piang (*nē* « ») 勁 丨 匕, zeer stijf.

Piàng *tsing piàng*, met geweld stelen, gewelddadig inbreken.

hoai piàng piàng (*hoā* » ») zeer onbillijk, (in handeling.)

pin pin piàng piàng, geluid van hard loopen.

P'iang *toā bú p'iang*, groote jongen.

tsoáh tsat ē p'iāng, het verschil veel.

p'iāng kó (*p'āng* ») 泡 鼓, tamboerijn.

Piao

縹 Piao *piao tì*, 丨 緻, schoon, fraai (van vrouwen.

表 Piaó Buitenkant, buiten; bekend maken, ter kennis brengen, toonen; voorbeeld, teeken; gedachtenis, gedenkteeken; neven, nichten.

hoat piaó ē ioh, 發 丨 之 藥, zweetmiddel.

piaó bing, 丨 明, bekend maken ten-, toon spreiden.

piaó sut, 丨 率, voorbeeld.

it piaó ē dzin bút, 一 丨 人 物, een voorbeeldig fraai mensch.

bó piaó, 墓 丨, beschreven steenen, (om een graf.)

tsing piaó, 貞 丨, eene eereteeken gedenkteeken oprichten.

piaó kì, 丨 記, gedachtenis, souveni

piaó hiā, 丨 兄, neef.

ko piaó hiā tī, 姑 丨 兄 弟, neo (zoon van moeders broeders.)

i piaó hiā tī, 姨 丨 兄 弟, moeder zuster's zoon

piaó sió tī, 丨 小 弟, tante's zoon jongere broeder vader'szijde.

piaó toā tsi 丨 大 姊, tante's dochte oudere zuster vader'szijde.

piaó sió bē (» » *moē*) 丨 小 妹, tante's doch ter, jongere zuster vader'szijde.

piaó peh (» *pēh*) 丨 伯, oud tante's kin oudere vader'szijde.

piaó tsik, 丨 叔, oud tante's kin jongere vader'szijde.

piaó miā, 丨 名, noemen, den naam geven van . . . den naam drage van . . . .

婊 Piaó Lichtekooi, hoer.

piaó king, 娼 館, bordeel.

piaó kiá, 丨 子, hoerenkind, (scheldw.

piaó p'ó, 丨 婆, hoerenwaardin.

bān dzin piaó, 萬 人 丨, publiek hoer, (scheldw.)

piaó tsú ts'ùi, 丨 子 嘴, leugen achtig spreken.

laū piaó, 老 丨, oude hoer, (scheldw.

飄 P'iao *p'iao liû*, 丨 流, wegstroomen, weg drijven, wegdwalen, overal rondzweven

p'iao ioh, 丨 藥, zweetmiddel.

p'iao sàn ē ioh, 丨 散 之 藥, af drijven, zweetmiddel.

p'iao iét (» it) | 逸, kwispelen, in zijn schik, opgeruimd zijn.

p'iao p'iet, | 撇. levendig, (van aard.)

ts'ing p'iao. 清 |. zacht en levendig, (van aard.)

p'iao t'aô, | 頭. papier op goederen geplakt met den naam van de fabriek enz. er op.

laī p'iao. 內 |, binnenste papier waarop de fabrieksnaam staat, naam van den maker, enz. enz.

hong p'iao, 封 |. papier waarin iets geplakt is.

Hoereren.

p'iaô piaô, | 七. do.

p'iaô k'eh (» keh) | 客 |. hoereerder.

p'iaô tō im, | 賭 飲. hoereren, dobbelen en drinken (als het toppunt van een onbezorgd leven beschouwd.)

Pien

Zijde, kant; grens, grensplaats.

lióng pien. 兩 |. van beide kanten.

pông pien. 旁 |. ter zijde, omstanders.

pien kaì, | 界. grensplaats.

pien kiong. 疆 |. grenzen, (van een rijk.)

pé pien, 把 |. grensplaatsen bewaken.

Zamenstellen, opstellen, maken.

pien sûn, | 純. een rand aan iets maken.

pien koa, pien k'ik, | 歌, | 曲, een lied versje maken.

sin pien, 新 |. nieuw ingesteld.

pien hâm, | 銜. een groef (in hout enz.) maken, groef, sleuf.

鞭 Pien Penis van viervoetige dieren, pees.

攀 Pien (Pan) Trekken, naar zich toetrekken; zich vast houden aan.

pien king tsì, | 弓 箭. de boog spannen.

pien tsiū̄ tsûn, | 上 船, tegen een schip opklimmen.

匾 Pién Opschrift boven de deur van een huis.

koà pién, 掛 |. een opschrift (loftuiting) boven de deur hechten.

pai pién, 牌 |, uithangborden.

貶 Pién pī pién, | 被. afgezet zijn.

扁 Pién pién taō, | 豆, platte boonen die tegen diarrhoea gebruikt worden.

變 Pièn Veranderen, vervormen, eene andere wending nemen als zaken, ommekeer; opstand, omwenteling.

pièn hoà. | 化. veranderen, hervormen.

pièn oā, | 換, veranderen.

pièn ì, | 意. van plan veranderen.

pièn ts'ien, | 遷. veranderen.

bô pièn t'ong ê lâng, 無 | 通 之 人. een onpraktisch mensch.

tsoán pièn, 轉 |. veranderen, naar de omstandigheden handelen,

pièn bī. | 味. van smaak veranderen.

pièn lién, | 臉, van gelaatskleur veranderen, (door toorn of vreugde.)

pièn koà, | 卦, veranderen, eene andere wending nemen.

pièn tsìng, | 蒸, ommekeer in eene ziekte.

pièn hing, | 形, van gestalte of handelwijze veranderen.

pièn boē, | 賣, tot geld maken.

pièn sik, | 色, van kleur veranderen.

dziaó pièn, 繞 |, overal gebarsten.

bin pièn, 面 |, opstand (door verdrukking der overheden.)

pièn siong (» *siàng*) | 常, van voorkomen veranderen, van handelingen veranderen.

pièn t'ong, | 通, naar de omstandigheden weten te handelen.

癱 Pièn *pièn suī*, | 遂, verlamming.

遍 Pièn Alom, overal, geheel: rondgaan, eene keer rond.

pièn pièn sī, | 匕是, overal heeft men het, komt het voor.

pièn tē gim, | 地錦, mos; berekening op den grond of een stukje papier.

pièn sin, | 身, over het geheele ligchaam.

kui nā pièn, 數巡 |, verscheidene malen rond.

辯, 辨 Pien, Onderscheiden, onderscheid maken tusschen, redetwisten, twistredenen, disputéren, wederleggen, tegenspreken.

hun piēn, 紛 |, onderscheiden.

piēn tsin kè, | 眞假, het echte van het valsche onderscheiden.

piēn pok, | 駁, over en weer bespreken, wederleggen.

piēn lūn, | 論, bespreken.

piēn lai piēn k'ì, | 來 | 去, twistredenen, disputéren.

piēn tó, | 倒, wederleggen, omverpraten, overreden.

kióng piēn, 强 |, met geweld willen wederleggen, tegenspreken.

便 Piēn Gereed, klaar; gelegen, geschikt, doelmatig, bij de hand, handig, praktisch; bereidwillig, gewoon, alledaagsch, genoeg, waterlozing; dan, in dat geval

piēn piēn, | 匕, gereed, klaar.

piēn boé, | 買, klaar gemaakt koopen.

tsiáh piēn ts'ing piēn, 食 | 穿 | het slechts voor het eten en aantrekken hebben.

bī piēn, 未 |, lastig te . . .

bī piēn k'ui ts'ùi, 未 | 開口 nog niet gevoegelijk over iets kunnen spreken.

lī piēn, 利 |, handig, praktisch, doelmatig.

hiēn kà piēn, 現 日 |, voor de hand klaar.

sun piēn, 順 |, zoo als zulks het geschikste uitkomt, in éénе moeite

piēn tsiét, | 捷, handig, praktisch.

káng piēn, 簡 |, beknopt, praktisch

sui piēn, 隨 |, naar het uitvalt, naar het gelegen komt.

hong piēn, 風 |, bereidwillig.

k'oaì piēn, 快 |, gemakkelijk, zonder veel moeite, bereidwillig.

piēn tàng, , gewoon, alledaagsch (van zaken en voorwerpen.)

piēn pēng, *piēn tèng*, | 飯, dagelijksche pot, eten.

siaó piēn, 小 |, waterloozen, urine

tuā piēn, 大 |, zijn gevoegd doen ontlasting.

nā īm sī li t'ao piēn sī i t'ao k'ì 若不是汝偷 | 是伊偷去, als gij het niet gestolen hebt dan heeft hij het gestolen.

偏 P'ien Afwijken.

p'ien p'iah, | 僻, afgelegene.

p'ien p'ien, | 匕, bij voorkeur, uitsluitend, moedwillig.

p'ien kièn, | 見, private opinie.

p'ien tô̤ é giêp, | 途之業, een onbetamelijk beroep.

p'ien su, | 私, partijdig.

p'ien sim, | 心. do.

p'ien t'án, | 袒, partijdig, (onrechtvaardig.)

p'ien aì, | 愛, bij voorkeur boven de anderen, liefhebben.

p'ien p'ien beh | *(» » boeh)* } | 匕要. vast besloten zijn om.

tsoè lâng p'ien p'ien p'ien, 做人 | 匕匕, een wonderlijk mensch zijn.

ts'ú p'ien pâng, 取 | 房. bijzitten nemen.

p'ien kiong, | 宮, keizerlijke bijzitten.

皮 *p'i p'ién*, | 展, goederen of menschen
'ién ruim uit elkander schikken, ruim (van eene plaats.)

扁 Bedriegen, beetnemen, te kort doen.
'ièn *moâ̤ p'ièn*, 瞞 |. bedriegen.

k'it lâng p'ièn, 被人 |. bedrogen worden.

p'ièn lâng tsit k'o̤, | 人一圓, iemand voor een dollar bedriegen.

siet p'ièn, | 設. bedriegen.

koai p'ièn, 拐 |. oplichten, (mensch.)

p'ièn gín á, | 小兒. kinderen met mooie beloften paaijen.

p'ièn ts'uì, | 口, iets niet bijzonder lekker te eten geven.

p'ièn tsiáh p'ièn ts'ī̍ng, | 食 | 穿, iemand bedriegen voor voedsel en kleeding, (als gekochte kinderen die later wegloopen.)

p'ièn hān (of ān), | 限, iemand bedriegen in den termijn van betaling.

p'ah p'ièn pō̤, 打 | 步. bedriegerij plegen.

háng p'ièn, 喊 |, vrees aanjagen, bedriegen.

p'ièn lâng, | 人, iemand bedriegen.

gaû p'ièn, 善 |. bedriegelijk.

遍
P'ièn *tin tsit p'ièn* | *(» » pièn)* } 斟一 |. ééns rondschenken.

片
P'ièn Numer. voor dunne en kleine dingen strook, reep.

p'ièn tog, tsoá p'ièn, miâ p'ièn, | 單, 紙 |, 名 |, visitekaartje.

tsit p'ièn hûn, 一 | 雲. strook wolken.

hông p'ièn ko, 紅 | 餻. roode reepjes koek.

it p'ièn ê ts'iū nâ̤, 一 | 樹林, een geheel bosch.

ping p'ièn, 冰 |, Baros kamfer.

a p'ièn, 鴉 |, opium.

tsit p'ièn ê tsing lí, 一 | 情理, eene taal waar rede in is.

Piet

別
Piet *hun piet* 分 |, onderscheiden.

piet hó p'ai̤ | 好歹, het goede van het kwade onderscheiden.

piet ts'iem si, | 籤詩, een orakelversje uitleggen.

別
Piét *li piét*, 離 |. verlaten, afscheid nemen.

koat piét, 訣 |, afscheid nemen op zijn sterfbed.

tsiēm piét, 暫 ｜. voor korten tijd verlaten.

kiú piét, 久 ｜, voor langen tijd verlaten.

paì piét, 拜 ｜, afscheid van elkander nemen.

piét hō, ｜ 號, onderscheidings naam.

piét miâ, ｜ 名, do.

piét tsing, ｜ 情, andere zaken, uit andere reden voorkomende.

砵 Bord.
P'iet *p'iet á*, ｜ 仔, do.

p'iet á tû, ｜ 仔 厨, borden kast.

t'ng p'iet, 湯 ｜, soepbord.

丿 *k'a p'iet ts'ut*, 脚 ｜ 出, dwarstaan
P'iet van de voet.

撇 *p'iet ts'e* (» *ts'e*) in oneenigheid zijn.
P'iet *kap i p'iet ts'a*, do.

p'iet p'iet, ｜ 匕, do.

p'iet ih giet ih, ｜ 伊 囓 伊, iemand afsnouwen, niets van hem willen hooren.

nñg p'iet ts'ùi ts'u (*nō* » » ») 二 ｜ 嘴 鬚, de snor.

bô tsit p'iet, 無 一 ｜, geen trek kennen, volstrekt geene kennis van zaken hebben.

○ *p'iao p'iet*, 飄 ｜, levendig, (van aard.)
P'iet *p'iet t'aô*, ｜ 頭, niet naauw of bekrompen (in zijn handelen.)

翩 Klapwieken.
P'iét *p'iét p'iét pe* (» » *poe*) ｜ 匕 飛, fladderen, klapwieken.

p'iét p'iét haó, ｜ 匕 哮, wapperen als een vlag.

hi bé teh p'iét (» *boé* » ») 魚 尾 ｜, de staart van de visch zwaait.

p'i p'i p'iét p'iét, 披 匕 ｜ ｜, fladderen, (als een dier in het water.)

p'ah p'iét. 打 ｜. klapwieken.

Pin

檳 *pin ning*, ｜ 榔, siri.
Pin *pin ning áh*, ｜ 榔 鴨, siridoos.

濱 *haí pin ē sò tsaī*, 海 ｜ 之 所 在,
Pin zeeplaatsen, plaatsen aan zee gelegen.

pin pin pòng pòng, ｜ ｜ 滂 ｜, geluid van geschut en van iemand die hard stapt.

彬 *pin pin tsé tsé*, ｜ ｜ 濟 ｜. fatsoen-
Pin lijk, ordentelijk.

賓 *pin ping lai óng*, ｜ 朋 來 往, met
Pin gasten en vrienden omgang.

tsú tiong pin, pin tiong tsú, 主 中 ｜, ｜ 中 人, gastheer onder de gasten, (als iemand die in eene vreemde plaatsgasten ontvangt.)

禀 Bekendmaken, mededeelen aan hoogeren,
Pín een verzoekschrift indienen; verzoekschrift., petitie.

pin pò, ｜ 報. aan hoogeren bekendmaken.

pin bing, ｜ 明, door een verzoekschrift duidelijk uiteenzetten.

pin kì, ｜ 見, op audientie bij een mandarijn gaan.

pin ts'ing, ｜ 請, door een geschrift verzoeken.

pin t'iep, ｜ 帖. verzoekschrift.

pin k'é, ｜ 啟, do.

dzip pin, 入 ｜, een verzoekschrift indienen.
p'ah pin, 打 ｜, eene petitie inleveren.
su pin, 私 ｜. private brieven, (van lagere beambten aan hoogeren.)
pin sing. ｜ 性, aard, karakter.

編 Pin *pin tsiem*. ｜ 針, insteken als een naald.
pin tiaò, ｜ 着, vaststeken met.
tik pin, 竹 ｜, bamboezen deurscherm.
pin á, ｜ 子 do.

扁 Pin *pin ta* (*pin* ») ｜ 擔. juk. (om lasten aan te dragen.)

鬢 Pin *pin pi*, ｜ 旁, de slapen van het hoofd.
pin t'io, ｜ 挑, haarspeld.
pin sui, ｜ 毛, haar aan de slapen van het hoofd.
uī bai ts'at pin, 畫 眉 漆 ｜. de wenkbraauwen schilderen en de hoofd slapen bijteekenen.

篦 Pin *sat pin*, 虱 ｜. stofkammetje.
pin t'aò ming, ｜ 頭 毛, het haar met een stofkam uitkammen.

Pin *sì koè k'ì pin*, overal gaan rondzoeken.

儐 Pin *pin poā*, ｜ 絆. met elkander als vrienden omgaan en geschenken geven.

屏 Pin Scherm, schut.
ui pin, 圍 ｜, kamerscherm.
pin hong, ｜ 風, scherm, schut, afscheiden.
pin tó, ｜ 斗, middelste gedeelte in een schut of scherm.
pin péh, ｜ 白. schriftelijk dood bericht, (aan de deur geplaatst.)

憑 Pin Zich verlaten op, vertrouwen op; als bewijs, aannemen, volgens, naar; bewijs, afhangen van.
bòh tit pin i ê oē, 勿 ｜ 他 之 言. verlaat U niet op wat hij zegt.
pin kù (» *kì*) ｜ 據, bewijs.
bò pin, *bò pin kù*, 無 ｜, 無 據, de bewijzen ontbreken.
pin sìn, ｜ 信. geheel en al vertrouwen.
tsún pin, 準 ｜. tot maatstaf of bewijs dienen.
pin sim, ｜ 心, het hangt van U zelve af hoe het voor te doen komen.
pin toa, ｜ 單, certificaat.
bûn pin, 文 ｜, schriftelijke aanstelling.
pin li kóng, ｜ 汝 話, volgens Uw zeggen.
pin lâng ê tsō hoà, ｜ 人 之 造 化, het hangt van iemands geluk af.

重 Pin *pin t'aò tsoè*, ｜ 頭 作, van voren af, op nieuw doen.

貧 Pin Arm, behoeftig,
pin kiông, *pin hân*, ｜ 窮, ｜ 寒, arm.
pin tsing. ｜ 僧, arme Boeddha priester, (neder. term.)

Pin *pin toā lin*, 怠 惰

品 P'in Rang. rij, soort, kwaliteit, officiële rang; graad; handelingen, gedrag.
dzin p'in, 人 ｜. soort van mensch.
p'in dzī t'é, ｜ 字 體, in den vorm van het karakter *p'in*, (als gebouwen.)
kè p'in, 菓 ｜, koek soorten, koekjes in het algemeen.

58

t'ing p'in, 糖 |. suiker voorwerpen.
siōng p'in, 上 |, van den eersten graad, rang, kwaliteit.
koa p'in, p'in kip, 官 |, | 級, mandarijngraad, rang.
il p'in, 一 |, van den hoogsten graad.
p'in hīng, | 行. gedrag, levenswandel.
bô p'in, 無 |. geen onderscheid van rang maken.

約 Overeenkomen, beloven.
P'ín *bing p'in, p'in bing*, 明 |. duidelijk
P'ín overeenkomen beloven.
p'in tiā, | 定, vast overeenkomen.
bô p'in, 無 |. niet overeengekomen zijn.
p'in tsing ni, | 全 年. voor een geheel jaar overeenkomen, engagéren.

誇 Bluffen, zich verheffen op.
P'ín *p'in p'óng*, | 張. do.
p'in sè hē, | 世 係. op zijne afkomst pochen.
p'in i ē pún sū, | 伊 本 事, zich op zijne kundigheden verheffen.

笛 Dwarsfluit.
P'ín *pún p'in á*, 吹 | 仔, op de dwarsfluit spelen.

僛 Waggelen, (als een dronken man.)
P'in *p'in p'in*, | 匕, do. scheefgaan.
kiâ p'in p'in, 行 頗 匕, waggelen, zwaaijen, als een dronk mensch.
oai p'in, 歪 |. scheef, waggelen.
tsuì p'in p'in, 醉 | , waggelen van dronkenschap.
hong ts'e p'in lòh k'ì, 風 吹 | 落 去, de vlieger komt scheef neêr.
p'in p'iā, | 飄, onverwacht ontstuinig aankomend, (als wind of een slag.)

Ping

兵 *ping ling*, | 丁. soldaat.
Ping *tsng ping*, 當 |, soldaat zijn.
bé ping, 馬 |, cavallerie.
ping bé (» *bē*) | 馬, het leger, soldaten in het algemeen.
pō ping, 步 |, infanterie.
ping k'ì | 器, militaire wapenen.
k'ì ping, 起 |. soldaten op den been brengen.
ping tsûn, | 船, oorlogschepen.
taī ping, 大 |, groot leger.
ts'ut ping, 出 |, tenstrijde trekken.
ts'ao ping, 操 |. soldaten doen exerceren.
hók ping, 伏 , soldaten in hinderlaag leggen.
kiù ping, 久 |, hulptroepen.

氷 IJs, ijzel.
Ping *kien ping*, 堅 |, vriezen.
ping t'ing, | 糖, kandijsuiker.
ping t'ing boáh (» » *hún*) | 糖 末, fijn gestampte kandijsuiker.
ping ts'ù, | 厝, ijshuis.
ping k'ui, | 開, het ijs gaat los.
ping iû (» *iû*) | 鎔, het ijs smelt.
ping ts'ing, | 床, koelbed, (van marmer, enz.)
ping ping ping, | | |, zeerkoel.
ping sng seh tàng, | 霜 雪 凍, ijs en sneeuw, *d. i.* zeerkoud.
ping sng ê bah, | 霜 肉, geijsd vleesch.

hi ing ping ping, 魚用丨匕, visch met ijs ijzen, koelhouden.

反 Ping (Pán) Omkeeren, omdraaijen; omvallen, omslaan, onderste boven.

ping tó, 丨倒, omkeeren.

ping tin tńg, 丨翻轉, omkeeren, onderste, boven.

ping lâi ping k'ì, 丨輾丨去, zich over en weer draaijen, (als in bed.)

ping laī bīn ts'ut lai, 丨裏面出來, het binnenste buiten keeren.

ping ts'i̍ oā sik, 丨生換熟, het nieuwe voor het oude verruilen.

ping t'ing (» *t'ān*) 丨挺, steeds van zin veranderen, onstandvastig.

ping k'ap, 丨閤, voorover.

ping p'ak, 丨朴, op de buik liggen.

ping tsih tsoâ, 丨龟蛇, eene draai aan zijn woorden geven; zich zelven tegen spreken.

ping ts'iò poáh tó, 丨面跌倒, achterovervallen.

poáh ping, 跋丨, nergens rust hebben, veranderlijk.

ping pak, 丨腹, het gegetene uitbraken.

tsûn ping, 船丨, het vaartuig sloeg om.

ping ts'iù hō̤ lâng k'oà, 丨手與人看, de hand omkeeren en aan anderen laten zien, *d. i.* zijne eigene schande laten zien.

ping ts'iù hoe, 丨手花, met een handgreep weggoochelen.

ping lâng ê tsi̍, 丨人之錢, iemand in geld bedriegen.

ping tō̤, 丨肚, op de rug liggen. (van doode visschen.)

t'i̍ ping tsoè toē, 天丨做土, de hemel keert om tot aarde, (van lageren die hoogeren verdrukken.)

ping tsih koai, , een oogenblik te voren gezegd heeft; iets van plan zijn geweest te zeggen maar nog bij tijds eene andere rigting aan zijne woorden geven.

ping pì, 丨變, zich niet domweg aan iets houden, naar de omstandigheden veranderen.

ping t'án k'ap, 丨坦閤, onderste boven.

báh tsiu ping péh, 目丨白, alleen het wit van de oogen laten zien.

秉 Píng Ter hand nemen, vasthouden.

ping kong, 丨公, rechtvaardig, onpartijdig.

ping tsìng, 丨正, onpartijdig.

ping sim bû k'uì, 丨心無愧, volgens zijn geweten zich niet te schamen hebben.

ping sìn, 丨性, verstand.

并 Pìng Met, en, benevens.

ping īm sī, 丨不是, toch niet zoo.

goá pìng īm tsai, 我並不知, Ik weet het volstrekt niet.

it ping.... it ping, aan den eenen kant.... aan den anderen kant.....

却 Pìng Toch eigenlijk wel.

pìng īm mā̤, 丨不肯, maar toch niet alleen, slechts....

柄 Pìng *koân pìng*, 權丨, macht, gezag.

ū pá pìng, 有把丨, er is iets omzich aan te houden, om de zaak te besturen, dirigeren.

ū pìng kù, 有丨據, er is een bewijs.

秤 Ping Wegen; weegschaal.

ping tāng, 丨重, wegen.

t'ien ping ping loū tsoē tang, 天 | | 若 多 重, op een weegschaal wegen.

平 Ping Gelijk, effen, vlak; gelijkstaand, gelijksoortig, billijk, rechtvaardig; gewoon, ordinair, middelmatig, gewoonlijk; rust, vrede, rustig, vreedzaam; tot rust brengen.

ping tē k'i hong p'ō, | 地 起 風 波, op een effen weg storm verwekken, *d. i.* iemands vrede stooren.

ping poè, | 輩, gelijk van rang, gelijkstaand.

ping ting, | 等, van gelijken graad.

ping hing è lé, | 行 之 禮, beleefsheids manieren tusschen gelijken.

kong ping, 公 |, billijk, rechtvaardig.

ping ī, | 易, gemakkelijk.

ping kè, | 價, gewone prijs.

ping t'iò, | 糶, bij hongersnood rijst tegen den gewonen prijs verkoopen.

ping hò, | 和, middelmatig, juist goed.

ping k'ong, | 空, onverwacht, plotseling.

ping siòng, | 常, gewoonlijk, alledaagsch.

ping sò, | 素, van te voren, tot nog toe.

ping dzit, ping sing, ping si, | 日, | 生, | 時, do.

t'aì ping, 太 |, algemeene vrede.

ping an, | 安, rustig, op rust.

ping an mah? | 安 麽, hoe vaart gij?

ping ting, | 定, rustig, in vrede.

ping bin, | 民, rustig volk.

ping ts'át, | 賊, roovers, oproerlingen tot rust brengen.

朋 Ping Vriend.

ping iù. | 友, vriend.

hò ping ch, 好 | 者, een goede vriend.

ping iù tō, | 友 道, manieren tusschen vrienden.

硼 Ping *ping se* (» *se*) | 砂, borax.

邊 Ping Kant, zijde; partijen.

kui ping, 歸 |, ter zijde leggen, (als uitschot.)

nīng ping è lâng, 兩 | 之 人, beide partijen.

tsoè nīng ping, 做 兩 |, aan twee stukken.

弊 Pīng *pē pīng* / *pi* » / *maò pīng*, | 病 / 第 |, iets defects aan iets, niet geheel in orde.

烹 P'ing Braden, (van groote stukken.)

p'ing iù, | 油, door het vet halen er een weinig in laten braden.

p'ing tiaō, | 調, koken en braden in het algemeen.

併 P'ing *p'ing pé*, | 皮, de slechte plaatsen uit vachten snijden en met goede stukken lappen.

聘 P'ing Verzoeken, uitkiezen.

p'ing kim, | 金, huwelijks geld.

p'ing gi, p'ing lé, | 禮, huwelijks geschenken.

goàn p'ing, 原 |, eerste vrouw: voor afgaande huwelijks geschenken.

hing p'ing, 行 |, geschenken voor een huwelijk geven.

p'ing kim gûn / » » *gin* | 金 銀, geld bij een huwelijk geven.

p'ìng gaô lâng, | 賢人, knappe menschen in zijne dienst verzoeken.

騁 P'ing *p'ìng i ē tsai tiaū*, | 伊才技, zijne kennis aan den dag brengen.

p'ìng pit siá, | 筆寫, voor de hand wegschrijven.

苹 *p'ing kó*, | 果, appel.

P'ing *p'ing suí siong hông*, | 水相逢, het kroost en het water ontmoeten elkander; van vrienden die elkander op verschillende plaatsen en tijden ontmoeten.

評 P'ing *p'ing lūn*, | 論, onpartijdig over iets praten.

p'ing p'oe (» *p'e*) | 批, vergelijken; een besluit op eene compositie fo petitie zetten.

p'ing koai kē (» *koân kē*) | 高下, over het beste en mindere redeneren.

p'in p'ing, 品 |, de graad, kwaliteit onderscheiden.

p'ing tsing li, | 情理, onderscheiden, vergelijken wie ongelijk en wie gelijk heeft.

鵬 P'ing *taī p'ing tsiaó*, 大 | 鳥, fabelachtige monster groote vogel, (op den spiegel van groote schepen geschilderd.)

較 P'ing *pi p'īng*, 比 |, vergelijken.

p'īng toā liép, | 大粒, onderling vergelijken wie het sterkste is.

p'īng k'oà, | 看, onderling vergelijken.

kap li p'īng tseh, 與汝 | 之, met U vergelijken.

mih p'à p'īng, 物怕 |, dat voorwerp kan niet bij anderen vergeleken worden, het haalt er niet bij.

p'īng pān, | 辦, de monsters vergelijken.

祇 P'ing *p'īng tsō hoà*, | 造化, het hangt van het geluk af.

拚 P'īng *p'īng si miā*, | 生命, op leven of dood vechten.

p'ìnq hiong, 騁兇, verwoed.

Pio

鏢 Pio *pio á*, | 仔, horologie.

Pio *pio pio ts'iò ts'iò*, dartel zijn, gekheid maken en lachen.

驃 Pio Vet sterk, (van paarden.)

Pio *kaò pio*, 足 |, genoegzaam sterk, (van paard.)

tsiáng pio, 獎 |, al te vet.

sit pio, 失 |, te weinig vet.

標 Pio *pó pio*, 保 |, assurantie bewijs.

ts'ah pio, 插 |, bakens zetten.

pàng pio, 放 |, een baken zetten.

ts'iú pio, 奪 |, de bakens wegnemen, (bij een roei wedstrijd.)

ts'iú t'aô pio, 奪頭 |, het eerst de bakens wegnemen, *d. i.* de haantje de voorste willen zijn.

批 Pio *pio tsù*, | 註, aan den kant aanteekenen.

pio ti bé āu, | 在尾後, aan het eind opteekenen (als op eene rekening.)

鏢 Pio *pio hî*, | 魚, een visch harpoeneren.

t'ih pio, | 鐵, harpoen.

tiòng pio, 中 |, door een harpoen getroffen worden.

表 Pió *pió tsiu* (» *tsiang*) | 章, verzoekschrift aan den keizer.

tsìn pió, 進 |, een verzoekschrift aan den keizer indienen.

tsaò piò, 奏 ｜, do.

鰾 *hi piō ka*, 魚 ｜ 膠, vischlijm.
Piō *tiu̍ piō (tiu̍)*, ｜ 脹, door te veel gegeten te hebben op den rug gaan liggen als visschen.

票 Schriftelijk bewijs, briefje, lootje, vol-
P'iò macht.

tèng p'iò, 當 ｜, lombardbriefje.

p'iò kù, ｜ 據, schriftelijk bewijs.

ts'ut p'iò, 出 ｜, volmagt tot inhechtenis neming geven.

pò sit p'iò, 報 失 ｜, er kennis van geven dat men een bewijs, lootje enz. verloren heeft.

p'iò gûn, tsi̍ p'iò, ｜ 銀, 錢 ｜, papierengeld.

bi p'iò, 米 ｜, rijstbriefje, rijstbonnetje.

ū pai ū p'iò, 有 牌 有 ｜, van zijne papieren voorzien, (als een schip.)

漂 Drijven; licht, rank als schepen; bleeken.
P'iò *k'in p'iò*, 輕 ｜, licht, rank.

p'û p'û p'iò p'iò, 浮 匕 ｜ 匕, do. onsoliede in handelingen.

p'iò péh, ｜ 白, bleeken.

p'iò lō, ｜ 布, in den dauw bleeken.

p'iò pō, ｜ 露, goed bleeken.

萍 Kroost.
P'iò

瓢 *iâ p'iò*, 椰 ｜, schepper van cocosnoot.
P'iò *haō p'iò*, 匏 ｜, waterschepper van een *haō* gemaakt.

Po

玻 *po le*, ｜ 璃, glas.
Po *po lê kan*, ｜ 璃 矸, flesch.

po lê ao, ｜ 璃 甌, bierglas.

po lê tsoṅ, ｜ 理 盞, wijnglas.

pûn po lê, 吹 ｜ 璃, glasblazen.

tsú po lê, 做 ｜ 璃, glas maken.

褒 Prijzen, roemen, ophemelen.
Po *po so*, ｜ 唆, roemen prijzen.

po tsiáng, ｜ 獎, do.

hò po, 好 ｜, gaarne geprezen zijn.

po lo so, ｜ 囉 唆, zeer prijzen, ophemelen.

ko po, 過 ｜, overmatig prijzen.

po sioh, ｜ 惜, prijzen.

舷 De verschansing, het buitenboord van
Po een schip.

po pi, ｜ 邊, verschansing.

tsûn po, 船 ｜, do. buitenboord.

so po, ｜ 抹, het buitenboord verven.

保 Beschermen, bewaken; instaan, borg-
Pó staan, voor zijne verantwoording nemen; borg, borgtocht; verzekeren assuréren.

pó pì, ｜ 庇, beschermen, bewaken.

pó hō, ｜ 護, do.

pó iū, ｜ 佑, do.

t'aì tsú t'aì pó, 太 子 太 ｜, beschermheer, gouverneur van den kroonprins.

pó tsoân, ｜ 全, in goeden toestand bewaren.

pó kú, ｜ 舉, aanbevelen, recommanderen.

pó iòng, ｜ 養, zich ontzien, (om zijne krachten terug te krijgen.)

tē pó, pó tiú, 地 ｜, ｜ 長, soort wijkmeester.

pó hūn, ｜ 份, uitgestrektheid van een wijk, buurt.

pó niá, ｜ 領, instaan, borgstaan.

pó dzīn, | 認, borgtocht zijn.

pó dzīn eh, | 認 的, borg.

pó dzīn lâng, | 認 人, do.

pó pio ê dzī, | 票 之 字, assurantie biljet.

pó ke, | 家, assurantie.

dzip pó ke, 入 | 家, assuréren.

pó pio, | 票, assurantie-bewijs, polis.

liên hoân pó, 連 環 |, wederkeerig voor elkander borgstaan.

ts'ú pó, 取 |, borgtocht nemen.

寶 Pó Edele steen, kostbaarheid, kostbaar; waardéren; draaibord.

pó tsióh, | 石, edele steen.

pó poè, | 貝, kostbaarheid, kostbaar.

t'oân ka pó, 傳 家 |, familiekostbaarheden.

kok pó, 國 |, rijksgeld.

sam pó hút, 三 | 佛, de drie hoofdafgoden, (die naast elkander in tempels zijn.)

pó sioh, | 惜, waardéren, veel houden van (iemand of iets.)

pó taó, | 斗, bak waarin het draaibord is.

k'ui pó tiû, 開 | 場, een dobbelhuis opzetten, houden.

鴇 ó *pó dzi á*, | 兒 仔, hoerenkind, ondeugende drommel, (tegen kinderen gezegd.)

報 ò Vergelden, beloonen, betaald zetten; bericht geven, bekend maken, doen weten, mededeelen, opgeven, aangeven, berichtbrenger.

pò tap, | 答, vergelden.

pò ìng, | 應, do.

pò un, | 恩, eene weldaad vergelden.

pò siû, pò oan, | 仇, | 冤, wraaknamen.

t'ong pò, 通 |, alom bekend maken, aandienen (als een bezoeker).

pò ti, | 知, doen weten.

lai pò sìn, 來 | 信, bericht komen brengen omtrent iets.

pò seh, | 說, informatie brengen.

pò bing, | 明, duidelijk bekend maken.

pò p'oe, | 批, door een brief mededeelen.

ka pò, 家 |, brief tijding naar huis.

pò hi, | 喜, vreugde tijding aanbrengen.

pò tiaò, | 條, bericht van iemands officiele aanstelling.

pò á, | 仔, de berichtbrengers van iemands benoeming.

pò gê, 鬧 衙, in zwermen uitvliegen, (als bijen,)

sa pò sa sō, 相 | 相 掿, tegen elkander zeggen en elkander aanzetten, (als om te spijpelen.)

pò siaù, | 賬, verschillende posten ter boeking opgeven; de jaarlijksche rekening aan de aandeelhebbers mededeelen.

kia pò, 京 |, Peking courant.

pò hiòng, | 餉, voor de belasting aangeven.

pò sè koán, | 稅 舘, belastingkantoor.

pò mia, | 名, zijn naam opgeven.

pò tiém, | 點, het uur aangeven.

pò tsing lâng, | 衆, alom bekend maken.

暴 Pò *pò t'aô*, | 頭, storm.

婆 Oude vrouw, minachtend wijf.
Pô *ko pô*, 姑 丨. oudtante.

peh pô, 伯 丨, tante, (vrouw van (vader's ouderen broers.)

tsim pô, 嬸 丨, moeder van zijne tante; de vrouw van zijne jongere oom van vaderszijde.

ím pô, 姆 丨, moeder van zijne tante de vrouw van zijn oudere oom van vaderzijde.

pô tsiá bú, 丨 者 母, beschermgeest (van jongere kinderen), kindermeid.

laū pô, 老 丨, oude dienstmaagd.

k'it tsiáh pô, 乞 丐 丨, bedelares.

ts'át pô, 賊 丨, diefegge.

kīm pô, 妗 丨. oud tante, (vrouw van grootmoedes), (van moeders zijde) jongeren broeder.

kong pô, 公 丨. (de tabletten van) grootouders.

laū kong pô, 老 公 丨, oude aangetrouwde vader en moeder van manszijde.

蝠 *bit pô*, 蝙 丨, vleermuis.
Pô

暴 *k'i t'o pô*, 土 起 丨. onderzeesche aardbeving.
Pô

晡 Oorspr. van 3 tot 5 uur namiddag; vóór of namiddag.
Po

tsit po, 一 丨, één vóór- of namiddag.

ting po, *ē pō*, 上 丨, 下 丨, vóórmiddag, namiddag.

tsiâ po kú, 全 丨 久, een geheelen morgen lang, (wachten, enz-)

pòà po, 半 丨, één halve dag.

poà po aō, 半 丨 後, achtermiddag.

míng po, 晚 丨, do.

埔 Vlakte plateau.
Po *k'àng po*, 空 丨, uitgestrekte vlakte.

soa po, 沙 丨, zandvlakte.

soa po, 山 丨, bergvlakte, plateau.

ts'aó po, 草 丨, grasvlakte.

埠 *po t'aô*, 丨 頭, zeehaven.
Po

Po *po tiah á*, 丨 花 雀, winterkoninkje.

枯 Verdorren, verdroogen.
Po *po k'ì*, 丨 去, verdord, uitgedroogd. vermolmd.

po sim, 丨 心, inwendig uitgedroogd.

ts'ùi k'ì po, 齒 嘴 丨, holle kies.

補 Verstellen, lappen, repareren, inzetten.
Pó eene leegte of te kort aanvullen, voltallig maken; versterken, kracht geven versterkend (aan het ligchaam), voordeel geven.

pó sa, 丨 衫, kleêren verstellen, repareren.

pó t'ī, 丨 綻, repareren, lappen (kleederen) verstellen.

pó sa ím, 丨 衫 姆, verstelster.

pó t'at, 丨 剔, lappen, oplappen, repareren.

pó oá, 丨 碗, kommen krammen.

pik pó i. 衣 丨 百, bedelaarskleed.

pó koā, 丨 袞, mandarijn borstlap.

t'i p'oà ïng pó, 天 破 用 丨, toen de hemel stuk was repareerde men hem, *d. i.* eene beleediging kan hersteld worden.

pó siaò, 丨 數, eene post bijschrijven.

pó giáh, 丨 額, aanvullen, voltallig maken.

pó k'eh, 丨 缺, eene open gekomen mandarijns plaats aanvullen.

pó̤ hè, 丨貨, goederen aankoopen; het te kort komende met waren aanvullen.

pó̤ k'í, 丨齒, kiezen aanvullen, plombeeren.

sa̤ po̤, 相丨, elkander vergoeden; eene loopende rekening vereffenen.

pé pó, 賠丨, terуggeven, (tot dat het oorsp. getal, gewicht enz. er is.)

po̤ ióh. 丨藥. versterkende geneesmiddelen.

po̤ oân, 丨丸, versterkende pillen.

tsu im po̤, 滋陰丨. verzachtend, verkoelend en versterkend.

tsiáh po̤, 食丨, versterkende dingen eten.

ū so̤ po̤, 有所丨, voordeel gevend (als spijzen of handelingen.)

bô po̤, 無丨. het geeft geen voordeel.

Gedroogd vleesch.

bah po̤, 肉丨, gedroogd vleesch.

gô̤ k'i pó̤, 蜈蜞丨, uitgedroogde leege bloedzuiger, *d. i.* inhalig.

lâng po̤, 人丨, levend geraamte, zeer mager.

Bijl.

pó̤ t'aô, 丨頭. bijl.

géh pó̤, 月丨, maanvormige, ronde bijl.

Verdord, (als bloemen), gedroogd. verdroogd.

kien pó̤, 堅丨, verdord. verdroogd.

hoe pó̤, 花丨, gedroogde bloemen, (onder thee gemengd).

ts'ài po, 菜丨, gedroogde ingemaakte radijzen.

pó̤ pó̤ pó̤, 丨丨丨, ingedroogd, verdroogd.

布 Pò̤ Doek, linnen. laken, stof, geed: een doek; uitspreiden, uitzenden.

ki pò̤, 機丨. linnen weven.

pò̤ kui, 丨規, weefgetouw.

pò̤ li, 丨簾, gordijn.

pò̤ liaô, 丨條, zwachtel.

dzoáh pò̤, 夏丨, graslinnen.

ts'ià bûn pò̤, 斜紋丨, drill.

hoe pò̤. 花丨, sits.

pò̤ p'it, 丨疋, stukgoederen.

sik pò̤, 色丨, gekleurde stoffen, shirtings.

ìn hoe pò̤ (» *hoa* ») 印花丨, gebloemde stof.

toā hoe pò̤ (» *hoa* ») 大花丨, groot gebloemde stof.

sió hoe pò̤ (» *hoa* ») 小花丨, klein gebloemde stof.

pò̤ p'âng, 丨篷, linnen zeil.

pò̤ pi, 丨幔, legertent, zomertent.

pò̤ kao, 丨郊. manufactuur-lakenwinkel,

pò̤ pâng, 丨房. laken verwers, en lakenwinkel.

pò̤ tē hì, 丨袋戲. marionettenspel.

tsoè pò̤ tē siú, 做丨袋首, aan het hoofd van den (geld) zak staan *d. i.* mandarijnen personen aanduiden die zij geld kunnen afzetten

pò̤ tsìng si, 丨政司, provinciale schatmeester.

pò̤ kíng, 丨景, eene uitzicht, gezicht afdeeling. (voor dat men gaat schilderen.) een schets maken.

pò̤ kiòk, 丨局, maatregelen nemen, uitmaken.

賄 **Pè** — *pò̤ tah*, , | 搭, handlangers uitzenden om de bewoners op te ruien.

pò̤ lō̤, | 路, omkoopen.

播 — *pò tsing* } | 種, zaaijen.
(*pò* ») }

Pò̤ — *pò̤ ts'ân hoe*, | 田花, wilde witte roos.

晡 **Pò̤** — *pò pò̤*, | |, taai door ouderdom.

傅 **Pò̤.** — Familienaam.

暴 — Verdrukken.

Pō — *pō̤. dziók*, | 虐, do.

k'it làng pō̤, 被人 |, door iemand aan de kaak gesteld worden.

蒲 **Pô** — *ts'ang pô̤*, 菖 |, een riet den 5den dag van de 5de maand aan de deuren gehangen.

ts'ang pô̤ hiā̤, 菖 | 艾, de Acorus gramineus en de Arthemisia,(5de maand 5den dag aan de deuren ophangen.)

pô toân, (of *t'oân*) | 團, gevlochten mat waarop men bij offeren knielt.

pô̤ oê. | 鞋, stroosehoenen, pantoffels.

蒲 — Familienaam.

Pô̤ — *mî pô̤*, 綿 |. stijve nog niet gekamde watten.

胞 **Pô** — *tāu sī pô̤*, 荳豉 |, gekookte en opzettelijk beschimmelde boonen bij het maken van soja gebezigd.

ut pô̤ sih, 欝㧊 |, doodgaan door zich niet uit het ei te kunnen werken, (van kuikens),

袍 **Pô̤** — *lìng pô̤*, 龍 |. drakenjas. (keizerl.)

縩 **Pô̤** — *nó pō̤*, 莿 |, een omslag in kleederen leggen.

sàn pò̤ sa̤, 散 | 衫. kleed met gerafelde, ongezoomde kanten. (rouw voor eene moeder).

蔀 **Pō̤** — *ts'ì nā pō̤*, 莿林 |, doornboschje struik.

步 **Pō̤** — Voetstap, schrede, voet, te voet, zet in het schaakspel middel, manier, steek. list.

k'a pō̤, 脚 |, voetstap.

pō̤ kiā̤, | 行, te voet gaan.

pō̤ ping, | 兵, infanterie.

pō̤ tsièn, | 戰, gevecht van infanterie.

pō̤ tsì̤, | 箭, boogschutters te voet.

toā pō̤ kiā̤, 大 | 行, hardloopen.

k'ui pō̤, 䦧 |, groote stappen nemen.

lièn pō̤ dzip, 連 | 追, op de hielen zitten.

pō̤ sè̤, 行勢, manier van handelen. handelwijze.

k'ìng pō̤, 藏 |, de manier op iets verbergen.

pō̤ pō̤, | |, voetje voor voetje, elke bijzonderheid.

tsit pō tsit pō̤, 一 | 一 |, voetje voor voetje, voorzichtig.

hó pō̤, 好 |, goede manier.

kik pō̤, 極處, uiterste middelen laatste poging.

laò aū pō̤, 留後 |, eene kans voor het vervolg openlaten.

t'ao tsiáh pō̤, 偷食 |. slinksche streek.

p'ah p'ièn pō̤. 打騙 |, bedriegerij

tòk pō̤, 毒 |, schadelijke list streek.

bô pō̤ ìh, 不奈他. niet weten wat aan iemand te doen.

goá bô lí pō̤, 我無乃爾何 Ik weet niet wat aan U te doen. Ik geef U op.

部 **Pō̤** — Algemeen hoofd. departement, ministerie

klassenhoofd, (waaronder karakters gerangschikt zijn.)

liók pō̲, 六 〡, zes ministeries.

lī pō̲, 吏 〡, civiel departement.

hō̲ pō̲, 戶 〡, departement van financiën.

lé pō̲, 禮 〡, departement van de ceremoniën.

ping pō̲ (*piŋ* ») } 兵 〡, departement van oorlog.

hing pō̲, 刑 〡, departement van justitie.

kong pō̲, 工 〡, departement van publieke werken.

pō̲ tsiòng, 〡 衆, onderhoorige bevelhebbers.

ngó pō̲ ts'iu, 鬍 〡 鬚, baard, sik en knevels.

哺 Bijten op, kauwen.

Pō̲ *pō̲ hun hioh*, 嚼烟 棄, tabak pruimen.

pō̲ tsiáh, 〡 食, opvreten, (van wilde dièren.)

liên tsih soah pō̲ lòh k'ì, 連 舌 撒 〡 落 去, zijn tong er bij inslikken, (van iets lekker.)

pō̲ boē noō̲ (*bē* » ») } 〡 不 爛, niet zacht kunnen kaauwen, *d. i.* eene zaak niet ten einde kunnen brengen.

k'ang ts'uì pō̲ tsih, 空 嘴 〡 舌, met een leège mond op zijn tong kaauwen.

捕 Vatten, arresteeren.

Pō̲ *pō̲ t'iŋ*, 〡 爹, politieschout.

sùn pō̲, 巡 〡, politie adjudanten.

波 *p'o lōng*, 〡 浪, de golven.

P'o *hong p'o*, 風 〡, wind en golven, stormen des levens.

hai p'o, 海 〡, golven der zee.

p'un p'o, 奔 , overal rondzwerven.

p'o lò bit, 〡 羅 蜜, de broodvrucht.

ping tē k'i hong p'o, 平 地 起 風 〡, op eene effen vlakte wind en golven doen ontstaan, *d. i.* moeilijkheden veroorzaken waar ze niet bestonden.

tsui p'o hùn, 水 〡 痕, golfjes, kringetjes, op het water; gemarmerde kleur.

ling p'o, 寧 〡, Ningpo.

坡 *soa p'o*, 沙 〡, zandvlakte, strand.

P'o

灰 *p'ó á sik* (*p'ú*) » 〡 色, grijs, grauw.

P'ó

頗 Een weinig, tamelijk.

P'ó *p'ó liók* » (*liúk*) } 〡 畧, ongeveer, in het ruwe.

p'ó p'ó á, 〡〡 仔, een weinig.

p'ó oē k'ì tit, 〡 能 去 的, tamelijk, het kan er nog door.

破 Verwoesten, verstrooijen.

P'ò *p'ò ka tōng sán* » (*ke̱*) » » } 〡 家 蕩 產, zijne bezittingen verliezen.

p'ò siâ̱, 〡 城, eene stad innemen.

p'ò koa, 〡 瓜, ontmaagden.

k'àng p'ò, 間 〡, doorzien, (eene zaak.)

p'ò tīn, 〡 陣, de vijandelijke gelederen door breken.

sì niû̱ p'ò i ts'ien kun, 四 両 〡 之 千 斤, met vier oncen duizend pond te boven komen. *d. i.* geringe krachten goed weten aan te wenden.

青 *p'ò á ts'iū*, 〡 冬 樹, lindeboom.

P'ò

浮 P'ò — *p'ò á tsiòh*, | 子 石 . puimsteen.

p'ò p'ò, | |, zacht, (van suikerriet enz.)

t'o̲ k'ah p'ò, 土 更 |, de aarde is wat zachter.

p'ò sin, | 身, zacht (ais hout enz.)

鋪 P'o̲ — Uitspreiden, uitleggen, uitstallen, rangschikken; boven opleggen, beleggen, plaveien; bed, beddegoed.

p'o̲ pai, | 排, uitstallen; de mooie kant voorhangen, formeele beleefheid.

kap i p'o̲, 合 他 |, (door geschenken) beleefheid bewijzen.

p'o̲ siet. | 設, fraai rangschikken.

p'o̲ bīn, *p'o̲ oá bīn*, | 面, | 椀 面, het beste. fraaiste boven opleggen.

p'o̲ hè bin, | 貨 面, de beste waar boven opleggen, uitstallen.

p'o̲ bīn t'an, | 面 蟶, zijne mooie zijde voorhangen.

p'o̲ mi̲, | 棉, watteeren.

p'o̲ hoe, | 花, bloemen opleggen, borduren.

p'o̲ kiò, | 橋, een brug leggen.

p'o̲ lō, | 路, een weg plaveien.

p'o̲ tsng, | 磚, met tichels beleggen.

p'o̲ kaì, | 蓋, beddegoed.

ts'ng p'o̲, 床 |, ledikant en soort canapé.

pog p'o̲, 搬 |, (een lijk) uit het bed (in de zaal) overbrengen.

菩 P'o̲ — *p'o̲ sat*. | 薩, Boeddha afgoden.

蒲 P'o̲ — *p'o̲ t'oàn*. | 團, matten kussen, (in tempels gebruikt.)

桴 P'o̲ — *bèh p'o̲*, 麥 |, gerstdoppen.

t'aò p'o̲, 頭 |, roos op het hoofd.

ts'uì p'o̲ p'o̲, geen trek of smaak i[n] eten hebben.

譜 P'ó — Lijst, register, boek, leerboek, handboek.

tsók p'ó, 族 |, geslachts register.

gák p'ó, 樂 |, muziekboek.

bô p'ó, 無 |, zich niet aan de ma[at] of muziek houden.

k'ik p'ó, 曲 |, verzenboek.

uī é p'ó, 畫 |, handleiding d[er] teekenkunst.

ki p'ó, 棋 |, handleiding voor schaal spelers.

普 P'ó̲ — Gelijkelijk, wijd verspreid over.

p'ó̲ t'i̲ ē, | 天 下, over de gehe[ele] wereld.

p'ó̲ tō̲, *p'ó̲ sì*, | 度, | 施, alg[e]meene offerfeest aan de afgestorvene allerzielen: 7de maand.

p'ó̲ tō̲ kong, | 度 公, god over zielen in de onderwereld.

頗 P'ó — *p'ó p'ó* | |, een weinig, een beet[je].

p'ó̲ liok (» *(liák)*) | 畧, ongeveer, in het [al]gemeen.

鋪 P'ò̲ — *kog p'ò̲*, 官 |, mandarijn p'ò̲, kor[ter] dan de *sog* of *bin pò̲*.

ts'aò hī lâng p'ò̲, 臭 耳 聾 [|], een doove man's *p'ò̲*, *d. i.* zeer la[nge] weg.

tsit p'ò̲, 一 |, 10 li's.

tsit p'ò lō̲, 一 | 路, een weg [van] 10 li's.

p'ò̲ hūn, | 分, landerijen enz. [bin]nen een *p'ò̲* liggend.

tiàm pò̲, 店 | } winkel.
p'ò̲ hō̲, | 戶 }

laó p'ò̲, 老 |, van ouds beroe[mde] winkel, doorkneed in een vak.

扶 P'ō̤ Oplichten, (als een tafel om iets onder de pooten te zetten.)

p'ō̤ mîng » *(mûi)* } ｜門, een deur uittillen.

p'ō̤ tāng, ｜重, optillen om het gewicht te voelen.

p'ō̤ ih, ｜之, ophemelen, vleien.

gaô p'ō̤ lâng, 賢｜人, iemand ophemelen, vleien.

p'ō̤ t'á, ｜擎, wel op zijne handen willen dragen, vleien.

p'ō̤ k'a sáng ts'iú, ｜脚｜手, laag vleijen.

p'ō̤ k'oà, ｜看, iets optillen om te zien of het zwaar of licht is.

p'ō̤ lóh lai, ｜下來, onder steunen, oplichten, en naar beneden laten zakken.

p'ō̤ oá, ｜倚, dichter bij tillen,

p'ō̤ oá, 蟛蟹, een soort kreeft.

部 P'ō Boekwerk.

tsit p'ō ts'eh, 一｜書, een boekwerk.

蔀 P'ō Boschjes, bos.

tsit p'ō tik, 一｜竹, een bamboe boschje.

ts'ì á p'ō, 莿仔｜, doornboschje.

tsit p'ō ts'aò, 一｜草, een bos gras.

tsit p'ō t'aô mîng, 一｜頭毛, een bos haar.

抱 P'ō In de armen tegen de borst aan dragen, omarmen, omhelzen; beethouden.

p'ō kiá, ｜子, een kind in de armen dragen.

sa p'ō, 相｜, elkander omhelzen.

p'ō gûn, ｜銀, geld tegen de borst aan dragen.

p'ō sim k'uì, 心氣, aan den grond als vastgenageld staan.

p'ō k'i siak tó, ｜起跌倒, resoluut handelen.

p'ō ún, ｜穩, gerust zijn, securiteit hebben.

簿 P'ō̤ Register, boek, koopmansboek.

siaò p'ō̤, 數｜, koopmansboek.

tsóng p'ō̤, 總｜, grootboek.

tsiū p'ō̤, 上｜, boeken, inschrijven.

ts'ut dzip p'ō̤, 出入｜, boek van uitgaven en inkomsten.

tì hè p'ō̤, 置貨｜, magazijnboek.

ts'ó ts'ing ê p'ō̤, 草清｜, kladboek.

dzit ts'ing ê p'ō̤, 日清｜, koopmans journaal.

欂 P'ō̤ *p'ō̤ t'iaō*, ｜柱, pilaren.

㰖 P'ō̤ *tsià p'ō̤*, 蔗｜, suikermolen, suikerfabriek.

p'ō̤ tiá, ｜釜, groote pan om suiker in te koken.

Poa

般 Poa Soort, zaak, ding.

tsit poa iu, 一｜樣, gelijk, niet verschillend.

pah poa, 百｜, allerlei, velerlei zaken.

ts'ing poa bān poa, 千｜萬｜, allerlei dingen.

tsit poa taī, 一｜事, eene zaak.

搬 Poa Verplaatsen, verzetten, van plaats doen veranderen, verhuizen.

poa k'ang, ｜空, leegmaken, leegdragen, (als een vertrek).

poa ts'eh, ｜書, boeken verzetten, verleggen.

poa̤ nong k'ì, | 盡去, met alles verhuizen.

poa̤ ts'ù, | 厝, verhuizen.

poa̤ gū só, | 寓所, van tijdelijke woonplaats veranderen.

poa̤ ke, | 家, verhuizen, zich elders met ter woon vestigen.

poa̤ soá, | 徙, verhuizen.

poa̤ hè, | 貨, lading lossen, uitdragen.

poa̤ ts'ia, | 挺, verzeulen, onderste boven halen.

poa̤ kè tseng, | 嫁粧, de bruids geschenken overbrengen.

poa̤ ing oē, | 閒話, oude niets beduidende dingen ophalen.

演 Spelen, voorstellen, (comedie.)

Poa̤ *poa̤ hì*, | 戲, comedie spelen.

poa̤ hì lâng, | 戲人, comediant.

poa̤ toā ts'ut hì, | 大出戲, groote tooneelvoorstelling geven; groote ruzie hebben.

poa̤ ka tsoah hì, | 蟉蠘戲, kakkerlakken comedie voorstellen, (*d. i.* onbeduidende dingen doen.)

kap i poa̤ kaò oē, 與他 | 至能, iets zoolang met iemand overdoen tot dat hij het kent.

簸 Wannen.

Poà *t'ai poà*, 篩 |, wannen.

poà k'eng, | 糠, kaf uitwannen.

poà ki, | 箕, wan, zeef.

poà soa, | 沙, het zand uit rijst wannen.

○ Stampen, (van een schip.)

Poà

半 Half, helft, gedeeltelijk.

Poà *poà lō*, | 路, halverwege.

poà ló laū, | 老人, van gevorderden leeftijd.

tsit poà, 一 |, de helft.

poà pah, | 百, vijftig.

toā poà, 大 |, de grootste helft.

tùi poà pun, 對 | 分, ieder de helft van iets deelen.

poà bák sa k'oà, | 目相看, een oogje op elkander houden.

poà tsiū lō ē, | 上路坐, halverwege blijven zitten.

poà sìn poà gi, | 信 | 疑, half gelooven en half betwijfelen.

poà sì lâng, | 世人, een halve menschen leeftijd.

poà mi, | 夜, middernacht.

poà tsùi, | 醉, een weinig beschonken, aangewirt.

poà bīn siong sik, | 面相熟, elkander wel meer gezien hebben.

nēng ki poà tsûn, 二枝 | 船, een bark.

poà si poà oáh, | 死 | 活, tusschen leven en dood.

tsiet poà, 折 |, in de helft splitsen (als schuld), 50%.

pe kaò poà t'i, 飛高 | 天, een halve hemel hoog vliegen.

géh poà, 月 |, helft van de maand.

poà ni, | 年, halfjaar, helft van het jaar.

ni poà, 年 |, anderhalfjaar.

kiâ poà lé, 行 | 禮, met halve beleefdheid behandelen (als mandarijnen op private bezoeken).

poà poà ui, | | 桅, kotter.

poà t'aò ts'i, | 粗豪, ruw, onbeschoft.

poà iao pá, 丨 饑 飽, half genoeg gegeten hebben.

poà ts'i sik } 丨 生 熟, halfgaar.
» *ts'e* »

poà t'ong put, 丨 通 不, slechts half ervaren in iets zijn.

poà bák k'ui k'oeh, 丨 目 開 合, een weinig door de vingers zien.

poà t'áng tsui, (of *sui*) 丨 桶 水, slechts ter halve kennis van iets hebben.

p'ah kaò poà sio si, 打 到 丨 小 死, halfdoodslaan.

poà lō tsih pín ta } 丨 路 折 扁 擔
» » » (*pín*)

halverwege breekt de draagstok, *d. i.* halverwege met iets opgescheept blijven.

絆 Poà Valstrik, lasso; vangen, doen struikelen, struikelen.

poà bé soh, 丨 馬 索, lasso.

poà tó lâng, 丨 倒 人, menschen over lijnen doen vallen.

poà tó, 丨 倒, struikelen, over iets vallen.

poà k'a bák, 丨 脚 目, in iets struikelen.

pìn poà, 儐 丨, vriendelijke omgang hebben met.

poà k'a poà ts'iú, 丨 脚 丨 手, tegen voeten en handen aanstooten, *d. i.* in den weg liggen.

盤 Poà Schotel, schaal, bord, blaadje, schenkblad, assiette; zaak, affaire, ambt; markt, marktprijs, een vraag.

t'áng poà, 桶 丨, theeblad.

tsien poà, 煎 丨, braadpan.

kó poà, 古 丨, schaal uit de oudheid.

poà tà, 丨 担, bladen, bakken en manden, (met geschenken.)

kiō tsing poà, 轎 前 丨, bakken (met geschenken die) voor de draagstoel (door bruidegom worden uitgedragen.)

poà tī, poà huì, 丨 費, reisgeld.

siá poà, 寫 丨, schrijfbord, lei.

sìng poà, 筫 丨, rekenbord, abacus.

t'ien ping poà, 天 秤 丨, schalen van een balans.

moá poà, 滿 丨, over het geheel bord, schaakbord *d. i.* geheel en al, alles.

k'a poà, 脚 丨, wreef van de voet.

tsioh poà, 石 丨, vlakte op eene rots.

pō poà, 部 丨, onderbuik.

tsit poà ē sū, 一 丨 事, die eene zaak.

tsing poà, 全 丨, de geheele zaak, de geheele hoeveelheid waren.

kao poà, 交 丨, overdoen, (een ambt of affaire.)

k'ui poà, 開 丨, de markt voor iets openen, een prijs vragen.

kè poà, 價 丨, koopprijs, vraag.

ts'ut kè poà, 出 價 丨, meer dan den marktprijs betalen.

poà k'aó, 丨 口, vraag, prijs, (voor eene factuur goederen.)

poà si, 丨 時, met de teekens van den 12 deeligen cyclus en den datum der maand zijn lot op de vingers aftellen.

踰 Poà Overgaan, overklimmen; te boven, te buiten gaan.

poà kè soa, 丨 過 山, een berg overklimmen.

poà soa kè niá, ｜山過嶺, ver weggaan.
tsuí poà kè hoā, 水｜過岸, het water slaat over den dijk.
kè tsì poà ìh, 過錢｜伊, iemand overbieden.

搬 Poà Van plaats doen veranderen, verplaatsen, overdoen; verhuizen, zie ook *poā*.
poà tsai, ｜栽, overplanten.
poà kè k'a, ｜過缸, in een pot overplanten.
poà kè oá, ｜過碗, van het eene kopje in het andere overgooijen.
poà kè ts'iú, ｜過手, in andere handen overgaan.
poà tsiū tsûn, ｜上船, in een schip overladen.
poà siaò, ｜數, een post overboeken.
poà ts'uì poà tsih, ｜口｜舌, van den een aan den ander overtellen.
poà oē, ｜話, over en weerspreken, redetwisten.
poà poà soá soá, ｜｜徙匕, gedurig verhuizen
poà poà iô iô, ｜匕搖匕, de.

拌 Poà Door elkander mengen, omdraaijen in.
poà t'ing, ｜糖, suiker met meel vermengen.
poà poà. ｜｜, door elkander mengen.

紡 Poà Opleggen, stikken, afzetten, (met band, enz.)
poà bé k'i, ｜尾赳, met punten afzetten (als een zakdoek.)
poà oē, ｜鞋, schoenen stikken, met koord beleggen.

拂 Poā Afvegen, afslaan, uitslaan, uitschudden, schudden met.
poā ing ia, ｜蒙埃, de stof afslaan, afvegen.
poā sa, ｜衣, kleeren uitslaan, uitkloppen.
poā ts'ing k'i, ｜清氣, schoonschudden, uitschudden, (als een stofdoek).
poā sàm t'aò mîng, ｜撒頭髮, de loshangende haren schudden.
iô t'aò poā hī, 搖頭｜耳, verontwaardigd het hoofd schudden.
poā sit, ｜翼, klapwieken.
poā báng, ｜蚊, muskieten uitslaan, wegslaan.
īng ts'iú íng poā lòh k'i, 用手袖｜落去, met de mouw iets op den grond strijken.
tò poā lâng, 到｜人, iemands woorden verdraaijen, verkeerd voorstellen
sì koè poā lâng, 西處｜人, ieder een in zaken betrekken.

破 P'oà Gebroken.
p'ah p'oà, 打｜, breken.
p'oà lih, 劈裂, opengescheurd, opengespleten.
p'oà ts'uì, ｜碎, stukbreken, verbrijzelen.
p'oà k'ui, ｜開, openkloven.
kóng p'oà, 說｜, uitleggen, verklaren, verklappen.
p'oà sìng » (*suì*) ｝｜損, vervallen, stuk, kapot, versleten.
p'oà pò tiàm, ｜布店, voddenwinkel.
p'oà siù » (*siū*) ｝｜相, verminkt, mismaakt.
p'oà tsî, ｜財, geld verliezen bij iets
p'oà iū iū » (*iū iū*) ｝｜爛匕, aan stukken, flarden gescheurd.
p'oà ke, ｜家, zijn huis ten val brengen.

p'oà tsàm, | 譖 } door zijn praten maken dat iemand iets niet doet, iets afraden.
p'oà ts'uì tsàm, | 口 譖
p'oà ts'uì, | 口

p'oà hiàh, | 額. *lett.* het voorhoofd stukslaan, als bedelaars doen.

p'oà noā, | 爛, stuk en verrot, boosaardig, (van vrouwen.)

p'oà p'oà noā noā, | | 爛 匕, versleten en verrot, (van kleêren).

kong p'oà, 攻 |. stuk rammeien.

kiā p'oà tá, *kiā kaò p'oà tā*, 驚 | 胆, 驚 至 | 胆. doodsbevreesd zijn.

t'iah p'oà, 拆 |, stuk scheuren, (als een geschrift) slechten (als een schip, huis, enz.,) eene zaak uit elkander leggen, ontleden.

koé p'oà (*kė*) » } 解 |, eene twist vereffen, de gevolgen er van voorleggen.

p'oà huì tsi, | 費 錢 } geld bij iets verliezen.
p'oà tsi, | 錢

p'oà pī » (*pē*) } | 病, ziekte ongesteldheid.

p'oà ts'ù t'áng, | 厝 桶, bouwvallen van een huis.

p'oà pit, | 筆, voor het eerste leeren schrijven.

p'oà sàm, | 散, stuk en versleten.

p'oà ts'â, | 柴, hout kleinhakken.

p'oà ping, | 平, doormidden hakken, in tweeën gebroken.

p'oà k'ui sim koā, | 開 心 肝, zijn hart voor iemand open leggen.

siū p'oà sim koā (*siō*) » » » } 想 | 心 肝, met uiterste inspanning denken.

peh p'oà sim koā (*pēh*) » » » } 擘 | 心 肝, do.

peh p'oà bīn (*pēh*) » » } 擘 | 面, rond, onbeschaamd voor iets uitkomen.

p'oà lâng ê tāi tsì, | 人 之 事, iemands zaak niet doen gebeuren.

p'oà tsoè nīng kó » (*tsò nō*) } | 做 二 股, in tweeën verdeelen.

p'oà tsui, | 水, een dam van een rijstveld open hakken om er het water te laten uitloopen.

ts'ing k'ì p'oà 穿 棄 |, gescheurde kleederen aan hebben.

tsit kù oē p'oà ì, 一 句 話 | 意, met een enkel gezegde iemands meening in duigen laten vallen.

p'oà tsi iah miā, | 錢 益 命, geld verliezen maar er zijn leven voordeel meê doen.

k'oà p'oà, 看 |, doorzien, (eene zaak).

p'oà hui kim k'áp, | 瓷 金 磕, tegen gebarsten porselein kan men aanstooten als ware het goud, *d. i.* krakende wagens loopen het langst.

判 P'oà *p'oà àn*, | 案, vonnissen, eene zaak, rechterlijk onderzoeken.

p'oà koā, | 官, rechtsgeleerde bij de rechtbanken.

p'oà toàn, | 斷, uitspraak doen, vonnis uitspreken.

sim p'oà, 審 |, oordeelen, vonnissen.

p'oà hàp, | 合, uitspaak doen om weder bij elkander te komen, (van man en vrouw of van kooplieden.)

p'oà k'ui, | 開, uitspraak doen om van elkander aftegaan, te scheiden, (van dito.)

販 P'oā̤ p'oà hè (hoè) } ┃ 貨, kleinhandel drijven.
p'oā̤ hoàn, ┃ 販, in het klein verkoopen om te laten rondventer.
p'oā̤ lai boē, ┃ 來 賣, in het klein verkoopen.

伴 P'oā̤ Genot, medgezel; gezelschap houden, vergezellen.
lâng p'oā̤ ê lâng, 同 ┃ 之 人, medgezellen, kameraden.
lâng k'eh p'oā̤, 人 客 ┃, medegasten.
p'oā̤ k'eh, ┃ 客, gasten gezelschap houden
ū p'oā̤, 有 ┃, in gezelschap.
tsoè p'oā̤, 做 ┃, gezelschap houden. vergezellen.
sūn p'oā̤, 順 ┃, met anderen tegelijk, in ééne moeite doen enz.
p'oā̤ sàng, ┃ 送, een eindwegs vergezellen.
poê p'oā̤, 陪 ┃, gezelschap houden.
sa p'oā̤ kiâ, 相 ┃ 行, te zamen gaan, elkander vergezellen.
p'oā̤ sin niû, ┃ 新 娘, eene bruid uitgeleide doen.
p'oā̤ pao, ┃ 包, zakken voor sieraad, (bij hooge gelegenheden aangedaan.)
p'oā̤ tá, ┃ 胆, moed geven, (als een zwaard bij zich.)
p'oā̤ ts'iú, ┃ 手, *lett.* de hand gezelschap houden, iets nemen alleen om wat in de hand te hebben, (als een waaijer.)

Poah

鉢 Poah poah á, ts'ién poah, ┃ 仔, 淺 ┃, bord, ondiepe kom. (waarin men het bloed van beesten opvangt.)

鈸 Poah Cimbalen, bekkens.

撥 Poah pai poah, 擺 ┃, van eene ander plaats gaan leenen.
i poah, 移 ┃, bij een ander gaan leenen (als winkeliers.)
poah ts'ut, ┃ 出, afnemen van (als van geld.)
poah k'ui tsit pi, ┃ 開 一 邊, ter zijde leggen (van dingen of gesprekken.)
poah kang, ┃ 工, het eene werk voor een ander laten liggen.
poah kang poah p'āng, 乘 暇 竊 隙, van de minste gelegenheid gebruik maken om .....
hun poah, 分 ┃, verdeelen (naar verschillende plaatsen.)
p'aì poah, 派 ┃, over verschillende personen verdeelen.
poah ping, ┃ 兵, soldaten verdeelen, uitzenden.
poah lâng, ┃ 人, menschen uitzenden.

跌 Poáh Vallen, neervallen; omwentelen, verzeulen.
poáh tó, ┃ 倒, omvallen.
poáh loh tsuí, ┃ 落 水, in het water vallen.
poáh loh bé, ┃ 落 馬, van het paard afvallen.
poáh loh bé ê, ┃ 落 馬 者, van zijn paard gevallen zijn, *d. i.* zijn aanzien verliezen.
géh laī poáh loh lai, 月 內 ┃ 下 來, als uit de maan gevallen. (van een fraaije vrouw.)
ts'ia poáh, 倒 ┃, verleggen, verzeulen.
poáh ping, ┃ 反, nergens rust hebben.

poáh ts'iú, ｜手, onhandig doen.

pih poáh, heen en weer woelen. (als een zieke.)

p'ah poáh, 打｜, over en weer dragen, verzeulen; woelen.

敀 Overreden, weerleggen.

Poáh *poáh tó*, ｜倒, overreden, omverpraten.

poáh i kò bò oē, ｜他至無語, zoo weerleggen dat hij niets meer weet te zeggen.

tsing li poáh tó láng, 情理｜倒人, iemand door gezonde taal overreden.

bing poàh, 明｜, duidelijk met iemand overeenkomen.

poáh kun niū, ｜斤両, over het gewicht verschillen; twisten.

賭 Hazardspel spelen, dobbelen.

Poáh

poáh pai á, ｜牌仔, kaartspelen.

poáh taō á, ｜骰仔, dobbelsteenen werpen.

汲 *poáh t'áng*, ｜桶, emmer.

Poáh

卜 *poáh poe*, ｜筊, voorspelling met

Poáh bamboes wortels.

poáh koà, ｜卦, voorspelling met een schilpad.

斗 *tsit poáh hun*, —｜煙, een dot ta-

Poáh bak.

toā poáh hun, 大｜煙, een groote dot tabak.

鈸 *lá poáh*, 鐃｜, cimbalen.

Poáh *poáh kó*, ｜鼓, cimbalen en trommen bij begrafenis gebruikt.

弄 *poáh sai*, ｜獅, kunsten maken.

Poáh *poáh t'ui kui*, ｜槌鬼, verward, vol moeielijkheden.

潑 Werpen in.

P'oah *p'oah tsui*, ｜水, met water gooijen, water uitgooijen, (als over een land).

p'oah hō, ｜雨, door inkomende regen nat geregend worden.

hō tò p'oah dzip lai, 雨倒｜入來, de regen komt dwars in.

掛 Leggen over, (als kleeren over een stoel.)

P'oáh *p'oáh sa*, ｜衫, kleeren over de schouders of over een stoel leggen.

sa p'oáh king, 相｜肩, elkander de armen over de schouders leggen.

p'oáh ts'ing ts'ang, ｜糖葱, (gekookte) suiker uitgooijen en trekken.

p'oàn p'oáh, 盤｜, zich met (bezoekers) onderhouden.

Poan

搬 *poan t'io*, ｜挑, aanzetten tot (men-

Poan schen) tegen elkander ophitsen.

poan sɔ, ｜唆, tegen elkander ophitsen.

poan ts'ùi tsih, ｜口舌 } ma-
poan ts'ùi poan tsih, ｜口舌 }
ken dat iemand nog driftiger wordt dan hij reeds is, het vuurtje aanstoken.

poan t'io sū siong, tot aanklachten aanzetten; tot twist ophitsen.

半 *poàn suī*, ｜癱, verlamming.

Poàn *poàn tsiet*, ｜節, de helft voor iets krijgen van wat het gekost heeft, 50% van iets krijgen.

tsiet poàn, 節｜, do.

POAN

叛 Afvallen, afvallig worden.

Poān *koán poān*, 反 ｜, do.

poān gi̍k, ｜ 逆, oproerig worden, zich tegen het wettig gezag verzetten.

poē poān, 背 ｜, do.

poān ts'ut, ｜ 出, oproerig worden en afvallen.

poān kok, ｜ 國, van het rijk afvallen.

poān kut, ｜ 骨, niet te vertrouwen, (van pers.)

loē poān, 內 ｜, inwendig afvallen, (als de bezettting eener belegerde vesting.)

poān tóng, ｜ 黨, zamenzweerders voor afval.

P'oàn Gezelschap houden, zich onderhouden met, omgaan met.

p'oàn k'eh, ｜ 客, gasten onderhouden.

p'oàn p'oáh, ｜ 掛, zich onderhouden met

p'oàn soàn, ｜ 旋, vriendschappelijke omgang hebben met.

p'oàn tsa bó, ｜ 妻 婦, met vrouwen omgaan.

p'oàn tsú tē, ｜ 子 弟, met zonen van rijken omgaan.

p'oàn tióh hó kaô, ｜ 着 好 猴, met een rijken gast omgaan (van lichtekooien.)

toā p'oàn, sió p'oàn, 大 ｜, 小 ｜, zeer intieme en minder intieme omgang hebben met, (gew. met vrouw)

○ De beenen kruisen.

P'oàn *k'a p'oàn t'ui*, 脚 ｜ 腿, met de beenen kruiselings onder het lijf zitten.

p'oàn t'ui í, ｜ 腿 椅, stoel zonder zijleuning.

POAT

Poat

拔 Poát *ng̍ á poát*, 籃 仔 ｜, guava.

魃 Poát *hān poát*, 旱 ｜, geest van langdurige droogte.

hān poát ts'uì, 旱 ｜ 口, steeds ongeluk verkondigend.

拔 Poát *poát goân*, ｜ 元, de titel van den hoogsten *Lim sing*, uitkiezen, (examinatie.)

poát kòng, ｜ 貢, do. om *Poat kong* te worden.

soán poát, 選 ｜, uitkiezen, (uit menschen of voorwerpen.)

t'ê poát, 提 ｜, iemand opnemen, er boven ophelpen.

kiù poát, 救 ｜, iemand oprapen, optillen.

liên kun poát » *(kin)* », 連 根 ｜, met wortel en al uittrekken.

跋 Poát *poát poát siép siép*, ｜ ｜ 涉 ㄊ, te land en te water gaan.

丿 De trek, P'oat genaamd

P'oat P'iet *p'oat ts'e*, ｜ 叉, oneenig zijn met, overhoopliggen met.

bô poā p'oat » » *(p'iet)*, 無 半 ｜, geen enkele trek kennen; totaal niets waardig zijn.

k'a p'oat ts'ut, 脚 ｜ 出, de voeten dwars zetten.

nēng p'oat ts'iu *(nō p'iet)* », 二 ｜ 鬚, de snor.

潑 P'oat *sat p'oat* / *sàn p'oat*, 撒 ｜, slecht (van vrouwen).

p'oat hū, ｜ 婦, slechte gemeene vrouw, (scheldw.)

p'oat tsiēn, ｜ 賤, slecht, gemeen, (scheldw. tegen vrouwen).

Poe

杯 Poe *tsiú poe*, 酒 丨, wijnglas.
té poe (*tę́*) » 茶 丨, theekopje.

標 Poe *giò poe*, 橈 丨, korte roeispaan.
tik poe, 竹 丨, plak, (van de meesters.)
poáh poe, 筊 丨, met orakel blokjes gooijen.
siū poe (*siō*) » 聖 丨, orakelblokje in den vorm van een halve maan.
tsit siū poe » (*siō*) » 一 聖 丨, wanneer een orakelblokje op de platte zijde en het andere op. de bolle ligt dan hebben de goden het gebed verhoord.
im poe, 陰 丨, de beide orakelblokjes liggen op den platten kant.
ts'iò poe, 仰 丨, de beide orakelblokjes liggen op den bollen kant.
k'iā poe, 豎 丨, op den kant staan, van een orakelblokje.

輩 Poè *sien poè*, 先 丨, voorgaande geslacht.
tsit poè, 此 丨, tegenwoordige geslacht.
hō poe, 後 丨, nakomende geslacht,
laó tsien poè, 老 前 丨, ouder, van vroeger geslacht.
hā poè (*hō*) « 下 丨. daaropvolgend geslacht.
tióng poè (*tiáng* ») 長 丨. voorgaand geslacht.
pi (of *ping*) *poè* (*pę*) » 平 丨, van gelijken leeftijd of rang.

陪 Poè Gezelschap houden, vergezellen, omgang hebben met.
poè làng k'eh, 丨 人 客, gasten gezelschap houden.
kao poè, 交 丨, omgaan met.
poè p'oā, 丨 伴, gezelschap houden.
hōng poè, 奉 丨, do. vergezellen (bel. term).
sit poè, 失 丨, neem het mij niet kwalijk dat ik U alleen laat, (tot zijne gasten gezegd.)
poè sàng, 丨 送, uitgeleide doen.
poè pó, 丨 補, het te kort komende er zelf bijleggen.
poè tsoē, 丨 罪, eene beleediging goed maken (door een feest enz.)
poè lé, 丨 禮, door geschenken enz. eene beleediging goed maken.
poè ts'àn, 丨 襯, iets meer doen uitkomen.
poè tsám, 丨 斬, een minder schuldige vóór zijne verbanning enz. bij de onthoofding van den hoofdschuldige doen tegenwoordig zijn.

培 Poè *poè ióng* » (*ió*) 丨 養, opvoeden, opleiden.
tsai poè, 栽 丨, verzorgen, opvoeden, (kinderen.)

背 Poē Oproerig, afvallig worden, den rug keeren naar.
poē poān, 丨 叛, do.
poē pún kok, 丨 本 國, zijn vaderland verraden.
poē làng é un » » » (*in*) 丨 人 之 恩, ondankbaar zijn.
poē gī, 丨 義, den rug naar het betamelijke keeren, ondankbaar zijn.
hoán poē, 反 丨, den rug toekeeren, afvallig worden.

悖 Poē *poē gik*, 丨 逆, do.
poē biū, 丨 謬, niet overstemmen, overeenkomen, niet de ware beteekenis, ondankbaar.

狽 Poē *liông poē*, 狽 |, in verval, achter-uitgang, armoedig.

poē kut, | 骨, niet te vertrouwen, on-oprecht.

焙 Poē *taī poē*, 大 |, *Taī-poē* thee.

poē á, | 仔, mindere soort *Taī-poē*.

信 P'oe Brief.

p'oe sin (*p'e*) » } 書 |, brief.

p'oe lông, | 囊, enveloppe.

p'oe k'ak, | 殼, do.

tsip p'oe, 追 |, door een brief terug-roepen.

p'oe p'é, | 皮, buitenste adres op een brief.

kià p'oe, 寄 |, een brief verzenden.

tsaù p'oe, 走 |, een brief per cou-rier zenden.

p'oe gûn, | 銀, geld dat bij eene brief gezonden wordt.

lō poe, 路 |, open briefje.

tiēn p'oe, 佃 |, leenbrief, leencon-tract.

p'oe sìn ong lai, | 信往來, correspondentie.

kià p'oe ê lâng, 寄 | 之人, correspondent.

siá p'oe p'e, 寫 | 皮, een adres op een brief schrijven.

批 P'oe P'e Aanmerking maken op, critiséren; zijn besluit over een brief of verzoekschrift geven, dit besluit of antwoord zelve; aanteekening, randteekening.

p'oe pok, | 駁, verandering in het besluit van een lageren brengen.

p'oe p'ing, | 評, iemand critiseren, het kwade in hem zeggen.

p'oe tsún, | 准, goedkeurend ant-woord.

p'oe gú, | 語, inhoud van het ant-woord op een vezoekschrift.

p'oe tsiò, | 照, haven uitklaring.

pông p'oe, 傍 |, handteekening.

tsóng p'oe, 總 |, nabericht, (in een boek.)

剖 P'oe Horizontaal afsnijden.

p'oe bah, | 肉, vleesch dun snijden.

īng to p'oe tiòh, 用刀 | 着, met een mes afsnijden.

p'oe tsoéh » (*tséh*) } | 截, dun snijden en fijn hakken.

臉 P'oé P'é *ts'uì p'oé* » (*pé*) } 嘴 |, koonen, wangen.

k'a ts'ng p'oé, 脚穿 |, de billen.

oai p'oé, 歪 |, scheeve wang, scheef-gezicht.

配 P'oè Bevatten, passen aan, toevoegen aan, verdeelen over.

p'it p'oè, 匹 |, passen bij, (als man en vrouw.)

m̄ p'oè, 不 |, niet bij elkander pas-sen.

p'oè ts'in, | 親, tot vrouw geven aan . . . .

p'oè ts'ah, | 插, gelijkmatig ver-deelen, (als bloemen van verschillende kleuren.)

p'oè sik, | 色, de bij elkander pas-sende kleuren nemen.

p'oè háp, | 合, bij elkander, wat bij elkander past.

sù p'oè, 四 |, evenredig, gepropor-tioneerd van grootte zijn, inverhouding zijn.

hoat p'oè, 發 |, verdeelen op, zijne plaats aanwijzen.

sì miā p'oè ih, 性命 | 伊, een moord met zijn leven boeten.

稗 P'oè. Onkruid tusschen het graan.

Poh

薄 Poh. Dun, slap als thee, tinblad.

póh póh, | |, weinig beduidend.

bī póh, 味 |, weinig smaak, (aan iets).

kim póh, 金 |, goudblad.

tâng póh, 銅 |, koperblad.

póh póh ê lé, | | 禮, weinig beduidende beleefdheid, gierig geschenk, (door den schenker van iets gezegd.)

póh tún á tsi, | 盾仔錢, 8ste dollar.

póh tsiú, | 酒, lichte wijn.

tām póh, 淡 |, weinig.

lóh póh, 落 |, al minder en minder worden.

póh p'ê » (*p'oê*) } | 皮, licht beschaamd, kleinzeerig.

p'iā póh, 淡 |, zwak niet sterk.

soe póh (*se*) » } 衰 |, dun verspreid.

k'iu póh, 淺 |, onverdraagzaam.

ts'ēng pòh poh, 穿飄 |, zich dun aankleeden.

粕 P'oh. Grondsop, wat na het aftrekken overblijft.

tsià p'oh, 蔗 |, suikerriet vezels, uitkauwsel.

tsiú p'oh, 酒 |, uitwringsel van wijn.

ioh p'oh, 藥 |, afgetrokken medicijnen.

té sim p'oh, 茶心 |, afgetrokken theebladen.

ts'o p'oh, 粗 |, grof van gestalte.

k'ioh lâng ê tsao (of *sai*) *p'oh*, 拾人之屎, iemands mest oprapen, *d. i.* iemands idée stelen.

kaū oē p'oh, 厚話 |, veel maar nonsense spreken.

p'oh p'oh, | |, saploos, smakeloos.

bô beh p'oh ting ih (*bóh ts'iù* » ») } 不做探伊, bemoei U niet met hem, laat U niet met hem in.

ts'iù p'oh, 㩲 |, zich met iets inlaten, bemoeien.

Pok

駁 Pok. Discutéren, weêrleggen, tegenspreken, twistredenen; eene fout vinden in, aanmerking maken op; overschepen, overladen; springen (als drooghout.)

piēn pok, 辯 |, discutéren, weêrleggen.

pok i bô oē, | 他無語, zoo weerleggen dat iemand niets meer te zeggen heeft.

p'oe pok, 批 |, verandering brengen in het besluit van een lageren.

pok hîng ih, | 還伊, terug zenden (het niet deugende).

pok kè tsûn, | 過船, in een ander schip overladen.

pok hè, | 貨, goederen overladen.

pok á tsûn, | 仔船, laadboot.

𤖢 Pok. *pok k'ang*, | 孔, een gat in iets maken, een zaak doen uitlekken.

pok ts'ut lai, | 出來, uitspringen, (als glas uit een raam.)

熇 Pok *ïng ké pok bi*, 用 火 丨 米, rijst droog in een pan heeten.

北 Pok Noord.
tong se lâm pok, 東 西 南 丨, de 4 windstreken.

卜 Pok *pok koà*, 丨 卦, het orakel raadplegen, waarzeggen.

薄 Pók *pók gūn*, 丨 岸, steenen dam.
pòk lé, 丨 禮 } onbeduidend, (van een
pók ì, 丨 意 } geschenk.)
pók tsing, 丨 情, onhartelijk.
pók hò iû, 丨 荷 油, pepermuntolie.
tūm pók, 淡 丨, stil, eenvoudig van aard.
k'ing pók, 輕 丨, onbezadigd.

僕 P'ok *lō pók*, 奴 丨, slaaf.

縛 Pók *sok pók*, 束 丨, in elkander gedrongen, zich niet kunnen verroeren.

博 P'ok *p'ok hák*, 丨 學, geleerd.
p'ok kó, 丨 古, ervaren in de oudheid kunde; kleine vaas (antiquiteit.)
t'am p'ok, 貪 丨, veel houden van, gaarne eten.

凸 P'ok *p'ok p'ok*, 丨 丨, opgekruld.

朴 P'ok *p'ok sít*, 丨 實, eenvoudig, niet opgesmukt.

踼 P'ok *sim koa p'ók p'ók*, 心 肝 丨 丨, kloppen van het hart door vrees enz.
p'ók p'ók ts'ing, 心 跳, sterke hartklopping.
p'ók p'ók t'iaò, 丨 七 跳, springen, spartelen.

瀑 P'ók *p'ok p'ok haó*, 丨 丨 吼, kabbelen van het water.
p'ók pò tsoân, 丨 布 泉, waterval.

p'ah p'ók á, 打 丨 仔, in de handen klappen.

P'ok *p'ók á*, 丨 仔, proppenschieter.

爆 P'ók *p'ah p'ók á*, 打 丨 仔, proppenschieter afschieten.
p'i p'i p'ók p'ók, 丨 丨, Knetteren (als brandend hout.)

滂 P'ók kletteren in het water.

Pong

榜 Póng *póng gán*, 丨 眼, middelste graad van *Han-lin*.
póng siú, 丨 首, het hoofd eener afkondiging, (als de eerste bij een examen.)

帮 Póng *póng uì*, 丨 桅, eene mast dikker maken door aan de kanten palen aan te brengen.

謗 Pòng Vergrooten, grooter op geven dan het is.
huí pòng, 毀 丨, belasteren.
iao giên hui pòng } 妖 言 毀 丨,
» (*gàn*) » » } leugens vertellen.
hong pòng, 風 丨, een valsch gerucht. (dat zich alom verspreid.)
pòng hoán, 丨 反, valschelijk zeggen, dat er ergens oproer is.
soè pòng toā } 小 丨 大, vergrooten,
(*sè*) » » } bluffen.
ū pòng bò, 有 丨 無, zeggen dat het niet zoo is terwijl het werkelijk zoo is.
kè tsi pòng pòng k'i, 價 錢 丨 匕 起, de prijs stijgt schielijk.
pín pín pòng pòng, het geluid van vele voetstappen; ook van kanonschoten.

旁 *siù siú pòng koan* } 袖 手 丨 觀,
» (*ts'iú*) » » }

niet de handen in zijn mouwen staan te kijken, als of het hem niet aanging.

pông pien, | 邊, omstanders.

pông p'oe (» *p'e*) } | 批, kantteekeningen, (in Chin. boeken.)

pọng k'ao tsik kik, | 敲 側 擊, iemand niet recht streeks maar zijdelings tot iets aanzetten.

pông kong, | 胱, waterblaas, (bij menschen).

pông sū, | 事, lett. kamerzaken; de bijslaap (bel. term).

Unster; met een unster wegen.

pōng tsí, | 子, gewichten van een unster.

pōng ts'ioh, | 石, balans van een unsterarm.

pōng poā̤, | 盤, weegschaal van een unster.

pōng hè, | 貨, waren met een unster wegen.

ts'iong pōng, 猖 |, onvoorzichtig, onbesuisd.

tsoáh tsit pōng, 差 一 |, het verschilt veel.

pōng pōng kiò, | 乜 呌, geluid van voetstappen over eene holle plaats.

tsit p'óng á, 一 | 仔, een handvol.

p'óng, met beide handen opscheppen.

póng tsui, | 水, water met de handen opscheppen.

p'óng sai kọ bīn, | 屎 糊 面, zich zelven schaamte op den hals halen.

siang ts'iú p'óng, 雙 手 |, met beide handen opscheppen.

棒 P'óng *tin p'óng toé* (» » *té*) } 籐 | 底, rottingen onderlaag (in een bed.)

tin p'óng, 籐 |, baleh baleh, rottingen onderlaag.

p'ín p'óng, 誇 張, bluffen, overdrijven.

凸 P'òng Bol, convex, opgezwollen.

p'òng k'í, | 起, uitspringen.

p'òng sim, | 心, schuitjes geld.

p'òng kiạ̀, | 鏡, mikroskoop.

p'òng song, | 鬆; van grooten omvang, wijd uit elkander.

p'òng hún, | 粉, blanketselmeel.

p'ọ̀ng hong, 脹 風, winderig, (in de buik.)

sim koa̤ p'òng toā bú é, 心 肝 | 大 拇 个, groot opzwellen van het hart, *d. i.* zich groote winst voorstellen.

p'óng kè (» *kẹ̀*) } | 價, overvraagde prijs.

p'òng ts'ú, | 鼠, eekhorentje.

p'òng kóng, | 管, bol staan, opgezwollen, opzwellen, als een zeil door de wind, bladderen, (als verw.)

p'òng p'ā, | 胞, een blaar trekken.

p'òng dzī nèng, | 膩 膿, opzwellen van den onderhuid.

p'òng ling, | 乳, door de moedermelk opgezwollen, bol, (als jonge kinderen.)

p'òng ting, *pòng tioh i è ting*, | 丁 | 着 他 個 丁, tegen iemands spijker aankomen, *d. i.* hem over iets willen spreken op een oogenblik dat hij niet goed gehumeurd is.

p'òng tsō hoà, | 造 化, kans, avontuur, toevallig.

p'òng soe ōng, | 衰 旺, van het toeval afhangen.

p'òng tioh, | 着, onvoorziens ontmoeten, tegenkomen.

p'òng tioh lâng ê bé t'aô, | 着 人 之 馬 頭, tegen iemands paardenkop aanstooten, *d. i.* iemand die reeds knorrig was aanleiding tot toorn geven.

p'òng ūn k'ì, | 運 氣, van het geluk, toeval afhangend.

P'ong *p'ah p'în p'ông siû*, zwemmende met de handen op het water slaan.

p'ông tsit ê, ploffen (van een voorwerp dat in het water valt.)

Pu

富 Rijk.

Pù *pù lâng*, | 人, rijk mensch.

pù tsiâ t'i (» *tsiō* ») | 成 天, uiterst rijk.

pù siā, | 鄉, rijk dorp.

t'àn kaò pù, 賺 到 |, veel geld op iets verdienen.

ēm pù nî iā pù géh, 不 | 年 也 | 月, al is het geheele jaar niet rijk (overvloedig) er zijn toch rijke maanden (door landbouwers gezegd.)

pù hō, | 戶, rijke families.

炮 Heeten, in de asch braden.

Pù *pù kaò âng âng*, | 至 紅 紅, rood gloeijen.

pù lát tsí, | 栗 子, kastanjes in de asch braden.

匏 *pû á*, | 仔, kalabas.

Pu *pû hia*, | 靴, schepper van een kalabas gemaakt.

hô lô pû, 葫 蘆 |, kalabas; liegen, leugenachtig.

tsiáh pû bô laû tsíng, 食 | 不 留 種, kalabas eten en de pitten niet bewaren, *d. i.* niet voor de toekomst zorgen.

堆 Hoop, stapel.

Pû *tsit pû gû sai*, 一 | 牛 屎, een hoop koemest.

tsoè pû, 做 |, allen tegelijk, in eens.

sio hé pû, 燒 火 |, een vuurstapel aanleggen.

tsoè tsit pû, 做 一 |, op een hoop liggen.

婦 *sim pū* (*sin* ») 媳 |, behuwddochter.

Pū *sun sim pū* (» *sin* ») 孫 媳 |, neef's vrouw.

抱 Bedekken als een kip hare eijeren, broeien, uitbroeien.

Pū *pū nñg*, | 卵, eieren uitbroeien.

pū koe á, | 雞 仔, tot kuikens uitbroeien.

pū ah, | 鴨, eenden (eieren tusschen stroo) uitbroeien.

tsoè pū, 做 |, broeisch zijn.

菢 *ts'uì á pū pū*, 嘴 仔 | |, knorrig, boos, den mond dichthouden.

Pū *aò pū pū*, 惡 | |, boos, stilzwijgen.

pū noā, | 沫, schuim op den mond krijgen (als krabben of kinderen.)

tsìm kaò pū pū pū, 浸 到 | | |, doorweekt (zoo dat het opgezwollen en zacht is.)

甫 *t'i p'ú kng*, 天 | 光, het aanbreken van den dag.

P'ú *t'i p'ú p'ú á bē kng*, 天 | | 未 光, aanbreken van den dageraad.

埔 P'ù Grauw, grijsachtig.

p'ú sik, | 色, grijs van kleur.

Muf, beschimmeld.

si̱ p'ú, 生 |, beschimmelen.

ts'aò p'ú bí; 臭 | 味, muf van smaak.

bàk tsiu phú phú, 目 | 匕, zwakke oogen, door ouderdom, ziekte enz.

bàk tsiu beh phú beh phú, 目 將 | 將 |, oogen beginnen onduidelijk te zien, van ouderdom.

P'ú *p'ú ts'àng*, tooi, opschik, uiterlijke praal.

浮 P'ù Drijven, rijzen, zwellen, vlot worden, drijvend, niet vast, onzeker; oppervlakkig, uitstaand, uitsteken, uitspringen.

p'û tsioh, | 石, drijfsteen, puimsteen.

p'û tsui, | 水, op het water drijven.

tsui-tī̱-tsûn-p'û, 水 漲 船 |, is het water hoog dan raken de schuiten vlot, een onmiddelijk gevolg van iets.

p'û sū, | 嶼, eilandje.

p'û kiò, | 橋, hangbrug.

ts'uì k'i-p'û, 嘴 齒 |, de kiezen zijn gerezen, gezwollen.

p'û tsing, | 腫, opzwellen.

p'û t'aô k'i lai, | 頭 起 來, er bovenop komen, toenemen (in handel.)

p'û soa, | 沙, drijfzand.

k'i p'û soa̱, 起 | 線, een uitstekend bandje aanbrengen (als aan meubelen.)

p'û ku, | 居, tijdelijke woning.

p'û p'û iò iò, | | 搖 搖, waggelen, schommelen.

p'û p'iò, p'û p'û p'iò p'iò, | 漂, | 漂 漂, licht, rank; niet sekuur, onzeker, (als handel); onsoliede (van menschen.)

p'û tāng, | 重, bruto gewicht.

p'û dzī, | 字, uitstaande, verheven uitgesnedene karakters.

p'û hûn, | 痕, uitstekende streep, rand.

p'û tia̱, | 定, handgeld dat weer teruggenomen kan worden.

p'û siaò, | 數, voorloopige opteekening van goederen die niet zeker verkocht zijn.

p'û p'ō, | 薄, boek waarin wordt opgeteekend welke waren uitgegaan maar nog niet zeker verkocht zijn.

葡 P'û *p'û tô tsiú*, | 萄 酒, druivenwijn.

p'û tô ts'i̱ (ts'e̱), 萄 | 青, purperkleurig.

p'û tô (p'ô) », | 萄, druiven.

p'û tô koa̱, | 萄 乾, rozijnen.

P'ū *p'ū p'ū pe (» » poe)*, fladderen, vliegen als witte mieren.

P'ū *bê-p'ū k'i lai (moe̍ » »)*, de rijst borrelt op (kookt.)

Puh

發 Puh Ontspruiten, als zaad.

puh i̱, | 薏, do.

puh k'i, | 齒, tanden krijgen.

puh p'ā, | 胞, een blaar trekken.

puh p'éh (» p'oéh), | 沫, opborrelen.

puh ting, | 燈, opborrelen (als water.)

puh kóng á, | 管 呵, opborrelen (in het water.)
puh gê (» *gé*) } | 芽, ontspruiten.
puh liép á, | 粒, puistjes krijgen.
sì koè teh puh (» *kè* » ») } 四 處 |, overal ontspruiten, oprijzen (van puistjes, ook van dieven).
puh ìm, | 蔭, een bloemknop krijgen.

吹 Uitblazen met den mond.
P'uh *p'uh hūn*, | 烟, rook uitblazen.
p'uh dzip k'ì, | 入 去, inblazen in . . . .
p'uh ióh hún, | 藥 粉, poeder in iets blazen, in den mond enz.

堆 *tsit p'úh t'ǫ*, 一 | 土, een hoop aarde.
P'úh *tsit p'úh nā t'ē nịh*, 一 | 若 水 母 也, eene massa als een zee-kwal (van logge dikke menschen.)
tsit p'úh ǫ ǫ, 一 | 烏 烏, een zwarte massa (in donker.)
tsit toā p'úh, 一 大 |, een groot, gezet mensch.
bīn hàm p'úh, 面 腫 |, opgezwollen van gelaat.

Pui

拔 *puí k'í lai*, | 起 來, uithalen,
Puí uittrekken (als een haarspeld uit het haar, minder sterk dan puih.)

痱 *pùi á*, | 仔, puistjes door de warmte
Pùi veroorzaakt, roode hond.
hoat pùi á, 發 | 仔, warmte puistjes hebben.
ts'iu pùi, 秋 |, herfstpuistjes.

dziet pùi, 熱 |, warmtepuistjes.

肥 Vet.
Puî *puî p'àng*, | 胖, gezet, zwaarlijvig.
puî ts'ân, | 田, vruchtbare grond.
puî péh, *puî puî péh péh*, (*pẹ́h* » » » » ») } | 白 | | 白 白, vet en blank.
puî nîng (» *nńg*) } | 軟, vet en zacht.
puî toē (» *tē*) } | 地, vette, vruchtbare grond.
puî sio noā, | 熳 爛, vet, warm en zacht (goed, lekker eten.)
puî pùn, | 糞, mest en vuilnis.
ìng puî, *ak puî* / *hē* », *ŏh* » / (*hẹ̄* » ») } 壅 | 沃 |, bemesten, mest opbrengen.
kaoh puî, ○ |, tot verrotting, mest overgaan.
puî ti, | 猪, vet varken (tegen logge menschen gezegd),
puî bah, | 肉, vet, vet vleesch.
puî tsui, | 水, vet, sappig (van vruchten.)
hit é sọ́ tsaī k'ah puî, 彼 所 在 更 |, deze plaats is vetter, bloeijender.

吠 *puī*, , blaffen.
Puī *kaó puī*, 狗 |, de hond blaft.
sám puī, *loān puī*, 滲 | 亂 |, dom weg blaffen.
ngdọh ngdọh puī, 爻 爻 |, grommen (van honden), mompelen, (van menschen.)

唾 *p'ui noā̤* / *(p'oè »)* ┃涎, speeksel, spuwen.
P'ui

p'ui t'âm, ┃痰, slijmen, slijmspuwen.

p'ui t'âm p'ui noā̤, ┃痰┃涎, om op te spuwen (uit minachting) laag, slecht (van iemands reputatie.)

p'ui huih / *(» toeh)* ┃血, bloed spuwen.

p'ui hiet kák, ┃棄去, uitspuwen.

p'ui ih / *(poè »)* ┃他, in het gezicht spuwen, verdrukkken.

p'ui p'iák ih / *(» o »)* ┃樸伊, iemand beleedigen, (lett. in het gezicht spuwen en gooijen.)

p'ui noā̤ tsièm tiēn, ┃涎占殿, spuwende zich eene plaats toeëigenen, (van kinderen), do. over een koop in besprek zijn zonder handgeld te geven.

屁 *pàng p'ui* / *(» pui)* 放┃, een wind laten, do. bangmaken.
P'ui

pàng kuí á p'ui, 放鬼仔┃, leugenachtige taal.

tsit tè ná p'ui t'at m̄h, 一箇若┃塞耳, klein van persoon.

p'ui bīn / *(» p'ui)* ┃面, onbeschaamd.

p'ui t'aô p'ui bīn, ┃頭┃面, niettegenstaande men reeds beleedigd is nog met iemand willen spreken; zonder het minste gevoel van eer.

Puíh

拔 *puih* / *(pèh)* , met geweld uittrekken.
Puíh

puih k'í, ┃起, uitplukken.

puih kun / *(» kin)* ┃根, met wortel en al uithalen.

oê puih, / *(ê »)* 鞋┃, schoenhoorn,

puih oê / *(» ê)* ┃鞋, schoenen aantrekken.

puih tiaò o̤ / *(pèh »)* ┃吊湖, aan de putpomp trekken.

puih kièm / *(pèh »)* ┃劍, het zwaard trekken.

t'oa t'oa puih puih, 拖┃┃┃ lang op elkander moeten wachten om voort te gaan.

pī puih / *(pe̤ »)* 掀┃, gelijk trekken (als een kleed.)

puih sa̤ á ku / *(péh) (ki)* ┃衫仔裾, aan de panden van een kleed vasthouden (niet van zich willen laten afgaan.)

k'ui tsī puih tsoâ̤, 開井┃泉, iemands nering wegnemen.

sing li k'it i puih k'i, 生理被他┃去, zijne nering door iemand ontnomen worden.

sa̤ puih k'eh, 相┃客, elkanders klanten aftrochelen.

抽 *puih tàng soà*, ┃銅線, koperdraad trekken.
Puíh

Pun

分 Verdeelen, deelen (in rekenkunde.)
Pun *pun hō̤*, ┃與, deelen met . . . .

pun k'ui, ┃開, verdeelen, splitsen, scheiden.

pun p'oe, ┃信, brieven uitdeelen.

pun tsai, ┃栽, uitplanten. (als rijst.)

pun lī, ┃離, van elkander afscheid nemen.

PUN

pun pi }
(» *pi*) } ｜平, gelijkelijk verdeelen.

pun ping, ｜平, in tweeën verdeelen.

pun ke hé, }
» (*ke hóe*) } ｜家伙, de bezittingen verdeelen.

pun tsiáh, ｜食, bedeelen.

pun ts'iū oé, ｜樣鞋, door de bruid gemaakte schoenen onder de familie verdeelen.

ū pun tiu, 有｜讓, mededeelzaam zijn (van kinderen.)

tsiaò pun, 照｜, volgens elks deel.

pun gù t'iah t'ui, ｜牛折腿, een spreekwoord. Zie *t'ui*.

本 Pún — Wortel; stam, oorsprong, aanleidende oorzaak, oorspronkelijk, in den grond; eigen, eigenste, zelf, tot zich zelven behoorend; hoofdsom, kapitaal; numerale voor boekdeelen.

pun toē, ｜地, inlandsch.

pún kok, ｜國, vaderland.

pún ke, ｜家, geboorteplaats,

pún lai, ｜來, oorspronkelijk.

pún dzién, ｜然, do.

pún goàn, ｜源, do.

goàn pún, 源｜, do.; het oorspronkelijke, zelfde boekdeel.

poē pún, 背｜, tegen zichzelven inzijn, zijn vaderland verzaken.

pún sin, ｜身, zelf, in eigen persoon.

pún lâng, ｜人, de eigenste man, de man zelve.

kò pún, 顧｜, voor zijn eigen zaken, belang zorgen.

pún hūn, *pún tsit*, ｜分｜職, plicht.

pún tóe, ｜底, oorspronkelijk.

P'UN

pò pún, *ti un pò pún*, 報｜, 知恩報｜, een weldaad vergelden.

pún koa, ｜官, de mandarijn bij wien men behoort.

pún géh, ｜月, de tegenwoordige maand.

pún sú, *pún lng*, ｜事｜領, bekwaamheid.

pún tsi, *pún bu*, ｜錢｜母, kapitaal.

siáo pún to li, 少｜多利, veel interest van een klein kapitaal.

sit pún, 失｜, geld verliezen, er geld bij toeleggen.

toā pún, *sió pún*, 大｜小｜, evenredig grooter of kleiner.

k'ui pún, 貴｜, zijn kapitaal moeten aanraken.

tāng pún, 重｜, veel geld vereischend, kostbaar.

tsaò pún, 奏｜, een verzoekschrift aan den keizer inzenden.

tsit pún ts'eh, 一｜書, één boekdeel.

ts'iú pún, 手｜, verzoekschrift, visitekaartje aan hoogeren.

h pún sin, 爾｜身, gijzelve.

pún sik sai iū, ｜色西洋, grijze shirtings.

kun pún }
(» *kin*) } 根｜, vaste bezitting.

糞 Pùn — *pùn sò*, ｜掃, vuilnis.

pùn sò tui, ｜掃堆, vuilnis, mesthoop.

pùn sò tsûn, ｜掃船, vuilnisschuit.

pùn taò, ｜斗, vuilnisschop.

loh pùn, 下｜, bemesten.

pui pùn, 肥｜, mest en vuilnis.

kaoh pùn, ◯ 丨, tot verrotting overgaan (van vuilnis.)

pùn ki, 丨 箕, mest-aarde mandje.

pùn k'aó, 丨 口, aars, anus.

pùn ki beh k'iù ū hī ē (» » *boeh* » » » ») 丨 箕 要 楸 有 耳 兮, voor aardmandjes moet men zulken nemen die ooren hebben, *d. i.* voor onbekenden moet men securiteit nemen.

吹 Pùn Blazen.

pùn pi á, 丨 口 吹, fluiten (op een mondfluitje.)

pùn lìng, 丨 冷, koelblazen.

pùn tōng siao, 丨 洞 簫, blazen (op een muziekinstrument.)

pùn tát á / *pùn p'in á* 丨 笛 仔, fluit spelen.

pùn po lē, 丨 玻 璃, glasblazen.

pùn lē, 丨 螺, horenblazen (als vleeschverkoopers.)

pùn ts'e, 吹 茄, de klarinet blazen.

pùn ts'ut, 丨 出, aspireren, met eene aspiratie uitspreken.

k'uì pùn ts'ut, 氣 丨 出, uitademen.

k'uì pùn dzìp, 氣 丨 入, inademen.

pùn tàng, 丨 筒, blaaspijpje om glas te blazen enz., erwtenblazer.

pùn hong, 丨 風, opblazen, do. in korten tijd opschieten (van menschen en beesten.)

pùn hé, 丨 火, vuur, een vlammetje uit- of aanblazen.

pùn tóh, *pùn hoa*, 丨 灼 丨 熄, aanblazen, uitblazen.

taī tsì si koè pùn, 事 四 處 丨, eene zaak overal rondbazuinen.

笨 Pūn Nalatig, lomp, plomp (van lichaam), onpraktisch (van voorwerpen)

pūn ti bú (» » *bó*) 丨 猪 母, logge zeug (van een log mensch gezegd.)

ts'ún pūn, 蠢 丨, log, onvoorzichtig, onbesuisd.

ts'o̱ pūn, 粗 丨, grof en lomp.

pūn ts'ing, 丨 松, dom en oninschikkelijk.

tiong pūn, 中 丨, tusschendeks.

siang pūn ē tsûn, 双 丨 之 船, een schip met twee dekken.

pūn ting, 丨 頂, halfdek, op het dek.

潰 P'un Rijstwater.

p'un tai, 丨 滓, bezinksel van rijstwater.

sτng p'un (*sui* ») 酸 丨, zuur rijstwater, spoeling.

奔 P'un *p'un tsáo*, 丨 走, verward wegloopen, rondzwerven.

p'un p'o, 丨 波, rondzwerven (als zeelieden.)

sì lō̱ p'un soà, 四 路 丨 散, naar alle kanten wegvluchten.

p'un song, 丨 喪, zich naar de plaats van een sterfgeval spoeden.

滚 P'ún *p'ah p'ún*, 打 丨, spartelen.

lām sám p'ún, 濫 滲 丨, roekeloos gebruiken (kleêren, geld enz.)

灑 P'ùn Spatten.

p'ùn tioh, 丨 着, bespat worden door...

p'ùn hō̱, 丨 雨, door regen nat gespat worden.

hoa p'ùn, 花 丨, fraai, sierlijk.

p'ùn noā ts'iu, 丨 涎 鬚, spatten uit den mond (onder het spreken.)

p'ùn seh hoe, 丨 雪 花, het sneeuwt.

p'ùn tion t'ǫ, |着土, door aarde slijk bespat worden.

p'ùn kim, |金, met goud bespikkelen.

kap i p'ùn tiém, 與他|點, iemand bespikkelen, *d. i.* iemand met eenige geschenken lekker maken.

tsiaò p'ùn tioh, 齊|着, allen iets (van zijne rijkdom) mededeelen (als eene mandarijn die rijk bij zijne familie terugkeert.)

盆 P'ùn *bīn p'ùn*, 面|, waschkom.

hoe p'ùn (*hoa* ») 花|, bloempot.

lim p'ùn, 臨|, in barensnood zijn.

p'ah p'ùn, 打|, flodderen (als kinderen), voor de aardigheid doen, van tijd tot tijd ook eens gebruiken zonder er eene gewoonte van te maken (als het rooken van opium.)

p'ùn king, |景, dwergplanten, waaraan bepaalde vormen gegeven zijn, bloemen in potten.

p'ah hì p'ùn, 打戲|, voorstellingen uit de hel geven.

kiáo-k'og p'ùn k'aó, 賭看|口 bij het dobbelen zien aan welken kant de beste kans voor dien dag is.

Put

不 Put Niet.

put tsi, |止, zeer . . . .

put tsi hó, |止好, zeer goed.

put tsi tát tsi̱, 甚值錢, zeer duur, kostbaar.

put gi, |宜, onbetamelijk.

put gī, |義, ongepast.

put lūn, |論, zonder in aanmerking neming van . . .

put lūn sim mih (» » *mi̱h* ») |論甚麽, wat ook.

put lūn tī tsit si, |論在何時, onverschillig wanneer.

put lūn tī tsit é, |論那個, onverschillig wie.

put lūn ta lóh sǫ tsaī, |論那個所在, waarook, onverschillig waar.

put pit, |必, niet mag men.

put bién, |免, onvermijdelijk.

put tik i, 不得已, do.

put kò, |過, slechts, maar.

put dzit, |日, in korten tijd.

put ì, |意, onverwachts.

put k'u (» *k'i*) |拘, onverschillig, het komt er niet op aan.

扒 Put *put soa*, |沙, zand met de beide handen bij elkander strijken.

put pùn sò, |糞掃, vuil opvegen.

ts'in ts'iū put gûn (» *ts'iō̱* » *gin*) 如|銀, (zooveel verdienen) alsof men het geld opschepte.

hām hǫ̂ put, 含糊|, voor de hand wegstrijken (als vruchten enz. zonder uit te kiezen.)

佛 Pút *pút kaò* (*hút* ») |教, boeddhisme.

pút (*hút*) , boeddhistische afgoden.

pút á t'ǒ (*ang*» ») |仔土, klei.

ts'eng pút (» *hút*) 粧|, afgodsbeelden maken.

ná pút nih, 如|的, als een afgod oprecht, zonder listen.

hē̱ pút } *(hē̱ »)* } 許 ｜, aan een afgod bidden.

pút tsō̱, ｜ 祖, de godin Koan-im.

pút sià̱, sià̱ pút, ｜ 聖 聖 ｜, heilige afgod.

oáh put, 活 ｜, (als) een levende afgod.

tiong hō̱ ná̱ pút nḁ̂h, 忠 厚 如 ｜, oprecht als een Boeddha.

hē sin t'ok pút, 許 神 托 ｜, zeer vurig bidden.

斫 Neèrvellen, neèrsabelen.

P'ut *p'ut ts'iū ki*, ｜ 樹 枝, snoeien (boomen.)

p'ut liaó liáó, ｜ 了 了, geheel en al afsnoeien, opmaken (van zijne bezitting.)

lām sám p'ut, 濫 滲 ｜, niet goed hakken (van timmerlieden), roekeloos gebruiken.

p'ut p'ut tiò, spartelen, springen.

Sa

摸 Tasten, rondtasten, bij elkander krabben,
Sa strijken.

lām sám sa, ts'ìn ts'ái sa, 濫 滲 ｜, 隨 便 ｜, in den blinde rondtasten, nemen wat het eerst voor de hand komt.

àm bong sa, 暗 ｜, in donker rondtasten.

iao sa la, 飢 ｜ 拉, van honger alles eten wat voor de hand komt.

sa liáh, ｜ 拿, rondzoeken en vatten.

sa la tsiáh, ｜ 拉 食, kwistig eteu (zonder aan zuinigheid of betaling te denken.)

sa bò liâo á mìng, ｜ 無 寮 仔 門, lett. de deur van de hut niet kunnen vinden, in haast of verwarring niet weten wat te doen.

sa tsoè tsit pé, ｜ 做 一 把, bij elkander strijken.

sa tsi̱ gùn, ｜ 錢 銀, overal geld zien te leenen.

bò tè t'ang sa, 無 地 可 ｜, nergens kunnen krijgen (waren, geld enz.)

摳 *sa k'í*, ｜ 起, oplichten. opnemen (zijn
Sa kleed.)

砂 *dziaò sa* } *(naò se̱)* } 磠 ｜, ammoniak zout.
Sa

沙 *sa* } *se̱* } familienaam.

Sa *sa lòng*, ｜ 籠, sarong.

栅 *sa lân*, ｜ 欄, houten omheining (gew.
Sa voor mandarijnbureau.)

衫 Jas, kleed.

Sa̱ *té sa̱*, 短 ｜, hemd, overkleed.

tîng sa̱, 長 ｜, lange jas.

moâ̱ sa̱, 麻 ｜, hennepen kleed, begrafenis kleed.

hà sa̱, 孝 ｜, rouwkleed.

sa̱ á bín, ｜ 刡, kleerenborstel.

sa̱ á kè } *(» » kè̱)* } ｜ 架, kapstok.

sa̱ á láng, ｜ 籠, vuilegoed's mand.

k'ùn sa̱, 睡 ｜, slaapjas.

ka sa̱, 鉸 ｜, een kleed knippen.

三 Drie.

Sa̱ *sa̱ tsàn*, ｜ 層, derde verdieping.

sa̱ bé tsit tìng hê, ｜ 尾 一 段 蝦, slordig en verkwistend

62

sa ki ui, | 枝桅, driemastschip.

sa làng beh sì láng t'ó bô hūn, | 人欲四人討無分, drie menschen willen het hebben en vier kunnen er geen deel van krijgen, *d. i.* iedereen is er maar al te graag op.

tsaì sa kóng, 再三說, herhaaldelijk zeggen.

tsaì sa kám siā, 再 | 感謝, herhaaldelijk dankbetuigen.

sa kóng nīng hē (» » *nō̤ hoē*) | 言二止, zich herhaaldelijk verontschuldigen.

sa k'a tu, | 脚猪, leugenachtig.

liàh sa k'a tu, 掠 | 脚猪, zich van de beantwoording van iets afmaken.

sa k'a bé (» » *bé*) | 脚馬, op drie pooten, (een schraag.)

sa sim nīng ì (» » *nō̤* ») | 心二意, van gelijke gezindheid.

sa pó lak dzīn, | 保六認, vele getuigen.

sa kóng sì īm tióh, |說四不着, gedurig, geheel en al de plank mishebben.

相 Wederkeerig, elkander.

Sa *sa p'ah*, | 打, vechten.

Sio *sa tsi* (» *tse*) | 爭, vechten, twisten, wedijveren, den strijd strijden.

sa k'iú, | 扭, worstelen.

sa t'ià, | 愛, elkander beminnen, wederkeerige liefde.

sa ts'am, | 雜, door elkander mengen.

sa tsi k'ioh (» *tse* ») | 爭拾, om iets grabbelen.

sa su, | 輸, eene weddingschap aangaan.

sa tú tióh, | 遇; elkander ontmoeten.

sa kià baī (» » *maī*) | 寄候, naar elkanders gezondheid laten vragen.

sa háp, | 合, vereenigen, overeenstemmen.

sa soà, | 續, opvolgen, het eene op het andere.

sa liên (*sio* ») 相連, vereenigen, bijvoegen.

sa kap, | 合, gezamenlijk.

sa kap kia, 同行, gezamenlijk loopen, elkander vergezellen.

sa kap k'iā, 同居, te zamen wonen.

sa kap k'aó tsaò, 同口灶, te zamen eten.

sa tsì (*sio tsè*) 相諍, redetwisten.

灑 *siao sá* (» *soá*) 瀟 | , opgeruimd, in zijn

Sá schik zijn.

sá t'oat, | 脫, levendig, zich niet zoo aan beleefdheid houdend.

Sá *sá sū*, waarom? *sá mih*, wat!

Sà Grijpen, vangen, (als naar muskieten grijpen.)

Sah

煠 Koken, (als eieren.)

Sáh *sáh koe nīng*, | 雞蛋, eieren koken.

sáh sik, | 熟, gaarkoken.

sáh poà ts'i sik (» » *ts'e* ») | 半生熟, halfgaarkoken.

péh sáh kaó t'aô, 白 | 狗頭, lett. een hondenkop alleen koken, *d. i.* steeds nederig lief zijn al wordt men zelfs beleedigd.

sa sáh, kap i sáh } (*sio* » » » ») } 相｜, 與他｜, met iemand raadplegen, praten over.

kap i siao sáh, 與他相｜, met iemand over iets praten, (als over den prijs.)

sah lai sah k'ì, ｜來｜去, onzamenhangend, van de hak op de tak springen.

sah tióh hong, 感着風, koude vatten.

sah iá, ｜影, naar de schaduw grijpen, *d. i.* onwaarheid spreken.

sah hô sin, ｜蝴蠅, een vlieg vangen.

him sah tióh tik kóng, 熊｜着竹管, de beer grijpt de bamboestok, *d. i.* sterk verlangen iets te hebben.

sah tióh pak tó pi, ｜着腹肚邊, een stomp, duw in de zijde krijgen.

sah ih, ｜伊, iemand foppen, voorgeven iemand iets te hebben zien doen om de waarheid uit hem te lokken.

sah k'ùi, ｜氣, aan den grond als vastgenageld staan.

sah sim, ｜心, plotseling ontstellen (als bij een doodsbericht.)

put tsi sah, 不止｜, sterk verlangen naar iets hebben.

sah sah haó, 匕｜吼, sterk om iets verzoeken, verlangen.

Sai

Baas, meester, geverseerd in een vak.

sai hū, ｜阜, baas, werkman.

bák sai, 木｜, timmerman, timmermansbaas.

sai á, ｜仔, leerling, leerjongen.

sai hia tī, ｜兄弟, leermakkers.

sai hū pō, ｜阜步, meesterstuk, meesterlijk, listig.

kóng oē ū sai hū, 說語有｜阜, meesterlijk, listig spreken.

bē òh sai sing òh sùt, 未學｜前學術, voordat men baas wil worden moet men de manieren leeren.

sai kong, 道士, Taöistische priester, toovenaar.

獅 Sai Leeuw; groot.

tsióh sai, 石｜, steenen leeuwen, (bij tempels of offergebouwen.)

hé sai, 火｜, leeuw van vuurwerk.

hong sai, 風｜, windleeuw, (steenen leeuw op huizen gezet.)

lāng sai, 弄｜, een leeuw voorstellen (bij processien.)

ū t'aô sai bô bé laô, 有頭｜無尾樓, wel een voor- maar geen achtersteven, niet in volkomen orde.

hô sai kaó, 鬍｜狗, langharige hond; nieuwsgierigaard.

iô sai, 搖｜, schuddebollen, (van kinderen.)

t'ai sai, 殺｜, den leeuw dooden, *d. i.* over een zaak beraadslagen.

tsiú sai, tê sai, 酒｜, 茶｜ groote wijn, theedrinker.

p'ī t'aô sai sai sai, 鼻頭｜｜｜, groot van neus.

西 Sai West, westelijk, het westen van waar het Boedhisme naar China gekomen is.

sai iû, ｜洋, de wester oceaan, Portugal, Europeesch.

sai pak hō, ｜北雨, NW. regen, regenbui.

sai pak tsoè liáo tsiah hè lâm (» » » » » (*hoé* »)) 丨北做了方向南, toen de NW. wind over was kwam een Z. wind, *d. i.* van boos weder goed worden.

sai iû̠ pò̠, 丨洋布, shirtings.

sai koe, 丨街, de weststraat.

dzit lóh sai, 日落丨, de zon gaat in het westen onder.

îng sai iû̠ (*ui̠* » *iô*) 黄丨洋, gele shirtings.

sai sì, *sai bīn*, *sai hᵉng*, 丨方, het westen.

dzit ts iâ sai (» *siâ* ») 日斜丨, de zon gaat in het westen onder.

kiâ̠ tang k'ì sai, 行東去丨, overal heengaan.

sai t'i̠ kò lò hàn, 丨天告羅漢, (even dwaas als) in de Boedh. taal de *lohàn* te gaan aanklagen, *d. i.* tegen aanzienlijken is het moeilijk iets te doen.

私 Sai — Privaat.

sai k'ia, 丨已, privaat, egoïstisch, zelfzuchtig.

犀 Saí — *sai gû*, 丨牛, rhinoceros.

sai gû bāng géh (» » » *goeh*) 丨牛望月, als een rhinoceros die naar de maan uitziet, *d. i.* sterk naar iets verlangen.

使 Saí — Bevelen, in zijn gebruik hebben; gebruiken, zich bedienen van, behoeven; verbruiken, verteren, onkosten.

saí kúi i pī̠, 丨鬼醫病, een duivel zenden om eene ziekte te genezen, *d. i.* eene zaak nog erger maken.

ts'e sai, 差丨, zenden, bevelen.

sai ts'at, 丨漆, verven.

bô gû saí bé, 無牛丨馬, h[...] men geene koe dan bedient men [...] van een paard, *d. i.* bij gebrek [...] het eene gebruikt men het ander[...]

sai sō, 丨唆, aanhitsen, verleiden.

saí lō̠, 丨路, omkoopen.

saí sìng, 丨性, driftig.

sai t'aô ts'i̠, 丨頭爭, met [...] hoofd stompen.

saí ts'iú hoe, 丨手花, met [...] handgreep doen.

sai tò k'ao k'i, 丨到鉤刺, [...] weerhaak gebruiken, *d. i.* eene [...] om den arm houden.

kâ̠ tsiáh kâ̠ sai, 敢食敢丨, alles verteren wat men verdient.

saí p'aì, 丨派, zich opsmukken, [...] dosschen.

saí kien sik, 丨見識, verstand, [...] streek bij iets gebruiken.

oē sai til, 可丨得, het is te [...] bruiken, het gaat.

īm sai, 不丨 het behoeft niet, onn[...] dig.

mi̠h sai, 麽丨, waarvoor zou men [...] het doen? het behoeft niet.

hé iū sai kòng, behoeft men dat nog zeggen?

sai an ni̠ si̠, 何用如此, waar[...] toch zou men het doen? het is onnood[...]

sai tsoá, 丨紙, papier gebruiken, [...] branden.

sai ts'uì ts'iok, 丨嘴錯, met [...] mond (niet inderdaad) doen.

sai īng, 丨用, gebruiken, verbruike[...] onkosten.

駛 Saí — Een schip besturen, zeilen.

sai tsûn, 丨船, zeilen.

sai tog p'àng, ǀ 單 篷, met één enkel zeil zeilen, *d. i.* slechts één goed kleed hebben.

saí ts'ia, ǀ 車, wagen mennen.

屎 Mest, drek; overblijfsel, vuil.

Saí *sai hák*, ǀ 礐, mestput, geheim gemak.

sai t'áng, ǀ 桶, mestemmer.

sai kun, *sai pò*, *sai tè*, ǀ 巾, ǀ 布, luier.

sai pi tsiù, ǀ 比 醬, mest bij soja vergelijken, *d. i.* een domme bij een kundige vergelijken.

bīn boah sai, 面 抹 ǀ, onbeschaamd.

tsit tō sai, 一 肚 ǀ, een nietswaardig mensch.

ts'aò sai kè, 臭 ǀ 計, domme list.

ts'oah sai ping, 瀉 ǀ 兵, schijtebroeken, (van soldaten.)

boē sai m kui àng, 賣 ǀ 不 全 甕, mest niet bij een geheelen pot verkoopen, *d. i.* geen geld hebben om iets degelijks te doen.

tām póh sai bé, 淡 薄 ǀ 尾, een weinig overschot.

hī sai, 耳 ǀ, oorvuil.

bák sai, 目 ǀ, tranen.

tsik sai, 燭 ǀ, vuil van de kaars.

k'iep sai, 㩼 ǀ, onmeededeelzaam.

史 *sai* / (*sú*) , familienaam.

Sai *p'ah sai eh* / (» *o*) » , de hik hebben.

婿 *ang saì*, 翁 ǀ, echtgenoot, man.

Saì *lú saì* / (*lí* ») 女 ǀ, schoonzoon.

kiá saì, 囝 ǀ, behuwdzoon, schoonzoon.

sin saì, 新 ǀ, bruidegom.

bē saì / (*boē* ») 妹 夫, jongēre zuster's man.

sun saì, 孫 ǀ, man zijner nicht, (oomszuster.)

賽 *saì tsu*, ǀ 珠, valsche paarlen.
Saì

曬 *saì tai*, ǀ 臺, vlak (bordes) boven een huis, dakvlak met een koepeltje er op.
Saì

祀 *hoe kan gō saì*, 花 矸 ǀ, bloemvazen, kandelaars en reukwerkpot, (op 't altaar gezet.)
Saì

殺 *saì biēn* / *bo k'ì* verwerpen, met iets wegdoen.
Saì

hit ê hong siok i king saì k'ì, 此 個 風 俗 已 經 ǀ 去, die gewoonte is reeds verworpen.

事 *hok saī*, 服 ǀ, dienen.
Saī

saī pút, ǀ 佛, een Boeddha beeld ter aanbidding zetten, aanbidden, (ook *ts'aī*.)

saī p'oà noā, ǀ 破 爛, zich moedwillig slordig voordoen (ook *ts'aī*.)

使 *saī* (ook *ts'aī*) *kò ì*, ǀ 固 意, moedwillig.
Saī

姒 *tàng saī*, 娣 ǀ, aangehuwde zusters, (vrouwen van broeders.)
Saī

似 *sik saī*, 熟 ǀ met elkander bekend, kennissen, familiaar.
Saī

Sak

推 Schuiven, stooten, duwen.

Sak *sak lóh*, ǀ 下, neêrduwen.

sak lóh lai, | 下 來, neerstorten.

sak tó, | 倒, omduwen.

sak oá, | 近, aanschuiven.

sak k'ui, | 開, openduwen.

sak k'ì, | 去, wegschuiven, verschuiven.

ts'ia ts'ia sak sak (» » (*siak*) } 奢 匕 | 匕, van den eenen naar den anderen kant geduwd worden (als in een gedrang.)

sak k'ah dzip (*sak* » ») } | 更 入, een weinig inschuiven, indringen, (als een voorwerp dat zou vallen.)

sak lī (*sak* ») } 離, afduwen, (als een boot van strand), vlot (adj.)

sak p'ù, | 浮, vlot (adj.)

sak tsûn, | 船, een schuit voortduwen, vlotduwen.

oe oe sak sak, 挨 匕 | 匕, dringen (in een gedrang.)

sak hō lâng tsē siaò, | 與 人 坐 數, iets aan een ander toeschrijven, de schuld van iets op een ander schuiven.

拂 Sak *báng sak* (» *sut*) } 文 |, voorwerp om muskieten uit te slaan.

sak t'áng (*siak* ») | 桶, dorschkuip, beter *siak*.

sak t'aò (*siak* ») } | 頭, beter *siak*, gedurig met het hoofd knikken, (als kinderen die weenen.)

sak sin (*siak* ») } | 身, beter *siak*, zijn ligchaam afmatten door te zware lasten.

pàng sak (*o*) ») } 放 |, weggooien, laten loopen.

sak báng, | 蚊, muskieten weglaan.

Sam

杉 Pijnboom, pijnhout; hout, timmerhout
Sam *sam ts'à*, | 柴, pijnhout.

sam á, *sam liaō*, | 料, timmerhout.

p'ā sam á, 冇 | 仔, licht poreus hout.

sam pai, | 簰, houtvlot.

sam á liaò, | 寮, houtschuur, loods.

sam hâng, | 行, houtwinkel.

p'ō sam t'aò, 拖 | 頭, de kop (dikste gedeelte) van het hout heet hebben, *d. i.* het moeijelijkste gedeelte voor zijne verantwoording hebben.

三 Drie.
Sam *sam kaò*, | 教, de drie sekten, (Conf., Tao en Boeddh.)

put sam put sù, 不 | 不 四, noch het een noch het ander, niet in orde.

sam put si, 多 少 時, nu en dan, ongelijk.

k'oā sam sik, 看 | 色, de kat uit den boom kijken.

sam sing, | 牲, de drie offeranden, (uit vleesch en visch bestaande.)

sam put hók, | 不 服, niet met elkander harmonieren.

sam háp t'ō, | 合 土, metselkalk.

sam pán, | 舨, sampan, boot.

sam pa lang, | 寶 壟, Samarang.

sam k'i ts'ít kaò siao, | 起 弋 到 銷, alles verloren, even als een pand in een pand in een pandjeshuis.

sam it sam sip it, ｜一三十一, geld onder elkander verdeelen.

sam tsai, ｜才, de drie machten (hemel, aarde en de mensch.

滲 Sám Rondstrooijen met de vingers, (als peper.)

lām sám, 濫｜, onbezonnen, onbesuisd, verkwistend, zonder nadenken, leugenachtig.

sám liēm (*lām* » ») ｜念, raaskallen, ijlen.

sám lai, ｜來, onbehoorlijk, onbesuisd komen.

sám tióh, ｜着, morsen, (van drooge waren.)

sám ioh boáh, ｜藥末, poeder strooijen.

sám hô̤ tsióh, ｜胡椒, peper strooien.

逢 Sàm *t'aô mêng sàm sàm* (» *mô̤*) 頭毛｜｜, verward haar.

p'ah sàm t'aô mêng, 打｜頭毛, met loshangende haren.

dzû dzû sàm sàm (*dzi dzi* » ») 絮七｜｜, verward door elkander, van het haar.

sàm iā̤ iā̤, ｜颺七, in franjes ook in flarden afhangend.

sàm pô̤, ｜線, gerafeld, (als een rouwkleed zonder zoom.)

hô̤ hô̤ sàm sàm, 鬍七｜｜, slordig.

sàm mêng kuí (» *niô̤* ») ｜毛鬼, als een duivel met loshangend haar.

sàm k'ô̤ k'a, ｜褲脚, de broekspijpen buiten de kousen dragen.

p'oà sàm, 破｜, stuk en versleten.

三 am *sàm su*, ｜思, herdenken, overdenken, rijpelijk nadenken.

森 Sàm *lā sàm*, 濫｜, vuil.

lā sàm siáh, 濫｜席, vuil, ook spookachtig.

Sām *sām sām*, in elkander gedrukt, (als oude menschen.)

kòng oē sām lâng, iemand toujouwen, toesnouwen.

San

删 San *san k'ì*, ｜去, uitlaten, (als een zin), verkorten.

san k'ah té, ｜更短, verkorten.

san koé (» *ké*) ｜改, verkorten en verbeteren (als bij eene correctie), uitlaten.

san tsio, ｜少, verkorten, (als een te lange zin.)

星 San *lân san*, 零｜, kleinigheden, overschot, uitschot.

山 San *kang san*, 江｜, stroomen en bergen in een land, rijk.

t'aì san, 太｜, groote berg in Soatang, do. invloedrijke persoon om op te steunen.

san kun, ｜君, vorst van het gebergte, *d. i.* de tijger.

san á àh, roep tegen apen, gelijk ons »kees"!

瘦 Sán Mager, schraal, onvruchtbaar.

siao sán, 消｜ mager, afgevallen.

sán giên, ｜峭, do.

sán gû toā kak, p'oà ts'ù toā mêng ak, ｜牛大角, 破室大門枙, een magere koe heeft groote horens, een vervallen huis heeft groote deurkozijnen, een mensch in vervallen staat.

sán t'iu, ｜抽, mager en lang.

sán toē, ｜地, schrale grond.

sán ts'àn, | 田, schraal rijstveld.

產 Sán Voortbrengen, voortbrengselen; bezittingen, vermogen; baren.

t'ó sán, 土 |, voortbrengselen van den grond.

sing sán, 生 |, kinderen baren.

siaó sán, 小 |, miskraam.

sán bùn, | 門 vulva.

san giëp, *giëp sán*, | 業, 業 |, bezittingen.

tiën sán, 田 |, landerijen, bezittingen.

bút sán, 物 |, vermogen, bezittingen.

散 Sàn Verspreiden, verdrijven.

sàn ioh, | 藥, zweetmiddel.

hoat sàn, 發 |, verdrijven, (als eene gevatte koude.)

sàn tá, | 胆, moedig aan.

tsaî sàn dzîn bòng, 財 | 人 亡, schatten verstrooid en menschen gedood.

sù sàn, 絮 |, verspreiden.

hun sàn, 分 |, zich verdeelen en verspreiden.

sàn-koah ts'iah, onverschrokken, arm.

lòng ien sàn bū, 濃 烟 | 霧, dikke wolken en verwarde mist, *d. i.* benarde donkere omstandigheden

sàn sim, | 心, onverschrokken tot alles in staat.

p'iao sàn ê ióh, 飄 | 藥, zweetmiddel.

put tsí sàn, 不 止 |, onverschokken, do. zeer arm.

Sang

鬆 Sang Slap, los, (niet strak aangehaald.)

sang sang, | 匕, droog, (niet zamenhangend.

k'in sang, 輕 |, licht en los.

pàng sang, 放 |, los laten hangen.

pàng lāng sang, 放 拵 |, do.

sang sang lāng lāng, | | 拵 匕, los, niet stevig in elkaar.

sang sang p'à p'à, | | 冇 匕, los en hol, niet stevig ingestampt.

k'a sang ts'iú lāng, 脚 | 手 拵, los te voet en met de handen zwaaien als wanneer men een vriend te gemoet treedt.

sang p'ò sang p'ò, | 破 | 破, los, niet vastgestampt, (als aarde.)

hoan tsû sang, 番 薯 |, meelig, van aardappelen.

雙 Sang *sang si mêng* (*siang si mui*) | 扇 門, dubbele deur.

sang kó kièm, | 股 劍, snijdende dolk.

tsiâ sang tsiâ tuì (» *siàng* » ») 成 | 成 對, gepaard zijn, een paar uitmaken, (als man en vrouw.)

sang si, | 生, tweelingen.

sang koan ê ì sù (*song* » » » ») | 關 的 意 思, dubbele beteekenis.

k'in k'in á sang k'í lai, 輕 匕 | 起 來, voorzichtig bij elkander schrappen, opscheppen.

p'ò k'a sáng ts'iú (» » *sáng* ») , vleien. zeer in zijn schik zijn.

送 Sàng Geschenken geven, cadeau geven, schenken; uitgeleide doen, uitlaten.

sàng lé, | 禮, geschenken geven.

sàng lé toa, | 禮 單, lijst van geschenken.

hōng sàng, 奉 |, cadeau geven, voor niet geven.

sàng hong, | 風, iemand geschenken bij zijn vertrek geven,

sàng ni̱, | 年, nieuwejaars geschenken geven.

sáng tsoeh, | 節, geschenken op de jaarlijksche feestdagen geven.

sàng tiṉ, | 定. handgeld geven.

sàng dzit, | 日, den huwelijksdag aan de bruidsfamilie mededeelen.

sàng tiṉ, | 錨, het anker uitbrengen met een kleine boot.

ah sàng, 押 |, begeleiden, escorteeren.

hu̱ sàng, 後 |, begeleiden.

sàng tsòng, | 塟, eene begrafenis bijwonen.

sàng k'eh, | 客, bezoekers uitlaten.

sàng kè, | 嫁, eene bruid uitgeleide doen, (door de koppelaarster of oude dienstmaagd.)

sàng kè ḿ, | 嫁 姆, bruidsvrouw.

sàng kè k'ah suí sin niṉ, | 嫁 更 美 新 娘, de bruidsvrouw is fraaier dan de bruid,

sàng sin-tsiṉ t'i̱, | 神 上 天, de geesten uitgeleide ten hemel doen, den 24en dag van de 12e maand.

bé aō sàng, 尾 後 |, bezaanzeil.

sàng dzit t'aò á, | 日 頭 仔, aan de ouders van de bruid een geschrift zenden waarop geschreven staat welke dagen worden voorgesteld voor het huwelijk enz.

宋 Sàng Familienaam.

Sao

Sao *Sao phi*, sarkastisch.
sao i á phi, sarkastisch tot hem spreken om hem beschaamd te maken.

蚩 Klein insekt dat hout eet.

Sao *kim hi sao*, 金 魚 |, insekt om goudvisschen te voeden.

Sao *Sao-sao*, los, onzamenhangend.
Gebarsten, *sao hûn*, gebarsten.
hūm sao, , , gebarsten.

Sao *sao ku̱ i ts'ut láng*, door pappen, een puist tot rijpheid brengen en doen etteren.
sao oá, de gebroken kanten tot elkaar brengen.

嗄 Schor.

Sao *sao siṉ*, | 聲, schor.

消 Krimpen.

Sao *sao hong*, | 風, krimpen, (door de wind zaamgetrokken.)

掃 Saò Vegen, wegvegen; bezem; wegnemen, doen verdwijnen.
saò tē, | 地, den grond vegen.
ts'ing saò, 筅 |, stoffen en vegen.
piṉ saò, 併 |, uithalen en schoonvegen.
saò pùn sò é, | 糞垢者, voddenraper.
saò laò laò k'i, | 流 匕 去, schoon wegvegen, alles opkoopen.
saò tsiú, | 箒, bezem.
tik saò, 竹 |, bamboezen bezem.
t'ih saò tsiú, 鐵 | 箒; ijzeren bezem, *d. i.* onheilaanbrengend.
saò tû, | 除, wegvegen, uitroeijen.
saò hìng, | 興 alle verlangen naar iets wegnemen, (als eene ongelukstijding).

哨 Saò Kruisen, (tegen roovers.)

saò tsûn, | 船, oorlogsjonk, boot om roovers te vatten, kruisboot.
k'oaì saò, 快 |, snelle kruisboot.
ts'ut saò, 出 |, op kruistocht uitgaan.
sûn saò, 巡 |, rondkruisen.
saò ping, | 兵, soldaten van een kruisboot.
saò kak (*siaò* ») } | 角, trompet, hoorn, soort schuiftrompet.

譟 Toejouwen, snauwen; brutaal.
Saò *saò lâng*, | 人, iemand toesnaauwen.
p'ai̱ sia̱ saò, 歹 聲 |, uitjouwen, wegjouwen.

嗽 Verkouden, hoesten.
Saò *k'ām saò*, 咳 |, hoesten.

Saoh

Saóh *saóh saóh liām*, achtereen aframmelen.
ts'è saóh saóh, zeer broos, ritselend (als klatergond.)
saóh saóh á kia̱, langzaam, voetje voor voetje loopen.

Sap

Sap *sap sap*, kruimels.
sap sòe, fijn gruis, kruimels.
iù sap sap, fijn, tot gruis.
tè k'ah sap, de thee is te veel met poeder gemengd.
Sap *hō̱ á sap sap*, fijne regen.
Sap *lap sap*,, liederlijk, vuil.
Sáp *kō̱ sáp sáp*, vuil., smerig, (als iemands baard.)

Sat

虱 Luis.
Sat *sat bú* (» *bó*) } | 母, luis.
bát sat, 木 |, weegluis.
bàt sat ts'iò ts'iū guī, de weegluis lacht om de boomluis; *d. i.* de pot verwijt den ketel dat hij zwart is.
sat pìn, | 篦, luizenkam.
sat pìn t'at, | 篦 托, kammenkrabber.
sat pìn kim, | 篦 金, Japansche kobang.
t'ō̱ sat, 土 |, soort meerval (met platten kop.)
t'ō̱ sat t'aô, 土 | 頭, een plat hoofd
liáh sat, 拿 |, luizen vangen; de zwarigheden uit den weg ruimen.
liáh kiaó sat, 拿 賭 |, alle bedriegerijen bij het dobbelen uit den weg ruimen.
t'ō̱ sat àng (» » *à̱*) } 土 | 甕, een gat met katvisch.

薩 Familienaam.
Sat *pō̱ sat*, 菩 |, Boedh. afgoden.

殺 Dooden, vermoorden; onverschrokken
Sat *hò̱ sat*, 好 |, moordlustig.
tsám sat tsū iû, 斬 | 自 由, macht over leven en dood hebben.
iók kat iók sat, 欲 結 欲 |, van plan zijn iemand te vermoorden
sat ki, | 機, moorddadig plan
kiep sat, 刼 |, uitplunderen en vermoorden; geweldig, sterk als medicijnen.
sat ts'iú, | 手, onverschrokken, (als een chirurgijn.)

塞 Verstoppen, verstopt.
Sat *p'ī̱ sat*, *sat p'ī̱*, 鼻 |, | 鼻, verstopte neus.

[illegible] *sat p'oat, sal naī*, 丨 潑, 丨 奈, boosaardig, slecht (van vrouwen.)

[illegible] *sat bûn*. 番 鹼, zeep, savon.

Se

Se *tsing kah se* (*tsing* » ») , nagelriem.

紗 Zijden gaas, katoen garen.
Se *se iang*, haspel.
se hō (*o* ») , do.
hō se, haspelen.
mi se, 丨 棉, katoen garen.
dziaò se, 縐 丨, krip, floers.
ts'ia se, 車 丨, katoen haspelen.
p'áng se, 紡 丨, katoen spinnen.
se ting (*sē* ») 丨 燈, met katoen bekleede lamp.
tsiang se, 漳 丨, zijden stof uit Tsiang tsioe.
oā se, 換 丨, katoen inruilen.

裟 Se *ka se*, 袈 裟, overjas van een Boeddha priester.

砂 Se *tsu se*, 硃 丨, cinnaber, vermiljoen.
ping se, 硼 丨, borax.

西 Se *se hong*, 丨 方, Indië (Britsch)

稅 Sè Soe Huren, huur, rente, belasting.
ts'ut sè, 出 丨, verhuren.
sè ts'ù, 丨 厝, een huis huren.
sè k'oè (» *kè*) 丨 契, belastingbrief.
t'iu sè (» *soè*) 抽 丨, belasting heffen.
hiòng sè, 餉 丨, belasting, rechten.
pō sè koàn, 報 丨 館, belastingkantoor.
laō sè, 漏 丨, belasting ontduiken, smokkelen.
lō taò sè, 路 頭 丨, kaaigeld.

勢 Sè Sì Macht, gezag, invloed; voorkomen, gesteldheid, toestand, de omstandigheden.
koàn sè, 權 丨, macht, gezag.
ū sin sè, *ū sè lik*, *ū sè t'aô*, 有 身 丨, 有 丨 力, 有 丨 頭, een ruggesteun hebben in iets, iets hebben om zich op te verlaten.
sit sè, 失 丨, zijne macht, invloed verliezen.
uì sè, 畏 丨, voor iemands macht vreezen.
siep sè, 涉 丨, invloedrijken vleier.
k'ò sè, 靠 丨, op zijne macht steunen.
sè lik, 丨 力, macht.
k'oà sè, 看 丨, de omstandigheden afzien.
taī sè, 大 丨, naar alle waarschijnlijkheid.
hó sè (» *si*) 好 丨, goed, geschikt.
sè bīn, 丨 面, voorkomen, toestand,
tē sè, 地 丨, gesteldheid van een land.
t'ok sè bīn, 託 丨 面, aan iemand van grooten invloed opdragen.
sūn sè, 乘 丨, volgens den toestand, de omstandigheid.
níng sè, 軟 丨, zachtzinnig, zonder geweld.
ts'iú sè, 手 丨, de toestand, houding van de hand, (als bij het schrijven.)
k'iâ bé sè, 騎 馬 丨, houding bij paardrijden, met de beenen wijd van elkander.
p'ai sè, 歹 丨, onbetamelijk, niet goed.
sai sè, 使 丨, van zijne macht gebruik maken.

SE

tsai sè lik-tsing } 財 | 力 全,
(» *sì* *tsui*)
schatten, macht en kracht, volledig bezitten.

世 Menschenleeftijd, geslacht, generatie; de
Sè eeuw; wereld, de aarde; erfelijk.
Sì *būn sè*, 萬 |, alle generatiën, door alle eeuwen heen.

sè sū, | 事, wereldsche zaken.

sè tsing taī, | 情 事, eenmaal aangenomen gebruiken.

sè kan, | 間, de wereld, aarde.

sè tsiū è lâng, de menschen op aarde.

sè siók, | 俗, de gewoonte der eeuw; gewoon, alledaagsch.

sè hong; | 風, gewoonten, gebruiken.

sè ka è lâng, | 家 之 人, iemand van oude aanzienlijke familie.

sè tsit, | 職, erfambt.

sè sip } | 襲, erfelijk.
(» *sit*)

細 *sè sim*, | 心, voorzichtig, omzichtig.
Sè *tsú sè*, 仔 |, do.

Sè Afschuiven, afschudden.
sè tsuí, het water afschudden, (van eene parapluie.)

Sè *bōe tsáp sè* } , naaibehoeften, garen en
(*bē* » ») band verkoopen.

Sè *sa sè*, *kap i sè*, elkander niet toegeven.

垂 Nederhangen, slaphangen, nêerbuigen
Sè als de uiteinden van een juk.
Soé *sé sé* } | |, slap, slaphangen.
(*soé soé*)

sè lòh k'i, | 落 去, neêrhangen.

sè bé kaó, | 尾 犬, hond met nêerhangende staart.

hoe t'aô sè sè } 花 頭 | |, de bloem
(*hoa* » » ») hangt neêr.

SE

tàm sé, 俯 |, het hoofd neerhangen van ouderdom.

laō sé } 老 |, de »oude heer",
(*laō tàm soé*) vader.

sé sui, | 鑵, langs de tuit neêrloopen (als bij een trekpot waarvan de tuit verstopt is.)

Sè *nōa sé* } , slabbetje voor kinderen.
(*ām sé*)

Sè *o lièn sé lô ién sé*, rammelaars, tamboerijn's enz. bij processiën.

麝 *sē kaó* } | 犬, muskusdier.
(*siā* »)

Sē *sē lóh k'i* } , langs iets heenglijden,
Sē (*sōe* » ») heenschuiven.

Sē *kiā lō kiā k'i sē lah* } , uitgeput van
(» » » » (*sōe*) ») het loopen.

Sē *sē giò sē giò* } , slaphangend, ver-
(*sè* » » ») flaauwend, langzaam.

誇 *sē miā* } , | 名, naam aan iemand
(*sī* ») na zijn dood gegeven.
Sē

Seh

雪 Sneeuw.
Seh *lóh seh*, 落 |, het sneeuwt.

seh hoe } | 花, sneeuwvlok.
(» *hoa*)

péh seh seh } 白 | |, sneeuwwit.
péh » »)

seh bō, | 帽, windhoed (van kinderen.)

說 Zeggen, spreken.
Seh *seh siā*, *seh to siā*, | 謝, 多 謝,
Soeh dankzeggen, bedanken.

seh oē } | 話, spreken.
(» *oā*)

k'in siā soè seh } 輕 聲 細 |,
(» » *sè* ») zachtjes en omzichtig spreken.

国家出版基金项目
NATIONAL PUBLICATION FOUNDATION

海上絲綢之路文獻集成

總主編　陳支平　陳春聲

科技與文化編 92

主編　王揚宗　葉農

海峽出版發行集團
THE STRAITS PUBLISHING & DISTRIBUTING GROUP
福建人民出版社

本册目次

客法大辭典

（*Dictionnaire chinois-français, dialecte hac-ka: précédé de quelques notions et exercices sur les tons*）

〔法〕賴嘉禄（Charles Rey）編

《客法大辭典》，法國賴嘉祿編。賴嘉祿（Charles Rey，一八六六—一九四三），法國巴黎外方傳教會會士。生於法國里昂，一八八九年來華。此書前含引言、標音説明、語法説明、用法説明等。正文依客家方言羅馬字音節排序，依次羅列漢字字頭、斜體羅馬字拼音、法文字義、漢字例詞例句。末附部首檢字索引，及干支、節氣、民俗節日、親屬稱謂、珠算基礎、度量衡、歷史朝代及國家與地區、常見人名等。據一九〇一年香港版影印。

客法大辭典

DICTIONNAIRE

CHINOIS-FRANÇAIS

DIALECTE HAC-KA

客法大辭典

DICTIONNAIRE
CHINOIS-FRANÇAIS
DIALECTE HAC-KA

PRÉCÉDÉ DE QUELQUES NOTIONS ET EXERCICES SUR LES TONS.

PAR CH. REY

Missionnaire Apostolique du KOUANG-TONG

HONGKONG
IMPRIMERIE DE LA SOCIÉTÉ DES MISSIONS ÉTRANGÈRES
1901

AVANT-PROPOS.

COURTES NOTIONS SUR LE PEUPLE HAC-KA.

I.— Le mot Hac-ka veut dire hôte, étranger.

Les Hac-ka sont donc des étrangers: leur langage, leurs us et coutumes, leur généalogie le prouvent suffisamment.

Ils parlent le mandarin, mélangé de patois. Au cours de leurs pérégrinations, ici leur langue s'est corrompue, là elle s'est enrichie au contact des diverses peuplades qu'ils ont traversées; et les montagnes qu'ils habitent lui ont donné ce cachet spécial et rude, qui la distingue des autres dialectes.

Le Hac-ka est parlé par quatre millions de personnes, dans la province de Canton seulement.

II.—Les Hac-ka ont des mœurs patriarcales; simples, hospitaliers et superstitieux, ils vivent de peu, s'entr'aident dans la bonne et la mauvaise fortune, et gardent avec un soin jaloux le culte des ancêtres.

Obligés de batailler pour se frayer un chemin ou pour se maintenir dans les pays conquis, ils ont un grand attrait pour la boxe et le bâton. Chicaneurs et procéduriers, ils ne reculent pas devant la perte de leurs biens pour gagner un procès et *sauver la face*.

Le costume et les bijoux des femmes et des enfants diffèrent totalement du costume et des bijoux des Poun-ti (本 地) et des Hoc-lo (學 老).

Ce peuple abhorre la mode des petits pieds. Cela prouverait qu'ils ont quitté leur pays d'origine avant que cette mode fût en vogue.

III. — Par leur généalogie on voit que les Hac-ka viennent du Nord de la Chine: trois siècles avant Jésus-Christ, on les trouve dans le Chan-tong (山 東) et le Chan-si (山 西).

Sous la dynastie des Ts'in 秦 (249-209 av. J.-C.), ils furent contraints d'émigrer au Ho-nam (河 南) et au On-fi (安 徽).

Sous une autre dynastie celle des Tsin 晉 (419 ap. J.-C.), une nouvelle révolution les chassa de ces pays, et ils gagnèrent les régions montagneuses du Kiang-si (江 西) et du Fou-kien (福 建).

Au commencement de la dynastie des T'ong 唐 (618 ap. J.-C.), une nouvelle révolution les poussa vers le Sud: les uns s'établirent dans la chaîne de montagnes qui sépare le Kiang-si (江 西) du Kouang-tong (廣 東); les autres cherchèrent un refuge dans l'extrême Nord du Fou-kien (福 建).

Sous la dynastie des Soung 宋 (960-1278 ap. J.-C.), ils se firent soldats, et dans une bataille livrée en 1279 aux Mongols, à l'Ouest de Macao, des milliers d'entre eux trouvèrent la mort avec le dernier prince des Soung.

C'est vers cette époque qu'ils firent leur première apparition sur les côtes de la province de Canton; mais ils ne s'y établirent définitivement que sous la dynastie des Min 明 (1368 ap. J.-C.).

Un changement de dynastie est toujours une cause de troubles et de désordres. Les montagnards du Fou-kien (福建) et du Kiang-si (江西) ne purent que subir les déprédations répétées des soldats des deux partis. Pour en finir, ils résolurent d'aller planter leur tente sur des rivages plus hospitaliers.

Ceux du Kiang-si (江西) passèrent les frontières du Kouang-tong (廣東), et vinrent s'établir dans les sous-préfectures de Lioung-tch'on (龍川), de Hin-nen (興寧), et du P'in-yan (平遠). Ceux du Fou-kien descendirent le fleuve Min (明) et le fleuve de Tchong-tchou (漳州), et, arrivés à la mer, firent voile vers le Sud, s'éparpillant sur toutes les côtes jusqu'aux sous-préfectures de Sin-on (新安) et de Hiong-san (香山), etc. etc.

Les Hac-ka, qui habitaient auparavant la sous-préfecture de Nen-fa (寧化), s'arrêtèrent aux environs de Swatow. Trouvant le pays occupé, ils remontèrent le fleuve de l'Est jusqu'à la ville de Ka-yn-tchou (嘉應州), dont ils firent leur quartier général. Du N.E. du Kouang-tong (廣東) ils se répandirent peu à peu dans les autres parties de la province.

C'est à l'époque de la rébellion des T'ai-p'in (太平) (1850-62) qu'ils furent admis aux examens et aux emplois du gouvernement.

En 1864-66, une guerre cruelle éclata entre les Poun-ti et les Hac-ka; 150,000 de ces derniers trouvèrent la mort sur les différents champs de bataille. Le gouvernement, par d'énergiques mesures, mit fin à ces sanglants combats, et fournit de fortes sommes d'argent à ceux qui voulurent passer dans les régions inhabitées du Kouang-si (廣西), de l'île de Hoï-nam (海南) et de Oui-tchou (圍州).

Aujourd'hui, trop nombreux dans les pays qu'ils occupent, torturés par la faim, et étouffant dans un espace trop resserré, ils n'émigrent plus guère dans l'intérieur de la Chine. Attirés par les mines d'or de la Californie, de l'Australie et du Transvaal, par celles de charbon du Tonkin, et celles d'étain de la presqu'île de Malacca, de Batavia et de Bornéo, ils se fixent dans ces régions.

引言

廣東人民大致三大類曰本地曰客家曰學老各類源流不一而語言亦異此書所載即嘉應州客家之土語此地人民讀字常有兩音一書音一俗音書上見其字則讀之與官話之音相近與同類交言則別其音比如我字別讀作涯或雅你字作愚嘴字作載等皆是更亦間時按事變音變聲譬如那字隨其所指那個或那人或那裡讀秣個或瞞人或奈裡之音上字變爲平聲或上聲隨其所指事義之不同下字被字聽字等亦然

課教西人或別省客商之語師見此書內各字當照土音讀之

土語中有許多無字可表者凡遇此宗話句則用同音之字以代之字旁加一口字示明此字單表其音而無義比如㰺字但取歡字之音而忽其義

學習異國之語言非容易事惟望此小書畧助各位君子以成其功焉

客法大辭典

INTRODUCTION.

I.—Variantes dans la prononciation.

On a souvent contesté l'utilité d'un dictionnaire Hac-ka, à cause des variantes de prononciation dans les divers dialectes. La différence pourtant n'est pas si grande qu'elle paraît de prime abord; on la remarque principalement dans les finales de certains mots, ou bien à la manière plus ou moins dure de rendre les mêmes sons.

Les Chinois n'ayant pour guide que l'oreille et ne connaissant pas notre méthode de fixer les sons par des lettres, prononceront les mêmes voyelles de différentes façons, selon que leur oreille les percevra. Ainsi, à Ka-yn-tchou, le son *a* dans *kian*, ailleurs sera prononcé *kien*; le mot *yan* se changera en *yen* ou *yon;* le son *e* deviendra *i* dans le mot *tchi*, pour *tche*.

On trouve en diverses parties de la France un langage plus ou moins dur; de même on trouvera en Chine une dureté plus ou moins grande, en telle localité plutôt qu'en telle autre. L'*y* à Ka-yn-tchou n'est qu'un *i* mouillé; il sera tellement mouillé, p. ex. à Lioûng-tch'ōn (龍川), qu'il se changera en *j*, dans les mots *jan* ou *jon*, pour *yan* ou *yon*. Dans un autre endroit, la lettre *j* se transformera en *ch*, et l'on dira *tche* pour *tje;* et, par analogie, *tch'i* pour *tche*, *tse* pour *tze*, *ts'e* pour *tse*.—Ailleurs, ce sera le contraire, et l'on ne fera aucune distinction entre les lettres *j* et *z*, comme dans *tze* pour *tje*.

Faisant une étude de la langue de Ka-yn-tchou, on a écrit d'après la prononciation de ce pays, tout en notant les différences.

Les exemples précédents montrent bien que ces différences ne sont pas essentielles et il sera facile de s'y reconnaître.

Il y a des expressions locales, des idiotismes que l'on ne trouvera pas dans cet ouvrage; impossible de faire un livre complet. Puisse ce premier essai, toutefois, servir de canevas aux missionnaires étudiant le dialecte Hac-ka, et leur épargner une partie de leur peine!

2

II. — De l'orthographe.

Chaque langue a une manière particulière de prononcer les mêmes lettres: on reconnaît tout de suite un Anglais parlant français et un Français parlant anglais. Chacun garde son accent. On comprend dès lors que l'orthographe française ne puisse jamais bien rendre l'accent chinois. Il est donc absolument nécessaire de se faire lire les caractères par un Chinois, pour reproduire exactement le son.

Voici quelques remarques et explications nécessaires:

a	o	y	ang	se prononcent comme en français;
oua	ouo	ou	ong	
ya	yo	you	yong	
oung				a un son particulier qu'il faut entendre pour le saisir;
ai	oi	oui		comme dans *aïe*, la langue *d'oïl*, *oui*;
am	an			,, ,, Amérique, analyse.
en	yen	ien		,, ,, ennemi, moyenne.
on	yon	ion		,, ,, bonheur, Bayonne.
e				dans le corps d'un mot, est toujours ouvert.
e				à la fin d'un mot, est toujours muet, comme dans les mots français *je*, *me*, à moins qu'il ne soit pointé (e˙), alors il se prononce comme dans *aimé*.
mg				à peu près comme dans l'*m* finale de *Siam*;
ng				à peu près comme dans l'*n* finale des mots latins *an*, *forsan*;
tch				il faut faire sentir les deux lettres, mais sans siffler.
h initiale				indique simplement une forte aspiration.

Les autres consonnes ont la même valeur qu'en français. Leur aspiration dans le corps d'un mot, est indiquée par une apostrophe.

Il faut remarquer avec soin la manière dont se font les aspirations. Car, si chaque langue a sa manière de prononcer les mêmes lettres, chacune aussi a sa manière d'aspirer.

III. — Des tons.

On distingue six tons représentés par les signes suivants:

1er ton	*chóng p'in*	上平	c.-à.-d.	recto tono élevé	—
2e ,,	*há p̣'in*	下平	,,	,, ,, bas	^
3e ,,	*chóng chăng*	上聲	,,	montant	╲
4e ,,	*k'í chăng*	去聲	,,	descendant	╱
5e ,,	*chóng gnĭp*	上入	,,	rentrant élevé	◡
6e ,,	*há gnĭp*	下入	,,	rentrant bas	⌒

Les tons ne se font pas partout de la même manière, et ne se prononcent pas toujours comme leur dénomination semblerait le faire supposer. Ainsi le 3e ton (chóng chăng), qui signifie « élever la voix,» s'exprime à Ka-yn-tchou en la baissant; le *chŏng p'in*, qui signifie « recto tono,» se fera en élevant la voix. Ailleurs il en sera autrement. Il est donc de toute nécessité d'avoir pour professeur un homme originaire du pays que l'on habite.

La seule difficulté pour arriver à bien parler, c'est d'apprendre à distinguer les tons. Pour cela, il faut les diviser et avoir soin de n'étudier qu'un ton à la fois. Il ne faut pas croire qu'on perde le temps à cette première étude; tout le succès dépend de ce travail préliminaire, qu'on ne saurait assez recommander.

Pendant plusieurs jours, s'il le faut, on se fait lire par un Chinois les caractères dont le mot est marqué par le signe du premier ton (—); et on le répète sans se lasser jusqu'à ce qu'on puisse, ex abrupto, c'est-à-dire, sans trop réfléchir, imiter l'accent et le ton chinois. Alors seulement on passe au deuxième ton, et ainsi de suite.

Cet exercice prolongé sur le même ton fera très bien sentir la différence d'un ton à un autre. Pour se guider, qu'on suive attentivement le mouvement des lèvres de celui qui parle, sans oublier que tous les mots sont monosyllabiques et ne se prononcent que par une émission de voix.

Quand on est capable de saisir tous les tons à la simple audition de l'orateur, on apprend alors des phrases, mais sans en composer jamais soi-même. Ne connaissant pas la tournure chinoise, on parlerait français en chinois, ce qu'il faut absolument éviter.

Il faut écrire d'abord en brouillon les phrases que l'on aura entendues; puis reprenant les mots un à un, les chercher dans le dictionnaire et se faire indiquer le caractère par un Chinois. Le caractère trouvé, on sera fixé sur le sens, le ton et l'aspiration, s'il y en a. En somme, ne jamais apprendre une phrase par cœur, sans avoir bien exactement écrit la prononciation, le ton et l'àspiration. Sans cette précaution, on apprendrait mal, et il serait très difficile de se corriger.

Par cette méthode, certainement suffisante et confirmée par l'expérience, on arrivera à posséder la phraséologie chinoise mieux que toutes les grammaires ne pourraient jamais l'enseigner.

NOTA.—Prendre garde à la prononciation défectueuse de certains Chinois. On en trouve en effet qui prononcent indifféremment *sa* et *cha*; *tsa* et *tcha*; *tsong* et *tchong*; *tje* et *tze*.

IV. — Dernières remarques.

1. — La traduction des mots et des locutions chinoises renfermés dans ce Dictionnaire, n'est pas toujours absolument littérale. On a visé surtout à rendre exactement le sens. Bien des nuances ont dû nous échapper; mais c'est inévitable entre deux langues dont le génie est si différent. Le style de la conversation est très elliptique: on omet souvent le sujet ou le régime du verbe, le sens de la conversation suffit pour faire comprendre. Ainsi, dans beaucoup de phrases, on a mis *je*, *tu*, *il*, un peu au hasard. Le sujet du verbe n'étant pas exprimé en chinois, on pouvait tout aussi bien en sous-entendre un autre.

2. — Le langage populaire ne s'écrit point ordinairement en caractères chinois; la langue écrite est différente, et ceux qui n'ont point étudié la comprennent peu. On a cependant écrit (sauf de rares exceptions) en caractères chinois tous les mots et toutes les phrases de ce Dictionnaire. C'est une vraie traduction; et elle n'était pas sans offrir de nombreuses difficultés.

D'abord, il y a quelques mots de la langue parlée qui n'ont pas dans la langue écrite de caracteres correspondants. Dans ce cas on a employé un caractère qui représente le son plutôt que le sens.

Ensuite on trouve des caractères qui changent de ton, et même de prononciation, dès qu'ils rentrent dans le domaine de la langue parlée. Par exemple le caractère 你 *toi:* tout Chinois, en le lisant, prononcera «*nī*», et en parlant, pour dire, *toi*, il prononcera «*gnî*». Le caractère 我 *moi:* se prononce «*ngō*» en langue écrite, mais dans la langue parlée on dira «*ngaî*». De même les caractères 上 *chóng* et 下 *há* changeront de ton et l'on dira *chōng*, *hā*, ou *chòng*, *hà*, selon le sens.

On pourrait faire la même remarque pour les mots qui sont aspirés en langue écrite et non en langue parlée ou vice-versà. Quand ces cas se présentent, le Dictionnaire donne entre parenthèses le mot tel qu'il se prononce.

Cette remarque était à faire: en effet, le Chinois qui indiquera le caractère, le prononcera certainement dans le langage des livres, et l'on pourrait être surpris de ne pas voir concorder sa prononciation avec celle qui est notée.

Enfin il y a d'autres caractères employés d'une façon si diverse, selon les pays, que l'on rencontrera certainement des contradicteurs. Dans ce cas nous avons choisi le caractère le plus généralement employé dans le district de *Ka-yn-tchou*.

3. — On trouve, dans le langage populaire, une foule de finales dont les unes influent plus ou moins sur le sens, et les autres ne servent qu'à la conson-

nance. C'est par le bon emploi de ces finales que notre parler sera tout à fait correct et plaira aux Chinois.

Ces finales sont des émissions de voix qui varient beaucoup selon les pays. Elles déterminent quelquefois les temps dans les verbes; d'autres fois elles sont une espèce d'article, et souvent sont simplement euphoniques.

Il ne faut pas, dès le principe, trop s'en préoccuper; on risquerait de les employer mal à propos, et alors le langage, au lieu d'être élégant, tendrait au ridicule. Seule une longue expérience peut en faire sentir les nuances, et en donner l'usage régulier.

EXERCICES SUR LES TONS.

Remarque générale.—Se faire lire par le maître, et répéter tout le temps nécessaire, avant de passer au ton suivant.

Sur le premier ton.

燒	*Chāo.*	Chaud.
身	*Chīn.*	Le corps.
傷	*Chōng.*	Blesser.
收	*Choū.*	Recevoir.
花	*Fā.*	La fleur.
番	*Fān.*	Etranger.
飛	*Fī.*	Voler.
灰	*Fōe˙.*	Cendre.
方	*Fōng.*	Carré.
夫	*Foū.*	Aider.
分	*Foūn.*	Partager.
風	*Foūng.*	Le vent.
圩	*Hī.*	Le marché.
香	*Hiōng.*	Parfum.
兄	*Hioūng.*	Frère aîné.
衣	*Ȳ.*	Habit.
烟	*Yān.*	Tabac.
有	*Yoū.*	Avoir.
家	*Kā.*	Famille.
羹	*Kāng.*	Bouillie.
交	*Kāo.*	Livrer.
謙	*K'iām.*	Humble.
輕	*K'iāng.*	Léger.
恭	*Kioūng.*	Respecter.
科	*K'ō.*	Examen.
瓜	*Koūa.*	La courge.
空	*K'oūng.*	Vide.
官	*Koūon.*	Le mandarin.
懶	*Lān.*	Paresseux.
冷	*Lāng.*	Froid.
鑥	*Loū.*	La rouille.
免	*Mēn.*	Dispenser.
尾	*Mī.*	La queue.
母	*Moū.*	Mère.
蚊	*Moūn.*	Le moustique.
拿	*Nā.*	Apporter.
盃	*Pī.*	La tasse.
帮	*Pōng.*	Aider.
西	*Sī.*	Ouest.
箱	*Siōng.*	Boîte.
修	*Sioū.*	Orner.
[illegible]	*T'ām.*	Fade.
刀	*Tāo.*	Le couteau.
傘	*Tchā.*	Le parapluie.
車	*Tch'ā.*	La voiture.
深	*Tch'īm.*	Profond.
眞	*Tchīn.*	Vrai.
吹	*Tch'oī.*	Souffler.
中	*Tchoūng.*	Milieu.
燈	*Tēn.*	La lampe.
添	*T'iām.*	Ajouter.
梯	*T'oī.*	L'échelle.
湯	*T'ōng.*	Bouillon.
吞	*T'oūn.*	Avaler.
尖	*Tsiām.*	Pointu.
千	*Ts'iēn.*	Mille.
親	*Ts'īn.*	Parent.
倉	*Ts'ōng.*	Grenier.
往	*Vōng.*	Aller.
烏	*Voū.*	Noir.

Sur le deuxième ton.

蛇	*Châ.*	Le serpent.
城	*Châng.*	Ville murée.
時	*Chê.*	Epoque.
神	*Chîn.*	Esprit.
常	*Chông.*	Toujours.
薯	*Choû.*	Patate.
浮	*Feoû.*	Flotter.
和	*Fô.*	Concorde.
湖	*Foû.*	Trou.
紅	*Foûng.*	Rouge.
鞋	*Haî.*	Souliers.
寒	*Hôn.*	Froid.
鹽	*Yâm.*	Sel.
羊	*Yông.*	Chèvre.
油	*Yoû.*	Huile.
奇	*K'î.*	Surprenant.
鉗	*K'iâm.*	Pinces.
勤	*K'iôun.*	Diligent.
窮	*K'ioûng.*	Pauvre.
狂	*K'ông.*	Idiot.
藍	*Lâm.*	Bleu.
欄	*Lân.*	Barrière.
鈴	*Lâng.*	Clochette.
涼	*Leông.*	Frais.
連	*Liên.*	Unir.
流	*Lioû.*	Couler.
來	*Lôi.*	Venir.
雷	*Loûi.*	Tonnerre.
埋	*Maî.*	Enterrer.
門	*Moûn.*	Porte.
泥	*Naî.*	Boue.
南	*Nâm.*	Sud.
能	*Nên.*	Puissance.
魚	*Ng.*	Poisson.
牙	*Ngâ.*	Dent.
年	*Niân.*	Année.
牛	*Nioû.*	Buffle.
耙	*P'â.*	Herse.
排	*P'âi.*	Disposer.
棚	*P'âng.*	Baraque.
刨	*P'aô.*	Rabot.
皮	*P'î.*	Peau.
漂	*P'iaô.*	Flotter.
平	*P'în.*	Paix.
賠	*P'oî.*	Restituer.
愁	*Scoû.*	S'inquiéter.
墻	*Siông.*	Muraille.
存	*Soûn.*	Conserver.
桃	*T'aô.*	Pêche.
塵	*Tch'în.*	Poussière.
傳	*Tch'ôn.*	Propager.
長	*Tch'ông.*	Long.
綢	*Tch'oû.*	Soie.
錐	*Tch'oûi.*	Marteau.
虫	*Tch'oûng.*	Insecte.
頭	*T'eôu.*	Tête.
田	*T'iên.*	Rizière.
臺	*T'oî.*	Trône.
堂	*T'ông.*	Temple.
同	*T'oûng.*	Avec.
茶	*Ts'â.*	Thé.
柴	*Ts'aî.*	Bois de chauffage.
泉	*Ts'ân.*	Source d'eau.
晴	*Ts'iâng.*	Serein.
錢	*Ts'iên.*	Sapèque.
從	*Ts'ioûng.*	Depuis.
財	*Ts'oî.*	Richesses.
床	*Ts'ông.*	Lit.
完	*Vân.*	Fini.
圍	*Vî.*	Entourer.
禾	*Vô.*	Riz en herbe.
黃	*Vông.*	Jaune.
無	*Voû.*	Aucun.
文	*Voûn.*	Littérature.

Sur le troisième ton.

啞	*À.*	Muet.
襖	*Ào.*	Habit doublé.
洒	*Chà.*	Asperger.
少	*Chaò.*	Peu.
審	*Chìm.*	Juger.
賞	*Chòng.*	Récompenser.
手	*Choù.*	La main.
火	*Fò.*	Le feu.
府	*Foù.*	Préfecture.
粉	*Foùn.*	Farine.
耳	*Gnì.*	Oreille.
好	*Haò.*	Bon.
起	*Hì.*	Aller.
響	*Hiòng.*	Bruit.
雨	*Ỳ.*	La pluie.
遠	*Yàn.*	Loin.
舀	*Yaò.*	Puiser.
永	*Yoùn.*	Perpétuel.
假	*Kà.*	Faux.
敢	*Kàm.*	Oser.
攪	*Kaò.*	S'amuser.
巧	*K'aò.*	Habile.
狗	*Keòu.*	Chien.
口	*K'eòu.*	La bouche.
己	*Kì.*	Soi-même.
解	*Kiaì.*	Expliquer.
澗	*Kiàn.*	Gouttière.
緊	*Kìn.*	Pressé.
九	*Kioù.*	Neuf.
改	*Koì.*	Corriger.
講	*Kòng.*	Parler.
苦	*K'où.*	Souffrance.
鬼	*Kouì.*	Diable.
捆	*K'oùn.*	Enrouler.
管	*Kouòn.*	Administrer.
欖	*Làm.*	Olive.
老	*Laò.*	Vieux.
李	*Lì.*	Prune.
買	*Maì.*	Acheter.
米	*Mì.*	Riz non cuit.
妙	*Miaò.*	Admirable.
五	*Ng.*	Cinq.
眼	*Niàn.*	Œil.
粄	*Pàn.*	Gâteau.
保	*Paò.*	Protéger.
比	*Pì.*	Comparer.
本	*Poùn.*	Principal.
使	*Sè.*	Employer.
寫	*Sià.*	Ecrire.
想	*Siòng.*	Penser.
打	*Tà.*	Battre.
扯	*Tch'à.*	Déchirer.
轉	*Tchòn.*	Revenir.
主	*Tchoù.*	Seigneur.
寵	*Tch'oùng.*	Grâce.
等	*Tèn.*	Attendre.
斗	*Teoù.*	Boisseau.
妥	*T'ò.*	En sûreté.
賭	*Toù.*	Parier.
採	*Ts'aì.*	Cueillir.
盞	*Tsàn.*	Godet.
草	*Ts'aò.*	Herbe.
走	*Tseòu.*	Marcher.
取	*Ts'ì.*	Extraire.
請	*Ts'iàng.*	Inviter.
酒	*Tsioù.*	Vin.
左	*Tsò.*	Gauche.
總	*Tsoùng.*	En général.
此	*Tsè.*	Cet.
子	*Tzè.*	Graine.
慰	*Vì.*	Consoler.
妄	*Vòng.*	A faux.
穩	*Voùn.*	Solide.
碗	*Vouòn.*	Bol.

Sur le quatrième ton.

暗	*Ám.*	Obscur.
凹	*Aó.*	Gorge de montagne.
赦	*Chá.*	Pardonner.
扇	*Chán.*	Eventail.
是	*Ché.*	Etre.
聖	*Chín.*	Saint.
上	*Chóng.*	Supérieur.
受	*Choú.*	Subir.
順	*Choún.*	Conforme.
話	*Fá.*	Parole.
飯	*Fán.*	Riz cuit.
會	*Fí.*	Société.
放	*Fóng.*	Déposer.
父	*Foú.*	Père.
二	*Gní.*	Deux.
下	*Há.*	Inférieur.
喊	*Hám.*	Appeler.
號	*Haó.*	Numéro.
氣	*Hí.*	Air.
汗	*Hón.*	Sueur.
意	*Ý.*	Intention.
夜	*Yá.*	Nuit.
要	*Yaó.*	Nécessaire.
印	*Ýn.*	Sceau.
樣	*Yóng.*	Espèce.
右	*Yoú.*	Droite.
告	*Kaó.*	Accuser.
彀	*Keoú.*	Assez.
鋸	*Kí.*	Scier.
勸	*K'ián.*	Exhorter.
敬	*Kín.*	Honorer.
救	*Kioú.*	Sauver.
近	*K'ioún.*	Près.
蓋	*Koí.*	Couvercle.
看	*K'ón.*	Regarder.
塊	*K'ouaí.*	Morceau.
貴	*Kouí.*	Noble.
棍	*Koún.*	Bâton.
過	*Kouó.*	Passer.
另	*Láng.*	En outre.
利	*Lí.*	Intérêt.
練	*Lién.*	S'exercer.
亂	*Lón.*	Confusion.
路	*Loú.*	Chemin.
罵	*Má.*	Injurier.
賣	*Maí.*	Vendre.
帽	*Maó.*	Chapeau.
味	*Mí.*	Saveur.
傲	*Ngaó.*	Orgueil.
念	*Niám.*	Réciter.
拜	*Paí.*	Saluer.
辦	*P'án.*	Gérer.
凭	*Pén.*	S'adosser.
鼻	*P'í.*	Nez.
病	*P'iáng.*	Malade.
破	*P'ó.*	Rompre.
舖	*P'oú.*	Boutique.
掃	*Saó.*	Balayer.
字	*Sé.*	Lettre.
笑	*Siaó.*	Rire.
送	*Soúng.*	Accompagner.
道	*T'aó.*	Raison.
蔗	*Tchá.*	Canne à sucre.
正	*Tchín.*	Juste.
臭	*Tch'oú.*	Puer.
銃	*Tch'oúng.*	Fusil.
凳	*Tén.*	Banc.
地	*T'í.*	La terre.
定	*T'ín.*	Certain.
造	*Ts'aó.*	Créer.
就	*Ts'ioú.*	Aussitôt.
賺	*Ts'ón.*	S'enrichir.
位	*Ví.*	Personne.
換	*Vouón.*	Changer.

Sur le cinquième et le sixième ton.

石	*Chăc.*	Pierre.
舌	*Chăt.*	Langue.
蝕	*Chăt.*	Se ruiner.
十	*Chĭp.*	Dix.
食	*Chĭt.*	Manger.
杓	*Chŏc.*	Cuillère.
熟	*Choŭc.*	Cuit.
罰	*Făt.*	Punir.
復	*Foŭc.*	De nouveau.
月	*Gnĕt.*	Lune.
合	*Hăp.*	Unir.
學	*Hŏc.*	Apprendre.
若	*Yŏc.*	Si.
屐	*K'iăc.*	Sabot.
狹	*K'iăp.*	Etroit.
極	*K'ĭt.*	Excessivement.
裂	*Liĕt.*	Déchirer.
力	*Lĭt.*	Force.
落	*Lŏc.*	Tomber.
麥	*Măc.*	Froment.
竻	*Nĕt.*	Epine.
白	*P'ăc.*	Blanc.
別	*P'iĕt.*	Autre.
薄	*P'ŏc.*	Mince.
踏	*T'ăp.*	Fouler aux pieds.
姪	*Tch'ĭt.*	Neveu.
着	*Tch'ŏc.*	Bien.
逐	*Tch'oŭc.*	Expulser.
特	*T'ĭt.*	Exprès.
讀	*T'oŭc.*	Etudier.
雜	*Ts'ăp.*	Divers.
賊	*Ts'ĕt.*	Voleur.
疾	*Ts'ĭt.*	Maladie.
昨	*Ts'ŏc.*	Hier.
滑	*Văt.*	Glissant.
鍋	*Vŏc.*	Poële.
物	*Voŭt.*	Chose, ustensile.
軛	*Âc.*	Joug.
鴨	*Âp.*	Canard.
設	*Chât.*	Proposer.
濕	*Chîp.*	Humide.
識	*Chît.*	Connaître.
遡	*Chôc.*	Aller à l'aventure.
叔	*Choûc.*	Oncle.
闊	*Fât.*	Large.
福	*Foûc.*	Bonheur.
嚇	*Hâc.*	Effrayer.
血	*Hiêt.*	Sang.
殼	*Hôc.*	Ecorce.
約	*Yôc.*	Régler.
隔	*Kâc.*	Séparer.
結	*Kêt.*	Nœud.
曲	*K'ioût.*	Tortueux.
角	*Kôc.*	Corne.
骨	*Koût.*	Os.
瀝	*Lâc.*	Rigole.
蕒	*Mâc.*	Laitue.
惡	*Ôc.*	Méchant.
百	*Pâc.*	Cent.
筆	*Pît.*	Pinceau.
駁	*Pôc.*	Réfuter.
答	*Tâp.*	Répondre.
織	*Tchît.*	Tisser.
著	*Tchôc.*	Vêtir.
粥	*Tchoûc.*	Soupe de riz.
滴	*Tît.*	Un peu.
托	*T'ôc.*	Trier.
啄	*Toûc.*	Becqueter.
摘	*Tsâc.*	Cueillir.
拆	*Ts'âc.*	Démonter.
則	*Tsêt.*	Mesure.
七	*Ts'ît.*	Sept.
桌	*Tsôc.*	Table.
屋	*Voûc.*	Maison.

Combinaison des deux premiers tons.

天堂	*T'iēn t'ông.*	Le Paradis.
金錢	*Kīm ts'iên.*	Bonne sapèque.
宗徒	*Tsoūng t'oû.*	Les apôtres.
新年	*Sīn niân.*	Le nouvel an.
番人	*Fān gnîn.*	L'étranger.
馬媽	*Mā mâ.*	La jument.
間房	*Kiān fông.*	La chambre.
蜂糖	*Foūng t'ông.*	Le miel.
上棚	*Chōng p'âng.*	Monter à l'étage.
聲名	*Chāng miâng.*	Réputation.
爭田	*Tsāng t'iên.*	Se disputer une rizière.
烟筒	*Yān t'oûng.*	La pipe.
花園	*Fā yân.*	Le jardin.
新聞	*Sīn voûn.*	Une nouvelle.
烏蠅	*Voū ŷn.*	Une mouche.
風琴	*Foūng k'îm.*	L'accordéon.
艱難	*Kiān nân.*	Difficile.
肩頭	*K'iān t'eôu.*	L'épaule.
功名	*Koūng miâng.*	Titre d'honneur.
馬蹄	*Mā t'âi.*	Le pied du cheval.
雞啼	*Kē t'âi.*	Le chant du coq.
朝辰	*Tchāo chîn.*	Le matin.
圩塲	*Hī tch'ông.*	La foire.
柱頭	*Tch'oū t'eôu.*	La colonne.
梯牌	*T'ōi p'âi.*	L'escalier.
齋期	*Tsāi k'î.*	Jour d'abstinence.
天晴	*T'iēn ts'iâng.*	Beau temps.
嬰孩	*Ȳn hâi.*	Bébé.
番薯	*Fān choû.*	Patate.
功勞	*Koūng lâo.*	Mérites.
波茶	*Pō ts'â.*	Cuire du thé.
燒紅	*Chāo foûng.*	Rougir au feu.
拿來	*Nā lôi.*	Apporter.
牽牛	*K'iān niôu.*	Conduire le buffle.
灰窰	*Foē yâo.*	Four à chaux.
猪油	*Tchoū yoû.*	Saindoux.
耕田	*Kāng t'iên.*	Labourer les champs.
黃蜂	*Vông foūng.*	Guêpe.
門框	*Moûn k'iōng.*	Monture de porte.
寒天	*Hôn t'iēn.*	Hiver.
頭尾	*T'eôu mī.*	La tête et la queue.
裁衫	*Ts'âi sām.*	Tailler un habit.
來往	*Lôi vōng.*	Allées et venues.
欄杆	*Lân kōn.*	Barrière.
擎傘	*K'iâng tchā.*	Porter son parapluie.
黃蟮	*Vông chān.*	Anguille de rizière.
蝦公	*Hâ koūng.*	Crevette.
墻差	*Siông ts'āi.*	Bâtisse à fouler les murs.
勞心	*Lâo sīm.*	Soucis.
濛沙	*Moûng sā.*	Brouillards.
人家	*Gnîn kā.*	Famille.
圓圈	*Yân k'iān.*	Cercle.
朋友	*P'oûng yoū.*	Amis.
塵灰	*Tch'în foē.*	Poussière.
長衫	*Tch'ông sām.*	Longue robe, toge.
劏猪	*Tchê tchoū.*	Saigner un porc.
良心	*Leông sīm.*	Reconnaissant.
淋花	*Lîm fā.*	Arroser les fleurs.
題經	*T'î kīn.*	Entonner les prières.
銅波	*T'oûng pō.*	Casserole de cuivre.
油罌	*Yoû āng.*	Bouteille d'huile.
名聲	*Miâng chāng.*	Réputation.
調羹	*T'iâo kāng.*	Cuillère.
蛇哥	*Châ kō.*	Serpent.
無終	*Voû tchoūng.*	Sans fin.
全心	*Ts'iên sīm.*	De tout cœur.
傳知	*Tch'ôn tī.*	Propager, faire savoir.
銀錶	*Nioûn piāo.*	Montre d'argent.
洋毯	*Yông tchān.*	Couverture.
常生	*Chông sēn.*	Vie éternelle.
唐山	*T'ông sān.*	Les montagnes de la Chine.
葵花	*K'oûi fā.*	Tournesol.
撈篩	*Leôu fī.*	Filet à pêche.
螺螄	*Lô sē.*	Vis, tire-bouchon.

Combinaison du premier ton avec le troisième.

車眼	*Tch'ā niàn.*	Percer un trou.
公所	*Koūng sò.*	Lieu public.
規矩	*Koūi kì.*	Règlement.
金鑛	*Kīm kouàng.*	Minerai d'or.
恭喜	*Kioūng hì.*	Salut !
番梘	*Fān kiàn.*	Savon.
堅振	*Kiān tchìn.*	La Confirmation.
燒火	*Chāo fò.*	Allumer le feu.
多少	*Tō chaò.*	Un peu.
領洗	*Leāng sè·.*	Recevoir le baptême.
斟酒	*Tchīm tsiòu.*	Verser du vin.
冷水	*Lāng choùi.*	De l'eau fraîche.
辛苦	*Sīn k'où.*	Pénible.
相彷	*Siōng fòng.*	Se ressembler.
相打	*Siōng tà.*	Se battre.
天主	*T'iēn tchoù.*	Dieu.
三斗	*Sām teòu.*	Trois boisseaux.
恩寵	*Ēn tch'oùng.*	La grâce.
癲狗	*Tiēn keòu.*	Chien enragé.
燈盞	*Tēn tsàn.*	Veilleuse.
燈籠	*Tēn loùng.*	Lanterne.
雞爪	*Kē· tsào.*	Pattes de poule.
鍖墩	*Tsēm toùn.*	L'enclume.
拿走	*Nā tseòu.*	Emporter.
天井	*T'iēn tsiàng.*	Cour intérieure d'une
清楚	*Ts'īn tsè.*	Clairement. [maison.
安慰	*Ōn vì.*	Consoler.
往擺	*Vōng pài.*	Autrefois.
釘穩	*Tāng voùn.*	Clouer solidement.
醫好	*Ȳ haò.*	Etre guéri.
偷米	*T'cōu mì.*	Voler du riz.
官府	*Koūon foù.*	Le mandarin.
帮手	*Pōng choù.*	Donner un coup de
歡喜	*Fōn hì.*	Content. [main.
燒酒	*Chāo tsiòu.*	Eau-de-vie.
勉强	*Miēn kiòng.*	A la rigueur.
冤枉	*Yān vòng.*	Vexation.

講書	*Kòng choū.*	Commenter un livre.
水泡	*Choùi p'aō.*	Ecume.
上鞍	*Chòng ōn.*	Mettre la selle, seller.
老兄	*Laò hioūng.*	Mon frère aîné.
請坐	*Ts'iàng ts'ō.*	Veuillez vous asseoir.
挽衫	*Vàn sām.*	Suspendre son habit.
搔癢	*Tsaò yōng.*	Se gratter.
點心	*Tiàm sīm.*	Frustulum.
洗衫	*Sè· sām.*	Laver les habits.
比方	*Pì fōng.*	Pour exemple.
閃開	*Chàm k'ōi.*	Se garer.
講差	*Kòng ts'ā.*	Parler à tort, se trom-
祖公	*Tzè koūng.*	Ancêtres. [per.
火燒	*Fò chaō.*	Incendier, brûler.
幾多	*Kì tō.*	Combien.
老公	*Laò koūng.*	Mari, époux.
水缸	*Choùi kōng.*	Amphore,
耳公	*Gnì koūng.*	Oreille.
火窻	*Fò ts'oūng.*	Chaufferette.
拼傘	*Màng tchā.*	Recouvrir un para-
暑天	*Tch'où t'iēn.*	Canicule. [pluie.
喜歡	*Hì fōn.*	Content.
守貞	*Choù tchīn.*	Observer la virginité.
使車	*Sè tch'ā.*	Conduire une voiture.
轉身	*Tchòn chīn.*	Se retourner.
煑湯	*Tchoù t'ōng.*	Cuire de la soupe.
紙灰	*Tjè foē·.*	Chaux de papier.
早晚	*Tsào vān.*	Matin et soir.
儘多	*Tsìn tō.*	Au plus.
兩両	*Lcòng leōng.*	Deux onces.
點鐘	*Tiàm tchoūng.*	Heure.
酒甖	*Tsiòu āng.*	Bouteille de vin.
水晶	*Choùi tsīn.*	Cristal.
眼珠	*Niàn tchōu.*	Prunelle de l'œil.
寫單	*Sià tān.*	Ecrire une liste.
打交	*Tà kāo.*	Se battre, se bouscu-
走風	*Tseoù foūng.*	S'ébruiter. [ler.

客法大辭典

Combinaison du premier ton avec le quatrième.

端正	*Tōn tchín.*	En vérité.
加增	*Kā tsén.*	Augmenter.
波飯	*Pō fán.*	Cuire le riz.
燒炭	*Chaō t'án.*	Brûler du charbon.
斷氣	*T'ōn hí.*	Rendre le dernier soupir.
坐轎	*Ts'ō k'iáo.*	Aller en palanquin.
懶惰	*Lān t'ó.*	Paresseux.
耕種	*Kāng tchoúng.*	Labourer et planter.
上岌	*Chōng ýn.*	Gravir la montagne.
綱鑑	*Kōng kám.*	Annales.
公道	*Koūng t'áo.*	Juste, équitable.
裝淨	*Tsōng ts'iáng.*	Nettoyer.
驕傲	*Kiāo ngáo.*	Orgueil.
偷盜	*T'eōu t'áo.*	Voler.
番豆	*Fān t'eóu.*	Arachides.
方便	*Fōng p'ién.*	Avantageux.
恭敬	*Kioūng kín.*	Honorer.
貂竇	*Tiāo teóu.*	Nid d'oiseau.
兄弟	*Hioūng t'í.*	Frères.
野獸	*Yā tch'óu.*	Animaux sauvages.
冷淡	*Lāng t'ám.*	Sans ferveur.
三寸	*Sām ts'oún.*	Trois pouces.
初次	*Tsē tsé.*	Pour la 1ère fois.
因爲	*Ȳn ví.*	Parce que.
禮貌	*Lī máo.*	Urbanité.
當面	*Tōng mién.*	En présence.
開胃	*K'ōi ví.*	Apéritif.
天地	*T'iēn t'í.*	Le ciel et la terre.
衫褲	*Sām foú.*	Habits et pantalons.
沙垻	*Sā pá.*	Banc de sable.
有病	*Yoū p'iáng.*	Etre malade.
樟樹	*Tchōng choú.*	Camphrier.
灣路	*Vān loú.*	Se détourner de son chemin.
忠厚	*Tchoūng heóu.*	Fidèle.
朝夜	*Tchāo yá.*	Matin et soir.
丁對	*Tēn toúi.*	En plein.
蚊帳	*Moūn tchóng*	Moustiquaire.
漏風	*Leóu foūng.*	Fuite d'air, s'ébruiter.
看書	*K'ón choū.*	Lire.
祭衣	*Tsí ȳ.*	Chasuble.
種花	*Tchoúng fā.*	Cultiver des fleurs.
猫公	*Miáo koūng.*	Un chat.
樹根	*Choú kīn.*	Racine d'arbre.
爛衫	*Lán sām.*	Habit déchiré.
覡公	*Cháng koūng.*	Sorcier.
畵花	*Fá fā.*	Peindre des enjolivures.
放下	*Fóng hā.*	Déposer.
聖母	*Chín moū.*	La S.Mère(S.Vierge).
令尊	*Lín tsoūn.*	Votre père.
練武	*Lién voū.*	Faire l'exercice militaire.
地方	*T'í fōng.*	Endroit.
萬里	*Ván lī.*	Dix mille *lī* (très loin).
用心	*Yoúng sīm.*	Mettre son cœur à.
赴圩	*Foú hī.*	Aller au marché.
大風	*T'ái foūng.*	Grand vent.
念經	*Niám kīn.*	Réciter des prières.
至多	*Tjé tō.*	Au plus.
麵包	*Mién pāo.*	Pain de froment.
教友	*Kaó yoū.*	Chrétiens.
丈夫	*Tch'óng foū.*	Mari.
罪宗	*Ts'oúi tsoūng.*	Péchés capitaux.
岌崗	*Ýn kōng.*	Colline.
飯湯	*Fán t'ōng.*	Eau de riz.
異端	*Ý tōn.*	Superstitions.
晒衫	*Sái sām.*	Sécher les habits au soleil.
四方	*Sí fōng.*	Carré.
病重	*P'iáng tch'oūng.*	Gravement malade.
造天	*Ts'aó t'iēn.*	Créer le Ciel.
外家	*Ngoé' kā.*	Parents d'une fille mariée.
盡兜	*Ts'ín teōu.*	Tous.
背書	*P'ói choū.*	Réciter sa leçon.
夏天	*Há t'iēn.*	Eté.
唱歌	*Tch'óng kō.*	Chanter un air.
鷓鴣	*Tchá koū.*	Perdrix.

Combinaison du premier ton avec le cinquième.

包袱 *Paō foŭc.* Toile à envelopper.
三十 *Sām chĭp.* Trente.
往日 *Vōng gnĭt.* Jadis.
書籍 *Choū sĭt.* Livres, régistres.
禮物 *Lī voŭt.* Présents.
家業 *Kā niăp.* Héritage, patrimoi-
蜂蠟 *Foūng lăp.* Cire d'abeille. [ne.
攤蓆 *T'ān ts'iăc.* Etendre la natte.
天熱 *T'iēn gnĕt.* Le temps est chaud.
三月 *Sām gnĕt.* La troisième lune.
釘屐 *Tāng k'iăc.* Faire des sabots.
灰石 *Foē chăc.* Pierre à chaux.
生活 *Sēn făt.* Vivant, vivace.
干協 *Kōn hiăp.* Relation, rapport.
通達 *T'oūng t'ăt.* Perspicace, intelli-
今日 *Kīn gnĭt.* Aujourd'hui. [gent.
煎熟 *Tsiēn choŭc.* Cuire à point.
薄被 *P'ŏc p'ī.* Légère couverture.
十三 *Chĭp sām.* Treize.
入間 *Gnĭp kiān.* Entrer dans sa cham-
讀書 *T'oŭc choū.* Etudier. [bre.
俗語 *Sioŭc nī.* Proverbe.
辣椒 *Lăt tsiāo.* Piment.
十分 *Chĭp foūn.* Dix parts, très.
莫聲 *Mŏc chāng.* Ne dites rien.
食朝 *Chĭt tchaō.* Déjeuner.
食烟 *Chĭt yān.* Fumer le tabac.
疊坐 *T'iăp ts'ō.* Coussin pour s'asseoir.
拆開 *Ts'ăc k'ōi.* Séparer.
直心 *Tch'ĭt sīm.* Cœur droit.
學生 *Hŏc sāng.* Etudiant, élève.
立春 *Lĭp tch'oūn.* Equinoxe du prin-
熱心 *Gnĕt sīm.* Fervent. [temps.
裂開 *Liĕt k'oī.* Se diviser, se séparer.

Combinaison du premier ton avec le sixième.

阿伯 *Ā pâc.* Oncle paternel.
上棹 *Chōng tsôc.* Monter sur la table.
差伯 *Ts'āi pâc.* Satellites.
中國 *Tchoūng kouĕt.* La Chine.
斟酌 *Tchīm tchôc.* Se consulter.
親戚 *Ts'īn ts'ĭt.* Parenté.
家室 *Kā chĭt.* Epouse.
方法 *Fōng fâp.* Moyen.
寬闊 *K'ōn fât.* Large.
賓客 *Pīn k'ĕt.* Hôte, convive.
東北 *Toūng pĕt.* Nord-Est.
鈎搭 *Kcoū tâp.* Agrafe, crochet.
三尺 *Sām tch'âc.* Trois pieds.
開目 *K'ōi moŭc.* Ouvrir les yeux.
三百 *Sām pâc.* Trois cent.
花缽 *Fā pât.* Pot de fleur.
金箔 *Kīm p'ôc.* Clinquant d'or.
百公 *Pâc koūng.* Grand oncle.
一盃 *Ŷt pī.* Une tasse.
百三 *Pâc sām.* Cent trente.
虐鳥 *Niôc tiaō.* Attraper les oiseaux
忒多 *T'iĕt tō.* Trop. [au filet.
脫衫 *T'ŏt sām.* Enlever son habit.
塞罌 *Sĕt āng.* Boucher la bouteille.
着衫 *Tchôc sām.* Mettre son habit.
薄硝 *P'ôc siāo.* Salpêtre.
肉身 *Nioŭc chīn.* Le corps humain.
摘花 *Tsâc fā.* Cueillir une fleur.
插花 *Ts'âp fā.* Bouturer une fleur.
屋下 *Voŭc hā.* A la maison.
發燒 *Fât chāo.* Avoir la fièvre.
赤馬 *Tch'âc mā.* Cheval brun.
鐵釘 *T'iĕt tāng.* Clou.
出心 *Tch'oŭt sīm.* Faire acte de bonté.

Combinaison du deuxième ton avec le troisième.

行李	*Hâng lì.*	Bagages.
辰早	*Chîn tsào.*	Le matin.
糊紙	*Foû tjè.*	Coller du papier.
魔鬼	*Mô kouì.*	Démon.
泉水	*Ts'ân chouì.*	Source.
棚板	*P'âng pàn.*	Planches de plancher.
財主	*Ts'ôi tchouì.*	Patron, maître.
尋倒	*Ts'îm taò.*	Avoir trouvé.
牙齒	*Ngâ tchè.*	Dent.
田水	*T'iên chouì.*	Eau de rizière.
凉爽	*Leông sòng.*	Fraîcheur agréable.
唔曉	*Mĝ hiào.*	Ne pas savoir.
强水	*K'iông chouì.*	Acide.
鑼鼓	*Lô kouì.*	Tam-tam et tambour.
窮苦	*K'ioûng k'où.*	Pauvre.
牛牯	*Nioû kouì.*	Taureau.
鞋底	*Hâi tài.*	Semelle de soulier.
浮水	*Feôu chouì.*	Surnager.
鉛粉	*Yân foùn.*	Blanc de céruse.
眠几	*Mîn ỳ.*	Chaise longue.
唔肯	*Mĝ hèn.*	Ne pas vouloir.
憑據	*P'în kì.*	Preuve.
洪水	*Foûng chouì.*	Déluge.
唔好	*Mĝ haò.*	Non; ce n'est pas
奇妙	*K'î miaò.*	Etonnant. [bon.
籮籠	*Lô loùng.*	Panier de voyage.
無始	*Voû tchè.*	Sans commencement.
愚蠢	*Gnî tch'oùn.*	Imbécile.
橋不	*K'iâo toùn.*	Pilier du pont.
剮狗	*Tchê keoù.*	Dépecer un chien.
元祖	*Niân tzè.*	Premier ancêtre.
雷火	*Loûi fò.*	Eclair.
長久	*Tch'ông kiouì.*	Longtemps.
停止	*T'în tjè.*	S'arrêter, cesser.
磁碗	*Tsê vouòn.*	Bol en porcelaine.
床板	*Ts'ông pàn.*	Planches de lit.
麼膽	*Mô tàm.*	Peureux.

打贏	*Tà yâng.*	Gagner la bataille.
好難	*Haò nân.*	Très difficile.
補鞋	*Poù hâi.*	Réparer les souliers.
酒壺	*Tsiòu foû.*	Cruche pour le vin.
可憐	*K'ò lîn.*	A faire pitié.
講和	*Kòng fô.*	Faire la paix.
拐人	*Kouài gnîn.*	Tromper quelqu un.
整橋	*Tchàng k'iâo.*	Réparer un pont.
捨財	*Chà ts'ôi.*	Abandonner ses ri-
狗嫲	*Keoù mâ.*	Chienne. [chesses.
守城	*Chouì châng.*	Garder la ville.
水湖	*Chouì foû.*	Gouffre.
打人	*Tà gnîn.*	Frapper quelqu'un.
紙煤	*Tjè moî.*	Papier-amadou.
火柴	*Fò ts'âi.*	Allumettes.
耳環	*Gnì p'ân.*	Boucles d'oreilles.
煮融	*Tchouì yoûng.*	Faire fondre.
檢錢	*Kiàm ts'iên.*	Acquitter, payer.
板頭	*Pàn t'eôu.*	Planche.
本錢	*Poùn ts'iên.*	Capital.
使牛	*Sè niôu.*	Conduire un buffle.
寫田	*Sià t'iên.*	Hypothéquer une ri-
鎖頭	*Sò t'eôu.*	Cadenas. [zière.
火鉗	*Fò k'iâm.*	Pincettes.
水銀	*Chouì nioûn.*	Mercure.
火鹽	*Fò yâm.*	Sel de cuisine.
水龍	*Chouì lioûng.*	Pompe.
隱藏	*Voùn ts'ông.*	Caché, secret.
打魚	*Tà nĝ.*	Pêcher.
紙牌	*Tjè p'âi.*	Cartes à jouer.
鎖題	*Sò chê.*	Clef.
小茴	*Siàc fî.*	Anis.
買成	*Mài châng.*	Marché conclu.
轉來	*Tchòn lôi.*	Revenir.
等我	*Tèn ngaî.*	Attendez-moi.
好行	*Haò hâng.*	Bonne route.
死人	*Sì gnîn.*	Un mort.

Combinaison du deuxième ton avec le quatrième.

而後	*Ý heóu.*	Dans la suite.
難做	*Nân tsó.*	Difficile à faire.
頭上	*T'coû hóng.*	Au commencement.
行路	*Hâng loú.*	Marcher.
皇帝	*Fông tí.*	Empereur.
時候	*Chê heoú.*	Epoque.
盤費	*P'ân fí.*	Dépenses de voyage.
來去	*Lôi hí.*	Allons.
麼用	*Mô yoúng.*	Inutile.
容易	*Yoûng ý.*	Facile.
河垻	*Hô pá.*	Plage du fleuve.
鄰舍	*Lîn chá.*	Voisin.
材料	*Ts'âi liáo.*	Matériaux.
吵鬧	*Ts'aô naó.*	Tapage.
隨便	*Soûi p'ién.*	A volonté.
明悟	*Mîn ngóu.*	Intelligence.
埋葬	*Mâi tsóng.*	Enterrer, ensevelir.
權柄	*K'iân piáng.*	Autorité.
神父	*Chîn foú.*	Père spirituel (prêtre).
鞋面	*Hâi mién.*	Le dessus du soulier.
和尚	*Vô chóng.*	Bonze.
禽獸	*K'îm tch'oú.*	Animaux (quadrupè-
徒弟	*T'oû t'í.*	Disciple. [des).
傳教	*Tch'ôn káo.*	Propager la religion.
涼帽	*Leông máo.*	Chapeau d'été.
頭路	*T'eoû loú.*	Moyen d'existence.
提案	*T'î ón.*	Citer en jugement.
嘩算	*Fâ són.*	Supputer.
松樹	*Ts'ioûng choú.*	Pin.
憂慮	*Yoû lí.*	S'inquiéter.
唔彀	*Mĝ keóu.*	Insuffisant.
唔係	*Mĝ hé·.*	Non.
棚上	*P'âng hóng.*	A l'étage.
脾氣	*P'î hí.*	Caractère, le naturel.
閒話	*Hân fá.*	Paroles oiseuses.
同陣	*T'oûng tch'ín.*	Ensemble, en com-
甜個	*T'iâm ké·.*	Sucré, doux. [pagnie.
令堂	*Lín T'ông.*	Votre mère.
過年	*Koúo niân.*	Le jour de l'an.
報仇	*Paó choû.*	Se venger.
病人	*P'iáng gnîn.*	Un malade.
泡茶	*P'áo ts'â.*	Infuser du thé.
勸人	*K'ián gnîn.*	Exhorter quelqu'un.
渡船	*T'oú chôn.*	Bac.
路程	*Loú tch'în.*	Route, chemin.
釣爐	*Tiáo loû.*	Encensoir.
號頭	*Haó t'eôu.*	Numéro.
到來	*Taó lôi.*	Arriver.
店頭	*Tiám t'eôu.*	Boutique.
跳皮	*T'iáo p'î.*	Taquin, importun.
去眠	*Hí mîn.*	Aller se coucher.
信皮	*Sín p'î.*	Enveloppe de lettre.
剃頭	*T'í t'côu.*	Raser la tête.
婦人	*Foú gnîn.*	Femme.
後來	*Heóu lôi.*	Ensuite.
慢行	*Mán hâng.*	Marcher doucement.
嘴唇	*Tchói choûn.*	Lèvres.
兆頭	*Cháo t'côu.*	Présage.
大陽	*T'aí yông.*	Le soleil.
應酬	*Ýn tch'oû.*	S'occuper de son hô-
灶頭	*Tsáo t'eôu.*	Foyer. [te.
撐船	*Ts'áng chôn.*	Faire avancer la bar-
賺錢	*Ts'ón ts'iên.*	S'enrichir. [que.
聖神	*Chín chîn.*	Le Saint-Esprit.
樹頭	*Choú t'eôu.*	Bloc de bois, tronc
聖人	*Chín gnîn.*	Un Saint. [d'arbre.
就來	*Ts'ióu lôi.*	Venir de suite.
另回	*Láng fî.*	Une autre fois.
貸人	*T'ói gnîn.*	Remplacer quelqu'un.
做田	*Tsó t'iên.*	Travailler aux champs.
辦和	*P'án fô.*	Arranger une affaire à
做完	*Tsó vân.*	C'est fini. [l'amiable.
大黃	*T'ái vông.*	Rhubarbe.
放糖	*Fóng t'ông.*	Mettre du sucre.

Combinaison du deuxième ton avec le cinquième.

靈薄	*Lîn p'ŏc.*	Les limbes.
財物	*Ts'ôi voŭt.*	Richesses, biens.
徉蝶	*Yông yăp.*	Papillon.
前日	*Ts'iên gnĭt.*	Avant-hier.
茶葉	*Ts'â yăp.*	Feuilles de thé.
湖蝶	*Foû t'iăp.*	Espèce de papillon.
和睦	*Fô moŭc.*	Concorde.
明白	*Mîn p'ăc.*	Clairement.
邪術	*Siâ choŭt.*	Magie.
盐局	*Yâm k'ioŭc.*	Régie du sel.
黄蠘	*Vông ts'ăt.*	Cancrelas.
蘿葍	*Lô p'ĕt.*	Rave.
來歷	*Lôi lĭt.*	Suite des faits.
籐蓆	*T'ên ts'iăc.*	Natte en rotin.
辭别	*Tsê p'iĕt.*	Prendre congé.
奇物	*K'î voŭt.*	Une chose extraor-
疑惑	*Gnî fĕt.*	Douter. [dinaire.
藥丸	*Yŏc yân.*	Pilule médicinale.
白糖	*P'ăc t'ông.*	Sucre blanc.
入門	*Gnĭp moûn.*	Rentrer.
殺人	*Săt gnîn.*	Tuer quelqu'un.
弱房	*Niŏc fông.*	Branche faible (d'une
疊平	*T'iăp p'iâng.*	Egaliser. [famille).
值錢	*Tch'ĭt ts'iên.*	Valoir de l'argent.
舌麻	*Chăt mâ.*	Langue.
合同	*Hăp t'oûng.*	Convention écrite.
學臺	*Hŏc t'ôi.*	L'examinateur.
石頭	*Chăc t'eoû.*	Pierre.
笏頭	*Nĕt t'eoû.*	Broussailles.
鹿茸	*Loŭc yoûng.*	Corne de cerf.
駱駝	*Lŏc t'ô.*	Chameau.
蝠婆	*P'ĕt p'ô.*	Chauve-souris.
石墻	*Chăc siông.*	Mur en pierre.
别人	*P'iĕt gnîn.*	Un autre.

Combinaison du deuxième ton avec le sixième.

牛角	*Nioû kôc.*	Corne de bœuf.
禾逼	*Vô pît.*	Moineau.
麻索	*Mâ sôc.*	Corde de chanvre.
明悉	*Mîn sît.*	Comprendre claire-
邪色	*Siâ sêt.*	Luxure. [ment.
牛梔	*Nioû âc.*	Joug de buffle.
傳帖	*Tch'ôn t'iâp.*	Envoyer sa carte.
油漆	*Yoû ts'ît.*	Huiler et laquer.
形迹	*Hŷn tsît.*	Apparences.
湖鴨	*Foû âp.*	Canard sauvage.
留客	*Liôu hâc.*	Retenir un invité.
頭髮	*T'eôu fât.*	Chevelure.
和約	*Fô yôc.*	Traité de paix.
牌骨	*P'aî koût.*	Côte, côtelette.
鞋刷	*Haî sôt.*	Brosse à souliers.
鉛筆	*Yân pît.*	Crayon.
零六	*Lâng lioûc.*	Plus six.
吃人	*Ngât gnîn.*	Mordre quelqu'un.
捉人	*Tsôc gnîn.*	Attraper quelqu'un.
桌圍	*Tsôc vî.*	Devant de table.
膝頭	*Ts'ît t'eoû.*	Genou.
竹頭	*Tchoûc t'eoû.*	Bambou.
骨頭	*Koût t'eoû.*	Os.
搭船	*Tâp chôn.*	Prendre le bateau.
接人	*Tsiâp gnîn.*	Recevoir quelqu'un.
鐵錐	*T'iĕt tch'oûi.*	Marteau de fer.
出門	*Tch'oût moûn.*	Sortir, voyager.
撮人	*Ts'ôt gnîn.*	Filouter, extorquer.
託錢	*T'ôc ts'iên.*	Trier les sapèques.
笠麻	*Lîp mâ.*	Chapeau de jardinier.
骨牌	*Koût p'âi.*	Domino.
發財	*Fât ts'oî.*	S'enrichir.
剝皮	*Pôc p'î.*	Dépecer.
摘茶	*Tsâc ts'â.*	Cueillir le camélia.

Combinaison du troisième ton avec le quatrième.

打對	*Tà toúi.*	Tirer juste.
老店	*Laò tiám.*	Ancienne boutique.
火利	*Fò lí.*	Flamme.
講話	*Kòng fá.*	Parler.
審判	*Chìm p'án.*	Juger.
左右	*Tsò yoú.*	Gauche et droite.
改過	*Kòi koúo.*	Corriger.
買賣	*Mài mái.*	Acheter et vendre.
透氣	*T'eòu hí.*	Respirer.
寫信	*Sià sín.*	Ecrire une lettre.
苦像	*K'où sióng.*	Crucifix.
體面	*T'ì mién.*	Gloriole.
走路	*Tseoù loú.*	Voyager.
古怪	*Koù kouái.*	Rusé.
老妹	*Laò moé·.*	Sœur cadette.
响銃	*Hiòng tch'oúng.*	Tirer un coup de fusil.
手帕	*Choù p'á.*	Mouchoir.
洗面	*Sè· mién.*	Se laver la figure.
煑菜	*Tchoù ts'ói.*	Cuire les aliments.
打棍	*Tà koún.*	Jouer du bâton.
扯爛	*Tch'à lán.*	Déchirer.
口胃	*K'eoù ví.*	Appétit.
紙炮	*Tjè p'aó.*	Pétard.
反教	*Fàn kaó.*	Apostasier.
穩當	*Voùn tóng.*	Solide.
依靠	*Ỳ K'aó.*	Se confier en.
賞賜	*Chòng sé.*	Récompenser.
轉向	*Tchòn hióng.*	Se retourner.
整正	*Tchàng tcháng.*	Réparer.
感謝	*Kàm ts'iá.*	Merci.
少欠	*Chaò k'iám.*	Il manque.
九歲	*Kioù sé·.*	Neuf ans.
擺貨	*Pài fó.*	Etaler la marchandise.
主教	*Tchoù káo.*	Evêque.
小帽	*Siaò máo.*	Petit chapeau.
講笑	*Kòng siáo.*	Plaisanter.
請瞓	*Ts'iàng liáo.*	Veuillez vous reposer.
大險	*T'ái hiàm.*	Grand danger.
救火	*Kióu fò.*	Eteindre un incendie.
賣紙	*Mái tjè.*	Vendre du papier.
菜種	*Ts'ói tchoùng.*	Semence de légume.
判死	*P'án sì.*	Condamner à mort.
奧妙	*Aó miaò.*	Mystère.
告解	*Kaó kiài.*	Se confesser.
聖洗	*Chín sè·.*	Le Saint baptême.
聖水	*Chín choùi.*	Eau bénite.
下手	*Há choù.*	Se mettre à l'œuvre.
大姊	*T'ái tsì*	Sœur aînée.
靠儿	*Kaó ỳ.*	Fauteuil.
熨斗	*Yoún teòu.*	Fer à repasser.
要緊	*Yáo kìn.*	Nécessaire.
漏水	*Leoú choùi.*	Dégoutter.
大譜	*Tái p'où.*	Environ.
發筍	*Ts'án soùn.*	Produire des rejetons.
戴頂	*Tái tàng.*	Porter le globule.
看倒	*K'ón tào.*	Avoir vu.
病死	*P'iáng sì.*	Mourir de maladie.
聖寵	*Chín tch'oùng.*	La grâce.
聖體	*Chín t'ì.*	Eucharistie.
地保	*T'í pào.*	Maire.
字典	*Sé tièn.*	Dictionnaire.
枉了	*Nóng liào.*	C'est dommage.
糯米	*Nó mì.*	Espèce de riz.
露水	*Loú choùi.*	Rosée.
近遠	*K'ioún yàn.*	Près ou loin.
大雨	*T'ái ỳ.*	Grande pluie.
順手	*Choún choù.*	A portée de la main.
遇倒	*Gní taò.*	Avoir rencontré.
釣頸	*Tiáo kiàng.*	Se pendre.
過矮	*Koúo ài.*	Plus bas.
鑽眼	*Tsón niàn.*	Faire un trou avec un poinçon.
彀擺	*Keóu pài.*	Assez.
拱子	*Kioúng tzè.*	Faire des petits.
詐死	*Tsá sì.*	Faire le mort.

Combinaison du troisième ton avec le cinquième.

白紙	*P'ăc tjè.*	Papier blanc.
着火	*Tch'ŏc fò.*	S'enflammer.
鑿眼	*Ts'ŏc niàn.*	Faire un trou au ci-
姪子	*Tch'ĭt tzè.*	Neveu. [seau.
糴米	*T'ăc mì.*	Acheter du riz.
落雨	*Lŏc ỳ.*	Il pleut.
極好	*K'ĭt haò.*	On ne peut mieux.
麥粄	*Măc pàn.*	Gâteau de froment.
蝕本	*Chăt poùn.*	Faire faillite.
藥草	*Yŏc ts'aò.*	Herbes médicinales.
族譜	*Ts'oŭc p'où.*	Livre généalogique.
入耳	*Gnĭp gnì.*	Comprendre et rete-
石板	*Chăc pàn.*	Dalle. [nir.
默想	*Mĕt siòng.*	Méditer.
鑊鏟	*Vŏc ts'àn.*	Petite pelle de cuisine.
搯死	*K'ăc sì.*	Tuer en ecrasant en-
姪女	*Tch'ĭt ǹg.*	Nièce. [tre ses doigts.
早穀	*Tsaò koŭc.*	Riz hâtif.
屯穀	*Toùn koŭc.*	Faire provision de
草蓆	*Ts'aò ts'iăc.*	Natte en herbe. [riz.
酒席	*Tsioù sĭt.*	Festin.
主日	*Tchoù gnĭt.*	Dimanche.
打獵	*Tà liăp.*	Chasser.
討食	*T'ào chĭt.*	Mendier.
鼎力	*Tìn lĭt.*	Supporter.
打棚	*Tà pŏc.*	Frapper le tambou-
好食	*Haò chĭt.*	Bon à manger. [rin.
澗鑿	*Kiàn ts'ŏc.*	Ciseau cannelé.
煑熟	*Tchoù choŭc.*	Cuit à point.
火藥	*Fò yŏc.*	Poudre à canon.
狡猾	*Kaò văt.*	Fourbe, trompeur.
九十	*Kioù chĭp.*	Quatre-vingt dix.
踩蓆	*Ts'aì ts'iăc.*	Mettre le pied sur la
火石	*Fò chăc.*	Pierre à feu. [natte.

Combinaison du troisième ton avec le sixième.

粉壁	*Foùn piâc.*	Crépir un mur.
總督	*Tsoùng toûc.*	Vice-roi.
省察	*Sèn ts'ât.*	S'examiner.
打鐵	*Tà t'iĕt.*	Battre le fer.
打錫	*Tà siâc.*	Travailler l'étain.
狗虱	*Keoù sĕt.*	Puce de chien.
賭博	*Toù pôc.*	Jouer aux jeux de
享福	*Hiòng foûc.*	Jouir. [hasards.
整屋	*Tchàng voûc.*	Réparer une maison.
掌屋	*Tchòng voûc.*	Garder la maison.
手鈪	*Choù âc.*	Bracelet.
首飾	*Choù chĭt.*	Ornements de tête.
海殼	*Hoì hôc.*	Coquille de mer.
肚渴	*Toù hôt.*	Avoir soif.
打缺	*Tà k'iĕt.*	Ebrécher.
打脈	*Tà mâc.*	Tâter le pouls.
掘窟	*Kòi foût.*	Creuser un trou.
瞎眼	*Hât niàn.*	Aveugle.
刻苦	*K'ĕt k'où.*	S'imposer des fati-
目瞶	*Moûc p'où.*	Myope. [gues.
貼紙	*Tiâp tjè.*	Appliquer du papier.
息火	*Sĭt fò.*	Eteindre le feu.
發癩	*Pôt t'ài.*	Avoir la lèpre.
夾襖	*Kâp aò.*	Habit doublé.
泌酒	*Pĭt tsioù.*	Distiller du vin.
避暑	*P'ĭt tch'où.*	Se garer de la cha-
作主	*Tsôc tchoù.*	Se décider. [leur.
跌倒	*Tiĕt taò.*	Etre tombé.
汁糝	*Tchĭp sàm.*	Bouillie de cochon.
摺子	*Tchâp tzè.*	Livret, carnet.
撥火	*P'ât fò.*	Attiser le feu.
則倒	*Tsĕt taò.*	Avoir expérimenté.
屋瓦	*Voûc ngà.*	Les tuiles de la mai-
一點	*Ŷt tiàm.*	Un point. [son.

Combinaison du quatrième ton avec le cinquième.

萬物	*Ván voŭt.*	Toutes choses.
樹葉	*Choú yăp.*	Feuilles d'arbres.
棄絕	*Hí ts'iĕt.*	Rejeter.
定着	*T'ín tch'ŏc.*	Sûrement.
地獄	*T'í nioŭc.*	Enfer.
大畧	*T'ái liŏc.*	Environ.
糶穀	*T'iáo koŭc.*	Vendre du riz.
鬪殺	*Teóu săt.*	Se battre.
貨物	*Fó voŭt.*	Marchandises.
鬧熱	*Naó gnĕt.*	Animation.
四末	*Sí măt.*	Les quatre fins dernières.
煉獄	*Lién nioŭc.*	Purgatoire.
犯族	*Fám ts'oŭc.*	Commettre l'inceste.
放入	*Fóng gnĭp.*	Faire entrer.
混雜	*Foún ts'ăp.*	En désordre.
暫別	*Ts'iám p'iĕt.*	Prendre congé.
做席	*Tsó sĭt.*	Donner un festin.
默念	*Mĕt niám.*	Prier tout bas.
食飯	*Chĭt fán.*	Manger le riz.
疾病	*Ts'ĭt p'iáng.*	Maladie.
特事	*T'ĭt sé.*	Exprès.
樂意	*Lŏc ý.*	Joyeux, content.
立會	*Lĭp fí.*	Former une société.
裂教	*Liĕt kaó.*	Hérétique.
力量	*Lĭt leóng.*	Puissance, force.
莫笑	*Mŏc siaó.*	Ne riez pas.
雜貨	*Ts'ăp fó.*	Marchandises diverses.
十字	*Chĭp sé.*	Croix.
岳父	*Ngŏc foú.*	Beau-père du mari.
白淨	*P'ăc ts'iáng.*	Blanc et propre.
食醉	*Chĭt tsoúi.*	S'enivrer.
逆命	*Niăc mín.*	Désobéir.
習慣	*Sĭp kouán.*	S'exercer, s'habituer.
物件	*Voŭt k'ián.*	Chose.

Combinaison du quatrième ton avec le sixième.

印蹟	*Ýn tsiâc.*	Trace, vestige.
待客	*T'ái hâc.*	Traiter un hôte.
利益	*Lí ŷt.*	Intérêt, avantage.
未必	*Ví pît.*	Est-ce bien sûr!
做得	*Tsó têt.*	Cela peut faire, oui.
問答	*Moún tâp.*	Catéchisme.
樹木	*Choú moûc.*	Bois, forêt.
第六	*T'í lioûc.*	Le sixième.
受屈	*Choú k'ioût.*	Etre opprimé.
唱曲	*Tch'óng k'ioûc.*	Chanter un air.
愛德	*Oí têt.*	Vertu de Charité.
認錯	*Gnín ts'ôc.*	Reconnaître ses torts.
利息	*Lí sît.*	Intérêt, gain.
樹殼	*Choú hôc.*	Ecorce d'arbre.
病脚	*P'iáng kiôc.*	Avoir mal au pied.
降福	*Kóng foûc.*	Bénir.
俸祿	*Foúng loûc.*	Appointements.
屋棟	*Voûc toúng.*	Faîte de la maison.
織布	*Tchît poú.*	Tisser la toile.
木匠	*Moûc sióng.*	Menuisier.
則正	*Tsêt tcháng.*	Expérimenter.
雪豆	*Siêt t'eóu.*	Petits pois.
不論	*Poût loún.*	N'importe.
卜卦	*Poûc koúa.*	Tirer l'horoscope.
襪帶	*Mât tái.*	Jarretières.
鐵鍊	*T'iêt lién.*	Chaîne de fer.
答信	*Tâp sín.*	Envoyer une lettre.
執照	*Tchîp tcháo.*	Passe-port.
摘菜	*Tsâc ts'ói.*	Cueillir des légumes.
歇店	*Hiêt tiám.*	Auberge.
洽味	*Kiâp mí.*	Apre au goût.
跌壞	*Tiêt fái.*	S'abîmer en tombant.
撥扇	*P'ât chán.*	S'éventer.
各樣	*Kôc yóng.*	D'un autre genre.

Combinaison du cinquième ton avec le sixième.

十尺	*Chĭp tch'âc.*	Dix pieds.	八月	*Pât gnĕt.*	La huitième lune.
讀識	*T'oŭc chît.*	Apprendre par cœur.	畢直	*Pît tch'ĭt.*	Directement, tout
石室	*Chăc chît.*	Maison en pierre.	跌落	*Tiêt lŏc.*	Tomber. [droit.
狹窄	*Hăp tsêt.*	Etroit.	出入	*Tch'oût gnĭp.*	Sortir et entrer.
綠色	*Lioŭc sêt.*	Couleur verte.	責罰	*Tsît făt.*	Punir.
食粥	*Chĭt tchoûc.*	Manger de la soupe	竹笏	*Tchoûc mĕt.*	Lanières de bambous.
蠟燭	*Lăp tchoûc.*	Chandelle. [de riz.	炙藥	*Tchâc yŏc.*	Cuire un remède.
落脚	*Lŏc kiôc.*	Anse à porter.	屋宅	*Voûc ts'ĕt.*	Habitation.
白鐵	*P'ăc t'iêt.*	Fer blanc.	捉賊	*Tsôc ts'ĕt.*	Attraper un voleur.
十七	*Chĭp ts'ît.*	Dix-sept.	七十	*Ts'ît chĭp.*	Soixante dix.
月鴿	*Gnĕt kâp.*	Pigeons.	押服	*Âp foŭc.*	Soumettre.
罰惡	*Făt ôc.*	Punir les méchants.	福樂	*Foûc lŏc.*	Bonheur.
鑊舌	*Vŏc toûc.*	Le fond de la poële.	出力	*Tch'oût lĭt.*	S'efforcer.
吸鐵	*Hiăp t'iêt.*	Fer aimanté.	咳嗽	*K'êt tch'oŭc.*	Tousser.
值得	*Tch'ĭt têt.*	Valoir.	著屐	*Tchôc k'iăc.*	Mettre ses sabots.
沓濕	*Tăp chîp.*	Trempé, tout mouil-	筆墨	*Pît mĕt.*	Plume et encre.
踏脚	*T'ăp kiôc.*	Appuyer du pied. [lé.	貼藥	*Tiâp yŏc.*	Appliquer un remède.

Nombres cardinaux.

REMARQUE.—L'expression chinoise qui indique l'absence d'une quantité ou le zéro, est 零 *lâng*, plus, reste.

一	*Ŷt.*	1	一百零一	*Ŷt pâc lâng ŷt.*	101
二 ou 両	*Gní* ou *leòng.*	2	二百 (ou 両百) 一十, ou 二百一	*Gní pâc* (ou *leòng pâc*) *ŷt chĭp,* ou *gní pâc ŷt.*	210
三	*Sām.*	3	三百四 ou 三百四十	*Sām pâc sí* ou *sām pâc sí chĭp.*	340
四	*Sí.*	4	一千	*Ŷt ts'iēn.*	1 000
五	*Ng̀.*	5	一千零零一 ou 一千零一個	*Ŷt ts'iēn lâng lâng ŷt* ou *ŷt ts'iēn lâng ŷt kó.*	1 001
六	*Lioûc.*	6	一千零一十 ou 一千零一	*Ŷt ts'iēn lâng ŷt chĭp* ou *ŷt ts'iēn lâng ŷt.*	1 010
七	*Ts'ĭt.*	7	一千一百	*Ŷt ts'iēn ŷt pâc.*	1 100
八	*Pât.*	8	一千三百八十八	*Ŷt ts'iēn sām pâc pât chĭp pât.*	1 388
九	*Kioù.*	9	一萬	*Ŷt ván.*	10 000
十	*Chĭp.*	10	十萬	*Chĭp ván.*	100 000
十一	*Chĭp ŷt.*	11	百萬	*Pâc ván.*	Un million.
十二	*Chĭp gní.*	12			
二十	*Gní chĭp.*	20			
二十一	*Gní chĭp ŷt.*	21			
四十	*Sí chĭp.*	40			
五十	*Ng̀ chĭp.*	50			
六十九	*Lioûc chĭp kioù.*	69			
九十	*Kioù chĭp.*	90			
一百	*Ŷt pâc.*	100			

Nombres ordinaux.

Les nombres ordinaux se forment, en chinois, par la simple addition du mot 第 *t'í* au nom de nombre cardinal.

第一	*T'í ŷt.*	Le premier.	第十	*T'í chĭp.*	Le dixième.
| 二	*T'í gní.*	Le deuxième.	| 一千	*T'í ŷt ts'iēn.*	Le millième.

Mais quand on parle des jours du mois, il y a une expression spéciale. Pour les dix premiers jours, on dit :

初一	*Tsē ŷt.*	Le premier.	初六	*Tsē lioûc.*	Le sixième.
| 二	*Tsē gní.*	Le deuxième.	| 七	*Tsē ts'ĭt.*	Le septième.
| 三	*Tsē sām.*	Le troisième.	| 八	*Tsē pât.*	Le huitième.
| 四	*Tsē sí.*	Le quatrième.	| 九	*Tsē kioù.*	Le neuvième.
| 五	*Tsē ng̀.*	Le cinquième.	| 十	*Tsē chĭp.*	Le dixième.

Ensuite on dit :

十一日	*Chĭp ŷt gnĭt.*	Le onzième jour.
十二日	*Chĭp gní gnĭt.*	Le douzième, etc.

客法大辭典

Particules numérales.

Aux nombres cardinaux se rattachent les particules numérales.

On nomme ainsi des mots qui expriment une idée caractéristique, ou une propriété frappante d'objets, et s'ajoutent aux noms de nombre.

Dans la langue française certains mots ressemblent beaucoup aux particules numérales des Chinois. Nous disons par exemple, une pièce de toile, une main de papier, un grain de sable, un monceau de paille, une pile de bois etc.

En chinois chaque généralité de mots a sa particule numérale qu'on ne peut omettre sans inconvénient. Voici les plus usitées groupées par ordre alphabétique pour qu'on y puisse recourir plus aisément.

幱 *Fōn*, s'emploie pour les couvertures, les tentures, ce qui ressemble à une couverture.

ŷt fōn p'ī, une couverture.

ŷt fōn tsí ÿ, une chasuble.

sām fōn ts'iăc, trois nattes.

副 *Foú*..... pour les cercueils, pour un ensemble d'objets de même espèce.

ŷt foú kouōn ts'oî, un cercueil.

ŷt foú k'eoú tzè, cinq boutons.

ŷt foú tjè p'ai, un jeu de cartes.

ŷt foú touí liên, deux bandes de papier portant deux phrases symétriques.

ŷt foú ts'ông pàn, les deux planches d'un lit.

幅 *Foŭc*..... pour les peintures, les cartes géographiques, les bannières et en général les objets étendus en long.

ŷt foŭc fá, une peinture.

ŷt foŭc tchaō p'aî, une enseigne de boutique.

sām foŭc k'î, trois drapeaux.

封 *Foūng*.... pour les lettres et les objets qui se mettent dans une enveloppe scellée ou cachetée.

ŷt foūng sín, une lettre.

ŷt foūng nioûn, un petit paquet cacheté contenant de l'argent.

D'un rouleau de cinquante piastres on dit : *ŷt t'oûng nioûn.*

口 *Heoù* (pour *k'eoù*).... pour les marmites, les poëles, les puits, les sacs.

leòng heoù vŏc t'eoû, deux poëles.

ŷt heoù tsiàng, un puits.

chĭp heoù t'oî, dix sacs.

On dit aussi *k'eoù* selon les pays.

穴 *Hiĕt*.... pour les tombeaux, les cavernes.

ŷt hiĕt t'î, un tombeau.

員 *Yân*.... pour les piastres, les mandarins.

ŷt yân kouōn, un mandarin.

sè nioûn ŷt yân, dépenser une piastre.

架 *Ká*.... pour les horloges, les voitures, les machines, les balances, les abaques.

ŷt ká tchoūng, une horloge.

個 *ké*.... pour les hommes et pour les choses. En principe, elle peut s'employer pour tous les substantifs, mais il est plus élégant de se servir, selon la nature même des mots, de la particule qui leur est propre.

ŷt ké· gnîn, un homme.
sām ké· gnĕt, trois mois.
ŷt ké· fā piēn, une piastre.

口 *K'eoù*.... pour les membres d'une famille.

sí k'eoù gnîn, quatre personnes.

支 *Kī* (pour *tjē*).... pour les baguettes, les choses longues et minces.

ŷt kī fā, une fleur.
ŷt kī tchā, un parapluie.
ŷt kī lăp tchoûc, un cierge.

間 *Kiān*.... pour les appartements, les maisons.

ŷt kiān tiám, une boutique.

件 *K'ián*.... pour les habits, les affaires, les colis.

ŷt k'ián sām, un habit.
ŷt k'ián sé, une affaire.

坵 *K'ioū*.... pour les rizières.

leòng k'ioū t'iên, deux rizières.

股 *Koù*.... pour les parties d'un tout.

ŷt koù chouì, un filet d'eau.
sām koù piēn, une tresse à trois branches.
ŷt koù foūng, une bouffée de vent.

塊 *K'ouaí*.... pour les fragments, les piastres, les pierres, les briques, les tuiles.

ŷt k'ouaí pō li, un morceau de verre.
ŷt k'ouaí nioûn, une piastre, (mais il ne faut pas dire *ŷt k'ouaí fā piēn*).
ŷt k'ouaí chăc t'eoû, une pierre.
ŷt k'ouaí ngà, une tuile.

款 *K'ouàn*.... pour les choses, de différentes espèces, les articles d'un contrat, les objets de commerce, les affaires.

haò tō k'ouàn toūng sī, beaucoup d'objets.
fô yôc yoū sām k'ouàn, le traité de paix contient trois articles.
ŷt k'ouàn sé, une affaire.

綑 *K'oùn*.... pour les fagots. et tout ce qui est lié en botte.

ŷt k'oùn ts'iaô, un fagot de bois.

管 *Kouòn*.... pour les pinceaux, les crayons, les tubes et ce qui y ressemble.

ŷt kouòn pît, un pinceau.

面 *Mién*.... pour les miroirs, les drapeaux, les tam-tam.

ŷt mién kiáng, un miroir.
ŷt mién lô, un tam-tam.

枚 *Moê·*....pour les petites boules, les perles, les aiguilles.

ŷt moê· tchoū, une perle.
ŷt moê· tchīm, une aiguille.

把 *Pà*.... pour les éventails, les verges, les cadenas, les parapluies, et en général les objets qui se prennent à la main.

ŷt pà chán, un éventail.
ŷt pà sò, un cadenas.

皮 *Pî*.... pour les plaques et ce qui ressemble à une plaque.
ŷt p'ì moûn, une porte.
sām p'i choú pàn, trois planches.
ŷt p'ì t'ièt pàn, une plaque de fer.

匹 *P'ĭt*.... pour les chevaux, les ânes et les animaux qui portent sur leur dos, pour les montagnes, les étoffes.
ŷt p'ĭt mā, un cheval.
ŷt p'ĭt lô, un mulet.
ŷt p'ĭt sān, une montagne.
ŷt p'ĭt (疋)*poú*, une pièce d'étoffe.

頂 *Tàng*.... pour les coiffures, les palanquins.
ŷt tàng maó, une chapeau.
ŷt tàng k'iaó, un palanquin.

隻 *Tchâc*.... pour certains animaux, pour l'un des deux objets qui font la paire, et pour la plupart des substantifs, hormis les hommes.
ŷt tchâc kē, une poule.
ŷt tchâc haî, un soulier.
ŷt tchâc mât, un bas.

張 *Tchōng*....... pour les feuilles de papier, les tables, les bancs, les lits, et en général pour les choses qui présentent une grande surface plane.
ŷt tchōng tjè, une feuille de papier.
ŷt tchōng tsôc, une table.
ŷt tchōng ts'ông, un lit.

條 *T'iaô*.... pour certains animaux, les arbres, les bambous, les fleuves, les routes, les cordes, et en général pour tout ce qui est long et mince ou étroit.
ŷt t'iaô nioû, un buffle.
ŷt t'iaô choú, un arbre.
ŷt t'iaô hô, un fleuve.
ŷt t'iaô sôc, une corde.

臺 *T'oî*.... pour les drames, les comédies, les messes.
ŷt t'oî hí, une comédie.
ŷt t'oî nì sât, une messe.

座 *Ts'ó*.... pour les tours, les ponts, les bâtiments.
ŷt ts'ó k'iaô, un pont.
ŷt ts'ó fông voûc, une maison.

位 *Ví*.... pour les personnes qu'on veut honorer.
leòng ví chîn foú, deux prêtres.

文 *Voûn*.... pour les sapèques, les sous.
sām voûn ts'iên, trois sapèques.

Exercice de lecture sous forme de dialogue.

神父在裡子嫽, *chîn foú ts'ōi lì tzè liaó.*	Le Père est ici à se reposer.
係,咁早, *hé·, kàn tsaò!*	Oui, te voilà déjà!
唔早,神父喊我來做那個, *mĝ tsaò, chîn foú hám ngaî loî tsó mâc ké·?*	Il n'est pas tôt (rép. de politesse); pourquoi le Père m'a-t-il appelé?
坐等來,我問爾,屋下還有爺哀麼, *ts'ō tèn loî, ngaî moún gnî, voûc hā hân yoū yâ oē· mô?*	Assieds-toi, je vais te le dire: chez toi as-tu encore ton père et ta mère?
還有, *hân yoū.*	Oui.
屋下耕有幾多担穀田, *voûc hā kāng yoū kì tō tām*(1) *koŭc t'iên?*	Chez toi, combien cultives-tu de charges(1) de rizières?
家事貧苦單單耕裡十過担, *kā sé p'în k'où tān tān kāng lî chĭp kouó tām.*	Ma famille est pauvre, je ne cultive que dix et quelques charges.
爾幾多歲, *gnî kì tō sé·?*	Quel âge as-tu?
十七歲, *chĭp ts'ĭt sé·.*	Dix-sept ans.
討裡老婆麼, *t'aò lî laò p'ô mô?*	As-tu pris femme?
唔曾, *mĝ ts'ên.*	Pas encore.
爾讀裡幾多年書, *gnî t'oŭc lî kì tō niân choū?*	Pendant combien d'années as-tu étudié?
讀裡三四年, *t'oŭc lî sām sí niân.*	J'ai étudié trois ou quatre ans.
個,你都識字, *ká! gnî toū chĭt sé.*	Oh! alors tu sais lire les caractères.
就係唔多識, *ts'ioú hé· mĝ tō chĭt.*	C'est-à-dire que je ne les sais pas beaucoup.
你噲款麼, *gnî voé· k'aī mô?*	Peux-tu porter (s. e. les fardeaux)?
我款得四五十斤起, *ngaî k'aī têt sí ng̀ chĭp kīn hì.*	Je puis porter quarante à cinquante livres.
你肯同我相帮麼, *gnî hèn t'oûng ngaî siōng pōng mô?*	Consens-tu à m'aider?
神父相愛做得,總係唔知曉得麼, *chîn foú siōng oí tsó têt, tsoùng hé· mĝ tī hiào têt mô?*	Le Père me témoignant cette affection, je le veux bien, mais je ne sais pas si je le pourrai.

(1) *Charge* a ici le sens de: mesure agraire. Voir le mot 担 *tām*, dans le Dictionnaire.

容易學, *yoûng ý hŏc.* — C'est facile à apprendre.

做那𠮶工夫, *tsó mâc ké· koūng foū?* — Quel travail faudra-t-il faire?

輔彌撒, 煑飯食, 洗衫, 掃地, 撿點各樣東西, *p'où nì sât, tchoù fán chĭt, sè· sām, saó t'í, kiàm tiàm kôc yóng toūng sī.* — Servir la Messe, faire (cuire) le dîner (le riz), laver les habits, balayer, mettre en ordre chaque chose.

神父食飯阿食麵包, *chîn foú chĭt fán á chĭt mién paō?* — Le Père mange-t-il du riz ou du pain?

食麵包, *chĭt mién paō.* — Je mange du pain.

個, 我唔曉得做麵包, *ká! ngaî mĝ hiaò tĕt tsó mién paō.* — Oh! je ne sais pas faire le pain.

麽相干, 我會敎你, *mô siōng kōn, ngaî voé· kaō gnî.* — Peu importe, je t'apprendrai.

個, 做得, *ká! tsó tĕt.* — Alors, je consens.

我算多少工錢別你, *ngaî són tō chaò koūng ts'iên poūn gnî.* — Je te donnerai quelque salaire.

聽神父安排, *t'în chîn foú ōn p'aî.* — Comme le Père le voudra.

係做得先讀讀彌撒經來, *hé· tsó tĕt siēn t'oŭc chĭt nì sât kīn loî.* — Si tu y consens, apprends d'abord les prières de la Messe.

好, 那久來, *haò, naí kioù loî?* — C'est bien; quand (faudra-t-il) venir?

就來也做得, *ts'ioú loî yā tsó tĕt.* — Tout de suite; je veux bien.

我轉下屋下來, *ngaî tchòn há voŭc hā loî.* — Je vais auparavant retourner chez moi.

你愛作緊來, *gnî oí tsôc kìn loî.* — Dépêche-toi (il faudra te dépêcher).

好, 神父愛借幾下個花邊別我, *haò, chîn foú oí tsiá kì há ké· fā piēn poūn ngaî.* — Entendu; je voudrais que le Père me prêtât quelques piastres.

借來做那個, *tsiá loî tsó mâc ké·?* — Te prêter, pour quoi faire?

麽衫著愛做衫褲, *mô sām tchôc oí tsó sām foú.* — Je n'ai pas d'habits, je veux me faire des habits.

唔使咁排長, *mĝ sè kàn p'aî tch'ông.* — Il n'est pas nécessaire d'être si beau.

同神父出門愛伶俐, *t'oûng chîn foú tch'oût moûn oí lāng lí.* — Pour sortir avec le Père il faut être propre.

到聖堂來做, 你嘩算那個日來, *taó chín t'ông loî tsó, gnî fā són mâc ké· gnĭt loî?* — Tu les feras de retour à la chapelle: quel jour comptes-tu venir?

樣都愛月半哼來得, *nióng toū oí gnĕt pán tsáng loî tĕt.* — De toutes manières, je ne pourrai venir qu'à la pleine lune (la moitié du mois).

個,你歸一下來, *ká! gnî kouī ŷt há loî.*	Eh bien, tu peux (d'abord) t'en retourner.
好,神父請𤍠, *haò, chîn foú ts'iàng liaó.*	Bien; Père, je vous invite à vous reposer.

Exemple de civilité chinoise dans une visite.

神父在裡子𤍠, *chîn foú ts'oī ỳ tzè liaó.*	Le Père se repose ici (manière de se dire bonjour).
係,你去那裡來, *hé·, gnî hí naí lī loî?*	Oui. D'où venez-vous?
唔曾去那裡,我特事來, *mĝ ts'ēn hí naí lī, ngaî t'ĭt sé loî.*	Je n'ai été nulle part, je viens tout exprès.
咁有心, 請坐, 食茶烟, *kàn yoū sīm.... ts'iàng ts'ō.... chĭt ts'à yān.*	Que vous êtes bon!... veuillez vous asseoir.... buvez le thé, fumez.
莫拘禮, *mŏc kī lī.*	Ne faites pas de politesse.
閣下貴處, *kôc há kouí tch'oú?*	Quel est le noble pays de Monsieur?
草舍平遠, *ts'aò chá P'în yàn.*	Ma chaumière est au P'în-yàn.
在城阿在鄉, *ts'aí châng á ts'aí hiōng?*	A la ville ou à la compagne?
在鄉, *ts'aí hiōng.*	A la campagne.
貴姓, *kouí siáng?*	Quel est votre illustre nom (de famille)?
小姓陳, *siaò siáng Tch'în.*	Mon humble nom est Tch'în.
那個大號, *mâc ké· t'aí haó?*	Et quel est votre honorable prénom?
細人子唔曾有, *sé· gnîn tzè mĝ ts'ēn yoū.*	Petit enfant que je suis, je n'en ai pas.
借問你, *tsiá moún gnî.*	Dites, je vous en prie.
我個賤字芳奎, *ngā ké· ts'ién sé Fōng K'ōuî.*	Mon méprisable nom est Fōng-k'ouî.
久仰, *kioū niòng.*	Depuis longtemps je vous attendais.
豈敢,(不堪), *k'ì kàm, (ou poût k'ām).*	Comment oserais-je? (ou) je ne suis pas digne (*s.-ent.* de tant d'honneurs).
你有那個貴幹, *gnî yoū mâc ké· kouí kón?*	Quelle importante affaire vous amene?
特事來拜候神父, *t'ĭt sé loî paí heoú chîn foú.*	Je viens tout exprès pour saluer le Père.
十分有心, *chĭp foūn yoū sīm.*	Vous avez un excellent cœur.

神父那個貴國, *chîn foú mâc ké· kouí kouêt?*	Quelle est le noble royaume du Père?
敝國就喊法國, *pí kouêt ts'ioú hám fâp kouêt.*	Mon humble royaume s'appelle la France.
到中國有幾多路程, *taó tchoūng kouêt yoū kì tō loú tch'în?*	Quelle est la distance jusqu'en Chine (*litt.* combien y a-t-il de route)?
大約有四五萬里, *t'aí yôc yoū sí ngg̀ ván lī.*	Il y a environ 40 a 50 mille *lī*.
神父到來有幾多年, *chîn foú taó loî yoū kì tō niân ?*	Depuis combien de temps le Père est-il venu?
到來有十零年, *taó loî yoū chīp lâng niân.*	Il y a plus de dix ans.
神父帶哩家眷來麼, *chîn foú taí lî kā kián loî mô?*	Le Père a-t-il amené sa femme?
唔曾, 淨自己來, *mĝ ts'ên, ts'iáng tsé kì loî.*	Non, je suis venu tout seul.
做那個唔帶家眷, *tsó mâc ké· mĝ taí kā kián?*	Pourquoi n'amenez-vous pas votre femme?
做神父個人一心傳教不能帶家眷, *tsó chîn foú ké· gnîn ŷt sīm tch'ōn kaó poût nên taí kā kián.*	Un prêtre n'a qu'un désir, qui est de propager la religion, il ne peut avoir de femme.
神父家下有幾多個人食飯, *chîn foú kā há yoū kì tō ké· gnîn chĭt fán?*	La famille du Père se monte à combien de personnes (*litt.* combien y a-t-il de personnes à dîner)?
一共有七個人, *ŷt k'ioúng yoū ts'īt ké· gnîn.*	En tout, nous sommes sept.
令尊還健麼, *lín tsoūn hân k'ián mô?*	Monsieur votre père est-il en bonne santé?
我先父過哩身, *ngā siēn foú kouó lì chīn.*	Mon père est mort.
令堂還健麼, *lín t'ông hân k'ián mô?*	Madame votre mère est-elle en bonne santé?
現下還借日, *hién há hân tsiá gnĭt.*	(Dieu *s.-ent.*) lui prête encore vie.
神父有幾多昆玉, *chîn foú yoū kì tō k'oūn nioûc?*	Combien le Père a-t-il de frères?
有兩賤兄弟, *yoū leòng ts'ién hioūng t'í.*	J'ai deux (méprisables) frères.
神父第幾, *chîn foú t'í kì?*	Le Père est-il l'aîné ou le cadet?
我過細, *ngaî kouó sé·.*	Je suis le plus jeune.

海上絲綢之路文獻集成 科技與文化编

令兄在家做那個, *lín hioūng ts'aí kā tsó mâc ké·?*	Que fait monsieur votre frère, à la maison?
我家兄屋下做生理, *ngaî kā hioūng voūc hā tsó sēn lī.*	Mon frère fait le commerce chez lui.
係生財, *hé· sēn ts'oî.*	C'est une grande source de richesses.
麽相干, 你閣下㨗生財, *mô siōng kōn, gnî kôc há tsáng sēn ts'oî.*	(Son commerce *s.-ent.*) n'a pas d'importance, c'est vous, monsieur, qui vous enrichissez.
我都唔曾做那個生理, *ngaî toū mĝ ts'ên tsó mâc ké· sēn lī.*	Mais moi, je ne fais pas le commerce.
你貴境地方出息係好, *gnî kouí kín t'í fōng tch'oūt sīt hé· haò.*	Votre noble pays donne de beaux revenus.
麽那個出息總係耕田, *mô mâc ké· tch'oūt sīt tsoùng hé· kāng t'iên.*	Il n'y a guère de revenus, je ne fais que cultiver les rizières.
今年個禾還大収成還好, *kīn niân ké· vô hân t'aí choū chîn hân haò.*	Cette année le riz était assez beau, la rentrée a dû être abondante.
照常, *tchaó chông.*	Comme à l'ordinaire.
你貴境有人奉敎麽, *gnî kouí kín yoū gnîn foúng kaó mô?*	Dans votre noble pays, y a-t-il des chrétiens?
現下麽, 我都就係想來奉敎, *hién há mô, ngaî toū hé· siòng loî foúng kaó.*	Jusqu'à présent, non; mais je voudrais bien, moi, me faire chrétien.
奉敎係好, *foúng kaó hé· haò.*	C'est très-bien de se faire chrétien.
奉敎愛帶那個來麽, *foúng kaó oí taí mâc ké· loî mô?*	Pour être chrétien faut-il apporter quelque chose?
唔使總係愛有心學道理, *mĝ sè tsoùng hé· oí yoū sīm hôc t'aó lī.*	Non, on ne vous demande que de la ferveur à étudier la doctrine.
神父有那個書麽借我看, *chîn foú yoū mâc ké· choū mô tsiá ngaî k'ón.*	Le Père pourrait-il me prêter quelque livre?
個, 有, 拿一本你看, *ká! yoū, nā ŷt poùn gnî k'ón.*	Oui, oui; en voilà un.
感謝神父, 我暫別一下來, 另回請神父到舍下來嫽, *kàm ts'iá chîn foú, ngaî ts'iám p'iĕt ŷt há loî, láng fî s'tiàng chîn foú taó chá há loî liaó.*	Merci, mon Père, je vous fais mes mes adieux, et vous invite à venir me voir un jour chez moi.
還早嫽一下添, *hân tsaò liaó ŷt há t'iām.*	Il est encore tôt, restez un peu.
另回來, *láng fî loî.*	Ce sera pour une autre fois.

食裡晝來歸, *chĭt ê· tchoú loî kouī.*

Vous dînerez avant de partir.

還早我歸一下來，請嫽, *hân tsaò ngaî kouī ŷt há loî, ts'iàng liaó.*

Il est encore tôt, je puis partir avant, ne vous dérangez pas.

個，你歸一下來，另回來到府拜候，漫行, *ká! gnî kouī ŷt há loî, láng fî loî taó foù paí heoú, mán hâng.*

Et bien, je vous laisse partir, (*litt.* une autre fois) un jour j'irai vous saluer (*litt.* saluer votre palais). Allez doucement.

Quelques phrases plus difficiles pour exercer la langue.

水打一雙屐，一打，打在石狹屐，唔知屐狹石石狹屐, *chouì tàŷt soūng k'iăc, ŷt tà, tà ts'aí chăc k'iăp k'iăc; mĝ tī k'iăc k'iăp chăc chăc k'iăp k'iăc.*

Le courant a emporté une paire de sabots, et ils se sont pris entre les pierres ; on ne sait pas si les pierres se sont prises dans les sabots, ou si les sabots se sont pris dans les pierres.

廣東東門當家種東瓜，香港中灣當家種西瓜，久聞廣東東門當家個東瓜大；追出香港中灣當家個西瓜大過廣東東門當家個大東瓜. *Koùong toūng toūng moûn tōng kā tchoúng toūng kouā, hiōng kouòng tchoūng vân tōng kā tchoúng sī kouā; kioù voûn koùong toūng toūng moûn tōng kā ké· toūng kouā t'aí; tchoūi tch'oût hiōng koùong tchoūng vân tōng kā ké· sī kouā t'aí koúo kouòng toūng toūng moûn tōng hā ké· t'aí toūng kouā.*

A *Canton*, à la porte de l'Est, le procureur cultive une courge ; à *Hong-kong* à *Tchoung-van*, le procuteur cultive un melon ; depuis longtemps on entend dire que la courge du procureur de la porte de l'Est à *Canton*, est grosse ; on a fini par trouver que le melon du procureur de *Tchoung-van*, à *Hong-kong*, était encore plus gros que la grosse courge du procureur de la porte de l'Est, à *Canton*.

蔗摵正擎蔗準傘遮日頭, *tchá tsât tcháng k'iâng tchá tchoùn tchā tchā gnĭt t'eoû.*

Fais une gerbe de canne à sucre et porte-la en guise de parapluie pour te garantir du soleil.

天晴借蓆聚做煎腈猪肉膀酒，麼酒就請食井水將就, *t'iēn ts'iáng tsiá ts'iăc ts'í ts'ioū tsiēn tsiāng tchoū nioûc pòng tsioù, mô tsiòu ts'iόu ts'iàng chĭt tsiàng chouì tsiōng ts'ioú.*

Il fait beau, empruntons des nattes et groupons-nous, nous rôtirons du porc que nous mangerons en buvant le vin, s'il n'y a pas de vin, et bien, ou vous priera de vous contenter de l'eau du puits,

客法大辭典

DICTIONNAIRE

CHINOIS-FRANÇAIS

DIALECTE HAC-KA

Ā

阿 *Ā*. Préfixe qui affecte les noms de personnes, à moins que le nom ait deux caractères.

丨善, ā chán. 丨鳳, ā foúng. 丨滿, ā mān.

On dit aussi.

丨叔, *ā choûc*, oncle.

丨哥, *ā kō*, frère aîné.

丨公, *ā koūng*, grand-père.

丨姆, *ā mē·*, maman.

丨巴, *ā pa*, papa.

你丨叔在屋下麽, *gnî ā choûc ts'ōi vouc hā mô ?* ton oncle est-il chez lui?

你有幾多個丨哥, *gnî yoū kì tō ké· ā kō ?* combien as-tu de frères aînés?

鴉 *Ā*. 老丨, *laò* 丨, corbeau.

丨鵲, 丨 *siăc*, pie.

À

啞 *À*. Muet. 丨嘴, 丨 *tchói*, muet.

Á

阿 *Á*. Particule employée à la place de 在 *ts'ái*, être dans, sur, dessus. Dans certains cas a le sens de la conjonction *ou*; dans d'autres est simplement euphonique.

攊丨桌上去, *fĭt á tsôc hóng hí*, jette sur la table.

蛇哥纏丨樹上去, *châ kō ts'ân á choú hóng hí*, le serpent s'enroule autour de l'arbre.

神父食飯丨食麵包, *chîn foú chĭt fán á chĭt mién paō?* le Père mange-t-il du riz ou du pain?

食丨帛就來, *chĭt á p'ĕt ts'ioú loî*, viens dès que tu auras mangé.

坐丨子, *ts'ō á tzè*, asseyez-vous.

瞭丨子, *liáo á tzè*, demeurez, reposez-vous.

ÂC

鈪 *Âc*. 手丨, *choù* 丨, bracelet.

牛丨(軛) *nioû* 丨, joug de bœuf ou de buffle.

I

ĀI

挨 *Aī.* Rencontrer un obstacle; atteindre, retard.

| **壞**, | *fái*, détérioré par un obstacle.

門框忒矮喑 | 倒人, *moún k'iōng t'iĕt aì voé* | *taò gnîn*, le montant de la porte est trop bas, on peut se heurter.

| **音**, *ȳm*, prononciation défectueuse; différence de prononciation.

莫咁 | 阿, *mŏc kàn* | *nā*, pas tant de lambinerie.

AÌ

矮 *Aì.* Bas, peu élevé.

裡張桌忒 |, *ỳ tchōng tsôc t'iĕt* |, cette table est trop basse.

| **凳子過好坐**, | *tén tzè kouó haò ts'ō*, on est mieux sur une chaise basse.

放 | 一滴, *fóng* | *ȳt tīt*, mettre un peu plus bas.

ĀM

掩 *Ām* (*yàm*). Clôturer, entourer.

| **園**, | *yân*, entourer le jardin d'un mur ou d'une haie.

ÂM

菴 *Âm.* **和尚** |, *vô-chóng* |, monastère de bonzes.

ÁM

暗 *Ám.* Obscur, ténébreux.

| **晡夜**, | *poū yá*, ce soir.

昨晡 |, *ts'ŏc poū* |, hier au soir.

容易喑 |, *yoúng ý voé* |, la nuit approche.

| **中做個事**, | *tchoūng tsó ké sé*, la chose s'est faite en secret.

| **病**, | *p'iáng*, maladie honteuse.

ÀN (Voyez *KÀN*).

ĀNG

罌 *Āng.* Bouteille, vase à petite ouverture.

酒 | 拿來洗淨來, *tsioù* | *nā loî sè ts'iáng loî*; lave la bouteille à vin.

一 | 酒, *ȳt* | *tsioù*; une bouteille de vin.

AŌ

嗷 *Aō.* Accuser, imputer.

| **人做賊**, | *gnîn tsó ts'ĕt*, accuser quelqu'un de vol.

| **我唔倒**, | *ngaî mĝ taò*, on ne peut m'en accuser; on ne peut pas dire que c'est moi.

凹 *Aō* (*aó*). Portion d'arc, courbure, dépression.

樹 |, *choú* |, arc formé par une branche courbée.

忒 |, *t'iĕt* |; la courbure est trop prononcée.

屐板愛 | 一滴嘩好著, *K'iác pàn oí* | *ȳt tīt tsáng haò tchôc*, la semelle du sabot doit avoir une légère dépression pour qu'il chausse bien.

ÀO.

拗 *Aò.* Plier, ployer, briser avec les mains.

| 斷, | *t'ōn*, rompre.

莫 | 一 | 就噲斷, *mŏc* | *ӯt* | *ts'ioú voé· t'ōn*, ne le ploie pas, si tu le ploies il se rompra.

我麼事 | 斷, *ngaî mô sé* | *t'ōn* je ne le romprai pas.

我 | 唔斷, *ngaî* | *mĝ t'ōn*, je ne puis le rompre.

| 曲, | *k'ioût*, tordre.

| 壞, | *faí*, abîmer en pliant.

襖 *Aò.* Habit doublé.

長 | , *tch'ông* | , longue robe doublée.

棉 | , *miên* | , habit ouaté.

AÓ.

奧 *Aó.* Caché, profond.

| 妙, | *miaò*, mystère.

天主教有好多 | 妙個道理, *t'iēn tchoù kaó yoū haò tō* | *miaò ké· t'aó lī*, dans la religion chrétienne il y a beaucoup de mystères.

凹 *Aó.* Gorge de montagne; contredire.

中國角 | 都有茶亭, *tchoūng kouêt kôc* | *toū yoū ts'â t'în*, en Chine, on trouve des kiosques à chaque gorge de montagne.

麼人敢同我 | , *mô gnîn kàm t'oûng ngaî* | , personne n'ose me contredire.

賭 | , *toù* | , parier.

我賭 | 你唔敢去, *ngaî toù aó gnî mĝ kàm hí*, je parie que tu n y vas pas.

ÂP

押 *Âp.* Garder, retenir, dompter, opprimer.

| 落班房貯, | *lŏc pān fông toù*, il est mis en prison.

小 | , *siaò* | , mont-de-piété où l'on engage de petits objets.

克苦 | 肉身, *k'ĕt k'où* | *nioûc chīn*, réduire son corps en servitude.

| 伏私慾, | *foŭc sē yoŭc*, dompter ses passions.

鴨 *Âp.* Canard.

泥 | , 番 | , 貨 | , *naî* | , *fān* | , *fó* | , différentes espèces de canards domestiques.

湖 | , *foû* | , canard sauvage.

ÂT

痖 *Ât.* Colère sourde, mécontent, de mauvaise humeur.

| 病, | *p'iáng*, malade par suite d'un mécontentement.

| 死, | *sì*, mourir de colère.

| 嚏, | *tsoùi*, éternument.

打 | 嚏, *tà* | *tsoùi*, éternuer.

CHÂ

(*Voir aussi les mots SA*).

蛇 *Châ.* Serpent.

一條 | , *ӯt t'iâo* | , un serpent.

狗媽 | , *keoù mâ châ*, lézard.

CHÀ

捨 *Chà.* Abandonner, se défaire de.

你｜得麼，*gnî ｜têt mô?* en fais-tu le sacrifice?

｜身，｜命，｜*chīn*, ｜*mín*, sacrifier sa vie, martyr.

一個錢都｜唔得，*ŷt ké· ts'iên toū ｜mĝ têt*, il ne donnerait pas même une sapèque.

我｜你唔得，*ngaî chà gnî mĝ têt*, je ne puis consentir à me séparer de vous.

洒 *Chà*. Asperger, répandre.

｜聖水，｜*chín chouì*, asperger d'eau bénite.

｜阿地下起，｜*á t'í hā hì*, répandre par terre.

酒壺轉帛裡酒｜帛一半，*tsioù foû tchón p'ĕt lê· tsioù ｜p'ĕt ŷt pán*, le pot de vin est tombé et la moitié du vin s'est répandu.

耍 *Chà*. S'amuser, jouer, demeurer quelque temps dans un endroit sans occupation bien déterminée. Ne s'emploie qu'ajouté à un autre mot qui en complète le sens.

嫽｜，*liáo*, ｜, flâner, se récréer.

遊｜，*yoû* ｜, se promener, errer.

玩｜，*ngán* ｜, s'amuser.

CHÁ

舍 *Chá*. Maison.

草｜，*ts'aò* ｜, ma chaumière, (polit.).

｜弟，｜*t'í*, mon frère cadet. Ce mot «*chá*» n'est employé dans ce sens que lorsqu'il s'agit d'un parent au moins d'un degré au-dessous de celui qui parle; ainsi on ne pourrait pas dire ｜兄，｜*hioūng*, mon frère aîné, mais on dira 家兄，*kā hioūng*, ou de même 家父，*kā foú* mon père.

赦 *Chá*. Pardonner.

｜罪，｜*ts'oúi*, absoudre, faire grâce d'une peine.

恩｜(ou 大｜)，*ēn* ｜(ou *t'ái* ｜), indulgence.

全｜，*ts'iên* ｜, indulgence plénière.

係有痛悔麼有｜唔得個罪，*hé· yoū t'oúng fí môyoū ｜mĝ têt ké· ts'oúi*, avec la contrition il n'y a pas de péché sans pardon.

射 *Chá*. Tirer de l'arc, lancer.

｜箭，｜*tsién*, lancer des flèches.

粒石｜阿我眼珠仁起，*sé· chăc ｜á ngaî niàn tchoū ŷn hì*, j'ai reçu une petite pierre dans l'œil.

CHĂC

石 *Chăc*. Pierre; Mesure de dix boisseaux.

一條｜頭，*ŷt t'iaô ｜t'eoû*, une pierre.

打｜，*tà* ｜, travailler la pierre.

｜人，｜*gnîn*, statue de pierre.

刀｜，*taō* ｜, pierre à aiguiser.

金鋼｜，*kīm kōng* ｜, diamant.

火｜，*fò* ｜, pierre à feu.

玉｜，*nioŭc* ｜, jade.

｜膏，｜*kaō*, gypse. (Les Chinois s'en servent pour faire leurs fromages de haricots, 豆腐，*t'eoú foú*.)

一｜穀，*ŷt* ｜*koŭc*, dix boisseaux de riz, un picul.

CHĂI

䑛 *Chaï* (ou *sē·*). Lécher.

狗｜毛, *keòu* | *maō*, le chien se lèche.

CHÂM

(*Voir aussi les mots* SAM)

蟾 *Châm* (ou *sâm*). | **蜍蠦**, *châm choû lô*, crapaud.

CHÀM

閃 *Chàm*. Se garer, s'écarter.

｜開來, | *k'oï loî*, garez-vous.

｜阿裡邊去, | *á ỳ piēn hí*, écartez-vous de ce côté,

船一想｜別個船撞倒石頭撞壞, *chôn ŷt siòng* | *p'ĭĕt ké· chôn ts'óng taò chăc t'eoû ts'óng faí*, la barque, en voulant éviter une autre barque, s'est brisée contre un rocher.

CHĀN

鱔 *Chān*, Petite anguille de rizière.

白｜, *p'ăc* |, anguille blanche.

黃｜, *vông* |, anguille jaune.

剪黃｜, *tsièn vông* |, pêcher les anguilles avec des ciseaux.

CHÀN

擅 *Chàn*. Arbitraire, disposer à son gré, exceller.

你自｜做個, *gnî tsé* | *tsó ké·*, tu as agi à ta guise, c'est toi-même qui as pris ce parti.

你｜長做那個工夫, *gnî* | *tch'ông tsó mâc ké· koūngfoū?* en quoi excellez-vous ? que faites-vous habituellement ?

CHÁN

善 *Chán*. Bon, bien, doux, probe, vertueux. (On dit aussi *chān*).

行｜, *hâng* |, faire le bien.

分｜惡, *foūn* | *òc*, distinguer le bien du mal.

｜功, | *koūng*, bonne œuvre.

｜講, | *kòng*, parler sans s'emporter, paisiblement.

｜心人, | *sīm gnîn*, homme paisible, droit, honnête.

｜教子女, | *kaō tzè ǹg*, bien élever ses enfants.

用｜法, *yoúng* | *fâp*, employer la douceur.

騸 *Chán*. Châtré.

｜馬, | *mā*, cheval châtré. (Ce mot ne s'emploie que pour le cheval; d'un chapon on dit **䥫雞**, *sién kē·*).

扇 *Chán*. Eventail; battant de porte.

一把 (ou **一枝**) |, *ŷt pà* (ou *ŷt kī*) *chán*, un éventail.

撥｜, *pă't* |, s'éventer.

寫｜, *sià* |, écrire sur un éventail. (L'éventail n'est pas complet sans quelques caractères écrits dessus.)

一｜門, 雙｜門, *ŷt* | *moûn*, *soūng* | *moûn*, porte à un battant, porte à deux battants.

CHĀNG

聲 *Chāng*. Voix, son, ton.

小 |, *siaò* |, à voix basse.

莫 |, *mŏc chāng*, taisez-vous.

莫咁大 |, *mŏc àn t'aí chāng*, ne parlez pas si fort.

名 |, *miâng chāng*, réputation, renommée.

CHÂNG

成 *Châng* (*chîn*). Accompli, terminé, conclu.

事講 |, *sé kòng châng*, l'affaire est conclue.

買 |, *maì* |, le marché est conclu, j'ai fini par acheter.

唔 | 人, *mĝ* | *gnîn*, ce n'est pas un homme, c'est un vaurien.

那個事都做唔 |, *mâc kĕ· sé toū tsó mĝ* |, il ne mène aucune affaire à bonne fin, il ne réussit en rien.

| 下, *châng há*, quelquefois. (Pop.).

做豆腐愛落鹽水哮 | 得, *tsó t'coú foú oí lŏc yâm chouì tsáng* | *têt*, pour faire du fromage, il faut mettre de la présure pour faire cailler.

城 *Châng*. Ville murée.

| 內, | 外, | *nouí*, | *ngoé·*, dans les remparts, en dehors des remparts.

出 |, 入 |, *tch'oūt châng, gnĭp châng*, sortir de la ville, entrer dans la ville.

京 |, 省 |, 州 |, 縣 |, *kīn* |, *sèn* |, *tchoū* |, *yán* |, la capitale de l'empire, la capitale d'une province, la sous-préfecture, le chef-lieu d'une sous-préfecture.

CHÁNG

覡 *Cháng*. | **公**, | *koūng*, sorcier. magicien,

CHĀO

燒 *Chaō*. Bruler, rôtir, chaud, chaleur, chauffer.

好 | 火, *haò chaō fò*, il est temps de faire le dîner, (d'allumer le feu).

| 唔着, | *mĝ tch'ŏc*, le feu ne prend pas, cela ne peut pas brûler.

雞子拿來 |, *kē· tzè nā loî chaō*, fais rôtir la poule.

| 紅, *chaō foûng*, rougir au feu.

| 融, *chaō yoûng*, faire fondre.

| 料個, | *liaó ké·*, verroterie.

發 |, *fât* |, fièvre, chaleur intérieure.

| 窰, | *yaō*, chauffer un four.

CHAÒ

少 *Chaò*. Peu, moins, manquer.

多 |, *tō* |, un peu, quelques.

至 |, *tjé* |, à tout le moins.

| 見多怪, | *kián tō koudi*, qui a peu vu s'étonne beaucoup.

| 講個人, | *kòng ké· gnîn*, c'est un homme qui parle peu.

| 一個錢, | *ŷt kĕ· ts'iên*, il manque une sapèque.

減 | 一半, *kàm* | *ŷt pán*, diminuer de moitié.

| 唔得個, | *mĝ têt ké·*, c'est indispensable.

一個錢都 | 唔得, *ŷt ké. ts'iên toū* | *mĝ têt*, je ne te fais pas grâce d'une sapèque.

CHÁO

兆 *Chaó.* Million, présage.

一 ｜ 銀, *ŷt* ｜ *nioûn*, un million de piastres.

｜ 頭, ｜ *t'eoû*, pronostic, présage.

CHĂP

叶 *Chăp.* ｜ 音, *chăp ŷm*, articuler, bien parler, sans difficulté de langue ou de gosier.

涉 *Chăp.* ｜ 水, *chăp chouì*, nager debout, passer une rivière à gué ayant de l'eau jusqu'au genou.

好難去愛上岌 ｜ 水, *haò nân hí oí chōng ŷn* ｜ *chouì*, le voyage est très pénible, il faut gravir les montagnes et passer les rivières.

CHÂP

眨 *Châp.* Mouvement des paupières.

｜ 目, ｜ *moûc*, fermer les yeux.

CHĂT

舌 *Chăt.* Langue.

— 嫲, *chăt mâ*, la langue.

｜ 嫲伸出來, ｜ *mâ chīn tch'oût loî*, tire la langue.

｜ 嫲縮倒去, *chăt mâ souc ts'ioū hí*, retire ta langue.

大 ｜, *t'aí chăt*, se dit de celui qui a un défaut de langue.

蝕 *Chăt.* Se ruiner, perdre.

｜ 本, ｜ *poùn*, faire faillite.

我 ｜ 三個花邊, *ngaî* ｜ *sām kè fā piēn*, j'y perds trois piastres.

CHÂT

設 *Chât.* Instituer, établir.

｜ 法, *chât fâp*, imaginer un moyen, instituer des lois.

｜ 規矩, *chât kouī kì*, faire un règlement, établir des règles.

｜ 一個公所好念經, ｜ *ŷt kè koūng sò haò niám kīn*, établir un oratoire, lieu public pour prier.

｜ 席服禮, ｜ *sīt foûc lī*, donner un dîner en réparation d'une injure.

CHĒ

(*Voir aussi les mots SE*)

詩 *Chē.* Vers, poésie.

｜ 經, ｜ *kīn*, Le livre des vers. (Un des livres sacrés des Chinois.)

屍 *Chē.* Cadavre.

驗 ｜, *niám chē*, examiner juridiquement un cadavre. En dehors de cette expression, ce mot est peu employé; on dit 死人, *sì gnîn*, ou 死佬, *sì laò*, un mort. (Pop.)

CHÊ

匙 *Chê.* 鎖 ｜, *sò chê*, clef,

時 *Chê.* Temps, saison, époque.

｜ ｜, ｜ ｜, toujours, en tout temps.

起 ｜, *hì chê*, commencer.

幾 ｜, *kì chê*? quand?

｜ 辰鏢, ｜ *chîn piaō*, montre.

那個丨候, *mâc ké· chê heoú?* à quelle époque?

CHÈ

屎 *Chè*. Excréments, résidu, bouse, fiente, crotte.

屙丨, *ō chè*, évacuer. (Mot trivial).

屙黎丨, *ō laî chè*, évacuer sans s'en apercevoir.

拈狗丨, *niām keoù* 丨, ramasser les crottes de chien. (Métier souvent très lucratif en Chine).

耳丨, 鼻丨, *gnì* 丨, *p'í* 丨, le cérumen, morve.

丨背尾, 丨*poé· mī*, derrière, à la fin.

丨囊公, 丨 *nâng koūng*, le rectum.

CHÉ

氏 *Ché*. Famille d'une femme. L'unique usage de ce mot, dans la langue parlée, est de servir pour l'appellation officielle des personnes mariées. P. ex. dans 張陳丨, *Tchōng Tch'în* 丨, *Tchōng* est le nom de famille du mari, *Tch'în* est le nom de famille des parents de la femme; on ajoute *ché*, ce qui peut se traduire: Madame *Tchōng* issue de la famille *Tch'în*.

是 *Ché*. Etre. (Langue écrite).

示 *Ché*. Ordre, décret, avertissement.

出告丨, *tch'oût kaó* 丨, publier une ordonnance.

丨問你, 丨 *moún gnî*, je te demande un peu!

市 *Ché*. Marché.

丨鎮, 丨 *tchìn*, marché, lieu de vente.

照丨價, *tchaó* 丨 *ká*, d'après le prix courant.

好行丨, *haò hâng* 丨, qui se vend beaucoup, qui a cours.

利丨, *lí ché*, de bon augure, portebonheur.

試 *Ché*. Examiner.

考丨, *k'aò ché*, passer les examens.

世 *Ché*. Monde, vie, génération.

出丨, *tch'oût ché*, ou plus vulgairement *tch'oût sé·*, venir au monde.

丨上個福不長久, 丨 *chóng ké· foûc poût tch'ông kioù*, les joies du monde sont bien courtes.

丨界, 丨 *kiaí*, le monde matériel.

丨俗, 丨 *siouc*, les mœurs du monde.

百丨, *pâc ché*, toutes les générations, tous les siècles.

蒔 *Ché*. Planter le riz.

丨田, *ché t'iên*, planter le riz,

田丨完 (ou 丨下), *t'iên* 丨 *vân* (ou 丨 *hā*, la plantation du riz est achevée.

誓 *Ché* Serment.

發丨, *fât* 丨, jurer, faire serment.

發虛丨, *fât hī ché*, faire un faux serment, jurer en vain.

豉 *Ché*. 豆丨, *t'eoú* 丨, condiment fait avec une espèce de fève fermentée.

丨油, 丨 *yoû*, sauce faite avec des haricots fermentés.

CHÉ·

事 *Ché·* (sé). Travail, ouvrage.
做 |, *tsó ché·*, travailler.
做 田 |, *tsó t'iên ché·*, travailler aux champs.
做 重 還 |, *tsó tch'oûng p'ân* (pour *fân*) *ché·*, refaire ce que l'on vient de faire.

CHET (voir CHAT).
CHI (voir CHE et HI).

CHÌM

愼 *Chìm.* **謹** |, *kioùn chìm*, attentif, circonspect.

審 *Chìm.* Juger, examiner.
| **判** *chìm p'án*, juger.
私 | **判**, *sē chìm p'án*, jugement particulier.
公 | **判**, *koūng chìm p'án*, jugement général.
| **結** *chìm kiēt*, décider.

CHÍM

甚 *Chím.* Beaucoup, très, qui? quoi?
| **多**, *chím tō*, beaucoup.
| **好**, *chím haò*, très-bien.
| **麼**, *chím moût*, qui? quoi? (style écrit).

CHĪN

身 *Chīn*, corps.
肉 |, *nioûc chīn*, le corps humain.
| **體**, *chīn t'ì*, corps, santé.
一 |, *ŷt chīn*, tout le corps.
| **上**, *chīn hóng*, sur le corps, sur soi.
分 | **家**, *foūn chīn kā* (ou *poūn chīn kā*), diviser le patrimoine.
下 |, *há chīn*, partie inférieure du corps, mot poli pour désigner les parties honteuses.
本 |, *poùn chīn*, mon corps, ma personne, moi-même.
| **分**, *chīn foún*, rang, condition d'une personne, qualités personnelles, talents.
好 | **分 個 人**, *haò chīn foún ké· gnîn*, c'est un homme bien doué.

升 *Chīn.* Mesure de capacité, la dixième partie du boisseau. Monter, élever en grade, exhausser. Extraire les substances spiritueuses.
十 | **為 一 斗**, *chīp chīn vî ŷt teoù*, dix *chīn* font un boisseau.
| **天 堂**, *chīn t'iēn t'ōng*, monter au ciel, aller en paradis.
高 | (**陞**), *kaō chīn*, monter en grade.
| **主 教**, *chīn tchoù kaó*, être élevé à l'episcopat.
| **官**, *chīn kouōn*, promu à la dignité de mandarin.
| **高**, *chīn kaō*, exhausser.
屋 愛 | **高 來**, *voûc oí chīn kaō loî*, on doit exhausser la maison.
| **糖**, *chīn t'ōng*, raffiner le sucre.

伸 *Chīn.* Etendre.
舌 嘛 | **出 來**, *chât mâ chīn tch'oût loî*, tire la langue.
Voyez (**伸**) *tch'oūn*.

2

紳 *Chīn*. | 士, *chīn sé* (ou bien 鄉 | *hiōng chīn*), homme lettré, notable du pays, qui a quelque influence dans la région.

CHÎN

神 *Chîn*. Esprit, génie.
| 明, *chîn mîn*, les esprits.
純 |, *choûn chîn*, pur esprit.
天 |, *t'iēn chîn*, ange, esprit céleste.
| 父, *chîn foú* prêtre (père spirituel).
| 品, *chîn p'in*, le sacrement de l'ordre.
做 | 工, *tsó chîn koūng*, faire des œuvres de dévotion, faire ses exercices spirituels.
辦 | 工, *p'án chîn koūng*, se confesser. (Style chrétien).
精 |, *tsīn chîn*, esprits vitaux, énergie, ardeur.
佢講話有 | 氣, *kî kòng fá yoū chîn hí*, il y a de l'expression, de l'éloquence dans son discours.

成 *Chîn*. Devenir.
| 聖人, *chîn chín gnîn*, devenir un saint.
| 大, *chîn t'aí*, devenir grand.
Voir aussi les mots *châng*, *tcháng*, *tch'âng*.

辰 *Chîn*. Heure.
時 | 鐘, *chê chîn tchoūng*, horloge.
年 |, *niân chîn*, année.
生 |, *sēn chîn*, moment ou jour de la naissance.
我生 | 唔好, *ngā sēn chîn mĝ haò*, je suis né sous une mauvaise étoile (litt, à un mauvais moment).

晨 *Chîn*. Aurore, matin.
早 | 頭, *tsào chîn t'eoû*, le matin.
今早 |, *kīn tsào chîn*, ce matin.
| 朝日, *chîn tchāo gnĭt*, demain matin.

承 *Chîn*. Recevoir, flatter, supporter, servir de base.
| 認, *chîn gníu*, reconnaître, avouer.
受 | 家業, *choū chîn kā niăp*, hériter.
保 | 係, *paò chîn hé*, j'en réponds.
應 |, *ýn chîn*, s'occuper de, prendre sur soi.
奉 | 人, *foúng chîn gnîn*, honorer qqn. le flatter, lui faire des compliments.
樹板忒薄 | 咁重唔起, *choú pàn t'iĕt p'ŏc chîn àn tch'oūng mĝ hì*, les planches sont trop minces, elles ne peuvent supporter un poids si lourd.

CHÍN

聖 *Chín*. Saint, consacrer, bénir.
| 人, *chín gnîn*, un Saint.
| 衣, *chín ȳ*, le scapulaire.
| 龕 (ou | 櫃), *chín k'ām* (ou *chín k'oúi*), le tabernacle.
| 寵, *chín tch'oúng*, la grâce.
| 體, *chín t'ì*, l' Eucharistie.
| 跡, *chín tsĭt*, miracle.
| 事, *chín sé*, les sacrements.
主教有 | 神父個權, *tchoù káo yoū chín chîn foú ké k'iân*, l'évêque a le pouvoir d'ordonner les prêtres.

| 水, *chín choùi*, eau bénite.

求神父 | 過念珠子, *k'ioû chín foú chín kouó niám tchoū tzè*, je prie le Père de bénir mon chapelet.

盛 *Chín*. Abondant, florissant.

豐 | 年, *foūng chín niân*, année fertile.

茂 |, *miaó chín*, végétation luxuriante.

竹頭好快 |, *tchoūc t'eoû haò k'ouái chín*, les bambous se multiplient vite.

蜂子 | 阿唔知幾多, *foūng tzè chín á mĝ tī kì tō*, les abeilles se sont multipliées dans un nombre incalculable (litt. je ne sais combien).

勝 *Chín*. Vaincre.

打 | 仗, *tà chín tchóng*, remporter la victoire.

百戰百 |, *pâc tchán pâc chín*, être victorieux dans tous les combats.

CHIOU (Voir CHOU)

CHĬP

十 *Chĭp*. Dix.

| 個人, *chĭp ké· gnîn*, dix hommes.

| 字架, *chĭp sé ká*, croix.

| 字架個橫樹, *chĭp sé ká ké· vâng choú*, les bras de la croix.

| 字街, *chĭp sé kiāi*, rue croisée.

| 分, *chĭp foūn*, très, marque du superlatif.

| 分熱, *chĭp foūn gnĕt*, il fait excessivement chaud.

| 程有八程噲死, *chĭp tch'âng yoū pât tch'âng voé· sì*, il y a huit chances sur dix qu'il mourra.

拾 *Chĭp*. Dix (caractère employé dans les contrats). Ramasser, mettre en ordre.

収 | 東西, *choū chĭp toūng sī*, ramasse les effets. (Voir le mot 收 *choū*).

什 *Chĭp*. | 麼, *chĭp moût*, qui? quel? quoi? (style écrit).

CHĬP

濕 *Chĭp*. Humide, mouillé.

| 氣, *chĭp hí*, humidité,

我一身搭 |, *ngaî ȳt chīn tăp chĭp*, je suis complètement mouillé.

CHĬT

食 *Chĭt*. Manger.

| 朝, *chĭt tchāo*, dejeûner du matin.

| 晝, *chĭt tchoú*, dîner de midi.

| 夜, *chĭt yá*, dîner du soir.

好 | 飯, *haò chĭt fán*, le dîner est prêt.

好 | 個, *haò chĭt ké·*, bon à manger, chose comestible.

| 裡飯唔曾, *chĭt lî* (ou *chĭt ê·*) *fán mĝ ts'ên*, avez-vous dîné?

火 | 錢, *fò chĭt ts'iên*, frais de nourriture.

有病 | 唔起, *yoū p'iáng chĭt mĝ hì*, il est malade, il ne peut manger.

做唔倒 |, *tsó mĝ taò chĭt*, ne pouvoir vivre de son travail.

實 *Chĭt*. Vrai, sincère.

| 在, *chĭt ts'aí*, vraiment, très, d'aplomb.

| 在好, *chĭt ts'aí haò*, on ne peut mieux.

梯子愛放|在來唔係人會跌, *t'oī tzè oí fóng chĭt ts'aí loî, mģ ké· gnîn voé· tiêt*, il faut poser l'échelle bien d'aplomb, autrement on pourrait tomber.

老|人, *laò chĭt gnîn*, homme sincère, sans malice, facile à tromper.

講|話, *kòng chĭt fá*, parler sincèrement.

講|情, *kòng shĭt ts'în*, raconter les choses telles qu'elles sont.

CHÎT

失 *Chît*. Perdre, laisser échapper, manquer.

| 望, *chît vóng*, désespérer.

| 聲, *chît chāng*, perdre la voix.

銃子|火, *tch'oúng tzè chît fò*, le coup de fusil est parti par mégarde.

| 手, *chît choù*, manquer son coup.

| 脚, *chît kiôc*, faire un faux pas, trébucher.

| 信, *chît sín*, manquer de fidélité, ne pas tenir sa parole.

室 *Chît*. Maison, épouse.

石|, *chăc chît*, maison de pierre. (Les chinois donnent ce nom à la cathédrale de Canton).

家|, *kā chît*, épouse.

有家有|, *yoū kā yoū chît*, il a de la famil!e.

飾 *Chît*. Ornement.

首|, *choù chît*, ornements de tête. (S'emploie pour désigner en général toutes sortes d'ornements de femme, comme bracelets, boucles d'oreilles, épingles etc.).

式 *Chît*. Règle, modèle.

合|, *hăp chît*, convenable, en bon accord.

禮事唔多合|做, *yà sé mģ tò hăp chît tsó*, il n'est pas très convenable de faire cela.

兩個人唔合|, *leòng ké· gnîn mģ hăp chît*, les deux ne sont pas d'accord.

過唔同個様|, *koúo mģ t'oûng ké· yóng chît*, d'un autre genre, d'un autre modèle

識 *Chît*. Savoir, connaître.

你|字麼, *gnî chît sé mô*, connais-tu les caractères?

我唔|你, *ngaî mģ chît gnî*, je ne te connais pas.

認|, *gnín chît*, reconnaître.

我認你唔|, *ngaî gnín gnî mģ chît*, je ne te reconnais pas.

麼見|個人, *mô kián chît ké· gnîn*, un homme sans jugement.

釋 *Chît*. | 教, *chît kaó*, religion de bouddha.

| 典, *chît tièn*, livres de prières des bonzes.

悔|人, *fí chît gnîn*, faire réparation d'honneur.

CHŎC

(Voir aussi SOC)

杓 *Chŏc*. | 麻, *chŏc mâ*, grande cuillère en bois.

CHÔC

遡 *Chôc.* Aller à l'aventure.

| 嫽, *chôc liáo*, se promener, errer à l'aventure.

| 食, *chôc chìt*, mendier de porte en porte.

CHOÉ·

稅 *Choé·*. Douane, inpôt.

過 |, *kouó choé·*, acquitter les droits.

睡 *Choé·*. Se coucher, dormir.

好去 | 目, *haò hí choé· moûc*, il est temps d'aller se coucher, dormir.

| 唔着, *choé· mĝ tch'ŏc*, ne pouvoir s'endormir.

| 醒, *choé· siàng*, s'éveiller.

噴 |, *p'óún choé·*, ronfler.

CHÔN

船 *Chôn.* Barque, bateau.

渡 |, *t'oú chôn*, barque de passage.

火 |, *fò chôn*, bateau à vapeur.

上 |, *chōng chôn*, s'embarquer.

下 |, *hā chôn*, débarquer.

CHŌNG

上 *Chōng (chóng)*. Monter, inscrire, parvenir.

| 山, *chōng sān*, gravir la montagne.

| 水, *chōng chouì*, remonter la rivière, remonter le courant.

| 案, *chōng ón*, aller au jugement.

| 人個當, *chōng gnîn ké· tóng*, être pris au piège, être désagréablement surpris.

| 馬, *chōng mā*, monter à cheval.

| 轎, *chōng k'iáo*, monter en palanquin.

| 簿, *chōng p'oū*, enregistrer.

| 摺, *chōng tchâp*, inscrire sur son carnet.

| 教友人個名, *chōng kaó yoū gnîn ké· miâng*, inscrire les noms des chrétiens.

還唔曾 | 三十歲, *hân mĝ ts'ên chōng sām chìp sé·*, il n'a pas encore atteint l'âge de 30 ans.

商 *Chōng.* Commerçant.

| 量, *chōng leông*, délibérer.

傷 *Chōng.* Blesser, blessure.

打 |, *tà chōng*, blesser en frappant.

內 |, *noúi chōng*, lésion interne.

| 害人, *chōng hói gnîn*, nuire à quelqu'un.

| 風, *chōng foūng*, refroidissement, rhume.

| 人個禾, *chōng gnîn ké· vô*, endommager les champs de riz.

CHÔNG

常 *Chông.* Toujours.

| |, *chông chông*, toujours.

平 |, *p'în chông*, ordinaire.

| 用個, *chông yoúng ké·*, usuel, dont on se sert toujours.

裳 *Chông.* 衣 |, *ȳ chông*, habits en général.

嘗 *Chông.* Goûter.

你｜阿子我酒, *gnî chông á tzè ngā tsioù*, goûte un peu mon vin.

CHÒNG

賞 *Chòng*. Récompenser.

｜善罰惡, *chòng chán făt ôc*, récompenser les bons et punir les méchants.

｜賜人, *chòng sé (*ou *tsé) gnîn*, donner en récompense.

我｜你一百錢, *ngaî chòng gnî ŷt pâc ts'iên*, je te donne cent sapèques de gratification.

上 *Chòng (chóng)*. Ajuster les différentes parties d'un tout, enduire.

｜鞋底, *chòng haî taì*, mettre une semelle, ressemeler.

桌做成唔曾｜成, *tsôc tsó tcháng mĝ ts'ên chòng tcháng*, la table est finie mais elle n'est pas encore montée.

｜馬鞍, *chòng mā ón*, mettre la selle.

時辰鐘死帛裡愛｜過, *chê chîn tchoūng sì p'ĕt lî oí chòng koúo*, l'horloge s'est arrêtée il faut la remonter.

｜油, *chòng yoû*, huiler.

｜色, *chòng sêt*, colorier.

CHÓNG

上 *Chóng*. En haut, supérieur.

上｜背, *chōng chóng poé*, aller du côté le plus haut.

坐｜面, *ts'ō chóng mién*, être assis à la place d'honneur.

｜輩人, *chóng pí gnîn*, nos supérieurs, les anciens.

｜等, *chóng tèn*, première qualité, superfin.

｜下, *chóng há*, à peu près, environ.

｜早, *chóng tsaò*, autrefois, jadis.

尙 *Chóng*. 和｜, *vô chóng*, bonze.

CHÔT

(Voir aussi SOT)

說 *Chôt*. Parler, dire.

｜話, *chôt fá*, parler. (Ce mot est peu employé dans le langage parlé, voyez 講 *Kòng*, 話 *vá*).

CHOŪ

收 *Choū*. Percevoir, recueillir, mettre en ordre, détruire.

｜信, *choū sín*, recevoir une lettre.

｜穀利, *choū koŭc lí*, percevoir les revenus de riz.

東西好｜起, *toūng sī haò choū hì*, ramasse les affaires.

火燒屋｜帛有十過個人, *fò chaō voûc choū p'ĕt yoū chĭp kouó ké gnîn*, la maison a brûlé, plus de dix hommes ont péri.

我｜拾你, *ngaî choū chĭp gnî*, je vais te mettre à la raison.

輸 *Choū*. Perdre au jeu, être vaincu, avoir le désavantage.

官司打｜裡, *kouōn sē tà choū lî*, le procès est perdu.

書 *Choū*. Livre.

｜房, *choū fông*, école.

敎｜, *kaō choū*, enseigner (les livres), faire l'école.

｜敎, *choū kaó*, la loi Judaïque.

背｜, *p'oí choū*, réciter sa leçon.
看｜, *k'ón choū*, lire.
一部｜有三本, *ŷt p'oú choū yoū sām poùn*, l'ouvrage est en trois volumes.

CHOÛ

仇 *Choû*. Ennemi, haïr.
｜恨人, *choū hén gnîn*, détester quelqu'un.
報｜, *paó choû*, se venger.
唔做得報人個｜, *mĝ tsó têt paó gnîn ké· choû*, il est défendu de se venger.
對｜, *toúi choû*, adversaire, antagoniste.

薯 *Choû*. Espèce de tubercule comestible.
番｜, *fān choû*, patate.
荷蘭｜, *hô lân choû*, pomme de terre.

CHOÙ

署 *Choù*. Faire l'interim.
｜任官, *choù ŷm kouōn*, mandarin intérimaire.

守 *Choù*. Observer, surveiller.
｜貞, *choù tchīn*, garder la virginité.
｜節, *choù tsiēt*, garder la viduité ou le célibat.
｜主日, *choù tchoù gnĭt*, observer les Dimanche.
｜規矩, *choù kouī kì*, observer les convenances, se bien conduire.
｜城門, *choù châng moûn*, garder la porte de la ville.

首 *Choù*. Tête, principe.
會｜, *fí choù*, nom donné aux chefs d'une corporation.
｜飾, *choù chĭt*, ornement de femme. (Voir *chĭt*).

手 *Choù*. Main.
｜掌, *choù tchòng*, paume de la main.
｜背, *choù pí* (pour *poé·*), revers de la main.
｜指, *choù tjè*, doigts de la main.
｜巾, *choù kīn*, ou ｜帕, *choù p'á* mouchoir, serviette.
｜藝, *choù gní*, métier.
｜尾, *choù mī*, souvenir.
起｜, *hì choù*, commencer, mettre la main à l'œuvre.
到｜, *táo choù*, obtenir.
｜脚長, *choù kiŏc tch'ông*, (litt. avoir les mains et les pieds longs). Gens portés au vol.
打空｜, *tà k'oúng choù*, marcher les mains vides, ne rien porter.
下｜多, *há choù tō*, l'opération est compliquée; il y a trop de monde.
兩下｜做得倒, *leòng há choù tsó têt taò*, cela peut se faire en un tour de main, (litt. deux tours de main).

CHOÚ

受 *Choú*. Recevoir, subir.
｜傷, *choú chōng*, recevoir une blessure.
｜苦, *choú k'où*, souffrir.
｜單, *choú tān*, reçu, quittance.
我｜佢唔下, *ngaî choù kî mĝ hā*, je ne puis l'endurer, le supporter.

丨人個氣, *choú gnîn ké· hí*, avoir à supporter la mauvaise humeur de quelqu un.

恕 *Choú*. Pardon, miséricorde.

寬丨人, *k'ōn choú gnîn*, pardonner à quelqu'un.

壽 *Choú*. Longévité.

丨木, *choú moŭc*, cercueil.

上丨,中丨,下丨, *chóng choú, tchoūng choú, há choú*, 120 ans, 100 ans, 80 ans, de vie.

做丨酒, *tsó choú tsiòu*, festin donné par un vieillard le jour de sa fête.

樹 *Choú*. Arbre, bois.

一條丨, *ŷt t'iâo choú*, un arbre.

丨木, *choú moŭc*, les arbres en général.

丨頭, *choú t'eoû*, tronc de l'arbre, bloc de bois.

丨節, *choú tsiĕt*, les nœuds de l'arbre.

丨扒, *choú p'à*, les branches d'arbre.

撐丨子, *ts'áng choú tzè*, étayer un arbre.

拿一塊丨子來楔桌, *nā ŷt k'ouái choú tzè loî siăp tsŏc*, caler la table avec un morceau de bois.

庶 *Choú*. **丨民**, *丨mîn*, le peuple.

CHOŬC

贖 *Choŭc*. Racheter.

補丨, *poù choŭc*, satisfaction d'une offense.

天主降生為丨衆人個罪, *t'iēn tchoù kóng sēn ví choŭc tchoúng gnîn ké· ts'oúi*, Dieu s'est fait homme pour racheter les péchés de tous les hommes.

丨轉一坵田, *choŭc tchòn ŷt k'iōu t'iên*, racheter une rizière que l'on avait hypothéquee.

去當舖丨轉東西, *hí tóng p'oú choŭc tchòn toūng sī*, aller au Mont-de-piété pour racheter des objets.

熟 *Choŭc*. Cuit, expérimenté. (Mûr, voyez *sioŭc*).

豬肉煮丨唔曾, *tchoū nioŭc tchoù choŭc mĝ ts'ên*, la viande de porc est-elle cuite à point?

讀書讀丨, *t'oŭc choū t'oŭc choŭc*, apprendre par cœur.

丨識人, *choŭc chĭt gnîn*, ou bien, **相丨個人**, *siōng choŭc ké· gnîn*, homme bien connu, avec qui on a de fréquents rapports.

屬 *Choŭc*. Dépendre de, subordonné, tributaire.

東石丨平遠縣管, *toūng-chăc choŭc p'în-yàn yán kouòn*, *Toūng-chăc* est du ressort de la sous-préfecture de *P'în-yán*.

丨那個主教管, *choŭc mâc ké· tchoù káo kouòn*, de quel évêque dépend-il?

CHOÛC

叔 *Choŭc*. Oncle paternel, frère cadet du père.

阿丨, *ā choŭc*, mon oncle.

丨伯兄弟, *choŭc pâc hioūng t'í*, cousins germains.

丨公, *choŭc koūng*, grand-oncle (cadet du grand-père).

速 *Choûc*. Vite.
| 迅, *choûc sìn*, vite, immédiatement.
| 卽, *choûc tsīt*, à l'instant.
| 行, *choûc hâng*, aller de suite.

誰 *Chouî*. Quel ? qui ? (style écrit).

水 *Choùi*. Eau.
落 |, *lŏc choùi*, il pleut.
| 車, *choùi tch'ā*, noria.
| 龍, *choùi lioûng*, pompe.
打 坪 |, *tà p'iâng choùi*, se servir du niveau d'eau.
| 銀, *choùi nioûn*, mercure.
風 |, *foūng choùi*, situation et disposition d'un emplacement considérées au point de vue de l'influence qu'on lui attribue sur le bonheur ou le malheur de la famille.
死 |, *sì choùi*, eau stagnante.
| 土, (v. | 色), *choùi t'où*, (v. *choùi sĕt*), climat.
合 | 色, *kăp choùi sĕt*, s'acclimater.
銀 |, *nioûn choùi*, ou simplement *choùi*, taux de l'argent, titre de l'argent, perte d'argent sur le change. (Voir 銀 *nioûn*).

水 *Choùi*. Espèce, forme. (Se prononce plus souveut *hì*, *voir ce mot*).

CHOÛN
(*Voir aussi* SOUN).

唇 *Choûn*. Lèvre, bord.
嘴 |, *tchói choûn*, les lèvres.
莫 行 咁 |, *mŏc hâng kàn choûn*, ne marche pas si près du bord.

淳 *Choûn*. Doux, d'un bon naturel, apprivoisé.
| 善 人, *choûn chán gnîn*, homme doux et bon.
老 虎 畜 唔 | 個, *laò foù hioūc mĝ choûn ké·*, le tigre ne s'apprivoise pas.

CHOÚN

順 *Choún*. Se conformer, mettre en ordre.
我 | 你 意, *ngaî choún niā ý*, je me conforme à tes désirs.
| 便, *choún p'ién*, profiter de l'occasion.
| 路, *choún loú*, sur son chemin.
| 手, *choún choù*, à la portée de la main.
| 口, *choún k'eoù*, facile à prononcer.
| 風, *choún foūng*, vent favorable.
| 水, *choún choùi*, naviguer dans le sens du courant.
| | 流 流, *choún choún lioû lioû*, tout va à souhait.

CHOŬT

述 *Choŭt*. Publier, raconter.
所 | 個 書 有 好 多 假 個, *sò choŭt ké· choū yoū haò to kà ké·*, ce que les livres racontent n'est pas toujours vrai.

術 *Choŭt*. Artifice.
邪 |, *siâ choŭt*, magie, sorcellerie.

É·

係 *É·* (ou *í* pour *hé·*). Beaucoup, très.

3

| 好, *é· haò*, très bien.

| 多, *é· tō*, beaucoup.

裡個馬 | 淳, *ỳ ké· mā é· choûn*, ce cheval est très doux.

ĒM

Ēm. Porter sur son sein.

| 細人子, *ēm sé· gnîn tzè*, porter un petit enfant sur son sein.

| 細人睡, *ēm sé· gnîn choé·*, endormir un enfant en le portant sur son sein.

| 燒, *ēm chaō*, réchauffer sur son sein.

ĒN

恩 *Ēn*. Bienfait, grâce.

| 寵, *ēn tch'oùng*, grâce.

| 典, *ēn tièn*, bienfait.

| 赦, *ēn chá*, indulgences.

開 | 別我, *k'oī ēn poūn ngaî*, soyez indulgent envers moi.

EOÙ

嘔 *Eoù*. Vomir.

我想 |, *ngaî siòng eoù*, j'ai envie de vomir.

EOÚ

熰 *Eoú*. Réduire en cendres, enfumer.

| 灰, *eoú foē·*, réduire en cendres.

| 竻頭, *eoú nĕt t'eoû*, brûler des broussailles.

| 蚊, *eoú moūn*, enfumer les moustiques.

漚 *Eoú*. Conserver.

牛奶 | 唔得, *nioû nén eoú mĝ tĕt*, le lait ne se conserve pas.

| 壞, *coú faí*, se détériorer par le temps.

猪肉 | 臭, *tchoū nioŭc coú tch'oú*, la viande de porc a pris une mauvaise odeur.

ÊP

Êp. Lancer, jeter.

| 石頭, *êp chăc t'eoû*, lancer des pierres.

Êp (ou *ĕt*) Retenu par un obstacle.

船 | 等裡, *chôn êp tèn lî*, la barque s'est ensablée,

ĔT

呃 *Ĕt* (*k'ĕt*). | 啄, *ĕt toŭc*, hoquet.

打 | 啄, *tà ĕt toŭc*, avoir le hoquet.

FĀ

花 *Fā*. Fleur, fleuri.

摘 |, *tsâc fā*, cueillir des fleurs.

| 園, *fā yân*, jardin.

開 |, *k'ōi fā*, fleurir.

春天樹開 |, *tch'oūn t'iēn choú k'oī fā*, les arbres fleurissent au printemps.

| 布, *fā poú*, toile de diverses couleurs.

| 狗, *fā keoù*, chien à la peau tachetée.

| 娘, *fā niông*, femme débauchée, courtisanne.

| 眼, *fā niàn*, troubler la vue, jeter de la poudre aux yeux.

一個 | 邊, *ĭt ké· fā piēn*, une piastre.

FÂ

華 *Fâ*. Pompeux, splendide.

中 |, *tchoūng fâ*, la Chine.

嗶 *Fâ*. Chercher ou trouver dans son esprit un expédient, prévoir.

｜正愛幾多本錢來做, *fâ tcháng oí kì tō poùn ts'iên loî tsó*, calculer d'avance ce qu'il faut de capital pour une entreprise.

裡擺生理麼｜, *ỳ paì siēn lī mô fâ*, cette fois le commerce ne répond pas aux prévisions.

｜唔定, *fâ mĝ t'ín*, on ne peut pas prévoir.

｜算, *fâ són*, calculer, prévoir.

｜拳, *fâ k'iân*, jouer à la mourre.

FÁ

畫 *Fá*. Peindre, tracer des lignes, dessiner.

｜像, *fá sióng*, peindre des portraits.

｜花, *fá fā*, peindre des fleurs, des enjolivures, etc...

｜虎｜皮難｜骨, *fá foù fá p'ì nân fá koût*, on ne peut pas juger des gens sur la mine.

｜壁, *fá piâc*, rayer ou barbouiller les murs.

｜圖, *fá t'oû*, tracer un plan.

化 *Fá*. Transformer, fondre, dissoudre.

消｜, *siaō fá*, digérer.

｜灰, *fá foē·*, éteindre la chaux.

你放忒多白糖｜唔得盡, *gnî fóng t'iēt tō p'ác t'ông fá mĝ têt ts'ín*, tu mets trop de sucre, il ne pourra pas tout fondre.

｜胎, *fá t'oī*, arrière-cour des maisons.

(叫)｜, *káo fá*, mendier, mendiant.

話 *Fá*. Parole, mot.

講｜, *kòng fá*, parler.

一句｜, *ŷt kí fá*, un mot.

我麼两句｜, *ngaî mô leòng kí fá*, je n'ai pas deux paroles.

講閑｜, *kòng hân fá*, dire des paroles oiseuses, (signifie aussi faire des médisances).

你講冇｜, *gnî kòng p'áng fá*, tu dis des paroles vides de sens.

｜不投機, *fá poût t'eoû kī*, les paroles ne concordent pas, la discussion tourne en dispute, parole qui n'est pas dite à propos, coq-à-l'âne.

FÂC

發 *Fâc* (*fât*). Rebondir, se détendre, parer un coup.

｜阿上, *fâc á chóng*, rebondir.

搣阿起｜阿開, *măc á hì fâc á k'oī*, donner un coup de bâton et en parer un.

法條唔正噲｜走, *fâp t'iáo mĝ tcháng voé· fâc tscoù*, le ressort n'est pas bien mis, il va se détendre.

FAÎ

懷 *Faî*. Sein, garder dans le cœur.

｜胎, *faî t'oī*, porter un fruit dans son sein, femme enceinte. (Style relevé).

FAÍ

壞 *Faí*. Se gâter, corrompre.

打｜, 跌｜, *tà faí, tiēt faí*, abîmé par un choc, par une chute.

| 事, *faí sé*, gâter une affaire, affaire gâtée.

| 表樣, *faí piào yóng*, scandaliser, donner le mauvais exemple.

| 人個名聲, *faí gnîn ké· miâng chāng*, perdre la réputation d'autrui.

FÂM

凡 *Fâm*. Quiconque.

| 主日, *fâm tchoù gnĭt*, chaque Dimanche.

FÁM

犯 *Fám*. Transgresser, violer, résister.

| 罪, *fám ts'oüi*, pécher.

| 小齋, *fám siào tsaī*, violer la loi de l'abstinence.

| 人, *fám gnîn*, criminel, acusé. On dit *fām gnîn* d'un homme importun, agaçant.

患 *Fám*. Malheur, calamité.

| 難, *fám nán*, calamité.

FĀN

番 *Fān*. Etranger, espèce, nombre de fois.

| 人, *fān gnîn*, étranger.

過 |, *kouó fān*, aller à l'étranger.

| 禾, *fān vô*, riz d'automne.

賊來裡三 | 一夜, *ts'ĕt loî lì sām fān ŷt yá*, les voleurs sont venus trois fois en une nuit.

翻 *Fān*. Changer, tourner, retourner.

書 | 轉來, *choū fān tchòn loî*, retourne le livre.

| 案, *fān ón*, annuler un jugement.

一夜緊 | 去 | 轉, *ŷt yá kìn fān hí fān tchòn*, toute la nuit je n'ai fait que me tourner de côté et d'autre.

Lât-lât fān, sens dessus dessous.

細人子(係) |, *sé· gnîn tzè é· fān*, cet enfant est très espiègle.

FÂN

煩 *Fân*. Importuner, triste, pénible.

| 勞你, *fân láo gnî*, pardon! je vous ai fort importuné.

| 勞你同我帶一封信子, *fân láo gnî t'oûng ngaî taí ŷt foūng sín tzè*, veuillez prendre la peine de me porter une lettre.

藩 *Fân*. | 臺 *fân t'ôi*, grand trésorier d'une province. (On dit mieux 布政司 *póu tchín sē*).

繁 *Fân*. Beaucoup, embrouillé.

事情 | 雜, *sé ts'în fân ts'ăp*, beaucoup d'affaires, affaires embrouillées.

礬 *Fân*. Sels métalliques.

白 |, *p'ăc fân*, alun.

青 |, *ts'iāng fân*, sulfate de fer.

膽 |, *tàm fân*, sulfate de cuivre, vitriol bleu.

FÂN

還 *Fân* Rendre. (En ce sens on dit plus souvent «*vân*». *Voyez ce mot)*.

Encore, (en ce sens on dit mieux «*hân*» *Voyez ce mot*).

FÀN

反 *Fàn* Se révolter, contraire.

| 敎, *káo*, abjurer, apostasier.

病又 | , *p'iang yóu fàn*, la maladie l'a repris.

FÁN

飯 *Fán* Riz cuit, repas.

一飡 | , *ŷt ts'ōn fán*, un repas.

蔽 | , *pí fán*, séparer le riz de son eau après une première cuisson.

| 好裡, *fán hào lê·*, le repas est servi.

販 *Fán*. Revendeur.

米 | , *mì fán*, marchand de riz.

馬 | , *mā fán*, maquignon.

FÂP

法 *Fâp*. Méthode, moyen, règle.

麼 | , *mô fâp*, impossible, il n'y a pas moyen.

有那個方 | 麼, *yoū mâc ké· fōng fâp mô*? y a-t-il quelque moyen?

| 水, *fâp chouì*, eau bénite des sorciers.

犯 | , *fám fâp*, violer la loi.

| 塲, *fâp tch'ông*, le lieu du supplice.

| 國, *fâp kouĕt*, la France.

| 條, *fâp t'iaô*, ressort.

FĂT

活 *Făt*. Vivant, vivre.

復 | , *foŭc făt*, ressusciter.

你信德唔 | , *nia sín têt mg făt*, ta foi n'est pas vive.

咁 | 潑, *àn făt pât!* qu'il est agile!

罰 *Făt*. Punir, peine.

天主 | 惡, *t'iēn tchoù făt ôc*, Dieu punit les méchants.

| 三個花邊, *făt sām ké· fā piēn*, une amende de trois piastres.

FÂT

闊 *Fât*. Large.

寬 | , *k'ōn fât*, large, spacieux.

開 | , *k'oī fât*, élargir, agrandir.

髮 *Fât*. 頭 | , *t'eoû fât*, chevelure.

發 *Fât*. Produire, surgir, envoyer.

| 痛悔, *fât t'oúng fí*, faire un acte de contrition.

| 燒, *fât chaō*, avoir la fièvre.

| 財, *fât ts'ôi*, devenir riche.

| 錢, *fât ts'iēn*, distribuer des sapèques.

打 | 人去買菜, *tà fât gnîn hí maì ts'ói*, envoyer quelqu'un acheter des légumes.

FÊN

衡 *Fên*. Balance, joug. Ne s'emploie que dans le sens de 權 | *k'iân fên*, autorité.

FEOÛ

浮 *Feoû*. Flotter, surnager.

樹子 | 水, *choú tzè feoû chouì*, le bois surnage.

| 橋, *feoû k'iaô*, pont flottant, pont de bateau.

FEOÙ

否 *Feoù*. Particule interrogative, finale de phrase.

Ne s'emploie que dans les livres.

FEÓU

埠 *Feóu* | 頭, *feóu t'eôu*, ville non murée.

FĔT

或 *Fĕt*. Ou, peut-être. 倘 | , *t'òng fĕt*, si, à condition.

倘 | 唔肯, *t'òng fĕt mĝ hèn*, si par hazard il ne veut pas.

惑 *Fĕt*. 疑 | , *gnî fĕt*, douter, soupçonner.

獲 *Fĕt* Obtenir, trouver.

拉 | , *là fĕt*, trouver.

FĪ

飛 *Fī* (ou *pī*). Voler.

| 走裡, *fī tseòu lê*, il s'est envolé.

銀 | , *nioûn fī*, billet de banque, billet à ordre.

非 *Fī* Négation, faux, mal.

| 禮之言, *fī lī tjē nián*, paroles déshonnètes.

唆是懂 | , *sò ché toùng fī*, dire ce que l'on ne pense pas, dire bon ce que l'on sait être mauvais. (Style relevé).

匪 *Fī*. Mauvais, dépravé.

土 | , *t'où fī*, voleurs.

會 | , *fí fī*, mauvaise société, se dit des sociétés secrètes.

緋 *Fī* | 紅, *fī foûng*, rouge.

揮 *Fī*. Faire mouvoir.

愛 | 轉水裡向來, *oí fī tchòn chouì ỳ hióng loî*, il faut conduire l'eau de ce côté.

FÎ

回 *Fî*. Revenir; nombre de fois.

| 信, *fî sín*, répondre à une lettre, rendre réponse.

來 | , *loî fî*, les allées et venues.

頭 | , *t'eoû fî*, la première fois.

好多 | , *haò tō fî*, bon nombre de fois.

茴 *Fî*. | 香 (ou 小 |), *fî hiōng* (ou *siaò fî*), anis.

FÍ

廢 *Fí*. Inutile, abandonner.

| 物, *fí voŭt*, chose inutile, bonne à jeter.

人 | 帛裡個, *gnîn fí p'ĕt lî kć*, cela a été jeté, abandonné. (Voir *fĭt*).

費 *Fí*. Dépenser, employer.

所 | (ou 用 |), *sò fí* (ou *yoúng fí*), dépenses ordinaires.

盤 | , *p'ân fí*, viatique, argent de voyage.

| 心, *fí sīm*, soucis, se donner de la peine.

肺 *Fí*. Poumons.

心 | , *sīm fí*, le cœur et les poumons.

(Plus vulgairement, 氣膈 *hí kâc*, les poumons).

悔 *Fí*. Regretter, se repentir.

痛｜, *t'oúng fí*, contrition.

｜心, *fí sīm*, regretter ce que l'on a fait.

｜釋人, *fí chĭt gnîn*, faire réparation d'honneur.

會 *Fí*. Société, occasion, se rencontrer.

聖教｜, *chín kaó fí*, la Sainte Eglise.

｜匪, *fí fī*, mauvaise société secrète.

機｜, *kī fí*, occasion.

自唔曾｜過面, *tsé mĝ ts'ên fí kouó mién*, nous ne nous sommes jamais vus.

｜官, *fí kouōn*, visiter le mandarin.

｜元, *fí niân*, un des degrés du doctorat.

惠 *Fí*. Bienfait.

恩｜, *ēn fí*, bienfait.

FĪN

Fīn. Egratignure.

手掛倒係多｜, *choù kouà tào é· tō fīn*, j'ai la main toute égratignée.

FÍN

Fín. Remuer, agiter.

馬｜頭 (呀), *mā fín t'eoû-ná*, le cheval agite sa tête.

牛尾緊｜, *nioû mī kìn fín*, la queue du bœuf ne fait que remuer.

FĬT

廢 *Fĭt*. (pour *fí*). Jeter, rejeter, lancer, abandonner.

｜帛佢, *fĭt p'ĕt kî*, jette-le.

｜石頭, *fĭt chăc t'eoû*, lancer, jeter des pierres.

裡生理我｜唔得, *ỳa siēn lī ngaî fĭt mĝ tĕt*, je ne puis abandonner ce commerce.

FÔ

和 *Fô*. Concorde, accord, modéré.

｜睦, *fô moŭc*, être d'accord, en bonne intelligence.

講｜, *kòng fô*, terminer une querelle, faire la paix.

｜裡十個花邊, *fô lî chĭp ké· fā piēn*, c est accommodé moyennant dix piastres.

你唱曲我｜你, *gnî tch'óng k'ioûc ngaî fô gnî*, chante-moi un air je t'accompagnerai.

温｜, *voūn fô*, tiède, douce chaleur.

夥 *Fô*. ｜計, *fô kí*, compagnon, collègue, associé.

FÒ

火 *Fò*. Feu.

好燒｜, *haò chaō fò*, il est temps d'allumer le feu.

｜忒很, *fò t'iĕt hên*, le feu est trop ardent.

｜利 (ou 焰), *fò lí* (ou *liám*), flamme.

｜煋, *fò sēn*, étincelle.

｜柴, *fò ts'aî*, allumettes.

藥, *fò yŏc*, poudre à canon.
| 窗, *fò ts'oūng*, chaufferette.
| 箭, *fò tsién*, fusée.
| 管, *fò kouòn*, le verre d'une lampe.
家 |, *kā fò*, ustensile, instrument.

FÓ

賀 *Fó*. Féliciter.
恭 | 人, *kioūng fó gnîn*, adresser des félicitations à quelqu'un.

貨 *Fó*. Marchandises.
| 物, *fó voŭt*, marchandises en général.
雜 | 生理, *ts'ăp fó siēn lī*, commerce aux cent articles.

禍 *Fó*. Malheur, calamité.
細人子麼孝敬父母天主有降 | *sé· gnîn tzè mô haó kín foú moū t'iēn tchoū yoū kóng fó*, Dieu euvoie des malheurs aux enfants qui n'honorent pas leurs parents.

Fōc gnîn (pop.) tromper.

FOĒ·

灰 *Foē·*. Chaux, cendre.
石 |, *chăc foē·*, chaux.
塵 |, *tch'în foē·*, poussière.
| 色, *foē· sĕt*, couleur cendrée, ils appellent souvent ainsi le violet.

FŌN

歡 *Fōn*. Particule numérale des couvertures, des ornements.
一 | 洋氈, *ŷt fōn yông tchān*, une couverture.
一 | 祭衣, *ŷt fōn tsí ȳ*, une chasuble.

歡 *Fōn*. Se réjouir, consentir.
| 喜, *fōn hì*, content.
| 樂, *fōn lŏc*, plaisir, se réjouir.
佢唔多 | 喜, *kî mĝ tō fōn hì*, il n'a pas l'air très content.

FÓN

換 *Fón*. Changer, échanger (on dit mieux *vouón* voy. ce mot).

緩 *Fón*. Différer, peu à peu.
| | 子來, *fōn fōn tzè lôi*, allez doucement.

FŌNG

方 *Fōng*. Carré, pays, moyen.
四 |, *sí fōng*, carré.
地 |, *t'í fōng*, pays, endroit, terrain.
一 | 一俗, *ŷt fōng ŷt sioŭc*, chaque pays a ses coutumes.
| 法, *fōng fâp*, moyen.
| 便, *fōng p'ién*, commode, avantageux.
比 |, *pì fōng*, par exemple.

荒 *Fōng*. désert, famine, vide.
| 地瀝, *t'í lăc*, terrain inculte.
饑 | 年辰, *kī fōng niân chîn*, année stérile.

慌 *Fōng*. Précipité.
咁 | 忙, *àn fōng mông*, que vous êtes empressé! (manière de remercier ou de reconnaître un service).

FÔNG

坊 *Fông*. Boutique, atelier, fabrique.

酒 |, *tsioù fông*, boutique où l'on fait le vin.

油 |, *yoû fông*, boutique où l'on fait l'huile, moulin à huile.

印書 |, *ýn choū fông*, imprimerie.

牌 |, *p'aî fông*, arcs de triomphe, (monuments en pierre qne l'on rencontre parfois sur les grandes routes).

房 *Fông*. Maison, chambre, appartements particuliers.

間 |, (ou | 間), *kiān fông* (ou *fông kiān*), chambre.

廚 |, *tch'oû fông*, cuisine.

親 |, 遠 |, *ts'īn fông, yàn fông*, branches d'une même famille, rapprochées (ou) éloignées (de la souche commune).

一隻屋有三 | 人, *ȳt tchâc voûc yoū sām fông gnîn*, la famille comprend trois branches.

過 |, *kouó fông*, être adopté par une autre branche.

通 |, *t'oūng fông*, expression honnête pour désigner l'acte conjugal.

門 |, *moûn fông*, loge du portier d'un tribunal.

衙貯裡有三班六 |, *ngâ toù lî yoū sām pān lioûc fông*, au prétoire il y a trois escouades de satellites et six bureaux (dont voici les noms): 吏 |, 戶 |, 禮 |, 兵 |, 刑 |, 工 |, *lí fông, foú fông, lī fông, pīn fông, hȳn fông, koūng fông*, bureau des dignités, de l'impôt, des rites, des affaires militaires, des affaires criminelles, des travaux publics.

妨 *Fông*. Empêcher, nuire.

無 |, *voû fông*, cela ne nuit pas, sans inconvénient.

無 | 來嫽, *voû fông loî liaó*, que cela ne vous empêche pas de venir me voir.

防 *Fông*. Se mettre en garde, pourvoir.

裡個人靠唔住愛 | 佢, *ỳ kó gnîn k'aó mĝ tch'oú, oí fông ki*, on ne peut se fier à cet homme, mettons-nous en garde contre lui.

| 備, *fông p'í*, prévoir et pourvoir, se prémunir contre.

| 身, *fông chīn*, prendre des mesures pour sa propre sûreté, faire attention.

皇 *Fông*. Empereur.

| 帝, *fông tí*, l'Empereur.

做 | 帝, *tsó fông tí*, être empereur.

| 太后, *fông t'aí heoú*, l'Impératrice.

中國 | 帝喊天子, *tchoūng kouĕt fông tí hám t'iēn tzè*, on appelle l'empereur de Chine le Fils du Ciel.

凰 *Fông*. 鳳 |, *foúng fông*, phénix, oiseau fabuleux.

FÒNG

紡 *Fòng* (ou *p'iòng*). Filer au virolet.

| 線, *fòng sién*, filer, faire du fil.

| 綿花, *fòng miên fā*, filer le coton.

訪 *Fòng*. S'informer.

| 問, *fòng moún*, prendre des renseignements.

4

彷 *Fòng*. Ressembler.

兩個人相|, *leòng ké· gnîn siōng fòng*, ils se ressemblent tous les deux.

謊 *Fòng*, Tromper,

莫|人, *mŏc fòng gnîn*, dites la vérité, ne me trompez pas.

|角, *fòng kôc*, oublier.

FÓNG

放 *Fóng (ou pióng)*. Déposer, lâcher, placer, mettre.

|學, *fóng hŏc*, cesser l'école, aller en vacances.

你|心佢唔會死, *gnî fóng sīm kî mĝ voé· sì*, soyez sans inquiétude, il ne mourra pas.

我|心唔下, *ngaî fóng sīm mĝ hā*, je ne puis m'empêcher d'être inquiet.

我釣個魚子忒細我|走佢, *ngaî tiaó ké· nĝ tzè t'ièt sé· ngaî fóng tseòu kî*, le poisson que j'ai pris est trop petit, je le relâche.

|痘, *fóng t'eóu*, vacciner.

担子|下來, *tām tzè fóng hā loî*, dépose ton fardeau.

FOŪ

夫 *Foū*. Aider ; mari.

担|, *tām foū*, porteurs de bagages.

轎|, *k'iaó foū*, porteurs de chaise.

馬|, *mā foū*, palefrenier.

做工|, *tsó koūng foū*, travailler.

丈|, *tch'óng foū*, mari.

敷 *Foū*. Appliquer.

|膏藥, *foū kaō yŏc*, appliquer un cataplasme.

呼 *Foū*. Crier.

|天|地, *foū t'iēn foū t'í*, remplir le ciel et la terre de ses cris.

FOÛ

扶 *Foû*. Soutenir par le bras. (Voir *k'oû* et *p'oû*).

|彌撒, *foû nì săt*, servir la Messe.

湖 *Foû*. Mare, grande excavation. Lac.

脚踏阿|起, *kiôc t'ăp á foû hì*, mettre le pied dans une flaque d'eau.

|洋田, *foû yông t'iên*, mare sans fond, rizière qui ne se dessèche jamais.

|蜞, *foû k'î*, sangsue.

|鰍, *foû ts'ioū*, petite anguille qui vit dans la boue.

|南, *foû nâm*, la province du *Foûnâm*. (Sud du lac).

江|, *kōng foû*, vagabond.

蝴 *Foû*. |蝶, *foû t'iăp*, espèce de gros papillon.

葫 *Foû*. |豆, *foû t'eóu*, espèce de fève.

椈 *Foû*. |椒, *foû tsiāo*, poivre.

糊 *Foû*. Coller, badigeonner.

|紙, *foû tjè*, coller du papier.

|石灰, *foû chăc foē·*, mettre une couche de chaux.

|壁, *foû piăc*, tapisser un mur.

| 窗子, *foû ts'oūng tzè*, mettre du papier aux fenêtres.

| 塗, *foû t'oû*, imbécile, brouillon, étourdi.

| 說, *foû chôt*, déraisonner.

鬍 *Foû*. Barbe, favoris.

留 | 鬚, *lioû foû sī*, laisser croître les favoris.

狐 *Foû* | 狸, *foû lî*, renard.

壺 *Foû*. Vase pour liquides.

茶 | , *ts'â foû*, théière.

酒 | , *tsiòu foû*, pot à vin.

夜 | , *yá foû*, vase de nuit.

FOÙ

府 *Foù*. Préfecture, préfet.

潮州 | , *tch'aô tchoū foù*, préfecture de *Tch'ao-tchou*.

下 | 落狀, *hā foù lŏc ts'óng*, aller à la préfecture porter une accusation.

官 | , *kouōn foù*, le mandarin.

尊 | , *tsoūn foù*, votre noble palais, (manière polie de demander où l'on demeure).

虎 *Foù*. Tigre.

老 | , *laò foù*, le tigre.

寶 | , *paò foù*, léopard.

琥 *Foù*. | 珀, *foù p'ĕt*, ambre.

苦 *Foù* (pour *k'où*). Amer.

我畏 | , *ngaî ví foù*, je n'aime pas l'amertume.

裡個藥十分 | , *ỳ ké· yŏc chĭp foūn foù*, ce remède est très amer.

FOÚ

父 *Foú*. Père.

孝敬 | 母, *haó kín foú moū*, honorer son père et sa mère.

繼 | , (v. 後 |), *kí foú*, (v. *heoú foú*), second mari de la mère.

代 | , *t'oí foú*, parrain.

神 | , *chîn foú*, prêtre (père spirituel).

| 兄, *foú hioūng*, notables.

戽 *Foú*. Répandre de l'eau.

地泥愛 | 濕呼好掃地, *t'í naî oí foú chĭp tsáng haò saó t'í*, il faut humecter le parterre avant de balayer.

| 水飲田, *foú choùi ým t'iên*, inonder une rizière en y jetant de l'eau au moyen d'un seau suspendu.

赴 *Foú*. Aller avec empressement à.

| 圩, *foú hī*, aller au marché.

| 瞻禮, *foú tchām lī*, arriver pour la fête.

你做事 | 我唔倒, *gnî tsó ché· foú ngaî mĝ taò*, tu travailles sans pouvoir aller aussi vite que moi.

戶 *Foú*. Porte, famille.

門 | , *moûn foú*, porte.

烟 | , *yān foú*, foyer, famille.

裡個地方有好多烟 | , *ỳ ké· t'í fōng yoū haò tō yān foú*, dans cette localité il y a beaucoup de familles.

賦 *Foú*. Donner, distribuer, répartir.

| 聖體, *foú chín t'ì*, donner la Sainte Communion.

| 洗, *foú sè·*, baptiser.

肉身就係父母生個靈魂就係天主 | 個, *nioŭc chīn ts'ioú hé· foú moū sēn ké· lîn foūn ts'ioú hé· t'iēn tchoù foú ké·*, nos parents ont engendré notre corps, mais Dieu nous a donné l'âme.

付 *Foú.* Livrer, donner, confier.

吩 | (v. 附). *foūn foú*, ordonner.

| 貨, *foú fó*, livrer la marchandise.

| 託, *foú t'ŏc*, confier, charger de.

拊 *Foú.* Frapper légèrement.

| 手, *foú choù*, donner un coup de main.

到我罪愛 | 心, *táo ngō ts'oúi oí foú sīm*, arrivé à *mea culpa* il faut se frapper la poitrine.

傅 *Foú.* Précepteur, transmettre, oindre.

師 | , *sē foú*, patron d'apprentis, maître ouvrier.

終 | , *tchoūng foú*, Extrême-Onction.

| 終油, *foú tchoūng yoû*, donner l'Extrême-Onction.

褲 *Foú.* Pantalon.

著 | , *tchŏc foú*, mettre son pantalon.

負 *Foú.* Ingrat.

辜 | , *k'oū foú*, ingrat.

辜 | 天主個恩, *k'oū foú t'iēn tchoù ké· ēn*, abuser de la grâce.

欺 | , *k'ī foú*, tromper et vexer.

啞馬噲欺 | 人愛小心, *yà mā voé· k'ī foú gnîn, oí siaò sīm*, ce cheval est méchant par moment, faites attention.

副 *Foú.* Aider, seconder, particule numérale pour l'ensemble d'objets de même espèce.

| 主教, *foú tchoù káo*, coadjuteur, propréfet.

| 爺, *foú yâ*, petit mandarin militaire.

一 | 對聯, *ŷt foú toúi liên*, deux bandes de papier portant une sorte de distique formé de deux phrases symétriques.

一 | 紙牌, *ŷt foú tjè p'aî*, un jeu de cartes.

一 | 鈕子, *ŷt foú k'eóu tzè*, cinq boutons d'habit.

婦 *Foú.* Femme mariée.

| 人家, *foú gnîn kā*, femme en général, épouse.

做夫 | , *tsó foū foú*, faire l'acte conjugal.

富 *Foú.* Riche, richesse.

| 貴人, *foú koúi gnîn*, homme riche et noble.

護 *Foú.* Garder, protéger.

| 守天神, *foú choù t'iēn chîn*, ange gardien.

保 | , *pào foú*, protéger.

FOŬC

服 *Foŭc.* Habit, accoutumé, servir.

衣 | , *ȳ foŭc*, habits.

| 事, *foŭc sé*, servir, soigner.

心十分唔 | , *sīm chìp foūn mĝ foŭc*, je ne puis digérer cette affaire.

袱 *Foŭc.* 包 | , *pāo foŭc* carré de toile pour envelopper ses objets de voyage.

伏 *Foŭc.* Etre prosterné.

壓 | , *âp foŭc,* dompter.

| 地, *foŭc t'í,* prosterné à terre.

| 天, *foŭc t'iēn,* le mois de la canicule.

| 望, *foŭc vóng,* implorer humblement.

復 *Foŭc.* Retourner à, revenir.

| 活, *foŭc făt,* ressusciter.

| 仇, *foŭc choû,* se venger.

| 轉來, *foŭc tchòn loî,* revenir, retourner.

FOÛC

福 *Foûc.* Bonheur.

| 樂, *foûc lŏc,* jouissance, bonheur.

永 | , *yoūn foûc,* bonheur éternel.

受 | , *choú foûc,* soyez heureux, (salutation).

降 | , *kóng foûc,* bénir.

| 氣, *foûc hí,* chance.

有 | 送財無 | 送氣, *yoū foûc soúng ts'oî, voû foûc soúng hí,* celui qui est heureux donne son argent, le malheureux donne son travail.

五 | , *ng̀ foûc,* les cinq félicités chinoises; qui sont (d'après leurs livres): 壽, 富, 康寧, 攸好德, 考終命, *choú, foú, k'ōng nên, yoū haó têt, k'aò tchoūng mîn,* longévité, richesses, santé, persévérance dans la vertu, heureuse mort; (plus vulgairement) 妻, 子, 富, 貴, 壽, *ts'ī, tzè, foú, koúi, choú,* avoir une femme, des enfants, de la richesse des dignités et une longue vie.

幅 *Foûc.* Particule numérale des peintures, des inscriptions.

一 | 聖像, *ŷt foûc chín sióng,* une image.

一 | 招牌, *ŷt foûc tchaō p'aî,* une enseigne de boutique.

FOUI. (Voir FI.)

FOŪN

分 *Foūn.* Partager, centième partie de l'once.

| 開, *foūn k'ōi,* diviser, séparer.

| 別, *foūn p'iĕt,* différence.

一 | 銀, *ŷt foūn nioûn,* centième partie de l'once, et dixième du «*ts'în v. ts'iên*» valeur de 12 à 15 sapèques, un sou.

| 明, *foūn mîn,* clairement, évident.

十 | , *chĭp foūn,* au plus haut degré.

十 | 好, *chĭp foūn haò,* parfaitement bien.

紛 *Foūn.* Embrouillé, pêle-mêle.

| 雜, *foūn ts'ăp,* objets de différents genres mêlés ensemble.

線 | 帛 𥚃 (解) 唔得倒, *sién foūn p'ĕt lè· kè· m̂g têt taò,* le fil est tout embrouillé, je n'arriverai pas à le démêler.

昏 *Foūn.* Troublé, obscur, soir.

黃 | 時候, *vông foūn chê héou,* le temps du crépuscule.

發 | , *fât foūn,* tomber en pamoison, trouble d'esprit.

頭 (呀) | , *t'eôu nâ foūn,* mal de tête.

婚 *Foūn.* | 配, *foūn p'í*, mariage, se marier.

葷 *Foūn.* Aliments gras, c. à d. la viande, le poisson, ail, oignons, poireaux etc.

食 |, *chĭt foūn*, faire gras, par opposition à 食齋, *chĭt tsāi*, faire abstinence.

FOÛN

墳 *Foûn.* Tombeau.

地 |, *t'í foûn*, tombeau.

| 山, *foûn sān*, cimetière.

掃 |, *sáo foûn*, balayer, c.-à-d. entretenir le tombeau.

魂 *Foûn.* 靈 |, 覺 |, 生 |, l'âme raisonnable de l'homme, l'âme sensitive des bêtes, l'âme végétative.

FOÙN

粉 *Foùn.* Farine, poudre, poussière.

米 |, *mì foùn*, farine de riz.

|, *foùn*, ils appellent encore ainsi les pâtes en filaments, vermicelle, macaronis etc.

鉛 |, *yân foùn*, blanc de céruse.

| 壁, *foùn piăc*, blanchir une cloison avec la chaux.

藥 |, *yŏc foùn*, poudre médicinale.

FOÚN

分 *Foún.* Devoir; dose.

本 |, *poùn foún*, devoir.

守 (v. 做) 本 |, *chòu (v. tsó) poùn foún*, remplir son devoir.

過 |, *koúo foún*, dépasser la mesure.

天 |, *t'iēn foún*, part d'intelligence donnée à chaque homme.

好天 | 個人, *hào t'iēn foún ké gnîn*, un homme qui a beaucoup de moyens naturels.

FOÚN

忿 *Foún.* | 怒, *foún nóu*, colère.

發 | 怒, *făt foún nóu*, se mettre en colère.

混 *Foún.* Confus, en désordre.

世亂亂 | |, *ché lón lón foún foún*, le monde est tout révolutionné.

| 帳, *foún tchóng*, orgueilleux, qui se mêle de ce qui ne le regarde pas.

| 沌, *foún t'oún*, chaos.

憤 *Foún.* Faire des efforts.

發 |, *făt foún*, faire des efforts.

| 志, *foún tjé*, mettre de la bonne volonté.

FOŪNG

風 *Foūng.* Vent, mœurs, renommée.

| 琴, *foūng k'îm*, accordéon, harmonium.

| 領, *foūng leōng*, capuchon.

| 波, *foūng pō*, persécution.

| 箱, *foūng siōng*, soufflet de forge.

| 車, *foūng tch'ā*, moulin à vent.

| 俗, *foūng sioŭc*, mœurs, coutumes.

蜂 *Foūng.* Abeille, guêpe.

| 子, *foūng tzè*, abeille commune.

| 娘, *foūng niông*, abeille mère.

黃 |, *vông foūng*, guêpe.

| 糖, *foūng t'ông*, miel.

鋒 *Foūng*. Aigu, pointu.

| 利, *foūng lí*, aigu et tranchant.

當先 |, *tōng siēn foūng*, avant-garde d'un bataillon.

| 馬, *foūng mā*, cheval fougueux.

FOŪNG

封 *Foūng*. Cacheter, numéral des lettres et petits paquets.

愛 | 信, *oí foūng sín*, il faut cacheter la lettre.

| 聖堂, *foūng chín t'ông*, mettre les scellés sur une église (en temps de persécution).

一 | 信, *ŷt foūng sín*, une lettre.

| 印, *foūng ýn*, fermer les sceaux (vacances du mandarin).

| 包, *foūng pāo*, argent donné en cadeau, étrennes, gratification.

我拿裡兩百錢 | 包別其, *ngâi nā lê leòng pâc ts'iên foūng pāo poūn kî*, je lui ai donné deux cents sapèques d'étrennes.

豐 *Foūng*. Abondant, prospère.

年辰 | 熟, *niân chîn foūng choŭc*, année fertile.

楓 *Foūng*. | 樹, *foūng chóu*, arbre qui ressemble à l'érable.

FOÛNG

逢 *Foûng*. Rencontrer.

我路上 | 倒佢, *ngaî loú hóng foûng taò kî*, je l'ai rencontré en chemin.

| 倒係圩日我來唔得, *foûng taò hé· hī gnît ngaî loî mģ têt*, s'il se trouve que c'est un jour de marché je ne pourrai pas venir.

縫 *Foûng*. 裁 |, *ts'aî foûng*, tailleur d'habits.

紅 *Foûng*, Rouge.

| 色, *foûng sēt*, couleur rouge.

| 毛人, hommes aux poils rouges (les Anglais).

掛 |, *koúa foûng*, suspendre du rouge, c. à d. afficher un voile rouge, marque de solennelle réparation, ou signe de fête.

洪 *Foûng*. | 水, *foûng choùi*, inondation, grande crue, déluge.

FOÙNG

哄 *Foùng*. Tromper.

| 噠人, *foùng t'ât gnîn*, tromper quelqu'un.

FOÚNG

奉 *Foúng*. Suivre, se conformer à, servir.

| 教, *foúng káo*, embrasser la religion.

| 教人, *foúng káo gnîn*, chrétien.

| 事, *foúng sé*, servir, suivre les ordres.

| 承人, *foúng chîn gnîn*, flatter quelqu'un.

俸 *Foúng*. | 祿, *foúng loŭc*, traitement, viatique.

FOUT

佛 *Foŭt*. Bouddha. | **敎**, *foŭt káo*, bouddhisme.

FOUT

窟 *Foût*. Trou, fosse.

掘 |, *kòi foût*, creuser un trou.

忽 *Foût*. La millionième partie d'une once. (Voir **毫** *haô*).

| **然**, *foût yân*, soudain.

| **然死**, *foût yân sì*, mourir de mort subite.

惚 *Foût*. Troublé, hébété.

咁恍 |, *àn fòng foût*, comme tu es embarrassé! troublé! inconsidéré!

GNĒ·

你 *Gnē· (ni)*. Ton, tien. (Voyez *nīa*).

GNĔT

月 *Gnĕt*. Lune, mois lunaire.

| **光**, *gnĕt koūong*, la lune.

有 | **光**, *yoū gnĕt koūong*, il y a clair de lune.

日 |, *gnĭt gnĕt*, les jours et les mois.

那個 | **日**, *mâc ké· gnĕt gnĭt*? quel est le mois et le jour? quelle est la date?

光緒二十年三 | **初七日**, *koūong sī gní chĭp niân sām gnĕt tsē ts'ĭt gnĭt*, vingtième année de *Koūong sī*, le 7eme jour de la troisième lune. (Manière de dater.)

正 |, *tchíng gnĕt*, nom de la 1ere lune.

做 |, *tsó gnĕt*, faire ses couches.

| **曆**, *gnĕt lăc*, calendrier.

熱 *Gnĕt*. Chaud.

| **天**, *gnĕt t'iēn*, temps de l'été.

鬧 |, *náo gnĕt*, grand concours, apparat.

生理鬧 |, *siēn lī náo gnĕt*, le commerce est animé, a de la vogue.

| **氣**, *gnĕt hí*, chaleur.

| **心**, *gnĕt sīm*, fervent.

| **心學道理**, *gnĕt sīm hŏc t'áo lī*, apprendre la doctrine avec ardeur.

| **鴿**, *gnĕt kâp*, pigeon.

GNÎ

你 *Gnî (ni)*. Toi, tu. Ce terme ne s'emploie pas seul quand on s'adresse à des supérieurs. On l'évite en se servant de la troisième personne.

唔干 | **事**, *mĝ koūon gnî sé*, cela ne te regarde pas.

愛 |, *ói gnî*, comme tu voudras.

| **等**, *gnî tèn*, vous autres, vous, (*nĝ tèn*, par abréviation).

疑 *Gnî*. Doute, soupçon.

| **惑**, *gnî fĕt*, douter.

半信半 |, *pán sín pán gnî*, hésitant, ne savoir que croire.

儀 *Gnî*. Loi, rite.

禮 |, *lī gnî*, cérémonie, présents de cérémonie.

彌撒禮 |, *nì sât lī gnî*, honoraires de Messe.

愚 *Gnî*. | **蠢**, *gnî tch'oùn*, sot, stupide.

GNÌ

耳 *Gnì*. Oreille, anse.

丨公, *gnì koūng*, l'oreille.

丨爬, *gnì p'â*, cure-oreille.

丨鐶, *gnì p'ân*, boucles d'oreille,

畚箕丨, *poún kī gnì*, l'anse du panier.

木丨, *moûc gnì*, espèce de champignon comestible qui pousse sur de vieux arbres.

GNÍ

二 *Gní*. Deux.

丨丨一四, *gní gní ŷt sí*, deux fois deux font quatre.

第丨, *t'í gní*, le deuxième.
Le mot **第** *t'í* se sous-entend dans les expressions suivantes:

丨號, *gní haó*, numéro deux.

我丨哥過番, *ngā gní kō kouó fān*, mon second frère aîné est allé à l'étranger.

義 *Gní*. Jutice; adoptif, commun, public.

天主個公丨, *t'iēn tchoù ké· koūng gní*, la Justice de Dieu.

丨父, **丨子**, *gní foú, gní tzè*, père adoptif, fils adoptif.

極有丨氣個人, *k'ĭt yoū gní hí ké· gnîn*, homme au cœur excellent, fidèle en tout.

發丨怒, *fât gní noú*, se mettre dans une juste colère.

丨井, *gní tsiàng*, puits commun.

丨塚, *gní tch'oùng*, cimetière commun acheté par cotisation.

議 *Gní*. Délibérer.

商丨, *chōng gní*, tenir conseil.

丨事, *gní sé*, délibérer des affaires en conseil.

丨學關, *gní hŏc kouān*, délibérer pour fixer les honoraires d'un maître d'école.

藝 *Gní*. Arts et métiers.

做手丨, *tsó choù gní*, exercer un métier.

學手丨, *hŏc choù gní*, apprendre un métier.

文丨咁好, *voûn gní kàn haò!* comme il est fort en littérature!

遇 *Gní*. Rencontrer par hazard.

丨倒機會, *gní tào kī fí*, rencontrer une occasion.

丨倒險事, *gní tào hiàm sé*, tomber dans un danger.

寓 *Gní*. Logement, habiter.

尊丨在那里, *tsoūn gní ts'oī naí lī?* où se trouve votre hôtel? (Se dit entre voyageurs).

我暫丨東石, *ngaî ts'iám gní Toūng chăc*, je reste pour le moment à *Toung chac*.

GNÎN

人 *Gnîn*. Homme. S'emploie comme pronom indéfini.

主丨, *tchoù gnîn*, patron, propriétaire.

丨類, *gnîn louí*, la race humaine.

大丨, *t'aí gnîn*, grand homme, se dit en parlant à un mandarin.

5

老大｜, *laò t'aí gnîn*, Votre Excellence, se dit en parlant à un gouverneur de province. On l'emploie aussi en parlant à un vieillard, terme plus honorable que le suivant.

老｜家, *laò gnîn kā*, un vieillard.

有｜來, *yoū gnîn loî*, quelqu'un vient.

我聽｜講過, *ngaî t'āng gnîn kòng kouó*, je l'ai entendu dire.

有｜話, *yoū gnîn vá*, on dit.

各｜各事, *kôc gnîn kôc sé*, chacun ses affaires.

今日｜唔好, *kīn gnĭt gnîn mĝ haò*, aujourd'hui je ne suis pas bien.

GNÍN

認 *Gnín*. Prendre connaissance, connaître, avouer.

｜字, *gnín sé*, connaître les caractères.

愛｜眞事來, *oí gnín tchīn sé loî*, il faut prendre une connaissance exacte de la chose.

｜錯, *gnín ts'ôc*, reconnaître ses torts.

｜罪, *gnín ts'ouí*, avouer sa faute.

誤｜, *ngoú gnín*, prendre une chose pour une autre.

GNĬP

入 *Gnĭp*. Entrer, à l'intérieur.

｜來, *gnĭp loî*, entre, (en appelant de l'intérieur.).

｜去, *gnĭp hí*, entre, (en parlant de l'extérieur).

忒出忒｜你話我知, *t'iĕt tch'oŭt t'iĕt gnĭp gnî vá ngaî tī*, dis-moi si c'est trop en dehors ou trop en dedans.

出｜愛關門, *tch'oŭt gnĭp oí kouān moûn*, en entrant ou en sortant il faut fermer la porte.

｜會, *gnĭp fí*, devenir membre d'une association.

｜學, *gnĭp hŏc*, être reçu bachelier.

GNĬT

日 *Gnĭt*. Jour, temps.

｜｜, *gnĭt gnĭt*, tous les jours.

今｜, *kīn gnĭt*, aujourd'hui.

明｜ (v. **晨朝｜**, v. **天光｜**), *miâng gnĭt* (v. *chîn tchaō gnĭt*, v. *t'iēn kouōng gnĭt*), demain.

後｜, *heoú gnĭt*, après-demain.

昨晡｜, *ts'ŏc poū gnĭt*, hier (cette expression varie beaucoup selon les pays. On dit: *ts'ī poū gnĭt*, *ts'ioū poū gnĭt*, *ts'ō poū gnĭt*, *ts'āng poū gnĭt*, *sō tō gnĭt*, etc.).

日頭, **｜鬚**, *gnĭt t'coû*, *gnĭt sī*, le soleil, les rayons de soleil.

生｜, *sāng gnĭt*, jour anniversaire de la naissance.

HĀ

下 *Hā (há)*. Descendre, en bas.

｜｜背, *hā hā poé*, aller d'un lieu à un autre moins élevé.

｜崀, *hā ýn*, descendre une côte.

｜船, *hā chôn*, descendre de bateau.

放｜來, *fóng hā loî*, déposer.

｜身, *hā chīn*, partie inférieure du corps, mot honnête pour désigner les parties naturelles de l'homme.

在底｜, *ts'oī taì hā*, c'est tout en bas, dans le bas.

桌底｜放等來, *tsôc taì hā fóng tèn loî*, mettez sous la table.

地 | (v. 地泥 |), *t'ī hā (v. t'ī naî hā)*, par terre.

天 | , *t'iēn hā*, l'empire chinois, l'univers.

HÂ

鰕 *Hâ.* | 公, *hâ koūng*, crevette.

蝦 *Hâ.* | 蟆, *hâ má*, espèce de grenouille.

HÀ

下 *Hà (há).* Mettre bas.

狗媽 | 裡四個子, *keoù má hà lî sí ké· tzè*, la chienne a fait quatre petits.

| 乳, *hà nén*, prendre des médecines pour avoir du lait.

| 鳥竇, *hà tiaō teóu*, prendre un nid d'oiseau.

暇 *Hà.* Loisir, repos.

閒 | 無事, *hân hà voû sé*, n'avoir rien à faire.

HÁ

下 *Há.* Inférieur; particule numérale des coups.

| 等, *há tèn*, de seconde qualité, de qualité inférieure.

| 賤, *há ts'ién*, vil, dégradant.

| 九溜, *há kioù lioû*, les neuf arts mécaniques.

打佢一 | , *tà kî ŷt há*, donne-lui un coup.

一 | 工夫做得倒, *ŷt há koūng foū tsó tĕt taò*, cela peut se faire en un rien de temps.

| 使 (ou | 手) 多, *há sè* (ou *há choù*) *tō*, l'opération est compliquée.

夏 *Há.* Eté. | 天, *há t'iēn*, l'été.

| 至, *há tjé*, le solstice d'été.

| 布, *há póu*, fine toile de chanvre pour habits d'été.

廈 *Há.* Grande maison.

老兄大 | 在那裡, *laò hioūng t'ái há ts'ái nái lī*? (mot à mot) où est la grande maison de mon frère aîné?

HÂC

客 *Hâc (k'ĕt).* Celui qui reçoit l'hospitalité, étranger, passager.

人 | , *gnîn hâc*, hôte.

應酬 | , *ýn tch'oû hâc*, recevoir les visiteurs, s'occuper de son hôte, lui rendre les civilités.

待 | 待得好, *t'aí hâc t'aí tĕt haò*, il traite bien ses hôtes.

| 家人, *hâc kā gnîn*, homme de la tribu qui porte ce nom.

| 家人山地方核過多, *hâc kā gnîn sān t'í fōng hĕt kouó tō*, les Hacka habitent de préférence les pays montagneux.

HÂC

膝 *Hâc.* Testicules.

| 卵, *hâc lòn*, glande testiculaire.

嚇 *Hâc.* Effrayer.

| 死人, *hâc sì gnîn*, frayeur mortelle.

海上絲綢之路文獻集成 科技與文化編

HĀI

溪 *Hāi*. Ruisseau, torrent de montagne. 小｜, *siào hāi*, petit ruisseau.

HÂI

孩 *Hâi*. Petit enfant.
｜童, *hâi t'oûng*, 嬰｜, *ȳn hâi*, idem,

鞋 *Hâi*. Souliers, chaussure.
皮｜, *p'î hâi*, souliers en cuir,
布｜, *poú hâi*, souliers en étoffe.
鑲｜, *siōng hâi*, souliers fleuris, brodés.
｜梁, *hâi leông*, les cordes ou coutures du dessus.
著｜, *tchôc hâi*, se chausser.
｜底, *hâi taì*, la semelle du soulier.

HAÌ

蟹 *Haì*. 老｜, *lào haì*, écrevisse, crabe.

HÂM

咸 *Hâm*. Tout, complet.
｜巴冷, *hâm pā lāng*, (ailleurs 一巴連, *ȳt pā liên*) le tout ensemble.

含 *Hâm*. Tenir à la bouche, contenir, renfermer.
狗｜骨頭, *keoù hâm koūt t'eoû*, le chien tient un os dans sa gueule.
我㧒一個石頭狗噲｜轉來, *ngaî fīt ȳt ké· chăc t'eoû keoù voé· hâm tchòn loî*, je jette une pierre et le chien me la rapporte dans sa gueule.
包｜, *paō hâm*, renfermé, compris dans.
記｜, *kí hâm*, mémoire.

｜忍, *hâm nioūn*, supporter avec patience.
你愛話清楚來莫｜｜糊糊, *gnî oí vá ts'īn tsè loî mŏc hâm hâm foû foû*, parle clairement sans cacher ta pensée.
水｜, *chouì hâm*, conduit d'eau.
烟｜, *yān hâm*, cheminée.

銜 *Hâm*. Titre, grade.
官｜, *koūon hâm*, titre de mandarin,
愛寫那個｜頭, *oí sià mâc ké· hâm t'eou?* quel titre faut-il écrire? (par ex: en tête d'une pièce).

涵 *Hâm*. ｜養, *hâm yōng*, soigner sa santé.

鹹 *Hâm*. Salé.
｜味, *hâm mí*, saveur salée.
｜過頭, *hâm koúo t'êou*, c'est trop salé.
｜菜, ｜魚, *hâm ts'oí*, *hâm ngˆ*, légumes salés, poisson salé.

HÁM

喊 *Hám*. Appeler.
｜佢來, *hám kî loî*, dis-lui de venir.
｜佢走, *hám kî tseòu*, dis-lui de s'en aller.
我｜佢唔來, *ngâi hám kî mgˆ loî*, je l'appelle sans pouvoir le faire venir.
你｜那個名, *gnî hám mâc ké· miâng?* comment t'appelles-tu?
｜冤, *hám yān*, demander justice au mandarin en criant devant le prétoire.
｜賊, *hám ts'ĕt*, crier au voleur.

陷 *Hám*. Tomber dans.

| 氐誘感, *hám ȳ yóu kàm*, (dans le *Pater*) succomber à la tentation.

| 害人, *hám hoí gnîn*, causer du dommage à quelqu'un.

HÂN

閒 *Hân*. Avoir le temps, non occuppé, oisif.

唔得 | , *mĝ têt hân*, je n'ai pas le temps.

講 | 話, *kòng hân fá*, dire des paroles oiseuses, ou bien selon les circonstances se quereller, faire des médisances.

| 人免進, *hân gnîn mēn tsín*, défense aux flâneurs d'entrer.

咁清 | , *kàn ts'īn hân!* comme vous avez du loisir!

還 *Hân (fân)*. Encore, de nouveau.

| 有麼, *hân yoū mô*? y en a-t-il encore? | 好多, *hân haò tō*, il y en a encore beaucoup.

| 早, *hân tsaò*, encore trop tôt.

HÁN

莧 *Hán*. | 菜, *hán ts'oí*, espèce d'amarante comestible.

限 *Hán*. Terme, limites.

無 | , *vôu hán*, infini, sans limites.

| 定一年, *hán t'ín ȳt niân*, au terme d'une année.

有 | , avoir des limites, peu considérable.

HĀNG

坑 *Hāng*. Vallon, ruisseau, canal.

聖堂在石灰 | , *chín t'ông ts'oī chăc foē˙ hāng*, l'église est à *chăc foē˙ hāng* (le vallon des pierres à chaux). Dans les pays de montagnes, les noms de village sont le plus souvent désignés sous le mot de vallon.

| 公, *hāng koūng*, canal, rivière; se dit aussi des digues de la rivière.

| 圳, *hāng tsoún*, ruisseau plus petit, canal qui conduit l'eau dans les rizières.

HÂNG

行 *Hâng*. Marcher, agir.

| 路, *hâng loú*, marcher, voyager à pied.

先 | , *siēn hâng*, marcher devant.

| 前, *hâng ts'iên*, s'approcher.

慢 | , *mán hâng*, allez doucement, (politesse adressée à ceux qui vous quittent).

好生 | , *haó sēn (v.siēn) hâng*, prenez garde, marchez avec précaution.

耶穌言 | , *yâ sē niân hâng*, vie (paroles) de Jésus.

看佢 | 事人都咁巧, *k'ón kiâ hâng sé gnîn toū àn k'aò*, d'après ce qu'il fait on voit qu'il est industrieux.

| 醫, *hâng ȳ*, exercer la médecine, médecin.

| 通, *hâng t'oūng*, aller à la selle.

| 李, *hâng lì*, bagages.

桁 *Hâng*. Poutres du toit d'une maison.

| 頭瓦角, *hâng t'eoû ngà kôc*, les poutres, les tuiles et les lattes (tout ce qui compose le toit).

HAŌ

(Voir aussi les mots HO)

耗 *HAŌ*. Détruire.

衫子裁差丨帛裡, *sām tzè ts'aí ts'ā haō p'ĕt lî*, tu as mal taillé l'habit, il ne vaut plus rien.

一看倒信就丨帛佢, *ŷt k'ón taò sín ts'ioú haō p'ĕt kî*, déchire la lettre après l'avoir lue.

丨靡錢財, *haō fî ts'iên ts'oî*, dissiper ses biens.

HAÔ

毫 *Haô*. Quantité infime, dixième partie du *lî*, poil.

絲丨不錯, *sē haô póût ts'ŏc*, il n'y a pas la moindre erreur.

両,錢,分,厘,丨,絲,忽, *leōng, ts'iên, foūn, lî, haô, sē, foût*, une once, le dixième, le centième, le millième, le dix millième, le cent millième, le millionième d'une once.

十丨爲一厘, *chĭp haô vî ŷt lî*, dix *haô* font un *lî*.

一丨子, *ŷt haô tzè*, une pièce de 10 cents.

丨毛, *haô maō*, fin poil, duvet.

HAÒ

好 *Haò*. Bon, bien, très, facile.

丨食, *haò chĭt*, bon à manger.

丨唔丨都愛去, *haò mĝ haò toū oí hí*, il faut y aller coûte que coûte.

菜煮丨裡, *ts'oí tchoù haò lî*, les légumes sont cuits à point.

病丨裡, *p'iáng haò lî*, guéri de sa maladie.

丨處, *haò tch'oú*, utilité, bénéfice.

丨笑, *haò siaó*, c'est risible.

頂丨個, *tìn haò ké·*, tout-à-fait bon, de première qualité.

丨得多, *haò tĕt tō*, beaucoup mieux.

丨做, 丨讀, *haò tsó, haò t'oŭc*, facile à faire, à étudier.

丨看, 丨聽, *haò k'ón, haò t'āng*, agréable à la vue, à l'oreille.

HÁO

好 *Háo*. Aimer, désirer.

丨食, *háo chĭt*, gourmand.

丨色, *háo sĕt*, aimer la volupté.

丨酒, *háo tsiòu*, aimer le vin.

效 *Háo*. Exemple, effet.

丨法, *háo fâp*, exemple.

丨驗, *háo niám*, effet.

HAÓ

號 *Haó*. Désignation, nom, signe, marque.

你那個大丨, *gnî mâc ké· t'aí haó?* quel est votre nom? (Politesse).

那個字丨, *mâc ké· sé haó*, quelle est la marque de fabrique?

寶丨, *paò haó*, votre maison de commerce, votre boutique.

記丨, *kí haó*, signe, marque.

丨頭, *haó t'eoû*, titre, enseigne.

畫丨, *fá haó*, tracer un signe, mettre sa signature.

請聖丨, *ts'iàng chín haó*, faire le signe de la croix, (le saint signe).

孝 *Haó*. Piété filiale, deuil.

| 敬, *haó kín*, honorer.
| 順父母, *haó choún foú moū*, être respectueux et obéissant envers ses parents.
守 | , *choù haó*, prendre le deuil.
你 | 服滿程麼, *niā haó foŭc mān lī mô?* votre deuil est-il achevé?

HĂP

合 *Hăp*. Joindre, unir; fermer; ensemble; être d'accord.
| 手, *hăp choù*, joindre les mains.
| 口, *hăp k'coù*, fermer la bouche, trouver bon au goût.
| 書, *hăp choū*, fermer un livre.
打 | 同, *tà hăp t'oúng*, faire un pacte, écrire une convention en partie double.
| 共, *hăp k'ioúng*, somme totale.
唔多 | 理, *mĝ tō hăp lī*, ce n'est pas très convenable.

盒 *Hăp*. Boîte, coffret.
烟 | , *yān hăp*, tabatière.
紙 | , *tjè hăp*, boîte en papier, en carton.

狹 *Hăp* (ou *k'iăp*). Etroit, resserré.
地方忒 | , *t'í fōng t'iĕt hăp*, l'endroit est trop petit.

HÂP

瘖 *Hâp*. Asthme.
(發) | , *pôt hâp*, devenir, être asthmatique.

HÂT

瞎 *Hât*. Aveugle.
| 子, *hât tzè*, homme aveugle.
| 一目, *hât ўt moŭc*, devenir borgne.
| 鬧, *hât naó*, faire ses embarras.

HÉ·

係 *Hé·*. Oui; appartenir à; si.
| 唔 | , *hé· mĝ hé·?* oui ou non? n'est-ce-pas?
| 你書唔 | , *hé· niā choū mĝ hé·?* est-ce ton livre?
| 你你好拿去, *hé· niā gnî haò nā hí*, si c'est à toi tu peux l'emporter.
| 有錢我肯借, *hé· yoū ts'ién ngaî hèn tsía*, si j'avais de l'argent je t'en prêterais volontiers.

HĒM

哼 *Hēm*. Crier, se plaindre.

HĒN

痕 *Hēn*. 傷 | , *chōng hēn*, plaie, blessure.
| 迹, *hēn tsĭt*, égratignure, écorchure.

HÊN

狠 *Hên*. Excéder, très fort.
毛辮編倒忒 | , *maō piēn p'ìn taò t'iĕt hên*, mes cheveux sont tressés trop serrés.
臭味十分 | , *tch'oú mí chĭp foūn hên*, une puanteur excessive.
程酒好 | 個, *yà tsioù haò hên ké·*, ce vin est très fort.

HÈN

肯 *Hèn (k'èn)*. Consentir.

丨唔丨, *hèn mĝ hèn?* veux-tu? consens-tu?

佢唔丨借, *kî mĝ hèn tsiá*, il ne veut pas prêter.

HÉN

杏 *Hén*. (ou *hém*). Amandier.

丨仁, *hén ŷn*, amande.

恨 *Hén*. Haïr, détester.

惱丨, *nāo hén*, détester.

幸 *Hén*. Avoir le bonheur de.

僥丨, *hiaō hén*, avoir de la chance, du succès.

不丨, *poût hén*, pas de chance (style relevé).

HEOÛ

侯 *Heoû*. Titre honorifique.

丨爺, *heoû yâ*, qui a le titre de *heoû*, marquis.

喉 *Heoû*. 丨嚨, *heoû loûng*, gosier.

猴 *Heoû*. 丨哥, *heoû kō*, singe.

HEOÙ

口 *Heoù (k'eoù)*. Bouchée, ouverture; particule numérale des marmites, des poêles.

丨液, *heoù lān*, salive.

一丨肉, *ŷt heoù nioûc*, une bouchée de viande.

一丨吞得落, *ŷt heoù t'oūn têt lŏc*, on n'en ferait qu'une bouchée.

傷丨, *chōng heoù*, ouverture d'une plaie.

刀子割倒唔知幾大丨, *taō tzè kôt taò mĝ tī kì t'aí heoù*, il s'est fait, avec son couteau, une plaie béante.

河丨, *hô heoù*, embouchure d'un fleuve.

三丨鍋頭, *sām heoù vŏc t'eoû*, trois poêles.

HEÓU

后 *Heoú*. Reine, impératrice.

皇大丨, *fông t'aí heoú*, impératrice-mère.

厚 *Heóu*. Epais, grand.

肥丨, *p'î heóu*, gras et gros, bien portant.

丨重, *heóu tch'oūng*, digne, grave.

寬丨個人, *k'ōn heóu ké gnîn*, c'est un homme au cœur large et généreux.

候 *Heóu*. Temps, attendre, s'informer.

時丨, *chê heóu* temps.

等丨, *tèn heóu*, attendre.

拜丨, 問丨, *paí heóu*, *moún heóu*, saluer, s'informer de la santé.

後 *Heóu*. Après, ensuite.

丨日, *heóu gnĭt*, après-demain.

丨來, *heóu loî*, dorénavant.

丨生, *heóu sāng*, jeune, peu âgé.

麼丨, *mô heóu*, n'avoir pas de descendants.

HĔT

核 *Hĕt.* Habiter, demeurer, repos.

你在那里｜, *gnî ts'oī naí lī hĕt?* où habites-tu?

神父來中國｜得慣麼, *chîn foú loî tchoūng kouĕt hĕt tĕt kouán mô*, est-ce que le Père s'habitue en Chine?

狐狸㰍貯｜, *foú lî loúng toù hĕt*, le renard demeure dans sa tanière.

核 *Hĕt.* ｜**桃**, *hĕt t'aô*, noix, noyer.

HĪ

虛 *Hī.* Vain, vide, faux.

發｜誓, *fât hī ché*, faire un faux serment, jurer en vain.

｜**言假話**, *hī niân kà fá*, parole vide de sens, mensonge.

｜**字**, *hī sé*, lettre employée seulement comme particule explétive ou euphonique.

圩 *Hī.* Marché, foire.

｜**塲**, *hī tch'ông*, lieu du marché.

出｜, (v. **赴｜**), *tch'oût hī* (v. *foú hī*), aller au marché.

稽 *Hī.* ｜**首**, *hī choù*, incliner profondément la tête.

HÌ

喜 *Hì.* Content, se réjouir.

歡｜, *fōn hì*, se réjouir, être content.

恭｜, *kioūng hì*, féliciter.

｜**酒**, *hì tsioù*, repas de réjouissance.

你做那個｜事, *gnî tsó mâc ké· hì sé?* quelle fête y a-t-il?

許 *Hì.* Promettre, permettre. Espèce, genre, forme.

｜**願**, *hì nián*, faire le vœu.

你｜過我一個花邊, *gnî hì koúo ngâi ŷt ké· fā piēn*, tu m'as promis une piastre.

自來火有好多｜, *tsé loî fò yoū hào tō hì*, il y a beaucoup d'espèces d'allumettes.

我坐理｜過好, *ngaî ts'ó ỳ hì koúo hào*, j'aime mieux cette forme.

起 *Hì.* Aller, commencer (et une foule d'autres sens très variés que l'usage apprendra).

｜**手**, *hì choù*, mettre la main à l'œuvre.

｜**身**, *hì chīn*, se mettre en route.

做唔｜, *tsó mĝ hì*, je ne puis faire cela.

｜**火**, *hì fò*, allumer le feu.

檢｜東西, *kiàm hì toūng sī*, ramasser les objets.

HÍ

氣 *Hí.* Air, temps, odeur, vapeur.

節｜, *tsiĕt hí*, les 24 divisions de l'année.

天｜, *t'iēn hí*, température.

福｜, *foŭc hí*, bonheur.

透｜唔出, *t'eòu hí mĝ tch'oût*, avoir de la peine à respirer.

脾｜, *p'î hí*, caractère, naturel de qq.

器 *Hí.* Ustensile, vase.

｜**皿**, *hí mēn*, instrument en général.

軍｜, *kioūn hí*, armes de soldat.

6

磁 | 個, *tsê hí kè*, en porcelaine.

小 | , *siào hí*, susceptible.

棄 *Hí*. Rejeter, mépriser.

| 絕異端, *hí ts'ièt ý tōn*, rejeter les superstitions.

丟 | 老婆, *tioū hí laò p'ô*, abandonner sa femme.

戲 *Hí*. Comédie, théâtre.

唱 | , *tch'óng hí*, jouer la comédie.

一本 | , *ŷt poùn hí*, une pièce de comédie.

一台 | , *ŷt t'ôi hí*, un acte de comédie.

撮把 | , *ts'ôt pā hí*, faire des tours de passe-passe.

去 *Hí (ou k'í)*. Aller, verbe auxiliaire signifiant que l'action du verbe va se faire.

我 | 來, *ngâi hí loî*, j'en reviens.

快出 | , *k'ouái tch'oût hí*, sors vite d'ici.

上 | 來, *hóng hí loî*, lève-toi.

來數 | 數, *loî sé hí sé*, recettes et dépenses.

HIÂM

嫌 *Hiâm*. Se plaindre de, avoir du dégoût pour, reprocher.

裡馬好麼那個 | , *yà mā haò mô mâc kè hiâm*, ce cheval est bon, il n'a pas de défauts.

我 | 佢胸唔彀開, *ngaî hiâm kiā hioūng mĝ keoú k'oī*, moi, je lui reproche d'avoir la poitrine trop étroite.

| 少, *hiâm chaò*, | 多, *hiâm tō*, trouver trop peu, trouver trop.

HIÀM

險 *Hiàm*. Danger, péril; être sur le point de.

遇倒 | 事, *gní taò hiàm sé*, tomber dans un danger.

| | 跌倒, *hiàm hiàm tièt taò*, j'ai failli tomber.

好得我先看倒唔係鵰子係人, | | 別我開銃, *haò têt ngaî siēn k'ón taò mĝ hé tiaō tzè hé gnîn, hiàm hiàm poūn ngaî k'oī tch'oúng*, heureusement que je me suis aperçu à temps que ce n'était pas un oiseau, mais un homme, j'étais sur le point de faire feu.

HIAŌ

僥 *Hiaō*. Faux, trompeur.

你同我作棋做得單單你莫用 | , *gnî t'oûng ngaî tsôc k'î tsó têt tān tān gnî môc yoúng hiaō*, je veux bien te laisser jouer aux échecs avec moi, à condition que tu ne fasses pas de filouteries.

HIAÔ

姣 *Hiaô*. Charmes, caresses.

莫咁 | , *môc àn hiaô*, pas tant de mignardises.

HIÀO

曉 *Hiào*. Savoir.

我 | 得, *ngaî hiào têt*, je le sais.

你 | 騎馬麼, *gnî hiào k'î mā mó*, sais-tu monter à cheval?

病阿唔 | 食飯, *p'iáng á mĝ hiào chĭt fán*, il est malade à ne pas pouvoir manger.

HIÁO

𧁲 *Hiáo*. Relevé en pointe.

唐人個屋兩面｜起, *t'ông gnîn ké· voûc leòng miến hiáo hì*, les maisons des Chinois ont les deux côtés relevés en pointe.

眠床板噲｜起愛楔坪來, *mîn ts'ông pàn voé· hiaó hì oí siăp p'iăng loî*, les planches du lit font bascule il faut les caler.

HIĂP

協 *Hiăp*. S'entraider, se conformer.

｜力同心, *hiăp lìt t'oûng sīm*, agir d'un commun accord.

裡事我麼那個干｜, *yà sé ngaî mô mâc ké· kōn hiăp*, cette affaire ne me concerne pas.

吸 *Hiăp*. Aspirer, humer.

｜石, *hiăp chăc*, pierre à aimant.

｜鐵, *hiăp t'iĕt*, fer aimanté, aimant.

挾 *Hiăp* (ou *kiăp*). Presser un objet des deux côtés; placer un objet entre deux autres.

聖像我｜阿經書貯裡, *chín sióng ngaî hiăp á kīn choū toù lì*, j'ai mis l'image dans mon livre de prières.

Voir *kiăp*.

HIÂP

脇 *Hiâp*. Jointure du dessous des bras, aisselle.

我書｜下挾等裡, *ngaî choū hiâp hā hiăp tèn lì*, j'ai mon livre sous le bras.

HIÊN

弦 *Hiên*. Corde d'arc.

弓弦上起來好掷, *kioūng hiên chòng hì loî haò pāng*, mettre la corde à l'arc pour tirer.

月光十五日㫌前爲上｜，十五㫌後爲下｜, *gnĕt kouōng chìp ngˋ gnìt ȳ ts'iên vî chóng hiên, chìp ngˋ ȳ heoú vî há hiên*, on dit que la lune a la corde de son arc (croissant) en haut pendant les 15 premiers jours du mois et en bas pendant les 15 derniers jours.

絃 *Hiên*. Violon.

彈｜, *t'ân hiên*, pincer un instrument à corde.

鋸｜, *kí hiên*, jouer avec l'archet.

賢 *Hiên*. Sage, vertueux.

｜智, *hiên tjé*, la sagesse.

你賴子咁｜惠, *niā laí tzè kàn hiên fí*, votre enfant est très vertueux.

懸 *Hiên*. Suspendre, suspendu, relevé en bordure.

｜｜吊, *hiên hiên tiáo*, suspendu en l'air.

｜上, *hiên hóng*, sur le rebord.

鍋鏟麼｜剷油唔起, *vŏc ts'àn mô hiên ts'àn yoû mˊ hì*, la pelle n'a pas de rebord, je ne puis puiser l'huile.

HIÈN

顯 *Hièn*. Faire paraître, manifester, visible, évident.

丨 聖蹟, *hièn chín tsĭt*, faire des miracles.

丨 出來, *hièn tch'oŭt loî*, montrer, faire voir.

丨 揚天主個榮光, *hièn yông t'iēn tchoù ké· yoûng kouōng*, manifester la gloire de Dieu.

蚿 *Hièn.* 丨 公, *hièn koūng*, ver de terre.

憲 *Hièn.* Titre de grand mandarin.

三大丨, *sām t'ái hièn*, les trois grands mandarins civils préposés à l'administration d'une province; ce sont:

1° 制臺, *tjé t'oî*, le vice-roi. 撫臺, *voù t'oî*, le gouverneur d'une province.

2° 布政司, *poú tchín sē*, le trésorier général.

3° 按察司, *ón ts'ât sē*, le grand juge.

HIÉN

楦 *Hién.* 丨 頭, *hién t'eôu*, forme de souliers.

鞋子丨唔開, *haî tzè hién mĝ k'oī*, les souliers ne peuvent être élargis à la forme.

HIÉN

現 *Hién.* Qui apparaît, manifeste.

丨 下, *hién há*, à présent.

買賣丨錢, *mài mái hién ts'iên*, acheter, vendre argent comptant.

看得係丨倒, *k'ón têt é· hién tào*, on peut le voir très distinctement.

獻 *Hién.* Offrir à un supérieur.

祭丨, *tsí hién*, offrir un sacrifice.

HIĔT

穴 *Hiĕt.* Numéral des tombeaux.

一丨地, *ŷt hiĕt t'í*, un tombeau.

丨 精, *hiĕt tsīn*, (vulg. *ts'în*), le point vital d'un être vivant.

丨 精别佢打倒, *hiĕt ts'in poūn kî tà taò*, il l'a frappé au point vital.

HIÊT

血 *Hiêt.* Sang.

打出丨, *tà tch'oŭt hiĕt*, frapper jusqu'au sang.

死丨, *sì hiĕt*, sang coagulé.

丨 洗, *hiĕt sè·*, baptême de sang.

歇 *Hiĕt.* Se coucher, passer la nuit.

丨 宿, 丨 店, *hiĕt sioŭc*, *hiĕt tiám*, auberge.

麼那裡丨, *mô nái lī hiĕt*, n'avoir pas où passer la nuit.

HĪN

興 *Hīn.* Inaugurer, commencer.

丨 過一個樣子, *hīn koúo ŷt kè· yóng tzè*, inaugurer une autre mode.

丨 動多人, *hīn t'oúng tō gnîn*, attirer beaucoup de monde.

某日丨工, *meoū gnĭt hīn koūng*, on commencera tel jour.

HÎN

形 *Hîn.* Forme, image.

丨 像, *hîn sióng*, image.

山 | , *sān hîn*, configuration des montagnes.

無 | 無像, *voû hîn voû siông*, sans forme ni figure, spirituel.

刑 *Hîn*. Supplice, peine.

受 | , *choû hîn*, subir le supplice.

| 部, *hîn p'oú*, tribunal des châtiments.

HÍN

興 *Hín*. Verve, entrain.

食酒就發 | , *chĭt tsìou ts'ióu fât hín*, il a bu du vin et le voilà plein d'entrain. On dit aussi *hìn* 咁 | , *àn hìn!* quel tapageur tu fais!

釁 *Hín*. Cause d'un procès, d'une haine.

爲小事就爭 | , *vî siào sé ts'ióu tsēn hín*, pour une bagatelle les voilà tout de suite brouillés.

在前我同佢有 | 隙, *ts'aí ts'iên ngaî t'oûng kî yoū hín hĭt*, autrefois j'ai eu des différends avec lui.

HIŌ

靴 *Hiō*. Bottes.

著 | , *tchôc hiō*, mettre des bottes.

HIÔC

𠺝 *Hiôc*. Gauchir, se déformer, se dit d'une planche qui a perdu sa forme.

裡個板頭做唔得𠺝 | | 起, *ỳ ké pàn t'eôu tsó mĝ têt voé hiôc hiôc hì*, cette planche ne va pas, elle gauchirait.

HIŌNG

鄉 *Hiōng*. Territoire, canton.

| 紳, *hiōng chīn*, les notables du pays.

| 鄰, *hiōng lîn*, voisin du même canton.

平遠有十五 | , *p'în yàn yoū chĭp ngè hiōng*, le *P'în yàn* a 15 cantons.

聖堂係東石 | 管個, *chín t'ông hé toūng chăc hiōng kouòn ké*, l'église est du ressort du canton de *Toūng chăc*.

香 *Hiōng*. Bonne odeur, parfum.

乳 | , *ȳ hiōng*, encens.

丁 | , *tēn hiōng*, clou de girofle.

| 員, *hiōng yân*, citron.

燒 | , *chāo hiōng*, brûler de l'encens aux idoles.

| 料, *hiōng liáo*, parfums, épices.

HIÒNG

響 *Hiòng*. Son, bruit.

我聽 | 一下, *ngâi t'āng hiòng ȳt há*, j'ai entendu un bruit.

紙炮十分 | , *tjè p'áo chĭp foūn hiòng*, les pétards ont un éclat très retentissant.

享 *Hiòng*. Jouir.

| 福, *hiòng foŭc*, être heureux, jouir.

| 用, *hiòng yoúng*, user à son gré.

| 壽七十年, *hiòng chóu ts'ĭt chĭp niân*, il a joui de la vie pendant 70 ans.

餉 *Hiòng*. Vivres et solde de l'armée.

發 | , *fât hiòng*, distribuer la solde.

HIÓNG

向 *Hióng*. Vers, but, intention.

方 | , *fōng hióng*, direction.

志 | , *tjé hióng*, résolution.

| 我檢錢, *hióng ngâi kiàm ts'iên*, adresse-toi à moi pour réclamer l'argent.

轉 | , *tchòn hióng*, se retourner, changer de côté.

HIOŪ

休 *Hioū*. Cesser, finir.

| 想, *hioū siòng*, (litt. tu as cessé de désirer), tu désires en vain.

朽 *Hioū*. Pourrir.

| 壞, | 爛, *hioū fái*, *hioū lán*, c'est pourri, c'est gâté.

HIOÛC

畜 *Hioûc*. Animal domestique, élever, apprivoiser.

| 牲, *hioûc sāng* (on dit aussi *tch'oûc sāng* ou *t'côu sāng*), animal domestique.

| 雞, | 猪, *hioûc kē*, *hioûc tchoū*, élever des poules, des porcs.

| 唔淳, *hioûc mĝ choûn*, ne pouvoir apprivoiser.

HIOŪN

熏 *Hioūn*. Sécher au feu.

| 飯, *hioūn fán*, faire réchauffer le riz après en avoir versé l'eau.

HIOÚN

訓 *Hioún*. Enseigner, élever.

敎 | 人, *kāo hioún gnîn*, exhorter quelqu'un.

HIOŪNG

兄 *Hioūng*. Frère aîné.

| 弟, *hioūng t'í*, frères en général.

叔伯 | 弟, *choûc pâc hioūng t'í*, les enfants de deux frères, c.-à-d. cousins.

家 | , *kā hioūng*, mon frère aîné. (Voir le mot 舍 *chá*).

凶 *Hioūng*. Malheur, péril.

| 惡, *hioūng ôc*, malheur.

吉 | , *kît hioūng*, faste et néfaste.

恐怕有那個 | 險, *k'ioùng p'á yoū mâc ké hioūng hiàm*, je crains qu'il n'y ait quelque danger.

兇 *Hioūng*. Violent, méchant.

| 惡人, *hioūng ôc gnîn*, homme méchant, violent.

病好 | , *p'iáng hào hioūng*, sa maladie est bien grave.

胸 *Hioūng*. Poitrine, thorax.

好馬 | 愛開, *hào mā hioūng oí k'oī*, un bon cheval doit avoir la poitrine large, ouverte.

HIOÛNG.

雄 *Hioûng*. Courageux, fort, oiseau mâle en général.

英 | , *ȳn hioûng*, homme d'un grand courage.

鱅 *Hioûng*. Espèce de poisson d'étang.

HÎP.

噏 *Hîp*. Opprimer, vexer.

大姓 | 小姓, 大官 | 小官, *t'ái siáng*

hîp siào siáng, t'ái houōn hîp siào kouōn, les grandes familles oppriment les petites familles, les grands mandarins oppriment les petits mandarins.

熻 *Hîp.* Cuire à l'étouffé.

飯噲好愛丨一下, *fán voé· hào ói hîp ŷt há,* dès que le riz est à point il faut l'étouffer un moment (en fermant le couvercle).

HÎT.

隙 *Hît.* Crevasse, fente, espace vide; manque, défaut; grief.

墻子有縫丨, *siông tzè yoū p'oúng hît,* le mur est crevassé.

前時我同佢有釁丨, *ts'iên chê ngâi t'oûng kî yoū hín hît,* j'ai déjà eu lieu d'être mécontent de lui.

我去打鵰麼丨, *ngâi hí tà tiāo mô hît,* j'ai été à la chasse sans succès.

HŌ.

(Voir aussi les mots *Hao*).

呵 *Hō.* Souffler, attirer.

丨燒手, *hō chāo choū,* souffler dans les mains pour les réchauffer.

丨唔倒人來, *hō mg̀ taò gnîn lôi,* je ne puis attirer les gens.

Hō. Être, demeurer, (selon les pays on dit encore *hoī, t'oī, t'ō, etc.* ces mots ne sont que des déformations du mot **在** *ts'ái*).

神父丨屋下麼, *chîn foú hō voûc hā mô?* le père est-il chez lui?

還丨個看書, *hân hō ké· k'ón choū!* vous êtes encore là à lire!

HÔ.

何 *Hô.* Qui? quel? pourquoi? comment?

丨爲, *vî hô,* **如丨**, *ŷ hô,* comment?

今年生理如丨, *kīn niân siēn lī ŷ hô?* comment va le commerce cette année?

你在丨處, *gnî ts'ái hô tch'oú?* en quel endroit habitez-vous?

丨必惹事, *hô pît niā sé?* à quoi bon se créer des affaires?

河 *Hô.* Fleuve, rivière.

丨垻, *hô pá,* plage du fleuve.

過丨, *koúo hô,* traverser le fleuve.

一條丨, *ŷt t'iâo hô,* un fleuve.

豪 *Hô* (ou *hâo*) **丨猪**, *hô tchoū.* porc-épic.

丨箭, *hô tsién,* piquants du porc-épic.

HŎC

學 *Hŏc.* Etudier, apprendre, imiter.

丨習, *hŏc sîp,* étudier.

文丨, *voûn hŏc,* science des lettres, littérature.

武丨, *voū hŏc,* science militaire.

丨生, *hŏc sāng,* étudiant.

丨院, v. **丨臺**, *hŏc yán* v. *hŏc t'ôi,* grand examinateur envoyé de Pékin.

入丨, *gnîp hŏc,* être reçu bachelier.

丨人, *hŏc gnîn,* imiter, singer.

丨人個樣子, *hŏc gnîn ké· yóng tzè,* singer les manières d'autrui.

丨人知, *hŏc gnîn tī,* rapporter, moucharder.

我丨先生知, *ngâi hŏc sīn sāng tī,* je vais le rapporter au maître.

鶴 *Hŏc*. Héron, aigrette, nom générique des oiseaux échassiers.

HÔC.

殼 *Hôc*. Écorce, enveloppe.
春 | , *tch'oūn hôc*, coquille d'œuf.
樹 | , *choú hôc*, écorce d'arbre.
蛇哥退 | , *châ kō t'oúi hôc*, le serpent change de peau.
船 | , *chôn hôc*, carcasse d'un bateau.

烙 *Hôc*. Frire avec très peu d'huile ou de graisse.
| 粄, *hôc pàn*, frire des gâteaux.

HŌI

在 *Hōi (ts'ái)*. Être, demeurer, (selon les pays on dit encore *hō, t'ōi, etc.*, ces mots ne sont que des déformations du mot 在 *tsái.) hōi ngái lī*, où est-ce? *hōi ỳ lī*, il est là, c'est là.

HOÎ

Hoî sōi, ouïes des poissons.

HÒI

海 *Hòi*. Océan, mer.
| 帶, *hòi tái*, algues marines.
| 浪, *hòi lóng*, vagues de la mer.

HÓI.

害 *Hói*. Nuire, porter dommage.
| 處, *Hói tch'oú*, préjudice, affront.
利 | , *lí hói*, violent, fort.
山猪傷 | 人個田, *sān tchōu chōng hói gnîn ké· t'ién*, les sangliers font du dégât dans les champs.

HÔN.

寒 *Hôn*. Froid.
| 天, *hôn t'iēn*, l'hiver, le temps des froids.
| 燒病, *hôn chāo p'iáng*, fièvre intermittente.
風 | 暑濕, *foūng hôn tch'òu chīp*, le vent, le froid, la chaleur, l'humidité, (quatre causes de maladies, célèbres dans la médecine chinoise.)
作 | , *tsôc hôn*, ressentir des frissons.

HÒN.

罕 *Hòn*. Rare, peu.
希 | , *hī hòn*, rare.
| 見, *hòn kián*, cela se voit rarement.

HÓN

漢 *Hón*. Nom d'une dynastie.
豪 | , *haô hón*, puissant, audacieux (peu employé).

汗 *Hón*. Sueur.
出 | , *tch'oūt hón*, suer.

釬 *Hón*. Souder.
| 銅, | 錫, *hón t'oūng, hón siāc*, souder le cuivre, l'étain.

翰 *Hón*. | 林, *hón lîm*, docteur académicien.
| 墨, *hón mĕt*, encre d'une qualité supérieure.

旱 *Hón*. Sécheresse, dessécher.

天 | , *t'iēn hón*, sécheresse.

田 | 壞 了, *t'iên hón faí liaò*, les rizières ont été gâtées par la sécheresse.

行 | 路, *háng hón lóu*, voyager par voie de terre.

| 塘, *hón t'ông*, dessécher un étang.

HŌNG.

糠 *Hōng*. Son, balle de riz.

穀 | , *Koŭc hōng*, balle de riz.

米 | , *mì hōng*, son de riz. 糟 | , *tsāo hōng*, résidus de grains distillés.

HÔNG

行 *Hông*. Magasin, entrepôt; ligne, rangée, file.

開 洋 | , *k'ōi yông hông*, ouvrir un magasin de marchandises européennes.

外 | , *ngóe' hông*, qui n'est pas du métier, qui n'y entend rien.

內 | , *noúi hông*, ou 在 | , *ts'aí hông*, capable, qui comprend les choses.

唔 在 | , *mĝ ts'aí hông*, incapable, qui ne s'y entend pas.

一 | , *ŷt hông*, une ligne.

一 | 樹, *ŷt hông choụ́*, une rangée d'arbres.

HÓNG

項 *Hóng*. Classe, un article, un ensemble; particule numérale des choses en général.

桌上幾多 | 東西, *tsôc hóng kì tō hóng toūng sī*, que de choses différentes il y a sur la table!

正 | , 雜 | , *tchín hóng, ts'ăp hóng*, choses prévues, auxquelles on s'attendait, choses imprévues, non comptées.

巷 *Hóng*. Corridor, passage, petite rue, cul-de-sac.

過 一 條 | 就 到, *koúo ŷt t'iâo hóng ts'ioú táo*, passez un corridor et vous y êtes.

| 角 頭, *hóng kôc t'eoû*, au fond de l'impasse.

上 *Hóng* (*chóng*). Dessus, lever.

| 起 來, *hóng hì loî*, lève-toi.

| 唔 起, *hóng mĝ hì*, je ne puis me lever.

上 棚 | , *chōng p'âng hóng*, monter à l'étage.

放 阿 桌 | 起, *fóng á tsôc hóng hì*, mettre sur la table.

HOT.

渴 *Hôt*. Soif, altéré.

肚 | , *toù hôt*, j'ai soif.

止 | , *tjè hôt*, apaiser la soif.

| 慕, *hôt móung* ou | 想, *hôt siòng*, désirer ardemment.

Ȳ

以 *Ȳ*. Se servir de, à cause de cela, jusqu'à.

可 | , *K'ò ȳ*, pouvoir employer, pouvoir servir à, être convenable, être permis.

所 | , *sò ȳ*, c'est pourquoi, donc, par conséquent.

自 古 | 來, *tsé koù ȳ loî*, depuis l'an-

7

tiquité jusqu'à maintenant, de tout temps.

丨前, *ȳ ts'iên*, auparavant.

丨後, *ȳ heoú*, désormais.

於 Ȳ. A, dans.

祭獻丨天主, *tsí hién ȳ t'iēn tchòu*, offrir un sacrifice à Dieu.

Ȳ dans le langage vulgaire se sous-entend presque toujours, on dit aussi bien *tsí hién t'iēn tchòu*.

與 Ȳ. Donner, à, comme, avec.

今日丨我, *kīn gnĭt ȳ ngō*, donnez-nous aujourd'hui (dans le Pater).

相丨, *siōng ȳ*, être lié d'amitié. (Peu employe), se sous-entend dans la langue vulgaire.

衣 Ȳ. Nom générique des habits.

丨裳 (v. 丨服). *ȳ chông* (v. *ȳ foŭc*), habits en général.

一件丨服, *ȳt k'ián ȳ foŭc*, un habit.

聖丨, *chín ȳ*, scapulaire.

簑丨, *sō ȳ*, petit manteau en écorce de palmier pour préserver de la pluie.

祭丨, *tsí ȳ*, ornements sacerdotaux.

醫 Ȳ. Guérir, exercer la médecine.

丨生, *ȳ sēn*, médecin.

丨好裡, *ȳ hào lè*, il a été guéri.

丨死, *ȳ sì*, mourir à cause des mauvais soins ou des remèdes du médecin.

Ŷ

而 Ŷ. Et. 從今丨後, *ts'ioûng kīn ŷ héou*, désormais.

如 Ŷ. Comme, semblable à.

丨何, *ŷ hô*, (v. 何 *hô ŷ*,), comment?

今年不丨舊年, *kīn niân poût ŷ k'ioú niân*, cette année, ce n'est pas comme l'année passée.

丨今, *ŷ kīn*, présentement.

深丨海, *tch'īm ŷ hòi*, profond comme la mer.

儒 Ŷ. 丨教, *ŷ kaó*, religion des lettrés.

丨書, *ŷ choū*, livres classiques.

丨家, *ŷ kā*, famille de lettrés.

咁丨雅, *kàn ŷ ngā*, comme vous êtes distingué!

餘 Ŷ. Superflu, excédant.

有丨剩, *yoū ŷ chín*, il y en a de reste.

丨外, *ŷ ngóe*, en outre.

兒 Ŷ. Fils, enfants; comme particule, il s'ajoute à beaucoup de mots pour en faire des diminutifs, ou simplement par euphonie.

Dans ce dernier cas, on prononce *ŷ* ou *gnî*. 耳覺覺丨聽, *gnì kôc kôc gnî t'ăng*, prêter une oreille attentive, ouvrir l'oreille.

丨女, *ŷ ng̀*, enfants en général.

有幾多個令郎, *yoū kì tō ké lín lòng?* manière polie de demander: combien avez-vous de fils? Rép. 三個小丨, *sām ké siào ŷ*, trois petits enfants (quand même ils auraient vingt ans).

Ŷ

移 Ŷ. Transporter, émigrer.

丨走, *ý tsèou*, émigrer.

丨文, *ý voûn*, lettre officielle entre mandarins.

裡 Ỳ ou *lì* ou *yè·* ou *yà*. Ici, là, ce, cette (parlant du plus proche).

放裡子, *fóng ỳ tzè*, mets ici.

神父在丨子麼, *chîn foú ts'oī ỳ tzè mô?* le Père est-il ici?

丨裡來, *ỳ lî loî*, ici, viens ici.

唔係丨子個子 (ou 個裡) *mĝ hé· ỳ tzè ké· tzè* (ou *ké· lî*), pas ici, là.

丨個, *ỳ ké·* (ou *yè· ké·* ou *yà ké·*), ce, ceci (parlant du plus proche).

丨個東西拿來, *ỳ ké·* (ou *yà ké·*) *toūng sī nā loî*, apporte cette chose-ci.

唔係丨個, 個個, *mĝ hé· ỳ ké·, ké· ké·*, pas celle-ci, celle-là.

羽 Ỳ. Plumes.

丨扇, *ỳ chán*, éventail de plumes (ne s'emploie à peu près que dans cette expression. On dit d'ordinaire: *maō* 毛).

丨翼, *ỳ ÿt*, aide, assistance.

你淨自己做唔來有幾多丨翼好佢出來, *gnî ts'iáng tsé kì tsó mĝ loî yoū kì tō ỳ ÿt haò kioūng tch'oût loî*, tu n'as pas pu faire cela tout seul, déclare tes complices.

神父麼丨翼難傳教, *chîn foú mô ỳ ÿt nân tch'ôn kaó*, le missionnaire sans aides peut difficilement propager la religion.

雨 Ỳ. Pluie.

落丨, *lŏc ỳ*, pleuvoir.

丨毛, *ỳ maō*, pluie fine.

會落丨, *voé· lŏc ỳ*, il va pleuvoir.

丨水多, *ỳ choùi tō*, les pluies sont abondantes.

依 Ỳ (ou *ȳ* ou *ý*). Consentir à, se conformer à.

丨我意思, *ỳ ngā ý sé*, conforme-toi à mon avis.

丨神父安排, *ỳ chîn fóu ōn p'âi*, s'en tenir aux dispositions du Père.

丨舊, *ỳ k'ióu*, comme auparavant.

丨靠天主個仁慈, *ỳ k'áo t'iēn tchoù ké· ŷn tsê*, s'appuyer sur la miséricorde de Dieu.

几 Ỳ. Chaise en général, qu'il y ait, ou non, dossier.

竹丨, *tchoŭc ỳ*, chaise de bambou.

靠丨, *kaó ỳ*, chaise à dossier.

馬叉丨, *mā tsá ỳ*, chaise pliante.

眠丨, *mîn ỳ*, chaise longue, chaise à dormir.

Ý

意 Ý. Pensée, idée, opinion, attente, désir, intention, volonté, sentiment.

深丨, *tch'īm ý*, pensée profonde.

照我丨思, *tchaó ngā ý sé*, d'après mon opinion.

佢丨思唔好, *kiā ý sé mĝ haò*, son idée n'est pas bonne.

中丨, 合丨, *tchoúng ý, hăp ý*, selon notre attente, conforme au désir.

出主丨, *tchoût tchoù ý*, prendre une détermination, donner son avis.

故丨, *koú ý*, à dessein, de propos délibéré.

過丨唔得, *kouó ý mĝ tĕt*, supporter

avec peine; tant de bonté pour moi me confond.

唔好｜思, *mĝ hào ý sé*, répugnance à faire une chose nuisible ou désagréable à quelqu'un.

咁大個人樣得好｜思來相打, *àn t'aí ké· gnîn nióng têt haò ý sé loî siōng tà?* vous n'avez pas honte de vous battre à votre âge?

天主保佑事事如｜, *t'iēn tchoù paò yoú sé sé ŷ ý!* que Dieu vous protège et que tout aille à vos souhaits!

異 Ý. Différent.

｜端, *ý tōn*, superstition, vaine observance.

做｜端, *tsó ý tōn*, faire des superstitions.

樣班你就過｜樣, *nióng pān gnî ts'ioú kouó ý yóng*, comment! mais vous n'êtes plus le même!

易 Ý. Facile; changer.

容｜, *yoúng ý*, facile.

｜得話, *ý têt vá*, facile à dire.

｜經, *ý kīn*, le livre des Mutations (classique chinois).

預 Ý. Préparer, prévoir.

｜備, *ý p'í*, préparer.

｜備領聖體, *ý p'í leāng chín t'ì*, se préparer à la communion.

｜先, *ý siēn*, avant tout.

愛｜防裡個惡人, *oí ý fông ỳ ké· ôc gnîn*, il faut se garder de ce méchant.

諭 Ý. Signifier, exhorter.

上｜ ou ｜旨, *chóng ŷ*, ou *ý tjè*, décret impérial.

YĀ

也 Yā. Et, aussi.

｜有好個｜有唔好個, *yā yoū haò ké· yā yoū mĝ haò ké·*, il y en a de bons il y en a aussi de mauvais.

我｜係咁樣想, *ngâi yā hé· àn yóng siòng*, moi aussi, je pense ainsi,

野 Yā (yà). Sauvage.

｜獸, *yā tch'oú*, animaux sauvages.

｜猪, *yā tchoū*, sanglier.

揶 Yā. Une des salutations chinoises (qui consiste à abaisser plus ou moins les deux mains rapprochées et fermées, puis à les relever jusqu'à la poitrine ou au front.

倡｜, *tch'óng yā*, faire ce salut.

YÂ

耶 Yâ. Finale de phrase, s'emploie dans le Saint nom de Jésus, 耶穌, *Yâ sē*.

爺 Yâ. Père, seigneur, monsieur.

你｜子還健麼, *niā yâ tzè hân k'ián mō?* ton père se porte-t-il bien?

三子｜, *sām tzè yâ*, le père et ses deux fils.

｜門, *yâ moûn*, les domestiques du mandarin.

師｜, *sē yâ*, le conseiller officiel du mandarin.

Yâ particule respectueuse ajoutée au nom d'une personne notable ou constituée en dignité. *Lì tēn yâ*, monsieur *Lì t'ēn*.

YÀ

裡 *Yà* (pour *lì* ou *ỳ* ou *yè·*). Ce, ceci (le plus proche) celui-ci.

| 字你識麼, *yà sé gnî chĭt mô?* connais-tu ce caractère?

| 個罌子拿去洗, *yà ké· āng tzè nā hí· sè·*, va laver cette bouteille-ci. (Voir *ỳ*).

乜 *Yà*. Dérober, attraper à la volée, une poignée, gratter.

鷂婆 | 走一隻雞子, *yáo p'ô yà tsèou ŷt tchâc kē· tzè*, l'épervier a enlevé un poulet.

一 | 米, *ŷt yà mì*, une poignée de riz.

| 癢, *yà yōng*, se gratter pour apaiser une démangeaison.

食生芋子噲 | 人, *chĭt sāng voú tzè voé· yà gnîn*, les tarros crus sont très âpres au gosier.

YÁ

夜 *Yá*. Nuit, soir, tard.

| 晡頭, *yá poū t'eôu*, la nuit.

半 | , *pán yá*, minuit.

做 | , *tsó yá*, faire le dîner du soir.

讀 | 書, *t'oŭc yá choū*, étudier à la lampe.

YĀI

挨 *Yāi*. Pousser, forcer à avancer.

| 倒城門, *yāi taò châng moûn*, à force de marcher, je suis arrivé à la porte de la ville.

| 輪子, *yāi loûn tzè*, faire tourner une roue, (ou bien) faire avancer une brouette.

YÂI

椰 *Yâi*. Coco. | 子, *yâi tzè*, coco.

| 子樹, *yâi tzè choú*, cocotier.

YĀM

閹 *Yām*. Châtrer.

| 雞, | 猪, *yām kē·*, *yām tchoū*, châtrer les coqs, les porcs.

YÂM

炎 *Yâm*. Flamme, flamber; brûler, brûlant.

火燒山 | 上唔知幾高, *fò chaō sān yâm chōng mĝ tī kì kaō*, la montagne est en feu, les flammes s'élancent à une hauteur incalculable.

| 燒, *yâm chaō*, chaleur étouffante, très chaud.

燄 *Yâm*. Eclat rapide et intermittent d'une lumière.

雷火緊 | , *loûi fò kìn yâm*, les éclairs ne cessent de sillonner les nues.

簷 *Yâm*. Saillie d'un toit.

屋 | , *voŭc yâm*, saillie du toit.

| 頭, *yâm t'eôu*, trottoir que garantit la saillie du toit.

鹽 *Yâm*. Sel.

火 | , *fò yâm*, sel fin, recuit.

硝 | , *siāo yâm*, salpêtre.

粗 | , *tsē yâm*, gros sel.

閻 *Yâm*. | 羅王, *yâm lô vông*, le dieu des enfers.

螢 *Yâm.* 火 | 虫, *fò yâm tch'oûng*, ver-luisant, luciole.

YÀM

淹 *Yàm* ou *yām*. Immergé, inondé.

河水大田都 | 倒𠰲, *hô choùi t'ái t'iên toū yàm taò lê·*, la crue des eaux a inondé toutes les rizières.

| (醃) 生菜食, *yàm sāng ts'oí chĭt*, faire de la salade.

掩 *Yàm*. Couvrir, voiler.

遮 | , *tchā yàm*, cacher, dissimuler.

遮 | 實情, *tchā yàm chĭt ts'în*, cacher la vérité.

屋看唔倒樹子 | 等𠰲, *voûc k'ón mĝ taò choú tzè yàm tèn ê·*, on ne peut pas voir la maison, les arbres la cachent.

YÁM

厭 *Yám*. Avoir en dégoût, satiété.

聽你講去十分 | 等𠰲, *t'áng gnî kòng hí chĭp foūn yám tèn ê·*, je suis dégoûté de t'entendre parler.

嫽阿煩 | , *liaó á fân yám*, je suis ennuyé d'un si long repos.

艷 *Yám*. Beau, belle couleur.

花咁 | , *fā àn yám!* quelle vivacité de couleur dans ces fleurs!

氣像好 | , *hí sióng hào yám*, elle a une figure de toute beauté.

Yám. Exciter, remuer.

莫 | 等梯我怕跌, *mŏc yám tèn t'oī ngâi p'á tiĕt*, ne remue pas l'échelle, j'ai peur de tomber.

Yám yám tchoūn, trembler de tous ses membres.

YĀN

冤 *Yān*. | 枉, | 屈, *yān vòng*, *yān k'ioŭt*, injustice, vexation, faire tort, opprimer.

喊 | , *hám yān*, crier à la porte du tribunal pour demander justice.

| 仇, *yān choû*, | 家, *yān kā*, ennemi.

結 | , *kiĕt yān*, devenir ennemi.

咽 *Yān*. | 喉, *yān heôu*, gosier, larynx.

烟 *Yān*. Fumée, tabac, opium.

火 | , *fò yān*, fumée.

黃 | , *vông yān*, tabac à fumer.

食 | , *chĭt yān*, fumer.

洋 | , *yông yān*, opium.

鴉片 | , *ā pĕn yān*, opium.

| 筒, *yān t'oûng*, pipe.

水 | 筒, *choùi yān t'oûng*, pipe à eau.

| 油, *yān yoû*, jus de tabac, nicotine.

蔫 *Yān*. Se flétrir, se faner.

花 | 帛𠰲, *fā yān p'ĕt lê·*, les fleurs sont fanées. On dit plutôt *ts'iá*, 謝, *voir ce mot*.

揠 *Yān*. Feuilleter un livre.

| 書來看, *yān choū loî k'ón*, cherche dans le livre, pour voir.

YÂN

員 *Yân*. Particule numérale des mandarins.

一｜官, *ŷt yân koūon*, un mandarin.
大小官｜, *t'ái siào koūon*, les grands et les petits mandarins.
委｜, *vī yân*, mandarin délégué.
生｜, *sēn yân*, titre de bachelier.

圓 *Yân*. Rond, numéral des piastres.
｜個, *yân ké·*, rond, c'est rond.
｜圈, *yân k'iān*, un rond, un cercle.
使裡花邊三｜, 錢三十文, *sè lê· fā piēn sām yân, ts'iên sām chīp voûn*, j'ai dépensé 3 piastres et 30 sapèques.

丸 *Yân*. Pilule, globule.
藥｜, *yŏc yân*, pilules médicinales.
肉｜, *nioûc yân*, boulettes de viande hachée.

延 *Yân*. Faire durer longtemps.
遲｜, *tchê yân*, ｜擱, *yân kôc*, tarder, mettre obstacle.

筵 *Yân*. Numéral des tablées de vin.
罰裡佢三｜席, *făt lê· kî sām yân sĭt*, on l'a puni de trois tablées de vin.

園 *Yân*. Jardin, verger.
花｜, *fā yân*. jardin à fleurs.
菜｜, *ts'ói yân*, jardin potager.

垣 *Yân*. Mur d'enceinte.
城｜, *châng yân*, mur de la ville.
四圍有墻｜, *sí vî yoū siông yân*, un mur entoure les quatre côtés.

轅 *Yân*. ｜門, *yân moûn*, portes latérales des prétoires.

鉛 *Yân*. Plomb.
｜筆, *yân pĭt*, crayon.
｜瑪, *yân mā*, balle de fusil.
｜粉, *yân foùn*, blanc de céruse.

緣 *Yân*. Cause, parce que.
｜由, 因｜, ｜故, *yân yoû*, *ȳn yân*, *yân koú*, cause, origine, circonstances.
那個｜故, *mâc ké· yân koú*, pour quelle raison?
無｜無故, *voû yân voû koú*, sans rime ni raison.

然 *Yân*. Idée générale d'être, d'exister; ne s'emploie jamais seul.
所以｜, *sò ȳ yân*, ce par quoi une chose existe, cause, motif.
自｜, *tsé yân*, exister par soi-même, spontané, naturel, naturellement.
了｜, *liaò yân*, clair, évident.
聽(v. 盡)佢自｜, *t'ín* (v. *ts'ín*) *kî tsé yân*, laisser agir la nature, laisse-le faire à sa guise; se résigner à son sort.
斷｜, 必｜, *tōn yân*, *pĭt yân*, certes, certainement.
旣｜, *kí yân*, puisqu'il en est ainsi,
雖｜, *souī yân*, bien qu'il en soit ainsi,
｜後, *yân heoú*, après qu'il en fut ainsi, après cela, ensuite.
隔遠嚮銃人先看火｜後哱聽嚮, *kâc yàn hiòng tch'oúng gnîn siēn k'ón fò yân heoú tsáng t'āng hiòng*, quand quelqu'un tire un coup de fusil au loin, on voit le feu avant d'entendre le bruit.
忽｜, 忽｜間, *foŭt yân*, *foŭt yân kiān*, soudainement, en un instant.

YÀN

遠 *Yàn*. Loin, éloigné.

| **近**, *yàn k'ioún*, éloigné ou rapproché c.-à-d. distance.

唔知 | **近**, *mĝ tī yàn k'ioún*, je ne connais pas la distance.

愛看 | **近**, *oí k'ón yàn k'ioún*, cela dépend de la distance.

永 | , *yoùn yàn*, éternellement, éternel.

| **三步路**, *yàn sām p'oú loú*, éloigné de trois lieues.

爭得 | , *tsāng tĕt yàn*, il s'en faut de beaucoup.

YÁN

燕 *Yán*. Hirondelle.

| **窩**, *yán vō*, nid d'hirondelle.

院 *Yán*. Grande maison, villa, édifice public.

學 | , *hŏc yán*, examinateur pour le degré de **秀才**, *sioú ts'oî*.

撫 | , (ou **撫台**), *voù yán* (ou *voù t'oî*), gouverneur d'une seule province.

兩 | **來到**, *leòng yán loî taó*, les deux gouverneurs, le *tsoùng toûc* et le *voù t'oî*, sont arrivés.

怨 *Yán*. Ressentiment, avoir en aversion, se plaindre.

我麼那個 | **佢**, *ngaî mô mâc ké· yán kî*, je n'ai aucun grief contre lui.

神父唔知那人唔着又緊 | **我**, *chîn foú mĝ tī màn gnîn mĝ tch'ŏc yoú kìn yán ngaî*, le Père ne sait pas qui a tort et ne fait que s'en prendre à moi·

積 | **人**, *tsĭt yán gnîn*, en vouloir à quelqu'un (*litt.* accumuler des haines sur quelqu'un).

硯 *Yán*. Pierre sur laquelle on broie l'encre.

墨 | **拿來**, *mĕt yán nā loî*, apporte l'encre et la pierre.

縣 *Yán*. Sous-préfecture dépendant d'un **州** *tchoū* ou d'un **府** *foù*.

| **城**, *yán châng*, chef-lieu d'une sous-préfecture ou ville de 3[cme] ordre.

貴 | , *kouí yán*, Monsieur le sous-préfet (quand un égal ou un supérieur s'adresse au mandarin de cette ville).

YĀNG

宛 *Yāng* (*vàn*). Enrouler, entortiller.

| **毛辮**, *yāng maō piēn*, enrouler sa tresse autour de la tête.

樹上 | **下轉**, *choú hóng yāng á tchòn*, enroulé autour de l'arbre.

一 | **鐵線**, *ŷt yāng t'iĕt sién*, un rouleau de fil de fer.

YÂNG

贏 *Yâng*. Avantage, gagner, l'emporter.

官司打 | , *koūon sē tà yâng*, le procès est gagné.

打得佢 | , *tā tet kî yâng*, il est de taille à l'emporter dans la lutte.

麼 | **麼輸**, *mô yâng mô choū*, la partie

est nulle (*litt.* ni avantage ni désavantage).

講唔｜, *kòng mĝ yâng*, avoir le dessous dans une discussion.

賭｜, *toù yâng*, gagner au jeu.

營 *Yâng* (*ŷn*). **｜盤**, *yâng p'ân*, camp retranché.

紮｜盤, *tsâp yâng p'ân*, établir un camp retranché.

YÀNG

影 *Yàng*. Ombre, trace.

日｜, *gnĭt yàng*, ombre d'un corps qui intercepte la lumière du soleil.

人｜, *gnîn yàng*, l'ombre de l'homme.

麼｜, *mô yàng*, il n'y a pas l'ombre de cela, ce n'est pas vrai.

｜一下唔曾看分明, *yàng ŷt há mĝ t'iên k'ón foūn mîn*, je l'ai entrevu, je ne l'ai pas vu clairement.

人有名樹有｜, *gnîn yoū miâng choú yoū yàng*, l'homme a sa réputation comme l'arbre a son ombre.

映 *Yàng*. Photographier, réfléchir.

像｜, *yàng sióng*, photographier.

YĀO

妖 *Yāo*. Magique, prodigieux.

｜怪 v. **｜精**, *yāo kouái* v. *yāo tsīn*, sorcier.

｜魔, *yāo mô*, fantôme.

腰 *Yāo*. Milieu du corps, reins.

｜骨, *yāo koût*, épine dorsale.

猪｜, *tchoū yāo*, rognons de porc.

有官犯死罪愛同佢切｜, *yoū koūon fám sì ts'ouí oí t'oûng kî ts'iĕt yaō*, on scie les reins à un mandarin qui a encouru la peine de mort.

｜帶, *yaō taí*, ceinture que l'on met par dessus les habits.

邀 *Yaō*. Inviter.

｜兩個人同陣行, *yaō leòng ké· gnîn t'oûng tch'in hâng*, inviter deux hommes pour faire route ensemble.

係主教來東石愛｜多人來, *hé· tchoù kaó loî toūng chăc oí yaō tō gnîn lôi*, si l'évêque vient à *Toung chac* il faudra faire venir beaucoup de monde.

YÂO

遙 *Yaô*. Loin, long.

路｜, *loú yaô*, la route est longue, c'est loin.

山｜水遠, *sān yaô chouì yàn*, être séparés par des montagnes et des rivières c.-à-d. par une grande distance.

窰 *Yaô*. Four à chaux, à briques, à poterie etc.

燒｜, *chaō yaô*, chauffer un four.

瓦唔曾出｜, *ngà mĝ ts'ên tch'oūt yaô*, les tuiles sont encore au four.

灰｜, *foē· yaô*, four à chaux.

搖 *Yaô*. Exciter, remuer.

｜鈴, *yaô lāng*, agiter la clochette.

｜樹, *yâo choú*, secouer un arbre.

｜｜擺擺, *yaô yaô pài pài*, n'être pas solide sur sa base, se dandiner.

｜船架槳, *yaô chôn ká tsiòng*, faire

8

avancer la barque à forces de rames.

謠 *Yaô.* | 言, *yaô niân*, faux bruits, vaine rumeur.

麼個事淨 | 言, *mò ké· sé, ts'iáng yâo niân*, ce n'est pas vrai, ce ne sont que de vaines rumeurs.

YAÒ

舀 *Yaò.* Puiser à l'aide d'une cuiller ou d'un petit vase ce qui est contenu dans un vase plus grand.

| 水, *yaò choùi*, puiser de l'eau.

| 一杓麻水, *yaò ŷt chôc mâ choùi*, puiser une cuillerée d'eau.

| 一盃酒, *yaò ŷt pī tsioù*, puiser une tasse de vin.

YAÓ

要 *Yaó.* Nécessaire.

| 緊, *yaó kìn*, nécessaire.

| 緊個人, *yaó kìn ké· gnîn*, homme dont on ne peut pas se passer.

鷂 *Yáo.* | 婆, | *p'ô*, épervier.

角 | , *kôc yáo*, milan.

紙 | , *tjè yáo*, cerf-volant.

放紙 | , *fóng tjè yáo*, lancer le cerf-volant.

YĂP

葉 *Yăp.* Feuille d'une plante, ce qui ressemble à une feuille.

樹 | , *choú yăp*, feuille d'arbre.

茶 | , *ts'â yăp*, feuilles de thé.

洋 | 絞, *yông yăp káo*, charnière.

百 | 窗, *pâc yăp ts'oūng*, persienne.

頁 *Yăp.* 書 | , *choū yăp*, feuillet de livre.

讀書讀識三 | , *t'oŭc choū t'oŭc chît sām yăp*, j'ai appris par cœur trois pages.

蝶 *Yăp.* 洋 | , *yông yăp* (pour *yông t'iăp*), papillon.

YÂP

醃 *Yâp* (*yām*). Saler, dessécher par le sel.

| 猪肉, *yâp tchoū nioŭc*, saler du porc.

淋菜淋裡忒培就 | 死, *lîm t'sói lîm lì t'iĕt p'î ts'ióu yâp sì*, les légumes ont été arrosés avec de l'engrais trop fort, les voilà tous desséchés.

壓 *Yâp* (ou *niâp* pour *âp*). Déprimé, écrasé. Voyez *niâp*

𥉻 *Yâp* (ou *niâp*). Scintillement des étoiles. Voyez *niâp*.

YĂT

越 *Yăt.* Outre-passer, plus.

超 | 人性, *tch'aō yăt gnîn sín*, surpasser la nature humaine, surnaturel.

| 多 | 好, *yăt tō yăt hào*, plus il y en aura, mieux cela vaudra.

| 發好, *yăt fât hào*, d'autant mieux.

| 食水 | 作渴, *yăt chĭt choùi yăt tsôc hôt*, plus on boit plus on a soif.

YÂT

日 *Yât.* Dire. 嚷嚷｜｜, *yông yông yât yât*, se dit de quelqu'un qui est toujours à marmotter.

揭 *Yât.* Déboucher, découvrir.

｜開來, *yât k'oī loî*, déboucher.

田缺｜開來好過水, *t'iên k'ièt yât k'oī loî haò kouó chouì*, rouvrir le passage à l'eau des rizières.

窗紙莫去｜, *ts'oūng tjè mŏc hí yât*, ne va pas décoller le papier de la fenêtre.

YÊ·

涎 *Yê·.* Bave.

蝴鰍吐｜, *foû ts'ioū t'óu* (ou *t'oúi*) *yê·*, le *foû ts'ioū* crache de la bave.

馬跑熱噲出｜, *mā p'aō gnĕt voé· tch'oût yê·*, le cheval a couru au point d'en écumer.

Yê·. Lambin, lambiner.

｜官, *yê· koūon*, un mandarin paresseux qui laisse traîner les affaires en longueur.

YÈ·

裡 *Yè·* (ou *ỳ*). Ici, là, ceci, celui-ci; voyez : *ỳ*.

YÉ·

Yé· (ou *vé·*). Jeter, éparpiller.

｜菜仁, *yé· ts'ói ŷn*, semer à la volée des graines de légumes.

YEN (voir *YAN*)

ȲM

音 *Ȳm.* Son, prononciation.

弦｜好聽, *hiēn ȳm hào t'āng*, le son du violon est agréable.

字一樣｜唔同, *sé ŷt yóng ȳm mĝ t'oûng*, le caractère est le même, mais la prononciation diffère.

聲｜嘹喨, *chāng ȳm liaô leóng*, sa voix est claire et distincte.

陰 *Ȳm.* Principe imparfait, par opposition au mot 陽 *yông*, qui désigne le principe parfait; ombre. *Voir* 陽 *yông*.

｜間, *ȳm kiān*, l'enfer des païens.

｜涼, *ȳm leông*, ombragé et frais.

天｜, *t'iēn ȳm*, ciel nuageux.

地方忒｜, *t'í fōng t'ièt ȳm*, l'endroit est trop ombragé.

ŶM

淫 *Ŷm.* Luxure.

｜慾, *ŷm yoŭc*, passions impures.

犯邪｜, *fám siâ ŷm*, commettre un péché de luxure.

邪｜個念頭, *siâ ŷm ké· niám t'eôu*, pensées impures.

歌唱｜詞, *kō tch'óng ŷm tsê*, chanter des airs lascifs.

｜人家婦女, *ŷm gnîn kā foú ngò*, corrompre la femme ou la fille d'autrui.

ỲM

飲 *Ỳm.* Boire. ｜酒, *ỳm tsiòu*, boire du vin. Ce mot est peu employé; on dit simplement: 食酒, *chĭt tsiòu*.

ÝM

蔭 *Ým.* Mouiller, humecter.

掃地愛先｜濕地泥來, *sáo t'í ói siēn ým chīp t'í nâi loî*, avant de balayer il faut d'abord humecter le sol.

灌｜塘, *kouón ým t'ông*, étang pour les irrigations.

任 *Ým.* Emploi public. Etre libre de, laisser libre de.

上｜,赴｜, *chōng ým, foú ým*, se rendre à son poste.

接｜, *tsiâp ým*, recevoir les sceaux et entrer en fonctions.

現｜, *hién ým*, celui qui est actuellement en charge.

前｜, *ts'iên ým*, celui qui était précédemment en charge.

五年做一｜官, *ǹg niân tsó ȳt ým kouōn*, les pouvoirs d'un mandarin durent cinq ans.

｜你做, *ým gnî tsó*, fais comme tu voudras.

ȲN

慇 *Ȳn.* **｜勤** (ou **懃**), *ȳn k'iôun* (ou *k'în*), servir avec empressement.

咁｜勤, *àn ȳn k'iôun*, comme vous êtes empressé à me servir ! *(Politesse).*

英 *Ȳn.* **｜雄**, *ȳn hioûng*, homme vaillant et courageux, héros.

｜國, *ȳn kouêt*, Angleterre.

引 *Ȳn.* Attirer par un appât, amorce; conduire, indiquer.

｜人犯罪, *ȳn gnîn fám ts'ouí*, entraîner quelqu'un à pécher.

｜線, *ȳn sién*, mèche de pétard ou autre.

紙煤麼｜火石打唔着, *tjè moê· mô ȳn fò chăc tà mĝ tch'ŏc*, le papier allumette n'est pas amorcé, la pierre à feu ne pourra pas le faire prendre.

指｜路, *tjè ȳn loú*, indiquer la route.

小｜, *siào ȳn*, courte préface.

嬰 *Ȳn.* **｜孩**, *ȳn hâi*, petit enfant.

因 *Ȳn.* A cause, parce que.

｜此, *ȳn tsè*, à cause de cela.

｜爲, *ȳn ví*, parce que.

痐 *Ȳn.* Mal de tête, **頭哪｜**, *t'eôu nâ ȳn*, j'ai mal à la tête.

ŶN.

營 *Ŷn.* Projet, dessein, expédient.

｜生, *ŷn sēn*, moyen de gagner sa vie.

咁噲｜謀, *kàn voé· ŷn meoû !* comme vous savez vous tirer d'embarras !

仁 *Ŷn.* Commisération, pépin, noyau, graine.

｜心, *ŷn sīm*, **｜慈**, *ŷn tsê*, miséricorde, miséricordieux.

賴天主個｜慈, *lái t'iēn tchoù ké· ŷn tsê*, implorer la miséricorde de Dieu.

菜｜, *ts'ói ŷn*, graines de légumes,

桃｜, *t'âo ŷn*, noyau de pêche.

仍 *Ŷn.* Comme auparavant.

｜舊, *ŷn k'iôu*, comme auparavant.

｜然不改, *ŷn yân poût koì*, il persiste à ne pas se corriger.

蠅 *Ŷn*. 烏｜, *voū ŷn*, mouche commune.

ỲN

癮 *Ỳn* (pour *yoùn*). Besoin périodique et impérieux que fait éprouver une habitude, spécialement celle de fumer l'opium.

還唔曾上｜, *hân mĝ tsên chōng ỳn*, je n'éprouve pas encore cette nécessité, (l'habitude n'est pas encore prise.)

過｜, *koúo ỳn*, fumer pour satisfaire ce besoin.

孕 *Ỳn*. 受｜, *chóu ỳn*, devenir enceinte.

我自細｜育大來, *ngaî tsé sé· ỳn yoûc t'aí loî*, je l'ai conçu et élevé depuis son plus bas âge.

ÝN

印 *Ýn*. Cachet, sceau; imprimer, empreinte.

打｜, *tà ýn*, apposer le sceau.

接｜, *tsiâp ýn*, recevoir les sceaux, entrer en charge.

封｜, *foûng ýn*, fermer les sceaux; vacances des tribunaux, du 20 de la dernière lune au 20 de la première.

｜書, *ýn choū*, imprimer un livre.

｜板, *ýn pàn*, planche gravée pour imprimer.

脚｜, *kiôc ýn*, empreinte du pied.

火｜, *fò ýn*, marque faite au fer rouge.

應 *Ýn*. Répondre, donner une réponse; se charger de, consentir, rendre service à quelqu'un.

有人喊愛｜一下來唔係樣得知你聽倒裡麼, *yoū gnîn hám oí ýn ŷt há loî, mĝ hé· nióng têt tī gnî t'àng taò lî mô*, quand on t'appelle il faut répondre, autrement comment savoir si tu as entendu ou non.

我答｜裡佢唔使來, *ngaî tâp ýn lî kî mĝ sè loî*, je lui ai répondu que c'était inutile de venir.

請人答｜, *ts'iàng gnîn tâp ýn*, chercher un répondant.

｜酬, *ýn tch'oû*, rendre la pareille, se faire mutuellement des politesses, traiter un étranger.

有人來就愛｜酬佢, *yoū gnîn loî ts'ioú oí ýn tch'oû kî*, dès qu'il vient quelqu'un, il faut s'occuper de lui.

｜聲, *ýn chāng*, écho.

Le ton change dans ces expressions:

｜當, ｜該, *ŷn tōng, ŷn koī*, il faut, il convient, infaillible.

｜承人, *ŷn chîn gnîn*, se charger de, accepter, consentir.

崟 *Ýn*. ｜崗, *ýn kōng*, colline, montagne.

上｜, *chōng ýn*, monter une côte.

｜頂, *ýn tàng*, le sommet de la montagne.

YŎC

浴 *Yŏc* (*yoŭc*). Se baigner, se laver.

| 堂, *yǒc t'ông*, salle de bain.

| 帕, *yǒc p'á*, linge à se laver le corps.

藥 *Yǒc*. Médicament, poudre, drogue quelconque.

| 草, *yǒc ts'ào*, plantes médicinales.

膏 |, *kāo yǒc*, emplâtre, onguent.

毒 |, *t'oǔc yǒc*, poison.

| 水, *yǒc choùi*, drogue liquide.

火 |, *fò yǒc*, poudre à canon.

開 | 單, *k'ōi yǒc tān*, écrire une ordonnance.

若 *Yǒc*. Si, que si.

| 有方便, *yǒc yoū fōng p'iên*, s'il y a une occasion.

| 是, *yǒc ché*, si, s'il est vrai que. Il y a une foule de manières d'exprimer le conditionnel, et il ne faut user que rarement de ce mot *yǒc*.

YÔC

約 *Yôc*. Régler, contrat.

| 定那個日, *yôc t'ín mâc ké· gnĭt*, assigner tel jour.

大 |, *t'ái yôc*, (on dit aussi 大畧, *t'ái liôc*), en général.

和 | (v. 條 |), *fô yôc* (v. *t'iâo yôc*), traité de paix ou de réglementation.

籲 *Yôc*. Invoquer, appeler au secours.

| 告吾主, *yôc káo nĝ tchoù*, humblement (*supplicicer*) je m'accuse devant mon Dieu (prière du confiteor).

YON (voir *YAN*)

YONG

養 *Yōng*. Nourrir, élever, entretenir, mettre bas, allaiter.

生 | 之恩, *sēn yōng tjē ēn*, le bienfait de la vie et de la conservation.

| 身, *yōng chīn*, entretenir la vie, fortifier le corps.

| 唔大, *yōng mĝ t'ái*, ne pouvoir élever jusqu'à la croissance complète.

| 糧, *yōng leông*, nourriture.

聖體係靈魂個 | 糧, *chín t'ì hé· lîn foûn ké· yōng leông*, l'Eucharistie est la nourriture de l'âme.

狗 | 裡子, *keòu yōng lê· tzè*, la chienne a mis bas.

狗 | 子, *keòu yōng tzè*, la chienne allaite ses petits.

癢 *Yōng*. Prurit, démangeaison.

搔 |, *tsào yōng* (ou *yà yōng*), se gratter pour apaiser une démangeaison.

一身都 |, *ŷt chīn toū yōng*, tout le corps me démange.

秧 *Yōng*. Jeune plant de végétaux qu on peut repiquer.

| 子, *yōng tzè*, même sens, s'entend surtout du riz.

| 田, *yōng t'iên*, | 地, *yōng t'í*, rizière, terrain réservés pour la semence du riz.

菜 |, *ts'ói yōng*, semis de légumes.

幾時落 |, *kì chê lǒc yōng ?* quand sème-t-on le riz ?

YÔNG

羊 *Yông*. Brebis, chèvre, mouton.

| 牯, *yông koù*, bouc, bélier.

草 | , *ts'ào yông*, chèvre.

棉 | , *miên yông*, brebis, mouton.

掌 | 子, *tchòng yông tzè*, paître les brebis.

洋 *Yông*. Mer, pays au delà des mers.

東 | , *toūng yông*, le Japon, mer orientale.

西 | ,. *sī yông*, mer occidentale, les pays d'occident.

| 人, *yông gnîn*, étranger, européen, américain.

| 貨, *yông fó*, marchandises européennes.

| 油, *yông yôu*, pétrole.

| 氈, *yông tchān*, couverture de lit.

楊 *Yông*, | 柳樹, *yông lioù choú*, saule pleureur.

揚 *Yông*. Produire au grand jour

名 | 四海, *miāng yông sí hoì*, votre nom est connu des quatre mers.

陽 *Yông*. 陰 | , *ȳm yông*, deux principes qui en s'unissant constituent tous les êtres matériels. Le principe 陽 *yông* correspond au plus parfait, et le principe 陰 *ȳm* au plus imparfait de deux êtres qui sont opposés entre eux ou qui vont naturellement ensemble, comme sont le ciel et la terre, le soleil et la lune, le souverain et le sujet, l'homme et la femme, le mâle et la femelle, le jour et la nuit, la lumière et les ténèbres.

大 | , *t'ái yông*, le soleil.

| 間, *yông kiān*, sur la terre des vivants, par opposition à 陰間 *ȳm kiān* dans les enfers.

| 瓦, *yông ngà*, les tuiles qui recouvrent les autres et sont exposées au soleil, par opposition à 陰瓦 *ȳm ngà* les tuiles qui sont placées dessous et cachées au soleil.

YÓNG

嚷 *Yóng*. Foule, animé, fréquenté.

今日墟好 | , *kīn gnīt hī haò yóng*, aujourd'hui il y avait foule au marché.

大瞻禮聖堂咁 | , *t'aí tchām lī chín t'ông àn yóng*, pour la grande fête il y avait beaucoup de monde à l'Eglise.

樣 *Yóng*. Forme, manière, espèce.

一 | 個, *ȳt yóng ké·*, semblable, de même forme.

一 | 大, 一 | 細, *ȳt yóng t'ái, ȳt yóng sé·*, également grand, également petit.

咁 | 講, *àn yóng kòng*, parler comme ceci.

拿一頂帽做 | 子, *nā ȳt tàng máo tsó yóng tzè*, prendre un bonnet pour modèle.

| | 都有, *yóng yóng toū yōu*, il y a de tout.

讓 *Yóng* ou *nióng*. Se mettre au

dessous d'un autre par un sentiment de respect, céder.

謙 | , *k'iâm yóng*, condescendance.

忍 | , *nioūn yóng*, patience.

麼賣個東西做人情我 | 畀你, *mō mái ké· toūng sī, tsó gnîn ts'în ngâi yóng poūn gnî*, cette chose n'est pas à vendre, par amitié je te la cède.

| 位, *yóng ví*, céder sa place.

YOŪ

有 *Yōu (yoù)*. Avoir, être, exister.

| 錢麼, *yōu ts'iên mō?* as-tu des sapèques?

| 話同神父講, *yōu fá t'oûng chîn foú kòng*, j'ai un mot à dire au Père.

| 事, *yōu sé*, j'ai des affaires, je suis occupé.

你 | 幾多歲, *gnî yōu kì tō sé·*, quel âge as-tu?

天主自 | 個, *t'iēn tchoù tsé yōu ké·*, Dieu existe par lui-même.

天主 | 三位, *t'iēn tchoù yōu sām ví*, il y a trois personnes en Dieu.

| 病, *yōu p'iáng*, être malade.

| 人來, *yoū gnîn loî*, quelqu'un vient.

友 *Yōu (yoù)*. Ami, compagnon.

朋 | , *p'oûng yōu*, amis.

親 | , *ts'în yōu*, parents et amis.

教 | , *káo yōu*, ami en religion c.-à-d. chrétien.

酒肉朋 | , *tsioù nioûc p'oûng yōu*, ami jusqu'à la bourse (*litt.* ami seulement pour la table).

我個知己朋 | , *ngā ké· tjē kì p'oûng yōu*, c'est mon meilleur ami.

YÔU

由 *Yôu*. Point d'origine, de départ, dépendre.

情 | v. 緣 | , *ts'în yôu* v. *ŷan yôu*, circonstance, cause, origine.

| 東石來, *yôu toūng chăc loî*, venir de *Toūng chăc*.

| 天不 | 人, *yôu t'iēn poût yôu gnîn*, cela est au pouvoir du ciel et non des hommes.

油 *Yôu*. Graisse, huile, essence, graisser, huiler.

茶 | , *ts'â yôu*, huile de camélia.

猪 | , *tchoū yôu* graisse de porc.

打 | , *tà yôu*, faire de l'huile, acheter de l'huile en détail.

添 | , *t'iām yôu*, ajouter de l'huile à la lampe.

牛乳 | , *nioû nén yôu*, beurre.

| 窗, *yôu ts'oūng*, enduire d'huile les barreaux d'une fenêtre.

幽 *Yoû*, Lentement, doucement.

| | 來, *yoû yoû loî*, allons doucement (expression des porteurs de palanquin lorsqu'ils montent une côte à pas ralentis).

遊 *Yoû*, Errer, se promener,

| 耍, *yoû chá*, | 玩, *yoû liaó*, se promener.

外 | , *ngoé·yoû*, voyager à l'étranger.

遠 | , *yàn yoû*, voyager dans le pays.

憂 *Yoû*. Triste, affligé, avoir souci de.

| 愁, *yoû seoû*, être triste.
| 慮, *yoû lí*, avoir souci de.

YOÚ

又 *Yoú*. De nouveau, encore, et.
| 來, *yoú loî*, revenir.
| 一個, *yoú ŷt ké·*, encore un.

右 *Yoú*. Droite.
走 | 手片, *tseòu yoú choù p'ièn*, prendre le chemin de droite.

幼 *Yoú*. Jeune, délicat, menu; poli des murs ou autre chose.
還 | 唔知那個, *hân yoú mĝ tī mâc ké·*, il est encore jeune, sans discernement (paroles d'excuses).
做粗事也噲, | 事也噲, *tsó tsē ché· yā voé·, yoú ché· yā voé·*, il sait faire un travail délicat comme un travail plus grossier.
| 石, *yoú chăc*, pierre à polir les murs blanchis.
擟 | *nô yoú*, polir en frottant.

佑 *Yoú*. Protéger, secourir.
庇 | , *p'ī yoú*, 保 | , *paò yoú*, même sens.
天主保 | , *t'iēn tchoù paò yoú*, que Dieu vous protège (c'est le souhait de bonjour des chrétiens).

誘 *Yoú*. Attirer, tenter.
| 感, *yoú kàm*, tenter, tentation.
引 | 人, *ŷn yoú gnîn*, tenter, porter quelqu'un à faire une chose.

柚 *Yoú*. | 子樹, *yoú tzè choú*, pamplemousse.

賄 *Yoú*. Présents corrupteurs.
官府受賄 | , *koūon foù choú lê· yoú*, le mandarin a reçu des pots-de-vin.

YOŬC

欲 *Yoŭc*. Désirer, concupiscence.
私 | , *sē yoŭc*, désir déréglé, concupiscence.
從心所 | , *ts'ioûng sīm sò yoŭc*, à votre choix.

辱 *Yoŭc*. Affront, outrager.
被人污 | , *p'ī gnîn voū yoŭc*, j'ai été injurié, violée.
羞 | 人, *siōu yoŭc gnîn*, homme dégradé qui ne pense qu'à faire des bassesses.

YOŪC

育 *Yoūc*. Nourrir, élever.
生男 | 女, *sēn nâm yoūc ǹg*, avoir des enfants des deux sexes.
你生 | 幾多個人, *ngî sēn yoūc kì tō ké· gnîn*? combien avez-vous d'enfants?

YOŪN

允 *Yoūn*. Permettre, accorder.
甘心 | 服, *kām sīm yoūn foŭc*, je te l'accorde de bon cœur.
| 諾人, *yoūn nōc gnîn*, promettre, permettre.

YOÛN

匀 *Yoûn*. Egal, uniforme.

分唔｜, *foūn mĝ yoûn*, on ne peut diviser en parts égales.

蒔禾蒔得好｜, *ché vô ché têt haò yoûn*, le riz a été planté bien régulièrement.

上色上倒唔多｜, *chòng sĕt chòng taò mĝ tō yoûn*, la couleur n'est pas très uniforme.

脉都還｜, *mâc toū hân yoûn*, le pouls est encore régulier.

雲 *Yoûn*. Nuage.

一朵｜, *ŷt tò yoûn*, un nuage.

｜遮日頭, *yoûn tchā gnĭt t'eôu*, les nuages cachent le soleil.

耘 *Yoûn*. Sarcler.

｜田, *yoûn t'iên*, enlever les herbes, sarcler les rizières.

YOÙN

永 *Yoùn*. Perpétuel.

｜遠, **｜久**, *yoùn yàn*, *yoùn kiòu*, éternel, éternellement.

詠 *Yoùn*. Chanter, hymne.

｜詩, *yoùn chē*, déclamer des vers.

歌｜, *kō yoùn*, chant, chanter.

隱 *Yoùn*. Cacher,

｜藏, *yoùn ts'ông*, cacher.

一句話都｜唔得, *ŷt kí fá toū yoùn mĝ têt*, ne pouvoir garder un secret.

做｜修, *tsó yoùn siōu*, se faire ermite.

YOÚN

閏 *Yoún*. **｜月**, *yoún gnĕt*, lune intercalaire.

潤 *Yoún*. Humecter, humide, onctueux.

｜濕, *yoún chĭp*, humecter.

黄烟轉｜, *vông yān tchòn yoún*, le tabac a pris de l'humidité.

蜂糖食裡係｜, *foūng t'ông chĭt lê· ké· yoún*, le miel est un adoucissant pour l'estomac.

運 *Yoún*. Mouvoir ou se mouvoir en rond; transporter.

日月｜行, *gnĭt gnĕt yoún hâng*, le soleil et la lune tournent.

四｜, *sí yoún*, les quatre saisons.

｜氣, *yoún hí*, les vicissitudes de la fortune.

佢｜氣唔好, *kiā yoún hí mĝ haò*, la fortune lui est contraire, il n'a pas de chance.

東西｜倒裡子來, *toūng sī yoún taò ŷ tzè loî*, transporter les affaires jusqu'ici.

｜兵, *yoún pīn*, transporter des soldats d'un endroit à un autre.

韻 *Yoún*. Consonnance, harmonie.

㨍風琴係落｜, *pāng foūng k'îm hé· lŏc yoún*, jouer de l'accordéon donne une belle harmonie.

調｜, *t'iâo yoún*, rimer.

熨 *Yoún*. Repasser au fer à chaud.

| 斗, ***yoún teòu***, fer à repasser.

| 衫褲, ***yoún sām foú***, repasser les habits au fer.

YOÛNG

容 *Yoûng*. Supporter avec patience; aisé; apparence extérieure.

含 | , ***hâm yoûng***, supporter avec patience, pardonner.

天理不 | , ***t'iēn lī poūt yoûng***, le ciel ne le pardonne pas.

不 | 後, ***poūt yoûng heoú***, l'affaire ne souffre pas de délai.

| 易, ***yoûng ý***, aisé, facile.

| 易做, ***yoûng ý tsó***, facile à faire.

唔係咁 | 易, ***mĝ hé· àn yoûng ý***, ce n'est pas si facile que ça.

| 貌, ***yoûng maó***, tenue du corps, contenance, air.

正 | 貌, ***tchín yoûng maó***, composer son extérieur.

| 貌唔正, ***yoûng maó mĝ tcháng***, sa tenue a trop de laisser-aller.

榕 *Yoûng*. | 樹, ***yoûng choú***, banıang.

熊 *Yoûng*. Ours.

狗 | , ***keoù yoûng***, ours à tête de chien, ours ordinaire.

| 家, ***yoûng kā***, ours fabuleux qu on dit ressembler à l'homme.

融 *Yoûng*. Fondre, se liquéfier.

煮 | , ***tchoù yoûng***, faire fondre par la cuisson.

雪雨日唔曉 | , ***siĕt leòng gnĭt mĝ hiaò yoûng***, au bout de deux jours la neige n'était pas encore fondue.

庸 *Yoûng*. Constant, invariable.

中 | , ***tchoūng yoûng***, le juste milieu (un des livres classiques chinois).

| | 碌碌, ***yoûng yoûng loŭc loŭc***, se dit d'un homme qui ne réussit en rien.

傭 *Yoûng*. Travailler à la journée.

| 工過日, ***yoûng koūng kouó gnĭt***, travailler à la journée pour gagner sa vie.

榮 *Yoûng*. 光 | , | 福, ***koūong yoûng***, ***yoûng foŭc***, gloire, honneur.

天主個 | 福, ***t'iēn tchoù ké· yoûng foŭc***, la gloire de Dieu.

咁 | 寵佢, ***kàn yoûng tch'oùng kî***, vous lui faites beaucoup d'honneur.

絨 *Yoûng*. Velours.

| 帽, ***yoûng máo***, bonnet de velours.

| 鞋, ***yoûng haî***, souliers de velours.

毧 *Yoûng*. | 毛, ***yoûng māo***, duvet.

鷂婆 | 好斷血, ***yáo p'ô yoûng haò tòn hiĕt***, le duvet de l'épervier est bon pour arrêter le sang.

茸 *Yoûng*. 鹿 | , ***loŭc yoûng***, corne de cerf (appréciée en médecine).

YOÙNG

湧 *Yoùng*. Jaillir avec force.

水 | 出來, ***choùi yoùng tch'oūt loî***, l'eau sortit avec impétuosité.

壅 *Yoùng*. Couvrir, entourer d'une butte de terre, le pied d'une plante.

|等泥去, *yoùng tèn naî hí*, recouvrir de terre.

勇 *Yoùng*. Fermeté d'âme, brave, bravoure.

剛|, *kōng yoùng*, bravoure, énergie.

麼剛|個人, *mô kōng yoùng ké· gnìn*, homme sans énergie.

當壯|, *tōng tsóng yoùng*, faire le métier de soldat.

帶|, *taí yoùng*, commander des soldats.

YOÚNG

用 *Yoúng*. Employer, dépenses.

|心, *yoúng sīm*, mettre du soin.

|費, *yoúng fí*, dépenses.

彀|, *keóu yoúng*, suffisant.

麼|, *mô yoúng*, cela ne vaut rien.

|唔着, *yoúng mĝ tch'ŏc*, impropre au service réclamé.

我唔|酒, *ngâi mĝ yoúng tsioù*, je ne bois pas de vin.

冒|, *maó yoúng*, **枉|**, *nóng yoúng*, abuser.

亂|, *lón yoúng*, user sans discernement.

YOÛT

鬱 *Yoût*. Triste, oppressé par le chagrin.

心十分憂|, *sīm chĭp foūn yoû yoût*, j'ai le cœur tout à fait mal à l'aise, je suis accablé de tristesse.

裡個事我十分|氣, *ỳ ké· sé ngai chĭp foūn yoût hí*, je suis tout à fait mécontent de cette affaire.

熱氣|積等裡愛藥酒來食, *gnĕt hí yoût tsĭt tèn ê· oí yŏc tsioù loi chĭt*, (*litt.*) un échauffement m'oppresse, il me faut prendre de la médecine.

ŶP

揖 *Ŷp*. Salutation chinoise.

作|, *tsôc ŷp*, faire cette salutation. (On dit mieux **唱瑯**, *tch'óng yā*.)

YT

佚 *ў̆t*. Repos, à l'aise.

今日唔多安|, *kīn gnĭt mĝ tō ōn ў̆t*, aujourd'hui, je ne me trouve pas très bien.

役 *ў̆t*. **差|**, *ts'āi ў̆t*, satellites.

翼 *ў̆t*. Ailes.

鵰|, *tiaō ў̆t*, ailes d'un oiseau.

唦|, *siā ў̆t*, déployer les ailes.

拔|, *păt ў̆t*, battre des ailes.

附|, *foú ў̆t*, complice. (Voir **羽** *ỳ*).

亦 *ў̆t*. Aussi, et (se sous-entend dans le langage ordinaire).

ŶT

一 *Ŷt*. Un, entier, le même, aussitôt que,

第|, *t'í ŷt*, le premier, le plus parfait.

| 両 個 人, *ŷt leòng ké· gnîn*, un ou deux hommes.

| 年 | 次, *ŷt niân ŷt tsé*, une fois l'an.

| 生 人, *ŷt sēn gnîn*, toute la vie.

| 心, *ŷt sīm*, de tout cœur.

| 心 | 意, *ŷt sīm ŷt ý*, d'un commun accord.

| 路, *ŷt loú*, continuellement.

| 把 連, *ŷt pà liên*, le tout réuni.

| 醒 就 愛 上, *ŷt siàng ts'ioú oí hóng*, aussitôt éveillé il faut se lever.

益 *Ŷt*. Utilité, avantage.

利 |, *lí ŷt*, profit, gain.

| 處, *ŷt tch'oú*, utilité.

天 主 道 理 有 | 於 人, *t'iēn tchoù t'aó lī yoū ŷt ȳ gnîn*, on a des avantages à se faire chrétien.

億 *Ŷt*. Cent mille.

縊 *Ŷt*. 自 |, *tsé ŷt*, se suicider.

JEN (voir *YAN*)
JON (voir *YAN*)

KĀ

加 *Kā*. Placer un objet sur un autre, ajouter, augmenter, conférer.

愛 | 一 個 樹 板 來, *oí kā ŷt ké· choú pàn loî*, il faut ajouter une planche.

| 增 功 勞, *kā tsén koūng laô*, augmenter ses mérites.

愛 | 補 一 百 錢, *oí kā poù ŷt pâc ts'iên*, il faut ajouter un supplément de cent sapèques.

| 五 錢, | 六 錢, *kā ng̀ ts'iên, kā lioûc ts'iên*, augmenter le taux ordinaire de cinq sapèques, de six sapèques. Etant posé comme principe que 10 sapèques, font 1 *foun*, 一 分 銀, *ŷt foūn nioûn*, 100 sapèques 1 *ts'ien*, 一 錢 銀, *ŷt ts'iên nioûn*, 1000 sapèques un taël, 一 両 銀, *ŷt leōng nioûn*, si les sapèques sont plus ou moins bonnes, on ajoutera 2, 3, 4, 6 etc. sapèques pour faire le *foun*. Si l'on compte 加 五 錢, *kā ng̀ ts'iên*, le *foun* sera donc de 15 sapèques, ainsi du reste.

| 恩, *kā ēn*, conférer une grâce.

枷 *Kā*. Cangue.

戴 |, *k'āi kā*, porter la cangue.

家 *Kā*. Famille, classe d'individus.

一 | 人, *ŷt kā gnîn*, toute une famille.

| 眷, *kā kián*, femme et enfants.

| 父, | 母, | 兄, *kā foú, kā moū, kā hioūng*, mon père, ma mère, mon frère (quand il s'agit d'un parent au-dessus de celui qui parle. *Voir* 舍 *chá*).

婦 人 |, *foú gnîn kā*, épouse, femme en général.

| 室, *kā chît*, épouse.

東 |, *toūng kā*, supérieur, patron, maître.

當 |, *tōng kā*, procureur, celui qui gère les biens ou les affaires du patron.

自 |, *tsé kā*, soi-même.

大 |, *t'aí kā*, tous, tous ensemble.

老 人 |, *laò gnîn kā*, vieillard.

傢 *Kā*. | 伙, *kā fò*, ustensile quelconque, outil.

| 事, *kā ché·*, même sens.

木匠個 | 事, *moūc sióng ké· kā ché·*, les outils de menuisier,

猳 *Kā.* 駁 | , *pôc kā*, s'accoupler, faire le coït (ne se dit que des animaux).

雞公打 | , *kē· koūng tà kā*, le coq monte la poule.

K'Ā

迦 *K'ā.* Réprimander, gronder, crier contre quelqn'un.

官府 | 佢, *koūon foù k'ā kî*, le mandarin lui fit des objurgations.

咁起 | 我我唔准, *àn hì k'ā ngâi ngâi mĝ tchoùn*, vous aurez beau me gronder, je ne consentirai pas.

K'Â

卡 *K'â.* Emprisonné; charpente qui maintient les planches qui servent à fouler les murs; entraves que l'on met aux pieds ou aux mains des prisonniers pour les empêcher de s'enfuir.

官府 | 拷人. *koūon foù k'â k'aó gnîn*, le mandarin fait mettre les entraves.

墻 | 子, *siông k'â tzè*, charpente à fouler les murs.

KÀ

假 *Kà.* Faux, altéré.

攏總 | 個, *loūng tsoùng kà ké·*, le tout est faux.

講 | 話, *kòng kà fá*, mentir.

唔曉得真 | , *mĝ hiào têt tchīn kā*, je ne sais si c'est vrai ou faux.

| 借, *kà tsiá*, métaphore.

麽幾多貨唔係 | 個, *mô kì tō fó mĝ hé· kà ké·*, on trouve peu de marchandises qui ne soient pas altérées.

| 人個名, *kà gnîn ké· miâng*, emprunter le nom de quelqu'un.

鰕 *Kà.* | 魚, *kà nĝ*, espèce de poisson de rivière.

KÁ

架 *Ká.* Echafaudage, charpente, étagère, particule numérale des machines.

十字 | , *chĭp sé ká*, la croix, échafaud en forme de croix.

找 | , *tsào ká*, monter un échafaudage.

床 | , 書 | , *ts'ông ká, choū ká*, montants de bois de lit, pupitre ou bibliothèque.

一 | 鐘, *ŷt ká tchoūng*, une horloge.

嫁 *Ká.* Marier sa fille, prendre un époux.

| 與發財人, *ká ÿ fât ts'oî gnîn*, mariée à un homme riche.

你妹子幾時行 | , *niā moé· tzè kì chê hâng ká?* quand marierez-vous votre fille?

價 *Ká.* Prix, valeur.

| 錢, *ká ts'iên*, même sens.

照市 | , *tchaó ché ká*, d'après le prix courant.

定 | , *t'in ká*, fixer un prix.

講 | , *kòng ká*, débattre le prix.

駕 *Ká*. Titre de politesse.

尊 |, *tsoūn ká*, monsieur *(politesse)*.

個 *Ká (ké·)*. Cela. Voir *ké·*.

quand à ça! alors, eh bien! oh!

| 事我唔答, *ká sé ngâi mĝ tâp*, de cela je ne m'en mêle pas.

| 做得, *ká tsó tĕt*, alors, oui.

| 係, *ká hé·*, oh! oui.

| 我唔知, *ká ngaî mĝ tī*, oh! je n'en sais rien.

K'ĂC

掐 *K'ăc*. Pincer, serrer fortement avec les doigts.

有一擺行夜路忽然間被人頸頸上 | 阿來, *yoū ȳt pài hâng yá loú foût yân kiān p'í gnîn kiàng kīn hóng k'ăc á loî*, une fois je voyageais la nuit, quand tout à coup, quelqu'un me prit à la gorge.

莫 | 咁狠, *mŏc k'ăc àn hên*, ne serre pas si fort.

你 | 穩來, *gnî k'ăc voùn loî*, tiens solidement.

KÂC

隔 *Kâc*. Séparer, ce qui sert à séparer, rayon d'armoire,

| 麼幾遠, *kâc mô kì yàn*, il n'y a pas très loin.

| 縣城三十里, *kâc yán châng sām chĭp lī*, distant de la ville de 30 lys.

| 壁, *kâc piâc*, mur de séparation.

兩 | 壁, *leòng kâc piâc*, de l'autre côté de la cloison, voisin d'à côté.

| 兩三十里路聽得倒, *kâc leòng sām chĭp lī loú t'āng tĕt taò*, on pouvait l'entendre à une distance de deux à trois lieues.

拖 |, *t'ō kâc*, tiroir.

櫃子有三 |, *k'oúi tzè yoū sām kâc*, l'armoire a trois compartiments.

KAĪ

(Voir anssi les mots KIAI)

雞 *Kaī* (ou *kē·*). Poule. *Voyez kē·*.

K'ĀI

欵 *K'āi*. Porter un fardeau sur l'épaule à l'aide d'un bâton.

| 水, | 泥, *k'āi chouì, k'āi naî*, porter de l'eau, de la terre.

| 唔起, *k'āi mĝ hì*, je n'ai pas la force de porter.

KAÍ

個 *Kaí*. Voir *Ké·*.

KĀM

甘 *Kām*. Saveur douce mêlée d'une légère et agréable amertume.

好茶有 | 味, *haò ts'â yoū kām mí*, le bon thé a une saveur agréable.

| 草, *kām ts'aò*, réglisse.

| 心, *kām sīm*, de bon cœur.

你 | 願麼, *gnî kām nián mô?* y consens-tu?

柑 *Kām*. Orange à peau non adhérente; orange en général.

酸 | , *sōn kām*, espèce d'orange aigrelette.

| 子皮, *kām tzè p'ī*, écorce d'orange.

疳 *Kām*. | 積, *kām tsît*, maladie des vers.

感 *Kām (kàm)*. Imposer, faire violence morale.

我請你來唔係 | 你來, *ngaî ts'iàng gnî loî mĝ hé· kām gnî loî*, je t'invite à venir, mais je ne t'en fais pas une obligation.

路上佢 | 我同佢款担, *loú hóng kî kām ngaî t'oûng kî k'aī tām*, en route il m'a obligé à porter son fardeau.

監 *Kām*. Prison.

坐 | , *ts'ō kām*, être en prison.

| 禁三年, *kām kím sām niân*, faire trois ans de prison.

K'ĀM

堪 *K'ām*. Digne, capable.

不 | , *poût k'ām*, je n'en suis pas digne; (réponse de politesse quand on reçoit un compliment).

| 當如此, *k'ām tōng ŷ tsè*, il méritait cela.

龕 *K'ām*. Niche.

神 | , *chîn k'ām*, niche d'idole.

聖體 | , *chín t'ì k'ām*, tabernacle.

KÀM

敢 *Kàm*. Oser, hardi.

佢唔 | 來, *kî mĝ kàm loî*, il n'ose pas venir.

唔 | 當, *mĝ kàm tōng*, je n'ose accepter un pareil honneur (*politesse.*)

咁 | , *àn kàm*, quelle hardiesse!

感 *Kàm*. | 謝, *kàm ts'iá*, remercier.

誘 | , *yóu kàm*, tenter, tentation.

減 *Kàm*. Diminuer, omettre.

| 少幾下個錢, *kàm chaò kì hā ké· ts'iên*, faire un rabais de quelques sapèques.

| 一個小齋, *kàm ŷt ké· siaò tsaī*, omettre, oublier un jour d'abstinence.

K'ÀM

砍 *K'àm*. Ecraser par un poids, une chute de corps.

一倒樹樹子 | 倒佢 | 死裡, *ŷt taò choú, choú tzè k'àm taò kî k'àm sì lî*, en abattant un arbre, l'arbre l'a écrasé et il en est mort.

KÁM

嚂 *Kám*. Intercaler.

| 日, *kám gnît*, de deux en deux jours.

| 三日, *kám sām gnît*, de trois en trois jours, à trois jours d'intervalle.

監 *Kám*. Grade acheté, eunuque.

| 生, *kám sēn*, titre de celui qui a acheté un grade.

大 | , *t'aí kám*, eunuque du harem impérial.

鑒 *Kám*. Miroir, exemplaire.

綱｜, *kōng kám*, annales de l'empire.

聖敎綱｜, *chín káo kōng kám*, histoire de l'Eglise.

K'ÁM

坎 *K'ám*. Rebord, tertre.

田｜, *t'iên k'ám*, bord des rizières.

｜上, *k'ám hóng*, sur le tertre, le monticule.

門｜脚, *moûn k'ám kiôc*, madrier qui passe sous la porte et qu'il faut enjamber pour entrer.

勘 *K'ám*. Examiner juridiquement, examiner et décider.

官府親自去｜過, *koūon foù ts'īn tsé hí ｜ kouó*, le mandarin est allé en personne sur les lieux, pour examiner.

KÀN

(Voir aussi les mots KIAN)

咁 *Kàn* (ou *àn*). Que ! combien ! autant, comme.

｜多蚊, *kàn tō moūn*, que de moustiques !

我唔愛｜多, *ngaî mĝ oí kàn tō*, je n'en veux pas tant.

唔係｜樣, *mĝ hé· kàn yóng*, ce n'est pas comme cela.

KĀNG

庚 *Kāng*. Caractère du cycle, âge.

貴｜, *kouí kāng*, quel âge avez-vous ?

打年｜, *tà niân kāng*, écrire l'extrait de naissance.

更 *Kāng*. Les cinq veilles de la nuit. Elles sont de deux heures chacune, et vont de sept heures du soir à cinq heures du matin.

打｜, *tà kāng*, frapper pour annoncer les différentes veilles; faire la garde de nuit.

半夜三｜起火燒屋, *pán yá sām kāng hì fò chaō voūc*, à minuit, à la troisième veille, un incendie s'est déclaré dans une maison.

羹 *Kāng*. Bouillie, colle.

麼乳食細人子食｜, *mô nén chìt sé· gnîn tzè chìt kāng*, faute de lait l'enfant mange de la bouillie.

同我煮｜糊東西, *t'oûng gnaî tchoù kāng foû toūng sī*, cuis-moi de la colle de farine pour coller quelque chose.

調｜, *t'iaô kāng*, cuiller pour prendre le bouillon.

耕 *Kāng*. Travailler la terre, tisser.

｜田人, *kāng t'iên gnîn*, laboureur, agriculteur.

｜種, *kāng tchoúng*, l'agriculture.

｜布, *kāng poú*, tisser de la toile.

KÀNG

鯁 *Kàng*. Arête de poisson qui est restée dans le gosier; obstacle, difficulté, embarras.

骨頭｜倒裡, *koût t'eoû kàng taò lî*, un os s'est arrêté dans mon gosier.

10

老虎一丨倒線就弩倒裡, *laò foù ŷt kàng taò sién ts'ioú noù taò lì*, dès que le tigre donne dans le fil, il est aussitôt atteint par la flèche empoisonnée.

丨人個脚, *kàng gnîn ké· kiŏc*, embarrasser les jambes, faire un croc-en-jambe.

KAŌ

教 *Kaō*. Enseigner.

丨書, *kaō choū*, faire l'école.

丨打, *kaō tà*, donner des leçons de boxe ou de bâton.

丨佢唔倒, *kaō kî mĝ taò*, on ne peut rien lui apprendre.

丨佢唔聽, *kaō kî mĝ t'āng*, il ne tient aucun compte de mes enseignements.

交 *Kaō*. Donner de main à main, livrer, échanger, avoir des relations, contigu, près de.

丨定頭, *kaō t'ín t'coû*, livrer des arrhes.

鎖匙丨別你, *sò chê kaō poūn gnî*, je te confie les clefs.

你契丨出來看, *niā k'é· kaō tch'oût loî k'ón*, montre-moi ton contrat.

求神父丨過一串念珠別我我個壞帛裡, *k'ioû chîn foú kaō kouó ŷt tch'ón niám tchoū poūn ngaî ngā ké· faí p'ĕt lì*, je prie le Père de me changer mon chapelet, le mien est cassé.

相丨, *siōng kaō*, amis, union réciproque.

丨接, *kaō tsiâp*, avoir des relations.

丨觀, (v. 丨易), *kaō kouōn (v. kaō ŷt)* relations de commerce, client, clientèle.

絕丨, *ts'iĕt kaō*, rompre les relations d'amitié.

丨界地方, *kaō kiaí t'í fōng*, pays limitrophes.

細人子打丨, (pour 架), *sé· gnîn tzè tà kaō*, (pour *tà ká*), les enfants se battent.

高 *Kaō*. Haut, élevé, noble.

一滴丨矮都麼, *ŷt tît kaō aì toū mô*, ils sont tout à fait égaux entre eux.

兩丈丨, *leòng tch'óng kaō*, haut de vingt pieds.

丨陞, *kaō chīn*, monter en grade, être élevé en dignité.

丨姓, *kaō siáng*, votre nom ?

丨壽, *kaō choú*, votre âge ?

跌一丨, *tiĕt ŷt kaō*, tomber de sa hauteur.

篙 *Kāo*. Gaffe, perche.

竹丨, *tchoûc kāo*, perche de bambou.

撑丨, *ts'áng kāo*, faire avancer (v. gr. une barque) à l'aide d'une perche.

膏 *Kāo*. Substance grasse, onguent, pommade.

丨藥, *kāo yŏc*, onguent.

石丨, *chăc kāo*, gypse, plâtre.

虎骨丨, *foù koût kaō*, gélatine de tigre.

膠 *Kāo*. Colle forte, coller.

牛丨, 魚丨, *nioû kāo, nĝ kāo*, colle de bœuf, colle de poisson.

羔 *Kāo.* | 羊, *kāo yông*, agneau.
天主 | 羊者, *t'iēn tchoù kāo yông tchà*, Agneau de Dieu (prières chr.).

糕 *Kāo.* Gâteaux, sucreries.
| 餅, *kāo piàng*, croquette, gâteau.
雞蛋 | , *kē· t'án kāo*, gâteau fait avec des œufs.
糖 | , *t'ông kaō*, confiture.

K'ĀO

蹺 *K'āo.* Croisé, entrelacé.
| 腳, *k'āo kiôc*, croiser les jambes.
| 叉, *k'āo ts'ā*, croisé en forme d'X.
竹篾 | 差, *tchoûc mĕt k'āo ts'ā*, les lanières de bambou sont mal entrelacées.

KAÒ

稿 *Kaò.* Manuscrit, copie, brouillon.
打 | 子, *tà kaò tzè*, écrire en brouillon.

絞 *Kaò.* Enrouler une corde autour de quelque chose, enchevêtrer, attacher, garrotter.
毛辮 | 唔知様班, *maō piēn kaò mĝ tī nióng pān*, je ne sais comment ma tresse est embrouillée.
剨猪愛先 | 佢 | 穩來, *yām tchoū oí siēn kaò kî kaò voùn loî*, avant de châtrer un porc il faut le garrotter solidement.
| 刑比斬刑輕一層, *kaò hîn pì tsàm hîn k'iāng ŷt ts'ên*, le supplice de la strangulation est un peu moins infamant que celui de la décapitation.

狡 *Kaò.* | 猾, *kaò vât*, rusé, roué.

攪 *Kaò.* S'amuser, faire, agir (dans un sens large).
| 壞, *kaò fái*, s'abîmer, se pervertir.
| 唔贏, *kaò mĝ yâng*, je n'en viens pas à bout.
| 那個, *kaò mâc ké·*? à quoi t'amuses-tu?
做生理 | 裡两年, *tsó siēn lī kaò lî leòng niân*, j'ai passé deux ans à faire le commerce.

K'AÒ

考 *K'aò.* Examiner, examen.
| 試, *k'aò ché*, examen ou concours pour les degrés dans les lettres ou dans les armes.
縣 | , 州 | , 府 | , *yán k'aò, tchoū k'aò, foù k'aò*, examen préliminaire pour le degré de 秀才, *sioú ts'oî*, devant le sous-préfet, devant le préfet.
| 秀才, *k'aò sioú ts'oî*, concourir pour le degré de bachelier.
| 舉人, *k'aò kì gnîn*, concourir pour la licence.
大主 | , *t'aí tchoù k'aò*, examinateur nommé pour conférer le degré de 舉人 *kì gnîn*, au chef-lieu d'une province.

巧 *K'aò.* Adresse, industrie.
| 工夫, *k'aò koūng foū*, ouvrage habilement fait.
番人十分 | , *fān gnîn chĭp foūn k'aò*

les européens sont très industrieux.

咁 | 妙, *àn k'aò miaó!* quelle merveilleuse habileté!

烤 *K'aò.* | 酒, *k'aò tsiòu,* distiller du vin.

KAÓ

教 *Kaó.* Enseignement, religion.

天主 |, *t'iēn tchoù kaó,* la religion catholique.

外 | 人, *ngoé· kaó gnîn,* étrangers à la religion, païens.

| 友, *kaó yoū,* ami de la religion, chrétien.

主 |, *tchoù kaó,* maître de la religion, évêque.

告 *Kaó.* Avertir, accuser.

| 示, *kaó ché,* ordonnance, décret.

亂 | 人, *lón kaó gnîn,* accuser les gens à tort et à travers.

| 解, *kaó kiài,* se confesser.

| 狀, *kaó ts'óng,* écrire une accusation, accusation écrite.

原 |, *niân kaó,* l'accusateur, le plaignant.

被 |, *p'ī kaó,* l'accusé.

窖 *Kaó.* Enfouir, cacher sous terre, cave, fosse.

| 阿泥鼓裡起, *kaó á naî t'eoû lì hì,* enfouir sous terre.

粗 |, *tsē kaó,* fosse à purin.

| 銀, *kaó nioûn,* cacher de l'argent.

古 |, *koù kaó,* trésor caché.

我𢯎倒一個古 |, *ngaî koì taò ȳt ké· koù kaó,* en creusant la terre, j'ai découvert un trésor.

靠 *Kaó (k'aó).* | 几, *kaó ỳ,* chaise à dossier, fauteuil.

洋葉 |, *yông yăp kaó,* charnière de porte ou autre.

酵 *Kaó.* Levûre, levain.

| 餅, *kaó piàng,* levûre vendue sous forme de gâteau.

麼 | 子麵包唔得發, *mô kaó tzè mién paō mĝ têt fât* (ou *pôt*), le pain ne peut fermenter sans levûre.

K'AÓ

拷 *K'aó.* Blâmer, frapper, torturer.

呾 | 人, *k'ā k'aó gnîn,* blâmer sevèrement quelqu'un.

| 問, *k'aó moún,* torturer quelqu'un pour lui arracher un aveu.

靠 *K'aó.* S'appuyer sur, se confier.

裡個人 | 唔住, *ỳ ké· gnîn k'aó mĝ tch'oú,* on ne peut pas se fier à cet homme.

麼那個 | 頭, *mô mâc ké· k'aó t'eoû,* n'avoir plus d'appui.

愛 | 天主個恩, *oí k'aó t'iēn tchoù ké· ēn,* il faut se confier en la grâce de Dieu.

| 自巳個力量, *k'aó tsé kì ké· līt leóng,* s'appuyer sur ses propres forces.

敲 *K'aó*. Frapper contre, heurter contre.

丨門, *k'aó moûn*, frapper à la porte.

丨鐘, *k'aó tchoūng*, frapper sur une cloche.

KÂP

合 *Kâp* (*hăp*). Dixième partie du *chīn*, s'unir, se joindre.

十丨做一升, *chĭp kâp tsó ŷt chīn*, dix *kâp* (ou *k'âp*) font un *chīn*.

丨棺材, *kâp kouōn ts'oî*, faire un cercueil.

到那裡丨路, *taó naí lī kâp loú*? à quel endroit se réunissent les deux routes ?

兩條河丨阿攸, *leòng t'iaô hô kâp á ts'ioū*, les deux rivières se réunissent.

手骨打斷丨唔轉, *choù koût tà t'ōn kâp mĝ tchòn*, l'os du bras est brisé, et l'on ne peut le remettre.

丨水色唔倒, *kâp chouì sêt mĝ taò*, ne pouvoir s'acclimater.

甲 *Kâp*. Lettre du cycle, ongle, cuirasse.

La première des dix lettres du cycle, qui combinées avec les douze caractères des heures, forment les soixante branches du cycle appelé 甲子, *kâp tzè*, qui sert à compter non seulement les années, mais aussi les mois, les jours et même les heures.

我個丨子就係丁卯, *ngā ké· kâp tzè ts'ioú hé· tēn maō*, je suis né en l'année *tēn maō* (1866).

丨子你背得出麼, *kâp tzè gnî p'oí têt tch'oût mô?* peux-tu réciter par cœur les caractères du cycle ?

手指丨, *choù tjè kâp*, ongles des doigts de main.

脚趾丨, *kiôc tjè kâp*, ongles des doigts de pied.

手指丨花, *choù tjè kâp fā*, bâlsamine.

竹丨帽, *tchoûc kâp maó*, casque en bambou.

鐵丨, *t'iĕt kâp*, cuirasse en fer.

丨書, *kâp choū*, relier un livre.

袷 *Kâp*. 丨襖, *kâp aò*, habit doublé.

K'ÂP

掐 *K'âp*. Pincer, saisir avec les ongles.

丨狗虱, *k'âp keoù sêt*, écraser une puce avec les ongles.

丨死, *k'âp sì*, tuer en écrasant entre les doigts. *Voir* 掐 *k'ăc*.

恰 *K'âp*. A point, juste, calculer de mémoire, supputer.

丨當, *k'âp tóng*, comme il faut.

丨丨彀, *k'âp k'âp keoú*, cela suffit juste.

丨子算你曉得麼, *k'âp tzè són gnî hiaò têt mô?* sais-tu calculer de mémoire ?

我丨倒佢錢唔彀用, *ngaî k'âp taò kiâ ts'iên mĝ keoú yoúng*, je crois que son argent ne suffira pas.

KÂT

咖 *Kât*. 麼丨煞, *mô kât sât*, il n'y

a pas moyen, je ne sais comment faire.

樣 | 煞, *nióng kât sât*, comment faire! que vais-je devenir!

KĒ·

街 *Kē·*. Rue. *Voir kiaī.*

雞 *Kē·* (ou *kaī*). Poule, coq.

| 公, *kē· koūng*, coq.

| 媽, *kē· mâ*, poule qui a déjà pondu.

| ?, *kē· lón*, poule qui n'a pas encore pondu.

鐵 |, *sién kē·*, chapon.

| 啼, *kē· t'aî*, le chant du coq.

劏 |, *tchê kē·*, tuer une poule.

| 胲, *kē· koī*, le gésier de la poule.

| 脛, *kē· k'īn*, l'estomac de la poule.

田 |, *t'iên kē·*, espece de grenouille.

K'Ê·

K'ê·. Nigaud, stupide.

你樣咁 |, *gnî nióng àn k'ê·*, oh! que tu es nigaud!

KÈ·

解 *Kè·* (*kiaì*). Délier, détacher, déboutonner.

| 索, *kè· sôc*, détacher, enlever la corde.

紇打十分狠我 | 唔脫, *kēt tà chĭp foūn hên ngaî kè· mĝ t'ôt*, on a fait le nœud très serré je ne puis le défaire.

褲頭帶 | 鬆來, *foú t'coû taí kè· soūng loî*, desserrer la ceinture du pantalon.

衫 | 脫來, *sām kè· t'ôt loî*, déboutonner son habit.

Kè· Puceron des légumes, maladie des légumes.

菜發 |, *ts'oí pôt kè·*, les légumes prennent la maladie.

KÉ·

個 *Ké·* Particule numérale qui peut remplacer la plupart des autres particules.

一 | 人, *ŷt ké· gnîn*, un homme.

一 | 桌, *ŷt ké· tsôc*, une table.

Marque du génitif, on peut aussi prononcer *kē·*.

神父 | 衫, *chîn foú ké· sām*, l'habit du Père.

Signifie aussi en langue parlée; cela, celui-là, en parlant du plus éloigné.

唔係裡個 | 個, *mĝ hé· ỳ ké·, ké· ké·*, ce n'est pas celui-ci, c'est celui-là.

唔係裡擺 | 擺, *mĝ hé· ỳ paì ké· paì*, ce n'est pas cette fois-ci c'est l'autre fois. *Voir* 個 *ká*.

計 *Ké·*. Ruse, stratagème, combinaison.

算 |, *són ké·*, imaginer des ruses.

魔鬼個 | 謀, *mô kouì ké· ké· miaô*, les ruses du diable.

| 跳咁好, *ké· t'iaó àn haò*, le stratagème est bon.

千方百 |, *ts'iēn fōng pâc ké·*, mille moyens et cent stratagèmes (toutes sortes de combinaisons).

芥 *Ké·* (ou *kiaí*). | **菜**, *ké· ts'oí*, espèce de légume dont les Chinois font les légumes salés.

K'É·

契 *K'é·*. Contrat, titre de propriété; ami.

印 |, *ýn k'é·*, timbrer un contrat.

紅 |, *foúng k'é·*, contrat muni du sceau officiel.

白 |, *p'ăc k'é·*, contrat sous seing privé.

| **哥**, *k'é· kō*, amoureux, amant en dehors du mariage.

KÈM

Kèm. Couvrir, couvercle.

鍋頭愛 | **等來**, *vŏc t'eoû oí kèm tèn loî*, il fallait couvrir la marmite.

| **鍾**, *kèm tchoūng*, couvercle en forme de coupe.

燈子個 | **鍾打帛裡**, *tēn tzè ké· kèm tchoūng tà p'ĕt lî*, le globe de la lampe est brisé.

KĒN

根 *Kēn*. Racine, origine (au fig. seulement, au propre on dit *kīn*).

天主個道理有 | **有原**, *t'iēn tchoù ké· t'aó lī yoū kēn yoū niân*, la doctrine de Dieu a son origine et son fondement.

| **由**, *kēn yoû*, origine, source.

| **本**, *kēn poùn*, en réalité, principal, base, fondement.

跟 *Kēn*. Suivre, chercher.

| **問**, *kēn moún*, s'informer.

| **尋**, *kēn ts'îm*, chercher, s'enquérir.

| **班**, *kēn pān*, satellite, valet de pied.

| **前**, *kēn ts'iên*, en présence de.

K'ÊN

凝 *K'ên*. Se congeler, se coaguler.

猪油 | **等裡**, *tchoū yoû k'ên tèn lî*, la graisse de porc s'est congelée.

K'ÈN

懇 *K'èn*. Demander avec instance, être mécontent, de mauvaise humeur, travailler avec acharnement.

| **求天主**, *K'èn k'ioû t'iēn tchoù*, supplier ardemment le bon Dieu.

做那個咁 |, *tsó mâc ké· àn k'èn?* pourquoi es-tu de si mauvaise humeur?

發 |, *fât k'èn*, s'acharner à un travail; se mettre en colère.

頃 *K'èn*. | **刻**, *k'èn k'ĕt*, en un clin d'œil.

肯 *K'èn*. Consentir, vouloir. *Voir hèn.*

KÉN

凝 *Kén* (*k'ên*). Tremper les métaux; sensation de froid par attouchement.

鋼愛 | **水啫硬**, *kóng oí kén chouì tsáng ngáng*, il faut tremper l'acier pour qu'il soit dur.

水十分冷噲｜人, *chouì chĭp foūn lāng voé· kén gnîn*, l'eau est très froide elle vous glace (les doigts).

更 *Kén*. Marque du comparatif, changer d'emploi.

｜多｜好, *kén tō kén haò*, plus il y en aura, mieux cela vaudra.

咁樣子｜好, *àn yóng tzè kén haò*, comme cela c'est encore mieux.

｜變, *kén pién*, changer.

K'ÉN

冰 *K'én (pēn)*. Glace, givre, grêle, se geler.

塘水｜帛裡, *t'ông chouì k'én p'ĕt lì*, l'étang est gelé.

落｜, *lŏc k'én*, il tombe du givre ou de la grêle.

做｜都做得倒, *tsó k'én toū tsó tĕt taò*, on peut même fabriquer de la glace.

KEŌU

勾 *Keōu*. Attirer, effacer.

｜引人犯罪, *keōu yǹ gnîn fám ts'ouí*, porter quelqu'un au péché.

｜佢唔來, *keōu kî mǵ loî*, je ne puis l'attirer.

前時先｜通裡, *ts'iên chê siēn keoū t'oūng lì*, il s'était déjà laissé séduire autrefois.

一筆｜消, *yt pĭt keōu siāo*, effacer d'un trait de pinceau.

裡個字寫差愛｜帛佢寫過, *ỳ ké· sé sià ts'ā, oí keōu p'ĕt kî sià koúo*, ce caractère n'est pas le bon, il faut l'effacer et en écrire un autre.

｜淨, *keōu ts'iáng*, nettoyer, enlever les saletés.

鈎 *Keōu*. Anneau non fermé, crochet, accrocher.

搭｜, *keōu tāp*, agrafe, broche.

錨｜, *nâo keōu*, ancre de bateau.

釣｜, *tiáo keōu*, hameçon.

水桶跌落井底下愛｜起來, *choùi t'oùng tiĕt lŏc tsiàng taì hā oí keōu hì loî*, le seau est tombé au fond du puits, il faut l'en retirer.

溝 *Keōu*. Canal, fossé.

｜瀝, *keōu lāc*, canal, fossé.

水｜窟, *choùi keoū foūt*, même sens.

鳩 *Keōu*. tourterelle et ses espèces.

璞｜, *p'oŭc keoū*, tourterelle commune.

班｜, *pān keoū*, ramier.

鬮 *Keoū*. 拈｜, *niām keoū*, tirer au sort.

K'EOŪ

箍 *K'eoū*. Cercler, anneau.

水桶拿來｜起來, *choùi t'oùng nā loî k'eoū hì loî*, vous allez cercler ce seau.

鐵｜, *t'iĕt k'eoū*, cercle de fer.

拿竹篾來｜, *nā tchoŭc mĕt loî k'eoū*, cercler avec du bambou.

KEOÙ

狗 *Keoù.* Chien.

一條｜, *ŷt t'iâo keoù,* un chien.

｜螞蛇, *keoù mâ châ,* lézard.

｜虱, *keoù sêt,* puce de chien, puce en général.

苟 *Keoù.* **｜且**, *keoù ts'ià,* témérairement.

莫咁｜且, *mŏc àn keoù ts'ià,* n'agis pas tant à la légère.

K'EOÙ

口 *K'eoù.* Bouche, entrée, numéral des personnes.

｜胃, *k'eoù ví,* estomac, appétit.

開｜胃, *k'oī k'eoù ví,* ouvrir l'appétit.

｜才, *k'eoù ts'oî,* talent de la parole.

｜信, *k'eoù sín,* nouvelle de vive voix.

｜角, *k'eoù kŏc,* se quereller.

一家人七｜, *ŷt ka gnîn ts'ĭt k'eoù,* une famille de 7 personnes.

KEOÚ

殼 *Keoú.* Suffire, assez.

｜擺, *keoú pài,* c'est suffisant.

儘｜, *tsìn keoú,* c'est largement suffisant.

能｜, *nên keoú,* puissant, habile, pouvoir, vouloir.

不能｜個人, *poût nên keoú ké· gnîn,* homme incapable.

K'EOÚ

鈕 *K'eoú.* Bouton d'habit.

一付｜子, *ŷt foú k'eoú tzè,* cinq boutons.

｜襻, *k'eóu p'án,* boutonnière.

衫子｜等來, *sām tzè k'eoú tèn loî,* boutonne ton habit.

簆 *K'eoú.* Peigne du métier de tisserand.

扣 *K'eoú.* Déduire une quantité d'une autre, escompte, agrafer, boutonner.

｜除, *k'eoú tch'oû,* retrancher.

｜三七, *k'eoú sām ts'ĭt,* retenir trente du cent et ne donner que 70. (On sous-entend le mot **十** *chĭp ; litt.* moins 30 reste 70).

兩個花邊｜頭, *lcòng ké· fā piēn k'eoú t'eoû,* un escompte de deux piastres.

一石穀同我｜算幾多錢, *ŷt chăc koŭc t'oûng ngaî k'eoú són kì tō ts'iên,* faites-moi le compte, à combien revient le picul de riz ?

叩 *K'eoú.* **｜問**, *k'eoú moún,* interroger.

｜頭, *k'eoú t'eoû,* saluer en baissant la tête.

｜求人, *k'eoú k'ioû gnîn,* implorer quelqu'un.

KÊP

鈒 *Kêp.* Mettre en bas la partie concave d'un objet, encapuchonner.

｜酒盃, *kêp tsioù pī,* placer un verre à vin la partie concave tournée en bas.

冒子別我｜倒一隻鵰, *maó tzè*

poūn ngaî kēp taò ŷt tchâc tiāo, j'ai attrapé un oiseau en l'enfermant dans mon chapeau.

菜碗拿來｜等來, *ts'oí vouòn nā loî kēp tèn loî*, recouvre (d'un bol renversé) le bol qui contient les légumes.

墨盤拿來｜轉起, *mĕt p'ân nā loî kēp tchòn hì*, remettre le couvercle de l'encrier.

｜子, *kēp tzè*, capsule de fusil.

｜子唔過引, *kēp tzè mĝ kouó ŷn*, la capsule a raté.

打｜子, *tà kēp tzè*, frapper sur la capsule. *Voir kèm*.

KÊT

格 *Kĕt*. Loi, règle, approfondir.

｜外, *kĕt ngoé·*, en outre, en surplus (en dehors de la règle).

｜外有一百錢, *kĕt ngoé· yoū ŷt pâc ts'iên*, il y a en outre 100 sapèques.

｜物, *kĕt voŭt*, approfondir les choses, sciences naturelles.

紇 *Kĕt*. Nœud, embrouillé.

打｜, *tà kĕt*, faire un nœud.

打雙活｜, *tà soūng fāt kĕt*, faire un nœud coulant.

線子打｜, *sién tzè tà kĕt*, le fil est tout embrouillé.

革 *Kĕt*. Destituer.

阻｜, *tzè kĕt*, empêchement.

｜功名, *kĕt koūng miâng*, destituer quelqu'un de son titre.

｜官, *kĕt kouōn*, casser un mandarin.

K'ÊT

刻 *K'ĕt*. Graver, un moment, opprimer, tourmenter.

｜書板子, *k'ĕt choū pàn tzè*, graver les planches d'un livre.

一｜, *ŷt k'ĕt*, un quart d'heure.

即｜愛來, *tsĭt k'ĕt oí loî*, il faut venir de suite.

｜薄人, *k'ĕt p'ŏc gnîn*, traiter durement les gens, vexer, exiger arbitrairement.

｜苦, *k'ĕt k'où*, affliger son propre corps; mortifier ses passions; s'imposer beaucoup de peine ou de fatigue.

克 *K'ĕt*. Dompter, maîtriser.

不能自｜, *poût nên tsé k'ĕt*, ne pouvoir se maîtriser soi-même.

客 *K'ĕt*. Convive, hôte. (Voir *hâc*).

賓｜, *pīn k'ĕt*, hôte.

｜官, *k'ĕt kouōn*, mandarin de passage.

咳 *K'ĕt*. Tousser.

｜嗽, *k'ĕt tch'oŭc*, même sens.

｜嗽藥, *k'ĕt tch'oŭc yŏc*, remède contre la toux.

｜唔出, *k'ĕt mĝ tch'oût*, faire des efforts pour tousser sans le pouvoir.

乞 *K'ĕt*. **｜食**, *k'ĕt chĭt*, mendier.

KĪ

機 *Kī*. Force motrice, occasion.

| 器, *kī hí*, machine, moteur quelconque.

攬 | , *lām kī*, (vulg. *lām kí*), métier de tisserand.

茶 | 桌, *ts'â kī tsôc*, petite table à thé.

| 會, *kī fí*, occasion.

撞倒 | 會, *ts'óng taò kī fí*, rencontrer une occasion.

不投 | 個話, *poŭt t'eoû kī ké· fá*, parole qui n'est pas dite à propos, coq-à-l'âne.

家 | 布, *ka kī poú*, kaki, espèce d'étoffe.

饑 *Kī*. Faim, famine.

| 荒年辰, *kī fōng niân chîn*, année stérile.

肚 | , *toù kī*, avoir faim.

譏 *Kī*. Se moquer.

| 誚人, *kī ts'iaò gnîn*, se moquer de quelqu'un (peu employé).

居 *Kī*. | 住, *kī tch'oú*, habiter, être.

拘 *Kī*. Réprimer.

莫 | 禮, *mŏc kī lī*, ne faites pas de cérémonies.

不 | , *poŭt kī*, n'importe qui, qui que ce soit.

枝 *Kī* (*tjē*). Particule numérale des choses longues que l'on peut tenir à la main. Branche.

一 | 筆, *ŷt kī pĭt*, un pinceau.

一 | 花, *ŷt kī fa*, une fleur.

聖 | , 聖 | 主日, *chín kī*, *chín kī tchoù gnĭt*, les rameaux bénits, le Dimanche des rameaux.

基 *Kī*. 地 | , *t'í kī*, base, emplacement, fondement.

箕 *Kī*. 糞 | , *poún kī*, instrument de bambou qui a la forme d'un van et dans lequel on recueille les balayures, on porte le fumier, la terre etc.

簸 | , *paí kī*, van.

萁 *Kī*. 鹵 | , *loū kī*, fougères, grandes herbes.

K'Ī

欺 *K'ī*. Mépriser, faire injure, opprimer.

有功名人過唔敢 | 負, *yoū koūng miâng gnîn kouó mĝ kàm k'ī foú*, quand on a un titre d'honneur, on n'ose pas tant vous chercher noise.

嶇 *K'ī*. Escarpé, montant; se tenir debout.

十分 | 個嵐, *chĭp foūn k'ī ké· ýn*, cette côte est excessivement raide.

| 唔穩, *k'ī mĝ voùn*, ne pouvoir se tenir debout.

放 | 來, *fóng k'ī loî*, mettre droit, perpendiculaire à l'horizon.

| 倒來, *k'ī taò loî*, tiens-toi droit.

KÎ

佢 *Kî*. Il, elle, lui. (*Voir kia*).

丨有病, *kî yoū p'iáng*, il est malade.

你話丨知, *gnî vá ki tī*, dis-lui.

K'Î

期 *K'î*. Période de temps déterminé.

日丨, *gnĭt k'î*, jour fixé.

齋丨日, *tsaī k'î gnĭt*, jour d'abstinence.

定丨, *t'ín k'î*, fixer un terme.

關丨, *kouān k'î*, échéance.

節丨, *tsiĕt k'î*, division de l'année.

今日我係打擺個丨日, *kīn gnĭt ngaî hé· tà paì ké· k'î gnĭt*, c'est aujourd'hui mon jour de fièvre.

旗 *K'î*. Drapeau, bannière.

插丨, *ts'âp k'î*, planter le drapeau.

扯丨, *tch'a k'î*, hisser le drapeau.

棋 *K'î*. Jeu d'échecs, de dames, ou autres.

象丨, *sióng k'î*, échecs.

作象丨, *tsôc sióng k'î*, jouer aux échecs.

麒 *K'î*. 丨麟, *k'î lîn*, animal fabuleux, licorne.

耆 *K'î*. 丨老, *k'î laò*, terme respectueux pour dire vieillard.

六十歲爲丨, *lioŭc chĭp sé· vî k'î*, un homme de soixante ans s'appelle *k'î*. Voir 歲 *sé·*.

奇 *K'î*. Extraordinaire, surprenant.

咁丨妙, *àn k'î miaò!* que c'est admirable!

丨怪, *k'î kouaí*, curieux, étrange.

麽那個出丨, *mô mâc ké· tch'oût k'î*, il n'y a rien d'extraordinaire.

離離丨丨個人, *lî lî k'î k'î ké· gnîn*, homme extravagant, bizarre.

騎 *K'î*. Aller à cheval.

丨馬, *k'î ma*, même sens.

馬十分鋒唔敢丨, *mā chĭp foūn foūng mĝ kàm k'î*, le cheval est très fougueux, je n'ose pas le monter.

祈 *K'î*. 丨求, *k'î k'ioû*, prier, demander.

丨求天主, *k'î k'ioû t'iēn tchoù*, prier Dieu.

丨神作福, *k'î chîn tsôc foŭc*, demander le bonheur aux esprits.

千丨莫添忘, *ts'iēn k'î mŏc t'iām piόng*, je vous en prie, de grâce, n'oubliez pas.

鬐 *K'î*. 丨觚, *k'î koū*, nageoire de poisson.

KÌ

紀 *Kì*. Annales, années.

愛顧等綱丨來, *oí koú tèn kōng kì loî*, il faut vérifier sur les annales.

年丨大, *niân kì t'aí*, d'un âge avancé.

舉 *Kì*. Promouvoir à un degré ou à une charge.

丨人, *kì gnîn*, licencié.

裡個人好愛｜起佢來做官, *ỳ ké· gnîn haò oí kì hì kî loî tsó kouōn*, cet homme est bon, il faut l'élever au grade de mandarin.

佢功名係保｜來個, *kiā koūng miâng hé· paò kì loî ké·*, son titre d'honneur lui a été donné en récompense.

一｜两得, *ŷt kì leòng têt*, faire d'une pierre deux coups.

矩 *Kì*. **規｜**, *kouī kì*, règle, loi, usage.

守規｜, *choù kouī kì*, observer les convenances.

麼規｜, *mô kouī kì*, malhonnête, impoli, sans convenances.

據 *Kì*. Preuve, gage.

憑｜, *p'în kì*, même sens.

有憑有｜, *yoū p'în yoū kì*, il y a des preuves, des gages.

麼憑｜, *mô p'în kì*, il n'y a pas de preuves.

｜你所講你有理｜佢所講你麼理, *kì gnî sò kòng gnî yoū lī kì kî sò kòng gnî mô lī*, d'après toi (litt. d'après les preuves que tu avances) tu as raison, d'après lui tu as tort.

幾 *Kì*. Quel? combien? quelques.

有｜多個人, *yoū kì tō ké· gnîn?* combien y a-t-il de personnes?

愛｜多錢, *oí kì tō ts'iên?* combien faut-il de sapèques?

愛十｜個花邊, *oí chĭp kì ké· fā piēn*, il faut dix et quelques piastres.

｜時來, *kì chê loî?* quand viendra-t-il?

有｜大, *yoū kì t'aí?* de quelle grandeur?

己 *Kì*. Soi-même.

我自｜做個, *ngaî tsé kì tsó ké·*, c'est moi-même qui l'ai fait.

天主自｜有個, *t'iēn tchoù tsé kì yoū ké·*, Dieu existe par lui-même.

自｜個人, *tsé kì ké· gnîn*, gens à soi, de la famille.

K'Ì

啟 *K'ì*. Informer, faire connaître.

天主默｜的, *t'iēn tchoù mĕt k'ì tît*, inspiré par Dieu.

簡神父收｜, *kiàn chîn foú choū k'ì*, au Père *Kiàn* pour qu'il en prenne connaissance (adresse d'une enveloppe de lettre).

豈 *K'ì*. Comment? pourquoi? est-ce?

｜有此理, *k'ì yoū tsè lī?* est-ce raisonnable?

｜敢, *k'ì kàm?* comment oser?

懼 *K'ì*. **恐｜**, *k'oùng k'ì*, craindre.

莫｜唔使｜佢, *mŏc k'ì mĝ sè k'ì kî*, n'ayez pas peur, vous n'avez rien à craindre de lui.

KÍ

句 *Kí*. Particule numérale des mots; phrase, mot.

還有一｜話愛講, *hân yoū ŷt kí fá oí kòng*, j'ai encore un mot à dire.

｜｜, *kí kí*, en détail, de point en point.

唔成｜, *mĝ châng kí*, ne pas former un sens complet.

到裡斷｜, *taó lì t'ōn kí*, la phrase finit là.

記 *Kí*. Mémoire, se souvenir.

｜含, ｜財, *kí hâm, kí ts'oî*, la mémoire.

｜得, *kí têt*, je me rappelle.

｜念, *kí niám*, garder le souvenir.

常常愛｜念天主, *chông chông oí kí niám t'iēn tchoù*, il faut toujours penser à Dieu.

忘｜, *mòng kí*, oublier.

｜號, *kí haó*, signe, marque.

｜認, *kí gnín*, indice, marque.

打一個｜認, *tà ŷt ké· kí gnín*, faire une marque secrète; (on dit aussi par corruption de mot *kín lín*).

鋸 *Kí*. Scier, scie.

｜屎, *kí chè*, sciure de bois.

｜斷, ｜唔斷, *kí t'ōn, kí mĝ t'ōn*, scier en deux, ne pouvoir scier en deux.

｜齒, *kí tchè*, les dents de la scie.

寄 *Kí*. Confier, livrer.

｜信, *kí sín*, confier une lettre.

東西｜阿天和堂店, *toūng sī kí á t'iēn fô t'ông tiám*, j'ai déposé les affaires à la boutique *t'iēn fô t'ông*.

繼 *Kí*. Succéder.

｜父, *kí foú*, nom qu'un fils donne à celui que sa mère a épousé en secondes noces.

｜母, *kí moū*, marâtre.

我｜續簡神父個位, *ngaî kí sioŭc kiàn chîn foú ké· ví*, j'ai succédé au Père *Kiàn*.

我賴子過｜別我阿哥, *ngaî laí tzè kouó kí poūn ngaî a kō*, mon fils a été adopté par mon frère.

髻 *Kí*. Chignon de femme, crête de coq, huppe.

梳｜, *sē* (ailleurs *sō*) *kí*, faire son chignon.

雞｜, *kē· kí*, crête de coq.

雞公｜花, *kē· koūng kí fa*, amarante crête de coq.

既 *Kí*. ｜然, *kí yân*, puisque.

｜然係咁樣你唔使去, *kí yân hé· àn yóng gnî mĝ sè hí*, puisqu'il en est ainsi, tu n'as pas besoin d'y aller.

K'Í

去 *K'í*. Aller. *Voir hí*.

KIÂ

佢 *Kiâ* (*kî*). Son, sa, sien.

｜個, *kiâ ké·*, c'est le sien.

唔知係我唔知係佢, *mĝ tī hé· ngâ mĝ tī hé· kiâ*, je ne sais pas si c'est le mien ou le sien.

K'IÂ

K'iâ. *Lâ-k'iâ*, Araignée.

?｜絲, *lâ k'iâ sē*, toile d'araignée.

? | 牽絲, *lâ k'iâ k'iān sē*, l'araignée fait sa toile.

? | 網倒烏蠅, *lâ k'iâ miòng taò voū ŷn*, l'araignée a pris une mouche dans sa toile.

K'IÁ

? *K'iá*. | 把, *k'iá pà*, râteau.

跨 *K'iá* ou *k'iám (k'oūa)*. Écarter les jambes, enjamber quelqu'un, à califourchon.

| 人, *k'iá gnîn*, passer par dessus quelqu'un.

行去 | 也 | 子, *hâng hí k'iá yā k'iá tzè*, se dit de quelqu'un qui marche les jambes écartées.

細妹子莫脚 | | 子麼規矩, *sé· moé· tzè mŏc kiŏc k'iá k'iá tzè, mô kouī kì*, n écarte pas les jambes, ma petite, ce n'est pas convenable.

KIĂC

彶 *Kiăc*. Vite, s'empresser.

| | 來, *kiăc kiăc loî*, vite ! vite ! arrive.

走得十分 | , *tseoù tĕt chĭp foūn kiăc*, il peut aller très vite.

行 | 阿子, *hâng kiăc á tzè*, empresse-toi.

K'IĂC

屐 *K'iăc*. Sabot, chaussure de bois.

釘 | , *tāng k'iăc*, clouer la bande de cuir qui recouvre le sabot.

KIAĪ

街 *Kiaī* (ou *kē·*). Rue, bourg, ville.

一條 | , *ŷt t'iaô kiaī*, une rue.

出 | , *tch'oūt kiaī*, sortir en ville, au bourg.

通 | , *t'oūng kiaī*, par toute la rue.

| 上去尋佢, *kiaī hóng hí ts'îm kî*, va le chercher dans la rue.

KIAÌ

久 *Kiaì (kioù)*. Longtemps. *Voir kioù*.

解 *Kiaì*. Expliquer, raconter, déboucher. *(Voir kè·)*.

| 說, *kiaì chôt*, expliquer.

你曉 | 麼, *gnî hiaò kiaì mô ?* sais-tu le sens ?

你寫個字麼 | , *gnî sià ké· sé mô kiaì*, ce que tu écris n a pas de sens.

告 | , *kaó kiaì*, se confesser.

酒瓶拿起 | 開來, *tsioù p'în nā hì kiaì k'oī loî*, débouche-moi la cruche de vin.

出 | , *tch'oūt kiaì*, aller à la selle.

| 元, *kiaì niân*, le premier à l'examen de la licence.

| 耳, *kiaì gnì*, curer les oreilles.

KIAÍ

解 *Kiaí*. Couper du papier en long ; conduire un criminel d'un lieu à un autre.

| 一張紙, *kiaí ŷt tchōng tjè*, couper une feuille de papier.

| 犯人下省, *kiaí fám gnîn hā sèn*, conduire un criminel à la capitale de la province.

界 *Kiaí*. Limite, terme.

兩省交 |, *leòng sèn kaō kiaí*, rencontre des limites de deux provinces.

| 址分明, *kiaí tjè foūn mîn*, les limites sont bien déterminées.

安 | 石, *ōn kiaí chăc*, poser des pierres comme limites.

各有各 |, *kôc yoū kôc kiaí*, chacun a son terrain limité.

世 |, *ché kiaí*, le monde.

兼 |, *kiām kiaí*, proche des limites, hazardeux (en ce dernier sens on dit aussi *kiām ké·*).

芥 *Kiaí*. | 辣, *kiaí lăt*, moutarde.

| 蘭菜, *kiaí lân ts'oí*, choux.

戒 (誡) *Kiaí*. Défendre, s'abstenir.

天主十 |, *t'iēn tchoù chĭp kiaí*, les 10 commandements de Dieu.

犯六 |, *fám lioūc kiaí*, pécher contre le sixième.

| 酒, *kiaí tsioù*, s'abstenir du vin, y renoncer.

| 洋烟, *kiaí yông yān*, ne plus user, s'abstenir de l'opium.

| 指, *kiaí tjè*, bague.

KIĀM

兼 *Kiām*. Unir, ensemble, en même temps.

船 | 前來, *chôn kiām ts'iên loî*, aborder, amener la barque auprès.

| 岸, *kiām ngán*, aborder au rivage.

| | 子, *kiām kiām tzè*, à peu près, presque.

| 界, *kiām kiaí* (ou *kiām ké·*), hazardeux.

| 兩個事, *kiām leòng ké· sé*, remplir deux fonctions à la fois, faire deux choses à la fois.

K'IĀM

謙 *K'iām*. Humble, humilité.

| 卑, | 遜, *k'iām pī*, *k'iām soún*, humilité.

| 讓, *k'iām yóng* (ou *nióng*), modestie, céder par modestie.

| 虛, *k'iām hī*, affabilité, modestie.

| 忍, *k'iām nioūn*, patience.

K'IÂM

鉗 *K'iâm*. Pinces, tenailles.

火 |, *fò k'iâm*, pincettes.

鐵 |, *t'iĕt k'iâm*, tenailles.

手 |, *choù k'iâm*, petite pince.

KIÀM

劍 *Kiàm*. Recueillir, ramasser.

| 錢, *kiàm ts'iên*, percevoir sa paye, acquitter.

我去 | 錢佢又唔肯 |, *ngai hí kiàm ts'iên, kî youí mĝ hèn kiàm*, je vais percevoir ma paye et il ne veut pas m'acquitter.

| 碗筷, *kiàm vouòn k'ouaí*, desservir la table.

| 屋, | 瓦, *kiàm voūc*, *kiàm ngà*, réparer la maison, réparer la toiture

en remplaçant les mauvaises tuiles.

｜點東西, *kiàm tiàm toūng sī*, mettre les objets en ordre.

KIÁM

儉 *Kiám.* Epée, glaive.

手｜, *choù kiám*, poignard.

K'IÁM

儉 *K'iám.* Epargner.

勤｜, *k'ioûn k'iám*, économe. *(Voyez k'iáng).*

欠 *K'iám.* Faire défaut, être insuffisant.

｜人個錢, *k'iám gnîn ké· ts'iĉn*, devoir de l'argent à quelqu'un.

你｜我三十個錢, *gnî k'iám ngaî sām chīp ké· ts'iên*, tu me dois trente sapèques.

我｜[illegible]｜個主日, *ngaî k'iám lî ŷt ké· tchoù gnĭt*, il y a un dimanche que je n'ai pas observé.

｜債, *k'iám tsaí*, dette.

｜主, *k'iám tchoù*, débiteur.

寫｜字, *sià k'iám sé*, écrire une obligation.

開｜, *k'oï k'iám (ou kiám)*, bâiller.

跨 *K'iám (k'ouā).* Enfourchure des jambes, empan, enjamber, se mettre à califourchon.

手｜, *choù k'iám*, empan.

爭一｜, *tsāng ŷt k'iám*, il s'en faut d'un empan.

｜過, *k'iám kouó*, enjamber.

麼橋就愛｜阿過, *mô k'iaô ts'ioú oí k'iám á kouó*, puisqu'il n'y a pas de pont il faut enjamber. Voir *k'iá.*

KIĀN

間 *Kiān.* Chambre, au milieu, dedans, particule numérale des compartiments de maison.

入｜, *gnĭp kiān*, rentrer dans sa chambre.

｜貯[illegible], *kiān toù liaó*, demeurer dans sa chambre.

內｜, *nouí kiān*, appartements des femmes.

日｜, *gnĭt kiān*, en plein jour.

平時｜, *p'în chê kiān*, en temps ordinaire.

天地｜, *t'iēn t'í kiān*, en ce monde.

世｜, *ché kiān*, même sens (se dit mieux).

一｜房屋, *ŷt kiān fông voûc*, un compartiment de maison.

艱 *Kiān.* ｜難, *kiān nân*, difficile, ardu.

｜辛, *kiān siĉn (pour kiān sīn)*, ennuyeux.

姦 *Kiān*, Fornication, adultère.

犯｜, *fám kiān*, commettre la fornication ou l'adultère.

奸 *Kiān.* Entêté, rusé, tenace.

｜雄, *kiān hioûng*, tenace, dur de cœur.

｜惡, *kiān ôc*, même sens.

｜刁梟惡, *kiān tiaō hiaō ôc*, entêté, agaçant, filou, méchant.

裡個人做事倸丨計, *ỳ ké· gnîn tsó sé hé· kiān kí*, cet homme est très têtu.

堅 *Kiān*. Solide, fort, fortifier.

丨穩, *kiān voùn*, solide.

丨固, *kiān koú*, fortifier, solide.

領丨振, *lcāng kiān tchìn*, recevoir la Confirmation.

慳 *Kiān*. Avare.

丨恡, *kiān nín*, avare, tenace.

捐 *Kiān*. Souscription, surtaxe, achat d'une charge.

丨題錢, *kiān t'î ts'iēn*, souscrire une somme.

丨功名, *kiān koūng miāng*, acheter un titre honorifique.

丨官, *kiān kouōn*, acheter une place de mandarin.

肩 *Kiān* (ou *kīn*). L'épaule.

丨頭, *kiān t'eoû*, même sens.

鬆丨, *soūng kiān*, se soulager l'épaule en déposant son fardeau.

麼幾遠一丨路, *mô kì yàn, ŷt kiān loú*, ce n'est pas loin, une épaulée (c'est-à dire le temps de porter un fardeau sans changer d'épaule).

上丨, *chōng kiān*, mettre le fardeau sur l'épaule.

K'IĀN

牽 *K'iān*. Conduire par la main, tirer, amener quelqu'un à ses projets.

丨牛, 丨馬, *k'iān nioû, k'iān mā*, conduire un buffle, un cheval.

丨手, *k'iān choù*, se donner la main.

丨佢上, *k'iān kî hóng*, aide-le à se lever.

丨我過橋, *k'iān ngaî kouó k'iaô*, donne-moi la main pour passer le pont.

丨葡萄藤上樹, *k'iān p'oû t'aô t'ên chōng choú*, faire monter une vigne sur un arbre.

丨門索, *k'iān moûn sôc*, faire l'intermédiaire pour amener des femmes de mauvaise vie.

丨會, *k'iān fí*, monter une société.

圈 *K'iān*. Cercle, circonférence, circuit fermé (rond ou non); marquer une lettre d'un petit cercle.

鐵丨, *t'iēt k'iān*, anneau de fer.

畫丨, *fá k'iān*, tracer des ronds.

打一個圓丨, *tà ŷt ké· yân k'iān*, tracer un cercle, un zéro.

丨一個字, *k'iān ŷt ké· sé*, tracer un petit cercle sur le côté d'un caractère (pour avertir qu'il change de ton).

三角丨, *sām kôc k'iān*, triangle.

丨丨轉, *k'iān k'iān* (ou *k'ouān k'ouān*) *tchòn*, tourner tout autour.

K'IÂN

權 *K'iân*. Autorité, pouvoir.

丨柄, *k'iân piáng*, même sens.

交丨, *kaō k'iân*, donner le pouvoir.

神父代天主個丨赦罪, *chîn foú t'oí t'iēn tchoù ké· k'iân chá ts'oui*, le prêtre tient de Dieu le pouvoir de remettre les péchés.

丨衡, *k'iân fên*, autorité, justice.

| 家, *k'iân ka*, administrer les affaires de la famille.

虔 *K'iân*. S'appliquer à.

| 心 | 意, *k'iân sīm k'iân ý*, avec ferveur et application.

拳 *K'iân*. Poing.

打 | , *tà k'iân*, boxer.

打一個 | 頭, *tà ŷt ké· k'iân t'eoû*, donner un coup de poing.

KIÀN

簡 *Kiàn*. Abréger, concis.

從 | , *ts'ioûng kiàn*, en définitive, bref.

| 便, *kiàn p'iên*, court et commode.

| 慢人, *kiàn mán gnîn*, traiter sans respect, (réponse de politesse aux remerciements que fait un hôte au moment du départ).

| 筆寫個, *kiàn pît sià ké·*, écrit en caractères abrégés.

筧 *Kiàn*. Conduit d'eau, gouttière.

水 | 噲漏, *chouì kiàn voé· leoú*, la gouttière a des fuites.

繭 *Kiàn*. Cocon de ver à soie, faire son cocon.

蠶子 | 竇, *ts'âm tzè kiàn teoú*, le ver à soie fait son cocon.

| 綢, *kiàn tch'oû*, fort tissu fait avec une espèce de soie.

鹻 *Kiàn*, Savon, potasse.

| 水, *kiàn chouì*, eau de lessive.

番 | , *fān kiàn*, savon européen.

揀 *Kiàn*. Choisir.

| 選, *kiàn sièn*, même sens.

天主 | 選童貞瑪利亞爲母, *t'iēn tchoù kiàn sièn t'oûng tchīn Mā lí ā vî moū*, Dieu a choisi la Vierge Marie pour mère.

K'IÀN

犬 *K'iàn*. Chien (on dit mieux 狗 *keoù*).

卷 *K'iàn* ou *kiàn*. Cahier, dossier, tome. Ce mot n'est guère usité que dans le dernier sens, et encore on dit mieux 本 *poùn*.

倦 *K'iàn*. Fatigué.

| 怠, *k'iàn t'aí*, même sens, (peu employé).

KIÁN

見 *Kián*. Percevoir par les yeux du corps ou de l'âme; remarquer, comprendre.

看唔 | , *k'ón mĝ kián*, ne pouvoir pas percevoir par la vue.

病唔 | 好, *p'iáng mĝ kián haò*, on ne voit pas d'amélioration dans sa maladie.

舞倒咁樣個事我唔敢 | 神父, *moù taò àn yóng ké· sé ngaî mĝ kàm kián chîn foú*, après une telle affaire je n'ose pas me présenter devant le Père.

少丨多怪, *chaò kián tō kouaí*, qui a peu vu s'étonne facilement.

丨罪唔得, *kián ts'ouí mĝ têt*, on ne peut y voir aucun mal.

丨証人, *kián tchín gnîn*, témoin.

免丨, *mēn kián*, je le dispense de venir me voir (signifie un refus d'audience).

刀子唔丨, *taō tzè mĝ kián*, mon couteau a disparu.

麽丨識個人, *mô kián chĭt ké gnîn*, homme sans expérience.

丨唔得火, *kián mĝ têt fò*, cela ne peut être exposé au feu.

丨人都有, *kián gnîn toū yoū*, tous en ont.

眷 *Kián*. Parenté, famille.

家丨帶來裡, *kā kián taí loî lì*, j'ai amené ma famille.

細人同我丨顧阿子, *sé gnîn t'oúng ngaî kián koú á tzè*, veillez sur mon enfant.

建 *Kián*. Bâtir.

丨造聖堂, *kián ts'aó chín t'ông*, bâtir une église.

K'IÁN

件 *K'ián*. Particule numérale des affaires, des habits, des colis.

物丨, *voŭt k'ián*, ustensile, objet.

一丨事, *ȳt k'ián sé*, une affaire.

两丨衫, *lcòng k'ián sām*, deux habits.

箱子大細有十丨, *siōng tzè t'aí sé yoū chĭp k'ián*, caisses grandes et petites, il y en a dix en tout.

案丨愛留心, *ón k'ián oí lioû sīm*, occupez-vous avec soin de mon procès.

勸 *K'ián*. Exhorter, pousser à faire.

丨人奉教, *k'ián gnîn foúng kaó*, exhorter quelqu'un à se faire chrétien.

我想丨佢莫打官司丨佢唔倒, *ngaî siòng k'ián kî mŏc tà kouōn sē k'ián kî mĝ taò*, j'ai fait tout mon possible, mais inutilement, pour l'engager à ne pas intenter le procès.

健 *K'ián*. Dur, fort.

丨旺, *k'ián vóng*, vigoureux, bien portant.

康丨, *k'ōng k'ián*, même sens.

神父個母親還丨麽, *chîn foú ké moū ts'īn hân k'ián mô?* votre mère se porte-t-elle bien? (chrétien parlant au missionnaire).

硬丨, *ngáng k'ián*, solide, dur.

KIĀNG

驚 *Kiāng*. Craindre, s'effrayer.

得人丨, *têt gnîn kiāng*, effrayant.

着丨, *tch'ŏc kiāng*, avoir une frayeur, un soubresaut.

嚇丨, *hăc kiāng*, faire peur.

K'IĀNG

輕 *K'iāng* (*k'īn*). Leger, alléger.

丨丨, *k'iāng k'iāng*, légèrement, léger.

担子唔知丨重, *tām tzè mḡ tī k'iāng tch'oūng*, je ne sais pas si la charge est légère ou lourde.

丨身, *k'iāng chīn*, accoucher.

看丨人, *k'ón k'iāng gnîn*, regarder quelqu'un avec mépris.

K'IÂNG

擎 *K'iâng*. Tenir à la main, porter droit.

丨傘, *k'iâng tchā*, porter son parapluie.

丨旗, *k'iâng k'î*, porter, tenir un drapeau.

丨燭, *k'iâng tchoûc*, tenir un cierge à la main.

KIÀNG

頸 *Kiàng*. Cou. 丨頸, *kiàng kìn*, cou.

吊丨, *tiaó kiàng*, se pendre.

KIÁNG

鏡 *Kiáng*. Miroir, glace, lunettes.

照丨, *tchaó kiáng*, se regarder dans un miroir.

戴眼丨, *taí niàn kiáng*, porter des lunettes.

千里丨, *ts'iēn lī kiáng*, longue-vue, lunette d'approche.

西洋丨, *sī yông kiáng*, stéréoscope.

K'IÁNG

儉 *K'iáng* (*k'iám*). Économe, parcimonieux.

省丨, *sèn k'iáng*, user avec économie.

燒炭比燒柴麼過丨, *chaō t'án pì chaō ts'iaô mô kouó k'iáng*, brûler du charbon n'est pas plus économique que be brûler du bois.

我丨倒兩百錢, *ngaî k'iáng taò leòng pâc ts'iên*, j'ai épargné 200 sapèques.

KIAŌ

嬌 *Kiaō*. Gentil, délicat.

細人子做丨, *sé gnîn tzè tsó kiaō*, l'enfant fait le gentil, le mignard.

丨嫩, *kiaō noún*, tendre et délicat.

驕 *Kiaō*. Orgueil.

丨傲, *kiaō ngáo*, même sens.

發丨傲, *fât kiaō ngáo*, commettre un acte d'orgueil.

K'IAŌ

敲 *K'iaō* (ou *k'aó*). Frapper. (Voyez *k'aó*).

蹺 *K'iaō* (ou *k'aō*). Croiser, entrelacer. (Voyez *k'aō*).

K'IAÔ

橋 *K'iaô*. Pont.

石丨, *chăc k'iaô*, pont de pierre.

樹板丨, *choú pàn k'iaô*, simples planches posées au-dessus d'un ruisseau ou d'un ravin.

浮丨, *feoû k'iaô*, pont flottant, pont de bateau.

| 墩, *k'iaô toūn*, piles du pont.
過 | . *kouó k'iaô*, passer le pont.

繳 *Kiaò*. Donner du travail, dépenses de ménage.

做生理愛好多來 |, *tsó siēn lī oí haò tō loî kiaò*, faire le commerce réclame beaucoup de dépenses.

出門盤 | 大, *tch'oūt moûn p'ân kiaò t'aí*, dans les voyages, les dépenses sont grandes.

| 人做生理, *kiaò gnîn tsó siēn lī*, donner le capital nécessaire pour faire le commerce en son nom.

| 人畜牛, *kiaò gnîn hioūc nioû*, faire élever un buffle, donner un buffle à nourrir, affermer son buffle.

| 細人讀書, *kiaò sé· gnîn t'oŭc choū*, faire les dépenses nécessaires pour permettre à l'enfant d'étudier.

KIAÓ

叫 *Kiaó*. Pleurer, crier, chant ou cri des animaux.

細人子 |, *sé· gnîn tzè kiaó*, l'enfant pleure.

鬼 |, *kouì kiaó*, le diable crie.

貓 | 公, *miaó koūng kiaó*, le chat miaule.

K'IAÓ

轎 *K'iaó*. Chaise à porteur, palanquin.

| 夫, *k'iaó foū*, porteurs de chaise.

| 帷, *k'iaó vî*, tente, couverture de la chaise.

一頂 |, *ŷt tàng k'iaó*, un palanquin.

坐 |, *ts'ō k'iaó*, être en palanquin.

撬 *K'iaó*. Soulever avec un levier.

| 石頭, *k'iaó chăc t'eoû*, soulever des pierres avec un levier.

釘子拿來 | 脫, *tāng tzè nā loi k'iaó t'ôt*, arrache les clous.

㨢唔脫愛 | 脫, *pāng mĝ t'ôt oí k'iaó t'ôt*, on ne peut les arracher en tirant, il faut faire levier.

竅 *K'iaó*. 七 |, *ts'ĭt k'iaó*, les 7 ouvertures du corps humain (signifie plutôt en langage vulgaire, les moyens, les capacités de l'esprit.

靈魂出 |, *lîn foûn tch'oût k'iaó*, l'âme est sortie par les ouvertures (c.-à-d. il est mort).

開 |, *k'oī k'iaó*, bâiller.

七孔八 |, *ts'ĭt k'oùng pât k'iaó*, se dit d'un homme ingénieux qui a toutes sortes de moyens.

| 妙, *k'iaó miaò*, admirable d'ingéniosité.

KIĂP

夾 *Kiăp*. Tenir des deux côtés, occuper les deux côtés.

| 一塊猪肉, *kiăp ŷt k'ouaí tchoū nioûc*, prendre un morceau de viande avec les bâtonnets.

| 書, *kiăp choū*, presser un livre.

火 |, *fò kiăp*, pincettes.

K'IĂP

狹 *K'iăp*. Étroit, resserré.

地方忒｜, *t'í fōng t'iĕt k'iăp*, l'endroit est trop petit.

溝瀝鑊｜, *keoū lâc t'iĕt k'iăp*, le ruisseau est trop étroit.

石｜, *chăc k'iăp*, petit détroit entre deux rochers.

KIÂP

刦 *Kiâp*. Prendre par force, piller.

路上賊｜走我個東西, *loú hóng ts'ĕt kiâp tseoù ngâ ké· toūng sī*, en route les voleurs ont pillé mes effets.

路上有人打｜愛老成, *loú hóng yoū gnîn tà kiâp oí laò chîn*, on pille sur les routes, faites attention.

洽 *Kiâp*. Apre, acerbe.

有｜味, *yoū kiâp mí*, cela a un goût âpre.

K'IĔT

竭 *K'iĕt*. S'épuiser, de toutes ses forces.

一心｜力, *ŷt sīm k'iĕt lĭt*, faire tous ses efforts.

｜崑崗, *k'iĕt ýn kōng*, grimper à travers une montagne.

KIÊT

抉 *Kiĕt*. Châtrer.

｜猪, ｜雞, *kiĕt tchoū, kiĕt kē·*, châtrer un porc, une poule.

決 *Kiĕt*. Statuer.

｜主意, *kiĕt tchoù ý*, prendre une résolution.

｜斷, *kiĕt tón*, décider, porter une sentence.

結 *Kiĕt*. Edifier, s'unir, union morale, terminer une affaire, fructifier, se coaguler.

｜墻, *kiĕt siông*, construire un mur en briques ou en pierres.

你做個屋係舂得子｜得子, *gnî tsó ké· voŭc hé· tchoūng tĕt tzè kiĕt tĕt tzè ?* la maison que tu fais est-elle en terre foulée ou en briques ?

｜親, *kiĕt ts'īn*, contracter une alliance par le mariage.

｜朋友, *kiĕt p'oûng yoū*, lier amitié.

｜約櫃, *kiĕt yŏc k'ouí*, arche d'alliance.

｜案, *kiĕt ón*, terminer un procès, porter une sentence définitive.

事還唔曾了｜, *sé hân mĝ ts'ĕn liaò kiĕt*, l'affaire n'est pas encore terminée.

｜菓, ｜子, *kiĕt kouò, kiĕt tzè*, produire des fruits, des graines.

｜實, *kiĕt chĭt*, ferme, solide, durable.

屋做得｜實, *voŭc tsó tĕt kiĕt chĭt*, la maison a été faite solidement.

｜羮, *kiĕt kāng*, faire de la colle de farine.

做豆腐愛鹽水㖸｜得成, *tsó t'eoú foú oí yâm chouì tsáng kiĕt tĕt châng*, il faut de la présure pour faire coaguler le *t'eoú foú*.

潔 *Kiĕt*. Pur, propre.

｜淨, *kiĕt ts'iáng*, même sens.

貞｜, *tchīn kiĕt*, pureté, virginité.

K'IÊT

缺 *K'iĕt*. Manque, omission, brèche.

| **本分**, *k'iĕt poùn foún*, manquer à son devoir.

| **少經文**, *k'iĕt chaò kīn voún*, avoir omis des prières.

一吊錢 | 少 (ou | **欠**) **三十個**, *ŷt tiaó ts'iĕn k'iĕt chaò* (ou *k'iám*) *sām chĭp ké*, il manque 30 sapeques à la ligature.

| **牙齒**, *k'iĕt ngâ tchè*, qui a perdu ses dents.

| **嘴**, *k'iĕt tchoí*, homme qui a un bec-de-lièvre.

碗公打一個 |, *vouòn koūng tà ŷt ké k'iĕt*, le bol est ébréché.

KĪM

金 *Kīm*. Or, doré.

| **子打個**, *kīm tzè tà ké*, fait en or.

| **沙**, *kīm sā*, sable aurifère.

| **薄**, *kīm p'ŏc*, or en feuilles.

| **針**, *kīm tchīm*, espèce de lis jaune comestible.

| **銀花**, *kīm nioûn fā*, chèvre-feuille.

| **鋼石**, *kīm kōng chăc*, diamant.

KĪM

(*Voir aussi les mots KIN*)

K'ĪM

欽 *K'īm*. Honorer, respecter.

| **命**, *k'īm mín*, mandat impérial.

| **崇天主萬有之上**, *kīm ts'oúng t'iēn tchoù ván yoū tjē chóng*, honorer Dieu par-dessus toutes choses.

| **差**, *k'īm ts'aī*, commissaire impérial.

| **使**, *k'īm sè*, ambassadeur.

衾 *K'īm*. **衣** |, *ȳ k'īm*, habits dont on revêt les cadavres.

衣 | 棺槨, *ȳ k'īm kouōn kôc*, les habits et le cercueil, (tout ce qu'il faut pour la sépulture).

衿 *K'īm*. Le devant d'un habit.

大 |, *t'aí k'īm*, habit qui se boutonne par le côté.

小 |, *siaò k'īm*, habit qui se boutonne sur le devant.

矜 *K'īm*. | **憐**, *k'īm lîn*, avoir pitié.

哀 |, *oī k'īm*, faire l'aumône, aumône.

K'ÎM

禽 *K'îm*. Nom générique des oiseaux.

| **獸**, *k'îm tch'oú*, les animaux volatiles et quadrupèdes.

琴 *K'îm*. Instrument de musique, harpe.

風 |, *foūng k'îm*, harmonium, accordéon.

自彈 |, *tsé t'ân k'îm*, boîte à musique.

KÌM

錦 *Kìm.* Tissu de soie à fleurs de différentes couleurs.

｜花, *kìm fā*, broder des fleurs.

KÍM

禁 *Kím.* Défendre, prohiber.

食｜猪肉, *chı̆t kím tchoū nioûc*, manger de la viande défendue.

｜屠, *kím t'oû*, abstinence de viande, commandée dans un malheur public.

K'ÎM

擒 *K'îm* (pour *k'îm*). Prendre d'assaut, saisir, appuyer, peser sur, empressé, presser.

洋狗曉得｜鳥子, *yông keoù hiaò tĕt k'îm tiaō tzè*, les chiens européens savent happer les oiseaux.

｜重重來, *k'îm tch'oūng tch'oūng loî*, appuie fortement.

｜等裡上唔起, *k'îm tèn lî hóng mĝ hì*, il pèse sur moi, je ne puis me relever.

咁｜, *àn k'îm*, se dit de quelqu'un qui s'acharne au travail.

打｜頭, *tà k'îm t'eoû*, faire la culbute.

KĪN

根 *Kīn* (*kēn*). Racine.

樹｜, 草｜, *choú kīn, ts'aò kīn*, racine d'arbre, d'herbe.

樹倒吊裡還愛䀠｜頭, *choú taò p'ĕt lî hân oí koì kīn t'eoû*, l'arbre est abattu, il reste à creuser les racines.

巾 *Kīn.* **手｜**, *choù kīn*, mouchoir, serviette.

今 *Kīn.* maintenant.

｜日, *kīn gnı̆t*, aujourd'hui.

｜朝, *kīn tchaō*, ce matin.

｜年, *kīn niân*, cette année.

｜早晨, *kīn tsaò chîn*, ce matin.

｜晡夜, *kīn poū yá*, ce soir.

如｜, *ŷ kīn*, présentement.

從｜ (v. **自｜**) **以後**, *ts'ioùng kīn* (*v. tsé kīn*) *ȳ heoú*, désormais.

斤 *Kīn.* Livre, mesure de poids.

十六兩爲一｜, *chı̆p lioûc leōng vî ŷt kīn*, 16 onces font une livre.

｜半, *kīn pán*, une livre et demie.

半｜, *pán kīn*, une demi-livre.

四｜少兩兩, *sí kīn chaò leòng leōng*, quatre livres moins deux onces.

打｜頭 (v. **擒頭**), *tà kīn t'eoû* (*v. k'îm t'eoû*), faire la culbute.

京 *Kīn.* Capitale, résidence du gouvernement.

北｜, 南｜, *pĕt kīn, nâm kīn*, Pékin (la cour du Nord), Nankin (la cour du Sud).

筋 *Kīn.* Nerfs.

一身｜骨作痛, *ŷt chīn kīn koŭt tsōc t'oúng*, tout le corps me fait mal.

血｜, *hiĕt kīn*, artères, veines.

手掌個|紋, *choù tchòng ké· kīn voûn*, les linéaments de la main.

肩 *Kīn* (ou *kiān*). |頭, |膀, *kīn t'eoû v. kīn pòng*, épaule. (*Voyez kiān*).

經 *Kīn*. Prière, livres sacrés, règle constante.

五|, *ng̀ kīn*, les cinq livres canoniques des Chinois, qui sont: 易|, 詩|, 書|, 禮記, 春秋, *ý kīn, chē kīn, choū kīn, lī kí, tch'oūn ts'ioū*.

|書, |本, *kīn choū, kīn poùn*, livre de prière.

念|, *niám kīn*, prier, réciter des prières.

題|, *t'ì kīn*, entonner les prières.

唔正|, *mĝ tchín kīn*, faux, erroné, de mauvais aloi.

|期, *kīn k'ì*, les règles des femmes.

K'ĪN

卿 *K'īn*. Appellatif des grands mandarins.

三品以上爲|, *sām p'ìn ỳ chóng vì k'īn*, au-dessus du troisième grade, les mandarins ont le titre de *k'īn*.

輕 *K'īn*. Mépriser, faire affront.

|慢人, *k'īn mán gnîn*, faire affront à quelqu'un.

兢 *K'īn*. Tremblant, craintif.

戰戰||, *tchán tchán k'īn k'īn*, trembler de peur (plus vulgairement on dit *t'án t'án tchoūn*).

脛 *K'īn*. Estomac des oiseaux.

雞|肝我唔愛, *kē· k'īn kōn ngaî mĝ oí*, je ne veux pas de l'estomac et du foie de la poule.

KÌN

緊 *Kìn*. Pressé. Se joint à beaucoup de mots avec l'idée d'effort, d'insistance .

要|, *yaó kìn*, nécessaire, urgent.

|急, *kìn kīp*, urgent.

咁|做那個, *àn kìn tsó mâc ké·?* pourquoi es-tu si pressé?

|做, |話, |賴人, *kìn tsó, kìn vá, kìn laí gnîn*, travailler sans relâche, parler sans cesser, implorer avec insistance.

黏|, *niâm kìn*, avec, adhérer à.

黏|佢行, *niâm kìn kì háng*, marcher à côté de lui.

石頭夾|佢脚, *chăc t'eoû kiăp kìn kiă kiôc*, son pied est resté pris entre deux pierres.

景 *Kìn*. Situation, état, paysage, panorama.

光|, *kouōng kìn*, état, disposition.

|緻, *kìn tjé*, beau paysage, beau site.

儆 *Kìn*. Exciter à agir.

|戒人, *kìn kiaí gnîn*, avertir quelqu'un de se tenir en garde contre.

|醒人, *kìn siàng gnîn*, réveiller quelqu'un de sa torpeur, exciter l'attention, exciter à agir.

KÍN

敬 *Kín*. Respecter, adorer, vénérer.

孝 | 父母, *haó kín foú moū*, respecter ses parents.

恭 | 天主, *kioūng kín t'iēn tchoù*, honorer Dieu.

| 神, *kín chîn*, vénérer les esprits.

竟 *Kín*. 究 |, 畢 |, *kioú kín*, *pît kín*, enfin.

究 | 我錢有㨃麼㨃, *kioú kín ngā ts'iên yoū kiàm mô kiàm?* décidément, me payeras-tu oui ou non?

境 *Kín*. Frontières, pays.

| 界, *kín kiaí*, même sens.

出 |, *tch'oût kín*, sortir des limites d'une juridiction.

勁 *Kín*. Force, se servir de ses forces.

有 | 氣, *yoū kín hí*, il a de la force.

使 |, 趱 |, *sè kín*, *tsán kín*, déployer ses forces, s'efforcer.

K'ÍN

慶 *K'ín*. Feliciter, fêter, célébrer.

| 賀人, *k'ín fó gnîn*, féliciter, fêter quelqu'un.

喜 |, *hì k'ín*, fête, féliciter.

尊家咁閙熱有那個喜 | 事麼? *tsoūn kā àn náo gnĕt, yoū mâc ké hì k'ín sé mô?* votre maison est bien animée, y a-t-il une fête?

K'IÔ

茄 *K'iô*. Aubergine. (On dit aussi *tiaó ts'oí*).

跏 *K'iô*. Paralytique, perclu des jambes.

KIÔC

脚 *Kiôc*. Pied, patte, résidu, lie.

一隻 |, *ŷt tchâc kiôc*, un pied.

雙 |, *soūng kiôc*, les deux pieds.

| 板, | 䏲, *kiôc pàn*, *kiôc tsāng*, la plante des pieds, le talon.

| 跡, *kiôc tsiâc*, trace du pied, vestige.

墻 | 下放等來. *siông kiôc hā fóng tèn loî*, pose-le au pied du mur.

三 | 凳, *sām kiôc tén*, trépied.

一步 |, *ŷt p'oú kiôc*, un pas.

你合 | 步唔倒, *gnî hăp kiôc p'oú mĝ taò*, tu ne vas pas au pas.

打赤 |, *tà tch'âc kiôc*, aller les pieds nus.

| 盆, *kiôc p'oûn*, baquet pour se laver les pieds.

油 |, 酒 |, *yoû kiôc*, *tsioù kiôc*, résidu d'huile, lie de vin.

| 子, *kiôc tzè*, portefaix, courrier.

算 | 錢, *són kiôc ts'iên*, payer le port.

| 頭, *kiôc t'eoû*, pioche.

K'IÔC

却 *K'iôc*. Rejeter, dédaigner.

推 |, *tch'oui k'iôc*, ne pas accéder à une demande.

失 |, *chît k'iôc*, oublier.

K'IOÍ

騎 *K'ioí* ou *k'oí*. Fatigué, las.

行 | , 攰 | , *hâng k'ioí, k'aī k'ioí,* fatigué d'avoir marché, d'avoir porté.

唔知 | , *mĝ tī k'ioí,* ne pas sentir la fatigue.

KIŌNG

薑 *Kiōng*. Gingembre.

| 麻, *kiōng mậ,* gingembre.

疆 *Kiōng*. | 界, *kiōng kiaí,* limites, confins.

剛 *Kiōng* (pour *kōng*). Juste, à l'instant.

| | 啱到, *kiōng kiōng* (ailleurs *kōn kōn*) *ts'áng taó,* je ne fais que d'arriver.

| | 八個, *kiōng kiōng pât ké·,* tout juste huit.

K'IŌNG

腔 *K'iōng*. Creux, son de voix.

眼珠 | , *niàn tchoū k'iōng,* l'orbite, creux de l'œil.

各地方口 | 唔同, *kôc t'í fōng k'eoù k'iōng mĝ t'oûng,* l'accent diffère dans chaque pays.

框 *K'iōng*. Cadre, monture.

門 | , *moûn k'iōng,* cadre, monture d'une porte.

眼鏡 | , *niàn kiáng k'iōng,* monture d'une lunette.

聖像 | , *chín sióng k'iōng,* cadre d'une image.

K'IÔNG

強 *K'iông*. Violent, fort.

| 房, 弱房, *k'iông fông, niŏc fông,* branche (d'une famille) forte (si elle a plus d'argent ou plus de personnel), branche faible (par opposition à branche forte).

| 水, *k'iông chouì,* (plus vulg. *kiòng chouì*), acide, eau-forte.

K'IOŪ

臼 *K'ioū*. Mortier.

碓 | , *toí k'ioū,* mortier à piler.

舂 | , *tchoūng k'ioū,* petit mortier de pharmacien.

新 | , *sīm* (pour *sīn*) *k'ioū,* bru. Voir *sīn*.

坵 *K'ioū*. Particule numérale des rizières.

我耕三 | 田, *ngaî kāng sām k'ioū t'iên,* je cultive trois rizières.

舅 *K'ioū*. Oncle maternel.

阿 | , *a k'ioū,* mon oncle.

| 姆, *k'ioū mē·,* femme de l'oncle maternel.

K'IOÛ

求 *K'ioû*. Demander, prier.

| 天主個仁慈, *k'ioû t'iēn tchoù ké· ŷn tsê,* implorer la miséricorde de Dieu.

| 神父寬免, *k'ioû chîn foú k'ōn mēn,* demander une dispense au Père.

| 唔倒, *k'ioû mĝ taò,* ne pouvoir obtenir ce que l'on demande.

毬 *K'ioû.* Balle à jouer, petite sphère.

打 | , *tà k'ioû,* jouer à la balle.

球 *K'ioû.* 地 | , *t'í k'ioû,* globe terrestre.

KIOÙ

九 *Kioù.* Neuf.

第 | 個, *t'í kioù ké·,* le neuvième.

| 歸 算, *kioù kouī són,* table de Pythagore.

久 *Kioù.* Longtemps.

好 | , *haò kioù,* très longtemps.

打 一 個 長 | 個 主 意, *tà ŷt ké· tch'ōng kioù ké· tchoù ý,* prendre une résolution durable.

不 | 會 來, *poût kioù voé· loî,* il viendra sous peu.

| 不 | , *kioù poût kioù,* de temps en temps.

| 見, *kioù kián,* il y a longtemps que nous ne nous sommes vus.

韮 *Kioù.* | 菜, *kioù ts'oí,* ciboulette.

KIOÚ

救 *Kioú.* Sauver, secourir, mettre un terme à un mal.

| 世 主, *kioú ché tchoù,* le Sauveur du monde.

| 命, *kioú miáng,* sauver la vie à quelqu'un.

| 贖, *kioú choŭc,* racheter, sauver.

两 個 人 相 打 麼 人 去 | , *leòng ké· gnîn siōng tà mô gnîn hí kioú,* tous les deux se battent et personne ne va les séparer.

| 火, *kioú fò,* éteindre un incendie.

佢 病 麼 | , *kiā p'iáng mô kioú,* sa maladie est sans remède.

究 *Kioú.* Examiner, chercher, enfin.

嚴 | , *niâm kioú,* punir sevèrement.

講 | , *kòng kioú,* approfondir et expliquer une question.

咁 講 | , *àn kòng kioú,* quelle élégance! quel luxe!

| 竟, *kioú kín,* enfin, décidément.

| 竟 樣 班, *kioú kín nióng pān,* en fin de compte, comment est-ce ?

柩 *Kioú.* Cercueil contenant le cadavre.

棺 | , *kouōn kioú,* même sens.

K'IOÚ

舊 *K'ioú.* Vieux, ancien.

| 年, *k'ioú niân,* l'an passé.

| 衫, | 屋, | 鞋, *k'ioú sām, k'ioú voŭc, k'ioú haî,* vieux habits, vieille maison, vieux souliers.

| 帛 裡, *k'ioú p'ĕt lî,* c'est vieux, c'est usé.

依 | , *ŷ k'ioú,* comme auparavant.

KIOŬC

逐 *Kioŭc (tch'oŭc).* Pourchasser, s'empresser pour arriver à un but.

| 走 佢 (ou | 佢 走), *kioŭc tseoù kî*

(ou kioŭc kî tseoù), chasse-le, mets-le à la porte.

| 轉來, *kioŭc tchòn loî*, rappeler, rappelle-le.

| 倒陣來, *kioŭc taò tch'ín loî*, rattraper les compagnons.

| 水, *kioûc chouì*, conduire l'eau, se dit des siphons, des jets d'eau, etc.

K'IOŬC.

局 *K'ioŭc*. Comité, bureau d'affaires publiques, mairie ; prendre au piège, retenir, contraindre.

| 官, *k'ioŭc kouōn*, maire.

當 | 紳, *tōng k'ioŭc chīn*, les notables qui s'occupent ordinairement des affaires.

鹽 |, *yâm k'ioŭc*, régie, douane du sel.

洋務 |, *yông voú k'ioŭc*, tribunal qui s'occupe des affaires des Européens.

| 烏蠅, *k'ioŭc voū ŷn*, prendre les mouches au piège.

老鼠 |, *laò tch'où k'ioŭc*, ratière.

我間貯 | 等裡樣得慣, *ngaî kiān toù k'ioŭc tèn-ê' nióng têt kouán?* contraint de rester dans ma chambre, comment puis-je m'y habituer ?

K'IOÛC

曲 *K'ioûc*. Chanson.

唱 |, *tch'óng k'ioûc*, chanter des airs.

菊 *K'ioûc*. Marguerite.

| 花, *k'ioûc fā*, toutes les fleurs du genre marguerite, chrysanthème, zinnia, etc.

麯 *K'ioûc*. Espèce de riz rouge qui, fermenté, sert à donner de la couleur au vin de 糯米, *nó mì*.

KIOŪN

君 *Kioūn*. Roi, prince, chef, le plus important.

國 |, | 王, *kouĕt kioūn, kioūn vông*, chef d'un Etat, souverain.

先到爲 | 後到爲臣, *siēn taó vî kioūn heoú taó vî chîn*, celui qui arrive le premier est le roi, celui qui arrive après est son sujet.

夫 |, 細 |, *foū kioūn, sé' kioūn*, mon mari, ma femme.

同 | 一夜話勝讀十年書, *t'oûng kioūn ŷt yá fá chín t'oŭc chĭp niân choū*, passer une nuit d'entretien avec un sage vaut mieux que dix ans d'étude (*proverbe*).

唐人食飯爲 |, *t'ông gnîn chĭt fán vî kioūn*, le riz est le principal aliment des Chinois.

我早晨頭加非爲 |, *ngaî tsaò chîn t'eoû kā fī vî kioūn*, le café est mon principal aliment du matin.

軍 *Kioūn*. Armée, militaire.

| 器, *kioūn hí*, équipement militaire, engins de guerre.

將 |, *tsiōng kioūn*, maréchal. (Il y en a 4 dans toute la Chine).

充 |, *tch'oūng kioūn*, condamner ou être condamné à un exil et à un service gratuit au-delà des frontières des dix-huit provinces.

均 *Kioūn*. Égaliser, proportionner.

三個人 | 分, *sām ké· gnîn kioūn foūn*, divisons également en trois parts.

愛 | 分一半, *oí kioūn foūn ȳt pán*, il faut diviser également en deux parts.

K'IOÛN

芹 *K'ioûn*. | 菜, *k'ioûn ts'oí*, céleri.

菌 *K'ioûn*. Champignon.

羣 *K'ioûn*. Se grouper, multitude, foule, troupeau.

| 湫, *k'ioûn ts'ioū*, se grouper.

Voir 陣 *tch'ín*.

裙 *K'ioûn*. Habit de femme, tablier de cuisine.

圍身 |, *vî chīn k'ioûn*, tablier.

勤 *K'ioûn*. Diligent.

| 擒, *k'ioûn k'îm*, actif, diligent.

殷 | 人, *ȳn k'ioûn gnîn*, servir avec empressement, être aux petits soins.

| 勞, | 苦, | 儉, *k'ioûn laô, k'ioûn k'où, k'ioûn k'iám*, faire diligence, se donner de la peine.

KIOÙN

謹 *Kioùn*. Attentif, soigneux.

愛 | 愼, *oí kioùn chìm*, il faut être attentif, sur ses gardes.

| 等來, *kioùn tèn loî*, fais attention.

僅 *Kioùn*. Juste ce qu'il faut.

| | 彀, *kioùn kioùn keoú*, cela suffit juste.

| 可彀用, *kioùn k'ò keoú yoúng*, cela suffit pour mon usage.

K'IOÚN

近 *K'ioún*. Près, approcher.

遠 |, *yàn k'ioún*, distance.

我唔知遠 |, *ngaî mĝ tī yàn k'ioún*, je ne sais pas si c'est loin ou près, c.-à-d. la distance.

| 時, *k'ioún chê*, récemment.

| 山, | 水, *k'ioún sān, k'ioún choùi*, près des montagnes, près des eaux.

KIOŪNG

弓 *Kioūng*. Arc, courbé en forme d'arc.

| 弦, *kioūng hiên*, la corde de l'arc.

挷 |, 開 |, *pāng kioūng, k'oī kioūng*, bander un arc.

背 | |, *poé· kioūng kioūng*, se dit de celui qui a le dos voûté.

天 |, *t'iēn kioūng*, arc-en-ciel.

宮 *Kioūng*. Pagode, palais.

天后 |, *t'iēn heoú kioūng*, pagode de la reine du ciel.

皇 |, *fông kioūng*, le palais de l'Empereur.

恭 *Kioūng*. Respecter, révérer.

丨敬天主, *kioūng kín t'iēn tchoù*, vénérer Dieu.

丨賀人, *kioūng fó gnîn*, honorer quelqu'un par des présents.

丨喜, *kioūng hì*, saluer, salut! bonjour!

出丨, *tch'oût kioūng*, aller à la selle.

供 *Kioūng*. Avouer de sa propre bouche.

官府打佢唔丨, *kouōn foù tà kî mĝ kioūng*, le mandarin a beau le frapper, il n'avoue pas.

供 *Kioūng*. Nourrir, donner à manger.

丨猪, 丨牛, 丨馬, *kioūng tchoū, kioūng nioû, kioūng mā*, donner à manger au porc, au buffle, au cheval.

丨乳, *kioūng nén*, allaiter.

狗媽丨子, *keoù mâ kioūng tzè*, la chienne allaite ses petits.

我丨裡你十年, *ngaî kioūng lî gnî chĭp niân*, je t'ai nourri pendant dix ans.

丨應人, *kioūng ýn gnîn*, pourvoir à la nourriture de quelqu'un.

K'IOÛNG

窮 *K'ioûng*. Pauvre, terme, sans limites.

貧丨人, *p'în k'ioûng gnîn*, pauvre.

丨苦, *k'ioûng k'où*, misérable, très pauvre.

無丨, *voû k'ioûng*, sans limites, infini.

世界丨盡, *ché kiaí k'ioûng ts'ín*, la fin du monde.

到東石神父個裡山丨水盡, *taó toūng chăc chîn foú ké· lî sān k'ioûng choùi ts'ín*, arrivé à Toung chac où est le missionnaire (*litt.*) on est au bout des montagnes et des sources (au bout du monde).

KIOÙNG

拱 *Kioùng*. Saluer en joignant les mains convexes. Bombé, en arc, voûté.

丨手, *kioùng choù*, joindre les mains.

丨手作揖, *kioùng choù tsôc ŷp*, joindre les mains pour saluer.

丨橋, *kioùng k'iâo*, pont arqué.

橋愛丨走來過主固, *k'iaó oí kioùng hì loî kouó tchoù koú*, il faut faire le pont en voûte c'est plus solide.

恐 *K'ioùng*. Craindre, de peur que, peut-être.

丨怕係, *k'ioùng p'á hé·*, je pense que oui.

丨怕噲死, *k'ioùng p'á voé· sì*, il est à craindre qu'il ne meure.

KIOÚNG

拱 *Kioúng*. Engendrer, mettre au monde.

丨一個賴子 *kioúng ŷt ké· laí tzè*, mettre un fils au monde.

丨子, *kioúng tzè*, faire des petits.

唔知那個丨個, *mĝ tī mâc ké· kioúng ké·*! je ne sais pas qui est-ce qui t'a engendré (imprécation)!

K'IOÚNG

共 *K'ioúng*. Ensemble, avec, la somme totale.

三位丨一個天主, *sām ví k'ioúng ȳt ké· t'iēn tchoù*, les 3 Personnes ne font qu'un Dieu.

丨三百錢, *k'ioúng sām pâc ts'iēn*, au total, 300 sapèques.

丨下食飯, *k'ioúng há chĭt fán*, dîner ensemble.

統丨, 總丨, *t'oùng k'ioúng, tsoùng k'ioúng*, somme totale, le tout ensemble.

K'IOÛT

屈 *K'ioût*. Opprimer.

冤丨好人, *yān k'ioût haò gnîn*, opprimer les braves gens.

受丨, *choú k'ioût*, être victime d'une injustice.

委丨, *vī k'ioût*, être comme courbé et accablé sous un poids; contrainte, malaise, oppression.

曲 *K'ioût*. Plié, tortueux.

彎彎丨丨個路, *vān vān k'ioût k'ioût ké· loú*, route sinueuse.

拗丨, *aò k'ioût*, tordre.

K'ĬP

及 *K'ĭp*. Et, parvenir.

千丨千丨, *ts'iēn k'ĭp ts'iēn k'ĭp*, va vite vite.

赴得丨, *foú têt k'ĭp*, arriver à temps.

赴不丨, *foú poût k'ĭp*, ne pouvoir arriver à temps, c'est trop tard.

大過不丨, *t'aí kouó poût k'ĭp*, ne pas faire les choses comme les autres.

KÎP

給 *Kîp*. Donner, livrer.

丨酒錢, *kîp tsioù ts'iēn*, donner un pourboire.

急 *Kîp*. Pressé, prompt, réduit aux abois.

性丨, *sín kîp*, vif de caractère.

丨病, *kîp p'iáng*, maladie subite.

丨事, *kîp sé*, affaire pressante.

K'ĬT

極 *K'ĭt*. Marque du superlatif, le point le plus élevé.

丨多, 丨好, *k'ĭt tō, k'ĭt haò*, excessivement nombreux, très bien.

北丨 南丨, *pêt k'ĭt, nâm k'ĭt*, le pôle boréal, le pôle austral.

大丨, *t'aí k'ĭt*, le principe de toutes choses, la loi qui régit tous les êtres.

KÎT

吉 *Kît*. Heureux, de bon augure.

大丨利市, *t'aí kît lí ché*, bon présage, bon augure.

丨祥, *kît siông*, félicité.

納丨, *năp kît*, présenter les 八字 *pât sé* huit lettres qui désignent l'année, le mois, le jour et l'heure de la naissance d'un jeune homme, afin que les comparant avec les *pât sé* de la jeune fille qu'il recherche en mariage, on examine si leur union sera heureuse.

橘 *Kît*. Espèce d'orange.

14

金丨, *kīm kīt*, espèce d'orange.

丨餅, *kīt piàng*, orange confite.

KŌ

哥 *Kō*. Frère aîné, cousin paternel.

大丨, *t'aí kō*, le premier des frères aînés.

二丨, 三丨, *gní kō, sām kō*, le deuxième, le troisième des frères aînés, etc.

阿丨, *a kō*, mon frère. Cette expression sert aussi à interpeller les étrangers de même âge, ou à peu près, que soi. S'ils sont plus âgés on dit: 老兄 *laò hioūng*, ou 大伯 *t'aí pâc*.

Si celui qui est interpellé est connu, on ajoute *kō* à son nom: 天祿丨, *T'iēn loûc kō*, 捷二丨, *Ts'iâp gní kō*.

On trouve encore ce mot après le nom de certains animaux: 猴丨, *heoû kō*, le singe, 蛇丨, *châ kō*, le serpent.

歌 *Kō*. Chant, chanson.

唱丨, *tch'óng kō*, chanter.

聖誕丨, *chín tán kō*, chant de Noël.

唱山丨, *tch'óng sān kō*, chanter des airs de montagnes. (Chansons légères).

K'Ō

戈 *K'ō*. Lance.

干丨, *kōn k'ō*, le bouclier et la lance, les armes, la guerre.

科 *K'ō*. Degré dans les lettres.

赴丨, *foú k'ō*, aller aux examens supérieurs.

醫丨, *ȳ k'ō*, art de la médecine.

外丨, *ngoé' k'ō*, médecin qui s'occupe des maladies de peau, des plaies, fractures, etc.

內丨, *nouí k'ō*, médecin qui s'occupe des maladies internes.

銀丨, *nioûn k'ō*, ou 銀鍋子, *nioûn vŏc tzè*, creuset à éprouver les métaux.

K'Ò

可 *K'ò*. Convenir, pouvoir, permettre.

丨以, *k'ò ȳ*, cela peut aller, possible, permis, passable.

丨憐, *k'ò lîn*, digne de pitié.

丨愛, *k'ò oí*, aimable.

K'Ó

課 *K'ó*. Travail, tâche, devoir.

日丨, *gnĭt k'ó*, devoir journalier.

經丨, *kīn k'ó*, prières réglementaires.

國丨, *kouêt k'ó*, revenus de l'état, impôts.

K'ŎC

磕 *K'ŏc*. Frapper, heurter.

丨頭, *k'ŏc t'eoû*, grande salutation qui se fait en se mettant à genoux et en baissant la tête jusqu'à terre.

入間門框丨倒我, *gnĭp kiān moûn k'iōng k'ŏc taò ngaî*, en entrant dans ma chambre je me suis heurté à la porte.

丨烟屎, *k'ŏc yān chè*, frapper sur un corps dur avec une pipe pour en faire tomber la cendre.

KÔC

角 *Kôc.* Corne, cornet, coin, angle.

牛 |, 羊 |, *nioû kôc, yông kôc,* corne de buffle (ou bœuf), de chèvre,

吹 |, *tch'oī kôc,* sonner du cornet.

壁 |, *piâc kôc,* coin de mur.

口 |, *k'eoù kôc,* se quereller.

豆 |, *t'eoú kôc,* espèce de haricot.

| 菜, *kôc ts'oí,* épinards.

三 | 圈, *sām kôc k'iān,* triangle.

桷 *Kôc.* Lattes pour supporter les tuiles du toit.

各 *Kôc.* Chaque, chacun.

| 人 | 意, *kôc gnîn kôc ý,* chacun ses idées, autant d'hommes autant d'opinions.

| 樣 事, *kôc yóng sé,* c'est un autre genre d'affaire, une autre affaire.

覺 *Kôc.* Remarquer, s'apercevoir.

耳 | | 見 聽, *gnì kôc kôc gnî t'āng,* prêter une oreille attentive.

| 魂, *kôc foûn,* âme sensitive.

慌 |, *fōng kôc,* oublier.

不 |, *poût kôc,* sans s'en apercevoir, instinctivement.

閣 *Kôc.* Conseil impérial, tour, belvédère.

內 |, *nouí kôc,* conseil privé de l'empereur.

文 淵 閣, *voûn yān kôc,* le palais du 正 宰 相, *tchín tsaì sióng,* premier ministre.

體 仁 |, *t'ì ŷn kôc,* le palais du 副 宰 相, *foú tsaì sióng,* ministre en second.

殿 |, *t'ién kôc,* palais des ministres tartares.

| 下, *kôc há,* votre seigneurie, vous, Monsieur (politesse).

樓 |, *leoû kôc,* tour, belvédère.

躭 | (ou 擱) *tām kôc,* différer, retarder, empêcher. *(Voir* 躭 *tām.)*

K'ÔC

確 *K'ôc.* Certain, sûr.

| 係, ou (的 | 係), *k'ôc hé·,* (ou *tît k'ôc hé·,* c'est certain, en effet.

我 聽 得 詳 |, *ngaî t'āng têt siông k'ôc,* j'ai entendu clairement.

殼 *K'ôc* (ou *hôc*). Écorce, enveloppe. *(Voyez h'ôc.)*

KOĪ

該 *Koī.* Devoir, falloir.

| 罰 個, *koī fât ké·,* digne de châtiment.

| 死, *koī sì,* digne de mort.

| 當, *koī tōng,* cela doit être, cela devait arriver.

應 |, *ýn koī,* il y a obligation.

頦 *Koī.* Gésier des oiseaux.

雞 |, *kē· koī,* gésier de la poule.

K'OĪ

開 *K'oī.* Ouvrir, commencer, entreprendre, payer.

打 | 門, *tà k'oī moûn*, (ou 門打 | 來, *moûn tà k'oī loî*), ouvre la porte.

揭 |, *yât k'oī*, découvrir, déboucher.

分 |, *poūn k'oī*, diviser.

两兄弟分 |, *leòng hioūng t'í poūn k'oī*, les deux frères ont fait la division des biens, se sont séparés.

| 田, *k'oī t'iên*, défricher un terrain pour en faire une rizière.

| 山, *k'oī sān*, commencer l'exploitation d'une forêt.

| 齋, *k'oī tsaī*, fin du Carême.

| 船, *k'oī chôn*, démarrer.

| 茶錢, *k'oī ts'â ts'iên*, payer son écot.

| 工錢, *k'oī koūng ts'iên*, payer la main-d'œuvre.

| 單, *k'oī tān*, écrire un billet, une liste.

KOÌ

改 *Koì*. Changer, corriger.

| 變, *koì pién*, changer en bien ou en mal.

| 主意, *koì tchoù ý*, changer d'avis.

| 日, *koì gnĭt*, remettre à un autre jour.

| 地, *koì t'í*, changer un tombeau de place.

| 過, *koì kouó*, se corriger de ses défauts.

定 |, *t'ín koì*, prendre la résolution de se corriger.

| 文章, *koì voûn tchōng*, corriger une composition littéraire.

畡 *Koì*. Piocher, creuser.

| 泥, *koì naî*, piocher la terre.

| 一個湖, *koì ŷt ké· foû*, creuser un trou.

地堰我 | 倒一缸銀, *t'í lăc ngaì koì taò ŷt kōng nioûn*, en piochant mon terrain, j'ai trouvé un vase plein de piastres.

K'OÌ

暨 *K'oì*. Tout, et.

一 | 都係, *ŷt k'oì toū ké·*, tout cela en est.

一 | 邪妄之事, *ŷt k'oì siâ vòng tjē sé*, toutes les superstitions.

凡主日 | 諸瞻禮之日, *fâm tchoū gnĭt k'oì tchoū tchām lī tjē gnĭt*, chaque Dimanche et tous les jours de fête... (commandements de l'Eglise).

概 *K'oì*. En général.

大 | 幾多錢, *t'aí k'oì kì tō ts'iên ?* environ, combien de sapèques ?

KOÍ

蓋 *Koí*. Couvrir, couvercle, surpasser.

| 被, *koí p'ī*, couverture, se couvrir d'une couverture.

| 瓦, *koí ngà*, mettre les tuiles, couvrir de tuiles.

鍋 |, *vŏc koí*, le couvercle de la marmite.

鋪 |, *p'oū koí*, literie de voyage.

你帶有鋪 | 麼, *gnì taí yoū p'oū koí mô, ?* as-tu apporté ta literie ?

遮 |, *tchā koí*, protéger, aider.

望神父遮 | 阿子, *móng chîn foû tchā koí á tzè*, désirer l'aide du Père.

天主道理｜天下好, *t'iēn tchoū t'aó lī koí t'iēn há haò*, la doctrine chrétienne surpasse toutes les autres.

那人｜縣有錢, *màn gnîn koí yán yoū ts'iên, ?* quel est le plus riche de la sous-préfecture ?

KŌN

(*Voir aussi les mots KOUN*)

干 *Kōn*. Concerner, relation.

有相｜, 麼相｜, *yoū siōng kōn, mô siōng kōn*, il y a conséquence, intérêt, il n'y a pas de conséquence, intérêt.

｜你那個事, *kōn gnî mâc ké· sé, ?* en quoi cela te regarde-t-il ?

唔｜你事, *mĝ kōn gnî sé*, ça ne te regarde pas.

麼｜碍, *mô kōn ngoé·*, il n'y a pas d'empèchement.

我麼｜涉, *ngaî mô kōn chăp*, cela ne me concerne pas.

一｜人証提齊來, *ŷt kōn gnîn tchín t'î tsê· loî*, appeler tous les témoins au jugement.

竿 *Kōn*. Tige de bambou.

担｜, *tám kōn*, bâton de bambou dont on se sert pour porter les fardeaux.

釣｜, *tiaó kōn*, ligne de pêcheur.

肝 *Kōn*. Foie.

猪｜, *tchoū kōn*, foie de porc.

杆 *Kōn*. Perche, bâton en bois.

桅｜, *mî kōn*, mât de barque; mât d'honneur.

欄｜, *lân kōn*, balustrade, balcon, garde-fou ; galon d'habit.

乾 *Kōn*. Desséché, sec.

猪肉｜, 牛肉｜, *tchoū nioŭc kōn, nioû nioŭc kōn*, viande de porc ou de bœuf, salée et desséchée.

晒｜, *saí kōn*, dessécher au soleil.

｜柴好燒, *kōn ts'iaô haò chaō*, le bois sec est bon à brûler.

K'ŌN

寬 *K'ōn*. Large (au pr. et au fig).

｜闊, *k'ōn fât*, large, ample, vaste.

｜恕人, *k'ōn choú gnîn*, pardonner à quelqu'un.

｜免, *k'ōn mēn*, dispenser.

KÒN

稈 *Kòn*. Paille de riz ou de blé.

一揸｜, *ŷt tsā kòn*, une poignée de paille.

趕 *Kòn*. A temps, sans retard, se presser, chasser, profiter de l'occasion.

｜快來, *kòn k'ouaí loî*, presse-toi.

愛｜倒大瞻禮, *oí kòn taò t'aí tchām lī*, il faut presser (le travail) pour achever avant la grande fête.

｜醫生, *kòn ȳ sēn*, aller chercher le médecin.

｜佢走, *kòn kî tseoù*, fais-le sortir d'ici, mets-le à la porte.

｜神父在裡子好辦神工, *kòn chîn foú t'oī ỳ tzè haò p'án chîn koūng*, profiter de la présence du Père pour e confesser.

KÓN

幹 *Kón*. Affaire, agir.

有那貴｜, *yoū mâc ké· kouí kón?* quelle affaire vous amène ?

能｜, *nên kón*, habileté, habile, puissant.

那個事都唔｜, *mâc ké· sé toū mĝ kón*, il ne s'occupe de rien.

我有事｜, *ngaî yoū sé kón*, j'ai une affaire; quelque chose à faire.

K'ÓN

看 *K'ón*. Voir, regarder, apprécier.

｜得倒, *k'ón tĕt taò*, je vois, je puis voir, on peut voir.

｜唔倒, *k'ón mĝ taò*, je ne vois pas.

唔曾｜, *mĝ t'iên* (ou *mĝ ts'ên*) *k'ón*, je n'ai pas vu.

｜病人, *k'ón p'iáng gnîn*, visiter les malades.

｜日, *k'ón gnĭt*, choisir un jour favorable.

｜阿剩, *k'ón á chín*, voyons un peu (pop).

KŌNG

(Voir aussi les mots KOUONG)

綱 *Kōng*. Loi, règle.

｜常, *kōng chông*, lois fondamentales de la société.

｜鑑, *kōng kám*, annales, histoire.

狗嬷一年下两｜, *keoù mâ ŷt niân hà leòng kōng*, la chienne a deux portées par an.

剛 *Kōng*. Ferme, dur, fort, juste, au moment même.

金｜石, *kīm kōng chăc*, diamant.

｜｜啱好, *kōng kōng tsáng haò*, c'est tout juste ce qu'il faut.

｜｜走, *kōng kōng tseoù*, il vient de partir.

崗 *Kōng*. Sommet d'une montagne,

崑｜, *ýn kōng*, montagne, colline.

缸 *Kōng*. Vase à large ouverture.

水｜, *chouì kōng*, grand vase ou bassin à contenir l'eau.

尿｜, *niaó kōng*, urinoir.

扛 *Kōng*. Porter un fardeau à plusieurs au moyen d'un long bâton; au fig. aider quelqu'un.

愛三個人｜, *oí sām ké· gnîn kōng*, il faut trois hommes pour porter ce fardeau.

｜樑, *kōng leông*, maîtresse poutre.

｜幫人, *kōng pōng gnîn*, aider quelqu'un, parler ou agir en sa faveur.

江 *Kōng*. ｜河, *kōng hô*, fleuve (peu employé).

｜湖, *kōng foû*, vagabond, qui court partout sans avoir de domicile fixe. On désigne aussi sous ce nom, les franc-maçons.

K'ŌNG

康 *K'ōng*. Prospère, fort.

老人家還｜健麼, *laò gnîn kā hân k'ōng k'ián mô ?* mon bon vieux, la santé est-elle bonne ?

K'ÔNG

狂 *K'ông*. Fou, sot.

發｜, *fât k'ông*, accès de folie.

｜狗, *k'ông keoù*, chien enragé.

KÒNG

講 *Kòng*. Parler, discuter, délibérer, expliquer.

｜話, *kòng fá*, parler, causer.

｜笑, *kòng siaó*, plaisanter.

｜理, *kòng lī*, parler raison, discuter une affaire.

｜唔贏, *kòng mĝ yâng*, ne pouvoir tenir tête à son adversaire dans la dispute.

亂｜, *lón kòng*, parler à tort et à travers.

｜書, *kòng choū*, expliquer un livre, le commenter.

｜白話, *kòng p'ăc fá*, dire des mensonges.

｜分明 (v. **｜明白**, v. **｜清楚**), *kòng foūn mîn* (*v. kòng mîn p'ĕt v. kòng ts'īn tsè*), parler clairement.

｜道理, *kòng t'aó lī*, prêcher.

｜衰人, *kòng soī gnîn*, décrier, dénigrer quelqu'un.

KÓNG

鋼 *Kóng (kōng)*. Acier, garnir d'acier.

脚跟拿去｜過, *kiŏc t'eoû nā hí kóng kouó*, garnir la pioche d'une couche d'acier.

降 *Kóng*. Descendre, s'abaisser.

天主聖子｜生, *t'iēn tchoù chín tzè kóng sēn*, le Fils de Dieu descendant (du ciel) s'est fait homme.

｜福, *kóng foûc*, bénir.

｜禍, *kóng fó*, maudire.

K'ÓNG

匟 *K'óng*. **｜床**, *k'óng ts'ông*, lit de repos, espèce de sofa.

炕 *K'óng*. Faire sécher au feu, cuire à sec.

｜麵包, *k'óng mién paō*, cuire le pain.

｜燥, *k'óng tsaō*, sécher au feu.

抗 *K'óng*. Résister.

頑｜, *ngân k'óng*, résister, ne pas obtempérer.

｜糧, *k'óng leông*, refuser de payer les impôts.

KÔT

葛 *Kôt*. Nom de plusieurs plantes grimpantes.

生｜, *sāng kôt*, une espèce de ces plantes.

｜薯, *kôt choû*, le tubercule d'une de ces plantes.

｜布, *kôt poú*, toile faite avec les feuilles d'ananas.

割 *Kôt*. Couper, reporter une dette sur un tiers.

丨禾, *kôt vô*, couper la moisson.

丨斷索, *kôt t'ōn sôc*, couper une ficelle en deux.

手丨倒裡, *choù kôt taò lî*, je me suis coupé le doigt.

某人少我錢我啥丨别你儉, *meoū gnîn chaò ngā ts'iên, ngâi voé· kôt poūn gnî kiàm*, un tel me doit de l'argent, je lui reporterai (ma créance) pour qu'il te paye.

KOŪ

姑 *Koū*. Tante paternelle, sœur du père.

丨子 (ou 丨 丨), *koū tzè* (ou *koū koū*), ma tante.

姑娘, *koū niông*, fille, femme; on appelle aussi de ce nom, les religieuses.

孤 *Koū*. Orphelin, seul.

丨哀子, *koū oī tzè*, orphelin de père et de mère.

丨單, *koū tān*, seul, sans appui.

入丨老院, *gnĭp koū laò yán*, entrer à l'hospice des vieillards.

豇 *Koū*. Accroupi.

丨倒食飯, *koū taò chĭt fán*, manger, assis sur ses talons. Voir *poū*.

K'OŪ

枯 *K'oū*. Desséché, gâté, tourteau.

梨子丨帛裡, *lî tzè k'oū p'ĕt lî*, le poirier est mort, desséché.

茶丨, *ts'â k'oū*, tourteau fait avec le résidu des fruits du camélia dont on a fait l'huile.

辜 *K'oū*. Faute, ingratitude.

丨負, *k'oū foú*, ingrat, abuser.

丨負天主個恩, *k'oū foú t'iēn tchoù ké· ēn*, abuser de la grâce de Dieu.

KOÙ

古 *Koù*. Ancien, antique.

丨時, *koù chê*, les temps antiques.

自丨以來, *tsé koù ȳ loî*, de tout temps.

丨董人, *koù toùng gnîn*, homme singulier, qui n'est pas de son siècle; nain.

丨怪, *koù kouaí*, rusé, aux manières étranges.

講丨, *kòng koù*, raconter des histoires, des romans.

股 *Koù*. Partie d'un tout, cuisse, fesse.

三丨索, *sām koù sôc*, une corde composée de trois torons.

分三丨, *foūn sām koù*, diviser en trois parties.

你生理幾多丨做, *niā siēn lī kì tō koù tsó?* de combien d'actions se compose ton commerce?

有二十丨我賸三丨, *yoū gní chĭp koù ngaî t'ên sām hoù*, il y a vingt actions et j'en ai trois.

屁丨, *p'í koù*, fesses.

兩丨泉, *leòng koù ts'ân*, deux veines d'eau, deux sources.

牯 *Koù*. Mâle.

牛丨, *nioû koù*, taureau, buffle.

狗丨, *keoù koù*, chien.

鼓 *Koù.* Tambour; enflé.

打鑼｜, *tà lô koù*, battre du tambour et du tam-tam.

｜起來, *koù hì loî*, faire ventre, bomber, devenir convexe.

被人家｜弄(ou **｜惑)**, *p'ī gnîn kā koù loùng (* ou *koù fĕt)*, on s'est joué de moi.

K'OÙ

苦 *K'où.* Souffrance, douleur.

困｜, 病｜, *k'oún k'où, p'iáng k'où*, fatigue, maladie.

受｜, *choú k'où*, souffrir.

｜像, *k'où sióng*, crucifix.

｜修聖人, *k'où sioū chín gnîn*, les saints pénitents.

辛｜, *sīn k'où*, application soutenue des facultés de l'âme, travail, fatigue.

貧｜, *p'în k'où*, pauvre, indigent.

KOÚ

故 *Koú.* Parce que, à cause.

緣｜, *yân koú*, cause, motif.

｜所以, *koú sò ÿ*, c'est pourquoi.

｜意做個事, *koú ý tsó ké· sé*, c'est fait exprès.

固 *Koú.* Fortifier, opiniâtre, ferme.

堅｜信德, *kiān koú sín tĕt*, affermir la Foi.

主｜, *tchoù koú*, solide.

雇 *Koú.* Louer, location.

｜一條船, *koú ÿt t'iaô chôn*, affréter une barque.

｜人工, *koú gnîn koūng*, louer des ouvriers.

顧 *Koú*, Pourvoir à, prendre soin,

看｜, *k'ón koú*, veiller à.

管｜教友, *kouòn koú kaó yoū*, s'occuper des chrétiens, régir avec soin les chrétiens.

不｜人個臉, *poūt koú gnîn ké· liēn*, (*litt.* ne pas soigner la face des autres) parler ou agir d'une manière offensante.

不｜自己個臉, *poūt koú tsé kí ké· liēn*, homme sans vergogne (qui ne soigne pas sa face).

｜家, *koú kā*, subvenir aux besoins de la famille.

K'OÚ

庫 *K'oú.* Trésor.

｜房, *k'oú fông*, chambre où l'on met les trésors, les richesses.

當財｜, *tōng ts'oî k'oú*, trésorier.

扶 *K'oú (foû).* S'appuyer sur.

老人家愛杖子｜等來, *laò gnîn kā oí tch'òng tzè k'oú tèn loî*, un vieillard a besoin b'un bâton pour s'appuyer. *Voir p'oû* et *foû*.

KOUĀ

瓜 *Kouā.* Cucurbitacées.

東｜, 金｜, 節｜, *toūng kouā, kīm kouā, tsiĕt kouā*, diverses espèces de courges.

黃｜, 苦｜, 西｜, *vông kouā, foù kouā, sī kouā*, concombre, courge amère, pastèque ou melon.

| 片, *kouā p'ièn*, tranches de courge confites dans le sucre.

詿 *Kouā*. Tromper.

莫 | 人, *mŏc kouā gnîn*, ne me trompe pas.

K'OUĀ

誇 *K'ouā*. Se vanter, vantard.

| 奬自己, *k'ouā tsiòng tsé kì*, se vanter.

| 人, *k'ouā gnîn*, vantard.

跨 *K'ouā*. Enjamber. (Voyez *k'iá* et *k'iám*).

KOUÀ

寡 *Kouà*. Veuve, peu, modique.

| 婦, *kouà foú*, veuve.

守 |, *choù kouà*, garder la viduité.

鰥 | 孤獨, *kouān kouà koū t'oŭc*, veuf, veuve, orphelin, sans enfants.

不論多 |, *poŭt loún tō kouà*, peu ou beaucoup, n importe.

剮 *Kouà*. Écorcher, supplice des cent plaies.

受 |, *choú kouà*, subir ce supplice.

喎 *Kouà*. Mot qui marque l'excès.

撥倒一身 | 泥, *p'ât taò ўt chīn kouà nâi*, éclabousser tout le corps de boue.

滿草坪 | 花, *mān ts'aò p'iâng kouà fā*, la prairie est toute émaillée de fleurs.

| 賊個地方, *kouà ts'ĕt ké· t'i fōng*, il n'y a que des voleurs dans ce pays !

掛 *Kouà (kouá)*. Accroc, déchirure.

衫子剐你 | 爛, *sām tzè poūn gnì kouà lán*, tu as fait un accroc à ma robe.

笏子 | 倒, *nĕt tzè kouà taò*, une épine m'a écorché.

K'OUÀ

扒 *K'ouà (ou p'à)*. Branche d'arbre. *Voir p'à*.

KOUÁ

卦 *Koua*. Lignes servant à la divination.

八 |, *pât kouá*, les huit figures fondamentales faites avec ces lignes.

卜 |, ou 占 |, *poŭc kouá*, ou *tchám kouá*, exercer la divination au moyen de ces lignes.

掛 *Kouá*. Suspendre, accrocher.

| 號, | 像, *kouá haó, kouá sióng*, suspendre des cartes de visite, des images.

| 招牌, *kouá tchāo p'aî*, exposer une enseigne.

官府 | 牌某日審事, *kouōn foù kouá p'aî meoū gnĭt chìm sé*, le mandarin a exposé le tableau, tel jour on jugera.

褂 *Kouá*. Pardessus, veste.

馬 |, *mā kouá*, pardessus court à larges manches.

皮馬 |, *p'î mā kouá*, pardessus fourré.

KOUAĪ

乖 *Kouaī.* Gentil, rusé.

細人子係 |, *sé· gnîn tzè hé· kouaī,* l'enfant est bien gentil, (s'entend aussi de sa santé) il se porte bien.

唔多 |, *mĝ tō kouaī* il ne va pas très bien.

| | 兒莫叫, *kouaī houaī gnî mŏc kiaó,* sois gentil, ne pleure pas.

性情 | 古, *sín ts'în kouaī koù,* fourbe, rusé, mauvais caractère.

KOUAÌ

拐 *Kouaì.* Tromper, engager à suivre, séduire, obtenir par fraude.

| 細人, *kouaì sé· gnîn,* obtenir par quelque ruse, la paix à un enfant qui pleure.

| 帶婦人家, *kouaì taí foú gnîn kā,* attirer par ruse et emmener avec soi une femme.

打眼 |, *tà niàn kouaì,* faire les yeux doux (*litt.* trompeurs).

蛞 *Kouaì.* **| 子**, *kouaì tzè,* espèce de petite grenouille.

KOUAÍ

怪 *Kouaí.* Extraordinaire, merveilleux, s'étonner.

| 物, *kouaí voŭt,* monstre.

古 |, **奇 |**, *koù kouaí, k'î kouaí,* extraordinaire, merveilleux.

古 | 人, *koù kouaí gnîn,* homme aux manières étranges.

你唔守主日難 | 天主麽降福你, *gnî mĝ choù tchoù gnĭt nân kouaí t'iēn tchoù mô kóng foŭc gnî,* si tu n'observes pas le dimanche, rien d'étonnant que Dieu ne te bénisse pas.

| 唔得, *kouaí mĝ tĕt,* il n'y a pas de quoi s'étonner.

麽 | 我, *mô kouaí ngaî,* excusez-moi (politesse).

佢作 | 唔得, *kî tsôc kouaí mĝ tĕt,* il ne peut rien contre, il ne peut rejimber (*litt.* ne peut faire le monstre).

少見多 |, *chaò kián tō kouaí,* qui a peu vu s'étonne facilement.

K'OUAÍ

塊 *K'ouaí.* Morceau, fragment; particule numérale des pierres, des masses compactes.

一 | 石頭, *ŷt k'ouaí chăc t'eoû,* une pierre.

一 | 火磚, **一 | 瓦**, *ŷt k'ouaí fò tchōn, ŷt k'ouaí ngà,* une brique, une tuile.

打碎了唔成 |, *tà souí liaò mĝ châng k'ouaí,* c'est réduit en poussière, cela ne forme pas de morceaux.

血 |, *hiĕt k'ouaí,* caillot de sang.

稗 *K'ouaí (ou p'aí).* **| 子**, *k'ouaí tzè,* ivraie.

快 *K'ouaí.* Plaisir, rapide, vite.

爽 |, *sòng k'ouaí,* à l'aise, sans chagrin, dispos.

| 活, *k'ouaí făt,* heureux, dans le bien-être, avoir la joie dans le cœur.

| | 來, *k'ouaí k'ouaí loî,* viens vite.

火船都還 | 火車又過 |, *fò chôn*

toū hân k'ouaí fò tch'ā yoú kouó k'ouaí, le vapeur va dejà bien vite mais le chemin de fer est encore plus rapide.

輕 |, *k'iāng k'ouaí*, agile, leste.

筷 *K'ouaí*. Bâtonnets dont on se sert pour manger.

一雙 | 子, *ŷt soūng k'ouaí tzè*, une paire de bâtonnets.

| 子夾一塊猪肉, *k'ouaí tzè kiăp ŷt k'ouaí tchoū nioŭc*, prendre un morceau de viande avec les bâtonnets.

劊 *K'ouaí*. | 子手, *kouaí tzè choù*, bourreau chargé de couper la tête.

KOUĀN

關 *Kouān*. Fermer, douane, conséquence, échéance.

| 門, *kouān moûn*, fermer la porte.

門 | 等來, ou | 門, *moûn kouān tèn loî*, ou *kouān moûn*, ferme la porte.

| 唔尾, *kouān mĝ mī*, cela ne ferme pas complètement.

唔 | (ou 干) 你事, *mĝ kouān*, (ou *kōn*) *gnî sé*, cela ne te regarde pas.

| 係, *kouān hé·* (ou *kouān hí*), conséquence.

過 |, *kouó kouān*, passer la douane.

| 稅, *kouān choé·*, droits de douane.

| 期, *kouān k'î*, échéance.

| 節, *kouān tsiĕt*, point important, chose nécessaire.

議學 |, *gní hŏc kouān*, s'entendre sur les appointements d'un maître d'école.

寫 | 帖, *sià kouān t'iăp*, écrire ce dont on a convenu pour le paiement d'un maître d'école.

K'OUĀN

圈 *K'ouān (k'iān)*. | | 轉, *k'ouān k'ouān* (pour *k'iān k'iān*) *tchòn*, tourner tout autour, tout autour.

K'OUÀN

欵 *K'ouàn*. Libéral, particule numérale des choses de différentes espèces, des contrats, etc.

| 待人, *k'ouàn t'aí gnîn*, traiter quelqu'un avec libéralité.

一 | 事, *ŷt k'ouàn sé*, une affaire.

第九 |,... *t'í kioù k'ouàn*,... l'article neuvième....

| 式, *k'ouàn chĭt*, manière de tourner une phrase, art de faire une chose.

有做狀子個 | 式, 有寫信個 | 式, *yoū tsó ts'óng tzè ké· k'ouàn chĭt, yoū sià sín ké· k'ouàn chĭt*, il y a le style des pièces d'accusation, il y a le style littéraire.

KOUÁN

慣 *Kouán*. S'habituer, accoutumé

神父 | 唔 |, *chîn foú kouán mĝ kouán?* le Père s'habitue-t il ?

攪 |, *kaò kouán*, avoir l'habitude.

攪 | 鴉片烟, *kaò kouān ā pèn yān*, il a l'habitude de l'opium.

賭 |, *toù kouán*, avoir l'habitude de jouer.

食得 |, *chĭt tĕt kouán*, s'habituer à la nourriture.

K'OUÁN

歀 *K'ouán*. Porter en bandoulière.

唔曉款|得子過好, *mĝ hiaò k'aī k'ouán tĕt tzè kouó haò*, je ne sais pas porter avec un bâton, j'aime mieux porter en bandoulière.

婦人家|大肚, *foú gnĭn kā k'ouán t'aí toù*, femme enceinte.

KOUĀNG

桄 *Kouāng*. Barreau, échelon, tige d'une plante.

窗|, 梯|, *ts'oūng kouāng, t'oī kouāng*, barreau de fenêtre, echelon d'une échelle.

草|, 花|, *ts'aò kouāng, fā kouāng*, tige d'une plante, d'une fleur.

胱 *Kouāng*. Gonflé, enflé.

牙齒痛面都|帛裡, *ngâ tchè t'oúng mién toū kouāng p'ĕt lê*, j'ai mal aux dents, j'en ai la figure toute enflée.

膨|, *p'āng kouāng*, gonfler en soufflant.

KOUÀNG

鑛 *Kouàng*. Minerai.

金|, 銀|, *kīm kouàng, nioûn kouàng*, minerai d'or, d'argent, etc.

KOUĂT

啒 *Kouăt*. Mot qui marque l'excès.

|爛, *kouăt lán*, tout abîmé.

|融, *kouăt yoûng*, tout en morceaux.

KOUÂT

刮 *Kouât*. Racler, ratisser.

蘿蔔拿來|淨皮來, *lô p'ĕt nā loî kouât ts'iáng p'î loî*, racle proprement les navets.

|猪毛, *kouât tchoū maō*, racler les soies d'un porc saigné.

|削, *kouât siŏc*, tourmenter quelqu'un par des présents pour en obtenir de l'argent.

K'OUÂT

闊 *K'ouât*. Large. *Voir fât.*

KOUĊ

喖 *Kouc*. Étouffé par l'eau, engorgé, suffoqué.

我跌落水底下險險|死, *gnaî tiĕt lŏc chouì taì hā hiàm hiàm kouc sì*, je suis tombé au fond de l'eau et j'ai failli me noyer.

灶下燒火火烟|等裡透氣唔得, *tsaó hā chaō fò fò yān kouc tèn ê· t'eoù hí mĝ tĕt*, quand j'allume le feu à la cuisine, la fumée me suffoque, je ne puis pas respirer.

谷 *Kouc*. Vallée.

山|, 窩|, *sān kouc, vō kouc*, vallée, ravin.

穀 *Kouc*. Riz non décortiqué.

打|, *tà kouc*, battre le riz.

打一石|做得五斗米, *tà ȳt chăc kouc tsó tĕt nĝ teoù mì*, le rendement du battage d'un *chăc* de riz est de 5 boisseaux.

糴 |, *t'ăc kоŭc*, acheter du riz.
糶 |, *t'iaó kоŭc*, vendre du riz.

KOÛC

緝 *Koûc*. Serré, dru.

打索打倒好 |, *tà sôc tà taò haò koûc*, cette corde a été faite bien serrée.

布耕倒係 |, *poú kāng taò hé· koûc*, l'étoffe a un tissu très serré.

毛辮編 | 來, *maō piēn p'īn koûc loî*, fais ma tresse serrée.

KOUÊN

誑 *Kouên*. Aboyer, cri du chien quand il a senti le gibier.

狗一 | 有定着鼻倒蹟, *keoù ŷt kouên yoū t'ín tch'ŏc p'í taò tsiâc*, dès que le chien aboie, on est sûr qu'il a flairé une piste.

KOUÊT

國 *Kouêt*. Royaume.

中 |, *tchoūng kouêt*, la Chine.
| 家, *kouêt kā*, le gouvernement.

KOŪI

歸 *Kouī*. Se diriger vers, appartenir à, réunir, retourner.

| 屋下, *kouī voûc hā*, retourner à la maison, chez soi.

來 |, *loî kouī*, se dit d'une fille nouvellement mariée qui retourne à la maison paternelle saluer ses parents.

| 除, *kouī tch'oû*, l'addition et la soustraction.

平遠縣 | 嘉應州管, *p'în yàn yán kouī kā ýn tchoū kouòn*, la sous-préfecture du *P'în yàn* dépend de la ville de *Kā ýn*.

| 做, *kouī ts'ioū*, réunir, grouper,

九 |, *kioù kouī*, la table de Pythagore.

龜 *Kouī*. Tortue.

問 |, *moún kouī*, consulter la tortue. (La carapace de la tortue est censée donner des présages).

| 殼, *kouī hôc*, carapace de la tortue.

閨 *Kouī*. Appartement de femme.

| 閫, *kouī koùn*, même sens.

規 *Kouī*. Règle.

聖教四 |, *chín kaó sí kouī*, les 4 commandements de l'Eglise.

| 條, *kouī t'iaō*, articles d'un règlement.

| 矩, *kouī kì*, règle, loi, usage, convenances.

麼 | 矩, *mô kouī kì*, malhonnête, impoli, sans convenances.

立 | 矩, *līp kouī kì*, faire un règlement.

K'OUĪ

虧 *K'ouī*. Manque, dommage, nuire.

缺 | 經文, *k'iĕt k'ouī kīn voûn*, omettre ses prieres.

| 人個錢, *k'ouī gnîn ké· ts'iên*, avoir des dettes.

唔怕,麼事丨人, *mĝ p'á, mô sè k'ouī gnîn,* n'aie pas peur, on ne te nuira pas.

丨本, *k'ouī poùn,* vendre à perte.

K'OUÎ

魁 *K'ouî.* Qui tient le 1er rang,

丨首, *k'ouî choù,* même sens.

葵 *K'ouî,* 丨菜, *k'ouî ts'oí,* espèce de légume.

丨花, *k'ouî fā,* tournesol, soleil.

KOUÌ

鬼 *Kouì.* Diable, génie, mânes.

魔丨, *mô kouì,* le diable, le démon.

丨倒路, *kouì taò loú,* (*litt.* le diable a détourné le chemin) le diable nous a égaré.

見丨, *kián kouì,* voir des fantômes.

丨叫, *kouì kiaó,* bruit causé par un revenant.

詭 *Kouì.* Rusé, trompeur.

用丨計, *yoúng kouì ké·,* user de ruse.

做丨事, *tsó kouì ché·* faire un travail inutile, ou que l'on devra défaire.

你講丨話, *gnî kòng kouì fá,* tu dis des blagues.

晷 *Kouì.* Ombre du soleil.

日丨, *gnĭt kouì,* cadran solaire.

K'OUÌ

毀 *K'ouì.* Médire, détruire.

丨謗, *k'ouì pòng,* calomnier, dénigrer.

字紙唔在我丨帛裡, *sé tjè mĝ ts'oī ngaî k'ouì p'ĕt lî,* il n'y a plus d'écrit, je l'ai détruit.

丨拆房屋, *k'ouì ts'âc fông voûc,* démolir une maison.

跪 *K'ouì.* S'agenouiller.

丨倒來, *k'ouì taò loî,* agenouille-toi.

丨凳, *k'ouì tén,* agenouilloir, prie-Dieu.

丨唔下, *k'ouì mĝ hā,* ne pouvoir se mettre à genoux.

丨鍊, *k'ouì lién,* s'agenouiller sur des chaînes (torture).

丨體聖, *k'ouì chín t'ì,* s'agenouiller devant le Saint Sacrement.

愧 *K'ouì.* Honte, pudeur, remords.

自卑自丨, *tsé pī tsè k'ouì,* s'humilier et être confus.

丨心, *k'ouì sīm,* avoir des remords de conscience.

KOUÍ

桂 *Kouí.* Cannellier.

肉丨, *nioûc kouí,* espèce de cannelle dont l'écorce sert en médecine.

丨秋, *kouí ts'ioū,* la huitième lune.

瑰 *Kouí.* 玫丨花, *moê· kouí fā,* rose, rosier.

玫丨經, *moê· kouí kīn,* les prières du Rosaire.

季 *Kouí* (pour *kí*). Saison.

上｜，下｜，*chóng kouí, há kouí*, la 1ère et la 2ème partie de l'année.

四｜，*sí kouí*, les 4 saisons.

四｜齋，*sí kouí tsaī*, abstinence des Quatre-Temps.

貴 *Kouí*. Riche, noble, illustre, prix élevé. S'emploie par politesse comme vocatif dans le sens de *Votre* ou de *Monsieur*.

富｜，*foú kouí*, riche, richard.

尊｜，*tsoūn kouí*, ｜重，*kouí tch'oúng*, noble, de grande estime.

聖體係至尊｜個聖事，*chín t'ì hé· tjé tsoūn kouí ké· chín sé*. L'Eucharistie est le plus noble des sacrements.

買十分｜，*maì chĭp foūn kouí*, c'est acheté très cher.

｜姓，*kouí siáng?* ｜國，*kouí kouĕt?* ｜處，*kouí tchoú?* quel est votre nom? votre royaume? où est votre habitation?

｜縣，｜府，*kouí yán, kouí foù*, Monsieur le sous-préfet, Monsieur le préfet.

好得我遇倒一個｜人唔係我躪走裡，*haò t'ĕt ngaî gní taò ŷt ké· kouí gnîn m̂g ké· ngaî t'óng tseoù lì*, heureusement j'ai rencontré un brave homme, sans quoi je m'égarais.

K'OUÍ

櫃 *K'ouí*. Armoire, buffet.

鐵｜，*t'iĕt k'ouí*, coffre-fort en fer.

米｜，*mì k'ouí*, armoire, buffet où l'on met le riz.

內｜，*nouí k'ouí*, celui qui est chargé des écritures et de la caisse, dans un commerce.

外｜，*ngoé· k'ouí*, celui qui est chargé de la vente dans un commerce.

K'OŪN

昆 *K'oūn*. Frère plus âgé que soi.

有幾多個｜玉，*yoū kì tō ké· k'oūn nioŭc?* combien avez-vous de frères? (*politesse.*) Rép. 三賤兄弟，*sām ts'ién hioūng t'í*, trois *méprisables* frères.

KOÙN

滾 *Koùn*. Bouillant, bouillonner, très chaud; se rouler, dégringoler.

煲｜水，*pō koùn chouì*, faire bouillir de l'eau.

水｜，*chouì koùn*, l'eau bout.

瀝瀝｜，*lâc lâc koùn*, bruit que fait l'eau en bouillant.

一晡夜雷公瀝瀝｜，*ŷt poū yá louî koūng lâc lâc koùn*, le tonnerre a grondé toute la nuit.

两個細人子在個裡緊｜，*leòng ké· sé· gnîn tzè ts'oī ké· lì kìn koùn*, les deux enfants sont là à se battre.

狗打｜，*keoù tà koùn*, le chien se roule.

石頭崁崗上｜阿下，*chăc teoû ýn kōng hóng koùn á há*, une pierre a dégringolé de la montagne.

裩 *Koùn*. ｜身衫，*koùn chīn sām*, habit étroit avec manches étroites.

K'OÙN

捆 *K'oùn*. Lier, plier, enrouler; part. num. de ce qui est lié en botte.

被骨拿來丨正來, *p'ï koût nâ loî k'oùn tcháng loî*, enroule, plie cette couverture comme il faut.

一丨樹扒, *ŷt k'oùn choú p'à*, un fagot de branches d'arbre.

KOÚN

棍 *Koún*. Bâton.

打丨, *tà koún*, jouer du bâton.

扶等丨來行, *p'oû tèn koún loî hâng*, s'appuyer sur un bâton en marchant.

K'OÚN

困 *K'oún*. Las, fatigué, misérable.

丨睡, *k'oún choé·*, dormir de fatigue.

丨苦, *k'oún k'où*, malheureux, misérable.

丨倦, *k'oún k'iàn*, fatigué, las.

閫 *K'oún*. 都丨府, *toū k'oún foù*, chef d'un bataillon, dans une sous-préfecture.

KOŪNG

工 *Koūng*. Travail, ouvrier.

做丨夫, *tsó koūng foū*, travailler.

人丨, *gnîn koūng*, journées de travail.

一丨, 半丨, 丨半, *ŷt koūng, pán koūng, koūng pán*, une journée de travail, une demi-journée, une journée et demie.

長丨, *tch'ông koūng*, domestique à l'année.

開丨, 停丨, *k'oī koūng, t'în koūng*, commencer l'ouvrage, cesser le travail.

公 *Koūng*. Public, juste, mâle.

丨所, *koūng sò*, édifice public, lieu de réunion.

丨事, *koūng sé*, affaire officielle.

丨道, *koūng t'aó*, juste, équitable.

丨義, *koūng gní*, justice.

兩丨婆, *leòng koūng p'ô*, le mari et la femme.

相丨, *siōng koūng*, appellation honorifique pour désigner un serviteur, ou quelquefois le fils de celui à qui l'on parle.

雞丨, *kē· koūng*, coq.

貓丨, *miaó koūng*, chat.

功 *Koūng*. Mérite, œuvre.

立丨, *lĭp koūng*, faire une action méritoire.

做善丨有丨勞, *tsó chán koūng yoū koūng laô*, on acquiert des mérites en faisant des bonnes œuvres.

諸聖相通丨, *tchoū chín siōng t'oūng koūng*, la Communion des Saints.

丨名, *koūng miâng*, titre d'honneur, grade.

攻 *Koūng*. Attaquer.

四面丨阿來, *sí mién koūng á loî*, attaquer des quatre côtés à la fois.

丨城, *koūng châng*, attaquer, assiéger une ville.

K'OŪNG

空 *K'oūng*. Vide.

丨中, *k'oūng tchoūng*, le vide, l'air, le ciel.

16

箱子｜個, *siōng tzè k'oūng ké·*, la boîte est vide.

｜心, *k'oūng sīm*, à jeun.

｜手, *k'oūng choù*, avoir les mains vides.

KOÙNG

拱 *Koùng (kioùng)*. Bombé, en dos de chameau.

｜阿起, *koùng á hì*, qui va en bombant.

｜｜個, *koùng koùng ké·*, qui est bombé.

K'OÙNG

孔 *K'oùng*. Trou, ouverture, espace vide.

七｜來血, *ts'ĭt k'oùng loî hiĕt*, le sang lui sort par tout le corps (*litt.* par les sept ouvertures du corps).

｜雀, *k'oùng tsiŏc*, paon.

｜明燈, *K'oùng mîn tēn*, ballon, mongolfière.

｜夫子, *k'oùng foū tzè*, Confucius.

KOÚNG

貢 *Koúng*. Tribut, payer le tribut.

進｜, *tsín koúng*, offrir, payer le tribut.

｜生, *koúng sēn*, un des grades de bachelier.

捐一個｜生, *kiān ȳt ké· koúng sēn*, acheter un titre de *koúng sēn*.

K'OÚNG

空 *K'oúng*. Libre, loisir, vide.

｜唔｜, *k'oúng mĝ k'oúng?* avez-vous le temps ? êtes-vous libre ?

事情多唔得｜, *sé ts'în tō mĝ tĕt k'oúng*, j'ai trop d'affaires, je ne suis pas libre.

麼｜間, *mô k'oúng kiān*, il n'y a pas de chambre libre, disponible.

KOUŌ

過 *Kouō (kouó)*. S'user par le frottement.

脚頭使來使去噲｜, *kiŏc teoû sè loî sè hí voé· kouō*, à force de se servir de la pioche, on l'use.

刀麻使｜裡, *taō mâ sè kouō lì*, le couteau de cuisine est usé.

KOUÒ

果 *Kouò*. Certain, en effet.

｜然係眞, *kouò yân hé· tchīn*, c'est en effet la vérité.

裡個事好同佢結｜, *ỳ ké· sé haò t'oûng kì kiĕt kouò*, il faut en finir avec son affaire.

菓 *Kouò*. Fruits.

五穀百｜, *ǹg koŭc pâc kouò*, toute espèce de céréales et de fruits (*litt.* les 5 céréales et les 100 fruits).

摘｜, *tsâc kouò*, cueillir des fruits.

裹 *Kouò*. Envelopper, rouler.

｜脚布, *kouò kiŏc poú*, petit carré d'étoffe dont les Chinois s'enveloppent les pieds pour ne pas salir leurs bas.

過 *Kouò (kouó)*. Livrer, donner, faire passer de main en main.

| 定頭, *kouò t'în teoû*, donner des arrhes.

| 銀, *kouò nioûn*, livrer de l'argent.

新聞紙 | 別佢, *sīn voûn tjè kouò poūn kî*, fais-lui passer le journal.

KOUÓ

過 *Kouó*. Passer d'un lieu à un autre, excéder, trop ; s'adjoint aux verbes pour faire le prétérit ; a des sens multiples qu'apprendra l'usage.

| 橋, *kouó k'iaô*, passer sur le pont.

| 河, *kouó hô*, passer le fleuve.

| 路個人, *kouó loú ké· gnîn*, un passant.

| 年, *kouó niân*, passer l'année, le jour de l'an.

| 後, *kouó heoú*, après coup.

病人怕佢 | 夜唔得, *p'iáng gnîn p'á kî kouó yá mĝ tĕt*, le malade ne passera probablement pas la nuit.

| 頭, *kouó teoû* (ou | 分, *kouó foún*), outre-mesure.

買得 |, *maì tĕt kouó*, ce n'est pas trop cher.

耐得 |, *naí tĕt kouó*, c'est supportable.

比我 | 大, *pì ngaî kouó t'aí*, plus grand que moi.

做 |, 去 |, 食 |, 見 |, *tsó kouó, hí kouó, chĭt kouó, kián kouó*, j'ai fait cela autrefois, j'y suis allé jadis, j'en ai mangé autrefois, j'ai déjà vu.

一 |, 兩 |, *ŷt kouó, leòng kouó*, une rangée, deux rangées.

一 | 石頭一 | 石灰, *ŷt kouó chăc t'eoû ŷt kouó chăc foē·*, une couche de pierres, puis une couche de chaux.

| 失, *kouó chĭt*, manquement, faute.

KOUŌN

(*Voir aussi les mots KON*)

官 *Kouōn*. Mandarin, officier.

一員 |, *ŷt yân kouōn*, un mandarin.

文 |, 武 |, *voûn kouōn, voū kouōn*, mandarin civil, mandarin militaire.

| 府, 州 |, 縣 |, *kouōn foù, tchoū kouōn, yán kouōn*, préfet de 1ere classe, de 2eme classe, sous-préfet.

打 | 事, *tà kouōn sé*, (ou 打 | 司, *tà kouōn sē*), soutenir ou intenter un procès.

五 |, *nĝ kouōn*, les cinq moyens de perception, les cinq sens.

棺 *Kouōn*. | 材, | 木, *kouōn ts'oî, kouōn moŭc*, cercueil.

一副 | 材, *ŷt foú kouōn ts'oî*, un cercueil.

觀 *Kouōn*. Considérer de loin, observer.

旁 | 去探分明, *p'ông kouōn hí t'àm foūn mîn*, aller voir ou entendre pour prendre des renseignements.

照旁 | 人講, *tchaó p'ông kouōn gnîn kòng*, d'après ce que j'ai entendu dire.

| 音, *kouōn ŷm*, la déesse des Chinois.

冠 *Kouōn*. Couronne, chapeau.

茨 |, *tsé kouōn*, couronne d'épines.

衣 | 帶來禮麼, *ŷ kouōn taí loî lî mô ?* avez-vous apporté vos habits et votre chapeau ? (Se dit surtout des vêtements de cérémonie).

KOUÒN

管 *Kouòn*. Gouverner, administrer, étui, petit manche.

丨事, *kouòn sé*, s'occuper des affaires.

唔丨事, *mĝ kouòn sé*, ne pas s'occuper des affaires, ou bien, cela n'a pas de rapport avec cette affaire.

丨帶五百兵, *kouòn taí ǹg pâc pīn*, commander à 500 soldats.

東石係平遠丨個, *toūng chăc hé· p'in yàn kouòn ké·*, *Toūng chăc* dépend de la sous-préfecture de *P'in yàn*.

筆丨, *pĭt kouòn*, manche de pinceau.

玻璃丨, *pō lî kouòn*, le verre d'une lampe.

針丨, *tchĭm kouòn*, étui pour les aiguilles.

一丨筆, *ŷt kouòn pĭt*, un pinceau.

一丨銃, *ŷt kouòn tch'oúng*, un coup de fusil.

館 *Kouòn*. Hôtel, auberge.

公丨, *koūng kouòn*, hôtel de mandarin, autre que le prétoire.

打公丨, *tà koūng kouòn*, prendre logement dans un hôtel de ce genre.

那個貴丨, *mâc ké· kouí kouòn*, où habitez-vous ? (à quelqu'un qui est en voyage. *Politesse*.)

酒丨, *tsioù kouòn*, cabaret.

鴉片丨, *a pèn kouòn*, salle publique où l'on fume l'opium, fumoir public.

KOUÓN

貫 *Kouón*. Enfiler.

丨串, *kouón tch'ón*, complice.

一丨錢, *ŷt kouón ts'iēn*, une enfilade de sapèques.

灌 *Kouón*. Emboquer.

丨藥, *kouón yŏc*, faire avaler de force des remèdes.

唐人剛牛先丨佢唔知幾多水, *t'ông gnîn tchê nioû siēn kouón kî mĝ ti kì tō choui*, les Chinois, avant de tuer un buffle, lui font avaler une grande quantité d'eau.

罐 *Kouón*. Cruchon, bouteille.

一丨酒, *ŷt kouón tsioù*, une bouteille de vin.

酒丨, 油丨, *tsioù kouón*, *yoû kouón*, cruchon à vin, à huile.

鑵 *Kouón*. 丨嘴, *kouón tsouì*, espèce de pioche pointue.

KOUŌNG

光 *Kouōng*. Brillant, lumière, éclat, nu, gloire.

丨明, *kouōng mîn*, lumière éclatante, évidence.

丨鮮, *kouōng siēn (ou sāng)*, brillant et neuf, qui a le brillant du neuf, net, propre, poli.

伶丨, *lîn kouōng*, nu, net.

照丨, *tchaó kouōng*, réfléchir la lumière, éclairer, illustrer.

天丨, *t'iēn kouōng*, l'aurore.

月｜, *gnĕt kouōng*, le clair de lune.

榮｜, *yoûng kouōng*, gloire, honneur, glorifier.

增｜聖教會個名, *tsén kouōng chín kaó fí ké· miâng*, augmenter la gloire de l'Eglise.

KOUÒNG

廣 *Kouòng*. Grand, vaste.

｜東, ｜西, *kouòng toūng, kouòng sī*, province du Kouang-tong, province du Kouang-si.

K'OUÒNG

况 *K'ouòng* (ou *k'òng*). ｜且, *kouòng ts'ià*, d'autant plus.

KOÛT

骨 *Koût*. Os, la partie la plus ferme d'un corps.

｜頭, *koût t'eoû*, os.

牌｜, *p'aî koût*, côtes.

｜筒油, *koût t'oûng yoû*, moëlle des os.

烟皮｜, *yān p'î koût*, côtes des feuilles de tabac.

豆子老咇裡有｜, *t'eoú tzè laò p'ĕt lî yoū koût*, les haricots sont passés, ils ont des côtes.

K'OŬT

𡲢 *K'oŭt*. Tronqué, sans queue.

｜尾狗, *k'oŭt mī keoù*, chien sans queue.

裡枚針｜咇裡, *ỳ moê· tchīm k'oŭt p'ĕt lî*, cette aiguille est émoussée.

LĀ

拉 *Lā*. Tirer, attirer. Dans ce sens, ce mot est peu employé à *Kā ýn tchoū*, on dit plutôt : 攋 *laī*, 拿 *nā*, 挷 *pāng*.

｜｜扯扯, *lā lā tch'à tch'à*, tirer de de côté et d'autre, encombrer, encombrant.

LÂ

迾 *Lâ*. Visiter, aller au devant, pour se rendre compte.

｜地方, *lâ t'í fōng*, visiter le pays.

｜病人, *lâ p'iáng gnîn*, visiter les malades.

｜𨑨, *lâ liaô*, se promener, errer à l'aventure.

Lâ. *Lâ k'iâ*, araignée. *Voir k'iâ*.

LÁ

椏 *Lá*. Ouverture, fente.

手指｜, *choù tjè lá*, jointure des doigts.

馬蹄麼｜唔比牛蹄, *mā t'aî mô lá mĝ pì nioû t'aî*, le sabot du cheval n'est pas fendu comme celui du bœuf.

棚板唔尾還有｜, *p'âng pàn mĝ mī hân yoū lá*, les planches ne sont pas bien jointes, on voit des ouvertures.

LĂC

曆 *Lăc*. Ordre du temps, calendrier.

月｜, *gnĕt lăc*, calendrier.

癧 *Lăc.* Tumeur au cou, maladie des glandes.

瀝 *Lăc.* Bruit de l'eau qui bout.

水｜｜滾, *chouì lăc lăc koùn,* l'eau bout avec force.

壢 *Lăc.* 地｜, *t'í lăc,* terrain plat, sans eau.

荒地｜, *fōng t'í lăc,* terrain abandonné, non défriché, ou stérile.

剌 *Lăc.* Couper, fendre.

｜開玻璃, *lăc k'oī pō lî,* couper du verre.

｜柴, *lăc ts'iaô,* fendre du bois.

LÂC

瀝 *Lâc.* Ruisseau, rigole.

圳｜, *tsoún lâc,* petit ruisseau, comme ceux qui bordent les champs ou les rizières.

坑｜, *hāng lâc,* ruisseau un peu plus grand, comme ceux d'une vallée.

河｜, *hô lâc,* petite rivière.

界｜, *kiaí lâc,* rigole servant de limite.

LAĪ

攋 *Laī.* S'efforcer, attirer.

相打緊｜, *siōng tà kìn laī,* ils se battent tant qu'ils peuvent.

夾死緊｜, *kâp sì kìn laī,* dût-il en mourir, il va de l'avant.

臭肉｜烏蠅, *tch'oú nioûc laī voū ŷn,* la viande qui pue attire les mouches.

LAÎ

犁 *Laî.* Labourer, charrue.

｜田, *laî t'iên,* labourer une rizière.

｜頭, *laî t'eoû,* le fer de la charrue, le soc, ou la charrue elle-même.

｜壁, *laî piâc,* le fer d'arrière de la charrue.

㗝 *Laî.* Peser sur.

｜屎, ｜尿, *laî chè, laî niaó,* évacuer ou uriner sans s'en apercevoir.

秤忒｜, *tch'ín t'iĕt laî,* peser trop lourd, (le poids penchant trop).

烏｜｜, *voū laî laî,* d'un noir sale.

LAÍ

賴 *Laí.* Mettre son appui ou sa confiance en; demander avec insistance; fils.

｜天主仁慈, *laí t'iēn tchoù ŷn tsê,* mettre sa confiance en la miséricorde de Dieu.

來去向神父｜倒一個聖像來, *loî hí hióng chîn foú laí taò ŷt ké· chín sióng loî,* allons demander une image au Père, au risque de l'importuner.

誣｜人, *moû laí gnîn,* accuser faussement, nuire à quelqu'un par une accusation fausse.

食藥圖｜人, *chĭt yŏc t'oû laí gnîn,* s'empoisonner pour nuire à quelqu'un (par le soupçon de meurtre qu'on aura laissé sur cette personne, lui occasionnant un procès ruineux).

雞媽 | 哺, *kē mâ laí p'oú*, la poule s'obstine à couver sans avoir des œufs.

| 子, *laí tzè*, fils.

你有幾多個子, *gnî yoū kì tō ké· laí tzè ?* combien avez-vous de fils ?

LĀM

攬 *Lām.* Réunir, rassembler.

| 攸來, *lām ts'ioū loî*, rassembler le tout, ramasser le tout.

| 機, *lām kí (pour kī)*, métier de tisserand.

| 倒賊, *lām taò ts'ĕt*, attraper un voleur.

LÂM

藍 *Lâm.* Indigo, plante qui sert à la teinture, bleu.

| 色, *lâm sêt*, couleur bleue.

籃 *Lâm.* panier, corbeille.

| 箕, *lâm kī*, espèce de petit panier dont se servent les femmes.

LÀM

揇 *Làm (ou nàm).* Adopter. *(Voyez nàm).*

欖 *Làm.* Olive chinoise.

LÁM

纜 *Lám.* Corde de bambou dont on se sert pour hâler les barques.

濫 *Lám.* | 官, *lám kouōn*, mandarin cupide qui gruge le monde, ne s'occupe des affaires qu'à condition d'être payé, ou ne donne raison qu'au plus offrant.

LĀN

涎 *Lān.* 口 |, *heoù lān*, salive.

吐口 |, *t'ouí heoù lān*, cracher.

懶 *Lān.* Paresseux, paresse.

犯 | 惰, *fám lān t'ó*, faire le paresseux, commettre un acte de paresse.

LÂN

欄 *Lân.* Barrière, enclos, bordure d'habit.

| 杆, *lân kōn*, balcon, garde-fou ; bordure d'habit, galons.

牛 |, *nioû lân*, étable à bœufs.

攔 *Lân.* Arrêter, barrer le passage, intercepter.

| 等佢, *lân tèn kî*, arrête-le, empêche-le de passer.

| 日頭, *lân gnìt t'eoû*, intercepter les rayons du soleil.

蘭 *Lân.* Nom de plusieurs plantes odorantes assez communes.

LÀN

零 *Làn (pour lâng).* | | 散散, *làn làn sàn sàn*, dispersés d'ici de là.

教友 | 散, *haó yoū làn sàn*, les chrétiens sont à distance les uns des autres, non groupés.

LÁN

爛 *Lán.* Brisé, détérioré, déchiré, usé; bien cuit, blet.

打｜, *tà lán*, briser.

扯｜, *tch'à lán*, déchirer.

｜疤, *lán pā*, plaie, blessure.

裡個藥噲｜肉, *ỳ ké· yŏc voé· lán nioûc*, cette drogue attaque les chairs.

衫子｜(𨑨)帛裡, *sām tzè lán p'ĕt lê·*, l'habit est déchiré.

著｜衫, *tchŏc lán sām*, porter des guenilles.

牙齒軟牛肉愛煲來, *ngâ tchè niōn nioû nioûc oí pō lán loî*, il faudra faire bien cuire le bœuf, parce que j'ai mal aux dents.

桃子漚阿忒久｜做帛裡, *t'aô tzè eoú á t'iĕt kioù lán ts'ioū p'ĕt lî*, on a conservé les pêches trop longtemps, elles sont toutes blettes.

LĀNG

冷 *Lāng.* Froid.

發｜, *fât lāng*, frissonner, avoir la fièvre.

菜｜帛裡, *ts'oí lāng p'ĕt lî*, les légumes sont refroidis.

｜淡教友, *lāng t'ám kaó yoū*, chrétien tiède, sans ferveur.

｜落, *lāng lŏc*, négligent, peu actif.

LÂNG

伶 *Lâng (pour lîn).* **｜俐**, *lâng lí*, propre, net.

洗衫洗｜俐, *sè· sām sè· lâng lí*, lave proprement les habits.

鈴 *Lâng.* Clochette, grelot.

搖｜, *yaô lâng*, agiter la clochette.

零 *Lâng.* Reste, fraction.

一百｜三個錢, *ŷt pâc lâng sām ké· ts'iên*, 103 sapèques.

一兩三, *ŷt leōng sām*, un taël 3 (*ts'iên*).

一兩｜三, *ŷt leōng lâng sām*, un taël plus 3 (*foūn*).

留多少錢｜用, *lioû tō chaò ts'iên lâng yoúng*, conserver un peu d'argent pour les menues dépenses.

｜｜生生, ou **｜｜碎碎**, *lâng lâng sāng sāng* ou *lâng lâng souí souí*, menus détails.

䁁 *Lâng.* Sécher à l'air.

麼日頭晒衫拿來｜燥來, *mô gnĭt t'eoû saí sām nā loî lâng tsaō loî*, il n'y a pas de soleil, sèche les habits à l'air.

LÁNG

烺 *Láng.* Lisse, brillant.

壁粉倒咁｜, *piāc foùn taò àn láng*, le mur a été crépi très uni.

刀子磨倒咁｜溜, *taō tzè nô taò àn láng lioú*, le couteau a été aiguisé d'un brillant très vif.

另 *Láng.* En outre, différent, autre.

｜回來, *láng fî loî*, tu reviendras une autre fois.

｜外有那個事麼, *láng ngoé· yoū*

mâc ké· sé mô? y a t-il encore autre chose ?

| 事行, *láng sé hâng*, aller seul, séparé de la compagnie.

LAŌ

挔 *Laō*. Mêler, ajouter, avec, rassembler, réunir.

沙灰 | 合來, *sā foē· laō kâp loî*, mêler le sable avec la chaux.

菜餚 | 一個蛋來, *ts'oí teoú laō ŷt ké· t'án loî*, ajoute un œuf dans les légumes.

| 差, *laō ts'ā*, ajouter à tort, se tromper en mêlant.

| 神父講䬸, *laō chîn foú kòng liaó*, causer avec le Père.

| 湫, *laō ts'ioū*, rassembler, réunir.

LAÔ

勞 *Laô*. Travail, peine.

煩 | 你, *fân laô gnî*, je vous demande pardon de la peine que je vous donne.

唔使 | 心, *mĝ sè laô sīm*, inutile de vous inquiéter.

功 | , *koūng laô*, action méritoire.

伯 | , *pâc laô*, pie-grièche.

癆 *Laô*. | 病, *laô p'iáng*, phtysie, maladie de poitrine.

發 | 瘦, *pôt laô seoú*, être phtysique.

牢 *Laô*. Prison.

監 | , *kām laô*, prison. On dit plutôt 班房, *pān fông*.

LAÒ

老 *Laò*. Vieux, ancien, respectable.

| 人家, *laò gnîn kā*, vieillard.

| 公, *laò koūng*, | 婆, *laò p'ô*, mari, femme, épouse.

| 兄, *laò hioūng*, | 弟, *laò t'aí*, mon frère aîné, mon frère cadet.

| 妹, *laò moé·*, ma sœur cadette.

| 手, *laò choù*, expérimenté, qui s'y entend.

| 實, *laò chĭt*, sincère, simple, débonnaire.

| 虎, | 鼠, | 鴉, *laò foù, laò tch'où, laò ā*, tigre, rat, corbeau.

LAÓ

挔 *Laó*. Peser, soupeser.

一担一担愛 | 等來, *ŷt tām ŷt tām oí laó tèn loî*, il faut peser toutes les charges l'une après l'autre.

咾 *Laó*. Espacé, peu serré.

米篩忒 | , *mì sī t'ièt laó*, le crible est trop gros.

種菜種 | | 來, *tchoúng ts'oí tchoúng laó laó loî*, plante les légumes peu serrés.

LĂP

攋 *Lăp*. Demander, implorer.

| 一滴別我, *lăp ŷt tĭt poūn ngaî*, donne-m'en un peu.

| 食, *lăp chĭt*, se dit de quelqu'un qui vous importune par ses demandes incessantes.

臘 *Lăp*. Saler, dessécher.

丨猪肝, *lăp tchoū kōn*, saler un foie de cochon.

丨乾, *lăp kōn*, saler et dessécher.

蠟 *Lăp*. Cire d'abeilles ou d'insectes.

蜂丨, *foūng lăp*, cire d'abeilles.

丨樹, *lăp choú*, espèce d'arbre qui donne de la cire.

丨燭, *lăp tchoûc*, chandelle, cierge.

洋丨, 白丨, *yông lăp, p'ăc lăp*, bougie de suif ou de stéarine.

LÂP

合 *Lâp* (*hăp*). Ajuster bout à bout.

酒透丨阿酒罌起, *tsioù t'eoú lâp á tsioù āng hì*, ajuster l'entonnoir à la bouteille.

邋 *Lâp*. 丨遢, *lâp sêp*, saletés, résidus secs, comme des brindilles d'herbe etc.

丨遢, *lâp sâp*, sordide.

LĂT

Lăt. Bas côtés d'une maison.

一丨屋, *ŷt lăt voûc*, un bas côté d'une maison, bâtiment latéral.

辣 *Lăt*. Saveur piquante, âcre.

芥丨, *kiaí lăt*, moutarde.

你放忒多加里十分丨, *gnî fóng t'iĕt tō kā lī chĭp foūn lăt*, tu as mis trop de kari, c'est trop piquant.

LÂT

Lât. Ardeur du soleil, brûler, croûte.

日頭十分丨, *gnĭt teoû chĭp foūn lât*, le soleil est très ardent.

火忒丨, *fò t'iĕt lât*, le feu est trop ardent.

菜燒丨, *ts'oí chaō lât*, les légumes sont brûlés.

爛疤脫丨, *lán pā t'ŏt lât*, la plaie a formé une croûte.

Lât. 丨丨翻, *lât tât fān*, sens dessus dessous.

丨丨倒, *lât lât taò*, même sens.

LEĀNG

領 *Leāng*. Recevoir, gouverner, col; particule numérale des habits; là.

禮物官府唔曾丨, *lī voŭt kouōn foù mĝ ts'ĕn leāng*, le mandarin n'a pas reçu les présents.

丨洗, *leāng sè˙*, le baptême, recevoir le baptême.

丨事官, *leāng sé kouōn*, consul.

丨撿, *leāng kiàm*, facile à avoir, à prendre.

細人子拿竹篙來打桃子跌下來我丨撿, *sé˙ gnîn tzè nā tchoûc kaō loî tà t'aô tzè tiĕt hā loî ngaî leāng kiàm*, l'enfant abattait les pêches avec une gaule, je n'avais qu'à les ramasser.

衫丨, *sām leāng*, col d'un habit.

一丨褲, *ŷt leāng foú*, un pantalon.

神父在丨麼, *chîn foú ts'oí leāng mô*? le Père est-il là (expression particulière à certains pays)?

嶺 *Leăng*. Colline.
丨崗, *leăng kōng*, colline.

LEÁNG

領 *Leáng*. Charade.
做丨, *tsó leáng*, faire une charade.
團丨, *t'ôn leáng*, deviner une charade.

LEN
(*Voir* LANG et LIEN)

LEŌNG

両 *Leōng*. Once, taël.
一丨銀, *ŷt leōng nioûn*, un taël.
两丨猪肉, *leòng leōng tchoū nioûc*, 2 onces de viande de porc.

LEÔNG

良 *Leông*. Bon, excellent.
丨善, *leông chán*, d'un caractère doux, vertueux.
丨心人, *leông sīm gnîn*, homme de conscience, reconnaissant.
死絕丨心, *sì ts'ĭĕt leông sīm*, qui a perdu toute conscience.
背丨心, *p'oí leông sīm*, agir contre sa conscience.

凉 *Leông*. Frais.
丨爽, *leông sòng*, fraîcheur agréable.
井水陰丨, *tsiàng chouì ŷm leông*, l'eau du puits est très fraîche.
天過丨, *t'iēn koúó leông*, le temps s'est rafraîchi.
丨帽, *leông maó*, chapeau léger que les femmes portent en été.

量 *Leông*. Mesurer, délibérer.
丨有幾長, *leông yoū kì tch'ông*, mesurer la longueur.
拿來丨一下, *nā loî leông ŷt há*, mesurons un peu.
商丨, *chōng leông*, délibérer, se consulter.
好商丨個人, *haò chōng leông ké gnîn*, homme de bonne composition.

糧 *Leông*. Nourriture, impôts, régiment.
養丨, *yōng leông*, nourriture.
丨餉, *leông hiòng*, impôts.
還丨, *vân leông*, solder les impôts.
丨房, *leông fông*, bureau des impôts.
帶一個丨子, *taí ŷt ké leông tzè*, conduire un régiment (500 soldats).

粱 *Leông*. 高丨粟, *kaō leông sioûc*, sorgho.
高丨酒, *kaō leông tsioù*, vin de sorgho.

樑 *Leông*. Maîtresse poutre.
某日放扛丨, *meoū gnĭt fóng kōng leông*, tel jour on posera la maîtresse poutre (ce qui se fait solennellement).
買屋看丨討薪臼看娘, *maí voûc k'ón leông t'aò sīm k'ioū k'ón niông*, en achetant une maison il faut examiner la maîtresse poutre, pour choisir une bru il faut considérer ce qu'est la belle-mère.

鞋 |, *haî leóng*, arète ou côte des souliers, sur le dessus du pied.

LEÒNG

兩 *Leòng*. Deux (ne s'emploie pas dans les nombres ordinaux).

一 | 三, *ŷt leòng sām*, 1, 2, 3.

| 十, *leòng chìp*, 20.

| 百, *leòng pâc*, 200.

LEÓNG

量 *Leóng*. Mesure, capacité.

力 |, *lìt leóng*, degré de force (physique ou morale).

度 |, *t'oú leóng*, habileté, intelligence, générosité.

大 | 個人, *t'aí leóng ké· gnîn*, homme au cœur grand, large, généreux.

福大 | 大赦宥阿子佢, *foûc taí leóng t'aí chá yoú á tzè kî*, vous, qui avez le cœur large et magnanime, pardonnez-lui.

我 | 倒佢麼來, *ngaî leóng taò kî mô loî*, je pense qu'il ne viendra pas.

亮 *Leóng*. Clair, lumineux.

光 |, *kouōng leóng*, brillant, clair.

月係 |, *gnĕt hé· leóng*, la lune est très claire.

燈火唔 |, *tēn fò mĝ leóng*, le feu de la lampe n'est pas vif, ne donne pas de lumière.

LEOÛ

撈 *Leoû*. Retirer de l'eau, tirer hors de.

桶跌落井底下 | 唔起, *t'oùng tiĕt lŏc tsiàng taì hā leoû mĝ hì*, le seau est tombé au fond du puits, on ne peut pas le repêcher.

| 箠, *leoû fī*, filet à pêcher.

樓 *Leoû*. Tour, grenier, étage supérieur.

上 | 上, *chōng leoû hóng*, monter à l'étage.

| 梯, *leoû t'oī*, escalier.

門 |, *moûn leoû*, portail.

LEOÚ

漏 *Leoú*. Laisser passer l'eau, s'échapper à travers de.

屋 | 雨, *voûc leoú ỳ*, la pluie passe à travers le toit.

桶 | 水, *t'oùng leoú chouì*, le seau a une fuite.

| 風, *leoú foūng*, fuite d'air; laisser échapper un secret.

裡件事莫 | 風, *ỳ k'ián sé mŏc leoú foūng*, que cette affaire reste secrète.

陋 *Leoú*. Abject, honteux.

| 漱, *leoú seoú*, se dit d'un homme malpropre et grossier.

醜 |, *tch'où leoú*, vilain, honteux.

摟 *Leoú*. Appeler, attirer.

| 雞, | 狗, *leoú kē·, leoú keoù*, appeler les poules, le chien.

| 唔聽, *leoú mĝ t'āng*, ne pouvoir faire venir en appelant.

牛媽吽 | 佢子, *nioû mâ kiaó leoú kiā tzè*, la vache mugit pour appeler son petit.

｜雞米, *leoú kē· mì*, du riz pour attirer les poules (se dit des présents que l'on donne, en vue de toucher le cœur de quelqu'un et d'obtenir ce que l'on désire).

LÊP

㩉 *Lep*. Dérober, enlever furtivement, chiper, saisir rapidement un objet.

LĔT

扐 *Lĕt*. Soulever, soupeser.

｜得起, ｜唔起, *lĕt têt hì, lĕt mĝ hì*, je puis le soulever, je ne puis le soulever.

LĪ

(Voir aussi les mots LOUI)

里 *Lī* (pour *lì*). Mesure itinéraire d'environ 1000 pas.

行裡三十｜, *hâng lì sām chĭp lī*, j'ai fait 30 *lī*.

隔聖堂三｜路, *kâc chín t'ông sām lī loú*, à trois *lī* de la chapelle.

十｜為一步, *chĭp lī vî ÿt p'oú*, dix *lī* font une lieue.

萬｜長城, *ván lī tch'ông châng*, la grande muraille de 10 000 *lī*.

鄉｜間個事唔干你事, *hiōng lī kiān ké· sé mĝ kōn gnî sé*, c'est l'affaire du village, cela ne te regarde pas.

理 *Lī*. La droite raison, régler, administrer, gouverner.

天｜, *t'iēn lī*, la droite raison, la raison d'être d'une chose; justice, équité.

天｜良心, *t'iēn lī leông sīm*, la raison et la conscience.

合｜, 唔合｜, *hăp lī, mĝ hăp lī*, conforme, non conforme à la raison, convenable, pas convenable.

有｜, 麼｜, *yoū lī, mô lī*, avoir raison, n'avoir pas raison.

道｜, *t'aó lī*, vérité, doctrine.

講道｜, *kòng t'áo lī*, prêcher.

生｜, *sēn lī* (vulg. *siēn lī*), moyen de vivre, métier, commerce.

做生｜, *tsó siēn lī*, faire le commerce.

｜事, 料｜, *lī sé, liaó lī*, gérer une affaire, arranger, prendre soin de.

求神父打｜我事, *k'ioû chîn foú tà lī ngâ sé*, je prie le Père de s'occuper de mon affaire.

各人個事各人料｜, *kôc gnîn ké· sé kôc gnîn liaó lī*, que chacun s'occupe de ses affaires.

總｜衙門, *tsoùng lī ngâ moûn*, le ministère des affaires étrangères à Pékin.

條｜, *t'iaô lī*, arrangement, disposition ; diviser par articles.

天文地｜, *t'iēn voûn t'í lī*, l'astronomie et la géographie (*ou géomancie*).

地｜先生, *t'í lī sīn sāng*, jongleur prétendant découvrir les terrains qui portent bonheur.

鯉 *Lī*. Carpe.

紅｜嫣, *foûng lī mâ*, espèce de carpe.

禮 *Lī*. Politesse.

｜節, *lī tsiĕt*, rites, cérémonies.

補｜節, *poù lī tsiĕt*, suppléer les cérémonies.

| 貌, *lī máo*, urbanité.

| 物, *lī voŭt*, présents de politesse.

行官 | , *hâng kouōn lī*, observer le cérémonial d'usage entre mandarins.

| 部, *lī p'oú*, tribunal des Rites.

裡 (裏) *Lī* ou *lì* ou *lî*. Doublure d'habit, mettre une doublure.

烏衫藍 | , *voū sām lâm lī*, habit noir avec une doublure bleue.

布係靨愛拿來 | 過, *poú hé· ngôc oí na loî lī kouó*, l'étoffe est bien mauvaise, il faudra y faire mettre une doublure.

LÎ

裡 *Lî*. Intérieur, dans ; son final employé dans certains pays.

我心 | 唔安樂, *ngaî sīm lî mĝ ōn lŏc*, je n'ai pas le cœur à l aise.

屋貯 | , *voŭc toù lî*, dans la maison.

我個 | , *ngā kḗ· lî*, c'est à moi, c'est le mien.

Comme son final, ce mot est prononcé de diverses manieres, selon les pays. A *Ka-yn-tchou* on dit surtout *lê·*, et on l'emploie aussi comme marque du passé, dans le sens du caractère 了 *liaò*.

你去 | 麼, *gnî hí lê· mô?* y es-tu allé?

我去 | , *ngaî hí lê·*, j'y suis allé.

Lorsque le mot précédent finit par une consonne, la lettre *l* de *lê·* est supprimée, mais on fait une légère liaison avec le mot précédent.

食 | 飯唔曾, *chĭt-ê· fán mĝ ts'ên ?* avez-vous dîné ?

掌羊 | , *tchòng yông-ê·*, garder les chèvres.

Cette remarque ne doit pas être prise pour une règle générale; l'usage seul peut en faire comprendre l'à-propos.

離 *Lî*. Se retirer, être séparé.

| 開犯罪個機會, *lî k'oī fám ts'oúi ké· kī fí*, écarter l'occasion de pécher.

遲早都愛相 | , *tchê tsào toū oí siòng lî*, tôt ou tard il faudra se séparer.

| 唔開, *lî mĝ k'oī*, ne pouvoir se passer de.

| 別, *lî p'ĭĕt*, se séparer, prendre congé.

璃 *Lî*. Pierre transparente.

玻 | , *pō lî*, verre, vitre.

剌 ou 劃玻 | , *lăc* ou *văc pō lî*, fendre ou rayer un verre.

玻 | 窗, 玻 | 盃, 玻 | 瓦, *pō lî ts'oūng, pō lî pī, pō lî ngà*, fenêtre à vitres, verre à boire, tuile en verre.

籬 *Lî*. Enclos, haie.

園 | , *yân lî*, enclos de jardin.

梨 *Lî*. Poire.

| 子樹, *lî tzè choú*, poirier.

厘 *Lî*. Mesure de poids (millième de l'once), contribution.

十 | 爲一分, *chĭp lî vî ўt foūn*, 10 *lî* font 1 *foūn*.

| 戥, *lî tĕn*, petite balance pour peser l'argent.

| 金, *lî kîm*, droits de douane.
收 | 金, *choū lî kīm*, exiger la contribution.

狸 *Lî*. 狐 | , *foû lî*, renard.
貓 | *miaó lî*, chat sauvage.

驪 *Lî*. Âne.
一匹 | , *ŷt p'ît lî*, un âne.
| 哥 豕, *lî kō tôc*, nom vulgaire de l'âne.

Lì

裡 *Lì*. Ici. (Voyez *ỳ*.)

李 *Lì*. Prune.
| 子 樹, *lì tzè choú*, prunier.
當 | , *tōng lì*, espèce de prune sauvage ; ailleurs on l'appelle aussi 當|楠 *tōng nèm*.

Lí

利 *Lí*. Utilité, profit, gain ; tranchant, aigu.
| 益, *lí ŷt*, avantage, utilité.
| 息, *lí sît*, profit, gain.
裡 個 生 理 麼 | 息 , *ỳ ké· siēn lī mô lí sît*, ce commerce n'est pas lucratif.
| 錢, | 穀, *lí ts'iên, lí koŭc*, intérêt en argent, en riz.
三 分 | , *sām fōun lí*, intérêt au taux de 30 pour cent, profit de 30 pour cent.
對 本 | , *touí poùn lí*, intérêt à 100 pour 100.
| 害, *lí hoí*, violent, dangereux, nuisible.
婦 人 家 個 嘴 係 | 害, *foú gnîn kā ké· tchoí hé lí hoí*, les femmes ont méchante langue.
刀 子 唔 | , *taō tzè mĝ lí*, le couteau ne coupe pas.
牽 馬 索 忒 粗 嗆 | (厲) 人 , *k'iān mā sôc t'iĕt tsē voć· lí gnîn*, les rênes sont trop rugueuses, elles vous écorchent.
火 | , *fò lí*, flamme (ailleurs 火 燄, *fò yám* ou *liám*).

例 *Lí*. Règle, loi.
| 書, *lí choū*, code.
犯 | , *fám lí*, violer la loi.
照 | 辦 事, *tcháo lí p'án sé*, juger une affaire d'après la loi.

痢 *Lí*. Dyssenterie.
| 症, *lí tchín*, même sens.
屙 | 肚, *ō lí toù*, dyssenterie (s'emploie au figuré pour se moquer de quelqu'un qui ne sait pas retenir sa parole, parle à tort et à travers).

吏 *Lí*. Magistrat.
官 | , *kouōn lí*, magistrat.
| 部, *lí p'oú*, tribunal des magistrats à Pkéin.
| 房, *lí fông*, tribunal correspondant dans chaque sous-préfecture.

櫐 *Lí* ou *louí*. Support pour fleurs ou légumes.
豆 | , *t'eóu lí*, support pour haricots.
花 拿 來 | 過, *fā nā loî lí koúo*, mets des supports aux fleurs. Voir *louí*.

荔 *Lí*. | 菓, *lí koùo*, prune ou poire sauvage.

利 *Lí.* Langue des animaux.

牛 | , 猪 | , *nioû lí, tchoū lí,* langue de bœuf, langue de porc. Nom inventé par les bouchers pour remplacer le mot 舌 *chăt* langue, qui ressemble trop au mot 蝕 *chăt,* faire faillite !

LIÂM

廉 *Liâm.* Désintéressé, intègre.

| 恥, *liâm tchè* , pudeur.

不顧 | 恥, *poût koú liâm tchè,* n'avoir pas de pudeur.

簾 *Liâm.* Rideau, voile, store.

門 | , *moûn liâm,* store ou rideau de porte.

掛 | , *kouá liâm,* suspendre un voile ou un store.

告解 | , *kaó kiaì liâm,* voile de confessionnal.

鐮 *Liâm.* Faucille.

草 | , *ts'ào liâm,* faucille à couper l'herbe.

LIÀM

澰 *Liàm.* Desséché.

塘 | 帛 禮, *t'ông liàm p'ĕt lê·,* l'étang est desséché.

田 晒 | 水, *t'iên sái liàm choùi,* la rizière est desséchée par le soleil.

扭 | 衫, *nioù liàm sām,* dessécher un habit en le tordant.

LIÁM

廉 *Liám.* Côte, arête d'un corps solide.

開柑子拿一 | 別我就好, *k'oī kām tzè nā ŷt liám poūn ngaî ts'ioú haò,* ouvre l'orange et donne-m'en une tranche, cela me suffit.

六 | 洋 桃 罕 見, *lioŭc liám yông t'aô hòn kián,* les caramboles à six côtes sont rares.

殮 *Liám.* Habiller un mort.

殯 | ou | 葬, *pín liám,* ou *liám tsóng,* ensevelir un mort.

入 | , *gnĭp liám,* mettre le mort dans le cercueil.

燄 *Liám.* 火 | , *fò liám,* flamme vacillante, traînée de lumière (ailleurs 火 利 *fò lí,* flamme).

LIĀO

衤了 *Liāo.* Particule numérale des pantalons.

一 | 褲, *ŷt liāo foú,* un pantalon (ailleurs on dit: 一 領 褲 *ŷt leāng foú*).

LIÂO

寮 *Liâo.* Hangar, abri contre la pluie, cabanes que les laboureurs dressent dans leurs champs.

搭 一 個 | , *tâp ŷt ké· liaô,* faire ou construire un abri de ce genre.

撩 *Liâo.* Provoquer, taquiner par des attouchements, ou des tapes.

| 婦 人, *liâo foú gnîn,* avoir des jeux de mains avec une femme.

我 唔 曾 | 你, 你 打 我 做 乜 個,

ngâi mĝ ts'în liâo gnî, gnî tà ngaî tsó mâc ké· ? je ne t'ai pas taquiné, pourquoi me bats-tu ?

LIAÒ

了 *Liaò*. Terminer, conclure, signe du passé.

丨事, *liaò sé*, terminer une affaire.

官丨帛程, *koūon liaò pĕt lê·*, le mandarin a perdu sa place.

丨然, *liaò yân*, c'est clair, évident.

做丨, *tsó liaò*, c'est fait.

忘了, *móng liaò*, jai oublié.

丨程, *liaò lê·*, 丨淨, *liaò ts'iáng*, tout est perdu.

丨不得, *liaò poût têt*, ça n'en finira pas! on n'y peut rien.

LIÁO

料 *Liáo*. Matériaux, compter, prévoir.

材丨, *ts'âi liáo*, matériaux, ingrédients.

木丨, *moûc liáo*, bois de charpente ou de menuiserie.

丨想唔定, *liáo siòng mĝ t'ín*, on ne peut pas prévoir.

丨理, *liáo lī*, s'occuper des affaires.

LIAÓ

嫐 *Liaó*. flâner ; se promener ; n'a pas de correspondant bien exact en français, l'usage fera comprendre le sens.

迣丨, 丨耍, *lâ liaó, liaó chà*, se promener, flâner.

我去同神父丨, *ngâi hí t'oûng chîn foú liaó*, je vais tenir compagnie au Père.

天光到暗丨, *t'iēn koūong táo âm liaó*, ne rien faire du matin au soir.

LIĂP

獵 *Liăp*. Chasser avec des chiens.

打丨, *tà liăp*, même sens.

丨狗, *liăp keoù*, chien de chasse.

粒 *Liăp* ou *lĭp*. Particule numérale des grains.

一丨米, *ŷt liăp mì*, un grain de riz.

LIÂP

頰 *Liâp*. 丨牙齒, *liăp ngâ tchè*, pris entre les dents.

細骨丨倒牙齒, *sé· koût liâp taò ngâ tchè*, un petit os s'est arrêté entre mes dents.

細炮子拿阿褲頭上丨等程, *sé· p'aó tzè nā á foú t'eoû hóng liâp tèn ê·*, suspendre son revolver à sa ceinture.

LIĒN

臉 *Liēn*. Face, visage.

丨面, *liēn mién*, même sens, au propre et au figuré.

麼丨面, *mô liēn mién*, il n'a pas de face, il est déshonoré.

傷丨, *chōng liēn*, déshonorer, humilier. *Voir mién.*

LIÊN

連 *Liên*. Unir, ensemble, consécutif.

18

兩坵田相｜, *leòng k'ioū t'iên siōng liên*, les deux rizières sont contiguës.

一把｜, *ŷt pà liên*, le tout ensemble.

｜兩日, *liên leòng gnǐt*, deux jours de suite.

｜你都同來去, *liên gnî toū t'oûng loî hí*, toi aussi viens avec nous.

縺 *Liên*. Coudre, point de devant.

｜一件衫, *liên ŷt k'ián sām*, coudre un habit.

蓮 *Liên*. ｜花, *liên fā*, nénuphar.

｜肉, ou ｜子, *liên nioûc* ou *liên tzè*, graine de nénuphar.

鰱 *Liên*. Espèce de poisson.

｜鯉, *liên lī*, espèce de fourmilier à fortes écailles.

LIÉN

練 *Lién*. S'exercer.

唔曉騎馬唔曾｜過, *mĝ hiào k'î mā, mĝ ts'ên lién koúo*, je ne sais pas aller à cheval, je ne m'y suis jamais exercé.

操｜, *ts'āo lién*, s'exercer au métier des armes, faire l'exercice.

團｜, *t'ôn lién*, se réunir pour s'exercer, s'exercer ensemble.

鍊 *Lién*. Chaîne en métal.

鐵｜, *t'iēt lién*, chaîne de fer.

鎖｜, *sò lién*, enchaîné et cadenacé.

煉 *Lién*. Purifier par le feu.

｜獄, *lién nioŭc*, le purgatoire.

戀 *Lién*. Tromper, surprendre par artifice; être attaché à une personne ou à une chose.

撮把戲緊係｜人個, *ts'ōt pà hí kìn hé· lién gnîn ké·*, les tours de prestidigitation ne sont que des tromperies.

｜人個錢, *lién gnîn ké· ts'iên*, filouter les sapèques d'autrui.

｜｜不捨, *lién lién poût chà*, s'attacher à une chose, ne pouvoir s'en séparer.

蹍 *Lién*. Piétiner.

菜都｜死, *ts'ói toū lién sì*, les légumes ont été tellement piétinés, qu'ils en sont morts.

牛｜泥好出磚, *niôu lién nâi hào tch'oūt tchōn*, le buffle piétine la terre pour en faire des briques.

LIĔT

列 *Liĕt*. Ordre, rang.

｜品天神, *liĕt p'ìn t'iēn chîn*, hiérarchie des anges.

｜位教友, *liĕt ví káo yoū*, tous les chrétiens, chrétiens de tout rang.

烈 *Liĕt*. Violent, méchant.

性情好｜, *sín ts'în hào liĕt*, d'un caractère emporté, porté à la colère.

馬十分｜, *mā chĭp foūn liĕt*, le cheval est très fougueux.

裂 *Liĕt*. Diviser, déchirer.

｜開, *liĕt k'oī*, se séparer, se fendre.

| 教, *lìt káo*, schisme, hérésie.

LĪM

廩 *Līm.* | 生, *līm sēn*, bacheliers choisis au concours dans chaque (縣 *yán*) sous-préfecture, et recevant de l'administration publique une subvention annuelle.

補 |, *poù līm*, être admis dans cette catégorie de bacheliers.

LÎM

林 *Lîm.* Forêt.

樹 |, *choú lîm*, forêt d'arbres.

竹 |, *tchoûc lîm*, forêt de bambous (peu employé, on dit plutot : 樹山, 竹山, *choú sān, tchoûc sān*).

淋 *Lîm.* Arroser, mouiller.

| 菜, *lîm ts'oí*, arroser les légumes.

秋 | 夜雨田禾噲好, *ts'ioū lîm yá ý t'iên vô voé· haò*, les nuits d'automne sont pluvieuses, la moisson sera bonne.

臨 *Lîm.* Approcher, près de.

聖神降 |, *chín chîn kóng lîm*, la Pentecôte.

| 終, *lîm tchoūng*, proche de la fin, agonie.

早安排 | 尾攪唔贏, *tsào ōn p'âi, lîm mī kào mĝ yâng*, prends tes mesures d'avance, au moment venu tu ne pourrais y suffire.

| 尾來, *lîm mī lôi*, à la fin, en dernier lieu.

| 夜就發冷, *lîm yá ts'ioú fât lāng*, les frissons de la fièvre viennent dès la nuit tombante.

LĪN

鱗 *Līn.* Écaille de poisson.

湖鰍麽 | 子, *foû ts'ioū mô līn tzè*, le *foû ts'ioū* (petite anguille de boue) n'a pas d'écailles.

LÎN

鄰 *Lîn.* Voisin, contigu, limitrophe.

| 舍, *lîn chá*, voisin, proche voisin.

| 近, *lîn k'ioún*, voisinage, tout près.

四 | 八家, *sí lîn pât kā*, tout le voisinage.

憐 *Lîn.* Avoir pitié.

矜 | 我等, *k'īm lîn ngō tèn*, ayez pitié de nous (litanies).

實在可 |, *chìt ts'aí k'ò lîn*, c'est à faire pitié.

精 |, *tsīn lîn*, qui a l'intelligence ouverte.

| 通, *lîn t'oūng*, intelligent, ingénieux.

靈 *Lîn.* Substance spirituelle, faculté de comprendre.

| 魂, *lîn foûn*, l'âme spirituelle.

| 魂三司, *lîn foûn sām sē*, les trois facultés de l'âme.

| 性, *lîn sín*, intelligence, instinct.

麽 | 性, *mô lîn sín*, qui manque de jugement.

燒 | 屋, *chāo lîn voûc*, brûler (après 3 ans) la maisonnette, en papier ou en bois, dans laquelle est censée résider l'âme du défunt.

凌 *Lîn*. Nuire, outrager.

| 辱, *lîn yoŭc*, injurier, outrager.

依勢 | 人, *ỳ ché lîn gnîn*, profiter de sa force, ou de son autorité pour nuire à quelqu'un.

綾 *Lîn*. | 羅, *lîn lô*, 羽 | , *ỳ lîn*, espèce d'étoffe de soie.

翎 *Lîn*. | 子, *lîn tzè*, plume de paon portée en plumet comme insigne de mandarin.

戴 | 子, *tái lîn tzè*, porter ce plumet.

花 | , *fā lîn*, 藍 | , *lâm lîn*, insigne d'un grand mandarin.

輪 *Lîn* (*loûn*). Successif, alterner.

| 等來掌屋, *lîn tèn loî tchòng voŭc*, garder la maison, chacun à son tour.

| 去 | 轉, *lîn hí lîn tchòn*, aller et venir à tour de rôle, faire la navette.

Lîn lîn (ou *līn līn*) *lāng lāng*, aller çà et là.

LÌN

Lìn. Membre viril. Sans doute à cause de l'obscénité même de ce mot, les Chinois l'emploient très fréquemment. On ne peut en ignorer le sens; voici les expressions les plus communes.

Àn lìn koún ! correspond à l'expression vulgaire : que tu es bête !

Gnî ts'ioŭc ngā lìn, tu m'embêtes (*litt.* tu me piques le membre).

Gnî naí ngā lìn mĝ hô, tu ne pourras rien contre moi (*litt.* tu ne pourras pas même supporter la force de mon membre).

Kî voé· kōt lìn, il va te couper le membre. Se dit souvent pour effrayer les enfants, comme on dirait : voilà le croque-mitaine.

LÍN

令 *Lín*. Ordre, loi, noble.

皇帝個命 | , *fông tí ké· mín lín*, l'ordre de l'Empereur.

| 尊, | 堂, | 郎, | 兄, *lín tsoūn, lín t'ông, lín lông, lín hioūng*, Monsieur votre père, Madame votre mère, Monsieur votre fils, Monsieur votre frère.

| 旗, *lín k'î*, drapeau confié à un chef de bataillon.

王 | 旗牌, *vông lín k'î p'aî*, autorité absolue donnée par l'Empereur.

· 畧 *Liŏc*. Un peu.

| | , 大 | , *liŏc liŏc, t'aí liŏc*, en général, environ, en résumé.

大 | 有幾多擺, *t'aí liŏc yoū kì tō paì ?* combien de fois environ ?

| | 曉得, *liŏc liŏc hiaò tĕt*, je sais à peu près.

LIOŪ

溜 *Lioū* (*lioû*). Ramper.

蛇哥 | 等來, *châ kō lioū tèn loî*, le serpent s'avance en rampant.

LIOÛ

留 *Lioû*. Retenir, garder, réserver.

| 客, *lioû hâc*, retenir un hôte par politesse.

猪肉丨阿天光日食，*tchoū nioûc lioû á t'iēn kouōng gnĭt chĭt,* réserve la viande de porc pour demain matin.

丨毛辮，丨鬚，*lioû maō piēn, lioû sī,* laisser croître ses cheveux, sa barbe.

丨心，*lioû sīm,* faire attention.

榴 *Lioû.* 石丨，*chăc lioû,* grenadier.

硫 *Lioû.* 丨磺 *lioû vông,* soufre.

流 *Lioû,* Couler, suivre le courant, changer de place; classe d'hommes.

丨水，*lioû chouì,* eau courante, opposé à : *sì chouì* (eau stagnante).

丨血，*lioû hiĕt,* écoulement de sang.

蠟燭噲丨，*lâp tchoûc voé· lioû,* le cierge coule.

放丨，*fóng lioû,* envoyer ou être envoyé en exil.

上丨個人，*chóng lioû ké· gnîn,* homme de la haute classe.

下丨個人，*há lioû ké· gnîn,* homme de la basse classe.

丨丨溜溜，*lioû lioû lioú lioû,* errer à l'aventure.

打丨郎，*tà lioû lông,* vagabonder.

LIOÙ

柳 *Lioù.* 丨樹，*lioù choú,* Saule pleureur.

LIOÚ

溜 *Lioú.* Etre entraîné par le courant, glisser.

丨滑，*lioú văt,* glissant, poli.

桌唔坪東西噲丨走，*tsôc mĝ p'iâng toūng sī voé· lioú tseoù,* la table n'est pas d'aplomb, les objets vont glisser.

捉魚子捉唔噲丨走，*tsôc nĝ tzè tsôc mĝ voùn voé· lioú tseoù,* on peut difficillement tenir un poisson, il vous glisse des mains.

丨馬，*lioú ma,* promener le cheval après une course.

LIOǓC

綠 *Lioǔc.* Vert, vert pâle.

丨色，*lioǔc sĕt,* couleur verte.

丨竹，*lioǔc tchoûc,* espèce de bambou.

菉 *Lioǔc.* 丨豆，*lioǔc t'eóu,* espèce de pois.

錄 *Lioǔc.* Inscrire, copier.

丨上簿上起，*lioǔc chōng p'oū hóng hì,* inscrire au registre.

同我丨到一張，*t'oûng ngâi lioûc tào ŷt tchōng,* copie-m'en un exemplaire.

目丨，*moûc lioǔc,* table d'un livre.

LIOÛC

六 (陸) *Lioûc.* Six.

丨個，第丨個，*lioûc ké·, t'í lioûc ké·,* six, le sixième.

丨丨續續，*lioûc lioûc sioǔc sioǔc,* successivement, à mesure.

LIOŪNG

矓 *Lioūng*. Approcher, courir dessus.

行快來野猪緊｜等來, *hâng k'ouái loî yā tchoū kìn lioūng tèn loî*, va donc vite, le sanglier nous vient dessus.

鷓鴣難打一聽倒响就｜走, *tchá koū nân tà ŷt t'āng taò hiòng ts'ioú lioūng tseoù*, la perdrix est difficile à chasser, dès qu'elle entend du bruit elle piète.

LIOÛNG

龍 *Lioûng*. Dragon, animal fabuleux auquel les Chinois attachent la fortune d'une famille ou d'un pays,

迎｜燈, *niâng lioûng tēn*, faire la procession avec d'immenses lanternes à forme de dragon (amusement superstitieux du nouvel an).

｜眼, *lioûng niàn*, espèce de fruit.

馬｜頭, *mā lioûng t'eôu*, licou du cheval.

LĬP

立 *Lĭp*. Eriger, établir.

｜皇帝, *lĭp fông tí*, instituer un empereur.

吾主耶穌親｜個, *ng̃ tchòu yâ sē ts'īn lĭp ké·*, institué par N. S. Jésus-Christ lui-même.

｜功, *lĭp koūng*, faire des actions méritoires.

｜和約, *lĭp fô yôc*, faire un traité de paix.

｜借字, *lĭp tsiá sé*, dresser un contrat de prêt.

LÎP

笠 *Lîp*. **｜麻**, *lîp mâ*, large chapeau en feuilles de bambous.

粒 *Lîp* (ou *liăp*). Part. num. des grains (*voir liăp*).

LĬT

力 *Lĭt*. Force, puissance.

盡｜, *ts'ín lĭt*, faire son possible.

用｜, *yoúng lĭt*, **出｜**, *tch'oût lĭt*, déployer ses forces, faire des efforts.

有幾百斤｜, *yōu kì pâc kīn lĭt*, il est de force à manier plusieurs centaines de livres.

我麼咁大個｜量, *ngaî mô àn t'aí ké· lĭt leóng*, je n'ai pas cette puissance.

肋 *Lĭt*. Côte (peu employé, on dit: **牌骨** *p'aî koût*).

栗 *Lĭt*. Châtaigne.

勒 *Lĭt*. Presser, forcer, faire une violence morale.

取錢盡｜, *ts'ì ts'iên ts'ín lĭt*, tourmenter, presser quelqu'un, afin d'obtenir son payement.

官府｜佢到案, *kouōn foù lĭt kî taó ón*, le mandarin l'a contraint de se présenter au jugement.

｜索人個錢, *lĭt sôc gnîn ké· ts'iên*, faire une violence morale à quelqu'un, pour avoir son argent.

律 *Lĭt.* 法 | , *fâp lĭt,* loi, règle.

一 | 判佢, *ŷt lĭt p'án kî,* punissez-le suivant la même règle, de la même manière.

歷 *Lĭt.* Ordre, suite de faits.

| 代, *lĭt t'oí,* les générations successives.

| 年都有裡個規矩, *lĭt niân toū yoū ỳ ké· kouī kì,* cette règle existe depuis une série d'années.

來 | , *loî lĭt,* origine et suite de faits, ordre.

樣個來 | 你講我知, *nióng ké· loî lĭt gnî kòng ngaî tī,* raconte-moi les faits, comme ils se sont passés.

LŌ

囉 *Lō.* | 唆, *lō sō,* se dit d'un homme importun, ennuyeux.

LÔ

羅 *Lô.* Filet, tissu à mailles peu serrées.

紗 | *sā lô,* tissu en soie, clair et léger.

| 盤, *lô p'ân,* boussole.

波 | 麻, *pō lô mâ,* tissu fait avec les feuilles d'ananas.

籮 *Lô.* Corbeille, panier qui sert à porter les céréales.

| 籠, *lô loùng,* corbeille, panier de voyage.

一担 | , *ŷt tam lô,* une paire de corbeilles (pour une charge).

蘿 *Lô.* | 蔔, *lô p'ĕt,* rave, navet, carotte.

紅 | 蔔, 黃 | 蔔, *foûng lô p'ĕt, vông lô p'ĕt,* radis, carotte.

| 蔔絲, *lô p'ĕt sē,* navet coupé en filets menus.

鑼 *Lô.* Tam-tam, gong.

打 | 鼓, *tà lô kòu,* frapper du tamtam et de la grosse caisse.

螺 *Lô.* 田 | , *t'iên lô,* escargot de rizière.

| 螄, *lô sē,* vis, tire-bouchon.

扭 | 螄, *nioú lô sē,* tourner une vis pour l'enfoncer ou la retirer.

騾 *Lô.* Mulet.

一匹 | , *ŷt p'ĭt lô,* un mulet.

| 係奸, *lô hé· kiān,* le mulet est têtu.

LÓ

Ló-só, sale, malpropre.

LŎC

落 *Lŏc.* Tomber, descendre ; demeurer.

| 雨 ou | 水, *lŏc ỳ* ou *lŏc chouì,* pleuvoir, il pleut.

| 三日雨, *lŏc sām gnĭt ỳ,* il a plu pendant trois jours.

失落, *chĭt lŏc,* laisser perdre, perdre.

| 船, *lŏc chôn,* s'embarquer.

你那裡 | 店, *gnî naí lī lŏc tiám ?* où vas-tu loger ?

麼那裡 | 脚, *mô naí lī lŏc kiŏc,* n'avoir pas où poser le pied, où loger.

鵰子｜阿樹上𠝹, *tiaō tzè lŏc á choú hóng liaó*, l'oiseau s'est posé sur l'arbre.

放唔｜, *fóng mĝ lŏc*, ne pouvoir faire tenir dans.

｜多一個字, *lŏc tō ŷt ké· sé*, ajouter un caractère.

吞唔｜, *t'oūn mĝ lŏc*, ne pouvoir avaler.

駱 *Lŏc*. ｜駝, *lŏc t'ô*, chameau.

絡 *Lŏc*. ｜脚, *lŏc kiôc*, espèce d'anse pour porter les sacs.

樂 *Lŏc*. Plaisir, joie.

｜意, *lŏc ý*, content, satisfait.

安｜, *ōn lŏc*, bien-être.

心唔安｜, *sīm mĝ ōn lŏc*, je n'ai pas le cœur à l'aise.

LÔI

來 *Lôi*. Venir, arriver; se joint comme auxiliaire à beaucoup de verbes, avec un sens vague de venir, approcher, habile, etc.

｜唔得, *lôi mĝ têt*, ne pouvoir venir.

唔得｜, *mĝ têt lôi*, que ne peut-il venir!

｜裡, *lôi lê·*, être venu, voici.

你去那裡｜, *gnî hí naí lī lôi*, d'où viens-tu?

｜銀十二両, *lôi nioûn chĭp gní leōng*, reçu en argent 12 taëls (terme de compte).

自｜, *tsé lôi*, venir de soi, naturellement.

自｜火 (ou 自得火), *tsé lôi fò* (ou *tsé têt fò*), allumettes chimiques.

本｜, *poùn lôi*, à proprement parler.

做得｜, 做唔｜, *tsó têt lôi, tsó mĝ lôi*, pouvoir ou savoir faire, ne pas savoir ou pouvoir faire.

｜歷, *lôi lĭt*, suite de faits, origine.

｜往, *lôi vōng*, venir et aller, fréquenter.

嫖賭食烟那個都｜, *p'iaô toù chĭt yān mâc ké· toū lôi*, luxure, jeux, fumeur d'opium, il est de tout (il vient pour tout).

一｜, 二｜, *ŷt lôi, gní lôi*, d'abord, ou premièrement; ensuite, ou secondement.

LOÍ

睞 *Loí*. Trou, ouverture.

賊挖裡｜入間, *ts'ĕt vât lì loí gnĭp kiān*, les voleurs ont fait un trou pour entrer dans la chambre.

我衫子火燒一個｜, *ngā sām tzè fò chāo ŷt ké· loí*, le feu a fait un trou à mon habit.

袋子有一個｜, *t'oí tzè yoū ŷt ké· loí*, le sac est troué.

補一個｜, 塞一個｜, *poù ŷt ké· loí, sĕt ŷt ké· loí*, raccommoder un trou avec une pièce, boucher un trou.

老鼠｜, 蛇｜, *laò tch'où loí, chá loí* trou de rat, trou de serpent.

LÒN

卵 *Lòn*. Œuf, glande.

雞嫲生｜, *kē· mâ sāng lòn*, la poule fait son œuf.

魚子撥｜, *nĝ tzè p'ât lòn*, les poissons frayent.

䝙｜, *hâc lòn*, testicules.

LÓN

亂 *Lón.* Trouble, confusion, rébellion, à tort et à travers.

念經心 |, *niám kīn sīm lón,* prier avec distraction.

作 |, *tsôc lón,* révolutionner, rébellion.

米貴怕 |, *mì kouí p'á lón,* quand le riz est cher, les troubles sont à craindre.

| 講, *lón kòng,* parler à tort et à travers.

| 看, | 想, *lón k'ón, lón siòng,* regarder ce qu'il ne faut pas, penser à mal.

| 打, *lón tà,* frapper indistinctement.

LÔNG

郎 *Lông.* Terme honorifique employé pour désigner un jeune homme.

令 |, *lín lông,* Monsieur votre fils.

幾多個令 |, *kì tō kè· lín lông ?* combien avez-vous de fils ?

婿 |, *sé· lông,* gendre.

等 | 嫂, *tèn lông sào,* bru achetée en prévision d'un fils à venir.

廊 *Lông.* Bas côtés des maisons chinoises.

兩廳兩 | 個屋, *leòng t'āng leòng lông kè· voûc,* maison à deux salles et à deux bas côtés.

榔 *Lông.* **檳 |**, *pīn lông,* noix d'arec.

狼 *Lông.* **豺 |**, *sâi lông,* loup.

心十分 | 毒, *sīm chīp foūn lông t'oŭc,* méchant cœur.

LÓNG

朗 *Lóng.* Clair, net.

佢聲咁 |, *kīa chāng àn lóng,* comme sa voix est haute et nette !

勁 |, *kín lóng,* même sens.

月 |, *gnĕt lóng,* clair de lune.

浪 *Lóng.* Flot, vague.

海 |, *hoì lóng,* les vagues de la mer.

大風 |, *t'ai foūng lóng,* grand vent, bourrasque.

麼個事嗷人你算麼風起 |, *mô ké· sé aō gnîn gnî són mô foūng hì lóng,* tu m'accuses à tort, et *(litt.)* tu soulèves une vague sans vent.

LÔT

劣 *Lôt.* Vil, méprisable, sans valeur.

醜 |, *tch'où lôt,* vilain, pervers, de mauvaise réputation.

| 官, *lôt kouōn,* mandarin incapable.

| 生, *lôt sēn,* bachelier sans valeur.

| 紳, *lôt chīn,* notable sans valeur, homme de paille.

捋 *Lôt.* Faire glisser la main le long d'un objet, effeuiller ou égrener une plante en la tenant d'une main et en faisant glisser l'autre main le long de la tige ou de l'épi ; dépouiller, nettoyer.

| 牛乳, *lôt nioû nén*, traire une vache.

| 衫袖, *lôt sām ts'ioú*, relever avec la main la manche de son habit.

猪肉骨頭別你 |, *tchoū nioûc koût t'eoû poūn gnî lôt*, je te donne mon os de porc à grignoter.

鉢頭 | 淨來好裝水, *pât t'eoù lôt ts'iáng loî haò tchōng chouì*, nettoie l'écuelle pour y mettre de l'eau.

剆 *Lôt*. Couper, trancher.

| 雞, *lôt kē*, saigner une poule.

LOŪ

Loū. Gale des chiens.

狗發 |, *keoù pôt loū*, le chien a la gale.

蔨 *Loū*. | 萁, *loū kī*, fougères.

滷 *Loū*. Marais salant; rouille.

| 鏡水, *loū kiáng chouì*, eau stagnante dont la surface est chargée de plaques luisantes.

生 |, *sāng loū*, se rouiller.

擄 *Loū*. Capturer, faire prisonnier.

| 捉, | 搶, *loū tsôc, loū ts'iòng*, prendre, piller, capturer.

LOÛ

爐 *Loû*. Réchaud, fourneau.

燒 | 子, *chāo loû tzè*, allumer le fourneau.

吊 |, *tiáo loû*, encensoir.

香 |, *hiōng loû*, brûle-parfums.

鸕 *Loû*. | 鶿, *loû tsê*, cormoran.

LOÚ

路 *Loú*. Chemin, route, moyen d'arriver à une fin.

一條 |, *ŷt t'iâo loú*, un chemin.

指 | 碑, *tjè loú pī*, inscription sur pierre qui indique la route.

麼岔 |, *mô ts'á loú*, route sans bifurcation.

修 |, *sioū loú*, réparer une route.

走水 |, *tseoù chouì loú*, voyager par eau, prendre la voie de l'eau.

| 程遠, *loú tch'în yàn*, il y a beaucoup de chemin à faire.

頭 |, *t'eôu loú*, emploi, gagne-pain.

我同你開一條 |, *ngaî t'oúng gnî k'oī ŷt t'iaô loú*, je t'ouvre un chemin, je t'indique un expédient.

破石頭愛看 |, *p'ó chăc t'eoû oí k'ón loú*, pour fendre une pierre il faut suivre la veine.

露 *Loú*. Rosée, divulguer un secret.

| 水大, *loú chouì t'ái*, la rosée est abondante.

神父麼事 | 人個罪, *chîn foú mô sé loú gnîn ké ts'oúi*, le prêtre ne divulgue pas les péchés des pénitents.

| 出馬脚, *loú tch'oût mā kiôc*, on voit le bout de l'oreille (*litt.* le pied du cheval) qui passe, la vérité se fait jour.

LOŬC

鹿 *Loŭc*. Cerf.

| 茸, *loŭc yoûng*, corne de cerf (médecine).

熝 *Loŭc*. Brûler par attouchement, ou immersion.

火管 | 倒我, *fò koüon loŭc tào ngâi*, le verre de lampe m'a brûlé.

滾水 | 倒我, *koùn choùi loŭc tào ngâi*, l'eau bouillante m'a brûlé.

LOÛC

碌 *Loûc*. Remuer un liquide, peiner, se donner de la peine.

两個春拿來 | 合, *leòng ké· tch'oūn nā loî loûc kâp*, battre deux œufs.

差 | 人家, *ts'āi loûc gnîn kā*, les satellites ennuient le monde par leurs exigences.

勞 |, *lâo loûc*, qui ne perd pas un instant, bûcheur.

祿 *Loûc*. 俸 |, 食 |, *foúng loûc, chìt loûc*, traitement, appointement.

LOŪI

(Voir aussi les mots LI)

擂 *Loūi*. Battre, frapper.

| 鼓, *loūi koù*, battre le tambour.

| 背, *loūi poé·*, frapper légèrement sur le dos, masser le dos.

屢 *Loūi*. Fréquemment, souvent.

| 次 (ou | 常) 領聖體, *loūi tsé*, (ou *loūi chōng*) *leāng chín t'ì*, recevoir fréquemment la Communion.

LOUÎ

雷 *Louî*. Tonnerre.

| 公呌 (ou 响), *louî koūng kiaó* (ou *hiòng*), le tonnerre gronde (ou retentit).

| 火, *louî fò*, éclair.

打 | 公, *tà louî koūng*, faire danser l'anse du panier.

擂 *Loúi*. Écraser, broyer.

| 火藥, *loúi fò yŏc*, fabriquer de la poudre.

| 色料, *loúi sĕt liáo*, broyer des couleurs.

LOUÌ

簏 *Louì*. | 公, *louì koūng*, espèce de panier à petite ouverture, où les pêcheurs mettent leurs poissons.

酒 |, *tsioù louì*, petit panier faisant filtre, et servant à séparer le vin du riz fermenté.

LOÚI

類 *Loúi*. Race, espèce.

人 |, *gnîn loúi*, le genre humain.

同 |, *t'oûng louí*, de la même espèce.

同 | 相求, *t'oûng louí siōng k'ioû*, qui se ressemble s'assemble.

累 *Loúi*. Entraîner dans une mauvaise affaire, créer des embarras à quelqu'un.

拖 | 人家, *t'ō loúi gnîn kā*, envelopper autrui dans son infortune.

命案拖 | 人多, *miáng ón t'ō loúi gnîn tō*, un procès où il s'agit de mort d'homme, nuit à beaucoup de monde.

彙 *Loúi*. Espèce, touffe, concentrer, réunir.

字 | , *sé loúi*, dictionnaire.

| 部 字 | , *ŷt p'oú sé loúi*, un dictionnaire en plusieurs volumes.

| 倣 , *loúi ts'ioū*, réunir, rassembler.

濾 *Loúi* (ou *louî*). Filtrer.

| 豆 腐 , *loúi t'eoú foú*, passer par un linge le fromage liquide de haricots.

| 加 非 , *loúi kā fī*, filtrer le café.

LOÛN

倫 *Loûn*. Ordre, rapport.

人 | , *gnîn loûn*, les rapports des hommes entr'eux.

五 | , *ng̀ loûn*, les cinq rapports sociaux, savoir : 君臣, 父子, 夫婦, 兄弟, 朋友, *kioūn chîn, foú tzè, foū foú, hioūng t'í, p'oûng yoū* ; entre le prince et le sujet, le père et le fils, le mari et la femme, les frères, les amis.

輪 *Loûn*. Roue, charrette.

| 子 麼 轉 , *loûn tzè mô tchòn*, la roue ne tourne pas.

拖 | , *t'ō loûn*, tirer une charrette.

日 | . 月 | , *gnĭt loûn, gnĕt loûn*, disque du soleil, de la lune.

火 | 船 , *fò loûn chôn*, vapeur à roues.

車 | 子 , *tch'ā loûn tzè*, roue de machine, volant, turbine.

LOÚN

論 *Loún*. Parler de, quant à.

理 | ou 講 | , *lī loún* ou *kòng loùn*, parler, discuter.

| 道 理 唔 着 , *loún t'áo lī mĝ tch'ĕ*, au point de vue de la raison, ce n'est pas soutenable.

不 | 那 人 , *poŭt loún màn gnîn*, qui que ce soit.

LOŪNG

攏 *Loūng*. Rassembler.

| 倣 來 , *loūng ts'ioū loî*, réunir, rassembler.

| 總 , *loūng tsoùng*, tout, tout ensemble.

聾 *Loūng*. Sourd.

耳 | 麼 , *gnì loūng mô ?* es-tu sourd?

籠 *Loūng*. Cage, panier qui sert à porter les porcs, les poules.

鵰 | , *tiaō loūng*, cage d'oiseau.

LOÛNG

嚨 *Loûng*. 口 | , *heòu loûng*, gosier.

礱 *Loûng*. Ecorcer le riz, meule à écorcer

| 穀 , *loûng koŭc*, écorcer le riz.

釘 | , *tāng loûng*, fabriquer une meule à écorcer.

壠 *Loûng*. Creux, trou, tunnel.

兎 子 打 | , *t'oú tzè tà loûng*, les lapins creusent des trous.

開 | 過 火 車 , *k'oī loûng koúo fò tch'ā*, creuser un tunnel pour le chemin de fer.

LOÙNG

籠 *Loùng.* 籮 \|, *lô loùng*, panier, corbeille de voyage, corbeille à transporter le riz.

燈 \|, *tēn loùng*, lanterne ronde, en bambou garni de papier transparent.

LOÛT

捋 *Loût.* S'échapper, glisser, tomber.

你 褲 \| 帛 裡, *niā foú loût p'ĕt lĕ·*, ton pantalon ne tient pas.

睡等裡目洋氈 \| 阿地下去, *choĕ· tèn ê· moûc yông tchān loût á t'í hā hí*, pendant mon sommeil, ma couverture est tombée à terre.

MĀ

馬 *Ma.* Cheval.

一 匹 \|, *ŷt p'ĭt mā*, un cheval.

上 \|, 下 \|, *chōng mā, hā mā*, monter à cheval, descendre de cheval.

\| 蹄, *mā t'âi*, sabot du cheval.

\| 騌, *mā tsoūng*, crinière du cheval.

騷 \| (ou 生 \| 牯), *sāo ma* (ou *sāng ma kòu*), cheval entier.

\| 牸, \| 娘, *mā tsé, ma niông*, jument ; jument qui a porté.

\| 夫, *ma foū*, palefrenier.

木 \|, *moûc mā*, chevalet de menuisier.

\| 齒 莧, *mā tchè hán*, pourpier.

碼 *Ma.* Port, débarcadère, poids d'une balance, mesure, chiffre.

\| 頭, *ma t'eôu*, port, débarcadère.

你 \| 子 過 大, *niā ma tzè koúo t'aí*, les poids de ta balance sont plus forts.

\| 號, *mā háo*, chiffres secrets (d'un commerçant).

司 \| 秤, *sē ma tch'ín*, balance dont les poids ont la vraie mesure réglementée par le mandarin.

瑪 *Mā.* \| 瑙, *mā nào*, cornaline.

喊 \| (ou 霸 \|), *hám mā* (ou *p'ŏc mā*), avoir le monopole. Plus exactement on dit : 承 餉 \| *chîn hiòng mā.*

\| 利 亞, *ma lí ā*, nom de la Sainte Vierge Marie.

MÂ

媽 *Mâ* (*ma*). Femelle, mère.

雞 \|, *kē· mâ*, poule qui a déjà pondu.

狗 \|, 牛 \|, *keòu mâ, niôu mâ*, chienne, vache qui ont déjà porté.

麻 *Mâ.* Espèce de chanvre, sésame.

\| 索, *mâ sôc*, corde faite avec ce chanvre.

蟆 *Mâ.* 蝦 \|, *hâ mâ*, grenouille.

MÁ

罵 *Má.* Gronder, injurier, maudire.

\| 人 個 話, *má gnîn ké· fá*, paroles injurieuses.

唔 好 去 阿 巴 噲 \|, *mĝ haò hí a pā voé· má*, n'y allons pas, papa nous gronderait.

MĂC

麥 *Măc*. Froment et ses genres.

大丨 (ou 穀丨), *t'aí măc (ou koŭc măc)*, orge.

丨粲, *măc ts'án*, épi de blé.

嚜 *Măc*. Donner un coup de bâton (populaire).

丨一下, *măc ўt há*, donner un coup de bâton.

MÂC

擘 *Mâc* ou *pâc*. Déchirer, arracher.

丨爛衫, *mâc lán sām*, faire un accroc à son habit.

丨番豆殼, *mâc fān t'eóu hôc*, décosser les arrachides.

脈 *Mâc*. Pouls.

看丨, 打丨, *k'ón mâc, tà mâc*, tâter le pouls.

咁大氣丨, *àn t'ái hí mâc*! quel souffle! quelle patience! (par ex. dans un travail de longue haleine.)

藚 *Mâc*. Laitue et ses espèces.

那 *Mâc (nà)*. 丨個, *mâc ké·* (ou *kē·*) quoi? quel? Ce mot est prononcé de bien des manières selon les pays: *mâc kāi* (ou *kái*) *nà kōi*, etc.

丨個東西, *mâc ké· toūng sī*? qu'est-ce? quoi?

做丨個, *tsó mâc ké·*? pourquoi? que fais-tu?

丨個都有, *mâc ké· toū yoū*, il y a de tout.

丨個都知, *mâc ké· toū tī*, il sait tout.

MAÎ

埋 *Maî*. Ensevelir, 丨葬, *maî tsóng*, ensevelir.

丨死老, *maî sì lào*, enterrer un mort.

鷶 *Maî* (ou *moĉ·*). Oiseau qui sert d'appeau.

畜鷓鴣做丨子, *hioŭc tchá kōu tsó maî tzè*, élever une perdrix pour en attirer d'autres.

MAÌ

買 *Maì*. Acheter.

丨賣, *maì maí*, acheter et vendre, c'est-à-dire faire le commeree.

丨成, *maì châng*, c'est acheté, marché conclu.

我丨來賣, *ngâi maì loî mái*, je l'ai acheté pour le revendre.

丨服人心, *maì foŭc gnîn sīm*, gagner le cœur des gens avec de l'argent.

MAÍ

賣 *Maí*. Vendre.

爭買爭丨, *tsāng maì tsāng maí*, se faire concurrence dans l'achat ou la vente.

三百錢我唔丨, *sām pâc ts'iên ngâi mĝ maí*, pour 300 sapèques, je ne le vends pas.

丨成, *maí châng*, c'est vendu, marché conclu.

MĀN

滿 *Mān* (màn). Plein, remplir.

莫倒咁丨, *mōc tào àn mān*, ne verse pas trop plein.

丨間䁖泥磚, *mān kiān kouà nâi tchōn*, toute la chambre est pleine de mottes de terre.

丨心 ou 丨意, *mān sīm* ou *mān ý*, être pleinement satisfait, au comble de ses vœux.

做丨月, *tsó mān gnĕt*, finir le mois, (se dit d'une femme qui a enfanté et ne peut sortir avant ce temps).

MÂN

瞞 *Mân*. Déguiser, tromper, cacher sa pensée.

告解丨一個罪做唔得, *káo kiaì mân ўt ké· ts'oúi tsó mĝ tĕt*, en confession, on ne doit pas cacher un seul péché.

丨昧頁心, *mân mí leông sīm*, se fausser la conscience.

你事丨我唔過我知, *nia sé mân ngaî mĝ kouó ngaî tī*, tu ne pourras pas me tromper, je connais ton affaire.

蠻 *Mân*. Barbare, entêté, cœur dur.

丨人, *mân gnîn*, ils appellent ainsi tous les peuples de Mandchourie, et même les étrangers.

十分丨個人, *chĭp foūn mân ké· gnîn*, homme très entêté, sans cœur.

合丨(ou 打丨)食, *kâp mân* (ou *tà mân*) *chĭt*, manger de force.

用丨 *yoúng mân*, s'obstiner.

MÀN

那 *Màn* (*nà*). Quel ? qui ?

丨人, *màn gnîn ?* qui est là ?

丨人話, *màn gnîn vá ?* qui l'a dit ?

MÁN

慢 *Mán*. Lentement, mépriser, peu obligeant.

丨丨來, *mán mán loî*, allez doucement.

丨丨看, *mán mán k'ón*, on verra peu à peu.

丨行, *mán hâng*, allez doucement (souhait de bon voyage).

輕丨人, *k'īn mán gnîn*, mépriser, faire affront.

大丨, *t'ái mán*, (ou 簡丨 *kiàn mán*), je vous ai traité bien indignement ; réponse de politesse à un hôte qui s'en va.

MĀNG

蟒 *Māng*. Taon, grosse mouche qui tourmente les chevaux et les buffles.

丨子多掌馬唔得, *māng tzè tō tchòng mā mĝ tĕt*, il y a trop de taons, je ne puis paître le cheval.

丨袋, *māng p'âo*, habit de cérémonie.

MÂNG

芒 *Mâng*. Pas encore (abréviation de 唔講 *mĝ hân*).

| 愛, *mâng oí*, pas encore, je n'en veux pas encore.

| 去, *mâng hí*, je n'y vais pas encore.

| 好, *mâng hào*, ce n'est pas encore le moment.

| 怕, *mâng p'á*, il n'y a pas encore de danger.

懵 *Mâng*. Esprit inculte, peu intelligent.

十分 | 個人, *chĭp foūn mâng ké· gnîn*, c'est un homme absolument bouché.

忙 *Mâng*. Empressé, vite.

| 風, *mâng foūng*, grand vent, bourrasque.

Mais on dit : 煞 |, *săt māng*, se dépêcher, s'empresser.

MÀNG

漭 *Màng*. Couvrir, recouvrir.

傘子拿來 | 過, *tchā tzè nā loî màng koúo*, changer l'étoffe d'un parapluie.

頭哪 | 等裡, *t'eôu nâ màng tèn ê·*, la tête couverte d'un voile.

蜢 *Màng*. Sauterelle, criquet,

草 |, *ts'ào màng*, criquet.

MĀO

毛 *Māo*. Cheveu, poil, défectueux.

| 辮子, *māo piēn tzè*, la tresse des cheveux.

生 |, *sāng māo*, pousser des poils.

鵰 |, *tiāo māo*, plume (poil d'oiseau).

眉 |, *mî māo*, sourcils.

| 虫, *māo tch'oūng*, chenille à poils.

| 病, *māo p'iáng*, défaut, vice, mauvaise habitude.

MAÔ

麼 *Maô*. Négation. (Voir *mô*).

茅 *Mâo*. Herbe, chaume.

絲 |, *sē mâo*, chiendent, espece d'herbe.

MAÓ

貌 *Maó*. Figure, forme.

像 |, *sióng maó*, mine de quelqu'un.

禮 |, *lì maó*, politesse, manières polies.

看佢年 | 還輕, *k'ón kî niân maó hân k'iāng*, il paraît jeune à voir sa figure.

冒 *Maó*. Usurper, téméraire, donner à l'entreprise.

| 領聖體, *maó leāng chín t'ì*, recevoir indignement la sainte Communion.

| 用天主個恩, *maó yoúng t'iēn tchoū ké· ēn*, abuser des bienfaits de Dieu.

| 工夫, *maó kōung foū*, donner un travail à l'entreprise.

| 倒裡風, *maó tào lè· foūng*, (*litt.*) j'ai attrapé un coup de vent, j'ai pris froid.

帽 *Maó*. Bonnet, chapeau.

一頂｜, *ŷt tàng maó*, un chapeau.

草｜, *ts'ào maǒ*, chapeau de paille à larges bords.

｜頂, *maó tàng*, pompon, bouton du bonnet.

風｜, *foūng maó*, capuchon.

MĂT

末 *Măt.* Extrémité, fin ; poudre fine.

四｜, *sí măt*, les 4 fins dernières.

胡椒｜, *foû tsiāo măt*, poivre en poudre.

Le ton change dans :

麼｜有, *mô mât yoū*, il n'y en a guere.

MÂT

抹 *Mât.* Oindre, enduire, essuyer.

｜一點色料就好看, *mât ŷt tiàm sēt liáo ts'ioú hào k'ón*, passez-y un peu de couleur, et ce sera beau.

｜聖油, *mât chín yoû*, faire les saintes Onctions.

淨來, *mât ts'iáng loî*, essuiye proprement.

襪 *Mât.* Bas, chaussette.

一雙｜, *ŷt soūng mât*, une paire de bas.

｜帶, *mât tái*, jarretières.

MĒ·

姆 *Mē·.* Femme, femelle.

｜｜, *mē· mē·*, mère adoptive.

阿｜, *a mē·*, maman, mère.

你阿｜在屋下麼, *gnî à mē· ts'ōi voûc hā mô ?* ta mère est-elle à la maison ?

伯｜, *pâc mē·*, tante paternelle par alliance.

牛｜, *nioû mē·*, veau.

MÉ·

浼 *Mé·.* Sale, sordide.

｜細, *mé· sé·* ou *gné· sé·*, même sens.

衫打｜, *sām tà mé·*, tu as taché ton habit.

MĒN

(Voir aussi les mots MIEN)

猛 *Mēn* ou *māng.* Méchant, violent.

｜獸, *mēn tch'oú*, bête féroce.

免 *Mēn* (ou *miēn*). Eviter, dispenser.

｜不得, *mēn poût tēt*, inévitable, cela arrivera certainement.

｜債, *mēn tsaí*, remise d'une dette, pardonner.

寬｜小齋, *k'ōn mēn siào tsai*, dispenser de l'abstinence.

｜糧, *mēn leông*, dispenser des impôts.

｜見, *mēn kián*, refuser de voir quelqu'un.

皿 *Mēn.* **器｜**, *hí mēn*, ustensile en général.

MÈN

緬 *Mèn.* Réfléchir, penser.

| 正來, *mèn tcháng loî*, pensez-y ; j'y réfléchirai.

還𢱑 | 我唔分明, *hân hì mèn ngâi m̂g foūn mîn*, j'ai beau réfléchir je ne comprends pas.

| 得出, | 唔出, *mèn têt tch'oût, mèn m ĝtch'oût*, comprendre, ne pas comprendre, se rappeler ou non le souvenir de, saisir ou non un plan, une idée.

MÉN

孟 *Mén*. | 子, *mén tzè*, Mencius, célèbre philosophe chinois.

亞 |, *a mén*, Amen.

MEŌU

某 *Meōu*. Un tel, un certain.

| 年 | 月 | 日愛寫分明, *meōu niân meōu gnĕț meōu gnĭt oí sìa foūn mîn*, il faut écrire clairement telle année, tel mois, tel jour.

畝 *Meōu* (ou *meòu*). Arpent de terrain d'environ deux 担 *tām* et demi. Cette mesure n'est plus guère employée, on compte par charge de 100 livres. D'une rizière qui donne 3 charges de riz, on dira : j'ai acheté trois charges (三 担 *sām tām*) de terrain.

MEÔU

謀 *Meôu* (ou *miâo*). Combiner un plan, machiner, délibérer secrètement.

| 害人, *meôu hoí gnîn*, méditer de nuire à quelqu'un.

| 事在人成事在天, *meôu sé ts'aí gnîn, châng sé ts'aí t'iēn*, l'homme propose et Dieu dispose.

| 生理, *meôu siēn lī*, chercher un commerce.

MEOÙ

貿 *Meoù* (ou *miào*). | 易, *meoù ÿt*, le commerce en général, faire le commerce.

MĔT

默 *Mĕt*. Secret, silencieux, retiré.

𠹌件事同我 | 探一下, *ỳ k'ián sé t'oûng ngâi mĕt t'àm ŷt há*, prends des informations en secret sur cette affaire.

做 | 想, *tsó mĕt siòng*, faire la méditation.

| 念, *mĕt niám*, prier à voix basse.

| | 𠹌來莫別人知, *mĕt mĕt lì loî mŏc poūn gnîn tī*, faisons la chose en secret, que personne n'en sache rien.

墨 *Mĕt*. Encre.

| 水, *mĕt choùi*, encre liquide.

| 盤 (ou | 硯), *mĕt p'ân* (ou *mĕt yán*), encrier presque plat, pour broyer l'encre.

| 斗, *mĕt teòu*, instrument des menuisiers, pour encrer le cordeau à tracer des lignes.

密 *Mĕt*. Serré, dense.

種菜莫種咁 |, *tchoúng ts'ói mŏc tchoúng àn mĕt*, ne plante pas les légumes trop serrés.

織布織得咁 |, *tchĭt poú tchĭt têt àn mĕt*, la toile a été tissée très serrée.

工夫咁 |, *koūng foū kàn mĕt*, qui ne perd pas son temps dans son travail.

蜜 *Mĕt*. Miel.

蜂 |, *foūng mĕt*, miel d'abeille.

| 糖, *mĕt t'ông*, miel.

篾 *Mĕt*. Ecorce de bambou, divisée eu bandes étroites.

剖 |, *p'ó mĕt*, détacher ces lanières du bambou.

拿竹 | 來綁架, *nā tchoŭc mĕt loî pòng ká*, lier les échafaudages avec des lanières de bambou.

滅 *Mĕt*. Mettre fin, détruire.

消 |, *siāo mĕt*, détruire, exterminer.

| 天主教, *mĕt t'iēn tchoù káo*, exterminer la religion chrétienne.

MÊT

搣 *Mêt*. Achever, finir, faire.

| 成你工夫來, *mêt tcháng nīa koūng foū loî*, achève ton ouvrage.

今日我來 | 乜個, *kīn gnĭt ngaî loî mêt mâc ké·?* maintenant, à quoi vais-je m'occuper ?

MĜ

唔 *Mĝ* (abréviation du mot 麼 *mô*). Non, ne pas; particule interrogative à la fin d'une phrase.

| 曾, *mĝ t'sên*, pas encore.

Cette expression est prononcée de diverses manières selon les pays: *mĝ t'iên*, *mĝ t'iêng*, etc.

| 曾來, *mĝ ts'ên loî*, il n'est pas encore venu.

Les Chinois abrègent, et l'on comprend quelquefois: *mĝ ńĝ hê· loî*, ou *mĝ nê· loî*, il n'est pas venu.

| 使, *mĝ sè*, inutile, pas nécessaire.

| 奈何, *mĝ nái hô*, pas moyen de faire autrement.

你來 |, *gnî loî mĝ ?* viens-tu ?

使得 |, *sè têt mĝ ?* peut-on s'en servir ?

MĪ

每 *Mī*. Chaque.

| 年 | 月 | 日, *mī niân ,mī gnĕt, mī gnĭt*, chaque année, chaque mois, chaque jour.

告解 | 年一次, *káo kiài mī niân ŷt tsé*, se confesser une fois chaque année.

美 *Mī* (*mí*). Bon, beau.

| 貌, *mī máo*, belle figure, aux traits fins.

讚 |, *tsán mī*, louer, glorifier.

讚 | 耶穌, *tsán mī yâ sē* ! loué soit Jésus !

尾 *Mī*. Queue, extrémité, bien joint.

| 巴, *mī pā*, queue.

二月 | 來, *gní gnĕt mī loî*, à la fin de la 2eme lune.

臨 |, *lîm mī*, (ou par déviation 粘 |, *niâm mī*, ou *niâp mī*), à la fin, en dernier lieu.

頭 |, *t'eoû mī*, la tête et la queue, le

premier et le dernier, le commencement et la fin.

麼頭麼|個話, *mô t'eoû mô mĭ ké· fá*, discours sans suite.

我從頭至|做阿起, *ngaî ts'ioûng t'eoû tjé mĭ tsó á hì*, c'est moi qui l'ai fait, depuis le commencement jusqu'à la fin.

門愛關|來, *moûn oí koūan mĭ loî*, il faut fermer la porte complètement.

棚板唔||, *p'âng pàn* (ou *pièn*) *mĝ mĭ*, les planches ne sont pas bien jointes.

桅 *Mĭ*. |杆, *mĭ koūon*, mât d'honneur que l'on met devant les maisons de ceux qui ont obtenu un grade. Mât de bateau.

MÎ

沬 *Mî*. Laver, essuyer avec un linge mouillé.

|淨桌來, *mî ts'iáng tsŏc loî*, lave proprement la table.

眉 *Mî*. |毛, *mî mao*, sourcils.

微 *Mî*. Peu considérable, peu, modique.

做生理十分|末, *tsó siēn lì chĭp foūn mî măt*, dans le commerce on ne gagne que peu à la fois.

|罪, *mî ts'oúi*, péché véniel.

|嫌, *mî hiâm*, peu respectueux.

|意, *mî ý*, petite attention.

|妙, *mî miaò*, délicat et admirable, mystérieux, caché, impénétrable.

迷 *Mî*. Aveuglé (au moral), troublé.

|色, *mî sĕt*, luxure.

|魂藥, *mî foûn yŏc*, médecine qui fait perdre conscience de ses actes.

MÌ

米 *Mì*. Riz décortiqué, non cuit.

赤|, *tch'âc mì*, riz de montagne à teinte rougeâtre.

糙|, *ts'áo mì*, riz grossièrement écossé.

|糉, *mì tch'àng*, espèce de gâteau de riz torréfié.

|粉, *mì foùn*, vermicelle.

MÍ

味 *Mí*. Goût, saveur, sel fondu.

麼|道, *mô mí t'áo*, cela n'a pas de goût.

|道唔清楚, *mí t'áo mĝ ts'ĭn tsè*, le goût n'est pas franc.

菜蔬裡你唔曾放|, *ts'oí teoú lì gnî mĝ ts'ên fóng mí*, tu n'as pas assaisonné les légumes.

昧 *Mí*. Obscur, obscurcir.

瞞|良心, *mân mí leông sīm*, agir contre sa conscience.

汨 *Mí*. S'enfoncer dans l'eau, plonger.

|水, *mí choùi*, plonger.

|幾久唔倒, *mí kì kioù mĝ taò*, ne pouvoir rester longtemps sous l'eau.

媚 *Mí*. Basse complaisance, flatter.

｜等婦人家, *mí tèn foú gnîn kā*, ne penser, n'avoir des attentions que pour les femmes.

MIĀ

㑴 *Miā.* Caresser avec la main, tâter, toucher.

｜狗, *miā keoù*, caresser uu chien.

｜唔倒, *miā mĝ taò*, ne pas pouvoir reconnaître la nature d'une chose au simple toucher.

｜阿𠮶跟簕去裡, *miā á nĕt t'eoû p'oûng hí lê·*, en allant à tâtons, je me suis jeté dans les épines.

—路, *miā loú*, aller à tâtons, chercher son chemin.

MIÂNG

名 *Miâng* Nom d'une personne ou d'une chose, titre, renommée.

安｜, *ōn miâng*, imposer un nom.

小｜ ou 肉｜, *siào miâng* ou *nioŭc miâng*, nom que les parents donnent à leur enfant après sa naissance.

學｜, *hŏc miâng*, nom que le maître donne à son élève.

考｜, *k'aò miâng*, nom que le candidat prend en se présentant aux examens.

官｜, *kouōn miâng*, nom qu'un officier prend en entrant en charge.

地｜, *t'í miâng*, nom de pays.

書｜, *choū miâng*, titre d'un livre.

聖｜, *chín miâng*, le nom de baptême

你喊那個｜, *gnî hám mâc ké· miâng ?* comment t'appelles-tu ?

點｜, *tiàm miâng*, faire l'appel nominal.

傳人個｜, *tch'ôn gnîn ké· miâng*, rendre célèbre le nom de quelqu'un.

｜聲, *miâng chāng*, réputation.

壞人個｜聲, *fái gnîn ké· miâng chāng*, briser, perdre la réputation d'autrui.

出｜, *tch'oût miâng*, se rendre célèbre.

出｜字, *tch'oût miâng sé*, s'inscrire, donner son nom.

父神｜下, *chîn foú miâng hā*, au nom, au compte du Père.

明 *Miâng* (*mîn*). ｜年, *miâng niân*, l'année prochaine.

MIÁNG

命 *Miáng* (*mín*). Vie, destin. (Voyez aussi 命 *mín*).

｜都唔愛, *miáng tōu mĝ oí*, risquer sa vie (plutôt que de renoncer à une chose).

短｜鬼, *tòn miáng kouì*, diable qui mourra jeune (*malédiction*) !

致｜聖人, *tjé miáng chín gnîn* (dans cette expression on dit plutôt *tjé mín*), les saints Martyrs.

捨一條唔愛, *chà ŷt t'iâo miáng mĝ oí*, je donne ma tête à couper que...

喊救｜, *hám kioú miáng*, crier au secours.

MIÂO

Voir aussi les mots MEOU)

苗 *Miâo.* Tige et feuillage des plantes.

番薯 |，番豆 |，*fān choû miâo, fān t'eoú miaô*, feuillage de patate, d'arachides.

蘿蔔 |，*lô p'ĭt miâo*, feuilles de rave.

謀 *Miâo* (ou *meôu*). 計 |，*ké· miâo*, ruse, stratagème.

MIÀO

藐 *Miào*. Regarder avec mépris.

| 視人家，*miào sé gnîn kā*, regarder avec mépris autrui.

貿 *Miào* (ou *meòu*). | 易，*miào ўt*, commerce, faire le commeree.

妙 *Miào* ou *miaó*. Admirable, excellent.

天主奇 | 個安排，*t'iēn tchòu k'î miào ké· ōn p'âi*, la Providence admirable de Dieu.

奧 |，*áo miào*, mystère, mystérieux.

微 |，*mî miào*, subtil, caché, impénétrable.

MIÁO

猫 *Miáo*. Chat.

| 公，*miáo koūng*, chat.

| 頭鵰，*miáo t'eôu tiāo*, chouette.

| 狸子，*miáo lî tzè*, espèce de chat sauvage.

茂 *Miáo*. | 盛，*miáo chín*, végétation luxuriante.

廟 *Miáo*. Temple, pagode.

文昌 |，*voûn tch'ōng miáo*, temple de Confucius, pagode des lettrés.

關帝 |，ou 武 |，*kouān tí miaó* ou *voū miáo*, pagode des mandarins.

MIĒN

免 *Miēn* (ou *mēn*). Dispenser, éviter. *(Voyez mēn).*

勉 *Miēn*. S'efforcer.

| 力，*miēn lĭt*, s'efforcer.

| | ou | 强，*miēn miēn* ou *miēn kiòng*, à la rigueur, ça peut aller.

MIÊN

棉 *Miên*. | 花，*miên fā*, coton.

| 被，*miên p'ī*, couverture de coton.

綿 *Miên*. Mou, tendre.

猪肉唔曾煮 |，*tchoū nioûc mĝ ts'ên tchoù miên*, la viande de porc n'est pas cuite à point.

| 羊，*miên yông*, mouton.

| 紗，*miên sā*, fil de coton.

MIÉN

麵 *Mién*. Farine de froment ou autres, vermicelle.

| 粉，*mién foùn*, farine.

| 包，*mién pāo*, pain.

| 餅，*mién piàng*, pain de froment, hosties.

打 | 餅，*tà mién piàng*, faire des hosties.

面 *Mién*. Visage, face, surface; particule numérale des miroirs, des tam-tams, etc.

洗｜, *sè· mién*, se laver le visage.

｜前, *mién ts'iēn*, ou 當｜, *tōng mién*, en présence.

體｜, *t'ì mién*, considération, honneur, pompe.

｜目, *mién moûc*, honneur, considération.

辦事麼體｜, *p'án sé mô t'ì mién*, il a réglé un différend, sans honneur, l'honneur n'étant pas sauf.

麼｜目見神父, *mô mién moûc kián chîn foú*, j'ai honte de me présenter (dans de pareilles conditions) devant le Père.

救｜目 (ou ｜皮), *kióu mién moûc* (ou *mién p'î*), sauver sa face, c'est-à-dire l'honneur.

外｜, *ngoé· mién*, le dehors, partie extérieure.

桌｜上放等來, *tsôc mién hóng fóng tèn loî*, mettez sur la table.

兩｜差唔多, *leòng mién ts'ā mḡ tō*, les deux faces sont à peu près pareilles.

一｜鑼, *ŷt mién lô*, un tam-tam.

一｜鏡, *ŷt mién kiáng*, un miroir.

MÎN

民 *Mîn*. Peuple.

天下萬｜, *t'iēn hā ván mîn*, tous les peuples du monde.

教｜, *káo mîn*, nom sous lequel sont désignés officiellement les chrétiens.

四｜, *sí mîn*, les 4 classes de la société : 士 *sé*, les lettrés, 農 *noûng*, les agriculteurs, 工 *koūng*, les artisans, 商 *chōng*, les commerçants.

明 *Mîn*. Clair, évident, intelligent, prochain.

｜悟, *mîn ngoú*, intelligence.

愛講｜白, *oí kòng mîn p'ăc* (ou *p'ĕt*), il faut parler clairement.

我話裡｜｜白白, *ngâi vá lê· mîn mîn p'ăc p'ăc*, je l'ai dit très clairement.

各人｜白, *kôc gnîn mîn p'ăc*, chacun sait à quoi s'en tenir.

聰｜ *ts'oūng mîn*, intelligent.

｜天, ｜早晨, ｜月, ｜年, *mîn t'iēn*, *mîn tsào chîn*, *mîn gnĕt* (ou *miâng gnĕt*), *mîn niân* (ou *miâng niân*), demain, demain matin, le mois prochain, l'an prochain.

眠 *Mîn*. Se coucher.

一｜就睡, *ŷt mîn ts'ioú choé·*, aussitôt couché je m'endors.

｜床, *mîn ts'ông*, lit.

有人話馬麼｜麼睡, *yoū gnîn vá mā mô mîn mô choé·*, il y en a qui disent que le cheval ne se couche et ne dort jamais.

共下｜, *k'ioúng há mîn*, coucher ensemble (est quelquefois employé en confession pour désigner le péché de fornication ou d'adultère).

MÍN

命 *Mín*. Ordre, ordonner, destin, vie; dans ce dernier sens on dit plutôt *miáng* (*voir* 命 *miáng*), excepté dans l'expression suivante :

爲天主致｜, *vî t'iēn tchòu tjé mín*, donner sa vie pour Dieu.

神父｜個, *chîn foú mín ké·*, c'est le Père qui l'a ordonné.

天主有｜, *t'iēn tchoù yoū mín*, Dieu l'ordonne.

奉｜, *foúng mín*, être chargé d'exécuter un ordre.

天｜, *t'iēn mín*, l'ordre du ciel, le destin, la fatalité (selon les païens).

死生有｜富貴在天, *sì sēn yoū mín, foú koúi ts'ái t'iēn*, la vie et la mort sont soumises au destin; les richesses et les honneurs dépendent de la volonté du ciel.

MIÔNG

芒 *Miông*. Espèce de grande herbe.

｜頭, *miông t'eôu*, buisson de ces herbes, hallier.

MIÒNG

網 *Miòng*. Filet, épervier.

打｜, *tà miòng*, jeter l'épervier

｜倒裡, *miòng taò lì*, il a été pris au filet.

… … ｜倒虫, *lâ k'iâ miòng tào tch'oûng*, l'araignée a pris un insecte dans sa toile.

MŌ

摩 *Mō*. Toucher, tâter.

｜得倒, ｜唔倒, *mō têt tào, mō mĝ tào*, on peut le toucher, on ne peut pas le toucher.

｜等裡行, *mō tèn ê· hâng*, marcher à tâtons.

｜欄, *mō lân*, grande corbeille à faire sécher les grains.

MÔ

麼 *Mô*. Particule interrogative à la fin d'une phrase; particule négative au commencement ou dans le corps d'une phrase ; non, aucun, nul.

今日過好｜, *kîn gnît koúo hào mô?* aujourd' hui cela va-t-il mieux?

有錢｜, *yoū ts'iên mô*, avez-vous de l'argent ?

神父｜來, *chîn foú mô lôi*, le Père ne vient pas.

｜相干, *mô siōng kōn*, peu importe.

mô kât sât, il n'y a pas moyen, je ne sais plus comment faire.

｜末有, *mô mât yoū*, il n'y en a guère.

魔 *Mô*. Démon ｜鬼, *mô koùi*, le démon.

邪｜, *siâ mô*, le démon impur.

MÓ

攠 *Mó*. Frotter, tourmenter, moudre, meule à aiguiser (en ce dernier sens on dit plutôt: *nô*, voyez ce mot).

肩頭｜痛, *kiān t'eôu mó t'oúng*, l'épaule est endolorie par le frottement de la charge.

牛｜癢, *nioû mó yōng*, le buffle se gratte.

｜光, (ou 滑) *mó* ou *mō kouōng* (ou *vât*), polir en frottant.

｜麵, ｜加非, *mó mién, mó kā fī*, moudre de la farine, du café.

｜石, *mó châc*, meule, pierre à moudre.

｜房, *mó fōng*, moulin.

MǑC

莫 *Mǒc*, Ne pas, il ne faut pas.

丨來, *mǒc loi*, ne viens pas.

丨聲, *mǒc chāng*, taisez-vous, silence.

丨信佢話, *mǒc sín kì vá*, il ne faut pas croire ce qu'il dit.

MOÊ·

梅 *Moê·*. Espèce de prune sauvage.

媒 *Moê·*. Entremetteur de mariage.

做丨人, *tsó moê· gnìn*, faire l'entremetteur.

丨人婆, *moê· gnìn p'ô*, entremetteuse.

煤 *Moê·*. Charbon de terre.

丨炭, *moê· t'án*, charbon de houille, anthracite.

紙丨, *tjè moê·*, papier roulé, dont les Chinois se servent en guise d'amadou, d'allumettes.

霉 *Moê·*. Moisi.

羹漚起丨, *kāng eoú hì moê·*, la colle finit par se moisir.

鶥 *Moê·* (ou *maî*). Oiseau qui sert d'appeau. (Voir *mâi*).

枚 *Moê·*. Particule numérale des petites boules, des aiguilles, des épines.

一丨珠, *ȳt moê· tchoū*, une perle.

猜丨, *ts'āi moê·*, jouer à pair ou impair, à la mourre.

一丨針, *ȳt moê· tchīm*, une aiguille.

玫 *Moê·* Pierre précieuse.

丨瑰, *moê· koúi*, rosier, rose.

丨瑰經, *moê· koúi kīn*, prières du Rosaire.

MOÉ·

妹 *Moé·*. Petite fille, sœur cadette.

有幾多個丨子, *yoū kì tō ké· moé· tzè*, combien avez-vous de filles?

係賴子丨子, *hé· laí tzè moé· tzè?* est-ce un garçon, ou une fille ?

老丨, *lào moé·*, sœur cadette.

有大姊麼老表丨, *yoū t'ái tsì mô lào moé·*, j'ai des sœurs aînées, mais pas de sœur cadette.

表姊丨, *piào tsì moé·*, cousine.

MÔNG

亡 *Mông* (ou *vông*). Mourir.

先丨, *siēn mông*, les défunts.

追思先丨, *tchoūi sē siēn mông*, faire commémoraison des morts.

MÓNG

忘 *Móng* (*mông*). Oublier.

丨了一件事, *móng liào ȳt k'ián sé*, j'ai oublié une chose.

On dit aussi, plus vulgairement:

添丨, *t'iām p'ióng* ou *t'iām móng*, ou encore: 丨記, *móng kí*, oublier, j'ai oublié.

丨恩, *móng ēn*, qui oublie les bienfaits, ingrat.

望 *Móng* (ou *vóng*). Espérer, désirer.

失丨, *chīt móng*, désespérer, être trompé dans son attente.

21

有｜頭麼，*yōu móng t'eôu mô?* y a-t-il de l'espoir ?

｜升天堂，*móng chīn t'iēn t'ông*, désirer aller au ciel.

我｜你好，*ngâi móng gnî hào*, je désire (cherche) ton bien.

MOŪ

母 *Moū*. Mère.

｜親，*moū ts'īn*, mère.

繼｜，ou 後｜，*kí moū*, ou *heoú moū*, marâtre.

乳｜，*nén moū*, nourrice.

聖｜瑪利亞，*chín moū mā lí ā*, la Sainte Mère (de Dieu) Marie.

字｜，*sé moū*, racines ou clefs des caractères chinois.

MOÛ

模 *Moû*. Moule, forme, règle.

鑄銅鑄鐵麼｜子做唔得，*tchoú t'oûng tchoú t'iĕt mô moû tzè tsó mĝ tĕt*, pour couler du cuivre ou du fer, il faut absolument un moule.

巫 *Moû*. Magicien, sorcier.

師｜邪術，*sē moû siâ choŭt*, sorcier qui fait des sorcelleries.

誣 *Moû*. Importuner, calomnier.

｜衰人，*moû soī gnîn*, importuner quelqu'un.

｜告，*moû káo*, calomnier, accuser faussement en justice.

MOÙ

舞 *Moù* (*voù*). Faire, agir.

昨晡日做個嘢｜成來，*ts'ŏc poū gnĭt tsó ké· oí moù tchâng loî*, il faut achever ce que tu faisais hier.

｜猴哥，*moù heôu kō*, faire travailler des singes.

｜龍燈，*moù lioûng tēn*, faire la procession aux flambeaux.

MOÚ

墓 *Moú*. ｜墳，*moú foûn*, tombeau.

打醮｜，*tà tsiáo moú*, rendre un culte solennel aux ancêtres devant leur tombeau.

慕 *Moú*. Penser avec affection.

仰｜天主，*niōng moú t'iēn tchoù*, penser avec affection à Dieu.

夢 *Moú* (ou *moúng*). Rêver, songe.

發｜，*pôt moú*, rêver, faire un songe.

你發｜麼，*gnî pôt moú mô ?* rêves-tu ? tu n'y songes pas ?

解｜，*kiaì moú*, interpréter un songe.

MOŬC

睦 *Moŭc*. 和｜，*fô moŭc*, être d'accord, paix.

莫咁多官｜，*mŏc àn tō koŭon moŭc*, ne fais pas tant de manières.

牧 *Moŭc*. Pasteur.

耶穌善｜者，*yâ sē chán moŭc tchà*, Jésus le Bon Pasteur.

｜士，*moŭc sé*, dénomination que l'on donne aux ministres protestants.

MOÛC

目 *Moŭc*. Œil, bourgeon.
單|人, *tān moŭc gnin*, borgne.
|珠仁, *moŭc tchoū ŷn*, prunelle de l'œil.
篤|睡, *toŭc moŭc choé*, avoir sommeil.
桃子闢|, *t'aô tzè pĭt moŭc*, les pêchers bourgeonnent.

木 *Moŭc*. Arbre, bois.
樹|, *choú moŭc*, arbres, bois.
|料, *moŭc liáo*, bois de construction.
棺|, *kouōn moŭc*, cercueil.
|匠, *moŭc sióng*, menuisier.
|耳, *moŭc gnì*, espèce de champignon d'arbre.

MOŪN

蚊 *Moūn*. Moustique.
|帳, *moūn tchóng*, moustiquaire.
|香, *moūn hiōng*, ingrédients aromatiques pour chasser les moustiques.

MOÛN

門 *Moûn*. Porte.
一扇|，雙扇|, *ŷt chán moûn*, *soūng chán moûn*, une porte simple, une porte à deux battants.
|樓, *moûn leoû*, grande porte d'entrée, portail.
|頭瞭, *moûn t'eoû liaó*, rester à l'entrée de la porte.
閂|，撐|，鎖|, *ts'ōn moûn*, *ts'áng moûn*, *sò moûn*, fermer la porte au verrou, au contrefort, à clef.
出|, *tch'oŭt moûn*, sortir de chez soi.
|上, *moûn chōng* (ou *hōng*), 1er des domestiques du mandarin, son portier.
|生, ou **|徒**, *moûn sēn* ou *moûn t'oû*, disciple.
教|, *kaó moûn*, religion, secte.

們 *Moûn*. Marque du pluriel.
我|，你|, *ngō moûn*, *gnî moûn*, nous, vous. (Plus vulg. **我等** *ngā tèn*, **你等** *gnî tèn*).

問 *Moún*. Demander, s'informer.
有字你唔識愛|先生, *yoū sé gnî mĝ chĭt oí moún sīn sāng*, s'il se trouve un caractère que tu ne connaisses pas, demande au maître.
|唔聲, *moún mĝ chāng*, ne pouvoir obtenir de réponse.
|候, *moún heoú*, saluer en passant, envoyer un bonjour.
|答, *moún tăp*, dialogue, catéchisme.

MOÛNG

矇 *Moûng*. Vue trouble.
眼|, *niàn moûng*, myope, aveuglé.

朦 *Moûng*. Caché.
暗||, *ám moûng moûng*, il fait tout noir.
|山原崁唔敢去, *moûng sān heoú ŷn mĝ kàm hí*; les gorges sont obscures et les fourrés épais (les montagnes

sont noires et les bois épais), je n'ose pas m'y aventurer.

| 沙, *moûng sā*, brouillard.

蒙 *Moûng*. Etre redevable d'un bienfait.

叨 |, *t'āo moûng*, je vous serais obligé...., je vous serais reconnaissant....

承 |, *chîn moûng*, même sens.

| 古, *moûng koù*, la Mongolie.

MOŬT

沒 *Moŭt*. Particule négative (style écrit). Plein, jusqu'au bord, plongé dans l'eau, submergé.

裝倒一 | 盃子來, *tchōng taò ŷt moŭt pī tzè loî*, remplis une pleine tasse.

牛咁大個東西都 | 唔下佢噲漂, *nioû àn t'aí ké· toūng sī toū moŭt mĝ hā voé· p'iaō*, le buffle, malgré sa grosseur, ne peut enfoncer dans l'eau, il surnage.

天融地 |, *t'iēn yoûng t'í moŭt*, la fin du monde.

MOÛT

𠾍 *Moût*. Pourri, gâté, décomposé.

柑子 | 了, *kām tzè moût liào*, les oranges sont toutes pourries.

| 綿, *moût miên*, réduit en boullie.

NĀ

拿 *Nā*. Prendre, apporter, emporter, donner.

| 來, *nā loî*, apporte.

| 轉來, *nā tchòn loî*, rapporte.

| 去, | 轉去, *nā hí, nā tchòn hí*, emporte, remporte.

—起來, *nā hì loî*, prendre en bas, à terre, soulever, élever.

| 得出, | 唔出, *nā têt tch'oût, nā mĝ tch'oût*, pouvoir, ne pas pouvoir produire au dehors, v. gr. payer, rembourser.

NÂ

哪 *Nâ*. Particule finale employée après certains mots, ou à la fin d'une phrase. L'expérience seule peut en apprendre l'usage régulier.

頭 |, *t'eôu nâ*, la tête.

來 |, *loî nâ*, viens donc.

NÀ

那 *Nà*. Où? quel? (Vulgairement *naí* on *ngaí*. Voir ces mots.)

NÂC

Nâc. Rire (populaire).

Nâc. | 腰, *nâc yāo*, courbature de reins, effort.

NĀI

乃 *Nāi*. Mais, certes, et (style écrit).

奶 *Nāi*. Nourrice.

| 母, *nāi moū*, nourrice.

請人來 | 乳, *ts'iàng gnîn loî nāi nén*, inviter une nourrice.

NÂI

泥 *Nâi*. Terre, boue.

落地｜下, *lŏc t'í nâi hā*, tomber à terre.

做｜水師傅, *tsó nâi choùi sē foú*, maître maçon.

NÂI

奈 *Naí*. Moyen, remède.

唔｜何, *mĝ naí hô*, malgré soi, pas moyen de faire autrement.

｜佢唔何, *naí kî mĝ hô*, je ne puis venir à bout de lui.

耐 *Naí*. Endurer, solide, durable,

｜得過, *naí têt kouó*, supportable, tolérable.

忍｜, *nioūn naí*, patience, patienter.

你屋係唔粉壁就唔｜, *niā vouĉ hé· mĝ foùn piâc, ts'ioú mĝ naí*, si vous ne crépissez pas votre maison, elle ne durera pas. *Voyez ngaí.*

那 *Naí* (ou *ngái* pour *nà*).

｜裡, *naí lī*, où, quel ?

你去｜裡來. *gnî hí naí lī loî*, d'où viens-tu ?

｜個人來, *naí ké· gnîn loî*, qui est celui qui vient d'arriver ?

｜久, *naí kiòu*, quand ?

Selon les pays, on dit encore : *naí-vòng*; *ní vòng*; *naí vòng t'áng*; *naí t'áng*; où ? dans quel endroit ?

NÂM

南 *Nâm*. Sud.

指｜針, *tjè nâm tchīm*, aiguille qui indique le sud, boussole.

男 *Nâm*. Mâle, masculin.

｜子人, *nâm tzè gnîn*, homme (par opposition à femme).

｜色, *nâm sêt*, sodomie.

NÀM

揇 *Nàm* (ou *làm*). Porter dans ses bras ; adopter.

｜細人子, *nàm sé· gnîn tzè*, porter un enfant dans ses bras.

佢唔愛我｜, *kî mĝ oí ngâi nàm*, il ne veut pas que je le porte dans mes bras.

有两個賴子一個自己拱個一個｜個, *yōu leòng ké· laí tzè, ŷt ké· tsé kì kioúng ké·, ŷt ké· nàm ké·*, j'ai deux fils, j'ai engendré l'un, et adopté l'autre.

NÂN

難 *Nân*. Difficile.

｜做, ｜話, *nân tsó, nân vá*, difficile à faire, à dire.

作｜, *tsôc nân*, se trouver dans l'embarras.

刁｜人, *tiaó nân gnîn* donner de l'embarras à quelqu'un.

艱｜, *kiān nân*, difficile, ennuyeux.

｜爲你, *nân vî gnî*, tu as pris de la peine pour moi, merci (politesse).

｜耐, *nân ngái* (pour *nái*), difficile à supporter.

做那個咁｜來, *tsó mâc ké· kàn nân loî* ? pourquoi tardes-tu tant à venir ?

丨得倒, *nân têt taò*, difficile à obtenir.

NÁN

難 *Nán*. Souffrance, calamité.

受丨, *choú nán*, souffrir.

你家娘來你丨度到徲, *niā kā niông loî niā nán t'oú taó lê*, ta belle-mère vient, (le temps de tes peines commence) tu n'es pas au bout de tes peines.

NÂNG

壤 *Nâng*. Petite dépression.

玻璃丨, *pō lî nâng*, la dépression, ou l'étranglement du col de la bouteille de verre.

一丨一極, *ŷt nâng ŷt k'ĭt*, une dépression et une dilatation.

NÁNG

躟 *Náng*. Écraser du pied.

丨人個脚, *náng gnîn ké· kiŏc*, marcher sur le pied de quelqu'un.

丨死, *náng sì*, tuer en écrasant.

莫丨倒蓆, *mŏc náng taò ts'ĭăc*, ne marche pas sur la natte.

NĀO

惱 *Nāo*. Haine, haïr.

丨恨, *nāo hén*, détester.

得人丨, *têt gnîn nāo*, détestable, haïssable.

NAÔ

錨 *Naô*. Ancre de bateau.

下丨, *hā naô*, jeter l'ancre.

起丨, ou 拖出丨, *hì naô* ou *t'ō tch'oût naô*, lever l'ancre.

丨鈎, *naô keoū*, bâton armé d'un crochet, croc, gaffe.

NAÒ

瑙 *Naò*. 瑪丨, *mā naò*, cornaline.

腦 *Naò*. Cerveau, cervelle.

猪丨, *tchoū naò*, cervelle de cochon.

丨髓, *naò chè* (pour *sòi*), cervelle.

NAÓ

殰 *Naó*. Empoisonner.

尋藥丨老鼠, *ts'îm yŏc naó lào tch'où*, chercher des drogues pour empoisonner les rats.

鬧 *Naó*. Bruyant, animation, faire du bruit.

吵丨, *ts'âo naó*, se quereller, se disputer à grands cris.

丨事, *naó sé*, susciter une affaire, une rébellion.

丨人家, *naó gnîn kā*, faire du charivari devant une maison.

生理丨熱, *siēn lī naó gnĕt*, le commerce est animé, il y a foule.

NĂP

納 *Năp*. Prendre, recevoir, payer ses intérêts.

丨財, *năp ts'oî*, amasser des richesses.

丨福, *năp foŭc*, être heureux.

令尊丨福, *lín tsoūn năp foŭc* ? M. votre père est-il en bonne santé (*litt.* jouit-il de tous les bonheurs)?

丨糧，丨穀利，*năp leông, năp kŏuc lí*, payer les impôts, payer le revenu de riz.

NÂT

燵 *Nât.* Brûler par attouchement.

火管丨倒我，*fô kouòn nât taò gnaî*, le verre de lampe m'a brûlé.

丨倒一個皰，*nât taò ỹt ké· p'iaó*, la brûlure m'a fait une ampoule.

NÊM

腩 *Nêm.* Tendre, mou, blet.

番薯熠丨𠲜，*fān choû sâp nêm ē·*, les patates sont assez cuites (assez tendres).

肘子丨𠲜噲穿，*tch'oî tzè nêm-ê· voé· tch'ōn*, l'abcès est mûr, il va percer.

丨柿子，*nêm sē tzè*, nèfles du Japon (kaki), mûres, blettes.

NÈM

楠 *Nèm.* Prune sauvage, fruit d'une espèce de rhododendron.

當丨子，*tōng nèm tzè*, prune d'hiver.

摘當丨子，*tsâc tōng nèm tzè*, cueillir de ces fruits.

NÉM

腩 *Ném.* Sans consistance.

行起係丨，*hâng hì hé· ném*, il marche comme s'il ne pouvait se tenir sur ses jambes.

丨雞，*ném kē·*, se dit d'une poule malade, qui a de la peine à marcher.

你豆腐忒丨，*niâ t'eoú foú t'ïêt ném*, ton fromage n'a pas assez de consistance.

NÊN

能 *Nên.* Puissance, pouvoir.

全丨天主，*ts'iên nên t'iēn chòu*, Dieu tout-puissant.

丨幹，*nên kón*, puissance, habileté.

不丨彀，*poût nên kéou*, c'est impossible; je n'y puis consentir (suivant le contexte).

寧 *Nên.* Aimer mieux, plutôt.

丨受萬苦不敢犯罪，*nên choú ván k'où, poût kàm fám ts'oúi*, plutôt souffrir tous les tourments que de commettre un péché.

NÉN

乳 *Nén.* Lait.

細人子食丨，*sé· gnîn tzè chĭt nén*, l'enfant tète,

丨姑，*nén koū*, téton, pis.

牛丨，羊丨，*nioû nén, yông nén*, lait de vache, de chèvre.

丨母，*nén moū*, nourrice.

斷丨，*t'ōn nén*, sevrer.

NEÔU

粈 *Neôu.* Epais, gluant.

你煲倒粥十分丨，*gnî pō tào tchoŭc chĭp foūn neôu*, tu as cuit la soupe de riz beaucoup trop épaisse.

墨水忒丨噲粘筆，*mĕt chouì. t'ïêt neoû voé· niâm pīt*, l'encre est trop épaisse, elle se colle au pinceau.

NEÒU

扭 *Neòu*. Empoigner, saisir avec la main.

丨等來, *neòu tèn loî*, empoigne-le.

鈕 *Neòu*. 丨襻, *neòu p'án*, boutonnière.

蒟 *Neòu*. 丨葉, *neòu yăp*, feuille de bétel.

NÊP

妠 *Nêp*. Gras, embonpoint.

咁丨個人, *àn nêp ké· gnîn* ! comme cet homme a de l'embonpoint !

NĔT

捞 *Nĕt*. Pincer, saisir du bout du doigt.

丨人, *nĕt gnîn*, pincer quelqu'un avec les doigts.

丨花, *nĕt fa*, cueillir une fleur.

笏 *Nĕt*. Epine.

丨頭, *nĕt t'eôu*, buisson.

丨頭蓬, *nĕt t'eôu p'oûng*, fourré, broussailles.

杉子丨, *ts'ám tzè nĕt*, aiguilles de sapin.

NĜ

魚 *Nĝ*. Poisson.

一條丨, *ŷt t'iâo nĝ*, un poisson.

鹹丨, *hâm nĝ*, poisson salé.

油丨, *yôu nĝ*, la sèche.

鱷丨, *ngŏc nĝ*, crocodile.

打丨, *tà nĝ*, pêcher d'une manière quelconque.

nĝ hoî soī, ouïes du poisson.

nĝ k'ì koū, nageoires du poisson.

吾 *Nĝ*. Moi, mon, notre (style écrit).

丨主耶穌, *nĝ tchòu yâ sē*, Notre Seigneur Jesus-Christ.

蜈 *Nĝ*. 丨公虫, *nĝ hoūng tch'oûng*, scolopendre, mille-pieds.

你 *Nĝ*, Abréviation du mot : 你 *gnî*, *toi*, dans quelques cas, et dans certains pays.

愛丨, *oí nĝ*, comme tu voudras.

Le ton change dans cette seule expression :

丨等, *ngtèn*, vous, vous autres.

NG̀

女 *Nġ*. Femme, par opposition à 男 *nâm*, homme.

不論男女儕儕都去得, *poŭt loún nâm nġ sâ sâ toū hí têt*, hommes ou femmes, tout le monde peut y aller.

姪子姪丨, *tch'ĭt tzè tch'ĭt nġ*, neveu et nièce.

孫子孫丨, *soūn tzè soūn nġ*, petit fils et petite fille.

五 *Nġ*. Cinq

丨個, *nġ ké·*, 第丨, *t'í nġ*, cinq, le cinquième

午 *Nġ*. Midi.

| 時, *ng̀ chê*, heure chinoise, de 11h du matin à 1h après midi.

| 時花, *ng̀ chê fā*, espèce de fleur qui éclot tous les jours à midi précis.

仵 *Ng̀*. | 作, *ng̀ tsôc*, expert du prétoire, chargé de constater les blessures et les causes de mort.

忤 *Ng̀*. | 逆, *ng̀ niăc*, désobéir, rebelle.

| 逆不孝, *ng̀ niác poŭt háo*, manquer gravement à la piété filiale.

NǴ

Ńg. Abréviation du mot 二 *gní*, deux. Ce mot ne s'emploie que pour dire: *ńg chĭp*, vingt.

NGĀ

我 *Ngā (ngō)*. Mon, le mien.

|, 你, 佢, *ngā, niā, kiā*, le mien, le tien, le sien.

| 錢, *ngā ts'iên*, mon argent.

| 個, *ngā ké·*, c'est à moi, c'est le mien.

| 等, *ngā tèn*, nous, nous autres.

| 等唔慣食粥, *ngā tèn mǵ kouán chĭt tchoŭc*, nous ne sommes pas habitués à manger de la soupe de riz.

NGÂ

牙 *Ngâ*. Dent.

| 齒, *ngâ tchè*, même sens.

| 齒痛, *ngâ tchè t'oúng*, avoir mal aux dents.

缺一個 | 齒, *k'iĕt ȳt ké· ngâ tchè*, il manque une dent.

脫 | 齒, *t'ôt ngâ tchè*, arracher une dent.

象 |, *sióng ngâ*, ivoire.

做 | 人, *tsó ngâ gnîn*, faire l'entremetteur dans les marchés de grains, de poules, de porcs.

芽 *Ngâ*. 豆 |, *t'cóu ngâ*, haricots que l'on fait germer, pour les manger en guise de légumes verts.

娃 *Ngâ*. 阿 |, *ō ngâ*, petit enfant qui vient de naître.

衙 *Ngâ*. | 門, *ngâ moûn*, prétoire, tribunal.

進 | 門, *tsín ngâ moûn*, entrer au prétoire.

| 門八字開有理麼錢莫進來, *ngâ moûn pât sé k'oī yoū lī mô ts'iên mŏc tsín loî*, le tribunal ressemble au caractère 8, si vous n'avez pas d'argent, même ayant le droit pour vous, n'y entrez pas.

NGÀ

瓦 *Ngà*. Tuiles.

一塊 |, *ȳt k'ouaí ngà*, une tuile.

溝 |, *keoū ngà*, rigole que forment les tuiles, à l'intersection de deux toits qui se rencontrent.

陰 |, 陽 |, *ȳm ngà..., yông ngà*, tuiles placées en sens convexe..., en sens concave.

NGÂI

我 *Ngâi (ngō)*. Je, moi.

| 知, *ngaî tī*, je sais.

| 愛, | 唔愛, *ngaî oí, ngaî mĝ oí*, je veux, je ne veux pas.

NGAÍ

耐 *Ngaí* (*naí*). Supporter, tenir bon.

| 了二百小板子, *ngái liào gní pâc siào pàn* (ou *pièn*) *tzè*, il a reçu 200 coups de verges (sans broncher).

| 得苦個人, *ngaí têt k'où ké gnîn*, il est de force à supporter la fatigue.

難 |, *nân ngaí*, difficile à supporter. *Voyez naí.*

那 *Ngaí* (*nà*). Où, quel ?*Voir naí.*

NGĀM

喦 *Ngām*. Cloison, mur, ce qui ressemble à un mur, escarpement à pic.

| 下, *ngām hā*, au pied du mur.

| |, *ngām ngām*, tout juste, ni trop, ni trop peu.

嘴 |, *tchoí ngām*, le menton.

NGÂM

岩 *Ngâm*. 石 |, *chăc ngâm*, caverne, grotte.

NGÀM

喦 *Ngàm*. Incliner, s'incliner.

| 頭, *ngàm t'eoû*, incliner la tête, faire un salut de tête.

風吹禾盡 |, *foūng tch'oī vô ts'in ngàm*, le vent agite les champs de riz.

NGĀN

(*Voir aussi les mots NIAN*)

研 *Ngān*. Broyer, réduire en morceaux, écraser.

番薯拿來 | 綿, *fān choû nā loî ngān miēn*, écrase les patates en bouillie.

| 墨, *ngān mĕt*, délayer l'encre de Chine, en la frottant sur la pierre.

NGÂN

頑 *Ngân*. Résister.

| 抗, *ngân k'óng*, résister.

| 丟丟, *ngân tiôu tiôu*, se dit d'un enfant désobéissant.

NGÁN

岸 *Ngán*. Rivage, rive.

兼 |, *kiām ngán*, aborder le rivage.

上 |, *chōng ngán*, monter sur le rivage.

市 |, *ché ngán*, ville non murée, petite ville.

鴈 *Ngán*. | 鵝, *ngán* (ou *nián*) *ngô*, grue.

NGÁNG

硬 *Ngáng*. Solide, dur. opiniâtre, raide, rigide.

| 樹, *ngáng choú*, bois dur.

| 健, *ngáng k'ián*, solide, fort, bien portant.

| 性, *ngáng sín*, entêté, dur de caractère.

春煎忒 |, *tch'oūn tsiēn t'iĕt ngáng*, les œufs sont trop cuits.

丨愛, *ngáng oí*, il faut absolument, je veux absolument.

丨係, *ngáng hé·*, c'est bien vrai, vraiment.

講丨話, *kòng ngáng fá*, parler avec fermeté et dureté.

NGĀO

咬 *Ngāo*. Mordre.

狗丨人, *keòu ngāo gnîn*, les chiens mordent.

NGÂO

㘭 *Ngâo*. Tordu, tourné, biscornu.

鞋丨帛裡, *haî ngâo p'ĕt lî*, les souliers sont déformés.

丨...., *ngâo tîn tîn*, se dit de quelque chose biscornu, sans forme.

熬 *Ngâo*. Faire fondre, faire cuire longtemps.

丨虎膏, *ngâo foù kāo*, faire de la gélatine de tigre.

丨糖糕, *ngâo t'ông kāo*, cuire de la marmelade.

丨火鹽, *ngâo fò yâm*, faire évaporer l'eau salée, pour en faire du sel fin.

NGÁO

敖 *Ngáo* ou *ngāo*. Lancer.

丨石頭, *ngáo chăc t'eôu*, lancer des pierres.

傲 *Ngáo*. Orgueil, obstiné.

驕丨, *kiāo ngáo*, orgueil, orgueilleux.

丨性, *ngáo sín*, caractère hautain, obstiné.

NGĂT

齧 *Ngăt*. Pincer, pris dans un engrenage.

手丨倒裡, *choù ngăt tào lê·*, mon doigt est pris (à un engrenage, à une jointure de porte, etc.).

GNÂT

Ngât. Avare, parcimonieux, qui n'aime pas à donner.

個個人好丨, *ké· ké· gnîn hào ngât*, cet homme est très avare.

吃 *Ngât*. Mordre.

丨倒一口來, *ngât tào ȳt heòu loî*, donner un coup de dent (en emportant le morceau), mordre une bouchée.

狗會丨人, 小心, *keòu voé· ngât gnîn, siào sīm*, le chien mord, attention !

Ngât. Mauvaise odeur d'un goût caractéristique.

老鼠臭丨, *lào tch'où tch'oú ngât*, le rat pue cette odeur.

NGEOU voir NIOU

NGŌ

我 *Ngō*. Je, moi, (voir *ngâi*).

NGÔ

鵝 *Ngô*. Oie.

丨毛, *ngô māo*, plume d'oie.

雁丨, *ngán* (ou *yán* ou *nián*) *ngô*, grue.

NGÓ

餓 *Ngó*. Avoir faim, endurer la faim.

丨兩日, *ngó leòng gnǐt*, je n'ai rien mangé de deux jours.

丨瘦, *ngó seoú*, maigrir par insuffisance de nourriture.

丨死, *ngó sì*, mourir de faim.

臥 *Ngó*. Être couché, ou adossé comme pour dormir.

坐丨, *ts'ō ngó*, se tenir adossé sans mouvement.

NGǑC

樂 *Ngǒc*. Musique.

丨器, *ngǒc hí*, instrument de musique.

作丨, *tsôc ngǒc*, orchestre, faire un orchestre.

奏丨, *tseoú ngǒc*, jouer de la musique, en avant la musique!

岳 *Ngǒc*. 丨父, *ngǒc foú*, beau-père du mari.

丨母, *ngǒc mōu*, belle-mère du mari. (Plus vulg. 丈人老, 丈人婆, *tch'óng gnîn laò, tch'óng gnîn p'ô*.

NGOC

噩 *Ngôc*. Mauvais, vilain, sans valeur.

佧工夫係丨, *kiā koūng foú hé· ngôc*, son travail (main d'œuvre) est mauvais.

丨錢, *ngôc ts'iên*, mauvaise sapèque.

丨貨, *ngôc fó*, mauvaise marchandise.

NGŌE·.

呆 *Ngōe·*. Idiot, stupide.

NGÓE·

碍 *Ngoé·*. Obstacle, empêcher, embarrasser.

並無丨, *p'ín vôu ngoé·*, il n'y a absolument aucune difficulté.

丨事, *ngoé· sé*, embarrasser, gêner.

丨路, *ngoé· loú*, embarrasser la route.

丨我唔倒, *ngoé· ngaî mĝ tào*, cela ne me gêne pas, (ou bien,) cela ne m'empêchera pas de...

丨唔倒聖母個凈血, *ngoé· mĝ taò chín moū ké· ts'iáng hiĕt*, sans nuire à la pureté de la Sainte Vierge (*catéch*).

外 *Ngoé·*. Extérieur, dehors, excepté, non compris.

出丨背, *tch'oūt ngoé· poé·*, sortir dehors.

出丨頭, *tch'oūt ngoé· t'eôu*, même sens; s'emploie aussi pour désigner les lieux d'aisance, aller à la selle.

轉丨家, *tchòng* (pour *tchòn*) *ngoé· kā*, aller voir ses parents (se dit d'une fille mariée qui retourne chez ses parents).

另丨, *láng ngoé·*, en outre.

丨教, *ngoé· kaó*, en dehors de la religion, payens.

我工錢以丨我聽倒兩個花邊, *ngā koūng ts'iên ỹ ngoé· ngaî ts'ón taò*

leòng ké· fă piēn, j'ai gagné deux piastres en plus de mon salaire.

NGOÚ

誤 *Ngóu*. Se tromper, erreur nuisible.

丨倒一個字, *ngóu taò ŷt ké· sé*, je me suis trompé de caractère.

丨了工夫, *ngóu liào koūng foū*, avoir négligé son travail, avoir perdu son temps.

個人噲丨事, *ké· gnîn voé· ngoú sé*, cet homme gâtera les choses.

悟 *Ngoú*. Comprendre.

明丨, *mîn ngoú*, intelligence.

NGOÛI

危 *Ngoûi*. 丨險, *ngoûi hiàm*, danger extrême.

病將丨, *p'iáng tsiōng ngoûi*, malade à l'extrême.

NĪ

語 *Nī*. 俗丨, *sioŭc nī*, proverbes, dictons.

蟻 *Nī* ou *nié·* ou *ní* ou *gnī*. 丨公, *nī koūng*, fourmi.

白丨, *p'ăc nī*, fourmi blanche, termite.

蠹丨, *nông nī*, libellule.

疑 *Nî* (*gnî*). Douter, imaginer.

丨懦, *nî noûc*, penser, supposer. *Voir gnî*.

丨人不用, 用人不丨, *nî gnîn poût yoúng, yoúng gnîn poût nî*, n'employez pas un homme dont vous doutez, et si vous employez un homme, ne doutez pas de lui.

尼 *Nî*. 丨姑, *nî koū*, bonzesse.

呢 *Nî*. Flanelle, drap ; terminaison de phrases dans les livres.

丨衫, 丨馬褂, *nî sām, nî mā koúa*, veste de flanelle, pardessus en drap.

宜 *Nî*. Convenable, raisonnable.

丨防險事, *nî fông hiàm sé*, il faut se précautionner contre le danger.

不丨, *poût nî*, il ne convient pas.

NIĀ

你 *Niā* (*nī*). Ton, tien.

係丨個麼, *hé· niā ké· mô* ? est-ce à toi ?

丨事, *niā sé*, c'est ton affaire.

惹 *Niā*. Exciter, provoquer.

丨事, *niā sé*, susciter des affaires.

丨人相打, *niā gnîn siōng tà*, provoquer les gens à se battre.

丨火, *niā fò*, causer un incendie.

NIĂC

逆 *Niăc*. Contraire, en opposition.

丨風, *niăc foūng*, vent debout.

丨命, *niăc mín*, résister à un ordre

忤丨, *ng niăc*, rebelle, désobéir.

NIÂC

額 *Niâc*. 丨頭, *niâc t'eôu*, front.

匾 | ,*pièn niâc*, pancarte de boutique, inscription sur un tableau.

| 分, *niâc foūn*, part, portion.

麼 | , *mô niâc*, il n'y a plus rien, il ne reste rien.

NIĂM

拈 *Niăm*. Prendre, ramasser.

| 石頭, *niăm chăc t'eôu*, ramasser des pierres.

| 鬮, *niăm keōu*, tirer au sort.

你手帕跌落地 | 起來, *niă choù p'á tiĕt lŏc t'í hă niăm hì loî*, ton mouchoir est tombé par terre, ramasse-le.

NIÂM

嚴 *Niâm*. Qui impose une obligation, sévère, intense.

威 | , *vī niâm*, majesté, gravité.

| 命, *niâm mín*, ordre sévère, formel.

| 辦, *niâm p'án*, juger sévèrment.

酒好 | , *tsioù hào niâm*, le vin est fort, très alcoolisé.

茶忒 | , *ts'â t'iĕt niâm*, le thé est très trop fort.

黏 *Niâm*. Collé, adhérent ; avec.

糞煮倒忒鮮 | 唔穩, *kăng tchoù taò t'iĕt siēn niâm mĝ voùn*, la colle est trop claire, elle ne prend pas.

| 人草, *niâm gnîn ts'aò*, espèce d'herbe qui s'attache aux vêtements.

兩條狗 | 等 (ou | 緊) 佢去, *leòng t'iaô keoù niâm tèn* (ou *niâm kìn*) *kì hí*, deux chiens l'accompagnaient.

| 尾 (ou 臨尾), *niâm mī* (ou *lîm mī*), à la queue, à la fin.

NIÀM

儼 *Niàm*. De la même manière, comme.

佢講起 | 然一樣, *kì kòng hì niàm yân ŷt yóng*, il raconte d'une manière tout à fait vraisemblable.

| 然婦人家一樣, *niàm yân foú gnîn kă ŷt yóng*, il a absolument les manières d'une femme.

NIÁM

念 Réciter, penser, lire.

| 輕心亂, *niám kīn sīm lón*, prier avec distraction.

| 頭, *niám t'eôu*, pensées.

雜 | *ts'ăp niám*, distractions.

| 珠子, *niám tchoū tzè*, chapelet, rosaire.

| 書, *niám choū*, lire un livre à haute voix.

| 我聽, *niám ngaî t'ăng*, récite-moi, lis-moi.

你事我時時掛 | ou 記 | , *niă sé ngaî chê chê kouá niám* ou *kí niám*, je pense constemment à ton affaire.

驗 *Niám*. Examiner, vérifier juridiquement.

| 屍, | 傷, *niám chē*, *niám chōng*, examiner un cadavre, une blessure.

仵作 | 出來十二傷, *ǹg tsôc niám tch'oŭt lôi chĭp gní chōng*, l'expert a constaté 12 blessures.

染 *Niám*. Teindre.

丨布，丨衫褲，*niám poú, niám sām foú*, teindre de la toile, des habits.

丨紅個，藍個，*niám foûng ké·, lâm ké·*, teindre en rouge, en bleu.

開丨房，*k'oī niám fông*, tenir une teinturerie.

NIÂN

年 *Niân*. Année.

今丨，明丨，後丨，前丨，*kīn niân, mîn* (ou *miâng*) *niân, heoú niân, ts'iên niân*, cette année, l'an prochain, dans deux ans, l'an passée.

前兩丨，*ts'iên leòng niân*, il y a deux ans.

頭丨，(ou 前頭丨，) *t'eôu niân*, (ou *ts'iên t'eôu niân*) autrefois, les années précédentes.

丨丨都係一樣，*niân niân toū hé. ŷt yóng*, chaque année il en est ainsi.

拜新丨，*paí sīn niân*, souhaiter la bonne année.

過丨，*hoúo niân*, passer l'année (pour désigner le jour de l'an).

丨紀大，*niân kì t'aí*, vour êtes âgé.

少丨紀，*chaò niân kì*, il est encore jeune.

元 *Niân*. Premier, principe, commencement.

丨年，*niân niân*, première année d'un règne.

狀丨，*ts'óng niân*, le 1er sur la liste des académiciens.

解丨，*kiái niân*, le 1er sur la liste des licenciés.

言 *Niân*. Parole.

謠丨，*yâo niân*, faux bruits, rumeurs.

俗丨，*sioŭc niân*, dicton.

話汚丨，*vá voū niân*, dire des paroles grossières.

顏 *Niân*. Couleur.

丨色，*niân sĕt*, couleur, coloris.

丨色幾好看，*niân sĕt kì hào k'ón*, le coloris est assez joli.

原 *Niân*. Source, origine.

根丨，*kēn niân*, même sens.

萬有眞丨，*ván yōu tchīn niân*, la vraie origine de toutes choses (titre inscrit au frontispice des églises).

丨罪，*niân ts'oúi*, péché originel.

丨係我做個，*niân hé ngâi tsó ké·* c'est bien moi qui ai fait la chose.

NIÀN

眼 *Niàn*. Œil, petit trou.

丨珠仁，*niàn tchoū ŷn*, la prunelle des yeux.

丨皮，*niàn p'î*, les paupières.

丨屎，*niàn chè*, chassie des yeux.

瞎丨，*hât niàn*, arracher les yeux, aveugle.

眨丨，*châp niàn*, cligner des yeux, fermer les yeux.

丨鏡，*niàn kiáng*, lunette.

車丨，*tch'ā niàn*, pratiquer un trou en tournant.

鑽 |, *tsón niàn*, faire un trou en enfonçant un poinçon.

鑿 |, *ts'ŏc niàn*, faire un trou en se servant du ciseau.

| 下, *niàn há*, à présent, présentement.

Niàn. Appuyer, presser, pincer.

消息 | 阿起就開, *siāo sĭt niàn á hì ts'ioú k'oī*, en appuyant sur le loquet cela s'ouvre tout de suite.

鎖頭 | 尾來, *sò t'eôu niàn mī loî*, presser bien sur la serrure pour la fermer.

NIÁN

願 *Nián*. Consentir, désirer.

你 | 唔 |, *gnî nián mĝ nián?* veux-tu oui ou non?

你咁 | 麼, *gnî kăm nián mô?* y consens-tu?

| 死, *nián sì*, accepter la mort de bon cœur.

許 |, *hì nián*, faire un vœu

還 |, *vân nián*, accomplir un vœu.

NIÂNG

迎 *Niâng*. Aller en procession, aller au devant.

| 聖體, *niâng chín t'ì*, porter le Saint Sacrement en procession.

| 龍燈, *niâng lioûng tēn*, promener d'immenses lanternes en forme de dragon.

| 春, *niâng tch'oūn*, aller inviter le printemps, cérémonie qui se fait au commencement du printemps.

NIAŌ

鳥 *Niaō*. Oiseau.

| 雀, *niaō tsiŏc*, oiseau en général.

| 銃, *niaō tch'oúng*, fusil de chasse chinois.

NIAÔ

饒 *Niâo*. Pardonner.

| 得你一擺, *niâo tĕt gnî ŷt paì*, je te pardonne pour cette fois.

NIÁO

尿 *Niáo*. Urine.

阿 |, *ō niáo*, uriner.

| 桶, *niáo t'oùng*, seau qui sert à porter les urines.

| 缸, *niáo kōng*, urinoir.

| 壺, *niáo foû*, vase de nuit.

猪 | 袋, *tchoū niáo t'oí*, vessie de porc.

NIĂP

業 *Niăp*. Héritage, état de vie.

家 |, 產 |, *kā niăp, sàn niăp*, biens de famille, héritage paternel.

佢麼事 |, *kî mô sé niăp*, il n'a pas d'emploi, d'occupation.

尋那個正 |, *ts'îm nâc ké· tchín niăp*, chercher quelque occupation régulière et honnête.

NIÂP

䁝 *Niâp* ou *yâp*. Scintillement, vibration d'un corps.

星子 | | 濽, *sēn tzè niâp niâp ts'án*, les étoiles scintillent.

眼珠仁 | | 攢, *niàn tchoū ŷn niâp niâp ts'án*, les yeux clignent.

嘴子 | | 條, *tchoï tzè niâp niâp t'iaô*, il est toujours à marmotter quelque chose.

niōng niōng niâp niâp, même sens.

壓 *Niâp* (*âp*). Déprimé, écrasé.

帽子別你打 |, *máo tzè poūn gnî tà niâp*, tu m'as bosselé mon chapeau.

攝 *Niâp* (ou*yâp*). Tirer à soi, tenir.

| 衫袖, *niâp sām ts'ióu*, retrousser les manches de son habit.

| 鼻公, *niâp p'í koūng*, se boucher le nez.

| 尿, *niâp niáo*, retenir son urine.

NIEN voir NIAN

NIEOU voir NIOU

NIET voir GNET

NÍN

悋 *Nín*. **慳 |**, *kiān nín*, avare, avarice.

NIŎC

弱 *Niŏc*. Faible.

病阿十分 |, *p'iáng á chĭp foūn niŏc*, il est très affaibli par la maladie.

| 房, *niŏc fông*, branche faible (d'une famille). Voyez **强** *k'iông*.

NIÔC

虐 *Niôc*. Prendre les oiseaux au filet ; tyranniser.

| 鳥子, *niôc tiāo tzè*, prendre les oiseaux au filet.

官府殘 | 百姓, *kouōn foù ts'ân niôc pâc siáng*, le mandarin tyrannise tout le monde.

Niôc. Démanger, piquer.

布十分粗噲 | 人, *poú chĭp foūn tsē voé· niôc gnîn*, cette étoffe est trop rude, ça vous gratte.

衫敨裡唔知有那個噲 | 人, *sām teoú lì mĝ tī yoū mâc ké· voé· niôc gnîn*, je ne sais ce qu'il y a dans mon habit, ça шə picote.

NIŌN

軟 *Niōn*. Faible ; qui fléchit.

| 弱, *niōn niŏc*, sans vigueur, faible.

脚 |, *kiôc niōn*, douleur dans la jambe, les jambes fléchissent.

受 |, *choú niōn*, céder son droit par conciliation.

桁子忒細噲 |, *hâng tzè t'iĕt sé· voé· niōn*, les poutres sont trop petites, elles fléchiront.

床板忒硬愛攤稈來放 |, *ts'ông pàn t'iĕt ngáng ói t'ān kòn loî fóng niōn*, les planches de lit sont trop dures, il faut les radoucir en étendant de la paille.

NIŌNG

仰 *Niōng* ou *niòng*. Désirer, attendre.

| 慕天主, *niōng moú t'iēn tchoù*, soupirer après Dieu.

久 |, *kiòu niōng*, depuis longtemps je vous attendais!... (Rép.) **豈敢**, *k'ì kàm*, comment oserais-je? c.-à-d. c'est trop d'honneur (*politesse*).

NIÔNG

娘 *Niông*. Mère de famille, terme honorifique pour appeler les femmes d'un certain âge.

家 |, *kā niông*, belle-mère.

你討裡姑 | 麼, *gnì t'ào lê· koū niông mô?* as-tu pris femme ?

新 |, *sīn niông*, appellatif des jeunes mariées.

馬 |, *mā niông*, jument qui a son poulain, ou qui a déjà porté.

NIÓNG

讓 *Nióng*. Céder (voir *yóng*).

樣 *Nióng* (*yóng*). Comment ?

| 班做得, *nióng pān tsó têt ?* comment cela se peut-il ?

我唔知 | 班做, *ngaî mĝ tī nióng pān tsó*, je ne sais pas comment faire.

| 都愛去, *nióng toū oí hí*, quoi qu'il arrive (ou) de toutes manières, il faut y aller.

NIÔU

牛 *Niôu*. Bœuf, buffle.

| 牯, *niôu koù*, bœuf ou taureau.

| 牸, *niôu tsé*, vache, bufflonne.

| 嫲, *niôu mē·*, petit d'une vache ou d'une bufflonne.

牽 |, *k'iān niôu*, conduire un buffle.

撑 |, *tchòng niôu*, garder, paître le buffle.

撑 | 賣 |, *tchòng niôu mái niôu*, vendre le buffle que l'on vous a donné à garder (proverbe).

犀 |, *sī niôu* rhinocéros.

水犀 |, *choùi sī niôu*, hippopotame.

NIÒU

扭 *Niòu*. Tordre, tourner.

衫拿來 | 湳, *sām nā loî niòu liàm*, tordre un habit pour égoutter l'eau.

| | 揪揪, *niòu niòu tsiòu tsiòu*, contourné, tourné en spirales.

| 風車, *niòu foūng tch'ā*, tourner le moulin à vanner.

Mais on dit : | 螺螄 *niòu lô sē*, tourner une vis pour l'enfoncer ou la retirer.

NIŎUC

獄 *Niŏuc*. Prison.

地 |, *t'í niŏuc*, l'enfer.

煉 |, *lién niŏuc*, le purgatoire.

罰下地 |, *făt hā t'í niŏuc*, envoyer en enfer.

玉 *Niŏuc*. Pierre précieuse.

| 石, *niŏuc chăc*, jade.

| 體, *niŏuc t'ì*, votre honorable personne.

昆 |, *k'oūn niŏuc*, M. votre frère.

褥 *Niŏuc* (ou *yŏuc*). Tapis, matelas pour siège, ou lit.

攤 | 疊眠, *t'ān niŏuc t'iăp mîn*, étendre un tapis pour se coucher.

NIOÛC

肉 *Nioûc*. Chair, viande.

| 身, *nioûc chīn*, le corps humain.

猪 |, 牛 |, 羊 |, *tchōu nioûc, niôu*

niouc, yông niouc, viande de porc, de bœuf, de chèvre.

| 桂, *niouc koúi*, espèce de cannelle.

骨 |, *koût niouc*, les os et la chair, la matière et la forme, le fond et la forme.

NIOŪN

忍 *Nioūn*. Patienter, supporter.

| 耐, *nioūn nái*, supporter avec patience.

| 讓, *nioūn yóng*, céder patiemment.

| 唔下, *nioūn mĝ hā*, ne pouvoir supporter.

NIOÛN

銀 *Nioûn*. Argent.

| 錢, *nioûn ts'iên*, argent et sapèques, biens, fortune, argent monnayé.

汞 | *choùi nioûn*, mercure.

| 硃, *nioûn tchoū*, vermillon.

| 水, *nioûn choùi*, argent pur, titre de l'argent.

| 水高 (v. 底), *nioûn choùi kāo* (ou *taì*), argent à titre élevé (ou faible).

| 水有幾多呈, *nioûn choùi yoū kì tō tch'âng?* combien y a-t-il de parties d'argent pur ?

我算十二水, *ngaî són chĭp gní choùi*; je compte àu taux de 12 (sapèques le *foūn* = 1200 pour un taël).

九呈 |, *kioù tch'âng nioûn*, argent au titre de $\frac{9}{10}$ ou $\frac{90}{100}$. On dit de même: 八呈, 七呈, *pât tch'âng, ts'ĭt tch'âng*, pour les titres de $\frac{8}{10}$ et $\frac{7}{10}$.

一錠 |, *ŷt t'ín nioûn*, un lingot d'argent.

鍍 |, *t'oú nioûn*, argenter.

平 |, *p'în nioûn*, peser de l'argent.

| 行, *nioûn hông*, banque.

NIOÚN

Nioún. Ferme, coriace, dur sans être cassant, solide par son élasticité.

雞肉唔曾煮熟還係 |, *kē· niouc mĝ ts'ên tchoù chouc hân hé· nioún*, la poule n'est pas cuite à point, elle est encore dure.

樟樹係 |, *tchōng choú hé· nioún*, le bois de camphrier est solide (plutôt par son élasticité que par sa rigidité).

NIOÛNG

濃 *Nioûng*. Épais, fourni.

樹山幾 |, *choú sān kì nioûng*, la forêt est bien épaisse.

番薯苗幾 |, *fān choû miaō kì nioûng*, le feuillage des patates est bien fourni.

你酒十分 |, *niā tsioù chĭp foūn nioûng*, ton vin est très fort.

竻頭蓬係 |, *nĕt t'eoû p'oûng hé· nioûng*, les fourrés sont très épais.

NIOÚNG

Nioúng (ou *nióng*, ou *ým*, ou *gním*).

| 管, *nioúng koùon*, partout, de tous côtés. Dérivé du mot 任 *ým*, à volonté.

NÔ

攞 *Nô* (ou *mô*). Aiguiser, frotter.

| 刀子, *nô taō tzè*, aiguiser un couteau.

| 刀石, *nô taō chăc*, pierre à aiguiser.

唔會 | 利, *mĝ ts'ên nô lí*, il n'est pas bien aiguisé.

NÓ

糯 *Nó*. | 米, *nó mì*, espèce de riz glutineux qui sert à faire le vin.

NON

暖 *Nōn* (*nòn*). Tiède, réchauffer.

天氣過 |, *t'iēn hí koúo nōn*, la température s'est radoucie.

| 水洗身, *nōn choùi sè· chīn*, faire chauffer de l'eau pour se laver le corps.

著過 | 個衫, *tchôc koúo nōn ké· sām*, porter des vêtements plus chauds.

NÓNG

枉 *Nóng* (*vòng*). Gaspiller, inutilement, en vain.

| 了, *nóng liào*, c'est dommage!

| 費心, *nóng fí sīm*, c'est en vain que je me suis donné de la peine.

咁好個馬死 | 鳥裡, *àn hào ké· mā sì nóng fĕt lê·*, quel excellent cheval! c'est dommage qu'il soit mort.

NOÛ

奴 *Noû*. Esclave.

| 才, *noû tsoî*, esclave, serviteur.

NOÙ

弩 *Noù*. Flèche empoisonnée; tuer avec ces flèches.

| 藥, *noù yŏc*, poison qui sert à faire ces flèches.

| 老虎, *noù lào foù*, tuer le tigre avec des flèches empoisonnées.

NOÚ

怒 *Noú*. Colère.

忿 |, *foún noú*, même sens.

發忿 |, *fât foún noú*, se mettre en colère.

天主個義 |, *t'iēn tchoù ké· gní noú*, la juste colère de Dieu.

NOŬC

Noŭc. Frayeur, sursaut.

| 驚一吓, *noŭc chāng ŷt há*, j'ai eu un sursaut.

NOÛC

讷 *Noûc* ou *noŭt*. Penser, douter.

疑 |, *nî noûc*, douter, soupçonner.

我 | 倒佢唔敢來, *ngâi noûc tào kî mĝ kàm loî*, je pensais qu'il n'oserait pas venir.

NOÛI

内 *Noûi*. Dedans, intérieur.

| 肚, *noûi toù*, dedans, au milieu.

心 |, 城 |, *sīm noûi, chăng noûi*, dans le cœur, dans la ville.

在 |, *ts'ái noûi*, y compris.

NOÚN

嫩 *Noún*. Tendre, délicat, ténu.

| 草, *noún ts'ào*, herbe tendre.

人還係 | , *gnîn hân hé· noún*, il est encore bien jeune.

綫子忒大有過 | 個麼, *sién tzè t'iĕt t'aí yoū koúo noún ké· mô ?* ce fil est trop gros, y en a-t-il de plus fin ?

NOŪNG

Noūng ou *noúng*. Cheveux en désordre, boursoufflé, enflé.

毛辮 | 阿起, *māo piēn noūng á hì*, ta tresse est toute ébouriffée.

| 絲狗, *noúng sē kèou*, chien qui a les poils hérissés.

NOÛNG

農 *Noûng*. Agriculteur.

| 學, *noûng hŏc*, l'art, l'étude de l'agriculture.

膿 *Noûng*. Pus, humeur.

肘子出 | , *tch'ôi tzè tch'oût noûng*, il sort du pus de l'abcès.

| 頭, *noûng t'eoû*, bourbillon du furoncle.

鼻 | , *p'í noûng*, morve.

NOŬT

訥 *Noŭt*. Cacher sa pensée en parlant.

| 等來講, *noŭt tèn loî kòng*, hésiter à parler, parler sans faire connaître sa pensée.

Ō

屙 *ō*. S'effondrer.

屋 | 帛裡, *voûc ō p'ĕt lè·*, la maison s'est effondrée.

屎, *ō chè*, évacuer par les voies naturelles.

| 尿, *ō niáo*, uriner.

| 肚, *ō toù*, dévoiement, dyssenterie.

Ô

阿 *Ô* (*ō*). | 頭, *ô t'eoû*, dénomination de celui qui crie lorsque le mandarin est en route.

ÔC

惡 *Oc*. Mal, mauvais, méchant.

分善 | , *foūn chán ôc*, distinguer le bien du mal.

| 事, *ôc sé*, mauvaise action.

| 心, *ôc sīm*, mauvaise intention.

狗係 | , *keoù hé· ôc*, le chien est très méchant.

OĪ

哀 *Oī*. Mère (ne se dit pas des animaux.)

還有 | 子麼, *hân yōu oī tzè mô ?* avez-vous encore votre mère ?

兩子 | , *leòng tzè oī*, les deux, la mère et le fils ou la fille.

麼爺麼 | , *mô yâ mô oī*, sans père ni mère.

哀 *Oī*. Compatir.

| 矜, *oī k'īm*, faire l'aumône, faire une œuvre de miséricorde.

| 憐, *oī lin*, compatir.

OÍ

愛 Aimer, vouloir, il faut.

| 德, *oí tĕt*, vertu de charité.

| 天主萬有之上及愛人如己, *oí t'iēn tchòu ván yoū tjē chóng k'ĭp oí gnîn ŷ kì*, aimer Dieu par-dessus tout, et le prochain comme soi-mème.

相 |, *siōng oí*, s'aimer mutuellement.

| 走, *oí tsèou*, il faut partir.

我 | 走, *ngâi oí tsèou*, je veux partir.

你 | 唔 |, *gnî oí mĝ oí* (par abréviation on dit ordinairement : *gnî oí moé·* ou *moē·) ?* veux-tu ? en veux-tu ?

唔 |, *mĝ oí (moé·)*, je n'en veux pas.

硬 |, *ngáng oí*, je le veux absolument; il le faut absolument.

ŌN

安 *ōn*. Tranquille, disposer.

| 樂, *ōn lŏc*, content, bien dispos.

| 然, *ōn yân*, tranquille.

平 |, *p'în ōn*, en bonne santé, en paix.

請 |, *ts'iàng ōn*, souhait de bonne santé ; présenter ses civilités.

| 神, *ōn chîn*, reposer ses esprits.

| 慰, *ōn vì*, consoler.

| 排, *ōn p'âi*, disposer, arranger.

做 | 所, *tsó ōn sò*, faire une absoute.

| 所彌撒, *ōn sò nì-sât*, Messe de Requiem.

盡天主 | 排, *ts'ìn t'iēn tchoù ōn p'âi*, à la volonté de Dieu.

隨神父 | 排, *soûi chîn foú ōn p'âi*, à la disposition du Père.

| 聖像, *ōn chín sióng*, placer nne image.

| 十四苦路, *ōn chĭp sí k'où loú*, placer un chemin de Croix.

| 着 *ōn tch'ŏc*, considérer, selon.

鞍 *ōn*. Selle de cheval.

| 韂, *ōn ts'án*, harnais, harnachement.

上馬 |, *chòng mā ōn*, seller le cheval.

下馬 |, *hà mā ōn*, ôter la selle.

ÓN

按 *Ón*. Donner en gage.

| 察司, *ón ts'ăt sē*, grand juge criminel de toute une province.

你田 | 俾我我就肯借, *niā t'iên ón poūn ngaî ngaî ts'ioú hèn tsiá*, donne-moi ta rizière en gage, alors je te prêterai.

案 *Ón*. Procès, jugement, sentence.

| 件, *ón k'ián*, procès, cas dans la loi.

到 |, *táo ón*, comparaître devant le tribunal.

審 |, *chìm ón*, juger un procès.

問 |, *moún ón*, interroger les partis.

結 |, *kiĕt ón*, solution définitive d'un procès.

PĀ

巴 *Pā*. 尾 |, *mī pā*, queue d'un animal.

| 不得, *pā poŭt tĕt*, plût à Dieu que !

| 不得落雨, *pā poŭt tĕt lŏc ŷ*, plût à Dieu qu'il pleuve !

疤 *Pā*. Cicatrice.

爛 |, *lán pā*, plaie, blessure.

裡個人頭哪上有 | 子就係, *ŷ ké· gnîn, t'eôu nâ hóng yoū pā tzè ts'ioú hé·*, cet homme qui a une cicatrice sur la tête, hé bien c'est lui !

腳上發一個爛｜，*kiôc hóng pôt ŷt ké lán pā*, il me vient une plaie au pied.

P'Â

琶 *P'â*. 琵｜，*p'î p'â*, espèce de harpe, guitare.

杷 *P'â*. 枇｜樹，*p'î p'â choú*, 枇｜子，*p'î p'â tzè*, bibassier, son fruit.

爬 *P'â*. Ramper, se traîner, escalader.

｜得子行，*p'â têt tzè hâng*, ramper, aller à quatre pattes.

｜阿樹上去，*p'â á choú hóng hí*, grimper sur un arbre (on dit aussi *k'iâ* corruption du mot *p'â*).

｜唔倒來食，*p'â mĝ taò loî chĭt*, ne pas pouvoir gagner sa vie.

鈀 *P'â*. Râteau, râteler.

｜乜，*p'â yà*, râteau (ordinairement de bambou).

耙 *P'â*. Herse.

｜田，*p'â t'iên*, herser une rizière.

鈀 *P'â*. ｜頭，*p'â t'eoû*, trident de combattant.

耳｜子，*gnì p'â tzè*, cure-oreille, épingle de femmes.

PÀ

把 *Pà*. Prendre, poignée ; particule numérale des manches, verges, parapluies, couteaux, éventails.

｜人個地方，*pà gnîn ké· t'í fōng*, prendre, empiéter sur le terrain d'autrui.

｜守，*pà choù*, en sentinelle, veiller.

｜門，*pà moûn*, garder la porte.

等日｜來，*tèn gnĭt pà loî*, attends quelques jours.

擺｜，*paì pà*, quelquefois.

賣一｜柴，*maí ŷt pà ts'iâo*, vendre un fagot de bois (*litt.* une poignée).

一｜稈，*ŷt pà kòn*, une botte de paille.

打一個｜掌，*tà ŷt ké· pà tchòng*, donner une gifle.

一｜刀，一｜扇子，一｜傘，*ŷt pà tāo*, *ŷt pà chán tzè*, *ŷt pà tchā*, un couteau, un éventail, un parapluie.

靶 *Pà*, Cible.

射對｜子來，*chá toúi pà tzè loî*, tirer juste dans la cible.

P'À

扒 *P'à*. Branche.

樹｜，*choú p'à*, branche d'arbre.

裡條河分三｜水，*ỳ tiâo hô foūn sām p'à choùi*, ce fleuve se divise en trois branches.

我屋下三｜開，*ngâi voŭc hā sām p'à k'oī*, chez moi, la famille se divise en 3 branches.

PÁ

霸 *Pá*. Régner par violence, usurper.

｜佔各國，*pá tchám kôc kouĕt*, conquérir injustement un royaume.

丨人倒地方, *pá gnîn ké· t'í fōng*, usurper le terrain d'autrui.

垻 *Pá*. Plaine, aire.

太平丨, *t'aí p'iâng pá* (ou simplement *t'aí p'iâng*), grande plaine, grande prairie.

河丨, *hô pá*, quai, rivage en terrain plat.

沙丨, *sā pá*, rive sablonneuse, banc de sable.

P'Á

帕 *P'á*. Mouchoir, serviette, linge quelconque.

手丨, *choù p'á*, mouchoir.

拭桌丨, *ts'oūt tsôc p'á*, torchon pour essuyer la table.

怕 *P'á* Craindre.

丨唔丨, *p'á mĝ pá?* as-tu peur ?

得人丨, *têt gnîn p'á*, effrayant.

丨畏個人, *p'á ví ké· gnîn*, homme peureux, timide.

PĂC

Păc. Eclat, éclabousser.

滚猪油捞水噲丨人, *koùn tchōu yoû lāo choùi voé· păc gnîn*, si vous mêllez de l'eau à la graisse bouillante, elle vous éclaboussera.

畢丨聲, *pît păc chang*, bruit soudain, explosion.

P'ĂC

白 *P'ăc*. Blanc ; vain, sans réalité.

丨淨, *p'ăc ts'iáng*, blanc et propre, d'un beau blanc.

寫丨水字, *sià p'ăc chouì sé*, écrire des caractères fautifs.

講丨話, *kòng p'ăc fá*, dire des choses vides de sens.

明丨, *mîn p'ăc* (ou *p'ĕt*), clair, manifeste, évident.

客話講得係丨, *hâc fá kòng têt hé· p'ăc*, il parle très bien la langue *hac-ka*.

PÂC

百 *Pâc*. Cent.

一丨二, *ŷt pâc gní*, 120.

一丨零二, 102.

丨姓, *pâc siáng*, le peuple.

擘 *Pâc*. Déchirer, arracher.

丨爛衫, *pâc lán sām*, faire un accroc à son habit.

丨我聖像別人丨爛, *ngâi chín sióng poūn gnîn pâc lán*, quelqu'un a déchiré mon image.

伯 *Pâc*. Oncle, frère aîné du père.

大丨, *t'aí pâc*, mon oncle.

叔丨兄弟, *chouĉ pâc hioūng t'í*, cousins germains.

丨公, *pâc koūng*, frère aîné du grand-père ; grand-oncle.

P'ÂC

魄 *P'âc*. Partie matérielle de l'âme selon les philosophes chinois.

三魂七丨, *sām foûn ts'ĭt p'âc*, les 3 principes supérieurs et les 7 principes inférieurs de l'âme. (Nul ne peut dire ce qu'il entend exactement par ces principes.)

PĀI

跛 *Pāi*. Boiter, boiteux.

丨脚子, *pāi kiôc tzè*, boiteux.

脚打丨裡, *kiôc tà pāi lê*, il a été frappé au point d'en boiter.

箄 *Pāi*. Rotin des bourreaux, verge plate des maîtres d'école.

我愛打你兩丨竹箄好, *ngâi oí tà gnî leòng tchoûc pāi tcháng hào*, je vais te donner deux coups de verge, et ce sera bien fait.

P'ĀI

剫 *P'āi*. Tailler, découper.

丨尖筆子來!, *p'āi tsiām pît tzè loî*, taille le crayon en pointe.

丨番薯, *p'āi fān choû*, peler des patates.

砒 *P'āi*. 丨霜, *p'āi sōng*, arsenic (on l'appelle aussi 人信 *gnîn sín*).

P'ÂI

排 *P'âi*. Rang, ranger, disposer.

一丨, 兩丨, *ŷt p'âi, leòng p'âi*, une rangée, deux rangées.

丨丨行, *p'âi p'âi* ou *pâi pâi hâng*, marcher en rang.

丨安, *p'âi tch'ông*, beau, apparat.

好丨塲, *háo p'âi tch'ông*, aimer l'apparat, le luxe.

牌 *P'âi*. Bouclier, enseigne, médaille, radeau, cartes à jouer.

丨藤, *t'ên p'âi*, bouclier en rotin.

招丨, *tchāo p'âi*, enseigne de marchand.

掛招丨, *koúa tchāo p'âi*, exposer l'enseigne.

聖丨, *chín p'âi*, médaille.

祖公丨, *tzè koūng p'âi*, tablette où sont écrits les noms des ancêtres, et où leurs âmes sont censées résider.

樹丨, 竹丨, *choú p'âi*, *tchoûc p'âi*, radeau de bois, de bambous.

紙丨, *tjè p'âi*, cartes à jouer.

骨丨, *koût p'âi*, domino.

打紙丨, *tà tjè p'âi*, jouer aux cartes.

丨坊, *p'âi fông*, arc-de-triomphe.

PAÌ

擺 *Paì*. Etaler en ordre, fièvre, fois.

丨出貨來賣, *paì tch'oût fó loî maí*, étaler de la marchandise à vendre.

打丨子, *tà paì tzè*, avoir la fièvre intermittente.

丨把, *paì pà*, quelquefois, de temps en temps.

幾多丨, *kì tō paì ?* combien de fois ?

搖丨丨, *yâo paì paì*, se dandiner.

PAÍ

拜 *Paí*. Saluer, adorer.

丨天主, *paí t'iēn tchoù*, adorer Dieu.

丨人做先生, *paí gnîn tsó sīn sāng*, reconnaître quelqu'un pour maître, se déclarer son disciple.

丨新年, *paí sīn niân*, souhaiter la bonne année.

禮|, *lī paí*, rendre un culte religieux.

禮|日, *lī paí gnĭt*, dénomination du dimanche chez les protestants.

簸 *Paí.* |箕, *paí kī*, van.

|米, *paí mì*, vanner le riz.

P'AÍ

敗 *P'aí.* Détruire, gâter.

|壞人家, *p'aí faí gnîn kā*, faire mépriser le monde, faire perdre son honneur.

|壞聖教會個名聲, *p'aí faí chín káo fí ké· miâng chāng*, perdre, gâter la bonne renommée de l'Eglise.

|壞事, *p'aí faí sé*, gâter une affaire.

仗|打, *tà p'aí tchóng*, perdre la bataille.

|家子, *p'aí kā tzè*, se dit de celui qui, par ses prodigalités, cause la ruine d'une famille.

派 *P'aí.* Distribuer, partager.

照人|, *tcháo gnîn p'aí*, distribuer d'après le nombre des gens.

|人工, *p'aí gnîn koūng*, distribuer à chacun sa part de travail.

官|兩名差去, *koūon p'aí leòng miâng ts' āi hí*, le mandarin a envoyé deux satellites.

稗 *P'aí* |子, *p'aí tzè* (ou *k'ouái tzè*), ivraie.

PĀN

班 *Pān.* Escouade, disposer, mettre en ordre.

共|人, *k'ioúng pān gnîn*, de la même compagnie, travaillant au même ouvrage.

炭廠有兩|人, *t'án tch'òng yōu leòng pān gnîn*, la mine de charbon a deux escouades d'ouvriers.

大|, *t'aí pān*, porteurs de chaise.

請兩|人, *ts'iàng leòng pān gnîn*, louer deux escouades de porteurs.

平|個, *p'iâng pān ké·*, de même degré en âge, ou en dignité.

四|, *sí pān*, les 4 escouades de satellites.

戲|子, *hí pān tzè*, comédiens de la même troupe.

|房, *pān fông*, prison.

|正桌凳來, *pān tcháng tsôc tén loî* mets en ordre les tables et les bancs.

般 *Pān.* Manière, espèce.

一|都係, *ŷt pān toū hé·*, tout cela en est.

百|先理都難做, *pâc pān siēn lī toū nân tsó*, toute espèce de commerce est difficile à entreprendre.

搬 *Pān.* Emigrer, déménager, porter un objet d'un endroit à un autre.

由潮州府|上平遠縣, *yoû tch'áo tchoū foù pān chōng p'în yàn yán*, de la préfecture de *Tchao-tchou* émigrer à la sous-préfecture du *P'in-yan*.

|東西, *pān toūng sī*, transporter ses objets d'un lieu à un autre.

|石頭, *pān chăc t'eôu*, transporter des pierres.

|家, *pān kā*, déménager.

扳 *Pān.* Attirer à soi, saisir un objet élevé.

丨樹子丨斷, *pān choú tzè pān t'ōn,* en ployant l'arbre, on l'a brisé.

丨穩來, *pān voùn loî,* tiens bon.

丨船, *pān chōn,* attirer une barque à soi.

P'ĀN

拚 *P'ān.* Frapper, battre.

鞋隻丨阿去, *haî tchâc p'ān á hí,* je vais te donner un coup de soulier.

丨壞, 丨死, *p'ān faí, p'ān sì,* blessé, tué par une chute, ou par des coups.

東西丨了, *toūng sī p'ān liaò,* tout est brisé.

P'ÂN

攀 *P'ân.* Saisir un objet élevé et s'en aider pour monter.

丨架, *p'ân ká,* faire de la gymnastique.

擊 *P'ân.* Dérouler, étendre.

箱肚個東西拿來丨出來, *siōng toù ké· toūng sī nā loî p'ân tch'oût loî,* enlève les objets qui sont dans la caisse.

丨開, *p'ân k'oī,* débarrasser, déblayer, éparpiller.

丨開沙灰來晒, *p'ân k'oī sā foē· loî saí,* éparpiller la chaux pour la sécher au soleil.

盤 *P'ân.* Assiette, soucoupe (sens large).

拿一個深丨一個淺丨來, *nā ŷt ké· tch'īm p'ân ŷt ké· ts'ièn p'ân loî,* apporte une assiette creuse et une assiette plate.

算丨, *són p'ân,* abaque.

丨錢, 丨費, *p'ân ts'iên, p'ân fí,* argent de voyage, viatique.

丨問, *p'ân moún,* prendre des informations, tourner un accusé en tous sens, pour savoir toute la vérité.

鐶 *P'ân* 耳丨, *gnì p'ân,* boucles d'oreilles.

PÀN

板 *Pàn* (ou *pièn*). Planche.

丨頭, *pàn t'eôu,* même sens.

一圍丨頭, *ŷt vî pàn t'eôu,* planches d'une surface de 10 pieds carrés; unité de mesure pour les planches.

棚丨, *p'âng pàn,* planches à plancheier.

銅丨印個書, *t'oûng pàn ýn ké· choū,* livre imprimé sur planches métalliques.

店老丨, *tiám lào pàn,* patron de la boutique.

石丨, *chăc pàn,* dalle de pierre.

粄 *Pàn.* Gâteau, pâtisserie.

煎麥丨, *tsiēn măc pàn,* frire des gaufres.

丨帕, *pàn p'á,* crible fin en toile métallique.

PÁN

半 *Pán* Moitié.

一儕一丨, *ŷt sâ ŷt pán,* chacun la moitié.

| 個, *pán ké·*, la moitié.

一 個 |, *ŷt ké· pán*, un et demi.

| 夜, *pán yá*, minuit.

| 生 | 死, *pán sāng pán sì*, à demi-mort.

| 斤, *pán kīn*, une demi-livre.

斤 |, *kīn pán*, une livre et demie.

行 倒 | 路 就 起 病, *hâng taò pán loú ts'ioú hì p'iáng*, à mi-chemin, il tomba malade.

絆 *Pán* (ou *p'án*). Lier, ligotter, embarras.

馬 龍 頭 | 穩 來, *mā lioûng t'coû pán voùn loî*, attache solidement le licou du cheval.

有 人 | 等 裡 走 唔 得, *yoū gnîn pán tèn ê· tseòu mĝ têt*, je suis retenu par quelqu'un, je ne puis sortir.

P'ÁN

伴 *P'án*. Compagnon.

我 同 你 同 |, *ngâi t'oûng gnî t'oûng p'án*, je vais te tenir compagnie.

辦 *P'án*. Gérer, préparer.

| 事, *p'án sé*, gérer les affaires.

| 席, *p'án sīt*, préparer un festin.

| 倒 有 體 面, *p'án tào yoū t'ì mién*, il a fait cela grandement.

你 | 那 個 貨, *gnî p'án mâc ké· fó?* quelle espèce de marchandise vends-tu ?

咁 多 錢 我 | 唔 出, *àn tō ts'iên ngaî p'án mĝ tch'oût*, je ne puis fournir autant d'argent.

判 *P'án*. Juger, distinguer.

| 案, *p'án ón*, rendre la sentence.

堂 |, *t'ông p'án*, minute de l'interrogatoire.

前 官 斷 後 官 |, *ts'iên koūon tón heóu koūon p'án*, le mandarin précédent et le suivant ont jugé de la même manière.

天 主 審 | 生 死 者, *t'iēn tchòu chìm p'án sēn sì tchà*, Dieu jugera les vivants et les morts.

襻 *P'án*. 鈕 |, *neoù* (ou *k'coú*) *p'án*, boutonnière.

衫 鈕 脫 吊 裡 轉 來 |, *sām k'coú t'ōt p'ēt lé· p'án tchòn loî*, ton habit s'est déboutonné, reboutonne-le.

盼 *P'án*. Espérer, s'attendre à.

顧 | 人 家, *koú p'án gnîn kā*, s'intéresser à quelqu'un, lui faire du bien.

| 望, *p'án vóng* (ou *móng*), désirer ardemment.

PĀNG

邦 *P'āng*. Petit royaume.

番 |, *fān pāng*, en pays étranger. Vulgairement on dit : *fān p'ièn*.

挷 *Pāng*. Tirer, arracher.

| 索, *pāng sôc*, tirer la corde.

| 斷, *pāng t'ōn*, rompre en tirant.

| 草, *pāng ts'ào*, arracher l'herbe.

P'ĀNG

膖 *Pāng*. Gonfler en soufflant.

| 脹 牛, *p'āng tchóng niôu,* gonfler le buffle (avant de le dépecer).

猪 尿 袋 拿 來 | 胱 來 晒, *tchoū niáo t'oí nā loî p'āng kouāng loî saí,* gonfle la vessie de cochon pour la faire sécher.

胮 *P'āng.* Mot qui, devant un autre, marque l'excès.

| 臭, *pāng tch'oú,* air empesté, quelle puanteur!

P'ÂNG

棚 *P'âng.* Etage d'une maison.

上 | 上, *chōng p'âng hóng,* monter à l'étage.

橫 |, *vông* (pour *vâng*) *p'âng,* planchéier.

天 |, *t'iēn p'âng,* dernier étage.

膨 *P'âng.* | 脹, *p'âng tchóng,* grave constipation. (D'une légère constipation, on dit mieux: 大便唔通, *t'aí p'ién mĝ t'oūng, litt.* les grandes commodités sont bouchées.

| 屎 猪, *p'âng chè tchōu,* porc malade de constipation.

P'ÁNG

冇 *P'áng.* Creux, sans résistance; espèce de cruche à petite ouverture.

| 蘿 蔔, *p'áng lô p'ĕt,* rave creuse.

| 樹, *p'áng chóu,* arbre, bois creux à l'intérieur, ou léger, sans consistance.

講 | 話, *kòng p'áng fá,* dire des mots vides de sens, des insanités, des paroles inutiles.

| 子裝等裡, *p'áng tzè tchōng tèn è·,* c'est dans la cruche.

埲 *P'áng.* Embourber.

路 係 濕 噲 | 人, *lóu hé· chīp voé· p'áng gnîn,* les routes sont détrempées, on s'embourbe.

係 湖 洋 田 唔 好 去 | 得 人 係 深 倒, *hé· foû yông t'iên, mĝ hào hí, p'áng tĕt gnîn hé· tch'îm tào,* c'est une rizière à fond marécageux, n'y vas pas, tu peux t'embourber très profondément.

| 泥, *p'áng naî,* vase.

PĀO

包 *Pāo.* Envelopper, paquet, répondre de.

| 東 西, *pāo toūng sī,* envelopper, empaqueter des objets.

| 袱, *pāo foŭc,* toile à envelopper.

| 鐵, | 銅, *pāo t'iĕt, pāo t'oûng,* garni de fer, de cuivre.

一 | 棉 花, *ŷt pāo miên fā,* un paquet, un ballot de coton.

| 含, *pāo hâm,* le tout ensemble, y compris.

| 在 內, *pāo ts'aí noúi,* y compris.

| 心 菜, *pāo sīm ts'oí,* chou pommé, légume pommé.

石 灰 賣 得 兩 錢 銀 | 到, *chăc foē· mái tĕt leòng ts'iên nioûn pāo táo,* la chaux se vend deux *ts'în* d'argent, livrée à domicile.

我 | 你 麼 事, *ngâi pāo gnî mô sé,* je réponds que tu n'auras pas d'affaire.

| 一 年, *pāo ŷt niân,* répondre pour un an.

丨工, *pāo koūng*, prendre à forfait une construction, s'engageant à fournir les matériaux et la main-d'œuvre.

胞 *Pāo*. Matrice.

丨衣, *pāo ȳ*, même sens.

同丨兄弟, *t'oûng pāo hioūng t'í*, frères consanguins.

P'ĀO

跑 *P'āo*. Courir.

丨走裡, *p'āo tsèou lî*, il s'est enfui.

丨馬, *p'āo mā*, courir à cheval, galoper.

丨文書, *p'āo voûn choū*, porter des dépêches.

泡 *P'āo*. Ecume.

水丨, 酒丨, écume d'eau, de vin.

拋 *P'āo*. Lancer, jeter.

丨石頭, *p'āo chăc t'eôu*, lancer des pierres.

P'ÂO

袍 *P'âo*. Habit long.

蟒丨, *māng p'âo*, habit de cérémonie.

丨套, *p'âo t'áo*, habit complet, avec la veste de dessus.

刨 *P'âo*. Rabot, râcler,gratter.

丨子, 丨花 (ou 丨屎), 丨 *p'âo tzè*, *p'âo fā* (ou *p'âo chè*), rabot, copeaux de menuisier.

丨馬, *p'âo mā*, étriller le cheval.

PAÒ

飽 *Paò*. Rassasié.

食丨唔曾, *chĭt paò mĝ tsĉn* ? avez-vous bien mangé ?

肚丨 (ou 丨肚), *toù paò* (ou *paò toù*), gêne de l'estomac, provenant d'un manque de digestion.

保 *Pào*. Protéger.

天主丨佑, *t'iēn tchòu pào yóu*, que Dieu vous protège (salut des chrétiens), grâce à Dieu, Dieu aidant.

主丨聖人, *tchoù pào chín gnîn*, saint Patron.

丨自己個身子, *pào tsé kì ké· chīn tzè*, défendre son corps, sa vie.

里丨, *lī pào*, maire de village.

丨家, *pào kā*, assureur, répondant.

寶 *Pào*. Précieux.

丨貝, *pào pí*, chose de grand prix.

耶穌丨血, *yâ sē pào hiĕt*, le Précieux Sang de Jésus-Christ.

丨號, *pào háo*, votre noble nom.

取丨, *ts'ì pào*, extraire des trésors.

PAÓ

苞 *Paó*. Eclater, se briser, crever, éclore.

銃子打丨裡, *tch'oúng tzè tà paó lê·*, le fusil a éclaté.

傘子掙倒忒狠噲丨, *tchā tzè màng tào t'iĕt hĉn, voé· paó*, la couverture du parapluie est trop tendue, il va se déchirer.

花容易噲丨出來, *fā yoûng ý voé·*

paó tch'oût loî, les fleurs vont bientôt éclore.

䶌 *Paó*. 丨牙, *paó ngâ*, dent proéminente.

豹 *Paó*. 丨虎, *paó foù*, léopard.

報 *Paó*. Annoncer; rendre la pareille.

打發人丨信, *tà fât gnîn paó sín*, envoyer un messager porter la nouvelle.

聖母領丨, *chín moū leāng paó*, l'Annonciation.

日丨, 月丨, *gnĭt paó, gnĕt paó*, journal quotidien, mensuel.

丨恩, 丨仇, *paó ēn, paó choû*, être reconnaissant; se venger.

我愛丨佢仇, *ngaî ói paó kiă choû*, je veux me venger de lui.

P'ÁO

炮 *P'aó*. Faire explosion, pétard, canon.

丨石頭, *p'aó chăc t'eoû*, faire sauter un rocher avec la poudre.

西瓜丨, *sī koūa p'aó*, canon.

水雷丨, *choùi loûi p'aó*, torpille.

丨臺, *p'aó t'oî*, fort, emplacement de la batterie sur les remparts.

紙丨 *tjè p'aó*, pétard.

打紙丨, *tà tjè p'aó*, faire partir des pétards.

暴 *P'aó*. Violent.

起丨風, 丨雨, *hì p'aó foūng, p'aó ŷ*, il s'élève un vent violent et une forte pluie.

裡官丨虐百姓, *yà koūon p'aó niôc pâc siáng*, ce mandarin traite durement son peuple.

泡 *P'aó*. Infuser, macérer.

丨茶, *p'aó ts'â*, infuser du thé.

抱 *P'aó*. Porter dans ses bras.

聖母丨耶穌, *chín moū p'aó yâ sē*, la Ste Vierge portant l'Enfant Jésus. (Vulgairement on dit 揇 *nàm*).

PĂT

迫 *Păt*. 丨翼, *păt ŷt*, battre des ailes.

撥 *Păt*. Rejaillir, étendre (mot dont le sens vague change suivant les pays).

莫擲石頭水噲丨人, *mŏc jĭt chăc t'eôu choùi voé· păt gnîn*, ne jette pas de pierres, tu fais rejaillir l'eau jusque sur moi.

丨灰, *păt foē·*, étendre la chaux, soit pour crépir un mur, soit pour bâtir.

P'ĂT

拔 *P'ăt*. Extirper, arracher.

一毛不丨, *ŷt maō poût p'ăt*, on ne peut rien obtenir de lui.

丨劍, *p'ăt kiám*, dégainer.

丨貢生, *p'ăt koúng sēn*, titre du premier lauréat des examens qui ont lieu tous les 10 ans, entre tous les bacheliers et les licenciés.

鈸 *P'ăt*. Cymbales.

打鑼 | , *tà lô* vulg. *lâ p'át,* jouer des cymbales.

PÂT

八 *Pât.* Huit.

百 | , *pâc pât,* 180.

百零 | , *pâc lâng pât* 108.

| 百, *pât pâc,* 800.

| 字頭, *pât sé t'eôu,* les 8 caractères tirés du cycle, dont 2 pour l'année, 2 pour le mois, 2 pour le jour et 2 pour l'heure de la naissance. (On s'en sert pour tirer l'horoscope).

我個 | 字頭唔好, *ngâ ké· pât sé t'eoû mĝ hào,* mes 8 caractères ne donnent pas un heureux présage.

撥 *Pât.* Distribuer, donner de l'ouvrage, assigner un rôle, envoyer.

神父 | 你去那里做先生, *chîn foú pât gnî hí naí lī tsó sīn sāng ?* où est-ce que le Père t'envoie comme catéchiste ?

官府 | 幾多名差, *kouōn foù pât kì tō miāng ts'aī ?* combien de satellites le mandarin a-t-il envoyés ?

鉢 *Pât.* Terrine, pot évasé.

| 頭, *pât t'eōu,* baquet de terre.

花 | , *fā pât,* pot de fleur.

P'ÂT

潑 *P'ât.* Eventer, faire du vent. Eclabousser, épandre. Faucher, couper.

| 蚊, *p'ât moūn,* chasser les moustiques en éventant.

| 扇, *p'ât chán,* s'éventer.

| 火, *p'ât fò,* attiser le feu.

| 人, *p'ât gnîn,* jeter de l'eau sur quelqu'un.

雨 | 阿窗子上來裡, *ỳ p'ât á ts'cūng tzè hóng lôi lê·,* la pluie est renvoyée (par le vent) jusque sur la fenêtre.

| 糞, *p'ât poún,* épandre du fumier, fumer.

細人子打 | 賴, *sé· gnîn tzè tà p'ât laí,* se dit d'un enfant qui crie, se roule, fait ses caprices pour obtenir quelque chose.

爛 | 婦, *lán p'ât foú,* femme méchante ; mégère, harpie.

竻頭 | 阿開, *nĕt t'eôu p'ât á k'oī,* faucher, abattre les épines à coup de serpe.

| 路, *p'ât loú,* émonder la route ; p. ex. : couper les branches et les herbes qui s'avancent sur le chemin.

魚子 | 卵, *nĝ tzè p'ât lòn,* les poissons frayent.

PÈ·

鄙 *Pè·.* Vil, abject, en mauvais état.

| 人, *pè· gnîn,* homme bas, vil.

| 貨, *pè· fó,* mauvaise marchandise.

講 | 話, *kòng pè· fá,* dire des paroles honteuses.

講人個 | 處, *kòng gnîn ké· pè· tch'óu,* raconter les défauts d'autrui.

PĒN

冰 *Pēn.* | 糖, *pēn t'ông,* sucre candi.

崩 *Pēn*. S'écrouler, s'ébouler.

岌崗 | 了, *ýn kōng pēn liào*, la montagne s'est éboulée.

田坎 | 帛 裡, *t'iēn k'ám pēn p'ĕt lē·*, le talus de la rizière a croulé.

P'ĒN

烹 *P'ēn*. | 茶, *p'ēn ts'â*, faire cuire du thé.

P'ÊN

朋 *P'ên*. Ami. Voyez *p'oúng*.

硼 *P'ên*. | 砂, *p'ên sā*, borax.

PÉN

凭 *Pén*. S'adosser, s'appuyer.

裡竹几唔好 | 人, *yà tchoŭc ỳ mĝ hào pén gnîn*, on ne peut pas s'adosser commodément sur cette chaise.

我屋 | 山, *ngâi voŭc pén sān*, ma maison est adossée à une montagne.

莫 | 倒我, *mŏc pén tào ngâi*, ne t'appuie pas sur moi.

麽後 | 山, *mô heóu pén sān*, manière de dire : je n'ai pas de rejeton, pas d'enfants.

| 山食山 | 水食水, *pén sān chĭt sān pén choùi chĭt choùi*, celui qui habite la montagne vit de la montagne ; celui qui habite près des eaux, vit de l'eau (c.-à-d.) des industries exercées sur l'eau.

P'ĔT

蔔 *P'ĕt*. 蘿 | *lô p'ĕt*, rave.

蝠 *P'ĕt (ou p'ĭt)*. | 婆, *p'ĕt p'ô*, chauve-souris.

別 *P'ĕt (p'iĕt)*. | 何, *p'ĕt hô*, ailleurs.

嘉應州係咁樣話 | 何我唔知, *kā ýn tchoū hé· kàn yóng vá, p'ĕt hô ngâi mĝ tī*, à Ka-yn-tchou on dit comme cela, ailleurs je ne sais pas. *Voir p'iĕt*.

PÊT

北 *Pĕt*. Nord.

| 斗星, *pĕt tèou sēn*, étoile polaire.

坐 | 向南, *ts'ō pĕt hióng nâm*, maison adossée au Nord et exposée au Sud.

P'ÊT

帛 *P'ĕt*. Particule qui indique l'achèvement complet d'une action, ou le passé, et qui remplace le mot 了 *liào*. Pour l'harmonie, on lui ajoute la particule 裡 *lì* ou *lē· (voir ce mot)*, qui a presque la même valeur que lui. L'usage seul apprendra les cas où l'on ne se sert que de l'un de ces mots.

食就食裡唔曾食 |, *chĭt ts'ióu chĭt-ē· mĝ ts'ên chĭt p'ĕt*, j'en ai mangé, mais je n'ai pas tout mangé.

我工夫做 | 裡, *ngā koūng foū tsó p'ĕt lē·*, j'ai fini mon travail.

容易喒 |, *yoûng ý voé· p'ĕt*, cela va être bientôt fini.

PĪ

悲 *Pī*. | 哀, *pī ōi*, commisération, affection.

天主個慈 | , *t'iēn tchoù ké· tsê pī*, la miséricorde de Dieu.

盃 *Pī*. Tasse, verre à boire.

茶 | , *ts'â pī*, tasse à thé.

玻璃 | , *pō lî pī*, verre à boire.

一 | 茶, *ŷt pī ts'â*, une tasse de thé.

一個茶 | , *ŷt ké· ts'â pī*, une tasse à thé.

卑 *Pī*. Vil, bas.

謙 | , *k'iâm pī*, humble.

| 賤人, *pī ts'ién gnîn*, homme grossier.

碑 *Pī*. Inscription sur pierre.

愛放 | 石, *oí fóng pī chăc*, il faut mettre une pierre gravée.

指路 | , *tjè loú pī*, pierre gravée qui sert à indiquer le chemin aux passants.

坡 *Pī*. | 頭, *pī t'eôu*, barrage, pour élever l'eau d'une rivière.

萆 *Pī*. | 麻, *pī mâ*, ricin.

| 麻油, *pī mâ yôu*, huile de ricin.

飛 *Pī* (pour *fī*). Voler.

| 走𠊎, *pī tsèou lê·*, il s'est envolé.

打 | 雕, *tà pī tiāo*, tirer les oiseaux au vol.

P'Ī

批 *P'ī*. Réponse sommaire d'un supérieur; allouer.

官府唔曾出 | , *hoūon foù mĝ ts'ên tch'oût p'ī*, le mandarin n'a pas encore sorti la réponse (à l'accusation).

| 得好, *p'ī tĕt hào*, la réponse est bonne.

| 山 | 三年, *p'ī sān p'ī sām niân*, il a loué (donné à exploiter) sa forêt pour trois ans.

婢 *P'ī*. Servante, esclave.

買使 | 子, *mài sè p'ī tzè*, acheter une servante.

老 | , *lào p'ī*, même sens.

主之 | 女在玆, *tchoù tjē p'ī ng̀ ts'aí tzē*, voici la servante du Seigneur.

庇 *P'ī*. Protéger.

| 佑, *p'ī yóu*, protéger, secourir.

被 *P'ī*. Couverture de lit; marque du passif; (en ce dernier sens on prononce *p'í*; voir ce mot.)

| 骨, *p'ī koût*, couverture chinoise sans sa doublure.

| 皮, *p'ī p'î*, doublure, toile qui enveloppe la couverture.

On dit aussi: | 單, *p'ī tān*.

P'Î

皮 *P'î*. Peau, écorce, cuir.

樹 | , *choú p'î*, écorce d'arbre.

牛 | , *niôu p'î*, peau de buffle, cuir.

| 鞋, *p'î hâi*, souliers de cuir.

鐵 | , *t'iĕt p'î*, mince feuille de fer.

耗 | , *hō p'î*, planche arrondie d'un côté, la 1ere sciée du tronc d'arbre.

肥 *P'î*. Gras.

| 豬肉, *p'î tchoū nioûc*, le gras de la viande.

| 大, *p'î t'ái*, gras et gros.

脾 *P'î.* | 胃, *p'î ví*, estomac, naturel, bile.

| 氣唔好, *p'î hí mḡ hào*, qui a mauvais caractère.

琵 *P'î.* | 琶, *p'î p'â*, espèce de violon, guitare.

枇 *P'î.* | 杷, *p'î p'â*, bibassier.

培 *P'î.* Engrais, engraisser, prendre soin.

| 田, *p'î t'iên*, fumer les champs.

禾麼 | 唔跷大, *vô mô p'î mḡ hiào t'aí*, le riz qui n'est pas engraissé ne peut grandir.

好得有人栽 | 你, *haò têt yoū gnîn tsāi p'î gnî*, heureusement que quelqu'un prend soin de toi.

Pì

彼 *Pì.* Lui, là.

| 此, *pì tsè*, réciproquement.

時常渴慕, *chê chông hôt moú....* sans cesse je soupirais après vous....

Rép. | 此一樣, *pì tsè ŷt yóng*, c'est réciproque (*politesse*).

比 *Pì.* Comparer, mesurer.

| 方, *pì fōng*, par exemple.

講一個 | 方, *kòng ŷt ké· pì fōng*, donner un exemple.

唔 | 往時, *mḡ pì vōng chê*, ce n'est pas comme autrefois.

我唔 | 別人, *ngâi mḡ pì p'iĕt gnîn*, je ne suis pas comme les autres.

| 我過高大, *pì ngâi koúo kāo t'ái*, plus grand que moi.

| 正有幾長, *pì tcháng yōu kì tch'ông*, mesure exactement la longueur.

髀 *Pì.* Avant-jambe, cuisse.

手 | , 脚 | , *choù pì, kiôc pì*, avant-bras, cuisse,

猪 | , 雞 | , *tchoū pì, kē· pì*; cuisse de porc, cuisse de poule.

| 褲, *pì foú*, jambières, cuissards.

妣 *Pì.* Nom de la mère défunte.

考 | , *k'aò pì* nom du père et de la mére défunte (inscription sur la pierre tombale).

P'ì

鄙 *P'ì.* Vil, abject.

| 陋, *p'ì leoú*, même sens.

| 視人, *p'ì sé gnîn*, regarder quelqu'un avec mépris, dédain.

裡個人可 | 至極, *ŷ ké· gnîn k'ò p'ì tjé k'ĭt*, cet homme mérite le plus profond mépris.

Pí

貝 *Pí.* Perle, précieux.

寶 | , *pào pí*, chose précieuse, bijou, richesses.

萁 *Pí.* | 子, *pí tzè*, noix de galle.

疿 *Pí* (pour *fí*). Boutons de chaleur.

出熱 | , *tch'oût gnĕt pí*, il me vient des boutons de chaleur.

輩 *Pí*. Ordre, rang, génération.

信 |, *sín pí*, les fidèles (style relevé entre chrétiens).

等 |, *tèn pí*, toutes ces sortes de gens (après énumération).

老 |, 小 |, *lào pí, siào pí*, ceux qui sont plus rapprochés de la source commune; ceux qui en sont plus éloignés.

佢上 |, 我下 |, *kì chóng pí, ngaî há pí*, il est d'une génération (ou d'un rang) au-dessus, et moi d'une génération (ou d'un rang) au-dessous.

篦 *Pí* (ou *pín*). Peigne fin.

賣梳 |, *mái sē* (ou *sō*) *pí*, vendre des démêloirs et des peignes fins.

梳裡愛 | 過, *sē lè· oí pí koúo*, après avoir peigné au démêloir, il faut encore peigner au peigne fin.

弊 *Pí*. Fraude.

衙門藪 | 病多, *ngâ moûn teóu pí p'iáng tō*, il y a beaucoup de fraudes, de roueries, dans les prétoires.

你麽還我你脫 | 唔得, *gnî mô vân ngâi, gnî t'ōt pí mĝ tēt*, si tu ne me restitues pas, je ne te manquerai pas (ta faute ne sera pas impunie).

閉 *Pí*. Fermer.

| 戶 | 俶來, *pí fóu pí ts'ioū loî*, ferme bien toutes les portes.

| 汗, *pí hón*, sueur rentrée.

敝 *Pí*. Vil, de peu de prix; rejeter, mettre de côté.

| 國, *pí kouēt*, | 室, *pí chīt*, ma patrie, ma femme *(politesse)*.

| 飯, *pí fán*, séparer le riz de son eau.

祕 *Pí*. Secret, caché.

| 跡, *pí tsīt*, sacrement (style chrétien.)

沸 *Pí*. Bouillir.

水 | 裡, *chouì pí lè·*, l'eau bout.

背 *Pí*. Porter sur le dos, ou sur une seule épaule.

| 細人子, *pí sé· gnîn tzè*, porter un enfant sur le dos.

| 人過河, *pí gnîn koúo hô*, porter quelqu'un sur le dos, pour passer la rivière.

| 樹子, *pí chóu tzè*, porter un arbre, une poutre sur l'épaule.

P'Í

倍 *P'í*. Doubler.

雙 | 價錢你都唔賣, *soūng p'í ká ts'iên gnî toū mĝ mai?* on t'en donne le double de son prix, et tu ne veux pas le vendre?

我出兩個花邊, *ngâi tch'oūt leòng ké· fā piēn*, j'en donne deux piastres...

唔彀 | 加兩個來, *mĝ kéou, p'í kā leòng ké· loî*, cela ne suffit pas, ajoutes-en deux autres.

被 *P'í* (*p'ī*). Marque du passif.

| 釘十字架, *p'í tāng chīp sé ká*, il a été crucifié.

| 人𪭢我, *p'í gnîn kĩp ngaî*, j'ai été opprimé.

| 人打𠺢, *p'í gnîn tà lê*, j'ai été battu.

| 告, *p'í kaó*, l'accusé, le prévenu.

屁 *P'í*. Pet, vesse.

打 | 卵, *tà p'í lòn*, faire un pet, une vesse.

佢想得我錢得倒 | 卵, *kî siòng têt ngâ ts'iên têt tào p'í lòn*, il croyait me soutirer de l'argent, il a remporté une veste.

鼻 *P'í*. Nez, flairer, percevoir l'odeur.

| 公, *p'í koũng*, nez, narine.

| 屎 ou | 膿, *p'í chè* ou *p'í noúng*, morve du nez.

| 公塞等𠺢, *p'í koũng sêt tèn ĉ*, avoir le nez bouché.

你話咁香個花我 | 都唔倒, *gnî vá àn hiõng ké fã ngaî p'í toũ mĝ taò*, tu dis que cette fleur sent si bon, je ne sens rien.

我 | 係香, *ngaî p'í hé hiõng*, je trouve que cela sent bon.

備 *P'í*. Préparer, pourvoir.

預 |, *ý p'í*, préparer d'avance.

預 | 領聖體, *ý p'í leãng chín t'ì*, prépare-toi à faire la sainte Communion.

防 |, *fông p'í*, prendre garde, se munir contre.

防 | 旱天, *fông p'í hón t'iẽn*, prendre ses mesures contre la sécheresse.

配 *P'í*. Unir, assortir.

婚 |, *foũn p'í*, mariage.

唔相 |, *mĝ siõng p'í*, choses qui ne s'accordent pas.

| 一對熱鴿, *p'í ŷt toúi gnẽt kâp*, assortir un couple de pigeons.

PIÂC

壁 *Piâc*. Mur, cloison.

粉 |, *foùn piâc*, blanchir, crépir un mur.

間 |, *kiãn piâc*, cloison qui divise les chambres.

兩隔 |, *leòng kâc piâc*, voisins, séparés par un mur.

Piâc. *Mĝ piâc*, maladroit (pop.).

P'IAC

劈 *P'iâc*. Fendre d'un coup de serpe ou de hache.

| 笏頭, *p'iâc nẽt t'eoû*, abattre les broussailles à coups de serpe.

| 開路, *p'iâc k'õi loú*, se frayer un passage (à travers les fourrés).

PIÃNG

Piãng. | 生理, *piãng siẽn lĩ*, se faire concurrence dans le commerce.

两儕工夫有 |, *leòng sâ koũng foũ yoũ piãng*, ils se font concurrence.

P'IÂNG

坪 *P'iâng*. Plat, uni.

| 埔, *p'iâng p'oũ*, 草 |, *ts'ào p'iâng*, clairière, pré.

禾 | , *vô p'iâng*, aire à sécher le riz.
| 水 , *p'iâng choùi*, niveau d'eau.
| 大 , *p'iâng t'aí*, également grand.
| 地 , *p'iâng t'í*, terrain uni, plat.
桌唔 | , *tsôc mĝ p'iâng*, la table n'est pas d'aplomb.
唔 | 心個人 , *mĝ p'iâng sīm ké· gnîn*, homme partial.
| 班人 , *p'iâng pān gnîn*, de même rang, égal en dignité.

PIÀNG

餅 *Piàng*. Gâteau, pâtisserie.
打麵 | , *tà mién piàng*, faire des hosties.
柿 | , 橘 | , *sē piàng*, *kīt piàng*, kaki confit, orange confite.

PIÁNG

柄 *Piáng*. Manche, autorité.
脚頭 | , *kiôc t'eôu piáng*, manche de la pioche.
刀 | , *taō piáng*, manche de couteau.
權 | , *k'iân piáng*, autorité, pouvoir.

屏 *Piáng*. Cacher, se cacher.
| 人個東西 , *piáng gnîn ké· toūng sī*, cacher les objets de quelqu'un.
唔知 | 阿那理去 , *mĝ tī piáng á naí lī hí*, je ne sais pas où il est allé se cacher.

P'IÁNG

病 *P'iáng*. Maladie, malade.
疾 | , *ts'īt p'iáng*, légère maladie, malade.
| 好凶, *p'iáng hào hioūng*, maladie grave.
急 | , *kīp p'iáng*, maladie subite.
醫唔得個 | , *ȳ mĝ tēt ké· p'iáng*, maladie incurable.
毛 | , *māo p'iáng*, défaut, mauvaise habitude.

P'IĀO

驫 *Piaō*. Bondir, sauter, courir.
馬盡 | , *mā ts'în piaō*, le cheval court à fond de train.
| 阿河去 , *piaō á hô hí*, se jeter dans le fleuve.
| 下來 , *piaō hā loî*, sauter en bas.
一想心就噲 | , *ȳt siòng sīm ts'ioú voé· piaō*, rien que d'y penser, le cœur me bat. (Voir 跳 *t'iaó*.)

票 *Piāo*. Maison de jeu.
開 | , *k'oī piāo*, ouvrir une maison de jeu.
白鴿 | , *p'ăc kāp piaō*, loterie.

膘 *Piāo*. 宗 | 肉 , *tsoūng piāo nioūc*, graisse des animaux, lard.

錶 *Piāo*. Montre.
時辰 | , *chê chîn piaō*, montre.

P'IĀO

飄 *P'iāo*. Poussé par le vent, flottant.
| 洋過海, *p'iāo yông koúo hoì*, sillonner les mers.
| 海, *p'iāo hoì*, traverser la mer, voyager sur mer.

P'IAÔ

漂 *P'iâo.* Porté sur les flots, surnager.

樹子噲｜水, *choú tzè voé· p'iâo choùi*, le bois surnage.

嫖 *P'iâo.* Fréquenter les maisons de débauche, faire la fornication.

｜賭那個都來, *p'iâo toù mâc ké· toū loî*, débauche, jeu, il est de tout.

PIÀO

表 *Piào.* Extérieur, modèle; consanguinité;

｜意, *piào ý*, symbole, emblème, figure.

做好｜樣, *tsó hào piào yóng*, donner le bon exemple.

｜像, ｜對聯, *piào sióng, piào toúi liên*, cartonner des images, des inscriptions, pour pouvoir les suspendre.

｜姊妹, *piào tsì moé·*, cousines germaines.

｜姪子, *piào tch'ìt tzè*, neveu, par les femmes.

婊 *Piào.* ｜姊, *piào tsì*, prostituée.

當｜姊, *tōng piào tsì*, c'est une prostituée.

｜姊館, *piaò tsì kouòn*, maison de prostituées.

P'IÁO

票 *P'iáo.* Billet commercial, mandat, certificat.

當｜, *tóng p'iáo*, reçu, facture venant du Mont-de-piété.

銀｜, *nioûn p'iáo*, valeur au porteur, créance.

扯｜, *tch'à p'iáo*, se faire délivrer un reçu.

官府出裡｜, *koūon foù tchoût lê· p'iáo*, le mandarin a sorti un mandat d'arrêt.

漂 *P'iáo.* Blanchir par exposition au soleil.

｜蠟, *p'iáo lăp*, blanchir de la cire.

｜布, *p'iáo poú*, blanchir la toile.

皰 *P'iáo.* Ampoule.

行路行阿起｜, *háng loú hâng á hì p'iáo*, à force de marcher, j'ai des ampoules.

PIĒN

邊 *Piēn.* Côté, bord.

左｜右｜, *tsò piēn yoú piēn*, côté gauche, côté droit. (On dit aussi *tsò p'ièn, yóu p'ièn.*)

身｜麼錢, *chīn piēn mô ts'iên*, je n'ai pas d'argent sur moi.

聽旁｜人講 ... *t'āng p'ông piēn gnîn kòng*,... à entendre les gens du voisinage....

唇｜, *choûn piēn*, au bord, le bord.

鞭 *Piēn.* Fouet, cravache.

馬｜, *mā piēn*, cravache de cheval.

馬｜搊一下, *mā piēn sioū ŷt· há*, donner un coup de cravache.

褊 *Piēn.* Bordure d'habit, ourlet.

丨手帕, 丨衫子, *piēn choù p'á, piēn sām tzè,* ourler un mouchoir, un habit.

辮 *Piēn.* Tresse des cheveux.

編毛丨, *p'iēn* (ou *p'īn*) *māo piēn,* tresser les cheveux.

宛毛丨, *yāng māo piēn,* enrouler sa tresse autour de la tête.

P'IĒN

編 *P'iēn* (ou *p'īn*). Tresser, lier ensemble (voir *p'īn*).

篇 *P'iēn.* Chapitre, articles d'un chapitre. Dans certains pays, s'entend aussi des feuillets d'un livre.

丨丨文章, *ŷt p'iēn voûn tchōng,* une dissertation.

偏 *P'iēn.* Incliné, dépravé.

丨情, *p'iēn ts'în,* les passions déréglées.

押伏丨情, *âp foŭc p'iēn ts'în,* vaincre ses passions.

一話你就頸頸丨丨兒, *ŷt vá gnî, ts'ióu kiàng kīn p'iēn p'iēn nî*; dès que l'on te fait une observation, ton cou est tout penché (c.-à-d.) tu nous regardes de travers, de mauvais œil.

相丨, *siōng p'iēn,* je vous ai manqué de politesse: (réponse de politesse à celui qui demande si on a déjà dîné).

P'IÊN

便 *P'iên.* 丨人, *p'iên gnîn,* (pour 便人 *p'iên gnîn*), de bas prix, avantageux. Cette expression prend, par corruption, diverses formes: *p'iên gnî*; *p'iên ŷ*; ou simplement *p'iâng.*

買丨人, *maì p'iên gnîn,* acheter à bon marché.

PIÈN

貶 *Pièn.* Destituer (style relevé).

丨官, *pièn koūon,* dégrader un mandarin.

扁 *Pièn.* Aplati des deux côtés, retourner sens dessus dessous.

丨丨個石頭, *pièn pièn ké· chăc t'eôu,* pierre bien plate.

丨轉石頭, *pièn tchòn chăc t'eôu,* retourner une pierre sens dessus dessous.

丨額, *pièn niâc,* inscription placée horizontalement au frontispice d'un bâtiment, ou au-dessus d'une porte.

P'IÈN

片 *P'ièn.* Carte de visite; tranche.

名丨 (ou 丨子) *miâng p'ièn,* (ou simplement *p'ièn tzè,* carte de visite.

飛名丨, *fī miâng p'ièn,* envoyer sa carte.

一丨玻璃, *ŷt p'ièn pō lî,* un verre de vitre.

棚板要落丨縫, *p'âng pàn oí lŏc p'ièn p'óung,* il faut faire des rainures juxtaposées aux planches.

切成｜子, *ts'iĕt châng p'ièn tzè*, couper en tranches.

番｜, *fān p'ièn* (pour 邦 *pāng*), l'étranger.

PIÉN

變 *Pién*. Changer, passer ou faire passer d'un état à un autre, transformer.

｜心, *pién sīm*, changer de sentiment.

話｜了, *fá pién liào*, il se contredit.

事｜壞, *sé pién faí*, l'affaire a mal tourné.

人唔曉｜神, *gnîn mĝ hiào pién chîn*, l'homme ne peut se transformer en esprit.

徧 *Pién*. Tour, fois, tout.

念五｜在天, *niám ǹg pién ts'aí t'iēn*, réciter cinq *Pater*.

｜山都係人, *pién sān toū hé· gnîn* (peu employé, on dit plutot 滿山 … *mān sān* …) toute la colline est couverte de monde.

P'IÉN

騙 *P'ién*. Tromper, faire tort.

｜人家, *p'ién gnîn ka*, tromper, nuire à quelqu'un par quelque rouerie, le faire tomber dans un piège.

｜背, *p'ién poé·*, furtivement, en cachette.

面前講好話｜背講衰人, *mién ts'iên kòng hào fá p'ién poé· kòng soī gnîn*, il vous loue en face et déblatère contre vous par derrière.

便 *P'ién*. Commode, facile, avantageux.

水方｜, *choùi fōng p'ién*, l'eau est à portée.

隨｜, *souî p'ién*, à volonté, à votre guise.

順｜, *choún p'ién*, profiter de l'occasion.

行大｜行小｜, *hâng t'ái p'ién, hâng siào p'ién*, aller à la selle (aux grandes commodités), uriner.

大｜唔通, *t'ái p'ién mĝ t'oūng*, il y a constipation.

食｜飯, *chĭt p'ién fán*, à la fortune du pot.

係有方｜, *hé· yōu fōng p'ién*…s'il y a une occasion favorable…

辨 *P'ién*. Discuter, expliquer, distinguer.

｜道理, *p'ién t'áo lī*, expliquer, raisonner la doctrine.

｜駁, *p'ién pôc*, discuter, réfuter, répondre aux objections.

神鬼两樣愛｜分明, *chîn kouì leòng yóng oí p'ién foūn mîn*, il faut bien distinguer entre un esprit et un démon.

P'IĔT

別 *P'iĕt*. Autre, différent, être séparé.

｜人, *p'iĕt gnîn*, un autre homme.

有｜樣麼, *yoū p'iĕt yóng mô ?* y en a-t-il d'une autre sorte ?

有大分｜, *yoū t'aí foūn p'iĕt*, il y a une grande différence.

辭 | , ou 暫 | , *tsê p'iĕt, ts'iám p'iĕt,* dire adieu, se séparer.

| 處 , *p'iĕt tch'oú,* ailleurs.

分 | ,*foūn p'iĕt,* distinguer, différence.

P'IÊT

撇 *P'iĕt.* Virgule, apostrophe.

唐字難記 | 畫多 , *t'ông sé nân kí p'iĕt vâc tō* ! les caractères chinois sont difficiles à retenir, il y a tant d'apostrophes et de traits !

PĪN

兵 *Pīn.* Soldat.

| 頭 , *pīn t'eóu,* chef militaire.

紮得有 | , *tsâp têt yoū pīn,* il y a des soldats campés.

調 | , *tiáo* (pour *t'iáo*) *pīn,* recruter des soldats.

別 *Pīn* (ou *poūn*). Donner, partager (voyez *poūn*).

賓 *Pīn.* | 客 , *pīn hâc,* hôte (celui qui reçoit l'hospitalité).

檳 *Pīn.* | 榔 , *pīn lông,* noix d'arec.

P'ĪN

編 *P'īn* (pour *p'iēn*). Entrelacer, tresser.

| 毛辮 , *p'īn māo piēn,* faire la tresse des cheveux.

| 絲線 , *p'īn sē sién,* tresser les cordons qui font la fausse queue.

拚 *P'īn* ou *p'ín.* Courir un risque.

| 命 , *p'īn miáng,* exposer sa vie.

我同佢 | 命 , *ngaî t'oûng kî p'īn miáng,* je veux me battre avec lui jusqu'à ce que l'un des deux meure.

刀子 | 阿起 , *taō tzè p'īn á hì,* donner un coup de couteau (au risque de se le faire rendre).

P'ÎN

平 *P'în.* Calme, paix; balance, peser.

大家 | 安 , *t'aí kā p'în ōn,* tout le monde va bien.

| 時 , *p'în chê,* en temps de paix, en temps ordinaire.

| 安 , *p'în ōn,* bonne santé, paisible, content.

天 | , *t'iēn p'în,* petite balance romaine.

| 銀 , *p'în nioûn,* peser de l'argent.

評 *P'în.* | 論 , *p'în lóun,* délibérer.

貧 *P'în.* Pauvre.

| 窮 , *p'în k'ioûng,* même sens.

家 | , *kā p'în,* ma famille est pauvre.

瓶 *P'în* ou *p'iâng.* Cruche, bouteille, vase.

一 | 酒 , *ŷt p'în tsiòu,* une bouteille de vin.

花 | , *fā p'iâng,* vase de fleurs.

屏 *P'în.* Paravent, châssis quelconque monté.

| 風 , ou 門 | , *p'în foūng,* ou *moûn*

p'in, devanture d'une boutique ou d'une salle, toute en portes.

丨風簾, *p'in foūng liâm*, paravent.

憑 *P'in*. Preuve, gage.

丨據, *p'in kì*, même sens.

有丨有據, *yoū p'in yoū kì*, il y a de bonnes preuves.

講話麼丨, *tchói vá mô p'in*, une simple parole n'est pas une preuve.

丨上頭, *p'in chóng t'eôu*, s'en remettre à ses supérieurs.

PÌN

稟 *Pìn*. Informer un supérieur ; accuser.

丨神父知, *pìn chîn foú tī*, en informer le Père, le consulter.

丨明, *pìn mîn*, consulter.

丨人, *pìn gnîn*, accuser quelqu'un.

秉 *Pìn*. Tenir, prendre une poignée.

丨公判理, *pìn koūng p'án lī*, juger d'après la justice.

丨淨, *pìn ts'iáng*, enlever une ordure, nettoyer.

丨屎, *pìn chè*, s'essuyer, après une selle.

P'ÌN

品 *P'ìn*. Grade, ordre.

神丨, *chîn p'ìn*, le sacrement de l'Ordre.

陞四丨,五丨,六丨,七丨, *chīn sí p'ìn, ǹg p'ìn, lioūc p'ìn, ts'īt p'ìn*, être promu aux Ordres mineurs, au sous-diaconat, au diaconat, à la prêtrise.

列丨聖人, *lièt p'ìn chín gnîn*, les différentes classes de Saints.

並 *P'in* (pour *p'ín*). Certainement.

丨麼一個錢, *p'ìn mô ȳt ké· ts'iên*, il n'y a absolument pas une sapèque.

丨麼個事, *p'ìn mô ké· sé*, il n'y a certainement rien de cela.

聘 *P'ìn*. 丨金, *p'ìn kīm*, cadeaux de fiançailles aux parents de la fille.

PÍN

并 *Pín*. Et, aussi, tous.

丨佢丨我, *pín kî pín ngâi*, lui et moi.

一丨同來去, *ȳt pín t'oûng loî hí*, allons-y tous ensemble.

殯 *Pín*. Ensevelir provisoirement·

丨葬, *pín tsóng*, ensevelir un mort.

P'IÒNG

紡 *P'iòng* (pour *fòng*). Filer au virolet. Voir *fòng*.

PIÓNG

放 *Pióng* (pour *fóng*). Poser, placer. Voir *fóng*.

PĪT

必 *Pīt*. Certain.

丨定係眞個, *pīt t'ín hé· tchīn ké·* bien sûr, c'est vrai.

未丨會來, *ví pīt voé· loî*, vraiment

il viendrait (dans le sens négatif), il n'est pas si sûr qu'il vienne.

何丨咁樣做, *hô pĭt àn yóng tsó* ? pourquoi agir ainsi ?

泌 *Pĭt*. Distiller.

丨酒, *pĭt tsioù*, distiller du vin, vin distillé.

筆 *Pĭt*. Pinceau, plume, écriture.

一枝丨, *ўt tjē pĭt*, un pinceau (on dit plus vulgairement: 一管丨, *ўt kouòn pĭt*.)

丨尖, 丨管, 丨筒, 丨架, *pĭt tsiām*, *pĭt kouon*, *pĭt t'oúng*, *pĭt ká*; pointe, manche du pinceau, tube dans lequel on le dépose.

蘸丨, *tsiàm pĭt*, tremper le pinceau dans l'encre.

代丨人, *t'oí pĭt gnĭn*, écrire au nom d'autrui.

畢 *Pĭt*. 丨竟, *pĭt kín*, en fin de compte.

丨直, *pĭt tch'ĭt*, tout droit, directement.

丨(嗶)吱, *pĭt kī*, espèce d'étoffe.

逼 *Pĭt*. Presser, exiger, contraindre.

取錢麽咁樣丨人, *ts'ì ts'iên mō àn yóng pĭt gnĭn*, tu pourrais réclamer ton argent sans presser à ce point les gens.

勒丨, *lĭt pĭt*, contraindre.

廹 *Pĭt*. Presser, urger.

咁急丨, *kàn kĭp pĭt*, c'est bien si pressant.

丨切, *pĭt ts'iĕt*, même sens.

Pĭt. Moineau, nom générique des passereaux.

禾丨 *vô pĭt*, moineau commun.

劈 *Pĭt* (pour *p'iăc*). Se fendre, fente.

玻璃丨爬裡, *pō lî pĭt p'ĕt lé*, la vitre est fendue.

酒盃打丨裡, *tsiòu pī tzè tà pĭt lí*, le verre est fêlé.

P'ĬT

譬 *p'ĭt*. Comparer.

比丨, *pì p'ĭt*, ou 丨如, *p'ĭt ŷ*, par exemple, pour comparaison.

避 *P'ĭt*. Eviter, fuir.

丨雨, *p'ĭt ỳ*, se garer de la pluie.

躲丨罪惡, *tò p'ĭt ts'oúi ôc*, éviter le péché.

丨世俗, *p'ĭt ché sioŭc*, fuir le monde.

闢 *P'ĭt*. Commencer, ouvrir.

開丨之初, *k'oī p'ĭt tjē tsē*, au commencement de toutes choses.

丨妄, *p'ĭt vòng*, dissiper, réfuter les erreurs.

辨丨異端, *p'ién p'ĭt ý tōn*, réfuter les superstitions.

僻 *P'ĭt*. Retiré, tranquille.

丨靜地方, *p'ĭt ts'ín t'í fōng*, lieu retiré et tranquille.

匹 *P'ĭt.* Particule numérale des chevaux, des ânes.

一 | 馬, *ӯt p'ĭt mā,* un cheval.

疋 *P ĭt.* Particule numérale des toiles.

一 | 布, *ӯt p'ĭt poú,* une pièce de toile.

PŌ

保 *Pō.* Cuire à l'eau,

| 飯, *pō fán,* cuire le riz.

| 綿, *pō miên,* cuire à point, réduit en bouillie.

| 滾 水, *pō koùn choùi,* faire bouillir de l'eau.

沙 | *sā pō,* casserole de terre, d'argile, pour cuire l'eau.

波 *Pō.* Vague. | 羅 渦, *pō lô tsióu,* tourbillon d'eau.

| 浪, *pō lóng,* vagues.

| 蘿 麻, *pō lô mâ,* étoffe faite avec des feuilles d'ananas.

玻 *Pō.* | 璃, *pō lī,* verre, vitre.

P'Ō

蔸 *P'ō.* Particule numérale des arbres.

倒 一 | 樹, *tào ӯt p'ō choú,* abattre un arbre.

P'Ô

婆 *P'ô.* Vieille femme, grand-mère; appellation des femmes mariées.

阿 | , *ā p'ô,* ma grand'mère.

| 大, *p'ô t'aí,* arrière-grand-mère.

大 |, 小 |, *t'aí p'ô, siào p'ô,* femme légitime, concubine.

兩 公 |, *leòng koūng p'ô,* les deux époux.

老 |, *lào p'ô,* femme, épouse.

P'Ó

破 *P'ó.* Rompre, déchirer, ouvrir avec un couteau.

| 柴, *p'ó ts'iâo,* couper, fendre du bois de chauffage.

| 石 頭, *p'ó chăc t'eôu,* casser des pierres à coups de massue.

打 | 船, *tà p'ó chôn,* briser la barque, faire naufrage.

打 | 城, *tà p'ó châng,* prendre une ville d'assaut.

看 | 世 俗, *k'ón p'ó ché sioŭc,* mépriser les affaires du monde, en reconnaître la vanité.

| 雞, | 猪, | 魚, *p'ó kē, p'ó tchoū p'ông,* écorcher, vider une poule, un porc, un poisson.

PŎC

梆 *Pŏc* (*pōng*). Tambourin de bois ou de bambou sur lequel on frappe pour annoncer les veilles ou donner un signal quelconque.

打 |, *tà pŏc,* frapper sur cet instrument.

P'ŎC

雹 *P'ŏc.* Grêle. 落 |, *lŏc p'ŏc,* tomber de la grêle.

薄 *P'ŏc*. Mince, grêle. Clinquant, feuille de métal.

忒丨個紙, *t'iĕt p'ŏc ké· tjè*, ce papier est trop mince.

刮丨, *kouât p'ŏc*, amincir.

金丨,銀丨,錫丨, *kīm p'ŏc, nioûn p'ŏc, siâc p'ŏc*, feuille d'or, d'argent, d'étain.

菲丨, *fī p'ŏc*, très mince.

丨荷, *p'ŏc hô*, menthe.

刻丨待人, *k'ĕt p'ŏc t'aí gnîn*, traiter quelqu'un sans égard, à la légère.

PÔC

博 *Pôc*. Jouer; ample, grand.

賭丨, *toù pôc*, jouer aux jeux de hazard.

丨學, *pôc hŏc*, très savant.

剝 *Pôc*. Dépouiller, dénuder.

丨樹皮, *pôc choú p'î*, dépouiller un arbre de son écorce.

丨人個衫, *pôc gnîn ké· sām*, dépouiller quelqu'un de ses habits.

駁 *Pôc*. Contredire, rétorquer, opposer, réfuter, ajouter, rajuster.

丨道理, *pôc t'áo lī*, discuter et réfuter la doctrine.

辨丨異端, *p'ién pôc ý tōn*, réfuter les superstitions.

丨船, *pôc chôn*, changer de barque, prendre une correspondance.

丨長索, *pôc tch'ông sôc*, ajouter une corde de plus.

索斷帛裡愛丨轉起, *sôc t'ōn p'ĕt lĕ·, oí pôc tchòn hì*, la corde est cassée, il faut la rajuster.

丨猳, *pôc ka*, s'accoupler, faire le coït (ne se dit que des animaux).

P'OC

拍 *P'ôc*. Frapper avec les mains.

丨手, *p'ôc choù*, battre des mains.

丨門, 丨桌 *p'ôc moûn, p'ôc tsôc*, frapper à la porte, frapper sur la table.

衫子丨淨來, *sām tzè p'ôc ts'iáng lôi*, frappe les habits pour en faire sortir la poussière.

丨一下, *p'ôc ȳt há*, frapper un coup.

泊 *P'ôc*. 淡丨, *t'ám p'ôc*, simple, content de peu, frugal.

先理淡丨, *siēn lī t'ám p'ôc*, le commerce rapporte peu.

食著淡丨, *chĭt tchôc t'ám p'ôc*, manger et se vêtir pauvrement.

朴 *P'ôc*. 丨硝, *p'ôc siāo*, salpêtre.

POÉ·

背 *Poé·*. Dos, revers.

丨囊, *poé· nông*, le dos,

丨囊上 *poé· nông hóng*, sur le dos.

屋丨夫, *vouc poé· foū* (ou simpl. *vouc poé·*), derrière la maison.

屎丨尾, *chè poé· mī*, derrière, à la fin, en dernier lieu.

丨紙, 丨聖像, *poé· tjè, poé· chín sióng*, doubler le revers d'un papier, d'une image.

騙丨, *p'ién poé·*, en cachette, à l'insu.

P'ÔI

賠 *P'ôi*. Restituer, réparer un dommage.

| 銀, *p'ôi nioûn*, restituer de l'argent.

| 唔起, *p'ôi mĝ hì*, je n'ai pas de quoi rembourser.

佢認 |, *kî gnín p'ôi*, il promet de restituer.

P'ÓI

背 *P'ói*. Renier, apostasier, trahir; détourné.

| 天主, | 教, *p'ói t'iēn tchoù*, *p'ói káo*, renier Dieu, la religion, apostasier.

| 頁心, *p'ói leông sīm*, agir contre sa conscience.

地方十分 |, *t'í fōng chĭp foūn p'ói*, l'endroit est par trop retiré, tranquille.

裡地方過 | 風, *yà t'í fōng kouó p'ói foūng*, cet endroit est plus à l'abri du vent.

| 書, *p'ói choū*, tourner le dos au livre, c'est-à-dire réciter sa leçon.

狗 |, *keòu p'ói* le chien aboie.

焙 *P'ói*. Griller, sécher au feu.

P'ŌN

翻 *P'ōn*. Vomir. Retourner l'un dans l'autre.

一食倒藥就 | 帛裡, *ŷt chĭt tào yŏc ts'ióu p'ōn p'ĕt lê*, dès qu'il eut avalé son remède, il le vomit.

雞腸愛 | 出來呼好洗淨, *kē tch'ông oí p'ōn tch'oût loî tcháng haò sè ts'iáng*, il faut retourner les boyaux de la poule, pour pouvoir les laver.

| 襪, *p'ōn mât*, retourner ses bas.

PŌNG

帮 *Pōng*. Aider, contribuer, corporation, caravane.

相 | 我, *siōng pōng ngâi*, aide-moi.

| 助異端, *pōng tsé ý tōn*, contribuer aux superstitions.

各人 | 錢也好 | 人工也好, *kôc gnîn pōng ts'iên yā hào pōng gnîn koūng yā hào*, chacun peut y contribuer (par ex: à bâtir une église) soit par son argent soit par sa main-d'œuvre.

打 | 人, *tà pōng gnîn*, implorer l'aide de quelqu'un (voir 瞻 *tchām*).

來到一 | 米, *loî táo ŷt pōng mì*, il est arrivé une caravane de (porteurs de) riz.

| 船, *ŷt pōng chôn*, une flotte.

梆 *Pōng* (ou *pŏc*). Petit tambourin de bois (voir *pŏc*).

P'ŌNG

碰 *P'ōng*. Heurter, frapper.

| 石頭, *p'ōng chăc t'eôu*, briser ou fendre des grosses pierres à coup de massue.

| 錐, *p'ōng tch'oûi*, massue à briser les rochers.

| 門, *p'ōng moûn*, frapper à la porte.

蚌 *P'ong*. Espèce d'huitre.

P'ÔNG

旁 *P'ông*. A côté, approcher.

| 邊人, *p'ông piēn gnîn*, les gens du voisinage.

| 觀, *p'ông kouōn*, voir, considérer, juger une chose qui ne nous concerne pas.

照 | 觀人講, *tcháo p'ông kouōn gnîn kòng*, d'après ce que j'ai entendu dire, d'après les racontages.

兩 |, *leòng p'ông*, des deux côtés.

PÒNG

榜 *Pòng*. Tableau, liste.

發 |, *fāt pòng*, afficher la liste des noms de ceux qui sont reçus aux examens.

| 眼, *pòng niàn*, celui qui est reçu académicien avec le numéro 2.

兩 | ou 進士, *leòng pòng* ou *tsín sé*, docteur.

綁 *Pòng*. Lier, attacher.

拿索來 | 起, *nā sôc lôi pòng hì*, attache-le avec une corde.

膀 *Pòng*. Epaule.

肩 |, *kiān pòng*, épaule.

前 | 猪肉, *ts'iēn pòng tchoū nioūc*, épaule de cochon.

謗 *Pòng*. 毀 |, *k'oùi pòng*, dénigrer, calomnier.

䅭 *Pòng*. Ajouter au riz, au vin.

麽菜 |, *mô ts'ói pòng*, n'avoir pas de légumes pour manger avec le riz.

番豆好 | 酒, *fān t'eoû haò pòng tsioù*, les arachides sont bonnes avec le vin.

P'ÓNG

傍 *P'óng* Etre à côté; s'appuyer, s'attacher à.

| 人個地, *p'óng gnîn ké· t'í*, faire un tombeau tout près de celui d'un autre, (pour profiter du même vent du bonheur).

| 人家有錢個, *p'óng gnîn kā yoū ts'iēn ké·*, s'attacher à une famille riche.

差 | 官府個勢, *ts'aī p'óng kouōn foù ké· ché*, les satellites mettent leur confiance dans le mandarin.

PÔT

發 *Pôt*. Surgir, fermenter, devenir.

| 大水, *pôt t'aí chouì*, il y a inondation.

麵包唔 |, *mién pāo mĝ pôt*, le pain ne fermente pas.

個隻屋幾 |, *ké· tchâc voūc kì pôt*, cette famille est très riche.

| 病, | 癲, | 癩, | 夢, *pôt p'iáng pôt tiēn, pôt t'ài, pôt moúng*, devenir malade, fou, lépreux, rêver.

| 人瘟, *pôt gnîn voūn*, la peste a éclaté.

POŪ

豇 *Poū* (ou *koū*). Accroupi.

雞嫲 | 倒噲生春, *kē· mâ poū tào, voé· sāng tch'oūn*, la poule est accroupie, elle va faire l'œuf.

麽凳坐 | 倒來燉, *mô tén ts'ō poū tào loî liáo*, puisqu'il n'y a pas de banc, mettons-nous sur les talons.

P'OŪ

鋪 *P'oū.* Préparer, arranger, étendre.

｜排, *p'oū pài* (pour *p'âi*), arranger, mettre en ordre.

攤｜板幷｜稈, *t'ān p'oū pàn pín p'oū kòn,* préparer un lit et y étendre de la paille.

｜置, **｜路**, *p'oū tjé, p'oū loú,* (on peut aussi dire **布置**, *poú tjé* ou **補置**, *poù tjé,* **補路**, *poù loú*) disposer, arranger; réparer une route (en y mettant des pierres).

普 *P'oū.* Grand, immense.

｜天下, *p'oū t'iēn hā,* le monde entier, partout.

簿 *P'oū.* Registre, cahier.

一本｜, *ỹt poùn p'oū,* un registre.

訂｜ (ou **上｜**), *tāng p'oū* (ou *chōng p'oū*), inscrire sur le registre.

P'OÛ

葡 *P'oû.* **｜萄**, *p'oû t'âo,* vigne, raisin.

菩 *P'oû.* **｜薩**, *p'oû sāt,* idole.

葫 *P'oû.* **番｜**, *fān p'oû,* espèce de courge, gourde.

鍋 *P'oû.* **｜鑼**, *poû lô,* marmite à faire cuire le riz.

扶 *P'oû* (*foû*). Soutenir par le bras, aider.

｜等佢上, *p'oû tèn kî hóng,* aide-le à se lever.

唔使人｜, *mĝ sè gnîn p'oû,* je n'ai pas besoin d'être soutenu.

POÙ

補 *Poù.* Raccommoder, réparer, suppléer.

｜衫, **｜鞋**, **｜鍋頭**, *poù sām, poù hâi, poù vōc t'eôu,* raccommoder les habits, les souliers, les marmites.

｜錢, *poù ts'iên,* compléter un nombre de sapèques.

｜罪; **做｜贖**, *poù ts'oúi; tsó poù choŭc,* satisfaire à ses péchés; faire pénitence.

斧 *Poù.* **｜頭**, *poù t'eôu,* hache.

P'ÒU

瞨 *P'où.* Myope, qui n'y voit pas clair.

年紀大我目｜, *niân kì t'aí ngaî moŭc p'où,* je suis âgé et mes yeux faiblissent.

輔 *P'où.* Aider, servir.

｜彌撒, *p'où nì sāt,* servir la Messe.

甫 *P'où.* **菜｜**, *ts'oí p'où,* navets salés.

譜 *P'où.* A peu près, approximatif.

我大｜知得, *ngâi t'ái p'où tī tēt,* je sais à peu près.

大｜算一下, *t'aí p'où són ỹt hā,* calculer en gros, approximativement.

十分麼｜個人, *chīp foūn mô p'où*

ké· gnîn, homme sans idées, sans jugement, sans combinaisons.

族丨, *ts'oŭc p'où*, livre généalogique des descendants d'une même souche.

POÚ

布 *Poú*. Toile, étoffe; disposer.

一疋丨, *ŷt p'ĭt poú*, une pièce d'étoffe.

剪丨, *tsièn poú*, acheter (découper) de la toile.

丨置好, *poú tjé hào*, c'est bien disposé, ordonné.

丨政司, *poú tchín sē*, trésorier général d'une province.

P'OÚ

哺 *P'oú*. Couver.

雞麻丨子, *kē mâ p'oú tzè*, la poule couve ses petits.

捕 *P'oú*. Se mettre en embuscade.

猫公丨老鼠, *miáo koūng p'oú lào tch'où*, le chat guette un rat.

丨狗, *p'oú kcoù*, renard.

步 *P'oú*. Pas; mesure itinéraire de dix 里 *lī*.

一丨脚, *ŷt p'oú kiŏc*, un pas.

一丨一丨, *ŷt p'oú ŷt p'oú*, pas à pas, graduellement.

幾下丨脚, *kì hā p'oú kiŏc*, à quelques pas.

脚丨長, *kiŏc p'oú tch'ông*, avoir le pas allongé.

地丨, *t'í p'oú*, situation, sort heureux ou malheureux.

到裡個地丨, *taó ỳ ké· t'í p'oú*,...... réduit à cette situation....

丨路, *p'oú loú*, mesure itinéraire, une lieue, environ six kilomètres, dix 里 *lī*.

一日我行得十丨路到, *ŷt gnĭt ngaî hâng tĕt chĭp p'oú loú taò*, je puis faire dix lieues en un jour.

部 *P'oú*. Collection; tribunal.

一丨書有四本, *ŷt p'oú choū yoū sí poùn*, l'ouvrage a 4 volumes.

聖教禮丨, *chín káo lī p'oú*, la Sacrée Congrégation des Rites.

丨院, *p'oú yán* (ou 總督 *tsoùng toŭc*), gouverneur général de plusieurs provinces.

六丨, *lioŭc p'oú*, les six tribunaux supérieurs de la capitale ou ministères: à savoir: le 吏丨, *lí p'oú*, tribunal ou ministère des officiers civils, le 禮丨, *lī p'oú*, ministère des Rites, le 戶丨, *foú p'oú*, ministère des revenus publics, le 兵丨, *pīn p'oú*, ministère de la guerre, le 刑丨, *hîn p'oú*, ministère des châtiments, enfin le 工丨, *koūng p'oú*, ministère des travaux publics.

Aprés le traité de 1862, on y a ajouté le 總理衙門, *tsoùng lī ngâ moûn*, ministère des affaires étrangères; et récemment on a formé le 海丨, *hoì p'oú* ministère de la marine.

舖 *P'oú* Boutique, magasin.

一間丨, *ŷt kiān p'oú*, une boutique.

看 ou 掌丨, *k'ón* ou *tchòng p'oú*, garder la boutique.

坐丨, *ts'ō p'oú*, tenir boutique.

P'ŎUC

僕 *P'oŭc*. Serviteur. Employé seulement dans les lettres à un supérieur, pour se nommer.

璞 *P'oŭc*. Crochet, agrafe.

丨孤釘, *p'oŭc koū tăng*, crochet qui sert de charnière aux portes.

PÔUC

卜 *Poûc*. 丨卦, *poûc koúa*, consulter les sorts, tireur d'horoscope.

腹 *Poûc*. Ventre. Peu employé en parlant.

講心丨話, *kòng sīm poûc fá*, se dire des secrets.

我同佢至丨個朋友, *ngaî t'oûng kî tjé poûc ké· p'oûng yoū*, c'est un ami de cœur.

P'OÛC

仆 *P'oûc*. Abouché, replié sur soi la face contre terre.

丨倒來睡目, *p'oûc tào loî choé· moûc*, dormir accoudé sur une table, la tête dans les bras.

丨倒來念經, *p'oûc tào loî niám kīn*, prier la face prosternée contre terre.

脚頭忒丨唔好使, *kiŏc t'côu t'iĕt p'oûc mĝ hào sè*, la pioche est trop recourbée et d'un usage incommode.

POŪN

分 *Poūn* (ou *pīn*). Donner, distribuer, pour, à.

求神父丨多少白糖丨我, *k'ioû chîn fŏu poūn tō chào p'ăc t'ông poūn ngâi*, je prie le Père de me donner un peu de sucre.

兩個人丨, *lcòng ké· gnîn poūn*, à partager entre deux.

愛拿丨那人, *oí nā poūn màn gnîn ?* à qui faut-il le donner ?

愛拿丨我, *oí nā poūn ngaî*, donne-le moi.

Poūn (pour 被 *p'í)* marque du passif.

丨人打裡, *poūn gnîn tà lé·*, j'ai été battu. (Voir 被 *p'í)*.

P'OŪN

P'oūn. Epaisseur, épais.

量有幾丨, *lcông yoū kì p'oūn*, mesurer l'épaisseur.

噴 *P'oūn (foún)*. Souffler, déborder.

丨烏火, *p'oūn voū fò*, éteindre le feu (par ex. d'une lampe) en soufflant.

丨着火, *p'oūn tch'ŏc fò*, attiser le feu en soufflant dessus.

丨出, *p'oūn tch'oût*, déborder.

發大雨噲丨塘, *pôt t'aí ỳ voé· p'oūn t'ông*, l'averse va faire déborder l'étang.

P'OÛN

盆 *P'oûn*. Cuvette, bassin.

面丨, *mién p'oûn*, cuvette de toilette.

脚丨, *kiŏc p'oûn*, bassin à se laver les pieds.

去丨菓, *hí p'oûn koùo*, envoyer les cadeaux de noce (composés de porc, poule, canard, poisson, donnés aux parents de la jeune fille).

POÙN

本 *Poùn.* Fondement, principe, propre, personnel ; particule numérale des livres.

丨錢, *poùn ts'iēn*, somme d'argent mise dans le commerce.

麼丨錢做生理, *mô poùn ts'iēn tsó siēn lī*, n'avoir pas de capital pour faire le commerce.

對丨利, *touí poùn lí*, intérêt égal au capital, 100 du 100.

丨來, *poùn loî*, primitif, originaire, naturellement.

丨丨個, *poùn poùn ké·*, c'est le même, c'est le primitif, celui dont on vient de parler.

丨地人, *poùn t'í gnîn*, aborigène.

人個丨性, *gnîn ké· poùn sín*, le naturel, le caractère de quelqu'un.

有丨事個人, *yoū poùn sé ké· gnîn*, homme qui a des capacités, des moyens naturels.

POÚN

体 *Poún.* Lourd, grossier.

咁丨氣個人, *àn poún hí ké· gnîn*! quel lourdeau que cet homme !

糞 *Poún.* Fumier, excréments.

牛欄丨, *niôu lân poún*, fumier d'étable à buffle.

丨箕, *poún kī*, panier dont les laboureurs se servent pour porter la terre ou le fumier.

P'OÚN

噴 *P'oún.* Rejeter avec force l'air des poumons par le bouche; rejeter quelque chose de le bouche avec l'air des poumons ; exhaler une odeur.

丨睡, *p'oún choé·*, ronfler.

丨水, *p'oún choùi*, rejeter de l'eau de la bouche avec force, sous forme de pluie.

丨香, *p'oún hiōng*, exhaler une agréable odeur.

丨臊, *p'oún sāo* (ou *p'āng sāo*), cela pue le fauve.

P'OÛNG

朋 *P'oûng.* 丨友, *poûng yoū*, ami.

結丨友, *kiĕt p'oûng yoū*, contracter amitié.

有錢丨友多, *yoū ts'iēn p'oûng you tō*, les riches ont beaucoup d'amis.

篷 *P'oûng* (*foûng*). Toit de barque, tente.

船丨, *chôn p'oûng*, toit de barque.

布丨, *poú p'oûng*, toile d'abri, tente.

搭一個丨, *tâp ŷt ké· p'oûng*, construire un hangar, un appentis.

艻頭丨, *nĕt t'eoû p'oûng*, fourrés, broussailles épaisses.

POÙNG

捧 *Poùng.* Porter dans les deux mains, présenter des deux mains.

丨去菜托來, *poùng hí ts'oí t'ŏc loî*, emporte le plateau à légumes.

P'OÚNG

縫 *P'oúng* (pour *foûng*). Couture d'un habit, fente, jointure.

莫掤我衫一掤噲𡊨丨, *mŏc pāng ngâi sām, ŷt pāng voé· páo p'oúng*, ne tire pas mon habit, il pourrait se découdre.

棚橫倒唔好,還有丨唔知幾大, *p'âng vông taò mĝ hào, hân you p'oúng mĝ tī kì t'aí*, le plancher n'a pas été bien fait, il y a encore beaucoup de fentes (les planches ne sont pas jointes).

落片丨, *lŏc p'ièn p'oúng*, faire des rainures sur les tranches pour emboîter et unir les planches entre elles.

墻有丨壁有耳, *siông you p'oúng piăc yoū gnì*, les murs ont des fentes, les cloisons des oreilles.

POǓT

Poǔt ou *pŏc*. 丨滿, *mān*, archi-plein.

P'OǓT

噴 *P'oǔt*. Déborder. Même sens que *p'oūn*. On dit *p'oūn* ou *p'oǔt* selon les pays.

莫擺咁滿噲丨出, *mŏc saī àn mān voé· p'oǔt tch'oût*, ne verse pas si plein cela va déborder.

POÛT

不 *Poût*. Négation adverbiale.

了丨得, *liào poût têt*! cela ne finira pas !

丨拘, *poût kī*, 丨論, *poût loún*, sans distinction.

En langue vulgaire le mot *poût* est remplacé par le mot *mĝ*, *mĝ hào* pour *poût hào*, ce n'est pas bien, non.

SĀ

沙 *Sā*. Sable, gravier.

丨坝, *sā pá*, plaine sablonneuse, se dit surtout d'une plage de fleuve ou de mer.

丨子, *sā tzè*, plombs de chasse.

丨煲, *sā pō*, vase d'argile, casserole en argile.

丨梨, *sā lî*, nom de poire.

粆 *Sā*. 丨糖, *sā t'ông*, cassonade, sucre en poudre.

紗 *Sā*. Gaze.

雨丨, *ỳ sā*, 綿丨, *miēn sā*, différentes étoffes plus ou moins grossières.

丨燈, *sā tēn*, lanterne recouverte de gaze.

痧 *Sā*. Défaillance subite.

發丨, *pôt sā*, être pris de ce mal.

拈丨 (ou 捉丨), *niām sā* (ou *tsŏc sā*), pincer les veines de celui qui est pris de ce mal, pour activer le sang.

SÂ

儕 *Sâ*. Chacun, unité de personne.

一丨一個, *ŷt sâ ŷt ké·*, chacun un.

一丨一半, *ŷt sâ ŷt pán*, chacun la moitié.

丨丨都有分, *sâ sâ tou you foún*, chacun y a part, nous sommes tous solidaires.

來三四丨, *loî sām sí sâ*, nous sommes venus trois ou quatre.

SÂC

磜 *Sâc*. Morceau, quartier ; côté.

玻 璃 丨, *pō lî sâc*, débris de verre.

瓦 丨, *ngà sâc*, morceau de tuile.

一 丨 作 痛, *ŷt sâc tsôc t'oúng*, tout un côté me fait mal.

SĀI

揌 *Sāi*. Verser un liquide.

丨 酒, *sāi tsiòu*. verser du vin.

賽 *Sāi* (*soí*). Actions de grâces aux ancêtres, culte aux ancêtres.

丨 地, *sāi t'í*, rendre ce culte sur le tombeau.

SAÎ

Saî. Avoir l'estomac creux, besoin de viande.

久 唔 曾 食 猪 肉 肚 係 丨, *kiòu mĝ ts'ên chĭt tchōu nioûc toù hé· saî*, quand il y a longtenps qu'on n'a pas mangé de viande on a le ventre desséché.

豺 *Saî*. 丨 狗, *saî keòu*, loup.

SAÌ

徙 *Saì*. Changer de lieu, de domicile, transporter une chose d'un lieu à un autre.

猫 媽 丨 竇, *miáo mâ saì teoú*, la chatte change son nid de place.

我 上 間 丨 倒 下 間 去, *ngaî chóng kiān saì tào há kiān hí*, de la chambre du haut où j'étais, j'ai transporté mes pénates à la chambre d'en bas.

SAÍ

晒 *Saí*. Sécher au soleil, exposer au soleil.

丨 衫, *saí sām*, sécher les habits au soleil.

愛 帶 帽 嘚 日 頭 麼 事 丨 壞 人, *oí taí máo tcháng gnĭt t'eoû mô sé saí fai gnîn*, il faut porter un chapeau, pour que l'ardeur du soleil ne vous fasse pas mal.

帥 *Saí*. Grand chef militaire.

丨 官, *saí kouōn*, même sens.

元 丨, *niân saí*, généralissime.

SĀM

衫 *Sām*. Habit, veste, robe chinoise.

一 件 丨, *ŷt k'ián sām*, un habit.

着 丨, 脫 丨, *tchôc sām*, *t'ôt sām*, mettre son habit, l'ôter.

三 *Sām*. 丨 個, *sām ké·*, trois.

丨 萬 丨 千 丨 百 丨 十 丨, *sām ván sām ts'iēn sām pâc sām chĭp sām*, 33333·

丨 丨 爲 九, *sām sām vî kiòu*, 3 fois 3 font 9.

SÂM

蟬 *Sâm*. Cigale.

SÀM

糝 *Sàm*. 汁 丨, *tchĭp sàm*, bouillie pour les cochons.

飯 丨, *fán sàm*, riz cuit, grains de riz cuit.

SĀN

山 *Sān.* Montagne, bois, forêt; montagneux.

一面 | , *ŷt mién sān*, une montagne.

| 脚下 , *sān kiŏc hā*, au pied de la montagne.

樹 | , *choú sān*, bois, forêt.

| 塲 , *sān tch'ŏng*, même sens.

墳 | , *foûn sān*, cimetière (peu importe qu'il soit sur la montagne ou dans la plaine).

| 羊 , *sān yŏng*, chèvre sauvage.

地方好 | , *t'í fōng hào sān*, le pays est très montagneux.

珊 *Sān.* | 瑚 , *sān foû*, corail.

SÀN

產 *Sàn.* Héritage, patrimoine.

家 | ou | 業 , *kā sàn* ou *sàn niăp*, même sens.

生 | , *sēn sàn*, engendrer un héritier.

姍 *Sàn.* Prospère, bien portant, beau.

樹子咁 | , *choú tzè àn sàn*, la forêt, le bois est beau (par sa prospérité.)

裡馬好肥 | , *yà mā haò p'î sàn*, ce cheval est gras et bien portant.

散 *Sàn.* Séparé, épars, distribuer.

教友係零 | , *kaó yoū hé làn sàn*, les chrétiens sont loin les uns des autres, non groupés.

毛辮 | 鳥裡 , *maō piēn sàn p'ĕt lê*, la tresse de tes cheveux s'est déliée.

| 錢 , *sàn ts'iên*, distribuer des sapèques.

SÁN

散 *Sán.* Disperser, dissiper.

| 兵 , *sán pīn*, renvoyer les soldats.

風吹 | 了 , *foūng tch'oī sán liaò*, le vent a tout dispersé.

行嫽 | 一吓心來 , *hâng liaó sán ŷt hā sīm loî*, se promener pour se distraire un peu.

| 血 , *sán hiĕt*, faire circuler le sang.

SĀNG

生 *Sāng* (*sēn*). Vivant, cru, naître, pousser, pondre.

煎猪肉半 | 半熟 , *tsiēn tchoū nioŭc pán sāng pán choŭc*, cuire du porc moitié cru moitié cuit (un bifteck).

先生, *sīn* (pour *siēn*) *sāng*, né avant; on donne ce titre à ceux qui exercent une profession libérale, ou à ceux que l'on veut honorer.

| 日 , *sāng gnĭt*, jour de naissance, jour anniversaire de la naissance.

寫年 | , *sià niân sāng*, écrire un extrait de naissance.

草都唔 | , *ts'ào toū mĝ sāng*, l'herbe même n'y pousse pas.

雞媽 | 春 , *kē mā sāng tch'oūn*, la poule pond son œuf.

後 | *heóu sāng*, jeune, adolescent.

SĀNG

鉎 *Sāng.* Fonte.

| 鍋頭 , *sāng vŏc t'eôu*, poële en fonte.

丨子, *sāng tzè*, plombs de chasse, grenaille.

牲 *Sāng* (ou *sēn*). 頭 丨, *t'eôu sāng*, animaux domestiques.

甥 *Sāng* (ou *sēn*). 外丨, *ngoé sāng*, neveu (fils de la sœur).

外丨女, *ngoé sāng* (ou *sēn*) *ng̀*, nièce (fille de la sœur).

SĀO

臊 *Sāo*. Forte odeur de sauvage.

臭狐狸丨, *tch'oú foū lî sào*, ça pue l'odeur de renard.

羊牯也十分丨, *yông koù yā chĭp foūn sāo*, le bouc pue aussi cette odeur.

騷 *Sāo* (*saô*). 丨馬, *sāo mā*, étalon, cheval entier.

筲 *Sāo*. 馬丨, *mā sāo*, besace, sac que l'on peut mettre en bandoulière.

飯, *fán sāo*, petite poche où l'on met le riz, que l'on fait cuire tout enfermé.

SAÔ

騷 *Saô*. 牢丨, *laô saô*, inquiet, soucieux.

SAÒ

Saò. Fouetter, coup de flanc.

嫂 *Saò*. Femme d'un frère plus âgé; qualificatif des femmes mariées.

我大丨, 二丨, *ngâi t'aí saò, gní saò*, la femme de mon frère aîné, de mon second frère (aîné).

兩子丨, *leòng tzè saò*, les deux belles-sœurs.

SAÓ

掃 *Saó*. Balai, balayer.

丨笆, *saó pà*, balai.

稈丨, 芒丨, *kòn saó, miông saó*, balai de paille, balai de joncs.

丨間房, *saó kiān fông*, balayer la chambre.

丨人個面目, *saó gnîn ké mién moûc*, (*litt.*) balayer la figure à quelqu'un, faire affront à quelqu'un.

SÂP

烚 *Sâp* Cuire dans l'eau.

丨春, 丨番薯, *sâp tch'oūn, sâp fān choû*, cuire des œufs à l'eau, cuire des patates à l'eau.

SĂT

殺 *Săt*. Tuer, couper la tête.

五毋丨人, *ng̀*, *voū săt gnîn*, cinquième (commandement du décalogue), vous ne tuerez pas.

官府犯死罪麽丨頭愛切腰, *kouōn foù fám sì ts'ouí mô săt t'eoû oí ts'iĕt yāo*, on ne coupe pas la tête d'un mandarin qui s'est rendu coupable d'un délit capital, mais on lui scie les reins.

唔丨鼠個貓公, *mg̊ săt tch'où ké miaó koūng*, c'est un chat qui ne tue pas les rats.

煞 *Săt*. Hermétiquement fermé.

銲丨, *hón săt*, souder hermétiquement.

關 | , *kouān săt*, ferme en joignant bien, hermétiquement.

| 忙 , *săt māng* (pour *mâng*), empressé, affairé, se dépêcher.

SĒ

(Voir aussi les mots CHE)

師 *Sē*. Maître, qui enseigne.

一傅 , *sē foú*, ouvrier expérimenté.

出 | , *tch'oût sē*, sortir d'apprentissage, devenir maître ouvrier.

從 | 傅, *ts'ioûng sē foú*, se mettre sous la conduite d'un maître.

| 爺 , *sē yâ*, conseiller officiel du mandarin.

| 鐸 , *sē t'ŏc*, nom du prêtre catholique, dans les livres de prières.

老 | , *laò sē*, titre que l'on donne à un maître d'école en lui parlant.

獅 *Sē*. Lion.

打 | 子, (ou | 頭) *tà sē tzè* (ou *tà sē t'eoû*), la danse du lion, jeu du nouvel an.

柿 *Sē*. Nèfle du Japon, kaki.

| 餅 , *sē piàng*, nèfle sèche.

思 *Sē*. Penser, méditer.

日夜 | 想 , *gnĭt yá sē siòng*, penser, réfléchir jour et nuit.

我 | 量你咁苦 , *ngâi sē leông gnî àn k'où*, je te plains, j'ai compassion de tes malheurs.

妄 | 妄想 , *vòng sē vòng siòng*, avoir des mauvaises pensées.

鰓 *Sē*. Ouïes des poissons.

| 耳, *sē gnì*, même sens. (Vulgairement, on dit *hoî soī*).

穌 *Sē*. 耶 | , *yâ sē*, Jésus.

施 *Sē*. Donner gratuitement.

| 恩 , *sē ēn*, accorder un bienfait.

布 | , *poú sē* ou *sé*, faire plaisir.

我拿兩個錢布 | 阿子你 , *ngaî nā leòng ké· ts'iên poú sē á tzè gnî*, voilà deux sapèques pour te consoler.

絲 *Sē*. Fil sans torsion, fibre, le cent-millième de l'once.

| 線 , *sē sién*, fil de soie pour coudre.

蘿蔔 | , *lô p'ĕt sē*, navets découpés en fils, et desséchés au soleil.

扭 | 手鈪 , *nioù sē choù âc*, bracelet en filigranes.

一個 | 毫都唔愛 , *ȳt ké· sē haô toū mĝ oí*, je ne veux absolument rien. (Voir 毫 *haô*).

司 *Sē*. Présider, président.

都 | , *toū sē*, major (grade militaire).

靈魂有三 | , *lîn foûn yoū sām sē*, l'âme a trois facultés.

打官 | , *tà kouōn sē*, procès, être en procès.

布政 | , *poú tchín sē*, grand trésorier d'une province.

私 *Sē*. Particulier, privé.

| 審判 , *sē chìm p'án*, jugement particulier.

| 恩 , *sē ēn*, grâce actuelle.

| 下去做 , *sē há hí tsó*, aller faire une chose en cachette, en particulier.

| 用, *sē yoúng*, user d'une chose en son particulier.

| 欲, *sē yoŭc*, passion, concupiscence, aiguillon de la chair.

梳 *Sē*. Démêloir, peigne.

| 毛辮, *sē māo piēn*, démêler la tresse.

| 頭, *sē t'eôu*, arranger la chevelure d'une jeune fille à la manière des femmes.

| 髻, *sē kí*, taire son chignon.

疏 *Sē*. Eloigné, séparé, n'avoir ensemble aucune relation; friable, sec et peu résistant.

| 遠, *sē yàn*, éloigné.

親 |, *ts'īn sē*, les proches parents et les parents éloignés.

日遠日 | 日近日親, *gnĭt yàn gnĭt sē gnĭt k'ioún gnĭt ts'īn*, la séparation refroidit de jour en jour l'amitié, la fréquentation mutuelle la rend plus intime.

| 財仗義, *sē ts'oî tch'óng gní*, ne pas chercher à s'enrichir et s'appliquer à pratiquer la justice.

麵包炕倒忒 |, *mién pāo k'óng tào t'ĭēt sē*, le pain a été grillé trop friable.

SÈ

史 *Sè*. Historien.

聖 |, *chín sè*, les Evangélistes.

| 書, *sè choū*, livres d'histoires.

使 *Sè*. Employer, se servir, faire que; guider.

| 錢, *sè ts'iên*, dépenser des sapèques.

| 用, | 費, *sè yoúng, sè fí*, dépenses ordinaires.

番錢 | 唔得, *fān ts'iên sè mĝ tĕt*, les sous étrangers ne passent pas.

唔曉 | 脚頭, *mĝ hiào sè kiŏc t'eôu*, ne pas savoir se servir de la pioche.

| 牛, *sè nioû*, faire marcher, faire travailler le buffle.

| 馬, *sè mā*, guider le cheval.

唔 |, *mĝ sè*, la chose n'est pas nécessaire, c'est inutile.

唔 | 來, *mĝ sè loî*, inutile de venir.

SÉ

思 *Sé*. Sens, signification, idée, pensée.

有意 |, *yoū ý sé*, il y a une signification.

多人讀書唔知得意 |, *tō gnîn t'oŭc choū mĝ tī tĕt ý sé*, beaucoup lisent des livres sans en comprendre le sens.

伺 *Sé*. | 候, *sé heóu*, attendre.

咊人 | 候, *vò gnîn sé heóu*, dites-leur d'attendre.

事 *Sé*. Affaire, chose, occupation.

一件 |, *ўt k'ián sé*, une affaire.

| 情, *sé ts'în*, affaire, procès.

唔得閑有 |, *mĝ tĕt hân yoū sé*, je n'ai pas le temps, je suis occupé.

多 | 個人, *tō sé ké· gnîn*, homme brouillon, remuant, toujours à créer des affaires.

服 | 人, *foŭc sé gnîn*, servir quelqu'un.

服 | 病人, *foŭc sé p'iáng gnîn*, soigner un malade.

士 *Sé*. Magistrat, lettré.

學 | , *hŏc sé*, lettré, savant.

傳敎 | , *tch'ôn káo sé*, nom officiel donné aux missionnaires.

道 | , *t'áo sé*, dénomination des sectateurs de la doctrine de la Raison. Secte de 老子 *Laò tzè*.

仕 *Sé*. Magistrature.

出 | 做官, *tch'oût sé tsó koūon*, aller prendre possession d'une magistrature.

數 *Sé* (ou *choú*). Nombre, quantité, compter, calculer, énumérer.

| 目, *sé moûc*, nombre, chlffre.

總 | (ou 共 |), *tsoùng sé* (ou *k'ioúng sé*), au total, somme totale.

| 錢, *sé ts'iên*, compter les pièces de monnaie.

同我算 | , *t'oûng ngaî són sé*, faites-moi le compte.

| 着, *sé tch'ŏc*, le compte est juste.

打死無 | 幾多, *tà sì voû sé kì tō*, tuer un nombre infini.

| 唔得幾多, *sé mĝ têt kì tō*, en nombre incalculable.

訴 *Sé* (ou *chóu*). Se défendre d'une accusation.

别人告你就愛 | 呈子, *p'iĕt gnîn káo gnî ts'ióu ói sé tch'în tzè*, quelqu'un t'a-t-il accusé, il faut aussitôt y répondre par une pièce de défense.

賜 *Sé* (ou *tsé*). Faire don (un supérieur à un inférieur).

賞 | , *chòng sé*, récompenser, donner libéralement.

勢 *Sé* ou *ché*. Force, autorité, influence.

你逞自己有錢依 | 欺人, *gnî tch'în tsé kì yoū ts'iên ỳ ché k'ī gnîn*, c'est parce que tu es riche que tu te crois permis d'opprimer les gens.

你無錢無 | 唔好打官司, *gnî voû ts'iên voû ché mĝ haò tà kouōn sē*, tu n'as ni argent ni influence, il ne faut pas intenter le procès.

打把 | , *tà pà ché* ou *hí*, faire un petit cadeau, dans l'intention d'en recevoir un plus considérable.

佢過有 | 頭, *kî kouó yoū ché t'eoû*, il a plus d'influence, plus d'autorité.

| 必同佢打官司, *ché pît t'oûng kî tà kouōn sē*, nous sommes obligés, par la force des choses, de faire un procès.

生理時 | 唔好, *siēn lī chê ché mĝ haò*, les circontances ne sont pas bonnes pour le commerce.

視 *Sé*. Regarder.

藐 | 人 ou (鄙 | 人), *miào sé gnîn*, (ou *p'ì sé gnîn*), regarder quelqu'un avec mépris.

字 *Sé*. Lettre, caractère, écrit.

正 | , 草 | , *tchín sé*, *ts'ào sé*, lettres écrites en entier et de forme régulière, caractère cursif.

輩 | , *pí sé*, lettre qui entre dans le nom d'un individu, et qui indique son rang de génération.

丨彙, ou 丨典, *sé loúi* (ou *sé tièn*), dictionnaire.

丨眼, *sé niàn*, locution, sens d'un mot.

丨母, *sé moū*, clefs ou radicaux des caractères chinois.

立丨, *lìp sé*, écrire un billet ou un contrat.

名丨, 丨號, *miâng sé*, *sé haó*, nom d'une boutique, marque.

似 *Sé*. Semblable, comme.

有相丨, *yoū siōng sé*, il y a quelque ressemblance.

SĒ·

舐 *Sē·* (ou *chāi*). Lécher.

狗媽丨佢子, *keòu mâ sē· kiā tzè*, la chienne lèche ses petits.

SÈ·

洗 *Sè·*. Laver, baptiser, effacer, anéantir.

丨衫, *sè· sām*, laver les habits.

丨淨, *sè· ts'iáng*, laver proprement.

領丨, 領過丨, *leāng sè·*, *leāng kouó sè·*, recevoir le baptême (signifie aussi administrer le baptême), avoir reçu le baptême.

付丨, *foú sè·*, administrer le baptême en cas de nécessité, à la place du prêtre ; ondoyer.

丨心, *sè· sīm*, purifier son cœur.

丨一村人, *sè· ŷt ts'oūn gnîn*, raser un village.

SÉ·

細 *Sé·*. Petit, menu, fin.

丨人子, *sé· gnîn tzè*, petit enfant.

丨丨人子, *sé· sé· gnîn tzè*, tout petit enfant.

有粗有丨, *yoū tsē* (ou *tch'oū*) *yoū sé·*, il y en a du gros et du fin.

丨聲講話, *sé· chāng kòng fá*, parler à voix basse.

細茶, *sé· ts'â*, thé de meilleure qualité (dont les feuilles sont plus tendres).

婿 *Sé·* 丨郎, *sé· lông*, gendre.

老妹丨, *laò moé· sé·*, beau-frère (mari de la sœur cadette).

歲 *Sé·* (ou *soúi*). Année, âge.

比我大一丨, *pì ngâi t'aí ŷt sé·*, plus âgé que moi d'une année.

有幾多丨, *yoū kì tō sé·* ? quel âge as-tu ?

到十丨曰幼, *taó chìp sé· yât yoú*, jusqu'à l'âge de dix ans on est enfant; à vingt ans c'est 弱 *nioc*, l'adolescence; à trente ans, on est 壯 *tsóng*, adulte ; à quarante ans, on est 强 *k'iông*, à cinquante ans, on est 艾 *niaí*, à 60 ans, on est 耆 *k'î*, à 70 ans, on est 稀 *hī*, à 80 ans, on est 耋 *tiêt*, à 90 ans, on est 耄 *maò*, à cent ans, on est 悼 *laò*, ou 期頤 *kî hī*.

Sé· 穢丨, *vé· sé·*, sale, sordide.

SĒM

参 *Sēm*. Plante médicinale.

洋丨, 高麗丨, *yông sēm*, *kaō lí sēm*, diverses espèces de *sēm*.

海丨 *hoì sēm*, limace de mer.

SĒN

生 *Sēn.* Naître, engendrer, vivre, produire.

Ce mot ce prononce *sēn* ou *sāng* selon les pays ; et tantôt *sēn* tantôt *sāng*, selon les cas, lesquels varient dans chaque pays. (Voir *sāng* 生).

天主降 |, *t'iēn tchoù kóng sēn*, Dieu s'est fait homme.

門 |, *moûn sēn*, disciple.

一 | 人, *ŷt sēn gnîn*, toute la vie d'un homme.

甥 *Sēn* (ou *sāng*). **外 |**, *ngoé· sēn*, neveu (fils de la sœur).

外 | 女, *ngoé· sēn ǹg*, nièce (fille de la sœur).

焺 *Sēn.* **火 |**, *fò sēn*, étincelle.

星 *Sēn.* Etoile, astre.

| 宿, *sēn sioûc*, étoiles, planètes.

| 屎, *sēn chè*, étoiles filantes.

| 河, *sēn hô*, Voie lactée. (On dit aussi **河溪** *hô haî.*)

北斗 |, *pêt teoù sēn*, étoile polaire.

SÈN

省 *Sèn.* Province, examiner, économiser.

廣東 |, *kouòng toūng sèn*, la province de Canton.

| 城, *sèn chāng*, la capitale de la province.

出 v. **下** v. **上 |**, *tch'oût* v. *hā* v. *chōng sèn*, aller à la capitale de la province (monter, y descendre selon la position).

| 察, *sèn ts'ât*, s'examiner.

| 儉阿子, *sèn k'iáng á tzè*, sois économe.

我 | 倒一個花邊, *ngaî sèn taò ŷt ké· fā piēn*, j'ai économisé une piastre.

SEOŪ

搜 *Seoū.* Fouiller, chercher.

身上 | 出來, *chīn hóng seōu tch'oût loî*, trouvé sur lui en le fouillant.

我身上 | 一個錢唔出, *ngaî chīn hóng seou ŷt ké· tsiên mĝ tch'oût*, je ne trouve pas une sapèque sur moi.

餿 *Seou.* Odeur et goût de ranci.

猪油 | 了, *tchoū yoû seoū liào*, la graisse de porc a pris une odeur de ranci.

茶過夜唔得噲 |, *ts'â koúo yá mĝ têt voé· seoū*, le thé ne peut passer la nuit sans se gâter.

SEOÛ

愁 *Seoû.* S'attrister, s'inquiéter.

憂 | *yoû seoû*, s'attrister, avoir du souci.

唔使 | 麼錢, *mĝ sè seoû mô ts'iên*, il n'y a pas à s'inquiéter du manque d'argent.

你 | 那個, *gnî seoû mâc ké·?* de quoi es-tu triste ?

SEOÚ

瘦 *Seoú.* Maigre, amaigrir.

鴉片烟越食越 |, *ā p'iēn yān yát*

chĭt yăt seoú, plus on fume l'opium, plus on maigrit.

田 | , *t'iên seoú*, la rizière est maigre, sans engrais.

病十日我 | 裡兩斤, *p'iáng chĭp gnĭt ngâi seoú lê· leòng kĭn*, dans une maladie de 10 jours, j'ai maigri de deux livres.

SÊP

澀 *Sêp*. Apre, astringent, pas lisse.

柿子亡熟還係 | , *sē tzè màng sioûc hân hé· sêp*, la nèfle n'est pas assez mûre elle est encore très âpre au goût.

眼珠係 | , *niàn tchoū hé· sêp*, les yeux me picotent.

嗇 *Sêp*. Avare.

吝 | , *lín sêp*, même sens.

澁 *Sêp*. 邋 | , *lâp sêp*, saleté, résidus secs.

SÊT

色 *Sêt*. Couleur, volupté.

淡淡個紅 | , *t'ám t'ám kê· foúng sêt*, couleur rose.

迷 | , *mî sêt*, luxure, volupté.

犯手 | , 男 | , 女 | , *fám choù sêt*, *nâm sêt*, *ng sêt*, commettre le péché solitaire, la sodomie, la fornication.

虱 *Sêt*. Pou, puce.

狗 | , | 媽, *keòu sêt*, *sêt mâ*, puce commune, pou commun.

發 | 媽, *pôt sêt mâ*, avoir des poux.

Sêt. Arrière-petit-fils. | 子, | 女, *sêt tzè*, *sêt ng*, arrière-petit-fils, arrière-petite fille.

塞 *Sêt*. Bouchon, boucher.

酒 | , *tsioù sêt*, bouchon de bouteille à vin.

水 澗 | 等 裡, *choùi kiàn sêt tèn lè·*, le conduit d'eau est obstrué.

骰 *Sêt* (ou *t'eoû*). Dés à jouer.

質 | , *tchĭt sêt*, jeter les dés.

SĪ

西 *Sī*. Occident.

坐東向 | , *ts'ŏ toūng hióng sī*, situe à l'Est et tourné vers l'Guest.

東 | , *toūng sī*, chose, objet quelconque.

犀 *Sī*. Rhinocéros.

水 | 牛, *choùi sī nioû*, hippopotame.

| 角, *sī kôc*, corne de rhinocéros, estimée en médecine.

須 *Sī*. Certes.

必 | 告解, *pĭt sī káo kiaì*, il faut nécessairement se confesser.

需 *Sī*. | 索銀, *sī sôc nioûn*, exiger injustement, extorquer de l'argent.

篩 *Sī* (ou *ts'ī*). Tamis gros, tamiser.

| 米, | 沙, *sī mì*, *sī sā*, tamiser du riz, du sable.

鬚 *Sī*. Barbe, poils, ce qui ressemble à la barbe ; barbillons d'un poisson ; étamines d'une fleur ; vrilles de la vigne ; filaments déliés d'une racine ; houppe, frange, etc.

留 |, *lioû sī*, conserver la barbe.

葡萄藤有 |, *p'oû t'âo t'ên yoū sī*, les sarments de vigne ont des vrilles.

日頭 |, *gnīt t'eoû sī*, les rayons de soleil.

噓 *Sī*. Diminutif qui s'ajoute à certains mots.

笑 | |, *siáo sī sī*, sourire.

繻 *Sī* (ou *soūi*). Effiler, faire de la charpie.

| 豆角, *sī t'eóu kôc*, enlever les fils de haricots.

布 | 絨來, *poú sī yoûng loî*, effiler de la toile, faire de la charpie.

sì

死 *Sì*. Mourir.

| 吊裡, *sì p'ēt lē·*, il est mort.

| 老, *sì laò*, un mort.

我 | 都唔去, *ngâi sì toū mĝ hí*, dût-il m'en coûter la vie, je n'irai pas.

| 都唔甘願, *sì toū mĝ kām nián*, plutôt la mort que d'y consentir.

打 |, *tà sì*, assommer, tuer.

燒 |, *chāo sì*, brûler vif.

跌 |, *tiēt sì*, mourir d'une chute.

sí

四 *sí*. Quatre. | 萬 | 千 | 百 | 十, *sí ván sí ts'iēn sí pâc sí chīp*, 44440.

| 方, *sí fōng*, carré.

絮 *Sí*. Garnir de coton, ouater.

| 綿花 | 勻來, *sí miên fa sí yoûn lôi*, étendre le coton bien également.

| 雞竇, *sí kē· tcóu*, préparer un nid à la poule, en garnissant un panier de paille.

敘 *Sí*. Raconter, tenir une conversation.

| 話 ou 談 |, *sí fá* ou *t'âm sí*, entretien, conversation.

我 | 分明你知, *ngâi sí foūn mîn gnī tī*, je vais t'expliquer clairement.

相 |, *siōng sí*, s'entretenir.

暢 |, *tch'òng sí*, s'égayer par des conversations joyeuses.

序 *Sí*. Ordre, ranger en ordre; préface d'un livre.

次 |, *tsé sí*, ordre.

間房個東西極有次 |, *kiān fông ké· toūng sī k'ìt yoū tsé sí*, tout est bien en ordre dans la chambre.

| 齒, *sí tchè*, ranger par ordre d'âge.

唔知那人過老兩儕 | 一下齒來, *mĝ tī màn gnîn kouó laò leòng sâ sí ŷt há tchè loî*, je ne sais pas quel est le plus âgé de vous deux, dites votre âge, mettez-vous selon votre âge.

簿 |, 書 |, *p'oū sí, choū sí*, préface de registre, de livre.

緒 *Sí*. Ordre, succession, suite.

你講個話麼頭麼 |, *gnî kòng ké· fá mô t'eôu mô sí*, ce que tu dis n'a pas de suite.

SIĀ

Siā. Déployer, étendre.

鵰子丨開翼, *tiāo tzè siā k'oī ўt*, l'oiseau déploie ses ailes.

些 *Siā*. Peu. (Plus vulg. *siām*, *voir* ce mot).

丨小事情 *siā siaò sé ts'în*, c'est une bagatelle.

SIÂ

斜 *Siâ*. Incliné, dévier, obliquer.

日頭丨帛𡍲, *gnĭt t'eoû siâ p'ĕt lê·* le soleil est au couchant.

丨線, 丨布, *siâ sién, siâ poú*, diagonale, toile rayée en diagonale.

大路丨阿左手去, *t'aí loú siâ á tsò choù hí*, la grande route oblique à gauche.

邪 *Siâ*. Dépravé, mauvais.

丨念頭, *siâ niám t'côu*, pensées deshonnêtes.

丨淫, *siâ ŷm*, luxure, action obscène.

丨敎, *siâ káo*, religion perverse, sorcellerie.

講丨話, *kòng siâ fá*, dire des paroles obscènes.

SIÀ

寫 *Sià*. Ecrire.

丨字, *sià sé*, écrire.

丨信, *sià sín*, écrire une lettre.

丨田, *sià t'iên*, hypothéquer une rizière.

SIÁ

卸 *Siá*. Quitter, se dissiper.

丨白衣主日, *siá p'ăc ȳ tchoù gnĭt*, le Dimanche de Quasimodo (déposition des habits blancs).

賊子打丨𡍲, *ts'ĕt tzè tà siá lé·*, les brigands ont été dispersés.

官丨任, *kouōn siá ým*, le mandarin quitte sa charge.

瀉 *Siá*. Couler, diarrhée.

丨肚, *siá toù*, avoir la diarrhée.

止唔倒丨, *tjè mĝ taò siá*, ne pouvoir arrêter la diarrhée.

SIÂC

䳭 *Siâc*. 鴉丨, *a siâc*, pie.

錫 *Siâc*. Etain.

打丨, *tà siâc*, travailler l'étain.

丨壺, *siâc foû*, bidon, cruchon en étain.

惜 *Siâc (sĭt)*. Aimer, caresser.

丨細人, *siâc sé· gnîn*, aimer les enfants, les gâter, les caresser.

得人丨, *tĕt gnîn siâc*, aimable.

SIĀM

些 *Siām (siā)*. Peu, bagatelle.

一嘘, *siām sī*, tant soit peu, quelque peu.

丨嘘有那個病佢就唔肯做事, *siām sī yoū māc ké· p'iáng kî ts'ioú mĝ hèn tsó ché·*, dès qu'il est tant soit peu malade, il ne veut pas travailler.

SIÂM

暹 *Siâm.* | 羅國, *siâm lô kouĕt,* le royaume de Siam.

SIĀNG

腥 *Siāng.* Mauvaise odeur comme celle du poisson et du chien.

魚,狗,蛞,咁多都|個, *nĝ, keoù, kouài, àn tō toū siāng ké·*, le poisson, le chien, la grenouille, tout cela a cette odeur.

SIÀNG

醒 *Siàng.* Etre éveillé, sortir de l'ivresse, sortir de l'ignorance, de l'inadvertance.

睡|, *choé· siàng,* se réveiller.

|睡, *siàng choé·*, dormir peu profondément.

我講|你知, *ngâi kòng siàng gnî tī,* je vais t'expliquer clairement.

食醉還唔|, *chĭt tsouí hân m̂g siàng,* il n'est pas encore sorti de son ivresse.

SIÁNG

姓 *Siáng.* Nom générique de famille.

你|那個, *gnî siáng mâc ké·* ? comment t'appelles-tu (*familier*)?

貴| *v.* **高|** *v.* **尊|**, *koúi siáng, v. kāo siáng, v. tsoūn siáng,* Votre noble nom? (*Politesse.*)

Rép: **小|賴**, *siào siáng Laí,* mon humble nom est Laí.

改|, *koì siáng,* changer de nom.

百|, *pâc siáng,* toutes les familles, le peuple.

SIĀO

消 *Siāo.* Détruire, dissiper, dissoudre.

|滅, *siāo mĕt,* détruire, anéantir.

|化, *siāo fá,* dissoudre, fondre, digérer.

|息, *siāo sĭt,* artifice, truc mécanique.

門肚放|息, *moûn toù fóng siāo sĭt,* mettre un appareil caché dans la porte (pour qu'on ne puisse ouvrir).

硝 *Siāo.* Salpêtre.

朴|, *p'ôc siāo,* même sens.

煎|, *tsiēn siāo,* retirer par la cuisson, le salpêtre de la terre; salpêtrière.

簫 *Siāo.* Sorte de flûte, sifflet.

吹|, *tch'oī siāo,* jouer d'un de ces instruments.

SIÀO

小 *Siào.* Petit, piètre, vil.

|聲講話, *siào chāng kòng fá,* parler à voix basse.

|事, *siào sé,* affaire de peu d'importance.

行|路, *hâng siào loú,* passer par la petite route.

討|, *t'ào siào,* prendre une concubine.

|心, *siào sīm,* attention! attentif, soigneux.

|引, *siào ŷn,* préface d'un livre, préambule.

| 便, *siào p'ién*, terme poli pour dire uriner.

| 茴, *siào fi*, anis.

SIÁO

笑 *Siáo*. Rire.

滯人 |, *tché gnîn siáo*, provoquer le rire, faire rire de soi.

| 嘘嘘, *siáo sī sī*, sourire.

講 |, *kòng siáo*, plaisanter.

得人 | ou 好 |, *tĕt gnîn siáo* ou *haò siáo*, risible, qui porte au rire.

肖 *Siáo*. Ressembler.

妻賢子 |, *ts'ī hién tzè siáo*, quand la femme est sage les enfants le deviennent.

不 | 子, *poŭt siáo tzè*, qui ne ressemble pas à son père (se dit d'un enfant mal élevé).

你學人學得咁恰 |, *gnî hŏc gnîn hŏc tĕt kàn k'ăp siáo*! comme tu sais bien singer le monde!

鞘 *Siáo*. Fourreau en cuir.

刀 | 子, *taō siáo tzè*, fourreau de coutelas.

SIĂP

Siăp. Nom d'une espèce de riz qui se sème un peu plus tard que le riz ordinaire.

蒔 | 子, *ché siăp tzè*, planter ce riz.

楔 *Siăp*. Caler.

桌子唔坪愛 | 穩來, *tsŏc tzè mĝ p'iâng oí siăp voùn loî*, la table n'est pas d'aplomb, il faut la caler.

SIĒN

先 *Siēn*. Avant, auparavant, d'abord, autrefois.

我 | 到兩日, *ngâi siēn táo leòng gnĭt*, je suis arrivé deux jours avant.

我 | 到嘉應州後來上東石, *ngâi siēn táo kā ýn tchoū heóu loî chōng toūng chăc*, je suis d'abord arrivé à la ville de Ka-yn, par après je suis monté à Toung chac.

| 知, *siēn tī*, savoir avant, prophète.

先生, *siēn sēn* (ou *sīn sāng*), plus âgé. Titre que l'on donne à ceux qui exercent une profession libérale; équivaut à maître, monsieur.

| 父, *siēn foú*, feu mon père.

| 理, *siēn lī* (pour 生理 *sēn lī*), (*litt.*) raison de vivre, c.-à-d. moyen d'existence, et plus particulièrement le commerce.

做 | 理, *tsó siēn lī*, faire le commerce.

| 理唔好, *siēn lī mĝ hào*, le commerce ne va pas.

仙 *Siēn*. Immortel, génie.

| 人, *siēn gnîn*, génie, fée.

| 姑, | 媽, *siēn koū, siēn mâ*, sorcier, sorcière qui se chargent de prophétiser.

問 |, *moún siēn*, demander, appeler le prophète.

| 人粄, *siēn gnîn pàn*, espèce de gâteau de gélatine rafraîchissante, fait avec du froment et certaines herbes.

鮮 *Siēn*. Frais, récent, limpide.

新 | 魚, *sīn siēn nĝ*, poisson frais.

新丨猪肉, *sīn siēn tchoū nioūc*, porc frais.

丨水, *siēn choùi*, eau limpide.

SIÈN

Sièn Fermer à la targette.

門丨等來, *moûn sièn tèn loî*, ferme la porte à la targette (ou avec le clou).

癬 *Sièn* Dartre.

發丨, *pôt sièn*, avoir des dartres.

鮮 *Sièn*. Eclat de bois, fragment.

手上撳倒一個丨子, *choù hóng toún tào ŷt ké· sièn tzè*, j'ai attrapé un éclat de bois dans la main.

選 *Sièn*. Choisir.

丨過來; *sièn koúo loî*, choisir, trier.

宗徒係耶穌親自丨個, *tsoūng t'oû hé· yâ sē ts'īn tsé sièn ké·*, les Apôtres ont été choisis par Jésus lui-même.

天主揀丨童貞女爲毋降生, *t'iēn tchoù kìan sièn t'oûng tchīn ngò vî moû kóng sēn*, Dieu a choisi une vierge pour mère.

SIÉN

鐁 *Sién*. 丨雞, *sién kē·*, chapon.

線 *Sién*. Fil à coudre, fil composé de plusieurs brins ; ligne.

絲丨, 棉丨, *sē sién, miên sién*, fil de soie, de coton.

鐵丨, 銅丨, *t'iĕt sién, t'oûng sién*, fil de fer, de cuivre.

打丨 *tà sién*, tirer une ligne au cordeau encré, ou bien, faire des moulures avec le rabot.

SIĔT

洩 *Siĕt*. Jet, s'échapper en jet, seringue.

水丨阿起, *choùi siĕt ā hì*, l'eau a rejailli en jet.

丨筒, *siĕt t'oûng*, seringue.

丨氣, *siĕt hí*, l'air, le gaz s'échappe.

SIET

雪 Neige.

落丨, *lŏc siĕt*, il neige.

丨融帛裡, *siĕt yoûng p'ĕt lè·*, la neige est fondue.

棉花丨, *miên fā siĕt*, neige qui tombe en flocon.

丨豆, *siĕt t'eóu*, petits pois d'automne.

丨粉, *siĕt foùn*, espèce de poudre dont on fait une drogue rafraîchissante.

泄 *Siĕt*. Dévoiement, diarrhée.

又嘔又丨, *yóu coù yóu siĕt*, il a des vomissements et de la diarrhée.

SĪM

心 *Sīm*. Cœur, conscience, affection, application de l'intelligence ou de la volonté ; centre.

耶穌聖丨, *yâ sē chín sīm*, le Saint Cœur de Jésus.

兩個人同丨, *leòng ké· gnîn t'oûng sīm*, ils sont tous les deux unis de cœur, ou de volonté.

放｜, *fóng sīm*, bannir toute inquiétude.

｜口唔對, *sīm k'coù mĝ touí*, parler contre sa pensée.

我｜肝, *ngā sīm kōn*, la moitié de moi-même.

用｜, *yoúng sīm*, avec application.

留｜, *lioū sīm*, faire attention, graver dans sa mémoire.

小｜, *siaò sīm*, faire attention, prendre garde.

有｜麼｜, *yoū sīm, mô sīm*, avoir ; n'avoir pas bonne intention, pas de générosité, d'affection.

人唔齊｜, *gnîn mĝ ts'ê· sīm*, ils ne s'entendent pas.

你｜忒大, *niā sīm t'iĕt t'aí*, tu portes tes visées trop loin.

中｜, *toúng sīm* (pour *tchoúng sīm*), le milieu, le centre.

菜｜,樹｜,車｜, *ts'oí sīm, choú sīm, tch'ā sīm*, le cœur d'un légume, d'un arbre, l'essieu d'une roue.

SĪN

薪臼, *sīn k'ioū (vulg. sīm k'ioū)*, bru. (*Litt.* bois et mortier, ainsi appelée parce que c'est elle qui est chargée de couper le bois de chauffage et de blanchir le riz au mortier.)

辛 *Sīn*. Amer ; fatigue.

｜苦, *sīn k'où*, souffrances, fatigues, pénible.

艱｜, *kiān sīn*, difficile, ardu, ennuyeux.

新 *Sīn*. Nouveau, récent, neuf.

｜神父, *sīn chîn foú*, un nouveau Père.

｜教友, *sīn kaó yoū*, néophyte.

｜衫, ｜鞋, *sīn sām, sīn haî*, habit neuf, souliers neufs.

｜聞, *sīn voûn*, nouvelle, journal.

從｜ (ou 重｜), *ts'ioúng sīn*, (ou *tch'oûng sīn*), renouveler, à neuf.

｜鮮, *sīn siēn*, frais, récent (se dit des viandes fraîches).

SÌN

訊 *Sìn*. Interroger judiciairement.

官傳｜, *koūon tch'ôn sìn*, le mandarin cite à comparaître pour être interrogé.

候｜, *héou sìn*, attendre l'interrogatoire.

迅 *Sìn*. Vite, prompt.

｜速, *sìn choŭc*, très vite, promptement.

SÍN

信 *Sín*. Croire, avoir confiance, lettre, nouvelle.

｜天主, *sín t'iēn tchoù*, croire en Dieu.

｜德, *sín têt*, vertu de Foi.

我｜你, *ngâi sín gnî*, j'ai confiance en toi.

我唔｜唐人個藥, *ngaî mĝ sín t'ông gnîn ké· yŏc*, je n'ai pas confiance aux remèdes des Chinois.

我｜唔來, *ngaî sín mĝ loî*, je ne puis y croire.

搭｜, *tâp sín*, envoyer une lettre, annoncer une nouvelle.

寫一封｜, *sìa ŷt foūng sín*, écrire une lettre.

人｜, *gnîn sín*, arsenic.

性 *Sín*. Nature, caractère.

｜情, *sín ts'în*, même sens.

人｜, 天主｜, *gnîn sín, t'iēn tchoù sín*, nature humaine, nature divine.

人｜情難改, *gnîn sín ts'în nân koì*, on corrige difficilement son caractère.

硬｜個人, *ngáng sín ké· gnîn*, homme d'un caractère dur, entêté,

硬｜個樹, *ngáng sín ké· choú*, bois très dur.

｜教, *sín káo*, la loi naturelle.

SIÔC

削 *Siôc*. Tailler, râcler.

｜筆, *siôc pît*, tailler un crayon.

｜筷子, *siôc k'ouái tzè*, fabriquer des bâtonnets.

刮｜人個錢, *kouât siôc gnîn ké· ts'iên*, attirer à soi l'argent des autres.

SIŌNG

相 *Siōng*. Réciproque, mutuel, d'accord.

｜和, ｜愛, *siōng fô, siōng oí*, s'aimer d'un amour réciproque.

我同佢｜好, *ngaî t'oūng kì siōng hào*, je suis en bons termes avec lui.

兩個屋｜連, *lcòng ké· vouc siōng liên*, les deux maisons sont attenantes.

唔｜同 (v. 似), *mĝ siōng t'oûng* (v. *sé*), ne pas se ressembler.

｜幫 (ou 襄), *siōng pōng*, aider, s'entr'aider.

｜生, *siōng sēn*, se mêler.

油同酒唔｜生, *youû t'oûng tsiòu mĝ siōng sēn*, l'huile ne se mèle pas avec le vin.

箱 *Siōng*. Boîte, caisse, malle.

風｜, *foūng siōng*, soufflet de forge.

廂 *Siōng*. Aile de bâtiment.

｜房, *siōng fòng*, chambres de côté.

鑲 *Siōng*. Insérer, incruster, enchâsser, relier.

｜骨, *siōng koūt*, incruster de l'ivoire.

｜聖像, *siòng chín siông*, enchâsser une image.

｜牙齒, *siōng ngâ tchè*, se mettre un râtelier.

｜鞋, *siōng haî*, souliers garnis de brodures.

｜馬蹄, *siōng mā t'aî*, ferrer un cheval.

SIÔNG

墻 *Siông* (ou *ts'iông*). Mur, muraille.

舂｜, *tchoung siông*, élever un mur en foulant.

｜角邊, *siông kôc piēn*, au coin du mur.

｜脚下, *siông kiôc hā*, au pied du mur.

結｜, *kiēt siông*, élever un mur en maçonnerie.

詳 *Siông*. Examiner clairement

｜敘, *siông sí*, expliquer à fond, raconter en détail.

丨文, *siông voûn*, relation envoyée à un supérieur.

講得丨明, *kòng têt siông mîn*, vous parlez très clairement.

SIÒNG

想 *Siòng*. Penser, désirer.

丨唔倒, *siòng mĝ tào*, ne pouvoir se rappeler.

你丨一下, *gnî siòng ŷt há*, réfléchis un peu.

丨差, *siòng ts'ā*, se tromper.

丨做生理, *siòng tsó siēn lī*, désirer faire le commerce.

丨食飯, *siòng chĭt fán*, désirer manger, avoir faim.

丨嘔, *siòng eòu*, avoir envie de vomir.

唔我丨發財, *ngaî mĝ siòng fât tsoî*, je ne désire pas devenir riche.

我丨同神父講两句話, *ngaî siòng t'oûng chîn foú kòng leòng kí fá*, je voudrais dire deux mots au Père.

SIÓNG

相 *Sióng*. Aider.

宰丨, *tsaì sióng*, ministre de l'Empereur.

丨公, *sióng koūng*, terme honorifique pour désigner un serviteur ou le fils de celui à qui, ou de qui l'on parle. On appelle ainsi les séminaristes.

匠 *Sióng*. Ouvrier, fabricant.

木丨師傅, *moûc sióng sē foú*, menuisier.

泥丨, *naî sióng*, maçon.

象 *Sióng*. Eléphant.

丨鼻, *sióng p'í*, trompe d'éléphant.

丨牙, *sióng ngâ*, ivoire.

像 *Sióng*. Image, figure.

石丨, *chăc sióng*, statue.

映丨, *yàng sióng*, photographier.

聖丨, *chín sióng*, sainte image, image religieuse. (Voir 像 *ts'ióng*).

SIŌU

羞 *Siōu*. Honte, pudeur.

全麼丨恥, *ts'iên mô siōu tchè*, absolument sans pudeur.

丨死你, *siōu sì gnî*, honte à toi!

丨死人, *siōu sì gnîn*, à faire mourir de honte.

遮丨, *tchā siōu*, couvrir, cacher sa honte, c.-à-d. les parties honteuses de l'homme.

修 *Siōu*. Orner, ajuster, réparer, bâtir.

丨道院, *siōu t'áo yán*, monastère.

丨道, *siōu t'áo*, s'exercer aux vertus, perfectionner sa voie, ses actions.

隱 ou 獨丨, *yoùn* ou *toŭc siōu*, moine, ermite.

丨田坎, *siōu t'iên k'àm*, râtisser le bord d'une rizière.

丨路, *siōu loú*, réparer une route, la paver.

SIÔU

囚 *Siôu*. Emprisonner.

丨犯, *siôu fám*, criminel emprisonné.

SIÒU

扨 *Siòu.* Fouetter, donner un coup de verge.

丨馬, *siòu mā,* donner un coup de verge au cheval.

SIOÚ

秀 *Sioú.* Fleurir ; beau, agréable.

文武丨才, *voûn voū sioú ts'oî,* bachelier civil et militaire.

丨氣, 丨雅, 丨嫩, *sióu hí, sióu ngā, sióu noún,* joli, élégant, délicat.

繡 *Sioú.* 錦丨, *kìm sióu,* broder.

丨花, *sióu fā,* même sens.

SIOŬC

俗 *Sioŭc.* Coutume, vulgaire.

風丨唔好, *foūng sioŭc mĝ haò,* les mœurs ne sont pas bonnes.

丨語 ou 話, *sioŭc nī* ou *fá,* langage vulgaire, proverbe, dicton.

世丨, *ché sioŭc,* le vulgaire, le monde.

續 *Sioŭc.* Continuer, suivre.

丨絃, *sioŭc hiên,* rattacher la corde: se remarier après la mort de sa femme.

陸陸丨丨, *lioŭc lioŭc sioŭc sioŭc,* sans interruption.

繼丨人個位, *kí sioŭc gnîn ké· ví,* succéder à quelqu'un.

SIOÛC

熟 *Sioûc (choŭc).* Mûr.

漚丨, *eoú sioûc,* conserver jusqu'à maturité.

桃子唔丨, *t'âo tzè mĝ sioûc,* les pêches ne sont pas mûres.

粟 *Sioûc.* Millet.

高粱丨, *kāo leông sioûc,* sorgho.

包丨, *pāo sioûc,* maïs.

狗尾丨, *keoù mī sioûc,* panais.

鴨脚丨, ou 三角丨, *âp kiôc sioûc,* ou *sām kôc sioûc,* sarrasin, blé noir.

宿 *Sioûc.* Etoile; habiter.

星丨, *sēn sioûc,* étoile.

丨夜, *sioûc yá,* passer la nuit.

尋店丨夜, *ts'îm tiám sioûc yá,* chercher une auberge pour y passer la nuit.

今晡夜那里歇丨, *kīn poū yá naí lī hiêt sioûc ?* où allons-nous passer la nuit ce soir ?

SIOÚNG

誦 *Sioúng.* Réciter, lire à haute voix.

丨經, *sioúng kīn,* réciter des prières.

丨書, *sioúng choū,* lire à haute voix.

訟 *Sioúng.* Contester, plaider, accuser.

與詞起丨, *hín tsè hì sioúng,* en venir à la dispute.

自丨自呈, *tsé sioúng tsé tch'în,* s'accuser soi-même, se trahir.

頌 *Sioúng.* Louer.

丨揚, *sioúng yông,* louer, proclamer les louanges.

SĬP

夕 *Sĭp*. Soir. **朝 |**, *tchāo sĭp*, le matin et le soir.

集 *Sĭp*. Réunir, ensemble.
齊 |, *ts'ê· sĭp*, réunis au complet.

習 *Sĭp*. S'exercer, s'habituer, s'adonner, choisir.
| 生 理, *sĭp siēn lī*, s'adonner au commerce.
學 |, *hŏc sĭp*, s'exercer, s'adonner à l'étude.
| 慣 (ou **慣 |**), *sĭp koúan* (ou *koúan sĭp*), s'habituer, s'exercer.
| 好 地 方, *sĭp hào t'í fōng*, choisir un bon endroit.
好 馬 難 |, *hào mā nân sĭp*, un bon cheval est difficile à trouver.

SĬT

席 *Sĭt*. Festin.
酒 |, *tsiòu sĭt*, même sens.
辦 |, *p'án sĭt*, préparer un festin.
唔 成 |, *mĝ chāng sĭt*, mauvais dîner qui ne mérite pas le nom de *sĭt*.

籍 *Sĭt*. Registre, rôle du cens.
書 |, *choū sĭt*, livres en général.
入 法 國 個 |, *gnĭp fâp kouēt ké· sĭt*, se faire naturaliser Français.
嘉 應 州 人 上 平 遠 入 |, *kā ȳn tchoū gnîn chōng p'în yàn gnĭp sĭt*, un habitant de Ka yn tchou s'est fait mettre au nombre des habitants du P'în yan.

SÎT

昔 *Sît*. **| 日**, *gnĭt sît*, autrefois.

瑟 *Sît*. **琴 |**, *k'îm sît*, espèce d'instrument à cordes.

惜 *Sît*. Epargner, aimer, prendre soin.
| 錢, *sît ts'iên*, économiser les sapèques.
愛 | 父 母, *oí sît foú moū*, aimer ses parents.
憐 | 病 人, *lîn sît p'iáng gnîn*, prendre soin des malades (voir *siâc*).

息 *Sît*. Tranquille, apaiser, gain.
平 |, *p'în sît*, tranquille, calme.
舊 年 大 家 亂，今 年 大 家 平 |, *k'ioú niân t'ái kā lóu, kīn niân t'ái kā p'în sît*, l'année passée la population était en révolution, cette année elle est très tranquille.
止 | (ou **| 止**), *tjè sît* (ou *sît tjè*), se reposer.
| 止 安 所, *sît tjè ōn sò*, qu'il repose en paix.
裡 生 理 麼 耶 個 出 |, *yà siēn lī mô mâc ké· tch'oût sît*, ce commerce n'est pas très lucratif.
利 | 大, *lí sît t'ái*, le profit est considérable.
小 |, *siāo sît*, mécanique secrète, cachée.
門 上 個 消 | 壞 帛 裡, *moûn hóng ké· siāo sît fái p'ĕt lê·*, le secret de la porte est abîmé.
佢 走 好 久 麼 信 |, *kî tseòu haò*

kioù mô sín sĭt, il est parti depuis longtemps et n'a pas donné de ses nouvelles.

聖堂下來往人日日不｜, *chín t'ông hā loî vōng gnîn gnĭt gnĭt poŭt sĭt*, à la chapelle, les allants et venants ne cessent pas.

媳 *Sĭt*. Bru.

｜婦, *sĭt foú*, même sens.

令｜, *lín sĭt*, votre bru (*politesse*).

熄 *Sĭt*. Eteindre.

火打｜佢, *fô tà sĭt kî*, éteins le feu.

噴｜, *p'oūn sĭt*, éteindre en soufflant.

悉 *Sĭt*. Savoir.

明｜, *mîn sĭt*, savoir clairement, comprendre.

裡個人我熟｜, *ỳ ké· gnîn ngaî choŭc sĭt*, je connais très bien cet homme.

詢｜, *soún sĭt*, s'informer.

我詢｜佢緣由, *ngaî soún sĭt kiā yân yoû*, je vais lui demander ses raisons.

領｜一切, *leāng sĭt ŷt ts'ièt*, j'ai tout bien compris (dans une réponse à une lettre).

你事我早都耬｜, *niā sé ngaî tsào toū lcoù sĭt*, je connais déjà ton affaire par ouï-dire.

蟋 *Sĭt*. ｜蟀, *sĭt soŭt*, grillon (vulgairement 草｜, *ts'ào sĭt* ou *ts'ào tsĭt* selon les pays).

滴 *Sĭt* (pour *tĭt*). Peu.

｜扐, *sĭt pà*, un peu.

一｜, *ŷt sĭt*, une goutte, une larme.

SŌ

蓑 *Sō*. ｜衣, *sō ȳ*, espèce de manteau fait avec des feuilles de 松樹, *ts'ioûng choú*. On s'en sert à la campagne contre la pluie.

梭 *Sō*. Navette de tisserand.

唆 *Sō*. Exciter.

挑｜, *t'iāo sō*, qui sème la discorde.

SÒ

所 *Sò*. Lieu, endroit, pronom relatif, qui, que, lequel.

｜在, *sò ts'ái*, endroit, lieu.

公｜, *koūng sò*, lieu de réunion publique.

安｜, *ōn sò*, lieu de repos (style chr.)

天主無｜不在, *t'iēn tchoù voû sò poŭt ts'ái*, Dieu est partout.

無｜不爲, *voû sò poŭt vî*, il n'y a rien qu'il ne fasse, il est capable de tout.

你｜講個話, *gnî sò kòng ké· fá*, les paroles que tu as dites.

｜以, *sò ȳ*, c'est pourquoi.

—費, *sò fí*, argent de voyage, dépenses en général.

鎖 *Sò*. Cadenas, serrure, cadenasser.

一把｜, *ŷt pà sò*, un cadenas.

｜頭, *sò t'eôu*, le cadenas tout entier

｜鬚, *sò sī*, la partie rentrante d'un cadenas chinois.

｜匙, *sò chê*, la clef.

SÔC

索 *Sôc*. Corde, ficelle.

一條|, *ŷt t'iâo sôc*, une corde.

打|, *tà sôc*, faire une corde.

|斷帛裡, *sôc t'ōn p'ĕt lĕ·*, la corde est rompue.

三股|, *sām koù sôc*, corde composée de trois torons.

SŌI

衰 *Soī*. Déchu, misérable, faible. Dans la bouche des Chinois, ce mot semble être l'expression de toutes les calamités : pauvreté, misère, honte, insuccès, etc.

打官師打|, *tà koūon sē tà soī*, en faisant son procès, il s'est appauvri, ou bien, s'est rendu ridicule, ou, n'a pas réussi (selon les circonstances).

講|人, *kòng soī gnîn*, ridiculiser quelqu'un, dire toutes sortes de mal de lui.

SOÍ

歲 *Soí*. Agé, âge. Voir *sé·*.

賽 *Soí*. Concourir.

|馬, *soí mā*, faire la course aux chevaux.

|那人過嗜, *soí màn gnîn koúo voć·*, concourir au plus habile.

SŌN

酸 *Sōn*. Aigre, acide, aigri.

|酯, *sōn tsé*, vinaigre.

酒|裡帛, *tsioù sōn p'ĕt lĕ·*, le vin a tourné à l'aigre.

|味, *sōn mí*, saveur acide.

漚|, *coú sōn*, aigri par le temps.

SÓN

算 *Són*. Calculer, compter, considérer.

一學, *són hŏc*, mathématiques.

|盤, *són p'ân*, abaque, machine à calculer.

打|盤, *tà són p'ân*, calculer sur l'abaque.

裡個錢麼|, *yà ké· ts'iên mô són*, cette sapèque ne compte pas.

都|好, *toū són hào*, c'est encore bien comme cela.

好打|, *hào tà són*, tu peux commencer, agir, entreprendre.

蒜 *Són*. Ail.

|頭, *són t'eoû*, tête d'ail.

|仁, *són ŷn*, gousse d'ail.

SŌNG

桑 *Sōng*. |樹, *sōng choú*, mûrier.

霜 *Sōng*. Gelée blanche.

露水|, *loú choùi sōng*, grosse rosée d'automne.

喪 *Sōng*. Deuil, funérailles.

居|, *kī sōng*, être en deuil (au moment des funérailles).

做|事, *tsó sōng sé*, faire les cérémonies de l'enterrement.

SÒNG

喪 *Sọng*. Prodigue, perdre.

我麼咁｜, *ngaî mô àn sòng*, je ne suis pas si prodigue, si dépensier.

｜帛裡, *sòng p'ĕt lê·*, perdre son œuvre, c'est perdu, c'est dommage !

爽 *Sòng*. **｜快**, *sòng k'oúai*, heureux, à l'aise.

地方咁涼｜, *t'í fōng àn leōng sòng*, l'endroit est assez frais et agréable.

SÔT

刷 *Sôt*. Brosse, brosser.

鞋拿來｜淨, *haî na loî sôt ts'iáng*, brosse proprement les souliers.

SOÛC

縮 *Soûc*. Se rétrécir, se raccourcir.

布一洗噲｜佽, *poú ŷt sè· voé· soûc t'sioū*, la toile se rétrécit par le lavage.

你脚｜佽來, *nia kiôc soûc ts'ioū loî*, retire tes jambes.

SOŪI

雖 *Soūi*. Quoique, bien que, supposons que.

｜然有病, *soūi yân yoū p'iáng*, quoiqu'il soit malade.

繻 *Souī* (ou *sī*). Effiler (Voir *sī*).

SOÛI

隨 *Soûi*. Selon, se conformer à.

｜時, *soûi chê*, selon les circonstances.

｜意, *soûi ý*, volontiers, comme vous voudrez.

｜便, *soûi p'ién*, à votre guise, vaille que vaille.

｜後還有來過, *soûi heóu hân yoū loî koúo*, par après, il est encore revenu.

SOÙI

髓 *Soùi* (ou *soì*). Cervelle.

腦｜, *nào soùi* (vulg. *nào chè*), même sens.

SOÚI

歲 *Soúi* (ou *sói* ou *sé·*), année, âge. Voir *sé·*.

碎 *Soúi*. En menus morceaux.

打｜切｜, *tà soúi, ts'iĕt soúi*, réduire en menus morceaux ; couper en petits morceaux.

｜銀, *soúi nioûn*, menus morceaux d'argent.

玻璃｜, *pō lî soúi*, débris de verre.

遂 *Soúi*. **｜意**, *soúi ý*, qui convient, de son gré, à souhait.

你做個文章我唔｜意, *gnî tsó ké· voûn tchōng ngaî mĝ soúi ý*, la composition littéraire que tu viens de faire n'est pas de mon goût.

SOŪN

孫 *Soūn*. Petit-fils, descendants.

｜子, **｜女**, *soūn tzè*, *soūn ǹg*, petit-fils, petite-fille (enfants du fils).

外｜, **外｜女**, *ngoé· soūn, ngoé· soūn ǹg*, petit-fils, petite-fille (enfants de la fille).

姪 |, *tch'ĭt soūn*, petit-fils des frères (ligne masculine).

子 |, *tzè soūn*, descendants en général.

SOÛN

旬 *Soûn*. Espace de 10 jours, 10 ans, etc.

一個月分上中下 |, *ŷt ké· gnĕt foūn chóng tchōung há soûn*, un mois se divise en trois dizaines, la première, celle du milieu, la dernière.

巡 *Soûn*. Examiner, inspecter.

| **查**, *soûn ts'â*, même sens.

存 *Soûn*. Garder, conserver.

| **銀**, | **穀**, *soûn nioûn*, *soûn koŭc*, conserver de l'argent, du riz.

| **起來**, *soûn hì loî*, conserve-le.

SOÙN

筍 *Soùn*. Jeunes pousses de bambous ou d'arbres.

竹 |, *tchoŭc soùn*, pousse de bambou.

禾 |, *vô soùn*, espèce de plante aquatique dont on mange la tige.

濽 |, *ts'án soùn*, pousser des rejetons.

榫 *Soùn*. Tenon.

| **頭**, *soùn t'eôu*, même sens.

鑿眼好榫 |, *ts'ŏc niàn haò tcóu soùn*, faire un trou avec le ciseau pour y adapter le tenon.

SOÚN

遜 **謙** |, *k'iâm soún*, humble, humilité.

SOŪNG

雙 *Soūng*. Double, une paire.

| **手**, | **脚**, *soūng choù*, *soūng kiŏc*, les deux mains, les deux pieds.

一 | **鞋**, *ŷt soūng haî*, une paire de souliers.

| **關語**, *soūng kouān nī*, paroles à double sens.

鬆 *Soūng*. Relâché, peu serré.

寬 |, *k'ōn soūng*, même sens.

放 |, *fóng soūng*, desserrer.

地方咁 | **容**, *t'í fōng àn soūng yoûng*, l'endroit est assez vaste, on y est au large.

SOÙNG

搡 *Soùng*. Pousser.

一個人挷一個人 |, *ŷt ké· gnîn pāng ŷt ké· gnîn soùng*, il y en a un qui tire et un qui pousse.

| **門**, *soùng moûn*, pousser la porte.

莫 | **人**, *mŏc soùng gnîn*, ne nous pousse donc pas.

| **人跌**, *soùng gnîn tiĕt*, faire tomber quelqu'un en le poussant.

SOÚNG

送 *Soúng*. Offrir, faire un cadeau, accompagner.

| **禮物**, *soúng lī voŭt*, offrir des présents.

我麼秣個 | **神父**, *ngâi mô mă: ké· soúng chîn foú*, je n'ai rien à offrir au Père.

| **聖體**, *soúng chín t'ì*, donner, porter la Communion.

| 人去, *soúng gnîn hí*, accompagner quelqu'un, le reconduire.

| 葬, *soúng tsóng*, aller à l'enterrement, enterrer.

唔使錢我 | 别你, *mĝ sè ts'iên ngaî soúng poūn gnî*, je ne veux pas d'argent, je t'en fais cadeau.

T'Ā

他 *T'a*. Lui, elle, il (employé dans les livres seulement). *Voyez kî* 佢.

TÀ

打 *Tà*. Battre, frapper de quelque manière que ce soit; s'emploie dans une foule de sens que l'usage apprendra.

| 死人, | 壞人, *tà sì gnîn, tà fái gnîn*, tuer, blesser quelqu'un.

| 鐵, | 銅, *tà t'iĕt, tà t'oúng*, travailler au marteau le fer, le cuivre.

| 油, *tà yoû*, puiser de l'huile, en acheter en détail.

| 理, *tà lī*, gérer une affaire, s'occuper de.

| 算, *tà són*, commencer, se mettre à l'œuvre.

| 帮你, *tà pōng gnî*, je vous prie, faites-moi l'obligeance.

| 早, *tà tsào*, dès le matin.

| 重重 (ou 長長) *tà tch'oúng tch'oúng* (ou *tch'ông tch'ông*), se balancer, balançoire.

| 退累, *tà t'oúi louí*, marcher à reculons.

| 眺望, *tà tiáo móng*, faire le guet.

百 | 百人都有, *pâc tà pâc gnîn toū yoū*, il y avait bien une centaine d'hommes.

T'ĂC

笛 *T'ăc*. Flûte.

吹 |, *tch'oī t'ăc*, jouer de la flûte.

| 鼓手, *t'ăc koù choù*, joueurs de flûte.

糴 *T'ăc*. Acheter des grains.

| 穀 | 豆, *t'ăc koŭc, t'ăc t'éou*, acheter du riz, des haricots.

T'ÂC

搭 *T'âc*. Attacher, lier.

捉倒個賊 | 等裡, *tsôc tào ké ts'ĕt t'âc tèn ê*, le voleur que l'on a pris est attaché.

| 黃獐, *t'âc vông kiāng*, attraper un chevreuil au lacet.

TĀI

低 *Tāi*. Bas, peu élevé.

東石地方過高嘉應州過 |, *toūng chăc t'í fōng koúo kāo kā ýn tchoū koúo tāi*, le pays de Toung-chac est plus élevé, la ville de Ka yn est plus basse.

| 一寸, | 一丈, *tāi ŷt ts'óun, tāi ŷt tch'óng*, plus bas d'un pouce; d'un *tch'óng* (10 pieds).

T'ĀI

弟 *T'āi* (*t'í*). 老 |, *laò t'āi*, frère puîné.

| 賴, *t'āi laí*, esclave, domestique acheté.

當 | 賴, *tōng t'aī laí*, être esclave.

T'AÎ

蹄 *T'aî*. Sabot de cheval.

馬｜，牛｜, *mā t'aî, niôu t'aî*, sabot de cheval, de bœuf.

洋｜箄, *yông t'aî pāi*, espèce de maillet long et plat, à l'usage des maçons.

馬發｜, *mā fât t'aî*, le cheval rue.

啼 *T'aî*. Chant du coq.

雞｜, *kē· t'aî*, le coq chante.

雞｜裡就上身, *kē· t'aî lê· ts'ióu hóng chīn*, se lever au chant du coq.

TAÌ

抵 *Taì* (ou *tì*). Couvrir, cacher.

看唔倒樹子｜等裡, *k'ón mĝ taò choúi tzè taì tèn ê·*, je ne peux pas voir, les arbres me cachent la vue.

傘子驚去來｜日頭, *tchā tzè k'iāng hí loî taì gnĭt t'eoû*, prend ton parapluie pour te garantir du soleil.

底 *Taì*. Bas, fond, fondement, surface inférieure.

打唔倒｜, *tà mĝ taò taì*, on ne peut atteindre le fond.

鞋｜, *haî taì*, semelle de soulier.

｜下, *taì hā*, dessous.

放阿桌｜下起, *fóng á tsôc taì hā hì*, mettre sous la table.

裡件事根｜我都明白, *ỳ k'ián sé kēn taì ngâi toū mîn p'ĕt*, je connais l'origine et le fond de cette affaire.

T'ÀI

癩 *T'ài*. Lèpre.

發｜, *pôt t'aì*, avoir la lèpre.

TAÍ

戴 *Taí*. Porter sur la tête.

｜帽, *taí máo*, porter le chapeau.

｜頂, *taí tàng*, porter un globule ou un bouton d'honneur.

帶 *Taí*. Ceinture, attache, porter un objet sur soi, conduire avec soi une personne ou une chose.

褲頭｜, *foú t'eôu taí*, ceinture de pantalon.

襪｜, *mât taí*, jarretière.

草鞋｜, *ts'aò haî taí*, attaches de sandale.

｜來，｜去, *taí loî, taí hí*, apporter, emporter.

｜轉來｜轉去, *taí tchòn loî, taí tchòn hí*, rapporter, remporter.

｜好多人來, *taí hào tō gnîn loî*, amener beaucoup de monde.

你｜有錢麼, *gnî taí yoū ts'iên mô?* as-tu apporté de l'argent sur toi ?

｜貨, *taí fó*, transporter des marchandises.

｜兵, *taí pīn*, conduire avec soi des soldats, être chef militaire.

T'AÍ

大 *T'aí*. Grand, gros, superlatif, surpasser.

我鞋忒｜, *ngā haî t'iĕt t'aí*, mes souliers sont trop grands.

比我｜一歲, *pì ngaî t'aí ỹt sé*, plus grand que moi d'un an.

｜不相同, *t'aí poût siōng t'oúng*, c'est très différent.

| 方, *t'aí fōng*, le grand genre, générosité.

去 | 便, *hí t'aí p'ién*, mot poli pour dire : aller à la selle.

| 家, *t'aí ka*, tout le monde.

待 *T'aí*. Traiter.

| 客 | 得 好, *t'aí hâc t'aí têt haò*, il traite bien ses hôtes.

| 慢, *t'aí mán*, je vous ai traité peu poliment (expression polie adressée à ceux qui vous quittent).

剃 *T'aí* (ou *t'í*). Raser.

| 頭, *t'aí t'eoû*, raser la tête.

TĀM

擔 *Tām*. Porter, fardeau (au propre et au fig). Dans le sens de porter on dit plutôt : 攲 *k'aī*.

攲 |, *k'aī tām*, porter un fardeau.

| 子 重, *tām tzè tch'ōung*, le fardeau est lourd.

On dit par exception :

| 竿, *tám kōn*, bâton qui sert à porter les fardeaux.

一 | 穀, *ŷt tām koŭc*, une charge de riz, c'est-à-dire deux corbeilles contenant dix boisseaux. Mesure agraire employée à la place du mot 畝 *meoū*, elle représente, soi-disant, un terrain suffisant. pour donner un revenu de dix boisseaux.

三 | 穀 田, *sām tām koŭc t'iên*, une rizière qui donne trente boisseaux.

我 買 裡 八 | 穀 田 十 四 兩 一 |, *ngaî maì lî pât tām koŭc t'iên chîp sí leōng ŷt tām*, j'ai acheté huit charges de rizières à quartoze taëls la charge.

| 承, *tām chîn*, se porter caution, répondre de.

躭 *Tām*. Différer, tarder.

| 擱, *tām kôc*, différer, retarder, empêcher.

有 事 | 擱, *yoū sé tām kôc*, une affaire m'a retardé.

| 起 頭 來 看, *tām hí t'eôu loî k'ón*, avancer la tête pour voir.

| 脚, *tām kiôc*, avancer la jambe allonger les jambes.

T'ĀM

貪 *T'ām*. Convoiter, cupide.

| 人 家 個, *t'ām gnîn kā ké*, convoiter le bien d'autrui.

| 心, *t'ām sīm*, cupide, ambitieux.

| 餐, *t'ām ts'ōn*, gourmand, gourmandise.

醈 *T'ām*. Fade, insipide, sans sel.

菜 忒 |, *ts'oí t'iĕt t'ām*, les légumes ne sont pas assez salés.

T'ÂM

燂 *T'âm*, Chauffer au feu.

樹 棍 拿 來 | 直, *choú koún nā loî t'âm tch'ĭt*, chauffer un bâton pour le dégauchir.

竹 頭 愛 | 軟 哞 物 得 倒 |, *tchoŭc t'eoû oí t'âm niōn tsáng voŭt têt taò*, il faut ramollir le bambou en le chauffant, afin de pouvoir le tordre.

痰 *T'âm*. Gros crachat, humeurs, pituite.

發｜火, *pôt t'âm fò*, être poitrinaire, phthisique.

吐｜, *t'ouí t'âm*, cracher.

談 *T'âm*. Langage.

土｜話, *t'où t'âm fá*, la langue vulgaire, le patois.

｜論, *t'âm loún*, discuter, causer.

潭 *T'âm*. Gouffre, eau profonde.

一失脚就噲跌落｜, *ŷt chĭt kiôc ts'ioú voé· tiĕt lŏc t'âm*, il suffit d'un faux pas pour tomber dans le gouffre.

TÀM

膽 *Tàm*. Fiel, courage.

蛇｜好做藥, *châ tàm hào tsó yŏc*, le fiel du serpent est bon pour faire des remèdes.

咁大｜, *àn t'aí tàm*, quelle audace !

T'ÀM

探 *T'àm*. Espionner, éprouver.

打｜, *tà t'àm*, aller aux informations, espionner.

｜人個心, *t'àm gnîn ké· sīm*, sonder les sentiments de quelqu'un.

T'ÁM

淡 *T'ám*. Modéré, tempéré.

顏色｜帛裡, *niân sĕt t'ám p'ĕt lé·*, la couleur n'est plus vive.

冷｜, *lāng t'ám*, tiède, sans ferveur, languissant.

生理｜帛裡, *siēn lī t'ám p'ĕt lé·*, le commerce languit.

掞 *T'ám*. Poutre transversale, traverse, poser une traverse.

｜一個板頭, *t'ám ŷt ké· pàn t'eôu*, jeter une planche en travers.

｜橋, *t'ám k'iâo*, jeter un pont.

TĀN

丹 *Tān*. 紅｜, *foûng tān*, minium.

紅靈｜, *foûng lîn tān*, médecine en poudre.

單 *Tān*. Seul, seulement, mais, à condition.

｜｜我一個人, *tān tān ngaî ŷt ké· gnîn*, moi tout seul.

｜身人, *tān chīn gnîn*, homme qui est seul, célibataire.

我｜｜賣米, *ngaî tān tān maí mì*, je ne vends que du riz.

曕禮｜, *tchām lī tān*, calendrier.

藥｜, *yŏc tān*, formule de médecine.

開藥｜, *k'oī yŏc tān*, écrire une ordonnance de médecine.

收｜, *choū tān*, reçu, facture.

不｜麽益還有害, *poût tān mó ŷt hân yoū hoí*, non seulement il n'y a pas d'avantage, mais eucore il y a préjudice.

我噲算两個花邊工錢單單你莫犯懶惰, *ngaî voé· són lcòng ké· fā piēn koūng ts'iĕn tān tān gnî mŏc fám lān t'ó*, je te compterai deux piastres de salaire à condition que tu ne fasses pas le paresseux.

袒 *Tān.* 被 \|, *p'ī tān*, ou 被皮, *p'ī p'ī*, enveloppe de la couverture chinoise, drap de lit.

T'ĀN

灘 *T'ān.* Rapide de fleuve.

放船下 \|, *fóng chôn hā t'ān*, lancer la barque dans le rapide.

攤 *T'ān.* Etaler, répartir.

\| 子, *t'ān tzè*, étalage de marchandises.

擺 \|, 收 \|, *paì t'ān, choū t'ān*, faire un étalage, le rentrer.

\| 開, *t'ān k'oī*, étendre.

開 \| 館, *k'oī t'ān kouón*, tenir une maison de jeux.

T'ÂN

檀 *T'ân.* Santal ou sandal.

香 \|, *t'ân hiōng*, bois de sandal employé comme parfum.

彈 *T'ân.* Pincer un instrument à cordes ; carder le coton.

\| 琴, \| 絃 *t'ân k'îm, tân hiên*, jouer de la harpe, du violon.

\| 棉花, *t'ân miên fā*, carder le coton.

壇 *T'ân.* 神 \|, *chîn t'ân*, tertre, ou autel quelconque élevé en plein air pour les sacrifices.

T'ÀN

坦 *T'àn.* Plat, uni.

地方係坪 \|, *t'í fōng hé· p'iâng t'àn*, le terrain est très uni.

鍋頭忒窩係過 \| 就過好, *vǒc t'eôu t'ïĕt vō hé· koúo t'àn ts'ioú koúo hào*, la poêle est trop concave, si elle était plus évasée ce serait mieux.

但 *T'àn.* \| 係, *t'àn hé·*, seulement, mais (vulg. 單 *tān* voir ce mot).

毯 *T'àn.* \| 子, *t'àn tzè*, tapis tissé.

攤 \| 子, *t'ān t'àn tzè*, étendre le tapis.

TÁN

旦 *Tán.* Nom donné aux comédiens qui jouent le rôle de femmes.

老 \|, 小 \|, 正 \|, *lào tán, siào tán, tchín tán*, différents rôles de femmes dans les comédies. Les Chinois se servent de ce mot pour s'insulter.

誕 *Tán.* Naissance.

\| 辰, *tán chîn*, jour de naissance.

耶穌聖 \|, 聖母聖 \|, *yâ sē chín tán, chín moū chín tán*, Noël, Nativité de la Sainte Vierge.

T'ÁN

炭 *T'án.* Charbon.

石 \| v. 煤 \|, *chăc t'án* v. *moê· t'án*, charbon de houille.

火 \|, 香 \|, *fò t'án* ou *hiōng t'án*, charbon de bois.

蛋 *T'án.* Œuf.

雞 \|, 鴨 \|, *kē· t'án, âp t'án*, œuf de poule, de cane. *Voir* 春 *tch'oūn.*

歎 *T'án*. Pousser un soupir (style relevé).

嗟 | ou 讃 | 一口氣, *tsiā t'án* ou *tsán t'án ŷt heòu hí*, pousser un soupir, respirer un peu, se reposer un instant (plus vulg. **透氣** *t'eoù hí*).

怨 |, *yán t'án*, se plaindre, gémir, murmurer.

彈 *T'án*. Globule, balle.

鉛 |, *yân t'án*, balle de plomb.

戰 *T'án* (*tchán*). Ebranler, secouer, trembler.

梯子緊 |, *t'oī tzè kìn t'án*, l'échelle ne fait que branler.

| | 震, *t'án t'án tchoūn*, trembler, tremblant.

TĀNG

釘 *Tāng*. Clou, clouer, cheville.

鐵 |, 竹 |, *t'iĕt tāng, tchoûc tāng*, clou en fer, cheville de bambou.

| 穩, *tāng voùn*, clouer solidement.

| 秤, *tāng tch'ín*, accorder une balance romaine.

| 死, *tāng sì*, mourir cloué, tuer en clouant.

拿鐵鉗來 … 脫 |, *nā t'iĕt k'iâm loî k'iaó t'ŏt tāng*, arracher les clous avec des tenailles.

疔 *Tāng*. Furoncle.

發 | 瘡, *pŏt tāng t'sōng*, avoir un furoncle qui empêche de s'asseoir.

訂 *Tāng*. Annoter, inscrire.

| 簿, *tāng p'oū*, inscrire sur le registre.

買幾多那個要 | 分明, *mài kì tō mâc ké ói tāng foūn mîn*, tout ce que tu achètes il faut le noter exactement.

T'ĀNG

聽 *T'āng* (*t'ín*). Ecouter, entendre, obéir.

| 人講, *t'āng gnîn kòng*, entendre dire, j'ai ouï dire.

| 人話, *t'āng gnîn vá*, obéir, écouter les avis de qqn.

| 差, *t'āng ts'ā*, comprendre de travers, mal compris.

好 |, 唔好 |, *hào t'āng, mĝ hào t'āng*, agréable, désagréable à entendre, ou comme son s'il s'agit de musique, ou comme sens s'il s'agit de paroles.

你 | 我話, *gnî t'āng ngâi vá*, écoute mes avis.

我講你 |, *ngâi kòng gnî t'āng*, je vais t'expliquer (*litt.* je te dis que tu entendes.)

廳 *T'āng*. Salle principale.

| 堂, *t'āng t'ông*, cour judiciaire.

下 |, *hā t'āng*, corps de bâtiment qui suit la porte d'entrée et est comme le vestibule du **上 |**, *chóng t'āng*, lequel est la salle principale.

花 |, *fā t'āng*, salon de réception, kiosque.

客 |, *hăc t'āng*, salle de réception, parloir.

食飯 |, *chĭt fán t'āng*, salle à manger.

TÀNG

頂 *Tàng*. Particule numérale des bonnets, des palanquins ; sommet, superlatif.

一丨帽, *ŷt tàng máo*, un bonnet.

一丨轎, *ŷt tàng k'iáo*, une chaise à porteurs.

丨子, *tàng tzè*, globule ou bouton d'honneur, insigne qui se porte au haut du chapeau de cérémonie.

戴丨, *tái tàng*, porter le chapeau de cérémonie avec son globule.

紅丨，藍丨，水晶丨，銅丨, *foûng tàng, lâm tàng, chouì tsīn tàng, t'oûng tàng*, globule rouge (de corail), bleu, de cristal, de cuivre.

摘丨, *tsâc tàng*, enlever le globule, dégrader.

佢丨𠳞官府摘帛𠮩, *kīa tàng poūn kouōn foù tsâc p'ĕt lĕ·*, le mandarin lui a enlevé le bouton d'honneur.

岌崗丨上, *ýn kōng tàng hóng*, au sommet de la montagne.

屋丨上, *voûc tàng hóng*, au sommet de la maison.

頂頂高, *tìn tàng kāo*, excessivement haut.

T'ÁNG

T'áng t'ī. Terminaison finale usitée dans certains pays, et qui marque le participe présent. Elle s'emploie comme le mot **等** *tèn*. Voir ce mot.

Tsó t'áng t'ī, chĭt t'áng t'ī, il travaille, il mange.

TĀO

刀 *Tāo*. Couteau, part. num.

一把 ou **一張 丨子**, *ŷt pà* (ou) *ŷt tchōng tāo tzè*, un couteau.

剪丨，剃頭丨, *tsièn tāo, t'í t'eoû tāo*, ciseaux, rasoir.

使丨個, *sè tāo ké·*, celui qui manie le couteau, dans les boucheries, soit pour tuer, soit pour débiter la viande.

丨尖，丨嘴，丨背, *tāo tsiām, tāo tchoí, tāo poé·*, la pointe, le tranchant, le revers du couteau.

一丨紙, *ŷt tāo tjè*, une main de papier.

T'ĀO

叨 *T'āo*. Désirer ardemment.

丨蒙神父, *t'āo moûng chîn foú*, je serais reconnaissant au Père.

T'AÔ

淘 *T'aô*. Curer, nettoyer, laver; se fatiguer.

鑛沙拿來丨淨, *koùang sā nā loî t'aô ts'iáng*, lave proprement le minerai.

米有沙愛丨淨, *mì yoū sā oí t'aô ts'iáng*, le riz est plein de sable, il faut le laver.

丨神, *t'aô chîn*, se fatiguer l'esprit.

萄 *T'aô*. **葡丨**, *p'oû t'aô*, raisin, vigne.

桃 *T'aô*. Pêche, pêcher.

丨子樹，丨子, *t'aô tzè choú, t'aô tzè*, pêcher, pêche.

核丨, *hĕt t'aô*, noix.

逃 *T'aô*. Fuir, déserter, éviter.

丨走𠮩, *t'aô tsèou lĕ·*, il s'est enfui.

| 到聖堂下, *t'aô táo chín t'ông hā*, il s'est réfugié à l'église.

| 難, *t'aô nán*, s'évader, s'échapper.

綯 *T'aô*. Attacher, retenu par une corde.

拿索來 | 馬, *nā sôc loî t'aô mā*, apporte une corde pour attacher le cheval.

| 穩, *t'aô voùn*, attacher solidement.

狗 | 等裡唔怕, *keoù t'aô tèn ē· mĝ p'á*, le chien est attaché, n'aie pas peur.

TAÒ

倒 *Taò*. Renverser, verser, tomber, répandre; auxiliaire marquant le passé, l'impératif, souvent simplement euphonique.

| 樹子, *taò choú tzè*, abattre un arbre.

米 | 了裡, *mì taò liaò lé·*, le riz a versé.

| 水, | 酒, *taò choùi, taò tsioù*, verser de l'eau, du vin, remplir d'eau, de vin.

| | ..., *taò taò tsiáng*, sens dessus dessous.

| 草, *taò ts'aò*, ruminer.

做得 |, 做唔 |, *tsó têt taò, tsó mĝ taò*, pouvoir faire, ne pas pouvoir faire.

我餓倒阿唔曉食, *ngaî ngō taò á mĝ hiào chĭt*, j'ai tellement enduré la faim que je n'ai plus la force de manger.

我聽 | 唔曾看 |, *ngaî t'āng taò mĝ ts'ên k'ón taò*, j'ai entendu, mais je n'ai pas vu.

你跂 | 來, *gnî k'ī taò loî*, tiens-toi debout.

拿 | 來, 打 | 來, *nā taò loî, tà taò loî*, prends cela; frappe.

| 轉來, *taò tchòn loî*, revenir sur ses pas.

T'AÒ

討 *T'aò*. Demander, chercher.

| 食, *t'aò chĭt*, mendier, mendiant.

| 人個東西, *t'aò gnîn ké· toūng sī*, demander à quelqu'un quelque objet (gratis).

| 唔倒, *t'aò mĝ tào*, ne pouvoir obtenir en demandant.

| 親 v. | 老婆 v. | 婦人家, *t'aò ts'īn v. t'aò laò p'ô v. t'aò fóu gnîn kā*, prendre femme.

| 新臼, *t'aò sīm k'ioū*, prendre une bru.

TAÓ

到 *Taó* Jusque, arriver, parvenir.

| 如今, *taó ŷ kīn*, jusqu'à maintenant.

| 個時來看, *taó ké· chê loî k'ón*, alors (arrivé là) je verrai (ce que j'ai à faire).

你 | 那里去, *gnî taó naí lī hí ?* où vas-tu ?

汕頭 | 嘉應有四百過里路, *sān t'eoû taó kā ýn yoū sí pâc koúo lī loú*, de Swatow à Ka yn il y a plus de 400 *lī*.

道 *Táo (t'áo)*. Fois.

一 |, 兩 |, *ŷt táo, lèòng táo*, une fois, deux fois.

過河幾下 |, *koúo hô kì hā táo*, passer le fleuve plusieurs fois.

T'AÓ

道 *T'aó.* Raison, doctrine; route.

講｜理, *kòng t'aó lī,* prêcher, expliquer la doctrine.

公｜, *koūng t'aó,* juste, équitable.

試馬大｜, *ché mā t'aí t'aó,* la grande route.

路｜(ou 路程) 唔遠, *loú t'aó (* ou *loú tch'în) mĝ yàn,* la route n'est pas longue.

做｜塲, *tsó t'aó tch'ông,* faire des superstitions pour les morts, par le ministère des bonzes.

｜臺, *t'aó t'ôi,* nom donné à plusieurs officiers, entre autres à celui dont l'autorité administrative s'étend sur deux ou trois préfectures.

人唔｜地, *gnîn mĝ t'aó t'í,* n'être pas très bien portant.

盜 *T'aó.* 偷｜, *t'eōu t'aó,* voler.

｜賊, *t'aó ts'ĕt,* voleur, brigand.

套 *T'áo.* Enveloppe, étui.

信｜, *sín t'áo,* enveloppe de lettre.

｜褲, *t'áo fóu,* jambières, cuissards.

袍｜, *p'áo t'áo,* pardessus de cérémonie.

TĂP

沓 *Tăp.* Frapper légèrement ; mot qui, placé devant un autre, marque l'excès.

杉拿來｜淨來, *sām nā loî tăp ts'iáng loî,* frapper les habits pour les nettoyer.

｜濕, *tăp chĭp,* tout mouillé, trempé.

攞攞｜｜, *lăp lăp tăp tăp,* négligent, sale.

T'ĂP

踏 *T'ăp.* Fouler aux pieds.

聖母｜蛇, *chín moú t'ăp châ,* la Vierge foule le serpent à ses pieds.

踐｜ ou 蹧｜, *ts'ién t'ăp* ou *tsāo t'ăp,* mépriser, traiter indignement.

｜碓, *t'ăp toí,* faire manœuvrer le mortier à fouler le riz.

你買田愛去｜過來, *gnî maì t'iên oí hí t'ăp koúo loî,* si vous achetez des rizières, il faut d'abord (vous rendre sur les lieux pour) les visiter.

一隻脚｜两條船噲浸死, *ŷt tchăc kiŏc t'ăp leòng t'iâo chôn voé· tsím sì,* si vous avez un pied sur deux barques, vous risquez de vous noyer.

TÂP

答 *Tâp.* Répondre; promettre.

一問一｜, *ŷt moún ŷt tâp,* l'un fait la demande, l'autre fait la réponse.

盡你罵我唔｜你, *ts'ín gnî má ngaî mĝ tâp gnî,* injurie-moi tant que tu voudras, je ne te répondrai pas.

報｜, *páo tâp,* reconnaissance, rendre la pareille.

你｜應一句, *gnî tâp ýn ŷt kí,* réponds un mot.

我｜應做, *ngaî tâp ýn tsó,* je promets de faire.

搭 *Tâp.* Suspendre, appuyer, assembler les pièces d'une charpente ; et, avec.

釣 | , *keōu tâp*, crochet, agrafe.

門 | 等來, *moûn tâp tèn loî*, ferme la porte (en la retenant soit avec un clou, soit avec le verrou extérieur).

拿黄烟 | 烟 筒, *nā vông yān tâp yān t'ôung*, apporte le tabac et la pipe.

| 船, *tâp chōn*, prendre place sur un bateau.

| 一 個 寮, *tâp ӯt ké· liâo*, construire un abri, un hangar.

| 信, *tâp sín*, envoyer une lettre.

我 船 唔 | 人 淨 | 貨, *ngā chōn mĝ tâp gnîn ts'iáng tâp fó*, ma barque ne prend pas de voyageurs, mais seulement des marchandises.

担 子 重 | 唔 得 東 西, *tām tzè tch'oūng tâp mĝ têt toūng sī*, le fardeau est lourd, on ne peut rien ajouter par-dessus.

T'ÂP

塔 *T'âp*. Tour.

象牙寶 |, *sióng ngâ pào t'âp*, Tour d'ivoire (litanies de la Ste Vierge).

上 |, *chōng t'âp*, monter à la tour.

T'ĂT

達 *T'ăt*. Intelligent, connaître.

通 | ou 明 |, *t'oūng t'ăt*, ou *mîn t'ăt*, intelligent, perspicace.

TÂT

笪 *Tât*. 簟 |, *t'iám tât*, grosse natte pour faire sécher les grains.

T'ÂT

噠 *T'ât*. Tromper.

哄 | 人, *foúng t'ât gnîn*, tromper quelqu'un.

| 人 個 錢, *t'ât gnîn ké· ts'iên*, filouter les sapèques d'autrui.

TCHĀ

傘 *Tchā* (*chàn*). Parapluie, dais.

擎 |, *k'iâng tchā*, porter le parapluie. On dit mieux *chàn* dans le sens de dais.

官 出 門 有 洋 |, *kouōn tch'oût moûn yoū yông chàn*, quand le mandarin sort, il y a un dais (qui le précède).

遮 *Tchā*. Couvrir, cacher.

| 日 頭, *tchā gnît t'eôu*, garantir du soleil.

| 雨, *tchā ỳ*, garantir de la pluie.

| 羞, *tchā siōu*, cacher sa honte, les parties honteuses.

TCH'Ā

車 *Tch'ā*. Char, roue, nom de machines, d'instruments.

火 | 路, *fò tch'ā loú*, chemin de fer.

| 心, *tch'ā sīm*, essieu d'une roue.

馬 |, *mā tch'ā*, voiture à chevaux.

踏 脚 |, *t'âp kiôc tch'ā*, bicyclette.

水 |, *choùi tch'ā*, noria, turbine.

風 |, *foūng tch'ā*, moulin à vanner.

| 眼, *tch'ā niàn*, faire un trou avec une vrille, un foret, un vilebrequin.

| 樹, *tch'ā choú*, tourner du bois.

抓 *Tch'ā*. Grappe; porter à la main, tirer, empoigner, dresser.

一 | 葡萄子, *ŷt tch'a p'oû t'aô tzè*, une grappe de raisin.

| 倒, *tch'ā taò*, attraper, porter.

包袱同我 | 來去, *pāo foŭc t'oûng ngaî tch'ā loî hí*, porte-moi mon paquet.

| 歧, *tch'a k'ī*, dresser, faire tenir droit.

| 旗, *tch'ā k'î*, hisser le drapeau.

| 下來, *tch'ā hā loî*, abaisser en tirant.

| 出來, *tch'ā tch'oût loî*, enlever, sortir en tirant.

伸 |, *tch'oūn tch'ā*, lisse, sans pli.

你摺倒衫唔伸 |, *gnî tchâp taò sām mĝ tch'oūn tch'ā*, tu as mal plié ton habit (il y a des plis, il est chiffonné).

賒 *Tch'ā*. Acheter ou vendre à crédit.

| 來, *tch'ā loî*, acheter à crédit.

| 去, *tch'ā hí*, vendre à crédit,

TCHÀ

者 *Tchà*. Auxiliaire marquant l'adjectif; souvent n'est qu'euphonique (employé surtout dans les livres).

善 |, 惡 |, *chán tchà, ôc tchà*, les bons, les méchants.

或 |, 再 |, *fĕt tchà, tsaí tchà*, ou bien, encore.

TCH'À

扯 *Tch'à*. Déchirer.

| 爛, *tch'à lán*, déchirer.

我褲 | 爛, *ngaî foú tch'à lán*, mon pantalon est déchiré.

TCHÁ

蔗 *Tchá*. Canne à sucre.

攪 |, *kào tchá*, broyer la canne à sucre pour en extraire le jus.

鷓 *Tchá*. | 鴣, *tchá koū*, perdrix.

TCHÂC

隻 *Tchâc*. Particule numérale pour beaucoup d'objets différents (en général, s'emploie quand il s'agit de l'un des objets qui font la paire).

一 | 手, 一 | 脚, 一 | 鞋, *ŷt tchâc choù, ŷt tchâc kiôc, ŷt tchâc haî*, une main, un pied, un soulier.

炙 *Tchâc*. Cuire, rôtir, chauffer.

| 子, *tchâc tzè*, pot à cuire.

| 藥, *tchâc yŏc*, cuire des médecines.

| 火, *tchâc fò*, se chauffer.

| 日頭, *tchâc gnĭt t'eoû*, se chauffer au soleil.

TCH'ÂC

尺 *Tch'âc*. Pied (mesure de longueur qui varie suivant les lieux et les professions).

十寸爲一 |, *chĭp ts'oún vi ŷt tch'âc*, dix pouces font un pied.

曲 |, *k'ioût tch'âc*, équerre de menuisier.

| 寸, *tch'âc ts'oún*, mesures de longueur en général ; dimensions d'une chose ; juste milieu ; exactitude.

有 | 寸, *yoū tch'âc ts'oún*, avoir les dimensions voulues, être fait d'après une règle.

一 | 地都麽, *ŷt tch'âc t'í toū mô*, n'avoir pas un pied de terrain.

赤 *Tch'âc*. Rougeâtre; nu.

| 馬, *tch'âc mā*, cheval couleur brune, rougeâtre.

打 | 剝, *tà tch'âc pôc*, être nu, ou avec le pantalon seul.

打 | 脚行, *tà tch âc kiôc hâng*, marcher pieds nus.

TCHĀM

瞻 *Tchām*. Regarder avec espoir ; honorer.

| 帮人, *tchām pōng gnîn*, (plus vulg. (打) *tà pōng gnîn*), implorer l'aide de quelqu'un.

| 帮神父同我辦清楚, *tchām pōng chîn foú t'oûng ngaî p'án ts'īn tsè*, j'implore l'aide du Père pour terminer cette affaire.

| 禮, *tchām lī*, honorer par des cérémonies, honorer d'un culte ; fête chrétienne ; jour de la semaine.

四大 | 禮, *sí t'ái tchām lī*, les 4 grandes fêtes de l'année.

| 禮二, | 禮三, *tchām lī ŷt, tchām lī sām*, 2ème férie, 3ème férie (lundi, mardi).

粘 *Tchām*. | 米, *tchām mì*, espèce de riz.

TCHÁM

占 *Tchám*. Consulter les sorts; | 卦, *tchám koúa*, consulter les sorts, tirer l'horoscope.

佔 *Tchám*. Usurper, empiéter.

霸 | 人個地方, *pá tchám gnîn ké· t'í fōng*, usurper, occuper injustement le terrain d'autrui.

TCHĀN

氈 *Tchān*. Laine travaillée, feutre.

洋 |, *yông tchān*, couverture européenne.

鞋 |, *haî tchān*, semelle épaisse des souliers chinois.

TCHÁN

戰 *Tchán*. Bataille, combattre.

相 |, *siōng tchán*, se battre.

| 船, | 馬, *tchán chôn, tchán mā*, navire de guerre, chevaux de cavalerie.

TCH'ÂNG

呈 *Tch'âng* (*tch'în*). Quantité, partie.

今年個穀晒得四 | 倒, *kīn niân ké· koŭc sái tĕt sí tch'âng tào*, cette année, on ne pourra obtenir que 4 parties du riz (sur 10).

三 | 錢, 對 | 錢, *sām tch'âng ts'iên, touí tch'âng ts'iên*, signifie qu'il y a les 3 dixièmes ou la moitié de bonnes sapéques (voir 鏍 *nioûn*).

十 | 有九 | 喑死, *chĭp tch'âng yoū kioù tch'âng voé· sì*, on peut parier neuf sur dix qu'il mourra.

神父講話我聽得識五 | 倒, *chîn foú kòng fá ngaî t'ang tĕt chĭt ng tch'âng taò*, je ne comprends que les cinq dixièmes de ce que le Père dit.

橙 *Tch'âng*. Orange à écorce adhérente.

TCHÀNG

整 *Tchàng* (*tchìn*). Réparer, mettre en ordre, disposer.

丨屋, *tchàng voûc*, réparer une maison.

丨時辰鐘, *tchàng chê chîn tchoūng*, réparer une horloge.

丨成, *tchàng tcháng*, la réparation est faite.

丨大, 丨細, *tchàng t'aí, tchàng sé*, agrandir, rapetisser.

TCHÁNG

正 *Tcháng* (*tchín*). Précis, comme il faut, droit, juste.

丨好, *tcháng hào*, tant mieux, c'est bien fait, justement.

唔多丨, *mĝ tō tcháng*, ce n'est pas très précis, pas bien à sa place.

丨月, *tcháng gnĕt*, nom de la 1ere lune.

心思唔丨, *sīm sé mĝ tcháng*, n'avoir pas des intentions droites.

成 *Tcháng* (*chîn*). Fini, accompli.

做丨, *tsó tcháng*, finir, achever.

預備丨, *ý p'í tcháng*, c'est prêt, la préparation est terminée.

整丨, *tchàng tcháng*, c'est raccommodé, la réparation est faite.

TCHĀO

朝 *Tchāo*. Matin, jour.

丨夜, *tchāo yá*, matin et soir.

今丨, 明丨, *kīn tchāo, mîn tchāo*, aujourd'hui, demain.

食丨, *chĭt tchāo*, déjeûner.

招 *Tchāo*. Avouer, avertir.

丨牌, *tchāo p'aî*, enseigne, inscription.

丨呼, *tchāo foū*, prévenir, avertir, répondre d'une affaire, patronner.

我唔敢過番怕麼人丨呼, *ngaî mĝ kàm kouó fān p'á mô gnîn tchaō foū*, je n'ose pas aller à l'étranger, je crains que personne ne s'occupe de moi.

TCH'ĀO

超 *Tch'āo*. Surpasser.

丨過, *tch'āo kouó*, même sens.

丨過人性, *tch'āo kouó gnîn sín*, qui surpasse la nature de l'homme, surnaturel.

TCH'AÔ

朝 *Tch'aô*. Dynastie ; cour impériale.

大清丨, *t'aí ts'īn tch'aô*, la dynastie actuelle des *Ts'īn*.

丨庭, *tch'aô t'în*, la cour impériale.

潮 *Tch'aô*. Flux et reflux, mouvement de la mer.

海水有兩丨漲丨退丨, *hoì choùi yoū leòng tc'haô tchóng tch'aô t'ouí tch'aô*, la mer a deux mouvements, le flux et le reflux.

丨泥, *tch'aô nâi*, la vase laissée par le fleuve en se retirant.

TCHAÓ

照 *Tchaó*. Eclairer, réfléchir, d'après.

燈 | 光 | 得 遠, *tēn tchaó kouōng tchaó tĕt yàn*, la lampe éclaire au loin.

拿 鏡 來 | 你 面, *nā kiáng loî tchaó niā mién*, regarde-toi au miroir.

| 應 人, *tchaó ýn gnîn*, avoir égard, prendre les intérêts de qqn.

| 舊, | 前, *tchaó k'ióu, tchaó ts'iên*, comme autrefois.

| 理 辦, *tchaó lī p'án*, juger d'après le droit, la justice.

| 你 話, *tchaó gnî vá*, d'après ce que tu dis.

| 常, *tchaó chông*, d'ordinaire, ordinaire.

| 會, *tchaó fí*, communications officielles entre grands mandarins.

TCH'AÓ

兆 *Tch'aó*. Million. (Voir *chaó*).

TCHÂP

摺 *Tchâp*. Plier.

| 一 張 紙, *tchâp ŷt tchōng tjè*, plier une feuille de papier.

| 衣 裳, *tchâp ȳ chông*, plier les habits.

TCHĂT

蜇 *Tchăt*. | 皮, *tchát p'î*, espèce d'herbe marine, ou champignon de mer comestible.

TCH'ĂT

徹 *Tch'ăt*. Comprendre, pénétrer.

透 |, *t'cóu tch'ăt*, perspicace, intelligent.

TCHÂT

拆 *Tchât*. Réduire, déduire une quantité.

一 吊 錢 同 我 來 | 七 呈, *ŷt tiáo ts'iên t'oûng ngaî loî tchât ts'ĭt tch'âng*, reduis-moi cette ligature au $\frac{7}{10}$ (en enlevant les mauvaises sapèques).

| 實, *tchât chĭt*, franc, loyal.

裡 個 事 我 領 單 單 每 百 圓 我 愛 扣 你 十 個 | 實 每 百 圓 你 僅 得 九 十 個, *ỳ ké· sé ngaî leāng tān tān mī pâc yân ngaî oí k'eoú gnî chĭp ké· tchât tchĭt mī pâc yân gnî kioùn tĕt kioù chĭp ké·*, j'accepte l'affaire à condition de prendre 10% (de commission), tu n'auras que 90.

TCH'ÂT

徹 *Tch'ât*. Enlever, faire disparaître.

| 席, *tch'ât sĭt*, débarrasser la table (après un festin).

食 唔 |, 做 唔 |, *chĭt mĝ tch'ât, tsó mĝ tch'ât*, ne pouvoir arriver à manger, à faire assez vite.

細 人 相 打 | 開 來, *sé· gnîn siōng tà tch'ât k'oī loî*, séparez ces enfants qui se battent.

Tch'ât. Douleur de tête.

頭 哪 噲 |, *t'eôu nā voé· tch'ât*, la tête me fait mal.

TCHĒ

Les mots *tche* ne paraissent être que les mots *tje* aspirés. Dans certains endroits, ils sont prononcés comme *tse*; ailleurs, il serait peut-être mieux d'écrire *tche* pour *tje*, et *tch'e* pour *tche*.

Voir l'introduction, page IX.

雉 *Tchē*. 丨雞, *tchē kē·*, faisan.

痴 *Tchē*. Stupide.

丨呆, *tchē ngōe·*, idiot, hébété.

TCHÊ

遲 *Tchê*. Lent, tard, tarder.

手脚丨慢, *choū kiōc tchê mán*, lent dans le travail.

丨鈍個人, *tchê t'oún ké· gnîn*, homme à intelligence lente.

忒丨, *t'ïet tchê*, c'est trop tard.

剮 *Tchê*. Dépecer, déplumer.

丨猪, *tchê tchōu*, dépecer un porc, saigner un porc, l'échauder pour enlever les poils.

丨雞, *tchê kē·*, plumer, dépouiller une poule.

池 *Tchê*. Etang, vivier, réservoir.

湯丨, *t'ōng tchê*, cuiller.

塘丨, *t'ông tchê*, réservoir, étang.

魚丨, *nĝ tchê*, vivier.

天丨, *t'iēn tchê*, cour intérieure d'une maison, par où s'échappent les eaux pluviales.

硯丨, *yán tchê*, petit vase qui accompagne l'encrier chinois.

持 *Tchê*. Tenir d'une main ferme, garder.

丨平辦理, *tchê p'în p'án lī*, traiter une affaire selon la stricte justice.

把丨地方, *pà tchê t'í fōng*, occuper la place, embarrasser le chemin.

TCHÈ

齒 *Tchè*. Dent.

牙丨, *ngâ tchè*, dent de la mâchoire.

鋸丨, *kí tchè*, dents d'une scie.

輪丨, *loún tchè*, les dents d'une roue de machine.

恥 *Tchè*. Pudeur, honte.

麼廉丨個人, *mô liâm tchè ké· gnîn*, homme sans pudeur.

丨笑人, *tchè siáo gnîn*, se moquer de quelqu'un.

羞丨, *sioū tchè*, avoir honte, rougir de honte.

始 *Tchè*. Commencement.

無丨無終, *voû tchè voû tchoūng*, sans commencement ni fin.

TCHÉ

試 *Tché* (*ché*). Essayer, sonder, éprouver.

丨看, *tché k'ón*, examiner, vérifier.

裡個馬我丨過麼用, *yà ké· ma ngâi tché koúo mô yoúng*, j'ai essayé ce cheval, il ne vaut rien.

你唔信來丨阿剩, *gnî mĝ sín ? loî tché á chín*, tu ne me crois pas ? viens essayer.

治 *Tché*. Régir, gouverner, soigner.

丨國, *tché kouĕt*, gouvernement, gouverner un royaume.

調丨病, *t'iaô tché p'iáng*, ou simplement *tché p'iáng*, soigner une maladie.

盲丨外先丨內, *mâng tché ngoé· siĕn tché nouí*, il veut dominer sur sa famille, avant d'avoir dominé sur les étrangers.

痔 *Tché.* Hémorrhoïdes. Dans certains endroits, on appelle ainsi la chute du rectum.

TCHÉ·

砌 *Tché·* Elever une maçonnerie. Construire un mur en brique ou en pierre.

丨石坎, *tché· chác k'ám*, construire un mur de soutènement.

丨墻, *tché· siông*, construire un mur en brique ou en pierre.

滯 *Tché·*. Contagieux, se propager, retenir, empêcher.

裡病哈丨人, *yà p'iáng voé· tché· gnîn*, cette maladie est contagieuse.

阻丨, *tzè* (ou *tchoù*) *tché·*, empêchement, obex.

丨語, *tché· nī*, on appelle ainsi les mots ou particules qui s'ajoutent, pour l'euphonie à d'autres mots sans en changer le sens.

丨人笑, *tché· gnîn siáo*, exciter le rire.

丨人耻笑, *tché· gnîn tchè siáo*, exciter la dérision.

TCHI voir TJE

TCH'I voir TCHE

TCHĪM

針 *Tchīm.* Aiguille, petite épine.

丨眼, *tchīm niàn*, trou d'une aiguille.

丨嘴, *tchīm tchoí*, pointe de l'aiguille.

使丨, *sè tchīm*, travailler à l'aiguille.

穿丨, *tch'ōn tchīm*, enfiler une aiguille.

南北丨, *nâm pĕt tchīm*, boussole.

風雨丨, *foūng ỳ tchīm*, baromètre.

斟 *Tchīm.* Transvaser, verser, délibérer.

丨酒, *tchīm tsioù*, verser du vin.

丨酌, *tchīm tchôc*, délibérer.

TCH'ĪM

深 *Tch'īm.* Profond.

唔知丨淺, *mĝ tī tch'īm ts'ièn*, je ne sais pas la profondeur (ou 不知丨淺如何, *poŭt tī tch'īm ỳ hô*, même sens, style plus relevé).

丨奥, *tch'īm áo*, profond, mystérieux.

丨睡, *tch'īm choé·*, profond sommeil.

丨色, *tch'īm sĕt*, couleur voyante et vive.

愛啲丨來, *oí koì tch'īm loî*, il faut creuser profondément.

TCH'ÎM

沉 *Tch'îm.* Submergé, plongé dans l'eau.

船丨下, *chôn tch'îm hā*, la barque a été submergée.

丨唔下, *tch'îm mĝ hā*, ne pouvoir être submergé.

TCHÌM

枕 *Tchìm.* | **頭**, *tchìm t'côu*, oreiller.

| **箱**, *tchìm siōng*, espèce de cassette servant d'oreiller.

TCHÍM

針 *Tchím (tchīm).* Dard, aiguillon d'abeille, de guêpe, etc.

死蜂生 |, *sì foūng sāng tchím*, quand la guêpe est morte, son aiguillon ne l'est pas.

TCHĪN

眞 *Tchīn.* Vrai, véritable.

| **實**, *tchīn chĭt*, vrai, sincère, positif.

| **福八端**, *tchīn foŭc pât tōn*, les huit béatitudes de l'évangile.

聽唔 |, *t'āng mĝ tchīn*, ne pas entendre clairement.

分唔倒 | **假**, *foūn mĝ tào tchīn kà*, ne pas distinguer le vrai du faux.

| **心**, *tchīn sīm*, en toute vérité, de tout cœur.

| **容**, *tchīn yoûng*, visage très ressemblant.

萬有 | **原**, *ván yōu tchīn nián*, *(omnium est vera origo,)* Il (Dieu) est l'origine de tout.

貞 *Tchīn.* Virginité, chasteté.

| **節**, *tchīn tsiĕt*, même sens.

童 | **女**, *t'oûng tchīn ǹg*, fille vierge.

| **節牌坊**, *tchīn tsiĕt p'âi fông*, arc-de-triomphe élevé aux veuves qui ont gardé la chasteté, ou aux filles qui ont gardé la virginité après la mort de leur fiancé.

珍 *Tchīn.* Précieux.

| **珠**, *tchīn tchoū*, perle fine.

| **寶**, *tchīn pào*, bijou, objet précieux.

烝 *Tchīn.* Cuire à la vapeur d'eau.

| **菜**, **飯**, **酒**, *tchīn ts'oí, fán, tsioù.* cuire à la vapeur d'eau, des légumes, du riz, du vin.

TCH'ĪN

稱 *Tch'īn.* Donner un titre, exalter, publier.

愛 | **佢大老爺**, *oí tch'īn kî t'ái lào yâ*, il faut l'appeler: Monseigneur, Monsieur.

自 |, *tsé tch'īn*, se vanter.

| **讚人家**, *tch'īn tsán gnîn kā*, louer quelqu'un.

| **人個名**, *tch'īn gnîn ké miâng*, donner du renom à quelqu'un.

三字 | **呼麼規矩**, *sām sé tch'īn foū mô kouī kì*, il n'est pas convenable d'appeler (quelqu'un) par ses trois caractères (c.-à-d. par son nom de famille suivi de son nom de personne).

TCH'ÎN

呈 *Tch'în.* Acte d'accusation, pièce d'un procès.

一張 | **子**, *ўt tchōng tch'în tzè*, un acte d'accusation.

做 |, **遞** | **子**, *tsó tch'în, t'í tch'în tzè*, composer, présenter un acte d'accusation.

訴 |, *sé* (ou *choú*) *tch'în*, réfutation d'une pièce d'un procès.

程 *Tch'în* ou *tch'âng*. Ordre, route.

照章 |, *tcháo tchōng tch'în*, d'après le règlement.

幾日路 |, *kì gnĭt loú tch'în*, route de plusieurs journées.

陳 *Tch'în*. Avarié, vieux.

黄烟 | 帛裡, *vông yān tch'în p'ĕt lê*, le tabac est avarié.

| 年老酒, *tch'în niân lào tsiòu*, vin vieux de plusieurs années.

老 | 皮, *lào tch'în p'î*, vieilles écorces d'oranges (employées en médecine).

塵 *Tch'în*. Poussière.

人死了變 | 灰, *gnîn sì liào pién tch'în foē*, l'homme devient poussière après sa mort.

掃 | 灰, *sáo tch'în foē*, épousseter, balayer.

TCHÌN

賑 *Tchìn*. Secourir, faire l'aumône.

| 濟窮人, *tchìn tsí k'ioûng gnîn*, donner pour secourir les pauvres.

整 *Tchìn*. Arranger, réparer.

修 | ou 打 | 間房, *sioū tchìn* ou *tà tchìn kiān fông*, arranger, réparer une chambre.

擺得齊 |, *pài tĕt ts'ê tchìn*, c'est bien orné, agencé (voir *tchàng*).

振 *Tchìn*. Exciter, affermir.

領堅 |, *lìng kiān tchìn*, recevoir la Confirmation.

震 *Tchìn*. Tremblement.

地 |, *t'í tchìn* tremblement de terre. (Voir *tchoūn*.)

一州 | 動, *ўt tchoū tchìn t'oúng*, toute la ville est en émoi.

鎮 *Tchìn*. Citadelle, tenir garnison.

| 守, *tchìn choù*, mettre une garnison dans une place pour la garder.

市 |, *sé tchìn*, nom donné à certains grands marchés quotidiens.

懲 *Tchìn*. Réprimer, se maîtriser, se tenir en garde.

| 治人 ou | 責人, *tchìn tché gnîn* ou *tchìn tsĭt gnîn*, réprimander quelqu'un.

罵佢打佢那個也 | 佢唔倒, *má kî tà kî mâc kó yā tchìn kî mĝ tào*, on a beau le gronder, le frapper, rien ne peut le corriger.

| 一儆百, *tchìn ўt kìn pâc*, en réprimer un si bien, que les cent autres en soient terrorisés.

TCH'ÌN

逞 *Tch'ìn*. Se vanter, faire étalage d'une chose.

自 | 有能幹, *tsé tch'ìn yoū nên kón*, faire parade de son habileté.

| 强, *tch'ìn k'ióng*, affectation, se vanter d'être le plus fort.

| 手勢, *tch'ìn choù ché*, montrons notre force.

正 *Tchín.* Droit, juste, irréprochable, principal. (Voir *tcháng.*)

佢心不｜, *kiâ sīm poût tchín*, ses intentions ne sont pas droites.

端｜個, *tōn tchín ké*, c'est bien vrai.

｜道, *tchín t'aó*, la voie droite, légitime.

｜夫｜妻, *tchín foū tchín ts'ī*, mari et femme légitime.

｜主教, *tchín tchoù kaó*, l'Ordinaire (par opposition à son coadjuteur).

症 *Tchín.* Maladie.

｜頭, *tchín t'eôu*, maladie, vice.

那個｜頭都有, *mâc ké tchín t'eôu toū yoū*, il a tous les vices.

醫生看佢｜頭唔識, *ȳ sēn k'ón kīa tchín t'eôu mĝ chĭt*, le médecin ne peut diagnostiquer sa maladie.

痢｜, *lí tchín*, dyssenterie.

政 *Tchín.* Lois, gouvernement.

國｜, *kouĕt tchín*, le gouvernement du royaume.

布｜司, *poú tchín sē*, trésorier général.

証 *Tchín.* Témoin, rendre témoignage, preuve.

對｜, *touí tchín*, témoigner en face.

死無對｜, *sì voû touí tchín*, le témoin étant mort, il n'y a plus de confrontation possible.

見｜人, *kián tchín gnîn*, témoin oculaire.

TCH'ÍN

陣 *Tch'ín.* Ensemble ; moment ; ordre de bataille.

同｜來去, *t'oûng tch'ín loî hí*, allons ensemble.

係有｜我敢去, *hé yoū tch'ín ngaî kàm hí*, si j'ai de la compagnie, j'oserai y aller.

痛裡一｜, *t'oúng lî ȳt tch'ín*, cela m'a fait mal pendant un moment.

一｜雨, *ȳt tch'ín ỳ*, une averse.

一｜烟, *ȳt tch'ín yān*, une bouffée de fumée.

一｜風, *ȳt tch'ín foūng*, un coup de vent.

一｜一｜, *ȳt tch'ín, ȳt tch'ín*, de temps en temps, par moment.

一｜璞鳩, *ȳt tch'ín p'oŭc keoū*, une volée de tourterelles.

一｜羊子, *ȳt tch'ín yông tzè*, un troupeau de chèvres.

出｜, *tch'oūt tch'ín*, aller au combat.

秤 *Tch'ín.* Balance romaine ; peser.

一支｜, *ȳt kī tch'ín*, une balance.

｜杆，｜鈎，｜砣，｜扭, *tch'ín kōn, tch'ín keōu, tch'ín t'ô, tch'ín neòu*, le levier de la balance, crochet pour suspendre les objets à peser, poids de la romaine, sa poignée.

釘｜, *tāng tch'ín*, faire (*litt.* clouer) une romaine.

壓｜頭, *âp tch'ín t'eoû*, frauder en pesant, en appuyant sur la balance.

裡個｜子｜得幾重倒, *ỳ ké tch'ín tzè tch'ín tĕt kì tch'oūng tào* ? jusqu'à quel poids peut peser cette romaine ?

｜子忒嘞, *tch'ín tzè t'iĕt laî*, la balance est trop lourde (le poids est trop fort).

| 子忑準, *tch'în tzè t'iĕt tchoùn*, la balance est trop légère (le poids est trop faible).

| 一字過, *tch'în ŷt sé koúo*, peser juste.

TCHÎP

汁 *Tchîp*. Jus, sauce, bouillie pour les cochons.

| 糣, *tchîp sàm*, bouillie pour les cochons.

煮 |, *tchoù tchîp*, faire cuire la bouillie.

執 *Tchîp*. Administrer ; obstiné.

| 照, *tchîp tcháo*, passeport ou titre délivré par l'autorité.

| 事人, *tchîp sé gnîn*, ceux qui ont la direction d'une affaire.

| 定愛去, *tchîp t'în oí hí*, je veux absolument y aller.

咁固 |, *kàn koú tchîp* ! quel entêté !

TCH'ĬT

姪 *Tch'ĭt*. Neveu (ne se dit que des enfants d'un frère et non d'une sœur).

| 子, | 女, | 孫, | 孫女, *tch'ĭt tzè, tch'ĭt ǹg, tch'ĭt soūn, tch'ĭt soūn ǹg*, neveu, nièce, petit-fils, petite-fille des frères.

內 |, *nouí tch'ĭt*, le neveu de ma femme.

直 *Tch'ĭt*. Droit, direct, juste, sincère.

山中有 | 樹世上無 | 人, *sān tchoūng yoū tch'ĭt choú ché chōng voû tch'ĭt gnîn*, dans les montagnes il y a des arbres droits, en ce monde il n'y a pas d'homme droit.

| 心人 *tch'ĭt sīm gnîn*, homme aux intentions droites.

行 | 路, *hâng tch'ĭt loú*, suivre le droit chemin.

那個路過 |, *naí ké· loú koúo tch'ĭt*? quelle est la route la plus directe ?

畢 |, *pĭt tch'ĭt*, tout droit, directement.

值 *Tch'ĭt*. Coûter, valoir, mériter.

| 錢, 唔 | 錢, *tch'ĭt ts'iên, m̂g tch'ĭt ts'iên*, avoir du prix, n'en pas avoir.

| 得幾多錢, *tch'ĭt tĕt kì tō ts'iên*? combien cela peut-il valoir ?

照時 |, *tchaó chê tch'ĭt*, au prix ordinaire.

TCHÎT

只 *Tchît*. Seulement, mais.

| 有一個, *tchît yoū ŷt ké·*, il n'y en a qu'un.

織 *Tchît*. Tisser.

| 布, *tchît poú*, tisser la toile.

職 *Tchît*. Charge, office, profession.

本 |, *poùn tchît*, office propre de quelqu'un.

佢麼那個 | 業, *kî mô mâc ké· tchît niăp*, il n'a pas d'emploi.

有官 |, *yoū kouōn tchît*, il a une charge de mandarin.

TCHÎT

質 *Tchît*. Substance, nature d'une chose, témoignage.

氣 |, *hí tchît*, nature, constitution, humeur.

| 朴, *tchît p'ŏc*, simple, sans apprêt, sans déguisement.

對 |, *touí tchît*, confronter les témoins.

有人 | 証麼, *yoū gnîn tchît tchín mô?* y a-t-il des témoins?

TCH'ÎT

拭 *Tch'ît*. Essuyer.

TCH'ŎC

着 *Tch'ŏc*. Envoyer, atteindre un but, apparent, manifeste, vrai, bien. Auxiliaire employé dans certains cas comme *tào* 倒.

| 人搭信, *tch'ŏc gnîn tâp sín*, envoyer quelqu'un porter une nouvelle.

|, 十分 |, *tch'ŏc, chîp foūn tch'ŏc*, c'est vrai, c'est bien vrai.

遇 | (v. 倒), *gní tch'ŏc* (v. *tào*), rencontrer.

| 火, *tch'ŏc fò*, s'enflammer.

火燒唔 |, *fò chāo mĝ tch'ŏc*, le feu ne prend pas.

TCHOC

著 *Tchôc*. Vêtir.

| 得着, | 唔着, *tchôc têt tch'ŏc, tchôc mĝ tch'ŏc*, (l'habit) me va, ne me va pas.

| 衫, | 鞋, *tchôc sām, tchôc hâi*, mettre son habit, ses souliers.

酌 *Tchôc*. Délibérer, verser.

斟 |, *tchīm tchôc*, délibérer.

| 酒, *tchôc tsiòu*, verser du vin.

TCH'ŌI

吹 *Tch'ōi* Souffler, souffler d'un instrument.

風 | 壞人, *foūng tch'ōi faí gnîn*, le vent, en soufflant, vous rend malade.

燈子俾風 | 烏, *tēn tzè poūn foūng tch'ōi voū*, le vent a éteint la lampe.

| 笛子, *tch'ōi t'ăc tzè*, flûte, jouer de la flûte.

TCH'ÔI

肘 *Tch'ôi*. Furoncle, abcès.

發 |, *pôt tch'ôi*, avoir un abcès.

| 子會穿, *tch'ôi tzè voé· tch'ōn*, l'abcès va percer.

TCHÓI

載 *Tchói*. Transporter en bateau, ou en voiture, chargement de bateau, ou de voiture.

| 人, | 貨, *tchói gnîn, tchói fó*, transporter en bateau, des hommes, des marchandises.

佢船 | 得萬過斤倒, *kiâ chôn tchói têt ván koúo kīn tào*, sa barque supporte un chargement de plus de dix mille livres.

嘴 *Tchói (pour tsoùi)*. Bec, museau, embouchure.

丨角，丨唇，丨啱，*tchói kôc, tchói choûn, tchói ngām,* les joues, les lèvres, le menton.

親丨，*tsīm tchoí,* embrasser, baiser.

刀丨，*tāo tchói,* le tranchant du couteau.

丨甜心苦，*tchói t'iám sīm foù,* sa bouche est douce, mais son cœur est amer.

两個人講丨，*leòng ké· gnîn kòng tchói,* ils se querellent ensemble.

酒壺丨，烟筒丨，*tsiòu foû tchói, yān t'oûng tchói,* bec d'une cruche de vin, embouchure d'un tuyau de pipe.

講爛丨，*kòng lán tchói,* dire des paroles blessantes

TCHŌN

專 *Tchōn.* S'appliquer à, uniquement, exprès.

丨心念經，*tchōn sīm niám kīn,* prier attentivement.

丨門做筆，*tchōn moûn tsó pît,* fabriquer exclusivement des pinceaux.

自丨，*tsé tchōn,* selon son gré.

不可自丨自主，*poût k'ò tsé tchōn tsé tchoù,* il faut éviter de ne prendre conseil que de soi-même.

丨做一件事，*tchōn tsó ŷt k'ián sé,* s'appliquer uniquement à une affaire.

磚 *Tchōn.* Brique.

一塊丨，*ŷt k'oúai tchōn,* une brique.

火丨，泥丨，*fò tchōn, nâi tchōn,* brique cuite au feu, brique de terre(cuite au soleil).

丨頭，*tchōn t'eôu,* brique de terre, moule à faire des briques.

TCH'ŌN

穿 *Tch'ōn.* Pénétrer de part en part, percer. *Voir* 串 *tch'ón* enfiler.

打丨，*tà tch'ōn,* percer de part en part.

丨針，*tch'ōn tchīm,* enfiler une aiguille.

裡件事我辦不來愛一個人丨透 *ỳ k'ián sé ngâi p'án poût loî, oí ŷt ké· gnîn tch'ōn t'eóu,* je ne puis régler seul cette affaire, il faut un intermédiaire.

裡個山丨阿過就係，*ỳ ké· sān tch'ōn á koúo ts'ióu hé·,* passez ce bois, et vous y êtes.

TCH'ÔN

傳 *Tch'ôn.* Propager, communiquer.

丨教，*tch'ôn káo,* propager la Religion.

係宗徒丨下來個，*hé· tsoūng t'ôu tch'ôn hā loî ké·,* cela vient, par tradition, des Apôtres.

一個丨一個，*ŷt ké· tch'ôn ŷt ké·,* se transmettre de l'un à l'autre.

丨謠言，*tch'ôn yâo niân,* semer de faux bruits.

丨話，*tch'ôn fá,* faire interprète.

好事不出門惡事丨千里，*hào sé poût tch'oût moûn, ôc sé tch'ôn ts'iēn lī,* le bien reste secret, le mal est connu à mille *li.*

TCHÒN

轉 *Tchòn.* Revenir, retourner, tourner, faire un circuit, nombre de fois, de tours.

請丨，*ts'iàng tchòn,* je vous invite à

vous en retourner (à ne pas me reconduire).

一去一｜, *ŷt hí ŷt tchòn,* un aller et un retour.

佢倒｜來, *kî tào tchòn loî,* il revient.

｜身, *tchòn chīn,* s'en retourner. Se dit aussi dans le sens de revenir sur son fait.

佢唔敢｜身, *kî mĝ kàm tchòn chīn,* il n'ose pas revenir sur son fait, (ou sur son dire).

螺螄｜, *lô sē tchòn,* pas de vis.

團｜, *t'ôn tchòn,* tout autour, dans tous les environs.

｜角, *tchòn kôc,* un tournant (par ex. de route).

走一｜, *tseòu ŷt tchòn,* faire un tour, un circuit.

｜北風, *tchòn pêt foūng,* le vent tourne au Nord.

圈圈｜, *k'iān k'iān* (ou *k'ouān k'ouān*) *tchòn,* tourner tout autour.

TCH'ÒN

喘 *Tch'òn.* Respiration haletante.

｜氣病, *tch'òn hí p'iáng,* asthme.

TCHÓN

轉 *Tchón.* Tomber de sa hauteur, renverser.

屋｜了䂮, *voûc tchón liào lê·,* la maison s'est écroulée.

打｜, *tà tchón,* renverser.

TCH'ÓN

篆 *Tch'ón.* ｜字, *tch'ón sé,* écriture antique carrée.

傳 *Tch'ón.* ｜子, *tch'ón tzè,* histoire, roman historique.

左｜, *tsò tch'ón,* nom d'un livre classique historique.

串 *Tch'ón.* Enfiler, ligature, particule numérale; entente secrète.

｜珠子, *tch'ón tchoū tzè,* enfiler des perles.

一｜珠子經, *ŷt tch'ón tchoū tzè kīn,* un chapelet.

｜通, *tch'ón t'oūng,* se mettre d'intelligence, conspirer.

兩個人｜通做事, *leòng ké· gnîn tch'ón t'oūng tsó sé,* il y a eu complicité entre eux deux.

一｜錢, *ŷt tch'ón ts'iên,* une ligature de sapèques.

TCHŌNG

張 *Tchōng.* Ouvrir, étendre, particule numérale.

開｜, *k'oī tchōng,* ouvrir, étendre.

｜揚, *tchōng yōng,* publier, divulguer, faire resplendir.

今日還唔曾開｜, *kīn gnĭt hân mĝ ts'ên k'oī tchōng,* aujourd'hui, je n'ai encore rien vendu.

一｜紙, *ŷt tchōng tjè,* une feuille de papier.

一｜桌, *ŷt tchōng tsôc,* une table.

麼主｜個人, *mô tchoù tchōng ké· gnîn,* homme sans décision, sans volonté.

章 *Tchōng.* Composition littéraire, division de livre.

做文｜, *tsó voûn tchōng*, faire une composition littéraire, une dissertation.

照｜程辦事, *tcháo tchōng tch'in p'án sé*, arranger une affaire d'après les règles établies.

裡書分四｜, *yà chōu foūn sí tchōng*, ce livre se divise en quatre parties.

裝 *Tchōng* (*tsōng*). Enfermer, mettre dans.

｜起來, *tchōng hì loî*, enferme-le, mets-le en lieu sûr.

麽那個來｜, *mô mâc ké loî tchōng*, je n'ai rien dans quoi le mettre.

一個罌子｜咁多唔得, *ŷt ké āng tzè tchōng àn tō mĝ têt*, tout cela ne peut tenir dans une bouteille.

樟 *Tchōng*. ｜樹, *tchōng choú*, camphrier.

TCH'ŌNG

昌 *Tch'ōng*. Prospérer, splendide.

永不能｜盛, *yoùn poût nēn tch'ōng chín*, que jamais tu ne prospères! (imprécation).

文｜宮, *voûn tch'ōng kiōung*, temple des lettrés.

娼 *Tch'ōng*. Prostituée.

當｜, *tōng tch'ōng*, se prostituer.

鬧｜家, *náo tch'ōng kā*, fréquenter les mauvaises maisons.

TCH'ÔNG

長 *Tch'ông*. Long, de longue durée.

三丈｜, *sām tch'óng tch'ông*, 30 pieds de long.

｜衫子, *tch'ông sām tzè*, toge, longue robe chinoise.

｜短, *tch'ông tòn*, le long et le court, longueur, le bien et le mal, qualités et défauts.

比｜短, *pì tch'ông tòn*, mesurer la longueur.

講人｜短, *kòng gnîn tch'ông tòn*, médire, parler du prochain à tort et à travers.

請｜年, *ts'iàng tch'ông niân*, louer un domestique à l'année.

不｜久, *poût tch'ông kiòu*, pas longtemps.

腸 *Tch'ông*. Intestins, boyaux.

大｜, 小｜, *t'aí tch'ông, siào tch'ông*, gros intestin, intestin grêle.

釀｜, *nióng* (ou *yóng*) *tch'ông*, boudin, saucisson.

場 *Tch'ông*. Marché, foire, place; particule numérale.

好大個圩｜, *hào t'aí ké hī tch'ông*, c'est un grand marché.

山｜, *sān tch'ông*, bois, forêt, montagne.

山｜樹木, *sān tch'ông chóu moûc*, tous les arbres d'une propriété.

法｜, *fâp tch'ông*, place des exécutions.

佢唔在｜, *kî mĝ ts'aí tch'ông*, il n'était pas de la partie.

麽那個看｜, *mô mâc ké k'ón tch'ông*, il n'y a pas grand'chose à voir.

佢做我個過丨, *kî tsó ngā ké· koúo tch'ông*, il me joue des tours.

一丨官司, *ŷt tch'ông kouōn sē*, un procès.

𩟗一丨, *liáo ŷt tch'ông*, se reposer un moment.

兩個人打一丨, *leòng ké· gnîn tà ŷt tch'ông*, ils se donnent une rossée.

丨屋, *tch'ông voûc*, lieu des examens.

逢丨作興, *foûng tch'ông tsôc hín*, l'occasion fait le larron (traduction large).

TCHÒNG

轉 *Tchòng* (*tchòn*). S'en retourner. Ce mot ne s'emploie que dans le sens de : 丨外家, *tchòng ngoé· kā*, s'en retourner dans sa famille (se dit d'une fille mariée, qui retourne chez ses parents).

長 *Tchòng*. Grandir, grossir.

丨成, *tchòng chîn*, adulte, homme fait.

麵包丨起了, *mién pāo tchòng hì liào*, le pain a levé.

掌 *Tchòng*. Paume de la main, garder, veiller à, conserver, gouverner.

手丨, 打手丨, *choù tchòng, tà choù tchòng*, paume de la main, donner sur les doigts.

丨屋, 丨牛, *tchòng voûc, tchòng nioû*, garder la maison, garder (paître) le buffle.

丨管, *tchòng kouòn*, gouverner, gérer, avoir la charge ou le soin de.

男人出門婦人家丨管家裏個事, *nâm gnîn tch'oût moûn foú gnîn kā tchòng kouòn kā lì ké· sé*, les hommes voyagent, et les femmes gèrent les affaires de la famille.

TCH'ÒNG

廠 *Tch'òng*. Chantier, aire sans clôture.

搭丨, *tâp tch'òng*, installer un abri.

船丨, *chôn tch'òng*, chantier pour les bateaux.

煤炭丨, *moē· t'án tch'òng*, dépôt de charbon.

杖 *Tch'òng*. Bâton, canne.

老人家愛丨子扶等來, *laò gnîn kā oí tch'òng tzè koú* (pour *foû*) *tèn loî*, un vieillard doit s'appuyer sur une canne.

孝丨, *háo tch'òng*, bâton de deuil sur lequel s'appuie le fils du défunt, lors des funérailles.

暢 *Tch'òng*. Content, gai.

人唔多伸丨, *gnîn mĝ tō tch'oūn tch'òng*, je ne suis pas bien portant, pas à l'aise.

丨敘, *tch'òng sí*, s'égayer par des conversations joyeuses.

丨𨈆, *tch'òng liáo*, s'entretenir joyeusement.

TCHÓNG

漲 *Tchóng*. Inondation, crue.

河水丨一丈高, *hô choùi tchóng ŷt tch'óng kāo*, l'eau du fleuve a monté de 10 pieds.

丨潮, *tchóng tch'âo*, marée montante.

脹 *Tchóng*. Enfler. Voir 腫 *tchoùng*.

發 | 牛, *pôt tchóng nioû*, buffle malade et dont le ventre se gonfle.

帳 *Tchóng*. Tente, courtine.

蚊 |, *moûn tchóng*, moustiquaire.

賬 *Tchóng*. Dette, créance, comptes.

開 |, *k'oî tchóng*, payer ses dettes.

取 |, *ts'ì tchóng*, réclamer sa créance.

放 | 取 利, *fóng tchóng ts'ì lí*, prêter à intérêts.

| 目 唔 分 明, *tchóng moûc mĝ foûn mîn*, les comptes ne sont pas en règle.

息 ou 塞 官 |, *sît* ou *sêt koûon tchóng*, payer les droits de bureau au mandarinat, pour arrêter les poursuites d'une affaire.

仗 *Tchóng*. Armes, combat.

打 |, 開 |, *tà tchóng, k'oî tchóng*, combattre, commencer la bataille.

打 勝 |, 打 輸 |, *tà chín tchóng, tà choû tchóng*, être vainqueur, être vaincu.

TCH'ÓNG

唱 *Tch'óng*. Chanter.

| 歌, *tch'óng kō*, chanter des airs.

| 經, | 戲, *tch'óng kīn, tch'óng hí*, chanter les prières, chanter (jouer) la comédie.

| 山 歌, *tch'óng sān kō* chanter des airs montagnards, airs libres.

丈 *Tch'óng*. Mesure de longueur (10 pieds).

十 尺 爲 一 |, *chìp tch'âc vî ŷt tch'óng*, dix pieds font un *tch'óng*.

長 兩 | 四, *tch'ông leòng tch'óng sí*, long de 24 pieds.

長 兩 | 零 四, *tch'ông leòng tch'óng lâng sí*, long de 20 pieds plus deux (pouces).

| 夫, *tch'óng foū*, mari, époux.

| 人 老, *tch'óng gnîn lào*, beau-père (père de l'époux).

TCHOŪ

周 *Tchoū* (*tcheōu* dans certains endroits). Tourner autour, circuit.

| 圍 一 轉, *tchoū vî ŷt tchòn*, faire un tour, un circuit.

一 | 年, *ŷt tchoū niân*, une année révolue.

| 濟 人, *tchoū tsí gnîn*, faire l'aumône.

| 年 一 分 利, *tchoū niân ŷt foūn lí*, intérêt annuel d'un *foūn* pour cent.

| 圍 舂 墻, *tchoū vî tchoūng siông*, construire un mur d'entourage.

州 *Tchoū*. Préfecture de second ordre (ou sous-préfecture de premier ordre, selon d'autres).

嘉 應 |, *kā ýn tchoū*, la préfecture de *kā ýn*.

出 | *v.* 下 | *v.* 上 |, *tch'oût tchoū* (*v. hā tchoū v. chōng tchoū*, selon qu'il faille monter ou descendre), aller à la préfecture.

洲 *Tchoū*. Partie du monde.

天 下 有 五 大 |, *t'iēn hā yōu ng t'ái*

tchoū, la terre se divise en (*litt.* a) cinq parties.

硃 *Tchoū.* Couleur rouge, vermillon.

土 |, *t'où tchoū*, vermillon.

銀 |, *nioûn tchoū*, minium de plomb.

珠 *Tchoū.* Perle, précieux.

念 |, *niám tchoū*, chapelet, rosaire.

珍 |, *tchīn tchoū*, bijou, perle précieuse (employée aussi en médecine.)

誅 *Tchoū.* Exterminer.

| 滅九族, *tchoū mĕt kiòu ts'oūc*, exterminer toute la parenté.

諸 *Tchoū.* Tous.

| 聖瞻禮, *tchoū chín tchām lī*, fête de la Toussaint.

| 位, *tchoū ví*, vous tous, messieurs.

猪 *Tchoū.* Cochon, porc.

| 哥, *tchoū kō*, verrat.

生 | 牸, *sāng tchoū tsé*, truie.

| 媽, *tchoū mâ*, laie.

| 絛, *tchoū t'iâo*, truie châtrée, cochon.

豪 |, *hô tchoū*, porc-épic.

租 *Tchoū* (ou *tzē*). Revenus. Voir *tzē*.

TCH'OŪ

柱 *Tch'oū* Colonne de bois ou de pierre, poteau, support.

| 墩, *tch'oū toùn*, colonne, pieu.

一 絛 | 墩, *ŷt t'iâo tch'oū toùn*, une colonne.

苧 *Tch'oū.* Ortie blanche (employée comme le chanvre).

| 索, *tch'oū sōc*, corde faite avec cette plante.

抽 *Tch'oū.* Tirer, serrer; frais de douane.

一身個筋頭 | 倣, *ŷt chīn ké kīn t'eôu tch'oū ts'iou*, tous les nerfs de mon corps sont tendus.

燈子忒少油 | 唔上, *tēn tzè t'iĕt chào yoû tch'oū mĝ chōng*, la lampe a trop peu d'huile, elle ne peut monter.

唔曾綁穩愛 | 狠來, *mĝ ts'ên pòng voùn oí tch'oū hên loî*, ce n'est pas attaché solidement, il faut serrer fort.

| 稅, *tch'oū choé*, passer la douane, payer les frais de douane.

| 子, *v.* | 頭, *tch'oū tzè*, ou *tch'oū t'eoû*, tiroir d'un meuble.

TCH OÛ

酬 *Tch'oû.* Rendre une politesse, répondre à un bienfait.

| 謝人, *tch'oû ts'iá gnîn*, remercier par des cadeaux.

應 | 人, *ýn tch'oû gnîn*, s'occuper de quelqu'un, lui donner l'hospitalité, lui rendre les civilités.

籌 *Tch'oû.* Compter, supputer, réfléchir à ce qu'il faut faire.

裁 |, *ts'âi tch'oû*, pourvoir d'une chose, combiner un plan.

| 託, *tch'oû t'ōc*, supputer.

除 *Tch'oû*. Soustraire, exclure, à moins que.

一百錢｜五十還有五十, *ŷt pâc ts'iên tch'oû ǹg chĭp hân yōu ǹg chĭp*, de 100 sapèques, ôtez-en 50, il en reste encore 50.

打歸｜, *tà kōui tch'oû*, faire une division.

我｜你工錢, *ngâi tch'oû nĭa koūng ts'iên*, je retiens de ton salaire.

｜裡俾麽那個話, *tch'oû ỳ ké· mô mâc ké· vá*, à part cela, il n'y a rien à dire.

｜了佢我行唔得, *tch'oû liào kî ngâi hâng mḡ têt*, sans lui, je ne puis rien faire.

｜免, *tch'oû mēn*, condonner, épargner.

｜帛有病日日愛來, *tch'oû p'ĕt yōu p'iáng gnĭt gnĭt oí loî*, il faut venir tous les jours, à moins que tu ne sois malade.

廚 *Tch'oû*. Cuisine, cuisinier.

｜房, *tch'oû fông*, cuisine.

｜子, *tch'oû tzè*, cuisinier.

企｜, *k'ī tch'oû*, armoire.

壁｜, *piâc tch'oû*, placard.

棧｜, *ts'án tch'oû*, garde-manger.

綢 *Tch'oû*, Soie, tissu de soie.

紡｜四圍齊, *fòng tch'oû sí vî ts'ê·*, longue robe de soie.

TCHOÙ

主 *Tchoù*. Maître, disposer en maître.

天｜, *t'iēn tchoù*, maître du ciel, Dieu.

｜日, *tchoù gnĭt*, jour du Seigneur, dimanche.

一個｜日, *ŷt ké· tchoù gnĭt*, une semaine.

｜人, *tchoù gnîn*, le propriétaire, le maître.

｜敎, *tchoù káo*, l'Évêque.

｜保, *tchoù pào*, protecteur, patron.

自｜, *tsé tchoù*, maître de ses actions, libre arbitre.

作｜, *tsôc tchoù*, statuer, disposer en maître.

出｜意, *tch'oût tchoù ý*, prendre une détermination.

｜固, *tchoù kóu*, solide, ferme.

煮 *Tchoù*. Cuire à l'eau.

｜好裡, *tchoù hào lê·*, c'est cuit.

｜熟, *tchoù choŭc*, cuit à point.

TCH'OÙ

暑 *Tch'où*. Chaleur.

｜天, *tch'où t'iēn*, l'été.

避｜, *p'ĭt tch'où*, se garantir de la chaleur.

鼠 *Tch'où*. Rat et autres animaux rongeurs.

老｜, *lào tch'où*, rat, souris.

裡個貓公唔殺｜, *yà ké· miáo koūng mḡ sât tch'où*, ce chat ne tue pas les rats.

醜 *Tch'où*. Vilain, honteux.

｜陋, *tch'où leóu*, vilain, honteux.

講｜話, *kòng tch'où fá*, dire des paroles obscènes.

處 *Tch'où.* Châtier.

官｜治佢, *kouōn tch'où tché kî,* le mandarin l'a puni sévèrement.

｜死人, *tch'où sì gnîn,* mettre à mort, punir de mort.

｜拚清楚, *tch'où p'án ts'īn tsè,* trancher un différend.

TCHOÚ

晝 *Tchoú.* Jour, le temps qui s'écoule depuis le lever du soleil jusqu'à son coucher.

上｜, 下｜, *chóng tchoú, há tchoú,* la matinée, la soirée.

半｜, *pán tchoú,* la matinée avancée.

忒｜赴圩唔倒, *t'iĕt tchoú foú hī mĝ taò,* la journée est trop avancée, nous n'arriverons pas pour la foire.

食｜, *chĭt tchoú,* dîner.

做｜, *tsó tchoú,* faire le dîner de midi.

咒 *Tchoú.* Faire des imprécations.

｜罵人, *tchoú má gnîn,* injurier qqn.

著 *Tchoú.* Publier.

｜書, *tchoú chou,* publier un livre.

註 *Tchoú.* Expliquer, commentaire.

｜解, *tchoú kiài,* commentaire, expliquer.

｜子也愛讀, *tchoú tzè ya ói t'oŭc,* il faut aussi étudier les commentaires.

｜得明白, *tchoú tĕt mîn p'ĕt* (*p'ăc*), c'est très bien expliqué.

鑄 *Tchoú.* Couler du métal.

｜鍋, *tchoú vŏc,* fondre des marmites.

｜鉎, *tchoú sāng,* couler de la fonte.

｜鐵廠, *tchoú t'iĕt tch'òng,* fonderie.

裡塑像係｜倒個係鑿倒個, *yà chín sióng hé· tchoú taò ké· hé· ts'ŏc taò ké·*? cette statue a-t-elle été coulée au moule ou bien sculptée?

蛀 *Tchoú.* Teigne, ronger.

尼衫｜了裡, *nî sām tchoú liào lê·,* ma robe de drap est toute rongée des vers.

TCH'OÚ

臭 *Tch'oú.* Puanteur, sentir mauvais (au propr. et au fig.).

唔知香｜, *mĝ tī hiōng tch'óu,* ne pas savoir distinguer la bonne odeur de la mauvaise (ne pas savoir distinguer le bien du mal).

猪肉｜帛裡, *tchou nioûc tch'oú p'ĕt lĕ·,* la viande sent mauvais, elle est gâtée.

獸 *Tch'óu.* Quadrupèdes, animaux sauvages.

禽｜, *k'îm tch'óu,* oiseaux et quadrupèdes, les animaux en général.

野｜, *yā tch'óu,* animaux sauvages.

住 *Tch'óu.* Habiter, demeurer, s'arrêter.

你在那裡｜, *gnî ts'ái nái lī tch'óu,* (ou bien: *gnî hōi* v. *hō* v. *t'ōi ngái lī tch'oú*)? où habites-tu?

留｜幾天, *liòu tch'óu kì t'iēn,* retenir (un hôte) quelques jours.

對人唔｜, *toúi gnîn mĝ tch'oú*, ne pouvoir se présenter devant quelqu'un (à cause d'une impolitesse).

歇店｜一夜, *hiĕt tiám tch'oú ŷt yá*, passer une nuit à l'auberge.

處 *Tch'oú*. Lieu, endroit.

｜｜都在, *tch'oú tch'oú toū ts'ái*, il est partout.

到｜走, *táo tch'oú tseòu*, aller partout.

别｜, *p'iĕt tch'óu*, ailleurs.

各｜地方唔同, *kôc tch'óu t'í fōng mĝ t'oûng*, chaque pays est différent.

貴｜?... 敝｜在石正, *koúi tch'óu ?... pí tch'óu ts'ái chăc tchín*, où habitez-vous ? je demeure à *Chac tchin*.

TCH'ŎUC

掓 *Tch'oŭc*. Agiter, remuer.

稈掃唔伶俐拿來｜淨來, *kòn sáo mĝ lâng lí nā loî tch'oŭc ts'iáng loî*, le balai n'est pas propre, secoue-le.

騎馬噲｜人一身, *k'î mā voé tch'oŭc gnîn ŷt chīn*, l'équitation vous secoue tout le corps.

嗽 *Tch'oŭc*. Tousser.

我受裡風緊｜, *ngâi choú lê foūng kìn tch'oŭc*, j'ai pris froid, je ne fais que tousser.

逐 *Tch'oŭc*. Chasser, expulser.

驅｜人, *k'ī tch'oŭc gnîn*, chasser qqn.

趕｜魔鬼, *kòn tch'oŭc mô koùi*, chasser le diable. (Voir *kioŭc*.)

TCHÔUC

粥 *Tchoûc*. Soupe de riz.

食鮮｜, *chĭt siēn tchoûc*, manger de la soupe claire de riz.

我食兩飡一飡飯一飡｜, *ngâi chĭt leòng ts'ōn, ŷt ts'ōn fán, ŷt ts'ōn tchoûc*, je fais deux repas, un repas au riz, un repas à la soupe de riz.

囑 *Tchoûc*. Confier, recommander.

叮｜, *tēn tchoûc*, recommander avec instance.

主教｜我去平遠傳教, *tchòu káo tchoûc ngâi hí p'în yàn tch'ôn káo*, l'évêque m'a envoyé évangéliser le *P'in yan*.

我至｜你裡件事, *ngaî tjé tchoûc gnî lì k'ián sé*, je te recommande cette affaire.

築 *Tchoûc*. Battre le terrain, tasser.

｜墻，屋, *tchoûc siông, tchoûc voûc*, élever un mur, bâtir une maison.

祝 *Tchoûc*. Bénir.

｜聖水, *tchoûc chín choùi*, faire de l'eau bénite.

｜壽, *tchoûc choú*, féliciter qqn. le jour de son anniversaire.

｜文, *tchoûc voûn*, prières païennes ressemblant à des litanies.

燭 *Tchoûc*. Torche, chandelle.

黃蠟｜, *vông lăp tchoûc*, cierge de cire.

｜臺, *tchoûc t'ôi*, chandelier, bougeoir.

竹 *Tchoûc*. Bambou.

一墩｜頭, *ŷt toūn tchoûc t'eôu*, une touffe de bambous.

| 節, *tchoûc tsiĕt*, les nœuds du bambou.

| 箱 *tchoûc siōng*, longueur du bambou, comprise entre deux nœuds.

TCH'OÛC

觸 *Tch'oûc*. Attaquer, exciter.

| 父母個怒, *tch'oûc foú moū kê· noú*, exciter, provoquer la colère de ses parents.

細人莫吵一吵嚕 | 惱人, *sé· gnîn mŏc ts'aô ўt ts'aô voé· tch'oûc naō gnîn*, enfants, ne faites pas de tapage, sinon vous allez nous mettre en colère.

束 *Tch'oûc*. | 修, *tch'oûc siōu*, honoraires d'un maître d'école.

畜 *Tch'oûc* (*hioûc*). | 生, *tch'oûc sāng*, animaux domestiques.

TCHOŪI

(*Voir aussi TSOUI*)

追 *Tchouī*. Poursuivre, remonter dans le passé.

我 | 𠊎佢好遠, *ngâi tchouī lê· kì hào yàn*, je l'ai poursuivi bien loin.

| 跡, *tchoūi tsiâc*, suivre à la piste.

愛 | 等根頭來, *oí tchoūi tèn kēn t'eoû loî*, il faut en rechercher la cause.

| 思唔倒, *tchoūi sē mģ taò*. ne pouvoir rappeler ses souvenirs.

| 思先亡, *tchoūi sē siēn vōng*, rappeler le souvenir des défunts, commémoration des morts.

我錢愛 | 取轉來, *ngaî ts'iĕn oí tchoūi ts'ì tchòn loî*, il faut me faire rendre mon argent.

TCH'OŪI

推 *Tch'ouī* ou *t'ouī*. Prétexter, s'excuser. Voir *t'ouī*.

TCH'OÛI

錐 *Tch'oûi*. Marteau.

鐵 | , *t'iĕt tch'oûi*, marteau de fer.

搥 *Tch'oûi*. Frapper, piler, broyer.

| 綿, *tchoûi miĕn*, piler, réduire en miettes.

| 鐵, *tchoûi t'iĕt*, forger le fer.

墜 *Tch'oûi*. Poids qui attire en bas.

砣子忒輕 | 唔下, *t'ô tzè t'iĕt k'iāng tch'oûi mģ hā*, le poids est trop léger il ne peut attirer.

線 | , *sién tch'oûi*, fil à plomb.

TCHOÚI

墜 *Tchoúi*. Tomber, céder (peu employé, on dit plutôt 落 *lŏc*).

| 星, *tchoúi sēn*, bolide.

TCHOŪN

震 *Tchoūn* (*tchìn*). Trembler.

一身戰戰 | , *ўt chīn t'án t'án tchoūn*, trembler de tous ses membres.

TCH'OŪN

春 *Tch'oūn*. Printemps.

| 天, *tch'oūn t'iēn*, le printemps.

立 | , *lĭp tch'oūn*, équinoxe du printemps.

春 *Tch'oūn*. Œuf.

雞 | , 鴨 | , *kē· tch'oūn, âp tch'oūn*, œuf de poule, de cane.

| 黃 , | 白, *tch'oūn vông tch'oūn p'ăc*, le jaune d'œuf, le blanc d'œuf.

| 殼 , *tch'oūn hôc*, coquille d'œuf.

伸 *Tch'oūn* (*chīn*).Uni,lisse, tendu.

我毛辮 | 帛裡, *ngā māo piēn tch'oūn p'ĕt lê·*, ma tresse de cheveux s'est défaite.

| 腰 , *tch'oūn yāo*, s'étirer (*litt*. détendre les reins).

綫子紇帛裡愛 | 抓 , *sién tzè kĕt p'ĕt lì oí tch'oūn tch'ā*, le fil est tout embrouillé, il faut le débrouiller.

行得 | , 行唔 | , *hâng tĕt tch'oūn, hâng mĝ tch'oūn*, pouvoir marcher jusqu'au bout, ne pas pouvoir.

講話唔 | 抓 , *kòng fá mĝ tcho'ūn tch'ā*, se contredire dans ses paroles, dire des mots sans suite.

人唔 | 暢 , *gnîn mĝ tch'oūn tch'òng*, n'être pas très bien portant.

TCHOÙN

准 *Tchoùn*. Permettre, approuver, ratifier.

主教 | , *tchòu káo tchoùn*, l'évêque le permet.

官 | 呈子 , *kouōn tchoùn tch'în tzè*, le mandarin a admis son accusation.

父母降福賴子天主有 | , *foú mōu kóng foŭc laí tzè t'iēn tchoù yoū tchoùn*, Dieu exauce les bénédictions des parents.

準 *Tchoùn*. Juste; tenir la place de.

手藝係 | , *choù sé hé· tchoùn*, être adroit.

時辰鐘唔 | , *chê chîn tchoūng mĝ tchoùn*, l'horloge n'est pas juste.

番人食麵包 | 飯 , *fān gnîn chĭt mién pāo tchoùn fán*, les étrangers mangent du pain en guise de riz.

| 定那個日來去 , *tchoùn t'ín mâc ké· gnĭt loî hí*, déterminer le jour du départ.

TCH'OÙN

蠢 *Tch'oùn*. Stupide, imbécile.

十分 | 個人 , *chĭp foūn tch'oùn ké· gnîn*, cet homme est très borné.

TCHOUNG

(*Voir aussi* TSOUNG)

中 *Tchoūng*. Milieu, centre.

| 門 , | 堂 , *tchoūng moûn, tchoūng t'ông*, porte du milieu d'une maison, la salle du milieu d'un prétoire, ou d'une maison.

| 等 , *tchoūng tèn*, du commun.

| 人 , *tchoūng gnîn*, entremetteur d'affaire.

| 間人 , *tchoūng kiān gnîn*, médiateur de rencontre, qui se mêle à une affaire sans y être intéressé.

| 國 ou **| 華** , *tchoūng kouĕt* ou *tchoūng fâ*, l'empire du milieu, la Chine.

Dans le sens de centre on emploie de préférence le mot **心** *sīm*. Voir ce mot.

忠 *Tchoūng*. Fidèle.

| 厚 個 人, *tchoūng heóu ké· gnîn*, homme fidèle.

春 *Tchoūng*. Piler, fouler.

| 墻, *tchoūng siông*, construire un mur en terre foulée.

藥草拿來 | 綿, *yŏc ts'ào nā loî tchoūng miên*, piler des herbes médicinales (pour cataplasmes).

終 *Tchoūng*. Fin, terme, mort.

| 傅, *tchoūng foú*, l'Extrême-Onction.

傅 | 油, *foú tch'oūng yoû*, administrer l'Extrême-Onction.

得 善 |, *têt chán tchoūng*, obtenir une bonne mort.

天 主 無 始 無 |, *t'iēn tchoù voû tchè voû tchoūng*, Dieu n'a ni commencement ni fin.

天 地 | 窮, *t'iēn t'í tchoūng k'ioûng*, la fin du monde.

鐘 *Tchoūng*. Cloche, horloge, couvercle en forme de globe.

打 |, *tà tchoūng*, frapper la cloche, sonner.

時 辰 |, *chê chîn tchoūng*, horloge, pendule.

一 點 |, *ŷt tiàm tchoūng*, une heure.

? |, *kèm tchoūng*, couvercle en forme de cloche ou globe.

燈 子 個 |, *tēn tzè ké· tchoūng*, le globe de la lampe.

念 三 | 經, *niám sām tchoūng kīn*, réciter l'Angelus.

撞 *Tchoūng* (*ts'óng*). Pousser.

莫 緊 | 門, *mŏc kìn tchoūng moûn*, ne poussez pas la porte ainsi.

TCH'OŪNG

Voir aussi TS OUNG

充 *Tch'oūng*. Exiler, confisquer.

辦 | 罪, | 軍, *p'án tch'oūng ts'oúi, tch'oūng kioūn*, condamé à l'exil, exilé.

地方拿來 | 公, *t'í fōng nā loî tch'oūng koūng*, confisquer une terre, le terrain est devenu propriété publique.

冲 *Tch'oūng*. Verser, mêler, s'élever dans les airs, jaillir.

| 酒 | 滿 來, *tch'oūng tsiòu tch'oūng mān loî*, verse-moi du vin, verse plein.

酒 敱 裡 | 等 水 去, *tsiòu teóu lî tch'oung tèn choùi hí*, mêler de l'eau au vin.

火 利 | 阿 起, *fò lí tch'oūng á hì*, la flamme s'est élevée très haut dans les airs.

日 日 灶 下 燉 火 氣 嗆 | 壞 人, *gnĭt gnĭt tsaó hā liaó fò hí voé· tch'oūng faí gnîn*, obligé de rester tous les jours à la cuisine, les vapeurs qui s'élèvent du foyer me font mal.

| 身, *tch'oūng chīn*, se doucher.

| 涼, *tch'oūng leông*, se rafraîchir par des lotions d'eau froide.

重 *Tch'oūng*. Lourd.

有 幾 |, *yoū kì tch'oūng*? combien cela pèse-t-il ?

有 一 百 斤 |, *yoū ŷt pâc kīn tch'oūng*, cela pèse 100 livres.

TCH'OÛNG

虫 *Tch'oûng.* Vers, insecter.

丨子吃了裏, *tch'oûng tzè ngâc liào lê*, c'est mangé par les vers.

毛丨, *mâo tch'oûng*, chenille velue.

重 *Tch'oûng.* De nouveau, répété.

雙丨, *soûng tch'oûng*, double, boublé.

两丨樓, *leòng tch'oûng leôu*, maison à deux étages.

做丨還事, *tsó tch'oûng p'ân (pour fân) ché*, refaire le même ouvrage une seconde fois.

TCHOÙNG

腫 *Tchoùng.* Tumeur, enflure, se gonfler.

丨起來, *tchoùng hì loî*, se gonfler, tuméfier.

一身都丨了, *ŷt chīn tōu tchoùng liào*, tout son corps est enflé.

種 *Tchoùng.* Semence, espèce.

留穀丨, *liôu koŭc tchoùng*, conserver de le semence de riz.

浸穀丨, *tsím koŭc tchoùng*, tremper la semence de riz dans l'eau, pour le faire germer.

大丨狗, *t'ái tchoùng keòu*, chien de grosse race.

丨丨罪惡, *tchoùng tchoùng ts'ouí ôc*, toutes les espèces de péché.

TCH'OÙNG

寵 *Tch'oùng.* Faveur, grâce.

丨教, *tch'oùng kaó*, la loi de grâce.

恩丨 ou **聖丨**, *ēn tch'oùng* ou *chín tch'oùng*, grâce sanctifiante.

天主所丨愛個, *t'iēn tchoù sò tch'oùng oí ké*, ceux que Dieu aime, aimé de Dieu.

塚 *Tch'oùng.* Tombeau commun.

義丨, *gní tch'oùng*, cimetiere commun acheté par cottisation.

TCHOÚNG

中 *Tchoúng.* Atteindre le but.

打丨, *tà tchoúng*, même sens.

丨舉, *tchoúng kì*, devenir docteur.

丨意, *tchoúng ý*, cela me va, satisfaisant, conforme à mes vœux.

丨靶丨紅心, *tchoúng pà tchoúng foûng sīm*, tirer en plein centre (*litt.* dans le rouge du milieu de la cible).

種 *Tchoúng.* Planter, cultiver.

耕丨, *kāng tchoúng*, cultiver la terre.

丨花, 丨菜, 丨樹, *tchoúng fā, tchoúng ts'oí, tchoúng choú*, cultiver des fleurs, des légumes, planter des arbres.

丨得生, 丨唔生, *tchoúng tĕt sāng, tchoúng m̂g sāng*, pouvoir pousser, ne pas pouvoir pousser.

眾 *Tchoúng.* Tous.

天主降生爲救丨人, *t'iēn tchoù kóng sēn ví kióu tchoúng gnîn*, Dieu s'est fait homme pour sauver tous les homnes.

丨心難一丨口難齊, *tchoúng sīm nân ŷt, tchoúng k'èou nân ts'ê*, il est difficile que tous pensent et parlent de la même façon.

TCH'OÚNG

重 *tch'oúng*. Grave, considérable, important.

看佢看得 | , *k'ón kî k'ón têt tch'oúng*, il fait grand cas de lui.

敬 | , *kín tch'oúng*, avoir en haute considération.

| 罰, *tch'oúng făt*, punir sévèrement

| 罪, *tch'oúng ts'ouí*, péché grave.

四 *Tch'oúng*. Odeur piquante.

芥辣噲 | 人, *kiái lăt voé· tch'oúng gnin*, la moutarde vous monte au nez.

銃 *Tch'oúng*. Fusil, pistolet.

鳥 | , **洋 |** , *niāo tch'oúng*, *yông tch'oúng* fusil chinois, fusil étranger.

| 頭劍, *tch'oúng t'eôu kiám*, baïonnette.

打 | , *tà tch'oúng*, tirer des coups de fusil.

雙管 | , *soūng koùon tch'oúng*, fusil à deux coups.

打一管 | , *tà ȳt koùon tch'oúng*, tirer un coup de fusil.

打幾下管 | , *tà kì há koùon tch'oúng*, tirer quelques coups de fusil.

TCH'OÛT

出 *Tch'oût*. Sortir, produire, émettre.

| 來, **| 去**, *tch'oût loî*, *tch'oût hí*, sortir dehors, aller dehors.

喊佢 | 來, *hám kî tch'oût loî*, dis-lui de venir au dehors.

| 恭, *tch'oût kioūng*, aller à la selle.

你拿 | 來看, *gnî nā tch'oût loî k'ón*, montre-le.

錢拿唔 | , *ts'iên nā mĝ tch'oût*, n'être pas à même de donner des sapèques.

| 歲, *tch'oût sé·*, naître, venir au monde.

| 名, *tch'oût miâng*, célèbre, avoir de la renommée.

有錢敢 | 衆無衣難 | 門, *yōu ts'iên kàm tch'oût tchoúng voû ȳ nân tch'oût moún*, le riche ose se montrer, celui qui n'a pas d'habit n'ose pas passer le seuil de sa porte.

TĒN

丁 *Tēn*. Ce mot n'a pas, en langue parlée, de sens bien déterminé ; il exprime la force, la vigueur.

兵 | , *pīn tēn*, les soldats.

門 | ou **門閥**, *moûn tēn* ou *moûn foūn*) les familiers du mandarin.

白 | , *p'ăc tēn*, un homme du simple peuple.

今年添裡幾多個 | , *kīn niân t'iām lî kì tō ké· tēn ?* cette année, de combien de personnes s'est augmentée votre famille ?

家裏麼有一個白 | , *kā lî mó yōu ȳt ké· p'ăc tēn*, dans la famille il n'y en a pas un qui ne soit globulé.

| 對, *tēn toúi*, en plein, comme il faut.

食裡藥 | 對, *chĭt tê· yŏc tēn toúi*, il a pris un remède très efficace.

日頭 | 對, *gnĭt t'eôu tēn toúi*, en plein soleil.

| (ou **叮**) **囑**, *tēn tchoûc* , ordonner, commander.

丨香, *tēn hiōng*, clou de girofle.

恭喜你財丨與旺, *kiōung hì gnî ts'oî tēn hīn vóng*, bonjour, puissent tes richesses s'accroître avec ta famille.

燈 *Tēn*. Lampe, lanterne, fanal, falot.

點丨, *tiàm tēn*, allumer la lampe.

丨拿來上油, *tēn nā loî chòng yoû*, mets de l'huile dans la lampe.

天丨, *t'iēn tēn*, lampes que les païens allument en certaines occasions, au sommet d'un mât.

丨籠, *tēn loûng* lanterne, falot.

孔明丨, *k'oùng mîn tēn*, ballon gonflé à l'air chaud et portant son feu.

丨心, *tēn sīm*, mèche de lampe.

丨盞, *tēn tsàn*, petite soucoupe qui contient l'huile de la lampe.

丨摘, *tēn tsâc*, petit disque de métal pesant sur la mèche pour l'assujettir.

T'ĒN (*voir T'ien*).

T'ÊN

T'ÊN

謄 *T'ên* ou *t'én*. Concorder, suivre.

個隻籮丨唔倒, *ké· tchâc lô t'ên mĝ taò*.la charge est plus lourde d'un côté que de l'autre.

你算數來看丨得倒麼, *gnî són sé loî k'ón t'ên têt taò mô*, fais tes comptes et voyons si tes chiffres concordent avec les miens.

丨脚蹟, *t'ên kiôc tsiâc*, suivre une piste.

丨會, *t'ên fí*, s'associer.

丨分, *t'ên fōun*, avoir part, prendre part.

藤 *T'ên*. Liane, tige rampante, rotin.

番薯丨, *fān choû t'ên*, tiges de patates.

丨几, *t'ên ỳ*, chaise en rotin.

葡萄丨, *p'oû t'aô t'ên*, branches de vigne.

TÈN

等 *Tèn*. Mot final qui marque ordinairement le participe présent.

神父食丨裡, *chîn foú chĭt tên lê·*, le Père est après manger.

佢做丨裡事, *kî tsó tên lê· ché·*, il est à travailler, il travaille.

On l'emploie aussi pour marquer l'impératif.

食丨來, *chĭt tèn loî*, mange, mangez.

做丨來, *tsó tèn loî*, faites, travaillez.

Ailleurs on emploie dans le même sens le mot: 緊 *kìn*, (voir ce mot).

等 *Tèn*. Attendre, qualité, marque du pluriel.

丨下來, 丨下就來, *tèn hā loî, tèn hā ts'ióu loî*, attends un instant, j'arrive.

丨唔久, *tèn mĝ kiòu*, je ne puis attendre longtemps ; sous peu, dans peu de temps.

丨佢好裡來, *tèn kî hào lê· loî*, attends qu'il soit guéri, laisse-le jusqu'à ce qu'il soit guéri.

丨我看, 丨我做, *tèn ngâi k'ón, tèn ngâi tsó*, laisse-moi voir, laisse-moi faire.

有上｜中｜下｜, *yoū chóng tèn tchoūng tèn há tèn*, il y a première qualité, qualité moyenne, qualité inférieure.

我｜, 你｜, 佢｜, *ngā tèn, gnî tèn, kî tèn*, nous, vous, ils ou eux.

我｜人唔係咁樣做, *ngā tèn gnîn mĝ hé· àn yóng tsó*, nous autres, nous ne faisons pas ainsi.

我｜唔比佢｜, *ngā tèn mĝ pì kî tèn*, nous ne sommes pas comme eux.

戥 *Tèn*. Petite romaine à un seul plateau, pour peser l'argent et autres petits objets de prix.

釐｜, *lî tèn*, même sens.

拿｜子來秤, *na tèn tzè loî tch'în*, apporte la balance pour peser.

TÉN

凳 *Tén*. Banc, escabeau.

一張｜, *ȳt tchōng tén*, un banc.

馬｜, *mā tén*, étrier.

TEOŪ

桪 *Teoū*. Porter devant soi des deux mains.

凳子｜出來, *tén tzè teoū tch'oût loî*, apporte le banc.

兜 *Teoū*. Bassin, auge; provoquer; marque du pluriel.

猪｜, *tchoū teoū*, auge de porc.

地｜, *t'í teoū*, bassin à recueillir les ordures.

肚｜, *toù teoū*, poche que les Chinois portent sur le ventre.

同細人子｜屎｜尿, *t'oûng sé· gnîn tzè teoū chè teoū niáo*, faire aller les petits enfants, provoquer leurs selles ou leurs urines à la manière des mamans. (Dans le sens de provoquer, ce mot ne s'emploie que dans cette expression).

有｜子, *yoū teoū tzè*, il y en a un peu.

聽得｜倒, *t'āng tēt teoū taò*, je puis entendre quelque peu.

佢｜人, *kî teoū gnîn*, eux.

盡｜, *ts'în teoū*, tous.

T'EOŪ

偷 *T'eōu*. Voler, dérober.

犯｜盜, *fám t'eōu t'áo*, commettre un vol.

還細｜針大裡｜金, *hân sé· t'eōu tchīm t'ái lî t'eōu kīm*, celui qui, tout jeune, vole une aiguille, devenu grand, volera de l'argent.

｜走, *t'eōu tsèou*, s'en aller à la dérobée.

｜看, ｜聽, *t'eōu k'ón, t'eōu t'āng*, regarder, entendre à la dérobée, guetter.

｜食, *t'eōu chīt*, voler quelque chose à manger.

好貓公噲｜食, *haò miaó koūng voé· t'eōu chīt*, les bons chats sont voleurs.

T'EÔU

骰 *T'eôu* (ou *heôu* ou *sēt* selon les pays). Dés à jouer.

擲｜, *tchīt t'eôu*, jeter les dés.

頭 *T'eôu*. Tête, chef, premier, commencement; finale de bon nombre de substantifs.

| 哪, *t'eôu nâ*, la tête, par rapport aux autres membres.

喏 |, *ngàm t'eôu*, faire un petit salut de tête, un signe d'assentiment.

搖 |, *yâo t'eôu*, branler la tête (en signe de dénégation, ou autre chose).

佢在 (ou 坐) |, *kî ts'ái* (ou *ts'ó*) *t'eôu*, il est le premier.

| 一, *t'eôu ŷt*, même sens.

酒 |, *tsioù t'eôu*, vin de 1ere qualité, le premier alcool qui sort de l'alambic.

| 麵, *t'eôu mién*, farine de première qualité.

| 上, *t'eôu hóng*, au commencement.

兩 |, *leòng t'eôu*, les deux extrémités.

我坐一 |, *ngaî ts'ó ŷt t'eôu*, je tiens un bout, j'ai droit à une part.

賭博塲 | 家抽 |, *toù pôc tch'ông t'eôu kā tch'oú* (pour *tch'oū*) *t'eôu*, dans les maisons de jeu, les patrons prélèvent une prime sur les enjeux.

走裡 |, *tsèou ỳ t'eôu*, aller de ce côté-ci.

外 |, *ngóe' t'eôu*, marcher du côté opposé, en dehors.

| 回, *t'eôu fî*, l'autre fois.

| 緒, *t'eôu sí*, continuité, suite.

你話麼 | 麼緒, *niâ fá mô t'eôu mô sí*, tes paroles n'ont pas de suite.

| 路, *t'eôu loú*, place, emploi quelconque.

嫩過頭, *noún koúo t'eoú*, trop tendre.

投 *T'eôu*. Se jeter, aller trouver, conforme.

| 河, *t'eôu hô*, se jeter à l'eau.

自 | 羅網, *tsé t'eôu lô miòng*, se prendre à ses propres filets.

| 案, *t'eôu ón*, se présenter au tribunal.

兩個人極相 |, *leòng ké' gnîn k'ït siōng t'eôu*, ils sont tous deux en très bon accord.

話不 | 機, *fá poût t'eôu kī*, paroles en dehors de la question, coq-à-l'âne.

愛先 | 鄉紳呼好告狀, *oí siēn t'eôu hīong chīn tsáng haò káo ts'óng*, il faut d'abord confier votre affaire aux notables avant de lancer votre pièce d'accusation.

TEOÙ

斗 *Teoù*. Boisseau (le 10eme d'un picul).

十 | 爲一石, *chĭp teoù vî ŷt chăc*, dix boisseaux font un picul.

刮 |, *kouât teoù*, niveler le boisseau.

熨 |, *yoún teoù*, fer à repasser.

墨 |, *mĕt teoù*, instrument de menuisier, pour encrer le cordeau à tracer les lignes.

T'EOÙ

透 *T'eoù* (*t'eóu*). | 氣, *t'eoù hí*, respirer.

| 氣唔出, *t'eoù hí mĝ tch'oût*, ne pouvoir respirer.

| 大氣, *t'eoù t'ái hí*, pousser un long soupir.

TEOÚ

鬥 *Teoú*. Ajuster, emboîter, concorder.

| 得着, | 唔着, *teoú tĕt tch'ŏc, teoú mĝ tch'ŏc*, pouvoir réunir, ajuster, ne pas pouvoir réunir.

丨唔穩, *teoú mĝ voùn*, ne pouvoir faire tenir solidement, en ajustant.

丨倒主日, 丨倒有人來, *teoú tào tchoù gnĭt, teoú tào yoū gnîn loî*, s'il se trouve que c'est un dimanche, s'il se trouve qu'il arrive quelqu'un.

丨錢, *teoú ts'iên*, se cotiser.

丨多, *teoú tō*, plus ou moins! tout au juste!

鬭 *Teoú*. Lutter, contester.

丨殺, *teoú săt*, s'entretuer.

相丨是非, *siōng teoú ché fī*, être en contestation, en discussion.

牛噲丨人, *niôu voé· teoú gnîn*, le buffle donne de la tête.

藪 *Teoú*. Nid, cocon, dedans.

鳥丨, *tiāo teoú*, nid d'oiseau.

虫丨, *tch'oûng teoú*, cocon de ver, nid d'insecte.

樹丨裡有虫, *choú teoú lî yoū tch'oûng*, il y a des vers dans le bois.

酒丨裏放等香料來, *tsiòu teoú lî fóng tèn hiōng liáo loî*, mettre des parfums dans le vin.

T'EOÚ

豆 *T'eoú*. Pois, haricots, fèves.

丨腐, *t'eoú foú* (pour *foù*), fromage fait avec le 黃丨, *vông t'eoú*.

磨丨腐, *mó t'eoú foú*, fabriquer ce fromage.

讓丨腐, *nióng* (ou *yóng*) *t'eoú foú*, ce fromage mélangé avec de la viande et des légumes.

丨殼, *t'eoú hôc*, cosse de fèves, de haricots.

丨芽, *t'eoú ngâ*, germes de haricots.

四季丨, *sí koúi t'eoú*, haricot des quatre saisons.

痘 *T'eoú*. Variole, vaccin.

出丨子, *tch'oût t'eoú tzè*, avoir la petite vérole.

丨種, *t'eoú tchoùng*, vaccin.

種洋丨, *tchoúng yông t'eoú*, ou 放丨, *fóng t'eoú*, vacciner.

放丨放唔出, *fóng t'eoú fóng mĝ tch'oût*, le vaccin n'a pas pris.

透 *T'eoú*. Pénétrer, s'infiltrer, traverser.

丨徹, *t'eoú tch'ăt*, perspicace, intelligent.

穿丨一件事, *tch'ōn t'eoú ŷt k'ián sé*, voir clair dans une affaire.

丨過, *t'eoú koúo*, traverser.

裡個銅線信丨落省去, *ỳ ké· t'oûng sién sín t'eoú lŏc sèn hí*, ce fil télégraphique va au chef-lieu de la province.

T'EOÚ

𠵘 *T'eoú*. Empoisonner.

丨死人, *t'eoú sì gnîn*, empoisonner un homme.

T'ĔP

揲 *T'ĕp*. Entassé, serré.

舂丨, *tchoūng t'ĕp*, tasser en foulant.

地壢泥十分丨, *t'í lăc nâi chĭp foūn t'ĕp*, la terre de ce jardinet est par trop tassée.

擒丨, *k'îm t'ĕp*, tasser en appuyant.

家裡係丨, *kā lê· hé· t'ĕp*, sa famille est bien fournie (d'argent).

TÊT

(*Voir aussi TIET*).

得 *Têt*. Obtenir, avoir, pouvoir, jouir de ; mot souvent employé comme auxiliaire.

丨倒, 丨唔倒, *têt tào, têt mĝ tào*, obtenir, ne pas obtenir.

心大不丨, *sīm t'aí poūt têt*, qui trop embrasse mal étreint.

丨病, *têt p'iáng*, contracter une maladie.

唔丨知, 唔丨見, 唔丨好, *mĝ têt tī, mĝ têt kián, mĝ têt hào*, ne pas parvenir à savoir, à voir, à guérir.

做丨, 做唔丨, (ou 唔做丨,) *tsó têt, tsó mĝ têt*, (ou *mĝ tsó têt*), pouvoir faire, ne pas pouvoir, il est permis, il n'est pas permis.

來丨, 來唔丨, *loî têt, loî mĝ têt*, pouvoir venir, ne pas pouvoir.

不丨不, *poūt têt poūt*, forcément, ne pouvant faire autrement.

好丨多, *hào têt tō*, beaucoup mieux.

大丨多, *t'ái têt tō*, beaucoup plus grand.

丨人畏, *têt gnîn ví*, effrayant.

丨人惱, *têt gnîn nāo*, haïssable.

巴不丨, *pā poūt têt*, Dieu veuille que !

德 *Têt*. Vertu, bienfait.

信丨, 望丨, 愛丨, *sín têt, vóng têt, oí têt*, la vertu de foi, d'espérance et de charité.

功丨, *koūng têt*, mérite et vertu.

修丨立功, *siōu têt lîp koūng*, s'adonner à la vertu, et acquérir des mérites, se sanctifier.

T'ÊT

(*Voir aussi T'IET*)

踢 *T'êt*. Frapper, pousser du pied.

脚丨一傷, *kiôc t'êt ŷt chōng*, donner un coup de pied.

丨脚趾, *t'êt kiôc tjè*, trébucher.

TĪ

Tī. 丨背, *tī poé·*, en dedans, par opposition à 外背, *ngoé·poé·*, en dehors.

衫子還在丨背, *sām tzè hân ts'oï tī poé·*, mon habit est encore dans (la maison).

丨間, *tī kiān*, dans l'autre chambre (indéterminée).

丨肚有消息, *tī toù yoū siāo sît*, en dedans, il y a une mécanique.

知 *Tī* (*tjē*). Savoir, connaître.

樣得丨, *nióng têt tī ?* comment pourrait-on le savoir ?

我先丨 *ngâi siēn tī*, je le savais.

先丨聖人, *siēn tī chín gnîn*, les saints prophètes.

唔丨痛, *mĝ tī t'oúng*, ne pas sentir la douleur.

T'Î

題 *T'î*. Titre ou préface d'un livre, entonner, citer, souscrire.

出丨目, *tch'oūt t'î moūc*, donner le sujet de composition.

丨經, 丨禱文, *t'î kīn, t'î tào voûn*, entonner les prières, les litanies.

丨起來講, *t'î hì loî kòng*, je dirai comme citation.... je citerai...

我丨兩十個大圓修路, *ngaî t'î*

leòng chĭp ké· t'aí yân sioū loú, je souscris 20 dollars pour réparer la route.

提 *T'ì.* Extraire, faire sortir.

｜案, *t'ì ón,* citer en justice, appeler le prisonnier pour se présenter au jugement.

｜督, v. **｜臺**, *t'ì toûc* v. *t'ì t'oî,* général qui commande toutes les troupes d'une province.

｜拔人, *t'ì p'ăt gnîn,* prêter secours, aider.

｜防人, *t'ì fông gnîn,* prendre garde, se mettre en garde.

Tì

抵 *Tì.* Résister, empêcher, valoir, donner en échange.

｜擋魔鬼, *tì tòng mô kouì,* résister au diable.

｜日頭, *tì gnĭt t'eôu,* mettre à l'abri du soleil, empêcher le soleil (d'arriver, en mettant un obstacle devant ses rayons).

寫田作｜, *sìa t'iên tsôc tì,* hypothéquer une rizière en caution.

係有事我｜擋, *hé· yōu sé ngâi tì tòng,* s'il y a des affaires (procès), c'est moi que cela regarde.

｜得, 唔｜得, *tì têt, mĝ tì têt,* cela vaut son prix, ne vaut pas son prix.

你馬唔｜錢, *niā mā mĝ tì ts'iên,* ton cheval n'a pas grande valeur.

T'ì

體 *T'ì.* Corps, substance.

聖｜, *chín t'ì,* la Sainte Eucharistie.

成聖｜, 領聖｜, *chîn chín t'ì, leāng chín t'ì,* consacrer l'Eucharistie, recevoir la Communion.

身｜平安麼, *chīn t'ì p'în ōn mô?* vous portez-vous bien ?

｜面, *t'ì mién,* honneur, gloriole, mine, luxe, pompe, considération, apparat.

｜待人, *t'ì t'ái gnîn,* traiter quelqu'un avec considération.

Tí

帝 *Tí.* Empereur.

皇｜, *fông tí* (pour *vông tí*), l'Empereur.

｜, *chóng tí,* dominateur suprême. Nom que les protestants emploient, pour désigner Dieu. (Les païens désignent une idole sous ce nom, et pour cette raison, il est défendu aux chrétiens de l'employer pour le nom de Dieu.)

T'í

遞 *T'í.* Remettre de main à main.

｜年, *t'í* ou vulg. *t'ín niân,* l'année suivante.

｜呈子, *t'í tch'în tzè,* présenter un acte d'accusation.

｜日來講, *t'í gnĭt loî kòng,* nous en parlerons un autre jour.

弟 *T'í.* Frère cadet.

兄｜, *hioūng t'í,* frères en général.

親兄｜, *ts'īn hioūng t'í,* propres frères, du même père.

徒｜, *t'oû t'í,* apprenti, disciple.

子 | , *tzè t'í*, fils et frères cadets.

叔伯 (ou 堂) 兄 | , *choŭc pâc* (ou *t'ông*) *hioūng t'í*, cousins germains.

剃 *T'í* (ou *t'ái*). Raser.

| 頭, *t'í t'eôu*, raser la tête.

| 鬚, *t'í sī*, faire la barbe.

第 *T'í*. Mot employé pour faire les nombres ordinaux.

| 幾, *t'í kì*? quel quantième? quel numéro?

| 十 個, *t'í chĭp ké'*, le dixième.

| 一, *t'í ŷt*, le premier, en premier lieu, avant tout, particulièrement, principal.

地 *T'í*. Terre, champ, lieu, tombeau.

天 |, *t'iēn t'í*, le ciel et la terre.

| 基, *t'í kī*, terrain, terre.

整 | 基, *tchàng t'í kī*, aplanir, préparer un terrain, un emplacement.

| 方, *t'í fōng*, lieu, endroit, place, site, pays.

| 泥 下, *t'í nâi hā*, par terre, sur le sol.

| 保, *t'í pào*, chef de quartier, maire.

| 名, *t'í miâng*, nom d'endroit à la campagne.

| 獄, *t'í nioŭc*, l'enfer.

| 墳, *t'í foûn* (ou simplement *t'í*), tombeau.

TIĀ

爹 *Tīa*. Père, papa.

你 | 在 屋 下, *niâ tīa ts'ōi voŭc hā*, ton père est à la maison.

TIĀM

兼 *Tiām* (pour *kiām*). | |, *tiām tiām*, doucement, avec attention, avec ensemble.

T'IĀM

添 *T'iām*. Ajouter, augmenter.

| 飯, *t'iām fán*, servir le riz (se dit aux garçons d'auberge, aux serviteurs).

愛 | 幾 多, *oí t'iām kì tō?* combien faut-il ajouter en plus?

放 兜 |, *fóng teōu t'iām*, mettre un peu plus.

打 佢 一 下 |, *tà kî ŷt há t'iām*, donne-lui encore un coup, frappe-le encore.

| 多, | 補, *t'iām tō*, *t'iām poù*, augmenter, compléter.

| 忘, *t'iām p'ióng* ou *móng*, oublier.

| 丁, *t'iām tēn*, augmenter le nombre d'hommes.

恭 喜 新 年 | 多 丁, *kioūng hì sīn niân t'iām tō tēn*, bonne année! que votre famille s'accroisse!

T'IÂM

甜 *T'iâm*. Doux, sucré.

| 個, *t'iâm ké'*, c'est sucré.

| 酒, *t'iâm tsiòu*, vin doux; se dit aussi pour désigner le vinaigre.

TIÀM

點 *Tiàm*. Un peu, goutte, point, noter, heure, allumer.

一 | 水, 酒, *ŷt tiàm choùi*, *tsiòu*, un peu d'eau, de vin, ou une goutte d'eau, de vin.

一 | 都麼, *ȳt tiàm toū mô*, il n'y a rien du tout.

打 | 心, *tà tiàm sīm*, prendre une collation, un goûter, un frustulum.

| 書, *tiàm choū*, ponctuer un livre, marquer d'un point un caractère.

打 一 |, *tà ȳt tiàm*, faire un point au pinceau.

我 | 過 麼 差, *ngaî tiàm koúo mô ts'ā*, j'ai compté, c'est exact.

| 名, *tiàm miâng*, nommer, enregistrer les noms.

| 聖 水, *tiàm chín choùi*, prendre de l'eau bénite.

| 火, *tiàm fò*, allumer.

| 燭, *tiàm tchoūc*, allumer le cierge.

三 | 鐘, *sām tiàm tchoūng*, il est trois heures.

TIÁM

玷 *Tiám*. Tache, déshonorer.

無 | 之 母, *voû tiám tjē moū*, Mère sans tache (litanies).

| 衊 聖 教 會, *tiám mé· chín káo fí*, déshonorer la sainte Eglise.

店 *Tiám*. Boutique, auberge.

一 間 |, *ȳt kiān tiám*, une boutique.

開 |, *k'oī tiám*, tenir, ouvrir une boutique.

酒 |, 歇 |, *tsiòu tiám, hiēt tiám*, boutique, auberge où l'on vend du vin, où l'on peut coucher.

T'IÁM

T'iám. | 筆, *t'iám pīt*, humecter le pinceau.

簟 *T'iám*. | 子, *t'iám tzè* (pour 墊 *tiám* qui se dit moins), coussin que l'on met sur un siège.

| 笪, *t'iám tāt*, grande et grosse natte en bambou, pour sécher les grains.

TIĀO

Tiāo. Piquer, darder (se dit des mouches à dard).

黃 蜂 | 人, *vông foūng tiāo gnîn*, les guêpes piquent.

刁 *Tiāo*. Pervers, qui excite la discorde.

| 惡, | 唆, | 拐, *tiāo ôc, tiāo sō, tiāo kouài*, pervers, qui excite, qui débauche.

| 難, *tiāo nân*, qui cherche à causer du désagrément.

鵰 *Tiāo*. Oiseau.

打 |, *tà tiāo*, se livrer à la chasse aux oiseaux.

| (貂) 鼠, *tiāo tch'où*, espèce d'écureuil, ou rat volant.

虐 | 子, *niôc tiāo tzè*, prendre les oiseaux au filet.

T'IĀO

挑 *T'iāo*. Porter un fardeau sur l'épaule à l'aide d'un bâton, choisir.

| 水, | 泥, *t'iāo choùi, t'iāo naî*, porter de l'eau, de la terre (s'emploie comme 㧡 *k'aī*).

等 我 | 過 好 個 來, *tèn ngâi t'iāo koúo hào ké· loî*, laisse-moi choisir le meilleur.

愛｜倒一個細人嗆輔彌撒個來, *ói t'iāo tào ŷt ké· sé· gnîn voé· p'où nì sǎt ké· loî*, il faut choisir un enfant qui sache servir la Messe.

雕 *T'iāo*(ou *tiāo*). Sculpter, graver.

｜花, *t'iāo fā*, sculpter des fleurs.

｜字, *t'iāo sé*, graver des caractères.

｜印, *t'iāo ýn*, graver un cachet.

｜書板子, *t'iāo chōu pàn tzè*, graver les planches d'un livre.

T'IÂO

條 *T'iâo*. Particule numérale des bancs, des cordes, des fils, des serpents, des chemins, des rivières, et en général de tout ce qui est long et mince ou étroit. Article ou paragraphe d'un écrit, loi, règle, principe.

鐵｜, *t'iět t'iâo*, baguette, barre de fer.

一｜蛇, 一｜石頭, 一｜路, 一｜牛, *ŷt t'iâo châ, ŷt t'iâo chǎc t'eôu, ŷt t'iâo loú, ŷt t'iâo niôu*, un serpent, une pierre, une route, un buffle.

一｜命, *ŷt t'iâo miáng*, une vie.

第十五｜, *t'í chǐp nǵ t'iâo*, le quinzième article.

｜理, *t'iâo lì*, mettre en ordre.

調 *T'iâo*. Mêler, tempérer, préparer.

｜舂, *t'iâo tch'oūn*, battre les œufs pour les mélanger.

｜羹, *t'iâo kāng*, cuillère.

｜和, *tiâo fô*, tempéré, se radoucir, modérer.

天氣｜和, *t'iēn hí tiâo fô*, le temps s'est radouci.

身體｜和, *chīn t'ì t'iâo fô*, la santé est assez bonne.

｜菜｜得好, *t'iâo ts'oí t'iâo tět hào*, les mets sont assez bien préparés.

｜ ?, *t'iâo t'iám*, bien disposé, bien arrangé, coordonné.

布置｜ ?, *póu tjé t'iâo t'iám*, arranger convenablement.

TIÀO

Tiào. Violer, copulam facere. Mot dont les Chinois se servent constamment, soit comme injure, soit comme parole d'impatience. Voici quelques expressions qu'il est bon de savoir:

Tiào kiā tsì tjē (ou simplement *tiaò kiā*), je viole sa sœur (ou simplement je la viole). Parole d'impatience dite à tout propos contre les êtres soit animés, soit inanimés; elle répond aux mots grossiers b.. f.. cr.. etc.

Tiaò niā mē·, je viole ta mère.

Niā mē· poūn ngaî tiaò tsáng haò, je violerais ta mère que ce serait bien fait.

Kcoù tiaò ké· toūng sī, c'est un chien qui a engendré ça ! race de chien !

TIÁO

弔 v. 吊 *Tiáo*. Suspendre, peser la grande romaine, diviser; particule numérale des monnaies enfilées.

｜起來打, *tiáo hì loî tà*, frapper un homme qu'on a suspendu par les mains.

索｜下來, *sôc tiáo hā loî*, descends

la corde (en retenant un bout fixé en haut).

丨墨線, *tiáo mĕt sién*, tendre le fil à plomb.

丨爐, *tiáo loû*, encensoir.

你丨有幾重, *gnî tiáo yōu kì tch'ōung?* combien as-tu trouvé à la balance ?

丨起來賣, *tiáo hì loî maí*, vendre séparément.

丨起來審, *tiáo hì loî chìm*, instruire un procès en interrogeant séparément les partis.

一丨錢, *ŷt tiáo ts'iên*, une ligature de sapèques.

丨菜, *tiáo ts'oí*, aubergine.

釣 *Tiáo*. Accrocher, tirer à soi avec un crochet.

丨魚, *tiáo nĝ*, pêcher à la ligne.

水桶跌落井愛丨起來, *choùi t'oùng tiĕt lŏc tsiàng oí tiáo hì loî*, le seau est tombé dans le puits, il faut l'en retirer.

丨穀上棚, *tiáo koŭc chōng p'âng*, monter le riz au grenier (en tirant le sac avec une corde).

T'IÁO

T'iáo. Oublier, omettre.

丨帋上名, *t'iáo p'ĕt chōng miâng*, j'ai oublié d'inscrire les noms.

你丨一個字, *gnî t'iáo ŷt ké· sé*, tu as omis une lettre.

跳 *T'iáo*. Sauter, danser; corniche de maison.

丨下來, *t'iáo hā loî*, sauter en bas.

丨過瀝, *t'iáo koúo lăc*, franchir un ruisseau.

丨唔過, *t'iáo mĝ koúo*, ne pouvoir franchir.

丨板, *t'iáo pàn*, passerelle.

丨蚤, *t'iáo tsào*, puce.

丨皮人, *t'iáo p'î gnîn*, espiègle, importun, chicaneur, filou.

丨脚, *t'iáo kiŏc*, sauter sur une jambe.

丨子, *t'iáo tzè*, pickpocket.

調 *T'iáo*. Echanger, permuter, troquer.

包丨, *pāo t'iáo*, promettre de changer la marchandise, si elle ne convient pas.

裡個花邊唔好愛同我丨過, *ỳ ké· fā piēn mĝ hào oí t'oûng ngâi t'iáo koúo*, cette piastre n'est pas bonne, veuillez me l'échanger.

糶 *T'iáo*. Vendre des grains.

丨穀, 丨米, 丨豆, *t'iáo koŭc*, *t'iáo mì*, *t'iáo t'eóu*, vendre du riz non écossé, du riz écossé, des haricots.

T'IĂP

疊 *T'iăp*. Etager, étendre.

田子有一丨一丨, *t'iên tzè yoū ŷt t'iăp ŷt t'iăp*, les rizières sont en étagères.

雲子一丨一丨, *yoûn tzè ŷt t'iăp ŷt t'iăp*, les nuages sont les uns sur les autres (comme en rayons).

丨阿地下, *t'iăp á t'í hā*, étendre par terre.

Le ton change dans l'expression:

丨坐, 丨眠, *t'iâp ts'ō*, *t'iâp mîn*, mettre

36

un tapis, ou autre chose sur un siège, sur un lit, pour s'asseoir ou se coucher.

蝶 *T'iăp.* 瑚 | , *foû t'iăp*, espèce de papillon.

碟 *T'iăp.* Petite assiette,soucoupe.

擺 | 子 , *paì t'iăp tzè*, servir des petites assiettes (des hors-d'œuvre, dans un grand dîner).

劈 *T'iăp* (pour *p'iăc*). Tailler à coup de hache.

| 平 , *t'iăp p'iâng*, aplanir (un bois) avec la hache.

| 樹 頭 , *t'iăp choú t'eoû*, équarrir un arbre, une poutre.

疊 *T'iăp.* Plier, serrer, mettre en ordre.

| 整 擔 子 來 , *t'iăp tchàng tām tzè loî*, préparer les objets pour une charge à porteur.

東 西 | 齊 麼, *toūng sī t'iăp ts'ê· mô ?* les objets sont-ils prêts ?

TIAP

貼 Afficher, coller.

| 告 示 , *tiâp káo ché*, afficher un décret, une proclamation.

| 對 聯 , *tiâp toúi liên*, afficher les tablettes en vers.

| 錢 , *tiâp ts'iên*, ajouter de l'argent (se dit dans le sens de graisser la patte à quelqu'un. Dans le sens de suppléer à ce qui manque, on dit 帖 *t'iâp*).

| 膏 藥 , *tiâp kāo yŏc*, appliquer un emplâtre.

T'IÂP

帖 *T'iâp.* Ecrit, diplôme, carte d'invitation, billet, à point, ajouter, numéral des potions de médecine.

一 張 | 子 , *ŷt tchōng t'iâp tzè*, une carte de visite , un billet d'invitation.

散 | 子 , *sàn t'iâp tzè*, lancer des billets d'invitation.

傳 | , *tch'ôn t'iâp*, présenter sa carte à domicile.

裡 件 事 唔 妥 | , *ỳ k'ián sé mĝ t'ò t'iâp*, cette affaire n'est pas bien sûre, pas encore réglée.

唔 彀 我 噲 | , *mĝ keóu ngâi voé t'iâp*, je suppléerai de ma bourse à ce qui manque.

我 食 裡 三 | 藥 , *ngâi chĭt ê· sām t'iâp yŏc*, j'ai pris trois potions de médecine.

TIĒN

顛 *Tiēn.* | | 倒, *tiēn tiēn tào*, sens dessus dessous.

| 倒 是 非 , *tiēn tào ché fī*, sens dessus dessous, faire les choses à rebours.

癲 *Tiēn.* Fou, toqué.

| | 董 董, *tiēn tiēn toùng toùng*, qui radote, qui a un peu perdu la tête.

發 | , *fât tiēn*, (plus vulgairement *pôt tiēn*), devenir fou, avoir un accès de folie.

T'IĒN

天 *T'iēn.* Ciel, jour.

喊 | 喊 地 , *hám t'iēn hám t'í*, en appeler au ciel et à la terre.

憑 | 吩附, *p'în t'iēn foūn foú*, à la volonté du ciel.

| 理頁心, *t'iēn lī leông sīm*, la conscience droite, telle qu'elle est donnée par le ciel.

| 主, *t'iēn tchoū*, maître du ciel, Dieu (style chr.).

| 主保佑, *t'iēn tchòu pào yoú*, que Dieu vous protège.

| 堂, *t'iēn t'ông*, paradis, Ciel.

| 上還有 |, *t'iēn chóng hân yoū t'iēn*, au dessus du ciel il y a encore un autre ciel. (Se dit en parlant du mandarin : au dessus de lui il y a encore d'autres mandarins plus élevés à qui on peut s'adresser).

| 晴, *t'iēn ts'iáng*, le temps est beau, le ciel est serein.

| 井, *t'iēn tsiàng*, cour intérieure des maisons chinoises.

| 光, | 光日, *t'iēn koūong, t'iēn koūong gnĭt*, l'aurore, demain matin. (Voir *gnĭt* 日)

T'IÊN

田 *T'iên*. Rizière, champ de riz.

一坵 |, *ŷt k'ioū t'iên*, une rizière.

開 |, *k'oī t'iên*, défricher pour faire des rizières.

垻 |, 山 |, *pá t'iên, sān t'iên*, rizières riveraines, rizières de montagne.

湖洋 |, *foû yông t'iên*, rizières qui ne sont jamais à sec.

捉 | 唇, 背 ou 糊 | 坎 (ou 唇), *tsŏc t'iên choûn, poé* ou *foû t'iên k'ám* (ou *choûn*), préparer le talus de la rizière en y rapportant de la terre, en le crépissant avec de la boue.

塡 *T'iên*. Boucher, combler.

| 滿湖窟, *t'iên mān foû foût*, combler les trous.

唔使我 | 你賬, *mĝ sè ngâi t'iên niā tchóng*, ce n'est pas à moi à payer tes dettes.

曾 *T'iên* (pour *ts'ên*). Encore (n'est employé que précédé de la négation *mĝ*).

佢唔 | 來, *kî mĝ t'iên loî*, il n'est pas encore venu.

| 係, *t'iên hé*, ce n'est pas possible! serait-ce vrai ?

Ce mot est plus ou moins déformé, selon les pays. La prononciation vraie est *ts'ên* ; voir ce mot.

TIÈN

典 *Tièn*. Règle, loi, bienfait.

字 |, *sé tièn*, dictionnaire.

恩 |, *ēn tièn*, bienfait.

點 *Tièn* (*tiàm*). 一 |, *ŷt tièn*, un tout petit peu. Voir *tiàm*.

墊 *Tièn*. 坐 |, 凡 |, *ts'ō tièn, ŷ tièn*, coussin ou tapis que l'on met sur un siège.

拜 |, *paí tièn*, coussin que l'on met pour s'agenouiller.

T'IÉN

墊 *T'ién*. Payer pour un autre, avancer de l'argent à quelqu'un.

代 |, *t'oí t'ién*, payer pour un autre.

裡個錢麼帛裡我咸你｜, *ỳ ké ts'iên mô p'ĕt lé ngaî kăm gnî t'ién*, si cet argent est perdu, tu en es responsable.

賠｜, *p'oí t'ién*, compenser une perte.

佃 *T'ién*. Louer, affermer.

｜戶, *t'ién foú*, fermier, locataire.

換｜戶, *voûon t'ién foú*, changer de locataire, de fermier.

｜字, *t'ién sé*, contrat de loyer, de ferme.

｜田, *t'ién t'iên*, vendre sa terre, en se réservant la faculté de la racheter.

電 *T'ién*. Eclair, électricité.

｜氣, *t'ién hí*, électricité.

｜線, ｜信, *t'ién sién*, *t'ién sín*, fil télégraphique, télégramme.

打 ou 搭｜信, *tà* ou *tâp t'ién sín*, envoyer un télégramme.

殿 *T'ién*. Temple, palais.

皇｜(ou mieux 金鑾｜ ou 輪｜), *vông t'ién* (ou mieux *kĭm lân t'ién* ou *loûn t'ién*), Palais impérial.

十｜閻君, *chĭp t'ién yâm kioûn*, les dix dieux de l'Enfer. (Le mot *t'ién* a ici le sens de personnalité).

奠 *T'ién*. Sacrifice pour les morts, la veille de l'enterrement, ou en d'autres circonstances.

開｜, *k'ōi t'ién*, faire ce sacrifice, qui consiste à verser qqs. gouttes de vin par terre, après avoir adoré.

靛 *T'ién*. Indigo.

｜花, *t'ién fā*, plante qui donne l'indigo.

打｜, *tà t'ién*, faire coaguler l'indigo dissous dans l'eau.

TIÊT

跌 *Tiêt*. Tomber, choir, glisser.

｜倒, ｜下, *tiêt tào*, *tiêt hā*, être tombé, tomber.

｜死, *tiêt sì*, mourir d'une chute.

｜價, *tiêt ká*, baisser de prix, rabais.

米｜三十個錢, *mì tiêt sām chĭp ké ts'iên*, le riz a baissé de 30 sapèques.

T'IÊT

忒 *T'iêt*. Trop.

｜多, ｜少, *t'iêt tō*, *t'iêt chào*, trop, trop peu.

｜難, *t'iêt nân*, trop difficile.

鐵 *T'iêt*. Fer.

打｜, *tà t'iêt*, battre le fer, forger.

熟｜, 白｜, *choŭc t'iêt*, *p'ăc t'iêt*, fer doux, fer blanc.

｜個, ｜打個, *t'iêt ké*, *t'iêt tà ké*, en fer, fabriqué en fer battu.

｜皮, ｜板, *t'iêt p'î*, *t'iêt pàn*, feuille de fer, plaque de fer.

TĪN

Tīn. Tourner autour.

｜去｜轉, *tīn hí tīn tchòn*, tourner tout autour.

T'ÎN

亭 *T'în*. Kiosque, belvédère.

茶｜, *ts'â t'în*, pavillon ouvert, destiné aux voyageurs qui veulent prendre du repos.

停 *T'în*. S'arrêter, cesser.

丨脚, *t'în kiôc*, s'arrêter.

丨工, *t'în koũng*, cesser le travail.

鐘子丨吊裡, *tchoũng tzè t'în p'ēt lê*, l'horloge s'est arrêtée.

丨當, *t'în tóng*, arrêté, fixé.

那個事講丨當, *mâc ké sé kòng t'în tóng*, tout est bien arrêté, c'est bien convenu.

愛算丨當, *ói són t'în tóng*, il faut bien compter, bien prendre ses mesures.

廷 *T'în*. Palais impérial.

朝丨, *tch'âo t'în*, le palais d'un souverain.

庭 *T'în*. Intérieur de la maison.

家丨, *kā t'în*, intérieur de la famille.

霆 *T'în*. 雷丨, *loûi t'în*, le tonnerre.

TÌN

鼎 *Tìn*. Ferme, résistant, soutenir un fardeau.

丨力, *tìn lĭt*, fort, qui dépense de la force, point de résistance.

裡個人丨苦唔得, *ỳ ké gnîn tìn k'où mĝ tĕt*, cet homme n'est pas endurant, ne peut résister à la fatigue.

丨丨, *tìn tìn*, paisiblement, doucement.

小心丨丨子來, *siào sīm tìn tìn tzè loî*, attention, doucement.

TÍN

Tín toũng. La luette du gosier.

T'ÍN

定 *T'ín*. Certain, sûr, déterminer, fixer, statuer, décision, sur commande.

一丨係, *ŷt t'ín hé*, c'est absolument vrai.

麼丨着, *mô t'ín tch'ŏc*, ce n'est pas sûr.

丨時候, *t'ín chê hcóu*, déterminer le temps.

丨案, *t'ín ón*, prononcer la sentence, rendre le verdict.

丨錢, 丨頭, *t'ín ts'iên*, *t'ín t'eôu*, arrhes.

拿五十個錢丨頭, *nā ǹg chĭp ké ts'iên t'ín t'eôu*, donne-lui 50 sapèques d'arrhes.

丨做, *t'ín tsó*, faire faire sur commande.

丨做一雙鞋, *t'ín tsó ŷt soũng haî*, faire faire une paire de souliers sur commande.

聽 *T'ín*. Entendre, écouter, comprendre.

丨命, *t'ín mín*, obéir.

丨我做, *t'ín ngâi tsó*, laisse-moi faire. (Voir *t'āng*.)

錠 *T'ín*. Lingot d'argent.

TIŌU

丢 *Tiōu*. Abandonner, jeter.

丨生理, *tiōu siēn lī*, abandonner le commerce.

丨吊佢, *tiōu p'ēt kî*, jette-le, laisse-le. (Mot peu usité, on emploie de préférence les mots 放 *fóng*, 捨 *chà*, *fĭt*, voir ces mots).

T'ĬT

特 *T'ĭt*. Exprès, à dessein.

丨事來, 丨事做個, *t'ĭt sé loî, t'ĭt sé tsó ké·*, venir exprès, fait à dessein.

敵 *T'ĭt*. Ennemi, résister.

仇丨, *choû t'ĭt*, ennemis.

丨戰, *t'ĭt tchán*, résister.

TÎT

的 *Tît*. 丨確係, *tît k'ôc hé·*, en effet, c'est manifeste.

丨當人, *tît tóng gnîn*, homme honnête, sur lequel on peut compter.

En langue parlée, ce mot ne s'emploie que dans ce sens. Il est beaucoup employé en langue écrite, pour former les adjectifs, ou marquer le génitif.

滴 *Tît*. Goutte, peu.

一丨, *ŷt tît*, un tout petit peu.

TJĒ

Tjē. Parties sexuelles de la femme.

知 *Tjē*. Savoir, connaître. (Voir *tī*).

丨人丨面不丨心, *tjē gnîn tjē mién poût tjē sīm*, on ne peut juger des gens sur la mine.

之 *Tjē*. Cela, marque du génitif (inusité en langue parlée).

肢 *Tjē*. Membre.

四丨百體, *sí tjē pâc t'ì*, les quatre membres et tout ce qui constitue le corps.

支 *Tjē*. Branche, tribut, portion, aider, résister.

宗丨, *tsoūng tjē*, descendants d'un même aïeul, même branche de famille.

一丨人馬, *ŷt tjē gnîn mā*, une troupe de cavaliers.

丨錢用, *tjē ts'iên yoúng*, avancer de l'argent, par portion.

我愛丨兩百錢, *ngâi oí tjē leòng pâc ts'iên*, je veux percevoir 200 sapèques, sur ce qui m'est dû.

丨不住, *tjē poût tch'oú*, ne pouvoir tenir, ou résister.

枝 *Tjē* (ou *kī*). Branche, numéral des rameaux, des pinceaux, des flèches.

樹丨, *choú tjē*, branches d'arbre.

聖丨主日, *chín tjē tchoù gnĭt*, le dimanche des Rameaux.

一丨筆, 一丨花, 一丨箭, *ŷt tjē pĭt, ŷt tjē fā, ŷt tjē tsién*, un pinceau, une fleur, une flèche.

TJÈ

止 *Tjè*. Cesser, faire cesser, seulement.

二月起五月丨, *gní gnĕt hì, ǹg gnĕt tjè*, à partir de la 2ème lune jusqu'à la 5ème.

界址裡子起到個子丨, *kiái tjè ỳ tzè hì táo ké· tzè tjè*, les limites commencent ici et finissent là.

丨渴, 丨痛, 丨怒, 丨瀉, 丨血, *tjè*

hôt, tjè t'oúng, tjè noú, tjè siá, tjè hiĕt, calmer la soif, la douleur, la colère, arrêter la diarrhée, le sang.

唔丨三百錢, *mĝ tjè sām pàc ts'iĕn,* il y a plus de 300 sapèques.

有一百錢麼? ... 唔 丨, *yoū ŷt pâc ts'iĕn mô?.... mĝ tjè,* y a-t-il 100 sapèques? .... il y a plus (*litt.* non seulement.

吥佢丨步, *vò kî tjè p'oú,* dis-lui de s'arrêter.

址 *Tjè.* Fondement, emplacement.

界丨, *kiái tjè,* emplacement, limites.

趾 *Tjè.* 脚 丨, *kiôc tjè,* doigts des pieds.

指 *Tjè.* Doigts de la main, indiquer.

手丨, *choù tjè,* doigts de la main.

手丨公, 手 丨 尾, 中手 丨, *choù tjè koūng, choù tjè mī, toúng* (pour *tchoūng*) *choù tjè,* le pouce, le petit doigt, le doigt du milieu.

手丨甲, *choù tjè kâp,* les ongles.

丨人, *tjè gnîn,* indiquer qqn. en le montrant du doigt.

丨 人 知, *tjè gnîn tī,* indiquer à quelqu'un, montrer, faire voir.

請神父 丨 教我, *ts'iàng chîn foú tjè kaó ngâi,* je prie le Père de vouloir bien m'instruire.

旨 *Tjè.* Volonté, ordre.

諭丨 *v.* 聖丨, *ý tjè* v. *chín tjè,* ordre, décret impérial.

紙 *Tjè.* Papier, contrat.

一張丨, *ŷt tchōng tjè,* une feuille de papier.

貢白丨, *koúng p'ăc tjè,* bon papier à écrire, 1ere qualité.

連四丨, 官邊丨, *liĕn sí tjè, koūon piēn tjè,* autres espèces de papier, assez bon.

書 丨, *choū tjè,* papier ordinaire à écrire.

粗丨, 草丨, *tsē tjè, ts'ào tjè,* espèces de papier grossier, jaunâtre, employé à une foule d'usages, entre autres à faire le:

丨煤, *tjè môe',* papier allumette, amadou.

出一張丨, *tch'oût ŷt tchōng tjè,* donner un écrit.

補丨, *poù tjè,* présenter une requête par écrit, après l'avoir faite de vive voix.

黹 *Tjè.* 針丨, *tchīm tjè,* couture.

TJÉ

至 *Tjé.* Superlatif.

丨好, *tjé hào,* le meilleur.

丨多, 丨少, *tjé tō, tjé chào,* au plus, au moins.

致 *Tjé.* Arriver au point de, livrer.

唔丨倒, *mĝ tjé tào,* il n'est pas arrivé à ce point.

莫丨倒生病, *mŏc tjé taò sēn p'iáng,* ne vas pas attraper une maladie.

丨命死, *tjé mín sì,* mort martyr.

丨衰人, *tjé soī gnîn,* rendre qqn.

malheureux par ses méchancetés, ses tracasseries, le livrer à la dérision.

智 *Tjé*. Prudence, sagesse.

賢 | , *hièn tjé*, le don de sagesse.

志 *Tjé*. Volonté, intention.

麽 | 氣 個 人 , *mô tjé hí ké· gnîn*, c'est un homme qui n'a pas de volonté forte.

立 | , *lìp tjé*, prendre la résolution.

| 意 , *tjé ý*, dessein, proposition, résolution.

痣 *Tjé*. Verrue, grain de beauté.

制 *Tjé*. Conduire, gouverner.

| 臺 , *tjé t'ôi*, vice-roi, gouverneur d'une ou plusieurs provinces.

製 *Tjé*. Confectionner, se procurer, accommoder.

| 家 事 , *tjé kā ché·*, faire faire ou acheter des meubles, des outils.

| 衣 裳 , *tjé ȳ chōng*, faire faire des habits.

藥 愛 | 過 , *yŏc oí tjé .koúo*, il faut accomnoder les remèdes.

置 *Tjé*. Placer, disposer.

安 | , 布 | , *ōn tjé, poú tjé*, mettre à sa place, arranger, disposer.

看 樣 班 安 | 法 , *k'ón nióng pān ōn tjé făp*, voyons comment il faudra disposer.

你 屋 布 | 布 得 好 , *niā voŭc poú tjé poú têt hào*, ta maison est bien faite, tout est bien disposé.

TŌ

多 *Tō*. Beaucoup, très, plus, trop.

| (*v.* 好 |) 人 來 , *tō (v. hào tō) gnîn loî*, il vient beaucoup de monde.

| 年 , *tō niân*, beaucoup d'années.

好 得 | , *hào têt tō*, c'est beaucoup mieux.

| 少 , *tō chào*, un peu.

| 少 酒 , | 少 水 , | 少 病 , *tō chào tsioù, tō chào choùi, tō chào p'iáng*, un peu de vin, d'eau, quelque peu malade.

幾 | , *kì tō ?* combien ?

幾 | 個 人 , 幾 | 個 錢 , *kì tō ké· gnîn? kì tō ké· ts'iên ?* combien d'hommes? combien d'argent ?

咁 | , *àn tō*, combien! que! quantum!

我 唔 愛 咁 | , *ngâi m̀g oí* (prononcez *moé·*) *àn tō*, je n'en veux pas autant.

咁 | 講 個 人 , *àn tō kòng ké· gnîn*, quel babillard !

麽 | 個 , *mô tō ké·*, il n'y en a pas trop.

| 過 頭 (ou simplement 忒 |), *tō koúo t'eôu* (ou simplement *t'ièt tō*), il y en a trop.

| 個 畀 你 , *tō ké· poūn gnî*, je te donne le restant.

T'Ō

拖 *T'ō*. Tirer de force, entraîner.

| 車 , *t'ō tch'ā*, tirer une voiture.

| 上 來 , *t'ō chōng loî*, tirer, monter en tirant.

我 | 你 上 省 , *ngâi t'ō gnî chōng sèn*, je te ferai aller jusqu'à la capitale (pour ce procès).

官 司 儘 | , *koūon sē tsìn t'ō*, prolonger indéfiniment un procès.

| 累人, *t'ō loúi gnîn*, porter préjudice à quelqu'un, l'envelopper dans son infortune.

| 梆, *t'ō pāng*, en moyenne.

| 隔, *t'ō kâc*, tiroir.

T'Ô

佗 *T'ô*. Bosse, bossu.

背 |, *poé· t'ô*, bossu.

砣 *T'ô*. Poids, masse.

鐘 |, 秤 |, *tchoūng t'ô, tch'ín t'ô*, poids d'une horloge, d'une romaine.

駝 *T'ô*. 駱 |, *lŏc t'ô*, chameau.

馱 *T'ô*. Porter à dos d'animal.

| 炭, | 米, *t'ô t'án, t'ô mì*, porter du charbon, du riz. (Ne se dit que des animaux.)

堂 *T'ô* (pour *t'ông*). Lieu, endroit.

一 | 地方, *ŷt t'ô t'í fōng*, un endroit.

一 | 一 | 唔同, *ŷt t'ô ŷt t'ô mĝ t'oûng*, à chaque endroit ce n'est pas la même chose.

TÒ

島 *Tò* (ou *tào*). 海 |, *hoì tò*, île. On dit aussi 海墩, *hoì toūn*.

躲 *Tò*. | 避, *tò p'ĭt*, éviter, fuir.

| 避人, *tò p'ĭt gnîn*, éviter quelqu'un, fuir sa présence.

| 避雨, *tò p'ĭt ỳ*, se garer de la pluie.

T'Ò

妥 *T'ò*. En sûreté, en repos.

裡件事唔 | 當, *ỳ k'ián sé mĝ t'ò tóng*, cette affaire n'est pas en règle.

T'Ó

惰 *T'ó*. Paresse, paresseux.

懶 |, *lān t'ó*, paresseux.

柁 *T'ó*. | 尾, *t'ó mī*, gouvernail d'un bateau.

TŎC

Tŏc. Réitérer, ennuyer par des répétitions, molester par des avis ou des demandes réitérées.

| 等佢去取佢錢, *tŏc tèn kì hí ts'ì kiā ts'iên*, surveille toutes les occasions de lui réclamer son argent.

T'ŎC

鐸 *T'ŏc*. Clochette.

| 德 v. 司 |, *t'ŏc têt* v. *sē tŏc*, nom du prêtre catholique, dans les livres chrétiens.

托 *T'ŏc*. Choisir, trier.

一吊錢我 | 倒兩百過噩錢, *ŷt tiaó ts'iên, ngai t'ŏc taò leòng pâc kouó ngôc ts'iên*, sur une ligature, j'ai trié plus de 200 mauvaises sapèques.

TOC

啄 *Tôc* (ou *toûc*). Becqueter, frapper du bec. *Voir toûc*.

T'OC

託 *T'ôc*. Recommander, confier.

我｜付你同我帶一封信, *ngâi t'ôc fóu gnī t'oûng ngâi tái ŷt foūng sín*, c'est à toi que je m'en rapporte, pour me porter une lettre.

我拜｜你相幫我一下, *ngâi pái t'ôc gnī siōng pōng ngâi ŷt há*, je te prie de vouloir bien m'aider.

你｜佢管, *gnī t'ôc kî koùon*, confie-lui la direction, le soin, la gestion (de telle affaire).

｜人做事, *t'ôc gnîn tsó sé*, charger quelqu'un de faire une chose.

托 *T'ôc*. Soutenir.

｜盤, *t'ôc p'ân*, plateau pour porter les tasses.

落落｜｜, *lŏc lŏc t'ôc t'ôc*, se dit d'une chose qui remue, qui ne tient pas au manche.

TŌI

堆 *Toī*. Monceau, tas, entasser.

一｜石頭，一｜草, *ŷt toī chăc t'eoû, ŷt toī ts'ào*, un tas de pierres, une meule d'herbe.

｜起來, *toī hì lôi*, entasser.

T'OĪ

在 *T'oī* (pour *ts'ái*). Etre dans.

｜那里起身, *t'oī nái lī hì chīn?* d'où viens-tu ?

神父｜屋下麼, *chîn fóu t'oī voûc hā mô?* le Père est-il à la maison ?

Selon le cas et les pays, ce mot se prononce encore *ts'oī*, *ts'ái*, *hōi*, voir ces mots.

胎 *T'ōi*. Sein, matrice, fœtus.

有｜個婦人家, *yōu t'oī ké· fóu gnîn kā*, femme enceinte.

跌｜, *tiĕt t'oī*, avortement.

細人有｜毒, *sé· gnîn yoū t'oī t'oŭc*, se dit des enfants qui ont la tête couverte de plaies.

梯 *T'ōi*. Echelle.

｜牌, *t'ōi p'âi*, escalier d'un intérieur de maison.

｜桄, *t'ōi koūang*, échelons de l'échelle.

T'ÔI

臺 *T'ôi*. Trône, estrade, tour, titre de grand mandarin, part. num. des messes.

祭｜, *tsí t'ôi*, autel.

天主｜前, *t'iēn tchoù t'ôi ts'iên*, en présence de Dieu.

礮｜, *p'áo t'ôi*, fort, tour servant de fort.

燭｜, *tchoûc t'ôi*, chandelier, bougeoir.

父｜, *foú t'ôi*, nom que les lettrés donnent au mandarin.

臬｜, (ou **按察司**) *gnĕt t'ôi*, (ou *ón ts'ât sē*), grand juge criminel d'une province.

一｜彌撒, *ŷt t'ôi nì săt*, une messe.

擡 *T'oî*. Porter à plusieurs; ériger.

｜石頭, *t'oî chăc t'eôu*, porter à

plusieurs une pierre (par ex: une grosse pierre de taille).

丨棺材子, *t'oî koūon ts'oî tzè*, civière.

丨頭, *t'oî t'eôu*, revenir à la ligne en écrivant.

愛丨一個字, *oí t'oî ŷt ké· sé*, il faut mettre à la ligne, d'un caractère au dessus.

苔 *T'oî*. Mousse.

流丨, *lioū* (pour *liôu*) *t'oî*, mousse qui croît dans l'eau.

青丨, *ts'iāng t'oî*, mousse verte qui se trouve dans les endroits humides.

TÒI

堆 *Tòi* (pour *tōi*). En gros, en bloc.

丨買, 丨賣, *tòi mài. tòi mái*, acheter, vendre en gros.

TOÍ

Toí. Objecter, pousser à bout par des arguments.

我緊丨佢丨倒唔曉聲, *ngâi kìn toí kî toí tào mĝ hiào chāng*, je l'ai tellement poussé par mes objections qu'il ne savait plus que dire.

碓 *Toí*. Mortier à piler, à blanchir le riz.

丨臼, *toí k'iōu*. mortier à piler.

踏丨, *t'áp tói*, mortier à blanchir le riz.

T'OÍ

袋 *T'oí*. Poche, sac, mettre en poche.

米丨, 烟丨, *mì t'oí, yān t'oí*, sac à riz, blague à tabac.

丨等來, (ou 丨起來), *t'oí tèn loî*, (ou *t'oí hì loî*), mets-le dans ta poche.

代 *T'oí*. Génération, postérité, tenir la place de.

一丨人, *ŷt t'oí gnîn*, une génération.

前丨, 後丨, *ts'iên t'oí, heoú t'oí*, les ancêtres, les descendants.

丨天主個權, *t'oí t'iēn tchoù ké· k'iân*, tenir ses pouvoirs de Dieu.

丨管, 丨理, *t'oí kouòn, toí lī*, gouverner, régir par intérim.

丨父, 丨母, *t'oí foú, t'oí moū*, parrain, marraine.

丨子, 丨女, *t'oí tzè, t'oí ng̀*, filleul, filleule.

貸 *T'oí*. Emprunter.

告丨, 丨借, 助丨, 寬丨, *kaó t'oí, t'oí tsiá, tsé t'oí, k'ōn t'oí*, emprunter, assister, aider , exempter.

TŌN

端 *Tōn*. Article, division, porter devant soi d'une ou de deux mains.

做異丨, *tsó ý tōn*, faire des superstitions.

愛分三丨, *oí foūn sām tōn*, il faut diviser en trois articles.

眞福八丨, *tchīn foûc pât tōn*, les 8 béatitudes.

丨茶, 丨飯, *tōn ts'â, tōn fán*, apporter le thé, le riz.

忒重丨唔起, *t'iêt tch'oūng tōn mĝ hì*, c'est trop lourd je ne puis le porter

| | (ou | 正), *tōn tōn* (ou *tōn tchín*), exactement, intégralement, en vérité.

T'ŌN

斷 *T'ōn* (pour *tón*). Rompre, interrompre.

打 | , *tà t'ōn*, rompre en frappant.

割 | , *kôt t'ōn*, couper en deux.

| 擺子, *t'ōn paì tzè*, couper la fièvre.

病還唔曾 | 根, *p'iáng hân mĝ ts'ên t'ōn kīn*, la racine de la maladie n'est pas encore coupée.

| 火烟, *t'ōn fò yān*, cesser les feux (pour dire : n'avoir plus rien à faire cuire, être dans la misère.

| 氣, *t'ōn hí*, rendre le dernier soupir.

T'ÔN

團 *T'ôn*. Rond, rassembler, environner.

泥 | , *nâi t'ôn*, boule de terre, morceau de terre.

一 | 泥, *ŷt t'ôn nâi*, une motte de terre, une boule de terre.

| 近, *t'ôn k'ióun*, aux alentours.

| 圓, *t'ôn yân*, être unis, rassemblés.

| 齊, *t'ôn ts'î*, être réunis.

教友唔 | 圓, *káo yoū mĝ t'ôn yân*, les chrétiens ne sont pas groupés.

TÒN

短 *Tòn*. Court, bref.

忒 | , *t'iĕt tòn*, trop court.

| 兩寸, *tòn leòng ts'oún*, trop court de deux pouces.

講人長 | , *kòng gnîn tch'ông tòn*, dire les longues et les brèves de quelqu'un, médire.

有長有 | , *yoū tch'ông yoū tòn*, il a ses qualités et ses défauts.

斷 *Tòn* (pour *tón*). Arrêter.

| 血, *tòn hiĕt*, arrêter le sang (d'une blessure).

| 水, *tòn choùi*, intercepter, arrêter l'eau (v. g. cesser l'irrigation).

快去 | 佢米, *k'oúai hí tòn kiā mì*, va vite arrêter son riz, (l'empêcher de passer plus loin pour pouvoir l'acheter avant d'autres. Se dit aussi des voleurs qui arrêtent le riz au passage).

TÓN

斷 *Tón*. Trancher une question, adjuger.

| 定, *tón t'ín*, définir, trancher la question.

不遵官 | , *poŭt tsoūn koūon tón*, ne pas s'en tenir à la sentence du mandarin.

地方官 | 畀我, *t'í fōng koūon tón poūn ngâi*, le mandarin m'a adjugé le terrain.

| 得公道, *tón tĕt koūng t'áo*, il a porté une sentence juste.

墩 *Tón*. Escalier, marche.

上 | , *chōng tón*, monter les escaliers.

路忒𢰅愛結 | , *loú t'iĕt k'ī oí kiĕt tón*, la route est trop raide, il faut construire des escaliers.

T'ÓN

段 *T'ón.* Partie, fragment, numéral des paragraphes.

一 | 經, *ŷt t'ón kīn,* une prière.

你讀到裡子一 |, *gnî t'oŭc táo ỳ tzè ŷt t'ón,* lis jusqu'ici, cela fait une phrase.

做事麼 | 落, *tsó sé mô t'ón lŏc,* agir sans continuité, sans méthode.

一 | 田, *ŷt t'ón t'iên,* un ensemble de rizières groupées.

緞 *T'ón.* Satin, soie damassée.

| 鞋, *t'ón haî,* souliers en satin.

TŌNG

當 *Tōng.* Il faut, gérer, supporter, actuel.

該 | 受苦, *koī tōng chóu k'où,* il fallait qu'il souffrit.

| 用個恩, *tōng yoúng ké· ēn,* les grâces dont on a besoin.

| 家, | 家人, *tōng kā, tōng kā gnîn,* gérer les intérêts d'une famille, chef de famille.

| 相公, | 賊, *tōng sióng koūng, tōng ts'ĕt,* être séminariste, ou domestique, être voleur.

| 兵, | 差, *tōng pīn, tōng ts'aī,* être soldat, satellite.

裡個苦難 |, *ỳ ké· k'où nân tōng,* ces peines sont difficiles à supporter.

| 不得, *tōng poût têt,* impossible à supporter.

| 日, | 時, *tōng gnĭt, tōng chê,* alors, en ce temps-là.

| 面, *tōng mién,* en présence, face à face.

| 面話, *tōng mién vá,* parler en face, dire de vive voix.

T'ŌNG

湯 *T'ōng* Bouillon, jus.

煮 |, *tchoù t'ōng,* cuire du bouillon.

猪肉 |, *tchoū nioŭc t'ōng,* bouillon de porc.

飯 |, *fán t'ōng,* eau de riz.

燙 *T'ōng.* Laver, rincer, échauder.

| 淨來, *t'ōng ts'iáng loî,* rincer proprement.

| 猪, | 雞, *t'ōng tchoū, t'ōng kē,* échauder un porc, une poule, pour enlever plus facilement les poils, les plumes.

| 脚, *t'ōng kiŏc,* se laver les pieds.

| 嘴, *t'ōng tchói,* se rincer la bouche.

T'ÔNG

堂 *Tông.* Lieu, endroit, boutique, salle, temple, famille.

天 |, 地 |, 聖 |, *t'iēn tông, t'í t'ông, chín t'ông,* le Ciel, le paradis terrestre, le lieu saint, c.-à-d. l'église.

三 | 屋, *sām t'ông voŭc,* maison à 3 corps de bâtiments l'un derrière l'autre, et séparés par 2 cours.

祠 |, *tsê t'ông,* pagode des ancêtres d'une même famille.

大 |, *t'ái t'ông,* tribunal ouvert dans la partie antérieure du prétoire, où est admis le public.

二丨, *gní t'ông*, tribunal intérieur où ne sont admis que les intéressés.

官坐太丨, *koũon ts'ō t'ái t'ông*, le mandarin siège au tribunal public.

令丨, *lín t'ông*, votre mère (*polit.*).

丨兄弟, *t'ông hioũng t'í*, cousins, fils de frères ou de cousins.

唔係親個係丨兄弟, *mĝ hé· ts'în ké· hé· t'ông hioũng t'í*, ils ne sont pas frères utérins, ils sont cousins.

TÔNG

唐 *T'ông*. Nom d'une dynastie célèbre (520 av. J.C.).

丨朝, *t'ông tch'aô*, dynastie des *T'ông*.

丨人, *t'ông gnîn*, les Chinois.

講丨話, *kòng t'ông fá*, parler la langue chinoise.

塘 *T'ông*. Etang, réservoir ; distance d'un relai à un autre.

丨池, *t'ông tchê*, même sens.

開 v. 挖丨, *k'oī* v. *vă t'ông*, creuser un étang, un réservoir.

旱丨, *hón t'ông*, dessécher un étang.

行一丨路, *hâng ŷt t'ông loú*, faire une course d'un *t'ông* (une lieue de 6 kilomètres).

糖 *T'ông*. Sucre.

白丨, 黃丨, *p'ăc t'ông, vông t'ông*, sucre blanc ; sucre jaune ou mélasse.

放丨, *fóng* ou *pióng t'ông*, sucrer.

蜂丨, *foũng t'ông*, miel.

TÒNG

黨 *Tòng*. Compagnon, bande.

惡丨, *ôc tòng*, mauvaise engeance.

都係一丨個, *toū hé· ŷt tòng ké·*, c'est tout de la même clique.

擋 *Tòng*. Empêcher, faire obstacle, résister.

你唔使阻丨佢, *gnî mĝ sè tzè tòng kî*, ne l'empêche pas, laisse-le faire.

領婚配唔得有阻丨, *leăng foũn p'í mĝ têt yoũ tzè tòng*, ils ne peuvent pas contracter mariage, il y a empêchement.

担子拿開去莫丨等路, *tām tzè nā k'oī hí mŏc tòng tèn loú*, enlève ta charge de là et n'obstrue pas la route.

丨風, 丨雨, *tòng foũng, tòng ŷ*, abriter contre le vent, contre la pluie.

抵丨魔鬼, *tì tòng mô kouì*, résister au démon.

T'ÒNG

倘 *T'òng*. 丨或, 丨若, *t'òng fĕt, t'òng yŏc*, si, s'il en est ainsi.

TÓNG

當 *Tóng*. Tenir place de ; hypothéquer, donner en gage (a des sens multiples que l'usage apprendra).

飯丨唔得麵包, *fán tóng mĝ têt miĕn pāo*, le riz ne vaut pas le pain.

佢自己丨得兩個人, *kî tsé kì tóng têt leòng ké· gnîn*, lui seul en vaut deux.

上丨, *chŏng tóng*, être désagréablement surpris.

一回上了丨二回莫照樣, *ŷt fî chŏng liào tóng gní fî mŏc tcháo yóng*, attrapé une première fois, une autre fois n'allez pas faire la même sottise.

停 |, *t'în tóng*, définitivement, sûrement.

主意打停 |, *tchoù ý tà t'în tóng*, ma résolution est définitivement arrêtée.

| 舖, 開 | 舖, *tóng p'oú, k'oī tóng p'oú*, mont-de-piété, tenir un mont-de-piété.

| 東西, *tóng toūng sī*, engager des objets au mont-de-piété, hypothéquer.

小押 |, *siào âp tóng*, espèce de mont-de-piété non reconnu, tenu par des particuliers.

T'ÓNG

燙 *T'óng*. Réchauffer.

酒拿去 | 燒來, *tsioù nā hí t'óng chāo loî*, va chauffer le vin (sans le faire bouillir).

踼 *T'óng*. Se tromper de route, glisser, manquer.

| 路 | 程兩里, *t'óng lóu t'óng lê· leòng lī*, je me suis trompé de route, et me suis allongé de deux *lī*.

我 | 一下險險跌, *ngaî t'óng ŷt há hiàm hiàm tiĕt*, j'ai glissé et failli tomber.

| 人工, *t'óng gnîn koūng*, perdre du temps.

我 | 倒兩工, *ngaî t'óng tào leòng koūng*, j'ai perdu deux journées.

鎕 *T'óng*. 斗 | 子, *teòu t'óng tzè*, instrument pour niveler les grains dans le boisseau.

輷 *T'óng*. Un moment, un espace de temps, particule numérale des courses.

一 | 夫工做得成, *ŷt t'óng koūng foū tsó têt tcháng*, ce sera fait en un rien de temps.

佢走程有一 |, *kî tseòu lê· yoū ŷt t'óng*, il est parti, il y a un moment.

馬 |, *mā t'óng*, piste où l'on fait courir les chevaux.

跑一 |, *p'āo ŷt t'óng*, courir une fois la piste.

T'ŎT

奪 *T'ŏt*. Enlever de force.

衫褲畀佢搶 | 了, *sām foú poūn kî ts'iòng t'ŏt liào*, on l'a dépouillé de tous ses habits.

TÔT

掇 *Tôt*. Apporter, vendre pour être revendu, vendre en gros, exciter.

| 前來, *tôt ts'iên loî*, apporte ici.

佢唔肯 | 出來看, *kî mĝ hèn tôt tch'oût loî k'ón*, il ne veut pas l'exhiber.

| 酒賣, *tôt tsioù mái*, vendre du vin en gros.

| 婦人家, *tôt foú gnîn kā*, vendre une femme pour être revendue ailleurs.

你莫去 | 佢話來講, *gnî mŏc hí tôt kiā fá loî kòng*, ne vas pas l'exciter à parler.

T'OT

脫 *T'ôt*. Enlever, ôter, quitter.

| 一件衫, *t'ôt ŷt k'ián sām*, enlever, quitter un habit.

| 牙 齒, *t'ôt ngâ tchè*, arracher une dent.

你 帽 頂 | 帛 秷, *niä máo tàng t'ôt p'ĕt lê·*, le pompon de ton chapeau s'est détaché.

解 |, 解 唔 |, *kè· t'ôt, kè· mĝ t'ôt*, dénouer, ne pouvoir dénouer.

| 担 (v. | 身), *t'ôt tām* (v. *t'ôt chīn*), ôter sa charge (se décharger d'une responsabilité).

退 唔 |, *t'oúi mĝ t'ôt*, ne pouvoir se décharger.

| 神, *t'ôt chîn*, s'évanouir.

走 |, *tsèou t'ôt*, s'échapper.

| 字, | 像, *t'ôt sé, t'ôt sióng*, décalquer une lettre, une image.

TOŪ

都 *Toū*. Même, aussi, tout.

鬼 | 唔 怕 個, *koùi toū mĝ p'á ké·*, il n'a peur de rien, pas même du diable.

一 齊 | 係, *ŷt ts'ê· toū hé·*, tout cela en est.

病 重 | 麼 事 死, *p'iáng tch'oūng toū mô sé sì*, sa maladie est grave, malgré tout il n'en mourra pas.

| 司, *toū sē*, chef de bataillon.

T'OÛ

圖 *T'oû*. Désirer, avoir en vue' plan, carte.

只 | 救 靈 魂, *tchĭt t'oû kióu lîn foûn*, n'avoir en vue que le salut de son âme.

萬 國 全 |, *ván kouĕt ts'iên t'oû*, carte générale de tous les royaumes, mappemonde.

打 |, *tà t'oû*, tracer un plan.

| 料, *t'oû liáo*, plan, combinaison.

| 賴 人, *t'oû lái gnîn*, calomnier, réclamer à tort.

屠 *T'oû*. Tuer.

| 夫, *t'oû foū*, boucher.

開 |, *k'ōi t'oû*, (v. 打 |, *tà t'oû*) exercer le métier de boucher, lever la défense du : 禁 | *kím t'oû*, (voir *kím*).

塗 *T'oû*. Crépir, biffer.

| 壁, *t'oû piăc*, crépir un mur.

| 一 個 字, *t'oû ŷt ké· sé*, biffer une lettre.

糊 |, *foû t'oû*, sot, imbécile, brouillon.

途 *T'oû*. Route, chemin.

路 |, *loú t'oû*, chemin, route.

半 | 而 廢, *pán t'oû ŷ fí*, abandonner une entreprise à mi-chemin.

徒 *T'oû*. Disciple, apprenti.

木 匠 師 傅 帶 兩 個 | 弟, *moûc sióng sē foú tái leòng ké· t'oû t'í*, le maître menuisier a deux apprentis.

十 二 宗 |, *chĭp gní tsoūng t'oû*, les douze apôtres.

TOÙ

肚 *Toù*. ventre, estomac, intérieur de l'homme, dedans.

| 痛, | 饑, *toù t'oúng, toù kī*, avoir mal au ventre, avoir faim.

看 佢 行 實 係 好 | 裡 十 分 鄙, *k'ón kì hâng chĭt hé· hào toù lì chĭp foūn pè·*, à voir ses manières il paraît bon, au fond il est très mauvais.

丨兜 (ou 丨 搭) *toù teoū* (ou *toù tâp*, bourse, poche que les Chinois portent sur le ventre.

行 丨 ou 走 丨, *hâng toù* ou *tseoù toù*, avoir le dévoiement.

神父還在間丨裏, *chîn foú hân ts'aí kiān toù lî*, le Père est encore dans sa chambre.

消息在 ? 丨, *siāo sīt ts'ái tī toù*, la mécanique est à l'intérieur.

堵 *Toù*. Particule numérale des murs, fermer le passage.

一丨墻, *ȳt toù siông*, un mur.

隔一丨壁, *kâc ȳt toù* ou *ȳt t'oú piâc*, séparé par une cloison.

丨水, *toù choùi*, fermer le passage de l'eau.

丨口子, *toù k'eòu* (v.*heòu*) *tzè*, garder un défilé.

賭 *Toù*. Jouer aux jeux de hazard, parier.

丨博, 丨錢, *toù pôc*, *toù ts'iên*, jouer à ces jeux, jouer de l'argent.

我丨你食咁多唔下, *ngâi toù gnî chĭt àn tō mĝ hā*, je parie que tu ne mangeras pas tout cela.

T'OÙ

土 *T'où*. Terre.

泥丨唔好, *nâi t'où mĝ hào*, la terre n'est pas bonne.

沙丨, *sā t'où*, terre sablonneuse.

本丨出個, *poùn t'où tch'oūt ké·*, produit indigène.

丨談 (v. 丨話) *t'où t'âm* (v. *t'où fá*), patois, langage populaire.

TOÚ

睹 *Toú*. Regarder.

耳聞目丨, *gnì voûn moûc toú*, entendre de ses propres oreilles, voir de ses propres yeux.

妬 *Toú*. Envie, jalousie.

嫉丨, *ts'ĭt toú*, jalouser, être envieux.

T'OÚ

吐 *T'oú*. Cracher, vomir.

丨口液, 丨血, *t'oú heoù lān*, *t'oú hiĕt*, cracher de la salive, cracher le sang.

丨藥, *t'oú yŏc*, vomir la médecine.

兎 *T'oú*. Lapin, lièvre.

野丨子, *yā t'oú tzè*, lièvre.

度 *T'oú*. Mesure, régler, degré, passer.

食酒過丨, *chĭt tsioù koúo t'oú*, boire du vin outre mesure.

有量丨個人, *yoū leóng t'oú ké· gnîn*, c'est un homme généreux, magnanime.

地理圖愛分丨數, *t'í lī t'oû oí foūn t'oú sé*, sur les cartes géographiques, il faut distinguer les degrés (de longitude et de latitude).

站前一丨, *tsám tsiên ȳt t'oú*, avancer d'un cran.

丨日, *t'oú gnĭt*, passer les jours, vivre.

鍍 *T'oú*. Dorer ou argenter.

丨金, 丨銀, *t'oú kīm*, *t'oú nioûn*, dorer, argenter.

渡 *T'oú*. Traverser un fleuve.

38

丨船, *t'oú chôn*, bac ou barque de passage.

過丨船, *koúo t'oú chôn*, passer le fleuve dans la barque de passage.

同船過丨, *t'oûng chôn koúo t'oú*, passer le fleuve ensemble sur la même barque.

T'OǓC

毒 *T'oǔc*. Poison, venin.

食丨藥死, *chĭt t'oǔc yǒc sì*, mourir empoisonné.

丨蛇, *t'oǔc châ*, serpent vénimeux.

解丨藥, *kiài t'oǔc yǒc*, contre-poison.

丨心人, *t'oǔc sīm gnîn*, homme au cœur pervers, au cœur haineux.

獨 *T'oǔc*. Unique, seul.

丨有一個人, *t'oǔc yoū ȳt ké gnîn*, il n'y a qu'un seul homme.

丨門生理, *t'oǔc moûn siēn lī*, commerce qu'on est seul à faire dans l'endroit.

孤丨人, *koū t'oǔc gnîn*, homme seul, sans enfants.

讀 *T'oǔc*. Etudier.

丨書人, *t'oǔc choū gnîn*, lettré, homme d'étude.

問答愛丨熟來, *moún tâp oí t'oǔc choǔc loî*, il faut étudier le catéchisme par cœur.

我丨到裡子, *ngâi t'oǔc táo ỳ tzè*, j'ai étudié jusque là.

丨得, 丨唔得, *t'oǔc têt, t'oǔc mĝ têt*, avoir de l'aptitude pour l'étude, n'en pas avoir.

TOÛC

督 *Toûc*. Examiner, gouverner.

總丨, *tsoùng toûc*, vice-roi.

丨工, *toûc koūng*, diriger et surveiller les travaux.

啄 *Toûc*. Becqueter.

鳥子丨菜, *tiāo tzè toûc ts'oí*, les oiseaux becquètent les légumes.

丨樹鳥, *toûc choú tiāo*, espèce d'oiseau qui frappe les arbres de son bec, pour en faire sortir des insectes.

沰 *Toûc*. Peu, goutte, mouiller, eau qui tombe par gouttes.

一丨水, *ȳt toûc choùi*, une goutte d'eau.

雨丨倒我一身, *ỳ toûc tào ngâi ȳt chīn*, la pluie m'a tout mouillé.

唔怕雨丨, *mĝ p'á ỳ toûc*, qui ne craint pas la pluie.

启 *Toûc*. Le bas, le fond.

鍋丨, *vǒc toûc*, le fond extrême de la marmite.

窩丨, *vō toûc*, le fond du ravin, la partie la plus avancée dans la montagne.

T'OUĪ

兌 *T'oúi*. Se défaire d'une marchandise, vendre en gros, au rabais.

咁多貨我丨別你, *àn tō fó ngâi t'oúi poūn gnî*, je te vends toutes ces marchandises.

丨行, *t'oúi hông*, magasin en gros.

推 *T'ouī* ou *tch'ouī*. Pousser des mains devant soi, s'excuser, prétexter.

| 出去, *t'ouī tch'oût hí*, pousser.

| 開, *t'ouī k'oī*, écarter, rejeter.

| 唔開, *t'ouī mĝ k'oī*, ne pouvoir se débarrasser.

| 辭, *t'ouī tsê*, refuser, s'excuser.

| 三 | 四, *t'ouī sām t'ouī sí*, apporter divers prétextes pour refuser.

| 故個話, *t'ouī koú ké· fá*, paroles d'excuses.

| 阿人身上去, *t'ouī á gnîn chīn hóng hí*, rejeter sa faute sur autrui.

| 脫, *t'ouī t'ôt*, s'excuser.

| 唔脫, *t'ouī mĝ t'ôt*, ne pas parvenir à s'excuser.

T'OÙI

腿 *T'oùi*. Jambon, cuisse.

火 |, *fò t'oùi*, jambon salé.

TOÚI

對 *Toú*. En face, répondre, comparer, couple, paire.

| 門, *toúi moûn*, en face, vis-à-vis.

| 面話佢, *toúi mién vá kî*, dis-le lui en face.

| 苦像跪倒, *toúi k'où sióng k'oùi tào*, s'agenouiller devant le crucifix.

| 神父講, *toúi chîn foú kòng*, dire, parler au Père.

| 手, *toúi choù*, adversaire, antagoniste.

| 本利, *toúi poùn lí*, intérêt égal au capital $\frac{100}{100}$.

| 證 *toúi tchín*, confronter les témoins.

| 人唔住, | 得住, *toúi gnîn mĝ tch'oú, toúi têt tch'óu*, ne pouvoir se présenter (ne pas recevoir l'approbation des hommes), pouvoir se présenter (sans reproches).

兩個字紙愛 | 過, *leòng ké· sé tjè oí toúi koúo*, il faut comparer l'écrit avec l'original.

| 子 (v. | 聯), *toúi tzè* (v. *toúi liên*), sentences, épitaphes, inscriptions en distiques parallèles que les Chinois posent sur leurs murs comme ornement.

一個 | 年, 一個 | 時, *ŷt ké· toúi niân, ŷt ké· toúi chê*, une année révolue, une heure chinoise révolue (à partir d'une époque fixe.

一 | 白鴿, 一 | 燭, *ŷt toúi p'ác kâp, ŷt toúi tchoûc*, un couple de colombes, une paire de cierges.

T'OÚI

吐 *T'oúi* (pour *t'oú*). Cracher, rejeter de la bouche.

| 口液, *t'oúi heòu lān*, cracher.

呑唔下我 | 帛𥚃, *t'oūn mĝ hā ngâi t'oúi p'ēt lê·*, ne pouvant l'avaler, je l'ai recraché.

退 *T'oúi*. Reculer, rétrocéder.

你 | 兩步, *gnî t'oúi leòng p'oú*, recule de deux pas.

打 | 彙, *tà t'oúi loúi*, marcher à reculons.

| 担, *t'oúi tām*, rejeter une responsabilité.

| 某人身上, *t'oúi meōu gnîn chīn hóng*, rejeter la faute sur un tel.

進 | 兩難, *tsín t'oúi leòng nàn*, avancer ou reculer, les deux sont difficiles (être dans une position difficile).

兌 *T'oúi*. Echanger, payer.

| 田, *t'oúi t'ién*, sous-hyppothéquer une rizière.

我少佢一吊錢我 | 某人去, *ngâi chào kiā ŷt tiáo ts'iên, ngâi t'oúi meōu gnîn hí*, je lui dois une ligature, je l'ai passée à un tel.

TOŪN

炖 *Toūn*. Mitonner, cuire à petit feu.

| 猪肉, | 雞, cuire du porc, une poule,

墩 *Toūn*. Monticule dans une plaine, touffe, pile.

我屋在 | 下, *ngā voûc ts'aí toūn hā*, ma maison est au pied du monticule.

一 | 竹頭, 一 | 草, *ŷt toūn tchoûc t'eôu, ŷt toūn ts'ào*, une touffe de bambous, une touffe d'herbe.

橋 | , *k'iaô toūn*, pile de pont.

T'OŪN

吞 *T'oūn*. Avaler.

| 落, (v. | 下), *t'oūn lŏc* (v *t'oūn hā*), avaler.

| 唔落, (v. | 唔下), *t'oūn mĝ lŏc* (v. *t'oūn mĝ hā*), ne pouvoir avaler.

囤 *T'oūn* (ou *t'oùn*). Remplir, combler.

裡湖愛 | 滿來, *yà* (ou *ŷ*) *foû oí t'oūn mān loi*, il faut combler ce trou.

TOÙN

墩 *Toùn*. Bloc équarri, pieu, piquet.

樹 | , *choú toùn*, bloc de bois, pieu, piquet.

釘等來三四個 | 爲界, *tāng tèn loî sām sí ké· toùn vî kiái*, plante 3 ou 4 piquets, pour marquer les limites.

柱 | , *tch'oū toùn*, colonne.

鐵 | , *tsēm toùn*, enclume.

屯 *Toùn* (ou *t'oùn*). Amasssr pour revendre, approvisionner.

| 貨, | 穀, *toùn fó, toùn koŭc*, faire provision de marchandises, de riz, pour les revendre en temps opportun.

今年 | 穀愛帖本, *kīn niân toùn koŭc oí t'iâp poùn*, cette année, on n'amassera du riz qu'avec perte.

頓 *Toùn*. Saluer en inclinant la tête.

| 首拜, *toùn choù paí*, baisser profondément la tête pour saluer.

T'OÙN

腯 *T'oùn*. Préparer les peaux d'animaux.

| 牛皮, *t'oùn nioû p'î*, tanner une peau de buffle.

TOÚN

Toún. Particule employée dans certains endroits pour marquer le passé.

我看｜，聽｜，去｜, *ngâi k'ón toún, t'âng toún, hí toún*, je l'ai vu jadis, je l'ai entendu, j'y suis allé.

撴 *Toún*. Piquer, se heurter, recevoir un choc.

手上｜倒一枚釘, *chou hóng toún tào ŷt moê· tchîm*. attraper une épine dans le doigt.

門框忒矮噲｜人, *moûn k'iông t'ièt aì voé· toún gnîn*, la porte est trop basse, on peut se heurter.

T'OÚN

鈍 *T'oún*. Emoussé (au propre et au figuré).

刀子使｜了, *tao tzè sè t'oún liào*, le couteau est émoussé.

裡個細人子係｜, *ỳ ké· sé· gnîn tzè hé· t'oún*, cet enfant est très borné, a l'esprit obtus.

TOŪNG

中 *Toūng* ou *toúng* (pour *tchoūng*). Centre.

｜心, *toūng sīm*, le milieu, le centre.

｜手子, *toūng choù tzè*, le doigt du milieu.

冬 *Toūng*. Hiver.

｜下, *toūng ha*, en hiver.

立｜，｜至, *lĭp toūng, toūng tjé*, le commencement de l'hiver, solstice d'hiver.

東 *Toūng*. Est, Orient.

｜西南北, *toūng sī nâm pĕt*, l'Est le Sud l'Ouest le Nord.

｜西, *toūng sī*, chose, objet quelconque.

那個｜西, *mâc ké· toūng sī?* quoi? qu'est-ce?

｜家, *toūng ka*, le maître de la maison, patron.

T'OŪNG

通 *T'oūng*. Communiquer, comprendre, tout.

｜功念經, *t'oūng koūng niám kīn*, prier en commun.

｜行(v.｜用)個錢，｜行個貨, *t'oūng hâng (v. t'oūng yoúng) ké· ts'iên, t'oūng hâng ké· fó*, monnaie courante, marchandise qui a du débit.

｜風, *t'oūng foūng*, ventilation, aérer.

裡條路｜到東石, *ỳ t'iâo loú t'oūng táo toūng chăc*, cette route conduit à *Toung Chac*.

不｜世情個人, *poŭt t'oūng ché ts'în ké· gnîn*, qui ne connaît rien aux choses du monde.

唐話還唔｜, *t'ông fá hân mĝ t'oūng*, il ne comprend pas encore le chinois.

｜體, *t'oūng t'ì*. tout.

｜身大汗, *t'oūng chīn t'aí hón*, le corps tout en sueur.

｜城都曉得, *t'oūng châng toū hiaò têt*, toute la ville le sait.

動 *T'oūng* (pour *t'oúng*). Toucher, bouger.

東西莫起｜佢, *toūng sī mŏc hì t'oūng kî*, ne touche pas à mes affaires.

那個都愛起丨, *mâc ké· toū oí hì t'oūng*, il faut qu'il touche à tout.

你坐倒來莫丨, *gnî ts'ō tào loî mŏc t'oūng*, assieds-toi et ne bouge pas.

T'OÛNG

同 *T'oûng*. Ensemble, avec, aussi.

兩儕丨行, *lcòng sá t'oûng hâng*, ils marchent tous les deux ensemble.

丨神父去, *t'oûng chîn foú hí*, aller avec le Père.

丨行生理, *t'oûng hông siēn lī*, du même commerce.

丨房, *t'oûng fòng*, habiter la même chambre, terme poli pour désigner l'acte conjugal.

我等兩個丨年, 丨月, *ngā tèn lcòng ké· t'oûng niân, t'oûng gnĕt*, nous sommes tous les deux nés la même année, le même mois.

咁樣講事唔丨, *àn yóng kòng sé mĝ t'oûng*, comme tu le dis, ce n'est plus la même chose.

丨我帶一封信去, *t'oûng ngaî taí ўt foūng sín hí*, va me porter une lettre.

桐 *T'oûng*. Abrasin, arbre dont la noix fournit une excellente huile.

丨子, 丨樹, *t'oûng tzè, t'oûng choú*, noix de l'abrasin, abrasin.

丨油, 丨油灰, *t'oûng yoû, t'oûng yoû foē·*, huile d'abrasin, mastic fait avec de la chaux et cette huile.

筒 *T'oûng*. Tube, tuyau, cylindre.

烟丨, *yān t'oûng*, pipe.

火丨, *fò t'oûng*, tube de bambou dont on se sert pour attiser le feu.

一丨銀, *ўt t'oûng nioûn*, un rouleau de piastres.

銅 *T'oûng*. Cuivre.

丨打個, *t'oûng tà ké·*, fait en cuivre.

白丨, *p'ăc t'oûng*, cuivre blanc (alliage de cuivre).

丨貨, *t'oûng fó*, articles en cuivre.

丨青, *t'oûng ts'iāng*, vert-de-gris.

童 *T'oûng*. Enfant, non marié.

孩丨, *haî t'oûng*, petit enfant, nouveau-né.

丨身, 丨貞, *t'oûng chīn, t'oûng tchīn*, corps qui a l'intégrité virginale, vierge.

丨貞女, *t'oûng tchīn ǹg*, fille vierge.

TOÙNG

懂 *Toùng*. Comprendre.

丨書 丨得明白, *toùng choū toùng tĕt mîn p'ĕt*, comprendre les livres, comprendre clairement.

咁不丨個人, *àn poût toùng ké· gnîn*, quel homme borné!

董 *Toùng*. 古丨, *koù toùng*, qui n'a pu atteindre son développement naturel.

古丨人, *koù toùng gnîn*, nain.

T'OÙNG

統 *T'oùng*. Gouverner, présider.

佢丨帶幾多人, *kì t'oùng taí kì tō gnîn?* combien d'hommes commande-t-il?

歸我丨下，*koũi ngaî t'oùng hā*, il est sous mon commandement.

丨共，*t'oùng k'ioúng*, la totalité, en tout.

丨身，*t'oùng chīn*, entièrement.

桶 *T'oùng*. Seau, baquet, tonneau, enveloppe.

水丨，酒丨，*choùi t'oùng, tsiòu t'oùng*, seau d'eau, tonneau de vin.

一丨蜂子，*ȳt t'oùng foūng tzè*, une ruche d'abeilles.

信丨，*sín t'oùng*, enveloppe de lettre.

TOÚNG

棟 *Toúng*. Faîte de maison.

作屋丨，*tsôc voûc toúng*, faire, construire le faîte d'une maison.

凍 *Toúng*. Avoir froid.

丨死，*toúng sì*, mourir de froid.

我丨倒丨壞，*ngâi toúng taò toúng faí*, j'ai pris froid, j'en suis malade.

猪肉丨，*tchoū nioûc toúng*, gelée de porc.

猪肉丨唔起，*tchoū nioûc toúng mĝ hì*, ne pouvoir congeler la viande de porc.

疼 *Toúng*. Plaie causée par le froid.

手上起寒丨，*choù hōng hì hôn toúng*, avoir des engelures aux mains.

T'OÚNG

洞 *T'oúng*. Défilé, gorge de montagne.

石丨，*chac t'oúng*, gorge, défilé entre deux rochers.

痛 *T'oúng*. Douleur, souffrance.

頭哪丨，肚丨，*t'eoû nà t'oúng, toù t'oúng*, avoir mal à la tête, au ventre.

打丨，燒丨，*tà t'oúng, loûc t'oúng*, battre, brûler à faire mal.

看佢咁苦我心丨，*k'ón kî àn k'où ngā sīm voé· t'oúng*, en le voyant si malheureux, je me sens pris de commisération.

丨悔，發丨悔，*t'oúng fí, fāt t'oúng fí*, contrition, faire un acte de contrition.

動 *T'oúng*. Remuer, émouvoir, mettre en mouvement.

丨手丨脚，*t'oúng choù t'oúng kiôc*, remuer mains et pieds, s'agiter.

講道理丨人個心，*kòng t'áo lī t'oúng gnîn ké· sīm*, émouvoir en prêchant.

丨兵．*t'oúng pīn*, mettre les soldats en campagne, marche militaire.

走丨一下人就鬆，*tseòu t'oúng ȳt hā gnîn ts'ioú soūng*, une petite promenade vous rend de suite dispos.

T'OÛT

凸 *T'oût*. Boursouflure, relevé en bosse.

丨起來，*t'oût hì loî*, saillant, saillir.

TSĀ

渣 *Tsā*. Résidu, lie.

酒丨，加非丨，葯丨，*ts'iòu tsā, kā fī*

tsā, yŏc tsā, lie de vin, marc de café, résidu de médicaments.

揸 *Tsā.* Tenir en main, une poignée, petite gerbe.

丨權, *tsā k'iân,* tenir le pouvoir.

我話唔倒唔係我丨權, *ngâi vá mĝ tào mĝ hé· ngâi tsā k'iân,* je ne puis dire oui, ce n'est pas moi qui en ai le droit.

丨穩, *tsā voùn,* tiens bon.

一丨菜, 一丨稈, *ŷt tsā ts'oí, ŷt tsā kòn,* une poignée de légumes, une poignée de paille.

TS'Ā

叉 *Ts'ā.* Fourche, fourchette, fourchu.

刀丨拿來, *taō ts'ā nā loî,* apporte les couteaux et les fourchettes.

樹丨, *choú ts'ā,* fourche, branche fourchue.

三丨路, *sām ts'ā loú,* routes à trois bifurcations.

馬丨椅, *mā ts'ā ỳ* ou (*mā tsá ỳ*), chaise pliante.

差 *Ts'ā.* Errer, se tromper.

麼丨個, *mô ts'ā ké·,* il n'y a pas d'erreur.

丨得遠, *ts'ā têt yàn,* se tromper de beaucoup.

丨唔多, *ts'ā mĝ tō,* à peu près, il s'en faut de peu.

丨唔多死帛裡, *ts'ā mĝ tō sì p'ĕt lê,* il a failli mourir.

丨唔多噲暗, *ts'ā mĝ tō voé· ám,* il va faire nuit.

丨唔多做完, *t'sā mĝ tō tsó vân,* il a presque fini.

TS'Â

茶 *Ts'â.* Thé, camelia.

請丨, *ts'iàng ts'â,* je vous invite à boire le thé.

泡丨, *p'áo ts'â,* infuser le thé.

復水丨, *foûc choùi ts'â,* thé infusé pour la 2eme fois.

一點丨水不能食, *ŷt tiàm ts'â choùi poût nên chĭt,* il ne faut rien avaler (ni une goutte de thé ni une goutte d'eau).

出丨錢, *tch'oût ts'â ts'iên,* payer le thé, donner un pourboire.

有丨有酒多兄弟, *yoū ts'â yoū tsioù tō hioūng t'í,* ayez du thé et du vin, les amis ne vous manqueront pas.

摘丨子, *tsâc ts'â tzè,* cueillir les fruits du camélia.

打丨油, *tà ts'â yoû,* faire de l'huile de camélia.

查 *Ts'â.* Examiner.

丨一件事, *ts'â ŷt k'ián sé,* examiner une affaire.

丨明自己個罪, *ts'â mîn tsé kì ké· ts'oúi,* examiner clairement ses péchés.

丨出來, *ts'â tch'oût loî,* découvrir en cherchant.

丨唔出那個罪, *ts'â mĝ tch'oût mâc ké· ts'oúi,* je ne puis découvrir aucun péché.

搽 *Ts'â.* Enduire, oindre.

丨藥油, *ts'â yŏc yoû,* oindre avec de l'huile médicinale.

丨聖油, *ts'â chín yoû*, oindre avec les Saintes Huiles.

TSÁ

竈 *Tsá* ou *tsâc* (pour *tsáo*). 丨下, *tsá hā*, cuisine, chambre où l'on fait la cuisine.

詐 *Tsá*. Tromper, feindre.

丨病, 丨死, *tsá p'iáng, tsá sì*, feindre, faire le malade, faire le mort.

丨得子, *tsá têt tzè*, frauduleusement, il fait semblant.

咁奸丨, *kàn kiān tsá*! quel avare!

岔 *Tsá* (pour *ts'á*). Traverser, passer par.

上縣愛丨阿大畲過, *chōng yán oí tsá á t'ái ts'iâ koúo*, pour aller à la sous-préfecture, il faut passer par *T'ai ts'ia*.

丨阿河頭做得丨阿東石做得, *tsá á hô t'eôu tsó têt tsá á toūng chăc tsó têt*, on peut y aller, soit par *Ho t'eou*, soit par *Toung chac*

丨人轉, *tsá gnîn tchòn*, prendre la défense de quelqu'un, en renchérissant sur ses paroles.

醡 *Tsá*. Presser, comprimer.

油丨, *yoû tsá*, pressoir à huile.

丨唔出油, *tsá mĝ tch'oût yoû*, ne pouvoir tirer de l'huile en comprimant.

洗裡衫愛丨渷來, *sè· lê· sām oí tsá liàm loî*, les habits lavés, il faut les presser pour les dessécher.

煠 *Tsá*. Frire à l'huile.

番薯拿來丨, *fān choû nā loî tsá*, fais frire les pommes de terre à l'huile.

油丨餅, *yoû tsá piàng*, gâteaux frits à l'huile.

TS'Á

岔 *Ts'á*. Bifurquer.

直去麼丨路, *tch'ĭt hí mô ts'á loú*, allez tout droit, il n'y a pas d'embranchement.

路丨走唔知那裡去, *loú ts'á tseòu mĝ tī nái lī hí*, la route se bifurque et s'en va je ne sais où.

TS'ĂC

牐 *Ts'ăc*. Barricader.

丨間房, *ts'ăc kiān fông*, faire une séparation dans une chambre.

丨開, *ts'ăc k'ōi*, barricader, séparer.

TSÂC

摘 *Tsâc*, Cueillir.

丨花, 丨菜, 丨茶子, *tsâc fā, tsâc ts'oí, tsâc ts'â tzè*, cueillir des fleurs, des légumes, des fruits de camélia.

壓 *Tsâc* (pour *âp*). Comprimer, peser sur, écraser.

丨書, 丨紙, *tsâc choū, tsâc tjè*, presser des livres, du papier.

拿石頭來丨, *nā chăc t'eôu loî tsâc*, presser sous une pierre.

你丨倒我脚, *gnî tsâc tào ngā kiôc*, tu me marches sur le pied.

墻轉帛裡丨死一個人, *siông tchón p'ēt lê· tsâc sì ȳt kê· gnîn*, le mur, en s'écroulant, a écrasé un homme.

TS'ÂC

册 *Ts'âc.* Cahier, registre.

印契愛上｜簿, *ýn k'é oí chōng ts'âc p'oū,* quand on fait timbrer ses contrats, on l'inscrit au registre.

入程學老師愛註｜, *gnîp lî hŏc laò sē oí tchoú ts'âc,* l'examinateur doit enregistrer les noms de ceux qui sont reçus bacheliers.

拆 *Ts'âc.* Démonter, séparer les parties, défaire, démolir, déchirer, dissoudre.

｜開書信, *ts'âc k'oī choū sín,* décacheter une lettre.

｜衫, *ts'âc sām,* découdre un habit.

｜時辰鐘, *ts'âc chê chîn tchōung,* démonter une horloge.

｜壞了, *ts'âc faí liào,* gâter en démontant.

｜婚姻, *ts'âc foūn ȳn,* dissoudre un mariage.

｜債, *ts'âc tsái,* payer ses dettes.

TSĀI

齋 *Tsāi.* Jeûne, abstinence.

大｜，小｜, *t'aí tsāi, siào tsāi,* jeûne, abstinence.

封｜，開｜, *foūng tsāi, k'oī tsāi,* commencer le Carême, le finir.

求寬免大｜, *k'iôu k'ōn mēn t'ái tsāi,* demander dispense du jeûne.

做｜, *tsó tsāi,* faire un ensemble de superstitions, durant plus ou moins longtemps, avec force tapage d'instruments.

栽 *Tsāi.* Planter, cultiver.

｜花, *tsāi fā,* cultiver des fleurs.

｜培人, *tsāi p'î gnîn,* prendre soin, prendre les intérêts de quelqu'un, l'entourer de soins.

災 *Tsāi.* Malheur, calamité.

｜難，｜殃, *tsāi nán, tsāi yōng,* malheur, catastrophe.

水｜，火｜, *choùi tsāi, fò tsāi,* désastre causé par l'inondation, par l'incendie.

除死無大｜, *tch'oû sì voû t'aí tsāi,* à part la mort, il n'y a pas de grand malheur (dicton païen).

TS'ĀI

搓 *Ts'āi.* Brasser, pétrir la farine.

｜麵包, *ts'āi mién pāo,* faire le pain.

｜灰, *ts'āi foē,* gâcher le mortier.

墻｜, *siông ts'āi,* charpente à fouler les murs.

墻｜卡, *siông ts'āi k'â,* la partie qui maintient les planches de cette charpente.

差 *Ts'āi.* Satellite, corvée, envoyer.

出｜, *tch'oût ts'āi,* envoyer les satellites.

交房｜, *kāo fông t'sāi,* mettre en prison préventive.

當｜事, *tōng ts'āi sé,* subir une corvée.

裡頭路｜事重, *yà t'eôu loú t'sāi sé tch'oūng,* cet emploi demande un service très compliqué.

| 佢去辦𠮶個事, *t'sāi kì hí p'án ỳ ké· sé*, envoie-le pour traiter cette affaire.

釵 *Ts'āi*. Aiguille de tête pour les femmes.

金 | 玉環, *kīm ts'āi nioũc p'àn*, aiguille en or et pendants en jade.

猜 *Ts'aī* (*ts'aî*). Deviner, conjecturer, résoudre des énigmes, pressentir.

人心難 |, *gnîn sīm nân ts'aī*, il est difficile de deviner ce que pensent les gens.

| 枚, *ts'aī moê·*, jeu de la mourre, jouer à pair ou impair.

我 | 佢麼來, *ngâi ts'aī kî mô loî*, je m'imagine qu'il ne viendra pas.

TS'AÎ

纔 *Ts'aî*. Alors, seulement, juste alors. (Ce mot est corrompu par l'usage ; dans la langue pop. on dit 睜 *tsáng*, *voir ce mot*). On trouve ce mot dans le catéchisme : | 妥, *ts'aî t'ò*, comme cela, c'est bien.

柴 *Ts'aî* (ou *ts'iâo*). Bois à brûler, bois de chauffage.

一担 |, 一捆 |, *ŷt tām ts'aî*, *ŷt k'oùn ts'aî*, une charge de bois, un fagot de bois.

你燒 | 阿燒炭, *gnî chāo ts'aî á chāo t'án ?* brûles-tu du bois ou du charbon ?

材 *Ts'aî* (ou *ts'oî*). Matière, matériaux.

枉 | 料, *nóng ts'aî liâo*, gaspiller les matériaux.

𠮶樹子鋸得三 | 倒, *yà choú tzè kí tēt sām ts'aî tào*, on peut faire trois morceaux (matériaux) de cet arbre.

棺 |, *kouōn ts'aî*, cercueil.

葯 |, *yŏc ts'aî*, médicaments bruts, matière pour les produits pharmaceutiques.

裁 *Ts'aî*. Couper, tailler, choisir.

學 | 縫, *hŏc ts'aî foûng*, apprendre le métier de tailleur.

會縺唔會 |, *voé· liên mĝ voé· ts'aî*, il sait coudre mais il ne sait pas faire la coupe.

| 一件衫, *ts'aî ŷt k'ián sām*, faire la coupe d'un habit.

| 籌, *ts'aî tch'oû*, pourvoir à une chose, déterminer son plan.

樣來 | 籌做聖堂, *nióng loî ts'aî tch'oû tsó chín t'ông ?* quel plan de chapelle avez-vous en vue ?

| 一個妥當人, *ts'aî ŷt ké· t'ò tóng gnîn*, choisir un homme sûr.

TSAÌ

宰 *Tsaì*. Gouverner, tuer.

萬物個大主 |, *ván voŭt ké· t'aí tchoù tsaì*, le Dominateur, maître de toutes choses.

| 相, *tsaì sióng*, ministres de l'Empereur.

| 雞, | 猪, *tsaì kē·*, *tsaì tchoū*, tuer une poule, un porc (peu employé).

| 犯人, *tsaì fám gnîn*, décapiter un criminel.

崽 *Tsaì*. Petits des animaux.

猪 |, *tchoū tsaì*, petits cochons.

細滿 |, *sé· mān tsaì*, on apppelle ainsi les petits enfants, dans certains endroits.

爛 |, *lán tsaì*, se dit d'un homme méchant, qui cherche noise à tout le monde.

載 *Tsaì*. Année.

一年半 |, *ŷt niân pán tsaì*, une année ou une demi-année (un temps indéterminé).

TS'AÌ

採 *Ts'aì*. Choisir et cueillir, butiner.

蜂子 | 花, *foūng tzè ts'aì fā*, les abeilles butinent.

| 藥草, *ts'aì yŏc ts'ào*, cueillir des plantes médicinales.

踩 *Ts'aì*. Fouler aux pieds.

| 爛, | 壞, *ts'aì lán, ts'aì faí*, déchiré, gâté, pour avoir été foulé aux pieds.

| 十字, *ts'aì chĭp sé*, fouler la croix aux pieds, apostasier.

馬 | 死一個人, *mā ts'aì sì ŷt ké· gnîn*, le cheval a écrasé un homme sous ses pieds.

TSAÍ

再 *Tsaí*. Encore, de nouveau, davantage, désormais.

| 多我唔怕, *tsái tō ngâi mĝ p'á*, seraient-ils plus nombreux encore, je ne les crains pas.

| 三我話你知, *tsaí sām ngâi vá gnî tī*, pour la troisième fois je te le dis.

我 | 不敢食酒, *ngâi tsaí poût kàm chĭt tsiòu*, désormais, je n'oserai plus boire de vin.

| 者, *tsaí tchà*, en outre.

債 *Tsaí*. Dette, obligation.

| 賬, *tsaí tchóng*, dette active, créance.

取 |, *ts'ì tsaí*, réclamer ses dettes, une créance.

拆 (v. 還) |, *ts'âc* (v. *vân*) *tsaí*, payer ses dettes.

| 主, *tsaí tchoù*, créancier.

欠 |, *k'iám tsaí*, avoir une dette.

收 |, *choū tsaí*, recevoir le paiement d'une dette.

磜 *Tsái*. Rochers abrupts.

石 |, 水 |, *chăc tsaí, choùi tsaí*, rochers, cascades.

TS'ÁI

在 *Ts'ái*. Exister, être dans. (Selon les pays et les circonstances, la prononciation de ce mot varie beaucoup. On dit: *ts'oī, t'oī, hoī*, ... voir ces mots).

| 屋下, *ts'ái voûc hā*, à la maison.

| 前, *ts'ái ts'iên*, auparavant, jadis.

自 |, 唔自 |, *tsé ts'ái, mĝ tsé ts'ái*, être (ou) n'être pas à l'aise.

| 佢手麼裡個事, *ts'ái kî chòu mô ỳ ké· sé*, sous lui, il n'y avait pas cette affaire, il n'en était pas ainsi.

｜我意思唔係咁樣做，*ts'ái ngâ ý sé mĝ hé· àn yóng tsó*, d'après mon idée, (selon moi) ce n'est pas comme cela qu'il faut faire.

盡｜你，*ts'ín ts'ái gnî*, comme tu voudras, à ta guise.

寨 *Ts'ái*. Fortification de montagne, camp retranché.

賊子一來一家人上｜，*ts'ĕt tzè ŷt loî ŷt kā gnîn chōng ts'ái*, dès que les rebelles arrivent, toute la famille monte aux fortifications.

TSĀM

簪 *Tsām*. Epingles de tête dont se servent les femmes pour retenir leurs cheveux.

｜環首飾，*tsām p'ân chouì chĭt*, épingle de tête, pendants d'oreilles, ornement de tête (se dit pour désigner tous les ornements d'une femme).

入裡秀才愛｜花，*gnĭp lî sioú ts'oî oí tsām fa*, on épingle une fleur à celui qui vient d'être reçu bachelier.

沾 *Tsām*. ｜恩，*tsām ēn*, recevoir un bienfait.

裡個事我｜光你，*lì ké· sé ngaî tsām kouōng gnî*, je vous en suis redevable.

TS'ĀM

參 *Ts'ām*. Mêler, ajouter, dégrader.

｜酒，*ts'ām tsioù*, vin que l'on a additionné d'eau.

｜風話，*ts'ām foūng fá*, ajouter, glisser un mot.

｜官，*ts'ām koūon*, dégrader, casser un mandarin.

｜將，*ts'ām tsióng*, colonel.

｜謀．*ts'ām meoû*, comploter, tenir conseil.

TS'ÂM

讒 *Ts'âm*. Calomnier, murmurer.

莫聽人個｜言，*mŏc t'āng gnîn ké· ts'âm niân*, n'écoutez pas les mauvaises langues.

蠶 *Ts'âm*. Ver à soie.

｜子牽絲，*ts'âm tzè k'iān sē*, le ver à soie fait sa soie.

｜子繭藪，*ts'âm tzè kiàn teóu*, le ver à soie fait son cocon.

TSÀM

斬 *Tsàm*. Couper d'un coup sec.

｜頭，*tsàm t'eôu*, décapiter.

｜斷，*tsàm t'ōn*, couper en deux.

｜鐵，*tsàm t'iĕt*, couper un morceau de fer au ciseau.

TS'ÀM

慘 *Ts'àm*. Souffrir, avoir du chagrin.

病十分｜，*p'iáng chĭp foūn ts'àm*, sa maladie est très douloureuse.

冤｜，*yān ts'àm*, être dans la peine, la souffrance.

TSÁM

滲 *Tsám*. S'infiltrer, s'imprégner.

裡坵田唔好水噲｜走，*ỳ k'iōu t'iên mĝ hào chouì voé· tsám tseoù*, cette rizière n'est pas bonne, l'eau ne tient pas.

外背個水｜阿間房去, *ngoé· poé· ké· choùi tsám á kiān fòng hí*, l'eau de dehors s'infiltre jusque dans chambre.

TS'ÁM

站 *Ts'ám (tsàn)*. Etape, relais.

到東石打路｜, *táo toūng chăc tà loú ts'ám*, on relachera à *Toung chac*.

｜房, *ts'ám fòng*, auberge, hôtel.

｜前一度, *ts'ám ts'ién ŷt t'oú*, avancer d'un degré, d'un cran.

打飛鵰愛｜前一度, *tà pī tiāo oí ts'ám ts'ién ŷt t'oú*, quand on tire au vol, il faut viser un peu en avant.

杉 *Ts'ám*. Sapin.

｜樹做個, *ts'ám choú tsó ké·*, fait en bois de sapin.

｜笏, *ts'ám nĕt*, aiguilles du sapin.

鏨 *Ts'ám*. Ciseau pour tailler les pierres. Sculpter, graver avec cet instument.

石頭上｜字, *chăc t'eōu hóng ts'ám sé*, graver des caractères sur la pierre.

像 *Ts'ám (sióng)*. Ressembler.

佢唔｜病人, *kî mĝ ts'ám p'iáng gnîn*, il ne ressemble pas à un malade.

隔遠看｜人, *kâc yàn k'ón ts'ám gnîn*, de loin, on dirait un homme. Voir 像 *ts'ióng*.

TS'ĀN

剗 *Ts'ān (ts'àn)*. Couper à rebrousse-poil.

剃頭｜毛, *t'í t'eōu ts'ān māo*, raser la tête en coupant à rebrousse-poil.

TS'ÂN

泉 *Ts'ân*. Source d'eau.

水｜, *choùi ts'ân*, source d'eau.

山脚下有｜水, *sān kiōc hā yoū ts'ân choùi*, il y a une source au pied de la montagne.

纏 *Ts'ân*. Enrouler, entortiller.

線拿來｜阿竹子上, *sién nā loî ts'ân á tchoŭc tzè hóng*, enrouler le fil autour d'un bambou.

蛇哥｜阿樹上去, *châ kō ts'ân á choú hóng hí*, le serpent est allé s'enrouler autour de l'arbre.

殘 *Ts'ân*. Nuire, restes.

｜疾, *ts'ân ts'ĭt*, maladie incurable.

官｜虐百姓, *koūon ts'ân niôc pâc siáng*, le mandarin tourmente tout le monde.

｜菜, *ts'ân ts'ói*, restes des légumes.

｜舊, *ts'ân k'ioú*, vieux, avarié.

TSÀN

站 *Tsàn*. Se tenir, renvoyer, remettre.

｜起來, *tsàn hì loî*, tiens-toi droit, fixe!

｜前三日, ｜後三日, *tsàn ts'ién sām gnĭt, tsàn heóu sām gnĭt*, remettre à trois jours plus tôt, renvoyer à trois jours plus tard.

大官出門小官兩旁｜班, *t'aí kouōn tch'oŭt moûn siaò kouōn leòng*

p'ông tsàn pān, quand un grand mandarin sort, les petits mandarins se tiennent sur deux rangs (font la haie).

盞 *Tsàn*. Petite écuelle, godet.

燈 |, *tēn tsàn*, petite lampe à huile toute montée, veilleuse.

趲 *Tsàn*. Presser, urger, se hâter.

| 勁, *tsàn kín*, s'efforcer, employer toutes ses forces.

| 齊來, *tsàn tsê· loî*, empressons-nous tous ensemble.

TS'ÀN

鏟 *Ts'àn*. Râcler, pelle.

| 草皮, *ts'àn ts'ào p'î*, râtisser l'herbe.

| 坪, *ts'àn p'iâng*, aplanir en râclant.

鍋 |, *vŏc ts'àn*, petite pelle pour la cuisine.

TSÁN

攢 *Tsán* (pour *tsàn*). Rouler.

| 石頭, *tsán chăc t'eôu*, faire rouler des pierres (v. gr. du haut d'une montagne).

| 錢, | 柑, *tsán ts'iên, tsán kām*, faire rouler des sapèques, des oranges (jeux des enfants).

讚 *Tsán*. Louer.

| 美, | 頌, *tsán mī, tsán sioúng*, louer, glorifier.

TS'ÁN

濺 *Ts'án*. Rejaillir.

水花 | 天, *choùi fa ts'án t'iēn*, l'eau rejaillit (litt. les fleurs d'eau rejaillissent au ciel).

火煋 | 天, *fò sēn ts'án t'iēn*, jaillir des étincelles.

| 笋, *ts'án soùn*, bourgeonner, pousser des rejetons.

碾 *Ts'án*. Laminer.

| 布, *ts'án póu*, lisser la toile avec une pierre faisant l'office de laminoir.

| 紙爆, *ts'án tjè p'áo*, faire des pétards, en roulant les papiers avec un laminoir *ad hoc*).

石 | *chăc ts'án*, pierre à laminer, laminoir en pierre.

棧 *Ts'án*. | 廚, *ts'án tch'ôu*, garde-manger.

| 房, *ts'án fông*, hangar, dépôt, baraque.

粲 *Ts'án* ou *tch'án*. Epi.

麥 |, 穀 |, *măc ts'án, koŭc ts'án*, épi de blé, épi de riz.

拈穀 |, *niām koŭc ts'án*, glaner le riz.

TSĀNG

踭 *Tsāng*. 脚 |, *kiŏc tsāng*, le talon du pied.

手 |, *choù tsāng*, le coude.

爭 *Tsāng* (*tsēn*). Contester, disputer, concourir, il s'en faut.

| 買, *tsāng maì*, se disputer à qui achètera.

| 賣, *tsāng mái*, vendre à l'enchère.

| 田, | 地方, *tsāng t'iên, tsāng*

t'í fōng, se disputer une rizière, un terrain.

佢｜起｜走, *kî tsāng hì tsāng tseòu*, à force de disputer, il a fini par s'en emparer.

｜得遠, *tsāng têt yàn*, il s'en faut de beaucoup.

｜三十個錢, *tsāng sām chĭp ké· ts'iên*, il s'en faut de 30 sapèques.

TS'ÂNG

睜 *Ts'âng*. Briller, réfléchir la lumière.

月光就係日頭｜光個, *gnĕt kouōng ts'ioú hé· gnĭt t'eôu ts'âng kouōng ké·*, c'est le soleil qui éclaire la lune.

看日頭唔倒噲｜眼, *k'ón gnĭt t'eôu mĝ tào voé· ts'âng niàn*, on ne peut regarder le soleil, il vous éblouit.

TS'ÀNG

爭 *Ts'àng* (*tsēn*). S'efforcer.

｜光, *ts'àng kouōng*, agir d'une manière ostensible, pour s'attirer des compliments.

TSÁNG

睜 *Tsáng* ou *tcháng* (mot *ts'âi* 纔 corrompu). Récemment, enfin, afin que.

｜唔久, *tsáng mĝ kioù*, récemment.

｜兩日, *tsáng leòng gnĭt*, il n'y a que deux jours.

剛剛｜來, *kōng kōng* ou *kiōng kiōng tsáng loî*, il ne fait que d'arriver.

干 (*v.* 剛) ｜在裡子, *kōn* ou *kiōng tsáng t'oî ỳ tzè*, il n'y a qu'un instant il était là.

裡本書唔係我裡個｜係, *ỳ poùn choū mĝ hé· ngā yà ké· tsáng hé·*, ce livre-ci n'est pas le mien, c'est bien celui-là.

粉壁愛擠｜磨事劈, *foùn piâc oí nô tsáng mô sé pĭt*, quand on blanchit un mur il faut le frotter, afin qu'il ne se fendille pas.

TS'ÁNG

掙 *Ts'áng*. Faire de grands efforts.

猪｜飽, *tchoū ts'áng pào*, le porc a mangé à n'en pouvoir plus.

唱經唔好｜板, *tch'óng kīn mĝ hào ts'áng pàn*, en chantant les prières il ne faut pas forcer sa voix.

｜釀腸, *ts'áng nióng tch'ông*, faire des saucissons.

諍 *Ts'áng*. Se disputer, répliquer.

｜嘴, *ts'áng tchói*, se disputer, se quereller.

佢｜兩句話, *kî ts'áng leòng kí fá*, il a riposté par quelques paroles.

撐 *Ts'áng*. Pousser, étayer, soutenir, contrefort, étai.

｜船, *ts'áng chôn*, faire avancer une barque avec une perche.

棍｜子, *koún ts'áng tzè*, bâton dont se servent les porteurs, pour soutenir leurs fardeaux, bâton de vieillard.

打｜, *tà ts'áng*, se servir de ce bâton, en portant les fardeaux.

｜門, *ts'áng moûn*, mettre un bâton en contrefort derrière la porte.

｜樹子, *ts'áng choú tzè*, étayer un arbre.

樽 *Ts'áng* ou *tch'áng*. Meuble dont se servent les Chinois pour porter les mets, soit aux noces soit aux sacrifices.

TSĀO

燥 *Tsāo*. Sec, desséché.

晒 | , 炕 | , 眼 | , *saí tsāo, k'óng tsāo, lâng tsāo,* sécher au soleil, au feu, à l'air.

你洗裡個衫褲 | 麼, *gnî sè· lê· ké· sām foú tsāo mô* ? les vêtements que tu as lavés sont-ils secs.

遭 *Tsāo*. Rencontrer, trouver sur son chemin, hasard.

| 難, *tsāo nán*, éprouver des malheurs.

| 火, *tsāo fò*, être incendié, incendie.

| 水荒, *tsāo chouì fōng*, inondation.

| 逢貴人, *tsāo foûng kouí gnîn*, rencontrer un homme illustre (se dit d'un homme qui vous a tiré d'un mauvais pas, ou rendu un service signalé).

| 來個, *tsāo loî ké·*, par hasard.

糟 *Tsāo*. 酒 | , *tsioù tsāo*, résidu de grains distillés ou fermentés.

TS'ĂO

操 *Ts'āo*. S'exercer.

| 練武, *ts'aō lién voū*, se livrer aux exercices militaires.

| 練道理, 字, *ts'āo lién t'áo lī, sé*, apprendre la doctrine, l'écriture.

| 守, *ts'āo choù*, fidèle observateur du devoir.

裡個人有 | 持, *ỳ ké· gnîn yoū ts'aō tchê*, cet homme est plein de sollicitude.

抄 *Ts'āo*. Transcrire.

| 一張契, *ts'āo ŷt tchōng k é·*, copier, transcrire un contrat.

官出個批愛 | 倒來, *koūon tch'oūt ké· p'ī oí ts'āo tào loî*, il faut copier la réponse que le mandarin sort.

TS'ÂO

槽 *Ts'âo*. Cabane, rigole creusée dans le bois.

馬 | , *mā ts'âo*, mangeoire pour les chevaux.

耶穌在馬 | 降生, *yâ sē ts'aí mā ts'aô kóng sēn*, Jésus est né dans une étable.

烟 | , 紙 | , *yān ts'âo, tjè ts'âo*, fabrique, usine de tabac, de papier.

一 | 烟, *ŷt ts'âo yān*, une fournée de tabac.

研 | , *ngān ts'âo*, rigole où passe la roue qui écrase les arachides, dans les fabriques d'huile.

打一個 | , *tà ŷt ké· ts'âo*, creuser une rainure, une rigole.

吵 *Ts'âo*. Bruit, vacarme, quereller.

莫 | 人, *mŏc ts'âo gnin*, ne m'ennuie pas par ton vacarme.

| 鬧, *ts'âo náo*, tapageur, turbulent.

兩個人緊相 | , *leòng ké· gnîn kìn siōng ts'âo*, ces deux sont toujours à se disputer.

40

海上絲綢之路文獻集成 科技與文化編

TSÀO

蚤 *Tsào.* 跳 | , *t'iáo tsào,* puce.

棗 *Tsaò.* 烏 | , *voū tsaò,* jujube.

搔 *Tsào.* Se gratter, griffer.

| 癢, *tsào yōng,* se gratter pour faire passer une démangeaison.

| 爛 , *tsào lán,* s'écorcher en se grattant.

貓公噲 | 人 , *miaó koūng voé· tsào gnîn,* le chat griffe.

爪 *Tsào.* Griffes.

虎 | , 貓 | , *foù tsào, miáo tsào,* griffes de tigre, de chat.

雞 | , *kē· tsaò,* pattes de poule.

早 *Tsào.* Matin, tôt.

今 | , | 辰頭 , *kīn tsào, tsào chîn t'eôu,* ce matin, le matin.

咁 | 上 , *àn tsào hóng,* si tôt levé ! (*politesse,* manière de se dire bonjour, le matin).

| 知我唔去, *tsào tī ngâi mĝ hí,* si j'avais su je n'y serais pas allé.

你 | 唔話 , *gnî tsào mĝ vá,* que ne le disais-tu plus tôt.

| 穀 , *tsào koŭc,* espèce de riz qui mûrit plus tôt.

找 *Tsào.* Echanger la monnaie, suppléer, construire.

| 一個花邊錢 , *tsào ŷt ké· fa piēn ts'iên,* changer une piastre en sapèques.

愛 | 三十個錢別我 , *oí tsào sām chĭp ké· ts'iên poūn ngâi,* il faut me rendre 30 sapèques (sur ma monnaie).

| 紙人, 紙屋 , *tsào tjè gnîn, tjè voŭc,* fabriquer des hommes en papier, une maison en papier (dont les païens se servent aux enterrements).

| 時辰鐘 , *tsào chê chîn tchoūng,* fabriquer une horloge.

TS'ÀO

草 *Ts'ào.* Herbe.

㧊 | , *pāng ts'ào,* arracher l'herbe.

割 | 皮 , *kôt ts'ào p'î,* couper de l'herbe à faire la litière.

糞 | , *poún ts'ào,* engrais provenant d'herbes, de pailles mélangées avec le fumier d'animaux.

藥 | , *yŏc ts'ào,* plante médicinale.

| 蜢, *ts'ào màng,* sauterelle, criquet.

寫正字莫 | 得子 , *sià tchín sé mŏc ts'aò tĕt tzè,* écris en lettres régulières, et non en écriture courante.

炒 *Ts'ào.* Griller, rôtir, frire.

| 加非 , | 黃豆 , *ts'ào ka fī, ts'aò vông t'eoú,* griller le café, des haricots.

| 猪肉 , *ts'ào tchoū nioŭc,* rôtir du porc.

TSÁO

竈 *Tsáo.* Foyer, cuisine.

打 | 頭 , *tà tsáo t'eôu,* construire un fourneau.

| 神 , *tsáo chîn,* dieu du foyer.

倒 | , *tào tsáo,* renverser son fourneau (signifie qu'une famille est éteinte, sans rejetons).

TS'ÁO

造 *Ts'áo*. Créer, inventer.

｜萬物的主, *ts'áo ván voŭt tît tchoù*, le Seigneur, Créateur de toutes choses.

新｜個東西, *sīn ts'áo toūng sī*, chose nouvellement inventée.

番人｜倒好多奇物,- *fān gnîn ts'áo taò haò tō k'î voŭt*, les étrangers ont inventé beaucoup de choses merveilleuses.

掉 *Ts'áo*. Chercher, fouiller.

｜出來, *ts'aó tch'oût loî*, découvrir.

定着係佢偷, ｜佢身上看｜得出麼, *t'ín tch'ŏc hé· kî t'eoū, ts'aò kî chīn hóng k'ón ts'aò têt tch'oût mô*, c'est sûrement lui qui l'a volé, qu'on le fouille et l'on verra si on ne le découvre pas sur lui.

到山頭過關愛聽佢｜, *taó sān t'eoú kouó kouān oí t'ín kî ts'áo*, à la douane de Swatow il faut se laisser fouiller.

｜山, *ts'áo sān*, fouiller un bois avec force vacarme, pour faire sortir le gibier.

糙 *Ts'áo*. Riz imparfaitement décortiqué, grossier.

米忒｜, *mì t'iĕt ts'áo*, le riz est trop grossier, pas assez blanc.

咁粗｜個人, *àn tsē ts'áo ké· gnîn!* quel homme rustique! grossier!

耖 *Ts'áo*. Labourer une seconde fois.

｜田, *ts'áo t'iên*, donner un second labour à la rizière.

躁 *Ts'áo*. Agitant, être agité, excitant.

裡茶咁｜昨晡日我食裡一盃就一夜睡唔得, *ỳ* (ou *yà*) *ts'â àn ts'áo ts'ŏc poū gnĭt ngai chĭt ê· ŷt pī ts'ióu ŷt yá choé· mĝ têt*, que ce thé est excitant! hier j'en ai bu une tasse et je n'ai pas pu dormir de toute la nuit.

TS'ĂP

雜 *Ts'ăp*. Mêlé, divers.

｜字書, *ts'ăp sé choū*, petit livre où l'on a compilé tous les caractères les plus usuels.

｜貨舖, *ts'ăp fó p'oú*, bazar, boutique aux cent articles.

｜念, *ts'ăp niám*, distractions, divagation de la pensée.

混｜, *foún ts'ăp*, en désordre.

TSÂP

鍤 *Tsâp*. Long fourchon à quatre dents, et recourbé, pour brasser la chaux ou travailler la terre.

裡鐵｜唔好使, *yà t'iĕt tsâp mĝ hào sè*, ce fourchon n'est pas commode.

裡鐵｜忒仆, *yà t'iĕt tsâp t'iĕt p'oûc*, ce fourchon est trop recourbé.

札 *Tsâp*. Ordre écrit d'un supérieur.

｜子 ou **｜文**, *tsâp tzè* ou *tsâp voûn*, lettre officielle d'un mandarin supérieur à son inférieur.

上頭有｜下來, *chóng t'eôu yōu tsâp hā loî*, les (mandarins) ont envoyé un ordre.

丨子, *tsâp tzè*, livret chinois formé d'une feuille plissée.

挓 *Tsâp*. Retrousser.

衫袖丨等來, *sâm ts'iôu tsâp tèn loî*, retrousse tes manches d habits.

劮 *Tsâp*. Fort, sans relâche.

生理唔丨勁, *siēn lī mĝ tsâp kín*, le commerce ne va pas fort.

師傅做事咁丨, *sē foú tsó ché· àn tsâp*, l'ouvrier travaille bien, sans perdre de temps.

絷 *Tsâp*. Se fixer, demeurer.

神父到那理丨, *chîn foú táo nái lī tsâp ?* où le Père va-t-il se fixer à demeure ?

東石丨有五千兵, *toūng chăc tsâp yoū ňg ts'iēn pīn*, 5000 soldats sont fixés à *Toung chac*.

丨營盤, *tsâp yâng p'ân*, établir un camp.

TS'ÂP

Ts'âp. Espèce de corbeille en forme de cuillère, pour ramasser les grains.

插 *Ts'âp*. Planter, ficher.

丨樹扒, 丨花, *ts'âp choú p'à, ts'âp fa*, planter une bouture d'arbre, de fleur.

丨得生, 丨唔生, *ts'âp têt sāng, ts'âp mĝ sāng*, pouvoir pousser par bouture, ne pas pouvoir.

愛丨三個樹墩來, *oí ts'âp sam ké· choú toùn loî*, il faut planter trois piquets.

婦人家頭上丨花, *foú gnîn kā t'eoû hóng ts'âp fā*, les femmes se mettent des fleurs sur la tête.

TS'ĂT

蠟 *Ts'ăt*. Cancrelas, cafards.

黃丨, *vông ts'ăt*, cancrelas.

TSÂT

扎 *Tsât*. Bander, attacher.

丨羽扇, *tsât ỳ chán*, faire un éventail de plumes.

丨掃把, *tsât saó pà*, faire un balai.

你怕風愛丨頭哪, *gnî p'á foūng oí tsât t'eoû nâ*, si tu crains le vent bande-toi la tête.

你臂褲解吊裡愛丨過, *nîa pì foú kè· p'ĕt lê· oí tsât koúo*, tes jambières sont dénouées, il faut les rattacher.

撫 *Tsât*. En bon ordre.

做得丨實, *tsó têt tsât chĭt*, cela est fait solidement, *litt*. bien ordonné, de manière à être solide.

裡個人丨實, *ỳ ké· gnîn tsât chĭt*, cet homme fait bien les choses.

T'SÂT

察 *Ts'ât*. 省丨, *sèn ts'ât*, examiner, rechercher.

省丨自己個罪, *sèn ts'ât tsé kì ké· ts'oúi*, examiner sa conscience (ses péchés).

擦 *Ts'ât*. Frotter, frictionner.

丨淨來, *ts'ât ts'iáng loî*, frotter pour nettoyer, polir.

拿灰來丨, *nā foē· loi ts'ât*, frotter avec de la cendre.

獺 *Ts'ât.* Loutre.

丨子皮, *ts'ât tzè p'i*, fourrure en peau de loutre.

TSĒ

(Ces mots ne sont que les mots *tze* aspirés; le *z* se change en *s*. Ailleurs on écrirait mieux *ts'e* au lieu de *tse.*)

初 *Tsē.* Commencement, principe.

丨次, *tsē tsé*, la première fois.

丨來到今, *tsē loî táo kīn*, depuis son arrivée jusqu'à présent.

丨領聖體, *tsē leāng chín t'ì*, communier pour la 1ere fois.

丨一, 丨五, 丨十, le 1er, 5eme, 10eme jour de la lune.

今日丨幾, *kīn gnĭt tsē kì*? aujourd'hui, le combien sommes-nous?

粗 *Tsē.* Grossier, rude.

裡布式丨做衫唔得, *yà poú t'ièt tsē tsó sām mĝ tĕt*, cette étoffe est trop grossière, on ne peut pas en faire un habit.

佢做丨事做得做嫩事做唔得, *kî tsó tsē ché· tsó tĕt tsó noún ché· tsó mĝ tĕt*, il est bon pour un travail grossier, et non pour un travail délicat.

丨窖, *tsē káo*, latrines, fosse à purin.

TSÊ

慈 *Tsê.* Miséricorde.

仁丨, 丨頁, *ŷn tsê, tsê leông*, miséricorde, bonté.

你唔丨心, *gnî mĝ tsê sīm*, tu n'es pas charitable, clément.

磁 *Tsê.* Porcelaine.

丨器東西, *tsê hí toūng sī*, objets en porcelaine.

鋤 *Tsê.* Pioche, piocher.

山丨, *sān tsê*, espèce de pioche.

丨泥, 丨石, *tsê nâi, tsê chăc*, piocher la terre, extirper les pierres avec la pioche.

祠 *Tsê.* 丨堂, *tsê t'ông*, temple ou pagode des ancêtres.

林家丨堂, *Lîm kā tsê t'ông*, temple des ancêtres de la famille des *Lîm*.

辭 *Tsê.* Récuser, se démettre.

丨別, *tsê p'ièt*, prendre congé (formule de politesse en quittant son hôte).

佢來丨走神父, *kî loî tsê tseoù chîn foú*, il vient dire adieu au Père, prendre congé de lui.

官丨任, *koūon tsê ým*, le mandarin donne sa démission, abdique.

丨謝不收, *tsê ts'iá poŭt choū*, refuser un présent en remerciant.

詞 *Tsê.* Parole.

衆口一丨, *tchoúng k'eoù ŷt tsê*, ils n'eurent qu'une voix pour dire..... ils disent tous la même chose.

你言丨話裡麼差, *niā niân tsê vá lê· mô ts'ā*, les paroles que tu viens de dire sont bien vraies.

TSÈ

此 *Tsè.* Ce, cela.

丨人，丨地，丨處，*tsè gnîn, tsè t'í, tsè tch'oú,* cet homme, ce pays, ce lieu (style plus relevé).

既然到丨來裡，*kí yân tào tsè loî lê·....* puisqu'on en est venu jusqu'à ce point.....

楚 *Tsè* ou *tch'où* ou *ts'ò.* Disposé, à point.

清丨，*ts'īn tsè,* fini, bien net, bien clair (voir *ts'īn*).

TSÉ

自 *Tsé.* Soi-même, dès, depuis.

丨己個，*tsé kì ké·,* sien, à soi.

丨家個人，*tsé kā ké· gnîn,* gens de la famille.

丨己好個，*tsé kì hào ké·,* il s'est giuéri tout seul, sans remèdes.

丨己跌落，*tsé kì tiĕt lŏc,* c'est tombé tout seul, sans force étrangère.

丨八月到十月，*tsé pât gnĕt táo chĭp gnĕt,* de la 8^em lune à la 10eme.

丨今以後，*tsé kīn ỹ heóu,* dorénavant.

丨然，*tsé yân,* cela va sans dire, naturellement, bonne situation, confortablement.

丨主，*tsé tchoù,* le libre arbitre.

丨縊，*tsé ŷt,* se suicider.

次 *Tsé.* Fois, ordre.

一丨，兩丨，幾丨，*ŷt tsé, lcòng tsé, kì tsé,* une fois, deux fois, quelquefois.

一年一丨，*ŷt niân ŷt tsé,* une fois l'an.

裡宗貨過丨，*ỳ tsoūng fó koúo tsé,* cette marchandise est d'une qualité inférieure.

丨錢，*tsé ts'iên,* mauvaise sapèque.

牸 *Tsé.* Femelle non châtrée.

牛丨，馬丨，豬丨，狗丨，*nioû tsé, mā tsé, tchoū tsé, keoù tsé,* vache, jument, truie, chienne (qui n'ont pas encore porté).

助 *Tsé.* 幫丨，*pōng tsé,* aider.

醋 *Tsé.* Vinaigre.

酸丨，*sōn tsé,* même sens.

裡酸丨好兇，*yà sōn tsé hào hioūng,* ce vinaigre est très fort.

寺 *Tsé.* 廟丨，*miáo tsé,* pagode, bonzerie.

賜 *Tsé* (ou *sé*). Donner gratuitement (voir *sé*).

字 *Tsé* (pour *sé* dans certains endroits). Lettre. Voir *sé.*

TSĒ·

姐 *Tsē·* (*tsià*). 阿丨，*a tsē·,* femme publique, prostituée.

奚 *Tsē·* Petit, grêle.

細人子咁丨，*sé gnîn tzé àn tsē·,* comme cet enfant est délicat.

丨尾子，*tsē· mī tzè,* le dernier né, le Benjamin.

TS'Ê·

齊 *Ts'ê·* (ou *ts'ĭ*). Complet, ensemble, égal.

人來｜麼, *gnîn loî ts'é· mô?* les gens sont-ils tous venus?

｜心做事, *ts'ê· sīm tsó sé*, agir d'un commun accord.

書頁唔｜愛剪｜來, *choū yăp mĝ ts'ê· oí tsièn ts'ê· loî*, les feuilles du livre ne sont pas égales, il faut les couper égales.

腫｜到心肝, *tchoùng ts'ê· táo sīm kōn*, l'enflure est montée jusqu'au cœur.

TSĒM

砧 *Tsēm*. **手｜**, *choù tsēm*, petit maillet de fer dont se servent les tailleurs d'habits.

｜頭, *tsēm t'eoû*, planche à hâcher, à découper la viande.

鐵 *Tsēm*. **｜墩**, *tsēm toùn*, enclume.

TSĒN

爭 *Tsēn* ou *tsāng*. Voir *tsāng*.

罾 *Tsēn*. Long et large filet à pêcher.

箏 *Tsēn*. Instrument de musique à plusieurs cordes, que l'on fait vibrer au moyen d'ongles artificielles adaptées aux doigts.

TS'ÊN

(Voir aussi TS'IEN)

Ts'ĕn. Epais, fourni.

岌崗十分｜, *ýn kōng chĭp foūn ts'ên*, la montagne est très fournie (en arbres et hautes herbes qui barrent le passage).

錢 *Ts'ĕn* (pour *ts'iên* dans certains pays). Sapèque. Voir *ts'iĕn*.

曾 *Ts'ên*. **唔｜**, *mĝ ts'ên*, pas encore.

佢還唔｜來, *kî hân mĝ ts'ĕn lôi*, il n'est pas encore venu.

食理唔｜, *chĭt tê· mĝ ts'ĕn?* avez-vous dîné (ou pas encore)?

佢唔｜領洗, *kî mĝ ts'ĕn leāng sè·*, il n'est pas encore baptisé.

(A Ka-yn tchou ce mot est prononcé *t'iên* ou *t'iêng*.)

層 *Ts'ên*. Etage, couches superposées.

三｜樓, *sām ts'ĕn leôu*, maison à trois étages.

一｜一｜個, *ŷt ts'ĕn ŷt ts'ên ké·*, par couches superposées.

一｜石頭一｜泥, *ŷt ts'ĕn chăc t'eoû, ŷt ts'ĕn nâi*, une assise de pierres, une couche de terre.

還有一｜你唔曾想倒, *hân yoū ŷt ts'ên gnî mĝ ts'ĕn siòng tào*, il y a encore un point auquel tu n'as pas songé.

TSÉN

增 *Tsén* (*tsēn*). Augmenter, accroître.

加｜天主個榮光, *ka tsén t'iēn tchòu ké· yoûng koūong*, augmenter la gloire de Dieu.

| 田, *tsén t'iên*, ajouter l'argent nécessaire, pour acheter à fonds perdu une rizière dont on n'a que l'hypothèque.

甑 *Tsén*. 飯 |, *fán tsén*, espèce de tonnelet dans lequel on fait cuire le riz à la vapeur.

飯 | 閉子, *fán tsén pí tzè*, fond du tonnelet qui forme claie, de manière à laisser passer la vapeur d'eau.

TSEÒU

走 *Tseòu*. Aller, marcher, partir.

| 路, *tseòu loú*, voyager à pied, marcher.

路好 |, *loú hào tseòu*, la route est bonne.

| 下府, *tseòu hā foù*, aller à la préfecture.

好 |, *hào tseòu*, il est temps de partir.

佢拿 | 我烟筒去, *kî nā tseòu ngā yān t'oūng hí*, il a emporté ma pipe.

葯 | 裡性, *yŏc tseòu lê· sín*, le remède, la drogue s'est éventée.

| 風, (v. 漏 v. 通風) *tseòu foūng*, (v. *leoú* v. *t'oūng foūng*), divulguer, ébruiter.

裡件事 | 風做唔得, *ỳ k'ián sé tseòu foūng tsó mĝ têt*, il ne faut pas que cette affaire transpire au dehors.

TSEÓU

奏 *Tseóu*. Faire un rapport à l'Empereur; jouer de la musique.

| 皇上, *tseóu fông chóng*, faire part à l'Empereur.

| 樂, *tseóu ngŏc!* en avant la musique!

TS'EÓU

湊 *Ts'eóu*. Réunir, assembler.

| 唔起一百錢, *ts'eòu mĝ hì ŷt pâc ts'iên*, il n'arrive pas à réunir cent sapèques.

| 倒十過個人來打野猪, *ts'eóu tào chĭp koúo ké· gnîn loî tà yā tchoū*, réunissons une dizaine de gens, pour chasser le sanglier.

你來得 | 巧, *gnî loî têt ts'eóu k'ào*, tu arrives bien à propos.

TSEP

捻 *Tsêp*. Une pincée, prendre une pincée.

一 | 鹽, 一 | 黄烟, *ŷt tsêp yâm, ŷt tsêp vông yān*, une pincée de sel, de tabac.

| 一滴茶葉畀我, *tsêt ŷt tīt ts'á yăp poūn ngái*, prends-moi une petite pincée de feuilles de thé.

TS'EP

Ts'êp. Blanchir le riz en le frappant, pour lui enlever sa première couche grisâtre.

| 米 | 白來, *ts'êp mì ts'êp p'ăc loî*, frapper le riz, le frapper jusqu'à blanc.

TS'ĔT

宅 *Ts'ĕt*. 屋 |, *voŭc ts'ĕt*, maison. habitation.

擇 *Ts'ĕt*. Choisir.

丨倒好地方來, *ts'ĕt tào hào t'í fōng loî*, choisissons un bon endroit.

丨唔倒好個, *ts'ĕt mĝ tào hào ké·*, on n'en trouve pas de bon.

賊 *Ts'ĕt*. Brigand, voleur.

盜丨, *t'áo ts'ĕt*, même sens.

捉丨, *tsôc ts'ĕt*, saisir un voleur.

當丨, *tōng ts'ĕt*, être voleur, exercer le brigandage.

走丨, *tseoù ts'ĕt*, fuir les brigands.

TSÊT

則 *Tsĕt*. Règle, mesure.

比一個丨子, *pì ŷt ké' tsĕt tzè*, prendre une mesure.

炕麵包愛丨正火色來, *k'óng mién pāo oí tsĕt tcháng fò sĕt loî*, pour cuire le pain, il faut bien calculer la mesure de feu qu'il faut.

我丨過個事, *ngaî tsĕt kouó ké· sé*, c'est une chose que j'ai apprise par expérience.

側 *Tsĕt*. Incliné, de côté.

丨眠, *tsĕt mîn*, être couché sur le côté.

丨近, *tsĕt k'ioún*, tout près, tout à côté.

屋丨角, *voŭc tsĕt kôc*, à côté de la maison.

窄 *Tsĕt*. Etroit.

間房十分丨, *kiān fông chĭp foūn tsĕt*, la chambre est par trop étroite.

丨狹狹個 *tsĕt k'iăp k'iăp ké·*, très étroit.

天堂個丨路, *t'iēn t'ông ké· tsĕt loú*, le chemin étroit du paradis.

TS'ÊT

測 *Ts'ĕt*. Conjecturer.

我丨倒佢麼來, *ngaî ts'ĕt tào kî mô loî*, je crois qu'il ne viendra pas.

人心難丨, *gnîn sīm nân ts'ĕt*, il est difficile de connaître à fond le cœur de l'homme.

策 *Ts'ĕt*. Stratagème, exercice littéraire.

計丨, *ké· ts'ĕt*, stratagème, ruse.

對丨, *toúi ts'ĕt*, réponse donnée par écrit.

TSĪ

嚌 *Tsī* ou *tsí*. Voix confuses.

天光到暗丨丨嘖嘖, *t'iēn koūong táo ám tsī tsī tsiá tsiá*, du matin au soir c'est un bavardage continuel.

擠 *Tsī*. Presse, encombrement.

聖堂丨滿, *chín t'ông tsī mān*, l'église est pleine, comble.

街上十分丨擁, *kiaī hóng chĭp foūn tsī yoúng*, les rues sont encombrées.

TS'Ī

妻 *Ts'ī* Epouse.

夫丨, *foū ts'ī*, mari et femme.

討 v. 娶丨, *t'ào* v. *ts'í ts'ī*, prendre femme.

丨賢子肖, *ts'ī hiên tzè siáo*, si la femme est sage les enfants le seront aussi.

41

TS'Î

齊 *Ts'î* (ou *ts'ê·*). Ensemble, complet. Voir *tsê·*.

臍 *Ts'î.* Nombril.

肚一帶, *toù ts'î taí*, cordon ombilical.

糖 *Ts'î.* | 粑 粄, *ts'î pā pàn*, espèce de gâteau.

TSÌ

姊 *Tsì.* Sœur aînée.

大 | 老 妹, *t'ái tsì lào moé·*, sœur aînée, sœur cadette.

| 妹, *tsì moé·*, frères et sœurs en général.

我有一個阿哥一個大 | 三 | 妹, *gnaî yoū ŷt ké· ā kō ŷt ké· t'ái tsì sām tsì moé·*, j'ai un frère aîné et une sœur aînée, nous sommes trois, frère et sœurs.

| 丈, *tsì tch'óng*, beau-frère.

TS'Ì

取 *Ts'ì.* Exiger, prendre, ôter, extraire.

我 唔 | 佢 錢, *ngâi mĝ ts'ì kiā ts'iēn*, je ne lui réclame pas son argent.

| 泥, | 石 頭, *ts'ì naî, ts'ì chăc t'eoû*, prendre, extraire de la terre, des pierres.

魚 骨 | 出 來, *ñĝ koût ts'ì tch'oût loî*, enlève les os du poisson.

| 唔 脫, *ts'ì mĝ t'ôt*, ne pouvoir enlever, extraire.

| 耳, *ts'ì gnì*, nettoyer, curer l'oreille.

| 寶, *ts'ì pào*, extraire des trésors.

TSÍ

濟 *Tsí.* Secourir, aider.

賑 | 人, *tchìn tsí gnîn*, faire l'aumône.

做 牙 |, *tsó ngâ tsí*, faire un bon dîner (*litt.* faire une aumône aux dents). Se dit du repas des ouvriers, auquel, selon l'usage, ils ont droit deux fois par mois.

祭 *Tsí.* Sacrifice, sacrifier.

| 獻 天 主, *tsí hién t'iēn tchoū*, sacrifier à Dieu, offrir à Dieu en sacrifice.

| 臺, *tsí t'oî*, autel.

下 | 臺, 上 | 臺, *hā tsí t'oî, chōng tsí t'oî*, descendre de l'autel, monter à l'autel,

| 衣, *tsí ȳ*, vêtements sacerdotaux.

霽 *Tsí* (ou *tsoúi*). Sécher par absorption.

| 紙, *tsí tjè*, papier brouillard.

拿 紙 | 淰 水 來, *nā tjè tsí liàm choùi loî*, emboire l'eau avec du papier.

擠 *Tsí.* Chatouiller.

畏 |, *vi tsí*, craindre le chatouillement.

TS'Í

趣 *T'sí.* Plaisant, agréable, drôle.

裡 個 人 咁 |, *ŷ ké· gnîn àn ts'í*, cet homme est il drôle !

細 人 子 咁 | |, *sé· gnîn tzè àn ts'í ts'í*, que l'enfant est gentil, agréable.

娶 *Ts'í.* Prendre femme.

| 親, | 老 婆, | 婦 人 家, *ts'í ts'īn, ts'í lào p'ô, ts'í foú gnîn kā*, prendre femme.

| 媳子, *ts'í sĭt tzè*, prendre une bru, plus vulg. 討新臼, *t'aò sīm k'ioū*.

聚 *Ts'í*. Rassembler.

| 㑋來商量, *ts'í ts'iōu loî chōng leông*, s'assembler pour délibérer.

| 兵, *ts'í pīn*, assembler des soldats.

TS'IÂ

𨀝 *Ts'iâ*. En pente douce, penché.

岌崗 | | 個, *ýn kōng ts'iâ ts'iâ ké·*, la montée n'est pas très raide.

屋 | 帛 裡, *voûc ts'iâ p'ĕt lê·*, la maison penche, n'est pas droite.

TSIÀ

姐 *Tsià*. Epouse, sœur (selon les pays), en général, toute parenté féminine.

婆 |, *p'ô tsià*, grand'mère.

討 | 子, *t'aò tsià tzè*, prendre femme.

TS'IÀ

且 *Ts'ià*. Mais, d'ailleurs.

| 看, *ts'ià k'ón*, vous n'avez qu'à voir...

| 等一輌就看, *ts'ià tèn ŷt t'óng ts'ióu k'ón*, d'ailleurs, attendez un moment, et vous verrez.

況 |, *k'ouòng ts'ià* de plus, *a fortiori*.

TSIÁ

借 *Tsiá*. Prêter, emprunter.

| 錢, | 米, *tsiá ts'iên, tsiá mì*, prêter de l'argent, du riz.

| 去, | 唔去, *tsiá hí, tsiá mĝ hí*, prêter, emprunter, ne pouvoir prêter, emprunter.

向人 | 東西, *hióng gnîn tsiá toūng sī*, demander à emprunter.

| 人個名, *tsiá gnîn ké· miâng*, emprunter le nom de quelqu'un.

籍 *Tsiá* (*siá*). Se servir de, profiter de.

| 倒機會, *tsiá taò kī fí*, profiter de l'occasion.

佢 | 倒神父做彌撒偷東西, *kî tsiá taò chîn foú tsó nì săt t'coū toūng sī*, il a profité de ce que le Père disait la messe pour voler des objets.

TS'IÁ

謝 *Ts'iá*. Remercier; se faner.

| 多, *tō ts'iá*, merci!

| 禮, *ts'iá lī*, honoraires d'un médecin, cadeaux de remerciements.

酬 | 人, *tch'oú ts'iá gnîn*, remercier quelqu'un par un festin, un cadeau.

感 | 天主身體平安, *kàm ts'iá t'iēn tchoù chīn t'ì p'în ōn*, j'en rends grâces à Dieu, je me porte bien (réponse de politesse chrétienne).

花 | 帛 裏, *fā ts'iá p'ĕt lə·*, les fleurs sont passées, fanées.

TS'IĂC

蓆 *Ts'iăc*. Natte.

床上攤等 | 來, *ts'ông hóng t'ān tèn ts'iăc loi*, étends une natte sur le lit.

TSIÂC

績 *Tsiâc*. Tailler le chanvre.

｜麻, *tsiâc mâ*, travailler, tailler le chanvre.

蹟 *Tsiâc* (pour *tsît*). Trace, vestige.

印｜, *ýn tsiâc* vestige, trace.

脚｜, *kiôc tsiâc*, empreinte de pied.

賸脚｜, *t'ên kiôc tsiâc*, suivre une piste.

TS'IÂC

Ts'iâc. Filocher, travailler au crochet.

｜撈䉡, *ts'iâc leoû fi*, faire un filet à pêcher.

｜一雙襪, *ts'iâc ŷt soūng mât*, tricoter une paire de bas.

Ts'iâc. Courir, s'enfuir.

盡｜, *ts'ín ts'iâc*, il court de toutes ses forces.

TSIĀM

尖 *Tsiām*. Pointe, pointu.

刀｜, 針｜, 脚｜, *tāo tsiām, tchīm tsiām, kiôc tsiām*, pointe d'un couteau, d'une aiguille, bout, pointe du pied.

｜｜去, *tsiām tsiām hí*, qui va en pointe.

簽 *Tsiām*. Cheville, coin, cheviller.

做 ou 削一個竹｜, *tsó* ou *siôc ŷt ké· tchoûc tsiām*, faire ou tailler une pointe de bambou.

桌円成拿來｜狠, *tsôc teóu tcháng nā loî tsiām hén*, la table une fois montée, cheville-la fortement.

地方狹愛｜等來, *t'í fōng k'iăp oí tsiām tèn loî*, le local est petit, il faut se serrer.

TS'IĀM

簽 *Ts'iām*. Fiche, bande de papier rouge collée sur l'enveloppe d'une lettre ou sur un autre objet, et portant le nom du destinataire. Bâtonnets de bambou réunis dans un tube, et dont se servent les juges pour faire connaître le nombre de coups à donner aux coupables, les sorciers pour consulter les sorts...

火｜, *fò ts'iām*, mandat pressant.

官出爽｜, *koūon tch'oût lé· tsi'ām*, le mandarin a lancé un mandat très pressant (écrit sur une fiche).

官愛打人丢｜, *koūon oí tà gnin tioū ts'iām*, quand le mandarin veut faire frapper, il lance une fiche (sur laquelle est inscrit le nombre de coups à donner).

打｜, ou 下｜, *tà ts'iām* ou *há ts'iām*, faire une génuflexion.

抽｜, *tch'oū ts'iām*, interroger les sorts.

TSIÀM

蘸 *Tsiàm*. Tremper dans un liquide.

筆拿來｜墨水, *pît nā loî tsiàm mĕt choùi*, tremper son pinceau dans l'encre.

猪肉拿來｜豉油, *tchoū nioûc nā loî tsiàm ché yoû*, tremper la viande dans la sauce.

TS'IÁM

暫 *Ts'iám*. Temporaire.

｜時, ｜下, *ts'iám chê, ts'iám há*, momentanément.

| | 上, | | 下, *ts'iám ts'iám chōng, ts'iám ts'iám hā*, aller en montant graduellement, en descendant graduellement, peu à peu.

| 別一下, *ts'iám p'ièt ўt há*, adieu, prendre congé de quelqu'un.

TSIĀNG

腈 *Tsiāng*. Partie maigre de la viande ; joli.

| 猪肉, *ts'iāng tchoū niōuc*, partie maigre de la viande de porc.

聖堂好 |, *chín t'ông hào tsiāng*, l'église est très jolie.

| | 個聖像, *tsiāng tsiāng ké· chín sióng*, une très jolie image.

TS'IĀNG

靑 *Ts'iāng*. Couleur verte, vert de feuillage.

| 草, | 菜, *ts'iāng ts'ào, ts'iāng ts'oí*, herbe verte, légumes.

梨子還忒 |, *lî tzè hân t'ièt ts'iāng*, les poires sont encore trop vertes.

| 礬, *ts'iāng fân*, sulfate de fer, vitriol vert.

銅 |, *t'oûng ts'iāng*, vert-de-gris.

TS'IÂNG

晴 *Ts'iâng*. Serein, beau temps.

天 |, *t'iēn ts'iâng*, il fait beau temps, le temps est beau.

| 唔久, *ts'iâng mĝ kioù*, le temps ne restera pas longtemps beau, serein.

TSIÀNG

井 *Tsiàng*. Puits.

| 水, *tsiàng chouì*, eau de puits.

開, v. 挖 |, *k'oī*, v. *vā tsiàng*, creuser un puits.

| 嘴, *tsiàng tchói*, bord, orifice d'un puits.

水桶跌落 |, *chouì t'oùng tièt lŏc tsiàng*, le seau d'eau est tombé dans le puits.

天 |, *t'iēn tsiàng*, cour intérieure d'une maison.

TS'IÀNG

請 *Ts'iàng*. Inviter, faire venir, louer.

|, *ts'iàng*... je vous invite... veuillez vous donner la peine... (Se dit à l'hôte qui se présente, ou bien pour laisser passer quelqu'un devant soi, ou quand on fait à quelqu'un une politesse quelconque, ou lorsqu'on quitte quelqu'un ou une compagnie).

| 坐, *ts'iàng ts'ō*, veuillez vous asseoir (si l'on parle à un hôte qui arrive). Ne vous dérangez pas, restez assis (se dit au maître de la maison, au moment du départ).

| 轉, *ts'iàng tchòn*, veuillez vous en retourner, ne vous donnez pas la peine de m'accompagner plus loin.

| 茶, | 酒, *ts'iàng ts'â, ts'iàng tsioù*, veuillez boire le thé, le vin (politesse de table).

| 問一句話, *ts'iàng moún ўt kí fá*, je voudrais vous faire une petite question.

| 醫先生, *ts'iàng ӯ sīn sāng*, demander le médecin.

｜木匠, *ts'iàng moūc sióng*, faire venir le menuisier.

｜唔倒人, *ts'iàng mĝ tào gnîn*, on ne peut trouver du monde, des ouvriers à louer.

｜衆同禱, *ts'iàng tchoúng t'oúng tào*, nous vous invitons tous à prier (prières chrétiennes *oremus*).

TSIÁNG

Tsiáng. (Objet mis) le haut en bas, à la renverse.

倒倒｜, *tào tào tsiáng*, mettre le haut en bas.

頭哪｜下起做工, *t'eôu-nâ tsiáng hā hì tsó koūng*, travailler la tête en bas.

TS'IÁNG

淨 *Ts'iáng*. Propre, net, seulement, absolument.

洗｜, 刮｜, *sè· ts'iáng, kouāt ts'iáng*, nettoyer en lavant, en grattant.

洗唔｜, *sè· mĝ ts'iáng*, ne pouvoir nettoyer en lavant.

｜酒唔曾挠水, *ts'iáng tsioù mĝ ts'ên laō choùi*, il n' y a que du vin, je n'y ai pas ajouté d'eau.

滿聖堂｜男子人麼婦人, *mān chín t'ông ts'iáng nâm tzè gnîn mô foú gnîn*, toute l'église était pleine d'hommes seulement, pas de femmes.

｜我自己 (*v.* 自家) *ts'iáng ngâi tsé kì (v. tsé kā)*, rien que moi.

東西畀賊偷｜, *toūng sī poūn ts'ĕt t'eoū ts'iáng*, les voleurs ont absolument tout volé.

TSIĀO

蕉 *Tsiāo*. Banane, bananier.

芎｜, *kioūng tsiāo*, banane.

椒 *Tsiāo*. Poivre.

胡｜, *foû tsiāo*, poivre ordinaire.

辣｜, *lát tsiāo*, piment.

TS'IĀO

捎 *Ts'iāo*. Ourler.

衫縺成還唔曾｜邊, *sām lièn tcháng hân mĝ ts'ên ts'iāo piēn*, l'habit est tout cousu, mais les bordures ne sont pas encore ourlées.

簫 *Ts'iāo (siāo)*. Traverse qui relie plusieurs planches.

｜板頭, *ts'iāo pàn t'eôu*, mettre une traverse à des planches.

｜床板, *ts'iāo ts'ông pàn*, mettre une traverse aux planches de lit.

TS'IÂO

柴 *Ts'iâo* ou *ts'âi*. Bois de chauffage. Voir *ts'âi*.

TSIÀO

剿 *Tsiào*. ｜滅, *tsiào mĕt*, détruire, exterminer.

TSIÁO

醮 *Tsiáo*. Superstitions publiques.

打｜, *tà tsiáo*, faire ces superstitions. Elles consistent en prières récitées par un bonze entouré d'une ou plusieurs idoles de papier; ces idoles sont brûlées à la fin des cérémonies, qui durent plusieurs jours. Pendant ce temps les païens observent l'abstinence.

TS'IÁO

嚼 *Ts'iáo*. Mâcher.

丨綿, *ts'iáo miên*, mâcher, amollir en mâchant.

就好吞落唔好丨, *ts'iόu hào t'oūn lŏc mĝ hào ts'iáo*, avale tout de suite, sans mâcher.

TSIÂP

接 *Tsiâp*. Recevoir, attraper au vol, remplacer, succéder, joindre.

丨人, 丨信, *tsiâp gnîn, tsiâp sín*, recevoir quelqu'un, recevoir une lettre.

打發轎子去丨, *tà fât k'iáo tzè hí tsiâp*, envoyer un palanquin au devant de quelqu'un.

䕶阿上去我喑丨, *fìt á chōng hí, ngâi voé· tsiâp*, lance en l'air, j'attraperai.

你丨唔倒, *gnî tsiâp mĝ taò*, tu ne pourras pas attraper.

丨位, *tsiâp ví*, remplacer, succéder.

丨主敎個位, *tsiâp tchoù káo ké· ví*, succéder à l'évêque, prendre sa place.

我米丨唔倒明年, *ngā mì tsiâp mĝ tào miâng niân*, mon riz ne suffira pas (ne rejoindra pas) jusqu'à l'an prochain.

丨生婆, *tsiâp sēn p'ô*, accoucheuse.

TS'IÂP

妾 *Ts'iâp*. Concubine.

一妻一丨, *ŷt ts'ī ŷt ts'iâp*, une femme légitime, et une concubine.

竊 *Ts'iâp*. Voler furtivement.

偷丨東西, *t'eoū ts'iâp toūng sī*, dérober furtivement, chiper.

TSIĒN

煎 *Tsiēn*. Frire, rôtir, cuire à la graisse.

丨春, *tsiēn tch'oūn*, cuire des œufs en omelette, ou au miroir.

丨粄, *tsiēn pàn*, frire des gâteaux.

丨猪油, *tsiēn tchoū yôu*, faire cuire la graisse de porc, pour en faire du saindoux.

TS'IĒN

千 *Ts'iēn*. Mille.

一丨, 幾丨, *ŷt ts'iēn, kì ts'iēn*, mille, quelques milliers.

丨苦萬難, *ts'iēn k'où ván nán*, tous les tourments.

丨里馬, *ts'iēn lī mā*, courrier officiel.

丨里鏡, *ts'iēn lī kiáng*, longue-vue, jumelle.

遷 *Ts'iēn*. Changer, transférer.

家業丨阿東石去, *kā niăp ts'iēn á toūng chăc hí*, transporter son domaine à *Toūng chăc*.

地丨阿 v. 攺過另事去, *t'í ts'iēn á v. koì koúo láng sé hí*, le tombeau a été transferé ailleurs.

TS'IÊN

錢 *Ts'iên*. Sapèque, monnaie, 10eme partie de l'once.

一個 v. 一文｜, *ŷt ké* v. *ŷt voûn ts'iên*, une sapèque.

金｜v. 好｜; 次｜ou 𠎝｜, *kīm ts'iên* v. *hào ts'iên*; *tsé ts'iên*, ou *ngôc ts'iên*, bonne sapèque, mauvaise sapèque.

算｜, *són ts'iên*, faire un compte, faire payer.

你講幾多｜, *gnî kòng kì tō ts'iên ?* quel prix as-tu fait ?

信｜, 脚｜, 工｜, *sín ts'iên*, *kiôc ts'iên*, *koūng ts'iên*, prix d'un port de lettre, d'une course, salaire.

找｜, *tsào ts'iên*, changer une piastre en sapèques.

一｜銀, *ŷt ts'iên nioûn*, un *ts'iên* d'argent, 10ème partie de l'once.

一両五｜三, *ŷt leōng ngè ts'iên sām*, une once (plus) 5 *ts'iên* 3 *foūn*.

交火｜, *kaō fò ts'iên*, soudoyer, graisser la patte à qqn.

全 *Ts'iên* (ou *ts'iôn*). Entier, complet, parfait.

｜能, *ts'iên nên*, tout-puissant.

｜心, *ts'iên sīm*, de tout son cœur.

｜赦, *ts'iên chá*, indulgence plénière.

｜家有病, *ts'iên kā yoū p'iáng*, toute la famille est malade.

｜｜麽用個, *ts'iên ts'iên mô yoúng ké*, cela ne vaut absolument rien.

前 *Ts'iên*. Avant, auparavant.

｜日, 大｜日, *ts'iên gnĭt*, *t'aí ts'iên gnĭt*, avant-hier, trois jours avant.

我在｜, *ngâi ts'aí ts'iên*, je suis avant.

｜來個, ｜話個, *ts'iên lọî ké*, *ts'iên vá ké*, venu avant, dit précédemment.

｜十日, *ts'iên chĭp gnĭt*, 10 jours auparavant.

以｜, (ou 在｜) 我去過, *ȳ ts'iên* ou *ts'aí ts'iên*), *ngâi hí koúo*, autrefois j'y suis allé.

TSIÈN

剪 *Tsièn*. Couper avec des ciseaux.

｜刀, *tsièn taō*, ciseaux.

｜手指甲, *tsièn choù tjè kăp*, se couper les ongles.

｜斷, *tsièn t'ōn*, détacher avec des ciseaux.

TS'IÈN

淺 *Ts'ièn*. Eau peu profonde, peu profond (au propr. et au fig.)

河水｜｜過得, *hô choùi ts'ièn ts'ièn koúo têt*, l'eau du fleuve est très peu profonde, on peut passer.

我唔知深｜, *ngâi mĝ tī tch'īm ts'ièn*, je ne connais pas la profondeur.

佢道理｜薄, *kiâ t'áo lī ts'ièn p'ŏc*, il est peu instruit.

TSIÉN

餞 *Tsién*. Repas d'adieux.

｜行, *tsién hâng*, faire des présents ou donner à manger à quelqu'un qui va partir, coup de l'étrier.

箭 *Tsién*. Flèche.

射｜, *chá tsién*, lancer des flèches.

射步｜, 射馬｜, *chá p'oú tsién*, *chá mā tsién*, lancer des flèches étant à pied, étant à cheval.

𢫫 *Tsién*. Arc-bouter, étayer.

跌唔下有樹子｜等裡, *tiĕt mğ hā yoū choú tzè tsién tèn ê·*, il ne peut tomber (par ex. : un arbre que l'on vient de couper), il est retenu par un arbre.

｜門板, *tsién moûn pàn*, arc-bouter la porte. (Synonyme du mot **撐** *ts'áng*).

薦 *Tsién*. Proposer quelqu'un pour une charge, recommander, patronner; pressé.

｜人去同神父當相公, *tsién gnîn hí t'oûng chîn foú tōng sióng koūng*, proposer quelqu'un à un Père comme domestique.

我唔識你又麼人｜你來... *ngâi mğ chĭt gnî yoú mô gnîn tsién gnî loî*... je ne te connais pas, et tu n'es recommandé par personne...

聖堂擠滿人｜等裡, *chín t'ông tsī mān gnîn tsién tèn ê·*, l'église était pleine, on était les uns sur les autres.

TS'IÉN

踐 *Ts'ién*. Traiter indignement, fouler aux pieds (au fig).

｜踏耶穌的聖體, *ts'ién t'ăp yâ sē tĭt chín t'ì*, profaner le corps de Notre-Seigneur Jesus-Christ.

賤 *Ts'ién*. Vil, avilir, de peu de valeur.

輕｜人, *k'īn ts'ién gnîn*, mépriser quelqu'un.

咁｜個人, *àn ts'ién ké· gnîn*, quel homme bas!

裡樣樹子係｜, *ỳ yóng choú tzè é· ts'ién*, ces sortes d'arbres prennent facilement.

TSIĔT

Tsiĕt. Lancer.

｜石頭, *tsiĕt chăc t'côu*, lancer des pierres.

｜唔遠, *tsiĕt mğ yàn*, ne pouvoir lancer loin.

TS'IĔT

絕 *Ts'iĕt*. Rejeter, manquer, finir.

棄｜各樣異端, *hí ts'iĕt kôc yóng ý tōn*, rejeter toutes sortes de superstitions.

｜房, *ts'iĕt fông*, famille éteinte.

一家人｜了裡, *ȳt ka gnîn ts'iĕt liào lê·*, de toute la famille, il ne reste plus personne.

糧食｜了裡, *leông chĭt ts'iĕt liaò lê·*, les vivres sont épuisés.

｜來往, *ts'iĕt lôi vōng*, rompre les relations avec quelqu'un.

TSIÊT

節 *Tsiêt*. Tempérance, fraction.

守｜，｜婦, *choù tsiêt, tsiêt foú*, garder le veuvage, veuve.

｜用, *tsiêt yoúng*, user avec économie.

骨｜，樹｜，竹｜, *koût tsiêt, choú tsiêt, tchoûc tsiêt*, articulation des os, nœud du bois, du bambou.

一年有二十四個｜氣, *ȳt niân yoū gní chĭp sí ké· tsiêt hí*, l'année (chinoise) est divisée en 24 époques.

過｜, *koúo tsiêt*, passer la fête d'une

de ces époques (se dit surtout du 5eme jour de la 5eme lune).

TS'IÊT

截 *Ts'iĕt*. Couper, diviser en morceaux.

路愛同佢|斷, *loú oí t'oúng kî ts'iĕt t'ōn*, il faut lui intercepter, barrer le chemin.

樹頭拿來破兩|, *choú t'eoû nā loî p'ó leòng ts'iĕt*, fendre un bloc de bois en deux parties

工錢做三|撿, *koūng ts'ièn tsó sām ts'iĕt kiàm*, payer le salaire en 3 termes.

一|書, *ŷt ts'iĕt choū*, une division d'un livre.

切 *Ts'iĕt*. Couper, hacher, pressant, important.

|碎, *ts'iĕt souí*, couper en menus morceaux.

|成片, *ts'iĕt chāng (ou chîn) p'ièn*, couper en tranches.

|愛, *ts'iĕt oí*, aimer de toutes ses forces, vouloir absolument.

咬牙|齒, *ngāo ngâ ts'iĕt tchè*, grincer des dents.

|要, *ts'iĕt yaó*, nécessaire, important.

裡事我係關|, *yà sé ngâi ké kouān ts'iĕt*, j'attache une grande importance à cette affaire.

TSĪM

親 *Tsīm* (pour *ts'īn*). |嘴, *tsīm tchoí*, se baiser, s'embrasser.

|苦像, *tsīm k'où sióng*, baiser le crucifix.

TS'ÎM

尋 *Ts'îm*. Chercher.

|唔倒, *ts'îm mĝ tào*, ne pouvoir trouver en cherchant.

我|東西|唔轉, *ngâi ts'îm toūng sī ts'îm mĝ tchòn*, je cherche quelque chose sans pouvoir la trouver.

TSÍM

浸 *Tsím*. Tremper, imprégner.

|水, *tsím choùi*, tremper, imbiber.

|死, *tsím sì*, être noyé.

衫褲|濕, *sām foú tsím chĭp*, les habits sont tout mouillés.

落大水屋|等裡, *lŏc t'ái choùi voŭc tsím tèn é*, l'inondation a fait monter l'eau jusqu'à ma maison.

TSĪN

Tsīn. Tige.

鐵|, 竹|, 芒|, *t'iĕt tsīn, tchoŭc tsīn, mióng tsīn*, tige de fer, tige, petit bâton de bambou, tige de grandes herbes.

精 *Tsīn*. La partie la plus subtile d'une chose, perspicace, habile, principes de la génération.

|神, *tsīn chîn*, vigueur naturelle, entrain.

今日我麼|神, *kīn gnĭt ngâi mò tsīn chîn*, aujourd'hui je suis sans entrain, languissant.

|工, |致, *tsīn koūng, tsín tjé*, habile, subtil.

|怪, *tsīn kouái*, démons aériens.

|巧, *tsīn k'aò*, habile dans un art.

漏 | , *leoú tsīn,* perte de semence, pollution involontaire.

晶 *Tsīn.* Cristal.

氷 | 石 , *choùi tsīn chăc,* cristal de roche.

睛 *Tsīn.* 眼 | , *niàn tsīn,* prunelle des yeux.

TS'ĪN

親 *Ts'īn.* Parents, parenté.

父 | , 母 | , *foú ts'īn, moū ts'īn,* père, mère.

外 | , *ngoé· ts'īn,* parent par alliance.

討 | , *t'ào ts'īn,* contracter mariage.

| 戚 , *ts'īn ts'īt,* parents en général (par alliance).

你 同 其 有 | 麼 , *gnî t'oûng kî yoū ts'īn mô?* avez-vous quelque parenté avec lui?

人 | 財 不 | , *gnîn ts'īn ts'oî poŭt ts'īn* on est parent, mais l'argent ne connaît pas de parenté.

| 自 , | 身 , | 手 , *ts'īn tsé, ts'īn chīn, ts'īn choù,* soi-même, en personne, de ses propres mains.

| 眼 看 個 , *ts'īn niàn k'ón ké·,* vu de mes propres yeux.

淸 *Ts'īn.* Pur, limpide, mettre au clair, vérifier.

| 水 , *ts'īn choùi,* eau limpide.

| 楚 , *ts'īn tsè* (ou *tch'où*), clair et net, achevé, conclu.

講 | 楚 , *kòng ts'īn tsè,* parler clair et net, clairement.

事 辦 | 楚 , *sé p'án ts'īn tsè,* l'affaire est terminée.

| 官 , *ts'īn koūon,* mandarin intègre, qui ne gruge pas.

數 愛 | 過 來 , *sé oí ts'īn koúo loî,* il faut vérifier les comptes.

TS'ÎN

情 *Ts'în.* Passion, sentiment, affection.

愛 | , 欲 | , *oí ts'în, yoŭc ts'în,* passion de l'amour, affection, passion du désir, concupiscence.

性 | , *sín ts'în,* le caractère, le naturel.

| 分 , *ts'în foūn,* égards, complaisance.

| 理 , *ts'în lī,* raisonnable.

麼 | 麼 理 , *mô ts'în mô lī,* déraisonnable, injuste.

| 願 , *ts'în nián,* volontiers, de bon gré, spontanément.

| 願 討 食 我 唔 同 佢 做 工 , *ts'în nián t'aò chĭt ngaî mĝ t'oûng kî tsó koūng,* plutôt mendier que de travailler pour lui.

奉 人 | 個 話 , *foúng gnîn ts'în ké· fá,* ce sont des paroles de respect humain.

求 | , *k'iôu ts'în,* demander la paix.

事 | , *sé ts'în,* affaire, chose.

用 | , *yoúng ts'în,* témoigner son affection, par des paroles ou par des actes.

唔 知 | 個 人 , *mĝ tī ts'în ké· gnîn,* homme insensible aux bienfaits.

人 | 還 人 | 財 上 愛 分 明 , *gnîn ts'în vân gnîn ts'în ts'oî hóng oí foūn mîn,* les bons comptes font les bons amis.

TSÌN

儘 *Tsìn*. Tout à fait.

｜多, *tsìn tō*, tout au plus, au plus.

｜彀, *tsìn keoú*, cela suffit amplement.

｜做得個, *tsìn tsó tĕt ké·*, cela peut très bien faire, très bien aller comme cela.

TSÍN

進 *Tsín*. Entrer, pénétrer.

｜教, *tsín káo*, embrasser la religion.

｜屋, **｜城**, *tsín voŭc*, *tsín chăng*, entrer dans une maison, en ville.

｜唔去, *tsín mĝ hí*, ne pouvoir entrer, pénétrer.

｜士, *tsín sé*, un grade littéraire au-dessus de la licence, lettré qui peut être élevé à une charge.

TS'ÍN

盡 *Ts'ín*. Entièrement, sans cesser, laisser, à volonté.

講唔得｜, *kòng mĝ tĕt ts'ín*, je ne pourrai jamais tout dire.

唔曾大｜, *mĝ t'iên t'ái ts'ín*, il n'a pas fini de grandir.

｜大, **｜好個**, *ts'ín t'ái*, *ts'ín hào ké·*, c'est tout ce qu'il y a de plus grand, de meilleur.

｜走, **｜笑**, **｜𡡉**, *ts'ín tseoù*, *ts'ín siáo*, *ts'ín liáo*, courir, rire, s'amuser sans fin.

｜在佢, *ts'ín ts'ái kî*, laisse-le, comme il voudra.

｜佢做, **｜佢走**, *ts'ín kî tsó*, *ts'ín kî tseoù*, laisse-le faire, aller à sa guise.

｜本分, *ts'ín poùn foún*, faire tout son devoir.

靜 *Ts'ín*. Tranquille, calme.

地方平｜, *t'í fōng p'în ts'ín*, le pays est en paix, tranquille.

夜晡頭讀書過｜, *yá poū t'côu t'oŭc choū koúo ts'ín*, quand on étudie la nuit, on est plus tranquille, on a moins de distractions.

TSIÔC

爵 *Tsiôc*. Coupe, dignité.

聖｜, *chín tsiôc*, calice.

｜位, **｜祿**, *tsiôc ví*, *tsiôc loŭc*, haute dignité (comme celle de mandarin, de prêtre), traitement qui y est attaché.

我唔修人｜我修天｜, *ngái mĝ sioū gnîn tsiôc ngâi sioū t'iēn tsiôc*, je ne m'exerce pas à acquérir les dignités humaines, je cherche à obtenir celles du ciel.

雀 *Tsiôc*. Oiseau.

鳥｜, *niào tsiôc*, oiseau en général.

TS'IÔC

蹤 *Ts'iôc*. Sauter, voltiger.

三張桌｜得過, *sām tchōng tsôc ts'iôc tĕt koúo*, il peut sauter trois tables.

猫公｜阿窗子上去, *miáo koūng ts'iôc á ts'oūng tzè hóng hí*, le chat a sauté sur la fenêtre.

TS'IŌN

吮 *Ts'iōn*. Sucer, **｜乳**, *ts'iōn nén*, teter.

TS'IÔN

全 *Ts'iôn (ou ts'iên).* Tout, entièrement. Voir *ts'iên.*

TSIŌNG

將 *Tsiōng.* Bientôt, d'après; marque du futur.

| 暗, *tsiōng ám,* il va faire nuit, crépuscule.

| 來, *tsiōng loî,* bientôt, ultérieur, qui va arriver.

| 來噲發財, *tsiōng loî voé' fât ts'oî,* il va devenir riche.

| 理辦理, *tsiōng lī p'án lī,* opposer à quelqu'un son propre raisonnement.

| 心比心, *tsiōng sīm pì sīm,* juger les autres d'après soi.

| 就, *tsiōng ts'ióu,* se conformer à la volonté des autres, se contenter d'une chose faute d'une meilleure.

| 臨主日, *tsiōng lîm tchoù gnìt,* dimanches de l'Avent.

| 軍, *tsiōng kioūn,* Gouverneur militaire (il y en a quatre dans toute la Chine), Maréchal.

漿 *Tsiōng.* Suc, sève; empois, amidonner, colle de farine, ou de riz.

番薯 | , *fān choû tsiōng,* suc de patate.

拿飯湯來 | , *nā fán t'ōng loî tsiōng,* empeser avec de l'eau de riz, amidonner.

TS'IŌNG

Ts'iōng. Ts'iōng chît koī, pomme d'Adam.

鎗 *Ts'iōng.* Fusil, lance, pique.

旂 | , *k'î ts'iōng,* lance.

拿旂|來刺死人, *nā k'î ts'iōng loî ts'ioûc sì gnîn,* percer quelqu'un de sa lance.

鳥 | , *niāo ts'iōng,* fusil de chasse.

當 | (搶) , *tōng ts'iōng,* faire par fraude la composition d'un autre (moyennant finances).

TS'IÔNG

墻 *Ts'iông (ou siông).* Mur, muraille. *Voir siông.*

TSIÒNG

奬 *Tsiòng.* Louer, vanter.

| 賞人, *tsiòng chòng gnîn,* faire des compliments à quelqu'un, le louer.

槳 *Tsiòng.* Rames, aviron.

| 船, *tsiòng chôn,* ramer, faire aller la barque à la rame.

| 脚, *tsiòng kiôc,* cheville à laquelle on attache la rame.

TS'IÒNG

搶 *Ts'iòng.* Prendre par force, ravir, piller.

| 劫地方, *ts'iòng kiâp t'í fōng,* piller, saccager, se rendre maître d'un pays par la force.

| 人, | 婦人家, *ts'iòng gnîn, ts'iòng foú gnîn kā,* dépouiller un homme, rapt d'une femme.

| 那人先到, *ts'iòng màn gnîn siēn táo,* se disputer à qui arrivera le premier.

TSIÓNG

將 *Tsióng*. Chef militaire.

参｜, *ts'ām tsióng*, colonel.

醬 *Tsióng*. Saumure, espèce de sauce pour assaisonner les mets.

菜拿來醮｜, *ts'oí nā loî tsiàm tsióng*, tremper son morceau dans la saumure.

菜｜, *ts'oí tsióng*, sorte de conserve alimentaire.

TS'IÓNG

像 *Ts'ióng* (pour *sióng*). Ressembler, semblable.

佢映倒我像咁｜麽, *kî yàng tào ngā sióng àn ts'ióng mô ?* m'a-t-il photographié ressemblant ?

｜討食個, *ts'ióng t'ào chĭt ké·*, on dirait un mendiant.

做事唔｜, *tsó sé mĝ ts'ióng*, ne pas faire les choses comme les autres, original, mauvaise apparence.

TS'IOŪ

偢 *Ts'ioū*. Tout, tous, rassembler, tout ensemble.

做｜帛裡, *tsó ts'ioū p'ĕt lĕ·*, tout est fait.

殺｜帛裡, *săt ts'ioū p'ĕt lĕ·*, ils ont tous été décapités.

聚｜來, *ts'í ts'ioū loî*, rassembler, réunir.

撿｜東西來, *kiàm ts'ioū toūng sī loî*, ramasse les objets, mets tout en ordre.

秋 *Ts'ioū*. Automne.

｜天, *ts'ioū t'iēn*, en automne.

立｜, *lĭp ts'ioū*, commencement de l'automne.

鰍 *Ts'ioū*. **湖｜**, *foû ts'ioū*, toute petite anguille de rizière, qui se conserve en hiver dans la terre sèche, pour reprendre vie au temps des pluies.

TS'IÔU

泅 *Ts'iôu*. Nager, grimper.

｜水, *ts'iôu choùi*, nager.

｜阿樹上去, *ts'iôu á choú hóng hí*, grimper sur les arbres.

｜唔上, *ts'iôu mĝ chōng*, ne pouvoir grimper.

TSIÒU

酒 *Tsiòu*. Vin, alcool, festin.

糯米｜, *nó mì tsiòu*, vin ordinaire des Chinois, fait avec une espèce de riz appelé *nó mì*.

燒｜, *chāo tsiòu*, vin distillé, alcool.

烝｜, *tchīn tsiòu*, faire le vin, cuire les grains pour faire le vin.

泌（ou **烤**）**｜**, *pĭt* (ou *k'ào*) *tsiòu*, distiller le vin.

打｜醉, *tà tsiòu tsoúi*, s'enivrer.

｜錢, *tsiòu ts'iĕn*, pourboire.

討新娘｜, *t'ào sīn niông tsiòu*, festin de noces.

做｜悔釋人, *tsó tsiòu fí chĭt gnîn*, faire un festin pour réparer l'honneur de quelqu'un, pour réparer une offense.

肘 *Tsiòu*. Coude.

打一斷｜, *tà ўt tón tsiòu*, donner un coup de coude. (Vulg. on dit plutôt: *choù tsāng*, le coude.)

揪 *Tsiòu*. Tordre, tordu.

扭扭｜｜, *nioù nioù tsiòu tsiòu*, tordu, contourné, en spirales.

｜耳公, *tsiòu gnì koūng*, tordre les oreilles (tirer les oreilles).

螺螄｜ *lô sē tsiòu*, tire-bouchon.

TSIÓU

縐 *Tsióu*. Crispé, frisé, ridé, pli, se contracter.

毛十分｜唔好梳, *māo chĭp foūn tsioú mĝ hào sē*, les cheveux très frisés sont difficiles à peigner.

衫子摺倒唔好｜帛裡, *sām tzè tchâp tào mĝ hào tsióu p'ĕt lĕ·*, l'habit a été mal plié, il est tout froissé.

｜紗, 湖｜長衫, *tsióu sā, foû tsióu tch'ông sām*, crêpe de soie chinoise, robe de cette étoffe.

TS'IÓU

袖 *Ts'ióu*. **衫｜**, *sām ts'ióu* manches d'habit.

攝衫｜, *niâp sām ts'ióu*, retrousser ses manches d'habit.

就 *Ts'ióu*. Aussitôt, pour lors, sans retard, groupé, serré.

｜係, *ts'ióu hé·*, oui, justement, à savoir, c'est-à-dire, quoique.

｜來, ｜愛, ｜轉, *ts'ióu loî, ts'ióu oí, ts'ióu tchòn*, j'arrive de suite, il le faut immédiatement, reviens de suite.

｜係咁樣, *ts'ióu hé· àn yóng*, c'est bien comme cela.

｜係佢, *ts'ióu hé· kî*, c'est justement lui.

教友唔｜難教, *kaó yoū mĝ ts'ióu nân kāo*, si les chrétiens ne sont pas groupés, il est difficile de les instruire.

銃子愛｜銃嘅好, *sāng tzè oí ts'ióu tch'oúng tsáng hào*, les plombs doivent être groupés (serrés), alors le fusil est bon.

TSIOÛC

足 *Tsioûc*. Suffisant, à point.

人心不｜, *gnîn sīm poût tsioûc*, le cœur de l'homme n'est jamais satisfait.

｜用, *tsioûc yoúng*, suffisant, suffire.

檢｜錢, *kiàm tsioûc ts'iên*, donner le nombre suffisant de sapèques.

一個｜月, *ŷt ké· tsioûc gnĕt*, un mois complet.

TS'IOÛC

刺 *Ts'ioûc*. Piquer, percer, découper.

一個竻｜倒我, *ŷt ké· nĕt ts'ioûc tào ngâi*, une épine m'a piqué.

｜牙齒, *ts'ioûc ngâ tchè*, se curer les dents.

｜菜, *ts'ioûc ts'oí*, découper les légumes.

旂鎗拿來｜死人, *k'î ts'iōng nā loî ts'ioûc sì gnîn*, tuer quelqu'un en le perçant d'une lance.

TSIOŪNG

蹤 *Tsioūng* **｜蹟**, *tsioūng tsiâc*, trace, vestige.

無影無｜, *voû yàng voû tsioūng*, sans le moindre vestige.

縱 *Tsioūng*. Pas droit, de travers.
看去屋壁丨走裡, *k'ón hí vouc piâc tsioūng tscòu lì*, on dirait que le mur de la maison n'est pas droit.

丨布, *tsioūng poú*, étoffe coupée en biais.

TS'IOÛNG

從 *Ts'ioûng*. Suivre, se conformer, émaner, de, depuis.

丨天主教, *ts'ioûng t'iēn tchoù káo*, suivre la religion chrétienne.

丨官斷個, *ts'ioûng koūon tón ké*, se conformer à la sentence du mandarin.

丨宗徒傳下來, *ts'ioûng tsoūng t'oû tch'ôn hā loî*, qui descend des apôtres.

丨今以後, *ts'ioûng kīn ỳ heóu*, dorénavant.

丨先, *ts'ioûng siēn*, autrefois.

松 *Ts'ioûng*. Pin.
丨樹, *ts'ioûng choú*, pin, bois de pin.
丨仁, *ts'ioûng ŷn*, résine de pin.
丨毛, *ts'ioûng maō*, aiguilles de pin.

TSIOÙNG

縱 *Tsioùng*. Malgré, quand même.
丨然有個事你唔使打官司 *tsioùng yân yoū ké sé gnî mĝ sè tà koūon sē*, quand bien même il en serait ainsi, tu n'as pas à faire de procès.

十分放丨個人, *chĭp foūn fóng tsioùng ké. gnîn*, rien ne peut le retenir.

丨賊, *tsioùng ts'ĕt*, relâcher un voleur.

TSĬT

責 *Tsĭt*. Réprimander.
懲丨人, 丨罰人, *tchĭn tsĭt gnîn, tsĭt făt gnîn*, gronder, punir quelqu'un.

丨成人, *tsĭt chîn gnîn*, réprimander.

鯽 *Tsĭt* 丨魚, *tsĭt nĝ*, brème, petit poisson de rivière.

TS'ĬT

疾 *Ts'ĭt*. Maladie.
殘丨, *ts'ân ts'ĭt*, maladie incurable.

嫉 *Ts'ĭt*. 丨妬, *ts'ĭt toú*, envie, jalousie.

丨妬人, *ts'ĭt toú gnîn*, porter envie à quelqu'un.

TSÎT

卽 *Tsît*. Aussitôt.
丨刻, 登丨, *tsît k'ĕt, tēn tsît*, aussitôt, immédiatement, à l'instant.

積 *Tsît*. Amasser, accumuler.
丨財, *tsît ts'ôi*, thésauriser.
丨米, 丨穀, *tsît mì, tsît koŭc*, amasser du riz.

蹟 *Tsît*. Signe, vestige.
形丨唔像, *hîn tsît mĝ ts'ióng*, il n'a pas bonne apparence.
聖丨, *chín tsît*, miracles.
顯聖丨, *hièn chín tsît*, faire des miracles. (Voir *tsiâc*.)

楖 *Tsît*. Frapper, piquer, donner un coup de bâton ou autre dans le sens de la longueur, c.-à-d. comme on donne un coup d'épingle.

眼刓你｜倒裡, *niàn poūn gnî tsĭt tào lê·*, tu m'as attrapé dans l'œil.

TS'ĬT

七 *Ts'ĭt.* Sept.

｜十, ｜百, *ts'ĭt chĭp, ts'ĭt pâc*, 70, 700.

講｜講八, *hòng ts'ĭt kòng pât*, parler à tort et à travers.

｜罪宗, *ts'ĭt ts'oúi tsoūng*, les sept péchés capitaux.

戚 *Ts'ĭt.* 親｜, *ts'ĭn ts'ĭt*, parents, parents par alliance.

膝 *Ts'ĭt.* ｜頭, *ts'ĭt t'eôu*, le genou.

雙｜跪倒, *soūng ts'ĭt k'ouì tào*, s'agenouiller des deux genoux.

漆 *Ts'ĭt.* Laque, vernis, vernir.

｜過個, *ts'ĭt koúo ké·*, c'est verni.

｜一過, *ts'ĭt ŷt koúo*, passer une couche de vernis.

TS'Ō

(Voir aussi TSE)

坐 *Ts'ō (ts'ó).* Etre assis, s'asseoir, demeurer.

｜倒來, 請｜, *ts'ō tào loî, ts'iàng ts'ō*, assieds-toi, veuillez vous asseoir.

｜轎, ｜車, ｜船, *ts'ō k'iáo, ts'ō tch'ā, ts'ō chôn*, aller (être assis) en palanquin, en voiture, en barque.

｜上頭, *ts'ō chóng t'eôu*, être assis à la première place, la place d'honneur.

屋子｜下裡, *voŭc tzè ts'ō hā lê·*, la maison s'est affaissée.

｜堂, *ts'ō t'ông*, siéger au tribunal, séance.

搓 *Ts'ō* ou *ts'ó.* Frotter, limer, gratter.

｜滑, ｜淨, *ts'ō vă̆t, ts'ō ts'iáng*, polir en frottant, nettoyer en frottant.

銼子拿來｜, *ts'ó tzè nā loî ts'ō*, limer.

｜牙齒, *ts'ō ngâ tchè*, se brosser les dents.

TSÔ

漕 *Tsô (ou tsáo).* Eau qui tombe de haut.

屋簷水｜｜下, *voŭc yâm choùi tsô tsô hā*, l'eau des gouttières tombe en douche.

TSÒ

左 *Tsò.* Gauche.

｜手, ｜脚, *tsò choù, tsò kiôc*, main gauche, pied gauche.

中國尙｜西國尙右, *tchoūng kouĕt hióng tsò sī kouĕt hióng yoú*, en Chine la 1ere place est à gauche, en Europe elle est à droite.

｜右, *tsò yoú*, à droite et à gauche, les assistants.

TSÓ

做 *Tsó.* Faire, agir, fabriquer.

｜手藝, *tsó choù gní*, exercer une profession, un métier.

｜生理, ｜工夫, *tsó siēn lī, tsó koūng foū*, faire le commerce, travailler.

｜得，｜唔得，*tsó têt, tsó mĝ têt*, cela est possible, oui, n'est pas possible, non.

｜那個，*tsó mâc ké·?* quoi? pourquoi? qu'est-ce?

你｜那個，*gnî tsó mâc ké·?* que fais-tu?

TS'Ó

跧 *Ts'ó.* Glisser, tomber en glissant.

路十分滑噲｜人，*loú chĭp foūn vǎt voé· ts'ó gnîn*, la route est par trop glissante, on risque de tomber.

坐 *Ts'ó.* Demeurer, préférer.

向南｜北，*hióng nâm ts'ó pêt*, le devant (d'une maison) regardant le Sud, le dos tourné au Nord.

你在那裡｜家，*gnî t'oī naí lī ts'ó kā?* où habites-tu en famille?

兩枝扇子我｜裡個過好，*leòng kī chán tzè ngâi ts'ó ỳ ké· koúo hào*, de ces deux éventails, je préfère celui-ci.

你｜做泥水我｜做木匠，*gnî ts'ó tsó nâi chouì ngâi ts'ó tsó moûc sióng*, tu préfères être maçon, moi j'aime mieux être menuisier.

座 *Ts'ó.* Siège. Partic. numérale des maisons.

係神父個｜位，*hé· chîn foú ké· ts'ó ví*, c'est la place du Père.

一｜聖堂，*ŷt ts'ó chín t'ông*, une église.

銼 *Ts'ó.* Lime, limer.

一枝｜子，*ŷt kī ts'ó tzè*, une lime.

三角｜子，圓｜了，*sām kôc ts'ó tzè, yân ts'ó tzè*, lime triangulaire, lime ronde.

TS'ŎC

鑿 *Ts'ŏc.* Ciseau de menuisier.

三分｜，*sām foūn ts'ŏc*, ciseau de la largeur de trois lignes.

筧｜，*kiàn ts'ŏc*, ciseau dont la pointe est en gouttière.

｜眼，*ts'ŏc niàn*, faire un trou au ciseau.

昨 *Ts'ŏc.* Hier.

｜日，ou ｜天，*tsŏc gnĭt* ou *ts'ŏc t'iēn*, hier. —Plus vulgairement:

｜晡日，｜晡夜，*ts'ŏc poū gnĭt, ts'ŏc poū yá*, hier, hier au soir.

On trouve ce mot plus ou moins déformé selon les pays: *Ts'ī poū gnĭt*, ou *ts'iōu pōu gnĭt*, ou *ts'ō poū gnĭt* etc..

TSÔC

作 *Tsôc.* Faire (synonyme de 做 *tsó* mais moins employé), s'imaginer que.

｜田唇，*tsôc t'iên choûn*, faire les bords d'une rizière.

｜主，*tsôc tchòu*, se déterminer, prendre une résolution, agir en maître.

｜善，｜惡，*tsôc chán, tsôc ôc*, faire le bien, faire le mal.

我｜為你話唔係，*ngâi tsôc vî gnî vá mĝ hé·*, je croyais que tu disais non.

我｜為(ou｜倒)係水我一下吞落一大盃火酒，*ngâi tsôc vî* (ou *tsôc tào*) *hé· chouì ngâi ŷt há t'oūn lòc ŷt t'aí pī fò tsiòu*, croyant que c'était de l'eau, j'ai avalé d'un seul coup une grande tasse d'eau-de-vie.

桌 *Tsôc*. Table.

一張｜, *ŷt tchōng tsôc*, une table, une tablée de 8 personnes.

條｜，脫｜, *t'iâo tsôc, t'ôt tsôc*, table plus longue que large, table qui se démonte.

三張｜席, *sām tchōng tsôc sĭt*, un festin de trois tablées.

｜圍, *tsôc vî*, antipendium, devant de table.

｜面, *tsôc mién*, surface de la table.

捉 *Tsôc*, Saisir, prendre.

賊子別我｜倒, *ts'ĕt tzè poūn ngâi tsôc tào*, j'ai attrapé le voleur.

忒噲走｜唔倒, *t'iĕt voé tsèou tsôc mĝ tào*, il court trop vite, on ne peut pas l'attraper.

｜狗虱, *tsôc kèou sĕt*, attraper des puces.

TS'ÔC

錯 *Ts'ôc*. Errer, se tromper (style relevé).

認｜, *gnín ts'ôc*, reconnaître ses torts.

不｜, *poût ts'ôc*, c'est cela, il n'y a pas d'erreur.

千｜萬｜, *ts'iēn ts'ôc ván ts'ôc*, j'ai eu mille et dix mille fois tort.

TSŌI

Tsoī. Parties honteuses de l'homme. (Mot trivial très souvent employé dans les malédictions.)

Gnî ts'iōn ngā tsoī, tu me suces la verge (tu m'agaces).

Tsoī maō voé· tch'ŏc fò, les poils de ma verge vont prendre feu (pour exprimer une grande colère).

TS'ŌI

Ts'oī. **｜過**, *ts'oī koúo*, malheureux, qui est dans la peine.

在 *Ts'oī (ts'ái)*. Etre, exister.

你姆還｜麼, *niā mē· hân ts'oī mô ?* ta maman existe-t-elle encore ?

神父｜裡, *chîn foú ts'oī lì*, le Père est présent.

TS'OÎ

Ts'oî. Frapper d'un coup de couteau.

刀子｜阿起, *tāo tzè ts'oî á hì*, donner un coup de couteau (de haut en bas).

才 *Ts'oî*. Capacités, talent.

三｜, *sām ts'oî*, les trois puissances, le ciel, la terre et l'homme.

口｜，文｜, *k'eòu ts'oî, voûn ts'oî*, talent de la parole, talent d'écrivain.

裡個道理超過人個｜, *ŷ ké· t'áo lì tch'aō koúo gnîn ké· ts'oî*, cette doctrine surpasse les capacités de l'homme.

材 *Ts'oî* (ou *ts'aî*). Matériaux. Voir *ts'aî*.

財 *Ts'oî*. Richesses, biens.

發｜, ou **生｜**, *fât ts'oî*, ou *sēn ts'oî*, s'enrichir.

當 | 庫, *tōng ts'oî k'oú*, trésorier.

| 主, *ts'oî tchoù*, maître, patron, chef de commerce.

有 | 喜, *yoū ts'oî hì*, avoir de la chance, du succès.

TS'OÌ

睬 *Ts'oì*. Faire attention (ne s'emploie qu'au négatif).

唔 | 人, *mĝ ts'oì gnîn*, affecter de ne pas s'occuper de quelqu'un.

TS'OÍ

菜 *Ts'oí*. Légumes, mets en général.

青 |, *ts'iāng ts'oí*, légumes verts.

| 秧, *ts'oí yōng*, plants de légumes.

冇 |, *mô ts'oí*, il n'y a rien à manger (réponse de politesse à un invité qui se met à table).

請 |, *ts'iàng ts'oí*, veuillez vous servir (politesse de table).

| 仁, *ts'oí ŷn*, graines de légumes.

脆 *Ts'oí*. Fragile, peu résistant.

玻璃十分 | ,*pō lî chĭp foūn ts'oí*, le verre est très fragile.

裡個花好看單單十分 |, *ỳ ké· fa hào k'ón tān tān chĭp foūn ts'oí*, cette fleur est belle, mais elle ne dure pas.

TS'ŌN

閂 *Ts'ōn*. Verrou, fermer au verrou.

門 |, *moûn t'sōn*, verrou de la porte.

| 門, *ts'ōn moûn*, fermer la porte au verrou.

飧 *Ts'ōn*. Repas.

一日食三 |, *ŷt gnĭt chĭt sām ts'ōn*, faire trois repas par jour.

兩 | 飯一個點心, *leòng ts'ōn fán ŷt ké· tiàm sīm*, deux repas complets et un goûter.

犯貪 |, *fám t'ām ts'ōn*, commettre un péché de gourmandise.

TSÒN

纂 *Tsòn*. Chapeau d'enfant.

| 絨, *tsòn yoûng*, pompon du chapeau.

TSÓN

鑽 *Tsón*. Pénétrer, vrille.

魔鬼 | 佢心, *mô koùi tsón kiā sīm*, le diable s'est emparé de son cœur.

那裡都緊 | 等去, *nái lī toū kìn tsón tèn hí*, se faufiler partout.

| 眼, *tsón nian*, faire un trou avec une vrille.

| 穿, *tsón tch'ōn*, percer de part en part.

| 唔入, *tsón mĝ gnĭp*, ne pouvoir faire entrer la vrille.

TS'ÓN

賺 *Ts'ón*. Gagner de l'argent, faire du profit.

| 錢, *ts'ón ts'iên*, gagner de l'argent.

過番過好 |, *koúo fān koúo hào ts'ón*, à l'étranger on gagne plus facilement.

囤穀 | 倒五呈, *toùn koŭc ts'ón tào ǹg tch'âng*, en amassant du riz j'ai eu un bénéfice de 50 %.

TSŌNG

庄 (*v.*莊) *Tsōng*. Orné, distingué, entrepôt, magasin, territoire.

咁端｜個人, *àn tōn tsōng ké· gnîn*, quel homme distingué, modeste, qui inspire le respect.

｜子, *tsōng tzè*, villa, ferme avec ses dépendances, maison de campagne avec ses propriétés.

寫｜子, *sià tsōng tzè*, hypothéquer une propriété.

｜頭, *tsōng t'eôu*, marque de magasin.

一樣一樣個｜頭, *ŷt yóng ŷt yóng ké· tsōng teôu*, chaque magasin a sa marque.

貨｜, 銀｜, *fó tsōng, nioûn tsōng*, entrepôt de marchandises, d'argent.

粧 *Tsōng*. Ornement de femme.

嫁｜咁齊, *ká tsōng àn tsê·*, la dot mobilière est considérable.

女扮男｜, *ǹg p'án nâm tsōng*, homme qui s'habille en femme.

裝 *Tsōng*. **｜淨, ｜抨, ｜壞, ｜爛**, *tsōng ts'iáng, tsōng p'iāng, tsōng fái, tsōng lán*, nettoyer, aplanir, abîmer, écrabouiller.

軍｜, *kioūn tsōng*, armements, équipement militaire.

TS'ŌNG

倉 *Ts'ōng*. Grenier.

穀｜, *koŭc ts'ōng*, grenier à riz.

官｜, *koūon ts'ōng*, greniers publics, pour secouirr le peuple en temps de famine.

穀拿來上｜, *koŭc nā loî chōng ts'ōng*, mettre le riz dans le grenier.

蒼 *Ts'ōng*. Couleur d'azur.

｜天, *ts'ōng t'iēn*, le ciel bleu.

｜蠅子, *ts'ōng ŷn tzè*, (ou **青蠅** *ts'iāng ŷn*), espèce de mouche azurée, qui pique les bestiaux.

瘡 *Ts'ōng*. Gale, furoncle.

發｜, *făt (ou pŏt) ts'ōng*, avoir la gale.

發疔｜, *pŏt tāng ts'ōng*, avoir un furoncle à la partie postérieure, un clou.

艙 *Ts'ōng*. Compartiment de barque, cale.

四｜船, *sí ts'ōng chôn*, barque à quatre compartiments.

貨拿來下｜, *fó nā loî hā ts'ōng*, mettre les marchandises dans la cale.

｜面上, *ts'ōng mién hóng*, le dessus de la cale, où se mettent les passagers.

愴 *Ts'ōng*. **｜惶**, *ts'ōng fông*, souci, préoccupation.

你莫咁｜惶, *gnî mŏc àn ts'ōng fông*, ne te mets pas tant en soucis.

TS'ÔNG

床 *Ts'ông*. Lit.

｜鋪, *ts'ông p'oū*, literie.

｜板, ｜架, *ts'ông pàn (ou pièn), ts'ông ká*, planches de lit, bois, échafaudage du lit.

病稱三日唔曾上｜, *p'iáng lê· sām gnĭt mĝ ts'ên hóng ts'ông*, il est tombé malade et a gardé le lit trois jours.

匟 |, *k'ong ts'ông*, lit de repos, canapé.

藏 *Ts'ông*. Cacher, garder secret.

唔知 | 阿那裡去, *mĝ tī ts'ông á nái lī hí*, je ne sais pas où il est allé se cacher.

一句話 | 唔核, *ŷt kí fá ts'ông mĝ hĕt*, il ne peut garder secrète une seule parole.

TSÓNG

壯 *Tsóng*. Fort, robuste.

| 身, *tsóng chīn*, d'une santé robuste.

| 旺個人, *tsóng vóng ké· gnîn*, homme d'un embonpoint vigoureux.

葬 *Tsóng*. Ensevelir, enterrer.

埋 |, *mâi tsóng*, ensevelir.

生養死 |, *sēn yōng sì tsóng*, pourvoir à l'entretien pendant la vie, et à l'enterrement après la mort.

TS'ÓNG

狀 *Ts'óng*. Accusation, pièce d'accusation.

做 | 子賺倒錢, *tsó ts'óng tzè ts'ón tào ts'iên*, il s'est enrichi en faisant des pièces d'accusation.

佢告裡我三 |, *kî káo lê· ngaî sām ts'óng*, il m'a accusé trois fois.

| 元, *ts'óng niân*, le plus haut grade parmi les docteurs.

形 | 唔好, *hîn ts'óng mĝ haò*, se dit d'un homme de mauvaise constitution.

藏 *Ts'óng*. Trésor.

西 |, *sī ts'óng*, le Thibet (trésor de l'Occident).

臟 *Ts'óng*. Viscères.

五 | 六腑, *ng̀ ts'óng lioûc foù*, les 5 viscères supérieures et les 6 viscères inférieures.

撞 *Ts'óng*. Rencontrer, heurter.

我路上 | 倒神父, *ngâi loú hóng ts'óng tào chîn foú*, j'ai rencontré le Père sur mon chemin.

愛 | 倒呼有, *oí ts'óng tào tsáng yoū*, on n'en trouve que de rencontre.

| 倒機會, *ts'óng tào kī fí*, rencontrer l'occasion.

船 | 倒石頭, *chôn ts'óng tào chăc t'eôu*, la barque s'est heurtée à un rocher.

火船對火船 | 倒, *fò chôn toúi fò chôn ts'óng taò*, deux vapeurs se sont heurtés l'un contre l'autre.

白 |, *p'ăc ts'óng*, pickpoket, escroc.

| 目珠, *ts'óng moûc tchoū*, autre espèce d'escroc.

TSŎT

咄 *Tsŏt*. Sucer, téter, force aspirante.

細人 | 乳, *sé· gnîn tsŏt nén*, l'enfant tète.

| 得穩, *tsŏt tĕt voùn*, tenir par la la force aspirante.

| 田螺, *tsŏt t'iên lô*, manger des escargots.

TS'ÔT

撮 *Ts'ôt*. Escamoter, extorquer, commettre de petits vols, ramasser.

｜人個錢, *ts'ôt gnîn kè· ts'ièn*, extorquer de l'argent par ruse ou fraude.

｜把戲, *ts'ôt pà hí*, faire des tours de passe-passe sur les tréteaux.

｜箕, *ts'ôt kī*, espèce de petite corbeille pour ramasser les grains.

啜 *Ts'ôt*. Aspirer les aliments.

｜粥, *ts'ôt tchoŭc*, manger la soupe de riz sans se servir des bâtonnets, en aspirant les aliments et les prenant avec les lèvres.

TS'OUC

族 *Ts'oŭc*. Famille, race.

一｜人, *ŷt ts'oŭc gnîn*, tous les descendants d'une même souche.

｜譜, *ts'oŭc p'où*, livre généalogique d'une grande famille, avec toutes ses branches.

犯｜, *fám ts'oŭc*, commettre l'inceste.

滅｜, *mĕt ts'oŭc*, anéantir une famille.

嗽 *Ts'oŭc*. Tousser.

我受冷風緊｜, *ngaî choú lĕ· foūng kìn ts'oŭc*, j'ai pris froid, je ne fais que tousser.

火烟噲｜人, *fò yān voé· ts'oŭc gnîn*, la fumée vous prend à la gorge.

TS'OŪI

催 *Ts'ōui*. Presser, stimuler, hâter.

｜人還賬, *ts'ōui gnîn vân tchóng*, presser quelqu'un de payer ses dettes.

｜佢來, **｜工夫**, *ts'ōui kî loî, ts'ōui koūng foū*, presse-le de venir, presser le travail.

打發人去｜, *tà fât gnîn hí ts'ōui*, envoyer quelqu'un pour dire de se dépêcher.

TS'OÛI

隨 *Ts'ouî* (*souî*). **｜便**, *ts'ouî p'ién*, volontiers. Voir *souî*.

TSOÙI

嘴 *Tsoùi* (ou *tchói*). Bouche, bec, embouchure.

鵰｜, *tiāo tsoùi*, bec d'oiseau.

茶壺｜, *ts'â foû tsoùi*, bec d'une cruche à thé.

TSOÚI

濟 *Tsoúi* ou *tsí*. Emboire. Voir *tsí*.

最 *Tsoúi*. Très, absolu.

｜要緊, *tsoúi yáo kìn*, absolument indispensable.

醉 *Tsoúi*. Ivre, ivresse.

食｜, *chĭt tsoúi*, s'enivrer.

打酒｜, *tà tsiòu tsoúi*, boire jusqu'à s'enivrer.

我唔曉｜, *ngâi mĝ hiào tsoúi*, je n'éprouve pas l'ivresse, je supporte bien le vin.

酒噲｜人, *tsiòu voé· tsoúi gnîn*, le vin enivre.

TS'OUÍ

翠 *Ts'oúi*. Martin-pêcheur.

| 花, 做 | 花, *ts'oúi fā, tsó ts'oúi fā*, fleurs faites avec les plumes de cet oiseau, faire de ces fleurs.

罪 *Ts'oúi*. Péché, offense.

犯 |, *fám ts'oúi*, faire un péché.

得 | 天主, 得 | 人, *tēt ts'oúi t'iēn tchòu, tēt ts'oúi gnîn*, offenser Dieu, offenser quelqu'un.

| 歸於我, *ts'oúi koūi ȳ ngō*, à moi revient la faute, j'en porte le péché.

原 |, 本 |, *niân ts'oúi, poùn tsoúi*, péché originel, péché actuel.

重 v. 大 |, 小 |, *tch'oūng* v. *t'aí ts'oúi, siào ts'oúi*, péché grave, mortel, péché véniel.

TSOŪN

尊 *Tsoūn*. Noble, vénérer.

| 號, *tsoūn háo?* quel est votre noble nom (*politesse*)?.

| 敬老人家, *tsoūn kín lào gnîn kā*, respecter les vieillards.

聖體係至 | 貴個聖事, *chín t'ì hé· tjé tsoūn koúi ké· chín sé*, l'Eucharistie est le plus respectable des Sacrements.

遵 *Tsoūn*. Obéir avec respect.

| 命, *tsoūn mín*, même sens.

| 守規誡, *tsoūn choù koūi kiái*, observer fidèlement les règles.

罇 *Tsoūn*. Bouteille, carafe.

酒 |, 玻璃 |, *tsiòu tsoūn, pō lî tsoūn*, bouteille de vin, bouteille en verre.

TS'OŪN

村 *Ts'oūn*. Village, hameau.

一 | 都知, *ȳt ts'oūn toū tī*, tout le village le sait.

TSOÚN

圳 *Tsóun*. Petit ruisseau, rigole.

| 瀝, *tsóun lâc*, rigole, petit ruisseau.

| 瀝拿來勾淨, *tsóun lâc nā loî keōu ts'iáng*, débarrasser la rigole des saletés qui l'obstruent.

TS'OÚN

寸 *Ts'oún*. Pouce, dixième partie du pied.

有尺 |, *yoū tch'âc ts'oún*, il y a la mesure.

三 | 二, *sām ts'oún gní*, trois pouces et deux (lignes).

得一 | 入一尺, *tēt ȳt ts'óun gnìp ȳt tch'âc*, on leur donne un pouce, ils en prennent un pied.

TSOŪNG

宗 *Tsoūng*. Ancêtre, principal, catégorie.

祖 |, *tzè tsoūng*, ancêtres.

| 廟, *tsoūng miáo*, temple des ancêtres,

同 |, (ou 同祖 |), *t'oûng tsoūng*, (ou *t'oûng tzè tsoūng*), de la même souche, descendants du même ancêtre.

頭一 |, *t'eoû ȳt tsoūng*, tout d'abord, surtout.

第二 |, 第三 |, *t'í gní tsoūng, t'í*

sâm tsoūng, en deuxième lieu, en troisième lieu.

一｜一｜愛算我聽, *ŷt tsoūng ŷt tsoūng oí són ngâi t'ang*, il faut que m'énumères tout, point par point.

還有一｜事愛問神父, *hân yoū ŷt tsoūng sé oí moún chîn foú*, j'ai encore une question à poser au Père.

騌 *Tsoūng*. Crinière de cheval.

馬｜, ｜毛, *mā tsoūng, tsoung māo*, crinière de cheval, crins.

棕 *Tsoūng*. Espèce de palmier.

｜皮, *tsoūng p'ī*, gaine qui se forme autour de cet arbre, et dont les fibres servent à faire des cordes, des nattes, etc.

｜毛, ｜索, *tsoūng māo, tsoūng sôc*, fibres de cette gaine, cordes faites avec ces fibres.

TS'OŪNG

聰 *Ts'oūng*. Intelligent.

｜明個人, *ts'oūng mîn ké· gnin*, homme intelligent.

窗 *Ts'oūng*. Fenêtre.

｜桄, *ts'oūng kouāng*, barreaux de la fenêtre.

開｜, *k'oī ts'oūng*, pratiquer une fenêtre dans le mur.

｜子打開來, *ts'oūng tzè tà k'oī loî* ouvrir la fenêtre.

囱 *Ts'oūng*. 烟｜, *yān ts'oūng*, cheminée.

葱 *Ts'ōung*. Oignon.

｜子, ｜頭, *ts'ōung tzè, ts'oūng t'eôu*, oignons.

TS'OÛNG

崇 *Ts'oúng*. Respecter grandement.

欽｜天主, *k'īm ts'oúng t'iēn tchòu*, honorer Dieu de toute son âme.

TSOÙNG

總 *Tsoùng*. En général, en somme.

共｜, *k'ioúng tsoùng*, (ou *loūng tsoùng*), en tout.

｜告解, *tsoùng káo kiài*, confession générale.

賬愛拿來歸｜, *tchóng oí nā loî kouī tsoùng*, il faut faire le total des comptes.

｜督, *tsoùng toûc*, vice-roi.

TSOÚNG

粽 *Tsoúng*. 米｜, *mì tsoúng*, espèce de gâteau de riz.

TS'OǓT

拭 *Ts'oǔt* (*tch'īt*). Essuyer.

｜淨｜桌, *ts'oǔt tsôc ts'oǔt ts'iáng*, essuyer la table proprement.

TSOÛT

卒 *Tsoût*. 兵｜, *pīn tsoût*, soldats.

｜世, *tsoût ché*, toute la vie.

TZĒ

(Ces mots sont, dans certains pays, prononcés comme *tjē*, et vice- versa).

咨 *Tzē.* 丨文, *tzē voûn*, pièce officielle entre grands mandarins.

丨奏, *tzē tséou*, rapport officiel fait à l'Empereur.

資 *Tzē.* Biens, richesses.

丨本, *tzē poùn*, richesses, possessions.

酒丨錢, *tsioù tzē ts'iên*, pourboire.

滋 *Tzē.* Succulent, tendre, qui s'étend facilement.

丨味, *tzē mí*, savoureux, succulent.

泥丨潤好做事, *nâi tzē yoún hào tsó ché*, la terre étant molle et humectée est facile à travailler.

丨事 (*v.* 鬧事), *tzē sé (v. náo sé)*, susciter des troubles.

租 *Tzē (ou tchoū).* Revenu, rente, affermer.

收丨, *choū tzē*, percevoir ses revenus.

納丨, 讓丨, *năp tzē, nióng tzē*, payer le revenu, faire remise sur la redevance.

年辰唔好丨都打唔起, *niân chîn mĝ hào tzē toū tà mĝ hì*, l'année est mauvaise, la récolte ne suffit pas même pour la redevance.

丨東西, 丨牛, *tzē toūng sī, tzē nioû*, louer, emprunter des objets, un buffle, à tant par jour ou par mois.

丨屋, *tzē voŭc*, louer, affermer une maison.

TZÈ

子 *Tzè.* Fils, graine, finale de la plupart des substantifs, en guise d'article.

丨孫, *tzè soūn*, fils et petits fils.

天主聖丨, *t'iēn tchoù chín tzè*, le Fils de Dieu.

扇丨, 袋丨, 衫丨, *chán tzè, t'oí tzè, sām tzè*, l'éventail, le sac, l'habit.

L'usage (qui varie souvent d'un lieu à un autre) peut seul apprendre quels substantifs requièrent ou admettent *tzè* comme finale.

一丨烟, *ŷt tzè yān*, une pincée de tabac.

丨牛, 丨狗, 丨猫, *tzè nióu, tzè keoù, tzè miáo*, jeune buffle ou veau, jeune chien, jeune chat.

仔 *Tzè.* S'appliquer à.

丨細, *tzè sé*, avec soin.

莫咁丨細, *mŏc àn tzè sé*, n'ayez pas tant d'égards envers moi (*politesse*).

紫 *Tzè.* 丨色, *tzè sĕt*, violet. (Le plus souvent, on appelle ainsi la couleur rose, et 灰色 *foē sĕt*, le violet.)

祖 *Tzè.* Ancêtres.

丨公 (*v.* 丨宗), 原丨公, *tzè koūng (v. tzè tsoūng), niân tzè koūng*, ancêtres, nos premiers parents.

丨業, *tzè niăp*, héritage transmis de père en fils, depuis plusieurs générations.

阻 *Tzè (ou tchoù).* Empêcher.

丨攔, 丨擋, 丨隔, *tzè lân, tzè tòng, tzè kăc*, empêcher, mettre obstacle.

領婚配唔得有丨擋, *leăng foūn p'í mĝ tĕt yōu tzè tòng*, il y a empêchement de mariage.

VĀ

挖 *Vā* (ou *vât*). Ouvrir, creuser, excaver, creux, échancrure.

| 脥, *vā loí*, pratiquer une ouverture, faire un trou.

| 塘, *vā t'ông*, creuser un réservoir d'eau.

嘴 | |, *tchoí vā vā*, bouche béante.

| 叉, *vā ts'ā*, fourche, piquet en fourche.

| 口, *vā heoù*, échancrure, col de montagne.

VÁ

話 *Vá* (pour *fá*). Dire, parler. (Synonyme de 講 *kòng*.)

我 | 你知, *ngâi vá gnî tī*, je te le dis, que je te dise.

佢唔曉 |, *kî mĝ hiào vá*, il ne sait pas ou ne peut pas parler.

你噲 |, *gnî voé· vá*, tu es habile à parler (sous-entendu : cela ne prouve pas que tu aies raison).

麼那個 |, *mô mâc ké· vá*, je n'ai rien à dire, il n'y a rien à dire.

VĂC

畫 *Văc*. Trait, dessiner, esquisser, couper le verre.

唐字有好多撇 |, *t'ông sé yoū hào tō p'iĕt văc*, les caractères chinois ont beaucoup de virgules et de traits.

| 十字, *văc chìp sé*, tracer une croix.

| 一個圓圈, *văc ŷt ké· yân k'iān*, tracer un cercle.

| (劃) 玻璃, *văc pō lî*, fendre le verre.

| 玻璃金鋼石, *văc pō lî kīm kōng chăc*, diamant à couper le verre.

VAĪ

歹 *Vaī*. Mauvais.

有好 |, *yoū hào vaī*, il y a du bon et du mauvais.

| 心, *vaī sīm*, mauvais cœur, méchant.

| 事, *vaī sé*, mauvaise affaire.

VÀI

Vài. Crier.

細人子莫 | 咁大聲, *sé· gnîn tzè mòc vài àn t'ái chāng*, enfants, ne criez pas si fort.

| | 跳, *vài vài t'iáo*, tapageur, importun par son bavardage, son tapage.

VĀN

鯇 *Vān*. Espèce de poisson d'étang qui se nourrit d'herbe.

灣 *Vān* (*vân*). Contourner, courbé, circuit.

| 路, *vān loú*, prendre un chemin détourné.

我蹓路 | 阿州城去, *ngâi t'óng loú vān á tchōu chāng hí*, je me suis égaré et j'ai passé par la ville.

| | 轉, *vān vān tchòn*, tourner autour, circuits, détours, prétextes.

| | 曲, *vān vān k'ioūt*, sinueux, détourné.

晚 *Vān*. Soir.

早 | 課, *tsào vān k'ó*, prières du matin et du soir.

念｜課，*niám vān k'ó*, réciter la prière du soir.

｜間嘹，*vān kiān liáo*, à ce soir (style relevé).

VÂN

完 *Vân*. Achevé, fini.

食｜，食唔｜，*chĭt vân, chĭt mĝ vân*, avoir tout mangé, ne pouvoir tout manger.

我工夫做｜，*ngā kōung foū tsó vân*, j'ai achevé mon travail.

｜粮，*vân leông*, payer l'impôt.

還 *Vân* (*fân*). Rendre, restituer.

｜賬，*vân tchóng*, payer ses dettes.

｜唔起，*vân mĝ hì*, n'avoir pas de quoi rendre.

借人個東西愛｜，*tsiá gnîn ké· tōung sī oí vân*, quand on emprunte il faut rendre.

灣 *Vân*. Circuit, contour.

路轉｜，*loú tchòn vân*, la route fait un détour.

VÀN

挽 *Vàn*. Accrocher, pendre, entortiller.

｜衫，*vàn sām*, pendre l'habit.

｜阿鐵釘上起，*vàn á t'iĕt tāng hóng hì*, accroche-le au clou.

衫上有竻｜等裡，*sām hóng yoū nĕt vàn tèn é·*, des épines se sont prises à ta robe.

宛 *Vàn* (ou *vān* ou *yàn*). Replié sur soi-même comme un serpent ; semblable.

路｜阿去｜阿轉，*loú vàn á hí vàn á tchòn*, la route est très tortueuse.

｜｜轉轉，*vàn vàn tchòn tchòn*, faire beaucoup de détours.

｜像，*vàn ts'ám*, vraisemblable.

佢講古講得係｜像，*kî kòng koù kòng tĕt é· vàn ts'ám*, il raconte si bien son histoire qu'elle paraît vraisemblable.

VÁN

萬 *Ván*. Dix mille, tout, universalité.

一｜三千，*ÿt ván sām ts'iēn*, 13000.

｜國｜民，*ván kouĕt, ván mîn*, tous les royaumes, tous les peuples.

｜歲，*ván sé·*, (dix mille années) Empereur, Sa Majesté, vive le Roi !

｜有真原，*ván yoū tchīn niân*, *omnium est vera origo*. Il est la vraie source de tout (inscription ordinaire au frontispice des chapelles).

｜不敢犯罪，*ván poŭt kàm fám ts'oúi*, jamais je n'oserai pécher.

｜不能，*ván poŭt nên*, absolument impossible.

VÂNG

橫 *Vâng*. En travers, dans le sens de la largeur, pas droit, au propr. et au fig.

｜桄，*vâng kouang*, traverse, bois mis en travers.

｜眠個，*vâng mîn ké·*, se coucher dans le sens de la largeur du lit.

老蟹｜｜走，*lào hài vâng vâng tseòu*, les crabes marchent de travers.

丨路過, *vâng loú koúo*, prendre un chemin de traverse.

丨心人, *vâng sīm gnîn*, homme fourbe, déloyal.

咁强丨 *kàn k'iông vâng*, quel homme déloyal.

VÂNG

横 *Váng*. Renverser, tomber (synonyme de 跌 *tiĕt*).

樹子丨下裡, *choú tzè váng ha lì*, l'arbre est tombé.

人丨阿地下去, *gnîn váng á t'í ha hí*, l'homme est tombé à terre.

VĂT

滑 *Văt*. Poli, glissant.

路十分丨, *loú chĭp foūn văt*, la route est très glissante.

魚子係丨捉唔穩, *nĝ tzé é· văt tsôc mĝ voùn*, le poisson est très glissant, on ne peut le tenir.

衫子唔曾挽穩就走, *sām tzè mĝ ts'ên vàn voùn ts'ioú văt tsèou*, l'habit n'a pas été accroché solidement, et il a glissé.

VÂT

猾 *Vât*. Trompeur, fourbe.

狡丨, *kào vât*, même sens.

裡個人十分狡丨唔好惹佢, *ỳ ké· gnîn chĭp fōun kào vât mĝ hào niā kí*, cet homme est un filou, il ne faut pas s'y frotter.

挖 *Vât* (ou *vā*). Creuser, faire une une ouverture. (Voir 挖 *vā*).

丨開, *vât k'oī*, ouvrir en creusant.

丨大, *vât t'aí*, agrandir en creusant.

丨心肝, *vât sīm kōn*, arracher le cœur. (Crime que l'on impute aux chrétiens).

丨眼珠仁, *vât niân tchoū ŷn*, arracher les yeux.

VÉ·

Vé· ou *yé·*. Semer à la volée.

丨菜仁, *vé· 's'oí ŷn*, semer à la volée des graines de légumes.

穢 *Vé·*. Sale, sordide.

Vé· sé·, sale, malpropretés.

VĪ

威 *Vī*. Gravité, majesté.

當不得天主個丨嚴, *tōng poŭt tĕt t'iēn tchòu ké· vī niâm*, ne pouvoir soutenir la majesté de Dieu.

咁丨嚴個人, *àn vī niâm ké· gnîn*, quel homme grave, sévère, sérieux !

委 *Vī*. Confier une affaire, déléguer.

丨員, *vī yân*, mandarin délégué.

打發丨員, *tà fât vī yân*, envoyer un délégué.

難丨人, 丨屈人, *nân vī gnîn, vī k'ioŭt gnîn*, opprimer quelqu'un.

丨丨曲曲個事, *vī vī k'ioût k'ioût ké· sé*, affaire très embrouillée.

VÎ

惟 *Vî*. Seulement.

丨有天主做得來個, *vî yoū t'iēn tchoù tsó tĕt loî ké·*, il n'y a que Dieu qui puisse le faire.

帷 *Vî*. Rideaux, toile, tenture disposée autour d'une table ou d'un autre objet.

窗 |, 桌 |, *ts'oūng vî, tsôc vî*, rideaux de fenêtres, devant de table.

祭臺 |, *tsí t'oî vî*, devant d'autel, antipendium.

爲 *Vî*. Etre, faire.

天主敎 | 正, *t'iēn tchoù káo vî tchín*, la religion catholique est la seule véritable.

好 | 難, *hào vî nân*, c'est bien difficile.

不 | 多, *poût vî tō*, il n'y a rien de trop.

我作 | 攪得子, *ngái tsôc vî kào têt tzè*, je croyais que c'était pour s'amuser (pour rire).

無所不 |, *voû sò poût vî*, il n'y a rien qu'il ne fasse.

遺 *Vî*. Abandonner, laisser à la postérité.

| 下背天主命, *vî hā p'oí t'iēn tchoù mín*... que nous a transmis (Adam) en violant les ordres de Dieu (catéchisme).

聖堂下個事我 | 兩個·先生管, *chín t'ông hā ké· sé ngaî vî leòng ké· sīn sāng kouòn*, j'ai laissé les affaires de la chapelle entre les mains de deux catéchistes.

| 下個祖業, *vî há ké· tzè niăp*, laissé en héritage.

圍 *Vî*. Entourer, bloquer.

週週 |, *tchoū tchoū vî*, tout autour.

賊刮佢 | 倒裡, *ts'ĕt poūn kî vî tào lê·*, les voleurs l'ont entouré.

| 墻, *vî siông*, mur d'enceinte, clôture.

違 *Vî*. Désobéir.

| 命, *vî mín*, désobéir.

陽奉陰 |, *yông foúng ȳm vî*, extérieurement faire mine d'obéir, et désobéir en cachette.

VÌ

緯 *Vì*. Franges, trame d'une étoffe.

| 帽, *vì máo*, ou 帽 |, *máo vì*, franges des chapeaux de cérémonie.

經 |, (ou | 線), *kīn vì* (ou *vì sièn*). trame d'une étoffe, lignes régulières.

慰 *Vì*. Consoler.

安 | 人家, *ōn vì gnîn kā*, consoler le prochain.

VÍ

未 *Ví*. Pas encore.

| 有天地, *ví yoū t'iēn t'í*, avant que le ciel et la terre ne fussent.

| 必, *ví pît*, c'est douteux, est-ce-que ? forme interrogative avec un sens négatif.

| 必有來, *ví pît yoū loî*, est-ce qu'il vient (dans le sens négatif) ?

位 *Ví*. Personne, dignité.

三 | 一體, *sām ví ȳt t'ì*, trois personnes en une seule substance.

一 | 天神, 一 | 聖人, *ȳt ví t'iēn*

chîn, ŷt ví chín gnîn, un Ange, un Saint.

來 裡 兩 | 客, *loî lè· lìong ví hâc*, il est arrivé deux hôtes.

地 | (ou | 分), *t'í ví (ou ví foún)*, condition, dignité.

各人個地 | 唔同, *kôc gnîn ké· t'í ví mĝ t'oûng*, la condition de chacun n'est pas la même.

爲 *Ví*. Pour, à cause de.

| 小事就相打, *ví siào sé ts'ioú siōng tà*, pour une bagatelle, les voilà qui se battent.

天主 | 何造人, *t'iēn tchoù ví hô ts'áo gnîn ?* pourquoi Dieu a-t-il créé l'homme ?

因 | 有病來唔得, *ŷn ví yoū p'iáng loî mĝ têt*, je ne puis venir, parce que je suis malade.

| 你方便, *ví gnî fōng p'ién*, c'est commode pour toi, pour ta commodité.

衛 *Ví*. Protéger, défendre.

麼一個人 | 護佢, *mô ŷt ké· gnîn ví foú kî*, pas un qui prenne sa défense.

侍 | *ché ví*, garde impériale.

胃 *Ví*. Estomac (vulg. 飯包 *fán pāo*).

噲翻 |, *voé· fān ví*, cela donne envie de vomir.

開 |, *k'oī ví*, appéritif.

| 口唔好, *ví k'eoù mĝ hào*, je n'ai pas d'appétit.

謂 *Ví*. Appeler, signifier.

何 | 全能, *hô ví ts'iên nên*, qu'appelle-t-on tout-puissant ?

樣 | 聖人, *nióng ví chín gnîn*, comment peut-on dire que c'est un saint ?

樣 | 善人, *nióng ví chán gnîn*, comment peut-on l'appeler homme de bien ?

十分無 |, *chĭp foūn voû ví*, tu n'as absolument rien à dire, tu ne peux donner aucune raison.

畏 *Ví* Craindre, avoir peur.

咁怕 | 個人, *àn p'á ví ké· gnîn*, quel homme peureux.

鬼都唔 | 個, *koùi toū mĝ ví ké·*, il n'a peur de rien, ce serait le diable que je n'aurais pas peur.

得人 |, *têt gnîn ví*, effrayant.

餵 *Ví* Nourrir les animaux (et aussi les enfants qui ne peuvent pas encore manger seuls).

| 猪, | 雞, | 馬, *ví tchōu, ví kē·, ví mā*, donner à manger au porc, aux poules, au cheval.

| 細人, *ví sé· gnîn*, faire manger l'enfant.

VŌ

窩 *Vō*. Ravin ; creux, concave ; repaire.

山 |, *sān vō*, ravin de montagne.

| | 子, *vō vō tzè*, en creux, concave.

| 家, *vō kā*, recéleur.

| 賊, | 娼, *vō ts'ĕt, vō tch'ōng*, repaire de brigands, maison de femmes publiques.

| 藏, *vō ts'ông*, recéler.

| 藏賊子, *vō ts'ông ts'ĕt tzé*, donner asile aux voleurs.

VÔ

禾 *Vô*. Riz en herbe.

丨容易噲出穀, *vô yoûng ý voé· tch'oût koŭc*, le riz va sous peu donner ses grains.

丨坪, *vô t'âng*, aire à sécher le riz.

丨 *pĩt*, moineau commun.

丨倉, *vô ts'ōng*, grenier à riz.

和 *Vô*. 丨尚, *vô chóng* (pour *fô chóng*), bonze.

VÒ

咊 *Vò*. Appeler, inviter, dire.

丨佢來, *vò kî loî*, appelle-le, dis-lui de venir.

丨神父來傅終由, *vò chîn foú loî foú tchoūng yoû*, inviter le Père à venir donner l'Extrême-Onction.

丨佢唔來, *vò kî mĝ loî*, je ne puis le faire venir.

丨佢作緊, *vò kî tsôc kìn*, dis-lui de se dépêcher.

VŎC

Vôc. Lancer (usité dans certains endroits).

丨石頭, *vôc chăc t'eôu*, lancer des pierres.

鍋 *Vŏc*. Poêle à frire.

丨頭, *vŏc t'eoû*, poêle à frire.

丨𥐻, *vŏc toŭc*, le fond de la poêle.

一口丨, *ŷt hcòu vŏc*, une poêle.

VOĒ·

煨 *Voē·*. Cuire sous la cendre.

丨薑, *voē· kiōng*, rôtir du gingembre sous la cendre.

VOÉ·

噲 *Voé·*. Habile à ; marque du futur.

曉都曉得唔多丨, pour savoir faire, je sais faire, mais je ne suis pas très habile.

邦個都丨做, *mâc ké· toū voé· tsó*, il sait tout faire.

我丨去, *ngâi voé· hí*, j'irai.

神父辰朝日丨來, *chîn foú chîn tchāo gnĭt voé· loî*, le Père viendra demain.

VŌNG

往 *Vōng*. Aller.

來丨, *loî vōng*, venir et aller ; fréquentation, relations suivies.

佢丨等兩家麼那個來丨, *kî tèn leòng kā mô mâc ké· loî vōng*, les deux familles n'ont pas de relations.

丨丨, *vōng vōng*, fréquemment.

丨年, 丨回, *vōng niăn*, *vōng fî*, les années précédentes, les autres fois.

丨日, 丨擺, *vōng gnĭt*, *vōng paì*, les jours passés, les autres fois.

你丨那裡去, *gnî vōng ngái lī hí ?* où vas-tu ?

VÔNG

皇 *Vông* (pour *fông*). Empereur.

教化丨, *káo fá vông*, l'empereur de la religion, c.-à-d. le Pape.

(Voir *fông*).

癀 *Vông (pour fông)*. | 疸, *vông t'án*, jaunisse.

王 *Vông*. Roi, prince.

三 | 來 朝, *sām vông loî tch'āo*, les trois Rois qui viennent adorer : Epiphanie.

| 爺, *vông yâ* (ou 親 |, *ts'īn vông*), titre des frères et des oncles de l'Empereur.

亡 *Vông* (ou *môug*). Mourir. S'emploie indifféremment comme *mông*. Voir ce mot).

黃 *Vông*. Jaune.

| 色, *vông sĕt*, couleur jaune.

穀 還 唔 |, *koŭc hân mĝ vông*, le riz n'est pas encore jaune (pas mûr).

上 咁 高 眼 噲 |, *chōng àn kāo niân voé vông*, on a le vertige (*litt.* on voit jaune) de monter si haut.

魚 子 翻 |, *nĝ tzè fān vông*, les poissons tournent au jaune (maladie des poissons d'étang, qui les portent à humer l'air à la surface de l'eau).

| 牛, *vông nioû*, bœuf commun.

| 鱔, *vông chān*, petite anguille de rizière.

大 |, *t'aí vông*, rhubarbe.

橫 *Vông* (pour *vâng*). Planchéier.

| 棚, *vông p'âng*, planchéier l'entresol.

| 棚 | 得 尾, *vông p'âng vông tĕt mī* c'est bien planchéié, les planches sont bien jointes.

磺 *Vông*. Soufre.

硫 |, *lioû vông*, soufre.

| 強 水, *vông kiòng choùi* pour *vông k'iông choùi*, acide sulfurique.

VÒNG

枉 *Vòng*. Mauvais, pas droit.

| 然, *vòng yân*, en vain, inutilement.

你 | 然 說 話, *gnî vòng yân chŏt fá*, c'est en vain que tu prêches.

冤 |, *yān vòng*, vexant, être opprimé.

冤 | 人, *yān vòng gnîn*, vexer quelqu'un, l'opprimer sans motif.

Voir le mot *nóng*.

妄 *Vòng*. A faux, à tort, mensonge.

| 証 人, *vòng tchín gnîn*, calomnier quelqu'un, prêter faux témoignage.

| 思 | 想, *vòng sé vòng siòng*, se laisser aller à de mauvaises pensées.

| 告 人 家, *vòng káo gnîn kā*, accuser autrui à tort.

VÓNG

望 *Vóng* (ou *móng*). Espérer, espérance.

信 | 愛, *sín vóng oí*, la foi, l'éspérance et la charité.

Ce mot s'emploie indifféremment comme *móng*.

旺 *Vóng*. Clair, beau.

興 |, *hīn vóng*, prospère, prospérer.

蜂 子 唔 興 |, *foūng tzè mĝ hīn vóng* les abeilles ne prospèrent pas, languissent.

血 | , *hiĕt vóng*, sang des animaux égorgés.

猪 | 子, *tchōu vóng tzè*, sang de porc.

咁健 | 個人, *àn k'ián vóng ké· gnîn*, quel homme robuste, bien portant.

VOŪ

毋 *Voū*. Ne pas, défense de.

| 殺人, | 偷盜, *voū săt gnîn, voū t'eoū t'áo*, défense de tuer son prochain, de voler.

烏 *Voū*. Noir, éteint.

| 色, *voū sĕt*, couleur noire.

| 蠅, *voū ŷn*, mouche commune.

| 蚊, *voū moūn*, petit moustique noir.

火 | 帛 裡, *fò voū p'ĕt lè·*, le feu s'est éteint.

燈子畀風吹 |, *tēn tzè poūn foung tch'oī voū*, le vent a éteint la lampe.

正音講得係 |, *tchín ŷm kòng tĕt é· voū*, il parle la langue mandarine bien clairement (noire, par opposition à l'expression :

客話講得係白, *hăc fá kòng tĕt é· p'ăc*, il parle la langue hacka bien (blanche) clairement .

汚 *Voū*. Dépravé, sordide.

| 穢, *voū vé·*, sordide, saletés, immondices.

講 | 言, *kòng voū niân*, dire des paroles dépravées, de sales mots.

| 辱婦人, *voū yoŭc foú gnîn*, violer une femme.

武 *Voū*. Militaire, vaillant.

| 官, *voū kouon*, mandarin militaire.

| 童生, *voū t'oūng sēn*, aspirant au baccalauréat ès armes.

| 秀才, | 舉, | 侍衛, *voū sióu ts'ôi, voū kì, voū ché ví*, bachelier, licencié, docteur ès armes.

好 | 藝個人, *hào voū gní ké· gnîn*, athlète, homme très versé dans le métier des armes.

VOÛ

無 *Voû*. Sans, nul, rien, aucun, manque.

| 始 | 終, *voû tchè voû tchoūng*, sans commencement ni fin, éternel.

| 所不在, *voû sò poût ts'ái*, nul endroit où il ne soit, partout.

| 所不爲, *voû sò poût vî*, il n'y a rien qu'il ne fasse, capable de tout.

| 形 | 像, *voû hîn voû sióng*, nul apparence ni figure, spirituel, immatériel.

| 別事, *voû piĕt sé*, nulle autre chose.

VOÙ

撫 *Voù* (ou *moù*). Entretenir, faire.

| 育, *voù yoŭc*, nourrir et élever.

| 一個細人, *voù ŷt ké· sé· gnîn*, adopter un enfant.

| 院 (ou | 臺), *voù yán* (ou *voùt 'ôi*), sous-gouverneur de province, préfet.

Voir *moù*.

VOÚ

務 *Voú*. S'appliquer à, affaire.

你做那個｜藝, *gnî tsó mâc ké· voú (* ou *moú) gnî,* à quoi t'occupes-tu ?

事｜, *sé voú,* affaire.

鹽｜, 敎｜, *yâm voú, káo voú,* affaires se rapportant au monopole du sel, à la religion.

幾百錢個事｜, *kì pâc ts'iên ké· sé voú,* c'est une affaire de quelques centaines de sapèques.

芋 *Voú.* Taro.

｜子, ｜頭, *voú tzè, voú t'eoû,* taro, tubercule du taro.

｜梡, *voú koūang,* tiges de taro, queue des feuilles.

VOÛC

屋 *Voûc.* Maison.

神父在｜下麼, *chîn foú ts'ōi voûc hā mô ?* le Père est-il à la maison ?

一間｜, *ŷt kiān voûc,* un compartiment de maison.

VOUI (Voir *Vi*)

VOŪN

溫 *Voūn.* Tiède, tempéré.

｜｜個水, *voūn voūn ké· choùi,* eau tiède.

｜和, *v.* ｜厚個人, *voūn fô v. voūn heoú ké· gnîn,* homme paisible, doux.

瘟 *Voūn.* Peste.

發｜死, *pôt voūn sì,* mourir de la peste.

VOÛN

文 *Voûn.* Littérature.

做｜章, *tsó voûn tchōng,* faire des compositions littéraires.

｜童生, *voûn t'oûng sēn,* aspirant au baccalauréat ès lettres.

｜書, *voûn chōu,* dépêche officielle.

搭｜書, *tâp voûn chōu,* envoyer une dépêche officielle.

天｜地理, *t'iēn voûn t'í lī,* l'astronomie et la géographie.

斯｜人, *sē voûn gnîn,* homme bien élevé, délicat, civil. Se dit aussi de la beauté du visage.

裡個婦人家咁斯｜, *ỳ ké· foú gnîn kā àn sē voûn,* cette femme est jolie, aux traits délicats.

一｜錢, *ŷt voûn ts'iên,* une sapèque.

汶 *Voûn.* Eau trouble.

水係｜, *choùi é· voûn,* l'eau est toute trouble.

炆 *Voûn.* Mitonner, cuire à petit feu.

｜豬肉, ｜牛肉, *voûn tchoū nioûc, voûn niôu nioûc,* cuire à petit feu du porc, du bœuf.

紋 *Voûn.* Linéaments des mains, veines des bois, des pierres.

手｜, *choù voûn,* linéaments des mains.

聞 *Voûn.* Entendre, percevoir.

新｜, *sīn voûn,* nouvelles, journaux.

新｜紙到裡, *sīn voûn tjè táo lī·,* les journaux sont arrivés.

耳不｜心不亂, *gnì poût voûn sīm*

poût lón, ce dont je n'entends pas parler ne me trouble pas le cœur.

風 | , foūng voún, la rumeur, on dit.

VOÙN

穩 Voùn. Ferme, solide stable.

釘 | tāng voùn, clouer solidement.

桌唔 | , tsôc mĝ voùn, la table n'est pas solide, stable.

裡個棍拿來手上直放你放得 | 麼, ỳ ké· koún nā loî choù hóng tch'ĭt fóng gnî fóng tĕt voùn mô ? pourrais-tu faire tenir ce bâton tout droit sur ta main ?

生理唔 | 當, siēn lî mĝ voùn tóng, le commerce n'est pas sûr.

你做事唔 | 當, gnî tsó sé mĝ voùn tóng, tu agis trop à la légère.

VOÚN

Voún Enfermer.

牛拿來 | 阿牛欄起, nioû nā loî voún á nioû lân hì, enferme le buffle dans l'écurie.

| 等裡走唔得, voún tèn ê· tseoù mĝ têt, il est enfermé et ne peut sortir.

汶 Voún. Se vautrer, se baigner (ne se dit que des animaux), barbouiller.

牽牛 | 水, k'iān nioû voún choùi, aller faire baigner le buffle.

猪泥鼓緊 | , tchōu naî tcoú kìn voún, le cochon se vautre tant qu'il peut dans la boue.

衫 | 倒裡泥, sām voún tào lê· naî, mon habit est tout souillé de boue.

VOŪNG

翁 Voūng. 老 | , lào voūng, nom qu'on donne par honneur aux vieillards.

老 | 還健麼, lào voūng àn k'ián mô venérable vieillard, votre santé est-elle bonne ?

VOÚNG

甕 Voúng. Grand vase à petite ouverture.

| 菜, voúng ts'oí, espèce de légume.

VOUÔN

渾 Vouôn (foûn). Entier, complet, tout.

| 下, vouôn há, tout, tout ce qui est là.

| 身都癢, vouôn chīn toū yōng, tout le corps me démange.

| 個都愛來, vouôn ké· toū oí loî, il faut que tous viennent.

VOUÒN

碗 Vouòn. Bol, tasse, écuelle.

食一 | 飯, chĭt ŷt vouòn fán, manger un bol de riz.

同我舀一 | 飯, t'oûng ngâi yào ŷt vouòn fán, remplis-moi un bol de riz.

洗 | 盤, sè· vouòn p'ân, laver la vaisselle.

撿 | , kiàm vouòn, ramasser les bols après le repas.

腕 Vouòn. | 子骨, vouòn tzè koût, rotule du genou.

脚子走 | , *kiôc tzè tsèòu vouòn*, avoir une entorse au pied.

VOUÓN

換 *Vouón*. Changer, troquer.

| 衫 褲 , *vouón sām foú*, changer d'habit.

| 毛 , *vouón māo*, changer de poils, muer.

| 水 土, *vouón choùi t'où*, changer de climat.

愛 | 過樣子來 , *oí vouón koúo yóng tzè loî*, il faut changer de manière, varier.

VOǓT

勿 *Voǔt*. Ne pas.

切 | 遲延 , *ts'iĕt voǔt tchê yân*, ne tardez pas (style relevé).

物 *Voǔt*. Chose, ustensile.

| 件 , *voǔt k'ián*, choses, matériel, affaires.

天 地 萬 | , *t'iēn t'í ván voǔt*, le ciel la terre et toutes choses.

貨 | , 財 | , *fó voǔt, ts'ôi voǔt*, marchandises, biens, richesses.

VOÛT

扐 *Voût*. Plier, courber, entorse.

| 樹子做靠倚 , *voût choú tzè tsó káo ỳ*, courber un bois pour faire un fauteuil.

愛拿火來燂焞 | 得轉 , *oí nā fò loî t'âm tsáng voût têt tchòn*, il faut le faire chauffer pour pouvoir le courber.

脚 | 倒裡 , *kiôc voût tào lē·*, je me suis tordu le pied, fait une entorse.

握 *Voût*. Ramasser à la pelle.

| 穀 , | 泥 , *voût koǔc, voût naî*, ramasser, puiser du riz avec un panier, une pelle ou autre chose.

NOMS DE BAPTÊME.

Voici une courte liste des noms de baptême les plus employés. Elle peut être utile au missionnaire qui, dans les premiers temps, se trouve souvent embarrassé, lorsqu'un chrétien lui apporte son fils à baptiser sous tel ou tel nom.

亞納	*A năp*	Anna
亞加大	*Ā kā t'aí*	Agatha
亞肋叔	*Ā lĭt choûc*	Alexius
亞肋山	*Ā lĭt sān*	Alexander
奧斯定	*Aó sē t'ín*	Augustinus
恩理格	*Ēn lī kĕt*	Henricus
歐瑟伯	*Eoú sît pâc*	Eusebius
斐理伯	*Fī lī pâc*	Philippus
斐理斯	*Fī lī sē*	Felix
方濟各	*Fōng tsí kôc*	Franciscus
福禮濟大	*Foûc lī tsí t'aí*	Felicitas
熱羅尼莫	*Gnĕt lô nî mŏc*	Hieronymus
依理亞	*Ÿ lī a*	Julia
儒畧	*Ý liŏc*	Julius
依肋奈	*Ȳ lĭt naí*	Irenæus
依納爵	*Ȳ năp tsiôc*	Ignatius
於爾新	*Ȳ nī sē*	Agnes
若翰	*Yŏc hón*	Joannes (Baptista)
若望	*Yŏc vóng*	Joannes Apostolus
若瑟	*Yŏc sît*	Joseph
盎博羅削	*Yóng pôc lô siôc*	Ambrosius
依撒伯爾	*Ȳ sât pâc nī*	Elisabeth
如斯定	*Ý sē t'ín*	Justinus
如斯弟納	*Ý sē t'í năp*	Justina

嘉辣	*Kă lăt*	Clara
加祿	*Kă loûc*	Carolus
嘉俾阨爾	*Kă pi âc nĭ*	Gabriel
加大利納	*Kă t'ai lí năp*	Catharina
老楞佐	*Laò lîn tsò*	Laurentius
辣法阨爾	*Lăt fâp âc nĭ*	Raphael
良	*Leông*	Leo
留納多	*Lioû năp tō*	Leonardus
羅撒	*Lô sât*	Rosa
路加	*Loú kă*	Luca
類斯	*Louí sĕ*	Aloyzius Gonzagæ
路濟亞	*Loú tsí a*	Lucia
瑪而弟納	*Ma ŷ t'í năp*	Martina
瑪加利大	*Ma ka lí t'aí*	Margarita
瑪利亞	*Ma lí ā*	Maria
瑪爾谷	*Mă nĭ koŭc*	Marcus
瑪達勒納	*Ma t'ăt lĭt năp*	Magdalena
瑪爾大	*Mă nī t'aí*	Martha
瑪爾定	*Mă nĭ t'ín*	Martinus
瑪竇	*Mā t'coú*	Matthæus
瑪弟亞	*Ma t'i a*	Mathias
默辣尼亞	*Mĕt lăt nî ă*	Melania
莫尼加	*Mŏc nî kă*	Monica
味增德	*Mí tsén tĕt*	Vincentius
雅各伯	*Ngă kôc pâc*	Jacobus
額我略	*Niăc ngō liŏc*	Gregorius
尼各老	*Nî kôc laò*	Nicolaus
彌額爾	*Nì niăc nĭ*	Michael
安德助	*Ōn têt lĭt*	Andreas
安當	*Ōn tōng*	Antonius
伯多祿	*Pâc lō loûc*	Petrus
巴爾納伯	*Pā nĭ năp pâc*	Barnaba
巴爾多祿茂	*Pă nĭ tō loûc miaó*	Bartholomœus
伯爾納鐸	*Pâc nĭ năp t'ŏc*	Bernardus
保辣	*Paò lăt*	Paula
保祿	*Paò loûc*	Paulus
巴西略	*Pă sī liŏc*	Basilius
彼理日大	*P'í lĭ gnĭt t'aí*	Birgitta

本大	*Poùn ta'í*	Benedicta
本篤	*Poùn toûc*	Benedictus
斯德望	*Sē tĕt vóng*	Stephanus
西滿	*Sī mān*	Simon
西默翁	*Tī mĕt voúng*	Simeon
西爾物斯得助	*Sī nī voŭt sē tĕt lĭt*	Silvester
達陡	*T'ăt teoù*	Thaddæus
德肋撒	*Têt lĭt sàn*	Teresia
多默	*Tō mĕt*	Thomas
多明我	*Tō mîn ngō*	Dominicus
多納前	*Tō năp ts'iên*	Donatianus et Rogatianus
羅加前	*Lô kā ts'iên*	
則濟理亞	*Tsêt tsí lī a*	Cæcilia
文多辣	*Voûn tō lăt*	Bonaventura

VOCABULAIRE

FRANÇAIS-CHINOIS

Pour apprendre la langue chinoise, un commençant ne doit jamais suivre le système de traduire des phrases françaises. Ce Vocabulaire n'est donc pas destiné à aider dans un tel travail; mais il doit servir soit à trouver une quantité de mots que l'on ne saurait où chercher dans le Dictionnaire même, soit à retenir des expressions déjà vues mais oubliées. Aussi ne donne-t-il pas la traduction complète en chinois, mais simplement le mot et le caractère à cherchér.

Il ne donne pas davantage les termes qui, en chinois, ne se peuvent rendre que par une périphrase, ceux qui expriment des idées générales et abstraites, enfin la plupart des mots composés ou dérivés. Il suffira, dans ces occasions, de recourir au mot simple ou au mot-racine, ou bien à un autre mot analogue, pour le sens, au mot désiré.

A, prép. Se sous-entend. Aller à la ville, 出州 *tch'oût tchoū,* 下州 *hā tchoū.* Il viendra à midi, 十二點鐘噲來 *chĭp gní tiàm tchoūng voé· loî.* || Marque du datif. 別 *poūn,* ou se sous-entend selon les circonstances. J'ai donné 100 piastres au mandarin, 我拿裡一百花邊別官府 *ngâi nā lê· ŷt pâc fā piēn poūn koūon foù.* Donne-moi ce livre, 裡本書拿別我 *ỳ* (ou *lì* ou *yà*) *poùn choū nā poūn ngâi.* Ce mouchoir est à moi, 裡個手巾係我個 *yà* (ou *ỳ* ou *lì*) *ké· choù kīn hé· ngā ké·.* || *Voir* dans, vers, jusqu'à, etc.

Abandonner. 捨 *chà, fĭt,* 丢 *tioū,* 唔愛 *mĝ oí (moé·),* 棄 *hí.*

Abaisser. *Voir* bas, baisser.

Abaque. 算盤 *són p'ân.*

Abattre. 倒 *taò,* 打轉 *tà tchón,* 拆 *ts'âc.*

Abcès. 瘡 *ts'ōng,* 腊 *tch'ôi.*

Abdiquer. 辭任 *tsê ým.*

Abeille. 蜂子 *foūng tzè.*

Abîmer. 打壞 *tà fái*, 裝爛 *tsōng lán*. = S'abîmer 沉落 *tch'îm lŏc*.

Abject. 下賤 *há ts'ién*, 鄙 *pè·* (ou *p'ì*), 卑 *pī*.

Abjurer. 反教 *fàn káo*, 棄絕 *hí ts'ĭĕt*.

Abolir. 除 *tch'oû*, 改 *kòi*, 消滅 *siāo mĕt*.

Abominable. 得人惱 *tĕt gnîn nào*.

Abondant. 多 *tō*, 盛 *chín*.

Abord (d'). 第一 *t'í ŷt*, 先 *siēn*. || *Voir* commencement.

Aborder. 兼岸 *kiām ngán*.

Aborigène. 本地人 *poùn t'í gnîn*.

Aboutir. 到 *taó*, 成 *cháng*.

Aboyer. 背 *p'ói*.

Abréger. — un récit, 畧畧講 *liŏc liŏc kòng*. || Concis, 簡 *kiàn*, 放短 *fóng tòn*, 少 *chào*.

Abreuver. — un buffle 牽牛食水 *k'iān niôu chĭt choùi*. || Imbiber, 淋濕 *lîm chĭp*. || S'—, 食水止渴 *chĭt choùi tjè hôt*.

Abriter. 遮 *tchā*, 抵 *tì* (ou *tài*), 蓋 *kói*.

Abrupt. 岐 *k'ī*.

Absenter (s'). 出門 *tch'oût moûn*.

Absolument. 一定 *ŷt t'ín*, 全 *ts'iên*, 十分 *chĭp foūn*.

Absorber, avaler. 食 *chĭt*, 吞 *t'oūn*. || S'—, 濟 *tsí*.

Absoudre. 赦罪 *chá ts'oúi*.

Abstenir (s'). Se traduit par une négation. || S'— de manger, 唔食 *mĝ chĭt*; — de travailler, 唔做事 *mĝ tsó ché·*.

Abstinence. 小齋 *siào tsāi*. || Jour d'—, 齋期 *tsāi k'î*.

Absurde. 唔合理 *mĝ hăp lī*.

Abuser. 枉用 *nóng yoúng*, 辜負 *k'oū foú*.

Académie. 翰林院 *hón lîm yán*.

Accablant. 難鼎 *nân tìn*.

Accabler. 壓 *tsâc* pour *âp*. || Importuner, 賴 *lái*.

Accaparer. 屯 *toùn* ou *t'oùn*, 霸 *pá*, 佔 *tchám*, 把 *pà*.

Accélérer. 趕快 *kòn k'ouái*.

Accent. 聲 *chāng*, 音 *ȳm*.

Accepter. 收 *choū*, 領 *leāng*, 接 *tsiâp*. || *Voir* consentir, répondre, recevoir.

Accessoires. 共下個 *k'ioúng há ké·*, 零碎 *lâng soúi*.

Accident. 患難 *fám nán*. || Par accident, 遇倒 *gní taò*, 撞倒 *ts'óng taò*.

Acclimater (s'). 合水色 (ou 水土) *kâp choùi sĕt* (ou *choùi t'où*).

Accommoder. 合意 *hăp ý*, 講和 *kòng fô*.

Accompagner. 同行 *t'oûng háng*, 同陣 *t'oûng tch'ín*, 帶 *tái*, 送 *soúng*.

Accomplir. 做完 *tsó vân*, 守 *choù*, 做成 *tsó tcháng*.

Accord. 合同 *hăp t'oûng*, 和氣 *fô hí*, 和約 *fô yôc*, 齊心 *ts'ê· sīm*.

Accorder. *Voir* permettre, accord.

Accoucher. 輕身 *k'iāng chīn*; *kioúng*.

Accoupler. 配 *p'í*, 對 *toúi*.

Accourcir (s'). 縮 *soûc*, 變短 *pién tòn*.

Accourir. 快來 *k'ouái lôi*.

Accoutumer. 習慣 *sĭp koúan*, 習學 *sĭp hŏc*, 做慣 *tsó koúan*, 教 *kāo*.

Accrocher. 挽 *vàn*, 吊 *tiáo*, 掛 *koúa*, 鈎 *keoū*.

Accroupi. 互倒 *koū taò*.

Accueillir. 答應 *tâp ýn*, 招呼 *tchāo foū*, 待 *t'ái*.

Accumuler. 堆 *tōi*, 加 *kā*, 屯 *toùn*, 積 *tsĭt*.

Accusation. 呈子 *tch'în tzè,* 案 *ón,* 狀 *ts'óng.*
Accuser. 告 *káo,* 稟 *pìn.*
Acerbe. 澁 *sêp,* 洽 *kiâp.*
Acéré. Qui est d'acier, 鋼做個 *kóng tsó ké·.* || Affilé, 鋒利 *foūng lí,* 尖 *tsiām.*
Acharner (s'). 緊做 *kìn tsó,* 趲勁 *tsán kín,* 盡力 *ts'ín lĭt.*
Acheter. 買 *mài;* — des grains 糴 *t'ác;* — du porc 割猪肉 *kôt tchoū nioûc;* — de la toile 剪布 *tsièn poú;* — de l'huile 打油 *tà yoû;* — du sucre 稱白糖 *tch'în p'ăc t'ōng;* — du charbon 吊炭 *tiáo t'án;* — des meubles 製家事 *tjé ka ché·.*
Acide. 酸 *sōn.*
Acier. 鋼 *kóng.*
Acquiescer. 遵 *tsoūn.*
Acquitter. *Voyez* payer, rendre, absoudre.
Âcre. 辣 *lăt,* 乜嘴個 *yà tchói ké·.*
Acte. *Voyez* action || Ecrit, 契 *k'é·,* 紙 *tjè,* 守 *sé.*
Actif, adj. 勤擒 *k'ioûn k'îm*; *săt mang.* || Subs. m. 來數 *loî sé.*
Action. 事 *sé,* 行實 *hàng chĭt.*
Actuel. 現下 *hién há,* 如今 *ŷ kīn.*
Adapter. 鬥 *teóu,* 對 *toúi,* 安 *ōn,* 合 *kâp, lâp.*
Additionner. 歸總 *koūi tsoùng.*
Adhérer. 黏 *niâm,* || Consentir, 願 *nián.*
Adieu. 暫別 *ts'iám p'iĕt.*
Adjacent. *Voyez* attenant.
Adjuger. 斷 *tón.*
Admettre. 領收 *leāng choū.* || Permettre, 準 *tchoùn,* 許 *hì.* || Croire 信 *sín.* || Reconnaître pour véritable, 認 *gnín,* 供 *kioūng.*
Administrer, régir. 管 *koùon,* 打理 *tà lī.* || Conférer, 付 *foú,* 傅 *foú;* — l'Eucharistie, 送聖體 *soúng chín t'ì;* — une médecine, 下藥 *hā yŏc,* 灌藥 *koúon yŏc.*
Admirable. 奇妙 *k'î miào,* 好妙 *haò miào.*
Adolescent. 後生 *heóu sāng,* 少年人 *chaò niân gnîn.*
Adonner (s'). 專務 *tchōn vóu,* 擅長 *chàn tch'ông,* 好 *háo.*
Adopter. — un fils, 揹細人 *nàm sé· gnîn.* || Choisir de préférence, 坐 *ts'ó.*
Adorer. 恭敬 *kioūng kín,* 欽崇 *k'īm ts'oūng,* 拜 *pái.*
Adosser. 凭 *pén,* 靠 *k'áo.*
Adoucir, rendre doux. 放甜 *fóng t'iâm.* || Rendre moins froid, 溫和 *voūn fô.* || Polir, 搓滑 *ts'ó văt.*
Adresse, adroit. 會 *voé·,* 巧 *k'aò,* 活 *făt.* || — d'une lettre, 信皮 *sín p'î,* 信封 *sín foūng.*
Adulte. 長成 *tchòng chîn,* 成人 *châng gnîn.*
Adultère. 姦 *kiān.*
Adversaire. 對頭 *toúi t'eôu.*
Aérer. 通風 *t'oūng foūng,* 通氣 *t'oūng hí.*
Affable. 好脾氣 *haò p'î hí,* 淳 *choûn.*
Affaiblir. *Voyez* faible.
Affaire. 事 *sé,* 事情 *sé ts'în,* 事務 *sé voú.*
Affaisser (s'). 坐下去 *ts'ō ha hí,* 屙 *ō.*
Affecter, faire à dessein. 故意 *koú ý,* 特事 *t'ĭt sé.* || Feindre, 詐 *tsá.* || Affliger, 心痛 *sīm t'oúng,* 憂愁 *yoū seōu.*

Affection. 愛情 *ói ts'în,* 心 *sīm.* || Maladie, 病 *p'iáng.*
Affermer. 寫 *sià,* 佃 *t'ién,* 租 *tzē.*
Affermir. *Voyez* solide.
Affiche. 帖 *t'iăp,* 報單 *páo tān.* || — officielle, 告示 *káo ché.*
Afficher. 貼 *tiăp,* 發榜 *fât pòng.*
Affiler. 磨利 *nô lí,* 磨尖 *nô tsiām.*
Affilier (s'). 入會 *gnĭp fí.*
Affinité. 外親 *ngoé· ts'īn.*
Affirmer. 講定 *kòng t'ín,* 眞眞係 *tchīn tchīn hé·.*
Affliger. 傷心 *chōng sīm.* || S'affliger, 憂愁 *yoū scoû,* 憂慮 *yoū lí.*
Affluer. 流下 *liôu hā,* 歸 *koūi,* 來得多 *loî têt tō.*
Affluent. 小河 *siào hô.*
Affolé. 攪惛 *kaò foūn.*
Affreux. 十分唔好看 *chĭp foūn mĝ haò k'ón,* 醜 *tch'où.*
Affront. 傷臉 *chōng liēn,* 得罪人 *têt ts'oúi gnîn,* 污辱 *voū yoŭc,* 凌辱 *lîn yoŭc.*
Affronter. 不怕 *poŭt p'á,* 去鬬 *hí teóu.*
Afin. 因爲 *ȳn ví.*
Agacer. 惹 *niā.*
Agate. 瑪瑙 *mā naò.*
Âge. 歲數 *sé· sé,* 年紀 *niân kì,* 庚 *kāng,* 壽 *choú,* 時候 *chê heóu.*
Agé, avancé en âge. 老 *laò,* 有年紀 *yoū niân kì.* || Plus — d'un an, 大一歲 *t'ái ȳt sé·;* moins — d'un an, 小一歲 *siào ȳt sé·.*
Agencer. *Voyez* ajuster, ranger.
Agenouiller (s'). 跪 *k'oùi.*
Agile. 活潑 *făt pât,* 輕快 *k'iāng k'ouái.* || *Voyez* actif.
Agir. 行 *hâng,* 爲 *vî,* 做 *tsó,* 作 *tsôc.*

Agiter. 搖 *yâo,* 動 *t'oūng,* 動 *t'oúng, tch'oŭc.*
Agneau. 羔羊 *kāo yông,* 細羊子 *sé· yông tzè.*
Agonie. 臨終 *lîm tchoūng.*
Agrafe. 鈎搭 *keōu tâp,*
Agrafer. 扣 *k'eóu,* 搭 *tâp.*
Agrandir. 做大 *tsó t'ái,* 整大 *tchàng t'ái.*
Agréable. 好 *haò,* 得人愛 *têt gnin oí,* 合意 *háp ý,* 中意 *tchoúng ý.*
Agréer, approuver. 准 *tchoùn.* || Plaire, 合意 *háp ý,* 歡喜 *fōn hì.*
Agreste, sauvage. 山 *sān,* || Grossier, 粗 *tsē.*
Agriculture. 耕種 *kāng tchoúng;* l'art de l'agriculture, 農學 *noûng hŏc.*
Aider. 相幫 *siōng pōng,* 幫助 *pōng tsé,* 幫手 *pōng choù.*
Aïeul. — paternel, 阿公 *ā koūng;* — maternel, 外阿公 *ngoé· ā koūng.*
Aïeule. — paternelle, 阿婆 *ā p'ô;* — maternelle 外婆 *ngoé· p'ô.*
Aigre. 酸 *sōn,* 餿 *seōu.*
Aigu. 尖 *tsiām.*
Aiguille. 針 *tchīm.*
Aiguiser. 磨利 *nô lí.*
Ail. 蒜 *són.*
Aile. 翼 *ȳt;* — d'une maison *lăt,* 橫屋 *vâng voŭc.*
Ailleurs. 別處 *p'iĕt tch'oú.* || D'ailleurs, 另外 *láng ngoé·,* 格外 *kēt ngoé·.*
Aimant. 吸鐵 *hiăp t'iĕt.*
Aimer. 愛 *oí,* 好 *háo,* 貪 *t'ām.*
Aîné. Frère aîné, 阿哥 *ā kō,* 大哥 *t'ái kō.* || Sœur aînée, 大姐 *t'ái tsì.* || Plus âgé, 過大 *koúo t'ái.*
Ainsi. 咁樣 *kàn yóng,* 故所以 *koú sò ȳ.* || *Voyez* comme.

Air, élément. 氣 *hí*. || Vent, 風 *foūng*. || Dans les airs, 天頂上 *t'iēn tàng hóng*. || *Voyez* manière.
Aire. 禾坪 *vô t'áng* (pour *p'iâng*), 坝子 *pá tzè*. || Surface plane, 面子 *mién tzè*.
Aisance, facilité. 容易 *yoûng ý*, 鬆用 *soūng yoúng*. || Fortune, 有財 *yoū ts'ôi*, 有錢 *yoū ts'iên*. || Lieux d'aisances, 便桶 *p'ién t'oùng*.
Aise. *Voyez* content.
Aisselle. 手腋下 *choù hiâp hā*.
Ajouter. 加 *kā*, 添 *t'iām*, 堆 *tōi*, 補 *poù*.
Ajuster. 鬥 *teóu*, 安 *ōn*, 合 *lâp*.
Alcool. 泌酒 *pît tsiòu*.
Alêne. 鑽子 *tsón tzè*.
Alentour. 週週圍 *tchoū tchoū vî*, 隣近 *lîn k'ioún*.
Alerte, vigilant. 勤擒 *k'ioûn k'îm*, 小心 *siào sīm*.
Aligner. 齊 *ts'ê*, 排 *p'âi*, 行 *hông*.
Aliment. *Voyez* nourriture.
Alité, 床上眠 *ts'ông hóng mîn*.
Allaiter. 供乳 *kioūng nén*.
Allée. 路道 *loú t'áo*, 巷子 *hóng tzè*.
Aller. 走 *tseòu*, 去 *hí*, 往 *vōng*, 到 *táo*. || Sur le point de, 將來 *tsiōng loî*, 噲 *voé*, 臨 *lîm*. || *Voyez* convenir, se porter.
Alliage. 銀水 *nioûn choùi*.
Alliance. 親 *ts'īn*.
Allumer. 點 *tiàm*. || S'—, 着火 *tch'ŏc fò*.
Allumette chimique. 自來火 *tsé loî fò*, 火柴 *fò ts'âi*. || — de papier, 紙煤 *tjè moē*.
Alors. 就 *ts'ioú*, 單 *tān*, 晔 *tsáng*.
Alphabet. 字母 *sé moū*.
Altérer. 假 *kà*, 變 *pién*, 壞 *fái*, 害 *hói*. || *Voyez* soif.
Alterner. 換 *voúon*, 一回一回 *ŷt fî ŷt fî*, 一轉一轉 *ŷt tchòn ŷt tchòn*.
Alun. 白礬 *p'ăc fân*.
Amande. 仁 *ŷn*.
Amarrer. 綯 *t'âo*.
Amasser. 積 *tsît*, 堆 *tōi*, 屯 *toùn*.
Ambassadeur. 欽差 *k'īm ts'āi*.
Ambition. 貪心 *t'ām sīm*, 圖 *t'oû*.
Âme. 靈魂 *lîn foûn*.
Amende. 罰 *făt*. || — honorable, 認錯 *gnín ts'ôc*, 悔釋 *fí chît*.
Amener. 牽 *k'iān*, 帶 *tái*, 引 *ŷn*, 送 *soúng*, 解 *kiái*, 拿 *nā*.
Amer. 苦 *foù*.
Ameuter (s'). 鬧 *naó*, 作亂 *tsôc lón*, 造反 *ts'áo fàn*.
Ami. 朋友 *p'oûng yoū*, 相好 *siōng haò*, 熟 *choŭc*.
Amiable, s'arranger à l'—, 講和 *kòng fô*.
Amict. 盖頭布 *kói t'eôu poú*.
Amincir. 削薄 *siôc p'ŏc*.
Amnistie. 皇恩大赦 *vông ēn t'ái chá*.
Amollir. 放軟 *fóng niōn*.
Amonceler. 堆 *tōi*.
Amour. 愛情 *ói ts'în*.
Ample. 寬闊 *k'ōn fât*, 太 *t'ái*.
Ampoule. 皰 *p'iáo*.
Amuser (s'). 嫽 *liáo*, 攪 *kaò*, 笑 *siáo*.
An, année. 年 *niân*, 歲 *sé*.
Anarchie. 亂 *lón*.
Ancêtres. 祖公 *tzè koūng*, 祖宗 *tzè tsoūng*, 先人 *siēn gnîn*.
Ancien. 古 *koù*, 老 *laò*, 舊 *k'ióu*, 在前 *ts'ái ts'iên*.
Ancre. 鈎錨 *keoū nâo*.

Âne. 驢子 *lî tzè.*
Anéantir. 消滅 *siāo mĕt,* 收 *choū.*
Ange. 天神 *t'iēn chîn.*
Angelus. 三鍾經 *sām tchoūng kīn.*
Angle. 角 *kôc.*
Angoisse. 艱難 *kiān nân,* 憂慮 *yoû lí.*
Anguille. 黃鱔 *vông chān,* 白鱔 *p'ăc chān.*
Animal. 禽獸 *k'îm tch'óu,* 頭生 *t'eôu sāng.*
Animer. 勸 *k'ián. Voyez* exciter.
Anis. 茴香 *fî hiōng,* 小茴 *siào fî.*
Annales. 綱鑑 *kōng kám,* 綱紀 *kōng kì.*
Anneau. 圈 *k'iān,* 戒指 *kiái tjè.*
Anniversaire. 滿年 *mān niân;* — de naissance, 生日 *sāng gnĭt.*
Annoncer. 報信 *páo sín.* || *Voyez* avertir, prédire.
Annuler. *Voyez* abolir.
Anse. 耳 *gnì;* — à porter les bagages, 落脚 *lŏc kiôc.*
Antérieur. 前 *ts'iên,* 先 *siēn,* 頭上 *t'eôu hóng,* 上早 *chóng tsào.*
Anthracite. 石炭 *chăc t'án.*
Antidote. 解毒 *kiái t'oŭc.*
Antipendium. 桌帷 *tsôc vî;* — d'autel 祭臺帷 *tsí t'ôi vî.*
Antre. 石岩 *chăc ngâm,* 洞 *t'oúng.*
Anus. 屎窟 *chè foût; chè nâng koūng.*
Anxieux. *Voyez* inquiet.
Apaiser. 平 *p'în,* 息 *sĭt.* || —la douleur, 止痛 *tjè toúng;* — la soif, 止渴 *tjè hôt.*
Apercevoir. *Voyer* voir.
Aplanir. 裝坪 *tsōng p'iâng.*
Aplatir. 扁 *pièn,* 坪 *p'iâng.*
Apostasier. 反教 *fàn káo,* 背天主 *p'ói t'iēn tchoù.*
Apostiller. 批 *p'ī.*
Apôtre. 宗徒 *tsoūng t'oû.*
Apparaître. 發顯 *fât hièn,* 顯出來 *hièn tch'oût loî.*
Apparat. 排塲 *p'âi tch'ông,* 體面 *t'ì mién.*
Appareiller. 配 *p'í,* 對 *toúi.* || Mettre à la voile, 開船 *k'ōi chôn.*
Apparence. 樣子 *yóng tzè,* 形像 *hîn sióng.*
Apparent. 現 *hién,* 清楚 *ts'īn tsè,* 明白 *mîn p'ăc.*
Appartement. 間房 *kiān fông,* 屋 *voŭc.*
Appartenir. Cela m'appartient, 係我個 *hé· ngā ké·.* || Etre l'affaire, le devoir de, 係我事 *hé· ngā sé,* 我管個事 *ngâi kouòn ké· sé.* || Faire partie de, 做 *tsó,* 屬 *choŭc,* 歸 *koūi.*
Appauvrir. 窮帛裡 *k'ioûng p'ĕt lé·. Voyez* pauvre, ruiner.
Appeau. 媒子 *moê· tzè,* 嘹鵰個 *leoú tiāo ké·.*
Appeler. 喊 *hám,* 稱 *tch'īn,* 招呼 *tchāo foū.*
Appétissant. 合口味 *hăp k'eòu mí,* 開胃 *k'ōi ví.*
Appétit. Avoir bon—, 想食 *siòng chĭt.* || — sensuel 私欲偏情 *sē yoŭc p'iēn ts'în.*
Applaudir. 拍手 *p'ôc choù.* || *Voyez* louer.
Appliquer. 放 *fóng,* 貼 *tiâp.* || S'appliquer, 用心 *yoúng sīm,* 專心 *tchōn sīm.*
Appointements. — d'un mandarin, 俸祿 *foúng loŭc;* — d'un maître d'école, 束修 *tch'oŭc siōu.* || *Voyez* salaire.
Apporter. 拿來 *nā loî,* 擒 *tōn,* 帶 *tái.*
Apposer. — un sceau, 打印 *tà ýn;* — sa signature, 畫號 *fá haó.*

Apprécier. *Voyez* estimer.
Apprendre. 學 *hŏc*, 讀 *t'oŭc*. ‖ Entendre dire, 聽知 *t'ăng tī*. ‖ *Voyez* enseigner.
Apprenti. 徒弟 *t'oû t'í*; 新手 *sīn choù*.
Apprêter. 安 *ōn*, 布置 *poú tjé*; — les aliments 煮菜 *tchoù ts'oí*. ‖ S'apprêter, 預備 *ý p'í*.
Approcher, v. a. 拿前 *nā ts'iên*, 端前 *tōn ts'iên*. ‖ V. n. 近 *k'ioún*, 臨 *lîm*; la nuit approche, 𠊎夜 *voé· yá*. ‖ Peu différent, 差不多 *ts'ā poût tō*.
Approuver. 准 *tchoùn*, 許 *hì*.
Appui, support. 撐 *ts'áng*. ‖ Aide, 帮手 *pōng choù*, 扶 *p'oû*.
Appuyer, soutenir. 撐 *ts'áng*. ‖ *Voyez* appui. ‖ Peser, v. n. 擒 *k'îm*, 壓 *tsăc*.
Âpre. 洽 *kiăp*. ‖ Rude, raboteux, 唔坪 *mĝ p'iâng*, 粗 *tsē*.
Après, prép. 後 *heóu*. ‖ L'un — l'autre, 一個一個來 *ŷt ké· ŷt ké· loî*. ‖ — tout, 總係 *tsoùng hé·*, 都係 *toū hé·*. ‖ *Voyez* derrière, dessous, selon. ‖ — adv. 過後 *koúo heoú*, 以後 *ȳ heoú*, 後來 *heoú loî*; huit jours —, 過八日 *koúo pât gnĭt*, 八日後 *pât gnĭt heoú*; peu —, 後麼幾久 *heoú mô kì kioù*.
Apte. 𠊎 *voé·*, 合式 *hăp chĭt*.
Aqueduc. 水筧 *choùi kiàn*.
Arachide. 番豆 *fān t'eóu*.
Araignée. *Lâ k'iâ*.
Arbitraire. 自擅 *tsé chàn*, 隨意 *soûi ý*.
Arbitre. 中間人 *tchoūng kiān gnîn*. ‖ Libre —, 主張 *tchoù tchòng*, 自主 *tsé tchoù*.
Arbre. 樹 *choú*.
Arc. 弓 *kioūng*, 彎 *vân*.
Arc de triomphe. 牌坊 *p'aî fōng*.
Arc-en-ciel. 天弓 *t'iēn kioūng*.
Archange. 大天神 *t'ái t'iēn chîn*.
Arche. — d'un pont. 橋弓 *k'iâo kioūng*. ‖ Arche d'aillance, 結約之櫃 *kiĕt yŏc tjē k'oúi*.
Archives. — d'un tribunal, 案卷 *ón k'iàn*.
Arçonner. 彈 *t'ân*.
Ardent, chauffé au rouge. 燒紅個 *chaō foûng ké·*. ‖ Chaud, 熱 *gnĕt*, 滾 *koùn*. ‖ Caractère —, 急性 *kĭp sín*. ‖ Fervent, 熱心 *gnĕt sīm*.
Arec. Noix d'—, 檳榔 *pīn lông*.
Arête, os de poisson. 魚骨 *nĝ koût*. ‖ Angle saillant, 角 *kŏc*.
Argent. 銀 *nioûn*. ‖ — comptant, 現錢 *hién ts'iên*.
Argile. 黃泥 *vông nâi*.
Arithmétique. 算學 *són hŏc*.
Arme. 軍器 *kioūn hí*.
Armée. *Voyez* soldat.
Armoire. 櫃子 *k'oúi tzè*.
Arpent. 畝 *meoū*.
Arpenter. 量地方 *leông t'i fōng*.
Arracher. 扯 *tch'à*, 掹 *pāng*, 取 *ts'ì*, 脫 *t'ŏt*.
Arranger. 安排 *ōn p'âi*, 補置 *poù tjé*, 修 *sioū*.
Arrêter, empêcher. 攔 *lân*. ‖ Faire cesser, 止 *tjè*, 停 *t'în*. ‖ — des voleurs, 捉賊 *tsŏc ts'ĕt*. ‖ S'—, 停脚 *t'în kiŏc*.
Arrhes. 定頭 *t'ín t'eoû*.
Arrière (en). 屎背尾 *chè poé· mī*, 後背 *heóu poé·*. ‖ Faire un pas en —, 退一步 *t'oúi ŷt p'oú*.
Arrière-neveu (lignée masculine), 姪

孫 *tch'ĭt soūn;* arrière-nièce, 姪孫女 *tch'ĭt soūn ng̀.*

Arrière-petit-fils (lignée masculine) 虱子 *sēt tzè;* arrière-petite-fille, 虱女 (ou 虱媽) *sēt ng̀* (ou *sēt mâ*, pop.).

Arriver. 到 *taó; lioūng.* ‖ — à temps, 赴 *foú,* 趕 *kòn.* ‖ Survenir, 遇 *gní.*

Arroser. 淋 *lîm,* 飲 *ým,* 噴水 *p'oún choùi,* 㕽水 *foú choùi,* 潑水 *p'ât choùi.*

Arsenic. 砒霜 *p'aī sōng,* 信石 *sín chăc.*

Art. 法則 *fāp tsēt,* 憑則 *p'în tsēt.* ‖ Métier, 手藝 *choù gní.*

Artère. 血筋 *hiēt kīn.*

Article. un —, 一節 *ŷt tsiēt,* 一欵 *ŷt k'ouàn.* ‖ Objet, 一件 *ŷt k'ián.* ‖ — de foi, 一端 *ŷt tōn.*

Articulations (les). 骨節 *koūt tsiēt.*

Articuler. 念明白 *niám mîn p'ăc.*

Artifice. 術 *choūt,* 計 *ké',* 巧 *k'aò.* ‖ Feu d'—, 花筒 *fā t'oūng.*

Artisan. 工人 *koūng gnîn,* 師傅 *sē foú,* 做手藝個 *tsó choù gní ké'.*

Ascendants. 上輩 *chóng pí,* 老輩 *laò pí.*

Ascension. — de J. C. 耶穌升天 *yâ sē chīn t'iēn.*

Ascète. 修道人 *sioū t'aó gnîn.*

Asie. 亞西亞洲 *ā-sī-ā tchoū.*

Asile. — pour les vieillards, 孤老院 *koū laò yán;* — pour les enfants trouvés, 嬰孩堂 *ŷn haî t'ông.* ‖ Refuge, 避處 *p'ĭt tch'oú.*

Aspect, apparence 樣式 *yóng chĭt.* ‖ Visage, 臉面 *liēn mién.*

Asperger. 洒水 *chà choùi,* 潑水 *pât choùi.*

Aspersoir. 洒聖水刷 *chà chín choùi sōt.*

Aspirer, attirer l'air dans les poumons, 咄氣 *tsŏt hí.* ‖ Désirer, 貪 *t'ām.*

Assaisonner. 放香料 *fóng hiōng liáo.*

Assassin. 殺人個 *săt gnîn ké'.*

Assemblée. 會 *fí,* 大家 *t'ái kā,* 衆人 *tchoúng gnîn.*

Assembler. 聚做 *ts'í ts'ioū,* 連 *liên.* ‖ *Voir* réunir.

Asseoir (s') 坐 *ts'ō.*

Assez. 彀 *keóu.*

Assiéger. 圍 *vî,* 攻 *koūng.*

Assiette. 盤子 *p'ân tzè.*

Assise, par assises. 一層一層個 *ŷt ts'ên ŷt ts'ên ké.*

Assister, être présent. 在 *ts'ái;* — à la Messe, 聽彌撒 *t'āng nī sât.* ‖ — à la comédie, 看戲 *k'ón hí.* ‖ *Voyez* soigner, aider.

Associé. 夥計 *fô kí,* 同辦 *t'oûng p'án.*

Associer (s'). 打夥 *tà fô,* 做會 *tsó fí,* 縢會 *t'ên fí.*

Assommer. 打死 *tà sì.*

Assomption, fête de l'—, 聖母升天 *chín moū chīn ch'ēn.*

Assoupi. 半睡半醒 *pán choé' pán siàng.*

Assouvir. — la faim, 食飽 *chĭt paò;* — la soif, 止渴 *tjè hôt,* — sa passion, 滿意 *mān ý.*

Assurer, garantir. 保 *paò,* 躭認 *tām gnín.* ‖ *Voir* affirmer.

Assurer (s'), se garantir. 防備 *fông p'í.* ‖ Examiner, 查 *ts'â.*

Asthme. *Hāp.*

Astringent. 澁 *sēp.*

Astronomie. 天文 *t'iēn voûn.*

Attacher. *Voyez* coller, clouer, lier, aimer.

Attaquer. 下手 *hâ choù,* 攻 *koūng,* 惹 *niâ.*

Atteindre. 挨 *āi*, 摸得倒 *mō têt taò*, 打倒 *tà taò*. || Attraper en chemin, 趕倒 *kòn taò*.

Attendre. 等 *tèn*. || *Voyez* prévoir, espérer.

Attention. 小心 *siào sīm*, 專心 *tchōn sīm*. || Ne pas faire — à quelqu'un, 唔睬人 *mĝ ts'òi gnîn*.

Attirer. — de force, 攋 *lāi*; — par artifice, 摟 *leoú*, 呵 *hō*, 勾引 *keōu ȳn*. || — des malheurs, 惹禍 *niā fó*.

Attraper. 捉 *tsôc*. || Etre attrapé, 上當 *chōng tóng*.

Attribuer. 歸 *koūi*. || Imputer, 怪 *kouái*, 嗷 *aō*.

Aubaine. 財喜 *ts'ôi hì*.

Aube. — du jour, 天光 *t'iēn kouōng*. || — pour la Messe, 長白衣 *tch'ông p'ăc ȳ*.

Aubergine. 茄 *k'iô*, 吊菜 *tiáo ts'ói*.

Aucun, nul. N'être d'aucun usage, 麼用個 *mô yoúng ké·*. || Pas un; il n'y en a pas un, 一個都麼 *ȳt ké· tōu mô*.

Audace. 胆子 *tàm tzè*.

Audience. Avoir une — particulière, 相見 *siōng kián*, 相會 *siōng fí*. || Tribunal; tenir —, 坐堂 *ts'ō t'ông*.

Auge. 兜 *teōu*, 盆 *p'oûn*.

Augmenter. 加增 *kā tsén*, 多 *tō*, 大 *t'ái*. *Voyez* ajouter.

Augure. 兆頭 *chaó t'cóu*.

Aujourd'hui. 今日 *kīn gnĭt*, 今朝 *kīn tchaō*. || A présent, 如今 *ŷ kīn*, 現下 *hién há*.

Aumône. 哀矜 *oī k'īm*, 賑濟 *tchìn tsí*.

Auparavant. 先 *siēn*, 前 *ts'iên*, 預先 *ý siēn*.

Auprès. 近 *k'ioún*. || *Voyez* chez, vers, avec.

Aussi, de même. 都 *toū*, 也 *yā*. || C'est pourquoi, 故所以 *koú sò ȳ*. || Autant, 一樣 *ȳt yóng*, 一般 *ȳt pān*; pas aussi grand, 麼咁大 *mô kàn t'ái*; dix fois plus grand, 大十分 *t'ái chĭp foūn*.

Aussitôt. 就 *ts'ióu*, 當時 *tōng chê*, 卽刻 *tsĭt k'ĕt*.

Austérités. Pratiquer des —, 克苦肉身 *k'ĕt k'où nioŭc chīn*.

Autant. 咁多 *àn tō*. *Voyez* aussi.

Autel. 祭臺 *tsí t'ôi*; (païen) 香机 *hiōng kī*.

Automne. 秋 *ts'iōu*.

Autoriser. 准 *tchoùn*, 許 *hì*.

Autorité. 權 *k'iân*; être sous l'— de quelqu'un, 在人名下 *ts'ái gnîn miâng hā*.

Autour. 週圍 *tchoū vî*, 圍近 *t'ôn k'ioún* 四面 *sí mién*.

Autre. 別個 *p'iĕt ké·*, 唔同樣 *mĝ t'oûng yóng*. || L'un.... l'autre, 裡個 *ý ké·*.... 個個 *ké· ké·*. || Les autres (en dehors de ceux dont il vient d'être parlé), 餘 v. 另外 *ý* v. *láng ngoé·*.

Autrefois. 在前 *ts'ái ts'iên*, 從前 *ts'ioûng ts'iên*, 往擺 *vōng pài*.

Autrement. 別樣 *p'iĕt yóng*.

Autrui. 別人 *p'iĕt gnîn*, 人家 *gnîn kā*.

Avaler. 吞 *t'oūn*.

Avance (d'). 預先 *ý siēn*, 早 *tsào*.

Avancement. 高陞 *kaō chīn*.

Avancer. — la main, 伸手 *tch'oūn choù*. || — l'heure du repas, 早點食飯 *tsaò tiàm chĭt fán*. || — de l'ar-

gent, 賒 *tch'ā*. || Aller en avant, 行前去 *hâng ts'iên hí*. || L'horloge avance, 鍾子忒快 *tchoūng tzè t'iĕt k'ouái*. || Faire saillie, 走出 *tseoù tch'oût*.
Avant (d'une barque), 船頭 *chôn t'eôu*.
Avant, adv. et prép. 以前 *ỳ ts'iên*, 先 *siēn*, 早 *tsaò*. || — un an, 等唔倒一年 *tèn mĝ taò ŷt niân*. || — tout, 弟一 *t'í ŷt*.
Avantage. 利益 *lí ŷt*, 好處 *haò tch'oú*.
Avare. 慳悋 *kiān nín*, 嗇 *sép*.
Avec. 同 *t'oûng*, 㧯 *laō*, 連 *liên*. || Par le moyen, 用 *yoúng*, 使 *sè*.
Avenir. 將來 *tsiōng lôi*, 後來 *heoú lôi*.
Aventure. 遇 *gní*, 撞 *ts'óng*.
Aversion. 唔愛 *mĝ oí*, 得人惱 *tĕt gnîn naō*, 見唔得個 *kián mĝ tĕt ké*.
Avertir. 話知 *vá tī*, 報 *paó*, 禀 *pìn*, 告 *kaó*, 學 *hŏc*.
Aveugle. 瞎 *hât*, 瞙目 *mô moŭc*.
Avis, opinion, 意思 *ý sé*. || Donner des —, 敎 *kaō*, 勸 *k'ián*. || Nouvelle, 信 *sín*. || — officiel, 告示 *kaó ché*.
Aviser. 打主意 *tà tchoù ý*, 嘩算 *fâ són*.
Avoir, v. a. 有 *yoū*.
Avoir, patrimoine, 家業 *kā niăp*, 身家 *chīn kā*. || Richesses, 財帛 *ts'ôi p'ĕt*.
Avorter. 跌子 *tiĕt tzè*, 落胎 *lŏc t'ōi*.
Avouer. 認 *gnín*, 承認 *chîn gnín*, 親口講 *ts'īn k'eoù kòng*.

B

Bac. 渡船 *t'oú chôn*.
Bachelier. 秀才 *sioú ts'oî*.
Badigeonner. 刷 *sōt*, 糊 *foû*.
Bagage. 行李 *hâng lì*, 東西 *toūng sī*.
Bagatelle. 小事 *siào sé*, 小東西 *siào toūng sī*.
Baguette. — de bambou, 竹𥯨 *tchoŭc tsīn*; tige de fer, 鐵𥯨 *t'iĕt tsīn*.
Baie. 海灣 *hoì vân*.
Baigner. 浸 *tsím*. || Se baigner, 洗身 *sè chīn*.
Baiser. 親嘴 *tsīm tchói*; — le Crucifix, 親苦像 *tsīm k'où siông*.
Baisser, v. a. — un peu, 放矮一的 *fóng ài ŷt tīt*, 放下 *fóng hā*. || — la tête, 啱頭 *ngàm t'eoû*. || V. n. — de prix, 跌價 *tiĕt ká*. || L'eau du fleuve a baissé, 河水退了 *hô choùi t'oúi liaò*. || Se baisser, 𠐴起 *koū (ou poū) hì*.
Balai. 掃把 *saó pà*.
Balance. — à deux plateaux, 平 *p'în*; — romaine, 秤 *tch'ín*, 戥子 *tèn tzè*.
Balancer. 搖 *yaô*, 擺 *pài*. || Se —, 打重重 *tà tch'oûng tch'oûng*.
Balayer. 掃地 *saó t'í*.
Balle. — de fusil, 鉛彈 *yân t'án*. || — à jouer, 毬 *k'ioû*. || Paquet, 包 *paō*.
Ballon. 孔明燈 *k'oùng mîn tēn*.
Ballotter. 搖 *yaô*, 𢱢 *tch'oŭc*.
Balsamine. 手指甲花 *choù tjè kâp fā*.
Balustrade. 欄杆 *lân kōn*.
Bambou. 竹頭 *tchoŭc t'eoû*; jeune pousse de —, 竹笋 *tchoŭc soùn*; lanière de bambou, 竹篾 *tchoŭc mĭt*.
Bananier. 芎蕉樹 *kioūng tsiaō choú*.
Banc. 凳 *tén*.
Bande. 帶 *tái*; — de cuir, 牛皮帶(ou 條) *nioû p'î tái (ou t'iaô)*. || Troupe, 陣 *tch'ín*, 羣 *k'ioûn*.
Bander. 纏 *ts'ân*, 包 *paō*. || Tendre avec effort, 㩧緊 *pāng hèn*.

Bannière. 旗 *k'î.*
Banque. 銀行 *nioûn hông.*
Baptême. 浸洗 *chín sè·.* || Baptiser, 付洗 *foú sè·.* || Etre baptisé, 領洗 *leāng sè·.*
Baquet. 盆 *p'oûn.*
Baraque. 篷 *p'oûng,* 寮 *liaô.*
Barbe. 鬚 *sī.*
Barbier. 剃頭師傅 *t'í t'eoû sē foú.*
Barbouiller. 搽 *ts'â,* 刷 *sôt,* 糊 *foû.*
Baril. 桶 *t'oùng.*
Baromètre. 風雨錶 *foūng ỳ piāo.*
Barque. 船 *chôn.*
Barrage. 坡頭 *pī t'eoû.*
Barre. 棍 *koún;* — de fer, 鐵棍 *t'iĕt koún,* 鐵條 *t'iĕt t'iaô.* || — de porte, 門扛 *moûn kōng.* || Trait de pinceau, 一畫 *ŷt văc.*
Barrer. — la porte, 閂門 *ts'ōn moûn.* || *Voyez* empêcher, intercepter, effacer.
Barrière. 栅 *ts'ăc.* || *Voyez* balustrade.
Bas. 矮 *aì,* 下 *há,* 淺 *ts'ièn,* 底 *taì,* 小 *siào,* 賤 *ts'ién.*
Bas (vêtement). 襪 *măt.*
Bassin. 盆 *p'oûn,* 盤 *p'ân,* 池 *tchê.*
Bât. 鞍 *ōn.*
Bataille. 仗 *tchóng.*
Bâtir. 結 *kiĕt,* 修 *siōu,* 做 *tsó,* 砌 *tché·.*
Bâton. 棍 *koún,* 杖 *tch'òng.*
Bâtonnet. — dont on se sert pour manger, 筷子 *k'ouái tzè.* || Jeton, 籤 *ts'iām.*
Battant. — de porte, 門扇 *moûn chán.*
Batterie. — de cuisine, 廚房個傢伙 *tch'oû fông ké· kā fò.*
Battre. 打 *tà.* || Etre battu, 俾人打 *p'í (ou poūn) gnîn tà.* || Le cœur bat, 心拍拍跳 *sīm p'ôc p'ôc piaō.* || Se battre (en bataille), 打仗 *tà tchóng.* || Se quereller, 相打 *siōng tà,* 鬥 *teóu.*
Bazar. 雜貨舖 *ts'áp fó p'oú.*
Béatitude. 眞福 *tchīn foûc.*
Beau. 好看 *haò k'ón,* 排長 *p'aî tch'ông.*
Beaucoup. 多 *tō.*
Beau-frère, mari d'une sœur, 姊丈 *tsì tch'óng.* || Frère de la femme, ou du mari, 阿伯 *ā pâc* (s'il est plus âgé), 阿叔 *ā choûc* (s'il est moins âgé, cadet).
Beau-père, père de la femme, 丈人老 *tch'óng gnîn laò,* 岳父 *ngŏc foú.* || Second mari de la mère, 繼父 *kí foú.*
Bec. 嘴 *tsoùi.* || Pointe, 尖 *tsiām.*
Becqueter. 啄 *toûc.*
Bélier. 羊牯 *yông koù.*
Belle-mère, mère de la femme, 丈人婆 *tch'óng gnîn p'ô,* 家娘 *kā niông,* 岳母 *ngŏc moū.* || Marâtre, 繼母 *kí moū.*
Belle-sœur, sœur aînée du mari, 阿姐 *ā tsià;* sœur cadette, 阿姑 *ā koū.* || Femme d'un frère (aîné), 大嫂 *t'ái saò.* S'ils sont plusieurs frères on dira, 二嫂, 三嫂 *gní saò, sām saò.*
Belvédère. 亭子 *t'in tzè,* 樓 *leoû.*
Bénin, doux. 良善 *leông chán,* 淳 *choûn.*
Bénir. 降福 *kóng foûc.* || *Voyez* consacrer.
Berge. 坎 *k'ám.*
Berger. 掌羊子個 *tchòng yông tzè ké·.*
Besace. 馬胥 *mā saō.*
Besoin. 缺 *k'iĕt,* 欠 *k'iám,* 愛 *oí,* 要緊 *yaó kìn.* || Pas — de, 唔使 *mĝ sè,* 唔愛 *mĝ oí.*
Beurre. 牛乳油 *nioû nén yoû.*

Biais (de). 斜起 *siâ hì.*
Bible. 聖經 *chín kīn.*
Bibliothéque. 書架 *chouō ká,* 書櫃子 *chouō k'oúi tzè.*
Bien. 好 *haò.* || *Voyez* qualité, plaisir, très, beaucoup.
Bienfait. 恩 *ēn.*
Bientôt. 不久 *poût kiouù,* 將來 *tsiōng loî,* 容易 *yoûng ý.*
Bifurquer. 岔 *ts'á.*
Bijou. 寶貝 *paò pí,* 珍寶 *tchīn paò.*
Bile. 胆 *tàm.*
Billet. 票 *p'iáo,* 字紙 *sé tjè,* 帖 *t'iâp.*
Bizarre, 奇 *k'î,* 怪 *kouái.*
Blanc, adj. 白 *p'ăc.* *Voyez* net. || Subst. — de céruse, 鉛粉 *yân foùn,* — d'œuf, 春白 *tch'oūn p'ăc.*
Blanchir. — par exposition au soleil, 漂白 *p'iaó p'ăc.* || — un mur, 粉壁 *foùn piâc.* || *Voyez* laver.
Blasphémer. 咒罵天主 *tchoú má t'iēn tchoù.*
Blé, froment. 麥 *măc.*
Blesser. 傷 *chōng,* 打壞 *tà fái.*
Bleu. 藍色 *lâm sĕt.*
Bloc. — de bois, 樹頭 *choú t'eoû.* || Morceau, 塊 *k'ouái.* || Amas, 堆 *tōi.* || En —, 一下 *ŷt há.*
Bœuf. 黃牛 *vông nioû.*
Boire. — de l'eau, 食水 *chĭt chouì;* — du vin, 食酒 *chĭt tsiouù.*
Bois. 木 *moûc,* 樹料 *choú liáo.* || — de chauffage, 柴 *ts'iaô* (ou *ts'âi*). || Forêt, 樹山 *choú sān.*
Boisseau. 斗 *teoù;* dix boisseaux, 一石 *ŷt chăc;* dixième d'un —, 一升 *ŷt chīn;* centième d'un —, 一合 *ŷt kâp* (ou *k'âp*).

Boîte. 盒 *hâp,* 箱 *siōng,* 筒 *t'oûng.*
Boiter. 跰脚 *pāi kiôc.*
Bol. 碗 *vouòn.*
Bombe. 西瓜炮 *sī kouā p'aó.*
Bon. 好 *haò,* 善 *chán.* || — à rien, 麽用 *mô yoúng,* 不中用 *poût tchoúng yoúng.* || Tout de bon, 端眞個 *tōn tchīn ké·.*
Bondir. 發 *fât* (ou *fâc*) 跳 *t'iáo.*
Bonheur. 福 *foûc,* 樂 *lŏc.*
Bonjour. *Voyez* saluer.
Bonnet. 帽 *maó.*
Bonze. 和尙 *vô chóng.*
Bonzesse. 尼姑 *nî koū.*
Borax. 硼砂 *p'ên sā.*
Bord. 邊 *piēn,* 唇 *choûn.* || *Voyez* limite.
Borgne. 獨眼 *t'ŏuc niàn.*
Borne. — en pierre qui sépare deux champs, 界石 *kiái chăc;* — qui sépare deux sous-préfectures, 界牌 *kiái p'aî.*
Borné. 有限 *yoū hán.*
Borner (se), ne pas dépasser la mesure, 不過分 *poût kouó foún.* || Se contenter de, 不過 *poût kouó,* 單單 *tān tān.*
Bossu. 背佗 *poé· t'ô.*
Botte, chaussure. 靴 *hiō.* || Paquet, une —, 一把 *ŷt pà,* 一捆 *ŷt k'oùn,* 一揸 *ŷt tsā.*
Bouc. 羊牯 *yông koù.*
Bouche. 口 *k'eòu,* 嘴 *tsoùi* (ou *tchói*).
Bouchée, une —. 一口 *ŷt heoù.*
Boucher, v. a. 塞 *sĕt,* 封 *foūng,* 堵 *toù.*
Boucher, subst. 屠戶 *t'oû foú,* 打屠 *tà t'oû.*
Boucles. — d'oreilles, 耳鐶 *gnì p'ân.*
Bouclier. — en rotin, 籐牌 *t'ên p'aî.*

Boue. 泥 *naî.*
Bouger. 動 *t'oūng,* 動 *t'oúng*; *yám,* 震 *tchoūn.*
Bougie. 蠟燭 *lăp tchoûc.*
Bouillir. 滾 *koùn,* 沸 *pí.*
Bouillon. 湯 *t'ōng.*
Boule. 球 *k'ioû,* 團 *t'ôn,* 圓 *yân.*
Bouleverser. 亂 *lón,* 翻 *fān,* 倒 *taò.*
Bourg. 大村 *t'ái ts'oūn.*
Bourgeon. 目 *moûc,* 芽 *ngâ.*
Bourreau. 劊子手 *k'ouái tzè choù.*
Bourse. 銀袋 *nioûn t'oí,* 肚兜 *toù teōu.*
Boussole. 指南針 *t,è nâm tchīm.*
Bout, extrémité. 尾 *mī,* 頭 *t'eoû.*
Bouton. — de fleur, 花包 *fā paō.* ‖ — d'habit, 鈕 *neoù* ou *k'eóu.* ‖ Insigne chinois, 頂子 *tàng tzè.*
Boutonnière. 鈕襻 *k'eóu p'án.*
Boyau. 腸 *tch'ông.*
Bracelet. 手鈪 *choù âc.*
Branche. — d'arbre, 樹扒 *choú p'à.* ‖ — de famille, 房 *fông.*
Branler. 搖 *yaô,* 動 *t'oúng; yám.*
Bras. 手 *choù,* 手臂 *choù pì.* ‖ Tenir dans ses bras, 揇 *nàm.*
Brave, courageux. 有胆個 *yoū tàm ké*·. ‖ Honnète, 好 *haò,* 忠厚 *tchoūng heoú.*
Brèche. 口 *heoù,* 缺 *k'iĕt.*
Bref. 短 *tòn.* ‖ En un mot, 總係 *tsoùng hé*·.
Bride. Partie du harnais d'un cheval composée de la têtière, du mors et des rênes, 馬哽 *mā kàng.* ‖ Rênes, 牽馬帶 *k'iān mā tái.* ‖ Licou, 馬籠頭 *mā lioûng t'eoû.*
Brigand. 賊 *ts'ĕt.*
Brillant. 光 *kouōng,* 亮 *leóng.* ‖ Fastueux, 體面 *t'ì mién.*
Brique. — cuite au feu, 火磚 *fò tchōn.* ‖ — cuite au soleil, 泥磚 *naî tchōn.*
Briser. 打爛 *tà lán,* 打壞 *tà fái,* 打破 *tà p'ó,* 打碎 *tà soúi,* 打斷 *tà t'ōn.* ‖ — la réputation, 敗壞名聲 *p'ái fái miâng chāng.*
Brosser. 刷 *sôt.*
Brouillard. 濛沙 *moûng sā.*
Brouillon, perturbateur. 多事個 *tō sé ké*·, 糊塗 *foû t'oû.* ‖ Ecrit à mettre au net, 稿子 *kaò tzè.*
Broyer. 研碎 *ngān soúi,* 研綿 *ngān miên.*
Bru. 薪臼 *sīm k'ioū.*
Bruit, son. 响聲 *hiòng chāng.* ‖ Rumeur, 聲名 *chāng miâng,* 謠言 *yaô niân.*
Brûler, consumer par le feu. 燒 *chaō.* ‖ Causer une vive douleur par le feu, 熝痛 *loŭc t'oúng.* ‖ Dessécher, 晒燥 *sái tsaō,* 晒乾 *sái kōn.* ‖ Etre allumé, 燒着 *chaō tch'ŏc.*
Bruyant. 鬧熱 *naó gnĕt.*
Buffle. 水牛 *choùi nioû.*
Bureau. 桌 *tsôc.* ‖ Les six Bureaux, 六房 *lioûc fông.*
Burette. 細罌子 *sé*· *āng tzè,* 壺 *foû.*

C

Ça. *Voyez* cela.
Çà. *Voyez* ici, là.
Cabane. 寮 *liaô,* 篷 *p'oûng.*
Cabaret. 酒店 *tsioù tiám.*
Cacher. 屏 *piáng,* 藏 *ts'ông,* 瞞 *mân.*
Cacheter. 封 *foūng.*

Cadavre. 死老 *sì laò*, 屍 *chē*.
Cadeau. 禮物 *lī voŭt*.
Cadenas, un —. 一把鎖頭 *ўt pà sò t'eoû*.
Cadran. — solaire, 日晷 *gnĭt koùi*. ‖ — d'horloge, 鐘面 *tchoūng mién*.
Cadre. 框 *k'iōng*, 架 *ká*.
Cage. 籠 *loūng*.
Cahier. 書 *choū*, 簿 *p'oū*.
Caille. 禾鶉 *vô t'oùn*.
Caisse. 樹箱 *choú siōng*.
Calamité. 禍 *fó*, 患難 *fám nán*, 災害 *tsāi hói*.
Calculer. 算 *són*, 打算盤 *tà són p'àn*.
Calendrier. 月曆 *gnĕt lăc*. ‖ — chrétien, 瞻禮單 *tcham lī tan*.
Caler. 楔 *siăp*.
Calice. 聖爵 *chín tsiôc*.
Calmer. *Voyez* apaiser.
Calomnier. 妄証 *vòng tchín*, 誣告 *moû kaó*.
Calotte. *Voyez* bonnet.
Calquer. 脫字 *t'ôt sé*.
Camarade. 朋友 *p'oûng yoū*, 夥計 *fò kí*.
Camp. 營盤 *yâng p'ân*.
Canal. 河 *hô*, 坑瀝 *hāng lâc*, 溝瀝 *keoū lâc*, 水澗 *choùi kiàn*.
Canapé. 匟床 *k'óng ts'ông*.
Canard. 鴨嫲 *âp má*.
Cancrelas. 黃蠘 *vông ts'ăt*.
Cangue. 枷 *kā*.
Canicule. 伏天 *foŭc t'iēn*.
Cannelle. 肉桂 *nioŭc koúi*.
Canon. 炮 *p'aó*.
Cantique. 聖歌 *chín kō*.
Canton. 鄉 *hiōng*.
Capable. 㖸 *voé·*, 有能幹 *yoū nên kón*, 有才能 *yoū ts'oî nên*.

Capital, adj. Crime —, 死罪 *sì ts'oúi*; cause —, 命案 *miáng ón*. ‖ Péchés capitaux, 罪宗 *ts'oúi tsoūng*. ‖ *Voyez* principal, important.
Capital, subst. m. — de commerce, 本錢 *poùn ts'iên*.
Capitale. — d'un royaume, 京城 *kīn châng*. ‖ — d'une province, 省城 *sèn châng*.
Car. 因爲 *ўn ví*.
Caractère. 性情 *sín ts'în*, 脾氣 *p'î hí*.
Caravane. 幫 *pōng*.
Carboniser. 燒變炭 *chaō pién t'án*.
Carcasse. 殼 *hôc*.
Caresser. 惜 *siâc*.
Carotte. 黃蘿蔔 *vông lô p'ĕt*.
Carpe. 鯉嫲 *lī mâ*.
Carré. 四方個 *sí fōng ké·*.
Carte. — à jouer, 紙牌 *tjè p'aî*. ‖ — de visite, 名片 *miâng p'ièn*, 拜帖 *paí t'iâp*. ‖ — de géographie, 圖 *t'oû*.
Cas, affaire. 事 *sé*. ‖ En tout —, 不論 *poŭt loún*, 樣樣 *yóng yóng*. ‖ *Voyez* pouvoir, estimer, circonstance.
Casque. 甲帽 *kâp maó*.
Cassonade. 白糖 *p'ăc t'ông*.
Catéchisme. 問答書 *moún tâp choū*.
Catholique. 奉教人 *fcúng kaó gnîn*.
Cause. 緣故 *yân koú*, 根由 *kēn yoû*. ‖ A — de, 因爲 *ўn ví*.
Causer. ‖ *Voyez* parler, exciter.
Caution. 保人 *paò gnîn*.
Cavalier. 騎馬個 *k'î mā ké·*.
Caverne. 石岩 *chăc ngâm*.
Ce, cet, cette, ceci, celui-ci. 裡個 *ў ké*, *yà ké*, *yè· ké·*, *lì ké·*, *lè· ké·* (selon les pays).

Céder. 讓 nióng (ou yóng). || *Voyez* consentir, inférieur.
Ceinture. 帶子 *taí tzè.*
Cela, celui-là. 個個 *ké· ké·, ká ké.*
Célèbre. 出名 *tch'oût miáng.*
Cendre. 灰 *foē·.*
Cent. 百 *pâc.*
Centre. 心 *sīm,* 中心 *toúng sīm.*
Cependant. 總係 *tsoùng hé·,* 都係 *toū hé·,* 到底 *taó tài.*
Cercle. 圓圈 *yân k'iān,* 箍 *k'eoū.*
Cercueil. 棺材 *kouōn ts'oî,* 壽木 *choú moûc.*
Cérémonies. 禮節 *lī tsiĕt.*
Certain. 一定 *ŷt t'ín.*
Certificat. 憑據 *p'în kì.*
Cervelle. 腦 *naò.*
Cesser. 停 *t'în,* 止 *tjè.*
Chacun. 個個 *ké· ké·,* 各人 *kôc gnîn.*
Chagrin. *Voyez* affliger.
Chaîne. 鍊 *lién.*
Chair. 肉 *nioûc.*
Chaise. 凡 *ŷ,* 櫈 *tén.* || *Voyez* palanquin.
Chambre. 間 *kiān.*
Chameau. 駱駝 *lŏc t'ô.*
Champ. 地壢 *t'i lăc.* || Rizière, 田 *t'iên.*
Champignon. 菌 *k'ioûn,* 木耳 *moûc gnì.*
Chance. 福氣 *foûc hí,* 財喜 *ts'oî hì.*
Chandelier. 燭台 *tchoûc t'oî.*
Changer. 換 *vouón,* 調 *t'iaó,* 變 *pién.*
Chanson. 曲 *k'ioûc,* 歌 *kō;* — champêtre, 山歌 *sān kō.*
Chanter. 唱 *tch'óng.*
Chantier. 廠 *tch'òng.*
Chanvre. 蔴 *mâ,* 苧 *tch'oū.*
Chapeau. Un —, 一頂帽 *ŷt tàng maó;* — d'ouvrier, 笠麻 *lĭp mâ.*

Chapelet. Un —, 一串念珠 *ŷt tch'ón niám tchoū.*
Chapitre. Un — de livre, 一節書 *ŷt tsiĕt choū.*
Chapon. 鐓雞 *sién kē·.*
Chaque. — jour, 每日 *mī gnĭt,* 日日 *gnĭt gnĭt.* || *Voyez* chacun.
Charbon. — de bois, 香炭 *hiōng t'án,* 火炭 *fò t'án;* — de terre, 煤炭 *moê· t'án,* 石炭 *chăc t'án.*
Charge. 担 *tām.* || — de bateau, 載子 *chói tzè.* || *Voyez* devoir, dignité.
Charger. *Voyez* confier, répondre, soigner.
Charité. 愛德 *oí têt.* || *Voyez* aumône.
Charlatan. 撮把戲 *ts'ôt pà hí.*
Charpentier. 木匠 *moûc sióng.*
Charrue. 犁頭 *laî t'eoû.*
Chasser. 逐 *kioŭc,* 逐 *tch'oŭc,* 趕走 *kòn tseoù.* || Aller à la chasse, 打獵 *tà liăp,* 打鵰 *tà tiāo.*
Chasteté. 貞節 *tchīn tsiĕt.*
Chat. 貓公 *miaó koūng.*
Chatouiller. 擠 *tsí.*
Châtrer. 閹 *yām;* 抉 *kiĕt.*
Chaud. 熱 *gnĕt,* 滾 *koùn,* 溫 *voūn,* 燒 *chāo.*
Chauffer. 燒 *chāo,* 燙 *t'óng,* 炕 *k'óng.* || — au soleil, 晒 *saí,* 炙日頭 *tchâc gnĭt t'eoû.* || Se —, 炙火 *tchâc fò.*
Chaufferette. 火窗 *fò ts'oūng.*
Chausser (se). 著鞋 *tchôc haî.*
Chaux. 石灰 *chăc foē·.*
Chavirer. 船轉了 *chôn tchón liaò,* 翻船 *fan chôn.*
Chemin. 路 *loú,* 道 *t'aó.*
Cheminée. 烟窗 *yān ts'oūng.*
Chenille. 毛虫 *maō tch'oûng.*

Cher, aimé. 愛個 *oí ké·*. ‖ Coûteux, 貴 *koúi*, 值錢個 *tch'ĭt ts'iên ké·*.

Chercher. 尋 *ts'îm*, 掉 *ts'aó*.

Cheval. 馬 *mā*.

Cheveu. 頭髮 *t'eoû făt*, 頭毛 *t'eoû maō*.

Chèvre. 草羊 *ts'aò yông*.

Chèvre-feuille. 金銀花 *kīm nioûn fā*.

Chien. 狗 *keoù*. ‖ — de fusil, 銃子殼 *tch'oúng tzè hôc*.

Chinois. 唐人 *t'ông gnîn*, 中國人 *tchoūng kouĕt gnîn*.

Chirurgie. 外科 *ngoé· k'ō*.

Chœur. Se diviser en deux chœurs pour chanter, 分兩班唱經 *foūn leòng pān tch'óng kīn*. ‖ Les neuf — des Anges, 九品天神 *kioù p'ìn t'iēn chîn*.

Choisir. 擇 *ts'ĕt*, 託 *t'ôc*, 挑 *t'iāo*, 揀選 *kiàn siĕn*.

Chômer. 停工 *t'în koūng*, 放工 *fóng koūng*.

Chose. 物件 *voŭt k'ián*, 東西 *toūng sī*, 事 *sé*.

Chou. 芥蘭菜 *kiái lân ts'ói*, 苞菜 *paō ts'oí*, 白菜 *p'ăc ts'oí*.

Ci. Ce jour-ci, 今日 *kīm gnĭt*; cette année-ci, 今年 *kīm niân*; en ce temps-ci, 如今 *ŷ kīm*.

Cible. 靶子 *pà tzè*.

Ciboire. 聖體爵 *chín t'ì tsiôc*, 聖體盒子 *chín t'ì hâp tzè*.

Ciel, régions supérieures. 天 *t'iēn*. ‖ Température, 天氣 *t'iēn hí*. ‖ Séjour des Bienheureux, 天堂 *t'iēn t'ông*.

Cierge. 蠟燭 *lăp tchoūc*.

Cil. 目毛 *moūc maō*.

Cime. — de montagne, 山頂 *sān tàng*. ‖ — d'un arbre, 樹尾 *choú mī*.

Ciment. 沙灰 *sā foē·*, 紅毛泥 *foúng maō naî*. ‖ *Voir* mastic.

Cimetière. 墳山 *foûn sān*, 聖山 *chín sān*, 義塚 *gní tch'oùng*.

Circoncision. 割損禮 *kôt soùn lī*.

Circonstance. 情由 *ts'în yoû*, 緣由 *yân yoû*.

Circuler. 過 *kouó*, 走去走轉 *tseoù hí tseoù tchòn*, 通 *t'oūng*.

Cire. 蠟 *lăp*.

Ciseau. — de menuisier, de sculpteur, 鑿子 *ts'ŏc tzè*.

Ciseaux. 剪刀 *tsièn taō*.

Ciseler. 鑿花 *ts'ŏc fā*, 雕花 *t'iaō fā*, 刻 *k'ĕt*.

Citerne. 塘池 *t'ông tchê*, 魚塘 *ngŷ t'ông*, 井 *tsiàng*.

Civil, opposé à militaire. 文個 *voûn ké·*. ‖ Poli, 有禮貌 *yoū lī maó*, 有規矩 *yoū kouī kì*.

Clair, luisant, bien éclairé. 亮 *leóng*. ‖ Net, 明白 *mîn p'ác*, 清楚 *ts'īn tsè*. ‖ Serein, 晴 *ts'iâng*. ‖ Peu foncé, 淡色 *t'ám sĕt*.

Classe. 班 *pān*, 樣 *yóng*, 行 *hông*, 等 *tèn*, 水 *hì*.

Clef. — d'une serrure, 鎖匙 *sò chê*. ‖ — d'un caractère chinois, 字母 *sé moū*.

Clochette. 鈴子 *lâng tzè*.

Cloison. 間壁 *kiān piăc*.

Clou. 鐵釘 *t'iĕt tāng*. ‖ Clouer, 釘 *tāng*.

Coaguler (se). 成餅 *châng piàng*, 結做 *kiĕt ts'iōu*.

Cochon. 猪 *tchoū*.

Cocon. 麩 *teoú*, 繭子 *kiàn tzè*.

Cœur. 心 *sīm*.

Coffre. 櫃子 *k'oúi tzè*, 箱 *siōng*.

Cohabiter. 同房 *t'oúng fông*, 共下核 *k'ioúng hā hĕ̀t*.
Coin, angle. 角 *kôc*.
Col. 衫領 *sām leāng*. ‖ — de montagne, 山凹 *sān aó*.
Colère. 忿怒 *foún noú*, 氣 *hí*.
Colique. 肚痛 *toù t'oúng*.
Colle. 𥻘 *kāng*, 膠 *kaō*.
Coller. 糊 *foú*, 貼 *tiâp*, 黏 *niâm*.
Colline. 岌崗 *ýn kōng*; 山 *sān*.
Colonne. 柱墩 *tch'oū toùn*.
Combien. 幾多 *kì tō*, 咁多 *àn* (ou *kàn*) *tō*.
Comédie. 戲 *hí*.
Comestible. 好食個 *haò chĭ̀t ké·*.
Commander. 命 *mín*, 吩咐 *foūn foú*. ‖ Faire une commande, 請做 *ts'iàng tsó*; 𠹌 *vò*.
Comme. 像 *ts'ióng*, 如 *ŷ*; — lui, 比佢一樣 *pì kî ŷt yóng*. ‖ De quelque manière que, 不論 *poŭ̂t loún*.
Commencement. 頭上 *t'eoû hóng*. ‖ Au —, 起時 *hì ché*, 當初 *tōng tsē*, 先 *siēn*.
Commencer. 起時 *hì chê*, 下手 *hā choù*.
Comment. 樣斑 *nióng pān*.
Commerce. 買賣 *maì maí*, 生理 *siēn lī*.
Commettre. 犯 *fám*, 做 *tsó*, 作 *tsôc*.
Commissaire. — impérial, 欽差 *k'īm ts'aī*. ‖ Délégué, 委員 *vī yân*.
Commode. 方便 *fōng p'ién*, 順便 *choún p'ién*.
Commun, qui appartient à tous, 大家個 *t'aí kā ké·*, 通體 *t'oūng t'ì*, 公 *koūng*. ‖ Vulgaire, 平常個 *p'în chông ké·*, 照常 *tchaó chông*.
Communion. Recevoir la —, 領聖體 *leāng chín t'ì*.
Communiquer, transmettre, 傳 *tch'ôn*, 通 *t'oūng*. ‖ Avoir des relations, 來往 *loî vōng*, 交覯 *kaō kouōn*.
Compagnon. 陣 *tch'ìn*, 夥計 *fô kí*.
Comparer. 比 *pì*. ‖ Confronter, 對 *toúi*.
Compartiment, case. 隔 *kâc*. ‖ Un — de maison, 一間屋 *ŷt kiān voŭ̂c*.
Compassion. Avoir —, 心痛 *sīm t'oúng*, 心動 *sīm t'oúng*, 哀憐 *oī lîn*. ‖ Digne de —, 可憐 *k'ò lîn*.
Compenser. 補 *poù*, 賠 *p'oî*.
Complet. 全 *ts'iên*, 齊 *ts'ê·*.
Compléter. 補 *poù*. ‖ Achever, 做完 *tsó vân*.
Compliment. 奉承人個話 *foúng chîn gnîn ké· fá*, 獎賞人個話 *tsiòng chòng gnîn ké· fá*.
Comploter. 謀 *meoû*.
Composition. — littéraire, 文章 *voûn tchōng*.
Comprendre, renfermer. 包含 *paō hâm*. ‖ Saisir par la pensée, 分明 *foūn mîn*, 明白 *mîn p'ăc* (ou *p'ĕt*), 懂 *toùng*.
Compromettre. 拖累 *t'ō loúi*.
Comptant. Argent —, 現錢 *hién ts'iên*, 現撿 *hién kiàm*.
Compte, nombre. 數目 *sé moŭ̂c*, 賬目 *tchóng moŭ̂c*.
Compter. 算數 *són sé*, 點 *tiàm*. ‖ Penser, 嘩算 *fâ són*, 打算 *tà són*, 想 *siòng*.
Concubine. 妾 *ts'iâp*, 小婆 *siaò p'ô*.
Concupiscence. 私慾偏情 *sē yoŭ̂c p'iēn ts'în*.
Condescendre. 順人個意 *choún gnîn ké· ý*, 將就 *tsiōng ts'ioú*.
Condisciple. 同學 *t'oûng hŏ̀c*, 共下讀書 *k'ioúng hā t'oŭ̂c choū*.

.3

Condition, rang. 地位 *t'í ví*, 身分 *chīn foún*, 位分 *ví foún*, 光景 *kouōng kìn*. ‖ A —, 單單 *tān tān*; se tourne par une périphrase: 你領得全大赦單單敬皇命個善功愛做完 *gnì leāng tēt ts'iên t'ái chá tān tān kaó vông mín kē chán koūng oí tsó vân*, tu gagneras l'indulgence plénière, à condition que tu accomplisses les les bonnes œuvres qu'a ordonné le Pape. *Voyez* si.

Conduire. 牽 *k'iān*, 帶 *tái*, ‖ Accompagner, 送 *soúng*.

Confession. 告解 *kaó kiài*, 辦神工 *p'án chîn koūng*.

Confiance. 相信 *siōng sín*, 靠望 *k'aó móng*.

Confier. 交 *kaō*, 付託 *foú t'ŏc*, 寄 *kí*.

Confirmation. 堅振 *kiān tchìn*.

Confisquer. 充公 *tch'oūng koūng*.

Confiture. 糖糕 *t'ông kaō*, 糖菓 *t'ông kouò*.

Confondre, brouiller. 混雜 *foún ts'ăp*, 攪亂 *kaò lón*. ‖ Ne pas discerner, 唔分想 *mĝ foūn siòng*.

Conforme. 照樣 *tchaó yóng*, 相同 *siōng t'oûng*.

Congé. — à des écoliers, 放學 *fóng hŏc*. ‖ Renvoi d'un domestique, 算數 *són sé*.

Conjecturer. 猜 *ts'aī*, 恐怕 *k'ioùng p'á*, 嚀 *fâ*.

Connaître. 曉得 *hiaò tēt*, 知 *tī*, 認 *gnín*, 識 *chĭt*, 熟 *choŭc*.

Consacrer, offrir à Dieu. 献與天主 *hién ȳ t'iēn tchoù*. ‖ Changer au Corps de J. C., 成聖體 *chîn chín t'ì*. ‖ Bénir, 聖 *chín*.

Conscience. 良心 *leông sīm*.

Consécutif. 麼停 *mô t'în*, 連緊 *liên kìn*.

Conseil. 意事 *ý sé*, 主意 *tchoù ý*.

Conseiller, subst. m. 當君師 *tōng kioūn sē*; — d'un mandarin, 師爺 *sē yâ*.

Conseiller, v. a. 勸 *k'ián*, 出主意 *tch'oŭt tchoù ý*.

Consentir. 敢願 *kàm nián*, 肯 *hèn*, 許 *hì*, 准 *tchoùn*, 答應 *tăp ýn*.

Conséquence. 關係 *konān hé*, 隋後 *souî heoú*.

Conserver. 存 *soūn*, 留 *lieû*, 漚 *eoú*.

Considérer. 看 *k'ón*, 想 *siòng*.

Consoler. 安慰 *ōn vì*.

Constant. 硬心 *ngáng sīm*, 長久 *tch'ông kioù*.

Constater. 則 *tsēt*, 看 *k'ón*, 查 *ts'â*, 驗 *niám*.

Constipé. 大便唔通 *t'aí p'ién mĝ t'oūng*.

Consul. 領事官 *leāng sé kouōn*.

Consulter. 問 *moún*. ‖ Délibérer, 商量 *chōng leông*. ‖ Examiner, 查 *ts'â*.

Contagieux. 滯人個 *tché gnîn kē*.

Conte. 古事 *koù sé*, 傳子 *tch'ón tzè*.

Contempler. 看 *k'ón*, 想 *siòng*.

Contenir. 裝 *tchōng*, 包含 *paō hâm*.

Content. 歡喜 *fōn hì*, 自在 *tsé ts'aí*, 滿意 *mān ý*.

Contester. 爭 *tsāng*.

Continuer. 接倒 *tsiăp taò*, 騰 *t'ên*, 接手 *tsiăp choù*.

Contracter. — alliance, 結親 *kiĕt ts'īn*. ‖ — des dettes, 該賬 *koī tchóng*, 生賬 *sēn tchóng*. ‖ — une maladie, 生病 *sēn p'iáng*, 得病 *tēt p'iáng*.

Contraire, opposé. 反 *fàn*, 相反 *siōng fàn*. || Vent —, 逆風 *niăc foūng*. || Dire tout le —, 反轉來講 *fàn tchòn loî kòng*.
Contrat. 契 *k'é·*, 字紙 *sé tjè*, 合同 *hăp t'oûng*.
Contre, opposé. 逆 *niăc*, 邊背 *piēn poé·*. || Près de, 凭 *pén*, 近 *k'ioún*, 兩隔壁 *leòng kâc piâc*.
Contre-cœur (à). 唔奈何 *mĝ naí hô*.
Contredire. 凹人 *aó gnîn*.
Contribuer. 錢鐵 *tch'oût ts'iên*, 滕分 *t'ên foūn*.
Contrition. 痛悔 *t'oúng fí*.
Convaincre. 問倒 *moún taò*, 講倒 *kòng taò*.
Convenir, admettre. 認 *gnín*. || Décider ensemble, 定 *t'ín*, 約定 *yôc t'ín*, 講成 *kòng châng* ou *tcháng*. || Plaire, 中意 *tchoúng ý*, 合式 *hăp chĭt*, 遂意 *soúi ý*.
Convention. 合同 *hăp t'oûng*.
Converser. 講話 *kòng fá*, 講撇 *kòng liáo*.
Convertir (se). 改過 *koì koúo*.
Convexe. 拱起個 *kioùng hì ké·*.
Convive. 坐席個 *ts'ō sĭt ké·*, 客 *hâc*.
Convoiter. 貪 *t'ām*.
Copeau. 鉋屎 *p'aô chè*.
Copier. 抄 *ts'aō*, 錄 *liŏuc*.
Coq. 雞公 *kē· koūng*.
Coque. 殼 *hôc*.
Corbeau. 老鴉 *laò a*.
Corbeille. 籃子 *lâm tzè*, 籃箕 *lâm kī*, 籮籠 *lô loùng*.
Corde. 索 *sôc*. || — de halage, 欖頭 *lám t'eoû*. || — de violon, 弦線 *hiên sién*.
Cordeau. — de charpentier. 墨線 *mĕt sién*.
Cordon. 絲線 *sē sién*, 絛子 *t'aō tzè*, 帶子 *taí tzè*.
Corne. 牛角 *nioû kôc*. || Sabot du cheval, 馬蹄 *mā t'aî*.
Corps, être organisé. 身 *chīn*, 體 *t'ì*. || Opposé à l'esprit, 肉身 *nioûc chīn*.
Correspondre, être conforme. 對 *toúi*, 合 *hăp*. || Communiquer, 通 *t'oūng*, 透 *t'eoú*.
Corriger, réformer. 改 *koì*. || Réprimander, 懲責 *tchìn tsĭt*. || Punir, 責罰 *tsĭt făt*.
Corrompre. 壞 *faí*, 帶壞 *taí faí*, 敗壞 *p'aí faí*. || Se —, 學壞 *hŏc faí*.
Côte, os. 肋骨 *lĭt koŭc*, 牌骨 *p'aî koŭc*. || Colline, 岌崗 *ýn kōng*.
Côté. 邊 *piēn*, 膀 *pòng*. || *Voyez* face, auprès.
Coton. 棉花 *miên fā*.
Cou. 頸筋 *kiàng kīn*.
Couché, placé horizontalement. 放坪個 *fóng p'iâng ké·*, 眠個 *mîn ké·* || — pour dormir, 眠起睡 *mîn hì choé·*.
Coude. 手踭 *choù tsāng*, 肘 *tsioù*.
Coudre. 縺 *liên*.
Couler, suivre sa pente. 流 *lioû*. || Laisser échapper, 漏 *leoú*. || Jeter au moule, 鑄 *tchoú*.
Couleur. 色 *sĕt*, 色料 *sĕt liaó*.
Coup. Un —, 一下 *ŷt há*; un — de couteau, 一刀 *ŷt taō*; un — de pied, 一脚 *ŷt kiôc*; un — de fusil, 一管銃 *ŷt kouòn tch'oúng*.
Coupable. 犯人 *fám gnîn*, 罪人 *ts'oúi gnîn*.

Couper. 割 *kôt,* 切 *ts'iĕt,* 裁 *ts'aî;* — avec des ciseaux, 剪 *tsièn.*
Couple. 一雙 *ŷt soūng,* 一對 *ŷt toúi.*
Cour. — d'une maison, 天井 *t'iēn tsiàng.* || Résidence du souverain, 朝廷 *tch'aô t'în.*
Courage. 好胆子 *haò tàm tzè.* || Dureté de cœur, 硬心 *ngáng sīm.*
Courber. 彎 *vān,* 拗曲 *aò k'ioūt;* — la tête, 啱頭 *ngàm t'eoû.*
Courir. 跑 *p'aō,* 盡走 *ts'ín tseoù.*
Courrier. 千里馬 *ts'iēn lī mā,* 信脚 *sín kiôc.*
Courroie. 皮帶 *p'î tái.*
Court. 短 *tòn,* 小 *siaò,* 細 *sé·.*
Cousin, cousine; fils, fille d'un oncle paternel, 叔伯兄弟 *choûc pâc hioūng t'í,* 叔伯姊妹 *choûc pâc tsì moé·.* Fils, fille d'un oncle maternel ou d'une tante paternelle, 表兄弟 *piaò hioūng t'í,* 表姊妹 *piaò tsì moé·.* Fils, fille d'une tante maternelle, 姑表兄弟 *koū piaò hioūng t'í.*
Cousin, moucheron. 蚊子 *moūn tzè.*
Couteau. 刀 *taō.*
Coûter, valoir. 値 *tch'ît,* 抵 *tì;* — cher, 貴 *koúi;* — bon marché, 便人 *p'iên gnîn.*
Coutume. 規矩 *koūi kì,* 風俗 *foūng sioŭc.*
Couver. 哺 *p'oú.*
Couvercle. 盖 *koí; kèm tchoūng.*
Couverture. 被 *p'ī,* 被盖 *p'ī koí,* 羊毡 *yông tchān.* || Enveloppe de la couverture, 被皮 *p'ī p'î;* — sans son enveloppe, 被骨 *p'ī koūt.*
Couvrir. *kèm,* 盖 *kói,* 遮 *tchā,* 抵 *tài.*
Crabe. 老蟹 *laò haì.*
Cracher. 吐 *t'oú,* 吐口液 *t'oúi heoù lān,* 吐痰 *t'oúi t'âm.*
Craindre. 怕 *p'á,* 畏 *ví,* 驚 *kiāng.*
Crayon. 鉛筆 *yân pīt.*
Créancier. 賬主 *tchóng tchoù.*
Crédit. Vendre ou acheter à crédit, 賒 *tch'a.*
Créer, tirer du néant. 造 *ts'aó.* || Nommer à un titre, 封 *foūng,* 立 *līp,* 安 *ōn.*
Crêpe. 縐紗 *tsioú sā.*
Crépir. 粉石灰 *foùn chăc foē·.*
Crête. — de coq, 雞公髻 *kē· koūng kí.* || — de montagne, 山頂 *sān tàng.*
Creuser. 啄 *koì,* 挖 *vā,* 挖 *vât.*
Creux. 空個 *k'oūng ké·,* 冇 *p'áng.*
Crevasse. 縫 *p'oúng,* 口 *heoù.*
Crever, faire rompre. 炮 *paó,* 打破 *tà p'ó.*
Cribler. 篩 *sī.*
Crier. 叫 *kiaó,* 喊 *hám.* || Faire du tapage, 吵鬧 *ts'aò naó.*
Crime. 大罪 *t'ái ts'oúi.*
Criminel. 犯人 *fám gnîn.*
Crinière. — de cheval, 馬騌 *mā tsoūng.*
Cristal. 水晶 *choùi tsīn.*
Croc, crochet. 鈎子 *keoū tzè,* 鈎搭 *keoū tâp.*
Croire. 信 *sín.*
Croiser. — les bras, 蹺手 *k'aō choù;* — les jambes, 蹺脚 *k'aō kiôc.*
Croître, grandir. 長 *tchòng,* 大 *t'aí,* 生 *sāng,* 出 *tch'oût.*
Croix. 十字 *chîp sé.*
Crouler. 屙 *ō,* 轉 *tchón,* 倒 *taò,* 崩 *pēn.*
Cru, non cuit. 生個 *sāng ké·.*
Crucifix. 苦像 *k'où sióng.*
Cueillir. 摘 *tsâc,* 採 *ts'aī.*

Cuiller. 調羹 *t'iaô kāng*, 湯匙 *t'ōng tchê*, 杓 *chôc*.
Cuir. 牛皮 *nioû p'î*.
Cuire. 煮 *tchoù*; — à petit feu, 燉 *toūn*; — sous la cendre, 煨 *voē*; — à la vapeur, 蒸 *tchīn*; — au four 炕 *k'óng*; — jusqu'à la décoction, 熬 *ngaô*; — dans la graisse, 煠 *tsá*; — dans l'eau, 煲 *pō*; griller, frire, 煎 *tsiēn*, 炙 *tchâc*.
Cuisine. 廚房 *tch'oû fông*, 灶下 *tsaó hā* (ou *tsá hā*).
Cuisinier. 廚子 *tch'oû tzè*, 火頭 *fò t'eoû*.
Cuisse. 髀 *pì*.
Cuivre. 銅 *t'oûng*.
Cultiver. — la terre, 耕 *kāng*, 種 *tchoúng*, 栽培 *tsaī p'î*, 服事 *foŭc sé*.
Curer. 勾淨 *keoū ts'iáng*; — les oreilles, 解耳 *kiài gnì*.
Cure-dent. 牙刺 *ngâ ts'ioŭc*; cure-oreille, 耳鈀 *gnì p'â*.
Cuvette. 盆 *p'oûn*.
Cycle. 甲子 *kâp tzè*.
Cymbale. 鈸 *p'ăt*, 鑼 *lô*.

D

Dalle. 石板 *chăc pàn*.
Damner. 罰下地獄 *făt hā t'í nioŭc*.
Danger. 凶險 *hioūng hiàm*.
Dans. 在內 *ts'ái noúi*, ? 貯 *tī toù*, 心內 *sīm noúi*.
Dartre. 癬 *sièn*.
Davantage. 過多 *koúo tō*, 多兜 *tō teoū*.
De, marque du génitif. 個 *ké*; — marque du point de départ, 由 *yoû*, 從 *ts'ioûng*.
Débarcadère. 碼頭 *mā t'eoû*.
Débarquer. 下船 *hā chôn*.
Débarrasser. 撿開 *kiàm k'ōi*, 收拾 *choū chìp*.
Déboîter. 走腕 *tseoù vouòn*, 拆 *ts'âc*.
Déborder. 噴出 *p'oūn tch'oŭt*, 浡出 *p'oŭt tch'oŭt*.
Déboucher. 開 *k'ōi*, 揭 *yât*.
Debout. 幅倒 *k'ī taò*, 直 *tch'ĭt*.
Débris. 碎東西 *soúi toūng sī*.
Décapiter. 殺 *săt*, 斬頭 *tsàm t'eoû*.
Décharger. 脫担子 *t'ōt tām tzè*. || — une barque, 起貨 *hì fó*. || — un fusil, 開銃 *k'ōi tch'oúng*.
Déchirer. 扯爛 *tch'à lán*, 擘 *mâc*.
Décider. 打定主意 *tà t'ín tchoù ý*, 斷 *tón*.
Découvrir. 打開 *tà k'oī*. || *Voyez* trouver, déboucher.
Décret. — impérial, 上諭 *chóng ý*, 聖旨 *chín tjè*. || Ordonnance affichée d'un mandarin, 告示 *kaó ché*.
Dédaigner. 嫌 *hiâm*, 看唔起 *k'ón mĝ hì*, 輕慢 *k'īn mán*.
Dédire (se). 反口 *fàn k'eoù*, 反轉來講 *fàn tchòn loî kòng*.
Déduire. 除 *tch'oû*, 扣 *k'eoú*, 折 *tchât*.
Défaire. 拆 *ts'âc*.
Défaut. 毛病 *maō p'iáng*.
Défendre, protéger. 保護 *paò foú*, 保佑 *paò yoú*. || Interdire, 禁 *kím*, 不准 *poŭt tchoùn*.
Définir. 定 *t'ín*, 講成 *kòng tcháng*.
Défunts (les). 先亡 *siēn vông*.
Dégât. 傷 *chōng*, 害 *hoí*.
Dégoût. 厭煩 *yám fân*, 看唔起 *k'ón mĝ hì*.
Dégrader. 革 *kĕt*, 參 *ts'ām*.
Degré. 一步 *ŷt p'oú*, 度 *t'oú*, 斷 *tón*.

Dehors. 外 *ngoé·*. || En — de, 除外 *tch'oû ngoé·*, 格外 *kĕt ngoé·*, 另外 *láng ngoé·*.
Déjà. 咁早 *àn tsaò*.
Déjeuner. 食朝 *chĭt tchaō*, 食早飯 *chĭt tsaò fán*.
Délai. 遲 *tchê*, 慢 *mán*, 延 *yân*, 緩 *fón*.
Délasser (se). 撫健 *liaó k'ián*, 撫鬆 *liaó soūng*, 透氣 *t'eoù hí*.
Délayer. — de l'encre, 研墨 *ngān mĕt*.
Délégué. *Voyez* commissaire.
Délibérer. 商量 *chōng leông*.
Délicat. 細 *sé·*, 嫩 *noún*, 柔 *tsē·*.
Délier. 解開 *kè· k'oī*.
Délivrer. 放 *fóng*, 救 *kioú*.
Déluge. 洪水 *foûng choùi*.
Demain. 明天 *mîn t'iēn*, 辰朝日 *chîn tchaō gnĭt*; *sō tō gnĭt*; 天光日 *t'iēn kouōng gnĭt*.
Demander. 問 *moún*, 求 *k'ioû*.
Démanger. 癢 *yōng*.
Démarrer. 開船 *k'oī chôn*.
Déménager. 搬家 *pān kā*.
Demeurer. 住 *tch'oú*, 核 *hĕt*, 在 *ts'ái*, 站 *tsàn*.
Demi. 半 *pán*.
Demoiselle. 姑娘 *koū niông*, 妹子 *moé· tzè*.
Démolir. 拆 *ts'âc*.
Démon. 魔鬼 *mô kouì*.
Démonter. 拆 *ts'âc*, 下 *hà*, 下脫 *hà t'ōt*.
Dent. 牙齒 *ngâ tchè*.
Dépasser. 過 *kouó*, 出 *tch'oūt*.
Dépêche. — officielle, 文書 *voûn choū*. || Lettre, 信 *sín*.
Dépendre, détacher. 下 *hà*, 放下 *fóng hā*. || Etre sous l'autorité de quelqu'un, 屬 *choŭc*, 管 *kouòn*, 由 *yoû*, 在 *ts'ái*.

Dépense. 使 *sè*, 用 *yoúng*, 費 *fí*.
Déplaire. 唔合意 *mĝ hăp ý*, 唔中意 *mĝ tchoúng ý*.
Déposer. 放 *fóng*, 寄 *kí*.
Dépouiller. 搶 *ts'iòng*, 奪 *t'ŏt*, 脫 *t'ōt*. || Enlever la peau, 剝 *pôc*.
Depuis, prép. 從 *ts'ioûng*, 自 *tsé*. || Adv. *Voyez* ensuite.
Déraisonner. 發癲 *pōt tiēn*, 發狂 *fât k'ông*.
Dernier, qui est après tous les autres. 尾上 *mī hóng*, 黏尾 *niâm mī*. || Qui précède immédiatement ; la dernière fois, 上次 *chóng tsé*, 頭擺 *t'eoû paì*, 頭一回 *t'eoû ȳt fî*.
Dernièrement. 近日 *k'ioún gnĭt*, 先麼幾久 *siēn mô kì kioù*, 臨尾 *lîm mī*.
Dérober. 偷 *t'eoū*.
Derrière. 後 *heoú*, 背後 *poé· heoú*.
Descendre. 下 *hā*.
Désert. 荒地 *fōng t'í*, 空地 *k'oúng t'í*.
Déserter. 偷走 *t'eoū tseoù*.
Désespérer. 失望 *chĭt móng*.
Déshonnête. 邪淫個 *siâ ŷm ké·*, 醜陋 *tch'où leoú*.
Déshonorer. 傷臉 *chōng liēn*, 乜面目 *yà mién moŭc (pop.)*.
Désigner, indiquer. 指 *tjè*. || Fixer, 定 *t'ín*.
Désir. 心意 *sīm ý*, 慾 *yoŭc*.
Désirer. 想 *siòng*, 貪 *t'ām*, 圖 *t'oû*, 願 *nián*.
Désœuvré. 閒人 *hân gnîn*.
Désordre (en). 亂個 *lón ké·*, 混雜 *foún ts'ăp*.
Désormais. 從今以後 *ts'ioûng kīn ȳ heoú*, 後來 *heoú loî*.

Dessein. 主意 *tchoù ý*, 必事 *sīm sé*. || A —, 特意 *t'ìt ý*, 故意 *koú ý*.
Desserrer. 放鬆 *fóng soūng*.
Dessous. 下 *hā*, 底下 *taì hā*.
Destin. 天命 *t'iēn mín*.
Détail. 零碎 *lâng souí*.
Détenir. 留 *lioû*, 存 *soûn*.
Déterrer. 𠲖出 *koì tch'oût*, 挖出 *vā tch'oût*.
Détour. 灣 *vân*, 轉 *tchòn*.
Détruire. 拆 *ts'âc*, 滅 *mĕt*, 收 *choū*.
Dette. 債賬 *tsaí tchóng*.
Deuil. 孝 *haó*, 喪事 *sōng sé*.
Devancer. 先行 *siēn hâng*.
Devant, subst. m. 前頭 *ts'iên t'eoû*, 面子 *mién tzè*, 面上 *mién hóng*. || Adv. et prép. 前 *ts'iên*, 在前 *ts'aí ts'iên*, 面前 *mién ts'iên*.
Devenir. 成 *châng*, 做 *tsó*, 變 *pién*.
Devin. 算命個 *són miáng ké·*, 問先 *moún siēn*.
Dévisser. 扭脫螺螄 *nioú t'ōt lô sē*.
Devoir, subst. m. 本分 *poùn foún*.
Devoir, v. a. Avoir à payer. 少人個 *chaò gnîn ké·*, 欠人個 *k'iám gnîn ké·*. || Etre sur le point de, 愛 *oí*.
Dévotion. 熱心 *gnĕt sīm*.
Diamant. 金鋼石 *kīm kōng chăc*, 算石 *són chăc*.
Diarrhée. Avoir la —, 屙肚 *ō toù*, 瀉 *siá*.
Dictionnaire. 字典 *sé tièn*.
Dieu. 天主 *t'iēn tchoù*.
Diffamer. 壞名聲 *faí miâng chāng*, 毀謗 *k'ouì pòng*.
Différer, retarder. 緩 *fón*, 慢 *mán*. || Etre différent, 唔同 *mĝ t'oûng*, 唔一樣 *mĝ ȳt yóng*.
Difficile. 難 *nân*.
Digérer. 消化 *siaō fá*.
Digne. — d'amour, 可愛個 *k'ò oí ké·*, 得人愛 *tĕt gnîn oí*, 得人惜 *tĕt gnîn siâc*; — de châtiment, 該罰個 *koī făt ké·*. || Je n'en suis pas digne, 唔敢當 *mĝ kàm tōng*, 不堪 *poŭt k'ām*.
Dignité, charge éminente. 高位 *kaō ví*. || Air de grandeur, 威嚴 *vī niâm*.
Digue. 坎 *k'ám*.
Diligent. 擒 *k'îm*, 快 *k'ouái*, 小心 *siaò sīm*.
Dimanche. 主日 *tchoù gnĭt*.
Diminuer. 減少 *kàm chaò*. || Baisser de prix, 跌價 *tiĕt ká*. || Devenir plus petit, 細了 *sé· liaò*, 短了 *tòn liaò*.
Dîner. 食晝 *chĭt tchoú*.
Dire. 講 *kòng*, 話 *vá*.
Direct. 直 *tch'ĭt*.
Direction. 向 *hióng*. || Changer de —, 轉向 *tchòn hióng*.
Discerner. 看清楚 *k'ón ts'īn tsè*, 分出來 *foūn tch'oût· loî*.
Disciple. 徒弟 *t'oû t'i*, 門生 *moûn sēn*, 學生 *hŏc sāng*.
Discuter. 講論 *kòng loún*, 辨 *p'ién*.
Disparaître. 唔見 *mĝ kián*, 唔在 *mĝ ts'cī*.
Dispenser. 寬免 *k'ōn mēn*.
Disperser. 撒 *sán*.
Dispos. 爽快 *sòng k'ouái*, 安樂 *ōn lŏc*.
Disposer. 安排 *ōn p'aî*, 擺 *paì*, 布置 *poú tjé*.
Disputer (se). 相罵 *siōng má*, 相吵 *siōng ts'aô*.
Distance. A quelle —, 隔幾遠 *kâc kì yàn*. || *Voyez* près, loin, différer.
Distiller. 烤 *k'aò*, 泌 *pĭt*.

Distinguer. 分 *foūn.* || Se —, 出名 *tch'oût miâng.*

Distrait. 心雜亂 *sīm ts'ăp lón,* 心亂 *sīm lón.*

Distribuer. 分 *foūn,* 撒 *sàn.*

Diviser. 分 *foūn,* 分均 *foūn kioūn.*

Division (arithmétique). 歸除 *kouī tch'oú.*

Divulguer. 傳 *tch'ôn,* 走 ou 漏風 *tseoù* ou *leoú foūng.*

Docile. 聽話 *t'āng vá,* 聽命 *t'in mín.*

Docteur. 進士 *tsín sé.*

Doctrine. 道理 *t'aó lī.*

Doigt. — de la main, 手指 *choù tjè;* — du pied, 脚趾 *kiôc tjè.*

Dommage. 害 *hoí,* 傷 *chōng.* || C'est—, 枉了 *nóng liaò.*

Dompter. 押伏 *âp foŭc.*

Donner. 㓦 *poūn,* 交 *kaō,* 送 *soúng,* 拿 *nā.*

Dorer. 上金 *chòng kīm,* 鍍金 *t'oú kīm.*

Dormir. 睡目 *choé· moŭc.*

Dos. 背 *poé·.*

Dose, une — de médecine, 一副藥 *ŷt foú yŏc.*

Douane. 稅關 *choé· kouān.*

Double, deux fois autant, 多一半 *tō ŷt pán.* || Deux choses pareilles, 雙 *soūng.*

Doublé (habit). 袷襖 *kâp aò.*

Doucement. 慢慢 *mán mán.* || A voix basse, 小聲 *siaò chāng.*

Douleur. 痛 *t'oúng.*

Doute. 疑惑 *gnî fĕt.*

Doux, saveur. 甜 *t'iâm,* 甘 *kām.* || Bon, affable, 良善 *leông chán,* 淳 *choûn.*

Dragon. 龍 *lioûng.*

Drapeau. 旗 *k'î.*

Dresser. 抓歧 *tch'ā k'ī.*

Droit, adj. 幅倒 *k'ī taò,* 直 *tch'ĭt.* || Opposé à la gauche, 右 *yoú.*

Droit, subst. m. Selon le —, 照理 *tchaó lī,* 論理 *loún lī.* || Avoir le bon droit pour soi, 有理 *yoū lī.* || Lois, 例 *lí.*

Dur. 腮 *nioún,* 硬 *ngáng.* || Insensible, 硬心 *ngáng sīm,* 忍心 *nioūn sīm.*

Durable. 長久個 *tch'ông kioù ké·,* 耐 *nái.*

Duvet. 毧毛 *yoûng maō.*

Dynastie. 朝 *tch'aô.*

Dyssenterie. 痢症 *lí tchín.*

E

Eau. 水 *choùi.*

Eau-de-vie. 燒酒 *chaō tsioù.*

Ecaille. 鱗 *lîn,* 殼 *hôc.*

Ecarter. 閃開 *chàm k'oī,* 撿開 *kiàm k'oī.*

Echauder. 燙 *t'óng.*

Echauffant. 熱性 *gnĕt sín.*

Echéance. 日子 *gnĭt tzè,* 限期 *hán k'î.*

Echecs. 棋 *k'î.*

Echelle. 梯子 *t'oī tzè.*

Echo. 應嘴 *ýn tsoùi.*

Eclairer. 照光 *tchaó kouōng.*

Eclat, fragment. 鲜 *sièn.* || Brillant, 體面 *t'ì mién.*

Eclater. 苞 *paó;* faire —, 炮 *p'aó.*

Eclore. 苞出來 *paó tch'oût loî.* || S'épanouir, 開花 *k'oī fā.*

Ecole. 學堂 *hŏc t'ông.*

Ecolier. 學生 *hŏc sāng.*

Econome, adj. 儉 *k'iáng.* || Subst. m. 當家 *tōng kā.*

Ecorcer. 剝皮 *pôc p'ĭ.* || — le riz, 礱穀 *loûng koŭc.*

Ecorcher, enlever la peau. 剝皮 *pôc p'ĭ,* 剖 *p'ó.* || Déchirer la peau, 掛爛 *kouà lán.*

Ecouter. 聽 *t'āng.*

Ecraser. 壓 *tsâc* pour *âp.*

Ecrire. 寫 *sià.*

Ecuelle. 碗 *vouòn,* 盞 *tsàn,* 鉢 *pât.*

Ecume. 泡 *p'aō.*

Ecurie. — pour bœufs, 牛欄 *nioû lân.*

Eduquer. 教 *kaō,* 教訓 *kaō hioún.*

Effacer, biffer, 勾 *keoū,* 塗 *t'oû.*

Effet. 效法 *haó fâp.*

Effleurer. 爭一點動倒 *tsāng ȳt tiàm t'oūng taò.*

Efforcer (s'). 趲勁 *tsán kín,* 出力 *tch'oût lĭt,* 用力 *yoúng lĭt.*

Effrayer. 嚇人 *hâc gnîn.* || Effrayant, 得人畏 *têt gnîn ví.*

Egal, pareil. 一樣 *ȳt yóng.* || Qui ne dépasse pas, 齊 *ts'ê·,* 坪 *p'iâng,* 匀 *yoūn.*

Eglise. La Ste Eglise, 聖教會 *chín kaó fí.* || Temple, 聖堂 *chín t'ông.*

Electricité. 電氣 *t'ién hí.*

Eléphant. 象 *sióng.*

Elever, lever en l'air. 升起 *chīn hì.* || Promouvoir, 陞 *chīn.* || *Voyez* nourrir, éduquer.

Eloquence. 口才 *k'eoù ts'oî.*

Emballer. 包 *paō,* 裝在箱貯 *tchōng ts'aí* (ou *á*) *siōng toù.*

Emblême. 記號 *kí haó,* 表意 *piaò ý.*

Embouchure. 嘴 *tchói,* 口 *k'eoù,* 口 *heoù.*

Embrasser. 抱 *p'aó,* 揞 *nàm,* 親嘴 *tsīm tchói.*

Emeute. 亂 *lón,* 鬧 *naó.*

Emigrer. 搬 *pān,* 遷 *ts'iēn.*

Emmagasiner. 裝貨 *tchōng fó,* 堆貨 *toī fó.*

Emmancher. 鬥柄 *teoú piáng.*

Emmener. 牽 *k'iān,* 帶去 *taí hí.*

Emoussé. 鈍 *t'oún.*

Emouvoir, attendrir. 動人個心 *t'oúng gnîn ké· sīm.*

Empêcher, mettre obstacle. 阻擋 *tzè tòng.* || Retenir, 攔 *lân,* 堵 *toù.* || Défendre, 禁 *kím,* 不准 *poût tchoùn.*

Empereur. 皇帝 *fông tí.*

Empeser. 漿 *tsiōng.*

Empiéter. 爭 *tsāng,* 把 *pà.*

Emplâtre. 膏藥 *kaō yŏc.*

Employer. 用 *yoúng,* 使 *sè.*

Empois. 漿 *tsiōng.*

Empoisonner. 透死 *t'eóu sì,* 㵠 *naó.*

Emporter. 拿去 *nā hí,* 拿走 *nā tseòu,* 帶去 *taí hí.*

Emprisonner. 押落班房 *âp lŏc pān fông.*

Emprunter. 借 *tsiá.*

Enceinte. Mur d'—, 圍墻 *vî siōng,* 垣墉 *yân châng.*

Enceinte (être). 嗽大肚 *k'ouán t'aí toù.*

Encens. 乳香 *ȳ hiōng.*

Encensoir. 吊爐 *tiaó loû.*

Enchaîner. 鎖鍊 *sò lién.*

Enchérir. 起價 *hì ká.*

Enclin. Etre — à, 噲 *voé·,* 好 *haó.*

Enclume. 鐵墩 *tsēm toùn.*

Encore. 再 *tsái,* 又 *yoú.* || — plus, 過多 *kouó tō.*

Encourager. 勸 *k'ián.*

Encre. 墨水 *mĕt choùi.*

4

Endormir (s'). 睡着 *choé· tch'ŏc.*

Endroit. 地方 *t'í fōng.*

Enduire. 上 *chòng,* 油 *yoû,* 糊 *foû,* 搽 *ts'â.*

Enfant. 嬰孩 *ȳn haî,* 細人 *sé· gnîn.*

Enfer. 地獄 *t'í nioŭc.*

Enfiler. 串 *tch'ón.*

Enfin. 總係 *tsoùng hé·,* 到底 *taó taì,* 究竟 *kioú kín.*

Enflé. 腫 *tchoùng,* 脹 *tchóng,* 胱 *kouāng.*

Enfoncer. 放下 *fóng hā,* 擒下 *k'îm hā,* 釘 *tang,* 插 *ts'âp.*

Enfouir. 埋 *maî,* 窖 *kaó.*

Enfumer. 熰 *eoú.*

Engelure. 寒疼 *hôn toúng.*

Enivrer (s'). 食醉 *chĭt tsouí,* 打酒醉 *tà tsioù tsoúi.*

Enlever. 拿去 *nā hí,* 拿脫 *nā t'ôt.*

Ennuyer (s'). 唔慣 *mĝ kouán,* 嫽煩 *liaó fân.*

Enraciner (s'). 生根 *sāng kīn.*

Enrouler. 纏 *ts'ân,* 捆 *k'oùn.*

Enseigne. 招牌 *tchaō p'aî,* 字號 *sé haó.*

Enseigner. 教 *kaō.*

Ensemble. 共下 *k'ioúng há,* 一齊 *ȳt ts'ê·.*

Ensevelir. 埋葬 *maî tsóng.*

Ensuite. 過後 *kouó heoú,* 然後 *yân heoú,* 以後 *ȳ heoú.*

Entasser. 堆 *toī,* 囤 *toùn.*

Entier. 全個 *ts'iên ké·.*

Entonner. — les prières, 題經 *t'î kīn.*

Entonnoir. 酒透 *tsioù t'eoú.*

Entourer. 圍 *vî,* 掩 *am.*

Entraîner. 拖 *t'ō,* 抓 *tch'ā.*

Entre. 中心 *toúng sīm,* 中間 *tchoūng kiān.*

Entremetteur. 中人 *tchoūng gnîn.* ‖ — de mariage, 媒人 *moê· gnîn.*

Entrer. 入 *gnĭp,* 進 *tsín.*

Enveloppe. — de lettre, 信桶 *sín t'oùng,* 信皮 *sín p'î.* ‖ Ecorce, 殼 *hôc,* 皮 *p'î.*

Envelopper. 包 *paō.*

Envers. — lui, 别佢 *poūn kî,* 佢面前 *kî mién ts'iên.*

Envie. 嫉妬 *ts'ĭt toú.*

Environ. 差唔多 *ts'ā mĝ tō,* 大畧 *t'ái liŏc.* ‖ Les —, 隣近 *lîn k'ioún.*

Envoyer. 打發 *tà fât,* 搭 *tâp,* 送 *soúng.*

Epais, pas mince. *p'oūn.* ‖ Peu fluide, 稠 *neoû,* ‖ Dru, 密 *mĕt,* 濃 *nioûng.*

Epaule. 肩頭 *kiān t'eoû,* 肩膀 *kiān pòng.*

Epidémie. 瘟 *voūn.*

Epine. 竻 *nĕt,* 針 *tchīm,* 簕 *sièn.*

Epouser, prendre pour épouse, 娶 *ts'ì,* 討 *t'aò;* (pour époux) 嫁 *ká.*

Eprouver. 試 *tché,* 探 *t'àm.*

Equinoxe. — de printemps, 立春 *lĭp tch'oūn;* —d'automne, 立秋 *lĭp ts'ioū.*

Errer, se tromper. 做差 *tsó ts'a,* 話差 *vá ts'a,* 錯 *ts'ôc.*

Escalier. 墩子 *tón tzè,* 梯牌 *t'oī p'aî.*

Escorter. 送 *soúng.*

Espèce. 樣 *yóng,* 類 *louí,* 彙 *louí.*

Espérer. 望 *vóng.*

Esprit. 神 *chîn.*

Essayer. 試 *tché.*

Essuyer. 拭 *ts'oŭt; tch'ĭt,* 抹 *mât.*

Estimer, évaluer. 嘩 *fâ,* 猜 *ts'aī.* ‖ Faire cas, 看重 *k'ón tch'oúng.*

Estomac. 肚 *toù,* 飯包 *fán paō.*

Etablir. 立 *lĭp,* 安 *ōn.*

Etage, un —, 一層 *ȳt ts'ĕn.*

Etagère. 架子 *ká tzè.*
Etain. 錫 *siâc.*
Etaler. 攤 *t'ān,* 擺 *paì.*
Etape. 路站 *loú ts'ám,* 塘 *t'ông.*
Eté. 夏 *há,* 熱天 *gnĕt t'iēn.*
Eteindre. 熄火 *sĭt fò,* 噴烏火 *p'oūn voū fò,* 救火 *kioú fò.*
Etendre, déployer, 打開 *tà k'oī,* 伸 *chīn,* 伸 *tch'oūn.*
Eternel. 永遠 *yoùn yàn,* 無始無終 *voû tchè voû tchoūng.*
Etincelle. 火煋 *fò sēn.*
Etoffe. 布 *poú.*
Etonnant. 奇 *k'î,* 怪 *kouái.*
Etranger, subst. m. 番人 *fān gnîn,* ‖ Hôte, 客 *k'ĕt (*ou *hâc).*
Etrangler. 搯頸 *t'âc kiàng.*
Etre. 在 *ts'aí,* 有 *yoū,* 係 *hé·.*
Etrier. 馬凳 *mā tén,* 馬踏 *mā t'ăp.*
Etroit. 狹 *hăp,* 狹 *k'iăp,* 窄 *tsĕt.*
Etudier. 讀書 *t'oŭc choū.*
Eucharistie. 聖體 *chín t'ì.*
Evangile. 新聖經 *sīn chín kīn.*
Evangélistes. 聖史 *chín sè.*
Eveiller. — en appellant, 喊醒 *hám siàng.* ‖ S'—, 睡醒 *choé· siàng.*
Eventail, un —, 一把 (ou 支) 扇 *ȳt pà (*ou *kī) chán.*
Eventer. 撥扇 *p'ât chán.*
Evêque. 主教 *tchoù kaó.*
Eviter. 閃 *chàm,* 躲避 *tò p'ĭt,* 免 *mēn.* ‖ Ne pouvoir —, 不得不 *poŭt tĕt poŭt,* 免不得 *mēn poŭt tĕt.*
Exact. 對 *toúi,* 着 *tch'ŏc,* 合式 *hăp chĭt,* 麼差 *mô ts'ā.*
Examen. 省察 *sèn ts'ât,* 考 *k'aò.*
Examinateur. 學院 *hŏc yán,* 學臺 *hŏc t'oî.*
Examiner. 看 *k'ón,* 查 *ts'â.* ‖ — juridiquement, 驗 *niám.* ‖ S'—, 省察 *sèn ts'ât.*
Exaucer. 准 *tchoùn.*
Excéder. 過分 *kouó foún,* 過度 *kouó t'oú.*
Excepter. 除 *tch'oû,* 麼算個 *mô són ké·.*
Excuser (s'). 辭 *tsê,* 脫罪 *t'ôt ts'ouí.*
Exemple, modèle, 樣子 *yóng tzè.* ‖ — moral, 表樣 *piaò yóng.* ‖ Par —, 比方 *pì fōng,* 好比 *haò pì.*
Exercer. 教 *kaō,* 操練 *ts'aō lién.* ‖ S'—, 學慣 *hŏc kouán,* 操 *ts'aō.*
Exhorter. 勸 *k'ián,* 教訓 *kaō hioún.*
Exhumer. 改地 *koì t'í.*
Exil. Condamner à l'—, 罰充軍 *fât tch'oūng kioūn,* 罰流 *fât lioû.*
Exorciser. 逐魔鬼 *kioŭc mô houì,* 驅魔 *h'ī mô.*
Expérience. 見識 *kián chĭt.* ‖ Avoir l'— de, 試過個 *tché kouó ké·,* 則過個 *tsĕt kouó ké·.*
Expier. 補贖 *poù choŭc.*
Expirer, mourir. 斷氣 *t'ōn hí.*
Expliquer. 解 *kiaì,* 講 *kòng.*
Explorer. 打探 *tà t'àm,* 看 *k'ón.*
Exposé, 擺出個 *paì tch'oŭt ké·.* ‖ Tourné vers, 向 *hióng.*
Exposer 擺 *paì,* 攤 *t'ān.* ‖ — à l'air, 眼 *lâng;* au soleil, 晒 *saí.*
Exprimer, tirer le suc en pressant. 醡 *tsá.*
Extérieur. 外頭 *ngoé· t'eoû,* 外面 *ngoé· mién.*
Exterminer. 消滅 *siaō mĕt,* 殺盡 *sât ts'ìn,* 收 *choū.*
Extorquer. 撮 *ts'ôt,* 騙 *p'ién,* 戀 *lién.*

Extraire. 拿 (v. 取 v. 掷 v. 抓 v. 攺) 出來 *nā* (v. *ts'ì* v. *pāng* v. *tch'ā* v. *koì*) *tch'oût loî*.

Extrême, dernier. 尾上個 *mī hóng ké·*, 臨尾個 *lîm mī ké·*. || Très grand, 至太個 *tjé t'aí ké·*.

Extrême-Onction. 終傅 *tchoūng foú*, 終油 *tchoūng yoû*.

Extrémité. 尾 *mī*.

F

Façade. 面子 *mién tzè*.

Face, visage. 面 *mién*. || En— (en présence), 當面 *tōng mién*. || En— de (vis-à-vis), 對面 *touí mién*.

Facile. 容易 *yoûng ý*, 易得 *ý têt*. || — à étudier, 好讀 *haò t'oŭc*.

Fade. 餤 *t'ām*, 麽味 *mô mí*.

Fagot, un—de branches d'arbres, —捆樹扒 *ŷt k'oùn choú p'à*.

Faible, sans force. 弱 *niŏc*, 麽力 *mô lĭt*. || Sans fermeté, 軟 *niōn*.

Faillir, n'être pas éloigné de. 爭一滴 (v. 點) *tsāng ŷt tît* (v. *tiàm*). *Voyez* se tromper, pécher.

Faillite. 蝕本 *chăt poùn*.

Faim. Avoir —, 肚餓 *toù kī*, 餓 *ngó*.

Faire. 做 *tsó*, 爲 *vî*, 作 *tsôc*. || Mettre bas, 下 *hà*. || Constituer un tout, 上 *chòng*, 成 *chîn*.

Falloir. Il faut, 愛 *oí*, 該當 *koī tōng*.

Familier, subst. m. 熟人 *choŭc gnîn*. || Adj. 熟 *choŭc*, 慣 *kouán*, 平常個 *p'în chông ké·*.

Famille. 家 *kā*, 烟戶 *yān foú*, 族 *ts'oŭc*.

Famine. 荒年 *fōng niân*.

Fané. 萎了 *yān liaò*, 謝了 *ts'iá liaò*.

Fantôme. 精怪 *tsīn kouaí*, 鬼 *kouì*.

Fardeau. 担 *tām*.

Farine. 麵粉 *mién foùn*.

Fatigue. 辛苦 *sīn k'où*, 蹄 *k'ioí*.

Faucille. 鐮子 *liâm tzè*.

Faute. 罪 *ts'ouí*, 過失 *kouó chĭt*.

Fauteuil. 靠椅 *kaó ỳ*.

Faux, adj. 假個 *kà ké·*, 詐 *tsá*.

Faveur. 恩典 *ēn tièn*. || Obtenir une —, 得賞 *têt chòng*.

Favoriser. 栽培 *tsaī p'î*, 保佑 *paò yoú*.

Fécond. 肯生 *hèn sāng*, 肯出 *hèn tch'oût*.

Feindre. 詐 *tsá*.

Féliciter. 恭賀 *kioūng fó*, 恭喜 *kioūng hì*.

Femelle. 嫲 *mâ*, 牸 *tsé*.

Femme. 婦人家 *foú gnîn kā*, || Vieille femme, 婆 *p'ô*, 老伯姆 *laò pâc mē·*. || Epouse, 妻 *ts'ī*, 姐 *tsià*, 老婆 *laò p'ô*, 家室 *kā chĭt*. 家眷 *kā kián*.

Fendre. 劈 *pĭt*. || —du bois, 破柴 *p'ó ts'iaô*; —du verre, 畫玻璃 *văc pō li*.

Fente. 縫 *p'oúng*, 口 *heoù*, 隙 *hĭt*.

Fer. 鐵 *t'iĕt*, || — à repasser, 熨斗 *yoún teoù*.

Ferment. — pour faire le vin, 酒餅 *tsioù piàng*. || —Levain, 酵 *kaó*.

Fermenter. 發 *fât*, *pôt*; 起 *hì*, 長 *tchòng*.

Fermer. 關 *kouān*.

Fertile. 盛 *chín*. 茂盛 *miaó chín*.

Ferveur. 熱心 *gnĕt sīm*.

Festin. 酒席 *tsioù sĭt*.

Fête. 喜事 *hì sé*, 瞻禮 *tchām lī*.

Feu. 火 *fò*.

Feuille. 葉 *yăp*. || —de papier, 一張紙 *ŷt tchōng tjè*.

Feuillet, un.—, 一頁 *ŷt yăp*, —篇 *ŷt p'iēn*.

Feuilleter. — un livre, 揜書 *yān choū*, 翻書 *fān choū*.
Feutre. 氈 *tchān*.
Fève. 豆 *t'eoú*.
Fiançailles. Faire des fiançailles (pour un garçon), 定親 *t'ín ts'īn*, 討親 *t'aò ts'īn*; (pour une fille), 放 *fóng*. ‖ Présents de —, 聘金 *p'ín kīm*. ‖ Rompre les —, 退親 *t'ouí ts'īn*.
Ficher. 插 *ts'ăp*, 釘 *tāng*.
Fidèle. 忠厚 *tchoūng heoú*, 忠實 *tchoūng chĭt*, 妥當 *t'ò tóng*.
Fièvre. 寒燒 *hôn chaō*, 發燒 *fât chaō*; — intermittente, 打擺子 *tà paì tzè*.
Figure, forme extérieure. 樣子 *yóng tzè*, 形像 *hîn sióng*. ‖ Comparaison, 比方 *pì fōng*, 表意 *piaò ý*.
Fil. 線 *sién*, 絲線 *sē sién*, ‖ — de fer, de cuivre, 鐵線 *t'iĕt sién*, 銅線 *t'oûng sién*.
Filer. 紡線 *p'iòng sién*.
Filet. 網 *miòng*, 撈筐 *leoû fī*. ‖ Pris dans les filets de qqn., 上人個當 *chōng gnîn ké· tóng*.
Fille. 妹子 *moé· tzè*.
Filleul. 代子 *t'oí tzè*; filleule, 代女 *t'oí ng̀*.
Fils. 賴子 *laí tzè*.
Filtrer. 濾 *loúi*.
Fin, bout. 尾 *mī*. ‖ Menu, 細 *sé·*, 仔 *tsē·*. ‖ Rusé, 精伶 *tsīn lîn*.
Fixe, immobile. 麼動 *mô t'oūng*, 穩 *voùn*. ‖ Certain, 定着 *t'ín tch'ŏc*, 靠得住 *k'aó têt tch'oú*.
Fixer, déterminer, 定 *t'ín*. ‖ Rendre stable, 釘穩 *tāng voùn*.
Flamme. 火利 *fò lí*, 火燄 *fò liám*.
Flaque. — d'eau, 水湖 *choùi foû*.
Flatter. 奉承 *foúng chîn*, 稱說人 *tch'īn chŏt gnîn*. ‖ Se flatter, 自誇 *tsé tch'ìn*, 自說 *tsé chŏt*.
Flèche. 箭 *tsién*.
Fleur. 花 *fā*.
Fleurir. 開花 *k'oī fā*.
Fleuve. 河 *hô*.
Flotter. 浮水 *feoû choùi*, 漂 *p'iaô*.
Flûte. 笛子 *t'ăc tzè*.
Foi. 信德 *sín têt*.
Foie. 肝 *kōn*.
Foire. 圩 *hī*, 圩場 *hī tch'ông*.
Fois, une —, 一次 *ŷt tsé*, 一回 *ŷt fî*, 一擺 *ŷt paì*. ‖ Chaque —, 擺擺 *paì paì*.
Foncé, bleu —, 深藍 *tch'īm lâm*.
Fond. 底 *taì*.
Fondement. 地基 *t'í kī*, 地脚 *t'í kiŏc*.
Fondre, liquéfier, 化 *fá*, 煮熔 *tchoù youńg*. ‖ Couler, 鑄 *taó*; *tchoú*.
Fontaine. 水泉 *choùi ts'ân*.
Fonte. 生鐵 *sāng t'iĕt*.
Force. 力 *lĭt*, 力量 *lĭt leóng*.
Forcer. 勉 *kām*. ‖ Se forcer, 趲勁 *tsán kín*, 用蠻 *yoúng mân*.
Foret. 鑽子 *tsón tzè*.
Forêt. 樹山 *choú sān*.
Forgeron. 打鐵師傅 *tà t'iĕt sē foú*.
Forme. 樣子 *yóng tzè*. ‖ Moule, 模子 *moû tzè*. ‖ — de cordonnier, 楦頭 *hién t'eoû*.
Fort, adj, solide. 主固 *tchoù koú*, 硬健 *ngáng k'ián*. ‖ Robuste, 壯旺 *tsóng vóng*, 健 *k'ián*. ‖ A plus forte raison, 況且 *k'òng ts'ià*.
Forteresse. 炮台 *p'aó t'oî*, 寨 *ts'aí*.
Fortifier, réparer les forces, 補人 *poù gnîn*. ‖ Affermir, 堅固 *kiān koú*.

Fortune. 錢財 *ts'iên ts'oî.*
Fosse. 窟 *foût.*
Fossé. 坑公 *hāng koūng*, 溝 *keoū*, 瀝 *lâc.*
Fou, subst. 狂人 *k'ông gnîn*, 呆人 *ngoē· gnîn.* || Devenir —, (發)癲 *pôt tiēn.*
Fouiller. 搜 *seoū.*
Foule. 人多 *gnîn tō*, 壅 *yóng.*
Fouler. 踩 *ts'aì*, 蹍 *lién*, 踏 *t'ăp*, 舂 *tchoūng.*
Four. 窰子 *yaô tzè*, 炕爐 *k'óng loû.*
Fourche, fourchette, 叉子 *ts'ā tzè.*
Fourmi. 蟻公 *gnī (ou nī) koūng.*
Fourreau. 袋子 *t'oí tzè.* || — de couteau, 刀鞘 *taō siaó.*
Foyer. 灶頭 *tsaó t'eoû.* || Famille, 烟戶 *yān foú.*
Fraction. 零頭 *lâng t'eoû.*
Fragile, qui se brise aisément. 脆 *ts'oí.* || Pas solide, 唔主固 *mĝ tchoù koú.*
Frais. 涼 *leông.* || Récent, 新鮮個 *sīn siēn kė·.*
Franc. 老實 *laò chĭt*, 忠值 *sīm tch'ĭt.*
Frange. 鬚 *sī.*
Frapper. 打 *tà.* — du pied, 踢 *t'ĕt.*
Fréquenter. 來往 *loî vòng.*
Frère, (plus âgé). 阿哥 *ā kō*; (moins âgé), 老弟 *laò t'aí.* Ils sont frères, 佢同佢兄弟 *kî t'oûng kî hioūng t'í.*
Friche (terre en). 荒地 *fōng t'í.*
Frire. 煎 *tsiēn.*
Froid, adj. 冷 *lāng*, 寒 *hôn.*
Froisser. 扭縐 *nioù tsioú.*
Fromage. — de lait, 牛乳餅 *nioû nén piàng*; — de haricots, 豆腐 *t'eoú foú.*
Froncer. 縐 *tsioú.*
Front. 額頭 *niâc t'eoû.*
Frontière. 邊界 *piēn kiaí.*
Frotter. 擦 *ts'ât*, 拭 *ts'oŭt*, 摩 *nô*; *mó*, 搓 *ts'ō.*
Fructifier. 結子 *kiĕt tzè*, 結菓 *kiĕt kouò.*
Fruit. 菓 *kouò.*
Fuir. 跑走 *p'aō tseoù*, 偷走 *t'eoū tseoù.*
Fumée. 烟 *yān.*
Fumer. 食烟 *chĭt yān.* || Epandre du fumier, 潑糞 *p'ât poún.*
Furoncle. 釘瘡 *tāng ts'ōng*, 肘 *tch'oî.*
Furtivement. 偷倒 *t'eoū taò*, 暗商做事 *ám chōng tsó sé.*
Fusée. 火箭 *fò tsién*, 花筒 *fā t'oûng.*
Fusil. 銃 *tch'oúng.*
Futur. 後來 *heoú loî*, 將來 *tsiōng loî.*

G

Gage. 當頭 *tóng t'eoû.*
Gager. 賭 *toù*, 打賭 *tà toù.*
Gagner. 賺錢 *ts'ón ts'iên*, 得 *tĕt.* || L'emporter, 贏 *yâng.*
Gain. 利息 *lí sĭt.*
Gale. 瘡 *ts'ōng.*
Garçon. 癩子 *laí tzè.*
Garde-fou. 欄杆 *lân kōn.*
Garder, veiller sur. 掌 *tchòng*, 看守 *k'ón choù.*
Gardien. — d'une porte, 掌門個 *tchòng moûn kė·.* || Ange —, 護守天神 *foú choù t'iēn chîn.*
Garer (se). 閃開 *chàm k'oī*, 防 *fông.*
Gaspiller. 枉用 *nóng yoúng.*
Gâteau. 餅 *piàng*, 糕 *kaō.*
Gâter. 壞 *faí*, 爛 *lán.* || — les enfants, 惜壞細人 *siâc faí sé· gnîn.*

Gauche. 左 *tsò.*
Gaz. 氣 *hí.*
Gaze. 紗 *sā.*
Gélatine. 膠 *kaō.*
Geler. 凍 *toúng*, 氷 *k'én*, 凝 *k'ên.*
Gendre. 婿郎 *sé· lông.*
Général (en). 一總 *ŷt tsoùng*, 大畧 *t'aí liŏc*, 大概 *t'aí k'oì.*
Génération. 代 *t'oí*, 輩 *pí.*
Généreux. 大方 *t'aí fōng*, 大量 *t'aí leóng.*
Genou. 膝頭 *ts'ĭt t'eoû.*
Gentil. 乖 *kouaī*, 得人惜 *têt gnîn siâc.*
Génuflexion. Faire une —, 打篏 *tà ts'iām.*
Gérant. 管事 *kouòn sé.*
Germe. 芽 *ngâ.*
Gigot. 羊髀 (v. 腿) *yông pì* (v. *t'ouì*).
Gilet. 裩身衫 *k'oùn chīn sām.*
Gingembre. 薑 *kiōng.*
Girofle (clou de). 丁香 *tēn hiōng.*
Givre. 白霜 *p'ăc sōng.*
Glace. 氷 *k'én.*
Glisser. 滑 *văt*, 溜 *lioú.*
Globe. — terrestre, 地球 *t'í k'ioû.*
Gloire. 榮光 *yoûng kouōng.* || Gloriole, 面目 *mién mouĉ*, 體面 *t'ì mién.*
Gorgée, une —, 一口 *ŷt heoù.*
Gosier. 喉嚨 *heoû loûng.*
Gourmand. 好食 *haó chĭt.*
Goût. 味道 *mí t'aó.*
Goûter. 嘗 *chông.*
Goutte, une —, 一滴 *ŷt tĭt*, 一點 *ŷt tiàm.*
Gouttière. 水筧 *chouì kiàn.*
Gouvernail. 敗柁 *chôn t'ó*, 柁尾 *t'ó mī.*
Gouverner. 管 *kouòn*, 掌 *tchòng*, 主事 *tchoù sé.*

Grâce, don surnaturel. 聖寵 *chín tch'oùng*, 恩 *ēn.*
Grade, dignité. 功名 *koūng miâng*, 官銜 *kouōn hâm.*
Graine. 子 *tzè*, 仁 *ŷn*, 種 *tchoùng.*
Graisse. 油 *yoû.*
Grand, étendu. 大 *t'aí.* || Haut, 高 *kaō.* || Long, 長 *tch'ông.*
Grandir. 長 *tchòng*, 大 *t'aí.*
Grappe, une — de raisin, 一抓葡萄 *ŷt tch'a p'oû t'aô.*
Gras, adj. 肥 *p'î.*
Gras, subst. m. 肥肉 *p'î nioûc*; faire —, 食葷 *chĭt foūn.*
Gratter. 刮 *kouât*, 搓 *ts'ō*, 乜 *yà.*
Grave. 重 *tch'oúng*, 大 *t'aí.*
Graver. 刻 *k'ĕt*, 雕 *t'iaō.*
Greffer. 駁 *pôc.*
Grêle, subst. f. 雹 *p'ôc.*
Grelot. 鈴 *lâng.*
Grenade. 石榴 *chăc lioû.*
Grenier. 倉 *ts'ōng.* || Etage, 天棚 *t'iēn p'âng.*
Grenouille. 蝦蟆 *hâ mâ*, 蛞子 *kouaì tzè.*
Griffe. 爪 *tsaò.*
Griffer. 搔 *tsaò*, 搔爛 *tsaò lán.*
Griller. 炕 *k'óng*, 炒 *ts'aò.*
Grimper. 爬 *p'â*, 泅 *ts'ioû.*
Grincer. 搓牙齒 *ts'ō ngâ tchè.*
Gris, cendré. 灰色 *foē· sĕt.*
Gros. 大 *t'aí.* || Acheter en —, 堆買 *toì maì.*
Grossier. 粗 *tsē*, 笨 *poún.* || Riz —, 糙米 *ts'aó mì.* || Paroles grossières, 醜話 *tch'où fá.*
Grue. 鴈鵝 *ngán ngô.*
Guêpe. 黃蜂 *vông foūng.*

Guérir, v. a. 醫病 *ȳ p'iáng.* || V. n. 病好 *p'iáng haò.*
Guerre. Faire la —, 相打 *siōng tà,* 相戰 *siōng tchán,* 打仗 *tà tchóng.*

H

Habile. 噲 *voé·,* 熟 *choŭc,* 巧 *k'aò,* 有工夫 *yoū koūng foū.*
Habiller (s'). 著衫 *tchôc sām.*
Habit. 衣服 *ȳ foŭc,* 衫 *sām.*
Habiter. 核 *hĕt,* 住 *tch'oú.*
Habitude. 慣習 *kouán sĭp;* — mauvaise et invétérée, 老毛病 *laò maō p'iáng.*
Hache. 斧頭 *poù t'eoû.*
Hacher. — menu, 切碎 *ts'iĕt soúi.*
Haie. — d'épines, 竻頭掩 *nĕt t'eoû ām.*
Haïr. 惱恨 *naō hén.*
Haleine. 氣脉 *hí mâc.*
Hameçon. 釣鈎 *tiaó keoū.*
Hangar. 寮 *liaô,* 廠 *tch'ŏng.*
Haricot. 豆子 *t'eoú tzè.*
Hasard. Rencontrer par —, 逢 *foûng,* 遇 *gní,* 撞 *ts'óng.*
Hâte. 快 *k'ouái,* 忙 *mâng.*
Haut, adj. 高 *kaō.* || A voix haute, 大聲 *t'aí chāng.*
Haut, subst. m. 上面 *chóng mién,* 頂上個 *tàng hóng ké·.*
Herbe. 草 *ts'aò.*
Hérésie. 裂教 *lĭĕt kaó.*
Héritage. 家業 *kā nĭăp,* 身家 *chīn kā.*
Heure, une heure, 一點鐘 *ȳt tiàm tchoūng.* || De bonne heure, 早 *tsaò.*
Heureusement. 好得 *haò tĕt.*
Heureux. 有福 *yoū foŭc.* || Favorable, 好 *haò.*
Heurter. 撞 *tchoūng,* 撞 *ts'óng,* 碰 *p'ōng.*
Hideux. 醜 *tch'où.*
Hier. 昨日 *ts'ŏc gnĭt; ts'ioū poū gnĭt; ts'ī poū gnĭt; ts'āng poū gnĭt* (selon les pays).
Hirondelle. 燕子 *yán tzè.*
Hisser. 抓上 *tch'ā chŏng.*
Histoire. 綱鑑 *kōng kám,* 傳子 *tch'ón tzè.*
Hiver. 冬 *toūng,* 寒天 *hôn t'iēn.*
Homme. 人 *gnîn,* 男人 *nâm gnîn.*
Homonyme. 同姓 *t'oûng siáng.*
Honnête. — homme, 好人 *haò gnîn,* 正大 *tchín t'aí.*
Honneur, estime des hommes, 臉 *liēn,* 面 *mién,* 聲名 *chāng miâng.*
Honorable. Homme —, 有體面個 *yoū t'ì mién ké·.*
Honoraires. — d'un maître d'école, 束脩 *tch'oŭc sioū,* 學錢 *hŏc ts'iēn;* — d'un médecin, 謝禮 *ts'iá lì.*
Honte. Avoir —, 怕羞 *p'á sioū,* 唔好意思 *mĝ haò ý sé.*
Hoquet. Avoir le —, 打嗝厥 *tà hĕt toŭc.*
Horizontal. 坪 *p'iâng.*
Horloge. 時辰鐘 *chê chîn tchoūng.*
Hostie. Pain d'autel, 麵餅 *mién piàng.*
Hôte, celui qui donne l'hospitalité, 主人 *tchoù gnîn.* || Celui qui la reçoit, 客 *hâc.*
Hôtellerie. 店子 *tiám tzè.*
Huile. 油 *yoû.*
Humble. 謙卑 *k'iām pī,* 謙遜 *k'iām soún.*

Humecter. 潑濕 *p'ât chîp*, 噴濕 *p'oún chîp*.
Humide. 濕 *chîp*, 潤 *yoún*.
Hypothèque. 當 *tóng*.

I

Ici. 裡 *lì*, 裡 *ỳ*, 裡子 *lì tzè*, 裡裡 *ỳ lì*.
Idée. *Voyez* pensée, intention, avis.
Idole. 菩薩 *p'oû sât*.
Ignorer. 唔知 *mĝ tī*, 唔曉得 *mĝ hiaò têt*.
Il, pron. 佢 *kî*. ‖ Ils, 佢等 *kî tèn*.
Ile. 海墩 *hoì toùn*, 海島 *hoì tò* (v. *taò*).
Illégitime, contre la loi, 唔合國法 *mĝ hăp kouĕt fâp*. ‖ Contre la raison, 唔合理 *mĝ hăp lī*. ‖ *Voyez* injuste.
Image. 像 *sióng*, 花 *fā*.
Imaginer. 嘩 *fâ*, 想 *siòng*.
Imiter. 學樣 *hŏc yóng*, 效法 *haó fâp*.
Immédiatement. 立刻 *lĭp k'ĕt*, 卽刻 *tsĭt k'ĕt*, 就 *ts'ioú*, 當時 *tōng chê*.
Immiscer (s'). 鑽 *tsón*, 管閑事 *kouòn hán sé*.
Immortel. 永不死 *yoùn poût sì*, 常生不死 *chông sēn poût sì*.
Impair. 單 *tān*. ‖ Nombre —, 單數 *tān sé*.
Impartial. 坪心 *p'iâng sīm*.
Impératrice-mère. 皇大后 *fông t'ai heoú*.
Impétueux. Vent —, 忙風 *mâng foūng*. ‖ Caractère —, 急性 *kĭp sín*.
Implorer. 求 *k'ioû*, 懇求 *k'èn k'ioû*, 賴 *lái*.
Important. 要緊 *yaó kìn*, 重 *tch'oúng*.
Importer. 關 *kouān*. ‖ Peu —, 麼要緊 *mô yaó kìn*, 麼相干 *mô siōng kōn*. ‖ N'importe qui, 不論那人 *poût loún màn gnîn*; n'importe quoi, 不論那個 *poût loún mâc ké·*.
Importun. 跳皮人 *t'iaó p'î gnîn*, 混帳 *foún tchóng*.
Impossible. 人做唔來個 *gnîn tsó mĝ loî ké·*, 萬不能個 *ván poût nên ké·*.
Imprimer. 印 *ýn*; — à la brosse, 刷 *sŏt*.
Impudique. 邪 *siâ*.
Impur. 唔乾淨 *mĝ kōn ts'iáng*.
Inanimé. Chose —, 死物 *sì voŭt*.
Incarner (s'). 降生 *kóng sēn*.
Incendie. 火燒屋 *fò chaō voûc*, 失火 *chĭt fò*.
Incertani. 麼定 *mô t'ín*.
Incliner. 放斜 *fóng siâ*, 方畬 *fóng ts'iâ*. ‖ — la tête, 啱頭 *ngàm t'eoû*.
Indifféremment, indifférent. 不論 *poût loún*, 不拘 *poût kī*.
Indigène. 本地人 *poùn t'í gnîn*.
Indigo. 靛 *t'ién*; (la plante), 藍子 *lâm tzè*.
Indiquer. 指 *tjè*; — par gestes, 比 *pì*.
Indisposé, légèrement malade. 唔伸暢 *mĝ tch'oūn tch'òng*, 唔道地 *mĝ t'aó t'í*, 唔自然 *mĝ tsé yân*.
Indulgence. — accordée par l'Eglise, 恩赦 *ēn chá*, 大赦 *t'aí chá*. ‖ Facilité à pardonner, 仁慈 *ŷn tsê*.
Inépuisable. 麼盡個 *mô ts'ín ké·*.
Infect. 臭 *tch'oú*.
Inférieur, placé au dessous. 下 *hā*. ‖ Moindre, 下 *há*, 下等 *há tèn*.
Infiltrer (s') 浸 *tsím*, 抽 *tch'oū*.
Inflammation. Avoir une —, 有火 *yoū fò*, 腫 *tchoùng*.

Influence, qui a de l'—, 話得事 *vá tĕt sé*, 有勢頭 *yoū sé t'coū*.
Informer (s'). 訪問 *fòng moún*.
Infuser. 泡 *p'aó*.
Ingénieux. 巧 *k'aò*, 精伶 *tsīn lîn*.
Ingrat (être). 麽頁心 *mô leông sīm*, 失恩 *chĭt ēn*.
Injurier. 罵 *má*, 汚辱 *voū yŏuc*.
Inné. 生成個 *sāng chĥng ké*.
Innocent. 麽罪 *mô ts'ouí*,
Inoccupé. 閒 *hân*, 空 *k'oúng*.
Inonder. 淹 *yàm*, 飲 *ým*, 浸 *tsím*.
Inquiet. 憂慮 *yoū lí*.
Inscription. 字 *sé*, 匾額 *pièn niâc*. || Deux — correspondantes sur deux tablettes verticales, 對子 *touí tzè*. || — sur une pierre commémorative, 碑石 *pī chăc*.
Inscrire. 訂 *tāng*, 寫 *sià*, 上 *chōng*.
Insecte. 虫 *tch'oúng*.
Inspecter. *Voyez* examiner.
Inspirer. Dieu l'inspire, 天主默照佢 *t'iēn tchoù mĕt tchaó kî*. *Voyez* conseiller.
Instant, un —, 一下 *ŷt há*. || Il n'y a qu'un instant, 剛剛 *kiōng kiōng*.
Instinct. 本性 *poùn sín*, 靈性 *lîn sín*.
Instituer. 立 *līp*, 定 *t'ín*.
Instrument. 傢事 *kā ché*, 傢伙 *kā fò*, 器皿 *hí mìn*.
Insu. A l'— de qqn. 麽話佢知 *mô vá kî tī*, 騙背 *p'ién poé*.
Intelligent 聰明 *ts'oūng mîn*.
Intention. 意事 *ý sé*, 心事 *sīm sé*, 主意 *tchoù ý*. || Avec —, 故意 *koú ý*.
Intercalaire, mois —, 閏月 *yoún gnĕt*.
Intercéder. 轉求 *tchòn k'ioû*.
Intercepter. 隔 *kâc*, 攔 *lân*, 抵 *tì* ou *taì*, 堵 *toù*, 擋 *tòng*.
Intérêt. 利 *lí*, 益處 *ŷt tch'oú*.
Intérieur. 內 *nouí*, 貯 *toù*, 肚 *toù*.
Intérim. 署任 *choù ým*, 代理 *t'oí li*.
Interroger. 問 *moún*.
Interrompre. 斷 *t'ōn*, 止 *tjè*, 停 *t'în*.
Interprète. 傳話 *tch'ôn fá*.
Intervalle. 隔 *kâc*, 減 *kám*. || Espace vide, 孔 *k'oùng*.
Intestin. 腸 *tch'ông*,
Introduction. 小引 *siaò ŷn*, 序 *sí*.
Introduire. 放入 *fóng gnìp*, 帶 *taí*, 引 *ŷn*.
Inusité. 麽人愛 *mô gnîn oí*, 少用 *chaò yoúng*, 唔通行 *mĝ t'oūng hâng*.
Inutile. 麽用 *mô yoúng*, 廢物 *fí voŭt*.
Inutilement. 枉了 *nóng liaò*.
Inventer. 造 *ts'aó*, 緬出來 *mèn tch'oŭt loî*.
Invétéré. 慣 *kouán*, 老毛病 *laò maō p'iáng*.
Inviter. 請 *ts'iàng*, 吙 *vò*.
Invoquer. 喊 *hám*. *Voir* implorer.
Irriter. 惹 *niā*.
Issue. 出路 *tch'oŭt loú*, 口 *hcoù*, 脒 *loí*, || Moyen, 方法 *fōng fâp*.
Ivoire. 象牙 *sióng ngâ*.

J

Jadis. *Voir* autrefois.
Jailllir. 湧 *yoùng* 濽 *ts'án*. 潑 *păt*, 潑 *p'ât*.
Jamais, 自唔啱 *tsé mĝ ts'ĕn*. || A—, 永遠 *yoùn yàn*, 永久 *yoùn kioù*.
Jambe. 脚臂 *kiŏc pì*.
Jambières. 套褲 *t'aó foú*, 臂褲 *pì foú*.
Jambon. 火腿 *fò t'ouì*.

Jardin. — de fleurs, 花園 *fā yân;* — potager, 菜園 *ts'oí yân.*

Jarre. 罌 *āng,* 甕 *voúng,* 甏 *p'áng.*

Jarrètières. 襪帶 *mât taí,*

Jaune. 黄 *vông.*

Jeter. 擲 *fìt,* 丟 *tioū,* 敖 *ngaó.* || Se —, *piaō,* 跳 *t'iaó* 投 *t'eoû.*

Jeune. 後生 *heoú sāng,* 年輕 *niân k'iāng.*

Jeûner. 守大齋 *choù t'aí tsaī.*

Joie. Etre dans la —, 快活 *k'ouaí fát,* 歡喜 *fōn hì,* 心安樂 *sīm ōn lŏc.*

Joindre. 合 *hăp,* 合 *kâp,* 合 *lâp,* 搭 *tâp.*

Jointure. — des os, 骨節 *koût tsiĕt,*

Joue. 嘴角 *tchoí kôc.*

Jouer. — de l'argent, 賭錢 *toù ts'iên.* || — d'un instrument (avec les lèvres), 吹 *tch'oī;* (avec les doigts), 彈 *t'ân,* 鑼 *kí,* 打 *tà.* || S'amuser, 攪 *kaò.*

Jour, clarté, 光 *kouōng,* 亮 *leóng.* || Espace de 24 heures, 日 *gnĭt,* 天 *t'iēn.* || — et nuit, 日夜 *gnĭt yá.*

Journal. 新聞紙 *sīn voûn tjè,* 日報 *gnĭt paó.*

Jugement, faculté de l'âme. 靈性 *lîn sín.* || Action de juger, 審判 *chìm p'án.*

Juger. 審 *chìm,* 斷 *tón,* 判 *p'án.*

Jurer. *Voir* serment.

Jus. 湯 *t'ōng,* 漿 *tsiōng,* 水 *chouì,* 汁 *tchĭp.*

Juste, adj. 公道 *koūng t'aó,* 照理 *tchaó lī.* || Adv. 準 *tchoùn,* 對 *touí,* 着 *tch'ŏc,* 正 *tcháng.*

Jusque. 到 *taó.*

L

Là, adv. 裡子 *ỳ tzè* ou *lì tzè,* 裡邊 *ỳ* ou *lì piēn,* 個裡 *ké· lì,* 個邊 *ké· piēn,* 個頭 *ké· t'eoû.* || En ce temps-là, 當時 *tōng chê,* 裡個時候 *ỳ* ou *lì ké· chê heoú.* || Jusque là, 到個時 *taó ké· chê.*

Labourer. 犁 *laî,* 耕 *kāng,* 耖 *ts'aó.*

Lac. 細海 *sé· hoì,* 大水湖 *t'aí chouì foû.*

Lacet. 帶子 *taí tzè,* 索 *sôc;* prendre au —, 搭 *t'âc.*

Lâche, non tendu. 鬆 *soūng.* || Poltron, 麼膽 *mô tàm.* || Sans cœur, 歹心 *vaī sīm.*

Lâcher, détendre. 放鬆 *fóng soūng,* || Laisser échapper, 放 *fóng,* 擲 *fìt.*

Laid. 唔好看 *mĝ haò k'ón,* 醜 *tch'où.*

Laine. 綿羊毛 *miên yông maō.*

Laisser, ne pas emmener avec soi, 留 *lioû.* || Ne pas empêcher, 准 *tchoùn;* laisse-le faire, 等佢做 *tèn kî tsó,* 聽佢做 *t'ín kî tsó,* 儘佢做 *ts'ín kî tsó.* || Abandonner, 放 *fóng,* 遺 *ûi,* 捨 *chà.*

Lait. 乳 *nén.*

Laitue. 萵菜 *mâc ts'oí.*

Lame. Une — de couteau, 一張刀 *ŷt tchōng taō.* || Plaque, 板 *pàn* ou *pièn.*

Lampe. 燈 *tēn.*

Lance. 旂鎗 *k'î ts'iōng.*

Langage. 語 *fá,* 土談 *t'où t'âm,* 講話 *kòng fá.*

Langue. 舌 *chăt.*

Lanière. 皮帶 *p'î taí,* 皮條 *p'î t'iaô.* || — de bambou, 竹篾 *tchoûc mĕt.*

Lanterne. 燈籠 *tēn loûng.*

Lapin. — domestique, 兎子 *t'oú tzè.* || — sauvage, lièvre, 野兎子 *ya t'oú tzè.*

Lard. 肥猪肉 *p'î tchoū nioûc.*

Large. 寬 *k'ōn*, 闊 *fât*, 大 *t'aí*.
Larme. 目水 *moûc chouì*.
Latrines. 粗窖 *tsē kaó*, 畚缸 *poún kōng*, 屎窖 *chè kaó*.
Laver. 洗 *sè*, 洙 *mî*, 盪 *t'ōng*.
Lécher. 舐 *chaī* ou *sē*.
Légaliser. — un contrat, 稅契 *choé k'é*.
Léger. 輕 *k'iāng*.
Légumes. 小菜 *siaò ts'oí*.
Lendemain. 明天 *mîn t'iēn*, 第二日 *t'í gní gnĭt*.
Lent. 慢 *mán*, 遲 *tchê*, 延 *yân*.
Lèpre. 癩 *t'aì*.
Lequel, laquelle, 那個 *naí ké*.
Lettre, caractère d'écriture, 字 *sé*. ‖ Epître, 書信 *choū sín*.
Lettré. 紳士 *chīn sé*, 讀書人 *t'oŭc choū gnîn*.
Leur. 佢等個 *kì tèn ké*.
Levain. 酒餅 *tsioù piàng*, 醒 *kaó*.
Lever, soulever. 拏起來 *nā hì loî*, 抓起來 *tch'ā hì loî*, 扐 *lĕt*. ‖ Germer, 生起來 *sāng hì loî*. ‖ Fermenter, 發 *pôt*. ‖ Se —, 上起來 *hóng hì loî*, 軀倒來 *k'ī taò loî*. ‖ Le vent se lève, 起風 *hì foūng*.
Lèvre. 嘴唇 *tchoí choûn*.
Lézard. 狗螞蛇 *keoù mâ châ*.
Libéral. 大方 *t'aí fōng*, 大量 *t'aí leóng*.
Libre, indépendant. 自主 *tsé tchoù*. ‖ Inoccupé, 空 *k'oúng*, 閒 *hân*.
Licencié. 舉人 *kì gnîn*.
Licite. 可以 *k'ò ȳ*, 使得 *sè tĕt*, 做得 *tsó tĕt*.
Lie. 渣 *tsā*, 脚 *kiŏc*.
Lier. 搭 *t'âc*, 綯 *t'aô*, 綁 *pòng*, 揰 *tsât*.
Lieu. *Voir* endroit. ‖ Tenir — de, 當 *tóng*, 準 *tchoùn*.
Ligne, trait. 線 *sién*, 畫 *văc*. ‖ Rangée, 行 *hông*. ‖ Pêcher à la ligne, 釣魚 *tiaó ńg*.
Limaille. 銼屎 *ts'ó chè*.
Lime. 銼子 *ts'ó tzè*.
Limite. 界 *kiaí*. ‖ Fixer uue — de temps, 限期 *hán k'î*. ‖ Dépasser les —, 過度 *kouó t'oú*. ‖ Sans —, 無限 *voû hán*.
Limpide. 清 *ts'īn*.
Lion. 獅子 *sē tzè*.
Liqueur. 甜酒 *t'iâm tsioù*.
Lire. — un livre, 看書 *k'ón choū*. ‖ Savoir —, 識字 *chĭt sé*. ‖ — à haute voix, 讀 *t'oŭc*, 念 *niám*.
Liste. 單子 *tān tzè*. ‖ — (des candidats admis), 榜 *pòng*.
Lit. 床 *ts'ông*.
Litanies. 禱文 *taó voûn*.
Littérature, art d'écrire, 文法 *voûn fâp*.
Livre, s. m. 書 *choū*.
Livre, s. f. 斤 *kīn*.
Livrer. 交 *kaō*, 寄 *kí*, 撿 *kiàm*, 拿 *nā*.
Locataire. 佃戶 *t'ién foú*.
Locution, une —, 一句話 *ȳt kí fá*.
Loger. 歇 *hiĕt*, 住 *tch'oú*, 站 *tsàn*.
Loi. 國法 *kouĕt fâp*, 例 *lí*. ‖ Règle, 規矩 *kouī kì*.
Loin. 遠 *yàn*,
Long. 長 *tch'ông*, 久 *kioù*. ‖ *Voir* lent.
Longtemps. 久 *kioù*.
Lors. — des troubles, 亂個時候 *lón ké chê heoú*. ‖ Lorsque, 時候 *chê heoú*.
Lot. 分子 *foūn tzè*, 股子 *koù tzè*.

Louer. En parlant de meubles, d'animaux, 租 *tzē* ou *tchoū*. || En parlant d'ouvriers, 請 *ts'iàng;* 和 *vò*. || S'il s'agit de barques, de chaises, 寫 *sià*, 雇 *koú*.

Louer (laudare). 稱說人 *tch'în chôt gnîn*, 奬慣人 *tsiòng chòng gnîn*, 讚美人 *tsán mī gnîn*.

Lourd. 重 *tch'oūng*.

Lourdeau. 忲 *poún*, 粗 *tsē*.

Loyer. 佃錢 *t'ién ts'ên*.

Lui. 佢 *kî*.

Lumière. 光 *kouōng*, 火 *fò*.

Lune. 月 *gnĕt*, 月光 *gnĕt kouōng*.

Lunettes. 眼鏡 *niàn kiáng*.

Luxure (péché de). 邪淫個罪 *siâ ŷm ké· ts'ouí*, 六誡個罪 *lioŭc kiaí ké· ts'ouí*.

M

Macérer. 浸 *tsím*, 泡 *p'aó*.

Mâcher. 嚼 *ts'iaó*.

Machine. 車 *tch'ā*, 架 *ká*, 機器 *kī hí*.

Maçon. 泥水師傅 *naî choùi sē foú*.

Magasin. 舖子 *p'oú tzè*, 行 *hông*.

Magie. 邪術 *siâ choŭt*. 邪法 *siâ fâp*, 邪敎 *siâ kaó*.

Maigre. 瘦 *seoú*. || Partie maigre de la viande, 腈肉 *tsiāng nioŭc*.

Main. 手 *choù*.

Main-d'œuvre. 工 *koūng*, 人工 *gnîn koūng*.

Maintenant. 今 *kīn*, 現下 *hién há*.

Maire. 地保 *t'í paò*.

Mais. 單單 *tān tān*, 到底 *taó taì*.

Maïs. 包粟 *paō sioŭc*.

Maison. 屋 *voŭc*. || Famille, 家 *kā*, 烟戶 *yān foú*.

Maître. 主人 *tchoù gnîn*. || — d'école, 先生 *sīn sāng*, 老師 *laò sē*. || — ouvrier, 師傅 *sē foú*.

Maîtriser. 押伏 *âp foŭc*, 懲 *tchìn*, 擒 *k'îm*.

Mal. 唔好 *mĝ haò*, 歹 *vaī*, 惡 *ôc*. || *Voir* souffrir, malade.

Malade (être). 病 *p'iáng*, 苦 *k'où*, 唔好 *mĝ haò*, 唔伸暢 *mĝ tch'oūn tch'òng*, 唔道地 *mĝ t'aó t'í*.

Maladroit. 唔嗆 *mĝ voé·* ... *mĝ piâc*.

Mâle; (en parlant des hommes), 男 *nâm;* (en parlant des animaux), 公 *koūng*, 牯 *koù*.

Malgré. — Soi, 唔奈何 *mĝ naí hô*, 不得不 *poŭt têt poŭt*, 雖 *souī*.

Malheur. *Voir* calamité.

Maltraiter. 大慢人 *t'aí mán gnîn*, 待人唔好 *t'aí gnîn mĝ haò*, 踐踏 *ts'ién t'âp*.

Maman. 阿姆 *ā mē·*, 哀子 *oī tzè*.

Mamelle. 乳姑 *nén koū*.

Manche, poignée. 柄 *piáng*. || — d'habit, 衫袖 *sām ts'ioú*.

Mandarin. 官 *kouōn*.

Mandat. 票 *p'iaó*.

Manger. 食 *chĭt*.

Manière, façon. 樣子 *yóng tzè*. || De quelle manière? 樣班 *nióng pān ?* || Procédé, 法子 *fâp tzè*, 方法 *fōng fâp*.

Manifester. 發顯 *fât hièn*, 顯出來 *hièn tch'oŭt loî*.

Manœuvre, s. m. (ouvrier), 土工 *t'où koūng*.

Manquer, faire défaut. 缺 *k'iĕt*, 爭 *tsāng*, 欠 *k'iám*, 忒少 *t'iĕt chaò*.

Marâtre. 後母 *heoú moū*, 繼母 *kí moū*.
Marc. 渣 *tsā*, 脚 *kiôc*.
Marchand. 買賣人 *maì maí gnîn*, 做生理 *tsó siēn lī*, 販 *fán*.
Marchander. 講價 *kòng ká*.
Marchandise. 貨 *fó*.
Marché. 圩塲 *hī tch'ông*. || *Voir* prix, contrat.
Marchepied. 踏脚凳 *t'âp kiôc tén*.
Marcher. 行路 *hâng loú*, 走 *tseoù*.
Mare. 水潮 *chouì foû*, 湖洋田 *foû yông t'iên*.
Marée. 海潮 *hoì tch'aô*. || — basse, 退潮 *t'ouí tch'aô*. || —haute, 漲潮 *tchóng tch'aô*.
Mari. 丈夫 *tch'óng foū*, 老公 *laò koūng*.
Mariage. 婚配 *foūn p'í*. || Demander en —, 求親 *k'ioû ts'īn*.
Marié, nouveau —, 新郎 *sīn lông*. || Nouvelle —, 新娘 *sīn niông*.
Marier. — (sa fille), 嫁 *ká*; (son fils), 討新臼 *t'aò sīm k'ioū*, 講親 *kòng ts'īn*. Se —, 婚配 *foūn p'í*.
Marmite. 鋪鑼 *p'oū lô*.
Marque, empreinte. 印 *ýn*, 蹟 *tsiâc*, 踪 *tsioūng*. || Signe, 記號 *kí haó*. || Indice 憑據 *p'în kì*.
Marquis. 侯爺 *heoú yâ*.
Marteau. 鐵鎚 *t'iĕt tch'ouî*.
Martyr 致命 *tjé mín*.
Masque. 鬼像 *kouì sióng*, 鬼面殼 *kouì mién hôc*.
Masse. 墜 *tch'ouî*, 砣 *t'ô*, 堆 *toī*.
Massepain. 雞蛋糕 *kē· t'án kaō*.
Mastic. — à l'huile, 桐油灰 *t'oûng yoû foē·*.
Mât. 桅杆 *mī kouōn*.
Matelas. 褥子 *nioŭc tzè*.
Matière. 材料 *ts'aî liaó*.
Matin. 早辰 *tsaò chîn*, 天光 *t'iēn kouōng*.
Maudire. 罵 *má*.
Mauvais. 唔好 *mĝ haò*, 謌 *pè·*, 嚚 *ngôc*, 惡 *ôc*.
Méchant. 惡 *ôc*, 唔好 *mĝ haò*.
Mèche. — de lampe, 燈芯 *tēn sīm*. || — de pétard, 火引 *fò ýn*.
Médaille. — pieuse, 聖牌 *chín p'aî*.
Médecin. 醫生 *ȳ sēn*, 行醫個 *hâng ȳ ké·*.
Médecine. Art de la —, 醫法 *ȳ fâp*. || Livres de —, 葯書 *yŏc choū*. || Remède, 葯 *yŏc*.
Médire. 講人長短 *kòng gnîn tch'ông tòn*, 講閒該 *kòng hân fá*, 講人個 *kòng gnîn ké·*.
Méditer. 默想 *mĕt siòng*, 緬道理 *mièn t'aó lī*.
Meilleur. 過好 *kouó haò*. || Bien —, 好得多 *haò têt tō*. || Le —, 第好個 *t'í haò ké·*, 至好個 *tjé haò ké·*, 最好個 *tsouí haò ké·*.
Mêler. 撓 *laō*.
Membre. Les — du corps, 手脚 *chouì kiôc*, 四肢 *sí tjē*. || Etre — d'une société, 膯會 *t'ēn fí*.
Même, semblable, 一樣 *ȳt yóng*, 同 *t'oûng*, 像 *ts'ióng*. || Identique, 本本個 *poùn poùn ké·*. || Soi—, 自己 *tsé kì*. || quand —, 既然 *kí yân*, 雖 *souī*.
Mémoire. 記才 *kí ts'oî*, 記含 *kí hâm*.
Ménager. 儉 *k'iám*, 省 *sèn*.
Mendiant. 討食個 *t'aò chĭt ké·*, 叫化 *kaó fá*, 江湖 *kōng foû*.
Mensonge. 白話 *p'ăc fá*, 假話 *kà fá*.
Menthe. 薄荷 *p'ŏc hô*.
Mentionner. 題 *t'î*.

Menton. 嘴啱 *tchoí ngām.*
Menuisier. 木匠 *moũc sióng.*
Mépriser. 輕慢 *k'īn mán*, 看輕 *k'ón k'iāng*, 看破 *k'ón p'ó*, 看衰 *k'ón soī*, 看唔起 *k'ón mĝ hì.* || Ne pas craindre, 唔怕 *mĝ p'á.*
Mer. 海 *hoì*, 洋 *yông.*
Merci. 多謝 *tō ts'iá*, 感謝 *kàm ts'iá.*
Mercure. 水銀 *chouì nioûn.*
Mère. 母親 *moū ts'īn*, 娘 *niông*, 姆 *mē*, 媽 *mâ.*
Mérite. 功勞 *koūng laô.*
Mériter. *Voyez* digne.
Merveilleux. 奇妙 *k'î miaó*, 怪 *kouaí.*
Messe. 彌撒 *nì sât.*
Mesure, objet qui sert à mesurer. 則 *tsĕt*; — longueur, 尺 *tch'âc*, 寸 *ts'oún*; — de capacité, 升 *chīn*, 斗 *teoù.* || Dimension, 尺寸 *tch'âc ts'oún*, 長短 *tch'ông tòn.* || Prendre une —, 則正 *tsĕt tcháng*, 比一個則 *pì ŷt ké· tsĕt.* || Faire sur —, 比等來做 *pì tèn loî tsó*, 量等來做 *leông tèn loî tsó.* || A —, 輪等來 *lîn tèn loî*, 陸陸續續 *lioûc lioûc sioŭc sioŭc.* || Outre —, 過分 *kouó foún*, 過度 *kouó t'oú.*
Mesurer. 比 *pì*, 量 *leông*, 則 *tsĕt.*
Méthode, moyen. 方子 *fōng tzè*, 方法 *fōng fâp*, 法則 *fâp tsĕt.* || Règle, 規矩 *kouī kì.* || Ordre, 次序 *tsé sí*, 欵式 *k'ouàn chĭt.*
Métier. 手藝 *choù gní.* || Occupation, 事業 *sé niăp*, 頭路 *t'eoû loú.* || — de tisserand, 攬機 *lām kí.*
Mets. 菜 *ts'oí*, 食用 *chĭt yoúng.*
Mettre, placer. 放 *fóng*, 安 *ōn.* || — (un objet entre deux autres), 夾 *kiăp.* || — (dans un récipient), 裝 *tchōng.* || Enfouir, 窖 *kaó.* || Revêtir, 著 *tchôc.* || Porter sur soi, 帶 *taí.*
Meuble. 傢伙 *kā fò.*
Meule. 磨石 *mó chăc.* || Tas, 堆 *toī.*
Meurtre. 命案 *miáng ón.*
Meutrir. 搪痛 *mó t'oúng*, 打痛 *tà t'oúng*, 打傷 *tà chōng.*
Midi. 午時 *ng̀ chê.* || Sud, 南 *nâm.*
Miel. 蜂糖 *foūng t'ông*, 蜜糖 *mĕt t'ông*, 蜂蜜 *foūng mĕt.*
Mien. 我個 *ngā ké·.*
Miette. — de pain, 麪包碎 *mién paō souí.* || Peu, 滴 *tīt* ou *sīt*, 微 *mî.*
Mieux. *Voyez* meilleur, préférer.
Mijoter. 炆 *voûn*, 炖 *toūn.*
Milan. 角鷂 *kôc yaó.*
Milieu. 中 *tchoūng*, 心 *sīm*, 半 *pán.*
Mille, un —, 一千 *ŷt ts'iēn*, dix —, 一萬 *ŷt ván*; cent —, 十萬 *chĭp ván.*
Million. 一百萬 *ŷt pâc ván.*
Mince. 薄 *p'ŏc*, 細 *sé·.*
Mine. 廠 *tch'òng.* *Voyez* visage.
Minerai. 鑛 *kouàng.*
Ministre. — d'Etat, 宰相 *tsaì sióng.*
Minuit. 半夜 *pán yá.*
Minute. 一分鍾 *ŷt foūn tchoūng.* || *Voyez* brouillon.
Minutieux. 仔細 *tzè sé·.*
Miracle. 聖跡 *chín tsīt.*
Mirer (se). 照鏡 *tchaó kiáng.*
Miroir. 鏡子 *kiáng tzè.*
Misérable. 可憐 *k'ò lîn*, 窮苦 *k'ioûng k'où.* || Méprisable, 得人惱 *tĕt gnîn naō.*
Miséricorde. 仁慈 *ŷn tsê*, 慈心 *tsê sīm.*
Missionnaire. 傳敎士 *tch'ôn kaó sé.*
Mitoyen. 隔壁 *kâc piâc.*

Mobile. 曉動個 *hiaò t'oúng ké·*, 噲走個 *voć· tscoù ké·*, 唔穩 *mĝ voùn.* || *Voyez* motif.
Mode, usage. 風俗 *foūng sioŭc*, 慣 *kouán.*
Modèle. 樣式 *yóng chît*, 模子 *moû tzè.*
Modeste. 謙虛 *k'iām hī*, 端莊 *tōn tsōng.*
Moelle. 骨油 *koût yoû.*
Mœurs. — publiques, 風俗 *foūng sioŭc.* || — d'un individu, 行爲 *hâng vî*, 行式 *hâng chît.*
Moi. 我 *ngaî.*
Moindre. 過小 *kouó siaò*, 小 ou 細一滴 *siaò* ou *sé· ŷt tît.* || Le —, 至小個 *tjé siaò ké·*, 至細個 *tjé sé· ké·.*
Moineau. 禾 ? *vô pît.*
Moins. 過少 *kouó chaò*, 莫咁多 *mŏc àn tō.* || Au —, 至少 *tjé chaò.* || A — que, 除 *tch'oû.* On emploie mieux une périphrase. A — qu'il ne soit malade, 係有病麼話 ou 麼算 ou 唔使 *hé· yoū p'iáng mô vá* ou *mô són* ou *mĝ sè.*
Mois. 月 *gnĕt.*
Moisir, 生 ou 起霉 *sāng* ou *hì moê·.*
Moisson. 禾 *vô.*
Moissonner. 割禾 *kôt vô*, 割麥 *kôt măc.*
Moitié. 半 *pán.*
Moment. 刻 *k'ĕt*, 時候 *chê heoú.* || Attendre un —, 等一下 *tèn ŷt há.* || *Voyez* occasion.
Mon. 我個 *ngā ké·.*
Monceau. 堆 *toī.*
Monde, univers. 天下 *t'iēn hā.* || Terre, 地 *t'í*, 世界 *ché kiaí.* || La vie du siècle, 世俗 *ché sioŭc.*

Monnaie. 錢 *ts'iên.*
Monopole. 瑪 *mā*, 獨門子生理 *t'oŭc moún tzè siēn lī.*
Monsieur. 閣下 *kôc há*, 先生 *sīn sāng*, 老兄 *laò hioūng*, 老爺 *laò yâ.*
Monstre. 怪物 *kouaí voŭt*, 妖怪 *yaō kouaí.*
Montagne. 山 *sān*, 岌崗 *ýn kòng*, 嶺 *leāng.*
Mont-de-piété. 當舖 *tóng p'oú.*
Monter. 上 *chōng.* || — en grade, 高陞 *kaō chīn.*
Montre. 鏢 *piaō.*
Montrer, faire voir. 拿出來看 *nā tch'oût loî k'ón*, 顯 *hièn*, 指 *tjè.*
Monture. 騎個頭牲 *k'î ké· t'coû sāng.* || Ce qui sert à assembler les parties d'un tout, 架 *ká*, 框 *k'iōng.*
Moquer (se). 笑人 *siaó gnîn*, 恥笑 *tchè siaó.*
Morceau. 塊 *k'ouaí*, 截 *ts'iĕt*, 碎 *souí.*
Mordre. 咬 *ngaō*, 吃 *ngât.*
Mort, subst. f. 死 *sì*, 終 *tchoūng.* || Subst. m. 死人 *sì gnîn.* || Adj. 死個 *sì ké..*
Mortier. 臼 *k'ioū.*
Mot, un —, 一句話 *ŷt kí fá.*
Motif. *Voyez* cause.
Mou. 軟 *niōn*, 綿 *miên.*
Mouche. 烏蠅 *voū ŷn.*
Moucher. 拭鼻屎 *ts'oŭt p'í chè.*
Mouchoir. 手巾 *choù kīn*, 手帕 *choù p'á.*
Moudre. 攠 *mó.*
Mouiller. 蔭 *ým*, 裝濕 *tsōng chîp.*
Moule. 模子 *moû tzè.*
Mouler. — (en métal), 鑄 *tchoú*; (en argile), 作 *tsôc*, 找 *tsaò.*

Moulin, meunerie. 磨房 *mó fóng.* ‖ — à vent, 風車 *foūng tch'ā.*
Mourir. 死 *sì,* 過世 *kouó ché,* 過身 *kouó chīn.*
Mourre (jouer à la). 猜枚 *ts'aī moé·,* 嘩拳 *fâ k'iân.*
Mousse. 青苔 *ts'iāng t'oî,* 流苔 *lioū t'oî.*
Moustache. 八字鬚 *pât sé sī.*
Moustiquaire. 蚊帳 *moūn tchóng.*
Moustique. 蚊子 *moūn tzè.*
Moutarde. 芥辣 *kiaí lât.*
Mouton. 綿羊 *miên yông.*
Mouvoir. *Voyez* remuer.
Moyen, subst. m. 方法 *fōng fâp.* ‖ Aptitude, 力量 *lĭt leóng,* 才 *ts'oî.*
Moyen, adj. 中等 *tchoūng tèn.*
Muet. 啞子 *à tzè.*
Mulet. 騾子 *lô tzè.*
Mur. 墻 *siông,* 壁 *piăc.*
Mûr. 熟 *sioŭc.* ‖ Le riz est —, 穀子黃了 *koŭc tzè vông liaò.*
Mûrier. 桑樹 *sōng choú.*
Murmurer. 怨 *yán.*
Museau. 嘴 *tsouì* ou *tchoí.*
Musicien. 吹手 *tch'oī chouì.*
Myope. 眼矇 *niàn moûng,* 目瞶 *moŭc p'où.*

N

Nager. 泅水 *ts'ioû chouì.* ‖ Habile à —, 噲水 *voé· chouì.*
Nain. 古董人 *koù toùng gnîn.*
Naître. 生 *sāng,* 出歲 *tch'oût sé·.*
Nappe. — d'autel, 祭台布 *tsí t'oî poú.*
Narine. 鼻孔 *p'í k'oùng.*
Natte. 蓆 *ts'iác.* ‖ Grande et grosse —, 簟笪 *t'iám tât.*
Nature. 性 *sín,* 光景 *kouōng kìn.*
Naturel, subst. m. 本性 *poùn sín,* 脾氣 *p'î hí.*
Naturel, adj. qui va de soi. 自然 *tsé yân.* ‖ Inné, 生成個 *sāng châng ké·.*
Naufrage (faire). 打壞船 *tà faí chôn,* 沉船 *tch'îm chôn.*
Navet. 蘿菖 *lô p'ĕt.*
Navette. — de tisserand, 梭子 *sō tzè.*
Naviguer. 行船 *hâng chôn,* 飄海 *p'iaō hoì.*
Navire. 船 *chôn.*
Ne. 麼 *mô,* 唔 *mĝ,* 不 *poût,* 莫 *mŏc* (impératif). ‖ — faire que, 單單 *tān tān,* 淨 *ts'iáng.* ‖ — faire que de, 綱 *kiōng.*
Néanmoins. 到底 *taó taì.*
Nécessaire. 要緊 *yaó kìn.*
Négligent. 唔用心 *mĝ yoúng sīm,* 冷落 *lāng lŏc,* 冷淡 *lāng t'ám.*
Négliger. 不管 *poût kouòn.*
Neige. 雪 *siĕt.*
Nénuphar. 蓮花 *liên fā.*
Nerf. 筋 *kīn.*
Net, propre. 淨 *ts'iáng,* 清楚 *ts'īn tsè.*
Neuf, adj. num. 九 *kioù.* ‖ Nouveau, 新 *sīn.*
Neveu, fils du frère, 姪子 *tch'ĭt tzè;* fils de la sœur, 外甥 *ngoé· sēn.*
Nez. 鼻公 *p'í koūng.*
Ni. 也麼 *yā mô,* 也唔 *yā mĝ.*
Niche. — d'idole, 神龕 *chîn k'ām.*
Nichée, une —. 一竇 *ŷt teoú.*
Nier. 唔認 *mĝ gnín.*
Niveau, instrument. 坪水 *p'iâng chouì.* ‖ De —, 坪 *p'iâng.*

6

Niveler. 裝坪 *tsōng p'iâng.*
Noce. 筵席酒 *yân sīt tsioù*, 新娘酒 *sīn niông tsioù*, 好事 *haò sé.*
Nœud. 紇 *kĕt.* || — dans le bois, 樹節 *choú tsiĕt.*
Noir. 烏 *voū.*
Noix. 核桃 *hĕt t'aô.*
Nom, appellation. 名 *miâng.* || Avoir le — de, 喊 *hám.* || — de famille, 姓 *siáng.* || Réputation, 名聲 *miâng chāng.*
Nombre. 數目 *sé moŭc.* || Un grand —, 多 *tō.*
Nombreux. 多 *tō.*
Nommer, imposer un nom. 安名 *ōn miâng.* || *Voir* appeler.
Non. 唔係 *mĝ hé*, 麼個事 *mô ké sé.*
Nord. 北 *pĕt.*
Notables. 鄉紳 *hiōng chīn*, 紳士 *chīn sé.*
Notre. 我等個 *ngā tèn ké.*
Nourrice. 阿奶 *ā naī*, 乳母 *nén moū.*
Nourrir. 養 *yōng*, 供 *kioūng.* || — (des animaux), 餧 *ví.*
Nourriture. 食用 *chĭt yoúng*, 養糧 *yōng leông*, 飯 *fán.*
Nous. 我等 *ngā tèn.*
Nouveau. 新 *sīn.*
Nouvelle. 新聞 *sīn voûn.* || Demander des — de la santé, 問候 *moún heóu*, 問安 *moún ōn.*
Novice. 徒弟 *t'oû t'í*, 生手 *sāng choù*, 唔熟手 *mĝ choŭc choù*, 新 *sīn.*
Noyau. 忽 *foŭt*, 仁 *ŷn.*
Noyer, v. a. 浸 *tsím*, 浸死 *tsím sì*, 淹 *yàm.*
Nu. 麼衫褲 *mô sām foú*, 赤剝 *tch'ăc pôc.*
Nuage. 雲 *yoûn.*
Nuire. 害 *hoí*, 傷害 *chōng hoí.*
Nuit. 夜 *yá*, 暗 *ám.*
Numéro. 數號 *sé haó*, 碼 *mā.*

O

Obéir. 聽命 *t'ín mín*, 聽話 *t'āng vá*, 順 *choún.*
Objet. 東西 *toūng sī*, 物件 *voŭt k'ián.*
Obliger, imposer un devoir. 感 *kām.* || *Voir* commander.
Obscur. 暗 *ám.*
Observer, accomplir ce qui est prescrit. 守 *choù.* || Regarder, 看 *k'ón.*
Obstacle. 碍 *ngoé*, 阻擋 *tzè tòng.*
Obstiné. 蠻 *mân*, 硬性 *ngáng sín*, 奸 *kiān.*
Obtenir. 得 *tĕt*, 倒 *taò.*
Occasion, moment favorable. 機會 *kī fí.* || Par —, 順便 *choún p'ién.*
Occupé (être). 有事 *yoū sé*, 唔閒 *mĝ hân*, 唔空 *mĝ k'oúng.*
Occuper, s'emparer. 佔 *tchám.* || *Voir* habiter. || S' — de, 打理 *tà lī*, 管 *kouòn.*
Odeur. 氣色 *hí sĕt.* || Bonne —, 香 *hiōng*; mauvaise —, 臭 *tch'oú*,
Odieux. 得人惱 *tĕt gnîn naō.*
Œil. 眼 *niàn*, 目 *moŭc.*
Œuf. 春 *tch'oūn*, 卵 *lòn*, 蛋 *t'án.*
Œuvre. 工 *koūng*, 事 *ché.*
Offenser. 得罪 *tĕt ts'oui*, 得失 *tĕt chĭt.*
Offrir. — en présent, 送 *soúng*; — à un supérieur, 獻 *hién.* || — en sacrifice, 祭 *tsí*,
Oie. 鵝 *ngô.*
Oignon. 葱 *ts'oūng.*
Oindre. 搽 *ts'â*, 抹 *mât* 拭 *ts'oŭt.*

Oiseau. 鳥 *tiaō*.
Oisif. 閒 *hân*, 空 *k'oúng*, 麼事 *mô sé*,
Ombre. 影 *yàng*.
On. 人 *gnîn*.
Once. 兩 *leōng*.
Oncle, frère du père, 阿伯 *ā pâc*, 阿叔 *ā choûc*, frère de la mère, 阿舅 *ā k'ioū*.
Ongle. 手指甲 *choù tjè kâp*.
Onguent. 膏藥 *kaō yŏc*.
Onze. 十一 *chĭp ŷt*.
Opinion. 意思 *ý sé*, 心意 *sīm sé*.
Opium. 鴉片烟 *a pèn yān*, 洋烟 *yông yān*.
Opportun. 鬥着 *teoú tch'ŏc*, 對 *toui*.
Opposer. 對 *toui*. || *Voir* arrêter, empêcher, résister.
Opprimer. 脅 *hĭp*, 委屈 *vī k'ioût*, 欺負 *k'ī foú*.
Or 金 *kīm*.
Orange. 柑子 *kām tzè*; — à peau adhérente, 橙 *tch'âng*; — à peau non adhérente, 柑橘 *kām kĭt*.
Ordinaire. 平常 *p'în chông*, 勉强 *miēn kiòng*, 中等 *tchoūng tèn*.
Ordonnance. — de médecin. 藥單 *yŏc tan*; écrire une —, 開藥單 *k'oī yŏc tān*.
Ordres, conférer les SS. Ordres, 聖 *chín*. || *Voir* disposer, commander.
Ordre. 次序 *tsé sí*. || Sacrement de l'—, 聖品 *chín p'în*.
Oreille. 耳公 *gnì koūng*.
Oreiller. 枕頭 *tchìm t'eoû*.
Orfèvre. 打銀個 *tà nioûn ké·*, 銀匠 *nioûn sióng*.
Orgueil. 驕傲 *kiaō ngaó*.
Orient 東 *toūng*.
Origine. 根由 *kēn yoû*, 根底 *kēn taì*, 根原 *kēn niân*, 來歷 *loî lĭt*.
Originel, péché —. 原罪 *niân ts'ouí*.
Orner. 修 *sioū*, 布置 *poú tjé*, 擺 *paì*.
Orphelin. 獨子 *t'oŭc tzè*, 孤哀子 *koū oī tzè*.
Orphelinat. 嬰孩堂 *ȳn haî t'ông*.
Os. 骨頭 *koūt t'eoû*.
Osciller. 搖 *yaô*; *yám*, 擺 *paì*.
Oser. 敢 *kàm*.
Oter 脫 *t'ŏt*.
Ou. 阿 *á* (le plus souvent ne s'exprime pas), 或 *fĕt*.
Où. 那裡 *naí lī*.
Ouater. 放綿花 *fóng miên fā*.
Oublier. 忘記 *móng kí*, 添忘 *t'iam p'iông* ou *móng*, 慌覺 *fōng kôc*.
Ouest. 西 *sī*.
Oui. 係 *hé·* (s'exprime plus souvent en répétant le verbe). As-tu de l'argent ? R. 有 *yoū*.
Ourler. 揹 *ts'iaō*.
Ours. 狗熊 *keoù yoûng*.
Outil. 傢伙 *kā fò*, 傢事 *kā ché·*.
Outrager. 凌辱 *lîn yoŭc*, 污辱 *voū yoŭc*, 蹧蹋 *ts'ién t'ăp*.
Outre, au delà. 個邊 *ké· piēn*, 外背 *ngoé· poé·*. || — mesure, 過度 *kouó t'oú*, 過分 *kouó foún*. || En —, 另外 *láng ngoé·*, 格外 *kĕt ngoé·*. || D'— en —, 穿過 *tch'ōn kouó*.
Ouvertement. 明明 *mîn mîn*, 實心 *chĭt sīm*, 外面 *ngoé· mién*.
Ouverture. 睞 *loí*, 孔 *k'oùng*. || *Voir* trou, commencement.
Ouvrage, livre. Un —, 一部書 *ȳt p'oú choū*. || *Voir* travail.

Ouvrier. 師傅 *sē foú*, 工人 *koūng gnîn*.
Ouvrir. 開 *k'oī*, 揭 *yât*.

P

Pacifier. — (par les armes), 打平 *tà p'in;* (par un accord), 講和 *kòng fô*.
Page, une —, 一張 *ŷt tchōng*, 一面 *ŷt mién*.
Pagode. 廟子 *miaó tzè*, 宮 *kioūng*.
Païen. 外教人 *ngoé kaó gnîn*.
Paillasse. 疊眠個 *t'iâp mîn ké*.
Paille. — de riz, 禾稈 *vô kòn;* — de blé, 麥稿 *măc kaò*.
Pain. 麵包 *mién paō*.
Pair, nombre —, 雙數 *soūng sé*.
Paire, une —, 一雙 *ŷt soūng*, 一對 *ŷt touí*.
Paix. 平 *p'în*, 和 *fô*, 安 *ōn*.
Palais. 府 *foù*, 公館 *koūng kouòn*. || — de l'Empereur, 殿 *t'ién*.
Palanquin. 轎 *k'iaó*.
Pâle. 白 *p'ăc*, 淡色 *t'ám sĕt*.
Palefrenier. 馬夫 *mā foū*.
Palpiter. 心 ? *sīm piaō*.
Panier. 籃子 *lâm tzè*, 籠 *loūng*, 籠 *loùng*.
Pantalon. 褲 *foú*.
Panthère. 豹虎 *paó foù*.
Paon. 孔雀 *k'oùng tsiŏc*.
Papa. 阿巴 *ā pā*, 阿爹 *ā tiā*.
Pape. 教皇 *kaó vông*, 教宗皇 *kaó tsoūng vông*.
Papier. 紙 *tjè*.
Papillon. 洋蝶 *yông yăp*.
Pâques. 復活瞻禮 *foŭc făt tchām lī*.

Paquet. 包 *paō*.
Par, marquant le mouvement, le passage, 從 *ts'ioûng*, 由 *yoû*. || En, dans, 在 *ts'aí*. || *Voir* cause, motif, etc.
Parabole. 比方 *pì fōng*, 表意 *piaò ý*.
Paradis. — terrestre, 地堂 *t'í t'ông*. || Ciel, 天堂 *t'iēn t'ông*.
Paraître. 現 *hién*, 像 *ts'ióng*, 像 *ts'ám*.
Paralytique. 跏 *k'iô*.
Parapluie. 傘 *tchā*.
Parce que. 因爲 *ȳn ví*.
Parcourir. 走過 *tseoù kouó*.
Pardonner. 寬恕 *k'ōn choú*, 赦 *chá*, 饒 *niaô*.
Pareil. *Voir* égal.
Parent. 家內人 *kā nouí gnîn*. || — par affinité, 親戚 *ts'īn ts'ĭt*.
Paresse. 懶惰 *lān t'ó*.
Parfait. 十分好 *chĭp foūn haò*, 全 *ts'iên*.
Parier. 賭凹 *toù aó*.
Parjure. 虛誓 *hī ché*, 虛言 *hī niân*.
Parler. 講話 *kòng fá*, 話 *vá*.
Parmi. 在 *ts'aí*, 中 *tchoūng*.
Parole. 話 *fá*. || *Voir* éloquence, promettre.
Parrain. 代父 *t'oí foú*.
Part. 分 *foūn*, 分 *foún*, 股 *koù*, 塊 *k'ouaí*. || De — en —, 穿透 *tch'ōn t'eoú*. || *Voir* endroit, partout, excepter, séparément.
Partager. 分 *foūn*, 均 *kioūn*, 派 *p'aí*.
Parti, un —, 一黨 *ŷt tòng*. || Détermination, 主意 *tchoù ý*. || *Voir* moyen, avantage.
Partialité. 唔坪心 *mĝ p'iâng sīm*.
Participer. 謄分 *t'ēn foūn*, 有名 *yoū miâng*.

Particulier, qui appartient à des particuliers, 私個 *sē ké·*. || *Voir* chaque, propre.

Partie. *Voir* part, morceau, endroit, adversaire.

Partir. 走 *tseoù*, 去 *hí*, 起身 *hì chīn*. || Commencer, 起手 *hì choù*.

Partout. 處處 *tch'oú tch'oú*, 各處 *kōc tch'oú*, 那裡都 *naí lī toū*.

Pas, subst. m. Un —, 一步 *ȳt p'oú*.

Pas, négation. 麼 *mô*. || *Voir* ne.

Passable. 可以 *k'ò ȳ*, 勉強 *miēn kiòng*, 做得 *tsó tēt*.

Passage, ruelle. 巷 *hóng*. || *Voir* chemin.

Passager, adj. 不長久 *poūt tch'ông kioù*, 一下 *ȳt há*, 一陣 *ȳt tch'ín*.

Passager, subst. m. 客 *hâc* ou *k'ēt*, 過路個 *kouó loú ké·*.

Passé, adj. Qui remonte à l'antiquité, 古 *koù*, 舊 *k'ioú*, 老 *laò*. || Ecoulé, 先個 *siēn ké·*, 過帛裡 *kouó p'ēt lê·*.

Passe-port. 路票 *loú p'iaó*, 執照 *tchīp tchaó*.

Passer. 過 *kouó*. || *Voir* couler, pénétrer.

Passion. — de J. C. 耶穌個苦難 *yâ sē ké· k'où nán*.

Passion, sentiment de l'âme. 心 *sīm*, 情 *ts'în*. || Les mauvaises —, 私慾偏情 *sē yoŭc p'iēn ts'în*.

Pâte. 麵 *mién*.

Pâté. 包 *paō*, 餅 *piàng*.

Pater (prière). 在天經 *ts'aí t'iēn kīn*.

Patience. 忍耐 *nioūn naí*. || Perdre—, 忍唔下 *nioūn mĝ ha*.

Patrie. 本國 *poùn kouēt*, 鄉村 *hiōng ts'oūn*.

Patrimoine. 家業 *kā niăp*, 家產 *kā sàn*, 產業 *sàn niăp*.

Patron. Le saint —, 聖主保 *chín tchoù paò*. || Maître, 東家 *toūng kā*, 主人 *tchoù gnîn*. || *Voir* modèle, moule.

Patronner. 保舉 *paò kì*, 招呼 *tchaō foū*, 薦 *tsién*.

Patte. 脚 *kiōc*. || Marcher à quatre —, 爬 *p'â*.

Paume (de la main). 手掌 *choù tchòng*.

Paupière. 眼皮 *niàn p'î*.

Pauvre. 窮 *k'ioûng*, 苦 *k'où*, 貧窮 *p'în k'ioûng*.

Paver. 修石路 *sioū chăc loú*, 放石板 *fóng chăc pàn*.

Pavillon. 茶亭 *ts'â t'în*. || *Voir* drapeau.

Paye. — des ouvriers. 工錢 *koūng ts'iên*; — des soldats, 兵餉 *pīn hiòng*.

Payer. 開錢 *k'oī ts'iên*, 還賬 *vân tchóng*, 撿錢 *kiàm ts'iên*.

Pays. 地方 *t'í fōng*.

Paysan. 鄉下人 *hiōng hā gnîn*.

Peau. 皮 *p'î*.

Pêche (fruit). 桃子 *t'aô tzè*.

Péché. 罪 *ts'ouí*.

Pêcher. 打魚 *tà nĝ*; — à la ligne, 釣魚 *tiaó nĝ*.

Peigne. — fin. 篦 *pí* ou *pín*; démêloir, 梳子 *sē tzè*.

Peindre. 畫 *fá*, 上色 *chòng sēt*.

Peine, châtiment. 罰 *făt*. || Etre en—, 作難 *tsōc nân*. || Homme de —, 耐苦個 *naí* ou *ngaí k'où ké·*.

Peintre. 畫像師傅 *fá sióng sē foú*.

Peler. 削皮 *siōc p'î*, 刮皮 *kouāt p'î*, 剝 *pōc*.

Pelle. — à feu. 火鏟 *fò ts'àn;* — pour la poële, 鍋鏟 *vŏc ts'àn.*
Pendant. 時候 *chê hcoú;* — qu'il est encore vie, 趕佢還在 *kòn kî hân ts'oī.* || Souvent ne s'exprime pas, v. gr. — un an, 一年 *ŷt niân.*
Pendre. 吊 *tiaó,* 挽 *vàn.*
Pénétrer. 進去 *tsín hí,* 入 *gnĭp,* 透 *t'eoú.*
Pénitence. 補贖 *poù choŭc.*
Pensée. 意思 *ý sé,* 念頭 *niám t'eoû.*
Penser. 想 *siòng,* 諗 *mèn.* || Garder le souvenir, 記念 *kí niám.*
Pente. 畬 *ts'iâ,* 斜 *siâ,* 崛 *k'ī.*
Pépin. 仁 *ŷn,* 子 *tzè.*
Perçant. 利 *lí,* 尖 *tsiām.*
Percer. 穿 *tch'ōn.* || — avec une vrille, 鑽 *tsón.* || — avec le ciseau, 鑿 *ts'ŏc.*
Perche. 竹篙 *tchoŭc kaō,* 桅杆 *mī kōn.*
Perdre. 失 *chĭt,* 落 *lŏc,* 跌 *tiĕt,* 唔見 *mĝ kián.* || — au jeu, 輸 *choū.* || — dans le commerce, 蝕本 *chăt poùn.*
Perdrix. 鷓鴣 *tchá koū.*
Père. 父親 *foú ts'īn.* || — spirituel, 神父 *chîn foú.*
Perle. 珠 *tchoū.*
Perméable. 過得 *kouó tĕt.*
Permettre. 許 *hì,* 准 *tchoùn.*
Perpétuel. 永遠 *youn yàn.*
Perquisition (faire une). 掉 *ts'aó,* 搜 *seoū.*
Perruquier. 剃頭師傅 *t'í t'eoû sē foú.*
Persécution. 風波 *foūng pō.*
Persévérer. 耐心 *naí sīm,* 麼變 *mô pién.*
Personne. 位 *ví,* 人 *gnîn,* 口 *k'eoù.* || En —, 自己 *tsé kì,* 親自 *ts'īn tsé,* 本人 *poùn gnîn.* || Aucun, 麼人 *mô gnîn.*
Personnel, adj. 本個 *poùn ké·,* 各人個 *kŏc gnîn ké·.*
Persuader. *Voir* croire, exhorter.
Peser. — (à la romaine), 秤 *tch'ín,* 吊 *tiaó;* (à une balance à deux plateaux), 平 *p'în.* || — beaucoup, 重 *tch'oūng.*
Peste. 瘟 *voūn.*
Pet. 屁 *p'í,* 屁卵 *p'í lòn.*
Pétard. 紙炮 *tjè p'aó.*
Petit, adj. 小 *siaò,* 細 *sé·.* || De — taille, 矮 *aì.* || — à —, 慢慢 *mán mán.*
Petit, subst. m. 子 *tzè.*
Petite-fille, fille du fils, 孫女 *soūn ngì.* || Fille de la fille, 外孫女 *ngoé· soūn ngì.*
Petit-fils, fils du fils, 孫 *soūn.* || Fils de la fille, 外孫 *ngoé· soūn.*
Pétition. 稟帖 *pìn t'iâp,* 呈子 *tch'in tzè.*
Pétrir. 搓 *ts'aī.*
Pétrole. 洋油 *yŏng yoû.*
Peu. 少 *chaò.* || Un —, 多少 *tō chaò,* 一點 *ŷt tiàm,* 一滴 *ŷt tĭt.*
Peuple. 百姓 *pâc siáng.*
Peur. Avoir —, 怕 *p'á,* 驚 *kiāng.* || Faire —, 嚇 *hâc.*
Peut-être. 恐怕 *k'ioùng p'á,* 唔敢話 *mĝ kàm vá.*
Pharmacie. 藥店 *yŏc tiám,* 藥舖 *yŏc p'oú.*
Photographie. 照個像 *tchaó ké· siông.*
Phrase. Une —, 一句話 *ŷt kí fá.*
Pie. 鴉鵲 *a siâc.*
Pièce. *Voir* morceau.
Pied. 脚 *kiŏc.* || — de certains animaux, 蹄 *t'aî.* || Mesure de longueur, 尺 *tch'âc.*

Piédestal. 腳 *kiôc*, 台 *t'oî*.
Piége, embûches. Tomber dans un—, 上當 *chōng tóng*, 落網 *lŏc miòng*.
Pierre. 石頭 *chăc t'eoû*.
Piété. Avoir de la—envers Dieu, 熱心恭敬天主 *gnĕt sīm kioūng kín t'iēn tchoù*. ‖ Avoir de la piété filiale, 孝敬父母 *haó kín foú moū*.
Pieu. 樹墩 *choú toùn*.
Pigeon. 熱鴿 *gnĕt kâp*.
Pile. 墩 *toūn* 堆 *toī*
Piler 舂 *tchoūng*.
Piller. 搶 *ts'iòng*, 刦 *kiâp*, 奪 *t'ŏt*.
Pilule. 丸 *yân*.
Piment. 辣椒 *lăt tsiaō*.
Pin. 松樹 *ts'ioûng choú*.
Pince. 夾子 *kiăp tzè*, 鉗 *k'iâm*.
Pinceau. — à écrire, 筆 *pĭt*. ‖ Gros— pour badigeonner, 刷子 *sôt tzè*.
Pincée. Une —, 一捻 *ȳt tsĕp*.
Pincer. 掐 *k'ăc*, 夾 *kiăp*, 搦 *nĕt*.
Pioche. 腳頭 *kiôc t'eoû*, 山鋤 *sān tsê*.
Pipe. 烟筒 *yān t'oûng*.
Piquer. 刺 *ts'ioûc*. ‖ — au goût, 辣 *lăt*.
Pirate. 水賊 *chouì ts'ĕt*.
Pire. 過唔好 *kouó mĝ haò*, 更唔好 *kén mĝ haò*.
Piscine. 魚池 *nĝ tchê*. ‖ — sacrée, 聖井 *chín tsiàng*.
Pistolet. 短銃 *tòn tch'oúng*.
Pitié. *Voir* miséricorde, compassion.
Place. 地方 *t'í fōng*. ‖ Tenir la — de, 代 *t'oí*. ‖ Prendre—, 坐 *ts'ó*.
Placer *Voir* mettre.
Plafond. 棚 *p'âng*.
Plaider. 打官司 *tà kouōn sē*.
Plaie. 爛疤 *lán pa*.
Plaindre. *Voir* compassion. Se—, 嫌 *hiâm*, 怨 *yán*.
Plaine. 垻 *pá*, 坪 *p'iâng*.
Plaire. 中意 *tchoúng ý*, 得人惜 *têt gnîn siâc* ‖ Comme il vous plaira, 隨意 *souî ý*, 盡在你 *ts'ín ts'aí gnî*.
Plaisanter. 攪 *kaò*, 講笑 *kòng siaó*.
Plaisir, 快活 *k'ouaí făt*, 快樂 *k'ouaí lŏc*, 歡喜 *fōn hì*.
Plan, subst. m. 圖 *t'oû*. ‖ *Voir* forme, dessein.
Planche. 板頭 *pân t'eoû*.
Plancher. — supérieur, 樓 *leoû*; — inférieur, 地坪 *t'í p'iâng*.
Plant. 秧子 *yōng tzè*.
Plante, — du pied, 腳板 *kiôc pàn*. ‖ Les —, 草木 *tsaò moûc*.
Planter. 種 *tchoúng* ‖ Ficher, 釘 *tāng*, 插 *ts'âp*.
Plaque. 板 *pàn*.
Plat, adj. Uni, 坪 *p'iâng*, 勻 *yoûn*. ‖ Aplati, 扁個 *pièn ké*.
Plat, subst. m. 盤子 *p'ân tzè*.
Plateau. 盤 *p'ân*. 托 *t'ôc*.
Plâtre. 石膏 *chăc kaō*.
Plein. 滿 *mān*.
Pleurer. 叫 *kiaó*, 出目水 *tch'oût moûc chouì*.
Pleuvoir. 落水 *lŏc chouì* 落雨 *lŏc ỳ*.
Plier 疊 *t'iăp*, 摺 *tchâp*. ‖ Courber, 拗 *aò*, 曲 *k'ioût*.
Plomb. 鉛 *yân*. ‖ — de chasse, 沙子 *sa tzè*.
Pluie. 雨 *ỳ*.
Plume. 毛 *maō*. ‖ —à écrire, 番筆 *fan pĭt*, 鐵筆 *t'iĕt pĭt*.
Plumeau. 雞毛掃 *kē maō saó*.
Plumet. 翎子 *lîn tzè*.

Plùpart (la). 過多 *kouó tō.*
Plus, comparatif. 過 *kouó.* ‖ Pas—de, 麽多 *mô tō,* 單單 *tān tān,* 不過 *poût kouó.* ‖ Trois fois.—qu'auparavant, 比先多三擺 *pì siēn tō sām paì.* ‖ De—, 另外 *láng ngoé˙,* 還 *hân.* ‖ —(répété), 越 *yǎt.* ‖ A—forte raison, 况且 *k'òng ts'ià.* ‖ Au—, 至多 *tjé tō.* ‖ Le plus, superlatif, 最 *tsouí,* 頂 *tìn,* 至 *tjé.* ‖ Plus, négatif, 永久麽 *youn kiou mô,* 再不 *tsaí poût.*
Plusieurs. 幾下個 *kì há ké˙.*
Plutôt. *Voir* préférer.
Poche. 袋子 *t'oí tzè,* 肚兜 *toù teoū,* 肚搭 *toù tâp.*
Poids. 重輕 *tch'oūng k'iāng.* ‖ —d'horloge ou autre, 砣 *tô.* ‖ — de balance, 碼子 *mā tzè.*
Poignard. 刀 *taō,* 手劍 *choù kiám.*
Poignée, ce que l'on peut tenir dans la main. 一揸 *ŷt tsā,* 乜 *yà,* 把 *pà,* ‖ Manche, 柄 *piáng.*
Poil. 毛 *maō.*
Poinçon. 鑽 *tsón.*
Poing. 拳 *k'iân.*
Point, petite marque. 點 *tiàm.* ‖ *Voir* endroit, instant, affaire, faillir.
Pointe. 尖 *tsiām.* ‖ Petit clou. 細釘 *sé˙ tāng.*
Poire. 梨子 *lî tzè.*
Poison. 毒藥 *t'oǔc yǒc.*
Pois. 豆 *t'eoú.*
Poisson. 魚 *ngˆ.*
Poitrine. 胸 *hioūng.*
Poivre, 胡椒 *foû tsiaō.*
Poli, uni. 坪 *p'iâng,* 光生 *kouōng sāng,* 滑 *vǎt,* 幼 *yoú.* ‖ Civil, 有禮貌 *yoū lī maó,* 有規矩 *yoū kouī kì.*
Polir. 過幼 *kouó yoú,* 搓滑 *ts'ō vǎt,* 搓光 *ts'ō kouōng.*
Pomme. — de terre 荷蘭薯 *hô lân choû.* ‖ Patate douce, 番薯 *fān choû.*
Pompe, machine pour élever l'eau, 水龍 *choùi lioûng,* 水車 *choùi tch'ā.*
Pompe, magnificence, 體面 *t'ì mién,* 排長 *p'aî tch'ông.*
Pondre. 生春 *sāng tch'oūn;* (en parlant des poissons), 撥卵 *p'ât lòn.*
Pont. 橋 *k'iaô.*
Porcelaine. 磁器 *tsê hí.*
Port. 碼頭 *mā t'eoû.* ‖ Prix de transport, 脚錢 *kiôc ts'iên.*
Portail. 門樓 *moûn leoû.*
Porte. 門 *moûn.*
Porter. — à la main, 抓 *tch'ā,* 拿 *nā.* ‖ — en bandoulière, 㪞 *k'ouán.* ‖ — avec soi, 帶 *taí.* ‖ — sur la tête, 戴 *taí.* ‖ — dans les bras, 揞 *nàm.* ‖ — directement sur l'épaule 背 *pí.* ‖ — sur l'épaule en balançoire, 㩒 *k'aī,* 挑 *t'iaō.* ‖ — sur l'épaule, à plusieurs, 扛 *kōng.* ‖ Aller présenter, 送 *soúng.* ‖ Se bien —, 平安 *p'în ōn,* 好 *haò.* ‖ *Voir* produire, exciter.
Portier. 掌門個 *tchòng moûn ké˙.*
Poser. *Voir* mettre.
Possédé. 鬼上身個 *kouì chōng chīn ké˙.*
Posséder. *Voir* avoir, savoir.
Poste. — aux lettres, 信幫 *sín pōng.*
Postérité. 後人 *heoú gnîn,* 後代 *heoú t'oí,* 子孫 *tzè soūn.*
Pot. 罌 *āng,* 缽 *pât,* 瓶 *pîn,* 壺 *foû.*
Potion, une —, 一副藥 *ŷt foú yǒc.*
Pou. 虱嫲 *sêt mâ.*

Pouce. 手指公 *choù tjè koūng.* || Dixième partie du pied, 寸 *ts'oún.*

Poudre. 藥 *yŏc,* 粉 *foùn.*

Poule. 雞嫲 *kē· mâ.*

Poulet. 雞 ? *kē· lón,* 細雞 *sé· kē.*

Pouls. 脈 *mâc.*

Poumon. 氣膈 *hí kâc.*

Poupe. 船尾 *chôn mī.*

Pour, en vue de. 爲 *ví;* se sous-entend quelquefois, ou se tourne, v.gr.: voyager pour sa santé, 出門醫病 *tch'oût moûn ȳ p'iáng.* Ouvrir la fenêtre pour aérer la chambre, 開窗好通風 *k'oī ts'oūng haò t'oūng foūng.* || En considération, v. gr.: pour l'amour de toi, 做情 *tsó ts'în.* || Au lieu de, en guise de, 作爲係 *tsôc vî hé·,* 當 *tóng,* 准 *tchoùn;* v. gr.: prendre une épée pour (croyant prendre) un bâton, 拿劍作爲係棍 *nā kiám tsôc vî hé· koún;* ... (en guise de bâton)... 准棍 *tchoùn koún.* || A cause de, 因爲 *ȳn ví.*

Pourboire. 酒錢 *tsioù ts'iên,* 茶錢 *ts'â ts'iên.*

Pourquoi. 做那個 *tsó mâc ké·.* || C'est —, 故所以 *koú sò ȳ,* 故此 *koú tsè.*

Pourrir. 漚壞 *eoú faí,* 爛 *lán,* 嚒 *moût.*

Poursuivre. 追 *tchouī,* 趕 *kòn,* 逐 *kioŭc,* 騰 *t'ên.*

Pourtant. 總係 *tsoùng hé·,* 到底 *taó taì.*

Pourvoir. 打理 *tà lī,* 顧 *koú,* 安排 *ōn p'aî.*

Pourvu que. 單愛 *tān oí.*

Pousser. 㧐 *soùng.* || *Voir* croître.

Poussière. 塵灰 *tch'în foē·.*

Poutre. 桁 *hâng,* 扛梁 *kōng leông.*

Pouvoir, puissance. 能幹 *nēn kón.* || Force, 力量 *lĭt leóng.* || Autorité, 權柄 *k'iân piáng.*

Pouvoir, v. a. 能彀 *nēn keoú,* 做得倒 *tsó tĕt taò.*

Prairie. 草坪 *ts'aò p'iâng.*

Pratique, chaland. 交觀 *kaō kouōn.* || *Voir* usage.

Précaution. 小心 *siaò sīm.* || Prendre des —, 防備 *fông p'í.*

Précédent. 以前 *ȳ ts'iên,* 在前 *ts'aí ts'iên,* 往時 *vōng chê.*

Précepte. 規誡 *kouī kiaí,* 誡命 *kiaí mín.*

Précepteur. 師傅 *sē foú.*

Prêcher. 講道理 *kòng t'aó lī,* 傳教 *tch'ôn kaó.*

Précieux. 寶 *paò,* 貴 *kouí.*

Précipiter. 放下去 *fóng hā hí,* 廢下去 *fít hā hí.* || Se —, ? 下 *piaō hā,* 投 *t'eoû,* 跳下 *t'iaó hā.* || *Voir* hâte.

Prédire. 先話 *siēn vá.*

Préface. 書序 *choū sí,* 小引 *siaò ȳn.*

Préfecture. 府 *foù.*

Préférer. 情願 *ts'în nián,* 坐 *ts'ó,* 寧 *nên.*

Préfet. 府官 *foù kouōn.*

Prélever. 除 *tch'oû,* 扣出 *k'eoú tch'oût.*

Prématuré. 早 *tsaò,* 忒早 *t'ĭet tsaò.*

Prémices. — du riz, 新米 *sīn mì.*

Premier. 第一 *t'í ȳt,* 頭上 *t'eoû hóng,* 先個 *siēn ké·.*

Prendre. 捉 *tsôc,* 拈 *niām,* 拿 *nā.*

Préparer. 預備 *ý p'í.* 布辦 *poú p'án.*

Près. 近 *k'ioún.*

Présage. 兆頭 *chaó t'eoû.*

Présence (en). 面前 *mién ts'iên,* 當面 *tōng mién.*

Présent, adj. 在 *ts'aí; ts'oī*, 有 *yoū*. || A —, 現下 *hién há*.
Présent, subst. m. 禮物 *lī voŭt*. || *Voir* maintenant.
Présenter. || *Voir* offrir, introduire.
Président. 爲頭 *vî t'coú*, 坐頭 *ts'ó t'eoú*. || — d'un ministère à Pékin, 尚書 *chóng choū*.
Presque. 差唔多 *ts'ā mĝ tō*.
Pressant, urgent. 緊 *kìn*, 急 *kīp*.
Pressé, très occupé. 麽閒 *mô hân*, 攪唔贏 *kaò mĝ yâng*, 事多 *sé tō*. || Troublé, 慌忙 *fōng mông*.
Presser, peser sur, 壓 *tsâc*, 擒 *k'îm*; 眼 *niàn*. || Serrer de près, 擠 *tsī*, 薦 *tsién*. || Urger, 催 *ts'ouī*, 逼 *pīt*.
Pressoir. 酢 *tsá*.
Prêt, adj. 成 *tcháng*, 成 *châng*. || *Voir* préparer.
Prêter. 借出去 *tsiá tch'oūt hí*.
Prétexter. 推 *t'ouī*.
Prétoire. 衙門 *ngâ moûn*.
Prêtre. 神父 *chîn foú*, 鐸德 *t'ŏc tēt*.
Preuve. 憑據 *p'în kì*.
Prévenir. || *Voir* avertir.
Prévoir. 先想 *siēn siòng*, 嘩 *fâ*, 猜 *ts'aī*.
Prier. 求 *k'ioû*, 念經 *niám kīn*.
Prière. 經文 *kīn voûn*.
Primitif. 原 *niân*, 本 *poùn*, 舊 *k'ioú*.
Prince. 王爺 *vông yâ*.
Principal. 頭一 *t'eoû ȳt*, 最要緊個 *tsouí yaó kìn ké* 君 *kioūn*.
Principe. *Voir* commencement, cause.
Printemps. 春 *tch'oūn*.
Prison. 班房 *pān fông*.
Priver. *Voir* enlever, s'abstenir.
Privilège. 私恩 *sē ēn*, 格外個恩 *kāt ngoé ké ēn*.

Prix, valeur d'une chose. 價錢 *ká ts'iên* || — de la main d'œuvre, 工錢 *koūng ts'iên*.
Probable. 係過多 *hé kouó tō*.
Proces. 官司 *kouōn sē*, 案 *ón*.
Procession. 迎神 *niâng chîn*.
Prochain, adj. La semaine —, 後個主日 *heoú ké tchoù gnĭt*; l'an —, 明年 *miâng niân*.
Prochain, subst. m. 人家 *gnîn kā*, 別人 *p'iĕt gnîn*.
Procurer. *Voir* donner, livrer, exciter.
Prodige. 奇事 *k'î sé*. || *Voir* miracle.
Prodiguer. 喪 *sòng*, 盡使錢 *ts'ín sè ts'iên*.
Produire, engendrer, 生 *sāng*, 發 *fāt*; *pôt*. || — des fruits, 結子 *kiĕt tzè*. || — des rejetons, 攢笋 *ts'án soùn*.
Proéminent, élevé. 高 *kaō*. || Qui ressort en bosse, 凸去來 *t'oūt hí loî*, 鼓去來 *koù hí loî*. || Qui dépasse, 走出來 *tseoù tch'oūt loî*.
Profaner. 輕慢 *k'īn mán*, 踐踏 *ts'ién t'ăp*.
Profit. 利息 *lí sīt*.
Profiter (d'une occasion). 趕機會 *kòn kī fí*, 順便 *choún p'ién*.
Profond. 深 *tch'īm*.
Progrès. *Voir* mieux, augmenter.
Projeter. 謀 *meoû*, 打主意 *tà tchoù ý*, 想 *siòng*.
Promener (se). 行嬲 *hâng liaó*.
Promettre. 許 *hì*, 答應 *tāp ýn*. || Donner des espérances, 有望 *yoū móng*.
Prompt, vite. 快 *k'ouaí*. || Vif. 急 *kīp*.
Prononciation. 口音 *k'eoù ȳm*.
Propager. 傳 *tch'ôn*.
Prophète. 先知 *siēn tī*.
Propice. 順 *choún*.

Proportionné. 相配 *siōng p'í*, 對 *touí*.
Propos. A —, 着 *tch'ŏc*, 對 *touí*, 丁對 *tēn touí*, 合式 *hăp chĭt*. || *Voir* dessein, mot.
Propre, particulier. 本 *poùn*, 自己個 *tsé kì ké'*. || *Voir* net.
Propriétaire. 主人 *tchoù gnîn*.
Prospère. 盛 *chín*, 興旺 *hīn vóng*, 爛 *sàn*.
Prosterner (se). 仆倒 *p'oŭc taò*, 磕頭 *k'ŏc t'eoû*.
Protéger. 保佑 *paò yoú*, 保護 *paò foú*.
Protestant. 裂敎 *lĭĕt kaó*.
Proverbe. 俗話 *sioŭc fá*, 俗語 *sioŭc nī*.
Province. 省 *sèn*.
Provoquer. 惹 *niā*, 致倒 *tjé taò*.
Prudent. 有見識 *yoū kián chĭt*, 小心 *siaò sīm*.
Prune. 李子 *lì tzè*.
Prunelle. 眼珠仁 *niàn tchoū ŷn*.
Public. 公 *koūng*, 衆人個 *tchoúng gnîn ké'*. || Cimetière—, 義塚 *gní tch'oùng*.
Publier. 述 *choŭt*, 傳 *tch'ôn*.
Puce. 狗虱 *keoù sĕt*, 跳蚤 *t'iaó tsaò*.
Pudeur. 廉恥 *liâm tchè*, 羞恥 *sioū tchè*.
Puer. 臭 *tch'oú*.
Puiser. — de l'eau, 打水 *tà chouì*, 舀水 *yaò chouì*.
Puisque. 旣然 *kí yân*.
Puissance. 能 *nên*, 權 *k'iân*. || Influence, 勢頭 *sé t'eoû*.
Puits. 井 *tsiàng*.
Punaise. 乾皮 *kōn p'î*.
Punir. 罰 *făt*.
Pupitre. 書架 *choū ká*.
Pur, sans mélange. 淨 *ts'iáng*. || Chaste, 潔淨 *kiĕt ts'iáng*.
Purgatif. 涼藥 *leông yŏc*, 好泄個藥 *haò siĕt ké' yŏc*.
Purgatoire. 煉獄 *lién nioŭc*.
Purifier. *Voir* laver.
Pus, 膿 *noûng*.

Q

Qualité, manière d'être. 樣子 *yóng tzè*. || — supérieure, 上等 *chóng tèn*; de mauvaise —, 部 *pè'*, 醜 *ngôc*. || Bonnes —, 好處 *haò tch'oú*.
Quand, dans quel temps? 幾時 *kì chê*; 那久 *naí kioù*. || Dans le temps que, 時候 *chê heoú*, 當時 *tōng chê*. || Après que, 以後 *ȳ heoú*. || Toutes les fois que, 擺擺 *paì paì*.
Quant. — à, 照 *tchaó*, 論 *loún*.
Quarante. 四十 *sí chĭp*.
Quart. Prendre le —, 四分拿一分 *sí foūn nā ŷt foūn*.
Quatorze. 十四 *chĭp sí*.
Que. *Voir* qui, quel, pourquoi, combien.
Quel. 那個 *mâc ké'*. || Le quantième v. gr. quel jour? 初幾 *tsē kì*. || Exclamatif, 咁 *kàn*, 咁多 *kàn tō*. || — qu'il soit, 不拘 *poŭt kī*, 不論 *poŭt loún*.
Quelque, un. 一個 *ŷt ké'* || Plusieurs, 幾個 *kì ké'*.
Quelquefois. 幾下擺 *kì há paì*, 幾回 *kì fî*.
Quelqu'un. 人 *gnîn*.
Querelle. 口角 *k'eoù kôc*, 相駡 *siōng má*, 相吵 *siōng ts'aô*.
Quêter 討 *t'aò*.

Queue. 尾 *mī.*
Qui, interrogatif. 那人 *màn gnîn.* || Relatif, 個 *ké·*, 所 *sò.*
Quiconque. 不論那人 *poût loún mān gnîn.*
Quittance. 收單 *choū tān.*
Quitter, s'éloigner de. 離 *lî*, 離開 *lî k'oī*, 走 *tseoù.* || Enlever, 脫 *t'ôt.* || *Voir* abandonner.
Quoi. *Voir* qui, quel.
Quoique. 雖 *souī*, 雖然 *souī yân*, 唔怕 *mĝ p'á.*

R

Rabot. 刨 *p'aô.*
Raboter. 刨 *p'aô.*
Raccommoder. 補 *poù*, 整 *tchàng.*
Race. *Voir* espèce.
Racheter. 贖轉來 *choŭc tchòn loî.*
Racine. 根 *kīn.*
Racler. 刮 *kouât.*
Radeau. 樹牌 *choú p'aî.*
Radicaux, clefs de l'écriture chinoise, 字母 *sé moū.*
Radoter. 湖說 *foû chôt.*
Rafraîchir (se). — en buvant. 食涼 *chĭt leông.* || — en se lavant, 洗涼 *sè· leông.* || Devenir froid, 冷帛裡 *lāng p'ĕt lé·*, 噲涼 *voé· leông.*
Rage. 癲 *tiēn.*
Raide. 硬 *ngáng.*
Rainure. 縫 *p'oúng*, 線 *sién*, 槽 *ts'aô.*
Raisin. 葡萄 *p'oû t'aô.*
Raison, faculté de comprendre. 明悟 *mîn ngoú.* || Droit, équité, 理 *lī.* || *Voir* cause.
Raisonner. 講理 *kòng lī.* || Répliquer, 推論 *t'ouī loún*, 駁 *pôc.*
Ramasser. 拈 *niām*, 檢 *kiàm*, 收 *choū.*
Rame. 槳 *tsiòng*,
Rameau. 樹扒 *choú p'à*, 支 *tjē*, 枝 *kī.*
Ramener. 送轉來 *soúng tchòn loî*, 帶轉來 *taí tchòn loî.*
Rampe, 欄杆 *lân kōn.*
Ramper. 爬 *p'â.*
Rang, ligne. 行 *hông*, 排 *p'aî*, 列 *liĕt.* || Ordre, 次序 *tsé sí.* || Classe, dignité, 等 *tèn*, 位 *ví*, 品 *p'ìn.*
Ranger, étaler en ordre. 擺 *paì*, 檢點 *kiàm tiàm.* || Se —, (céder la place), 讓路 *nióng loú*, 讓位 *nióng ví*, 閃 *chàm.*
Râpe. 銼 *ts'ó.*
Rapide (de fleuve). 灘 *t'ān.*
Rapide. 快 *k'ouaí.*
Rappeler. 喊轉來 *hám tchòn loî.* || Faire souvenir, 提 *t'î*, 幫記 *pōng kí.* || Se — 記得 *kí tĕt*, 想倒 *siòng taò.* || Ne pouvoir se —, 想唔倒 *siòng mĝ taò.*
Rapport, relations. 來往 *loî vōng*, 交親 *kaō kouōn.* || *Voir*, comparer, convenir, motif.
Rapporter, 拿轉來 *nā tchòn loî.* || *Voir* dire, raconter, produire.
Rare. 罕 *hòn*, 少見 *chaò kián.*
Ras. 抨 *p'iâng*, 短 *tòn.*
Raser, couper avec un rasoir, 剃 *t'í.* || Effleurer, 爭一點動倒 *tsāng ŷt tiàm t'oūng taò.*
Rassasier. 飽 *paò.*
Rat. 老鼠 *laò tch'où.*
Râteau. 耙也 *p'â yà.* || Ratisser les feuilles, 耙葉 *p'â yăp.*

Raturer. *Voir* effacer.
Ravager. 傷害 *chōng hoí.*
Ravin. 坑公 *hāng koūng*, 溝 *keoū*, 山窩 *sān vō.*
Ravir. 奪 *t'ôt*, 偷 *t'eoū*, 搶 *ts'iòng*,
Rayer. 劃 *văc*, 剌 *lăc.*
Rayon. — de lumière, 光 *kouōng*, 日鬚 *gnĭt sī*, ‖ — d'armoire, 隔 *kâc.*
Réaliser. 做出來 *tsó tch'oūt loî*, 成 *châng.*
Rebelle, subst. 賊 *ts'ĕt.*
Rebours (à). 倒 ? *taò tsiáng*, ... 翻 *lât lât fan.*
Recéleur. 窩家 *vō kā.*
Récemment. 近日 *k'ioún gnĭt*, 啱 *tsáng.*
Recette, argent reçu. 來數 *loî sé*, 來銀 *loî nioûn*, 入 *gnĭp.* ‖ Moyen, 方法 *fōng fâp.*
Recevoir. 收 *choū*, 受 *choú*, 領 *leāng*, 接 *tsiâp*, 得 *têt.*
Réchaud. 爐 *loû.*
Réciter. 念 *niám.* ‖ — sa leçon, 背書 *p'oí choū.*
Récolte. 收成 *choū chîn*, 收穀 *choū koŭc.*
Recommander. 託付 *t'ôc foú*, 拜託 *paí t'ôc.* ‖ *Voir* confier, exhorter.
Récompense. 賞 *chòng.*
Réconcilier. 勸和 *k'ián fô.* ‖ Se — 做和睦 *tsó fô moŭc.*
Reconduire. 送轉 *soúng tchòn.* ‖ *Voir* conduire.
Reconnaissance. 知恩 *tī ēn*, 頁心 *leông sīm.* ‖ Montrer de la—, 報恩 *paó ēn.*
Reconnaître 認識 *gnín chĭt.*
Recourir, se mettre sous la protection de. 投 *t'eoû.* ‖ *Voir* invoquer, employer.
Recouvrer. 拿轉來 *nā tchòn loî*, 尋轉來 *ts'îm tchòn loî.*

Récréer (se). 嫽 *liaó*, 攪 *kaò.*
Reçu, subst. m. 收單 *choū tān.*
Recueillir, donner asile. 應酬 *ýn tch'oû* ‖ *Voir* ramasser.
Reculer. 退 *t'ouí.*
Rédemption. 救贖 *kioú choŭc.*
Redresser. 挷直 *pāng tch'ĭt*, 拗直 *aò tch'ĭt.*
Réduire. 扣 *k'eoú*, 折 *tchât*, 除 *tch'oû.*
Réel. 實在 *chĭt ts'aí*, 眞 *tchīn.*
Réfléchir. 想 *siòng*, 緬 *mèn.* ‖ — la lumière, 照光 *tchaó kouōng.*
Réfugier (se). 投 *t'eoû*, 閃 *chàm*, 避 *p'ĭt.*
Refuser. 唔甘願 *mĝ kām nián*, 唔收 *mĝ choū*, 辭 *tsê.*
Réfuter. — une accusation, 訴 *sé.* ‖ — une erreur, 辨 *pién*, 駁 *p'ôc*, 闢 *p'ĭt.*
Regarder. 看 *k'ón*, 望 *móng.* ‖ Concerner, 干 *kōn.* Cela ne te regarde pas, 唔干你事 *mĝ kōn gnî sé.*
Registre. 簿 *p'oū*, 冊 *ts'âc.*
Règle, précepte. 規矩 *kouī kì*, 法 *fâp.* ‖ Manière d'agir, 憑則 *p'în tsĕt.*
Reglisse. 甘草 *kām ts'aò.*
Régner. 做皇帝 *tsó fông tí.*
Regretter, penser à. 記念 *kí niám.* ‖ Se repentir: (d'y être allé), 早知我唔去 *tsaò tī ngaî mĝ hí.* Je regrette le temps perdu, 枉咁多閑我唔願 *nóng kàn tō hân ngaî mĝ nián.*
Reins. 腰 *yaō*, 腰骨 *yaō koŭt.*
Reine. 皇后 *fông heoú*; reine-mère, 皇太后 *fông t'aí heoú.*
Rejaillir. 濺 *ts'án*, 潑 *p'ât.*
Réjouir (se). 歡喜 *fōn hì.* ‖ *Voir* plaisir.
Réjouissance. 喜事 *hì sé.* 好事 *haò sé.*

Relâche (prendre un peu de). 撇一下 *liaó ŷt há*, 透氣 *t'coù hí*. ‖ *Voir* cesser, loisir.

Relativement. 看 *k'ón*, 照 *tchaó*, 論 *loún*. ‖ En comparaison, 比 *pì*.

Religion. 教 *kaó*. ‖ Ordre religieux, 會 *fí*.

Remarier (se); en parlant d'un homme. 討過一個婦人家 *t'aò kouó ŷt ké' foú gnîn kā*; en parlant d'une femme, 再嫁 *tsaí ká*.

Remarquer. 看分明 *k'ón foūn mîn*, 看正來 *k'ón tchín loî*.

Remède; médecine en poudre, 藥粉 *yǒc foùn*, 藥散 *yǒc sàn*, médecine liquide, 藥水 *yǒc choùi*, 藥酒 *yǒc tsioù*; médecine en herbes. 藥草 *yǒc ts'aò*.

Remercier. 感謝 *kàm ts'iá*, 多謝 *tō ts'iá*.

Remettre. *Voir* livrer, pardonner, différer, confier.

Remonter. 到上 *taó chōng*. ‖ Barque qui remonte le courant, 上水船 *chōng choùi chôn*. ‖ — l'horloge, 上鐘 *chòng tchoūng*, 開鐘 *k'oī tchoūng*.

Remords. Eprouver du —, 知罪 *tī ts'ouí*, 良心唔平 *leông sīm mĝ p'în*, 愧心 *k'ouì sīm*.

Rempart, mur d'une ville. 城 *châng*.

Remplacer. 代 *t'oí*. ‖ Tenir lieu de, 當 *tóng*, 准 *tchoùn*. ‖ *Voir* changer.

Remplir. 裝滿 *tchōng mān*. ‖ Accomplir, 做 *tsó*, 守 *choù*.

Remuer. 搖 *yaō*, 動 *t'oúng*.

Renard. 捕狗 *p'oú keoù*, 狐狸 *foû lî*.

Rencontrer. 遇 *gní*, 逢 *foûng*, 撞 *ts'òng*.

Rendre, restituer 還 *vân*, 賠 *p'oî*.

Renier. 唔認 *mĝ gnín*, 背 *p'oí*.

Renom. 名 *miâng*, 名聲 *miâng chāng*.

Renoncer, rejeter. 棄絕 *hí ts'ĭĕt*, 捨 *chà*, 唔愛 *mĝ oí*.

Renouveler. 再 *tsaí*, 又 *yoú*, 從新 *ts'ioûng sīn*.

Rentrer. — chez soi. 轉家 *tchòn kā*, 回家 *fî kā*. ‖ *V*. a. 收 *choū*, 撿 *kiàm*.

Renverser. 倒 *taò*, 轉 *tchón*, 翻 *fān*.

Renvoyer. *Voir* envoyer, différer.

Repaire. 窩 *vō*.

Répandre. 洒 *chà*, 散 *sán*, 倒 *taò*. ‖ Propager, 傳 *tch'ôn*.

Réparation. Faire réparation d'honneur, 認錯賠禮 *gnín ts'ŏc p'oî lī*, 悔釋人 *fí chĭt gnîn*.

Réparer. 補 *poù*, 整 *tchàng*.

Repas, un —, 一飧飯 *ŷt ts'ōn fán*; grand repas, 酒席 *tsioù sĭt*.

Repasser. — (du linge), 熨 *yoún*. ‖ *Voir* aiguiser, réfléchir.

Répentir (se). 痛悔 *t'oúng fí*.

Répéter. 話過 *vá kouó*, 再講 *tsaí kòng*. ‖ Refaire, reproduire, 做過 *tsó kouó*.

Répliquer. 應嘴 *ýn tchoí*, ... *toí*, 講嘴 *kòng tchoí*.

Répondre. 答 *tâp*, 答應 *tâp ýn*. ‖ Ecrire une lettre en réponse, 回信 *fî sín*. ‖ Etre caution, 保 *paò*, 躭承 *tām chîn*.

Reposer, s'appuyer. 凭 *pén*, 靠 *k'aó*.

Reprendre. — connaissance, 醒 *siàng*. ‖ — vie, 反生 *fàn sāng*. ‖ *Voir* prendre, continuer, réprimander.

Représenter, tenir la place de. 代 *t'oí* 准 *tchoùn*. ‖ *Voir* indiquer.

Réprimander. 罵 *má*, 責備 *tsĭt p'í*, 責成 *tsĭt chîn*, 嫌人 *hiâm gnîn*, 話 *vá*.

Réprimer 押 *âp*, 懲 *tchìn*, 懲治 *tchìn tché.*
Reprocher. 嫌 *hiâm.* || *Voir* réprimander.
Réprouver, blâmer. 嫌 *hiâm*, 唔允 *mĝ youn*, 講唔着 *kòng mĝ tchŏc.* || *Voir* damner.
Reptile. 蛇 *châ.*
Répudier. — sa femme. 丟老婆 *tiou laò p'ô.*
Répugnance. Avoir de la —, 唔甘愛 *mĝ kâm oí*, 畏 *ví*, 愛唔得 *oí mĝ tĕt.*
Réputation. || *Voir* renom.
Requête 呈子 *tch'în tzè*, 禀帖 *pìn t'iâp.*
Réserver. 留 *lioû. Voir* conserver, laisser, excepter.
Résilier. 退 *t'ouí*, 磨算 *mô són.*
Résister, opposer la force. 抗 *k'óng*, 耐 *naí* ou *ngaí*, 抵擋 *tì tòng*, || Ne pouvoir —, 奈唔何 *naí mĝ hô.*
Résolution. *Voir* dessein.
Respecter. 敬 *kín*, 尊 *tsoūn*; — ses parents, 孝敬父母 *haó kín foú moū*,
Respirer. 出氣 *tch'oût hí*, 透氣 *t'eoù hí.*
Responsable. Il est —, 佢事 *kiā sé*, 担承 *tām chîn*, 担保 *tām paò.*
Ressembler. 像 *ts'iông*, 像 *ts'ám*, 相似 *siōng sé.* || Se —, 相同 *siōng t'oûng.*
Ressemeler. 上鞋底 *chòng haî taì.*
Ressort, subst. m. 法條 *fâp t'iaô.*
Ressusciter. 復活 *foŭc făt*, 反生 *fàn sāng.*
Reste. 剩 *chín*, 餘剩 *ŷ chín*, 多個 *tō ké·.*
Restituer. *Voir* rendre.
Rétablir. 做轉 *tsó tchòn.* || Il est complètement rétabli, 醫好哩 *ŷ haò lê·.*
Retard. 躭擱 *tām kôc.* || *Voir* différer.
Retenir, faire rester. 留 *lioû.* || *Voir* empêcher, retrancher, se rappeler, supporter.
Retirer, tirer de qq. endroit. 抓出 *tch'ā tch'oût*, 取 *ts'ì.* || Recueillir, 收 *choū.* || Se — (s'en aller), 走 *tseoù*, 離開 *lî k'oī*, 轉 *tchòn.*
Retour. 轉 *tchòn.* L'aller et le retour, 來回 *loî fî.*
Retourner. Tourner d'un autre côté, 翻轉 *fān tchòn*, 倒轉 *taò tchòn.* || — l'un dans l'autre, *p'ŏn.*
Retraite. Battre en —, 退走 *t'ouí tseoù.* || Endroit solitaire, 僻靜地方 *p'ĭt ts'ín t'í fōng.* || Faire une —, 做神功 *tsó chîn koūng*, 停工 *t'în koūng.*
Retrancher. 除 *tch'oû*, 扣 *k'eoú.* || *Voir* couper.
Rétrécir (se). 縮 *soŭc.*
Retrousser. 扎 *tsâp*, 攝 *niâp.*
Réunir. 湊 *ts'eoú*, 聚 *ts'í*, 收俬 *choū ts'ioū*, 集 *sĭp*, 齊 *ts'ê·.*
Réussir. 成 *châng*, 做着 *tsó tch'ŏc*, 鬥着 *teoú tch'ŏc*, 好 *haò*, 對 *touí.*
Rêve. 夢 *móng* ou *moúng.*
Revêche, caractère —, 固執 *koú tchĭp*, 奸計 *kiān kí.*
Réveille-matin. 鬧鐘 *naó tchoūng.*
Réveiller (se). 睡醒 *choé· siàng.*
Révéler. 講出來 *kòng tch'oût loî*, 露 *loú.* || *Voir* divulguer.
Revendeur. 販 *fán.*
Revenir. 轉來 *tchòn loî*, 回 *fî.*
Revenu. 租 *tzè*, 利 *lí*, 出息 *tch'oût sĭt.*
Revers. 背 *poé·.* || *Voir* calamité.
Revêtir. 著 *tchôc.* || *Voir* enduire.
Révolte. 亂 *lón*, 反 *fàn.*

Rhume. Attraper un —, 傷風 *chōng foūng*. || *Voir* tousser.
Riche. 富貴 *foú kouí*, 發財 *fât ts'oï*, ...*pôt*.
Ricin. 萆痲 *pī mâ*.
Ride. 縐 *tsioú*.
Rideau. 帷 *vî*, 簾 *liâm*.
Rien. 麽那個 *mô mâc ké·*. || Donné pour —, 送個 *soúng ké·*, 唔使錢 *mĝ sè ts'iēn*.
Rincer. 盪 *t'ōng*, 洗 *sè·*.
Rire. 笑 *siaó*.
Rite. 禮 *lī*.
Rive. 岸 *ngán*, 河邊 *hô piēn*.
Rivière. 河 *hô*.
Riz. — en herbe, 秧子 *yōng tzè*; — non écossé, 穀 *koŭc*; — écossé, 米 *mì*; — cuit, 飯 *fán*.
Robe. 長衫 *tch'ông sām*; — doublée, 長襖 *tch'ông aò*. || — de cérémonie, 袍 *p'aô*.
Rocher. 石 *chăc*, 石礫 *chăc tsaí*.
Rogner. *Voir* couper, tailler.
Roi. 王 *vông*.
Roman. 古 *koù*, 傳 *tch'ón*.
Rompre. 拗斷 *aò t'ōn*, 打斷 *tà t'ōn*.
Rond. 圓 *yân*.
Ronfler. 噴睡 *p'oún choé·*.
Ronger. 吃 *ngât*; rongé par les vers, 蛀 *tchoú*.
Rosaire (prières du). 玫瑰經 *moê· kouí kīn*.
Rose. 玫瑰花 *moê· kouí fā*.
Rosée. 露水 *loú chouì*.
Rotin. 籐子 *t'ên tzè*.
Rôtir. 炕 *k'óng*, 燒 *chaō*.
Roue. 車輪 *tch'ā loûn*.
Rouet. 車子 *tch'ā tzè*.
Rouge. 紅 *foûng*.
Rougeole (avoir la). 出痲 *tch'oūt mâ*.
Rougir. *Voir* honte.
Rouille. 鏽 *loū*.
Rouler. 滾 *koùn*. || Plier en roulant, 捆 *k'oùn*.
Route. 路 *loú*, 道 *t'aó*.
Royaume. 國 *kouĕt*.
Ruban. 欄杆 *lân kōn*. || Lacet, 帶子 *taí tzè*.
Ruche, une — d'abeilles, 一桶蜂子 *ŷt t'oùng foūng tzè*.
Rue, une —, 一條街 *ŷt t'iaô kiaī*.
Ruelle. 巷子 *hóng tzè*.
Rugueux. 澁 *sĕp*, 唔坪 *mĝ p'iâng*.
Ruiner. 敗家 *p'aí kā*. || Tomber en ruine, 𡁻崩 ou 屙 *voé· pēn* ou *ō*; 害 *hoí*. || Etre ruiné, perdre sa fortune, 蝕本 *chĭt poùn*, 窮帛裡 *k'ioúng p'ĕt lî*.
Ruisseau. 瀝 *lâc*, 坑瀝 *hāng lâc*, 河溪 *hô haī*, 溝 *keoū*.
Ruse. 詭計 *kouì ké·*.
Rusé. 狡猾 *kaò vât*, 古怪 *koù kouaí*, 精 *tsīn*.

S

Sable. 沙 *sā*.
Sabot. 屐 *k'iăc*. || — d'animal, 蹄 *t'aî*.
Sabre. 刀 *taō*, 劍 *kiám*.
Sac. 袋 *t'oí*.
Sacré. 聖 *chín*.
Sacrement. 聖跡 *chín tsĭt*, 聖事 *chín sé*.
Sacrifice. 祭 *tsí*. || Privation, ne pouvoir se résoudre à faire le —, 捨唔得 *chà mĝ tĕt*.

Sacrilège (commettre un). 冒領 ou 冒做聖事 *maó leāng* ou *maó tsó chín sé.*
Sage. 賢 *hiên.* || Cet enfant est —, 細人子係乖 *sé· gnîn tzè hé· kouāi.* || Le —, 君子 *kioūn tzè.* || *Voir* bon, prudent, intelligent.
Sage-femme. 接生婆 *tsiâp sēn p'ô.*
Saigner, v. a. 放血 *fóng hiĕt.* || v. n. 流血 *lioû hiĕt;* — du nez, 出鼻血 *tch'oût p'í hiĕt.*
Sain. 好 *haò,* 麼病 *mô p'iáng.*
Saint. 聖 *chín.* || Une — mort, 善終 *chán tchoūng.*
Saisir. *Voir* prendre, comprendre, profiter.
Saison, époque. 時節 *chê tsiĕt.* || Les quatre —, 四季 *sí kouí.*
Salaire. 工錢 *koūng ts'iên.*
Sale. 唔伶俐 *mĝ lāng lí,* 浼 *mé·,* 穢 *vé·,* 邋遢 *lâp sâp.*
Salé. 鹹 *hâm.*
Saletés. 攋澁 *lâp sĕp.*
Salive. 口液 *heoù lān.*
Salle. 廳 *t'āng.*
Salpêtre. 朴硝 *p'ŏc siaō,* 硝鹽 *siaō yâm.*
Saluer. 拜 *paí,* 問候 *moún heoú,* 請安 *ts'iàng ōn.* || — des mains, 唱耶 *tch'óng yā.* || Faire la prostration, 磕頭 *k'ŏc t'eoû.*
Salut, bénédiction du S[t]. Sacrement. 聖體降福 *chín t'ì kóng foûc.* || Penser à son —, 想救靈魂 *siòng kioú lîn foûn.* || *Voir* sauver, vie.
Sang. 血 *hiĕt,* 旺 *vóng.*
Sanglier. 野猪 *yā tchoū,* 山猪 *sān tchoū.*
Sangsue. 湖蜞 *foû k'î.*
Sans, négation. 無 *voû,* 麼 *mô.* || — même demander, 問都麼問 *moún toū mô moún.*
Santé (avoir une bonne). 平安 *p'în ōn,* 健 *k'ián.*
Sapèque. 錢 *ts'iên.*
Sapin. 杉樹 *ts'ám choú.*
Sarcler. 耘 *yoûn,* 椰草 *pāng ts'aò.*
Sarrasin, blé noir. 三角粟 *sām kŏc sioŭc,* 鴨脚粟 *âp kiŏc sioŭc.*
Satellite. 差 *ts'aī.*
Satin. 緞子 *t'ón tzè.*
Satisfaire. 補贖 *poù choŭc.* || *Voir* accomplir, payer, content.
Sauce. 湯 *t'ōng,* 醬 *tsiōng.*
Saucisse. 讓腸 *nióng tch'ông,* 貫腸 *kouón tch'ông.*
Saule. 柳樹 *lioù choú.*
Saumure. 鹽水 *yâm chouì.*
Sauter. 跳 *t'iaó,* ... *piaō.* || *Voir* éclater.
Sauvage. 野個 *yā ké·.*
Sauver. 救 *kioú.* || Se — (faire son salut), 救靈魂 *kioú lîn foûn.* || *Voir* fuir.
Savant. 有才學 *yoū ts'oî hŏc.*
Saveur. 味 *mí.*
Savoir. 知 *tī,* 曉 *hiaò,* 噲 *voé·,* 熟 *choŭc.*
Savon. 番鹼 *fān kiàn.*
Scandale. 壞表樣 *faí piaò yóng.*
Scapulaire. 聖衣 *chín ȳ.*
Sceau. 印 *ýn.*
Scellé. 封 *foūng,* 印 *ýn.*
Schisme. 裂敎 *liĕt kaó.*
Scie. 鋸 *kí.*
Sciure. 鋸屎 *kí chè.*
Sculpter. 雕 *t'iaō.*
Se. *Voir* soi.

8

Seau. 水桶 *chouì t'oùng.*

Sécher. — à l'air, 㫰燥 *lâng tsaō;* — au soleil, 晒 *saí;* — au feu, 炕 *k'óng.*

Secouer. 搖 *yaô,* 㧾 *tch'oŭc.*

Secourir. *Voir* aider, sauver.

Secret (en). 暗上 *ám chóng,* 背 *poé·,* 默默 *mĕt mĕt.*

Secrétaire. 內櫃人 *nouí k'ouí gnîn.*

Secte. 教 *kaó,* 黨 *tòng.*

Séculier. 世俗個 *ché sioŭc ké·.*

Séduire. 勾引 *keoū ÿn,* 牽 *k'iān.* || *Voir* tromper, corrompre.

Sein, poitrine. 胸 *hioūng,* 心肝 *sīm kōn.* || *Voir* mamelle.

Sel. 鹽 *yâm.*

Selle. — de cheval, 馬鞍 *mā ōn.* || Garde-robe, aller à la —, 行大便 *hâng t'aí p'ién,* 出恭 *tch'oût kioūng,* 屙屎 *ō chè.*

Selon. 照 *tchaó,* 看 *k'ón.*

Semaine, une —, 一個主日 *ŷt ké· tchoù gnĭt.*

Semblable. 一樣 *ŷt yóng. Voir* égal, prochain, ressembler.

Semelle. — de soulier, 鞋底 *haî taì.*

Semence. 種 *tchoùng.*

Semer. 種 *tchoúng,* ? *yé·* ou *vé·,* 落 *lŏc.*

Sens. Les cinq —, 五官 *ǹg koūon.* || Homme de bon —, 懂事個人 *toùng sé ké· gnîn,* 有見識 *yoū kián chĭt.* || En—opposé, ? ? 翻 *lât lât fān,* 倒 ? *taò tsiáng.* || Signification, 意思 *ý sé.*

Sensible, qui tombe sous les sens. 看得倒個 *k'ón tĕt taò ké·,* 有形有像 *yoū hîn yoū sióng.* || Avoir le cœur—, 心軟 *sīm niōn.*

Sentence (rendre une). 斷 *tón,* 結案 *kiĕt ón.*

Sentier. 小路 *siaò loú.*

Sentiment. 心 *sīm,* 情 *ts'în.* || *Voir* avis, sentir, comprendre.

Sentir, éprouver une impression. — la douleur, 知痛 *tī t'oúng.* || Ne pas — la faim, 唔曉肚餓 *mĝ hiaò toù kī.* || *Voir* flairer, comprendre.

Séparément. 另事 *láng sé,* 一個一個 *ŷt ké· ŷt ké·.* || Interroger les parties —, 吊問 *tiaó moún.*

Séparer. 分開 *foūn k'oī.*

Sept. 七 *ts'ĭt.*

Sépulcre. 墳 *foûn,* 地墳 *t'í foûn.*

Serein. 晴 *ts'iâng.* || Calme, 平 *p'în,* 和 *fô.*

Sérieux. 唔係講笑個 *mĝ hé· kòng siaó hé·,* 有相干 *yoū siōng kōn.* || *Voir* grave, important.

Seringue. 洩筒 *siĕt t'oúng.*

Serment (faire). 發誓 *fât ché,* 願 *nián.*

Sermon. *Voir* prêcher.

Serpent. 蛇哥 *châ kō.*

Serré, fortement tendu. 狠 *hên.* || Dru, 密 *mĕt.* || Comprimé, 擠 *tsī,* 尖 *tsiām,* 薦 *tsién.*

Serrer, lier fortement. 絞狠 *kaò hên,* 捆 *k'oùn.* || Mettre en lieu sûr, 收 *choū,* 撿 *kiàm.* || *Voir* pincer, presser.

Serrure. 鎖頭 *sò t'eoû.*

Service. *Voir* aider, bienfait, usage.

Servir, aider comme domestique. 幫人 *pōng gnîn.* || — un malade, 服事病 *foŭc sé p'iáng gnîn.* || — la table, 擺桌 *paì tsôc,* 擺飯 *paì fán.* || — comme soldat, 當兵 *tōng pīn.* || — Dieu, 奉事天主 *foúng sé t'iēn tchoù.* || *Voir* utile, usage, remplacer, employer. || Se — de, 使 *sè,* 用 *yoúng.*

Seuil. 門頭 *moûn t'eoû*, 門脚下 *moûn kiôc hā*.
Seul, unique. 浄一個 *ts'iáng ŷt ké·*, 獨 *t'oŭc*, 單 *tān*, 浄自己 *ts'iáng tsé kì*.
Seulement. 單單 *tān tān*, 不過 *poŭt kouó*. || Pas —, 唔止 *mǵ tjè*. || A l'instant, 啍 *tsáng*.
Sève. 醬 *tsiōng*, 汁水 *tchĭp choùi*.
Sévère. 嚴 *niâm*, 狠 *hēn*, 緊 *kìn*.
Sexe (sans distinction de). 不論男女 *poŭt loún nâm ǹg*.
Si, conj. 若 *yŏc*, 係 *hé·* (se sous-entend le plus souvent). || Adv. 咁 *àn* ou *kàn*.
Siècle, un —, 一百年 *ŷt pâc niân*.
Siège. 凳 *tén*, 几 *ỳ*, 座位 *ts'ó ví*. || *Voir* assiéger.
Siéger. — dans un tribunal, 坐堂 *ts'ō t'ông*.
Sien. 佢個 *kiâ ké·*, 自己個 *tsé kì ké·*.
Sifflet. 簫 *siaō*.
Signe, marque. 記號 *kí haó*, 記認 *kí gnín*. || Le — de la croix, 聖號 *chín haó*. || Indice, 憑據 *p'în kì*, 兆頭 *chaó t'eoû*.
Signe, 畫號 *fá haó*.
Signifier. *Voir* dire, expliquer, indiquer, commander.
Silence. 麼聲麼氣 *mô chāng mô hí*; faites —, 莫聲 *mŏc chang*.
Simple, adj. opposé à double, 單 *tān*. || Non rusé, 老實 *laò chĭt*. || *Voir* seul, facile, ordinaire, franc, droit.
Sincère. *Voir* franc, droit, vrai.
Singe. 猴哥 *heoû kō*.
Singulier. *Voir* différer, extraordinaire, étrange, merveilleux.
Sinon. 唔係 *mǵ hé·*.
Sinueux. 彎 *vān*, 曲 *k'ioŭt*.
Site. 地勢 *t'í ché*, 景緻 *kìn tjé*.
Sitôt. 咁早 *kàn tsaò*, 咁快 *kàn k'ouaí*.
Situé. 在 *ts'aí*.
Six. 六 *lioŭc*.
Soc. 犁頭 *laî t'eoû*.
Société. 會 *fí*.
Sœur. — plus âgée, 大姊 *t'aí tsì*; — moins âgée, 老妹 *laò moé·*.
Soi. 自己 *tsé kì*. || En —, 本來 *poùn loî*. || Cela va de —, 自然 *tsé yân*.
Soie. 綢 *tch'oû*.
Soif. Avoir —, 肚渴 *toù hôt*. || Etancher la —, 止渴 *tjè hôt*.
Soigner. 管 *kouòn*, 顧 *koú*, 服事 *foŭc sé*. || Faire avec soin, 用心 *yoúng sīm*, 仔細 *tzè sé·*.
Soir. 暗 *ám*; ce soir, 今晡夜 *kīn poū yá*. || Prière du —, 晚課 *vān k'ó*.
Soit, je le veux bien. 做得 *tsó tĕt*, 好 *haò*. || Conj. 不論 *poŭt loún*, 或 *fĕt*.
Soixante. 六十 *lioŭc chĭp*.
Sol. 地基 *t'í ki*, 地泥 *t'í naî*.
Soldat. 兵 *pīn*, 勇 *yoùng*.
Soleil. 日頭 *gnĭt t'eoû*, 大陽 *t'aí yông*.
Solide, ferme, durable. 穩當 *voùn tóng*, 主固 *tchoù koú*, 硬 *ngáng*, 鐵實 *t'iĕt chĭt*.
Solitaire adj. Endroit — (tranquille). 僻靜地方 *p'ĭt ts'ín t'í fōng*.
Solitaire, subst. m. 隱修 *yoùn sioū*.
Solstice. — d'été, 夏至 *há tjé*. || — d'hiver, 冬至 *toūng tjé*.
Sombre, noir. 暗 *ám*, 烏 *voū*. || Nuageux, ciel —, 陰天 *ȳm t'iēn*.
Somme, total. 總共 *tsoùng k'ioúng*, 統共 *t'oùng k'ioúng*. || Nombre, 數目 *sé moŭc*.

Sommeil. 睡目 *choé· mouc*. ‖ Avoir—, 篤目睡 *touc mouc choé·*.
Sommet. 頂 *tàng*.
Son, adj. poss. 佢個 *kiā ké·*.
Son, subst. — de riz, 米糠 *mì hōng*. ‖ — musical, 音 *ȳm*, 聲 *chāng*.
Sonder. 看深淺 *k'ón tch'īm ts'ièn*, 試 *tché*, 探 *t'àm*.
Songe. 夢 *moúng*.
Sonnette. 鈴 *lāng*.
Sorcier. 覡公 *cháng koūng*, 仙姑 *siēn koū*.
Sorgho. 高粱粟 *kaō leông siouc*.
Sort. Tirer au —, 拈鬮 *niām keoū*. ‖ Interroger les —, 抽籤 *tch'oū ts'iām*, 占卜 *tchám pouc*, 問仙 *moún siēn*.
Sortilège. 邪法 *siâ fâp*.
Sortir. 出 *tch'oût*. ‖ Etre issu, 出身 *tch'oût chīn*.
Sot. 癲 *tiēn*, 蠢 *tch'oùn*.
Souche (d'arbre). 樹頭 *choú t'eoû*, 樹脚 *choú kiōc*.
Souci. 勞心 *laô sīm*, 費心 *fí sīm*. ‖ *Voir* inquiet.
Soucoupe. 碟 *t'iăp*, 細盤 *sé· p'ân*.
Soudain. 忽然 *foût yân*.
Souder. 銲 *hón*.
Souffle, vent. 風 *foūng*. ‖ Respiration, 氣 *hí*.
Souffler. 吹 *tch'oī*. ‖ Le vent souffle, 風吹 *foūng tch'oī*, 起風 *hì foūng*. ‖ Respirer, 透氣 *t'eoù hí*.
Soufflet. — de forge, 風箱 *foūng siōng*. ‖ Donner un —, 打巴掌 *tà pā tchòng*.
Souffrir. 受苦 *choú k'où*, 痛 *t'oúng*. ‖ *Voir* supporter.
Soufre. 硫磺 *lioû vông*.

Souhaiter. — la bonne année, 拜新年 *paí sīn niân*. ‖ — le bonjour, 問候 *moún heoú*, 請安 *ts'iàng ōn*. ‖ *Voir* désirer.
Soulager. 鬆 *soūng*, 寬 *k'ōn*. ‖ *Voir* consoler, aider.
Soulier. 鞋 *haî*.
Soumettre. 押伏 *âp foŭc*, 打伏 *tà foŭc*. ‖ Se —, 准 *tchoùn*, 遵 *tsoūn*.
Soupçonner. 猜 *ts'aī*, 猜疑 *ts'aī gnî*.
Soupe. 麵包湯 *mién paō t'ōng*.
Souper. 食夜 *chĭt yá*.
Souple. 軟 *niōn*.
Source. 水泉 *chouì ts'ân*. ‖ *Voir* origine.
Sourcil. 眉毛 *mî maō*.
Sourd. 耳聾 *gnì loūng*.
Sourire. 笑嘻嘻 *siaó sī sī*.
Sous. — la table, 桌底下 *tsôc taì hā*. ‖ Les gens qui sont — moi, 我手下個人 *ngaî choù hā ké· gnîn*. ‖— tel mandarin, 某官管個 *meoū kouōn kouòn ké·*.
Soustraire. *Voir* dérober, enlever, retrancher.
Soutenir. 扶 *p'oû* ou *foû*, 撐 *ts'áng*.
Souvenir (se). 記得 *kí tĕt*.
Souvent. 好多擺 *haò tō paì*.
Spacieux. 寬闊 *k'ōn fât*.
Spirale. 螺螄 *lô sē*.
Spirituel, incorporel. 無形無像個 *voû hîn voû sióng ké·*. ‖ Choses spirituelles, 靈魂個事 *lîn foûn ké· sé*. ‖ *Voir* intelligent.
Station, centre de chrétiens, 公所 *koūng sò*. ‖ Les 14 Stations (du Chemin de la Croix), 十四處 *chĭp sí tch'oú*. ‖ *Voir* étape.

Statue. 像 *sióng*.
Stérile. Terre —, 荒地 *fōng t'í*. || Femme —, 麼子個 *mô tzè ké'*..
Subalterne, subordonné. 手下個人 *choù hā ké' gnîn*.
Suborner. 貼錢 *tiâp ts'iên*, 交火錢 *kaō fò ts'iên*.
Substance. 體 *t'ì*. || — spirituelle, 神體 *chîn t'ì*.
Subtil, menu. 細 *sé'*.
Succéder. 接位 *tsiâp ví*, 接手 *tsiâp choù*, 繼 *kí*. || *Voir* remplacer.
Succomber. || *Voir* consentir, mourir.
Sucer. 咄 *tsŏt*.
Sucre. 糖 *t'ông*.
Sud. 南 *nâm*.
Suer. 出汗 *tch'oût hón*.
Suffire. 彀 *keoú*, || *Voir* pouvoir.
Suggérer, parler de. 提 *t'î*. || Exciter, 引 *ȳn*, 勾 *keoū*.
Suif. 油 *yoû*.
Suite. 緒 *sí*, 尾 *mī*. || Tout de —, 就 *ts'ioú*. || *Voir* accompagner, après, conséquence, ordre.
Suivant. Le jour —, 第二日 *t'í gní gnĭt*. || Adv. *Voir* selon.
Suivre, aller dans la direction de, 滕 *t'ên*. || Se conformer à, 順 *choún*, 從 *ts'ioûng*. || *Voir* accompagner, poursuivre, observer. || Se —, 相連 *siōng liên*.
Sujet. — de composition, 題目 *t'î moûc*. || *Voir* cause, objet.
Superficie. 面 *mién*.
Supérieur. 上 *chóng*, 上 *hóng*, 大 *t'aí*.
Superstition. 異端 *ý tōn*.
Suppléer. 補 *poù*, 帖 *t'iâp*. || *Voir* remplacer.

Supplice. 刑 *hîn*, 苦 *k'où*.
Supplier. 求 *k'ioû*, 懇求 *k'èn k'ioû*.
Supporter. 鼎力 *tìn lĭt*, 承 *chîn*. || Souffrir, 受 *choú*. || Endurer, 耐 *ngaí* ou *naí*, 忍 *nioūn*.
Supposer. Supposons, 好比 *haò pì*, 比方 *pì fōng*. || *Voir* conjecturer, feindre.
Sur, prép. — la table, 桌上 *tsôc hóng*; — soi, 身上 *chīn hóng*. || *Voir* près de, vers, parmi, quant à, à cause de.
Sûr. 穩當 *voùn tóng*, 妥當 *t'ò tóng*. || Certain, 定着 *t'ín tch'ŏc*.
Surface. 面 *mién*.
Surlendemain. 後日 *heoú gnĭt*.
Surnaturel. 超性個 *tch'aō sín ké'*.
Surpasser. 超過 *tch'aō kouó*, 大過 *t'aí kouó*, 蓋過 *koì kouó*.
Surtout. 頭一宗 *t'eoû ȳt tsoūng*, 第一 *t'í ȳt*.
Susceptible, qui s'offense facilement. 小氣 *siaò hí*. || *Voir* apte.
Suspendre. 吊 *tiaó*, 搭 *tâp*, 挽 *vàn*. || *Voir* interdire, interrompre.

T

Tabac. 黃烟 *vông yān*.
Table. 桌 *tsôc*.
Tablette. 牌 *p'aî*.
Tablier. 圍身裙 *vî chīn k'ioûn*.
Tabouret. 矮凳子 *aì tén tzè*.
Tache. Faire une —, 打浼 *tà mé'*, 玷 *tiám*.
Tâcher. *Voir* s'efforcer.
Tacheté. 花個 *fā ké'*.
Taël, un —, 一兩銀 *ȳt leōng nioûn*.

Tailler, amincir, 削 *siôc*, 剕 *p'aī*. || E-monder, 撥 *p'ât*. || Découper, 裁 *ts'aî*. || — la pierre, 打石 *tà chăc*.
Tailleur. — d'habits, 裁縫 *ts'aî foûng*. || — de pierres, 打石師傅 *tà chăc sē foú*.
Taire. 麼話 *mô vá*. || Se —, 莫聲 *mŏc chāng*.
Talent. 才 *ts'oî*. || Avoir du —, 噲 *voé'*. || *Voir* capable.
Talon. 脚睜 *kiôc tsāng*.
Talus. 坎 *k'àm*.
Tambour. 鼓 *koù*.
Tamis. 篩 *sī*.
Tam-tam. 鑼 *lô*.
Tandis que. || *Voir* pendant, au contraire.
Tanière. 壟 *loûng*, 洞 *t'oúng*.
Tanner. 腯 *t'oùn*.
Tant. 咁多 *kàn tō*. || — mieux, 唨好 *tsáng haò*. || *Voir* si, tellement.
Tante. Sœur du père, 姑姑 *koū koū*; sœur de la mère, 阿姨 *ā ŷ*. || Femme d'un oncle paternel, 伯姆 *pâc mē'*; femme d'un oncle maternel, 舅姆 *k'ioū mē'*.
Tantôt. Tantôt..., tantôt. 一時..., 一時 *ŷt chê*..., *ŷt chê*. 一下..., 一下 *ŷt há*..., *ŷt há*. || *Voir* bientôt.
Tapis. 毡子 *t'àn tzè*.
Tapisser. 糊紙 *foû tjè*, 貼紙 *tiâp tjè*.
Tarare. 簸箕 *paí kī*.
Tard. 遲 *tchê*, 暗 *ám*, 夜 *yá*.
Tarder. 躭擱 *tām kôc*, 遲延 *tchê yân*, 難 *nân*.
Tare. Défalquer la —, 除皮 *tch'oû p'î*.
Tas. 堆 *toī*.
Tasse. 盃 *pī*, 碗 *vouòn*.
Tâter. 摩 *mō*, *miā*. || *Voir* essayer.
Teindre. 染 *niám*.
Tel, un —, 某人 *meoū gnîn*.
Télégraphe. — électrique, 電線 *t'ién sién*.
Télescope. 千里鏡 *ts'iēn lī kiáng*.
Tellement. 倒 *taò* (ajouté au verbe). J'ai — mangé du lard que j'en ai le dégoût, 食肥猪肉食倒畏 *chĭt p'î tchoū nioûc chĭt taò ví*.
Témoin. 証 *tchín*, 見證 *kián tchín*.
Témoignage (rendre un faux). 妄證 *vòng tchín*.
Température. 天氣 *t'iēn hí*.
Tempéré. 溫 *voūn*, 淡 *t'ám*.
Temple. *Voir* église.
Temps, époque, durée, 時候 *chê heoú*. || Etat du ciel, 天 *t'iēn*. || *Voir* loisir, température.
Tenailles. 鉗子 *k'iâm tzè*.
Tendre, adj. 嫩 *noún*, 軟 *niōn*, 綿 *miên*.
Tendre, présenter en avant. 伸 *chīn*, 伸 *tch'oūn*. || *Voir* bander.
Tendresse. Avoir de la — pour qqn. 惜 *siâc*, 心動 *sīm t'oúng*.
Tenir. 拿穩 *nā voùn*. || — dans la bouche, 含 *hâm*; — dans les bras, 揹 *nàm*. || *Voir* résister, maîtriser, désirer, dépendre.
Tentation. 誘感 *yoú kàm*.
Tente. 帳 *tchóng*, 布篷 *poú p'oûng*.
Tenter. 誘感 *yoú kàm*, 勾引 *keoū ŷn*. || *Voir* essayer, attirer, entraîner.
Tenue. 樣子 *yóng tzè*.
Terminer. 做成 *tsó tcháng*, 做完 *tsó vân*.
Terrain. 地方 *t'í fōng*.

Terre, globe terrestre. 地球 *t'í k'ioû.* ‖ Sol, 泥 *naî,* 土 *t'où.*
Territoire. 地方 *t'í fōng,* 鄉 *hiōng.*
Tête. 頭 *t'eoû.*
Thé. 茶 *ts'â.*
Théâtre. 戲 *hí.*
Tiède. 溫溫 *voūn voūn,* 淡 *t'ám.*
Tien. 你個 *niā ké·.*
Tige. ... *tsīn,* 梲 *kouāng.*
Tigre. 老虎 *laò foù.*
Timide. 麼膽 *mô tàm.*
Tirer. 抓 *tch'ā,* 拖 *t'ō.* ‖ — le canon, 響炮 *hiòng p'aó,* 放炮 *fóng p'aó.* ‖ — de l'arc, 射箭 *chá tsién.*
Tiroir. 拖隔 *t'ō kâc.*
Tisane. 水藥 *chouì yŏc,* 茶 *ts'â.*
Tisser. 織 *tchĭt,* 耕布 *kāng poú.*
Titre. 名 *miâng,* 號 *haó,* 銜頭 *hâm t'eoû,* 功名 *koūng miâng.* ‖ *Voir* contrat.
Toi, tu, te. 你 *gnî.*
Toile. 布 *poú.*
Toit. 屋下水 *voŭc hā chouì,* 屋頂 *voŭc tàng.*
Tombe. 地墳 *t'í foûn.*
Tomber. 落 *lŏc,* 跌 *tiĕt,* 下 *hā,* 屙 *ō,* 崩 *pēn.*
Ton ta, tien. 你 *niā.*
Ton, subst. m. 聲 *chāng,* 暗 *ȳm.*
Tonneau. 桶 *t'oùng.*
Tonnerre. 雷公 *louî koūng.*
Torche. 火 ... *fò tsīn,* 火把 *fò pà.*
Tordre. 扭 *nioù.*
Tort. *Voir* faute, dommage, se tromper.
Torturer. 拷 *k'aó.*
Tôt. 早 *tsaò.*
Total. *Voir* somme.
Toucher. 動 *t'oūng,* 摩 *mō.* ‖ *Voir* attenant, émouvoir, regarder, aborder.

Toujours, 常 *chông,* 長久 *tch'ông kioù.*
Tour, subst. f. 樓 *leoû,* 塔 *t'âp.*
Tour, subst. m. mouvement circulaire. Un —, 一轉 *ȳt tchòn.* ‖ Promenade, 行一下 *hâng ȳt há,* 走一轉 *tseoù ȳt tchòn.* ‖ Circonférence, 週圍 *tchoū vî.* ‖ — à —, 輪去輪轉 *lîn hí lîn tchòn.* ‖ — de tourneur, 車子 *tch'ā tsè.* ‖ — d'adresse 把戲 *pà hí.* ‖ — de force, 武戲 *voū hí.*
Tourbillon. 波羅綹 *pō lô tsioú.*
Tourmenter. 難委人 *nân vī gnîn,* 賴人 *laí gnîn.* ‖ *Voir* torturer, affliger.
Tournant. 彎 *vân,* 角 *kôc.*
Tourner. — la meule, 礱 *loûng;* — la roue, 扭車 *nioù tch'ā.* ‖ — la tête, 轉面 *tchòn mién.*
Tourterelle. 璞鳩 *p'oŭc keoū.*
Tousser. 咳 *k'ĕt,* 嗽 *tch'oŭc.*
Tout, tous. 咸巴冷 *hâm pā lāng,* 一巴連 *ȳt pā liên,* 攏總 *loūng tsoùng,* 渾個 *vouôn ké·,* 一齊 *ȳt ts'ê·,* 盡兜 *ts'în teoū.*
Tout-puissant. 全能 *ts'iên nên.*
Trace. — de pas, 脚蹟 *kiŏc tsiâc.*
Tradition. 傳下個 *tch'ôn hā ké·.*
Traduire. — en chinois, 轉唐話 *tchòn t'ông fá.*
Traîner. 拖 *t'ō.* ‖ *Voir* tirer, différer.
Traire. 捋乳 *lôt nén.*
Traité. — de paix. 和約 *fô yôc.*
Traitement. — d'un dignitaire, 俸祿 *foúng loŭc.* ‖ — d'un employé, 工錢 *koūng ts'iĕn.* ‖ *Voir* honoraires.
Traiter. — des hôtes, 待客 *t'aí hâc.* ‖ — durement les gens, 刻薄人 *h'ĕt p'ŏc gnîn.* ‖ — une affaire, 辦事 *p'án sé.* ‖ *Voir* soigner, délibérer.

Tranchant, adj. 鋒利 *foūng lí.*
Tranchant, subst. m. — d'un couteau, 刀嘴 *taō tchoí.*
Tranche. 片 *p'ièn,* 塊 *k'ouaí.*
Tranquille. 平安 *p'în ōn,* 靜 *ts'ín.*
Transcrire. *Voir* copier.
Transparent, adj. 透得光 *t'eoú tĕt kouōng.*
Transplanter. 種過另事去 *tchoúng kouó láng sé hí.*
Transporter. 搬 *pān,* 徙 *saì.* || *Voir* porter.
Transversal. 橫個 *vâng ké·.*
Travail. 工 *koūng,* 工夫 *koūng foū,* 人工 *gnîn koūng.*
Travailler. 做事 *tsó ché·,* 做工 *tsó koūng.*
Travers (en) 橫個 *vâng ké·,* 斜個 *siâ ké·.* || A tort et à —; 亂 *lón.*
Traverser. 過 *kouó,* 透 *t'eoú,* 穿 *tch'ōn.*
Traversin. 枕頭 *tchìm t'eoû.*
Treillis. 竹簾 *tchoŭc liâm.*
Trembler. 震 *tchoūn.* || *Voir* branler.
Tremper. 浸 *tsím,* 蘸 *tsiàm.*
Trente. 三十 *sām chĭp.*
Très. 十分 *chĭp foūn,* 極 *k'ĭt,* 至 *tjé.*
Tresser. 編 *p'īn.*
Tribunal, résidence d'un mandarin. 衙門 *ngâ moûn.* || Salle de justice, 堂 *t'ông,* 六部 *lioŭc p'oú.*
Trident. 鈀頭 *p'â t'eoû.*
Trier. 托 *t'ŏc,* 挑 *t'iaō.*
Trinité. 聖三 *chín sām.*
Triste. *Voir* inquiet, affliger.
Tromper. 謊 *fòng,* 𧩰 *t'ăt,* 戀 *lién,* 騙 *p'ién.* || Se —, 做差 *tsó ts'ā,* 錯 *ts'ŏc.*
Tronc. — d'arbre, 樹墩 *choú toùn,* 樹頭 *choú t'eoû.*
Trop. 忒多 *t'ĭĕt tō.*
Trou. 窟 *foŭt,* 湖 *foû,* 孔 *k'oùng,* 睞 *loí,* 眼 *niàn.*
Trouble, adj. pas limpide. 汶 *voûn.*
Trouble, subst. m. 亂 *lón,* 鬧事 *naó sé.*
Troupe, une. — 一陣 *ŷt tch'ín,* 一班 *ŷt pān,* 一羣 *ŷt k'ioûn.*
Trouver. 尋倒 *ts'îm taò.* || *Voir* ramasser, rencontrer, imaginer, estimer.
Truie. 猪媽 *tchoū mâ.*
Tube. 筒 *t'oûng.*
Tuer. 打死 *tà sì,* 殺 *săt,* 洗 *sè·.*
Tuile. 瓦 *ngà.*
Tumeur. 肘 *tch'oî.*
Turban. 布帶 *poú taí.*
Turbulent. 多事個 *tō sé ké·.*

U

Ulcère. 爛疤 *lán pā,* 肘 *tch'oî.*
Ultérieur, qui est au delà, 個邊個 *ké· piēn ké·.* || Qui vient après, 後來個 *heoú loî ké·.*
Un, qui est seul. 一個 *ŷt ké·.* || —, article indéfini, s'exprime de beaucoup de manières par les particules numérales; et souvent ne s'exprime pas.
Unanime. 齊心 *ts'ê· sīm,* 同心合意 *t'oûng sīm hăp ý.*
Uni, sans aspérités, 坪 *p'iâng.* || Egal, 勻 *yoûn.* || D'accord, 和睦 *fô moŭc.*
Union, unir. *Voir* accord, réunir, uni.
Uniquement, exclusivement. 專 *tchōn,* 單 *tān.*
Urine. 尿 *niaó.*
Uriner. 屙尿 *ō niaó,* 行小便 *hâng siaò p'ién.*

Usage, emploi, utilité. 用 *yoúng*, 使 *sè*. || Etre d'un— universel, 通行 *t'oūng hâng*. || *Voir* coutume.

User, diminuer par le frottement. 使過 *sè kouō*. || *Voir* employer, dépenser, gâter.

Ustensile. 傢伙 *kā fò*.

Usurper. 霸佔 *pá tchám*.

Utérin. 親兄弟 ou 胞兄弟 *ts'īn hioūng t'í* ou *paō hioūng t'í*.

Utile. 有用 *yoū yoúng*, 有益處 *yoū ŷt tch'oú*.

V

Vacances. — des écoliers. 放學 *fóng hŏc*. || — des tribunaux, 封印 *foūng ýn*.

Vacant. 閒 *hân*, 空 *k'oúng*, 麼事 *mô sé*.

Vaccin. 痘種 *t'eoú tchoùng*.

Vache. 牛嫲 *nioû mâ*, 牛牸 *nioû tsé*.

Vagabond. 江湖 *kōng foû*, 流 *lioû*.

Vague, adj. 唔明白 *mĝ mîn p'âc*, 唔淸楚 *mĝ ts'īn tsè*.

Vague, subst. f. 水浪 *chouì lóng*.

Vain. 虛 *hī*. || *Voir* inutile.

Vaincre. 勝 *chín*, 贏 *yâng*. || *Voir* surpasser.

Vaincu. 輸 *choū*.

Vaisseau. *Voir* barque, vase.

Valeur. 價錢 *ká ts'iên*. || Avoir de la —, 值錢 *tch'ĭt ts'iên*, 抵錢 *tì ts'iên*. || *Voir* courage.

Vallée. 坑 *hāng*, 山窩 *sān vō*.

Valoir. *Voir* valeur, égaler.

Vanner. 簸 *paí*.

Vanter. 稱說人 *tch'īn chôt gnîn*, 獎賞人 *tsiòng chòng gnîn*.

Vapeur. — d'eau. 水氣 *chouì hí*.

Varier. *Voir* différer, changer.

Variole. 痘子 *t'eoú tzè*.

Vase, subst. f. 埲泥 *p'áng naî*.

Vase, subst. m. 缽 *pât*, 瓶 *p'în*, 罌 *āng*. || — de porcelaine, 磁器 *tsê hí*. || — de nuit, 夜壺 *yá foû*.

Vaste. 寬 *k'ōn*, 闊 *fât*, 大 *t'aí*.

Vaurien. 麼用個人 *mô yoúng ké gnîn*, 壞人 *faí gnîn*.

Vautrer (se). 汶泥 *voún naî*.

Veille. — de nuit. 更 *kāng*. || Le jour précédent, 頭一日 *t'eoû ŷt gnĭt*.

Veiller, se privor de sommeil. 瞭夜 *liaó yá*, 守夜 *choù yá*. || *Voir* soigner, garder.

Veine. 血筋 *hiĕt kīn*.

Velours. 絨 *yoûng*.

Vendre. 賣 *maí*.

Vénéneux. 有毒 *yoū t'oŭc*.

Venger, v. a. et v. pronom. 報仇 *paó choû*.

Véniel (péché). 小罪 *siaò ts'ouí*.

Venir. 來 *loî*, 到 *taó*.

Vent. 風 *foūng*.

Ventre. 肚 *toù*.

Ver. 虫 *tch'oûng*. || — de terre, 蛇公 *hièn koūng*; — à soie, 蠶子 *ts'âm tzè*.

Verge. *Voir* baguette.

Verger. 菓木園 *kouò moŭc yân*.

Vérifier. *Voir* examiner.

Vermicelle. 粉 *foùn*.

Vermifuge. 畴虫藥 *t'eoú tch'oûng yŏc*, 猱虫藥 *naó tch'oûng yŏc*.

Vermillon. 銀硃 *nioûn tchoū*.

Vermoulu. 蛀了 *tchoú liaò*, 爛 *lán*.

Vernis, laque. 漆 *ts'ĭt*.

Verre 玻璃 *pō lî*. ‖ — de vin, 酒盃 *tsioù pī*.

Vers, uue pièce de —, 一首詩 *ŷt choù chē*.

Vers, prép. 向 *hióng*, 對 *touí*, 近 *k'ioún*, 到 *taó*, 邊 *piēn* (après le mot).

Verser. 倒 *taò*, 轉 *tchón*. ‖ — à boire, 斟 *tchīm*, 充 *tch'oūng*.

Vert. 綠 *lioŭc*, 青 *ts'iāng*.

Vert-de-gris. 銅青 *t'oûng ts'iāng*.

Vertical 直 *tch'ĭt*.

Vertige (avoir le). 眼黃 *niàn vông*.

Vertu 德 *t'ĕt*. ‖ *Voir* nature, effet.

Vessie. 尿袋 *niaó t'oí*.

Vêtement. *Voir* habit.

Veuve. 寡婦 *kouà foú*.

Viande. 肉 *nioŭc*.

Viatique. 盤錢 *p'ân ts'iên*.

Vice. 毛病 *maō p'iáng*. ‖ *Voir* défaut.

Vice-roi. 總督 *tsoùng toŭc*, 制臺 *tjé t'oî*.

Vider.—en versant, 倒 *taò*; — en puisant 舀出來 *yaò tch'oŭt loî*. ‖ — un poisson, 破魚 *p'ó ngˆ*.

Vie. 命 *miáng*. Toute la —, 一生人 *ŷt sēn gnîn*.

Vieillard. 老人家 *laò gnîn kā*.

Vieillir. 老 *laò*. ‖ En parlant des choses, 舊 *k'ioú*, 陳 *tch'în*.

Vierge, 貞女 *tchīn ngˋ*, 童貞 *t'oûng tchīn*. ‖ La Ste Vierge, 聖母 *chín moū*.

Vieux, ancien. 老 *laò*, 古 *koù*. ‖ Usé, 舊 *k'ioú*.

Vif. 生 *sāng*, 生活 *sāng făt*. ‖ Irascible, caractère —, 急性 *kĭp sín*. ‖ *Voir* actif, ardent.

Vigne. 葡萄 *p'oû t'aô*.

Vigueur. 精神 *tsīn chîn*. ‖ *Voir* force.

Vil, abject. 賤 *ts'ién*, 鄙 *pè˙*, 卑 *pī*, 敝 *pí*.

Vilain. 醜 *tch'où*, 唔好看 *mĝ haò k'ón*.

Village. 村 *ts'oūn*.

Ville. 城 *châng*.

Vin. 酒 *tsioù*.

Vinaigre. 酸醋 *sōn tsé*, 甜酒 *t'iâm tsioù*.

Vingt. 二十 *gní chĭp*.

Violence 强 *k'iông*, 蠻 *mân*, 力 *lĭt*.

Violent 狠 *hèn*, 兇 *hioūng*, 利害 *lí hoí*.

Violer, enfreindre. 犯 *fám*, 背 *p'oí*. ‖ — (une femme), 犯姦 *fám kiān*; *tiaò*. *Voir* profaner.

Violet, couleur violette. 灰色 *foē˙ sĕt*, 茄色 *k'iô sĕt*.

Violon. 絃 *hiên*.

Vis, subst. f. 螺螄釘 *lô sē tāng*.

Visage. 面 *mién*, 臉 *liēn*.

Vis-à-vis. 對面 *touí mién*.

Viser, mirer. 指 *tjè*, 向 *hióng*. ‖ — juste, 指對 *tjè touí*. ‖ Avoir en vue, 想 *siòng*, 貪 *t'ām*.

Visiter. 迓 *lá*, 看 *k'ón*, 會 *fí*. ‖ Aller saluer, 迓 *lá*. 拜候 *paí heoú*. ‖ *Voir* examiner.

Visiteur. 客 *hâc*.

Vite. 快 *k'ouaí*, 忙 *mâng*, 亟 *kiăc*.

Vitre. 玻璃片 *pō lî p'ièn*. ‖ Une —, 一塊玻璃 *ŷt k'ouaí pō lî*.

Vivier. 魚塘 *ngˆ t'ông*.

Vivant. 生 *sāng*, 活 *făt*.

Vivre. 生 *sāng*, 在 *ts'aí*.

Vœu. 愿 *nián*. ‖ *Voir* désir.

Voici, voilà. 就係 *tsioú hé˙*.

Voile, subst. m. — de tête, 遮面帕 v. 簾 *tchā mién p'á* v. *liâm*. ‖ — de calice, 盖聖爵布 *koí chín tsiôc poú*. ‖ *Voir* rideau.

Voiler. 遮 *tchā*, 抵 *taì*, 蒙 *moûng*. ‖ *Voir* cacher, couvrir.

Voir. 看 *k'ón*, 見 *kián*. ‖ *Voir* comprendre, estimer, examiner.

Voisin, limitrophe. 連 *liên*, 交界 *kaō kiaí*. ‖ Qui demeure auprès, 鄰舍 *lîn chá*, 隔壁 *kâc piâc*, 近 *k'ioún*.

Voiture. 車 *tch'a*.

Voix. 聲 *chāng*, 音 *ȳm*.

Voler, dérober. 偷 *t'eoū*. ‖ Prendre de vive force, 搶 *ts'iòng*. ‖ Commettre de petits vols, 撮 *ts'ôt*.

Voleur. 賊 *ts'ĕt*, 盜賊 *t'aó ts'ĕt*.

Volonté. 主意 *tchoù ý*, 心 *sīm*. ‖ *Voir* désir, intention.

Volontiers. 做得 *tsó têt*, 中意 *tchoúng ý*, 隨便 *souî p'ién*.

Volume, livre. Un —, 一本 *ŷt poùn*.

Vomir. 嘔 *eoù*, 翻 *p'ōn*, 吐 *t'oú*.

Vouloir, avoir l'intention de. 想 *siòng*. ‖ Demander, exiger, 愛 *oí*. ‖ Etre disposé à, 肯 *hèn*, 愛 *oí*.

Vous. 你等 *gnî tèn*.

Voyage. -- aller et retour. 來回 *loî fî*, 去轉 *hí tchòn*. ‖ Tout le temps du —, 一路 *ŷt loú*.

Voyager. 走路 *tseoù loú*, 出門 *tch'oût moûn*.

Vrai. 眞 *tchīn*, 實在 *chĭt ts'aí*.

Vrille. 鑽 *tsón*.

Vue. *Voir* œil, voir, considérer, site.

Vulgaire. *Voir* commun, vil.

Z

Zèle. 熱心 *gnĕt sim*.

GÉNÉALOGIE.

嫡脈 *tît mâc.* LIGNE DIRECTE.

Côté paternel.	**Côté maternel.**
Trisaïeul. 高祖 *kaō tzè*, vulg. 公白 *koūng p'ăc.*	Trisaïeule. 高祖母 *kaō tzè moū*, vulg 婆白 *p'ô p'ăc.*
Bisaïeul. 曾祖 *tsēn tzè*, vulg. 公大 *koūng t'aí.*	Bisaïeule. 曾祖母 *tsēn tzè moū*, vulg. 婆大 *p'ô t'aí.*
Aïeul ou grand-père. 祖 *tzè*, vulg. 阿公 *ā koūng.*	Aïeule ou grand'mère. 祖母 *tzè moū*, vulg. 阿婆 *ā p'ô.*
Père. 父親 *foú ts'īn*, vulg. 阿巴 *ā pā.*	Mère. 母親 *moū ts'īn*, vulg. 阿姆 *ā mē·.*
Fils. 子 *tzè*, vulg. 頼子 *laí tzè.*	Fille. 女 *ǹg*, vulg. 妹子 *moé· tzè.*
Petit-fils. 孫 *soūn.*	Petite-fille. 孫女 *soūn ǹg.*
Arrière-petit-fils. 曾孫 *tsēn soūn*, vulg. 虱子 *sêt tzè.*	Arrière-petite-fille. 曾孫女 *tsēn soūn ǹg*, vulg. 虱嫣女 *sêt mâ ǹg.*

LIGNE COLLATÉRALE.

旁支 *p'ông tjē.* **Côté paternel.**	外支 *ngoé· tjē.* **Côté maternel.**
Arrière-grand-oncle,	**arrière-grand'tante.**
Frère { aîné 伯公大 *pâc koūng t'aí.* / cadet 叔公大 *choûc koūng t'aí.* } du bisaïeul.	Frère aîné ou cadet de la bisaïeule. 舅公大 *k'ioū koūng t'aí.*
Sœur du bisaïeul. 姑婆大 *koū p'ô t'aí.*	Sœur de la bisaïeule. 姨婆大 *ŷ p'ô t'aí.*
Grand-oncle,	**grand'tante.**
Frère { aîné 伯公 *pâc koūng.* / cadet 叔公 *choûc koūng.* } du grand-père.	Frère de la grand'mère. 舅公 *k'ioū koūng.*
Sœur du grand-père. 姑婆 *koū p'ô.*	Sœur de la grand'mère. 姨婆 *ŷ p'ô.*

Oncle, tante.

Frère { aîné 阿伯 *ā pâc.*
{ cadet 阿叔 *ā choûc.*
du père.

Sœur du père. 阿姑 *ā koū* ou 姑姑 *koū koū.*

Frère de la mère. 阿舅 *ā k'ioū.*

Sœur de la mère. 阿姨 *ā ŷ,* ou 姨母 *ŷ moū.*

Cousin, cousine issus de germains.

Fils des cousins. 堂兄弟 *t'ông hioūng t'í.*

Fille des cousins. 堂姊妹 *t'ông tsì moé'.*

Cousin germain, cousine germaine.

Fils des frères du père. 嫡堂兄弟 *tīt t'ông hioūng t'í* ou 叔伯兄弟 *choûc pâc hioūng t'í.*

Fille des frères du père. 叔伯姊妹 *choûc pâc tsì moé'.*

Fils des sœurs du père. 姑表兄弟 *koū piaò hioūng t'í.*

Fille des sœurs du père. 姑表姊妹 *koū piaò tsì moé'.*

Fils des frères de la mère. 母表兄弟 *moū piaò hioūng t'í.*

Fille des frères de la mère. 母表姊妹 *moū piaò tsì moé'.*

Fils des sœurs de la mère. 姨表兄弟 *ŷ piaò hioūng t'í.*

Fille de sœurs de la mère. 姨表姊妹 *ŷ piaò tsì moé'.*

Frère, sœur.

Terme général: 親兄弟 *ts'īn hioūng t'í* ou 胞兄弟 *paō hioūng t'í.* 胞姊妹 *paō tsì moé'.*

Frère aîné. 阿哥 *ā kō.*
Frère cadet. 老弟 *laò t'aī.*

Sœur aînée. 大姊 *t'aí tsì.*
Sœur cadette. 老妹 *laò moé'.*

Neveu, nièce.

Fils des frères. 姪子 *tch'ĭt tzè.*
Fille „ 姪女 *tch'ĭt ǹg.*

Fils des sœurs. 外甥 *ngoé' sēn.*
Fille „ 外甥女 *ngoé' sēn ǹg.*

Petit neveu, petite nièce.

Fils des neveux. 姪孫 *tch'ĭt soūn.*
Fille „ 姪孫女 *tch'ĭt soūn ǹg.*

Fils des nièces. 外甥孫 *ngoé' sēn soūn*
Fille des nièces. 外甥孫女 *ngoé' sēn soūn ǹg.*

外親 *ngoé· ts'īn.* AFFINITÉS.

Grand-père mat. 外阿公 *ngoé· ā koūng.*	Grand'mère mat. 外阿婆 *ngoé· ā p'ô*
Oncle maternel. 阿舅 *ā k'ioū.*	Tante maternelle. 阿姨 *ā ŷ.*
Oncle mat. par alliance (mari de la tante m.). 姨丈 *ŷ tch'óng.*	Tante mat. par alliance (femme de l'oncle m.). 舅姆 *k'ioū mē·.*
Oncle paternel par alliance (mari de la tante paternelle). 姑丈 *koū tch'óng.*	Tante pater. par all. (femme de l'oncle paternel). aîné 伯姆 *pâc mē·*. cadet 叔姆 *choūc mē·.*
Mari. 丈夫 *tch'óng foū* ou 老公 *laò koūng.*	Femme. 妻子 *ts'ī tzè* ou 老婆 *laò p'ô.*
Beau-père du mari (frère de la femme). 岳父 *ngŏc foú* ou 丈人老 *tch'óng gnîn laò.*	Beau-père de la femme (père du mari). 家官 *kā kouōn* ou 阿巴 *ā pā.*
Belle-mère du mari (mère de la femme). 岳母 *ngŏc moū* ou 丈美婆 *tch'óng mī p'ô.*	Belle-mère de la femme (mère du mari). 家娘 *kā niông* ou 阿姆 *ā mē·* ou 姆姆 *mē· mē·.*
Beau-frère du mari (frère de la femme). 阿舅 *ā k'ioū.*	Beau-frère de la femme (frère du mari.) aîné 大郎 *t'aí lông.* cadet 小叔 *siaò choūc.*
Belle-sœur du mari (sœur de la femme). 阿姨 *ā ŷ.*	Belle-sœur de la femme (sœur du mari). 阿姊 *ā tsì.*
Bru. 新臼 *sīm k'ioū.*	Gendre. 婿郎 *sé· lông.*
Belle-sœur (femme du frère). 阿嫂 *ā saò.*	Beau-frère (mari de la sœur). ainée 姊丈 *tsì tch'óng.* cadette 老妹婿 *laò moé· sé·.*

EXAMENS LITTERAIRES.

Dans la hiérarchie littéraire il y a quatre degrés: le Baccalauréat, la Licence, le Doctorat et l'Académie.

L'examen pour le Baccalauréat est appelé 歲試 *souí ché*. Il a deux parties. L'admission à la première partie donne le titre de 秀才 *sioú ts'oï*, ou 生貢 *sēn koúng*, ou 附生 *foù sēn*. On dit: 入秀才 *gnĭp sioú ts'oï*, ou 入學 *gnĭp hŏc*, obtenir le premier degré.

L'admission à la seconde partie confère le titre de 廩生 *lîm sēn*. On dit: 補廩 *poù lîm*, subir avec succès la seconde partie du Baccalauréat.

L'examen à la Licence s'appelle 鄉試 *hiōng ché*. Celui qui est admis prend le nom de 舉人 *kì gnîn*, licencié. On dit: 中舉 *tchoúng kì*, obtenir ce grade.

L'examen au Doctorat est appelé 會試 *fí ché*. L'élu prend le nom de 進士 *tsín sé*. On dit: 中進士 *tchoúng tsín sé*, devenir docteur.

L'examen pour le titre d'académicien s'appelle 殿試 *t'ién ché*. Les lauréats sont appelés 翰林 *hón lîm*. On dit: 中翰林 *tchoúng hón lîm*, devenir académicien.

Reprenons chacun de ces points. — Tout aspirant aux grades littéraires doit, au préalable, subir, dans sa préfecture ou sa sous-préfecture, un examen présidé par le mandarin du lieu. S'il habite une sous-préfecture de second ordre, c.-à-d. un 縣 *yán*, il devra, après cet examen devant son mandarin, en passer un second devant le mandarin de la sous-préfecture de premier ordre, c.-à-d. du 州 *tchoū* dont il dépend, ou bien devant le préfet, s'il ne dépend que d'une préfecture, c.-à-d. d'un 府 *foù*. C'est ce qu'on appelle le 縣考 *yán k'aò*, 州考 *tchoū k'aò*, 府考 *foù k'aò*. Les candidats qui sont reçus ont leurs noms affichés (出榜 *tch'oût pòng*), et sont appelés 童生 *t'oūng sēn*. Ils ont par-là (et eux seuls) le droit de se présenter au concours pour le Baccalauréat. — Voilà pour les préliminaires.

I. — Le concours pour le Baccalauréat (1e partie) a lieu tous les trois ans, dans les préfectures et les sous-préfectures de premier ordre. Il est présidé par un envoyé de Pékin nommé 學臺 *hŏc t'oî*. Le nombre des candidats admis ou 秀才 *tsioú ts'oî*, est fixé pour chaque sous-préfecture et peut varier selon les différentes provinces. Les noms suivants sont inscrits sur une liste à part. Si, entre deux examens, un bachelier vient à mourir, le premier de la seconde liste est, *ipso facto*, promu bachelier en remplacement du défunt, et peut, en conséquence, se présenter à la seconde partie du Baccalauréat sans recommencer la première épreuve. Il prend le titre de 增生 *tsén sēn*.

Pour la seconde partie, le concours se passe à la préfecture entre tous les bacheliers 秀才 *sioú ts'oî*. Comme pour l'examen précédent, le nombre des admissions est fixé d'avance; et le premier de la seconde liste (comme ci-dessus) qui vient après, est admis, lorsque la mort d'un élu laisse une place vacante. On dit qu'il est 補增 *poù tsén*.

Tous les trois ans, il y a entre tous les bacheliers 秀才 *sioú ts'oî*, 增生 *tsén sēn*, 廩生 *lîm sēn* et 補增 *poù tsén*, un concours général obligatoire appelé 接歲 *tsiâp souí*. Les quatre premiers dans la composition reçoivent le titre de 優貢 *yoû koúng*. Tous doivent s'y présenter (sous peine d'être radiés), jusqu'à ce qu'ils aient obtenu le degré de 舉人 *kì gnîn* (licencié).

Tous les dix ans, dans chaque préfecture et sous-préfecture, nouveau concours général entre tous les bacheliers, sans excepter les 優貢 *yoû koúng*. Au premier dans la composition est conféré le titre de 拔貢 *p'ăt koúng*.

II. — Pour la Licence, les examens se tiennent tous les trois ans, au chef-lieu de la province. Ils sont présidés par deux examinateurs appelés 主考 *tchoù k'aò*. Le nombre des admissions varie selon les provinces. Il y en a environ quatre-vingt dans celle de Canton. Ces quatre-vingts noms sont affichés au tableau d'honneur; le premier de la liste a le titre de 解元 *kiaí niân*, et les autres reçoivent celui de 舉人 *kì gnîn*. Les noms de la seconde liste, comme pour le Baccalauréat, sont affichés sur un autre tableau; et les vingt premiers sont appelés 副貢 *foú koúng*.

III. — Le concours pour le Doctorat, n'a lieu, tous les trois ans, qu'à Pékin, entre tous les licenciés de l'Empire. Il y a environ, pour toute la Chine, trois cents admissions, parmi lesquelles dix-huit à peu près pour la province de Canton. Le jury se compose de quatre examinateurs appelés 總差 *tsoùng ts'aī*. Le premier admis (de tous) reçoit le titre de 會元 *fí niân*; les autres sont appelés 進士 *tsín sé*.

IV. — Le concours pour le titre d'académicien se tient tous les trois ans, à Pékin, entre tous les docteurs 進士 *tsín sé*; il est présidé par l'Empereur ou son délégué, et au sortir du concours, tous sont honorés d'un titre de plus:

Le premier de la liste est appelé 狀元 *ts'óng nián;* le deuxième, 榜眼 *pòng niàn;* le troisième, 探花 *t'àm fā;* le quatrième, 傳臚 *tch'ôn loú.* — Les cinquante suivants sont appelés 翰林庶吉士 *hón lîm choú kīt sé.* — Tous les autres sont répartis en trois classes: 1° les 部主事 *p'oú tchoù sé* (chefs des tribunaux ou ministres. Voir 部 *p'oú* dans le Dictionnaire); 2° les 知縣 *tjē yán* (sous-préfets; ils ont droit à un mandarinat dans une sous-préfecture de second ordre); et 3° les 中書 *tchoūng choū,* titre du dernier degré.

Il est clair que les 54 premiers académiciens ci-dessus (*ts'óng nián, pòng niàn,* etc.) peuvent recevoir les dignités et être admis aux emplois que le gouvernement confère aux *p'oú tchoù sé, etc.*

Dans les examens militaires, on a suivi, du moins jusqu'à présent, une marche parallèle, et les lauréats ont reçu les mêmes titres. La seule différence est que le candidat, au lieu de faire une dissertation littéraire, doit tirer cinq flèches à pied, et trois autres à cheval; il doit en outre manier un énorme coutelas et soulever un gros bloc de pierre. On examine aussi la force musculaire de chaque individu, en comparant la tension plus ou moins grande de son arc.

Le nombre des admissions est fixé d'avance, et si, parmi les concurrents, personne n'a atteint le but, on prend ceux qui en ont approché le plus près. Du reste, il est question sérieusement de réformer tout ce qui concerne cette théorie des exercices pour obtenir des grades militaires, et de dresser de nouveaux programmes plus modernes.

NOM DES CENT FAMILLES CHINOISES.

百家姓 *Pâc kā siáng.*

庫 *Chá.*
石 *Chăc.*
韶 *Chảo.*
邵 *Cháo.*
時 *Chê.*
沈 *Chìm.*
愼 *Chìm.*
申 *Chîn.*
成 *Chîn.*
盛 *Chín.*
商 *Chōng.*
常 *Chông.*
上 *Chóng.*
尙 *Chóng.*
舒 *Choū.*
仇 *Choû.*
壽 *Choú.*
水 *Choùi.*
歐 *Eoū.*
花 *Fa.*
華 *Fâ.*
懐 *Faī.*
范 *Fám.*
樊 *Fân.*
衡 *Fên.*
弘 *Fên.*
費 *Fí.*
惠 *Fí.*
和 *Fô.*
賀 *Fó.*
官 *Fón.*
方 *Fōng.*
房 *Fông.*
符 *Foû.*
胡 *Foû.*

扶 *Foû.*
富 *Foú.*
扈 *Foú.*
傅 *Foú.*
伏 *Foŭc.*
賁 *Foún.*
封 *Foūng.*
豐 *Foūng.*
酆 *Foūng.*
洪 *Foúng.*
紅 *Foúng.*
逢 *Foúng.*
鳳 *Foúng.*
倪 *Gnî.*
羿 *Gní.*
下 *Há.*
夏 *Há.*
咸 *Hâm.*
杭 *Hāng.*
幸 *Hén.*
侯 *Heôu.*
後 *Heóu.*
郝 *Hĕt.*
郗 *Hī.*
奚 *Hī.*
稽 *Hī.*
許 *Hì.*
祁 *Hí.*
邢 *Hîn.*
向 *Hióng.*
邱 *Hioū.*
何 *Hô.*
韓 *Hôn.*
項 *Hóng.*
家 *Kā.*

賈 *Ká.*
甘 *Kām.*
湛 *K'ām.*
闞 *Kàm.*
高 *Kaō.*
郜 *Kaó.*
郟 *Kâp.*
勾 *Keōu.*
苟 *Keóu.*
寇 *K'eóu.*
居 *Kī.*
姬 *Kī.*
紀 *Kì.*
璩 *Kì.*
懼 *K'ì.*
計 *Kí.*
季 *Kí.*
冀 *Kí.*
暨 *Kí.*
解 *Kiài.*
甄 *Kiān.*
權 *K'iân.*
簡 *Kiàn.*
喬 *K'iaô.*
闕 *K'iĕt.*
金 *Kīm.*
岑 *K'îm.*
經 *Kīn.*
荆 *Kīn.*
景 *Kìn.*
靳 *Kín.*
姜 *Kiōng.*
匡 *K'iōng.*
强 *K'iông.*
丘 *K'iōu.*

裘 *K'iôu.*
鞠 *K'ioûc.*
麴 *K'ioûc.*
弓 *Kioūng.*
龔 *Kioūng.*
汲 *Kĭp.*
吉 *Kĭt.*
戈 *K'ō.*
柯 *K'ō.*
郭 *Kôc.*
蓋 *Kói.*
干 *Kōn.*
江 *Kōng.*
康 *K'ōng.*
葛 *Kôt.*
古 *Koù.*
顧 *Koú.*
庫 *K'óu.*
關 *Kouān.*
谷 *Koŭc.*
國 *Kouĕt.*
桂 *Koúi.*
公 *Koūng.*
空 *K'oūng.*
孔 *K'oùng.*
貢 *Koúng.*
管 *Koùon.*
廣 *Koùong.*
賴 *Lái.*
藍 *Lâm.*
欒 *Lân.*
冷 *Lāng.*
勞 *Laô.*
梁 *Leông.*
婁 *Leôu.*

黎 *Lī.*
李 *Lì.*
呂 *Lì.*
利 *Lí.*
厲 *Lí.*
鬲 *Lí.*
酈 *Lí.*
虞 *Lí.*
廉 *Liâm.*
廖 *Liáo.*
連 *Liên.*
林 *Lîm.*
凌 *Lîn.*
劉 *Liôu.*
柳 *Lioù.*
陸 *Lioŭc.*
龍 *Lioûng.*
羅 *Lô.*
駱 *Lôc.*
郎 *Lông.*
魯 *Loū.*
盧 *Loû.*
路 *Loú.*
祿 *Loûc.*
逯 *Loûc.*
雷 *Loûi.*
龐 *Loūng.*
隆 *Loûng.*
馬 *Ma.*
麻 *Mâ.*
滿 *Mān.*
毛 *Māo.*
茅 *Mâo.*
孟 *Mén.*
糜 *Mī.*

米 *Mì.*
苗 *Miâo.*
繆 *Miáo.*
明 *Mîn.*
宓 *Mĕt.*
莫 *Mŏc.*
梅 *Moê·.*
毋 *Moū.*
慕 *Moú.*
牧 *Moŭc.*
穆 *Moŭc.*
閔 *Moūn.*
蒙 *Moûng.*
那 *Nà.*
能 *Nên.*
鈕 *Neòu.*
魚 *Nĝ.*
吳 *Nĝ.*
伍 *Ng̀.*
阮 *Ngán.*
敖 *Ngâo.*
岳 *Ngŏc.*
鄂 *Ngŏc.*
危 *Ngoûi.*
魏 *Ngoúi.*
冉 *Niām.*
嚴 *Niâm.*
元 *Niân.*
顏 *Niân.*
饒 *Niâo.*
聶 *Niăp.*
甯 *Nín.*
藺 *Nín.*
仰 *Niòng.*
牛 *Niôu.*
艾 *Nói.*
芮 *Noúi.*
農 *Noûng.*
安 *Ōn.*
晏 *Ón.*
巴 *Pā.*
白 *P'ăc.*
柏 *Pâc.*
班 *Pān.*
潘 *P'ān.*
卞 *P'àn.*
彭 *P'âng.*
包 *Paō.*
鮑 *Paō.*
暴 *P'áo.*
裴 *P'ī.*
皮 *P'î.*
貝 *Pí.*
邴 *Piàng.*
邊 *Piēn.*
別 *P'iĕt.*
平 *P'în.*
畢 *Pît.*
薄 *P'ŏc.*
簿 *P'oū.*
浦 *P'où.*
步 *P'oú.*
卜 *Poûc.*
僕 *P oûc.*
馮 *P'oûng.*
蓬 *P'oûng.*
沙 *Sā.*
山 *Sān.*
司 *Sē.*
師 *Sē.*
蘇 *Sē.*
施 *Sē.*
史 *Sè.*
須 *Sī.*
胥 *Sī.*
昝 *Siàm.*
蕭 *Siāo.*
宣 *Siēn.*
薛 *Siĕt.*
辛 *Sīn.*
莘 *Sīn.*
相 *Siōng.*
宿 *Sioûc.*
習 *Sĭp.*
席 *Sĭt.*
藉 *Sĭt.*
索 *Sôc.*
桑 *Sōng.*
孫 *Soūn.*
宋 *Soúng.*
戴 *Tái.*
談 *T'âm.*
譚 *T'âm.*
車 *Tch'ā.*
詹 *Tchām.*
晁 *Tch'aô.*
趙 *Tch'áo.*
鄭 *Tch'áng.*
池 *Tchê.*
陳 *Tch'în.*
程 *Tch'în.*
張 *Tchōng.*
章 *Tchōng.*
昌 *Tch'ōng.*
諸 *Tchoū.*
朱 *Tchoū.*
周 *Tchoū.*
儲 *Tchoū.*
褚 *Tchoū.*
屠 *Tch'oû.*
堵 *Tchoù.*
楚 *Tch'où.*
竺 *Tchoûc.*
祝 *Tchoûc.*
束 *Tch'oûc.*
終 *Tchoūng.*
鍾 *Tchoūng.*
充 *Tch'oūng.*
仲 *Tch'oúng.*
丁 *Tēn.*
鄧 *Tēn.*
滕 *T'ên.*
鈄 *T'eōu.*
竇 *T'eóu.*
刁 *Tiāo.*
田 *T'iên.*
狄 *T'ĭt.*
支 *Tjē.*
邰 *T'ōi.*
段 *Tón.*
湯 *T'ōng.*
唐 *T'ông.*
党 *Tòng.*
都 *Toū.*
涂 *T'oû.*
杜 *T'oú.*
東 *Toūng.*
通 *T'oūng.*
童 *T'oûng.*
董 *Toùng.*
查 *Ts'â.*
柴 *Ts'âi.*
宰 *Tsài.*
蔡 *Tsaí.*
曹 *Ts'âo.*
巢 *Ts'âo.*
曾 *Tsēn.*
鄒 *Tseōu.*
徐 *Ts'î.*
齊 *Ts'î.*
謝 *Ts'iá.*
焦 *Tsiāo.*
譙 *Tsiāo.*
井 *Tsiàng.*
全 *Ts'ién.*
錢 *Ts'iên.*
秦 *Ts'în.*
晉 *Tsín.*
蔣 *Tsiòng.*
秋 *Ts'iōu.*
松 *Ts'ioūng.*
從 *Ts'ioûng.*
戚 *Ts'ĭt.*
左 *Tsò.*
翟 *Ts'ŏc.*
卓 *Tsôc.*
莊 *Tsōng.*
蒼 *Ts'ōng.*
臧 *Ts'ông.*
崔 *Ts'oūi.*
祖 *Tzè.*
訾 *Tzè.*
萬 *Ván.*
滑 *Văt.*
蔚 *Vì.*
韋 *Ví.*
衛 *Ví.*
霍 *Vôc.*
汪 *Vōng.*
黃 *Vông.*
王 *Vông.*
武 *Voū.*
毋 *Voū.*
烏 *Voū.*
鄔 *Voû.*
溫 *Voūn.*
文 *Voûn.*
聞 *Voûn.*
翁 *Voūng.*
于 *Ȳ.*
伊 *Ȳ.*
於 *Ȳ.*
禹 *Ȳ.*
余 *Ý.*
茹 *Ý.*

俞 *Ý.*
庾 *Ý.*
喻 *Ý.*
也 *Yà.*
閻 *Yâm.*
燕 *Yán.*
沃 *Yāo.*
姚 *Yâo.*
陶 *Yâo.*
葉 *Yăp.*
越 *Yăt.*
陰 *Ȳm.*
任 *Ým.*
般 *Ȳn.*
印 *Ýn.*
應 *Ýn.*
樂 *Yŏc.*
養 *Yōng.*
羊 *Yông.*
楊 *Yông.*
尤 *Yoû.*
游 *Yoû.*
雲 *Yoûn.*
尹 *Yoún.*
雍 *Yoūng.*
容 *Yoûng.*
融 *Yoûng.*
勞 *Yoûng.*
戎 *Yoûng.*
熊 *Yoûng.*
郁 *Yoût.*
鬱 *Yoŭt.*

CORRESPONDANCE

DE L'ANNÉE DU CYCLE AVEC CELLE DE L'ÈRE CHRÉTIENNE.

		甲 乙 *kâp* 4 *yât* 5	丙 丁 *piàng* 6 *tēn* 7	戊 己 *vóu* 8 *kì* 9	庚 辛 *kāng* 0 *sīn* 1	壬 癸 *gnîm* 2 *koúi* 3
子 丑	*tzè tch'où*	0. 6	1. 7	2. 8	4.	5.
寅 卯	*ŷn māo*	5.	0. 6	1. 7	3. 9	4.
辰 巳	*chîn sé*	4.	5.	0. 6	2. 8	3. 9
午 未	*ǹg vî*	3. 9	4.	5.	1. 7	2. 8
申 酉	*chīn yōu*	2. 8	3. 9	4.	0. 6	1. 7
戌 亥	*soût hói*	1. 7	2. 8	3. 9	5.	0. 6

Rien de plus facile que de trouver l'année de N. S. correspondant à une année quelconque du Cycle. Par exemple : il s'agit de trouver à quelle année de N. S. correspond l'année du cycle, *sīn hói*. Je cherche d'abord le mot *sīn* au haut d'une des cinq colonnes verticales. Je vois à côté le chiffre **1**, qui sera le dernier chiffre de l'année qu'il s'agit de trouver.

Je cherche ensuite, dans une des six colonnes horizontales, le mot *hói*. Je suis cette colonne jusqu'au petit carré qui forme la jonction avec la colonne verticale. J'y trouve le chiffre 5 qui est l'avant dernier chiffre de l'année en question. L'année chechée est donc 1851.

En suivant la méthode inverse, on trouverait aussi facilement le nom de l'année du cycle correspondant à l'année 1851.

Quant aux carrés contenant 2 chiffres, ils correspondent à deux années distantes de 60 ans. Par ex.: en cherchant l'année correspondant à *piàng chīn* on trouverait à la fois 1836 et 1896, le même nom du Cycle revenant tous les 60 ans.

Il faut remarquer en outre que le tableau ci-dessus ne donne directement que les années du 19eme siècle.

Il serait facile de faire un tableau semblable pour le 20eme siècle, en ajoutant 6 au chiffre de chaque carré (au chiffre le plus élevé, dans les casiers où il y en a deux). Si l'addition atteint ou dépasse 10, on néglige le premier chiffre, pour ne garder que le chiffre des unités. Ainsi pour les carrés de la 1ere colonne horizontale, on aurait, de gauche à droite, les chiffres 2 (de $6+6=12$), 3 (de $7+6=13$), et ainsi de suite 4, 0, 1.

PAYS ÉTRANGERS A LA CHINE

Europe.

羅瑪 *Lô mā,* Rome. Siège de la
— Chrétienté: 教宗國 *Káo tsoūng kouēt.*
法國 *Făp kouēt,* France.
— Cap. 巴理 *Pā lī,* Paris.
— 馬賽 *Mā sái,* Marseille.
英國 *Ȳn kouēt,* Angleterre.
— Cap. 倫敦 *Loûn toūn,* Londres.
德國 *Tēt kouēt,* Allemagne.
布國 *Poú kouēt,* Prusse.
奧國 *Áo kouēt,* Autriche.
俄國 *Ngô kouēt,* Russie. (俄羅斯 *Ngô lô sē*)
瑞國 *Choúi kouēt,* Suède. (瑞典 *Chouí tièn*)
那國 *Nà kouēt,* Norvège. (那威 *Nà vī*)
丹國 *Tān kouēt,* Danemark.
荷蘭國 *Hô lân kouēt,* Hollande.
比國 *Pì kouēt,* Belgique.
瑞士 *Choúi sé,* Suisse.
意國 *Ý kouēt,* Italie. (意大利亞 *Ý t'aí lí ā*)
葡國 *P'oû kouēt,* Portugal. (葡萄牙 *P'oû t'aô ngâ*)
日國 *Gnĭt kouēt,* Espagne. (西班亞 *Sī pān ā*)
— ou: 大呂宋 *T'á lì soúng.*

希國 *Hī kouēt,* Grèce. (希臘) *Hī lăp.*
土國 *T'oû kouēt,* Turquie. (土耳基 *T'oû gnì kî*)
— vel: 回子國 *Fî tsè kouēt.*
地中海 *Tí tchoūng hòi,* Mer Méditerranée.

—

Afrique.

挨及 *Āi kĭp,* Egypte. (阨日多國 *Āc gnĭt tō kouēt*)
穌彝 *Sē ŷ,* Canal de Suez.
紅海 *Foûng hòi,* Mer Rouge.
太浪山 *T'ái lóng sān,* Cap de Bonne Espérance.

—

Océanie.

呂宋 *Lì soúng,* Iles Philippines [(Luçon)]
加拉巴 *Kā lā pā,* Batavia.
波羅州 *Pō lô tchōu,* Bornéo.
蘇門答臘 *Sē moûn t'ăp lăp,* Sumatra.
萬丹 *Ván tān,* Java. (呀瓦 *Yà ngà.*)
摩鹿加 *Mō loŭc kā,* Les Moluques.
新金山 *Sīn kīm sān,* Australie.
新西蘭 *Sīn sī lân,* Nouvelle-Zélande.
檀香山 *T'ân hiōng sān,* Iles Sandwich.

—

Asie.

日本國 *Gnĭt poùn kouĕt*, Japon (東洋 *Toūng yông*)
— Capitale: Tokio. 東京 *Toūng kīn*.
— Port: Nagasaki: 長崎 *Tch'ông k'î*.
— id. Kobé: 神戶 *Chîn foú*.
— id. Yokohama: 橫濱 *Vâng pīn*.
— id. Hakodaté: 箱館 *Siōng kouòn*.
東京 *Toūng kīn*, Tonquin. (交阯 *Kāo tjè*).
— Capit.: Hanoi. 河內 *Hô noúi*.
— Port: Haiphong. 海防 *Hòi fông*.
安南 *Ōn nâm*, Annam. (越南 *Yăt nâm*).
西貢 *Sī koúng*, Saïgon, (Coch. Française).
眞臘 *Tchīn lăp*, Cambodge.
南掌 *Nâm tchòng*, Laos. (*Laò vā*)
木來由 *Moŭc lâi yôu*, Malaisie.
— Singapour (Angl.) 新嘉波 *Sīn kā pō*.
— Malaka. 瑪拉加 *Mā lā kā*.
— Klang: Kuala Lumpur 吉冷 *Kĭt lāng*.
Seramban 湖洋 *Foû yông*.
— Grd. Pérak: Ipoh 巴羅 *Pā lô*.
Batu Gajah 巴肚加也 *Pā toù kā yā*.
— Petit Pérak: Taiping 小北曆 *Siào pĕt lăc*.
— Pinang: (Angl.) 檳榔酥 *Pīn lông sē*.
Mattang Tinggi 山崽 *Sān tsài*.
Macham Buboo 打錫土 *Tà siăc t'où*.
Buket Mertajam 大山脚 *T'aí sān kiŏc*.
Balek Pulan 山背 *Sān poé*.
暹羅 *Siâm lô*, Siam.
緬甸 *Mièn tién*, Birmanie.
印度 *Ýn t'oú*, Inde. (小西洋 *Siaò sī yông*)
Les Indiens 吉伶人 *Kĭt lîn gnîn* (pop.)
不丹 *Poŭt tān*, Boutan.
尼波羅 *Nî pō lô*, Népaul. (*Pī p'ông tsè*)
西藏 *Sī ts'óng*, Thibet.
巴馬 *Pā mā*, Pamir.
阿富汗 *Ō foú hón*, Afghanistan.
俾路芝 *Pì loú tjē*, Bélouchistan.
波斯 *Pō sē*, Perse.
大秦 *T'ái ts'în*, Ancienne Syrie.
如達國 *Ý t'ăt kouĕt*, Judée. (如德亞 *Ý tĕt ā*)
— Cap. Jérusalem: 日路撒冷 *Gnĭt loú sàn līn*.
天方 *T'iēn fōng*, Arabie.
— 默伽 *Mĕt kā*, La Mécque.
— 阿丹 *Ā tān*, Aden (Angl.).

Amérique.

美國 *Mī kouĕt*, Etats-Unis. (花旗國 *Fā k'î kouĕt*)
— New York: 紐約 *Niòu yŏc*.
— Californie: 舊金山 *K'ióu kīm sān*.
墨西哥 *Mĕt sī kō*, Mexique.
巴拿馬 *Pā nā mā*, Panama.
祕魯 *P'ĭt loū*, Pérou.
智利 *Tjé lí*, Chili.
巴西 *Pā sī*, Brésil.

圖書在版編目（CIP）數據

海上絲綢之路文獻集成.科技與文化編.第十一輯/
王揚宗，葉農主編. -- 福州：福建人民出版社，
2024.7. -- ISBN 978-7-211-09491-2

Ⅰ. K203

中國國家版本館CIP數據核字第2024JA5506號

海上絲綢之路文獻集成·科技與文化編（第十一輯）

主　　　編　王揚宗　葉　農
文化卷主編　葉　農
責 任 編 輯　趙遠方
美 術 編 輯　白　玫
出 版 發 行　福建人民出版社
電　　　話　0591-87533169（發行部）
電 子 郵 箱　fjpph7221@126.com
地　　　址　福建省福州市東水路 76 號
經　　　銷　福建新華發行（集團）有限責任公司
印 刷 裝 訂　上海中華印刷有限公司
地　　　址　上海市青浦區匯金路 889 號
電　　　話　021-69213456
開　　　本　787 毫米 ×1092 毫米　1/16
印　　　張　266.5
版　　　次　2024 年 7 月第 1 版第 1 次印刷
書　　　號　ISBN 978-7-211-09491-2
定　　　價　3200.00 元（共 8 冊）

国家出版基金项目
NATIONAL PUBLICATION FOUNDATION

海上絲綢之路文獻集成

總主編　陳支平　陳春聲

科技與文化編 89

主編　王揚宗　葉農

海峽出版發行集團
THE STRAITS PUBLISHING & DISTRIBUTING GROUP
福建人民出版社

本册目次

厦荷大辭典［二］

（*Chineesch-Hollandsch woordenboek van het Emoi dialekt*）

〔荷〕佛蘭根（J. J. C. Francken） 赫萊斯（C. F. M. de Grijs）編

seh tsing (*soeh* ») | 情, toegevendheid, vergiffenis voor iemand vragen.
seh péh (*soeh péh*) | 白; sprekende (niet zingende) zeggen.
seh ts'iò, | 笑, aardigheden, uien vertellen.
pò seh, 報 |, kennis geven van, komen zeggen.

屑 Seh Sèh Kruimels, gruis; kruimelen, afkruimelen; kruimels.
hō á seh seh, 雨 | |, stofregen.
p'ah seh, 打 |, verkruimelen, vermorsen, (als graan.)
k'ioh seh, 拾 |, het gruis, de kruimels oprapen.
k'ioh hoan tsû seh, 拾番薯 |, een aardappelveld nalezen.

刷 Seh Soeh *ts'at seh*, 漆 |, verfkwast.

轉 Séh Séh Rondom, rondgaan.
seh siâ tíng, | 城頂, op een vesting, stadsmuur rondloopen.
i i séh, 圓 |, ronddraaien.
séh lin tíng (» *lièn tuì*) | 旋返, omdraaien.
séh tsit lin, | 一轔, éèns rondgaan, ronddraaien.
séh tsit lin pièn (*séh tsit pièn*) | 一轔遍, éèns rondgaan.
moâ koe séh (» *ke* ») 滿街 |, de geheele markt rondloopen.
séh lin long, | 轔琅, ronddraaien, rondgaan.
séh t'íng á, | 糖仔, naar suikerpopjes draaien.
t'íng á séh, 糖仔 |. draaibord.

p'ièn i i i séh, 諞至圓匕 |, iemand om den tuin leiden, bedriegen.
hō lâng íng teh séh, 被人諞的 |, door iemand misleid worden.

Seng

酸 Seng Sni Zuur, wrang, scherp; stijf in de lenden, rhumatisch; talmend, langzaam; inwendig aangedaan, weedoen.
eh seng, | 呃, het zuur hebben.
seng bī, | 味, zuur van smaak.
seng noā, | 沫, zuur speeksel.
ts'iah seng, *p'ah tsaò seng eh*, 赤 |, 打臭 |, zuur oprispen.
kiêm seng k'ó tsiá, 鹽 | 苦淡, wederwaardigheden, het bittere des levens.
kiêm sí seng è lâng, 鹽死 | 的人, een gierig mensch.
seng seng siep siep, | | 澁匕, schraal in de keel, wrang.
ám seng, 涪 |, verzuurd rijstwater,
seng sa, | 衫, kleeren stijven.
seng ts'aì, *ts'aì seng*, | 菜 菜 |, salade.
seng ts'ò kè, | 醋架, olie en azijnstel.
seng níng t'iâ, *níng seng t'iâ*, | 軟痛, 軟痛, stijf in de leden.
níng seng kiâ, 軟 | 行, langzaam loopen.
níng seng k'ok, 軟 | 說, langzaam praten.
seng soé, | 洗, stijf, rhumatisch.
íng seng hàm, *íng seng tsíng*, 黄 | 烘, 黄 | 腫, geelzucht, waterzucht.

hō̤ (en *tsoū*) *lâng sim-seng*, 與人心 |, iemand inwendig wee doen.

霜 Seng — IJzel, rijp; ook van dingen die door hunne kristallen naar ijzel gelijken.

ping seng, 冰 |, ijs en ijzel.

seng hong, | 風, ijzel en wind.

ts'in kaò ná seng nih, zeer koel, koud.

kien seng, 堅 |, tot ijzel stremmen.

seng kàng, | 降, tijd waarop de rijp neerkomt, 10de maand.

t'ing seng, 糖 |, kandijsuiker.

p'ī seng, 砒 |, rattekruid.

孀 Seng — Weduwe, alleenstaand.

ko̤ seng, 孤 |, eenzelvig, excentriek, niet met anderen omgaan.

攢 Seng — Steken, insteken.

t'ih seng, 鉄 |, els, (ijzeren pin.)

mîng seng, 門 |, pin op een deurbout.

īng oē seng lâng, 用話|人, iemand een steek onder water geven.

孫 Seng, Suị — Familienaam.

[illegible]

桑 Seng — *seng ts'iū*, | 樹, moerbeziënboom.

seng tsai (*ts'ing sui*) } | 材, do.

喪 Seng — Rouw, sterfgeval.

ting seng ê dzit, 重|之日, dag die een dubbel sterfgeval met zich sleept.

損 Séng, Suị — Bederven, schaden; verkwisten, verspillen, onnuttig gebruiken, verslonsen, verknoeien.

p'ah séng, 打 |, verkwisten; hoe jammer, het is zonde dat!

séng gō̤ kak, | 五谷, het graan bederven, schaden.

séng sin miā, | 身命, geen zorg voor zijn leven dragen.

séng tsi̤ gûn, | 錢銀, geld verkwisten.

séng k'uì tióh lát, | 氣着力, zijne krachten verspillen.

séng hoaī, | 壞, vervallen, (als een huis.)

séng sin, | 神, geestvermoeiend.

pah séng ts'uì, *séng ts'uì*, 打|嘴, | 嘴, vruchteloos spreken.

séng tīng, | 斷, verwaarloozen.

Séng — *séng k'ièn séng*, bijgeloof.

Séng — *k'ùn séng*, van iemands behoefte aan iets, misbruik maken.

爽 Séng — *níng séng*, 軟 |, fijn, subtiel, (van werk of beroep.)

筭 Séng, Suị — Rekenen, berekenen, tellen; denken, bedenken, het er voor houden.

séng siaò, | 賬, rekenen, berekenen.

kiōng séng, 共 |, berekenen.

séng poâ, | 盤, rekenbord, (Chin.)

tsiaò séng, 照 |, volgens berekening.

tiém séng, 點 |, natellen.

at séng, 按 |, op de vingers tellen.

ts'ui séng, 推 |, berekenen, uitrekenen.

gaò séng ê lâng, 善|人之, iemand die alles wil verantwoord hebben.

séng liâo lîng, juist een zeker uur berekenen om te komen.

séng si séng dzit, | 時 | 日, den tijd voor iets berekenen.

séng hîng, | 行, met berekening handelen.

séng sik, | 色, do.

sìng miā̤, 丨命, waarzeggen.

boē sìng tit sī lâng, 未丨做人, niet als een mensch beschouwd kunnen worden.

àm sìng, 暗丨, bij zich zelven berekenen.

p'ah sìng, 打丨, denken, bedenken.

sìng lai sìng k'ì, 丨來丨去, over en weer denken, beraadslagen.

sìng k'í lai, 丨起來, het er voor houden.

sìng ī̆m tiòh, 丨不着, verkeerd rekenen.

束 Sìng Trekken, aanhalen, stijfbinden.

sìng ân, 丨緊, vast aanhalen.

īng soà̤-sìng si, 用線丨死, met een draad doodbinden, afbinden, (als wratten.)

sìng io, 丨腰, het middel stijf aanrijgen.

siao sìng, 消丨, kramp in de buik.

床 Sìng *lâng sìng*, 籠 , kookkorf.

tsit sìng ké, 一丨粿, een koek uit een kookben.

Sìng *lâng sing bō*, 籠丨帽, ronde Mongoolsche muts.

Sìngh *sìngh p'ī̤*, de neus ophalen, (niet snuiten.)

sìngh p'ī̤, hun. Snuiven.

Si

詩 Si Vers, gedicht.

si king, 丨經, de si king, van Confucius.

si ong, 丨翁, dichter.

si hù-bûn tsiṳ̄, 丨賦文章, verzen en litterarische opstellen.

絲 Si Zijde, zijden draad, dunne draad, een draadje, haartje, weinig, een weinigje.

si soà̤, 丨線, zijden draad.

si soà̤ tiàm, 丨線店, garen- en bandwinkel.

niṳ̂ á si (*ts'âng si*) 蠶仔丨, zijde van de zijdewormen.

t'âng si, 蟲丨, rupsenzijde, (voor vischlijnen gebruikt.)

hô̤ si, 湖丨, ruwe zijde, *hô̤ si k'eh*, 湖丨客, koopman, reiziger in ruwe zijde.

si mî̤, 丨綿, zijden watten.

p'áng si, 紡丨, zijde spinnen.

kī̤ si, 經丨, zijde, een web spinnen; eene zaak ingewikkeld maken.

lièm si, 繹丨, zijde van de cocon afwinden; aan draden afhalen.

si pò̤, 丨布, half zijde. half katoenen stof.

t'iu si, 抽丨, zijde uitspinnen, opschieten, (van kinderen.)

ti tu si, 蜘蛛丨, spinneweb.

pe si, 飛丨, vliegende herfstdraden.

tâng si, 銅丨, zeer fijn koperdraad.

t'ao meng si, 頭毛丨, een hoofdhaar.

bé bé si, 馬尾丨, haar van een paardenstaart.

luô bé si hē teh, 留尾丨在耳, een eind draad overlaten, onafgedaan laten.

tīng si, 斷丨, zelfs geen haartje.

si hô, *li si*, 丨毫, 厘丨 een weinigje.

tsit si si á, 一丨丨也, een beetje.

si si á, | | 仔, klein.

tsit si á k'ùi teh t'èh, 一 | 氣的出, op zijn uiterste liggen.

sīn tsit tiaô k'ùi si, 剩一條氣 |, er blijft hem nog slechts een weinig levenskracht over.

西 Si *si koe* (» *koa*) | 瓜, watermeloen.

si koe oá toā pîng, | 瓜倚大平, zich scharen bij de machtigsten.

鷥 Si *péh līng si* (*pèh* » ») 白鷺 |, kraanvogel.

lō si, 鷺 |, ijsvogel.

屍 Si Lijk.

sin si, *sí si*, 身 |, 死 |, lijk.

lō pòng si, 路旁 |, lijk aan den kant van den weg.

si tiû, *si pī*, | 埸, | 棚, plaats voor lijkschouwing.

giēm si, 驗 |, een lijk schouwen.

t'iah si, 折 |, men zal mijn lijk uit elkander trekken (voor eigen schulden.)

sin si, 埋 |, een lijk begraven.

biét si, 滅 |, een lijk vernietigen.

i si, 移 |, een lijk naar eene andere plaats brengen.

si ts'in, | 親, de betrekkingen van een lijk.

tsoân si, 全 |, het lichaam in zijn geheel laten, niet onthoofden.

施 Si Verspreiden, geven, bedeelen. Familienaam.

si siá, | 捨, beschenken, geven ronddeelen.

si un, | 恩, weldaden bewijzen.

si dzio, | 尿, een klein kind laten wateren.

Si *si si siák siák*, haastig, gaauw.

si sí sút sút, elkander geheime teekens geven.

死 Sí Dood, de dood, dood zijn ook in het spel, sterven, door den dood verliezen. vóór z. n. duidt het in eenige gevallen eene verachting aan evenals ons gemeenzaam »verduiveld"; doodelijk. den dood ten gevolge hebben, crimineel, ter dood veroordeeld; doodloopend als een haven, stilstaand als water; vastaangehaald als een knoop in tegenoverstelling van een strik. onveranderlijk, voor geene verandering of wijziging vatbaar, vast; door geene bijkomende omstandigheden te influenceren, vasthoudend, onpraktisch, stil, suf; achter werkwoorden geplaatst om den dood als gevolg van de handeling aan te duiden verliest het doorgaans zijn toon als *táh sih* doodtrappen.

īm kiū si, 不驚 |, den dood niet vreezen, onverschrokken.

kiū si lâng, vuil, smerig.

īm tsai si oáh, 不知 | 活, niet weten of iemand dood of levend is.

p'e si 配 |, den dood niet ontzien.

si k'iaò k'iaò, | 蹺 ; *si tít tít*, | 直 ; *si nī nī*, | 㔹 — dood vulgo: hardstikke dood.

sí lâng koan kaò oáh, *oáh lâng koan kaò si*, | 人拐至活, 活人拐至 |, Talent om iemand te overreden die bepaald van plan was iets niet te doen.

ka kī sàng si, *tó si*, 自己送 | 討 |, zich ten dood wijden, den dood berokkenen.

poàⁿ sio si, 小半｜, halfdood.

goāⁿ si, 愿｜, gewillig sterven, nu toch eindelijk tevreden zijn, (spijtig gezegd.)

k'èh si } 揢｜, doodsmoren.
ké »)

ké si, 哽｜, do.

táh si, 踏｜, doodtrappen.

tsūn si, 撰｜, den nek omdraaien, (als van een kip.)

si kat, ｜結, een dubbelde knoop.

sàng si, *kakī sàng si*, } 送｜自
t'ó si. *kakī t'ó si*.
已送｜, zich zelven den dood berokkenen.

sí sim noā sìng, 心爛性, bedaard doen, niet driftig te werk gaan (hoe driftiger gij wordt des te minder gaat het.)

si mêng } ｜門, doode deur *d. i.* vaste
(» *mui̤*)
winst, loon waar buiten men niets meer kan verdienen.

si sim, ｜心, niets meer aan iets denken.

si bai, stil, niet levendig, (van personen.)

tàng si̤ tàng sí } 仝生仝｜,
(» *se* » »)
gelijkelijk leven en sterven, (man en vrouw.)

si īm goāⁿ, ｜不愿, zelfs na zijn dood zal hij niet toestemmen.

si bô kiù, ｜無救, er is niets meer aan te doen.

īm si īm oàh, 不｜不活, noch dood noch levend, ongeneeslijk gekwetst.

si bák īm k'oeh, ｜目不合, na zijn dood de oogen niet sluiten, ongewillig sterven.

tsiù si-tsèh tsoē, 詛｜這罪, zweren dat men sterven mag als het niet waar is.

si tit put bîng, ｜得不明, aan onbekende oorzaken gestorven.

hó si, 好｜, zijn natuurlijken dood sterven.

si tsèh bô lâng, ｜絶無人, mogen al uwe betrekkingen sterven, (scheldw. van vrouwen.)

si lóh, ｜落, even na iemands dood, zoodra iemand gestorven is.

ts'ám sí, 慘｜, een ellendigen dood sterven.

si soah si soah, ｜煞｜煞, met den dood is het afgedaan.

si koat, *tsip si koat*, ｜决, 執｜决, zich dom, onveranderlijk aan iets houden.

si bó̤ eh, ｜妻的, weduwenaar.

si sit, ｜失, door den dood verliezen, sterfgeval.

si gín á, *si kaó á*, ｜仔狗, ｜仔女, verduiveld kind, verduivelde hond, (scheldw.)

si tsa-bó̤ kui á, ｜女鬼仔, ondeugende duivel van een meid!

si tá̤, ｜胆, moed die den dood niet vreest.

si tsoē, ｜罪, doodmisdaad, doodstraf.

si àn, ｜案, criminele regtspraak.

si hoāⁿ, *si siû*, ｜犯, ｜囚, ter dood veroordeelde.

si bah, ｜肉, dood vleesch.

si káng, ｜港, doodloopende haven.

si huih, ｜血, stilstaand bloed.

si tsui, ｜水, do. water.

tsíng t'aò á si ngī̤ (en *ngī̤ si*), 手指死勁, de fijt in de vingers hebben.

p'ah ts'it kat sí, 打一結｜, een knoop leggen, eene zaak onveranderlijk vaststellen.

kat sí tiā, 結｜定, do.

sí ts'uì, ｜嘴. met zijn mond vol tanden.

tsip sí pán, 執｜板, zich dom aan iets houden, niet naar omstandigheden weten te veranderen.

sí lâng tit, ｜人直, lichtgeloovig, dom.

sí k'oà, ｜看, in den letterlijken zin des woords opnemen (als eene vergelijking.)

sí tsú, ｜主, iemand die zich alles laat welgevallen.

sí sng, ｜酸, eenzelvig, excentriek.

始 Sí Aanvang, begin.

sí tsiong, ｜終, begin en eind, van begin tot eind.

ki sí iā, 其｜也, in den beginne.

四 Sì Vier, *toē sì*, 第｜, de vierde, *sì tsáp ho*, ｜十號, *sì tsáp it* of *siáp it*, ｜十一, 41.

sì kak, ｜角, vierhoekig, vierkant; oprecht, rechtvaardig.

sì kuì, ｜季, de 4 jaargetijden.

sì soà, ｜散, verspreiden.

sì koè (» *kè*) ｜處, alom.

sì koè iû (» *kè* ») ｜處游, rondzwerven.

sì koè t'oân, ｜處傳, alom verkondigen.

sì koè ûn ûn, ｜處巡行, heen en weer drentelen.

sì bīn, ｜面, van alle kanten.

sì hng, ｜方, overal, alom.

sì ui, ｜圍, do.

sì pi, ｜邊, aan de vier kanten.

sì bīn soa, ｜面山, overal op de bergen.

sì mîng t'aô (» *muî* ») ｜門頭, (aan) de vier poorten.

sì siâ mîng (» » *muî*) ｜城門, de vier stadspoorten.

世 Sì *tsit sì lâng*, 一｜, zijn leven lang.

kè sì (*koè* ») 過｜, sterven.

sì tíng sì ê lâng tíng sì kú (*ē* » ») 上｜人, Noordelijke bewoners.

tsiū sì hong, 上｜風, de wind uit de bovenhand krijgen, do. het meest sympathie ondervinden.

ē sì hong, 下｜風, de wind uit de tweede hand krijgen, do. het minste sympathie ondervinden.

hong sì, 風｜, kant van den wind.

pak sì, 北｜, het Noorden.

Sì *hiēn sì*, 現｜, openlijk voor iets uitkomen, zijne familie onteeren, (als lichte kooien.)

施 Sì *sì tsú*, ｜主, onderhouders, donateurs van Buddh. priesters, (door hen zoo genoemd.)

siá sì, 捨｜, aalmoezen enz. geven.

pò sì, 布｜, aalmoezen geven, (aan Boeddh. priesters.)

試 Sì *k'ó sì*, 考｜, in een examen meedoen.

時 Tijd, tijdstip, door een aanw. voornaamw. of het partikel *ê* met het voorgaande verbonden, beteekent het »ten tijde van . . . , toen . . . "; een Chin. uur = 2 Europeesche; de gewoonten van den tijd, de smaak, mode.

ū si, somtijds, 有 丨, de eene of andere tijd.

tsit si, 此 丨, nu.

hiēn si, 現 丨, thans.

tsik si, 卽 丨, onmiddelijk.

aō sí, 後 丨, later, naderhand.

tī si, 何 丨, wanneer?

si tsūn, 丨 候, tijd.

si tsoeh, 丨 節, do., tijdstip.

sī si, *kip si*, *kaò si*, 是 丨, 及 丨, 至 丨, de tijd is daar, op zijn tijd

si tsing, 丨 鐘, klok, uurwerk.

si piò, 丨 鏢, horologie.

siông si, 常 丨, steeds; vroeger.

si siông, 丨 常, steeds.

si si k'ik k'ik, 丨 丨 刻 匕, steeds.

put si, 不 丨, steeds.

bô si, 無 丨, nimmer.

si ūn, 丨 運, lot, noodlot.

si àh ūn àh bīng àh, 丨 也 運 也 命 也, het hangt van den tijd en het noodlot af.

tong si, 當 丨, toen ter tijd.

tong si ê mịh, 當 丨 之 物, algemeen gevraagde goederen.

si kè, 丨 價, loopende prijs, marktprijs.

si kè ê dzī } 丨 價 字, prijs-courant.
(» *kẹ̀* » ») }

si kiû, *kiû si*, 丨 行, 行 丨, algemeen gezocht, gewild.

si k'ì tsing, 丨 氣 症, algemeen heerschende ziekte.

tsit tùi si, 一 對 丨, een wijzertje van 12 Chin. uren rond, juist na verloop van een dag.

t'è si, 退 丨, uit den tijd, smaak zijn.

si p'aì, 丨 沛, gewoonte, mode van

k'ong hi hit (of *ê*) *si*, 康 熙 那 丨, ten tijde van Kànghi.

baó si, 卯 丨, 5—7 uur 's morgens.

sin si, 辰 丨, 7—9 » »

tsī si, 巳 丨, 9—11 » »

gō si } 午 丨, 11—1 » s' middags.
(*ngō* ») }

bī si, 未 丨, 1—3 » »

sin si, 申 丨, 3—5 » »

iú si, 酉 丨, 5—7 » s' avonds.

sut si, 戌 丨, 7—9 » »

haī si, 亥 丨, 9—11 » »

tsú si, 子 丨, 11—1 » s' nachts.

t'iú si, 丑 丨, 1—3 » »

in si, 寅 丨, 3—5 » s' morgens.

匙 Lepel; sleutel.
Si
só si, 鎖 丨 sleutel.

tsōan si, 㩛 丨, do.

tê si, 茶 丨, theelepeltje.

tsien si, 煎 丨, braadlepel, spaan.

pēng si, 飯 丨, rijstlepel.

t'ng si, 湯 丨, soeplepel.

pīng si kut, 飯 丨 骨, schouderblad.

k'iao si, 蹻 丨, uitstekende vleugels aan een hoed uit de Ming dynastie.

辭 Sì — Weigeren, zich verontschuldigen, bedanken voor; niet te doen willen hebben met, afscheid nemen, verlaten.

t'e sì, 推 ｜, zich verontschuldigen, weigeren.

sì koa, ｜ 官, voor een ambt bedanken.

sa sì, 相 ｜, afscheid nemen van elkander.

sì si̱, ｜ 生, afscheid nemen van de levenden, gezegd van een lijk dat vóór de kisting op een stoel wordt geplaatst en aan wien ieder thee aanbiedt.

paì sì, 拜 ｜, groeten en weggaan, iets aan een ander overlaten, zich er niet mede inlaten.

是 Sī — *sī*, het is. *tsiṳ̀ sī*, 正 ｜, het is zoo.

sī īm sī, ｜ 不 ｜, is het zoo niet?

īm sī, 不 ｜, het is niet, neen.

kóng sī oē (» » *oā*) } 說 ｜ 話, redelijk spreken.

kóng īm sī oē (» » » *oā*) } 說 不 ｜ 話, onredelijk spreken.

bóng bī sī, 惘 未 ｜, het is niet zeker of het zoo is of niet.

sī k'a siaò, ｜ 脚 俏, een geloofwaardig persoon.

sī ē siaò (» *e* ») } ｜ 下 俏, geschikt, dat gaat goed.

bān bān á sī 緩 匕 也 ｜, langzamer-

tsō hoà sī 造 化 ｜, gelukkig.

tsō hoà īm sī 造 化 不 ｜, ongelukkig.

t'aò tióh bé sī (» » *boé*) } 頭 着 尾 ｜, van begin tot eind, geheel en al goed.

hièm sī tsiah sī, als ik roep kan er begonnen worden gezegd b. v. door koelies voor zij een last oplichten.

li sī, 屢 ｜, in alles toestemmen.

īm sī lâng, 不 ｜ 人, niet als mensch kunnen gerekend worden.

寺 Sī — *sī ī*, ｜ 院, Boeddhistischklooster.

li ko sī, 尼 姑 ｜, nonnenklooster.

侍 Sī — *sī nèng*, ｜ 郎, vice-president van een departement.

視 Sī — *kūn (kīn) sī*, 近 ｜, bijziende.

恃 Sī — *tsū sī*, 自 ｜, op zich zelven steunen, zich op zijne kennis enz. verlaten.

生 Si̱ — Voortbrengen, doen ontstaan, baren, scheppen, opmaken als leugens; geboren worden, ontstaan, geboorte; leven, levend; onbekend, vreemd.

si̱ kiá, ｜ 子, een kind baren.

si̱ nīng, ｜ 卵, eijeren leggen.

t'ao si̱, 偷 ｜, onecht kind.

si̱ ko, ｜ 菰, beschimmelen.

si̱ sien, ｜ 銑, roesten.

haō si̱, zoon.
haō si̱ ke, jongelingen.

t'aò si̱, 畜 ｜ } , huisdieren.
tsing si̱, 鍾 ｜ }

hoan si̱, 回 ｜, weder leven krijgen, d. i. werken, omzetten (als harde suiker die smelt.)

si̱ hī á lâng, ｜ 耳 濃, loopende ooren hebben.

bē tsù si̱ sing tsù sì, 未 註 ｜ 先 註 死, vóór iemands geboorte is zijn dood reeds bepaald.

ts'ut si̱ dzip sì, 出 ｜ 入 死, levensgevaar (voor iemand) loopen.

si̱ laī, ｜ 利, op interest zetten, interest geven.

ts'ut si̱, 出 ｜, spruiten, schieten (als zaad.)

si̱ dzit, ｜ 日, geboortedag.

si kun tìng tiaó, |根訂緊, vast-ingeworteld zijn.

si taī tsì, twist, moeielijkheden maken.

si tsiâ, |成, van nature.

si ts'òng. |創, opmaken, (een leugen.)

si k'a si ts'iú, |脚|手, er veel bijmaken.

ké si ké sí, 假|假死, zijne zaak vergrooten, erger voorstellen dan het is.

oē si oáh sit, 能|活的, uit elkander genomen kunnen worden. er kan naar verkiezing meé gehandeld worden,

si oē, *si gièn tsō gú*, |話, |言狀語, leugens opmaken.

ta pō si tiu, 男子形狀, manwijf.

boē tit t'ang si sí, *bōe tit t'ang si*, *boe tit tang sí*, 未得生|, 未得生未得死, te weinig om te leven en te veel om te sterven.

kià si, 寄|, parasiet, woekerplant.

ki si sí, 見|死, op leven of dood vechten.

hó si tsòe, 好|做, welgeschapen.

si bak bē bat k'oà ki, |目未曾見過, van zijn leven nog niet gezien hebben.

moà si lâng bàk, 瞞|人目, iemand voor zijne oogen bedriegen.

si hūn, |疎, onbekend met iets.

si hūn ê lâng, |面人, onbekeude, vreemdeling.

si lâng, |膿, etteren, zweren.

鍟 Si Gegoten ijzer, ruwijzer.

tiá si, ruw panijzer.

ing si tsui lâmtiâo, 用|水粘在, met gesmolten ijzer vast, dicht gieten.

böe ōe ing si tsuí lâm si tiâo, 不能用|水粘在, niet steeds iemand er bovenop kunnen houden.

肘 Si *ts'iú si*, 手|, elleboog.

si si soaih soaih, kraken als een draagstoel.

si, bekrompen. *ni si*, bekrompen in handelwijze.

扇 Sì Waaier, nummer voor deuren, vensters, scherven, enz.

si tē, |袋, waaierdoosje.

géh si / *goéh »* } 月|, ronde waaier.

tsoá si, 紙|, papieren do.

iét si, 搧|, met een waaier waaien.

tsiáo ming sì / (» *mô* ») } 鳥毛|, veéren waaier.

hong si, *ts'iu ts'ien si*, 鞦韆|, poenka.

si hióh, |葉, waaierblad.

tsit sì ming / (» » *mûi*) } 一|門, een deurvleugel.

si kut, |骨, stokjes van een waaier.

姓 Sì Sè Familienaam in 't algemeen.

peh si / *peh sè* } 百|, het volk.

dzī si, 字|, familienaam.

tsáp ke kaó dzī si / (» *ke* » » ») } 十家九字|, van de 10 huizen zijn er 9 verschillende families. *d. i.* niet eenparig handelen.

hok si. 覆|, dubbele familienaam, (uit twee karakters bestaande.)

Si *t'ô á si*, 桃仔|, gezouten perziken.

ka ná si, 橄欖|, gezouten olijven.

ts'ui̤ iém si̤, 起鹽｜, salpeter uitslag, (als op een muur.)

常 Si̤ — *i̤ i̤ si̤ si̤*, 圓｜｜, dralen, niet tot een besluit kunnen komen.

豉 Sī̤ — Inmaken, pekelen.

sī̤ kiém, ｜鹽, zouten, pekelen.

sī̤ iém, ｜鹹, zouten.

sī̤ tioh, ｜着, bijtende stof in iets krijgen.

taō sī̤, 豆｜, gepekelde boonen.

sī̤ he, ｜灰, in kalk leggen, (als eieren.)

sī̤ koé, ｜鮭, visch inzouten, pekelen.

sī̤ ts'aì, ｜菜, groenten inmaken.

Sia

賒 Sia — Op crediet geven.

t'am sia kuì boé (» » » *bé*) 貪｜貴買, wegens crediet duur moeten koopen.

sia siaò, ｜賬, op crediet gekocht.

sia k'iém, ｜欠, op crediet gekocht en nog schuldig blijven.

sia hè, ｜貨, goederen op crediet verkoopen.

些 Sia — *sia tam po*, een weinigje, een haartje.

寫 Siá — Schrijven.

siá dzī, ｜字, do.

siá dzī eh, ｜字的, klerk.

siá dzī toh, ｜字棹, lessenaar, schrijftafel.

ts'ao siá, 抄｜, kopieeren.

siá p'oe (» *p'e*) ｜批, een brief schrijven.

siá hō̤ làng, ｜與人, met schriftelijke bewijzen aan iemand geven.

ts'ó siá, 草｜, in cursiefschrift schrijven.

捨 Siá — *si siá*, 施｜, cadeau doen, weggeven aan.

t'ao koah tiu siá si bē, 偷割稠｜世粥, iets van iemand ontnemen om het aan een ander te geven.

siá sim, ｜心 niet meer aan iets denken.

boē oē pàng siá tit (*be* » » » ») 不能帮｜的, niet van zich af kunnen gooien.

siá sin, ｜身, zich niet ontzien.

siá ì siá ì, ｜意｜意, van niet veel belang achten.

koah siá, 割｜ } , afhakken en weggooien, do. niet meer met iemand omgaan.
koah liaó siá, 割了｜ }

hí siá, 喜｜, met vreugde afstaan, geven.

oē siá tit tsiáh, oē siá tit ts'ìng (*ē* » » » *ē* » » ») 能｜的食, 能｜的穿, veel geld voor eten en kleeding durven uitgeven.

赦 Sià — Vergeven, kwijtschelden, amnestie.

sià bién, ｜免, vergeven.

sià tsoē, ｜罪, een misdaad vergeven.

taī sià t'ien hā, 大｜天下, algemeene amnestie.

瀉 Sià — Water laten afvloeien; ontlasting hebben, purgeren, diarrhee.

laò sià, 泄｜, diarrhee.

sià ióh, ｜藥, purgeermiddel.

siel sià, 洞｜, een weinig diarrhee hebben.

t'ò sià, 吐 ｜, braken en diarrhee, cholera.
hoat sià, 發 ｜. ontlasting krijgen.
p'ah sià, 打｜, ontlasting veroorzaken, (door medicijnen.)
tsi sià, 止 ｜, diarrhee stoppen.
tsui sià, 水 ｜, waterachtige ontlasting.
sià tsui, ｜ 水, do. hebben.
sià pak, ｜ 腹, diarrhee hebben.

Van zich af, ter zijde leggen, van zich afschuiven, overgeven, opgeven; afnemen, aflichten, afdoen; overschuiven op, overdoen aan; hellend.
sià sū, ｜ 事, zijn ambt overgeven; eene zaak van zich afschuiven.
sià dzīm, ｜ 任, do.
sià kah, ｜ 甲, het harnas afgooien.
sià oa, ｜鞍, het zadel afdoen, afnemen.
sià hè, ｜ 貨, goederen van den rug van een mensch of beest afnemen.
sià king, ｜ 肩, op een anderen schouder overleggen, (als stoeldragers.)
sià tà, ｜ 擔, de last, schuld van iets van zich afschuiven.
sià ts'ing, ｜ 銃, een geweer schoonschieten, een oud schot er afschieten.
sià ts'ɛng, ｜ 瘡, venerische ziekte aan een ander overdoen.
soa sià sià, 山 ｜ ｜, sterk afhellend (van een berg.)

Verblijf, woning, huis; eeretitel gevoegd achter den naam van personen wier voorouders aanzienlijke ambten bekleed hebben; nederige term voor »mijn."
ts'ó sià, *pē sià*, *tsiān sià*, 草 ｜, 敝 ｜, 賤 ｜. nederige termen voor »mijn huis."
hân sià, 寒 ｜. do.
sià dzin, ｜ 人, iemand wiens voorouders hooge beambten waren.
t'iòng sià, 暢 ｜. een vrolijke, kwistige klant.
sià tē, *sià ts'in*, ｜弟, ｜親, nederige termen voor mijn jongere broeder, mijne betrekkingen.

辱 Sià
Schande berokkenen, oneer aandoen.
sa sià, 相 ｜, elkander schande aandoen.
sià sam tāi, ｜ 三 代, zijne 3 generatien schande berokkenen.
sià tsó dziòk tsong, ｜ 祖 ｜ 宗, zijne voorouders oneer aandoen.
sià tsiàh, ｜ 食, laaghartig iemand de keeren verwijten die hij bij u gegeten heeft.

邪 Sià
Kwaad, verkeerd.
sià kaò, ｜ 教, valsche leer.
sià im, ｜ 淫, ontuchtig.
sià sút, ｜ 術, valsche manieren.
sià sin, ｜ 神, valsche geesten.
sìn sià, 信 ｜, bijgeloovig, (aan spoken enz. gelooven.)
kai sià kui tsìng, 改 ｜ 歸 正, van slecht tot het goede veranderen.
p'ik sià, 辟 ｜, den boozen geest (besmetting enz.) van iets afweren.
li m t'ang hō i sià k'ì, 汝不可被伊｜去 laat u niet door hem verleiden.
sià koài, ｜ 怪, wonderlijk.
sià hoat, ｜ 法, wonderlijke, duivelsche manier.
iao sià, 妖 ｜, wonderlijk.
kiā sià lō, 行 ｜ 路, een verkeerden, slechten levenswandel hebben.

佘 Siâ　Familienaam.

賒 Siâ　*liâo siâ*, 遼 ｜, zeer overvragen.

put tsi siâ, *siâ siâ*, 不 止 ｜,｜｜, zeer overvragen.

siâ ê mih, ｜ 的 物, goed van onbepaalden prijs.

Siâ　*siâ ui*, de mast strijken.

siâ lòh lai, ｜ 落 來, laten neerkomen, naar beneden halen, (als een mast.

謝 Siā　Afzien van, opgeven, zich onttrekken aan, voorlichten, te kennen geven; bedanken, dankzeggen, dankbetuigen; verwelken.

siā sū, ｜ 事, van eene zaak afzien.

siā goān, ｜ 願, gelofte doen.

to siā, 多 ｜, bedanken, dank u.

kám siā, 感 ｜, bedanken.

siā lé, *siā gi*, ｜ 禮, ｜ 儀, geschenken als dankbetuiging.

seh siā, 說 ｜, dankzeggen, bedanken.

k'aò siā, 叩 ｜, knikkend dankzeggen.

kóng siā, 講 ｜, bedanken.

paì siā, 拜 ｜, buigende danken.

siā paì, ｜ 拜, bedanken voor de eer een overledenen aangedaan.

siā pō, ｜ 步, lett. (voor de voetstappen bedanken *d. i.* knielende bedanken aan de deur van hen die eene begrafenis hebben bijgewoond) door de hoofdrouwers gedaan.

siā sin, ｜ 神, de geesten bedanken (na eene genezing enz.)

siā kim, ｜ 金, bedanken door eene geldelijke belooning.

ts'iá sin siā, 請 伸 ｜, een dankmaal geven.

hoe-siā, 花 ｜, de bloem verwelkt.

社 Siā　De beschermgod eener plaats; een dorp, gehucht, vereeniging van personen, societeit.

hiu siā, *siā li*, 鄉 ｜, ｜ 里, dorp, gehucht.

siā laī, ｜ 內, in het dorp.

siā k'aó, ｜ 口, aan den ingang van het dorp.

siā tiú, ｜ 長, dorpshoofd.

siā tsìng sū, ｜ 衆 事, zaken die een geheel dorp aangaan, (als processiën.)

kiet siā, 結 ｜, eene vereeniging, clan vormen.

射 Siā　Met een pijl schieten, treffen, boogschieten.

siā tsì, ｜ 箭, een pijl afschieten, boogschieten.

tsoân siā, 全 ｜, bij elk pijlschot raken.

sin siā, 神 ｜, zuiver boogschieten.

麝 Siā　Muskusdier.

siā kaó, ｜ 狗, do.

siā hiu, ｜ 香, muskus.

石 Siā　*siā liû* (*sē* ») ｜ 榴, granaatappel.

卸 Siā　*kong siā*, 工 ｜; stoeldragers.

聲 Sia　Geluid, do. nummer, voor schoten, keeren roepens.

sa siá, 三 ｜, 3 schoten, 3 maal geroepen.

miá sia, 名 ｜, beroemdheid.

sia im, ｜ 音, geluid.

sia sia kù kù, ｜｜ 句 匕, elk oogenblik van hetzelfde oude spreken.

ts'ut sia, 出 ｜, kraken, geluid geven.

siạ seh (» *soeh*) ｜說, geluid van iemands spreken.

siạ saò, p'aị siạ saò, ｜嗽, 歹｜嗽, uitjouwen, wegjouwen.

hong siạ, 風｜, gerucht.

t'oân miạ seh siạ (» » *oeh* ») 傳名說｜, veel valsch laten spreken.

t'iạ siạ, 聽｜, naar het algemeen zeggen luisteren.

t'iạ siạ bāng iạ, 聽｜望影, van hooren zeggen hebben.

gûn siạ (*gîn* ») 銀｜, waarde, prijs van het zilvergeld, do. hoeveelheid geld die iemand bezit.

kè siạ (*kẹ̀* ») 價｜, prijs van de waar.

ū siạ bô iạ, 有｜無影, wel gezegd worden maar niet waar zijn.

k'ui siạ, 開｜, zijn stem verheffen.

何 Siâ

siâ sū (*sâ* ») ｜事, waarom!

siâ mịh, ｜物, wat!

siâ lâng, ｜人, wie!

nā ū siâ sū, 若有｜事, als er het een of ander is.

bô siâ t'ang kóng, 無｜所說, er is niets te zeggen, te vertellen.

siâ oē ah (» *oā* ») ｜話, wat voor taal!

聖 Siạ̀ Heilig, uitwerking hebbend, krachtdadig.

siạ̀ dziah, ｜蹟, waar voorteeken.

siạ̀ koah tiā, ｜幷定, stellig uitwerking hebben, uitkomen, (als waarzeggers enz.)

ū ling siạ̀, 有靈｜, bovennatuurlijke kracht bezitten, (van geesten gezegd.)

tsiù tsoā boē siạ̀, 呪罪未｜, vervloekingen komen niet uit.

tsit pai siạ̀ nīng pai tiā-sạ pai lóng bô iạ, 一次｜二次定三次無影, voor de eerste maal komt het uit, voor de tweede is het stellig zoo, maar voor de derde maal is er niets van waar, (tegen waarzeggers gezegd.)

koē siạ̀ koē t'è, 易｜易退, zoo in trek en zoo weer in verval raken, (als afgodsbeelden, kooplieden enz.)

k'ì kaò siạ̀, 去到｜, zeer lang voor iets uit, weggebleven zijn.

tạ̀ tsit ē iū siạ̀ siạ̀ siạ̀, 粧一樣｜｜｜, zich zeer oprecht, welmeenend voordoen.

城 Siâ Stad, fort, vesting.

siâ ts'ī, ｜市, stad.

siâ laô, ｜樓, toren.

kiạ siâ, 京｜, hoofdstad (des rijks.)

sing siâ, 省｜, hoofdstad eener provincie.

siâ k'ang, ｜孔, geschutspoorten (op eene vesting.)

siâ k'iah, ｜缺, geschutsgaten (op een vestingmuur.)

t'ô siâ, 土｜, loopgraaf.

siâ goā, ｜外, buitenstad.

siâ tî, 池｜, stads-, vestinggrachten.

siâ tó tsi, ｜斗址, burgmuren.

siâ meng laô (» *miâ* ») ｜門樓, wachthuis boven een poort.

siâ àng, ｜甕, zijdeurtje in een vestingdeur, do. vestinggeschutspoorten.

hām siâ, 陷｜, eene stad innemen.

kong siâ, 攻｜, eene vesting, stad bestormen.

ui siâ̤, 圍 ｜, eene stad belegeren, do. eene vesting, stad bouwen.

siâ̤ ts'iṳ̂ (» *ts'iô̤*) } ｜ 墻, stadswallen.

k'ùn siâ̤, 困 ｜, eene stad belegeren.

sûn siâ̤, 巡 ｜, de rondte door de stad doen.

soa̤ siâ̤, 山 ｜, binnenlandsche vesting.

bān li tîng siâ̤ (» » *tîng* ») } 萬 里 長 ｜, de groote Chineesche muur.

城 — *siâ̤ kao*, ｜ 郊, stadsgrachten.

Sià̤ — *kui siâ̤*, 幾 ｜, hoeveel deelen, graden zuiver.

tsiok siâ̤, 足 ｜, volkomen zuiver (van goud enz.)

su siâ̤, 輸 ｜, voor iets anders in degelijkheid onderdoen.

誘 Sià̤ — Lokken, aantrekken.

sa̤ siâ̤ (*sio* ») } 相 ｜, elkander lokken, uitlokken.

siâ̤ hia̤, ｜ 兄, gasten lokken, (als lichtekooien doen.)

siâ̤ lâng, ｜ 人, iemand verlokken, (als lekker eten.)

櫼 Siā̤ — *siā̤ koà*, ｜ 蓋, luik (van een schip.)

ts'ik siā̤, 粟 ｜, graankist.

siā̤ nâ̤, ｜ 籃, groote mand, ben.

houten bak met étages waarop offeranden en geschenken gedragen worden.

siā̤ tsàn, ｜ 層, de afdeelingen in een houten bak.

tsit kìng siā̤, 一 扛 ｜, een vracht in twee bakken.

Siah

削 Siah — Afsnoeien, afschrappen, afsnijden.

siah p'è (» *p'oè*) } ｜ 皮, schillen.

siah ts'â, ｜ 柴, houthakken.

siah ts'â á, ｜ 柴 仔, houtsnijden.

siah tsiem, ｜ 尖, een punt snijden aan.

k'oe siah (*k'e* ») } 刮 ｜, afschrappen, afsnijden.

siah hiáh, ｜ 額, een scheefloopend voorhoofd.

tsiem t'aô siah t'ih, 針 頭 ｜ 鉄, ijzer van de punt van een naald afschrappen, *d. i.* zeer weinig geld verdienen.

siah kut-loh bah, ｜ 骨 落 肉, afgevallen, (als waren de beenderen afgeschraapt en het vleesch afgevallen.)

k'ao siah, 敲 ｜, afschrapen, do. een weinig bedriegen.

錫 Siah — Tin, *siah soa̤*, ｜ 山, tinberg.

siah k'òng (en *k'ìng*), ｜ 礦, tinmijn.

siah póh, ｜ 薄, bladtin.

p'ai̤ tâng kū siah, 歹 銅 舊 ｜, oud koper en tin.

席 Siáh — Namen voor feesten, bijeenkomsten enz.

iên siáh, 筵 ｜, feestmaal.

tsit siáh tsiú, 一 棹 ｜, één gastmaal.

榭 Siáh — *pn̄g siáh*, 飯 ｜, maaltijd.

siáh tsióh (*siā̤* ») } ｜ 石, marmer, speksteen.

siáh hùn, ｜ 粉, schrapsel van speksteen.

siáh i, siáh toh, ｜ 椅, ｜ 棹, marmeren stoelen en tafels.

Siáh — *siáh á* (en *ts'iáh á*), lepel, schepper.

laō siáh, schuimspaan.

t'ih siáh, ijzeren schuimspaan.

Vijl, scherper van messen.

siáh á schaaf.

siáh á king (· o ·) ｜, schaafstaal, *d. i.* best staal.
siáh siáh siáh, gelijk en glad, helder (als van verw.)

Siak

倒 *siak tó*, ｜跌, omvallen.
Siak *siak loh bé*, ｜下馬, van het paard vallen.
siak lóh k'i, ｜下去, neêrwerpen.
p'ah siak, 打｜, rusteloos, niet kunnen slapen of liggen, van een zieke.
boē kam tit p'ah siak, 未堪打｜, niet veel verzeulen kunnen velen.
siak sin, ｜身, iemands lichaam folteren, te veel van iemands krachten vergen.
siak si, ｜死, doodgooien.
siak si pan, ｜死班, iemand laten buitelen, (in komedies).
Siak *siak p'ah*, vast uitmaken.
p'ah siak, do.
拂 *siak tiū*, ｜禾, rijst dorschen, neerslaan (zoodat de korrels er uitvallen.)
Siak *siak t'áng*, ｜桶, dorschkuip.
siak béh, 麥｜, tarwe dorschen.
擲 *siak saō*, ｜譟, brutaal spreken.
Siak *p'ah siak pō (en ē)* (» » » (» ē)) 打｜步, laatste hulpmiddel, beslissende stap.
tsoè sing li ká p'ah siak, 做生理較拋｜, in het groot, roijaal handel durven drijven.
siak t'aô, siak taō, ｜頭, slaan met met het hoofd van pijn.
piā ao siak tih, 拋碟｜砥, kopjes en schoteltjes op den grond gooien.
tsiong gûn tuì hing k'ám siak loh k'i 將銀胸坎｜落去, iemand geld tegen den borst gooien, *d. i.* door geld iemand doen zwijgen.
t'eh gûn teh sa siak (» gin » sio ») 取銀相｜｜, met geld voor elkander niet willen onderdoen.
sai kong siak ts'ióh, 司公｜席, de Taoist. priester slaat met de mat, *d. i.* de uiterste middelen' gebruiken.
siak k'i siak tó, ｜起｜倒, verwerpen en instellen, (van iemand die durft te handelen).
siak iêm bi, ｜鹽, met zout gemengde rijst achternagooijen, (als een onheilaanbrengend mensch.)
siak pò, ｜布, goed slaan, (op een steen.)
漱 *siak k'áo*, ｜口, den mond spoelen.
Siak
屑 *siák siák haó*, ｜｜吼, fluiten door
Siák snelheid, (als een pijl.)
si si siák siák, 絲匕｜｜, door de lucht gonzen, zeer gaauw, haastig.

Siang

雙 Nummer, voor dingen aan paren.
Siang *siang si* (» se) ｜生, tweelingen.
siong aó, ｜拗, dubbelgevouwen.
siang aó tsih, ｜拗, dito.
siang tsiū (» tsiō) ｜槳, boot voor één man met 2 riemen.
bô kui siang, 不全｜, niet tot een zelfde paar behoorend, ongelijkparig.
tsiā siang tsiā tuì, 成｜成對, een paar uitmaken (als man en vrouw.)
ká siang, 消｜, dubbel nemen, (als een touw, enz.)

p'ah siang, 甲 |, dubbel nemen, aan tweeën, dubbel.
tsit p'ah-siang tiòh, 一打兩着, twee vliegen in één klap.
siang t'aô t'út, | 頭禿, aan beide uiteinden afvallen.
siang koan è ì sù, | 關意思, eene dubbele beteekenis.
siang k'oân, | 環, dubbele hoepel enz.
siang k'a k'ui, | 脚開, met de beenen nog uit elkander staan, *d. i.* nog niet bepaald weten wat van beide te doen.
siang géh / (» *goéh*) | 月, even maand, als 2de, 4de, 12de.

卸 Laten neervallen.
Siàng *siàng lóh k'ì*, | 落去, dito.

上 *ìm tang siàng i è tàng*, 不 | 可伊
Siàng 凍, gooi zijne stutten niet om, *d. i.* laat u niet door hem opruien, beet nemen.

同 *bô siāng* / (» *kang*) 無 |, van dezelfde soort.
Siāng *siāng iū* / *kāng iū* | 樣, van dezelfde soort.
siāng tsit lâng / (*kāng* » ») | 一人, dezelfde man.
siāng k'iā laī, | 居住, te zamen wonen.
siāng t'ò / (*kēng* ») | 套, tot een zelfde nest behoorende, (als manden.)
bô siāng k'a / (» *kāng* ») 不 | 脚, ongelijkparig, (van schoenen.)

Siao

消 Dooien, smelten; ophouden te bestaan,
Siao doen ophouden als eene verbindtenis, eindigen, afmaken, uit den weg ruimen, uitdoen als eene betaalde rekening; krampachtig optrekken, krimpen, slinken, doen slinken; verteren, digereren, spijsvertering; in hoeveelheid afnemen, verminderen, afvallen, mager worden, afgevallen; verbruiken, consumeren, veel gebruikt, gezocht.
siao hoà, | 化, verteren, digereren.
ts'at siao, *kao siao*, 擦 |, 到 |, eene post uitschrappen, doorhalen.
siao àn, | 案, een rechtsgeding eindigen, afmaken.
siao kun, | 筋, kramp.
siao sing, | 簨, kramp in de buik.
siao sit, | 息, tijding, berichten van; oorpeutertje.
siao sit hoe, | 息花, Acacia.
siao sih, | 蝕, verminderen, in hoeveelheid afnemen.
siao t'aò, | 透, doorloopen, voortgang hebben.
hā siao, 下 |, vuile urine, soort gonorrhee.
siao tiā, | 定, iemands handgeld nemen en de goederen aan een ander verkoopen, (daar de bepaalde tijd voor bedenking reeds over is.)
siao p'iā, | 兵, scheef zijn, loopen (door pijn); omkrullen, kromtrekken.
siao kui, | 圭, eten in de krop verteren.
siao láp, | 納, geregelde ontlasting hebben, gezond van harte.
siao k'ì, | 去, ontlasting bevorderen.
siao sán, | 瘦, afgevallen, mager.
siao tiaô, | 條, do.
siao ko, | 膏, pleister.
siao sat, | 束, afgevallen.

ū siao, *ū siao t'aô siao tsoē tsoē*, 有｜, 有｜頭, ｜多匕, veel gebruikt worden, goed te verkoopen.

siao hoa, ｜化, verteren, digereren, ontlasting hebben.

硝 Salpeter.

Siao *gé siao*, 牙｜, do.

iém siao, 鹽｜, do. op muren.

siao hông, ｜礦, salpeter en zwavel.

宵 Nacht.

Siao *goân siao*, 元｜, het lantaarnfeest op den 15den van de eerste maand.

t'ong siao lah tsik, 通｜蜡燭, groote waskaars die een nacht doorbrandt.

蕭 Familienaam.
Siao

簫 Fluit.

Siao *ts'e siao*, 吹｜, fluit spelen.

tōng siao, 洞｜, hoboë.

灑 *siao sá* („ *soá*) ｜瀟, opgeruimd, in zijn schik.
Siao

小 *siaó soat*, ｜說, verhaaltje, novelle.
Siaó

siaó k'ì, ｜器, spoedig tevreden gesteld, bekrompen (van geest.)

siaó sì, ｜試, examen voor siù tsai.

siaó kúi bīn, ｜鬼面, slot van een deur; do. vuilik.

tì siaó kuí bīn, 戴｜鬼面, zich schamen.

siaó sán, ｜產, miskraam.

tsik siaó-sing to, 積小成多, veel (lett. opstapelen van) kleintjes maken een groote.

siaó kiok, 小局, verlegen wanneer men hoogeren ziet.

siaó k'ó, 可｜, weinig beduidend, niet veel om het lijf hebbend.

siaó sū, ｜事 weinig beduidende zaak.

taī siaó kiem, 大｜兼, groot en klein bij elkander.

siaó k'ién, ｜犬, mijn zoon. } beleefde nederige termen.
siaó dzi, ｜兒, do.
siaó lú („ *lí*) ｜女, mijne dochter.

siaó k'ai, ｜楷 kleine karakters.

siaó kui á k'eh („ „ „ *k'ēh*) ｜鬼仔客, iemand die met weinig tevreden is.

siaó tsì k'ì, ｜志氣, niet veel grootsche plannen voor den toekomst gemaakt hebben.

siaó só kièn („ *sé* „) ｜所見, van weinig ondervinding, doorzicht.

siaó dzîn, 人｜, de gemeene man, beschaamd zijn.

siaó hàn, ｜寒, geringe kleine koude, (begin van den winter.)

siaó sú, ｜暑, geringe, kleine hitte, (begin van den zomer.)

siaó piēn, *siaó kai*, ｜便, ｜改, wateren, (beleefde term.)

㺀 Krankzinnig, krols.
Siáo *siaó lák lák*, ｜吷匕, snakig, grappig, zich niet zoo strak aan de beleefdheid houdend.

poà tien siaó, 半顛｜, half krankzinnig.

siaó dzip tsut, ｜入出, van geilheid heen en weêr draaien.

hiáo siaó, ｜｜, geil, (van vrouwen.)

siaó sin, | 神, een weinig krankzinnig, voor uitspanning iets doen wat men niet gewoon is te doen, (als dobbelen.)

siaó niau, | 貓, krolsche kat.

Siaó *siaó loé* (» *lé*), beschaamd zijn, zich schamen.

數 Siaò Tellen, optellen, rekenen, berekenen; rekening, post, in te vorderen schuld; geldelijke of koopmanszaken; lijst; de vooruitzichten, gevolgen van; verscheidene, elk.

siaò siaò, 算 |, tellen, optellen.

sing siaò, 算 |, berekenen, rekenen.

siaò ts'ò, siaò tā (*suì* » *suì* ») | 錯, | 差, fout rekenen.

at siaò (» *suì*) 按 |, op de vingers tellen.

tuì siaò, 對 |, de rekeningen vergelijken, onderling afrekenen.

hoē siaò, 會 |, in elkanders tegenwoordigheid berekenen.

siaò gûn (*suì* ») | 銀, geld tellen.

siaò si siaò dzit (*suì* » » » ») | 時 | 日, de tijd voor iets berekenen.

siaò siū, | 想, berekenen, bedenken.

siaò koe lō tsióh, | 街 路 石, de straatsteenen tellen, *d. i.* leegloopen.

siaò liēm, | 念, denken aan.

tsiū goá ē siaò, 上 我 之 |, zet het op mijne rekening.

siu siaò, pàng siaò, 放 | 賒 |, op crediet geven.

siaò p'ō, 數 簿, koopmansboeken.

siaò hāng, | 項, geldelijke zaken.

siaò hāng óng lai (en *lai óng*), | 項 往 來, een loopende rekening met elkander hebben.

siaò kuī, | 櫃, boekhouder.

pik siaò, | 迫, op betaling aandringen, manen.

ts'ing siaò, 清 |, oene rekening voldoen.

ts'at siaò, 察 |, eene rekening uitschrappen.

poā siaò, 抄 |, eone post overbrengen.

siaò pàng, 賬 房, rekenbureau, rekenkamer.

siaò toé, | 底, het nog schuldig geblevene.

tsiū siaò (*tsiō* ») 上 |, bij de rekening voegen.

tsiaò siaò toé, 照 | 底, volgens vroegeren prijs.

oân siaò, 完 |, schuld afbetalen.

siu siaò, | 收, schulden ophalen, invorderen.

tsa (en *ts'à*) *siaò* (*tse* *ts'ē* ») 查 |, eene rekening nazien.

siao kun, | 巾, doek waarin men opgehaalde gelden doet.

su hun siaò, 輸 份 |, in kwaliteit onderdoen, minder in rang staan.

bò giáh siaò. 無 額 |, te weinig om geteld te worden.

si ka siaò, 是 脚 |, knap in zijn vak zijn.

siaò bák, | 目, lijst van....

hó ē siaò, 好 毅 |, goed voorkomen, vooruitzicht, (van zaken.)

k'oà ē siaò, 看 下 |, de omstandigheden, gevolgen in aanmerking nemen.

siaò ē, elkeen.

少 Siaò Jeugdig, jong.

siaò liên, | 年, jong van jaren, jong.

siaò liên ke, 丨年家, jongelieden.

siaò iâ, 丨爺, titel voor mandarijn-kinderen, jongeheer.

誚 Siaò Laken.

kièn siaò, 見丨, zich schamen, schandelijk.

笑 Siaò *hâm siaò hoe*, 含丨花, de ingehouden lach, de magnolia fuscata.

肖 Siaò Gelijken.

siaò sin, 丨神, sprekend gelijkend, levend, natuurlijk, (van schilderijen.)

put siaò, 不丨, ontaard, (van kinderen.)

ı̄m bat siaò, 不識丨, de manieren nog niet kennen, (van kinderen gezegd.)

精 Siaô Zaad, (lage term.)

tsáp tsing siaô, 雜種丨, hoerenkind, (scheldwoord.)

giét siaô, 逆丨, van slecht zaad, ras, (scheldwoord tegen kinderen.)

siaô bé kiá, 丨尾子, scheldwoord.

haô siaô, 呼丨, liegen, leugenachtig, (lage term.)

soe siaô, 衰丨, ongelukkig, niet voorspoedig.

招 Siaō Slaan, (schuins weg.)

siaō bé pı̱, 丨馬鞭, met een zweep slaan.

邵 Siaō Familienaam.

紹 Siaō *siaō hin tsiú*, 丨興酒, Siaōhinwijn.

Siem.

siem siem, 纖, maar juist . . . , op het nippertje af.

siem siem á ı̄ kaò, maar juist genoeg.

閃 Siém *siem k'ì k'oà̱*, even ter sluiks gaan zien.

siem, 閃, wijken voor, ontwijken.

siém pī, 丨避, do. vermijden.

tò siém, 避, do. do.

siém k'ui, 丨, do.

seim hō̱, 避雨, voor den regen schuilen.

siém tioh, 丨着, een lichaamsdeel verwringen.

siém pı̱, *siém pi k'ì*, op zijde gaan.

siém bih, wegschuilen.

siém bát, zich verschuilen.

siém hı̄ng hı̄ng » *(huı̱)* », zich ver weg verschuilen.

sı̱ siem (*sio*) », 相丨, voor elkander uit den weg gaan.

hoah siém, roepen om menschen uit den weg te doen gaan.

siém íng, 丨影, in de schaduw schuilen, uit de zon gaan.

siém dzít, 丨日, uit de zon gaan, voor de zon schuilen.

siém hong, 丨風, uit de wind, tocht gaan.

siém ı̄m kı̱ it, iemand niet willen ontvangen, te woord staan.

siém sai hong, iemand ontloopen, vermijden.

siém ts'iú, 丨, de hand doen neerzakken door zwaarte.

滲 Sièm *toā laō put dzû sió sièm*, een groot lek is niet zoo erg als eene kleine doordruppeling is, veel in eens (wegnemen enz.) is niet zoo erg als onophoudelijk een weigin.

sièm ts'ut, 丨出, doorzijpelen.

sièm tsui, 丨水, in of uitzijpelen van water.

siėm sai, | 糞, zijne ontlasting niet hebben kunnen ophouden.
siėm dziō, | 尿, bij dropjes wateren
siėm tseh siėm tseh, bij kleine hoeveelheden teruggeven.
ùn á siėm, do.
siėm tsing, gonorrhee, druiper.

尋 *tsit siėm*, 一 尋, vadem.
Siėm *tsit siėm tìng ts'im*, een vadem lang, diep.
siėm ti'aò, | 着, omvademen.
kui siėm ts'im, hoeveel vadems diep?
mih-hō li siėm teh, |, ik geef u dit tot onderpand.

Siėm *siėm sà* » *(si)* | |, fabelachtige kikvorsch

贍 *iòng siēm*, » *(iáng)* 養 贍, geld voor zijn
Siėm ouden dag, pensioen.

暹 *siēm lô*, 暹 羅, Siam.
Siėm *sì siēm sui*, » *(lam)*, van alle kanten afdruipen (als regen).
siēm tsu, rood, roode verfstof.

Sien

仙 Iemand die door een afgezonderd leven
Sien en meditatiën tot onsterfelijkheid geraakt. een onsterfelijke; genius, fee; numeraal partikel voor afgodsbeelden, poppen enz.
oàn sien būng, een droom uitleggen dien een genius u gegeven heeft.
sien k'a dziah, voetstappen van genii.
siet sien, foppen.
sien tan, levensmedicijn (der Taoïsten).
hó sien hoat, goede manier om iets te doen.
pat sien kè hai-sui làng piėn sin t'ong, gaan de acht genii over de zee (eene proef die zij om de 500 of 1000 jaar moeten doorstaan) dan moet elk voor zich zelven zijne kunde aanwenden *d. i.* in tijd van nood zorge iedereen voor zich zelven.

sam sien tan, een soort van medicijn.
sien ts'èng, groote bank, canapé.
k'ah kuì oàh sien king, beter, fraaier dan een geniiverblijf, elysium.
tó teh t'iao sien, achterover liggen met de beenen, krom, (om te rusten).
pat sien toh, sì sien toh, tafel voor acht en voor vier personen.
tsit sien pút, een afgodsbeeld.
tsiú sien, buitengewoon groote wijndrinker.
a p'ièn sien, verslaafde opiumschuiver.

先 Vooropgaan, voorgaan, het eerst; vroe-
Sien ger, te voren, voorafgegaan, overleden. wijlen.
sien hē ts'iú, het eerst de hand aan iets leggen, bijnemen.
sien hong, aanvoerder der voorposten.
sien si, meester, onderwijzer, dokter. mijnheer; drukt een fatsoenlijk bestaan uit.
sien si niû, mevrouw.
sien dzin, vroegere menschen, overledenen.
lîng sien tòng, wijlen uwe moeder.
sien, vroegere, wijlen.

銹 Roest, ijzerroest.
Sien *si sien*, roesten, roestig.
t'ih sien, ijzerroest.
sin k'u si sien *(hin su si sien)*, zoor vuil over het ligchaam.

珊 *sien hô* *(san)* » |, roode koraal.
Sien

鮮 *sin sien*, glans van nieuwheid. (als op
Sien zijde).

癬 Schurft.
Sién *si sién* *(se)* », schurft hebben.
noū sién, vochtige schurft.
ta sien, drooge do.

tè sién, bordje onder een theepot gelegd.
sién pa, laatste afgetrokken opium.
sién ú!, uitroep van ontsteltenis, ah!

掮 Siên Slaan.
sièn ts'uì p'oé » » *(p'è)* }, een slag op de wangen geven.
sièn koah kout, slaan en tikken.
sièn hong, door de wind bewaaid worden, in de wind staan.
sièn ièn taö, met jonge lieden gemeenschap hebben (van bejaarde vrouwen).

蟬 Siên *Siên t'oè*, larve eener cicade.
ts'iu sièn, kleine sprinkhaan.

禪 Siên *Siên ts'ìng*, bank van een Boedh. priester.
tsē siên, met de voeten kruiselings in overpeinzing zitten, (van Boedh. priesters gezegd).

倦 Siēn Vermoeid, uitgeput.
siēn siēn, do.
siēn siēn t'ih t'ih, afgemat, ziek.
ià ià siēn siēn, moede van iets zijn, tegenzin in iets krijgen.
siēn hō, aanhoudende regen.

Siēn *Siēn làng* (*sīn*) » }, hagedis.

Siēn *Siēn tsí* (*siēn*) » }, de ballen (fats. term).
toā soè siēn, een groot en een klein testiculum.

鱔 Siēn *Siēn hi*, paling.

善 Siēn *Hing siēn*, het goede doen.
siēn tsiong sí, zijn natuurlijke dood sterven.
k'i siēn p'ò ok, de goeden verdrukken en de slechten vreezen.
sin siēn, tot het goede verbeterd zijn.
siēn liòng è làng, een goed, braaf mensch.
hò siēn è làng, iemand die aan goede dingen wil mede doen.

擅 Siēn *siēn tsū*, op eigen gezag, eigendunkelijk.

Siep

澁 Siep Ruw, ongelijk, niet geleidelijk, stroef, wrang, loom, lusteloos.
seng seng siep siep, wrang, schraal in de keel.
siep tī toah, zeer wrang.
ts'o siep; *ts'o siep ts'o siep*, grof en ruw.
àn siep, strak en stroef.
k'a-siep siep, stroef, loom in de voeten, geen lust hebben om uit te gaan.
bák tsiu-siep, lusteloos, slaperige oogen.
ts'uì siep siep, geen eetlust hebben.
bák t'aò siep, niet willen zien.
kièm siep, gierig.
ts'iú t'aò siep, schrap in geld zitten.
k'ó siep, bitter en wrang.
siep siep á kào, maar juist genoeg.
tsiáh siep, het sap van de »ka tia" laten doortrekken.
siep siep, stroef stroefgaan.

梜 Siep *Siep tiép*, stevig in elkander.
siep bát, dichtstoppen.
siep toh k'a, de poot van een tafel vastzetten (door er iets onder te plaatsen).

攝 Siep *Siep aū ts'iú*, heimelijk in de hand stoppen, omkoopen.
soè siep, iemand heimelijk iets geven.

Sièp Zamentrekking van sì tsáp veertig, siep it 41.

Sièp *Siép làng è tsi gún*, iemand geld aftroggelen (als Boedh. priesters of nonnen).
k'it làng siép k'ì, door iemand misleid, verleid worden.
hō kui siép k'ì, door een spook of geest weggetooverd, weggenomen zijn.
ùn á siép ts'ut lai, langzamerhand doorzijpelen (als water door een waterkan).
àm tsī siép hō i, heimelijk in de hand stoppen.

涉 Sièp *Siép sè*, (*sì*) » }, vleien, zich bij invloedrijken indringen.

66

siép liép } , bijeenzamelen.
(*láp*) »
siép su, oneerlijk, partijdig, onrechtvaardig
kan siép, betrekking (hebben) op, aangaan.
koan siép, do.
ū kao siép, zeer intiem met iemand verbonden door banden van vriendschap of handelszaken.

Siet

設 Siet Oprichten, instellen, tot stand brengen, aanrichten; rangschikken, plaatsen; vooronderstellen; bedriegen, beetnemen.
siet lip, oprichten, instellen.
sin siet, nieuw ingesteld, ingevoerd.
siet hoat, eene vaste manier instellen.
siet king, nieuw instellen
siet bô king, voor leugenachtig houden.
siet àm kè, eene heimelijke streek bedonken, strik leggen.
siet iên, een feestmaal aanrichten.
siet ts'ùi táo, *siet ts'ùi taó mē̤ lang*, iemand uitschelden.
siet sim, hardvochtig.
p'o̤ siet, *pai siet*, rangschikken.
siet sū, *ká siet*, vooronderstelt dat....
siet sióng, vooronderstellender wijze denken.
siet sien, knap bedriegen.
siet p'ièn lâng, bedriegen, beet nemen.
ts'il siet poeh siet, *t'ien siet tē siet*, *ts'i̤ siet péh siet*, steeds handig bedriegen, beet nemen.

洩 Siet Lekken, uitvloeien; uitlekken, openbaar worden.
laū siet, uitlekken, bekend worden.
siet k'ì, de kracht, geur ontsnapt er uit.
būng siet, nachtelijke zaadvloed.
siet sià, diarrhee hebben.

褻 Siet Oneerbiedig behandelen, ontheiligen, bezoedelen.
siet tòk, ontheiligen, godslastering.
ap siet, bezoedelen, verguizen.
k'ó̤ siet ê sū, een zaak die moeielijk te beslissen valt.
Siet *tùn hô̤ ts'i siét*, lip, keel, tand en tongklanken.
kao̤ k'aó siét, veel over en weer pratens kosten vóórdat het geregeld is.
koat siét, tong schrapper.
siét siét kiò, geluid van scherpe messen.

Sih

閃 Sih Vonkelen, (als een ster.)
sih tseh sih tseh, flikkeren als weerlicht of muurvliegen, ook het kloppen van de hersenkas van kinderen.
sih nḡ, bliksem, weerlicht.
nìng sih sih, zoo zacht dat het trilt.
kim sih sih, helder, flikkerend, (als een glad mes.)
k'a p'ù ts'iú sih, aan handen en voeten trillen, (van vrees, toorn of ziekte.)

薛 Sih Familienaam.

時 Sih *Dzit sih*, dag.
mi̤ sih } , nacht.
mē̤ »)
Sih *nih sih*, wurgen.
kik sih, verdrinken.

蝕 Sih *Sih pún*, verlies van kapitaal.
siao sih, verminderen, afnemen.
sih tūng, in gewicht verliezen.
ū sih pún tsai tsú bô ū sih pún kioh ku al verliest men ook op zijne koopwaar het koelieloon moet toch betaald worden, *d. i.* het verlies moet drukken op den baas niet op den werkman.
sing li k'ah sih, geen geld op zijn handel verdienen.
sih loh k'ih, zamenpakken, als aardewerk.)

k'ui sik, het verlies over de partijen verdeelen.
sik hùn, afnemen, dalen (als water), zakken (als voedsel.)

Sik

Kleur, kleurig; gelaatskleur, tint, uiterlijk, voorkomen; toestand, gesteldheid; soort, slag van . . . ; fraai, schoonheid; wellust, wellustig.
lik sik, groen.
sik tsui, kleur, tint.
bò sik tsui, niet gerespecteerd worden, beschaamd staan.
sik tì, soort van kleur, kleur.
bīn sik, gelaatskleur, uiterlijk.
sik liaō, stukjes verf.
bing sik tsióng, eene beste theesoort.
tsoát sik, uiterst fraai, (van eene vrouw).
kok sik ê hè mịh, allerhande waren.
it sik, eenkleurig, gelijksoortig.
sim mịh hō ê lâng sik, wat soort, slag van mensch?
sik iók, wellustige begeerten.
hò sik, veel van het schoone geslacht houden, wellustig.
ts'iah sik, vleeschkleurig
tsang sik, bruin.
sit sik, bleek worden.
k'ì sik, gelaatskleur.
huih sik (*hoeh* ») }, bloedkleurig.
tsit áh ê sik liaō, een verfdoos.
bák sik, vermogen der oogen.
dziém sik, kleuren, de kleuren geven aan teekeningen.
ts'aì (en *tsàn*) *sik*, door eene donkere omgeving beter laten uitkomen.
kap sik liaō / *kiáo sik* » }, kleuren mengen.
hoán sik, verkleuren.
t'è sik, verschieten.
bīn-sit sik, ontstellen, bleek worden.
ut sik, de kleuren vermorsen: het is zonde zoo iets goeds voor zulk een gering doeleinde te gebruiken.
tsáp hoe gō sik, , veelkleurig.
o tsí sik, roodachtig zwart.
gán sik, vermogen der oogen, gezicht.
hó bák sik, goed, scherp van gezicht.
bák sik-k'á, een vernuftig gezicht hebben, *d. i.* iets kennen zoodra men het ziet.
ū k'í sik, toenemen, bloeiender worden, (als handel.)
tsaī sik lú / (» *sit lí*) }, maagd, ongehuwd meisje,
tì sik ka / (» *sit ke*) }, gehuwd zijn, (beleefde term.)

適 Sik
sik ts'ù, aangenaam, levendig.
sim sik, aardig, voor amusement.

俗 Sik
Oud, (van hout, zaad enz.)
sik tsoh, zich in alles en overal goed schikken, goed op zijn plaats vinden.
sik sin, rijp, (van hout.)

首 Sik
tsik (ook *siú sik*), gouden of zilveren vrouwen versierselen.
keh sik / (*kēh sit*) }, vaste vorm, regel.

席 Sik
tsē sik, *dzip sik*, aan tafel gaan, (beleefde term.)
tsē siú sik, op de eerste plaats aan tafel zitten.
toā sik bīen, gewoon zijn in het publiek op te treden, te spreken.

釋 Sik
sik kaò, Buddhisme.

蟋 Sik
sik sut / (*sik* ») }, krekel.
sik k'ò, korte zwachtel door vrouwen boven de schoen gedragen.

熟 Sik
Rijp, gaar.
bò sik / *īm si* }, onrijp, ongaar.
sik saī, familiaar, bekend.

sik saī làng, kennis, iemand dien men kent.

sik p'iáh, geheel gebranden steenen.

tsaī ts'iū sik, aan den boom rijp worden.

sik lō, bekende weg.

sik ts'iá, gewoon zijn aan, den slag van iets hebben.

sik làng, een kennis.

siong sik / (*siang* »), met elkander bekend.

sik liù liù, zeer bekend (op eene plaats) zeer goed kennen.

sik hàng, zeer bekend in eene plaats zijn.

sik hè / (» *hoè*), gare, gekookte waar.

hoân sik bók hoân ts'i / (» » » » *t'se*), waar men bedreven in is moet men niet verruilen tegen hetgeen waarvan men niets afweet.

sik hoan, inboorling van Formosa die reeds met Chineezen omgang gehad hebben.

sik hun, zwarte tabak.

làng t'aô-sik, met de menschen van de plaats bekend zijn.

sik tsoá, rijp, *d. i.* gelijmd papier.

sik ts'uì, gewoon zijn iets te zeggen.

Sim

心 Sim — Het hart als zetel der gedachte, hartstochten en neigingen; de geest, het gemoed, de gedachten, het denkvermogen, verstand; het hart, binnenste, inwendige, midden van iets.

sim koa, hart en lever, binnenste.

goá sim koa, mijn hartje, mijn liefje.

sim t'aô, hart, gemoed.

t'am sim, hebzuchtig.

k'ùn sim, vlijtig.

sió sim, voorzichtig, omzichtig, gedienstig.

sè (en *soè*) *sim*, voorzichtig, naauwkeurig.

hó sim, *p'aī sim*, goed, slecht van harte.

sit sim, krankzinnig.

hiao sim, ondankbaar.

k'ui sim, zich vorgooien, slecht gedragen.

sim hoe-k'ui, vol verwachting, opgeruimd.

hòng sim, *pàng sim*, zich geruststellen.

ts'ing sim, opgeruimd.

hó sim hīng, goed van harte.

toā sim hīng, voor groote zaken geschikt.

t'ao sim boē hīng / (» » *t'ao* »), heimelijk handelen.

ts'ìn sim, koel behandelen.

lô sim / *hoân sim*, zijn geest afmatten.

k'ō sim, zijn geest uitputten.

ū sim k'iaò, van helder doorzicht.

sim sin toā, van groot vernuft.

sim koa ts'àn, hardvochtig.

tiém sim, klein maal, tusschenmaal.

sim sū, iets dat iemand zwaar op het hart ligt.

sim su, doordenkend.

sim sik, aardig, voor amusement.

k'ang sik, nuchter, (zonder iets gegeten te hebben.)

si sik noā lìng, geduldig verdragen.

bô sim tsiō, geen lust, trek hebben.

tsit sim tsit ì, vast voorgenomen.

siū sim siū koa, met inspanning denken.

sim sim liēm liēm, zeer aan iets denken.

īm kè sim, (eene gedachte) niet van zich kunnen afgooien.

sim laī taī / (» » *sū*), inwendige gedachte. (wat in iemands binnenste omgaat.)

gi sim tāng, ongeloovig, achterdochtig.

sim pak oē, vertrouwelijke, openhartige taal.

sim sì kin, haastig van aard.

ū sim kiang, veel tegenwoordigheid van geest, doorzicht hebben.

kien sim, vastvoorgenomen.

toā sim koa, niet met weinig tevreden zijn.

sim hé-tóh, in vuur, toorn ontsteken.
koan sim, met oplettendheid.
kiⁿ sim, vreesachtig, voorzichtig.
tsoan sim, met geheel zijn geest, uitsluitend (zich bezig houden met iets).
t'iu sim, opschieten, (als graan.)
in sim, staartje, lont.
tê sim, theebladeren.
ting sim, lampenpit.
hoe sim, hart van een bloem; vulva.
ts'iú tiong sim, palm van de hand.
ka tsiah sim, midden van den rug.
p'àⁿ sim, inwendig hol.
po sim, inwendig uitgedroogd.
an sim, rustig van gemoed, op zijn gemak.
sim ti tsiok, tevreden zijn.
sim sa ing / (» *sio hiàng ing*) }, sympathiseren.
sim tì è, zeer met iets ingenomen zijn.
hu sim / *hi* » }, nederig.
sí sim, niet meer aan iets denken.
sí sim hoa ting, nog maar niet kunnen opgeven, geduldig verdragen.
hūn sim, haatvoedend in het hart.
ts'ûn sim, zich vertederen.
hòng sim, *pàng sim*, gerust zijn, niet bevreesd.
sim huih-kiét / (» *hoek* ») } het bloed gestolt, (door het denken.)
ts'aò sim koa, slecht van harte.
tsoan sim, uitsluitend (zich bezig houden met iets.)
hiao sim, ondankbaar, (elkander later niet meer willen kennen.)
káng sim, midden eener haven.
sim sin toā, van groot vernuft.
sim koa hong, onbesuisd, onvoorzichtig.

新 Sim
sim pū / (*sin* ») }, behuwddochter.

參 Sim
hai sim (en *som*) / (» *som* » ») }, Biche de mer.

審 Sím
Verhooren, vonnissen, rechten.
sim p'oàⁿ, oordeelen, verhooren.
sim toàn, uitspraak doen over.
sim àn / *sim mīng* / (» *muī*) }, eene regtszaak beoordeelen.
sim sit, naar de waarheid ondervragen.
tuì sím, in elkanders tegenwoordigheid ondervragen.
hoē sim, gezamenlijk vonnissen.
sim sū, eene zaak gerechtelijk onderzoeken.
sim ts'at, gerechtelijk onderzoeken.
sim bōe ts'ut, een verhoor niet kunnen uitmaken.

沈 Sim
Familienaam.

顉 Sìm
Op en neer gaan (als de veeren van een rijtuig), schudden als in een draagstoel.
níng sìm, *níng níng sìm sìm* / (*nuí* » *niū nuī* » ») }, slap, zwabberend, (als een lange dunne plank.)
sìm tseh tsiah kiâ, bij rukjes voortloopen (als stoeldragers), langzaam handelen.
sìm lát bé / (*siàng* » *boé*) }, iemands laatste krachten beproeven.
sìm taò kú, zien wie het langst uit kan houden, (als twee personen die voor elkander niet willen inwilligen.)

尋 Sîm
sîm siông / (» *siâng*) }, gewoon, alledaagsch.

愖 Sīm
sīm sīm, rustig, stil.
siū-kaò sīm k'ì / (*siū* » » ») }, tot versuffens toe denken.
sīm tseh tsiah kóng, na een oogenblik rustens zeggen.
sīm sīm tsīng tsīng, zeer stil, even ophouden (om na te denken enz.)

甚 Sīm
Zeer, grondig.
t'aì sīm, zeer, uiterst.

sīm dzién, uiterst, zeer.
i sīm, reeds al te....
sīm ts'ió...., tot nog...., en daarenboven....
sīm tsoē, zeer veel.
sīm sī īm hó, het is volstrekt niet goed.
Símh *Símh mih*, wat!
simh mih lâng, wie?
simh mih si, wanneer?
simh mih ién kò, waarom?

Sín

新 Sin Nieuw, nieuwelings, kortelings.
sin k'oán, nieuwe vorm.
sin niō, *sin kiá sai*, bruid en bruidegom.
sin lâng, jong echtpaar.
sin tsin, *sin ni*, nieuwjaar.
sin kū kao piō, het nieuwe met het oude vermengen.
sin siō, nieuwe vorm.
sin bûn, nieuws, nieuwstijding.
tsoè sin, om als nieuw te gebruiken, b. v. kleederen voor hooge gelegenheden.
sin tseh á-kū láh dzit, een nieuw geestenbriefje en een oude almanak dat is altijd met hetzelfde aankomen, oude koeien uit de sloot halen.
sin bī, nieuwe zeldzame spijs.
sin ien, glans van nieuwheid.
sin sien, nieuw en frisch uitziend.
sin siet, nieuw ingesteld.
ts'oā sin pū, eene schoondochter huwen, (tegen de mans ouders gezegd.)
sin (en *sim*) *pū*, schoondochter.
sin hok, nieuw geluk, naam van eene offerande aan de geesten.
ting sin, van nieuw af aan.
tsiông sin k'i t'aô, van voren, van nieuw af aan.

身 Sin Lichaam, lijf, romp, stam; persoon, persoonlijk, zich zelf; de vrucht bij zwangerschap.
sin k'u }
(*hin sin*) } , lichaam.
sin t'é, lichaam, lichaamsgesteldheid.
sin si, lijk.
ē sin, onderste gedeelte van het lichaam of andere voorwerpen.
téng sin, zich omdraaien.
p'ai téng (en) *tsoán sin*, zich slecht kunnen roeren, in een lastig parket zitten.
hoan sin, zich omdraaien, omkeeren.
hoan sin á, in een ommezien.
kè sin, voorbijgaan.
pún sin, zelf, in persoon.
ta sin, zelfstandig.
lī sin, verlaten, van iets afgaan.
k'in sin, licht.
ts'iū sin boomstam.
sin io, lendenen, middel.
sin bát, gekist (van een lijk.)
ts'ut sin, van afkomst, geboorte.
sin hūn, fatsoen, stand.
gin á sin, gekochte jonge slavin.
k'iā sin, op de voeten, regtop staande (van een beeld).
k'iā k'i sin, opstaan.
toō sin, eenig kind.
an sin, uitrusten; ergens neêrleggen.
tī sin, zich om iemand strengelen, *d. i.* het iemand lastig maken met vele zaken tegelijk.
pák sin, strak om het lijf spannend.
tsiong sin, zijn levenlang.
p'e tsit sin si, zijn leven voor iemand niet ontzien.
si sin p'e, veel kans hebben om nog eens doodgeslagen te worden (scheldwoord).
soé sin, zich van iets vrij wasschen, alle verantwoording van zich afwerpen.

tàm sin, nog een sleep achter zich hebben, met anderen betrokken zijn.
tsiā sin, het eigenlijke hoofd (van eene zaak enz.)
t'oè sin, van papier gemaakte pop van iemand die ziek is (deze wordt tot verteedering der geesten verbrand.)
sin īn, zwanger.
ū sin, bevrucht, zwanger.
ka laóh sin, een miskraam hebben.
t'út sin, de bevallen door medicijnen hevorderen.

辛 Sin Bitter, ellendig, smartvol, moeitevol, familienaam.
sin k'ó, ellende, smart.
sin kim, *sin lô*, loon, traktement, gage (van bedienden enz.)

申 Sin *sin si*, 3—5 uur namiddag.
sin ts'ing, verzoeken (van lage aan hoogere beambten).

紳 Sin *sin sū*, titel van eenig geleerde die een knoop mag dragen.
hiong sin, de geleerden en de gegoede stand.
sia k'im, titel van gegradueerde geletterden.

伸 Sin *sin oan*, een kwaad herstellen,
iú oan bû sin, ongelijk ondervinden en niemand hebben om het te herstellen.

信 Sìn Geloofwaardig, te vertrouwen; geloofhechten aan, gelooven, vertrouwen; zich houden aan, nakomen; brief, bericht.
sìn pin, geloofwaardig bewijs.
pīn sìn, gelooven, als authoriteit aannemen.
sìn sít, de waarheid.
sìn sim, gelooven, niet in twijfel trekken.
k'ing sìn, lichtgeloovig.
īm sìn siā, voor niet waar houden.
sìn iok, eene overeenkomst nakomen.
p'oe sìn, brief.
sìn tsoá, briefpapier.
gûn sìn, brief met geld er bij.
pò sìn, bericht brengen.
hong sìn, vaste wind.
tíng hong sìn, *hong-tíng sìn*, de wind draait.
sìn tsióh, rattekruid, van Sìn tsiu afkomstig.

訊 Sìn Onderzoek doen, ondervragen, verhooren.
sìn mīng, ondervragen, verhooren.
sìn kiet, verhooren en vonnis uitspreken.
tìng sìn, in de rechtzaal ondervragen.
hāo sìn, wachten totdat men verhoord zal worden.
t'oân sìn, iemand den tijd voor zijn verhoor doen weten.

汛 Sìn Militair station, wachtstation, wachtpost.
sìn tē, wachtstation.
lī k'ui sìn tē, lett. van zijne wachtpost afgaan zich buiten zijn terrein begeven als zeeroovers die aan land komen.
k'iū sìn, ter bewaking van (grensplaatsen enz.) zijn.
sìn hóng, grenswachter, wachters aan landingsplaatsen gesteld.

迅 Sìn Gaauw, snel, plotseling.
sìn sok, vroeg bij tijds, een man van de klok.
sìn lui put kip iém dzī, bij eene plotselinge dondorslag heeft men geen tijd de ooren dicht te doen; iemand onverhoeds met iets op het lijf vallen.
sìn pit-sia, vlug wegschrijven.

顖 Sìn De vereeniging van de hersenpan.
sìn tsang, kleine hoofdstaart op de hersenpan van kinderen.
sìn ming, bekkeneelnaad, pijlnaad.

愼 Sīn eig. *sīn*, voorzichtig, oplettend.
kín sìn, voorzichtig, zorgvuldig.

神 Sîn De etherische leven gevende kracht, levenskracht, levensgeesten; onlichamelijk zelfbewust wezen, geest, bo-

vennatuurlijke, hemelsche wezens, de goden; gemoedstoestand, geest, stemming.
sin hùn, de ziel.
tsing sin, levenskracht; geest.
sit sin, moedeloos, neerslachtig (door rampen).
k'ùn tsing sin, slapen om nieuwe levenskracht te krijgen.
sin bing, de goden.
hē sin-t'ok pút, de goden en Boeddha afbidden.
sàng sin, de geesten, goden uitgeleide doen (op den 24sten dag van de 12de maand).
tsih sin, de geesten inhalen (op den 4den dag van de eerste maand.
niâ sin, de geesten in processie inhalen.
ming sin, de deurgoden; rood plakkaat op eene deur.
mēng sin, aan de goden vragen.
ts'ó bók sin, geest, god der planten: iemand die met weinig tevreden is of ook, wiens winst niet lang zal duren.
sin ūi, plaats voor een afgodsbeeld.
sin siōng, afgodsbeelden.
sin tsú, tablet van een overledene.
tsing sin, geestdrift.
sin pút, geesten en afgoden.
k'ai lō̤ sin, eene papieren pop die bij eene groote begrafenis als wegbaner vooruitgeleid wordt.
bò tse sin iá, er is niets van aan.
oúh sin, sí sin, levendig en stil van aard.
koâ kaò dzip of *ts'ut sin*, zoo lang op iets staren dat men er zich als ware het mede vereenzelvigt.
sin sin sin, diep in gedachten verzonken.
siào sin, sprekend als gelijkenis.
sin ts'ai, uiterlijk, voorkomen.
bò sin ts'ai, bò sin bò ts'ai, onopgeruimd.
bò sin bò sin, neerslachtig.

k'ùn sin, slaperig.
toā bīn sin, niet schuw of bedeesd (van eene vrouw).
sin ì, inwendige, eigenlijke bedoeling.
k'ám sin }
gōng sin }, dom, idiotisch.
p'ai sin k'ì, moeielijk, slecht gaan. een gek figuur slaan.
gìn sin, tegen iemands zin aandoen.
siáo sin, voor de aardigheid doen.

臣 Sin
Minister, dienaar van een vorst, vassal.
dzìn sin, minister, hooge beambten.
kun sin ióh, bijkomende, assisterende geneesmiddelen, adjuvans.

承 Sin
Vangen, opvangen.
sin tióh, vangen.
sin īm tióh, niet goed vangen, misvangen.
sin hō̤, regen opvangen.

辰 Sin
sin si, 7—9 uur 's morgens.

蠅 Sin
Vlieg.
hō̤ sin, vlieg.
kim sin, paardevlieg.
ts'aì ts'o-siâ sin, stinkend en zout goed trekt vliegen aan.

腎 Sīn
Sīn, de nieren.
goū sīn, de teelballen.
sīn tsui, semen.
pō̤ sīn, semen aanzettend.

剩 Sīn
Sīn, overschot overschieten.
ū sīn, overschot, er schiet van over.
sīn hè bé, overschot van koopwaren.
bò sīn tsít hāng, er is niets meer van over.

Sīn
kin sīn, zorgvuldig omzichtig.

Sing

生 Sing
Voortbrengen, doen ontstaan, baren; geboren worden, leven, groeien; opleveren; acteur.

sin sing, van nature.
sing bút, levende wezens.
t'ai sing, zoogdieren.
hák sing, leerling.
sing k'ik, voortbrengen en verdelgen als elementen elkander doen.)
tsoè sing lí, koophandel drijven.
sing lí lâng, koopman, handelaar.
sing lí tsûn, koopvaardijschip.
sing sik, interest geven.
sing sán, baren.
sing tiong, opgroeien (van menschen).
it sing, zijn levenlang.
ping sing, te voren, steeds.
sing sū, aanleiding tot twist geven twistziek.
goē sing, neef (zoon van eene zuster).
sing oân, de laagste litteraire graad.
lím sing, de eerste van den laagsten litterairen graad.
kàm sing, een graad die met geld gekocht is.
sing toan, aanleiding tot iets geven.
sing gièn tsō gú, leugens opmaken.
sing hoát kè, manier om aan de kost te komen.
sing tsing, tot betere gedachten tegen over iemand komen.
sing-toā, acteurs en actrices.
siò sing, *laū sing*, *bū sing*, jonge, oude en militaire acteurs.

陞 Sing Stijgen, rijzen, verhoogd worden.
ko sing, stijgen (in rang), moogt gij tot hooge posten opklimmen.
ka sing, stijgen, rijzen in rang of prijs.
t'iaò kip sing, een rang overspringen.
sing p'aò, saluutschoten geven (voor beambten).

笙 Sing Mondorgel.

升 Sing *Sing*, ophijschen
sing ki, een vlag ophijschen.

pik dzit sing t'ien, op klaar lichten dag ten hemel varen *i. e.* in korten tijd tot hoog aanzien en rijkdom komen.

牲 Sing *Sing lé*, offeranden, offerdieren.

星 Sing *Sing sing*, orang-outang.

先 Sing *Taī sing*, vroeger, te voren.
Sing *k'í sing*, in vroeger tijd, te voren.
Sing *Sing k'ó*, ellende smart.

省 Sing *Síng siá*, provinciale hoofdstad.
síng, provincie.
sing k'òng, in de hoofdstad van de provincie gaan aanklagen.
sing ts'at (*sing*), onderzoeken.
īng k'ah síng (*iōng k'ah sí*), zuinig zijn met gebruiken.
síng síng, matig, weinig.
síng sū, zoo weinig mogelijk twist trachten te hebben.
kiém sing, zuiniger zijn.
liém síng, zuiniger worden, minder verteren.
tsiū hú tsiū síng (*tsō hú tsi ūsé*), eene zaak voor alle mogelijke gerechtshoven brengen.
síng ts'at kaò kik, tot in de minste bijzonderheden toe onderzoeken.
kán síng, in den ruwen omtrek.
síng siaò, goedkooper.
síng kiâ, een loopen uithalen, besparen.
síng tit goá k'ì, het haalt mij een gaan uit.
síng pit, verkort schrijven.

Sing *Sa sing hē* (*ō* »), met elkander verzoenen, weêr goede vrienden worden.
pin ning sa sing hē (*o*), onder het gebruiken van siri zich verzoenen.

醒 Sing *Sing gō*, tot een juist inzicht komen.
bing sing, ontwaken, opwekken.

聖 Sing Heilig als het toppunt van moreele en intellectuele bekwaamheden, wijs; keizerlijk.
sìng, heilig.
sìng dzin, een heilige, wijze.
sìng biaō, tempel aan Confucius.
sìng siū, geboortedag des keizers.
sìng dzin k'am, kompashuisje.
sìng ts'eh, de bijbel.

性 Sìng Natuurlijke gesteldheid, aangeboren aard, inborst, gestel; hoedanigheid.
sìng p'iah, *p'iah sìng*, aard eigenschap, eigenaardigheid, gesteldheid, hoofdneiging.
sìng tē, *sìng tsing*, inborst, aard.
noō sìng, *sìng tē-noō*, langzaam van aard.
kin sìng, *sìng tē-kin*, haastig van aard.
kip sìng, *sìng-kip*, do.
sò sìng, do.
si sìng, zonder veerkracht.
t'è sìng, van zijne kracht verliezen (als geneesmiddelen)

姓 Sìng Familienaam, familie.
kuì (en) *ko sìng*, welke is uwe geëerde familienaam?
taī sìng, *siaò sìng*, groote machtige en kleine zwakke familie.

勝 Sìng Overwinnen, het winnen op, overtreffen uitmunten.
tik sìng, de overwinning behalen; behouden terugkomen als een schip.
hò sìng, steeds anderen willen overtreffen.

成 Sing Voltooien, afmaken, voleindigen; maken tot, daarstellen, vormen; helpen zijn doel te bereiken ondersteunen; komen tot, worden; volmaakt, uitstekend.
sing sū, eene zaak voltooien, afmaken.
sing kong, voltooien; zich verdienstelijk maken.
sing sing, van nature; er boven op helpen.
tsok sing, ondersteunen, helpen.
k'an sing, zich iemand aantrekken, er boven op helpen.
bù sing, tot niets kunnen worden, voor niets te gebruiken zijn.
sing tsiū ìh, iemand helpen, bijstaan.
sing ting, meerderjarig (15 j.) worden.
tióng sing, een mensch (geen kind meer) zijn.
sing hút, in Boeddha opgenomen worden.
sing ts'in, een huwelijk aangaan.
sing ke tì hé, zich een stand en bezittingen verwerven.
hōng sing, aanraden te doen.
sing gú, spreuk.
ū kaò sing sing sing, sprekend gelijkend teekenen.
sing poā, voltooien, tot een eind brengen.

誠 Sing Oprecht, eerlijk; in waarheid, wezenlijk.
sing sit, oprecht; wezenlijk.
sing king, oprecht eeren, vereeren.
sing sim, oprecht van harte.
taò sing, zich overgeven, onderwerpen.
sing hóng sing k,ióng, oprechtelijk eerbiedigen en vreezen.

城 Sing Ommuurde stad, vesting.
sing hóng iâ, beschermgod eener stad.
sing hóng biō, tempel voor sing hóng iâ

承 Sing Ontvangen, aannemen, in handen krijgen, overnemen.
sing siū, (*sing*) }, ontvangen.
sing tsiep, in handen krijgen.
sing poā, eene zaak overnemen; voltooijen tot een eind brengen.
siong sing, aan elkander overleveren.
tsit ts'iú-sing kè tsit ts'iú, van den eene aan den ander overgeleverd.
ìng sing, toestemmen, belooven.
hōng sing, vleien, gedienstig behandelen; aanraden iets te doen.

縱 Sīng Den vrijen teugel laten aan, toegeven (zijne kinderen enz.)
t'ing sīng, do.
sīng koàn, door te veel toegeeflijkheid aan iets gewend zijn.
sīng hing, tengelloos te werk gaan.

盛 Sīng *Sīng*, overvloedig, veel.
ōng sīng, overvloedig = sīng ōng.
liōng sīng, meer dan genoeg, overvloedig.
iōng sīng, in groote hoeveelheid komen (als menschen of koop waar).
to siā lí ê sīng tsing (of) *sīng siet*, ik dank u voor uw ruim onthaal.

乘 Sīng *Sīng*, vermeerderen, vermenigvuldigen.
sīng hoat, vermenigvuldiging (*d. i.* optelling en vermenigvuldiging).
sīng ki, van de gelegenheid gebruik maken.

Sio

燒 Sio *Sio*, branden, warm.
sio ts'aò ta, zengen, verzengen.
hé sio, brand.
hé sio tsiú / (*hoé* ») }, gedestilleerde wijn.
sim laī sio dziét, inwendig gejaagd.
sio kim, goudpapier branden en offeranden doen.
sio koah, gebraad.
sio t'ìng / (*t'ìng tioh*) }, zich branden.
praten, iemand polsen.
sio hu, tot asch verbranden.
kap i sio sàh, met iemand over iets praten: iemand polsen.
sio tīng / (*tuī*) }, afbranden.
sio lio k'ì, door brand verwoesten.
là lùn sio, leukwarm, laauw.
hé sio ts'ù, brand in een huis.
sio hé, kok.
(*hoé*) *hé sia soa*, (het gewas op) een berg verbranden; brandend heet.
sio hiū, reukstokjes branden
sio t'oà, kolenbranden
sio bah, vleesch roosteren.
sio t'ng, warm water.
sio hé pû / (*hoé* ») }, zich om een vuurstapel warmen.
sio dzī tsoá, beschreven papier verbranden.
kip sio, steenen ketel (voor wijze of thee).
sio hui, aardewerk bakken.

煨 Sio *Kah sio*, zich warm toedekken.
sio k'ùi, warme gloed (geringe warmte).
poà sio, laauw, afgekoeld.
ts'īng sio, zich warm aankleeden.
ùn sio, warm houden (als de hen hare kuikens onder de veêren).
hāng sio, warm roosteren.
sio dziét, warm, heet.
sio hōng hōng, warm, heet tot stoomens toe.
k'oeh sio / (*k'eh* ») }, tegen elkander aankruipen voor de warmte.
p'ák sio, door de zon verwarmd.
sio kún kún, brandend heet.
sio sio bīn ù lâng ts'iù k'a ts'ng (*ts'ui*), bedaard tegen twistende menschen spreken.

蕭 Sio Eene familienaam.

誚 *Ts'ut sio*, uitvallen: zich niet kunnen inhouden om haren man te bekijven.
sio lâng, iemand tegen een ander opzetten.

相 Sio *Sio*, elkander, wederkeerig.
sio p'ah, vechten.
sio tsì / (*tsè*) }, kibbelen, kijven.
kap i sio sàh, met iemand over iets praten: iemand polsen.

sio ts'am, door elkander mengen.
sio p'oā, vergezellen.

小 Sió *Sió tī*, jongere broeder.
sió bē (*moē*), jongere zuster.
sió tsím, vrouw van een jongeren broeder.
sió ko, man's jongere zuster.
tsoè sió bák (*tsò* »), het fijne timmermans-werk doen.
sió ping, linkerkant.
sió sió k'ì làh, ga links af.
sió tsì k'ì (*siaó* »), niet veel groote plannen voor de toekomst hebben.
sió ki kut, dun, fijn van beenderen.
sió sim, bescheiden, uiterst omzichtig, vleiend, gedienstig.
sió tá, lafhartig, kleingeestig.
sió bèh (*bèh*), tarwe.
sió lī, dissenterie.
sió kang, assistent ambtenaren.
sió k'oá, niets beduidend, onbeduidend.
sió k'aó, klein van eten.
sió lóh (*sió*), klein van persoon.
sió ts'át, kleine dieven.
sió lō, zijweg.
sió tsiá, titel voor mandarijn dochter.
sió toā, jonge mannelijke actrice.

徐 Si *Sió sū*, geringe onbeduidende zaak.
néng néng si si (*nuí nuí* »), zacht en slap.
tsoè lâng si si, langzaam, in zijne handelingen zijn.
si lat si k'ì, langzaam, dralend te werk gaan.

Sioh

惜 Sioh Beminnen.
sioh sioh īm t'ang haó, sus! sus! huil niet (tegen kinderen gezegd).
sioh pún hūn, zijn plicht betrachten.
iao koe īm sioh ts'è-iao lâng īm sioh bīn p'è, eene hongerige kip geeft niet om de plak en een hongerig mensch geeft niet om zijn fatsoen.
sa sioh (*sio*), elkander beminnen.
gaó sioh, lief, toegenegen jegens
k'ó sioh, jammer dat.....
sioh lièh, hart hebben voor...., in waarde houden.
t'iá sioh, beminnen.
aì sioh, beminnen.
pó sioh, beschermen, verzorgen.
sioh p'è (*p'oè*), kleinzeerig.
sioh bīn p'è (*p'oè*), spoedig beschaamd zijn
sioh t'é biān, voor zijn fatsoen zorgen
t'aó (*iū*) *sioh bè* (*iā*) *sioh* (*boè*), volstrekt niets van iets willen afstaan.
po sioh, prijzen, aanmoedigen.
sioh tioh tsī, hart voor zijn geld hebben
sioh p'è īm sioh kut, voor het vel maar niet voor de beenderen zorgen (als een moeder die vreezende hare kinderen te slaan hun karakter bederft).

Sióh *Ts'iú sióh*, zweeterige, kleverige handen
k'a sióh, zweeterige voeten.
ts'aò sióh, stinkend zweeterig (van een gezegde dat men gedurig herhaalt).

Sióh *Sióh k'ì* (» *o*), verminderen, minder worden, (van dingen).
pún tsī ùn á sióh k'ì, langzaam zijn kapitaal verminderen.
sióh pī, het inwendige koud laten (ordinair, niet zoo buitengewoon).
sióh oē (» *oā*), ordinair gezegde.
sióh sióh è mīh, ordinaire dingen.
sióh bī, ordinaire smaak, van gewone middelmatige stand.

tsīng tsīng siòh siòh, stil, rustig.
siòh k'ièn, voorgevoel hebben, zeer bijgeloovig zijn.

Siok

縮 Siok *Lim tīn-t'oè siok*, op het punt van strijden gekomen zijnde van bangheid terugtrekken.

叔 Siok *Siok tit*, familiebetrekking (niet aangetrouwde).
siok tit tig tī, dito.
pao siok, ooms (vader's volle broeders).

屬 Siók Behooren tot, een deel uitmaken van; toebehooren aan, passen aan: ondergeschikt, onderhoorig.
ka siók, huis, familiegenooten.
ts'in siók, familiebetrekking.
hū s ók, *siók hū* (ē), onderhoorigen, ondergeschikten.
siók kok, onderhoorige landen, koloniën.
siók oàn, ondergeschikte beambten.
siók bók, liefde, respect voor iemand hebben
siók li é, aan u toebehoorend.
siók i ts'īng, het past aan hem om dit aan te trekken.

熟 Siók Gaar; gewoon aan, bedreven in.
koàn siók (*sik*), gewoon aan.
siók sik, gewoon, bedreven in.

俗 Siók Gemeen, van slechte kwaliteit, vulgair, ruw, ongemanierd; gewoon, alledaagsch; gewoonten, gebruiken; de wereld, de leeken in tegenoverstelling van den priesterstaat.
siók gú, volksgezegde, spreekwoord.
ts'o̱ siók, onbeschoft, grof, ruw.
siók kut, grof van uiterlijk.
siók sū, zaken van het dagelijksch leven.
put siók, niet alledaagsch, buitengewoon.
hong siók, zeden en gewoonten, gebruiken.
sè siók, gewoonten der eeuw.
t'o̱ siók, plaatselijke gewoonten.
ok siók, slechte gewoonten.
sip siók é só̱ tsaī, plaatsen waar men allerlei gewoonten ziet.
sui siók, de plaatselijke gewoonten opvolgen.
t'oat siók, zich niet aan de gewoonten houden.
hoàn siók, uit den priesterstand wéer in de wereld terugkeeren.

續 Siók Vereenigen, verbinden; vereenigd, achtereenvolgens.
siók hièn, een tweede huwelijk aangaan (van mannen).
siók ts ù, tweede huwelijk.
tsiep siók, achtereenvolgens.
liók siók, do.; ongeveer, nagenoeg.

贖 Siók Vrijkoopen, loskoopen, afkoopen, lossen als verpande goederen.
siók sin, iemand vrijkoopen, loskoopen.
siók tsoē, eene straf afkoopen.
siók hoè, een verpand goed lossen.
ts'ú siók, afkoopen, lossen.

Siong

傷 Siong *Siong* (*siang*), wonden, verwonden, kwetsen; wond, kwetsuur, benadeelen, schade aandoen; grieven, droevig aandoen, bedroefd.
siū siong, gewond zijn.
siong ióh, geneesmiddelen voor wonden.
giām siong, wonden schouwen.
siong hùn, litteeken.
tāng siong, *k'in siong*, zware, lichte verwonding.
to siong, wond met een zwaard.
p'ah siong, wond door een slag veroorzaakt.

siong tiōng, kostbaar, veel geld of moeite kostend.
siong-tiōng, de wond is zwaar.
siong pún, veel geld kostend.
siong haī, benadeelen.
tiòng siong, schaden, benadeelen.
siong gaī, mede schade doen lijden.
siong hong, eene koude vatten.
siong sú, eene zonnesteek hebben.
siong sit, zich ziek eten.
kóng oē k'ì siong tioh ih, in zijn gesprek, iemand kwetsen, beleedigen.
kièn kíng siong tsing, door het gezicht van iets getroffen worden.
siong sim, bedroefd.
siong pi / *ai siong*, inwendig getroffen, bedroefd.

商 Siong — *Siong* (*siang*), beraadslagen, raadplegen; handeldrijven, handelaar.
siong liòng (» *liàng*), beraadslagen
siong gī, raadplegen, bespreken.
siong tsùn, kustjonk, koopvaardijjonk.
k'eh siong, reizende koopman.
kao siong, handeldrijven.
siong tiào de *Siong* dynastie, 1766—1122 j. v. Chr.

相 Siong — *Siong* (*siang*), wederkeerig; elkander.
siong hó, goede vrienden zijn.
siong sik, elkander goed kennen.
siong ts'ú, zamenwonen, met elkander omgaan.
siong t'aī, met elkander omgaan.
bô siong kan, dat doet er niets toe, onbeduidend.

想 Sióng — *Siet sióng* (» *siáng*), bedenkingen inbrengen tegen.
sióng liōng, denken, het er voor houden.
sióng ki li, de omstandigheden, toestand in aanmerking nemende.
sióng tú liòng, tegen elkander weggaan (als wederkeerige schuld).

賞 Sióng — *Tsit tsi̱ á sióng goah*, geef mij een centje.
sióng hoát, belooning en straf (van den hemel, van een vorst enz).

上 Sióng — *Sióng si̤*, de opgaande, de 2° toon.

相 Siòng — *Pì siòng*, van handelwijzen veranderen.
siòng (*siòng*), kijken op, zien naar.
tuì siòng, elkander aankijken.
tsaí siòng (» *siàng*), eerste minister.
siòng miā (*siàng* »), waarzeggen (uit de gelaatstrekken).
tsiēn siòng, laag uiterlijk, karakter.
siòng sū (*siàng* »), gelaatskundige.
kim kim siòng (» *siàng*), onbewegelijk, onwrikbaar op iets kijken.
siòng k'ang siòng p'āng, naar eene goede kans voor iets (winst, twist enz.) uitzien.
p'ai siòng (» *siàng*), slecht, hebzuchtig van karakter.
siòng maō, uiterlijk, gelaat.

常 Siông — *Siông* (*siâng*), altijd, steeds, gewoon, gewoonlijk, ordinair.
siông siông, altijd, steeds.
siông si, steeds, gewoonlijk.
si siông, steeds.
tsiaò siông, als gewoonlijk.
hui siông, buitengewoon, zeldzaam.
ping siông, gewoon, ordinair.
siông dzin, ordinair mensch.
sim siông, gewoonlijk.
hoân siông / *pièn siông*, van zijne vroegere (goede) geaardheid veranderen.
siông k'oā, te voren dikwijls gezien hebben.

嘗 Sióng *Sióng k'oŋ*, van iets proeven; te voren dikwijls gezien hebben.

詳 Sióng *Sióng* (*siâng*) }, zorgvuldig onderzoeken; een naauwkeurig rapport inzenden; bespreken.
sióng sè, naauwkeurig, zorgvuldig.
sióng sè sín ts'at, naauwkeurig onderzoeken.
sè sióng, naauwkeurig.
sióng bùn, uitvoerig rapport.
sióng kik, uitvoerig de redenen opgeven om iemand te doen afzetten.
ts'am sióng, bespreken.

祥 Sióng *Sióng* (*siâng*) }, geluk, gelukkig.
sióng suī, gelukkig teeken.
put sióng, ongelukkig.

松 Sióng *Sióng*, Pijnboom.
sióng ka, hars.

潃 Sióng *Ts'uì k'i sióng*, tandenvuil.
laô sióng, naam van een beruchten vuilik; onverschillig, vuil op zijne kleeding zijn.

裳 Sióng *Sióng* (*o*) }, een onderkleed.
moâ sióng, hennepenkleed (bij zwaren rouw).

上 Siōng Hoog.
siōng k'òng, op eene hoogere authoriteit appelleren.
siōng hó, opperbest.
tíng siōng hó, opperbest.
siōng dzin, superieuren.
siōng hai, Shanghai.
Siōng tē, God.
siōng tsìn, hooger van rang worden.
sū siōng tsiep hā (» *siāng* » *hē*) }, hoogeren dienen en lageren ontvangen.
siōng kuì, uiterst duur.
siōng tiong hā, bovenst, middel en laag (van graad, kwaliteit).
put siōng put hā, niet te hoog noch te laag, middelmatig (van prijs, gestalte enz).

象 Siōng *Hing siōng*, voorkomen (van persoon), beeldtenis.
nó siōng (» *ts'iāng*) }, afbeeldsel van, afgodsbeeld.

尚 Siōng *Siōng* (*siāng*) }, toch noch, nog steeds.
siōng ts'iā (*siāng* ») }, maar toch.
siōng iáo, toch nog.
siōng kú, toch nog (niettegenstaande) toch nog.

誦 Siōng *Siōng king*, zijne gebeden lezen (van een Boeddhistisch priester).

Sip

濕 Sip Indringen als fijne motregen, door vocht doortrokken worden, vochtig.
sip kaò ts'i ts'i ts'i, geheel en al doorbrengen van vocht.
sip sip á kaò, maar juist genoeg.
sip k'ì, vochtig.
sip lūn, vochtig.
sò sip, half droog en nat, vochtig.
sip toē (» *tē*) }, vochtige grond.
ts'i sip / *tâm sip* }, vochtig.
sip ts'ù, lett. Het vochtige huis, *i. e.* lijkenhuis.
sip noā, vochtig en zacht.
sip bī, vochtige lucht (begin van bederf).
sip t'aò, door vocht doortrokken.
ts'iū sip, vochtig worden, beslaan.

習 Sìp *Hák sip*, aanleeren.
un sip, repeteeren, overleeren.
kaò sip, onderwijzen, leeren.
ok sip, (van elkander) slechte manieren leeren.

sip koǒn sing tsū dziên, gewoonte een tweede natuur.

十 Sìp — *Sìp gē kiú put sing*, van alles wat, maar niets grondig kennen.
sip ok, de 10 hoofdmisdaden.
sip hong ê sò tsaī, plaats waar menschen van alle streken komen.

拾 Sìp — *Sin sìp*, bij elkander doen, pakken, opbergen.
k'ioh sip, bij elkander garen, oprapen.

襲 Sìp — *Sè sip*, door erfenis aan een ambt komen, erfambt.

Sit

失 Sit — Verliezen, kwijtraken; verzuimen, te kort komen in; zich vergissen, eene fout, verkeerdheid, vergissing begaan.
sit lóh, verliezen.
sit sū, verlies.
sit toa, lijst van verloren goederen.
sit iok, eene overeenkomst verbreken.
sit sik, bleek worden.
sit t'aô tuì, haar echtsgezel verliezen (van een weduwe).
sit sim, krankzinnig.
sit k'ì, flaauw vallen, schijndood zijn.
sit sin, mismoedig, neerslachtig.
sit bōng, zijne hoop opgeven.
sit tá, zijn moed verliezen.
sit hé, vuur laten vallen, door onvoorzichtigheid brandstichten.
sit tsì, mismoedigd.
sit lō, de moed verliezen, verdwalen.
sa sit lō, elkander misloopen.
sit bin, niet kunnen slapen.
sit si, uit den smaak, mode zijn.
sit ts'ò, zich vergissen.
sit gō, zich vergissen, bij vergissing.
sit tsui, gebrek aan water hebben.
pò sit tsui, aangifte van een averij doen.
sit lé, in beleefdheid te kort komen, onbeleefd; ik ben onbeleefd jegens u (bel. tern).
sit lé lâng, iemand onbeleefd behandelen.
sit ts'iá, bij ongeluk.
sit k'a lóh ts'iá, door onhandigheid in iets te kort komen (in beleefdheid enz.)
sit ts'uì, *sit giên*, zich verpraten, zeggen wat men niet zeggen moest.
kè sit, overtreding, verkeerdheid, fout.
sit pit, vergeten, overgeslagen hebben te schrijven.
sit tsin, van het oorspronkelijk ware afwijkend.
sit ts'at, verzuimen te onderzoeken.
sit soàn, verzuimen aan iets te denken.
sit k'oà, verzuimen, vergeten te kijken naar.

蝕 Sit — Eten, opeten.
sit dsit, lett. opeten van de zon (door den draak) de zonsverduistering.
sit géh, maansverduistering.

息 Sit — *Sit t'aô-tsió*, niet veel werk aan den hand hebben.
tsoh sit ê lâng / (*tsò* » »), landbewoners.
siao sit, bericht omtrent 2e; oorpeutertje.

熄 Sit — Uitdooven, uitgedoofd, uitgaan.

式 Sit — Vorm, manier, wijze.
k'oán sit, vorm, manier, uiterlijk, wijze.
háp sit, betamelijk, gepast.
k'iaó sit, fraai schrander van uiterlijk.
kàn toā sit ê lâng, iemand die voor groote zaken geschikt is.
m̄ sī sit, het is onveilig, niet raadzaam gevaarlijk.

實 Sít — Solide, degelijk, vast, stevig in elkander, kompakt, hard; waar, wezenlijk, inderdaad, het ware, de waarheid, waar, effectief, zuiver, netto vast, vastgesteld, bepaald; eerlijk oprecht.

厦荷大辭典

kiet sit, stevig instampen.
t'iëp sit, kompakt op elkander gestapeld, gepakt; eenvoudig, onopgewerkt.
sit pī, degelijke ziekte (niet door zwakte veroorzaakt).
sit sit, wezenlijk, in waarheid.
sit sit, de wezenlijkheid niet bezitten.
sing sit, wezenlijk, waar; oprecht.
sit sū, ware gebeurtenis.
tsiaò sit, *kù sit*, naar waarheid.
sit tsaī, *sit sit tsaī tsaī*, wezenlijk, voorzeker.
lip sit / *k'ak sit* }, inderdaad, wezenlijk.
sit sìn, wezenlijk, waar.
k'aò sit, *tù sit*, netto bedrag met alle onkosten er af.
sit giáh, netto hoeveelheid, bedrag.
sit sin, zuiver, netto ontvangen.
tù ts'o̤ pak sit, na afrekening van alle bijkomende zaken.
sit kè, vaste, ware prijs.
sit huì, vaste uitgaven.
sit sim, oprecht.
sit ì, *sit tsing*, oprechte meening, bedoeling.
laó sit, oprecht, eerlijk.

翅 Sit
Vleugel, vlerk, vin van een visch.
p'ah sit, klapwieken.
t'ién sit, *t'ı sit*, de vleugels uitspannen.
high sit, eensklaps schrikken.
sit ko̤-ta lī, *sit ko̤ bé-ta*, de vlerken zijn reeds droog, (de vogel kan alleen uitvliegen) *d. i.* op zijne eigene wieken kunnen drijven.
si̤ k'a si̤ sit, er pooten en vleugels *d. i.* veel leugens bijmaken.
hi sit, vinnen (van een visch).

食 Sit
Eten; voedsel, levensmiddelen.
sit bút, voedsel in het algemeen.
hé sit, levensmiddelen.
siong sit, zich ziek eten.
keh sit / (*kik* ») }, het gegetene uitbraken.
dzit sit, dagelijksch voedsel.

Sít
Ui sit, voorteeken van geluk.

[口+息] Sít
Sit lát, Singapore.

Siu

收 Siu
Ontvangen, opzamelen, bijeenbrengen, ophalen, inhalen, binnenhalen als oogst; oogsten, bergen, opbergen, verbergen; inkorten, intrekken, zich terugtrekken, gaan schuilen (als in een haven), eene zaak afdoen, voleindigen.
siu sip, opzamelen, verzamelen.
siu siào, schulden ophalen.
siū to̤g, kwitantie.
siu tē tso̤, belasting op landerijen innen.
siu liû, opnemen, bij zich houden (uit medelijden).
siu k'ìng, wegbergen.
siu ki kiáh ko̤, niets meer van iets laten hooren.
siu liêm, (een lijk) kisten.
siu tai, ter aarde bestellen.
siu ping, zijne soldaten bijeen brengen.
siu kìm, vatten en gevangen zetten.
siu ko̤, in de gevangenis opsluiten.
siu tiàm, uitgestalde waren binnenhalen.
siu toh, de tafel afnemen.
siu tang, de winteroogst inhalen.
sit siu, onvoordeelige oogst.
siu pi̤g, de oude oogst voor de nieuwe ontruimen.
ts'ut siu, buitengewoon goede oogst.
siu tsaī, lading voor een schip bij elkander brengen, opleggen, (voor een bepaalde plaats).
siu p'ák oogsten en te droogen leggen (van granen).
siu tso̤ tsiáh so̤g, van de opbrengst zijner huizen en landerijen leven.
bōe ōe siu so̤g, lett. een berg kan men niet opbergen *d. i.* aan die zaak is geen eind te maken.

68

siu liêm, zijne uitgaven verminderen.
siu sok, verminderen, inkrimpen (van uitgaven enz.)
siu dzip káng, *siu og*, in een haven, schuilhaven binnenloopen.
siu sū, eene zaak afmaken.
siu kang, werk eindigen.
siu tiâ, eene zaak afdoen; de menigte doen uiteengaan.
siu kiók, een eind aan iets maken.
siu soah, voleindigen.
siu i, het nog onafgedane afmaken.
siu k'a, zich aan iets onttrekken; het onderste, minst in het oog loopende van een voorwerp afmaken.

修 Siu Verfraaien, in orde brengen, repareeren; regelen, verbeteren.
siu tsing, verfraaien, repareren.
siu lí, repareeren, opredderen.
siu kiô, een brug repareren.
toā siu, *sió siu*, groote en kleine reparatie.
siu tsin, Taoistische priester worden.
siu hīng, zijne handelingen regelen; zedelijk, zedig.
siu siēn, ten goede verbeteren.
laō put siu, oud en nog zoo slecht.
siu sìng, van levenswandel verbeteren.
sok siu, salaris van meesters.
sin tsíng kah, nagels knippen, afsnijden.
siu k'a lan, eksteroogen afsnijden.
siu tsʻuì tsʻiu, de kantharen van een baard wegscheren.
siu bīn ming, de haren op het gelaat afscheren.

相 Siu *Siu si pī* / (*siŋ si pē̤*) }, liefdesmart.

守 Siú Bewaken, zich houden aan.
siú hoat, zich aan de wet houden.
siú kí, zijn plicht betrachten.
siú sîâ, eene stad bewaken.
siú hūn, zijn plicht betrachten.
siú pī, majoor.
siú kui tō kú, zich aan de gewone gebruiken houden.
tsoè lâng siú siú, omzichtig, sekuur.
pé siú / *tìn siú* }, bewaken (als grensplaatsen).
sit siú, verzuimen te bewaken, niet kunnen houden (als eene vesting).
siú tsiet, de weduwe staat bewaren.

首 Siú *Ui siú é lâng*, de hoofdaanlegger.
siú kip, het hoofd van een gesneuvelde.
ù siú ù bí, schroomvallig, niet ferm handelen.
sīú sīk, hoofdsieraden.
tsē siú uī, op de eerste plaats zitten (*b. v.* aan tafel.)
tsē siú sìk, aan de hoofdtafel zitten.

手 Siú *Siú tsiok*, als handen en voeten (van oudere en jongere broeders gezegd.)
tsʻìng siú, kanonniers.
pʻao sīú, dito.
tsuí siú, matroos.
hō siú, bazuinblazers.
koè tsú siú, de beul.
to pó̤ siú, de beulen die bij het gevolg van een mandarijn behooren.

繡 Siù *Siù hoe* / (» *hoa*) }, borduren, geborduurd, borduurwerk.
tsʻiah siù, borduren.
siù soâ, borduurzijde.
siù kui, borduurraam.
siù kim soâ, met gouddraad borduren.
ûn á teh siù, langzaam in handelinge zijn.
siù pi, geborduurde rand (aan een kleed
siù kûn, een rok borduren.

秀 Siù *Siù tsai*, laagste litter, graad.
iù siù, fijn, fatsoenlijk.
tsʻing siù, do.
siù, fijn, smaakvol.
siù tik á, fijne bamboezen roede.
siù siù, slap (als eene lange dunne tak).

獸 Siù — *Siù*, viervoetig dier.
k'îm siù, vogels en viervoetige dieren.
iá siù, wilde beesten.

守 Siù — *Sûn siù*, eene inspectiereis door het rijk doen.

首 Siù — *Ts'ut siù*, iets komen aangeven (een oproer enz.)

鞘 Siù — *To ts'ut siù*, het zwaard uit de schede trekken.

泅 Siû — *Siû*, zwemmen.
tiêm t'aò siû, onderwater zwemmen.
bók bók siû, met het water aan de lippen, water inkrijgen bij het zwemmen, 2e in moeielijke omstandigheden zijn.
k'iā siû, staande zwemmen.
t'aò hō-siû laèh, door den regen heen waden, komen.

囚 Siû — *Ka siû*, gevangenen, 2e veelvraat.
siû ts'ia, houten kooi (waar gevangen in vervoerd worden).

讎 Siû — *Pò siû*, wraak nemen.
oan siû, vijandschap.
siû dzin, iemand met wien men in vijandschap is.
kiêt siû, onverbiddelijke vijandschap aanknoopen.

受 Siū — Ontvangen, krijgen; lijden, te verdragen hebben, aanduider van den lijdenden vorm.
siū un, weldaden ontvangen.
siū tsing, wilwillendheid ondervinden.
siū ìm kiá, een kind dat steeds ontzien is.
siū iū, zich laten omkoopen.
siū dziók, verdrukt worden.
sing siū (*sin* ») }, ontvangen, opnemen (een pers).
dzím siū, bij zich houden.
siū k'ui, bij iets lijden, schade lijden.

壽 Siū — Ouderdom, leeftijd, levensjaren, lang leven; verjaardag.
hè siū, ouderdom, leeftijd.
siū goân, levensjaren.
bān siū, *sìng siū*, 's Keizers verjaardag.
ts'ik hè siū, zijne jaren verkorten (door slechte handelingen).
paì siū, *hō siū*, iemand op zijn verjaardag gelukwenschen.
iaó siū, kort leven, vroegstondig sterven.
siū so-kai tsiong, zijn levensbaan afgelegd hebben.
taī siū, groot portret (van oudere menschen).
siū pán, doodkist die men nog bij zijn leven laat maken.
siū hik, plaats voor een graf (nog bij zijn leven uitgekozen).

巢 Siû — Vogelnest, nest; schuilhoek, roofnest.
tsiaó siū, vogelnest.
p'ang siū, bijennest.
tsoh siū, een nest bouwen.
tsit siū kqe, een stel kippen.
p'ah p'oà siū, het nest is gebroken, die familie is uit elkander.
kui siū, naar zijn nest teruggaan; het geheele nest.
lóh siū, in zijn nest zijn, geïnstalleerd zijn (op een nieuwe plaats).
ts'át siū, roofnest.

愁 Siū — Toorn.
siū k'ì, toorn, vertoornd.
k'oài siū k'ì, gaauw vertoornd.

袖 Siū — *Ts'iú siū*, polsmofje.
ts'iú-t'ong siū, de handen in de mouw steken.

Siū — *Siū* (*siù*) }, schede van een zwaard.
kiàm siū, schede van een zwaard.
to siū, schede van een mes.
gûn siū, geldkistjes bestaande uit twee uitgeholde stukken hout met ijzeren banden aan elkander bevestigd (voor het transporteeren der belasting).

授 Siū Geven.
su siong siū siū (» *siang* » ») }, heimelijk (gestolen) goed voor aan elkander bewaren of aan elkander geven.

鑲 Siŋ *Siŋ* (*siŋ*) }, inleggen, beleggen.
siŋ ting kin (» » *kan*) }, aan de borst overslag van het kleed met band afgezet.
siŋ kim, met goud inleggen.

箱 Siŋ *P'ė siŋ* (*p'oė* ») }, leêrenkoffer.
siŋ, kist, koffer.
(*siŋ*) *i siŋ*, kleêrenkoffers, reiskoffers.
siŋ láng, kisten en koffers, bagage.
tsim t'aô siŋ, kistje door reizigers als hoofdkussen gebruikt.

過 Siŋ *Siŋ hó* (*siŋ* ») }, zeer goed, al te goed.
siŋ ts'ut lát, zich overspannen.

傷 Siŋ *Siŋ*, belagchelijk maken.
Hì siŋ (» *siŋ*) }, verslaafd aan comediespel.
siŋ si pī (*siŋ* ») }, liefdeziekte, verliefdheid.

賞 Siŋ́ *Siŋ́ sù* (*siŋ́* ») }, belooven, schenken aan.
siŋ́ (*siŋ́*) }, kijken naar, bekijken van maan en bloemen gezegd).
siŋ́ hoe, bloemen bekijken.
siŋ́ hong, een fooi geven (aan bedienden).
siŋ́ lién, de gunst bewijzen (beleefdelijk) de schande van iets besparen).
niá siŋ́, eene belooning gaan ontvangen.
iû siŋ́, rondwandelen en rondkijken.
siŋ́ tín tai, iemand een mandarijngraad schenken.
siā siŋ́, voor eene belooning dank zeggen.
ts'ut siŋ́ keh (» » *keh*) }, prijs zetten op het terug vinden van een persoon of voorwerp.
ts'iŋ siŋ́, om de uitgeschreven belooning vragen.
siŋ́ tsi, met geld beloonen.
ts'ut siŋ́ t'iep, eene belooning voor iets uitlooven, uitschrijven.
bô niŋ́ siŋ́, niet zeer veel, in kleine hoeveelheid.

想 Siŋ́ *Su siŋ́*, steeds aan iemand denken.
liaō siŋ́, het er voor houden, van meening zijn.

相 Siŋ̀ *Siŋ̀ kang* (*siŋ̀ kang*) }, beleefde term tegen geleerde of fatsoenlijke menschen.
p'ai k'oŋ siŋ̀, leelijk van uiterlijk, een mal figuur slaan.
si siŋ̀ (*se* ») }, gedeelte van den cyclus waarin men geboren is.
m̄ t'ang hō kāo siŋ̀ hó k'ih, pas op dat de honden het niet opeten.
bô laō siŋ̀, niet lang kunnen duren (als onsterke dingen, zwakke menschen.)
iŋ siŋ̀ (*iŋ* ») }, voorkomen, vorm.
tsáp dzī si siŋ̀ (*se* ») }, de twaalf dierenwanden cyclus *d. i.* muis, koe, tijger, haas, draak, slang, paard, schaap, aap, kip, hond, zwijn.

常 Siŋ̂ *Pi siŋ̂* (*ping siâng*) }, algemeen, gewoon, alledaagsch.

漦 Siŋ̂ *Siŋ̂* (*siŋ̂*) }, kleverig, vuil, smerig 2e slijm van visch.
iŋ iŋ siŋ̂ siŋ̂ (*iŋ*) }, dom, stomp, dralend, langzaam.
t'ai ko siŋ̂, lepra etter.
moŋ siŋ̂ (» *se*) }, slijm van de aal.
noŋ noŋ siŋ̂ siŋ̂ (*siŋ̂*) }, slijmerig, nat.
ko ioh siŋ̂, slijmerig vuil dat een pleister achterlaat.

想 Siu̥ — ***Siū̥***, denken, bedenken.
tsīng tsīng siū̥, rustig overdenken.
siū̥ lat siū̥ k'ì, overdenken.
siū̥ beh tsò, van plan zijn om te doen.
siū̥ bô kaò, onverwacht, buiten berekening.
siū̥ k'ì lai, herdenken, in de gedachten terugroepen.
siū̥ boē ts'ut, niet op iets kunnen komen.
aē siū̥ tit kaò, begrijpelijk: niet boven's menschen verstand.
siū̥ ts'ut, iets in de gedachten krijgen op iets komen.
siū̥ īm ts'ut, niet op iets kunnen komen.
siū̥ sīm siū̥ kog, steeds plannen beramen.
ū siaò siū̥, aan iets denken met verlangen het te hebben.
siū̥ hīng, niets meer doen dan men volgens de letter doen moet.
bô liēm si siū̥, niet op het oogenblik op de gedachten van iets komen.
siū̥ k'ang, over een goede kans voor iets denken.
ts'im siū̥, diep denken, doordenken.
siū̥ kè, een plan beramen.
siū̥ lō̥, over eene goede manier voor iets, denken.
siu̥ t'ang siū̥ sai, naar alle richtingen denken.
īm bat siū̥, heen begrip, inzicht hebben.

尙 Siū̥ — ***Hé siū̥***, Boeddhistische priester.
siū̥ su, president van een ministerieel departement.

鯗 Siū̥ — ***Ts'aò kiēm siū̥***, stinkende gezouten visch lucht.

授 Siū̥ — ***Siū̥ ts'eh***, een les opgeven.

So

搔 So — Wrijven, inwrijven, jeuken, krabbelen, strijken over; rollen, draaien.
so ts'iú, in de handen wrijven, met leége handen.
so bák tsiu, de oogen wrijven.
so iù, met olie inwrijven.
so i̥-tī̥ pi̥, rondwrijven en plat drukken *d. i.* naar goedvinden met iets kunnen handelen.
so k'a so ts'iú, de voeten en handen wrijven, streelen (als eene moeder haar kind).
so o̥ bīn, zijn gelaat zwart wrijven; iemand niet meer willen kennen.
so soh á, tot een touw-koord rollen.
siang so ê sò̥, dubbel gedraaid getwijnd garen.
t'ao so lâng ê mi̥h, iemands goed heimelijk wegstrijken, wegnemen.

慅 So — ***Lô so***, lastig, verward.

唆 So — Oorspr. het gesnap van kinderen; aanzetten, aanhitsen.
so lōng, aanhitsen, opruien.
kiao so, tweedracht zaaien, tegen elkander opruien.
so loáh, liefkozen.
po so, prijzen.

梭 So — Spoel, weversspoel, schietspoel.
ts'iah so, spoel, navette, om te knoopen.
būng so, do. om netten te knoopen.

蘇 So — ***So bák***, sapanhout.
so bák ko, sapanhout gekookte verw.

騷 So — ***Hong so***, als het geluid van de wind, van pierewaaien, uitgaan, houden.

鎖 Só — ***Só***, een chin. slot dichtdoen.
só tiaò, vastsmeden.
só si, sleutel.
tsit p'ì̥ só, een slot (deurslot).
só pat, plaatje (gew. van zilver) door kinderen op de borst gedragen.
t'ih só, ijzeren slot.
só ts'i, de veer in een chin. slot.
só liēn, aan een ketting leggen (als schuldigen).

koñ t'ih só, een ijzeren ketting dragen (als misdadigers).
lòh só, op slot doen
só ming (» *mui*), een deur op slot doen.

嫂 Só
Hiə só, vrouw van zijn ouderen broeder.
só, eerenaam aan getrouwde vrouwen gegeven.

Só *Só tsuì ė taī tsì*, eene zaak waarover veel woorden moeten gewisseld worden voor dat die in orde is.

Sò Inzuigen, intrekken (als water in hout).
tė sò, theedoekje van katoen of zijde of spons, tusschen het kopje en het schoteltje gelegd.
tsuì ta sò, zeer dorstig.
sing k'u ko sò, droog van huid, koortsig.
àn sò, droog, gebrek aan geld.
sán ts'àn kaō sò tsui, een schraal rijstveld trekt veel water aan.

Sò Driftig, opvliegen, onbesuisd.
sò kip, driftig, ongeduldig.
sò sut, onbesuisd, onvoorzichtig.
sò pō, koppig en stijfhoofdig en driftig van aard.

掃 Sò
Tsè sò, de graven vegen en reinigen en er offeranden opbrengen.
pùn sò, vuil, mest, opveegsel.
sò àm, een kolk (overdekte).
sò tsi, een vuilnisput.
pė pùn sò, het vuil aanvegen.

緩 Sò
Sò, kruipen (als insekten).
sò sò sò, langzaam, slepend (in handelingen).
tíng lò sò, zeer lang.
sò, heen en weergaan, rondtrekken.
sò lai sò k'ì, do.
sò tsáo, wegkruipen (als een paling enz.)

唆 Sō
Sō, aanhitsen (als honden of pers.)
saí sō, aanhitsen, tegen elkander opstooten.
sō lai sō k'ì, beide partijen aanhitsen.
t'in i sō, naar iemands aanhitsen luisteren, er gehoor aangeven.

Sō *ing sō*, deining.

Sō *o pa lī sō*, zeer zwart.

搜 So
Visiteeren, huiszoeking houden, doorzoeken.
sō ka, huiszoeking houden, een huis plunderen.
so so, *so lo*, doorzoeken.
so kiėm, (een schip bij zijne aankomst) visiteeren.

蘇 So
Familienaam; naam van de hoofdstad van Kangsai; fraai, net.
so tsiu, Soochow, het Parijs van China.
so k'oán, *so k'ì*, fraai, eenvoudig.

酥 So
Droog, kruimelig van brood of koek; schraal van de lippen.
so so, schraal van de lippen.
ts'uì k'aó so, naam van koekjes die onmiddelijk in de mond smelten.
so so á dziét, gloeien (als bij koorts enz.

疎 So
Ts'in so, na, en ver verwant.
So io, stijve, kromme rug.

所 Só
Plaats, oord; dat wat; het middel waardoor.
só tsaī, plaats.
dzīm só, plaats waar men aangesteld is.
kong só, publieke vergaderplaats.
king i só, vertrek waarin een rouwdragers bezoekers ontvangt.
só i, daardoor, het middel om.
só i dzién, de oorzaak waarom iets zoo is.
só huì, uitgaven, onkosten.
só ū ė mih, de voorhanden zijnde dingen, de voorwerpen die men heeft.
bù só put tsì, tot alles in staat zijn.
só ts'ut put dzû só tsū, op de plaats waar iets van daan komt is het niet zoo goed of goedkoop als waar het heen gevoerd wordt.

li sǫ́ kóng, dat wat gij zegt.
k'it i sǫ́ haī, door iemand benadeeld, in het verderf gestort worden.
bò hō̤ lé sǫ̀-sǫ́ k'u, zich niet door beleefdheids vormen laten binden zich er niet streng aanhouden.

素 Sǫ̀ — *Sǫ̀*, eenvoudig, onopgesierd.
ptng sǫ̀, tot nog toe, te voren.
p'ak sǫ̀ } (*p'ak*) }, eenvoudig.
sǫ̀ i, civiele kleeding.
sǫ̀ si, te voren.
sǫ̀ sióng, te voren.
sǫ̀ tsu, koralen rozenkrans door Boeddh. pr. gedragen.

訴 Sǫ̀ — *Sǫ̀ oan*, verdedigen (in een gerechtshof.)
sǫ̀ tsīng, eene aanklachte weerleggen, zich voor eene aanklachte verontschuldigen.
sio sǫ̀ tiëp, het verzoekschrift dat men aan een afgod geeft verbranden.
hun sǫ̀, zich verdedigen, zijne onschuld betoogen.
ts'ut sǫ̀, do.

Sǫ̀ — *Put kè ki sǫ̀*, ontelbaar.
t'ien sǫ̀, vastgesteld raadsbesluit des hemels.
sǫ̀ tiā, do.
bû sǫ̀, ontelbaar.

Soa

沙 Soa — *Soa*, zand.
soa soā, zandbank.
soa pǫ, zandvlakte.
soa p'o, zandig strand.
soa hìng, zandveld.
kim soa, stofgoud.
soa tāng, ballast.
k'oe soa } (*k'e* ») }, rivierzand.
soa laō, filtreer toestel.
kaǫ soa tiém, vol zand stipjes (als aardewerk dat niet zuiver gebakken is).
p'ah ka soa, op den grond, in het zand vallen.
ki̤ soa, bezinksel van potasch.
soa t'ing, ruwe bruine suiker.
ts'iah soa, bruine suiker.
soa lik pǫ̀, onder zand gedroogde groene stof.
lâm soa, met zand overdekken (als een lijk tegen verrotting).
toâ soa, het zand uit iets schudden, ziften.
soa bák, gaatjes die bij het bakken van aardewerk er in komen.
soa soa, zanderig, ruw, niet glad (als aardewerk.)
tsi̤ soa kui, de krop met zand volstoppen (als kippen om ze zwaarder te maken).
haí soa p'o, groot zandig zeestrand.

鯊 Soa — *Soa hi*, haai.
soa sìt } (*hi ts'ì*) }, haaienvinnen.
soa tō̤, haaienbuik van iemand die alles onverschillig goed of slecht eet of koopt.
gōng á soa, domme haai *d. i.* domme kerel.

痧 Soa — *Tióh soa*, snijdingen in de buik, koliek.
tióh ǫ soa, een koliek krijgen.
é kaó soa } (*ę* » ») }, eene beroerte.
liáh soa, iemand die eene beroerte heeft wrijven en knijpen.
giah soa, iemand die eene beroerte heeft aderlaten (met een speld).
kuih soa, iemand die koliek heeft met scherven enz. schrappen.
p'uh soa ióh, iemand die eene beroerte heeft medic. in de neus blazen.

徙 Soá — *Soá k'ui*, uit den weg nemen, wegschuiven.
oe soá, door dringen voortschuiven *d. i.* eene zaak langzaam, bij horten en stooten doen.

bò soá pō̤, geen voet verroeren, verzetten.
soá uī, van plaats veranderen, naar eene andere plaats gaan.
oa̤ soá, do. verhuizen.
ts'ien soá, verplaatsen, verhuizen.
tsit dzit soá tsai sa̤ dzit k'iā ing, verplaatst men (planten) den eenen dag dan verdorren zij den derden *d. i.* door verhuizen verliest men de nering voor een tijd.
tseng-soá tsióh, van bakpannen op rotssteen komen *d. i.* van kwaad tot erger.
soá k'ah dzip, meer naar binnen verplaatsen.
pa̤ soá, verhuizen, verplaatsen.
kia̤ soá, rondtrekken.
soá pō̤, *soá k'a*, de voeten verzetten.
i soá, verhuizen.
soa tè, do. van plaats veranderen.
tsit dzit soá kè tsit dzit, van den eenen dag op den anderen schuiven.

砂 Soá — *Soá*, vermolmde, verweerde vergane rotssteenen.
t'ō̤ soá, verweerde rotssteen met aarde.
tsioh soá, verweerde rotssteen.

續 Soà — Soà *i īng*, iemand steeds in zijne behoeften voorzien (door geld te geven als hij het noodig heeft).
lièn soà, aan elkander (gevoegd).
sa̤ soà (*sio* ») }, aan elkander binden, achtereenvolgens.
soà, *sūn soà*, van die gelegenheid gebruik maken aan ...., met een.....
soà tsoè (» *tsò*) }, daarna, in ééne moeite door doen maken.
soà kang, in ééne moeite van het werk, tot voortzetting van het werk.
soà ts'iú, in dezelfde moeite door.
soà lai, in eene moeite komen.
soà tsáng, eene valsche staart aanvoegen.
boē oē sa̤ tsiep soà, niet geregeld na elkander, niet in geregelde opvolging.
sa̤ lièn sa̤ soà, achtereenvolgens.

Soā — *Soā*, ruischen, ritselen.
si si soā soā, ritselen (als vallende bladen).

Soā — *Sī soā tsoè* (*tsò*) }, snel, onafgebroken doen.

山 Soa̤ — *Soa̤*, berg, heuvel.
soa̤ kok, vallei.
soa̤ k'i (» *k'e̤*) }, ravijn.
soa̤ ki̤, afgrond.
soa̤ ting, vastewal.
tsiṳ̄ soa̤, een berg opgaan, aan wal gaan.
soa̤ tsiem, piek.
soa̤ ka tsoáh (*o*) }, iemand die voor anderen naar eene goede plaats voor een graf uitziet.
soa̤ kui, do.
ts'ut soa̤, begraven.
soa̤ ti, wild varken.
soa̤ t'ō̤, haas.
soa̤ niá, berghelling.
hé (*hoé*) *soa̤*, vuurspuwende berg.
soa̤ t'aò, bergtop.
soa̤ kaó, vos.
kim soa̤, Californie.
soa̤ k'a, voet van den berg.
soa̤ haō, onbeschaafd mensch die zelden in steden is geweest.
soa̤ hong, landwind.
sùn soa̤, de rondte op de bergen doen.
p'ak soa̤, een graf afmaken (3 dagen na de begrafenis).
soa̤ giêm, bergtempel.
soa̤ tōng, spelonk, grot.
k'ui soa̤, een berg ontginnen.
sin lóh soa̤, nieuwelings uit het binnenland gekomen.
soa̤ ien, de bergstof *d. i.* onbeleefdheid, ongemanierdheid.

soa̤ ts'át, landroovers.
soa̤ tsē, bergvesting.
dzip soa̤, op de bergen gaan.
soa̤ laī lâng, bergbewoner.
k'iā soa̤ t'aò, zich op de bergen ophouden (als dieven).
soa̤ bīn, voorste gedeelte van een berg.
soa̤ k'a ts'ɛng, *soa̤ poè* (*ts'ui̤*), achterste gedeelte van een berg.
toā soa̤ bú (» » *bó*), hoogste berg van een bergketen.
soa̤ lō̤, bergweg.
lóh soa̤ hong, wind die van een hoogen berg neërgeslagen wordt.
soa̤ k'im iá siù, wild (gevogelte enz.)
poà soa̤ koaī̤ (» *koān*), afgelegene distrikten.
soa̤ koaī̤ (» *koān*). binnenlandsche, in het gebergte liggende distrikten.
soa̤ siā̤, binnenlandsche stad.
soa̤ k'iah, vallei, diepte tusschen twee bergen.
soa̤ sin t'ó tī, berg, aardgod (voor onbewoonde plaatsen).
soa̤ lâng, bergbewoners, inlanders.
aō piah soa̤ t'ang k'ò, een berg in den rug om op te steunen *d. i.* eene steun in anderen hebben.

散 Soá̤ *Soá̤ soá̤* (*soá̤*), hier en daar (weinigen).
ioh soá (» *sán*), poeder van medicijnen.
pàng soá̤ iā, overal naar willekeur laten gaan, niet in toom houden.
tsoē-kaò ts'ut soá̤, zooveel dat het overal verstrooid ligt.
soá̤ kiep (*soá̤* »), op verschillende plaatsen plunderen.
soá̤ ts'át, uit elkander verspreidene gelegene dieven, hier en daar wat.

Soà̤ *Soá̤ pâng*, kraamkamer gedurende de eerste maand na de bevalling.

散 Soà̤ Verspreiden, verstrooien, uitdeelen, uitgeven; zich verspreiden, uiteen gaan, van elkander gaan, uiteen vallen.
sì soà̤, verspreiden, verstrooid.
iā soà̤, uitstrooien (als zaad).
soà̤ soà̤, *soà̤ noà̤*, overal verspreid.
p'ah soà̤, uit elkander gaan.
sì soà̤ t'âng (*t'âng-sìsoà̤*), als een uiteen gevallen emmer, eener familie waarvan de leden uit elkander zijn.
t'iah soà̤, uit elkander scheuren; uit elkander gaan.
lō ke soà̤ t'eh, verspreid onder den blooten hemel wonen.
soà̤ ts'ī, afloopen, eindigen van de markt.
soà̤ hé, een' compagnieschap opheffen.
hiṳ-soà̤, de processie is afgeloopen.
soà̤ tóng, het verbond is uiteen.
soà̤ koán, uiteen gaan van de leden eener leercursus.
soà̤ óh, de jaarlijksche cursus eindigen.
soà̤ kang tsi̤, werkloon uitdeelen.
soà̤ hiông, soldij uitdeelen.
soà̤ taó, de dingen eener (maat uiteen doen vallen *d. i.* uiteen gaan) van een compagnieschap of gezelschap.
kóng oē-soà̤ soà̤, in het algemeen, onbepaald spreken.

線 Soà̤ Draad, garen, koord.
si soà̤, zijden draad, zijde.
se soà̤ (*se̤* »), katoendraad.
siù soà̤, borduurgaren.
dziòng soà̤, floszijde.
kim soà̤, gouddraad.
t'ih soà̤, ijzerdraad.
ts'ing tsiem bān soà̤, met veel zorg, moeite genaaid.
kao tsiem tó soà̤, met veel inspanning doen.

tâng soậ, koperdraad.
tâng soậ p'oe, een draadbericht; een telegram.
soậ soh siong t'ong, heimelijk met elkander in verbindtenis staan.
boé soậ, verraderlijk (door omkooping) vatten enz.
soa soậ, zandbank.
kap soậ, garen aan elkander spinnen.
p'áng soậ, garen spinnen.
tsít in ê soậ, *soậ kiù*, *tsít kiù ê soậ*, een klos garen.
ts'ɛng soậ, een draad in (de naald) steken.
soậ hì, marionettenspel.
hong soậ p'ah tioh, door een dwarlwind, windhoos getröffen worden.
mī soậ, vermicellie.
hièn soậ, snaren.
kap i bô oh soậ (*o*) }, niet met iemand omgaan.

汕 Soậ *Soậ t'aò*, Swatow.

傘 Soậ Scherm, zonnescherm, parapluie.
hō soậ, parapluie.
niậ soậ, roode pajong voor hooge ambtenaren uitgedragen.

Soah

撒 Soah Indoen, tusschenvoegen, vermengen.
soah t'ing, suiker indoen.
soah p'ang, iets geurigs instrooien.
soah kièm, zout indoen.

息 Soah Ophouden, doen ophouden, een eind maken aan, eindigen, afdoen, afgedaan; rusten, roesten, uitrusten, zich nederzetten, nederzetten.
soah sū, eene zaak afdoen, eene twist vereffenen.
soah kang', het werk afbreken.
soah hì, de komedie is gedaan.
ah soah, doen ophouden, tegengaan.
soah kiók, eindigen, afgedaan.
hoah soah, roepen om twistenden te doen ophouden.
sí soah, onveranderlijk afgedaan.
hoậ soah, de macht inhouden hebben om iets te doen ophouden.
soah bé, einde, aan het einde, ten laatste.
bô soah bé, eindeloos.
tsiaó-soah tī hit ê uī, de vogel roest daar.
soah k'a, tijdelijk zijn, verblijven.
aō k'a-soah k'i tsaī, de achterste voet stevig neerzetten *d. i.* eene zaak gunstig voor de toekomst schikken.

殺 Soah Dooden, slachten.
soah sìh, dooden.
soah koe, een kip slachten.
soah huih, bloed vergieten *d. i.* slachten (als kippen).
ū soah tioh, berekend, afgemeten, volgens eene zekere regel (als een zet in het schaakspel, van handelingen enz.

煞 Soah Onheil, ramp; door een ramp treffen.
hong soah, windramp, ongunstige ligging door blootstelling aan de wind.
soah sin-tāng, zeer vele onheilen hebben
ts'il soah poeh paī, steeds ongelukkig zijn, ongeluksvogel.
sam soah, drie ongelukken die iemand dood kunnen veroorzaken.
sin soah, een onheil afweren.
boē t'aó soah, een onheil niet kunnen afwenden.
k'it soah sin soah tioh, door den geest van onheil getroffen worden.

Soáh *Bák tsít soàh*, in een oogenblik.
soàh tseh, in een oogenblik.
k'in á soàh tseh, in een oogenblik.
bák soàh, even indutten.

Soai

Soai̯ *Soai̯* ook *sòng* (*soai̯*), onbeschoft, dom.
tsiáh lāng sòng soai̯, van iemands domheid misbruik maken.

Soai̯ *Soai̯ á*, manga.
si̯ soai̯ á (*se̯*), een bubo krijgen.

Soaih

喧 Soaih *Soaih soaih kiò*, kraken.
si̯ si̯ soaih soaih, kraken (als een oude stoel).

Soan

Soan *Līng soan tòng*, moeder (bel. term).

酸 Soan *Hàn soan*, bedeesd, verlegen met zich zelven.
soan bō bò lièm k'ang, niet uit iemands spreken wijs kunnen worden.

宣 Soan *Soan tiaò*, ter audientie roepen (van den keizer).
t'ìng soan put t'ìng tiaò, wachten tot dat men verzocht wordt niet tot dat men ontboden wordt *d. i.* zich wel laten verzoeken maar niet laten bevelen.
soan lò̯, koperen reukpot.
soan kun, wortels uitschieten.
kun-soan put tsi tīng, de wortels strekken zich zeer ver uit.

諠 Soan *Soan nā̯* (» *nā̯*), leven maken.
soan hoa, do.

鑽 Soan *Soan lai soan k'ì*, woelen (als iemand die niet slapen kan).
ìng kún tsui-soan (*iōng*), met warm water doorgieten.
soan dzìp k'ì, doordringen (als kwik in zand).

soan to, met de hand aan het zwaard staan; met een zwaard in de zijde staan (als wanneer mandarijnen uitgaan).

樼 Soàn *Soán k'a*, de voet knellen (als een schoen of door een strafwerktuig.
soán ts'iú, de handen knellen (door een strafwerktuig).
soán tsí, kneller (waartusschen handen of voeten gezet worden).

選 Soàn *T'iao soán*, uit velen uitkiezen.
tik soán, boven anderen uitkiezen.
soán poát, den knapsten onder de knappen uitkiezen.
soán dzìp king, uitkiezen om in het paleis te zijn (als de keizer vrouwen tot zijne bijzitten).
soán kiá̯ sai, een behuwdzoon uitkiezen

Soàn *Tsì̯ soán*, langwerpige oliekoek.

蒜 Soán *Soàn t'aò*, knoflook.
soàn bān, de afdeelingen in knoflook.
soàn koai̯ (» *koá̯*), knoflook stengel.

算 Soán *Put tsiā̯* en *siōng soàn* (*o*) (*siāng*), niet kunnen gerekend worden als....
soàn hoat, rekenkunst.
ts'ien soàn bān soàn, herhaaldelijk, onophoudelijk over iets denken.
tá̯ soàn, denken, bedenken.
sit soàn, misrekenen, verkeerd denken.

旋 Soàn *Tsiu soán*, twee personen weer goede vrienden maken.
tsó soàn, links omdraaien.
p'oán soán, omgaan met, verkeeren met (gew. met lichte kooien).

璇 Soān *Soān tsióh*, diamant.
soān k'eh, diamant verkooper.
soān pit, diamantstift.
hé soān (*hoé* »), diamant.

Soān *Him soān*, prijzen, ophemelen met verlangen, hetzelfde geluk te hebben.

ts'ing soān, prijzen.

Soān *Gaó soān lâng*, *gaò lién soān*, iemand knap bedriegen om geld uit hem te krijgen, voorwendsel ophalen.

Soat

說 Soat *Siaó soat*, novellen, roman, vertelsels.

soat ts'iaò (» *ts'iaò*) }, uien, comieke dingen vertellen.

soat háp, iets door over en weer spreken tot stand brengen (als een huwelijk door de middelares).

sing soat, eene zaak schikken, afmaken.

Soat *Soat bùn*, zeep.

雪 Soat *Taī soat*, groote sneeuwtijd, de elfde maand.

siaó soat, 10de maand.

Soe

梳 Soe *Soe* (*se*) }, kam; kammen, het haar opmaken.

ts'â soe, houten kam.

taī pē soe, schildpadden kam.

soe t'aó, het haar kammen.

soe tseng, zijn toilet maken (van vrouwen).

p'oà ping soe, eene scheiding in het haar leggen.

soe boē tit, niet recht kunnen kammen *i. e.* niet uit een te warren (van eene zaak.)

衰 Soe *Soe* (*soe*) }, in achteruitgang zijn, wegkwijnen, in verval geraken; achteruitgang verval, ongeluk, ongelukkig.

soe lám, verzwakken, wegkwijnen.

soe dziók, in verval, zwak (als een rijk)

soe bi, in achteruitgang, ongelukkig (als eene familie).

soe t'è, in achteruitgang, in verval, verzwakt.

soe póh, een weinig, dun verspreid.

soe sap, armoedig, niet fraai.

kaí soe, iemand plagen door hem allerlei ongelukken voor te houden.

ko soe bò p'oā, alleen zonder gezelschap (wonen enz. gew. van vrouwen gezegd).

soə sin, geest van ongeluk, voorteeken van verval.

kaó-kā soe lâng, honden bijten de zwakste lieden *d. i.* zwakken durft een ieder aan.

ts'ik soe, ongelukkig voorteeken.

疏 Soe *Soe*, ver van verwantschap.

hun ts'in soe (*se*) }, onderscheid maken tusschen dichte- en verre verwanten.

蔬 Soe *Kim hi soe*, Chara vulgaris (aan goudvisschen gegeven).

pao soe, mossen die op een lijkkist of urn groeien.

洗 Soé *Soé* (*sé*) }, wasschen.

soé k'aó, den mond spoelen.

tè soé (*tē sien*) }, theedoekje (dat tusschen het kopje en schoteltje gelegd wordt).

soé sin, zich het ligchaam wasschen 2e. alle verantwoordelijkheid van zich afwasschen.

soé ts'iú bīn, handen en het gelaat wasschen.

tsâng soé (» *sé*) }, baden en wasschen.

soé oan, zich van eene valsche beschuldiging vrijspreken.

soé i ē t'é bīn, iemands fatsoen wegnemen.

bò soé bīn, beschaamd, met schaamte overladen.

k'oe soé (*k'e* ») }, bij kleine hoeveelheden van iets afnemen, afbrokkelen.

sap soé, kruimels, gruis, vuil.
soé tsīng, een huis van de besmetting zuiveren (na een sterfgeval enz.) ook eene verdenking van iemand afnemen.
soé hút, geld ophalen om een afgodsbeeld lett. te reinigen (voor onderhoud van tempel enz.)
soé bīn gaī tioh hī, bij het wasschen van het gelaat de ooren raken.
i. e. bij het bespotten van iemand ook de omstanders treffen.
tsiū tsoū soé sin, door een eed alle verdenking van zich afnemen.
hoè soé lâng é pīng tìng, overal eenmaal zien op te loopen.
soé k'a tsiū tsûn, zijne voeten wasschen en op een schuit gaan *i. e.* alle verdenking, verantwoordelijkheid van zich afnemen.
soé mìng hong, door een gastmaal enz. de verdenking die op een huis licht wegnemen.
soé tīng tsú tsiáh, wasschen (als borden, de vloer) en kooken; het werk van vrouwen.

黍 Soé — *Soé* (*sé*), gierst.
hoan soé, bezemkoren.
lō soé, do.

Soé — *Kong ōe soé lâng* (*ōū*), uit het spreken iemand belagchelijk maken.

Soé — *Sīng soé* (*suī* »), rhumatiek.

小 Soè — *Soè* (*sè*), klein.
soè hàn, klein van gestalte, dwergachtig.
soè i, bijzit.
soè kiá, klein kind.
oé soè (*é* »), klein, jong.
sī soè é lâng, lageren.
soè tsik, mans jongere broeder.
soé tsiáh, klein van eten.

細 Soè — *Soè dzī* (*sè* »), zorgvuldig, voorzichtig, zorgdragen 2e nederig.
soè tsoh, spion.
soè sia, zachtjes.
soè k'eh, spion, raadgever in een leger.
soè k'a, kleine (gebonden) voeten.
tsú soè (» *sè*), voorzichtig.
soè sim, do. omzichtig.

Soè — *Soè* (*o*), dreggen, visschen naar.

說 Soè — *Soè* (*soè*), aandringen op, uitlokken tot.
īng ōē kì soè ih (*ōū*) (*soè*), door woorden tot iets uitlokken.

歲 Soè — *Bān soè*, *bān soè iâ*, eerenaam aan den keizer gegeven.

Soeh

塞 Soeh — *Soeh*, inschuiven, instoppen, tusschen inzetten, invoegen (als een stuk hout in een reet).
soeh, toestoppen als een gordijn.
tsa bó soeh, iemand die altijd bij de vrouwen zit.
soeh hé íng (» *hoé íng*), van de duisternis gebruik maken om een huis in te sluipen.
soeh aū ts'ù, achter's hands heimelijk geven.
soeh toh k'a, iets onder den poot eener tafel schuiven om ze vast te doen staan.
soeh k'i tsaī, een voorwerp (als eene tafel) vastzetten.
soeh k'i, tusschen de kiezen blijven zitten.
soeh siap, heimelijk in de hand stoppen (om iemand tot iets over te koopen).

oéh oéh soeh soeh, naauw en smal.
koh soeh, gezwel in de armholte.
(*seh*) *soeh dzìp k'ì*, inschuiven, instoppen.

Soh

索 Soh — *Soh*, touw.
tah soh, koorddansen.
ti lak soh, varkenstouw (met lus).
tsūn soh á kǿ, omdraaien, omwringen (als ware het een touw).
p'ah soh, touw slaan.
liaò soh (*á*), wand en weeflijnen.
tiạ̀ soh, ankerkabel.
soh á t'ui, touwladder.
tsúi tò soh, peillijn.
poạ̀ bé soh (*poạ̀ bẹ́ soh*), lasso.
k'an mîng soh (*muị*), touw van een deurkatrol.
hē liù soh (*hẹ̄* »), een valstrik, lus leggen.
lóh soh, een touw onder iets laten zakken 2e touw dat men onder iets doet om het op te tillen.
ki soh, vlaggelijn.
soh lō̤, de touwen, de werking der touwen op een schip.
kaò-tīng liáo soh, de aap breekt zijn touw af (zoodat hij er niet tegen op naar boven kan klimmen) *i. e.* door eigen schuld iemands vertrouwen verliezen.

棟 Soh — *Soh tsiu̱ ts'iū* (*tsiō̤*), in een boom klimmen.
soh ân ân, vastaanhalen; sterk op iets aandringen.
gın á-put tsı gaò soh lâng, kinderen klouteren iemand zeer op het lijf.
ts'iú ı̂ng-soh soh soh, zeer strak gespannen van mouwen.

鐲 Sóh — *Sóh*, armband (van oude vrouwen).
ts'iú sóh, do.
p'ûng sóh, een armband aanbieden (door de moeder van den bruidegom aan de bruid gedaan).
koà sóh, een armband aandoen.

Sóh — *Sóh*, rondtrekken, alom gaan.
sì koè sóh (*kè*), rondreizen, rondtrekken.

Sóh — *Ts'un tsıt tiaô sóh koh*, (oorspr. soh) er blijft niets (lett. dan het touw) over (als na het opmaken van balans).

Sok

束 Sok — *Sok*, binden, tot een bundel maken, aanhalen; beteugelen, bedwingen; bundel bosje.
sok ts'iú, de handen gebonden hebben niets kunnen doen.
sok k'a sok ts'iú, aan handen en voeten gebonden zijn.
sok pók, in elkander gedrongen, gebonden, niet vrij in zijne handelingen.
iok sok, beteugelen (menschen).
k'u sok, bedwingen.
sok kim, salaris van een meester.
sok ı kín, vastaanhalen, binden.
kiet sok, strak, stijf.
sin sok, in een bundel bij elkander doen
hiu sok, zakje, bundeltje reukstokjes.
tsıt sok á, een bundeltje, dun van middel.
hao pao sok, koperen of edelsteene plaatje als sluiting op eene zak of beurs.
hō̤ saạ̀ sok, paraplui foudraal.
hun sok, sigaren koker.
to sok, schede van een zwaard.
ts'iú sok, handschoenen.

肅 Sok — *Sok*, stil van aard; gaauw.
sok tsīng, stil, rustig.

速 Sok *Sok*, snel, gaauw.
sìn sok, *sok sìn*. snel, in allerijl.
sok ts'â, soort van sandelhout.

Som

Som *Ginseng*, Panax quinquefol.
Haí som, Biche de mer.
Dzin som, Ginseng.

Song

喪 Song *Song sū*, begrafenis plechtigheden.
tiaò song, met offeranden komen condoleren.
song kiet sū, droevige en vrolijke zaken (*b. v.* dood en huwelijk).
ku song } (*ki* ») }, in den rouw zijn.
baī song, condoleren.

鬆 Song *P'ōng song*, niet stevig in elkander, los.

爽 Sóng *Sóng k'oaì*, gezond (van menschen en plaatsen).
hò sóng, opgeruimd, vrijgevig.
sóng, fraai (van eene plaats) fraai, zindelijk, rustig.
ts'ing sóng, gezond (van eene plaats).
k'òng sóng ê lâng, een onbekrompen mensch (in handelingen).
sóng iok, eene belofte niet nakomen.
Sóng *Lōng sóng lâng*, iemand aanhitsen, tegen een ander opstoken.
Sóng *Tsoè tsit ts'uì-sóng lòh k'ì*, in ééns inslikken zonder te kaauwen.

喪 Sòng *Sòng*, arm.
sòng giēn giēn, doodarm.
sòng hiong, behoeftig, arm.
kiông sòng, arm.
sòng ts'iah, doodarm
sòng hiong kiá, arme lieden.
king sòng, arm.

sòng sim pīng kòng, zich geheel en al vergetende en als krankzinnig (dobbelen enz.)

宋 Sòng *Sòng tiâo*, De Song dynasti.
sòng bōng, graf uit de sòng dynastie.
lū sòng, Manilla.
sòng bí, *sòng bah*, gedroogde garnalen en vleesch van Manilla.
Sòng *Sòng hing*, uitgeleide doen (op eén reis.)
Sóng *Sóng*, onbeschoft, dom, van niets afweten.
t'ǫ sông, do.
sông tai, do.
tsiáh lâng sông, misgebruik maken van iemands domheid om hem te bedriegen.
Sōng *Sōng*, onderschuiven.
tuì aō piah sōng lòh k'ì, van achteren naar beneden schuiven.
Sōng *Lok sōng*, neergedrukt door armoede, kleeren aanhebben die te wijd en te lang zijn (de teekenen van armoede dragen).
sōng tseh·sōng tseh, log loopen (als een karbouw).

Su

私 Su *Su*, privaat, particulier, persoonlijk; partijdig, onrechtvaardig; heimelijk, geheim; eigendunkelijk.
poà kong su, half voor het algemeen en half privaat.
su tsū, willekeurig, naar eigen goed denken.
su tsièm, heimelijk in bezit nemen.
su t'ong, in geheime verstandhouding zijn met.
su p'oe, geheime brief.
p'ien su, *su k'ia*, *su sim*, *siép su*, partijdig, onrechtvaardig.
su tsing, geheime verstandhouding.
su k'ang, lett. heimelijk gat, geheime handelingen.

su lē, eigenmachtige instellingen.
su hū, partijdig, in het geheim.

輸 Su — *Su*, onderdoen voor, niet gelijk komen aan, verliezen, eene weddingschap, een spel of strijd verliezen; wedden.
su siaò, *su hun siaò*, in hoedanigheid onderdoen.
su lâng bò su tīn, wel als privaat mensch maar niet in het publiek voor iemand onder doen.
su siā, in gehalte, kwaliteit onderdoen.
su iâ, verliezen en winnen, wedden.
sa su gûn, om geld wedden.
k'ang sa su, om niets wedden.
sa su, wedden.
su kiaó, *poáh su kiáo*, met het dobbelen verliezen.

思 Su — *Su*, denken, overdenken, terugdenken naar, verlangend, denken aan; gedachten.
sàm su, herhaaldelijk overdenken.
su niū, overdenken, beraadslagen.
su siū, bedenken, denken over.
su hiu, aan zijne geboorteplaats terugdenken.
su ling, de borst willen hebben (van kinderen.
sim su, inwendige gedachten, doordenken.

師 Su — *Su*, meester, iemand die in iets geverseerd is.
tsīng su, advokaat.
kun su, raadgever in een leger,
su iâ, secretaris van een beambte.
bút-kok i i su, alles heeft zijn meester.
su hū, eerenaam aan Boeddh. priesters.

伺 Su — *Su hāo*, *su kì*, zijne opwachting maken bij.

書 Su — *Su* (*si*), boek, schrijver.
su pūn, secretaris, schrijver.
su king,

須 Su — *Su* (*si*), moeten.
su tioh, moeten, behooren.

需 Su — *Su* (*si*), levensbehoeften.
kun su (» *si*), legerfourage, soldij voor het leger.

史 Sú — *Sú kog* en *koan* (*s.*), geschiedschrijver (die dagelijks opteekent wat er in het rijk voorvalt).
sú kì (*sú*), geschiedboeken.
t'aì sú, geschiedschrijver (van het hof.

使 Sú — *Siet sú*, verondersteld dat....
ko sú, do.
sú huì (*sú*), onkosten.

暑 Sú — *Pī sú* (» *sì*), de warme plaatsen ontvluchten.
tuī sú, *siaó sú*, groote en kleine hitte

Sú — *Kám sú kun*, onverschrokken troepen.

四 Sù — *Sù hong*, vierkant, de vierstreken van het kompas.
sù tsì, op de vier uiteinden.
sù biēn siū tik (*sù*), van alle kanten aangevallen worden.
sù ui, overal, alom.
sù tsìng, rechtvaardig, onpartijdig.
sù si, de vier jaargetijden.
sù su, de vier klassieke boeken.
sù li boát, Soerabaia.
sù sik pai, vierkleurige platen (wit, zwart rood, geel).
sù koán tsìng, geheel en al volledig (van muziek instrumenten) ook van ander dingen gebruikt.
sù kò gán, een levendig afbeeldsel dat iemand in alle richtingen schijnt aan te kijken.
sù biēn pat tát, van alle kanten zichtbaar, openlijk.
sù tsi, handen en voeten.

賜 Sù — *Sù*, toelaten dat, geven aan.

siù sù (*siû*), geschenken geven, begiftigen.
k'im sù, keizerlijk geschenk.

絮 Sù
Sù k'ih, uitrafelen.
sù sù (*sì sì*), versleten.

恕 Sù
Sù sim (*sì* »), medelijdend, zich in iemands toestand verplaatsen.

Sù
Sù ing (*sù*), jasmijn.

Sù
Sù bù k'ī tūn (*kī*), voor niets vreezen.
sù bù (oig. *bú*), verdrukken.

Sù
Sù (*sì*), excrementen (van insekten.
pàng sù (» *sì*), excrementen uitwerpen (van insekten).
hō sin pàng sù, als een vlieg die zijne excrementen neerlegt *i. e.* overal iets onafgedaans laten liggen.

庶 Sù
Sù bú (*sì bó*), naam door de kinderen der wettige vrouw aan hun vader's bijzitten gegeven.
sù ts'ut (*sì* »), kinderen van bijzitten.

使 Sù
Sù tsiá, gezant.

嗣 Sù
Hō sù, erfgenamen, nakomelingen.
bò tsú sù, tempeltje voor overledenen zonder kinderen of nakomelingen.
ts'ut sù, door een ander tot zijn kind aangenomen worden.
bò sù ê giép, bezittingen waarvoor geene naaste erfgenamen zijn.

祠 Sù
Sù tîng, vooroudertijke tempel.

殊 Sù
Sù put ti, alleen niet weten dat....., onwetend zijnde van.

辭 Sù
Gién sù-té té (*gân*), niet wel bespraakt zijn.
sù hing, afscheid nemen.

事 Sū
Sū giép, beroep, ambacht.
to sū, twistziek.
pún sū, verstand, kennis.
dziá sū, aanzetten, ophitsen.
sing sū, twistziek.
sim sū, zaken die in het hart omgaan.
su sū, alles, elke zaak.
sià sū, een zaak van zich afschuiven.
tsú sū, het opzicht over iets hebben, opzichter.
ts'ióng sū, zaken twist enz. doen ontstaan.
sū li, gesteldheid, aard van eene zaak.
laū ts'ut sū, eene twist veroorzaken.
tsáp sū, allerlei zaken.
sū hō, later, naderhand.
sè sū, wereldsche zaken.
dzîn sū, omstandigheden van een persoon.
tsip sū, de stoet volgelingen van een mandarijn (die zwaarden enz. voor hem uitdragen.

署 Sū
Sū, waarnemend (van ambtenaren).
sū lí, waarnemen.

嶼 Sū
Sū, eiland.
soŋ sū, een eiland (in zee).
p'ù sū, een klein eiland.
têng iû lō sū, de zee is lang en de eilanden groot *d. i.* het is verder af dan het u zoo toeschijnt.

序 Sū
Ts'ú sū, volgorde.

伺 Sū
Sū hun, wachten bij, klaar staan met tabak.
su tsiú, dito met wijn.
sū tê, dito met thee (als bedienden doen).

緒 Sū
Sū, het begin, het voorbeeld voor iets.

似 Sū
Sū sī dzi hui, schijnen zoo te zijn en het eigenlijk toch niet zijn.
siong sū, op elkander gelijkend.

70

祀 Sū *Tsè sū*, offeranden aan de voorouders.

士 Sū *Sū lŏng kong siong*, de 4 standen, geletterden, landbouwers, handwerkslieden, kooplieden.
sū tsut, soldaat.
taī hàk sū, rijkskanselier.

Suh

吸 Suh *Suh* (*soh*), zuigen (aan de borst).
suh hŏng, de kwade stof uit iets zuigen.
súh ta, opzuigen, inzuigen als papier de inkt droog zuigt.
suh tâm, inzuigen, natzuigen.
suh hun, tabak sigaren rooken, trekken.
suh tiaô tiaô, zich vastzuigen (als een bloedzuiger).
tsē teh-suh-ts'ùi k'i siŏng, het vuil uit de tanden zitten zuigen *i. e.* zonder bezigheid over nietswaardige dingen spreken.
suh ling, moedermelk zuigen.
suh huih, bloed zuigen.
suh lâng, etter uitzuigen, uittrekken (als medic.)
suh lâng suh huih, etter en bloed uitzuigen 2° iemand op allerlei manieren uitzuigen.
suh lâng t'aô k'ak oḁ ts'é, iemands hersenen uitzuigen 2° iemand op allerlei manieren uitzuigen.

Súh *Súh giēn*, stomp, dof (van aard).
súh súh, do.
tsit iū̩ nḁ́ súh koh (*iō̩*), evenals een suf mensch.

Sui

雖 Sui *Sui dziēn*, alhoewel.
sui bóng, do.
sui sī án nḭ, ofschoon het zoo is.

髼 Sui *Ming sui* (*niō̩* »), harenkrans later bij de hoofdstaart ingevlochten.

蓑 Sui *Tsang sui*, grove regenmantel.

荽 Sui *Iên sui*, koriander zaad.

鑵 Sui *Ū sui bô koū̩*, een tuit maar geen hengsel hebben (waar niets aan is om vast te houden) *i. e.* nietswaardig (van pers. en dingen.)
sui, een kraan, tuit.
t'ut sui, verstopte tuit.
dziō sui, urine kanaal.
tê koàn sui (*tḙ*), tuit van een trekpot.
kip sio sui, tuit van een wijnkan.

水 Suí *Suí*, water.
suí gûn (» *gin*), kwikzilver.
suí gû, karbouw.
suí koe, kikvorsch.
suí koe lêh, ironiesch gezegd van iets dat niet zeer mooi is.
lók suí t'o dzin, anderen met zich mede in het water slepen *d. i.* anderen in zijn val ongeluk medeslepen.

觜 Suí *Tsiah ts'ùi suí* (*tsuí*), behendig, knap spreken.
ti ts'ùi suí, varkenssnuit.

Suí *Pìn suí* (» *suí*), haar aan de slapen van het hoofd.

美 Suí *Suí*, fraai.
suí ts'ong, niet zeer fraai, toch niet zoo mooi.
suí k'oán, *suí iū̩*, fraaie vorm.
suí sik, fraaie, standvastige kleur.

隨 Sui *Sui*, volgen, volgens, in overeenstemming met, zich schikkende naar; ach tervolgens, elk, stuk voor stuk, één voor één, afzonderlijk; vervolgens, daarop, dadelijk.

kun sui
(*kin* ») }, volgen (als eene bediende).

sui kè kán
(*kè*) }, eene slavin die hare meesteresse bij haar huwelijk volgt.

sui bú kè, zijne moeder in haar tweede huwelijk volgen.

ts'in sui, persoonlijk volgen.

sui sin pi, tot iemands gevolg behooren, iemand overal vergezellen (als eene bijzit).

sui dzīm, (eene beambte) naar de plaats zijner bestemming volgen.

sui p'oā k'ì, in gezelschap gaan.

sui aū, naderhand, later.

sui piēn, naar het uitvalt, zonder omslag.

sui ki-ìng piēn, naar omstandigheden handelen.

sui tsui k'ì-sui tsui lai, met stroom gaan en met stroom terugkomen.

sui k'ì-sui lai, zoo gaan en zoo terugkomen.

sui mīng sui ìn
(*muī*) }, zoo gevraagd zijn en zoo antwoorden.

sui dzī t'ák, karakter voor karakter afzonderlijk lezen.

sui kù, woord voor woord, zin voor zin.

sui pō kiā, voetje voor voetje loopen.

sui ts'iú, onmiddelijk, zonder tusschenpoozen, in eene moeite door.

sui é, *sui làng*, elk afzonderlijk, elkeen.

sui géh, *sui ni*
(*goéh*) }, elke maand, elk jaar, bij het jaar.

sui tsit (en) *tsik*, onmiddelijk.

sui si, terstond.

垂 Sui — *Sui*, afhangen, neêrhangen, naar beneden hangen.

sui tī hi aū piah nih, van achteren afhangen (als een sjerp).

liú sù-sui hi tsui nih, de wilgenranken hangen in het water neêr.

sui ts'iú, de handen laten neêrhangen.

hō-sì lâm sui, de regen stroomt van alle kanten af.

穗 Suī — *Suī*, korenaar.

béh suī, tarweaar.

béh-ts'ut suī, de tarwe schiet door.

Suī — *Suī hi*, lip die op een kram wordt vastgehaakt.

祟 Suī — *Kui suī ê làng*, een wonderlijk, bedriegelijk mensch.

癱 Suī — *Piàn suī*, verlamming.

poàn suī, halve do.

瑞 Sui — *Siōng suī*
(*siāng* ») }, fraai, gelukkig voorteeken.

Suī — *Sui mīng suī ìn*
(*muī*) }, zoo gevraagd zijn en zoo antwoorden.

sui kù suī kù, woord voor woord, zin voor zin.

sui suī, *iō kiā*
(*sui*) }, voetje voor voetje loopen.

遂 Suī — *Suī tì*, onmiddelijk komen tot: geraken tot.

Sun

孫 Sun — *Sun*, klein kind, nakomeling.

kiá sun, nakomelingen.

koe sun
(*ke* ») }, kuiken.

laī sun, kleinzoon van zoonskant.

goā sun, kleinzoon van dochterskant.

laī tsa bó sun, kleindochter van zoonskant.

goā tsa bó sun, kleindochter van dochterskant.

tsa bó sun, 1e kleindochter 2e hoer.

sun sim pū (*sin*) , vrouw van zijn neef.
sun sài, aangetrouwde kleinzoon.

笱 笋 Sún *Sún*, de jonge kegelvormige knoppen van bamboes, zwaluwstaarten, elk puntig wigvormig hout dat in eene voeg of groef moet; sponning.
tik sún, bamboesknoppen.
sèng sún, zure bamboesknoppen, aspergieknoppen.
sún kon, gedroogde bamboesknoppen.
tsiep sún, door zwaluwstaarten aan elkander doen; in elkander grijpen (van woorden.)
tsiep sún k'ak, iemand naar de mond spreken.
sún k'ang, gat voor eene pin, zwaluwstaart.
lòh sún, de zwaluwstaarten indrijven, in de voegen drijven.
ts'ák sún, een gat voor een wigje of pin hakken.
t'út sún, uit elkander schieten van zwaluwstaarten.
ts'oà sún, *sún ts'oà*, dwars lat of balk over iets.
taò sún, in elkander grijpen (van woorden).
bā sún, met zwaluwstaarten bevestigen.
sún hâm, groef voor een wig of insluitend hout.
tsiòh sún, hooge kegelvormige rots.
tsiòh-p'ah sún, gaten in een rots slaan om ze te laten springen.

損 Sún *Sún*, verminderen, vervallen; schaden, beschadigen.
sún pī, wegkwijnende ziekte.
sún tsìn, do.
haī dzi sún, ziekte van kinderen enz.
sún haī, schaden, benadeelen.
sún hoaī, beschadigd, vervallen.
sún siong, wond, kneuzing.
sún iú, schadelijke vriend.

Sùn *K'iem sùn*, nederig.

舜 Sùn *Sùn tè*, de keizer Sùn (uit de oudheid).

巡 Sûn *Sûn*, rondgaan, de rondte doen, kruisen; eene inspectiereis doen.
sûn ki, wachtloopen.
sûn iā, de nachtelijke rondte doen.
sûn tsìng, visites bij zieken afleggen (van doktoren).
sûn soa, de rondte op de bergen doen.
sûn lō, een weg inspecteren.
sûn tsa, de rondte doende onderzoeken.
sûn sī, *sûn k'oà*, de rondte doen en nakijken (als beambten, doktoren).
sûn hiu, met een reukstokje in de hand de rondte bij zijne donateurs doen (van Boeddh. pr.)
sûn àn, inspectiereis doen om de rechtszaken na te zien die in zijn distrikt hebben plaats gehad; ommegaande rechter.
ts'ut sûn, eene inspectiereis maken.
sûn tioh, door overal rond te gaan, krijgen of vinden.
sûn iû, op zee kruisen.
sûn saò, kruisen (als een kanonneerboot).
sûn pō, naam van lage mandarijnen die de rondte moeten doen.
sì koè sûn sûn, overal rondgaan, rond wandelen.
sûn kiêm, schout, lagere assistent.

循 Sûn *Sûn*, volgen; geleidelijk, goed van harte.
sûn sûn, geleidelijk, zuiver van harte, volmaakt in orde.
un sûn (*in* ») , do.

純 Sûn *Sûn*, zuiver, onvermengd; gelijkmatig; volmaakt in orde.
sûn tsoân, volmaakt.
sûn siòk, gelijkmatig, gestadig.
sûn sûn ê sik, eene gelijke kleur.

旬 Sùn — *Sùn*, een tiental jaren of dagen; een tijd van zeven dagen gedurende den rouw.
liók sùn, 60 jaar.
tsoì sùn, de zevendaagsche offeranden gedurende den rouw doen.

惇 Sùn — *Sùn*, familienaam.

𤸫 Sùn — Plooi, vouw, geplooid.
lik sùn, met plooien, geplooid.
bák tsiu ting sùn, een plooi in het ooglid hebben.

順 Sūn — *Sūn sūn*, zachtmoedig, toegevend, geleidelijk, zacht (van smaak).
īm sūn, ongehoorzaam.
sūn liông (» *liàng*), plichtbetrachtend.
sūn laô, met de stroom meêgaan.
sūn hong, goede wind, met de wind mede.
hô sūn, in harmonie.
sūn lō, den weg volgende, 2e in zijn weg.
sūn ts'iú, naar de hand.
sūn kang, zonder tusschenpoozen, in de zelfde moeite met een.
sūn ts'uì-kóng, uitspreken zooals het hem voor de mond komt.
si k'ì put sūn, ongeregeld, ongestadig weêr.
haò sūn, ouderlievend en gehoorzaam.
sūn tsuí hing tsiu, met de stroom meêvaren 2e zonder moeielijkheden geregeld zijn gang gaan.
sūn ki tsū dzién, laat hem zijn eigen gang gaan.
sūn sè (» *sì*), naar de toestand van zaken, naar de omstandigheid....
sūn piēn, met één, in eene moeite.
sūn géh (» *goéh*), voldrachtig.
sūn aò, geleidelijk in de keel gaande (als zachte wijn).
sū dzī, karakters natrekken.
sūn bōng pai dzi, de karakters van een grafsteen ophalen.
sūn sūn á k'i lai, gelijkelijk oplichten (als een kist met breekbare waar).
kóng oē-sūn ìh, met iemand meespreken, hem gelijk geven.

Sut

拂 Sut — *Sut*, zweepen, geesselen, stoffen, uitstoffen.
sut bé pì (*bé*), met een zweep klappen.
bút sut, slaan en zweepslagen geven.
bé sut (*bé*), lange koetsiers zweep.
tsit è sut-siang è tióh, twee vliegen in een klap raken.

瞬 Sut — *Sut bák*, met de oogen toewenken.
sut t'aò-tāng bák, met hoofd en oogen toewenken = tāng t'aò sut bàk.

恤 Sut — *T'é sut*, medelijdend behandelen.
un sut (*in* »), do.

戌 Sut — *Sut si*, 7—9 uur 's avonds.

率 Sut — *Sò sut*, onbesuisd, onvoorzichtig.
sut tit, rechtuit, onbewimpeld, ronduit spreken.
sut tsin, do. naar waarheid.
ts'o sut, onvoorzichtig, onbesuisd.
ts'ó sut, vlug weg, zonder veel zorg.

Sut — *T'óng sut*, aanvoeren (soldaten).
sut ping, soldaten aanvoeren.

屑 Sut — *Tsit sut á*, een kruimeltje.
kù sut, zaagsel.
piá sut, koekkruimels.

蟀 Sut — *Sik sut*, krekels.

述 Sút — *Sút*, verhalen, vertellen.
hok sút, oververtellen.

術 Sút *Hoat sút*, listige manieren om.
Sút *siù sút*, listige, wonderlijke streken.
sút, beetnemen, bedriegen; tooverstreek, hekserij.
sút-p'ièn, bedriegen.
sim sút put toan, zijn hart is niet goed.
si si sút sút, elkander stil geheime teekens geven.
īn ts'ùi sút làng, iemand beetnemen; iemand toefluiten.

Sút *Sút t'ó tī kong*, spel waarbij de duim de aardgod is, de derde vinger tijger enz. de vingers tegen elkander opstekende ziet men wie het weet.

Sút *Sút tsch tsiū k'ì*, in een ommezien weggaan.
háng sút p'ièn sút, bedreigen (vrees aanjagen) en bedriegen.

Ta

男 Ta *Ta po* (*tsa* ») }, mannelijk (bij menschen).
ta po làng, man.
ta po gín á, jongetje.

礁 Ta *àm ta*, blinde zandbank.
loè tioh ta, op een zandbank loopen.
ta, zandbank, droogte.
k'oà ta, op een zandbank blijven vastzitten.

乾 Ta *Ta*, droog.
ta sin, zelfstandig zijn, onafhankelijk.
ta sò, droog (niet vochtig).
ta sim, inwendig droog.
ta ts'è, droog en broos.
ta la k'ì, geheel en al verdroogd.
ta ts'aó, hooi.
ts'ùi ta, dorstig.
kan ta, alleen, op zich zelven zonder iets anders er bij.
ta mo (*o*) }, gedroogde zeeolijven.

t'ao siu tàm ta, alles wegstelen w... slechts voor de hand komt.
ts'aò ta, aangebrand.
ìm ta, in de schaduw droogen
ta lī, droog en loslatend (niet voch... en kleverig).
p'ák ta, in den zon droogen.
ta tiú, gedwee, lief, stil (als een ki... dat begint te loopen).
k'a ta ts'iú ta é sing lí, een zindelij... koophandel (waarbij men zich niet v... behoeft te maken).
sít kó bé-ta, de vlerken droog hebb... *i. e.* zelfstandig mensch zijn.
tsiáh īm ta, niet droog, schoon ope... *i. e.* eene zaak niet geheel en al t... einde kunnen brengen.

Ta *Bò ta oà* / *bò ta til oà* / *bò koat ta oà* }, er is niets aan te do..., het kan niet and... of.... onvermijdelij...

大 Ta *Ta ko* (*toā* ») }, mans vader.
ta ke (*toā ke*) }, mans moeder.

Tá *Tá kú á*, oogenblikkelijk, aanstonds.
Tá *Tá lóh*, waar?
Tá lóh só tsaī, waar?
tá lóh tī tsit é, wie? welke?
Tá *Tá tá*, geluid van kinderen die pas b... ginnen te spreken.

罩 Tà *Tà*, overdekken, bedekken met.
tà bīn, het gezicht bedekken (als m... een sluier).
báng tà, muskieten gordijn.
tà pi (» *pè*) }, een tooneel opslaan en ove... dekken.
tà p'è á, een sluier overdoen.
koe tà, kippen dekmand.
tà koe, kippen onder een mand doen.
kiong lú tà (*li*) }, met lange franjes a... hangende geborduurde kraag, door ... bruid gedragen.

Tà, springen (als tijgers).

sì koè tà (*kè*), overal in den blinde rondtasten, overal crediet zien te krijgen.

tà koạị k'ì lâi, zich op de achterste pooten oprichten (als honden).

Kọ tà, verdorren (van planten) uitdroogen, afgevallen (van menschen).

ts'ùi-tít tít tà k'ì, langzamerhand meer en meer dorst krijgen.

lâng tít tít tà k'ì, hoe langer hoe magerder worden.

ọ tà, donker van kleur en mager.

hoe-tà k'ì, verdorren, verflensen van bloemen.

kien tà, verdroogen, verdorren.

Tā i boé (*kā*), van iemand koopen.

tā i kóng, tot iemand zeggen.

Tạ, thans, nu.

kaò tạ, tot nu toe....

teng tạ pėh dzit (*pẹ̄h*), op klaarlichten dag.

Tạ su iêm, zout smokkelen.

tạ teh (*tẹh*), dragen en door zware lasten gedrukt worden (als rondventors).

pin tạ, lange houten draagstok.

tạ, dragen (een last); aannemen, pachten.

hit ê taī tsì-kā i tạ k'ih lâi, iets op zich nemen.

tik tạ, bamboezen draagstok.

ts'iâng tạ, een draagstok met scherpe ijzeren uiteinden.

gû tạ, juk.

tạ tạ́, de last dragen.

t'oè lâng tạ tạ̀ (*t'è*), iets voor een ander op zich nemen.

tạ ị, in dwarsche richting van de balken (als de plaatsing van een bed, voor ongelukkig gehouden).

膽 Tạ́ *Tạ́*, gal, galblaas; moed, dapperheid.

him tạ́, beerengal (als medic. gebruikt).

toā tạ́, moedig, dapper.

sió tạ́, lafhartig = bô tạ́.

pàng tạ́, *hòng tạ́*, moedig.

sàn tá, onverschrokken.

tạ́ t'aò, moed.

hó tạ́ t'aò, moedig.

kia̤ p'oà tạ́, zeer bevreesd.

lún tạ́, zijne moed, voortvarendheid inhouden, nog eens van te voren onderzoeken.

tsòng tạ́, zijne moed versterkend, kracht bijzetten (als een zwaard).

sí tạ́, doodelijke moed (zoodat men den dood niet vreest).

kā t'ị tsioh tạ́, van den hemel moed leenen, op eens moedig worden.

打 Tạ́ *Tạ́*, slaan; vechten, strijden; doen, in werking brengen; voor een ander nw. duidt het de handeling aan.

tạ́ tsièn, strijden, vechten.

aó tạ́, slaan.

tạ́ soàn, bedenken.

tạ́ tiêm, stuk voor stuk optellen: door mooie praatjes tot iets krijgen.

tạ́ t'ing, afluisteren.

tá tiōng (» *tiāng*), vechten.

tsoè lâng bô tạ́ kìn (*tsò*), hulpvaardig, bereidwillig zijn.

tạ́ pai ê pị̄ (*pẹ̄*), koorts.

tạ́ tsị, alles in geld afbetalen, zich niet met het eten enz. van werklieden bemoeien.

lóng tsóng kā tạ́ ná ná lâi, do. zich met niets anders dan het geld bemoeien.

tạ́ ts'aó tsí, festonneren.

tạ́ tsien, afstappen om iets te gebruiken.

tá siong }
(» *siang*) }, wonden.

k'ok tá-sing tsiao, door slaan tot bekentenis brengen.

tiém tá, iemand tot iets overreden, te praten, aanraden.

kong tá, aanvallen (als een vesting),

tá tsiàh tá ts'ing, eten en kleeren in geld uitbetalen.

tá, *tá tsiet*, geld in plaats van de geschenken geven.

tá t'áng, een laag verf of kalk over iets leggen als over lijkkisten enz. breeuwen 2° plagen, treiteren.

tá sing }
(» *sui*) }, denken, meenen.

tá tōng, bewegen om.

tá tiép, repareren.

tá hoat, in orde brengen.

擔 Tà — *Tà*, pikol, vracht, last, gang (als water 2 emmers).

tà t'aó, vracht last; gewicht van een vracht.

ké tsí tà, vracht, manden van vruchten rondventers.

tsit tà hoàn á tà ta tó kui nā king hàng tièm, die rondventers vracht heb ik reeds gedragen terwijl verscheidene handelshuizen gesprongen zijn (door rondventers gezegd).

tà tà, de last van iets dragen, de verantwoording op zich nemen.

tsaó tà, hard met een last loopen.

t'ao ni tà t'aó, heimelijk van een vracht afnemen (als leegloopers van een rondventermand).

tà uī, ruimte voor lading.

hoàn á tà, vracht, last van een rondventer.

tsit tà tsui, een gang (2 emmers) water.

tsit t'aó tsit tà, alles wat er is, groot of klein.

tsiáh tà, de verantwoordelijkheid (lett. last) van iets op zich nemen.

tsē tà, do.

Tà — *Boē kóng boē tà*, niet kunnen zeggen, spreken (als een jong kind dat pijn heeft).

Tà — *Tà*, in (als een motje in de vlam),

tà hé }
(» *hoé*) }, in of om het vuur, de vlam vliegen.

k'it hé tà k'ih }
(*hoé*) }, vlam vatten.

tà tsùn, een schuit branden (om ze schoon te maken).

tà soé }
(» *sé*) }, een schuit schoon branden en wasschen.

sa tà gō, elkander verkeerd begrepen hebben.

Tà — *Tà lâng*, het iemand lastig maken, kinderen.

tìng tà, in de war brengen (als iemand die aan het rekenen of denken is).

tà tuì pát uī k'ì, eene andere richting aan een gesprek geven, over iets anders spreken (als men ziet dat twee personen twist zouden krijgen.)

錯 Tā — *Tā*, }
(*ts'ò*) }, verkeerd, fout.

k'it lâng tā bák k'ì }
(*o*) }, door iemand beetgenomen worden in het zien van iets.

tā boé bô tā boē, men kan zich wel vergissen bij het koopen maar niet bij het verkoopen.

sing tā }
(*sui ts'ò* }, fout rekenen.

t'ia tā, verkeerd, misverstaan.

k'oà tā, verkeerd zien.

tā siaò, verkeerd rekenen.

tā dzīn, in vergissing voor het zijne aanzien.

tā̤ bák / *(o)* }, zich vergissen in het zien, verkeerd zien.

k,oà̤ tā̤ bák / *(o)* }, do.

'a *T'a hiṳ goā lí* / *(t'a hio̤)* }, in andere dorpen, op andere plaatsen.

'á *P'ô̤ t'á̤*, wel op zijne handen willen dragen, vleien.

tuì hing k'ám kā i t'á̤ k'ì, iemand een duw tegen de borst geven.

tsṅg t'á̤, iets opheffen om het laten zien.

t'á̤ koai̤ / *(koân)* }, opheffen, omhoog houden.

kā i t'á̤ k'ì, do.

boé kaò tsit t'á̤, een handstapeltje koopen (zoo veel als men op zijn hand kan stapelen).

'à *T'à lā*, in iets roeren om te zien wat er in is, visiteeren, nakijken.

t'à hé / *(» hoé)* }, een weinig vuur van iets afnemen.

t'à k'ui, met een stok enz. uit den weg schuiven (als vuilnis).

t'à ké tsí / *(o)* }, vruchten van den boom aftikken.

hō̤ i t'à lóh lai / *(o)* }, door iemand neergehaald zijn (als vruchten).

t'à hn̂g, een tuin omwoelen (om de grond losser te maken).

ǐng oē t'à i ê ì sù, een onderwerp aanroeren om iemands opinie er over uit te lokken.

'ā *Tsng t'ā̤*, zich opsmukken, opgesmukt.

Tah

'ah Opscheppen met een lepel; koopen (wijn, olie enz.)

tah taō iù, soja opscheppen.

tah iù, olie koopen.

tah tsiú, wijn koopen.

拍 Tah Met de platte hand slaan, in de handen slaan, slaan op.

tah ts'iú, in de handen slaan.

tah ka tsiah, iemand op den rug kloppen (om iemand te prijzen).

tah hing, *tah hing k'ám*, zich op de borst slaan; de verantwoordelijkheid van iets op zich nemen.

tah toh, op de tafel slaan.

tah hiah, ontstellen.

搭 Tah *Tah*, vastklampen aan; zich vasthouden aan; zich aan boord begeven, scheepspassagier zijn; oprichten, opslaan (als een tent.)

tah kao, boothaak.

tah hoā̤, houvast om tegen op te klimmen.

ū tah t'aô, in verbindtenis staan.

tah tsûn, aan boord gaan, inschepen.

tah k'eh, passagier.

tah bā, stijf, sluitend.

tah tah, dicht tegen elkander aan (als schepen).

koai̤ tah tah, stevig dicht.

tah liép, intiem met elkander.

kià tah, met iemand overzenden (als geld.)

tah ts'ù koà, het dak opleggen.

tah ts'aò liaô, een hut bouwen.

tah hì pi̤, een tooneel opslaan.

tah liâng pi̤, een tent voor de luchtigheid opslaan.

貼 Tah *Tah*, aanplakken; bevestigen aan.

tah dzī péh, eene advertentie, biljet aanplakken.

tah ts'ut sè / *(soè)* }, te huur aanplakken.

tah boah, doen als of men zich zeer inspande.

tah lién, geldbeurs.

pak tó̤ iao káo tah ka tsiah, zoo uitgehongerd dat de buik tegen den rug aankomt.
tah sin, strak om het lijf sluitend.

踏 Táh *Táh*, de voet zetten op, betreden, trappen op; beslag leggen op (in goeden zin) afnemen, aftrekken, afzonderen, afhouden.
ts'aó táh, vertrappen.
t'ún táh, do.
táh sìh, doodtrappen.
táh soh, koorddansen.
k'a táh, iets om de voeten op te zetten (als steenen in een beek gelegd om er over te gaan.)
k'a táh i, voetenbankje.
k'a táh boē (en) *m̄ tuà toē*, de voeten niet op den grond kunnen houden d. i. springen van vreugde.
táh tsiā̤ pi̤ toē, zoo vertrappen, vernielen dat het een gelijken grond wordt (als een ingenomen stad).
bé táh t'ìng, stijgbeugels.
táh sit, de wezenlijke toestand onderzoeken.
táh k'àm, opnemen, opmeten (eene plaats.)
táh sit toē, beproeven of de grond vastgenoeg is om te betreden.
táh pang, vlonder.
kiā̤ táh, de voet zetten te, komen te..., omgaan met...., handelingen.
hó kiā̤ táh, goed te betreden, begaan.
táh t'ūm, achteruit gaan (in handel).
tsiaó táh, *tsiáo táh ki*, stokje voor vogels om op te zitten.
tsiaó táh làng (en *tuì*, *táh tuì làng*, vogelknip.
koe-sṳ táh (*ke-sio táh*), de kippen treden.
kū i táh tsit hūn, een deel in iets aan iemand geven (als in handel).
táh só̤ huì, de onkosten er afhouden.
táh pun tsi̤ k'i lai, zijn oorspronkelijk kapitaal van kapitaal en winst aftrekken, afnemen.
táh sièm ló, (bij de verdeeling zijner bezittingen) iets voor zijn ouden dag er afhouden.
táh kong tsi̤, een gedeelte als algemeen fonds afhouden (van een erfenis).

塔 T'ah *T'ah*, pagoda.
ts'it tsàn t'ah, pagoda met zeven verdiepingen.
hiṳ t'ah, reukwerk pagoda (lange kring reukwerk in het midden met een hooge punt eindigende).
tsō t'ah, eene pagoda bouwen.
t'ah tsiem, punt eener pagoda.
tsùn t'ah, vuur, lichttoren voor schepen.

T'ah *T'ah bi*, rijst voor de tweede maal stampen.
tsit tsing tsit t'ah, stampen en nog eens overstampen (rijst).

疊 T'ah *Sa t'áh* (*sio*), op elkander liggen, elkander overtreffen.
ting ting t'áh t'áh, hoog op elkander gestapeld.
tsit t'áh ē sṳ-ts'eh (*ts'e̤h*), een stapel kleeren. boeken.
k'ah t'áh ih, iemand overtreffen.
ke t'áh tsit niṳ́ sṳ, één jas meer aantrekken.
koh t'áh tsit tsàn laó, nog eene verdieping er boven op bouwen.
kè tsi̤-t'áh ih, meer geld dan een ander voor iets willen geven.
t'áh sṳ, kleeren op elkander stapelen 2° nog een kleed er over aantrekken.
làng t'áh làng, de eene man op den ander, massa menschen (als bij eene komedie).

Tai

Tai *Tai tai*, dom.
gōng tai, *tai gōng*, dom, idioot.

tai k'ì, dom.

sòng tai, dom, niet veel fatsoenlijks gezien hebben.

Tai *Ling tai k'ì*, melklucht; praten als een pas geboren kind.

ts'aò ling tai, stinkende, zure (moedermelk) lucht.

Tai *Ko̤ tai tsí*, lange strepen geel geldpapier (bij festiviteiten vóór tempels gehangen).

滓 *Iù tai*, olie droesem.

Taí *tse taí*, droesem, bezinksel 2e onoverkomelijke zwarigheden in eene zaak.

tai bī, eene troebele lucht.

tsē taí, bezinken.

lò taí, *taí*, zeer troebel.

帶 *Taì*, gordel; een strook, streek; mede-

Taì nemen, medevoeren, bij zich dragen, bezwaard zijn met.

it taì ē sò̤ tsaī, de geheele streek.

kaò taì, belasten met, opdragen.

koai taì, oplichten, wegvoeren (kinderen enz.)

taì pī (en) *pīng* (*pī*) }, eene ziekte, kwaal met zich voeren.

taì tsit, eene kwaal hebben.

taì tsoē, eene straf met zich voeren (als een banneling).

taì tsit-hoē ka (*kē*) }, in het privaat leven terugkeeren maar zijn ambtstitel behouden.

taì àn, een rechtszaak hangende hebben.

pik taì, fluor albus.

戴 *Taì*, op het hoofd dragen.

Taì *ting taì*, mandarijnknoop (op de muts).

koan taì, hoofddeksels.

埋 *Tâi*, begraven.

Tâi *tâi àn toé* (*té*) }, rechterlijke aangifte van iets doen.

oàh oàh tâi, levend begraven.

tâi tsí gûn (*gîn*) }, geld begraven.

k'it ing tâi lòh k'ì, door de golven bedolven worden.

liàh lâng tò t'aò tâi, iemand met het hoofd naar beneden begraven (waardoor hij immer in de hel blijft (scheld.)

lí m̄ sai tâi àn, gij behoeft geen vischje uit te gooien, naar iets te spellen (als om geld te leenen).

tâi bát, in de aarde begraven, verstoppen.

tâi sí lâng, een doode begraven.

īng gûn k'in tâi lâng (*gîn*) }, door, onder zijn geld iemand begraven.

臺 *Tâi oân*, Formosa.

Tâi *tsing tâi* (*tsâng* ») }, voorste gedeelte van het tooneel.

aū tâi, achterste gedeelte; waar de muziekanten zitten.

laū tâi, door het slaan op trom en gong toeschouwers bij het tooneel brengen.

p'aò tâi, batterij.

tsik tâi, kandelaar.

bú tâi, ondergouverneur.

tsiàng tâi (*tiàng* ») }, bevelhebbers tent.

hì tâi, tooneel.

hièn tâi, eere titel aan hooge mandarijnen gegeven.

taī tsì-hō̤ i lòh tâi, eene zaak doen voltrekken.

Tâi *K'eng tâi*, kafinsekt.

koe tâi, kippenluizen 2e kleingeestig, bekrompen (van idée).

代 *Taī*, generatie, geslacht; voor, ten be-

Taī hoeve van, in de plaats van...

sè taī siong t'oân, van geslacht tot geslacht overleveren.

taī taī, elke generatie.

taī pān, zaakgelastigde, agent.

taī su (» *si*) }, schrijver (voor anderen die niet schrijven kunnen).
taī li, voor een ander doen, waarnemen,
taī tsoè (» *tsò*) }, voor iemand doen.
taī dzīn, voor iemand instaan.
kao taī, aan iemand opdragen.
taī i ts'ut, voor iemand betalen.

玳 Taī — *Taī poē*, schildpadschild.

鮘 Taī — *Taì hi*, karper.

大 Taī — *Taī*, groot; edel als eeretitel; grootendeels, algemeen.
taī dzin, edele heer, Excellentie.
taī ke (» *ke*) }, alle.
taī sè (» *sì*) }, algemeen voorkomen.
taī k'aì, over het algemeen.
taī k'aì ē tsing hing, algemeen voorkomen (eener zaak).
taī iok, *taī liók* (» *iak*) (» *liák*) }, in het algemeen, ongeveer.
taī hông, rabarber.

在 Taī — *Taī sing* (» *san*) }, eerst, te voren, het eerst.
taī séng kiá (» *san* ») }, vooruitloopen.

事 Taī — Zaak.
taī tsì, zaak.
p'ai taī, slechte zaken.
t'ó bò taī, zich zaken, moeielijkheden op den hals halen.

舦 Taī — *Taī*, roer van een schip; achtervoegsel achter den naam van schippers.
taī kong, schipper, stuurman.
sa taī, schipper Sa.

篩 T'ai — *T'ai*, zeef, ziften.
t'ai taó, zeefbak.
bi t'ai, rijstzeef.
t'ai k'ng, kaf uitziften.
p'ai ē mih t'ai t'ai ts'ut k'ì, het slechte er uit ziften.
ná t'ai ná tsió, hoe meer men het zift des te minder wordt het *i. e.* zoolang uitkiezen, sorteeren dat er zeer weinig overblijft.
bi t'ai bák ē toū, zoo groot als een gaatje in een zeef *i. e.* zeer klein.
kóng oē tioh īng bi t'ai lai t'ai, zoo spreken dat zijne woorden eerst moeten gezift worden (om het van leugens te zuiveren).
t'ai bi, rijst ziften, door een zeef gooien.

胎 T'ai — *T'ai sing*, zoogdieren.
siū t'ai, bevrucht worden (van vrouwen).
tsē t'ai, in de moeder buik zijn (van kinderen).
an t'ai ióh, medicijn die men aan eene zwangere vrouw geeft wanneer haar kind niet rustig is.
t'ai sin, baarmoedergeest (gezegd in voorwerpen te zijn die eene zwangere vrouw lang onaangeroerd heeft laten liggen, verplaatst men ze dan kan zij eene ontijdige bevalling hebben).
tsiong tsûn ui t'ai, bodemerij.
tsiong ts'ù hō i ui t'ai, hijpotheek op een huis geven.
t'ai tsioh, onder onderpand van iemand leenen.

颱 T ai — *Hong t'ai*, orkaan.

T'ai — *T'ai kú*, er iemand boven op helpen.

癩 T'aí — *T'aí ko*, melaatschheid (hooge graad van
t'ai ko iá, lazaret, pesthuis.
t'ai ko kuí, vuile, smerige duivel.

T'aí — *T'aí t'ó*, hoe toch zou?
beh t'ai (*boeh*) }, hoe toch zou...?

T'aí — *Siet t'ai*, uitschelden (gemeen).

大 T'aì — *T'aì*, te..., al te...
t'aì tsú, kroonprins.

t'ài pîng, vrede.
t'ài kò, te zeer...
k'ah t'ài kò, al te zeer...
t'ài tsoē, al te veel...
t'ài kàm, besnedene; eunuch.
t'ài t'ài, oude mandarijns vrouw.
toā t'ài, *dzī t'ài*, hoofdvrouw, en tweede vrouw (bijzit).
t'ài hō, keizerin moeder.
t'ài siong lò kun, god der tooveraars.
an dzû t'ài san, rustig, gerust als de T'ài san in Soa tang.

T'ai *T'é t'ài*, voorkomen, uiterlijk (bel. term)

T'ài *Beh siá ĭm-t'ài k'ì (boeh)*, schrijf het of schrijf het niet zooals gij wilt.
beh tsiū siá ĭm tsiū t'ài k'ì (boeh), do.
p'ai-lí t'ài k'ì boé (bé), als het niet goed is dan behoeft gij het niet te koopen, waarom komt gij het dan koopen.
k'ó i t'ài k'ì, men kan het ook laten, laten loopen, niet doen.
nū ĭm-t'ài k'ì, zoo niet, laat het dan maar loopen.

殺 T'ai *T'ai lai sih*, geheel en al, in massa dooden.
t'ai tō é lâng (» tō tsai é lâng), slager.
t'ai k'ui, opensnijden (van pompelmoezen en alle groote vruchten gebruikt).
t'ai paī, nederlaag lijden.
t'ai sai, een leeuw dooden *i. e.* (met iemand) redetwisten, de zaak uit elkander leggen.
t'ai t'aò hoān (en) *p'e (p'oe)*, tot onthoofding veroordeelde, vorm voor onthoofding (scheld term).
ká kap lâng t'ai lān p'oà hiáh, als men twist met iemand heeft, zich niet bekommeren wat de gevolgen voor zich en zijn eer kunnen zijn.

t'ai tō hó boé loē, slachters hebben gemakkelijke handel (zij hebben niet lang over prijs en kwaliteit te spreken) *d. i.* menschen die beiden kennis van iets hebben komen gemakkelijk tot een resultaat.
t'ai sih, vermoorden.
t'ai lâng, iemand vermoorden.
t'ai hiôh, snijden, kwetsen (het ligchaam.)
t'ai t'aò, onthoofden.
sa t'ai (sio »), vechten.
t'ai iâ, overwinnen (in een slag).
t'ai su, verliezen (in een slag.)
t'ai p'ah ts'ò, vechten slaan en hakken.
kè tsi-kap i t'ai siuh, met iemand over den prijs dingen.
t'ai sit, tot eene billijken prijs afdingen.
kóng oē t'ai siuh ìh, in zijn spreken iemand benadeelen, treffen.

待 T'aī *K'oán t'aī*, behandelen.
t'aī, do. 2e wachten tot dat...
tíng t'aī, *t'ìng t'aī (tíng t'aī) (o)*, wachten.
t'aī si t'aī dzit, een zekeren tijd wachten.

迨 T'aī *T'aī*, toen, juist toen.
t'aī lâng tsiep k'eh, menschen ontgen en met gasten omgaan.
t'aī k'eh, gasten ontvangen 2e op kalanten, koopers wachten.
t'aī goá lai i tō k'ì lah, toen ik kwam was hij reeds weg.

T'aī *Pîng t'aī (pán t'ān)*, niet standvastig zijn, steeds van zin veranderen.

Tak

錄 Tak Opteekenen, aanteekenen, opschrijven.
tak siàò, eene post boeken.
tak bé tsi, met verkorte cijfers schrijven.

觸 Stooten met de hoorns, aanstooten tegen,
Tak aanbotsen, moeielijkheden maken, over hoop liggen met, belemmeren.

tak tioh, stooten tegen.

gù sa tak (*sio*) }, de koeien stooten elkander.

tioh k'a tak, de voet stooten tegen, struikelen.

tak sìh, doodknappen (als eene vloo).

ts'uì tak tioh tsìh, de mond ligt met de tong over hoop *i. e.* de beste vrienden kunnen wel eens twisten.

tak ti̲, moeielijkheden maken, in den weg liggen.

Tak *Tak tak k'áp k'áp*, tegen iemand aanstooten, hem willen belemmeren.

kap lâng tak, ruzie met iemand hebben.

Tak *Put tak put ts'it*, ongeregeld in zijne handelingen of kleeding.

毎 *Ták*, elk.
Ták *ták pai*, telkens, herhaaldelijk.

ták ē, elk een.

ták dzit, dagelijks.

tak géh (» *goéh*) }, maandelijks.

ták ni̲, jaarlijks.

ták ūī, overal.

bák tsiu-ták, op het eerste gezicht iemand doorgronden.

毒 *Ták*, vergift, vergiftig.
Ták *ták kù nú ts'át bák*, vergiftig, slecht als het oog van een dief.

ták sim, gevaarlijk, vergiftig van hart.

tsiáh ták, vergif innemen.

pàng ták, 1e vergift afgeven, uitwerpen 2e iemand door een streek er in laten laten loopen.

ts'uì t'aò ták, vergiftig van mond (scheldnaam).

dzoáh ták ták, zeer warm (van het weder).

dzoáh ták t'i̲, heete dag.

hē ták ts'iú, eene vergiftige hand neer laten *d. i.* iets doen waardoor men anderen zeer benadeelt.

燭 *Ko̲ ták*, eenzelvig.
Ták

Ták *Ták á hi p'ē* (*p'oē*) }, vel van een visch, even als haaien vel bij ons, voor glad schuren gebruikt.

濁 *Iù ták*, bezinksel van olie.
Ták

T'ak *Ing sat pìn t'at lai t'ak* (*iōng*) (*t'ok*) (*t'ok*) }, met een kammenschoonmaker schoonkrabben.

t'ak p'ăng (eigl.) *t'at p'ăng* (*t'at p'ăng*) }, tot aanvulling van, in een ledig oogenblikje.

T'ak *T'ak siaò* (*sùi̲ siaò*) }, rekenen (op het rekenbord).

t'ak sìng poā (*t'ak sui̲ poā*) }, op het rekenbord rekenen.

讀 *T'ák*, lezen.
T'ák *t'ák k'ì mē̲ ìh*, iemand uitschelden als of men het voor las (als bejaard menschen doen).

gû-bīn tsing-t'ák k'oè, eene koe een papier voorlezen *d. i.* met domme menschen over diepe onderwerpen spreken.

t'ák ts'eh (» *ts'e̲h*) }, studeren.

t'ák ts'eh lâng (*ts'e̲h*) }, een geletterde.

t'ák-kaò oē̲ liām (*ē*) }, uit het hoofd leeren.

t'ák dzī̲, (in de) boekentaal (lezen).

k'ùn t'ák (*k'in* ») }, vlijtig leeren.

oē̲ t'ák tit (*ē*) }, geschikt zijn om te studeren.

Tam

擔 Tam *Tam*, op de schouders dragen, dragen, verdragen; op zich nemen, instaan voor.

tam tńg, instaan voor.

tam niá, *tam dzīn*, *tam sing*, instaan, borg staan voor.

ī̇m tam su iá̤, niet tegen zijn verlies kunnen.

tam tsing, eene weldaad gedachtig zijn, verplichting aan iemand hebben.

tam sin miā̤, volgens zijne krachten kunnen dragen, bestand zijn tegen.

tam ti-bóh tam ts'ok, bij borgstelling moet men met overleg en niet verkeerd te werk gaan.

耽 Tam *Tam koh*, ophouden, vertragen, uitstellen.

tsit dzit tam koh kè tsit dzit (*koè*), van den eenen dag op den anderen verschuiven.

tam gō̤, teleurstellen.

啖 Tam *Tam*, eten, proeven van.

tam k'oà̤, *tam tsiáh k'oà̤*, proeven.

k'in k'in á tam tseh, even van iets proeven.

与 Tam *K'a-tam tioh hit ê só̤ tsaī*, met de voet ergens op rusten; eene vaste voet ergens hebben.

膽 Tám *Tám hóng*, zich onbeschaamd valschelijk uitgeven, eigenaar van.

tám hoân, blaauwe vitriool.

tám hân, niet moedig, vreesachtig.

tám liōng (» *liāng*), moedsgesteldheid.

tám tám, vreezen.

tám tì, moed en kennis.

tám lik, moedskracht.

頕 Tàm *T'aò k'ak tàm tàm*, het hoofd laten hangen en bedenken.

tàm t'aò, do. goedkeurend, toeknikken.

tàm sè (» *soè*), gebukt (van ouderdom).

淡 Tâm *Tâm*, nat, vochtig.

p'ah tâm, nat maken.

tâm sip, *tâm lūn*, nat, vochtig.

tâm lok lok, nat, modderig, slikkerig.

tâm kun (» *kin*), eene natte doek.

tâm tsuí hè (*hoè*), door water beschadigde goederen.

tâm sin, nog een sleep na zich hebben, met anderen betrokken zijn, niet zelfstandig zijn.

tâm ta, nat en droog, alles wat maar voorkomt.

tâm ,ta-goá tsē taō, wat er ook van kome ik neem de verantwoordelijkheid op mij.

談 Tâm *Tâm*, spreken over, een gesprek voeren, converseeren; plaatselijk dialect, patois.

tâm lūn, spreken over, converseren.

tâm kaò ki̤ ts'im, tot diep in den nacht blijven praten.

ts'iaò tâm, lachverwekkende, komieke vertelsels.

hân tâm, gesprek over onbeduidende zaken.

tâm t'ien soat tē, over koekjes en kalfjes praten.

hiṳ tâm (*hiang*), plaatselijk dialect, patois.

些 Tām *Tām póh*, een weinigje.

tām tām, middelmatig.

tām tām kè dzit, middelmatig door zijn dag, aan de kost komen.

tām pók, stil eenvoudig van aard.

tām tām sò̤ sò̤, eenvoudig (van kleeren enz.)

tsing ì k'ah tām, minder intiem, koeler met iemand zijn.

tām tsui Tāmsui, (haven in het N. van Formosa).

tăm tsong, eenvoudige kleeding (van vrouwen).
tăm, eenvoudig (van kleur).
lăng tăm, koel (van dingen) en menschen ook van handel.
ts'ing tăm, het niet zeer breed hebben.

貪 T'am *T'am*, hebzuchtig, begeerig zijn naar.
t'am p'oh, veel houden van..., gaarne eten.
t'am ts'ùi / (*t'am ts'ùi tsui*), gulzig.
siò t'am, met weinig tevreden, in zijn schik.
t'am tsai, begeerig zijn naar geld.
tam dzìh pin dzī k'ek, het karakter »hebzuchtig" heeft den vorm van het karakter »arm" *i. e.* hebzucht heeft gewoonlijk armoede tot gevolg.
t'am sim, hebzuchtig.
t'am ts'òng, gulzig.
t'am tsiáh, gulzig.
t'am tsiáh siòng / (*siàng*), do.
t'am tioh, begeerig zijn naar.
t'am bin, slaperig, slaapziek.
t'am k'ùn, do.
t'am sik, wellustig.
t'am kè / (» *kè*), hebzuchtig wegens den (mooien) prijs.
t'am tsiú, verlangend zijn naar wijn, gaarne wijn drinken.
t'am làng ê pín sū, verlangend naar iemands kunde zijn (en daardoor veel van hem verdragen).

速 Tám *T'ám mê*, verhaasten, spoeden.

探 Tàm *T'àm*, peilen, vademen; bezoeken, eene visite afleggen bij.
t'àm hoe / (» *hoa*), laagste graad van Han lìm.
t'àm t'aù, het hoofd vooroversteken.
t'àm mēng / (» *muī*), uitvragen, vragen naar.
t'àm ts'im k'in, de diepte van het water peilen.
ts'át t'àm, dieven spion.
t'àm t'aò tsai loh k'ì, te ver overkijkende voorover naar beneden vallen.
t'àm k'oà, gluren nazien, nakijken (als door er in te booren).
t'àm t'iā, afluisteren.
t'àm k'oà, bezoeken (komen kijken naar iemand).
īng oē t'àm làng ê ì / (*iōng oā*), iemand polsen.
t'àm t'aò t'àm naó (en *taō*) / (*taō*), inkijken. heen en weer, rondkijken.
t'àm baī, iemand bezoeken.
kià t'àm, iemand opdragen naar een ander te informeeren.
t'àm kè / (» *kè*), naar den prijs informeeren.
t'àm k'a, met de voet beproeven of iets hard genoeg is om op te loopen.
t'àm k'a kiā, voorzichtig loopen.
t'àm siā t'àm iá, naauwkeurig onderzoek naar iets of iemand doen.
bô t'àm t'iā ih, niet veel om iemand geven.
t'àm pàng, de bruid gaan bezoeken (3 dagen na het huwelijk door haren jongeren broeder gedaan).
t'àm ts'in, zijne familie bezoeken.
t'àm tsí, voorover in een put kijken.

癲 T'âm *T'âm loān*, gek, krankzinnig.

痰 T'àm *Hân t'àm*, koud slijm.
t'àm, slijm.
t'àm koàn, kwispeldoor.
p'ùi t'àm, slijm uitspuwen.
p'ī t'àm noā, neusslijm, snot.
t'àm-tū, door slijm verstopt (als een aanborstige).

hong t'âm, slijm als van een krankzinnige.

t'âm iên, slijm en speeksel.

T'âm, diepe waterkuil.

t'âm á kut á, waterkuilen en gaten.

Tsít t'âm tsiú, een pot wijn.

Táh t'ām, achteruit gaan (in eene affaire).

ts'im t'ām, nog dieper in schuld komen.

t'ūm t'uī k'ì, opgaan door dat velen er van moeten hebben enz.

t'ūm tsít ēh, eens indompelen (als een akertje in een watervat).

Tan

Hông tan, menie.

tan tiên, borst, plaats waar het geluid van daan komt.

tan ts'ing, gekleurd (van eene teekening).

tan ko-ióh soạ-sin sien lân piēn, levens medicijn zalf en poeder kunnen geesten zelfs moeielijk uitmaken (door apothek. gezegd).

p'ah tan tók, uitslaan, uitslag krijgen door het overmatig gebruik van medicijnen.

sien tan, geesten, *i. e.* voortreffelijk geneesmiddel.

Tan ting, eenig kind.

tan tan, maar niet grooter worden (van kinderen vruchten enz.)

tan sin-p'it bé, alleen (zonder gevolg.)

tan dzin-tók mạ́, do.

Tán ih (*o*), op iemand wachten.

tán làng koē laō ting) (*k'oaì*), wacht men op iemand dan is een minuut als een uur lett. is men spoedig oud.

ts'ia̤ tán tseh (*ting*), eilieve wacht even.

tán si tán k'ik (*t'ìng haō si k'ik*), tot den (waren) tijd wachten.

tán ko̤ k'ang, op eene enkele kaart wachten (bij het kaart spelen); op ééne enkele gelegenheid uitzien.

tán tsú, de overledene's tablet te gemoet gaan, inhalen (door de betrekkingen na de begravenis gedaan).

tán tsih (*tán tsih*), opwachten en ontvangen.

tán t'aī (*o*), wachten op..., tot...

但 Tàn — *Tàn*, slechts.

旦 Tàn — *It tàn*, op een goeden dag, de een of andere dag.

boán tàn, Nieuwjaarsdag.

響 Tàn — *Tàn*, ratelen (als de donder) knallen, afgaan, klinken.

tsị-bô nīng ē-boē tàn, wanneer men geen twee duiten heeft kan er geen geluid van komen *d. i.* waar twee twisten hebben beiden schuld.

lui-tàn, donderen, het dondert.

k'ū k'ū tàn, rommelen (als donder of in de buik).

oē-kong liaó oē tàn (*oā*), door iedereen aangehoord worden.

kóng oē boē tàn (*oā bē*), geen weerklank vinden (van zijn woorden).

ts'ing-boē tàn (*bē*), het geweer gaat niet af.

p'é-tàn tsóng oē tàn (*p'oé*) (*ē*), gij zult, of hij zal nog slaag krijgen.

pe'-teh beh tàn lah (*p'oé*) (*boeh*), hij komt er niet zonder slaag af.

t'àn ap (*t'àn ap*), ten onder brengen (als een opstand).

陳 Tân, familienaam.
Tàn *t'ien hā-tàn lîm kò poàn*, onder den hemel (in Tsiang en Tsoan tsiu) maken de fam. Tàn en Lîm meer dan de helft uit.

但 *Put tān*, niet slechts.
Tān *tān sī*, slechts is het...
sù bù k'ī tān { (*kī*) }, volstrekt niet bevreesd zijn.
put tān hoân, niet bang zijn, er tegen op zien, zich veel moeite te geven.

蟶 *T'an*, Solen: een weekdier.
T'an *t'an tiū*, beddingen waar men Solen teelt.
hiao t'an, krom trekken (door wind enz.)
hiao t'an k'ak, krom getrokken.
si t'an, lett. doode Solen *i. e.* lijk langs den weg liggend.
k'iaò t'an, krom leggen *i. e.* dood zijn.
k'ah hiao t'an á k'ak, nog meer krom trekken dan een Solen schelp *i. e.* zeer spoedig vriendschap of weldaden vergeten.

攤 *Pai t'an*, eene stalletje opzetten (op
T'an een markt).

毯 *T'án á*, vloerkleed, wollendeken.
T'án

縱 *T'án hoai* { (» *hoā*) }, overdwars.
T'án *t'án tit*, recht (niet dwars).
t'án tó, op zijde liggend.
t'án k'ap, *ping t'án k'ap* { (*pún*) }, voorover, onderste boven.
t'án k'iā, overlangs.
t'án p'in sin { (*pī*) }, waggelen, scheefloopen (als een beschonken mensch).
t'án dziēn, rechtuit, onbewimpeld, onverschrokken.
T'án *T'án mē*, onmiddelijk, oogenblikkelijk.
t'án tsá, zeer vroeg.

疸 *Hông t'án*, geelzucht.
T'án

T'án *T'án hō*, iemand partijdig helpen.
p'ien t'àn, partijdig, onrechtvaardig.

賺 *T'àn*, winnen, verdienen.
T'àn *t'àn tsī*, geld verdienen, winnen.
toā t'àn, groote winst.
t'àn tsiáh, de kost verdienen.
bô t'ó t'àn, niets voor de kost doen.
tsaó t'àn, overal rondgaan om geld te verdienen.
t'àn pá, *t'àn ts'uì pá*, niets meer dan de kost verdienen.

趁 *T'àn*, volgen, opvolgen, navolgen; zich
T'àn benutten, gebruik maken van.
t'àn iū { (*iō*) }, een voorbeeld volgen.
oe làng t'àn tīn { (*e*) }, met de groote hoop meëgaan, meëdoen.
sa t'àn ts'uì { (*sio*) }, elkander naar de mond praten.
t'àn làng ts'uì bé { (*boé*) }, iemand naar de mond spreken, instemmend zijne laatste woorden herhalen.
t'àn laū pē ē bīng līng, het bevel van zijn vader opvolgen.
sa t'àn sa hán, elkanders voorbeeld volgen.
t'àn ki hoē, van eene goede gelegenheid gebruik maken.
t'àn ing { (» *ân*) }, van vrijen tijd gebruik maken.
t'àn tsá, van de vroegte gebruik maken. vroeg....
t'àn si (en) *ē siaò* { (*ē*) }, van de gunstige gelegenheid gebruik maken.
t'àn làng bô ing { (*ân*) }, er van gebruik maken dat iemand bezig is (om hem te bestelen enz.)
t'àn ah, eenden hoeden.

嘆 'àn *T'àn*, zuchten.

t'oè lâng t'àn k'ì (*t'è*) }, een verdrukt mensch helpen, ruimer adem doen halen.

tiông u toán t'àn (*tiàng hì*) }, zuchten en snikken.

Tang

東 'ang *Tang*, oost, oostelijk.

tang hong, oostenwind.

tang sì, *tang hıng*, *tang bīn*, *tang ping* (spr. *pình*) het oosten, oostelijk.

ìng tang, naar het oosten gewend.

tang iû (» *iô*) }, lett. 'de oostelijke oceaan, Japan.

tang iû ts'at, jap. verlakt.

tang it sai it, de eerste plaats in het oosten en de eerste in het westen *i. e.* de 1[e] en de 2[e] gastenplaats.

kiû tang tsaó sai, overal rondzwerven.

tang tang sai sai, velerlei bezigheden.

bô tang bô sai, niets hebben.

tangtó sai oai, links of rechts neervallen.

冬 'ang *Tang*, winter; oogst.

tang t'i, winter.

lip tang, begin van den winter.

tang tsoeh (» *tseh*) }, winter solstitium.

kè tang (*koè*) }, den winter overblijven.

ah tang, den winter (op eene vreemde plaats) overblijven van schepen.

tang koe (» *koa*) }, winterpompoen.

ts'ìng tang, sterke N. wind (des winters).

tsè tang, de winterofferanden (aan de voorouders) doen.

tang kuì, wintergetij.

tsiáh tang, het wintermaal eten (in de 11de maand).

pò toā tang, het wintergraan zaaien (8ste maand).

siu tang, het wintergraan, de winteroogst binnenhalen.

hó nî tang, voorspoedig, vruchtbaar jaar.

tsá tang, eerste oogst (6de maand).

ùn tang, late oogst.

hó tang tō (*o*) }, goede oogst.

tsit tang, ééne oogst.

苳 Tang *Tang o ts'aì*, peterselie.

中 Tang *Tang ıng*, midden, midden in, in.

璫 Tang *Tin tin tang tang*, geluid van de guitaar.

tsit ê ts'uì tang tang kiò (en) *háo*, boven allen uit te hooren zijn.

sik tang tang, zeer glad, geslepen (van personen.)

sin tang tang, splinter nieuw.

suí tang tang, uiterst fraai.

蹾 Tang *K'a-tang tioh*, de voet tegen iets stuk schaven.

tsûn-tang tioh tsióh t'aò, het schip is op een klip geloopen.

Tang *Bân tang á*, winterkoninkje.

董 Táng *Táng sū*, opzichter, architect; commissaris.

toā táng, *sió tang*, hoogste en lagere opzichters.

蕫 Táng *Táng*, familienaam.

凍 Táng *Huih táng*, zwarte stukken bloed.

擋 Táng *Táng kù*, eene hoogere persoon gaan ontvangen.

táng tioh, aantreffen, tegen iets (eene gelegenheid enz.) aanloopen.

當 Tàng *Tàng tsin*, voorzeker, in waarheid, stellig.

tàng tsoè (» *tsò*), verkeerdelijk houden voor zich verbeelden alsof...
ún tàng, *t'ò* (en *t'ó tàng* (*t'ò*)), veilig, sekuur.

凍 Tàng *Kien tàng*, stremmen, bevriezen.
koā kaò tàng lâng, zoo koud dat men er van bevriest.
bah tàng, gelei.
tàng sȩng, bevroren.

Tàng *Īng tsíng kah tàng lâng* (*iōng tsing*), iemand de nagels in het vleesch duwen.
tàng tsih, op de tong bijten, prikkelen (als heete dingen).

儅 Tàng *Lí tȩng sim mih hàng tàng*, wat neemt gij waar? (in een mandarijn bureau of handelshuis).

同 Tâng *Tâng*, vereenigd, gezamelijk, gelijk, dezelfde.
sȩ tâng, gelijk, hetzelfde.
tâng sì (» *sȩ̀*), van denzelfden familienaam.
tâng nȋ eh, van hetzelfde jaar, van denzelfden leeftijd.
tâng tī tâng k'ó, lief en leed gezamenlijk deelen.
tâng sim tâng ì, één van zin.
tâng oā, van dezelfde examinatie zijn.
tâng k'í hong p'aì ê lâng, personen die gezamelijk fortuin en aanzien verworven hebben.
tâng mȇng (» *muî*), dochters uit hetzelfde huis gehuwd hebben.
k'ao su háp tâng, gelijkluidende afschriften van een testament die een gemeenschappelijk stempel hebben.

銅 Tâng *Tâng*, koper, koperen.
péh tâng (*pȩ́h* »), witkoper.
âng tâng, roodkoper.
téng ts'ī, kopergroen.
tâng tsing, koperen bel.
sig-nā tâng tsing, schelle stem, geluid.
tâng toé, koperen bodem, kiel (van schepen).
tâng hông, koperrood.
tâng gûn, met koper vervalscht zilver.
tsiáh tâng, lett. koper geld eten (onderdanen) uitzuigen.
ts'iū tâng sien, roesten van koper.
p'oà tâng kū siah, gebroken koper en oud tin *i. e.* van geener waarde.
tâng gê tsô-t'ih ts'uì kí, koperen zaken en ijzeren tanden *i. e.* hardnekkig volhouden.
tâng kòng, koperen kanon.

筒 Tâng *Tâng*, buis, koker.
tik tâng, bamboezen koker.
pit tâng, penseelenkoker.
tsī tâng, geldkoker.
ien tâng, schoorsteen.
hiā tâng, kokervormige dakpannen.
tsút tâng pò, een rol goed.

童 Tâng *Tâng tsí*, *tâng ki*, (*sin*), tooveraar.
tsiū tâng (*tsiō*), den geest hebben (van tooveraars).
koan tâng, (door papier te offeren) een tooveraar den geest doen krijgen.
t'iaò tâng (*o*), springen (van een tooveraar.)

䯨 Tâng *K'a tâng kut*, scheenbeen.

東 Tâng *Tâng gák biō*, tempel voor den rechter uit de onderwereld.

橦 Tâng *K'iā tâng*, stutten onder een dwarsbalk zetten.

重 Tāng *Tāng*, zwaar, wichtig; zwaarte, gewicht; zwaar, in hooge mate, zeer, groot, belangrijk.
k'in tāng, zwaarte, gewicht.

tāng tsaī, zwaar geladen.
sit tāng, netto gewicht.
sit tāng, tarra gewicht.
ku tāng (*ki* »), bruto gewicht = p'ù tāng.
tsing tā, *ka tāng* (*ke̱*), overwicht.
tāng sin, soortelijk zwaar.
hāng tāng, zeer zwaar.
tìm tāng, zwaar (specifiek).
īng ts'iú tìm tāng, op de hand wegen.
t'uī tāng, aan beide kanten even zwaar maken.
ts'ut tāng, het gewicht te boven gaan.
tāng ts'ìn, zware, valsche weegschaal.
hē tāng, *teh tāng*, *teh tó̱ tāng* (*hē̱*) (*le̱h*) (*te̱h*), ballast innemen.
hē soa tāng (*hē̱*), zand als ballast innemen.
tāng kut, soortelijk zwaar.
tāng pún, veel geld, een groot kapitaal vereischend (als eene onderneming).
tāng laī, lett. zware interest, woeker.
pàng tāng tsè (*tsè*), met woeker uitzetten.
pī-tim tāng, zwaar, ernstig ziek.
tāng siong (*siang*), ernstige, gevaarlijke wond.
tāng tāng è hìng hoat, zware straf.
kóng oē oē tāng (*oā ē*), geloofwaardig, degelijk spreken.
hī k'ang-tāng, hardhoorig, doof.
tāng bin, vast slapen.

Tāng, bewegen, in beweging brengen, zich bewegen; aanraken, aanroeren, een begin maken met.
tin tāng, bewegen, zich bewegen.
tāng t'aô sut bák, met hoofd en oogen wenken.
oáh tāng, levendig, vlug (van aard).
t'aô bák tsai tāng, naar de omstandigheden weten te handelen.
ngiaóh ngiaóh tāng, krioelen, wemelen (als insekten).
hong ts'e ts'aó tāng (*ts'oe*), bij het minste geruis.
tāng t'ó̱, aan den grond roeren, den grond open hakken.
tāng hong, iets openmakende de lucht er bij laten komen.
k'i tāng, iemand iets opdragen, lastig vallen met (beleefde term).
tsaó (en) *kiá̤ tāng*, zijn gevoeg doen.
tāng kang, het werk beginnen.
tāng ts'iú, het eerst de hand aan iets leggen, met iets beginnen.
ts'o̱ tāng, ruw werk.

⿰重瓦 *Tāng*, pot, urn.
Tāng *àn á tāng á*, potten en pannen.
kim tāng (» *taó*), beenderen urn.
hong tāng, pot ter afwering van windrampen op de daken gezet.

可 *T'ang*, mogen, het mag, om te... het
T'ang is te...
ēm t'ang, het mag niet.
t'ang ts'iò, belachelijk.
bò t'ang hó tsiáh, niet lekker om te eten.
bò t'ang hó, niet bijzonder goed.
bò t'ang, niet willen toelaten... 2° niet in de mogelijkheid zijn om.
bò t'ang tiáh tioh, geene mogelijkheid om hem te vatten.
i bô t'ang hō̱ goá k'oà̤, hij wil het mij niet laten zien.
i bò t'ang hō̱ goá k'ì, hij wil mij niet laten weggaan.
bò k'ó̱ siá̤ tang, het is niet zeker dat het mag.

牕 *T'ang á tsí*, bouten voor een raam.
T'ang *t'ang á*, venster, raam.

t'i t'ang, dakvenster.

ts'iū tièm t'ang (*ts'iō*) , de winkelblinden sluiten, inzetten.

keng t'ang (*kui*) , verlicht, knap.

t'ang keng (» *kui*) , doorzichtig transparent.

piah t'ang, kastje in den muur.

se t'ang, met doek bekleed vensterraam.

t'ang á mêng, vensterdeuren, blinden.

t'ang lāng / *lān t'ang* / (*t'ang lāng*) , door en door (als gebeeldhouwd gesneden voorwerpen.)

桶 T'áng *T'áng*, vat, kuip, ton, tobbe; fig. voor eene vereeniging van personen of eene familie gebruikt waarvan de leden door de duigen worden voorgesteld.

t'ang á, kuip, emmer.

poáh t'áng, emmer.

tsui t'áng, wateremmer.

bīn t'áng, waschkom.

k'a t'áng, voetkuipje.

t'áng kao, puthaak.

t'án poā, presenteerblaadje.

t'áng niā, dwarshout in een emmer (om een touw aan te binden).

hō t'áng, emmer waarmede men water op het land giet.

t'áng toé (» *té*) , bodem van een kuip.

t'áng ts'iā (» *ts'iō*) , duigen van een vat of emmer.

k'iā t'áng, in een ton staan en zoo doodhongeren (straf).

p'ai t'áng, slecht vat, slecht gesteld (met eene zaak).

laò t'áng, een uiteen gevallen kuip 2° eene uit elkander gegane familie.

t'áng k'o, hoepel om een kuip.

toā t'áng k'o. iemand die de geheele familie nog bij elkaår houdt.

kā làng k'o hó t'áng, eene zaak tusschen personen bijleggen.

p'ah p'oà t'áng, een kuip stuk maken; twist tusschen personen doen ontstaan.

poā t'áng sai è làng (*tsui*) , iemand die weinig kennis bezit.

put t'ong t'áng, niet praktisch, niet naar de omstandigheden weten te handelen.

kùn t'áng, doortrapte schelm.

tá t'áng, eene laag verf of kalk over lijkkisten enz leggen 2° plagen, sarren.

p'aò t'áng laī, in het fort.

hia t'áng, laarzenschacht.

béh t'áng (*boéh* ») , het been, de kuit van eene kous.

T'áng *P'é t'áng* (*p'oé*) , huid, vel (als kleeding) pels.

iā ko t'áng, schapenvacht (voor kleeding bereid).

p'aò t'áng, pelsvoering van eene lange overjas.

疼 T'àng *T'àng t'iā*, pijn doen, zeer doen.

k'ó t'àng, bedroefd, inwendig hartzeer.

透 T'àng *T'àng*, doorloopen in... tot...

t'àng kè, doorgaan (als een priem door papier enz.)

sa t'àng (*sio*) , corresponderen met (als kamers, wegen) in verbinding staan met

sa t'àng làng (*sio*) , door en door, (als een wond enz.) in elkander loopen (als kamers) met elkander corresponderen.

sa làng t'àng (*sio*) , do.

趟 T'àng *P'ao tsit t'àng*, één rit rijden.

paó tsit t'àng bé (*bē*) , do.

kiā tsit piên (en) *lìn t'àng* (*piên*) (*o*) , ééns rondgaan.

虫 *T'âng*, worm, rups, insekt.
T'âng *bīn* en *būn t'âng* (*būn*), wormen (in het lichaam).
t'âng kién (» *kán*), insektenpop.
t'âng si, rupsenzijde (als vischlijn gebruikt).
báng t'âng, muskiet.
tsiù t'âng, invretende wormen, mot.
hiā t'âng, kleine soort duizendpoot (op de dakken gevonden).
tsiēn t'âng, ondeugende duivel (tegen kinderen die overal aanzitten).
t'âng á, dreumes (door moeders tegen hare kinderen gezegd).
t'âng t'oā, insekten (in het algemeen).
ts'ì ming t'âng, zeer behaarde rups.
o tō t'âng, rups met zwarte buik; nietige worm (als de mensch op aarde).
p'ai t'âng ts'ì, slechte, boosaardig mensch.
iêm âng-si t'âng, in een zoutpot ontstaan wormen *i. e.* moeielijkheden maken of wantrouwen zonder dat er reden voor bestaat.

桐 *T'âng iù*, olieverf.
T'âng *t'âng iù he* (*hoe*), kalefaterkalk, soort van stopverf.

筩 *T'āng*, boei, ton; dobber.
T'āng *hi t'āng*, dobber.
tiō t'āng, ankerboei.
T'āng *T'iu t'āng*, aan de marionetten trekken. *i. e.* onderwijzen, leeren (gew. door vrouwen gezegd).

Tao

兜 *Tao*, naar zich toe halen.
Tao *tao oá*, do.
tsiū tao, nader bijkomen.
tao liù, met geweld terug houden.
tao ân, vast aanhalen.
oè-tao tī (*te*), strak om de hiel sluitend van schoenen.
bò tao bò sao, *bò tao sao*, onbepaald, onzeker over iets spreken.
tao hún, meel met water mengen.

處 *Tao*, huis, woning.
Tao *lí k'ì in tao*, ga naar zijn huis.
tsit tao, hier.
nī tao, *nī tao pí* (*nī tao*) (*o*), eind van het jaar.
ts'ù pī tao, dicht bij huis.
tsù k'a tao, do.
kūn tao (*kīn* »), dicht bij, niet ver afgelegen.
siā tao k'iā k'í, dicht bij de stad wonen.
pē bú k'a tao (*pē bó*), bij de ouders in huis zijnde, nog ongehuwd.

兠 *Tao su*, brutaal, onverschrokken.
Tao

斗 *Taó*, vat; inhoudsmaat van drooge waren,
Taó bak enz. om iets te bevatten. Het sterrebeeld Sagit tarius.
bí taó, rijstmaat.
sing taó siā, bij de inhoudsmaat berekenen.
koā taó, de standaard taó.
taó t'aó, maat, inhoud van een taó.
taó kai, strijkhout van een taó.
taó sui, vaste meter in een handelshuis.
bák taó, inktdoos (door timmerlieden gebruikt.)
pùn taó, vuilnis schepper.
ts'ia pùn taó, *ts'ia p'a līn taó*, ombuitelen, duikelen.
pit taó, penseelenkoker.
ki koā taó, bak halverwege of boven aan een vlaggestok.
hé taó, stoof.
ut taó, strijkijzer,
hō taó, gietemmer 2° opgewipte kin.

toā taó tsį bō, een groote vilten hoed.
k'a ts'ɛng taó, bodem, onderste gedeelte van een voorwerp.
k'a ts'ɛng taó-toā, eene machtige steun hebben.
p'è (en) *sut aō taó*, iemand heimelijk de gelegenheid afsnijden.
ts'ù aō taó, achterplaats van een huis.
tāng taó, zwaar, veel; voorspoedig, bloeiend.
pak taó, de Groote Beer.
lâm taó, Zuidpoolsterren.

脰 Taó
ts'uì ē taó (*ẹ̄*) }, de kin.
ē taó ts'iu (*ẹ̄*) }, de kinbaard.
p'ai̤ ts'uì taó, gemeen uitschelden.

鬥 Taò
Taó, strijden, wedijveren, om strijd.
taò tsoè tsing (» *tsò tsàn*) } wedijveren om de voorste zijn.
taò su iâ̤, wedijveren.
taò ling tsûn (*liông*) }, wedroeien van drakenbooten.
taó pó, kostbaarheden tegen elkander vergelijken.
taò sa̤ tsi̤ (» *sio tsẹ*) }, om strijd doen.
taò boé (» *bé*) }, om strijd koopen.
taò ūn k'ì, van het geluk afhangend.
taò tsō hoà, bij geluk, gelukkig.

湊 Taò
Taò (*tsò̤*) }, bij elkander brengen, vereenigen, in elkander zetten, doen in één grijpen; gezamelijk, met elkander.
taò t'i̤, bijleggen, aanvullen.
taò hù, het stel volledig maken.
taò hì, eene tooneeltroep bijeen brengen.
tsáp taò laò, van allerlei plaatsen bij elkander gehaald.
taò ts'ī, bij elkander hetzelfde beroep uitoefenen, als schoenmakers die dezelfde straat bewonen.
taò kọ, gezamelijk aandeel hebben in.
taò tóng, gemeenschappelijk verbond vormen, zamenspannen.
taò siū, gezamelijk overdenken.
taò sún, in de sponning sluiten, in elkander grijpen (van woorden).
taò ts'ìng, een geweer in elkander zetten.
taò pang k'ì in, karavaan, gezamelijk gaan.
taò pang ìh, gezamelijk iemand helpen.
taò sa̤ tsūn, elkander helpen.
taò k'a ts'iú, een handje helpen.
taò ts'aò, toevallig.

午 Taò
12 uur 's middags.
dzít taò, middag.
ē taò, namiddag.
tɛng taò, vóórmiddag.
tiong taò, middag 11—1 uur.
dzít oṳ̀ taò, tegen den middag.
tsiáh taò, het middagmaal eten.
hioh taò, eene middagrust nemen.
soah taò, eene middagschoft nemen.

罩 Saò
Taò, met een bol voorwerp bedekken. bedekken.
taò koe, kippen onder een mand doen.
koe taò, kippenmand.

到 Taò
Láo taò, ervaren, bedreven in.

投 Taò
Taò, het verkeerde aantoonen van; beschuldiging inleveren tegen....
taò hânq, zich overgeven aan, zich aansluiten aan, zich onderwerpen.
taò sing, zich overgeven, onderwerpen.
taò ki, overeenstemmen in idée.
taò hioh (» *hẹh*) }, overnachten te...
taò sù, aangifte doen van.
taô kun, op de lijst der soldaten zetten zich bij het leger doen inschrijven inlijven.
taô tsúi, zich verdrinken.

taò si̤ bò taò sí (se̤), geeft men zich over dan is het om het leven te behouden en niet om te sterven.

taò so̤, zijne onschuld aan den dag brengen, zich verdedigen.

taò kò, het ware van eene zaak openleggen (aan mandarijnen).

goá taò lih, ik zal het u zeggen hoe het is.

taò i ê laō pē, zijn vader kennis van iets geven (als van het slechte gedrag zijner kinderen.)

taò t'ai, in de buik eener vrouw ontvangen worden (als zielen uit de onderwereld).

taò t'iep, eene visitekaart afleveren, afgeven.

taò pin, een verzoekschrift indienen.

taò bùn su, eenen mandarijnbrief afgeven.

taò t'i̤ taò toē, tot hemel en aarde spreken (als iemand die in zich zelven spreekt).

Taò *Bák taò* (eig. *táo*), inktdoos (door timmerlieden voor hun inktlijn gebruikt).

骰 *Taò á*, dobbelsteenen.

Taò *ts'iet taò á toā*, aan dobbelsteenen snijden.

poáh taò á, met dobbelsteenen gooien.

taò á tìng, lantaarn in den vorm van een dobbelsteen.

Taò *Tsē taò (ts'ē)*, de verantwoordelijkheid op zich nemen.

豆 *Taō*, boonen, peulvruchten.

Taō *taō ngoeh (keh* of *ne̤h)*, erwten.

taō tsiù (» tsio̤), soja.

ho lin taō (lan), doperwten.

pèh taō (pe̤h ook *hū)*, witte boonen.

o̤ taō, zwarte boonen.

lik taō, groene erwten.

taō ts'aì (ook ge̤), spruitjes, boonenspruitjes.

taō hū, boonenwrong.

k'ah nṅg taō hū, zachter dan boonenwrong *i. e.* zwak, machteloos.

taō piá, boonenkoekjes.

taō iù, soja.

taō á hoe (taō á hoa), blokjes, ruitjes (dobbelsteen).

kouh taō á liép (taò), aan dobbelsteentjes snijden.

taō k'o̤, taō piá (taō), oliekoeken, lijnkoeken.

taō sī po̤, gekookte en opzettelijk beschimmelde boonen, bij het maken van soja gebezigd.

bah taō, peulen.

to taō, soort Roomsche boonen.

bí taō, soort lange tuinboonen.

taō gè, boonenspruitjes.

taō kog, gedroogd boonenmeel.

脰 *Taō lāng*, de hals, nek (van beesten ook
Taō van menschen).

taō ām, do. (van beesten).

niá taō, halskraag van een kleed.

Taō *Taō taō lai*, steeds, gedurig komen.

Kù taō-īm sī án ni̤, dat is geen zin, dat
Taō wordt zoo niet gezegd.

讀 *I tsoè sim mıh taū tè*, wat doet hij,
Taō welke bezigheid heeft hij aan de hand.

偷 *T'ao t'eh*, stelen.

T'ao *t'ao k'oġ*, loeren.

t'ao t'iġ, heimelijk afluisteren.

t'ao si̤ (» se̤), onwettig, onecht 2e huisdieren.

sġ t'ao (sio »), verdraaien (als woorden of de wet).

海上絲綢之路文獻集成 科技與文化編

t'ao tsiáh, snoepen.
t'ao laō, heimelijk ontstelen, van iets afstelen.
t'ao tsiáh pō, slinksche draai, streek.
t'ao sim àm kīng, heimelijk, dievelings, ter sluiks.
t'ao tâm ta, alles stelen wat slechts voor de hand ligt.
t'ao ni t'ao liēm (lièm), afstelen.
t'ao kang, iemand met werk bedriegen, niet soliede maken.
t'ao tsiem, zoo naaien of borduren dat er van achteren bijna geen garen te zien is.

解 T'aó
T'aó, ontknoopen.
t'aó kat, losbinden, losmaken.
t'aó k'ui, ontrollen, losmaken.
t'aó toà, ontgorden.
t'aó k'uì, zijn hart lucht geven (door toorn); lucht doorlaten.
t'aó t'oah, naar de omstandigheden handelen, zich niet stijfhoofdig aan zijn idée houden.
t'aó, doorloop hebben (als water).
siao t'aó, uit elkander gaan, omgezet worden (als waren); geregeld doorgang hebben (als ontlasting).
t'aó k'iò, eene door anderen gedane gelofte voor zijn ongeluk, krachteloos maken.

T'aó
Miâ dzī-t'aó, dzī hō-t'aó, algemeen bekend.
tsui-p'oà ū tsit lō t'aó, waar opstapeling van water is moet men het toch ergens heen laten loopen *i. e.* wanneer men zeer in schuld is moet men toch eene manier of tijd opgeven wanneer men het terugbetalen zal.

透 T'aò
T'aò, doorloopen, doorgaan, uitkomen te, correspondeeren, in verbinding staan met; door, door en door, geheel en al; grondig door en door kennen; hevig van wind, regen enz.
tse nīng king ts'ù sa t'aò (nō kan) (sio), deze twee huizen loopen in elkander uit.
t'aò tsit sì koè (kè), niet alle plaatsen corresponderen (als een weg) 2e overal, alom.
sa làng t'aò (sio), met elkander correspondeeren (als aangrenzende kamers).
p'ah t'aò, een doorgang maken.
tsaó t'aò, overal rondgaan informeeren.
t'aò siao sit, berichten over en weer brengen.
kiâ t'aò t'aò, overal (in eene plaats rond geweest zijn.
bat t'aò t'aò, door en door kennen.
mîng-k'ui t'aò t'aò, de deur wagen wijd open doen.
hoan k'i t'ao, door en door omwoelen (als aarde).
t'aò á, spion.
ū làng t'aò lai, een spion is komen mededeelen...
t'aò hō lai, door den regen komen.
t'aò mi k'ì (mê), den nacht doorgaan.
t'aò t'iet, grondig inzien.
t'aò sin, over het geheele lichaam.
t'aò sin hoan, geheel en al veranderen (als een huis).
t'aò k'oah, de geheele breedte (als van een stuk goed).
t'aò tiaò, de geheele strook.
hong t'aò tsui t'aò, sterke wind en golfslag.
hō-t'aò, hevige regen.
tsit t'aò hō, een duim diepe regen.
laò tsui-t'aò, de stroom is zeer sterk.

趁 T'aò
T'aò tsá, 's morgens vroeg.
t'aò hong, in den wind, met den wind.
t'aò dzít, op klaarlichten dag.
t'aò dzít taò, op het midden van den dag.

ò Door doen, vermengen met, vervalschen met.

t'aò tsui, met water vermengen.

t'aò gû ling-tsiáh, met melk drinken (als koffij.)

ò *T'aô*, hoofd; bovenste gedeelte; hoofdpersoon, aanvoerder; het eerst, voor het eerst, de eerste, beste, voornaamste.

t'aô k'ak, hoofd.

t'aô k'ak t'ià, hoofdpijn,

t'aô ts'é (» *ts'oê*) }, hersenen.

t'aô tíng, kruin van het hoofd.

t'aô hiáh, voorhoofd.

t'aô bín, haarborstel.

sim t'aô, het hart.

t'aô tsing (» *tsûn*) }, van voren.

king t'aô (*kan* ») }, schouder.

gê tsò t'aô (*gê*) }, de kinnebakken.

t'aô tsang, hoofdhaar (vrouwelijk).

t'aô tsang bé, hoofdstaart.

tsím t'aô, hoofdkussen.

t'aô mîng (» *mô*) }, hoofdhaar.

t'aô mîng (» *muî*) }, hoofddeur, voordeur.

tsím t'aô tē, peluwsloop.

kûn t'aô, vuist.

tsíng t'aô á, vinger.

p'ai liēm t'aô, slechte gedachten.

k'a t'aô u, de knie.

ts'aì t'aô, radijs.

soàn t'aô, knoflook.

lō t'aô, landingsplaats.

po t'aô, haven.

pó t'aô (*p'ú* ») }, bijl.

loê t'aô (*lê* ») }, ploegschaar.

tsûn t'aô, voorsteven.

t'aô ui, voorste mast, fokkemast.

t'aô p'àng, voorste zeil, fok.

t'aô kun tíng (*kin*) }, marszeil.

t'aô lō, broodwinning, kostwinning.

t'aô k'ak tàm tàm, het hoofd laten hangen en denken.

kè t'aô (*koè* ») }, overschrijden, al te. .

tuì t'aô, gelijkelijk.

t'aô ke (» *ke*) }, heer des huizes.

ts'át t'aô, rooversheofd.

t'aô lâng, hoofd (van eene zaak).

t'aô si (» *se*) }, huisdieren.

ĭm tsai t'aô, neem mij niet kwalijk, bij ongeluk.

t'aô pò, hoofddoek.

pao t'aô pò, de hoofddoek omdoen.

k'iao t'aô, krom uiteinde, knop.

tit t'aô, rechte uiteinde 2° rechtstreeks, rechtuit.

î t'aô, rond uiteinde.

tsiem t'aô, spits uiteinde.

ū t'aô bô bé, onzamenhangend.

t'aô tsit ē, voor de eerste maal.

t'aô tsit kiā, in de eerste plaats.

t'aô bák, hoofd van iets 2° titel.

t'aô tsit pai, voor de eerste maal.

t'aô tuì t'aô, tegenover elkander.

t'aô t'aô, in den beginne.

t'aô k'í, in den wind opzwaaien.

t'aô kiáh ĭm k'í, het hoofd niet durven opheffen van schaamte.

boé t'aô ts'ī, iemand het eerst handgeld op een dag geven.

t'aô sing, te voren, zoo juist.

pao t'aô péh, een witte rouwdoek om het hoofd doen.

t'aô sū, het begin, voorbeeld van iets.

De titel van een boek.

dzit t'aô, de zonschijf

dzit t'aô ting of *té*, lang of kort van de dagen.
ts'iú t'aò t'àn tsiáh, met handenarbeid de kost verdienen.
kak t'aò, kant, zijde, hoek.
hong t'aò, in, op den wind.
t'aô bák, belhamel.
ts'ut t'aò ts'ut laó, zich niet langer kunnende inhouden zich met eene zaak bemoeien.
ts'iú t'aò hiù, de voorste van iets zijn.
poáh t'aô, omkeeren, achterste voren zetten.
t'aò ting hó, ts'ut t'aò hó, uiterst goed.
tsiū t'aô, naar het Noorden opgaan (van schepen, koopwaren enz.)
hė t'aô, van het Noorden terugkomen.
ming t'aò, adjudant van mandarijnen.
tsá k'i t'aô, 's morgens vroeg.
ē po t'aò, 's namiddags.
t'aò dzit, de eerste dag.
oē t'aô ting, lang om te vertellen.
hō t'aô, trompet, hoorn.
sai t'aò tsì, met het hoofd stooten.
iò t'aò, het hoofd schudden (afkeurend of medelijdend).
tìm t'aò, het hoofd knikken.
gû t'aò bé bīn, beest van een mensch.
k'a t'aò ts'iú bé, kleine, onbeduidende handelingen (van personen).
sim t'aô īm tiū, niet goed bij zijn verstand zijn.
t'aò ló (en) *laó*, hoofdschedel.
koū t'aô, mandarijngevolg.
tsit t'aò ts'in, siang t'aò ts'in, familie door een enkel of door een wederzijdsche huwelijk.
tsit t'aò tsit tùi, met beiden een geheel uitmaken (zonder bijzitten te hebben).
t'aò tò k'eh, pas getrouwde vrouw die voor de eerste maal hare ouders gaat bezoeken.

T'aū *T'aū*, vergiftigen.
t'aū hi, visschen vergiftigen.
t'aū sih, vergiftigen.
ti of *kiêm kaò t'aū lah*, zoet of zout tot schadens toe.
t'aū k'ì, iemand vertoornd maken.

Taoh

搭 Taoh *Taoh*, klink, wervel, knip, dichtknippen, neerslaan (als de haan van een geweer).
mîng taoh á, klink, knip van de deur.
ts'â taoh á, houten wervel.
taoh tioh, in den klem van iets komen, tusschen iets komen.
taoh tioh bo lâng, met zeker iemand heimelijk slechte omgang hebben.
niaú ts'ú taoh (*ts'i*), rattenklem.
taoh tioh niaú ts'ú, ratten in eene klem vangen.
īm t'ang hō lâng taoh k'ì, laat u niet in strikken vangen, bedriegen.
té taoh, korte wervel. 2° niet aan de toekomst denken, alleen voor het oogenblik zorgen.
àm taoh, knip (van een deur, slot enz.)
p'ah tìh taoh á, heimelijk beraadslagen.
tsih k'it ts'ùi k'i taoh tioh, op de tong bijten.
tìng taoh, loeren om in zijn val, strik te krijgen.
mîng-k'an taoh ts'ùt k'ì, haal als gij uitgaat de deur op de klink.
táoh táoh haò, knakken, kraken (als de vingers).
hō á taoh taóh, dropregen.
taóh taóh á kiâ (en) *lai*, langzaam loopen, komen.
taóh taóh á kóng, zeer langzaam spreken.
ti ti taóh taóh, voorttrippelen; achter elkander.

Tap

答 *Tap*, antwoorden.
Tap *in tap*, do.
būn tap, vragen en antwoorden.
pò tap, vergelden.
tap siā, dankbetuigen.
tap lé, beleefdheid beantwoorden.
tuì tap, elkander antwoorden.
tap paì, eene visite beantwoorden; eene buiging beantwoorden.
tap tsoá, iemand door geschenken bedanken voor het offerpapier dat hij aan een lijk geofferd heeft.
Tap *Put tap nó (ts'it)*, niet betamelijk handelen, met ouderen als met zijn's gelijken omgaan.
𠯗 *T'ap*, afmeten op.
T'ap *t'ap lai t'ap k'ì*, do.
t'ap u, holletje (van de hand), kuil (in den grond); diep instaand (van oogen).
t'ap lap, ingevallen, met deuken.
t'ap k'ọ̀ k'a, de broekspijpen in de kousen gestopt.
t'ap bák, ingevallen oogen.
t'ap dzī, karakters afdrukken, aftrekken) (van steenen enz.)
sa t'ap k'a (sio), in elkander gedrongen loopen, onmiddelijk achter elkander loopen (als soldaten) de voet tegen den enkel van den anderen aanstooten.
sa t'ap k'i (sio), in elkander grijpen als de tanden van een rad.
t'ap béh (» boèh), de broek in de kousen gestopt.
pit t'ap, penseelendopje.
T'ap *Toā-t'ap soè*, het kleine in het grootere doen sluiten (als kopjes).
t'ap k'ang t'ap p'ūng, de gaatjes dichtstoppen; van het minste oogenblik dat men tijd heeft gebruik maken om iets anders te doen.

Tat

結 *P'ah tat*, de platte grond voor een huis,
Tat de plaatsing der kamers enz. uitleggen, verdeelen 2e eene zaak te voren overwegen en beramen.
ū soah tat, berekend, geregeld (van eene zaak).
oé kó tat, klein, dwergachtig (van menschen en voorwerpen).
達 *Tát*, doordringen, doorgronden, door en
Tát door verstaan; kundig, verstandig; open, openlijk.
tēn tát, door en door verstaan.
t'ong tát, knap, kundig.
tát tō li, iemand die de zaken verstaat.
tát ì, begrijpen.
hién tát, algemeen bekend, alom beroemd.
hoat tát, er boven opkomen, in bloeienden staat.
sù biēn pat tát, van alle kanten zichtbaar, openlijk.
値 *Tát*, waard zijn, kosten; het waard zijn,
Tát verdienen.
tát tsị, geld kosten, duur.
kè tát (koé »), meer dan de waarde.
tsiaò tát, volgens de waarde.
īm tát, niet waard zijn, der moeite niet waardig.
tiōng tát, het is billijk, betamelijk dat...
i tát tit goá, hij verdient het aan mij, ik heb verplichting aan hem.
笛 *Tát á*, fluit.
Tát
幸 *Tát tit...*, gelukkig dat...
Tát

tát tit kín kín i, gelukkig dat het spoedig genezen is.

塞 T'at *T'at*, stoppen, dichtstoppen, toestoppen; verstoppen, versperren; stop, kurk.

t'at bát, dichtstoppen.

t'at laō, een lek stoppen.

t'at ts'uì, water stoppen.

ts'uì t'at, een stop.

t'at tsè, lett. schulden stoppen, afbetalen.

liáh si̥ t'at sí, lett. met levenden de dooden aanvullen *i. e.* het eene gat maken om het andere te stoppen.

t'at k'ang, een gat stoppen; 2° hulp of een uitweg verloren hebben.

t'at ts'iú p'ūng, lett. de ruimte tusschen de vingers stoppen *i. e.* door de handen gaan, ongemerkt opgaan.

t'at tḙ kiah, (voor niets anders goed zijn dan om) in een aardkloof gestopt te worden (scheld. tegen een nietswaardig mensch).

pḙ t'at, repareeren, stoppen.

kan t'at, stop van een flesch.

tsít tè ná kan tat nīh, als een stop van een flesch (van een klein mensch gezegd).

踢 T'at *T'at*, schoppen; doen opspringen.

t'at k'a, *k'í k'a t'at*, schoppen.

lâm kûn pak t'at, de Zuidelijke (Chineezen) boksen, de Noordelijke schoppen (bij hun vechten).

sai pe t'at (*poe*) }, op eene hooge plaats springen als of men vloog.

遢 T'at *Tsaò t'at*, nalatig, slordig, zorgeloos met...

t'at t'ó, hoe toch! kan het waar zijn!

達 T'at *T'at á to*, lans.

t'at á oè, sandalen.

托 T'at *Sat pìn t'at* (*t'ok*) }, kammenkrabber.

T.àt *T'át* ook *tát ta* (*t át*) }, droogschenken, afschenken.

t'át, (kinderen) baren (lage scheldterm door vrouwen tegen elkander gebruikt).

ti bú t'át ti á, de zeug werpt biggen.

Te

Te *ò te tsi̥* (*tsi̥ ò piá*) }, oestergebakjes,

t'aò tsang ts'in ts'iū k'ok á te, een hoofdkapsel (vrouwen) als een oestergebakje *d. i.* klein.

béh te ké, koekjes van tarwemeel en suiker.

低 Te *Kièn ko te*, zien wie de eerste, de winner is en wie de verliezer (als bij veldslagen, examinatie, wedrennen.)

短 Té *Té*, kort.

té sū, kort onderkleed.

té taoh, onbetamelijk (er niet aandenken of anderen door zijne handelingen benadeeld worden).

kiū té lō (ook *siū*) }, een eind aan zijn leven maken.

té kè siū (*té hoè siū*) }, kortstondig leven, vroegtijdige dood.

té kang, een kort werk.

té k'ièm, te kort komen, in schuld bij iemand zijn.

té k'eh (» *k'oeh*) }, een te kort bij iemand hebben.

té lō, kort.

pák k'ah té pō, te kort binden.

tsing li-té, weinig begrip van billijkheid hebben.

té pún, weinig kapitaal.

lūn ting té, over het verschil in prijs spreken.

ū ting té siaò, nog een weinig in schuld bij iemand zijn.

tè bih pák ts'â, met een te kort eind rotting hout bij elkander (willen) binden *i. e.* met een te klein kapitaal groote handel willen drijven.

從 Tè
Tè (*toè*), volgen.
kun tè (*kin toè*), volgen.
tè i k'a aō, op de hielen zitten.
sŋ tè (*sio*), elkander volgen.
k'a tè k'a, elkander op den voet volgen.
tè aō, naderhand.
tè hé-hoa (*hoé*), ik mag uitgaan (sterven) als het vuur.
tè lâng tsáo, zich laten schaken.

地 Tè
Tè (*tè*), de grond, vloer, plaats.
saò tè, den grond wegen.
hó tè, eene goede plaats.
kè tè (*koè*), naar eene andere plaats gaan, van plaats veranderen.
tè tè tióh-tè tè sī, overal gaat dat zoo, dat is overal de gewoonte.

塊 Tè
Tè (*tè*), een stuk, numeraal partikel voor vierkante dingen, tafels, stoelen enz.
sui tè, elk stuk.
kui tè, een geheel stuk, het geheel.
tsit tè toh, een tafel.

帝 Tè
Tè (*tè*), regeerder, opperheer, albestuurder, vorst, keizer.
hông tè, de keizer.
siōng tè (*siāng*), God.
ts'ing ông ts'ing tè, de voornaamste persoon op eene plaats zijn.
tè tsing, Boeddh. en Taoistische priesterbel.

笮 Tè
Filtreren.
tè tāo hū (*tẹ̀*), boonenwrong laten doorlekken.

戴 Tè
Tè (*tè*), familienaam.

茶 Tè
Tê (*tệ*), aftreksel van... thee.
tê sim, thee (de bladeren).
tê hióh, theebladen.
tê ts'iū, theeboom.
tê aō, theekopje.
tê hoe (» *hoa*), camellia.
tê p'iet (» *poā*), schoteltje.
ì dzin tê, aftreksel van gepaarlde gerst.
tê si, theelepeltje.
ko p'i tê, aftreksel van koffij.
tê koàn, trekpot.
sin k'ak tê, naam van een medicijn.
tê kọ́, theeketel.
tê kì, laag tafeltje.
tê sò, theedoekje ook wel spons tusschen het kopje en het schoteltje gelegd.
hō̤ ī boé tê (*bé tệ*), vergoeden, schadeloosstellen (iemand bij zijn ontslag).
bán tê, ts'ai tê (*tệ*), thee plukken.
tsoè tê (*tsò*), thee bereiden.
pē tê (*poē*), thee roosteren.
tê p'è (» *p'oè*), bijspijzen bij thee.
tê liaō, zoetigheden, confituren bij de thee gebruikt.
p'aò tê, thee zetten.
ts'iong tê, thee opschenken.
tsoŋ tê, thee zetten.
iet tê, het vuur van het theewater aanwaaieren.
tê pâng, theezetters (bij mandarijnen).
tê su, theeproever.
tê sai hū, theebereider.
tê koán, theehuis.
tê tsui, theewater *i. e.* zeer goed, zuiver water.

pūng tė, thee in groote hoeveelheid aankoopen.
tė láng }
(*tė̤* ») }, theemand.
tė t'áng, theekist.
tė sim koàn, theebusje.
tė soé }
(» *sé* }, doekje onder de trekpot gelegd.
te sò, do.
tė tsùn, theeschuitje, looden schoteltje onder het theekopje.
tė sim p'oh, afgetrokken theebladen.
tė p'iah, verslaafd aan thee.
tė kū }
(» *kī*) }, theegereedschap, theegoed.
tė tȯ̤, vracht van theegoed (door mandarijn bedienden gedragen).
soa̤ tė, wilde, slechte thee.
tė soa̤, theeberg.
tė k'eh, theekoopman (die jaarlijks thee gaat opkoopen).
tė á iû, theeolie, van de zaden gemaakt.
tė lō̤, sterk afgetrokken thee.

Tė　*Taō tė* (*kàn sim mi̤h*), wat doet hij?

地 Tē　*Tē*, aarde, grond; terrein, plaats; gesteldheid, toestand.
tē ki, fondamenten, grondvesten.
tē tso̤, grondbelasting.
tē k'ì, dampkring.
tē pán, vloerplanken, houten vloer.
tē sè, gesteldheid van een land of terrein.
tē lui, loopgraaf; bromtol.
tē gik, hel.
p'ah tē gik, voorstellingen uit de hel geven.
tē pó, wijkmeester.
tē hing koa̤, plaatselijke overheden.
tē tso̤, grondbelasting.
tē tȯ̤, landkaart.
tē tsien, vloerkarpet.
hoat tē é sȯ̤ tsuī, eene plaats die onder de wet staat.
tē lí su, een aardwichelaar, iemand die de goede plaats voor een huis, een graf etc., aanwijst.
tē pō̤, manier van leven, handelingen.
tē uī, kring van iemands bestaan.
gan tē, vermogen van het oog, gezicht (om goeden van kwaden te onderscheiden).
sim tē, gesteldheid van het hart, karakter.
bīn tē, voorkomen, gelaat.

袋 Tē　*Tē*, zak.
tē á, zak.
tē á pi̤ pi̤, een platte zak, *d. i.* zonder geld.
pò̤ tē, balen zak.
pò̤ tē toé, van onderen wijd van boven naauw.
tē sai, vol drek (scheldw. tegen stijfhoofdige menschen).

埭 Tā　*Tē hoa̤*, dijk.
tē t'aò, bij hoogwater door de zee bespoelde plaatsen.

弟 Te　*Tē*, jongere broeder.
lìng tē, uw of zijn jongere broeder (beleefd).
sià tē, mijn jongere broeder (nederig).
tē hū, jongeren broeder's vrouw.
tē tsú, leerlingen, volgelingen (van zich zelven tegen afgoden gebruikt.)
tsú tē tsit, plichten van jongeren.

第 Tē　*Tē*, rangaanduidend partikel; gebouw, huis.
tē it, de eerste; zeer uiterst.
tē kui é, de hoeveelste?
hú tē, huis van hooge ambtenaren (hun door den keizer geschonken).

推 T'e　Van zich afstooten, afschuiven; weigeren, zich verontschuldigen.
t'e si, weigeren, afslaan, zich verontschuldigen.
t'e t'ok }
(» » en *t'oah*) }, zich verontschuldigen.

t'e óh, uit school blijven.

胎 T'e Baarmoeder.
tsē t'e, in de baarmoeder ontvangen zijn.
siang t'e, bevalling van tweelingen.
si nīng t'e (*se nō*), twee kinderen gebaard hebben.
lab t'e, ontijdig ter wereld brengen (van beesten).
ka laòh t'e, ontijdige bevalling.
t'e laī-toà laìh, van zijne geboorte af hebben, met iets geboren zijn.
t'e ming, haar dat men reeds bij zijne geboorte heeft.

俫 T'e Leunen tegen, leuning; steunen op.
kao í t'e, rugleuning van een' stoel.
t'e kiō, achterover in een draagstoel zitten.
t'e tī goá ê sin k'u, tegen mijn lijf aan leunen (als kinderen) op mij steunen.

撐 T'e *T'e* (*t'e*), voortduwen, voortboomen (als een boot).
t'e tsûn (*t'e*), een schuit voortboomen.
t'e k'o, do. 2° schuitenboom.

茶 T'e *T'e hang tsióh* (*té*), veelkleurige steen.

體 T'é *T'é*, lichaam, vorm, voorkomen, gedaante; verwezenlijken, zich in iemands toestand verplaatsen; fatsoen, decorum, waardigheid, beleefdheidsvormen.
sin t'é, lichaam.
siet sin lō t'é, geheel naakt.
it t'é, gelijkelijk, niet verschillend.
kuì t'é-hó mah, hoe vaart gij? (bel. term).
t'é hō, benaming.
t'é hō làng, iemand een bijnaam geven.
taī t'é, in het algemeen, algemeen voorkomen.
t'é t'aì, voorkomen, uiterlijk.
t'é sik, *t'é keh* (» *sit*) (» *keh*), vorm, gedaante.
t'é sut, medelijden, consideratie hebben met.
t'é hoē, eene bedoeling, beteekenis vatten, opmaken.
t'é t'iep, *t'é t'iep dzin tsing*, inschikkelijkheid, consideratie gebruiken.
t'é liōng (» *liāng*), inschikkelijk zijn jegens.
t'é ts'at, onderzoeken, navorschen.
t'é dzīn, zich een helder begrip van iets vormen.
tsit t'é kap hit t'é bò sa tâng, deze twee vormen zijn niet gelijk.
t'é biēn, fatsoen, fatsoenlijk, aanzienlijk
sit t'é, onfatsoenlijk, ongepast.
bò lé k'é, onbeleefd, onfatsoenlijk.
t'ien t'é, zijn aanzien ten toon spreiden, op grooten voet leven.
tik t'é, voor zijn stand passend.
koa t'é, de waardigheid van een overheidspersoon.
kok t'é, de waardigheid van een rijk.
t'é t'óng, uitwendige beleefdsheidvormen.
bò t'é t'óng, geene beleefdheidsvormen in acht nemen.

退 T'e *T'è aō*, teruggaan, terugtrekken.
t'è k'ì, wijken, terugtrekken.
t'è hing, terugzenden.
t'è sik, verschieten (van kleuren).
t'è ts'ī (*soà ts'ī*), van de markt afgaan, de markt is afgeloopen.
tsui-t'è (*t'è*), eb.
soe t'è, achteruit gaan (in bezittingen).
kiā tò t'è, achteruit loopen.
tò t'è kiā, achteruit loopen.
t'è si, uit den smaak zijn.
sa tó t'è (*sio*), langs elkander gaan.
tsi-k'ah t'è, achteruit gaan in geld.

74

t'è laō ping, oude soldaten uit den dienst ontslaan.

t'è t'aô hun, afspringen van een huwelijk (door de dood van den aanstaanden man).

t'è tsį, de prijs verminderen, minder geld voor iets betalen.

t'è hé, het vuur verminderen.

t'è king, staal uit het vuur halen en laten bekoelen (om het buigbaar te hebben).

t'è tsui, door het water halen (als nieuwe kleêren om ze zacht te maken).

t'è lôh lai, naar beneden halen (als een vlag).

p'ah t'è tàng kǫ, verflaauwen in het trom slaan *i. e.* in lust voor iets verminderen.

p'ah tè gō nį, vijf jaren teruggaan, terugtellen, vijf jaren vroeger.

提 T'ê *T'ê*, omhoog heffen, opheffen, oplichten, opnemen; er boven op helpen.

t'ê ts'į, tot bewustzijn, inzicht brengen.

t'ê hông, waken tegen, op zijne hoede zijn.

t'ê àn, eene rechtszaak uit de handen van een lageren nemen.

t'ê sim, *t'ê sìn*, do.

t'ê tok, bevelhebber der land en zeemacht.

tsui t'ê, admiraal.

liók t'ê, generaal.

t'ê tiaō, (soldaten) oproepen en hunne plaats in de slagorde aanwijzen.

t'ê poah, (soldaten) roepen en verdeelen.

t'ê poáh, *t'ê hê*, uit den nood helpen, er boven op helpen.

t'ê k'í, ophalen, aanhalen (eene zaak); tot onderwerp van een gesprek nemen.

t'ê kǫ koan, zaken van vroegeren tijd ophalen, vertellen.

t'ê koāį (» *koân*) }, hooger zetten, hooger schrijven.

t'ê t'aô, bovenuitsteken (als de karakters voor den naam van een rijk, vorst enz.)

T'ē *T'ē* (*t'ę̄*) }, zeekwal.

t'ē tē (*t'ę̄ t'ę̄*) }, log.

níng t'ē t'ē (*nuį*) }, niet van zich durven afspreken.

sí t'ē, als een doode kwal, onbewegelijk blijven.

noą̄ t'ē, do.

t'ē-liáh hè tsoè bák, de zeekwal huurt het oog van een garnaal *d. i.* een dom mensch dat op het oordeel van een ander afgaat.

tsit p'úh ná t'ē nìh, een stuk als een zeekwal, log.

Teh

壓 Teh Drukken op, liggen op; zetten, leggen op; drukken, duwen op of tegen, stoppen, instoppen, indoen.

teh ìn (*tęh*) }, een stempel zetten op, bezegelen.

king teh (*kuį* ») }, papierdrukker.

teh tsoá, papier (op de graven) leggen (bij het feest der gravenreiniging).

teh k'òng, (geld enz.) in een graf leggen.

teh pak, de leegte in den buik aanvullen.

teh tǫ́ tāng, ballast indoen.

teh ts'iém, de kiel voor een schip leggen.

teh toē gún (*tē gìn*) }, geld in de fondamenten voor een gebouw leggen; geld vooruitgeven om de voorkeur bij iets te hebben.

teh toh, (eene fooi) op tafel leggen (voor de bedienden).

teh tó, omvergooien; uitmunten, overtreffen.

teh ki, stekken planten (als aardappelen).
teh han tsû t in, aardappelstekken zetten.
teh moǵ, volstoppen.
teh tiā̤, vastleggen; geld geven om de voorkeur bij een koop te hebben.
bò teh, onovertreffelijk.
teh toé, op den bodem leggen, lang in pakhuizen liggen (als koopwaren).
teh toé hè, waren die tot het laatst overblijven.
teh pún, zijn kapitaal hebben liggen (aan goederen die men niet kan omzetten).
teh piah kak, (voor niets goed zijn dan om) in een hoek gestopt te worden.
teh tsi̤, geld opzetten (bij het spel).
teh siaò, steeds eene post achterstallige schuld hebben, het oude betalen en het nieuwe op crediet koopen.
siaò-tsít ni̤ teh kè tsit ni̤, de achterstallige schuld van jaar tot jaar transporteeren.

Teh (*teh*) }, pikken, oppikken (als vogels doen).
teh tsiù, stukpikken.
teh tsiáo koà, zijn noodloot door vogels trekken.
tsiem teh teh, zeer puntig, scherp.
pe teh, rondvliegen en (eten) oppikken, overal wat zien te verdienen.

Teh, juist bezig zijn met.
teh tsiáh, aan het eten zijn.
teh tsē, gezeten zijn.

Téh tò lai, gestolen goederen terugnemen, aan de dieven ontnemen.
ts'iṳ́ téh (*ts'ió̤ t'èh*) }, uitplunderen, uitrooven.

téh (*teh*) }, afbinden (als takken van een boom).
téh tsai, binden en overplanten.
(*te̤h ki*) *téh ki*, takken afbinden en overplanten.

汚 *Tsuí-téh k'ì* (*té̤h*) }, het water stroomt uit,
Téh het is eb.
haí tsuí téh k'ì, de zee trekt terug, eb.
liaô téh (*té̤h*) }, op het door de zee bespoelde loopen.

裼 *T'ìng pak t'eh*, naakt.
T'eh *tsit laī bīn-t'eh liu liu*, gansch naakt in huis zijn *d. i.* arm.
soe kɛng t'aò-soé t'eh bīn, het hoofd glad kammen en het gezicht schoon wasschen.
t'ìng t'eh t'eh, gansch naakt.

取 *T'éh*, nemen.
T'éh *t'éh lai* (*t'éh*) }, brengen.
t'éh k'ì, wegnemen.
t'éh ts'ut lai, uithalen (als uit een doos).
t'éh ts'ut k'ì, uitbrengen (als uit een huis).
t'éh lóh lai, neêrbrengen (van eene hooger plaats).
boē bong boē t'éh tit, niet aangeraakt of opgenomen kunnen worden (als teêre of vermolmde dingen).
T'éh *Tsít tiaò k'uì teh t'éh*, op zijn uiterste liggen.
t'éh king (*kan*) }, de schouders ophalen.

宅 *Ts'ù t'éh* (» *t'é̤h*) }, huis.
T'éh *t'éh sîn*, huisgod.
t'éh bú, huisgodin.
an t'éh, een huis inwijden (door priesters gedaan).
ts'á ke lā t'éh, ruzie in huis hebben.
ké tsí t'éh, boomgaard.

Teng

當 *Tɛng*, dragen, verdragen, verduren; op
Tɛ̨ng zich nemen, voor iets instaan, de verantwoordelijkheid op zich nemen; te-

genover, ten overstaan van, voor; ten tijde van, tijdens, gedurende; het beroep uitoefenen van, zijn.

tɛng boē tiaô, niet kunnen uithouden, weerstaan.

tɛng ı̄m k'i, boē t'ɛng tit k'i (*bē*) }, on-uitstaanbaar, (zoovele eerbewijzingen) niet kunnen dragen.

tɛng hong ing, wind en golven te verduren hebben; verantwoordelijk zijn voor alles wat er gebeurt.

tam tɛng, er voor instaan.

tɛng kong, de zaken voor het algemeen op zich hebben (als de leden eener familie die beurtelings de familiezaken besturen).

ti tɛng, op zich nemen, voor iets instaan.

tɛng tîng. voor de overheden.

tɛng t'i̱ kóng oū, tegenover den hemel spreken, den hemel als getuige van zijne woorden nemen.

tɛng ko̱ kiet àn, voor den rechter beslissen.

tɛng t'aò tuì bīn, in iemands gezicht (zeggen enz).

tɛng si, tɛng ki si, toen der tijd.

tɛng ts'oe, in den beginne.

tîng goân ts'oe, do. ; in zijne jeugd.

tɛng hò t'i̱, bij goed weder.

tɛng t'aò péh dzıt, op klaarlichten dag.

tɛng kiū, tɛng ióng, in de kracht des levens.

tɛng bīng àn, eene crimineele rechtszaak.

tɛng ping, soldaat zijn.

tɛng ts'e, mandarijnbode zijn.

ts'iong tɛng, in betrekking komen (als soldaten enz.)

Tɛng *Tɛng*, heimelijk kijken, loeren op; lagen of strikken leggen aan, verstrikken.

tɛng tán, loeren op (als op een vogelknip).

tɛng tiòh, verstrikken.

tɛng tsiaó, vogels verstrikken, vangen.

tɛng sin tɛng báng, op vliegen en muskieten loeren, *i. e.* zorgvuldig onderzoeken, nagaan.

轉 *Tɛ́ng sin* (*tui̱* ») }, zich omdraaien.

Tɛ́ng *oát tɛ́ng lai*, do.

i̱ i̱ tɛ́ng, ronddraaien.

tɛ́ng séh, rondslingeren.

(*hè sim*) *tɛ́ng ì*, van plan veranderen.

tɛ́ng pi̱, in overgang van kind tot man zijn.

tɛ́ng (*tui̱*) }, vereffenen (een geschil).

tò tɛ́ng, terugkeeren.

tɛ́ng sik, verkleuren (in aanverwante kleuren overgaan).

tɛ́ng pi̱, over de kinderjaren komen, mensch worden.

p'ai̱ tɛ́ng sin (*bai tui̱ sin* }, zich slecht kunnen roeren, in een leelijk parket zitten.

tɛ́ng ts'iū, van kind man worden.

óat lìn tɛ́ng, omkeeren, omdraaien, in een ommezien.

tɛ́ng tsih koan, een draai aan zijne woorden geven.

tɛ́ng tsìng (» *tsìn*) }, eene ommekeer krijgen (van eene ziekte).

tɛ́ng toā làng, man worden.

tɛ́ng sū, eene zaak, twist vereffenen.

ho̱ kong ts'iu tɛ́ng, door een middelaar laten vereffenen.

hoan tɛ́ng sin-tsiū lai, in een ommezien komen.

tɛ́ng âng, rood worden, in rood veranderen 2e uit den rouw gaan.

tɛ́ng ts'ù, naar zijn huis terugkeeren (door de bruid eenige dagen na haar huwelijk gedaan).

boē tíng k'ang, niet uit het gat kunnen (geen geld kunnen leenen om reeds gekochte goederen te betalen).

tíng hong bīn, omdraaien van den wind 2e eene andere richting aan eene zaak geven.

tíng p'aį t'į, slecht, leelijk weder worden.

當 Tèng *Tìng*, als pand geven, verpanden; verhijpothekeeren, lombard, pandjeshuis.

tìng tiàm, pandjeshuis.

tìng p'iò, lombardbriefje.

tiàn tìng, pandjeshuis.

hiòng tìng, gepatenteerd pandjeshuis.

tsún tìng, waarborg, onderpand.

tìng t'aò, verpande goederen.

sìn tìng, op goed vertrouwen verpanden. (voor meer zelfs dan het voorwerp waard is).

tìng ts'ù, een huis verpanden, met hijpotheek belasten.

搥 Tèng *Tìng hing* (*tuį*), zich op de borst slaan (van smart of spijt).

t'oè lâng tìng hing (*t'è*), voor iemand instaan.

tìng sim koŋ, zich op de borst slaan.

gûn-tuì hing k'ám tìng k'ìh, iemand geld tegen de borst werpen (om iets van hem gedaan te krijgen.)

tìng toē (*tuį tē*), vaste plaats die men voor zijne woonplaats heeft.

Tèng *Kiém toā tìng*, 's morgens vasten (en zijn rijst of geld daarvoor aan priesters en nonnen geven of aan de afgoden offeren).

tìng hē, neerzetten.

tìng í tìng toh, op stoel en tafel slaan (in woede).

tìng teh tsē (*tuį*), zitten, gezeten zijn.

ìng tìng ê lâng (*ùn t'ùn*), een ongezeggelijk mensch.

tú tìng (*o*), toevallig tegen (eene gelegenheid enz.) aanloopen.

頓 Tèng *Tìng*, numerale voor maaltijden.

sŋ tìng, 3 maaltijden.

長 Tìng *Tîng*, lang, uitgestrekt.

tîng sŋ, lange jas.

tîng tu (*» ti*), langwerpig.

tîng k'a ts'ìng, lang blijven zitten, plakken.

tîng bé ts'į, staartster, komeet; 2e ongeluk aanbrengend mensch.

hō i k'ah tîng tseh, wat langer maken; iemand een weinig toegeven.

tîng tsį tī i tao, nog geld bij iemand blijven staan.

t'éh tîng k'į, meer nemen dan men u schuldig is (van personen die eene loopende rekening hebben).

ts'ūn tîng, eene gelegenheid voor later open laten (als door eerlijk met iemand te handelen).

kóng lâng ê tîng té, veel op iemand aan te merken hebben, zijn doopceël lichten.

oē t'aò-tîng, lang om te vertellen.

tîng té siaò, wederzijdsche rekening. Rekening-courant.

goá kap i ū tîng té siaò, ik ben met hem in rekening-courant.

腸 Tîng *Tîng*, darm, ingewanden.

tîng á, darmen, ingewanden.

tîng tō, ingewanden, buik.

sį tîng, baarmoederzak (bij dieren).

bô pak tîng, zonder doorzicht.

bô tîng bô tō-tsiah tsít pé tą, niet door zijn doorzicht maar door zijn wagen voordeel behalen.

tîng tō tít, zonder doorzicht, niet naar de omstandigheden weten te handelen.

tsít tiaò tîng t'àng k'a ts'ìng, rechtuit, zonder doorzicht.

海上絲綢之路文獻集成 科技與文化編

唐 Tîng, *Tîng*, Chineesche dynastie v. Ch. 618—913, Chinees; familienaam.
tîng lâng, Chinees.
tîng oā, het Chineesch.
tîng soa, China.

堂 Tîng, *Tîng*, groot gebouw, tempel; hoofdvertrek, zaal, rechtszaal.
kong tîng, rechthuis.
tîng tíng, do.
óh tîng, school.
tîng tîng, voor de overheden.
sù tîng, voorouderlijk huis, tempel.
toā tîng, rechtszaal.
t'è tîng, van den rechterstoel afgaan; de rechtszitting sluiten.
lé paì tîng, Christen-kerk.
k'im tîng, rechterzetel (eerenaam.)
tsē tîng, op den rechterstoel zitten.
tít tîng, mandarijntolk voor het plaatselijk dialect.
k'iā tîng, aan beide kanten van den rechter staan (als zijn gevolg).
háng tîng, de rechterstoet een geschreeuw doen aanheffen om de misdadigers ontzag en vrees in te boezemen.
tsit tîng tsiū kiet àn, in één zitting eene zaak beslissen.

段 Tīng, *Tīng* (*tuī*) }, stuk, gedeelte, deel.
tsit tīng, een stuk.
lâng tīng, stuk van een mensch (scheldterm).
gín á tīng, tusschen kind en man in (15—18 jaar).

塘 Tîng, *Tîng*, vijver.
tí tîng, vijvertje.

斷 Tīng, *Tīng* (*tuī*) }, in tweeën breken.
tīng ling (*tuī*) }, van de melk afwennen.
tīng k'uì, den geest geven, sterven.
tīng tsit hāng, totaal weg.
tīng lō, den weg afsnijden, 2° geen omgang hebben met iemand.
tīng aō lō, do.
tīng poā lâng, tīng tsit lâng (*tuī*) (*tuī*) }, volstrekt niemand te huis.
tīng nīng k'ì (*nuī*) }, geheel en al, overal afgebroken.
lō tīng, druk bezochte plaats, plaats waar langs een ieder komt.
tīng ts'ùn ts'aó (*o*) }, uiterst arm lett. geen grasje hebben (niets te kooken hebben).
tīng hé hun (*hoé*) }, do.
bô tīng lâng, geen enkel mensch, niemand.
tīng tsíng, volstrekt niets meer.
tīng hûn hê (*hē*) }, geen wolkje aan de lucht.
tīng hùn iá, niets van iemand vernemen of zien.
tīng tsit ts'i (*ts'ē*) }, volstrekt niets.
tīng tiā, van zijn anker los gaan, 2° alle omgang met iemand aftrekken 3° zijn laatsten steun verliezen.
tīng kun (*tuī kin*) }, de wortel van iets uitroeien (als van eene ziekte).
ts'iong tīng (*tuī*) }, invallen en afbreken (als eene legerafdeeling.)
kat tīng (*tuī*) }, eene zaak met iemand afdoen, 2° alle verdere omgang afbreken.
siá tīng hō ih (*tuī*) }, iemand een schriftelijk bewijs geven dat hij niet meer met u te maken heeft.
tīng tsat (*tuī*) }, afbreken.

boē tīng, geheel en al verkoopen (zoodat men er later niets meer meê te maken heeft.)

tīng sin pe tīng báng haó, geen vlieg vliegt er, geen muskiet gonst er *d. i.* doodstil, eenzaam (als een weg).

撞 T'ing *Sa tīng tióh* (*sio tīng tióh*) }, tegenaan stooten (2° ontmoeten.

sa tīng t'aô (*sio tīng t'aô*) }, tegen elkander aanloopen, elkander ontmoeten.

tsoè koe tīng (*tsò ke tīng*) }, (den geheelen dag niets doen dan) rondloopen.

tīng lai tīng k'ì (*tīng*) }, heen en weer gaan.

tīng mîng (*tīng muî*) }, tegen de deur aanduwen (als honden).

丈 Tīng *Tīng* (*tīng*) }, 10 voet.

tīng dzī t'ui tsaī lâng kiáh, het hangt van den persoon af die een 12 voet lange ladder draagt (of zij waggelt of niet).

tsit tīng ts'a kaó ts'ioh, het verschilt veel.

bān tīng ts'un k'i, zeer diepe afgrond.

湯 T'ing *T'ing*, soep, saus 2° familienaam.

t'ing p'iet, soepbord.

t'ing si, soeplepel.

t'ing ti, warme badplaats (bij warme bronnen), warme bronnen.

t'ing pâng, badkamer (met warme baden.)

ióh t'ing, een drankje.

t'ing t'aô, soep, drankje.

ám t'ing, rijstwater, boeboer.

sa á ts'ing kaò ts'ut t'ing, zoolang zijne kleeren dragen totdat het sap er uit loopt.

脫 T'ing *T'ing* (*t'uì*) }, afdoen, afleggen, uittrekken; uitdoen; uitnemen.

t'ing sa, zijne kleêren uittrekken.

t'ing pak t'eh, naakt.

t'ing keng keng, gansch naakt.

t'ing k'ak, vervellen (als een slang).

t'ing k'ò ni hai, de zee met zijn broek willen bedekken.

p'é-t'ing k'ak, de huid vervelt.

t'ing hà, uit den rouw gaan.

t'ing oā, verruilen, verwisselen.

t'ing ts'uì k'í, tanden wisselen.

t'ing liú á, losknoopen (als een jas).

t'ing mîng, *mîng-t'ing k'í lai*, een deur uitnemen, uitlichten.

t'ing ui, een mast uitnemen.

t'ing ts'iah k'a eh dzip lók, *ts'ing hia eh tsiáh bah*, die blootvoets zijn, vervolgen het hert en die laarzen aanhebben eten het vleesch *i. e.* de paarden die de haver verdienen, krijgen ze niet.

燙 T'ing *T'ing*, branden, zich branden, (aan heet water).

sio t'ing, zich branden.

t'ing sim koa, zijn binnenste branden.

sio-kaò t'ing ts'iú, zoo heet dat men er de handen aan brandt.

t'ing p'ông p'ā, zich een blaar branden.

t'ing kún tsui, door kokend water halen (als groenten zonder ze te laten koken).

iû-t'ing tiòh, zich aan kokende olie branden.

販 T'ing *T'ing* (*t'uì*) }, overdoen aan.

t'ing hè (*t'uì hoè*) }, goederen aan een ander overdoen.

sa t'ing, aan elkander overdoen.

t'ing lâng, aan een ander overdoen.

糖 T'ing *T'ing* (*t'ing*) }, suiker.

péh t'ing (*péh* ») }, witte suiker.

kak t'ing, witte broodsuiker.

ping t'ing, candijsuiker.

bit t'ing | *(bit o)* } , honig.
t'ing tsui, suikerwater, siroop.
soah t'ing, zoet maken.
t'ing koàn, suikerpot.
t'ing sing, kandijsuiker.
soa t'ing, korrelsuiker.
laō bé t'ing | *(boé)* } , bruine suiker.
t'ing laō, suikertrechter, filtreer.
k'oeh t'ing | *(k'eh »)* } , suiker persen (uit het suikerriet).
t'ing p'o̤, suikerperserij, suikerfabriek.
t'ing ts'ia, suikerpers.
tò t'ing, gesmolten suiker in vormen gieten.
t'ing ang á, suikerpopje *i. e.* iemand die iedereen besmet, benadeeld die met hem te maken heeft.
t'ing á, suikerfiguren, popjes enz.
t'ing oân, suikerballen.
kuī t'ing sai, knielen als een suikerleeuw *d. i.* knielen (als voor den rechter).
t'ing tiàm, suikerwinkel.
t'ing pàng, suikerfabriek.
t'ing pang, reepen suiker.
t'ing ang á gaò luī lâng | *(o)* } , suikerbeeldjes kleven lichtelijk, *i. e.* die met pek omgaat, wordt er door besmet.

溫 T'ĭng
T'ĭng | *(t'ui̤)* } , opwarmen (eten).
t'ĭng ts'aì, groenten opwarmen.
t'ĭng sio, warm maken.
bòh tit tsiép tsiép t'ĭng | *(t'ui̤)* } , warm dat niet zoo gedurig op, herhaal dat niet zoo dikwerf.
koh teh t'ĭng, weder opwarmen, weer over iets spreken.

杖 T'ĭng
T'ĭng hui | *(t'ĭng)* } , porcelein verglazen.
t'ĭng tiá | *(t'ĭng)* } , een pan verglazen.
kè t'ĭng, verglazen.
t'ĭng oá, kopjes verglazen.

杖 T'ĭng
Hà t'ĭng | *(t'âng t'ĭng)* } , rouwstok die de oudste zoon achter het lijk zijns vaders draagt.
sik t'ĭng, de sleutel van de onderwereld, door Boeddha. priesters gebruikt om geesten te verjagen.

T'ĭng *Ts'in t'ĭng* | *t'ĭng)* } , gewicht van de hand
2° voorwerp zonder hetwelk men niets kan doen.

T'ĭng *T'ĭng*, een dwarsbalk.
mìng t'ĭng, een sluithout om deuren dicht te houden: in 't maleisch palang-pintoe.

Ti

知 Ti
Ti, weten, kennen verstaan; kennis geven, bekend maken aan.
siong ti, elkander ('s karakter) kennen.
ti tsiok, lett. weten wat genoeg is, te vreden zijn.
put ti put tsoē, onwetend zondigt niet.
ti kí, intieme vriend.
ti sim oē, intieme mededeeling.
ti im, verstand hebben van.
tsoè ti ki̤, gezien hebben, ooggetuige zijn.
ti to̤, lijst der gasten van wier komst men verzekerd is.
ti tsing, erkentelijk zijn.
t'ong ti, bekend maken, doen weten.
pò ti, do.
ti hoē, do. (van ambtenaren).
t'oân ti tsìng lâng, aan allen bekend maken.
ti hú, departements magistraat.

猪 Ti
Ti, varken; varken (als kenmerk van domheid).
ti bah, varkensvleesch.
ti bú, zeug.

gōng ti, *toā ti*, dom, groot varken, domoor.

pūn ti bú, logge zeug (van een log dom mensch).

ti ko, beer, m. varken.

dzú ti, speenvarken.

ti p'e (*» p'oe*), jonge varkens.

soŋ ti, wild varken.

hai ti á, zwart zeezwijn.

hô ti, egel.

ti tiem, hakblok, spekslagerswinkel.

ti kaó-tsing si, (als) een beest (scheldterm).

ti tsô, varkenstrog.

ti lak soh, varkenstouw.

a p'ièn ti, groote opium rooker.

ti bú ts'aì, een soort van eetbare groente.

Ti tu, spin.

ti tu si, spinweb.

Ti ti taóh taóh, druppelen (als regen); trippelen; aframmelen.

ti hong ŋg, iemand in moeielijkheden beschermen.

Taò ti (*» tì*), toch eigenlijk.

bô ti tsi, zonder eind, eindeloos, onputtelijk.

ti hā (*» hē*), later, daarna, in het vervolg.

ti hā dzin (*hē*), bedienden, dienstboden.

ti li, de eigenlijke gesteldheid van eene zaak.

kun ti (*kin »*), iemands geslachtsboom.

sŋ tâng ti (*sio tâng tì*), van gelijken leeftijd.

Taì ti (*» tú*), remplaceeren door, van goederen.

ti tik (*ti en tú*), het uithouden tegen, bestrijden, strijden.

ti sik (*ti »*), in de plaats zijn van iemand die het beter verdient: beter tot iets geschikt is.

ti t'ông, in de plaats stellen.

ti giáh (*ti en tú*), aanvullen met, remplaceeren door.

ti tng (*ti »*), afweren.

ti tng, voor iets instaan.

戴 Tì *Tì*, op het hoofd dragen; opzetten, ophebben.

tì bō, een hoed, muts opzetten, ophebben.

tì tng, een knoop op de muts hebben (als overheden en aanzienlijk personen.)

lo' t'aò tì tiā, ondanks alle moeielijkheden een zaak aanvatten.

tì siaò kui bīn, een mombakkes opzetten *d. i.* beschaamd zijn.

tì oai toā bō, iemand iets zonder goede gronden ten laste leggen.

智 Tì *Tì*, kennis, verstand, kundigheden; kundig, verstandig.

bing tì, wijsheid, kennis.

tì sik, do.

ū tì huī, verstandig.

siōng tì ê lâng, een allerverstandigst mensch.

siet kè tì, listen bedenken.

蒂 Tì *Tì*, vruchtbodem.

hoe tì, vruchtbodem.

bô hing tì, geen lust, trek van iets hebben.

致 Tì *Tì*, gaan naar, komen tot aan; in aanraking komen met, geraken tot; als natuurlijk gevolg hebben, met zich slepen, berokkenen.

sǫ tì, door.... tot.... gekomen.

tì miā ê pō uī, *tì miā ê siong*, eene doodelijke plaats, eene doodelijke wond.

i tì, daardoor, het gevolg daarvan is.
put tì, dan komt het niet tot...., om te voorkomen dat....
tì ìm, beschermen, begunstigen.
tì pī, zich eene ziekte berokkenen.
tsū tì, zich op den hals halen.
tì tiōng, hoogschatten.
tì sim tì ì, zich steeds bezig houden met...., steeds gedachtig zijn.
tì sim tì koa, do.
tì ì, zich ongerust, bezorgd maken.

置 Tì — *Tì*, in orde brengen, tot stand brengen, daarstellen; zich aanschaffen.
kièn tì, daarstellen, oprichten, instellen.
ts'ú tì (*ts'ì* ») }, regelen, in orde brengen.
tì hè (» *hoè*) }, goederen koopen.
tiaò tì, opzettelijk.
toé tì, beginselen, principes.
p'ah tóe tì, fondamenten leggen, de eerste indruk die men maakt.

綴 Tì — *King tì*, uitzicht, ligging (van eene plaats).

遲 Ti — *Ti*, langzaam, traag; laat, te laat; dralen, vertragen, uitstellen.
i king ti, te laat.
hoán hoé k'ah ti (*hoè*) }, berouw komt te laat.
ti oān, dralen, uitstellen.
ti bān, vertalmen, dralen.
ièn ti, uitstellen.
ling ti, langzaam doodmartelen.
ti gi, dralen met.
tam ti bók tam ts'ok, men mag wel borg zijn wanneer er uitstel zal plaats hebben (als bij betaling) maar niet wanneer het geheel en al zal misloopen.

池 Ti — *Ti*, vijver, kom, poel, familienaam.
hi ti, vischvijver.
ti tìng (» *tòng*) }, vijvertje.
ik ti, gemetselde badkom.
t'ing ti, warme bronnen.
ti tàn (» *tìng*) }, gebouw, torentje in een vijver.
siâ ti, vestings (stads) grachten.
ti nìh bô tsui-bē io til hi, in een vijver waarin geen water is kan men geene visschen houden *i. e.* waar geene middelen zijn, kan men niet bestaan.

堤 Ti — *Ti hông*, op zijne hoede zijn tegen.

墀 Tî — *Tan ti*, de roode trappen naar den keizerlijken zetel.

Tī — *Kì ti*, geheugen.
hó kì tī, goed van geheugen.

在 Tī — *Tī*, zijn te.
tī hit é ūi, op die plaats, daar.
tī teh, aanwezig, tehuis.

治 Tī — *Tī*, regeeren, besturen; heerschen over. goed zijn tegen, genezen (als medicijnen).
tī kok, het rijk besturen.
tī ke, een huisgezin besturen.
ping tī, iemand valsch beschuldigen.
tī hā, onderhoorigen.
i tī, genezen, eene ziekte behandelen.
tī iao, honger stillen; den boozen geest uitdrijven.
ts'òng tī, plagen, lastig maken.
tiaò tī lâng (*k'iaò*) }, iemand plagen, lastig maken.

雉 Tī — *Tī*, fesant.
tī koe (» *ke*) }, fesant.

何 Tī — *Tī si*, wanneer?
tī tsit é, wie, welke?

箸 Tī — *Tī*, Chineesche eetstokjes.
tī k'a, eetstokjes.

tī lâng, koker voor eetstokjes.

gê tī, *gûn tī* (*gê*) (*gîn*), ivoren, zilveren, eetstokjes.

hê tī (*hoê*), tang.

ts'ìng tī, laadstok.

痔 Tī *Tī*, aambeien.

tī ts'ɛng, aambeien.

laī tī, *goā tī*, inwendige, uitwendige aambeien.

kiêm tī ts'ɛng, gierig.

弟 Tī *Hia tī*, oudere en jongere broeder, broeders.

sió tī, jongere broeder.

Tī *Kā goá bô tī taī ê sū*, het heeft met mij niets te maken, het gaat mij niet aan.

甜 Tị *Tị* (*tị*), zoet, (lekker.)

kam tị, zoet.

kiêm sɛng tị (*suị*), confituren.

t'ìng tị bit tị, fraailuidend, uitwendig fraai (van woorden enz.)

tị kiêm-tsiá bô hiêm, geen aanmerking maken op zoet, zout of flaauw *d. i.* alles eten wat voorgezet wordt).

họ sin t'am tị, de vliegen houden van zoet (gezegd van iemand die veel van zoetigheid houdt.)

跟 Tị *K'a aō tị* (*tɛ*), de hiel.

ts'iù tị (*tɛ*), elleboog.

tùn tị (*tẹ*), terugtrekken, niet vooruit willen (als een paard) niet willen weggaan (van personen).

kak tị (*o*), schoenhoorn 2e = kak ts'ia.

oê tị (*o*), schoenenlip 2e schoenhoorn.

táh tó tị, de hielen van de schoen plat trappen.

纏 Tị *Tị*, omwinden, omwikkelen, inwikkelen; omkronkelen, zich slingeren om ingewikkeld, lastig maken, hinderlijk, in den weg zijn.

tị soị, garen omwinden.

tin-tị ts'iū, de slingerplant kronkelt zich om den boom.

tị sin, in vele zaken gewikkeld zijn, met iets opgescheept zijn.

tị sin tsoā, slang die zich om iemands lijf kronkelt.

ị tị, ingewikkeld, lastig uit te maken = ị ị tị tị.

tị kang, lang duren, veel tijd kosten.

tị t'aô pọ, de hoofddoek omdoen.

kao tị, zich inwikkelen in (zaken), zich in moeielijkheden brengen (door slechte omgang).

tak tị, moeielijkheden ontmoeten.

tị lâng, iemand belemmeren, in den weg zitten.

ts'it tị pɔeh tị lâng, iemand gedurig moeielijkheden bezorgen.

tị k'a tị ts'iú, handen en voeten belemmeren, in den weg staan.

tị k'a poā ts'iú, do.

tsoè lī, *tsoè ị tị*, chronische diarrhee hebben.

錢 Tị *Poā tị*, reiskosten.

扼 Tī̤ *Tī̤* (*tē̤*), vastgrijpen.

kui-tī̤ nā̤ aô, een duivel greep mij bij de keel *i. e.* ik kon of durfde het niet te zeggen.

tī̤ ân, stevig vasthouden.

tī̤ kûn t'aô bû (*lô*), de vuist ballen.

tī̤ si-lâng ê kaô, iemands aap dood knijpen *i. e.* iemand de gelegenheid, om voordeel te doen, benemen.

tī̤ aō ts'iú, heimelijk in de hand stoppen (geld om iemand tot iets over te halen).

滀 Tī — *Nā aò-tī, aò-tī*, de keel vol hebben (voor dat men gaat schreien).
tsui tī (» *tī*), vloed.
tsui tiēm tī, het water is op zijn hoogste punt.
tī, vol, boordevol.
pá tī (*tī*), propvol 2e overvloedig (in bezittingen).
tsit tī oá (*tsit oá tī*), (de hoeveelheid van) één kopje vol.
tī kaò laò ts'ut lai, zoo vol dat het er uitloopt.

鄭 Tī — *Tī* (*tē*), familienaam.

擋 Tī — *Tī ming* (*tīng mui*), nog iets tegen de deur aanzetten.
sá tī k'a ts'ɛng (*sio tīng k'a ts'ui*), met de achtersten tegen elkander aan staan, gezamelijk een derden aanvallen.
sa tī pa tsiah (*sio tīng k'a tsiah*), met de ruggen enz. do.

黐 T'i — *T'i*, lijmen (vogels).
t'i tsiaó, vogels lijmen.
t'i k'a vogellijm.
īng t'i-t'i tsiaó, met vogellijm vogels lijmen.
liēm t'i t'i zeer kleverig.
lā lī t'i (*lō*), onafgedaan, verward.

展 T'i — *T'i*, uitspannen (als een stuk papier, als een vogel zijn vleugels enz.) openen als het oog, een waaier, paraplui enz.
T'i — *T'i sit* = *t'i sit*, de vleugels uitspannen.
t'i hō soà, eene paraplui open doen.

恥 T'í — *Liēm t'i*, schaamte, gevoel van schaamte.

剃 T'i — *T'i*, scheren.
t'i t'aò, het hoofd scheren.
t'i t'aò sai hū, barbier.
t'i t'aò to, scheermes.
t'i t'aò tà, barbiers vracht.
t'i t'aò ts'iū (*ts'iū*), vaste barbier.
t'i ts'ui ts'iu, de baard scheren.
tsiū t'i, met de vleug (van het haar) scheren.
tò t'i, tegen de vleug in scheren.
pút-t'i bīn, een afgodsbeeld het gelaat scheren, het oude verguldsel afkrabben om er nieuw op te doen.

啼 T'i — *T'i* (*t'i*), kraaien.
t'i k'aò, schreien, weenen.
t'i haò, schreien.
t'i t'i k'aò k'aò, zeer schreien (als bij een lijk).
ts'oeh ts'oeh t'i (*ts'eh ts'eh*), snikken huilen.
koe-t'i (*ke*), de haan kraait.
koe-t'i sā lóh (*ke*), de haan heeft reeds 3 maal gekraaid (de dag zal spoedig aanbreken).
t'i t'i eh k'i-ts'iò ts'iò eh lai, gaan de huilenden weg dan komen de lachenden *i e.* wat deze voor niet zeer goed houdt, houdt een ander voor goed enz.

苔 T'i — *Ts'ī t'i* (*ts'ē* »), korstmossen.
ho t'i, eetbaar zeewier.

罈 T'i — *Tsit t'i tsiú* (*o*), een pot wijn.

雉 T'ī — *T'ī koe* (» *ke*), fesant.
tsit t'ī sa (*t'ih sa*), een kloen, kluive vlas.

天 T'ī — *T'ī*, hemel.
t'ī-kɛng (» *kuī*), dageraad.
t'ī-p'ù kɛng (*kuī*), aanbreken van den dag.

t'i-im im } , bewolkte lucht.
(*o im*)

bö t'i li, van slechte beginselen zijn.

t'i lui p'ah si, moge de donder treffen.

t'i lō, onder den blooten hemel.

hó t'i, *p'ai t'i*, mooi, slecht weder.

t'i tsi } , gat in het dak van een vertrek om licht door te laten.
(» *tsè*)

t'i tsi tà, lantaarn in het dak van een huis ook tot bedekking van een binnen plaats.

t'i pi, horizon, gezichtseinder.

t'i pi hai kak, ver afgelegene (plaats).

ü t'i bö dzit t'aò, onwaar, geen gevoel van billijkheid hebben.

t'i-t'iah hák, ochtendschemering.

t'i k'i, weêrsgesteldheid.

t'i kong, hemelheer, god.

t'i bö bák, (het is als of) de hemel niet zien kan (dat Hij zulk een slecht mensch zoo ongestraft laat).

īm tsiā t'i, de hemel komt niet uit, de zon komt niet door.

tsiáh t'i lō, dauw intrekken (als planten); niets bepaald voor de kost doen.

k'oà t'i ts'ân, een rijstveld dat alleen door regen bevochtigd worden.

k'oà t'i k'oà toē, van den hemel afhangen (als geluk of ongeluk).

t'i o-toē àm, hemel en aarde worden donker (roepen er wraak over als over een zeer onrechtvaardig zaak).

t'i hoán toē loān, oproer, verwarring in het rijk.

hong tioh t'i bak-ts'in ts'in ts'in, *d. i.* nog niets van de moeielijkheden in de wereld afweten.

t'i t'ang, dakraam (in den top van een kamer).

t'i ts'ioh, kwadrant of sextant.

t'i t'iaō, hemelpilaar (van zeer lange menschen).

sai t'i kò lò hàn, in den Boeddh. hemel een leerling van Boeddha. gaan aanklagen *i. e.* iemand willen aanklagen zonder dat men weet waar hem te vinden.

ts'un t'i, lente.

t'i si, jaargetijden, gesteldheid van het weder.

sī i e t'i, het is zijn hemel, hij is op het toppunt van zijn macht enz.

添 T'i *T'i* uitscheppen, opscheppen.

t'i pīng } , rijst opscheppen.
(» *puī*)

ke t'i } , vermeerderen.
(*ke* »)

t'i k'ah ke } , bijvoegen.
(*ke*)

t'i t'iep, bijdoen, bijvoegen, vermeerderen.

t'i ts in t'aò, overwicht, toegift geven.

t'i t'aò t'iep bé } , er nog een weinig bij verdienen (als eene vrouw door handwerken bij het kleine loon van haar man).
(*boé*)

t'ó t'i, om meer vragen (als bij gewicht).

t'i t'aò, toegift, overwicht.

t'i ts'ùi t'i tsih, iemand nog erger tegen een ander aanzetten.

t'i tāng, gewicht bijvoegen, nog erger maken (als verkeerde medicijn eene ziekte te doen.)

撐 T'i *T'i* } , stutten.
(*t'è*)

t'i k'i lai, opzetten als een hangend voorwerp als een deurscherm.

t'i } , balanceeren op de hand.
(*t'è*)

t'i t'ui } , stijf in de beenen.
(*t'è* »)

ts'ù t'i } , steunpilaar van een huis.
(» *t'è*)

t'ang á t'i, stuthout voor een raam, luik (om het open te houden).

t'i̤ sai | *(t'ḛ hṳ̍)* }, leggen als een leeuw (van honden).

hṳ̍ t'i̤ t'ah | *(hṳ̍ t'ḛ t'ah)* }, op de achterpooten liggen en op de voorpooten steunen als een tijger.

t'i̤ tī hi p'ī nih, op de neus balanceeren.

aō t'i̤, achterstut (door een vader van zijn zoon als steun in zijn onderdom gezegd).

kap i t'i̤, met iemand in twist, ruzie zijn, vechten.

眩 T'i̤ *T'i̤ dzit* | *(t'ḛ »)* }, niet in de zon kunnen opzien.

t'i̤ bák, in de oogen, schitteren (als in de zon op te kijken).

hé-put tsi t'i̤ lâng bák | *(hoé)* }, het vuur schittert zeer in de oogen, is zeer fel, hel.

縫 T'ī *T'ī* | *(t'ī)* }, naaien, vastnaaien, toenaaien.

t'ī sa̤, kleeren naaien.

pó t'ī, verstellen, repareeren (van kleeren).

tsáp pó poeh t'ī, veel gelapt (van kleeren).

t'ī oá, aan elkander naaien, vastnaaien.

t'ī ts'eh, een boek innaaien.

Tia

爹 Tia *A tia*, vader! (door kinderen tot hun vader gezegd).

ló tia, mandarijn.

ló tia ni̤, mevrouw (van mandarijnsvrouwen).

peh tia, oom (tegen vader's ouderen broeder gezegd).

打 Tia̤ *Ka tia̤*,

ka tia̤ p'é | *(p'oé)* }, bast voor leerlooien gebruikt Avicennia: Terminalia: Rhizophora.

ka tia̤ siep, sap dier planten.

顛 Tia̤ *Tia̤ lai tia̤ k'i*, waggelen.

k'ōng k'ōng tia̤, waggelen (als dronken lieden).

tia̤ dzit, in de zon loopen.

tia̤ hō, in den regen loopen.

ts'i̤ tia̤, eensklaps, onverwachts.

tiem tia̤, zoo juist, daar even.

鍛 Tiá̤ *Tiá̤*, ijzeren pan.

tiá̤ tsai, middelste gedeelte van een pan.

tiá̤ ts'oè | *(» ts'è)* }, panboender (van rotting of cocosschil).

ts'oè tiá̤ | *(ts'è »)* }, eene pan boenen.

tiá̤ pi̤ | *(» pè)* }, steel van eene pan.

tiá̤ ien, roet van eene pan.

tiá̤ koà, pandeksel.

k'ao tiá̤, eene pan afkrabben (het roet er van).

pó tiá̤, pannen repareeren | soorten van

oā tiá̤, pannen inruilen | beroep.

tsù tiá̤, pannen gieten.

tiá̤ lō, pannengieterij.

tiaò tiá̤, de pan ophangen *i. e.* geen geld hebben om eten te koken.

kòng p'oà tiá̤, de pan stuk slaan *i. e.* door te veel overhaasting eene zaak bederven.

īm tsai tiá̤ toé sī k'ih eh, niet weten dat de bodem van de pan van ijzer is *i. e.* de moeielijkheden niet kunnen waarmede zijne ouders fortuin verworpen hebben.

吋 Tiá̤ *Tiá̤ of tá̤ má̤ iù* | *(tiēm)* }, teer.

錨 Tià̤ *Tià̤*, anker.

tsit king (en) *ming tiá̤* | *(mui)* }, één anker.

p'a tià̤, ankeren.

k'í tiā̤, het anker winden, lichten.
tiā̤ soh, ankerkabel.
tiā̤ t'ûng, ankerboei.
tiā̤ k'i, ankerarm.
tiā̤ sin, lange gedeelte van het anker.
tiā̤ tā̤, dwarshout van het anker.
tiā̤ t'aò kim, ankergeld.
tsūm tiā̤, het anker laten slippen.
t'oa tiā̤, voor zijn anker wegdrijven, drift gaan.
tíng tiā̤ (*i*), om zijn anker draaien.
kià tiā̤, een tros op het anker van een ander schip uitbrengen.
hó tiā̤ to͘ (*tè*), goede ankergrond.
ts'ia tiā̤, het anker opwinden.
p'a tiā̤-gē (*gē*), het anker houdt.
tīng tiā̤ (*tuī* »), loslaten van het anker 2e alle verdere omgang met iemand afbreken 3e zijn laatsten steun verloren hebben.
p'a tiā̤ loh k'ì, neerknielen.
p'a p'ù tiā̤, een anker in het water hebben hangen zonder dat het nog grond raakt.
Sa tiā̤ (*o*), veel beweging maken.
Tsit tiā̤, een kant van eene bladzijde (soms ook meer).
dzip tiā̤, eene aanklachte inleveren, aanklagen.
tsoè tiā̤ (*tsò* »), eene beschuldiging opmaken aanklachten.
kuī tiā̤, knielende, een schriftelijke aanklachte inleveren.
Ming k'aó tiā̤ (*mui*), werf vóór een huis plaats vóór een huisstoep.
tsioh tiā̤, geplaveide plaats voor een huis.
tiā̤ laī, onbedekte binnenplaats.
ô tiā̤, oestervisscherij.

t'an tiā̤, plaats aan zee waar men Solens aankweekt.
iêm tiā̤, plaats waar men zout droogt.
bōng tiā̤, stoep vóór een graf.

定 Tiā̤ — *Tiā̤*, in rust, rustig, stil; vast, vastgesteld, zeker, bepaald, stellig, onveranderlijk; handgeld, godspenning.
sīm tiā̤, rustig, stil.
sim sin m̄ tiā̤, inwendig niet rustig.
t'i-tsù tiā̤, de hemel beschikt.
tiā̤ tiā̤, stil (van geluid of beweging).
tiā̤ tioh, stellig, vast, bepaald, uitgegemaakt.
kat si tiā̤, eene vaste knoop leggen *i. e.* niets meer aan eene zaak kunnen veranderen verloren.
tiā̤ tsi, *tiā̤ gin*, handgeld.
kao tiā̤, handgeld overhandigen.
kè tiā̤, het handgeld reeds gegeven hebben.
sàng tiā̤, handgeld geven.
tsò tiā̤, als handgeld geven.
gīm tiā̤, handgeld ontvangen = t'éh tiā̤.
tiā̤ tsoe, expresselijk, besteld gemaakt.
p'ù tiā̤, handgeld dat weer kan terug genomen worden.

錠 Tiā̤ — *Tiā̤*, numeraal voor staven goud en zilver.
gûn tiā̤ (*gin*), zilver in baren.

Tiā̤ — *Tiā̤ tiā̤*, *nā̤ tiā̤*, alleen, slechts (op het eind van den zin geplaatst.)

舵 Tiā̤ — *Hoā̤ tiā̤*, het roer in handen hebben, aan het hoofd eener zaak staan.

聽 T'ia̤ — *T'ia̤*, hooren, luisteren; gehoor geven aan, gehoorzamen.
t'ia̤ kì, hooren.
t'àm t'ia̤, onderzoeken, vragen naar.
t'ia̤ m̄ kì, niet verstaan = t'ia̤ m̄ ts'ut.
t'ia̤ m̄ tioh, misverstaan, verkeerd verstaan.
t'ia̤ ts'ò, *t'ia̤ gō̤*, *t'ia̤ tā̤*, verkeerd hooren, misverstaan

t'ia̤ kong, naar een gerucht luisteren.
t'ia̤ kia̤, naar de woorden der voorbijgangers luisteren om er zijn geluk of ongeluk uit op te maken (door vrouwen op den 15den dag der 1ste en 8ste maand gedaan).
hī k'ang iah laī laī teh t'ia̤, zorgvuldig luisteren.
t'ia̤ sia̤ bāng ia̤, verlangend naar iemand wachten op.
t'ia̤ hī t'ia̤ piah, overal afluisteren.
t'ia̤ īm ki̤ sit tsit p'i̤, hoort men het niet dan verliest men er (slechts) een stuk meê *i. e.* dan verliest men er toch niet veel bij.
t'ia̤ koai̤ bô t'ia̤ kē, gehoor geven aan den hoogen niet aan den lagen (prijs), *i. e.* nog altijd den hoogsten prijs vragen die vroeger geboden is.
bô t'àm t'ia̤ lìh, ik zal geen navraag naar u doen *i. e.* ik ben niet bang voor u.
bô beh t'ia̤ lâng, geen gehoor geven aan iemands vermanningen of betoogen.
t'ia̤ ts'ùt, uitkomen zooals men gezegd of voorspeld had.

廳 T'ia̤ — *T'ia̤*, zaal, hoofdvertrek, receptiekamer.
toā t'ia̤, receptiekamer.
k'eh t'ia̤, do.
t'ia̤ têng, zaal.
tsiáh pēng t'ia̤, eetzaal.
koa̤ t'ia̤, mandarijnzaal 2e kajuit.
koe t'ia̤, gastenvertrek in bijgebouwen.
t'ia̤ aō pâng, achterkamer (achter de receptiekamer.
sin niû ts'ut t'ia̤, de bruid komt in de zaal (op den trouwdag).
pū t'ia̤, politieagenten.

痛 T'ià — *T'ià*, pijnlijk.
bák tsiu t'ià, zeere oogen, oogpijn.
ts'ùi k'i t'ià, kiespijn.
bák tsiu tsoè t'ià (*tsò*), oogpijn (gew. een rood plekje) hebben.
t'ià t'ià, pijn.
si t'ià (*sè* ») , een zweertje enz. krijgen.
ui ui t'ià, indringende pijn.
tiuh tiuh t'ià, schoksgewijze pijn.
t'àng t'ià, pijn, smart.
sèng nìng t'ià (*sui nui*), stijf in de leden.
haò t'ià, hard schreeuwen (van angst of pijn) (lage volkstaal).
īm tsai t'ià, niet van de pijn afvoelen.

愛 T'ià — *T'ià*, beminnen.
t'ià sioh, lief hebben.
īm tsai t'ang t'ià, niet weten te waardeeren, geen hart voor iets hebben als geld dat men niet zelf verdiend heeft.
t'ià tioh tsi, zijn geld lief hebben, waardeeren.

程 T'ià — *T'ià* (*t'ê*), familienaam.
t'ià tsing sin, bij zijne volle gedachten komen (als na een droom om zich te verzekeren dat men nu wakker is).

T'iā — *Sio k'oá t'iā pak tô*, den buik een weinig bederven, een klein maal nemen.
t'iā tsing sin, iets versterkends nemen.

Tiah

摘 Tiah — *Tiah*, afbreken (als een boomtak.)
tiah in, zijne ambtzegels afnemen, ontslaan, afzetten.
tiah i ê koân, iemand zijn macht ontnemen.
tiah hoe (» *hoa*), bloemen plukken.
tiah, uitkiezen, uitzoeken (bij koopen).
t'aò tiah bé tiah (*boé*), het beste van iets uitkiezen 2e van voren en van achteren vast maken (als een schip).
tiah kù, een zin uit een boek nemen, aanhalen.
tiah ts'ùi ts'iu, de baardharen uittrekken.

tiah ming (» *mỏ*) , plukken, de haren uittrekken (scheldterm).
tiah hì, tiah ts'ut, een komediestuk uitkiezen.
toa tiah, er uitpikken, een persoon uit de massa op het oog hebben.
tiah sik, zijn naam uit een rechtsgeding doen schrappen door omkooping enz.
tiah bién (*o*) , do.
tiah miâ tiah sì (*sè*) , met naam en toenaam (spreken van..., uitschelden enz.)
toa tù tiah, man tegen man.
tiah nẹh á, knijptang, pincette.
tiah ts'iū ki, een boomtak afbreken.
ing soh á tiah tī sog ting, trossen op het land uitbrengen.

糶 Tiáh *Tiáh*, koopen (van granen.)
tiáh bí, rijst koopen.
ts'ai tiah bí, in groote hoeveelheid rijst koopen.
ping tiáh, in tijd van schaarschte tegen den ouden prijs rijst verkoopen.
tún tiáh, rijst opkoopen en opstapelen, opzolderen.
ts'iū tiáh (*ts'iō* ») , do.

Tiáh *Pog tiáh*, ruzie, twist met iemand hebben.

拆 T'iah *T'iah*, stuk scheuren.
t'iah bō, sloopen.
t'iah tsûn, een schip sloopen.
t'iah k'ui, een brief openbreken.
t'iah ts'uì, aan stukken scheuren.
t'iah hé lō (*hoé*) , de brand stuiten door huizen om te halen.
t'iah kó, eene compagnieschap ontbinden.
t'iah hé kì (*hoè*) , do.
t'iah hé (» *hoè*) , do.

t'iah lih, ophalen, scheuren.
tsit làng t'iah tsit lō, ieder zijn eigen weg gaan.
t'iah bah-ts'uì nih pō (*iah*) , zijne naaste aanverwanten mishandelen of benadeelen.
t'iah liah k'ì, geheel en al omhalen, stuk scheuren.
t'iah p'oà, slechten (een schip, huis enz.) stuk scheuren.
t'iah p'oà-hō i t'ia, eene zaak uit elkander leggen, ontleden.
t'iah koah, zich verdeelen (van een troep menschen).
t'iah soà, uit elkander gaan, uit elkander scheuren.
t'iah k'ui, van elkander gaan, uit elkander nemen scheiden (van man en vrouw).
pun t'iah, over allen verdeelen.
t'i-t'iah háh, doorbreken, doorkomen (van de zon).
koé t'iah (*ké* ») , uit elkander nemen en veranderen.
t'iah k'a lō, uit den weg nemen.
p'ah t'iah, geheel slechten.
tuì t'iah, gelijkelijk gezamelijk verdeelen.
t'iah tsoá, lett. papier verscheuren, eene overeenkomst vernietigen, eene compagnieschap ontbinden enz.
t'iah ké hióh, de bladen waarin de koek gebakken wordt stuk scheuren *i. e.* ophouden iemands leerling te zijn en nu zelfstandig baas worden.
t'iah t'ui, de dijen, billen uittrekken (als van kikvorschen) 2e wijdbeens staan.
t'iah si, aan draden, vezels trekken.
t'iah toa, een passagebiljet bij den scheepsagent of een biljet voor uitlading aan het belastingkantoor gaan halen.

76

t'iah ióh, medicijnen koopen.
t'iah dzī sṳ̄, iemands noodlot uit karakters voorspellen.

Tiang

Tiang *Tiang tiang haó* (en *tán (tiang)*), rammelen, snateren.
voor Tiang zie onder Tiong.

Tiao

雕 Tiao *Tiao*, klein houden als boomen, dwergplanten.
tiao tok, vormen, leiden, onderwijzen.
tiao k'ik, uitsnijden, beeldhouwen.
tiao p'ûn king, dwergplanten binden, leiden.
tiao ts'iū ki, een tak neertrekken.
tiao k'i k'iao, krom buigen.
tiao king (» *kiong*), een boog terugbrengen.
tiao king á, achterover gebogen.
soè hàn īm kà sī-toū hàn tsiū boē tiao tit, wordt men jong zijnde niet onderwezen dan is men grooter geworden niet te vormen.

刁 Tiao *Tiao bân*, onhandelbaar (van menschen).

特 Tiao *Tiao ti*, met opzet.
tiao kò̤ ì, met opzet.
tiao ts'òng, uitsluitend om.... opzettelijk om.
tiao ì, opzettelijk, uitsluitend om...
tiao tì, do.
tiao ì kò̤, *tiao tì kò̤*, opzettelijk.
tiao kang, do. uitsluitend om.
tiao lai, expresselijk komen om...
tiao tat, strak om het lijf spannend.
tiao ts'oân, opzettelijk, bij voorkeur uitkiezen.

Tiao *Pàng tiao*, iemand bedreigen, vrees aanjagen.
Tiao *Ts'iū bák-tiao lah*, de boom is verdord.

貂 Tiao *Tiao ts'ú* (*ts'ì*), *tiao p'è* (*p'oè*), marter, marterel.
ts'iah tiao, bruin martervilt.

朝 Tiao *Tsoè sam* (ook) *ts'it tiao*, op den derden of zevenden dag na de geboorte van een kind geschenken komen brengen.
sam tiao tsiò, drie dagen lange offerande.

Tiaó *Kóng oē tiaó tiaó*, lispelen, stotteren in het spreken.

召 Tiaò *Tiaò*, roepen, oproepen, ontbieden.
tiaò ping, soldaten oproepen.
tiaò hì, een troep komedianten ontbieden.
tiaò siaò p'o̤-lai k'où, de koopmansboeken ter bezichtiging ontbieden.

縣 Tiaò *Tiaò*, ver verwijderd.
tiaò oán, plaatsen die ver van elkander liggen.

弔 Tiaò Hangen, ophangen.
koà tiaò sim koa, bezorgd angstig.
tiaò oai, schuins hangen.
tiaò koh, het armsgat van een kleedingstuk dat nauw is.
tiaò koe, groote cochen-china kippen.
toū tiaò, het touw dat het roer in bedwang houdt.
tiaò kak, langwerpig vierkant.
tiaò kè, den prijs hoog houden (in tijden van schaarschte.
koà tiaò, zeer aan iets denken.
bàk sin tiaè tiaè, scheeve opgetrokken oogen.
tsiū tiaò pi, de galg, het schavot beklimmen.
tiaò o̤, de bamboetoestel om water uit een put te halen.
tiaò kiò, een hangende brug, een draaibrug.

tò tiaò, onderste boven.
liaò tiaò, dood als een pier, geheel ter zijde gesteld of afgedaan.
tiaò tsoá, condoleeren, offeren aan de dooden gedurende de eerste tien dagen.
tiaò oán, te ver om te bereiken, moeielijk te bereiken, te beroepen.

廐 *Tiaô*, stal, hok.
Tiaô *bé tiaò*, paardenstal.
koe tiaò, kippenhok.
tsit tiaò ti, een stal varkens, een dom huisgezin.
kaò tiaò, hondenhok, verblijf der kinderen naast het lijk der ouders.

Tiaò *Tiaô* ook *tiao*,
tiaô lai, opzettelijk komen.
tiaò tì, met voordacht.
tiaò kò ì, met opzet.

條 *Tiaô*, twijg; streep, reep, strook; num.
Tiaô part: voor lange dunne voorwerpen, op elkander volgende zaken enz. afdeeling in een boek of wetsbepaling, artikel, post (in een boek) enz.
kim tiaò, reep gouds.
tin tiaò, rottingen roede.
bák tiaò, stukje inkt.
hong tiaò, reep papier waarmede iets verzegeld is.
hoat tiaô, horologeveer.
liú tiaò, fijne vensterboutjes.
tsi̱ tiaô, karpet.
tiaò kiṉ, bepaling van een kontrakt.
tiaò toṉ, dito.
tiaò bák, bladwijzer, index.
tiaò liét, gerangschikt, gespecificeerd.
tiaô kui, reglement, bepaling.
tiaô lē (" *lī*), wetsbepaling.
tiaô tién, do.
pò tiaô, aangiftsbiljet, besluit (van iemand die een graad behaald heeft).
tsit tiaô tsi̱, eene zekere som gelds.
tsit tiaô sū, eene zaak.

tiaô iok, voorwaarden, bepalingen.
tiaô k'oán, bepaling van een kontrakt.
ts'ùi tiaô, afzonderlijke posten, één voor één.
tsóng tiaô, de verschillende posten bij elkander.

朝 *Tiaô*, het hof, keizerlijk paleis; keizer-
Tiaô lijke audientie, audientie houden, ter audientie gaan; regeerend stamhuis, dynastie.
tiaô ting, het hof; de keizer.
tiaô sin, ministers aan het hof.
tiaô tsu, parelsnoer van ministers.
tiaô ki̱, op audientie bij den keizer gaan.
dzip tiaô, do.
tiaô pâng, wachtkamer bij eene audientie.
kièn tiaô, op audientie komen.
tsē tiaô, audientie houden.
pún tiaô, de tegenwoordige dynastie.
ts'ing tiaô, de Ts'ing dynastie.
kok tiaô ts'o̱, begin eener dynastie.
paī tiaô, eene dynastie ten val brengen.
tiaô tē, dynastie.

Tiaô *Tiaô*, vastblijven, vasthouden, uithouden, houden aan.
si̱ kun tìng tiaô, ingeworteld, vastgeworteld op.
tìng tiaô, vastspijkeren.
k'an tiaô tiaô, stevig voorttrekken, niet loslaten.
boē tiaô, niet vastblijven, niet houden, niet kunnen uithouden.
tiaô hun, verslaafd aan opium.
tsiáh tiaô lah, verslaafd aan het rooken (van tabak, opium enz.)
tiaô koṉ tiaô dziét, een weinig binnenkoorts hebben.

刁 *Tiaô tī lâng* (*k'iaô* len.), iemand plagen, kwel-
Tiaô len.

調 *Tiaō ts'ú* (*tiaô ts'ɪ*), scheidsrechter zijn.
Tiaō

tiaō tō̤ (*tiaò* »), maatregelen nemen.

tiaō iòng (*tiaò iáng*), zich ontzien, voor zich zorgen (na eene ziekte).

tiaō ping (*tiaō* »), soldaten onderwijzen.

t'é tiaō, roepen, ontbieden.

k'ik tiaō (*tiaō*), melodie van een lied.

ū tiaò ū tiaō, in de maat en de melodie volgen.

p'a̤i sing tiaō, op een onaangenamen toon (antwoorden enz.)

hó sing tiaō, een goede stem.

ting tiaō (*tui* »), veranderen van de melodie.

tuì tiaō, met elkander omwisselen (als mandarijnen).

tiaō dzīm, zijn mandarijn ambt op eene andere plaats voortzetten.

兆 Tiaō *Tiaō t'aò* (*tiaō*), voorteekens.

kiet tiaō (*kit* »), gelukkig voorteeken.

凋 Tiaō *Tiaō* (*tiaō*), verdorren, sterven (als boomen).

tiaō tiaō teh k'iā (*k'iā kaò tiaō k'ih*), aan den grond als vastgenageld staan.

tiaō k'ih, do.

tiaō tsáng (*tiaō* »), verdorren, dood gaan (van boomen).

桃 T'iao *T'iao hu*, koelie.

kien t'iao poè hū, lasten dragen.

it kien t'iao (» » *t'iao tsīn*), alle verantwoording op zich hebben.

t'iao soán, uitkiezen (uit velen).

taī tsì-kā i t'iao k'i lai, zich verantwoordelijk, aansprakelijk voor iets stellen.

T'iao *T'iao k'ò* (*tiao k'ò*), er van profiteeren dat iemand bij niemand anders terecht kan dan bij u om hem veel te laten betalen.

t'iao t'ìng (*o*), iemand kwellen, last aandoen.

t'iao bàn (*tiao*) *t'iao làn*, onhandelbaar (van menschen), ruw (ongemanierd).

T'iao *T'iao t'iao* (*t'iao t'iao*), uitsluitend om..., opzettelijk om.

t'iao t'iao, toch maar (met alle geweld).

t'iao kang lai (*t'iao*), uitsluitend komen om, opzettelijk.

窕 T'iao *T'iao lāng* (*t'iao lāng*), luchtig, ruim (van een huis), net gekleed (van vrouwen).

挑 *T'iaó làng*, iemand uitkiezen.

T'iaó *kè t'iaó* (*koè* »), de besten uit de besten kiezen (van menschen of waren).

跳 T'iaò *T'iaò*, springen, sprong.

t'iaò bú, dansen.

t'iò t'iaò, huppelen, springen = tiò tiò t'iaò t'iaò.

oáh t'iaò t'iaò, springlevend.

t'iaò tsit dzī, een karakter overgeslagen hebben.

t'iaò tsiēn, spelen, huppelen (van kinderen).

t'iaò kip sing, een rang, graad overspringen.

t'iaò kui, het iemand lastig maken (als kinderen).

t'iaò pang, vlonder, overlegplank.

tah t'iaò, een vlonder neêrleggen.

t'iaò kè (» *koè*), overspringen.

sa̤ pō̤ tsit t'iaò, bij elke 3 stappen eens springen (als kinderen).

t'iaò hàn (en) *kui* (*kui*), ondeugende drommels (tegen kinderen).
k'ing t'iaò ê làng (*k'ing t'iaò*), een onbezadigd, lichtzinnig mensch.
sim kog p'ók p'ók t'iaò (*t'iaò*), sterk kloppen van het hart (uit vrees).
t'iaò hé (» *hoé*), door het vuur springen.
t'iaò k'a hoe (o), heen en weer hinkelen.
t'iaò ts'ù (» *ts'i*), haasje overspringen.
p'ah t'iaò, een overloop, vlonder over een afgrond enz. leggen, een steiger opslaan.
poáh loh t'iaò, van een steiger vallen.
t'iaò tàng, springen van een tooveraar (door wien men de meening van den afgod te weten komt).
t'iaò ts'it ts'i, over de zeven sterren springen, hinkelen over 7 steentjes in plaatsing als de groote beer, men schopt er telkens een van weg.
p'ut p'ut t'iaò, spartelen, springen (als visch of kinderen).
t'iaò kù, een zin overspringen, overslaan.
t'iaò k'ì, iets overslaan, uitlaten.
t'iaò kè ts'iû, een muur overspringen.

迢 T'iaò *Liaò t'iaò*, *t'iaò oán*, ver af, niet bij de hand.

瘯 T'iaò *T'iaò á* (*t'iao á*), puistjes op het gelaat.

柱 T'iaō *T'iaō*, post (van de deur) pilaar.
toā t'iaō, steunpilaren.
t'iaō tsu, steenen basis waar de pilaren rusten.
t'iaō, aandeelhebbers in eene zaak.
sa t'iaō, drie takken van één stamvader.
ū t'iaō hó-ū t'iaō p'aí, sommige familietakken gaat het goed, anderen gaat het slecht.
toā ki t'iaō, de steunpilaar van eene familie.
i t'iaō, ronde pilaar.
tsút sien nṳ́ t'i t'iaō, groot als een hemelpilaar (van lange personen).
p'ṳ t'iaō, steunpilaar in een vertrek.
tiém kim t'iaō, vier van boven met goud bespikkelde pilaren (in een huis).

Tiem

砧 Tiem *Tiem*, hakblok.
t'ih tiem, aanbeeld.
kùn t'aò tiem, hakblok voor de vuist i. e. steeds slaag krijgen.
ti tiem, vleeschblok, spekslagerswinkel.
bah tiem, spekslagerswinkel.
to tiem, hakblok.
tsoá tiem, blok waarop men papier afsnijdt.

補 Tiem *Tiem oé sai hū* (*ê*), schoenlapper.
tiem p'ê, met leder lappen (als schoenen.)
tiem p'ê oê eh, schoenlapper.

纔 Tiem *Tiem tiu*, juist zoo even.

沾 Tiem *Tiem tiem tiòk tiòk. tiem tiòk* (o), zich onveranderlijk aan zijn voornemen houden.
tiem, blijven kleven aan (als zand aan de voeten.)
tiem tioh soa, zand in of aan iets krijgen.
tiem tioh, in het lichaam dringen, er aan blijven zitten als een rond voorwerp waarop men zit.
tiem sim kog, in zijn binnenste blijven zitten (als eten dat men niet goed gekaauwd heeft).
tiem tioh k'a, iets aan de voet krijgen (als steentjes wanneer men blootvoets loopt).

點 Tiém **Tiém**, numer. voor druppels, sterren enz. uur; opteekenen, optellen.

tiém hè (*» hoè*), een inventaris maken van.

tsi tiém, uit den dwaalstroom brengen.

tiém hé (*» hoé*), licht aansteken.

tiém ting, de lamp opsteken.

tiém ting kat ts'ui, illumineeren en guirlandes uithangen.

tiém sim, een lichtmaal.

tiém sim áh, etenstrommel.

tiém tin ė lâng, iemand die niets over zijn kant laat gaan.

kui tiém tsing, hoe laat?

tiém ping, inspectie houden (over soldaten).

tiém baó, opteekening van al de menschen die een mandarijn in zijn huis heeft.

p'ah tiém, glazen slaan; het uur slaan.

tiém hiét, eene plaats voor een graf aanwijzen.

tiém sip dzī kè, een kruis slaan.

tiém tiém kim, alles in de uiterste puntjes, volmaaksten toestand 2e regen van vuurwerksterren.

tiém-tsiah kòng, eerst aantikken en dan slaan (als bij het spijkeren) 2e met voorzorg te werk gaan.

tá tiém, aanraden, 2e nazien, natellen.

tiém ts'i (*» ts'ė*), iemand uit den droom brengen.

kiem tiém, nakijken en natellen.

tsa tiém (*tse »*), do.

tiém miâ, de namen aflezen en aanteekenen.

tiém iù tsoè ki hō (*tsò*), een merk op iets zetten (als op schapen) 2e iets of iemands handeling niet licht vergeten.

ki tiém (*ke »*), uren van den wacht.

tiém ts'eh (*» ts'eh*), een boek puncteeren.

tiém kù, zinnen puncteeren.

tiém ki, wratten toucheeren.

tsit tiém á, een dropje, een weinig.

ts'ut ming si tiém kim, bij het uitgaan een parasoldrager en vier andere bedienden hebben.

hiém tsit tiém, het scheelde zeer weinig of....

hiém hiém k'iém tsit tiém, do.

tīng tiém (*tuī »*), volstrekt niets.

tiém t'aô tsai tíng bė (*tui boé*), tikt men hem op den kop dan weet hij den staart om te draaien (van iemand die eene zaak spoedig begrijpt).

tiém kao ìh, nazien en dan aan iemand overhandigen.

kouį tiém, hoog aangeschreven, beroemd.

tiém tsit ė t'aô hō i tsai, door het begin aan te raken iemand aan den gang helpen.

tiém tá, iemands moed aanprikkelen, tot iets aanzetten.

tiém hō i tóh, aansteken (vuur).

tiém hiu tsik, reukwerk en kaarsen aansteken.

sió tiém, een klein maal nemen.

tiém ien tsi, met rouge bestrijken (als vrouwen de lippen).

sìng ke kah tiém lâng giáh, de buurten tellen en de bevolking opteekenen *d.i* volkstelling houden.

店 Tièm **Tièm**, winkel.

tièm á, komenijswinkeltje.

tièm tó, bankroet.

tièm hō, naam van een winkel.

tièm t'aô, winkels (in het algemeen).

tièm p'ò, do.

k'ui tièm, een winkel opzetten.
toà tièm, in een winkel zijn (als bedienden).
tsē tièm, in den winkel zitten.
tièm bīn, voorste gedeelte, front van een winkel.
tsiú tièm, wijnwinkel, wijnhuis.
pīng tièm } , restauratie.
(*puī* ») }
k'eh tièm, *kioh t'ièm* } , logement.
(*k'e̱h*) (*he̱h*) }
tièm tsú pīng tièm pò, logementhouder, logementhoudster.
pai tièm bīn, voor zijn winkel uitstallen.
p'ah tièm bīn, voor de winkels bedelen.
tièm toé, inventaris van een winkel.
tièm tsioh-p'ui̱, winkel waarvan de huurders gedurig bankroet gaan.

在 Tièm
Tièm, wonen te, zich verstoppen, verschuilen.
ts'iá tièm teh, wacht nog even.
tièm teh tsē, gezeten zijn, zitten.
tièm sim mi̱h sú̱ tsaī, waar woont hij in wiens dienst is hij?

潛 Tièm
Tièm bī, onder duiken.
tièm sa̱ ts'ē } , wegkruipertje spelen.
(*sio ts'oē*) }
tièm bát bát, zich verstopt houden.
bih k'ì tièm, zich verstoppen, wegschuilen.
tièm k'ang, zich in een gat houden 2° volstrekt niet buiten 's huis komen.
tièm k'ang ku, iemand die steeds in huis blijft.
tièm hō̱, voor den regen schuilen.

沈 Tièm
Tièm, zinken, indompelen meer *tîm* uitgesproken.
tièm laū, lek stooten (van een schip).
tièm toé, naar den bodem zinken; bezinken.
tsûn-tièm loh k'ì, het schip zinkt.
hō̱-loh kaò beh tièm, het regent als of de grond neer zal zinken.
tièm làng ê p'oe gûn, een brief met geld van iemand niet bezorgen maar voor zich zelven houden.
toā tièm = *toā tìm*, zeer, hevig.
tièm làng ê mi̱h, iemands goed niet teruggeven.
lòh tsui pi̱ pi̱ tièm, vallen ze in het water dan zinken ze gelijkelijk *i. e.* de een is niet veel beter dan de ander.
k'ik tièm loh k'ì, insnijden zoodat de karakters niet uit, maar instaan.

墊 Tiēm
Tiēm k'ì lai, iets hooger zetten (door er iets onder te plaatsen).
tiēm pō̱. er bijleggen (als geld).
tiēn pê } , er bijleggen, bijvoegen.
(» *poê*) }
í tiēm, stoelkussen.
p'ê tiēm } , leeren stoelkussen.
p'oê ») }
í dziók tiēm, stoelkussen.
ts'ng tiēm, bedmatras.
paì tiēm, knielkussen (vóór afgodsbeelden).
tiēm koai̱ k'ì lai, hooger zetten.
bô tiēm toé ê làng, iemand die niets door erfenis heeft.

恬 Tiēm
Tiēm tī, hoogste stand van den vloed, kentering van den stroom.
bák sin-tiēm tiēm, niet overal heen kijken.
tiēm tiēm, bedaard (van aard) stil (van personen).
tiēm tiēm sīm sīm, do.
tiēm tī, stil, bedaard (van eene vrouw).
tiēm tsát (en *tsat*), naauwgezet, punctueel in zijne handelingen.
tiēm tiēm bô tsoè sia̱, wees stil en maak geen leven.

添 T'iem
Ka t'iem } , bijvoegen, vermeerderen.
(*ke̱* ») }
t'iem pō̱, bijvoegen.
t'iem tsng, bruidsgeschenken geven.
t'iem hok t'iem siū, geluk en lang leven toewenschen.

t'iem tsai, schatten toevoegen.

諂 T'iém
T'iém bī / *(mī)*, vleien.

甚 T'iém
Sih kaò t'iém t'iém t'iém, zeer veel geld verliezen.
tsing put tsi t'iém, zeer hard slaan 2°. zeer hard (rijst) stampen.
t'iém, ernstig (van eene ziekte), deerlijk hard, zeer.
t'iém t'iém tsik pī, streng straffen, zwaar straffen.
pī kaò t'iém t'iém t'iém / *(pē)*, uiterst ziek.
p'ah kaò t'iém t'iém t'iém, uiterst fijn slaan.
t'iém t'iém mē, *t'iém t'iém p'ah*, hevig schelden, slaan.

倘 T'iém
T'iém ts'ai, wellicht.
t'iém mih / *(» mé)*, spoedig.

恬 T'iém
T'iém tsīng, bedaard (van aard).
t'iém t'iém è lâng, een bedaard, bezadigd mensch.

墊 T'iēm
T'iēm, indompelen.
t'iēm pó, aanvullen, dempen, bijleggen.
t'iēm sih, iemand verdrinken.
t'iēm lóh tsi / *(tsé)*, in de put dompelen.
t'iēm t'uī ook *t'ūm* / *(t'ūm t'uī)*, voor velen zijner familie te zorgen hebben.
t'iēm hai / *(t'iēm »)*, val in zee (scheldterm.)
hong ts'e soū-t'iēm tó / *(t'âm t'âm)*, het vliegertouw hangt met een bocht.
t'iēm pún, steeds van zijn kapitaal moeten bijleggen.
oáh oáh t'iēm, levend verdrinken.
péh t'iēm è tsiú, ongebrouwen alleen gegiste wijn.

Tien

癲 Tien
Tien kòng, krankzinnig, razend.
hong tien, krankzinnig.
ts i tien, suf (van studeeren enz.)
tien gōng, suf, idiotisch.
su tien / *(si »)*, suf, onnoozel (door studeeren.)
soū tien, dom (door niet veel in de wereld geweest te zijn).

酊 Tien
Koū koū tien, waggelen.
tien tien tó tó, bij elke gelegenheid achteruit gaan (als handel).
tien lai tien k'i, zwaaien als een dronken man, waggelen.
tien tó, achteruit gaan (in handel) omvallen, verliezen (in handel).
tien tien tsuì / *(tsuì tien tien)*, beschonken.
tien bé / *(. bé)*, een paard laten draven, trippelen.

典 Tién
Tién, hijpotheek hebben op.
tién k'oè / *(» k'è)*, hijpotheekbrief.
tién tsú, hijpotheekhouder.
ts'ut tién è lâng, hijpotheekgever.
dzī tién, woordenboek.
tién tìng, pandjeshuis, verpanden.
toū tién, *sió tién*, pandjeshuis waar men voor langen, en waar men voor korten tijd verpandt.
kò tién, boeken der oudheid 2° boeken over de oudheid.
ts'ut king dzip tién, zeer geleerd.
ts'ut tién, hijpotheek op iets geven.
tién ts'ù, hijpotheek op een huis hebben
ú tién-ú siók, er bestaat hijpotheek geven en loskoopen *i. e.* bij leenen enz. moet men securiteit hebben.
tiaò tién, reglementen, bepalingen.
king tién, klassieke boeken.

展 *Tién pó*, pronken met.
Tién *tién sè bīn* (*sì*) }, zich in postuur zetten voor iets.
tién i é suí, zijne schoonheid doen voorkomen, uitkomen.
tién ui, de haren doen rijzen (als tijgers).
tién pún sū, zijne kennis ten toon spreiden.

𨘥 *Tién tō̤*, graden op eene globe.
Tién

田 *Tién sán*, landerijen en bezittingen.
Tién *tién sī lí tién-put háp tsuī nō̤ bûn tsién*, het rijstveld is het uwe, maar het gaat niet wel dat het vóór mijne deur is *i. e.* hij die iets in handen heeft is er meer baas over dan de eigenlijke bezitter.
Tién *Tién tsiṳ̄ bók tsú*, (iemands naam) op het tablet des overledenen schrijven, invullen.

殿 *Tsáp tiēn ê giêm ông*, de rechters van de
Tiēn tien departementen uit de onderwereld.
tiēn sì, plaats voor de examinatie der Han lin.
tsē tiēn, op den troon zitten (van den keizer).
p'ien tiēn, zijdelingsche audientiezaal van den keizer.
toā tiēn, *tsiā̤ tiēn*, groote keizerlijke audientiezaal.

典 *Tiēn p'oe* (» *p'e*) {, leenbrief, leencontract (van
Tiēn landen en huizen).
kiú tiēn sing giép tsú, na langen huur of leen, wordt men als eigenaar (van het pand).
tiēn hō̤, landwerker, landbebouwer (die den eigenaar een gedeelte der opbrengst geeft.)
tuì tiēn, een land in tegenwoordigheid van den bebouwer aan een ander overdoen.
k'í t'iēn, iemands leencontract (van land) opheffen.
oā̤ tiēn, een leencontract aan een ander geven.
teh tiēn, geld aan den eigenaar van een land geven om het te bebouwen ten einde minder gevaar te loopen ontzet te worden.

電 *Tiēn k'ì*, electricieteit.
Tiēn *tiēn k'ì ín*, telegraaf.
Tiēn *Tiēn tsiú*, wijn plengen (bij offeranden).

天 *T'ien tóng*, de hemel.
T'ien *t'ien sin*, hemelsche geest, engel.
t'ien saì (» *sù*) }, engel.
t'ien tsú kaò, Catholicismus.
tsiáh t'ien tóng, onrechtvaardig geld verdienen.
t'ien ping, weegschaal, balans.
t'ien ping oá, de schalen aan een balans.
t'ien ping ts'ìu, de boom aan een balans.
t'ien ping tsiem, aanwijzer op een balans.
t'ien sī̤, vastgestelde wet des hemels.
t'ien hó pán (*hou*) }, zoldering, plafond.
t'ien t'ien tsuì, elken dag beschonken.
t'ien lò tē bóng, ratteval.
t'ien k'ì, weêrsgesteldheid.
t'ien kong tē tō, zeer rechtvaardig, billijk.
t'ien lí, hemel's beginsel (straf, belooning enz.)
t'ien p'aò, bom.
t'ien dzién, natuurlijk, van zelf.
t'ien hoan tē hok, alles in verwarring (als in een rijk) chaos.

偏 *T'ien t'ien*, bij voorkeur, uitsluitend,
T'ien moedwillig.
t'ien t'óh ê lâng, iemand die zich alles laat gezeggen zonder er iets om te geven.
t'ien t'ien á beh (*boeh*) }, toch met alle geweld willen.

77

展 *t'ien t'ien á īm*, toch maar niet willen.
T'ien *T'ien t'é*, op te grooten voet leven.
T'ién *T'ién sit* / (*tién* ») , de vleugels uitspannen, uitstrekken (als een vogel).
t'ién k'ui / (*tién* ») , open doen (als een paraplui) uitspannen (als een stuk papier.)
hó p'i t'ién / (*tién*) , uitgestrekt, ruim van plaats).
t'ién tìng, pandjeshuis, verpanden.
toā t'ién sió t'ién, pandjeshuis waar men voor langen tijd en waar men voor korten tijd verpandt.

塡 T'ièn *T'ièn miâ*, iemands naam invoegen.

Tiep

Tiep *Tiep á toā*, een stipje, een weinigje, een kleine dreumel.
tiep á kú, in een oogenblik.
k'ah tiep á, straks, aanstonds.
tsit tiep tiep á, een weinigje.
Tiép *Tsit tiép*, nu, op het oogenblik.
nn̄g tiép, tweemaal, twee keeren.
Tiép *Hō tiép*, scharnier.
Tiép *Ting ting tiép tiép*, op elkander gestapeld, op elkander stapelen.
tiép tiép, verscheidene rijen achtereen.
siep tiép, kompact, praktisch
tiép tâ, verwondingen (in het algemeen).

牒 Tiép *Tiép*, geschreven gebed.
sio tiép, een geschreven gebed verbranden.

貼 T'iep *T'iep*, bedekken, weghouden; bijvoegen, bijpassen, aanvullen, een deel aan iets betalen; aanplakken; een komiek.
iep t'iep, weghouden niet laten zien.
t'é t'iep, inschikkelijk, toegevend zijn.
t'i t'aò t'iep bé, een weinig bijvoegen.
t'iep tse li tsi, (aan verscheidene personen) een weinig geven.
t'iep kang sih tsiáh, bij een werk geld moeten bijpassen, er op verliezen.
sa pn̄g t'iep, pang tiép / (*sio*) , gezamenlijk het te kort komende er bijpassen.
t'iep ts'ù sè, in de huishuur meebetalen.
t'iep ts'ìn t'aò á, een overwicht op de weegschaal leggen, gezegd van eene vrouw die de kinderen uit haar vorig huwelijk meebrengt.
t'iep hé sit, zijn deel in het eten metbetalen.
t'iep ts'ut lai, aanplakken (als de verwijdering van iemand uit zijn huis).

帖 T'iep *T'iep*, geschrift, bekendmaking; kaart visitekaart, schriftelijke invitatie.
tah t'iep á, een geschrift spotschrift enz. aanplakken.
pín t'iep, verzoekschrift.
miâ t'iep, naampapier, visitekaart.
tsaò (en *tsip*) *t'iep é lâng*, bediende die met de visitekaart vooruit loopt.
tsng pit t'iep sik, schrijver zijn in een mandarijnbureau.
t'iep sik / (» *sit*) , betiteling in eene invitatie.
pàng t'iep, invitaties rondzenden.
ts'ut lō t'aò t'iep, eene annonce aanplakken.
hun tsu lé t'iep, het huwelijkscontract en de lijst der geschenken.
t'iep lông, enveloppe voor invitatiekaarten.
tsit t'iep é kim poh, een pakje goudblad.
tsit t'iep ióh, een pakje medicijnen.

疊 T'iép *T'iép*, op elkander stapelen, opstapelen.
t'iép hè / (» *hoè*) , goederen op elkander stapelen.
t'iép ts'â, hout opstapelen.
t'iép sit, compakt, geregeld bij elkander.
ting ting t'iép t'iép, op elkander gestapeld.

t'iép k'g p'è (p'oè), panscherven op een muur steken (tegen dieven).

Tiet

Tùn tiét, moeielijkheden ontmoeten, met horten en stooten gaan.

tiét tá, verwondingen (in het algemeen.)

T'aò t'iet, door en door kennen, grondig verstaan.

t'ong t'iet, do.

t'iet ti, grondig, grondig doorzien.

t'ò t'iet é lâng (t'ó t'iep), een degelijke kerel die zich niet zoo aan de vormen houdt.

t'iet hoé (t'iet hoé), terugkeeren, terugbrengen (eene afdeeling soldaten, koopwaren enz.)

t'iet k'ì, wegnemen, opredderen (als spijzen na het eten).

T'iet hàn, een ijzeren kerel, iemand die wat hij eenmaal op zich heeft genomen ten uitvoer brengt

Tih

Tih, druppelen, droppelen, droppel (vocht) morsen.

bák sai-ná tih, de tranen vallen dropsgewijze af.

bô tsit tih á hong, geen droppeltje (zuchtje) wind.

tīng tih (tuī »), geen enkel dropje.

hō-tah-tih, dropsgewijze, lekken bij regen.

tih tsui kì, regendrempel (even buiten de groote zaal).

tih tioh bák tsui, door inkt bespet worden.

Tih *Tih tūng koe*, de zwakkere kippen op den kop pikken *i. e.* een zwakkere plagen.

aì tih lâng, steeds zwakkeren op den kop zitten.

碟 Tíh *Tih*, (saus) schoteltje = tíh á.

ui tih, de schoteltjes (saus of vruchten) rond de tafel zetten.

oá p'iet tih tū (eig. *tī*), kopjes, borden, schoteltjes en eetstokjes.

Tih *Tih tih túh túh*, stotteren, zijne woorden inslikken.

kóng oē tih túh (oā), zijne woorden inslikken.

kóng oē tih tih haó, stotteren.

要 Tíh *ēm tih (» tih)*, niet willen hebben, niets aan iets willen, iets verwerpen.

beh tih ēm tih, wilt gij het hebben of niet?

扯 Tih *Tih (tē)*, uitwringen, uitpersen (als een limoentje).

tih tsiep (tē »), sap uitpersen, uitwringen.

tih tsi (tē »), vasthoudend aan geld zijn.

tih sa á ku (tē ki), iemand bij de slip van zijn kleed pakken.

鐵 T'ih *T'ih*, ijzer.

t'ih k'oe, helm.

t'ih ting, spijkers.

t'ih ts'ai, spil.

t'ih tiem, aanbeeld.

bé k'aò t'ih, bladtin, blik.

p'ah t'ih, ijzer smeeden.

t'ih sai, ijzervijlsel.

ná t'ih t'áng, als een ijzeren kuip *i. e.* sterk.

ts'in t'ih t'ih (pi pi), koud als ijzer, kil.

k'ah nē t'ih (t'ih), harder dan ijzer *i. e.* hardvochtig.

t'ih kòng t'ih, twee aan elkander gewaagden die twist hebben.
t'ih lâng, een ijzeren, onverschrokken kerel.
t'ih kut á si / *(sè)*, mager en sterk.
t'ih pán sik, bruin van gelaatskleur.
t'ih k'í, ijzeren tanden, halsstarrig twist volhouden.
t'ih ts'ùi, ijzeren mond, do.
koà t'ih p'ī, een ijzeren helm ophebben (als een minister in de Hán dynastie die den keizer alles zeggen mocht). *d. i.* ronduit zijne meening durven uiten.
t'ih pi, ijzeren beuker.

T'íh *T'ih t'ih kiò*, stotteren.

T'íh *Pî kaò t'ih t'ih*, buiten kennis (in eene ziekte).
siēn siēn t'ih t'ih, afgemat, ziek.
t'oa t'ih, lang buiten kennis blijven voor dat men sterft; eene zaak rekken, langzaam doen.
ts'in t'ih t'ih / *(pi pi)*, koud, kil.

Tik

竹 Tik *Tik*, bamboes; bamboezen.
tik í, bamboezen stoel.
tik ko, bamboezen stok, schuitenboom.
tik sún, bamboesknoppen.
tik háh, bladschede van bamboes.
tik tsià, suikerriet (dat niet gegeten wordt).
tik ts'ìng, bamboezen koker waarin men klappers afsteekt.
tik lê, hoorn, schelp (waarop vleesch verkoopers blazen.)
tik tsoá, bamboespapier.
péh tik tsoá, wit papier.
tik ts'ú / *(» ts'í)*, voetzoekers.
tik nâ, bamboesbosch.

得 Tik *Tik*, krijgen, verkrijgen, behalen.
tik lī, winst behalen.
tik sìng / *(» sìn)*, overwinnen (in den strijd); behouden aankomen (als van eene reis.)
tik ì, zijn wensch hebben, in zijn schik zijn.
tik hoat, de goede manier op iets vinden.
tik k'iaò, *tik koat*, de goede manier, het geheim op iets vinden.
tik kai, verheugd, in zijn schik.
tik sim, intiem, elkanders meening kennen.
tik tō, den waren weg gevonden hebben (van Boeddh. priester die boven natuurlijke krachten hebben).
tik kè, juist goed, juist wat men hebben moet.
tik tsoē, misdoen, zondigen jegens, beleedigen, zich onbeleefd gedragen jegens, excuseer mij!

的 Tik *Tik k'ak*, zeker, stellig.
tik tik sī án ni, zeer stellig is het zoo.
tik sit, waar, wezenlijk.

德 Tik *Tik*, deugd.
tik hīng, deugd, braafheid.
tsit (en) *tsik tik*, deugden opstapelen, in deugd toenemen; thans ook: hoe langer hoe slechter worden.
sit tik, het is verkeerd, slecht dat....
bô tik tiū, niet streng van zeden (van vrouwen).

嫡 Tik *Tik*, wettige vrouw.
tik ts'ut, kind van zijne wettige vrouw.

澤 Tik *Un tik* / *(in »)*, weldaad.
sik tik, glanzend.
lūn tik / *(dzūn)*, zacht (van haar, de huid enz.)

敵 Tik *Tuì tik*, vechten, strijden, bestrijden.
bû tik, onovertreffelijk, onvergelijkelijk.

tí tik, bestrijden, vechten.

擇 Tik *Tik dzit*, een (gelukkigen) dag uitkiezen.

T'ik *T'ik mē*, bekijven.

kaì t'ik, bestraffen, schelden.

T'ik kut, de beenderen uit (kippen enz.) halen.

T'ik *Hú-t'ik koaī* (*t'it koān*), de Hú stuurt een bevel aan den Koaī.

Tim

精 Tim *Tim*, gaar, glad.

擲 Tim *Tim*, gooien, werpen (als met steenen).

Tim *tim tsióh t'aô*, met steenen gooien.

Tìm *Tìm*, zwaar.

tìm tāng, do.

tìm, donkerkleurig.

tìm sik, donkere kleur.

tāng tìm, specifiek zwaar.

īng ts'iú tìm tāng, in de hand wegen.

tìm t'aô zie *t'ìm*, goedkeurend knikken 2e voor iemand instaan.

tìm ts'ī, donkerblaauw.

toā tìm, niet zuiver zwart (als stof die niet genoeg geverfd is).

沉 Tim *Tim*, zinken.

tim lóh tsuí, in het water vallen of werpen.

tim gim, zich bedenken.

tim tāng, gevaarlijk, ernstig ziek.

ts'im tim, diep.

tim hiu (» *hio*), lignum aloës.

k'it lâng tim k'i (*tiem*), door iemand gehouden, niet overgeven worden (van iets dat hem was opgedragen aan een ander te geven).

tim lik lâng ē mih / *tim » » » »*), iemands goederen heimelijk houden.

toā tim, zeer.

tim lâng ē mih, iemands goed achterhouden.

p'ù p'ù tim tim ê sing lí, onzekere handel.

bī sò-tim tim tim, hoe langer hoe meer uitkomen van smaak (als bij goede thee).

燉 Tīm *Tīm*, gaar smeulen (als iets in een flesch in het kokende water).

tīm sio, in warm water dompelen, opwarmen.

tīm koàn, kan waarin datgene gedaan wordt dat men in kokend water gaar wil krijgen.

ts'ìn tīm lâng, iemand koel ontvangen.

tīm ióh, medicijnen koken door ze in een gesloten voorwerp (flesch enz.) in kokend water te doen.

tīm-tsiáh k'ah pó, langzamerhand gaar gesmeuld is versterkender om te eten.

kap i tīm taò kú, zien wie het het langst kan volhouden (met plagen enz.)

Tīm *Tīm iu* (» *io*), stil leggen op zee (zonder wind).

T'im *Im t'im*, ondoorgrondelijk (van menschen.)

im t'im tók, stil maar gevaarlijk, inwendig listen bedenkende.

T'ím *T'ím ih*, iemand stompen, stooten.

īng ts'iú t'im t'aô k'ak, iemand met de hand op het hoofd slaan.

t'im túh, stompen, slaan.

T'ìm *T'ìm t'aô*, iemand toeknikken, (toestemmend), Europeesche buiging maken.

t'aô t'ìm bé t'ìm (*t'aô t'ìm boé t'ìm*), met kop en staart op en neer wippen (als vogels).

Tin

Tin *Tin tin tang tang*, tokkelen.

珍 Tin *Kóng kaò tin tin iú bī*, lang en smakelijk vertellen.

siù tin, mooie editie (van boeken).
tin pó, kostbaarheid, edele steen.
siōng tin (*siāng* ») }, bovenst beste waar, goed.
tin tiōng, hoog schatten, zeer zorg dragen voor.
tin tin tiōng tiōng, zeer waardeeren.
san tin, landvoortbrengselen.

津 Tin — *Sing tin* (» *tsin*) }, watertanden (als vruchten).

Tin — *K'ui bò tin*, uitgaven, onkosten gemaakt hebben zonder dat men eigenlijk weet waaraan het gegaan is.
k'ai (en) *īng bò tin*, geheel en al opgebruiken zonder dat men er ten slotte eenig voordeel van heeft.

陳 Tin — *Tin lé* (eig. *tin lé*), geschenken geven.

Tín — *Tin tāng*, bewegen, verroeren.
īm t'ang hō̤ láng tin tāng k'ì, laat u niet bestelen (lage volk staal).

鎮 Tin — *Tin piah kak*, in een hoek werpen (als een onnuttig voorwerp of mensch).
tìn bát bát, opgepropt, vol.
tìn siù, gestationneerd zijn te (als een oorlogschip).
tìn káng, in eene rivier haven gestationneerd zijn (als een oorlogschip).
tìn tai, een luitenant generaal of vice-admiraal.
tìn tè (» *gè*) }, in den weg liggen.
tìn k'a tìn ts'ú, in den weg staan, hinderlijk zijn (als kinderen).
tsáp é tìn poeh é sī p'ai (*peh*) }, van de tien zijn er acht slechten.
tìn k'a lō̤, in den weg staan.
tìn t'éh (» *t'ẹ́h*) }, om, in een huis gestationneerd zijn, bij een huis wacht houden.
tiōng tìn é sọ̄ tsaī, eene voorname plaats.

si ti-tìn tiem, als een dood varken op het hakblok blijven liggen *d. i.* ziende dat men ergens te veel is toch niet weggaan.

陳 Tin — *Tin p'í*, oranjeschillen (medicijn).

Tin — *in in tin tin*, overal ingewikkeld als een slingerplant, 2e verward, moeielijk uit te maken.
k'ing kaò tin k'ì, zoolang opbergen dat het zijn kracht verloren heeft.
tuì i bīn tsing tin tsèh, iemand persoonlijk aan iets herinneren (als aan eene nog te betalen rekening).

籐 Tin — *Tin*, rotting, 2e stengel (kruipende, als van meloenplanten.)
tin í, rottingstoel.
tin pai, schild.
tin tiaò, rottingen roede.
tin pi, rottingen zweep.

藤 Tin — *Tin ing* (» *ui*) }, guttagom.

塵 Tin — *Tin ai*, stof, vuil.
ien tin, stofwolk.

纏 Tin — *i i taō tin*, door elkander als erwtenstruiken, 2o ingewikkeld (van eene zaak).

陣 Tīn — *Tin bōng*, sneuvelen.
tīn, numer voor reien soldaten, voor vluchten vogels, wolken, kudden schapen.
kao tīn, aanvallen (elkander).
tsiep tīn (*tsiep* ») }, den vijand afwachten.
tuì tīn, in slagorde tegenover elkander staan.
paī tīn, nederlaag lijden.
pai tīn, in slagorde stellen.
ts'o̤ kao tīn, den aanval beginnen.
ts'o̤ kì tīn, dito.
lak tīn, uit de rij gaan, uiteengaan.
tīn k'a, met de voeten in één lijn staan (als soldaten).

tîn t'aô, het hoofd, de aanvoerder van gelederen.

dzī tîn, rij van karakters.

ts'im tîn, diep in de vijandelijke gelederen indringen.

t'am tîn, hoe langer hoe meer in de gelederen indringen.

hām tîn, te ver in de vijandelijke gelederen gaan en ingesloten worden.

kiâ tîn, in gelederen loopen.

ah tîn, achter een troep aankomen.

pò tîn, *pai ping pò tîn*, de gelederen scharen.

ts'oàn tîn, dwars door een troep heen gaan.

t'àn tîn, *oe làng t'àn tîn*, met de troep meégaan.

tsit tîn ê toā hong, een sterke windvlaag.

tîn tîn ts'ut, bij elken aanval meégaan 2° met alles meêdoen.

T'in *Goá teh beh t'in ìh* / *(o)* }, ik zal hem negeren, donderen (lage volkstaal).

īm t'ang hō lâng t'in k'ì / *(o)* }, laat u niet bedriegen, beetnemen (lage volkstaal)

斟 *T'in*, schenken, inschenken.

T'in *t'in tsiú*, wijn inschenken.

lim t'in, zoo uitdrinken en zoo weer inschenken.

hō-nā t'in, de regen gutst neder.

saí dziō tó teh t'in, zoo ziek zijn dat men niet op kan staan en zich steeds bevuilt.

配 *Sù t'în* / *(sì »)* }, geproportioneerd zijn.

T'în *t'în t'aô*, gelijkelijk zwaar maken.

t'în tāng, aan beide kanten even zwaar maken.

ìn t'în, bij elkander passen, goed bij elkander komen.

sa t'în / *(sio »)* }, een paar uitmaken (als een vrouw).

t'în tuì, bij elkander zijn, een geheel uitmaken.

ták ki t'în t'în, elk haar even lang en recht.

Ting

燈 *Ting*, lamp, lantaarn.

Ting *ting kiû*, lampenballon.

ting hé / *(hoe)* }, kleine lamp.

lō ting, straatlantaarn.

ting t'io, lampenpituithaalder.

ts'iú ting, handlantaarn.

ting sim, lampenpit.

k'óng bing ting, luchtballon.

ting ts'ai, raadsel.

ting kaô, lampenstellaadje van hout.

ting ē / *(» ē)* }, bij lampenlicht.

tsiôh ting, steenen lantaarnpaal.

ting hoe, gespleten pit van de kaars.

t'ien ting, lantaarn die men 's avonds voor de deur hangt om aan den hemel te offeren.

登 *Ting kik*, een bestuur aanvaarden.

Ting *ting si*, toen, terstond.

ting kì, opteekenen, opschrijven.

釘 *Ting á*, spijkertjes.

Ting *t'ih ting*, spijker.

tik ting, bamboezen spijkers, pennen.

tsoá lien ting, rondgedraaid papier (om boeken in te naaien) ook in olie gedoopte fidibus.

lō si ting, schroef.

ting á t'ui, hamer.

ts'ùn ting gû káng lát, een duimsspijker heeft de kracht van een stier.

ting á t'aô (en) lèh / *(léh)* }, kop van een spijker.

丁 *Ting*, familienaam.

Ting *ting hiu* / *(» hiō)* }, kruidnagelen.

ka ting / (*ke* ») }, huisknecht.
sing ting, meerderjarig (16 jaar).
ting iu, rouw voor zijne ouders.
ting bú (en) *pē iu* / (*bó*) (*pē*) }, rouw voor moeder of vader.
tan ting / (» *ting*) }, eenigst kind.
iù ting, jongelieden.
ts'o ting, ruwe, onbehouden lieden.
tsòng ting, mannen in de kracht van hun leven.
dzin ting, menschen, zielen.
ts'ut ting, in bewoners toegenomen zijn.
ting-ōng, bloeiend in bewoners.
sún ting, in bewoners afnemen.
ping ting, soldaat.
mèng ting / (*miŋ* ») }, deurwaker.
ts'ing ting, stukjes vermicellie ('s zomers gegeten) 2e matrozen.
ts'in ting, aanverwanten.

疔 Ting — *Ting*, zweer, venerische zweer.
si ting, zweeren.
puh kóng á ting, opborrelen (als water).

叮 Ting — *Ting ling*, nog eens zeggen, op zijn gemoed drukken.
kóng oē-ting ih, iemand nog eens duidelijk zeggen (als de voorwaarden van een koop).
koh ting ih, nog eens tot iemand zeggen, herhalen.

Ting — *Ting hiòng* / (*tin hiàng*) }, belasting opleggen, heffen.

頂 Tíng — *Ting*, numer. voor hoeden, 2e mandarijnknoop.
ū ting tuì é lâng, mandarijn, ieder die een knoop mag dragen.
ting bīn, boven, op.
tī ting bīn, boven.
ting taò, voor den middag.
ting tsat, bovenste gedeelte van den arm.
ting tsân, tweede verdieping.
ting bé kop, te paard zittende mandarijnen (die voor hooge mandarijn uitrijden.)
ts'ù ting, dak.
soŋ ting, vastland.
ting t'oè / (» *t'è*) }, in de plaats van.
ting hó, best.
pūn ting, half dek.
bé laò ting / (*boē*) }, kajuit.
ting siōng siōng / (*siūg siāng*) }, allerbovenst.
siōng ting / *siāng* ») }, van de eerste kwaliteit.
kik ting, *lut ting*, iemand zijn mandarijnknoop ontnemen.
sik ting, gekleurde mandarijnknoop.
mō ting, zich valschelijk in de plaats stellen van.
ts'ìng ting, schurft op de kruin van het hoofd.
ting t'uì / (» *t'è*) }, de plaats nemen van..... remplaceeren.
ting sin, de vroegere, vorige...
ting dzit, vorige dagen.
ting t'aī, wachten.
it ting, uiterst, bovenst.
ting tē, volgorde.
ting kip, hooger in rang.
ping ting, van gelijken rang.
put ting, niet van gelijke waarde, prijs.
ts'iao ting / (*t'iao* ») }, den hoogsten graad behalen.
koàn ting, de beste uit de besten.

Tìng — *Tìng*, zilver en goud wegen, geldschaaltjes.
ting hoe / (» *hoa*) }, afdeelingen op een geldschaaltje zilver, goud.

釘 Tìng — *Tìng*, vernagelen (als een kanon).
tìng ts'eh / (» *ts'eh*) }, boekbinden, steken (van insekten).

tìng ts'eh sai kū (*ts'eh*) }, boekbinder.
tìng tiaò, vast spijkeren.
tìng tiòh, gestoken worden door, steken.
tìng sì, onveranderlijk.
tìng tâng, koperslager.
tìng liēn, geketend zijn.
tìng tìng, een spijker inslaan.
tìng tìng tiaò leh, als een vastgeslagen spijker *i. e.* niet verroeren.
tìng tsûn, een schip timmeren, bouwen.
tìng k'ang, een gat inslaan om den spijker in te drijven.
tìng ts'in, een weegschaal, balans maken.
tìng kō, stempelen (als munt).
ka tsaó tìng, vlooienbeet.
tìng ì, naar iemands zin zijn.
tìng lâng ì, iemands zin doen.
sa tìng ì (*sio*) }, sijmpathiseeren, harmonieeren.
kóng oē sa tìng t'ia (*oū sio*) }, in het spreken met elkander sijmpathiseeren.
tìng tók, iemand in moeielijke positie, verlegenheid brengen.
tìng sa, kleeren stikken.
tìng hoe, borduren (bloemen enz. op iets vastnaaien.)

重 ing *Ting*, numer voor aardlagen: zeeën, rotsen
ting ting, verscheidene rijen achtereen.
ting kù, stotteren.
sa ting (*sio* ») }, voor minder dan een ander verkoopen.
sa tìng, tegen elkander opbieden, concurreeren.
tìng kè, hoogere prijs voor iets geven, overbieden.
ting tá, overtreffen.
tìng tìng tiép tiép, op elkander gestapeld.
ting ting t'áh t'áh, do.

ting t'aò kóng, herzeggen, nog eens zeggen.
ting pē (» *poē*) }, dubbel zoo...
ting t'aô, van voren af aan.
ting t'aô tsoè, van voren af aandoen.
ting sùn, rand onmiddelijk boven het oog.
ting kù' stotteren = ting tsíh.
ting king (» *kan*) }, overslag aan een kleed (aan de borst).
ting kúm, op nieuw koude vatten, instorten in eene ziekte.
ting kì, nog eens opschrijven.
ting sin, van nieuw, voren af aan.
ting k'ì, achter elkander gegroeide tanden.
ting p'ē, ting sa (*p'oē*) }, een deken weer op zich leggen, een jas weer aandoen.
kui nā ting ming (*muī*) }, verscheidene deuren, apartementen van een huis.
ting tā, verward spreken, zich vergissen.
ting sing, een dubbel sterfgeval met zich slepende (als een ongelukkige dag).

亭 Ting *Ting*, loods, schuur.
lák kak ting, zeskant torentje.
poeh kak ting, pat koà ting (*peh*) }, achtkant torentje.
tsih kong ting, huis om nieuw aankomende mandarijnen te ontvangen.
kùn ting, soort tabernakel, kastje waarin men de tablet van den overledene draagt.
sog ting á, koepeltje, rustplaats in het gebergte.
tiaô ting, het hof.
ka ting (*ke* ») }, huisselijke (zaken).
ting ts'ing, bezakken, bezinken (als troebel water).

78

海上絲綢之路文獻集成 科技與文化編

有 Tīng | *Tīng* (*tān*) }, hard.
tīng ts'â, hard hout.
tīng sin, inwendig hard (als hout).
tīng taoh, stevig, sterk (van voorw. handel enz.)
tīng k'ok k'ok, klinken, geluid van zich geven.
kien tīng (» *tān*) }, stevig, hard.
pá pui tīng (*tān*) }, van goede familie, rijk.
t'aò k'ak tīng (*tān*) }, hardhoofdig, zelden ziek zijn (van kinderen).
tīng ê tiaò, stevige, sekure, schuld (die men zeker terug krijgt).
tīng lē, tīng kui (*tīng lī* }, vaste regel, vast gebruik.
tīng tsoē (*tīng* ») }, veroordeelen.
tīng sìng, vast (van karakter).
tīng pi, gelijkhangen als een schaal.
tīng kièn, vast, vastberaden.
tīng kè, eenen vasten prijs bepalen.
tīng sì (*tīng* ») }, raadsbesluit des hemels.
tīng tiók (*tīng tsiáh*), afgedaan, beredderd, bepaald.
tīng tòng, veilig, bepaald, sekuur.
it tīng, zeker, zonder twijfel, bepaald.
pit tīng sī, zeker, zonder twijfel is het....
tīng si, tīng k'ik, den tijd bepalen, aangeven (als een uurwijzer.)
tīng sin, tot bedaren komen (zijne bedaardheid terug krijgen.)
hō tīng, deurkozijn.

鄧 Tīng | *Tīng*, familienaam.
bóh tit tīng ih (*o*) / *bò beh p'oh tīng ih* (*o*) }, bemoei u niet met hem, laat u niet met hem in.

T'ing | *Nī ki siong t'ing*, overeenkomen in jaren.

逞 T'ing | *T'ing*, toegeven (kinderen enz.)
t'ing sīng, den vrijen teugel laten aan.
t'ing hiong, kwaadaardig.
t'ing ts'iu (» *ts'io*) }, zijn zwaard vooruitsteken.
t'ing á tsûn, lorcha, half Chineesch half Europeesch model.
hoe t'ing (*hoan* ») }, bloemen boot, bordeel.
tsa bó, do.
t'ing i ê k'ì, zijn toorn doen uitkomen bot vieren.
t'ing sin, te voorschijn treden.

等 T'ing | *T'ing*, toelaten, toestaan dat.
t'ing ki tsū dziēn, laat hem zijn eigen gang gaan.
t'ing t'ien, aan den hemel overlaten.
tú t'ing sino sit, bericht omtrent iets gaan inwinnen.
t'ing hān, wachten, staan wachten.
t'ing t'aī, do.
t'ing ts'e (» *ts'e*) }, wachter zijn in een mandarijnbureau.
t'ing ih (*tìng* ») }, bijleggen, betalen (in het spel).
tsī i t'ing i sī i, voor een duit 3 duiten geven (aan den winner).
bé táh t'ing (*bé táh tìng*) }, stijgbeugel.

停 T'ing | *T'ing*, wachten, ophouden, doen ophouden.
t'ing kang, het werk staken, schorten.
t'ing k'a, ophouden, stil staan (onder het loopen).
t'ing pū, blijven staan, ophouden, wachten.
hō i t'ing t'ing, langzaam laten gaan (als paarden), langzaam doen (van zaken).

t'ing ts'iú, wachten met, staken.
t'ing t'ing-tiep á kú, wacht even.
k'ah t'tng, straks, na weinig wachtens.
sing li-t'ing k'ih laih, handel staken.
tiaò t'ing, (eene zaak) regelen, schikken.

T'ing *T'ing*, rijzen (als een luchtballon, vliegeren).
t'ing sin, rechtop gaan zitten.
t'ing hing, met de borst vooruit.
t'ing hing bán king, met de borst vooruit en de schouders opgetrokken (als manke lieden enz).

Tio

釣 *Tiò á*, vischhaak.
tiò hi, visschen, hengelen.
tiò hi ang, ijsvogel.
īng dzī tiò i, iemand door lokaas vangen.
tiò kog, hengel.
tiò ki, schaakspelen.
tiò soà, vischsnoer.
tiò kao, vischhaak.
hē tiò (*hē* ») }, de haak uitleggen.
tsiáh tiò, van de haak eten.
tsit á tiò i toā taī, een schelvischje uitgooien om een kabeljauwtje te vangen.
pàng tiò, een vischsnoer uitvieren, een lokaas uitwerpen.
ēm t'ang tsiáh tióh i ê tiò, laat u niet in zijn strik vangen.
tiò bát, dichtnaaien.
tiò bō hoe, een sieraad op een muts naaien.

跳 *Tiò*, springen op dezelfde plaats blijven.
tiò t'iaò, springen, van plaats veranderen.
tiò tiò t'iaò t'iaò, huppelen (als kinderen.)
tiò k'a koe (*ts'īng k'a ke*) }, hinkelen.
tiò lóh tsui (*tiò*) }, in het water springen.
tiò tiò tsaò k'i, huppelend weggaan.
tiò tàng, als een tooveraar huppelen, springen, tooveraar zijn.
tiò k'a tèng toè (*tuì tè*) }, trappelen, stamp-voeten (van woede).
ts'iák ts'iak tiò, huppelen, op heete kolen staan.
k'i kà mí teh tiò, stampvoeten, trappelen van woede.
tiò tsit ē (*ē*) }, opspringen, ontstellen.
tiò t'i p'ùn toè, opspringen en stamp-voeten.
tò tiò, achteruit springen.
ts'io tiò, levendig, dartel (van beesten).
sim kog-p'ók p'ók tiò, bonzen van het hart.

Tiō *Tiō*, dreunen.
k'éh k'éh tiō, dreunen sidderen, rillen, (van koude of vrees).

挑 *Pìn t'io*, haarspeld.
T'io *t'io tām poh ióh hún*, een weinig poeder opnemen (als op de punt van een mes.)
t'io hoe (» *hoa*) }, borduren.
ts'ut t'io, statie stokken uitsteken enz.
t'io hé (» *hoé*) }, de pit van de lamp uithalen.
ting t'io, lampenpit uithaalder.
poan t'io (*pan* ») }, aanzetten, aanhitsen (menschen).
t'io bing, tot een eindsbesluit komen.
t'io p'oà, stuk steken, doorsteken (als een zweer of eene zak).

îng tsiem t'iò k'i lai, met een speld uithalen.

糶 T'iò *T'iò bí*, rijst verkoopen.
t'iò nó kok, graan verkoopen.
ping t'iò, in tijd van schraalte van levensmiddelen opgestapelde rijst tegen den ouden lagen prijs verkoopen.
Kè t'iò eh (*koè*) }, de beste uit de besten gekozen.
hē hi ts'iú bé oē t'iò, legt men het op de hand dan kan het springen *d. i.* het is fraai, allerliefst (van voorwerpen.)

Tioh

扽 Tioh *Tioh*, naar zich toehalen.
tioh án, strak uitspannen, uittrekken.
puih puih tioh tioh (*tioh péh péh*) }, met geweld trekken.
àm tsī kā i tioh (*tsē*) }, iemand heimelijk een duw, teeken geven.
tioh lóh tsui, in het water trekken.
tioh béh (» *boéh*) }, kousen aantrekken.
tioh tsûn, een schuit voorttrekken.
tioh sa á ku, bij den slip van zijn kleed (terug) trekken.
sa k'an sa tioh, elkander meetrekken.

Tih *Tioh* spelen bv. schaakspelen: *ki tioh*, zet in het schaakspel.
tsit pō ki tsit pō tioh, voor elke zet in het schaakspel is een tegenzet *d. i.* tegen elke handeling van deze zijde kan gene er een ander inbrengen.

是着 *Tioh* ja, juist zoo, zoo is het.
īm tióh, niet goed.
tióh lah, juist zoo, ja.
sit (*tioh*) *sīt tsit tioh* }, eene goede gelegenheid laten voorbij gaan.

ts'ē tioh, vinden.
gū tioh (*gī* ») }, gebeuren.
tú tioh, ontmoeten.
tióh boā, werken.
bak tióh, smerig maken.
tióh soè dzī (*sè*) }, draag zorg voor.
dzip tióh (*dzik* ») }, achterhalen.
tioh iao, betooveren.
tióh k'a tak, struikelen.
tióh tak, struikelen.
tióh kip, ongeduldig wachten op iets.
sim laī tióh kip, do.
t'aò tioh bé sī (*boé*) }, volkomen goed.
t'aò īm tióh bé īm sī (*boé*) }, volstrekt niet goed.
tióh soa, koliek.
tióh iáh, weggevreten neus.
oē tit sa tióh (*ē*) (*sio*) }, elkander kunnen ontmoeten, weêr zien.
tióh kia, door vrees bevangen worden.
tióh dzit, beurtdag.
tióh pé (» *pē*) }, het doel, de schijf raken, treffen.
tióh ts'ìng, door een schot getroffen, geraakt 2e venerische ziekten krijgen.
tióh ióh, de juiste medicijnen voor eene ziekte.
tiòh pī, eene ziekte krijgen, ziek worden.
tióh siong, verwond worden.
tióh kong, (volgens de beurt) de zaken voor het algemeen te doen hebben.
tióh pan, de dienstbeurt in een bureau hebben.
tióh lō tsú, de beurt hebben om voor

een gemeenschappelijken afgod te zorgen.
tiòk kòng, razend, dol worden.

Tiok

Tiok *Tiok it* (*tiòk*), elk, stuk voor stuk.

Tiòk *Tiēm tiòk* (*tiòk*), instaan voor, 2° vastbesloten zijn om.

sim laî tiòk kip (*tsiák*), ongeduldig (op iets) wachten.

tiòk sit (*tsiák*), inderdaad, het ware eener zaak toch eigenlijk, toch wezentlijk.

iú tiòk, iemand of iets waar men op aan kan, waarop men vertrouwen kan

ū tiòk lòk (*tsiák*), bepaald, naauwkeurig, geregeld, iemand die een thuiskomen heeft.

bò tiòk lòk, onbepaald, onnauwkeurig, verward.

tiòk ì (*tsiák*), vast voorgenomen zijn.

tiòk sit, de ware toedracht eener zaak.

ū tiòk lòk ê lâng, iemand waar men op kan, die te vertrouwen is, aan die eene vaste woning enz. heeft.

hoăn put tiok (*tsiák*), verkeerd, niet goed handelen.

Tiók *Tiók tuì* (*o*), verbannen.

tuì i kun tiók (*kin kiù*), uitgaande van iets op het spoor van iemand zien te komen (b. v. wetende waar gestolen goederen zijn de dieven zien te ontdekken.)

kik tiók (*tiok*), uitjagen.

Tiok *T'iok t'iok* (*tsik t'iok* ook *hiok*), opzamelen.

t'iok sè, zijn kracht voor iets verzamelen (als iemand die over iets heen zal springen).

liòk t'iok, de zes huisdieren.

giét t'iok, slecht beest (scheldw.)

Tiong

中 *Tiong kan*, te midden van.

Tiong *tiong ng*, do. onder, tusschen.

tiong pān, middelmatig.

tiong kun, centrum van het leger.

tiong tiong, middelmatig.

tiong iū, do.

tiong lâng, middelaar.

tiong ui, middelste mast, groote mast.

tiong k'í, voorste tanden.

tiong liên, middelbare leeftijd.

tiong tsai (» *tsai*), tweede vinger, middelste.

tiong iông (» *iâng*), midden, midden in, het gelukkige, juiste midden.

tiong tsi, halve dollar.

tiong ts'iu, 8ste maand 15de dag.

tik tiong (*tiong*), middelmatig.

kui tiong, in het midden, naar het midden toe.

sin tiong, in het lichaam, inwendig.

dzin tiong, gleuf tusschen neus en lip.

tiong pó, als middelaar voor iets instaan.

tiong tsun, de middelste, hoofdpriester (bij lijkdiensten enz.)

ki tiong, daaronder, onder het getal van dezen.

tiong ting, middelmatig.

k'ai tiong (» *tiang*), beginnen (een affaire), een winkel openen.

tiong ting (*tiang* »), lantaarns (die men uit

kan zetten, bij huwelijken gebruikt.)
tióng kok, china.

忠 Tiong *Tiong tit* (*tiong*), oprecht.
tsīn tiong, do.
tiong tùn, do.
tiong hō, oprecht, te vertrouwen.
gù tiong (*gi* ») , dom.
tiong sin, oprechte minister; oprecht.
poà tiong kan, half oprecht en half bedriegelijk.

長 Tióng *Tióng sing* (*tiáng* ») , groot geworden, opgewassen van menschen.
sing tióng (» *tiáng*), afkomstig (geboortig van) geleefd hebben te.
tióng taī (*tiáng* »), groot worden.
tsun tióng (» *tiáng*), eerwaardige oude.
tióng kè (*tiáng kè*), toenemen, opslaan in prijs.
ke tióng koá kè, een weinigje meer geven, opslaan.
tióng tsi, oudste zoon.
tióng sun, oudste zoon van zijn oudsten zoon.
tsit é ná tióng koh nīh, een groote lummel.

中 Tiòng *Tiòng*, raken, het doel treffen, eene litter: graad krijgen.
tiòng kú dzin, Kú dzin worden.
tiòng tsì, door een pijl getroffen worden.
tiòng k'ing, de spijker op de kop slaan.
tiòng kè (*tiòng*), zijn plan bereiken.
tiòng siong (*siang*), gewond zijn.
tiòng hong put gú, door een beroerte getroffen en niet kunnen spreken.
put tiòng iōng (*tiòng*), niet te gebruiken, nietswaardig (van pers.)

tiòng tám, door verrassing, verwondering, getroffen worden.
tiòng hūn, haten.
tiòng tók, vergiftigd worden.
tiòng tók làng, iemand vergiftigen.
tiòng pé, het doel, mikpunt treffen, juist goed treffen.

漲 Tiòng *Haó tiòng* (*tiàng*), springvloed.

脹 Tiòng *Ko tiòng* (*tiàng*), water in den buik.

Tiòng *Tiòng iòng dzit* (*tiàng iàng*), 9de maand 9de dag.
tiòng hok (*tiòng* »), herhalen, herhaling.

腸 Tiòng *Taī tiòng* (» *ts'iàng*), de groote ingewanden.
siaó tiòng (*ts'iàng*), de kleine ingewanden.
tuì tiòng (» *ts'iàng*), breuk, fistel.
siaó tiòng tuì (*ts'iàng*), do.
tit tiòng (*tìng*), ronduit (dom).
sim tiòng, inwendige gedachten, karakter.

Tiòng *Tiòng kiú* (*tiàng*), steeds, lang, eeuwig.
tiòng todn (*tiàng*), goed en kwaad: laag en kort.
kièn tiòng (*tiàng*), zijne hoofdstudie van iets maken.
làng-kok iú sò tiòng, iedereen heeft iets waarvan hij zijn vak maakt.

Tiōng *Tin tiōng*, hoog schatten, op prijs stellen.
kìng tiōng, do. eeren.
pó tiōng, do. zorgdragen voor.
tuì tiōng (*tì* »), do.
siong tiōng, erg, deerlijk (als van een woord) hoog (van prijs), veel geld kostend.

tiōng tiōng | *(tiōng »)* | , veel gewicht aan iemand hechten.

tiōng dzīen, zware ambtsverantwoordelijkheid.

tsun tiōng, hoogschatten, zorgdragen voor.

hō tiōng, bezadigd (niet lichtzinnig). aan.

tsū tiōng, zich zelven hoogschatten, schat u zelven hoog (beleefdheidsterm.)

gién tiōng | *(gân »)* | , uwe woorden zijn te zwaar, ik ben zooveel beleefdheid niet waard.

Tiōng *Tiōng gân*, makelaars loon.

tiōng tsi, commissiegeld 2e geld hoog achten, waardeeren.

Oiōng *Tá tiōng* | *(» tiāng)* | , vechten.

t'ok tiōng | *(tiāng)* | , belasten met, opdragen.

hō goá tiōng tsèh | *(tiāng)* | , laat ik u opdragen om....., ik zou u willen opdragen om.....

boē tiōng tit, niet op te vertrouwen, te verlaten.

hing tiōng | *(» tiāng)* | , straftoepasser in een mandarijn bureau.

sik tiōng, stok van Boeddh. priester.

hong tiōng, hoofdzaal in een Boeddh. tempel.

k'un tiōng kui uī, hoeveel broeders hebt gij? (beleefde term).

Tiong *Tsiet t'iong* | *(tsiet t'iong)* | , het midden tusschen een verschil nemen, een verschil midden door deelen.

寵 T'ióng *T'ióng aì*, tot zijn gunsteling, maken.

tik t'ióng, de favoriet van iemand zijn.

kuì t'ióng, uwe of zijne bijzit (beleefde term).

塚 *T'ióng*, begraafplaats.

T'ióng *t'ióng toē* | *(» tē)* | , algemeene begraafplaats.

gī t'ióng, do. (voor armen).

bān dzin t'ióng, do.

t'ióng soa, heuvel waar een ieder begraven mag.

T'iòng *T'iòng lòk* | *(t'iàng)* | , vreugde, verheugd.

t'iòng sóng | *(»)* | , vrolijk, opgeruimd.

t'iòng im | *(t'iàng)* | , vrolijk (wijn) drinken.

ham t'iòng, vrolijk, verheugd.

t'iòng sià, iemand die een vrolijk, zorgeloos leven leidt.

kóng t'iòng, gekheid vertellen, schertsen.

t'iòng sià ê lâng, iemand die van geen droefheid afweet maar steeds vrolijk is en zijn werk niet doet.

T'iông *T'iông t'iông*, soort modderworm.

sat t'iông ê ioh, medicijnen om wormen (in het lijf) te verdrijven.

mī t'iông, onvermoeid iets doen (als geld vragen, handeldrijven enz.)

Tit

得 Tit *Tit tioh*, verkrijgen, krijgen, ontvangen.

tit lâng t'iā, zich bemind maken bij anderen.

tit i sioh, zich door iemand bemind maken.

tát tit | *hīng tit* | , gelukkig dat, bij geluk.

bô t'ang tiò'h lán tit, wij kunnen er geen aandeel in krijgen.

boē tit t'ang k'ì, wij kunnen niet gaan

oh tit kóng, het gaat moeielijk het te zeggen.

oē tsoè tit | *(ē tsò* | , het gaat.

tsoè tit k'i, (*tsò*) }, kunnen volvoeren.
pūn tit k'i, kunnen beredderen.
koán tit k'i, kunnen behoeren.
tsoè boē tit k'i (*tsò bē*) }, niet kunnen volbrengen.
siá tit lai
siá oē tit lai (*ē*) }, kunnen schrijven.
Tit, malsch (van weder) iets beter van eene ziekte.
k'ah tit, beter uit te houden van weer enz.

直 Tít *Tit*, recht, (niet krom).
tit tit kiâ, rechtuit gaan.
tiaò tit, rondborstig, 2e afgedaan.
tiong tit, do. oprecht.
k'iok tit, gesteldheid van eene zaak, geschil enz.
hoai tit (*hoâ* ») }, vierkante grootte.
tit tit tsoē (*tsē*) }, hoe langer hoe meer.
hong tit k'i tit koâ, hoe meer de wind toeneemt des te kouder wordt het
tit tit, zonder ophouden.
tit tit kóng, onafgebroken spreken.
si lâng tit, lichtgeloovig dom.
p'ah boē tit (*bē*) }, niet tot een eind kunnen komen.
boē tit tit (*bē*) }, tot geen eind kunnen komen.
tsiáh tit, naam van een spel.
kiâ tit, do.
hoai kiâ tit tîng (*hoâ*) }, dwars, en rechts, over en weêr gaan.
tit toàn, rechtuit uitspraak doen.
k'a ts'iú puih tit tit (*ts'un*) }, met handen en beenen rechtuit gestrekt liggen *i. e.* dood zijn.
ts'un tit, rechtuit steken.
toā k'uì tit pùn, zwaar hijgen.
tit giên bô po (*gân*) }, ik zeg de waarheid en vlei niet.
tit bák, niet dan rechtuit voor zich uitkijken.
sut tit, oprecht, eenvoudig (zonder streken), ronduitspreken.
nḡ tit, rechtuit, ronduit, onbewimpeld.
put tit, ongelijk hebben.
it tit, rechtstreeks, onmiddelijk.
tit tú tit, rechtuit.
tit lō, rechteweg, rechtuit, niet ingewikkeld.
tit li tit lō, rechtuit, zonder moeielijkheden.
li lō tit, die manier is goed, daar kan later geen moeielijkheid mede zijn.
tit oò, in eenen gelijken toon door (zonder wending aan de stem te geven als bij zingen).

姪 Tit *Tit*, neef (oom zegger) = tít á broeders zon.
tit lú (» *li*) }, nicht, broeders dochter.
siok tit, van denzelfden familienaam.
tsú tit, jongens van het dorp (door het dorpshoofd aldus genoemd).
sè tit, door kinderen van intieme vrienden tegen elkander gebruikt.
tóng tit, achterneef (zoon van zijn cousin.)

遊 T'it *T'it t'ô*, uitspanning nemen, spelen gekheid maken met.
t'it t'ô king (*kan*) }, hoerenhuis, hoereeren.
hò t'it, *aì t'it*, veel houden van hoereeren.
kap lâng k'i t'it, met iemand gaan wandelen.
t'it k'a, iemand die veel van hoereeren houdt.
t'it 'o kiá, doordraaier.

t'it t'ô lâng, do. 2e boer.
t'it pát lâng ê t'ô, op een andermans zak loopen.
t'it tsa bó, bij lichtekooien loopen.
t'it t'it t'iòng t'iòng, veel van uitgaan, zwieren houden.
nn̄g lâng tuì t'it, tegen elkander wedden, op spelen (als bij dobbelen, wijnen drinken enz.)
kap lâng t'it, twisten (met iemand).

直 T'it
T'it, recht buigen.
t'it tit, do.
t'it t'it k'i bing pik, eene zaak duidelijk uitmaken, uiteenzetten.
t'it k'i tiaò tit, recht maken, eene zaak duidelijk uiteenzetten.
t'it io, de lendenen rechtuit strekken (als op een bank).

Tiu

丢 Tiu
Tiu tsui, over boord gooien, in het water gooien.
tiu k'ì, weggooien.
hiet tiu, do.
tiu tiu tsaó, recht doorloopen zonder om te kijken (van kinderen).
kiēn tiu, klein maar stevig (van kinderen) vriendelijk en vrijmoedig van kinderen.
tiu tsit pi̍, terzijde gooien, terzijde stellen (van voorw. en zaken).
tiu biēn, schande aangedaan, beschaamd gemaakt worden, zijn fatsoen te grabbelen gooien.
tiù tsih bé (boé), stamelen korttongig.
k'a tiù toē, een weinig stijf, mank gaan.

Tiù
Tiù iā, dag en nacht.

綢 Tiû
Tiû, zijde.
tiû toūn, algemeene naam voor zijde.
tiû toūn tièm, zijdewinkel.
tiû nńg ê mi̍h, zachte zijden stoffen.
mi̍ tiû, een geel weefsel van zijde en katoen, zeer sterk.
so̍ tiû effen zijde.
hoe tiû gím tiû, gebloemde zijde.

稠 Tiû
Tiû, k'aren (helder maken) ziften.
kè tiû (koè), klaren (als meel enz.)
tiû tsui hún, watermeel, witsel klaren, blanketsel wasschen.

籌 Tiû
Pàng tiû, afleveringsstokjes (aan koelies) afgeven.
pun tiû, do. afgeven.
toā tiû, groote afleveringsstok (voor meerdere kleinere tellend).
ki̍ tiû, wachtstokje (dat men aan wachtloopers geeft).
tsiōng goân tiû, een bazardspel met dobbelsteenen en staafjes.

躊 Tiû
Tiû tû, niet weten wat te doen, aarzelen, in bedenking staan hoe of wat!

䄻 Tiū
Tiū, rijststengel.
tiū kó, stroo van de rijst.
tiū t'aò, rijststoppels.
tiū kó tsáng, do.
koah tiū, maaien.
tiū ts'aó, graanstoppels.
tiū ts'un, roos.
pò tiū het graan pooten.
tiū-lâng hoe, de rijstaren zijn in bloei.

張 Tiu̍
Tiu̍ (tio̍), numer. voor stukken papier, brieven, zeilen, bedden 2e familienaam.
tiu̍ iū (io̍), den schijn aannemen van.
tiu̍ bāng, een net uitspannen.
tiu ti, op zijne hoede zijn, zich tegen eene gebeurtenis in gereedheid brengen.
bô tiu̍ ti, onverwachts.
tiu tiû (tiû tû), aarzelen.

tiụ hui sìng, een karakter als Tiụ hui d. i. opvliegend, driftig.

tiụ t'ien su / (*tiọ*) }, eerste sterrewichelaar der chineezen.

tiụ sin sè / (*sì*) }, zich in aanvallende houding stellen.

ts'it làng tsú tiụ sm tát nṅg làng su niụ (*nṅ*) (*niò*), het is beter dat twee personen elkander raadplegen dan dat één alleen te werk ga.

tiụ sin tiụ báng, i. e. voorzichtig loeren, naauwkeurig, voorzichtig onderzoeken lett. op vliegen en muskieten loeren.

tiụ tiém sim, een weinig eten meênemen.

tiụ bi, *tiụ ts'à*, rijst en hout medenemen (als op een tocht).

siang (of) *sṇ k'a tiụ ti*, voor beide, alle gevallen voorzorgen nemen.

tiụ ting kat ts'ai / (*tiang*) }, illumineeren en guirlandes ophangen.

tiụ k'aò niụ, proviand, levensmiddelen medenemen.

tiụ kè tsṇg, de huwelijksgeschenken, uitzet in gereedheid brengen.

tiụ kè, als bruidschat geven.

tiụ t'é biⁿn, den schijn van fatsoenlijk aannemen.

tiụ hūn, aan koopen leggen.

tiụ k'oạ kui è tsị, waardeeren, schatten hoeveel iets waard is.

tiụ king keh, in appartementen afdeelen (als een groot vertrek).

tiụ sṇ li sì, die en die, so and so, deze of gene.

騎 Tiụ　*Tiụ làng*, iemand onder bedreiging kwellen, iemand uit de hoogte behandelen.

sị tiụ / (*sio*) }, elkander treiteren.

tiụ tioh làng, *tiụ tiụ tioh tioh*, iemand treiteren.

Tiụ　*U pun tiụ* / (*tiọ*) }, aan de andere (kinderen) mededeelen, hun er ook wat van geven.

tsin tiụ, in werkelijkheid, als het op doen aankomt.

長 Tiụ　*Pó tiụ* / (*tiọ*) }, wijkmeester.

ke tiụ / (*ke* ») }, dorpshoofd 2e hoofd eener firma.

siā tiụ, dorpshoofd.

tiụ lō, dorpsoudere.

li tiụ, do. dorpshoofd.

漲 Tiụ　*Tiụ* / (*tiọ*) }, opgezwollen, dik (van de buik) 2e verstopte (buik).

tiụ làng, opstopping van etter.

tiụ hong, wind vatten.

tiụ ling, opstopping van melk.

tiụ k'i laih, lichten (een gezonken schip enz.)

tiụ piⁿ, opgezwollen buik (van visch) door te veel gegeten te hebben.

siao tiụ / (*siao tsui tiọ*) }, eene verstopping doen verdwijnen 2e eene zaak afmaken.

tiụ kui / (*tiọ* ») }, verstopt, opgepropt in de krop.

tsui-tiụ kaò ām, het water komt tot aan de keel, de nood is zeer hoog.

tú tiụ / (*o*) }, iemand weerleggen, zijn mond stoppen.

kóng oⁿ tiụ làng, iemand door een enkel gezegde de mond snoeren.

pá tiụ, verstopping (slechte spijsvertering).

tiụ sìh, barsten (van verstopping (gew. als scheldwoord.)

帳 Tiụ　*Tsiong kun tiụ* / (*tsiang*) }, bevelhebberstent.

báng tiụ, muskietengordijn.

sin tiû, gordijn vóór een afgodsbeeld.

塲 Tiû *Dzip tiû (tiô)*, examen gaan afleggen.

kà tiû, exercitieplein, executieplein.

soû tiû, bergstreek.

siu tiû, een eind aan eene zaak maken.

kiaó tiû, speelhuis, dobbelhuis.

bé (bē) tiû, paardenspel.

hì tiû, komediegebouw.

hiâ tiû, beschaamd, verlegen in het publiek.

bàng tiû, do.

sik tiû, gewoon zijn iets in het publiek te doen.

tsit tiû kang (tiô), uitsluitend, niets anders (doen).

oân tiû, afgemaakt (als een huis enz.)

tsièn tiû, slagveld.

pó tiû, dobbelhuis.

tsit tiû ê taī tsì, deze zaak, dit punt.

丈 Tiū *Tiū ím (tiō »)*, behuwd-moeder.

tiū làng, behuwd-vader (vrouw's vader.)

toā tiū, oom (man van moeder's oudere zuster).

kō tiū, oom (man van vader's zuster).

i tiū, oom (man van moeder's zuster).

抽 T'iu *T'iu ts'ut*, uitplukken, afnemen, afhouden, uittrekken.

t'iu ts'iem, orakel door middel van bamboezen stokjes.

t'iu hun, commissie, zijne percenten van iets krijgen.

t'iu t'iâ, trekken (als een zweer).

t'iu k'ao, loten, een lot uittrekken.

t'iu sè, t'iu hìng (soè) (hìng), belasting heffen.

t'iu ping, soldaten lichten.

t'iu tsui, water inzuigen (als bij eenspuit).

tsii t'iu, hevel.

tsui t'iu, spuit.

t'iu si, zijde uitspinnen 2e groot worden, opschieten van kinderen.

t'iu sim, opschieten (als graan).

sán t'iu, mager en lang.

t'iu to boē tit dzip siù (bē) (siù), zijn zwaard getrokken hebben en het niet meer in de schede kunnen steken *i. e.* woorden die men gezegd heeft moeielijk weer kunnen intrekken.

ioh t'iu, lavementspuit.

t'iu t'aò, percenten van iets afnemen.

t'iu kun (» kin), de peezen uitrekken.

t'iu ka lé, de marionetten doen spelen.

t'iu tseh-tsiah tin tāng, als er aan getrokken wordt bewegen zij (de marionetten) zich; *i. e.* niets uit zich zelven doen.

t'iu t'āng, onderwijzen, leeren.

T'iu *Kiuh kiuh t'iu*, zonder ophouden schreien, angstig tjilpen.

丑 T'ú *T'iú si (t'ió)*, 1—3 uur 's nachts.

t'iú (t'iú en t'ió), comiek (op een tooneel).

t'iú á kioh, comieke kerel.

Tiú *Ta tiú*, vlug, gedwee, stil (van kinderen).

Tiú *tsè tiú (tsè »)*, tegenhouden, verhinderen, in den weg staan (beleefde term).

Tiuh

㬹 Tiuh *Tiuh tiuh*, tintelen (als handen en voeten enz.)

tiuh tiuh toū, tintelen (als een zweer).

ân tuih tiuh, zeer strak aangehaald.

tiuh tsih kun (kin en boé), woorden gedeeltelijk inslikken.

t'iâ tiuh tiuh, tintelend pijn doen.

tiuh tiuh t'iâ, pijn bij schokken.

tiuh toé, een weinig mank gaan.

Tiūh *Sáu tiúh tiúh* zeer mager.

To

刀 To Een mes.

té to, een kort mes, een dolk.

to ts'ui, het lemmet van een mes.

to pi, het heft van een mes.

to k'oân, het gevest van een zwaard.

to tsiem, punt van een mes.

to siù, de scheede van een zwaard.

to pó siú, zwaarddrager van een mandarijn, beul.

to tiem, een hakblok.

k'ao to, een schaaf.

ts'ai to, snijmes om papier af te snijden.

gé to, vouwbeen.

to tsiòh, slijpsteen.

to k'ìng, rug van een mes.

hé to, vuurslag.

io to, zijdgeweer.

koan to, speer.

ts'iu to bák pé, zwaarden en harken (zwaarden in 't algemeen).

to t'ui, messentrap, messen door een paal gestoken waartegen de toovenaars oploopen.

p'ī to to, scherpe neus, arendsneus.

sio to hoe, geheim genootschap der chineezen.

tsit ki to, één mes.

t'ì t'aò to, een scheermes.

k'a to, een schaar.

siang bīn to kui, een dubbelhartig mensch die over en weer kwaad spreekt.

多 To *To*, veel.

to siā, wel bedankt.

to su, veel zaken, bemoeial.

ts'a put to, ongeveer, zoo wat juist genoeg, »letterlijk, vergissing niet veel".

To *To*, een aanvangspartikel aanduidende dat iets tegenvalt, wel zoo, wel wel, inderdaad.

to bô lah, wel er is er niets van.

to kò, dat is genoeg, voldoende.

koe nīng bát bát, to ū phāng, het ei is wel dicht maar heeft toch ook openingen, iets moeielijk geheim te houden.

īm to, wel inderdaad; het ware beter dat.

倒 Tó *Tó*, op zijde liggen 2° omgekeerd, in het tegendeel.

tó ló k'ì, geheel en al omvallen.

poáh tó, vallen over, omvallen.

siak tó, do.

sak tó, omtrekken.

ts'ia tó, omkeeren, onderste boven keeren.

tó t'aò, do.

tó t'ui, trap.

kút tó, uitglijden.

tó toà ts'ìng, bedlegerig (van een zieke).

tó iông, impotent.

tó píng (*tò pán*), omkeeren.

sa tó t'è (*o*), langs elkander gaan.

tó tsai ts'ìng (*to*), bedlegerig zijn.

tó ts'ìng, do.

tó ūn, zijne fortuin is gekeerd, de fortuin heeft hem den rug toegekeerd.

p'ah tó, omgooien.

kè tsì k'ì tó (*kè*), bij af, of opslag van den prijs.

p'ai k'ì tó (*bai*), moeielijk, slecht te hanteeren (van zware voorwerpen).

piān tó, weêrleggen, overtuigen.

tó tièm, bankroet gaan (van een winkel).

tó siaò, bankroet gaan.

k'ó tó, iemand overreden, met de mond vol tanden laten staan.

tó àn, een rechtsgeding verliezen.

a (t) put tó, tuimelaar.

tó pâng, uitsterven van eene familietak.

tó lâng ê tsi̍, anderen door zijn bankroet laten lijden.

島 Tó *Hai tó* } (*tó*), eiland.

tó sū } (*sī*), do.

禱 Tó *Ki tó*, bidden.

Tó *Kui tó gûn* } (*gîn*), hoeveel maal het gewicht in zilver.

Tó *T'ai ti tó iû* } (*iô*), varkens en geiten slachten.

回 Tò *To lai* } (*tu* „), terugkomen.

tò k'ì, teruggaan.

tsi̍t tò tsûn, éene scheepsreis (vice versa).

tsiáh tò, zijne woorden terughalen.

倒 Tò *Kiâ tò t'è* } (*tò*), achteruitloopen, 2e teruggaan.

tò t'è kiâ, achteruitloopen.

tò tiô } (*tò*), terugspringen.

tò tsiò, weêrschijn.

tò pon̄ lâng, zijn eigen woorden tot die van anderen maken.

tò t'aò tsai, voorover naar beneden vallen.

tò t'aò t'àn, verliezen (van zijn kapitaal).

tò t'aò tsoè, omgekeerd handelen.

tò kao k'i, weêrhaak.

tó k'ao (ook *kao*) *k'i* } (*kao*), do. 2o slinksche draai.

tò t'ap toé } (*tè*), ziel van een flesch.

tò tōng, stooten als een geweer.

tò tiaò liên, passiebloem.

tò pîng } (*pân*), omkeeren, omgekeerd.

tò kóng, omgekeerd zeggen, het tegenovergestelde zeggen van wat iets is.

k'ì tò, heen en weerom.

k'ì k'ì tò tò, zijne woorden inhalen.

kóng oē-k'ì tò } (*oā*), zijne woorden inhalen, terugnemen 2e niet stellig beloven.

tò kiâ, terugloopen.

左 Tò *Tò ts'iú*, linkerhand.

īng tò ts'iú } (*iōng*), linksch zijn = sai tò ts'iú.

傾 Tò *Tò ts'ut*, ledig maken.

tò tsui, water uitgooien.

tik tâng tò ka ná, (als of men) olijven in een bamboezen koker omkeerde *i. e.* rad spreken.

到 Tò *Tò dzīm*, zijn ambt aanvaarden.

hok tò, terugkrijgen wat men te voren verloren had, 2e zijne woorden terug roepen.

si-tò-hoe-piēn k'ui } (*hoa*), als de tijd daar is openen zich de bloemen *i. e.* het verstand komt met de jaren.

逃 Tô *Tô tsaó*, vluchten.

to p'iah, vermijden.

tô pī, do.

tô siém, do. ontwijken.

tô si̍ } (" *se̍*) *tô miā*, zijn leven redden.

to bōng sú tsoát, eenigen zijn gevlucht anderen gestorven.

tô t'oat, heimelijk ontvluchten, ontsnappen.

tô hoān, gevluchte misdadiger.

柁 Tô *Tô tsik*, kaars.

度 Tô *Tsui tô soh*, loodlijn, peilloodlijn.

tsui tô, peillood.

tuì tô, gelijkelijk.

多 Tô *Tô lóng* } (*o*), begunstigen, vooruithelpen.

鉈 Tô *Tô tí*, de gewichten van een balans.

ts'in tô, gewichten.

pōng tó, do.
k'ọ̄ tó, de algemeene geldschaal.
hā tó (*hẹ̄*) }, Emoi geldschaal 4 hun lichter dan de k'ọ̄ tó.
Lók tó, muilezel.

駝 Tó *Tó*, muilezel.
lók tó,tó hè, de muilezels dragen goederen.
Tó *Lû tó* ezelsvracht.

萄 Tó *P'û tó* (*p'ó*) }, druiven.
iû tó, carambola, (blimbing).

襟 Tó *Tó t'aó*, overslag bij de borst van een kleed.

淘 Tó *Tó tsi* (*tsẹ̄*) }, een put uitbaggeren, schoon maken.

道 Tō *Tō li*, leer, manier.
tō tai, superintendent, Taō tai.
tō iâ, do.
tō kaò, Taoïsme.
tō sū, Taoistische priester.
tō kọ, Taoistische non.
tō dzin. Taoistische priester (soort van)
tik tō, den waren weg gekregen hebben (van priester gezegd).
kong tō, rechtvaardig.
k'ui tō, den weg banen (voor mandarijnen), vóór hen uitroepen.
tō hák ė lâng, iemand die volgens de rede, billijkheid, handelt.
hoah tō, uitschreeuwen om uit den weg te gaan (als wanneer mandarijn aankomt).
tsì tō, boogschuttersplaats.
bû tō, niet behoorlijk, volgens recht en billijkheid handelen.
tō tik king, boek der rede en deugd.
tō koạ̄, Taoistische klooster.
tō toạ̄, Taoistische altaar 2e woning van Taoistische priesters.

tō á, de muziekanten enz. die bij Taoistische priester zijn.

都 To *Tọ t'óng*, luitenant-generaal.
tọ si, majoor.
tọ sī, toch immers is het..., volkomen is het.
lm tọ sī h, gij zijt het toch eigentlijk.

肚 Tó *Pak tọ́*, de buik.
tọ́ koā, zak (voor de buik gedragen).
k'a aō tọ́, kuit van het been
tọ́ laī, ruim (van een schip).
tsùn tọ́, do.
tọ́ ting, dek (van een schip).
koā pak tọ́, zwanger.
toā sai tọ kui, gezwollen buik (van kinderen).
io tọ, breede lendengordel.
keh tsoè nn̄g tọ́ (*kẹh tsè nọ̄ tọ́*) }, in twee hokjes, afdeelingen scheiden.
ts'iú tọ́, dikke van de arm.

賭 Tọ́ *Tọ́ k'i*, met alle geweld niet voor een ander willen onderdoen.
tọ́ k'ùi lát, worstelen.
tọ́ nī, vast aan zijne meening houden en er op wedden.
kap i tọ́, met iemand op iets wedden.

堵 Tọ́ *Hóng tọ́*, bewaken (als eene plaats tegen roovers).
tsit tọ́ ė uī, ééne teekening.

妬 Tọ̀ *Oàn tọ̀*, misgunnen, jaloersch zijn.
tsik tọ̀, do.
tọ̀ k'i, haten, misgunnen, jaloersch zijn op.
tọ̀ bak, misgunnende oogen.
tọ̀ hū, jaloersche vrouw.
tọ̀ hièn, knappe menschen misgunnen.

濕 Tọ̀ *Tọ̀ tâm*, beschadigd (door water).
tọ̀ tsui, door water beschadigd (van goederen).
tọ̀, vloeien (van inkt)
tọ̀, zich mededeelen aan (als olie aan papier) besmetten (als eene ziekte).

sn tô (*sio*), besmettelijke (ziekte).
tô tsing, druiper.
tô bák tsui, vloeien, vlekken van inkt.

鬭 Tò *Haī tò*, met wapens vechten.
tò k'ó, elkander uitschelden.

圖 Tô *Tô bô*, plannen maken, intriges bedenken.
tô su (» *si*), zegel.
tē tô, kaart landkaart.
hai tô, *tsui tô*, zeekaart.
ui tô (*oā*), den platten grond voor iets maken.
tô su tsióh (*si*), speksteen.
t'am tô, begeerig naar de middelen uitzien om iets te krijgen.
tô làng ê mih, plannen beramen om zich van een andermans goed meester te maken.
ui ìng hing tô (*oā*), het signalement van een vluchteling overal verspreiden.
ts'i tô, *t'ien bûn tô* (*ts'e*), kaart van den sterrenhemel.
tô i ê siōng (*ts'iūng*), iemands physionomie teekenen.
tô tsiêm, zich met een streek, van grond meester maken.

徒 Tô *Liù tô*, verbannen.
bûn tô, leerling.
tô tē, leerling (in eenig vak).

屠 Tô *Tô tsi tièm* (*tô*), restauratie.
kìm tô, slachten verbieden.
tô p'ú (*tō* »), pissebed.

塗 Tô *Hô tô*, verward, onduidelijk; ongeregeld in handelingen.
lō tô, weg.

肚 Tō *Tō tsai*, de navel.
hi tō, vischbuiken (handelsartikelen).
toā tō kui, dikbuikige kinderen.
p'oà tō, uitgelekt (van eene zaak).
k'in tō tīng (*ts ién*), niet diep denkend en spoedig boos wordend.
sio tō, blaas (urine).
k'iām tìng neh tō, uit zijn mond sparen om het aan anderen te geven.
tsit tō hīng, steeds plannen beramen.
toā tō kán, zwangere slavin.

度 Tō *Tō dzit*, zijn dagelijksch eten hebben.
tō kè tsit mî (*koè*) (*mê*), overnachten.
tō tiép, paspoort (aan Boeddh. priester door mandarijn gegeven).
p'ó tō, zielenfeest, 7de maand.
sio bē tō (*boē*), verzengd.
k'oan hông taī tō, verdraagzaam.
tsè tō (*tsì*), 's rijksinstellingen.
tiān tō, graden op een globe.
tō sò, aantal graden.
tō tsè laī, nog in den schoot gedragen wordende *i. e.* nog geen jaar oud.
tiao tō, opleiden, vormen (als kinderen).
ts'iao tō, uit de onderwereld helpen en weder doen geboren worden.
tō liōng, verdraagzaam.
tsiām tō, tijdelijk, zoolang ergens verblijven.
tō pá, juist genoeg hebben om door zijn dag te komen (maar niets meer).
hoat tō, manier, wijze.

荳 Tō *Tō k'ò*, nootmuskaat.
tō k'ò hoe (*hoa*), foelie.
péh tō k'ò (*éh*), cardamon.

渡 Tō *Tō tsûn*, passagierboot.
kè (*koè*) *tō ê tsûn*, pont, overhaal.

kè tō̠ (koè) }, overzetten over eene rivier.
tō̠ t'aô, landingsplaats.
k'eh tō̠ ê tsûn (k'e̠h) }, passagiersboot.
hè tō̠ (hoè) }, goederenboot, beurtschuit.

鍍 Tō̠ — *Tō̠ kim*, vergulden.

蓖 Tō̠ — *Tō̠ pi iû*, castorolie.

Tō̠ — *Tō̠ tîng*, groote hagedis.

Tō̠ — *Tō̠ im (» kin)* }, aardpier.
tō̠ kaô, molkrekel.
tō̠ kaó á, kleine krulhond.

竇 Tō̠ — *Tō̠*, familienaam.

杜 Tō̠ — *Tō̠*, do.
tō̠ tsoān, volgens eigen idée maken, uit zich zelven opmaken.

投 To̠ — *Kui-tō̠ lâng ê sin kóng oē*, de duivel gaat in iemands lichaam over en spreekt (bij comedies).

燼 To̠ — *Tō̠*, (geheel en al). verbranden.

叨 T'ō̠ — *T'o*, opslobberen (als eenden).
ts'iú- k'it ah t'o tioh, door een eend in de hand gebeten worden.
ah bú ts'ut bong t'o, de eend slobbert (alles) maar op d: i: beproef het maar, men kan nooit weten waar het nog goed voor is.

T'o — *Liók sui t'o dzin*, in het water vallende een ander medetrekken *i. e.* anderen in zijn val medeslepen.

討 T'ó — *T'ó*, vragen om...., 2e aanvallen (een rijk).
kū i t'ó, van iemand vragen.
t'ó tsi̠ sai hū, een knappe schuldeischer.
t'ó siab, opmaken, de verschillende posten optellen.

t'ó tsè (» tsè̠) }, een schuld invorderen.
t'ó tsi̠ niū̠ (niû̠) }, belasting heffen.
t'ó hi, visschen.
t'ó hi lâng, visscher.
t'ó hi tsûn, visschersschuit.
t'o hai, op vischvangst uitgaan.
t'ó t'àng, geld zien te verdienen, kost zien te verdienen.
t'ó tsa bō̠, overspel bedrijven.
t'ó bô oē ê lâng (oū) }, praatziek.
t'ó bô oē t'ang mīng (oū) (mui̠) }, uit nieuwsgierigheid (praatlust) vragen naar.
t'ó ts'ik, de oogst van zijne bezittingen (landgoederen) ophalen.
t'ó sū, zich onnoodig zaken op den hals halen.
t'ó bô in, zonder reden zich met iets bemoeien.
t'ó tsiáh, zien te eten te krijgen (als vogels, bedelaars enz.)
t'ó k'a-k'it lō̠ kiā̠, vruchteloos gegaan zijn.
ts'ú t'ó (ts'i ») }, invorderen, terugvorderen.
t'ó k'an t'aô (têng) }, verpande goederen lossen.
t'ó tsûn, de zekerheid van iets wenschen te weten (als door het orakel te raadplegen.)
t'ó tsui tsiáh iā bô, zelfs water kan men er niet krijgen (van eene ellendige plaats).
tong tsing pak t'ó, in het oosten en in het noorden bestrijden.
t'ó t'aô lō̠, eene betrekking, dienst zien te krijgen.
t'ó tsing, een gunst verzoeken.
t'ó ū sa̠ têng tsiāh, genoeg hebben om te eten.

t'ó p'é-t'iā̤, zich een pak slaag op de hals halen.

T'at t'ó (*t'ai* ») , hoe toch!

t'ó tī kong = *t'ó̤ tī kong* (*t'ó̤ tē* of *tī kong*) , de god van de aarde en van de graven.

T'ó, gebruik makende van...

t'ó tsûn tsaì, in een schip laden.

t'ó kiō kng lai, in een draagstoel komen aandragen.

P'ah t'ò, intriges bedenken.

k'oàn t'ò, do. strikken leggen.

kóng t'ò, van te voren bepaald afspreken, beraadslagen.

p'ah t'ong t'ò, do.

t'ong t'ò, heimelijke verstandhouding.

siòng t'ò ê oē (*siâng*) (*oā*) , gewoonlijk bij elkander gebruikte woorden.

t'ò t'aò gú (en) *oē* (*oā*) , beleefdsheidstermen als men iemand ziet.

t'ò gú (» *gí*) , do.

k'eh t'ò, beleefdsheidsvormen tegen gasten.

goā t'ò, overjas.

t'ò sa̤, een jas overdoen; de kleêren voor den overledene aantrekken (door den hoofdrouwer gedaan.)

kui t'ò, een geheel stel.

tsit t'ò oè (*oā*) , eene geheele redenering.

tsit t'ò sa̤, een stel kleêren.

tsit t'ò hì, een geheel komediestuk (van begin tot eind).

kóng kaò kui t'ò, zoo weten te vertellen dat het een geregeld geheel vormt (onwaarheid).

nn̄g lâng tsoè t'ò, met elkander in verstandhouding zijn.

Tik t'ò, iets veiligs hebben, iets waar men op aan kan.

t'ò tòng (*t'ó* ») , veilig, sekuur, in goede handen.

t'ò t'iet (*t'o* ») , vastberaden, resoluut.

t'ò t'iet ê lâng, een degelijke kerel.

桃 T'ô *T'ô âng tsoá*, roodpapier voor visitekaartjes.

tı̤ t'ô, *k'ó̤ t'ô*, zoete en bittere perziken.

t'o á si̤, gepekelde perziken.

t'ô á, perziken.

hût t'ô, okkernoten walnoten.

t'ô hoe bīn (*hou*) , een gezichtje als een perzikbloem (fraai).

t'ô hoe (» *hoa*) , perzikenbloem die aan den weg groeiende voor iedereen te krijgen is 2e lichtekooi.

t'ô hoe siaó, wellustig, geil (van vrouwen).

哺 T'ô *Koe t'ô á* (*ke*) , grooie kuikens.

玩 T'ô *T'it t'ô*, spelen, uitspanning nemen, wandelen, zie t'it.

土 T'ó *T'ó̤*, aarde 2e onbeschoft, onbeschaafd.

t'o̤ sán, voortbrengselen van den grond.

t'ó̤ siā̤, loopgraaf.

t'o̤ hók, Chinawortel (smilax china).

t'ó̤ toē (» *tē*) , plaats.

t'ó̤ si̤ (*se̤*) *á*, van gemengd ras.

t'ó kong, doodgraver (vernederende term) gemeen, ongemanierd.

t'ó̤ sòng, onbeschaafd.

ts'it t'ó̤ poeh t'ó̤ (*peh*) , laag, gemeen.

t'ó̤ t'aò t'ó̤ bīn, een laag, gemeen uiterlijk hebben.

t'ó̤ pù, op eens van lagen stand rijk geworden.

t'ó tī kong, aardgod.

t'ó̤ hō, bijnaam.

t'ó̤ pô, onbeschoft wijf (scheldwoord).

t'ō lō, onbeschofte manieren.
t'ó bin, onbeschoft volk.
t'ó oē } , lage volkstaal.
(» *oā*) }
t'ō siók, *bin tsing-t'ō siók*, zeden en gewoonten eener plaats.
tsui t'ō water en voortbrengselen (eener plaats), klimaat.
hō t'ō, aardgod.
t'ō sin, aardgeesten.
siā t'ó, den aardgod dank zeggen, op het eind van een werk aan hem offeren.
tsién t'ō, den grond omkrabben, de plaats voor een graf omtrekken.
p'oà t'ō, de grond openhakken (en er goud papier indoen als goed voorteeken bij het begin van een werk).
ts'ut t'ō, zelf zijne weinige kennis van dingen aan het licht brengen.
kui sog kui t'ō, ter aarde bestellen, begraven.

吐 T'ó
T'ó k'ùi, zuchten.
kig kaò m̄ ká t'ō k'ùi, geen adem durven halen van vrees.

吒 T'ó
T'ó t'aò, uitsteken uit, boven den horizont komen.
t'ó lui } , uitpuilende oogen.
(*t'ō* en *t'ò*) }
t'ō tsih, de tong uitsteken (van verbazing).
kig kaò bák-péh-tsih t'ō, zoo verschrikt dat de oogen wit worden en de tong uit de mond komt.
t'ō bah tsì, oprijzen van het vleesch als bij een zweer of wond.

吐 T'ò
T'ò, braken.
t'ò huih } , bloedspuwen.
(» *hoeh*) }
aó t'ò, braken.
t'ò hun, rooken als een kachel.
ū t'un t'ò, verdraagzaam.
ts'iah t'ò, braking bevorderen door iets in de keel te steken 2e iemand met geweld (geld) doen teruggeven.
t'ò sià tsing } , cholera.
(*tsìn*) }
laò t'ò tsing } , do.
(*tsìn*) }
t'ò gók, meeldraden (tusschen de bloembladen in.)
t'ò tsih, de tong uitsteken (als een opgehangene, hijgende honden enz.)
t'ò lō, aan het licht komen.
tò t'ò ts'ut k'ì, uitbraken, 2e terug moeten geven (als onrechtvaardig geld.
t'ò ts'ut tsin tsing, de waarheid zeggen. de geheele zaak onbewimpeld voorleggen.
t'ò bák, uitpuilende oogen.
t'ò bū, mist afwerpen (als bergen).
t'ò tsui, water braken, opgeven.
t'ò huih t'ò tò, bloed en bloeddraden uitbraken, 2e leugenachtig er uitgooien.

兎 T'ò
T'ò, konijn.
sog t'ò, haas.
t'ò á ting, lantaarn in den vorm van een konijn.
t'ò-būng géh, de konijnen zien uit naar de volle maan (om te jongen.)

土 T'ô
T'ô, klei, ongeprepareerde opium.
t'ô bé } , modder, slijk, modderig. slikkerig.
(» *moē*) }
t'ô t'oâ, steenkolen.
t'ô k'a, steenen vloer.
t'ô tsui ts'iū, een metselaar.
t'ô kat } , ongebakken steenen.
(» *kak*) }
t'ô pit, griffel.
t'ô sat, katvisch.
t'ô lâng, pelmolen.
t'ô sou pùn sò, vuilnis (in het algemeen.
tē t'ô, (niets dan) aarde inhebben scheldterm tegen een nietswaardig mensch).

ko t'ọ ko tọ̄, zich in het vuil wentelen, zich vuil maken (als kinderen die op den grond kruipen.)
t'ọ laó, wachttoren (in een dorp).
péh he t'ọ / (*pẹ́h siēn t'ọ*), kalkaarde.
keh t'ọ, t'ọ keh / (*kẹh*), laag aarde.
ngó sik t'ọ, veelkleurige aarde.
t'ọ t'iông, modderworm.
hiā t'ọ, aarde van een mierennest.
a p'ièn t'ọ, ongeprepareerde opium.
âng t'ọ, turksche ongeprepareerde opium.
t'ọ tsûn, schuit voor opiumvervoer.
kaoh t'ọ kaoh pùn, tot aarde en mest (vuilnis) overgaan (als het lichaam na den dood.)

Toa

帶 Toà *Toà*, gordel; medebrengen, met zich brengen.
toà tī sin k'u, bij zich dragen, hebben.
toà lai, brengen.
toà tò lai / (*tuị*), terugbrengen.
toà sok, schuif voor een band.
oē toà / (*ē* »), schoenveter.
toà hà, in den rouw zijn.
kaó sṇ toà / (*sio*), spelen van honden, paren.
toà pī / (» *pẹ̄*), eene ziekte onder de leden hebben.
toà tsoē, eene straf bij zich dragen, nog onder straf staan.
toè gi, iets vermoeden, in twijfel over iets zijn.
toà luī, opgehouden, teruggehouden worden door (opgescheept zitten met)
si liēm toà, aan de vier kanten met banden voorzien.
kat sṇ á toà, kinderen een fooitje geven.
kā i toà lai, medebrengen, vatten.
nī toà / (*nẹ̄* »), harde, stijve gordel.
nṅg toà / (*nuị* »), zachte gordel.
kak toà, hoornen, van het middel afstaande gordel (door vrouwen van mandarijnen gedragen).
toà hè, goederen medenemen.
toà to, een zwaard bij zich hebben.
kóng oē toà kut, in zijn spreken een been hebben *i. e.* eene diepe bedoeling in zijn spreken hebben.
kóng oē bô tah toà, niet passend spreken, den spijker niet op den kop slaan.
toà t'aò, sluiting, gesp enz. van een gordel.

念 Toà *Toà tioh*, in aanmerking nemen, gedachtig zijn aan.
toà tioh sī toā lâng ė bīn tsiṇ̄, zijne ouderen gedachtig zijn (en daarom iets niet doen wat men anders wel zou gedaan hebben.)

住 Toá *Toà*, wonen te....
toà tièm, in een winkel zijn (als bedienden).
toà t'aó lọ̄, eene betrekking hebben.
kīm toà / (*gīm* »), eene zekerheid, onderpand in iets hebben.

洵 Toà *Toà* ook *tsoá soa*, het zand uit iets schudden, ziften.
bi toâ / (» en *loà*), rijstzeef.
kiêm toà tsiṇ́ ts'aì, gezoute spijzen en versche groenten.

大 Toā *Toā*, groot, zeer.
i toā goá tsit nị, hij is een jaar ouder dan ik.
boē toā / (*bē* »), dwergachtig.
toā lát, machtig.

toā toā soè soè, groot en klein.
kóng toā oē, groot spreken.
toā ts'ut lát, zijn uiterste best doen.
toā ts'ìng, kanon.
toā hoáh kiā, lange stappen nemen, hard loopen.
toā ts'uì tsiáh, gulzig eten.
toā sia, luid.
toā sia háo, hard schreeuwen.
toā ko, groote roeiboot (frikboot).
toā hoe pò (hoa), groot gebloemd goed.
toā tsíh kaó, lispelen.
toā tsui iáh, groote molenaar (insekt).
toā tsuí, overstrooming.
toā béh (» bé), gerst.
toā p'àng, groot zeil.
toā hong, storm.
toā pō bú, duim.
toā bú sì koè (bóng) (kè), uiterst veel.
toā sì koè ū (kè), overvloedig, in overvloed.
toā tsóng tsai (tsat), examinator der *Tsin sū*.
toā tsú k'ó (tsí), eerste » » *Kú dzin*.
toā ku vrouw's oudere broeder.
toā i » » zuster.
tòng toā tsí oudere nichten (dochter van broeder.
toā hia oudere broeder.
toā tsí oudere zuster.
toā píng rechterkant.

舵 Toā *Toā* het roer.
hoa toā het roer in handen hebben, aan het hoofd staan van.
toā gè (gé), roerpin.
toā ling (ling), roerlijn.

拖 Toā *Toā* voortslepen, op sleeptouw nemen.
īng soè tsiák tsûn toā tsít kīng lia hit nī p'a ga in een kleine boot een anker naar die plaats uitbrengen.

單 Toa *Toa*, briefje, bewijs en rekening.
gûn toa, wissel.
tuì toa, do.
siá tuì toa, een wissel schrijven, geven.
iok toa (iàk), verbindtenis (schriftelijke).
siu toa, ontvangstbiljet, kwitantie.
kì hè toa (hoè), cognossement
tsaì hè toa (hoè), cognossement
pín toa, certifiaat.
tsáp mih toa, catalogus.
k'ui toa, eene rekening opmaken.
ko toa, alleen, alleen staand.
p'ē toa (p'oē), deken.
toa sì mìng (mui), enkele deur.
toa sin, het eenigste kind, — alleen.
toa kiā, op zich zelven gebruiken.
bô toa kiā, niet op zich zelven gebruiken (als een hulpwoord).
toa kù (kì), schriftelijk bewijs.
k'iem toa, schriftelijke schuldbekentenis.
tsiòh toa, leen acte.
tsē toa, een wissel accepteeren.
si toa, rechterlijk bewijs van eigendom.
tsu toa, rood geschrift.
pò toa koán, aangeven aan het kadaster.
toa k'a ts'iú, alleen zonder hulp zijn.
toa pe (poe), alleen zijn, gaan enz.
pàng toa, rekeningen afgeven.
hoē toa, wissel.
poáh toa, een comediestuk uitkiezen oorsp. door met een orakelblokje den afgod te raadplegen.

端 Toa̤ *In toa̤*, reden waarom — waaruit iets wat gesproten is.

彈 Toa̤ *Nn̄g toa̤*, eieren aan den eierstok (van kippen).
k'o̤ toa̤, kakelen (als de hen die een ei gaat leggen).

欵 Toá̤ *Toá̤ toá̤*, steeds, gedurig — vol.
toá̤ toá̤ k'ang, waarop veel aantemerken valt.
tsi bīng toá̤ toá̤ bák, over zijn geheele gelaat één oog en al zijn *i. e.* sproetig.
toá̤ toá̤ béh án n̤ tsoè, steeds aldus willen doen.

旦 Toà̤ *Hì toà̤*, mannelijke actrice, man die voor vrouw speelt.
koh toà̤ (gē), kinderen die bij eene op tocht op een paal gezeten zijn.
laō toà̤, oude actrice (mannel.)
hoe toà̤ (hoa), jeugdige schoone actrice (mannel.)
sio toà̤, jonge actrice van middelbaren leeftijd.
toà̤ k'ó̤, mannelijke actrice voor droevige rollen.
toà̤ kiā̤, verwijfd loopen.
bú toà̤, actrice die een militaire rol speelt.

壇 Toâ̤ *Toâ̤*, altaar..
pút toa, altaar voor een afgod.
kat toâ̤, een altaar opslaan.

Toâ̤ *Tsū toâ̤-tsū ts'iṳ̄*, zelf spelen en zingen 2e geen hulp van anderen noodig hebben.
toâ̤ tsi (toā̤), proppenschieter, erwtenschieter.
toâ̤ k'im (toâ̤), op de luit spelen.
toâ̤ mi̤ hoe (toa), watten kammen.
toâ̤ tsin de inktlijn doen afspringen om een lijn te trekken.
k'a kut toâ̤ sam hièn, *i. e.* verstomd, ontsteld staan op het gezicht van iets.
k'in kìn á kā i toâ̤ tseh, de snaar van iets tegen iemand aanroeren.

檀 Toâ̤ *Toâ̤ hio̤*, sandelhout.

惰 Toā̤ *Pin toā̤* lui *toā̤* do.
(sio̤ toā̤) siū toā̤ (sio̤), lui.
kut t'aò toā̤, lui van aard.
ts'aī toā̤, moedwillig, lui zijn.

彈 Toā̤ *Toā̤*, wegschieten knippen met de vingers, opspringen als een bal.
hō̤ tsióh t'aò toā̤ tioh, door een opspringende steen getroffen worden.
p'ah pang toā̤ t'iaō, op een plank slaan en ze tegen een pilaar laten aanspringen *i. e.* eene verkeerdheid in een anderlaken tegen iemand die er zelf aanschuldig is.
sì koè toā̤, overal tegen aankomen en terugspringen (als een kogel).

Toā̤ *Ū tiâo ū toā̤*, geregeld, in volgorde.
toā̤, numerale voor langdurende handelingen.
hó ts'iú toā̤, iets goeds verstaan.
tsi toā̤ ē oē (oā), een geheel gesprek, redenering.
tsit toā̤ ē taī tsì (sū), een geheele zaak.
tinh tinh toā̤, tintelen (als een zweer).

拖 T'oa *T'oa*, naar zich toe trekken.
t'oa bē (boē), eene zaak rekken.
toa kang, het werk verlengen, rekken.
toa k'ièm, schuldig zijn, steeds in schuld blijven.
toa ts'ut k'ì, buiten leiden, buiten brengen.
toa (oē), sloffen (werkwoord).

toa boā, werken.

toa king / *(kiong)* , een boog spannen.

toa soa, langdradig.

toa ts'ià, wagen nemen.

ts'ien t'oa, muilen.

t'oa luī, anderen in eene zaak bdtrekken.

t'oa moǹ koā soh, in zwaren rouw zijn.

t'oa pī̲ / *(pē̲)* , zich tegen eene ziekte verzetten — niettegenstaande zijne ziekte nog werken.

t'oa t'ô̤, over den grond slepen (als een lang kleed).

t'oa t'oa puih puih / *(péh péh)* , lang op elkander moeten wachten om voort te gaan.

sa̲ k'an sa̲ t'oa / *(sio) (sio)* , elkander voorttrekken (als bij een oploop).

t'oa ts'ut, 1e uittrekken- uithalen 2e een comediestuk rekken.

t'oa t'uī, allen wat van iets moeten hebben — tot zijn last komen (als arme familiebetrekkingen).

t'oa siaò, langzamerhand zijne schuld afbetalen.

k'ang t'oa, de schuld op een ander zien te schuiven.

t'oa loā, dito.

tsìt toā t'oa, eene groote rist, rij.

t'oa sai liên, een staart achter zich slepen- niet afgedaan zijn.

t'oa si dzìt, den tijd rekken dralen uitstellen.

t'oa tsûn een schuit voorttrekken.

káo t'oa, mogen de honden (uw lijk) wegsleuren (scheldwoord).

t'oa t'iêm, mogen (de honden uw lijk in het water) sleuren (scheldwoord).

t'oa bé ts'ī̲ / *(beé ts'ī̲)* , staartster komeet. 2e scheldwoord.

t'oa bāng, netten ophalen.

t'oa bō, in den molen loopen.

t'oa loè, voor den ploeg loopen.

tsoè gù teh t'oa, als een koe trekken i. e. zwaar te werken hebben.

t'oa t'ih lang aanhouden, slepend (al eene ziekte).

t'oa p'àng, het zeil door het water slepen 2e met een vlerk langs den grond strijken (als kalkoenen).

t'oa bák bé, veelbeduidend aanzien (vrouwen).

īng tsoá t'oa k'i lai, met papier (vui van eene vloeistof) afhalen.

拖 T'oā *Sa̲ ts'oā sa̲ t'oā* / *(sio) (sio)* , elkander leiden — het voorbeeld geven om iets te doen.

in t'oā, sa̲ ìn sa̲ t'oā / *(sio sio)* , elkander leiden meêslepen, op het idée van iets brengen.

ná t'oā ná oē, hoe meer men iets doe des te meer gaat men het verstaan.

īng soè tiâo soh lai t'oā kè k'it, / *(rūng sè) (koè)* , me klein touw (een grooter) door een ga halen.

t'oā lóh k'ì / *(t'o̲ ?)* , (medicijnen) met- of in iets innemen.

t'oā ióh oân, pillen met eenig vocht innemen.

T'oā *T'àng t'oā*, insekten in het algemeen.

汰 T'oā *T'oā*, wasschen, spoelen als kleederen.

soé t'oā / *(sé)* , wasschen en overspoelen.

t'oā sa̲, kleeren overspoelen (na dat ze reeds gewasschen zijn).

T'oa̲ *T'oa̲*, uit elkander spreiden, uit elkander zetten.

t'oa̲ k'ui, ieder zijn deel krijgen van.

t'oa̲ k'ì, door elkander gerekend, over het geheel verdeeld.

kong t'oa, ieders te betalen deel aan iets berekenen.

tsiàu t'oa, volgens het deel dat ieder aan iets moet betalen.

pai t'oa, ieder zijn deel van iets geven - krijgen.

mì t'oa (*mī*), aan hoopjes leggen.

t'oa kè, de prijs over de verschillende partijen verdeelen.

t'oa k'ah tsió, minder voor zijn deel krijgen.

kun t'oa, evenveel deel in iets hebben.

灘 *Hai t'oa*, landbank, modderig strand.

tsiū t'oa (*tsō*), een waterhelling op gaan van (schepen).

lòh t'oa, een water neergaan.

t'oa tsûn, een schip de helling ophalen.

予 *T'oá ts'áu*, onkruid wieden.

T'oá *t'oá k'ui*, openhakken (een weg).

t'oá sang, loshakken (als een te harden weg).

炭 *T'oà*, kolen.

T'oà *hé t'oà* (*hoé*), houtskool.

hé t'oà boàh (*hoé*), houtskoolpoeder.

t'ô t'oà, steenkolen.

muī t'oà (*boé*), steenkolen.

p'à t'oà, zachte houtskool.

t'oà tsao teh hun (*lí*), rooken door dat het nog niet goed aan is.

tīng t'oà, harde houtskool.

T'oà *T'oà*, afgeven (van kleuren), in een loopen door elkander loopen (van kleuren).

t'oà k'ui, uitdijen, uitzetten.

t'oà k'ui, uitvloeien (als olie, inkt enz.)

t'oà k'a, vloeien uitvloeien (als olie inkt enz).

孳 *Si t'oà* (*sī*), veel voortbrengen, zich sterk

T'oà vermenigvuldigen.

ná t'oà ná tsoē, zich hoe langer hoe meer voortplanten.

T'oà *Tò t'oà*, terugkrabbelen, minder bieden dan men reeds geboden heeft.

ná t'ák ná tò t'oà, hoemeer men studeert des te meer in bevattelijkheid achteruitgaan.

t'oà i ê kè tsī, terugkrabbelen in den prijs die men voor iets geven wil.

Toah

掇 *Toah k'ui*, zich losrukken.

Toah *kiao toah*, boos weggaan.

toah toah ts'oah ts'oah, boos- trotsch weggaan.

toah ts'iú, de hand losrukken.

tiu toah, boos weggaan na het eerste bod niet verder met den kooper willen spreken.

toah tseh tsoè i k'ì, niet verder willen luisteren en boos weggaan.

獺 *T'oah*, otter.

T'oah *tsui toah*, do.

toah p'ê (*p'oê*), ottervel.

T'oah *T'oah*, uitstellen.

ū t'oah langdurend, stevig, niet spoedig kunnen bederven, lang gerekt van een ziekte.

toah t'ang, scheel kijken.

toah, lade, schuif, schuiven.

toah dzip k'ì, inschuiven, dicht schuiven.

t'oah ts'ut lai, openschuiven.

tù t'oah, kastladen.

kan t'oah, het er maar mée doen.

kan boà péh t'oah (*péh*), zich zonder vergoeding afwerken.

bóng t'oah bong kè, het er nog zoo lang maar mée doen.

t'oah si dzit, van dag tot dag uitstellen.
pī lâng t'oah tsoeh k'ùi, de zieke rekt zijn leven van het jaarfeest op het andere 2e hoe langer hoe meer uitstellen.
t'oah tièm t'ang, de winkelblinden in schuiven.
t'oah á, lade.
t'oah tù, laden kast.
t'oah bi, rijst in water schoon rooren.
T'oah *T'oah se*, tong (een soort van visch).

Toan

端 Toan *Toan tsiâ* (*toan*), rechtschapen.
ts'ing toan bān toan (*tsièn*), volop in de bezigheden zijn, het druk hebben.
toan toan k'ai k'ai, in orde- in behoorlijken vorm.
toan tsong, ernstig (vooral van vrouwen gebruikt).
toan hong sì tsiâ (*toan*), recht, niet scheef.
sū toan, aanleiding oorsprong van eene zaak.
sing toan, aanleiding tot eene zaak (twist om) geven.
ī toan ê kaò, vreemde leerstellingen.
ī toan ê lâng, zonderling mensch.
to toan ê lâng, iemand die veel aan de hand heeft.
īng t'ui á lai toan (*o*), met een hamertje gelijkkloppen.
toan k'i sì tsiâ, rechtkloppen, rechtmaken.
ē toan, begin, oorsprong van rampen.
Toan *Toan tok*, nazien.
toan tok, *toan toan tok tok* (*tun*), op de kleinste puntjes letten 2e van iemands omstandigheden gebruik maken om hem te overvragen of weinig te bieden.
toan ih, overvragen wetende dat iemand dit noodig heeft.
Toán *Ngó toán*, klein van gestalte.
toán hīng, baldadig, onbetamelijk (niet aan anderen of aan den toekomst (denken).
toán kièn, van kort inzicht.
sim kog toán, steeds anderen willen be nadeelen.
斷 Toàn *Kout toàn*, vas besluiten.
p'og toàn, uitspraak doen over.
toàn iok (*iák*), een traktaat sluiten.
toàn dzièn, vast overgenomen om.....
toàn pit, conclusie — eindbesluit (in een geschrift)
toàn àn, een rechtsgeding uitmaken.
sim toàn, rechterlijk onderzoeken en uitspraak doen.
sìm toàn, do.
kong toàn, algemeene uitspraak, opinie.
tit toàn bô po, rechtuit zonder vleien.
toàn si, *toàn dzit*, den vasten tijd bepalen.
bô toàn ts'iâ eh (*o*), het is niet iets dat men maar zoo roekeloos kan wegnemen.
bing p'in bing toàn, vast duidelijk overeenkomen.
toàn kiet, einduitspraak in een rechtsgeding doen.
toàn su iâ, vastbesloten met iemand te wedden.
傳 Toàn *Sè toàn* (*toân*), voorouderlijke overlevering (als van een zeker geneesmiddelen.
緞 Toān *Kiök toān*, gebloemde zijde, brocaat.
kòng toān, satijn.
tiù toān, zijde.
ú toān (*t*), grein.
斷 Toān *Toān lō*, den weg afsnijden, versperren.

toān aō lō, den terugkeer afsnijden, versperren.
kat toān, eene zaak met iemand afdoen 2e alle verdere omgang afbreken.
tsám toān, afhakken, doorhakken.
it to liòng toān, met een mes beiden doorhakken *i. e.* in eens aan beide zaken een eind maken.
put toān bān dzī, het karakter duizend onafgebroken (als bij ornamenten).

煅 T'oân *T'oàn*, tot kalk branden.
t'oàn he, tot kalk branden.
t'oàn liēn, geverseerd zijn in, bekend zijn met.
t'oàn hin lò (hiɛ), een fornuis of wierook vat polijsten.
t'oàn dzī, karakters uit de oudheid.

傳 T'oán *T'oàn*, mededeelen.
liû toán, bekend maken, verkondigen.
t'oân aō taī (hō), overlaten aan de nakomelingschap.
t'oân tō, prediken.
t'oân tō eh, prediker.
t'oân kaò, leerstellingen verspreiden.
t'oàn làng, aan anderen mededeelen overleveren.
t'oân līng, kommando, bevel geven om....
t'oân ts'ut, k'ì, kommando geven.
t'oân miā seh sia (soeh), iemands naam en faam verspreiden.
sè t'oân (si), overlevering van zijne voorouders.
tsó t'oân, voorouderlijke overlevering.
k'ó t'oân, mondelingsche medeeling.
t'oân siū, aan anderen meedeelen, overleveren.
t'oân sin, kennis geven van den tijd waarop men iemand rechterlijk verhooren zal.
lik taī siong t'oân, van verscheiden generaties aan elkander overleveren.
t'oàn tog, eene bekendmaking, circulaire rondzenden.
t'oàn liēn, soldaten uit het volk oproepen en doen exerceeren.
t'oân uī, de troon aan een ander overgeven.
t'oân sè, de wereld bekend maken (als eene uitvinding).
t'oán ke pó, familiekostbaarheid.

團 T'oàn *P'o t'oân*, dikke ronde mat waarop Boedhistiesche priesters zitten.
t'oân in zijn volkomen geheel (als eene familie) vol als de maan.
t'oân t'oân ui tsū, van alle kanten omringen, insluiten.

Toat

奪 Toát *Ts'im toát*, diep ingrijpen in iets, meer van iets nemen dan hem toekomt.
kiòng toát, geweldadig bestelen.
tsing t'ien toát kok, den hemel bestrijden en rijken ontnemen (als een veroveraar).

脫 T'oat *T'oat tsáo*, ontsnappen, iemand laten ontsnappen.
tò t'oat, ontsnappen, ontkomen.
t'oat tò, wegloopen, ontsnappen.
t'oat li, zich losrukken (als iemand die gegrepen is).
t'oat sin lī, ontsnappen, ontkomen.
t'oat sin (t'uì k'ak), vervellen (als een slang); uit de schaal komen (als kuikens).
k'ì t'oat, den adem geven.

Toe

底 Toé *O toé (té)*, zwarte grond (van een muur enz).

p'ah toé, grondverwen.
p'ag o toé, o p'ah toé, zwart grondverwen.
k'a tsioh toé (té), zool van de voet.
hai toé, bodem der zee.
• *toé*, bodem (van iets).
Tsiang tsiu toé, In Tsiang-tsiu.
tsui toé, in het water.
tsùn toé, in het schip.
kaò toé, door en door, grondig.
ē toé, beneden, van onderen
lap toé (té), invallen van den bodem.
t'ap toé, do.
toé tsioh, fondamenten.
toé tì, beginselen, principes.
p'ah toé tì, fondamenten leggen, eerste impressie maken.
ū toé toé, degelijk soliede.
tiëm toé, naar den bodem zakken, zinken.
sim koa toé, inwendige van het hart.
tiàm toé, inventaris van een winkel.
hè toé (hoè), overschot van goederen.
sè ka toé (sì ke), van fatsoenlijken afkomst.
pù toé, van rijken oorsprong — oorspronkelijk.
kun toé (kin), oorspronkelijk beroep-stand.
tah toé, tot den bodem toe, ten uiterste (verdrukken enz.)
kì toé, den bodem zien (als bij een vat waarvan de inhoud bijna op is).

貯 Toé
Toé, in handen, in hebben, bevatten, doen in, indoen.
(té) toé iû, olie inhouden, indoen.

抵 Toé
Toé (té), afweren.
toé ts'iú, met de hand afweren.
bò toé ts'iú, het is geen partij voor..... (hij is te zwak).
ká toé ih, iemand het hoofd durven bieden.

蹄 Toè
Toè (sè), hoof (bij beesten).
bé toè (bē), paardenhoef.
bé toè ìng, mouw als een paardenhoef
k'a toè, zool van den voet.
ah bú toè (bó), eenden voet (van iemand wiens voeten uitstaan).
lok á toè, hertenhoeven, pooten van iemand die zeer hard loopen kan.
dziët toè, vurig in de voeten worden. (als een paard na een weinig draven.)

題 Toè
Toè ièn, voor geld inschrijven.
koan toè, voor eene zekere som op eene inteekeningslijst inschrijven.
toè bák, titel (van een boek).
toè tsàn, loffelijk opschift.
toè p'aì, (de betaling aan iets) over een aantal personen verdeelen.
ts'ut toè t'aò, een onderwerp voor een opstel geven.
kò toè, dzīn toè, zich aan het onderwerp houden, het onderwerp bij een opstel voor oogen houden.
toè si, een vers schrijven.
toè nēng pah k'o ē ièn, eene subscriptie van 200 dollars hebben.

地 Toē
Toē (tī), aarde.
toē ki, grondvest fondament.
toē tāng, aardbeving.
pún toē tsaī », plaatselijke.
toē hām, hinderlaag.
toē ē (ē), plaats der afgestorvenen.
tìng toē (tuì), op den grond trappen (van woede) stampvoeten.
toē méh (tē), aardaderen.
toē tiū (tiū), uitgestrektheid ruimte van plaats.

p'ah toē kè, iemand (als schadelijke personen) naar zijne geboorte plaats terugzenden).
tòng toē, *tìng toē*, eene plaats die men voor zijne vaste woonplaats heeft.
si toē, lett. doode plaats *i. e.* plaats als b. v. een eiland waar men van alle communicatie afgesloten kan worden.
sit toē, vaste harde grond.
p'à toē, zachte opgerulde grond.
bing ka toē (*ke*), beroemde plaats.

第 Toē *Toē it*, de eerste enz.
toē it hó, extra goed.
toē kui, de hoeveelste.
toē lòh k'i, hoe langer hoe lager komen (als een voorwerp dat van eene hooge plaats hand voor hand wordt neergelaten).

紵 Toē *Toē á sa*, vlasjas (lichte rouw bij begrafenissen).
toē (*tē*), vlas.
toē lao pao, rouwmuts (lichte rouw).
tseh toē (*peh*) (*ti*), vlas afhalen afspinnen.
toē pò, vlasdoek.

釵 T'oe *Kim t'oe* (*t'e*), gouden haarspeld.

刣 T'oe *T'oe hun*, tabak raspen, snijden.

體 T'oé *King t'oé* (*t'é*), vergelijken met (iemands uiterlijk.)
hing t'oé, uiterlijk, voorkomen als.
lú t'oé, *tsa bó t'oé* (*li ké*) (*tsa bó ké*), verwijfd, vrouwelijk.
níng t'oé (*hui*), zachtzinnig voorkomen.
kim t'oé bān dziók (*t'oé*), zich allerlei vernederingen en verdrukking laten welgevallen.

替 T'oè *T'oè* (*t'è*), in de plaats van, voor.
sa t'oè (*sio*), afwisselend.
t'oè oā, verruilen omwisselen als met kleeren.
t'oè lâng pān, voor een ander beredderen.
kió kao t'oè, roepen om afgelost te worden (wordt gezegd van den geest van drenkelingen die na drie jaar een ander mensch op dezelfde plaats zou doen verdrinken).
t'oè sin, van papier gemaakte pop van een ziek mensch (de pop lett. plaats vervanger wordt ter zijner herstelling verbrand).
tng t'oè, remplaceeren.
t'oè baó, voor een ander op de inspectie komen.
t'oè ts'iú, voor een ander dragen of waarnemen.

退 T'oè *T'oè pī*, schuw, verlegen wijken, uit den weg gaan.
t'oè pī (*t'è*), zich terugtrekken (als in een zijvertrek).
si-kong t'oè tsit, voor zijn mandarijnambt bedanken.
siën t'oè, het afgeworpen masker der cicaden.

Toeh

Toeh *Oéh toéh* (*éh téh*), nauw.
T'oéh *Oė t'oéh* (*ė t'éh*), achterlip aan een schoen
t'oéh = *t'éh*, nemen.

Toh

棹 Toh *Toh*, tafel

toh kun (*kin*), tafellaken.
pai toh, tafeldekken.
toh t'oah, ladentafel.
toh kuī, kabinet kast met deuren en laden.
toh t'aô, kant van een tafel.
toh t'aô ê siên si (*sin sī*), woordenboek.
toh ui, kleed aan een tafel.
pūn toh, een gastmaal aanrichten.
pat sien toh, sì siên toh, tafel voor acht en voor vier personen.
toh k'a, pooten van een tafel.
oā toh, lange rechterstafel.
toh koai (*koa*), dwarshouten tusschen de pooten van een tafel.
toh k'àm, tafeldeksel tafelblad over een kostbare tafel.
i oai toh, kleptafel (waarvan het blad genomen wordt en de pooten toeslaan).
gêh toh (*goêh*), ronde tafel.
tsit toh ê oē (*oā*), tafelkout tafelgesprek
moā toh ê oē (*oā*), do.
tsit toh tsiú, de wijn die aan een tafelmaal gedronken wordt.
saò toh, de tafel (als) schoonvegen, alles opgegeten hebben.
tsit toh saò keng keng (*kui kūi*), do.
tsē toh, aan tafel gaan zitten.
soā toh, van tafel opstaan.
sàng toh, iemand een maal toezenden.
kong tsō toh lange rechterstafel.
háp toh, tafels die tegen elkander aangezet worden om een vierkant uit te maken.

卓 Toh — *Toh*, familienaam.

灼 Tóh — *Tóh*, aangaan (van vuur).
hé-tóh (*hoé*), het vuur brandt.
pùn tóh, aanblazen.
sim hé tóh (*hoé*), in toorn ontsteken.

Tóh — *King tsiā tóh péh*, het magere uitkiezen en het witte (vette) er uitnemen (bij vleesch).
bó king bò tóh, niet uitkiezen of uitziften.

T'óh — *T'ien t'óh*, den schijn van gek dronken enz. aannemen.
t'óh t'óh, den schijn van doen aannemen niet geven om de beleedigingen die men hem aandoet.
t'óh kiá, ongezeggelijk kind of mensch.

Tok

督 Tok — *Tsóng tok*, onderkoning.
t'é tok, hoofd van de land en zeemacht.
tsik tok, beknorren.
tok tsièn, tot het gevecht aanzetten.
tok kang, tot werken aanzetten, narijden.
tok tuī, de gelederen overzien.
tók tīn, do.

篤 Tok — *Tok sit*, oprecht.
tok tok á lim, alleen zitten te drinken.

啄 Tok — *Tok*, oppikken (als vogel).
p'ī tò tok, p'ī á tok tok, haviksneus, papegaaineus.
tok kiaó, iemand die niet dobbelen kan *r* doen verliezen.
ké tsi tok pūn gi, van iemands omstandigheden misbruik maken, om goedkoop van hem te koopen.
hong ts'e tok loh lai, de vlieger schiet onderste boven naar beneden.

琢 Tok — *Tok*, bewerken (juweelen).
toan tok (*tun*), naauwgezet.

tiao tok, opleiden, vormen, leiden.
kaò tok, onderwijzen en vormen.
tok tsióh t'aò á, steentjes bijtelen.
tok sing, opleiden, vormen (kinderen).
tok iù, fijn kloppen, fijn bewerken (als steenhouwers).

毒 Tók *Tók*, vergift, vergiftig.
tók s h, vergiftigen.
ok tók, boosaardig.
aō bú tok (*bó*) }, slecht, stiefmoederlijk.
tók ióh, vergift.
k'ó tók, stiefmoederlijk behandelen.
tiòng tók, vergift inkrijgen, vergiftigd zijn 2e in reddeloozen toestand zijn.
tók oē, gifttaal.
tók pō, schadelijke helsche maatregel, streek.
tók kè, lett. vergiftig plan — schadelijke maatregel.
tók kong tok, met het eene vergift het andere verdrijven.
hoat dziét tók, warmte puisten hebben.
si ok tók mih, slechte veneerische zweeren enz. krijgen.
tsa bó tók, vrouwen vergift *i. e.* veneerische ziekte.
sià tók, veneerische ziekten afdrijven.
im t'im tók, stil maar gevaarlijk, boosaardig.
ng tók dzit, 5de maand 5den dag (waarop hemel en aarde, mannelijk en vrouwelijk beginsel gezegd worden te paren.
pàng tók, vergif neerwerpen (als vergiftige slangen) 2e iemand door laster enz. benadeelen.
p'ai sim tók hīng, slecht van hart en levenswandel.
tók k'ì-sīng vol vergif, vergiftige sappen.
kai tók, *ts'ing tók*, vergif afleidend vernietigend.

Tók *Tók tók*, slechts, maar.

ko hàng- tók ts'ī, de eenigste zijn die iets verkoopt, geene concurrentie hebben.
tók lik lân tsi, één man kan niet niet tegen de geheele massa op.
tók suī ts'ing, bed voor één persoon.
tók kak gē ming, éénig mandarijnbureau op een plaats.

T'ók *àn tók*, kast waar rechtspapieren in geborgen worden.
ts'ik tók, briefstijl.

託 T'ok *T'ok lâng*, iemand met iets belasten.
t'ok tiōng (*tiāng*) }, toevertrouwen aan, belasten met.
hù t'ok, toevertrouwen aan, belasten met.
kao t'ok, dito.
t'e t'ok, zich verontschuldigen, weigeren.
pài t'ok (*t'ok*) }, opdragen, belasten met.
kià t'ok, dito.
iong t'ok (*iang*) }, opdragen (om iets te doen.)
siū lâng t'ok, door iemand iets opgedragen zijn.
t'ok sè bīn (*si*) }, aan iemand van grooten invloed opdragen.
t'ok sin sè (*si*) }, dito.
ká t'ok (*ké*) }, het doen voorkomen als of.
t'ok pī, zich wegens ziekte verontschuldigen.

托 T'ok *T'ok king á*, chineesche schim.
t'ok k'i, de tanden uitpeuteren.
k'i t'ok, tandenstooker.
p'ah k'i t'ok, tandenstookers maken *i. e.* over onbelangrijke zaken spreken.

T'ok *T'ok kut*, Adamsappel.

T'ok *T'ok ts'ut lai*, doorduwen, uitduwen.

T'ok *T'ok pit á* (*t'ó pìt à*) }, musch (Munia malacca).

讀 T'ȯk *P'ūān t'ȯk*, gezamenlijk studeeren.
king tsiá king, t'ȯk tsiá t'ȯk, dat landbouwers landbouwen en studeerenden studeeren.

Tong

當 Tong *Tong kim*, thans, tegenwoordig.
tong sū, principaal van eene affaire.
tong si, toen ter tijd 2° in trek zijnde.
tong si ė mih, iets dat in trek, smaak is.
kám tsok kám tong, iets op zich durven nemen.
tong t'aò, onverschillig, kortaf, niet veel conplimenten maken (als kooplieden).
boē tong tit (bē), niet bestand zijn tegen....
ming hō̤ siong tong (sɥang), bij elkander komen, passen (als familien van gelijken stand).
ti tong, op zich nemen (de verantwoordelijkheid van iets).
sik kám, tong, de steen durft het op zich te nemen (op bescheimsteenen van steegjes geplaatst).

東 Tong *Tong ka (ke̤)*, patroon, van een meester tot zijn leerling.
án án tong tong, stijf aangehaald.
tong tong án, dito.
tin tin tong tong, tokkelen van snaar instrumenten.
hák tong, superieur-patroon, eerenaam door meesters gegeven aan hem, die hen geengageerd heeft.
kiaó tong ka (ke̤), hoofd, baas van een dobbelhuis.

黨 Tóng *Tóng luī*, soortgenooten.
kiet tóng, een verbond vormen (ten kwade).
tóng tsiòng, benden bij elkander brengen (om te stelen enz.).
tóng lâng, menschen bijeenroepen, bijeenbrengen.
ts'át tóng, dieven komplot.
taò tóng, zich bij een verbond-komplot aansluiten.

重 Tóng *Kó tóng*, rariteiten, antequiteiten.

懂 Tóng *Bóng tóng*, onvoorzichtig, roekeloos.
pūt tóng, (oorspr. mandarijnsch) niet begrijpen.
tóng sū ė lâng, iemand die kennis van zaken

擋 Tòng *Tòng*, duwtje, ruk, tegenhouden, verhinderen.
tòng (ook tìng) boē tiaó (bē), niet kunnen dragen.
tòng boē k'o̤ oē tiaó (bē) (ī), onverdragelijk, niet kunnen uithouden.
tsó̤ tòng, tegenhouden, terughouden van.
tòng tsū, tegengaan, verhinderen.
tòng lâng é tsi̤, iemand in de betaling verhinderen.
tòng boē ki̤ā, er niet in slagen om iets to verhinderen.
tòng siòng, iemand in iets verhinderen omdat men zelf er door benadeeld zou worden (als bij het bouwen van een huis)
tsaī tòng, steeds daar zijn, voorhanden zijn.

當 Tòng *Tò tòng (t'ò)*, toevertrouwd, veilig.
tòng toē (tē), vaste plaats waar men geboren is en nog leeft.
tik tòng, iets veiligs hebben.
tîng tòng, veilig sekuur.
t'ong kouh tòng, praktisch, doenbaar en sekuur.
tòng gōng, dom, sufferig.

棟 Tòng *Tòng liong (liang)*, voornaam, onmisbaar (van menschen).

堂 Tông *Tông hia*, oudere neef (kinderen van broeders).

tông tī, jongere „ „)

tông sió bē (moē), jongere nichts (dochter broeders).

tsīng tông peh (tsīng) (peh), oudste kind van zijn grootoom.

tsīng tông tsik, jonger kind van zijn groot oom.

tông tông, er fatsoenlijk uitzien.

tong tông, in het openbaar, openlijk.

tông sing, candidaat.

kong tông, publiek gebouw rechtszaal.

kong tông k'oà kì, gezamelijk, gelijkelijk zien.

gán tông k'oà kì, gelijkelijk gezien hebben.

ts'in tông, neven of nichten (zoon of dochters van broeders).

tsīng tông achterneven of nichten (zoons of dochters van neven).

līng tông, moeder (bel. term).

līng tsun tông vader en moeder (bel. term).

boán tông hông, hanglamp.

幢 Tông *Tông hoan*, lange afhangende beschreven strooken goed vóór Boeddha's gehangen, vaandels bij begrafenissen door kinderen gedragen.

同 Tông *Tông tō tiong*, tot hetzelfde beroep behoorende (meest door kooplieden gebuikt).

bâ ts'ú tông biēn, de kat en de rat slapen te zamen: twee handen op ééne buik.

tông tsú, pupil van het oog.

洞 Tōng *Tōng*, kloof.

tōng siao, fluit.

tōng siao kut, beenderen als een fluit *i. e.* mager.

tsióh tōng, rotskloof.

soa tōng, bergkloof spelonk.

kaò tōng, apenkuil (ook van een huis met vele hoeken en kamertjes).

動 Tōng *Naū tōng (naū)*, verwarring.

tōng tsīng, handelingen, maatregelen

sa tōng būn (sio), aan elkander introduceeren: elkander aanspreken.

tōng put tōng, steeds (elk oogenblik).

tōng sim, inwendig ontstellen, geprikkeld worden.

tōng kan ko, vechten strijden.

king t'ien tōng tē, hemel en aarde beroeren.

king tōng, allen beroeren (als de komst van een tijger) 2ᵉ wakker doen schrikken.

tōng tsing getroffen worden (als op het gezicht van eene schoone vrouw).

lô tōng, zich in beweging stellen, 2ᵉ lastig vallen.

tá tōng, iemand tot iets bewegen.

撞 Tōng *Sa tōng (sio)*, tegen elkander aanstooten 2ᵉ coïtus uitoefenen (lage term).

tōng, stooten (als een geweer) 2ᵉ stooten tegen, dringen.

tò tōng, do.

sa (sio) tōng, dringen.

tōng k'ang, een gat vinden om iets te verhinderen.

tōng tioh, stooten tegen.

tōng lai tōng k'i, heen en weer gaan (als leegloopers), heen en weer komen (als geld dat niet uit 't land gaat) in de wandeling blijven.

tōng p'oà sū, eene zaak bederven lett. stukstooten.

tōng mng, tegen de deur aanbonzen.

憧 Tōng *Tōng tút*, onverwachts, eensklaps.

蕩 *P'iao tōng*, overal rondzwerven.
Tōng *hòng tōng'* onbesuisd.
tōng tōng, no.

通 *T'ong*, doorsteken, praktisch, handig.
Tōng *t'ong ti*, mededeelen, bekendmaken.
t'ong hing, algemeen gangbaar, doorgaand.
t'ong tát, kennen, verstaan, knap.
t'ong t'aò, doordringen in.
t'ong hong, luchtig, windstroom. 2e heimelijk doen uitlekken.
t'ong su (*si*), kalender, almanak.
t'ong t'ò, algemeene (benaming enz).
ling t'ong, knap.
t'ong hiaó, grondig (door en door) verstaan.
t'ong niû (*niû*), balk.
t'sng t'i ē (*ē*), door de geheele wereld.
p'ah t'ong t'ò, elkander van te voren raadplegen.
t'ong sū, tolk.
kóng t'ong, van te voren bekendmaken, mededeelen.
poà t'ong put, slechts half ervaren in iets zijn.
t'ong hun ts'e (*t'oe*), een pijp doorsteken.
hun ts'e t'ong (*ts'oe*), pijpen doorsteker.
t'ong hit è uī, over die geheele plaats.
t'ong tsùn è làng, al de schepelingen.
su t'ong, geheime verstandhouding met den vijand, heimelijke slechte omgang met vrouwen.
t'ong pò, overal bekendmaken.
t'ong siông (*siông*), aan allen bekendmaken.
liù t'ong overal gaan, komen.
t'ong, doorloop, steegje.
t'ong t'iet (*t'aòh t'ièt*), door en door kennen, grondig verstaan.
t'ong t'ong tseh, doorsteken (als een verstopt gat.
t'ong siao sit, bericht omtrent iets mededeelen.
t'ong koan tsiet, geheime communicatie (met de vijandelijke partij).
t'ong k'iaò, praktisch, naar de omstandigheden weten te veranderen.
koàn t'ong, doorloopend, logisch.
t'ien hū t'ong, dievensleutel, looper.
t'ong óng (*t'ong*), naar andere plaatsen gaan (als goederen).
put t'ong t'áng, dom.
t'ong kiōng, met alles en alles, in het geheel, *t'óng kiōng*.
t'ong kiók è taī tsì, de geheele loop en afloop van de zaak.
t'ong poā, in het geheel, alles bij elkander genomen.
t'ong kan, overspel bedrijven.

蓪 *T'ong ts'ó*, rijstpapierplant, de Aralia
T'ong papyrifera.

倘 *T'óng nū beh an ni*, verondersteld dat
T'óng het aldus moet.

T'óng *T'óng ts'ùt*, voortstooten, uitsteken.
t'óng t'aô, boven uitsteken.

T'óng *T'é t'óng*, voorkomen, algemeen gewone manier gesteldheid.
t'óng niá, de aanvoerder zijn van, aanvoeren.
t'óng ping, soldaten aanvoeren order zijn commando hebben.
it t'óng, één geheel uitmakend, geheel en al.
t'óng kiōng, in het geheel, allen.
lóng t'óng, in het algemeen.
t'ong hat, onder zijne direktie, bestuur hebben.
paī t'ong è lâng. ongeluksvogel, iemand wien alles tegenloopt.
t'óng hūn (*hūn en hīn*), uiterst haten.

t'òng sim, uit den grond van het hart voortkomend.
t'òng hūn, ingekankerde haat.
t'òng k'ok, bitter weenen.
t'òng mē tsit tiŋ (tiŋ), iemand eens goed de huid vol schelden.

T'ōng *T'ōng*, een hoopje (als goed enz).
nīng t'ōng (nō), twee hoopjes.
t'ōng gûn, geld aan hoopjes leggen.
tsit t'ōng gûn, een hoopje geld.
t'ōng (eiŋ tōng) k'ang, een gat instooten *d. i.* eene gelegenheid vinden om iemand geld te doen verliezen.

Tu

蛛 Tu *Ti tu*, spin.
ti tu si, spinrag.
ti tu bāng, spinweb 2e net over draagstoelen enz.

抵 Tu *Tu*, durven.
tu ts'iú bé (boè), elkanders armenkracht meten.
tu hŏ ih, toereiken, geven aan iemand.
tu k'ui k'ì, uit den weg schuiven — zetten.
tu lai tu k'ì, over en weerschuiven (als een geschenk dat men uit beleefdheid niet wil aannemen).
kaò tu ook *kaò tú*, bamboezen koker aan de nek van valsche honden bevestigd.
tu tsai, met een knuppel tegen de buik elkander stooten.
tu sai lŏ, de russen (in Siberie) gaan bestrijden *d. i.* een lastig moeielijk ding gaan doen.
tu hong ing, wind en golven te weerstaan hebben *i. e.* voor alle moeielijkheden verantwoordelijk zijn.
tu gē mîng, de slechte handelingen van een mandarijn-bureau tegengaan.

Tu *Haî bô tsit tu*, zeer arm niets bezitten.
ô tu, oesterbanken.

適 Tú *Tú tú*, juist.
tú á tsiah, do.
tú hó, juist goed.
taī ke tú hó (ke), juist met elkander goed overeenstemmen.
ts'aò tú k'ám, juist toevallig.

遇 Tú *Tú tioh*, ontmoeten.
sŋ tú tióh (sio), elkander ontmoeten, tegenelkander aanstooten.
tú tīng, aantreffen (van dingen).
tú i boē tióh, iemand niet kunnen ontmoeten, aantreffen.

抵 Tú *Tú tsi*, geld afbetalen.
tú siàò, eene rekening afmaken, daarop afbetalen.
tú, stutten.
tú tèh, stutten, schragen.
tú tī, iemands mond volstoppen.
tsiáh kaò tú nâ aô, eten tot dat het aan de keel komt.
tú ts'ù tíng, tot aan het dak reikend (als opgestapelde waren).
tit tú tit, twee oprechten tegen over elkander.
sŋ tú ts'uì (sīō), elkander heimelijk van iets onderrichten.
tuì tú, quitte zijn, gebalanceerd, verevend.
pù tú t'ī, zeer rijk.
kóng oē tú ih, iemand met zijne eigene woorden den mond stoppen.

著 Tù *Tù bing (tì)*, ophelderen (omtrent).
tù ts'eh (ts'eh), zamenstellen (een boek).
tù ióh hng, recepten maken, schrijven.
tù miŋ ē p'ai lâng, een algemeen bekende schurk.

注 Tù *Hu hui toā tù tsi* (*hi*) (*tù*), veel geld verkwisten.

toā tù hè (*hoē*), groote hoeveelheid koopwaren.

tsit tù kiaò, een opzet-inzet bij het dobbelen 2e één spel.

ts'út tù goá kiò (*tù*), hij heeft er mij toe uitgelokt, ik ben niet uit mij zelven begonnen (met schelden enz).

tù i tao, bij iemand blijven zitten tot dat hij zijn schuld afbetaald heeft.

hūn tù, het betere van anderen voor het slechtere van zich zelven nemen.

Tù *Ping tù i boē tiaò*, de soldaten konden hem (den vijand) niet tegenhouden.

廚 Tû *Tû*, kast.

sā á tû, kleerenkast.

hong tû, vliegenkast.

niaó ts'ú tû (*ts'ì*), ratteval.

tû pâng, borden kamer, 2e kok.

ts'eh tû (*ts'eh*), boekenkast.

tû t'oah, kastladen.

k'iū tû, kooi waarin gevangenen staande vervoerd worden.

niao tû, kattenhok.

oá tû, bordenkast.

耡 Tû *Tû t'aô* (*tî*), krabber. ook *tî t'aô*.

躊 Tû *Tiû tû* (*tû*), aarzelen, weifelen.

陼 Tû *Tû* (*tî*), aftrekken (rekenterm), uitroeien.

tû ling (*tî*), de gemaakte toebereidselen na een sterfgeval verbranden. wordt ook gezegd als man en vrouw aan het vechten zijn en alles kapot smijten.

tû lù lù k'i (*tî lî lî k'i*), uitroeien.

tû lù, tû lù k'i, tû k'i, do.

tû ts'o pak sit (*tî*), al de bijkomend dingen er afgerekend.

tû sit, alle onkosten er afgerekend.

tû liaó i goā, behalve dat, met uitzondering daarvan.

tû i goā, do.

tû ts'ú i goā (*tî ts'í*), met uitzondering van dezen...... alles wat daar buiten gelegen is.

dzī kui it tû, door 21 deelen.

tsám tû uitroeien.

saò tû, do.

tû k'i, aftrekken.

ts'it tû poeh k'aò, alle onkosten er afrekenen.

tsám ts'aó tû kun, onkruid met den wortel uitroeien, *i. e.* kwaad met wortel en al uitroeien.

tû hui (*tî*), alleen ter oorzake van..... is het dat niet ......

塞 Tū *Tū sìh*, onder water houden en doen stikken; iemand het mes op de keel zetten.

tū tsui, onder water laten stikken.

tū kiém, door het zout halen.

īng oē tū ih (*iōng oā*), iemand door woorden weerleggen.

gaò ìn tū lâng, iemand knap weèrleggen.

gaò oē tū (*oē*), behendig iemand den mond stoppen.

t'âm tū, door slijm niet kunnen ademhalen.

tū mîng, iets tegen de deur aanzetten om het inkomen moeielijk te maken.

oá p'iet tih tū, borden-goed, tafelgereedschap.

T'ú (t'ì) }, familienaam.

T'ú 鋤 T'ù ts'áo (t'ì) }, gras weg schoffelen.

T'ù

T'ú U t'ù (uh t'ú) }, dom idiotisch.

T'ū T'ū kaò liáo, gebruiken tot er niets meer overschiet, verbruiken.

a p'ien t'ū kaò liáo, opium oprooken.

a p'ien toā poah t'ū, een groote dot opium rooken.

k'an t'ī t'ū, de blaasbalk trekken.

Tuh

着 Tuh Tiém tuh, waarschuwen, een heimelijke wenk geven.

tuk tuh kiâ, met het hoofd voorover voortstrompelen.

laō tuh tuh, voortstrompelend van ouderdom.

tuh bîn, dutten, kuikkebollen (van slaap).

tuh búk ka tsē (o) }, do.

tuh ku, sufferig dodderig stomp.

tuk ka tsē (tsoē) }, indommelen, op het punt zijn in slaap te vallen, dutten.

laō tuh ku, krom, sufferig door ouderdom.

ts'it laō poeh tuh (peh) }, alle oude menschen strompelen in het loopen.

着 Túh Ki ki túh túh, met de vinger op iemand wijzen uitschelden.

túh, stooten tegen, steken tegen.

túh ts'ut i ē p'ai (bai) }, iemands slechtheid aan den dag brengen.

túh k'ang túh p'āng, iemands gebreken zeggen, veel op iemand aan te merken hebben.

tuh kut p'āng, veel aanmerkingen op iemand te maken hebben.

túh tioh p'āng, iemands bedoeling juist raden, uitdrukken (zoodat hij niets meer weet te zeggen).

ts'un ts'ut túh tioh piah, de hand uitstekende tegen een muur aanstooten i. e. zoodra men iets wil gaan doen eene onoverkomelijke moeielijkheid ontmoeten.

Túh Kóng oē tìh túh (oā) }, zijne woorden inslikken.

鍷 T'uh T'uh á (t'uh }, spade.

t'uh t'ò, aarde afschoffelen.

托 T'uh T'uh k'i, de tanden uitpeuteren.

t'uh teh (t'uh) }, op zijn elleboog gaan liggen.

tuh ē taó, met de kin op de hand leunen.

t'uh, doorsteken, op de hand balanceeren.

t'uh p'òà t'in t'ong tien ts'ong, het dakraam (boven in het dak) doorstooten (zoodat men alles in huis zien kan) i. e. eene zaak aan het licht brengen.

T'uh T'uh koai (t'uh koān) }, plat op de hand omhoog steken.

tsit kiū tsit t'uh koai (t'oh) (koàn) }, zoo hoog, zoo lang zijn als men met de handen bereiken kan.

kap i t'uh tsiú bē, met iemand de kracht der armen beproeven i. e. zich met iemand meten.

T'úh T'úh t'úh, dom.

gām gām t'úh t'úh, dom, stomp.

tsīng tsīng t'úh t'úh, stil en dom, stomp (van aard).

t'úh koh, dommerik.

Tui

追 Tui Tui, vervolgen, achterna zitten.

tui koá, vervolgen.

tui pik, vervolgen, achterna zitten.
tui t'ó, achtervolgen en terugvorderen.
tui ts'át, dieven achterna zitten.
tui tsɛng, gestolen goederen terugvorderen.
tui ping, achterna zittende soldaten.
tui tòh lai, terug laten komen.
tui hoé, berouw hebben over vroegere verkeerdheden.

堆 Tui
Tsit tui, op een hoop.
t'o̱ tui, aardhoop.
ts'aó tui, hooiberg.
tui t'aô, wachtpost.
lui tui, onhandelbaar, lastig.
tsoè tui (*tsò* ») , een geheel uitmaken, paren.
k'ùn tui, met een troep nachtwacht gaan houden.
tui so̱a tui hai, opgestapeld als bergen en zee.
tui tsik, opstapelen.
ioh tui, raden hoeveel er zijn.
baóh tui (*baóh* ») , de geheele massa (opkoopen).
tsit tui làng, éene massa menschen.

拔 Tuì
Tuì t'aô k'ak kā i tuí k'i lai, uit het hoofd trekken (als haarspelden).

對 Tuì
Tuì, tegen, tegenover, gelijkelijk, even.
tuì bīn, tegenover.
tuì hoán, tegenovergesteld.
bô tuì pūn, niet overeenkomstig het monster.
tuì tiōng (» *tāng*) , voornaam, gewichtig, waardeeren.
tuì oā, inruilen tegen, van gelijke waarde.
tuì i kóng, aan iemand bekend maken, zeggen.
tuì t'aô, gelijkelijk.
tuì tù (» *tí*) , de rekening vereffenen.
tuì » goā siōng k'iàm, saldo nog schuldig of saldo nog te vorderen.
tuì to̱a, wissel.
tuì gùn (*gín* ») , wissel.
tuì, numer. voor dingen aan paren.
i kap goá tsoè tuì t'aô, hij is in onmin met mij.
tsoè tuì tik, *tsoè tuì t'aô*, tegenstander zijn van.
tuì liên, *liên tuì*, pendanten.
bô sa̱ tuì, niet met elkander overeenstemmen.
tuì k'ùn sa̱, van voren opengaande jas.
tuì ui, tegen elkander schaak spelen.
tuì lim, tegen, met elkander wijn drinken.
tuì tik, vechten, bestrijden.
tuì kia̱, spiegel.
tuì siu, in elkanders tegenwoordigheid ondervragen.
tuì kóng, tegen iemand persoonlijk zeggen.
tuì tâng, aan elkander gelijk.
tuì siaò, de rekeningen onderling vergelijken.
put tuì, niet gelijk, niet overeenstemmend.
tuì t'aô hó, gelijkelijk, even goed.
tuì t'iah, 1e met zijn beide de eenigste afstammelingen zijn 2e gelijkelijk onder beiden verdeelen.
ko̱ tuì k'a, man tegen man (dobbelen).
sit tuì, zijn man of zijne vrouw verloren hebben.
p'ah t'aô tuì, eene slavin uithuwelijken.
tuì tap, antwoorden.
tuì ni̱, juist één jaar geleden, een rond jaar.
tuì si tuì dzit, juist op denzelfden tijd.
tuì tuì tuì, juist gelijk, evenwijdig enz.
tuì ts'ien, zuiver gemikt.
tuì pé, do.
tuì tsìng, bewijzen tegen iemand inbrengen 2e juist voor de ziekte passend (van medicijnen).

tuì tīng, gelijkelijk zwaar, even zwaar.
tsiā̤ siang tsiā̤ tuì, een paar uitmaken (als man en vrouw).
tíng tuì, bij elkander passen (naar stand of jaren).
bó tuì ts'iú, zijn tegenstander, 's gelijke niet hebben.
tuì hū, iemand verwijten (als eene zaak die hij aangenomen heeft niet goed is uitgevallen.)
tsoè tuì, tegenoverstaande begrippen, zinnen maken.

Tuì *Tuì*, van uit, langs.
tuì hit tao (*a*), van daar, van daar uit.
tuì tsit tao (*a*), van hier, van hier uit.
tuì p'ai̤ nih siṳ̄ tò lai, bedenken, dubbele voorzorgen nemen voor het geval dat iets mis mocht loopen.

碓 Tuì *Tuì*, rijststamper.
ts'iú tuì, handmortier.
k'a tuì, voetmortier.
tuì k'ū, mortier.

搥 Tui *Tui*, met een voorwerp slaan, duchtig slaan.
tui hing t'ó̤ k'uì, op de borst slaan en zuchten.
tui sim koa̤, zich op de borst slaan.

Tui *Tui*, smeden.
tui t'ih, ijzer smeden.
tui sa̤, kleêren (bij het wasschen) schoon kloppen.

墮 Tuī *Tuī tsin*, waterpas.
tuī k'ì, gezwollen van de beenen.
tuī tiông (*t'út ts'iâng*), breuk.
siao tiông tuī, do.
tuī lòh, neêrvallen (van boven).
tuī lóh bé (*bé*), van het paard afvallen.
tuī lóh k'ì, neêrlaten (van boven naar beneden).

tuī tsing, druiper, zaadstrooming.

隊 Tuī *Toā tuī*, eene groote massa (soldaten).
tuī nó̤. gelederen.
hī tuī, oorbel.
tsing bé tuī (*bé̤ tuī*), een optocht te paard houden.
tsùn tuī, in orde staan (van gelederen).
pai tuī, in rangen plaatsen (van soldaten).
soà̤ tuī, uit elkander gaan (van soldaten, processie enz.)
k'o̤ tuī, door het blazen op de trompet de gelederen commandeeren.

兌 Tuī *Tuī kim*, tegen goud inruilen.
tuī gùn (» *gin*), tegen zilver geld inruilen (als eene massa koperen munt).

梯 T'ui *Laò t'ui*, ladder.
hùn t'ui, stormladder.
tó t'ui, trap.
oàn t'ui, wenteltrap.
tsûn t'ui, scheepstrap.
soh á t'ui, touwladder.
lè t'ui, wenteltrap.
pēh t'ui (*pe̤h* »), den trap opgaan.
t'ui tsí, sporten van een ladder.
laq t'ui koai̤ (*koa̤*), leuning van een trap.
tsit tiṳ t'ui (*tio̤*), een ladder, trap.
k'iā t'ui, ladder.
tik t'ui, bamboezen ladder.

推 T'ui *T'ui ui*, zich verontschuldigen, afslaan de schuld op een ander schuiven.
t'ui si, weigeren.
t'ui tó, omvergooien.
t'ui tī goá sin k'u, op mijne schouders schuiven, voor mijne verantwoording stellen.
t'ui hō̤ ìh, op een ander overschuiven 2e een deel in iets geven.

T‘ui *T‘ui*, inwrijven met (als met medicijnen.)

T‘ui *T‘ui*, verlakken.

t‘ui o̲ keng / *(kui̲)*, zwart verlakken.

t‘ui o̲ kim, do.

t‘ui keng, glad poetsen, wrijven, polijsten.

腿 T‘uí *Toā t‘uí*, de dijen.

ē t‘ui / *(ē̲ »)*, het been.

ien t‘ui, ham.

hé t‘ui / *(hoé »)*, do.

t‘uí t‘aò kut, heup, heupbeen.

gû t‘ui ts‘ìng, geweer als een koe dij (als de Europesche geweren).

k‘o̲ t‘ui, losse pijpen van een broek.

t‘i̲ t‘ui / *(t‘è »)*, stijf in de dijen.

tsiuó k‘a t‘ui, spillebeen (van een man met lange magere beenen.)

tsing toē-aū t‘ui, vóór- en achterpoot.

t‘ui sim bak, vleesch uit de dij *i. e.* vast kapitaal waarvan men leeft.

替 T‘uì *T‘uì*, verruilen voor (iets beters), vertellen met.

t‘uì oā̲, verruilen, verwisselen, ruien.

t‘uì pao, heimelijk in de plaats stellen van.

t‘uì ming, ruien (van vogels).

t‘ao t‘uì k‘i, heimelijk iets slechters in de plaats zetten.

t‘uì ts‘iú ìng, een nieuw onderstuk aan de mouw zetten.

鎚 T‘ui *T‘ui*, hamer.

ting á t‘ui, hamer.

t‘ih t‘ui, ijzeren hamer.

ts‘â t‘ui, houten hamer.

k‘ū t‘ui, stampen (van een mortier.)

lui t‘ui, stamper.

ko̲ t‘ui, trommelstokken.

lô t‘ui, stok om op de gong te slaan.

lōng t‘ui, ramei, beukhout.

s i t‘aò t‘ui, met het hoofd stooten.

k‘ùt t‘ui, lett. stompe hamer; stomp als de punt van een penseel, pen, enz.

kap i tu t‘ui, vijandelijk tegen over iemand staan, in vijandschap met iemand zijn (lage volkstaal.)

tsit t‘ui p‘ah tó, in één slag omslaan *d. i.* zeer sterk.

tsiem eh ho̲ goá, *t‘ui eh ho̲ li*, geef mij het scherpe uiteinde gij kunt het stompe in handen krijgen *d. i.* zelfs met ongelijke kansen ben ik niet bang voor u.

t‘ui kòng t‘ih, de hamer slaat op het ijzer *i. e.* twee personen die voor elkander niet onder doen.

kùn t‘ui, glad, schelmachtig, schurkachtig.

ts‘un tsit ki t‘ui, alleen over zijn, niet om zijn leven geven.

權 T‘ui *Niū t‘ui* / *(niō̲ »)*, gewicht van eene balans.

ts‘ìn t‘ui, klein gewicht, »

垂 T‘uī *T‘uī*, zwaar.

t‘uī tāng, aan beide kanten even zwaar maken.

lui t‘uī, zwaar van gehalte.

t‘oa t‘uī, opgeschept zitten met.

t‘uī t‘aô / *(t‘īn t‘aô)*, de beide uiteinden van een juk even zwaar maken.

t‘iēm t‘uī / *(t‘uī)*, verminderen van zijne bezittingen door de vele verwanten waarvoor men te zorgen heeft.

Tun

鈍 Tun *Tun*, stomp, bot.

ts‘ùi tsih-tun, niet goed ter spraak zijn.

bák tsin-tun, stomp, slecht van gewicht.

tun to ts‘ut laī ts‘iú, met een slecht stuk gereedschap fraaie dingen maken.

Tun *len tun*, vuurbaken, seinplaats bij elke 10 (tien) li's.

Tun *Tun tok*, eene zaak overzien.

屯 Tún *Tún tiáh*, veel rijst opkoopen en opstapelen.

tún hè (» *hoè*), goederen opstapelen, opbergen.

tún tiáh, opkoopen als het goedkoop is om te verkoopen als de markt hoog wordt.

tún tsàn, opstapelen, opzolderen.

tún tsiı̄ soa, opgestapeld als een berg, in groote hoeveelheid voorhanden.

盾 Tún *kō á tún*, molensteen.

tsióh tún, molensteen (straf).

tún làng, iemand vastzetten (aan een molensteen enz.)

ts'oı (en) *già tsióh tún*, een molensteen om de nek hebben (van misdadigers).

maū tún, tegenspreken (zich zelven).

tıng tún, bovenste molensteen, looper.

ē tún (*ē* »), onderste do.

kim tún á, gouden munt = kwart dollars.

tsit tún, één gulden.

頓 Tùn *Tùn ts'iú*, de hand geven.

tùn siú paì, het hoofd neêrbuigende groeten.

Tùn *Tùn*, ton (scheeps inhoudsmaat.)

tùn sè (» *soè*), tonnegeld.

tùn ts'ù, tonnegeld.

an tùn, een twist tusschen personen bijleggen.

tùn ti (» *tē*), terugtrekken, niet vooruit willen gaan (als een paard) niet willen weggaan.

tsıng tùn ping bé (*bē*), verstrooide soldaten bij elkander brengen.

tùn hō i tîng, een lang voorwerp door er aan te schudden, breken.

唇 Tûn *Tûn*, de lippen.

ts'uì tûn, do.

hī á tûn, oorlappen, oorlellen.

tûn, rand, kant (van wegen enz.)

bák tsiu tûn (»), onderste ooglid.

kâm tûn, de lip intrekken, den mond niet open doen.

ts'uì tûn p'ê sa k'oán t'aī (*p'oē si*), elkander voor den schijn beleefd behandelen.

遁 Tūn *Tùn lai*, hard komen aanloopen.

鈍 Tūn *Tūn*, dom, slecht van geheugen.

ti tūn, langzaam, dralend, stomp (van aard).

Tūn *Tūn si*, warm houden (als thee met een weinig vuur.)

tūn hé (» *hoé*), opwarmen, langzamerhand verwarmen.

īng hé-tūn, met vuur aan alle kanten gaar stoven.

tūn soan lō, een koperen offerpot met vuur en reukwerk verhitten (om ze fraai op te poetsen).

Tūn *Tūn hoat*, goochelmanier, goochelkunst.

Tūn *Tūn tsat* (» *tsap*), legeren, bij elkander komen (van soldaten).

tūn iı̄, een legerplaats opslaan, kampeeren.

tūn ping, soldaten op eene plaats verzamelen, post doen vatten.

呑 T'un *T'un*, verslinden, verzwelgen, slikken doorslikken.

t'un tsiáh, do.

t'un k'iem ook *hiao t'un*, schuldig blijven, niet teruggeven).

t'un k'ì, verzwelgen. opmaken.

ū t'un t'ō, zwijgen en spreken op zijn tijd.

t'un t'ō p'ù tim, naar de omstandigheden weten te handelen, verliezen en winnen enz.

t'un hün, verdragen, dulden (geduldig).

t'un dzim, verdragen, dulden.

t'un sig dzim k'ui (en) *k'i*, *dzim k'ui-t'un sig*, zijn toorn inhouden (niet durven uiten).

t'un boe lóh ē keh, inslikken maar niet in de ondermaag kunnen krijgen.

t'un ēm lóh (bē) }, niet kunnen inslikken *i. e.* er niet in slagen om zijne schuld onbetaald te laten.

pa lun t'un (pa laò lé t'un) }, inslikken zonder te kauwen.

t'un t'ih i, (als) een ijzeren pil inslikken *i. e.* met tegenzin eten.

hiao t'un, zijne schuld niet willen afbetalen.

péh péh t'un k'i (péh péh }, nooit terugbetalen.

t'un noū, zijn speeksel inslikken.

tsoè tsit ts'ui t'un-kiem bò kaò, ineens inslikken en aanmerking maken dat het niet genoeg is *i. e.* niet genoeg voor waar het voor dienen moet.

dzin sim put tsiok-tsoâ t'un ts'iū, 's menschen hart is nooit voldaan als een slang die een olifant wil inslikken.

T'un *Un t'un*, vuil, smerig, geelachtig vuil.

套 T'un *Tsit t'un*, een stel (als in elkander sluitende manden, potten enz.)

踐 T'ún *T'ún táh*, vertrappen (als een veld).

T'ún *Bú t'ún bú t'ún*, klein maar sterk.

T'ùn *T'ùn t'ùn*, lastig, zich aan zijn idée vasthouden, naar geene rede luisteren.

Ien t'ùn, roet.

T'ûn *t'ûn t'ûn*, dof.

ts'ing t'ûn, het vuil (spinwebben enz.) afragen.

T'ûn *T'ûn bú (» bó)* }, onvruchtbaar (van eene vrouw).

Tút *Tút*, oppoetsen, afwrijven.

kè tút (koè) }, gladpoetsen.

tút hō i keng, do.

突 *Tōng tút*, eensklaps.

Tút *tút dzièn*, do.

秃 *T'ut t'aò*, kaal van hoofd.

T'ut *t'ut meng (» niō)* }, kaal van hoofdhaar.

t'ut lù (» li) }, letterlijk, geschoren, kale ezel (scheldw. tegen Boeddh. priester).

t'ut ting, kale kruin.

T'ut *T'ut k'a*, met de beenen tegen elkander aanschrijnen.

t'ut, afwrijven.

t'ut bat, afwrijven, afpoetsen.

īng tsing t'aô kā i t'ut p'oà, met de vinger sterk wrijven (als het vlies van vruchten).

sū t'ut lō (sio ts'ut lō) }, elkander misloopen.

T'út lùn, verstuiken (als het been).

T'út *t'út ts'ut*, uit (iemands hand) vallen.

t'út k'ū, uit zijn verband zwikken.

t'út tsaò, uitvallen, uitschuiven.

t'út t'e (t'út t'ai) }, de vrucht verdrijven.

t'út sin, de bevalling door medicijnen bevorderen.

t'út king (» kang) }, van de schouders af laten glijden.

pàng t'út, uit de handen laten slippen (als het roer van een schuit).

t'út tsit dzī (kang tsit dzī) }, een karakter overslaan 1e ruimte voor een karakter overlaten.

脱 *T'út*, uitglijden.

T'út *táh t'út*, uitglijden.

k'a táh t'út, slechte omgang hebben (van vrouwen).

ts'ui táh t'út, zich verspreken (zeggen wat men had moeten verzwijgen).

Tsa

婦 **Tsa** *bó*, vrouwelijk, vrouw.
tsa bó lâng, vrouw.
(*tsa po lâng*), man.
tsa bo gín á, meisje.
tsa bó kiá, dochter.
īm tsiâ ta po īm tsiâ tsa bó, noch man noch vrouw zijn (hermaphrodiet) ook van eene ruwe vrouw gezegd.

Tsa *A tsa*, vuil, smerig = a a tsa tsa.

查 **Tsa** *Tsa ts'at* / (*tse* »), onderzoeken.
tsa giēm, visiteeren, onderzoeken.
tsa ts'ut, uitvinden, door onderzoek achter iets komen.
tsa k'àm, onderzoeken.
tsa tiém, nakijken en opteekenen.
sè tsa / (*sè tse*), naauwkeurig onderzoeken.
tsa hóng, heimelijk onderzoeken.
ts'e tsa / (*ts'e lâng k'ì tse*), iemand zenden om iets te onderzoeken.
k'e tsa / (*ke tse*), onderzoeken (of de behoorlijke belasting is opgebracht.)
tsa sit, het ware van eene zaak onderzoeken.
tsa bìng, duidelijk onderzoeken.

早 **Tsá** *Tsá tsá*, vroeg.
tsá k'i, 's morgens vroeg.
pàng tsá, vroeg; de ochtend les eindigen.
t'àn tsá / (*t'án*), bijtijds.
gaò tsá, vroeg (iemand prijzende gezegd).
tsá méng / (» *mui*), vroeg of later.
t'aò tsá, zeer vroeg.
ts'ing tsá, do.
tsá sí á, mocht gij jong sterven! (scheldterm door vrouwen gebruikt).
t'i kɛng tsá / (*kui*), morgenstond.
lóh tsá óh, naar de ochtendles gaan.
pàng tsá hē / (*hē*), de ochtendles eindigen (om de scholieren te laten ontbijten.)
bò tsá bò oâ, noch te vroeg noch te laat den waren tijd voor verschillende dingen niet kennen.
tsá k'í àm k'ùn, vroeg opstaan en laat, naar bed gaan.
tsá tsìng, vroeg zaaisel.
tsá bí, vroege rijst.
tsá nì, vroegere jaren.
tsaī tsá é lâng, de menschen uit de oudheid.
kó tsá, de oudheid.
tsá dzit, vroegere dagen, tijd.
(*maɔh tsá*), heden morgen.

詐 **Tsà** *Kan tsà* / (» *tsè*), bedriegelijk, arglistig.
tsà guī, bedriegelijk, valsch.
tsà hàng, in schijn zich onderwerpen.
tsà tsɛng, zich met het geld van het volk verrijken (van mandarijnen) zich laten omkoopen.
kaó tsà, onoprecht, valsch.
tsà p'ièn, bedriegen.
k'uí tsà, bedriegelijk, arglistig.
k'i tsà, bedriegen.

昨 **Tsā** *Tsā dzit*, gisteren.
tsā bō dzit, gisteren, ook eergisteren.
tsā bō tsá k'i, gistermorgen vroeg.

斬 **Tsâ** *Poâ tsâ*, kort zwaard.
tsâ-tsoè nīng tìng / (*tsò nō tuì*), in tweeën hakken.
tsoé tsá / (*tsè* »), gelijk, effen.

映 **Tsâ** *Tsâ dzit*, even in den zon te drogen leggen.
tsâ hé / (» *hoé*), even bij het vuur te drogen leggen.

83

tsà iù, even door het vet halen.

Tsà *Tsà k'i lai k'oà*, zich op de achterste pooten of teenen oprichten om te zien (als een tijger in een kuil of een mensch in gedrang).

燗 Tsà *Tsà bák*, in de oogen schitteren, flikkeren (als de zon of schel licht).

hé tsih-teh tsà / (*hoè nà*) }, de vuurtongen flikkeren.

tsà dzit, voor *tsà dzit*, even in den zon te drogen leggen.

k'it i tsà k'i, door iemand in de rede gevallen worden en daardoor vergeten wat men wilde zeggen.

Tsā *Tsā*, (droog goed) opscheppen.

tsā hi, visch scheppen.

hoai tsā tit tsā, op allerlei manieren geld verdienen.

tsā k'i lai, opscheppen, afscheppen (als vet op het soepwater.)

差 Ts'a *Ts'a liaoh* / (*ts'e* ») }, verkeerd, niet goed.

gien gú-ts'a / (*gàn gi-ts'e*) }, de verklaringen zijn verschillend.

ts'a ts'ok / (*ts'e* ») }, vergissing, zich vergissen.

ts'a put to / (*ts'a*) }, nagenoeg, het scheelt niet veel.

tsing ts'a / (» *ts'e*) }, zich vergissen, een fout maken.

kià ts'a lō / (*ts'e*) }, den verkeerden slechten weg opgaan.

bô ts'a / (*ts'e*) }, juist zoo (lett. er is geen vergissing in).

tsing ts'a, verschillen.

ts'a tit tsoē / (*ts'e tsē*) }, groot verschil, het verschilt veel.

ts'a tit hīng / (*huī*) }, do.

tsit tīng ts'a kaó ts'ioh, op tien voet scheelt het negen *i. e.* het verschil is zeer groot.

Ts'a *P'oat ts'a* / (*p'iet ts'e*) }, met elkander over weg liggen.

sa-ts'a k'i lai / (*ts'a*) }, zijn jas opnemen.

báng tà ts'a, plaats waar de beide kanten van een bedgordijn over elkander slaan.

炒 Ts'á *Ts'á*, schroeien, roosteren, branden (als koffie).

tsien ts'á, braden en roeren.

koē-kà ná ts'á tañ / (*o*) }, zeer gemakkelijk.

Ts'á *Ts'á táh*, verstrooien, door elkander gooien.

kiaó ts'á, door elkander gooien, lastig vallen.

ts'á ke lā t'éh / (*ke t'éh*) }, gekijf, ruzie (binnen 's huis.)

ts'á ook tsaó lao / (*ts'oó naō*) }, ruzie hebben.

ts'á lā / (*ts'á lā*) }, lastig vallen.

ká lá ts'á, vele zaken verward door elkander.

鈔 Ts'à *Ts'à p'iò*, muntbiljet.

tsi ts'à, muntbiljet, papiergeld.

tùn ts'à, tonnegeld.

Ts'à *Tá ts'à*, een kink in den kabel brengen.

柴 Tsâ *Tsâ*, hout.

tīng ts'â / (*tān* ») }, hardhout.

p'à ts'â, zachthout.

sam ts'â / (*sam* ») }, pijnhout.

ts'â k'o, brandhout.

ts'â t'ui, **houten hamer.**
ts'â k'oan, **handspaak.**
ts'â kiâh, **regenschoenen, klompen.**
ts'â oè (è), **do.**
ts'â ko tsûn, **houtboot.**
ts'â ts'aó, **hout en gewassen.**
tsit pé ts'â (pē), **een bos hout, takkebos.**
ts'â pai, **houtvlot.**
hiu ts'â (hio »), **reukhout.**
siah ts'â tsi, **een punt aan een hout snijden.**
ts'â tsi á, **houtsnippers.**
bân-kaò ná ts'â t'aò nih, **hardhoofdig, dom als een knoest hout.**
ts'â tsik, **dikke lange houten kaars waarin van boven een lampbrander.**
ts'â hâng, **houtmagazijn, hout bergplaats.**
ts'â ping, **gekloofd hout.**
ts'aò ts'â boē oē tiao tit, **verrot hout kan niet gefatsoeneerd worden *i. e.* een door en door slecht mensch is niet te hervormen.**

查 Ts'â — *Ts'â (ts'ê)*, **onderzoeken, onderzoek doen naar.**
ts'â mîng (» muī), **ondervragen.**
ts'â k'où, **nazien.**
ts'â k'ó, **onderzoeken, ondervragen.**
ts'â koe (ke), **klepperman, politiedienaar.**
ts'â iū, **de nachtelijke ronde doen.**
ts'â ke hé, **zijne bezittingen opnemen.**
ts'â aō ts'iú, **onderzoeken wat men nog te vorderen en te betalen heeft.**

s'â — *Ts'iú-ts'â nī (ts'â nē)*, **stijf, de handen verkleurd van koude.**
ts'â (ts'â), **de kramp hebben.**
bák tsiu ts'â ts'â, **gebroken van de oogen.**

si tsoè ts'â kang, **robust van gesteldheid zijn.**
koa ts'â, **lijkkist.**

吵 Ts'ā — *Hī k'ang ts'ā ts'ā haó*, **gonzen in het oor.**
ts'a ts'i ts'ā ts'ā (ts'i pù ts'i ts'ē), **fluisteren, mompelen = ts'i bú ts'ī ts'ā.**

Ts'à — *Ts'à ook t'à ts'iú (t'à ts'i »)*, **ruzie hebben en gebaren maken om te gaan vechten.**

Ts'ā — *Loān loān ts'ā*, **verward door elkander joelen.**
kap i ts'ā, **met iemand joelen, twisten en niet willen toegeven.**

Tsah

插 Tsah — *Tsah sa (ts'ao sa)*, **zijn kleed opnemen (op een smerigen weg.)**
tsah sai kun (tsah sai kin), **een luur omdoen.**
tsah lâng ē oē t'aò (tsáh oā) (tuì oē t'aò tsáh tsáh), **iemand in de rede vallen.**
kui kui tsah tsah, **zich volstoppen, zijn lijf volladen als arme menschen die veel gekregen hebben en met zich naar huis nemen.**
pih tsah, **strak om het lijf.**
tsah k'ò, **de broek ophalen.**
tsah tsi tsah gûn (gîn), **geld bij zich steken.**
tsah t'aò tsah bé (boe), **een weinig helpen, de hand leenen.**
tà tsah, **do.**
aō tsah, **steun voor zijn ouderdom (door vaders aan hun zoon gezegd).**

截 Tsáh — *Tsáh*, **tegenhouden.**
noā tsáh (nā noā), **verhinderen, bedekken.**

tsáh lō̤, onderscheppen, opvangen.

dzia tsáh, bedekken (als iemands kwaad).

tsáh dzit, een scherm tegen de zon zetten.

tsáh àm, in het licht staan.

tsáh hé (» *hoé*) }, do.

tsáh íng (» *íng*) }, schaduw geven.

tsáh kíng (» *kui̤*) }, in iemands licht staan.

íng tsáh (*ui̤* ») }, verbergen, verbloemen.

tsáh ts'iú, in de schaduw van zijn hand zitten (als bij het schrijven met het penseel).

pin tsáh, deurscherm.

tsáh tsoè nn̄g tíng, naar zich toe in tweeën hakken (als met een apothekers hakmes).

tuì lō̤ t'ạò-tsáh ih, iemand zijn weg afsnijden (als dieven die reeds wegliepen).

tsáh tsíng tsáh aō, iemand voor en achter den weg afsnijden.

tsi̤-kiém tsit tsáh, er ontbreekt een schuif cash (de cash worden bij 5 in de hand geteld).

Tsáh *Tsui tsáh*, sluisdeur.

siâ̤ tsáh, stads valdeur.

tsáh tsui, het water afsluiten.

míng tsáh (*mui̤* ») }, sluisdeur, poort van een vesting.

t'ih tsáh, ijzeren afsluiting (als aan vestingen of sluizen).

炙 Tsáh *Tsáh iù*, in het vet steken, door het vet halen.

tsáh bah, vleesch door water of vet halen.

插 Ts'ah *Ts'ah*, insteken, als bloemen in het haar.

ts'ah dzip, do.

ts'ah hoe (» *hoa*) }, bloemen insteken.

ts'ah tiā̤, met geschenken eene vrouw ten huwelijk vragen.

ts'oan ts'ah (*ts'ui̤* ») }, mechaniek.

loān ts'ah ts'ah, verward (van een rijk enz.)

t'aò ts'ah, hoofdtoilet, haarspelden, naalden enz.

ka̤i ts'ah (*kàn* ») }, met andere kleuren afzetten, breken.

ts'ah p'ai̤ tsi̤, slechte duiten er onder stoppen.

tsùn-ts'ah tsik, in de golf instorten en niet meer boven komen (van een schip.)

ts'ah hoe lé, behalve den vasten prijs voor werk of goederen nog voor zijn fatsoen wat geven.

ts'ah koh, met de handen in de zij staan.

hoe-tióh ts'ah t'aò tsing, bloemen moet men voorop steken *i. e.* eene belooning moet men bij de eerste gelegenheid geven.

ts'ah hī tsi̤, een pijl door het oor steken (aan boosdoeners).

ts'ah nō̤ hong ki, vlaggen van de vijf streken (N. Z. O. W. en het midden insteken (als op schepen) *i. e.* hoog in aanzien enz. zijn.

ts'ah hoe, lijzeils bijzetten.

ts'ah tī laī bīn teh k'iā̤, alléén in het midden (van een dorp of een slechte buurt) wonen.

持 Ts'ah *Hù hù ts'ah ts'ah*, ondersteunen, onder de armen houden.

ts'ah k'í ts'ah tó, helpen om op te komen en om te gaan liggen (zoo als men zieken doen moet).

Tsai

知 Tsai *Tsai*, weten, gevoelen.

sg tsai è ts'át (sio), een in dat huis bekende dief.
tsai iá, kennis van zaken hebben, ervaren zijn.
t'aò bák tsai tāng, goed naar de omstandigheden weten te handelen.
tsai tsáng, kennis van eene zaak hebben.
īm tsai t'aò, bij ongeluk, vergissing, neem het mij niet kwalijk.
īm tsai koā, niet van de koude afweten, de koude niet voelen.
kóng ts'ù tsai mîng ak, over een huis sprekende het deurportaal kennen *i. e.* na weinige woorden eene geheele zaak doorzien.

栽 Tsai *Tsai*, planten (als een boom).
pog tsai, overplanten.
tsai tsìng, zaaisel.
ts'aì tsai, even opgekomen groente.
gin á tsai, jong kind (van 7 à 8 jaar).
hoan tsû tsai (tsi), aardappelstekken, even opgekomen aardappel.
ah tsai, jonge eenden.
koe á tsai, kuikens.
hî tsai, kleine visschen, jong broed.
tò t'aò tsai, voorover naar beneden vallen.

災 Tsai *Tsai ē (eh)*, rampen.
tsai eh, do.
tsai lān, rampen, wederwaardigheden.
t'ien tsai, rampen des hemels.
hè tsai (hoé), vuurramp, brand.
tsuí tsai, rampen door water, overstrooming.
siū tsai iong (iang), door een ramp lijden.

齋 Tsai *Tsai kaì*, vasten en mediteeren.
ts'i tsai (ti »), vasten, geen geslachte wezens eten.
tsiah lìng tsai, zijn geheele leven vasten.
ts'i sg lák kaó tsai (ti), den 3en 6en en 9en dag vasten.
tsai tsing pò sì, Boeddh. priester op groenten onthalen en giften doen.

宰 Tsaí *Tsaí siòng (siàng)*, eerste minister.

載 Tsaì *Tsaì*, laden, inladen.
oē tsaì tik lâng (ē), het kan een mensch dragen.
tsaì mih k'ì, goederen vervoeren (per schip).
tsaì siū tsoē (siō tsū), overladen, te zwaar laden.
tsaì hè (» hoè), goederen inladen.
tsaì hè tog (hoè), reçu.
kì tsaì, opteekenen.
ūn tsaì, goederen vervoeren (aan schepen.)
tsaì tsiū ts'eh (tsiō ts'eh), in een boek opteekenen.
tsit nî poā tsaì, een jaar of een half jaar *d. i.* niet lang.
nēng nêng boē oē tsaì lát, onsterke voorwerpen kunnen geène sterke krachtsaanwending verdragen.
siaó tsûn put k'am tiōng tsaì, een kleine schuit kan geene zware lading dragen *i. e.* met geringe middelen kan men geene groote dingen doen.

再 Tsaì *Tsaì siū (» siō)*, overdenken.
koh tsaì, nogmaals.
tsaì k'oà, nogeens zien, bekijken.
tsaì sg, herhaaldelijk.
it dzī tsaì, herhaalde malen, onophoudelijk.
kai tsaì, bij geluk.

Tsài *Bin á tsài*, morgen, morgen ochtend.
財 *Tsai pit* (» *pik*) }, schatten.
Tsai
Tsai̤ *Tsi̤ tsai*, do.
tsai kù, boekhouder (op een schip.)
tsai tsú, rijk man.
tsai k'ì, geldelijk geluk.
ū tsai k'ì, gelukkig in finantieele zaken.
liên tsai ê hê kì (*hoê*) }, een compagnon die zijn geldelijk deel in de affaire heeft bijgelegd.
tsai-ōng-sing ko̤i, door grooten rijkdom zich een mandarijnambt koopen.
hoat tsai, schatten verwerven, rijk worden.
lún k'ì kiù tsai, zijn toorn inhouden om zijn geld te besparen.
tsiao tsai ông, koning, god der rijkdom (op schepen en in winkels vereerd).
tsai-put lō̤ gán, geld moet men niet op in het oog vallende plaatsen leggen.

才 *ū tsai tiaō*, bij machte zijn om...., vermogen de mogelijkheid zijn om...
Tsai *bô tsai tiaō*, niet vermogen.
tsai tsú, een genie.
ū tsai kàn, talenten bezitten, talentvol, bekwaam.
lō̤ tsai, slaaf ook scheldwoord.
bô ū hil ê tsai, niet de kennis voor iets hebben; niet voor een zeker doel geschikt zijn (ook van voorwerpen).

臍 *Tō̤ tsai*, de navel.
Tsai *tsai toà*, navelstreng.
tíng tsai (*tui* ») }, de navelstreng afknippen (bij eene bevalling).
tiṳ́ tsai, middelste gedeelte van een pan.
tu tsai, met een stok tegen de buik elkanders krachten meten.

儎 *Tsaī*, numer. voor cargo's, lading enz.
Tsaī *poà tsaī*, half geladen.
tsing tsaī, vol geladen.
tsaī tsi̤, vrachtgeld.
tsaī gùn (» *gîn*) }, do.
tsaī tsi̤, geld bij iemand hebben staan.
boán tsaī (*moā̤* ») }, vol geladen.
tāng tsaī, zwaar geladen.
k'in tsaī, licht geladen.
lám tsaī dzī, cognossement.
hē tsaī (*o*) }, lading inbrengen 2e bevrachten zijn.
in tsaī, vracht voor een schip zien te krijgen.
tsùn tsaī, vrachtgeld.
k'ioh tsaī, lading voor een schip bij elkander brengen.
kaò tsaī, zijne genoegzame lading hebben.

在 *Tsaī*, stevig.
Tsaī *tsaī tsá*, in de oudheid.
tsaī si̤ (» *se̤*) }, nog in leven zijn.
tsū tsaī, stevig staan (als een tafel), onverschrokken van menschen.
tsū tsū tsaī tsaī, onverschrokken, onbevreesd.
tsaī gùn (» *gîn*) }, nog geld te vorderen hebben van.
tsaī sik lú (*kui lí*) }, maagd.
īm tsaī hâng, met den loop van zaken onbekend zijn.
sit tsaī, inderdaad, wezentlijk.
tsaī kó̤, een aandeel inleggen.
tsaī pún, kapitaal inleggen.
ts'iàng tsaī si̤, vast afspreken, beloven om...
tsaī sim, in zijne gedachten hebben.
tsaī ka (» *ke̤*) }, te huis zijnde.
tsaī giáh, zijn getal, personeel volledig hebben.
tsaī tiṳ́ (» *tiṳ́*) }, 1e onder de menigte zijn 2e onbedeesd in het publiek.

tsaī nǒ } , niet bedeesd, onbeschroomd.
(o)

haī tsaī, do. onverschrokken.

tsaī kūn } , binnenkort, niet lang na
(» kīn)
deze; dicht bij.

tsaī goá p'ah sìng } , volgens mijn
(sui)
denken, naar ik denk.

k'og kín tsaī làng, langzaam of gauw hangt van de (gesteldheid der) personen af.

tsaī làng ì aì, al naar men het wenscht.

ts'ut tsaī lí, zooals gij wilt, het hangt van u af.

tsaī giáh, op het oogenblik voorhanden, beschikbaar hebben.

bô sō bô tsaī, geene plaats hebben (om te wonen of iets te zetten).

tsaī tsûn, aan boord gaan, inschepen.

tsaī ì tsaī ì, vast bij zijne opinie blijven.

tsaī k'a tsaī k'a, stellig, bepaald voor een deel kunnen tellen, gerekend worden.

bé sè k'iā tsaī, stevig in positie staan (om te vechten of iets zwaars op te lichten).

aī *Tsaī i sih* } , hoe moet het nu? ik heb
(o)
het u van te voren wel gezegd.

tsaī ni } , hoe moet het nu?
(tsaī ni)

tsaī kì sī hó p'aí, hoe kan men weten of het goed of kwaad is? = *hó p'ai tsaī k'ì*.

Ts'iú tsai, vinger.

ıi *ki tsai* } , de wijsvinger.
(» tsai)

tiong tsai, de tweede vinger.

bé dzī tsai } , de derde vinger.
(boé) laó á)

bé tsai } , de pink.
(boé »)

tsiem tsai } , vingerhoed.
(p'oè »)

k'a dzī tsai, tweede toon.

k'a tiong tsai, derde toon.

bé dzī tsai } , vierde toon.
(boé)

bé tsai } , kleine toon.
(boé »)

p'è tsai, *tàng tsai*, lederen, koperen vingerhoed.

tsáp it tsai, iemand met elf vingers.

pi làng tiong tsai, iemand de middelste vinger toewijzen (lage beleediging).

k'ik tsai, de verschillende vinger handgrepen die men bij het accompagneeren van een lied op een instrument moet doen.

pûn k'ik p'ǫ-tióh at tsai, blaast men eene melodie dan moet men de vingers bewegen.

Tsai *Tsai kú* } , hoe zou ik durven?
(tsai »)

li k'ì tsai iū, hoe is het er mee afgeloopen.

猜 *Ts'ai*, raadsel, raden.

Ts'ai *ting ts'ai*, raadsel (op lantaarns geschreven.)

ts'ai tioh } , raden, geraden hebben.
ts'ai ts'ut

ts'ai boē ts ut, niet kunnen raden.

ts'ai kún } , raden met het uitsteken
(o)
der vingers.

ts'ai lai ts'ai k'ì, heen en weer raden, gissingen maken.

ts'ai gi, gissen, betwijfelen.

si ts'ai, raadsel in vers.

彩 *Ts'ai t'aò*, voorteeken (oorspr. goed).

Ts'ai *p'ai ts'ai t'aò*, slecht voorteeken.

bô ts'ai, jammer dat..., ongelukkig.

nǫ ts'ai hûn, veelkleurige wolken, een gelukkig voorteeken.

hat ts'ai } , toejuichen, juichen.
(o)

ts'ai, guirlande.

ts'ai ki, vaandel met een lange smalle strook goed.

kì ts'ai, do.

bô ts'ai kang, vergeefsch werk, vergeefsche poging.

ts'ai lō̤, processie (bij avond).

sin ts'ai, uiterlijk, voorkomen.

ts'ai uī (» *oū*) }, gekleurde teekeningen.

hó ts'ai, gelukkig voorteeken.

ts'ai sik, met kleuren afzetten.

ts'ai kì kó, vlaggen en trommen (als bij eene processie).

ts'ai péh tièm (*pḛ́*) }, lijkwinkel (waar alles wat tot een lijk behoort verkocht wordt).

kat ts'ai, guirlandes ophangen.

koà ts'ai, guirlandes, festoenen aanhangen.

hoat ts'ai, een gelukkig voorteeken hebben, gelukkig zijn zoodra men iets begint.

ti sai nâ-kat ts'ai, aan een varkensmest mand guirlandes binden *i. e.* een vlag op een modderschuit.

Ts'aí *Kiém ts'ai* (*t'iém* ») }, wellicht.

採 *Ts'ai hoe* (» *hoa*) }, bloemen plukken, 2e van

Ts'aí de eene bloem op de andere gaan als een vlinder (ook als een jongen die van het eene meisje op het andere loopt).

ts'ai ts'ú (» *ts'ı*) }, opkoopen op eene andere plaats.

ts'ai tiáh, opkoopen (meestal van rijst.)

ts'ai tiáh bí, in groote hoeveelheid rijst opkoopen.

ts'ai tò tíng (*tṳ́i*) }, omwenden (zijn paard, schip enz.)

ts'ai hoè bé (*bḛ́*) }, zijn paard omwenden.

ts'ai pūn tê (*tḛ̂*) }, thee in groote hoeveelheid opkoopen.

ts'ai tê (» *tḛ̂*) }, thee plukken.

ts'aí ma̤i, uitkiezen en koopen (als benoodigdheden voor den keizer.)

t'aò tsing hoe k'it i ts'ai k'ì (*lni hoa*) }, door iemand in tegenwoordigheid van anderen beleedigd zijn.

ím ts'iù ts'aí ih, zich niet met hem inlaten bemoeien.

put ts'iù put ts'aí ih, do.

ts'ìn ts'ai, zooals, naar het uitvalt, het komt er niet op aan.

ts'ai làng ê sik tsuí, iemands fatsoen te grabbelen gooien.

ts'aí ts'ù, afhalen (als armen van rijken).

ts'aí ts'ai tsoaī tsoaī, onverschillig, onbeleefd behandelen.

菜 *Ts'aì*, groenten.

Ts'aì *ts'aì hîng* (» *hṳî*) }, moestuin.

ts'aì iû, salade-olie.

péh ts'aì (*pḛ́h* ») }, kool.

ts'aì kap bák, slecht van gezicht.

keh nâ ts'aì (*ke̤h mḛ̂ ts'aì*) }, groenten.

tang o ts'aì, peterselie.

k'ûn ts'aì (*k'în* ») }, selderij.

taū ts'aì, boonspruitjes.

ts'aì t'âng, rups.

ts'aì t'aô, radijs.

tsiáh ts'aì, vasten, geen vleesch of visch eten.

ts'aó ts'aì, groenten.

ts'aì kè á (*kḛ̀*) }, groenten stalletje.

k'ioh ts'aì seh (*se̤h*) }, groenten afval oprapen.

lō̤ ts'aì, reisvoorraad van drooge levensmiddelen.

tsiú ts'aì, bijspijzen bij wijn.

ts'aì nḡ, groenten en alles wat bij de rijst gebruikt wordt.

pān ts'aì, een feestmaal aanrichten.

tsú ts'aì / (*tsí* ») }, koken, eten bereiden.

haù ts'aì oá, aan de dagelijksche spijzen offeren.

ts'aì kị pīng / (» *kẹ puī*) }, groenten en rijst (na de begrafenis 's morgens en 's avonds aan den geest van den overledene geofferd.)

ts'aì kong, oppasser van Boeddh. priesters.

ts'aì pô, kookster voor nonnen.

ts'aì sin, voorspellende geest.

ts'aì toh, groentenmaal (zonder vet).

ts'aì nịh k'ioh tioh bah, in de groenten vleesch vinden *i. e.* voordeel krijgen waar men er niet opgerekend had.

ts'aì p'e, *ts'aì ti*, varken voor bij de groenten *d. i.* stommerik, nietswaardig mensch.

tsa bó kiá ts'aì tsi miā, meisjes hebben een lot als groentezaden, zij kunnen hoog in stand worden maar ook in lage standen geheel verloren gaan.

ts'aì soe, groenten.

tn ts'ang boē ts'aì, met uien loopen en groenten verkoopen, kleinhandel drijven.

裁 *Ts'ai hông* / (*tsai* ») }, kleêrenmaker.

Ts'ai *ts'ai ts'iū* / (» *ts'iọ̄*) }, vaste kleêrenmaker.

ts'ai to, mes om boeken af te snijden.

ts'ai ts'ioh, kleêrenmakers voet.

ts'ai, afsnijden (als papier).

ts'ai ts'eh / (*tsaì ts'ẹh*) }, een boek afsnijden.

ts'ai i, kleeren knippen (gew. van de bruidskleêren gezegd).

ts'ai tsiān, afknippen (van een stuk goed).

ts'ai liaū / (*tsoi* ») }, bouwstoffen, materialen.

sin ts'ai / (» *tsai*) }, voorkomen, uiterlijk.

ū tsú ts'ai / (*tsai*) }, eene zekere manier hebben om iets te doen.

ts'ai ts'ú, manier op iets, om iets te doen; schikken (eene zaak.)

ts'ai tók, bedenken, overpeinzen, afmeten (hoe iets te doen.)

tsū ts'ai sim ts'ai, zelf eene manier op iets bedenken.

豺 *Ts'ai lông* / (*ts'ai* ») }, wolf.

Ts'ai

纔 *Ts'ai tsiah* / (*ts'ai* ») }, juist, zoo even.

Ts'ai *hong ts'ai*, do.

ts'ai ts'ai ū, zoo juist, onlangs is.

Ts'aī *Ts'aī put* / (» *hút*) }, een afgodsbeeld neerzetten en er aan offeren.

ts'aī sin, aan de geesten offeren.

ts'aī ang, (Ts. ts.) dito.

置 *Ts'aī*, neerzetten, insteken (van een lang

Ts'aī voorwerp).

ts'aī hē teh / (*ts'ē*) }, neerzetten.

ts'aī k'il, palen, inzetten.

ts'aī t'iaū, een balk, paal in den grond zetten.

ts'aī sún, , door een tap, zwaluwstaart bevestigen.

ts'aī sng, door een pin vastzetten.

ts'aī lâng ê lók uī, een gelukstablet voor iemand oprichten *i. e.* door aan iemands tablet bij zijn leven te offeren zijne erkentelijkheid aanduiden.

ts'aī ts'aī teh tsē, onbeweeglijk zitten.

am kún-ts'aī ts'aī ts'aī, een stijve nek hebben.

ts'aī pọ̄, voorbedachtelijk, voorgenomen.

ts'aī kọ̄ ì, met opzet, voorbedachtelijk.

84

ts'aī ing ting, moedwillig eene zaak niet willen begrijpen.

採 *Ts'ai hoe* (*ts'ai* ») }, bloemen afrukken.

Ts'ai *p'ah ts'ai* (» *ts'án*) }, ruw, onvoorzichtig omgaan met.

襯 *Ts'aì* ook *ts,àn sik* (*ts'àn*) }, door eene zwarte

Ts'aì omgeving meer laten uitkomen.

Tsak

雜 *Tsak*, om het lijf dringen.

Tsak *tsô tsak* (*tsō* ») }, lastig vallen, het iemand lastig maken (door gedurig vragen enz.)

tsak tsō (» *tsō*) }, do.

sin tsak (*sio* ») }, opgepropt (nauwe ruimte voor elk).

ak tsak, benauwd (als eene nauwe plaats, onfrisch laag huis enz.)

tsak tsak tsoè tsit tui, op een hoop bij elkander dringen.

tsak làng kaò beh sí, iemand tot razend worden toe lastig vallen.

戳 *Ing ts'iu tsák sih* (*iōng ts'io* }, met een zwaard

Tsák dood steken.

tiòh ka tsák, zich verslikken.

軸 *Ts'ak*, afhangende teekeningen of ge-

Ts'ak schriften.

lièn ts'ak, do.

kó ts'ak dzī uī (*oū*) }, do. uit de oudheid.

tiaò ts'ak, do. ophangen.

pè ts'ak tièm, behangerswinkel.

Ts'ak *Ts'ak ts'ak* (*ts'ap ts'ap*) }, verward, zonder kop of staar.

ts'ak ts'ak dzû, dzû ts'ak ts'ak (*o*) }, verward door elkander.

ts'ak sún (*ts'ák* ») }, een gat hakken om een wig in te drijven.

ts'ák ts'ák ts'ak t'iaò (*o*) }, trappelen, springen.

ts'iaoh ts'ak tiò (*ts'iaoh ts'iaoh*) }, do.

Ts'ak *Ts'ak k'iā k'iā*, steeds op zijn post zijn (als het hoofd van een huis).

鑿 *Ts'ák*, doorboren, stooten met een wa-

Ts'ák pen.

ts'ák á, beitel.

ts'ak p'oà, opensteken, stuksteken.

ts'ák k'ang, een gat in iets maken, op iets vinden.

ts'ák sún, een gleuf voor een insluitend hout hakken, uitbijtelen.

tseng kah ts'ák (*tsing*) }, ronde bijtel.

ts'ì ts'ák (*ts'ì* ») }, vol uitstekende splinters.

ts'ák làng, iemand steken, prikken als doornen of de baard.

ka kī ts'ák kè lai già (*kè*) }, zich zelf den last op den hals halen.

nī ts'ák (*nē* ») }, stijf, niet meegevend, iemand rechtstreeks beleedigen.

Tsam

噆 *Tsam* (*tsam*) }, zich verzamelen op (als mieren,

Tsam vliegen enz. op suiker enz.) azen op...

Am tsam, vuil.

Tsam

斬 *Tsám*, onthoofden, afhakken.

Tsám *tsám tsoèh* (» *tséh*) }, vastberaden.

ū tsám tsoéh } *(tsih)* }, afdoend, beslissend, vastberaden, den knoop doorhakken.

tsám ting tsoéh t'ih, spijkers en ijzer doorhakken, vastberaden handelen.

kam tsám, bij eene onthoofding tegenwoordig zijn (van mandarijnen).

tsám sit, onthoofden.

tsám tû } *(» ti)* }, uitroeien.

tsám ts'aó tióh tù kun, bij het afhakken van onkruid moet men de wortelen uitroeien *i. e.* kwaad moet men met wortel en al uitroeien.

sian tsám hō tsaò, eerst onthoofden en dan aan den keizer berichten (door bevelhebbers met onbepaalde macht gedaan).

tsám sat tsū iû, onthoofden en dooden is in zijne macht *i. e.* onbepaald volmacht hebben.

跊 *Tsàm k'a en toē* } *(tē)* }, stampvoeten.

Tsàm *kiā lō tsàm tsàm*, trappelend loopen.

tiò k'a tsàm toē, trappelen en stampvoeten (van woede).

īng k'a tsàm tsìh, met de voet stuk trappen (als een plank).

tsàm kaò laò pang beh tsih, zoo stampen dat de vloer er van breken moet.

Tsàm *Sù-tsàm tsui*, door het water halen (als kleêren enz.)

tsàm sù, kleêren door het water halen.

嶢 *Tsàm*, iets afraden.

Tsim *p'oà tsâm* } *p'oà ts'uì tsâm* }, iemand iets afraden.

k'a tsiah aū tsàm lâng, achter iemands rug afraden.

tsàm i īm tsiū, iets afraden zoodat het niet tot stand komt.

嶒 Tsàm *Tsàm gàm*, steil (als een berg) stevig, sterk.

劖 *Tsām*, hakken.

Tsām *tsām tsíng t'aò á* } *(tsíng)* }, de vingers afhakken *i. e.* vastbesloten hebben iets nimmer meer te doen.

ts'iú toê-tsām hō lâng } *(tê)* }, zijn woord reeds aan iemand gegeven hebben, niet meer van iemand af kunnen.

tsām, afhakken.

tsām, inbijtelen, bijtel.

tsām tīng } *(» tuī)* }, afhakken.

tsām hoe } *(» hoa)* }, bloemen enz. uitbijtelen.

ū k'ám tsām, volgens den regel, ordelijk.

tsām tiā, het anker kappen, 2e allen verderen omgang met iemand afbreken.

tsām lō, allen verderen omgang afbreken.

tsām koe-tsiû tsoā, een kip de nek afhakkende een eed doen.

tsit p'iet ē péh tsām koe, een schaal alleen gekookte (niet gebraden) doorgehakte kip.

tsām tsíng t'aò á kè oá, zijne vingers afhakken om de schotel vol te maken *i. e.* voor iemand iets doende er nog van zich zelven bijleggen.

sim koā ts'in ts'iū tsioh tsām, een hart als een steenbeitel *i. e.* hardvochtig.

tsām lâng ē kè tsī, lett. iemands kooppijs afhakken *i. e.* wetende dat hij geld noodig heeft niet dan onder den prijs van hem willen koopen.

tsām k'a tsām ts'iú, lett. voeten en handen afgehakt hebben *d. i.* door anderen in de onmogelijkheid zijn iets te doen dat men zou willen doen.

sui koe tsām t'aò boē, kikvorschen met de koppen afgehakt verkoopen (en daardoor het gewicht der koppen in zijn nadeel hebben) *i. e.* (genoodzaakt zijn) het beste van waren te verkoopen en met het slechte te blijven zitten.

站
Tsām *Tsít tsām*, eene pleisterplaats, halt-station.

t'ing tsām, op eene pleisterplaats halthouden.

iáh tsām, pleisterplaats.

hioh tsām / (*h?h* »), op eene pleisterplaats overnachten.

t'aò tsām-tiong tsām bé tsām (*boe*), eerste, middelste en laatste pleisterplaats 2e eerste, tweede en derde afdeeling soldaten, reizigers enz.

iáh tsām pâng, huis aan eene pleisterplaats.

toā lō tsām, pleisterplaatsen aan den grooten weg.

tsām tsām ū k'eh tiém, bij elke pleisterplaats is een herberg.

kè ts'ām, eene pleisterplaats voorbij gaan.

tsām tsām ū tō li, op alles is er (of) heeft hij eene zekere manier.

參
Ts'am *Ts'am hú*, generaal-majoor (in vredes tijd).

ts'am tsiòng / (» *tsiàng*), do. kolonel

ts'am ts'am kik, van een mandarijnpost afzetten.

ts'am k'ó, vergelijken.

ts'am siông / (» *siàng*), gezamelijk raadplegen, bepraten.

ts'am bō, gezamelijk raadplegen.

ts'am bō tsō kè, gezamelijk raadplegen en listen bedenken.

sio ts'am, vermengen.

sa ts'am / (*siò* »), do.

ts'am ts'ap, verward door elkander.

ts'am tsáp loān loān, verward door elkander.

ts'am ts'u / (» *ts'i*), verward door elkander.

ts'am lam, verward, gemengd door elkander.

sa am ts'am / (*sio*), door elkander mengen.

ts'am kun, generaal, veldmaarschalk (in tijd van oorlog).

ts'am gī, gezamelijk bepraten.

ts'am kì, gezamelijk (ook) alleen, een hoogeren mandarijn bezoeken.

hoē ts'am, gezamelijk eene petitie indienen om een gelijken of hoogeren mandarijn afgezet te hebben.

i ts'am i i iā ts'am i, zij klagen elkander als slechte overheden aan.

Ts'am *Ts'am ts'ē* / (*o*), bekkens.

Ts'ám *Ts'i ts'ám lók p'ik*, ellendig en mismoedig (als na vele rampen).

ts'ám si, eene ellendige dood sterven.

ts'ám ts'ut, droevige acte in een tooneel, ellendige omstandigheden.

ts'ám ah, erbarmelijk, ellendig.

sīm ts'ám, do.

ts'i ts'ám / (*ts'i ts'ám*), ellendig, medelijdenswaardig.

ts'ám ts'oeh / (» *ts'eh*), erbarmelijk snikken.

ts'ám siong / (» *siang*), erbarmelijk bedroefd.

ts'ám king, erbarmelijke, ellendige toestand.

tsai ts'ám, de ellendige toestand inzien waarin men is.

gaō k'aò (en) *kiò ts'ám*, altijd roepen dat men het ellendig heeft.

讖
Ts'am *Kóng oē kā i ts'àm teh*, iemands toekomst voorzeggen, voorspellen.

ts'àm gú / (» *gí*), voorspelling.

tsō ts'àm, voorspellen.

lóh lâng ē ts'àm gú, (zich zoo gedragen dat iemands voorspelling uitkomt.

懺 *Ts'àm hoè* / *(» hoè)*, berouw hebben.
Ts'àm
king ts'àm, boete gebeden (van Boeddh. priesters).
k'ui lō ts'àm, lijkdienst houden (bij de begrafenis zelve door 5 of 7 Boeddh. priesters die het lijk vooruit gaan.)
paì ts'àm, om vergiffenis voor de zonden van een overledene bidden (als bij de lijkdienst.)
kong tik tse ts'àm / *(tsē)*, lijkdienst houden, vasten en boete doen.

鑱 *Toā ts'àm kó*, groote bekkens en trom.
Ts'àm *Hō-ts'àm ts'àm loh*, de regen valt zonder ophouden neer.

Tsan

罾 *Tsan*, schepnet.
Tsan *tsit tiū tsan*, een schepnet.
t'ó tsan, met een schepnet visschen.
k'an tsan, een schepnet ophalen.
tsan á tsûn, visschersschuit om met het schepnet te visschen.

層 *Aū tsan k'í*, achter kiezen.
Tsan *tíng tsan*, bovenste kaak.
ē tsan / *(ē »)*, onderste kaak.

曾 *Tsan*, familienaam.
Tsan

讚 *Ts'ing tsàn*, prijzen.
Tsàn

贊 *Tsàn gièn* / *(» gàn)*, iemand helpen spreken, voor iemand spreken.
Tsàn
tsàn siā, iemand helpen roepen.
tsàn sing, iemand helpen om iets tot stand te brengen.

站 *Tsàn tuī*, halthouden, in parade staan.
Tsàn *tsàn pan*, in rij, in parade staan.
tsàn teh k'iā, terzijde in een rij gerangschikt staan.

棧 *Tsàn pàng*, pakhuis, beteekent op Java ook handelshuis of firma.
Tsàn
tún tsàn, opstapelen, opzolderen.
tsàn hè / *(» hoè)*, goederen opbergen.
ts'ân k'ì laiʼi, goederen opbergen 2e nog hooger in bezitting doen rijzen.

層 *Tsàn*, numer. voor verdiepingen, treden van een trap enz.
Tsàn
kiā á tsàn, treden van een (steenen) trap.
lô t'ui tsàn, sporten, treden van een trap.
tíng tsàn, bovenste verdieping.

Tsàn *Tsàn*, numer. voor étages, afdeelingen in een mand, zaken enz.
ū tsàn ts'ù, in volgorde.
ē tsàn / *(ē »)*, benedenste étage.
tīng tsàn, tweede étage.
sa tsàn, derde étage.
ts'ing tsàn bān tsàn / *(ts'an)*, allerlei zaken.
nā á tsàn, étages van een mand. korf.
tsàn lòh k'ì, de verschillende étages later neerzakken (als van een mand).
tsit tsàn ē taī tsì, deze zaak.
tsàn tsàn- ū ì sù, in elke opvatting heeft het eene beteekenis.

殘 *Sa tsàn* / *(sio »)*, elkander doodsteken
Tsàn *tsàn ti*, varkens steken, slachten; varkens hebben.
kiáh to of (koeh si) á sa tsàn, vijandig tegenover elkander zijn.
tsàn dzim, wreed.

助 *Pang tsān*, helpen.
Tsān *tsān*, do.
sa tsān / *(sio »)*, elkander helpen.
tsān gièn / *(» gàn)*, iemand in het spreken helpen, voor iemand spreken.
tsān kang, iemand in zijn werk helpen.

tsān ts'iú, een handje helpen.
tsàn goá boé, help mij om (dit) te koopen.
tsān pút (» *ang*) }, aan eene processie mede helpen, meêdoen, contribueeren.

噆 *Ts'an*, kreunen, steunen.
Ts'an *hį hį ts'an*, kreunen = *hai hai ts'an*.
hiò ts'an, kreunen, kermen.
gaò k'aò ts'an, zeer spoedig, licht kreunen.

潺 Razen als water.
Ts'an *siò tsui-teh ts'an*, het water raast.

餐 *Boán ts'an*, het avondmaal, nachtmaal.
Ts'an *it dzit sām ts'an*, dagelijks drie malen.

燦 *Ts'àn lān*, fraai, prachtig, helder flikkeren.
Ts'àn

襯 *Oè ts'àn* (*o*) }, schoenvoering.
Ts'àn *ts'àn sik*, met kleuren afzetten, door eene donkere omgeving beter doen uitkomen.
poè ts'àn, iets meer doen uitkomen.
ts'àn ts'ah, afwisselen met, mengen met.
ts'àn dziém, afzetten met, afwisselen met (kleuren).
ts'àn kah (*k'ah ts'ah*) }, afwisselen met (spijzen, waren, menschen enz.) mengen met.
ts'àn teh kóng, in zijn gesprek iets zeggen, zoo maar zeggen zonder het bepaald te meenen.
hó lâng ts'àn ts'ah p'ai lâng, goede menschen met slechten vermengd, onder de goeden vindt men ook slechten.

田 *Ts'àn*, rijstveld, veld 2e familienaam.
Ts'àn *pui ts'àn*, een vruchtbaar veld.
sán ts'àn, onvruchtbaar veld.
lám ts'àn, mager, schraal veld.
soa ts'àn, zandig veld.
poh ts'àn, mager, schraal veld.
ts'àn kap á, een padde.
ts'àn lé, veldslak.
ots'àn ts'ú, veldmuis.
ts'àn hing (» *hui*) }, natte en drooge velden, velden in het algemeen.
pī ts'àn (*poē* ») }, een rijstveld doen indroogen.
pè ts'àn (*pē* ») }, eggen, bijharken (een veld.
pì ts'àn, een rijstveld beplanten.
sa k'u ts'àn, drie velden.
làm ts'àn, modderig veld.
ts'àn tsú, eigenaar van een veld.
ts'àn tsò (» *sòe*) }, landhuur.
ts'àn giep, bezitting in landerijen.
hì ts'àn, een veld bewateren.
ts'àn bò kōī, het karakter 田 zonder rand i. e. tien. 十
k'oì t'ì ts'àn, velden die alleen door den regen kunnen (bevochtigd worden.)

村 *Ts'o ts'àn*, ruw, ongemanierd (van menschen).
Ts'àn *ts'àn t'aò*, onbeleefd.

殘 *Sim kog ts'àn*, hardvochtig.
Ts'àn *ts'àn sim kog*, hardvochtig.
ts'àn ts'àn tsoì lòh k'ì, moedig aan. onverschrokken doen.

蜻 *ts'àn i* (*ts'àn ni*) }, Libellula krekel.
Ts'àn

Tsang

棕 *Tsang sik*, bruin.
Tsang *tsang ts'ing* (» *tsàn*) }, dikke mat van de Chamaerops gemaakt.
tsang ts'ing, Chamaerops boender, veger. stoffer.
tsang sui, grove regenjas.
tsang soh, touw van de Chamaerops gemaakt.

tsang pao lai, peeren (vóór dat ze rijp zijn in Chamaerops vezels gewikkeld).

鬃 Tsang *T'aô tsang*, hoofdhaar (van vrouwen en mannen.
t'aô tsang bé (boé), hoofdstaart.
bé tsang, de manen (van een paard).
sai tsang, leeuwenmanen.

椶 Tsang *Ing ts'i-tsang lah (iōng)*, beetpakken.
tsî- k'it i tsang k'ì, zijn geld is hem ontnomen, ontstolen.
p'ah tsang, touw slaan.
tsang lang lang k'ì, alles wegnemen.
tù t'aô tsang kā i tsang lai, bij de hoofdstaart beetpakken.

總 Tsáng *Tsáng t'aô*, aan het hoofd staan van, de directie hebben over.
tsáng kun t'aô (kin), aan het hoofd van iets staan.
tsáng siaò, de uitgaven en inkomsten nagaan, overzien.

鬃 Tsáng *Tsáng*, nagemaakt hoofdhaar, valsche staart.
soà tsáng, eene valsche staart aanhechten.
ts'aì tsáng á bé, struiken van groenten, koolstronken.

踪 Tsáng *Tsai tsáng*, kennis van zaken hebben.
tsai tsáng iá, do.
tsai tsáng dzē, op het spoor van iets zijn, de sporen kennen (als van gestolen goederen).
gō tsáng, de vijf teenen van de voet.

粽 Tsàng *Pák tsàng*, In bamboes bladeren inpakken.
tsàng, wigvormige in bamboesbladen gepakte gekookte rijst die den 5den dag 5de maand gegeten worden.
tsàng hióh, het blad waarin de tsàngs gepakt zijn.

愴 Tsàng *Tsàng tsàng tsàng*, verwaarloosd, er armoedig uitzien (als iemand die in verval is.)

叢 Tsàng *Tsàng*, numer. voor boomen, gras, graan, groenten enz.
ts'iū tsàng, boomen.
sin tsàng, nieuwe boom.
laū tsàng, oude boom.
hoe tsàng, bloemplanten. bloempotten (met bloemen er in).

沐 Tsàng *Tsàng ik*, baden.
tsàng soé (» sé), met water overgieten, wasschen.
tsàng hō, door regen nat gemaakt.
ièn lō tsàng tò lai, door (regen begoten) kletsnat te huis komen.

葱 Ts'ang *Ts'ang*, uien.
ts'ang king (» kui), ijzeren holle pijp, boor.
hong ts'ang, soort uien tegen gevatte koude gebruikt.
pō lè ts'ang, lampenglas.
ting ts'ang, do.
puh ts'ang (puh p'aóh á), opgisten.
k'i ts'ang, opgisten = *k'i ts'ang k'i ts'ang*.
ling ts'ang, openingen in de borsttepel.
ts'ang ts'ang, vol gaatjes.

怱 Ts'ang *Ts'ang ts'è*, onverwachts, plotseling (als een donderslag).
kóng oē put tsi ts'ang ts'è (oū), zeer plotseling, onverwachts spreken.
naū ts'ang ts'ang, woelig, veel getier (als op een feest.)

聰 Ts'ang *Ts'ang miā*, beroemd vernuftig.

菖 Ts'ang *Ts'ang pō (ts'iang pō)*, een riet in de 5e maand 5den dag aan de deuren gehangen.

Ts'áng *Dzū ts'áng ts'áng (dzi)* / *loān ts'áng ts'áng*, verward door elkander).

刺 Ts'àng *Ts'àng ming* / *(» mȯ)*, de veeren opzetten als een kalkoen enz.

ming king t'aô-ts'àng / *(mȯ kui)* / *ts'àng ming k'ing* de haren rijzen, te bergen van vrees, kippenvleesch hebben.

ts'àng ts'iu, *ts'ùi ts'iu-ts'àng ts'àng*, opstaande snor (ook als in toorn.)

Ts'àng *P'út ts'àng* / *(p'uh »)*, uiterlijke tooi, opschik.

Ts'àng *Sì koè ts'àng* / *(kè)*, zich overal verbergen (als dieven).

ts'àng lai ts'àng k'ì, dan hier dan daar zijn (als bij een oploop.)

緝 Ts'àng *Ts'àng* (ook) *tsàng tioh* / *(tsàng)*, betrapt worden (als bij smokkelen) betrappen, aantreffen.

hō bé k'oaì-ts'àng k'ì / *(tsàng)*, door den politiedienaar betrapt worden, in diens handen loopen.

Tsap

汁 Tsap *Tsuí tsap* / *(» tsiep)*, water.

t'eng tsap, dito.

十 Tsáp *Tsáp*, tien.

tsáp hun hó, allerbest.

tsáp dzī hun hó, opperbest.

tsáp mih tog, catologus.

kū tsáp hè tièm / *(hoè)*, uitdragerswinkel.

tsáp tsiok, volkomen, zuiver (van metalen).

tsáp tsing / *(» tsui)*, volkomen, volmaakt (bijwoord).

bô tsáp tsiok, onvolkomen.

tsáp dzī bīn á, dobbelbord.

tsoe tsáp / *(tsò »)*, een groot feest aanriel op den 60sten, 70sten enz. verjaardag v personen.

tsáp dzī lō t'aô, kruisweg.

tsáp ts'ùi-kaó k'a ts'eng, velen te ge en verward over iets spreken.

tsáp tsim kaó t'aô bák, allen het hoog woord in eene zaak willen hebben.

雜 Tsáp *Loān tsáp* / *(tsáp loān)*, vervalschen.

ts'am tsáp / *(ts'ap tsáp)*, verward door elkand

tsáp ts'e / *(» ts'e)*, koelie, boodschaplooper

tsáp ts'ùi, *tsáp tsáp ts'ùi ts'ùi*, allerlei soorten van...

tsáp ts'ùi áh, doos waarin men al kleine benoodigdheden doet.

gō hóe tsáp sik / *(hoa)*, veelkleurig, fraai.

tsáp tsai, algemeene kennis.

ts'ap tsáp, allerlei soort van...

tsáp sū, allerlei, onbeduidende dingen.

hun tsáp, verward door elkander.

p'ah tsáp kiáh / *(o)*, allerlei beroepen bij de hand nemen.

tsáp taò laò, allerlei door elkander gemengd.

tsáp tsóh é lâng, allerlei soort van menschen door elkander.

tsáp tsing, hoerekind.

tsáp hè tā, mars van een garen en band verkooper.

boē tsáp sè (en) *hè*, met een garen en band mars loopen.

tsáp lō tsing, van alle beroepen kennis hebben.

sim kog-tsáp tsáp tsáp, inwendig verward, niet rustig.

kiep tsáp, verward, niet geregeld (als een gesprek met zin en onzin).

Tsàp *Tsáp tsáp kaó*, medelijdend sussen.

[Chinese character] *Ts'ap taī tsì* (*tū*) }, zich met eene zaak bemoeien.
Ts'ap
ts'ap sū, zich met iets inlaten.
ts'ap ts'uì, zijn mond in een gesprek steken.
ts'ap ts'ap, verward door elkander.
ts'ap soeh (» *seh*) }, zich met iets inlaten, bemoeien.
bóh tit ts'ap ih, bemoei u niet met hem, laat hem loopen.
sa ts'ap (*sio* ») }, zich met elkander bemoeien, met elkander vermengen.
ts'ap pai á, de kaarten schudden.
ts'ap dzióng, woelig, vol gejoel en gedruisch (van eene plaats).
ts'ap tsáp, verward door elkander.
sa kao ts'ap, met elkander te maken hebben, met elkander in betrekking staan.

Tsao

[Chinese character] *Tsiú tsao*, wijndroesem, drab.
Tsao *tsao p'oh*, droesem en uitpersel (van wijn), bezinksel.
kiêm tsao (*iêm* ») }, zouten droesem.
âng tsao, roode drab.
k'ioh lâng ê tsao p'oh, iemands drab oprapen *i. e.* een gezegde of opinie van een ander stelen.

[Chinese character] *Tsao t'at*, verwaarloozen, nalatig, verTsao slonzen.
tsao t'at sin k'u (*hin sin*) }, zich zelven vergooien, niet ontzien.

[Chinese character] *Tsao tsao*, verflenst van kleur, versleten Tsao (oud).
tsao sim, inwendig gefolterd.
ao ao tsao tsao, verdrietig, neerslachtig, onopgeruimd 2e vuil.
tsiao tsao tso, do.
tsao tsao bin, niet kunnen slapen.
tsao sin, versleten, afgeleefd.
kaō aō tsao, inwendig zeer bedroefd.

溺 *Tsao a p'ièn*, verslaafd zijn aan, onderTsao mijnd zijn door opium.
tsao tsiú, verslaafd aan, ondermijnd door wijn.
tsao hun, verslaafd aan opium.
tsao kiaó, verslaafd aan spel.
Ts'â tsao, uitgedoofd hout, gedoofde kolen.

醃 *Tsao hi*, visch inleggen, inzouten.
Tsao *tsao ts'aì*, ingelegde groenten.

走 *Tsaó*, hardloopen, wegloopen.
Tsaó *tsaó k'ì k'èng*, wegloopen en zich verbergen.
tsaó k'ì tiêm, zich verbergen.
tsaó lī, ontvluchten, ontsnappen.
tsaó p'oe sìn (*p'ē*) }, brieven overbrengen.
tsaó p'oe ê lâng (*p'e*) }, brievenbezorger, looper.
tsaó hiòng (» *hiàng*) }, smokkelen.
tsaó hiòng ê lâng (*hiàng*) }, smokkelaar.
tsaó t'aò, overal rondsnellen om iets te krijgen.
tsaó pak, diarrhee hebben.
tsaó tāng, eene groote boodschap gaan doen.
tsaó k'iu (» *k'ī*) }, vreemd woord, vreemde uitspraak.
tsaó tsoáh, verschillend.
bô tsaó tsoáh, onveranderlijk, niet verschillend.
tsaó pi, wijken, uit den weg gaan.
t'ao tsaó, heimelijk wegloopen.
tsaó ka, uit de gevangenis vluchten.

tò tsaó si tséh } , eenigen zijn gevlucht
(*tò tsai*) } anderen zijn gestorven).

tsaó laó k'ì, geheel en al, spoorloos gevlucht.

tsaó-kaò bé-til } , zeer hard loopen.
(*boé*)

tsaó k'a p'ê } , het vel van zijne
(*p'oê*) } voeten af loopen *i. e.* onophoudelijk loopen.

tsaó tsui, per schip heen en weer reizen.

tsaó laō siao sit, spoedig een bericht gaan brengen.

tsaó pò, iets snel bekend gaan maken mededeelen.

tsaó bé ting } , lantaarn waarop paar-
(*bé*) } den geschilderd zijn die bij aansteking van de kaars gaan loopen.

tsaó lō, op weg gaan (van een koerier) 2e van iemand (winkelier enz.) weggaan, hem de clandisie ontnemen.

tsaó ts'i } , snel met iets wegloopen
(» *ts'i*) } (als met een lijk vóór dat het nog koud is).

tsaó hì ts'i } , hard met zijn visch
(*ts'e*) } loopen om ze nog versch te doen aankomen.

tsaó tà, met een vracht loopen (als rondventers).

tsaó ts'iú, vlug weg. loopend, (als schrift),

tsaó ts'iú-boē } , zonder lang dralen
bē) } verkoopen.

tsaó t'àn, overal rondgaan om geld te verdienen.

p'aó tsaó, iets nemen en er mede weg-loopen.

tsaó tsè } , voor schulden wegloopen.
(» *tsè*)

su dzip (en) *tsip tsaó* } , elkander ach-
(*tsáo sio dzik*) } terna loopen.

tsaó su liàh } , krijgertje spelen.
(*sio*)

tin tin tsaó, recht door wegloopen zonder om te kijken.

p'ah tsaó, verloren doen gaan = *p'ah tsaó lō k'ì*.

tióh tsaó bé t'ien kong } , stuipen heb-
(*bé*) } ben (van kinderen).

tsaó tsaó, papperig, dun (als rijst).

tsaó láng bi } , papperig dunne rijst.
(*o*)

tsaó tsui, water doen afloopen als een hellend dak.

tsaó of *p'ah tsaó tsú k'eh*, de klanten doen weggaan, verliezen.

tsaó bī, van zijne smaak verloren hebben.

tsaó iû, de olie, de etherische olie verliezen.

蚤 Tsaó *Ka tsaó*, vloo.

Tsaó *Tsaó á*, dochter.

tsaó á kiá, een dochtertje.

灶 Tsaò *Tsaò*, fornuis.

tsaò pi } , het kombuis.
(» *pē*)

tsaò k'a, keuken.

tsaò koe } , schoorsteenkrekel.
(» *ke*)

tsaò hiâh, steenen van een oven.

tsaò sin, fornuisgoden.

tsaò kun kong, fornuisgod.

tsaò sim t'ô, aarde uit het midden van een fornuis (als geneesmiddel gebruikt.

tsoh tsaò, een fornuis maken.

tsaò k'ang, *tsaò ts'uì*, vuurgat van een fornuis.

sien (en) *siang lièn tsaò*, dubbel fornuis.

k'aó tsaò, menschen die van één fornuis eten, huisgezinnen.

海上絲綢之路文獻集成 科技與文化編

lîn k'i lō̤ tsaò } , van elkander afgaan
(*lîn k'i lō̤ tsaò*) }
(als compagnons).

gû tsaò, ti tsaò, koe- en varkensslachthuis.

奏 *Tsaò*, tot den keizer zeggen.
Tsaò *tsao tsiṉ* } , bericht aan den keizer.
(» *tsiang* }

tsaò pêng } , bekendmaking aan den keizer.
(» *pún*) }

tsaò pán, ivoren reep die men vroeger voor zijn gelaat hield tegen den keizer sprekende.

㷮 *Tsaô biét*, uitroeien, vernielen, vernietigen.
Tsaô

tsaô ts'át, roovers uitroeien.

tsaô hiét, schuilhoek, rooversnest.

ts'át tsaô, rooversnet.

tsaô tsaô = *tsiâu tsiâu*, gelijkelijk.

找 *Tsaō*, er bijvoegen (het te kort komende.)
Tsaō

tsaō tsiok, er bijleggen tot dat het genoeg is.

tsaō oân, afbetalen hetgeen nog te kort kwam.

tsaō tsi̠, geld bijvoegen, bijpassen.

tsaō siaò bé } , het weinige, nog te kort schietende er bijvoegende.
(*boé*) }

tsaō kaò giáh, er bijvoegen tot dat er genoeg is.

tsaō bing, afrekenen, het te kort komende bijvoegen.

aō lai sa̠ tsaō, later met elkander verrekenen, afrekenen.

tsaō k'oè bé, bij de hijpotheekgelden nog zooveel vroeger totdat ze de waarde van het pand beloopen (waardoor het pand aan den hijpotheekhouder behoort).

抄 *Ts'ao*, een afschrift maken van.
Ts'ao *ts'ao siá*, do.

ts'ao p'oe } , brieven copieeren.
(» *p'e*) }

ts'ao laō (en) *aō̠* } , ruzie hebben.
(*ts'aó naō̠*) }

ts'ao kûn lik k'ō̤, de rok oplichten en de broek opstroopen (als bij het overgaan van een plas).

ts'iú ts'ao, manuscript.

kiṉ ts'ao, afgeschreven Peking Courant.

sió ts'ao, verkorten Peking Courant.

ts'ao sip, overschrijven, verzamelen (als mooie passages).

p'aò-ts'ao k'i lai, een lange jas oplichten.

ts'ao ke } , bezittingen verbeurd verklaren.
(» *ke̠*) }

ts'ao pi̠ li, een gordijn oplichten en ter zijde schuiven.

勦 *Ts'ao ping*, soldaten laten exerceeren, paradeeren.
Ts'ao

ts'ao liēn, zich oefenen in.

ts'ao kûn lōng pāng, boksen en batonneeren.

tsui ts'ao, manoeuvres te water.

soa̠ ts'ao, do. te land.

ts'aò ién, manoeuvres maken bij eene revue.

ts'ao sin peh pak } , inwendig gefolterd maken.
(*p̠eh*) }

Ts'ao *Laō ts'ao ts'ao* } , gejoel, gewoel (als bij een feest).
(*naō̠ ts'ao ts'ao*) }

Ts'ao *Báng tà* (of) *taò ts'ao*, koord waarmede men een muskietengordijn open houdt.

草 *Ts'aó*, gras.
Ts'aó *ts'aó ki*, grashalmpje.

ta ts'aó, hooi.

ts'aó bō } , strophoed.
(*o*) }

ts'aó loéh } , do.
(» *léh*) }

ts'aó liaò, strohut, schuur.

ts'aó męh, sprinkhaan.
ts'aó á tsùn, grasboot.
ts'aó p'ią, } *ts'aó p'i*, } graszode.
ts'aó lâng, vogelschrik (lett. gras mensch).
kiêm ts'aó, zeebies.
koah bé ts'aó (*bę*) }, gras voor de paarden snijden.
tsùm ts'aó tù kun (*ti kin*) }, met wortel en al uitroeien.
t'oą ts'aó, gras, onkruid wieden.
ts'aó toē (» *tē*) }, arme plaats.
ts'aó ts'ù, stroohuis 2e nederige term voor zijn eigen huis.
ts'aó liaō, gras.
nią ts'aó (*nią* ») }, legerfourage.
mîng ts'aó (*mę̂* ») }, beestenhuiden.
p'é ts'aó (*p'oé* ») }, do.
tîng sim ts'aó ts'aóh, stroomat.
ts'aó oê (» *ê*) }, sandalen.
ts'aó pę̂ oê, *pę̂ ts'aó oê* (*ê*) (*o*) }, strooschoenen.
ts'aó hoe tsuà (*hoa*) }, gevlekte slangen.
hoe ts'aó mih (*hoa*) }, dingen die gemakkelijk bederven.
ts'aó k'ę̀, struikroover.
ts'aó ts'àt á, struikroover (kleine).
ts'aó tsí, klis, klit.
tiū ts'aó, graanstoppels.
ts'aó ts'ìng, stroomatras.
ts'aó k'ùn, *ts'aó pū*, hooiberg, grashoop.
tsiáh toā ts'aó, groot gras eten *i. e.* alleen wanneer er veel meê te verdienen is iets willen doen.

ts'aó ki á poą tó lâng, een gras halmpje kan iemand doen omvallen *i. e.* een nietswaardig mensch kan u nog wel in moeielijkheden brengen.
ts'aó tsiaó, naam van kleine snelle goederen schuiten.

Ts'aó *Ts'aó táh*, trappen op, vertrappen.

Ts'aó *Ts'aó naū*, gejoel, gewoel, vertier, ruzie.

臭 *Ts'aò*, stinken, stinkend.

Ts'aò *ts'aò bī*, do.
ts'aò t'aô, zeerhoofd.
ts'aò noā, verrot.
ts'aò hī, loopende ooren.
ts'aò hī lâng, doof.
ts'aò ta, aangebrand, verzengd.
ts'aò hé lō bī (*hoé lō*) }, een aangebrande smaak.
p'ah ts'aò sêng eh (*suį*) }, oprispen (met eene onaangename smaak).
ts'aò sai hiem hiem, een vuile stank.
ts'aò ts'i k'ùi (*ts'ę*) }, stinkend (als onrijpe vruchten.)
tó-kaò bah t'ao ta, doorleggen.
ts'aò hīą (*hīę*) }, aangestoken (op een punt verrot als vruchten en enz.)
ts'aò hièn, stinkend (als onreine beesten).
ts'aò hiem hiem, erg stinkend.
ts'aò lò k'i, geheel en al bedorven verrot.
ts'aò tsiēn dzìn (*lâng*) }, stinkend verachtelijk mensch, scheldwoord tegen vrouwen.
aò t'aô ts'aò bin, knorrig boos uitzien *bīn ts'aò ts'aò*.
ts'aò ao bī, stinkende lucht.
ts'aò k'a ts'êng kią lâng iah (*ts'nį*) }, vreezen dat anderen zijne vorkeerdheid voor den dag zullen brengen.
ts'aò mią, slechte naam, *mią sią ts'aò*.
ts'aò sùn koą, slechts bedorven van harte (scheldterm).

ts'aò sim, inwendig verrot bedorven (van vruchten groenten enz.)

ts'aò tiá lo (lo̤), aangebrande lucht of smaak.

ts'aò hé lo (hoé lo̤), do.

tsaò ts'uì ia̤, zeere lippen.

ts'aò ts'uì kak (pi̤), zeere hoeken van den mond.

tsiáh ts'aò bi á, verrotte rijst eters (met minachting van soldaten gezegd omdat zij oude rijst de graanpakhuizen moeten eten).

ts'aò koa̤ seng, stinkende zure zweelucht.

ts'ao ts'o, stinkende vischlucht.

ts'aò ts'o si̤ sin, stinkende vischlucht trekt vliegen aan *i. e.* eene lichte vrouw trekt jongelieden aan.

ts'aò seng, bedorven en zuur.

kong ts'aò seng oē, onzin vertellen.

ts'aò bák, druipende oogen.

ts'aī ts'aò hīng, moedwillig, boosaardig.

Ts'aò *Ts'aò k'ám*, toevallig.

ts'aò k'aó (en *kiaó*), bij toeval.

ts'aò tú k'ám, do.

taò ts'aò, niet stellig van het toeval afhangend.

Ts'aò *Ts'aò tsia̤*, recht in zijn fatsoen zetten.

ts'aò lai ts'aò k'i of ts'iaò, het verschil deelen (als bij een koop).

Tsaoh

Tsaoh *Tsaoh dzi á*, opleggertje en vangertje spelen.

tsit ping i tsaoh kè hit ping i, van den stoel aan dezen kant op dien aan genen kant overwippen zonder met de voeten op grond te komen, door kunstenaars op het tooneel gedaan.

tsaoh kun, (kinderspel).

Tsaóh *Tsi tsi tsaóh tsaóh*, smekken.

tsaoh tsaóh liām, herhaaldelijk zeggen opnoemen prulen.

Ts'aoh *Ts'aóh ts'aóh tih*, droppelen (als een natte doek).

ts'aóh ts'aóh tiò, trappelen.

Tsat

節 Tsat *Tsat*, numer voor verzen, geledingen in bamboezen.

tik tsat, bamboes geledingen.

tsit tsat, één vers.

kut tsat, beengewrichten.

tsat, gewrichten.

tíng tsat, bovenste gedeelte van den arm.

ē tsat (e̤), onderste gedeelte van den arm.

laī tsat, binnengeleding van arm of been.

tsim tsat, afpassen.

tsat tsìm, afgepast afgemeten (niet teveel.

tīng tsat (tui̤ tsat), afbreken (als eene processie enz).

tsih tsat, afbreken, niet verder gaan (in een gesprek).

ū tsih tsat k'i lai, er is iets afgebroken uitgelaten.

tsit tsat ē taī tsì (sū), éene zaak ééncding.

tsat tsat ū tō lí, in elk zijner handelingen is reden, grond, gezond verstand.

ū tsat lo̤, afgemeten in handelingen, naar de omstandigheden weten te handelen.

tsat teh īng, afgemeten gebruiken (niet alles te gelijk).

tsat tsat ko, graad trapsgewijze hoogerworden (in aanzien of rijkdom).

tsat li ē k'uì lát, meet uwe krachten af, handel naar uwe krachten.

tsiù tsah, ingevreten vermolmde geleding (als van bamboes).

扎 Tsat *P'oe tsat* (*p'e*) (*tsap*), brief

扎 *Tsat*, omkluwen, omwinden.

īng pṳ̄ tsat (*iōng*) *tsat*, omzwachtelen.

tsat soà, garen om iets winden.

kun tsat, omzichtig, zorgvuldig.

k'ún tsat, aantrekken en vast aanhalen.

Tun *Tūn tsat* (*tsap*), gelegerd zijn (van soldaten).

tsū tsat (*tsrp*), do.

un iṳ̄ tsat tsē (*tsap tsē*), legeren.

Tsàt *Tsát tsát*, verstopt.

tsát p'ī (*sát*), verstopte neus.

tsát, vaststoppen stijfstoppen.

tsát pak, massief, (niet hol).

tsát tsi, hard.

tsát k'uì tsát k'uì, verstopt (als een pijp) geen adem kunnen halen (van ontsteltenis.

Bát tsát (*bát*), inktvisch.

Tsàt *bát tsát tsùn*, ossa sepia.

漆 Ts'at *Ts'at*, vernis (verv) verven.

sai ts'at, verven.

ts'at tsu ts'at, roodverven.

ts'at seh (*soeh*), verfkwast.

ts'at ts'ing, kwast waarmede men over het geverfde gaat om het gelijk te hebben.

hiaoh ts'at, *ts'at hiaoh*, bladderen van verf.

o kim ts'at (*pui*), zwart verlak.

iù ts'at, olieverf.

sai lik ts'at, groenverven.

ts'ī ts'at (*tsę*), ruwe verf.

sik ts'at, gekookte aangemaakte verf.

ts'at mī (*mī*), stopverw.

ts'at sai hū, verver.

ts'at pìn, haar aan de hoofdslapen bij bijverven.

uī o ts'at péh (*oū*) (*péh*), wit en zwart geklad oud besmeerd (als een muur het gezicht van een kind enz.)

ts'at toh-k'i bò ts'oı, op een geverfde tafel splinters willen vinden waar ze niet zijn *i. e.* moeielijkheden willen zoeken waar ze niet bestaan.

擦 *Ts'at*, uitwisschen uitschappen.

Ts'at *ts'at siaò*, afschrijven (van de rekening.

ts'at siaò bé, het restant op eene rekening vereffenen.

ts'at k'ì, uitschrappen, uitwisschen.

Ts'at *Sùn ts'at*, de rondte doen (als een wacht).

ts'at toát, onderzoeken en beslissen.

sè ts'at zorgvuldig nauwkeurig onderzoeken,

tsu ts'at, onderzoeken.

(*tsę*) *ting ts'at*, do.

ts'at ts'at tsi bing, alles nauwkeurig nagaande.

k'e ts'at (*ke*), onderzoeken ondervragen.

àm ts'at, heimelijk onderzoeken.

hóng ts'at, do.

賊 *Ts'át* dief.

Ts'àt *hai ts'át* zeeroover.

ts'át bé (*bę*), roovers.

ts'át ah, houd den dief!

ts'át tsùn rooversschuit.

ts'ú ts'át, kleine dieven.

ts'át tsē (*tsē*), rooversnest.

ts'át siū, do,

ts'át t'àm, dievenspion.

ts'át ts'át bák, dievenoogen,

ts'át sim ts'át hīng, als een roover.

ts'át t'aô, dievenhoofd.
ts'át k'a, onderhoorige dieven.
k'eh iá ts'át, slechter dan een roover.
ts'át tóng, dievenkomplot.
tsit hé (u) tóng ts'át (hoé), een komplot dieven.
kiep ts'át, struikroovers.
ts'át k'a lō, weg dien dieven in een huis nemen.
ts'át tsing, diefstal.
ts'át àn, rechtszaak over diefstal.
tsai iá ts'át, een dief die in huis bekend is.
ts'át tsng, gesloten goederen.
ts'át piā ts'át, elkander verklappen betichten van dieven.
soā ts'át, landdieven.
hoah ts'át, »dieven! dieven!" roepen.
tsiú ts'át, tegen dieven waken.
ts'át toā hiā, dieven breekijzer.
ke laī ts'át (ke), dief van binnen's huis.

Tse

此 Tse — *Tse*, dit.
tse taí (tse tsaí), bezinksel, bezinken droesem 2e onoverkomelijke zwarigheden in eene zaak.
tóh tse (tse), tweede aftreksel van medicijnen.
Tsé — *Tióh tse (tse)*, besmetting krijgen (van beesten).
p'ah tsit ê sa á tse hō i tsoè, een model voor een kleed knippen, om het iemand te laten maken.
姐 Tsé — *An tsé (á tsiá)*, betiteling van andermans slavin.
tsé á, betiteling voor eene slavin.

Tsé — *Tsé* dit, aldus, zoo.
債 Tsè — *Tsè (tsè)*, schuld.
k'ièm tsè, in schuld zijn.
tsè tsú, crediteur.
k'ièm tsè eh, debiteur, schuldige.
pàng tsè, op interest zetten.
tsing sì tsè (tsàng), schuld van vroegere generatie.
tsiò tsè (tsè), geld leenen.
tāng tsè, woekerwinst.
t'ó tsè, schuld invorderen.
t'ó tsè kiá, een kind dat veel gekost heeft
sa k'ièm tsè (sio), schuld bij elkander hebben (van deze of van de vorige wereld.)
moā ting tsè, schuld op afrekening na zijn vader's dood.
hing tsè, schuld betalen, vergoeden.
tsit sin k'u tsè (hin su), tot over de ooren toe in de schuld zitten.
pàng dzìk á tsè (tsè), geldleenen waarvan men dagelijks interest moet hebben.
hoe tsè (hoa tsè), schuld bij vrouwen (lichte kooien).
kiaó tsè, dobbelschuld.
tsaó tsè, voor schulden wegloopen.
pik tsè, op betaling van schuld sterk aandringen.
k'ièm hóng hing tsè, geld schuldig zijn aan een overbiddelijken schuldeischer.
獻 Tsè — *Hièn tsè*, offeren.
tsè sū, offeren.
tsè hièn, do.
tsè tang, winterofferande aan zijne voor ouders doen.
tsè saò (tsè), de graven reinigen (als op het gravenfeest).

tsè ki, aan een vlag offeren vóór den strijd.
tsè ko, aan de onverzorgde zielen offeren (ironisch voor eten gezegd).
tsè kò siào, voor zijne rekening, verantwoording nemen *i. e.* dooden, in dieventaal.

濟 Tsè *Tsín tsè (tsè)*, in tijd van hongersnood de behoeftigen helpen.
tsiu tsè, behoeftigen helpen.
put tsè sū (tsè), eene zaak die niet volbracht kan worden.

制 Tsè *Tsè tsok (tsì)*, maken doen.
tsè hoat (tsì), manier om iets te maken (medicijnen enz.)
hiêp tsè lâng (tsì), iemand treiteren door iets dwingen.
tsè ti i (tsì niû), tegenhouden, in den weg staan.
tsè iòh (tsè), medicijnen klaarmaken, mengen.
siú tsè, de gebruiken (bij rouw) in acht nemen.
in si tsè gi, de omstandigheden in aanmerking nemen.
ū hoat t'ang tsè ih, er is eene manier om het tegen te gaan.
tsé hoat bô sa tâng, de manier van behandeling is niet dezelfde.

Tsé *Si tsè*, mode, nieuw model.

Tsè *Tō tsè*, een jaar oud zijn (van kinderen.)

齊 Tsê *Tsê pī (tsê)*, geheel in orde.
tsê tsip, zich verzamelen (van soldaten).
tsê tsing, gelijkelijk.
tsê bi t'ui, stok die tot aan de wenkbrauw komt (in den strijd gebruikt).

蟬 Tsê *Am po tsê*, krekel.

這 Tsè *Tsè siah*, wat is dat!
tsè sī sim mih, wat is dat!

坐 Tsē *Teh tsē*, zitten.
ts'iū tsē, ga zitten.
tsē kiō, in een draagstoel zitten.
tsē bé ts'ia (bé), in een rijtuig rijden.
tsē ông tsē uī, op den troon zitten plaats nemen.
tsē t'i, regeeren (van den keizer).
tsē ts'ing, bezinken (als wijn).
tsē toé, bezinken.
tsē toē hun tsing (tsō tē), gestolen goederen ontvangen.
tsē taí (tsē té), bezinken.
tsē toa (ts'ē), eene wissel accepteeren.
īm tsē, eene wissel protesteeren.
tsē hiòng (tsē hiàng), ligging uitzicht van een huis.
tsē ki (ke), wacht houden.
tsē mi (mê), 's nachts blijven opzitten.
tsē siaò (ts'ē), eene schuld accepteeren.
tsē taô (tsē), de verantwoordelijkheid op zich nemen.
tsē tū, do.
tsiáh tsē, zich iets aantrekken op zich zelven toepassen.
tsē ka, in de gevangenis zitten.
tsē tùng, op den rechterstoel gaan zitten.
kap lâng lô tsē k'iā (pē), zich niet onder de menschen durven vertoonen *i. e.* beschaamd over zich zelven zijn.

t'iạ̀ k'ah tsē, de pijn is wat bedaard.
t'iạ̀ bōē tsē (*bē*), de pijn bedaart niet.
tsē t'e (*t'e*), in de baarmoeder zijn.
tsiaò ts'ù, volgens de ligging, richting van een huis.
tsē tsùn laī, tsē kiō, in een schuit, draagstoel komen.
tsē īm toà ì, geen rust op zijn stoel hebben, niet kunnen blijven zitten.
tsē giáh, zich verantwoordelijk stellen voor het geheele bedrag.
hoán tsē, de straf krijgen voor de misdaad waarvan men iemand valsch aangeklaagd heeft.
tsē tsōē de straf voor iets krijgen (bij valsche aanklachten).
tsē bé hē, het laatste uitkomen (bij een loterij).

寨 Tsē *Tsē* (*tsē̤*), fort.
ts'át tsē, rooversnest.
soạ tsē, bergfort (van roovers enz).
iạ̀ tsē, legerkamp.

Tsē *Tsē koà* (*tsē koà*), verkeerdelijk, misdadig.

吹 Ts'e *Ts'e* (*ts'oe*), waaien blazen (als de wind ook op een fluit of ander blaasinstument spelen).
ts'e siao, fluit blazen.
toā ts'e, soè ts'e, groote en klein hoboë.
hun ts'e, tabakspijp.
ts'e k'ì, wegwaaien.
ts'e pan, trommelslager, hoornblazer.
ts'e hong, in de wind droogen.
pùn ts'e, de hoboë blazen.
oe ts'e ts'iù (*e ts'oe ts'iọ̀*), viool strijken, hoboë blazen en zingen.
ts'e ts'ao (*ts'oe*), veel drukte (als bij een feest).
toā ts'e toā luī, groot blaas en ketelmuziek (als bij een huwelijk).

Ts'e *Hé ts'e*, tang.
ts'e (*ts'oe*), laten gaar smoken,
ts'e pīng (*ts'oe puī*), rijst gaar stoomen.
ts'e kè (*koè*), een koek gaar stoomen.
ts'e t'áng, kookbus.

差 Ts'e *ts'e sái* (*ts'e̤*), iemand zenden.
ts'e iáh, politie dienaar.
goān ts'e, politie dienaar.
ts'e k'ién zenden.
tsaó ts'e, koerier.
teng ts'e, ê làng, mandarijn loopers.
k'im ts'e, keizerlijke commissaris.
tsoan ts'e (*ts'e̤*), opzettelijk zenden.
ts'e īng, als bediende, boodschappenlooper gebruiken.
t'ing ts'e, wachters (bedienden die wachter tot er boodschappen te doen zijn).

叉 Ts'e *Sạ ts'e hô* (*ts'e̤*), eene in drieën vertakte rivier.
ts'e á, droogvork staak braadvork.
sip dzī ts'e (*ts'e̤*) *lọ̄*, kruisweg.
siang ts'e lọ̄ (*ts'e̤*), een in tweeën vertakte weg.
p'oà ts'e, aan de uiteinden in tweeën gespleten.
p'oat ts'e (*ts'ē*), doorschrappen.
kap i p'oah ts'e, met iemand kwade vrienden zijn.
tùi nạ̀ aò kíng ts'e teh, iemand met een vork tegen de keel stooten *i. e.* op het oogenblik dat iemand iets wil gaan zeggen hem zijn mond doen houden.

Ts'e *Tit tioh ts'e ka tsai* (*goā ke̤*), eene rijke vrouw huwen.

86

Ts‘e *Pàng hong ts‘e*, een vlieger oplaten.

髓 Ts‘é *Ts‘é* (*ts‘oé*), merg.

gû kut ts‘é (*t‘aò k‘ak oén ts‘é*), koemerg.

suh làng huih ts‘é (*soh* (*hoeh ts‘oé*), iemand uitmergelen, geld afzetten.

t‘aò k‘ak ts‘é, hersenen.

tsiáh si làng t‘aò k‘ak oa̤ ts‘é, de hersens van een lijk eten *i. e.* niet terugdeinzen voor de manier waarop men aan geld komt.

bé ts‘é (*ts‘oé*), zeer fijngestampte rijst.

péh-kaò ki̤ ts‘é (*pe̤h*) (*ts‘oé*), zeer wit (van rijst).

ìing koa̤ hōng ts‘é, drakenhart en phoeniksmerg *i. e.* allerzeldzaamst lekker eten.

諫 Ts‘é *Ts‘é ts‘é kiò* (*ts‘e̤h ts‘e̤h kiò*), kijven (van vrouwen).

Ts‘é *Sa̤ ts‘é ts‘iú* (*o*), de handen zamen vrouwen.

p‘ah ts‘é (»), een kruisband om iets leggen (?).

ts‘é kat; *p‘ah ts‘é kat* (»), een strik leggen

ts‘é lai ts‘é k‘ì, de een uitstekende de ander inspringende, de een (dag) meer de ander minder, gemiddeld.

sa̤ tò ts‘é (*sio*), om den ander uitstekend en inspringend.

ts‘é lìaō (*laō*), stuurman aan een vlieger.

bé soh ts‘é k‘ì lai, de leidstels ophouden.

k‘icn ts‘é k‘ì, door elkander gerekend.

脆 Ts‘è *Ts‘è* (»), broos breekbaar ook van's menschen broze leven gezegd.

ts‘è, droog (van vleesch).

ts‘è nga̤ñ nga̤ñ ts‘è sap sap, zeer broos.

tsûn sin ts‘è, het schip is rank.

ts‘i̤ ts‘è (*ts‘e̤ ts‘è*), eensklaps onverwachts.

ts‘ang ts‘è, do. (als een donderslag).

kóng oē put tsi ts‘ang ts‘è (*on̄*), plotseling eensklaps spreken.

lui ts‘è, de donder knettert.

Ts‘è *It ts‘è* (*ts‘iet*), geheel en al.

厠 Ts‘è *Ts‘è ti* (*ts‘e̤*), sekreet, No. 100

k‘û ts‘è (*tsio̤ñ ts‘e̤*), op het sekreet zitten

lóh ts‘è, do.

sai ts‘è, sekreet.

Ts‘è *P‘oà ts‘è* (*ts‘e̤*), gebroken — gebarsten en uit elkander gerafeld.

p‘oà ts‘è sia̤, geluid van gebarsten goed 2e krassend schel geluid.

Ts‘è *Ts‘è á* (*ts‘oè*), roede.

kiò koa̤ ts‘è, hevig onder de mandarijn roede schreeuwen *i. e.* zich erg beklagen wanneer er nog geen reden voor is.

hé ts‘è (*hoé ts‘oè*), pook.

尋 Ts‘è *Ts‘ē* (*ts‘oē*), zoeken.

ts‘ē k‘oa̤, opzoeken, zoeken naar.

ts‘ē tióh, vinden.

ts‘ē i t‘ó, van hem invorderen (schuld).

ts‘ē t‘aò sū (*sī*), eene zaak ontwarren.

sio ts‘ē (*sa̤*), elkander komen bezoeken.

ts‘iao ts‘ē (» *ts‘oē*), alle hoekjes en gaatjes doorzoeken.

ts‘ē bú (*o*), de krijger (bij het krijgertje spelen).

ts‘ē bô (*ts‘oē bô*) *ts‘ē īm kì* }, niet vindeu.

ts‘ē dzít, een gelukkigen dag uitkiezen.

bih (of) *tiàm sa ts‘ē* (*sio tièn ts‘oē*) }, wegkruipertje spelen.

ts‘ē k‘ang ts‘ē p‘ūng, een gat zoeken

ts‘ē siaò-k‘oà, een post, rekening opzoeken.

tsit lâng k‘ìng pah lâng ts‘ē, naar wat één man weggestopt heeft, moeten honderd zoeken.

pé ts‘ē, zoeken in alle hoekjes en gaatjes rondzoeken.

ts‘ē bê toē dzī ê, er is geen tweede zoo te vinden, eenig in zijn soórt, goed of slecht.

ts‘ē bô pún, zijn kapitaal, inkoop prijs niet van iets kunnen krijgen.

ts‘ē k‘an, met het lombard briefje het pand zoeken.

nā ū siá sū tsiah lai ts‘ē goàh, als er het een of ander is kom er mij dan over zoeken—spreken.

Ts‘ē *Ts‘ē ts‘ē haó*, ruischen als een bergstroom.

Ts‘ē ts‘ē laô, bij stroomen vloeien.

Tseh

仄 Tseh *Tseh* (*tseh*) }, de tonen met uitzondering der gelijken.

ho piâ tseh, de gelijke en de niet gelijke tonen opnoemen.

Tseh *Tseh* (*tseh*) }, opnemen (met een doek) (maar niet wrijven), betten.

Tseh *Tseh taī tsì* voor *tsit ê taī tsì* (*o*) }, deze zaak—dit.

tseh sìgh, wat is dat? verwondering.

Tseh *K‘ah t‘ing tseh*, wacht eens even.

k‘ah būn tseh, wat langzamer.

Tseh *Lap tseh lap tseh* (*tseh*) (*tseh*) }, slordig in kleeding van vrouwen.

laò tseh (*tseh*), slordig slonzig.

Tseh *Bák kiáh tseh*, hak van een vrouwenschoen.

絶 *Tséh*, uitgestorven van eene familie.

Tseh *tsèh kiá biét sun* (*tsoát tsú haī sun*) }, moogt gij geene nakomelingen hebben (scheldwoord).

si tséh (*tsóh*) }, moge uwe familie uitsterven.

tséh sam taī (*taī*) }, mogen 3 generaties uitsterven (scheldwoord).

tsèh aō taī (*tē*) }, mogen uwe volgende generaties uitsterven.

tséh tsing, geheel uit- of afgestorven (van familie en gewassen).

ko kút tséh tsing, alleen in de wereld en zijne geheele familie uitgestorven (scheldwoord).

書 Ts‘eh *Ts‘eh* (*ts‘eh*) }, boek.

ts‘eh pī, rug van een boek.

ts‘eh k‘a, onderkant van een boek.

ts‘eh t‘aô, bovenkant » » »

t‘ák ts‘eh, studeeren (hardop lezen).

k‘oà ts‘eh, lezen, een boek doorkijken zonder hardop te lezen.

liām ts‘eh, uit het hoofd opzeggen.

kó ts‘eh (*ts‘eh*) }, novellen.

poā ts‘ia sin ts‘eh á kú láh dzít, oude koeien uit de sloot halen.

tsō ts‘eh (*ts‘eh* }, in een boek opteekenen opschrijven.

póh ts‘eh á, dunne gemeene lijkkist.

t'ák si ts'eh (*ts'eh*), zich dom weg onveranderlijk aan de boeken houden.
ts'eh iép kim (*ts'eh iáh kim*), goudblad dat tusschen de bladen van een boek wordt uit gesmokkeld.
oé ts'eh (*o*), boek met patronen om schoenen te borduren.
k'oà ts'eh á, het boekje raadplegen waarin voor elken dag middelen voor kinderziekten worden gegeven.
haō peh ts'eh, zonneblinden, jaloeziën.

歠 Ts'eh — *Ts'eh* (*ts'oeh*), slurpen, opslurpen.
ts'eh t'eng, lepelkost opslurpen.
iā īm līm t'eng iā īm ts'eh tsiep, noch soep drinken noch sap opslurpen *i. e.* noch ja noch neen zeggen.

吸 Ts'eh — *Ts'eh k'ùi* (*ts'eh*), snikken.

Ts'eh — *loān ts'eh ts'eh* (*ts'eh ts'eh*), zeer verward (als de toestand van een rijk enz).

下 Ts'èh — *Ts'éh* (*ts'ē*), neèrhangen van een voorwerp verzakken.
ts'éh lóh k'ì, neèrzakken.
kè tsi k'ah ts'éh (*kè*) (*ts'éh*), de prijs is wat gedaald.
pī- tsit dzit tit tit ts'éh lóh k'ì (*pē*) (*ts'éh*), dagelijks erger worden van eene ziekte.
laò ts'éh, achteruitgang (als handel) 2e slordig.
sing li ts'éh lóh k'ì, achteruitgaan (van handel).

Ts'èh — *Tsi- ts'eh ts'éh háo*, het geld klettert (geluid van geldtellen).
oà p'ièt ts'i ts'i ts'éh ts'éh, gekletter gerammel van kommen en borden.

Tseng

莊 *Tseng*, familienaam.

裝 Tseng — *Tseng* (»), 1e bevatten 2e in kisten pakken.
tseng tsoè (*tsò*), namaken, 2e den schijn aannemen.
tseng i é siōng (*ts'iāng*), een aarden standbeeld van iemand maken.
tseng làng, een verkleede optocht houden.
tsit tseng hè (*tsong hoè*), eene hoeveelheid koopwaren.
sim mih tseng t'aò (*sám má*) (*tseg*) *t'aò*, wat soort van waren?
tseng hè (*hoè*), goederen inpakken.
tseng pùt (*ang*), afgodsbeelden maken.
tseng siōng (*tsūng*), bustes standbeelden maken.
tseng kim sin, een beeld van goud (of verguld) maken.
īn háp tseng, artikelen die niet voor de plaats of het volk tot verkoopen geschikt zijn.
tseng siong; een wond namaken.
tseng koh, bij eene processie op eene stellaadje rondgedragen worden, bij het koedah koedah feest op Java.

粧 Tseng — *Soe tseng* (*se*), garneeren, omzetten met, verkleeden, zijn toilet maken (van vrouwen.
tseng t'é biēn, zich voor doen als, er doekjes omwinden, pronken met het goed van anderen, groot van zich opgeven. den schijn van fatsoenlijk aannemen.

tsɛng t'á̱ (*tsɛ̀ng*), iets opheffen om het te laten zien.

tsɛng t'ṉ̄, zich opsmukken.

kè tsɛng (*kè̱*), uitzet bij een huwelijk.

tsɛng liêm, do.

t'ièm tsɛng, huwelijksgeschenken geven.

kiém tsɛng siy, doos waarin de bruidsgeschenken zijn.

磚 Tseng *Tsɛng* (*tsui̱*), vloersteen.

tsɛng pi̱ (*tsui pe̱*), geplaveid vlak op een huis.

tsɛng á hoe (*hoa*), groote blokken, ruiten.

tsɛng t'ṉ̱ hún piàh (*o*), binnen's huis fraai.

tsɛng hiā tsɛng p'iáh hiā (*tsúi̱*), steenen en pannen.

gūn tsi tsɛng, lange smalle steenen.

sṉ̱ kak tsɛng táh bē ū tsit kak tióh, nog niet op een hoek van een drie hoekige vloersteen staan *i. e.* op eene plaats nog niet geregeld gevestigd zijn.

tsɛng á t'aò (*tsui̱*), stukjes steen.

tsɛng soá tsioh, van steenen op rotsen komen (*i. e.* van kwaad tot erger komen).

庄 Tsɛng *Tsɛng ke* (» *ke̱*), eigenaar eener landhoeve.

tsi̱ tsɛng, wisselkantoor.

tsɛng, vlek gehucht.

tsɛng k'eh, kooplieden die in een gehucht gevestigd zijn.

贓 Tseng *Ts'át tsɛng* (»), gestolen goederen.

tsà tsɛng (*tsè̱*), geld afzetteu.

tui tsɛng, gesloten goederen zien terug te krijgen.

tsɛng tsìng (*tsìn*), bewijs in de gestolen goederen.

tsiū tsɛng kìu tō, door de gestolene goederen op het spoor der dieven komen.

Tsíng *Tsíng t'aò á* (*tsing*), vinger.

tsíng kah, nagels van de vingers.

k'a tsíng t'aò á, teen, toon.

鑽 Tsìng *Tsìng* (*tsùi̱*), boren.

tsìng á, priem, els, boor.

lak tsìng, drilboor.

tsìng teh (*tsùi̱*), zich verstoppen (als een muis in een gat).

tsìng sio, zich voor de warmte onder de dekens stoppen.

kiṉ̱ kaò bò k'ang t'ang tsìng dzìp k'ì, in uiterste benaauwdheid zijn.

t'iṉ̱-kao tsìng kut, tot in het been door dringend van pijn.

ui ui tsìng (*oe oe*), doorborend- indringend (van pijn).

tsìng k'aò kè k'ì, doorgeboord hebben.

lién tsìng inboren.

pi̱ tsìng (*pe̱*), boor met platte punt.

tsiem tsìng ê lâng, een man als een naald of boor *i. e.* iemand die in alles wat ziet te vinden.

ui tsiem tsìng soṉ̱, de naald doorsteken en het garen doorhalen *i. e.* hard vrouwen handwerk te doen hebben.

gaò nìng tsìng, behendig inkruipen *i. e.* bij de minste gelegenheid geld zien te maken.

sì koè tsìng, overal in en door kruipen (als kinderen, honden in een gedrang).

全 Tsìng *Tsìng dzièn*, volstrekt geheelen al.

tsiao tsìng (*tsui̱*), volledig kompleet.

tsè tsìng (*tsui̱*), volledig volkomen.

kɛng tsìng, volkomen kompleet gaaf (niet gebroken).

pah kāng tsēng (*pe̤h*) }, geheel volledig.
bô tsing iā tiòh pō̤, is het niet alles dan toch ten minste de helft (af betalen geven enz).
tsing ke, het geheele huisgezin.
tsing dzít tsing géh tsing ni̤, geheele dag maand jaar.
tsúp tsing, volledig zich in alle richtingen uitstrekkende (als bekwaamheden.)

從 Tsing *Tsing t'aô* (*ting*) }, van voren af aan op nieuw.
tsing sin tsoè (*ting tsò*) }, » » doen.

鑽 Tsing *Kaó lai teh tsing* (») }, de hond snuffelt rond, beruikt de lieden.
tsing tsak (*tsing*) }, rondsnuffelen ook aan menschen bet: lastig vallen.
boē k'am til ì tsing (*bē*) (*tsing*) }, op zijn onophoudelijk vragen smeeken toegeven.

螺 Tsīng *Tsīng* (*tsui̤*) }, hoofdkruin.
kíng níng tsīng (*kṳi nuí tsui̤*) }, draaien (als een draaikolk).
siang é tsīng, dubbele kringen op de hoofdkruin.

狀 *Tsīng* (») }, schriftelijke aanklacht, protest.
tsīng su, advokaat.
kò tsīng, aanklagen.
dzip tsīng (*tiḡ*) }, eene aanklachte inleveren.
tsīng tsoá (*tsīng*) }, schriftelijke aanklachte 2e papier voor aanklachten.
kò gū tsīng (*gi̤*) }, eene aanklachte bij den keizer doen.

Tsīng *Pa lun tsīng tsih* (*laó tsui̤*) }, op de lip zuigen en smekken.

p'iet hō̤ kaó tsīng, de borden aan den hond geven om aftelikken.
tsim kah tsīng
tsim tsim tsīng tsīng }, kussen en likken (als eene moeder haar kind).
tsīng ling, de borst aflikken (als een kind dat de borst gehad heeft).

Tsīng *Tsīng tī si* (*tsīng*) }, wanneer? op welken tijd van wanneer af?
tsīng t'aô kaò bé (*tsū » » boé*) }, van begin tot eind.
tsīng t'aô kóng (*tsiaò*) }, van voren af aan zeggen.
tsīng tsá (*tsīng*) }, van ouds af.

臟 Tsīng *Sió tsīng*, de ingewanden in de onder buik.

艙 Ts'ɛng *Ts'ɛng* (») }, het ruim (in een schip)..
k'ui ts'ɛng, de luiken openen (ontzegelen van een schip).
koá ts'ɛng k'do (») }, het hoofd over de luiken — over de lading.
tsùn ts'ɛng, ruim van een schip.
hong ts'ɛng, de luiken verzegelen.
tsui ts'ɛng, waterruim, ketel (aan boord van Chin. schepen).

Ts'ɛng *Ts'ɛng, hiu ts'ɛng* (») (*hiu* ») }, dorp vlek
ts'ɛng hàn (*ts'ùi*) }, ongemanierd, onbeschoft mensch.
ts'ɛng lâng (*ts'ui̤*) }, onbeschaafd mensch.
ts'ɛng t'ào ts'ɛng bīn (*ts'ui̤*) (*ts'ui̤*) }, een gemeen laag uiterlijk.
ts'ɛng ang ts'ɛng pò, een onbeschaafd echt paar.
ts'ɛng k'ì, boersch dorpsch lomp.

倉 Ts'ɛng *Bi ts'ɛng* (») }, graanpakhuis..

ts'ik ts'eng, do.

ts'eng k'o̤, graanpakhuizen en schat kamers.

gī ts'eng, publiek graanpakhuis.

ts'eng bi, graan uit de graanpakhuizen.

kaoh ts'eng bī, lucht van goederen die lang in een pakhuis of een schip geweest zijn.

屁 Ts'eng *K'a ts'eng* (*ts'ui*), fondament aars.

穿 Ts'eng *Ts'eng tsiem* (*ts'ui*), draad in de naald steken.

ts'eng soa̤, do.

tsiù ts'eng (*ts'ui*), doorgevreten van insekten.

ts'eng soa dzip tsióh (*ts'ui*), in bergen en in steenen gaan *i. e.* voor geene moeijelijkheden terugdeinzen.

ts'eng kun (*ts'ui kin*), wortels uitschieten.

瘡 Ts'eng *Ts'eng* (»), zweer.

tī ts'eng, aanbeien.

si ts'eng (*se* (»)), veneerische zweren hebben.

pán tseng, zweer op de bil.

伸 Ts'eng *Ts'eng ts'iú* (*ts'un*), de hand in iets steken.

ts'eng ting ts'iú (*ts'an*), de hand uitsteken (als bedelaars).

嚼 Ts'ing *Ts'ing kut* (*ts'ui*), beentjes kluiven.

tsiáh p'ui ts'ing kut, een wind eten en op de beentjes kluiven *i. e.* op alles aanmerking maken.

ts'ing koe tsí, meloenpitten kraken.

ts'ing p'ī (*ts'euh*), de neus ophalen.

tsing ts'ing, de neus snuiten.

Ts'ing *Ts'ing ts'iah* (*ts'ui*), rondsnuffelen op alle mogelijke manieren voordeel bejagen onvermoeid op iets uit zijn.

ts'ing k'ang ts'ing p'āng, een gat op iets zoeken.

beh k'ì ts'ing lâng, een gat gaan zoeken om geld uit iemand te krijgen.

貫 Ts'ing *Ts'ing* (*kui*), numerale voor paarlen en dingen aanritsen.

sa ts'ing (*kui*), aan elkander rijgen.

ts'ing ning tsoè tsit ē (*kui nui tsò ē*), aan elkander rijgen.

ts'ing tiaò (*kui*), aanrijgen, op iets rijgen.

ts'ing kè k'ì (*kui koè*), doorboren.

tsit ts'ing è tsu (*kui*), een rits paarlen.

ts'ing tsi, duiten aanrijgen.

Ts'ing *Ts'ing* (*ts'oàu*), steken op (als een hoofd op een paal).

床 Ts'ing *Bin ts'ing* (»), bed.

ts'ing á, wieg.

bin ts'ing tièm, schrijnwerkers winkel.

k'ong ts'ing (*k'ang*), gasten plaats.

sien ts'ing, canapé.

ts'ing kuī, bed met een vaste geldkist er onder.

k'ùn ts'ing, bed.

tók suī ts'ing (*sui*), bed voor één persoon.

toā ts'ing, groot bed.

poeh k'a bin ts'ing (*peh*), bed op 8 pooten dubbel bed.

k'àng ts'ing, gastenbank 2e vuurbed (waaronder gestookt kan worden).

tó ts'ing (*tó toà ts'ing*), bedlegerig zijn (van ziekte).

tiaò ts'ing, hangmat.

ts'ing p'o̤, reisbed.

tsiū ts'ing (*tsiō*), naar of in bed gaan.
hat tiáu ts'ing (*hoat*), springbed.
loh ts'ing k'a, opstaan ('s morgens).
an ts'ing, het huwelijksbed neêrzetten.
ts'ing t'aó p'ah-ts'ing bé hō (*boé hō*), twisten tusschen man en vrouw zijn spoedig bijgelegd.
pē ts'ing k'àng ts'ioh (*pē*), in bed liggen. kruipen van de pijn.
sio sin ts'ing, tsoè sin ts'ing (*o*) (*o*), op den 3den of 4den dag van het jaar aan overledenen offeren die gedurende het afgeloopen jaar gestorven zijn.

Tsi

枝 Tsi *Naī tsi* (*léh*), de *lai tsi* vrucht. Dimocarpus laitsi.
tsi tsiet, si ts'uh tsi tsiet (*sē*), ontstaan voor den dag komen van bijomstandigheden.

脂 Tsi *Ien tsi*, blanketsel.

Tsi *Tsai tsi taī*, van alles afweten-over alles meêpraten.
ts'aò tsi bai, *hiaò tsi*, scheldw. tegen vrouwen.
tsi ī, de clitoris (lagevolksterm).
tsi kui, glad geslepen sluw.
ké tsi tsiq, schijn van zeer geslepen aannemen.

支 *Tsi tsī*, geld gaan ontvangen.
tsi ts'ī, het roer van eene zaak in handen hebben.
tók lik lân tsi, één alleen is daar tegen niet bestand, niet opgewassen.
tsi lī, tsi tsi lī lī, met vele bijkomende omstandigheden moeielijkheden.
tsi lī beredderen (eene zaak).
hun tsi ts'ut lai, vertakkingen vormen (als eene familie).

肢 Tsi *Sù tsi*, armen beenen.

之 Tsi *Tsi*, genitief en adject partikel.

芝 Tsi *Lien tsi ts'ó*, paddestoel Boletus (voor geluk aanbrengend gehouden).

Tsi *Tsi tsi tsiuh tsiuh*, piepen van muizen.

指 Tsi *Tsi*, aanduiden, doelen op (pers. of zaken). te kennen geven.
tsi tiém, do.
tsi sī, uitduiden, aanduiden.
tsi miā tsi sī (*sè*), met naam en voornaam aanduiden.
tit tit tsi ih, rechtstreeks op iemand wijzen duiden.
ts'iú tsi (*tsai*), vingerring.
tsi bing, duidelijk uitduiden doelen op.
tsi kaò, uitduiden uitleggen verklaren.

子 Tsi *Ké tsi* (*koé*), vrucht.
tò tsi, gewrichten.
lâh tsi, kastanjes.
tsing tsi, zaad.
hi tsi, kuit van visch.
kiet tsi, vrucht zetten (van planten).
p'áh bé tsi (*bé*), verkorte cijfers zetten.
ts'aó á tsi, klit, klissen.
sat bú tsi luizen eieren.

止 Tsi *Tsi k'oah*, den dorst stillen.
tsi tsi tsiáoh tsiáoh (*tsi tsi tsuoh tsuoh*), smekken.
tsū tsi, zich nederzetten te ..., wonen t .
tsi pū, stilstaan, halthouden.
put tsi, zeer....
kìm tsi, verhinderen tegengaan.
tsi k'at, dorst lesschen.
tsi ki, honger stillen.

tsi tiên, hijpotheek aflossen.
tsò tsí, tegengaan, verhinderen.
dzū tsí (*dzī*) }, verbiedend tegengaan.
tsí huih (*hoeh*) }, bloedverlies stoppen.
bô ti tsí (*té*) }, onbegrensd-onbepaald (als winst enz).
tsí t'iâ, de pijn doen ophouden (als medic.)

紫 Tsí *Tsí king* (» ») }, een boom met scharlaken roode bloemen.
tsi sik, nanking kleur.
tsí hoe pò, nanking stof.
o tsi lo, bont en blaauw (geslagen).

此 Tsí *Tsí tao*, hier.

姊 Toā *Toā tsí*, oudere zuster.
tsi hu, zwager (oudere zuster's man).

只 Tsi *Tsi tit* (*tsi sī*) }, het kan niet anders of....
tsí koán (*tsí*) }, niets anders doen dan....
tsí hó (») }, wanneer slechts.
lâo (en) *liâo t'ui tsi* (*lob*) }, sporten van een ladder- trap.
t'ang á tsi, venstersbouten.
soe bák tsi, dichte tralies, uit gesneden traliewerk.
tiâ ts'â tsi, houtsprokjes branden (als arme lieden).
tsit tsi ê hiu ts'aò, een bundeltje welriekende planten.
tsit tsi ê dziông, een bundeltje, strengetje vloszijde.

址 Tsi *Kai tsi*, grensmerk.
tsō tsi, woonplaats.

siá tsō tsi, het adres (op een brief) schrijven.

Tsí *Tsi i*, keizerlijke wil-bevel.
sìng tsi, keizerlijk bevel.
kàng tsi, een bevel afvaardigen (van den keizer gezegd).

Tsí *Tsiem tsi*, naaldenwerk.

咫 Tsí *Tsi ts'ik kan* (*tsi ts'ik tsi tē*) }, zeer dichtbij.

至 Tsì *Tsì kik*, uiterst, zeer.
tsì hó, uiterst goed.
tsì u ... (*i*) }, wat aangaat ..., met betrekking tot.
tang tsì, wintersolstitium.
hē tsì, zomersolstitium.

贄 Tsì *Tsì kien*, visitegeld (voor een doktor).

志 Tsì *Sit tsì*, iets opgeven, niet meer aan iets denken.
loé tsì, beschaamd- neergedrukt zijn.
tsì k'ì, de wil.
ū tsì k'ì ê lâng, iemand die eergevoel naijver bezit.
tip tsì, het er opgezet hebben om,
sim tsì, bedooling, verlangen.
ū tsì k'ì, ondernemingsgezind.
bô tsì k'ì, dom bekrompen (van geest).

Tsì *I tsì* vuil, smerig.

Tsì *Taī tsì*, zaak.

志 Tsì *Koaī tsì*, de annalen van een *hiēn*.
sing tsì, annalen, beschrijving- geschiedenis eener provincie.

泥 Tsí *He tsi* (*hoe*) }, harde metselkalk *chunam*.
tsing oâ tsi, pleisterkalk met kopjesscherven fijnstampen.
t'ô bé tsi (*moai*) }, modderige aarde.

蹄 Tsí *Bé tsi* (*boé tsi*) }, kastanje Aesculus hippocastanum.

Tsi *Moâ tsi*, koekjes van fijne rijst met hennep er in (ook voor vulva gebruikt).
moâ tsi he, kalk met gestampte rijst en hennep.
ts'uì p'oé laò tsi, de wangen uitgezakt als een rijstkoekje.
aì tsiah tsi á ké ê, veel van koek, zoetigheid houden.

舐 Tsī *Tsī*, likken, aflikken.
tsit pù sai tsī boē ta, een hoop mest niet schoon kunnen oplikken *i. e.* eene zaak niet tot het eind toe kunnen volbrengen.
tsim tsim tsī tsī, kussen en likken (als eene moeder haar kind).

Tsī *Tsī bú tsī tsū* (*pú*), fluisteren.

Tsī *Tsī tsuī*, wie?
tsī tsuī á, do.
tsī » lâng, do.
ì īm sī goá ê tsī tsūi, hij gaat mij niet aan, ik heb niets met hem te maken.

巳 Tsī *Tsī si*, 9—11 uur 's morgens.

揵 Tsi̧ *Tsi̧*, wig, inwiggen, indrijven met geweld.
sai t'aô tsi̧ (*o*), met het hoofd stompen.
sai k'a tsi̧ t'at (*o*), een schop geven.
tsi̧ iù, olie slaan, persen.
tsi̧ àn, vast inslaan, stevig aandrijven 2e sterk aandringen op.
ts'à tsi̧, houten wig, kloof.
tsát tsi̧, hard (als aardappelen, als kluiten veeren in een matras).
īng ts'â tsi̧ tsi̧ pit, met een houten wig stukkloven.
tsi̧ lai kìn, stevig aanhalen, sterk op (geld) aandringen.
toā tè tsióh t'aô tsi̧ k'ì lai, een groot stuk rots doen spingen.

晶 Tsi̧ *Tsui tsi̧*, kristal.
tsui tsi̧ bák (»), doorschijnende heldere oogen.

凈 Tsi̧ *Tsi̧ tsui*, uitwasschen.

氈 Tsi̧ *Tsi̧ tiaò* karpet, beddesprei.
tsi̧ bō, muts (groote vilten).
iù tsi̧ oê (*ê*), geöliede vilten schoenen.
t'aô ming tsiâ tsi̧, het hoofdhaar verward in een klit (als gevangenen die zich in lang niet gekamd hebben).

揪 Tsi̧ *Tsi̧ hi̧ á* (»), bij de ooren trekken.

爭 Tsi̧ *Sa tsi̧* (*sio tsȩ*), twisten, wedijveren om strijd.

精 Tsi̧ *Iao tsi̧* (*tsiâ*), duivel, sater.
sik kaò ná tsi̧ nih (*tsùn tsiâ*), glad als een geest.
tsùâ tsi̧ (*tsiâ*), glad als een aal.
kui tsi̧ (*tsiâ*), slim glad.
tsiáo tsi̧ (*o*), listig, vol streken.
iao tsi̧ kui kouì, sluw vol streken.
k'ièm nn̄g ê kak tsiâ tsi̧, er ontbreken hem slechts twee hoorns om een duivel, sater te zijn *d. e.* zeer sluw.
tsi̧ tsi̧ tsi̧, zeer glad sluw 2e sterk vast in elkander gewerkt (als een karpet).

Tsi̧ *Tsī á* (*kap* (*tsi̧*)), duif.

Tsi̧ *Ké tsi̧ tsiáo* (*ké tsi̧* »), doen als of men geen kennis van iets had.
tsi̧ (»), kinderachtig (niet degelijk), jeugdig.
iù tsi̧ (»), jong, tenger, teeder.
tsi̧ ts'ioh, tenger, jeugdig, zwak.
k'uì lát tsi̧, jeugdige kracht *i. e.* spoedig afgemat.
tsi̧ tsi̧ tsi̧, jong, nog niet rijp (van vruchten).

tsi kiu, jonge gember (waarvan gemberbier gemaakt wordt).

井 Tsi — *Hé tsi* (*hoé tsè*), vuur brandput.

t'i tsi (*tsè*), lantaarn, dakraam.

tsi tsui (*tsè*), putwater.

tsi poâ (*o*), rand om een put.

tsui tsi, put.

kó tsi (*tsè*), do.

sò tsi kolk vuilnisput.

tsi noâ, omheining om een put.

k'ui tsi (*tsè*), een put graven.

tó tsi, een put uitbaggeren, schoonmaken.

箭 Tsì — *Tsì* (»), pijl.

hé tsì (*hoè*), vuurpijl.

tsì tē pijlkoker.

ts'iù tsì, werpspies.

tsì koai (*koý*), stok van een pijl, pijlstok.

tsì t'aô, *tsì bah* (*pe*), punt van een pijl.

pō tsì, pijlinfanterie.

bé tsì (*bē*), pijlcavalerie.

huih tsì, bloedstraal.

sai àm tsì, heimelijk benadeelen.

sai bák tsì, oogpijlen, lonkjes geven (tegen vrouwen enz.)

tsì ling, pijlstaart, veeren van een pijl.

tsì tō, boogschutterij, boogschuttersplein.

t'ó bah tsì, uitgroeien van nieuw vleesch na een wond.

tsit tsì tsiū tiòng pé, in een pijlschot het doel treffen *i. e.* de spijker op den kop staan.

諍 Tsì — *Sa tsì* (*sio tsè*), redetwisten.

tsng bin tsì (*tsè*), in iemands gezicht ontkennen heeten liegen.

si tsì oâh tsì (*tsè*), iemand brutaal voor liegen.

煎 Tsì — *Tsì* (»), in de olie bakken.

tsì iû, vetsmelten.

hoan tsû tsì (*tsi*), door het vet gehaalde aardappelen.

增 Tsì — *Tsì*, vergrooten, een stuk zetten in.

tsì k'ah k'oah, een stuk inzetten, wijder ruimer maken.

tsì k'ò k'a, een stuk aan de broekspijpen zetten om ze langer of wijder te maken.

掙 Tsì — *Tsì*, stoppen in.

kiông kiông tsì hū i tsiáh, met geweld in de mond duwen en laten eten.

tsì t'ih sai kui, een krop vol gestopt met ijzervijlsel (als van kippen om ze zwaarder te doen wegen).

tsì ts'ut lai kóng, invallen en iets zeggen.

tsì ts'ùi tsì tsih, de mond overal in steken.

錢 Tsî — *Tsî*, geld 2e familienaam 3e een gewicht, $^1/_{10}$ van een tail of chineesch once.

tsî gûn (*gin*), geld.

tsit tiao tsî, eene rist chineesche centen.

pún tsî, kapitaal.

laī tsî, interest.

bô tsî, arm.

tsî gûn tiâm (*gin*), geldwisselhuis.

tsî kik (*kiok*), munt.

tsî p'iò, bonnetje voor kopergeld.

tsî tâng, spaarpot.

tsî ts'á, oorspronkelijk papieren geld thans voor geld in het algemeen.

kang tsî, loon.

tsi̤ ts'ú (*tsi̤ ts'í*), geldrat.

tsi̤ ts'ú bák (*ts'í*), klein van oogen.

tsi̤ poeh á (*peh*), kwart dollar.

oā tsi̤ tièm, geldwisselhnis.

t'àn tsi̤ (*tsi̤*), geld verdienen.

háp tsi̤ t'àn, 100°/₀ verdienen.

káh gai tsi̤, slechte duiten instoppen.

tsi̤ kìng (*lūi*), duitenkoord, touw.

tsi tsai, geld, schatten.

pé tsi̤ kìng t'aô (*pe̤ kui̤*), de knoop van een rist duiten verdedigen *i. e.* goed op het geld passen.

tâng tsi̤, koperen duiten.

tsi nió (*nió*), belasting, soldij, fourage voor soldaten.

tsi bé (*boé*), het weinige overschietende geld.

siaò tsi̤ (*suì*), geld, duiten aftellen.

tsi̤ tsò, duitengleuf waarin men afgetelde duiten neêrlegt.

saí tsi̤ k'a. iemand die veel geld verbruikt.

gaò iṳ̀ tsi̤, (*o*), veel geld verbruiken.

nìng tsi̤ k'ang (*nui̤*), door het gat van een duit kruipen *i. e.* geldzuchtig zijn.

sìng tsi̤ siq (*sui̤*), volgens de waarde van de duit.

bák kim tsi̤ tsoè lâng (*tsò*), tegenwoordig maakt geld den man.

tsaī tsi̤, vrachtgeld 2e geld bij iemand hebben staan.

bú tsi̤ (*bó*), kapitaal, geleend geld (tegenover de interest).

Tsi̤ *Nī tsi̤* („), rand van het dak; goot.

Tsi̤ *Hō tsi̤* (*tse̤*), de regen houdt op.

pò̤ tsi̤ pò̤ im o̤ (*tse̤*), ongestadig weêr, nu eens regen een oogenblik later zonneschijn.

t'i̤ tsi̤ (*tsi̤*), de hemel klaart op (de regen is over).

靜 Tsī *Tsī* (*tsē*), stil (niet meer huilen van kinderen) bedaard (van de wind.)

tsī hong, *hong tsī* (*tsē*), de wind is gaan liggen.

háo tsī lah, opgehouden hebben met schreien.

ts'ù iáo kú īm tsī (of *tsīng*), houdt ge uw mond nog niet?

si īm tsī. nooit ophouden (met schreien).

tiēm tsī, bedaard, stil (van aard).

ki̤ ts'im tsip tsi̤ (of *tsīng*), diep in den nacht is het doodstil.

k'ùn tsī tsī (*tsīng tsīng*), alles in diepe rust.

àm tsī (*tsē*), stilletjes heimelijk.

àm tsoé tsi̤ (*tsò*), do.

t'iṳ̀ tsī boē, niet ophouden van pijn (scheldt).

腮 Ts'i *Hi ts'i*, kieuwen.

gê tsò ts'i (*ge̤*), uiteinden van de kaak.

sò ts'i (*ts'iu*), slot van een deur.

ts'iò kaò lī ts'i („), zich het kakebeen uit het gewricht lachen.

k'ah á ts'i, deksel van een vischkorf.

lim tê lim kaò bī ts'i, zooveel thee drinken dat men er zich in verslikt let'. dat het de kieuwen in loopt! (als iemand die duikende water inneemt).

Ts'i *Ts'i tien*, suf van studeeren enz.

ts'i tai, *ts'i gai*, *ts'i gōng*, *ts'i tsoat*, dom.

ts'i lóh k'ì, domweg vurig naar iets verlangen.

Ts'i *Ts'am ts'i*, verward door elkander.

Ts'i *Lóh tiá ts'i tsit eh* (eig. *e*), sissen zoodra het in de pan komt.

Ts'i *Ts'iet ts'i*, tandenknarsen (van woede).

刺 Ts,ì *Ts'ì*, stooten met een wapen, prikken, steken.

ts'ì ts'ák, doorsteken.

ts'ì k'ik, sluipmoordenaar, een sluip moord begaan.

ts'ì, angel.

tsít ki ts'ì, een doorn (een gevaarlijk persoon op eene plaats!

ts'ì á ts'iū, doornstruik.

ts'ì koe (*koa*), komkommer.

ts'ì nâ pô, doornbosch.

ts'ì á p'ō, doornboschje.

ts'oa ts'ì (*ts'iū*), vol moeielijkheden, lastig.

k'i ts'oa ts'ì (*ts'ia*), moeielijkheden, reden tot twist doen ontstaan.

ki ts'ì, uitlachen.

ts'aó ts'ì, doornen.

ts'ì p'è á (*p'oè*), doornstruiken..

ts'iah tioh ts'ì, een doorn in het vleesch krijgen.

ts'ì mìng t'âng, dikke sterk behaarde rups.

hoān tióh hit ê mâ t'âng ts'ì, zich vergrijpen tegen de rupsharige stekels van een visch die in den winter met fijne stekels bedekt is en die men bij het eten niet uit de mond kan krijgen (*i. e.* zaken doen met iemand die u in moeielijkheden zal brengen en van wien men niet af zal kunnen komen).

k'i hū noā t'ô bô ts'ì, met minachting denken dat in modder geen doornen zijn (*i. e.* een zwakkeren minachtend verdrukken niet denkende dat hij ook wel eens gevaarlijk voor u zoo kunnen zijn).

Ts'i *Ts'ì*, de smaak; proeven.

ts'ì k'oà, beproeven om....

ts'ì liēn, zich oefenen in.

ts'ì tsiáh k'oà, proeven.

ts'ì p'ī k'oà ruiken aan.

ts'ì ioh, een geneesmiddel (bij een zieke) beproeven.

t'aó mìng ts'ì hé, het hoofdhaar bij het vuur probeeren *i. e.* eene gevaarlijke zaak doen.

ts'i i ê ì sù, iemands bedoeling toetsen, trachten uit te vinden.

Ts'ì *Hî ts'ì*, visch vinnen.

Ts'ì *Bouh ts'ì iû*, met lijkolie besmeren (om iemand gehaat te maken).

滋 Ts'î *Ts'i*, vochtig.

ts'i sip, do.

ts'i lûn lûn, vochtig, nat.

ts'i lūn, vochtig en slap.

tâm ts'i, nat en vochtig.

ts'iū ts'i, vochtig worden (als meubelen bij vochtig weder) beslaan (door vochtigheid).

hoán ts'ì weêr slap, vochtig worden.

持 Ts'ì *Ts'ì teh*, nog onafgedaan.

ts'iá ts'ì teh, laat die zaak zoolang rusten.

ts'ì hē teh, zoolang terzijde leggen.

pá ts'i, een goed doorzicht hebben in.

ts'i tsai, vasten, geen geslachte wezens eten.

ts'i sè, op eens anders macht steunen.

i ts'i, helpen (als een doctor doet 2e eene zaak in handen nemen).

tsi ts'i, het roer van eene zaak in handen nemen.

徐 Ts'i *Ts'i*, familienaam.

市 Ts'ī *Ts'ī*, markt.

tsiū ts'ī, naar de markt gaan, het drukste van de markt.

koe ts'ī, do.
t'è ts'ī, de markt is afgeloopen.
paī ts'ī, niet gewild, niet te verkoopen.
ka iàh lī ts'ī, zeer gewild, goed te verkoopen.
pū ts'ī, oproer maken (de winkels sluiten).
hó en *p'ai ts'ī ts'ào* goed te verkoopen. gevraagd.
t'aò ts'ī t'aò ts'ai, het eerste handgeld op een dag is ook het voorteeken voor dien dag.
ti ts'ī, varkenmarkt.
gù ts'ī koemarkt.
ts'ī ts'aó, markt.
hi ts'ī vischmarkt.
ts'aì ts'ī, groenmarkt.
taò ts'ī op eenzelfde plaats dezelfde goederen verkoopen, b. v. eene straat met schoenmakers, een ander met kleermakers enz.
tièm ts'ī, marktplaats.
hu ts'ī, groote landmarkt.
hù ts'ī, naar de markt loopen.
ts'ī t'aò, begin van de markt.
tong ts'ī, goede stand (voor een winkel).
siâ ts'ī stadmarkt.
k'ui ts'ī, de markt openen, handgeld geven.
soâ ts'ī, afloopen uiteengaan van de markt.

養 Ts'ī — *Ts'ī*, opbrengen, opvoeden, voeren.
gaō ts'ī ts'iū, gelukkig zijn met de beesten die men opbrengt.
iû ts'ī (*iû*) }, voeden, opbrengen; houden (als beesten).
ts'ī kaó, honden voeden, honden houden.
ts'ī gù eh, veehoeder.
ts'ī kiá, kinderen opvoeden.
ts'ī ti, varkens houden.
ts'ī ts'iū, fokkerij- beestenhouderij.
tsi pǐng, met rijst voeden, van de borst afgenomen hebben, speenen.
ts'ī kiá bò lūn pǐng, bij het opvoeden van kinderen, spreke men niet over het geld dat zij nog zullen kosten.

Ts'ī — *Ts'iò ts'ī*, er vrolijk lacherig uitzien
ts'iò ts'iò ts'ī ts'ī. dito.

Ts'ī — *K'ùn ts'ī ts'ī*, slapen als eene roos.
ts ī ts'ī hoâ, snorken.

生 Ts'ị — *Ts'ị* (*»*) }, versch, rauw, ongekookt.
ts'ị bé (*bẹ̄*) }, wild paard, onhandelbaar ongemanierd man.
ts'ị kiạ (*ts'ẹ*) }, ontstellen.
ts'ị kiạ táh nìgh, zijne tegenwoordigheid van geest verliezen.
ts'ị sạ (*ts'ẹ*) }, weinig bekend met.
ts'ị ts'iû, onervaren, onbedreven.
ts'ị k'a k'eh (*k'ẹh*) }, vreemdeling op eene plaats.
kà tsiáh ts'ị tị lâng bah, tot alles in staat zijn.
poà t'aò ts'ị, half ervaren in iets.
ts'ị gi eng (als een onbewoond huis). twijfelachtig, ongerust worden.
ts'ị tsin haó peh leh (*o*) }, op eens hard beginnen te schreeuwen.
ts'ị kòng ê lâng, een krankzinnige, razende
ts'ị ts'è, eensklaps onverwachts.
tsaó ts'ị (*»*) }, snel met iets wegloopen als met een lijk dat op eene andere plaats te huis behoort.
tsaó hi ts'ị (*»*) }, hard met zijn visch loopen om ze versch te doen aankomen.
ts'ị tsin, onbedreven onbekend met.
ts'ị hàng, onbedreven, onbekend met den loop van zaken.
ts'ị hiong, onbedreven.
hoan sik bóh hoàn ts'ị, in koophandel houde men zich bezig met dat waarvan men verstand heeft.
ts'ị ts'òng, voor het eerst doen, opmaken.
ts'ị kòng lat, ruwe onbedreven onbesuisde aanwending van kracht.

ts'i kông kiā, sterk, robust, verhard (tegen ontberingen).

ts'i liáh īm tióh sik, onbedrevenen kunnen niet tegen bedrevenen op.

ts'i hoan, ruwe inboorlingen (als op Formosa).

ts'i bīn, *pi ts'i bīn*, van gelaatskleur veranderen (van woede).

bīn ts'i so, elkander niet kennen.

ts'i t'aò īm bat bīn, elkander volstrekt niet kennen.

hî ts'i (») , visch (in het algemeen).

hî- ts'i (») , de visch is versch..

ts'i- aò (») versch en verrot.

ts'i aò péh ut (*péh*) , iemand gewelddadig belasteren, valsch betichten.

ts'i tsin. eensklaps, onverwachts.

ts'i k'im oàh liáh, levend en wel pakken (als van iemand die eensklaps sterft of opgepakt wordt).

ts'i hāo hāo, zeer groen (onrijp of onbekend met zaken).

Ts'i *Ts'i ts'ám* (») , ellendig, medelijdenswaardig.

ts'i ts'ìn (*ts'e*) , schrikken, huiveren, bang zijn.

ts'i hìng, eng. huiverig (als een groot leeghuis).

ts'aò ts'i hìng, stinkend en verwoest als eene plaats waar moordtooneelen hebben plaats gehad.

Ts'i *Ts'i tsin hō* (*ts'iang kòng hō*) , regenbui.

星 Ts'i *Ts'i* (*ts'e*) , ster.

hé ts'i (*hoè*) , vonken.

ts'oah sai ts'i, vallende ster.

saò tsiú ts'i *tìng bé* » (*boé*) , komeet.

hé kim ts'i (*oá kim ts'e*) , vuurvlieg.

bo ts'i àm géh (*goéh*) , in donker (gaan — komen enz).

ts'ìn ts'i (*hoa*) , afdeelingen op eene balans.

ts'it ts'i pang (*ts'e*) , plank met zeven gaten in den vorm van het beeld *de groote beer* onder het lijk in de lijkkist gelegd.

青 Ts'i *Ts'i* (*ts'e*) , donkerblaauw bleek.

ts'i mi (*mê*) , blind.

ts'i kiàng kiàng (*kong kong*) , groen.

t'ák ts'i mi ts'eh (*mê p'er*) , de klanken leeren zonder de beteekenis der karakters te bestudeeren.

t'ut ts'i, uitspruiten, spruiten schieten.

hoan ts'i (*ts'e*) , indigo.

ts'i ioh (*ts'e*) , kleine groene kikvorsch.

ts'i n (*ts'e ni*) , blaauw en geel (van het gelaat).

ts'i lang lang, zeegroen.

ts'i ts'uì, lichtblauw, frissche kleur (als planten na regen).

ts'i t'aò sa á k'ò, lichtblauwe kleederen.

ts'i piàng piàng (*ts'e*) , onrijp, rauw.

p'ah ts'i (*ts'e*) , indigo aanmaken bereiden.

k'iā ts'i, indigo aanmaken, mengen.

ts'ah ts'i, boomtakken, of bladen aan de deur steken om het onheil weg te nemen van een lijk dat erlangs gevoerd is.

清 Ts'i̱ — *Ts'i̱ mŭi̱* / *(ts'ing bing)*, feest der graven reiniging 95 dagen na Europ. nieuwjaar, 5 April.

腈 Ts'i — *Ts'aò ts'i̱ bī* / *(ts'e̱)*, stinkende vischlucht.

ts'i̱ ts'o / *(ts'i̱* en *ts'e̱ ts'o)*, sterkriekend stinkend (als visch).

Ts'i̱ — *Ts'i̱ ím* / *(ts'e̱ ím)* moeders van man en vrouw.

Ts'i̱ — *Ts'i̱* / *(ts'é̱)*, wakker, wakker zijn, wakkermaken.

kiò ts'i̱, wakker roepen, wekken.

p'ah ts'i̱, wakker maken.

t'é ts'i̱, uit den droom helpen.

tiem ts'i̱, uit den droom helpen.

k'ùn ts'i̱, wakker worden, ontwaken.

ts'i̱ ts'uì / *(ts'é̱)*, de eetlust opwekken.

k'ùn ts'it ts'i / *(ts'é̱)*, in eens doorloopen.

ts'i̱ gō̱, tot bewustzijn, inzien komen.

ts'i̱ bin, zich wakker houden (door te drinken of te rooken).

tsiú tsuì ts'i̱, nuchter worden na dronkenschap.

ts'i̱ bák, de oogen ophelderende (als eene fraaie in het oog springende kleur).

Ts'i̱ — *Ts'i̱ sik pò̱* / *(»)*, lichtblauw goed.

tim ts'i̱, donkerblauw.

ts'iò ts'i̱, lichtblauw.

ts'in ts'i / *(ts'é̱)*, fraai (van vrouwen).

Ts'i̱ — *Ts'i̱ ming kào*, de haren rijzen te berge (van vrees).

ts'i̱ bák, in de oogen schitteren (als de zon) in het oog vallend (als geld).

ts'i̱ aò, in de keel blijven zitten, niet geleidelijk door de keel gaan.

ts'i̱ ts'ak ts'i̱ ts'ák, niet naar beneden willen (als harde spijzen) niet in orde zijn.

Ts'i̱ — *Ts'i̱ tsiū̱ koai̱ lai*, zich opheffen (als een tijger of menschen).

ts'i̱ boē tioh, zich opheffende, op de teenen staande, nog niet bij iets kunnen.

Tsia

此 Tsia — *Tsia*, hier.

tsia tsit sò̱ tsaī hier heen.

tsia taī ke / *(ke̱)*, deze allen.

lai̱ tsia tsē, kom hier zitten.

姨 Tsiá — *Tsiá hu*, echtgenoot zijner oudere zuster.

sió tsiá, jonge juffrouw, titel voor mandarijndochter.

k'ioh tsiá bú, vroedvrouw.

蔗 Ts'à — *Kam tsià*, suikerriet.

sik tsià, suikerriet dat niet gegeten wordt maar waarvan men suiker maakt.

soŋ tsià, suikerriet (hard en tot het maken van suiker gebruikt)

k'oeh tsià suikerriet uitpersen.

tsià p'ō̱, suiker perserij.

tsià ts'ia, suikerpers.

tsià ku, suikerriet tor.

Tsià — *Tsià ko̱*, patrijs.

Tsià — *Ka tsià* / *(ké̱)*, namaken.

tsià lâng é sin sè, op een anders macht steunen.

Tsià — *Bák tsià mi̱*, kippig (des avonds niet kunnen zien).

謝 Tsiā — *Tsiā*, familienaam.

Tsiā — *Tsiā lâng é sin sè*, op een anders macht steunen.

ká tsiā onwaar voorgeven dat..., als..

正 Tsia̱ — *Sin tsiŋ*, nieuwjaar.

tsiŋ geh / *(goéh)*, eerste maand do.

paì tsiŋ, *hō tsià*, nieuwjaar wenschen.

sin tsià géh, nieuwjaarsmaand.

tsiā sit sī án ni̱, het is inderdaad zoo.

赤 Tsia *Tsia̱ bah*, mager vleesch.
boé bah tsia̱ k'ah tsoē pui eh kah tsió, meer mager dan vet vleesch koopen.
bīn tsia̱ tsia̱, een rood gezicht hebben en daardoor zijne schaamte niet kunnen toonen.
iao tsia̱ (of *tsi̱*, duivel) scheldwoord.

淡 Tsiá *Tsiá̱*, smakeloos, flauw zonder zout, licht (van tabak enz).
tsiá̱ tsuí, zoetwater.
taī tsì k'ah tsiá̱ tsuí, die zaak is van niet veel gewicht.
kiêm tsiá̱, zoute en flauwe waren (in het huishouden).
tsiá̱ tí̱, flanw en zoet.
tsiá̱ tsiá̱, zeer flauw.
tsiá̱ tsiá̱ ê oē, flauwe taal 2e niet beleedigende taal.
péh tsiá̱ bô bī, flauw smakeloos.
néng tsiá̱ (*hui̱*), zwak.

正 Tsià *Tsià̱*, juist.
tsià̱ tsià̱, recht, niet scheef.
tsià̱ kaò, de ware leer.
tsià̱ gō̱ si, 12 uur middag.
tsin tsià̱, inderdaad.
tsià̱ sī, ja, zoo is het.
pi̱ tsià̱ (*pè̱*), middelmatig billijk *pi̱ pi̱ tsià̱ tsià̱*.
si tsià̱, rechtschapen, recht.
toan tsià̱, do.
tsià̱ ts'iú, de rechterhand 2e de eerste persoon in eene zaak zijn.
tsià̱ kóng, rechtuit zeggen.
tsià̱ kià̱, rechtuit recht doorloopen.
tsià̱ sin, het eigenlijke hoofd (van eene zaak bij eene rechtszaak enz).
tsià̱ bīn, de rechte- goede kant (van papier lakwerk).
tsià̱ lin lin, zeerrecht.
tit tit tsià̱ tsià̱, do.
tsià̱ dzī, uitspraak van het mandarijn dialekt.
tsià̱ im hì, komedie in het mandarijn dealekt.
tsià̱ ìn ko̱ng, hoofdmandarijn (die de ware hoofdzegels heeft en in zijn post zelfstandig is).
tsià̱ hoān, hoofdschuldige.
tsià̱ tō, van de ware plaats, van de plaats zelve.
tsià̱ pūn, ware monster.
oai ts'aì eh tsià̱ tsiah, de scheefmondige eet rechts *d. i.* zonder er rechtstreeks recht op te hebben, leven ten koste van iemand met wien men door huwelijk in betrekking staat.
iok tsià̱, pó tsià̱, hoofdlieden ouderen, scheids rechters in een dorp.

成 Tsiâ *Tsiâ̱*, worden, afmaken.
tsoè tsiâ̱ (*tsò*), voltooien, afmaken.
kóng ī̱m tsiâ̱ oē, het met iemand niet goed eens kunnen worden.
tsiâ̱ pah ni̱, volle honderd jaar.
tsiâ̱ dzít, den geheelen dag.
tsiâ̱ ni̱, een geheel jaar.
hō̱ lóh ī̱m tsiâ̱, het komt niet tot regenen.
tsiâ̱ t'i̱ si, opgeklaarde lucht.
tsiâ̱ lâng, volwassen zijn 2e reeds gehuwd zijn.
ī̱m tsiâ̱ lâng, niet gerekend kunnen worden mensch te zijn (als behoeftige menschen).
tsiâ̱ siâ̱ saò, het behoorlijke geluid (bij muziek) teruggeven.
pù tsiâ̱ t'i̱, zeer rijk.
tsiâ̱ siang tsiâ̱ tuì, een paar uitmaken.
ī̱m tsiâ̱ sin miā̱, geen mensch meer zijn (in vervallen toestand zijn).
ke hè tsoè tsiâ̱, zijne schaapjes op droog hebben.
tsiâ̱ k'it tsiáh, doodarm zijn.
tsiâ̱ piáo kiâ̱, lett. lichtekooi zijn *i. e.* in ellendige omstandigheden zijn, door iedereen geminacht worden.

ĩm tsiŋ̄ iŋ̄, niet goed staan, niet passen- niet voor den staat van den persoon passen.
tsiŋ̄ lók, in ellende zijn.
Tsiŋ̄ *Toŋ̄ háo tsiŋ̄*, leven maken (oorspronkelijk op het tooneel gewoonlijk ook daar buiten gebruikt).
o̤ âng tsiŋ̄, de zwarte roode acteur (die voor een robust mensch speelt).
推 *Ts'ia tó*, omstooten.
Ts'ia *ts'ia p'a lin taó*, buitelen.
ts'ia lin, buitelen.
ts'ia puáh (en) *poŋ̄*, van de eene plaats op de andere overleggen.
ts'ia ts'ia sak sak. van den eenen kant naar den anderen kant geduwd worden als in een gedrang.
ts'ia piŋ̄, beslissend (als een geneesmiddel).
ts'ia hŋ̄ ih, de schuld van iets op hem schuiven.
ts'ia tsit ē hŋ̄ i tó, door een stoot laten omvallen.
ts'ia k'i, schuinshouden, overhellen (als een schip).
ts'ia teh tò, schuinshouden en doen uit gudsen ook van harden regen gebruikt.
p'ah ts'ia tó, omgooien, omverstooten.
sa̤ ts'ia sa̤ p'ah, elkander stooten en stoeien (van kinderen).
硨 *Péh ts'ia kû*, witte mandarijnknop (van
Ts'ia den zesden graad).
Ts'ia *Ts'ia p'ang*, zeil zetten.
ts'ia, windas, wagen 2e familienaam.
ts'ia sai hu, wagenmaker.
ts'ia, draaibank.
ts'ia kui, draaibank.
ts'ia gê, ivoor draaien.
ts'ia kang, kunstdraaier.
ts'ú ts'ia, klein handspinnewiel.
bé ts'ia (*bê̤*) }, rijtuig.
tsui ts'ia, waterrad.
ká ts'ia, spil.
iû ts'ia, oliepers.
tsia ts'ia. suikerpers.
gû bô ts'ia, gangspil.
ts'ia hu, koetsier, wagenmenner.
ts'ia iep, rad (kamrad).
ts'ia k'i, tanden van een rad.
ts'ia tiŋ̄, het anker opwinden.
ts'ia k'oan, ankerspil.
ts'ia lién, overdekte wagen, rijtuig.
p'áng ts'ia, spinnewiel.
hé hun ts'ia, locomotief.
ts'ia bé, rijtuigen en paarden.
hé ts'ia k'i lai, goederen ophijschen.
tsui ts'ia ts'ia tsui, het waterrad maalt het water uit.
ts'ia k'i ts'ia tó, met een katrol ophijschen en laten zakken, helpen om op te rijzen en te gaan liggen (als een zieke)
ts'ia gık, edele steenen bewerken.
ts'in ts'iŋ̄ t'âng teh ts'ia, evenals rupsen die zich in iets werken (van hevige jeuking ook van kinderen die overal aan zitten).
péh hiŋ̄ ts'ia kaŋ k'ang k'ak, de witte mieren hebben het hol geboord, gevreten.
奢 *Ts'ia ts'i*, pronklustig, pronkziek.
Ts'ia *ts'ia hoa*, luisterrijk. prachtig.
ts'ia già (en) *kià*, verkwistend.
ts'ia iŋ̄, dito.
Ts'ià *Koai̤ ts'ià ts'ià*, hoog en hellend.
斜 *Ts'ià*, schuinsch.
Ts'ià *ts'ià bûn pŏ̤*, drill.
ts'ià k'i, schuins houden.
dzıt ts'ià sai, de zon gaat in het westen onder.
dzıt ts'ià soŋ̄, de zon gaat achter de bergen onder.
oai ts'ià scheef, schuins.
k'i ts'ià, do.
sai ts'ià sin, het lichaam scheef houdende schuins (ergens door gaan).

請 *Ts'iá*, uitnoodigen.
Ts'iá *hō lâng ts'iá* (*pō*), uitgenoodigd, geinviteerd worden.
ts'iá tsē, eilieve ga zitten.
ts'iá sien sī (*sin sē*), een meester engageeren.
ts'iá t'aò hiá, de voorste van iets zijn.
ts'iá hun, wees zoo goed te rooken (beleefdheidsterm).
ts'iá ts'iá, beleefdheidsterm eilieve ga uw gang drink wat enz. bij het weggaan. adieu.
ts'iá k'eh, gasten inviteeren.
ts'iá tsiú, gasten op wijn inviteeren.
ngiâ ts'iá, eerbiedig ontvangen inhalen (als afgodsbeelden of gasten).
ts'iá pût, een afgodsbeeld inhalen.
sā ts'iá gō ts'iá, er sterk op aandringen dat iemand toch eene invitatie moge aannemen.
sā lâng ts'iá sì lâng bô hūn van de 3 menschen die hem inviteeren kunnen 4 hem niet krijgen (van iemand die door een ieder geinviteerd wordt).
ts'iá hé kì, een klerk bediende engageeren.
ts'iá ts'ut t'iá, verzoeken in de hoofdzaal te komen: 3 dagen na het huwelijk door de bruidegom's zuster aan de bruid gedaan).
ts'iá pai, een scheepsbrief (voor een nieuw schip) vragen.
ts'iá dzī hō, (bij de overheden) een naam (voor een nieuwe winkel) vragen.

箕 *Pùn ts'iá*, kleine vuilnismand.
Ts'iá

且 *Ts'iá bóng*, toch nog maar.
Ts'iá *dzi ts'iá*, ... maar zelfs.
ts'iá hē teh, leg het zoolang néer.
ts'iá k'oà tseh, even zien, kijken.
ts'iá t'ing hāo, even wachten.
ts'iá t'ing k'a, wacht, blijf nog even.
tsiām ts'iá, tijdelijk zoolang.
ts'iá īng, tijdelijk zoolang maar gebruiken (tot dat men iets beters krijgt).

推 *Ts'iá ts'ià*, elkanders opgeheven handen
Ts'iá afslaan.

倩 *Ts'ià*, huren, in zijn dienstnemen.
Ts'ià *kò ts'ià*, huren (werklieden)
ts'ià ts'iá, bedriegerij door op examinatie zijn opstel door een ander te laten maken.
ts'ià pang ts'iú, helpers huren.
ts'ià t'oè ts'iú, iemand huren die het werk in uwe plaats doen moet.
ts'ià kang, een werkman huren.
tîng té ts'ià, voor langen, voor korten tijd huren (van werklieden).
ts'ià tîng kang, een vasten arbeider huren.
sā ts'ià ìng ū, elkanders hulp te gebruiken komt steeds voor (bel. term tegen iemand die u voor uwe assistentie bedankt).
ts'ià tsûn á een boot huren.

成 *Ts'iâ*, voltooien, afmaken.
Ts'iâ *tîng ts'iâ*, van kind man worden.
koé ts'iâ, veranderen verbeteren.
ts'iâ ih tsiâ lâng, verzorgen tot dat hij volwassen is (als van een wees).
koh ts'iâ tseh, de laatste hand aan iets leggen.
ts'iâ ti ìh, iemand opbrengen tot dat hij volwassen is.
ts'iâ kaò p'ai t'iâ, (een onnoozel gezegde) zoolang verdraaien, veranderen dat er eene slechte beteekenis uit komt.

Tsiah

Tsiah *Tsiah tsai iū* (*tsoá*) (*iū*), hoe?
àn tsiah iū, hoe?
tsiah sī, juist zoo ja.
it tsiah... dzī tsiah... in de eerste plaats... in de tweede plaats.
tsiah, dan, om zoo.

tsoē tsōe tsoē tsiah tióh, er zijn er toch zeker veel.

Tsioh *Tsiah ê*, deze.

tsiah kú, al dien tijd, zoo lang.

tsoē tsiah sī tsoē, zeer veel.

hoân tsiah sī hoân, zeer verward.

tsiáh tsiah ê hè, reeds zoo oud (en nog zoo dom).

Tsiah *Tú ú tsiah*, juist zoo even.

tsioh tsiah, do.

ts'ai tsiah, juist....

tsiah beh... op het punt zijn van te... juist zullen.

tsiah teh tsiáh, juist aan het eten zijn.

脊 Tsiah *Pa en ka tsiah*, rug.

隻 Tsiah *Tsiah* numer. voor schepen, beesten.

ko̱ tsiah bé, tsiáo, een enkel paard, vogel enz.

ko̱ tsiah teh pe, alleen vliegen (van een vogel).

tsit tsiah ts'iú, een enkele arm.

Tsiah mi̱, oogziekte waar door men 's avonds niet zienkan.

食 Tsiàh *Tsiáh*, eten.

tsiáh pīng (*pu̱ī*), eten.

ts'iáh ts'ai, vasten.

tsiáh ts'áo, grazen.

tsiáh pai, een kaart winnen.

tsiáh hun, tabak rooken.

tsiáh tê (*tē*), thee drinken.

tsiah liáh liáh k'i, geheel en al opgegeten door insekten enz.

tsiáh ioh, medicijnen innemen.

tsiáh tit, naam van een spel.

tsiáh lâng tit gōng sòng, misbruik van iemands domheid maken om hem te bedriegen.

tsiáh tiū, verloven, uithuwelijken.

tsiáh lâng ê tsi̱ / » *tsi̱ ê ko̱a*, mandarijnen die zich laten omkoopen.

tsiáh lâng ê dzī sì, de familienaam van een ander aannemen (als aangenomen kinderen of man).

tsiáh aò (» *koē*), toch zijn zin doordrijven.

tsiáh hong, wind vatten, windvangen (als een zeil).

tsiáh ts'im tsui, veel diepgang hebben.

tsiáh k'in tsúi, weinig diepgang hebben.

tsiáh dzīn, het op zich zelven toepassen, het opvatten als of het tegen hem zelven gezegd ware *i. e.* zich als eigenaar van iets opwerpen.

tsiáh tsē, zich iets aantrekken, op zich zelven toepassen.

t'ao tsiáh pō̱, verraderlijke valsche streek.

tsiáh ts'ùi sui, iemands laatste woorden opnemen en daar verder over gaan spreken.

tsiáh tsít ki ts'ùi, door zijn behendig spreken aan de kost komen.

tsiáh sin, versche waar eten.

ts'ùi ts'iáh tāng, steeds willen eten.

tsiáh ts'ùi ta, eten gebruiken tegen den dorst.

tsiáh ka tsiáh ts'iú, zijne bedienden benadeelen.

tsiáh làt, veel te dragen hebben (als een pilaar), met kracht aankomen.

tsiáh tō̱, de verantwoordelijkheid op zich nemen.

tsiáh ne̱ bò tsiáh ning, zich wel met sterken maar niet met zwakken willen meten.

tsiáh dzip bah kut, diep doordringen intrekken van kleuren, verf.

tsoá īm tsiáh bák, het papier neemt de inkt niet op, de inkt dringt niet in het papier.

sa̱ tsiáh ts'īng, juist in elkander grijpen goed in elkander sluiten.

tsiáh tioh hong, op de tocht staan 2° wind vatten (van een zeil).

k'it tsiáh, pun tsiáh, bedelaar.

t'ó tsiáh, op eten uit zijn.

kià tsiáh kià toā, bij een andere gevoed en opgebracht worden (als behoeftige kinderen).

t'àn tsiáh, de kost verdienen, aan de kost komen.

king tsiáh king ts'ing, keurig op zijn eten en kleeding zijn.

mi̤h tsiáh, spijzen.

tsiáh tsṳ̀ tìng, een geregeld groot maal gebruiken.

tsiáh liaō, in de bouwstoffen indringen (als een grondverf).

tsiáh iû k'ak boē tsiáh tsui, door olieverf laten doortrekken, op dat het water er niet inzuige.

tsiáh tsó̤, van de voorouderlijke bezitting eten (als na de gravenreiniging).

tsiáh kī, van de bezittingen zijner grootouders eten (als op een feest).

tsiáh sit, bijgerechten.

tsiáh làng è siaò, eene vervalsching (tot zijn eigen voordeel) in iemands rekening maken.

tsiáh aō ts'iú, achterhands geldkrijgen, omgekocht worden.

tsiáh k'ì tsiáh tsì, tegenzin, haat tegen iemand opvatten (als een arme die door zijne rijkere familiebetr. met minachting behandeld is en niet eer met hen wil omgaan voor dat hij zelf bemiddeld is).

tsiáh tò, zijne woorden terugnemen, zijn ongelijk bekennen.

tsiáh i tse p'iah, zich stijfhoofdig aan zijn idée houden.

tsiáh tsoà p'ē hó̤ huih, slangen eten en er tijgersbloed bij gebruiken *i. e.* onverschokken tot alles in staat.

tsiáh kun tîng, zijne broodwinning is afgesneden, heeft opgehouden, ligt op straat.

tsiáh pù bô lâo tsing, pompoenen eten en geen zaad bewaren *i. e.* onbesuisd, niet voor de toekomst zorgen.

ts'ut lai tsoán tsiáh, de wereld in gaan om zijn brood te verdienen.

刺 *Ts'iah*, knoopen.

Ts'ìh *ts'iah bāng*, een net knoopen.

ts'iah dzī, met karakters besnijden = brandmerken.

ts'iah bèh kousen breien.

ts'iah oē (ē), schoenmaken (van vrouw).

ts'iah siù, borduren.

ts'iah tiòh, zich steken met.

ts'iah tiòh tsiem, zich met een naald-steken.

ts'iah tiòh ts'o̤ (ts'ia̤), een splinter in zijn vleesch krijgen.

ts'iah t'ò̤, braking bevorderen 2e iemand met geweld iets doen teruggeven.

ts'iah huih, steken, slachten.

ts'iah sṳng, oprispen (met eene onaangename smaak).

ts'iah bák, verleidelijk voor het oog, in het oog vallend.

sa̤ ts'iah, elkander (met woorden) steken elkander iets slechts verwijten.

tuì ts'iah, elkander zijne slechtheden verwijten.

îng tsien si ts'iah, met een braadlepel losschuiven (uit de pan).

ts'ing ts'iah, glad, schoon afkluiven *i. e.* uit alle hoekjes en gaatjes geld zien te maken.

ts'iah oē tú tiòh goá ē k'a, uwe gemaakte schoenen passen mij juist *i. e.* iets van iemand leenende juist iets treffen dat geheel aan het doel beantwoord.

赤 *Ts'iah sik*, vleeschkleurig.

Ts'iah *ts'iah k'oat k'oat*, naakt (van armoede) dor bar.

tao ts'iah, arm en daardoor slecht.
ts'iah gû, koe.
ts'iah k'ō k'ō, bar, dor, niets bezittend.
ts'iah k'a, barrevoets.
ts'iah k'iét k'iét, dor, bar.
ts'iah bah, mager vleesch.
ts'iah iáh, onlekker onfrisch door warm te of stof enz.
ts'iah sin lō̤ t'é, gansch naakt.
ts'iah k'a ts'iah ts'iú, blootvoets.
sòng ts'iah ts'iah, doodarm.
ts'iah hàn, arm mensch, arme drommel.
ts'iah á arme drommels.
ts'iah á kiá, do.
ts'iah soa, bruine groffe suiker.
o̤ ts'iah, donkerbruin.
ts'iah koah ts'aò ta, bruin en aangebrand d. i. uitermate kijfachtig van vrouwen.
ts'iah pò, ongebleekt katoen.
bák tsiu ts'iah ting ting, staroogen, ontstellen (als een doodarm mensch op het gezicht van geld).
Ts'iah *Ts'iah tsa bó̤*, eene twistzieke vrouw.
ts'iah peh peh, boosaardig (van vrouwen).
Ts'iàh *Tuì hit ē uī ts'iáh kè k'ì*, van daar schuinsoversteken.

Tsiak

Tsiák *Tsí tsi tsiák tsiák*, geluid van uitspuitend water.
Ts'iàk *Ts'iak tsit ē (ē̤)*, eensklaps schrikken.
ts'iák tseh, eensklaps ontstellen schrikken (als bij een kanonschot).
Ts'iàk *Put tsi gaō ts'iák; aì ts'iak ē lâng*, bij het minste wat men heeft het terstond aan anderen willen mededeelen.

Tsiang

漳 *Tsiang tsiu*, Tsiang tsiu.
Tsiang *tsiang k'oán*, Tsiang tsiu vorm, fraai.
tsiang se, Tsiang tsiu gaas.
tsiang tsoân nêng hú ē lâng, menschen van de districten Tsiang en Tsoân.

掌 *Tsiáng kuī*, boekhouder.
Tsiáng *tsiáng koán*, beheeren.
tsiáng koán, de macht voor iets in handen hebben.
tsiáng lí, beheeren, besturen.
tsiáng t'aó, het hoofdbestuur over iets hebben (als een aannemer).
tsiáng poā, de loop van een handelshuis in handen hebben, besturen.

上 *Tsiáng kè*, stijgen in prijs.
Tsiáng *po tsiáng lâng*, iemand prijzen, roemen.
Tsiàng *Hun tsiàng*, verwarring veroorzaken (bv. door iets onechts onder echte voorwerpen te vermengen).

鎗 *Niao ts'iang*, geweer, ganzenroer.
Ts'iang

蹌 *Ts'iáng k'a*, hinken mankgaan.
Ts'iáng *ts'iáng tseh ts'iáng tseh*, strompelen, kreupelgaan.
Ts'iàng *Bô ts'iàng tsaī laī*. Niet daaronder begrepen zijn (als de meubelen bij een huis).

唱 *Ts'iàng bing*, uitschreeuwen (als een vendutie meester).
Ts'iàng
bing p'in bing ts'iàng, duidelijk genoeg gezegd duidelijk overeenkomen.
ts'iàng kè, een bod instellen (als een vendutiemeester.
ts'iàng kè ē lâng (kè̤), vendutiemeester.
ts'ut ts'iàng, nogmaals duidelijk zeggen (als een koopman met het sluiten van een koop).
ts'iàng hō, de nummers, de merken afroepen.
ts'iàng miâ, de namen afroepen.
ts'iàng tsaī siō, vast afspreken beloven om.
ts'iàng kah sí sí, duidelijk bepaald met iemand overeenkomen.

Ts'iâng *Pai ts'iâng*, pronken paradeeren opgesierd.

鎗 Ts'iâng *Ts'iâng tṳ*, een draagstok met scherpe ijzeren punten.

Ts'iâng *K'ut i ts'iâng tioh*, betrapt, gevat worden (als een dief).

kūng i ts'iâng lai, iemand betrappen en mèevoeren.

Ts'iâng *Lō̤ nih sa ts'iâng tioh*, elkander onderweg ontmoeten.

Tsiao

招 Tsiao *Tsiao an*, tot rust aanmanen.

tsiao dzīn, tot bekentenis komen, bekennen.

tsiao pat, uithangbord.

tsiao bō̤, afhuren.

tsiao iaô, alombekend, alombekend maken.

tsiao tsai ông, god van het geld.

昭 Tsiao *Tsiông bók tsiao tsiao*, vóór het gezicht van allen, in tegenwoordigheid van vele ooggetuigen.

pò ìng tsiao tsiao, duidelijke zichtbare belooning of straf (des hemels).

t'ien lí tsiao tsiao, de handelingen des hemels zijn duidelijk zichtbaar (als een roover die zelf vermoord is).

憔 Tsiao *Tsiao tsô*, bedroefd, akelig (als door een verhaal).

焦 Tsiao *Tsiao t'aô noū hī*, het hoofd verbrand en de ooren vergaan (als menschen die bij een brand zijn omgekomen).

鳥 Tsiaó *Tsiaó*, vogel.

ts'ik tsiaó á, musch.

k'eh tsiaó (») }, ekster.

tsiaó siū, vogelnest.

tsiaó lâng, vogelkooi.

tsiaó boē, lokvogel in een knip.

ko̤ ing tsiaó (ni) (o) }, groote uil.

âm kong tsiaó, kleine uil.

tsiaó á gûn, mexcaansche dollar.

tsiao á k'a t'ui, spillebeen.

gók tsiaó, belhamel, een sterke die de zwakkeren verdrukt.

gân tsiaó, do.

tsiaó á bák, ruitjes in rottingen zittingen gevlochten.

p'ah pe tsiaó, op een vliegenden vogel schieten *i. e.* op geluk rondgaan om te zien of men iets krijgen kan (als lichtekooijen).

tsiaó tah tuì, vogelknip.

姊 Tsiaó *Tsiaó hu*, zwager (man van zijne oudere zuster).

照 Tsiaò *Tsiaò iū* (iō̤) }, volgens het patroon, model.

tsiaò kò̤, zorgdragen voor.

tsiaò, volgens, overeenkomstig.

tsiaò ìng, ter assistentie staan, helpen.

tsiaò sìng (suì) }, volgens berekening.

tsiaò k'i kang, volgens den regel, zooals behoorlijk is.

tsiaò kui kú, volgens den regel.

tsiaò kū, hersteld, als te voren.

tsiaò goân, dito.

tsiaò k'ui, ieders te betalen deel in iets berekenen 2e gelijkelijk deelen.

tsiaò t'oṳ, do.

tsiaò sìng, do.

tsiaò sit kóng, onpartijdig, naar waarheid zeggen.

tsiaò t'aô tsoè, van voren af aan doen.

tsiaò tsing kiṳ lī̤, rechtmatig, rechtvaardig handelen.

koan tsiaò, naar beide zijden uitkijken, waken.

tsiaò hoē, brieven van gelijkstaande mandarijnen.

tsiaò tsit è iū, volgens deze manier, even als dit.

tsiaò li lō; *tsiaò li tsiaò lō*, volgens de betamelijke manier.
hok sing kióng tsiaò hh, de gelukster komt bij u schijnen (als een gelukkig mensch die bij u komt).

齊 *Tsiaò ùn*, gelijkelijk regelmatig.
Tsiaò *tsiaò tsing* (*tsui*) }, volledig kompleet.
tsiaò piēn, do.
bô tsiaô, onvolledig, inkompleet.
tsiaô tsiaò, gelijk (overal evenveel).
tsiaò ū, iedereen heeft, allen hebben.
tsiaò soe bát, fijn, net in elkander als een geweefd voorwerp.

Tsiaò *Tsiaò tsuì*, er akelig uitzien afgetobd.

Tsiaò *Ko tsiaò*, verdroogd uitgedroogd (van boomen), afgevallen van menschen.

Tsiaò *Tsiaô tsiò*, een weinig.

調 *Ts'iao*, door elkander doen (drooge
Ts'iao dingen).
ts'iao mī hún, deeg kneden.

Ts'iao *Ts'iao ts'ik*, levendig opgeruimd.
t'aò ts'iao, voorroer aan een schip om het sneller te kunnen omwenden.
ts'iao tō, zielen uit de hel bidden en weer op de wereld doen komen (door Bood. priester gedurende de7de maand gedaan).

搜 *Ts'iao* doorzoeken, visiteeren.
Ts'iao *ts'iao ts'ē* (*ts'oē*) }, do. huiszoeking houden.
ts'iao ke (*kē*), huiszoeking houden.
ts'iao ke biét tsok, vernietiging van goederen en familie.
ts'iao ū, al zoekende vinden.
ts'iao sin k'u, het lichaam visiteeren (of men ook iets bij zich heeft).
ts'iao tsûn, een schip visiteeren.
ts'iao ts'iao ts'ē ts'ē, overal rondzoeken.

Ts'iaó *Ts'iaó ts'iaó á kiā*, langzaam loopen.
ts'iaó ts'iaó á kè dzit, maar juist kunnen (genoeg hebben om te) leven.

Ts'iaó *Ts'ín ts'iaó*, woelig lastig speelziek (van kinderen).

移 *Ts'iaò tàm*, grappig gezegde vi.
Ts'iaò *ts'iaò iông*, vrolijk van uiterlijk.

跳 *Ts'iaò oá*, bijschuiven, dichterbij schuiven.
Ts'iaò *ts'ui ts'iaô* (*ts'i*) }, afdingen.
boē oē ts'ui ts'iaô tit (*bē ts'i*) }, onveranderlijk (van prijs of zaken),
kap lâng ts'ui ts'iáô. het met iemand over den prijs ééns zien te worden, met iemand raadplegen.
ts'iaò tú hó, gelijk zetten als een horologie, recht zetten als een kopje enz.
ts'iaò tuì tiém, gelijkzetten (uurwerk).
ts'ui ts'iaô, gelijkzetten (een uurwerk) overeenkomen (inprijs)
ts'iaô t'á, goed recht zetten (verbeteren).
ts'iaò kut, een been in het gewricht zetten.
ts'iaò boē oá, het niet met elkander over iets eens kunnen worden.
ts'iaò oá piah, tegen den muur aanzetten (schuiven.
kì tsi ts'iaô k'ah tsió, de prijs wat verminderen afslaan.
ts'iaò lai ts'iaô k'ì, het verschil deelen (bij het sluiten van een koop).

Tsiaoh

針 *Tsiaoh kè k'ì*, zonder loopje overspringen.
Tsiaoh

Tsiaoh *Hih hiaoh tsih tsiaoh*, met iedereen zonder onderscheid van onderdom of stand gekheid maken.

Tsiaoh *Tsiaoh kun*, *tsiaoh dzi á*, opleggertje spelen.

Tsiaòh *Tsiáoh tsiáoh kiò*, smekken.
tsi tsi tsaòh tsiaòh, smekken.
tsiaòh tsiaòh liēm, onophoudelijk opzeggen.

Tsiem

針 *Tsiem*, naald.

Tsiem *tsiem p'ī*, oog van een naald.

hân sú tsiem, thermometer.

tsiem tsaī, vingerhoed.

hong ú tsiem, barometer.

tsiem á t'aó ts'ah, hoofdsieraden.

tsiem tuì, doelen op, slaan op.

tsiem kóng, naaldenkoker.

pò tē tsiem, rijgnaald, paknaald.

kao tsiem tìng, kao tsiem tó soā }
ts'ing tsiem bān soā } , met
veel moeite naaien, veel moeite aan iets besteden.

tsiem soā, naald en draad.

tsiem k'ang, naaldenoog.

tsiem k'ang é toā, klein als het oog van een naald.

tsiem tsí, naaldenwerk.

hó tsiem tsí, gaô kiáh tsiem tsí, knap met de naald kunnen omgaan, knap de naald hanteeren.

tsiem tsiem tsìng é lâng }
tsiem tsìng tsìng } , iemand die op alles wat heeft aan te merken en over alles wil redetwisten.

tsí lâm tsiem, lô kì tsiem, kompasnaald.

tuì tsiem, volgens de kompasnaald gaan *i. e.* op iemand doelen.

kim tsiem }
(*tsam*) } , gouden haarspeld.

bô tsiem put ín soā, zonder naald kan men er den draad niet doorhalen *i. e.* zonder een middelaar kan de zaak niet tot stand komen.

尖 *Tsiem láī*, scherp puntig.

Tsiem *bák tsiem*, oogpuistje.

soā tsiem, bergpiek.

ts'ui tsiem tsih láī, welbespraakt.

tsiem teh teh, zeer puntig, scherp.

put k'i tsiem, met een punt opwerken (als meel in de maat).

sg tsiem lák kak é oē, é lâng, vol streken vol moeielijkheden; moeielijk met anderen overeenstemmend.

sin tsiem, de punt aan iets maken (als aan een potlood).

tsiem hong, puntig scherp van punt (oorsp. van een berg thans ook van voorwerpen, als penseelen enz. gezegd).

t'aô tsiem hī tùn póh, een puntig hoofd en dunne oorzomen *i. e.* slechte voorteekens om geld te maken.

tsiem bé liu, in een dun eind uitloopen (hoelanger hoe minder worden als handel).

k'ì ngó tsiem, de vijf punten weg doen (als de kop 2 pooten er 2 vlerken van een kip).

bīn bé tsiem tsī tsiem tsī, het onderste van het gelaat is eivormig.

tsiem k'a, iù ts'iú, puntige voeten en fijne handen als iemand die niet aan grof werk gewend is.

詹 *Tsiem*, familienaam.

Tsiem

Tsiem *Bák bé sió k'oá kē goá koan tsiem teh*, houd een weinig een oogje voor mij daarop.

占 *Tsièm*, zich nestelen te; in bezit nemen.

Tsièm *ts'im tsièm*, inbrenk maken op, zijn gebied overschrijden.

pà tsièm, overweldigen.

tsièm kù, zich van eene plaats meester maken, bezetten.

tsièm uī, eene (zit of staan) plaats innemen.

p'uì noā tsièm uī, spuwende zich eene plaats toeeigenen *i. e.* zonder genoegzame bewijzen of handgeld te geven zich als eigenaar opgeven.

oē boē oē ka kī tsièm teh kóng, men kan zelf niet alleen alle praats hebben *i. e.* men moet anderen ook vergunnen u te weêrleggen.

tsièm tē pō, eene woonplaats innemen *i. e.* behendig uitvluchten hebben om zich zelve geen schande aan te doen.
ts'ing o sq tsièm o t'iaō, die een zwarte jas aanheeft houdt zich bij den zwarten pilaar *i. e.* men trekt partij voor datgene waartoe men zelf behoort.
t'ai sin tsièm mêng, de geest der zwangerschap houd zich op in de deur (in een huis waar eene zwangere vrouw is, raadpleegt men het boekje der zwangerschap en datgene waar de geest zich dien dag ophoudt durft men niet te verzetten).

阻 Tsièm *Tsièm*, tusschenbeiden komen, scheiden (twee vechtende menschen).
sq tsièm, vechtende personen van elkander scheiden.

Tsiêm *Tsiêm sim*, met hart en ziel (studeeren enz).
ts'im tsiêm ê lâng, een stil maar kundig mensch.

Tsiēm *Tsiēm si*, tijdelijk.
tsiēm ts'iā / *(») koân*, tijdelijk.
tsiēm k'iā, tijdelijk ergens wonen.
tsiēm piét, voor korten tijd van iemand afscheid nemen.
tsiēm īng, tijdelijk zoolang maar gebruiken.

漸 Tsiēm *Tsiēm*, langzamerhand, trapsgewijze.
tsiēm tsìn, vorderen, vorderingen maken.
tsiēm tsiēm kè dzit, middelmatig van den eenen dag op den anderen kunnen leven.

簽 Ts'iem *Ts'iem miâ*, zijne handteekening zetten, endosseeren.
ts'iem dzī, onderteekenen (met of ander toepasselijk karakter).
ts'iem ah, onderteekenen.
ts'iem tsiem tsoè tsit tui, handteekeningen onder elkander plaatsen.
ts'iem tiaò á, titelpapier (een strook papier uit Chin. boeken met den titel er op, hangende).
ts'eh ts'iem, do.

籤 Ts'iem *T'iu ts'iem*, orakelstokjes uitrekken.
ts'iem tâng, koker voor orakelstokjes = *ts'iem kóng*.
ts'iem si, voorspellings versjes.
piet ts'iem si, een voorspellingsversje uitleggen.
taō ts'iem, reepen van boonenmeel.

槧 Ts'iém *Tsûn ts'iém*, kiel van een schip.
hē ts'iém, de kiel van een schip leggen.
ts'iém, de kiel (van een schip).
teh ts'iém, de kiel van een schip leggen.

插 Ts'iém *Ts'iém*, speld, rijgnaald 2e aanrijgen.
ts'iém kóng, een rijgnaald insteken.
ts'iém bí, rijst steken (om te probeeren).
īng to ts'iém dzìp k'ì, met een wapen steken.
hoe ts'iém, bloemen naald (die de vrouwen in het haar steken).
ts'iém hoe, bloemen aansteken aanrijgen.
hun ts'iém á, opiumnaald.
ts'iém á, vork.
t'ih ts'iém, ijzeren braadvork = *ts'iém kó*.
t'ing ts'iém, suikerboor.
īng tâng ts'iém-ts'iém bah, met koperen braadvork in vleesch steken.

僭 Ts'ièm *Ts'ièm*, te boven gaan (zijn rang).
ts'ièm uī, een hoogere plaats innemen.
ts'ièm hūn, zich meer aanmatigen dan tot zijn plicht behoort.
ts'ièm koân, eene te hooge plaats innemen, te hoog gezag voeren.
ts'ièm giēn, iets zeggen dat eigenlijk niet past voor de verhouding waarin men tot iemand staat (maar het toch willen zeggen als een vriend).
ts'ièm ts'ing ìh, iemand een te hoogen eerenaam geven.
tik tsōe k'ah ts'ièm, excuseer mij ik heb eene te hooge plaats ingenomen (beleefdheidsterm).

Tsien

煎 *Tsien*, met olie bakken (als visch).
Tsien *tsien poû*, braadpan.
tsien si, braadlepel.
tsien soán } , stoven.
» *tsoán* }
tá tsien, braden, in het algemeen eten klaarmaken (op reis).
tsien dzit, uitdroogen braden in den zon (als vleesch of het gezicht van werklieden).
tsien hi, vischbakken
tsien ts'á ê mih, gebakken en geroosterde spijzen.

氈 *Mo̱ tsien* } , deken van schapenvacht.
Tsien (*mô*) }
tē tsien, vloerkleed.
p'o̱ tsien, met een kleed bedekt (als de vloer).

箋 *Tsien tsoá*, fijn best papier.
Tsien

剪 *Tsién á*, schaartje.
Tsién *ka tsièn*, schaar.
tsién, knippen.
tsién to; hakmes (als in een apotheek gebruikt wordt)
tsik tsién, snuiters.
tsién t'aô ming, haarknippen.
tsién tsik sai, de kaars snuiten.
tsién liú, zakkenroller.
tsién ióh, medicijnen gereed maken.
tsién po̱, goed koopen.
tsién tiù, laken koopen.
tsién tsoè, verknippen tot ... (als een kleerenmaker).
ts'ai tsién, knippen (als een kleêren maker) afmeten bepalen.
tsién tsoè nn̄g tèng, in tweeën knippen.
ng tī tsién tèng, met de eetstokjes afbreken (als een lange vermicelliedraad.
tsién sa̱, goed voor kleêren laten afknippen, koopen.
siù tsién, borduurschaartje.

蟫 *Tsién á*, boekenworm.
Tsién *tsién t'âng*, boekenworm.
Tsién *Tsién ê lâng*, (Tsiang tsiu) menschen als dezen, zulke menschen.
Tsién *Kā i tsién king*, iemand een afscheidsmaal geven.

戰 *Kao tsièn*, strijden, gevecht, veldslag.
Tsièn *tsièn tsûn*, oorlogschip.
tsièn lām, groote oorlogsjonken.
tsièn kah, harnas.
sú tsièn } , dood vechten.
(*si*) }
tsièn tiû, slagveld.
tsièn tīn, slagorde.
tsuí tsièn, zeegevecht.
liók of *soa̱ tsièn*, landgevecht veldslag.,
tsièn paī, den slag verliezen.
tá tsièn, vechten strijden slag leveren.
hā tsièn tsu, een brief voor den dag van het gevecht geven.
tsièn tsiòng, een strijdbare dappere bevelhebber.
tsit ê tsièn tsiòng, een die voor een dapperen bevelhebber tellen kan *i. e.* een zeer knap koopman.
gaô ka lâng tsièn, steeds schelden en kijven van vrouweu.
ts'iú tsièn, de hand beeft (als van oude lieden).

薦 *Tsièn*, recommandeeren, aanbevelen.
Tsièn *kú tsièn* } , do.
(*kí*) }
tsièn tsu, recommandatie brief.
tsièn in, introduceeren, recommandeeren
tsièn áp, langwerpig vierkant confiturenblad (bij offeranden gebruikt).

棧 *Tsièn pàng*, pakhuis.
Tsièn

前 *Tsiông tsièn*, vroeger tevoren.
Tsiên *tsièn dzit*, vorige dagen.
sien tsièn, te voren vroeger.
í tsièn, van te voren.

tsién sin, te voren vroeger.
goân tsién, oorspronkelijk (van te voren).
tsién iạ̀, voorhoede.
bòk tsién gàn tsién vóór de oogen.
tsién dzīm koạ, mandarijn die vóór den tegenwoordigen, diens post bekleedde.
hiòng tsién, zonder aarzelen, moedig voorwaarts.
tsìn tsién, naar voren toe zetten (als een tafel enz).
tsién hạ hō̤ iòng, vóór een mandarijn uitroepen en van achteren antwoorden.
tsién hō̤ tsó iū, van voren van achteren rechts en links *i. e.* aan alle kanten.

蹁 *Tsiēn*, het iemand lastigmaken.
gaò tsiēn, overal met de handen aanzitten (van kinderen).
tsiēn k'a tsiēn ts'iú; *k'a ts'iú tsiēn*, met handen en voeten in beweging zijn.
tsiēn t'âng, laag insekt, ondeugende duivel (tegen kinderen).
t'iaò tsiēn, geen rust in zich hebben, altijd huppelen (van kinderen).

賤 Tsiēn *Hū tsiēn* (*hē̤*) }, verachtelijk, laag.
ts'aò tsiēn, gemeen (van menschen planten enz).
pin tsiēn, arm onaanzienlijk.
pi tsiēn, laag verachtelijk.
tsiēn pī, verachtelijke slavin (scheldw. tegen vrouwen in komediestukken gebruikt).
tsiēn kut t'aò, verachtelijk wezen (scheldwoord).
hù kuì pin tsiēn, rijkdom aanzien armoede en lage stand.
tsiēn dzin, laag verachtelijk mensch (fatsoenlijk scheldw. meestal tegen vrouwen).
k'ing tsiēn ih, iemand minachten, geringachten.
tsiēn siòng laag uiterlijk.
tsiēn siò, mijn (lett. verachtelijk) huis nederige beleefdheids termen.
tsiēn miạ̀, mijn naam, do.
tsiēn loē, mijne vrouw, do.

千 *Ts'ien kim*, uwe dochter (eernaam).
Ts'ien *ts'ien bān*, toch vooral.
ts'ien tsóng, kapitein.
tsien lí kiạ̀, verrekijker.
ts'ien lí bé, courier.
ts'ien īm sī-bān īm sī, duizendmaal excuus vragen.
ts'ien kun bān bé, duizende troepen en paarden (als in een gevecht).
ts'ien kun ts'ìn, hefboom.

遷 *Ts'ien i*, verplaatsen naar.
Ts'ien *ts'ien soá*, verplaatsen.
ts'ien iạ̀, het kamp verplaatsen.
ah ts'ien, met geweld doen verhuizen (uit overbevolkte plaatsen).
ts'ien to̤ bi o̤, naar *Bi o̤*, doen verhuizen (eene plaats in de samkok) *i. e.* van eene plaats verwijderen (als slechte lieden).

Ts'ien *Ts'iu ts'ien kè*, Russische schommel.
ts'ien ts'iu pi̤, schommel, wip.
p'ah ts'iu ts'ien, schommelen, wippen.

Ts'ien *Pí k'i ts'ien ts'ien*, zuiver aanleggen.
tuì ts'ien, zuiver gemikt.
ts'ien ts'ien ts'ien, zuiver (als een schot).

淺 *Ts'ién*, ondiep.
Ts'ién *ts'ién ts'ién*, oppervlakkig (niet diep).
ts'ién kièn, van weinig doorzicht.
iù ts'ién dzip ts'im, van het gemakkelijk tot het moeielijke overgaan.
ts'ién t'oa, muilen.
ts'ién ts'ien hiēn hiēn, gemakkelijk te begrijpen niet diep.
ts'ién hiēn, in het oog vallend.
ts'ién lō̤, blootgesteld, in het oog loopende
ts'ién sik, lichte kleur.
k'in ts'ién, ondiep niet diep (van eene plaats, van kennis).
ts'ién poạ̀, presenteer blaadje.
k'oà ts'ién, op eene ondiepte loopen (van een schip).

dzip ts'ién, op eene ondiepe plaats gaan (als een schip om anker grond te krijgen).

ts'ién tō̤ ting, van weinige, oppervlakkige kennis.

tsai lâng ê ts'im ts'ién, den staat van iemands kundigheden kennen.

aò ts'ién pouh (poā̤), verrot bakje (scheldw. tegen vrouwen).

ts'ién hák, oppervlakkige letterkennis.

Ts'ién *K'ioh ts'ién*, een offerandepot opstapelen (een pot waarin een lange bamboesstok geplaatst is die tot aan den top met gebraden kippen koeken enz. wordt opgestapeld).

遷 *lên ts'iên*, uitstellen.

Ts'iên *ts'iên kang*, langduren van een werk veel tijd kostende.

ts'iên i ts'iên dzit, van eenen dag op den anderen dralen verschuiven.

iên iên ts'iên ts'iên, dralend langdradig.

ts'iên lai ts'iên k'ì, over en weerschuiven (als bij het weigeren van een geschenk enz. aan te nemen).

ts'iên īm siu, uit beleefdheid geschenken weigeren aan te nemen.

Tsiep

汁 *Tsiep*, sap, etter.

Tsiep *ts'iū tsiep*, boomsap.

ū tsiep, sappig.

tsiep bák, *bák tsiu tsiep tsiep*, druipende oogen.

ling tsiep, melksap, melkvocht (van vrouwen).

tsiáh sí lâng tsiep, het druipend vocht van een lijk opdrinken *i. e.* van iemands dood gebruik maken om door valsche aanklachten geld van zijne betrekkingen te krijgen.

tsuí tsiep ts'ing k'ì, water is schoon, met water kan men alles schoon krijgen.

接 *Tsiep*, bij elkaâr binden insplitsen (als Tsiep touw) aanhechten enten op.

tsiep ìng, helpen, in reserve staan.

tsiep uī, een anderen vorst in een regeering opvolgen iemands openstaande plaats, betrekking innemen.

tsiep tsè, dieven heimelijk in de hand werken.

tsiép ts'iú eh, makelaar.

tsiep, zich aansluiten aan.

tsiep siók, achtereenvolgens, successievelijk geregeld, in volgorde.

tsiep dzīm, een post overnemen.

tsiep ts'uì, aanhechtingsplaats 2e met iemand over iets spreken.

tsiep ui, een mast verlengen.

tsiep sún, met wiggen (zwaluwstaarten) in elkander doen grijpen 2^e^ in elkander grijpen van woorden.

tsiep sún k'ak, iemand naar de mond spreken, gelijk geven zonder dat men zelf er iets van af weet.

ìng tsiep, ontvangen, als gasten behandelen.

t'aī lâng tsiep k'eh, gasten ontvangen en zich met hen bezighouden.

tsiep ts'iú, omgaan met, zaken hebben met.

sa̤ tsiep k'a, elkander op de voet volgen.

tsiep ìn, de ambtzegels overnemen.

tsiep láp, ontvangen.

kao t'aò tsiep dzī, met elkander fluisteren.

tsiep kut, een been inzetten.

kap lâng kao tsiep, met iemand omgaan zaken doen.

tsiep in, inhalen en leiden (als de ziel na den dood naar den hemel gaande).

t'ô tsiep lí, een perzik op een pruim enten.

tê hoe tsiep soa̤ tê, (camellia op wilde thee enten.

捷 *Tsiép tsiép*, vlug, snel rad, dikwijls, Tsiép steeds.

tsiép tsiép óh, vlug aanleeren.
tsiép lut lut, gauw rad spreken.
kin tsiép k'oai, gaauw rad.
kin t'in tsiep lim, zoo inschenken en zoo uitdrinken.
soè hō̤ tsiép lóh, eene kleine regen maar die gestadig aanhoudt *i. e.* kleine maar gestadige winst.

睫 Tsièp *Tsièp tsièp kiò*, smekken.
tsièp ts'uì tūn, met de lippen smekken.

妾 Ts'iep *Ts'iep*, bijzit.
boé (en) *ts'oā ts'iep*, een bijzit nemen.

Tsiet

節 Tsiet *Sù kuì pat tsiet*, de 4 jaargetijden en de 8 jaarfeesten.
tsiet iōng, zuinig.
tsiet kuì, onthouden van.
k'ì tsiet, goede handelingen.
tsing tsiet, kuisch.
tsiet liét, eerbaar kuisch.
tsiú tsiet, weduwe blijven.
tsīn tsiet, den eerbaren staat ten einde toe volbrengen, liever sterven dan zich over te geven.
paī bing sòng tsiet, zijn naam verliezen zich met schande bedekken.
tsiú k'ō̤ tsiet, haar ellendigen weduwe staat ophouden.
tsiú ts'ing tsiet, zuiver in weduwestaat blijven.
tsiet sing, zuiniger zijn.
tsi tsiet, *sì̤ ts'ut tsi tsiet*, ontstaan voor den dag komen, van bijomtstandigheden.
tsiet tsè, overheeren regelen besturen.

折 Tsiet *Tsiet*, deelen op; een tiende van.
sì tsiet $^4/_{10} = 40\%$ 3° weêrleggen iemand op zijne woorden vatten.
sṳ̄ tsiet, redetwisten.
ts'ú tsiet, percenten nemen.
p'ah tsiet, percenten bepalen.
tsiet t'iong, het verschil deelen, het verschil beslechten.
tsiet tsiet leh bô loū tsoē, na alle onkosten er of blijft er niet veel over.
tsiet sit, wezenlijke, zuivere (winst, gewicht enz).
kóng bô poàn tsiet ê oē, niet de helft waarheid vertellen van wat men zegt.
kóng oē tsiet ìh, door een enkel gezegde iemand weerleggen.

Tsiet *Bī tsiet tsiet*, wrang scherp van smaak.

截 Tsiét *Tsiét*, opvangen, onderscheppen (als roovers doen).
tsiét tsí, contraorder geven.
tsiét tō̤ ts'iṳ̄ kiep, iemand den weg afsnijden en uitplunderen.
k'ì tsiét i ê niṳ̄ ts'áo. (den vijand) zijne levensmiddelen afsnijden.
k'ì tsiét i ê tsī̤, vreezende zijn geld niet van iemand te krijgen zijne goederen in beslag nemen.
tsiét tīng bīn ê laò tsúi, het water boven op de rivier afsnijden.

捷 Ts'ièt *Bin tsiét*, vlug, handig.
liaó tsiét, afdoende (niet aarzelend).
kán tsiét, beknopt (niet langdradig).
tsiét koat, beknopte manier.
pò tsiét, bericht van eene overwinning geven.

切 Ts'iet *Kè tsī̤ kap i ts'iet ts'iet*, van iemands prijs afdingen verminderen.
ts'iet, ver.icaal doorsnijden, in stukken snijden.
ts'iet ts'iet, voornamelijk, toch, vooral.
ts'iet k'ah tsió, afdingen, verminderen.
ts'iet iaò, voornaam, belangrijk van groot belang.
ts'iet tīng, afsnijden, afhakken, af koopen.
ts'iet ì, zeer verlangend zijn naar.
ts'iet sim, do.
koan ts'iet, van belang zijn.

ts'in ts'iet, intiem.
kap i ts'iet tiū tiòh, bepaald met iemand afspreken tot een besluit komen, den knoop doorhakken.
ts'iet ts'í ê oàn hūn, eene knarstandende haat.
ts'iet ts'aì, groenten hakken.
tsiet k'ui tsoē tsoē tsí, eene meloen opensnijdende zijn er vele pitten.
Ts'ièt *T'oa oē*: *ts'iét tseh ts'iét tseh*, sloffen (op zijne schoenen of muilen).

Tsih

接 *Tsih*, aannemen ontvangen van.
Tsih *niû tsih*, (een) gast ontvangen tegemoet gaan.
tsih tiòh, aannemen, in handen nemen, ontvangen.
tsih ts'uì, oogenblikkelijk daarop zeggen.
tsih sin, de geesten ontvangen in de eerste maand vierden dag.
tsih tsiep, omgaan met, zich mengen met.
hiet hō i tsih, gooien en iemand laten vangen.

摺 *Tsih*, opvouwen.
Tsih *tsih sn̄*, kleêren opvouwen.
ts'iú tsih, zakpapier (zakboekje) waar in het kort al zijne schuldvorderingen zijn opgeteekend.
i tsih, plooien in kleêren.
tsih hûn, met plooien.
Tsih *Tsih tsih tsuh tsuh*, treiterachtig ondeugend zijn (als kinderen).

舌 *Tsìh*, de tong.
Tsìh *tsìh kun*, tongriem.
giang á tsìh, klepel van een bel.
tsìh á, lelletje in de keel.
bô ts'uì tsìh, geen tong in de mond hebben *i. e.* weinig spreken.
ts'uì tsiem tsìh laī, *ts'uì tsìh tsiem laī*, welbespraakt.
t'ò tsìh, de tong uitsteken (van verwondering of schrik).
tsīng tsih (*tsuī*), met de tong aflikken.
tìng tsih koan (*suī*), het gesprek op iets anders overbrengen, een andere wending aan zijne woorden geven.
tìuh tsìh kun (*kin*), lispelend spreken.
ts'ing ts'uì bān tsih oh hun piēn, met alle mogelijke betoogen toch niet tot overtuiging kunnen brengen.
ping tsih tsoā (*pán kouī*), het éene oogenblik tegenspreken wat men even te voren zeide.
koe tsih taoh, klink, veer (op een deur).
tsìh tsuì toà siang tsìh, een dubbele tong in de mond hebben *i. e.* wel spraakt zijn.
dzím hó tsìh, een tijger de tong uit de mond halen (*i. e.* uit dankbaarheid alles hoe onmogelijk ook voor iemand willen doen).

折 *At tsih*, door midden kraken.
Tsih *p'ah tsih ts'uì k'í*, zijne tanden op iets breken (op een hard ding).
at tsih kó pì (*pè*), een vertelsel afbreken.
tsih tsūm (*tuī*), de opeenvolging is afgebroken.
tsih tsat (*tuī*), afbreken niet verder gaan (in een gesprek).
p'ah tsih tsat (*tuī*), afbreken.
ū tsih tsat k'í lai, er is iets afgebroken uitgelaten.
tsih tìng, *tsih tsoè nn̄g tìng*, in tweeën breken.
poà lō p'ah tsih pìn tn̄, halverwege de draagstok stukbreken *i. e.* halverwege zijne belofte niet na komen.

Tsih *Lok tsih tsih*, modderig = *tsiúh tsiúh*.
ning tsih tsih (nui), zeer zacht ook *tsiúh tsiúh*.

低 Ts'ih *Ts'ih t'aô*, het hoofd laten hangen.
t'aô ts'ih ts'ih, met voorovergebogen hoofd druipstaartend beschaamd.
ts'ih lóh k'ì, neerschieten (als vogels doen).
bih bih ts'ih ts'ih, uiterst beschaamd.

電 Ts'ih *Ts'ih ts'oah*, het bliksemt.

蠘 Ts'ih *Ts'ih*, gevlekte groote krab.
âng ko ts'iah ts'ih, vleesch van krabben.

抑 Ts'ih *Ts'ih*, vasthouden de hand leggen op (als op iets dat anders weg zou gaan).
ts'ih lóh k'ì, neerdrukken.
kiòng kiòng eh ts'ih ih, gewelddadig iemand tot iets dwingen.
ìm t'ang ts'ih p'oà, druk het niet stuk (als een zwakke blikken doos).

Ts'ịh *Ts'ịh ts'áng*, snikken.
ím kạ ts'ịh ts'áng, niet durven snikken geen geluid van zich durven geven.

Tsik

燭 Tsik *Tsik*, kaars.
tsik tai, kandelaar.
iû tsik, zachte kaars.
gû iû tsik, vetkaars.
tsik sim, pit van de kaars.
láh tsik, waskaars.
tsik saí, vuil van de kaars.
tsik luī, afdruipsel van de kaars.
tô tsik, harde kaars van planten talk gemaakt.
tsik bâng, plant waarvan men kaarsenpitten maakt.
tsik hoe (hna), uitstaande kaarsenpit.
lâm tsik' iû tsik (o), kaarsen maken gieten.

tsùn-ts'ah tsik (tsik), voorover in een golf storten (van een schip).

責 Tsik *Tsik hoát*, straf, straffen.
tsik pī, straffen laken.
tsik mē, uitschelden.
k'ién tsik, bestraffen (van den hemel).

積 Tsik *Tsik tsū*, opstapelen, opgaren.
tsik t'iok, do.
tsik lai tsoē (tsē), in groote hoeveelheid aangevoerd, overvoerd zijn.
ok tsik (»), opstapeling van slechtheid.
liep tsik, opsprokkelen opsparen.
t'iòk tsik (hiok tsih), opgaren opstapelen.
tui tsik, opstapelen.
tsik tsá, van ouds (hoe langer hoe meer).
tsik tsọ í lai, van ouds her.
kam tsik, ziekte van kinderen waardoor zij veel eten, een opgezwollen buik krijgen en de hoofdharen uitvallen.
tsik tsik tsoè tsít tui, opstapelen.
tsik tik, deugden opstapelen steeds in deugden toenemen.

則 Tsik *Tsik lē (lé)*, wetsbepaling tarief.
it tsik, in de eerste plaats.
dzī tsik, in de tweede plaats.

跡 Tsik *Pit tsik*, handschrift, handteekening.
sìng tsik, heilige overblijfsels.
kọ́ tsik, overblijfsels uit de oudheid.

即 Tsik *Tsik si*, onmiddelijk.

塞 Tsik *Tsik*, instoppen.
tsik dzip k'ì, indrijven.
tsik huih (hoek), bloed uitknijpen.
kiòng kiòng kā i tsik ts'ut lai (» ») (dzik), met geweld geld uit hem, den gierigaard, knijpen.

tsik oá, dichterbij schuiven.

叔 Tsik *Tsik kong*, oudoom (jongere) van vaders zijde.

tsik peh (*peh*) }, oom (vaders oudere broeder).

pao tsik, oom (jongere) van vaders zijde.

tong tsik, neven nichten (kinderen van broeders).

piaó tsik, oudtante's kind, jongere van vaders zijde.

aō tsik, stiefvader.

tsik sun, neven en kleinkinderen.

笮 Tsik *Tsui tsik*, waterspruitje.

Ts'ik *Ts'ik soe*, een ongelukkig voorteeken ontmoeten.

ts'ik ò ē oē, vuile liederlijke taal.

ts'ik ò, bezoedelen.

粟 Ts'ik *Ts'ik*, ongepelde rijst.

bí ts'ik, gepelde en ongepelde rijst.

ts'ik gè, rijstspruiten.

ts'ik sṳ̄, rijstpakhuis.

tsiáh bi tsiáh ts'ik k'ah koai lâng, zij eten rijst en zijn toch gladder dan anderen (van gauwdieven of beesten gezegd).

雀 Ts'ik *Ts'ik tsiaó á*, musch.

促 Ts'ik *Ts'ik té*, een opnaaisel in een kleed leggen.

ts'ik kat, door een knoop er in te leggen korter maken.

ts'ik kē, lager maken.

ts'ik k'ah té, korter maken (door afknippen of innemen).

ts'ik k'a sa tsióng tsiū, de beenen korter maken en elkander toenaderen *i. e.* inwilligen, inschikkelijk zijn.

側 Ts'ik *Ts'ik sa kūn* (*k'ah kīn*) }, elkander naderen.

ts'ik bé sè, met de beenen wijd van elkander gaan staan om meer kracht te kunnen zetten.

ts'ik sik ts'ut eh, van eene bijzit geboren.

戚 Ts'ik *Ts'in ts'ik*, verwanten (aangetrouwde).

測 Ts'ik *Ts'ik tók*, peilbaar, doorgrondbaar.

boē oē ts'ik tók (*bē*) }, onpeilbaar, ondoorgrondelijk.

惻 Ts'ik *Ts'ik ún é sim*, medelijdend hart, gevoelens.

策 Ts'ik *Kè ts'ik*, plannen.

摵 Ts'ik *Ts'ik*, bewegen, op en neer gaan (als een draagstoel).

ts'iao ts'ik, levendig opgeruimd.

tiò k'a ts'ik, hinkelen.

p'ah ts'ik, uit elkander halen (als eene zaak, 2e verzeulen versjouwen).

iò iò ts'ik ts'ik, schudden sussen (als men een kind doet).

ts'ik kiá, een kindje sussen.

kap i ts'ik, met iemand het ware van eene zaak uitmaken.

kap i ts'ik siaò, met iemand het warebedrag van eene rekening uitmaken.

ts'ik lik lik leh (eene rekening of zaak) geheelenal uitmaken.

Tsim

Tsim *Tsim ts'ùi*, kussen, zoenen.

sa tsim, elkander kussen.

tsim tsīng tsīng, kussen, likken.

sa tsim ts'ùi, de monden bij elkander steken (als mieren die elkander ontmoeten).

t'iàⁿ kaò p'ō k'i lai tsim, zoo beminnen dat men het (kind) in de armen neemt en kust.

斟 Tsim *Tsim tsiok* (*tsiak*) }, beraadslagen over, omzichtig te werk gaan.

90

枕 *Tsim kut*, been van het achterhoofd.
Tsim *k'ò tsim*, armleuningkussen.
koe tsim, *koe tsi tsim*, schuins afloopend hoofdkussen.
siù tsim, geborduurd hoofdkussen.
tsim t'aò, peluw, hoofdkussen.
tsim t'aò tē, kussensloop.
tsim t'aò küi, peluwduivel, vrouw.
oan ig tsim, hoofdkussen voor twee personen.

Tsim *Tsím*, tante, vrouw van zijn oom van vaders zijde.
tsim pò, oudtante (vrouw van zijn grootvaders jongere broeder).
tsim ém, tante (vrouw van vaders broeder).
sió tsim, vrouw van zijn jongeren broeder.

浸 *Tsìm kaò ts'ut bī*, te trekken zetten (als
Tsìm medicijnen).
tsìm, weeken, in het water leggen.
tsìm k'ī, gele persimmon.
pit tsìm, penseelen standaard.
tsìm noā, doorweeken.
tsìm tsù, van water doortrokken.
tsìm k'a, een voetbad nemen.
tsìm hō, door regen doortrokken.
tsìm tsui, in het water zetten om te weeken enz.
hō lai tsui, langdurige harde regen.
tsìm t'aò, door en door doortrokken.
tsìm kaò oē, zoo doortrokken dat men het kan (als iemand die dagelijks ziende eindigt met het ook te konnen).
tsìm tsui tsìm tsiep, door water en vocht doortrokken (als groenten visch enz).

蟳 *Tsim*, krab.
Tsîm *àng tsim*, roode krab.
tsim kóng k'a, horrelvoet.
iao tsim sg nėh, hongerige krabben die elkander aangrijpen; de personen die gelijkelijk arm zijn en nog van elkander wat willen hebben.

Tsim *Tsim ts'ut lai*, er uithalen (van geld).

tsim tsį, geld uit de zak halen.
tsim t'àng t'àng, overal rondvoelen, bevoelen.

柑 *Ts'im tsièm*, inbreuk maken op, zijn
Ts'im grondgebied overschrijden vergrooten.
ts'im t'ėh / " *ts'a* / (*ts'ı*) }, langzamerhand ontvreemden.
ts'im īng / (*iōng*) }, te veel gebruiken.
ts'im k'ièm, te kortkomen bij.
ts'im hoān, een inval doen, aanvallen.
ts'im t'uī, dieper in schulden raken.
ts'im k'àm, meer en meer in schuld raken maar er zijn compagnon of baas niets van laten merken.
ts'im tīn, in de vijandelijke gelederen indringen.
ts'im haī, diep benadeelen.
ts'im kaì, inbreuk op een grens (van velden enz.) maken, zijne grenzen wederrechtelijk uitbreiden.
ts'im tsį, meer geld gebruiken dan men mag.
tit tit ts'im lai, hoe langer hoe meer inbreuk op iets maken, zijne grenzen overschrijden.

深 *Ts'im*, diep, ook van beteekenis.
Ts'im *ts'im tim*, do.
ts'im ts'ièn, perspectief.
ts'im hai hai, zeer diep.
ts'im siū, diepdenkend.
ts'im sim, do., van scherp doorzicht
ts'im ts'im ip dziā, eene diepe buiging maken.
ts'im tsį, binnenplaats (open of overdekt).
nį kù geh ts'im, voor langen tijd.
sik tì ts'im, diepe donkere kleur.
hák būn ts'im, diepe litterarische kennis.
dzī bak ts'im, do.
toā ts'im tiá, groote diepe pan.
goá ts'im tsai hit è lòng, ik ken dien man door en door.

kī ts'im, diep in den nacht.
ts'im soā lai, diep in het gebergte.
ts'im long long: *ts'im lang lang*, zeer diep.

滲 Ts'im *Ts'im k'a kiā*, voorzichtig voetje voor voetje loopen.
ts'im k'oā tseh, beproeven, iemand polsen.
ing oē kā i ts'im tseh, iemand polsen.

Ts'im *Ts'im nī*, dicht bij nieuwjaar.
k'ah ts'im tseh, nog wat wachten tot het dichterbij het nieuwjaar is (als tegen schuldeischers gezegd).

Ts'im *Taī tsi i king ts'im k'i*, die zaak is zoolang neer — terzijde gelegd.

Ts'im *Ts'im ts'im á kaò*, maar juist genoeg; juist gekomen zijn.

Ts'im *Toā ts'im*, de bekkens.

Tsin

眞 Tsin *Tsit tsin*, ongeveer een kattie.
tsui ts'in waterschepper.
升 *Tàng tsin*, stellig-zeker.
tsin tsing, de ware gestolen goederen.
tsin sim sit ì, oprecht van meening oprecht gemeend.
tsin tsiā, inderdaad.
tsin sit, do.
tsin tsin ts'ók ts'ók, ontwijfelbaar, zeker.
t'ā tsin tsing, zijn hart lucht geven, aan iemand openleggen.
sū tsin làn tit kè, eene ware zaak is moeielijk te verdraaien.
dzīn tsin, de wezenlijkheid van iets (zijn plicht enz.) vervullen 2e voor waarheid voor ernstig gemeend opvatten.
kī tsin bò tsit p'oat, als men hetzelf doen moet er niets van kennen.
tsin siā, ware natuurlijke stem.
tsin tiā, in werkelijkheid, als het op doen aankomt.
tsin ts'ó lē t'oàn, de vier soorten van schrift.
kòng tsin hiā, reukwerk dat de ware geesten doet weêrkomen.
tìng tsin, uiterst goed puik.
tsin kim put p'à hè, zuiver goud vreest het vuur niet *i. e.* wanneer ergens bedrog in iets is kan het gerust onderzoek velen.
tsin tsing poáh tsióh, de ware goederen vallen op den waren steen *i. e.* waar de goederen dezelfde zijn kan de prijs ook niet verminderd worden.
tsin làng boā kòng tit kè oē, een oprecht mensch kan geene leugens vertellen.

珍 Tsin *Tsin tsu*, paarlen.

Tsin *Ts'ì tsin*, eensklaps, onverwacht, zonder nadenken of voorzorgen.

Tsin *Bák tsiu tsin tsin tsin*, (op iets) staroogen.

Tsin *Tsē tsin*, bezinken.
ting tsin, van een bezonken stof het heldere afnemen bezinken 2e van een klad in het net schrijven.

蓁 Tsin *Kog tsin*, biesgewas.

振 Tsin *Tsin k'i*, er boven op helpen, een rijk uit zijn gevallen toestand ophelpen.
tsin tsè, noodlijdenden helpen (als bij hongersnood).

進 Tsin *Tsìn*, door een examen komen.
tsìn óh, do.
tsìn sū, derde litterarische graad.
tsìn t'ao tsing, voorgaan.
tsìn kòng, schatting komen opbrengen.
hō tsìn, nakomelingen.
tsìn tsoè, eene vrouw huwen (bij haar in huis genomen worden hetgeen soms door armoede van den man of door verwijderde woonplaats van de vrouw gebeurt).
tsìn iah, voordeel aanbrengend (als een gelukkig mensch in een huis aanbrengt).
ìn tsìn, introduceeren, leiden (als op een weg).

ĭm tsóng tsìng, ontaard (van kinderen).
tsìn tsòng, de lijkkist naar het graf brengen.
tsìn kièn é lé, geschenken bij een bezoek (aan hoogere mandarijnen).
t'iem ting tsìn tsai, vermeerdering van familie en schatten.
tsìn tsìn t'oè t'oè, toetreden en weer teruggaan, aarzelen.
dzit aò ng ū ts'ùn tsìn, als (ik) later wat vooruitkom (zal ik u zichtbare bewijzen mijner dank geven).

縉 Tsìn *Tsìn sin*, eeretitel voor elken gegradueerde.

繩 Tsin *Tsin*, lijn.
bak t'aò tsin / (*bak tsin*) }, inktlijn.
tuī tsin, waterpas.
toḁ tsin, de inktlijn spannen en loslaten.
k'an tsin, de inktlijn langs iets trekken.
uī tsin, *tsoè tsin*, een inktlijn trekken afperken.
tuì tsin in een rechte lijn.
tsiào tsin kiḁ lō̤, rechtmatig handelen.
tsún tsin, afgemeten, vastberekend.

瞡 Tsin *Tsin*, afmeten met een oog (als een timmerman).

Tsin *Tsin kap sòng bô siàng tiaò tē* de Tsin (204 v. Chr.) en de Sòng (950 na Chr.) zijn geene zelfde dynastie *i. e.* de personen of volken waarover gij spreekt, hebben niet met elkaar te maken kunnen niet met elkaår vergeleken worden.

盡 Tsīn *Tsīn*, uitputten zeer uiterst, waarschuwen, in bedenking geven.
tsīn tsaī, wezentlijk, inderdaad.
tsīn » tsoē / (*tsē*) }, zeer veel.
tsin hó, allerbest.
tsīn t'aò, tot het einde toe.
tsū tsīn, zelfmoord begaan.
tsīn tiong, oprecht, alles voor zijn heer of vorst veil hebben.

tsīn sim, oprecht, ter harte te nemen.
tsīn tsiet, tot het uiterste toe zich aan zijn plicht houden (vooral van vrouwen gezegd die niet ten tweeden male huwen).
tsīn lik, met krachtsinspanning.
tsing tsīn, wanhopig, zonder eenige verwaching.
tsīn tsing, met zijn uiterste best.
sḁ tsīn, elkander voor het laatst in bedenking geven.
ĭng oē tsīn làng, iemand nog voor het laatst in bedenking geven.
tsīn t'aò lah, zoover als mogelijk tot aan het eind.
tsīn ming, de geheele partij, menigte.
tsīn p'àng, met alle zeilen bij.
bô kióng tsīn, onmetelijk onbegrensbaar (als de hoogte des hemels).
kóng boē tsīn, onuitsprekelijk te veel om te vertellen (van eene verwarde zaak).
sìng boē tit tsīn, ontelbaar (als de sterren), onnoembaar van eene verwarde zaak.
it tsīn... geheel en al.
tsīn kai, geheel en al, allen.
tsīn ū t'eh ts'ut lai k'oḁ, alles wat er is laten zien (als monsters).
tsīn pūn, het uiterste (grootste of kleinste) model.
tsīn bé liu, het uiterste eind.
tsīn tsió, uiterst weinig.
tsīn i é k'ùi lát, al zijne krachten inspannen.
tsiáh kaò tsīn pàn, de wijnkan leègdrinken leègmaken.

親 Ts'in *Sing ts'in*, een huwelijk aangaan.
ts'in sin, zelve.
ts'in tsiḁ, familiebetrekking.
ts'in ts'ik, bloedverwanten.
goā ts'in, vrouwsfamilie.
ts'in ke / (*ke̤*) }, vader van zijne behuwd dochter.

ts'in im } , moeder van zijne behuwd
(*ts'e*) }
dochter.

tsoè ts'in ke, een huwelijk aangaan.

kiet ts'in, tsoè ts'in, do.

ts'in ts'iū } , even als, zooals.
(*ts'in ts'iō*) }

ū ts'in ts'iū } , gelijken op.
(*ts'iō*) }

ts'in bit, intiem.

ts'in dziét, intiem zijn met iemand, op goeden voet met hem zijn.

ts'in bák k'oà ki, met zijn eigen oogen zien.

ts'in siók, tot iemands familie behoorende.

kiong ts'in, dorpsgenooten (door uitlandige menschen gezegd).

ts'in aì, beminnen.

ts'in t'áh ts'in, door wederkeerige huwelijken aan elkander verwant.

ts'in ts'uì tuì láng kóng, eigenmondig mondelings persoonlijk tot iemand zeggen.

ts'in ts'iu t'éh hō ih, oigenhandig aan hem geven.

dzīn ts'in, uitvinden ontdekken dat men nog in de familie is.

ts'in ting, mannelijk familielid.

ts'in tòng, ooms enz.

dzi hun ts'in, weduwe die een tweede huwelijk aangaat.

kong ts'in, middelaar.

ts'in ts'iet, door innige vriendschap verbonden.

ts'in kūn tioh, naderen dichterbij komen.

ts'in ping, familie betrekkingen en vrienden.

liòk ts'in familiebetr. in het algemeen.

ts'in hiū ti, volle broeders.

tsì ts'in naaste verwanten.

hoé ts'in, van een engagement, huwelijk afzien.

Ts'in *Ts'in ts'i* } , fraai.
(*ts'é*) }

Ts'in *Ts'in ts'iaó*, woelig lastig, speelziek (van kinderen).

稱 *Ts'in*, wegen, unster.

Ts'in *ts'in kao*, haken van een unster.

ts'in t'ui, gewicht van een balans.

ts'in ke hé, zijne bezitting opnemen.

ts'in liaō, touw van een weegstok.

ts'in hè, goederen wegen.

ts'in koai, arm van een weegschaal.

ts'in hoe, merken afdeelingen op een balans.

ts'in ts'i, do.

ts'ien kun ts'in, hefboom.

ing ts'ien kun ts'in ts'in k'i lai, met een hefboom optillen.

tsit ts'in é tàng, 10 pond.

Ts'in *Ts'in ts'ai*, het komt er niet op aan onverschillig hoe ook, naar willekeur zoo als het uitvalt.

ts'in ts'ai làng, onverschillig wie ook.

ts'in » sū tsaī } , onverschillig waar.
(*sé*) }

Ts'in *Ts'in bīn*, somber (van uiterlijk en neerslachtig, ernstig uitzien van vrouwen).

ts'in, koud koel.

ts'i t'aò ts'in bīn } , opstuiven.
(*ts'e*) }

ts'in tim làng, iemand koel ontvangen.

ts'in sim, zijne vroegere lust voor iets laten varen.

ts'in sim, in ijver verkoelen, de moed laten zakken.

ts'in mūh ngh, huidziekte (door gevatte koude).

koā ts'in, koude, koud.

ts'i ts'in, kille huivering (van bangheid).

ts'in pi pi, koud kil.

ts'in sùng sùng, ijskoud = *ts'in t'ih t'ih* = *ts'in piang piang*.

ts'in k'ì, koel worden verkoelen.

ts'in ts'iò, koel lachen grijnzen.

poā sio ts'in, lauw.

ts'in líng, koud kil.

p'ah ts'in k'ì, koud doen worden.

爭 *Tsing kaò*, iemand een standje schoppen.
Tsing *tsing k'ì*, met boosheid (niet om geld) twisten = *tsing k'ì put tsing tsat.*
tsing ts'e todt tièn kièn sù dzù bièn, twist men over eene vrouw of ontneemt men elkanders veld beschouw dan den dood als eene slaap.

舂 *Tsing ts'iū* (*ts'iō*) }, een muur aanstampen.
Tsing *tsing*, met de vuist slaan, stompen.
tsing kòng p'ah, stompen, beuken en slaan.
tsing piàng, in een huis inbreken (als dieven).
tsing tiòh, stooten tegen.
tsing ming táh hō, met geweld de deur intrappen.
àm àm sg tsing tiòh, in donker tegen elkander aanstooten.
tsing noū, tot moes stampen.
tsing, in een mortier stampen.
tsing k'ū, rijstmortier.
tsing bi, rijst stampen.

貞 *Tsing tsiet*, kuisch.
Tsing *tsing tsiet hing*, eerepoort voor een brave vrouw.

精 *Tsing sè*, omzichtig te werk gaande, zorgvuldig.
Tsing *tsing kong*, buitengewoon ervaren zijn in.
tsing, juist getroffen geraakt, mannelijk zaad.
tsing sin, levendig, vrolijk, opgeruimd, helder van oogen.
tsing sin, wakker worden.
koh tsài tsing sin, weder bij komen van eene flauwte.
tsing kong, keurig net (van werk).
tsing hoa, opgesmukt.
tsing ing, er fiks stevig uitzien (van oude menschen en kinderen).
ji k'ì tsing tsing, zuiver aanleggen.
siòng tsing tsing, beproeven zien of het juist gaat (als een kanon).
ts'ì mì tsing é kaó līng, blinden zijn helder van geest, stommen zijn vernuftig.
gē tsing dzin pin, menschen die buitengewoon ervaren in iets zijn, zijn gewoonlijk arm.
tui tsing, zaadvloed valt, druiper.
ts'iū tsing sin, iemands levenskracht terughalen (als wanneer iemand flauw of stuipen heeft).
dzin tsit lō tsing, zich aan één bepaald vak wijden.
tò tsing, druiper
tsing bi ê tō li, eene fijne vernuftige manier op iets.

鐘 *St tsing*, klok.
Tsing *kòng tsing*, op de bel slaan.
iò tsing, schellen.
nà aò tsing á, lelletje in de keel.
k'ao tsing, de klok luiden (als Boeddh. pr).
tê tsing, theekopje.
tsiù tsing, wijnkop.
tsiáh làng t'aò tsing tsiù, de hoogste gas enplaats aan tafel hebben.
tsit tsing hiet kè sing, een wijnglas in eene andere provincie te werpen *i. e.* door met iedereen goed te zijn komt men verder dan met barsch te wezen.
tàng tsing, koperen bel of soort van gong.

增 *Tsing tsoàh*, verschillen.
Tsing *tsing tsa*, verschillen.
tsaò tsing, verschillen, niet juist in elkander passen.

征 *Tsing ping*, uitgelezen soldaten.
Tsing *ts'ut tsing*, ten strijde trekken.
tsing hoat, bestrijden, ten strijde trekken tegen.

曾 *Tsing tsō*, overgrootvader.
Tsing *tsing sun*, achter kleinzoon.

睛 *Bak tsiu tsing*, pupil van het oog.
Tsing

種 *Tsing*, soort van...
Tsing *tsing tsi*, bloemenzaad, zaad.

iū tsing, zaaien.
pò tsíng, do.
tsáp tsing á, onecht kind, kind van tien zaden.
tīng tsing, volstrekt niet meer.
tséh tsing, volstrekt niet meer over (van eene familie, van gewassen enz).
t'oân tsing, de generatie het ras voortzetten.
t'oâ tsing, uitplanten, voortplanten.
p'ai tsing tsák, van slecht ras scheldw).
tsu tsing, pokstof, inentstof.
t'ó tsu tsing, pokstof van iemand vragen.
iū tsing hoat k'i lai, zich zelven voortgezaaid hebben.

整 Tsing — *Tsing tsoè* (*tsé*), rangschikken, in orde brengen.
tsing tûn, geheel in orde brengen, repareeren.
tsing kò, beginnen iets te doen.
tsé tsing, geregeld regelmatig.
siu tsing, repareeren.
tsing lí, repareeren, er boven ophelpen.
t'aô tsing kaò bé, van top tot teen in het nieuw (letterlijk gerepareerd) zijn.
tsing sin ts'ī ng, zich in het pak steken zich kleêren aanschaffen.

腫 Tsing — *Tsing*, gezwel, opgezwollen.
tsing p'òng, gezwel.
p'òng tsing, gezwellen.
hàng tsing, gezwel, opzwellen.
âng tsing, roode opzwelling.
siao tsing, een gezwel doen verdwijnen.

種 Tsing — *Tsìng*, zaaien.
tsìng tsu, inenten, inenting.

政 Tsing — *Tsìng sū*, gouvernements zaken.

症 Tsing — *Pī tsìng*, soort ziekte, ziekte soort.
sùn tsìng, visites bij zieken gaan afleggen. (van dokter).
hoū tsìng, eene ziekte behandelen.
kè tsìng, ongeneeslijk.
si tsìng, do.
ok tsìng, slechte lastige ziekte.
p'ai tsìng t'aô, slechte gevaarlijke ziekte.
tui tsìng: eene ziekte genezend (van een medicijn).
laī goā k'e tsìng, inwendige uitwendige ziekte.
kip tsìng, gevaarlijke dringende ziekte, kwaal.
tsáp tsìng pī, altijd wat mankeeren.
kièn tsìng tsoē, veel ondervinding van ziekte hebben (als een oude dokter).
k'oà tsìng hoat ioh, de aard van de ziekte zien en daarna medicijn geven.

正 Tsing — *Tsìng king* (•), eerlijk, rechtschapen.
t ìng hoat, de wet toepassen op, dooden.
tsìng tsong, rechtschapen.
tsìng tit, onbewimpeld, rond (ronduit) (van personen.)
tsìng k'ì, eerlijk fatsoenlijk (zich met geene verkeerde dingen inlatend).
bìng tsìng giên-sūn, betamelijk volgens recht en billijkheid (waarmede zijn naam ongeschonden blijft)
tsìng p'aì, in rechte lijn afstammeling van.
tsìng tò, betamelijke levenswandel.
tsìng sik, hoofd, wettige vrouw (beleefdheidsterm).
ìng tsìng, vereerende term voor vrouw.

証 Tsing — *Kan tsìng*, getuigenis afleggen.
tsìng kù, bewijs.
ū tsìng ū kù, de bewijzen getuigen zijn voorhanden.
t'ih kan tsìng, ontegenzeggelijk bewijs.
nē kan tsìng, do.

衆 Tsing — *Tsìng lâng*, allen.
tsìng lâng ts'uì, volgens algemeen zeggen verklaring.
toā ke k'aò tsìng, vele huisgenooten.
boē kì tsìng tit, het daglicht niet kunnen zien (van verkeerde handelingen).

kong tsing, publiek gemeenschappelijk (niet privaat).

kong tsing kong iaō, het is gemeenschappelijk iets (en waarom zoudt gij alleen er u tegen verzetten).

tsing lâng t'aī it, het is gemakkelijker dat allen één wel geschenken geven (dan dat één het aan alle anderen doen zou).

tsing kong mi̍, (tempeltje der) publieke voorouders (de zielen van hen die geene nakomelingen hebben en wier tabletten in openbare tempeltjes vereerd worden).

前 Tsing *Bīn tsing k'iā*, voor iemand staand, in iemands gezicht, tegenwoordigheid, uit uitwendig.

tsing ni̍ / (*tsân*) }, vorige jaren.

tsing bīn, van voren.

tsing kun, de voorhoede.

tsing ia̍, do.

t'aô tsing, vooruit voor.

tsing dzìt, vroegere dagen.

tsing aō, van voren en van achteren, om en bij, ongeveer.

tsing mìng, voordeur.

tsing lâng kiá, kinderen uit een vorig huwelijk.

tsing k'i, *tsing sin*, een vorige keer.

ts'ut lâng tsing, boven ordinairen uitsteken.

gán tsing è taī tsì, zaken die voor oogen zijn.

bák tsiu tsing, voor iemands oogen in iemands tegenwoordigheid.

koan tsing kò̤ aō, van voren en van achteren oppassen (als bij het verdragen van iets).

tsing pai, eene vorige keer.

tsing pang, bij een vorigen keer, convooi, bezending.

tsing lóh aō lóh, het voor en het achtergedeelte van een huis (met meer dan één dak).

情 Tsing *Hâng tsing* / (") }, marktprijs.

lıng tsing, iemands gunst aannemen, zich overtuigd houden van iemands genegenheid (gezegd als men van iemands uitnoodiging geen gebruik kan maken).

ū tsing ti lâng tao, verplichting aan iemand hebben.

ts'it tsing, de zeven aandoeningen namelijk: tevredenheid, toorn, smart, vrees, liefde, haat en lust.

ū dzin tsing, gevoel voor weldaden enz. hebben.

sìng tsing, karakter aard.

tsoè tsing hò̤ ih, iemand om der wille van een ander kwijtschelden.

tsing li, gevoel van recht en onrecht.

tsing gī, menschlievendheid.

ts'át tsing, diefstal.

sū tsing, gesteldheid van eene zaak.

goân tsing, de omstandigheden in aanmerking nemende, zich in iemands plaats stellen.

kiù tsing, eene gunst van iemand verzoeken.

liōng tsing, zich in iemands toestand verplaatsen.

liēm tsing, verplichting jegens iemand in het geheugen houden.

bù tsing è lâng, een ondankbaar ongevoelig mensch.

hó tsing hó ì, met goede bedoeling.

tōng tsing, liefdes vuur doen ontsteken.

kao tsing, de gesteldheid van iemands genegenheid voor een ander.

kièn biēn sing tsing, op het gezicht van iets of iemand zich iets of iemand herinneren, genegenheid voor hem op vatten.

dzin-tsaī-dzin tsing tsaī, *dzin bông dzin tsing bông*, bij iemands leven is de genegenheid voor hem daar, sterft hij dan sterft ook de vroegere genegenheid.

sū tsīng, heimelijke betrekking verhouding (tusschen personen).
sọ kóng dzìp tsing dzìp lí, wat hij zegt dringt door, vindt plaats bij iemands gevoel voor recht en plichtmatigheid.

靜 *Tsīng tsīng*, stil.
Tsīng *k'ùn tsīng tsīng*, in diepe rust.
ts'ing tsīng, rein van levenswandel.
tsīng tsīng, houd u stil.
t'iem tsīng, bedaard stil (van aard).
siok tsīng, stil rustig (van plaatsen of personen).
ióng tsīng, zich door rust sterker maken.
ling ling tsīng tsīng, koel en stil, flauw (van handel).
tsīng tseh tseh en *tsiaoh tsiaoh*, zeer-rustig ook stilletjes (van handel).
tsīng tsaoh, stil rustig (van eene plaats).
tsīng tì, tsīng tì tsīng tì, stil rustig (van aard).

淨 *Kiet tsīng*, zindelijk rein (van levens-
Tsīng wandel.
tsīng sit tāng, netto gewicht.
soé tsīng, reinigen, zuiveren (als eene kraamvrouw of een huis waarin een lijk geweest is).
tsīng sin, een lijk zuiveren van de smetten der aarde voor dat het gekist wordt.
tsīng iû, olie branden (als Taoïstische priesters om booze geesten uit te drijven).
tsīng hiu, reukpoeder om eene plaats van booze geesten te zuiveren.

竫 *Pîng tsīng*, rustig, in vrede.
Tsīng *an tsīng*, do.
Tsīng *Sạ á tò tsīng ts'ut lai*, de (onder) kleeren komen boven de bovenkleêren uit.

清 *Ts'ing*, helder.
Ts'ing *ts'ing k'ì*, zindelijk.
ts'ing k'ì siù, do.
ts'ing kiet, zuiver (van gedrag).
ts'ing tsui, zoetwater.
ts'ing tsá, vroeg (in den morgen).

nīng ts'ing (nuī), wit van eieren.
ts'ing siaò, afrekenen, eene rekening voldoen?
ts'ing ts'ai, helder.
ts'ing ts'ó, afgedaan, afbetaald.
ts'ing ts'ó ts'ó en *ts'ọ ts'ọ*, duidelijk uitgemaakt eerlijk.
ts'ing kao á, een gracht uitbaggeren.
ts'ing ing ê tsị, gemakkelijk verdiend geld.
ts'ing ling k'ì, afgerekend hebben, geheel en al schoongemaakt.
ts'ing ing ê miạ, een onbezorgd leven.
ts'ing hân, niets te doen hebben.
ts'ing siù, net, keurig.
ts'ing goá tsai, alleen ik weet het.
ts'ing ts'ing lí tsit lâng, alleen gij.
ts'ing ts'ing m̄, alleen niet willen.
dzit ts'ing, journaal, dagboek (van een koopman).
ts'ó ts'ing, kladjournaal, memoriaal.
ts'ing tsa, telling houden van inwoners belasting enz.
ts'ing tām, klein van fortuin maar eerlijk.
lai ts'ing k'ì bing, eerlijk met iemand omgaan, handelen.
tsoè lâng ts'ing pik, een eerlijk man zijn.
ts'ing tsìng, zindelijk schoon.
ts'ing sóng, schoon zindelijk en mooi (van plaatsen huizen enz) rustig van eene plaats.
ts'ing tsīng, stil rustig (als eene plaats ook als weduwen enz).
tsiáh ts'ing ts'ài, niets dan groenten eten, vasten zooals de Boeddha priesters doen.
ts'in hân ê lâng, iemand die een rustig leven leidt (niet veel te doen heeft).
ts'ing pik, fatsoenlijk, onberispelijk.
t'ing ts'ing, bezinksel uitdruipsel van suiker.
ts'ut ts'ing, uitdruipen (gew. van suiker).
tsē ts'ing, bezinken.

91

ts'ing p'iao, regelmatig van uiterlijk welgemaakt.

ts'ing p'ang, sterke lucht.

ts'ing tê, beste thee.

ts'ing píng é sè kaì, eene vreedzame rustige wereld, eeuw.

sin ka ts'ing pik, hij en zijne familie zijn onbesproken smetteloos.

ts'ing tsui tsú pèh pīng, met schoon water kook ik witte rijst *i. e.* er is geen bedrog in mijne handelingen.

sui tiaô ts'ing, bij elk artikel, elken koop, afbetalen contant betalen.

ts'ing tsi, een put uitbaggeren schoonmaken.

ts'ing bing, feest der gravenreiniging.

千 Ts'ing *Ts'ing* (*ts'an*), duizend.

káng ts'ing, bij duizenden.

ts'ing bān, zeer veel.

sing ts'ing sing bān, bij duizenden en tien duizenden d; i: veel.

ts'ing giên bān gú, veel praten.

ts'ing tsiem bān soā, met veel zorgen genaaid (van kleêren).

k'iā ts'ing tó bān, duizenden hebben staan en tienduizenden hebben liggen (van een grooten handelaar gezegd).

Ts'ing *Ts'ing tìng* (*t'aô*), supercargo, ook voor matroos.

稱 Ts'ing *Tsū ts'ing*, zich noemen.

ts'ing ho, den eerenaam geven van.

ts'ing tsàn, prijzen roemen.

青 Ts'ing *Ts'ing t'ien pik dzit*, op klaarlichten dag.

筅 Ts'ing *Ts'ing*, stoffen.

koe méng ts'ing (*ke mō*), veêrenstoffer.

ts'ing he (*hoe*), witten.

tik ts'ing, bamboezen boender.

ts'ing saò, stoffen en vegen.

ts'ing, wegkrabben (als een kip aarde omkrabt), omwoelen.

p'ah ts'ìng, verslonzen, verknoeien.

ts'ap ts'ùi ts'ing (*ts'án*), verward slordig door elkander.

ts'ing laī bīn, het binnenste van een huis, kamer stoffen.

請 Ts'ing *Ts'ing kào*, om raad vragen.

ts'ing an, naar iemands gezondheid informeeren, zijn complimenten doen.

稱 Ts'ing *Aì ts'ing* (*ts'oán*), van opschik houden.

銃 Ts'ìng *Ts'ìng*, geweer.

toā ts'ìng, kanon.

ts'ìng sin, loop van het geweer.

ts'ìng ts'ing, kolf van het geweer.

ts'ìng k'aó, mond van den geweerloop.

ts'ìng t'uh, de laadstok.

ts'ìng tī, do.

ts'ìng tsí, kogel.

ts'ìng ióh, kruid.

té ts'ìng (*bé*), pistool.

pàng ts'ìng, een geweer afschieten.

ts'ìng bé, kanonnen, geweeren en wapens.

ts'ìng k'ang, geschutspoorten.

tióh ts'ìng, door een geweerschot getroffen worden.

p'aò ts'ìng, kanonnen.

laò ts'ìng, schoon schieten (als een vuil geweer).

pàng (of *laò k'ang ts'ìng*, een leeg kanon afschieten, vergeefsche moeite doen.

īng hé ióh ts'ìng tó siā, eene vesting door kruid in de lucht doen vliegen.

揖 Ts'ìng *Ts'ìng p'ī*, de neus snuiten.

Ts'ìng *Ts'ìng hiu*, reukwerk tusschen kleeren enz. leggen.

ts'ìng p'ang, reukstof tusschen iets leggen.

p'ang kaò ts'ìng lâng, sterkriekend, in de neus vliegend.

ien p'ū p'ū ts'ìng, de stoom stijgt borrelend op.

ien ts'ìng k'i lai, de stoom stijgt op.
ts'ìng k'ui, eene lucht aan iets mededeelen (als stank of geur aan voorwerpen).
ts'ìng hoe, bloemen tusschen iets leggen.

蓆 Ts'ìng *Ts'aú ts'ìng* (*tsûn*), dikke mat.

縱 Ts'ìng *Ts'ìng*, schieten als visch, ook pijlsnel om hoogvliegen als vogels.
ts'ìng tsiū koai, omhoog schieten (als een vogel).
huih si koè ts'ìng, het bloed spuit naar alle kanten uit.
ts'ìng ki tsi, vuurpijl.

筅 Ts'ìng *Koe ts'ìng bō*, pluimhoed (oorspronkelijk door mandarijnen thans ook door soldaten gedragen).

烝 Ts'ìng *Ts'ìng hoan tsù*, aardappelen met weinig water koken (tot het water opgedroogd is).

稱 Ts'ìng *Ts'ìng sin hūn*, afhangen van iemands stand (als zijne uitgaven).
ī̄m ts'ìng i, niet in zijn schik, humeur zijn.
ts'ìng teh tsiu tiaô, zet men ze in elkander dan houden ze (als zwaluwstaarten).

榕 Ts'ing *Ts'ing ts'iū*, vijgenboom, ficus.
Ts'ing *k'út ts'ing*, geene beleefdheid of manieren bezitten.

鍤 Ts'ing *Ts'ing*, ijzeren stooter, soort van spade (stok met platte ijzeren punt om aarde enz. af te stooten).
ts'ing hō i pi, gelijkstooten.

Ts'ing *Ts'ing peh* (*peh*), denneboom.

Ts'ing *Ts'ing tioh*, ontmoeten tegenkomen, betrappen.

穿 Ts'ī̄ng *Ts'ī̄ng*, aantrekken aan het lijf, dragen (als kleêren).
ts'ī̄ng sa, kleêren aantrekken, zich aan kleeden.
ts'ī̄ng oé, schoenen aandoen.
ts'ī̄ng k'oā, aanpassen (kleêren).
ts'ī̄ng sio, zich warm aankleeden, voor verwarming aantrekken.
tsiáh ts'ī̄ng ī̄ng, eten kleeding en dingen voor ander gebruik.
ts'ī̄ng bô toé k'ò, eene bodemlooze broek aantrekken. *i. e.* 1e in een put vallen 2e met iemand compagnieschap aangaan die enorme schulden meêbrengt.
ts'ī̄ng ts'ah hó k'oā, fraai in kleeding en in kapsel (van vrouwen).

逢 Ts'ī̄ng *Ts'ī̄ng tioh*, ontmoeten.

Ts'ī̄ng *ī̄m sa ts'ī̄ng* niet in elkander passen.
sa tsiáh ts'ī̄ng, in elkander sluiten grijpen.

Tsio

招 Tsio *Tsio*, roepen, bepraten om.
sa tsio (*sio*), elkander afhalen om....
tsio iú, aanzoek doen om.
tsio bō, huren (als hulptroepen).
tsió kun boé bé (*bé be*), een leger werven.
ui tsio (*oā*), zijne schuldbekentenis (procesverbaal) onderteekenen.
tsio ho, liefkozen, streelen.
tsio pai, uithangbord.
tsio ín, medenemen.
tsio boé tsio boē, een koopman moet menschen lokken om te koopen en te verkoopen.
tsio k'eh, koopers aanroepen lokken.
ts'ah tsio, bakens plaatsen.
tsio ang, een man trouwen, die daardoor in de familie van de vrouw komt.
sa tsio sa io, elkander afhalen en ge zamenlijk gaan.
tsio siong, vragen om handelsbetrekkingen met een huis aanteknoopen.

tsio sió tī, een broertje gekregen hebben (tegen den ouderen broeder gezegd).

芽 Tsio *Gīng tsio*, pisang (vrucht).
pa tsio, pisangboom.

椒 Tsio *Hō̤ tsio*, peper.

少 Tsió *Tsió*, weinig, verminderen.
tsió tsió, do.
tsió tsi̤, afslaan (den prijs).
k'ìt i tsió tsi̤, afgedongen worden.
kiém tsió, *kiém k'ak tsió*, minder.
liém tsió, weinig van iets afnemen.
tsió tsi̤ kā i boé, voor minder geld van iemand koopen.
ke tsió, meer of min, veel of weinig.

照 Tsiò *Tsiò*, verlichten mikken, aanleggen.
tsiò keng (*kui̤*) }, verlichten. 2e tegen het licht aanhouden.
p'oe tsiò (*p'e*) }, havenuitklaring van een schip.
ts'iò ts'ut lai, inschijnen, doorstralen (als de zon of het licht door een venster).
tsiò pé (*pe̤*) }, op een doel mikken.
tsiò ki̤, in den spiegel zien.
tsip tsiò, bewijs van aanstelling.
tsiò sin dzī, bewijs van afkomst, van zijn persoon.
pō̤ tsiò, aanstelling, bewijs van....
tsiò dzit, tegen het licht houden.
tò tsiò, dwarshoudende zien dwars het licht er laten gevallen.
pai tsiò, scheepsbrief.
tsiò sin, bewijs van aanstelling.
tsiò hé t'ang, zich bij een vuurkoker (soort bamb. stoof) warmen.
si̤ tuì tsiò, op elkander uitzien, tegen over elkander zijn (van huizen).
tsiò sin ki̤, groote spiegel (voor het geheele lichaam).
tsiò ts'i̤, muur voor een huis (als voor mandarijn huizen).

醮 Tsiò *P'ah tsiò*, eene offerande laten houden (bij vertrek of aankomst van een schip).
tsoè tsiò (*tsò*) }, Boeddhistische mis houden
tsio toā, altaar voor een Boeddhistische mis.

鵤 Ts'io *Ts'io koe* (*ke*) }, haan in tegenstelling van kapoen.
ts'iò gû káng, dekstier.
koá ts'io, door vetheid, geslachtsdrift gedreven (van beesten).

肖 Ts'io *Ts'io tsit* (») *kak tsit* }, uitstekende punten van van het dak.
tsùn t'ao tuì tsiak ts'io lai, het schip kwam van daar recht er op aanzetten.
tsit ki ts'uì ts'io kiák kiák, kakelen zwetsen (onvermoeid praten).
ts'io ts'io tiò tiò, springlevend, gezond en wel (en een oogenblik daarna dood).

笑 Ts'iò *Ts'iò*, lachen, uitlachen.
t'ang ts'iò, belachelijk.
kóng ts'iò, gekscheren.
kin ts'iò. do.
líng ts'iò, grijnzen.
gī gī ts'iò, glimlachen.
hō̤ láng ts'iò, zich belachelijk aanstellen.
t'i ts'iò, uitlachen.
ts'in ts'iò, grimlachen.
ts'iò bīn hó, iemand met een lachend uiterlijk maar een slecht hart.
hō̤ láng tsoè ts'iò pi̤, maken dat men door anderen uitgelachen wordt.
seh ts'iò, schertsen gekheid vertellen.
ti̤ ts'in ts'iò, valsch grijnzen.

仰 Ts'iò *Ts'iò ts'iò tó téh* *tó ts'iò* }, op zijn rug liggen.
lién k'ap ts'iò, munt of kruis omgooien.
ts'iò poe, de orakelblokjes liggen op den bollen kant.

tó ts'iò ts'iò, achterover op den rug liggen.
ts'iò ts'iú, met de palm van de hand boven.
kóng oē siang p'ak k'ui ts'iò, in het spreken twee munt hebben maar er een kruis bij omkeeren *i. e.* niet bepaald zeggen »ja" of neen.
k'ùn ts'iò ts'iò of *t'án ts'iò*, op den rug slapen.

淺 Ts'iò *Ts'iò ts'i*, lichtblaauw.
ts'iò lik, lichtgroen.

照 Ts'iō *Ts'iō* (*ts'iō*) }, bijlichten.
ts'iō keng, bijlichten.
ts'iō mih, naar iets bijlichten (dat men zoekt).
ts'iō lō, den weg bijlichten.

Tsioh

借 Tsiog *Tsioh lai*, leenen van.
tsioh lâng, aan iemand leenen,
tsioh tsi, geld leenen.
tsioh tsi hō lâng, geld uitleenen.
sing tsioh, voorschieten, leenen.
i tsioh, leenen van....
oā tsioh, leenen.
tsioh tog, leenbewijs.
tsioh dzī, schriftelijke verklaring van leening.
sa tsioh mēng, elkander aanspreken (als eene kennis die men op straat ontmoet).
sia tsioh, op crediet geven en leenen.
kiù tsioh, terleen vragen.
tsioh sè, op een anders macht steunen 2e van eene bijkomende kracht gebruik maken.
tsioh lát, van eene bijkomende kracht gebruik maken (als van een harde wind om een muur om te werpen).
tsioh to sat dzin, een mes leenen om iemand te dooden *i. e.* van eene gelegenheid gebruik maken om iemand te benadeelen (als bij een oproer).

㷛 Tsioh *Tsioh hé* (*hoé*) }, zich warmen, koesteren bij het vuur.
tsioh dzit, zich warmen, koesteren bij de zon.

跖 Tsioh *K'a tsioh toé* (*té*) }, zool van de voet.

Tsioh *Mi tsioh p ē*, gewatteerde deken.

跡 Tsioh *Toé tsioh hó*, de fundeering van een gebouw is goed, de principes van dien man zijn goed.

石 Tsióh *Tsióh*, 1e steen, rots 2e 10 katties 3e familienaam.
tsioh t'aò, steen, stuk graniet,
gik tsióh, juweel, edel steen.
hip tsióh (*hap*) }, magneet.
soān tsióh, diamant.
tsióh he, steenkalk.
hé tsióh (*hoé*) }, vuursteen.
tsióh soā, rif van rotsen.
siáh tsióh, marmer, speksteen.
tsióh tsām, steenbeitel.
tsióh piah, steile platte kant van een rots.
tsióh kàng, padde.
tsióh pi, steenen tablet.
k'ui tsióh, steenen (van de rotsen) afzakken.
p'ah tsióh, steenhouwer.
pó tsióh edele steenen.
tsióh nēng, ronde steenen (als in beekjes).
tsióh, familienaam.

尺 Ts'ioh *Ts'ioh*, duimstok.
tsit ts'ioh, een voet.
k'ut ts'ioh, winkelhaak.
keh ts'ioh, liniaal.
t'i ts'ioh, kwadrant.
ts'ioh t'aò, grootte van een voet.

ū ts'ùn ts'ioh, afgeweten, van bepaalde grootte.

鮮 Ts'ioh *Ts'ı̠ ts'ioh* (*ts'ı̠ ts'ioh*) }, versch.

Ts'ioh *Ts'ioh ts'ioh*, met water inwrijven.

tàm tàm (of) *ı̠ŋ ı̠ŋ ts'ioh ts'ioh*, modderig nat.

Ts'ioh *Ti ts'ioh* (*ti pi*), varkensmaag.

吸 Ts'ioh *K it già kang ts'ioh*, een duizendpoot krijgen die zich in het vleesch vastklemt.

蓆 Ts'ioh *Ts'iòh*, eene mat.

'ka bùn ts'iòh, een mat van Singapore.

tin ts'iòh, rottingen mat.

ts'aó ts'iòh, biezenmat.

p'àng ts'iòh soh lō̠, zeilen en touwen.

Tsiok

囑 Tsiok *Tsiok t'ok*, toevertrouwen aan.

tsiok dzī, testament.

tsiok su (*si*) }, do.

ting lin tsiok hù, nogmaals gelasten.

mai̠ ts'iok, omkoopen.

爵 Tsiok *Hong ts'iok* (*tsiok*) }, adeldom.

sè tsiok, erfelijke adelstand.

tsiú tsiok (» *tsiak*) }, drievoetige wijnbokaal.

祝 Tsiok *Tsiok*, familienaam.

tsiok siū, op iemands gezondheid drinken (op zijn verjaardag).

足 Tsiok *Tsiok kièn*, het is te voorzien dat....

ts'iong tsiok, overvloed, overvloedig.

ti tsiok, tevreden zijn.

tsiok siŋ̄, zuiver (van metalen).

tsiok tāng gûn, zilvergeld van zuiver gehalte.

tsiok sik, zuiver (van metalen).

sim boán ì tsiok, voldaan in zijne wenschen zijn.

pọ̄ tsiok tsaō tsiok, het tekortkomende er bijleggen.

hù tsiok, voldoende rijk.

tsiok o̠ kim, zuiver goud.

tsiok io̠ng, genoeg voor zijn gebruik.

tsiok giáh, voldoende genoeg.

tsiok sò̠, voltallig genoeg (van duiten enz).

tsiok tsiok, voldoende, voltallig volledig.

酌 Tsiok *Tsiok liōng*, eene beraming maken het er voor houden.

tsim tsiok, zorgvuldig naauwkeurig onder zoeken.

Tsiók *Tsi tsí tsiók tsiók*, geluid als men door eene modderige plaats slobbert.

觸 Ts'iok *Ts'iok tiok* (*ts'iōk*) }, iemand iets invallen, 2e op heeter daad betrappen ontmoeten.

ts'iok hoūn, beleedigen.

ts'iok lō̠, iemand boosmaken.

ts'iok lâng ê tóan, iemands verkeerdheid, zijn zwak punt aanroeren.

ts'iok kíng taī, juist een gelukkig ding voorteeken ontmoeteu.

雀 Ts'iok *K'óng ts'iok*, pauw.

k'óng ts'iok bé, pauwestaart.

濁 Ts'iók *Tâm ts'iók ts'iók*, modderig (als steegjes).

dziók dziók tsiók tsiók, modderig.

t'ō̠ k'a tsiók tsiók, modderig van den grond.

Tsiong

將 Tsiong *Tsiong kun* (») }, tataarsche generaal.

tsiong tsiū, het er maar mede doen.

tsiong teh teh si, op het punt zijn te sterven.

tsiong lai, toekomstig, voortaan.

ts'iong kè tsiū kè, anderman's plannen verijdelen.

tsiong sim pi sim, zijn eigen hart bij dat van anderen vergelijken, zich in iemands positie stellen.

終 Tsiong *Tsiong tsīm*, op een eind loopen (als levensmiddelen.

siū sò kai tsiong, het leven heeft een eind, iedereen moet sterven.

siēn tsiong (*tsiang*) }, een goed uiteinde, goede dood.

tsiong po, een geheele voor of namiddag.

tsiong dzit, den geheelen dag.

tsiong sin, zijn leven lang.

liên tsiong soè bō, op het eind van het jaar.

kaù liên tsiong, tot het eind van het jaar.

lim tsiong, op zijn eind gekomen, op zijn uiterste liggen.

iú sí iú tsiong, een begin en een einde hebben (van zaken).

鍾 Tsiong *Tsiong kui* (») }, koning der geesten.

tsiong (») }, familienaam.

種 Tsióng *Tsióng*, soort van, slag van... (in slechte) zien.

tsit tsióng ê lâng, dat slag van menschen.

bîng tsióng sió tsióng, fijne thee.

掌 Tsióng *Sien dzîn tsióng* (*tsiŋ*) }, jeukkrabbertje (gew. een ivoren of bamboezen handje).

tsiong koán (*tsiáng*) }, het beheer bestuur hebben over...

hiet tsióng (*tsiáng*) }, bloedroode palm van de hand.

it tsióng kim (*tsiáng*) }, op zijne vingers berekenen.

將 Tsiòng *Hù tsiòng* (*tsiòng*) }, adjudant generaal.

ts'am tsiòng, generaal majoor.

bîng tsiòng, een sterke moedige generaal.

ts'ut tsiòng dzíp siòng, uittrekkende bevelhebber en terugkomende eerste minister zijn.

衆 Tsiòng *Tsiòng bók tsiao tsiao* (*tsiòng*) }, (voor) aller oogen zichtbaar.

tsiòng k'ó it sû, allen zijn van dezelfde opinie allen zeggen het eenparig.

iòng tsiòng, met vele menschen (aankomen gaan enz).

dzîn tsaî ts'ut tsiòng, alle anderen in hoedanigheden bekwaamheden overtreffen.

瘴 Tsiòng *Ien tsiòng ê sọ tsaī*, een plaats met moerasdampen, verbanningsoord.

從 Tsiông *Tsiông*, van uit, van af.

tsiông kim í aū, van nu af aan.

tsiông tsiên, vroeger te voren.

tsiông t'âo kaù (of *tsì*) *bé*, van begin tot eind.

tsiông tsá, van oudster.

tsiông kín, spoedig snel.

sūn tsiông, opvolgen nakomen (gehoorzamen).

tsiông koŋ, in handen van de mandarijnen geven (eene zaak).

tsiông gōan, t'i tsiông dzîn gōan, de hemel heeft 's menschen wensch vervuld.

t'ìng tsiông hí piēn, laat aan hem over te doen zooals hem het beste uitkomt.

tsiông tsit tiaô lō k'ì, langs dezen weg gaan.

hū dzîn lâng iú sam tsiông, vrouwen hebben drie (menschen) die zij moeten opvolgen gehoorzamen (ongehuwd zijnde moeten zij hare ouders - gehuwd haar man en na diens dood haar zoon gehoorzamen).

tsiông liông (») }, den goeden weg volgen (als eene lichtekooi die wettig huwt).

狀 Tsiōng *Tsiōng goân* (») }, hoogste van de drie graden der Han lim.

冲 *Ts'iong*, opschenken als kokend water.
ts'iong hoūn tioh, zich vergrijpen tegen.
ts'iong tê, thee opschenken.
ts'iong tsiú, wijn opschenken.
ts'iong siong, schaden benadeelen door iemands licht te benemen enz. enz.
k'ùi ts'iong t'i, zwaar ademhalen (van woede).
tuì ts'iong, rechtstreeks tegenover elkander staan als water en vuur of als sommige dagen in het jaar.
siong ts'iong, elkander benadeelen door tegenover elkander te staan (als een steeg die recht op een deur uitloopt, slecht voorteeken).

衝 Tsiong *Ts'iong ts'ut lai* (») }, doorbreken, door het midden gaan.
ts'iong tút, doorbreken (door een vijandelijk leger).

猖 Ts'iong *Ts'iong kī* (» ») } lichtekooi.
piaò ts'iong, hoer (scheldw).
ts'iong piaò mē goàh, hij scheldt mij voor hoer uit.
ts'iong hū, hoer (scheldw).
tsoè ts'iong tsoè piaó, hoer zijn.

娼 Ts'iong *Ts'iong kóng* (*tsiang* en *ts'iong*) } woest, robust.
ts'iong kik, vechten (in eenslag).
ts'iong pōng, ruw onbehouden onvoorzichtig, onbesuisd.

從 Ts'iong *Ts'iong iông* (*ts'iong*) }, oogluikend toelaten uitstel geven.
ts'iong ts'iong iông tōng, op zijn gemak niet overhaast.

充 Ts'iong *Ts'iong tsiok*, overvloed, overvloedig.
ts'iong tēng, de plaats aanvaarden van.
ts'iong sīng, overvloedig veel.
ts'iong kong, aan het publiek geven (als een boete).

縱 Ts'ióng *Ts'ióng sū* (*ts'iáng*) }, zaken twist doen ontstaan.
ts'ióng hō, zich rampen op den hals halen.

縱 Ts'iòng *Hòng ts'iòng*, buitensporig.
ts'iòng i tsoè p'ai, iemand den vrijen teugel laten om het kwade te doen.
ts'iòng hing i lâng (*ts'iàng*) } een buitensporig mensch, een onverschokken booswicht.

倡 Ts'iòng *Ts'iòng siú*, zich aan het hoofd stellen.
ts'iòng si, het eerst uitvinden. het eerst de hand leggen aan.
hu ts'iòng hū sui, goede harmonie tusschen man en vrouw.

Tsip

執 Tsip *Tsip ì*, vastbesloten.
tsip it, vastbesloten.
tsip kó pán, zich aan de oude manieren houden, van den ouden stempel zijn.
tsip p'iah, halsstarrig.
tsip si koat zich onveranderlijk aan iets houden.
tsip aó, zich vast aan zijn idee houden, doordrijven.
aó tsip, do.
tsip bē, dom weg...., stijfhoofdig.
tsàp of *tsiep tsip kiò*, smekken.
k'u tsip (*k'i*) }, bekrompen (van geest) zich aan iets vasthoudend.
tsip tit, rechtuit onbewimpeld.
tsuó sg tsip en *dzip* (*sio dzip*) }, krijgertje spelen.
tsip sū (») }, gevolg, de dragers van mandarijnen.
tsip lé, zich aan de beleefdheid houden.

籍 Tsip *Bîn tsip*, geboorteplaats, plaats waar men geregistreerd is.
tsip (*tsik*) }, register.

集 Tsip *Tsū tsip* (*tsī*) }, bijeenzamelen.
tsip tsoè tui (*tsò*) }, verzamelen bijeenbrengen.
tsè tsip, zich verzamelen, bij elkander komen (van personen).
k'iu tsip, verzamelen ophalen bijeenbrengen.

咂 Tsip *Tsip*, smekken.
k'in k'in á tsip tseh, een weinig van iets eten, proeven.

濕 Ts'ip *Si ts'ip* (*ts'iū ts'ip*) }, met eene glad oppervlak bedekt als voorwerpen die lang in water gelegen hebben.
ts'ip k'a kiâ, voorzichtig loopen.
ts'ip tsip á tsuí ts'uí ts'ip ts'ip) }, juist zooveel water dat het oppervlak even bedekt is, (als een put beek enz. na lange droogte).
ts'ip ts'ip kaò, juist genoeg (maar niets te veel).
ts'ip tsip sip sip, glad en vochtig.

Ts'ip *O ko ts'ip*, aangegroeide oesters.

緝 Ts'ip *Ts'ip hik*, vatten (als dieven).
Ts'ip *tsa ts'ip*, nasporen en vatten.

Tsit

即 Tsit *Tsit tao*, hier.
tsit nih, hier.
tsit sǫ tsaī (*sé*) }, hier.
tsit uī, do.
tsit é, deze.
tsit k'ik, onmiddelijk nu.
tsit tiép, do.
tsit pō, do.
tsit sé, nu.
tsit tsūn, onmiddelijk nu.

織 Tsit *Tsit*, weven.
tsit pǫ, weven.
tsit kui, weefstoel.
tsit pǫ́, stoppen.
tsit bāng, een groot net knoopen.
tsit lú. de weefster: een ster in Lijra, door vrouwen op den 7den avond van de 7de maand aangebeden.

職 Tsit *Tsit dzīm*, plicht aan een mandarijnpost verbonden.
ts'ìng tsit. met zijn plicht overeenkomen.
tsit hūn, mandarijnbetekking.
tsit hâm, ambt, graad.
koā tsit, mandarijnambt.
dzīn tsit, zijn plicht vervullen.
tsīn tsit, volkomen zijn plicht vervullen.
t'è tsit, zijn mandarijnambt neerleggen.

鯽 Tsit *Tsit hi*, brasem.

脊 Tsit *Ts'ù tsit*, uitstekende gevel.
ka (en) *pa tsiah tsit* (*k'a*) *ling tsùn tsit* }, ruggegraat.
tiong tsit į, middelste dakbalk.

質 Tsit *Tsu tsit*, bevattelijkheid (voor leeren enz).

Tsit *Tsit*, één.
tsit taī, éėne generatie.
tsit làng tsit ē hoat tǭ, ieder heeft zijn eigen manier.
tsit bīn, zijne geheele gelaat.
tsit sin k'u, zijn geheele lichaam.
ū tsit bō nīng (*nḡ*) }, een van beiden slechts het behoeft niet beiden.
tsit iū (*iǭ*) }, gelijk.
tsit si, een oogeublik.
tsit tsūn, do, korten tijd.

tsit ē kóng i tsiū ki tit, nauwelijks was het gezegd of hij herinnerde het zich.

tsit sim kiu tsit sim iū ì aì, aan den eenen kant vreezen maar aan den anderen kant toch wenschen.

tsit dzit, één dag, den geheelen dag.

tsit lō, den geheelen weg.

tsit sì lòng, zijn leven lang.

tsit sim tsit ì, uitsluitend, zijn hart en gedachten op niet anders hebben dan op.

tsit si tsit sì, geen ander kind hebben dan.

tsit siang ts'iù, met niets anders dan een paar handen *i. e.* met leege handen zonder iets te bezitten.

疾 Tsìt — *Taì tsit*, lichaamsgebrek, kwaal.

k'i kò tsit, opkomen van eene oude vroegere ziekte, kwaal.

嫉 Tsìt — *Tsit tò*, benijden jaloersch zijn.

七 Ts'it — *Ts'it*, zeven.

ts'it tsáp, zeventig.

ts'it siáh, 7de maand 7den dag (avonds) ongeluksvogel.

ts'it ō poeh péh, zonder nadenken weg praten.

ts'it ku poeh koaì, zeer wonderlijk.

ts'it ts'og poeh ts'ì ē lòng, steeds moeielijkheden doen ontstaan.

ts'it tsáp sa poeh tsáp sì, 73 en 84 *i. e.* onbelangrijke taal.

ts'it kéng poeh kong, over allerlei zaken spreken.

ts'it k'aò poeh k'aò, dit er af en dat er af alle onkosten er af (blijft er niets over).

sam k'i ts'it kaò siao, na alle onkosten er af nog maar juist genoeg voor zijn onderhoud over hebben.

ts'it gèh poà kui, geest van het midden der 7de maand *i. e.* veelvraat.

tsit ē bīn ts'it k'ang aō piah tsit ē t'aò tsang, in haar gezicht heeft zij zeven gaten en van achteren een hoofdkapsel, zij is als alle andere vrouwen (tegen iemand gezegd die lang eene vrouw fixeert).

ts'it tien poeh tuh, voortstrompelen (als oude lieden).

ts'it tsing pī, ziekte door een der zeven gemoedsaandoeningen veroorzaakt.

tsap ts'it bē lai dzih dzī bē k'ì, tusschen de 17 en 22 jaar (jong van vrouwen).

擦 Ts'it — *Ts'it*, afwrijven (met een doek), afvegen.

ts'it toh, de tafel afvegen.

kū i ts'it ts'ui, lett. iemand de mond afvegen, *i. e.* door geld iemands mond stoppen.

ts'it ta, droogwrijven afvegen.

ts'it tām póh ts'at, een (deur) verfje over iets leggen.

Ts'it — *Magh ts'it k'ì*, iets voor zich houden dat men aan anderen moet geven.

Tsiu

周 Tsiu — *Tsiu*, familienaam.

tsiu ui, rondgaan, in omtrek.

tsiu tsì, volkomen, volmaakt.

kiū kiū tsiu tsì, alles volkomen in orde.

tsiu tsè, weldadigheid, schenken aan.

tsiu soàn, bijleggen (als twist).

tsìng lâng tsiu ti, allen weten het, iedereen weet het.

tsiu bit, volledig gedekt (van eene zaak), geheim.

tsiu tsat, solide volledig gedekt (van eene zaak).

tsiu liù, overal rondgaan rondreizen.

眼 Tsiu — *Bák tsiu*, het oog.

州 Tsiu — *Tsiu*, district.

ti tsiu, oppermagistraat van een Tsiu.

kun tsiu, assistent magistraat „ „

ē tsiu hu, lagere districten (van de plaatsen ten Z en W van Singapore).
kè tsiu hú k'ì, buiten 's lands gaan.

Tsiu *Ing to p'eà tsoè nñg tsiu*, met een mes in twee stukken snijden.

洲 *Hai tiong ing ē tsiu á*, een rots of verhevenheid in zee.
Tsiu

酒 *Tsiú*, wijn.
Tsiú *tsiú tsī*, port (brieven) fooi drinkgeld.
tsiú tsuì, beschonken.
tsiú poe, wijnglas.
tsiú ts'ī (*ts'ē*), nuchter (van wijn).
tsiú kui, dronkaard.
tsiú k'ì t'è, nuchter (na den wijn).
tsiú k'ut, kuiltjes in de wangen.
tsiú hàn, wijndrinker.
tsiú laó, wijnhuis.
tsiú t'iu (wijn) hevel.
tsiú laō, (wijn) trechter.
tsiú lóng, wijnhuis.
sio tsiú, warme wijn.
hé sio tsiú, brandewijn = *hé tsiú*.
kao liâng tsiú, brandewijn van kao liâng gemaakt.
ló tsiú, tarwewijn rood of geel.
ts'iá tsiú, gasten op wijn verzoeken.
tsiú king, begeerte naar wijn.
tsiú gièn, verslaafd aan wijn.
tsao tsiú, do.
tsiáh sán tsiú, enkel wijn zonder bijspijzen gebruiken.
koé tsiú, dronkenschap doen overgaan (als thee of vruchten doen 2e zijne gewoonte van veel wijn drinken opgeven).
tsiú p'è, bijspijzen bij wijn.
ts'ut tsiú, wijn overgeven braken.
tsiú hū kièn tsin tsing, in dronkenschap ziet men iemands wezenlijk karakter.
tsiú pàn, wijnkan.
tsiú tièm, wijnwinkel.
kik tsiú, wijnstoken.
kóng tsiú oē, opgewonden door wijn praten.
ts'aò tsiú, stinkende wijnlucht (als men te veel gedronken heeft).
eh tsiú hig, oprispen van wijn.
tah tsiú, wijnkoopen.
tsiáh hoe tsiú, met lichtekooien wijndrinken.
k'ìng tsiú, aanzetten om nog meer wijn te drinken.
koàn tsiú, met geweld wijn laten drinken.
tsiú pih, wijnworm (die gezegd wordt in het lichaam van een grooten wijn drinker te onstaan).
tsiú k'a, een goede wijndrinken.
tsiú lîng, regel op het wijndrinken.
tsiú ì, aangewit, een weinig beschonken
tsiú pì tsiū ts'ò, wijn verandert in azijn 2e na den dood van haren man den weduwestaat niet bewaren.

守 *Tsiú*, waken over.
Tsiú *tsiú kì*, nachtwacht houden.
tsiú koá, weduwe.
tsiú tsī lô, geldoppotter.
tsiú ts'át, voor dieven waken.
tsiú mī, nachtwacht houden.
tsiú bó, op zijne vrouw passen.
tsiú tsiet, haar weduwestaat ophouden.
tsiú ko toa, ongehuwd zijn of blijven.
tsiú kiá toā hàn, (in haren weduwestaat) haar kind opvoeden tot het volwassen is.
tsiú siâ, eene vesting bewaken, verdedigen.

帚 *Saò tsiú*, bezem.
Tsiú

呪 咒 *Tsiù mē*, vloeken, vervloeken.
Tsiù *liēm tsiù*, vervloeking over iemand uitspreken.
liēm king tsiù, belezen (als Boeddhh. priesters krankzinnigen of zieke beesten doen) ook voor overledenen.
tsiù liēm, uitschelden vervloeken.
hù tsiù, amulet en de belezing daarbij.

tsiù sin loé miŋ, zijn noodlot zich zelven vervloeken.
tsiù k'àng, dreinen zeuren om iets (als kinderen doen).

蛀 *T'iù*, invreten.
Tsiù *tsiù k'i*, holle kiezen.
tsiù, ingevreten door insekten.
tsiù t'âng, de mot, boekworm.
tsiù noŋ, vergaan vermolmd.
teh tsiù, eierschaal doorpikken (van kuikens).
tsiù k'ang, gaten in iets vreten als de mot) 2e met gaten doorvreten.
niaŋ tsiù tsiù, zeer mottig.

誓 *Tsiù tsoā*, een eed doen.
Tsiù *tsiù si tséh tsoā*, bij zijn leven zweren

就 *Tsiū*, dan, alsdan, toen, terstond.
Tsiù *tsiū sī*, juist zoo, dat is.
tsiū kūn (kīn), naderen, dichtbij.
tsiū kín, spoedig, gauw.
tsiū lai, onmiddelijk komen.
tsiū lai tsiū k'ì, naauwelijks gekomen of weer weggaan.
tsiū tao, naderbij komen.
sŋ tsióng tsiū, het verschil tusschen beiden middendoordeelen.
tsoè tsiū ih, iemand navolgen, toch maar dulden, toelaten.
sing tsiū ih, iemand helpen zijn doel te bereiken, iemand er boven ophelpen.
kóng oŋ k'ì tsiū ih, iemand gelijkgeven, met hem instemmen.
tsoè k'ì ih, iemand iets toelaten; toenaderen.
tsiong ts'ok tsiū ts'ok (tsiang), zich nu eenmaal vergist hebbende er maar het beste van maken.
tsiong kè tsiū kè, iemand met zijn eigenlist vangen.
tsō tsiū, iemand vooruithelpen, er bovenop helpen.

sing lì tsoè put tsiū, geen geld met den handel maken, verliezen.
in tsiū, nader bij iets brengen, tot iets doen toenaderen (zoodat het tot stand komt).
tsiū bò, eensklaps verdwijnen, weggaan (als rook door wind).
tsiū tsit ē mih kò kè, volgens (de waarde van) het voorwerp prijs bepalen.
tsiū tsit ē gûn k'ì boé, gaan koopen zooveel als men voor dat geld krijgen kan.

章 *Tsit tsiŋ (tsiŋ)*, een hoofdstuk.
Tsiŋ *bûn tsiŋ*, litterarisch opstel.

漿 *Hún tsiŋ (tsiŋ)*, stijfsel.
Tsiŋ *tsiŋ sŋ*, kleèren stijven.
t'ŋ bé tsiŋ, modder.
tsiŋ kŋ (tsiŋ), stijfsel.
ám tsiŋ, rijstwater, stijfsel.
tsuáh tsiŋ, stijfsel inzuigen (als kleèren).
kao á bé-tsiŋ, modder uit een gracht.
t'ŋ tsiŋ, modder (op een weg).
tsiŋ tsui, stijfselwater.

樟 *Tsiŋ ló*, kamfer.
Tsiŋ *tsiŋ ts'iū*, kamferboom.
tsiŋ ts'â, kamferhout.

蟾 *Tsiŋ tsû (tsi)*, pad.
Tsiŋ

槳 *Tsiŋ (tsiŋ)*, riem (van de boot).
Tsiŋ *kò tsiŋ*, roeien.
tsiŋ tiem, roeidol, roeipen.
tsiŋ koŋ, *tsiŋ hī*, touw waarmede de bootriem aan den staak vast zit.
siang tsiŋ á, een twee riems boot.
tsiŋ kah lŋ, met riemen en frikken i. e. in allerijl.
tah boah tsiŋ, aan de riemen hangen (niet hard meeroeien).

ah tsiŭ, achterste riem (tevens als roer dienende).

掌 *Tsiŭ* (*tsio*), familinaam.
Tsiŭ *ts'iú tsiŭ*. palm van de hand.
him tsiŭ, beeren klauwen.
p'ah ts i i tsiŭ, op de palm van de hand staan (aan mandarijnen en geletterden gedaan).
gô tsiŭ, *ah tsiŭ*. ganzen en eenden pooten.
tīng tsiú. doorloopende groef in het holle van de hand.

醬 *Tsiù liaū*, ingelegde groenten.
Tsiù *kiëm tsiù* zoute ingelegde waren.
tao tsiù, soja.
tsiù ts'ing, lichtgekleurde soort soja.
hoan kiù tsiù, ingelegde spaansche peper.
tsiù hoan kiù, spaansche peper inmaken.
tsiù tsiŭ, slikkerig, modderig.
tsiù kō kō, kleverig nat.
iŭ tsiu tsiù, slijmerig nat, vochtig.
noū tsiù tsiù, slijmerig nat.
tâm tsiù, kleverig nat.
tsiù kaò tsit si koè, alles bevuilen, besmeeren, smeerig maken.

此 *Tsiŭ ping*, hier, aan dezen kant.
Tsiŭ *un tsiŭ si*, aldus.

裳 *I tsiŭ*, kleederen (in het algemeen).
Tsiŭ

Tsiù *Tsiŭ tsi*, knijzen dreinen (van kinderen).

上 *Tsiū si*, bovenstaande, hoogergeplaatste
Tsiū ambtenaren.
tsiū toh, aan tafel gaan.
tsiū t'aò, naar het Noorden gaan (schepen en waren).
k'oŭ īm tsiū bák, voor gering achten.
k'oŭ īm tsiū bàk, niet voor zooveel gehouden hebben als het wezenlijk is.
īm tsiū ki ih, men kan hem niet als zoodanig rekenen.
t'éh īm tsiū ts'iù, te klein om in de handen genomen te worden.
t'èh īm tsiū ts'iù, opnemen maar het der moeite niet waard achten en het weer neerzetten.
tsiū ts'è, eene groote boodschap gaan doen.
tī goá sin tsiū, het berust bij mij, de verantwoordelijkheid ligt bij mij.
tsiū lō, op weg gaan.
tsiū soū, aan land gaan, den berg opgaan.
tsiū soū giëm, naar bergtempels gaan.
tsiū (*tsiō*) }, over, opgaan, beklimmen.
tsiū taò, de trappen opgaan.
tsiū laò t'ui, de trap opgaan.
tsiū láh, opgaan en neêrkomen.
tsiū kiu (*kio*) }, verhemelte.
tsiū siaò, op de rekening zetten, opteekenen, boekhouden van.
tsiū goá ē siaò, zet het op mijne rekening.
tsiū kiū, het examen voor Tsin sū doen.
tsiū tsui, lading lossen.
tsiū pan, gevlekt.
tsiū ē, in de buurt gelegen, omstreeks.
tsiū ē dzit, omstreeks dien dag.
tsiū tin, in het gevecht zijn.
kiŭ sai tsiū ts'iu ming, de bruidegom gaat de bruid in haar huis afhalen.
tsiū ts'ing tsiū bān, bij duizenden en tienduizenden.
tsiū kun tsiù niŭ, bij geheele ponden en oncen.
tsiū niū, *tsiu ping*, op de schaal zetten wegen.
sè tsiū ē lâng, de menschen op aarde.
si tsiū ē lâng, de menschen alom.
tsiū ts'im dzī, papieren bewijzende in hoeveel handen een pand is overgegaan.
ts'iū ni, vroegere vorige jaren.
tsih pah īm tsiū, ongeveer honderd, tegen honderd aan.
kui tsiū i ē sin, de geest, de duivel bezielt hem.

癢 *Tsiū̱* } (*tsiō̱*) } , jeuking, jeuken.
Tsiū̱ *tsiū̱ iah iah*, erg jeuken.
pè tsiū̱, krabben.
tsi tsiū̱, jeuking doen ophouden (van medicijnen).
tsiū̱ teh m pè bò tsiū̱ teh pè kào huih laò, op de plaats der jeuking niet krabben maar waar het niet jeukt zoo krabben dat het bloedt *i. e.* het noodige verzuimen en het onnoodige doen.
k'a t'âng tsiū̱ ts'ia ts'ia, zich niet kunnen weerhouden om ook eens te gaan kijken, uittegaan enz.

麞 *Tsiū̱*, klein soort hert, antiloop.
Tsiū̱ *tsiū̱ à p'è*, huid van een antiloop.

秋 *Ts'iu*, herfst.
Ts'iu *ts'iu t'i̱*, do.
ts'iu ts'in, frisch, koel.
tiong ts'iu, halfherfst 8ste maand 15 den dag.
p'ah ts'iu hōng, om ondersteuning komen vragen (zooals behoeftige betrekkingen doen).

鬚 *Ts'iu*, voelborens.
Ts'iu *ts'ui ts'iu*, snor en sik.
hê ts'iu, krabbehorens.
nī̱ng p'oat ts'iu, snor.
nó pō̱ ts'iu, baard bakkebaard.
hê ts'iu á soā̱, fijnkoord, garen (lett. als garnalen voelhorens).
hô̱ tsiu, baard.
k'ih ts'ui kiem hô̱ ts'iu, een hazelip en daarbij nog een baard (door chin. als niet zeer mooi beschouwd) *i. e.* niets van eene zaak verstaan en toch maar willen meêspreken.

絛 *Ts'iu*, franje.
Ts'iu *tsit p'a ts'iu*, een kwast.
bō á ts'iu, franje van een hoed.

鞦 *Ts'iu ts'ien*, wip, schommel.
Ts'iu *ts'iu ts'ien kè en pi̱*, schommel.

螙 *Hai ts'iu*, paalworm.
Ts'iu *tsûn ts'iu*, paalworm in schepen.

羞 *Goá kē li ts'iu teh*, ik zal u op uwe
Ts'iu wangen tikken, tegen ondeugende kinderen gezegd).

儦 *Tsit ts'iu ping*, eene afdeeling soldaten.
Ts'iu

湫 *Liu ts'iu è lâng*, *liu liu ts'iu ts'iu*, een nietswaardig mensch, een prul.

手 *Ts'iú*, de hand.
Ts'iú *ts'iú tsi* } (*tsai*) } , vingerring.
ts'iú k'oân, armband.
kióng ts'iú, de hand geven.
tah ts'iú, in de handen klappen.
tò ts'iú, linkerhand.
ts'iú tsiū̱ } (*tsiō̱*) } , palm van de hand.
ts'iú bák, de knokkels.
ts'iú kut, de arm.
ts'iú oân, armholte.
ts'iú k'ū, elleboog.
ts'iú kun } (*kin*) } , zakdoek.
iét ts'iú, met de hand wenken.
ts'iú gē, handwerk.
ts'iú t'ò, handschoen.
ts'iú pún, verzoekschrift.
ts'iú toū̱, knapheid (in zijn vak).
ts'iú lō̱, manier van werken, van doen.
ts'iú bīn t'àn tsiáh, met zijne handen de kost verdienen.
sui ts'iú, voor de hand weg.
bò tī goá ts'iú lai, het is niet in mijn macht, ik heb er niets over te zeggen.
lāo ts'iú, ervaren (in iets).
soeh aō ts'iú, achterhands in de hand stoppen om eene zaak gedaan te krijgen.
tsiáh (lâng è) aō ts'iú, zich laten om koopen.
tsiū̱ ts'iú k'oè, hijpotheekbrief.

gâo tsoè ts'iú, knap om iets na te maken.
hó en *p'ai ts'ut ts'iú*, goed en slecht te verkoopen.
hó en *p'ai ts'iú dziaô*, te vertrouwen niet te vertrouwen.
ts'iú t'aô k'aŋ k'ing, roijaal met zijn geld.
ts'iú t'aô lūng līng, roijaal, ruim in het geld zitten.
ts'iú t'aô ân, in moeielijke geldelijke omstandigheden zijn.
ts'iú t'aô nī, wreed, robust.
ts'iú pàng koai, zich ontfermen, de wrekende hand omhoog houden, niet laten neerkomen.
bô toé ts'iú, (hij is) geen partij (voor u) (hij is te zwak).
hō i tsit ê ts'iú sing tseh, geef hem eene douceur, fooi.
néng ts'iú, geen macht over zich hebben om iets te doen (als te vechten of het mes in iemands vleesch te steken).
pi ts'iú, met de handen gebaren maken gesticuleeren.
ts'iú tsiên, diefachtig.
toā ts'ut ts'iú, gul, roijaal.
sg gîm (of *kîm*) *ts'iú*, het onderling ééns zijn, elkanders handlangers zijn.
k'an ts'iú, eene plaatselijke vrouw huwen.
k'a k'in ts'iú kiā, gezond van lijf en leden.
tsaó ts'iú tsoè, loopend, vlugweg doen.
p'ah ts'iú, vechters (op het tooneel, ook in dobbelhuizen en bordeelen gebruikt om lastige gasten de deur uit te zetten).
kaó k'a kì ts'iú, onbestendig onstandvastig.
tsit ts'iú kang hu, een knap werkman.
tsit ts'iú dzī, een fraai schrijver.
ts'iú t'aô oē, met zijn eigenhand zelf kunnen doen.
gâu tsing ts'iú k'ong, behendig (als goochelaars of zakkenrollers).
ts'á ts'iú, elkander met de handen hedreigen (als personen die op het punt zijn van te vechten).
hiū ts'iú hiū kiok, met handen en voeten in beweging zijn (onder het spreken).
hē ts'iú, de hand aan iets leggen, iets beginnen.
hièn ts'iú, gul, roijaal.
pang ts'iú, een handje helpen 2e helper tweede hand.
ts'iú hûn, kringen streepen op de hand.
ts'iú ts'ia, spinnewiel.
t'ao kè ts'iú, bij diefstal de goederen reeds meester zijn.
m t'ang kè ts'iú, geef het niet uit uw hand, draag het niet aan een ander op.
kè kui nā tsiû, door verscheidene handen gegaan zijn.
sit ts'iú, onvoorzichtig, bij ongeluk.
ts'iú poā, bovenkant van de hand.
k'ong hi hi ts'iú nih tsoè hit ê sū, tentijde van Kanghi's bestuur is dit gebeurd.
tsit ts'iú kè tsi tsit ts'iú kè mih, geld bij de visch, kontant.
dzī ts'iú, tweede hand, helper.
iô ts'iú, met de hand afwijzen.
bô tuì ts'iú, geen partij zijn voor, geene koopers voor iets vinden.
ìng k'a ts'iú, helpers hebben, gebruiken.
bô ts'iú t'aô, niet in de mogelijkheid zijn aan geld te komen (als een zoon bij het leven zijns vaders).
tìng k'a bô ts'iú ìn, een stempel van zijne voeten en handen op iets zetten (als op een bewijs van echtscheiding).
ts'iú sè, de manier van de hand, iemands hand (als in schrift).
saí ts'iú hoe, behendig met de handen werken (als goochelaars).

k'a tè ts'iú, de voeten volgen de handen *i. e.* gauw onmiddelijk.
tit i ê ts'iu bé, het weinige achtergelatene van een overledene krijgen.

贖 Ts'iû — *Ts'iú k'an t'aò* (*s'ò*), een verpand goed loskoopen.

首 Ts'iú — *Nñg ts'iú ê si*, twee verzen.
ts'iú sik, vrouwelijke toiletbehoeften.

醜 Ts'iú — *Hièn ts'iú*, een bewijs van zijne domheid schande geven, (beleefde term als men iets voor iemand gedaan heeft).

倯 Ts'iù — *ĩm ts'iù ih*, niets met iemand te maken willen hebben.
ĩm ts'iù ts'ai, niet goed ontvangen.
ĩm ts'iù ts'ai ih, zich niet met hem inlaten bemoeien.
put ts'iù put ts'ai ih, zich volstrekt niet met hem inlaten.

嚏 Ts'iù — *P'ah k'á ts'iù*, niezen.

抽 Ts'iù — *Ts'iù* (*o*) (*t'iu*), oppalmen (als een touw).
ts'iù soh, een touw oppalmen.
p'où pak ts'iù ting, de buik opensnijden en de ingewanden er uithalen.
ĩng oē ts'iù ih, met woorden iets uit iemand lokken.
ts'iù ting ts'iù tō, lett. de ingewanden uithalen *i. e.* zich inwendig met iets folteren.
bán koe ts'iù tin, plukt men meloenen dan moet men den stengel ontwarren oppalmen *i. e.* de loop van eene zaak of diefstal ontwarren.

愁 Ts'iù — *In ts'iù*, bedroefd.
t'aò iu bīn ts'iù, bedroefd knorrig van uiterlijk.
siao ts'iù koé būn, droefheid verdrijven.

樹 Ts'iū — *Ts'iū*, boom.
Ts'iū bák, boomen.
ts'iū bák, boomknoest.
ts'iū kun, wortel.
ts'iū sin, stam.
ts'iū ki, tak.
ts'iū p'ê (*p'oé*), boomschors.
ts'iū tsiep, boomsap.
ts'iū nà, bosch.
liú ts'iū, wilgeboom.
mi hoe ts'iū (*hoa*), katoenboom.
sêng ts'iū, moerbezieboom.
ts'ing ts'iū, vijgeboom.
lát tsi ts'iū, kastanjeboom.
pêng ts'iū (*pui*), palmboom.
bû hoa kó ts'iū, vijgeboom.
ts'iū ĩm (*ts'iu*), Arbutus eigenlijk Mijrica sapida.
kó ts'iū bák, dwergplanten.
iò tsi ts'iū, aan den geldboom schudden *i. e.* veel geld met iemand verdienen als met eene lichtekooi.
kó ts'iū t'aò, dwergachtig (van planten en menschen).

Ts'iū — *Tsit ts'iū ping*, eene troep soldaten.
tsit ts'iū kaó hiā, een troep mieren.
tsit ts'iū gû sai, een hoop koemest.

薔 Ts'iū — *Ts'iū bi hoe*, roos.

鎗 Ts'iu — *Ts'iu* (*ts'io*), speer.
ts'iù ts'iu, een ander verzoeken voor zich te schrijven (als een opstel).
kièm ts'iu, puntige palen (van hout op ijzer)
kièm ts'iu mńg, deur, hek van puntige palen.
ts'iu to bák pô, speeren, zwaarden er harken *i. e.* wapens.

像 T'iu — *P'ai bīn ts'iu* (*p'ai iō siō*), een gemeen uiterlijk.

鯧 — *Ts'iu hi*, eene visch, de Stromateus Argenteus.

搶 Ts'iú *Ts'iú* (*tsió*) }, plunderen, diefstal.
ts'iú t'éh, wegnemen.
ts'iú k'ì, iets wegslepen.
ts'iú kiep, rooven, plunderen.
ts'iú pak, van zijne kleederen berooven, uitplunderen.
ts'iú niú k'ì, geheel en al totaal wegstelen.
taò ts'iú, om strijd wegnemen, willen hebben (als waren).
ts'iú téh, stelen afplunderen.
bô toàn ts'iú eh, men kan het maar niet roekeloos wegnemen.
ts'iú t'aô pio, haantje de voorste willen zijn.
ts'iú ts'oah / *ts'iú ts'iú ts'oah ts'oah* }, in aller haast. hals over kop ten einde brengen, op bergen, uit de handen rukken, niet nauwkeurig laten bekijken.
ts'iú hông, de slechte stoffen uit een wond enz. trekken (van medicijnen gezegd).

廠 Ts'iú *Ts'iú*, werf. In Emoi, ook het beenderenhuis van overledene soldaten.
tsûn ts'iú, scheepswerf.
kog ts'iú, rijks 's lands timmerwerf.

揖 Ts'iú *Ts'iù dziū* (*ts'iò*) (*dziú*) }, buigen als de Chineezen

唱 *Ts'iù*, zingen.
o o ts'iù, zingen.
ts'iù k'ik, do.
ts'iù koa, do.
ts'iù koai kè (*koàn kè*) }, opslaan (de prijs van iets).
ts'iù liēm, zingen.
tsū toì tsū ts'iù, zelf spelen en zingen 2e geen hulp van anderen noodig hebben.
ts'iù koai tiaū, in een hoogeren toon zingen *i. e.* meer en meer voorwaarden stellen, hooger prijs voor iets eischen.

墻 Ts'iû *Ts'iû* (*ts'iò*) }, muur..
ts'iû piah, muren.
tsaó koe ts'iû (*tsaó ni ts'iû*) }, muur om een huis.
ts'iû mîng kíng, kippenvleesch hebben.
poû ts'iû peh piah, over muren klimmen en tegen muren opklauteren.
siâ ts'iû, stadsmuur, wal.
tûng ts'iû t'ih piah, zeer sterk van een gebouw, vestingen.
tiok ts'iû, een muur, wal opbouwen.
tsing ts'iû, een muur opstampen.
hûn ts'iû, een muur witten, een gewitte muur.
ts'iû ki, de fundamenten: onderste lagen van een muur.
ts'iû k'a tióh tiok i tsaī, de voet van den muur moet stevig opgebouwd worden.
t'áng ts'iû, opstaande delen van een kuip.
k'ioh ts'iû, de delen van een uit elkander liggende kuip bij elkander zoeken, in elkander zetten.

縱 Ts'iû *Ts'iû lai*, komen uitschieten (als honden).
hé hong t'aô teh ts'iû, de wind blaast door het vuur.
ts'iû hé, door vuur of vonken verschroeid aangeslagen zijn.
ts'iû kūn oá, op toeschieten (als beesten op menschen enz).
kaó tò ts'iû lai, de hond keerde terug en kwam aanrennen, toeschieten.
ts'iû hiā, mieren aantrekken, lokken (als suiker) doet.
ts'iû iáh, vliegende mieren aantrekken (als licht doet).

Ts'iû *Sò tsaī k'ah kíng ts'iû*, die plaats is helderder, minder bedompt.

93

象 Ts'iū *Ts'iū* (*ts iū*), olifant.
ts'iū gê (*gê*), olifantstanden.
ts'iū p'ī, do. slurp.
ts'iū kíng, olifants slurp.
pīng ts'iū, groote eter.
ts'iū lô, olifantleider.
ts'iū ts'iu, olifantsbaard (waarvan de haren als tandenstokers gebruikt worden).
ts'iū kut, elpenbeen, ivoor.

上 Ts'iū *Ts'iū*, ophijschen.
ts'iū hiū, mieren aantrekkend lokkend.
ts'iū ts'i, nat door mist enz.
ts'iū līm, slap vochtig worden.
ts'iū sip, do.
ts'iū hún, met een stof-meellaag bedekt (als vruchten).
ts'iū tièn t'ang, winkelblinden inzetten
ts'iū mîng, een deur inzetten.

汲 Ts'iū *Ts'iū*, opslaan (als water).
ts'iū tsúi, water putten, water opslaan.

相 Ts'iū *Ts'in ts'iū*, evenals, gelijk.
īm ts'in ts'iū lâng, niet als gewone menschen (in armoede zijn).
tī it ts'iū, sprekend gelijkend.
uī tit ts'iū ts'iū ts'iū, zeer sprekend schilderen.

匠 Ts'iū *Bák ts'iū* timmerman.
t'ô tsui ts'iū, metselaar.
uī ts'iū schilder.
t'ô ts'iū, metselaar.
kang ts'iū, vaste werkman (rijks- of-stadwerkers enz).

棧 Ts'iū *Ts'iū tiáh*, opkoopen als het goedkoop is om te verkoopen als de markt hoog is, opzolderen.

Ts'iū *Ts'iū t'aò î*, bolvormige koeken bij een huwelijk uitgedeeld.
ts'iū t'aû tī kè, het haar van de bruid opmaken en haar de bruidsmuts opzetten.

Ts'iū *Ts'iū oê*, de zool aan het bovenste van de schoen naaien.

Tso

遭 Tso *Tso gū* (*gī*), voorval, ontmoetingen (in het leven).
tso tsien, door een ramp getroffen worden.
tso, ontmoeten.

燥 Tso *Būn būn tso tso*, inwendig gefolterd.
tso loūn, inwendig onwel, misselijk enz.
sim koū tso, geene ontlasting hebbende hongerig zijn.
tsuo tso, verdrietig, niet opgeruimd.

譟 Tso *Tso lô*, iemand lastig vallen, gedurig vragen om.

糟 Tso *Tso liaū*, kruiderijen, specerijen.

左 Tsó *Tsó*, linksch.
tsó iū, linkervleugel.
tsó kun, do.
tsó iū ê lâng, bedienden, (lett. ter zijde staanden).
tsó iū, hier of daar, daar ergens.
tsó ping, de linkerkant.
tsó bák, het linkeroog.
gō lák dzit tsó iū, ongeveer om en bij vijf of zes dagen.

棗 Tsó *Tsó á*, dadel.
âng tsó roode dadels.
o tsó, zwarte do.

槽 Tsô *Tsô*, familienaam.

曹 Tsó *Tsuí tsô*, regengoot.
bê tsô (*bê*), paardenruif.
tsô, luidruchtig, woelig (van eene plaats).
huih tsô, bloedbak door slachters gebruikt) bloedgroef (aan een zwaard).
tsî tsô, geld, duiten groef.

tso tsi, geld bij hoopjes aftellen.
tsit tsò gûn, een hoopje geld.
tsit tsò hiā, een stapeltje dakpannen.
嘈 Tsò *Tso tsak*, kwellen plagen, het iemand lastig maken.
tsò lâng hī, iemands ooren verdooven.
tsò p'oà hī k'ang, iemands ooren verdooven (als door hard schreeuwen).
tsak tsò, lastig vallen (door vragen enz).
tsò tsak, do. (met zaken of vele personen).
bô siū tit i tsò, zijn smeeken niet kunnen weêrstaan (en zoodoende toegeven).
遭 Tsò *Tsò koa hù*, procedeeren, een rechtsgeding hebben.
座 Tsō *Tsō*, numer voor heuvels, bergen, vestingen, fondamenten enz., bakje; voetstuk.
tsit tsō ê soa, één berg.
tsit tsō laô, één gebouw (numer voor alleenstaande gebouwen).
tsiū tsō, op eene verhevenheid gaan staan (als priesters doen om tot het volk te spreken) op het spreekgestoelte staan.
ting tsō, voet van een lamp.
put tsō, voet voor een afgodsbeeld.
tsit tsō put, een groep afgodsbeelden.
tsit tsō t'ah, éëne pagoda.
造 Tsō *Tsō hoà sī*, bij geluk.
hó tsō hoà, bij geluk.
tsō ts'eh (*ts'eh*), een lijst maken van.
si giên tsō gû (*se gàn tsō gi*), een leugen verzinnen.
tsō hoà, bij geluk, van het geluk afhangend.
p'ong tsō hoà, van het geluk afhangend.
īng gûn tit tit tsō k'i lai met geld opgebouwd d. i. veel geld gekost hebben.
tsō, maken, bouwen.
tsō t'ah, eene pagoda bouwen.
tsō tsûn, een schip bouwen.
tsō lō, wegen maken.
taù tsō hoà, toevallig van het geluk afhangend.
tsō ì, met voordacht, vast van plan zijn om.
t'ien tsō tē siet, door den hemel ingesteld.
tsō ke kah, huistelling, census houden.
tsō iao, wonderlijke dingen, leugens opmaken.
tsō tsiū, iemand er boven ophelpen, vooruithelpen.
hō lâng oē tsō tsiū tit, waard zijn door anderen opgenomen, vooruitgeholpen te worden.
kuì tsō, uw geluk (beleefde term).
k'ah hó tsō ts'it tsân ê pó t'ah, nog beter dan eene pagoda van zeven verdiepingen te bouwen.
Tsō *Tsō tsi*, adres op een brief woonplaats.
tsō hiòng, ligging, uitzicht van een huis.
kong tsō toh, rechtbank (de tafel).
皂 Tsō *Tsō hoân*, koperrood, groene vitriool.
tsō lē, mandarijn koelies (met hooge zwarte mutsen op).
Tsō o tsō pèh, zwart en wit bekladden.
tsō o bīn, zich zwart onkenbaar maken 2e iemand niet meer willen erkennen.
tsō t'ō kō tō, op den grond in het vuil wentelen (als kleine kinderen).
租 Tso *Tso*, landrente.
tē tso, grondbelasting, grondrente.
tso giép, renten en bezittingen.
tso, huren.
tso ts'ù, een huis huren.
ts'ù tso, huishuur.
tso ts'ik, rijst als landrente.
ts'ân tso, landrente.
siu tso tsiáh soá, van zijne renten leven.
tē tso k'e (*k'ò*), departement van grondbelasting (in een mandarijn bureau) kadaster.

祖 *Tsó*, overgrootvader van vaderszijde.
Tsó *goā tsó*, » » moederszijde.
tsó tsong, voorouders.
tsó kong, do.
tsó bú (bó), overgrootmoeder vaders zijde.
tsó ts'ù, voorouderlijke tempel.
tsó ke, geboorteplaats, vaderland.
tsó má, *tsó pô*, overgrootmoeder.
tsó giép, geërfde bezitting, erfgoed.
tsiáh tsó kong giép, van zijn erfgoed leven.
tsik tsó, van voorouders her.
tsó biō (en) *biaō*, voorouderlijke tempel.
si tsó, eerste van zijne voorouders die zich op eene plaats gevestigd hebben.
k'ai ki tsó, stamvader die zich het eerst op eene plaats gevestigd heeft.
kik ts'ut tsó, uit de familie verbannen niet willen erkennen (van een slecht persoon).
tsó sien, voorouders.
tsing tsó, overgrootvader.
tsing tsó má, overgrootmoeder.
ko tsó, over-overgrootvader.
ko tsó má, over-overgrootmoeder.
tsó dziah, woonplaats zijner ouders.

阻 *Tsó tsi*, verhinderen.
Tsó *tsó tòng*, do. hindernisseu in den weg leggen.
noā tsó, tegenhouden, in den weg staan.
tsó tsiét, onderscheppen, opvangen (als een brief.

Tsò *Tsò gák*, muziek maken.

助 *Pang tsō*, helpen.
Tsō *tsō*, do.
hó loē tsō, goede huisvrouw.
tsu tsō, helpen (door geld te geven).
tsō ok, helpen het kwade te doen.
ū sin tsō, bovennatuurlijke hulp.

臭 *Ts'aò ts'o*, sterke traan, tranige lucht
Ts'o of smaak (als visch vogels enz).
ts'i ts'o, *bī ts'o*, *ts'o k'i*, sterke visch lucht, tranige smaak.
tsiáh liaó ts'ut ts'ai ts'o, nadat men er van gegeten heeft eene sterke smaak in den mond hebben en nadat iets éénmaal goed bekomen of gelukt is, er weêr naar verlangen.

葷 *Bō tsiáh ts'o*, geen levende wezens eten
Ts'o (als Boeddh. pr. doen).

操 *Ts'o ts'ông ts'ut tsai goá*, nemen ofTs'o laten gaan is in mijne macht, het hangt geheel van mij af.

磋 *Sq kap ts'iet ts'o*, met elkander besproTs'o ken (als een geleerd onderwerp).

草 *Ts'ó kó*, ruwe schets, een klad van iets.
Ts'ó *ts'ó ts'ing*, kladboek.
ts'ó dzī, vlugschrift.
ló ts'ó, slordig weg.
ts'ó hoe (boa), van rijstpapier (Aralia papyrifera) gemaakte bloemen.
ts'ó sià, mijn huis (nederige term).
ts'ó liaó sū, eenvoudig weg kortweg een eind aan iets maken.
ts'ó tsu, cursiefschrift.
ts'ó sut, niet omzichtig, onbesuisd.
tsién ts'ó, de planten weghakken (om een graf op die plaats te maken).
it ts'ó it bók, een grasje een houtje d. i. in het geringste, kleinigheden.
t'ong ts'ó, de rijstpapier plant (Aralia papyrifera).

瑣 *Ts'ó ts'ui é tāi tsī*, verward (moeielijk
Ts'ó uittemaken.

万 *Tsit ts'ó*, tienduizend (alleen van geld
Ts'o gezegd).

楚 *Bō ts'ing ts'ó*, niet afgedaan, niet afgeTs'ó wacht.

錯 *Ts'ò*, verkeerd, foutief.
Ts'ò *ts'ò gō*, zich vergissing.
ū ts'ò, onjuist, bij vergissen.
sit ts'ò, zich vergissen.

bô ts'ò, juist zoo (er is geen vergissing).
ts'o ts'iú, bij ongeluk.
siá ts'ò, *ts'ò siá*, verkeerd fout schrijven.
ts'ò tn̄ siaò, verkeerd, zich vergissen met rekenen.
ts'ò toā bé, zich in de waarde, rang der cijfers vergissen (duizendtallen voor honderdtallen rekenen).
ts'ò boé bô ts'ò boē, men vergist zich wel bij het inkoopen maar niet bij het verkoopen.
dzìn ts'ò, zijne verkeerdheid erkennen 2e = *ts'ò dzīn*, verkeerdelijk houden voor, aanzien voor.
put ts'ò, lett. het is niet verkeerd, juist zoo.
ts'ien ts'ò ban ts'ò, wat was het toch verkeerd om....
ts'ò tsáh zich vergissen in het aftellen van cash.
bô ts'ò pán, geen verkeerde drukplanken hebben *i. e.* juist in zijne handelingen zijn.

剉 Ts'ò *Ts'ò* vellen, omhakken, fijnhakken.
ts'ò bah tsiū, vleesch fijnhakken.
ts'ò báh si, do.
ts'ò lò k'ì, geheel en al weghakken, afhakken.
t'ai ts'ò hakken.
t'ai p'ah ê lâng, vechtersbaas.
ts'ò ts'iū, een boom vellen.
bān to ts'ò, met tien duizend messen fijn hakken (b. v. al zou men er het leven bij verliezen niet willen toegeven).
ts'o ts'ò, (*o*) }, verwaarloozen, ruw (met iets omgaan).
k'áh ts'ám ts'ò k'a ts'ò ts'iu, nog erger dan beenen en handen afgehakt te hebben.

操 Ts'ò *Ts'ò k'im*, op de luit tokkelen spelen.
kaò hiah tsit ts'ò, tot zoover is het één (muziek) stuk.

糙 Ts'ò *Ts'ò bi*, gepelde rijst, nog niet gezuiverde rijst.

噪 Ts'ò *Ts'ò hī*, de ooren verdooven.
ts'ò lō, belet aandoen.
tsiaó á ts'ò nā pō, de vogels tjilpen in het boschje.

粗 Ts'o *Ts'o* ruw gemeen, laag, grof.
ts'o ts'o ê lâng, een gemeene kerel.
ts'o ts'ò, slordig zijn op.
ts'o lō, robust en lomp, ongemanierd.
ts'o k'ng, kaf.
ts'o tang, ruw (van werk enz).
ts'o sut, ongemanierd, ruw.
ts'o oē, iets oppervlakkig, onvolmaakt kunnen verstaan.
ts'o p'ê nī k'ak, robust.
ts'o sim toa tā, onverschrokken, robust.
ts'o hō, onbesuisd.
ts'o p'in, ruw grof (van pers).
ts'o kang, ruw werk.
ts'o siók, ruw van zeden.
ts'o kioh, ruwe onbeschofte kerel.
ts'o ting, ruwe kerels.
ts'o oē, gemeene taal.
ts'o pá, eenvoudig genoeg eten.
ts'o pi tìt, tamelijk middelmatig, in handel gelijk op spelen.
ts'o siap, ruw, grof (van voorwerpen, verf enz).
ts'o tsoá, grofpapier (gebruikt om vuur aan te steken).
ts'o p'e, ruwe omtrek, romp.
toā ts'o, zeer ruw, grof.
ts'o ts'ùi iá taó, iemand gemeen uitschelden.
ts'o k'ùi toā làt, ruw en sterk.
ts'o ts'ân, hardvochtig, wreed.
tāng ts'o hoat, ruwe, harde manier.
ing ts'o ts'o ts'o, de deining, golfslag is zeer sterk.

糞 Ts'o *Ts'o*, mest, drek.
tn ts'o ê lâng, mestdrager verkooper.

ts'o t'áng, mestemmer.
tò ts'o, mest uitscheppen.
ts'o dziō tsûn, mestschuit.

初 Ts'o *Ts'o ts'o*, nieuwelings, nog niet lang geleden.
k'i ts'o, in den beginne.
ts'o koā (*ts'e*), het begin van de koude.
ts'o lai, juist nieuwelings gekomen.
ts'o koān, zich voor het eerst aan iets vergrijpen.

楚 Ts'ó *K'ó ts'ó*, droefheid, smart.

Ts'ó *Ts'ó liók á oē k'i til* (*liák*), het kan nog eenigzins doorgaan.

醋 Ts'ò *Ts'ò*, azijn.
tsiú ts'ò, wijnazijn.
sng ts'ò, zure azijn.
sng ts'ò kè, olie en azijn stel.
k'iā ts'ò, azijn maken.
ts'ò bú, schimmel, hef van azijn.
ts'ò lâ, vel over azijn (schimmel).
tsiáh ts'ò, jaloersch zijn omdat haar man met andere vrouwen omgang heeft.
kòng p'oa ts'ò àng, het azijnvat stukslaan *i. e.* zeer jaloersch op haar man zijn.
ts'ò sin tāng, zeer jaloersch zijn (van vrouw op man en omgekeerd).

Tsoa

攡 Tsoa *Tsoa pai*, de kaarten schudden, een kaart afnemen.
tsoa ts'iem, door elkander doen (als kaarten enz).
tsoa gê pai, dobbelsteenen door elkander schudden schuiven.
tsoa lai tsoa k'i, over en weer door elkander schudden.

紙 Tsoá *Tsoá*, papier.
t'ô âng tsoá, rood kaartjes papier.
kim gûn tsoá (*gîn*), goud en zilver offer papier.
king i tsoá, olie papier met teekeningen van kleéren.
tsoá kun, snippers papier.
tsoá bīn (*tsoá āng á bīn*), mombakkes.
tsoá póh, dun goud of zilver offerpapier.
tsoá tsî, geldpapier (bij offeren gebruikt).
tsoá li, schuimspaan eig' rijstschepper.
pèh tik tsoá, wit papier (van bamboes gemaakt).
tsien tsoá, fijn best papier.
p'oe tsoá, briefpapier.
siaò p'ō tsoá, papier voor koopmansboeken met roode lijnen.
dzī tsoá, beschreven papier.
kō tsoá, papieren poppen, beesten enz. beplakken.
tsoá lién, fidibus (om lamp of pijp aan te steken).
tsoá lién ting, in olie gedoopte fidibus.
hièn tsoá papier offeren (verbranden).
hē tsoá t oè k iò, gelofte doen en papier offeren.
teh tsoá teh bōng tsoá, papier op de graven leggen (bij het feest der graven reiniging).
tsoá pai, speelkaarten.
bōng tsoá, graven papier dat bij de minste wind wegwaait, iemand die ongestadig. dan hier dan daar is.
iû tsoá, papier maken, uit de pap halen.
tsoá t'aò tsoá bé bô miâ dzī, noch aan het begin noch aan het einde van het geschrift staat zijn naam *i. e.* hij heeft geen aanspraak op wat er in dat papier staat.
tsoá kō t'ang, een papieren venster *i. e.* iets dat men gemakkelijk doorstooten doorzien kan.

tsoá ho kim bák tsiu, een papieren tijger maar glinsterende oogen *i. e.* al heeft hij zelf er niet veel verstand van, zijne tegenwoordigheid belet vele bedriegerijen.

k'ah ts'ám tsoá kō̤ eh, nog erger dan wanneer het van papier geplakt ware *i. e.* onsterk.

miā̤ dzī tsiáh tsoá, zijn naam dringt in het papier *i. e.* hij kan meer bij mandarijn of examinator gedaan krijgen dan een ander.

só̤ kóng tióh ing tsoá pao k'ì lai, wat hij gezegd heeft moet gij in papier opbergen *i. e.* niet vergeten — u herinneren.

蛇 Tsoâ *Tsoâ*, slang.

hun tsoâ, groote opiumrooker.

tsoâ siông, als een slang d. i. arglistig.

tsiàh tsoâ p'è hó̤ huih, slangen eten en er tijgerbloed bij drinken *i. e.* tot alles in staat zijn.

ok tók tsoâ, vergiftige slang.

sí tsoâ pô̤, als een slangengeraamte *i e.* onbewegelijk niets uitvoeren.

tsoâ bák, slangenoog.

tsoâ k'ak, slangenvel, huid.

tsoâ t'ìng k'ak, de slang schuift zijn vel af, beteekent het gestolene van een ander op zijn beurt wederafstelen.

Tsoà *Tsoâ*, ziften.

tsoâ li, rijstschepper van gevlochten bamboes.

Tsoā *Tsoā sún*, in de voegen wringen.

oê tsoâ l̄oh k'ì, schoenen aanwringen.

行 Tsoā̄ *Tsoā̄*, numer voor dingen op rijen als boomen, wegen enz.

tsit tsoā̄, een regel (ligne).

t'aò mîng tsoā̄, naad in het haar.

pò̤ tsoā̄, draad van goed.

tīng se tsoā̄, geen draadje goed hebben (om aan te trekken of te verkoopen).

tsē tsoā̄, naar den weg zoeken.

tsè bô tsoā̄, iemand volgende een verkeerden weg inslaan.

goá ū k'ì tsit nīng tsoā̄, ik ben een paar keeren gegaan.

Tsoā̄ *Tsiù tsoā̄*, zweren, een eed doen.

tāng tsoā̄, zware eed gelofte.

koé tsoā̄, een eed, gelofte veranderen.

tsiù tsoā̄ soé sin, door een eed alle verdenking van zich wegnemen.

煎 *Tsoa̤*, zacht koken, laten trekken.

Tsoa̤ *tsoa̤ tê* (*tê̤*) } thee te trekken zetten.

tsoa̤ ióh, medicijnen te trekken zetten, koken.

tsoa̤ tsui tsiáh, in water gekookt eten.

盞 *Fò lé tsoá̤*, glas.

Tsoa̤ *tsiú tsoá̤*, wijnglas.

tsit tsoá̤ ting, één lampje.

ting hé tsoá̤, lampbakje (bakte waarin een oliepit brandt).

kui tsáp tsoá̤ ting, eenige tientallen lampen.

sa tsoá̤ kan tê, drie kopjes drooge thee (zonder water er op geschonken bij offeranden gebruikt).

濺 Tsoà̤ *Tsoà̤ iû*, vet smelten.

泉 Tsoā̤ *Tsui tsoā̤*, wel, waterwel.

tsoā̤ tsui, welwater.

tsoā̤ bák, welader.

oáh tsoā̤, steeds loopende wel 2e gestadige verdiensten, voortdurende inkomsten.

sí tsoā̤, doode, niet steeds loopende, wel.

soa̤ k'a ts'ut tsoā̤, aan den voet van den berg welt het water op.

ts'uì tsoā̤, speeksel.

hé nā̤ tsoā̤, verschroeid.

賤 Tsoā̤ *Tsoā̤*, goedkoop.

noā̤ tsoā̤, goedkoop en veel, veel voor weinig geld.

siók kà tsoā̤, zeer goedkoop.

t'am tsoā̤ tsiáh p'oà ke, wegens het goedkoope van iets, zich er arm aan eten d. i. terwijl is goedkoop iets meer geld er aan besteden dan men anders doen zou.

tsoā pún, lage, goedkoope inkoopsprijs.

ts'un koá hō ná tsoā, hoe kouder de lente is des te overvloediger (lett. goedkooper) is de regen.

濺 Tsoā *Tsoā ts'ut*, uitgutsen, uitschommelen.

huih ki ki tsoā, het bloed gutst met een straal er uit.

tsoā dziō, heen en weer wateren (als beesten of kinderen).

Ts'oá *Loa ts'oá, lóa lóa ts'óa ts'óa (noá ts'oá)* }, slordig oppervlakkig, niet zorgvuldig.

蔡 Ts'oà *Ts'oà*, familienaam.

導 Ts'oā *Ts'oā*, geleiden.

in ts'oā, geleiden.

k'an ts iú ts'oā, bij de hand leiden.

ts'oā káng, loods.

hó ts'oā t'aò, een goed voorbeeld geven.

p'aį tsoā t'aò, een slecht » »

ts'oā lō, den weg wijzen, leiden.

ts'oā k'ang, iemand op de goede plaats voor iets leiden, eene goede gelegenheid voor iemand aanduiden.

sa in sa ts'oā, elkander leiden, lokken.

ts'oā kui lō, langs den waren weg leiden (als leerlingen rekruten).

娶 Ts'oā *Ts'oā bó*, eene vrouw huwen, trouwen (van een man).

aū ts'oā, hertrouwen (van een man).

kè ts'oā huwen, huwelijk.

kè ts'oā é lé, huwelijks plechtigheden, geschenken.

ts'oā ke aō, eene vrouw huwen (gew. buiten lands).

溢 Ts'oā *Ts'oā dziō*, in bed wateren.

ts'oā dziō pò, godin der stormen er zware regens.

芒 Ts'oą *Ts'oą ts'ì*, lastig vol moeielijkheid.

k'í ts'oą ts'ì, met splinters; moeielijkheden, reden tot twist doen onstaan.

k'it i ts'oą tioh, schuins weg door iets geraakt worden (als door een kogel die langs de wang vliegt).

sì koè ts'oą lâng, overal met een leuke streek iemands goed wegnemen.

giah k'ì tsit ki ts'oą, een splinter uithalen *i. e.* een schadelijk mensch verwijderen.

ts'oą, splinter.

giah ts'oą, een splinter uithalen.

ts'oą ts'ì, een splinter oploopen, zijne handen, vingers branden, moeielijk uit te maken, verward.

ts'iah tioh ts'oą, een splinter oploopen.

bák tsiu boē tióh tit tsit ki ts'oą, geen splinter in het oog kunnen velen *i. e.* geene groote zaken kunnen verdragen.

散 Ts'oá *Noá ts'oá*, dralend, langzaam (handelen).

Ts'oá *Tióh kaó ts'oá*, uitslag, soort schurft hebben.

閂 Ts'oà *Ts'oà*, de bout op een deur doen; bout voor een deur.

mîng ts'oà, deurbout.

ts'oà k'ui, de bout van een deur afnemen.

puih mîng ts'oà, de dwarsbout van een deur afhalen.

k'ui ts'oą, do.

ts'oà sún, *sún ts'oà*, dwarsbalk of dwarslat over iets.

ts'oà kun, dwarshout (aan deuren, onder het tafelblad enz).

ts'oà mîng, de bout op een deur doen.

闖 Ts'oà *Ts'oà*, slecht, robust, teugelloos.

hoai ts'oà, dwarshoofd, van een lastig mensch gezegd die moeielijk met anderen overeenstemt.

ts'oà tō, dwars over den weg loopen (wanneer een mandarijn er langs moet).

kik ts'oà é lâng, een teugelloos, roekeloos mensch.

Tsoah

搖 *Tsoah*, uitschommelen.

Tsoah *p'ah tsoah*, doen uitschommelen.
iò iò tsoah tsoah, uitschommelen (van vocht).
tsûn liah teh tsoah, de schuiten liggen te schommelen (als door een voorbijgaande stoomboot).
sì koè teh tsoah, overal trillen, in beroering zijn (als vóór het uitbreken van van een oproer).
dziòng kaò tsoah k'i lai, vreeselijk leven maken zoo dat alles er van trilt.
kè tsi̱ it tít tsoah k'i lai, de prijs komt eensklaps in beroering, stijgt.

Tsoah *Tsoah kú*, zoolang, al dien tijd.

差 *Tsaó tsoáh*, verschillen, verschuiven.

Tsoàh *kap i k'ah tsoáh*, wat koeler met iemand zijn.
tsing tsoáh, verschillen van.
tsoáh tsi̱, afdingen, minder betalen.
lóng bò tsoáh, het maakt geen verschil, geen onderscheid.
t'aò k'ak k'it i tsoàh tioh, zich het hoofd, den nek verwringen.
tsoáh kun, verdraaien, verwringen (uit het gewricht, het been enz).
tsoáh lùn, do.
tsiah kú k'ah tsoáh tiep tiep, het is in den laatsten tijd een weinigje beter, dragelijker (van ziekte, koude, warmte enz).
tsit iū bò tsoáh, gelijkelijk, niet verschillend.
tsoáh tsit dzit, het verschilt een dag (te vroeg of te laat).
ū tsit tè á tsoáh, tsoáh tsit tè à, er is een klein verschil in.
tsoáh pūn, een verschillend monster.

蠘 *Ka tsoáh*, kakkerlak.

Tsoàh *ts'ù tsoáh (o)* }, iemand die voor anderen naar huizen uitzien.
soa tsoáh (kui) }, iemand die voor anderen naar eene goede plaats voor een graf uitziet.
hai ka tsoáh, lett. zeekakkerlak *i. e.* een insekt dat veel in booten gevonden wordt.
tsit è nā péh ka tsoáh, evenals een witte kakkerlak (van iemand die in langen-tijd niet buiten geweest is).
ka tsoáh taó, stut voor een rek (tegen muren enz.

慄 *Ts'oah*, beven.

Ts'oah *giaòh giaòh ts'oah*, van vrees beven sidderen.
bah tsoah, het vleesch trilt (van schrik enz).
gōng bah teh ts'oah, er wacht hem een pak slaag.
k'a ts'iú tsoah, aan handen en voeten beven (van vrees).
k'a ts'oah ts'iú ts'oah, stuiptrekken, kramptrekken.
k'a ts'iú lák lák ts'oah, beven, trillen, als minderen tegenover meerderen.

爍 *Sih na ts'oah*, bliksemstraal.

Ts'oah *sih sih ts'oah*, trillen, fonkelen (als spiegelglas in de zon).
ts'oah tseh tsoè i k'ì, eensklaps boos weggaan.

𥊍 *Ts'oah*, kramp, de kramp hebben, kramp-

Ts'oah achtig trekken.
bák tsiu ts'oah, het oog trilt (als voorteeken van een ramp).

拔 *Ts'oah*, uitplukken als veeren van een

Ts'oah vogel.
ts'oah mêng, plukken (als een kip).
ts'oah tn̄g, stuk trekken, breken (als een touw).

94

tsi'ŋ́ ts'oah, in allerijl, hals over kop ten einde brengen opredderen.
ts'iŋ́ ts'oah, *ts'iŋ́ ts'iŋ́ tsoah ts'oah*, uit de handen rukken, niet nauwkeurig laten bekijken, beschouwen.
ts'ī ts'áo tīng ts'iŋ́ ts'oah, op het oogenblik dat er veel gejoel (en ook veel bedriegerij) op de markt is.

刷 *Ts'oah*, raspen.
Ts'oah *ts'aì t'aô ts'oah*, radijsrasp.
ts'oah á, rasp.
ts'o̱ ts'oah, *ts'o̱ ts'o̱ ts'oah ts'oah*, in allerijl overhaast den boel opredderen.
ts'oah ts'iem, schaven (als aardappelen).
hoan tsû ts'oah, aardappelenschaaf, rasp.
ts'oah iù iù, fijnraspen.

流 *Ts'oah sai ts'i̱*, vallende ster.
Ts'oah *ts'oah sai*, zich bevuilen (als kinderen).
ts'oah sai hoe, dunne ontlasting.
ts'oah sai tsui, do.

Ts'oah *Sa̱ ts'oah*, elkander bedriegen.
k'it i ts'oah k'ì, door iemand bedrogen worden.

斜 *Ts'oáh bák*, scheel kijken.
Ts'oàh *oai ts'oáh* / *oai oai ts'oáh ts'oáh* }, scheef 2e verschillen van
ts'oáh kak, een hoek afsnijden.
ts'oáh tit, schuinsweg, schuins af.
tuì hit tē ts'oah kè k'ì, van daaraf oversteken (een weg uithalen).
ts'ōah lō̱, een zijweg gaan.
sai ts'oáh sin, scheef gaan staan (als bij het schieten).
ts'oáh hûn, scheefloopende streep.
oai ts'uì ts'oáh bák, scheve mond en scheefstaande oogen, wenken geven.
tsít ê tsing tsoáh ts'oáh liao liáo, is één ding verschoven dan is het geheel scheef.

Tsoai

Tsoai *Oai oai tsoai tsoai* (*tsoáh*) }, scheef overhellen.

旋 *K'in á tsoat tseh* (*o*) } een weinigje kromwringen.
Tsoai
tsoai īm kè (*o*) }, stijf opdraaien, aanschroeven.

Tsoaī *Oé tsoaī i lóh*, schoenen aanwringen.
ts'iŋ́ k'it i tsoaī tioh, de hand verwringen.
ts'aí ts'aí tsoaī tsoaī, onverschillig, onbeleefd behandelen.

Tsoaih *Oaih oaih tsoaih tsoaih*, scheef overhellen.

Tsoan

專 *Tsoan sim*, oplettend, met geheel zijn
Tsoan hart.
tsoan tsí, doelen op.
tsū tsoan, zijne eigen zin volgen.
siēn tsū tsoan, *tók tsū tsoan*, volkomen zijn eigen meester zijn.
tsoan it, zich uitsluitend bezig houden met....
tsoan koán, uitsluitend, alleen, zonder anderen beheeren.
tsoan tsoan, uitsluitend.
tsoan ts'e, uitsluitend zenden om.....
tsoan tsoan tsoan, volstrekt, uitsluitend.
bí īm tsoan, de rijst is niet zuiver (er is iets anders door).
tsoan dzīm hit ê lâng, uitsluitend, geheel en al aan hem toevertrouwen, overlaten.
tsoan dzīm ì, zich uitsluitend aan zijn idée houden.

賺 *Tsoán*, voordeel hebben bij, verdienen.
Tsoán *tsoán tsiáh*, *tsoán tsiáh pō̱*, de kost verdienen.
lai tièm t'aò tsoán tsi̱, aan de winkels komen bedelen.
tsoán tsi̱, geld verdienen.
hoai̱ tsoán tit tsoán, op allerlei manieren, over en weer geld verdienen.

爋 *Tsièn tsoán*, stoven.
Tsoán *hoán tsoán*, omkeeren (als vleesch bij het braden).

轉 *Tsoán oan*, een eind aan een twist maken.
Tsoán *tsoán lîn têng (tuì)*, omdraaien.
tsoán piên, veranderen, vervormen, naar de omstandigheden handelen.
tsoán sin, zich omdraaien, omkeeren, in een oogenblik.
tsoán kao, bezorgen bij, geven aan.
tsoán sàng, bezorgen aan, geven aan.
tsoán kià, bezorgen aan een derden persoon.
tsoán t'ok, aan een derden persoon overgelasten.
gaô oán tsoán, behendig naar omstandigheden veranderen 2e zijdelings (niet recht uit) spreken.
tsoán séh, omdraaien, rechtdraaien (als een twist bijleggen).
bô tit t'ang tsoán sin, zich niet kunnen roeren (als door schulden).
tsoan tién, in de tweede hand hijpotheek op een huis geven.
tsoán koan, veranderen, verdragen 2e in overgang zijn.
tsoan gán, in een ommezien.
tsoán dzīm, van ambtsplaats veranderen 2e zijne reeds verlaten ambts plaats weder aanvaarden.

鑽 *K'it láng tsoàn k'i*, ontfutseld, ontstolen worden.
Tsoàn *t'aô lō k'it i tsoàn k'ì*, door iemand uit zijne betrekking verdrongen worden.

全 *Tsoàn dzièn*, geheel en al, volstrekt.
Tsoàn *oân tsoân*, volledig, in zijn geheel, voltallig.
tsoàn ke, het geheele huisgezin.
sip tsoàn, volledig.
lióng tsoàn, beiden hebben hun zin.
t'ien tē bû tsoàn kong, in het heelal is er niets volkomen helder gaaf *i. e.* hoe fraai iets ook is, er ontbreekt gewoonlijk iets aan.
tsoàn sik ê o, volkomen, geheel en al zwart.
bān tsoân bû pè (en) *sit*, er mankeert volstrekt niets aan (aan eene zaak).

泉 *Tsoàn tsiu*, distrikt van Fokkien.
Tsoàn

旋 *Tsoān*, met een sleutel sluiten, draaien, op-
Tsoān winden (als een horologie).
tsoān soh á ko, in elkander draaien (als een touw om het sterker te maken).
tsoān si, sleutel.
tsoān si k'ang, sleutelgat.
tsoān k'ui, openen met een sleutel.
tsiú tsoān, kurketrekker.
gaô lién tsoān, knap in het draaien *i. e.* glad zijn om geld uit iemand te krijgen (als arme lieden).
tsoān tioh ts'iú kut, de hand verdraaien verwringen.

撰 *Tō tsoān*, zelf maken (als een zin in een
Tsoān opstel, een leugen enz).

川 *San ts'oan*, bergen en bergstroomen,
Ts'oan landstreek.

穿 *Ts'oan*, een sleutel met een gat er in.
Ts'oan *ts'oan tin*, met slingerplanten begroeid.
ts'oan kun, door boomwortels omwoeld.
hoán ts'oan, omgekeerd, binnenste buiten aantrekken.
ts'it ts'oan pat t'ào, met alle kanten correspondeeren (als een weg of kamer).

餐 *Sam ts'oan nō bī*, dikwijls en lekker
Ts'oān eten.

喘 *Ts'oán*, hijgen.
Ts'oán *ts'oán k'ui*, ademhalen.
hioh ts'oán, uitrusten, uithijgen.
toā k'uì ts'oán boē tit, niet tot zijn adem kunnen komen.

ts'it k'ang bô kaò ts'oán, aan de zeven gaten (van het hoofd) niet genoeg hebben om adem te halen *i. e*, overladen met zaken zijn.

kik kaò boē ts'oán k'ùi, verstikken (door rook enz).

gaò ts'oán ê lâng, iemand die van hijgen houdt *i. e.* iemand die zeer gauw geagiteerd is en gaarne tegen anderen wedijvert.

串 Ts'oàn *Ts'oàn t'ong*, gemeenschap hebben met.

簒 Ts'oàn *Ts'oàn uī*, den troon overweldigen.

ts'oàn koàn, wederrechtelijk beheer; bestuur over iets aanmatigen.

ts'oàn t'aò lō, iemand door onderkruiping zijne broodwinning onttroggelen.

偏 Ts'oàn *Ts'oàn*, bij voorkeur.

ts'oàn ts'oàn, do.

闖 Ts'oàn *Ts'oàn ts'ut*, uitkomen snellen.

ts'oàn gê, een uitgroeiende tand.

ts'oàn tō, dwars over den weg steken (als zij reeds voor mandarijnen gebaand is).

loān loān ts'oàn: si koè ts'oàn, overal heen loopen, den weg niet houden (als paarden of schapen).

撰 Ts'oàn *Ts'oán*, uitkiezen, roepen, in gereedheid brengen.

ts'oàn lâng, menschen bij elkander brengen.

ts'oân piēn piēn, in gereedheid brengen, bij elkander zoeken (als bagage enz).

kā i ts'oàn lai, laat hij het klaar en wel hier brengen (als spijzen enz).

tiao ts'oàn, bij voorkeur, uitkiezen.

ts'oàn k'ang, een gat op iets zoeken (als om zijne schulden te betalen, goederen te verkoopen enz).

ts'oân tsoé, alles bij elkander gereed brengen.

ts'oàn k'a ts'iú, bedienden, helpers in gereedheid brengen, klaar hebben.

ts'oân lai ts'oân k'ì bô tsit ê hó, over en weer uitzoekende is er geen één goed.

ts'oân pūn, uitgezochte, gesorteerde partijen voor de verschillende plaatsen uitgekozen.

Tsoang

燦 Ts'oàng *Ts'oàng*, sierlijk, mooi, fraai, elegant.

ts'oàng kut, veel van opschik houden (in slechte beteekenis van lichte vrouwen gezegd).

aì ts'oàng, veel van opschik houden.

Ts'oàng *Ts'oàng kìm*, booswicht, zwendelaar.

hì ts'oàng, verzot op comedie.

ts'oàng hiṇ, schurk, brutale kerel.

Tsoat

拙 Tsoat *Tsoat*, dam.

tsoat loē, mijne vrouw (nederige term).

tsoat iaò, een uittreksel van een boek maken.

oat oat tsoat tsoat, niet rechtuit, gekronkeld (ook van woorden).

oai oai tsoat tsoat, scheef (van voorwerpen, huizen, schoenen enz).

ts'i tsoat, dom, vasthoudende aan zijn idée.

tsoat tìt, onbewimpeld, ronduit (dom).

ù tsoat, u tsoat, vasthoudend aan zijn idée.

lōng k'aó hoán tsoat, den schijn van vernuftig aannemende, integendeel dom zijn.

脫 Tsoat *Tsoat ts'ut lai*, uitknijpen, uitkomen (als ingewanden uit de buik).

tèng á tō tsoat tsoat ts'ut lai, de ingewanden wrongen zich er uit.

tsoat lai tsoat k'ì, over en weer wringen (als iets dat men niet dicht kan schroeven).

laó hióh pō kaò tsoat ts'ut lai, siri kauwen tot dat de sap er uit spritst.

絕 Tsoàt *Tsoát biaō*, uiterst fraai.

tsoát hó, uiterst goed.

tsoát ts'ù hòng sing, uitkomst in uitersten nood vinden.

kù tsoát } , do.
(*kì*)

koat tsoát, allen verderen omgang afbreken.

kat tsoát, do.

ts'oat tsing, de vroegere goede harmonie verbreken.

pē kiá bō tsoát tsing, vader en zoon breken (nooit) den omgang met elkander geheel af.

tsoát sui hó, laten doodhongeren lett. water en vuur onthouden.

tsoát niù ts'aó, den aanvoer van levensmiddelen afsnijden.

tsoát pō, uiterste middel (als van medic).

k'ì kaò tsoát k'uì, zoo toornig dat men geen adem kan halen.

tò bòng si tsoát, gevlucht of uitgestorven.

tsoát sù, geene erfgenamen, kinderen hebben.

tsoát ì, alle hoop opgegeven hebben.

ts'oát tsik, geen omgang meer hebben met..., niets meer van zich laten hooren of zien.

tsing kaò tsoát k'ì, alle hoop voor de toekomst opgeven, alle moed opgeven (als iemand die het bericht krijgt dat zijne bezittingen verloren zijn).

boē tsoát, boē tsīn tsoát, geheel en al verkoopen zoo dat men er alle betrekking op verliest.

tsīn tsoát dzī, bewijs van totalen verkoop.

tsoát sui, zeer fraai.

tsoàt kau, tsoàt lō, allen omgang met iemand afbreken.

k'ì tsoát, den laatsten snik gegeven hebben.

Tsoe

劑 Tsoe *Tsit tè tsoe* } , een stuk deeg (waarvan
(*tse*)
men maken kan wat men wil) 2e een kapitaal waarmede men alles doen kan.

mī tsoe } , deeg.
(*tse*)

Tsoé *Kóng oē beh lai tsoé goá* } , door woor-
(*o*)
den mij verdriet willen aan doen.

做 Tsoè *Tsoè* } , doen, maken, zijn.
(*tsò*)

tsoè k'ah té, korter maken.

tsoè kang è lâng, werkman.

tsoè tsoá sai hū, papier maker.

tsoè tiong lâng, middelaar zijn.

tsoè hun sai hū, tabaksverkooper.

tsoè bih » » mandenmaker.

tsoè sing lí, handel drijven.

tsoè hoē, bond voor wederkeerigen bijstand sluiten.

tsoè tit tsiâ, voltooien.

tsoè tsit ē } , alles bij elkander.
(*ē*)

tsoè k'ah hó } verbeteren.
(*tsò*)

tsoè pin kù } , getuigenis afleggen.
(*kì*)

tsoè oàn, een eind maken aan.

tsoè boē oē lai, het niet over zich kunnen verkrijgen, er niet toe kunnen besluiten om....

tsoé tsoh, den schijn van iets aannemen.

tsoè lóh k'ì, doen, ten uitvoer brengen.

tsoè hó, 1e het goede doen.

tsoè ts'iú, namaken.

tsoè toē tot onderwerp nemen (voor een opstel of gesprek, tot voorwendsel nemen om iemand te spreken enz).

tsoè toā lâng, volwassen (en getrouwd) zijn.

gaô tsoè lâng, een goed mensch zijn, hulpvaardig enz. zijn.

tsoè hó lâng, den goeden man uithangen, zich niet gaarne met iemand in onmin willen brengen al is het zelfs noodzakelijk.

tsoè p'aí lâng, de kat de bel omhangen.

tsoè ing lâng, doen als of het hem niet aanging, zich met iets niet willen inlaten.

tsoè kuì, gekheid maken, schertsen (van man en vrouw).

tsoè tsoè tsoh tsoh, valschelijk den schijn van iets aannemen.

tsoè tsing hō lâng, iemand eene gunst bewijzen.

tsoè tsui, overstroomen, overstooming.

tsìn tsoè, bij zijn huwen in het huis van zijne vrouw komen inwonen (als bij rijke vrouwen) bij zijn huwelijk zijne vrouw zelf afhalen.

tsoè k'ang twee handen op eenen buik zijn.

tsoè lâng oh, het is moeielijk zijne plichten als mensch te vervullen.

tsoè ts'in, familiebetrekking worden (door huwelijk).

tsoè pē tsoè kiá é lâng, vaders en zoons.

k'ioh tsoè tui, tot een hoop bij elkander rapen, brengen.

tsoè tsūn tsoè tsūn, bij vlagen (als pijn).

tsoè tsoeh, de jaarfeesten houden, op de jaarfeesten offeren.

tsoè hó, het goede doen, goed afmaken.

任 Tso'è *Tsoè li....*, ga uw gang met.

tsoè li k'ì, loop voort.

tsoè li tsiáh, ga voort met eten.

最 Tsoè *Tsoè kû*, zeer lang.

tsoè to, zeer veel, allermeest.

tsoè hó, uiterst goed.

Tsoê *Tsoê tsoê* (*tsê*), gelijkelijk.

tsoê tsoê toā, gelijk van grootte, evengroot.

tsoê tsing, gelijkelijk (verdeeld), evenredig (als ameublement enz).

tsit tsoê (*tsê*), allen te gelijk.

tsoê tsoê, do.

tsoê pī, in orde brengen.

m̄ tsoê tsê, niet gelijk, oneffen, ongelijk.

ts'ū tsoê (*ts'ī tsê*), zich verzamelen, bij een komen.

tsoê tsoê lai k'ì, tegelijk, met elkander gaan.

liâh tsoê, op eenzelfde lijn gelijk brengen (als paarden of schuiten bij een wedren).

tsoê t'aò, maak er een gelijk tiendeelig getal, ronde som, van.

ts'oân tsoê, alles in gereedheid brengen.

goá kap li tsoê tsit kọ (*sp. tsoê kọh*), ik zal een even groot aandeel als het uwe inleggen.

bah t'aô tsoê, zijne volle grootte en vetheid hebben (als varkens).

hē tsoê, in overeenstemming, gelijkelijk handelen (als bij een oproer).

多 Tsoē *Tsoē* (*tsē*), veel.

tsoē tsoē, zeer veel.

dzoā tsoē, hoeveel.

tsoē pai, dikwijls.

tsoē kat, vol knoopen.

tsoē oē (*oā*), praatziek.

tsoē tsió, veel of weinig, min of meer.

pūn tsoē, veel in gereedheid brengen.

罪 Tsoē *Tsoē* (*tsóē*), misdaad, zonde, straf.

ū tsoē, schuldig.

tsoē kò, fout, verkeerdheid.

hōān tsoē, misdoen, *tsoē hōān* schuldige, boosdoener.

tik tsoē, do. 2e excuseer mij.

tsoē siók, soort van misdaad, misdaad.

dzīn tsoē, eene misdaad bekennen.

tsoē dzín, schuldige, boosdoener (ook als scheldwoord).

gí tsoē, uitspraak over een misdaad doen.

pūn tsoē, eene misdaad bestraffen.

siók tsoē, eene misdaad, straf, afkoopen.

tsoē miâ, naam, graad van misdaad (straf) 2e vele namen, velen.

tsoē teh lâng, de misdaad drukt op iemand, doet zijn geweten knagen, doet hem ontstellen.

tsoē giét t'aì tāng, zijne misdaden waren zeer zwaar, grof.

tīng tsoē, de straf op eene misdaad bepalen.

Ts'oe *Ts'oe* (*ts'e*), rangschikkend telwoord.

ts'oe it, de eerste dag der maand.

k'i ts'oe (of *ts'o*), in den beginne.

tsng ts'oe (*ts'e*), do.

tsng goân ts'oe, do. in de jeugd.

刷 Ts'oè *Ts'oè* (*ts'è*), met zand schuren, gladpoetsen.

tiá ts'oè, panboender (van rotting of cocosschil).

ts'oè tiá, een pan boenen.

ts'oè k'ì kim, gladboenen.

ts'oè p'oà p'é k'ò, het vel of de broek stukschaven (als bij een val).

kè tsi kap i ts'oè k'ah tsió, met iemand over den prijs hebben (lett. boenen) om het goedkooper te hebben.

ts'oè suí gûn, met kwik bedekken (als koper om het als zilver te doen schijnen).

糝 Ts'oè *Bí ts'oè*, rijstendeeg.

bō ts'oè, het meel fijn malen.

tsing ts'oè, rijst, het meel stampen.

躖 Ts'oē *Ts'oē* (*ts'ē*), zijn voet na zich slepen (als menschen die verlamming in den voet hebben).

t'ô nìh ts'oē, op den grond kruipen, nog niet kunnen loopen.

bák kiáh tseh ná ts'oē, moogt ge uwe hakken hoe langer hoe meer voortslepen (als bedelaressen die gescheurde schoenen aan hebben (scheldwoord tegen vrouwen.)

k'a ts'oē tioh, met den voet tegen iets aanstooten.

tsûn k'ìn k'ìn á ts'oē tioh, het schip schoof even over (eene ondiepte of rots) heen.

īng kù á ts'oē tseh, met een kleine zaag glad zagen, schaven.

ts'oè k'i pi, glad, gelijk zagen.

Tsoeh

節 Tsoeh *Tsoeh kuì* (*tseh*), 24ste gedeelte van een jaar.

tsoeh k'uì (*k'ì*), de temperatuur van de verschillende halve maanden.

tang tsoeh, winter solstitium.

ni tsoeh, jaarlijksche feesten (om de halve maand).

tsoè tsoeh, spijzen enz. in gereedheid brengen voor de jaarlijksche feesten.

sàng tsoeh, elkander op de jaarlijksche feesten geschenken geven.

hioh tsoeh, rustdag houden op de jaarlijksche feesten.

pàng tsoeh, vacantie geven op de do.

截 Tsoèh *Tsoéh* (*tséh*), verticaal doorsnijden, afsnijden.

tsám tsoéh, resoluut, vastberaden.

ē tsoéh, onderste gedeelte / *tíng tsoéh*, bovenste » van het lichaam of andere voorwerpen.

p'oà tsoè nn̄g tsoéh, in twee stukken breken, snijden enz.

tsién tsoéh, handelen met (een kapitaal enz).

ts'ut tsaī lí tsién tsoéh, zooals gij daarmede handelen wilt.

戚 Ts'oeh *Ts'oeh* (*ts'eh*) }, misgunnen.
ts'oeh sim, teleurgesteld in zijne goede verwachting.
boē ts'oeh boē pì, geen berouw hebben of zich beteren.
k'ó ts'oeh, uiterst bedroefd zijn, het zich erg aantrekken dat....
ts'oeh miā, bedroefd zijn over, ontevreden zijn met zijn lot.
ts'ám ts'oeh, zich uit droefheid erg door iets folteren.
bóh tit ts'oeh pât làng ts'oeh ka kī, wees niet boos op anderen, maar wees het op u zelven.
ts'oeh sin ts'oeh miā, ontevreden met zijn lot zijn, er over morren.

Tsoh

作 Tsoh *Sik tsoh*, zich in alles en overal goed schikken goed op zijn plaats vinden.
hā tsoh, laag, verachtelijk.
tsoh sit, landbouwen.
gaò tsoè tsoh, iets knap namaken, nabootsen.
sik tsoh, gaar, glad geslepen (van pers.)
hoat tsoh, opkomen, voor den dag komen (als iets dat verborgen was of vroeger gegeten vergif).
gō tsoh, lijkschouwer.
soè tsoh, spion.
tsoh ts'àn, landbouwen.

築 Tsoh *Tsoh tsaò*, een fornuis bouwen.
tsoh ts'iū, een muur bouwen.
tsoh tsui, water naar een veld leiden.

塞 Tsoh *Sim kog tsoh tsoh*, inwendig onwel (door slechte digestie of verdriet).

擲 Tsóh *Tsóh*, op den grond werpen, toewerpen.
tsóh lóh, neêrwerpen.
tsóh tsióh t'aò, met een steen gooien.
làm sám tsóh, roekeloos overal neêrgooien.
gīm tsi sa tsóh, elkander met geld gooien d. i. voor elkander in geldzaken niet willen onderdoen.
gīm tsi tsóh lóh saí hák, geld in een mestput werpen *i. e.* zijn geld verkwisten.

射 Tsóh *Tsóh tsì*, met pijl en boog schieten.
tsóh tsiaó, scheel kijken.

作 Tsóh *Tsáp tsóh ê lâng*, allerlei slag van menschen.
tsáp tsóh ê só tsaī, eene plaats waar allerlei menschen komen (als een herberg).

昨 Tsóh *Tsóh dzit*, eergisteren.
lò tsóh dzit, vooreergisteren.

逐 Tsóh *Tsóh lai tsóh k'ì*, heên en weêr loopen.
tsing tsóh, onvermoeid snellen (als om geneeskundige hulp te halen of geld te leenen).
tsaó tsóh, hard, onvermoeid snellen.
ts'ì tsóh, schuw, bevreesd.
tsóh pút, een afgodsbeeld van eenen kant naar den anderen kant schudden (als bij een processie).

詛 Ts'oh *Ts'oh*, gemeen uitschelden.
ts'oh kàn kiaō làng, iemand gemeen uitschelden.
p'ai ts'uì ts'oh làng, do.
ts'oh làng pé t'aò bú kut, iemand over zijne ouders uitschelden.
ts'oh kaò īm sī ts'uì taó, zoo uitschelden dat het geen schelden meer is *i. e.* ongehoord gemeen uitschelden.

Tsok

作 Tsok *Tsok sū k'í t'aò làn*, alle begin is moeielijk.
tsok tsōng, een air van gezag aannemen.
tsok lōng, den gek steken met.

tsok ip, een buiging maken.
tsok koaì, lastig, hinderlijk maken.
tsok kaó koaì, do.
tsok ok, het kwade doen.
tsok sìng ih, iemand er boven op helpen, een buitenkansje geven.
tsok giét, slechte, verkeerde dingen doen.
tsìn tsok, vooruitgaan (in handel enz).
tsō tsok, doen maken, opmaken (als een leugen).
ui hui tsok taí, slecht handelen.
kám tsok kám tong, durven doen en op zich durven nemen.

濁 Tsók *Tsók*, walglijk, te veel van iets.
t'aì tsók, al te opgesmukt.
ts'aò tsok, te veel van hetzelfde en daar door gemeen, walglijk (als kleuren op een schilderij).

族 Tsók *Tsong tsók*, verwanten.
tsók p'ō, stamlijst.
ts'in tsók, familiegenooten.
kui tsong kui tsók, in geheele families bij elkander (wonend).
tsók tít, achterneven.
tsók siok, oudooms ooms.
tsók tsiū, familiehoofd.

呪 Tsók *Tsók tsók kiò haó*, sussen (geluid van iemand die pijn heeft of zeer verwonderd staat).

錯 Ts'ok *Kiā ts'ok*, verkeerd handelen.
ts'ok gō, zich vergissen.
ts'ok tsong, onverschillig welke.
ts'a ts'ok, verkeerd, fout.
ts'ièn ts'ok bān ts'ok, groote verkeerdheid, stommiteit.
ts'ok dzīn, verkeerdelijk voor het zijne aanzien.
ts'ok gók, ontstellen.

族 Ts'ok *Tsit ts'ok*, een bundel.
tsit ts'ok mñg, een vlok haar.
ts'it ts'ok ê lâng—ê hiā, een troep, hoop menschen, mieren.

齷 Ts'ok *Ok ts'ok*, vuil, liederlijk.

簇 Ts'ók *Ts'it ts'ók*, een troep, hoop (menschen) een dot (haar) enz.

鑿 Ts'ók *Ts'ók ts'ók k'ó kù*, het kan voorwaar als bewijs dienen.
tsin tsin ts'ók ts'ók, voorwaar, stellig.
ts'oan ts'ók, onnoodige dingen doen.

Tsong

宗 Tsong *Tsong tsók*, stamgenooten van: gelijken familienaam.
tsìng tsong, rechtschapen.
tsó tsong, voorouders.
tsong eh, van denzelfden familienaam.
hoa tsong, van denzelfden familienaam maar niet verwant.

装 Tsong *Tsít tsong hè*, eene vracht, factuur goederen.
kui tsong, in het groot, de geheele massa in eens.

踪 Tsong *Bô tsong bô tsik*, geene vaste woonplaats hebben, er zijn geene sporen van iemand of iets over.
tsong lièm, huwelijks uitzet.

粧 Tsong *Tām tsong*, eenvoudig (niet opgesmukt).
iēm tsong, zeer opgesmukt.

葬 Tsóng *Tsóng tok*, onderkoning.
tsóng ping tìn tai, luitenant-generaal.
pé tsóng (*pé* »), een hoofdman over honderd soldaten.
puh tsóng (*peh iā*), een hoofdman over honderd ruiters.
tsóng koā, bootsman.
tsóng p'ō, scheepskok.
tsóng p'ō, grootboek.
tsóng sìng (» *suì*), optellen.
tsóng miā, algemeene benaming.

tsóng bô, volstrekt niet.
tsóng īm sī, do.
lóng tsóng, geheel en al, alle.
tsóng k'áo, een door personen van verschillende streken bezochte plaats.
tsóng kiōng, in het geheel, alles bij elkander.
tsóng kun bú, de hoofdspier waarvan alle andere spieren uitgaan, het hoofd de wortel van eene zaak.
kiōng tsóng, allen bij elkander.
tsóng t'aò, de hoofdman van iets (van bedienden, matrozen enz.)
tsóng líng, hoofdaanvoerder, opperbevelhebber.
tsóng kun t'aò, de hoofdspier; de algemeene plaats van uitgang.
tsóng baóh, alles door elkander opkoopen.
tsóng sī, gewoonlijk, over het algemeen is het...

Tsóng *Put tsóng tsìn*, zonder principe, nietswaardig (pers.)
īm tsóng tsìn, ontaard (van kinderen).

總 Tsòng *Tsòng*, begraven.
ts'ut tsòng, gaan begraven.
bai tsòng, gaan begraven.
sàng tsòng, eene begrafenis bijwonen.
an tsòng, in het graf ter ruste leggen, begraven.
ts'ien tsòng, overbegraven (naar eene andere plaats).
hiong tsòng, spoedig na den dood begraven (na 7 of 14 dagen).

壯 Tsòng *lóng tsòng*, stevig, sterk (van pers.)
tsòng ting, mannen in de kracht van hun leven.
tsòng tá, zijn moed versterkend (als een wapen).
tsòng kiēn, stevig, kras (gew. van oude lieden).
tsòng liên ê si ê làng, in de kracht van zijn leven.

bin tsòng, sterke, stevige lieden uit het volk gekozen om vóór mandarijnen uit te gaan.
tsòng ióng, krachtige soldaten (vrijwilliger).
li-tit-k'i-tsòng, heeft men eene goede zaak voor, dan is zijne gesteldheid, inborst krachtig.

中 Tsòng *Put tsòng iōng*, niet te gebruiken, voor niets goed (van pers.)

撞 Tsông *Tsaó tsông*, overal rondsnellen (als om een dokter te vinden).
tsông tsóh, do.
tsông k'i lai, opspringen als paarden, honden enz.
tsông ts'ut lai, uitloopen, uitsnellen.
tsông koai, opspringen, hoog springen (als een hond die over een muur springt).
tsông p'oà bāng, het net stuk schieten (als een groote visch die door het net komt).
kín kín tsông ts'ut k'i k'oà, uitsnellen om te gaan zien.
kè tsi-k'it li tsông kè t'aò k'i, gij hebt te snel opgeboden (en daardoor te veel betaald).
k'a tsíng t'aò á tsông ts'ut lai, de toonen van den voet komen er door (door een kapotten kous).
gīm tsi tsông p'oà i ê io tó, iemands geldbuidel met geld stuk stoppen *i. e.* meer voor iets betalen dan het waardig.

藏 Tsông *Tsông k'ìng*, wegstoppen, verbergen.
ún tsông p'ai làng, slechte lieden herbergen, bij zich dulden.

臟 Tsōng *Ngó tsōng*, de vijf voornaamste inwendige lichaamsdeelen namelijk: hart, lever, longen, maag en nieren of blaas.

Tsōng *Bōng tsōng*, onvoorzichtig.

狀 Tsōng *īm tsiá tsōng*, niet goed staan (als kleeren).

ĩm tsiŋ̄ lâng tsōng, voor geen mensch kunnen gerekend worden (door slechtheid of mismaaktheid.)
hing tsōng, handelwijze, handelingen.
tsōng lâng, de verdenking op iemand laten vallen (als door goederen bij hem in huis te brengen waardoor het den schijn heeft als had hij ze gestolen).
ĩng oē tsōng lâng, iemands iets onwaars ten laste leggen.
tsok tsōng, wonderbaarlijk leven maken (als een muis in een doos enz.)
ĩm tsiŋ̄ tsi tsōng, den vorm der vulva niet hebben *i. e.* een air aannemen om iemand bang te maken.
si̤ giên tsōng gú, uit zich zelven opmaken (als een leugen).

傖 Ts'ong *Ts'ong pōng*, zorgeloos, onvoorzichtig, overijld, overhaast.
ts'ong kóng, overhaast, overijld.
ts'ong hóng, in der haast, in allerijl.
ts'ong hông tsaó, voorthollen, voortrennen.
ts'ong ts'ong bòng bòng, in drukte, overhaast.

蹌 Ts'ong *Ts'u ts'ong* / (*ts'i* ») }, vleien, kruipend behandelen.

聰 Ts'ong *Ts'ong bing*, knap, verstandig.
ts'ong ts'at, do.

蒼 Ts'ong *Liók ts'ong*, meeldraden.

窓 Ts'ong *tòng ts'ong*, studeermakkers.
ts'ong hing tē, intieme, studeermakkers.
ts'ong iú, do.

創 Ts'òng *Ts'òng*, gereedmaken, maken, 2e zich bedienende van..., met...
ts'òng k'ah k'oah, wijder maken.
ts'òng pi̤ / (» *pę̄*) }, gelijk maken.
ts'òng tsiŋ̄, in orde brengen.
ts'òng k'ì ts'òng piēn, in gereedheid brengen.
ts'òng sin, vernieuwen.
ts'òng king, plagen, kwellen.
ts'òng tī, lastig vallen, het iemand lastig maken, plagen.
ts'òng tsō, maken, scheppen.
tiaù ts'òng, opzettelijk maken.
ts'òng siet, nieuw instellen, invoeren.
si̤ ts'òng, opmaken, (als een leugen).
ts'òng oē lai kik i, iemand door woorden aanzetten, dwingen.
ts'òng tsiah ê ke si loū tsoē tsi̤, hoeveel kost het aanschaffen van deze meubelen?
ts'òng hiŋ / (*ts'oàng*) }, iemand die het anderen steeds lastig maakt (met twist enz.)

餸 Ts'òng *T'am ts'òng*, gulzig.
loū ts'òng, groot van eten, gulzig.

Tsu

書 Tsu *Tsu pâng* / (*si* ») }, school.
tsu ī / (*si*) }, collegie.
bīt tsu, geheime missieve.

疽 Tsu *Tsu* / (*tsu*) }, de pokken.
ts'ut tsu, de pokken hebben.
tsìng tsu, inenten.
tsu tsing, inentstof, pokstof.
t'ó tsu tsing, pokstof van iemand vragen.
tsu ùn, *tsu sùn*, gesteldheid van de pokken (gedurende een jaar)
ts'ut kiŋ tsu, voor het uitkomen der pokken ziek worden.
tsuí tsu, waterachtige pokken.

珠 Tsu *Giang á tsu*, klepel in een bel.
bák tsiu si̤ tsu, een paarl op het oog hebben.
tsu á, kralen.
tsin tsu, paarl.
hiŋ tsu / (*hio* ») }, welriekende kralen.

si tsu / *tsiaó tsu*, geweêrhagel.

tiaò tsu, parelsnoer (door hooge mandarijnen gedragen).

tsit ts'èng-ê tsu, een rits paarlen.

t'aô k'ak ū tsu, glad, gaar, vernuftig (schertsend gebruikt).

huih tsu á, bloeddroppel.

hī á tsu, lelletje aan het oor.

laô koā tsu á, zweetdroppels, zweeten.

iā bing tsu, in donker glinsterende paarlen.

k'i tsu, met paarlen opwerken (als ronde verhevenheden aan den rand van een tafel).

諸 Tsu *Tsu kat*, familienaam van een beroemden held.

孜 Tsu *Tsu tsu*, steeds, uitsluitend (willen denken aan).

tsu tsu it bī, niet anders (willen enz.) dan..., uitsluitend, volstrekt.

姿 Tsu *Tsu sik*, schoonheid, bevalligheid (van eene vrouw.)

• 朱 Tsu *Tsu*, familienaam.

tsu âng, scharlakenkleurig.

tsu kik, aardbeziën.

硃 Tsu *Tsu se* (*se*), bergrood, natuurlijk, vermiljoen.

gùn tsu (*gîn* »), vermiljoen, roode Chin. inkt.

tsu p'oe (*p'e*), keizerlijk besluit op een brief.

t'ô tsu, aard vermiljoen.

siēm tsu, sterk rood vermiljoen.

資 Tsu *Tsu tsit*, *t'ien tsu*, aangeboren geschiktheid, bevattelijkheid, om te leeren enz.

tsu tsō, helpen (door geld te geven).

滋 Tsu *Tsu bī*, smaak, geur.

主 Tsú *Tsú*, baas, meester, heer.

tsú lâng, gastheer.

ts'ù tsú, huisbaas.

tsú kò, vaste kalant.

giép tsú, eigenaar.

tsú k'eh, kalant.

tsûn tsú, scheepskapitein.

tsú ì, voornemens zijn, van plan zijn, over iets beschikken.

tsú soè, commandant en chef.

tsú soè, voorzichtig, omzichtig.

tsú sè, do.

bók tsú (*tsí*) / *sin tsú* (*tsí*), voorouders tabel, een houten plaatje waarop den naam des overleden geschreven staat en dat medegenomen wordt bij de begrafenis, om na de begrafenis geplaatst te worden in de zaal der voorouders.

tsú soè t'iaⁿ, luisteren naar.

tsú tiaⁿ, maatregelen nemen voor.... te zorgen hebben voor.

bô tsú tiaⁿ, niet gereed zijn voor, geene maatregelen genomen hebben.

tsú ts'ai, naar goedvinden kunnen handelen.

tsū tsú, zijn eigen meester zijn.

tsú hun, over een huwelijk beschikken.

tsú lĩng, het commando in handen hebben.

sim bô tsú, niet weten wat te doen.

hè tsú, eigenaar van goederen.

tsit tsú hè, eene geheele lading, massa factuur goederen.

si tsú, lett. doode heer *d. i.* zich alles laten gezeggen (zonder er iets tegen te doen).

sì tsú, *sì tsú niû*, donateur, donatrice.

tsú so, aanzetten, ophitsen.

boé tsú īm tsai boē tsú te. de kooper kent de plaats van den verkooper niet (als iemand die geene koopers voor zijne waar heeft kunnen krijgen, terwijl een ander er vruchteloos naar gezocht heeft).

tsú tsiòng (*tsiàng*), hoofdaanvoerder.

tsoè tsú, het hoofd van iets zijn, over iets beslissen, de stem voor iemand zijn.

sim mịh lâng tsú lih, wie is uw baas! op wien steunt gij? (dat gij zoo brutaal durft te zijn).

tsú kong, de heer, meester, baas (eere naam).

tsú p'ọ̀, administrateur.

子 Tsú — *Tsú*, burggraaf.

gī tsú, aangenomen zoon.

kè tsú, stiefzoon.

tsú tit, zoons en neven.

tsú tē, kinderen van rijke familie.

tsú si, 11—1 's avonds.

bô tsú sù, geene kinderen of nakomelingen hebben.

giét tsú. slecht mensch.

者 Tsú — *Tsú* (*tsí*), koken (als vleesch).

tsú tsiáh (*tsí* »), kok.

tsú po lê, glas maken.

ts'ut tsaī i tsien tsú, zooals hij daarmede handelen, daarover beschikken wil.

鑄 Tsù — *Tsù* (*tsù*), smelten (metalen).

tsù t'ih sai hū, ijzersmelter.

tsù ts'ìng » , geweermaker.

tsù tsị, munt slaan, munten.

ts'in ts'iū̱, bộ nịh tsù k'ì lai, als in één zelfde vorm gegoten, *i. e.* sprekend op elkander gelijkend.

註 Tsù — *Tsù*, opteekenen, commentaar.

tsù ts'eh (*ts'ẹh*), registreeren, opschrijven.

tsù bák k'ọ̀, staren, aanstaren.

tsù tiū̱, bevelen.

tsù á, commentaar.

tsù koé seh, door een commentaar verklaren.

tsù k'a, commentaar aan den voet van een boek.

tsù bing, duidelijkheidshalve er naast zetten (als naast een doorgeschrapt karakter).

注 Tsù — *Tsù ì*, uitsluitend denken aan, zijn vast voornemen gemaakt hebben.

tsù sim, do.

tsù sin, uitsluitend denken aan....

tsù tioh hai tsui, door zeewater doortrokken.

hō̱ tsui tsìm tsù, door regen doortrokken.

蔍 Tsù — *Ka tsù* (*tsì*), biezenmand of zak om geld of rijst in te doen.

慈 Tsû — *Tsû pi*, medelijden.

dzin tsû, do.

tsû sim, toegenegen.

番 Tsú — *Hoan tsû* (*hoan tsî*), aardappelen.

tsit k'ọ ná han tsû, dom als een aardappel.

hoan tsû ts'iem, aardappelschaaf, rasp.

咮 Tsû — *Tsû-tsû tsû* (*tsu*), roep naar kippen.

tsu beh, stellig, uitsluitend, willen.

自 Tsū — *Tsū dziên* (*tsū*), van zelf, natuurlijk.

tsū k'oa, bluffen.

tsū tsú, zijn eigen meester zijn.

tsū lai hé (*hoé*), lucifer, vuurstokje.

tsū tsoan, zelfstandig, zijn eigen meester zijn.

tsū tsok tsū tong, zelf doen en zelf de verantwoordelijkheid op zich hebben.

tsū tsok tsū tsoan, zijn eigen zin volgen.

tsū kọ̄, van ouds af.

tsū tsá, van vroeger af.

聚 Tsū — *Kiet tsū (tsī)*, bij elkander komen.
tún tsū (tū), do. (van soldaten).
tsik tsū, opzamelen, bijeenbrengen.
tsū tsí'' (tsī), vergaderen, bijeen komen.
tsū hoē, vergaderen, zich verzamelen.
tsū tsʻiú, ophouden (iets te doen.)
tsū tsat (tsū), zich stationneeren, post vatten te.
tsū ku, wonen, zijne woonplaats hebben te..
tsū tsí, woonplaats.
tòng tsū, tegenhouden, tegengaan.
tòng īm tsū, niet kunnen tegenhouden.
ui tsū, omsingelen, omringen.
tʻoân tʻoân ui tsū, dicht omsingelen.

套 Tsū — *Tsū (tsū)*, een doekje leggen tusschen of over iets.
tsū pọ̀, een doekje tusschen iets leggen.
bèh tsū, doek die men onder de kous draagt.

喁 Tsū — *Tsi tsi tsū tsū*, fluisteren.
tsū lai tsū kʻì, over en weer fluisteren.

趨 Tsʻu — *Tsʻu tsʻong (tsʻi)*, kruipen, vleien.

Tsʻu — *Kọ̄ ióh tsʻu (tsʻi)*, wormen die zich in zalf of pleister vormen (wanneer het lang op eenen wond geweest is).
tsʻu (tsʻi), larve.
tsuí si̤ tsʻu, er vormen zich larven (algen) in het water.

斜 Tsʻu — *Tsʻu tsʻu (tsʻu)*, hellend.
tsʻu kʻa, aan den voet schuins afloopend (van een berg, een hoop goederen enz.)

披 Tsʻu — *Tsʻu*, uitspreiden over... (als een mat, karpet enz.)
tsʻu tsi̤ tiâo, een karpet leggen.
tsʻu bín tsʻing, bed opmaken.

鼠 Tsʻú — *Niaġ tsʻú (tsʻi)*, rat.
tsʻú » á, muis.
tsʻiah tsʻú, wezel 2e gauwdief.
pʻòng tsʻú, eekhorentje.
tsʻú tsʻát (tsʻiep), kleine dieven.
gûn tsʻú, zilver, *i. e.* witte rat.
tsi̤ tsʻú, geldrat.
tsi̤ tsʻú bák, gezegd van iemand die het best in donker zien kan.
tiao tsʻú, rat wiens huid als vilt gebruikt wordt.
kaò tʻaò tsʻú hī, apenhoofd en rattenooren (van iemand die er leelijk uitzien.)

眛 Tsʻú — *Tsʻú báng (tsʻù tsʻíng)*, kippig, bijziende.

此 Tsʻú — *Tsʻú si (tsʻú)*, nu.
tsʻú tong kim, tegenwoordig, thans.

處 Tsʻú — *tiaō tsʻú (tsʻi) tsʻú hô*, verzoenen.
tsʻú lì, afdoen, regelen, afmaken (als eene twist met iemand).
siong tsʻú, met elkander in harmonie zijn.
kọ́ siong tsʻú, van ouds, oude kennissen.
tsʻú sū, eene zaak bijleggen, middelaar zijn.
tsʻut tsʻú, ū tsʻut tsʻú (tsʻi), iets waar men vat op kan hebben.
kʻui tsʻú, een punt ophalen langs hetwelk eene zaak geregeld bijgelegd kan worden.

取 Tsʻú — *Kʻó tsʻú (tsʻi)*, prijzenswaardig.
hō̤ lâng tsʻú tsʻiò, zich belachelijk maken.

ts'ai ts'ú (ts'ì), ontginnen, zoeken naar b. v. naar geneeskrachtige kruiden.
ts'im ts'ú, onttroggelen, aftroonen.
ts'ú tsiet, percenten van iets afnemen.

蜃 Ts'ú *Ts'ú bé (ts'ì)*, waterhoos.
ts'ú bé hong, windhoos.
k'i ts'ú bé, er komt een hoos op.

厝 Ts'ù *Ts'ù*, huis.
ts'ù ting, dak.
ts'ù hiā, dakpannen.
ts'ù kak, hoek.
ts'ù sè (soè), huishuur.
ts'ù pi t'aó bé, de buren.
ū ts'ù ū t'éh ê lâng, een gevestigd man.
ts'ù tiŋ sai hū, timmerman voor het grove werk in een huis (als ramen, deuren enz.)
k'iā bô tsi ts'ù, in het kostelooze huis wonen *i. e.* in de gevangenis zitten.
ū tō bô ts'ù, geene vaste woonplaats hebben.

趣 Ts'ù *Ts'ù bī (ts'ì)*, aller aangenaamst.
iú ts'ù, *ū ts'ù bī*, aangenaam.

次 Ts'ù *Ts'ù sū*, volgorde.
tsiaù ts'ù sū (ts'ù sī), volgens de rij, in volgorde.
tsit ts'ù, *nāng ts'ù*, éénmaal, tweemaal.
ts'ù tē, volgorde.
k'ah ts'ù eh, wat meer daaropvolgend, wat minder goed.
tsiet ts'ù, *tsat ts'ù*, bij termijnen afbetalen.

處 Ts'ù *Ts'ù ts'ù*, overal.
sù ts'ù ê lâng, de menschen, alom, overal.

疵 Ts'ū *Siáo ts'ū*, klein gebrek, weinig verkeerds.

hû ts'ù (hê), gebarsten (van edelsteenen.)
ū ts'ù hûn, gebarsten, met strepen (van edelsteenen).

趨 Ts'ū *Ts'ū*, uitglijden, glijden.
ts'ū loh k'ì, neerglijden.
k'it i ts'ū tòh, omverglijden, uitglijden.
ts'ū loh lai, naar beneden komen glijden (als langs een touw).
ts'ū ts'ū, glad (door afhelling.)
soh á-ts'ū k'ì, een touw aflaten, uitlaten (als van een vlieger).

放 Ts'ū *Ts'ū*, afgaan als een vuurpijl.
ts'ū tiòng tsai, de middelste vinger uitsteken (manier om iemand te beleedigen.)

Tsuh

茁 Tsuh *Tsuh ts'ut*, uitdruppelen.
tsuh í (puh), uitbotten.
tsuh gê, *tsuh ìm*, uitspruiten, ontkiemen.
tsit tsuh á, een druppeltje, stipje.
sì koè ū-tsuh tsuh ts'ut lai, overal voor den dag komen (als watten uit een gescheurd kussen, als dieven uit hunne schuilhoeken enz.)
bô ta tit oā tsiah tsuh ts'ut lai, er was niets aan te doen of hij moest het wel voor den dag halen (als een gierigaard met zijn geld).
tsuh tsit k'ang, een gat in iets steken (met een puntig voorwerp).

節 Tsuh *Tsih tsuh ê lâng*, een ondeugend, plaagziek mensch.

泏 Tsuh *Tsuì tsuh*, waterspuit.

焠 Ts'uh *Ts'uh tsuí*, blusschen (als gloeiend ijzer).
ts'uh, aansteken (doen ontploffen).

k'it ts'ing ióh ts'uh (ook *ts'úh*) *tioh*, door ontploffend kruit verzengd worden.
ts'uh p'aoh á, sissers afsteken.

Ts'uh *Tsûn k'i ts'úh tioh ta* (*o*), het schip schoof op een bank.

Tsui

堆 Tsui *Tsui tsui*, opgehoopt, met een kop.
tsiem koah tsui, puntig en opgehoopt.
tsui kah toā oá, opgehoopt er nog een groote kom *d. i.* zeer goedkoop.

鵻 Tsui *Ka tsui*, gevlekte duif.

Tsui *T'ih tsui*, ijzeren bijtel, priem door steenhouwers gebruikt.
kó tsui, liefje (tegen een kind gezegd).

推 Tsui *Koh k'i kā i tsui* (eig. *ts'ui*) *tseh*, iemand nog eens gaan aanzetten (als op den dag van betaling).

水 Tsuí *Tsuí*, water.
tsuí tsiep, lett. watervocht, water.
hō tsuí, regenwater.
kang tsuí, rivierwater.
kiêm tsuí, zeewater.
lō tsuí, dauw.
tsuí lō, waterweg, over water.
tsuí goân, bron.
ling tsuí, koud water.
sio tsuí, warm water.
kún tsuí, kokend water.
tsuí tìng of *tī*, vloed.
tsuí tiōng (*tiōng tiāng*), zeer hooge vloed.
tsuí k'ó of *t'è*, eb.
toā tsuí, overstrooming.
tsuí koàn, waterkan.
tsuí tó, peillood.
tsuí tò soh, peillood lijn.
tsuí kíng (*kuí*), maalstroom, draaikolk.
tsuí âm, watergeleider.
tsuí kao, waterweg langs de velden.
tsuí tsin, waterschepper.
tsuí t'iu, de pomp (op een schip).
ts'ut tsuí, goederen inladen.
tsuí im, rijzen van het water.
p'ī tsuí, snot.
tsuí siú, bemanning van een schip (matroos).
tsuí sien mîng (*muî*), de valreep.
tsáo tsuí, brievenbezorger.
tsuí tsī, kristal: zuivere kwartz.
tsuí tsī (*tsé*), wel, put.
tsuí tsièn, zeeslag.
tsuí ling (*liông*), brandspuit.
tsuí kuī, waterketel, watervat.
tsuí t'áng, wateremmers.
tsuí tuì, watermolen, waarvan rad door een stroom water in beweging wordt gebragt.
tsuí tsik, spuit, perspomp.
tsik tsuí, water persen, spuiten.
tsuí t'ó, klimaat, water en voortbrengselen eener plaats.
tsuí hoe, schuim van de zee.
tsuí p'o hûn, gemarmerd (geverfd), 1e. rimpels, golfjes op het water.
tsuí ts'ú, waterrat.
tsuí bō, watermolen.
taô tsuí, zich verdrinken.
tsuí ts'ia, waterrad.
p'ah tsuí, water opslaan.
taī tsì k'ah tsió tsuí, de zaak is van minder belang.
gûn tsuí, bijgelegd zilver voor het te lichte van een dollar. (*)
p'ah tsuí hoe, in het water flodderen.
bák tsiu-kim tsuí tsuí, zeer heldere oogen.
bah-tsuí tsuí tsuí, het vleesch is zeer slap.

(*) Bij gebrek aan een eigen zilveren munt worden alle vreemde munten in China in betaling genomen en gewogen.

hó tsuí sik, fraaie glans over iets.
kìng tsuí, glans over metalen.
ts'ut tsúi, 1e eene nieuwe glans over edelsteenen enz. brengen.
t'è tsuí, door het water halen, (als nieuwe kleëren).
tsuí si, watergetij.
toā (en) *sió laò tsuí*, sterk en zwak watergetij.
king tsui, maandelijksche vloed (bij vrouwen).
kaò tsuí, tot rijpheid, vruchtbaarheid zijn (van vruchten, beesten en menschen).
t'aò-dzī-sn̄g tsuí, 1e, 2e, 3e maal dat planten bloeien, aardappelen enz. rijp zijn.
t'aò tsuí ê kiá, het eerste kind.
tē sn̄g tsuí, het derde kind.
teh kui tsuí, de raddraaier van iets zijn.

醉 Tsuì *Tsuì*, beschonken.
tsiú tsuì, do.
poà tsuì, do.
tsuì hàn, dronkaard.
tsuì mn̄g mn̄g, stomdronken.
tsuì gán / *bák tsiu-tsuì tsuì* }, kleine oogjes (van vrouwen of mannen die wat te veel wijn gedronken hebben).
tsiú tsuì sim t'aò tiā, beschonken maar toch geregeld kunnen denken.
tsuì ì, zeer verlangen naar.
tit tit tsuì ih, sterk naar iets verlangen.

剉 Tsui *Tsui*, (rondom) afsnijden.
tsui tik, bamboes afsnijden.
tsui t'aò k'ak, het hoofd van het lichaam afsnijden.
tsui tsoè nn̄g tìng, in tweeën snijden (als suikerriet).
tsit ê oē tsui tit, deze is goed beet te nemen, te bedriegen.
tsui i k'ah tsió, (van den prijs) afknibbelen.

誰 Tsuī *Tsī tsuī*, wie?
sī tsuī, wie? wie is het?
tsuī lâng, welk mensch? wie?
tsuī á, wie?

Ts'ui *Ts'ui sìng* / (*sui*) }, berekenen.
ts'ui ts'ut, voor den dag brengen.
ts'ui tsun, boven allen uitkiezen.
ts'ui àn, aanhalen, stijftrekken (als een touw).
ts'ui sih, worgen,
ts'ui ts'ièn, verplaatsen, overbrengen op.
ts'ui pai, do.
kap lâng ts'ui ts'iaò / (*ts'i*) }, het met iemand over den prijs eens zien te worden, met iemand raadplegen.
ts'ui ts'ik, berekenen (als eene zonsverduistering enz.)
ts'ui sìng, berekenen (als bij het schaakspelen) 2e stijf aangehaald.)
ts'ut lát-ts'ui sìng, stijf aanhalen, afbinden.
tsiaò an nī sī ts'ui ts'ut k'ì, volgens dit (deel) de andere (deelen) berekenen (als de onkosten van 12 maanden naar die van één maand).

Ts'ui *Ts'ui pik*, aanzetten, haasten.
ts'ui, do.
ts'ui tiā, eene rechtszaak pousseeren.
ts'ui k'eh, gasten dringend uitnoodigen.
ts'ui ts'iok, aanzetten, haasten.

揣 Ts'uí *Ts'uí mō*, onderzoek doen naar.
ts'uí tók, van meening zijn, wedden dat....

Ts'uí *Ts'uí ts'uí n̄*, overal is het.

嘴 Ts'uì *Ts'uì*, de mond, bek.
tsit ts'uì, een mondvol, in één hap.
ts'uì k'í, het gebit.
ts'uì k'í-t'iā, kiespijn.
ts'uì p'oé, / (*p'é*) }, wangen.

ts'uì ē taó (ē) }, de kin.
ts'uì ts'iù, de baard.
ts'uì ta, dorst hebben, dorstig.
t'at ts'uì, den mond stoppen.
p'ai ts'uì taó, uitschelden, lekkerbekkig.
hun ts'e ts'uì, mondstuk van een pijp.
hó ts'uì táo, alles eten wat wordt voorgezet.
ts'uì sui, snuit (van varkens), mond (van menschen).
sūn ts'uì-kóng, gelijdelijk weg spreken.
p'ai k'ui ts'uì, moeielijk, gegeneerd om te zeggen.
tsit è ts'uì k'ui k'ui / *ū ts'uì bô tsih* }, met zijn mond vol tanden staan.
ts'ūi péh, lekkerbekkig.
p'oà ts'uì tsâm, iemand iets afraden.
p'oà ts'uì, iets iemand afraden, gebroken aan de mond, tuit.
ts'uì lâng ts'uì, zonder bepaalde reden met iemand over iets praten.
ts'uì t'aò-tūng, veel geld voor zijn waar willen hebben, brutaal zijn in het verkoopen.
k'ang ts'uì péh tsih (pō) }, hol, onbepaald spreken.
pi ts'uì, ts'uì pi pi, met de mond vol tanden staan.
ka tsaó ts'uì, vlooien beet.
k'ui ts'uì, de mond openen 2e den prijs van iets zeggen.
tú ts'uì, lett. de monden bij elkander brengen (als mieren) *i. e.* met iemand een weinig over iets spreken.
tsit ke-kui è t'aò ts'uì, hoeveel menschen zijn er in dat huis?
niū ts'uì, uit zijn mond sparen, (om aan anderen te geven).
k'iēm ts'uì, niet van iets durven eten, het uit zijn mond sparen.

TSUI

óh ts'uì óh tsih, overklappen, oververtellen.
ts'ap ts'uì, de mond in een gesprek steken, 2e verward door elkander.
ts'o ts'uì-mē lâng, iemand gemeen uitschelden.
siù ts'uì, knap in het voorspellen.
si ts'uì, zijn mond houden, niet meer durven tegenspreken.
p'ah ts'uì hoe / *p'ah ts'uì kó* }, over koetjes en kalfjes praten.
ts'uì t'ò, met den bek in de aarde wroeten (als ratten of merenster).
siah ah bú ts'uì, eene platte punt aan iets snijden.
k'i ts'uì, hazenlip.
hó t'aò ts'uì, gelukkig (van een schip) voorspoedige reizen makend.

碎 *Ts'uì*, kruimels.
Ts'uì *ts'uì ts'uì liáo*, in stukken gebroken.
p'ah ts'uì ts'uì, aan stukken breken, stuk slaan.
ts'uì iém iém, in kleine schilfers, gebroken.
ts'uì hún hún, tot gruis gebroken.
p'ah p'oà ts'uì ts'uì, aan kleine schilfers breken.
ts'uì sap sap, fijn.
ts'ó ts'uì, moeielijk, langdradig te vertellen, 2e diverse dingen enz.
ts'uì sut sut, tot gruis, fijn.
hún sin ts'uì kut, tot gruis, verpletterd doodvallen.
ts'uì bí, gebroken rijst (gebruikt om beesten te voeden).
lân san leh ts'uì, aan kleine hoeveelheden.
luì ts'uì è hè, diverse artikelen.

翠 *Huí ts'uì tsiáo*, ijsvogel.
Ts'uì *ts'i ts'uì*, frissche kleur (als planten na regen).

Tsun

尊 *Tsun pi*, hoog en laag (van stand).
Tsun *tsun king*, eeren.
tsū tsun, zich hooger titel geven dan dat ons volgens beleefdheid toekomt.
tsun kuì, eerwaardig.
tsun tiōng, hoogachten.
tsun tióng, ouderen van jaren.
līng tsun, uw vader (beleefdheids term).
tsun ong, do.
ka tsun, mijn vader.
ts'ui tsun, iemand boven anderen de hoogste eereplaats enz. geven.
tsun ts'ùn, uit respect iemands meening of toestemming vragen.
tsē tiong tsun, op de middelste eereplaats zitten (als de oudere priester bij plechtigheden).

遵 *Tsun i*, gehoorzamen aan eene rechterlijke uitspraak).
Tsun *tsun toàn*, de uitspraak van een mandarijn opvolgen.
tsun bīng, een bevel gehoorzamen (bel. term).

甯 *Tsún tsoè* (*tsò*), remplaceeren door, in de plaats nemen van.
Tsún *tsún tèng*, verpanden, als onderpand geven.
boē tsún kō tit, zich niet stellig op iemand kunnen verlaten.
tsún tsoè bô, doen als of niet, als of iets niet bestond.
tsún tiā, voor handgeld (bij een koop) geven.

撙 *Tsún tsat*, afpassen.
Tsún

准 *Ún tsún* (*ín* ») , vergunnen, toestaan).
Tsún *tsún*, do.
ēm tsún, niet toelaten, niet gedoogen, 2e niet gelijk, niet zuiver.

準 *Ū tsún tsin*, een vaste hand van iets
Tsún hebben, juist afweten.
Tsún *Tsún* (*tsún*), geraakt, juist.
ū tsún, juist gaan (als een horologie).
tsún pī, van te voren gereed maken.
tsún pin, *pin tsún*, tot maatstaf dienen.

戰 *Tsùn*, beven (van de hand).
Tsùn *niaǵh niaǵh tsùn*, beven, rillen.
tsùn kó, ijzeren veer.
tsùn ts'iú, *ts'iú-tsùn*, beven van de hand.
tsùn pit, beven van het penseel of pen (in de hand).
táh liáo oē tsùn, heeft men er op getrapt dan trilt het (als een vloer).

駿 *Pat tsùn ma*, een goed paard.
Tsùn

浚 *Tsuí tsùn*, bergstroom, waterleiding.
Tsùn *tsùn hoā*, dijk, kant van een stroom.

俊 *Ts'ong tsùn*, knap en fraai van uiterlijk.
Tsùn *tsùn siù*, beleefd, van fijne manieren.
ts'ing tsùn, beleefd.

峻 *Tsùn niá*, steile berghelling.
Tsùn *hiém tsùn*, gevaarlijk, (steil van een berg).

船 *Tsûn*, schip.
Tsûn *tsûn á*, boot.
tsûn tsiàh, schepen.
kap pán tsûn, schip met raas.
hé hún tsûn (*hoé lûn*), stoomboot).
iû tsûn (*iû* »), jonk voor buitenlandsch navigatie.
tsièn tsûn, oorlogschip.
tsûn hō, schepen.
ts'e tsûn (*ts'e* »), kruisboot.
siong tsûn (*siang* »), jonk voor kusthandel.
saò tsûn, jonk voor rooversvangst.

t'ó hî tsûn, visscherschuit.
má kaó tsûn, lorcha.
sing lí tsûn, koopvaardijschip.
tō tsún, passagierboot.
tsûn sè (soè), passagiersgeld.
tsún t'aò, voorsteven.
tsûn bé (boé), achtersteven.
tsùn tsú, kaptein.
tsûn pai, zeebrief.
tsûn p'oà, schipbreuk.
pák tsûn, een schip bevrachten.
tsiòng tsûn kó hō (tsiang), bodemerij op een schip nemen.
tsō tsûn sai hū, scheepmaker.
tsûn ts'aò è gûn (gin), tonnegeld.
k'ui tsûn, het anker lichten.
tsûn oá hâng, een schip consigneeren.
tsûn ù (ò), droogе dok.
ts'o dziō tsûn, mistschuit.
tìng tsûn, een schip timmeren, bouwen.
tsûn tsi, schuitengeld, overvaargeld.
tsûn tsìng, scheepszaken, scheepsaangelegenheden.
tê tsûn, theeschuitje, looden theeschoteltje.

存 Tsûn *Tsûn hè tog (hoè)*, goederenfactuur.
tsûn siaò, jaarlijksch balans opmaken.
tsûn sim, zich voorgenomen hebbenden.
tsûn k'ìng / tsûn toè, een afschrift bewaren.
tsûn sim, opzettelijk, met voordacht.
tsûn tsit è sim koi, opzettelijk.
tsûn pún tsi, kapitaal, in kas overhouden.
tsûn k'i k'ìng, opbergen (het overschietende geld).
tsûn hē, laten liggen.
tsûn hè, goederen opnemen, opteekenen (als bij het maken van balans).
tsûn t'ièn lí, het betamelijke, billijke in acht nemen.
liû tsûn, behouden, niet vernietigen, daar laten.
goân siu ts'ut tsûn, 原收出存 in kas, ontvangst, uitgaven, overschot (in koopmansboeken), in het journaal komt of om de tien dagen of om de maand een sluitpost voor waar deze vier woorden uitdrukken: *hoeveel er in kas was, hoeveel er bijgekomen hoeveel er afgegaan is* en *hoeveel er op heden in kas overblijft.*

前 *Tsûn ni*, twee jaren geleden.
Tsûn *lò tsûn ni* (eig. *ni*), 3 jaren geleden.

綾 *Tsūn*, draaien, herwringen.
Tsūn *tsūn sí*, de nek omdraaien.
tsūn sa, kleêren uitwringen.
kún lún tsūn, zich kronkelen (als een slang).
koaī tsūn, verdraaien, tegen iemands wil in handelen.
tsūn t'aò naó taō (iò), hoofd en hals in allerlei bochten wringen (als bij zingen).
kíng tsūn (kui »), verdraaien, verwringen.

陣 *Tsit tsūn*, een wijl, één oogenblik, een Tsūn wee.
tsit tsūn hong, een vlaag wind.
tsit tsūn hō, een bui regen.
hong tsoè (en) *kui tsūn*, het waait bij vlagen.
tsit tsū o àm hin, eene flaauwte van een oogenblik.
t'iù-tsoè tsūn, *tsoè tsūn t'iù*, pijn bij vlagen: weeën.

刻 *Hit tsūn*, toen, toen ter tijd.
Tsūn *tsit tsūn*, nu, op het oogenbl...
si tsūn, tijd, tijdstip...

春 *Ts'un*, lente, v...
Ts'un *ts'un t'i*, d...

moá bīn ts'un hong, er vrolijk opgeruimd uitzien.
ts'un ì, lente gedachten *i. e.* wellustige gedachten.
ts'un sim tōng, een weinig wellustige gedachten hebben.
ts'un t'aô, begin van de lente, het nieuwjaar.
sin ts'un, nieuwe lente *i. e.* nieuwjaar.
ts'ing ts'un dzoā tsoē, hoeveel lentes hebt gij, beleefd (tegen vrouwen of jonge menschen gezegd).
k'ui ts'un, verder in de lente, na het nieuwjaar.
ts'iá ts'un tsiú, gasten op lente malen verzoeken.
dzip ts'un, de lente ingaan.
ts'un kiong, lente *i. e.* wellustige, liederlijke teekeningen.

伸 Ts'un *Ts'un*, (de hand) uitsteken, uitsteken, rekken (als schoenen).
ts'un ùn, zich uittrekken.
ts'un, uitzetten als kwik door de warmte.
ts'un tsih, de tong uitsteken, laten zien.
ts'un io, zich de lendenen uittrekken.
ts'un tīng, zijn kapitaal vermeerderen (door het op interest te zetten).
ts'un tīng ts'iú, de hand uitsteken (als bedelaars).
ts'un t'aô, de kop, het hoofd uitsteken.
ts'un tit, uittrekken, recht maken.
ts'un ts'ùt lai, uitsteken, uitzetten.
īm ká ts'un k'a ts'iú, de handen of voeten niet durven insteken *i. e.* zich niet ruim durven roeren (als een lage in tegenwoordigheid van hoogeren of een koopman die nog niet veel geld heeft).

剩 Ts'un *Ts'un*, overblijven.
ū ts'un, overblijvend.
ts'un tsī, overschietend geld, batig saldo.
īng ū ts'un, na alle benoodigdheden er af nog overhouden.

蠢 Tsún *Ts'ún pūn*, onbezonnen, onvoorzichtig, log, onbesuisd.
gû ts'ún (*gi* »), log, lomp.

寸 Ts'ùn *Ts'ùn*, duim.
ū hun ts'ùn, bepaald, afgemeten (hoeveelheid geld enz.)
ts'ùn ts'ùn koah, hevig, inwendig gefolterd worden.
ū ts'ùn ts'ioh, met duimen en voeten *i. e.* afgemeten.
ts'ùn pō làn king, geen stapje verder kunnen gaan (van vermoeijenis).
tīng ts'ùn si, geen draadje meer overhebben (om aan te trekken of te verkoopen).
sui pō ts'ùn, kleine stapjes nemen (als vrouwen) 2e eene zaak stuk voor stuk afdoen.
ts'ùn tseh ts'ùn tseh, voetje voor voetje loopen, stuk voor stuk betalen enz.
tīng ts'it ts'ùn, volstrekt niets meer over hebben.
tìng ts'it ts'ùn, (voorwerpen van) zeven duim zelfs verpanden, tot ellende gebracht zijn.
ts'ùn pán bû tsûn, een duimsplankje was er zelf niet over (als van een verongelukt schip).

詢 Ts'ûn *Ts'ûn*, iemand waarschuwen, van te voren vragen.
ts'ùn làng, iemand voor het laatst in bedenking geven.
ts'ùn sim, zich verteederen.
ts'ùn sim, voorbedachtelijk, opzettelijk
ts'ùn piēn, alles in gereedheid brengen.
ts'ùn pūn, klaar maken 2e een model van iets bewaren.
ts'ùn tsú kò, maken dat men de kalandisie voor later behoudt.
ts'ùn giáh, een deel voor elk in gereedheid houden.

ts'ùn aō pai, eene gelegenheid voor de toekomst open laten (als bij handel.)

尊 *Ts'ùn kìng*, voorkomend zijn.
Ts'ùn *sa ts'ùn*, voorkomend zijn = sa tsun ts'ùn.

ts'ùn sī toā, voorkomend zijn voor ouderen hoogeren.

捘 *Ts'ūn*, met de vingers knijpen.
Ts'ūn *ts'ūn kaò o ts'ī*, bont en blauw knijpen.

ká lâng ts'ū lâng, iemand wringen en knijpen.

liēm kah ts'ūn (*e*), zeer taai, elastiek.

Tsut

卒 *Ping tsut*, soldaten.
Tsut *sū tsut*, bevelhebbers en soldaten.

抑 *Ut tsut*, neerslachtig, bedrukt, boos worden.
Tsut

秫 *Tsút bí*, kleverige rijst.
Tsút *toā tsút*, groote kleverige rijst.

tsút á, kleine do. (langer en harder).

tsút bí tsú é liaū k'ì, van tsut bí gekookte glasachtige voorwerpen (als doosjes).

拭 *Īng pò tsút tsút*, met een doek afvegen.
Tsút *īng ts'iú tsút*, met de hand afwrijven, afvegen (als tranen, de neus).

tsút tioh o, zich aan zwarte verf ophalen, vuil maken.

出 *Ts'ut*, uitkomen.
Ts'ut *ts'ut sì*, geboren worden.

ts'ut lát, zich inspannen.

ts'ut sia liāng, gillen.

ts'ut kè (*kè*), een bod doen.

ts'ut kè (*kè*), een man huwen.

ts'ut ke, Boeddh. priester of non worden.

ts'ut hai, in zee steken.

ts'ut goā, uitlandig gaan.

ts'ut dzip, in en uitgaan.

ts'ut dzip gûn (*gîn*), uitgaven en inkomsten.

ts'ut k'aó hè (*hoè*), uitgevoerde goederen, uitvoer.

ts'ut k'aó hiòng (*hiàng*), uitgaande rechten.

ts'ut sè (*soè*), verhuren.

ts'ut dzī péh (*péh*), aankondiging, advertentie, adverteeren.

ts'ut p'iò, volmacht geven, bevel tot in hechtenis nemen.

ts'ut pin kù (*kì*), getuigenis afleggen.

tsuh ts'ut, uitdruipen (als water uit een lek).

hièn ts'ut, aan den dag komen.

hiēn ts'ut, contant betalen.

ts'ut siù, aanklagea.

ts'ut sik é tsi (*sit*), profijt, voordeel.

ts'ut soa, begraven.

ts'ut tsòng, do.

ts'ut kiong, eene groote boodschap doen.

ts'ut siù, aanbrengen (aanklagen).

ts'ut tsing, ten strijde trekken.

ts'ut t'io, bakboordspieren uitsteken.

k'ah ts'ut sik, de kleuren komen beter uit.

ū ts'ut ts'ú, bewijs, authoriteit.

put ts'ut goá só liaū (*sé*), het is juist geschied zooals ik gedacht had.

ts'ut tsiú, wijn overgeven, braken.

ts'ut ts'iú, bij den aanvang.

ts'ut sin, van afkomst, van geboorte.

ts'ut tsoē, straf tot verbanning.

tsit ts'ut, een rol (in comedie).

ts'ut lut lut, geheel en al er uitkomen.

siū ts'ut, op iets komen, iets in de gedachten krijgen.

siū̱ īm ts'ut,, niet op iets kunnen komen.
k'oà īm ts'ut, niet kunnen zien.
kóng boē ts'ut, zijne meening niet in woorden kunnen uitdrukken.
sing boē ts'ut, niets op iets kunnen komen, geene goede manier op iets kunnen bedenken.
ts'ut siaò, crediet geven.
dzin tsai-ts'ut tsiòng, van buitengewoon fraai voorkomen zijn.
ts'ut ting, in mannelijke bewoners toenemen (van eene plaats of familie.)
ts'ut lō̱, op reis gaan.
ts'ūt t'aò, aan het hoofd staan van..., het eerst doen 2e zijne kennis, verdiensten voor den dag (kunnen brengen.
poa̱ sim mi̱h ts'ut t'aò, welk voorstel wordt er gedaan.
ts'ut t'aò t'i̱, eene opgeklaarde hemel, in verbeterde omstandigheden verkeeren.
ts'ut t'aò sing kak, die het hoofd voor uitsteekt beschadigt zijne hoornen *i. e.* die aan het hoofd eener zaak staat heeft de grootste verantwoordelijkheid.
ts'ut t'aò lō̱ bīn, zich onbeschaamd in het publiek vertoonen (van vrouwen).
ts'ut sū, mandarijn worden.
ts'ut ts'uì, de mond openen (en spreken).
ts'ut k'uì tiòh lát, zich zeer inspannen, moeite geven.
ts'ut tsuí, polijsten.
ū ts'ut tsuí, voordeel op iets hebben, er meer voor krijgen dan het gekost heeft.

任 Ts'ut — *Ts'ut tsaī*, naar dat, al naar dat.
ts'ut tsaī li, zooals gij dat wilt.

U

圍 U — *U su kùn* } (*ui*) } , schortje.

於 U — *Tsì u* } (*i*) } , met betrekking tot...., wat aangaat.
u sī, daarna, dan.

凹 U — *T'ap u* } (*o*) } , holletje (van de hand), kuil in den grond); diep in stand (van oogen).
lap u } (ook *o*) } , in een kuil vallen.
u, kuil, kuiltje.
(*o* ook *u*) *tiá toe u* } (*tiá̱ tè o*) } , holletje van een pan.

汙 U — *Pi u kō̱ tsiēn* } (*u*) } , vuil en laag (van pers.)
u piah kak, in de hoek van een muur, op de hurken zitten.
u tsout, vasthoudend aan zijn idée.
u k'u } (*k'i*) } , onveranderd (van aard) (een man) van etikette.
u t'ù, dom, idiotisch.
u dzù } (*dzi*) } , geleerde die zich onveranderlijk aan het oude houdt.

于 U — *U* } (*i*) } , familienaam.

盂 U — *K'a t'aò u*, de knie.

羽 Ú — *Ú se* } (*í se̱*) } , Engelsche polemieten, camlets, grijn.
ú toūn, Holl. do.
ú lin, bombazijn.
ú tiù, bombazijn.
ni̱ ú tiù toūn, flenel, camlets en zijde.

翼 Ú — *Ú ik* = *k'a ts'iú* } (*i*) } , helpers.

宇 Ú — *Ú tiū* } (*i* ») } , het heelal.

與 Ú *Ú ki... k'ah hó...* (*i*) }, beter... dan..

ú ku ú ts'ú (*í ki í ts'í*) }, steeds met elkander zijn, zeer intiem zijn.

澳 Ù *Tsùn ù* (*ò*) }, haven, droogdok.

oa ù, noodhaven.

Ù *Tsít ù* (*o*) }, een kuiltje, verzakking.

汚 Ù *Ú oè* (*ù*) }, vuil, smerig.

〇 Ù *Ú*, branden, brandmerken.

ù tióh hé (*ù » hoé*) }, verzengen.

ù sio, zich aan iets warmen.

sio ù ù, zeer warm.

ù ts'aò ta, verzengen, verschroeien, aanbranden.

迂 Ù *Ú tsoat* (*u »*) }, niet naar de omstandigheden weten te handelen, zich vasthouden aan zijn idée.

餘 Û *Kî û* (*î*) }, daar buiten nog.

û goā, daar buiten nog....

iû û, overig, overblijvend.

û tsu, buiten zijn vast inkomen nog verdiend geld.

û sîn, overschietend.

û tsîng, overblijvende genegenheid, dankbaarheid.

û ì, bijkomende, inbegrepen beteekenis.

佘 Û *Û* (*î*), familienaam.

有 Ū *Ū*, hebben, es giebt, er zijn, teeken van het verledene.

ū é, sommigen.

ū si, somtijds.

iaó ū, toch nog.

ū iao, honger hebben.

ū lí, redelijk, belangrijk.

ū lō̤ īng (*iōng*) }, nuttig.

ū hūn, een deel hebben in.

ū tsiep, sappig.

ū pī (*pē̤*) }, ziek.

ū ing, ledigen tijd hebben.

ū lát, sterk.

ū sū, bezig, bezet.

ū taī tsì (*o*) }, do.

ū pún sū, geschikt, bekwaam.

ū tì sik, wijs, verstandig.

ū tì huī, do.

ū iá̤, wezentlijk, waar.

ū sin īn, zwanger.

ū tsing tsoáh, verschillend.

ū tsoē, schuldig, strafschuldig.

ū kè sit (*koè*) }, verkeerd.

ū ts'ò, verkeerd, foutief.

ū gi na̤, twijfelachtig.

ū hok k'ì, gelukkig.

ū miâ̤ sia̤, beroemd.

ū miâ̤ bô sit (*iû bing bû sit*) }, in naam niet in daad.

ū siao t'aò, goed te verkoopen, gevraagd, gewild.

預 Ū *Ū sien ū pī*, van te voren klaar maken.

ū hóng, van te voren maatregelen tegen iets nemen.

ū sien (*ī sien*) }, in voorbaat doen.

Uh

Uh *Uh-kab boē tit k'í lat*, zich niet kunnen opwerken, niet kunnen opstaan (als oude menschen).

k'o̤ uh á, de hik hebben.

U i

威 Ui

Ui hing (*ui* ») } , ontzagwekkend voorkomen.

ui sit, gelukkig voorteeken.

bó ui sit, ongelukkig voorteeken.

ui giêm, deftig, ontzag inboezemend.

hó̤ ui, ontzag inboezemend.

ui hong, deftig, do.

ing ui, deftig, luisterrijk.

hā má ui, luister van een mandarijn bij het aanvaarden van zijn post.

bô ui ê lâng, een man voor wien niemand ontzag heeft.

tién ui, de manen opzetten (als een leeuw), de haren doen rijzen (als tijgers of katten).

háng ui, indruk maken, ontzag inboezemend (als een rechter die op de rechterstoel komt).

ui sui (*o*) } , met zich zelven verlegen (als iemand die zijne minderheid in een gezelschap ziet).

ui ui liét liét, ontzag inboezemend (als soldaten of kinderen van mandarijnen).

攢 Ui

Ui (*oe*) } , boren.

ui ui t'ià̤, indringende pijn.

t'ià̤-kaò ui ui tsìng, do.

ui k'ang, een gat inboren.

ui tsìng, boren, inboren.

ui iah, *ui oat*, boren en ondermijnen (als dieven een muur) heimelijk bestelen als een klerk in een handelshuis.

gaô ui lâng, iemand behendig bedriegen, bedotten.

ui k'àng, uitkrabbelen (als geld uit iemand halen).

toā tìng t'aô k'it lâng ui k'ì, achter zijn rug door iemand bedrogen, bestolen worden.

Ui *Pio á ui*, het werk, de raderen van een horologie.

胎 Ui

Ui, baarmoeder.

ui toà, navelstreng.

委 Uí

Uí oàn, officieele bode.

goā uí, sergeant.

ui k'iok, verward moeielijk uit te maken onduidelijk, ingewikkeld.

uí oán-k'ìng ih (*k'ṳ̀*) } , overtuigen, langzamerhand vermanen.

uí oán kiù, niet rechtuit solliciteeren om.

uí oán, niet rechtuit spreken, zeggen.

ui tik (*tit*) } , stellig, zeker.

uí sit, do.

ui tsin, do. voorwaar.

ui tsit ê lâng k'ì pūn, iemand gelasten, zenden om iets te doen.

uí t'ok, iemand gelasten, opdragen.

諉 Uí

T'ui uí, afslaan, zich verontschuldigen.

葦 Uí

Ló̤ uí, alang alang.

韋 Uí

Uí tô, Boeddh. god (die over de regels in een tempel waakt).

畏 Uì

Uì t'ià̤ (*ṳ̀* ») } , kleinzeerig.

uì lâng, bedeesd, verlegen.

kia̤ uì (*ṳ̀*) } , uit vrees dat.

k'iông uì, do.

m̄ uì, vrees niet, men behoeft er niet bang voor te zijn.

uì niao̤ ts'áo, kruitje roer me niet.

uì k'ì, niet houden van.

uì bó̤, zijne vrouw vreezen.

tsáp poeh ē k'ióng uì, lett. 18 maal vreezen; *i. e.* in alles, allerlei moeielijkheden vinden.

uì sū, bang zijn voor twist.

uì siú uì bi, vreesachtig, beschroomd zijn.

97

uì lâng tsai, bang zijn dat anderen het te weten zullen komen.

toā uì toā, soè uì soè, groote vreezen grooten, kleinen vreezen kleinen *i. e.* iets niet gaarne voor anderen willen weten.

慰 Uì *An uì* (*uì*), troosten, condoleeren, gerust-stellen.

壓 Uì *Uì ts'uì*, iemand tegenstaan (van spijzen).

尉 Uì *Mîng sin hō uì* (*o*), deurgoden, en deurwachters (huisgeesten).

桅 Uî *Uî*, mast.

t'aò uî, fokkêmast.

tiong uî, groote mast.

bé uî (*boé*), bezaansmast.

uî pîn, kamerscherm.

遺 Uî *Uî giép*, zijne bezittingen aan iemand vermaken.

uî laō, weglaten, niet opschrijven.

圍 Uî *P'ah uî*, een net omringen (en de visch opjagen).

uî k'ùn, belegeren, omsingelen.

tsiu uî, omringen.

uî tiòh, bezetten, omcirkelen.

uî teh, insluiten.

uî ts'iû (*ts'iû*), omwallen, ommuren.

uî kî, schaakspelen.

uî hān (» *ān*), afperken.

sì uî, alom.

sì long uî, sì lin long uî, rondom loopen.

tsaó uî ts'iû, buitenmuur om een huis, erf.

uî tsū, omsingelen, omringen.

hoe uî, bloemenkrans (meestal van zilver) door vrouwen om het hoofd ge dragen).

uî tsoè hoe tîng, tot een bloemtuin afperken.

違 Uî *Uî kéh* (» *kéh*), weerstreven.

uî gîk, tegenstreven, zich verzetten tegen.

uî lē, zich tegen de wet verzetten, met de wet strijdend.

uì kìm, tegen een verbod strijdend, verboden.

Uî *Toh uî*, afhangend tafelkleed.

ts'îng uî, katoenen of zijden afhangsel van een bed.

畫 Uī *Uī* (*oā*), schetsen, teekenen; beteekenen, bekladden, besmeren.

uī kang, schilder.

uī ts'iū, schilder.

uī kiû, schilderijen in lijsten.

uī hō, zijn merk zetten op.

uī ling uī hōng, allerlei uitvluchten zoeken, een bepaald antwoord ontduiken.

suí kaò ts'in ts'iū kiáh pit uī, fraai als ware het met een penseel geschilderd.

hó dzī uī, fraaie (afhangende) geschriften en teekeningen.

uī tsít é piâ hí piah nih, een koek op de muur teekenen *i. e.* holle beloften doen.

位 Uī *Uī* (*uī*), numer. voor leermeesters, priesters.

oā uī, van plaats veranderen.

tâ uī, ruimte voor lading 2e bedrag van eene belooning enz.

tang it uī sai it uī, de hoogste plaatsen aan de linker, en de rechterhand van den gastheer.

pát uī (*uī*), elders.

tē uī, plaats, stand, staat in de maatschappij.

ta lóh uī, waar?

tsē uī, den troon aanvaarden 2e aan tafel gaan zitten, gezeten zijn (van gasten).

kuì uī, op zijn eigen plaats gaan, tegen leerlingen gezegd.

hē kui uī, op zijne oorspronkelijke plaats zitten.
liét uī, gij allen (bel. term).
tsièm uī, een zit, of staanplaats innemen, bezeten.
t'è uī, afstand van den troon doen.

爲 Uī *In uī*, omdat.
í uī, het er voor houden dat..., denken dat...
uī i, iemand helpen.
sa uī, elkander helpen.
uī tiōng, hoogschatten, waardeeren.

胃 Uī *Pí uī*, de maag.
háh pi uī, met zijn maag, gestel overeenkomen 2e naar iemands zin handelen.
hoan uī, herkauwen (van beesten).

Uih

挖 Uih *Uih* (*oeh*), optillen, opwippen 2e afstrijken, afscheppen (als van stijfsel, boter enz.)

剜 Uih *Uih*, uitsnijden (als een beentje uit een vinger enz.)
uih ts'ùt, uittillen, uitsnijden.
uih he tsi, met pleisterkalk bestrijken.
kā i uih ts'ùi tseh, iemands mond afvegen *i. e.* door geld zijn stilzwijgen over eene zaak koopen.
uih bô tit t'ang k'í lai, zich niet kunnen opwerken, opstaan.
uih iû, olie afstrijken.
uih kọ ióh k'í lai p'ì, een lik zalf nemen om het (op een doek) uit te strijken.
uih tsit tè kọ, een lik stijfsel uitscheppen, nemen.
uih hoan tsû, aardappelen uit den grond wippen, rooien.
uih ts'iù p'oé tsiū ts'iò, streelt menschen (kinderen) tegen de wangen dan lachen ze.

畫 Uih *Uih* (*oáh*), lijnen trekken, linieeren, streep, trek (van een karakter).
it dzìh īm bat tsit uih, geen enkele trek van het karakter één kennen *i. e.* geene enkel karakter kennen.
ts'it uih poeh uih, verward opschrijven.
uih hûn, met strepen, krassen.
dzī uih sui, fraaie karakters.
uih tsiạ uih, k'iā tsiạ k'iā, fraai, ongedwongen, schrijven.

Uih *Uih* (*ui*), versleten, uitgesleten (als een mes, een steen enz.)
hoē uih (*oéh*), gemakkelijk verslijten.
p'oà uih (*oeh*), stuk en uitgesleten.
k'ih k'ih uih uih, gebarsten en uitgespleten.

裂 Uih *T'aò p'oà hī uih* (*oéh*), zich het hoofd bezeeren.
tạ-uih lah (*oéh*), het is er akelig mede gesteld.

挖 Uih *Gaò uih lâng ė siaò* (*o*), steeds veranderingen, vermeerderingen in iemands rekening maken.

Uih *Lọ-kiạ kaò uih k'i* (*éh*), een weg begaan hebben totdat hij uitgesleten is *i. e.* dikwijls een weg gegaan zijn.

Un

溫 Un *Un*, familienaam.
un dziû (*un*), zachtzinnig, toegevend.
un sip, aanleeren, repeteeren, overleeren.
un sio, leukwarm, warm maken.
un hô, middelmatig (van warmte.)
un tsiú, wijn lauwwarm maken.

un tī kiaó tiŋ niħ } , verslaafd aan het (*un* en *ùn*) dobbelhuis zijn.
un sùn, zachtzinnig, zacht van aard.
un ts'eh, een boek bestudeeren.

瘟 Un
Un ik (*iáh*) } , besmettelijke ziekte, pest.
tso un, door pest aangetast worden.
un ik ông (*iáh*) } , god der pest (ook van slechte geneesheeren gezegd).

恩 Un
Un tik (*in* ») } , weldadigheid.
kám un (*in*) } , dankbaar.
pò un, erkentelijk voor een gunst zijn.
un sut, medelijden, begunstigen.
un huī, weldaad.
un ìm, zijne gunsten over anderen uitstrekken.
ti un pò pún, dankbaar voor weldaden zijn.
bông un poē gī, ondankbaar.
un tsing, verplichting aan iemand, weldaden.
un dzin, *toā un dzin*, iemand aan wien men groote dankbaarheid verschuldigd is.

Un
Un un k'ùn k'ùn, gekronkeld.
un lun k'ùn k'ùn, gekronkeld.
un lùn k'ùn (*un*) } , zich kronkelen (als een slang).
un un k'ùn k'ùn (*in k'in*) } , vlijtig, gedienstig, liefderijk.
un k'ùn (*in k'in*) } , voorkomend, gastvrij.

殷 Un
Un (*in*) } , familienaam.
un sit, genoeg hebben om van te leven, ruimschoots de kost verdienen.

韞 Un
Un t'un, vuil, smerig.

Un
Sī un ai (*in*) } , eene opzwelling van het oor hebben.

穩 Ún
Ún tàng (*ún*) } , veilig, zeker.
an ún, veilig.
bò ún, onveilig.
ún ún tàng tàng, veilig, zeker.
ún tòng, veilig, sekuur.
ún t'ò, veilig, te vertrouwen.
ún piēn, veilig en klaar bij de hand.
ún sūn, veilig, sekuur.

隱 Ún
Ún ún (*in* ») } , onduidelijk, heel in de verte.
ún bi (*in* ») } , fijn, subtiel.
ún moā (*in* ») } , verborgen houden, geheim houden, bedekken.
ún k'ì k'ìng, wegbergen.
ún bit, geheim, verborgen.
ún gú, geheime taal, dieven taal.
ún iông, dulden, gedoogen, toelaten.
ún lik (*in* ») } , verzwijgen, verborgen houden.

痀 Ún
Ún ku (*ún*) } , bochel, gebocheld.
ún ku kiô, ronde brug.

翼 Ún
Ún koe á (*ún ke á*) } , kuikens onder hare vleugels koesteren.
ún sio, warm houden (als de hen hare kiekens onder de vlerken).

允 Ún
Ún tiŋ tiòh, stellig, vastbeloven.
ún (*ún*) } , toestaan, vergunnen.
ún ū, bepaald is het er, voorzeker.
ún hó, stellig, zonder twijfel is het goed.
ún ún, stellig, zonder twijfel, veilig.

蚓 Ún
T'ō ún (*tō kín*) } , aardpier, worm.

孕 Ún — *Ún hō i k'iao k'í lai* (*o*), zoo slaan, kloppen, pletten dat het ombuigt, als plaatijzer.
īng ún á-ún (*o*), met een klopper bol kloppen.

榅 Ùn — *Ùn tsiu* (*ùn*), stijven, in de stijfsel duwen.
ùn (*ùn*), indoopen in.
ùn t'ing, door de suiker halen.
ùn kiêm, in het zout stoppen, door het zout halen.
ùn tsuí, in het water doopen.
ùn pò, ruw geverfde stof.

Ùn — *Ùn* (*o*), afgedamde plassen waarin de visch met afnemend water op droog blijft liggen.
p'oà ùn (*o*), een afgedamde vischplas doorsteken.
ùn á hí (*o*), in plassen gevangene visschen.

韞 Ùn — *Ùn t'ùn* (*o*), log, lomp.

巡 Ûn — *Ûn*, rondloopen.
ûn k'ì, rondgaan (als een flesch aan tafel).
t'in tsit ûn, eens rondschenken, de flesch eens rond laten gaan.
ûn lai ûn k'ì, heen en weer wandelen.
ûn ûn, rondzwerven.
sì koè ûn ûn tseh, hier en daar rondloopen.

翔 Ûn — *Ûn*, zweven als vogels.

緩 Ûn — *Ûn ûn á*, langzamerhand.
ûn ûn á sī, do.
ûn ûn á kā, knabbelen aan.
ûn ûn á hé, langzaam er bijleggen.

Ûn — *It ûn k'ì* (*ûn*), gelijkelijk weg, voor de hand weg.
tsiaô ûn, gelijkelijk, regelmatig.
ûn lai ts'é k'ì, bij het te kort van het ééne, het te veel van het andere voegen, door elkander gerekend.
p'ah ûn k'ì, door elkander gerekend.

伸 Ûn — *Ts'un ûn*, zich uittrekken.

Ûn — *Ū ûn*, eene reeds te voren gebruikte streek om geld enz. te krijgen nogmaals aanwenden.

輩 Ûn — *Tíng ûn ē lâng*, menschen van vorige generatie (vader, grootvader enz.)
tíng tsit ûn, eene generatie hooger.
ē tsít ûn, eene generatie lager.
toā tsit ûn, eene generatie (30 jaren) ouder.
pī tú ûn, van gelijken leeftijd.

行 Ûn — *Dzī ûn*, rang die men in zijne familielijst bekleedt en die bij elke volgende generatie door een volgend karakter van een aangenomen tekst of vers wordt aangeduid.

運 Ūn — *Kiā-bô hó ūn*, nog niets dan ongeluk ontmoet hebben.
ūn k'ì tng sī, juist in gelukkige omstandigheden zijn.
tó ūn, tot elkander gebracht zijn.
taò ūn k'ì, van het toeval, geluk afhangend.
ūn tōng, ronddraaien, rondgaan.
ūn hing, omgaan, rondgaan.
ūn tsoán, stroomend, heen en weer gaand.
ūn hè (*hoè*), goederen vervoeren.
dzī ūn (*k'ì ūn*), levenswandel, lot, levensvoorvallen.
ūn tioh, vlakken.

韻 Ūn *Aò ūn*, geurig van thee, wanneer de geur in de keel terugkomt.
im ūn, klanken.
si ūn, rijmklanken (voor verzen).
kóng-kaò ū sia ūn k'i lai, zoo vertellen dat men het wezenlijk zou gaan gelooven.
ūn, eindklank.
ah ūn, rijmen.
sia ūn, geluid, klank.

沍 Ūn *Ūn*, smelten.

Ut

熨 Ut *Ut*, strijken als kleêren.
ut sa, kleêren strijken.
ut taó, strijkijzer.
ut kєng ut ut pi, glad, gelijk strijken.
ut king, de plooien strijken.

箢 Ut *Ing hé ut tik*, bamboes krombranden.
ut dziaó, gekreukeld.
ut tiò á, een haak krom buigen 2e neerknielen.
oan ut, valsch betichten.
ut tsut, bedrukt, neerslachtig, 2e boos worden.
ut k'iao, krom buigen.
ut ut, voorover zitten.
ut tioh, verzwikken.
ut aģ, lispelen, te korte tong hebben.
ut sik, het is zonde (dat zoo iets goeds voor zulk een min doeleinde gebruikt wordt).
iu ut, bedroefd, knorrig.
ut būn, niet in zijn schik, op zijn gemak zijn,
ut tsûn, eene reis in een schip maken.
ut lō, eene reis in een draagstoel maken.
oai ut, valsch betichten.
aó ut lâng, iemand valsch betichten.
ut si hit é lâng, iemand vreesselijk er onderhouden, verdrukken.
siū ut, valsch beticht worden 2e zijne bekwaamheden niet aan het licht kunnen brengen.
ut ik, inwendig boos.
ts'it ut poeh ut, allerlei onaangename dingen.
ut tsit hè, voor een jaar ouder geteld worden dan men wezentlijk is (door dat men op het eind van het jaar geboren is).
ut kut sì, bij de geboorte doodgewrongen worden.
ut boē lóh, zich niet naar iets kunnen wringen, in iets kunnen schikken, iets niet kunnen aanleeren, niet kunnen neêrknielen.
ut ku, kromme rug.
ut k'i, omwel door een al te zittend leven.

挨 Út *Út tióh*, strijken langs.
tuì hia út tseh, daar langs gaan.
út-tuì tsiah hè, daar langs heen gaan.
út tióh lâ sâm, vuil worden door langs iets heen te strijken.
út lai út k'i, heen en weer loopen, heen en weer zweven (als valken).
saò saò út út tseh, opvegen, afvegen.
út tseh sút tseh, zoo ongemerkt, zoo met heen en weer gaan is b. v. het jaar om.
t i út út, aarzelen.
út lìn téng, in een ommekeer, ommezien.

英漢潮州方言字典

（*A Chinese and English Vocabulary, in the Tie-chiu Dialect*）

〔美〕高德（Josiah Goddard）編

《英漢潮州方言字典》，美國高德編。高德（Josiah Goddard，一八一三—一八五四），美國浸信會傳教士。一八三八年派往新加坡，一八三九年至暹羅，次年抵曼谷，期間學習潮州方言，一八四二年編成此書，一八四八年來華，至寧波。此書前有引言，詳述潮州方言聲韻系統，正文所收字頭以潮州話羅馬字注音排序，皆標注聲調，並有簡要英文釋義。一八四七年初版，一八八三年上海美華書館二版。據一八八三年上海版影印。

英漢潮州方言字典

A CHINESE AND ENGLISH VOCABULARY,

IN THE

TIE-CHIU DIALECT.

BY JOSIAH GODDARD.

SECOND EDITION.

SHANGHAI:
AMERICAN PRESBYTERIAN MISSION PRESS.
1883.

INTRODUCTION.

THE following work, compiled originally to meet the wants of the writer, is offered to the public, simply with the desire that it may afford assistance in the studies of those who desire to make known the unsearchable riches of Christ to the numerous and interesting people who speak the dialect for which it is prepared. It is designed to embrace most of the words in common use, arranged according to their sounds and tones, with brief definitions, and thus form a convenient manual dictionary sufficient for the common purposes of the student. A large Dictionary must, of course, be at hand for reference in difficult and important cases. But a complete Dictionary in each of the Chinese dialects cannot be expected. The most that can be sought is a complete Dictionary in the Court dialect, and a convenient vocabulary in each of the several dialects which claim the attention of missionaries; and the earlier such a Vocabulary can be prepared the greater will be the saving of time and labor. It is believed that at least one third of the time and labor of acquiring a good knowledge of such a dialect as the Tie Chiu, with only a large Dictionary in the Court dialect, might be saved by the help of such a Vocabulary.

2. The *Orthography* employed in this work is intended to correspond with that in most common use, except where the peculiarities of the dialect require a difference. It is briefly exhibited in the following table:—

SOUNDS OF THE VOWELS, &C.

á as in *far*.
a the same sound shortened and approaching *u* in *but*.
à nearly as in *man*; intermediate between *a* in *hat* and in *far*.
e as in *they*; before a consonant it is shortened.
i „ „ *machine*; somewhat shortened before a consonant.
o „ „ *no*; *note*.
ó „ „ *lord*; *north*.
u „ „ *rule*; *put*.
ù „ „ *turn*.

w as *woo* in *wood*; or as *wu*; each letter being sounded short.
ai ,, in *aisle*.
au ,, *ow* in *now*.
iu ,, *ew* in *new*.
oi ,, in *going*.
^{n} small above the line represents the nasal sound.
^{u} ,, ,, ,, ,, ,, the indistinct sound of *u* in *but*.
ʻ the apostrophe denotes the *aspirate* sounds.

The third sound of *a* occurs in all those cases and those only in which it is preceded by *i* and followed by *ng* as *liáng*.

The sound of *e* in *they* and in *men* is usually regarded as the same in nature, differing only in length; it is not therefore marked in this work but is ascertained by its position.

The *i* shortened before a consonant is intermediate between its longest sound in *machine* and its shortest in *pin*, seldom becoming as short as in the latter.

The sound of *o* in *not* which has commonly been represented by the unmarked *o* never occurs in this dialect; the unmarked *o* is therefore used for the sound in *note*.

The termination *ou*, which has been employed by some, is not used in this work, as the sound which it represents does not seem to differ from the sound of *o* in *no*; if it has any *u* sound it is only the necessary turn of the voice in pronouncing the final *o*.

The *i* in *iu* has a more distinct sound than the *e* in *new*, and the *u* has the same sound as in *muse*.

The *w* retains both the consonant and vowel power. Its consonant power, however, is often very weak, sometimes scarely perceptible.

Y is used in but few words, and even concerning these it may be doubtful whether *i* would not be equally proper. It may also be remarked that many of the words under the initial *i* are sometimes spoken as if they commenced with *y*, especially in rapid pronunciation; as *iong* like *yong*.

It is to be observed that no attempt is made to mark the length of the vowels, but only the nature of their sounds; their length will vary in the same word according to the *tone*; and therefore if the word is pronounced correctly according to its *tone*, the *length* of the vowel will of course be correct. Hence, except in the case of *e* and *i* mentioned in the table as shortened before consonants, the length of the vowels may be said to be governed by the tones. This may easily be seen by pronouncing such words as *cham, che, kan, kiàng,* in each of the different tones.

The Tie Chiu dialect never exhibits the following initials, viz; *a,* *à*. *d, f, r, v, x,* and *z*; *c,* is used only in *ch,* and *q* is supplanted by *k.* The following terminations are never found; *à b, d, f, g* except in *ng, h, j*; *r, s, v, x* and *x*; *c, g, w* and *y* are not used as finals, their sounds being otherwise represented. With these exceptions all the vowel sounds exhibited in the table, and all the consonants with their usual English sounds are found both as initials and finals.

3. Eight varieties of TONE are marked in this work. This chief peculiarity is that the high and low, in the *even going* and *entering* are precisely the reverse of what they are called by the Chinese, and also of what thay have usually been marked by writers on other dialects. Yet the least observation will show that what the Chinese call the low is, in this dialect, really the high, and what they call the high is really the low tone. This peculiarity is, however, less manifest in the reading than in the common sound of the words, which often differ only in tone; the reading being more conformable to the tone as designated by the Chinese, whether high or low. But as the following work is designed to exhibit the common rather than the reading sounds, the really high is distinguished by a straight mark over the tonal semicircle as in the following table:—

TONES.

‘ˏ|	EVEN	*high*	下平	E p^{n}e.
˓|	,,	*low*	上平	Ch^{n}ie p^{n}e.
‘|	HIGH	TONE	上聲	Siang si^{n}a.
|’	GOING	*high*	下去	E kù
|’	,,	*medium*	去聲	Ku si^{n}a.
|²	,,	*low*	上去	Ch^{n}ie kù.
|ˏ	ENTERING	*high*	下入	E jip.
|,	,,	*low*	上入	Chi^{n}e jip.

The *low* EVEN, or *ch^{n}ie p^{n}e,* is strictly an even tone, being pronounced with a natural even voice and easy cadence at the close.

The *high* EVEN is usually found more difficult of utterance; the sound is high and somewhat prolonged, resembling a circumflex higher in the middle than at either end.

The peculiarity of the HIGH tone consists in a strong emphasis of the voice at the beginning of a word leaving the end to die away obscurely. Words in this tone are usually pronounced much shorter than in the *even*; but when followed by another word which is coupled to it and to be pronounced in connection with it, the sound is prolonged, rising, but not increasing in strength, to the close. In such cases it somewhat resembles the high Going.

The *high* GOING consists in a prolongation of sound continually *rising* to the end. The *medium* GOING comprises a class of words which Tie Chiu men commonly read in an even tone, somewhat lower than the *low* EVEN. The *low* GOING tone consists in a prolongation of the sound, very low but increasing in *strength* or *emphasis* to the close.

The ENTERING tone consists in an abrupt ending, and the *high* and *low* differ in the same manner as the high and low EVEN. all words ending in *k*, *p*, or *t* are of this class, and these are the only *consonants* which form the termination; when the vowels form the termination, they are pronounced as if a consonant was about to be added but is suddenly cut off. It is sometimes represented by adding a final *h*; but as the abruptness results from the nature of the tone, if the tonal mark is used the *h* is not necessary. The use of *h* also interrupts the uniformity of the orthogrophy, as words of this tone belong in the same class with others which do not end with *h*, and from which their sound differs only in tone. This may be seen by pronouncing such syllables as *chi*, *ti*, *te*, in each of the tones.

Though the preceding remarks may help to explain the nature of the tones in this dialect, yet the learner will need the assistance of a teacher with the living voice to enable him attain a perfectly correct use of them; and the earlier he learns to distinguish and pronounce them correctly the greater will be the saving of his future labor and the more accurate his use of the language.

4. We may here notice some varieties in the usage of persons who speak the Tie Chiu dialect.

Ch at the beginning of words is sometimes pronounced *ts*; and still more frequently intermediate between *ch* and *ts*.

The *i* in such words as *sin, tit,* is by some pronounced like *e* as *sen, tet.*

The termination *ie* is pronounced by many *io,* the *o* being somewhat short: as *bie, bio*; *ie io*; *chie chio.*

The termination *io* is often pronounced *iau*: as *lio, liau*; *mio, miau.*

The *oi* in such words as $ch^{n}oi$, *noi*, $t^{n}oi$, $o^{n}i$ is pronounced by many nearly like *ai*; as $ch^{n}ai$, *nai*, $t^{n}ai$, $a^{n}i$.

The initial *l* and *n* in such words as *lam, lan*; *nam, nan* are often interchanged; *i.e.* some persons will usually say *lam lan,* others usually *nam, nan,* without seeming to perceive any difference.

The terminations *n,* and *ng,* in such words as *kwan, kwang*; *tien, tiang,* are confounded by some who do not seem to notice any difference between them. Such persons will also usually confound the terminations *et* and *ak,* as *siet, siak.*

The *ù* in such words as 汝, 去, *lù, kù* is sometimes pronounced *u*; as *lu, ku.* Also *ù* in such words as 代, 塊 *tù kù* is often prononunced *ò*; as *tò, kò*; and it may be remarked that when the *ù* sound is given in this class of words it is a more open sound than when it occurs in the class just before mentioned; the difference is easily perceptible, but does not seem capable of being represented by Roman letters. The *ù* in such words as *ùn, ngùn* is sometimes pronounced *i*; as *in, ngin*; by others it is pronounced *e,* and the *n* changed to *ng*; as *eng,* ngeng.

The nasal sounds are used much more by some persons than by others. The words in which it is universally used are mostly those which in the Court dialect and also in the Tie Chiu reading sound end in *n* or *ng*; these terminations, in common usage, are often dropped, and the nasal sound inserted before the preceding vowel, which is also often changed to suit the new form of the word; as *Cheng*, $Ch^{n}e$; *Chiang*, $Ch^{n}ie$; *Chien*, $Ch^{n}ua$; *Hiong*, $H^{n}ia$.

5. The Tie Chiu, like most other dialects, has what is called a reading and also a common sound to the words. The common sound, however, to a considerable extent accords with the reading. There are also a large number of words whose reading and common sounds are used interchangeably both in reading and in conversation.

But in other cases the reading sound is used only in chanting the classics. Neither teachers nor common readers, in reading a common book, ever think of using any other than the common sound; nor do hearers expect any other. Hence reading in the Tie Chiu dialect corresponds, more than in some other dialects, with reading in other languages. The hearer is expected to understand the words as they are read, and whatever explanations are made are rather of the thought than of the words. It is therefore the common sound of the words which it is important for missionaries to know; it is well to acquire a knowledge of the reading sounds in order to trace analogies and make comparisons; but for the purpose of making known the Gospel it is of but little use. Hence in the following work the words are arranged according to the common sound; and where words have several sounds or tones with different meanings they are usually repeated under each respective sound or tone. In the second part or Index to the work, however, the reading sound will be found along with the common, where they differ from each other.

6. As the printing of this work has been performed under many disadvantages, it is presumed that severe criticism will be spared. If the work is capable of being, in the least degree, serviceable for the end designed let it be so used; and whatever can be done by any individual to render a future edition more useful will promote the great object of man's salvation. There will be different opinions among Chinese teachers as to the sound, and of course the collocation of many words. Instances have occured in which four different teachers have given as many different sounds to a word; hence it would not be strange if some words should be arranged incorrectly. It is hoped however, that, as much care has been taken, with the assistance of several native teachers, it will be found essentially correct, and will lead those who follow it to such a use of the language as will cause them to be readily understood, and will render them extensively useful to the people.

VOCABULARY.

A′ A′H A′I A′K A′M

A′.

亞 Inferior; an appellation of common men.

椏 Branches of a tree.

鴉 A crow; a raven.

鴨 A duck.

A′h.

啞 To dispute, wrangle.

A′i.

哀 Painful feelings; pity.

埃 Dust; sand.

餲 Spoiled food; corrupt.

藹 Shady; luxuriant.

噯 A breathing; a tone of disapprobation.

靉 Cloudy; obscure.

愛 Kind feeling; love.

欲 To wish for; desire; covet; a sign of the future.

A′k.

篕 A kind of bamboo.

惡 Wicked; sin.

A′m.

庵 菴 A small thatched cottage; a small monastery.

闇 Retired; sombre.

諳 Well acquainted with; to remember.

頸 The neck.

暗 Obscure; dark.

A'n.

安 Rest; tranquility.

鞍 A saddle.

按² According to; to try; to lay the hand on.

案² A bench; a case in law.

晏² Serene, cloudless and mild; harmony.

宴² A feast; banquet; repose.

鷃² A species of quail.

A'ng.

紅 Red.

洪 A deluge; great; abundant.

甕² A jar.

A'p.

匣5 A small box.

柙5 A cage.

盒5 A cover; a platter or dish; to cover over.

押 To escort; control: collect.

狎 Too familiar with; to make light of.

A't.

遏 To forbid; hinder; cause to desist; to press down.

抑 To press down; cause to stop: an interrogative particle.

Au.

喉 The throat.

歐 To spit out; vomit.

甌 An earthen cup; bowl.

拗 To sieze and drag with the hand; to break; obstinate; perverse.

嘔 To vomit; to nauseate; to spit.

毆 To strike or beat; to wrangle; beat unjustly.

後5 After; behind.

奧² Obscure; deep.

懊² Indignant; vexed; avaricious.

Bai.

眉 The eyebrows.

楣 Eaves of a house; the cross beam over a door.

Bák.

木5 Wood.

墨5 Ink; black.

Bát.

密 Secret; silent.

Bau.

卯 A horary character, from 5 to 7 o'clock A.M.

昴 The name of a constellation.

Be.

馬 A horse.

麥 Wheat.

Bi.

米 Rice.

未 A horary character, from 1 to 3 o'clock P.M.

味 Taste; scent; relish.

氽 To float on the surface of water; to swim.

篾 Reeds for making baskets.

Bie.

苗 Sprouts; grain growing; off-spring.

描 To sketch or draw pictures.

廟 A temple.

Bio.

妙 Delicate; small; excellent.

Bit.

蜜 Honey.

Bo.

畝 The Chinese acre of land.

姆 A female.

牡 The male of animals.

戊 An astronomical character; flourishing.

Bó.

無 No; not.

毋 Do not; a prohibitative particle.

帽 A cap or hat.

磨 A millstone.

母 A mother.

姆 An aged widow; a schoolmistress; a midwife.

牳 The female of cattle.

Boi.

買 To buy.

賣 To sell.

Bu.

꜁巫 A sorcerer or enchanter; magic.

꜁誣 To deceive; accuse falsely; superstitious.

꜁廡 A shade; porch; a vacant house.

꜁膴 Flesh dried without bones; fat; beautiful.

꜁蕪 Overgrown with weeds or wood; shady; dirty.

꜂侮 Neglect; disrespect.

꜂僬 Affection; love; also used for contempt.

꜂撫 To soothe; to hold; to keep down with the hand.

꜂憮 Affection; love.

꜂舞 Dancing; sleight of hand; tricks.

꜂武 Warlike; military; a foot-step.

꜂碔 Name of a valuable stone.

꜂鵡 A bird that can talk; a parrot.

務꜅ To apply the mind and strength to any object; effort.

婺꜅ A widow who does not marry again.

騖꜅ To run with haste and precipitation; violent.

꜁霧 Mist; fog: vapor.

Bua.

꜁磨 To rub or grind; to oppress.

秣꜇ To rub or brush in order to cleanse.

撥꜇ To spread out; select; disperse; expel or reject.

抹꜇ To blot out, rub out.

Buan.

꜀萬 Ten thousand; all.

Buang.

꜁亡 Lost; destroyed; dead.

꜁忘 To forget; disregard.

꜂罔 A net; impeded; to deceive.

꜂魍 A water sprite or demon.

꜂妄 False; confused; extravagant.

望꜅ Full moon.

Bue.

꜁枚 A small tree.

꜁梅 Name of a fruit; a prune.

꜁媒 A mediator in marriage affairs.

꜁煤 Coals; collection of soot.

˓尾 The tail; termination of.

未˭ Not; not yet.

襪˳ Stockings.

Bun.

文˱ Literature; letters; ornamental; ornament.

旻˱ An autumnal sky; pensive; melancholy.

紊˱ } Confusion.
紋˱ }

汶˱ Name of a river.

蚊˱ A flea; small insect.

捫˱ To touch with the hand; feel; to lay hold of; to shake.

聞˺ To hear.

悶˭ Grief; grieved.

們˭ A Particle added to nouns and pronouns to form the plural.

Chá.

柴˱ Fuel; to collect.

嗟˱ To sigh; lament; a tone of sorrow or surprise.

槎˱ To hew wood; pare; to fell.

渣˱ Settlings; dregs.

罝˱ A net for rabbits.

˓昔 Formerly; in former times.

˓昨 Yesterday; recently.

˓早 Morning; early; speedily.

˓蚤 A kind of insect.

乍˭ Suddenly; unexpectedly; for a short time.

搓˱ To rub in the hand.

怍˭ Ashamed; to blush.

怎˭ How? why?

詐˭ False; deceitful.

醡˭ A wine press.

仄˲ Rough tone.

Ch'á.

差˱ Error; erroneous; differing.

蹉˱ To slip; transgress; miss; slow.

˓炒 To fry; cook in a pan with lard or water.

閘˲ A gate at the head of a street or in a narrow pass.

柵 A railing; palisades.

插, 揷 To pierce; insert; stick into.

Chai.

臍 The navel; umbilical cord.

知 To know.

灾, 災 Great calamities; divine judgments.

菑 To clear land; to level a road to cut open; rend.

哉 An interrogative superlative exclamation.

栽 To plant.

烖 Calamities; divine judgments.

宰 To rule; a ruler; to kill and dress animals.

滓 Dregs; feces.

載 A year.

豸 A certain ravenous animal.

再 Again.

載 To contain; what is contained, as in a ship.

Ch'ai.

才 Talent; ability.

材 Materials; fit for use.

財 Wealth; property.

豺 A species of wolf.

蠆 A sting in the tail; a scorpion.

猜 Dislike; to suspect; to doubt; conjecture.

裁 To cut clothes; cut; tear.

采 Adorned with a variety of colors.

採 To pluck with the hand; to take.

綵 Colored silk; assemblage of every color.

纔 Just now; just then.

菜 Edible plants.

Chák.

窄, 笮 Narrow; compressed; a quiver: a punishment.

作 To act; make; do; begin.

Ch'ák.

鑿 A chisel; to bore or dig into.

英漢潮州方言字典

Chám.

針 A needle; any pointed instrument.

簪 A pin of metal or wood to fasten the hair.

箴 A needle; a surgeon's probe; to probe.

斬 To cut asunder; decapitate.

譖 To revile; slanderous speech.

Ch'ám.

儳 Irregular; rapid.

巉 A hill; a rocky, dangerous summit.

讒 To calumniate; to flatter those present and slander the absent.

慚 Ashamed; to blush.

參 叅 To mix together; to see; advise with; to give advice to a sovereign against inferior officers.

驂 Blended; three horses to one carriage.

慘 Painful feelings; distress of mind.

Chán.

層 An upper room or loft; a degree.

嶒 Mountains rising one above another.

罾 A fishing net.

贈 To present to; give; bestow.

棧 A scaffold; upper loft; a tent; stable; a railing.

贊 To see; to enter; discover; praise.

纘 To continue on in succession.

瓚 A kind of sceptre; a vessel to contain wine.

讚 To praise; assist.

站 To stand up; erect.

Ch'án.

田 A field.

殘 To rob; plunder; mangle; spoiled; killed; cruel.

棧 A sheepcote; stable.

餐 A meal of food.

孱 Weak; embarrassed; sighing.

僝 To see; to manifest; prepare.

樝 Name of a tree and fruit; a mattress.

鏟 A plane; to plane or level.

粲 A meal; to eat; many; excellent; to examine.

燦 Clear; luminous.

Cháng.

檣 A numeral of trees; a tree; bush.

臧 Good; faithful; generous.

莊 Sedate; stern; rigid.

棕 Name of a tree.

蓁 Small; trees with small branches.

鬃 The hair on a horse's neck; mane.

臟 The viscera of the animal body.

贓 To receive bribes; unjust gain; stolen goods; booty.

壯 Large; strong; affluent; manhood.

Ch'áng.

藏 To hide; conceal; store up.

葱 Green color; a vegetable.

愴 A wounded heart; grief.

蒼 Green; azure; abundant.

蹌 To step short and quick as in respect; fencing.

蔣 Name of a plant.

鏘 The sound of tones, bells etc.; notes of birds.

斨 A kind of hatchet; to wound with a hatchet.

創 A wound made by a knife; to begin; lay the foundation; make first; invent.

Cháp.

匝 To go round; perform the circuit of; revolve.

雜 襍 A mixture of colors or ingredients; mixed; confused.

卡 An important pass with a military station; a guard house.

十 Ten

汁 Juice; gravy; thick liquor

札 A board or tablet to write on.

扎 To bind; pluck up; eradicate.

Chát.

節 A limit; a joint; period of time; temperance; chastity.

櫛 A comb.

紮 To tie or bind together.

Ch'át.

賊 To rob; plunder; kill; a robber.

察 To investigate; examine; to judge; to manifest; careful.

擦꜁ To examine with the hand; to feel; to rub.

漆꜁ Resin; varnish; lacker.

㯃꜁ The varnish tree.

Chau.

꜀遭 To meet with; to occur; to happen; a time.

꜀糟 Grain from which spirits have been distilled; dregs.

꜂走 To walk; go; run.

皂[5] Inferiors; police runners.

造[5] To make; do; commence.

悼[5] Commiseration; to pity.

罩[5] A fishing basket; to cover over; to shade; a shade.

棹[5] To move; agitate; shake; to rectify.

奏[2] To give information to the emperor; to advise him.

灶[2] A furnace; fire place.

卓[5] To surpass, superior.

Ch'au.

[2]巢 A nest for birds or thieves; a lurking place.

[2]曹 A court or board of officers; a class; used to form the plural.

[2]傮 The whole; one complete round.

[2]嘈 Noise; clamor.

꜀勦 To fatigue; trouble; vex; light; active.

꜀剿 To cut off; exterminate.

꜀操 To grasp; hold fast; also the thing held.

꜀抄 To take or seize; to transcribe; to stir up.

꜂草 }
꜂艸 } Plants, grass, &c. — the running hand character; careless.

꜂藻 A water plant; elegant composition; joy.

懆[2] Vexatious; anxiety; sorrow.

澡[2] To wash; bathe.

燥[2] Fierceness of fire.

譟[2] Noise; clamor; disturbance.

躁[2] Precipitation; haste; fierce; to disturb.

慥[2] To act heartily and sincerely.

嗅[2] A strong smell; stink; to smell.

Che.

꜀齋 To fast; cleanse the heart; abstinence; respect.

這 This.

赭 Red earth; carnation color.

姐 An older sister.

寨 A camp; barracks; a sheep-fold.

債 To bear a burden; to be in debt; a debt.

職 To control; manage; the control of; care of.

責 To reprove; chastise; to be wrong; to inquire; to sustain an office.

勣 Meritorious service.

嘖 To cry out aloud; a tumultuous noise; a hissing.

簀 Mats; reeds; to collect.

績 Work performed; business; affair; meritorious deeds.

仄 Stooping; oblique.

昃 To descend; afternoon.

窄 Narrow; contracted.

漬 To soak, to steep.

Ch'e.

查 To examine into; inquire; a float or raft.

差 To send a messenger; a messenger.

叉 A fork.

厠 To cleanse and put in order; a place which needs cleansing; a privy; filthy.

册 A list; schedule; a book; a plan; to contrive.

策 A device; stratagem; to scheme; a switch.

Ch^{n}e.

晴 Clear sky after rain.

爭 To strive; wrangle.

井 A well; spring; order; land divided into parts.

阱 A pit; ditch; to fall into a pit.

靜 To judge; to be silent; quiet; stillness.

Ch'^{n}e.

青 A light green; azure; pale.

蜻 Name of an insect.

星 A star.

腥 Raw meat; fat.

菁 A kind of plant and flower.

惺 Fear; a tranquil, intelligent mind.

醒 To awaken or arouse, as from sleep, intoxication or stupidity.

Chek.

一 One; the first.

澤 Marshy; wet; softened; enriched.

叔 An uncle; a common appellation of Chinese; Mr.

則 Then; therefore; in that case; a rule; pattern.

嘖 To cry out aloud; tumultuous; wrangling.

漬 To drench; dye; steep.

積 To accumulate; hoard up; gather together.

稷 Best grain; the god of grain; the officer who presides over grain.

燭 A candle.

Ch'ek.

粟 Paddy; a small grain used for distillation.

斥 To break; lay open; expel; reprove; many.

側 By the side of; oblique; depraved; perverted.

惻 Acute pain.

測 To measure or fathom; pure; clear.

戚 Mournful; sorry; angry; relations; friends.

慼 Grief; mourning.

膝 The knees.

Cheng.

征 To go; to subjugate; conquer; punish.

鍾 A wine vessel; to collect; heavy.

鐘 A bell; a musical bell; tones of music.

貞 Chaste; pure; uncorrupted; a term in divination.

偵 To inquire; to spy; a spy.

楨 Name of a wood.

禎 A favorable omen.

精 Fine; thin; subtile; unmixed; spiritual; essence; semen.

睛 The pupil of the eye.

烝 To heat; or boil; to send; a multitude.

蒸 To ascend as vapor; a warm or hot vapor.

曾 A particle denoting that anything is already past or done.

僧 Budhist priests.

增 To add; increase; many.

憎 To dislike; to hate.

嘗 To taste; try; assay; already done; past.

舂 To beat as with a pestle; to pound.

꜀搼 To beat; to rush against.

꜀椿 A club or weapon; to strike; hit; to drive into the ground.

꜀箏 A musical instrument made of reeds.

‘腫 To swell; a swelling; inflated.

‘種 To plant; sow.

淨[5] To wash; clean; pure.

睜[5] To stare with displeasure; look with anger.

諍[5] To remonstrate; dissuade.

凊[5] Intense cold.

靖[5] Clean; fine; careful thought; to regulate; plan; order.

衆[2] The multitude; many.

政[2] Government; laws; to rule.

症[2] Sickness; a diseased state of body.

証[2] To remonstrate; to prove; testify; substantiate.

證[2] To testify; bear witness; evidence.

種[2] Seed; sort; class.

Ch‘eng.

꜀情 The passions; temper; disposition; circumstances.

꜀橙 Name of a tree; the orange tree.

꜀清 Pure; clear; tranquil.

꜀稱 To measure; weigh; adjust; to denominate; to praise.

銃[2] Hollowed or bored; a gun; cannon.

倩[2] Good; excellent; beautiful; instead of.

稱[2] A title or appellation.

Chi.

꜀躋 To ascend; climb a rugged hill.

꜀咥 A loud laugh; laughing.

꜀巵 A vessel to measure food or drink; a wine vessel.

꜀肢 The limbs of the body.

꜀脂 Fat animals; fatty substance; bones; to grease.

黹 To embroider, adorn.

꜀齎 To confer upon; bestow; supply; to store up.

‘旨 Excellent; the meaning or import of; will, purpose or decree.

‘指 To point with the finger; to refer to.

‘詣 To go in person.

‘齏 Variety of herbs blended together; broken; in confusion.

[c]止 To stop; only.

[c]址 Foundation.

[c]扯 To pull or tear with the hand; drag; pull open.

[c]祉 Happiness; felicity.

[c]芷 A fragrant medicinal plant.

[c]趾 A foundation; the toes.

[c]只 Only; singly; this and no more; merely.

[c]枳 A thorny wood of which hedges are made.

[c]咫 The ancient cubit, eight tenths of the present.

[c]紫 A nankin color; red; brown.

[c]姊 An older sister; a mistress.

巳[5] A horary character, from 9 to 11 o'clock A.M.

餂[5] Sweet taste; excellent.

舐[5] To lick with the tongue.

制[2] To cut and form; adjust; regulate; rule; make.

掣[2] To hinder; embarrass.

製[2] To make; fashion; regulate; decide.

幟[2] A banner; pendant; to attach to.

熾[2] A flame of fire; bright; splendor.

識[2] An inscription; epitaph; to remember.

躓[2] To stumble.

志[2] The will; purpose.

誌[2] Historical annals; to remember.

摯[2] To grasp with the hand; to hurt; to offer a present.

縶[2] To sew; tie or fasten together.

贄[2] A present made on being introduced to a superior.

至[2] To go or come to; arrive at; extreme; best.

祭[2] To carry human affairs before the gods; to sacrifice.

際[2] A limit; a place where two things meet; interval.

劑[2] To pare and clip; adjust; blend in due proportion.

擠[2] To push; press upon; put in order.

濟[2] Name of a river; to resist; help.

霽[2] To stop raining; fair sky after rain.

晰[2] Clear; bright.

瘛[2] A disease of children.

舌[5] The tongue; tongue of a bell, etc.

折 To pull or break open or in pieces; to diminish; to decide; reprove.

析 To split wood; to divide; discriminate.

淅 To wash rice; name of a river and province.

摺 To fold up; to destroy; a document sent to the Emperor.

Chʻi.

踟 Hesitation; embarrassment; irresolute.

齊 Even; regular; complete; to adjust; regulate; all together.

虒 Name of a place.

篪 Bamboo said to grow 1000 cubits high.

剺 Wounded skin.

墀 Vestibule in front of a hall; a path to the hall.

遲 Slow; dilatory.

池 A pool; pond; ditch.

阤 Degrees rising one above another; to advance.

馳 To run at full speed; gallop; to propel.

懝 Alarmed; apprehensive; to judge; intend.

妻 A wife; an equal.

凄 Intense cold.

悽 Sorrow; commiseration; anger; indignation.

棲 That on which a bird rests; a roost; a residence; to perch.

萋 Exuberance of foliage.

痴 Foolish; deranged.

恓 Much grieved; sorry; angry.

栖 Birds perched on trees; a roost; to rest; desist.

鴟 A certain bird.

蚳 A certain insect; a shell fish.

邸 The court; residence for court visitors; an inn; at the bottom; fundamental.

蚩 A worm; ugly; ignorant.

媸 A worthless woman; ugly and lewd; foolish.

恥 To be ashamed; shame.

侈 Large; profuse; prodigal.

齒 Teeth; the upper teeth.

市[5] Market place; street.

飼[2] To feed; nourish.

弒[2] To murder a superior.

試² To try; test; examine; compare.

莿² A device; stratagem.

妻² To give to wife; to marry.

Chⁿi.

꜀錢 Wealth; copper coin; money.

꜀瘵 Disease; contagious distemper.

꜀支 A branch; to branch out; to measure; the 12 divisions of time, of 2 hours each.

毡 A carpet for a floor.

꜀氈 Cloth or felt made of hair.

꜂穉 Young grain; young; small; tender.

擠² To push; to press upon; to put in order.

箭² An arrow; small bamboo.

Chʻⁿi.

꜀鮮 Fresh; not tainted nor salted.

Chia.

꜀遮 To cover over; to screen.

꜂者 A particle placed after verbs to denote the agent of the action.

꜂赭 Carnation color; red earth.

籍⁵ A list; register; book; to register.

藉⁵ To rely on; avail one's self of; to assist.

炙² To apply fire to; to broil; to dry; to approach near.

摭² To drag; to draw into notice.

蔗² Sugar cane.

鷓² A partridge.

樜² } A species of mulberry.
柘² }

跖² Lower part of the leg.

食⁵ To eat or drink; to retract; to endure an insult or injury.

隻꜆ Single; a numeral of things which are single.

蹟꜆ A footstep; to tread in the footsteps of.

跡꜆ } A trace; footstep; work of; examples for imitation.
迹꜆ }

Chʻia.

꜀車 A carriage.

꜀奢 Affluent; prodigal; wasteful.

꜀賒 To sell on credit; slow; remiss.

꜂且 And; then; also.

請 To invite; inquire after.

赤 Naked; flesh-color; reddish; vermilion.

Ch^{n}ia.

晶 Bright; luminous.

正 To rectify; put in order; to rule; execute laws; just at a given point of time.

整 To repair; put in order; to adorn.

正^{2} Upright; correct.

Chiak.

爵 A drinking cup; nobility; name of an office.

嚼 To bite; gnaw; chew.

勺 To take out with a spoon; a spoon.

妁 A mediator in marriage.

灼 To burn; to illumine.

芍 A medicine.

酌 To consult; deliberate.

靮 A bridle halter.

Chʻiak.

雀 A sparrow; small birds.

鵲 A fabled bird of joy.

綽 Slow; leisurely.

Chiam.

尖 Tapering; pointed; sharp; clever.

詹 Verbose; to examine into and give directions about.

瞻 To look up to with reverence.

襜 A curtain, cover or screen; garments which hang down and cover the knees.

贍 Plentiful; to give; bestow on the poor.

塹^{5} To arrange; spread out in order; ranks; army.

暫^{5} A short time; suddenly.

漸^{5} Gradually; to moisten; to dye; saturate.

占^{2} To prognosticate; divine; cast lots; to usurp.

佔^{2} To see; look at; to usurp.

踮^{2} To sit or stand still; stiff; dignified.

Chʻiam.

潛 To ford or pass through water; to enter deeply into.

僉 All; all united; the multitude.

簽 Slips of bamboo for drawing lots; to sign or subscribe.

懺[5] To repent; feel contrition.

籤[5] Slips of bamboo for drawing lots; used also as a permit or order.

纖[5] Pointed; sharp; clever.

僭[2] Erroneous; to overpass one's duty or sphere; to assume; usurp.

Chiàng.

꜀將 Take and do; to receive; a sign of the future.

꜀嫜 A husband's parents; to make obeisance to them.

꜀彰 Elegant composition; to manifest; exhibit.

꜀暲 Clear and bright.

꜀漳 Name of a stream.

꜀璋 A kind of sceptre made of chrysoprasus; a play thing.

꜀麞 A small species of deer.

꜂長 To increase by growth; to extend.

丈[5] A measure of ten cubits; an aged man.

仗[5] Weapons of war—as sword, spear, lance.

杖[5] A staff; a cudgel: to lean upon; hold; to beat with a staff; iron bar.

匠[5] A mechanic; artificer.

瘴[2] A distemper caused by pestilential vapors; a hot, feverish disease.

障[2] A separating dike; to separate; divide.

將[2] A general; captain.

獎[2] To assist; praise; encourage.

倀[2] Madly; blindly; to fall down.

悵[2] Regret; disappointment.

Ch'iàng.

꜀腸 Intestines; bowels; the seat of the affections.

꜀嬙 Female officers in the dynasty of Han.

꜀長 Long in time or space; a senior; superior.

꜀萇 Name of a plant.

꜀昌 Elegant; suitable; affluent; increasing.

꜀娼 A prostitute.

꜀猖 Wild and frightened; mad.

꜀菖 A water plant; sedge.

꜂廠 An open shed.

꜂氅 A bird's wing; a garment made of feathers.

倡[2] A showy person; singing girl; seducer; to accord with.

唱 To recite; sing.

Chiap.

捷 To obtain a victory; overcome; to complete; in haste.

洽 To blend with; instill gradually; to extend; saturated.

接 To receive; connect; come in succession; to unite.

Ch'iap.

妾 A concubine; an inferior wife.

竊 To steal; private; one's private opinion; to assume.

Chie.

招 To beckon; call by motion of the hand; to assume; confess.

樵 Fuel; a woodcutter.

蕉 A plantain; banana.

椒 Pepper.

照 To illumine; take care of; according to; like as.

譙 To censure; blame; to ridicule.

醮 To burn incense or victims & pour out oblations; to complete; to invite to take wine.

石 A stone.

借 To borrow or lend; to pretend; suppose.

質 The substantial part of; sincere; to realize; to substantiate.

Ch'ie.

笑 To laugh; deride.

蓆 A mat or carpet; large.

尺 A cubit.

Chnie.

章 A chapter; a prize essay; a complete piece.

樟 The camphor tree.

漿 Syrup; thick liquid; pus.

掌 The palm of the hand; to strike with the hand; to rule; to grasp.

槳 An oar; a short oar.

上 To ascend; go up; high.

癢 To itch; the itch.

醬 A kind of pickle; a mode of preserving meat, rice, &c.

Ch'nie.

墻 牆 A wall; that which defends.

鎗 A spear; lance; a tripod; a wine vessel.

匠 A mechanic; artificer.

搶 To seize by violence; to plunder.

象[5] An elephant.

Chien.

꜀顫 Trembling with cold; the head inclined to one side.

꜀鸇 A certain bird of prey.

꜀箋 To note down memoranda.

꜂殄 To end; terminate; destroy.

꜂畛 A dike that serves as a path and a division of fields; to terminate; to announce.

꜂疹 A disease that breaks out in pustules with fever; pox.

꜂紾 Bent; perverse; to twist; single garments.

꜂袗 A black garment; single raiment; garments with flowers.

꜂診 To examine; try or verify.

꜂趁 To walk briskly up to ; to embrace an opportunity.

꜂俴 Shallow; thin; thin metal.

꜂踐 To tread upon; to walk in a certain path.

꜂餞 To present with food or drink; to make a present.

꜂剪 To cut with scissors; shear.

꜂翦 Even and regular; scissors; to cut with scissors.

꜂燼 The residue of what is consumed by fire; ashes.

濺[5] A rapid purturbed current.

戰[2] To fight; war; battle; to be struck with fear.

Ch'ien.

꜀遷 To remove from one place to another; to change.

韆 Rope swinging for amusement.

꜀阡 A road running north and south; a road through the fields; luxuriant.

꜂淺 Shallow; superficial; easy.

꜂闡 To open; spread out; manifest.

Chiet.

即꜆ That is; then; forthwith; urgent.

Ch'iet.

切꜆ To cut; urgent; pressing; important; sincere; to spell words; the chief or important part of a thing in the whole.

Chim.

꜀斟 To pour out or into; to add; to deliberate.

꜂枕 A post or block to fasten cattle or horses to.

浸[2] To soak into; to soak.

濅[2] To water; to drench; to saturate; gradually

Ch'im.

꜀侵 To advance gradually; to invade secretly; to seek for to plunder.

尋 To search for.

撏 To take hold of; to draw.

深 Deep—as water, color, &c.; very; extremely.

寢 To sleep; to rest; a sleeping room.

Chin.

眞 True; sincere; genuine; truth.

津 A ford or ferry; a creek; to ford; to moisten.

薪 Fuel; brambles; to collect fuel.

榛 Trees; brushwood; a small fruit like a chestnut.

溱 Affluence; at ease; many; a multitude.

蓁 Exuberant foliage; a great accumulation; many.

臻 To extend to the utmost limit; highest degree.

搢 To insert; attach to; to introduce; to take.

拯 To deliver; draw out.

侲 Boys from ten to twelve years of age; good.

娠 To be pregnant; motion of the child in the womb.

振 To shake; excite; adjust; repair.

賑 Rich; to enrich; to supply the wants of; give to.

震 To shake; agitate; begin.

盡 To exhaust; finish; entirely; the extreme point.

進 To advance; to introduce; recommend, exert one's self.

薦 To introduce; recommend; pasture; grass.

荐 Grass; vegetables; pasture; to continue still as before.

晉 To increase; attach to; name of a Chinese dynasty.

縉 To attach to one; wrap around; carnation color; silk.

Ch'in.

臣 One who serves another; an officer under the Emperor.

秦 Title of the first universal monarch of China.

親 Affection for; one's own; near relations; to kiss.

嚫 To confer upon; bestow.

襯 Inner garments; to give to; bestow a largess.

Chio.

昭 Bright; splendid; light; to illumine.

焦 Burned; seared; vexatious; anxiety; distress.

僬 Clear discernment; having examined fully.

噍 To eat; chew; a hurried tone of voice.

憔 Lean from hunger and distress of mind.

椎 A bludgeon; club; hammer; mallet.

釗 Distant; to exert strength.

朝 Morning; to wait on the emperor or other high officers.

鳥 A bird; fowl.

詔 To declare; promulgate; teach; a proclamation

Ch'io.

朝 Court; a dynasty.

悄 Mournful; anxious; privately.

稍 In a small quantity; rather; gradually; a granary; the royal domains.

誚 Vexation; anxiety; distress.

嘲 To laugh; jest; ridicule.

Chip.

集 To collect; to mix.

執 To take hold of; grasp; apprehend; persecute.

縶 To tie; bind; fasten.

Ch'ip.

戢 To store up and lay aside weapons; put a stop to war.

楫 Trees in a forest; an oar.

緝 To follow in close succession; come often.

輯 To unite harmoniously; concord.

Chit.

疾 Urgent; vehement; to envy; to hate; disease; sick.

嫉 Jealous; envy.

蒺 A medicinal plant.

織 To weave.

脊 The spine; back; ridge of a house or mountain.

瘠 Lean; poor; to restrict.

鶺 A species of bird.

析 To split wood; to divide; to discriminate.

Ch'it.

七 Seven.

拭 To dust; wipe; rub; cleanse.

Chiu.

周 To provide for; to perform a circle; to complete; surround; a curve; circle.

賙 To bestow charity; relieve.

週 To turn or go round; circulate.

州 A province; a district.

洲 An island.

舟 A boat or vessel; to transfer.

輈 A certain pole in the fore part of a carriage.

酒 Wine; spirituous liquor.

肘 The fore arm; elbow; the muscles of the legs and arms

就 To go to; approach; immediately; then; to complete.

咒 To curse; to rail.

Ch'iu.

囚 To confine; imprison; a prison; a prisoner.

仇 To oppose; to return like for like; an enemy; a rival.

售 To sell; pay for.

雔 To wrangle; to hate; an enemy; hatred.

犨 A white cow; a cow lowing.

讐 To oppose; retaliate; hate; an enemy.

酬 To return the pledge or compliment in drinking; to recompense.

瘳 Convalescent; sudden removal of disease.

秋 Autumn;

揪 To seize; grasp; gather in the hand.

愀 Disconsolate; to change the countenance.

鞦 A wheel to sit on and turn round; a Chinese amusement.

鬚 The beard.

樹 A tree.

手 The hand.

醜 Deformed; hateful; shame; to hate; abhor.

Cho.

租 Grain paid as tax; tax; rent.

緅 Dark red color; dipped in red dye three times and then in black once.

鄹 Name of a country, where Confucius lived.

鄒 Name of a country.

祖 Ancestors; grandparents; to begin; the beginning.

驟 Swift; fleet; urgent; pressing.

Ch'o.

愁 Mournful; grieved.

粗 Coarse; vulgar; large.

麤 Same as the last; also to be afraid of and guard against.

醋[2] Vinegar; sour wine.

凑[2] Concurrence of circumstances; to collect and make up.

Chó.

꜀槽 A manger; a drain where liquor is run off; a place where wine is sold.

꜀艚 A small boat; a junk.

꜂棗 Dates; a species of cannarium.

꜂左 The left hand or side; a second or assistant; depraved; to degrade.

꜂阻 To hinder; stop; prevent.

꜂俎 A block on which meat is cut; a feast.

坐[5] To sit.

佐[5] To assist; an assistant.

助[5] To assist; succor; assistance.

座[5] A seat; a throne.

做[2] To make; to do; to be.

絕꜅ To break off; suspend; put an end to; a small quantity.

Ch'ó.

꜀剉 To trim off; chop to pieces; a mode of punishment.

꜀挫 To push down; break in pieces; maltreat.

꜀脞 Minced meat; minute; small bits.

꜀鋤 A hoe or iron instrument for turning up the ground.

꜀初 The first; beginning; to begin.

꜂楚 Brambles; a cluster of trees; sharp; painful.

꜂礎 The stone base of a pillar.

磋[2] To rub and polish.

鎈[2] Copper coin; money.

銼[2] A file; to rub.

錯[2] Mixed; confused; erroneous; mistaken.

撮꜅ A lump; small quantity.

撮꜅ To take with the fingers; to snatch; a small quantity.

蕞꜅ A bundle of reeds; to sprinkle wine in sacrifice, small.

Choi.

截꜅ To cut off; cut up; to trim.

節꜅ A festival; a set time.

Ch^{n}oi.

꜀前 Formerly; before.

Ch'^{n}oi.

꜀蠶 Silkworms.

千 A thousand; very many.

筅 A scrubber for cleaning rice; a broom.

Chok.

族 A kindred; family; clan; a class; a sort.

簇 Luxuriant plants; the metal point of an arrow.

鏃 Pointed; the point of an arrow.

足 The foot; enough; satisfied; complete.

祝 To bless; praise.

竺 A bamboo.

Ch'ok.

促 Near; close; urgent.

捉 To seize; grasp.

齪 Gnashing or grinding of the teeth; embarrassment.

蹙 Pressed upon; impelled; embarrassed; anxious.

噈 To expel the voice or breath; to taste; to lick.

蹴 Pressed upon; embarrassed; anxious.

矗 Upright; equal; equity; high.

躅 Footsteps; stamping with the foot.

觸 To gore; hit against; offend; oppose.

戳 To stamp with a seal; a seal; to stab.

Chong.

宗 Ancestors; an ancestral temple; a whole kindred or clan.

綜 Transverse threads in weaving; to collect together.

終 The end; termination; to end or terminate; to die.

螽 A species of locust.

蹤 A footstep; a trace.

總 All united together; the whole; general; altogether.

踵 The heel of the foot; to tread in the footsteps of.

從 To follow; comply with.

瘲 A disease; pain in the muscles and bones; rheumatism.

縱 Remiss; to connive at; although allowing it.

Ch'ong.

叢 欉 Crowded together; mixed assemblage; woody.

崇 Lofty; honorable; noble; to honor.

從 By; from; with; to follow.

꜀冲 Delicate; young; same as the next.

꜀沖 To agitate; shake; ascend; concord; deep; hollow.

꜀忡 Sorrowful; grieved.

꜀充 To fill; to carry to the utmost extent; sufficient; excellent; long; high.

꜀衷 Just and right; sincerity; moral rectitude; the heart, the mind; the center; inner garments.

꜀聰 Quickness of hearing and perception; discernment.

꜀怱 Agitation; hurry.

꜀衝 To excite; sudden motion; a path; a war chariot.

Chu.

꜀朱 Carnation or vermilion color.

꜀珠 A pearl; necklace; the ball of the eye.

꜀硃 Red oxide; vermilion.

꜀茱 Name of a medicine.

꜀銖 An ancient coin; a small coin.

꜀諸 Several; all; in; at; from.

꜀咀 To receive into the mouth and suck or taste.

꜀徂 To go; persevere; preserve.

覷' To spy out; look.

꜀沮 Water flowing into a pond, to overpass; to stop; injure.

꜀疽 A deep seated old sore.

꜀組 Silk fringe; silk cords to bind the hair.

꜀苴 Female hemp; the vegetable used in the soles of shoes.

꜀菹 Plants which grow in marshes.

꜀詛 Imprecations; to announce before the gods.

꜀趄 To walk with difficulty; having some impediment.

꜀諏 To take advice; to consult; to give information.

꜀陬 A corner or angle, as of a wall; to collect together and reside in.

꜂主 A lord; master; to rule.

住[5] To stop; to dwell; halt.

炷[5] The light or wick of a lamp.

駐[5] To stop and rest; a temporary residence.

聚[5] To assemble; to collect; to dwell; a crowd.

祚[5] Wealth; happiness; divine blessings; posterity.

胙[5] To offer flesh in sacrifice; offerings; to reward; blessings.

蚱[5] Name of an insect and of a fish.

酢[5] To return the pledge in drinking wine; to repay.

阼[2] The steps or mat appropriated to the chief person in sacrifices.

注[2] To lead; fix; that to which the mind is directed; record.

蛀[2] An insect which destroys wood.

註[2] To define; explain; illustrate; a definition; commentary.

足[2] Outward appearance; abundance.

鑄[2] To melt metals; to coin; to cast.

蠹[2] An insect that breeds in wood and books; a moth.

Ch'u.

徐 Leisurely; tardy; slow; steady; tranquil.

蜍 A species of frog.

除 The space inside the door but outside the screen; to remove, as disease, evil, &c., besides; to leave out.

芻 / 蒭 Plants; grass: to cut grass.

趨 To go in haste.

雛 Young fowls; chickens.

騶 To run swiftly; fleet.

鶵 Name of a bird.

取 To take; receive; assume; to approve; to be sought after.

娶 To take a wife; to marry.

處 A place; dwelling; to dwell; to place; decide; award.

厝[2] To place; to put; a large coarse stone.

措[2] To place; arrange; employ; a place.

趣[2] Celerity; quick; agreeableness; accommodating.

Chù

藷 The potato genus.

書 To write; a book or letter.

咨 To deliberate; consult; public documents; to sight; lament.

姿 Flattering; elegant; gait manner.

粢 Grain; a cake.

資 Goods; things necessary for one's own use.

諮 To plan; scheme; to ask questions

趑 To walk with difficulty; to make little progress.

茲 This; here; now.

孳 To bear or produce; ardent affection for; diligence.

鷀 Name of a water bird.

꜀緇 Dark colored silk.

꜀錙 Name of an ancient coin equal to eight Chinese ounces.

꜀貲 Wealth; property; money; a fine; to redeem with money.

꜀之 Sign of the possessive case; of; him; it; them; to go.

꜀芝 The budding forth of plants; a plant said to be incorruptible used as an emblem of happiness.

꜀孜 Sincere attachment to; diligent.

꜀⿰衤齊 To sew garments; to seam.

꜂子 A child; son; sages; an honorable appellation; a diminutive.

꜂仔 To sustain or attend to the duties devolving on one.

꜂耔 To weed; pluck out weeds.

꜂煮 To boil; cook.

꜂梓 Name of a valuable wood; to cut characters in wood.

自⁵ From; self; one's self; of itself; naturally; of course.

洎² Soup; a thick substance used in sacrifices.

滋² To increase; overflow; rich; to enrich; confused.

恣² Intrigue; levity; lewdness; profligate.

胾² A preparation of meat cut and minced.

Ch'ù.

꜁慈 Love; compassion; kind; compassionate.

꜁玼 Fresh and good; a fresh stone.

꜁疵 Disease; fault of temper; contracted feeling.

磁 Name of a stone.

꜁訾 To slander; dislike; animosity; licentious; to think.

꜁雌 }
꜁鴜 } The female of birds and fowls.

꜁徐 A dignified walk; leisurely; tranquil; sedate.

꜂此 This; these; here; now.

꜂鼠 A mouse; rat.

次² Second to; next in order; inferior; a place; an inn.

茨² Thatch; thorns; to collect; accumulate.

Chua.

꜁蛇 A serpent; snake; viper.

꜂紙 Paper.

Ch'ua.

꜁⿱⿱爫冖子 An heir; to inherit; to succeed.

‘歪 Aslant; distorted; depraved; incorrect.

蔡^{2} Plants or herbs; a proper name.

Ch^{n}ua.

‚泉 A fountain or spring of water; source; origin.

‘盞 A small cup for wine, oil &c.

賤^{2} Mean; low; cheap.

Ch‘^{n}ua.

閂^{2} To shut; bar a door; to fasten.

Chuak.

蠋$_{5}$ Name of an insect resembling a silk worm.

濁$_{5}$ Muddy; foul water.

濯$_{5}$ A fat, sleek appearance; to wash.

Chuan.

‹專 One; single; oneness of pursuit; to assume; usurp.

‹耑 The head or commencement; a hollow vessel.

‹湍 A narrow passage for water; rapids; to flow against.

‹顓 To regulate; direct; to pay close attention; correct; eminent.

‚遄 Haste; speed; to go and return with speed.

‘轉 To turn; revolve; to turn about.

‘囀 Modulations of voice; chirping.

撰^{5} To arrange; prepare; make; compose.

譔^{5} To make, write or compose a book.

饌^{5} Food; to eat and drink.

攢^{2} To collect; assemble; to cover a coffin without interring.

Ch‘uan.

‚全 Complete; entire; to finish.

‚牷 A bullock without blemish for sacrifice.

‚痊 To cure disease; convalescent; cured.

‚筌 A bamboo instrument for catching fish.

‚銓 To weigh; discriminate and select; to examine.

‹川 A stream; flowing; to flow.

‹穿 To bore through; perforate; to put on clothes.

‘喘 To pant; breathe short, as in asthma.

竄^{2} To run away and hide; pusilanimous; to seduce to vice.

串^{2} To connect as beads; to conspire; unite as accomplices.

篡^{2} To rebel and sieze by violence; to usurp.

爨² A furnace; fireplace; to eat.

Chuang.

꜀裝 To bind round or up; to dress; to put into a box.

狀⁵ From; fashion; to accuse; a letter; petition; a bed.

Ch'uang.

闖² To strike or hit against; to bolt out or in.

Chuat.

咄꜆ Mutual conversation; to rail or laugh at.

拙꜆ Unskillful; stupid.

茁꜆ To bud forth.

詘꜆ Stammering; to talk slowly.

啜꜆ To weep and sob; incessant talking; to taste.

惙꜆ Mournful; grieved.

掇꜆ To sieze; plunder.

歠꜆ To sip; swill down soup.

Ch'uat.

輟꜆ To desist; stop.

Chue.

罪⁵ Crime; sin; to criminate.

贅⁵ To give a pledge; addition; repetition; tautology.

嘬⁵ To eat with greediness; many eating all at once.

最² Important in the highest degree; superlative.

Ch'ue.

꜀吹 To breathe; to blow.

꜀炊 To boil or dress food by fire.

꜂髓 Marrow inside of bones; brains.

Chui.

꜀堆 A heap of earth; a pile; to accumulate; promiscuous.

꜀椎 A bludgeon; club; to strike; blunt; stupid.

꜀錐 An awl; sharp point.

꜀凸 Protuberant; jutting out; convex; a hillock.

꜂水 Water; tide.

꜂祟 Calamities; ill omens.

悴⁵ Grief visible in the countenance.

猝⁵ Abrupt; fierce; impetuous

瘁⁵ Labor; toil; pain; disease.

萃⁵ To collect; a rustling sound, as of leaves.

誶[5] To vilify; rail at; reprove; accuse: to interrogate.

醉[2] Intoxicated; stupified; highly fascinated.

Ch'ui.

꜀推 To push; impel; lead on; trace out; investigate; to overcome; excuse; to put off.

꜀睢 To stare; look angrily.

꜀崔 Lofty and large; mountainous.

꜀催 To urge; importune; impel.

꜂惴 Mournful; grief; difficulties.

꜂揣 To measure; try; essay; to put away.

꜂毳 Fur; down; a certain cap or crown; delicate.

嘴[2] The lips; mouth; beak of a bird; a snout.

碎[2] To rub or grind; break to pieces; small fragments.

粹[2] Unmixed; pure; complete; to rub or grind.

翠[2] Name of a bird with green feathers.

Chun.

꜀船 A ship; junk; boat; to follow the stream.

꜀尊 To honor; respect; honorable; venerable.

꜀蹲 A proud attitude; to sit in a reclining posture; to collect.

꜀遵 To follow; obey; comply with; obedience.

꜀樽, ꜀罇 } A wine vessel; luxuriant; to desist; stop.

꜀逡 To retire back abashed; to refuse.

꜂准 To approve; grant; allow; to decide.

꜂準 To equalise; adjust; weigh; measure.

撙[2] To adjust; direct; put in order; restrain.

俊[2] Superior talent; a high degree of excellence.

峻[2] Illustrious; high; dangerous.

梭[2] Name of a wood.

浚[2] Deep water; profound.

畯[2] A husbandman; an officer who presides over land.

竣[2] To complete one's work; to finish; retire and stand still.

餕[2] Hot food; the remains of food.

駿[2] A fine horse; dignified; illustrious; elegant.

雋[2] Beautiful; fine; good; fat

鐫[2] To carve; engrave; cut letters or words.

Chʻun.

存 To watch over and take care of; to preserve; retain.

春 The season of spring.

鶉 A bird of the quail species.

蠢 Simple; foolish; to move; crawl.

忖 To consider; reckon; conjecture; surmise.

舛 Confused; mixed; erroneous; to oppose.

寸 A Chinese inch.

Chᵘng.

庄 A farm-house; cottage; a country village.

粧 Ornamented; painted face; dowry; a lady's toilet.

莊 Grave; stern; firm; sedate.

妝 Dressed; ornamented; face painted; dowry.

磚 Brick; tile; square earthern ware.

狀 To declare; accuse; a letter; petition.

鑽 To bore into; search out; an instrument to bore with.

葬 To inter the dead; bury.

Chʻᵘng.

床 A bed or couch; to rest; eight cubits.

倉 A granary; storehouse; the overseer.

瘡 An ulcer; sore.

村 A hamlet; a village.

刺 To pierce; stab; to reprehend; satirise; to work with a needle; embroider.

Chut.

秫 A certain grain; a viscous substance made from grain.

糯 Name of a particular kind of rice.

卒 Soldiers; lictors; to cease; finish; die; haste; sudden; urgent.

倅 To assist; an assistant officer; a hundred men.

捽 To lead; direct; to follow sudden; prompt.

蟀 A cricket.

Chʻut.

出 To go out; to put out; eject.

E.

耶 An interrogative particle.

啞 Dumb; the noise of laughing; the voice of birds.

瘂 Dumb; the back of the neck.

厄 Knots of trees; to oppress; to be ill used; in distress.

扼 To seize with the hand; grasp; to pull.

軛 A yoke.

En.

楹 A post; pillar; support; rafters.

Ek.

懌 Pleased; gratified.

斁 To open; to destroy; put an end to.

繹 To arrange; state or explain; proceed in order; to end.

譯 To translate; a translation.

億 A hundred thousand; an immense, indefinite number.

憶 To remember; to consider.

臆 The breast; full; swelled out; puffed up.

溢 To overflow; inundate; a certain measure.

鎰 A certain quantity or weight; 20 or 30 ounces.

掖 To support or lead by the arm; the arm-pit.

液 Saliva or secretion from the nose; dregs.

腋 Under the arm; arm-pit; the side; near to one.

弋 An arrow with a string attached to it; to seize upon; to take possession of.

弈 A chess-boad; to play chess, large; extensive; of long continuance.

易 Change; alteration; transmutation.

翼 The wings of a fowl.

Eng.

英 Great talent and virtue; excellent; luxuriant; flourishing; English, England.

鍈 The sound of a bell.

嬰 A sucking child; a female infant; to add; to bind.

孾 A child.

攖 To take hold of with the fingers.

櫻 Name of a fruit; a cherry.

癭 A swelling in the neck.

纓 Strings or tassels; cap strings.

鸚 Name of a bird; a parrot.

膺 The breast; near related to; to sustain; to receive.

鷹 The eagle; hawk; falcon.

鶯 A certain bird; variegated feathers.

湧 To rise or bubble up as water from a spring.

孕 Pregnant; the fetus.

用 To use; employ; by; with.

應 Right; proper; ought; to answer; correspond to.

Gai.

碍 礙 To impede; hinder; oppose; an impediment.

Gau.

樂 Instrumental music.

Ge.

牙 A tooth; the incisor teeth.

芽 To bud forth; to begin; a bud; a germ.

衙 A civil or military court; a government office.

嫛 A woman affecting pretty airs.

Gek.

玉 A gem; a precious stone.

獄 A prison; jail.

Gi.

疑 To doubt; suspect; dislike; doubt; suspicion.

Gia.

呀 An interjection; tone of alarm.

訝 To deem strange; express surprise; to receive a visitor.

迓 To go forth to meet; to descend to.

Go.

吳 To talk loud; boast; a proper name.

蜈 A species of centipede.

悞 誤 Deceitful; false; erroneous; to err; fail; deceive; to lead astray.

Gó.

鵝 A goose.

餓 Hungry; hunger; famine.

Goi.

倪 An appellation of small children; to benefit; a limit.

藝 Business or occupation of life; any art or craft; the polite arts.

Gu.

牛 A cow; the bovine species.

Gù.

語 Words; speech; discourse; to speak; tell; discuss.

御 To drive a horse and carriage; whatever is done by the emperor is designated by this word.

禦 To oppose; hinder; cause to stop; to sacrifice.

馭 A horse keeper or driver; a charioteer.

Gua.

外 External; outside; over and above.

Gue.

月 The moon; a month.

Há.

合 To join; accord with; suit; united; agreeable to.

Hai.

咳 To cough; laughing of an infant; an infant.

孩 A small child.

欬 To belch from the stomach; cough; to call out aloud.

胲 The great toe; to prepare.

骸 The bones of the body; the body.

諧 To pair with; agree; harmony; peace.

海 The sea; an arm of the sea.

醢 Minced meat preserved in some liquor.

駭 Suddenly alarmed, agitated; surprised; to sound an alarm.

械 Weapons—as lance, spear, &c.; manacles.

亥 The last of the 12 horary characters, from 9 to 11 P.M.

懈 The heart loose and inattentive; remiss; careless.

邂 To meet without appointment; accidentally; pleased.

害 To injure; be injurious; hurtful; calamitous.

Hák.

學 To learn; receive instruction; to practice; a school.

壑 A ditch; valley; creek; bed of a torrent; a pit.

洫 A ditch for water in a field; moat round a city; to overflow.

涸 Dried up; exhausted.

Hám.

咸 All; the whole number; completely.

諴 Union; harmony; sincere; cordiality; to excite.

函 To contain; enfold; an envelope; a letter.

涵 To steep or soak in water; to contain.

啣 To contain or carry in the mouth; to sustain; receive.

銜 To contain in the mouth; a horse's bit; to guide; control.

含 To hold in the mouth; to restrain; endure; forbear.

頷 The jaws; chin.

蚶 Name of an insect.

酣 Excited by wine but not drunken; cheerful.

憾 To feel indignation, resentment or regret.

陷 To fall down; sink; to be ruined; to ruin or injure.

喊 To call aloud.

撼 To shake; to move.

Hán.

寒 Cold; winter; poor; solitary.

翰 Wings of a bird; ornaments; a pencil; quill; high; white.

韓 A wall round a well; name of an ancient state.

扞 A shield; to shield; keep off; oppose; desist.

罕 Infrequent; rare; seldom.

閈 A door or gate; a lane; to shut or close.

僴 A martial, commanding appearance.

看 To watch; look after.

悍 Ardent disposition; energy; fierce.

捍 To grasp; lift up; shake; to drive away; resist.

稈 Stubble; straw; dry stalks of grain.

旱 Drought; want of rain.

趕 To pursue after.

挭 To lead or drag along by force; to oppose.

限 To impede; to limit; to set a time; a limit.

漢 Name of an ancient Chinese dynasty; name of a river.

Háng.

行 A street; a factory; a storehouse; a kind or sort.

降 To yield; submit; be conquered.

杭 Name of a place.

航 A boat or ship; to sail in a boat or ship.

項 The back of the neck; large; a sort; species; item.

巷 A public path, lane or street.

Háp.

盍 Why? why not?

瘟 Shortness of breath; disease of the throat; lameness.

瞌 Sleepy; desire to sleep.

海上絲綢之路文獻集成 科技與文化編

Hát.

曷 Why? why not? to intimidate, as by a sharp question.

喝 To thirst; a guttural sound; an angry exclamation.

褐 Hair cloth; coarse cloth; poor.

謁 To state; to declare; to petition; to visit a superior.

害 An interrogative particle; who? what? why?

瞎 Blind; ignorant.

轄 Noise of wheels; the iron at the end of an axle; to rule; regulate; authority.

豁 A valley; enlarge; liberal; to open and expand.

Hau.

毫 豪 A small hair or down; small; very little.

豪 Eminent talents and virtue; great superiority; chief.

濠 A ditch round a city wall; name of a river and province.

昊 Appearance of summer; brilliant.

鴞 Name of a bird, not eatable and of unpleasant note.

號 The noise of weeping and crying; the roar of a tiger.

饕 Gluttonous; greedy; rapacious.

顥 Light and splendor of the sky; vast; numerous; happy.

哮 Calling out; a loud cry; roar of animals.

吼 The voice of any animal.

唬 To roar like a tiger; to intimidate.

浩 A deluge of water; vast; abundant; overflowing.

校 To compare; examine; a public school.

傚 To imitate; to regard as a law or rule.

候 To wait for; to inquire; expect.

鱟 The king crab.

効 To apply one's strength in obedience to some order or in imitation of a pattern; to aim.

效 Like; to learn of; imitate; effort; merit; efficacious.

好 To desire.

孝 Filial regard, obedience and service from children to parents.

He.

蝦 Lobsters; prawns; shrimps the cancer species.

嗄 Hoarseness; change of voice.

夏 Summer; name of an ancient Chinese dynasty.

厦 A piazza; side apartment of a house.

Hek.

黑	Black dark.
赫	Manifest ; plain ; clear ; red hot ; to burn ; anger.
嚇	To threaten ; the tone or voice of threatening.
核	The seed or kernel in fruit or grain ; the nucleus.
覈	To investigate ; put aside all glosses and ascertain the fact.

Heng.

刑	Punishment ; to punish ; a law.
型	To mould ; a mould ; pattern ; example.
形	Form ; figure ; bodily shape ; that which is visible.
恆	Constant ; perpetual ; unchanging.
行	To act ; do ; perform.
興	To rise ; flourish ; prosper ; to set up ; exalt ; high.
胸	The breast ; mind.
享	Pervading ; going through with ; success.
馨	Odors or spices ; perfume.
悻	Anger ; vexation ; very.
幸[5]	Fortunate ; lucky ; happy.
倖[5]	To be unremitting in the pursuit of gain.
行[5]	Actions ; conduct.
杏[5]	A sour plum ; an almond tree.

Hi.

奚	How ? why ? a servant.
徯	To wait ; stop with expectation.
希	To hope ; expect ; few ; seldom ; to stop ; scatter.
俙	To put on an honest face, when the heart is dishonest.
唏	To sigh or moan without shedding tears ; to pant ; snore.
欷	To sob ; timid ; snoring.
稀	Careless ; remiss ; few ; scattered ; apart.
絺	A species of hemp or flax, or the cloth made from it.
羲	Name of the founder of the Chinese empire.
犧	Victims for sacrifice ; pure ; spotless.
嘻	The sound of social pleasure ; laughing ; a sigh ; alas !
嬉	Handsome ; to ramble for pleasure.
熺	The joyful light of the stars ; to burn ; purify ; illumine.
熹	To apply fire to ; to heat ; hot ; pervading as light.

禧 Felicitous; happy; to announce or pray to the gods.

兮 A tone of interrogation or admiration.

頤 The chin; side of the mouth; to feed; nourish; deep.

熙 Light; splendor; increasing; flourishing; to dry.

醯 Sour.

喜 To be pleased; rejoice; to give joy to; to desire.

携 To lead by the hand; to take up.

繫 To connect or be connected; to follow in succession; related to; to bind or tie.

係 Is; am; to bind; connect; succeed to.

曳 To trail; an easy, leisurely gait; to drag the heel.

拽 To lead; draw; pull.

戲 A theatrical exhibition; to play or trifle with; to mock.

Hⁿi.

弦 The string of a bow or of a musical instrument.

絃 Strings of a musical instrument.

耳 The ear; an ear or handle of a cup, pitcher, etc.

Hia.

瑕 A stone fractured; error; fault; rent; split; remote.

瘕 A chronic disease of the abdomen; worms.

遐 Distant; remote.

霞 A halo; vapor; fog; variegated clouds.

靴 Boots.

下 Below; inferior; to descend; cause to descend.

瓦 Tiles; brick; earthernware.

暇 At leisure; unoccupied.

蟻 An ant; used for I.

額 The forehead; front; an inscription.

役 A servant; under officer; police runner.

歇 To desist; stop; rest; terminate.

Hⁿia.

邢 Name of a person and of a place.

兄 An older brother.

Hiam.

嫌 Jealousy; suspicious; to dislike.

獫 A hound; dog of chase.

險 Difficult; dangerous; deep abyss; steep; lofty.

Hiàng.

享 To enjoy; receive; accept; to offer to a superior.

響 Sound; noise; clamor; echo.

饗 To entertain a guest; to offer sacrifice.

向 Towards; directed towards the object to which the mind or desire is directed.

餉 Provisions for laborers or the army; duties paid to government.

嚮 Over against; towards; to press on towards.

Hiap.

協 Union; harmony; to unite.

恊 Fear; apprehension; to intimidate.

脇 脅 The sides of the body; ribs; to gather together; to receive.

夾 To carry secretly; hold fast; grasp; by the side.

俠 Generous and disinterested; to labor for the good of others.

挾 To conceal; protect; carry under the arm; store up.

梜 Wooden rails; sticks used as nippers; variegated wood.

浹 To penetrate with moisture; enrich; to instil instruction.

狹 Narrow; confined on each side.

蛺 A small butterfly or moth.

陜 Confined; a narrow pass.

叶 To accord with; unite; to rhyme with.

Hie.

頁 The head.

葉 Leaves of trees; foliage.

Hnie.

香 Incense; perfume.

鄉 A village; 12,500 families; former.

Hien.

俔 Like; to be compared to.

睍 Small pretty eyes; staring; to look furtively.

賢 A wise man; a sage; virtuous; worthy.

閑 A barrier; fence; a fold; to protect; great.

閒 Leisure; repose; unemployed; a crevice; interval.

嫻 Elegant; accustomed to.

譠 False; irregular; clamorous.

玄 Azure; the color of the sky; a dark sombre color.

伭 The strings of a bow.

炫 Luminous; splendid.

眩 Eyes wandering about; disorderly; disrespectful.

衒 Boasting; pedantic; offering for sale.

現 Manifestation; to manifest; exhibit; plain; clear.

顯 Light; manifest; apparent; to illustrate; exhibit.

絢 An ornamental binding or sash; black; swift.

憲 A ruler; officer; magistrate.

獻 To offer; present to a superior; to sacrifice.

釁 To smear with blood; fumigate; embalm; crime; wars; quarreling.

Hiet.

羯 A strong violent sheep; a ram; to castrate.

蝎 A scorpion.

Him.

熊 A bear.

歆 To desire; long for.

Hio.

僥 False; not genuine.

徼 To go round, either to ward off, circumvent or obtain; to assume; a fence.

邀 To screen; invite; seek to obtain; to want.

梟 A bird said to be cruel to its parents; strong; wicked; to hang a man's head on a pole.

曉 Light; clear; intelligent; morning; to understand.

Hiok.

郁 Elegant; name of a place.

勗 To stimulate to exertion.

馥 Fragrant odoriferous effluvia.

頊 Serious, attentive manner; gravity.

毓 To train up; educate; cause to grow.

旭 The light of morning; the rising sun.

Hiong.

雄 The male of fowls; bold; daring; violent.

凶 Great wickedness; evil; calamity; to ruin.

兇 Malevolent; cruel; fear.

酗 Drunk; in rage and mad with intoxication.

匈 The breast; thorax.

洶 Sound of water bubbling up from a spring or flowing fast

Hip.

翕 To unite together; harmonize; move; excite; abounding.

噏 To inhale; suck; drink.

搧 To strike, pull or drag.

歙 To snuff up the nose.

Hiu.

休 To cease; rest; repudiate; congratulate.

咻 To call to; to call in a confused manner; to mourn.

貅 A certain animal said to devour tigers.

鵂 A certain ominous bird.

幽 Shady; hidden; deep recess; retirement.

攸 To travel on water; cheerful; remote; who or which.

悠 Mournful; thoughtful; alas! remote; vast; at leisure.

麀 A roe; a female deer.

H^n iu.

朽 Rotten wood; offensive smell; to fail; rot; be forgotten.

復 Again; to return; send back; to answer.

臭 / 嗅 A strong smell; offensive; to smell.

Ho.

侯 A prince; viceroy.

褑 A small garment.

餱 Dry provisions; food previously dressed.

戶 A door; a family; to protect; chief.

戽 To take out with the hand or with a ladle; a ladle.

后 A prince; a queen; to succeed to; after.

逅 To meet by accident; gratified; insincere.

雨 Rain.

H^n o.

虎 A tiger.

否 No; not; not so.

Hó.

何 Which? who? what? how?

河 A river.

好 Good.

和 To respond; modify; cause to unite.

賀 To congratulate; to carry a burden; to bear.

號 A title; signature; appellation; trumpet; to cry.

耗 To injure; diminish; spoilt; confused.

訛 False; to spread a false report; to excite.

鶴 A bird that flies high, resembling a stork.

海上絲綢之路文獻集成 科技與文化編

Hoi.

蟹 A crab; lobster.

Hok.

伏 To lie prostrate on the face; hide; submit; secrete.

或 Uncertain; perhaps; either; or; this or that.

域 A boundary; a state; nation; the world; universe.

惑 To delude; tempt; excite doubt; cause to err.

棫 A bush of small thorny plants.

緎 A seam; to seam.

閾 The threshold of a door.

斛 A measure containing ten *tau;* to measure.

服 The abdomen; substantial; rich; to serve, to wait on; endure.

復 Again; to reiterate; restore; return.

幅 A roll; a piece of cloth or paper.

福 Divine protection; happiness; a blessing.

愎 Perverse; self-willed; resisting reproof.

蝠 A flying animal; a snake.

輻 The axle of a carriage.

蝮 Name of several insects and reptiles, as locusts, snakes.

複 Double garments.

覆 To subvert; ruin; defeat; to investigate; to overshadow and protect.

Hong.

弘 The sound of a bow string; great; large; to enlarge.

泓 Deep; clear; profound.

宏 Rest; repose; the echo in a large house; vast; large.

閎 The gate of a street or lane; the bar of a gate; wide; great.

洪 A deluge; great; vast.

烘 The flame of a torch.

鴻 Name of a bird similar to a goose; vast; large.

丰 Herbage shooting forth; a fine countenance; plump.

夆 To descend; submit; to cause to descend.

峯 The peak or summit of a hill.

烽 A hollow brick pyramid filled with combustables to be set on fire as a signal.

鋒 The point of a weapon, pencil or tongue; van of an army.

封 That which is given by the emperor or received from him; to receive; grant.

風 Custom; temper; spirit; disposition; wind.

英漢潮州方言字典

瘋 A kind of leprosy.

豐 Large numerous; affluent; exuberant; flourishing.

轟 The noise of carriages or of cannon.

蚌 An oyster from which pearls are procured.

俸 The salary to government officers.

棒 A staff; club.

蓁 Copious; luxuriant; substantial.

奉 To receive or offer in a respectful manner.

捧 To offer up with both hands; to receive in both hands.

鳳 An imaginary bird of good omen; a divine bird.

諷 To recite; compare and satirise; poignant allusions; satire.

哄 Voice of a crowd; to cheat; beguile; deceive.

鬨 To fight; the noise of fighting.

逢 To meet with; to occur; to run against; great, wide; to happen.

Hu.

符 To correspond; fit; to be credible; a book; charms.

互 Fitting into each other; mutual; reciprocal.

胡 An interrogative particle; how? why? remote; pepper.

椒 Pepper.

湖 A lake.

猢 An animal resembling a monkey.

瑚 Coral.

糊 Paste; to paste; daub; confused; stupid.

葫 A gourd or melon.

蝴 A butterfly.

餬 Food; gruel; congee; to depend on others for food.

鳧 A wild duck.

怙 To lean upon; support or be supported; a mother.

壺 A cup or pot for wine, tea &c.; name of an office.

狐 An animal possessed by demons; suspicious.

夫 A respectful appellation; a husband; a wife; used to introduce a new subject.

扶 To assist; support; protect.

砆 A certain valuable stone.

芙 Name of a flower.

鈇 A kind af axe or hatchet.

乎 A tone of interrogation, doubt or admiration.

꜀虖 To call out; a tone of lamentation; a sigh.

꜀嘑 To call out aloud; to speak angrily.

꜀嫭 Handsome; good; to boast of beauty.

꜀罅 Cracked, as an earthen vessel; rent; a crevice.

꜀膚 The skin; minced meat; beautiful; large.

꜀敷 To state before a sovereign; to diffuse by imperial orders.

꜀孚 Belief; trust; confidence; to hatch; nourish.

꜀俘 To take; take in war; a prisoner.

꜀桴 A raft; a certain beam in a house; a drumstick.

꜀傅 To annex; anoint; insert names; arrange; collect; a tutor.

꜀腐 Corrupted; rotten; broken; castrated.

꜂府 A book-store; a study; to collect; a place to meet in; the officers of the treasury; an officer.

꜂俯 To stoop the head and bend forward, to condescend.

꜂腑 The viscera; heart, lungs, liver, stomach, &c.

꜂釜 A vase without feet; a vessel to measure with.

꜂黼 Black and white; variegated; embroidered.

負[5] To bear on the back; to turn the back upon; ungrateful; to fail; render nugatory.

阜[5] A mound of earth; a hill; large; abundant.

煦[5] To boil; to heat; genial warmth; kind.

婦[5] A married woman; a wife; a woman; beautiful.

弣[2] The middle part of a bow which is taken in the hand.

拊[5] To apply the hand to; to beat; strike; a handle.

附[5] To be near to; lean against; to annex; to attach to, as to a party.

駙[5] An assistant horse.

矱[5] A marking line; to measure; adjust with a line.

穫[5] To cut down and gather in grain.

護[5] To watch over, assist and guard; name of an office.

鑊[5] An iron boiler without feet.

輔[5] The jaw bones; to assist; support.

訃[2] To announce the death of a person; to go hastily.

赴[2] To go to in person; to go speedily.

付[2] To offer; give; deliver to.

咐[2] To blow with the breath; to caution; to charge.

副[2] A second; an assistant; to assist; examine; inform; a suit of things.

賦[2] To exact; receive; give; to disturb; diffuse.

Hù.

魚 A fish.

漁 To fish; catch fish.

虛 Empty; vacant; unmeaning.

噓 To blow; breathe gently; recommend; speak in favor of.

墟 A mountain; a common; a place of concourse.

歔 Fearful; timid; to cry; to sigh; tone of sighing.

翊 To flap the wings; to assist.

詡 Boasting talk; to speak clearly and boldly; wide spreading.

許 To accede to; grant; permit; to promise; give.

Hua.

吪 Gaping; to arouse; agitate; threaten; convert; false.

Hue.

回 To revolve; turn round; return; curved; a chapter or section.

徊 Pacing back and forth in suspense or hesitation; irresolute; undetermined.

廻 To bend; turn round; irresolute; unsettled.

洄 An eddy; running back.

茴 Fragrant plants; a medicinal plant.

花 A flower; pleasure.

灰 Ashes; cinders; lime.

火 Fire; heat; to burn.

伙 A comrade; messmate.

夥 Many; a company; partners.

會 To assemble; associate; an association; to understand, a Church.

化 Change; mutation; to transform; reform.

貨 Articles of commerce; goods; to sell; bribe; expend.

悔 To be indignant; regret; repent; repentance.

晦 Last quarter of the moon; foggy; dim; obscure; evening.

誨 To instruct; admonish; induce; instruction.

血 Blood.

Hⁿue.

橫 A cross-bar; cross-wise; perverse; unreasonable.

Hui.

缶 A vessel of earthern-ware; a jar or basin.

揮 Impetuous effort; to shake; scatter; sprinkle; to move with the hand.

暉 Luminous; splendid.

翬 To fly rapidly with a noise.

輝 Fire; light; splendor; to shine.

非 Wrong; shameless; low; not.

扉 Folding doors made of wood.

騑 The two outer horses in a coach of four.

霏 Rain and snow; sleet.

妃 Royal concubines.

麾 A banner with which signals are made; to make a signal; speed.

匪 Not; not right; vagabonds; banditti.

悱 Endeavoring to speak out but unable.

棐 Name of a beautiful wood.

斐 Streaks or veins; variegated; fine and delicate.

翡 A small bird with reddish feathers.

腓 The calf of the leg; disease; change; to shun.

菲 Name of a vegetable; fasting; straw sandals.

蜚 Name of a disagreeable insect which destroys clothes, grain, furniture, &c.

誹 To speak against; slander.

卉 Plants; herbs; trees; thirty.

虺 A long snake; a man's name.

燬 Fire; a blaze.

毀 譭 To break in pieces; to ruin or be ruined; to slander; vilify.

彗 A comet; name of a plant.

嘒 Small; delicate; a soft, harmonious sound; clear; bright.

慧 Intelligent; clever; ingenious.

惠 Benevolence; kind; to bestow largesses; to show tenderness to the people.

繐 A kind of fine, open, cool cloth; cloth used in mourning.

蕙 A certain fragrant plant which grows in marshes.

肺 The lungs; the mental viscera.

費 To scatter wealth; expend; liberal; expense; waste; to hurt; injure.

廢 To fall to ruins; to fail; to annul; lay aside.

諱 To shun; avoid; dread; the name of a deceased person.

H^{n}ui.

懸 To suspend, physically or morally.

Hun.

雲 Clouds; fog.

꜀焚 To burn; consume by fire.

꜀渾 Water and mud; foul; confused; foolish; the whole.

꜀痕 A wrinkle in the flesh; a cut; a sore.

꜀魂 The spirit; soul; the spiritual part of *Iang*.

꜀馴 A gentle horse; yielding; docile; benign; harmless.

꜀昏 Twilight; obscure; indistinct.

꜀婚 Marriage; the bride's relations; dowry.

꜀惛 Intellectual darkness; confused ideas; forgetfulness.

꜀閽 To shut the gate at evening; a porter.

꜀分 To divide; distribute; give; a part; portion.

꜀吩 To snort; rage.

꜀紛 Many; confused; perplexed; hurry; bustle.

꜀芬 A bud first opening; to develope; harmonious.

꜀鼢 A field rat; a mole.

꜀葷 Odoriferous vegetables, as onions; strong meat.

꜂憤, ꜂忿 } Angry; vexed; indignation; anger; resentment; zeal; cruel.

꜂粉 Meal; flour; dust; powder for the face; to apply a color.

꜂朌 A large or numerous appearance; to distribute.

꜂悃 To plan; deliberate; sincere; faithful.

混꜄ Confused and in disorder; foul; dull.

溷꜄ Muddy water; unclean; impure; a privy.

訓꜄ To instruct; exhort; explain; instruction; doctrine.

奮꜄ Impetuous effort; to excite; to press forward to.

Hùn.

꜀殷 Diligent; flourishing; right; name of an ancient dynasty.

꜀慇 Mournful; careful.

꜀忻, ꜀欣, ꜀惞 } Joy; delight; to be pleased; to rejoice.

꜀掀 To pull or drag about; to lay hold of; grasp.

꜀軒 A carriage; the high front of a carriage; play; enjoyment.

꜀熏 Vapor; fumes; steam; to give offence to.

꜀勳 Well-deserving; loyal; meritorious.

꜀壎 A certain instrument of music.

꜀燻 To fumigate; to evaporate; apply fire to.

薰 Fragrance of plants; fragrant plants.

很 Disobedient; quarrelsome.

狠 Sign of the superlative degree; very.

恨 Indignation; anger; regret; repentance.

Hut.

佛 Buddha; examine; to turn aside; unreasonable; great.

核 The kernel, seed or stone in fruit; the truth or verity.

忽 惚 To forget; make light of; to do carelessly; suddenly; unexpectedly.

笏 A flattened reed; ivory or stone used as a badge of office.

弗 A strong negative or prohibitative particle; no; not.

咈 To deny; refuse; oppose; perverse.

彿 Resembling; an image or likeness.

怫 Mournful; sorry; disquietude of mind; anger.

拂 To brush or wipe; to wave; to oppose; perverse.

沸 To sprinkle with water; water bubbling up.

祓 To wash or bathe as a religious ceremony to drive away calamity and obtain happiness.

紼 Silk; raveled; disordered.

艴 An angry appearance; excess of color or show.

髴 Like; resembling; ornaments of a headdress; disheveled hair.

黻 Embroidered garments worn by high officers.

Hwa.

禾 Wheat; grain of any kind.

和 Mild; harmonious; harmony; peace; to accompany; unite with; together.

華 Flowers; elegant; adorned with virtue; splendor.

嘩 譁 Excessive talking; clamorous.

驊 A fine horse.

禍 Evil; calamity; curse from the gods; to afflict; destroy.

吪 To threaten; to shout or hoot at; to order in a rough angry tone.

Hⁿwa.

鼾 Snoring; hard breathing in sleep.

埢 A dike or raised foot-path that divides fields of grain.

Hwai.

懷 To cherish or contain in the mind, mouth, womb, &c.; thoughts.

淮 Name of a large river in central China.

槐 Name of a certain wood; name of an animal.

壞 [5] To spoil; ruin; injure; to go to ruin.

Hwam.

凡 All; commonly; whoever; whatever.

梵 Retirement; recitative.

患 [5] Vice; evil; calamity; grief.

犯 [5] To offend; violate; invade an offender; criminal.

笵 [5] A mould; rule; law.

范 [5] Herbage; grass.

範 [5] A pattern; rule; mould; strict and careful discipline.

汎 [2] To float; be driven about; levity.

氾 [2] To overflow; inundate; unsettled; agitated.

泛 [2] To float; flow down a stream; to overflow.

Hwan.

繁 Multitudinous; numerous; affairs that press upon and weary a person.

蘩 A certain edible plant.

樊 Hemmed in; unable to proceed; mixed; confused.

礬 Alum; also applied to other stones, as blue vitriol, &c.

煩 Excessively occupied; troubled; troublesome; to trouble.

圓 Round; globular; complete; to surround; circulate.

嬛 Sorrowful; without posterity; a female slave.

寰 The royal domain; the wall that surrounds the palace.

壆 環 A ring or circle; to surround; enclose.

還 To return to; give or pay back; still; yet; even till now.

鐶 A ring.

闤 A market-place; a wall surrounding a market.

垣 A low wall.

桓 Inscriptions or titles of honor applied to the deceased.

嚾 To call to; to clamor in disputation.

懽 Joy; joyful.

歡 Joy; satisfaction; delight; pleased.

讙 Clamor; vociferation; the voice of joy.

番 To rebel; oppose; a time or turn; foreign.

幡 A napkin or wiping-cloth; a streamer.

꜀旛 A long pendant streamer; a flag; banner.

꜀燔 To roast; flesh used in sacrifice.

꜀繙 To extend; widen; to translate.

꜀翻 To fly; to fly backwards.

꜀蕃 Luxuriant; exuberance; plenty.

꜂反 To turn back; return; contrary; on the contrary; rebel

꜂畈 A field; cultivated land.

꜂返 To return; come back; revert; cause to revert.

꜂飯 A meal; rice; food.

宦꜄ A servant of the crown; a eunuch of the palace; a servant.

奐[2] Large; easy; slow; colored; variegated.

喚[2] To call; to order; denominate.

換[2] To exchange; to remove from one place to another.

渙[2] Name of a river; spread out; scattered.

煥[2] Light of fire; clear, bright.

販[2] To traffic; buy and sell.

幻[2] Artifice; craft; fraud; magic arts; visionary appearance.

Hwang.

꜁妨 To impede; injure; impediment; injury; subjection.

꜁防 A like; boundary; to keep off; guard against; prohibit.

꜁皇 A title of dignity applied to heaven and sovereigns; royal.

꜁凰 An imaginary bird, ominous of peace.

꜁徨 Uncertainty; indecision; going backwards and forwards.

꜁惶 Fear; apprehension; alarm.

꜁煌 Light; luminous; splendid; a great fire.

꜁蝗 A locust.

꜁遑 Unoccupied; at leisure; pressed; urged.

꜁隍 Empty; a ditch round a city wall.

꜁黃 Yellow.

꜁潢 A lake; an accumulation of water.

꜁璜 A certain stone sceptre, called a half-sceptre.

꜁簧 An ancient musical reed.

꜁衡 A balance; measure; to weigh or measure; transverse.

꜀風 Wind; temper; feelings; to diffuse; scatter; haste.

꜀方 Square; regular; a region or place; then thereupon; connects cause & effect; a medical prescription; to compare.

芳 Fragrant; agreeable; excellent.

髣 Like; resembling.

㡃 Wide; vacant space; a place to dwell in.

慌 Confused; forgetful; hurried; agitated.

荒 Wild; empty; waste; barren; dearth; famine.

謊 What is spoken in a dream; unreal; false; lying.

駹 A horse running swiftly.

肓 A certain part of the thorax.

封 To seal or close any document; a seal; an envelope.

坊 A street; shop; tavern; to guard against; oppose; an impediment.

彷 An agitated state; indistinct; doubtful; similar.

訪 To inquire; examine; consult; ask advice; to see.

恍 Confused; unsettled; agitated; hurried.

放 To reject; send away; let loose; lay down; dissipated; to imitate.

倣 To imitate; copy; in imitation of; according to.

Hwap.

法 A law; rule; pattern; means; punishment.

Hwat.

伐 To strike; punish; reduce to subjection; lay waste.

閥 Meritorious services; degrees of honor or reward.

穴 A cave; a hollow among rocks or in a mountain; to dig through.

乏 Destitute; to want; fail; to spoil; defect.

罰 To punish; punishment; to fine; forfeit.

髮 Hair; beard; grass, vegetables, &c.

發 To send forth; bring out; produce; to advance.

I.

扅 The bar of a door; to bar the gate.

移 To remove from one place to another; to change; great.

佁 Impeded; obstinate stoppage; foolish; silly.

怡 Pleased; to please; harmony; joy.

詒 To hand down or continue in succession; a will or testament; to ridicule; remiss.

貽 To present or leave to; to bring upon one's self.

飴 Rice prepared into gruel or congee; to feed.

夷 Foreigners; to hurt; change; to equalize; class; great; good

姨 Sisters of a wife or mother

꜀痍 The hurt or wound; a sore or wound.

꜀洩 To spread out; disperse; ease expansion of mind; many.

꜀彝 Constant; invariable rule or principle; a law.

꜀於 In; on; place where; to.

꜀衣 Clothes; a cover; clothes for the upper part of the body.

꜀依 To rely on; trust to; according to; comparison.

꜀伊 He; she; it; they; a person or thing.

꜀咿 Violent laughter.

꜀噫 Alas! Ah! Oh!

異^{5} Different; strange; foreign; to oppose; another.

裔^{5} Posterity; descendants.

意^{2} Ideas; thoughts; opinion; meaning; intention.

薏^{2} Pearl barley.

縊^{2} To strangle; to suspend by a cord round the neck.

謚^{2} The name given to a person after his death.

噎^{2} Pain or stoppage in the throat.

饐^{2} Spoiled food; difficulty in swallowing.

肄^{2} Well acquainted with or versed in; to attend to carefully; weak.

I^{n}.

꜀員 Round; to circulate to every part; officers of government.

꜀圓 Round; a circle; a globe; a dollar.

꜀丸 Round; spherical; turning.

ʿ已 Done; finished; already; merely; only; to stop.

ʿ以 By; to the end that; cause; means; thereby; therefore.

ʿ苡 Name of a plant.

ʿ矣 A particle closing a sentence.

ʿ倚 To lean against; depend on; inclined to one side.

ʿ椅 A chair or seat; a certain kind of wood.

ʿ圉 Boundary; to oppose; a horse keeper.

院ʾ A public court; a mansion; palace; an official title.

硯ʾ A smooth stone that reflects light; a Chinese inkstone; to rub.

Ia.

꜀爺 A title of respect applied to kings, nobles, &c.

꜀亦 Also; moreover.

ʿ也 A final particle; also placed after an important word in the middle of a sentence.

ʿ野 Wilderness; wide extended.

冶 To melt; fuse metals; an artist who fuses metals.

易 Change; transmutation; name of one of the 5 classics.

馹 A fleet horse; a post horse.

驛 A post; government despatch; to applaud.

益 To add; increase; benefit; beneficial; abundant.

Iⁿa.

營 An intrenchment; a camp.

贏 Rich; powerful; to overcome; conquer; surpass.

影 Shadow; proof; truth.

Iam.

塩 Salt; salted.

扊 A bolt of a door.

炎 焰 Flame of fire; hot luminous; glorious.

豔 灩 Handsome; good; large; variegated; self-indulgent; dissipated.

奄 To cover over or shelter.

俺 I; me; great.

淹 To merge or soak in water; to detain; impede.

閹 Doorkeepers of the royal harem; an eunuch.

鵪 A quail.

饜 Satiated; fastidious.

弇 To screen; shade; obscure.

揜 掩 To gather together under a shelter; to screen; soothe.

偃 To cease; cause to cease; to lie down; to rest.

揠 To pluck up; eradicate; to force.

厭 To restrain; repress; subject; injure; obedient; united.

嚈 Satiated; to satisfy; to uncover; to dislike; hate; composed; steady.

Iàng.

佯 False; pretended; to feign.

徉 To stray; saunter.

揚 To spread out or abroad; to extend the fame of.

暘 Clear; bright; to dry in the sun.

楊 Name of a tree; a wide spreading tree.

煬 A blazing fire; to roast; to fuse metals.

瘍 Sores on the head; a wound.

陽 The superior or male principle in nature; the sun.

颺 Driven or fanned by the wind.

央 In the middle; divided in the middle; wide.

殃 Fault; punishment; calamity; ruin.

泱 Wide spread; vast; tossed about, as clouds, waves, &c.

鞅 Part of a bridle which hangs below the neck; violent.

養 To eat; nourish or take care of one's self.

恙⁵ Sorrow; disease; complaint.

養⁵ To feed; nourish; bring up.

癢⁵ To itch; the itch.

映² Clear; shining openly; the sun just past noon.

眏² To look; see; dullness of sight.

Iap.

壓 To throw down; crush; oppress; to guard; keep down.

Ie.

窰 A pottery; furnace to burn earthen ware.

陶 A potter; a furnace; agreeable; complying; to expel.

姚 Beautiful; elegant; lightsome.

腰 The loins; waist.

藥⁵ Medicine.

約 A treaty; contract; agreement.

$I^{n}e$.

羊 A sheep or goat.

洋 The ocean; vast; abundant.

痒 Diseased; an ulcer; a scab; to itch.

楊 Name of a tree; a wide spreading tree.

鎔 To fuse metals; melt; a mould.

融 Steam or vapor rising; clear; bright; knowledge.

鴦 The female of a certain bird famed for conjugal fidelity.

樣 A pattern; fashion; manner; way; mode.

Im.

婬 Luxurious ease; lewd; obscene.

淫 Excess; sexual excess; lewdness; lustful; to debauch.

霪 Long and excessive rains.

音 Sound; tone; news.

喑	Dumb; unable to speak from grief or weeping.
瘖	Dumb; a disease which disables from speaking.
陰	Obscure; the opaque, inferior or female in nature.
飲	To drink.
癊	Disease of the heart or mind.
蔭	Shady; to overshadow.

In.

寅	A horary character from 3 to 5 o'clock P. M.; strong; respectful.
夤	Respect; veneration; continued succession; remote.
演	Constant flowing; long protracted; to practice.
沿	Along the shore; to flow down the stream; to accommodate.
鉛	Lead and the like soft metals.
因	Because; for the sake of; on account of; as formerly.
姻	A bride; the families of the bride and bridegroom.
烟	Smoke; igneous vapor; fog.
絪	Hemp; warm genial air.
胭	The throat; to swallow down.
氤	Warm genial air or vapour; the generative stimulus.
湮	To fall; to be drowned or lost in the water.
甄	To form or burn earthen ware; to examine; illustrate.
禋	A clean pure sacrifice.
蘢	Name of a plant; a lily.
引	To lead; shew the way; introduce; seduce; introduction.
蚓	A worm.
印	A seal; to seal; stamp.
昇	To lift up; to bear.

Io.

缶	Earthen ware; a pitcher; to move; agitate; shake.
徭	To serve; perform service for government.
愮	Deflected; depraved; to seduce; impose upon.
搖	To shake; wave; agitate.
猺	A species of dog.
瑤	A certain valuable stone.
謠	To sing songs or ballads; to slander by idle stories.
䍃	To walk; go.
遙	Remote; distant.

窰	A pottery an empty, retired, silent place.
颻	The wind shaking or agitating anything.
夭	Feeble; winning; luxuriant.
妖	Strange; superhuman; elves; fairies; an omen.
殀	To die early; short lived; to kill the young.
祅	Things produced out of the proper season or in an unnatural manner.
窈	Deep; profound; retired; tranquil.
夭	Calamity; untimely death.
舀	To remove a liquid from one vessel to another; to lade or dip out.
曜	Light and splendor of the sun.
耀	To shine upon; dart forth rays; luminous.
要	To require; desire; requisite; important.

Iong.

容	Allow, permit, yield to contain; bear with; endure; countenance; manner.
榕	The banian tree.
溶	To fill; to contain; gentle flow; ease; leisure.
蓉	A certain plant whose flowers are said to change their color thrice a day.
塋	A grave or tomb.
嫈	Careful; attentive; good looking.
榮	To honor; rank; glory; beams under the eaves of a house.
熒	An illuminated house; name of a star and of a plant.
瑩	Lustre of gems; bright; clear perceptions.
縈	To wind or roll up.
罃	An earthern pitcher or vessel with a long neck.
螢	A fire fly; glow worm.
濴	A deep lake; marshy ground.
營	To explain and discuss; a camp.
庸	Constant; ordinary; simple; cordial; agreeing.
傭	To hire; to serve for hire; equal; impartial; to do.
墉	A small city; a wall; to make a mud wall.
慵	Indolent; lazy.
盈	Full; overflowing; complete.
噰	Notes of birds; harmonious sounds.
饔	Dressed food; to cook a morning meal; harmony.
雍 邕	Harmony; to assist; collect together.

雝	Name of a small bird; harmonious notes or sounds.
癰	A swelling; large offensive sore; an ulcer.
喁	A gaping appearance.
顒	A commanding, dignified, benevolent appearance.
永	Perpetual; eternal; distant; always.
泳	Always flowing; to dive and walk about under water.
甬	To issue forth; pass through; containing; constant.
俑	A wooden image buried with a dead person as his attendant or servant.
涌	To bubble up as water from a spring.
勇	Strong; brave; resolute; decided; to exert one's self.
踴 踊	To leap or skip in zeal or joy.
咏 詠	To sing; recite; chant.
壅	To stop up; prevent information; to add to.
擁	To grasp; embrace; carry; crowd around.

Ip.

邑	A city; a place where many dwell together.
唈	Panting; palpitation of the heart; short breathing.
挹	To remove out of one vessel into another; to pour out into.
浥	Wet; damp; dewy; water running down.
揖	To raise the folded hands and make a bow; to resign.

It.

佾	A band of eight musicians employed in sacrificing to ancestors.
逸	Unrestrained; to run to excess; luxurious ease; idle.
佚	Ease; rest; repose; retirement; to omit; neglect.
泆	To overflow; excess; licentious; dissipated.
乙	Bent; curved; one of the characters of the cycle; one.
一 壹	One; a; at once; as soon as; the whole; to unite.

Iu.

繇 由	From; by or through; by means of; to let.
油	Oil; lard; greasy oily extracts.

꜀游	To flow; float; go from home; to ramble for amusement.
꜀蝣	Name of an insect.
꜀遊	To saunter; roam; to go abroad with companions.
꜀尤	Very; still more; singular; strange.
꜀疣	A swelling; accumulation of muscular substance.
꜀蚘	Long worms found in human intestines.
꜀酋	A kind of Chinese liquor; hot; valiant.
꜀偤	To stand by and wait upon; attendant.
꜀猷	To plan; scheme; delineate; a path; road; virtue.
꜀猶	Like; similar; perhaps; even; still; doubtful.
꜀蕕	Stinking plants; rotten wood.
꜀褭	Rest; enjoyment; affluence; elegantly adorned.
꜀郵	A post office; place for relay of post horses; a cottage in a field.
꜀憂	Grief; sorrow; mournful; sad; sick.
꜀優	Abundant; affluent; luxurious ease; to trifle with.
꜀耰	A sort of harrow.
꜂友	An associate; friend; friendly; to love as brothers.
꜂酉	Matured; finished; satiated; old; the eighth moon; horary character, from 5 to 7 P.M.
꜂莠	Weeds; tares.
꜂誘	To mislead; seduce; tempt; to induce.
꜂牖	A latticed window; to lead; conduct the way.
꜂肘	The fore arm; elbow; the muscles of the legs and arm.
右[5]	The right hand or side; honor; to honor; assist; good.
佑[5]	To aid; help; protect.
祐[5]	Divine protection or assistance; help from the gods.
侑[5]	To assist; accompany; give mutually.
囿[5]	A garden enclosed; a park; aviary or menagerie.
宥[5]	To be indulgent to; relax; to assist; advise and encourage.
洧[5]	Name of a river; a garden with a pool.
賄[5]	To make presents; to bribe.
柚[2]	The pumelo.
又[2]	More; moreover; again.

I^{n}u.

幼[2]	Young and slender; small; tender affection; fine.

Jeng.

仍 According to; in consequence and in imitation of; again.

陾 Many; a multitude; the noise of beating a mud wall.

媵 A concubine; maid servant.

Ji.

兒 A child; infant; a boy.

字 A word; character; a title; to produce; love; a letter.

寺 Chambers or courts of public officers; an eunuch.

鉺 A hook; a barb.

餌 A bait; temptation; seduction.

廿 Twenty.

Jia.

惹 To excite; provoke; stir up; induce; cause.

Jiak.

若 If; as; such as.

弱 Weak; feeble; pliant.

Jiam.

冉 To walk; advance; invade; name of a disciple of Confucius.

苒 Luxuriant growth of plants.

髯 Whiskers; beard on the side of the face.

染 To dye; imbue; infect.

Jiàng.

嚷 Noise of many voices; wrangling; clamor.

壤 Soft, good soil; earth; a boundary; abundant.

攘 To seize; reject; cause trouble to; to stop.

讓 Yielding; complaisant; to give place to.

Jie.

橈 An oar; paddle.

尿 Urine.

Jien.

然 Yes; even so; thus; but; notwithstanding.

燃 To kindle; set fire to; to boil slowly; simmer.

Jim.

壬 One of the ten astronomical characters of the cycle; to be responsible for, to bear.

任 Trust committed to a person, to sustain; serve; be able to choose, a duty, a burden.

刃 A sharp pointed weapon or knife; edge; strong.

仞 A measure of eight cubits, to measure depth.

忍 Fortitude; patience; to bear; forbear; patient.

牣 A good sword; filled; crammed; overflown.

肕 Muscular flesh; tendons.

訒 To think; consider.

軔 Aparatus for stopping a wheel; to impede; stop.

恁 / 餁 Satiated; an entertainment; thoroughly cooked.

荏 A large kind of pulse; flexible; gradual progress.

衽 The front part of a garment which hangs down or laps over.

賃 To pay for a loan; rent; hire.

壬 To take upon one's self; to undertake.

妊 / 姙 Conception; pregnant; to become pregnant.

Jin.

仁 Benevolence; charity; virtue the seed, kernel or stone of fruit; the pupil of the eye.

人 A human being; man or woman.

認 To know; distinguish; recognise; to acknowledge.

Jio.

嬈 Pleasing; facinating; flattering; troublesome.

饒 Plenty of provisions; abundant; affluent; overplus; to spare; excuse.

爪 Claws; finger nails; to claw; scratch.

沼 A pool; fountain.

擾 To agitate; trouble; confusion; to soothe; nourish.

抓 To scratch gently; tickle; cajole.

皺 A wrinkled face; frowning eyebrows.

縐 A kind of Chinese crape.

繞 / 遶 To surround; go round; wind round.

Jip.

入 To enter; entering.

Jit.

日 The sun; day.

Jiu.

柔 Flexible; yielding; mild and tender: young plants.

揉 To bend; twist; to work.

揉皮 } To tan leather.

Jok.

辱 To disgrace; degrade; insult; debauch; defile.

蓐 Shoots from an apparently dead stalk, rush; straw; thick.

褥 氈 } A mat; matress; couch.

Jong.

戎 A military weapon or carriage; large; thou; you.

絨 Fine cloth; woolen cloth.

茸 Plants shooting up or growing thick; crowded.

氄 Mixed; confused; base; degenerated.

氄 Fine hair; fur or down; warm and soft.

Ju.

如 As; like; according to; if; to go.

筎 The bark of bamboo; a sort of medicine.

茹 Plants whose roots entangle with each other; soft; flexible; to covet; eat greedily.

臾 A moment; an instant.

腴 Big-bellied; soft; flabby; fat; entrails.

萸 A certain medical plant.

俞 To answer; assent; yes; well; still more.

愉 To please; be pleased; joy; gratification; luxurious.

腧 The back; loins.

窬 To bore or open a small hole or aperture; a small hole in the wall.

踰 逾 } To pass over; exceed; advance; distant.

儒 A scholar; the literati.

孺 An infant at the breast; to attach to; pertain to.

薷 Name of an herb and of a medicine.

乳 Milk; the breast; tender; soft.

愈 To overcome; heal disease; to advance; still more; better.

庾 A stack of grain or storehouse in the fields; abundant; affluent.

喻 To manifest; declare; instruct; proclaim.

諭 An edict; order; mandates; to declare; command.

覦 To desire; covet; look at; to attain.

諛 Flattery; adulation; to flatter.

裕 Plenty; affluent; generous; indulgent.

籲 To cry out in distress; to invoke with importunity.

Jù

而 And; as; but.

耳 The ear; handle to a cup; an euphonic and emphatic particle.

爾 An euphonic and emphatic particle; thou; you; your.

璽 A seal; a stamp.

邇 Near; at hand.

貳 Two; both; to divide; double-minded.

膩 Fat; glossy; smooth; congealed.

刵 To cut off the ears.

字 A title.

Jua.

熱 Hot; heat; ardent.

爇 To burn; blaze; set on a blaze.

Juan.

纂 Scarlet silk; to collect; arrange; abstract and form a compendium of; hand down.

Juat.

悅 Pleased; happy; to delight.

Jue.

睿 Profound intelligence; perspicacity; clear perception.

銳 Sharp-pointed; keen.

枘 The pointed end of a wooden handle fitted to enter the iron socket.

芮 Soft; flexible; plants growing; a shore; bank.

Jui.

遺 To leave; hand down; leave by will; to reject; base.

帷 A curtain; a tent.

惟 To think; consider; plan; to be; is; but; only.

維 To be connected, pertain or belong to; to consider.

唯 To answer; assent; yes; but; only; who?

Jun.

允 Sincerely; honestly; faithfull; to assent; promise.

吮 To suck; to lick.

狁 An opprobrious epithet.

潤 To enrich with rain or moisture; to instil; to benefit; riches.

閏 Intercalary; to add, or throw in.

Ká.

鉸 A hinge or joint; an instrument that turns on a hinge.

嫪 An excessive desire for or love to; hankering.

膠 Glue; to glue; adhere firmly; pertinacious; bigoted.

絞 To wrap round; twist; to strangle; a string or sash.

攪 To stir up; excite; shake.

咬 The voice of birds; moaning or crying in distress; bite.

齩 To bite or gnaw.

教 To teach; instruct; instruction; doctrine; precept.

較 To compare; a general view or statement of.

甲 Armor; coat of mail; finger nails; scales of fish, &c.; an astronomical character.

呷 To inhale; to swallow.

舺 A certain kind of boat.

K'á

脚 The foot; foundation; bottom of anything.

豈 How? implying the opposite or a denial of a proposition.

巧 Skill; ingenuity; skillful; craft; artifice; a genius,

扣 To strike; to knock; strike out; deduct.

Kⁿá.

柑 An orange; a bit or bridle.

敢 To be daring or bold; rash; to presume.

酵 Yeast; leaven; a fermenting substance.

Kai.

個 箇 An individual; one.

皆 All; taken together; collectively; all the preceding circumstances or things.

偕 With; together with; united.

喈 Voices or songs of birds.

楷 A pattern; example; mould; rule; straight and comely.

該 Ought; should; proper; the person place or thing refered to.

介 To assist; attend upon; great; firm; a boundary; only; single.

价 Great; good; to assist.

疥 To scratch; a scratch; a mere trifling sore or matter.

界 A boundary or limit; to limit; draw a line of separation.

芥 Mustard plant or seed; small; trifling.

戒 To warn; prohibit; to guard against; precepts; a limit.

誡 Commands; precepts; orders; to command; forbid.

蓋[2] 葢[2] To cover; screen; protect; a cover; for; because.

屆[2] A fixed or appointed time; utmost limit.

丐[2] To beg; take; give.

K'ai.

開 To open; unloose; separate from; to begin.

凱 愷 Good; excellent; victory; peace and joy.

剴 A large sickle or hook; to grind; assiduously.

覬 To hope for; desire; covet; fortunate; lucky.

鎧 A coat of mail; armor.

嘅[2] To sigh; lament.

慨[2] Magnanimous; generous; high minded.

概[2] To level; adjust; a leveler; in general.

溉[2] Rolling towards; to cleanse or wash with water.

暨[2] With; and; the termination, end, or extreme degree of.

Kák.

角 A horn; corner; quarter; division; to push with the horn.

桷 Name of a wood; a handle, club; mallet; to beat; examine.

各 Each; every; separately.

覺 To be roused; excited; to take notice; to perceive what was unknown before.

K'ák

雀 Aspiring; ardent; high toned.

確 Certainly; surely; indeed; the strict truth.

霍 Celerity; speed; alacrity; cheerfulness.

藿 Pulse; a fragrant plant.

売 殼 Thin skin of anything; empty and hollow; bark; a shell.

愨 Sincere; faithful; virtuous.

戞 A long spear or lance; usual; ordinary; stammering.

恪 Veneration and respect; commanding respect.

麯 A ferment for making spirits.

Kám.

甘 Sweet; pleasant; agreeable; voluntary; flattering.

泔 A decoction; rice-water.

疳 A disease of children from eating sweets; venereal sores.

꜀紺 Purple color; a kind of purple colored silk.

꜀苷 Liquorice plant.

꜀邯 Plenty; abundance; name of a place and of a river.

꜀監 A jail or prison.

꜂感 To move; rouse; excite indignation; thanks.

監꜄ To oversee; control; an overseer; inspector; an eunuch.

鑑꜄ 鑒꜄ A mirror; a precept or warning; to see.

噤꜄ To stop the mouth; refrain or be prohibited to speak.

K‘ám.

꜀堪 To sustain; be adequate to; worthy; tolerable.

꜀龕 To receive; contain; overcome; a temple; a niche in the wall for idols.

꜂戡 To pierce; overcome; kill.

꜂闞 To look with desire or expectation; to view.

꜂坎 A pit or dangerous place; to fall into a pit; to dig a pit.

꜂砍 To cut off, or down; to chop.

勘꜄ To investigate carefully; to try; judge; to be able for.

Kán.

꜀干 A shield; to fend off; to oppose; offend against; crime; a boundary; exposed to.

꜀奸 Immoral; improper; clandestine; fraudulent; corrupt.

꜀杆 Name of a wood; a post; club; stick; staff.

꜀玕 A certain valuable stone.

꜀訐 To charge with crime face to face; to bring to light clandestine proceedings.

꜀乾 Dry; dried up.

꜀閒 ꜀間 Between; a space either of time or place; in the midst of; empty; unoccupied.

꜀癇 Convulsions, fits; epileptic fits.

꜀姦 Fornication; adultery; unprincipled intrigues or plots.

꜀艱 Difficult; distressing; dangerous.

꜂簡 An official writing; to review; diminish; negligent; sincere.

꜂鐧 A military weapon.

꜂鹼 A kind of lye or soap.

꜂囝 A son or child.

꜂揀 To choose; select; discriminate.

諫꜄ To remonstrate; reprove a superior or a prince.

[illegible]꜄ 㵎꜄ Water running between two mountains; a stream in a valley.

⿰虫間 A kind of shell fish.

幹 Stem of a plant; original substance; business; affair.

澣 To wash clothes; ten days.

簳 Small bamboo.

⿱艹幹 Herbs; plants; the stem of grain.

Kʿán.

牽 To lead; pull; drag; connect; confined to.

刊 To cut; carve; engrave; to hew; to fell.

衎 Joy; rejoicing; feasting; ease; settled; sincere.

Káng.

工 Work; art; craft; a workman; artificer.

江 A large river.

岡 } The ridge of a mountain; top of a hill.
崗 }

剛 Hard; firm; stiff; strength; fortitude; violence; recently.

綱 The cord to draw up a net; that which regulates, controls or draws together, as prince, father, or husband.

罡 Name of a star; ursa major.

講 To speak; talk; discourse; explain; explanation.

港 Streams; canals; arms of the sea.

共 Together with; with; general; all together; the whole.

洚 Flowing in an irregular course or out of the channal.

絳 Deep red; crimson.

降 To descend; cause to descend; degrade; subdue.

釭 An urn.

Kʿáng.

康 Repose; joy; felicity; excellent; blessed; a road.

慷 Firm; elevated; energetic; strong; healthy.

糠 Chaff.

匡 Square; right; to rectify; assist; deliver.

空 Vacant; empty; exhausted; poor; to empty.

侃 Faithful; plain; unceremonious.

亢 The neck; throat; strong; to shelter; oppose; attack.

伉 To pair; match; a pair; to oppose; honest; blunt.

忼 High toned; aspiring; magnanimous; roused; to sigh.

抗 To raise with the hand; to shield; resist; oppose.

炕 To dry; dry hot.

K'áp.

恰 Seasonably; just at the time; fortunately; exactly.

祫 A sacrifice to ancestors which unites them all together.

蛤 A frog.

閤 A side door; small inner door.

鴿 A pidgeon; also a gourd; dove.

盍 To cover over.

瞌 Sleepy; eyes closed.

磕 Two stones striking against each other; to kneel and strike the head on the ground.

闔 A door; to shut; a whole family; all together; why not?

Kát.

結 To tie, bind; collect together; to contract; a contract; bond; to produce.

K'át.

剋 To overcome; injure; kill; to repress; to insist upon; urgent.

勊 Great effort; to force one's self to; to be adequate for.

尅 To cut; engrave; carve; peel; to use harshly.

Kau.

猴 The monkey species; name of a fruit.

高 Lofty; eminent; a high degree of.

篙 A pole for propelling boats.

交 To unite; connect; deliver over to; to exchange; intercourse; trade.

筊 Name of a musical reed; rope made of bamboos.

蛟 A kind of crocodile said to weigh 2000 catties.

郊 Common or waste land outside a city; region.

鮫 A species of dog fish.

勾 A hook; to hook; entice; to mark off and reject; a sentence.

鈎 A hook; a sickle; kind of spear; to hook; induce; drag.

羔 A lamb.

皐 To proclaim from the housetop; high; to sing; drawl.

槔 A machine for drawing water; name of a wood.

溝 A ditch; moat.

狗 }
犬 } A dog; a mean person.

攪 To throw into disorder or confusion; to trouble the mind.

狡 An animal resembling a dog; crafty; perverse; disorderly.

‘皎 White like the moon.

‘絞 To wrap round; twist; strangle.

‘皦 Clear; bright; white and luminous.

‘皓 Pure; white; unspotted; refulgence.

‘杲 The rising sun; clear; bright; eminent.

‘槁 Rotten wood; dried fish.

‘縞 Plain white silk.

‘燺 Dry; destitute of water.

‘藁 Straw; thatch; tablets on which government orders are written.

‘九 Nine.

‘玖 A black colored stone.

厚[5] Thick; large; abundant; liberal; generous.

告[2] To tell; inform; to order; to intreat; to accuse.

誥[2] To command; give directions; proclaim by writing.

到[2] To arrive at; extend to; reach to; full amount.

K‘au.

鬮‚ 鬮‚ To cast lots; to choose by writing names on slips of paper and drawing them out.

‘口 The mouth; entrance; narrow passage; speech; a numeral.

‘攷 ‘考 Aged; a deceased father; terminated; to question; to examine.

‘拷 To examine; inflict torture; to extort confession.

哭[2] To cry; lament; weep.

犒[2] To confer rewards or honors especially on the army.

叩[2] To strike; knock; discuss; ask; bow the head to the ground.

Ke.

枷‚ A flail; a wooden collar for criminals; shelves; cupboard.

家‚ A house; family; to dwell; a scholar of celebrity.

加‚ To add to; increase; confer; inflict; to charge.

伽‚ A budhist god; a dragon.

袈‚ Priests' clothes.

‘假 False; fictitious; to suppose; to borrow; excellent; leave of absence.

嫁[2] To marry or be married, applied to the woman; to take a husband.

稼[2] To sow grain; to plant.

架[2] A stand or frame; a case for books or other things.

駕[2] To ride on; to sit in; a carriage with horses; to ascend; Sir.

價[2] The price or value of a thing; to sell.

膈5 The breast; chest; stoppage in the chest or stomach.

隔5 A partition; something that comes between; to separate.

客) A guest; stranger; customer.

喀) To cough; retch; vomit.

Kⁿe.

(畊, (耕 — To plough; cultivate the ground; employ diligent effort.

(羹 Soup; broth.

(更 A watch of the night.

(庚 A horary character; the age of a person; to alter; a path.

(鶊 Name of a bird.

'哽 An impediment in speaking; choking; sobbing.

'梗 Straight; erect; to ward off; to prick; fierce.

徑[2] A narrow path; bye path; straight forward; hasty; to go.

涇[2] Flowing through in a straight course; permeable.

脛[2] Bones of the leg below the knee; straight forward.

逕[2] A foot-path; to approach near; go straight up to.

頸[2] The neck.

K'ⁿe.

(坑 A pit; cave; den; to put into a pit.

Kek.

局5, 侷5 — Restricted; cramped; confused; guarded; to crouch.

梮5 A carriage for provisions; sharp points under shoes to prevent slipping.

極5 The extreme point or degree; to carry to the utmost; exhausted.

殛) To criminate; punish; reject; to kill; leave to perish.

棘) Brambles; a hedge; fence.

戟) A spear with several points; a halberd.

革) Untanned skins; to take off; reject; degrade from office; a bridle.

格) To come or extend to; excite; rectify; a limit; rule.

菊) Name of a plant.

檄) A government order written on a small board; haste.

激) To excite; stir up; excitement.

鬲) An earthen vase or urn; a partition between.

翮 Wings of a bird spread out.

K'ek.

刻 To cut; engrave; carve; peel; to use harshly.

擊 To strike; knock; beat; to rouse; excite; attack; kill.

Keng.

宮 Palace; inner apartments: a wall; a note in music.

經 Classical books; what is excellent; rules; laws; to manage; to pass through.

莖 The stem of plants; handle of a sword or spear.

弓 A bow; cover of a carriage; a land measure, 8 cubits.

芎 A fragrant medicinal plant.

矜 Handle of a spear; to compassionate; respectful; conceited.

荆 A thorny bush; to punish.

更 To change; alteration; still move.

供 To place; arrange; give; declare; give evidence.

賡 Again; to respond to; continue in succession.

儆 To warn or caution against.

警 To warn; rouse; excite; to command with a penalty.

境 Boundary; frontier; place where one lives; one's condition.

景 Prospect; appearances; illuminated; boundaries.

竟 Finally; after all; the extreme point of; then.

競 Strong; violent; quarrelsome; precipitate; abundant.

敬 Attentive; respectful; to reverence; worship.

K'eng.

擎 To raise or lift up with the hand; to lift high.

鯨 A large fish; a sea monster.

扃 The bar of a door; to bolt a door.

兢 Attentive; cautious; respectful; anxious; alarm.

卿 A title conferred on high officers; a prince.

筐 A basket.

硜 Noise of stones dashing against each other; mean.

肯 Willing; pleased.

虹 A rainbow.

磬 The sound of a sonorous stone; to suspend.

罄 Empty; exhausted; to exhaust.

慶 To congratulate; good; happy.

Ki.

棋 A game of chess; the root or foundation.

旂 旗 A flag; banner; standard; a company under one standard.

朞 A foundation; a root; a game at chess.

幾 Nearly; rather.

機 The springs of action; causes; changes or permutations.

畿 鐖 A limit; boundary; the royal domain of 1000 *li*.

璣 Name of a speculum; name of a star.

磯 An impediment; stumbling block; to rub or excite.

譏 To slander; ridicule; reprehend; examine & report.

饑 飢 Dearth; famine; want; hunger.

肌 An animal or human body, including flesh & bones.

基 Foundation; commencement; to commence.

期 A year, day or month completed.

箕 A sieve or winnowing basket; a constellation.

綦 Strict; important; ornamented; variegated; strings for shoes or caps.

枝 A branch of a tree; joint of a finger; to branch out.

姬 A concubine; king's wife; a handsome woman.

稽 To examine into; compare; arrange; deliberate; to detain.

笄 A kind of bamboo.

己 One's own person or self; private; selfish; an astronomical character.

圮 To subvert; throw down; destroy; ruin.

杞 A wooden pin on which to hang anything.

紀 To arrange and number; to record; order; rule; twelve years.

几 A bench; stool; stand; table.

幾 How much, many or long?

筥 A small sheaf; a utensil for containing rice.

忌 To dislike; hate; envy; to fear.

惎 To be angry with; enraged against.

妓 Singing girls; prostitutes.

歧 Lofty; luxuriant; to diverge; branch off.

技 Clever; ingenious; contrivance; talent; ability.

歧 Forked; diverging; a road parting in two ways.

跂 A foot with many toes; reptiles walking; to stand tiptoe and look.

冀 Name of a place; to wish, hope for.

驥 An excellent horse.

寠 / **窶** Poor; rustic; rude; a certain cap for the head.

屨 Shoes or sandals.

踽 A stately gait in walking.

羈 A bridle or halter for a horse; to restrain; to economize.

企 To stand erect and look with expectation; to hope; expect.

廐 A stable for horses or cattle.

記 To record; remember; know.

繼 Coming one after another in course; successively; to continue the succession.

痣 A spot on the human body.

既 Already done; finished; past; since.

砌 Stone steps or stairs.

K'i.

奇 Strange; wonderful; mysterious; to wonder.

畸 Small pieces of waste land; surplus.

琦 A certain precious stone; fond of play.

綺 Variegated; striped with different colors.

其 He; she; it; they; his; its; any one; the; that.

期 An appointed time; to expect.

蜞 Name of a shell fish, similar to a crab, not eatable.

麒 A fabulous male animal which appears on the birth of great sages.

圻 A limit; boundary, 1000 *li* around the royal abode.

祈 To pray; invoke; supplicate of the gods; beg.

祇 The soul which animates the earth; the earth; respect; awe.

祁 Affluent; abundant; numerous; great; at ease.

耆 Aged; sixty years old; to direct; adjust.

欺 To deceive; impose upon; insult; deceive one's self; to slant; to tip.

谿 A valley with a stream running through it.

蹊 A road; a path.

崎 Mountainous path; dangerous precipice; dangerous.

踦 Incomplete; single; with but one foot.

英漢潮州方言字典

꜂起 To rise; to raise; lift up; to begin.

꜂啟 To open; explain; inform; instruct; distinguish.

꜂綮 An ensign of authority; a spear carried by a forerunner.

器꜄ A vessel; instrument; utensil; talent.

氣꜄ Breath; animal life; any subtle fluid; spirit or temper; feelings; ethereal; primary substance.

餼꜄ Provisions; grain for cattle, for presents or offerings.

亟꜄ Haste; speed; promptly.

棄꜄ To break off; forget; reject; give up; refuse.

Kia.

佳꜀ Excellent; beautiful.

嘉꜀ Good; excellent; to commend; be pleased.

袈꜀ Cloth; hair cloth; camlet.

葭꜀ A reed for a musical pipe.

豭꜀ A boar.

꜂賈 To buy and sell; a merchant.

寄꜄ To give in charge to another; to send to another.

屐꜅ A kind of wooden clog or shoe.

劇꜅ A great degree; difficult; distressing; to play; trifle.

揭꜅ To raise or lift up; bear; to be answerable for; to open.

K'ia.

꜀騎 To stride; to ride on the back of an animal; a rider.

隙꜅ A crevice; interstice; a cause: time of leisure.

Kⁿia.

꜀行 To walk; do; perform; practice; carry into effect.

꜀驚 To alarm; surprise; affright; excite; rouse.

꜀經 Authorised; rules; laws; classics; excellent.

꜀京 A capital city; great; lofty; eminent.

꜂子 A child; son; a diminutive appellation; also an honorable appellation.

件꜄ An item; a numeral of things.

鏡꜄ A mirror; clear; bright.

K'iak.

怯꜅ Cowardly; timid; weak.

刦꜅, 卻꜅ Behold; denotes certainty and surprise; to refuse; throw away; really; truly; therefore.

Kiam.

꜀鹹 A salt taste; salted.

兼 Together with; to connect, and; also.

蒹 Name of a plant.

撿 To gather and bind up; to restrict; restrain; search.

檢 Envelope of an official letter; to sort; arrange; compose; title of a book.

减 To diminish; injure; break off a part.

劍, 劒 } A double edged or pointed sword.

K'iam.

箝 To lock; shut and fasten; a lock; nippers.

鉗 Tongs; pincers; forceps; to pinch; gripe; injure.

緘 To bind with cords; close or fold up, as a letter; an envelope.

謙 Respectful; yielding; humble; quiet.

嗛 Deficiency; failure; a bird's craw; contents of the mouth.

慊 Indignation; dissatisfied; cherishing ill-will to.

歉 Deficiency; debt; to covet; not satisfied.

儉 Economical; sparing; niggardly.

欠 Want; insufficiency; to owe; be deficient.

Kiàng.

畺 A boundary; limit; to draw a limit.

僵 To lie down; stretched out; prostrate.

殭 Remaining uncorrupted after death.

韁 A bridle or halter.

疆 A limit; boundary; to fix a boundary.

姜 A famous surname.

羌 Western barbarians; shepherds; contrary; violent; gay.

強 To force one's self to do; to use force.

襁 The cloth used by females to bind infants on their backs.

K'iàng.

強 Strong; violent; obstinate; overbearing; an overplus.

Kiap.

峽 Mountains joining at the top forming a cover below.

筴 Slips of bamboo for writing on or for divination.

頰 The side of the face; jaw.

鋏 Nippers or tongs used by smelters; a kind of sword.

愜 Joyful; happy; prosperous.

篋 A basket or vessel to contain things.

刼 To take by violence; plunder; rob; a Budhist cycle.

Kie.

橋 A bridge; a carriage; proud; insolent.

蕎 Name of a place.

痂 A scab on a wound.

茄 A medicinal plant.

轎 A sedan chair carried on men's shoulders; a carriage.

叫 To call; name; cry out; call aloud.

$K^{n}ie$.

韁 A bridle or halter.

薑 } Ginger.
羌 }

$K^{\prime n}ie$.

腔 Tunes for songs; empty; puffed up.

Kien.

堅 To stablish; strengthen; confirm; solid; firm; determined.

慳 Sparing; parsimonious.

鏗 A ringing sound; to strike against.

娟 Beautiful; pleasing; excellent; sprightly.

悁 Angry; impetuous; hasty; mournful; anxious; sorry.

捐 To reject; put away; give up one's own for another.

涓 A small stream gradually increasing; to choose; purify.

建 To establish laws; to erect; build; establish.

健 Strong; indefatigable; difficult.

蠲 Clear; pure; bright; to illustrate; remit; haste.

絹 Fine silk; a net.

見 To see; observe; seeing; finding that; to manifest; forms the passive of verbs.

K'ien.

乾 Heaven; firm; diligent; advancing; dry.

拳 The fist; to grasp and hold fast; roll up; boxing.

騫 A girth for a horse; to fail, failure; disgraced.

愆 Error; transgression; excess; failure; disease.

虔 Firm; respectful; sincere; veneration; pious feeling.

遣 To send; commission; put away; reject; give liberty.

繾 Inseparably attached.

譴 To reprehend; blame; to scold.

褰 Garments that reach to the feet; to lift up the garments when stepping in water.

蹇 Lame; sick; crooked; stammering; difficult.

畎 A small stream; a water-course in a field; to diffuse.

Kiet.

竭 To try to the utmost; to exhaust; destroy; the highest degree.

桀 Cruel; fierce; murderous; banditti.

傑 Eminent virtue and talents; proud.

絜 Clean; pure; to adjust; measure; restrict.

潔 Pure; clear; clean.

K'iet.

孑 Single; one; only; a remnant; short; behind.

厥 An engine to throw stones; he; she; it; his; hers; its.

譎 False; intriguing; crafty; to impose upon.

喫 To eat; drink; receive an impression; to bear with.

楔 The two side posts of a door; a pillar; name of a wood.

恝 Without sorrow; dismissing whatever annoys.

挈 To take hold of with the hand; support; adjust.

[illegible] Noise of the teeth gnashing or grinding on each other.

攫 To take hold of; grasp.

躩 A short, quick, respectful step.

Kim.

今 Now; the present time.

金 Gold; metal; firm; hard.

錦 Ornamented or variegated silk.

妗 A wife's brothers and sisters; female gaiety and levity.

禁 To prevent; prohibit; guard against; be careful; prison.

噤 To stop the mouth; not to utter angry feelings.

K'im.

琴 A stringed instrument of music; to restrain.

襟 The parts of a garment which fold over or overlap.

禽 A fowl; feathered animal with two feet.

擒 To sieze; take alive; take prisoner.

欽 Imperial; majestic; respect.

衾 A large coverlet; a covering; a shroud.

衿 A small girdle or string; to fasten clothes; the collar.

Kin.

緊 Pressing; urgent; strict; to bind or tie tight.

K'in.

輕 Light; of little consequence; to despise.

Kio.

嘐 Boasting; alarm or surprise; the crowing of a cock.

嬌 Delicate tender; elegant; to bring up delicately.

驕 A wild horse; ungovernable; proud; self confident.

噭 To call out loud; a vociferating noise.

繳 To deliver up; give to a superior; a wrapper.

敽 To bind together.

矯 To straighten; rectify; also used for false; assuming.

K'io.

磽 Stony, stiff, barren land.

翹 Long feathers of a tail; numerous; to elevate; excite.

蹺 A strong martial appearance; prancing; to climb.

喬 High; curved; bent; proud; idle and dissipated.

敲 To beat or strike as a drum; a stout club or cudgel.

蹻 To raise the feet and walk or climb high.

竅 A cavity; interstice; aperture; orifice; fit time.

Kiok.

掬 To take hold of with both hands; a double handful.

鞠, 跼, 鞫 To bear; train up; small; young; an awl; to investigate fully; exhaust a subject; to question a criminal.

麴 A ferment for making vinegar; mother.

K'iok.

克 Able; adequate; to sustain; subdue; repress.

曲 Crooked; bent down; oppressed; accused falsely.

Kiong.

恭 Serious . respectful; reverential; affable; cordial.

躬 The body; one's own person or self.

洪 Congealed; coagulated.

拱 To raise the hands united, as in salutation; to take with both hands.

龔 To give; present to; supply with; respectful.

共 To give or supply with.

K'iong.

窮 To the last degree; to exhaust; impoverish; poor; the utmost.

邛 Labor; weariness; sickness; name of a place.

蛩 Name of an insect; mournful.

穹 Lofty and vast, as the canopy of heaven; to deprive of entrance.

恐 Fear; suspicion; anxious thought; to suppose; reckon.

鞏 To bind fast; maintain firmly; well secured; to dry.

Kip.

及 To extend to; have reference to; connect with; concerning; and; at; to.

急 Urgent; pressing; without resource; anxious; embarrassed.

給 To give; supply; provide; to give opportunity.

跲 For; instead of; to stumble.

K'ip.

吸 To draw in the breath; inhale; to drink.

扱 To take; receive; obtain; draw; lead; to courtesy or bow.

汲 To draw water from a well; to draw; lead; drag; laborious.

笈 A box for containing one's books.

級 Regular series; steps; degrees; classed; assorted; numeral of heads decapitated.

泣 To weep; shed tears silently.

Kit.

吉 Good; happy; fortunate; lucky; happiness.

劼 Endeavor; effort; firm; determined.

拮 To urge; perplex; embarrassed; distressed.

桔 A species of orange; the mandarin orange.

碣 A rock standing alone in the sea; a stone tablet.

橘 Name of a fruit of the orange species.

K'it.

詰 To interrogate; investigate; question with authority; to prohibit; reprove.

Kiu.

球 A sonorous stone; a globe; a sphere.

毬 A ball to play with; a kind of silk or cloth; staff; lamp.

絿 Hurried; pressed; urgent; precipitate.

玖 A precious stone of inferior value and black color; nine.

糾 A threefold cord; to combine; head a conspiracy; to examine into; prohibit.

赳 Possessing talents and strength; martial.

晷 A dial; a gnomon to show the declination of the sun; a day.

柩 A body laid in its coffin.

疚 Poor and diseased; chronic disease; perverse.

咎 Error; crime; quarrel, to hate wickedness; the judgments of heaven; hate.

鼛 A large drum twelve cubits long; to beat a drum.

究 To search; devise; investigate; to push to the utmost; finally; to hate.

救 To assist; protect; rescue; save; to prohibit; prevent.

K'iu.

求 To search for; endeavor to obtain; beg; intreat; pray.

裘 Skin garments.

賕 To bribe; to pervert justice for money.

逑 To pair; join; court or seek for in marriage; urgent.

丘 坵 A mound; hill; an area; hollow space; valley; great.

蚯 A worm.

虬 An animal of the lizard or dragon kind having a horn.

鳩 Name of a bird of the pidgeon species; to congregate; to rest.

Ko.

姑 A father's sisters; a husband's mother and sisters.

枯 Rotten wood; a dead tree; decayed; putrid.

沽 Name of a river; to buy; sell; abridge; retrench.

骷 Bones of the knee, loins and shoulder.

鴣 A partridge.

孤 Fatherless; an orphan; alone; destitute; poor.

菰 Name of a plant.

觚 A wine cup; a rule or law; a title of office.

古 Ancient; remote ages.

估 Tax; duty, custom paid to government; to reckon; to value; price.

牯 A bullock; also the male of swine and dogs.

詁 To explain; explanations.

酤 Liquor for drinking; to buy or sell wine.

苟 If; but; uncertainty; carelessly; illicitly; plants.

耇 An old person; very old.

股 The thighs; a branch of a stream; a division of; strong.

皷 鼓 To beat a drum; strike a sonorous body; to rouse or excite; a drum.

瞽 Blind; the master of a band of music.

蠱 Worms in the abdomen; poison; ghosts.

靠[5] To rely on; depend on.

詬[5] To revile.

垢[2] Dirt; filth; mire; mud; a disgrace; reproach.

姤[2] Meeting together; contact; union of the sexes.

冓[2] To connect together as the beams of a house; one hundred millions.

媾[2] Love; conjugal union; marriage; sexual intercourse.

搆[2] To draw; to pull; drag; to plot.

構[2] Wooden frame of a house; to join together; complete.

篝[2] A bamboo basket or utensil.

覯[2] To meet one's eye; to see; to happen; to effect; complete.

購[2] To buy; to seek to obtain for money.

遘[2] To meet; occur; happen; to bolt upon accidentally.

僱[2] To hire; borrow for money.

彀[2] To stretch a bow; an archer; enough; adequate.

轂[2] The name of a wheel; a wheel carriage.

够[2] Much collected together; satisfied; enough.

K'o.

苦 Bitter; unpleasant; distressing; urgent; to dislike.

楛 A wood of which shafts of arrows and spears are made; bad; weak.

庫[2] A storehouse; treasury.

褲[2] Pantaloons.

寇[2] Pirates; robbers; to plunder; pillage.

蔻[2] A nutmeg; a certain medicine.

Kó.

歌 To sing; recite in a musical tone; play on an instrument.

竿 A reed; cane; rod; staff; stick of bamboo.

哥 An elder brother used also by equals to each other.

鵝 A goose.

膏 Fat; lard; greasy; rich food; rich favors.

糕 A kind of pudding; dumpling; cake; bait.

槁 Rotten wood; dried fish; a certain medicine.

稿 Straw; rough sketch of any document; original copy.

告[2] To inform against; prosecute; to make known.

塊[2] A clod of earth; a lump; a piece.

閣, 擱 } A screen before a door; a case or press in which to lay up provisions; a gallery; council chamber.

K'ó.

戈 A spear or lance.

渦 To flow back; flow round; return.

呵 To interrogate; reprehend; blame; to yawn.

坷 Uneven; rugged; unfortunate; unsuccessful.

柯 Name of a wood; stalk of a plant; handle of an axe; means of effecting.

痾 Disease; sickness.

苛 Small; petty; troublesome; to reprehend; trouble; anger.

軻 An axle with wheels on it.

可 May; can; fit; competent; proper; worthy.

哿 Excellent; to commend; may; can; ornaments.

Koi.

街 A street; path; market.

雞 } A fowl; the fowl genus.
鷄 }

揩 To rub with the hand; to dust.

階 Stairs; steps; degrees; rank.

改 To change; alter; an alteration.

解 To cut open; unloose; explain; lay open; liberate.

易 Easy; not difficult; negligent; idle.

計 A complete number; to reckon; plan; devise; a plan.

解 To deliver up to an officer; to escort.

廨 An apartment near a *yamun*; a magastrate's lodging.

K'oi.

溪 A stream; river.

契 A written agreement; bond; deed; to unite; mournful.

Kⁿoi.

肩 The shoulders; back.

間 A house; room; tenement.

間 To separate; break off.

繭 The ball of silk as left by the silk worm.

Kok.

峪 A pool of water in a valley.

國 A nation; country; kingdom.

嘓 Chattering; troublesome loquacity.

幗 A woman's head-dress; a cap.

咯 Cackling of a fowl; coughing; wrangling.

谷 The channel of a stream; a valley; a cavern.

綌 Coarse hempen cloth.

穀 Grain of all sorts; real; good; substantial; wealthy.

K'ok.

梏 Manacles; a collar for the neck; correct conduct.

酷 Generous wine; hard hearted, as from wine; cruel.

鵠 A leather mark to shoot at; a water fowl; goose.

嚳 A hurried enunciation; to give information.

哭 To weep and cry aloud.

觳 A cup; a quiver; a small vessel; thin; a bludgeon; to rush against; trembling.

Kong.

功 Meritorious service; merit; praise; service; work.

攻 To attack; assault; rouse; apply closely to; put in order.

公 Public; not selfish; just; a title of nobility; male.

蚣 A poisonous insect; a medicine made of the centipede.

貢 Tribute; offerings of one's services; merit; to offer.

K'ong.

空 The firmament; great; wide; vacant; exhausted; poor; clearness of mind; abstraction.

倥 Ignorant; rude; hurry; urgent; weary.

悾 Unable to attain one's purpose; dissatisfied; ignorant; simple.

胸 Empty within; filled with wind; vain; ostentatious.

孔 An orifice; aperture; vacuum; great; very; high.

控 To draw or pull with the hand; to hold back; strike.

Ku.

劬 Labor; travail; distress; fatigue.

拘 To hook or take; to sweep or draw together.

朐 Dried meat; hams.

駒 A colt; fine young horse.

煦 To boil; to heat; genial warmth; kind; benevolent.

龜 A tortoise.

骷 Bones of the knee, loins and shoulder.

辜 Fault; crime; guilt; to monopolize.

俱 All; together; prepared.

舊 Old; not new; a long time; formerly.

賈 To buy and sell; a merchant.

久 A long time.

‘籃 Any vessel or utensil.

‘藍 Name of a plant,

‘羖 A sheep with black and white wool; a ram.

‘嘏 Great; remote; stable; happy; blessed; propitious.

具ˀ Arranged; prepared; to present to; a utensil.

颶ˀ A whirlwind; typhoon; a sea storm.

舅ˀ The brothers of a mother or wife; father of a husband.

懼ˀ Fear; apprehension.

句ˀ A sentence; period; to mark off; reject.

故ˀ A cause; reason; therefore; old; ancient; to die.

固ˀ Certainly; firm; solid; impervious; obstinate.

婟ˀ Excessive attachment to.

痼ˀ A chronic, deep rooted, obstinate disease.

錮ˀ To close or stop up firmly; to shut up a way.

顧ˀ To look to with care and regard; to protect.

K'u.

‚區 To discriminate; a place to lay up anything; a room; to class; a boundary.

‚傴 Bent forward in respect; hunch backed.

‚嶇 Rugged; an abrupt, peaked mountain.

‚摳 To lift up with the hand; to feel; to strike.

‚樞 A hinge; centre of motion; central; indispensable.

‚軀 To walk lame; an uneven path.

‚軀 The body.

‚驅 To drive; drive away; go before; a forerunner.

‚祛 To expel; drive away, as any noxious influences.

‚袪 The sleeve of a garment; the cuff.

‘罟 A net for fish or animals; an involvement.

臼ˀ A mortar for pounding rice or other things.

Kù.

‚籧 An ugly deformity of person; a man's name.

‚居 To dwell; reside; remain; to desist; an abode.

‚車 A wheel carriage; a wheel.

‘莒 Name of a plant and of a kingdom.

‘舉 To set up; elevate; raise.

‘矩 A square; a rule; usage; pattern; to square; adjust.

巨ˀ Great; vast; numberless; powerful.

- **拒** 5 To ward off; withstand; resist; defend; oppose.
- **秬** 5 A species of black millet.
- **距** 5 The spur of a cock; to oppose; be distant; large.
- **倨** 5 To stand erect; proud; indecorous.
- **据** 5 Hands diseased; restricted; embarrassed; precipitate.
- **踞** 5 To crouch; sit cross-legged.
- **據** 5 Proof; to lean or rest upon; according to; to take; seize.
- **遽** 5 Hurried; fluttered; irresolute; afraid; hasty.
- **鋸** 2 A saw; to saw.

K'ü.

- **瞿** Distrustful; timid; alarmed; anxious look; to stare.
- **衢** A street; thoroughfare.
- **渠** A gutter; large; gradual; name of a river.
- **去** 2 To go; going; to put away; reject; cut off.

Kue.

- **瓜** A cucumber; melon; the cucumis genus.
- **粿** Clean rice; rice food.
- **菓** Fruit of trees; really; truly.
- **過** 2 To pass; exceed; transgress; error; fault; crime; past.
- **髻** 2 Hair braided in a tuft on the top of the head.
- **郭** Waste land outside of cities.

K'ue.

- **科** A class; series; order; rank; a line.
- **魁** The chief; head; great.
- **恢** Great; greatness of mind; to enlarge.
- **盔** A vessel for rice; any vessel; a helmet.
- **詼** To jest; trifle with; seduce.
- **卦** 2 Divination; prognostic; to divine by lines.
- **課** 2 To essay; make trial; deliberate; plan; a task; tax.
- **闕** Empty; defective; wanting; disrespectful.
- **缺** Broken off; deficiency; want; a vacancy.

Kui.

- **圭** A gem or sceptre carried by officers as a badge of authority.
- **奎** Between the legs; striding.
- **跬** A pace or step; to step with one foot.
- **閨** Solitary apartments for women and children.

規 Compasses; a rule; custom; to rule; regulate; to plan.

窺 To spy; look; peep out of a cavern.

闚 To peep out at a door; to spy; observe narrowly.

歸 To return; go back; to attach one's self to; to send back.

鬼 Spirit of a dead man; ghost; demon; devil.

傀 Great; excellent; extraordinary; strange.

憒 Disquietude of mind; stupidity from sickness.

潰 Opposing currents clashing; in disorder; enraged.

瞶 To glance hastily; a dull eye; without a pupil.

蕢 Name of a vegetable; a clod of earth; utensil made of straw.

饋 Food; to prepare food; to offer it to superiors; to present to.

跪 To kneel as in worship.

桂 Name of a medicine; the laurus cassia.

癸 The last of the ten astronomical characters in the cycle.

季 Young; small; slender; the last of a series.

貴 Lofty; noble; costly; desirable valuable.

K'ui.

撅 To lift up the garments when fording water.

蹶 To walk fast; speedy motion; stumble; to step.

揆 To guess; conjecture; to examine; conclude.

睽 In opposition to; over against; distant.

䁱 To stare; look with displeasure; cast down.

葵 The malva or mallows; a variety of the hibiscus.

騤 A majestic horse; strong; violent; indefatigable.

馗 逵 The cheek or jaw bones; a road diverging in nine directions.

虧 Failure; deficiency; diminution; to injure; give trouble.

開 To open; unfold; spread open.

宄 Traitorous plots formed by external banditti.

軌 The rut of a wheel; a law; rule.

詭 To reprimand; to deceive; impose upon; perverse.

晷 A dial; a gnomon to show the sun's declination.

簋 A square vessel to contain grain used in sacrifice.

愧 Shame; ashamed; abashen.

Kⁿui.

匱 A large chest; a press with shelves and doors; exhausted.

櫃 A box; a press; a shop; counter.

縣 Chief town of a district; the officer who presides over it.

Kun.

裙 A petticoat; lower part of a dress.

軍 Many persons; an army; 12,500 men.

君 A chief; prince; king; to rule; honorable; virtuous.

袞 Imperial raiment; court dresses.

滾 Flowing water; moving rapidly; rolling; to roll.

鯀 A large fish.

郡 A principality.

棍 A stick; a staff; a rod.

K'un.

群 A flock of sheep; a company of persons; to accord.

坤 The earth; inferior; submissive.

昆 An elder brother; to take precedence; altogether.

崑 A fabulous mountain in central Asia.

鯤 The spawn of fish; a very large fish.

髡 To cut or shave off the hair; a leafless tree.

囷 A round granary; a place to collect grain.

捆 To beat and bind; to make firm; well made.

梱 The two sideposts of a door or gate; to finish; close.

綑 To tie up; bind; weave.

閫 Posts of a gate; apartments for the women.

麕 A species of deer very timid.

窘 Pressed by poverty or want; embarrassed; enfeebled.

困 Fatigued; exhausted; poor; weak; to weary; repress.

Kùn.

巾 A piece of cloth; a napkin.

斤 An axe; a catty; Chinese pound; to examine.

根 The root of a tree; radical; the source or origin of.

跟 The heel of the foot.

均 Equal; equally; all alike; to equalise; blend.

鈞 Thirty catties weight; to make, as a potter; nature.

筋 Tendons; strong muscular fibres; strong and nervous.

ˊ僅 Hardly; just about; just adequate; none to spare.

ˊ槿 A handle; name of a tree.

ˊ謹 Seriousness; respect; awe; care; attention; to guard against.

近⁵ Near, either in time or place; to approach.

覲² To see; to see or be introduced to a superior.

饉² Dearth; scarcity of vegetable diet.

巹² Wine vessels used at marriages.

艮² Perverse; firm; obstinate; a limit; boundary.

K'ùn.

ˏ勤 Diligent; laborious; to pay careful attention.

ˏ懃 Oppressed by circumstances.

ˏ芹 Name of a water plant; a vegetable much esteemed.

ˊ墾 To use effort, as in ploughing; to break; wound.

ˊ懇 Sincerely; earnestly; to beg or seek earnestly.

Kᵘng.

ˏ扛 To bear; to carry on a pole; the poles of a sedan chair.

ˏ缸 An earthenware vessel; an urn for the dead.

ˏ糠 Chaff; husk; fond of pleasure and remiss in duty.

ˏ綱 Refined iron; steel.

ˊ卷 A book; a part of a book; section; to roll up.

勸² To exhort; advise; comfort; excite.

Kut.

崛₅ A solitary mountain-top standing out singly.

掘₅ To dig into the ground; to hollow out; to spread out.

滑₅ Smooth; slippery; sharp; soap-stone.

骨ˎ A bone; hard and smooth parts of the body; fibres of plants.

猾ˎ Artful; crafty; tricky; deceitful; to gnaw.

汩₅ Flowing along; waves; agitated; confusion.

K'ut.

屈ˎ Bent; to stoop; to submit; to cause to stoop; to oppress.

堀ˎ A den; a cavern.

窟ˎ A cavern dug for a dwelling; a hole in the ground.

Kùt.

乞ˎ To beg; a beggar.

Kwa.

ʿ寡 Few; little; single; a widow; I, used by princes.

ʿ果 To surpass; overcome; really; truly.

割ˏ To cut; cut off; divide; wound; injure.

葛ˏ Creeping plants; plants of which thin cloth is made.

K'wa.

ˎ刳 To cut asunder; rip open; divide; kill.

ˎ胯 The legs or thighs.

ˎ袴 Pantaloons.

ˎ誇 To boast; vaunt; large.

ˎ跨 To pass over; surpass; to stride over.

挂² To suspend; hang up.

掛² To suspend; hang upon; anxious.

罣² An impediment; a net; to impede; fall into a net.

渴ˏ Thirsty; anxious to obtain or effect.

闊ˏ Open; wide; broad; distant; perverse; painful.

K^{n}wa.

ˎ官 An officer of government; a court.

ˎ棺 To close; shut up; a coffin.

ˎ肝 The liver.

ʿ赶 To pursue after; endeavor to overtake.

汗ˀ Sweat.

Kwai.

ˎ乖 To turn the back upon; perverse; wicked; strange.

ˎ劊 To cut or break asunder.

ʿ拐 To swindle; kidnap; to steal women and children.

ʿ柺 An old man's staff.

獪² Artful; crafty; fraudulent; causing disturbance.

繪² To draw pictures; to embroider; adorn with different colors.

膾² To cut or mince; very fine; minced meat or fish.

蒯² A certain kind of grass or rush for making cords.

怪² Strange; monstrous; fairies; to deem strange.

K'wai.

快² Flow of soul; joy; cheerfulness; speed.

Kwak.

槨ˏ The external coffin used by Chinese.

鵙ˏ Name of a water bird.

英漢潮州方言字典

蛞꜇ Name of an insect.

K'wak.

擴꜇ To stretch out; enlarge; to pound; beat.

Kwan.

꜀觀 To look; observe; to manifest; external appearance.

꜀鰥 A large fish; a bachelor; widower; few.

꜀祼 To pour out an oblation; to pour out wine for a guest.

꜀關 To bar a door; fasten; a bolt; a limit; consequence; a custom house.

꜀冠 A cap.

꜂管 To rule; control; guide; writing; a pencil; reed.

꜂倌 A charioteer; inferior officer.

꜂菅 Rushes and reeds fit for making mats and thatch.

꜂館, ꜂舘 } An inn; public hall; exchange; school; to lodge.

꜂逭 To exchange; turn pace; walk; go or run; away.

꜂捲 Robust; the fist; to roll up.

꜂綣 To bind as with a silk cord; strong attachment.

꜂盥 To wash the hands; to wash in a tub.

倦5 To desist from labor; idle; fatigue; lassitude.

貫2 To connect or string together; to pass through; involve.

慣2 Accustomed to; practiced in; having had experience of.

冠2 To cap or put a cap on the head, as at the age of twenty.

券2 A bond; deed of contract; a check; evidence.

眷2 To look to with regard; a family; near relation.

睠2 To turn round and look back.

惓2 Diligent; earnest; serious; mournful; to desist.

灌2 To flow to one place; to drink; pour out a libation; growing.

爟2 To kindle fire; to heat; fire flaming up; a fireman.

罐2, 鑵2 } A jar; mug; vessel for water, wine or oil; a tea caddy.

鸛2 A certain water fowl which sings at the approach of rain.

K'wan.

꜀權 Power; authority; circumstances which influence one.

꜀寬 Broad; large; easy; generous; forgiving; to enlarge.

꜀圈 A coop or pen; a prison; a small circle; to encircle.

꜂款, ꜂欵 } Sincere; affectionate; singleness of intention; to seek.

Kwang.

光 Light; splendor; shining; barely; only.

桄 A utensil used in weaving; a timber at the head of a boat.

胱 The urinary vessels; the bladder.

觥 A wine cup made of horn; crooked; large.

廣 Large; wide; extensive; widely; to widen.

耿 To see; light; a surname; large pendant ears.

褧 A single; external garment.

絅 To lead or drag impetuously; a single garment.

恍 Mad; wild; confused; disconcerted.

K'wang.

狂 Mad; foolish; ambitious; insanity.

煢 Desolate; alone; sorrowful; having none to depend on.

瓊 A flesh colored gem; a beautiful stone.

傾 Indirect; sideways; aslant; overturned; thrown down.

肱 Deaf; a noise in the ear; a great noise.

肱 The upper part of the arm; name of a country.

眶 The eye ball; margin of the eye.

頃 A moment; short time; timid.

況 More; further; still more.

貺 To confer upon; bestow; give to.

誑 Levity of speech; to seduce by lying speeches.

壙 A cave; grave; a desolate wilderness; extensive region.

曠 Clear; bright; empty; vacant; distant; of long duration.

矌 A colorless, lifeless eye; to stare; gaze.

纊 Raw silk; silk in a confused state, not formed into threads.

Kwat.

决 To decide; determine; fixed; intention; to open; spread out.

抉 To pluck; snatch; to pull, as a bow string.

訣 Parting words; farewell; a rule or precept; secrets of any craft.

駃 Fleet; swift; a frisking colt.

刮 To rub off; pare off; scrape; press.

括 To enclose; bundle or bind up; embrace; impede.

适 Fleet; hasty; a man's name.

英漢潮州方言字典

Lá.

喇 Precipitate utterance.

拉 To drag; pull; draw near; break; destory.

獵 To hunt wild animals; to hunt; pursue earnestly.

臘 The time when sacrifices are offered; to bind.

蠟 Wax; resin.

躐 To leap over; to overpass; overstep.

邋 Walking in a slow, pacing manner.

Lai.

來 To come; to effect; bring about.

徠 To encourage; reward; a precept; order; sincere.

萊 Name of a plant.

賚 To confer upon; give to an inferior.

騋 A tall horse; a mare.

梨 A pear; apple.

內 Within; inside; during.

籟 A wind instrument with tubes; an organ.

利 A sharp edge; acute; interest on money; profitable.

俐 Clever; ingenious.

Lák.

六 Six.

樂 Pleasure; joy; happiness.

Lâm or Nâm.

南 South; to go south.

喃 Incessant chattering.

楠 Name of a wood.

藍 Blue; a plant which colors blue.

襤 A single coverlet; garments; a collar or hem.

男 Male; the lowest of the five titles of nobility.

嵐 Mountain vapor or fog.

覽 To look at; observe; see; inspect.

攬 To grasp all one sees; to hoard up; monopolize.

欖 An olive; name of a fruit.

灠 A spring of water bubbling up.

婪 To covet.

檻 A baluster, or perpendicular rails; a cage; a fold.

ʿ艦 A ship of war so built as to defend those whithin.

檻⁵ Greedy; voracious; ardent desire; robust.

濫⁵ An overflowing; excess; to exceed due bounds.

Lán or Nán.

ˏ闌 A screen for a door or carriage; a railing; obscured.

ˏ攔 To stop or intercept with the hand; to prevent approach.

ˏ欄 Balusters or railing; railing to confine animals.

ˏ瀾 Streams flowing together and running in a continued course.

ˏ蘭 } Name of a fragrant plant, the class Gynandria.
ˏ𡅅 }

ˏ躝˙ To leap or pass over; to surpass.

ˏ難˙˙ Difficult; troublesome.

ˏ零 Residue; fragments; odd numbers; what is over.

ˏ鱗 Scales of fishes.

ʿ懶 Sleepy; remiss; idle; weak.

ʿ赧 To redden in the face; blush; ashamed; bashful.

爛⁵ Boiled or roasted excessively; torn; to tear; bright.

難⁵ Calamity; distress; to inflict suffering; difficult.

Láng.

ˏ浪 A wave; waves of the sea; unsettled; profligate.

ˏ狼 A wolf; cruel; abundant.

ˏ稂 Name of a plant; a tare.

ˏ廊 Small rooms on the sides of large houses.

ˏ螂 The male crab.

ˏ礱 To rub; grind corn or sharpen tools; to use effort; a stone.

ˏ籠 A basket; cage; quiver; to hoard up and monopolize.

ˏ聾 Deaf.

ˏ癑 Pain; disease.

ˏ膿 Ulcerous matter; pus.

ʿ曩 In former times; formerly; the other day.

ʿ囊 A bag; sack; to hold in a bag.

ʿ攮 To advance, or push forward violently.

朗⁵ Clear; bright; lofty; to solicit; to fill by force.

琅⁵ A certain valuable stone.

蜋⁵ Name of an insect; ineffectual effort.

弄 2 To play; trifle with; seduce; to perform; make; do.

Lát.

力 5 Strength; nerve; force; diligent effort.

Lau.

勞 To labor; wearied; to give trouble; merit; worthy deeds.

撈 To rake for in a river; to find and draw out of water.

牢 A prison; place to confine animals; cattle.

劉 A certain weapon; to kill; to arrange.

樓 The upper stories of a house; upper rooms; to collect.

老 Aged; venerable.

潦 An accumulation of water; heavy rains; to sink.

嫪 5 Excessive affection for; love to; hankering after.

漏 To leak; let out; lose; omit; a retired place; to instil.

鬧 Noise; tumult; bustle; to bustle about; business.

Le.

曆 The signs of heaven, sun, moon and stars which mark time.

歷 To pass through successive periods of time; next in order; to pass; transgress.

瀝 Dripping; dropping of water; to pour out.

讈 Artful; crafty speech.

靂 A crashing noise, like thunder.

Lek.

勒 5 A bridle with a bit; to bridle; restrain; force.

陸 5 High and dry; a dry path; dry ground.

綠 5 Green color; verdant.

菉 5 A plant of which cloth is made; shoots of bamboo.

癧 5 A swelling on the neck.

轢 5 A road for a cart; a wheel-rut.

Leng.

另 Besides; distinct from; another.

囹 A place of confinement formed by rails; a prison.

泠 The noise of wind and water.

玲 A certain valuable stone of an inferior kind.

羚 A species of antelope, resembling a sheep.

蛉 Name of an insect of the locust species.

軨 An axle; a hunting carriage; to hunt.

翎 Wings or feathers; feathers of an arrow; peacock's feathers.

鴒 Name of a bird of the lark species.

齡 The teeth, denoting a person's age; age.

寧 Tranquility; better; desiring this rather than that.

嚀 To direct; to caution; to give a charge to; to state fully.

凌 Ice; an ice house; struck with fear; to shame; insult.

稜 Name of a species of grain; a neighboring state; divinity.

綾 A fine sort of silk.

菱 Name of a vegetable; the trapa bicornis.

陵 A lofty mound; eminent; to aspire high; to insult; invade.

靈 Spiritual; etherial; the spirit of man; soul; efficacious, good.

龍 A dragon; crocodile.

隴 A large bank; a dike between fields; high.

令^{5} To order; warn; to cause; a law; rule; excellent; your.

伶^{5} Alone; to play; act the buffoon; to employ; be employed.

聆^{5} To listen to; yield obedience to.

苓^{5} Name of a medicinal plant.

佞^{5} Talents; insinuating address; artful language; flattering.

Li.

罹 Mournful; sorry; to occur; meet with.

璃 Glass; a shining appearance; a vitreous glaze.

離 To separate from; to leave; to divide; apart; distant.

籬 A fence of bamboo; a hedge; to keep off.

魑 A malevolent, diabolical spirit; fairy; elf.

厘 A kind of market place; shops; a small coin.

哩 A tone at the close of a sentence.

娌 A name by which brother's wives designate each other.

狸 A fox; wildcat.

黎 Glue; paste; black; black-haired, as young men.

藜 A certain plant; a stem or branch.

氂 / **釐** A small coin; cash; to regulate; govern.

嫠 A woman without a husband; a widow.

鸝 Name of a large, beautiful bird.

里 A measure; quarter of a mile; village; district.

俚 To trust; depend upon; rustic; vulgar.

理 To rule; direct; regulate; reason; principles; doctrine.

裡 裏 Inside of a garment; within.

鯉 The carp fish.

蠡 Name of an insect; also a shellfish.

李 A species of small plum; any small articles.

履 A shoe; to shoe; to tread upon.

旅 A stranger; guest; an army; many; arranged in order.

醴 Sweet wine; liquor distilled only one night.

詈 To implicate or blame others; to speak against.

利 Profit; profitable; gain; interest; sharp; felicitous.

唎 Sound; voice; noise.

痢 Dysentery; flux.

荔 A fragrant plant; a fruit; a rush fit for making brooms.

漦 Uninterrupted flow of water; name of a river.

涖 Water running down; to descend; go to; to supervise.

麗 Good; elegant; graceful; munificent; bright.

儷 Together with; a pair; couple; conjugal union.

灑 To sprinkle water; to wash; to scatter; disperse.

釃 To filter wine from the dregs; to separate.

厲 Severe; violent; rapid; excessive; cruel; to excite.

勵 To exert one's self; stimulate; rouse and encourage.

癘 A virulent sore; pestilence; noxious effluvia; to urge.

礪 A grindstone; whetstone.

糲 Coarse; rice not cleansed.

吏 A ruler; magistrate; an under officer.

例 To compare; adjust; laws; regulations; to compose.

裂 To rend; tear; burst.

Lia.

掠 To seize; to punish; to rob; plunder; compel.

Liak.

畧 A boundary; a plan; to abridge; little; to despise.

Liam or Niam.

帘 A tent; grog shop; a flag hung at a wine shop.

廉 Economical; moderate; uncorrupted; modest; to examine.

꜀簾 A curtain or screen.

꜀臁 The sides of the leg.

꜀薕 Name of a plant.

꜀鐮 A sickle; pruning knife.

꜀匳 A lady's toilet; box of perfume.

꜂斂 To collect; to harvest; to amass; hoard up.

꜂蘞 Name of a creeping plant.

念^{5} To ponder; consider; the thoughts; to read in a singing tone.

唸^{5} To sigh; a sigh; to recite.

捻^{5} To take work in the fingers.

殮^{5} To shroud the dead; dress for the grave.

稔^{5} Grain fully ripe; what has been long accumulating.

諗^{5} Thought; to consider; to give advice or reproof.

Liàng.

꜀良 Good; able; considerable.

꜀踉 To jump; proceed precipitately; to struggle.

꜀凉 Cool; sparing.

꜀梁 A bridge; beam or plank; the top beam of a house.

꜀粱 A species of grain; millet; tares.

꜂兩 Two; a pair; to double; an ounce weight; a two wheel carriage.

꜂倆 Art; craft; ingenuity.

꜂輛 A pair of wheels; one cart or carriage.

꜂魎 A kind of fairy or sprite; an apparition.

諒^{5} True speech; to believe; confide in; to know; to assist.

量^{5} A measure; to measure; the measure of; capacity of mind; ability to judge.

亮^{5} Clear; bright; splendid.

喨^{5} Clear distinct sound; to call plainly.

Liap.

粒$_{5}$ A grain; particle; kernel.

Lien.

꜀連 The rolling of a wheel; to return to; connect; and; also; even to.

꜀漣 A ripple on the water made by the wind; foul water.

꜀憐 To pity; compassionate; mercy.

꜀聯 Connected with; associated; to connect; arrange.

꜂璉 A vessel used in temples to contain grain.

꜂臉 The face; cheek; reputation.

靨 Handsome; beautiful; the jaws.

吝 5 / 悋 5 Niggardly; avaricious; sorry; disgraced.

煉 2 To refine metals by fire; to try; test.

練 2 To select; to make experiment; learn by experience.

鍊 2 To melt and refine metals; to try and thus benefit a man; matured; experienced.

鏈 2 A chain; connected or locked together; copper.

Liet.

列 5 To separate; arrange in order; rank; gradation.

冽 5 Cold air or vapor.

烈 5 Raging fire; impetuous; daring; fierce; excellent.

栗 5 A chestnut-tree; firm; commanding, severe; to exceed.

溧 5 Cold.

慄 5 Fear; apprehension; intimidated.

鬣 5 Name of a horse; a long beard; a brush; a pig.

Lim or Nim.

臨 To superintend; descend; come to; to commence.

林 A grove; a forest; luxuriant.

淋 Water dripping or falling; to wet or soak; to drench.

琳 Name of a stone.

痳 A stoppage of the urine; gravel.

霖 Long continued, incessant rains; abundant.

凜 Intense cold; a cold, stern manner; awe.

廩 A public granary; name of an office.

懍 Fear; respect; awe; danger; lassitude.

Lin.

隣 A neighborhood; near neighbors.

麟 A fabled animal said to appear when sages are born.

輦 The emperor's carriage; any carriage; to roll.

Lio.

僚 A companion; comrade; colleague; of the same rank.

寮 A small window; to study at the same window.

撩 To take hold of with the hand; to manage; support.

燎 Signal fires intended to rouse attention.

療 To resist disease; to cure; the practice of medicine.

瞭 Clear vision; a good eye.

繚 To wrap round; wind about; to manage.

譲 Artful, specious words; insidious language.

遼 Remote; far off.

廖 A hut; mean abode.

寥 Empty; vacant; wide; solitary.

瘳 To cure disease; convalescent.

蓼 Name of an acrid herb; name of a state.

聊 Carelessly; any how; to desire; to depend upon.

了 Finished; done; past; entirely; sign of perfect tense.

料 To measure; estimate; calculate; manage; provender; materials.

Lip.

立 Erect; to set up; establish; to fix; soon; speedily.

笠 A bamboo umbrella without a handle, like a cap.

苙 A kind of basket.

Liu.

旒 The streamers of a banner; pendent ornaments of a crown.

流 To flow; flow down; to cast off restraint; a class; clan.

琉 A pearl; vitreous substance or glaze; bright.

硫 Sulphur.

留 To stop; remain; detain; delay; slowly; a long time.

榴 The pomegranate.

溜 Name of a river; to flow; issue forth.

瑠 Vitreous substance; glass; a rice vessel.

瘤 A large swelling or tumour.

罶 A basket in which fish are taken.

遛 To linger or lurk about.

騮 A bay or chestnut horse with a black tail.

瀏 A gathering that swells and increases.

擲 To touch; lay the hand on; feel.

柳 The willow; weeping willow; a soft tree of free growth.

Lo.

盧 A furnace; a rice vessel; reeds that grow by the river.

爐 A furnace; stove; fireplace; a censer.

鑪 A vessel for wine.

蘆 Reeds that grow high on the banks of a river.

鑪 A furnace; a vase for incense; a wine vessel.

鱸 Name of a fish.

陋 Low; vulgar; obscure; petty; a narrow, dirty lane.

路 A path; road; passage; means; opportunity; way.

露 Dew; vapors in the night; genial dews.

露 To disclose; divulge; come to light.

Ló.

羅 Mournful; sorry; to occur; meet with.

羅 A net for taking birds; a species of silk; to arrange.

儸 Superior ability in the management of affairs.

囉 A tone in singing; prattle of a child; troublesome.

蘿 Creeping vines which entwine old trees.

鑼 A gong.

螺 A shellfish of the spiral form; a pearly snail.

騾 A mule.

裸 Naked; an inn.

顆 A small bead; a numeral of beads, gems &c.

惱 Something that vexes or disturbs; indignation.

瑙 Carnelian stone.

裹 To wrap up; bandaged; bundled up.

落 To fall; let fall; put down; a residence.

腦 Marrow, brains.

駱 A white horse with a black mane; a camel.

犖 A speckled cow; easily distingished; to excel.

Loi.

犁 To plough; a plough.

禮 Ceremony; rite; propriety; decorum; what is becoming.

Lok.

翏 To fly high.

勠 United strength and effort.

戮 To kill; slay; to cut in pieces; mangle; disgrace.

蓼 Long; large; mutually drawing each other.

洛 Dazzling glare of water.

烙 To burn; a red hot iron point.

絡 Thread of hemp or silk; the blood vessels; a net.

酪 Cream; the fat of milk.

雒 Name of a bird; a horse with a white mane.

碌 Stony; rocky and uneven; small.

祿 Official emoluments; salary; happiness.

錄 To transcribe; record; a record; a list.

稑 Grain, the latest planted and first ripe.

麓 The foot of a hill; a wood or forest at the foot of a hill.

Long.

農 To cultivate the ground; to plant; sow; agriculture.

儂 I; me; he; him.

濃 A thick liquid; rich; strong.

醲 Strong liquor; high flavored wine.

瓏 A large precious stone laid on the altar when praying for rain.

朧 A fat appearance.

隆 High and fertile; eminent; abundant; conspicuous.

鈴 A bell; a small bell suspended from banners.

壟 A grave; tomb; a high place in the midst of a field.

攏 To grasp; seize; use effort to effect some end; to work.

隴 A large natural bank; a dike between two fields.

竉 An aperture; a hole; a den.

Lu.

虜 To take alive; take captive as prisoners of war.

擄 To take captive; sieze; plunder.

廬 A cottage; thatch or mat huts; a temporary lodge.

[盧瓜] A species of gourd.

蘆 Name of a medicinal plant.

顱 The head; forehead; skull.

艫 A certain kind of boat; the end of a boat.

婁 An excessive number; many; stupid; simple.

僂 Curved; distorted; to bend.

摟 To draw; drag; pull; embrace.

[犭婁] A sow; female swine.

鏤 Hard iron or steel; to engrave; carve.

髏 The bones of the head; the calvaria.

鹵 Salt; salt land; natural salt.

[忄鹵] A deceived, perturbed mind; a hurried manner.

魯 Blunt; stupid; confused; name of a state.

櫓 A large shield; the large oar or skull in the stern of Chinese boats.

屢 Many times; reiterated; often.

縷 Silk thread; thread.

賂 To give; to bribe; presents; bribes.

輅 A carriage; harness; large; great.

鷺 Name of a white water-bird that flies in groups.

Lù.

攄 To extend; expand; open; spread out; to determine.

驢 A mule; an ass.

汝 }
你 } Thou; thee; you; your.

爾 Thou; thee; a euphonic and emphatic particle; a response.

呂 The spine; notes in music.

侶 An associate; companion; fellow.

閭 Gate of a village; a village of 25 families.

慮 To think on with desire, expectation or anxiety; concern; to devise; suspicion.

濾 Water; to wash, cleanse, purify; pure; to filtrate.

鑪 A heated iron with which to form or shape things.

Lua.

籮 A bamboo utensil for carrying things across the shoulders.

辣 Acrid, pungent taste; very sour.

Luan.

孌 Yielding; complying; warm affection for; longing after.

巒 The vertex or summit of a mountain.

攣 To bind or tie; to attach; interminable concatenation.

欒 Name of a tree with yellow wood, red branches and green leaves.

鑾 Bells attached to the imperial carriage; the imperial carriage.

鸞 A fabulous bird called divine.

戀 Warm affection for; ardent attachment to; devoted to.

亂 Confusion; rebellion; to confuse; make insurrection.

Luat.

劣 Infirm; weak; feeble; scarcely adequate.

閱 To inspect and take account of; to review; survey; examine.

埒 A low dike, wall or path in a field; to mark or draw limits; to class.

捋 To pluck; or take with the fingers; to rub or feel.

Lui.

雷 Thunder; a great noise; to echo.

擂 To rub or grind; to pound in a mortar.

羸 Lean; thin; meagre; emaciated.

鐳 A kind of vase.

累 To heap upon; pile up; bind; involve.

縲 A black cord; to bind or fasten with a cord.

儡 To injure; destroy; to injure mutually.

壘 A military wall; rampart; piled up; hilly.

礧 A hand-mill for grinding grain.

纍 To connect or bind together; concatenate; to implicate.

罍 A wine vessel with thunder clouds depicted on it.

藟 Name of a creeping plant.

磊 A great number of stones or rocks together.

誄 A eulogy on deceased persons; to eulogize.

蕊 The central part of a flower; pistils; suspicious.

戾 To stop; bend; crooked; perverse; wicked; to extend to.

淚 Tears; weeping; to flow rapidly.

累 To implicate; involve; injure.

彙 A hedgehog; porcupine.

類 A class; species; sort; kind.

Lun.

侖 To roll; think; arrange; spherical.

倫 Constant; regular; species; kindred; right and proper.

圇 Round; complete.

崙 Name of mountains in central Asia.

淪 Circular ripples on water; a whirpool; to perish; hell.

綸 To wind silk; to compare; classify and adjust; to sort.

輪 A wheel; large; great; to revolve; north and south.

論 To discourse about; discuss, reason; consult.

嫩 Weak; small; fine; delicate; soft; young; good.

Lut.

聿 A pen or pencil to write with; to narrate; forthwith; then; but; accordingly.

律 A law; constant rule; notes of music.

捭 To remove the dregs; to separate the pure from the impure.

綷 A large rope; a pulley; a tackle.

膟 Flesh used in sacrifices.

隼 Name of a bird of prey.

Má.

嗎 To chatter; talk much; to scold.

媽 Mother; mamma; female servants and nurses.

瑪 **碼** Carnelian stone; weights used in scales.

螞 A leech; blood-sucker.

Mai.

埋 To inter; bury; secrete; to harbour; lay up.

邁 To travel remotely; exceed; to rise supereminent.

勿 A prohibitive or hortative particle; do not.

Mák.

目 The eye; that which directs; an index; list; summary.

苜 A kind of grass to feed cattle.

Mán.

蠻 Southern barbarians; rude; barbarous.

閩 A species of serpent.

挽 To lead; draw; pull; draw back.

緩 Slow; leisurely; remiss; to delay; put off; late.

Máng.

龐 A lofty house; a mixed, confused appearance.

忙 Fluttered; hurried; pressed with business; precipitation.

汒 Wide; extensive; ocean-like,

芒 Sharp beard or point of grain; a sharp point.

茫 Vastness; vagueness; incertitude; vast as the ocean.

尨 Mixed; blended; confused.

厖 Large; abundant; affluent; a large rock.

哤 Confusion from diversity of language or dialect.

莽 Thick brushwood; confused; indistinct; disorderly.

憐 Perturbation of mind; suspicion.

蟒 The royal serpent; the largest of the serpent tribe.

虻 A mosquito.

網 A net.

夢 A dream; to dream; to see obscurely; obscure.

Mau.

矛 A kind of sword or spear.

茅 Reeds and rushes that grow high.

蟊 An insect that devours grain and the roots of plants.

眊 A dull eye; dull; stupid; drunk; old.

旄 A kind of banner; a cow's tail used to make signals.

耄 Thirty years of age; old.

髦 Hair of the head hanging down; mane of a horse; a locust.

冒 To advance blindfold; rush on heedless of consequences.

娼 Envious; to dislike; envy.

惛 Inordinate desire; covetous.

貌 External appearance; the air; manner; visage.

Me.

猛 Violent; fierce; quick; hasty; impatient.

蜢 A species of locust; a kind of light boat.

夜 Night; dark; obscure.

罵 To revile; rail at; scold; reprove.

脈 A vein; the pulse; current of blood.

咩 The voice of a sheep.

Mek.

貊 A northern tribe of barbarians; quiet; fixed.

陌 A raised path between fields; a street; road.

嘿 Quiet; silent; still; also disquieted in mind.

默 Dark; still; sombre.

霢 Small rain that falls without noise.

驀 To mount a horse; to leap or pass over.

Meng.

明 Clearness; brightness; clear; intelligent; to shed light on.

盟 An oath; imprecation; to bind one's self with an oath.

萌 To bud forth; spring up.

茗 The buds of the tea plant; tea; strong wine.

酩 A drink prepared from wheat or other grain.

銘 To remember; cause to remember; record; engrave.

冥 Obscure; gloomy; a silent recess; *hades*; darkness of mind.

暝 Dull; obscure; the shades of night.

꜀溟 A drizzling rain; cloudy vapors; immense waters.

꜀瞑 To shut the eyes; dullness of sight.

꜀蓂 Name of a fortunate plant.

꜀盲 Blind; precipitate.

꜀鳴 The note or voice of a bird; any sound, as of a bell, an insect.

꜂皿 Crockery and earthen ware; a vessel.

命⁵ Command; decree; fate; life; destiny of men.

孟⁵ A senior or superior; the beginning of; large.

Mi.

꜀迷 Deceived; tempted; led astray; a blind, stupid attachment to; to deceive.

꜀瞇 Dullness or obscurity of vision; badness of sight.

꜀麋 A large species of deer; a buffalo; water plants.

꜀糜 Rice boiled to gruel; to destroy entirely; soft; rotten.

꜀爢 Boiled to pieces; destroyed; torn; oppressed.

꜀棉 Name of a tree; the Bombax Pentandrum; Cotton.

꜂靡 Not; not having; not being; slowly; to stop; wasteful; prostrate.

꜂縻 A halter for a cow; to conduct or fasten; lead or drag.

꜂亹 Exertion; unwearied.

謎⁵ An enigma; a riddle.

媚⁵ Adulation; flattery; looks of love or seduction; smiling.

袂⁵ A sleeve or cuff; an embroidered sleeve; to open and spread out.

麪꜄ Wheaten flour.

乜꜆ Which one? what?

Mia.

꜀名 Name; reputation.

命² Life; what depends on the decree of heaven.

Mien.

꜀綿 Uninterrupted continuation; remote; enduring.

꜀勔 To endeavor; to encourage; stimulate.

꜀緬 Fine silk; remote; absent; to think over and over.

꜂閔 Mourners; grief; disease caused by grief; exertion.

꜂憫 Grief; commiseration; to compassionate; pity.

꜂黽 To strive; to force one's self; to constrain.

꜂免 To dispense with; prevent; avoid; put away.

‘勉 To endeavor; use effort; to force one's self to do; to persuade; stimulate.

‘娩 ‘挽 To bring forth offspring; parturition.

‘冕 A crown.

‘浼 An extensive sheet of water; exhausted; destroyed.

‘敏 Clearness and quickness of perception; respectful.

Min.

民 A people; the common people.

泯 To destroy; drown; perish.

眠 To shut the eyes; confused; bewildered.

緡 A fish line; a line or cord; a string of coin.

氓 People who leave their own country and become naturalized to another.

面 The face; face to face; front; towards.

Mio.

玅 Small; minute; abstruse.

苗 The first budding forth of a plant; sprouts; progeny.

錨 An anchor.

猫 A cat.

‘杪 The highest point of a tree; tips of the branches.

‘渺 White; glittering; vast; indistinct.

‘緲 Fine flowing; applied to style.

‘藐 Small; to esteem small; despise; contemptuous.

‘邈 Remote; to look at in a distant manner; contempt.

‘杳 Distant; obscure; profound; setting sun.

Mit.

威 To consume; destroy, as by fire.

滅 To consume; exterminate; cut off; extinguish.

宓 To stop; rest; repose; stillness; silent; secret.

蜜 Honey; sweet; flattering.

陌 A raised path between two fields; a road.

覓 To search; enquire after; seek for what is not seen.

Mno.

牟 To advance; encroach upon; invade; seize.

侔 Equal to; of the same rank or class; even.

眸 The pupil of the eye; the eye.

麰 Barley.

丘 The name of Confucius.

牡 The male of animals.

牳 A cow; the female of cattle.

貿 To barter; trade; buy and sell.

Mó.

痲 A cutaneous disease; measles; leprosy.

摩 To touch; rub; grind; to press; urge; destroy.

魔 Devils; demons supposed to afflict men.

毛 Hair.

模 A pattern or mould; the form; manner or figure of.

蟆 A frog.

謨 Plans fully matured; to devise; instruct.

麼 An interrogative particle.

募 To invite to do; a general invitation, as to join the army &c.

墓 A grave; a tomb.

幕 A private secretary; friends of an officer; tent.

慕 To desire ardently, to think of; hanker after; respect.

摹 To imitate a pattern; a form or rule.

暮 Evening; the sun setting.

望 To expect; hope; look for.

漠 Floating sands; a desert; a dry, careless manner.

膜 The delicate skin beneath the cuticle; to soothe; to touch delicately.

Mok.

莫 Not; is not; used to express the highest degree.

寞 Silence; stillness; quiet.

睦 Cordial; harmonious; kind; attached to.

穆 Pleasing deportment; commanding respect; cordial.

繆 Intimate intercourse; name of bad import applied to persons after death.

牧 A shepherd; to feed; to oversee; take care of.

沐 To wash and oil the hair; wash; to enrich; be enriched.

霂 Small rain that falls without noise.

Mong.

蒙 Dullness of perception; rash; rudely; to receive with gratitude; obtain; thanks.

幪 To cover over; shelter; a screen; abundant.

懞 Blind; stupid.

矇 The sun obscured by vapors; dull perception.

濛 Drizzling rain; thick; foggy.

朦 Dull; obscure; blind; ignorant.

朦 Fleshy; big; obscure; to obscure.

艨 A long narrow species of war junk.

霿 Small, drizzling rain.

摸 To seek by feeling with the hand; to feel; grasp.

謀 To deliberate; devise; contrive; consult; provide.

某 Used instead of the name of person or thing; I.

茂 Luxuriant; affluent; strong; elegant.

懋 The mind fully engaged; strenuous effort; abundant.

Mua.

麻 / 蔴 Hemp; a plant of which the skin is made into cloth.

饅 Cakes; bread; flour.

鰻 Name of a fish resembling an eel.

瞞 Dullness of sight; to blind; deceive; impose upon.

滿 Full; the whole; sufficient; the completion of a thing.

懣 Vexation and grief; sorrow and concern of mind.

Muan.

曼 A connective particle; and; therefore; vegetation.

嫚 Remiss; disrespectful; to insult; to defile.

幔 A kind of curtain; covering or screen.

慢 Leisurely; easily; remissly; disrespectful; proud.

漫 Excessive quantity of water; spreading and extending remotely.

蔓 Plants which creep and spread widely; intricate; extensive.

謾 To insult; disrespectful; to attempt to deceive.

Muat.

末 The end; last.

Mue.

痲 A cutaneous disease with fever and pustules; measles.

每 Each; every; always; constancy; although.

昧 Obscure; dull; sunset; blindly; without consideration.

沬 Name of a river; to wash the face.

眛 Dullness of sight; indistinct vision.

魅 A demon, fairy or elf that frightens and seduces men.

寐 To rest; shut the eyes; sleep; sleepily; stupid.

妹ˀ Younger sisters.

物ͻ A thing; anything; an item.

Mui.

꜀微 Obscure; abstruse; small; minute; delicate; slightly.

꜀薇 Vegetables for the table.

ˊ美 Excellent; beautiful; good; to praise.

Mᵘng.

꜀門 A door; gate; entrance; a family; disciple; sect.

ˊ晚 Evening; late; too late.

問ˀ To ask; enquire.

Mut.

歿ͻ To terminate; end; die; dead.

沒ͻ To exceed; transgress; to sink; drown; terminate; die; no; not; is not.

疫ͻ Pestilence; plague; distemper.

囫ͻ Complete; whole; round; undivided.

吻ͻ The sides of the mouth; the lips.

Ná.

꜀籃 A large basket.

ˊ那 That; there.

ˊ拏 } To take hold of; seize; apprehend; receive.
꜀拿 }

ˊ欖 An olive fruit or tree.

Nai.

ˊ乃 But; then; certainly; is; was; a connective particle.

ˊ奶 } The female breast; milk; to suckle.
ˊ嬭 }

ˊ鼐 A large vase or tripod.

耐ͻ To bear with; forbear; endure; patient forbearance.

奈ͻ To occur; meet with; as; like; how; resource.

賴ͻ To lean, depend or rely upon; that which supports.

Náng.

꜀人 A man; human being, male or female; an individual.

Náp.

納ͻ To present or offer to; to receive; accept.

喏ͻ } A tone of approbation, assent or promising; to answer.
諾ͻ }

Nau.

撓 To twist; wrench; disturb; vex; mix; confess.

惱 Indignation; grief.

腦 The marrow of the head; brains; glossy; soft.

弩 A cross-bow fitted to throw several arrows in succession.

Ne.

冷 Cold; solitary; lonely; careless.

Nek.

肉 Flesh; animal food; body.

搦 To lay the hand on; grasp; excite; provoke.

溺 To drown; sink down in water, vice, intoxication, &c.

匿 To hide; conceal; be hidden; abscond; clandestine.

慝 Feeling of shame; to be ashamed.

Neng.

能 Power; able; morally able; willing.

Ng.

黃 Yellow; the color of earth.

秧 The blade springing up; thick and close.

'Ng.

園 A garden; an enclosure.

方 A place; region; a plan; means; a recipe.

Ngai.

呆 Foolish; stupid.

涯 The bank of a river or stream; a shore.

刈 Shears; to cut herbs; reap; to regulate; put in order; talents.

艾 Name of a caustic plant; a person fifty years old.

岸 A high shore; bank of a river; eminent; the end.

崖 The side of a high hill; a precipice; a bank.

睚 To look at with suspicion, contempt or hatred; to squint at.

Ngák.

崿 A high, abrupt bank.

愕 Struck with sudden surprise; astonishment.

諤 Plain, straight forward language; honest.

鄂 A limit; boundary; surprise.

萼 The central parts of a flower.

噩 Alarm; fright; reverential awe; sincere.

英漢潮州方言字典

鱷 An alligator; sea-monster.

岳 嶽 Lofty or craggy summit of a mountain.

Ngám.

巖 A precipitous shore or cliff; lofty; mountainous.

誾 An inner gate; to stimulate; stir up; reform.

Ngán.

言 To speak; say; a word or sentence; words; discourse.

眼 The eye.

彥 Eminent; excellent; much extolled.

喭 To mourn and grieve for the sufferings of men.

諺 A proverb; maxim; a plain pithy saying.

鴈 Geese of the smaller sort.

Ngáng.

卬 Used by females for I; great; high; dear in price.

昂 To elevate; to rise as the sun; lofty; a dignified carriage.

Ngau.

爻 A character used in divination.

肴 Provisions of any kind except rice.

淆 Name of a river; confused; mixed.

翱 To fly or roam about; to spread the wings.

敖 To trifle and ramble about; proud; clamorous; rude.

熬 To dry or roast with fire; to bake, boil; broil.

遨 To ramble; wander.

鰲 Name of a fish.

驁 A spirited or untractable horse; proud; domineering.

囂 To make a noise; vociferation; clamor; reviling.

嗷 Incessant noise; clamoring for food.

傲 Uncivil; proud; to treat with neglect; haughty.

獒 A large species of dog.

樂 To be pleased; fond of; love.

殽 Mixed; blended; confused; pulse; flesh and bones.

Nge.

硬 Hard; firm; obstinate; perverse.

勁 Strong; unyielding; violent; overbearing.

Ngek.

逆 To meet; oppose; resist; withstand; rebel.

Ngeng.

꜀迎 To meet; escort; welcome; receive.

꜀凝 To congeal; freeze; coagulate; stern; rigorous; to fix.

Ngi.

꜀宜 Fit; right; proper; suitable to; ought; harmony; business.

꜀倪 Small children; to benefit; a limit; boundary.

꜀蜺 Name of certain insects; a rainbow.

꜀輗 A crossbar in front of a carriage.

꜀霓 A certain various colored animalcule; a rainbow.

꜀鯢 A certain kind of large fish.

꜀麑 A certain large animal like a lion; a deer.

꜀儀 Right; proper; a rule; pattern; a rite; manner.

꜂議 To consult; deliberate; dispute; to plan; select.

꜂儗 False; doubtful; suspicion; to compare.

꜂擬 To conjecture; surmise; to conclude; decide; similar.

羿[5] A master of archery.

義[5] Good; right; proper; righteousness; charitable.

毅[5] Fortitude; magnanimity; intrepid; unbending.

誼꜄ What is fit or proper for man; virtue; acquaintances; friends.

Ngia.

꜂雅 A species of crow; correct; decorous; learned; elegant.

Ngiak.

孽[5] Illegitimate children; the offspring or consequences of vice.

蘖[5] The roots or stump of a tree which is cut down.

糵[5] A fermenting substance.

軏[5] Part of a harness; a yoke.

虐[5] Unfeeling; harsh; cruel; tyranizing over; calamities.

瘧[5] A severe disease; ague and fever.

謔[5] To play or trifle with; to seduce; to ridicule.

臬[5] A mark to shoot at; a rule; a law; a judge.

闑[5] A pillar or small door in the middle of a gateway.

Ngiam.

꜀嚴 Cold; severe; stern; grave; strict; commanding; reverence.

꜂儼 Carrying a high head; stern; commanding; dignified.

驗꜄ To witness; verify; fulfillment of what has been said.

Ngiàng.

仰 To look up to, as with regard, admiration, or a sense of dependence; to rely on.

Ngiap.

業 An occupation; livelihood; patrimony; possessions; sign of the past tense.

Ngien.

妍 Elegant; beautiful; well versed or skilled in.

研 To grind; rub; dissolve in water; to investigate to the utmost.

Ngiet.

喫 To eat; drink; bear or put up with.

齧 To bite; gnaw; seize with the teeth.

Ngim.

唫 A hurried enunciation; to close up; shut.

吟 To sigh; moan; chaunt; recite.

岑 A high peak of a mountain; mournful.

黔 Black; black hair; a designation of the people of China.

Ngio.

堯 High; eminent; a famous ancient king of China.

蕘 Stubble or rushes used for fuel.

譊 Noisy; clamorous; contentious; debate.

鐃 A kind of bell used in the army; trumpets &c.

猫 A cat.

Ngo.

偶 A carved image of a man; two; a pair; of the same class; to pair; to happen.

耦 To plough or work in pairs; to pair; to occur; to meet.

藕 Name of a water plant.

伍 A file of five men; five families, mutually responsible.

午 A horary character, from 11 o'clock A. M. to 1. P. M.

忤 Disobedient; rebellious; undutiful.

迕 To meet; encounter; oppose; confused.

五 Five.

Ngó.

禺 Solitary; none to associate with.

愚 Simple; ignorant; stupid; used for I.

慪 Pleased; cheerful.

隅 A corner; an angle; a nook; rigid integrity.

俄 Hasty; momentary; sudden; appearing to fall.

哦 To recite; the tone of recitative.

娥 Good; a name.

峨 High; lofty.

莪 Name of an edible plant.

蛾 A silkworm; an insect.

虞 To consider; weigh; anxious thought; impediment.

圄 To detain; hold fast; to imprison; a prison.

梧 Name of a remarkable tree.

悟[5] To arouse or awaken the mind; to notice; perceive.

晤[5] Light; bright; to meet or speak together; explain.

寤[5] To awake from sleep; talking; to dream.

寓[5] A temporary lodging; to lodge; to pertain to.

遇[5] To meet unexpectedly; to occur; to happen.

Ngui.

危 Dangerous; situated on an eminence; ready to fall; danger.

峗 嵬 } Hilly; mountainous; danger.

巍 High; lofty; name of a kingdom.

僞[5] False; counterfeit; not genuine; fraudulent.

詭[5] To reprimand; deceive; impose upon.

Ngùn.

銀 Silver; money; metal.

誾 Cordial; respectful; upright; to debate in good temper.

嚚 Simple; stupid; silly; false.

Ngùt.

吃 To stammer; stutter; eat; swallow.

屹 A hill standing alone; a firm martial appearance.

汔 Water dried up; how? nearly.

矻 Constant and severe labor; determined effort.

圪 To stand erect.

訖 To come to a close; stop; finish; finished; closed; wound up.

迄 To reach or extend to; finally; at last.

齕 To bite or gnaw with the teeth; to eat.

兀 High and level at the top; to cut off the feet

Ngwan.

元 The first cause; origin; commencement; the first; the chief.

黿 A kind of fabulous tortoise.

原 A level waste ground or common; origin; commencement; again.

源 A source or spring of water; a source; cause.

顏 The countenance; forehead; color; appearance; reputation.

玩 A precious stone; to be fond of; play with; seduce.

阮 Name of a hill and of a certain kind of barrier.

頑 Simple; foolish; stupid; obstinate.

愿 Reverential; sincere; pious, virtuous; *used for the next.*

願 To desire; wish for; an object of desire; a vow; willing.

Ni.

尼 To accord with; concord; a budhist nun; stopped.

伲 Thou; thee; you.

坭 Soft earth; mire; name of a place.

妮 A slave girl; a budhist nun.

泥 Mire; miry; thick; adhesive; stagnant; bigoted.

涅 Mire; clay; miry; clayey.

年 A year; a person's age.

苨 Name of a tree which bears a small fruit.

瀰 To let go the string of a bow; to shoot; to extend remotely.

禰 Ancestral temple; hall of a father.

鮞 A species of small fish.

趍 To walk up hastily to; to embrace an opportunity.

女 To give a girl in marriage; to marry.

呢 An interrogative particle; also used for if; when.

昵 Related to; connected or associated with; near.

麑 A young deer; a young animal of any kind.

Nia.

聆 To hear; listen; obey.

領 The neck; a collar; to accept; receive; to govern.

嶺 The top or side of a hill; a mountain; a summit.

Niam.

拈 To take hold of with the fingers; to handle.

粘 黏 Paste; to paste; to be connected with.

Niap.

咡 The sides and corners of the mouth; side of the head.

聶 A whisper addressed to the ear of another.

囁 Chattering; vilifying; backbiting; loquacious.

懾 Timid; fearing.

攝 To take with the hand; to lift up as long garments.

躡 To tread upon; to ascend; walk up.

鑷 Tweezers; forceps; nippers.

捏 To take and collect with the fingers; to make a pretext.

涅 Black, dirty mud at the bottom of stagnant water.

Nie.

梁 A wooden bridge; a beam or plank; the top beam of a house.

樑 The ridgepole of a house.

量 To measure; to estimate; to judge; a measure; capacity.

糧 粮 Grain for food; daily rations; food; taxes.

娘 A respectful appellation of females.

兩 両 An ounce; a tael.

Nien.

年 A year; one's age.

Nio.

嫋 Long and slender; delicate; waving in the wind.

裊 Profound; remote; soft; delicate; to wind round.

Niu.

扭 To turn or twist with the hand; to wring; to grasp.

狃 A proud dog; a fox; accustomed; familiar; disrespectful.

紐 To bind; tie; a knot; jointure.

衄 To bleed at the nose; to wound.

鈕 A knob; a button.

恧 An internal feeling or sense of shame.

謬 Mistake; erroneous; falacious; false.

No.

奴 A slave.

伮 Great strength; murderous strength; desperate attack.

努 Exertion of strength; strenuous effort.

呶 Outcry; vociferation; clamor.

Nó.

孥 帑 Children and grand-children; delicate; a storehouse.

駑 An ugly old horse; a carriage horse.

懦 Weak; timorous; fearful; apprehensive.

儺 To drive away demons by certain rites; abundant; delicate.

耨 A hoe for rooting up weeds; to clear away weeds.

娜 Easy; leisurely; elegant; beautiful.

挪 To rub with the hand; to change from one use to another.

挼 To rub between both hands.

二 Two.

怒 Anger; displeasure; to be angry with.

Noi.

蓮 A water lily.

Nuan.

暖 Warm; temperate; mild; soft; bland.

煖 Warmth of fire; warm.

Nue.

餒 Hunger; famine; putrid fish or flesh.

Nui.

耒 A plough-handle; a plough.

Nⁿng.

郞 Name of an office; a respectful appellation of masters, husbands &c.

女 A woman; female; daughter.

軟 Soft; flexible; yielding; the wheel of a carriage.

卵 An egg.

Nut.

喏
訥 To stammer; slow of speech.

O.

湖 A lake; name of a river.

箶 A species of bamboo.

烏 A crow; black; an interrogative particle; how?

嫗 A mother; the fructifying influences of nature.

謳 To recite; sing verses or songs; to nourish.

鷗 A certain kind of water-fowl.

芋 An edible plant, with a solid root & large leaf; luxuriant.

O'.

蠔 The rough coarse oysters; a cluster of oysters.

荷 The water-lily; generic name of plants; burden.

呵 To speak angrily; reprehend; to interrogate; reiterated.

阿 O! ah! a familiar prefix to a person's name; who? what; distorted.

娿 Feeble; unsteady; weak.

猗 Soft; flexible; waving as a mulberry tree.

窩 A den; a cavern; a hollow place; solitary dwelling.

鍋 A boiler; a utensil for containing fat.

襖 A certain part of a dress; a short garment.

臥5 Sleeping; lying down; prostrate.

荷5 To bear or sustain; to bear a burden.

澳5 A deep river or bay; an entrance; a dock.

Oi.

鞋 Shoes.

挨 To place by the side of; to introduce; draw by force.

矮 A dwarf; of low stature.

隘5 A narrow pass; in narrow circumstances; urgent; straightened.

Oⁿi.

閒 A crevice; space between; interval; leisure; unoccupied.

閑 A barrier; a fence; to ward off; protect; large.

Ok.

屋 A habitation; house; a covering.

偓 To restrict; limit.

喔 Crowing of a cock.

幄 A curtain; a tent.

握 To grasp in the hand; to take a handful.

渥 Moistened; tinged; imbued; enriched; glossy.

齷 Closely pressed; embarrassed; to gnash the teeth.

澚 A bank; a shore.

沃 To water plants; flourishing; soft; fertile.

Ong.

翁 Feathers on the neck of a bird; a title of respect for old people.

(扌+翁)5 To tend a babe; toss up and down gently; embrace.

Pá.

巴 Wilderness; the country in distinction from the city.

吧 Large mouthed; angry; crying of an infant.

爸 Aged; an aged person; father.

笆 A thorny kind of bamboo; a hedge; fence.

芭 The blossoms and flowers of plants.

把 To take hold of; grasp; sieze; read *pe*, a numeral of things taken in the hand.

飽 Full; having eaten sufficient; satiated.

罷 To desist; put a stop to; a final particle; enough; well.

霸 To encroach; usurp; use force; compel; a prickly plant.

豹 A leopard.

Pʻá.

疱 A disease which causes swelling; swollen; a swelling.

冇 Empty, as grain without a kernel; withered; blasted.

怕 To fear; be afraid.

拍 To pat; touch; stroke.

打 To strike; beat; to reckon; commence; do.

Pai.

牌 A tablet; an order of government; a permit; passport; warrant; a shield.

排 To arrange; adjust; put in order; spread out.

擺 To separate; spread out; open; to strike; rouse.

敗 To subvert or be subverted; to break; spoil; ruin.

拜 To bow; worship; to bow in token of accepting anything.

湃 The sound of water increasing and rushing.

Pʻai.

徘 Dissolute play and amusement; irresolute; fickle.

派 To branch off; ramify; appoint to various departments.

沛 Increasing; copious; superabundant; rainy.

霈 Heavy rains; water flowing; marshy.

Pák.

縛 To bind; tie fast; roll up.

幅 A wide piece of cloth; roll of cloth or paper.

腹 The stomach; abdomen.

北 North; to go north.

剝 To split; tear; peel; flay; uncover; cut up.

Pʻák.

暴 To dry in the sun; scorch; bear the heat of the sun.

瀑 A heavy rain; water rushing down; in a spring.

爆 To dry by the fire; to heat; to fire crackers; to rend.

雹 Hail; frozen rain.

博 General; extensive; universal; profound.

搏 To strike with the hand; to touch; to fight; to wrest from.

膊 To strip and mangle slaughtered bodies; ribs and shoulders.

賻 To help; assist; assist with money.

Pán.

瓶 A large wine pitcher.

班 To confer; distribute; place in order; a series; rank; class.

斑 Streaks; stripes; variegated colors.

扳 攀 To pull back; to lead; draw to; reach up and grasp anything; pull down; climb up.

頒 To confer; distribute; disperse; numerous.

板 A flat board; a bastinade; a register; board for engraving words.

版 A board; plank; a list; register; tablet.

舨 A boat.

扮[2] To dress; set in order; a dress; apparel.

P'án.

盼[2] A beautiful eye; to look affectionately; to look about.

Páng.

房 A dwelling; a house; a room; an office.

枋 A certain wood fit for making carriages.

崩 To fall down from a high place; death of the emperor.

邦 A state; a nation; district.

幫 幇 To assist; help; an assistant; a second; to bind a shoe.

綁 To tie; to bind with cords.

榜 A splinter; the rule by which officers and literati are chosen; a notification.

傍[5] To approach; to lean against; lateral; to stand by the side.

搒[5] To screen; propel a boat; to strike; wrest from.

謗[5] To slander; vilify; to injure one's reputation.

放[2] To let go; send away; drive away; to put; lay down.

P'áng.

旁 Large; great; by the side; near to.

徬 To run by the side of, as a driver.

滂 Rain; water rushing down; a torrent.

磅 A stone falling; to rub or grind; a crash.

膀 The groin.

螃 A crab; a fish that goes side-ways.

帆 A sail; canvass; to sail.

龐 A lofty house; filled full; crammed.

蠭 A bee; a wasp; in swarms or crowed.

紡 Hempen threads; cords; to twist; spin.

Pau.

包 To wrap round; infold; envelope; contain.

胞 That which surrounds an infant in the womb; a bladder.

苞 Grass of which mats are made; the hull or husk of grain.

暴 Scorching; cruel; fierce; oppressive; violent wind.

菢 To cover over, as a bird its eggs.

鮑 Fish preserved in brine.

P'au.

刨 To pare off; to plane; to dig; a joiner's plane.

咆 To roar; the roar of a wild beast; angry.

庖 A kitchen; cook house; a cook.

泡 Bubbles on agitated or boiling water; blisters or pustules on the skin.

瓟 A gourd of which drinking cups are made.

袍 A cloak or large and long garment.

拋 To throw stones with the hand; to throw; cast; a cannon.

褒 To praise; to commend virtuous and proper conduct.

跑 To run; run away; to stamp; excavate the earth.

炮 A gun; cannon; rocket; to bake in the cinders.

砲 An engine for throwing stones; a gun; a mortar.

Pe.

爬 To scrape; scratch; crawl like a crab.

耙 鈀 A harrow; a rake; barbed arrow; military carriage.

筢 A rake.

琶 A three stringed instrument played with the hands.

抓 To scratch gently; tickle; to cajole.

杷 A handle; an instrument for levelling the ground.

父 A father.

白 White; clear; manifest; to explain; gratuitously.

帛 Silk; cloth goods; property; an official title; wealth.

百 A hundred; the whole number or species; many.

伯 A senior; superior; a father's elder brother.

栢 The cypress or fir; large; great; to urge.

擘 To beat the breast; break; to open; drive away.

P'e.

帕 A napkin; handkerchief; ornaments for the head.

袙 A turban; napkin to cover the forehead; apron.

P^{n}e.

棚 A temporary tent or shed.

病 Sickness; disease; defect; fault; to cause disease.

柄 A handle; authority; control.

P$^{\prime n}$e.

平 Even; level; smooth.

彭 Sound of a drum; appendages to military chariots; abundant; haughty; a path.

膨 A large swelled belly.

Pek.

迫 Urgent; pressing; to press hard upon and embarrass.

偪 To oppress; use ill; to compress; to fill; distend.

逼 To press upon; reduce to straits; tyrannize over.

P$^{\prime}$ek.

辟 A title of royal personages; majestic; punishment; laws.

劈 To strike or break open; to tear; split; cut.

擘 To open; break; the fingers.

癖 Indigestion; costiveness; a craving appetite; phlegm.

襞 To fold or plait garments.

闢 To shake; burst forth or open; to expand; retire.

霹 The shock and noise of thunder; crashing of an earthquake.

珀 Amber.

碧 A stone of azure or bluish color.

魄 The animal soul; sentient principle; form.

匐 To fall prostrate; to go on the hands and knees; to hasten.

蔔 A species of turnip.

Peng.

崩 Death of the emperor or high rulers.

駢 A pair of horses attached to a carriage; together.

胼 Hard, stiff, indurated skin; callous.

迸 To be dispersed; to wander idly; flow away; expel.

秉 A handful; to grasp; lay hold of; adhere to.

炳 The light of fire; luminous; perspicuous.

掽^{5} To expel; drive away.

竝^{5} **并**^{5} Together with; and; also; moreover; united.

併^{5} On a line with; even; together; to reject.

P'eng.

平 Even; equal; just; level; tranquil; to level; to subjugate.

坪 Level ground.

秤 To weigh; a certain weight.

評 To deliberate; arrange; decide; fix; criticise.

憑 Leaning on; proof; what may be proved.

朋 Of the same school, class or society; an equal; a friend.

鵬 A fabulous bird transformed into a fish.

烹 To boil water or other substances; to cook.

聘[2] To ask; inquire of; invite; to betroth; an embassy of peace.

騁[2] To walk; run; press forward at full speed.

Pi.

屁 To pass wind backwards; contempt for a person.

琵 To push from; name of a stringed instrument.

秕 Blasted grain; tares; chaff or grain not filled.

痺 A disease arising from damp.

脾 The internal membrane of the stomach; to stop.

碑 A stone tablet erected at tombs, in temples &c.

貔 Name of an animal resembling a hog.

匕 A spoon; a ladle.

比 To compare; classify; collate; prepare.

妣 A deceased mother; a female ancestor.

彼 That person, place, or thing; that; he.

俻[5], 備[5] Completed; ready; prepared; to prepare; provide.

俾[5] To cause that; to enable; to perform; accord.

婢[5] A female slave.

庳[5] A low cottage; low; short; the nose.

裨[5] To be benefited; to assist; supply what is deficient; to enable.

閉[5] To shut a door; to stop or close up; conceal.

枇[5] A fruit tree; a fine comb.

紕[5] Silk fringes and tassels applied to flags; a series.

陛[5] Stairs; steps; to ascend high.

敝[5] Bad; spoiled; poor; tattered raiment; evil; vice; crime.

幣[5] Silk; wealth; present.

蔽[5] To shade; shelter; conceal; screen; small.

斃 To die; dead.

被 A sign of the passive verb; is; a covering; to cover over.

貔 Name of a ferocious animal resembling a tiger.

毖 Careful; attentive; painstaking; laborious.

柲 The handle of a spear; a pair; stem of a pencil.

泌 Water flowing from a spring constantly increasing and widening.

避 To avoid; shun; retire from; escape.

獘 To fall prostrate or dead; to kill; wearied; vicious.

賁 Glossed over; ornamented; herbage.

秘 Mysterious; divine; abstruse; secret.

閟 Anything secret; mysterious; careful.

庇 Affording shade and shelter; to cover over; protect.

詖 Artful debate and litigation; insidious accusation.

轡 The reins by which a horse is guided.

臂 The arm from the elbow to the wrist.

鼈 A species of tortoise.

P'i.

疲 Fatigued; wearied; lassitude; weakness.

披 To open; spread out; spread over; cast off; break.

鄙 A small confined city; rustic; low; vulgar; vicious.

丕 Large; to present to; to receive with respect.

坯 To erect a mound; to fill up; add; increase.

邳 Name of a place.

痞 Pain; disease; a gathering in the abdomen; stoppage.

嬖 Partiality for; blind affection; depraved; a prostitute.

譬 To make a comparison; to compare; illustrate; a parable.

Pⁿi.

邊 On the frontier; border; by the side of; outside.

辮 To plait; twist; interweave.

鼻 The nose; nostrils; to smell.

Pia.

壁 A wall; a rampart; a rocky precipice.

璧 A round precious stone used as a badge of authority; an auspicious stone.

P'ai.

僻 Mean; low; depraved; licentious; deflected.

癖 See *P'ek.*

Pⁿia.

兵 Soldiers; an army; weapons of war; to attack.

冰 冰 Ice; gum, as camphor, rock sugar &c.

丙 An astronomical character used in the cycle.

餅 Food made of flour, as pastry, cakes, biscuit.

并 Together with; also; both together.

Pᵗⁿia.

聘 To betroth; espouse; ask; enquire of; invite.

Pie.

漂 To float; sail; moved and agitated as by the wind.

裱 A lady's kerchief; pictures pasted on anything.

P'ie.

萍 Moss-like substance which grows on stagnant water.

票 A goverment warrant; a broker's ticket; a written order.

摽 To strike; to beat or lay the hand upon the breast; to make a signal.

Pien.

綆 The rope of a well; a rope for drawing water.

鞭 A whip, lash or rod; to whip; flog.

籩 Name of an office; a basket used in sacrifice.

匾 A thin utensil; flat; a board; or tablet.

卞 Hurry; perturbed; hasty; a law; system of government.

忭 Gladsome; joyful.

抃 To touch with the hand; to strike the hands together, as in beating time, dancing etc.

便 Ease; convenient; advantageous; then; forthwith; thus.

辨 To divide; distinguish; discuss; ascertain.

瓣 The internal sections of fruit like an orange; petals of flowers.

辯 To distinguish; judge; discriminate clearly; to dispute.

變 A change; alteration; revolution; calamity.

徧 遍 To go round; extend every where; to pervade every place.

P'ien.

偏 Lateral; inclined; partial to; selfish; depraved; bent upon; side.

篇 A leaf or section of a book; writing on a slip of bamboo.

編 To arrange together in proper order; to bind; plait.

翩 To fly swiftly; crowd and bustle; troops and banners.

蝙 A bat; also the name of a fish.

褊 Small; straight; cramped; narrow.

蹁 Lame or distorted about the foot; the knee pan.

便 Continuous talking.

扁 A tablet with an inscription; flat.

片 A splinter; fragment; a bit; a slip; to divide; judge.

騙 To mount a horse; to cheat; deceive; take advantage of.

Piet.

別 To divide; separate; distinguish.

畢 The end; at last; finally.

Pin.

賓 A guest; a visitor; to receive a visitor.

儐 To accompany; to receive a guest with due ceremony; to pay respect to.

嬪 A woman; a beautiful woman; a deceased wife.

擯 To expel; reject; an envoy; to receive a national visitor.

濱 The margin of a river, lake or sea; contiguous; near.

繽 Numerous; crowded; mixed; variegated; in confusion.

鑌 Refined steel suitable for knives or swords.

邠 Name of a province or state.

斌 彬 A due mixture of plainness and ornament.

豳 Name of an ancient state.

品 A series; rank; class; actions; conduct; to arrange; a thing.

稟 To give; confer; receive; receive what is conferred; to state before a superior.

殯 To perform funeral rites; to inter.

鬢 The hair on the temples.

遍 See *Pien*.

篦 A comb; a bamboo rake; to lead; draw.

P'in.

屏 A screen inside a door; to screen; cover; reject.

缾 A pitcher or other utensil for containing wine.

貧 Indigent; poor.

頻 Urgent; pressing; precipitate; uninterrupted; continually.

嚬 To contract the eyebrows, as in smiling, anger or sorrow.

蘋 Name of a plant which grows on the surface of water.

顰 To frown; contract the eyebrows.

櫇 The apple-tree.

牝 Female; the female organ of generation.

砭 A stone needle; a probe; to probe.

貶 To censure; blame; detract from; injure.

Pio.

嫖 Levity; given up to prostitution; addicted to lewdness.

表 Exterior; external; to manifest; point out; a manifest.

俵 To give; distribute.

殍 To die of hunger; famished to death; decayed trees &c.

P'io.

剽 To prick an ulcer; to cut off; rob; plunder; swift; urgent.

嘌 Irregular; without rule, law or limit.

慓 Urgent; pressed; vehement.

標 The highest point of a tree; a signal; sign board; a warrant.

瓢 A species of gourd of which drinking cups are made.

螵 A species of spider.

驃 A fleet horse; strong and valorous.

飄 A whirlwind; a sudden and violent wind; blown about.

麃 Name of an animal resembling a deer; martial.

瀌 Rain and snow blended; a fall of sleet.

穮 To eradicate weeds from a field.

藨 A plant of which mats and sandals are made.

Pit.

畢 The end; close; termination; finished; at last.

篳 A hedge; an inclosure; a mean abode; a cart.

蓽 Name of a medicinal plant; a wicket gate.

蹕 To oblige to stop; to clear the way for the emperor; imperial travelling.

弼 A splice attached to a bow; to assist; add to; distorted.

觱 A horn blown to frighten horses.

筆 A pen, pencil or any utensil for writing with.

必 Decided; certain; necessary; must.

P'it.

匹 A pair; to correspond to; a husband or wife; intimate; single; a numeral of horses.

疋 A roll or piece of silk or cloth; a numeral of pieces of cloth.

Piu.

彪 Streaks, spots or veins, as of a tiger; a small tiger; a company.

Po.

埔 To extend widely; great; eminent; a field; a plain.

埠 A mart; place where ships and traders assemble.

脯 Meat dried and preserved; flesh of any kind.

‘補 To repair; mend; make up a deficiency; to strengthen.

‘斧 An axe; hatchet.

部⁵ A genus; tribe; a book or set of books; a council; public court; board of officers.

步⁵ A pace; a step; to travel; walk; go on foot.

布² Cotton or linen cloth; to spread out or abroad; diffuse.

P'o.

鋪 To spread out; arrange; a bed or table; a shop or store.

‘甫 To spread or extend everywhere; eminent; to begin.

‘匍 To go; creep on the hands & feet; crawl; strive to attain.

‘圃 A garden; orchard; cultivated field.

‘浦 Small streams; a creek or inlet.

‘莆 Name of a plant; the sword plant.

‘溥 Large; great; pervading everywhere; to spread abroad; proclaim.

‘普 Universally pervading; everywhere; great; uniform.

‘譜 A list; genealogy; biography; to write out a list; to arrange.

‘剖 To divide; split asunder in the middle; break open.

簿⁵ A register; account or memoranda book; a badge of office.

鋪² A shop; a store where things are sold.

Pó.

玻 A vitreous substance; glass; a gem.

波 Waves; water agitated by the wind; glossy; bright.

菠 Name of a fruit or vegetable.

陂 Uneven; not level.

‘保 To feed; nourish; protect; to be surety for; to sustain.

‘堡 A station for defence; a citadel; military post.

‘葆 Luxuriant herbage; to shade; cover; tranquil.

‘褓 A cloth to wrap up children or to carry them on the nurse's back.

‘寶 A gem; precious; felicitous; a national seal.

報² To reward; requite; a recompense; to inform.

薄⁵ Thin; slight; poor; bad; poor treatment; to despise.

泊⁵ The glare of water; a small wave; to anchor by the shore or in a bay.

駁 Particolored; diverse; to contradict; dispute.

P'ó.

坡 A bank; declivity; hill; mound; steep.

‘頗 Uneven; inclined to one side; in a small degree; rather.

跛 Lame; leaning on one side.

抱 To hold in the arms; infold; embrace.

粕 Feces or dregs of wine or other liquors.

Poi.

拔 To pull out; eradicate; draw forth.

八 Eight.

P'oi.

批 To strike; to compare; decide and declare officially; a petition; the reply; to pare off.

P^{n}io.

板 A flat board; a board on which lists are made.

秕 Blasted grain; tares; small; minute.

稗 Tares; weeds similar to grain.

辦 To adjust; judge; decide; punish.

Pok.

僕 A servant; slave; to follow; comply.

P'ok.

卜 To divine by means of a tortoise shell; to prognosticate; conjecture.

仆 Lying down; prostrate; bowing the head to the ground.

扑 A slight stroke; to strike; to flog.

朴 The bark of a tree; great; fundamental; separate.

菐 Luxuriant herbage; a case in which reeds are stuck.

撲 To lean towards; to fall; to pat; strike; flog.

樸 Plain, hard, close wood; substantial; without ornament.

璞 An unpolished gem; the external covering of a gem.

Pong.

篷 A mat covering for a boat; a utensil for straining liquor.

篷 A mat for a boat cover, sail, tent &c.

蓬 Name of an edible plant; luxuriant; in disorder.

縫 To sew; to unite by a seam; a seam; fissure; cleft.

鬔 Hair complicated and in disorder.

抔 To take up in the palm of the hands, as water.

Pu.

匏 A kind of melon or pumpkin.

晡 From 3 to 5 o'clock P. M.

捕 To take; pursue and seize; to catch; to persecute.

痡 Disease; an internal gathering or induration.

逋 To abscond; run away; fugitive; in debt.

餔 To feed; supply with food; dinner.

哺 To feed; put food into one's mouth; to nurse.

佈 To extend; extensive; filling the whole space.

怖 Afraid; alarmed; to cause fear.

富 Wealthy; rich; great possessions.

P'u.

浮 To float; to flow along with the stream; excess; light.

菩 Grass; herbage; thatch.

葡 The grape.

蒲 A species of water-rush of which mats are made.

簠 A round basket for grain.

Pua.

播 To sow; scatter; disseminate.

簸 A sieve for throwing up and winnowing grain.

鉢 A priest's rice dish; what is transferred from one to another.

P'ua.

婆 A designation of women, especially aged mothers.

破 Rent; broken; defeated; ruined; to break; defeat.

剖 To divide in the middle; split asunder; break open.

潑 To throw forth or sprinkle water; a shower; rain.

P^{n}ua.

盤 A tub-like vessel; a bathing tub; rice vessel; plate.

般 A manner; class; way; fashion.

搬 To put away; remove; transfer; pass over.

半 The half of anything; to divide in the middle.

P'^{n}ua.

潘 The dregs or washings of rice; dirty spots on the face.

伴 An associate; fellow; companion; to accompany.

Pue.

賠 To make up a deficiency or loss; to restore; repay.

陪 To accompany; attach to; assist; to second.

飛 To fly; to go or do with speed.

杯 盃 A wine cup; a drinking cup.

倍 To increase double; twofold; to oppose; low; vicious.

焙 To dry by the fire; to hatch eggs by the fire.

裴 Long garments or robes.

佩 Things attached to the girdle; to attach; to gird.

珮 A girdle with precious stones attached to it.

狽 An animal of the wolf kind said to be destitute of one or more feet; embarrassed.

背 To turn the back upon; to oppose; despise.

背 The back.

輩 A company; sort; class; series; forms the plural.

貝 Pearls; anything valuable and precious.

琲 Ornaments of tortoise shell; ornaments inlaid.

P'ue.

皮 Skin; bark; peel; wrapper; to skin; to peel.

培 To add earth or manure to; to assist; benefit; nourish.

配 Color of wine; a fellow; an equal; companion; to pair; unite; to accompany.

Pui.

肥 Fleshy; fat; abundant; rich land; to fatten.

悲 To commiserate; pity; tender compassion.

卑 Inferior; low; servile; below.

吠 The voice of a dog; to bark.

Pun.

噴 To blow or expel forcibly from the mouth.

分 To divide; distribute; give.

本 The root; original; substance; principal; foundation; this; mine; own.

畚 A basket for carrying earth or manure.

笨 The inside of bamboo; stupid; coarse.

糞 Excrement; ordure; filth; manure; to manure.

P'un.

盆 A jar, pitcher, basin, tub.

賁 Strenuous, impetuous effort.

墳 }
坟 } A tomb; grave; hillock; a bank; great; vast.

濆 The bank of a river; to overflow; to spirt forth water.

奔 To run away; to go in haste; precipitate; hurry.

Pung.

楓 Name of a peculiar kind of wood.

本 Original; natural; one's own; the root; fundamental.

飯 Boiled rice; food; a meal.

Put.

不 Not; no.

Pwan

叛 To revolt; separate from; desert.

畔 A path which divides fields.

P'wan.

般 To divide distribute; remove.

槃 A basin to wash in, or to drink from.

磐 A rock; large stone.

鞶 A small bag; a satchel.

鞶 A large girdle worn round the waist.

弁 A cap or bonnet to keep up the hair and show a person's rank.

拚 To take with the hand; to brush away; reject.

磻 Name of a stream; a stone fit for pointing arrows.

幡 A napkin for dusting; long streamers; to toss about.

燔 To roast; bake; flesh used in sacrifice.

蕃 Luxuriant; abundance; exuberance.

藩 A fence; boundary; frontier; to ward off.

蟠 Prostrate; writhing curling; burrowing in the ground.

判 To divide; distinguish; judge; decide; decision.

拌 To reject; throw away; disregard; to divide.

泮 A semi-circular pool in front of Chinese colleges; to bind.

絆 Ropes for entangling the feet; a snare; halter; to bind.

胖 The half of a victim; a slice of; large; fleshy.

Pwat.

孛 Plants shooting up luxuriantly; disobedient.

勃 Suddenly; a sudden change of countenance.

悖 Unsubmissive to just authority; rebellious; disobedient.

慹 誖 To delude; mislead by artful speeches; rebellion.

浡 Suddenly bursting forth; abundant; confused.

祓 To drive away calamity and supplicate blessings; to cleanse.

跋 To travel through shrubby paths; to walk laboriously.

鈸 Small bells used in the Budhist worship.

拔 To pull up, root out.

P'wat.

鉢 A small piece of money, in *Siam* used for a Tical.

Sá.

娑 To dance; make postures; garments tucked up.

砂 A small stone; pebbles; sand.

洒 To wash; cleanse; sprinkle; afraid.

Sná.

三 Three.

衫 A jacket; coat; upper garment; clothes.

Sai.

西 West; westward.

犀 An animal of the cow kind; a buffalo; rhinoceros.

獅 A lion.

腮 The side or lower part of the face; the jaws.

駛 Haste; to hasten; sail fast; run.

屎 Ordure; excrement.

使 To send; to cause; to manage; to succeed; use.

柹^{5} A fruit with red skin and soft pulp; the Diosypros.

使^{2} A messenger; one sent.

壻^{2} } 婿^{2} } A superior; a daughter's huband; a son-in-law.

賽^{2} To make a grateful return; to strive to surpass; contend.

Sám.

杉 The fir tree; any large good timber.

糝 Rice mixed with soup or with minced meat; mixed.

三^{2} Three times; to repeat three times.

Sán.

刬 To mow or shear.

芟 To cut herbs or plants; a large sickle or scythe.

刪 To pare off; expunge; decide what to retain and what to reject in a book revise.

疝 A disease in the lower part of the abdomen and organs of generation.

訕^{2} To slander; vilify; backbite.

[口散]^{2} To blow out from the mouth or nose.

撒^{2} To scatter; disperse; set loose; spread out.

Sáng.

雙 A pair; two; alike.

鬆 Disheveled hair; confusion; to relax; loose.

送^{2} To present to; to accompany a guest a short way on his return.

喪^{2} To lose; fail; die; be forgotten: to mourn for the dead.

Sáp.

颯 Wind; a sudden gust; fading; declining.

Sát.

虱 Fast running insects, as lice.

塞 To fill or stop up; obstruct; hinder; sincere.

薩 The gods of the heathen; idols: to assist; help; know.

Sau.

梢 The extreme top of a tree; the tips of branches; a pole; small: a rudder.

艄 The stern of a boat; a fast boat; swift; rapid.

慅 Moved; agitated; sorrowful; weariness.

搔 To scratch with the fingers: finger nails.

騷 Agitated; disturbed; lame; grieved.

蚤 A biting insect produced in dry soil: morning.

埽 To eject; put away; to sweep the ground: a dike.

掃 To brush away; sweep; to search by order of government.

嘯 The sound of roaring, hissing, or whistling: to blow.

Se.

儕 Order or class; company; group: forms the plural.

袈 A cloak worn by Budhist priests.

紗 Gauze; thin silk; crape.

些 Small; a few; a little.

S^n^e.

生 To be born; to live; to beget; produce; life.

鉎 Soft iron; cast iron; iron ore.

省 To examine into; to watch: watchful: to diminish; a province or state.

姓 Surname; family name.

性 A man's nature, disposition, constitution, ability, temper, &c.

Sek.

熟 Food cooked till quite done; ripe; mature; well acquainted with; experienced.

植 Planted; stuck into the ground; erected.

色 Color; quality; lust; sexual pleasure; appearance.

釋 To unloose; liberate; disperse: explain: to happen.

飾 To cleanse; set in; order; adorn; gloss; over; brighten.

嗇 Harvest gathered in; to accumulate; covetous; frugal.

穡 Grain fit to be gathered in; harvest; avaricious.

識 To know; recognise; wisdom; knowledge.

蹐 Walking; reverent; respectful: to step over.

碩 Large; full; ripe; mature; learned; virtuous.

瑟 A stringed instrument of music: many; stern.

悉 To know perfectly; to investigate; all; entirely.

蟋 A cricket; grasshopper.

息 To breathe; a breath; to stop; to rest; interest of money.

媳 Daughter-in-law; son's wife.

熄 To extinguish; to cover up embers to preserve them.

螫 The sting of an insect; a poisonous tooth.

式 A rule; pattern; specimen; to measure; to imitate.

軾 A crossbar in carriages and sedan-chairs to lean on.

蹐 Walking in a crooked manner.

適 To go to; to happen; to hit exactly; tranquility; joy.

晳 To distinguish; to discriminate clearly.

夕 Evening.

穸 A long dark night; the tomb.

Seng.

成 To effect; accomplish; complete; to perfect; to become.

誠 Without guile; true; honest; truth; sincerity.

承 丞 To be second to; to help; aid; an assistant; a second.

松 The pine or fir tree.

升 A certain measure about a quart; to accumulate; to ascend; advance.

昇 To ascend; peaceful; universal tranquility.

陞 To go up steps; to ascend; advance; be promoted.

勝 Adequate to; worthy of; to sustain; elevate.

牲 Domestic animals; victims for sacrifice.

猩 A species of monkey; an ape.

甥 A daughter's or sister's children; nephew or niece.

旌 A banner; to make signals; to cause to know.

笙 An instrument of music consisting of tubes.

眚 Something growing over the eye; error; excess; crime; calamity; to diminish.

惺 To arouse or awaken the mind.

乘 To ascend or sit upon; seize a good opportunity.

盛 Good in the highest degree; flourishing; abundant; full.

勝 To surpass; overcome; to win; to be superior to.

Si.

時 Time; a two hour period; a season: the proper time.

塒 A hen-roost formed in a wall; a roost.

辭 To decline; refuse: words. to decline an invitation to delay; to carry.

匙 A spoon; a key.

司 To have the control of; to rule; manage; an overseer.

伺 To wait for; attend upon; to observe; spy out; examine.

笥 A square bamboo chest; a trunk.

尸 A body; corpse; an effigy of a deceased person.

鳲 A species of pigeon.

屍 A dead body; a corpse.

꜀施 Expanded; spread out; to bestow; give; to use.

꜀系 Fine silk; small; fine; delicate; connected.

꜀絲 Raw silk; minute; small as a thread of raw silk.

꜀蓍 Name of a plant used in divination.

꜀詩 A verse; poetry; an ode; what may be sung.

꜀筮 Name of an herb used in divination; to divine.

꜀噬 To eat; gnaw; devour; grief.

꜂始 The beginning; origin; to begin; then; for the first time.

꜂死 To die.

꜂屣 Straw sandals; shoes that separate from the foot.

꜂蓰 Name of a plant: five fold.

꜀蹝 Straw sandals worn by wrestlers, dancers &c.

꜂豕 The bristles and tail of swine; swine.

꜂彖 A pig; a porcupine; a symbol used in divination.

꜂兕 A buffalo; rhinoceros.

꜂弛 To let go the string of a bow; set loose; unexerted.

꜂矢 An arrow; straight as an arrow; swift; true; to vow.

是^{5} Straight; right; is; am; this; that; yes; it is so.

侍^{5} To stand by the side of; to wait on; an attendant.

峙^{5} A lofty mountain; erect; high.

恃^{5} To rely or depend on.

氏^{5} A family name; an affix to the names of females.

示꜃ To declare; manifest; proclaim; teach; make known.

豉꜃ A jelly like condiment made of flour or pulse.

誓꜃ To swear; utter an oath or imprecation; to bind; a vow an oath.

逝꜃ To depart; die; go away.

視^{2} To look; view; examine; to teach; take knowledge of; behold.

四^{2} Four.

嗜^{2} To relish: desire ardently; indulge the animal lusts.

世^{2} An age; generation; mankind.

勢^{2} Strength; authority; influence; condition of.

蝕$_{5}$ To corrode; eat, as insects eat books, cloth &c.—to diminish; eclipse.

薛꜄ Name of a plant and of a state; a surname.

S^{n}i.

扇^{2} A wing; a door; a fan; to fan; to agitate.

煽^{2} To fan a flame; to inflame, seduce or delude.

Sia.

佘 A surname.

斜 Aslant; oblique; scattered; unsettled.

邪 Deflected; depraved; bad; corrupting; lewd; specious.

麝 The musk animal; the Moschiferus.

寫 To write; draw; paint; to lay down; put away.

舍 To expend; use; give up; give.

捨 To let go; give up; to give.

社[5] The deity who presides over any given region; local gods.

射 To shoot an arrow; to dart, as rays of light.

榭 A military school or store house; a case; to store up.

謝 To thank; express gratitude; to confess; to decline; take leave; thanks.

赦[2] To remit punishment; to forgive; pardon; let go.

卸[2] To put off; pull down; to ruin; give up.

舍[2] A cottage; a small, mean, broken house.

瀉[2] To drain water from land; a purging; dysentery.

席[5] A mat spread on the ground; a table; feast; repast; to rest.

錫 Pewter; tin; to confer; bestow.

S^{n}ia.

城 The wall of a town; a city.

聲 Sound; noise; voice; speech.

⿰木盛 A box or covered tray for containing food.

聖[2] Intuitive perception of all truth; wise; sacred; holy.

Siak.

削 To cut off; pare; to invade; sieze upon.

屑 Clear; remnant; observant; attentive; minute; to reduce to powder; to despise.

⿰扌屑 To take or throw out with the hand.

渫 To leak out; diminish; waste.

⿰氵業 To remove; to leak out; disperse.

Siam.

暹 The sun rising and increasing in splendor; *Siam.*

簷 The eaves of a roof hanging out over the wall.

蟾 A species of toad.

贍 Plentiful; sufficient for; to bestow; give to the poor.

參 Ginseng.

韱 Small; fine; wild leeks which grow on hills.

纖 Fine silk; delicate; small ornaments for clothes; neat

讖 A species of divination; a prognostic; to repent.

森 A forest; abundant; majestic; sombre; sham-wood.

閃 To shun; evade; pass away quickly, as lightning.

陝 Name of a province west of Honan.

Siàng.

嫦 A celebrated goddess in the palace of the moon.

庠 A village school; a college; to instruct; feed or nourish.

祥 Goodness; felicity; a prognostic; a good omen.

翔 To fly or look back; dignified; respectable.

詳 To examine, deliberate, and judge; to explain clearly; minute.

裳 Garments for the lower parts of the body; pantaloons.

商 A merchant; to devise; arrange; deliberate; consult.

徜 Disconcerted; irresolute; disappointed; extravagant.

襄 To assist; effect; accomplish; to praise; merit; fore-horses in a coach.

勷 In haste; urgent; hurried.

穰 The stock of grain; growing luxuriantly; abundance.

鑲 To inlay or plate with metal.

驤 A spirited horse; to elevate; remote.

殤 Untimely death; to die.

觴 A wine cup; a full cup; to cause to drink wine.

相 Mutually; reciprocally; to examine; to blend with.

湘 To boil; name of a river, lake and hill.

上 To ascend; go up; promote; high.

尙 Yet; still; nearly; probably; to add; title of officers about the court; to receive.

相 To assist; lead; direct; a minister of state; to reckon.

像 To imitate; similar; a likeness; an image.

Siap.

涉 To ford a stream; to pass through; to step upon; to implicate; involve.

洩 To desist or rest from; to be dissipated; leak out; diminish.

泄 To drain off; flow out; leak; to purge; put away; mixed.

倏 Hastily; rapidly; instantly; in a short time.

燮 To adjust; preserve order; to harmonize; to mature.

霎 A short time; a moment; small rain; a slight shower.

澀 Rough; not slippery or smooth.

澁 Rough; the ripple on the surface of water.

Sie.

燒 To burn; burn up; scorch.

惜 Regard or affection for; to compassionate; pity; sparing.

Snie.

常 Constant; usual; common; frequently; the five virtues.
嘗 To taste; assay.
償 To pay for; recompence; to revenge; to reply to.
傷 To wound; injure; grieve; grieved; injured.
廂 Side apartments; bed-rooms; rooms for females.
箱 A box; chest; bamboo basket; a store-room.
賞 To confer; bestow as a largess; to reward; a reward.
想 To think; consider; muse; expect; desire; a thought.
像 A likeness; image.
鞘 A scabbard; a sheath.

Sien.

墠 A place for sacrifice; a level place at the foot of the altar; wild or common ground.
嬋 Elegance or beauty of motion; beautiful.
蟬 An insect of the cricket kind; poison.
禪 To resign; to transfer; meditation; abstraction; sacrifice to heaven.
仙 Genii of mountains and hills; demigods.
珊 Coral; gems.
僊 Deathless; immortal.
銑 Metal which is burnished and glossy; a small chisel.
哂 To smile; to laugh at.
癬 Ringworms; a scab which spreads over the skin.
矧 To stretch still more; still more; how much more.
善 Good; excellent; virtuous; felicitous; dexterous; benevolent.
繕 To repair; put in order; to provide; to write out.
膳 The flesh of victims; good food duly prepared.
腎 The kidneys; to lead; to induce.
擅 To assume; usurp; to take or do without right or authority.

Siet.

設 To arrange; establish; institute; to suppose.
紲, 絏 To tie; bind; fasten with cords; bonds; a bridle.
褻 Rags; defiled; to defile; to treat with contempt; to insult.

Sim.

諶 True; sincere; truth; sincerity.
忱 Sincere; true; devoted.
心 The heart; mind; affections; intention; motive.

芯 Name of an herb or shrub.

審 To investigate clearly; to judge; decide; to restrain.

嬸 A younger brother's wife; also a father's brother's wife.

甚 In an extreme degree; very; superlative.

Sin.

神 Divinity; God; whatever is worshiped; spirit; divine; spiritual.

辰 Time; the sun, moon and stars; from 7 to 9 o'clock A.M.

宸 A retired apartment; the imperial apartments.

晨 The morning; dawn; light; clear; bright.

繩 A cord; a line; to line, or make a straight mark with a line; to warn; restrict.

蠅 Name of an insect; a specious, intriguing flatterer.

身 The body; trunk of a tree; hull of a ship; I; me.

申 To extend; stretch; explain; again; from 3 to 5 o'clock P.M.

伸 To spread out; straighten; to vindicate the cause of the injured.

呻 To recite; to sigh; moan.

紳 A girdle for the waist; to gird; gentlemen.

新 Fresh; new; to renew; to reform.

辛 Acrid; pungent; bitter; distress; toil; suffering.

莘 A medicinal sudorific plant; many; long.

騂 A horse of red and yellow color; carnation color.

愼 Careful; attentive; still; sincere; cautious.

剩 Overplus; surplus; remainder; not only.

信 Sincere; true to one's word; to believe; trust; a letter.

汛 To sprinkle with; speed; to expedite; haste.

訊 To interrogate; examine; accuse; reprove; direct.

迅 To go with speed; quick; hasty; sudden.

Sio.

瀟 Deep clear water; name of a river; rinsing rice.

簫 A reed; name of a musical instrument.

蕭 Name of a bitter herb; a barrier; waving; solitary.

宵 Obscure; night; small.

捎 To select from; to brush away; eradicate; reject.

消 To thaw; melt; digest; dissipate; consume.

硝 Nitre; salt-petre.

逍 To saunter about for amusement.

銷 To fuse metals; melt; dissolve.

霄 Vapor; clouds; halo; sleet; heaven.

搜 To shake; toss about; to search; to study the import of.

小 Small; petty; contracted; light; a few; young.

劭 Exertion; effort; to force one's self; excellence.

紹 To connect; to continue in succession; to succeed.

邵 High; eminent.

韶 An instrument of music; to continue the virtues of a predecessor.

髫 Tuft of hair which hangs down from a child's head.

肇 To commence; to correct; to devise; project; intelligent.

少 Few; small; young; to diminish; to owe; be wanting.

肖 Constitutional likeness as between parent and child; legitimate; filial.

數 To reckon; count; a number; several; fate; few.

櫢 To shake; agitate; brush or shake off.

Sip.

什 Ten; two files of five persons each; mixed.

襲 Double or outer garments: to continue in succession; to invade.

拾 To gather together; collect; to inquire about.

習 To practice; become accustomed to; repeat over and over; to learn thoroughly.

慴 Fearful; timid; cowardly.

摺 To fold up; a document folded up; to destroy.

熠 Glossy, shining feathers; lustre; effulgence.

濕 Damp; moist; hurried; depression of spirit.

隰 Low marshy land; a marsh.

Sit.

實 寔 Truth; true; sincere; real; full; solid; the kernel; grain; fruit.

殖 To fatten; to plant; cause to grow or flourish; erect.

失 To lose; fail; miss; neglect; failure; loss.

室 A dwelling; house; family; wife.

Siu.

泅 To swim.

收 To collect or receive; to bind or restrain.

修 To direct; regulate; adorn; cultivate the mind or heart.

梳 A comb; to comb; to dress.

羞 To be ashamed; conscious of having done wrong; to offer to a superior.

饈 To present food to a superior; to feed; food.

首 The head; a chief; a leader; to head; to manifest; origin.

ʿ守 To hold fast; guard; keep; protect; observe.

ʿ帚 Ordure; to sweep away filth.

ʿ箒 A besom; a broom; a certain kind of bamboo.

受ʾ To receive; accept; endure; forms the passive of verbs.

授ʾ To give to; to communicate.

綬ʾ A piece of silk to which official seals are suspended.

壽ʾ Longevity; age; a delicate term for death.

秀ʾ Flowery; splendid; elegant; luxuriant.

綉ʾ A section of cotton; to embroider.

銹ʾ Rust in metals.

妯ʾ Disquietude of mind; grief; the older of two wives.

岫ʾ A den or cavern in a mountain; a ravine.

袖ʾ The sleeve or cuff of a garment; valuable.

守ʾ 狩ʾ To hunt; to go round and examine, as an officer; to patrol.

獸ʾ A quadruped; a wild beast; an animal.

繡ʾ To variegate with different colors; embroidered.

So.

ʿ穌 ʿ甦 To desist and rest; tranquil; to resuscitate; come to life from the dead.

ʿ蘇 Name of a medicinal plant; cheerful; to rest; resuscitate.

ʿ蒐 A medicinal plant called earth's-blood; to hunt; to hide.

ʿ藪 A thicket in which are animals and lakes for fish.

ʿ廋 To conceal; hide; crafty; to search for what is hidden.

ʿ叟 A respectful epithet applied to aged persons.

ʿ瞍 An eye without a pupil; an aged person.

溲ʾ To steep in water; void urine.

瘦ʾ Lean; emaciated.

漱ʾ To wash the mouth; to rinse; spit out.

Só.

ʿ唆 To chatter; to whisper; sow discord; to misrepresent.

ʿ梭 A weaver's shuttle; name of a wood.

ʿ疎 Coarse; open; remiss; lax; careless.

ʿ疏 Open; wide apart; coarse; to explain.

ʿ蔬 Edible herbs; a species of grain; coarse, poor food.

ʿ所 A place; a thing; a cause or means; that which; what.

ᶜ嫂 A brother's wife; another person's wife.

ᶜ瑣 Minute; small; petty; troublesome; delicate; continuous.

ᶜ鎖 A lock; to lock; to fetter; rings; a chain.

疏² To explain; a statement or explanation sent up to the emperor.

索ↄ A string or cord; to bind; to extort from; extortion.

雪ↄ Snow.

Soi.

ᶜ洗 To wash; cleanse; purify.

細² Fine; small; delicate, as fine silk; petty; gentle; careful.

小² Small; little; young.

Snoi.

꜀先 First; before; to go before; lead; to put first.

Sok.

屬₅ 屬₅ To be connected with; belong or pertain to; a class; species; kindred; to cause.

斸₅ To chop; hew.

囑₅ To tell; direct; give orders to.

續₅ To follow in succession; continuous; successively.

贖₅ To ransom; redeem; atone for; a ransom.

俗₅ The lower walks of life; common; vulgar; customary.

孰₅ Who? what? which? mature; ripe.

塾₅ A school; an outer apartment; antechamber; lodge.

夙ↄ Early in the morning; speedily; respect and diligence.

束ↄ To bind as a bundle of sticks; to restrain; coerce; a bundle.

觫ↄ Afraid; afraid of death.

速ↄ Fleet; with haste; speedily; hurried.

餗ↄ Food contained in a boiler; rice food.

寂ↄ Silent; quiet; lonely; poor; stillness; repose; inactive.

淑ↄ Pure; limpid; uncorrupted; virtuous; accomplished.

菽ↄ Pulse; corn.

踧ↄ A respectful, sedate, easy manner or gait.

索ↄ To extort; extortion; to use violence; a cord; a rope.

縮ↄ To confuse; to contract in dimensions; to bind; confusion.

蓿ↄ Name of a wild root which cows and horses eat.

肅ↄ Dread; fear; awe; respect; stillness; with speed.

Song.

꜀嵩 A lofty mountain; highly elevated; eminent.

ᶜ悚 Double-minded; timorous; agitated by hopes and fe[illegible]

ʿ竦 Respect; awe; to stand in a stiff formal manner; to exalt.

ʿ嵸 The summits of hills or mountains.

ʿ聳 A sound in the ear; to stir up by advice; excite; inflame.

訟[5] Litigation; strife; contention; wrangling; disputation.

頌[5] The countenance; to praise; to publish the virtues of any one.

誦[5] To recite; chant; sing; to discuss; calumniate.

宋[2] Name of an ancient dynasty; a dwelling; to dwell.

Su.

˓殊 To kill; cut off; exterminate; to exceed; distinguish; superlative; very.

˓殳 A military weapon; the handle of a spear.

˓帤 A large cloth or napkin; a streamer; part of a bow.

˓輸 To rotate; to lose in any contest; be defeated; inferior; to offer to.

˓須 To need; necessary; requisite; to wait for or expect.

˓需 Necessary; what is necessary; to doubt; hesitate; stop.

˓濡 Enriched with moisture; to instil into; patient; mild.

˓胥 Altogether; mutually; to wait; fleshy.

˓糈 Grain given as a ration or used in sacrifice.

˓諝 To know; natural talent and acquired knowledge; wise; deceitful.

˓紓 Slow; remiss; procrastinating; calamitous.

˓舒 To open out; spread open; expand; leisure; ease; order.

˓鸀 A bird resembling a duck.

ʿ暑 Hot weather; summer.

ʿ楮 Name of a tree of the bark of which cloth and paper are made.

ʿ緒 The commencement; clue; course of events; to examine into.

ʿ褚 A clothes bag or basket; a pall; to cut and make clothes.

ʿ署 A public court; a temporary officer.

ʿ曙 The light of the rising sun; morning; clear.

ʿ黍 Grain; millet; a certain plant.

ʿ杵 A wooden beater or pestle.

序[5] Order; arrangement; a school-room; college; preface of a book.

敘[5] To arrange or explain in order; to converse about.

豎[5] To stand erect; to set up; establish; upright; chaste.

樹[5] To plant; erect; set on end.

庶[2] A great many; a multitude; nearly; probably.

恕[2] Benevolent; indulgent; to excuse an offence.

絮[2] The coarser part of silk; to compound; reiterate; verbose.

訴[2] To inform of; to accuse; to state in one's defence; calumny.

素[2] White; plain; not ornamented; originally; heretofore.

塐[2] To mould or form anything of earth or clay; an image.

愫[2] Sincere; true-hearted; one's real purpose.

愬[2] To inform of; accuse; defend; state to; calumny.

溯[2] To drive water back contrary to its natural course.

遡[2] To meet or go against; to urge; to accuse.

Sù.

꜀祀 To sacrifice to the gods or departed spirits; a sacrifice.

꜀祠 To offer sacrifice to ancestors; a hall dedicated to them.

꜀詞 To speak; speech; phrase; to request; announce to; accuse.

꜀嗣 To succeed; keep up the succession; inherit; offspring; hereafter.

꜀辭 Words; speech; to refuse; to decline; to take leave.

꜀思 To think; consider; desire; commiserate; thoughts.

꜀偲 To reprove or admonish with frankness; great talent.

꜀斯 This; that; these; forthwith; low; mean.

꜀厮 Servants; foragers; to fight and kill in the confusion of battle.

꜀嘶 The neighing of a horse; to belch.

꜀私 Peculiar; private; sai chiu; individual; selfish; clandestine.

꜀師 A master; teacher; a commander; a patron; soldiers.

꜁史 A historian; history.

士[5] A scholar; a gentleman; an officer; a literary title.

仕[5] To serve; to fill a public station; act as magistrate.

食[5] Food; to feed; nourish.

嶼[5] An island; a hill on a level plain.

耜[5] A harrow; to level the ground.

似[5] Like; similar to; as; as if; to continue in succession.

姒[5] A name by which brothers' wives designate each other.

俟[5] To wait; stay; until; great.

事[5] To serve.

事[5] Affair; employment; business.

賜[2] To confer; bestow on inferiors; give; distribute.

泗[2] Name of a river; secretion from the nose.

駟[2] Four horses attached to one vehicle.

肆 Excess; error; profligate; lawless; great; to act without regard to reason or law.

Sua.

沙 Sand; pebbles; anything small.

鯊 A shark.

徙 To remove or be removed from one place to another.

殺, 煞 To kill; to execute; to murder; to overcome; murderous.

宿 To pass the night; to sleep; a halting place; an inn.

S^{n}ua.

山 A mountain; hill; shore.

產 To produce or bear; what is produced; fruits of the earth; offspring; patrimony.

散 To scatter; disperse; dissipate; dismiss or break up an assembly; divorce.

線 Thread of any kind; to lead or draw; spy.

傘 To cover; shade off the sun and rain; an umbrella; parasol.

Suak.

朔 The first day of the moon; to begin; commence.

塑 An image; idol; to mould; form.

槊 A long spear; a railing; name of a wood.

數 Numerous; troublesome; hurried; irreverent.

Suan.

旋 To circulate; go round; return; to bring about; then; next.

璇, 璿 Name of a valuable stone; an astronomical instrument.

宣 To promulgate; proclaim; to summon; to spread abroad.

喧 Loud; clamorous; noise.

暄, 煊 Warmth of the sun; genial warmth; evening.

萱 Name of a plant which, when eaten, is said to ensure the birth of a son.

諠 False; irregular; clamorous.

選 To choose; select; appoint; timorous; apprehensive.

Suat.

梲 A short pillar or post on the top of a beam.

Suang.

爽 Light and cheerful; ease and health; to please; impetuous; to fail; miss.

顙 The middle of the forehead; the front.

Sue.

衰 To fade; decline; become weak; fall off; exterminate.

帥 A commander; a general; an army.

戍 [2] To guard the frontier; to banish to the frontier.

歲 [2] A year; one's age; the produce of a year.

稅 [2] Taxes; rent; custom; duties; to hire; to leave to, as by will.

說 To speak; converse; explain; speech; explanation.

刷 To scrape; rub; brush; cleanse; a brush.

Sui.

隋 Name of an ancient dynasty of China.

隨 To accord with; yield; follow; obey; forthwith.

遂 To accord with; not to oppose; forthwith; then.

燧 An instrument to obtain fire either by friction or from the rays of the sun.

璲 Name of a valuable stone attached to girdles and esteemed lucky.

穟 The flower or head of grain; the ear of corn.

垂 Suspended; to bow down; condescend; extend downwards.

諈 To implicate; connect or involve affairs; search into.

陲 The edge of a precipice; dangerous; a limit; frontier.

錘 A weight used in weighing; twelve taels of silver.

誰 Who? whose? what? who.

雖 Although; supposing that; admitting that.

綏 Steady; quiet; tranquil; to tranquilize; a battle.

荽 A fragrant plant beneficial in headaches.

蓑 Pendent flowers; a garment of leaves to defend from rain.

睡 [5] To sleep; to lie down.

瑞 [5] Auspicious; felicitous; a good omen.

穗 [2] The ear of grain; the flower of fruits and grass; elegant.

Sun.

旬 Ten days; a decade; to extend everywhere; all equally.

恂 Sincere; faithful; respectful; awe; reverence.

殉 To seek the attainment of any object at any risk.

洵 Faithful; sincere; distant; equal; even; to weep.

狥 To connive at; comply with in an evil sense.

荀 Name of a plant.

詢 To enquire; investigate; give information; to contrive.

循 To go as one is led; to comply or accord with; to go about; examine.

巡 To go about and examine; go the round; look after.

純 Pure; unmixed; without spot.

惇 Sincerity; plain, honest and kind.

鶉꜀ A species of quail.

孫꜀ A grandchild; remote descendants; posterity.

猻꜀ An animal of the monkey species.

飧꜀ An evening meal; flour and water mixed; dressed food.

꜂損 To diminish; injure; spoil; lose; give up.

꜂筍 } ꜂笋 } Young shoots of bamboo fit to be eaten; a sprout; a tenon.

順꜄ To obey; yield; comply; prosperous; harmonizing.

巽꜄ Humble; to select; a character used in divination.

孫꜄ } 遜꜄ } Complaisant; retiring; humble; yielding.

舜꜄ A Chinese king who lived B.C. 2100: sage; benevolent.

瞬꜄ The twinkling of an eye; an instant.

Sung.

酸꜀ Sour; debility; loitering.

霜꜀ Hoar frost; frigid; cold; grave; stern.

孀꜀ widow; solitary.

喪꜀ To mourn for the dead; mourning: to lose; to die.

桑꜀ The mulberry tree.

꜂耍 To play; sport; amuse; to trifle with; seduce.

算꜄ To reckon; to calculate; count; the abaccus.

蒜꜄ Garlic; a kind of small onions.

Sut.

術꜅ A path; a way of doing any thing; a rule; an art; a scheme.

述꜅ To narrate; rehearse; to collect, arrange and publish.

恤꜅ } 卹꜅ } Compassion; to pity; to have a tender care for.

戌꜅ A horary character for the ninth moon; also for from 7 to 9 o'clock P.M.

鉞꜅ The noise made by a saw; to saw.

帥꜅ To lead or head an army; to lead.

Swai.

蓑꜀ A mango.

Tá.

沓꜅ Reiterated; sound of dropping water; backbiting; rash.

踏꜅ To tread upon; to beat on the ground with the foot.

搭꜅ A thimble; to cover; add to; build up; to feel; rub; take passage; commit to.

T'á

他꜀ He; she; it; him; her; that; other; another.

疊꜅ To pile one above another.

英漢潮州方言字典

塔ɔ A tall spire, tower or pagoda.

T^{n}á.

꜀擔 To carry on the shoulder; to sustain; be responsible for; a burden.

ʿ胆 Gall; bile; courage; daring; fleshy; fat.

淡[5] Insipid; thin; light; volatile; unstable.

擲[5] To throw; throw away.

咀 To speak.

膽 To enquire.

担[2] A burden; picul; to strike; brush away; to lift; carry.

Tai.

ʿ歹 Perverse; evil; bad.

ʿ隶 To approach from behind; to extend unto.

大[5] Large; great; extensive; to enlarge.

怠[5] Supercilious; inattentive to; careless; negative rudeness.

殆[5] To begin; approach; to be near; dangerous; careless.

迨[5] 逮[5] } To pursue after and overtake; to extend to; adequate to; until.

岱[2] Name of a high mountain in China.

柋[2] A mallet or beater for beating silk.

貸[2] To confer upon; lend; lend on interest.

黛[2] Name of a medicine; to paint the eyebrows.

戴[2] To put one thing on another; wear or carry on the head; to sustain; to meet.

靆[2] Cloudy; dull; obscure.

T′ai.

꜀臺 臺 } An elevated terrace; a gallery; platform; the bar of a judge; an altar, table or stand.

꜀擡 To raise; lift up with the hand; to carry.

꜀台 Name of three stars or deities; eminent; exalted; Sir.

꜀抬 To raise; lift up, as a sedan chair; to shake; move.

꜀剖 To cut or pare anything.

꜀笞 To beat with a bamboo; to chastise; flog.

꜀苔 A species of moss or lichen.

꜀邰 Name of an ancient state.

꜀駘 An old, vicious horse; wild; waste; distant.

꜀篩 A sieve; a vessel to strain through; to sift or strain.

ʿ癩 A disease which breaks out in pustules or blotches; a sore; a kind of itch.

待[5] To wait for; until; to provide against; treat well or ill.

侍 To wait on; prepare; provide.

太 泰 } Great; extensive; name of a hill; the imperial altar.

汰 Slippery; waters rushing over and washing away; excess.

態 External manifestation of the thoughts and feelings by the gait and manner; behavior; treatment.

Ták.

度 To measure; estimate; reckon.

毒 Poison; poisonous; bad; malignity; noxious; vicious.

T'ák.

讀 To read; study; recite.

漯 Name of a river; waters rushing together.

宕 Eminent; to exceed; excess; profligate.

拓 To take up; lift or receive with the hand; push; break.

柝 A knocker; that on which a watchman strikes.

Tám.

躭 Addicted to pleasure; excessive indulgence; to linger; tarry.

菼 Young sprouts or rushes; green color.

啖 To taste; eat; swallow; entice with a bait; insipid.

T'ám.

痰 Phlegm; mucous.

談 譚 } Free conversation; chitchat; to converse; dispute.

覃 Extending to; spreading out far and wide.

潭 Name of a river; deep.

澹 Appearance of water, tranquil and sometimes agitated.

譫 Verbose; loquacity.

貪 To covet; desire; encroach upon the property of another; avaricious.

剡 Sharp; pointed; to sharpen; cut off.

探 To feel or search for; to spy; to visit and make enquiries about.

Tán.

丹 Carnation color; of but one color; simple; pure.

坍 The banks of a canal or river.

嘽 Joy; rejoicing; fullness; abundance.

癉 Disease arising from excessive labor; yellow jaundice.

簞 A small bucket to carry provisions in.

憚 Distress; afraid; worn out with fatigue; idle.

誕 Fables; nonsense; to deceive; extensive; a birth-day.

但 5 Only; but; especially; as soon as.

旦 2 Morning; clear; bright.

T'án.

彈 A bullet; ball; to draw the string of a bow; to play on a stringed instrument.

檀 Sandle-wood.

癱 Palsy; constriction of the mustles and tendons.

亶 Truth; to trust; sincere; abundant; plenty.

亘 To revolve; go round and return; extend to; promulge.

坦 Level; a plain; wide; composed; lightsome.

怛 Labor; fatigue; grief; commiseration; oppressed.

袒 To expose part of the naked body; to make bare.

嘆 2 } 歎 2 } A tone expressing strong feeling either of grief or admiration; to sigh; to praise.

賺 2 To gain, earn or acquire wealth.

Táng.

仝 } 同 } Together; united; the same; agreeing; similar; like.

筒 A tube open at both ends; a trumpet; a pipe; a reed.

筩 A tube; a pipe.

銅 Copper or brass.

東 East; the place of honor.

冬 Winter; the close; end.

中 Middle; midst; amongst; to hit the medium or mark.

洞 A ravine; den; cavern; deep; to pass through.

董 To rule; to correct; firm; recondite; a kind of root.

黨 Associates; a clan or party leagued together; a village of 500 families.

攩 A group or gang of persons; to strike; impede; screen.

重 5 Heavy; important; grave; respectable; heinous; to honor.

蛋 5 The egg of a bird; name of certain barbarous tribes.

盪 5 A vessel to bathe in; a tub; great; agitated.

蕩 5 Large; wide; extensive; unsettled; dissipated; remiss.

當 2 Firm; unwavering; a pledge; pawn.

T'áng.

虫 } 蟲 } Insects; reptiles; small animals.

膛 Fat; fleshy.

螳 A species of locust.

棠 Name of a wood; transverse bars of a carriage.

搪 To stretch or extend; fill up; offend; suddenly.

倘 儻 A conditional particle; if; should it be.

桶 A wooden vessel; bucket; tub; cask; barrel.

疸 Yellow jaundice.

閶 A bolt or fastening to a door.

Táp.

答 An answer; to reply to; to make a return; to recompence.

T'áp.

塌 Below the surface of the ground; to fall down.

榻 A couch; bed; a long narrow bed.

橐 A bag open at both ends; a mould; without a bottom.

凹 Hollow; concave; indented.

Tát.

達 Penetrable; intelligible; to understand; every; all.

鐸 A sort of bell or jingling instrument.

T'át.

達 A light playful gait; to frisk; to send a letter.

僌 To run away; to rebel against.

撻 To strike; beat; chastise.

蹅 To strike the foot against; to stamp the foot; to slip.

闥 A screen in a door-way; an inner door.

拓 To separate; divide; open.

Tau.

投 To throw or cast; to give one's self up to; to dip in water; to confer upon; to suit.

骰 A dice-box; also used for the thigh.

兜 To excite; stir up.

斗 A certain measure containing 12 catties.

抖 To shake up; rouse; excite; shake off.

找 To supply what is deficient; to seek for; to exchange money; a pole to propel a boat.

島 An island; a rock in the ocean.

搗 擣 To beat with the hand; to pound down or together.

禱 To pray; entreat; supplicate of the gods.

道 A way; path; a principle; good principles; nature of things; reason.

導 To point out the way; lead; direct; teach; rectify.

盜 To steal; rob; plunder; robbers.

蹈 To tread under feet; tread in the footsteps of; to agitate.

稻 Grain planted in water; paddy.

豆 荳 豆 A generic name for pulse, peas, beans &c.

痘 The small pox; pustules.

到 To arrive at; extend to; go or come to; everywhere; entire; complete.

T'au.

淘 洮 To wash; to stir about; to excite.

鼗 A small drum to be twirled in the fingers; a toy.

頭 The head; front; top; end; a numeral of affairs.

濤 Large waves; billows dashing on the shore.

偷 To steal; by stealth; clandestine; careless; weak.

幬 Canopy; the heavens; the sky, a curtain; a vail.

慆 Joy; indulgence; excess; doubt; suspicion.

滔 Water flowing rapidly and rising higher and higher.

焰 燄 The flame of fire; hot; burning; luminous.

韜 A sheath; a case or covering; broad; equitable.

叨 Inordinate desire; addicted to; ambitious; affected humility.

討 To direct; investigate; search; to rail at; mix; eject; kill.

套 A snare; a covering or case; large; wide.

褄 An outer garment or cloak.

透 To run away; pass over; to penetrate; to comprehend; alarmed.

逗 To stop; delay; dwell; remain; go circuitously.

Te.

茶 Tea; tea leaf.

宅 A dwelling place; the station one fills; a grave; to dwell; to fix; determine.

咤 Angry speech; to sputter; to make a noise when eating; to yearn over.

T^ne.

撐 To push with a pole; to pole a boat.

Tek.

値 To manage; transact; to occur; to take hold of.

特 Alone; only; especially; on purpose for; to pair; a victim for sacrifice.

狄 The northern regions or tribes; inferior officers; distant.

逖 To remove far off; put away; remote.

鹿 A deer.

蟄 Retirement; to retire to silence; dormant.

滌 To wash; cleanse; a vessel to wash in.

笛 A kind of flute or musical reed.

廸 To advance; tread in the steps of; to lead on; the right path of reason and virtue.

舳 The stern of a boat where the rudder is fastened.

軸 A part of the axle of a carriage; alacrity; cheerfulness.

翟 A pheasant with a long tail. to screen.

擢 To pluck up; select; promote; lead; excite.

敵 An enemy; one opposed to; to oppose; to attack.

嫡 The proper or true wife; correct; pertaining to the true wife.

竹 Bamboo; one of the tones of Chinese music; a thin slip of wood.

德 Virtue; power; abundance; benevolence; gratitude.

的 A target; mark to shoot at; bright; true; real.

T'ek.

勅 A precept; order; prohibition; sincere.

飭 A firm, respectful manner; adjusted; to give orders to; injunctions.

剔 To cut up; scrape off; to reject; to work up.

惕 Respect; awe; serious attention; active; cautious.

裼 To open the clothes and expose the breast in bravado.

禿 Bald; fallen off; the blunt end of.

陟 To ascend; to promote; advance; high; eminent.

忒 To change; alter; err; to doubt.

Teng.

亭 High; a shed by the wayside or in a garden; a watch-house; straight.

重 To repeat; a second time; again.

登 To ascend; advance; commence; record; to effect.

燈 A lamp; lantern; moral; light; precepts; laws.

徵 To testify; prove; manifest; fulfill; examine; verify; act; evidence; testimony.

癥 A disease of the stomach; cholic.

丁 A nail; pin; anything sharp; a sting; manhood; reiterated.

叮 Repeatedly; again and again.

町 A dike which serves for a path through fields.

疔 A venereal ulcer; a poisonous sore.

訂 To criticise; examine; collate; adjust; deliberate; to edit.

酊 Intoxicated.

釘 A nail, pin or bolt.

頂 The summit, vertex or top; the knob worn on the top of the head to distinguish rank.

等 Rank; class; series; forms the plural; to wait.

釘 To nail; to pin; fasten; to make nails.

凳 A seat; bench; stool; couch.

磴 Lofty; precipitous; a stone bridge.

蹭 Embarrassed; irresolute; going neither one way nor the other.

T'eng.

汀 A level shore by the side of a river.

停 To rest under; cease; stop; delay.

梃 A club; a stick; a branch or stalk.

渟 Stagnant water; a level shore.

霆 A clap of thunder; lightning.

棖 The two side-posts of a door; a staff; to follow.

澄 Pure, still water; clear; limpid.

瞪 To look straight forward.

騰 To leap upon; ascend; run fiercely; to propagate.

廷 A place of concourse or residence; a hall of audience; *His Majesty*; to rectify.

庭 A large hall in the midst of a house.

蜓 A dragon-fly.

窓 A window; a small door or aperture to admit light.

挺 To pluck forth; draw out; to stretch out; lead away.

艇 A boat.

逞 Presuming; forward; to extend to; precipitate.

頴 The ear of grain; point of an instrument; talent.

懲 To regulate; cause to stop; repress; to caution; correct.

聽 To hear and determine causes, as a judge.

Ti.

遞 To change; for; instead of; to transmit.

池 A pool; pond; receptacle for water.

治 To put in order; to rule; direct; chastise.

蜘 A spider.

氐 Below; low; mean; fundamental; to extend to.

低 Low; to bend down; droop to hang down.

羝 A ram; he-goat; buck.

底	At the bottom or foot of; the bottom; low; only.
抵	To oppose or stop; to bear opposition; to strike; push away.
柢	The root of trees or plants.
砥	A grindstone or whet-stone; level; even.
祇	Only; but; as introducing a qualifying clause.
詆	To vilify; slander; accuse falsely.
觝	To push with the horns; to gore; to oppose.
弟[5]	A younger brother; degrees; successive steps.
娣[5]	A younger sister; a younger brother's wife.
悌[5]	Dutiful conduct from a younger towards an older brother.
彘[5]	Swine; pigs; a sow.
棣[5]	Name of a wood; reiterated; accustomed to; skilled in.
隸[5]	To be attached to; attendants; under officers.
杕[5]	Name of a wood or shrub.
雉[5]	The fowl species; the pheasant.
稚[5]	Young; small; late.
薙[5]	To eradicate or burn grass and wild herbs.
地[5]	The earth; a place; the ground; seat of.
髢[2]	False hair; a false cue.
致[2]	To go or come to; carry to the utmost degree; to lead to; tend to; so that; minute.
置[2]	To appoint; establish; to place; put; to purchase.
智[2]	Wisdom; general information or science; wise.
帝[2]	A ruler; sovereign; emperor.
碟[5]	A plate; a bowl.
蔕	The stem of a plant or fruit; without root; unfounded.
滴	Water dropping; a drop.

T'i.

提	To lift up; take or bring up; introduce; to bring before a magistrate.
鞮	Leather boots or shoes.
啼 / 謕	To bewail; the note of a bird; crowing of a cock.
持	To grasp; hold fast.
痔[5]	Ulcers about the anus; to corrode; gnaw.
替[2]	To annul or reject; for; instead of; in behalf of.
翅[2]	Only; wings.
剃[2]	To shave off the hair or beard.

涕² Tears; to shed tears.

梯² Noxious grass; tares.

啻² Only; an excess; overplus.

揥² To grasp with the hand; to put away.

禘² Sacrifices to the royal ancestors.

嚔²
嚏² } To sneeze; a stoppage.

滯² Water impeded; congelation; stoppage; discordance.

褫² To put off one's clothes, or official robes; a fringe.

鐵 Iron.

Tⁿi.

縝 Silk prepared but not woven; close; thick; black.

Tia.

爹 Father.

糶 To buy rice; to procure food.

摘 To take with the hand; to pluck; pull; to set in order.

謫 To reprimand; blame; be angry with; punish.

T'ia.

折 To break asunder; to break off a part; to deduct; decide; repress; oppress; reprehend.

Tⁿia.

定 Settled; fixed; tranquil; certain; to settle; decide; only.

鼎 A tripod; stable; correct; to establish; make firm; a frying-pan or rice pot.

綻⁵ The seam of a garment; to open a seam.

錠⁵ White copper or tin; a certain piece of silver.

T'ⁿia.

呈 A statement in the form of a petition; to present or offer up to a superior.

程 To travel; journey; proceed; to offer to a superior.

聽 To hear; listen; comply; obey; to hear and decide a cause.

廳 A place where causes are heard; a court; office.

痛² Sick; in pain; painful; pain of mind; sorrow; pity.

Tiam.

甜 Sweet; excellent.

霑 A drizzling rain; to wet; damp.

坫 A screen in a door-way; a stand for food or drink.

沾 To moisten; to tinge; to receive favors; be affected by.

砧 A stone to beat clothes or plants upon.

苫 Thatch covering; a mourning garment.

玷 A gem that is broken; to stop; to disgra‹ e.

点 點 } A spot; a dot; a small quantity; to dot; to appoint; to blot out; to light a candle.

笘 A bamboo switch.

店 A shop; a stand; an inn.

T'iam.

恬 A peaceful, tranquil state of mind; repose.

聒 Clamorous; discordant; to hear; noisy.

添 To add to; increase.

忝 Feeling of shame; to cause shame; to disgrace.

悿 Weak; timorous; agitated.

諂 To flatter; praise; worship; mean adulation.

Tiáng.

暢 Expanding; pervading; to fill; joy; hilarity.

鬯 Name of a fragrant plant; odoriferous wine used in sacrifice.

Tiap.

喋 Loquacity; fluency of speech.

堞 A rampart; to fortify with a rampart.

揲 To take or grasp hold of; to take up.

楪 A window.

牒 A register; records; official document.

蝶 A butterfly.

諜 To excite mutiny or rebellion; to spy; a spy.

蹀 To step; tread upon; a short pace.

T'iap.

帖 A short written paper as a label, a card, a petition.

貼 To give a pledge; to attach to; to paste upon.

跕 To fall down; to drag the feet in walking.

Tie.

潮 The tide; rising tide; a district in the province of Canton; *Tie Chiu.*

趙 To go and announce to; to return what was borrowed.

着 Towards; at; to hit; to take effect; right; exactly.

T'ie.

挑 To stir up; excite; seduce; to carry on the shoulders.

糶 To sell grain.

T^{n}ie.

場 An arena or open space for sacrifices, military and literary contests &c.

張 To draw the string of a bow; to spread out; a numeral of things which spread out.

꜂長 Long; aged; elevated; to grow; increase.

丈^{5} Father-in-law; uncle; an aged person.

帳^{2} Curtain; to spread out; a tent.

脹^{2} Swelling of the abdomen.

賬^{2} To draw out accounts; reckon up; an account book.

漲^{2} Water extending and rising; higher; an inundation.

釣^{2} To catch fish with a hook.

Tien.

꜀顛 The vertex; head; forehead; subverted; cast down; insanity.

꜀癲 Insanity; frantic; convulsions; fits.

꜀珍 Valuable; precious; excellent.

꜂典 A standard classical work; canon; to rule; confer benefits; dictionary.

꜂腆 Much; many; abundant; good.

꜂覥 A bashful appearance; abashed.

꜂展 To unroll; spread out; inspect; sincere; agreeable.

꜂輾 To turn round as a wheel.

殿^{5} A large hall; fixed; the rear of an army.

簟^{5} Mats made of bamboo.

墊^{5} To put down; to sink; to pay down money; a cushion.

電^{5} Lightning.

奠^{5} Fixed; lofty; to discriminate; to present or offer up.

甸^{5} Space of 500 *li* about the court; divisions of land; to cultivate.

T'ien.

꜀畋 The level field; to till the ground; to hunt.

꜀鈿 Golden ornaments of a lady's head-dress.

꜀填 To fill up; make up deficiency; pay a debt; to stop up.

꜀廛 A shop where people buy and sell.

꜀纏 To wind round; tie; bind; wrap with silk.

꜀天 Heaven.

Tiet.

姪꜄ A nephew or niece.

垤꜃ High land; a hillock; an ant's hill.

桎꜃ Fetters; bonds; to stop; to pierce.

窒꜃ To stop or close up; fill; impede.

絰꜃ Pieces of white cloth worn in mourning.

耋꜃ A person eighty years of age.

蛭 A species of leech.

哲 Possessing great knowledge and keen discernment; wise.

帙 A cloth cover; a little bag.

瓞 A small species of melon; children and grandchildren.

秩 Order; series; succession; rank; wisdom; purity.

跌 To slip; stumble; fall; to move rapidly; to stamp.

軼 To rush forward; spread out; invade; sudden.

迭 Alternate; change; reciprocation; for; instead of.

輒 The sides of a chariot; suddenly; forthwith; without inquiry.

T'iet.

徹 Penetrable; to penetrate; penetration; perspicacious; passable; to cultivate.

撤 To dismiss; reject; send away; remove from office.

轍 The rut of a wheel; a track.

Tim.

沈 To sink; to put under water; to descend.

耽 Long ears; addicted to pleasure; formidable.

酖 Wine infused with poison; to delight in wine.

鴆 A species of bird rendered poisonous by eating serpents; poison.

琛 Natural gems of precious stones.

湛 To put in water; soak.

朕 Used by the emperor for I.

Tin.

塵 Dust; sand; effluvia; traces of a person.

籐 Rattan; vines; rushes; name of a medicine.

陳 To state in order; spread out; arrange; tell.

陣 An army; a file; company; ranks; to arrange; tell.

鎮 To press down; repress; keep in subjection; keep off any evil influence.

Tio.

條 A small twig; a string; an item; a section; a numeral.

刁 Perverse; violent; artful; wicked; restless.

凋 彫 Injured; falling off, as leaves of trees; debilitated.

剮 雕 To carve; work or polish stones; embellish; to be cut or fall to pieces.

忉 Grief; sorrow.

髫 The tuft of hair on a child's head; young.

貂 鼦 An animal of the mus species with fur.

齠 The period in which children change their teeth.

召[5] To call with authority; to summon; call.

兆[5] A tortoise shell used in divination; an omen; a mound or grave; a million.

弔[2] 吊[2] To mourn for the dead; wounded in the feelings.

T'io.

調 To mix; adjust in due proportions; to regulate; to nurse.

超 To step lightly; trip; leap over; surpass; excel; promote.

迢 Removed far off; lofty.

佻 Slender; weak; to steal; levity; slow; servile.

眺 To look aslant; look at a distance; to peep.

祧 Ancestral temples or tablets.

誂 To call or whisper to; to seduce; allure; seduction.

窕 Deep; profound; retired; elegant; delicate.

柱[5] A post; pillar; to sustain; support.

跳[2] To walk; to leap; skip; dance; to overpass.

T'iok.

畜 Domestic animals; to feed; to endure; to obey.

慉 To nourish; to induce; proud; to dislike; hate.

蓄 To accumulate; hoard up; to nourish; breed; bring up.

Tit.

直[5] Straight; correct; strict; just; directly.

得 Successful; to succeed; to attain; obtain; can.

Tiu.

紬 To select; take from; draw out; silk.

裯 A covering for a bed; bed curtains; a single garment.

丟 To throw away; throw.

冑 A helmet.

抒 To take by the hand; lead; to lay open; explain; to strain; to decant.

杼 Transverse part of a loom; thin; narrow; to pare thin.

紓 Slow; remiss; procrastinating.

宁 The space between the door and screen.

佇 To stand and wait for a long time.

竚 To stand for a long time; stand.

貯 To accumulate; store up; an accumulation.

苧^5 Name of a plant; a species of hemp.

宙^5 To contain; the earth or universe which contains all things.

晝^5 Day in distinction from night; day-light.

紂^5 Name of an infamous king of China.

T'iu.

儔 A number of persons; a company; a party; who?

疇 A cultivated field; a field of hemp; to cultivate.

籌 To calculate; reckon; devise; plan; arrange.

𧃒 Name of a plant.

躊 Embarrassed; irresolute; unable to proceed.

倜 Raised above others; unrestrained; noble freedom.

惆 Mournful; sorry.

稠 Grain growing thick; close; crowded together.

綢 Thick; close; to wrap round; hang with ornaments.

抽 To lead; take out from amongst; take a part.

丑 A horary character from 1 to 3 A. M.

To.

圖 To draw a map or picture; delineate; a map or delineation; to plan; to try; to contrive.

塗 To plaster; to ornament; to daub; to blot out.

厨 A quiver; a case for books; a cook-house.

蹰 Entangled; embarrassed.

屠 To butcher; kill; rend in pieces.

都 A metropolis; abundant; all; general; to dwell.

賭 To gamble; play; risk.

肚 The belly; stomach; seat of the sentient principle.

杜^5 To stop or fill up; shoot out; bark of which cords are made; name of a tree.

豆^5 A vessel used in sacrifice; a certain measure.

度 A law; rule; measure; limit; a degree; to measure; to think.

渡 To pass through or over; to ford a stream.

鍍 To wash or plate with silver or gold.

竇 An aperture; crevice; den; hole; aqueduct; channel.

鬭 To wrangle; fight; contest.

T'o.

塗 Clay; mud; earth.

土 Earth; the ground; a piece of ground; a country; a place.

吐 To spit out; vomit; reject; to utter; speak.

兎 A hare; rabbit.

菟 A medicinal plant.

Tó.

逃 To run away; abscond.

銚 A sauce-pan; a hoe; pick-axe.

刀 A knife; a sword.

多 Many; much; more; to add.

倒 To fall; subvert; turn up-side down; yet; after all; to pout out.

朶 Hanging pendent as fruit or flowers; to lead as a child.

垜 A target to shoot at; a side apartment or school-room.

躱 To hide; conceal; evade; the body.

惰 Disrespectful; remiss; lazy; lounging.

擇 To choose; select; pick out.

卓 To erect; establish; eminent; high and stable.

倬 Great; lofty; bright; manifest.

桌 A table; a stand.

琢 To work stones or gems; to cut; carve.

築 To beat down as mud into a wall; to build mud houses.

T'ó.

桃 A peach.

沱 A stream diverging from a river; tears falling; rain.

跎 To stumble; fall; to lose an opportunity.

陀 Irregular; dangerous.

鮀 Name of a fish; a shark.

萄 A grape.

鼉 A species of large fish; a kind of alligator.

唾 Spittle; to spit; to treat with contempt.

討 To investigate; search for; demand; to excite; kill.

妥 Tranquil; secure; firm; trusty; safe.

它 To bear; carry; a camel.

駝 A camel.

托 To take with the hand; also used for the next word.

託 To commit to the care of; to charge with; trust to.

Tó or Tù.

短 Short; to shorten; to come short.

在 To be in a place; to dwell; to be alive; to consist in.

代 An age; generation.

帒 袋 } A bag; sash; purse; packet.

奪 To seize upon by force; to take unjustly.

T'ó or Tù.

胎 The womb; pregnancy.

退 To decline; refuse; retire; draw back; yield.

Toa.

舵 A helm or rudder.

大 Great; large.

帶 A belt; girdle; to draw, lead or take along with.

T'oa.

拖 To drag; pull; lead; to steer a boat.

獺 A beaver, castor or otter.

T^{n}oa.

壇 An altar; an arena; a platform.

單 Single; alone; only; entirely; sincere; credible.

憚 Distress; afraid; wearied; difficulty.

惰 Remiss; lazy; lounging; disrespectful.

T'^{n}oa.

攤 To open; spread out; a stall; slow; remiss.

灘 Water rushing through a narrow pass; a rapid.

炭 Coals; charcoal.

Toi.

蹄 The foot or hoof of a quadruped; to kick.

題 The forehead; head; title of a book; a theme; to contribute; to praise.

堤 To stop or fill up; to raise a dike or barrier; firm.

底 Low; the bottom of; mean; only.

第 A degree; series; the ordinal of numbers; but; only.

苐 Name of a plant.

T'oi.

扠 To take, as with nippers; a harpoon; to strike.

釵 A large pin or bodkin to fasten up the hair.

體 Body; substantial; to realize; embody; to represent.

代 For; instead or in the place of.

T'^{n}oi.

佃 To cultivate the ground; to plough; to catch animals.

殿 A mansion; temple; hall; court.

靛 A blue dye; to color blue.

有 Solid; real; substantial; having a kernel.

T'ⁿoi.

看 To see; look at; consider.

Tok.

獨 Single; alone; only; one; one's self.

涿 Flowing down in drops; name of a stream.

逐 To propel; drive out; reject; each; one by one.

瀆 Foul; muddy; to defile; insult; annoy; disrespect.

匵 A box; case or press.

櫝 A case for a sword or any such thing; a coffin.

牘 A written document; a tablet; a card; small book.

犢 A calf; a heifer; a victim for sacrifice.

讟 Resentment; hatred and dissatisfaction; murmurs.

覿 To look; see; gaze at; to have an audience.

黷 Sordid; filthy; black; defiled.

啄 To peck; a bird eating; to take up food in the mouth; to choose.

斲 To cut; pare; hew.

督 To examine; reprove; rule; govern; lead; give orders.

篤 Thick; substantial; firm; real; sincere; superlative.

Tong.

中 The middle, centre; within.

忠 Faithful; honest; upright; not selfish; fidelity.

仲 The middle of three; younger; part of the name of *Confucius*.

動 To move; shake; to excite; agitate; stir up.

慟 The feelings moved to excess; extreme grief.

中 To hit the centre; right; exact; correct; to succeed.

凍 Ice; cold as ice; cold.

棟 Name of a kind of tree; a cross-beam in a house.

疼 Pain; acute feeling; affection; extreme regard.

T'ong.

童 A boy; lad; young girl; a virgin; chaste.

僮 A youth; silly; a slave girl or concubine.

幢 A kind of standard; screen; curtain; feathers attached.

曈 The sun about to shine forth; desire to shine.

潼 Name of several rivers; damp, wet appearance.

瞳 Pupil of the eye; to stare; a silly appearance.

艟 A kind of short boat.

蹱 To tread or walk upon; walking crooked as a child.

侗 Ignorant; rude; want of talent; plain; sincere.

恫 Pain; acute feeling; to sigh; grieved.

桐 Name of a wood.

洞 A ravine; deep; profound; to see through clearly; understand.

彤 Red; a red pencil.

通 To go through; penetrable; to comprehend; to succeed; all.

冢 A mound; summit of a hill; a grave.

塚 A grave; sepulchre.

統 The origin; clue; the whole; entire; general.

寵 Affection; tender regard; love; kindness.

撞 To pound; beat; strike suddenly; abrupt; to seize.

痛 Acute pain; disease; painful; wounded; sick.

Tu.

侏 A pigmy; low stature; small pillars.

蛛 A spider.

誅 To make inquisition; punish; destroy; exterminate.

堵 A low wall; to fend off; to shut; settled; tranquil.

暏 The morning light.

楮 Name of a tree of the bark of which cloth and paper are made.

渚 A small island.

睹, 覩 To look; observe; see.

闍 A battlement over a city gate; a tower for observation.

著 To manifest; make conspicuous; publish; to supply.

T'u.

儲 To provide; collect and assist; to be second to.

躇 Embarrassed; perplexed; at a loss how to proceed.

徒 To walk on foot; a footman; a disciple; pupil; a multitude; class; clan; only; futile; vain.

荼 Bitter; name of a bitter herb.

途 A path; road; way; means.

圖 To covet; desire; seek after.

Tú.

除 To exclude; subtract; put away; remove evil; besides.

猪 A swine; a pig.

箸 Chinese chop-sticks; sticks to eat with.

Tuan.

端 Straight; upright; decorous; commencement; first cause.

彖5 A pig; porcupine; symbols used in divination.

篆5 The ancient or seal character of writing.

斷5 To decide; determine; certainly; positively; to break off.

斷2 A decision; judgment.

煆2 鍛2 To fuse metals; to hammer; to work; to mature.

T'uan.

傳 To deliver to in succession; hand down; promulgate.

團 Collected together; a mass of; forming one whole.

Tue.

兌5 To exchange; compare; give an equivalent; pleased.

T'ue.

瘣 Possessed with the devil; diseased; a swelling.

魋 A divine animal resembling a boar.

癩 A boil; disease of the genital organs.

頹 Rushing down; falling; yielding; to be ruined.

駾5 A horse bolting forth suddenly.

Tui.

搥 To throw; to strike, as a drum or bell.

追 To escort; follow after; pursue; prosecute.

縋5 A cord or rope; to let down by a cord.

墜5 To slide or fall down; to fall over.

墮5 To fall; to fall into ruins, as a house, family or state.

懟5 譵5 Resentment and enmity; to hate and speak against.

隊5 To fall down; fall together; company; a hundred men.

對2 To answer; respond; to correspond to; to pair; a pair.

碓2 A pestle; to pound.

T'ui.

槌 To strike; beat; a beater; pestle; drum-stick; club.

鎚 A mallet; hammer; club; to beat; to hammer.

梯 Wooden steps; a ladder; steps or means to an end.

腿 The back part of the hip; the thigh.

褪 To put off one's clothes; undress; flowers fading.

Tun.

唇 The lips; mouth.

鈍 Blunt; dull; stupid.

敦 Angry; large; affluent; substantial; to urge; to rouse.

淳 Clear; pure; unmixed; to wash or cleanse; great.

諄 To state fully and impressively; to inculcate; instruct clearly.

醇 Generous wine; seminal matter; essence; respectful.

噋 Mere talk; repetition; a dull sound of a carriage.

堆 A pile; heap of earth; a multitude; to heap up.

塾 墩 } A hillock in a level place.

燉 A great flame; to steam; to place anything in steam.

鐓 The lower end of a spear-handle; low; to beat down; a beater.

盾 A kind of shield.

楯 A large railing round an orchard; a shield; name of a wood.

炖 Wind causing the fire to blaze.

頓 To bow the head to the ground; to desist; an inn; stupid.

腯 Covered with fat; fleshy.

瞓 Dullness of sight; sleepy.

T'un.

屯 To collect and station, as soldiers; beginning; sparing.

沌 Confused; rushing in confusion, as a torrent.

囤 A bamboo basket or wooden receptacle for grain; a granary.

肫 Earnest; honest; dried flesh; bones of the face.

豚 A pig; a fat hog for sacrifice.

遁 遯 } To skulk away; conceal one's self; withdraw.

吞 To swallow; swallow whole; to engross; sieze upon.

T'ung.

堂 A mansion; temple; hall; court; college.

腸 The intestines; bowels; the seat of the affections.

唐 Name of an ancient Chinese dynasty, and hence used for China or Chinese.

塘 An artificial pond.

長 Long.

當 What is proper; ought; to sustain; be adequate; to meet; oppose; a pledge; firm.

擋 To oppose; stand on the way of; impede; withstand.

斷 To break off; intermit; cease.

段 A piece, as of silk, of business or work; a section of history.

緞 Inside lining of a shoe; silk.

當 Firm; stable; a pledge.

儅 To cease; to stop.

T'ng.

糖 Sugar; honey; candy.

湯 Broth; soup; gravy; sauce.

Tut.

突 Abrupt; suddenly; to offend.

怵 Fear; reverence.

訹 To entice; lead astray; seduce.

脫 To fall off; to put off; to escape from; to get out.

黜 To blame; degrade; put out of office; exterminate.

U.

雩 Sacrifices intended to implore rain.

樗 Name of a certain wood.

娛 Joy; extacy; delight; to exult.

于 In; through; to; at; great; extensive.

吁 An interjection denoting disapprobation, concern or grief; to call.

旴 Morning; dawn; extending; great.

盂 A vessel to contain rice, wine, or water.

汙 污 Foul; dirty; name of a river.

訏 False; boasting; great.

迂 Wide; remote; vague; crooked; depraved; roving.

呼 To breathe out; call; invoke.

杅 A vessel for drinking with; large; self-sufficient.

嗚 Alas! to sigh; lament.

鷗 A certain water-fowl.

於 An interjection of grief or surprise; in; to consist in.

羽 Wings of a bird; feathers; a note of music.

禹 Name of an ancient Chinese emperor.

宇 To cover or spread over; the canopy of heaven; wide.

有 Is; to be; to possess; existence; affluent; further; more; truly.

惡 To hate; loathe.

塢 A bank, dike or wall; barracks; a village.

ù.

余 I; me.

畬 A field which has been cultivated only three years.

餘 Overplus; leavings; the rest.

予 To give; confer; bestow; to praise; I; me.

輿 The part of a carriage that contains the load; to sustain; contain.

歟 A particle closing a sentence denoting satisfaction or interest.

與 Together with; by; with; and; to; to reckon; wait for.

與 To give; to add to; to promise; comply with.

預^{5} 豫^{5} } Before-hand; previously prepared for; provided against; to deliberate; pleasure.

譽^{5} To praise; extol; speak highly of.

翳^{2} A kind of umbrella or fan made of a Pheasant's tail; to cover; screen.

飫^{2} To eat excessively; to gormandize; gluttonous.

瘀^{2} A local accumulation of blood; chronic disease.

Ua.

騧 A yellowish horse with a black mouth.

剮 To cut off the flesh and leave the skeleton bare.

呱 To cry as a child; crying; sobbing.

罛 A net for fish.

哇 A lascivious or flattering tone; a child sobbing; to vomit.

蛙 Frogs; a croaking noise as of frogs.

畦 Name of a place; a field containing 50 acres.

瓦 Earthen ware; tiles; bricks.

我 I; me; our; used emphatically when speaking of one's parents or country.

吾 I; me, when speaking of one's self; to guard; impede.

倚 To lean against; depend upon; inclined to one side.

活$_{5}$ Alive; lively; cheerful; moving.

Uⁿa.

安 Stillness; rest; tranquility; peace; how? what?

鞍 A saddle for a horse.

碗 A bowl, dish or plate.

旱^{5} Drought; want of rain.

案^{2} A table; a bench, as of a judge; a case in law.

晏^{2} The evening; tranquil; mild; benignant.

Ue.

鍋 An earthen rice pot; a pot for boiling food.

劃 A style or pointed instrument; to mark; split open.

衛[5] To escort; protect; a military station.

話 Words; speech; conversation; to talk; to tell.

尉[2] Name of an office; to settle tranquilize.

慰[2] To soothe; console; comfort.

蔚[2] Name of a plant; luxuriant foliage; thick and gloomy.

噦[2] The breath rising; to belch; voice of a bird; wide; light.

穢[2] Vice; filth; unclean; indecent; lewd; to defile.

畫[2] 畵[2] To mark; draw a line; to paint; draw pictures; to draw plans; devise. *Jip tone*; a line; a mark.

Ui.

爲 To do; to effect or make; to reckon or esteem; a reason; because.

圍 To surround; besiege; guard; limit.

幃 A single curtain; a bag to contain incense or perfume.

違 To oppose; turn the back upon; perverse; wicked.

闈 The door of the harem; the door to the ancestral hall &c.

桅 A short spear; the mast of a small boat.

威 Dignity; majesty; intimidating power; respectful.

醫 To heal; cure; the medical art.

委 To sustain a burden or office; to commit unto; to belong to; to send; reject.

蜲 Name of certain insects of the worm species.

諉 To implicate others; to involve; tautology; excuse.

韋 Perverse; insubordinate; leather thongs; soft leather.

偉 Great; extraordinary; surprising.

緯 The woof of a web; lines of latitude; transverse.

葦 Name of a flexible reed.

韙 To defend and illustrate the right and oppose the wrong.

喟 A tone expressing surprise, joy or praise.

渭 Water agitated; the noise of waves.

喂 To feed animals; to graze.

煨 Fire or any thing hot in a vessel.

爲[5] In consequence of; for; because of; to suffer the effect of an action.

位 A person; a place; a seat; right; regular; established.

痿 Weakness; lameness; impotency; to fade; rot; dead.

胃 } The stomach.
[illegible] }

畏 To fear; stand in awe of; reverence; submission.

謂 To say; speak of; to tell; to denominate.

Un.

運 To agitate; turn round; revolve; circulate.

云 To say; abundance; to turn round.

紜 A state of confusion.

芸 Plants budding forth; fragrant plants; to root out weeds.

耘 To pull out weeds and injurious plants from a field; to weed.

溫 Warm; genial; benign; cordial; mild; to warm.

熅 Fire and steam without smoke; genial warmth; vapor.

瘟 An epidemic disease; a pestilence.

縕 Confused like raveled silk; hemp; tattered; genial.

氳 Vapor; the generative influence or breath of nature.

蕰 An edible vegetable; an accumulation of.

蘊 Luxuriant; accumulated; repressed indignation.

韞 A reddish colour; yellowish; inside; a store room.

殞 To fade; fall; perish; die.

隕 To roll down; fall; fall into ruins.

刎 To cut; to cut the throat; to cut crosswise.

穩 To moisten grain for distillation; rest; safe; firm.

醞 To ferment liquor; to cherish or ferment in the mind.

慍 Hot, indignant feeling.

韻 Sounds which harmonize; rhyme; similar sounds.

搵 To obliterate; to absorb; soak; stain; dye; to wet; put into water.

U'n.

恩 To show kindness to; favor; benignity; gracious.

隱 Secret; hidden; settled; tranquil; small; to commiserate.

癮 A cutaneous disease; small pustules or blisters.

尹 Name of an office; to rule, grasp.

吚 To breathe; to moan.

Ut.

杌 A tree without branches; stunted; disquieted.

鬱 Fragrant herbs for sacrifice; anxious thoughts; vexations.

Wak.

獲 To obtain; to catch, as in hunting, or a thief.

穫 To reap grain; cut down and gather in a harvest.

Wan.

꜁緣 A cause; to connect as cause and effect; to accord with former circumstances.

꜁彖 Name of a wood; a branch.

꜁完 To complete; finish; close.

꜁捖 To strike; rub; work stones; to cut and pare.

꜁浣 To wash; cleanse; name of a river.

꜁莞 A kind of grass or rush of which mats may be made.

꜁員 Officers of government; round; to circulate; extend to every part.

꜁袁 Long garments or robes.

꜁猿 A monkey.

꜁轅 The poles or yoke of a carriage; a gate-way.

꜁淵 An eddy; whirlpool; deep abyss.

꜁宛 To cause to stoop; to oppress; to injure.

꜀鴛 The male of a certain bird considered an example of matrimonial fidelity.

꜀彎 To draw a bow and shoot; to bend; curved; bending.

꜀灣 A bay or curve in a shore; a place for boats or ships to anchor.

꜂腕 The wrist; to turn; twist.

꜂宛 Yielding; accommodating; to oppress; to injure; to repay; to redress.

꜂剜 To cut or pare; engrave; to cut deep into.

꜂婉 A yielding, complaisant woman; flattering; submissive.

꜂菀 Grass; pasture; name of a plant.

꜂踠 To bend the foot or leg; to bend the body.

꜂苑 Grass; pasture; luxuriant; herbage; delicate plants.

怨[2] Dissatisfaction; resentment; ill will; hatred; to repine.

Wang.

꜁王 A king; sovereign; royal; a title given to deceased ancestors.

꜁汪 A large, still expanse of water; tranquil; deep; vast.

꜁薨 Many; rapid; death of a prince; departed; died.

꜂往 To go; walk away; past; gone.

꜂枉 To rule by violence; bent down; oppressed; unjust.

旺[3] The sun shining forth with increasing splendor; to increase.

王[5] To rule; govern as a king; to flourish.

Wat.

越[5] To pass over; overstep; exceed; more; to lose.

鉞[5] A kind of large hatchet.

粤 A classical name for Canton; in; to say; that is.

刖 To separate entirely; to cut off the feet as a punishment.

穵 A den; deep hollow place; hollow; to explore with the hand.

曰 To speak; say; denominate; said; is called.

Yiak.

龠 籥 A musical instrument with three tables; a certain measure.

鑰 A lock; bolt to a door.

瀹 To boil; soup made of flesh and herbs.

躍 To skip; leap; dance; frisk about in joy.

鑠 爍 To fuse metals; to urge; impel; shining; bright.

Yien.

涎 Flowing of water; continued succession; saliva.

筵 A mat to sit upon; a feast; entertainment.

莚 Creeping plants; spreading far and wide; protracted.

蜒 Name of certain insects.

焉 A closing particle denoting settled opinion; thought completed.

嫣 Handsome; smiling; pleasing.

燕 A swallow; rest; repose; alone.

鳶 A bird of prey whose cry indicated wind.

遠 Remote in time or place.

胤 A continued line of posterity and inheritance; custom.

延 Long protracted; slow; remote; to spread far.

埏 A limit or boundary.

衍 Overflowing; wide spreading; prolix; diffuse.

羨 Covetous; desire; to desire; ardently; excess; praise.

爰 Slow; mournful; to remove; to lead.

媛 A beautiful woman who draws admirers; to seduce.

援 To lead; draw; rescue; save; assist; elevate.

遠 To remove to a distance; to put away; to regard as remote.

燕 To entertain a guest; to eat and drink.

Yok.

欲 To breathe after; desire; covet; lust.

浴 To bathe in a stream; to bathe.

慾 To lust after; desire inordinately; passion.

育 To bear; nourish; train up; to grow.

鬻 Gruel; natural food; to nourish; to sell.

煜 Shining; resplendent; moral lustre.

AN INDEX

CONTAINING A TABLE OF THE RADICALS

AND A LIST OF THE WORDS IN THIS VOCABULARY

ARRANGED ACCORDING TO THE RADICALS.

In this Index the tones are not marked, except that the *jip*, when it ends with a vowel, is indicated by a breve over the final letter.

In the TABLE of RADICALS the name of the radical is first given and then the name by which it is usually designated by *Tie Chiu* men, when it differs from the former, is given in Italic except when prevented by want of room. C. annexed to a Radical indicates that it is used only in composition with other characters; when prefixed to a secondary form of a Radical it indicates that that form is only so used.

In the LIST OF WORDS, the common sound, or that under which it is arranged in the Vocabulary, is first given, and then the Reading sound when it differs from the common, is given in Italic. The words under each Radical are arranged according to the number of strokes, but where there are only few words under a Radical the number of strokes is not indicated, as the eye will at once rest on the word sought without the trouble of counting. The list is believed to contain all the words in common use, and may therefore serve as a guide in the preparation of Chinese type, or of Vocabularies in other dialects.

TABLE OF RADICALS.

One Stroke.

一 1. It. *Chek.*
One; unity.

丨 2. Kun. *Tuicham.*
To pass through. C

丶 3. Chu. *Tiam.*
A point.

丿 4. Hék. *Puä.* C.
Bent.

乙 5. It.
One; curved.

亅 6. Kiok. C.
Hooked.

Two Strokes.

二 7. Ji. *Nó.*
Two.

亠 8. Tau. C.
A cover.

人 9. Nang. C. 亻.
Man; human.

儿 10. Jin. C.
A man.

入 11. Jip.
To enter.

八 12. Poi.
Eight.

冂 13. Keng. C.
Remote limits.

冖 14. Mit. *Kapbo.*
To cover. C.

冫 15. Peng. C.
Ice; cold.

几 16. Ki.
A bench or stand.

凵 17. K'ám. C.
A receptacle.

刀 18. Tó. C. 刂.
A knife.

力 19. Lát.
Strength.

勹 20. Pau. C.
To infold.

匕 21. Pi. To arrange.
A spoon or key.

匚 22. Hwang. C.
A square vessel.

匸 23. Hi. C.
To conceal.

十 24. Cháp.
Ten.

卜 25. Pok.
To prognosticate.

卩 26. Chát. 㔾 C.
A seal; credential

厂 27. Hán. C.
A shelter.

厶 28. Sù. *Ut* $m^{n}o$. C.
Deflected; selfish.

又 29. Iu.
Moreover.

Three Strokes.

口 30. K'au.
The mouth.

囗 31. Ui. *Kok kák.*
To inclose.

土 32. To.
Ground; earth.

士 33. Sù.
A scholar.

夂 34. Ti.
To follow.

夊 35. Sue. C.
Walk slowly.

夕 36. Sek.
Evening.

大 37. Tai. *Toa.*
Large.

女 38. $N^{u}ng$.
Female.

子 39. Chù.
A child.

宀 40. Mien. C.
A cover; roof.

寸 41. Chun.
An inch.

小 42. Sio. Small.

尢 43. Wáng. C. Distorted; strange.

尸 44. Si. A corpse.

屮 45. Tiet. A bud; sprout.

山 46. S^{n}ua. A mountain.

巛 47. Chuan 川. C. A stream.

工 48. Kong. *kang.* Work.

己 49. Ki. One's self.

巾 50. Kùn. Cloth.

干 51. Kán. A shield; to offend.

幺 52. Io. Small.

广 53. Iam. C. Shelter; roof.

廴 54. In. A journey.

廾 55. Kiong. C. To join hands.

弋 56. Ek. C. An arrow.

弓 57. Keng. A bow.

彐 58. Ki.彐. 彑. C. A swine's head.

彡 59. Sám. *sá podá.* Feathers; hair.

彳 60. Tek. C. A short step; pace.

Four Strokes.

心 61. Sim. C. 小.忄. The heart.

戈 62. Kó. A spear.

戶 63. Ho. A door.

手 64. Chiu. C. 扌. A hand.

支 65. Chi. A branch.

攴 66. Pok. 攵 C. A slight blow.

文 67. Bun. C. Letters; ornament.

斗 68. Tau. A measure.

斤 69. Kùn. A pound.

方 70. Hwang. Square.

无 71. Bu. C. Not; destitute.

日 72. Jit. The sun.

曰 73. Yet. *Wat.* To speak.

月 74. Guě. The moon.

木 75. Bák. Wood.

欠 76. K'iam. To owe.

止 77. Chi. To stop.

歹 78. Tai. C. 歺. Evil.

殳 79. Su. Weapons.

毋 80. Bó. Do not.

比 81. Pi. To compare.

毛 82. Mó. Hair.

氏 83. Si. A family.

气 84. K'i. Breath.

水 85. Chui. C. 氵 Water.

火 86. Hue. C. 灬. Fire.

爪 87. Jio. C. 爫. Claws.

父 88. Pe. A father.

爻 89. Ngau. To imitate.

爿 90. Chiang. A couch.

片 91. Pien. A splinter.

牙 92. Ge.
Teeth.

牛 93. Gu. C. 牜.
A cow.

犬 94. Kien. C. 犭.
A dog.

Five Strokes.

玄 95. Hien.
Azure; sombre.

玉 96. Gek. C. 王、
A gem.

瓜 97. Kue.
A melon.

瓦 98. Ua. *Hia*.
Earthen ware.

甘 99. Kám.
Sweet.

生 100. Seng. *$S^{n}e$*.
To produce.

用 101. Eng.
To use.

田 102. Tien. *chan*.
A field.

疋 103. Pit. C. 𤴓.
A roll or piece.

疒 104. Chit. C.
Diseased.

癶 105. Puă. C.
To separate.

白 106. Pĕ.
White.

皮 107. Pue.
Skin.

皿 108. Meng.
Crockery: dishes.

目 109. Mák.
The eye.

矛 110. Mau.
A hooked spear.

矢 111. Si.
An arrow; straight.

石 112. Chiĕ.
A stone.

示 113. Ki. *$P^{n}ua$ loi*.
To admonish.

禸 114. Nui.
To creep.

禾 115. Hwa.
Grain.

穴 116. Hwat.
A cave.

立 117. Lip.
To stand up.

Six Strokes.

竹 118. Tek. C. ⺮.
Bamboo.

米 119. Bi.
Rice.

糸 120. Si.
Silk.

缶 121. Hui.
Crockery.

网 122. Máng. 罒冗 冈.
A net.

羊 123. $I^{n}e$.
A sheep.

羽 124. U.
Wings.

老 125. Lau.
Aged.

而 126. Jù.
And.

耒 127. Lui.
A plough-handle.

耳 128. Jù. *$H^{n}i$*.
An ear.

聿 129. Lut.
A pencil.

肉 130. Nek. C. 月.
Flesh.

臣 131. Chʻin.
A minister.

自 132. Chʻù.
Self; from.

至 133. Chi.
To extend to.

臼 134. Ku.
A mortar.

舌 135. Chih.
The tongue.

舛 136. Chun.
Error.

舟 137. Chiu.
A boat.

艮 138. Kùn.
Perverse.

色 139. Sek.
Color.

艸 140. Chʻau. C. 艹
Shrubs; sprouts.

虍 141. U. *Hⁿo tau.* A Tiger.
虫 142. Táng. Reptiles.
血 143. Huĕ. Blood.
行 144. Kⁿia. To walk; do.
衣 145. I. Clothing.
襾 146. A'. *Sai tau.* To overshadow.

Seven Strokes.

見 147. Kien. To see.
角 148. Kák. A horn; corner.
言 149. Ngán. Words.
谷 150. Kok. A valley.
豆 151. To. *Tau.* Pulse.
豕 152. Si. Swine.
豸 153. Chai. Ravenous beasts.
貝 154. Pue. Pearls.
赤 155. Chiă. Flesh color.
走 156. Ch'au. To run.
足 157. Chok. C. ⻊. The foot.
身 158. Sin. The body.
車 159. Ku. A wheel carriage.
辛 160. Sin. Bitter.
辰 161. Sin. Time.
辵 162. T'ok. C. 辶. Going.
邑 163. Ip. C. 阝. A city.
酉 164. Iu. Distilled spirit.
釆 165. Pien. To discriminate.
里 166. Li. Chinese furlong.

Eight Strokes.

金 167. Kim. Metal.
長 168. Chiang 镸. Long.
門 169. Mⁿng. A door.
阜 170. Hu. C. 阝. A mound.
隶 171. Tai. *Ti.* To extend to.
隹 172. Chui. Short-tailed birds.
雨 173. Ho. Rain.
靑 174. Ch'e. Green; azure.
非 175. Hui. Not; wrong.

Nine Strokes.

面 176. Min. The face; surface.
革 177. Kek. Skin of animals.
韋 178. Ui. Insubordinate.
韭 179. Kiu. Leeks.
音 180. Im. Sound.
頁 181. Hiĕ. The head.
風 182. Hwang. Wind.
飛 183. Pue. To fly.
食 184. Chiă. To eat.
首 185. Siu. The head; chief.
香 186. Hiang. Incense; fragrant.

Ten Strokes.

馬 187. Be. A horse.

骨 188. Kut.
Bones.

高 189. Kau.
High.

髟 190. Pio.
Long hair.

鬥 191. To.
To quarrel; fight.

鬯 192. Tʻiang.
A fragrant plant.

鬲 193. Lek. *kek*.
A tripod; urn.

鬼 194. Kui.
A demon.

魚 195. Hù.
Fish.

Eleven Strokes.

鳥 196. Chʻio.
A bird.

鹵 197. Lu.
Salt.

鹿 198. Tek.
A deer.

麥 199. Bĕ.
Wheat.

麻 200. Mua.
Hemp.

Twelve Strokes.

黃 201. Hwang.
Yellow.

黍 202. Su.
Millet; adhesive.

黑 203. Hek.
Black.

黹 204. Chi.
To embroider.

黽 205. Mieu.
A frog.

Thirteen Strokes.

鼎 206. Teng. *T^{n}ia*.
A tripod; establish.

鼓 207. Ko.
A drum.

Fourteen Strokes.

鼠 208. Chʻù.
A mouse.

鼻 209. P^{n}i.
The nose.

Fifteen Strokes.

齊 210. Chʻi.
Even; correct.

Sixteen Strokes.

齒 211. Chʻi.
The teeth.

Seventeen Strokes.

龍 211. Leng.
A dragon.

龜 213. Ku.
A tortoise.

龠 214. Yiak.
A wind instrument.

LIST

OF THE

WORDS IN THIS VOCABULARY.

The design of the following list of words is to assist in finding any particular character when a teacher, from whom its sound may be learned, is not at hand. Being familiar with the radicals in the preceding table, the learner will readily discover one of them forming a prominent part of the word he wishes to find; and under that radical the word will be found in the following list, accompanied with the syllable under which it is arranged in the Vocabulary.

RADICAL 1.

一 Chek *It*
丁 Teng
七 Chʻit
丈 Chiàng
三 Sⁿa *Sam*
上 Siàng
下 Hia
不 Put
丐 Kai
丑 Tʻiu
且 Chʻia *Chʻe*
丕 Pʻi
世 Si
丘 Kiu
丙 Pⁿia *Peng*
丞 Seng
丢 Tiu
並 Peng

RADICAL 2.

丨 Kun
丫 A'
个 Kai
中 Tong
丰 Hong
串 Chʻuan

RADICAL 3.

丶 Tiam
丸 } Iⁿ
凡 } *Ien*
丹 Tán
主 Chu

RADICAL 4.

丿 Puă
乃 Nai
久 } Ku
乆 } *Kiu*
么 Mó
之 Chu
乍 Chá
乎 Hu
乏 Hwat
乖 Kwai
乘 Seng

RADICAL 5.

乙 It
九 Kau *Kiu*
乜 Mi,
乞 Kut
也 Ia *E*
乩 Ki
乳 Ju
乾 Kʻien
亂 Luan

RADICAL 6.

亅 Kiö,
了 Lío
予 U'
事 Su

RADICAL 7.

二 Nó *Jú*
于 U
云 Un
互 Hu
五 Ngo *U*
井 Chⁿe *Cheng*
況 Kʻwang
些 Se
亞 A
亟 Kʻi

RADICAL 8.

亠 Tau
亡 Buang
亢 Kʻáng
交 Kau *Kio*
亥 Hai
亦 Ia *Ek*
亨 Heng
克 Yien
享 Hiàng

1 一
2 丨
3 丶
4 丿
5 乙
6 亅
7 二
8 亠

英漢潮州方言字典

9 人

京 K^{n}ia *Keng*
亭 Teng
亮 Liàng
亶 Tʻán
亹 Mien

RADICAL 9.

人 Nang *Jin*
什 Sip
仁 Jin
仄 Cha, *Chek*
仆 Pʻók
仇 Chʻiu
今 Kim
介 Kai
仍 Jiong *Jeng*
仔 Chù
仕 Sù
他 Tʻá
仗 Chiang
付 Hu
仙 Sien
代 Tó *Tʻoi*
令 Leng
以 I^{n}

4

仰 Ngiáng
仞 Jim
仲 Tong
伉 Kʻáng
件 K^{n}ia *Kien*
仵 Ngo *U*
价 Kai
任 Jim
仿 Hwang
企 Ki
伊 I
伍 Ngo *U*
伏 Hok
伐 Hwat
休 Hiu
伙 Hue *Hó*

5

伯 Peh
估 Ko *Ku*
你 Lù *Ni*
伴 Pʻ^{n}ua *Puan*
体 Toi *Ti*
伭 Hien
伮 No *Nu*
伶 Leng
伸 Sin
似 Sù
伽 Kia
伺 Si
佁 Tai
佃 T^{n}oi *Tien*
佇 Tiu
佈 Pu
佚 It
但 Tan
位 Ui
低 Ti
住 Chu
佐 Chó
佑 Iu
佔 Chiam
何 Hó
佗 Tʻó
余 U *I*
佛 Hut
作 Chak

6

佞 Leng
佩 Pue *Pui*
佻 Tʻio
佾 It
佯 Iàng
佳 Kia
併 Peng
使 Sai *Sù*
來 Lai
侃 Kʻáng
侈 Chʻi
例 Li
侍 Si
侏 Tu
侓 Lut
侔 M^{n}o *Mong*
侗 Tʻong
供 Keng *Kiong*
依 I

7

侮 Bu
侶 Lù
侷 Kek *Kiok*
俄 Ngó
俑 Iong
侯 Ho
俙 Hi
俞 Jú
侵 Chʻim
便 Pʻien
俁 Go *U*
係 Hi
促 Chʻok
俊 Chun
俎 Chó
俏 Siak
俐 Li
俗 Sok
俘 Hu
俚 Li
保 Pó *Pau*
俟 Sù
俠 Kiap
信 Siap
俛 Mien

9 人

修 Siu

8

俯 Hu
俱 Ku
俳 Pai
俸 Hong
俾 Pi
倉 Ch'ang
個 Kai
倍 Pue
倮 Lui
倐 Siap
們 Bun
倒 Tó *Tau*
倖 Heng
倘 T'áng
候 *Hau* *Ho*
倚 In
借 Chie, *Sek*
倡 Ch'iang
倣 Hwang
値 Tek
倦 Kwan *Kien*
倨 Ku
倩 Ch'eng
倪 Goi *Ngi*
倫 Lun
俴 Chien
俵 Pio
俺 An
倀 Chiang
倆 Liang
倌 Kwan
條 Tio
倜 T'iu *Tio*
倥 K'ong
倬 Chau
倭 Ui

9

偃 Lam
偪 Pek
偵 Cheng
偫 T'ai
假 Ke *Kia*
偹 Pi
偈 Hat
偏 P'ien
偕 Kai
做 Chó
停 T'eng
健 Kien
偦 Su
側 Ch'ek
偶 Ngo
偷 T'au

10

傀 Kui
偉 Ui
僂 Lu
傅 Hu
傍 Páng
傑 Kiet
傘 S^{n}ua *San*
傚 Hau

11

催 Ch'ui
傭 Iong
僅 Han
傿 Yien
僉 Ch'iam
傲 Ngau
傳 T'uan
傴 K'u
債 Che *Chek*
傷 S^{n}ie *Siang*
傾 K'wang
備 Pi
僅 Kùn

12

像 S^{n}ie *Siang*
僝 Ch'án
僬 Chio
㒓 T'át
僭 Ch'iam
僕 Pok
僚 Lio
僞 Ngui
僥 Hio
僧 Cheng
㒋 Sù
僮 Tong
僑 Ko
價 Ke *Kia*
僵 Kiàng
儅 Tang
僻 P'ia *Pek*
儀 Ngi
儂 Long
億 Ek
儆 Keng
儉 K'iam

14

儒 Ju
儗 Ngi
儔 T'iu
儕 Se
儘 Chin *Chien*
償 S^{n}ie *Siang*
儡 Lui
優 Iu
儲 T'u
儳 Ch'ám
𠑊 Niap
儷 Li
儻 T'áng
儼 Ngiam
儺 Nó

RADICAL 10.

儿 Jin
兀 Kang

允 Jun
元 Ngwan *Yien*
兄 H^{n}ia *Hiong*
充 Chʻong
兆 Tio
兇 Hiong
先 S^{n}o *Sien*
光 Kwang
克 Kʻiok
兌 Tue
免 Mien
兒 Ji
兎 To *Tu*
兕 Si
兢 Kʻeng
兜 Tau

RADICAL 11.

入 Jip
內 Lai *Nui*
全 Chʻuan
兩 Liàng
両 Nie *Liang*

RADICAL 12.

八 Poi *Pak*
公 Kong
六 Lák *Lok*
兮 Hi
共 Káng *Kiong*
兵 P^{n}ia *Peng*
其 Kʻi
具 Ku
典 Tien
兼 Kiam
冀 Ki

RADICAL 13.

冂 Ki
册 Chʻie *Chek*
冉 Jiam
再 Chai
冑 Tiu
冒 Mau
冕 Mien
冓 Kau

RADICAL 14.

冖 Kap
冠 Kwan
冥 Meng
冢 Tʻong

RADICAL 15.

冫 Peng
冬 Táng *Tong*
冰 P^{n}ia *Peng*
冲 Chʻong
决 Kwat
况 Kʻwang
冶 Ja *E*
冷 Ne *Leng*
冸 Pʻwan
净 Cheng

8

准 Chun
凄 Chʻi
凌 Leng
涵 Ham
凉 Liàng
凋 Tio
凍 Tong
减 Kiam
淜 Peng
潔 Kiet
凛 Lim
凝 Ngeng
凟 Tok

RADICAL 16.

几 Ki
凡 凣 Hwam
凭 Peng
凰 Hwang
凴 Peng
凱 Kai
凳 Teng

RADICAL 17.

凵 Kam
凶 Hiong
凸 Chui
凹 Tʻáp
出 Chʻut
函 Hám

RADICAL 18.

刀 Tó *Tau*
刁 Tio
刃 Jim
分 Hun
切 Chʻiet
刈 Ngai *Ngi*
刊 Kʻán
刋 Kan
刎 Un *Mut*
刑 Heng
列 Liet
初 Chʻo
删 Sán
判 Pwan
別 Piet
刦 Kiap
刨 Pʻau
利 Li

6

刑 Heng
刮 Tiam Kwat
到 Tau
刲 Kui
制 Chi
刷 Sue *Siet*
刹 Sat
刺 Chù *Ch^{ʻu}ng*
券 Kwan *Kien*
刻 Kʻek

7

剃 Tʻi
則 Chek

10 儿
11 入
12 八
13 冂
14 冖
15 冫
16 几
17 凵
18 刀

18 刀
19 力
20 勹
21 匕
22 匚
23 匸
24 十

剉 Ch'ó
剋 Kut
削 Siak
剌 La,
前 Chⁿoi *Chien*

8

剗 Chien
剡 Iam
剖 P'o
剕 Pi
剛 Káng
剔 T'ek
剜 Wan *Wai*
剝 Pák
剞 Ki
剩 Sin
剪 Chien
剮 Ua *O'*
副 Hu

10

割 Kua *Kai*
創 Chang
剷 Chan
剚 Chi
剽 P'io
剿 Ch'au
劂 Kiet
劁 Chio
劇 Kia,
劈 P'ek
劉 Lau *Liu*
劚 Sok
劍 } Kiam
劒 }
劑 Chi
劓 Pi
劙 Li

RADICAL 19.

力 Lat *Lek*
功 Kong
加 Ke *Kia*
劣 Luat
助 Chó
劭 Sio
劬 Ku
努 No

6

劾 Hau *Kio*
勁 Nge *Keng*
劼 Kit
勃 Pwat
勅 T'ek
勇 Iong
勉 Mien
勒 Lek
動 Tong
務 Bu

10

勝 Seng
勞 Lau
募 Mó
勢 Si
勤 K'ùn
勦 Ch'au
勳 Hùn
勵 Li
勸 Kⁿng *Kien*
勷 Siang

RADICAL 20.

勹 Pau
勺 Chiak
勻 Un
勾 Kau
勿 Mai *Mut*
匆 Chong
包 Pau
匈 Hiong
匊 Pek
匍 Po
匏 Pu *Pau*
匐 Pek

RADICAL 21.

匕 Pi
化 Hue *Hó*
北 Pak *Pek*
匙 Si

RADICAL 22.

匚 Hwang
匠 Chⁿie *Chiang*
匝 Cháp
匡 K'áng
匣 Ap
匪 Hui
匯 Hwai
匱 Kⁿui
匧 Kiap

RADICAL 23.

匸 Hi
匹 Pit
匛 Kù
匿 Nek
匾 Pien
區 Ku
匵 Tok

RADICAL 24.

十 Chap
千 Chⁿoi *Chien*
廾 Ji
升 Seng
午 Ngo *U*
卍 T'un
卉 Pi
半 Pⁿua *Pwan*
卑 Pui *Pi*
卓 Tó *Tok*
卒 Chut
協 Hiap
南 Lám
準 Chun

英漢潮州方言字典

博 P'ák
犇 Po

RADICAL 25.

卜 P'ok
卞 Pien
卡 Kiok
占 Chiam
卦 K'ue *Kua*

RADICAL 26.

卩 Chat
卯 Bau
卮 Chi
印 In
危 Ngui
却 K'iak
卲 Sio
夘 Bau
卷 K^{n}ng *Kien*
卸 Sia
卽 Chiet
郤 Kiak
卺 Kun
卿 Keng

RADICAL 27.

厂 Han
厄 E, *Ek*
厘 Li
厖 Pang *Mang*
厚 Kau *Ho*
原 Ngwan *Yien*
厠 Ch'e *Chek*
厝 Ch'u
厥 K'iet
厦 He *Hia*
厩 Ki
厭 Iam
厮 Sù
厨 To *Tu*
厲 Li
廳 T^{n}in *Teng*

RADICAL 28.

厶 Sù
去 K'ù *Ki*
叁 Sa *Sam*
叄 Siam
參 Ch'ám

叅 Cham

RADICAL 29.

又 Iu
叉 Che
及 Kip
友 Iu
反 Hwan
収 Siu
叔 Chek *Sok*
受 Siu
取 Ch'u
叙 Su
叚 T^{n}ng *Tuan*
叛 P'wan
叟 So
叠 T'á,
叢 Chang *Chong*

RADICAL 30.

口 K'au *Ko*
古 Ko *Ku*
叭 Poi, *Pat*
句 Ku *Ki*
另 Leng

叩 Ku *Ko*
只 Chi
叫 Cie *Kio*
召 Tio
叮 Teng
叨 Tau
台 T'ai
可 K'ó
叱 Toa
史 Sù
右 Iu
叵 Pó
叶 Sip
司 Si

3

吁 U
吃 Ngùt
各 Kak *Hok*
合 Ha, *Hap*
吉 Kit
吊 Tio
同 Tang *Tong*
名 Mia *Meng*
吓 He *Hia*

后 Ho
吏 Li
吐 T'o *Tu*
向 Hiàng

4

君 Kùn *Kin*
吪 Hua
吻 Mut
吚 I
吝 Lien
吟 Ngim
吞 Tun
吠 Pui *Hui*
吧 Pá
否 H^{n}o
含 Hám
吮 Jun
吱 Ch^{n}i
吩 Hun
呈 T'^{n}ia *Teng*
吳 Go *U*
吵 Sau *Chau*
吶 Nut
吷 Kwat

24 十
25 卜
26 卩
27 厂
28 厶
29 又
30 口

30 口

吸 K'ip
吹 Ch'ue *Chui*
吼 Hau
吾 Ua *U*
告 Kau
呆 Ngai
呀 Gia
呂 Lù
听 Tⁿia *Teng*

5

咐 Hu
咖 Kia
呢 Ni
周 Chiu
咏 Iong
咆 P'au
咈 Hut
呪 Chiu
呱 Ua
味 Bi *Mi*
呵 Kó
呶 No *Nu*
呷 Ká *Kap*
呻 Sin
呼 U
命 Mia *Meng*
咀 Chu
咂 Chap
咄 Chuat
呡 Min
和 Hua *Hó*
咎 Kiu

6

咨 Chù
咬 Ka *Kio*
咫 Chi
咡 Jù
咤 Te *Tek*
咿 I
咥 Tiet
咭 Kit
咯 Kó, *Kok*
咳 Hai
咸 Ham
咽 In
哀 Ai
品 Pin
哂 Sien
哄 Hong
哆 Chⁿi *I*
咻 Hiu
咧 Li *Liet*
哇 Ua
咩 Iang
哈 Kap
哉 Chai

7

哥 Kó
員 Iⁿ *Ien*
哦 Ngò
呾 Tan
哩 Li
哨 Sau *Siet*
哭 K'au *Kok*
唈 Ip
哮 Hau
哼 Heng
哲 Tiet
哶 Chien
哺 Pu
哽 Kⁿe *Keng*
唆 So
唔 U
啍 Tun
唎 Li
唐 Tⁿng *Tang*

8

售 Ch'iu
唯 Jui
呿 Hwap
𠰻 Bun
唱 Ch'iang
㖼 Meng
唾 Tó
啁 Tiu *Chiu*
啄 Tó, *Tok*
商 Siang
啇 Tek
𠰄 Ti
問 Mⁿng *Bun*
啡 Hui
啓 Ki
啖 Tám
唷 Yok
啜 Chuat
唩 Ui

9

啞 E
啼 Ti
喈 Kai
喀 Ke *Kek*
喏 Nut *Nap*
喉 Au *Ho*
喨 Liàng
喭 Ngan *Yien*
喔 Ok
喟 Ui
喬 K'io
喑 Im
啻 T'i
喂 Ui
喃 Lam *Nam*
善 Sien
喇 La
喊 Ham
喋 Tiap
㖹 Eng
喘 Ch'uan
喚 Hwan
喜 Hi

30 口

喝 Hát
喞 Chiet
𠹗 Chek
喛 Tuan
喧 Suan
啣 Ham
喩 Ju
喪 Sᵘng *Sang*
喫 Kiet

10

單 Tⁿoa *Tan*
嗄 He *Hia*
嗱 Na
嗌 Ngek
嗔 Chin
嗅 Hⁿiu
嗇 Sek
嚠 Liu
嗎 Ma
嗐 Hat
嗑 Hap *Kap*
嗬 O'
鳴 Meng
嗛 Kiam

嗉 Su
嘗 Sⁿie *Siang*
嗜 Si
嗟 Chá
嗣 Sù
嗷 Ngau
嘀 Tek
嗸 Ngau
嘅 Kai *Ki*
嘆 Tan
嘏 Ku
嘖 Che *Chek*
嘒 Hui
嘓 Kok
嗽 So
嘈 Ch'au
嘉 Kia
嘑 U
嘔 Au
嘛 Mua *Mó*
嘘 Hù
嗶 Piet
嘩 Hua *Hó*

嘯 Sau
𠹇 San
嘬 Chui
嘹 Lio
嘲 Chio
嘰 Ki
嘴 Ch'ui
嘱 Sok
嘶 Soi *Sù*
嘸 Bu
嘷 Kau
嘻 Hi
噎 It
噏 Hip

13

噤 Kim
噦 Ue
器 K'i
噥 Long
噪 Ch'au
噹 Tang
噫 I *Ek*
噬 Si
噯 Ai

嚍 Ch'o *Chin*
噴 Pun
嚕 Lu
嚅 Su
嚟 Li
嚇 Hek
𡀯 Luai *Luat*
嚌 Chi
嚔 Ti
嚁 Ch'i
嚥 Yien
嚮 Hiang
嚫 Ch'in

15

嚨 Leng *Long*
嚴 Ngiam
嚶 Eng
嚳 Kok
嚷 Siang
嚼 Chiak
囀 Chuan
囁 Niap
囂 Ngau
囉 Ló

囊 Lang
囌 Só
囒 Lan
囓 Ngiet
囑 Sok

—

RADICAL 31.

31 口

口 Ui
囚 Ch'iu
四 Si *Sù*
回 囬 Hue *Hui*
因 In
囝 Kan
囤 T'un
囫 Mut
囮 Hue *Hó*
困 K'un
囷 K'un
囹 Leng
固 Ku
囿 Iu
圃 P'o
圄 U

31 口

32 土

圈 Kʻwan
圇 Lun
圉 I^{n}
國 Kok
圍 Ui
園 ʻNg *Yien*
圓 I^{n} *Yien*
圖 To *Tʻu*
團 Tʻuan
圜 Hwan

RADICAL 32.

土 Tʻo *Tu*
壬 Jim
在 Tó *Chai*
圩 U
圭 Kui
圮 Ki
圬 Kui
地 Ti

4

坊 Hwang
坟 Pʻun
圻 Tia *Kʻi*
址 Chi
坎 Kʻm
坍 Tán
坐 Chó
坑 Kʻ^{n}e *Keng*
均 Kun

5

坡 Pʻó *Pi*
坤 Kʻun
坼 Chʻek
坫 Tiam
坪 P^{n}ia *Pʻeng*
坭 Ni
坯 Pi
坦 Tʻán
坳 Hiu
垠 Kun
坷 Kʻó

6

垛 } 垜 } Tó
垡 Hwat
堭 Hwang
垤 Tiet
城 S^{n}ia *Seng*
垢 Ko
垣 Hwan
垂 Sui
埃 Ai
埕 Tʻ^{n}ia *Teng*
埔 Po *Pu*
埋 Mai
埉 Hiap
埇 Iong
埒 Luat
埠 Po *Pu*

8

埽 Sau *Chin*
堀 Kʻut
域 Hok
埤 Pui *Pi*
培 Pʻue *Pui*
基 Ki
執 Chip
堂 T^{u}ng *Tʻang*
堄 Ngi
堅 Kien
堆 Chui *Tun*
堇 Kùn
堤 Toi *Ti*
堡 Pó *Pau*.
堦 Koi *Kai*
墟 Chʻi
堞 Tiap
堳 Bai *Mi*
堪 Kʻám
堯 Ngio
堵 To *Tu*
報 Pó *Pau*
堸 Hong

10

塊 Kó *Kui*
塋 Iong
塒 Si
塐 Su
塢 U
塌 Tʻáp
塑 Suak
塔 Tʻá
塗 To *Tu*
塘 Tung
塚 Tʻong
塞 Sát
塟 Ch^{u}ng *Chang*
塡 Tien
墻 T^{n}ie *Chiang*
塵 Tin
墀 Chʻi
墉 Iong
墢 Chʻong
境 Keng
墊 Tien
墓 Mó
墜 Tui

12

墷 Ki
增 Cheng
墟 Hù
墨 Bák *Mek*
墪 } 墩 } Tun
墮 Tui
墳 Pʻun
墺 } 墺 } Au
墾 Kʻùn
壅 Iong
墻 Chʻ^{n}ie *Chiang*
壁 Pia *Pek*

英漢潮州方言字典

壇 T^{n}oa *Tan*
壑 Hák
壎 Hùn
壓 Iap
壙 K'wang
壕 Hau
壘 Lui
壞 Hwai
壟 Long
壤 Jiàng
壩 Pá

RADICAL 33.

士 Sù
壬 Jim
壳 K'ák
壯 Cháng
壹 It
壻 Sai *Su*
壺 Hu
壼 Kun
壽 Siu

RADICAL 34.

夂 Ti

RADICAL 35.

夊 Sue
夏 He *Hia*

RADICAL 36.

夕 Sek
外 Gua *Wai*
多 Tó
夜 Me *E*
够 Ko
夢 Máng *Mong*
夥 Hue *Hó*
夙 Sok
夤 In

RADICAL 37.

大 Tai
天 T^{n}i *T'ien*
太 T'ai
夫 Hu
夭 Io
央 Iáng
失 Sit
夷 I
夸 K'wa
夾 Hiap
奈 Nai
奇 K'i
奄 Iam
奉 Hong

6

奏 Chau
奎 Kui
奕 Ek
契 K'oi *Kiet*
奓 I
奔 P'un
套 T'au
奚 Hi
畚 Pun
奠 Tien
奢 Ch'ia *Che*
報 Pó
奧 Au
奩 Liam
奪 Tó, *Tuat*
獎 Chiang
獘 Pi
奮 Hun

RADICAL 38.

女 N^{n}ng *Ni*
奴 No
奸 Kán
妁 Chiak
好 Hó *Hau*
如 Ju
奶 Nai
妃 Hui
妄 Buang
妊 Jim
妗 Kim
妍 Ngien
妓 Ki
妖 Io
妙 Bio *Mio*
妝 Ch^{n}ng *Chuang*
妣 Pi
妥 T'ó
妨 Hwang

5

妬 Ko
妯 Iu
妮 Ni
姖 Kù
妹 Mue *Mui*
妻 Ch'i
妾 Ch'iap
姊 Che
始 Si
姆 Bó *Mu*
姐 Che
姑 Ko *Ku*
姓 S^{n}e *Seng*
委 Ui

6

姙 Jim
姤 Ko
姚 T'io
姜 Kiang
姦 Kán
姨 I
姪 Tiet
姿 Chù
姻 In
威 Ui
娃 Ua *Kui*

7

娉 P'eng
娌 Li
娣 Ti
娥 Ngo

32 土
33 士
34 夂
35 夊
36 夕
37 大
38 女

38 女
39 子
40 宀

娿 Hó / *Ú*
娜 Nó
娑 Sá
娘 Nie / *Niang*
娸 Ki
娛 U
娟 Kien
娩 Mien
娠 Chin

8

娼 Ch'iàng
姬 Ki
婟 Ku
婆 Pó
娶 Ch'u
婉 Wan
婐 Ló / *Kó*
婚 Hun
婢 Pi
婦 Hu
婪 Lam
婬 Im

9

婷 Teng
婿 Sai / *Su*

媒 Buo / *Mui*
媚 Mi
媛 Yien
媸 Ch'i
媢 Mau
媳 Sek
媽 Má
媾 Ko
嫁 Ke / *K'a*

10

嫂 Só / *Sau*
嫉 Chit
媵 Jeng
嫋 Nio
嫌 Hiam
嫗 O / *Au*
嫡 Tek
嫩 Lun
嫖 Pio
嫠 Li
嫜 Chiàng
嫣 Yien
嫦 Siàng
嬛 Hwàn

嫊 Sok
嫪 Lau

12

嬈 Jio
嬉 Hi
嬋 Sien
嬌 Kio
嬸 Sim
嫺 Hien
嬖 P'i
嬙 Ch'iàng

14

嬪 Pin
嬭 Nai / *Ni*
孃 Hwai
孀 Sⁿng / *Suang*
孋 Li
嫛 Ge
孌 Luan

RADICAL 39.

子 Chù
孑 Kiet
孔 Kong
孕 Eng
孖 Chù
字 Ji / *Jù*

存 Ch'un
孜 Chù
孝 Hau / *Hio*
孚 Hu
孛 Pwat / *Pui*
孟 Meng
孥 Nó / *Nu*
季 Kui
孤 Ko / *Ku*

6

孩 Hai
孫 Sun
孰 Sok
孳 Chù
㝃 Mien
孱 Ch'án
學 Hák / *Hiok*
孺 Ju
孻 Chien / *Chin*
孾 Eng

RADICAL 40.

宀 Kap / *Mien*
宂 Jong
它 T'ó
宁 Tiu

宄 K'ui
宅 Te / *Tek*
宇 U
守 Siu
安 An
宋 Song
完 Wan / *Yien*
宏 Hong

5

宕 Táng
宗 Chong
官 Kⁿwa / *Kwan*
宙 Tiu
定 Tⁿia / *Teng*
宛 Wan
宜 Ngi
客 Ke / *Kek*
宣 Suan
室 Sit
宥 Iu
宦 Hwan

7

密 Bát / *Mit*
宮 Keng / *Kiong*
宰 Chai

害 Hai
宴 An
宵 Sio
家 Ke *Kia*
宸 Sin
容 Iong
宿 Sua *Sok*
寂 Sok
寃 Wan
寄 Kia
寅 In
寇 K'o

9

富 Pu *Hu*
寐 Mue
寒 Hán
寓 Ngó *I*
寔 Sit
寞 Mok
寘 Ti
寥 Lio
寬 K'wan
察 Ch'át
寡 Kwa
寢 Ch'im
實 Sit
寧 Leng
賓 Pin
寤 Ngó *U*
寨 Che

12

審 Sim
寫 Sia *Se*
寮 Lio
寰 Hwan
寵 T'ong
寶 Pó
騫 K'ien
寖 Chim
寗 Leng
寠 Ki

RADICAL 41.

寸 Ch'un
寺 Ji *Jù*
封 Hong
射 Sia *Se*
尅 K'át
將 Chiàng
尉 Ue
專 Chuan
尊 Chun
尋 Ch'im
對 Tui
導 Tau

RADICAL 42.

小 Sio
少 Sio *Chie*
尖 Chiam
尔 Lù *Ni*
尙 Siáng

RADICAL 43.

尢 Wáng
尤 Iu
尨 Máng
就 Chiu

RADICAL 44.

尸 Si
尹 U'n
尺 Ch'ie *Chek*
尼 Ni
尽 Chin
尾 Bue *Mui*
局 Kek *Kiok*
屁 Pi
尿 Jie *Nio*
居 Kù
屈 K'ut
屇 Chun
屆 } Kai
届 }

6

屋 Ok
屎 Sai *Si*
屍 Si
屏 P'in
屐 Kia
屑 Siak
展 Tien

8

属 Sok
屠 To *Tu*
屢 Lu
履 Li
屣 Si
屨 Ki
層 Chán
屬 Sok

RADICAL 45.

屮 Tiet
屯 T'un

RADICAL 46.

山 S^{n}ua *Sán*
屹 Ngùt
岐 Ki
岑 Ngim
岳 Ngák *Ngiok*
岱 Tai
峙 Si
岡 Káng
岸 Ngai
岫 Siu

7

峭 Siak *Ch'io*
峪 Kok
峨 Ngó
峯 Hong
島 Tau
峗 Ngui
峽 Kiap
崇 Ch'ong
崛 Kut
崔 Chui
崎 K'i
崖 } Ngai
崕 }

40 宀
41 寸
42 小
43 尢
44 尸
45 屮
46 山

46 山 47 巛 48 工 49 己 50 巾 51 干 52 幺 53 广

崐 K'un
崗 Káng
崙 Lun
崩 Peng

9

崽 Sai *Sù*
嵐 Lám
嵯 Chà
嵬 Ngui
嵩 Song
嶺 Nia *Leng*
嶇 K'u
嶼 Sù
嶽 Ngák *Ngiok*
巍 Ngui
巉 Ch'ai
巒 Luan
巖 Ngam
巔 Tien

——

RADICAL 47.

巛 川 } Ch'uan
州 Chiu
巡 巡 } Sun
巢 Ch'au

——

RADICAL 48.

工 Káng *Kong*
左 Chó
巧 K'á *Kio*
巨 Kù
巫 Bu
差 Ch'á

——

RADICAL 49.

己 Ki
已 I^{n}
巳 Chi
巴 Pá
巵 Chi
巷 Háng
巽 Sun

——

RADICAL 50.

巾 Kùn
市 Chi
布 Po *Pu*
帆 P'áng *Hwan*
帋 Chui *Chi*
希 Hi
帑 Nó
帕 P'e *Bek*
帒 Tó *Tai*
帙 Tiet
帚 Siu
帖 T'iap
帘 Liam
帛 Pe, *Pok*

6

帝 Ti
𢂑 Sek
帥 Sue *Sui*
師 Sù
幇 Páng
席 Sia, *Sek*
𢃇 Li
帳 T^{n}ie *Chiang*
帶 Toa *Tai*
帷 Jui
常 S^{n}ie *Siang*
帽 Bó *Mau*

9

幅 Hok
幄 Ok
幫 Páng
幔 Muan
幗 Kok
幕 Mó
幣 Pi
幟 Chi
幡 Hwan
幢 T'ong

——

RADICAL 51.

干 Kán
平 P^{n}e *P'eng*
年 Ni *Nien*
并 幷 } Peng P^{n}ia
幸 Heng
幹 Kán

——

RADICAL 52.

幺 Io
幻 Hwan
幼 I^{n}u
幽 Hiu
幾 Ki

——

RADICAL 53.

广 Iam
庄 Ch^{n}ng *Chuang*
庇 Pi
床 Ch'^{n}ng *Chuang*
庌 Ge *Gia*
序 Su
底 Ti
庖 P'au
店 Tiam
庚 K^{n}e *Keng*
府 Hu
厏 Chá

6

庠 Siàng
度 To *Ták*
座 Chó
庫 K'o
庭 T'eng
庵 A'm
庶 Su
康 K'ang
庳 Pi
庸 Iong
庾 Ju
廂 S^{n}ie *Siang*

廉 Liam
廋 So
廈 He / *Hia*
廊 Láng
廒 Ngau
廕 Im
廚 To / *Tu*
廖 Lio
廄 Ki

12

廛 Li / *T'ien*
廝 Sù
廟 Bie / *Mio*
廠 Ch'iàng
廡 Bu
廢 Hui
廣 Kwang
廩 Lim
廬 Lu
龐 P'áng
廳 Tⁿia / *T'eng*

RADICAL 54.

廴 Iń
延 Yien
廷 T'eng
廹 Pek
廼 Nai
建 Kien
廻 Hue / *Hui*

RADICAL 55.

廾 Kiong
廿 Ji / *Ju*
弁 Pien
弄 Láng
弈 Ek
弇 Iam
奠 Tien
弊 P'i

RADICAL 56.

弋 Ek
弍 Nó / *Jù*
式 Sek
戕 Ch'án
弑 Ch'i

RADICAL 57.

弓 Keng / *Kiong*
引 In
弔 Tio
弘 Hong
弗 Hut
弛 Si
弝 Pá
弟 Ti

5

弦 Hⁿi / *Hien*
弧 Hu
弩 No
弱 Jiak
弣 Hu

8

張 Tⁿie / *Chiang*
强 K'iàng
弼 Pit
彀 Ko
彈 T'án
彊 Kiàng
彌 Ni
彎 Wan

RADICAL 58.

彐 Ki
彗 Hui
彖 Tuan
彘 Ti
彙 Lui
彝 I

RADICAL 59.

彡 Sám
形 Heng
彤 T'ong
彥 Ngán / *Yien*
彩 Ch'ai
彪 Piu
彫 Tio
彬 Pin
彭 Pⁿe / *Peng*
彰 Chiàng
影 Iⁿa / *Eng*

RADICAL 60.

彳 Tek
彷 Hwang
役 Hia / *Wak*
彺 Wang
彿 Hut
徂 Chu
往 Wang
彼 Pi
征 Cheng
徃 Wang

6

待 T'ai
很 Hùn
徉 Iàng
徊 Hui / *Hue*
律 Lut
後 Au / *Ho*
徐 Ch'u
徑 Kⁿe / *Keng*
徒 T'u

8

得 Tit / *Tek*
徠 Lai
徙 Sua / *Si*
徘 P'ai
徛 I / *Ki*
徜 Tang / *Siàng*
從 Ch'ong
御 Gù / *I*
徨 Hwang
徧 Pien
徭 Io

53 广 54 廴 55 廾 56 弋 57 弓 58 彐 59 彡

60 彳 16 心

復 Hok
循 Sun
徬 P'áng
徯 Hi
黴 Mui
徵 Teng
德 Tek
徹 Tiet
徼 Hio

—

RADICAL 61.

心 Sim
必 Pit
忉 Tio
忒 T'ek
忌 Ki
忙 Máng
忏 Chien
忍 Jim
忖 Ch'un
志 Chì
忘 Buang

4

忠 Tong
忤 Ngo *U*
忝 T'iam
忡 Ch'ong
快 K'wai
忭 Pien
忱 Sim
念 Liam
忻 Hùn
忿 Hun
忼 K'áng
忽 Hut

5

怎 Chá *Chak*
怍 Chá
怙 Hu
怳 Kwang
怖 Pu
怛 T'án
怱 Ch'ong
怏 Iàng
怒 Nó
怕 P'á
怗 T'iáp
思 Sù
怠 Tia
怡 I
急 Kip
性 Sⁿe *Seng*
怨 Wan *Yien*
怪 Kwai
怯 K'iak
怵 Tut

6

恇 Káng
恁 Jim
恂 Sun
恧 Nek
恆 Heng
恍 Hwang
恊 Hiap
恝 K'iet
恢 K'ue
恓 Ch'i
恐 K'iong
恃 Si
恒 Heng
恕 Su
恙 Iàng
恣 Chù
恤 Sut
恥 Ch'i
恨 Hùn
恩 U'n
恪 K'ák
恬 T'iam
恭 Kiong
息 Sek
恰 K'áp

7

悋 Lien
悄 Ch'io
悠 Hiu
恿 Iong
悅 Juat
悉 Sek
悌 Ti
悊 Chi
悔 Hue
悖 Pwat *Pui*
悚 Song
悞 Go *U*
悟 Ngo *U*
患 Hwam

8

悲 Pui
悻 Heng
悱 Hui
悼 Chau
惓 Kwan *Kien*
惕 T'ek
悴 Chui
悵 Chiàng
慘 Ch'ám
悶 Bun
悸 Kui
悽 Ch'i
惚 Hut
惞 Hùn
情 Ch'eng
惆 Tio *Chiu*
惇 Sun
惉 Tiam
惑 Hok
惘 Buang
惛 Hun
惜 Sie, *Sek*
惟 Jui
惡 A'k *Ok*
惡 U
悾 K'ong

惠 Hui

9

惱 Nau
想 S^{n}ie *Siang*
惶 Hwang
愀 Ch'o *Ch'iu*
惲 Hun *Hui*
惰 'Tó *Tai*
惻 Ch'ek
惺 Seng
愉 Ju
慍 Un
惹 Jia *Je*
愁 Ch'o *Ch'iu*
愆 Kien
愈 Ju
愍 Min
悿 T'iam
意 I
愕 Ngák
[illegible] Ngó
愚 Ngó *I*
愛 Ai
愜 Kiap

感 Kám

10

愧 Kui
[illegible] T'ai
慆 T'au
慅 Sau
慊 K'iam
[illegible] Máng
愷 K'ái
慌 Hwang
慇 Hùn
愽 P'ák
愴 Ch'áng
慎 Sin
愿 Ngwan *Yien*
慄 Liet
慈 Ch'ù
慉 T'iok
態 T'ai

11

慕 Mó
慥 Ch'au
[illegible] Lu
慻 Kwan *Kien*
慤 K'ak

慫 Chong
慟 Tong
憋 Pi
慝 Nek
慘 Ch'ám
慢 Muan
慙 } Ch'ám
慚 }
慠 Ngau
慧 Hui
慨 K'ai
慮 Lù
慰 Ue *Ui*
慳 Kien
慷 K'áng
慵 Iong
慴 Sip
慶 K'eng
慼 Ch'ek
慾 Yok
憑 P'eng
憂 Iu
憃 Cheng
憊 Pi

12

慣 Kwan
憎 Cheng
憮 Bu
憐 Lien
憑 P'eng
憒 Kui
憔 Chio
憚 Tán
憤 Hun
憨 K'ám
憫 Mien
憲 Hien

13

憶 Ek
懆 Ch'au
懌 Ek
懃 K'ùn
懈 Hai
懄 K'ùn
憾 Hám
懇 K'ùn
懋 Mong
應 Eng
懊 Au

懕 Iam
懣 Mua *Muan*
[illegible] Chiap
懞 Mong

14

懜 Máng *Mong*
懦 Nô
懯 Hu
懲 T'eng
懟 Tui
懵 Máng *Mong*
懶 Lán
懷 Hwai
懸 H^{n}ui *Hien*

18

懽 Hwan
懺 Siam *Ch'iam*
懼 Ku
懾 Niap
懿 I
戀 Luan
戇 Chuang

RADICAL 62.

—

戈 Ko
戊 Bo *Mo*

62 戈 63 戶 64 手 扌

戌 Sut
戍 Sue
戎 Jong
成 Seng
我 Ua *Ngó*
戒 Kai
或 Hok
戕 Chʻán
戚 Chʻek

8

戟 Kek
戞 Kʻák
戢 Chʻip
戥 Seng
戫 Hok
戡 Kʻám
戫 Jok
截 Choi
戮 Lok
㦰 Siam
戰 Chien
戲 Hi
戯 Hi
戳 Chʻok *Tek*

戴 Tai

—

RADICAL 63.

戶 Ho *Hu*
戹 I
戾 Lui
房 Páng *Hwang*
戽 Ho
所 Só
扁 Pʻien
扇 S^{n}i *Sien*
扈 Hu
扃 Kʻeng
扅 I
扊 Iam
扉 Hui

—

RADICAL 64.

手 Chʻiu
才 Chʻai
扎 Cháp
打 Pʻá
扒 Pán
扑 Pʻok
扠 Tʻoi *Chʻo*

托 Tó *Tek*
扛 K^{n}ng *Kang*
扞 Hán
扣 Kʻá *Ko*

4

扭 Niu
扮 Pán
抃 Pien
抒 Tiu
扱 Kʻip
抔 Pi
扯 Chi
扳 Pán
扲 I *U*
扶 Hu
批 Pai *Pi*
找 Tau
承 Seng
技 Ki
抄 Chʻau
抝 Au
抆 Bun
抉 Kwat
抅 Ku

把 Pá
抑 A't
抓 Jio
投 Tau
抖 Tau
抗 Kʻáng
折 Chi *Chiet*

5

披 Pʻi
抬 Tʻai
拓 Tʻat
抱 Pʻó *Pau*
抵 Ti
抹 Bua *Mok*
押 A'p
抽 Tʻiu
拂 Hut
担 T^{n}á *Tán*
拄 Chu
拆 Tʻia *Chek*
拇 Bó *Mu*
拈 Niam
拉 Lá
拊 Hu

拋 Pʻau
拌 Pwan
拍 Pʻá *Pek*
拏 Nà *Nu*
拐 Kwai
拒 Kù
拔 Pwat
拕 Tʻó *Tek*
拖 Tʻoa *Nui*
拗 Au
拘 Ku
拙 Chuat
拚 Pʻwan
招 Chio *Chio*
拜 Pai

6

拭 Chʻit *Sek*
括 Kwat
拮 Kit
挏 Tʻong
挌 Ke, *Kek*
拯 Chin
拱 Kiong
拳 Kʻien

拴 Chuan
挼 Só
拾 Sip
拷 Kʻau
拿 Ná
持 Tʻi
指 Chi
挈 Kʻiet
按 ʻAn
挑 Tʻio
挖 Wat

7

挨 Oi *Ai*
掜 Ngiak
捋 Luat
捍 Hán
挶 Kek *Kiok*
挼 Nó
捌 Poi *Pat*
挪 Nó
挫 Chʻó
挹 Ip
振 Chin
挺 Tʻeng
挽 Mán *Mien*
挾 Hiap
捆 Kʻun
捉 Chʻok
捐 Kien
捕 Pu

8

捧 Hong
掀 Hùn
捨 Sia *Se*
揔 Hut
掯 Kʻeng
捫 Bun
捬 Hu
捭 Pui
据 Kù
捱 Ngai
捲 K^{u}ng *Kʻien*
捷 Chiap
捻 Liam
捽 Chui
揕 Kʻám
掃 Sau
掇 Chuat
授 Siu
掉 Chau
掌 Ch^{n}ie *Chiàng*
排 Pai
掐 Hám
掟 Teng
掖 Ek
接 Chiap
掘 Kut
掙 Cheng
掛 Kʻwa *Kwai*
掠 Lia, *Lek*
採 Chʻai
探 Tʻám
掣 Chi
控 Kʻong
推 Chʻui
措 Chʻu
掩 Iam
掬 Kiok

9

揀 Kán
揸 Chá
揄 Ju
揥 Tʻi
揓 Si
揠 Iam
揾 Un
揲 Tiap
揦 Lá
揉 Jiu
描 Bie *Mio*
提 Tʻi
揑 Niap
插 Chʻá
揖 Ip
揚 Iàng
換 Hwan
𢯭 Lut
揜 Iam
握 Ok
揣 Chʻui
揪 Chʻiu
掽 Peng
揭 Kia, *Hak*
揮 Hui
援 Yien

10

搆 Ko
搇 Kʻim
搏 Pʻák
搠 Suak
搢 Chin
𢶠 Ong
搗 Tau *Nio*
搌 Tien
損 Sun
搐 Tʻiok
搕 Kʻáp
搔 Sau
搜 Sio *So*
搥 Tui
搦 Nek *Nio*
搧 S^{n}i *Sien*
搪 Tʻáng
搬 P^{n}ua *Pwan*
揱 Siak
搽 Tʻu
搶 Chʻ^{n}ie *Chʻiang*
携 Hi
摭 Chia

64 手 65 支 66 攴

11

捽 Lut
摧 Ch'ui
摯 Chi
摏 Cheng
摽 P'io
搖 Io
摘 Ti^n, *Tek*
擄 Lu
摟 Lu
摩 Mó
摳 K'u
摸 Mong *Mó*
摹 Mó
摺 Chi, *Sip*

12

撥 Bua
撈 Lau
㩉 Hip
撍 Chuan
撐 T^{n}e *Cheng*
撒 Sán
撓 Nau
撕 Sù
撚 Jien
撙 Chun
撞 T'ong
撣 Tán
撟 Kio
撤 T'iet
撥 Bua, *Hwat*
撦 Ch'ia *Ch'e*
撫 Bu
撩 Lio
搭 Tá, *T'áp*
播 Pua
撮 Ch'ó, *Chok*
撰 Chuan
撲 Pok
撻 T'át

13

擁 Iong
擕 Hi
擎 K'eng
撿 Liam
擂 Lui
擃 Long
擄 Lu
擅 Sien
擇 Tó, *Tuat*
擊 K'ek
操 Ch'au
擋 T^{n}ng *Táng*
擒 Kim
擔 T^{n}á *Tám*
擘 Pak
據 Kù

14

擠 Chi
擡 T'ai
擢 Ti^n, *Tek*
擣 Tau
擦 Ch'át
擧 Kù
擬 Ngi
擭 Hu
擱 Kó,
擯 Pin
擰 Leng
擲 T^{n}á *Teng*
擴 K'wak

15

擸 Lá, *Náp*
攄 Lù
擺 Pai *Pá*
擻 Sio
擾 Jio
攀 Pán
攔 Nán *Lán*
攖 Eng
攘 Jiàng
攙 Ch'ám
攢 Chuan
攛 Chun
攤 T'^{n}oa *Tán*
攝 Niap
攞 Ló
攩 Táng
攪 Ká *Kau*
攬 Lám
攣 Luan
攫 K'iet

RADICAL 65.

支 Chi

RADICAL 66.

攴 Pok
收 Siu
攷 K'au
攸 Hiu
改 Koi *Kai*
攻 Kong
放 Hwang
政 Cheng
故 Ku

7

效 Hau *Hio*
教 Ká *Kio*
敘 Su
敕 T'ek
敏 Mien
救 Kiu
敖 Ngau
敗 Pai
敝 Pi
敢 K^{n}á *Kám*
散 S^{n}ua *Sán*
啟 K'i
敦 Tun

9

敬 Keng
整 Ch^{n}ia *Cheng*
敲 K'io

敵 Tek
敲 Kio
敷 Hu
數 Sio *Su*
斂 Liam
斁 Ek
斃 Pi

RADICAL 67.

文 Bun
斑 Pán
斐 Hui
斌 Pin

RADICAL 68.

斗 Tau
料 Lio
斛 Hok
斜 Sia *Se*
斟 Chim

RADICAL 69.

斤 Kùn
斥 Chʻek
斧 Po *Pu*
斨 Chʻáng
斫 Kʻám
斬 Chám
斯 Sù
斷 Tuan
斴 Lin
斲 Tok

RADICAL. 70.

方 Hwang
於 I *U*
施 Si
斾 Hui
旁 Pʻáng
旄 Mau
旅 Li
旂 Ki
旋 Suan
旌 Seng
族 Chok
旒 Liu
旗 Ki
旛 Hwan *Pwan*

RADICAL 71.

无 Bó *Bu*
旣 Ki

RADICAL 72.

日 Jit
旦 Tán
早 Chá *Cho*
旨 Chi
旬 Sun
旭 Hiok
旰 Hán
旱 U^{n}a *Hán*

4

旺 Wang
旻 Bun
昇 Seng
昂 Ngáng
昆 Kʻun
昃 Che *Chek*
昊 Hau
昌 Chʻiàng
明 Meng
昏 Hun
易 Ek
易 Koi *I*
昔 Chá *Sek*
星 Chʻ^{n}e *Seng*
昵 Ni
昧 Mue *Mui*
映 Iang
昨 Chá *Cho*
昡 Hien
春 Chʻun
昬 Min *Mien*
昭 Chio
眙 I
是 Si *Sù*
昴 Bau

6

晒 Sai
時 Si *Sù*
晏 A'n
晉 Chin
晚 M^{u}ng *Mien*
晤 Ngò *U*
晡 Pu
晝 Tiu
晦 Hui
晨 Sin

8

普 Pʻo *Pu*
晴 Ch^{n}e *Cheng*
景 Keng
晣 Chiet
晳 Sek
晶 Ch^{n}ia *Cheng*
晷 Kʻui
智 Ti
晾 Liàng
暑 Su

9

暄 Suan
暈 Hun *In*
暉 Hui
暗 A'm
暘 Iàng
暢 Tiàng *Tien*
暇 Hia
暌 Kʻui
暖 Luan
暝 Meng
暮 Mó
暫 Chiam
暴 Pʻák
暹 Siam
曆 Lák *Le*

67 文
68 斗
69 斤
70 方
71 无
72 日

72 日
73 曰
74 月
75 木

曇 Hun *In*
曉 Hio
矇 Mong
曛 Hùn
曝 P'ák
曠 K'wang
曬 Sai
曜 Io
曙 Su
曩 Láng

RADICAL 73.

曰 Wat *Yet*
曲 K'iok
曳 Hi
更 K^{n}e *Keng*
曷 Hát
書 Chù *Su*
曹 Ch'au
曾 Cheng
替 T'i
最 Chue
會 Hue

RADICAL 74.

月 Gue, *Yet*
有 U *Iu*
朋 P'eng *Pong*
服 Hok
朔 Suak
朕 Tim
朗 Láng
望 Mó *Buang*
朝 Ch'io
期 K'i
朦 Mong
朧 Long

RADICAL 75.

木 Bák *Mok*
未 Bue *Mui*
末 Muat
本 Pun
札 Cháp
朱 Chu
朴 P'ok
朶 Tó
机 Ki
朿 Sok
朽 H^{n}iu

3

杈 T'oi
杉 Sám
杌 Ngùt
李 Li
杏 Heng
材 Ch'ai
村 Ch'^{u}ng *Chun*
杖 Chiàng
杜 To *Tu*
束 Sok
杠 Káng
呆 Ngai
杇 U
杆 Kán
杞 Ki

4

杯 Pue *Pai*
杰 Liet
東 Táng *Tong*
杳 Mio
杵 Su
杷 Pe
杼 Tiu
松 Seng
板 Pán
极 Kip
枇 Pue *Pi*
枉 Wang
析 Chi, *Sek*
林 Lim
果 Kwa
枝 Ki
杪 Sau *Mio*
杭 Háng
枚 Bue *Mui*
枕 Chim
枘 Jue

5

柝 T'ák
枯 Ko *Ku*
枱 T'ai
枳 Chi
枴 Kwai
枵 Hau *U*
架 Ke *Kia*
柢 Ti
某 Mong
柹 Sai
柋 Tai
枷 Ke *Kai*
柁 Toa
柄 P^{n}e *Peng*
柔 Jiu
柏 Pe, *Pok*
染 Jiam
柑 K^{n}á *Kám*
柒 Ch'it
柚 Iu
查 Ch'e *Chá*
柯 K'ó
柬 Kán *Keng*
柩 Kiu
柰 Nai
柱 T'io *Chu*
柳 Liu
柴 Chá *Chai*
柵 Ch'á,

6

栗 Liet
校 Ká *Hau*
栖 Ch'i
桀 Kiet

75 木

栢 Pe, *Pok*
栭 Tù
株 Tu
核 Hek
栓 Chʻuan
根 Kùn
栽 Chai
格 Kek
桁 Hang *Heng*
桂 Kui
桃 Tó *Tau*
桅 Ui *Ngui*
案 U^{n}a *An*
桊 Tu
桎 Tiet
桌 Tó, *Tok*
桐 Tʻong
桑 S^{n}ng *Suang*
桓 Hwan
桕 Kʻu
桔 Kit

7

桴 Hu
桶 Tong
梂 Kiu
桷 Kak *Hok*
梀 Sok
梵 Hwam
梜 Kiap *Hiap*
梲 Suat
桿 Han
梁 Nie *Liang*
桺 Liu
梅 Bue *Mui*
梏 Kʻok
梓 Chù
梗 K^{n}e *Keng*
條 Tio
梟 Hio
梧 Ngó *U*
梢 Sau
梨 Lai *Li*
梭 Só
梯 Tʻui *Ti*
械 Hai
梱 Kʻun
梳 Siu *Só*
梹 Pʻin

8

棄 Kʻi
棉 Mi *Mien*
棟 Tong
棋 Ki
棍 Kun
椆 Tʻiu *Chiu*
棒 Hong
棗 Chó *Co*
棘 Kek
棚 P^{n}e *Peng*
棠 Tʻáng
棣 Ti
棧 Chán
森 Siam
棲 Chʻi
棰 Sui
棹 Chau
棺 K^{n}wa *Kwan*
棕 Cháng
棖 Tʻeng
極 Kek
棨 Kʻi
棉 Mi
椅 I^{n}
植 Sek
椎 Chio *Chui*
椏 A'
椒 Chio
椓 Si
椰 Ia

9

楛 Ku
楫 Chʻip
椸 Si
楂 Cha
楊 Iàng
楓 P^{n}ng *Hwang*
楚 Chʻó
楞 Leng
榆 Ju
楣 Bai *Mi*
楥 Yien
業 Ngiap
楮 Tu
楹 E^{n} *Iong*
榔 Nó *Iáng*
楯 Tun

10

榕 Iong
槎 Chá
椽 Wan *Yien*
榛 Chin
樓 Lau *Liu*
槖 Tʻáp
榜 Páng
榧 Hui
榫 Chun
榭 Chia *Se*
榮 Iong
榴 Liu
榻 Tʻáp
槓 Kong
槁 Kau
槃 Pʻwan
構 Ko
槌 Tui
槐 Hwai
槤 Lien
槨 Kwak

11

樊 Hwan
⿰木產 Chʻán

75 木 76 欠 77 止 78 歹

樗 U
槿 Kùn
槳 Ch^{n}ie *Chiàng*
槪 K'ài
槔 Kau
槽 Chó *Chau*
椿 Cheng
樂 Lák *Lok*
樨 Ch'i
樑 Liàng
標 P'io
樜 Chia *Che*
樞 K'u
樟 Ch^{n}ie *Chiáng*
模 Mó
樣 I^{n}e *Iàng*

12

樵 Chio
樸 P'ok
櫨 S^{n}ia
樹 Ch'iu *Su*
橄 K^{n}á *Kám*
㯃 Ch'át
樽 Chun
櫐 Lui
橉 Lin
橋 Kie *Kio*
橘 Kit
橙 Ch'eng
橛 K'iet
機 Ki
橡 Siàng
橦 Tong
橫 H^{n}ue *Hwang*

13

檀 T'án
檄 Kio
檉 S^{n}ia *Seng*
檏 Ngiap
檑 Lui
檔 Táng
檜 Kwai
檯 Tai
櫂 Tek
檢 Kiam
檣 Chiàng
檳 Pin *Pien*
檻 Lám
櫃 K^{n}ui *Kui*

15

櫚 Lù
櫓 Lu
櫛 Chát *Chiet*
櫟 Yiak
欖 Lám
櫇 P'in
櫻 Eng
欄 Nán *Lán*
權 K'wan
欉 Cháng *Chong*
鬱 Ut
欒 Luan

RADICAL 76.

欠 K'iam
次 Chù
欣 Hún *Hien*
欬 Hai
欵 K'wan
欲 Ai *Yok*
欷 Hi

8

欹 K'i
欺 K'i
欽 K'im
款 K'wan
歇 Hia, *Hiet*
歆 Him

10

歃 Ch'á,
歉 K'iam
歁 Káp
歌 Kó
歎 T'án
歐 Au

13

歛 Liam
歔 Hù
歟 U'
歠 Chue, *Chuat*
歙 Niap
歡 Hwan

RADICAL 77.

止 Chi
正 Ch^{n}ia *Cheng*
此 Ch'ù
步 Po *Pu*
武 Bu
歧 Ki
歪 Ch'ua
𣦵 Lui
歲 Sue *Sui*
歷 Le, *Lek*
歸 Kui

RADICAL 78.

歹 Tai
死 Si *Sù*
歿 Mut
殀 Io
殃 Iàng
殆 Tái
殄 Chien
殊 Su
殉 Sun
殘 Ch'án
殖 Sit
殛 Kek *Ki*
殞 Un
殍 Pio
殤 Siàng
殮 Liam

殭 Kiàng
殯 Pin

—

RADICAL 79.

殳 Su
段 Tⁿng *Tuan*
殷 Hùn
殺 Sua, *Sát*
殼 K'ák
殽 Ngau
殿 Tⁿoi *Tien*
毀 Hui
毅 Ngi
毆 Au

—

RADICAL 80.

毋 Bó *Bu*
母 Bó *Mu*
每 Mue
毒 Ták *Tok*
毓 Hiok

—

RADICAL 81.

比 Pi
毗 Pi
毚 Ch'ám

—

RADICAL 82.

毛 Mó *Mau*
毧 Jong
毡 Chⁿi *Chien*
毫 Pák
毷 Hau
毬 Kiu
毳 Chui
毽 Kien
氄 Jok
氉 Jong
氅 Ch'iàng
氈 Chⁿi *Chien*

—

RADICAL 83.

氏 Si
氐 Ti
民 Min
氓 Min

—

RADICAL 84.

气 K'i
氛 Hun
氣 K'i
氤 In
氳 Un

—

RADICAL 85.

水 Chui *Sui*
永 Iong
氷 Pⁿia *Peng*
氾 Hwam
汀 T'eng
汁 Cháp *Sip*
求 K'iu

3

汎 Hwam
汐 Sek
汗 Kⁿwa *Kan*
汙 U
汚 U
汝 Lù *Jù*
汞 Hong
江 Káng *Kiàng*
汛 Sin
池 Ti *Chi*

4

汲 K'ip
汰 T'ai
汶 Bun
沓 Tá, *Tap*
汪 Wang
汩 Kut
決 Kwat
沂 K'i
沃 Ok
沈 Tim
沌 T'un
沒 Mut
沐 Mok
沖 Ch'ong
沙 Sua *Sá*
沠 P'ai

5

沮 Chu
沱 T'ó
沛 P'ai
沸 Hut
泮 P'wan
泆 Tiet *It*
泓 Hong
泱 Iàng
泔 Kám
泠 Ne *Leng*
泗 Sù
注 Chu
洄 Hue *Hwài*
河 Hó
油 Iu
沫 Bua, *Mut*
治 Ti *Chi*
沼 Jio
沽 Ko *Ku*
沾 Tiam
沿 In
泄 Siap
泅 Ch'iu *Siu*
泉 Chⁿua *Chuan*
泊 Pó, *Pok*
法 Hwap
泛 Hwam
泡 P'au
波 Pó
泣 K'ip
泥 Ni
泯 Min
泰 T'ai

6

洋 Iⁿe *Iàng*
洊 Chin
洮 Tio *T'au*
洶 Hiong

79 殳
80 毋
81 比
82 毛
83 氏
84 气
85 水

85 水 氵

洒 Sá *Si*
洗 Soi *Si*
洛 Lok
洨 Kau
洞 T'ong
津 Chin
洎 Chù
洩 Siap
洪 Hong
洫 Hák
洲 Chiu
活 Ua,
洽 Chiap *Sip*
派 P'ai
洧 Iu

7

流 Liu
涓 Kien
洚 Káng *Kiàng*
涖 Li
涇 K^{n}e
浙 Chi
浚 Chun
浥 Ip
浣 Wan
浦 Po *Pu*
浩 Hau
浪 Láng
浮 P'u *Piu*
浴 Yok
海 Hai
浸 Chim
浹 Hiap
浼 Mien
消 Sio
涌 Iong
涎 Yien

8

涕 T'i
涉 Siap
涯 Ngai
液 Ek
涿 Tok
淑 Sok
淮 Hwai
淅 Siak
淜 Páng
涵 Hám
涸 Hák
淆 Ngau
淋 Lim
淘 T'au
淚 Lui
游 Iu
淡 T^{n}á *Tám*
淤 U`
淨 Cheng
淪 Lun
淫 Im
深 Ch'im
淳 Tun
淵 Wan *Yien*
淹 Iam
混 Hun
清 Ch'eng
淺 Ch'ien

9

添 T'iam
渟 T'eng
渥 Ok
渭 Ui
湃 Pai
湮 In *Jien*
湣 Hun
湘 Siàng
減 Kiam
渠 K'ù
渦 K'ó
渡 To *Tu*
渣 Chá
温 Un
渫 Siak
測 Ch'ek
港 Káng
渴 Kw'a *Kát*
游 Iu
渺 Mio
渾 Hun
湎 Min
湍 Chuan
湖 O *Hu*
湛 Tim
湧 Eng
湲 Yien
湯 T^{n}ng *Táng*
渚 Tu
湴 Peng

10

源 Ngwan *Yien*
滌 Tek
溲 So
漱 So
準 Chun
溜 Liu
溝 Kau
溟 Meng
溢 Ek *It*
溺 Nek
溥 P'o *Pu*
溫 Un
溶 Iong
溪 K'oi *Ki*
溷 Hun
溯 Su *Suak*
溼 K^{n}e
滂 P'áng
滈 Kau
滅 Mit
滋 Chù
滑 Kut

英漢潮州方言字典

滓 Chai
滯 Tʻi *Tai*
溧 Liet
溦 Mui

11

滲 Sám *Chʻám*
漂 Pie
漳 Chiáng
漑 Kʻai *Ki*
滴 Ti,
滷 Lu
滾 Kun
滿 Mua *Muan*
漁 Hú *I*
漆 Chʻát
漏 Lau *Lo*
漓 Li
演 In
漕 Chau
漚 Au
漠 Mó, *Mok*
漢 Hán
漣 Lien
漯 Tʻák

漬 Che, *Chek*
漫 Muan
漲 T^{n}ie *Chiàng*
漸 Chiam
漿 Ch^{n}ie *Chiàng*

12

潑 Pʻua
潘 Pʻwan
潢 Hwang
潔 Kiet
潛 Chʻiam
澗 Kán *Kien*
潤 Jun
澍 Su
潦 Lau *Lio*
潭 Tʻám
潰 Kui
潮 Tie *Chʻio*
潺 Chʻán
澁 Siap
澄 Tʻeng
潚 Sio
澆 Kau *Kio*
澈 Tʻiet

13

澣 Kán
澡 Chʻau
澤 Chek
澀 Siap
澳 Ok *Au*
澾 Tʻát
澹 T^{n}á *Tám*
激 Kēk
濁 Chuak
濃 Long
濆 Pʻun *Pien*

14

濕 Sip
濘 Leng
濡 Su
濛 Mong
濟 Chi
濤 Tʻau
濠 Hau
濯 Chuak *Tek*
濫 Lám
濱 Pin *Pien*

15

瀉 Sia *Sek*
濺 Chien

瀘 Lù
瀑 Pʻák
瀆 Tok
瀚 Hán
瀝 Le, *Lek*
瀰 Ni
瀹 Yiak
灠 Lám
瀌 Pʻio
瀾 Lán
灌 Kwan
灑 Li
灩 Iam
灘 T^{n}oa *Tʻán*
灣 Wan

RADICAL 86.

火 Hue *Hó*
灰 Hue
災 Chai
灾 Chai
灶 Chau
灼 Chiak
炊 Chʻue *Chui*

炖 Tun
炳 Peng
炎 Iam
炕 Kʻáng *Háng*
炒 Chʻá
炙 Chia *Che*

5

炫 Hien
炮 Pʻau
炷 Chu
炤 Tio *Chio*
炬 Kù
炭 T^{n}oa *Tàn*
烈 Liet
烙 Lok
烕 Mit
烖 Chai
烏 O *U*
烘 Hong
烚 Kʻáp
烜 Hwan *Táng*
烝 Cheng
烟 In *Yien*

7

烰 Hu

85 水
86 火

86 火 87 爪 88 父 89 爻 90 爿 91 片 92 牙 93 牛

烹 P'eng
烽 Káng *Hong*
焉 Yien
焙 Pue *Pui*
焚 Hun
煥 Hwan
無 Bó *Bu*
焦 Chio
焰 Iam
然 Jien

9

煆 Tuan
煉 Lien
煴 Un
煜 Yok
煬 Iàng
煢 K'wang
煌 Hwang
煎 Chien
煏 Pek *Hok*
煮 Chù
煲 Pó *Pau*
煖 Nuan
煥 Hwan
煇 Hui

煙 In *Yien*
熙 Hi
煞 Sua, *Sát*
煦 Hu
煤 Bue *Mui*
煊 Suan
照 Chie *Chio*
煨 Ui
煩 Hwan

10

煽 S^{n}i *Sien*
熄 Sek
熊 Him
熏 Hùn
熒 Iong
熞 Kien
熟 Sek *Sok*
熨 Ui
熬 Ngau
熱 Jua, *Jiet*

12

熹 } Hi
熺 }
燔 Pwan *Hwan*
熾 Chi

燃 Jien
燄 T'au
燈 Teng
燉 Tun
燐 Lin *Lien*
燬 Hui
燋 Chio
燎 Lio
燒 Sie *Sio*
燮 Siap
燕 Yien
燙 Táng
營 I^{n}a *Iong*
燥 Ch'au
燦 Ch'án
燭 Chek *Sok*
燻 Hùn
燼 Chien
燺 Kau
燿 Io
爆 Pák *Pau*
爋 Hùn
爇 Jua *Sok*
爐 Lo *Lu*

爛 Lán
爢 Mi
燧 Sui
爨 Ch'uan

—

RADICAL 87.

爪 Jio
爬 Pe
爭 Ch^{n}e *Cheng*
爰 Yien
爯 Kwan
爲 Ui
爵 Chiak

—

RADICAL 88.

父 Pe *Hu*
爸 Pá
爹 Tia *Te*
爺 Ia *E*

—

RADICAL 89.

爻 Ngau
爼 Chó
爽 Suang
爾 Sù *Ni*

—

RADICAL 90.

爿 Chiàng
牀 Ch^{n}ng *Chuang*
牆 Ch'^{n}ie *Chiàng*

—

RADICAL 91.

片 Pien
版 Pán
牌 Pai
牒 Tiap
牖 Iu
牕 T'eng *Chong*
牘 Tok

—

RADICAL 92.

牙 Ge *Gia*
雅 Ngia *Nge*

—

RADICAL 93.

牛 Gu *Niu*
牝 P'in
牟 M^{n}o *Mong*
牢 Lau
牡 Bo *M^{n}o*
牧 Mok

物 Mue, *Mut*
牳 Bó *M^{n}o*
牯 Ko *Ku*
牲 Seng
特 Tek
牽 K'án
犀 Sai
犁 Loi *Li*
犇 P'un
犂 Loi
犎 Hong
犒 K'au
犛 Mau
犢 Tok
犧 Hi

——

RADICAL. 94.

犬 Kau *Kien*
犯 Hwam
狀 Chuang
狄 Tek
狂 K'wang
犭田 Tien
狎 A'p
狐 Hu
狒 Hui
狗 Kau *Kien*

6

狠 Hùn
臭 H^{n}iu
狥 Sun
犭休 Hiu
狡 Kau
狩 Siu
狸 Li
狹 Hiap
狼 Láng
狽 Puo *Pai*
猛 Me
猖 Chi'àng
猜 Ch'ai
猨 Yien

9

猺 Io
猢 Hu
猪 Tù *Chu*
猩 Seng
猫 Ngio *Mio*
猾 Kut
猴 Kau *Ho*
猶 Iu
猷 Iu
犭留 Liu
獃 Ngai
猿 Wan *Yien*
猻 Sun
獄 Gek *Ngiak*
獒 Ngau
獅 Sai *Sù*
獠 Lio
獎 Chiàng
獨 Tok
獬 Hai
獲 Wak
獵 Lá, *Nap*
獪 Kwai
獸 Siu
獺 T'oa, *Tat*
獻 Hien
獼 Ni
獮 Ni

——

RADICAL 95.

玄 Hien
玅 Mio
率 Chut

——

RADICAL 96.

玉 Gek *Ngiok*
王 Wang
玎 Teng
玕 Kán
玖 Kiu
玩 Ngwan
玲 Leng
玳 Tai
玷 Tiam
玻 Pó
珀 P'ek
珊 Sien *Sán*
珍 Tien

6

珧 Io
珪 Kui
班 Pán
玼 Ca'ù
珠 Chu
現 Hien
球 Kiu
理 Li
琲 Pue *Pai*
琉 Liu
琅 Láng *Liàng*

8

琥 H^{n}o *Hu*
琦 I *K'i*
琳 Lim
琢 Tó, *Tok*
琺 Hawp
琴 K'im
琵 Pi
琶 Pe

9

瑁 Mau
瑤 Io
瑇 Tui
瑋 Ui
瑕 Hia
瑙 Ló
瑚 Hu
瑞 Sui
瑜 Ju

93 牛
94 犬
95 玄
96 玉

96 玉
97 瓜
98 瓦
99 甘
010 生
101 用
102 田
103 疋
104 疒

瑟 Sek
瑣 Só
瑪 Má
瑩 Iong
瑰 Kui
瑯 Láng
瑳 Ch'á
璅 Chau
瑠 Liu
璃 Li
璞 P'ok
璇 Suan
璉 Lien
璋 Chiáng
璣 Ki
璫 Táng
璲 Sui
環 Hwan
璧 Pia, *Pek*
璽 Jù *Ni*
璿 Suan *Jui*
瓊 K'wang
瓏 Leng *Long*
瓚 Chán

RADICAL 97.

瓜 Kue *Kwa*
瓞 Tiet
瓠 Pu
瓟 P'au
瓢 P'io
瓣 P'^{n}oi *Pien*
瓥 Lu

RADICAL 98.

瓦 Hia *Ua*
瓷 Chù
瓨 Táng *T'ong*
甋 Tong
瓶 Pán
甄 In
甍 Meng
甎 Chun
甌 Au
甑 Cheng *Chán*
甕 A'ng
甖 Eng

RALICAL 99.

甘 Kám
甚 Sim
甜 Tiam
[illegible] Tim
甞 S^{n}ie *Siàng*

RADICAL 100.

生 S^{n}e *Seng*
產 S^{n}ua *Sán*
甥 Seng
甦 So *Su*

RADICAL 101.

用 Eng *Iong*
甬 Iong
甫 P'o

RADICAL 102.

田 Ch'án *Tien*
由 Iu
甲 Ká, *Kiet*
申 Sin
男 Lám *Nam*
甸 Tien
町 Teng
畇 Un
畆 Bo
畋 T'ien
畈 Hwan
界 Kai
畎 K'ien
畏 Ui

5

畔 Pwan
畛 Chien
畚 Pun
留 Liu
畜 Tiok
畝 Bo *Mo*
畢 Piet *Pit*
異 I
畦 Ua
略 Liak *Lok*
畧 Liak

7

畤 *Luat*
畬 U`
畯 Chun
番 Hwan
畫 Ue,
畵 Ue
畸 K'i *I*
畱 Liu
當 T^{n}ng *Táng*
畺 Kiàng
畿 Ki
疆 Kiàng
疇 T'iu
疊 T'á,

RADICAL 103.

疋 P'it
疎 Só
疏 Só
疑 Gi
疐 Chi

RADICAL 104.

疒 Chit
疔 Teng
疨 Hia
疝 Sán
疚 Kiu
疤 Pui *Pá*
疫 Mut

疥 Koi *Kai*

5

症 Cheng
疳 Kám
疴 K'ó
疱 P'á
疲 P'i
疸 T'án
疵 Ch'ù
疹 Chien
疼 Tong
疽 Chu
疾 Chit
痄 Chá *Chák*
疿 Hui

6

痍 I
痒 Iàng
病 Pⁿe *Peng*
痊 Ch'uan
痔 T'i *Si*
痕 Hun
痘 Tau
痣 Ki *Chi*
痞 P'i
痛 Tⁿia *T'ong*
痢 Li
痡 Pu
痚 Hi

8

痰 T'ám
痴 Ch'i
痲 Mue *Mó*
瘀 Ù
瘂 E
痳 Mue
痷 Iam
痺 Pi
痼 Ku
[illegible] I *Kó*
瘁 Chui
痿 Sui *Ui*

9

瘕 Hia
瘉 Ju
瘊 Ho
瘋 Hong
瘍 Iàng
瘖 Im
瘓 Hwan
瘟 Un
瘧 Ngiak
瘩 Háp
瘣 T'ue
瘤 Liu
瘥 Chó
瘠 Chit
瘛 Chi
瘜 Sek
瘡 Ch'ng *Ch'áng*

11

瘳 Ch'iu *Lio*
瘵 Chⁿi
瘻 Lau *Liu*
瘦 So
瘨 Chin *Tien*
瘰 Liu
瘴 Chiàng
瘲 Chong
瘼 Mó, *Mok*
癆 Lau
療 Lio
癇 Kán
癍 Pán
癈 Hui

13

癡 Chi
癖 Pia, *Pek*
癘 Li
癑 Láng *Long*
癢 Iàng
癧 Lek
癩 T'ai
[illegible] T'ue
癥 Teng
癬 Sien
癭 Eng
癯 K'ù
癰 Iong
癱 T'án
癲 Tien

RADICAL 105.

癶 Pua,
癸 Kui
登 Teng
發 Hwat

RADICAL 106.

白 Pe, *Pok*
百 Pe, *Pok*
皂 Chau
的 Tek
皈 Hwan
皆 Kai
皇 Hwang
皎 Kau
皓 Kau
皜 Kau *Hau*
皞 Hau *Kau*
皦 Kau

RADICAL 107.

皮 P'ue *P'i*
[illegible] Pì
皰 Pau
皷 Ko *Ku*
皺 Jio

RADICAL 108.

皿 Meng
盂 U
盃 Pue *Pai*
盅 Ch'ong *Chán*
盆 Pun

104 疒
105 癶
106 白
107 皮
108 皿

108 皿
109 目
110 矛
111 矢
112 石

盈 Iong
益 Ia, *Ek*
盍 Háp
盒 A'p
盔 K'ue
盖 Kai
盛 Seng
盜 Tau

8

葢 Kai
盐 Iam
盞 Ch^{n}ua *Chien*
盟 Meng
盡 Chin
監 Kám
盤 P^{n}ua *Pwan*
盥 Kwan
盧 Lo *Lu*
盬 Ku
醢 Hai

RADICAL 109.

目 Mák *Mok*
盱 U
眙 Ch'i *I*
盲 Meng
直 Tit
盼 P'án
眏 Iàng
相 Si^{n}e *Siàng*
盹 Tun
眄 Min *Kai*
盾 Tun
省 S^{n}e *Seng*
眇 Mio
眈 Tim
眉 Bai *Mi*
眊 Mau
看 T'oi *Hán*

5

眛 Mue
眞 Chin
眠 Min
眥 Chù
眩 Hien
督 No
眶 K'wang *K'áng*
眺 T'io
着 Tie *Chiet*
眷 Kwan
眸 M^{n}o *Mong*
眼 Ngán *Yien*

8

睛 Cheng *Chong*
睜 Cheng
睢 Ch'ui
睞 Lai
睡 Sui
督 Tok
睥 Pui *Pi*
睦 Mok
睨 Ngi
睫 Chiap

9

睿 Jue *Jui*
瞀 Bu
睹 To *Tù*
瞋 Tien
瞌 Háp
瞍 So
瞇 Mi
瞎 Hát
瞑 Meng
瞞 Mua *Muan*

12

瞧 Chio
瞪 T'eng
瞬 Sun
瞭 Lio
瞯 Kán *Kien*
瞳 T'ong *Chong*
瞶 Kui
瞻 Chiam
瞽 Ko *Ku*
矇 Mong
矃 Leng

RADICAL 110.

矛 Mau
矜 Kim *Keng*
矠 Ch'u *Sek*

RADICAL 111.

矢 Si
矣 I$_{n}$
知 Chai *Ti*
矧 Sien
矩 Kù
短 Tó *Tuan*
矮 Oi *Ai*
矯 Kio
矱 Hu

RADICAL 112.

石 Chie, *Sek*
矻 Ngùt
砂 Sá
砆 Hu
砒 Pi
砌 Ki, *Kiet*
硫 K'^{n}e *Keng*
砍 K'ám

5

砥 Ti
砤 Si
砵 Pua
砧 Tiam
砏 Pin
砞 Bua
砲 P'au
砶 Siu *Iu*
破 P'ua *Pó*
砦 Ch'ù
硃 Chu

研 Ngien

7

硝 Sio
硜 K'eng
硫 Liu
硬 Nge
硯 In / *Yien*
硼 Peng
硾 Sui
硺 Tó, / *T'.k*
碁 Ki
碌 Lok
碔 Bu
碍 Gai
碎 Ch'ui

9

碣 Kit / *Kiet*
碑 Pi
碟 Ti, / *Tiap*
碓 Tui
碗 Una / *Yien*
碡 Tàk / *Tok*
碩 Sok
碧 P'ek
碥 S"i / *Sien*
磊 Lui
確 K'ák
碼 Má
碾 Tien
磐 } Pwan
磐 }
磁 Ch'ù
磅 Páng
磋 Chó
磕 K'áp

11

磡 K'ám
磢 Suang
磨 Bua / *Bó*
磚 Ch"ng / *Chuan*
磬 K'eng
磽 K'io
磯 Ki
磻 P'wan
磴 Teng
磺 Hwang

13

礎 Ch'ó
礪 Li
礙 Gai / *Gi*
礦 K'wang
礫 Lek
礬 Hwan
礱 Láng / *Long*
礶 Kwan

RADICAL 113.

示 Si
社 Sia / *Se*
祀 Sù
祇 K'i
祈 K'i
祆 Io
祉 Chi

5

祐 Iu
祖 Cho / *Chu*
祗 Ti
祛 K'u / *Kiak*
祓 Pwat
祚 Chu
祝 Chok
神 Sin
祟 Chui
祠 Sù

6

祥 Siàng
祧 T'io
崇 Ch'ong
票 P'ie
祭 Chi
稟 Pin
禂 Tau / *Chiu*
禁 Kim
祿 Lok

9

禍 Hwa / *Hó*
禎 Cheng
福 Hok
禦 Gù / *I*
禘 T'i
禧 Hi
禪 Sien
禮 Loi / *Li*
禰 Ni
禱 Tau

RADICAL. 114

内 Nui / *Liàng*
禹 U
禽 K'im

RADICAL 115

禾 Hwa / *Hó*
秃 T'ek
秀 Siu
私 Sù
秉 Peng
秋 Ch'iu
秕 P"oi
科 K'ue / *Kó*
秘 Pi
秧 Ng / *Iàng*
秩 Tiet
秭 Chi
秦 Ch'in
租 Cho / *Chu*
秤 P'eng

6

䅈 I
稀 Hi
稅 Sue
移 I
稂 Láng / *Liàng*
稊 T'i
稴 Liam
稈 Hán

112 石
113 示
114 内
115 禾

115 禾 116 穴 117 立 118 竹

稇 K'un
稧 Hiap
程 T'ia *Teng*
稍 Ch'io

8

稠 T'iu
稜 Leng
稚 Ti
稗 P^{n}oi *Pi*
稟 Lim
種 Cheng *Chong*
稱 Ch'eng

10

稷 Chek
黎 Li
稿 Kó *Káu*
稻 Tau
稼 Ki *Kia*
稽 Ki
穀 Kok
穆 Mok
積 Chek
穌 So *Su*
穉 Ch^{n}i
穗 Sui *Hui*
穢 Ue *Ui*
穡 Sek
穩 Un
穫 Hu *Wak*
穰 Siàng
穮 P'io

—

RADICAL 116.

穴 Hwat
穵 Wat
究 Kiu
穸 Sek
穹 K'iong
空 K'áng
穿 Ch'uán
窀 T'un
突 Tut
穽 Ch^{n}e *Cheng*

5

窄 Chák
窈 Io
窊 Ua
窒 Tiet
窖 Kue *Kau*
窕 T'io
窓 T'eng
窟 K'ut
窘 K'un

9

窩 Ua
窬 Ju
窮 K'iong
窯 Ie
窺 Kui
竄 Ch'uan
窶 Ki
竅 K'io
竇 To
竈 Chau
竊 Ch'iap
窻 T'eng *Chong*

—

RADICAL 117.

立 Lip
站 Chán
竚 Tiu
竟 Keng
章 Ch^{n}ie *Chiàng*
竣 Chun
童 T'ong
竦 Song
竪 Su
竭 Kiet
端 Tuan
𥪰 Ch'u
競 Keng

—

RADICAL 118.

竹 Tek *Chok*
竺 Chok
竻 Lek
竿 Kó *Kán*
笄 Ki
笈 K'ip
笆 Pá
笋 Sun
笑 Ch'ie *Chio*
笏 Hut
笓 Pin *Pi*

5

笙 Seng
笵 Hwam
笘 Tiam *Chiam*
笮 Chák
第 Toi *Ti*
笞 T'ai
笠 Loi, *Lip*
笛 Tek
笥 Si
符 Hu
笨 Pun
笳 Kia

6

筆 Pit
筍 Sun
筅 Ch'^{n}oi
筎 Ju
筌 Ch'uan
筊 Kau
等 Teng
筄 Io
筋 Kùn
筐 K'eng *Káng*
筏 Hwat
筒 Táng *Tong*
筇 Kiong
答 Táp

筞 Chʻe, *Chek*
箁 Pu *Hu*
筥 Ki
筴 Kiap
筵 Yien
筪 A'k
⿱竹奉 Pong
筠 Un
筢 Pe *Pá*
筮 Si

8

箇 Kai
箳 Pin
箒 Siu
箏 Cheng
⿱竹插 Cháp
箋 Chien
箎 Chi
箕 Ki
算 S^{n}ng *Suan*
管 Kwan

9

箭 Ch^{n}i *Chien*
篋 Kiap
箱 S^{n}ie *Siàng*
箴 Chám
箸 Tù *Chu*
篝 Ko
篪 Chʻi
節 Chát *Choi*
範 Hwam
篆 Tuan
篇 Pʻien
⿱竹槖 Tó, *Tok*
篡 Chʻuan
篙 Kó *Kau*
篤 Tok
篩 Tai *Sù*
篱 Li
簑 Sui *Suai*
篳 Pit
篾 Bi, *Mit*
篷 Pong
簋 Kui
簇 Chok
簀 Che,
簍 Lu
篸 Chám
簝 Lio
簡 Kán
簠 Pʻu
簟 Tien
簧 Hwang
簪 Chám
簫 Sio

13

簳 Kán
簷 Siam
簸 Pua *Pó*
簽 Chʻiam
簾 Liam
簿 Pʻo
籐 Tin
籃 Ná *Nám*
籌 Tʻin
篼 Tau
籍 Chia *Che*
籓 Pwan
⿱竹畾 Lui
籙 Lok
籟 Lai *Nai*
籠 Láng *Long*
籩 Pien
籤 Chʻiam
籜 Ták *Tok.*
籥 Yiak
籬 Li
籮 Lua *Ló*
籲 Ju
籰 Kák

—

RADICAL 119.

米 Bi
粉 Hun
粃 P^{n}oi *Pi*
料 Lio
粒 Liap *Lip*
粕 Pʻó, *Pok*
粗 Chʻo *Chu*
粘 Niam *Chiam*

6

粟 Chʻek *Sok*
粵 Wat
粥 Chok *Kiok*
粧 Ch^{n}ng *Chuang*
粮 Nie *Liáng*
粢 Chù
粱 Liàng
粲 Chʻán

8

精 Cheng
粽 Cháng *Chong*
糊 Ko *Hu*
粹 Chʻui
粿 Kue *Kó*
糈 Su

10

糓 Kok
糕 Kó *Kau*
糙 Chʻau
糖 Tʻ^{n}ng *Táng*
糜 Mi
糞 Pun
糟 Chau
⿱將米 Ch^{n}ie *Chiàng*
糠 K^{n}ng *Káng*

12

糦 Hi
糧 Nie *Liàng*
糲 Li
糯 Chut
糴 Tia, *Tek*

118 竹
119 米

英漢潮州方言字典

119 米

糵 Ngiak

糶 Tʻie *Tik*

120 糸

—

RADICAL 120.

糸 Si

系 Si *Hi*

糾 Kiu

紂 Tiu

紀 Ki

約 Le, *Yiak*

紃 Hun

紅 A′ng *Hong*

4

紋 Bun

紊 Bun

紓 Su *Tiu*

紐 Niu

紏 Kiu

紕 Pi

納 Náp

純 Sun

紗 Se *Sá*

級 Kʻip

紙 Chua *Chù*

紛 Hun

紜 Un

素 Su

紡 Pʻáng *Hwang*

索 Sok

5

紫 Chi

紬 Tiu

組 Chu

絆 Pwan

紺 Kám

紘 H^{n}i *Hien*

紲 Siet

絅 Kwang

紼 Hut

紾 Chien

紮 Cháp

累 Lui

細 Soi *Tiu*

紳 Sin

紹 Sio

終 Chong

6

結 Kát *Kiet*

絰 Tiet

絶 Chó, *Chuat*

絢 Sun

絜 Kiet

絞 Ká *Kau*

絡 Lok

給 Kip

絨 Jong

絪 In

絮 Su

統 Tʻong

絲 Si

7

絹 Kien

絏 Siet

絳 Káng

綕 Choi *Chi*

絺 Hi

綆 Pien

綌 Kok

綏 Sui

綁 Páng

綑 Kʻun

綒 Hu

經 K^{n}ia *Keng*

8

綠 Lek *Lok*

緎 Hok

綢 Tʻiu

綜 Cháng *Chong*

綦 Ki

緅 Cho *Chu*

綺 Kʻi

緇 Chù

綣 Kwan *Kien*

綬 Siu

網 Máng *Buang*

維 Jui

綻 T^{n}ia *Teng*

綴 Tue

綵 Chʻai

綸 Lun

綱 Káng

綉 Siu

綽 Chʻiak

縄 Sin

綾 Lin *Leng*

綿 Mien

緬 Mien

9

緼 Un

緒 Su

緘 Kʻiam

線 S^{n}ua *Sán*

締 Ti

緝 Chip

緣 Wan *Yien*

編 Pʻien

緩 Mán *Yien*

緯 Ui

緞 T^{n}ng *Tuan*

緊 Kin

練 Lien

10

緻 Ti

縝 T^{n}i

縈 Iong

緲 Mio

縤 Só

緡 Min

縉 Chin

縋 Tui

縊 I

縐 Jio

縛 Pák
縞 Kau
縣 K^{n}ui, *Hien*
縫 Pong
縮 Sok
縶 Chip, *Chi*
縻 Mi
績 Che, *Chek*
縲 Lui
縱 Chong
縺 Lien
縷 Lu
總 Chong
繁 Hwan
繆 Mok
繇 Io, *Iu*

12

繒 Chán, *Cheng*
繢 Kui
繕 Sien
繐 Hui
織 Chit, *Sek*
繙 Hwan
繚 Lio
繞 Jio
繡 Siu
綦 Ki
繩 Sin

13

繪 Kwai
繫 Hi
繭 K^{n}oi
繳 Kio
繸 Sui
繹 Ek

14

辮 P^{n}i, *Pien*
繾 K'ien
繼 Ki
纊 K'wang
繽 Pin
纂 Juan, *Chuan*
續 Sok
纍 Lui
纏 T'ien
纜 Lám, *Nám*
纓 Eng
纖 Siam
纔 Ch'ai
纛 Tau
纘 Chán
纚 Si

RADICAL 121.

缶 Hui
缸 K^{n}ng, *Kụng*
䍃 Io
缺 K'ue, *Kiet*
缾 } P'in, *Pin*
絣 }
罅 Hu
罄 K'eng
罇 Chun
罋 A'ng
罌 Eng
罍 Lui
罏 Lo, *Lu*
罐 Kwan

RADICAL 122.

网 Máng
罔 Buang
罕 Hán
罛 Ua, *Hu*
罟 K'u
罝 Chu
罡 Káng
罩 Chau
罣 K'wa, *Kui*
罪 Chue, *Chui*
罧 Sim
置 Ti
罭 Ek

9

罰 Hwat
署 Su
罵 Me, *Má*
罷 Pá
罶 Liu
罹 Ló, *Li*
罾 Chán
羅 Ló, *Li*
羆 Pi
羈 Ki

RADICAL 123.

羊 I^{n}e, *Iàng*
美 Mui
羔 Kau
羌 Kiàng
羚 Leng
羜 Tiu
羝 Ti
羞 Siu
羖 Ku

6

着 Tie, *Chiet*
羨 Yien
義 Ngi
羣 } K'un
群 }
羯 Hiet
羹 K^{n}e, *Keng*
羶 Chien
羸 Lui
羲 Hi

RADICAL 124.

羽 U
羿 Ngi
翁 Ong, *Eng*
翅 T'i
翕 Hù, *Hi*
翎 Leng
習 Sip

120 糸
121 缶
122 网
123 羊
124 羽

124 羽
125 老
126 而
127 耒
128 耳
129 聿
130 肉

翔 Siàng
翌 Ek
翕 Hip

8

翠 Ch'ui
翡 Hui
翫 Ngwan
翦 Chien
翩 P'ien
翰 Hán
翳 U'
翻 Hwan
翬 Hui
翼 Ek
翹 K'io
翺 Ngau
耀 Io

RADICAL 125.

老 Lau
考 K'au
耇 Ko *Ku*
耄 Mau
者 Chia *Che*
耆 K'i

耋 Tiet

RADICAL 126.

而 Jù
耍 S^{n}ng
耑 Chuan
耐 Nai

RADICAL 127.

耒 Lui *Nui*
耔 Chù
耕 K^{n}e *Keng*
耖 Chau
耗 Hó
耙 Pe
耘 Un
耜 Sù
耡 Ch'ó
耦 Ngo
耬 Lu
耨 Nó
耰 Iu

RADICAL 128.

耳 Jù
耶 E
耻 恥 } Ch'i
耾 Hong *K'wang*
耽 Tim
耿 Kwang
聊 Lio

6

聆 Leng
聖 S^{n}ia *Seng*
聚 Chu
聘 P^{m}ia *Peng*
聞 Bun
聯 Lin *Lien*
聰 Ch'ong
聲 S^{n}ia *Seng*
聳 Song
聵 Kui
職 Che, *Chek*
聽 T^{n}ia *T'eng*
聾 Láng *Long*

RADICAL 129.

聿 Lut
肄 I
肅 Sok
肆 Sù
肇 Sio

RADICAL 130.

肉 Nek *Jok*
肋 Kùn
肖 Sio
肕 Jim
肘 Chiu
肚 To *Tu*
肛 Káng
肝 K^{n}wa *Kán*

4

⿰月少 Sua *Sá*
肴 Ngau
肦 Hun
股 Ko *Ku*
肢 Chi
肫 T'un
肥 Pui *Hui*
肨 Hong
肩 K^{n}oi *Kien*
服 Hok
肯 K'eng
肱 K'wang
育 Yok *Hiok*
肶 Pi

5

肺 Hui
胃 Ui
胄 Tiu
胆 T^{n}á *Tán*
胊 Ku *K'ong*
胥 Su
胤 Yien
背 Pue *Pui*
胗 Chien
胎 T'ó *Tai*
胙 Chu
胖 P'wan
胞 Pau
胚 P'i *Hwai*
胡 Hu
胋 Ku

6

胭 In
胱 Kwang
胼 Peng

脩 Siu
胷 } Heng
胸 } *Hiong*
能 Neng
胻 Háng *Heng*
腴 Ju
脂 Chi
脅 }
脇 } Hiap
脆 Kui
脈 Me, *Mek*
脊 Chit

7

脗 Mut
脚 K'á *Kiok*
腋 Ek
腆 Tʻien
腓 Hui
脛 K^{n}e *Keng*
脣 Sin
脢 Bue *Mui*
脫 Tut
脯 Po *Pu*
脤 Chin
脞 Chʻó

8

脹 T^{n}ie *Chiàng*
脾 Pi
腌 Iam
腊 Sit *Sek*
腎 Sien
腐 Hu
腑 Hu
腔 Kʻ^{n}ie *Kong*
腕 Wan

9

腥 Seng
腦 Nau
腫 Cheng *Chong*
胃 Ui
腭 Ngak
腮 Sai *Sú*
腰 Ie *Io*
腳 K'á *Kiok*
腧 Ju
腸 T^{n}ng *Chiàng*
腹 Pák *Hok*

10

腿 Tʻui
膆 Su
膀 Pʻáng
膈 Ke, *Kek*
膊 Pʻák
膉 Háp
膏 Kó *Kau*
膚 Hu
膛 Tʻáng
膜 Mó, *Mok*
膠 Ká *Kau*

12

膩 Jù
䐶 Chiạm
膴 Bu
膲 Chio
膨 P^{n}e
膳 Sien

13

膽 T^{n}á *Tám*
膝 Chʻek
膾 Kwai
膿 Láng *Long*
臁 Liam
臂 Pi
臉 Lien
臀 Tien
臊 Chau
膺 Eng
臆 Ek
臍 Chai *Chi*
朦 Mong

14

臝 Ló
臑 Ju
臢 Chán
臘 Lá, *Náp*
𦣃 Ló *Li*
臚 Lo
臟 Cháng

——

RADICAL 131.

臣 Chʻin
臥 O'
臧 Cháng
臨 Lim

——

RADICAL 132.

自 Chù
臭 H^{n}iu
臬 Ngiak

RADICAL 133.

至 Chi
致 Ti
臺 Tʻai
臻 Chin

——

RADICAL 134.

臼 Kʻu
臾 Ju
舂 Cheng *Chong*
舅 Ku *Kiu*
與 Ù
興 Heng
舋 Hien

——

RADICAL 135.

舌 Chi, *Siet*
舍 Sia *Se*
舐 Chi
舒 Su
舘 Kwan
舖 Pʻo

——

130 肉
131 臣
132 自
133 至
134 臼
135 舌

136 舛
137 舟
138 艮
139 色
140 艸

RADICAL 136.

舛 Ch'un
舜 Sun
舞 Bu

RADICAL 137.

舟 Chiu
般 P^{n}ua *P'wán*
舫 P'áng *Háng*
舨 Pán
航 Háng
舩 Song *Kong*
舵 Toa *Tai*
舶 Pek *Pok*
船 Chun *Chuan*
舳 Tek *Iu*
舺 Ká,
艄 Sau
艇 T'eng
艙 Ch^{n}ng *Chàng*
艚 Chó *Chau*
艟 T'ong
艨 Mong
艦 Lám
艫 Lo *Lu*

RADICAL 138.

艮 Kùn
良 Liàng
艱 Kán

RADICAL 139.

色 Sek
艴 Hut
艷 Iam

RADICAL 140.

艸 Ch'au *Ch'ó*
艻 Lek
艾 Ngai *Ngi*
芋 U
芍 Chiak
芒 芢 } Máng

4

芙 Hu
芰 Ch^{n}i
芟 Sán
芮 Jue *Jui*
芷 Chi
芯 Sim
芝 Chú
芥 Kai
芨 Kip
芫 Ngwan
芬 Hun
芭 Pá
花 Hue *Hwà*
芳 Hwang
芸 Uu
芹 K'ùn
芻 Ch'u
芽 Ge *Gia*

5

苑 Wan
苐 Toi *Ti*
苴 Chu
苒 Jiam
苕 Tiù
范 Hwam
苓 Leng
苔 T'ai
苗 Mio
苷 Kám
苛 K'ó
苞 Pau
苟 K'o *Ku*
苡 I^{n}
若 Jiak
苦 K'o *Ku*
苫 Tiam
英 Eng
苻 Hu
茀 Hut
茁 Chuat
茂 Mong
茅 Mau
茄 Kie
茉 Muat

6

苨 Ni
茗 Meng
荀 Sun
茱 Chu
茰 Ju
荏 Jim
荐 Chin
荔 Li
茨 Ch'ù
茫 Máng
茯 Hok
茲 Chù
茴 Hue *Hui*
茸 Jong
茶 Te *Ch'á*
茹 Ju
荆 Keng
荈 Ch'un
莽 Máng
草 Cha'u *Ch'ó*
荑 I
荒 Hwang

7

荳 Tau *Tu*
荷 O'
莒 Kù
莅 Li
萋 Ch'i
荸 Pwat
荼 T'u
荽 Sui
莉 Lie
莊 Ch^{n}ng

140 艸

莓 Mue
莖 Keng
莘 Sin
莪 Ngó
莞 Wan
莠 In *Sui*
莧 Hien
莩 Hu
莨 Láng *Liàng*
莫 Mok

8

莽 Máng
莚 Yien
萗 Cháng
萇 Ch'iàng
莿 Ch'i *Chù*
萊 Lai
菉 Lek *Lok*
菌 K'un
菊 Kek *Kiok*
菹 Chu
菓 Kue
菖 Ch'iàng
菜 Ch'ai
菠 Pó

菩 P'u
菫 Kùn
華 Hwa *Hó*
菱 Leng
菰 Ko *Ku*
菲 Hui
菴 A'm
菁 Ch'ⁿe
⿱艹掩 Pan
菑 Chai
萃 Chui
菽 Sok
萁 Ki
萄 T'ó
萆 Pui *Pi*
萌 Meng
菼 Tám
萍 P'ie *Peng*
萬 Buan

9

菟 T'o *Tu*
葭 Kia
董 Tang *Tong*
萺 Mong
葷 Hun

蓂 Meng
萱 Suan
萹 Pien
萼 Ngák
落 Ló, *Lok*
著 Tu
葉 Hie, *Hiap*
葚 Tim
葛 Kwa, *Kát*
葦 Ui
葩 Pui *Pá*
葡 P'u
葫 Hu
葸 Sù
葬 Chᵘng *Cháng*
葵 K'ui
葱 Ch'áng *Chong*
葺 Jong
蒂 Ti, *Ti*

10

⿱艹淑 Sok
蓑 Sui *Swai*
蒙 Mong
蒜 Sᵘng *Suan*
蔻 K'o

蓍 Si
蒺 Chit
蔥 Ch'ong
蓁 Chin
蒐 So
葆 Pó
蔣 Ch'iáng
蓖 Pi
蒟 Ku
蒔 Si
蒢 Chù *Chu*
蒲 P'u
蒸 Cheng
蒼 Ch'áng
蒿 Kau
蓄 T'iok *Tok*
蓉 Iong
蓆 Ch'ie, *Sek*
蓊 Ong
蓋 Kai
蓓 Pue *Pui*

11

蓪 Tong
蔡 Chua *Chai*
蓮 Lien

蔌 Sok
蓬 Pong
蓼 Lok
⿱艹欶 Lun
蔃 K'iàng
蔔 P'ek
蔓 Muan
蓰 Si
蔗 Chia *Su*
蔞 Lu
蔚 Ue *Ui*
蔟 Chok
蔬 Só
蔴 Mua *Mó*
蔭 Im
⿱艹勒 Lek

12

蔽 Pi
藜 Li
蕃 P'wan
蕕 In
蕭 Sio
蕞 Ch'ó, *Chui*
薈 Kwai
蕢 Kui

140 艸

141 虍

142 虫

藝 Goi *Ngi*
藥 Ie *Yiak*
藐 Mio
藤 Tin *Teng*

12

蕉 Chię
蕊 Lui
蕋 Lui
蕎 Kie
蕙 Hui
蕨 K'iet
蕩 Táng
蕪 Bu

13

藘 Kù
蕾 Lui
甍 Wang
蕹 Iong
薄 Pó, *Pok*
薆 Ai
薇 Mui
薏 I
薑 Kⁿie *Kiàng*
藚 Ch'ok
藹 Ai
薢 Kán
薤 Kiu *Hai*
薦 Chin
薩 Sát
薛 Si
薪 Chin

11

薯 Chù
薰 Hùn
藉 Chia *Che*
蘙 In
藪 So *Su*
藜 Li
藳 Kó *Kau*
蘄 Chi
藍 Kám
薱 Tui
藏 Ch'áng
藩 P'wan
藕 Ngo
藻 Ch'au
蘆 Lu
蘇 So *Su*
蘖 Ngiak
蘗 Ngiak
蘚 Sien
蘋 P'in
蘧 Kù
蘭 Lán
蘸 Chie
蘿 Ló

RADICAL 141.

虍 U
虎 Hⁿo *Hu*
虐 Ngiak
虔 K'ien
處 Ch'u
虛 Hù

7

虜 Lu
虞 Ngó *U*
號 Hó *Kau*
膚 Hu
虧 K'ui
虢 Kiak

RADICAL 142.

虫 T'áng *Chong*
虱 Sát
虯 K'iu
虺 Hui
虹 K'eng *Hong*
虻 Máng
蚌 Hong
蚊 Bun
蚓 In
蚘 Iu
蚩 Ch'i
蚣 K'ong
蚧 Kai
蚤 Chá *Cho*
蚚 Kùn
蚪 Tau

5

蚯 Kiu
蚱 Chá *Chu*
蚔 Ch'i *Ki*
蚶 Hám
蛉 Leng
蛀 Chu
蛅 Chiam
蛆 Chu
蛇 Chua *Tó*
蛋 Táng

6

蛙 Ua
蛛 Tu
蛞 Kwak
蛟 Kau
蛤 K'áp *Háp*
蛩 K'iong
蛣 Kit
蛭 Tiet

7

蛸 Siak *Sio*
蛺 Hiap
蜃 Sin
蛾 Ngó
蜀 Chuak
蜂 Hong
蜆 Hien
蜈 Go *U*
蜉 Hu *Pu*
蜋 Láng
蜍 Ch'u
蜓 T'ēng

8

蜘 Ti
蜚 Hui
蜜 Bit *Mit*

英漢潮州方言字典

蜲 Ui
蜄 Sin
蜞 K'i
蜢 Me
蟯 Kiàng
蜣 T^{n}ie *Chiàng*
蜻 Ch'^{n}e *Cheng*
蜹 Jue *Jui*
蜿 Wan
蜺 Ngi
蝀 Tong

9

蝏 Teng
蝨 Sát *Sek*
蝓 Ju
蝱 Máng *Meng*
蝌 Kue *Kó*
蝥 Bu
蝕 Si, *Siet*
蝗 Hwang
蝮 Hok
蝘 Iam
蝙 Pien
蝟 Ui
螮 Ti

蝠 Hok
蝣 Iu
蝦 He *Hia*
蝴 Hu
蝶 Tiap
蝸 Ua

10

螇 Hi
螃 Páng
螂 Láng
螄 Sù
融 I^{n}e *Iong*
螞 Má
螉 Ong
螟 Meng
螢 Iong
螭 Li

11

螫 Sek
螬 Chau
螯 Ngau
螲 Tiet
螳 T'áng
螺 Ló *Lui*
螻 Lu

蠭 P'áng *Hong*
螽 Chong
蟄 Tek
蟀 Chut
螵 P'io
蟅 Chia
蟆 Mó *Mok*
蟋 Sek

12

蟛 Páng *Peng*
蟠 P'wan
蠲 Kán
蟣 Ki
蟥 Hwang
蟬 Sien
蟮 Sien
蟲 T'áng *Chong*

13

蟷 Táng
蟶 Táng *Seng*
蟹 Hoi *Kai*
蟻 Hia *Ngi*
蟾 Siam
蠊 Li
蠅 Sin

蠆 Ch'ai
蠍 Hiet *Hát*
蠃 Wang

14

蠐 Chi
蠔 O' *Hau*
蠖 Wok
蠟 Lá, *Náp*
蠢 Ch'un
蠹 Chu
蠭 P'áng *Hong*
蠮 U`
蠱 Ko
蠡 Li
蠒 Kien
蠶 Ch'^{n}oi *Chám*
蠻 Mán

—

RADICAL 143.

血 Hue, *Hiap*
卹 Sut
衄 Niu
衆 Cheng *Chong*

—

RADICAL 144.

行 K^{n}ia *Heng*
衍 Yien
衎 K'án
衒 Hien
術 Sut
街 Koi *Kai*
衕 T'ong
衘 Hám
衙 Ge *Gia*
衚 Hu
衝 Ch'ong
衛 Ue *Ui*
衡 Hwang
衢 K'ù

—

RADICAL 145.

衣 I
表 Pio
衫 S^{n}á *Sán*
衰 Sue *Swai*
袁 Wan *Yien*
衽 Jim
衾 K'im
袂 Mi
衲 Náp
衷 Ch'ong

142 虫
143 血
144 行
145 衣

145 衣 146 襾 147 見 148 角 149 言

衸 Kai
衿 K'im
衮 Kun

5

袈 Ke *Kai*
袒 T'án
袗 Chien
袪 K'u
裊 Nio *Hio*
袋 Tó *Tai*
袍 P'au
袖 Sin
袞 Kun
被 Pue *Pi*

6

袣 Hi
袱 Hok
袵 Jim
袿 K'wa
袴 Ko *K'wa*
裀 In
裁 Ch'ai
裂 Li, *Lip*

7

裕 Ju
裔 I
裟 Se *Sá*
裝 Chuang
裙 Kun *Kien*
裘 K'iu
補 Po *Pu*
裡 Li
裏 Ló *Li*

8

裳 Siàng
褂 K'wa
製 Chi
裹 Ló
裸 Ló
⿰衤彔 Lok
裱 Pie *Pio*
裯 Tiu
裾 Kù
裨 Pi
裴 Pue *Hui*
裼 T'ek

9

褚 Su
褊 P'ien
褑 In
襃 P'o *Pau*
褒 P'au
⿰衤侯 Ho
複 Hok
褐 Kwa, *Hát*

10

褶 Sip
褧 Kwang
褫 T'i
褲 K'o
⿰衤弱 Jio
⿰衤貪 T'au
褸 Lu
褥 Jok
褪 T'ui
褰 Kien
襁 Kiàng
襍 Cháp
襄 Siàng
褻 Siet

13

襞 P'ek
襟 K'im
襚 Sui
⿰衤齊 Chù
襤 Lám
襖 O'
襢 Tán
襪 Bue *Mit*
襜 Chiam
襯 Ch'in
⿰衤囊 Láng
襲 Sip

RADICAL 146.

襾 A'
西 Sai *Si*
要 Io
覃 T'ám
覆 Hok
覈 Hek
覇 Pá
覊 Ki

RADICAL 147.

見 Kien
規 Kui
視 Si
覓 Mit
覕 Bu
覩 To *Tu*
覽 Lám
覦 Ju
親 Ch'in
覬 K'ai
覲 Kùn
覷 Chu
覽 Lám
覺 Kák *Kok*
觀 Kwan
覿 Tok

RADICAL 148.

角 Kák *Kok*
觔 Kùn
斛 Hok
觝 Ti
觚 Ko *Ku*
觟 Kui
觫 Sok
解 Koi *Kai*
觥 Kwang
觴 Siàng
觸 Ch'ok
觳 K'ok

RADICAL 149.

言 Ngán *Yien*

149 言

訂 Cheng *Teng*
訃 Hu
計 Koi *Ki*
討 T'ó *Tau*
訏 U
訒 Jim
訊 Sin
訓 Hun
訕 Sán
訖 Ngùt
託 T'ó, *Ták*
記 Ki

4

訛 Hó
訣 Kwat
訝 Gia
訟 Song
訥 Nut *Náp*
訪 Hwang
設 Siet
許 Hù *Hi*

5

詐 Chá
詁 Ko *Ku*
詒 I
詆 Ti
詎 Kù
詘 Chuat
訴 Su
訶 K'ó
診 Chien
註 Chu
証 Cheng
詈 Li
詔 Chio
評 P'eng
詖 Pi
詛 Chu
詠 Iong
訾 Ch'ù
詞 Sù

6

詢 Sun
詡 Hù *Hi*
詹 Chiam
詣 Chi
試 Ch'i
詤 Hwang
詩 Si
詬 Ko
詭 K'ui *Ngui*
詮 Ch'uan
詫 Tó *Tai*
詰 K'it
話 Ue *Hwa*
該 Kai
詳 Siàng
詶 Chiu
詼 K'ue
誄 Lui
誅 Tu
誆 Káng
誠 Seng
誇 K'wa

7

認 Jin
誌 Chi
誱 Hiap
誖 Pwat
誑 K'wang
誓 Si
誕 Tán
誘 Iu
語 Gù *I*
誚 Ch'io
誒 I^{n}
誡 Kai
誣 Bu
誤 Go *U*
誥 Kau
誦 Song
誨 Hue *Hui*
說 Sue *Suat*

8

談 T'ám
誰 Sui
諗 Liam
諕 Hau *Hu*
誾 Ngùn
諏 Cho *Chu*
誼 Ngi
課 Kue
誶 Chui
誹 Hui
調 Tio
諄 Tun
諒 Liàng
諈 Sui
論 Lun
諍 Cheng
請 Ch'ia *Cheng*
諉 Ui

9

諶 Sim
諛 Ju
諂 T'iam
諸 Chu
諤 Ngák
諝 Su
諮 Chù
諳 Ám
諴 Hám
諷 Hong
諧 Hai
諢 Hun
諻 Hui
諫 Kán *Kien*
謀 Mong
諾 Nut *Náp*
謚 I
謂 Ui
謁 Hát
謏 So
諱 Hui

149 言
150 谷
151 豆
152 豕
153 豸
154 貝

諠 Hien *Suan*
諺 Ngán *Yien*
諭 Ju

10

謓 Tien
講 Káng *Kien*
謙 Kʻiam
謎 Mi
謊 Hwang
謔 Ngiak
謇 Kʻien
謗 Páng
謝 Sia *Se*
謄 Teng
謠 Io
謕 Ti

11

謵 Sip
謨 Mó
譁 Hwa
謳 O
謹 Kùn
謬 Niu
謫 Tia *Tek*
譔 Chuan
證 Cheng
譙 Chie
譊 Ngio
䜍 Lio
譓 Hui
譚 Tʻám
譏 Ki
譎 Kʻiet
譜 Pʻo
識 Chi *Sek*
譖 Chám

13

議 Ngi
譫 Tʻám
譟 Chʻau
譬 Pʻi
警 Keng
譯 Ek
譸 Tʻiu *Tau*
譵 Tui
譭 Hui
護 Hu
譴 Kʻien
譽 Ù
變 Pien
讀 Tʻák *Tok*
讋 Long
讈 Le,
讚 Chán
讎 Chʻiu
讓 Jiàng
讖 Siam *Chiam*
讒 Chʻám
讘 Niap
讙 Hwan
讚 Chán
讟 Tok

RADICAL 150.

谷 Kok
豁 Hát
谿 Kʻi

RADICAL 151.

豆 Tau *To*
豈 Kʻá *Hi*
豉 Si
登 Teng
豎 Su
豐 Hong
豔 Iam

RADICAL 152.

豕 Si
豗 Ngùt
𧰴 Bue *Mu*
豨 Si
象 Ch^{n}ie *Siang*
豚 Tʻun
豫 Ù
豢 Hwan
豪 Hau
毅 Ngi
豭 Kia
豬 Tù

RADICAL 153.

豸 Chʻai
豹 Pá
豺 Chʻai
豼 Pi
貂 Tio
狐 Hu
豿 Ku *Kau*
貌 Mau
貅 Hiu
貊 Me,
貌 Mau
貓 Ngio *Mio*
貔 Pi
貘 Mó

RADICAL 154.

貝 Pue
貞 Cheng
貟 員 } Wan *Yien*
負 Hu
財 Chʻai
貢 Kong
貤 Chʻi

4

貧 Pin
貨 Hue *Hó*
販 Hwan
貪 Tʻám
責 Che,

5

貶 Chien
貺 Kʻwang
貯 Tiu

貫 Kwan
貰 Si
貲 Chù
貳 Jù
貴 Kui
貶 Pin *Peng*
買 Boi *Mai*
貸 Tai
費 Hui
貼 Tiap
貽 I
貿 Mⁿo *Mong*
賉 Hien
賀 Hó

6

賁 Pi
賂 Lu
賃 Jim
賄 Iu
資 Chù
賈 Kia *Ku*
賊 Ch'át *Chek*

7

賒 Ch'ia *Che*
賑 Chin
賕 K'iu
賓 Pin *Pien*

8

賙 Chiu
賛 Chán
賦 Hu
賚 Lai
賜 Sù
賬 Tⁿie
賞 Sⁿie *Siàng*
賠 Pue *Pai*
賤 Chⁿua *Chien*
賢 Hien
賣 Boi *Moi*
質 Chie *Sek*

9

賭 To
賴 Nai
賽 Sai
賻 P'ák
贄 Chi
賺 T'án *Chán*
贅 Chue *Ngau*

12

贈 Chán *Cheng*
贏 Iⁿa *Wang*
贊 Chán
購 Ko
贍 Siam
贐 Chin *Chien*
贖 Sok
贓 Cháng

RADICAL 155.

赤 Ch'ia, *Chek*
赦 Sia *Se*
赧 Lán
赫 Hek
赭 Che

RADICAL 156.

走 Chau *Cho*
赴 Hu
赶 Kⁿwa *Kán*
起 K'i
趁 趂 } Chien
趄 Chu
趈 Chiam
超 T'io
赳 Kiu
越 Wat
趦 Chù
趕 Kⁿwa *Kán*
趣 Chu
趙 Tie *Chio*
趨 Chu
趲 Chán

RADICAL 157.

足 Chu *Chok*
趾 Chi
跂 Ki
跋 Pwat
跖 Chia, *Ták*
跕 T'iap
跌 Tiet
跎 Tó
跐 Chù
跛 P'ó
跑 P'au
距 Kù

6

跬 Kui
跲 Kip
跟 Kùn
跡 Chia, *Chek*
跣 Soi *Sien*
跨 K'wa *Kó*
跪 Kui
路 Lo *Lu*
跴 Sien
跳 T'io
踈 Só
踉 Liàng *Láng*
踊 Iong

8

踏 Tá, *Táp*
跼 Kiok
踐 Chien
踦 K'i
踧 Sok
踪 Chong
踝 Kó
踖 Sek
踭 Cheng
踞 K'ù
踟 Ch'i
踠 Wan

9

踼 Iàng

154 貝
155 赤
156 走
157 足

157 足
158 身
159 車
160 辛

蹀 Tiap
踼 Iong
踖 Sek
踽 Ki
踰 Ju
踵 Chong
蹄 Toi, *Ti*

10

蹇 K'ien
蹈 Tau
蹌 Ch'áng
蹉 Ch'á
蹊 K'i
蹋 T'áp
蹙 Ch'ok
蹟 Chia, *Chek*
蹤 Chong
蹝 Sua, *Si*
蹣 Mua
蹡 Ch'áng
[illegible] K'u
蹠 Chia, *Che*

12

蹯 Pwan
蹴 Ch'ok, *Chiu*
蹻 K'io
躕 To
蹲 Chun
蹱 T'ong
蹶 Kui, *Kiet*
蹺 K'io
躁 Ch'au
躅 Chok
躇 T'u
躂 T'át
躉 Tun

14

躊 T'iu
躋 Chi
躝 Lán
躍 Yiak
躒 Lá, *Lek*
躡 Niap
躑 Teng
躓 Chi, *Sek*
躩 K'iet

RADICAL 158.

身 Sin
躬 Kiong
射 Sia
躭 T'ám
躰 T'oi, *T'i*
躱 Tó
躴 Láng, *Liàng*
軀 K'u
躿 K'áng

RADICAL 159.

車 Kù, *Ch'ia*
軋 Ngiak
軌 K'ui
軔 Jim
軒 Hùn, *Hien*
軍 Kun, *Kin*
軏 Ngiak
軟 N^{u}ng
斬 Chám
軛 E, *Ek*

5

軹 Chi
軸 Tek
軨 Leng
軻 K'ó
軼 Tiet
較 Ká, *Kio*
輈 Chiu
載 Chai
輅 Lu
軾 Sek
輔 Hu
輕 K'in, *Keng*
輒 Tiet

8

輓 Mien
輥 Kun
輗 Ngi
輛 Liàng
[illegible] Lek
輪 Lun
輝 Hui
輘 Leng
輞 Buang
輟 Ch'uat
輦 Lin
輩 Pue, *Pui*

9

輸 Su
輴 Tun, *Sun*
輻 Hok
輯 Ch'ip
轂 Ko
轅 Wan, *Yien*
轄 Hát
輿 U`
輾 Tien
轇 Lok, *Niu*
轆 Tek
轉 Chuan
[illegible] Siu
轍 T'iet
轎 Kie, *Koi*
轣 Le, *Lek*
轕 Kwa, *Kat*
轞 Kám
轟 Hong
轡 Pi, *Luan*
轢 Lek
轤 Lu

RADICAL 160.

辛 Sin
辜 Ku
辟 Pek
辠 Kau

辢 Lua, *Luat*
辦 Pnoi *Piēn*
辨 Pien
辭 Si *Sù*
辮 Pni *Pien*
辯 Pien

RADICAL 161.

辰 Sin
辱 Jok
農 Long

RADICAL 162.

辵 T'ok *Cho*
迀 Kán
迁 Ch'ien
迂 U
迄 Ngùt
迅 Sin
迍 Tun
迓 Gia
迎 Ngeng
迕 Ngo
近 Kùn
返 Hwan

5

迥 Kwang *Keng*
迨 Tai
迢 T'io
迪 Tek
延 Yien
迫 Pek
述 Sut
迭 It *Tiet*

6

迹 Chia, *Chek*
迸 Peng
迷 Mi
追 Tui
退 Tó *Tui*
逅 Ho
送 Sáng *Song*
逆 Ngek
逃 Tó *Tau*
适 Kwat

7

逍 Sio
逋 Pu
這 Che
逦 Li
逑 K'iu
逛 Kwang
透 T'au
逐 Tok
逓 Ti *Chi*
途 Tu
逕 Kne *Keng*
逗 T'au
通 T'ong
逝 Si
逖 Tek
逞 T'eng
速 Sok
造 Chau
逡 Chun
逢 Hong
連 Lin *Lien*

8

逮 Tai
逭 Kwan
週 Chiu
進 Chin
逰 Iu
逵 K'ui

9

逸 It
逾 Ju
遄 Chuan
遑 Hwang
逼 Pek
遁 T'un
遂 Sui
遇 Ngó *I*
遊 Iu
運 Un
遍 Pien
過 Kue *Kó*
遏 A't
遐 Hia
道 Tau
達 T'át
違 Ui

10

遙 Io
遡 Su
遘 Ko
遛 Liu
遜 Sun
遞 Ti
遠 Yien
遝 Táp

11

遣 K'ien
遨 Ngau
適 Sek
遭 Chau
遮 Chia *Che*
遯 T'un
遲 Ch'i
遵 Chun
遷 Ch'ien

12

選 Suan
遶 Jio
遺 Jui
遼 Lio
遽 Kù
避 Pi
邀 Hio
邁 Mai
邂 Hai
還 Hwan
邅 Tán
邇 Jù *Ni*
邊 Pni *Pien*
邋 Lá, *Náp*

160 辛
161 辰
162 辵

162 辵
163 邑
164 酉
165 釆
166 里
167 金

邈 Mio
邏 Ló

—

RADICAL 163.

邑 Ip
邕 Iong
邛 Kʻiong
邦 Páng
邪 Sia *Se*
那 Ná
邠 Pin
邢 H^{n}ia *Heng*
邸 Ki *Ti*
邳 Pʻi
邵 Sio

6

郊 Kau
郎 N^{n}ng *Láng*
郁 Hiok
郝 Hat
郡 Kun
部 Po
郭 Kue, *Kwak*
郵 Sui *Iu*

9

都 To *Tu*
鄂 Ngák
鄉 H^{n}ie *Hiàng*
鄒 Cho *Chu*
鄢 Yien
鄭 T^{n}e *Teng*
鄙 Pʻi
鄧 Teng
鄰 Lin *Lien*
鄹 Cho

—

RADICAL 164.

酉 Iu
酊 Teng
酌 Chiak
酎 Chiu
配 Pʻue *Pui*
酒 Chiu
酖 Tim
酢 Chá *Chau*
酗 Hiong
酥 So *Su*
酤 Ko
酣 Hám

6

酩 Meng
酬 Chʻiu
酧 Chiu
酪 Lok
酵 K^{n}á
酷 Kʻok
酸 S^{n}ng *Suang*
醃 Iam
醇 Tun
醉 Chui
醋 Chʻo *Chu*
醒 Ch^{n}e *Seng*

10

醞 Un
醜 Chʻiu
醢 Hai
醧 Kʻu
醫 Ui *I*
醬 Ch^{n}ie *Chiàng*

12

醮 Chie *Chio*
醴 Li
醯 Hi
醲 Long
醺 Hùn
釀 Jiàng
釂 Chiak
釃 Li
釁 Hien

—

RADICAL 165.

釆 Pien
采 Chʻai
釋 Sek

—

RADICAL 166.

里 Li
重 Teng
野 Ia *E*
量 Nie *Liàng*
釐 Li

—

RADICAL 167.

金 Kim
釘 Teng
釜 Hu
針 Chám
釣 T^{n}ie *Tio*
釵 Tʻoi *Chai*
釧 Hun
釬 Kán

4

鈞 Kùn
釿 Kùn
鈀 Pe
鈇 Hu
鈍 Tun
鈎 Kau
鈐 Ngim
鈒 Kip
鈕 Niu
鈔 Sua *Sá*

5

鈴 Long
鉎 S^{n}e
鉢 Pʻwat
鈹 Pʻi
鉅 Kù
鉈 Tó *Tek*
鈸 Pwat
鈿 Tʻien
鉋 Pʻau
鉞 Sut *Wat*

鉗 K'iam
鉛 In
鉢 Pua, *Pun*
鉤 Kau
鉄 T'iet
鉑 Pó, *Pok*

6

鉸 Ká *Kau*
鉺 Ji
銀 Ngùn
銃 Ch'eng *Chong*
銓 Chuan
銅 Táng *Tong*
銑 Sien
銚 Tó
銖 Chu
鉼 Páng
銘 Meng
銜 Hám

7

銲 Hán
銷 Sio
鋭 Jue *Jui*
鋏 Kiap
銼 Ch'ó
鋤 Ch'ó
鋒 Hong
鋃 Lang *Liàng*
鋪 Po *Pu*

8

鋷 Chu
錮 Ku
鋸 Kù
鋼 K^{n}ng *Kúng*
錄 Lok
錐 Chui
錘 Sui
錙 Chù
銹 Siu *Iu*
錠 T^{n}ia *Teng*
錦 Kim
錢 Ch^{n}i *Chien*
錫 Sia, *Sek*
錯 Ch'ó *Chu*

9

鍊 Lien
鍈 Eng
鍼 Chám
鍾 Cheng
鎭 Tin
鍋 Ue *Hwai*
鍛 Tuan
錨 Mio
鍍 To *Tu*
鍬 Ch'iu
鍤 Chá,
鑒 Kám
鍵 Kien

10

鎔 I^{n}e
鎰 Ek *It*
鏤 Lu
鎖 Só
鎗 Ch'^{n}ie *Chiàng*
鎈 Ch'ó
鎚 T'ui
鎛 P'ák
鎧 K'ai

11

鏖 Tek
鏗 Kien
鏢 Pio
鏝 Mua *Muan*
鏟 Ch'án
鏡 K^{n}ia *Keng*
鏈 Lien
鏨 Chám

12

鏽 Siu
鐐 Lio
鐃 Ngio
鐓 Tun
鐏 Chun
鐖 Ki
鐘 Cheng *Chong*
鐙 Teng

13

鐫 Chun
鐲 Chok
鐺 Táng
鐮 Liam
鐵 T'i *T'iet*
鐶 Hwan
鐸 Tát *Tok*
鑑 Kám
鐳 Lui
鑌 Pin *Pien*
鑄 Chu
鑛 Kwang
鑊 Hu

15

鑚 Ch^{n}ng *Chán*
鏠 Pong
鑠 Yiak
鑢 Liu *Lù*
鑰 Yiak
鑪 Lo *Lu*
鑱 Chám
鑲 S^{n}ie *Siàng*

18

鑴 Chui
鑵 Kán
鑷 Niap
鑼 Ló
鑽 Ch^{n}ng *Cháng*
鑿 Ch'ák *Chek*
鑾 Luan

RADICAL 168.

長 T^{n}ie *Chiàng*

RADICAL 169.

門 M^{n}ng *Bue*
閂 Ch'^{n}ua *Chuan*
閃 Siam
閑 Hán

167 金
168 長
169 門

169 門
170 阜
171 隶
172 隹

閉 Pi
閔 Mieng
閎 Hong
開 K‘ui, *K‘ai*
閏 Jun
閒 O^{n}i, Hien, *Kán*
閑 O^{n}i, *Hien*
間 K^{n}oi, *Kán*

5

閙 Lau
閟 Pi
閶 T‘áng
閘 Ch‘á,
閤 K‘áp
閧 Hong
閣 Kó, *Kok*
閥 Hwat
閨 Kui
閩 Mán

7

閫 K‘un
閭 Lù
閱 Luat
閹 Iam
閻 Ngám, *Ngiam*

閾 Hok
閽 Hun

9

闋 K‘ai, *Kiet*
闈 Ui
闇 Á'm
闌 Lán
闍 Tu
闊 K‘wa, *Kwat*

10

闒 T‘áp
闃 H^{n}iu
闑 Ngiak
闘 To, *Tu*
闔 K‘áp
闕 Kue, *Kiet*
闖 Ch‘uang
闚 Kui
闤 Hwan
關 Kwan
闟 Hip
闞 K‘ám
闢 P‘ek
闡 Ch‘ien
闥 T‘át

RADICAL 170.

阜 Hu
阡 Ch‘ien
阱 Ch^{n}e, *Cheng*
防 Hwang
阨 E, *Ek*
阝及 K‘ip
阮 Ngwan

5

阻 Chó, *Chu*
阼 Chu
陂 Pó, *Pi*
阿 A', *O'*
陀 T‘ó
附 Hu
陋 Lo
陌 Mek
降 Háng
限 Hán

7

陛 Pi
陜 Hiap, *Siam*
陞 Seng
陟 T‘ek
院 I^{n}, *Yien*
陣 Tin

除 Tù, *Ch‘u*

8

陪 Pue, *Pai*
陲 Sui
陬 Cho, *Chu*
陰 Im
陳 Tin, *Chin*
陵 Leng
陴 Pui, *Pi*
陶 Ie, *Io*
陷 Hám
陸 Lek, *Lok*

9

隄 Toi, *Ti*
隋 Sui
陽 Iàng
隍 Hwang
陰 Im
隅 Ngó, *I*
隆 Long
隊 Tui
階 Koi, *Kai*

10

隔 Ke, *Kek*
隕 Un

隘 Oi, *Ai*
隙 K‘ia, *K‘iak*
際 Chi
障 Chiàng

12

隤 Kui
隣 Lin, *Lien*
隨 Sui
險 Hiam
隧 Tui
隰 Sip
隱 Ùn
隴 Leng

RADICAL 171.

隶 Tai
隸 Tai
隷 Ti

RADICAL 172.

隹 Chui
隻 Chia, *Chek*
集 Sun, *Chun*
雀 Ch‘iak
雁 Ngán, *Yien*
雄 Hiong
雅 Ngia, *Nye*

集 Chip
雇 Ko
雉 Ti
雌 Chʻù
雎 Chui
雋 Chun
雍 Iong

8

雕 Tio
雖 Sui
雟 Chun
雙 Sáng *Suang*
雛 Chʻu
雝 Iong
雜 Cháp
雞 Koi *Ki*
離 Li
難 Lán

RADICAL 173.

雨 Ho
雪 Só *Sok*
雩 U
雲 Hun *In*
零 Lán
雷 Lui
雹 Pʻák *Pau*
電 Tien

6

需 Su
震 Chin
霆 Tʻeng
霄 Sio
霂 Mok
霉 Bue *Mui*
霍 Kʻák
霈 Pʻai
霑 Tiam
霏 Hui
霓 Ngi
霎 Siap
霖 Lim

9

霜 S^{u}ng *Suang*
霪 Im
霞 Hia
霧 Bu
霰 Sán

13

霸 Pá
靆 Tai
露 Lo *Lu*
霹 Pʻek
霽 Chi
霿 Mong
靂 Le, *Lek*
靈 Leng
靄 Ai

RADICAL 174.

青 Ch^{ʻn}e *Cheng*
靖 Cheng
靚 Ch^{n}ia
靛 T^{n}oi *Teng*
靜 Ch^{n}e *Cheng*

RADICAL 175.

非 Hui
靠 Ko
靡 Mi

RADICAL 176.

面 Min *Mien*
靦 Tien
靨 Lien *Lám*

RADICAL 177.

革 Kek
靫 Chiak
靴 Hia
靸 Kip
鞅 Iàng
鞋 Oi *Hia*
鞏 Kiong
鞍 U^{n}a *A'n*
鞘 S^{n}ie *Sio*

8

鞠 Kiok
鞱 Tʻau
鞦 Chʻiu
鞭 Pien
鞮 Tʻi
鞿 Ki
鞶 Pʻwan
韂 Siam
韁 K^{n}ie *Kiàng*
韆 Chʻien

RADICAL 178.

韋 Ui
韌 Jim
韜 Tau
韒 Sio
韓 Hán
韘 Tiap
韞 Un
韙 Ui
韜 Tʻau

RADICAL 179.

韭 Kui
韮 Hui

RADICAL 180.

音 Im
韶 Sio
韹 K^{n}ie *Kong*
韻 Un
響 Hiàng

RADICAL 181.

頁 Hie, *Hiap*
頂 Teng
頃 Kʻwang
項 Háng
順 Sun
須 Su
頑 Hùn
預 Uʼ

172 隹
173 雨
174 青
175 非
176 面
177 革
178 韋
179 韭
180 音
181 頁

181 頁
182 風
183 飛
184 食
185 首
186 香
187 馬

頑 Ngwan
頌 Song
頒 Pán
頊 Hiok
頓 Tun

5

頗 Pʻó
領 Nia *Leng*
頞 Áʼn
頤 Hi
頭 Tʻau *Tiu*
頰 Kiap *Hiap*
頲 Tʻeng
頷 Hám
頸 K^{n}e *Á'm*
頹 Tʻue

8

顆 Ló
頻 Pʻin
顋 Sai *Sù*
顒 Iong
顓 Chuan
題 Toi *Ti*
額 Hia,
顥 Hau
顏 Ngwan *Yien*

10

願 Ngwan *Yien*
顙 Suang
顛 Tien
類 Lui
顥 Hau
顧 Ku
顓 Chong
顫 Chien
顯 Hien
顰 Pʻin
顱 Lu

RADICAL 182.

風 Hwang *Hong*
颯 Sáp
颶 Ku
颺 Iàng
颻 Io
飄 Pʻio
飃 Pʻio

RADICAL 183.

飛 Pue *Hui*

RADICAL 184.

食 Chia, *Sù*
飡 Sun *Chʻán*
飢 Ki
飦 Kán
飧 Sun
飫 Uʻ *Ok*
飭 Tʻek
飪 Im
飲 Im
飯 P^{u}ng *Hwan*

6

飼 Chʻi *Si*
飴 I
飽 Pá *Pán*
飾 Sek
餂 Chi
餅 P^{n}ia *Peng*
餉 Hiàng
餌 Ji *Ju*
餁 Im
養 Iàng

7

餗 Sok
餐 Chʻán
餕 Chun
餒 Nue *Nui*
餓 Gó *Ngó*
餔 Po *Pu*
餘 Uʻ *I*
餞 Chien
館 Kwan
餧 Ui

8

餪 Nuan
餬 Hu
餵 Ui
餲 Ai
餱 Ho
饉 Kùn
餼 Kʻi *Kai*
餐 Chʻán
饈 Siu
饅 Mua *Muan*
餽 Kui

12

饋 Kui
饌 Chuan
饐 I
饍 Sien
饑 Ki
饒 Jio
饕 Hau
饔 Iong
饗 Hiàng
饘 Tʻán
饜 Iam

RADICAL 185.

首 Siu

RADICAL 186.

香 H^{n}ie *Hiáng*
馥 Hiok
馨 Heng

RADICAL 187.

馬 Be *Má*
馭 Gù *I*
馳 Chʻi
馴 Hùn
馹 Ia, *Ek*
駁 Pó, *Pák*

5

駒 Ku
駑 Nó

海上絲綢之路文獻集成 科技與文化編

駘 T'ai
馮 Me, *Má*
駕 Ke, *Kia*
駐 Ch'u
駝 Tó, *Tó*
駙 Hu
駛 Sai, *Sù*
駟 Sù

7

駾 T'ue
駭 Hai
駢 Pin, *Peng*
駱 Ló, *Lok*
駏 K'áng
駿 Chun
騭 Chit, *Tek*
騂 Sin
騜 Hwang

8

騐 Ngiam
騧 Ua
騎 K'ia, *Ki*
騑 Hui
騋 Lai
騙 P'ien

騁 P'eng
騖 Bu
騤 K'ui

10

騮 Liu
騰 T'eng
騫 K'ien
騶 Ch'o, *Chu*
騷 Sau
騸 S^{n}i, *Seng*
騣 Cháng, *Chong*
驄 Chong
驃 P'io
驀 Mek
驂 Ch'ám
騾 Ló, *Lu*
驁 Ngau
驅 K'u

12

驊 Hwa
驕 Kio
驚 K^{n}ia, *Keng*
驗 Ngiam
驛 Ia, *Ek*
驟 Cho
驢 Lù

驥 Ki
驤 Siàng
驪 Li

RADICAL 188.

骨 Kut
骭 Kán
骰 Tau
骷 Ko, *Ku*
骸 Hai
骹 Kau
髆 Hu
骾 Nge, *Keng*
髀 Pi
髁 Kó
髑 Tek
䯧 Hat
髏 Lu
髓 Ch'ue
體 T'oi, *Ti*
髖 Kwan

RADICAL 189.

高 Kau
豪 Hau

RADICAL 190.

髟 Hwat, *Pio*
髡 K'un
髣 Hwang
髯 Jiam
髢 Ti
髦 Mau
髫 Sio, *Tio*
髮 Hwat
髲 Pue, *Pi*
髭 Chù
髴 Hut
髸 Káng
髻 Kue, *Ki*
鬃 Cháng, *Chong*
鬂 Pin, *Pien*
鬆 Sáng, *Song*
鬍 Hu
鬋 Chien
鬐 Ki
鬚 Ch'iu, *Su*
鬔 Pong
鬣 Liet
鬟 Hwan

鬢 Pin, *Pien*
鬤 Siàng

RADICAL 191.

鬥 To
鬦 Tau
鬧 Lau
鬨 Hong
鬩 Ngi
鬪 To
鬭 To
鬮 鬫 } K'au

RADICAL 192.

鬯 T'iàng
鬱 Ut

RADICAL 193.

鬲 Kek
鬻 Yok

RADICAL 194.

鬼 Kui
魁 K'ue
魂 Hun
魅 Mue, *Mui*
魄 Pek

187 馬
188 骨
189 高
190 髟
191 門
192 鬯
193 鬲

194 鬼

魋 T'ue
魌 Ki
魏 Tue *Ngui*
魍 Buang
魎 Liàng
魑 Li
魔 Mó
魘 Iam

195 魚

RADICAL 195.

魚 Hù *I*
魯 Lu
魠 Toi *Ti*
鮫 Kau
鮀 T'ó
鮑 Páu

6

鮭 Koi *Ua*
鮞 Ni
鮮 Ch'^{n}i *Sien*
鯆 Po *Hu*
鯇 Wan
鯀 K'un
鯉 Li
䱍 Láng
䱂 Ni

鯊 } 鯊 } Sua *Sá*

8

鯤 Kun
鯢 Ngi
鯨 K'eng
鯪 Lin
鯧 Chiàng
鯬 Li
鰍 Chiu
鰓 Sai *Sù*
鯷 Ti

10

鰥 Kwan
鰢 Má
䲔 Cháng
鰲 Ngau
鰻 Mua *Muan*
鰾 Pio
鰽 Chó *Chau*
鱆 Chiàng

12

鱉 Pi, *Piet*
鱟 Hau
鱓 Tán *Sien*
鱔 Sien

鱗 Lán
鱲 Náp
鱷 Ngák
鱺 Li
鱸 Lo

196 鳥

RADICAL 196.

鳥 Chio *Nio*
鳧 Hu
鳩 K'iu
鳲 Si
鳳 Hong
鳴 Meng
鳶 Yien
鴂 Kwat
鴆 Tim
鴈 Ngán *Yien*
鴉 A'

5

鴒 Leng
鴞 Hau
鴛 Wan
鴕 T'ó
鴟 Ch'i
鴜 Ch'u
鴣 Ko *Ku*
鴨 A', *A'p*
鴦 Ie *Iàng*

6

鴻 Hong
鴿 K'áp
鵁 Kau
鵑 Kien
鴯 Jù
䳒 Jong
鵂 Hiu
鵙 Kwak
鵝 Gó *Ngó*
鵠 K'ok
鵳 Kien

8

鵡 Bu
鶄 Ch^{n}e *Cheng*
鵪 Iam
鵩 Hok
鵬 P'eng
鵰 Tiu *Chiu*
鵲 Chiak
鶃 Ngi
鶽 Sun *Ch'un*
鶊 K^{n}e *Keng*

9

鶖 Chiu
鶚 Ngák
鶩 Bu
鶬 Cháng

10

鷃 A'n
鶯 Eng
鶮 Kó
鶺 Chit
鶴 Hó,
鶷 Hát
鷥 Si *Chù*
鷄 Koi *Ki*

11

鷓 Chia *Che*
鷗 O *U*
鷑 Kit *Kiet*
鷦 Chio
鷯 Lio
鷲 Chiu
鷳 Hien

13

鷫 Su
鷹 Eng
鷿 Pek
鶡 Kát *Hat*

鷺 Lu
鸇 Chien
14
鸓 Lui
鸖 Kák
鸚 Eng
鸛 Kwan *Hwan*
鸞 Luan
鸝 Li

———

RADICAL 197.

鹵 Lu
鹹 Kiam *Ham*
鹽 Iam
鹼 Kán

———

RADICAL 198.

鹿 Tek *Lok*
麀 Hiu
麃 P'io
麋 Mi
麌 Go *U*
麑 Ngi
麓 Lok
麒 K'i
麕 K'un
麖 Kⁿia *Keng*
麗 Li
麚 Kia
麛 Ni
麝 Sia *Se*
麞 Chiàng
麟 Lin *Lán*
麤 Ch'o *Chu*

———

RADICAL 199.

麥 Be, *Mek*
麧 Kák
麴 Kiok
麵 Mi *Mien*

———

RADICAL 200.

麻 Mua *Mó*
麽 Mó
麾 Hui

———

RADICAL 201.

黃 Ng *Hwang*
黌 Ng *Hwang*

———

RADICAL 202.

黍 Su
黎 Li
黏 Niam

———

RADICAL 203.

黑 Hek
䵟 Kán
黔 Ngim
黛 Tai
默 Mek
黜 Tut
點 Tiam
黨 Táng
黭 Iam
黷 Tok
黶 Lien *Iam*

———

RADICAL 204.

黹 Chi *Hu*
黼 Hu
黻 Hut

———

RADICAL 205.

黽 Mien
黿 Ngwan
鼉 T'ó
鼈 Pi, *Piet*

———

RADICAL 206.

鼎 Ting *Teng*
鼐 Nai

———

RADICAL 207.

鼓 Ko *Ku*
鼕 Tong
鼗 Tio *T'au*
鼛 Kiu

———

RADICAL 208.

鼠 Ch'ù *Su*
鼢 Hun
鼦 Tio
鼯 Ngó *U'*
鼴 Kien *Iam*

———

RADICAL 209.

鼻 Pⁿi *Pi*
鼾 Hⁿwa

———

RADICAL 210.

齊 Ch'i
齋 Che *Chai*
齎 Chi

———

RADICAL 211.

齒 Ch'i
齕 Ngùt
齗 Tᵘng
齝 Si
齠 Tio
齡 Leng
齧 Ngùt *Ngiet*
𪗋 K'iet
齦 Ngùn
齩 Ká *Kau*
齪 Ch'ok
䶫 Hám
齷 Ok

———

RADICAL 212.

龍 Leng *Long*
龐 Márg
龕 K'ám
龔 Kiong

———

RADICAL 213.

龜 Ku
鼈 Pi, *Piet*

———

RADICAL 214.

龠 Yiak
龡 Ch'ue
龢 Hu
龥 Ju

196 鳥 197 鹵 198 鹿 199 麥 200 麻 201 黃 202 黍 203 黑 204 黹 205 黽 206 鼎 207 鼓 208 鼠 209 鼻 210 齊 211 齒 212 龍 213 龜 214 龠

海上絲綢之路文獻集成

總主編　陳支平　陳春聲

科技與文化編 90

主編　王揚宗　葉　農

海峽出版發行集團
THE STRAITS PUBLISHING & DISTRIBUTING GROUP
福建人民出版社

本册目次

福州方言拼音字典［一］

（*An Alphabetic Dictionary of the Chinese Language in the Foochow Dialect*）

〔美〕麥利和（Robert Samuel Maclay）　摩嘉立（Caleb Cook Baldwin）编

《福州方言拼音字典》，美國麥利和、摩嘉立編。麥利和（Robert Samuel Maclay，一八二四—一九〇七），美國美以美會傳教士。生於美國賓夕法尼亞州，一八四七年來華，次年至福州，一八七一年赴日，一八八一年在福州創辦鶴齡英華書院，一八八七年返美。摩嘉立（Caleb Cook Baldwin，一八二〇—一九一一），美國公理會傳教士。生於美國新澤西州，一八四八年來華，居福州達半世紀，一八九五年返美。是書前有使用説明，詳述注音法、聲調、連讀變調，並附聲韻調配合表。正文收文言字詞及土白九千三百九十，各頁下方録詞語，計三萬餘條。末附部首索引。據一八七〇年福州版影印。

福州方言拼音字典

ALPHABETIC DICTIONARY

OF THE

CHINESE LANGUAGE

IN THE FOOCHOW DIALECT.

BY

REV. R. S. MACLAY, D. D.
Of the Methodist Episcopal Mission;
AND
REV. C. C. BALDWIN, A. M.
Of the American Board Mission.

:o:

FOOCHOW:
METHODIST EPISCOPAL MISSION PRESS.
1870.

上古結繩而治後世聖人易之以書契

PREFACE.

As two names appear on the title-page of this dictionary, it is proper to indicate our respective shares in its preparation; and the more so, as it is due to the Rev. Mr. Baldwin to state that the larger portion of the labor of authorship has been freely performed by him, and that to his correct scholarship, extensive knowledge of the Foochow dialect, and indomitable perseverance, the dictionary is mainly indebted for the degree of thoroughness and accuracy it may possess. The manuscript for that portion of the dictionary comprised in pp. 1—631 was originally prepared by myself, but it was subsequently very carefully revised and improved by Mr. Baldwin, and a considerable portion of it (pp. 403—631) was entirely re-written by him. The portion comprised in pp. 632—1014, together with the Introduction to the dictionary, was prepared by Mr. Baldwin, and, as it was impracticable for me to revise his manuscript, it was printed just as it came from his hands. The general plan of the work and a responsibility for the whole are mine.

The design and scope of the dictionary are so fully set forth in the Introduction, given on subsequent pages, that it is unnecessary to make any extended remarks on the subject in this place. The aim has been to present a work that shall at once illustrate the Foochow dialect, and prove a valuable help to all students of the Chinese language. The definitions of the characters, and a large number of the phrases given under them, will apply equally well to any dialect through which the student seeks to acquire a knowledge of the general written language of China. Everything in the work that is peculiar to the Foochow dialect has been carefully marked, so that the student cannot be misled on this point. The large number of Romanized words appearing in the dictionary, and for which the written language furnishes no characters, is an interesting feature of this dialect, and indicates that modern Chinese thought is outgrowing the stereotyped forms of this ancient language. The same feature appears in other dialects.

It is difficult to assign exact geographical limits to the Foochow dialect, or to estimate with precision the amount of the population by whom it is spoken. In Foochow city, the capital of the Fookien province, and throughout the Foochow and Fooning prefectures, it is, with considerable variations, the vernacular of the people. Beyond these limits, it is spoken only by the Foochow merchants, artisans, &c. &c. who reside in most of the important cities of Fookien. Regarding Foochow city as the center of the dialect, we may say that it extends, *eastward* to the sea, a distance of about thirty miles; *northward*, to the Chehkiang province, two hundred miles; *westward*, to the Yenping prefecture, one hundred miles; and *southward*, to the Hinghwa prefecture, seventy miles. It is probable the dialect is spoken by five millions of people. The only native work on the dialect is a small Tonic dictionary, named the *Paik Ing* (Eight Sounds), and containing about 10,000 characters, which are distributed, according to their tones, under what are called the Initials and Finals of the dialect. The work is noticed more at length in the Introduction to this dictionary.

In the preparation of this dictionary, the results of the labors of Drs. Morrison, Medhurst, and Williams, in Anglo-Chinese lexicography, have been freely availed of, and this general acknowledgement of indebtedness is gratefully made. Sincere thanks are tendered to those members of the Missionary community in Foochow who have, in many ways, rendered valuable assistance—especially to the Rev. S. L. Baldwin, and Rev. L. N. Wheeler, whose opportune help made it possible to publish the work in Foochow, and under whose consecutive superintendence five hundred pages of it were printed. A large portion of the Mandarin sounds, which appear under the leading characters in the dictionary, were kindly furnished by Walter T. Lay

Esqr. of the Imperial Maritime Customs: Mr. Lay, however, is not responsible for any typographic errors in this department, as it was impossible for him to correct the proof-sheets while the work was passing through the press.

A brief list of Additions is placed at the end of the dictionary proper, and in it are given some additional uses of characters, and a few Romanized words and phrases which do not appear in the body of the work. A table of Corrections is given at the close of the volume, in which the more important errors occurring in the dictionary have been noted: the errors not corrected in the table are thought to be of an unimportant character, and their appropriate correction is readily suggested by the connection in which they occur. In the Index of Characters, where brackets have been used, it will be noticed that frequently the same character is repeated once or twice. In these instances the character has different tones which affect its meaning. The figures indicate where each form is found.

The printing of the dictionary, in view of the limited and imperfect appliances at command, has been a difficult and tedious task: the type-setting and press-work have been performed by Chinese hands; and, during the printing of the larger portion of the work, the supervision of the press and the drudgery of correcting the first "proofs", have unavoidably devolved on myself. A consideration of these circumstances will, perhaps, mitigate the severity of criticism, with regard to the defects and errors that may be detected in the work. The expenses of publication have been defrayed by the Mission Press connected with the Foochow Mission of the Methodist Episcopal Church, U. S. A.; and it is hoped that the proceeds arising from the sale of the book may reimburse the Office for the the heavy outlay.

The lexicographic elucidation of, at least, the more prominent dialects of China may, perhaps, be regarded as a pressing demand of the times. A knowledge of the proverbs, peculiar idioms, and common speech of a people so numerous as the Chinese will throw important light on questions connected with the general laws of language; and is absolutely necessary to all who seek to influence Chinese mind, or form a correct estimate of Chinese character. The materials for the following dictionary have gradually accumulated in our hands, from various sources, during twenty years of ordinary study and labor as missionaries. It has been our cherished hope that ultimately they might assume a permanent form, so as to be of service to others who may follow us in the study and use of the Chinese language; and it is with much satisfaction that we are now permitted, in the providence of God, to realize that hope: at the same time we recognize the entire truthfulness of Dr. Johnson's remark, that while "every other author may aspire to praise, the lexicographer can only hope to escape reproach".

The work is now offered to the public, with the earnest desire that it may be useful to students of the Chinese language; that it may tend to facilitate friendly intercourse between Western nations and China; and, above all, that it may promote the cause of Christian Missions among the Chinese.

R. S. MACLAY.

FOOCHOW, JUNE 14th 1870.

INTRODUCTION.

—:o:—

The design of this Dictionary is to assist the student in the acquisition both of the classic or written, and the vernacular or spoken, forms of the Foochow dialect. The former in style, idiom, and usage often differs widely from the latter. In orthography however all the tables of initials, finals, and words are precisely the same in both forms; and many single words and phrases that are strictly classic or common book-phrases are also used in the spoken language. A considerable part of such phrases are however confined to the literary class of the people. This has led some to style the more refined terms teachers' or scholars' patois. The common use of some phrases in the reading and colloquial styles appears in the plan of the work. It is farther evident that a fair proportion of the phrases in Chinese character at the foot of the page, as also the definitions of the leading classic or lexicographic characters are the common property of the mandarin and local dialects of the empire. It is hoped therefore that this volume will be of general use to students of the Chinese language.

The work contains 928 different syllabic divisions or sections, as written in Roman letters and numbered in the text. This of course does not include all the distinctions arising from difference in tone. The number of leading classic and colloquial characters, including the abbreviated and duplicate or alternate forms, and those repeated under different sounds is 9390. The number of paragraphs with one or more leading characters is 8311, and the number introduced by Romanized colloquial words, without Chinese characters to represent them, is 1242, making the whole number of paragraphs in the Chinese and English text 9553. Besides these two classes, some characters are found in the phrases at the foot of the page, which do not appear in the main text as leading characters. In such cases the meaning of the character appears in the *definition of the phrase* where its Romanized equivalent occurs, and this is often the only, or the most important, meaning it ever has in the language. There are also occasional instances of unimportant colloquial words or particles, in combination with other words in the Romanized phrases, which do not appear independently as leading words.

The arrangement of the work is alphabetic, excepting that the aspirate and composite initials are treated as single and independent letters. The order then is *a*, *ch*, *ch'*, *e*, *h*, *i*, *k*, *k'*, *l*, *m*, *n*, *ng*, *o*, *p*, *p'*, *s*, *t*, *t'*, *u*, *w*, *y*. The Chinese characters are arranged in the order of the tones, when the Romanized spelling for their sounds is the same. The *mandarin* sounds are in general according to Wade's system, and are placed under the characters. The general definitions are on the authority of Kanghi's Imperial Dictionary and native authors, as interpreted by teachers and lexicographers. The colloquial or unauthorized meanings are always clearly distinguished. Sometimes an additional reading of a leading character is given *before* the general definitions, when its definitions are the same in the different readings. When they are different, both the reading and definitions are usually given at the close of the paragraph or in the proper alphabetic place in the book. In the latter case reference is made to the different sound at the *end* of the general definitions.

The standard authority among native scholars for the readings of characters, as well as for their meanings, is Kanghi's Dictionary. The *Paik Ing*, a native tonic dictionary, is not classic authority, though prized as a convenient Manual of the Rudiments of this dialect and as furnishing brief definitions of characters. Usage however often disregards the readings of both these dictionaries. And in the present work such usage is frequently followed in assigning a character its Romanized alphabetic place, while the reading discarded by native usage is noted in the phrase "Read....in the dictionaries" immediately following the character. The readings of the *Paik Ing* are mostly used to introduce *colloquial* words and phrases. But even in this respect there is no strict rule followed by native teachers. They use much liberty, often choosing, either for its sound or its sense, some *classic* character, simpler than the one found in the *Paik Ing*.

The phrases are distinguished into three classes: (1) those following the general definitions are classic or book phrases; (2) those under COM., are *common* to the written and spoken languages, and include many refined terms and some epistolary phrases; (3) those under COLL., are such as, by reason of idiom, meaning, or colloquial characters used wholly or partly to represent them, may be more properly classed as *colloquial* phrases. The number of phrases in this dictionary is estimated at 30,000 to 35,000, of which $\frac{2}{3}$ or $\frac{3}{4}$ are comprised in the last two classes above mentioned, and are consequently used with more or less frequency in the ordinary business of life.

A slight acquaintance with the language will convince the student of the impossiblity of making a thorough and perfect distinction of the phrases into such classes. The literary tastes, knowledge, mental habits, and modes of speaking of different native teachers, as also the conceptions of the same teacher at different times, all tend to make the limits of the three classes somewhat variable, as found by actual experience in our work. Still there is ground for the distinction, and we hope that it will be useful in showing generally what phrases are spoken and what are not.

It should also be remarked in reference to the definitions of many of the colloquial phrases that there is no very fixed standard by which to test them. Usage varies to some extent in different places, while teachers and others often fail to agree in their explanations. This is peculiarly the case in reference to proverbial phrases. Some are universally known and used. Others are local, and others still are differently explained and applied in different localities.

ORTHOGRAPHY.

The system of orthography adopted in this Dictionary is essentially that known as the system of Sir William Jones. It was used in Romanizing the languages of India and the Pacific Islands, and the dialects of the North American Indians.

VOWELS.

1. *a*, as in *far, father*.
2. *á*, ,, ,, *care, fair*, or as *e* in *there*.
3. *ă*, ,, ,, *hat, sat, fathom*.
4. *e*, ,, ,, *they, prey*, or as *a* in *name*.
5. *é*, ,, ,, *met, seven, error*.
6. *ĕ*, ,, ,, *her*, or as *i* in *bird*.
7. *i*, ,, ,, *machine*.
8. *í*, ,, ,, *pin*, or as the second *i* in *infinite*.
9. *o*, ,, ,, *no, note, report*.
10. *ó*, ,, ,, *for, lord*, or as *a* in *fall*.
11. *u*, ,, ,, *bull*, but oftener as *o* in *move*, or *oo* in school.
12. *ü*, ,, ,, the French *l'une, jeune*.

DIPHTHONGS in the first tone.

1. *ai*, as in *aisle, aye, while*.
2. *au*, ,, *ow* in *now, howl*.
3. *eu*,
4. *iă*,
5. *ié*,
6. *io*, } have the sounds of the component vowels.
7. *iu*, as *ew* in *pew, chew*.
8. *oi*, has the sound of the component vowels.

TRIPHTHONG in the first tone.

1. *ieu*, has the sound of the component vowels.

CONSONANTS.

1. *ch*, as in church.
2. *ch'*, the aspirate *ch*, or the same as *ch* with an additional *h*, which is always represented by the Greek *spiritus asper*, or mark of rough breathing.
3. *h*, as in *hand* at the beginning of words, while at the end it is not fully enunciated, but marks an abrupt closing of the vocal organs.

B

4. *k*, as in *king* at the beginning of words, while at the end it is a suppressed *k* sound, an (like the *h*) marks an abrupt closing of the vocal organs.
5. *k'*, the aspirate *k*.
6. *l*, as in *lay*.
7. *m*, ,, ,, *may*.
8. *n*, ,, ,, *nay*.
9. *ng*, ,, ,, *singing*, both at the beginning and end of words.
10. *p*, ,, ,, *pay*.
11. *p'*, the aspirate *p*.
12. *s*, as in *say*.
13. *t*, ,, ,, *tame*.
14. *t'*, the aspirate *t*.
15. *w*, as in *want*, *wing*, *swan*, in the beginning and middle of words.
16. *y*, as in *yore*.

The native standard of pronunciation is a work called 戚林八音合訂 *Ch'ek Ling Paik Ing Hak Teng* or more simply the *Paik Ing*, or Eight Tone Book. As seen from the full title it is a compilation of the works of two authors, *Ch'ek* and *Ling*. The page is divided by a horizontal line. The lower section is by *Ling*, and the characters are arranged by a system of 20 initials and 35 finals. As a dictionary, it is somewhat more comprehensive than the upper part, but it is not used as a standard of pronunciation. The upper section is ascribed originally to *Ch'ek* (a military chieftain of the Ming dynasty, known familiarly as 戚叅將 *Ch'ek ch'ang chiong)*, and is the only standard of pronunciation for the Foochow dialect. It is a dictiionary in which all the characters are systematically arranged according to their sounds. Each simple word has three elements, an nitial sound, a final sound, and a tone. The initials are termed *che t'au*, word-heads. The finals are termed *che mó*, word-mothers, or fundamental generic sounds. To represent the former, 15 characters, having the 15 different initial sounds, are used. To represent the latter, 33 characters are in like manner employed. The original number was 36, but three of these became obsolete on account of identity in sound with other three in the list. This system of initials, finals, and tones constitutes the alphabet of the language. All the characters of the *Paik Ing* are arranged under the 33 finals, as the leading element or symbol, with the subdivision into 15 classes under each final according to the initial sounds of the characters, and the farther subdivision into 7 classes under each initial according to their tones. In practice, however, it will be found that for a considerable number of possible combinations of the Initials and Finals with their Tonic inflections, there are neither written characters nor colloquial words in this dialect. The above arrangement of characters with their definitions constitutes Chinese Alphabetic Dictionary.

By referring to the Tables below, the student will observe that an *initial* sound is a single consonant or two consonants combined, and that no vowel is ever used as an initial. (Words under the *eng* initial, however, may be regarded as beginning with the vowel of the final sound or with *w* or *y*). It is also seen that a *final* sound consists of a vowel or vowels, sometimes preceded by *w* or *y*, and sometimes followed by *h*, *k*, or *ng*.

TONES.

The tonic marks belong properly to the Romanized orthography of the language, as the tone is always an essential part of the word. In theory and as commonly spoken of, there are eight tones in this dialect, but practically only seven, as the second and sixth are identical, and the characters and spoken words having this peculiarity of sound are invariably referred to the second tone. The tonic marks are the same as those used in Williams' Tonic Dictionary. They consist of semicircles, and semicircles combined with horizontal strokes. Their position at the corners of characters and words indicates the tone, as seen in the following diagram:—

1.	2.	3.	4.	5.	6.	7.	8.
꜀丹	꜂胆	旦꜄	答꜆	꜁談	꜂胆	淡꜅	達꜇
꜀Tang.	꜂Tang.	Tang꜄.	Tak꜆.	꜁Tang.	꜂Tang.	Tang꜅	Tak꜇.

The poetical division of the tones is into 平聲 ꜁*ping* ꜀*siăng*, the even tones, and 仄聲 *chah*꜆ ꜀*siăng*, the deflected or oblique tones. The *first* and *fifth* tones belong to the former, and all the others to the latter class.

The tones are now commonly distinguished into two orders or grades, 上聲 *siong*² ꜀*siăng*, the *upper* or primary tones, and 下聲 *ha*² ꜀*siăng*, the *lower* or secondary tones. They are as follows:—

1. 上平 *siong*² ꜀*ping*, the upper even tone.
2. 上上 *siong*² ꜂*siong*, or *siong*² *siong*², the upper rising tone.
3. 上去 *siong*² *k'ëü*꜄, the upper departing or diminishing tone.
4. 上入 *siong*² *ik*꜇ " " entering or abrupt tone.
5. 下平 *ha*² ꜁*ping*, the lower even tone.
6. 下上 *ha*² ꜂*siong*, or *ha*² *siong*², the lower rising tone.
7. 下去 *ha*² *k'ëü*꜅ the lower departing or diminishing tone.
8. 下入 *ha*² *ik*꜇ " " entering or abrupt tone.

Description of the tones. The names given to the tones above are merely translations of the Chinese terms and furnish a very imperfect idea of their nature. The following very concise, lucid, and scientific description, with diagrams of the tones, is from the pen of Rev. Charles Hartwell of the American Board Mission.

"The tones have five elements, which are pitch, quality of voice, inflection, stress, and time.

The *first* tone has the pitch of a third, is the *head tone* in quality of voice, and is without inflection, without stress, and long in time.

The *second* tone is a minor third below the first, and has the pitch of sharp one. It is near the *orotund* in quality of voice, is without inflection, has the thorough stress, and is long in time.

The *third* tone begins on the pitch of a fifth below—as in diagram No. 1—and gradually rises to the key note. Or, with a consonant initial, begins on the key note of the voice—as in diagram No. 2—drops to a fifth below, and returns to the key note. It is long in time.

The *fourth* tone is like the third in pitch and inflection, but ends abruptly with a strong vanishing stress. It is pronounced more quickly than the third, but is properly long in time, as is shown by its changing to the first and second tones in combination, which are both long tones.

The *fifth* tone, beginning on the fifth of the voice in pitch with a strong radical stress, descends rapidly and is short in time. Sometimes, with consonant initials, it seems to take the form indicated in Diagram No. 2, the stress commencing with the vowel sound.

The *sixth* tone is the same as the second.

The *seventh* tone begins on the key-note of the voice, rises to the pitch of a second with strong emphasis, and descends with thorough stress to about a fifth below. It is long in time.

The *eighth* tone has the pitch of a third, is without inflection, and is short in time. It ends very abruptly, though with less stress than the fourth tone.

DIAGRAMS OF THE FOOCHOW TONES
IN THEIR FULL FORM.

No. 1. *Upper series.*

Lower series.

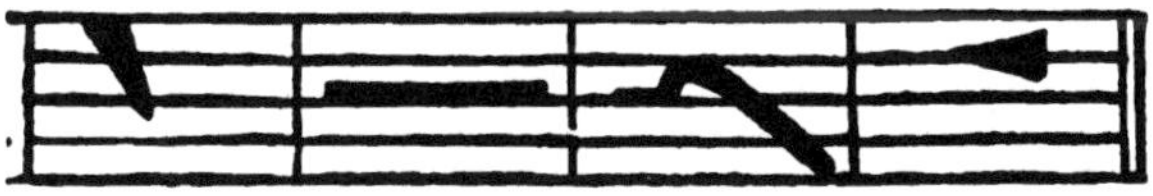

No. 2. Or, *Upper series thus.*

Lower series thus.

In the above diagrams the middle line is designed to represent the key-note of the speaker's voice".

The Rev. M. C. White, M. D., formerly a member of the Methodist Episcopal Mission, Foochow, now a Professor in Yale College, U. S. A. after careful study of the dialect, published the results of his investigations in the Methodist Quarterly Review. We quote his graphic delineation of the tones.—"The *first*, or *primary smooth tone*, called *siong*[3] *ˌping*, is a uniform even sound, enunciated a little above the ordinary speaking key, but neither elevated nor depressed, from the commencement to the close of the word. It is, in this respect, like the enunciation of a note in music; it may, therefore, be called the singing tone, or the musical monotone.

The *second*, or *primary high tone*, called *siong*[3] *ˈsiong*, is enunciated in the ordinary speaking key, and the voice usually falls a note at the close, as at the end of a sentence in unimpassioned discourse. In connected discourse, however, the second tone is sustained, and turns upward, like the vanishing stress of unaccented words in common conversation. In attempting to pronounce the letters *a-e*, we notice that *e* is pronounced either a note higher, or lower, than *a*. So, also, if we take the pains to listen attentively when *a* alone is pronounced, we shall notice that it has its ending, or vanishing movement, turned upward one note; or, if spoken like the close of a sentence, where the voice falls in the usual way, we shall perceive that the vanishing movement of *a* turns downward one note. This is exactly the variety of enunciation, distinguished by the *second*, or *siong*[3] *ˈsiong*, tone in this dialect.

The *third*, or *primary diminishing tone*, called *siong*[3] *k'ëü*[3], is what elocutionists call the *rising third*, and is heard in English on the emphatic word in a direct question, as, "Does it *rain?*" where the voice turns upward, through the interval of two notes of the octave.

The *fourth*, or *primary abrupt tone*, called *siong*[3] *ik*[3] turns the voice upward through the same interval as the *third tone;* but it terminates abruptly, as though the voice was suddenly interrupted in an effort to pronounce a final *h*. In words which, in other tones, end in *ng*, the abrupt close of the fourth tone sounds somewhat like a suppressed or half-uttered *k*, but the clicking sound of the *k* is not heard. If a person should attempt to ask the question, "Can you open the *lock?*" and be suddenly stopped before enunciating the final clicking sound of the *k*, he would give to the last word the *primary abrupt tone*.

The *fifth*, or *secondary smooth tone*, called *ha*[3] *ˌping*, is a quick, forcible enunciation, commencing about two notes above the ordinary key, and suddenly dropping down, at the close, to the key note. It is what is called by elocutionists the *falling third*, and, when emphatic, the *falling fifth*. It is sometimes called the scolding tone. It is heard in a petulant enunciation of the emphatic words in the sentence, "*No!* I'll do no such *thing*."

The *sixth tone* is identical with the *second*, and no words are arranged under it; that is, no *secondary high*, or *rising tone*, has yet been invented in this dialect.

The *seventh* or *secondary diminishing tone*, called *ha' k'ëü'*, is a guttural downward circumflex. It is, in English, expressive of peculiar emphasis, frequently indicating rebuke, scorn, or contempt, as,

" *Whence*, and what art thou, *execrable shape*?
. . . *Back* to thy *punishment*,
•*False fugitive*."

"You wrong me every way; you *wrong* me, Brutus."

The words *very many*, if spoken with forcible emphasis, would also exhibit the tone under consideration.

This is probably the most difficult tone in the language to enunciate correctly, under all circumstances.

The *eighth*, or *secondary abrupt tone*, called *ha' ik*, closes abruptly, like the *fourth tone*, but differs from it by being enunciated on a uniform pitch, a little above the ordinary key. The eighth tone is an abrupt termination of the first tone, in the same manner as the fourth tone is an abrupt termination of the third."

The tones in Combination

When words are enunciated singly, the tones appear in their full form and are marked in their elements and distinctive peculiarities. But in compound terms ornames, and inphrases whose component words are in regimen, or close construction, they assume striking peculiarities, which in some cases involve a radical change. *These peculiarities relate to the first or leading word of the term or phrase.* The only exception that we have noticed is when the following word is a mere suffix or unimportant word, in which case the leading word usually retains its ordinary character as to tone.

The *first* tone (leading) is usually spoken with a very strongly marked accent as in *꜀sing ꜀sang* (teacher), *꜀ki ʻchi* (a foundation).

The *second* tone (leading) has the peculiar inflection noticed above in the description of tones. It sometimes imparts to the voice a slightly sarcastic accent, especially when the following word is in the 3d or 7th tone, as in *ʻsiong sëü'* (reward), *ʻka mó'* (to feign).

The *third* and *seventh* tones (leading) cannot be distinguished form the *first* (leading). They have the same strongly marked accent. This is easily tested in colloquial terms which have no generally accepted character to represent the leading word. Native teachers, in *borrowing* a character for it, often disagree. One, perhaps, will use a first tone, another a third tone, and another a seventh tone, character.

The *fourth* tone (leading), when ending in *h*, has the quality of the *first* tone (leading); when ending in *k*, that of the *second* tone (leading). The following are familiar examples:—*tiăh*, *꜀hwa* (to pluck flowers), *k'ah*, *꜀t'iăng* (a parlor), *tóh*, *ʻkiăng* (a small table) spoken as *꜀tó ʻkiăng* (a small knife); *paik*, *꜀ing* (the eight tones), *ch'ek*, *ngwok*, the seventh month), *t'iék*, *liéng'* (an iron chain).

The *fifth* tone (leading) is spoken in a low or depressed tone of the voice without marked emphasis. The inexperienced student in his effort to speak words of this tone *in regimen*, according to the rules laid down for the tones *in their full form*, misses the sound entirely, and enunciates it like the *first* tone in regimen, saying *ˏniéng pwang'* instead of *ˏniéng pwang'* (a year and a half), *ˏpu sak*ˎ instead of *ˏpu sak*ˎ (a Budhist idol). The distinction is very apparent in the comparative pronunciation of such phrases as *ˏki ʻchi* (a foundation) and *ˏki ʻchi* (chess-men).

The *sixth* tone is obsolete, or the same as the *second*.

The *seventh* tone (leading) is the same as the *third* tone (leading), q. v.

The *eighth* tone (leading) has no marked distinction—as that prevailing in the *fourth* tone—between words ending in *h* and *k*. In the city of Foochow it is enunciated in a depressed tone of voice like the *fifth* tone (leading), while in the suburbs, and probably in the country, it is often heard with a strongly marked accent like the *first* tone (leading). This may be regarded as a kind of country brogue. In phrases having the *second* word in the *fifth* tone, this peculiar brogue is less evident, which is due to the strong radical stress or emphasis pertaining to that tone. Examples,—*pah*ˎ *ʻma* (a white horse), *sioh*ˎ *ˏpi* (a stone tablet), *siăh*ˎ *ˏta* (to drink tea), *pah*ˎ *t'ak*ˎ (the white pagoda), *hok*ˎ *ˏseng*, (a pupil), *hak*ˎ *e'* (agreeable), *nik*ˎ *ˏt'au* (the sun).

Tables.

The following Tables exhibit the system of Romanized Orthography, as used in writing the words or vocables of this dialect. An approximate representation of the sounds is all that can be hoped for in this department. Some students prefer *i* and *u* to *y* and *w* where these occur in the system. Good arguments may be adduced for either set of letters. But it should be observed that such arguments are partial in their application and do not affect the system as a whole, when the tones and their combinations, as well as the vowel and consonant sounds, are considered. It is hoped that the system adopted in this work will be readily acquired and prove serviceable to the student.

TABLE I. The initials and the finals, with the characters used in the Paik Ing to represent them, and their alphabetic value in Roman letters.

NOTE. The 11th initial (eng) denotes simply the absence of any initial consonant, hence the blank on the right in the column of alphabetic values.

FIFTEEN INITIALS.

1	Liu	柳	L
2	Piéng	邊	P
3	Kiu	求	K
4	K'e	氣	K'
5	Tá	低	T
6	P'ó	波	P'
7	T'a	他	T'
8	Cheng	曾	Ch
9	Nik	日	N
10	Si	時	S
11	Eng	鶯	
12	Mung	蒙	M
13	Ngü	語	Ng
14	Ch'ok	出	Ch'
15	Hi	喜	Hi

THIRTY-THREE FINALS.

1	Ch'ung	春	ung	17	Sieu (d)	燒	ieu
2	Hwa	花	wa	18	Ngüng	銀	üng
3	Hiong	香	iong	19	Kong	釭	ong
4	Ch'iu (d)	秋	iu	20	Chi	之	i
5	Sang	山	ang	21	Tëng	東	ëng
6	K'ai	開	ai	22	Kau	郊	au
7	Ka	嘉	a	23	Kwo (b)	過	wo
8	Ping	賓	ing	24	Sá	西	á
9	Hwang	歡	wang	25	Kio (c)	橋	io
10	Kó	歌	ó	26	Kié	雞	ié
11	Sü	須	ü	27	Siăng	聲	iăng
12	Pwí (a)	杯	wí	28	Ch'oi	催	oi
13	Ku	孤	u	29	Ch'ë	初	ë
14	Teng	燈	eng	30	T'iéng	天	iéng
15	Kwong	光	wong	31	K'iă	奇	iă
16	Hwi	輝	wi	32	Wai	歪	wai
				33	Keu	溝	eu

NOTE. Much difficulty is experienced in Romanizing some of the final sounds.

(a) Some would write the *pwí* final *pwe;* others prefer the form *pwoi.*

(b) Some give to the *kwo* final an additional slight *a* or *ë* sound, writing it *kwoa* or *kwoë.*

(c) Some would write the *kio* final *küo;* others prefer the form *kioa* or *kioë.*

Perhaps none of these forms fully represent the required sounds, which are accurately learned only by imitating the native mode of pronunciation.

(d) The vowel sounds of the *ch'iu* and *sieu* finals are often confounded—by teachers as well as others—especially in the suburbs and country. The same remark holds in reference to the *pwi* and *hwi* finals, the tendency being to use *wi* instead of *wí.*

c

TABLE II. Primary syllables or words, forn

Note. Words, composed of the *eng* initial and either of

		Liu 柳	Piéng 邊	Kiu 求	K‘e 氣	Tá 低	P‘ 波
Ch‘ung	春	lung	pung	kung	k‘ung	tung	p‘un
Hwa	花	lwa	pwa	kwa	k‘wa	twa	p‘wa
Hiong	香	liong	piong	kiong	k‘iong	tiong	p‘ion
Ch‘iu	秋	liu	piu	kiu	k‘iu	tiu	p‘iu
Sang	山	lang	pang	kang	k‘ang	tang	p‘an
K‘ai	開	lai	pai	kai	k‘ai	tai	p‘ai
Ka	嘉	la	pa	ka	k‘a	ta	p‘a
Ping	賓	ling	ping	king	k‘ing	ting	p‘in
Hwang	歡	lwang	pwang	kwang	k‘wang	twang	p‘wa
Kó	歌	ló	pó	kó	k‘ó	tó	p‘ó
Sü	須	lü	pü	kü	k‘ü	tü	p‘ü
Pwí	杯	lwí	pwí	kwí	k‘wí	twí	p‘wí
Ku	孤	lu	pu	ku	k‘u	tu	p‘u
Teng	燈	leng	peng	keng	k‘eng	teng	p‘en
Kwong	光	lwong	pwong	kwong	k‘wong	twong	p‘on
Hwi	輝	lwi	pwi	kwi	k‘wi	twi	p‘wi
Sieu	燒	lieu	pieu	kieu	k‘ieu	tieu	p‘ie
Ngüng	銀	lüng	püng	küng	k‘üng	tüng	p‘ün
Kong	釭	long	pong	kong	k‘ong	tong	p‘on
Chi	之	li	pi	ki	k‘i	ti	p‘i
Tëng	東	lëng	pëng	këng	k‘ëng	tëng	p‘ën
Kau	郊	lau	pau	kau	k‘au	tau	p‘au
Kwo	過	lwo	pwo	kwo	k‘wo	two	p‘wo
Sá	西	lá	pá	ká	k‘á	tá	p‘á
Kio	橋	lio	pio	kio	k‘io	tio	p‘io
Kié	雞	lié	pié	kié	k‘ié	tié	p‘ié
Siăng	聲	liăng	piăng	kiăng	k‘iăng	tiăng	p‘iăı
Ch‘oi	催	loi	poi	koi	k‘oi	toi	p‘oi
Ch‘ë	初	lë	pë	kë	k‘ë	të	p‘ë
T‘iéng	天	liéng	piéng	kiéng	k‘iéng	tiéng	p‘iéı
K‘iă	奇	liă	piă	kiă	k‘iă	tiă	p‘iă
Wai	歪	lwai	pwai	kwai	k‘wai	twai	p‘wa
Keu	溝	leu	peu	keu	k‘eu	teu	p‘eu

by combining each initial with each final.

finals *hiong*, *sieu*, *kio*, *siăng*, *t'iéng*, and *k'iă*, begin with *y*.

T'a 他	Cheng 曾	Nik 日	Si 時	Eng 鶯	Mung 蒙	Ngü 語	Ch'ok 出	Hi 非
t'ung	chung	nung	sung	ung	mung	ngung	ch'ung	hung
t'wa	chwa	nwa	swa	wa	mwa	ngwa	ch'wa	hwa
t'iong	chiong	niong	siong	yong	miong	ngiong	ch'iong	hiong
t'iu	chiu	niu	siu	iu	miu	ngiu	ch'iu	hiu
t'ang	chang	nang	sang	ang	mang	ngang	ch'ang	hang
t'ai	chai	nai	sai	ai	mai	ngai	ch'ai	hai
t'a	cha	na	sa	a	ma	nga	ch'a	ha
t'ing	ching	ning	sing	ing	ming	nging	ch'ing	hing
t'wang	chwang	nwang	swang	wang	mwang	ngwang	ch'wang	hwang
t'ó	chó	nó	só	ó	mó	ngó	ch'ó	hó
t'ü	chü	nü	sü	ü	mü	ngü	ch'ü	hü
t'wí	chwí	nwí	swí	wí	mwí	ngwí	ch'wí	hwí
t'u	chu	nu	su	u	mu	ngu	ch'u	hu
t'eng	cheng	neng	seng	eng	meng	ngeng	ch'eng	heng
t'wong	chwong	nwong	swong	wong	mwong	ngwong	ch'wong	hwong
t'wi	chwi	nwi	swi	wi	mwi	ngwi	ch'wi	hwi
t'ieu	chieu	nieu	sieu	yeu	mieu	ngieu	ch'ieu	hieu
t'üng	chüng	nüng	süng	üng	müng	ngüng	ch'üng	hüng
t'ong	chong	nong	song	ong	mong	ngong	ch'ong	hong
t'i	chi	ni	si	i	mi	ngi	ch'i	hi
t'ëng	chëng	nëng	sëng	ëng	mëng	ngëng	ch'ëng	hëng
t'au	chau	nau	sau	au	mau	ngau	ch'au	hau
t'wo	chwo	nwo	swo	wo	mwo	ngwo	ch'wo	hwo
t'á	chá	ná	sá	á	má	ngá	ch'á	há
t'io	chio	nio	sio	yo	mio	ngio	ch'io	hio
t'ié	chié	nié	sié	ié	mié	ngié	ch'ié	hié
t'iăng	chiăng	niăng	siăng	yăng	miăng	ngiăng	ch'iăng	hiăng
t'oi	choi	noi	soi	oi	moi	ngoi	ch'oi	hoi
t'ë	chë	në	së	ë	më	ngë	ch'ë	hë
t'iéng	chiéng	niéng	siéng	yéng	miéng	ngiéng	ch'iéng	hiéng
t'iă	chiă	niă	siă	yă	miă	ngiă	ch'iă	hiă
t'wai	chwai	nwai	swai	wai	mwai	ngwai	ch'wai	hwai
t'eu	cheu	neu	seu	eu	meu	ngeu	ch'eu	heu

TABLE III. FINALS, AS MODIFIED BY TONES.

Note. The *eng* initial is placed at the head of this table, as it denotes the absence of any initial consonant, and therefore gives the simplest form of all the finals through each tone. Hence all words spoken without an initial consonant, or beginning with *w* or *y*, are classed under this initial. See *Note* on preceding page.

Eng	鶯	上平	上上	上去	上入	下平	下上	下去	下入
Ch'ung	春	ung	ung	ong	ok	ung	ung	ong	uk
Hwa	花	wa	wa	wa	wah	wa	wa	wa	wah
Hiong	香	iong	iong	iong	iok	iong	iong	iong	iok
Ch'iu	秋	iu	iu	eu	euh	iu	iu	eu	iuh
Sang	山	ang	ang	ang	ak	ang	ang	ang	ak
K'ai	開	ai	ai	ai	aih	ai	ai	ai	aih
Ka	嘉	a	a	a	ah	a	a	a	ah
Ping	賓	ing	ing	eng	ek	ing	ing	eng	ik
Hwang	歡	wang	wang	wang	wak	wang	wang	wang	wak
Kó	歌	ó	ó	ó	óh	ó	ó	ó	óh
Sü	須	ü	ü	ëü	ëüh	ü	ü	ëü	üh
Pwí	杯	wí	wí	woí	woíh	uí	wí	woí	wíh
Ku	孤	u	u	o	oh	u	u	o	uh
Teng	燈	eng	eng	aing	aik	eng	eng	aing	ek
Kwong	光	wong	wong	wong	wok	wong	wong	wong	wok
Hwi	輝	wi	wi	oi	oih	ui	wi	oi	wih
Sieu	燒	ieu	ieu	ieu	ieuh	ieu	ieu	ieu	ieuh
Ngüng	銀	üng	üng	ëüng	ëük	üng	üng	ëüng	ük
Kong	釭	ong	ong	aung	auk	ong	ong	aung	ok
Chi	之	i	i	e	eh	i	i	e	ih
Tëng	東	ëng	ëng	aëng	aëk	ëng	ëng	aëng	ëk
Kau	郊	au	au	au	auh	au	au	au	auh
Kwo	過	wo	wo	wo	woh	wo	wo	wo	woh
Sá	西	á	á	á	áh	á	á	á	áh
Kio	橋	io	io	io	ioh	io	io	io	ioh
Kié	雞	ié	ié	ié	iéh	ié	ié	ié	iéh
Siăng	聲	iăng	iăng	iăng	iăk	iăng	iăng	iăng	iăk
Ch'oi	催	oi	oi	ói	óih	oi	oi	ói	oih
Ch'ë	初	ë	ë	aë	aëh	ë	ë	aë	ëh
T'iéng	天	iéng	iéng	iéng	iék	iéng	iéng	iéng	iék
K'iă	奇	iă	iă	iă	iăh	iă	iă	iă	iăh
Wai	歪	wai	wai	wai	waih	wai	wai	wai	waih
Keu	溝	eu	eu	aiu	aiuh	eu	eu	aiu	euh

It appears from Table III, and its note of explanation that there are 90 final syllables, which (as belonging to the *eng* initial) are also independent words or vocables. They may be arranged alphabetically as follows:—

a, á, aĕ, aĕh, aĕk, aĕng, ah, áh, ai, aih, aik, aing, aiu, aiuh, ak, ang, au, auh, auk, aung, e, ĕ, eh, ĕh, ek, ĕk, eng, ĕng, eu, ĕŭ, euh, ĕŭh, ĕŭk, ĕŭng, i, iă, (yă), iăh, (yăh), iăk (yăk), iăng, (yăng), ié, iéh, iék, (yék), iéng, (yéng), ieu, (yéu), ieuh, (yeuh), ih, ik, ing, io, (yo), ioh (yoh), iok (yok), iong, (yong), iu, iuh, o, ó, oh, óh, oi, ói, oih, óih, ok, ong, u, ŭ, uh, ŭh, ui, uí, uk, ŭk, ung, ŭng, wa, wah, wai, waih, wak, wang, wi, wí, wih, wíh, wo, woh, woí, woíh, wok, wong.

The tables II and III also furnish the data for ascertaining the number of vocables produced by the combination of initials with finals and the modification by tones. The whole number is (15X33X 7) 3465. Besides these, there are two words not strictly referable to the table of initial and final sounds, viz., the semi-vocal nasal *ng*ʾ (no, not) on p. 595, and the word ꜀*ngiau*, on p. 610, composed of the initial *ng* and a final compounded of *i* and *au*,—making the whole number of vocables 3467. But probably less than half of these are in actual use. This paucity of vocables or monosyllabic words is largely compensated by the very frequent union of two or more words, virtually forming polysyllables, to express simple ideas. Thus the number of words is in effect increased to several thousands, which give to this dialect "a richness and variety of expression but little inferior to that of many alphabetic languages".

Chinese phrases as foot notes. The expedient of placing the Chinese characters at the foot of the page was adopted because, while the dictionary was going through the press, we found it impracticable to combine our English and Chinese fonts of type in the same text. A fixed portion of the lower part of each page was, therefore, set apart for Chinese, the design being to place there the characters for the more important phrases occurring on the page. A new font of English type, which we could combine with the Chinese, arrived just in time to be used in printing the Introduction.

List of Radicals and Index of Characters. These are comprised in pages 1015—1104 at the end of the volume. Characters may usually be found by the alphabetic order of their sounds, as in English dictionaries. But when the sound of a character is unknown to the student, or the native teacher gives it a reading different from that under which it is classed in this Dictionary, reference must be made to the Index. The radicals are 214 in number, and the larger part of these are characters in common use. All other characters are composed of some one of these radicals and a certain number of additional strokes. To find a character in the Index, the student must first ascertain its radical and then the number of additional strokes made in writing it. To facilitate the search, it will be useful to observe the following suggestions, which are quoted with slight modifications from William's Tonic Dictionary, as being well adapted to our design in this part of the Introduction. "The best mode of impressing the forms of the characters on the memory is an important question; but in most cases, the union of the radical and primitive as *the* two parts to be remembered, has the advantage of simplicity, and the sound and meaning can be attached to these by the laws of association better than to a collection of strokes made apparently without plan. After learning the radicals, a careful examination of the primitives as given by Callery will show the principles on which the great mass of characters in the language are formed, and practice in reading and writing will then make them familiar. Many of the most common characters are the most difficult to find in the Index; they are generally placed under the simpler radicals, where they should be looked for first. For instance 以, 仝, 令, 仄, are all under 人; 井, 亞, are under 二; 兒, 先, are under 儿; all of which are referred to these radicals chiefly because they were prominent parts of the characters, and likely to catch the eye. Such anomalous instances amount to about two hundred, all of them primitives, while the remainder will give less trouble in ascertaining the proper radical. About one half (108) of the radicals are placed on the right or left of the primitive—constituting one half of the character and easily recognized. Others, like 二, 勹, 匚, 匸, 口, 行, 門, and 鬥, embrace the primitive and give no trouble. About 40 of them are placed on the top of the primitive, a few of which enter into combination with it, as in 奉, 夷, 彝, or 發, in such a manner as to give some hesitation as to the radical; while others, as 宀, 广, 疒, 爪, 穴, 竹, 罒, 艹, 虍, 雨, are more apparent. For many of the remainder, where the radical is either in combination, or the character is formed of two or three radicals as 相, 龔, or 現, practice will soon give the necessary facility in finding. . . . . . In counting the number of strokes in a character, the radical is not reckoned. After becoming familiar with the radicals themselves, and having a general acquaintance with the primitives, the number of strokes can be most quickly ascertained by inspection. For instance, the character 鬻 (rice - porridge), found under the radical 鬲, is made up of 弓, 米 and 弓, which severally number 3, 6, and 3 strokes, or 12 in all; the character 灧 (bubbling water), placed under the radical 水, is composed of 曲, 豆, 刀, 巴, numbering 11, 7, 2, and 4, strokes, or 24 in all. The number of characters formed of so many strokes as these is very few, and in most cases a glance at the word is sufficient to see how many make it". The following brief analysis may also be found useful in the more difficult task of memorizing *the general meanings* of characters. "The groups of characters under most of the radicals naturally refer to *the leading idea;* about one-third of them are more arbitrary, a large part of the characters under them having no reference to their radical. Those of the latter sort are usually primitives, of which there are about 1700 in the whole language".

In conclusion, the following practical suggestions are made, relating principally to the acquisition of the spoken language.

1. Study thoroughly the Orthography, comprising the rudiments of the language with the elements of initial, final, and tone in single words, as given in the Tables.

2. Practice on the rudiments and tables *with the native teacher*, learning to enunciate as he does. No extent or thoroughness of independent study can ever compensate for deficiency in such practice.

3. Notice the important changes which occur in the combination of tones, as given on pages xv and xvi.

4. Also observe how the final consonants *h*, *k*, and *g*, and some of the initials, are often half-suppressed or seem wholly to disappear in the easy, native mode of speaking. Very close attention should be given to these idiomatic changes, so soon as thoroughness is attained in enunciating words singly. This is essential to ease and accuracy in public address and common conversation.

5. It will be found useful to pratice writing out, in the Romanized form, simple phrases heard in conversation. This will serve to fix them in the memory, and to draw the attention to many important words or particles, which otherwise might not be thoroughly learned for years.

6. The student should by no means confine himself to his books and teacher, but should mingle with common people and observe carefully their modes of speaking. The union of study and observation will help to form a style, alike removed from coarseness and excessive refinement, while exclusive study with a teacher will tend to the formation of a book-colloquial style, not fully or readily understood by the people at large.

:o:

ALPHABETIC DICTIONARY

OF THE

FOOCHOW DIALECT.

(1) **A.**

鴉 鵶 ˓ Ya. A raven with a white streak on its breast: the former is used in the term for opium: [1]˓u ˓a, or [2]ˋlô ˓a, (coll. ˋlô ˓wa), a crow, a raven; COLL., [3]˓a p'iéng˒ opium; [4]˓a p'iéng˒ ˓hong, opium as prepared for smoking; [5]˓a p'iéng˒ ˋkwang, an opium shop; [6]˓a p'iéng˒ ˓t'u, crude opium, opium in balls; [7]˓a p'iéng˒ ngiéng˒ confirmed in the habit of smoking opium; [8]˓a p'iéng˒ ˋsai, dregs of opium, as adhering to the pipe in smoking.

丫 ˓ Ya. Forked, a fork, a crotch; the parting, of two fingers, branches, or tines: [9]˓a ˓k'wang, a slave-girl, a maid-servant; COLL., [10]˓a ˓t'au, a female slave; [11]˓a ˓t'au ˋkiáng, a slave girl.

阿 ˓ A. O. Read ˓ó; used for the coll. ˓a, as in [12]˓a ˓chi, a cicada, a locust; [13]˓a ˓pang, to chaffer, to haggle; [14]˓a ˓pang ˓hu, or ˓a ˓pang ˓k'a, a chafferer, a skinflint, a mean fellow.

˓A. A coll. word, as in ˓a ˓cha, used for ˓la ˓cha, dirty, foul, vile.

ˋ吓 A coll. character, used for the disjunctive or, as in o² ˓chiong wang² ˋa ˓mô, is it so or not? also euphonic and emphatic, as in [15]se² ˋa, yes, it is, right.

ˋ亞 Ya. Inferior, second, next, junior; to esteem lightly; hunchbacked, ugly; used as a prefix to names: [16]pok˒ ˋa, not inferior; COM., [17]ˋa ˓k'wi, the second class of Küjin literary graduates, comprising from the sixth to the twelfth, as their names stand on the official list; [18]ˋa seng˒ a secondary sage, as Mencius; [19]ˋa maing˒ another designation for Mencius.

ˋ啞 瘂 Ya. Dumb, unable to speak; dull, faded; a cracked sound, as of a bell; confused noise of children; wheezing; the nape of the neck: [20]ˋa ˋk'eu, dumb, a

[1]烏鴉 [2]老鴉 [3]鴉片 [4]鴉片煙 [5]鴉片館 [6]鴉片土 [7]鴉片癮 [8]鴉片屎 [9]丫鬟 [10]丫頭 [11]丫頭仔 [12]阿蠐 [13]阿邦 [14]阿邦夫○ [15]是吓 [16]不亞 [17]亞魁 [18]亞聖 [19]亞孟 [20]啞口.

dumb person; [1]*'a 'chü* (coll. *'a ,chü*), a mute; [2]*'a me^2* an enigma, a riddle; COM., [3]*pang^2 'a*, dumb, a mute; [4]*,siăng ,ing 'a*, the voice hoarse; *,t'iéng ,lëng te^2 'a*, deaf and dumb, incorrigibly stupid; COLL., *'a ,chü siăh, ,wong ,liéng*, the dumb eat the (bitter) *,wong ,liéng* herb; *met.*, one dumb with grief.

'娅 Ya. Brothers-in-law: [5]*,ing 'a*, relatives by marriage, especially brothers and parents.

'拗 Yao. Ao. Read *'au;* coll. *'o:* to snap, to break in two, to twist: [6]*'a siék,* to break in two; *'a ,hwa*, to pluck flowers; *'a chià^2* to break the sugar-cane; [7]*'a 'ch'iu*, to bend or wrench hands, as in a trial of strength; *met.*, perverse, refractory; *'a lang^2 ,tong*, or *'a tói^2 ,tong*, to snap or break in two.

吓 , A coll. word used at the end of a sentence; an exclamation of pain or surprise, spoken *,a* or *a^2* according to intensity of feeling: *,ai ,a*, or *,ai a^2* oh! ah! *se^2 ,a*, it is certainly; *'hó ,a*, good, excellent.

下^2 Hsia. Read *ha^2;* coll. *a^2:* down, inferior, low, mean; next, once, a time, a while; below, under, to descend; a little; a particle denoting fold or quantity: [8]*a^2 ,niéng*, the following year; *a^2 ngwok,* next month; *a^2 'tá*, below, under; *sioh, a^2* once; *lang^2 a^2* twice; *'ting sioh, a^2* wait a little; *a^2 pwang^2* one and a half; *lang^2 a^2 sô^2* twice as much; *a^2 kié^2* the following quarter of the year; [9]*a^2 'ngu*, or *a^2 tau^2* the afternoon; *a^2 chiéng^2* low, vulgar, mean; *a^2 chóh,* or *a^2 ,siă*, sordid, niggardly; [10]*a^2 kai^2* the lower regions, hades; *a^2 ,sing*, or *a^2 ,tong*, the lower portion of the human body; [11]*a^2 nik,* a future day; [12]*a^2 ,ing*, a menial, a servant; *a^2 ,húi*, or *a^2 ch'ëü^2* the next time; *a^2 ne^2 ,húi*, the very next time, another time, hereafter; [13]*a^2 'hu*, the lower prefectures (of Fookien); [14]*a^2 ,nang*, name given to the S. E. maritime districts of Fookien; [15]*a^2 ,k'wo*, the next literary examination; [16]*a^2 ,ch'ung*, the next primary examination; *p'ah, 'kwi a^2* to strike a few times, give a few blows; *a^2 ,ma tai^2* grasping, over-reaching; *na^2 sioh, a^2* just once; only, but, this only; this one point remains, as to be spoken of or considered; [17]*a^2 ,hai*, or *a^2 ,pa*, the chin; [18]*a^2 so^2* a secret, something concealed, a secret purpose or design, as *,i o^2 sié^2 nóh, a^2 so^2* what secret design has he? [19]*a^2 'ch'iu*, to put the hand to, to seize, to begin to do; *a^2 'ma yéng^2* a feast given to a friend on his arrival; *a^2 paik, taëng^2* a bully, a rough, a rascal.

廈^2 Hsia. Sha. Read *ha^2;* coll. *a^2* as in [20]*a^2 ,mwong*, Amoy; [21]*a^2 ,mwong 'hai ,wong*, the Amoy superintendent of Trade; [22]*a^2 ,mwong tô^2* the Tautai of Amoy.

娘^2 I. Read *,ngá;* used for the coll. *a^2:* the crying of a child.

1 啞子 2 啞謎 3 病啞 4 聲音啞 5 姻娅 6 拗折 7 拗手 8 下年 9 下午 10 下界 11 下日 12 下人 13 下府 14 下南 15 下科 16 下春 17 下頦 18 下數 19 下手 20 廈門 21 廈門海防 22 廈門道

*A*². A coll. word, perhaps a corruption of *au*²: behind, after, rear: *a*² ʻ*tau* (or ʻ*lau*), or *a*² ʻ*tau sié*² behind, in the rear; ˏ*kŭng a*² ʻ*tau*, to follow after; *tioh*ˎ *a*² ʻ*tau*, is behind, is in the rear.

(2) Á.

挨 挨 Ai. Yai. To delay, to detain, to hinder; late, slow; to push; to procrastinate, to put off; to pass time lazily; to beat, to strike on the back; to place at the side; to force, to crowd, as with the elbows; next, near: COM., ¹ˏ*á* ˏ*yong*, to delay, to wait, tardy, slow; ²ˏ*á* ˏ*si*, behind time, late; ˏ*á mó*² to push the querne; ³ˏ*á* ʻ*pó*, those acting as subordinate sureties for students; COLL., ⁴ˏ*á* ˏ*ti*, or ˏ*á* ˏ*sá*, to delay, to be late; ⁵ˏ*á sioh*ˎ *nik*ˎ to delay a whole day; ʻ*mwong* ˏ*á*, to keep putting it off, to delay from day to day; ˏ*á kau*ˀ *ang*ˀ to delay till dark; ⁶*móh*ˎ ˏ*á*, don't delay; ˏ*á* ˏ*si tio*² *nik*ˎ to procrastinate from day to day.

ˏÁ. A coll. word, as in ˏ*á* ˏ*mwong*, street night-gates; ˏ*á* ˏ*mwong* ˏ*piéng*, at the side of these gates.

ʻ矮 ʻ矮 Ai. Low, short, diminutive: COM., ⁷ʻ*á* ʻ*chŭng*, a small breed, applied to men and lower animals; ʻ*á* ʻ*á*, diminutive in stature; ʻ*á* ʻ*ma*, the crouching posture of a boxer; ʻ*á sá*ˀ low and small; COLL., ⁸ʻ*á* ˏ*chü*, a dwarf; ⁹ʻ*á kah*, a small frame — a small size or kind, as of fowls; ¹⁰ʻ*á paik*ˎ ʻ*kwi*, black dwarfish imps in the processions of the ʻ*ngu tá*ˀ; ʻ*á noh*ˎ *noh*ˎ (spoken ʻ*á* ˏ*nu noh*ˎ) very low in stature.

ˏ鞋 ˏ鞵 Hsieh. A shoe, shoes, slippers, brogans: COM., ¹¹ˏ*á wak*ˎ shoes and stockings; ¹²ˏ*á tai*ˀ shoe-strings; ¹³ˏ*á* ʻ*li*, shoe-lining; ¹⁴ʻ*ch*ʻ*au* ˏ*á*, straw shoes or sandals; ¹⁵*taung*² ˏ*á*, satin shoes; ˏ*siong* ˏ*á*, figured shoes; ˏ*á* ʻ*k*ʻ*au*, the mouth or opening of a shoe; ˏ*á chaung*ˀ a shoemaker's awl; ¹⁶ˏ*á yong*² a shoe-pattern; COLL., ¹⁷ˏ*á* ʻ*chiong*, the sole or bottom of the shoe (to beat one with); ˏ*á pek*ˎ a shoeing-horn, made of bone or brass; *süng*² ˏ*á*, to put on shoes, to wear shoes; ¹⁸ˏ*á t*ʻ*ó*ˀ wooden-soled shoes; ¹⁹ˏ*lung* ˏ*á*, or ˏ*lung* ˏ*á t*ʻ*ó*ˀ women's over-shoes; ˏ*á* ʻ*kiăng*, small shoes; ˏ*á meng*ˀ the uppers of shoes; ²⁰ˏ*á hwong*ˀ a shoe-last; ˏ*á p*ʻ*e*ˀ toe of a shoe; ˏ*á* ˏ*sa*, a shoemaker; ˏ*á* ˏ*tang*, the heel of a shoe; ˏ*á* ˏ*tang siăng*ˀ the heel cord of women's shoes; *k*ʻ*ek*ˎ ˏ*á* ʻ*chiong p*ʻ*ah*ˎ ˏ*nëng*, to beat one with a shoe-sole.

ˏÁ. A coll. word, used in formal affirmative answers; a sound of assent, yes, just so.

䆀² A coll. character: can, able to; apt, capable, competent; possibly, probably; as an auxiliary, am, is, do, does, will: *á*² ʻ*hieu*, or ²¹*á*² ʻ*hieu tek*, can comprehend, I understand it; *á*² ʻ*sai tek*, it will do, answers the purpose; yes,

¹挨延 ²挨時 ³挨保 ⁴挨遲 ⁵挨一日〇 ⁶莫挨 ⁷矮種 ⁸矮子 ⁹矮格 ¹⁰矮八鬼〇 ¹¹鞋襪 ¹²鞋帶 ¹³鞋裏 ¹⁴草鞋 ¹⁵緞鞋 ¹⁶鞋樣 ¹⁷鞋掌 ¹⁸鞋套 ¹⁹輪鞋 ²⁰鞋楦 ²¹䆀曉的〇

may do it; [1]*á chó* or *á chó tek*, can do it, it can be done, practicable, feasible; [2]*á ˛siăng*, able to finish; *á se* possibly, perhaps; *á se ʻma chai* it is so perhaps; *á ʻhó*, can improve, will get well; *á chó má chó* can you do it or not? is it practicable? [3]*á ˛tʻung*, can comprehend it; [4]*á ˛ming*, to understand clearly; plain, clear, perspicuous; *á siăh*, can eat; *á siăh tek*, eatable, fit to eat; *á pʻah*, can strike, pugnacious, contentious; *á má* or *á ʻa má* can you? will you or not? [5]*˛tu á* can do everything; *˛mó nóh á* cannot do anything; *˛i cheng á siăh* he is a great eater; *cheng á chó* a great worker; [6]*á piéng* can change or reform; [7]*á laung* confused, as in mind; tangled, as thread; *á yéng* satiated; *á chó ˛ka*, he'll build up his family — said of an industrious, frugal man; *á ˛lá ˛pa*, he plows and hoes; *met.*, industrious and saving; *á ʻsai sang* quick-tempered; *á ˛siăng ˛hwa má* can the bargain be closed or not? *á yék po ˛mó kang* he gets hot but don't sweat—applied to a person who is merely hasty in temper.

(3) Aĕh.

哊 Read *ĕük*; coll. *aĕh*: to eructate, to belch, to raise wind from the stomach; to vomit, noise of vomiting: *pʻah aĕh*, or *ʻau aĕh*, or *pʻah ʻsai aĕh*, to belch; *aĕh má hiok*, incessant belching; *aĕh sioh chʻoi* to belch up a mouthful.
Yu.

(4) Aĕng.

甕 A jar, a vase, an urn; a water amphora without spout or handle; a round window: COM., [8]*aĕng ˛kiéng*, and [9]*aĕng chʻoi* the brim and the mouth of a jar; COLL., [10]*aĕng ʻkiăng*, a small jar; [11]*aĕng ʻtié*, inside the jar; *aĕng ʻkiăng aĕng ˛nié*, small vases of various sizes; [12]*aĕng ˛siăng ˛tong*, the space between the outer and inner gates of a city wall; [13]*chʻoi aĕng aĕng tioh*, mouth agape like a jar—applied to infants.
Wêng.

Aĕng. A coll. word; a bustle, a great run of customers: *ʻyă aĕng* or *cheng aĕng* great bustle, a rush of business, lively times; *aĕng ʻkʻi ˛li*, the bustle begins as when customers in numbers patronize a shop.

(5) Ah.

揖 Read *ek*; coll. *ah*: to raise and lower the hands, with the palms placed together, as in saluting a friend or in worshiping an idol: *ah*, *˛chiă ah*, *˛chiă*, salute! salute!
Yi. I. Jung.

(6) Ai.

哀 Pity, grief, sorrow; to pity, to lament, to bewail, to mourn; to compassionate, to feel for, to condole with; sad, pained, grieved; lamentable; urgently, heartily: [14]*˛ai kʻok*, to lament and weep; [15]*˛ai tong* to grieve, in great distress; [16]*˛ai ˛ling*, or [17]*˛ai ˛siong*, to pity, to grieve for; [18]*ʻkʻó ˛ai*, lamentable; COM., [19]*ʻkü ˛ai*, to wail, to bewail; [20]*˛ai ˛chai*, alas!
Ai.

[1]能做 [2]能成 [3]能通 [4]能明 [5]都能 [6]能變 [7]能亂 [8]甕墘 [9]甕嘴 [10]甕仔 [11]甕裏 [12]甕城中 [13]嘴甕甕着 [14]哀哭〇 [15]哀慟 [16]哀憐 [17]哀傷 [18]可哀 [19]舉哀 [20]哀哉

[1]*'ai ꜀kiu 'k'u kó'* to make grievous complaints and beg piteously.

埃 ꜂Ai. Dust, fine dust, such as is raised by the wind: [2]*꜀ting ꜀ai*, dust.

欸 唉 ꜀Ai. Also read *'ai:* an ejaculation, ah! oh! to sigh; an expression of pain; to respond, to answer; to belch: in the coll. read *꜀ai*, q. v.: COLL., *꜀ai ꜀ó*, or *꜀ai ꜀a*, an expression of pain or surprise; *꜀ai a'* an expression of intense admiration.

靄 'Ai. Mist, fog; foggy, misty; the heavens obscured by fog or vapor; dense clouds.

藹 'Ai. Luxuriant vegetation; thick, shady, flourishing; dignified, personable; pleasing: [3]*꜀hwo 'ai*, dignified; [4]*'ai 'ai kek꜀ sëü'* accomplished scholars about a sovereign.

倚 'I. Read *'i;* coll. *'ai:* to trust, to rely or depend on, to confide in: [5]*'ai chiâ'* or [6]*'ai k'ó'* to trust in, to depend on; [7]*'ai wong'* to hope, to long after; *'ai paung'* to rest upon, to depend on; *'ai 'nü ché piêng'* hope you'll reform; *'ai ꜀ch'iong ꜀ch'iong ꜀pung, 'ai piâh꜀ piâh꜀ 'tó*, he leans on walls and they crumble, on partitions and they fall; *met.*, insufficient help; *ó' nóh꜀ 'ai chiâ'* something in which to trust; *꜀mó nóh꜀ 'ai chiâ'* nothing in which to trust.

'Ai. A coll. word, as in *'ai nai'* many, a plenty, great abundance! — as in replying to one who says there are none.

愛 Ai'. To love, to esteem highly, to take delight in, to feel attached to; to desire, to want; to be sparing of, forbearing, tender of; kind regard, love, attachment; the object of love, the beloved: used for the coll. *t'iàng'* q. v.: [8]*'che' ai'* dearly loved; [9]*'k'ó ai'* beloved, dear; COM., [10]*ai' sek꜀* to prize highly; [11]*꜀ing ai'* benevolence, compassion, love; [12]*ai' ꜀chai*, to love riches; [13]*ai' ꜀chai*, to admire talent; [14]*ai' ꜀ing ꜀ü 'ki*, to love others as yourself; [15]*ch'auk꜀ ai'* you mistake in loving, I am unworthy of your love—a polite phrase; COLL., [16]*se' ꜀i ꜀sing ai' ꜀ki ꜀nëng*, the person whom he tenderly loves.

噯 Ai'. Read *'ai;* coll. *ai':* an exclamation or ejaculation, about the same as *꜀ai*, q. v.: *ai' ꜀a*, an ejaculation expressive of pain or of severe labor, as in carrying a heavy burden.

嬡 Ai'. An unauthorized character: a girl: COM., [17]*leng' ai'* your daughter.

靉 Ai'. Cloudy, obscure, murky, clouds hiding the sun.

僾 Ai'. Like, similar; simulated; hard to see.

曖 Ai'. Cloudy, obscure, sun hidden by clouds: [18]*ai' tai'* cloudy, murky; *ai' ai'* obscured, as the moon; [19]*ai' mwoi'* confused, as the mind, to do anything confusedly or carelessly.

1 哀求苦告 2 塵埃 3 和藹 4 藹藹吉士 5 倚藉 6 倚靠 7 倚望 8 至愛 9 可愛 10 愛惜 11 仁愛 12 愛財 13 愛才 14 愛人如己 15 錯愛 16 是伊心愛其人 17 令嬡 18 曖曃 19 曖昧

曖' Ai. Dimness of sight, to see indistinctly.

隘' Ai. Yai. A pass, a defile; *met.*, contracted, narrow-minded, mean; exacting, rigid, stern; distressed, urgent; impeded, stopped up; confined, straitened: [1]*'hiéng ai'* a narrow, irregular valley; *met.*, partial, unjust.

欸 唉 Ai. Read *,ai* and *'ai*; coll. *,ai* (or *ai'*): an ejaculation of surprise; a prohibitory exclamation, stop! don't!

(7) Aik.

阨 厄 戹, O. Ai. An obstruction, a stop; a defile, a pass, a dangerous path; a calamity, accident, affliction, trouble; distressed, embarrassed, poor; the 3d also means a small door: [2]*aik, nang'* distress, sorrow, affliction; [3]*aik, ,küng*, extremely poor; [4]*,chai aik,* calamities and troubles; COLL., *aik, ,mó tek, kwo'* can't escape the calamity; inevitable, fatal, as disease.

扼 扼, To press the hand upon; to seize or hold with the hand; to repress; to gripe, to clutch; to grasp; to pull; to touch with the finger; to lay the hand on anything; also used in the sense of placed, put away: COLL., [5]*aik, 'ch'iu*, to press or touch with the hand; [6]*aik, ,wang*, to bend, to deflect, to make crooked; [7]*aik, 'king*, to press tightly, to secrete; [8]*aik, lóh,* to press down; *aik, aik,* press down! press on it! [9]*aik, 'piéng*, to flatten by pressure; [10]*aik, ,kiéng ,t'au*, to lay the hand on one's shoulder; [11]*aik, ,ch'iong aik, piăh,* to lean against walls, as small-footed women in walking; *aik, ,tĕng 'nĕ k'ó'* where has it been put?

軛, A yoke; the yoke of a carriage; a yoke, a restraint, a principle of conscience.

(8) Aing.

爓' Yen. Read *yék,*; coll. *aing'*: a dull fire; to smother, as a fire: [12]*aing' t'ang'* to smother burning coals in a jar; [13]*aing' 'hwi*, to extinguish fire; a dull fire, as olive-wood makes; *aing' tiĕng'* (the jar) filled; *aing' t'ang' aĕng'* a jar for extinguishing coals in.

限[2] Hsien. To limit, to fix or set a time; to settle, to determine; to assign, to adjust, to appoint, to agree upon; to impede, to moderate; a limit, an impediment, a boundary, a restriction; a few, a short time; a threshold: [14]*aing[2] 'chi*, to fix the limits as to time; COM., [15]*aing[2] nik,* to fix the day; [16]*kai' aing[2]* to establish the boundary; [17]*aing[2] ,ki*, to appoint the time; [18]*,kü aing[2]* to set a task; to appoint or set a time, as for executing a warrant, or collecting taxes; [19]*,niéng aing[2]* the term of years contracted for; [20]*aing[2] 'mwang*, expiration of the time; [21]*,u aing[2]* or *,u aing[2] liong[2]* unlimited, abundant

[1]險隘 [2]阨難 [3]阨窮 [4]災阨 [5]扼手 [6]扼彎 [7]扼緊 [8]扼落 [9]扼扁 [10]扼肩頭 [11]扼牆扼壁 ○ [12]爓炭 [13]爓火 [14]限止 [15]限日 [16]界限 [17]限期 ○ [18]拘限 [19]年限 [20]限滿 [21]無限

exhaustless, infinite; [1]'aing' lié' to fix regulations as to time and work; [2]'aing' ka' to limit prices, as officers do in times of scarcity; [3]'aing' 'wang, to limit one's eating, to diet; [4]'aing' ,hiong, to regulate time, as for study, by the burning of incense sticks; [5]'aing' ,k'wang, to set a large limit, as to time; [6]'aing' 'king, to set strict limits; aing' ,sang nik, limited to three days.

扂, **杲**, Hsien. Threshold of a door or gate: [7],mwong aing' (coll. ,mwong taing') a threshold.

(9) Ak.

鴨, Ya. A duck, a mallard: COM., [8],kié ak, chickens and ducks; [9],hwang ak, a Mandarin duck; [10]piéng ak, flat (dried) ducks; ak, laung' ducks' eggs; ch'ai' ak, a small, green-billed duck; COLL., ak, 'mó, the female duck; ak, koëk, the male duck; ak, 'kiăng, young ducks; ,mong ak, a large duck; lau' ak, an old duck; ak, 'mó ,chiu, a locality in Foochow, on the north bank of the Min, below the Great Bridge.

壓, Ya. To press down, to steady, to settle; to bend, to crush, to suppress; to repress, to intimidate, to oppress; to subject, to conquer, to destroy: used for the coll. tah, q. v.: [11]ak, 'tó, to throw down; met., to overthrow a person, as in a lawsuit; [12]ak, lek, to force, to compel, to constrain by violence; COM., [13]ak, chié' to prevent, to restrain; to subdue, to conquer; [14],tang ak, to suppress, as a riot; to stop, as a row; COLL., ak, 'tó ,nëng, to subvert one in his cause, to oppress; ak, ,kié ng' ,siăng po' you can't force a hen to hatch eggs; met., he cannot be forced to do it; ak, má' teu' can't be suppressed, irrepressible, as a conflict.

遏, O. To stop, to prevent, to bring to a stand-still; to reach, to arrive; to cut off; an unforeseen obstacle: [15]ak, 'chi, to stop; [16]ak, auk, to restrain the wicked, to prevent wickedness: COM., [17]ak, chié' ,sü ük, to subdue one's lusts.

呷, Also read hak,: to gulp, to swallow, to drink: [18],hwong ak, the clamor or buzz of a crowd.

押, Ya. To control, to govern, to rule; to pawn for a time, to reserve, to keep back; to affix; to escort, to guard; to lay hold of, to seize: [19]ak, taung' to mortgage, to pawn; COM., [20],ch'iéng ak, to affix the red strokes to official papers, to insert names, dates, etc., as a law-secretary does; [21]ak, ,teu, the accusation, placed on the back of a criminal when led to execution; ak, hwang' to escort criminals, to hand over in custody; ak, huk, to compel one to obey, constrained obedience; 't'ai ak, to give a pledge or pawn in borrowing money; ,kü ak, to put into close confinement; ak, hwo' to guard

1 限例 2 限價 3 限碗 4 限香 5 限寬 6 限緊 7 門扂 8 雞鴨 9 番鴨 10 扁鴨 11 壓倒 12 壓勒 13 壓制 14 彈壓 15 遏止 16 遏惡 17 遏制私慾 18 喤呷 19 押當 20 簽押 21 押條

merchandize in transportation; [1]*'sieu ak*, a small pawn shop; [2]*ak, ˛pwang*, to compel one to move, as when he fails to pay his rent; [3]*ak, nik, ‘chi*, to date official documents in red ink; [4]*ak, ˛pang ‘kwang*, to place in custody at an officer's; [5]*‘kwang ak*, to guard, to keep in custody; [6]*˛hwa ak*, a mark or signature to a deed or agreement; COLL., *ak, saëng’ ˛kwang ‘lá k‘ó’* to send one under arrest to the officer.

揠 Ya. To pull up, to eradicate.

閼 O. Also read *˛yéng* and *˛yéng*: to shut, to stop up; to obstruct; to suffocate; to prevent superiors knowing.

頞 O. The root of the nose; the frontal sinus; a saddle.

軋 Ya. Creaking of a wheel; a creaking, grating sound; punishment of the rack or wheel.

盒 Ho. Interchanged with the next: a box or vessel with a cover, as gallipots, caskets, pill-boxes; a covered platter: COM., [7]*˛king ak*, a gold box, as made of gold or simply to keep gold in; [8]*ak kai’* cover for a box; [9]*ak ˛chiéng*, gift of money to the person who brings the presents; COLL., [10]*ak ‘kiáng*, a small box; [11]*˛hong ak* a tobacco box; *paing’ se’ ak* to prepare the four boxes (of presents); [12]*ak lóh* a net-work sack in which presents are carried.

匣 Hsia. A chest, a trunk; a casket; a press for clothes, a coffer; a case for a set of books: COM., [13]*ngiêng’ ak* the box or case of an inkstone; [14]*pai’ t‘aik, ak* a card box, a small flat box used for various purposes; [15]*siu sek, ak* a dressing case, a coffer for female ornaments.

狎 Hsia. Intimate, familiar, accustomed, well-acquainted with; irreverent, disrespectful; to desecrate, to contemn; to change; to approach; to caress: [16]*ak nik* familiar, intimate with; [17]*ak ‘u*, to slight, to contemn, to insult; [18]*ak ngwang’* to sport with, lustful dalliance.

柙 Hsia. A cage or inclosure for wild animals or prisoners; to encage; a scabbard; a press; name of a tree.

阿 A. E. O. Wo. Read *˛ó*; coll. *ak*: a prefix to proper names, used by southern people: [19]*ak ˛tiá*, father; [20]*ak ˛ma*, mother; [21]*ak ˛kó*, brother; title of the heir apparent to the throne; [22]*ak ‘ná*, title given to an adopted mother.

Ak. A coll. word: swollen, puffed; *meng’ ak ak tioh* the face puffed, as of a child after sleep.

(10) Ang.

安 An. Still, settled; safe, calm, tranquil, peaceful, at ease, unconstrained; contented, harmonious, to tranquil-

---

[1]小押 [2]押搬 [3]押日子 [4]押班館 [5]管押 [6]花押 [7]金盒 [8]盒蓋 [9]盒錢 [10]盒仔 [11]煙盒 [12]盒絡 [13]硯匣 [14]拜帖匣 [15]首飾匣 [16]狎暱 [17]狎侮 [18]狎玩 [19]阿爹 [20]阿媽 [21]阿哥 [22]阿奶

福州方言拼音字典

ize; rest, peace, quiet, repose; to rest, to settle, to make easy, to remain at rest; an interrogative particle, how, how could? where? used for the coll. ˛eng, q. v.: ˛ang ˛ping, contented in poverty; ong˲ ˛ang, to inquire after one's health; ˛ang chaung˲ to deposit the coffin, to inter; COM., 1˛ang ˛hang, rest, leisure; still, quiet; 2˛ang cheng˲ silent, quiet, secluded; 3˛ang ˛sing, to compose one's mind; 4˛ang oi˲ to console, to comfort, to soothe; 5˛ang ˛ch'ong, to arrange the bridal bed—to put the cash of five reigns under its feet; ˛ang hiok˲ quiet, peaceful; 6˛ang ˊung, safe, secure, as a business, or as an investment; settled, arranged; ˛ang lok˲ happy, pleased; to rejoice; ˛ang sek˲ rest, repose; to rest; 7˛ang sek˲ nik˲ the Christian Sabbath; ˛Ang t'ai˲ ˛kio, name of a bridge in South Street, Foochow; pok˲ ˛ang, dissatisfied, discontented; 8ˊk'ieng˲ ˛ang, in need of repose; restless, in pain, as a sick person; ˛ang ˛ing, wife of an officer of the sixth rank; ˛ang ˛ming, to quiet the people; ˛ang tong˲ to arrange, to set in order; to do well, properly done; 9˛ping ˛ang, peace, quietness, well and happy; 10˛ang ˛nang, Annam; 11˛ang ˛hwi, the province of Nganhwi; 12˛Ming ˛ang, a pass in the Min river, about 18 miles below Foochow; ˛Ming ˛ang teng˲ a military post at the above pass; 13Hok˲ ˛ang, a district city in the Fooning prefecture, Fookien; 14˛Chung ˛ang, a district city in the Kienning prefecture, Fookien, a great mart for Teas; ˊIng ˛ang, a district city in the Yenping prefecture, Fookien; ˛Ang ˛k'á, a district in the Chinchew prefecture, Fookien; ˛ang hong˲ content with one's lot; 15˛ang hong˲ ˊsiu ˊki, to attend quietly to one's own duties; COLL., ˛ang ˊchiă oi˲ ch'ëü˲ place it here; ˛ang ˛ka, to leave means for support of the family during one's absence; ˛ang ˊk'ó ˛ti, how can I know that?

˛鵪鶉 An. A quail which the Chinese train to fight: ˛ang ˛sung, a quail under which two or three species of Coturnix are included.

˛鞍 An. A saddle: COM., 16ˊma ˛ang, a horse's saddle; ˊma ˛ang ˛kio, an arched bridge; ˊma ˛ang ˛ch'iong, a wall with a curving cap or top.

˛諳 An. Also read ang˲: accustomed to, skilled in, to know, to be fully acquainted with; to commit to memory; to recite, to rehearse: 17sŭk˲ ˛ang, skilled in, thoroughly acquainted with; 18˛ang lieng˲ mature, practised in; ˛ang sëüng˲ to repeat memoriter; 19pok˲ ˛ang sie˲ ko˲ not versed in worldly affairs; ˛ang sek˲ nŏi˲ ˊtieng, to be versed in the classics.

˛庵 An. Interchanged with the next: a round hut, a thatched cottage, a straw hovel for soldiers; a pig sty; a Budhist nunnery: COM., 20˛ang ˛tong se˲ kwang˲ the four kinds of temples, viz. nunneries, halls, Budhist and Tauist monasteries; ˛ná ˛ku ˛ang, a nunnery.

1安閒 2安靜 3安心 4安慰 5安床 6安穩 7安息日〇 8欠安 9平安 10安南 11安徽 12閩安 13福安 14崇安 15安分守己 16馬鞍 17熟諳 18諳鍊 19不諳世故 20庵堂寺觀

莽 ‘蓊 An. Also read ‘ang: a coarse grass: [1]‘ang ‚lang, St. John's wort, or ground pine, used for thatching buildings; the seeds of it are used for medicine.

腌 ‘Ang. Yen. Read ‚yéng, ‘yéng, and yék‚; coll. ‚ang, as in ‚ang ‚chang, dirty, filthy.

‚Ang. A coll. word, probably a corruption of ‚kang: to compel, to coerce, to force, to constrain one against his will: ‚ang ‚i chó' to make him do it; pwoh, ‚ang ‘ngwai chó' he wishes to force me to do it.

‘揞 An. Also read ang': to conceal, to screen; to cover, as with the hand; to suppress, to exterminate; also to grasp.

‘闇 An. Also read ang': to shut the door; to withdraw from society; an obscure recess; ignorant, dark-minded; badly lighted, the evening; an eclipse: [2]‘ang ‚mwong, to shut the door; [3]‘ang tang' very plain, unadorned, as dress; met., unassuming, modest, retiring, quiet; COLL., ‚mwong ‘ang ‚chiā, shut the door! ‚mwong ‘ang kwo' k‘ó' push to the door!

‘黯 An. Dark, pitchy dark; astonished and silent, as if lost in amazement: [4]‘Ngek, ‘ang, a famous statesman of the Han Dynasty.

‘唵 An. Also read ‚ang: to feed with the hands; to hold in the mouth: a word used by the Budhists.

‘泔 Kan. Read ‚kang; coll. ‘ang: broth of rice, congee; tasteless, insipid, tame: [5]pwong' ‘ang, congee; [6]‘ang chaik, or [7]‘ang ‚t‘ong, thin rice-broth; [8]‘ang ‘chiāng, weak, insipid; met., no taste or desire for, as when perceived to be useless or a failure.

‘Ang. A coll. word, as in ‘ang po' to decay, to rot; ‘ang lang' rotted all to pieces.

晏' Yen. Evening, sunset; a serene, clear sky; tardy, behindhand; peaceful, gentle; rich, full, as said of furs: [9]‚ti ang' late, slow; [10]ang' ‚hwa, late fruit; [11]ang' ‘k‘i, to get up late; [12]ang' ‘chü, a child born of aged parents: COLL., [13]ang' ‚kiāng, to go late, to go after the time; ang' ‚li, to come late, to delay; ang' k‘ó' to go late; [14]ang' ié' late planted, as vegetables; [15]ang' ‘kwi nik‚ a few days later, to wait a a few days.

暗' An. Sun obscured by clouds; dark, dimly-lighted, somber; gloomy; clandestine, unobserved, secret, underhanded; dull, stupid; private, mental: [16]ang' sek, a dark house; [17]ang' mwoi' ignorant, confused, dull; COM., [18]‚u ang' dark, cloudy, lowering; [19]‚kwong ang' light and darkness; [20]ang' k‘ang' a spirit-seer, one able to see evil spirits, as in a sick room; [21]ang' hó' a secret sign or signal; [22]ang' taing' the dark temple, applied to the recess where the ‘ngu tá' idols are placed; [23]ang' ‘hwi, a

[1]蓊藹 [2]闇門 [3]闇淡 [4]汲黯 [5]飯泔 [6]泔汁 [7]泔湯 [8]泔醬 [9]遲晏 [10]晏花 [11]晏起 [12]晏子 [13]晏行 [14]晏穧 [15]晏幾日○ [16]暗室 [17]暗昧 [18]烏暗 [19]光暗 [20]暗看 [21]暗號 [22]暗殿 [23]暗火

福州方言拼音字典

dull fire; ¹'ˏt'iĕng ang' darkness, night; COLL., ²ang' ˏmang, night, dark; ang' ˏmang chó' done by night; ³'ˏtong ang' in the darkness, in the night; ang' mang' secretly, privately, clandestinely; ang' mang' ˏmwang ˏnĕng, to cheat people slyly; ⁴ang' ˏcheng, dark needle—i. e., a secret injury; ang' mŏh, mŏh, or ang' ˏmwo ˏmwo, very dark, so dark that one must feel his way.

按' An. To put down, to lower; to stop, to prevent moving, to desist; to take hold of, to press down, to lay the hand on; to grasp, as a sword; to pull in or hold, as a horse; to rub, to chafe; to examine, to try a case, to inquire into; to act according to, to conform; according to, by: ⁵ang' pie' to hold the bridle-rein; ⁶'chëü' ang' to lay the hand on, as on the heart; *met.*, to examine yourself; ⁷ang' 'ch'iu, to lay the hand on; ⁸ang' ˏniëng, by the year; ⁹ang' haiu' according to the time; COM., ¹⁰ang' ˏsi, or ang' ch'ak, ˏsi, (also ang' ch'ak, soi' ˏsi), the provincial criminal judge; COLL., ang' 'chiă 't'á, or ang' 'chiă 'k'wang, or ang' 'chiă yong' or ang' 'chiă sie' according to this way or fashion; ang' ˏchiong wang' in this way, thus; ang' ˏchiong 'kong, thus saying, as to that utterance — *scil.*, it is right, true, wrong, &c., &c.

桉' **案'** An. A table, an official table, a bar or bench before a judge; that which is on his table, a case in law, an action; a sentence, a decision; to examine, to try judicially, to decide cases; placed in order, serial; a limit or frontier; a sacrificial table: ¹¹chai' ang' an accusation presented, the case entered or recorded; ang' ˏiu, the circumstances or merits of a case; ¹²huk, ang' to face the table, studious; ¹³p'ah, ang' to strike the table (to express admiration); to beat the desk angrily, as a judge does; COM., ¹⁴ang' tŏh, an official desk; ¹⁵ang' kwong' minutes of a judicial investigation; ¹⁶sing ang' to examine or try a case, to judge; ¹⁷hwak, ang' the official announcement of the names of the Siutsai graduates; ¹⁸ang' yong' a law suit; ¹⁹ˏhiong ang' the table with incense and offerings, as set out before an idol, or to greet an officer; COLL., ²⁰ang' ko' mwoi' hwak, the judge's decision not yet published; the names of the Siutsai not yet posted.

鷃' Yen. A small kind of partridge which breeds on the ground, and is said to crow in the morning.

桁 ˏHang. Read ˏheng; coll. ˏang: the rafters of a house: ²¹ngwa' ˏang, tiles and rafters; ²²ˏt'iong' ˏang, laths and rafters.

ˏ*Ang.* A coll. word: to equalize, to make equal: ˏang ˏli ˏang k'ó' or ˏang 'lá, or ˏang ˏli 'pwo k'ó' to equalize, to divide equally.

彈 ˏTan. T'an. Read ˏtang; coll. ˏang, as in ˏang tak, to quell a riot, to suppress a mob.

¹天暗 ²暗暝 ³當暗 ⁴暗針 ⁵按轡 ⁶自按 ⁷按手 ⁸按年 ⁹按候 ¹⁰按司 ¹¹在案 ¹²伏案 ¹³拍案 ¹⁴案棹 ¹⁵案卷 ¹⁶審案 ¹⁷發案 ¹⁸案件 ¹⁹香案 ²⁰案故 昧發 ²¹瓦桁 ²²椽桁 ○

旱^{2} Han. Dry weather, drought, dearth of rain; sunny sky; land travel: COM., [1]ʻ*ang*^{2} ꜀*tʻiêng*, or *chó*^{2} *ang*^{2} a drought; [2]*ang*^{2} ꜀*chai*, calamity of drought; [3]ʻ*kiu ang*^{2} or *twai*^{2} *ang*^{2} a protracted drought; [4]*ang*^{2} ꜀*tʻĕng*, drought insects in grain; [5]*ang*^{2} ꜀*tʻiêng* ꜀*tó* ʻ*ü kʻe*^{2} (or *e*^{2}), in a time of drought there are frequent appearances of rain; COLL., [6]*ang*^{2} ꜀*chʻeng ng*^{2} *kau*^{2} *só*^{2} the thirsty fields have not sufficient water.

銲^{2} **釬**^{2} Han. Read *hang*^{2}; coll. *ang*^{2}: to solder: [7]*ang*^{2} *laiu*^{2} solder; [8]*ang*^{2} ꜀*tʻau*, the place where the solder is applied; [9]*sek, ang*^{2} pewter solder; [10]꜀*tĕng ang*^{2} copper solder; ʻ*sai* ꜀*chiéng kʻó*^{2} *ang*^{2} to solder with money—use bribes or hush-money.

餡^{2} Hsien. Read *hang*^{2}; coll. *ang*^{2}: cakes stuffed with meat, sugar, dates, or other articles: [11]ʻ*kwí ang*^{2} a preparation for the inside of dumplings; [12]ʻ*piăng ang*^{2} a preparation for the inside of cakes; [13]꜀*tiêng ang*^{2} a sweetened preparation for cakes or dumplings; [14]꜀*keng ang*^{2} a salt preparation; *pwoh, tih, o*^{2} ꜀*tiêng ang*^{2} ꜀*ki*, he desires those with sweet stuffing.

Ang^{2}. A coll. word, used in urging infants to eat: *ang*^{2} *ang*^{2} take it in! take it in!

Ang^{2}. A coll. word: high embankments to keep out freshets: *ang*^{2} *pauk*, the embankment has burst.

(11) Au.

拗 Yao. A furrow, a hollow; an unevenness in the ground.

凹 Ao. Yao. Yeh. Wa. Indented; meandering; the dip of the horizon; the undulations in hills; a hole, a depression, a pit; concave: used for the coll. *nah*, and *náh*, q. v.: [15]꜀*sang* ꜀*au*, a valley.

嘔 Ou. Hsü. Read ꜀*eu* and ʻ*eu*; coll. ʻ*au*: to vomit, the noise of retching; to spit out: [16]ʻ*au tʻo*^{2} to vomit; ʻ*au aĕh*, to retch or vomit slightly; ʻ*au sioh, chʻoi*^{2} to belch up a mouthful; ʻ*au má*^{2} *chʻok*, can't vomit it; ꜀*i* ʻ*kong wa*^{2} *á*^{2} ʻ*au aĕh*, ꜀*nĕng*, his talk makes people retch! it is perfectly sickening! [17]ʻ*au* ꜀*neng*, to throw up milk, as an infant; [18]ʻ*au haik*, to vomit blood.

ʻ*Au*. A coll. word: dull, faded colors: ʻ*au* ʻ*au saik*, old faded colors.

拗 Ao. Yao. Also read ꜀*au*: to pull at, to twist, to break, to snap in two: also read *au*^{2} and in the coll. ʻ*a*, q. v.: used for the coll. ʻ*au*, as in [19]ʻ*au* ʻ*kau chaik*, a festival of the 1st moon, 29th day, when offerings of food are made at the shrines of idols and tablets: ʻ*au* ʻ*kau chĕük*, congee offered at this festival; [20]ʻ*au* ʻ*kau* ꜀*hang*, the cold weather of this festival.

拗^{2} Ao. Yao. Refractory, perverse, obstinate, self-willed; to rush madly against; in the coll.

1 旱天 2 旱災 3 久旱 4 旱蟲 5 旱天多雨氣 6 旱田伓殼燥 7 釬料 8 釬頭 9 錫銲 10 銅釬 11 粿餡 12 餅餡 13 甜餡 14 鹹餡 15 山凹 16 嘔吐 17 嘔乳 18 嘔血 19 拗九節 20 拗九寒

the same as ʻ*a*, to bend: also read ʻ*au*, q. v.: [1]*au*ʾ *p*ʻ*ek*, a wicked disposition, vicious, bad; *chek*, *au*ʾ vicious, wicked; [2]*au*ʾ ʻ*chü*, a disobedient, undutiful child; [3]*au*ʾ *ngik*, obstinate, stubborn; COLL., *au*ʾ ,*wang*, to bend; *au*ʾ *siék*, to break by bending; *ng*[2] ,*t*ʻ*ëng au*ʾ don't bend it! *au*ʾ ,*nau*, greedy, grasping; [4]*au*ʾ *nau*[2] noisy and refractory; *au*ʾ *ch*ʻ*wa*ʾ (or *swa*ʾ), to exorcise malign influences.

後[2] Hou. Read *hai*[2]; coll. *au*[2]: after, in time or place; behind, late; next, then; posterity, descendants: [5]*au*[2] *sié*ʾ succeeding state of metempsychosis; the future existence; [6]*au*[2] *tói*[2] succeeding generations; [7]*au*[2] ʻ*t*ʻ*oi*, the hind quarter; [8]*au*[2] ,*t*ʻ*iăng*, the rear parlor; [9]*au*[2] ,*mwong*, the back door; *au*[2] ,*ch*ʻ*iong*, the back wall; [10]*au*[2] ʻ*tu*, the rear suite of apartments; [11]*au*[2] ,*tiăng*, the rear court; *au*[2] ,*kiăng*, to walk behind; *au*[2] ʻ*ná*, step-mother; *au*[2] *pa*[2] step-father; *au*[2] *hiong*ʾ a back aspect; facing the other way; [12]*au*[2] ʻ*ch*ʻ*iu*, "back-hand,"—i. e., to clean up one's chips, to put things in order, as after finishing a job; ʻ*nü* ,*mó au* ʻ*ch*ʻ*iu*, you don't clean up after you; *au*[2] ʻ*mwi*, next, after, afterwards; *au*[2] *piăh*, ,*sang*, a back wall and hill; *met.*, a dependence, something to rely on; *au*[2] ,*tong* ,*pwo*, a second husband; *au*[2] *k*ʻ*aung*ʾ ,*seng* ,*pa* ʻ*k*ʻ*i*, last to bed but first up, to excel one though beginning after him; *chó*ʾ ʻ*kwi t*ʻ*ok*, ,*nëng au*[2] the devil falls in the rear—said jestingly, as to one coming late.

(12) Auk.

惡, O. Wu. E. Bad, vicious, depraved; wicked, cross, fierce; vile, ugly, deformed, ungracious; filthy, coarse, sordid; unfortunate, unlucky; in the coll. hard, difficult, unpleasant to get on with, intractable, perverse: also read ,*u* and *o*ʾ q. v.: [13]*auk*, *ngik*, perverse, refractory; [14]ʻ*üng auk*, ,*yong siéng*[2] to conceal his vices and proclaim his virtues; COM., [15]*sek*, *auk*, to commit suicide; [16]*auk*, *seu*ʾ ferocious beasts; [17]*auk*, ʻ*kwi*, evil spirits, vicious devils; [18],*hüng auk*, cruel, fierce, wicked; [19]*auk*, *sang*ʾ an evil disposition; [20]*chói*[2] *auk*, wickedness, sin, evil; [21]*auk*, *ngiék*, retribution for crimes (of a former state); [22]*auk*, ,*hing auk*, *chaung*[2] bad conduct, an evil example; *auk*, *tëk*, malice; *auk*, *pó*ʾ punishment of crime; *auk*, *puk*, a fierce servant, who backs up his master; COLL., ,*ngai auk*, wickedness; *auk*, ,*nëng*, bad people; *auk*, ,*ma* ʻ*kwang* ʻ*kau* ,*ka*, a savage cat watches nine houses — i. e., a fierce meddler; *auk*, ,*ing chëü*[2] ʻ*iu auk*, ,*ing* ,*mó*, a fierce fellow of course meets another to torment him—a bad man will always find his match.

握, Wo. Wu. Yo. Also read *ok*,: to grasp, to catch in the hand; to hold, to gripe, to seize; as much as the palm will hold: *auk*, ʻ*ch*ʻ*iu*, to shake hands; ʻ*chiong auk*, to hold in the palm of the hand.

齷, Wo. As in *auk*, *ch*ʻ*auk*, to urge, to crowd; to press, as the teeth against each

[1]拗癖 [2]拗子 [3]拗逆 [4]拗鬧 [5]後世 [6]後代 [7]後腿 [8]後廳 [9]後門 [10]後堵 [11]後埕 [12]後手 [13]惡逆 [14]隱惡揚善 [15]十惡 [16]惡獸 [17]惡鬼 [18]兇惡 [19]惡性 [20]罪惡 [21]惡孽 [22]惡形惡狀

other; in the coll. dirty, filthy, defiled; vile, in a moral sense: [1]*auk, ch'auk, 'si*, very filthy; [2]*auk, ch'auk, óh*, or *auk, ch'auk, kié'* meanness, low cunning; [3]*auk, ch'auk, k'e'* foul exhalations; *met.*, anger, fury; [4]*auk, ch'auk, ,t'iĕng*, bad weather; *auk, ch'auk, siăh,* *auk, ch'auk, ,pui*, gross food, gross fat—filthy habits of eating.

幄, Yo. Also read *ok,*: a curtain, a screen; a large tent, a marquee; to protect, to shelter; an awning to screen from the sun: [5]*,mi auk*, a decorated border at the top of curtains; [6]*,tiong auk*, to hang up curtains.

沃, Wu. Wo. To water, to irrigate; to bathe, to wet, to soften; to enrich, to mollify; to wash: used for the coll. *woh*, q. v.: [7]*auk, 'k'wang*, to wash the hands; [8]*'sá auk*, to wash; *met.*, to cleanse the heart; [9]*kwang' auk*, to water plants.

渥, Wu. Yo. Also read *ok,*: to moisten, to bedew, to water, to cause to increase or grow; to enrich with favors; to fertilize; to cover or daub thick; shining, rich; the noise of water: [10]*auk, tek,* enriched, as with favors; [11]*auk, ,tang*, to paint a deep red.

鋈, Also read *ok,*: to wash with silver or gold; to plate base metal; to overlay with finer metal, as the ornaments of a harness.

堊, O. Different colored clays; white or washed clay for crockery; to wash or plaster mud or unplastered walls; to whitewash; plaster; an unplastered wall; to paint on plaster, to ornament a wall.

喔, Wu. Yo. Also read *ok,*: the crowing of a cock: [12]*auk, auk,* the cackling of chickens; [13]*auk, ,i*, forced laughter.

(13) Aung.

Aung'. A coll. word: to watch, to herd, to guard, to look after, to care for: *aung' ch'io'* to watch the house; *aung' ch'ek,* to watch against thieves; *aung' nóh,* to guard anything; *,mó ,nĕng aung'* no one to watch; *aung' pang'* to watch with the sick; *aung' ,siăng ,lau*, to guard the city watch towers; *aung, ,mwong tŭk, 'k'eng p'ah, k'ĕük, siăh,* to guard the gate, drive away dogs, and beat beggars — are a porter's duties.

絖², 桁² Hang. The 1st read *,k'ong* and *haung'*, the 2nd read *,heng*: used for the coll. *aung'*: a bamboo pole; a pole, or support of wood: the 2nd used for the coll. *,ang, ,hong*, and *haung'* q. v.: [14]*tĕük, aung'* a bamboo pole; [15]*,i ,siong aung'* a pole for drying clothes on; [16]*tiong' aung'* poles for curtains; [17]*aung' ,ch'a*, a forked pole; [18]*aung' 'niong*, a limber pole; [19]*aung' siék,* the pole is broken; [20]*,ting aung'* the beam from which a lantern is suspended.

Aung'. A coll. word: to rub, to rub with the hands: *aung' aung'* to rub with the hands; *aung' ,hu*, torn, tattered, as the ends of worn sleeves; *aung' ,ta*, to rub dry; *aung' ĕü'* to wear away by rubbing.

---

1 齷齪死〇 2 齷齪智 3 齷齪氣 4 齷齪天 5 帷幄〇 6 張幄 7 沃盥 8 洗沃 9 灌沃 10 渥澤 11 渥丹 12 喔喔 13 喔咿 14 竹桁 15 衣裳桁 16 帳絖〇 17 桁叉 18 桁軟 19 桁折 20 燈桁

(14) Cha.

查 Ch'a. A raft, a float; to investigate, to examine, to inquire into; to search, to look for; it appears that, having investigated I find—used in official communications: [1]ˏ*cha hok*ˎ to cast up official accounts; COM., [2]ˏ*cha* ʿ*k'ó*, to investigate, to examine; [3]ˏ*cha ch'ak*, to examine, to search; [4]ˏ*cha* ˏ*ming*, to examine and make clear; [5]ˏ*cha ang*ˀ to examine officially; [6]ˏ*cha* ˏ*ching*, to examine truly; [7]ˏ*pwang* ˏ*cha*, a guard in charge of a post or gate; [8]*sé*ˀ ˏ*cha*, to search diligently; [9]ˏ*ch'á* ˏ*cha*, a police search; [10]ˏ*cha ch'ok*, to find out, to discover; [11]ˏ*cha yâ*ˀ ˏ*kwang*, an officer who patrols the streets at night; [12]ˏ*cha* ˏ*ch'ing*, to make inquiries before settling a betrothal; COLL., [13]ˏ*cha mwong*ˀ to inquire about; to investigate, to interrogate; ˏ*cha tioh*ˎ to find out; ˏ*cha tek*ˎ ʿ*king*, to examine rigidly; ˏ*eng* ˏ*cha*, to pester, to annoy one with questions.

楂 槎 Ch'a. Drift wood, a raft of timber; a small skiff; to fell trees, to hew wood.

渣 Cha. Name of a river; residuum, refuse, grounds, sediment, settlings, what remains after expressing the juice: COM., [14]ˏ*chiong* ˏ*cha*, residuum of rice ground wet, settlings or impurities of starch; [15]*yoh*ˎ ˏ*cha*, the refuse of medicinal herbs after steeping, a second decoction of herbs; COLL., [16]ˏ*cha p'óh*, sediments, settlings; [17]ˏ*cha* ˏ*yong*, reckless, beyond control; confused, failing, as a matter quarreled over; ˏ*mó p'óh*, ˏ*mó* ˏ*cha*, utterly false, wholly without reality; [18]ˏ*cha* ˏ*li*, confused, disarranged; *k'ëük*ˎ *niê*ˀ ʿ*kiäng* ˏ*tó tek*ˎ ˏ*cha* ˏ*li*, turned topsy-turvy by the children; [19]ˏ*cha* ʿ*tai*, sediment, settlings.

楂 樝 楂 柤 Cha. The first only is used in Foochow: a small, round, red fruit, with an acid taste, resembling the crab-apple; it grows in Shantung, and is much used for its acid: COM., [20]ˏ*sang* ˏ*cha*, the name of this fruit; [21]ˏ*nang* ˏ*cha*, a medicine prepared from sangcha; [22]ˏ*sang* ˏ*cha kó*, sangcha jelly; ˏ*sang* ˏ*cha* ˏ*t'ong*, sangcha sweet-meats.

皻 皶 Cha. Pimples on the nose, wine blotches; pimples on the skin: [23]ʿ*chiu* ˏ*cha*, wine blotches.

摣 揸 Cha. The 2d is an unauthorized character: to grasp, to clutch, to grab; to hold or take firmly; to work, as a bellows.

蹅 To put down the foot, to tread upon; the sound of trampling; to walk awry.

咱 Cha. Tsa. Tsan. Also read *chak*ˎ: a colloquial word used in the north: I, myself; the pronoun I in the Peking dialect.

1查	3查	5查	7盤	9差	11查	親	渣	粕	來	楂	楂
核	察	案	查	查	夜	13查	15藥	17渣	19渣	21南	糕
2查	4查	6查	8細	10查	官	僴	渣	洋	滓	楂	23酒
考	明	真	查	出	12查	14藥	16渣	18渣	20山	22山	皶

早 ʻ 蚤 ʻ Tsao. Read *ʻchó;* coll. *ʻcha:* the morning, early, soon; timely, formerly, anciently; betimes, beforehand, previously; just commenced: [1]*ʻcha ʻk'i*, or *ʻcha ʻk'i ˏt'au*, the morning; [2]*ʻcha ˏseng*, (spoken *ʻcha ˏleng*), a little while ago; [3]*ˏking tangʼ ʻcha*, this morning; *ʻcha ʻwang*, morning and evening; *ʻcha pwongʼ* early rice, breakfast; [4]*ëüʼ ʻcha*, early, timely, already, as a thing already prepared; [5]*ʻcha ˏtong*, morning audience, given by officers; [6]*chaiʼ ʻcha*, at a former period; *ʻcha ʻk'i kauʼ angʼ* from morning till night; *ʻcha siohˎ k'aikˎ* a little early; [7]*ʻcha ch'eʼ* the morning market; [8]*ʻcha hwakˎ* to gain a literary degree in youth; *ʻcha siohˎ pwoʼ* a little earlier; *ʻcha ʻwang ˏsi kaʼ pokˎ ˏtung*, the current prices differ morning and evening; *ʻcha ˏkwang*, or *ʻcha ˏtëng*, the harvest of the 6th moon; *ʻcha ʻmwong ˏtëng*, or *ʻcha ʻmwong ˏkwang*, the early and latter harvests.

乍ʼ Cha. Now, present, just now; quickly, suddenly, hastily; at first, for a moment; inadvertently, unexpectedly: in the coll. read *chaʼ* q. v.: [9]*chaʼ kiéngʼ* to happen to see, just seen; [10]*chaʼ chengʼ chaʼ t'óiʼ* to advance quickly, then suddenly retire.

疟ʼ Also read *ˏcha:* a severe disease, very sick; a running ulcer: [11]*chaʼ ˏsai*, a swelling or ulcer on the cheek.

詐ʼ Cha. To deceive, to cheat, to impose upon; artful, fraudulent, deceitful, treacherous; not real, illusory, fictitious: [12]*chaʼ ˏngiong*, to lie, to speak falsely; [13]*chaʼ ngoiʼ* fraudulent, deceitful, treacherous; [14]*chaʼ ˏmeu*, to plot, to beguile; COM., [15]*ʻk'ieu chaʼ* cunning, tricky, as a rogue; [16]*ˏkang chaʼ* false, lying, full of deceit; [17]*piéngʼ chaʼ* changeful, tantalizing, unreliable, Proteus-like; [18]*lekˎ chaʼ* to drive, to force, to extort from; COLL., *ˏngó chaʼ* to extort, to levy black mail, as in yamuns.

蚱ʼ Cha. Tsê. A sort of grasshopper; one says a large locust, called [19]*chaʼ ʻmeng;* [20]*chaʼ ˏsiéng*, a species of cicada; used for the coll. *t'aʼ* q. v.

迮ʼ Tsê. Read *chaik*, or *ch'aik*, in the dictionaries: pressing, urgent; to hasten, to drive, to force, to compel.

舴ʼ Tsê. As [21]*chaʼ ʻmeng*, a small boat, a pinnace, a gig.

炸ʼ Cha. An unauthorized character: to try in the fire; to purify, as metals; to refine.

醡ʼ Cha. Used for the next: a wine-press; to press or separate spirits: in the coll. read *taʼ* q. v.: [22]*ʻchiu chaʼ* a wine-press, a wine-vat.

榨ʼ Cha. An oil-press; a sugar-press; to press or extract juices: *ˏiu chaʼ* an oil-press.

Chaʼ. A coll. word: crushed, bruised, flattened, as a peg

1 早起 2 早先 3 今旦早〇 4 預早 5 早堂 6 在早 7 早市 8 早發 9 乍見 10 乍進乍退 11 疟腮 12 詐言 13 詐僞 14 詐謀 15 巧詐 16 奸詐 17 變詐 18 勒詐 19 蚱蜢 20 蚱蟬 21 舴艋 22 酒醡

福州方言拼音字典

driv n but not entering: ‘ch‘iu k‘ŭk, nóh, mô cha’ the hand crushed by a blow; ,tiăng cha’ bruised by something falling on it.

咋’ Cha. A loud sound, a rude noise.

齟齬 Cha. Read ,cha in the Paik, ,Ing in the sense of crooked, irregular teeth: COLL., [1],ma ,cha, to insist unreasonably; fretful, troublesome, as a child; confused, indistinct; che’ ‘siă cheng’ k‘ô ,ma ,cha, the words written very confusedly.

,Cha. A coll. word: clamor, confusion; to disturb by noise: ,cha ,cha kieu’ clamor, confused sounds, uproar; ,cha ,cha naung’ confused by noise; k‘ëŭk, ,i ,cha naung’ k‘ô’ my mind all confused by him.

,Cha. A coll. word: to fry in fat or vegetable oil: pong’ ,iu ‘lâ ,cha, fry it in oil; ,cha ,su ,su tioh, fry it crisp.

乍’ Cha. Read cha’: used in the Paik, ,Ing for the coll. cha’ as in pô’ cha’ now, just now, for the first time; unexpectedly; pô’ cha’ ,tiăng, hear it now for the first time; pô’ cha’ ch‘eng’ ch‘eng’ ‘si ,nëng, pô’ cha’ po’ ,k‘i ho’ ,nëng, a sudden cold freezes people to death, (so) one suddenly rich imposes on others.

(15) Chá.

齋 斋 Chai. A school; to abstain from animal food, vegetable diet; to revere, to respect; pure, reverential, serious; a closet: the 1st also read ,chai, q. v.: [2],chá kai’ to abstain from animal food, and vicious indulgence; COM., [3],chü ,chá, a school, a schoolroom; [4]ka’ ,chá, to teach school; [5]siong’ ,chá, to enter the school; [6],chá ,kié, rules of the school; [7],chá ‘iu, or [8],tŭng ,chá, schoolmates; [9],k‘wi ,chá, to open a school; [10],chá ‘su, a study; [11]sang’ ,chá, to discontinue a school; [12],nang ,chá, a boys' school; [13]‘nü ,chá, a girls' school; [14],chá ,kung, one in charge of a temple, a kind of laypriest; [15],chá ‘ma, a priestess, one who recites prayers in houses and in Kwanyin temples; COLL., [16]sói’ ,chá, to be a school-teacher; [17],kwong ,mwong ,chá, a private school; [18],kwong ,chá, or ,kong ,chá, to make offerings in school to Confucius in the 4th moon; [19]siăh, ,tong ,chá, a vegetarian; [20]siăh, ,hwa ,chá, a partial vegetarian; [21]siăh, ‘cha ,chá, to abstain from meat at breakfast; [22],chá ch‘ai’ a vegetable offering to the idols, vegetable diet; ,chá ‘k‘ë or ,chá ‘kë, the mischief-maker of a school.

饝 糬 Ch‘i. 糯 The last two are unauthorized, but are commonly used in Foochow: sweet cakes made of rice or wheat flour, stuffed with sugar and glutinous rice—offered to ghosts—i. e., spirits of the wretched dead, as

[1]嘛齟 [2]齋戒 [3]書齋 [4]教齋 [5]上齋 [6]齋規 [7]齋友 [8]同齋 [9]開齋 [10]齋所 [11]散齋 [12]男齋 [13]女齋 [14]齋公 [15]齋媽 [16]坐齋 [17]關門齋 [18]齋光 [19]食長齋 [20]食花齋 [21]食早齋 [22]齋菜

lepers, beggars, &c.: &c., COM., [1]꜀*chá* ꜁*yong*, a meal of cakes for ghosts; ʻ*miĕng*ʾ ꜀*chá*, wheaten cakes; *hwa*ʾ ꜀*chá*, to offer cakes; COLL., [3]꜀*pwong* ꜀*chá*, to distribute the cakes after offering them in worship; ʻ*kwi* ʻ*ch*ʻ*iong* ꜀*chá*, the spirits snatch the cakes; *met.*, avarice, greed; ꜁*ming* ꜁*t*ʻ*au* ꜀*chá*, large and small cakes for ghosts; ꜀*chá ang*ʾ stuffing of the ꜀*chá* cakes.

躋 躋 ꜀Chi. The first is more commonly used: to climb, to climb up high; to ascend, to go up, as stairs, to go aloft; to mount up a steep hill; to rise, as vapor; a rainbow: [4]꜀*p*ʻ*ang* ꜀*chá*, to climb up; [5]꜀*kó* ꜀*chá*, to ascend, to go up high; [6]꜀*chá* ꜁*tong*, to ascend to the hall.

臍 ꜀Ch'i. Also read ꜁*chá*: the navel; to cut off even: used for the coll. ꜁*sai*, q. v.: ʻ*siĕ*ʾ ꜀*chá*, to bite the navel; *met.*, to attempt impossibilities; [8]꜀*chá tai*ʾ the umbilical cord; [9]*twang*ʾ ꜀*chá*, to cut the umbilical cord.

懠 ꜀Ch'i. Angry, vexed, enraged; suspicious, envious; to doubt: [10]꜀*chá* ꜁*ngi*, suspicious.

賫 賷 ꜀Chi. To take or send a present; to present to, to offer; to dispatch, as documents; to send up, as to a superior; the first character also means to leave, to supply the necessaries for a journey; a sigh: [11]꜀*chá* ꜁*teu*, to hand in to; [12]꜀*ch*ʻ*ing* ꜀*chá*, to deliver in person; ꜀*chá song*ʾ to send, as a present; [13]꜀*chá chieu*ʾ ꜀*kwang*, a bearer of official dispatches.

蠐 ꜀Ch'i. A maggot: [14]꜁*iu* ꜀*chá*, the larvæ of a beetle, long white grubs that eat trees; [15]꜀*chá* ꜁*chó*, maggots in ordure.

齏 ꜀Chi. A sort of leek; to prepare and compound; to mix, to blend; to make dishes of vegetables, as the poor do; compounded, mixed; to compare, as opinions: [16]*hwo*ʾ ꜀*chá*, to blend in due proportions, as spices.

嚌 ꜀Chi. To taste, to sip; to wet the lips: [17]꜀*chá* ꜁*ngai*, to laugh. Read ꜁*chá*: a plaintive sound, as of birds.

儕 ꜀Ch'ai. A class, a group, a sort, a company; persons of the same class; also used as the plural first personal pronoun: [18]꜁*peng* ꜀*chá*, friends; [19]꜁*ngu* ꜀*chá*, we, us; [20]꜁*tung* ꜀*chá*, associates; [21]꜀*chá* ʻ*ngeu*, cronies, fellows.

霽 ʻChi. Rain ceasing; the clouds passing and the blue sky appearing: [22]꜁*ching* ʻ*chá*, the sky clearing; [23]*ngwok*꜇ ʻ*chá*, a bright moon; [24]꜀*k*ʻ*ai* ʻ*chá*, the clouds rolling away, showing the clear sky.

薺 ʻChi. Cress, shepherd's purse; a term for small esculent plants, as cress, pepper-grass, mint, &c.

穧 ʻChi. To reap grain; a handful of rice just cut; to put it together, to bind into sheaves.

1 穧筵 2 麪穧 3 分穧 4 攀躋 5 高躋 6 躋堂 7 噬臍 8 臍帶 9 斷臍 10 懠疑 11 賫投 12 親賫 13 賫送 14 蝤蠐 15 蠐螬 16 和齏 17 嚌啀 18 朋儕 19 吾儕 20 同儕 21 儕偶 22 晴霽 23 月霽 24 開霽

ʻ擠 Chi. Ch'i. To place, to spread out; to push, to push over; to upset; to press upon, to crowd: [1]ˌ*pai* ʻ*chá*, to press against; *met.*, to slander; COM., [2]*ëüng*ʼ ʻ*chá*, to elbow, to push, as a crowd.

ʻ齎 To bite, to gnaw; in the *Paik*ˎ ˏ*Ing*, the teeth uneven or irregular: COLL., [3]ˏ*cha* ʻ*chá*, a little more so, adding to, increasing, as a danger or risk; ˏ*cha* ʻ*chá sioh*ˎ *tek*ˎ ʻ*kiüng cheu*ʼ ʻ*tó*, press a little harder and it will fall, as a bank when a run is made on it for specie.

ʻ鱭 ʻ鮆 A thin fish, with a silvery body and a purplish tail, a mullet: *pek*ˎ ʻ*chá*, a greenish mullet, Mugil ventricosus; ʻ*ma* ʻ*chá*, a kind of anchovy, Coilia playfairii.

ʻ*Chá.* A coll. word, as in ʻ*chá* ʻ*chá kieu*ʼ garrulous, loquacious, talkative; ʻ*chá* ʻ*chá* ʻ*mó*, a garrulous old woman.

ʻ*Chá.* A coll. word: to wrench the foot: ʻ*chá* ˏ*wai*, to twist, to wrench; ʻ*chá p'wai*ʼ or ʻ*chá pauk*ˎ to burst (as a shoe) when you step awry.

濟ʼ Chi. To go over, to cross over, to ferry one over a stream; to assist, to aid, to succor; to give alms; to make successful, to effect, to bring about; able, capable, clever: [4]ʻ*iu chá*ʼ can be done, practicable; [5]*chá*ʼ ˏ*ch'iong*, to cross over a water; [6]*chá*ʼ ˏ*ing*, to ferry persons over; COM., [7]*sié*ʼ *chá*ʼ to give alms; [8]*keu*ʼ *chá*ʼ to relieve, to save; [9]ˏ*chiu chá*ʼ or ʻ*ching chá*ʼ to relieve by alms; [10]*chá*ʼ *sié*ʼ to aid people; [11]*chá*ʼ *söü*ʼ a business completed; COLL., *chá*ʼ ˏ*seng má*ʼ ʻ*pa seng*ʼ *kwo*ʼ *wak*ˎ ˏ*mai*, even inadequate relief to the living is better than burying them alive. Read ʻ*chá*: a river in Shantung.

纃ʼ A coll. character, found in the *Paik*ˎ ˏ*Ing*: a species of hemp (Bahmeria tenacissima) from the fiber of which the grass-cloth is made: *chá*ʼ ʻ*long*, a tunic or shirt of grass-cloth; [12]*chá*ʼ *k'o*ʼ grass-cloth trowsers; [13]*chá*ʼ *pwo*ʼ grass-cloth; *chá*ʼ ˏ*i*, garments of grass-cloth; [14]*chá*ʼ *tiong*ʼ grass-cloth curtains; ˏ*ch'u chá*ʼ coarse grass-cloth; [15]*chek*ˎ *chá*ʼ to weave grass-cloth; [16]*pah*ˎ *chá*ʼ ˏ*sang*, a white grass-cloth robe; [17]ˏ*kong* ˏ*sá chá*ʼ Kiangsi grass-cloth; *chá*ʼ ˏ*lá naung*ʼ in a snarl like tangled hempen fibers, as business or affairs.

ˏ齊 Ch'i. Even, level, plain surface, regular, flat, equal, uniform; to equalize, to tranquilize; to respect, decorous, correct; at once, all together; to adjust, to classify, to place in order, to arrange, to make even; quick, smart; good; to discriminate; an ancient feudal state, comprising that part of Shantung east of T'ai Shan; the 210th radical: also read ˏ*chai* and ˏ*chü*, q. v.: [18]ˏ*chá* ˏ*mi*, husband and wife grown old together; [19]ˏ*chá lik*ˎ to work together; COM., [20]ʻ*ching* ˏ*chá*, handsome, well dressed; to march in regular order like soldiers; [21]ˏ*chá* ʻ*ching*, prettily dressed, arranged with neatness; [22]ˏ*chá* ˏ*chiong*, all, entire, all present; [23]ˏ*chá ngié*ʼ to consult

[1]排擠 [2]擁擠 [3]齜齎 [4]有濟 [5]濟川 [6]濟人 [7]施濟 [8]救濟 [9]賙濟 [10]濟世 [11]濟事 [12]纃褲 [13]纃布 [14]纃帳 [15]織纃 [16]白纃衫 [17]江西纃 [18]齊眉 [19]齊力 [20]整齊 [21]齊整 [22]齊全 [23]齊議

together; [1]*‚chá ‚ka*, to govern a family; [2]*‚chá ‚ka te' kwok*, to harmonize the family and govern the empire; *‚chá 'hó*, both doing well; COLL., *‚chá k'ó'* to go together or in company; *mwoi' ‚chá*, not yet assembled, as a company; *‚chá ‚chá*, together, ready, in company; *‚chá chó' ‚chá siăh*, to work and eat in common; *‚chá móh, ch'ieu'* let us all not laugh! *‚chá siăh, ‚chá o' e'* eat and enjoy it together; *met.*, united in getting gain.

‚Chá. A coll. word, as in *‚chá siĕk*, to snap asunder, to break; *‚chá tói' ‚tong*, to break in two.

劑 [3] Chi. To pare, to trim, to make even, to equalize; to divide, to apportion, to adjust; to compound, as medicine; a dose, a recipe; used in the coll. for dough; *met.*, dull, stupid, unlucky: [3]*‚tieu chá'* to compound medicines; [4]*yoh, chá'* a dose of medicine; COLL., *chá' tioh, ‚nuí*, the dough must be kneaded; *met.* you are soft, unsophisticated; *chá' tek, 'heng*, incorrigibly dull, always imposed on. Read *'chá*, as in [5]*che' 'chá*, a bond such as can be divided and one part retained as evidence; [6]*‚tieu 'chá*, to regulate, to settle.

(16) Chaĕ.

助 [2] Chu. Read *cho'*; coll. *chaĕ'* as in [7]*‚pong chaĕ'* to help, to aid, to assist, to succor; [8]*chaĕ' lik*, to aid with strength; [9]*chaĕ' 'nü*, to help you; *chaĕ' 'ngwai* (or *‚nu*,) help me! [10]*chaĕ' ch'oi'* to back one in talking; [11]*chaĕ' ‚yăng*, to aid in overcoming; *chaĕ' ‚nĕng*, to assist people; *chaĕ' sioh, ‚ng'* to aid with a company; to help in a fight; *‚song chaĕ'* to assist each other.

(17) Chaĕk.

Chaĕk,. A coll. word, as in *‚chó chaĕk*, a sense of emptiness or indigestion, as from eating bamboo-sprouts, etc.

(18) Chaĕng.

糉 粽 Tsung. Three cornered dumplings of glutinous rice, done up in leaves: COLL., [12]*chaĕng' nioh*, leaves for wrapping dumplings; [13]*‚chiĕng 'mwoi chaĕng'* pointed dumplings; [14]*‚ngu ‚t'au chaĕng'* ox-head shaped dumplings; *'kwoi chaĕng'* to wrap and make up dumplings.

(19) Chah.

窄 Chai. Tsê. Read *chaik*, in the dictionaries: narrow, strait, small, diminutive; compressed; groveling, mean, narrow-minded: [15]*chah, 'sieu*, narrow and small; [16]*chah, keng'* a narrow path, a lane; COM., [17]*chah, pwo'* narrow cotton-cloth; *‚mwong chah*, the door narrow; *te' chah*, contracted ground, a small plat; a defile; [18]*to' liong' chah*, exacting, illiberal; COLL., *tio' chah*, the road narrow; [19]*chah, hek*, or *chah, kek*, much contracted; [20]*chah, ‚sié ‚mi*, a trifle narrow; *chah, chah, chó'* to do business on a small scale; *chah, tek, 'heng*, extremely contracted.

笮 Tsê. Read *chaik*, in the dictionaries; like the last: a quiver; ceiling of the roof; to hasten out; to press; to

[1]齊家 [2]治國齊家 [3]調劑 [4]藥劑 [5]質劑 [6]調劑 [7]帮助 [8]助力 [9]助汝 [10]助嘴 [11]助贏 [12]糉葉 [13]尖尾糉 [14]牛頭糉 [15]窄小 [16]窄徑 [17]窄布 [18]度量窄 [19]窄狹 [20]窄些微

tattoo, or brand, as a punishment: ¹*chah, ˛chiéng*, an ancient name of coin.

仄 ˏ Chai. Chua. Tsĕ. Read *chaik*, in the dictionaries: oblique, inclined, slanting, leaning; name of the six deflected tones: COM., ²*˛ping chah, ˛siăng*, the even and the oblique tones, all the tones of the Foochow dialect; ³*chah, ˛siăng*, the six deflected tones.

績 ˏ Chi. Read *chek,*; used for the coll. *chah*, as in ⁴*chah, siăng*ʾ to pick apart and make into threads; ⁵*chah, chá*ʾ to prepare the fiber for weaving grass-cloth.

Chah,. A coll. word: to slander, to defame: *chah, ˛nëng*, to slander people; *chah, ˛i kʻóʾ* or *chah, ˛i chʻok,* to slander him out of his place.

Chah,. A coll. word: to throw down, to pitch, as cash: *chah, ˛chiéng*, to pitch or throw cash so as to knock other cash out of a square—a game; *chah, piék, ˛ting*, to pitch nails instead of cash; *chah, ˛hang kʻaëk,* to pitch clam shells.

(20) Cháh.

Cháh,. A coll. word: sloppy: *langʾ cháh, cháh,* wet under foot, sloppy, plashy.

(21) Chai.

哉 ˛ Tsai. An interjection of praise or surprise; an interrogative particle, intimating doubt or conviction, according to scope; a superlative; a particle placed after important words to draw attention, but the regimen alters its meaning; to begin, to burst forth, as plants in the spring: ⁶*˛chai ˛seng ˛ming*, new moon of the 3d night; ⁷*taiʾ ˛chai*, oh, how great! ⁸*˛ai ˛chai*, alas! ⁹*˛hó ʻiu ˛chai*, how is it so? *˛ang chaiʾ ˛chai*, where is it? *˛chai ˛seng pʻaëk,* the moon on the 16th, just after the full.

栽 菑 ˛ ˛ Tsai. To cultivate, to plant, to tend, to raise; to set out plants or saplings; to hill, to heap earth at the roots; a sapling; to assist: ¹⁰*˛chai sik,* to set out plants, to plant and tend; COM., ¹¹*˛chai ˛hwa*, to cultivate flowers; *˛chai chʻaiʾ* to raise vegetables; ¹²*˛chai chëüngʾ* to plant; ¹³*˛chai ˛puí*, to manure, to enrich the soil; *ʻkʻó ʻi ˛chai ˛puí*, can improve him. Read *chaiʾ*: long planks for building earth walls.

災 灾 烖 菑 ˛ ˛ ˛ ˛ Tsai. The first two are most used: natural calamities, as floods and droughts; divine judgments, plagues, miseries, misfortunes, dangers; adverse, calamitous, unfortunate: COM., ¹⁴*˛chai hwoʾ* or *˛chai ˛yong*, calamities; ¹⁵*˛chai nangʾ* troubles, misfortunes; ¹⁶*˛tʻiéng ˛chai*, divine inflictions; *ʻchwi ˛chai*, floods, inundations; ¹⁷*ʻhwi ˛chai*, conflagrations; ¹⁸*˛chó ˛chai*, to meet calamity; ¹⁹*piéʾ ˛chai*, to avoid calamities; ²⁰*˛sieu ˛chai ʻkai aik,* to diminish afflictions and remove troubles; ²¹*yongʾ ˛chai*, sacrifices to avert

¹笮錢 ²平仄聲 ³仄聲 ⁴績線 ⁵績綪 ⁶哉生明 ⁷大哉 ⁸哀哉 ⁹何有哉 ¹⁰栽植〇 ¹¹栽花 ¹²栽種 ¹³栽培 ¹⁴災禍 ¹⁵災難 ¹⁶天災 ¹⁷火災 ¹⁸遭災 ¹⁹避災 ²⁰消災 ²¹禳災解厄

misfortune; [1]'ang' ,chai, a drought; COLL., ,*chai hwo' ,t'iéng siong'* ,*li*, judgments are from heaven.

齋 **齋** Chai. To restrain, to purify one's self, as when about to perform religious ceremonies; to abstain from eating flesh; to reverence; decorous; to chasten one's desires: the 1st also read ,*chá* and ,*chü*, and the 2d also read ,*chá*, q. v.: [2],*chai keng'* to abstain and revere, as in worship; ,*chai* ,*ming*, to purify by abstinence; [3],*chai lek*, cautious, prudent; COM., [4],*chai kai' muk*, *ük*, to fast, abstain from vice, and perform ablutions.

,*Chai*. A coll. word, as in ,*chai kaïk*, to perceive, to notice, conscious of; *ng'* ,*chai kaïk*, not to be aware of.

'宰 Tsai. To govern, to rule, to superintend; to fashion to one's liking; a ruler, a head man, a governor; to butcher, to skin and dress animals; to cook: [5]'*chai te'* to govern; [6]'*t'ung 'chai*, in ancient times the highest officer in the empire; [7],*ka 'chai*, a steward; [8]*'ek*, '*chai*, a district magistrate; ,*tio 'chai*, a butcher, a cook; '*chai sak*, to kill; '*chai kak*, to slice meat; [9]*uk*, '*chai* ,*keng* ,*ngiu*, kill not the ox that ploughs; COM., [10]'*chai siong'* a prime minister; [11]'*chü 'chai*, (coll. '*chio 'chai*), a ruler; the governing power, the mind; COLL., '*chai siong' pok*, '*ló 'hó* ,*t'ang* ,*sung*, a premier's capacity big enough to pole a boat; *met.*, a person of great forbearance and magnanimity.

'指 Chih. Read '*chi*; coll. '*chai*: a finger, a toe: [11]'*ch'iu 'chai*, the fingers; ,*k'a 'chai*, the toes; *twai' 'mó 'chai*, or *twai'* ,*mó 'chai*, the thumb; ,*kié kaïk*, '*chai*, the forefinger; *tai'* ,*tong 'chai*, the middle finger; ,*mó* ,*miäng 'chai*, the fourth finger; '*mwi 'chai*, the little finger; '*ch'iu 'chai 'mwi*, tip of the finger; [12]*sek*, *ek*, '*chai*, a double-thumbed person; *sek*, *ek*, '*chai 't'ó* ,*peng* ,*ngié*, "the double-thumbed cheapen things"—said of any one who haggles about prices.

'䆎 Tsai. To boil, to cook, to prepare food: [13],*p'eng 'chai*, to prepare food.

'滓 Tzŭ. Residuum, sediment; refuse, d r e g s; precipitate: [14]'*chaik*, '*chai*, sediment of liquids; COLL., *mëk*, '*chai*, or *mek*, '*chai*, tears; [15],*lau mëk*, '*chai*, to shed tears; *mëk*, '*chai* ,*ch'iäng* ,*tu* ,*mó*, not a tear.

'紙 Chih. Read '*chi* in the dictionaries: paper; a document, a writing: COM., [16]'*chai* ,*liéng*, narrow charts or scrolls; [17]'*chai* ,*kwong*, or '*chai taing'* a paper shop; [18]'*ngu saik*, '*chai*, five sorts of colored paper, variegated paper; [19]'*chai pek*, stationery; [20]'*chai* ,*i*, paper with figures of clothing on it, burnt in worship as offerings; [21]'*chai yeu'* a paper kite; [22]*che' 'chai*, written or printed paper; [23]*keng' sek*, *che' 'chai*, to revere lettered paper; '*chai* ,*p'wi*, pasteboard;

[1]旱災 [2]齋敬 [3]齋慄 [4]齋戒沐浴 [5]宰治 [6]冢宰 [7]家宰 [8]邑宰 [9]勿宰耕牛 [10]宰相 [11]主宰 手指 [12]十指 指一 [13]烹䆎 [14]汁滓 [15]流目滓 [16]紙聯 [17]紙坊 [18]五色紙 [19]紙筆 [20]紙衣 [21]紙鷂 [22]字紙 [23]敬惜字紙

福州方言拼音字典

'ₚpó ₍lá 'chai, transparent paper; 'chai 'tá, paper soles; "chai ₍pung, a paper manufactory or storing room; 'chai ₍teu, paper shavings; 'chai ₍t'au, selvedge of paper; 'chai ₍pau, done up in paper; ₍king 'chai, common writing paper; '₍kwong k'aiu' 'chai, a superior quality of paper; ngwok₍ kak₍ 'chai, wrapping paper; "ch'ó 'chai, or ₍ch'u 'chai, coarse paper; "chai ₍mui, (coll. 'chai ₍hëng), a paper match or lighter; "chai ₍chiëng, and ₍chiëng 'chai, two sorts of imitation money paper, as burnt in worship, scattered in funeral processions and placed at graves; '₍ing ₍ching póh₍ ₍ü 'chai, man's feelings are as thin as paper; 'chai ₍ch'iëng, a ticket, a label; COLL., '₍p'ië 'chai, note or letter paper; "kah₍ 'ngang 'chai, or 'ka 'lang 'chai, paper ruled in small squares; 'chai ₍nó, or 'chai t'ak₍, paper things, as burnt in worship or for toys, transparencies, etc.; 'chai 'kwi ₍t'iong, a few sheets of paper; how many sheets? 'chai 'ngiëng, paper tapers, as dipped in oil and lighted; 'chai 'ngiëng ₍ting, paper thongs, as used instead of thread to bind books; 'chai chô' ₍lang ₍tó, a railing made of paper—no means of support.

'載 Tsai. A year; to commence, as after a full revolution: also read chai' q. v.: "₍niëng 'chai, a year; COLL., sioh₍ ₍niëng pwang' 'chai, a year or half of a year; ₍sang ₍niëng ngo' 'chai, from three to five years.

載' Tsai. To contain, to hold, as a carriage or ship; to fill in, to load on, to bear, to sustain; to act, to do, to fulfill, to effect; to record; to adorn, to beautify; to load in and transport; written, recorded; filled, loaded; an auxiliary word, then, thereupon; an incalculably high number: also read 'chai, q. v.: COM., "ke' chai' to record; chai' ch'ah₍ to enter in a register or official list; chai' p'wo' to keep accounts or records; "su chai' what is recorded; COLL., o' chai' it is recorded; chai' tek₍ bearable, allowable; better; chai' tek₍ 'k'i, can bear it, as to buy that amount; chai' má' 'k'i, can't bear it, unable, as to expense.

再' Tsai. Again, doubled; to repeat, a second time; then, further, continued: "che' chai' che' ₍sang, two or three times, repeatedly; COM., "chai' 'kong, to say or explain again; "chai' ch'üä' to take a second wife; "chai' ka' to be married a second time, as a widow; "chai' pai' repeated compliments; "chai' ₍seng, to revive, as when near death; regeneration; COLL., chai' ₍sang, to sprout again; also used for a new spiritual birth, regeneration; chai' ₍li, to come again; chai' ₍sang chai' se' three or four times; chai' ₍k'wang 'kwi nik₍ to extend the time a few days; chai' ch'iong' ng' se' 'chiä ₍siäng, if I speak to you again it will not be in that tone!—said to a stubborn child.

儎' A coll. character, found in the Paik₍ ₍Ing: to stow away, as in a ship; the cargo or loading of a boat, termed sai' in the coll.; the ton-

1玻璃紙紙 房3京紙〇 4光扣紙〇 5草紙6紙煤 7紙錢8人情 薄如紙9批 紙10格眼紙 11年載12記載 13所載14至再 至三15再講 16再娶17再嫁 18再拜19再生

nage or capacity of a vessel; to record, "contains such an amount," —a term used on the backs of bank bills: [1]*'chai' hwo'* to receive cargo, as a ship.

債' (Chai.) To bear a burden, to owe; a debt; freight or passage money: COM., [2]*k'iéng' chai'* to be in debt; [3]*'li chai'* to pay one's debts; [4]*,chiéng chai'* money debts; [5]*,sü chai'* private debts; [6]*hó' chai' 'chü ,hwang,* the son pays the father's debts; [7]*'t'ó chai'* to collect dues; [8]*,sung chai'* fare, freight; *chai' 'mwi,* balance of a debt; *chai' 'mwang,* "the debt fully paid or canceled"—toils and troubles all past; COLL., [9]*,teng chai'* to pay a debt; *chai' má' hó'* owes nothing; [10]*chioh, chai'* to borrow money; *,ku 'ló chai'* debts due a leper—*scil.*, must be paid; *k'iéng' chai' wong' ,chai 'chio,* the debtor hates the creditor; *chai' 'mwi ko' mwoi' 't'ó ,wong,* you have not yet got the balance!—said to a mischievous child; *'nü ng' ,siu chai'* you'll not pay your debts—you are unfilial!

Chai'. A coll. word, as in *,mó ,kai chai'* contracted into *,ma chai'* (also spoken *'ma chai'* or *,ma tai'*), a peradventure, perhaps, uncertain.

才 (,Ts'ai.) Materials, stuff, or the substance of things, for which the next is also used; ability, capacity, talents, intelligence; endowments, genius, gifts; a person; a graduate: [11]*,chai tieu'* gifted; [12]*'sieu ,chai,* mediocrity; [13]*,tó ,chai,* largely endowed with capacity; adept; [14]*,sang ,chai,* the three powers, heaven, earth, and man; [15]*se' ,chai,* arrogant, conceited; *,chai hok,* learned; COM., [16]*,chai ,neng,* or [17]*,chai ,ching,* ability, capacity, talent; [18]*'k'eu ,chai,* eloquence, fluency; *,t'iéng ,chai,* native talent, natural endowment; [19]*seu' ,chai,* (coll. *seu' ,choi*), a Siutsai, graduate of the first degree—A. B.; *,ung ,chai,* literary talent; *pok, ,chai,* stupid; *,mi ,chai,* surplus talent; *met.*, a deferred Siutsai; *,chai chuok,* inferior talent.

材 (,Ts'ai.) Wood, timber, lumber; materials of which things are made, stuff; nature, qualities: [20]*,chai ngié'* skilled art; a trade, an occupation; *,chai muk,* wood, timber, lumber; *,liong ,chai,* good stuff; *met.*, genius, integrity; *sang' ,chai,* poor stuff; COM., *,chai lau'* stuff, building materials; *met.*, capability, accomplishments; *,chai ,kwang,* the guards of an officer's sedan; *,tó ,chai ,tó ngié'* very capable or versatile.

,Chai. A coll. word, as in *,chai 'kwi ,t'ui,* strike him a few blows; *,chai sioh, taung'* give him a beating.

財 貯 (,Ts'ai.) Wealth, goods, property; money, funds, possessions; whatever men can use; profits; bribes; presents: COM., [21]*hwo' ,chai,* goods; [22]*,chiéng ,chai,* wealth; *,chai 'pó,* riches; *,chai ,wong,* a wealthy person; *taik, ,chai,* to get gain, to succeed in a venture; [23]*hwak, ,chai,* to become wealthy; *,chai*

1 載貨	3 理債	5 私債	子還	8 船債	10 借債	12 小才	14 三才	16 才能	18 口才	20 材藝	22 錢財
2 欠債	4 錢債	6 父債	7 討債	9 還債	11 才調	13 多才	15 恃才	17 才情	19 秀才	21 貨財	23 發財

福州方言拼音字典

˛tung, a capitalist; ˛chai k'e˒ good luck; ˛chieu ˛chai, to amass wealth; ˛chai ˛sing, god of wealth, Plutus; [1]pok˒ ngie[2] ˛chieng ˛chai, wages of unrighteousness; [2]huing[2] ˛chai, sudden wealth; p'o˒ ˛chai, to lose riches; [3]˓ing ˛chai sek˒ ngie[2] to lose your integrity for money; ˛chai ˓lá, complimentary gifts to the bride before marriage; ˛chai ˛tó ˛sing yok˒ rich but infirm; COLL., k'ang˒ ˛chai ˛nu, a slave amassing riches; met., to toil for the benefit of others; ˛chai ˓chio, a man of wealth; ˛mó ˛chai ˓kwi, you beggar! ˛chai ˛sing chaung˒ securely rich.

豺 Ch'ai. A ravenous beast, a lynx, a wolf: read ˛ch'ai in coll. q. v.: [4]˛chai ˛long, a wolf; ˛chai ˛sing, a wolf's howl; met., fierce speech; [5]˛chai ˛long ˛tong tó[2] the wolf on the road; met., an oppressive ruler.

在[2] Tsai. To be in, to pertain to, to be at; to reside, to remain, to live, to dwell at; to belong to, to consist in; involved in, depending on; to be preserved or to continue; existing, being alive; in, is in, at; to examine; a place, a home; used in coll. for as, according to, as you please: [6]chai[2] sek˒ anciently; [7]chai[2] sek˒ in the house, at home; [8]˛su pok˒ chai[2] or ˛su ˓su pok˒ chai[2] omnipresent; chai[2] ˛king, the present; [9]˓kiu chai[2] to live long in a place; COM., [10]chai[2] ˛seng, living; chai[2] ˛ka, in the house; [11]˛ang chai[2] where is he! hence absent, gone, dead; [11]cheü[2] chai[2] quiet, peaceful; ˓su chai[2] a place; chai[2] ngwoi[2] besides, surplus; chai[2] kieng˒ to witness, to attest, a witness; chai[2] ˛chieng, before in time or place; COLL., chai[2] ˛ka ˛ch'ieng nik˒ ˓hó ch'ok˒ tio[2] pwang˒ ˛tieu ˛nang, at home, for a thousand days you have comfort, abroad, even for half a day you have trouble; chai[2] ˓nü, as you please; ng[2] chai[2] regardless of, indifferent to; ˛sing chai[2] ˓ié ˓lá, to lean against a chair.

寨[2] Chai. Also read sai˒; coll. chai[2]: a stockade, a palisade; an encampment; a stockaded village; a fortified place; a sheep-pen: [12]ch'ek˒ chai[2] a rendezvous for thieves; [13]chai[2] ˓chio, chief of the band; [14]˛niong ˓chü chai[2] a strongly fortified place in Changpwo district, Chiongchiu prefecture, Fookien; [15]˛sang chai[2] a fortified mountain retreat; [16]chai[2] ˓chio ˛t'au ˛tai˒ te[2] ˛kie ˛mó, the robber chief wears pheasant's feathers on his head! as scouting the idea of being rich—a play on the words chai[2] ˓chio and ˛chai ˓chio.

豸[2] Chai. A fabulous feline animal usually called [17]hai[2] chai[2]; its figure is embroidered on the robes of censors as indicating discrimination: also read ˓ti, as in poems, for the sake of rhythm.

(22) Chaik.

則˒ Tsĕ. A rule, a pattern, a law, an ordinance; a principle; a standard, a measure by which to test an act; to obey, to imitate, to conform to; an illative particle, where-

[1]不義錢財 [2]倖財 失義 [3]因財 [4]豺狼 [5]豺狼當道 [6]在昔 [7]在室 [8]無不在 [9]在在 [10]生安在 [11]在自 [12]賊寨 [13]寨主 [14]娘子寨 [15]山寨 [16]寨主頭戴雉雞毛 [17]獬豸 ○

fore, immediately, then; a conditional particle, after that, in that case; therefore, next, consequently: [1]*hwak, chaik,* a pattern, an example; [2]*ˏt'iéng ha^2 chaik,* an example for the whole world; [3]*ˏt'iéng chaik,* the heavenly model, as the rules of virtue in the classics; *song^2 tá' ˏchi chaik,* models of government for imitation; COM., [4]*chaik, ˏki ˏtüng,* the just medium; *ˋchung chaik,* a model, an example.

嵮, Tsê. A large, high mountain: *lik chaik, ˏhung,* the highest peak of a mountain.

側, Tsê. Read *ch'aik,;* coll. *chaik,:* [5]*chaik, ˏsing,* the person inclined, sidewise; *chaik, ˏsing k'aung'* to sleep on one side; *chaik, ˏsing sói^2* or *chaik, ˏpiéng sói^2* to sit sidewise.

責, Tsê. To reprove, to reprimand, to blame; to punish, to fine; to sustain, to be responsible for, to have charge of; to lay a weight on, to impose responsibility; to ask, to demand: [6]*chaik, ˋta,* to punish with blows; [7]*chaik, wong^2* to reprimand in hope of reformation; [8]*ke' chaik,* to record offences; [9]*chëü^2 chaik,* self-reproach; *tëüng^2 chaik,* to reprove severely; [10]*ˏkiu ˏchiong chaik, pe^2* to demand perfection in others; COM., *k'aik, chaik,* to exact, to extort; [11]*chaik, hwak,* to punish, to fine; [12]*chaik, pe^2* to rebuke, to reprimand; *chaik, eng^2* or *chaik, ˏsing,* an office, a trust, a duty.

幘, Chi. A head-tie, a headband, a turban.

嘖, Tsê. To call out loudly, to dispute, to quarrel noisily; garrulous, meddlesome; to admire, to praise loudly: [13]*chaik, chaik, ˏch'ing siéng^2* praised by everybody.

磧, Chi. Also read *chek,:* a sand-bank under water, a bar; rocks in water, a reef, a shoal, half-tide ledges: [14]*chaik, sik,* a reef of rocks; *chaik, ˏsa,* a sand-bar.

摘, Chai. Also read *tek,;* coll. *tiăh,* q. v.: to pluck, to pull, to cull, to gather, as fruit or flowers; to lay hold of; to move on, to start; to point out: [15]*chaik, ˏhwa,* to gather flowers; *chaik, ch'ai'* to pull vegetables; *chaik, kwo'* to collect sentences, to compile; *chaik, huk,* to investigate till the prisoner confesses; *chaik, ˏsing ˏleu,* star-plucking tower, a high tower; [16]*ˋch'ai chaik,* to select.

讁, **謫,** Chai. To blame, to reprehend; to degrade officers, to punish by degrading; to scold, to be angry at, to find fault with; a flaw, an error; a change of appearance: [17]*chaik, kaung'* to degrade; [18]*ˋk'iéng chaik,* to revile.

嘖, **賾,** Tsê. Inscrutable, occult; profound, hard to understand; the secret springs, hidden: [19]*che' chaik,* very abstruse; [20]*sauk, chaik,* to examine profound subjects.

[1] 法則 [2] 天下則 [3] 天則 [4] 則其中 [5] 側身 [6] 責打 [7] 責望 [8] 記責 [9] 自責 [10] 求全責備 [11] 責罰 [12] 責備 [13] 嘖嘖稱善 [14] 磧石 [15] 摘花 [16] 採摘 [17] 謫降 [18] 譴謫 [19] 至賾 [20] 索賾 ○

昃, Tsĕ. The declining sun; the afternoon; to wane, as the moon: *nik chaik꜁* the sun past the meridian; *ngwok chaik꜁* the moon waning; *nik ngwok ꜀sing chaik꜁* the sun and moon both have their zenith and decline.

簀, Chai. Tsĕ. A bed mat; boards for a bed; luxuriant growth; to collect, to gather; slips, small splints of reeds; read *chai꜃* a sort of wine-press or strainer.

汁, Chi'h. Gravy, juice, essence; thickened liquor, slosh; expressed juices or essences; sleety rain, wet snow: COM., [1]*꜀t'ong chaik꜁* warm gravy, soup; [2]*꜂chwi chaik꜁* juice, essence; *chaik꜁ ꜀keng*, the gravy is salt; COLL., *chaik꜁ ꜂chiŏng*, the gravy is fresh; *chaik꜁ ꜂tá*, or *chaik꜁ ꜀t'au chaik꜁ ꜂tá*, the leavings of gravy after a meal.

節, Chieh. Read *chiĕk꜁*; coll. *chaik꜁*: a joint of bamboo, a joint, a knot, a node; a feast, a festival; a limit, a solar term; a classifier of joints and limbs; all, every, in everything; in a *met.* sense, frugal, according to one's means: [3]*꜀sniĕng chaik꜁* annual festivals, of which there are eight; *chaik꜁ ꜂king* time of a festival; appearance, as of markets at festivals; *chaik꜁ ꜀piĕng*, or *chaik꜁ ꜀tau*, about the time of a festival; [4]*chaik꜁ so꜃* bills to be paid at festivals; *ngo꜄ nik chaik꜁* or [5]*ngo꜄ ngwok chaik꜁* a festival held on the first five days of the 5th moon; [6]*꜀ch'ing ꜀ming chaik꜁* festival of the tombs, in the 2nd or 3rd moon; [7]*꜀tĕng chaik꜁* festival at the winter solstice—time fixed by the almanac; *paik꜁ chaik꜁ ꜀ping ꜀ang*, peace during all the year!—a felicitous phrase; *nê꜄ sek sê꜃ chaik꜁ k'ê꜃* the 24 solar terms; [8]*chô꜃ chaik꜁* to celebrate a festival; [9]*saëng꜃ chaik꜁* to send presents at festivals; [10]*chaik꜁ keng꜃* presents of money given to employees at a festival; *tëük꜁ chaik꜁* a joint of bamboo; *nëük꜁ chaik꜁* a crumple, crumpled, shriveled; *met.*, bad luck; [11]*chaik꜁ ka꜃* festival holydays, vacations; *chaik꜁ chaik꜁ ꜀kó*, hooks linked in a chain to hang things on; *met.*, constantly rising or successful; [12]*꜀sniĕng chaik꜁ ha꜄* times of the festivals; *chaik꜁ chaik꜁* every joint; all, in general; [13]*chaik꜁ chaik꜁ nang꜄* always in distress; [14]*kauk꜁ chaik꜁ t'iăng꜃* every bone aches; *chaik꜁ chaik꜁ ꜂sai*, to use sparingly.

(23) Chaing.

諍, Chêng. To remonstrate with, to stop a wrong; to reprehend, to reprove, to rebuke for misconduct: also used for *꜀cheng*, to wrangle: [15]*kang꜃ chaing꜃* to reprove one's sovereign; [16]*꜀ting chaing꜃* to reprove the emperor in his palace.

譖, Chên. To traduce, to slander, to revile: [17]*chaing꜃ ꜀ing*, a slanderer; [18]*chaing꜃ ꜀ngi-ong*, slander, back-biting; *꜀ching ëüng꜄ ꜀chi chaing꜃* a plausible slander; COM., [19]*꜀chang chaing꜃* to slander, to traduce; COLL., *chaing꜃ ch'oi꜃ ꜂sieu ꜀ku*, a

[1]湯	[3]年	[5]五	明	[7]冬	[9]送	[11]節	下	[14]骨	[15]諫	[17]譖	[19]讒
汁	節	月	節	節	節	假	[13]節	節	諍	人	譖
[2]木	[4]節	節		[8]做	[10]節	[12]年	節	痛	[16]廷	[18]譖	
汁	數	[6]清	○	節	敬	節	難	○	諍	言	○

husband's sister who slanders his wife.

甑ʼ Tsêng. A boiler for distilling, an alembic, a still made of pewter; a steamer for rice; to steam: ʻ*hu chaing*ʼ a pan and boiler; *hwang*ʼ *chaing*ʼ a rice steamer.

苫ʼ Tsang. To cover a house with grass, to thatch; a mat; mourning: [1]*chai*² *chaing*ʼ during the time of mourning for one's parents; COLL., [2]*꜀schʻong chaing*ʼ a bed mat; [3]ʻ*chʻau chaing*ʼ a straw mattress; *꜀chĕng chaing*ʼ a palm-husk mat.

蹭ʼ Tsêng. To go aside, to lose the way, to wander; a stream diverging from the main channel: [4]*chaing*ʼ ʻ*taing*ʼ or *chaing*ʼ *taing*² in a flurry, unaptly; to leave the channel.

贈² Tsêng. To present, to bestow, to give; to confer, as by the crown; to add to: [5]*chaing*² ʻ*iu*, to make presents to friends; [6]*steu chaing*² to make presents; [7]*chaing*² *꜀ngiong*, a flattering recommendation; [8]*꜀hung chaing*² or *tʻek꜀ chaing*² to confer a meritorious degree; [9]*kó*ʼ *chaing*² to honor a meritorious officer's parents; *lië*² *chaing*² honorary degree; COLL., *chaing*² *pó*ʼ *ng*² *chaing*² *꜀küng*, he makes presents to the rich, not to the poor; [10]*chaing*² *ak* presents which the bride takes to her friends; *chaing*² *꜀pwang ꜀chiéng*, to present money as traveling expenses; *chaing*² ʻ*ngwai*, give me a present.

(24) Chaiu.

奏ʼ Tsou. To report to the emperor, to memorialize the throne; tell the sovereign, to cause him to hear or know; to present offerings to the gods; to play music; songs or tunes; muscular fibres: [11]*chaiu*ʼ *ngok* to play the music; [12]*chaiu*ʼ *saë*ʼ statements made in the memorial; [13]ʻ*nga chaiu*ʼ pleasant music; [14]*chiék꜀ chaiu*ʼ to mark time and harmony in music; [15]*chaiu*ʼ *kaik꜀ ꜀su ꜀ngiong*, offer to the gods with reverence and in silence; COM., [16]*chaiu*ʼ *siong*² or *chaiu*ʼ *꜀hwong tâ*ʼ to memorialize the emperor; *chaiu*ʼ *꜀chiong*, or *chaiu*ʼ ʻ*pwong*, a memorial to the emperor; *miéng*² *chaiu*ʼ a verbal statement to the emperor; [17]ʻ*chung chaiu*ʼ to grant the prayer of the memorial; *chaiu*ʼ *chiék꜀* memorial folded and ready; [18]*chaiu*ʼ ʻ*kó*, first draft of a memorial; [19]*tik chaiu*ʼ a candid memorial; COLL., *chaiu*ʼ *sioh* ʻ*pwong*, one memorial, to memorialize once.

縐ʼ Chou. Crape; rumpled, crenulated, crisp, frizzled; to corrugate, to wrinkle; used for next: COM., [20]*chaiu*ʼ *꜀sa*, crape; [21]*siáng*ʼ *chaiu*ʼ thick crape; COLL., *chaiu*ʼ *꜀sa pʻa*ʼ *꜀king ꜀nú nóh* a crape handkerchief bears rumpling; *met.*, one who bears teasing; *chaiu*ʼ *꜀sa meng*ʼ faced with crape, as a garment.

縐ʼ **皺**ʼ Chou. The skin wrinkled from age; wrinkled, creased, rumpled, crisped: [22]*chaiu*ʼ *꜀i*, rumpled garments; COM., [23]*chaiu*ʼ *꜀king*, imitation gold leaf; *chaiu*ʼ *shong*,

1 在苫 3 草苫 5 贈友 7 贈言 9 誥贈 11 奏樂 13 雅奏 15 奏假無言 16 奏上 18 奏稿 20 縐紗 22 皺衣
2 床苫 4 蹭蹬 6 投贈 8 封贈 10 贈盒 12 奏疏 14 節奏 17 准奏 19 直奏 21 綿縐 23 皺金

福州方言拼音字典

or *chaiu* *sung*, the marks of folding; *p'ui chaiu* wrinkled skin.

皺 Tsou. Read *cheu*; coll. *chaiu*: to knit the eye-brows, to frown, to scowl; a frown: *chaiu smi*, to frown.

腠 Ts'ou. Also read *ch'aiu*: [1]*chaiu li*, grain of the flesh, the divisions of the muscles, muscular fibres, the lines on the surface of the skin; the thin membrane between the skin and the flesh.

甃 Tsou. The brick walling of a well; to lay as bricks, to pile up, to finish off a well: [2]*ching chaiu* to wall up a well.

輳 Ts'ou. Also read *ch'aiu*: a wheel, centre of a wheel, focus where rays concentrate; to collect, to gather, to concentrate; assembled from all quarters; concentrated, as the spokes in the nave of a wheel: [3]*hok chaiu* converging, united in one.

驟 Tsou. Also read *chaiu*: a fleet horse; to run, swift, pressing, urgent; repeatedly, frequently; to reiterate: [4]*chaiu ü*, a heavy fall of rain; [5]*ma chaiu* a horse running swiftly; [6]*chaiu lai*, to come suddenly.

(25) Chak.

匝 迊 To make a circuit, to go the rounds like a watchman, a revolution; pervading, full, complete: [7]*chiu chak*, all-pervading, to go about; [8]*chak te* scattered all over the ground; COLL., [9]*lau chak*, to overflow, as water; [10]*sang chak*, to grow all over, like leaves on a tree; [11]*chak chak mek* close, dense, as foliage; [12]*chak chak k'wang*, full of circles or approval marks, as a composition; rounded, complete, as one's words.

帀 Tsa.

咂 Tsa. To open the mouth; a fish sucking.

扎 Cha. To pluck, to pull up; to draw out, as a sword; to make or cut out paper images; to bind, to bind around, to bundle up, a bundle, for which the next is more commonly used.

紮 Cha. To bind, to fasten, to tuck up; to wind round; to tie into a bundle; a bundle: COM., [13]*k'ung chak*, to bind, to tie in a bundle; [14]*chak tai* to fasten one's girdle; [15]*chak king*, to tie up tightly; [16]*chak tiong* to lift up or open the bed-curtains; [17]*chak i siong*, to tuck up one's sleeves or skirts; [18]*chak mwang*, wind it full; [19]*chak lüng kauk*, to wrap a corpse with red cloth or silk; COLL., *chak taing* to fasten securely.

札 Cha. A letter, a document, writings; a dispatch, an epistle; a tablet for writing; untimely death; a thin slip of wood; a paddle; a fold of armor: [20]*sung chak*, genuine dispatch; *pó chak* or *syeu chak*, a precious or valuable letter;

---

[1]腠理 [2]井甃 [3]輻輳 [4]驟雨 [5]馬驟 [6]驟來 [7]周匝 [8]匝地 [9]流匝 〇 [10]生匝 [11]匝匝密 [12]匝匝圈 [13]細紮 [14]紮帶 [15]紮緊 [16]紮帳 [17]紮衣裳 [18]紮滿 [19]紮龍骨 [20]文札 〇

[1]*꜀chiéng chak꜆* a former letter; [2]*꜁lai chak꜆* the letter just received; *꜀chü chak꜆* (coll. *꜀p'ié chak꜆*) a dispatch, a letter.

劄 Cha. Also read *tak꜆*: to prick, to embroider; a paper, a document; a particular kind of paper; a diploma; a contract; to write out, as a list of prices; a reply from a higher officer; a remonstrance to the emperor: COM., [3]*꜂chai chak꜆* official stationery; [4]*chak꜆ ꜀tang,* a purchase contract; *꜁mwong ꜀chü ꜂chai chak꜆* paper for edicts and dispatches; also used by priests in making images.

炸 Cha. An unauthorized character: to boil in fat or vegetable oil: COM., [5]*chak꜆ ꜁ngü,* to boil fish in oil; [6]*chak꜆ nük꜇* meat prepared in this way; *chak꜆ ꜂piéng,* flat doughnuts with meat stuffing; COLL., *꜁p'u chak꜆* or *꜀sieu chak꜆* to boil in oil, things so boiled; *꜁siu chak꜆ ꜂kwi,* a long kind of cruller; *꜀tiéng chak꜆* and *꜁keng chak꜆* doughnuts with sweet and salt stuffing.

浹 Hsia. Water flowing through; moistened, damp; to instill, to imbibe, to penetrate; a circuit, a complete turn of; in coll. a classifier of the fall, or gauged depth of rain: *kang꜄ ꜁diu chak꜆ pwoi꜄* perspiration streaming down the back; COM., [7]*chak꜆ hak꜇* to combine, to commingle; fully agreeing, as friends; [8]*꜀chiu chak꜆* all around, completed as a circuit or term; COLL., *꜁kiüng chak꜆* to walk all over or through; *꜂ü ha꜄ sioh꜇ chak꜆* a fall of rain.

雜 Tsa. A mixture of colors or ingredients; particolored, streaked; mixed, blended; confused, various, heterogeneous, fragmentary; to mix, to compound; to confuse, to revolve; to bore through: [9]*꜁sung chak꜇* suitable or unsuitable, fixed or vacillating, as the mind; [10]*꜁chó chak꜇* medley of loud sounds; COM., [11]*chak꜇ saik꜆* mixed colors; [12]*chak꜇ ëüng꜄* (coll. *chak꜇ ꜂sai,*) for general use; [13]*chak꜇ hwo꜄* different kinds of goods; [14]*hong꜄ chak꜇* confused, heterogeneous; [15]*chak꜇ ꜀chü,* miscellaneous books; [16]*chak꜇ pok꜆ ꜂teng,* different sorts, a medley; [17]*꜀sing chak꜇* the mind distracted; [18]*꜂ngu ꜀hwong chak꜇ ch'ëü꜄* everywhere, coming from all quarters; [19]*chak꜇ pwang꜄* to mix, a mixture; *chak꜇ hwoi꜄* to blend, to combine; *chak꜇ ꜀hwa,* mixed flowers; [20]*chak꜇ ó꜄* a public wharf; *chak꜇ ꜀ch'á,* low police; *chak꜇ ꜂chüng,* different species; COLL., *chak꜇ ch'ói꜄* a medley of little things; *chak꜇ ꜁pá ꜀t'ang,* a stall for all sorts of wares; *chak꜇ tio꜄* intersecting roads; *met.*, things from different places; *p'ah꜆ chak꜇* improper talk; *꜂nü kaëng꜄ ꜂ngwai p'ah꜆ chak꜇* you annoy me!

柵 Cha. Also read *ch'aik꜆* and *ch'ah꜆*; COLL., *chak꜇*: a stockade, a railing, a palisade; window-bars; a door made of slats: [21]*chak꜇ lak꜇* a kind of railing or palisade used to divide wards in cities and towns; *chak꜇ ꜁mwong,* or *chak꜇ lak꜇ ꜁mwong,* street-gates; [22]*siék꜆ chak꜇* to erect stockades or put up street-gates.

[1]前札 [2]來札 [3]紙劄 [4]劄單 [5]炸魚 [6]炸肉 [7]浹洽 [8]周浹 [9]純雜 [10]嘈雜 [11]雜色 [12]雜用 [13]雜貨 [14]混雜 [15]雜書 [16]雜不等 [17]心雜 [18]五方雜處 [19]雜秤 [20]雜澳 [21]柵欄 [22]設柵 ○

閘$_2$ Cha. A guarded gate, a barrier, a barricade, a dam; a barrier like a turn-stile, or a stockade; a lock, a flood-gate; to shut a gate; in Foochow, the front curtains of a sedan: COM., [1]*꜀kwang chak* a barrier, a sluice gate; [2]*꜂chwi chak* a sluice, a waste-weir; *paëk꜆ chak* northern canal lock in Foochow; COLL., *siong^2 chak* upper front curtain of a sedan; *a^2 chak* lower front curtain of a sedan.

卡$_2$ Ch'ia. A military post, a guard-house, usually called *chak ꜀pung*: COM., [3]*siĕk꜆ chak* to establish a military post; [4]*꜂siu chak* to guard a post.

⿱絕刀$_2$ Chüeh. Read *chiok*; coll. *chak*: to cut, to cut up, to mince, to cut to pieces: [5]*꜀tó chak* to cut with a knife; [6]*chak ꜂hung ch'ói꜄* to cut to pieces; [7]*chak ꜂tong*, to cut or lop off; [8]*chak siĕk* to cut in two; [9]*chak ꜂si*, to cut to death; *chak ꜀ch'a*, to chop wood; *chak lang^2 ꜀dong*, to cut into two lengths; *chak ꜀t'au*, to behead—used as a threat; *chak ꜀t'au ꜀mó ꜂hó ꜂si*, cut off your head and make you die wretchedly; *chak ꜀sang*, to slice up fresh, as crabs.

⿰扌⿸麻土$_2$ Sa. Mixed up; refuse, sweepings, dirt; sound of breaking things: COM., [10]*lak chak* refuse, odds and ends.

⿰口开$_2$ Hoi. Wrangling, noisy, clamorous, turbulent.

Chak. A coll. word; as *chak chó꜄* to slash and swear, like an infuriated woman.

(26) Chang.

꜀**簪** Tsan. A hair-pin, a clasp or bodkin used to confine the hair or fasten the coiffure; to insert in the hair, to stick on the head; quick, brisk, to collect speedily: [11]*꜀chang ꜀ing*, the gentry, the official class; [12]*꜀chang hwok꜆* hair-pin and ivory tablet formerly used at audiences; COM., [13]*꜀chang ꜀hwa*, to wear the golden flower as graduates do; [14]*꜀chang kwa꜄* to wear silk scarfs as graduates do; [15]*꜀chang ꜀hwa pai꜄ k'ak꜆* to put on the flower and go to salute friends; *꜀sang ꜀teu ꜀chang*, the three hair-pins as commonly worn; COLL., *꜀chang ꜂kiăng*, small hair-pins; [16]*ngwok ꜀chang ꜀hwa*, the white lily; *kwoi꜄ ꜀t'au ꜀chang*, hair-pin or ornament for front of the coiffure; *kwoi꜄ ꜂mwi ꜀chang*, ornament for back of the coiffure.

꜀**臢** Tsan. As in the common phrase *꜀ang ꜀chang*, dirty, filthy.

꜀**爭** Chêng. Read *꜀cheng*; coll. *꜀chang*; to contend, to dispute, to quarrel: [17]*꜀chang oi^2* to contend about a place or seat; *꜀chang ꜀ch'eng*, to dispute about fields; [18]*꜀song ꜀chang ꜀hung*, adulterous quarrels; [19]*꜀chang ꜀ka ngiĕk* to quarrel over the division of an estate; *꜀chang k'e꜄* quarrelsome; resolute, earnest; [20]*꜀chang che꜄ k'e꜄* to emulate; *꜀chang sié꜄ nóh꜆*

1 關閘 2 水閘 3 設卡 4 守卡 5 刀⿱絕刀 6 ⿱絕刀粉碎 7 ⿱絕刀斷 8 ⿱絕刀折 9 ⿱絕刀死 10 擸⿰扌⿸麻土 11 簪纓 12 簪笏 13 簪花 14 簪掛 15 簪花拜客 16 玉簪花 17 爭位 18 相爭風 19 爭家業 20 爭志氣〇

꜀ing ꜀chüng, what strife of talent or strength is it?—i. e., there's no need of quarreling about it; *꜀chang ꜀ch'á twakˎ ꜀tiëng kiëngʼ ʻsi ꜀sü ꜀miëng*, even to die is easy as sleeping to him who is striving to vindicate his wife's honor or save his land; *꜀chang ꜀ka ʻhwi*, to quarrel about property.

꜀*Chang.* A coll. word; as *꜀chang chëüʼ* a raw sore, as on a child.

ʻ井 Ching. Read *ʻching;* coll. *ʻchang;* a well: [1]*ʻchwi ʻchang* a well of water; [2]*ʻchang ʻchwi*, well-water; [3]*꜀t'iëng ʻchang*, an open court; [4]*ʻchang ꜀sing*, elfs of the well; [5]*ʻchang ꜀lau ꜀mwong*, one of the gates of Foochow; [6]*p'wakˎ ʻt'ëng kaëng^2 ʻchang*, bucket and well; *met.*, associated, connected; *ʻchang ꜀ch'ing mâ^2 lai^2 tekˎ sóhˎ ʻtoi*, when the well is deep don't blame the rope for being short; *met.*, don't require impossibilities.

ʻ斬 Chan. To behead, to cut, to cut in two, to dissever, to sunder; to root up, to break off, as intercourse; faded, forgotten, vanished: COM., [7]*ʻchang ꜀sià*, to destroy evil spirits; [8]*ʻchang hwang^2* to behead culprits; [9]*ʻchang twang^2* to cut asunder; [10]*ʻchang chekˎ* to expedite; to epitomize, an outline; [11]*kangʼ ʻchang*, officer in charge of an execution; [12]*ʻchang ʻch'ó ꜀tü ꜀kong*, to cut up root and branch; *met.*, to extirpate, as thieves.

琖 Chan. Also read *ʻchiëng:* a wine-cup, made of jade or other valuable stone.

ʻ昝 Tsan. A surname; used in the north for I, me, myself.

ʻ儹 Tsan. To accumulate, to collect together, to hoard up, to store.

ʻ寁 Tsan. Promptly, quickly, with haste; to hasten, to accelerate.

ʻ盞 Chan. A small wine-cup; a shallow cup for oil; the classifier of lamps: COM., [13]*ʻchiu ʻchang*, a wine-cup; [14]*ʻchang ꜀kó*, cup cakes; COLL., [15]*꜀ch'ang ꜀hwa ʻchang*, blue flowered wine-cup; [16]*ʻchiu ʻchang ʻkiäng*, a very small wine-cup; [17]*꜀ting ʻchang*, an oil-saucer; [18]*꜀ting siohˎ ʻchang*, one lamp.

醆 Chan. Muddy, unsettled spirits; liquor beginning to clear; a cup, a goblet.

ʻ聻 Chan. Also read *chiëng^2;* a prince of demons at sight of whom ogres and vampires flee; used as a charm.

ʻ棧 Tsan. Slips of wood placed between the fingers to squeeze them; a mode of torture like the thumbscrews; to torture; narrow: COM., *ʻchang ʻchi*, thumbscrews; [19]*ʻchang ʻchi kekˎ kongʼ* thumb and foot screws.

贊ʼ Tsan. To visit a superior, to come before an idol; to second, to assist in bringing forward; to introduce, to bring a present to one;

[1]水	[3]天	[5]井	桶	邪	斷	斬	根	糕	[16]酒	盞	[19]棧
井	井	樓	共	[8]斬	[10]斬	[12]斬	[13]酒	[15]青	盞	[18]燈	指
[2]井	[4]井	門	井	犯	截	草	盞	花	子	一	夾
水	神	[6]吊	[7]斬	[9]斬	[11]監	除	[14]盞	盞	[17]燈	盞	棍

to make clear, to bring to the light; to go out; to give evidence; to praise, to commend, in which sense it is interchanged with the next: [1]*ˏsiong chang'* to assist in completing, to forward a matter; *chang' chang'* to aid powerfully; COM., [2]*ˏch'ing chang'* to praise; [3]*chang' ˋlá*, a master of ceremonies at sacrifices.

讚 Tsan. To praise, to commend, to laud; to honor, to exalt, to magnify, to extol; to sing praises to, to record the praises of; to assist, to explain: [4]*chang' ˏyong*, to extol, to laud; COM., [5]*chang' ˋmi*, to praise; [6]*sëüng² chang'* to commend, to honor; [7]*chëük, chang'* to laud.

賺 Chuan. To impede, to hinder; to sell, to profit; to gain unfairly, to palm off poor goods.

醮 Chiao. To dip, as a pencil in ink, or sop a morsel in gravy.

Chang'. A coll. word: to contend, to dispute about, to quarrel: *chang' ˏsyŭng*, to overcome in a dispute; *chang' mā² kwo'* to succumb in a dispute.

孱 Ch'ien. Timid, afraid; weak, embarrassed: *ˏchang yok* feeble; *ˏchang liok*, incapable, stupid.

僝 To rail at; to manifest: *ˏchang chaiu²* to abuse, to vilify.

殘 Ts'an. To ruin, to destroy; to injure, to spoil, to mangle, to tread on; to kill, to slaughter; mischievous, wicked, cruel; spoiled, pillaged; broken food, leavings; deficient, nearly exhausted, ready to vanish: [8]*ˏchang k'wok*, scarce, nearly exhausted; COM., [9]*ˏchang hai²* to injure, to oppress; [10]*ˏchang pó²* fierce, vindictive; [11]*ˏchang p'ó'* devastated: [12]*ˏhüng ˏchang*, quarrelsome; [13]*ˏchang ˋüng*, harsh, cruel; [14]*ˏchang ˏhwang*, a light dollar; [15]*ˏchang uk* a worthless thing; [16]*ˏü ˏchang*, dregs; [17]*ˏchang chik* maimed, halt; [18]*ˏchang ˏtëng*, end of winter; COLL., *ˏchang chóh* to cast aside as worthless.

慙 慚 Ts'an. Ashamed, mortified, chopfallen; to feel ashamed of, to blush for; to be sensible of one's defects or failure: [19]*ˏchang saik*, or *ˏchang ˏngang*, shamefaced, bashful; [20]*pó² ˏchang*, to feel ashamed, mortified; [21]*ˏsiu ˏchang*, or *ˏchang k'oi'* ashamed.

巉 礹 Ch'an. A high inaccessible peak or cliff, a cloud-capped summit: [22]*ˏchang ˏngang*, a high craggy summit, also high rocks piled up; COLL., [23]*ˏchang ˏt'au ˏchang ˋnó*, a stern, forbidding look; *ˏchang ˏngiăng*, overgrown; big and coarse, as of persons or things.

讒 Ch'an. To adulate, to humor, to flatter; to misrepresent, to gloss over; to calumniate, to asperse, to traduce; servility, detraction,

1 襄贊	3 贊禮	5 讚美	7 祝讚	9 殘害	11 殘破	13 殘忍	15 殘物	17 殘疾	19 慚色	21 羞慚	23 巉頭
2 稱贊	4 讚揚	6 頌讚	8 殘缺	10 殘暴	12 兇殘	14 殘番	16 餘殘	18 殘冬	20 抱慚	22 巉巖	巉腦

malignity: [1]*schang ʻk'eu*, a foul-mouthed person; [2]*schang neng²* to asperse, as an adept in vulgar language; [3]*schang sing*, a reviler; [4]*schang sngiong*, abusive language; COM., [5]*schang chaing²* to abuse, to vilify; [6]*schang ssing*, an intriguing officer.

儳 Ts'an. Irregular, disorderly, as undrilled troops; unequal, uneven: *slang schang*, ugly, stubborn, sulky.

毚 Ts'an. Crafty, wily, cunning, as a hare: *schang t'o²* a crafty rabbit.

攙 Ch'an. To stab; to sustain, to support, to lead; to supply a want, to make up, as a deficiency; to pull out.

潺 Ch'an. The murmur of water: *schang schang ʻhiong*, sound of running water.

蠶 蚕 螗 Ts'an. The silkworm; caterpillars which weave cocoons: [7]*schang ʻkiëng*, raw silk; [8]*ˬch'ung schang*, spring silkworms; [9]*ʻyong schang*, to rear silkworms; [10]*schang ngwokˬ* "the silkworm month"—i. e., for rearing silkworms; *schang t'o² ˬsi*, the silkworm vomits forth the silk.

饞 Ch'an. To gormandize, fond of eating; greedy, gluttonous, voracious.

劖 Ch'an. To chisel, to cut, as stone; to mortise: *ˬchiéng schang*, to carve, to chisel.

暫² Chan. Short duration, a part of a day; to stop or cease for a while; briefly, shortly, in the interim; meanwhile, suddenly: COM., [11]*chang² ssi*, a brief space of time, a short period; [12]*chang² kié²* leave it awhile—till I return for it; [13]*chang² hiokˬ* to stop a little while, to rest or cease for a time; [14]*chang² spung*, a room rented temporarily, as a lodging; COLL., *chang² ssi lokˬ pokˬ* in distress only a while! *chang² siohˬ ha²* stop a while; to sojourn for a brief period.

鏨² (variant) **鏨**² Tsan. A stone-cutter's chisel, a small cold chisel; to pierce, as a thorn; to cut in, to cut or chisel out; to carve, as flowers: COM., [15]*chang² ˬtó*, a stone-cutter's chisel; [16]*chang² che²* to cut letters; COLL., *chang² ˬt'ëng t'au²* or *chang² ˬt'ëng slëng*, chisel it through, as thin metal.

站² Chan. To stand, to stand erect; to stop; a stage, a journey, a stoppage: [17]*yähˬ chang²* official post stations; COLL., *chang² st'au*, end of a stage, a caravansary.

棧² Chan. A warehouse, a godown, a hong; a workshop; a terrace, a covered loft; palisades; a scaffold; a covered plank road, cut out of the side of a hill; a hearse; a pen, a stable, a sheepcote; a wooden bridge or pathway: COM., [18]*chang² spung*, a warehouse, a godown; [19]*yohˬ chang²* a large medicine store; [20]*sta chang²* a tea hong; [21]*song chang²* a hong;

1 讒口 2 讒佞 3 讒人 4 讒言 5 讒譖 ○ 6 讒臣 7 蠶繭 8 春蠶 9 養蠶 10 蠶月 ○ 11 暫時 12 暫寄 13 暫歇 14 暫房 15 鏨刀 ○ 16 鏨字 17 驛站 18 棧房 19 藥棧 20 茶棧 21 行棧

福州方言拼音字典

COLL., *k'ô' chang² 'lá*, has gone to the hong.

輚² Chan. A tumbrel for carrying the wounded; a hearse.

虥² Chan. A tiger-cat: *chang² ꜀mau*, a tiger shedding its hair.

(27) Chau.

糟 Tsao. Read ꜀*chô;* coll. ꜀*chau:* the sediment, grains left after distilling spirits, dregs; the dregs of wine, the sediment of any liquor: ¹꜀*chau p'ôh*, dregs, sediment; ꜀*chau k'ong*, lees and husks; ²꜀*sing* ꜀*chau*, fresh lees; *sëng* ꜀*chau*, dull red lees; ꜀*chau ch'ai'* vegetables seasoned with distiller's dregs; ꜀*chau ch'ai' ak*, a dish of seasoned vegetables and duck.

蹧 Tsao. An unauthorized character, frequently used in posted bills and notifications; to spoil, to injure, to ruin: ꜀*chau t'ak*, or '*chau t'ak*, (spoken *chauk*, *t'ak*,) to waste, to injure wantonly.

嘈 Ts'ao. Read ꜀*chô;* coll. ꜀*chau:* as in ꜀*chau* ꜀*chau naung'* in confusion, disordered; perplexed in mind.

熿 Tsao. Charred; coals left after burning: COM., ³*t'ang'* ꜀*chau*, dead coals, embers; COLL., ⁴꜀*ch'a* ꜀*chau*, firebrands.

'爪 Chao. Chua. Nails, claws, talons; to scratch, to claw; to take up with the fingers; an agent, a minion; the 87th radical: ⁵'*chau* ꜀*nga*, nails and teeth; *met.*, servants, retainers; ⁶'*ch'iu* '*chau*, finger-nails; COM., ⁷'*hu* '*chau*, tiger's claws—shears so called; ⁸'*chau le²* sharp claws; COLL., '*k'a* '*chau*, toe-nails.

'抓 Chua. Interchanged with last; to scratch, to clutch, to claw; to titillate; to tear with the claws; to cajole.

'走 Tsou. Read '*cheu;* coll. '*chau:* to go; to travel; to run, to hasten, to flee, to escape; the 156th radical: ⁹꜀*tô* '*chau*, to fly, to escape; ¹⁰꜀*p'au* '*chau*, to run about; ¹¹'*chau* ꜀*hiong*, to go into the country to work; ¹²'*chau* ꜀*tiong*, to return home immediately after examination; ¹³'*chau* '*hui*, to fly from fire; ¹⁴'*chau nang²* to fly from trouble; ¹⁵'*chau e²* to lose its flavor; ¹⁶'*chau* '*ma*, to ride on horseback; ¹⁷'*chau* ꜀*tong*, a table-waiter, an attendant in a tavern; ¹⁸'*chau yong²* to vary from the pattern; '*chau* '*ma tô' eng²* "to ride to the office"—to bury immediately; '*chau k'ô'* to escape; '*chau* '*ma* ꜀*lau*, an upper verandah; '*chau* '*chau niäh* '*chau* '*chau k'ok*, hide and go seek; '*chau* '*chio*, to transfer your patronage from one shop to another; '*chau* ꜀*kong* ꜀*shu*, vagrants, as foreign jugglers and fortune-tellers.

找 Chao. To seek; to return a balance, as of money, to make change: COLL., ¹⁹'*chau* ꜀*chiêng* '*mui*, to return a balance of money; ²⁰'*chau tang²* to give wrong change; '*chau* '*tiê*, to receive a balance; '*chau ch'ok*, to pay a balance; '*chau*

¹糟粕 ²新糟 ³炭熿 ⁴柴熿 ⁵爪牙 ⁶手爪 ⁷虎爪 ⁸爪利 ⁹逃走 ¹⁰跑走 ¹¹走鄉 ¹²走塲 ¹³走火 ¹⁴走難 ¹⁵走味 ¹⁶走馬 ¹⁷走堂 ¹⁸走樣 ¹⁹找錢 尾 ²⁰找錯

sioh pah, to give back 100 cash. Read *shwa*, to pole a boat.

蚤 (with 虫爪) 蚤 Tsao. Read *'chó;* coll. *'chau:* a flea, sand-fleas or those produced in sandy ground: [1]*'ka 'chau*, a flea; *'ka 'chau 'sai*, flea-dirt; *hung smwong 'ka 'chau*, musquitos and fleas; *se' 'ka 'chau ka'* it is a flea-bite; *smó 'mwói 'ka 'chau*, "the agile flea"—an unreliable fellow, now here then off.

竈 灶 Tsao. The second is a vulgar character: a furnace, a kitchen range, a place for cooking: [2]*'ta chau'* a furnace for steeping tea; COM., [3]*chiong chau'* brick furnace; [4]*hung chau'* to cook separately; [5]*chau' laiu'* offerings to the kitchen god; [6]*chau' kung*, kitchen god; [7]*chie' chau'* to make offerings to the kitchen gods on 24th day, 12th moon; [8]*chau' 'ma*, kitchen goddess; [9]*chau' slong*, the top or face of the range; COLL., [10]*chau' seng*, a kitchen; [11]*ang chau' k'a*, presents made to a person when changing his place of residence; [12]*'tiäng chau'* pan and range; [13]*kiék, chau'* to build a range; *skiäng chau'* a portable furnace.

笊 Ch'ao. Also read *'chau:* a skimmer made of bamboo or iron wire; nests in caves: in coll. *chiă*, as *chiă slié*, q. v.

巢 Ch'ao. A nest on a tree; a den, a retreat; a lurking place; to nestle, to make a nest: [14]*schau hiék* nests and caves; [15]*sui schau*, to build retreats in trees or high places; COM., [16]*'cheu schau*, or *'cheu wo*, bird's nests; [17]*ch'ek schau*, a den of thieves; COLL., *smó schau*, houseless, homeless.

漅 Ch'ao. Name of a large lake in the southern part of the province of Nganhwi.

勦 剿 Ch'ao. To desolate, to destroy utterly, to ruin, to devastate, to exterminate, to cut off: [18]*schau sming*, to exterminate people; [19]*schau chiok* or *schau miék* to destroy utterly; [20]*ching schau*, to send troops against the enemy; COLL., [21]*schau 'sá spang te'* to desolate, to level to the ground.

轈 Ch'ao. A turret on a chariot, from the top of which to observe the troops.

嘲 Ch'ao. Sometimes read *hau:* to deride, to jeer at, to ridicule; raillery.

Chau. A coll. word; as *schau schau*, girt and ready, trim, ready to begin or to do expeditiously.

櫂 棹 Chao. A scull or oar for propelling vessels, a long oar; to shoot an arrow, to throw away: [22]*syeu chau'* to scull; *kie' chau'* a scull made of cassia wood; *wa' chau'* to make figures on a scull.

1 咬蚤 2 茶灶 3 磚灶 4 分灶 5 灶料 6 灶君 7 祭灶 8 灶媽 9 灶廊 10 灶前 11 安灶脚〇 12 鼎灶 13 結灶 14 巢穴 15 園巢 16 鳥巢 17 賊巢 18 剿民 19 剿絕 20 征剿 21 剿洗平地 22 搖櫂

福州方言拼音字典

掉[1] Chao. Interchanged with the preceding; to scull, to work the scull; to row, to propel a boat; to shake, to clash; correct, done or placed properly: *chau*[2] *'mwi*, to shake the tail; *chau*[2] *k'eng'* to strike musical stones together; *met.*, clashing, as opinions; *'mwi chau*[2] *'iu lik* the end of the scull has great force; *met.*, to finish a job well.

(28) Chauk.

作, Tso. To act, to do, to make; to begin, to discover, to invent; to arise, to appear; to rouse, to animate, as to a reformation; work, workmanship, to transact business: [1]*chauk*, *ˏkung*, the emperor; [2]*chauk*, *ˏsü*, a teacher; [3]*chiě' chauk*, to invent, to discover; [4]*chauk*, *sui*, to do, to perform; [5]*ˏtiéng chauk*, of heavenly origin; [6]*chauk*, *'ku*, to die; [7]*tong*[2] *chauk*, to move, to act, to work; [8]*peng*[2] *chauk*, a return of sickness; *chauk*, *sing*, to reform a wicked person; manly; *'ching chauk*, to set about, to do resolutely; *chauk*, *sëü*[2] to transact business; *ˏkeng chauk*, to till the soil; COM., [9]*chauk*, *ngiék* to act wickedly, to commit suicide; [10]*chauk*, *chik* tricky, treacherous; virulent, as eruptions; [11]*chauk*, *kwai'* strange, marvelous; very intelligent; *chieng*[2] *chauk*, rude, boisterous; *chauk*, *lok* to rejoice; *chauk*, *sing*, to aid in completing; [12]*sming ˏti ko' chauk*, willfully perverse; *chëü*[2] *chauk*, *shwang chëü*[2] *seu*[2] to reap the fruit of one's own doings; COLL., *chauk*, *ˏka*, handsome, beautiful; *chauk*, *'ch'au*, to annoy; *chauk*, *t'ak*, to injure, to destroy; *che*[2] *ˏka chauk*, *t'ak*, to ruin one's self by vice.

剟, 㓸, Chü. Read *ˏcheu* and *sauk*, ; used in the *Paik*, *ˏIng* for coll. *chauk*, : to pull; to snap, to break, as a cord with the hands: *chauk*, *'tong*, to sever; *chauk*, *tói' ˏtong*, to part into two lengths; *chauk*, *lóh sli*, to pull down violently, as a rope fastened aloft.

(29) Chaung.

壯' Chuang. Healthy, strong, robust, well, vigorous; hardy, bold, lusty, healthy; full-grown, manhood; age of thirty, full, flourishing: [13]*chaung' sëü*[2] a man of strength; [14]*chaung' che'* strong will, resolute; [15]*chaung' sniéng*, a young man; [16]*'u chaung'* a military cadet; *chaung' ˏsing*, vigorous in mind, industrious; COM., *chaung' kiong*[2] robust, powerful; *sming chaung'* an officer's runners; *shüng chaung'* sturdy; *skiong chaung'* fierce, turbulent; *chaung' ˏting*, a full-grown youth; *ˏing shüng 'ma chaung'* as strong as a horse.

葬' 塟' Tsang. To bury, to inter, to put under the ground: [17]*'pok*, *chaung'* to select a grave-site; [18]*ˏsung chaung'* ancient custom of burying a living person with a corpse; COM., [19]*smai* (or *smwai*) *chaung'* to bury; [20]*'k'i chaung'* to disinter; [21]*hau*[2] *chaung'* to bury in costly dress; [22]*ˏpong chaung'* to give money in aid of burial; to bury

[1] 作君 [2] 作師 [3] 製作 [4] 作爲 [5] 天作 [6] 作古 [7] 動作 [8] 病作 [9] 作孽 [10] 作疾 [11] 作怪 ○ [12] 明知故作 [13] 壯士 [14] 壯志 [15] 壯年 [16] 武壯 [17] 卜葬 [18] 殉葬 [19] 埋葬 [20] 起葬 [21] 厚葬 [22] 帮葬

in the same grave; *ho' chaung'* to bury an inferior in the vault of a superior; *haik, chaung'* to bury soon after death; *cheng' chaung'* act of placing the coffin in the grave; *saëng' chaung'* to attend a funeral; *hak chaung'* buried together, as husband and wife.

錐 錞 Chui. The first character is read *ˌch'wi;* coll. *chaung':* an awl, a borer; a sharp-pointed tool: [1]*'chaung' 'kiăng,* a small awl; [2]*'chaung' ˌt'au,* head of the borer; [3]*'chaung' 'mwi,* point of the borer; *siăng' chaung'* an awl for sewing; *ˌsá chaung'* a shoemaker's awl; *'piéng chaung'* a flat awl; *ˌcheng chaung'* small needle-like awl; *pak lak chaung'* a borer used by carpenters.

Chaung'. A coll. word: to run or creep into, to secrete, to hide away: *chaung' 'tié,* to run into; *chaung' k'aëng'* to run into holes; *chaung' ˌt'u 'tié,* to hide in the ground, as worms.

狀 Chuang. Appearance, form, fashion, shape, figure; to appear; to accuse, to declare in writing, to state; a complaint, an indictment: COM., [4]*ˌhing chaung'* form, shape, appearance; [5]*'kó' chaung'* to litigate, to go to law; [6]*'auk, chaung'* overbearing; [7]*'chaung' ˌsü,* a pettifogger, a notary; [8]*'këü' chaung'* to prepare and present a complaint to an officer; [9]*'pó chaung'* a bail or security for the accused party; *'kwi chaung'* like an imp, hence mischievous, tricky; [10]*'chaung' ˌngwong* (coll. *ˌchó ˌngwong* or *chó' ˌngwong*), the first of the Hanlin.

藏 Ts'ang. A store-house, a retreat; a casket, a strong box: also read *ˌchong,* q. v.: [11]*ˌking chaung'* a collection of Budhist books; COM., [12]*'pó chaung'* hoarded pearls, gems; [13]*ˌsá chaung'* Tibet; *te' chaung'* hades; [14]*te' chaung' ˌwong,* name of a certain deified Budhist.

臟 Tsang. The viscera, the entrails: COM., [15]*chaung' 'hu,* the five superior and six inferior viscera, all the inwards; [16]*'ngu chaung'* the five superior viscera; COLL., *twai' chaung'* large intestine, colon; *chaung' ˌt'au,* bottom of the rectum, the anus.

(30) Che.

志 Chih. The will, desire, inclination; purpose, intention, resolution; a sense of right; fixedness of purpose, strong determination; to record; history, annals; statistical and topographical works: [17]*che' sëü'* one aiming at excellence; [18]*'iu che'* a purpose, a design; [19]*teng' che'* fixed purpose; [20]*ek, che'* one purpose, concentration of mind; COM., [21]*che' k'e'* or *che' ch'ëü'* the will, purpose, intention; [22]*lik che'* to resolve; *taik, che'* to obtain one's object; *sek, che'* to fail, discouraged; *che' 'noi,* feeble purpose; *che' k'e' ˌngong ˌngong,* aspiring; *hong' che'* or *lá' che'* to animate, to stir one's self up to; COLL., *che' k'e' twai'* strong will; *ˌmó che' k'e'* fickle, irresolute.

1 錐子 2 錐頭 3 錐尾 4 形狀 5 告狀 6 惡狀 7 狀師 8 具狀 9 保狀 〇 10 狀元 11 經藏 12 寶藏 13 西藏 14 地藏王 〇 15 臟腑 16 五臟 17 志士 18 有志 19 定志 20 一志 21 志氣 22 立志

誌 識 ˀ **Chih.** To remember, to record, to write, to inscribe: used for the preceding; the 2d. character also read *sek*, q. v.: *keˀ cheˀ* to record; [1]*ˁku cheˀ* ancient records; [2]*kwok, cheˀ* annals of the country; COM., [3]*ˏsang kwok, cheˀ* annals of the Three States.

痣 ˀ **Chih.** A mole, a hair-mole; black or red spots on the body: COM., [4]*ˁcheˀ ˏsü*, hair growing out of a mole; *ˏu cheˀ* a black mole; COLL., *ˁteng cheˀ* or *cheˀ ˁteng kʻó* to remove a mole; *cheˀ sioh lak* a mole.

至 ˀ **Chih.** To come, to extend to, to arrive at, to reach to, to go to; the summit, the end, a limit; used as a preposition, to, at, even, till, up to; as to, respecting, in order to; as an adverb, most, greatly, much, very, the superlative degree; the solstice; the 133d radical: [5]*kʻaik, cheˀ* the arrival of guests; [6]*ˏsiéng cheˀ* to arrive first; [7]*cheˀ ˏing*, very benevolent; *cheˀ ˁli*, excellent doctrine; COM., [8]*cheˀ ˁsü pok, piéngˀ* while he lives will not change; [9]*séüˀ cheˀ* the four limits—viz., front, rear, right, and left; [10]*haˀ cheˀ* one of the 24 terms, summer; [11]*cheˀ ˏking*, to the present; [12]*cheˀ ˏchʻing*, very nearly related; COLL., [13]*cheˀ ˁchieu*, at the very lowest, *scil.*, it will cost so much.

郅 ˀ **Chih.** To ascend, to go up, as a hill; flourishing, as an age; very, exceedingly; name of a city: [14]*cheˀ ˏlüng*, grand, flourishing; [15]*cheˀ teˀ* well-governed, prosperous, as a state.

輊 ˀ **Chih.** Sometimes read *teˀ*: a carriage with a low front, lower than the back and turning down from the lading.

質 ˀ **Chih.** To bear witness, to give evidence, to testify; evidence, substance, proof; to ask, to inquire; a pledge, a hostage, a guarantee: also read *chek*, q. v.: [16]*ˏkau cheˀ* to exchange pledges, to contract; [17]*cheˀ chengˀ* to testify; to seek instruction or discuss subjects with one's teacher; [18]*cheˀ chaˀ* to give receipts for goods purchased; COM., [19]*tóiˀ cheˀ* to testify face to face, as plaintiff and defendant.

躓 ˀ **Chih.** To fall, to stumble, to trip and fall down: *ˏtiéng cheˀ* to fall headlong.

贄 ˀ **Chih.** A present designed to make way for one, given at an audience or first interview, or when entering school; a tablet anciently held in the hands at audiences: [20]*chek, cheˀ* to hold the tablet; COM., [21]*cheˀ kengˀ* contributions of money from female guests at a wedding; a present to a teacher; [22]*cheˀ kiéngˀ ˁlá*, bridal presents from female guests; presents to a superior.

摯 ˀ **Chih.** To grasp, to catch, to seize in the hand; to extend to; to present; to advance, to enter, to go to the edge; to break down,

1 古誌 2 國誌 3 三國誌 4 痣鬚 5 客至 6 先至 7 至仁 8 至死不變 9 四至 10 夏至 11 至今 12 至親 13 至少 14 郅隆 15 郅治 16 交質 17 質證 18 質劑 19 對質 20 執贄 21 贄敬 22 贄見禮

as trees from weight of snow: ꜀ching che꜄ warmly attached to.

鷙꜄ Chih. Birds of prey, accipitrine birds; violent, ruthless, hawk-like; to seize by violence.

觶꜄ Chih. A goblet, a wine-cup, containing 3 or 4 *ching* or gills; to fine one to drink so many cups: ꜀syong che꜄ to take the goblet.

Che꜄. A coll. euphonic prefix: *che꜄ cho꜄* to curse; *che꜄ chó꜄* to do, to continue doing.

字² Tzu. A character, a letter, a word; lettered, written on; a writing, a letter, an order; a symbol of thought; to love, to bear, to nourish, to suckle; the style or title taken at marriage; a name, a designation; to betroth a daughter: [1]꜂*u che²* to love and nourish; [2]*tai² che²* ꜂*sieu*, the great nourish the small; *tai² che²* to wait for marriage, as an affianced girl; COM., [3]꜂*sung che²* characters, letters; [4]꜀*pang che²* plainly written characters; [5]*che² p'wo²* copy-books; [6]꜂*ch'ó che²* running-hand characters; [7]*che²* ꜂*ngang*, words, set phrases; [8]꜂*k'ai che²* elegant or pattern characters; [9]*che²* ꜂*mó*, the finals; [10]*che²* ꜀*t'au*, the initials; copies written at top of the page; [11]*che² ngiê²* the literal meaning of words; [12]*che²* ꜂*tiéng*, a dictionary; [13]*che² hwak*꜀ rules for writing; [14]꜂*siă che²* to write; *che² t'aik*꜀ a book of writing-samples in different styles; COLL., *chiăng꜄ che²* the authorized characters, the mandarin pronunciation; *óh che²* to learn to read; *che²* ꜂*kiăng*, comments, marginal readings; *che² tang꜄* a copy placed under and showing through the paper written on.

孳² Tzu. As in *che²* ꜂*mói*, to procreate as birds. Usually read ꜀*chü*, q. v.

牸² Tzu. A cow, a mare; the female of domesticated animals.

自² Tzu. Read *chëü²*; coll. *che²*: self, one's self, I, personally: [15]*che²* ꜀*ka*, self; *che² chó꜄* to do yourself; [17]*che²* ꜀*ch'ing*, self-praise; [18]*che²* ꜂*chü taing꜄* taverns where you cook your own provisions; *che² ch'oi꜄ ch'iong²* ꜀*pu* ꜀*sing*, own mouth like a fly's—i. e., little to eat, *scil.* how then supply others? [19]*che²* ꜀*sing* ꜀*nang* ꜂*pó*, unable to protect itself—applied to an idol; [20]*che² ch'iong꜄* ꜀*mó* ꜀*siăng*, "no voice to sing for self"—to spend strength for others; *che² pok*꜀ *t'iăng꜄ che² pok*꜀ ꜀*mú*, it's your own stomach that aches, then rub it—i. e., repair your own blunders.

Che². A coll. euphonic prefix, as in *che² chaï²* to help, to assist.

(31) Chĕ.

꜀*Chĕ.* A coll. word; as ꜀*chĕ* ꜀*chĕ*, wet, soaked, as cakes; dull, stupid.

1 撫字 2 大字 3 小字 8 文字 ○ 4 平字 5 字薄 6 草字 7 字眼 8 楷字 9 字母 10 字頭 11 字義 12 字典 13 字法 14 寫字 15 自家 16 自做 17 自稱 18 自煮店 ○ 19 自身難保 20 自唱無聲

꜂Chĕ. A coll. word: to wrench the foot to one side; *met.*, to fail partially in business; stopped, interrupted, as from the plots of others.

꜂Chĕ. A coll. word: to crowd, to press forward, to force your way: *꜂chĕ kwoʾ* to crowd by; *꜂chĕ ꜂tó*, to throw down by pressing against.

(32) Cheh.

氵乚 Read *chek꜆*; coll. *cheh꜆*: to spirt out, to squeeze out, as soft things by the hand: *cheh꜆ ch'ok꜆ ꜂li*, to squeeze out; *cheh꜆ ꜀hwa ꜀seng*, to press out the peanut from its red film.

濈 Water rapidly flowing out; rapid; cordial, harmonious, agreeing; to accord with.

Cheh꜆. A coll. word: to stop, as a leak; to fill up: *cheh꜆ mekɔ* or *cheh꜆ ꜂mwang*, to fill up or stop closely, as leaks.

Cheh꜆. A coll. word; as *cheh꜆ cheh꜆ kieuʾ* (spoken rapidly *꜀chi ꜀chi kieuʾ*) to squeal, as rats.

(33) Chek.

織 Chih. To weave; woven; a general term for weaving: [1]*chek꜆ ꜂sü*, the thrum, ends of weaver's threads: com., [2]*chek꜆ pwoʾ* to weave cloth; [3]*chek꜆ ꜀si*, to weave silk; [4]*chek꜆ ꜂süng*, a coarse cloth of cotton and asses' hair, from Shantung; [5]*chek꜆ ꜀ki*, a loom; [6]*chek꜆ ꜂nü*, the star Wega, *a* in Lyra; [7]*chek꜆ cheuʾ* figures woven in the fabric; [8]*chek꜆ choʾ ꜂hu*, an officer at Soochow in charge of the duties on silks and satins.

緝 Ch'i. To spin, to twist a cord; to join, to connect, to continue; to come after, to follow, to succeed; to pursue, to search for; to apprehend: [9]*chek꜆ ꜀hi*, bright, splendid; perpetual, as doctrine; [10]*chek꜆ hekɔ* to seize; *angʾ chek꜆*, to watch at night, as for thieves.

職 Chih. Tribute, presents from other states; to govern, to attend to; to record; to act officially; official duty; title, rank, office, station; many, numerous: [11]*chek꜆ kangʾ* purchased degree of a kangseng; [12]*꜂siong chek꜆* steady employment; [13]*chek꜆ chek꜆* numerous; com., [14]*꜀kwang chek꜆* official title; [15]*chek꜆ hongʾ* official duty, one's employment; [16]*chek꜆ seüʾ* the duties of one's position; [17]*kaik꜆ chek꜆* to deprive of office, to degrade; [18]*꜀ka chek꜆* to confer a title; [19]*꜀pi chek꜆*, my title; [20]*sieʾ chek꜆* hereditary office or title; [21]*taiʾ chek꜆ ꜂hwoi ꜀ka*, a retired officer.

戢 Ch'i. To disband troops; to store up military supplies; to collect in an arsenal; to desist from, to lay aside, as arms; to fold, as wings: [22]*chek꜆ ꜂süng ꜀ping*, to disband troops; *chek꜆ ꜀kang ꜀k'wo*, to lay aside shields and spears; *chek꜆ ikɔ* to fold the wings; *hok꜆ chek꜆* ceaseless.

1織	3織	5織	7織	府	獲	職	職	事	職	職	家
餘	絲	機	就	9緝	11職	13職	15職	17革	19卑	21帶	22戢
2織	4織	6織	8織	熙	監	職	分	職	職	職	戎
布	絨	女	造	10緝	12常	14官	16職	18加	20世	冋	兵

葺, Ch'i. To put in order, to repair; to cover, to thatch; a spinous grass: *chek, ok,* to renew the thatch of a house.

輯, Ch'i. To collect the materials for a carriage; a car well-arranged; union, concord, agreement, to make everything agreeable; to collect, to gather, to compile; to act gently and cordially: [1]*ˏshwo chek,* to harmonize, concord; [2]*chek, ˏsiu,* peaceful, placid, as the countenance; [3]*ˏsü chek,* harmonizing words, to reconcile; *chek, ˏning,* placid, tranquil.

蛭, A leech, called *ˏchwoi chek,*: *ˏt'ong chek, ˏseng chik* swallowing a leech causes disease.

卽, **即**, Chi. About to eat; now, immediately; soon, presently; when, then, forthwith, near; if, perhaps; this, that is, or, alias; full, abundant: [4]*chek, ˏking,* now, the present; [5]*chai² chek,* close, near at hand; [6]*chek, chek,* full, an abundance; [7]*chek, ˏngu,* noon; COM., [8]*chek, k'aik,* instantly; [9]*chek, ˏch'ü,* or *chek, ˏli,* or *chek, ˏkwang,* then, *scil.* it's thus and so; [10]*chek, se²* that is, i. e.; [11]*chek, oi²* according to places, as at a feast; to ascend the throne; [12]*chek, sok,* quickly, hastily; [13]*chek, piéng²* at your convenience; [14]*ˏhi ˏch'ü chek, ˏpi,* if not this then that; COLL., [15]*chek, chek, hiéng²* brought out at once, as ready money; *chek, ˏkwang pong² ˏsing,* so just dismiss anxiety; [16]*chek, piéng² ˏkü ˏheng,* at convenience go and do.

喞, Chi. Noise of a crowd; hum of insects: *ˏch'iu chek,* a hum, a murmur; a hubbub; COLL., *chek, ˏnüng,* or *chek, chek, ˏnüng ˏnüng,* muttering, unwilling; *chek, chiăk,* or *chek, chek, chiăk, chiăk,* noise of lips in eating; *met.,* careless, slatternly.

堲, To make bricks; to make an arched grave; the snuff of a candle; embers; to dislike, to snuff at.

畟, A sharp agricultural utensil like a mattock; to attend to husbandry.

鯽, **鰿**, Chi. A species of bream (cyprinus gibelioides) with a long dorsal: *ˏch'iéng chek,* a fresh bream; COM., [17]*chek, ˏngü,* a small bream reared in ponds; *chek, ˏngü ˏkó,* a plaster made of the bream.

執, Chih. To take in the hand, to pick up, to lay hold of, to grasp, to apprehend, to catch; to maintain, to retain, to receive, to keep; to stop up; a handful; obstinate, bigoted: *chek, ˏch'iu,* to grasp; *chek, ˏsiu,* to receive, to keep; COM., [18]*chek, sëü²* to manage business, a manager; used for deacons; [19]*chek, sëü² ˏtang,* schedule of duties, as in a yamun; *chek, e²* heady, opinionated; [20]*kauk, chek, ek, ˏsü,* every one telling his own story; *chek, ek,* a man of one idea; *chek, pek,* to hold the pen—i. e., to write for another; *chek, ˏchu,* to hold the decanter, as the host

[1]和輯 [2]輯柔 [3]辭輯 [4]即今 [5]在即 [6]即即 [7]即午 [8]即刻 [9]即此 [10]即是 [11]即位 [12]即速 [13]即便 [14]非此即彼 [15]即即現 [16]即便舉行 [17]鯽魚 [18]執事 [19]執事單 [20]各執一詞

福州方言拼音字典

at a feast; *‸kü chek‸* set, obstinate; COLL., *chek‸ au'* perverse; *ko' chek‸ chê² ‸ka ê' sëü'* bigoted in opinion; *chek‸ ek‸ pok‸ ‸t'ung,* tenacious of one idea and blind to all others.

縶, To tie, to bind, to fasten, as a horse or cow; a cord, a thread: *chek‸ ‸mi,* to fasten, to bind to, as by kindness; *chek‸ ‘ma,* to tie a horse.

質, Substance, essence, nature of, the material of; rough, plain, unadorned, unpretending; sincere, honest; to confront, to cross-examine; to establish, to substantiate; opposite to; to appear in the presence of; firm, as a texture; a disposition, a habit; centre of a target: [1]*‘mi chek‸* brilliant, gifted; [2]*chek‸ tê²* plain; the mind, as endowed; [3]*‸sung chek‸* the adorned and the plain; [4]*‘p'auk‸ chek‸* plain; *‸chü chek‸* natural ability; COM., [5]*‸chai chek‸* original endowments; [6]*‘t'á chek‸* personality, nature of; [7]*‸hing chek‸* form, figure, sign.

鑕, An ax, a hatchet; an anvil or iron block used by smiths and others.

劕, A written agreement, a bond: *chek‸ chê²* long and short documents.

脊, The back, the backbone, the spine; convergent, as ribs; ridge of a house; a sierra, a ridge; a bone; in coll. used *met.* for a dependence, a ground of reliance: *chek‸ ‸ling,* the wagtail; [9]*‘iu ‸lung ‘iu chek‸* orderly and intelligent; *‸sung chek‸* crest of a hill or mountain; COLL., *‸p'iăng chek‸ kauk‸* the spine or backbone; *‸tong chek‸* the comb or apex of the roof; *ch'io' chek‸* the ridge of a roof; *‸p'iăng chek‸ kauk‸ mô² ngaing²* his spine is weak—can't safely rely on him.

瘠, Thin, lean, emaciated, reduced to a bone; poor, as land; to make lean, to impoverish; to retrench, to bring down; spoiled, as meat: [10]*chek‸ peng²* emaciated by sickness; [11]*chek‸ ‘ma,* a lean horse; *chek‸ ‘t'u,* thin soil.

鶺, A wagtail, called *chek‸ ‸ling;* it has a mottled black neck; also called *‸ũng ‸kü.*

稷, Panicled millet (milium), one of the five grains; quick, rapid; the god of agriculture: [12]*‘sü chek‸* rice and millet; [13]*ha² chek‸* evening; [14]*ke' ‸chai ke' chek‸* "offerings ready, present quickly"; COM., *haiu² chek‸* the god of harvests; *siâ² chek‸* gods of land and grain, the Ceres of China.

積, To gather, to hoard up, to accumulate; to increase, to add to, to pile upon: [15]*chek‸ ‸kung,* or *chek‸ taik‸* to acquire or lay up merit; [16]*chek‸ ‘lwi,* to pile up; [17]*chek‸ ‘sang,* to accumulate property; [18]*‸tung chek‸* to hoard up, as grain, etc; COM., [19]*chek‸ chiéng²* to increase gradually; [20]*‸chong chek‸* to hoard up; *chek‸ hëük‸* to gather; [21]*chek‸ ‘sieu sing ‸tó,* much from little;

1美質 2質地 3文質 4樸質 5才質 6體質 7形質 8脊令 9有倫有脊 10瘠病 11瘠馬 12黍稷 13下稷 14既齊既稷 15積功 16積累 17積產 18屯積 19積漸 20存積 21積小成多

chek, k'iéng to accumulate debts; [1]*chek, té* a stoppage, indigestion; *shang chek,* constipated from cold; [2]*hung shang 'sü chek,* sickness from wind, cold, heat, and constipation; COLL., *chek, siǎng toi sang,* grows to mountain size; *k'ŏ chek,* to cure constipation.

勣, Chi. Merit, praiseworthy acts, meritorious deeds, conduct worthy of reward: interchanged with next.

績, Chi. To twist hempen threads on the knee, to split hempen fibres; merit by laudable works; an affair, a business; to complete, to bring to a conclusion; to join, to piece: [3]*kung chek,* or *sëü chek,* or *chek, ngiék* meritorious deeds; [4]*pok, chek, ki ma,* unwilling to twist the fibres—i. e., lazy; [5]*sëü chek, shang hi,* a time of perfect tranquillity, a golden age.

迹, 跡, 蹟, Chi. A trace, a foot-mark, a footstep; vestiges, effects, consequences, signs; the results of previous conduct; to trace out, to follow up, to search for the effects of: [6]*chek, ch'iong* form, shape; [7]*mai chek, chëü sing,* to form your own character; [8]*pok, chek,* insubordinate; COM., [9]*sing chek,* traces of deity, miracles; [10]*'ku chek,* ancient signs, relics; [11]*chung chek,* foot-prints, traces of; [12]*shing chek,* form, shape.

跖, Sole of the foot; to step on, to tread on; to leap up, to dance; metatarsus of birds: [13]*tó chek,* the Robin Hood of China, in the days of Tsin; [14]*sik kié chek,* to eat the metatarsus of chickens.

蹠, Chi.

踖, Chi. To stride; to straddle or step over a thing; to walk reverently, to step in a formal manner, to measure one's steps.

蹐, To step carefully; short steps, a mincing walk; to walk here and there.

Chek,. A coll. euphonic prefix; as *chek, chiǎk,* to spatter, to splash; *chek, chak,* to wind about and bind, to tuck up as one's clothes.

擢, Chi. Read *chok; coll. chek:* to select, to raise, to promote; to employ in office: [15]*chek 'ch'ü,* to recommend a Küjin to the emperor for office; [16]*chek 'ch'ü ti kaing* to recommend to a district magistracy.

宅, Chai. Read *t'ek; coll. chek;* as [17]*chek mwong,* the door opening into the 2d. hall or private apartments of a yamun.

賊, A thief, a robber, a bandit, highwayman, a marauder; seditious, those who rise against the government; the enemy; a term of contempt; to murder, to maltreat; to rob, to pillage, to oppress; a fly in grain; in the coll. read *ch'ek* q. v.: [18]*k'ain chek*

[1]積滯 [2]風寒暑積 [3]功績 [4]不績其麻 [5]庶績咸熙 [6]蹟象 [7]邁迹自新 [8]不蹟 [9]神跡 [10]古跡 [11]踪跡 [12]形跡 [13]盜跖 [14]食雞跖 [15]擢取 [16]擢取知縣〇 [17]宅門 [18]寇賊

a bandit; [1]*schang chek₂* to plunder, to oppress; [2]*smau chek₂* a fly that destroys the stalks of grain; [3]*muk₂ chek₂* or *muk₂ chek₂ ˓ch'ó*, the equisetum hyemele, known as the Dutch rush or scouring rush, much used for scouring and polishing woods and metals.

截² Chieh. To cut, to cut in pieces; to cut asunder, to divide, to separate; to obstruct, to intercept, to stop; to cut off, to amputate; a portion; to discriminate, to make nice distinctions; in coll. a topic, a theme, a point, as of doctrine; always, everything: [4]*chek˳ chek˳* skilled in argument, making nice distinctions; [5]*chek₂ twang²* to cut off; COM., [6]*˓chu chek₂* to prevent, to stop; [7]*˓chang chek₂* moderate, temperate, as in words and acts; [8]*siong² chek₂* the upper portion of anything; COLL., [9]*chek₂ mah₂* to stop the pulse, to kill by pressing on a vital part as pugilists do; [10]*chek₂ so˒* to close an account; [11]*tik₂ chek₂* candid, bold; [12]*chek₂ chek₂ seu² k'e˒* angry about everything; [13]*chek₂ lung² ˓tu*, divided into two apartments; [14]*chek₂ ˓toi*, to make shorter; *˓chi sioh₂ chek₂ ki tô˒ ˓li*, this point of doctrine; *˓kong sioh₂ chek₂* to discuss a theme; *po² sioh₂ chek₂* one point more.

戳² Ch'o. Read *tauk˳*; coll. *chek₂*: a stamp or seal, such as used by constables and pettifoggers: [15]*chek₂ ke˒* a stamp; *kai˒ chek₂* or *kai˒ chek₂ ke˒* to stamp for authentication.

蝍² 蠽² Tsê. An insect that destroys the stalks of grain at the joints; a kind of Hessian fly.

鰂² 鱡² Tse. The cuttle fish; also called *˛u ch'ek₂* "black thief," and *mĕk₂ ngü*, "ink fish;" in medicine it is called *˓hai ˛p'ieu ˛sieu*, and sold in drug stores.

(34) Chëk.

Chëk₂. A coll. euphonic prefix; as *chëk₂ chëk₂ naing²* to talk incessantly.

(35) Cheng.

˛曾 ˛曾 Tsêng. To duplicate, to add; to fly high; a surname: also read *scheng*, q. v.: [16]*˛cheng ˛sing*, I, the inferior officer; COM., [17]*˛cheng ˓chu*, great-grandfather; [18]*˛cheng ˓chu ˓pi*, or *˛cheng ˓chu ˓mu*, great-grandmother; *˛cheng ˛song*, great-grandsons; *˛cheng ˛song ˓nü*, great-granddaughters; [19]*˛cheng ˓chü*, a celebrated disciple of Confucius.

˛增 Tsêng. To increase, to augment, to add; to repeat; repeated, doubled: [20]*˛cheng ˓mi*, to grow in virtue; *˛cheng ˛kó*, to exalt, to raise high; [21]*ho² ˓k'eu nik₂ ˛cheng*, population daily increasing; *˛cheng ek˳* (or COM., *˛ka ˛cheng*,) to increase, to add to; *˛cheng seu²* to prolong life.

1 殘賊 2 蝨賊 3 木賊 4 截截 5 截斷 6 阻截 7 斬截 8 上截 9 截脈 10 截數 11 直截 12 截截受氣 13 截二堵 14 截短 15 戳記 16 曾臣 17 曾祖 18 曾祖妣 19 曾子 20 增美 21 戶口日增

僧 ꜀Sĕng. A Budhist priest; a religious life: [1]*꜀siĕng ꜀cheng*, a devout priest; [2]*sŭk꜇ ꜀cheng*, a venial priest; [3]*mwak꜇ ꜀cheng*, I, the lowest priest; [4]*hwak꜇ ꜀cheng*, a priest of superior sanctity; [5]*꜀cheng sé꜄* a Budhist temple; [6]*꜀cheng sŭk꜇* clergy and laity, as used by Budhists; com., [7]*꜀cheng ꜀ka*, a bonze, a fraternity of priests.

憎 ꜀Tsĕng. To hate, to detest, to dislike, to abominate: [8]*꜂k‘ó ꜀cheng*, hateful, abominable; *seu꜄ ꜀sing ꜀cheng*, to be hated.

怎 ꜀Tsĕn. Also read *꜂cheng*: used in the Court dialect as an interrogative, how? what? in what way? [9]*꜀cheng tek꜇* how? *꜀cheng ꜂mó*, what? *꜀cheng ꜂meng*, how can it be done?

矰 䋫 ꜀Tsĕng. An arrow with a string tied to it, used for shooting birds; a short arrow; high: *꜀cheng ꜂ch‘i*, an arrow bound with a string; *꜀cheng ch‘iok꜇* to fasten the thread to the arrow.

罾 ꜀Tsĕng. A fishing net; a lifting net suspended by the corners: *há꜄ ꜀cheng*, a crab-net; *꜂teu ꜀cheng*, to cast the net.

爭 ꜀Chĕng. To wrangle, to dispute, to quarrel; to strive for precedence; to contest, to litigate; to reprove, to remonstrate, in coll. read *꜀chang*, q. v.: [10]*꜀hung ꜀cheng*, to divide and dispute; [11]*꜀siong ꜀cheng*, to wrangle; [12]*꜀cheng ꜀kiong*, overbearing; [13]*꜀cheng ꜀ngiéng*, anxious to excel, competitive; [14]*꜀cheng sĕŭng꜄* to contend at law; [15]*꜀cheng k‘é꜄* emulous, ambitious; [16]*꜀cheng ꜂k‘eu*, wrangling; [17]*꜀cheng ꜂sang*, to contest an estate; [18]*꜀cheng taiu꜄* to fight; [19]*꜀cheng ꜀siéng*, to strive to be first; [20]*꜀cheng nau꜄* noisy quarrels.

諍 ꜀Chĕng. Used for the preceding: to wrangle: *꜀cheng sĕŭng꜄* to litigate. Also read *chaing꜄* as *kang꜄ chaing꜄* to reprove a superior.

掙 ꜀Chĕng. To pierce, to prick; to force in; also read *chaing꜄* as in the coll. *ngaing꜄ chaing꜄* firm, stiff.

箏 ꜀Chĕng. A kind of guitar or harpsichord having 12 copper strings: [21]*꜀cheng tik꜇* guitar and flute; [22]*꜀cheng ꜀cheng*, loud piercing sounds; [23]*꜀hung ꜀cheng*, a kind of kite; jingling sounds of pieces of metal or glass hung in the wind.

睜 ꜀Tsĕng. A displeased look: *꜀ming ꜀cheng*, to look angrily.

錚 ꜀Chĕng. A small cymbal, a small-sized gong; the ringing sound of metals.

崢 ꜀Tsĕng. To rise above; conspicuous, eminent, lofty like a mountain: *꜀cheng ꜀ing*, lofty, dignified.

琤 ꜀Chĕng. Tinkling sound of gems or metals; the sound of gems when they are rung together.

1 禪僧	3 末僧	5 僧寺	7 僧家	9 怎的	11 相爭	13 爭妍	15 爭氣	17 爭產	19 爭先	21 箏笛	23 風箏
2 俗僧	4 法僧	6 僧俗	8 可憎	10 分爭	12 爭強	14 爭訟	16 爭口	18 爭鬭	20 爭鬧	22 箏箏	24 眳睜

臻 Tsêng. To arrive, to extend to; the utmost, the highest degree; many, numerous, a multitude; to collect, to congregate: *paik꜄ hok꜄ ꜂piéng ꜀cheng*, may every happiness come to you! *꜀ki këüngᵓ chiéngᵓ ꜀cheng*, a total famine; *꜂siong ꜀cheng*, to come swiftly.

꜀溱 Chêng. A small stream in Honan, one of the head waters of the Hwai river; to reach to; at ease, loose, at liberty; many, abundant: *paik꜄ kok꜄ ꜀cheng ꜀cheng*, may your granaries be filled!

꜀鍼 ꜀針 Chên. A needle; a cauterizing probe; to prick; to use the needle in acupuncture; pine leaves: [1]*꜀süng ꜀cheng*, pine leaves; [2]*꜀ong ꜀cheng*, sprouting rice; COM., [3]*꜀cheng ꜀p'wi*, unfinished needles; [4]*꜀ch'iong ꜀cheng*, to thread the needle; [5]*꜀cheng chiúᵓ* acupuncture; [6]*꜂ló ꜀king ꜀cheng*, or *ᶜchü ᶜngu ꜀cheng*, the compass-needle; [7]*꜀cheng siängᵓ* needle and thread; [8]*꜀hwa ꜀cheng*, needle used for embroidering; [9]*꜀cheng ch'engᵓ* a scale with the pointer on top; COLL., [10]*꜀cheng p'eᵓ* eye of the needle; [11]*꜀t'ieng ꜂pang ꜀cheng* pointer on middle of scales-beam; [12]*꜀cheng ᶜkwong*, a needle-case; *꜀cheng ᶜtiu ꜀cheng siängᵓ ᶜtiu siängᵓ* incessant stitching; *met.*, to work incessantly; *twai² ꜂pwoᵓ ꜀cheng*, or *twai² ᶜkwong ꜀cheng*, large needle; *꜀tü ᶜmó ꜀cheng*, darning needle; *꜂chiéng ꜀cheng*, a wire for stringing cash.

꜀棦 Chêng. A bundle of sticks, a number of sticks tied up into a faggot.

꜀榛 Tsêng. A fruit like the filbert or hazel; wood, brushwood; thorny bushes, as in a thick hedge; also a small sort of chestnut: [13]*ᶜsieu ꜀cheng*, a small filbert; [14]*꜀cheng ꜀cheng*, overgrown with bushes; COM., *꜂mau ꜀cheng*, a small filbert; COLL., [15]*꜀cheng ꜀kang*, dried filberts; [16]*꜀ch'ang ꜀cheng*, fresh filberts.

繒 Tsêng. A general name for common silken fabrics, as pongee, sarsnet, lutestring, &c., &c.

꜀蓁 Ch'in. Abundant, exuberant foliage, bushy trees; collected, an accumulation of: *꜀cheng ꜀cheng*, exuberant foliage.

鬇 Short hair: *꜂peng ꜀cheng*, the hair disheveled, tangled.

ᶜ翦 ᶜ剪 Chien. Even, regular, as feathers grow; to cut off smooth; to clip even; to shear; shears, scissors; to kill, to destroy; to reduce, to clip off; light, as a dye or a color: [17]*ᶜcheng miék꜄* to destroy utterly; [18]*ᶜcheng ᶜchau*, to trim the finger nails; [19]*꜂choi ᶜcheng*, to cut out, as garments; to consult, to reduce, as a price; COLL., [20]*ᶜcheng ch'óiᵓ* or *ᶜcheng ᶜhung ch'óiᵓ* to cut into bits; [21]*꜀ka ꜀tó ᶜcheng*, scissors, shears; [22]*ᶜcheng ᶜkeng*, to clip down, to reduce; *ᶜcheng ꜀t'ai*, a

1松	3針	5針	針	針	鼻	12針	14榛	16生	18剪	20剪	剪
針	砭	灸	7針	9針	11天	管	榛	榛	爪	碎	22剪
2秧	4穿	6羅	線	秤	平	13小	15榛	17剪	19裁	21剪	減
針	針	經	8花	10針	針	榛	乾	滅	剪	刀	○

sieve; ᶜ*cheng* ꜀*hwa yong*^{2} to cut flower patterns; *sk'wi* ᶜ*cheng*, to begin to cut the wedding dress; *ne*^{2} ᶜ*cheng*, medium-sized scissors; ꜀*hwa* ᶜ*cheng*, small scissors; ᶜ*cheng* ᶜ*tong*, to lop off; ᶜ*cheng* ᶜ*cheng kak*꜁, to pare the nails.

ᶜ譾 ᶜ譾 Chien. Shallow-pated, superficial, unskilled, not profound; sophistical: ᶜ*cheng kaiu*^{2} shallow-brained; *schai* ᶜ*cheng*, mediocre, of small capacity.

ᶜ*Cheng*. A coll. word; as ᶜ*cheng kak*꜁ (also ᶜ*chiéng kak*꜁) finger nails.

ᶜ*Cheng*. A coll. word; as ᶜ*cheng sheng* ᶜ*chiu*, a feast given to one about to go on a journey.

進ᵓ Chin. To advance, to enter; to go up or on, to get on; to walk before; to bring forward; to approach; to promote; to present; to introduce, to recommend; to come near; progress in, promotion, an advance: [1] ꜀*teng cheng*ᵓ to obtain office; [2] ᶜ*song cheng*ᵓ to select and promote; [3] *só*ᵓ *cheng*ᵓ inordinate ambition; COM., [4] *cheng*ᵓ *sëü*^{2} a Doctor of Laws, LL. D., the third literary or military degree; [5] *cheng*ᵓ *lük* to receive government salary; [6] *cheng*ᵓ ᶜ*pó*, to introduce wealth; to bring tribute to the emperor; [7] ꜀*siéng cheng*ᵓ first essay in second division of the Four Books; the ancients; the preceding class of siutsai; [8] *cheng*ᵓ *ek*꜁ to advance, to increase; [9] *cheng*ᵓ ꜀*hiong*, to offer incense, as on the hills on the 14th night of 8th moon; [10] ᶜ*ing cheng*ᵓ to introduce; [11] *cheng*ᵓ *chaung*ᵓ or *cheng*ᵓ ᶜ*k'wong*, to place the coffin in the grave; *cheng*ᵓ *t'ói*ᵓ to advance and retire; ꜀*sing cheng*ᵓ a student entering as a candidate; one having just obtained his degree; *cheng*ᵓ *pok*꜁, *cheng*ᵓ *t'ói*ᵓ *pok*꜁ *t'ói*ᵓ unable to advance or retreat, impracticable; *cheng*ᵓ *t'ói*ᵓ *su* ꜀*mwong*, no door to advance or retreat; i. e., in great straits; COLL., *cheng*ᵓ *óh* to obtain the siutsai degree; [12] *cheng*ᵓ ꜀*seng*, to advance; *cheng*ᵓ *sioh pwo*^{2} to take a step in advance.

正ᵓ Chêng. Correct, straight, square, right, not awry; erect, not inclined, even, not deflected; regular, usual, proper, to settle, to determine; the first, principal; just at the time of; constant, usual; genuine, real, as goods; to put in order; to assume, to enter on, as an office; to adjust, to govern, to execute the laws, to punish; also read ꜀*ching*, and in coll. ꜀*chiăng* and *chiăng*ᵓ q. v.: [13] ꜀*kü cheng*ᵓ to rest in the right; [14] *cheng*ᵓ *chói*^{2} to punish sin; [15] *cheng*ᵓ *hwak*꜁ to pronounce a judicial sentence; [16] *cheng*ᵓ ꜀*tong*, the tribunals of magistrates; [17] *cheng*ᵓ ᶜ*li*, or *cheng*ᵓ *tó*^{2} true doctrine, right reason; [18] *cheng*ᵓ *oi*^{2} the principal seat; [19] *cheng*ᵓ *k'e*ᵓ right feeling, a right spirit; [20] ꜀*hwong cheng*ᵓ or ꜀*tüng cheng*ᵓ upright, just; [21] ꜀*siéng cheng*ᵓ ancient sages; [22] ꜀*mi* ꜀*kwi cheng*ᵓ ꜀*chi*, to divine by the tortoise shell; *cheu*^{2} *cheng*ᵓ to compare and correct; ᶜ*ngu cheng*ᵓ the five elements; ꜀*p'iéng cheng*ᵓ

1 登進 2 選進 3 躁進 4 進士 5 進祿 6 進寶 7 先進 8 進益 9 進香 10 引進 11 進葬 12 進前 13 居正 14 正罪 15 正法 16 正堂 17 正理 18 正位 19 正氣 20 方正 21 先正 22 惟龜正之 ○

crooked and straight; ʻ*siu cheng*ʼ to obey the truth; *chengʼ* ͵*i* ͵*kwang*, to adjust the clothes and cap; COM., ͵*kiong sü twak cheng*ʼ ʻ*li*, to wrest the truth by violent talk; ʻ*li chengʼ* ͵*ngiong song*² the doctrine good, and the words appropriate.

症 ʼ Chêng. An unauthorized character, but found in the *Paik*, ͵*Ing*: disease, sickness, ailments, disorders: COM., ¹*chengʼ hau*² character of a disease; ²*chengʼ ngik* incurable disease; ³*song*² *chengʼ* a curable disease; ⁴ʻ*hwang chengʼ* disease growing worse; ⁵*auk, chengʼ* (coll. *ngai chengʼ*) violent disease; COLL., ⁶*pang*² *chengʼ* sickness; *chengʼ taëng*² serious illness; *mwok chengʼ* to cure sickness; *mwongʼ chengʼ* or *kʻangʼ chengʼ* to inquire into the nature of a complaint, as a physician.

政 ʼ Chêng. To rule, to govern; a standard, a regulator; a treatise, a guide on a subject; government, politics; laws, regulations: ⁷*chʻek, chengʼ* sun, moon, and five planets, or elements; *sheng chengʼ* to transact government business; ⁸*sing chengʼ* official clemency; ⁹*wong chengʼ* royal government—i. e., good rule; ¹⁰͵*kʻö chengʼ* a tyrannical government; ¹¹͵*ka chengʼ* family regulations; ¹²*chengʼ leng*² official orders; ¹³*laung*² *chengʼ* to discuss government matters; ¹⁴ʻ*i sui chengʼ* the authority is yours; COM., ¹⁵*hok chengʼ* Literary Chancellor; ¹⁶*kwok*, *chengʼ* or *chengʼ sëü*¹ the national government.

証 ʼ Chêng. To reprove, to reprimand; to remonstrate with, to admonish, to expostulate; to testify: interchanged with the following.

證 ʼ Chêng. To prove, to confront, to testify, to substantiate; to prove by authorities, to bear witness; evidence, testimony: ¹⁷*chengʼ chö*ʼ to confirm by evidence; ͵*ki ho*² ͵*yong yong si* ʻ*chü chengʼ* ͵*chi*, the father stole the sheep, and the son proved it; COM., ¹⁸*chengʼ kiëngʼ* to testify; ¹⁹*chengʼ ngiëng*² or *chengʼ këü*ʼ verification, proof; ²⁰͵*kang chengʼ* to testify; COLL., *chö*ʼ ͵*kang chengʼ* to bear witness.

晉 ʼ **晋** ʼ Chin. To advance, to increase, to flourish, to grow; to stick, as into a case, or about the person, in which sense the same as the next; to curb a horse; name of a dynasty, divided into the Western and Eastern Tsin, A.D. 265–419; a feudal state, now the southern part of Shansi; COM., ²¹*chengʼ lük* to receive a government salary; ²²*chengʼ* ͵*kong kaing*² a district in the Chinchew prefecture, Fookien.

搢 ʼ Chin. Also read *chiëngʼ*: to stick into, to insert, to put into, as a socket; to shake, to agitate: used for next: *chengʼ hwok*, to hold the pearly tablet, as at audiences; *chengʼ* ͵*sing lioh* book containing a list of the officers in the empire.

¹症 ³順 ⁵惡 ⁷七 ⁹王 ¹¹家 ¹³論 政 政 見 證 江
效 症 症 政 政 政 政 ¹⁵學 ¹⁷證 ¹⁹證 ²¹晉 縣
²症 ⁴反 ⁶病 ⁸仁 ¹⁰苛 ¹²政 ¹⁴爾 政 佐 驗 祿 ○
[illegible] 症 症 政 政 令 爲 ¹⁶國 ¹⁸證 ²⁰監 ²²晉

ALPH. DICT. 7.

縉 ˀ
Chin.
Carnation colored silk; a light red; to wrap around; to gird, as with a sash: [1]*ʻchengˀ ꜀sing*, the "red sashes"—i. e., the literati and gentry; *chengˀ ꜀sing ꜀siéng ꜀seng*, a literary gentleman.

瑨 ˀ
Chin.
A pebble, or secondary gem; a stone that may be considered a gem.

浸 ˀ
Chin.
To soak, to soak through, to penetrate; to macerate; to moisten, to mollify; to water, to bedew; to saturate; to steep in, to submerge, to immerse; to flood, to lay under water, as fields; drenched, wet, imbued with, watered; gradually, gently: [2]*chengˀ ëüng²* to saturate; [3]*tai² chengˀ* a great flood; [4]*chengˀ ʻpi tŏ² ꜀tiéng*, to lay the paddy fields under water; COLL., [5]*chengˀ ʻsi*, to drown; *chengˀ mauk*, to soak to pieces; [6]*chengˀ ꜀puí*, to swell by soaking; [7]*chengˀ ʻchwi*, to submerge in water; [8]*chengˀ chʻoˀ* to soak in vinegar; *chengˀ ʻsi ꜀chü ꜀nëng ʻkiăng*, to drown daughters; [9]*chengˀ hwaˀ* dissolved by steeping; [10]*chengˀ chʻauˀ* soaked till unsavory; [11]*chengˀ tʻauˀ* soaked through; *chengˀ ʻchwi ꜀tʻeng lang² ꜀tʻau loˀ* the solen steeped till the meat of its two ends appears; *met.*, failing, turning out badly.

Chengˀ. A coll. euphonic prefix; as *chengˀ chiéngˀ* to usurp; *chengˀ chiéngˀ* to tremble; *chengˀ chiăngˀ* yes, just so; *chengˀ chëüngˀ* to plant, to drop seeds.

曾 ꜁
Tsʻĕng.
An adverb of past time, past, gone by, already done; how! [12]*꜁cheng ʻpʻeu*, is it done or not? [13]*꜁hó ꜁cheng*, how can it be so! [14]*꜁cheng ꜀king*, already, past; [15]*e² ꜁cheng*, not yet; COLL., *paik, ꜁cheng* or *yaˀ ꜁cheng*, formerly, previously, already; *mwoi² ꜁cheng*, have not yet, never have.

層 ꜁
Tsʻĕng.
A story of a building; a shelf, a step, a round of a ladder; a layer, a strata, a tier, a stage; lamina, a plate or anything laid on; still more, added to; a step, a degree above; a classifier for steps, stories of buildings, &c.: COM., [16]*꜁cheng ꜁cheng*, every step; [17]*꜀tʻai ꜁cheng*, steps or rounds of a ladder; [18]*꜀chʻiéng ꜁cheng*, a thousand stories high—i. e., very high, as a mountain; [19]*꜁lai ꜁cheng*, a chow-chow basket with shelves or divisions; [20]*ʻkwi ꜁cheng*, how many steps? *꜁cheng chʻëüˀ* gradation, regular order; [21]*꜁cheng chʻëüˀ ꜀hung ꜁ming*, every step (of a business) plain; *꜁sing ꜁lai ꜁cheng*, a large basket with divisions; *꜀sang ꜁cheng ꜁lau*, a three storied house; an ancient bridal chair.

橙 ꜁
Chĕng.
Also read *꜁teng:* a variety of large coolie orange; the shaddock: *꜀chʻiu ꜁cheng*, autumnal shaddocks; *꜀kang ꜁cheng*, sweet shaddocks; *꜁wong ꜁cheng*, yellow shaddocks; *꜀sang ꜁cheng*, a melodinus, a woody climber belonging to the dogbane family. Read *taingˀ* a table, a desk; in the mandarin *ʻpang taingˀ* a bench.

---

1 縉紳 2 浸潤 3 大浸 4 浸彼稻田 5 浸死 6 浸肥 7 浸水 8 浸醋 9 浸化 10 浸臭 11 浸透 12 曾否 13 何曾 14 曾經 15 未曾 16 層層 17 梯層 18 千層 19 箂層 20 幾層 21 層次分明 〇

盡^2 儘^2 Chin. An empty vessel; to exhaust, to use all; finished, empty, exhausted; a quantity used up; all, entirely, wholly, fully, completely, to the utmost degree; to indulge, as one's grief; a superlative, very, most, exceedingly; a work brought to an end; to fill up, as time; to achieve, to accomplish; to stop, to conclude: [1]*cheng^2 nik*, the whole day; [2]*tai^2 cheng^2* a month of 30 days; [3]*ˌchü pok͵ cheng^2 ngiong*, I cannot write all I wish to say; COM., [4]*cheng^2 chiék͵* "exhaust chastity"—to commit suicide, as a widow does; [5]*cheng^2 ˊch'ü ˊhu*, drain this flagon, as the host says to guests; [6]*cheng^2 ˌsing*, to apply one's whole mind; [7]*cheng^2 ki tó^2* to try to do right only; [8]*u kùng cheng^2* inexhaustible, illimitable; [9]*cheng^2 ˊpwong hong^2* to discharge one's full duty; [10]*cheng^2 ˊsu ˊiu*, to use all of one's resources; COLL., [11]*cheng^2 ˌi sioh sié^2 meng^2* during his whole life, *scil.* I must support him; [12]*cheng^2 ch'eng*, or *cheng^2 ch'io^2* to solicit a bonus beyond the price of the property sold; *ˊkong mā^2 cheng^2* all cannot be told! *ˊsá cheng^2 chioh cheng^2* utterly destitute; *cheng^2 chioh, chö^2 tó^2 stiong*, to chant as Tauists, till the candle burns out; *met.*, to do so much and then stop; *cheng^2 ˊhó*, very good; [13]*cheng^2 hwai^2* very depraved; [14]*cheng^2 ˊmwói*, to the very end.

藎^2 Chin. A plant whose roots afford a yellow dye; residue, remainder, balance; to advance constantly; sincere, as in professions of friendship: [15]*cheng^2 ˊch'ó*, also called *wong ˊch'ó*, a plant used to dye yellow; *cheng^2 sing*, loyal officer.

燼^2 Chin. Ashes, embers, snuff, residuum after combustion; a quenched brand; relics; what is left, as of a conquered people, or after a conflagration: *sü cheng^2* the remainder, as of embers; [16]*ˊhwo cheng^2* quenched brands; *ˌsiu ne^2 kwok͵ ˌchi cheng^2* to receive what is left of the population of two kingdoms.

贐^2 Chin. Presents to one setting out on a journey; precious things: [17]*cheng^2 ngi*, or *cheng^2 keng^2* parting gifts; *koi^2 cheng^2* to make parting gifts.

凈^2 Ching. Cold, shivering: often used for next, but incorrectly.

淨^2 Ching. Also read *chiăng^2*: clean, pure, spotless, undefiled; upright, guileless; to wash, to cleanse; only; all; rapids in the river Han: [18]*ˌch'ing cheng^2* or *kiék͵ cheng^2* clean, pure; [19]*cheng^2 ˌsing*, to purify the heart; a clean heart.

靜^2 Ching. Still, silent, quiet, at rest; impassible, imperturbable; no bustle; mild, peaceable; pure, like water; to judge, to ponder, to meditate on; to desist: *st'iéng cheng^2* at rest, peaceful; *che^2 cheng^2* very still, solitary; *cheng^2 chö^2* to sit quietly; *cheng^2 ngiong*, quiet advice; *cheng^2 ˊnü*, a chaste virgin; *cheng^2 sek͵* to

[1]盡日 [2]大盡 [3]書不盡言 [4]盡節 [5]盡此壺 [6]盡心 [7]盡其道 [8]無窮盡 [9]盡本分 [10]盡所有 [11]盡伊一世面 [12]盡田 [13]盡壞 [14]盡尾 [15]藎草 [16]火燼 [17]贐儀 [18]清淨 [19]淨心

rest; [1]*cheng*^{2} *‛yong*, to nourish by repose: COM., [2]*ˏch‛ing cheng*^{2} clear and silent; [3]*ˏting cheng*^{2} correct, chaste, as females; [4]*‛hó*^{2} *cheng*^{2} fond of retirement, sedentary; [5]*sĕŭkˏ cheng*^{2} still and reverential; [6]*ˏping cheng*^{2} or *ˏang cheng*^{2} peaceful, tranquil; COLL., *cheng*^{2} *chiăhˏ cheng*^{2} very still, retired.

靚^2 Ching. To call, to invite; to allure; to ornament, to bedizen; handsome, bewitching; still, in which sense it is interchanged with the preceding.

靖^2 Ching. Small, fine, minute; to think, to plan, to devise, to scheme; to meditate on; to tranquilize, to harmonize, to restore peace, to clear, as the sea from pirates; to regulate, to settle disturbances; to become clear and quiet: [7]*cheng*^{2} *ˏmeu*, to plan, to devise; [8]*nikˏ cheng*^{2} *sĕŭ*^{2} *ˏhwong*, daily to plan for everything; [9]*cheng*^{2} *ˏsŭ*, to consider; [10]*cheng*^{2} *‛li*, to regulate; [11]*ˏpi sŭ cheng*^{2} *ˏchi*, allow me to manage it; [12]*cheng*^{2} *lwang*^{2} to settle disturbances; [13]*cheng*^{2} *ˏhwo*, to harmonize; [14]*chĕŭ*^{2} *chaukˏ hokˏ cheng*^{2} to act without a plan, reckless, fool-hardy.

婧^2 Ching. Also read *ˏching* and *‛ching*, but usually *cheng*^{2} and *ch‛aing*^{2}: chaste, as a virgin; to stand erect; weak, gentle, delicate, slender-waisted.

Cheng^2. A coll. euphonic prefix; as *cheng*^{2} *chang*^{2} to chisel, to engrave; to stamp, as dollars; *cheng*^{2} *chiŭng*^{2} to purify, to lustrate, as a Tauist priest does.

(36) Chĕng.

棕 ˏ 椶 ˏ Tsung. Read *ˏchung;* coll. *ˏchĕng:* a kind of gomuti palm; the chamoerops, whose bracts furnish coir for ropes, mats, coarse garments, &c.; the coir from the Borassus Gomutus; a dark brown, umber: [15]*ˏchĕng tĕŭkˏ* the palm-bamboo; [16]*ˏchĕng ˏsai*, rain garments made of coir; [17]*ˏchĕng chaing*^{2} coir-mats; [18]*ˏchĕng ˏsiong*, a box covered with coir; [19]*ˏchĕng ch‛eu*^{2} the palm tree; [20]*ˏchĕng ˏliĕ ˏpiéˏ* boughs of the palm; *ˏchĕng hokˏ* a coir-duster; *ˏchĕng sóhˏ lohˏ ‛chwi ˏka ‛king*, coir-rope put in water grows tighter; *met.*, increasing misery; *ˏchĕng saikˏ* umber color; *ˏchĕng p‛iĕng*^{2} palm-bracts; *ˏchĕng ˏsi*, palm-fibres.

鬃 騣 ˏ Tsung. Read *ˏchung;* coll. *ˏchĕng:* a horse's mane; bristles; leaves of the pine: *‛ma ˏchĕng*, or *lekˏ ˏchĕng*, a horse's mane; *ˏtŭ ˏchĕng*, bristles of a hog; *ˏsŭng ˏchĕng*, or *ˏsŭng pahˏ ˏchĕng*, leaves of the pine tree.

‛鬃 Tsung. Read *ˏchung;* used for the coll. *‛chĕng:* a high knot of hair, worn by females; the back lappet of a Chinese lady's head-dress, which extends over the neck; false hair; a periwig, a false cue: *ˏmang ‛chĕng*, wigs, or false cues for men; *‛nŭ ‛chĕng*, lady's wig; *ˏsĕ ‛chĕng*, to dress the wig; *‛chĕng ˏt‛au*, the end of the wig or lappet which is attached to the head; *‛chĕng siohˏ ‛liu*, a hair-roll, a lappet; *ch‛ai*^{2} *‛chĕng*, the

[1]靜養 [2]清靜 [3]貞靜 [4]好靜 [5]肅靜 [6]平靜 [7]靖謀 [8]日靖四方 [9]靖思 [10]靖理 [11]俾予靖之 [12]靖亂 [13]靖和 [14]自作弗靖 [15]棕竹 [16]棕蓑 [17]棕薦 [18]棕箱 [19]棕樹 [20]棕櫚枝 〇

tops of vegetables; [1]ʻchĕng taing꜄ a wig-shop.

꜂Chĕng. A coll. word: to pour or dash water on anything, to drench; to quench or extinguish, as fire; to cleanse with water: ꜂chĕng kwo꜄ kʻŏ throw it, dash it on! ꜂chĕng lŏh꜆ to pour down on; ꜂chĕng tʻah꜆ to cleanse by dashing water on; ꜂chĕng sioh꜆ ꜀sing, drenched all over the body; ʻsai ʻchwi ꜂chĕng, to dash water on; ꜂chĕng kwo꜄ to extinguish, as with water; ꜂chĕng lang² dash it wet.

(37) Cheu.

鄒 ꜀ Tsou. A district in the south-west of Shantung, on the Yellow river; an ancient city in Lu, where Mencius was born; a surname.

郰 ꜀ Tsou. The district in Lu where Confucius was born, situated in Yenchau-foo in Shantung, and not far from the preceding.

陬 ꜀ Tsou. An angle, or corner, as of a city wall; a bastion; a nook, a cove; to live together; abashed, ashamed: [2]꜀pi ꜀cheu, abashed; [3]maing² ꜀cheu, a name for the first month; [4]꜀sing ꜀cheu, corner of a city wall; [5]꜀ha ꜀cheu, a distant, lonely nook; [6]꜀hwong ꜀cheu, a sequestered cove; [7]꜀cheu ek꜆ the residence of Confucius, as in the preceding.

騶 ꜀ Tsou. A fabulous feline beast called [8]꜀cheu ꜀ngü, emblematical of kindness to animals; a royal groom or hostler: [9]chʻek꜆ ꜀cheu, the seven royal grooms.

緅 ꜀ Tsou. Silk first dyed red thrice, then twice dipped in black; a dark brown or brownish purple, puce.

諏 ꜀ Tsou. Also read ꜀chü: to consult with, to take advice; to inquire into matters of government; to deliberate in public assembly; to select, to choose: [10]꜀cheu kek꜆ to select a lucky day; [11]꜀chü ꜀cheu, take counsel; [12]꜀cheu ꜀chü, a constellation.

謅 ꜀ Tsou. To speak in an undertone, to whisper, to speak into one's ear: [13]꜀kʻing ꜀cheu, to speak privately, to whisper to.

掫 ꜀ Tsou. To strike the rounds at night, to pace the beat, as a watchman; to seize, to take with the hand.

鯫 ꜀ Tsou. Minnows, small white fish that skip over the water; met., a simpleton: [14]꜀cheu ꜀seng, a foolish fellow.

棷 ꜀ Tsou. Fire-wood; a kind of wood used for making combs, and watchmens' rattles; also used for fuel; a surname: ꜀cheu siong² the wood for making combs.

走 ꜂ Tsou. To run, to go, to travel; to sail; to hasten, to quicken one's steps; to flee, to run off, to escape; the 156th radical; in the coll. a menial, a runner: [15]ʻcheu seu꜄

---

[1] 鬃店 [2] 卑陬 [3] 孟陬 [4] 城陬 [5] 遐陬 [6] 荒陬 [7] 陬邑 [8] 騶虞 [9] 七騶 [10] 諏吉 [11] 咨諏 [12] 諏訾 [13] 輕謅 [14] 鯫生 [15] 走獸

quadrupeds, four-footed animals; ͵pwong ‘cheu, to abscond, to go abroad; ‘cheu ‘ma, to ride on horseback; ͵hi ͵sa ‘cheu sik͵ to make the sand and stones fly, as a strong wind; ͵loi ͵ting ‘cheu, rumbling of thunder; COLL., ‘cheu ‘keu, "running dogs,"—runners in brothels or other low places.

‘沼 **Chao.** A pool, or pond with crooked border; a water-tank used for a fish-pond: ͵leng ‘cheu, a water-lily pond; k‘ŭük͵ ‘cheu, an angular pool; ͵ling ‘cheu, a beautiful pond; ‘cheu ‘chi, ponds.

‘鳥 **Niao.** Read ‘neu; coll. ‘cheu: a bird, the feathered tribe: [1]‘cheu kaĕk͵ male of birds; [2]‘cheu ‘mó, female of birds; [3]‘cheu seu’ birds and beasts; [4]‘cheu ka’ a bird-roost; [5]‘cheu chiăh͵ a sparrow, a small bird; [6]‘cheu ‘kiăng, little birds, birdlings; [7]‘cheu taing’ a bird-shop; [8]‘chiĕng ‘cheu, birds just out of shell; *met.*, timid, unsophisticated; [9]͵ching ‘cheu, a small spotted bird caged by the Chinese; ‘cheu seu’ or [10]‘cheu ͵wo, birds' nests; [11]‘yong ‘cheu, to domesticate birds; ͵tong ‘cheu, to snare birds; [12]auk͵ ‘cheu, vicious birds; ‘chwi ‘cheu, aquatic birds; ‘ya ‘cheu, wild-fowls; p‘ah͵ ‘cheu, to shoot birds; [13]t‘ang’ ‘cheu, charcoal birds; [14]‘cheu ͵mui, a stool pigeon; [15]‘cheu ͵lĕng, bird-cage; [16]‘cheu kwang’ feeding cups in a bird-cage; [17]‘cheu ͵siăng, or ‘cheu ͵ing, a bird-like sound; ‘cheu kieu’ ch‘ok͵ ͵pung ͵mwong, when the birds sing, (ladies) must get up.

蛀’ **Chu.** Read chĕü’; coll. cheu’: an insect (Ptinus) that eats books; moths in clothes, wood, &c.; to eat as insects do; to decay, to rot: [18]siong² cheu’ worm-eaten; cheu’ ‘hung, dust from moth-eating; [19]͵chü cheu’ books worm-eaten; ‘ngai cheu’ decayed teeth; [20]cheu’ ͵t‘ĕng, a moth, a wood-worm; [21]͵i ͵siong cheu’ clothes moth-eaten; [22]cheu’ hok͵ small pitted, as a kind of Lichi fruit.

呪’ 咒’ **Chu.** To curse, to imprecate, to rail at, to swear; to recite spells, to curse; an oath; a charm, a spell, an incantation, an imprecation; a prayer: chó’ cheu’ or cheu’ ma’ to rail at; to curse.

͵Cheu. A coll. word, also spoken chiăk͵; same as ͵chieu q. v.: ͵cheu ͵cheu ͵siăng, loquacious, as beggars; to trouble by prating; ͵cha ͵cheu, to annoy; mŏh͵ lŏh͵ ͵chu wai’ ͵cha ͵cheu, don't stay here and trouble with your prating.

就² **Chin.** To complete, to make a circuit; to meet, to go towards, to go to, to draw near, to approach; to accompany, to follow, accommodated to; the place to which things tend, or culminate at; completed, finished; to come near in time; an adverb, then, immediately, at once, presently, forthwith; that is, the same as, just so; a conjunction, then, if, as if; able to do, willing: nik͵ cheu² daily progress; COM., [23]͵sing cheu² to finish, to complete; cheu² se²

1 鳥雄 2 鳥母 3 鳥獸 4 鳥架 5 鳥雀 6 鳥子 7 鳥店 8 茭鳥 9 精鳥 10 鳥窩 11 養鳥 12 惡鳥 13 炭鳥 14 鳥媒 15 鳥籠 16 鳥罐 17 鳥聲 18 上蛀 19 書蛀 20 蛀蟲 21 衣裳蛀 22 核蛀 23 成就 ○

the same as, that is; ¹*cheu² këüng²* to come near, close at hand; ²*cheu² oi²* to be put in a place; to occupy a seat; COLL., ³*cheu² ˌli*, to come at once; ⁴*cheu² chiăng²* straight, correct, as when placed in the middle; *ˌchiong cheu²* a make-shift, a stop-gap; *cheu² ˌi k'ó'* yield it to him, let him have it, as the house he occupies; *cheu² ˓ch'iu*, "at the hand,"—as to do by the way; *cheu² sioh ˌtoi*, come together; *cheu² ˓chiă sie²* after that fashion; ⁵*cheu² ch'iong²* exactly like, just as; ⁶*cheu² kiëng² hau²* instantly efficacious, as medicine.

鷲² Chiu. A large accipitrine bird, perhaps the eagle, or white-headed condor; said to have a yellow head, red eyes and beautiful plumage: ⁷*cheu² ˓neu*, an eagle; a condor; ⁸*ˌling cheu² ˌsang*, Eagle mountain, in the western part of China.

(38) Chëū.

注' Chu. Water disparting into streamlets; to lead water in channels; to pour, to soak, to saturate; to record; to comment; to collect; to strike; to fix the mind on a subject; to remember: ⁹*chëū' muh* to gaze at; ¹⁰*chëū' ˓ch'i ˌü ˌchiëng*, arrows set on the string; ¹¹*cheu² ˓king*, closely attentive; COM., ¹²*chëū' e'* to regard closely; ¹³*˓chwi chëū'* water flowing in; COLL., *lang² chëū'* to slough, to spread, as a diseased place.

漬' Chi. To soak, to steep; to dye; water-soaked, damaged by soaking: COM., ¹⁴*pek, chëū'* a cup to soak pens in; COLL., ¹⁵*chëū' lang²* soaked, or cooked soft; ¹⁶*chëū' ho²* soaked rotten; spoiled; *chëū' ˌt'ong*, softened in hot water, as food.

駐' Chu. To stop a horse; to rest, to tarry, to sojourn; a horse at rest; a halting-place: ¹⁷*chëū' chak,* or *chëū' teng²* to live at a place; stationed, appointed to a post; ¹⁸*chëū' chëük,* to stop; *chëū' pek,* halting place for the imperial cavalcade; COM., ¹⁹*chëū' ˌhwong*, the Manchus, because they guard the place.

足' Tsu. To obtain one's end by flattery; to increase, exceive; usually read *chëük,* q. v.: ²⁰*chëū' ˌküng*, to flatter by a respectful manner; ²¹*chëū' ˌngiong*, finical, fastidious, as about language.

蛀' Chu. An insect (Ptinus) which eats clothes, wood, books, &c.,; to eat, as insects do; in the coll. read *cheu'* q. v.: *chëū' ˌt'üng*, the Ptinus; worm-eaten.

剸' 傳' Tsu. To transfix, to stab, to thrust, to stick into the ground; to erect; to pierce with a sword; to put the plowshare into the ground; to dig up weeds; *chëū' ˌkeng*, to plow; *chëū' ˌsung*, to dig up weeds; *chëū' eng²* to pierce, as with a knife.

廁' 厠' T'së. A filthy place; a privy, a necessary; a place that requires cleansing; to wash, to cleanse; in order, to put in proper places, as guests; inclined, oblique;

¹就近 ²就位 ³就來 ⁴就正 ⁵就像 ⁶就見 效驗 ⁷鷲鳥 ⁸靈鷲山 ⁹注目 ¹⁰注矢於弦 ¹¹注緊 ¹²注意 ¹³水注 ¹⁴筆漬 ¹⁵漬𤀫 ¹⁶漬腐 ¹⁷駐扎 ¹⁸駐足 ¹⁹駐防 ²⁰足恭 ²¹足言 〇

a gorge through which a stream forces its way; [1]ˏchʻing chĕü' to cleanse a filthy place; [2]chĕü' ʻsu, a water-closet.

胾' To cut up meat into slices; steaks, bits of meat, slices of meat: [3]chĕü' ˏkeng, to cut up meat for soup; tai^2 chĕü' large slices of meat.
Tzu.

恣' Relaxation, dissipation; gay, loose, licentious; to follow one's passions, to throw off all restraint: chĕü' ˎsiu, gay, restless; [4]hwong' chĕü' profligate, dissipated; [5]chĕü' e' a restless, licentious disposition.
Tzu.

眥' Also read ˏchü: the canthus or corner of the eye; a fierce look; to look at angrily; a lappel, the place where it folds over; [6]ˎngang chĕü' to look at angrily.
Tzu.

Chĕü'. A coll. word: as in ˏka chĕü' or ˏka chĕü' ˏpau, a straw pouch to put things in; small bags to cook rice in; also called ʻchʻau ˏpau, q. v.

自^2 A preposition, from, commencing at, beginning from; a pronoun, I, my own, self, myself, personally; to use, to lead, to bring; 132d radical: [7]chĕü^2 ʻku kik ˏking, from ancient times to the present; [8]chĕü^2 ˏtʻiéng, from heaven; [9]chĕü^2 hong' to rouse, to animate one's self; COM., [10]chĕü^2 chai^2 at rest, peaceful, quiet; chĕü^2 ˏsing, one's self; [11]chĕü^2 ˏsing ˎnang ʻpó, cannot preserve himself; [12]chĕü^2 se^2 opinionated, conceited; [13]chĕü^2 chĕük$_2$ self-sufficient; [14]chĕü^2 ngwong^2 to consent, willing; [15]chĕü^2 ˏchʻing, self-styled; chĕü^2 wong' angry with one's self, remorseful; chĕü^2 kʻe' to throw one's self away; chĕü^2 ˎngiong chĕü^2 ʻngü, to soliloquize aloud; chĕü^2 chauk, ngiéka self-procured retribution; chĕü^2 ˏchiong, to assume, headstrong, presumptuous; chĕü^2 ˏti ʻli ʻtwang, conscious of fault; chĕü^2 cheng^2 to kill one's self; chĕü^2 tĕüng^2 to maintain self-respect; chĕü^2 ˎyong, of course; naturally, spontaneously; chĕü^2 ˏsing, to reform one's self; chĕü^2 ˎming ˏchüng, a clock; chĕü^2 eng' certainly, ought, should; chĕü^2 ko' pok, ha^2 cannot take care of self, *scil.*, how then look after others? COLL., chĕü^2 ˎdai ʻhwi, lucifer-matches.
Tzu.

聚^2 To assemble, to congregate, to gather; to meet; to tend to, to concur; to incline towards, popular; to collect, prepared, ready; to dwell together; a dwelling place, a village; a conjunction, a meeting; a place of meeting: [16]chĕü^2 ʻngü, to converse together; [17]chĕü^2 ˎmeu, to meet and form plans; [18]chĕü^2 sang' meeting and separating; [19]ˎming chĕü^2 an assembly of the people; [20]chĕü^2 liéng^2 to collect; to amass, as by official exactions; [21]chĕüng' ˏsing ʻsu chĕü^2 towards whom all hearts turn; COM., chĕü^2 chik, or chĕü^2 hwoi^2 to assemble; chek, chĕü^2 to hoard, as wealth; ek, ˏka ˎtʻwang chĕü^2 all the family met again; chĕü^2 ʻpó ˎpwong, a vase for
Chu.

1清厠 2厠所 3胾羹 4放恣 5恣意 6睚眥 7自古及今 8自天 9自訓 10自在 11自身難保 12自是 13自足 14自願 15自稱 16聚語 17聚謀 18聚散 19民聚 20聚斂 21衆心所聚

海上絲綢之路文獻集成 科技與文化编

precious things; a dish made of paper, carried about by beggars in the 12th month.

炷 [2] Chu. A wick; a stick of incense; to light: ˏhiong chēū² a lighted incense-stick; COM., ˏsang chēū² three incense sticks—usually burnt in worship.

住 [2] Chu. To stop, to desist from, to cease; to detain; to dwell, to stay, to live in; to endure; to withstand; to erect; after another verb it is often merely a sign of past time, or indicates that the action has rested: [1]ˏtung chēū² to dwell together; COM., [2]ˏkū chēū² to dwell in; [3]chang² chēū² to reside temporarily at; [4]chēū² ˋchi, to dwell, to live at; [5]chēū² pwo² to halt; [6]ˋk'ō pokˎ chēū² unreliable; COLL., chēū² ˋseng ˏsiŭng, to live in the provincial city; chēū² ˏk'a, to stand, to wait; chēū² ˋch'iu, to rest the hand—stop working.

柱 [2] Chu. A post, a pillar, an upright support, a joist; met., a main dependence, a statesman; to support, to uphold: [7]sēū² chēū² to place a post in position; [8]chēū² ha² ˋsū, emperor's historian; ˏtŭng ˏdiu ˋti chēū² a firm rock in the stream; met., person of ability; [9]ˏking ˏt'iéng chēū² "pillar of the heavens," i. e. able statesman, Atlas of the state.

(39) Chĕŭk.

足ˎ Tsu. The foot, the leg; sufficient, enough; full, satiated; surplus, too much; in full, entirely, wholly; to satisfy, to please, to supply the wants of; pure, as silver; actions, conduct; the 137th radical: also read chēū² q. v.: [10]chĕŭkˎ ˏping, a full complement of troops and arms; [11]chēū² chĕŭkˎ conceited; [12]pokˎ ˋngó chĕŭkˎ he disapproves of me; [13]sekˎ chĕŭkˎ to slip; to fall into sin, a fauxpas; [14]ˋkū chĕŭkˎ to raise the foot, as in walking; COM., [15]ho² chĕŭkˎ wealthy; [16]chĕŭkˎ ĕŭng² enough for use; pokˎ chĕŭkˎ not full, insufficient; [17]chĕŭkˎ ê² fully satisfied; [18]ˏti chĕŭkˎ contentment; pokˎ ˏti chĕŭkˎ never satisfied; chĕŭkˎ chĕŭkˎ or ˋmwang chĕŭkˎ or ˏch'ŭng chĕŭkˎ full, sufficient, ample; COLL., chĕŭkˎ ˋtá, full, as a string of cash; chĕŭkˎ ˏchié, to cash in full, as in redeeming bank bills; chĕŭkˎ chĕŭkˎ ˋchi sū² fully this much; chĕŭkˎ chēū² abundant, as food; chĕŭkˎ taĕng² full weight, as dollars; chĕŭkˎ saikˎ pure, without alloy, as metals.

粥ˎ Chu. Congee, gruel: [19]chĕŭkˎ ˏch'ing, thin gruel; [20]chĕŭkˎ lakˎ grains of rice in gruel; [21]ˏchiéng chĕŭkˎ rice porridge, or congee; COM., [22]ˋchū chĕŭkˎ to prepare congee; ˏt'ong chĕŭkˎ sweetened congee; sukˎ ˋmi chĕŭkˎ congee of the suk rice; ch'eng² chĕŭkˎ cold congee; nŭkˎ chĕŭkˎ meat congee; COLL., pwong² chĕŭkˎ rice gruel; chĕŭkˎ ˏsang ˋwang pwong² yă² ˏsang ˋwang, three bowls gruel, and also three bowls rice; met., to apply the same rule rigidly, to make no allowance for different circumstances.

[1]同住 [2]居住 [3]暫住 [4]住止 [5]住步 [6]靠不住 [7]豎柱 [8]柱下史 [9]擎天柱 [10]足兵 [11]自足 [12]不我足 [13]失足 [14]舉足 [15]富足 [16]足用 [17]足意 [18]知足 [19]粥清 [20]粥粒 [21]饘粥 [22]煮粥

燭, Chu. A candle; to illumine; to shine; in the coll. read *chioh*, q. v.: *sleng chëŭk*, the lotus-flower candle; *ʻcheng chëŭk*, to snuff a candle; *nika ngwoka ʻsu chëŭk*, illuminated both by the sun and moon.

叔, Chu. Read *sëŭk*; coll. *chëŭk*: a father's younger brother, an uncle; a respectful title applied to persons either older, or with whom you are slightly acquainted: [1]*pah chëŭk*, or [2]*chëŭk pah*, paternal uncles, uncles on the father's side; *chëŭk ʻchu*, a grandfather's younger brother; [3]*chëŭk pah ˏhing tá*[2] male cousins on the father's side; [4]*chëŭk pah ʻchiă mwoi*[2] female cousins on the father's side; [5]*chëŭk ʻsing*, wife of a father's younger brother; [6]*leng*[2] *chëŭk*, your junior paternal uncle; [7]*ˏka chëŭk*, my junior paternal uncle; [8]*ˏsiéng chëŭk*, my deceased junior paternal uncle; [9]*chëŭk tika* junior paternal uncles and nephews; [10]*ʻsieu chëŭk*, a husband's younger brother; [11]*ʻsó chëŭk*, elder brother's wife, and husband's younger brother; [12]*chëŭk ˏkung*, a grandfather's younger brother; also, husband's or wife's junior paternal uncle; *ˏtong chëŭk*, the sons of grandfather's younger brothers; *ˏpau chëŭk*, own junior uncles; *ˏniéng chëŭk*, father's junior fellow-graduate; my fellow-graduate's father, when junior to my father; [13]*ek chëŭk*, first uncle! [14]*ne*[2] *chëŭk*, second uncle!—as in addressing persons younger than your father.

囑, Chu. To order, to bid, to enjoin: *miéng*[2] *chëŭk*, to instruct him face to face; *ʻmá chëŭk*, to bribe; COM., *chëŭk tʻauk*, to commission one to do; COLL., *chëŭk ho*ʾ to order, to charge.

矚, Chu. To gaze, to look at earnestly; to fix the eyes on: *ʻwong chëŭk*, to look at distant objects.

柷, Chu. A sort of tub, with a stick in the center—musical instrument in Confucian worship: *chëŭk ʻngü*, instruments to direct a band of music.

祝, Chu. To pray, to supplicate; to recite prayers; joined to, connected with, attached to; to begin, to commence; the origin, the beginning; to cut off, to sever; to repeat, to reiterate: [15]*ʻsieu chëŭk*, an assistant at worship; [16]*chëŭk ˏsang ˏtó*, to pray for happiness, longevity and children; [17]*chëŭk ˏsüng*, the fire-god; COM., *chëŭk chang*ʾ to praise, to laud; [18]*miéu*[2] *chëŭk*, a temple-keeper, acolyth; [19]*meka chëŭk*, to repeat prayers silently; [20]*chëŭk siá*[2] to return thanks; *chëŭk seu*[2] birthday congratulations; to pray for long life; *chëŭk kó*ʾ to implore; [21]*chëŭk hok*, to bless, to bestow favors.

(40) Chëŭng.

衆, Chung. Sometimes written without the top stroke: a multitude, a concourse of at least three persons; many,

---

[1] 伯叔 [2] 叔伯 [3] 叔伯兄弟 [4] 叔伯姐妹 [5] 叔嬸 [6] 令叔 [7] 家叔 [8] 先叔 [9] 叔侄 [10] 小叔 [11] 嫂叔 [12] 叔公 [13] 一叔 [14] 二叔 [15] 小祝 [16] 祝三多 [17] 祝融 [18] 廟祝 [19] 默祝 [20] 祝謝 [21] 祝福 ○

福州方言拼音字典

a quorum, a majority; sign of the plural; they, much people; all, the people as distinguished from the officers: [1]*chëüngʾ ₍tó*, many, much; *chëüngʾ ʻkwa₎* much and little; [2]*chëüngʾ hóʾ* loved by the many; [3]*chëüngʾ ʻli*, many reasons; [4]*taik₎ chëüngʾ* to obtain the favor of all; com., *chëüngʾ loi²* many classes or kinds; [5]*₍kung chëüngʾ* the public; the assembly; *chëüngʾ ʻk'eu*, many mouths; many persons speaking; *₍chüng chëüngʾ* to go with the multitude; *chëü² chëüngʾ* to gather a crowd; [6]*hwang² chëüngʾ no²* hated by all; [7]*₍sang sing ₍sing chëüngʾ* three persons make a concourse; [8]*ʻkwa pok₎ tik₎ chëüngʾ* the few cannot resist the many; *ëü² chëüngʾ ₍t'ung ₍ti*, to make known to all the people; coll., *chëüngʾ ʻk'eu ₍ngong ₍ngong*, noisy declamation of a multitude; *chëüngʾ ₍nëng*, all, every one; *chëüngʾ pah₎ ₍sangʾ* all the people.

種ʾ (Chung.) To plant, to sow; to grow, to raise, to cultivate: *chëüngʾ hok₎* to bequeath happiness, as by one's virtues; [9]*chëüngʾ ngük₎ ₍lang ₍tiëng*, to raise pearls in the Blue Field (of Shensi)—i. e., to bring up good children; *chëüngʾ siëng²* to cultivate virtues; com., *₍chai chëüngʾ* to plant, to sow; [10]*chëüngʾ ʻngu kok₎* to raise grain; *chëüngʾ ʻchü ₍wong*, pills for the procreative powers; [11]*chëüngʾ tau²* or *chëüngʾ ₍chio*, to vaccinate; *chëüngʾ ₍yong tau²* to vaccinate in western style.

縱ʾ (Tsung.) Remiss, careless; extravagant, as in speech; to allow, to permit wrongfully; to indulge in; to let go; allowing, although, perhaps; to shoot an arrow: also read *₍chung*, q. v.: [12]*chëüngʾ ük₎* to give way to one's lusts; [13]*chëüngʾ sëüʾ* disorderly; profligate; [14]*chëüngʾ ʻsü*, or *chëüngʾ ₍yong*, although, even if, even though; *chëüngʾ ₍ngiong*, to talk extravagantly; *chëüngʾ songʾ* to shoot an arrow; [15]*chëüngʾ pai² ʻlé*, the disorderly violate propriety; com., [16]*₍süng chëüngʾ* to indulge in, to allow, as to do wrong.

從² (Tsung.) A clan, a family, a succession of, as posterity; inferior, a subordinate, second to, to follow after; secondary in rank; attached to: also read *₍chung*, *₍ch'üng*, and *₍chüng*: q. v.; [17]*chëüng² ʻchiä*, followers, retainers; [18]*se² chëüng²* a body servant; *puk₎ chëüng²* servants, menials; *₍ki chëüng² ₍sü ₍hung*, his followers were numerous as the clouds? *chëüng² ₍tong ₍hing tä²* term for second cousins; [19]*chëüng² ek₎ ʻp'ing*, the secondary-first grade of officers; com., *ʻing chëüng²* a female servant that escorts the bride; *chëüng² kaʾ* a female servant given to a bride.

Chëüng². A coll. word; to add on, to increase; to leave an additional space; as in *chëüng² sioh₎ ₍k'wang*, "add a circle"—as of hair left to increase the size of the cue.

(41) Chi.

之 (₍Chih.) A sign of the genitive; placed between two nouns or verbs it answers to who, which, that; a pronoun,

[1]衆 [3]衆 [5]公 怒 衆 衆 田 [11]種 [13]縱 [15]縱 縱 從
多 理 衆 [7]三 [8]寡 [9]種 [10]種 痘 肆 敗 [17]從 [19]從
[2]衆 [4]得 [6]犯 人 不 玉 五 [12]縱 [14]縱 禮 者 一
好 衆 衆 成 敵 藍 穀 慾 使 [16]容 [18]侍 品

he, she, it, they; this, that, these, those; often used in the abstract, after a noun, or as a relative particle in apposition; when doubled, the first refers to the antecedent subject, the second as a relative to the following substantive; to advance, to go to, to arrive at: ¹shó ꜀chi, going where? ²꜂siǎ ꜀chi, to let go, to relinquish; ³꜀chi ꜂chü, this person; ⁴꜂ming piéng² ꜀chi, discriminate it clearly; ⁵꜂iu taik꜆ ꜀chi ꜀ing, a virtuous person; ⁶꜀t'iéng tè ꜀chi tai² large as heaven and earth; ⁷꜂ch'ó muk꜆ ꜀seng ꜀chi, where plants and trees grow; ⁸꜀chi ꜂yǎ, to go to the country; ⁹꜀chi ꜂sü ꜂ch'i ꜂p'i ꜂t'a, faithful till death; kai꜄ ꜀chi kai꜄ ꜀chi, forbid it! forbid it! ꜀chi ꜂chü ꜀ü ꜀kwi, the virgin becomes a bride; song² ꜀chi ꜀chi ꜀ing, the person who conforms to this.

꜀Chi. A coll. word; as in ꜀chi ꜂p'á, the female secrets—used in vile expressions.

꜀Chi. A coll. word; as in ꜀chi che꜄ very, extremely; a superlative used at the end of phrases; pai² chi꜄ che꜄ utterly depraved or ruined.

꜀Chi. A coll. euphonic prefix; as in ꜀chi ꜀cha, to examine, to investigate; ꜀chi ꜀chwa, to draw out, as cards in playing.

꜀Chi. A coll. word; as in ꜀chi ꜀chi ch'ai꜄ cress, mint, or shepherd's purse—it is nailed on door-posts on 3d day of the 3d moon.

꜂止 Chih. To stop; to lodge, to dwell, to rest; only, but, however; politeness; to alight, as a bird; to seize, to detain, to prevent; interrupted, stopped; that which the mind rests in, an object; to cease from, to desist, to be still, to remain, to wait; the 77th radical: ¹⁰꜂keng꜄ ꜂chi, to be reverential; ¹¹꜂chi se² only thus; ¹²꜂chi ꜀liu, to detain; ¹³꜂chi sëük꜆ to stop for the night; ¹⁴꜀ang ꜂nü ꜂chi, rest satisfied with your object; ꜀chiong ꜂chi ꜀chi, about to stop; ¹⁵꜂chi ꜀ü che꜄ siéng² seek for the highest excellence; COM., ꜂kü ꜂chi, motion and rest; deportment, conduct; sheng ꜂chi, walking and stopping; shó ꜂chi, or pok꜆ ꜂chi, not only; keng꜄ ꜂chi, to restrain, to forbid, to prohibit; ¹⁶꜂chi pwo² ꜀yong ꜀sing, "stop and call out"—a notice over doorways; ꜀u ꜂ti ꜂chi, unlimited, boundless, no traces of; ꜂chu ꜂chi, to stop, to hinder; COLL., ꜂chi t'iǎng꜄ to soothe pain; ꜂chi taung꜄ "we stop receiving pawns"—notice on a pawnshop.

祉 Chih. Happiness, felicity: hok꜆ ꜂chi, happiness; sek꜆ ꜂chi, heaven-bestowed felicity; kek꜆ ꜂chi, good fortune; kę꜄ ꜀tó seu² ꜂chi, having already received great happiness.

꜂趾 Chih. The toes; the feet; to stop; the base, foundation, in which sense same as next: ꜀sing ꜂chi, foundation of a city wall; ꜀kau ꜂chi, Cochin China; COM., ꜂kü ꜂chi, to lift the feet in walking; met., to go and do.

꜂阯 ꜂址 A basis, a foundation: ꜀mi ꜂chi, the ruins of an old wall; COM., ꜀ki ꜂chi a foundation, that upon which any thing rests, or is built.

¹何之 ²捨之 ³之子 ⁴明辨之 ⁵有德之人 ⁶天地之大 ⁷草木生之 ⁸之之野 ⁹之死矢靡他 ¹⁰敬止 ¹¹止是 ¹²止留 ¹³止宿 ¹⁴安汝止 ¹⁵止於至善 ¹⁶止步揚聲 ○

子 Tsz. Read ʻchü; coll. ʻchi: seeds or slips, as of plants and fruit; nuts, as of lotus; dice; the roe or spawn of fishes: [1]ʻkwoi ʻchi, fruit; [2]chʻaiʾ ʻchi, seeds of vegetables; [3]ˌngü ʻchi, the spawn of fishes; [4]kiekˎ ʻchi, to produce seeds; [5]ˌkwa ʻchi, melon-seeds; chëüngʾ ʻchi, to plant seeds; ʻchi mwoi[2] taing[2] seeds not yet hardened; [6]ˌleng ʻchi, lotus-nuts; [7]ˌki ʻchi, chess-men; [8]ˌtau ʻchi, dice; [9]chʻiong[2] ˌki ʻchi, chess-men (32 in number); invented by Wu Wang, B. C. 1120; [10]ˌui ˌki ʻchi, kind of chess-men (360 in number) half black, half white, invented by Yau, B. C. 2300.

只 Chih. Only, merely; but, however, yet; this, a final particle: used in the coll. for thus, thus much; here, in this (place); this, this one: [11]ʻchi taikˎ only can or could; [12]ʻchi ʻiu, only have, merely; COM., [13]ʻchi ˏing, only for, simply on account of; [14]ʻchi ngwong[2] only wish; [15]ʻchi ʻkʻö, only ought or should; ʻchi ʻhü, only promised; ʻchi pʻaʾ only fearing lest; COLL., ʻchi waiʾ here, in this place; ʻchi sioh loi[2] this class or kind; ʻchi ʻtié, in here; ʻchi chiéng[2] so mischievous, so bad; ʻchi liüʾ or ʻchi chʻwoiʾ so fine, so showy; ʻchi ʻkwang, an illative, thus, then, hence; ʻchi ʻhü this and that, here and there; ˌmó ʻchi ˌmó ʻhü, neither this nor that, no trouble, nothing the matter; unprovoked, without cause; ʻchi ˏpeng, or ʻchi mengʾ this side, this way; ʻchi sioh ˌshui, or ʻchi sioh ˌdau, this once; ʻchi ʻhó, or ʻchi ʻmwang ʻhó, so very good; ʻchi ˏpong, or ʻchi nóʾ or ʻchi ˌseng nóʾ or ʻchi lóh now, this period of time; ʻchi ʻla ˌnëng, this person; ʻchi ˌtʻau siéʾ in this spot.

枳 Chih. A hedge-thorn, a spinous tree; a fruit like the pumalo with a thick rind; to injure, hurtful, like thorns: [16]ʻchi kekˎ a thorny bush; COM., [17]ʻchi sik the bitter medicinal seed of the ʻchi tree; [18]ʻchi kʻaukˎ (coll. ʻchi kʻaekˎ) a bitter medicinal bark (? the hovenia dulcis).

軹 Chih. The hole in the hub of a wheel, where the nave projects; the end of the nave projecting from the wheel; diverging, like the forks of a road: [19]ʻchi ʻsiu ˌsié, a two-headed snake, said to be found in the north.

咫 Chih. An ancient cubit of 8 inches, about equal to the English foot; a little, a few: ʻchi chʻekˎ ˏchi te[2] a little way, near, as one living close to me.

沶 Chih. Name of a river on the east coast of China; to strain spirits; a strainer made of plants.

沚 Chih. A small island, an islet; to dwell on an islet: [20]ʻchwi ˏtüng ʻchi, an islet in the water; ˏü ʻcheu ˏü ʻchi, on the lake and islet.

芷 Chih. A fragrant plant (pentandria digynia), it is also called [21]tek ˏhung, or ˏhwong ˏhiong: [22]pek ʻchi, angelica, a medicinal plant

[1]果子 [2]菜子 [3]魚子 [4]結子 [5]瓜子 [6]蓮子 [7]棋子 [8]骰子 [9]象棋子 [10]圍棋子 [11]只得 [12]只有 [13]只因 [14]只願 [15]只可 [16]枳棘 [17]枳實 [18]枳殼 [19]軹首蛇 [20]水中沚 [21]澤芬 [22]白芷

of which an ointment is made; the roots of the epidendrium are called ʻchi.

ʻ黹 Chih. To embroider; embroidered, braided; to put on braid or lace; the 204th radical: COLL., [1] ˏcheng ʻchi, embroidery, needle-work.

ʻ胏 Chih. The remnants of a meal; meat dried with the bones in it: ˏkang ʻchi, dried meat.

ʻ姊 Chih. An elder sister; a school mistress: in the coll. ʻchia, q. v.: [2]ʻchi mwoi˒ sisters; [3]paik˒ ʻchi, the eldest sister; [4]ngwok˒ ʻchi, lady in the moon, usually called ˓siong ˓ngó; [5]ʻchi ʻchi, elder sister; mother of the heir apparent, when a secondary wife of the emperor; [6]ʻchi t'iong˒ husband of an elder sister.

ʻ旨 ʻ旨 Chih. Meaning, intention; will, purpose, design; the subject, topic; the main drift, the sense; excellent, sweet, pleasant-tasted; delicate; a decretal, orders: [7]ˏchü ʻchi purport of the book; [8]tai˒ ʻchi, the main purport; [9]tá ʻchi, a topic, a text, a theme or thesis; [10]ˏkang ʻchi, sweet, luscious; ʻchi ʻchiu, excellent wine; [11]ʻchi ˏchai, how good! COM., [12]seng˒ ʻchi, the imperial commands; [13]ʻchi e˒ intention, will; the imperial rescript; [14]hong˒ ʻchi, to receive the imperial orders; [15]pwoi˒ ʻchi, to violate the teachings of.

ʻ指 Chih. A finger, a toe; to point, to refer to, to point out; to indicate, to teach, to command; a particular, a mode: interchanged with last: in the coll. ʻchai, q. v.: [16]ʻch'iu ʻchi, a finger; [17]ʻngu ʻchi, the fingers and thumb; [18]këü˒ ʻchi, the thumb; [19]sik˒ ʻchi, the forefinger; chëük˒ tai˒ ʻchi, the great toe; ʻchi ˏki ʻchiong, to point to the palm of the hand; met., very plain; ʻchi hek˒ to write with the finger, to calculate, to plan; [20]ʻchi ʻsü, to direct, to show how or what to do; [21]ʻchi ch'ek˒ to rebuke; COM., [22]ʻchi se˒ to teach, to instruct; [23]ʻchi ʻtiëng, to teach, to reveal to; ʻchi kak˒ finger-nails; [24]tik˒ ʻchi, to point directly to; title of an officer in the Han dynasty.

ʻ秭 Chih. A stack of corn; to number; the ninth place in notation; one hundred millions; a weight of 640 piculs.

ʻChi. A coll. euphonic prefix, as in ʻchi ʻchü, to stew, to boil, to cook.

˓鰣 Chih. Read ˓si; coll. ˓chi: a fish which enters the rivers from the ocean in May, and returns in September, probably the shad: ˓chi ˓ngü, the shad; ˓chi ˓ngwong ˓ngü, a large fish like the ˓wong ˏkwa.

焠 Used in the Paik˒ ˏIng, for the coll. ˓chi: to temper metal by dipping it while hot in water: ˓chi ʻchwi, to temper in water; ˓chi ch'o˒ to dip red-hot iron in vinegar—a restorative in fainting fits.

˓Chi. A coll. euphonic prefix, as in ˓chi ˓cha, to disturb, as by loud talking; ˓chi ˓chi kieu˒ singing of locusts.

[1] 針黹 [2] 姊妹 [3] 伯姊 [4] 月姊 [5] 姊姊 [6] 姊丈 [7] 書旨 [8] 大旨 [9] 題旨 [10] 甘旨 [11] 旨哉 [12] 聖旨 [13] 旨意 [14] 奉旨 [15] 背旨 [16] 手指 [17] 五指 [18] 巨指 [19] 食指 [20] 指使 [21] 指斥 [22] 指示 [23] 指點 [24] 直指

福州方言拼音字典

꜀Chi. A coll. word, as in ꜀chi ngak꜆, or ꜀chi ꜀chi ngak꜆, the locust after shedding it's coat in autumn—so called from its song.

꜀Chi. A coll. word, as in ꜀chi ꜀chi ꜀hwa, kind of fireworks, emitting variegated colors.

꜀Chi. A coll. word, as in ꜀chi cheh꜆, (spoken ꜀chi teh꜆ or ꜀chi deh꜆) to squeeze out; ꜀chi cheh꜆ ch'ok꜆ ꜀li, squeeze it out. See also cheh꜆.

(42) Chiă.

嗟 ꜀ Chê. A sigh; to sigh, to lament; painful regrets, ah! alas! an interjection of admiration: [1]꜀chŭ ꜀chiă, to bewail; [2]꜀chiă shu, or ꜀chiă t'ang꜄ to sigh; ꜀hŭ ꜀chiă, long-drawn sighs; chiok꜆ ꜀chiă, in an instant.

遮 ꜀ Chê. To cover, to screen, to vail, to conceal; to shade; to intercept, to stop; to overspread, to overshadow; a parasol: [3]꜀chiu ꜀chiă, extensive, much, as talk; COM., [4]꜀chiă ꜀kwong, to shut off the light; [5]꜀chiă pe꜄ to shade, to cover; [6]꜀chiă ꜂yĕng to hide, to conceal; [7]꜀chiă ꜀mwang, to deceive, to hide from one; [8]꜀chiă ꜀yong, a sunshade; [9]꜀chiă ꜂ŭ, a rain-screen; [10]꜂t'ang tŭak꜆ ꜀chiă ꜂sung, to cut down the bamboo and tend its sprouts; met., to discard the old for the new; COLL. [11]꜀chiă ꜂yĕng ngai tai꜄ to hide wickedness; ꜀chiă ang꜄ mók꜆ móh꜆ shaded till it's very dark.

罝 ꜀ Chih. A net for catching hares; a net for beasts; to stop the way, as a net does: t'o꜄ ꜀chiă, a net for catching hares; ꜀chiă ꜀p'eu, a small snare.

笊 ꜂ Chao. Read ꜂chau, or chau꜄; coll. ꜀chiă: a strainer, a cullender, a skimmer made of bamboo or wire: [12]꜀chiă ꜀lié, a bamboo ladle, a strainer, a skimmer; ꜀chiă ꜀lié pe꜄ a sieve placed in a vessel for steaming rice; ꜀chiă ꜀lié ꜀mó pang꜄ hau꜄ ꜀kié tok꜆ ꜀kwong, the ladle loses it's handle and the dipper usurps it's place; met., one losing a situation and another person getting it.

槎 ꜀ Ch'a. Also read ꜀cha, or ꜀ch'a: drift-wood; a small raft; to fell trees; to hew wood: ꜀sing ꜀chiă, to raft lumber.

姐 ꜂ 媎 ꜂ Tsu. Read ꜂chi, or ꜂chié; coll. ꜂chiă: elder sisters; a miss: [13]꜂chiă mwoi꜄ sisters; [14]꜂chiă ꜀hu, or ꜂chiă t'iong꜄ husband of an elder sister; [15]꜂sieu ꜂chiă, daughters of the gentry; [16]꜂pieu ꜂chiă, older female cousins of different surnames; [17]꜀pau ꜂chiă, own elder sister; [18]꜀ka ꜂chiă, my elder sister; [19]ngié꜄ ꜂chiă mwoi꜄ sworn-sisters—i.e. pledged friends; [20]ak꜆ ꜂chiă, a dwarfed duck; met., a stupid fellow; [21]꜂chiă ꜂ná, a father's concubine; ꜀i ꜂chiă, elder sister! a common mode of address; ꜀chiă ꜂chiă, or sa꜄ ꜂chiă, terms applied to concubines; ꜂chiă ꜂ma, grandfather's concubine.

---

1 咨嗟 2 嗟乎 3 周遮 4 遮光 5 遮蔽 6 遮掩 7 遮瞞 8 遮陽 9 遮雨 10 砍竹 遮筍 11 遮掩 歹事 12 笊篱 13 姐妹 14 姐夫 15 小姐 16 表姐 17 胞姐 18 家姐 19 誼姐妹 20 鴨 姐 21 姐奶 ○

ᶜ赭 Chê.
Ochre color; a carnation or reddish brown; a reddish soil: *ₑngang ₑtŭ auk*, *ᶜchiă*, countenance like the reddish soil; *ᶜchiă ₑi*, dress worn by felons; *ᶜchiă auk*, a reddish soil.

ᶜ者 Chê.
A relative or demonstrative pronoun, it, this, that, he, she; these, those; who, which, what; after verbs it forms a noun; after nouns it indicates a class; placed between two nouns or clauses, it puts them in apposition; makes an abstract sense; often a mere pause to arrest the attention: [1]*hok, ᶜchiă*, a student; [2]*ᶜsŭ ᶜchiă*, the dead; [3]*ᶜku ᶜchiă*, ancient, as time, men, things, &c.; *ₑung ᶜchiă*, a listener; [4]*seng' ᶜchiă*, nature; [5]*taik, ᶜchiă ᶜpwong yă'* virtue, that is the cardinal thing; COM., [6]*ₑhiĕng ᶜchiă*, a virtuous person; [7]*ₑti ᶜchiă ₑlai*, "let knowing ones come"—a common sign for shops.

ᶜ嗜
A coll. character, often used for the preceding; this, that, these, those: *ᶜchiă ₑnëng*, this person; *ᶜchiă ᶜk'wang*, this mode or way; *óh, ᶜchiă yong'* after this fashion; *ᶜchiă ₑchüi*, this, this thing; *ₑmó ᶜchiă sëü'* or *ₑmó ᶜchiă tai'* no such thing or matter; *ᶜchiă ₑk'wang ᶜk'wang*, or *ᶜchiă ₑt'á ᶜt'á*, this form or way; *ᶜchiă cheng' au'* this illness, *scil.* is serious, &c.; *ᶜchiă k'e' ₑnang seu'* this (cause of) anger is hard to bear; *ᶜchiă ch'oi' ₑnang ₑk'ei*, this is hard to utter, as from shame, fear, &c.

摭' Chă.
To take, to take out; to collect, to gather: *chiă' sek*, to gather; *ᶜch'ai ₑking chiă' tiong'* to cull (sentences) from books.

蔗' 樜' Chă.
The sugar-cane: COM., [8]*ₑkang chiă'* the sweet cane; name of a large town on the Min, 20 miles west of Foochow; [9]*chiă' p'óh*, refuse, shreds of the cane; [10]*chiă' ₑp'ui*, rind of the cane; [11]*chiă' ᶜmwi*, the slips or settings of the cane; [12]*ₑt'ong chiă'* sugar-cane; COLL., [13]*pah, chiă'* white cane; [14]*k'aik, chiă'* or *k'iă', chiă'* to express the cane juice; [15]*chiă' ₑch'iă*, a sugar-cane mill; [16]*chiă' sioh, chaik*, a joint of cane; [17]*chiă' sioh, t'iong'* a stalk of cane; [18]*chiă' hak,* tuft of leaves at top of the cane; [19]*chiă' kwok,* sections of the cane; [20]*ᶜtó chiă'* fallen cane; *met.*, adversity.

柘' Ch'ih.
Sometimes used for the preceding: a tree whose leaves are fed to silkworms; its wood is used for making musical instruments, bows, and arrows; from its roots is made a reddish-yellow dye used for the imperial garments: [21]*ₑsong chiă'* the mulberry and *chiă'* trees; *ₑnu chiă'* a species of the *chiă'* tree which is evergreen, and has thorns at its joints.

炙' Ch'ih.
To roast, to broil; to toast; to dry before the fire, to heat; warm, hot; near, to approach, to approximate; to fry in honey as some physic is; *kwoi' chiă'* a broiled hash of meat and fish;

[1]學者 [2]死者 [3]古者 [4]性者 [5]德者本也 [6]賢者 [7]知者來 [8]甘蔗 [9]蔗粕 [10]蔗皮 [11]蔗尾 [12]糖蔗 [13]白蔗 [14]刻蔗 [15]蔗車 [16]蔗一節 [17]蔗一杖 [18]蔗合 [19]蔗節 [20]倒蔗 [21]桑柘○

[1]'ₗhwang ch ă' to roast; [2]ₗch'ing chiă' to be intimate with: COM., [3]ₗcheng chiă' acupuncture and cauterizing: COLL., 'hwŏi chiă' lang[2] yék, burning with passion.

借' Chieh. Also read chiă[2]: to assist; to borrow, to lend; to ask, to beg for; to make a pretext of; to pretend, to suppose; if, for example, assuming; hypothetical, to use for an illustration; to praise: in coll. read chioh, q. v.: [4]chiă' ₗing, to lend to one; to use another person; [5]pok, chiă' straw sandals; [6]ka chiă' if, supposing that, to make use of, to assume; chiă' ₗming, to use another's name; [7]chiă' e' a pretext, a subterfuge; [8]chiă' ong[2] I beg to ask.

鷓' Chê. The partridge; francolins, grouse: COM., [9]chiă' ₗku, the common partridge.

ₗChiă. A coll. word, probably a corruption of ₗcha, as in ₗchiă ₗchiă kieu' clamor, confusion of sounds.

ₗChiă. A coll. word: an exclamation, there! there 'tis! there you have it!

藉[2] Chieh. To present or offer, as in worship; to borrow, to assist, to help; to trust in, to rely or depend on; ablative of cause, manner, or instrument, by, with, by means of; to avail of, to use, as a means; to use for a while; mild, generous, liberal; in confusion, disordered; to lead, as by a string: also read chik, q. v.: [10]oi' chiă[2] to comfort; [11]ₗchü chiă[2] to help, to aid; [12]pok, chiă[2] self-confident; COM., [13]ₗchiong chiă[2] to trust wholly; [14]tuk, chiă[2] to trust only in; [15]chiă[2] 'kwa, to presume on being a widow; COLL., 'ai chiă[2] to trust in, by, by means of; chiă[2] po' or chiă[2] o' ₗchiêng, purse-proud and overbearing; chiă[2] lau[2] ₗnëng, to presume on being old; chiă[2] ch'oi' to trust in one's gift of speech; chiă[2] ₗki-ong, or chiă[2] auk, to rely on strength, arbitrary; chiă[2] twai[2] ak, 'sieu, to presume on size and browbeat a smaller person; chiă[2] sié' or chiă[2] 'la sié' or chiă[2] o[2] sié' ₗt'au, to presume on one's authority or influence.

(43) Chiăh.

跡, 迹, Chi. Read chek,; coll. chiăh,: a track, a trace, a foot-mark; a spot, a stain: [16]ₗk'a chiăh, foot-prints: [17]ₗping ₗi ₗk'a chiăh, k'ó' ₗkăng, walk in his footsteps; [18]chiăh, tó'i' mark faded out; [19]ₗhong chiăh, traces, scars, marks; ₗmó ₗhong ₗmó chiăh, without mark, trackless, no trace (of him)—he never comes; chiăh, hiêng[2] ch'ok, ₗli, a spot appears on it; tau[2] chiăh, pock-marks.

雀, Ch'iao. Read ch'iok,; coll. chiăh,: a sparrow, a wren, a small bird: chiăh, 'ki-ăng, or ₗchiă chiăh, sparrows; ₗchiă chiăh, 'kiăng, little sparrows; [20]tau' chiăh, ₗseng, or tau' chiăh, ₗmang, to go to bed before the sparrows, as on the first night of the year; chiăh, 'mó, an

[1]燔炙 [2]親炙 [3]針炙 [4]借人 [5]不借 [6]假借 [7]借意 ○ [8]借問 [9]鷓鴣 [10]慰藉 [11]資藉 [12]不藉 [13]全藉 [14]獨藉 ○ [15]藉寡 [16]脚跡 [17]憑伊脚跡去行 [18]跡退 [19]痕跡 ○

old sparrow; *met.*, a person of experience and knowledge.

隻 ˎ **Chih.** One, single, not a pair or set, one of a pair; a classifier of men, animals, birds, vessels and of things in pairs or sets: COM., [1]*ˎtang chiăh*, single, only one; [2]*ˎsëng chiăh*, double, duplicated; COLL., [3]*chiăh, so'* counted one by one; *chiăh, so' nioh, wai'* how many are there? *sioh, chiăh,* one; [4]*chiăh, pwang'* one and a half; [5]*'chi chiăh*, this one; [6]*pek, chiăh*, another one; *chiăh, chiăh*, singly, every one; [7]*'kwi chiăh*, a few; how many? [7]*sá' chiăh*, or *naung' chiăh*, a small one; *ˎkó ˎlong chiăh*, entire, a whole one; *'cheu chiăh*, small birds in general; *chiăh, ˎchiéng 'pa*, one cash bundles of vegetables; *chiăh, ˎchiéng 'liong*, one cash per ounce; [9]*p'iéng' 'chai chiăh, che'* a bit of paper or a single word, *scil.* you are not to smuggle anything into examination.

Chiăh, A coll. word, for which the preceding is often used: just, just now; an illative particle, then; between adjectives it intensifies the meaning: *chiăh, ˎli*, or *chiăh, chiăh, ˎli*, has just come; *chiăh, 'si*, just dead; *chiăh, chiăh, 'hó*, just well; just now finished; *ˎchiong wang' chó' chiăh, 'sai tek*, do it thus and it will answer; *k'á' chiăh, k'á'* very quick.

(44) Chiăk.

汴 ˎ Read *chaik,;* coll. *chiăk,:* noise of water falling; to splash, to spill, to spill over as water: [10]*chiăk, k'ó'* spilled; *tiéng' chiăk*, to splash over from being brimfull; *chiăk, ˎwong*, all spilled; *yong' chiăk*, to spill by shaking; *chiăk, 'ch'iéng*, to spill out till only a little is left; [11]*chiăk, 'mwang te'* spilled all around.

Chiăk, A coll. word: to smack the lips as in eating, or in a quandary: *chiăk, ch'oi'* to smack the lips; *chiăk, chiăk, ˎsang ˎhung ˎtiéng*, smack! smack! it's somewhat sweet!

吃 ˎ **Chih.** Read *ch'ak,;* coll. *chiăk,:* sound of a hog eating; to smack the lips, as above: *chiăk, chiăk, kieu'* sound of a hog eating; *chiăk, chiăk, ˎsiăng*, sound, as of persistent begging; *ch'oi' naing' chiăk, chiăk,* to continue smacking the lips as in a quandary; *sioh, nik, chiăk, kou' ang'* smacking all day long till dark.

(45) Chiăng.

ˎ正 **Ching.** Read *ˎching;* coll. *ˎchiăng:* the first month of the year: [12]*ˎchiăng ngwok,* or *ˎsing ˎchiăng*, the first month; [13]*ˎlai ˎchiăng*, the next first month; [14]*pai' ˎchiăng*, New Year's compliments; [15]*ˎk'ai ˎchiăng*, to resume business after New Year's; [16]*ˎchiăng ngwok, 'chiu ˎkié ˎhwang tik,* must at once return the compliments of the New Year's feast—must make return presents; [17]*ch'ok, ˎchiăng*, on the opening of the first month; [18]*kwo' ˎchiang*, after the first month; [19]*ˎchiăng ngwok, ˎch'ë*, beginning

[1]單隻 [2]雙隻 [3]隻數 [4]隻半 [5]只隻 [6]別隻 [7]幾隻 [8]細隻 [9]片紙隻字 [10]汴去 [11]汴滿地 [12]正月 [13]來正 [14]拜正 [15]開正 [16]正月酒快還敵 [17]出正 [18]過正 [19]正月頭 ○

福州方言拼音字典

of the first moon (of the new year.)

精 Ching. Read ˌ*ching;* coll. ˌ*chiăng:* transformation; an apparition, form taken by spirits: [1]ˌ*yeu* ˌ*chiăng*, or ˌ*chiăng kwai*ˈ elfs, monsters, prodigies; [2]*piéng*ˈ ˌ*chiăng*, to change into an elf; *met.*, to become experienced; [3]ˌ*kau* ˌ*chiăng*, monkey-sprite; [4]ˌ*siăng* ˌ*chiăng*, to become a fairy; [5]ˌ*ha* ˌ*chiăng piék*, *kwai*ˈ shrimps and tortoises changing into elves; *met.*, insignificant fellows, as petty rebels, &c.

ˌ*Chiăng.* A coll. word: to frighten, to frighten away: ˌ*chiăng* ˈ*chau*, to frighten off, as pigs.

ˌ*Chiăng.* A coll. word, as in ˌ*chiăng* ˌ*chiăng* ˈ*tiong*, to glance hurriedly about.

䵘 Chan. Read ˈ*chang;* coll. ˈ*chiăng:* fresh, insipid, tasteless: [6]ˈ*chiăng* ˌ*sing*, fresh inside, as when the salt has not yet penetrated; [7]*e*ˀ ˈ*chiăng*, insipid; *pah*ˌ ˈ*chwi* ˈ*chiăng*, tasteless as water; ˈ*chiăng* ˈ*chiu*, weak wine; ˈ*chiăng lang*ˀ insipid; ˈ*chiăng* ˌ*niă nói*ˀ somewhat fresh; ˌ*keng* ˈ*chiăng*, salt and fresh; *ch'oi*ˀ ˈ*chiăng*, a tasteless mouth, as in sickness; ˌ*keng* ˌ*song* ˈ*k'u*, *lak*ˌ ˈ*chiăng* ˌ*tu* ˌ*siong kwo*ˀ have experienced all sorts of misery.

正 Ching. Read *cheng*ˀ; coll. *chiăng*ˀ: correct, straight, right, not awry, erect; even, not inclined, not deflected; regular, usual; proper, exactly, fitting, suitable; the first, the principal; just, at the time of, while, during; real, genuine, as goods: [8]*chiăng*ˀ ˌ*ung*, written or classic style; [9]*chiăng*ˀ *k'e*ˀ upright; [10]*chiăng*ˀ ˌ*king*, correct, virtuous; [11]*chiăng*ˀ *taung*ˀ or *chiăng*ˀ ˌ*kai*, right, moral; *chiăng*ˀ *chiăng*ˀ exactly, just right; *chiăng*ˀ *chiăng*ˀ ˈ*hó*, just the thing! [12]*chiăng*ˀ ˌ*sing*, the person himself; [13]*chiăng*ˀ *sai*ˀ chief imperial commissioner; [14]*chiăng*ˀ *se*ˀ right, yes; [15]*chiăng*ˀ ˌ*k'wo*, examination for Küjin degree; *chiăng*ˀ ˌ*miăng*, the principals, not proxies; [16]*chiăng*ˀ*ek*ˌ ˈ*p'ing*, the chief-first grade; [17]*chiăng*ˀ ˈ*kau* ˈ*p'ing*, the ninth or lowest rank; [18]*chiăng*ˀ ˌ*küng*, the empress; *má*ˀ *ch'iong*ˀ *chiăng*ˀ unlike, dissimilar; *chiăng*ˀ ˈ*lá* ˈ*kong*, while speaking.

ˌ*Chiăng.* A coll. word: to splash, to spatter: ˌ*chiăng lang*ˀ spattered; ˌ*chiăng sioh*ˌ ˌ*sing*, splashed all over the person.

ˌ*Chiăng.* A coll. word: to bounce, to bound: ˌ*chiăng* ˌ*mó*, to bounce away and be lost; ˌ*chiăng* ˌ*mó nói*ˀ ˈ*t'ó*, bounded off and can't be found.

淨 Ching. Read *cheng*ˀ and *chiăng*ˀ; coll. *chiăng*ˀ: clean, pure, spotless, undefiled; upright, guileless; to wash clean, to cleanse, to purify, to lustrate: [19]*chiăng*ˀ ˈ*t'u*, the pure region (of Budh); COM., *chiăng*ˀ *chiăng*ˀ unmixed, pure; [20]*chiăng*ˀ ˈ*chwi*, lustration water; [21]ˌ*sü ük*ˌ *chiăng*ˀ *cheng*ˀ to purify from fleshly lusts; COLL., *chiăng*ˀ *ch'io*ˀ to lustrate a house and exorcise spirits, as on occupying it.

[1]妖精 [2]變精 [3]猴精 [4]成精 [5]蝦精鼈怪 [6]䵘心 [7]味䵘 [8]正文 [9]正氣 [10]正經 [11]正當 [12]正身 [13]正使 [14]正是 [15]正科 [16]正一品 [17]正九品 [18]正宮 [19]淨土 [20]淨水 [21]私慾淨盡

(46) Chié.

芝 ꜀Chih. A sort of Boletus, or branched mushroom, said to be incorruptible, and to grow only in felicitous times: [1]꜀*chié* ꜀*i*, a sort of fungus, used as a condiment in the emperor's food; [2]꜀*ling* ꜀*chié*, the precious boletus; COLL., [3]꜀*chié* ꜀*mwai*, sesamum; ꜀*chié* ꜀*mwai p'iéng*꜄ wafer-like cakes, sprinkled with sesamum-seed; ꜀*chié* ꜀*mwai ang*꜄ stuffing of sesamum-seed; ꜀*chié* ꜀*mwai* ꜀*pau*, loaves stuffed with sesamum-seed.

巵 ꜀Chih. A goblet; a cup holding four gills; a syphon; a vessel for serving rations; a plant for dyeing a reddish color: *ngük*꜆ ꜀*chié*, the pearly cup; [4]*'laiu*꜄ ꜀*chié*, a syphon; *met.*, to waste, to squander; ꜂*chiu* ꜀*chié*, a wine-syphon.

梔 ꜀Chih. A tree used for dyeing yellow; a species of gardenia: COM., ꜀*chié* ꜂*chü*, the becho-nut, used in dyeing, and also as a febrifuge.

支 ꜀Chih. Interchanged with the next two: to branch, to diverge; to hold; to give, to pay; to prop, to succor; a branch, a bough of a tree; posterity, descendants; a sept or tribe; to attend to; to bear up, to stand firm; diverging, parting; the 12 horary characters; to measure; in the coll. to pay; also the correlative, to receive, to draw, as wages; the 65th radical: [5]*tė*꜄ ꜀*chié*, the 12 horary characters; COM., [6]꜀*chié p'wai*꜄ descendants, a tribe; [7]꜀*chié* ꜀*lié*, divergent; departing from the right, as in word or action; [8]꜂*pwong* ꜀*chié*, the original stock; [9]꜀*chié* ꜀*chiéng*, or ꜀*chié* ꜃*güng*, to pay out money; to draw money; [10]꜀*chié* *ëüng*꜄ to use, to expend; [11]꜀*chié* ꜀*t'i*, to succor; to bear, to sustain; [12]꜀*lié* ꜀*chié*, the lichi fruit (dimocarpus leche); [13]꜀*ting* ꜀*chié*, to suspend specie payments; [14]*haiu*꜄ ꜀*chié*, waiting to redeem its bills, as a bank; COLL., *mâ*꜄ ꜀*chié* ꜀*t'i tek*꜆ ꜂*k'i*, can't bear it, as expense; ꜀*chié* ꜀*këng* ꜀*chiéng*, to pay or draw wages; ꜀*chié nioh*꜆ *wai*꜄ pay or draw how much? ꜀*tong* ꜀*chié*, to overdraw money; ꜂*kung* ꜀*chié*, a rush for payment, as on banks.

枝 ꜀Chih. A branch, a twig; a slender post; to scatter, to branch off; a tributary of a river; sometimes used as a classifier of slender things, as pens, pencils, flowers, &c., &c.,: [15]꜀*chié yék*꜆ boughs and leaves; [16]꜀*chié chiék*꜆ joints of boughs; [17]꜀*ku* ꜀*chié*, withered boughs; ꜀*hwa* ꜀*chié*, flower-twigs; COM., [18]*kié*꜄ ꜀*chié*, twigs of cassia; [19]꜀*k'ai* ꜀*chié hwak*꜆ *yék*꜆ to branch and leaf out.

肢 ꜀Chih. The limbs of the body; hands and feet: COM., ꜀*chié* ꜂*t'á*, the whole body; *sëü*꜄ ꜀*chié*, the four limbs; [20]*sëü*꜄ ꜀*chié paik*꜆ ꜂*t'á*, all the members of the body.

脂 ꜀Chih. Grease, suet, lard, fat; hard gums of trees; *met.*, honors, glory; to grease; fat animals: [21]꜀*kó* ꜀*chié*, grease and suet; COM., [22]꜀*chié* ꜂*mi*, a reddish grain-like substance used for dyeing red; ꜀*yéng* ꜀*chié*,

[1] 芝栭 [2] 靈芝 [3] 芝蔴 [4] 漏巵 [5] 地支 [6] 支派 [7] 支離 [8] 本支 [9] 支錢 [10] 支用 [11] 支持 [12] 荔支 [13] 停支 [14] 候支 [15] 枝葉 [16] 枝節 [17] 枯枝 [18] 桂枝 [19] 開枝發葉 [20] 四肢百體 [21] 膏脂 [22] 脂米

福州方言拼音字典

rouge; ₍yong ₍chié, a white pearl; ¹₍ming ₍chié, the people's fat—i. e. their money.

₍呹 Chih. A sound, as of panting; used in coll., as in ²p'ek₎ ₍chié, a coarse kind of woolen cloth.

₍祇 ₍祗 Chih. To respect, to revere; to invocate; only, merely, but, however, yet; respect, reverence; great, important; to condole, to comfort: ₍chié keng' to venerate; ³₍chié 'ch'ü, only this.

'紫 Tzu. A reddish blue, a clay color, a nankeen tint; a fugacious, undecided hue: COM., ⁴'chié saik₎ a reddish blue, brown, purple; ⁵'chié ₍pó, a purple robe; ⁶'chié këük₎ the purple chrysanthemum; ⁷'chié ₍mi, the lagerstroemia or crape myrtle; 'chié ₍mi ₍sing, a star whose influences protect from malaria; ⁸'chié 'chai ₍kó, a plaster for boils; 'chié ₍ná ₍hung, the imperial certificate given to the first of the Hanlin; 'chié ₍hwa pwo' nankeen cloth; ⁹₍pien 'chié, fine nankeen; ₍ëng 'chié, a reddish purple; ¹⁰chiong' 'chié, a dark purple; ¹¹₍ch'ing ₍leng 'chié, a bluish purple; ₍nga ₍tang 'chié, a fine reddish purple; ¹¹'chié yéng' a kind of lily; the swallow—in poetic language; COLL., ¹²'chié ch'ai' the egg-plant; also the ₍tëng ch'ai' of the shops; 'chié meng' a purple facing of a garment; 'chié leu' leu' a pure, bright purple.

'呰 To oppress, to be unduly strict; to chide, to revile; weak; a fault, defect, flaw: ¹³'chié 'ü, lazy, careless.

'這 Chê. A demonstrative pronoun, this, that, these, those; the use of this word in the following phrases is in partial imitation of the mandarin: 'chié kó' this one; 'chié 'li, here; COM., ¹⁴'chié yong' thus, so; 'chié oi' ch'ëü' this place; 'chié ₍si haing' this time; COLL., 'chié ₍chong tai' contracted for 'chi sioh₎ ₍chong ₍ki tai' this affair, this one matter.

祭' Chi. To sacrifice, to offer slaughtered victims before the gods or penates, (these offerings are generally cooked;) to present offerings in worship; to bring an oblation, to come before the gods; the time of worship; an offering, a sacrifice: COM., ¹⁵chié' sëü' to present sacrifices; ¹⁶chó' chié' to offer sacrifices to the dead; ¹⁷chié' mwo' or chié' 'mwo, to make offerings at the graves; ¹⁸chié' 'lá, or chié' ₍ngi, sacrificial rites; ¹⁹chié' ₍ung, a prayer; an elegy hung up during the 49 days of mourning; ²⁰chié' 'chu ₍chung, or chié' 'chu ₍siéng, to sacrifice to ancestors; ²¹hiong' chié' to present an offering; ²²siong' 'ma chié' offerings when the corpse is placed in the coffin; COLL., chié' ₍ch'eng, fields reserved to sustain the ancestral worship; ₍pá chié' to arrange the offerings; ₍k'wi chié' first offerings at a grave.

際' Chi. To join, to cement, to unite, to connect; to form friendships; a limit, a border, a region; the line of juncture in things; the place where anything begins;

¹民脂 ²嗶吱 ³祇此 ⁴紫色 ⁵紫袍 ⁶紫菊 ⁷紫薇 紫微星 ⁸紫紙膏 ⁹紫花布 匾紫 ¹⁰醬紫 ¹¹青蓮紫 ¹²紫燕 ¹³紫茶 呰窳 ¹⁴這樣 ¹⁵祭祀 ¹⁶做祭 ¹⁷祭墓 ¹⁸祭禮 ¹⁹祭文 ²⁰祭祖宗 ²¹獻祭 ²²上馬祭

the time of occurring; now, since: [1]*chié' hwoi²* to join; [2]*kau chié'* friendships, associations; *ch'ok, ngiong chi chié'* at the time of speaking; [3]*t'iéng chié'* the zenith.

制 Chih. To cut out, to form; to adjust; to govern, to rule, to regulate; to limit, to hinder, to prevent; to make, to invent; a rule, a regulation, a law; to wear mourning: *'lá chié'* rules of politeness; *chié' chó²* to invent; COM., [4]*'hwak, chié'* a rule, statutes; *chié' to²* a pattern, a regulation; [5]*ch'aung' chié'* to discover; *chié' chauk,* to make; [6]*choi chié'* to adjust; [7]*hiék, chié'* to restrict, to exact; *aing² chié'* to fix the amount or time; [8]*chié' tai,* a viceroy; *king chié'* a low military officer—commands less than 100 men; [9]*siu chié'* to wear mourning for parents.

製 Chih. Interchanged with the last in some senses: to invent, to make; to cut out clothes; a fashion, a mode; to compound, as medicines; a pattern; a fur cloak: *chié' i siong,* to cut out clothes; COM., [10]*'k'ieu chié'* a fine model; an excellent compound; *sing chié'* a new pattern, a recent invention; [11]*chié' yoh,* to compound medicines; *chié' yoh, wong,* to prepare pills; [12]*p'au' chié'* to decoct medicines; [13]*choi chié'* to cut out, to make, as clothes; [14]*chié' p'au'* to cast cannon.

穄 Chi. Another name for panicled millet, grown in Shensi; it is not glutinous and resembles wheat: [15]*chié' 'mi,* panicled millet.

瘵 Chi. Also read *ch'ai':* weary, sick, diseased: [16]*ló chié'* consumption, a wasting disease.

掣 Che. To pull, to draw; to obstruct, to hinder from entering; to take, to choose, to select, to draw out; to raise up; to catch, to grasp: [17]*chié' 'tiu,* to grasp the elbow firmly; *met.,* rigid, severe; COM., [18]*k'eng chié'* to clutch and compel one.

(47) Chiék.

接 Chieh. To receive in the hand; to receive, to connect, to splice, to join; to succeed; combined with, united to; to take in, as jobs; to meet, to associate with; to take, as reflected light; quick; to graft, as a tree; to inherit, to come into the possession of: COM., [19]*kau chiék,* to fraternize; [20]*chiék, eng'* or *chiék, tai²* to entertain a guest; [21]*chiék, sŭk,* to connect, to join; *chiék, t'á'* to take another's place; [22]*chiék, 'mwi,* to take charge of a matter when nearly completed; [23]*chiék, ka'* to receive an idol or a superior; [24]*chiék, 'ch'iu,* to inherit a profession; to receive, as an unfinished job; *chiék, chong,* to honor (a graduate) with a feast; *chiék, kauk,* to set a fractured bone; *chiék, kwang ting,* a pavilion for meeting officers; COLL., *chiék, nëng k'ah,* to receive guests; *chiék, saëng'* to receive and dismiss, as guests; *chiék, meng'* an adopted daughter—second wife of a son-in-law; *chiék, ch'eu'* to graft trees; *k'ó' chiék, kieu'* to

[1]際會 [2]交際 [3]天際 [4]法制 [5]創制 [6]裁制 [7]挾制 [8]制臺 [9]守制 [10]巧製 [11]製藥 [12]炮製 [13]裁製 [14]製炮 [15]穄米 [16]癆瘵 [17]掣肘 [18]牽掣 [19]交接 [20]接應 [21]接續 [22]接尾 [23]接駕 [24]接手

go and bring one back in a sedan; *chiék, sioh, ˌtiong*, to get a job of work; [1]*chiék, kwóʾ ʿch'iu*, to receive, to take from another; *chiék, paingʾ* to manage for, to succeed another in the management of.

節, Chieh. A joint of bamboo; a joint, a knot, a node; a certificate, an article, a verse, a section of a chapter; a limit; a term, a holiday, a festival; a time, a regular interval; an emergency; the period or manner of doing a thing; economical, temperate, moderate; chastity, virtue, as in a widow; to limit a thing; to maintain; to restrain one's passions; to mark, as music; a classifier of limbs, joints, topics, affairs: in the coll. read *chaik*, q. v.: [2]*paik, chiék*, the eight festivals; *ˌch'ó chiék*, to maintain one's principles; [3]*chiék, ʿing sik*, to limit one's diet; [4]*chiék, sengʾ* to repress one's natural disposition; [5]*ˌhu chiék*, a certificate, a tally; COM., [6]*chiék, kiéngʾ* economical, frugal; *chiék, chiéʾ* to adjust, to control, to regulate; [7]*ˌsi chiék*, time, times and seasons; [8]*ˌchiong chiék*, chapter and verse; [9]*sek, chiék*, to lose integrity or chastity; *ˌting chiék*, chaste, as a female; *chiék, ëüngʾ* economy; *ʿsiu chiék*, chaste and virtuous—to remain a widow; *chiék, hauʾ* chaste and obedient to her husband's parents; [10]*chiék, hauʾ ˌhwong*, honorary portals to virtuous widows; [11]*chiék, ˌliéng*, uncorrupt, virtuous; [12]*ˌkwang chiék*, a limit, a restraint; *kengʾ chiék, ˌliong*, money for chaste widows.

摺, Chê. To fold, to double up; to break, to destroy, to injure; to pile up; to bend, as the knee; a fold, a doubling over: COM., [13]*ʿch'iu chiék*, folded paper for memoranda; [14]*chiék, liok*, a written digest or resumé; COLL., *p'ongʾ chiék*, to spirt water on stiffened clothes to fold them; *chiék, ˌi ˌsiong*, to fold clothes; *ʿsá ˌchiong pek, chiék*, to wash, starch, stretch, and fold.

折, Chê. To sunder, to snap in two, to break off; to fold, to bend; to oppress, to repress; to reprehend; to decide, to discriminate; to deduct; to stop; to injure; to lose one's heir; an act of a play; to exchange; to lose in trade; to make amends for, to set over against; to abase, to lower; unmarried: [15]*chiék, ˌtüng*, the just medium; [16]*chiék, huk*, to force one to submit; [17]*chiék, ʿsong*, to break; to injure; [18]*chiék, ük*, to shame one; *ˌchiong ˌkung chiék, chóiʾ* to make amends for misconduct by good works; COM., [19]*k'ëük, chiék*, crooked, deflected; *met.*, involved, as matters; [20]*chiék, pwangʾ* to reduce one half, as a debtor compounding with creditors; [21]*chiék, ˌchiéng*, or *chiék, kaʾ* to pay the value in money; COLL., *chiék, ˌt'au*, discount, reduction; *paik, chiék*, to pay only 80 in 100.

浙, Chê. A river in the Chehkiang province; the Chehkiang province; to wash rice; to rain; to cleanse: *chiék, ʿchwi*, river in Chehkiang; COM., [22]*chiék, ˌkong*, the Cheh-

[1]接	節	[4]節	[6]節	[8]章	[10]節	廉	摺	中	損	折	錢
過	[3]節	性	儉	節	孝	[12]關	[14]摺	[16]折	[18]折	[20]折	[22]浙
手	飲	[5]符	[7]時	[9]失	坊	節	畧	服	辱	半	江
[2]八	食	節	節	節	[11]節	[13]手	[15]折	[17]折	[19]曲	[21]折	○

福州方言拼音字典

kiang province; COLL., *chiĕk*, *꜀kong* *꜀pang* *꜁mó* *꜀song* *ʻch'ü*, the Cheh-kiang attendants (at the viceroy's) do not change (with those from Fookien); *met.*, let each one stick to his own business.

晢, 晣, The brightness of the stars; bright, luminous, splendid: *chiĕk*, *chiĕk*, brilliant, dazzling, splendid.

襵, ⿰衤得, Nieh. To fold garments; a seam; a plait; a frounce, a gather like those in the petticoat of a Chinese lady; plaited: COLL., [1]*chiĕk*, *꜀i* *꜁siong*, to fold clothes; [2]*chiĕk*, *p'woi*ʼ to fold bed-clothes.

楫, An oar, a paddle, or whatever is used to propel a boat; to row; swift; woody, forest-like: *꜀chiu* *chiĕk*, boat and oars.

櫛, Chien. A comb; to comb the hair; to clean: [3]*chiĕk*, *꜀hung* *muk*, *ʻü*, the wind combs his hair and the rain washes his face; *met.*, the hardships of traveling.

慴, Chieh. To lie prostrate; timid, cowardly: also read *sik* q. v.: *chiĕk*, *huk* to succumb dastardly.

癤, A small boil, a pimple, a sore.

捷, 㨗, Chieh. To conquer, to overcome, to triumph, to obtain a victory; successful, victorious; a victory; to complete; to announce, as a victory, or a promotion; hastily, quick, prompt, as a herald; joyful tidings: [4]*ʻhiong*ʼ *chiĕk*, to report, as a victory; [5]*chiĕk*, *chĕük*, swift, prompt; [6]*꜀ch'ung* *chiĕk*, spring examinations for the third degree; COM., [7]*chiĕk*, *ʻk'ieu*, (spoken *chiĕk*, *k'ieu*ʼ) precocious; [8]*chiĕk*, *꜀chai*, ready, clever, ingenious; [9]*chiĕk*, *꜁ló*, apt, ready at; [10]*꜁liĕng* *chiĕk*, to obtain degrees at successive examinations; [11]*ʻming* *chiĕk*, quick-witted; [12]*chiĕk*, *pó*ʼ to hasten to report good news.

睫, Chien. The eye-lashes; *met.*, the eye: [13]*꜁mi* *chiĕk*, the eye-lashes.

箑, Chieh. A fan; the word is usually seen on formal cards: [14]*꜀k'ing* *chiĕk*, a light fan; [15]*꜀küng* *chiĕk*, handkerchief and fan.

倢, 婕, Chieh. Handsome, elegant; a female officer: [16]*chiĕk*, *꜁ü*, a kind of palatial house-keeper.

(48) Chiĕng.

詹, Chan. Tattling, loquacious, wordy; to reach; at, extreme, such a time; to examine and direct; an officer; a surname; name of a mountain: used for *꜀chiĕng*, to divine; also for the next: [17]*ʻsieu* *꜁ngiong* *꜀chiĕng* *꜀chiĕng*, to tattle about trifles; COM., [18]*꜀chiĕng* *sëü*ʼ an officer in charge of the imperial harem.

譫, Chan. Wordy, loquacious: [19]*peng*ʼ *꜀chiĕng*, out of his head, incoherent; [20]*꜀chiĕng* *ʻngü*, wandering talk.

1 襵衣裳 2 襵被 3 櫛風沐雨 4 獻捷 5 捷足 6 春捷 7 捷巧 8 捷才 9 捷劵 10 連捷 11 敏捷 12 捷報 13 眉睫 14 輕箑 15 巾箑 16 婕好 17 小言詹詹 18 詹事 19 病譫 20 譫語

瞻 Chan. To look up to, to revere, to regard with respect: [1]*ˏchiéng ˊngiong*, to look up to; COM., [2]*ˏkwang ˏchiéng* to look at carefully; good-looking; [3]*ˏchiéng wong*ˋ to long for; to meditate with desire; [4]*ˏming ˏing ˊsu ˏchiéng*, to whom the people look up; [5]*sekˎ ˏkwang ˏchiéng*, to make a *faux-pas* in public ceremonies.

襜 Chan. An apron; a flap, a skirt; a curtain of a car; to adjust, to put the dress in order; flapping: [6]*ˏchiéng ˏchiéng*, trim, neat; flapping, as a curtain; [7]*pokˎ ˏing ekˎ ˏchiéng*, not enough to fill an apron.

幨 Chan. Similar to the last; a curtain of a carriage; a curtain over an opening; an overlap that hides a seam.

占 Chan. To divine, to cast lots; divination, casting lots; to observe, to wait for a verification of; to look towards; to judge of, to form an opinion of: also read *chiéng*ˋ q. v.: [8]*ˏchiéng pok*ˎ or *ˏchiéng kwa*ˋ to divine, to prognosticate.

佔 Chan. Superficial, trifling; low, vulgar; to look at carelessly; to skim over, as in reading fast: [9]*ˏchiéng söü*ˋ low, trifling; [10]*ˏchiéng pek*ˎ to read over and over without trying to understand.

沾 Chan. To moisten, to tinge; moist, damp, wet; to receive benefits; to participate in, to be a recipient of; obliged, benefited; imbued with; infected, affected: in the coll. to bestow, also the correlative idea, to receive gratuitously: [11]*ˏchiéng peng*ˋ taken sick; COM., [12]*ˏchiéng ˏkwong*, by your favor; [13]*ˏchiéng ˏong*, to receive favor; COLL., *ˏchiéng ˏk'á*, importunity, to force one to give; *ˏchiéng ˊch'a* or *ˏchiéng ˊcha*, to bestow gratuitously; to receive as a gift; *ˏchü ˏchiéng ˊchu siohˎ ˊmwong*, give me a book; [14]*k'aëng*ˋ *ˊnü ˏchiéng ˊcha*, let me get it of you as a gift; [14]*k'ëükˎ ˏnëng ˏka yâ*ˋ *ˏchiéng ˏkwong*, let me also be imbued with your favor.

湔 Chien. To sprinkle with the hand, to bespatter; to wash out spots; name of a river in Sz-chuen: [15]*ˊsá ˏchiéng*, to wash clean; COM., [16]*ˏchiéng ˏi ˏsiong*, to wash out spots from clothes.

濺 Chien. Also read *ˊchiéng* and *chiéng*ˋ: a swift current, a raceway; to flow swiftly; to spatter up, to dash against; to squirt out; to spurt out, as blood.

瀸 Chien. To soak, to moisten, to dampen; to overflow; a spring appearing and reappearing: [17]*ˏchiéng miék*ˎ to extirpate.

霑 Chan. Similar to the last: a dripping rain; to drizzle, to drip, to patter, to rain; to moisten, to wet by degrees; to wet through; soaked, saturated: [18]*ˏchiéng chëük*ˎ wet to the skin.

[1]瞻仰 [2]觀瞻 [3]瞻望 [4]民人所瞻 [5]失觀瞻 [6]襜襜 [7]不盈一襜 [8]占卜 [9]佔佢 [10]佔畢 [11]沾病 [12]沾光 [13]沾恩 [14]乞仈家也沾光 [15]洗湔 [16]湔衣裳 [17]瀸滅 [18]霑足 ○

氈 氊 毡 Chan. Hair or wool worked into a felt; coarse woolens, as blankets, carpets, rugs &c.: COM., te³ ˛chiéng, a carpet, a rug; ˛p'wo ˛chiéng, to spread a carpet; ˛chiéng ˛teu, a rug; ˛chiéng ˛teu ˛pau, a parcel done up in a rug; ˛chiéng ˛t'ang carpets and rugs; [1]˛chiéng mô³ a felt hat or cap; [2]˛chiéng ˊtá, felt soles; COLL., [3]˛p'wo ˛chiéng kaik˛ ˊch'ai, to spread rugs and tie up festoons.

鸇 Chien. A falcon, a goshawk, a yellow bird that chases pigeons; a sparrow-hawk: [4]˛ing ˛chiéng, hawks and falcons.

饘 Chien. Congee or gruel made from rice thoroughly boiled: [5]˛chiéng chëük˛ thick and thin congee.

邅 Chien. Unable to advance; to wind about: [6]˛tung ˛chiéng to make no progress; met., unlucky.

鱣 T'an. A sea-monster; a large sturgeon, or perhaps a grampus: ˛chiéng ˊwi, grampuses and sturgeons.

煎 Chien. To fry, to cook by frying in lard or oil; to stew, to decoct; to vex, to harass, to irritate: COM., [7]˛chiéng ˛t'ong, to boil water; [8]˛chiéng ˊpiäng, fried cakes; [9]˛chiéng ˊchü, to fry, adding water for gravy; [10]˛chiéng ˊch'a, to roast, to grill; COLL., ˛chiéng ˛su ˛su, or ˛chiéng ˛pa ˛pa, to fry crisp.

尖 Chien. Sharp, pointed, acute, peaked, conical; tapering to a point, wedge-like, pyramidal; needle-shaped; clever, ingenious: COM., [11]p'e³ ˛chiéng, sharp nose; [12]˛chiéng le³ sharp, grasping; [13]tëük˛ ˛chiéng, a medicine made of the bamboo leaf; [14]ˊting ˛chiéng, extreme, very, the prime, the best; [15]˛chiéng ˛t'au, the pointed end; [16]˛chiéng ˊmwi, the point; ˛ling ˛yong ˛chiéng, a medicine from the points of the horns of young goats; COLL., ˛sang kaëk˛ ˛chiéng, triangular; [17]˛chiéng ch'oi³ "protruding mouth," sticking a word in, officious; ˊkang ˊlang ˛chiéng, olive-shaped.

旃 Chien. A silken banner, a crooked flagstaff; to signalize one to come; careful, attentive.

鐫 Chien. Also read chong³: to engrave, to carve; to cut, to chisel; to censure, to degrade: [18]˛chiéng k'aik˛ to engrave; [19]˛sing ˛chiéng, new edition; [20]˛chiéng nyek˛ to degrade an officer.

覘 Chan. To peep, to spy at, to glance at; to look at stealthily; [21]k'ié ˛chiéng, to peep; [22]˛chiéng haiu³ to wait for.

˛Chiéng. A coll. word: a wedge, to drive a wedge; in a met. sense, smitten, cleaved; pressed, crowded in: ˛chiéng sioh˛ ˛chiéng, to drive a wedge, as in a tenon to fasten it; ˛chiéng sioh˛ oi³ to crowd into a place or seat; ˛chiéng sioh˛ hong³ (or ˊku,) to add another share; k'ëük˛ ˛lai

[1]氈帽 [2]氈底 [3]鋪氈結綵 [4]鷹鸇 [5]饘粥 [6]迍邅 [7]煎湯 [8]煎餅 [9]煎煮 [10]煎炒 [11]鼻尖 [12]尖利 [13]竹尖 [14]頂尖 [15]尖頭 [16]尖尾 [17]尖嘴 [18]鐫刻 [19]新鐫 [20]鐫級 [21]窺覘 [22]覘候 ○

福州方言拼音字典

ˏkung ˏchiéng ʻsi, cleaved to death by a thunder-bolt.

ˏChiéng. A coll. word, as in *ˏchiéng au²* perhaps a contraction of *ʻchi ˏseng au²* this time, now, the present.

ʻ僝 To rail at; to abuse; abusive language; to manifest, to make plain.

ʻ俴 Chien. Shallow, thin, beaten out, as a piece of metal; superficial, ignorant.

ʻ諓 Chien. To flatter; pleasant words, agreeable talk; sly insinuations: [1]*ʻchiéng ʻchiéng*, artful talk, shallow conversation.

ʻ餞 Chien. To present food to one; to give a farewell dinner to; parting presents of money or food; comfits: COM., [2]*ʻchiéng piék*, a parting dinner; [3]*ʻchiéng ˏheng ʻchiu*, farewell entertainment to one going on a journey.

ʻ翦 ʻ剪 Chien. Even, regular, as feathers grow; to cut off smooth, to clip even; to shear; shears, scissors; to kill, to destroy; to reduce, to clip off; light, as a dye: in the coll. read *ʻcheng*, q. v.

ʻ踐 Ch'ien. To tread upon, to trample on or over; to walk, to step; to arrange in order: [4]*ʻchiéng tak*, to tread upon; [5]*ʻchiéng chek*, to tread in another's footsteps; [6]*ʻchiéng ˏngiong*, to keep one's word; [7]*ʻchiéng yok*, to fulfill a contract.

ʻ戩 Chien. To destroy, to kill, to exterminate; to finish, to exhaust; to clip, to shear; entirely.

ʻ戔 Chien. Read *ˏch'iéng*; coll. *ʻchiéng*: young, young-looking, youthful, juvenescent; fresh, green, unripe: [8]*ˏsang tek ʻchiéng*, young-looking, boyish in appearance; *ʻchiéng ˏkwa ˏmó ˏnong ʻchiéng ʻkiăng ˏmó pok ˏtong*, unripe melons have no pulp, so children have no experience.

ʻ蝘 Read *ʻyéng*; coll. *ʻchiéng*: a harmless kind of house-lizard, of a livid color.

ʻ枕 Chĕn. Read *ʻching*; coll. *ʻchiéng*: as [9]*ʻchiéng ˏt'au*, a pillow; [10]*ʻchiéng ˏt'au ˏsiong*, a small trunk shaped like a Chinese pillow; *ʻchiéng ˏt'au ʻkiăng*, a small pillow; [11]*ʻchiéng ˏt'au pwo²* cloth wrappers for pillows.

ʻ槧 Boards for cutting books on; tablets for memoranda, tables to be written on with a pencil.

箭ˀ Chien. An arrow; an archer; a bow-shot; to dart out; to spring forth suddenly; swift like an arrow; a slender bamboo; bristling: [12]*tëük chiéngˀ* a slender bamboo; COM., [13]*chiéngˀ ʻch'i*, an arrow; [14]*chiéngˀ ʻkang*, unfinished arrow-shafts; [15]*ʻma chiéngˀ* mounted archers; [16]*pwo² chiéngˀ* foot-archers; [17]*chiéngˀ ˏpi*, target for archers; [18]*chiéngˀ tó²* target-course; [19]*ˏkŭng chiéngˀ* bows and arrows; [20]*leng² chiéngˀ* an arrow with a flag—

1 諓諓 2 餞別 3 餞行酒 ○ 4 踐踏 5 踐跡 6 踐言 7 踐約 8 生的戔 ○ 9 枕頭箱 10 枕頭 11 枕頭布 12 竹箭 13 箭矢 14 箭幹 15 馬箭 16 步箭 17 箭牌 18 箭道 19 弓箭 20 令箭 ○

a mandate; [1]*'chiéng' ,liong*, or *chiéng' hiong'* an archer's pay from the government; [2]*,kwong ,ing sëü' chiéng'* time flies like an arrow; COLL., [3]*sioh, chiéng'* to shoot arrows; [4]*'chiéng' tói'* an arrow-case; [5]*nge' chiéng'* arrows thrust through the ears—a punishment; [6]*paik, chiéng' paik, tëüng'* one hundred arrows all into the target.

僭 僣 Chien. To assume, to arrogate to one's self; to usurp; to overstep one's limit or rank; dubious, wrong, erroneous, false; usurped, despotic, assuming: [7]*chiéng' ,ch'ing*, surreptitiously styled; [8]*chiéng' ch'iék,* to assume, to get surreptitiously; COM., [9]*chiéng' chó'* "I usurp the seat," as in taking a higher place at a feast.

占 佔 Chan. The second character commonly, but erroneously, so used: to take precedence of; to trespass upon, to usurp, to seize, to supplant, to take by force; to assume, to arrogate, to take the liberty; to possess: also read *,chiéng*, q. v.: [10]*,ching chiéng'* to trespass on: COM., [11]*,kiong chiéng'* to take by force; [12]*chiéng' ,siéng*, to take the precedence of; [13]*pa' chiéng'* to take possession of forcibly; [14]*chiéng' te'* to incroach on the land of another; COLL., *chiéng' ,t'au teng'* to press to the front in battle; *chiéng' ,nëng ch'io'* to keep possession of a house without paying rent; *k'ëük, ,i chiéng' k'ó'* usurped by him.

瀳 洊 Chien. Interchanged with the next: water flowing on; a stream bursting forth again; repeatedly, again: *'chwi chiéng' che'* water flowing towards; *chiéng' lik,* successively.

薦 Chien. Grass eaten by animals, pasturage; to lead animals to good pastures; to introduce, to recommend; to guarantee, to insure; to lay out food; to adore, to worship without a victim; repetition, a succession: [15]*chiéng' ,chü*, a written recommendation; [16]*,ch'wi chiéng'* or *'kü chiéng'* to recommend, to introduce one; COM., [17]*'pó chiéng'* to recommend and be security for; [18]*chiéng' te' ,hwong*, to recommend to a place; [19]*chiéng' k'wok,* to commend to a vacant place; [20]*chiéng' 'kwang te'* to recommend to the post of teacher or secretary; [21]*'tiong chiéng'* to recommend one's employé to another party; COLL., *chiéng' 'chio*, the patron, one who recommends.

荐 Chien. Used for the last: to continue; some; to succeed, to recur repeatedly, as a famine; again, repeatedly: *chiéng' ,ki*, successive famines; *chiéng' ,kü*, to rough it in the bush.

栫 Chien. A prop; to shore up a leaning house, to support: a water-dam, made of stones and earth: COM., *chiéng' ,ch'iong*, to prop a wall; *chiéng' 'tó*, to throw down by too much pressure on the props; COLL., *chiéng' ch'io'* to

[1]箭	似	[4]箭	[6]百	[7]僭	[9]僭	[11]强	[13]霸	[15]薦	[17]保	方	館
糧	箭	袋	箭	稱	坐	占	占	書	薦	[19]薦	地
[2]光	[3]射	[5]耳	百	[8]僭	[10]侵	[12]占	[14]占	[16]推	[18]薦	鈌	[21]轉
陰	箭	箭	中	竊	占	先	地	薦	地	[20]薦	薦

福州方言拼音字典

prop a house; *chiéng' chiăng'* to shore up till erect.

戰 戦 Chan. To fight; to be alarmed, struck with dread; fearful, timid, afraid, anxious; a battle, an engagement; war, hostilities: military, pertaining to war: [1]*chiéng' kak*, armor; [2]*chiéng' lek*, afraid, terrified; [3]*chiéng' sĕă* a soldier; [4]*kiu chiéng'* protracted war; a veteran warrior; COM., [5]*ch'ok, chiéng'* to go forth to war; [6]*chiéng' taiu'* to fight; [7]*kau chiéng'* to fight, to go to war; [8]*tói' chiéng'* to join battle; [9]*chiéng' teng'* troops in platoons; [10]*chiéng' 'ku*, drums sounding the charge; [11]*chiéng' 'chü*, a challenge to fight; [12]*chiéng' tiong*, the field of battle; [13]*'miéng chiéng' pá*, a flag of truce; COLL., *chiéng' yăng*, a victory; *chiéng' sio*, or *chiéng' pat* a defeat; *p'ang p'ang chiéng'* or *'teu 'teu chiéng'* to tremble, to shake; *chiéng' 'ch'iu*, fine brass-wire.

顫 The head awry; to shiver with cold; fearful, trembling, affrighted: *hang chiéng'* shivering. Read *chiéng*, to smell.

前 Ch'ien. Before, in front of, in presence of; in advance; to advance, to go forward; to lead, to lead on; formerly, previously, anciently; the former, the past, the preceding: in the coll. read *seng*, q. v.: COM., [14]*chiéng haiu'* before and after, front and rear; [15]*chiéng ngwok*, the preceding month; *chiéng nik*, a former day; [16]*chiéng ing* the ancients; [17]*chiéng tieu*, former dynasties; [18]*chiéng ngiong*, old sayings, formerly said; [19]*chiéng pwo'* to walk first; [20]*'ngang chiéng*, visible, the present; [21]*chiéng 'ch'iu*, or *chŭng chiéng*, formerly, previously; *chiéng hu*, husband in a former life; [22]*chiéng pwoi'* seniors; venerable sir! *chiéng haiu' 'ch'iu*, before and after—in advance, beforehand, as in borrowing; [23]*chiéng liék*, selected students at Hien or Fu examinations—from the 2d to the 10th names; *chiéng hwang*, or *chiéng ch'ĕă'* a former occasion or time; *pok, chiéng pok, haiu'* just at the time; COLL., *á' 'kong chiéng Tong haiu' Hang' 'lü k'ó'* you 'll be talking of Tong and Han! i. e., wide of the mark; *chiéng tó' 'kong 'kong ki*, the one of whom I spoke.

潛 潜 Ch'ien. To ford, to cross water, to wade through; to dive, to walk on the bottom; to hide away, to abscond, to secrete one's self; deep, still, calm, placid, as deep water; ancient name of the river Han; carefully, cautiously, stealthily: *t'ing chiéng*, placid, still; reserved; *chiéng chong*, or *chiéng huk*, to secrete one's self; *chiéng pwo'* careful steps, a stealthy tread.

鼴 Read *'yĕng*; coll. *chiéng*, as in *chiéng 'ch'ü*, a mole; *chiéng 'ch'ü siéng*, the rank smell of a mole; *chiéng 'ch'ü chiăk, chiăk, kieu'* the squeak of a mole—is a bad omen.

[1]戰甲 [2]戰慄 [3]戰士 [4]久戰 [5]出戰 [6]戰鬬 [7]交戰 [8]對戰 [9]戰陣 [10]戰鼓 [11]戰書 [12]戰場 [13]免戰牌〇 [14]前後 [15]前月 [16]前人 [17]前朝 [18]前言 [19]前步 [20]眼前 [21]前手 [22]前輩 [23]前列

籛 ꜀Ch'ien. Also read ꜀ch'iéng: a person named ꜀Chiéng ꜀K'eng, who lived in the Shang and Chow dynasties to the age of 767, and then vanished.

錢 ꜀Ch'ien. A copper coin, cash, coppers; coin, money, currency, a piece of money; wealth, property; a tenth of a tael, a mace, which the cash once weighed: COM., [1]꜀tëng ꜀chiéng, copper cash; [2]꜀chiéng taing' a bank; [3]꜀chiéng yong² cash-signs (in front of a bank); [4]꜀chiéng p'ieu' bank-notes; [5]꜀hwang ꜀chiéng, foreign dollars; [6]꜀chiéng ꜀pwang, a grooved wooden plate for holding unstrung cash; ꜀chiéng ꜀cheng, a needle used in stringing cash; [7]꜀chiéng ʻmwi, a balance of money; [8]꜀chiéng kiéng' a charm made of cash strung in the form of a sword; [9]꜀chiéng ꜀pá, cash or silver medals (hung round the necks of children as charms); [10]꜀chiéng ꜀tëng, a bamboo for holding cash; [11]꜀siu ꜀chiéng, to receive money; [12]꜀chiéng ek, a mace and one tenth; [13]꜀chiéng le' interest; [14]꜀chiéng loi² immersed in gain; [15]ʻpwong ꜀chiéng, capital, stock in trade; [16]꜀chiéng lioh, history of coins; COLL., ꜀chiéng ʻchwi ꜀ch'üng chëük, monied; ꜀chiéng ʻchwi, premium on money; ꜀si ꜀chiéng, ordinary currency; ꜀tong pah, ꜀chiéng, good currency, all the cash good; ꜀chiéng ʻkiăng, or ꜀ngai ꜀chiéng, bad cash; ꜀chiéng ch'iong' or ꜀chiéng kwong' sóh, cord for stringing cash; ꜀chiéng taëk, a savings' box; ꜀chiéng tak, a cash-bag; ꜀chiéng ʻtau, a high wooden box for cash—used in shops; ꜀chiéng piéng² "cash braid"—i. e., the cue; ꜀chiéng tawng' miăng² money esteemed as life—excessively parsimonious; ꜀chiéng ꜀ch'iong pek, má² kwo' "can't pull it through the cash-hole;" met., he's so stingy I can get no money out of him!

賤² Chien. Worthless, mean, base, vile, low, ignoble, vulgar; cheap, low-priced; to depreciate, to lower; used for what is one's own: [17]chiéng² ꜀ing, a mean fellow; COM., [18]koi' chiéng² noble and base; [19]ʻa² chiéng² low, base; [20]꜀mi chiéng² insignificant; [21]chiéng² hwo' "miserable baggage!"—as a bad woman; [22]chiéng² nói² my wife; [23]chiéng² yong² my sickness; [24]chiéng² p'ek, my mean disposition—language of affectation; COLL., chiéng² miăng² life of drudgery; chiéng² chá² "mean dough"—a butt for ridicule; chiéng² ꜀p'wi, "low crude mass"—applied to depraved persons; chiéng² chauk, mischievous, as a child; cheng² chiéng² very depraved; very mischievous.

漸² Chien. Name of an affluent of the Yang-tsz-kiăng, near Ngan-king-fu; to find its way in, as water does; to increase by degrees, slowly, by little and little; stealthily, as decay; to flow, to imbibe; to tinge, to soak, to penetrate: chiéng² chëü² to soak gradually; chiéng² këüng² to approach by degrees; COM., chek, chiéng² by little and little; chiéng² chiéng² slowly, gradually.

[1]銅錢 [2]錢店 [3]錢樣 [4]錢票 [5]番錢 [6]錢盤 [7]錢尾 [8]錢劍 [9]錢牌 [10]錢筒 [11]收錢 [12]錢一 [13]錢利 [14]錢累 [15]本錢 [16]錢錄 [17]賤人 [18]貴賤 [19]下賤 [20]微賤 [21]賤貨 [22]賤内 [23]賤恙 [24]賤癖

塹꜃ 漸꜃ 壍 The moat around a wall, a fosse, a ditch; a sluice to lead water upon trees; to deepen, to dig out.

(49) Chieu.

招 Chao. To beckon, to motion to with the hand, to hail; to invite, to let people know; to induce, to lead in, to bring in, as converts; to raise, as troops; to confess; self-crimination; to excite; a hand-bill, a sign, a sign-board; a wave of the hand, a signal; to tie by the foot, to entangle: COM., [1]*꜀chieu ꜀ang*, to invite to peace—as rebels by offer of pardon; [2]*꜀chieu ꜂ing*, to introduce; [3]*꜀chieu ꜀hu*, to beckon and call; [4]*꜀chieu ꜀ping*, to recruit soldiers; [5]*꜀chieu ꜀hung*, or *chieu ꜀hong* (as spoken in Changloh), to bring back the soul—as of one who has died abroad; [6]*꜀chieu ꜀ch'ing* (coll. *꜀chieu ꜀nié sai꜃*), to invite one to be a son-in-law; [7]*꜀chieu ho꜃ ꜂ma*, to invite one to be the emperor's son-in-law; [8]*꜀chieu ngié꜃ ꜀ming*, or [9]*꜀chieu ꜀hiong ꜂ŭng*, to raise volunteers; [10]*꜀chieu ꜀pá*, a sign, a sign-board; [11]*꜀chieu chik꜁*, to call together; [12]*꜀chieu ꜀chai*, to prosper in business; [13]*꜀chieu neng꜃* to confess one's guilt; [14]*k'ok꜁ ꜂ta ꜀sing ꜀chieu*, extorted confession.

弨 Also read *꜀ch'ieu*: to fly back, as a bow; to spring back; a bow unbent.

昭 Chao. Brightness of the sun; bright, splendid, manifest; luminous, refulgent: [15]*꜀chieu ꜀ming*, refulgent; [16]*꜀chieu muk꜁*, order of precedence in the ancestral hall; [17]*꜀chieu ꜀kung tó꜃* an embroidered fillet, also called [18]*꜀hwa mó꜃*.

膲 The parts of the body between the heart and the groin, three imaginary organs which regulate the secretions.

焦 Chiao. Used for the last: burned, scorched; blackened, charred; smell of burning; vexed, harassed, anxious: COM., [19]*꜀chieu só꜃* parched, hot, feverish; *꜀sing ꜀chieu*, distressed; [20]*꜀chieu mong꜃* harassed, anxious.

燋 Chiao. Interchanged with last: to burn moxa; to scorch, to sear, to char wood: COLL., *꜀chieu tioh꜁* burnt, scorched; *꜀chieu ꜀ta*, scorched, as in being fried; [21]*꜀chieu ꜀pa*, burnt crust adhering to pans.

縿 Chiao. Raw hemp, hemp not yet cleansed: *꜀chieu ꜀i*, yellow hempen clothes, worn in mourning for grand-parents; *꜀chieu mó꜃* mourning caps.

蕉 Chiao. The banana or plantain: COM., *꜀pa ꜀chieu*, the plantain tree; *꜀pa ꜀chieu ꜂kwo*, plantains; *꜀pa ꜀chieu nioh꜁*, the plantain leaf; *꜀chieu kak꜁*, cloth made from the fibres of a kind of plantain.

鐎 A soldier's brass kettle or skillet, about the size of a peck measure; a brass pan.

[1]招安 [2]招引 [3]招呼 [4]招兵 [5]招魂 [6]招親 [7]招駙馬 [8]招義民 [9]招鄉勇 [10]招牌 [11]招集 [12]招財 [13]招認 [14]屈打成招 [15]昭明 [16]昭穆 [17]昭君套 [18]花帽 [19]焦燥 [20]焦悶 [21]燋疤

鷦 ꜀Chao. A wren, the tarin, the tody or some such small bird: [1]꜀*chieu* ꜀*lieu*, a little bird with an awl-shaped beak.

譙 Ch'iao. Read ꜀*chieu*; coll. ꜀*chieu*: a look-out loft or tower: [2]꜀*chieu* ꜀*ieu*, a look-out tower.

椒 ꜀Chiao. Pepper, peppery, hot: [3]꜀*chieu* ꜀*pung*, the peppery room—term applied to the queen's apartment; COM., [4]꜀*hu* ꜀*chieu*, common pepper; ꜀*hwa* ꜀*chieu*, chillies; ʻ*hwang* ꜀*chieu*, red-pepper; ꜀*kwa* ꜀*chieu*, melon-shaped peppers; [5]*k'aiuʼ* ꜀*chieu*, the button-pepper; *pah*꜁ ꜀*chieu*, white pepper.

少 ʻChao. Read ʻ*sieu*; coll. ʻ*chieu*: little, not much, few, not many; briefly, a little while; seldom, rarely; in a slight degree; limited; to owe, wanting, deficient, insufficient, destitute: *sá*^{2} ʻ*chieu*, much or little; how much? [6]ʻ*chieu k'iéngʼ* or ʻ*twang* ʻ*chieu*, to owe; *k'ak*꜁ ʻ*chieu*, too few, too little; [7]*k'wok*꜁ ʻ*chieu*, deficient, destitute; ʻ*chieu* ʻ*chieu*, very few; ʻ*ting* ʻ*chieu*, or *chengʼ* ʻ*chieu*, or ʻ*yǎ* ʻ*chieu*, very scarce, very little; [8]ʻ*chieu* ʻ*ch'ü* ꜀*tó* ꜀*lai*, small profits secure large gains; ʻ*chieu t'engʼ* to make small gains; ʻ*chieu* ꜀*nëng* ꜀*chiéng*, to owe money; [9]ʻ*chieu saungʼ* to reckon less, to cheapen; ʻ*chieu nioh*꜁ *wai*^{2} how much deficient? [10]ʻ*chieu siàh*꜁ ꜀*tó chëüʼ e*^{2} eat sparingly and it has fine flavor, *scil.*, eating much cloys.

照 炤 Chao. Light, brightness; to illuminate, to enlighten, to shine on; to patronize, to regard, to care for, to oversee, to assist; conformably to, according to; as, like, same as; to follow, as copy; to imitate, as a model: COM., [11]*chieuʼ* ꜀*lung*, by turns, rotation; *chieuʼ yeu*^{2} very bright; [12]*chieuʼ mengʼ* or *chieuʼ kiǎngʼ* to look in a mirror; *chieuʼ ko*^{2} or *chieuʼ k'angʼ* to oversee, to take care of; [13]ʻ*hwang chieuʼ* or *tó*^{2} *chieuʼ* reflected light; ꜀*sá chieuʼ* shines in from the west; [14]*chieuʼ engʼ* to patronize; *chieuʼ* ꜀*ch'iong*, a curtain-wall—in front of a yamun; [15]*chieuʼ hwoi*^{2} an official communication; *chieuʼ* ꜀*siong*, as usual, customary; *chieuʼ saungʼ* according to the calculation; [16]*chieuʼ lié*^{2} according to the law or regulation; [17]꜀*chong chieuʼ* fac-similes clipped from the ends of bank-notes when issued, and kept to detect counterfeits; [18]*chieuʼ* ꜀*t'iǎng*, sub-officers, as at the treasurer's; [19]꜀*kó chieuʼ* a large high lantern (in processions); *chieuʼ* ʻ*li*, according to reason; [20]*chieuʼ* ꜀*si kaʼ* according to current prices; COLL., *chieuʼ* ꜀*sing kiǎngʼ* "mirrors to illuminate hearts"—held before the breast by bride and groom; *chiǎngʼ chieuʼ* direct light; *chieuʼ yongʼ* one by one, articles reckoned singly; *chieuʼ nik*꜁ *p'woh*꜁ dried in the sun.

詔 Chao. To promulgate, to announce, to proclaim; to teach, to exhort, to instruct the empire; to encourage; a proclamation,

[1]鷦鷯 [2]譙樓 [3]棚椒 [4]番椒 [5]釦椒 [6]少欠 [7]缺少 [8]少取多來 [9]少算 [10]少食多注味 [11]照輪 ○ [12]照面 [13]返照 [14]照應 [15]照會 [16]照例 [17]存照 [18]照聽 [19]高照 [20]照時價 ○

imperial rescript, decree, royal mandate: COM., *chieu' ˓chü,* or [1]*'ngü²* *chieu'* a royal mandate; [2]*˓pung chieu'* to promulge the royal commands; *kaung' chieu'* to issue a royal decree; [3]*puo²* *chieu'* decree from one of the imperial boards; [4]*'chieu' ˓ting,* a pavilion-sedan in which imperial decrees are borne—as those ennobling one's ancestors; COLL., *˓ing chieu'* royal proclamation when an emperor ascends the throne; [5]*'pah˒ chieu'* proclamation announcing the death of the emperor.

譙 誚 Ch'iao. The second read *sieu'* but often used for the first: to scold, to blame, to reprehend; to bawl at: [6]*chieu' chaik˒* to rebuke; [7]*chieu' yong²* to scold. The first read *˓chieu,* a look-out tower, as in *˓chieu ˓leu,* the city-loft where the "watches" are beat.

醮 Chiao. To sacrifice to ancestors and to spirits; a sacrifice, a mass, a requiem; to give a cup of wine to a son at his wedding; finished, exhausted; to complete; to burn moxa: [8]*ho² chieu' 'chü,* the father gives the cup to his son; *chai' chieu'* to re-marry, as a widow; COM., [9]*˓ch'ing chieu'* a sacrifice; a religious festival; [10]*chieu' 'ngü,* prayers used at a sacrifice; COLL., *chó' chieu'* to offer sacrifices or requiems; *twai² chieu'* all-souls' festival; [11]*chó' 'hwi, chieu'* a sacrifice to avert conflagrations.

呪 咒 Chu. Read *cheu';* coll. *chieu':* to curse, to imprecate, to rail at, to swear; to recite spells; a curse, an imprecation: [12]*chieu' cho'* to curse; [13]*˓hu chieu'* charms and spells; *chieu' 'ngü,* spells; [14]*naing² chieu'* to repeat incantations.

樵 Chiao. Firewood, fuel, scattered wood; to cut wood; a wood-cutter; a look-out terrace, a watch-tower: [15]*'ch'ai ˓chieu,* to cut wood; *˓chieu tang'* pole and ropes for carrying wood; *muk˒ ˓chieu,* or [16]*˓chieu ˓leu,* a watch-tower; [17]*˓chieu ˓kó,* a wood-chopper's song; *˓chieu ˓hu,* a wood-cutter.

憔 Ch'iao. Lean, poor, anxious and starving: COM., [18]*˓chieu choi²* a lean, sallow look; distressed from want of food; [19]*˓chieu ch'ó'* anxious, perplexed.

噍 Chiao. Also read *˓chieu:* to chirp, as birds: harsh, dissonant; a husky, suppressed voice; to chatter; noise of voices: [20]*˓chiu ˓chieu,* to chirp, as birds; a harsh, dissonant cry; COLL., *˓chieu laĭ²* to disturb by clatter of voices; [21]*nge² ˓chieu ˓u,* chattering till my ears buzz! *˓chieu ˓nĕng k'aung' má² tioh˒* to keep folks awake by incessant talking. Read *chieu'* to chew, to gnaw.

瞧 To look at, to see; to look at furtively; to glance at: [22]*˓chieu ek˒ ˓chieu,* or (as spoken in mandarin) *˓ch'ieu ek˒ ˓ch'ieu,* I had a look at it.

1 御詔 2 頒詔 3 部詔 4 詔亭 5 白詔 6 譙責 7 譙讓 8 父醮子 9 清醮 10 醮語 11 做火醮 12 咒詛 13 符咒 14 念咒 15 採樵 16 樵樓 17 樵歌 18 憔悴 19 憔慒 20 啁噍 21 耳噍呼 22 瞧一瞧

(50) Chih.

*Chih*₂ A coll. word, as in *chih*₂ *ch'ok*₂ *꜀li*, to spirt out, as water from under a stone when trodden on.

*Chih*₂ A coll. word: same as *tih*₂ as in *chih*₂ *má*² *ch'ok*₂ unable to articulate, to stammer.

*Chih*₂ A coll. euphonic prefix, as in *chih*₂ *chóh*₂ to cast away, to throw aside.

(51) Chik.

集₂ Chi. To flock together; to gather, as clouds; to assemble, to come together, to congregate, to collect; to complete, to finish; to bring together; quiet, at rest, to rest; to go directly to the mark; to mix, to blend; to make a collection, to compile; a miscellany, ana; a place where people collect, as a market: [1]*꜀k'iu chik*₂ to collect; to take up, as subscriptions of money; [2]*꜀king chik*₂ a collection of the classics; COM., *chŭi*² *chik*₂ or [3]*hwói*² *chik*₂ to congregate, to assemble, as by appointment; [4]*꜀chá chik*₂ to come together; COLL., [5]*chik*₂ *sioh*₂ *꜀toi*, to collect, as persons or things.

疾₂ Chi. Used for the next: sickness, a disorder, a disease that comes suddenly upon one; calamities, afflictions; urgent, pressing, hasty; unlucky, infelicitous; to hate, to dislike, to envy: [6]*chik*₂ *peng*² ailments, disease; *chik*₂ *t'ong*² sickness and pain; [7]*꜀hang chik*₂ chilly, a cold; [8]*kek*₂ *chik*₂ urgent, hasty; *lá*² *chik*₂ a pestilence, a dangerous disease; [9]*mó*² *chik*₂ to hate, to envy; COM., [10]*꜀chang chik*₂ maimed; *ang*² *chik*₂ a secret disease; [11]*hwak*₂ *keu*² *chik*₂ return of an old disease; [12]*taik*₂ *chik*₂ to take a disease.

嫉₂ Chi. Envy, jealousy; to envy, to dislike, as a competitor: [13]*chik*₂ *o*² or *mó*² *chik*₂ to envy, to hate; *꜀ch'ing chik*₂ deadly hatred; COM., [14]*chik*₂ *to*² jealousy.

寂₂ 諔₂ Chi. Silent, still, quiet, as an empty house; solitary; unmoved, like a recluse; desolate, lonely: [15]*chik*₂ *cheng*² a dead silence; *chik*₂ *꜀yong pok*₂ *tong*² unmoved, imperturbable; COM., *chik*₂ *chik*₂ or *chik*₂ *꜀lieu*, or [16]*chik*₂ *chik*₂ *mok*₂ *mok*₂ silent, solitary.

蒺₂ Gorse, furze; a thorny shrub whose seeds are biting and spicy: [17]*chik*₂ *꜀lá*, a very spinous plant—the seeds used for diseases of the eye.

藉₂ Chi. Scattered, in confusion; wasteful; incessant, as talk; public fields cultivated by the people; trodden under foot; led, as by a string: also read *chiă*² q. v.: [18]*꜀long chik*₂ extravagant.

籍₂ Chi. A book for records, a tablet; a list, a register of the people; the place of enrolling, one's native place: [19]*꜀teng chik*₂ to enroll, to take a census; [20]*kiè*² *chik*₂ sojourners; COM., *꜀chü chik*₂ books;

[1] 鳩集 [2] 經集 [3] 會集 [4] 齊集 [5] 集一堆○ [6] 疾病 [7] 寒疾 [8] 急疾 [9] 冒疾 [10] 殘疾 [11] 發舊疾 [12] 得疾 [13] 嫉惡 [14] 嫉妬 [15] 寂靜 [16] 寂寂寞寞 [17] 蒺藜 [18] 狼藉 [19] 登籍○ [20] 寄籍○○

[1]*king chik* sacred books, classics; *chai*[2] *chik* to record; recorded; [2]*nik chik* naturalized citizens; *mó*[2] *chik* to assume falsely; *long chik* notorious, infamous; in disorder, as a table after a feast.

Chik A coll. euphonic prefix, as in *chik chiok* cut off, extirpated, as posterity; *chik chek* cut off, as a road; *chik chak* to cut up, to mince; *chik chiăk* to smack the lips, as in eating; also sound of falling rain, or of treading in slush.

(52) Ching.

眞 真 *Chin.* True, sincere, unfeigned, genuine, pure; in fact, truly, indeed, no mistake; a likeness; actual, not secondary; spiritual, pure, subtle, unmixed; used in coll. in sense of very, extremely: COM., [3]*ching 'ka*, true and false, genuine and spurious; *ching sik* true, really; [4]*ching meng*' or *ching 'chio*, one destined to be emperor; *ching wak* lively, true to life, as a likeness; *ching hwo*' genuine goods; [5]*ching 'pwong*, one's actual capital; [6]*sëü*' *pok ,mwang ,ching*, the truth cannot be hidden; *ching ching*, truly, really; [7]*ching pok, ne*' *ka*' positively not two prices—as on shop-signs; COLL., *ching 'hó*, very good; [8]*ching pok k'ang*, utterly unworthy; *ching chiăh, ching*, positively true; [9]*'ka paik, ching*, to pretend to know the truth of; *ching chiăng*' exactly right, just so; *ching hwang ching 'ka hwang 'ka*, if true then true, if false then false.

睛 The ball of the eye, the pupil: *'ngang ,ching*, or *muk ,ching*, the pupil of the eye, the eye; *ning ,ching*, a displeased look; COM., [10]*lo*' *,ching*, the eyeball prominent.

瞋 *Ching.* To stare at angrily, to glare at.

嗔 *Chen.* To get angry, passionate; to rail; angry: [11]*no*' *seng ,ching*, angry, passionate. Read *tieng*, to bully, to puff and bluster.

精 *Ching.* Cleaned rice; selected, ripe, mature; fine, subtle, delicate; the best, the finest; unmixed; devoted to, accustomed to, expert at; skillful, as in strategy; the pure parts of anything, etherial; essence of things; it is prefixed to other adjectives to indicate a high degree of; the animal spirits; the semen, germinating principle in nature; an apparition, form taken by spirits: in the coll. read *chiăng*, q. v.: *ching lik* earnest, energetic; [12]*ching mik* fine, polished; [13]*yong ,ching*, the sun; *ing ,ching*, the moon; [14]*ching ling*, intelligence; [15]*ching k'e*' ether, pure essence, first principle of; COM., [16]*ching ,ping*, picked soldiers; *ching t'ung*, highly intelligent, well-read; [17]*ching sung*, unmixed, uniform, as color; *ching sing*, energy, animal spirits; [18]*siék, ching*, involuntary emissions; [19]*ching ik* the vital secretions; COLL., [20]*ching kwong*, completely stripped, all gone, as property;

[1]經籍 [2]匿籍 [3]眞假 [4]眞命 [5]眞本 [6]事不瞞眞 [7]眞不二價 [8]眞不堪 [9]假八眞 [10]露睛 [11]怒生嗔 [12]精密 [13]陽精 [14]精靈 [15]精氣 [16]精兵 [17]精純 [18]洩精 [19]精液 [20]精光○

,ching eu' very fine, tender; *,mó ,ching ,sing,* spiritless; *,ching ,sing kiă'* "has gross spirits"—can see imps; *,ching 'cheng,* fitting, done just right.

鞕 Also read *'ching:* a bag to tie on a horse's head, in which his fodder is kept.

鉦 Cymbals set in a frame, used to signalize a halt in armies; a cymbal used by priests; a brass tambourine; center of a bell or drum: *,tung ,ching,* a brass cymbal; [1]*,sing ,ching,* the spiritual drum—it is of stone and said to give out a sound before rain.

征 (*,* Chêng.) To go, to take; to collect taxes; to go out to chastise, to reduce refractory states, to subjugate, to conquer: *,heng ,ching,* to go on a journey; [2]*,ching hwak,* to chastise a rebellious state; [3]*,ching swoi'* to collect customs; *,ching ,tŭ,* to exterminate; COM., [4]*,ching 'pi,* a private secretary who keeps account of taxes; [5]*,ching ,sá,* "expedition to the west"—in book of the Tang dynasty; [6]*ch'ok, ,ching,* to go out to war; [7]*,ching ,siu,* or *,ching ,diong,* to levy taxes.

正 (*,* Chêng.) The first: [8]*,chingngwok,* (coll. *,chiăng ngwok,*) the first-month of the year.

烝 (*,* Chêng.) A vapor made by heat, steam; vapor, mist; to steam, to cook by steaming, to distil; a multitude, all; to enter, to advance; clouds of dust; liberal, princely; a winter sacrifice; to commit incest with superiors in rank; to lay down; [9]*,hŭng ,ching,* to rise up, as steam; *,yéng ,ching,* vapors caused by heat; [10]*,ching ,li,* stewed pears; COM., [11]*,ching nŭk,* meat cooked moist; [12]*,ching ,tú,* a stewed quarter of pork; COLL., *,ching lang²* to boil soft; [13]*,ching ,su ,kó,* short-cakes, lunch; *,ching nong² 'piăng,* a kind of large biscuit; [14]*,ching ch'oi'* to kiss; *,ching sioh, ch'oi'* to imprint a kiss.

蒸 (*,* Chêng.) Used for last: twigs of hemp for burning; small firewood; hemp torches; vapor, steam; all, numerous; to rise, as vapor or steam: [15]*,ching ,ching nik, siong²* rising higher and higher, constantly improving, as a country.

菁 (*,* Ching.) Scallion blossoms; a kind of three-ribbed rush: [16]*,ching ,mau,* a three-ribbed rush; COM., [17]*,mwang ,ching,* a vegetable like a turnip. Read *,ch'ing,* flowery, elegant, flourishing.

斟 (*,* Chên.) To pour from or into, to lade out; to lighten; to deliberate, to adjust; a laddle, a spoon; to drink: [18]*,ching 'chiu,* to pour out wine to drink; COM., [19]*,ching chiok,* to deliberate, to plan.

旌 (Ching.) A banner, a standard having plumes, which are waved to encourage the troops; to make signals; ensignia, signals; to discriminate, to make manifest, to prove, to show forth: [20]*,ching ,ki,*

---

1 神鉦 ○ 2 征伐 3 征稅 4 征比 5 征西 6 出征 7 征收 8 正月 9 薰烝 10 烝梨 11 烝肉 12 烝蹄 13 烝酥糕 14 烝嘴 15 烝烝日上 ○ 16 菁茅 17 蔓菁 18 斟酒 19 斟酌 20 旌旗 ○

福州方言拼音字典

flags; ¹ˏ*ching chiĕk*, a passport; ²ˏ*ching* ˋ*pieu*, testimonials of merit granted by the emperor, and often hung up in the hall; ³ˏ*ching* ˋ*chiong chiĕk*, *hau*ˊ monuments to virtuous widows over fifty years of age.

津 ˏChin. A ford, a ferry; a landing-place; a ghaut; to ford, to cross a stream; to imbue, to moisten, to soften by soaking: ⁴ˏ*kwang* ˏ*ching*, an excise station, guard-houses at fords; COM., ⁵ˏ*t'iĕng*, ˏ*ching*, Tientsin, port of Peking; the constellation Cygnus; ˏ*ching ik*ˎ the secretions, as saliva, &c.

箴 ˏChĕn. A probe, a surgeon's needle; to probe; a caution, a check; pointed, urgent; to exhort, to rebuke; to urge to reform: ⁶ˏ*ching* ˏ*kié*, admonitions, cautionary maxims; ⁷ˏ*ching* ˏ*ngiong*, exhortations, good advice; ˏ*ching kai*ˊ to caution, to warn.

晶 ˏChing. Luster, brightness; pure, clear, light; crystal, crystalline; COM., ⁸ˋ*chwi* ˏ*ching*, a crystal, a quartz crystal; ˏ*ta* ˏ*ching*, the tea-stone, cairngorm stone; ⁹*haik*ˎ ˏ*ching*, smoky quartz; ˋ*chwi* ˏ*ching* ˏ*kŭng*, "crystal palace"—Neptune's abode; COLL., *sioh*ˎ ˏ*ching*, an inferior crystal; ˏ*t'au hwok*ˎ ˏ*ching*, "the hair crystal"—moss-agate.

升 ˏChĕng. Read ˏ*sing*; coll. ˏ*ching*: a Chinese pint containing ten *hak*ˎ and once made to hold a catty of rice; a pint measure: ¹⁰ˏ*ching* ˋ*tau*, a pint and a peck; ¹¹ˋ*mi* ˏ*ching*, a pint measure for rice; ¹²*tau*ˀ ˏ*ching*, a pint measure for beans; ¹³ˋ*mi sioh*ˎ ˏ*ching*, one pint of rice; ¹⁴ˏ*ching pwang*ˊ a ching and a half.

侵 ˏCh'in. To usurp, to encroach upon, to enter gradually; to appropriate, to plunder; to invade; possessed, as by a spirit; bad, calamitous, as a year; dwarfed, deformed, in which sense it is also read ˋ*ch'ing*: ¹⁵ˏ*ching chiĕng*ˊ to encroach upon; ¹⁶ˏ*ching* ˏ*t'ong*, to plunder, to devour; ¹⁷ˏ*ching twak*ˎ to take by force; ¹⁸*tai*ˀ ˏ*ching*, poor harvests.

駸 Used for the preceding: properly a swift horse: ¹⁹ˏ*ching* ˏ*ching*, a fast running courser.

祲 祲 ˏChĕn. To influence, to act upon; a malign halo; abundant, great, full.

ˏ*Ching*. A coll. euphonic prefix, as in ˏ*ching* ˏ*chiàng*, to stare at, to look about; ²⁰ˏ*ching* ˏ*chong*, to perform the toilet; ˏ*ching* ˏ*chong*, to pack, as in a trunk; ˏ*ching* ˏ*chiong*, to peer at slyly; ˏ*ching* ˏ*chŭng*, to pound, as in a mortar; ˏ*ching chiĕng*, to wedge; ²¹ˏ*ching chiĕng*ˊ *chiĕng*ˊ to tremble; ˏ*ching* ˏ*chang* ˏ*chang*, to quarrel.

枕 ˏChĕn. A pillow; to gather, to pick; a cross-bar at the back of a carriage; a bone in the midst of a fish's

¹旌節 ²旌表 ³旌奬節孝 ⁴關津 ⁵天津 ⁶箴規 ⁷箴言 ⁸水晶 ⁹黑晶 ¹⁰升斗 ¹¹米升 ¹²豆升 ¹³米一升 ¹⁴升半 ¹⁵侵佔 ¹⁶侵吞 ¹⁷侵奪 ¹⁸大侵 ¹⁹駸駸 ²⁰祲粧 ²¹祲戰戰 ○

brains; a stake for tethering a cow; to lie near to, contiguous, adjacent: [1]ʻ*ching ꜀piéng*, by the pillow; sleeping together; [2]ʻ*ching ꜀tʻeu*, (coll. ʻ*chiĕng ꜀tʻau*) a pillow; COM., [3]*seuʼ* ʻ*ching*, an ornamented pillow; [4]*tëük*꜇ ʻ*ching*, a bamboo pillow; [5]*kʻóʼ* ʻ*ching*, large pillows for couches; [6]*kʻaungʼ ꜀chʻong* ʻ*ching*, a square ottoman on a divan.

ʻ振 Chên. To shake, to move, to stir up, to agitate; to excite, to stimulate; to repair, to restore, to put in order; to rescue, to save; to joggle; to flap, as wings; to terrify; to uphold; to stop; to receive; to contain; used in the coll. in the sense of to move up; to reckon, as integers: [7]ʻ*ching ʻkʻi*, to resume; [8]ʻ*ching tong*ʼ to shake, to rouse up; [9]ʻ*ching ꜀hing*, to rise, to flourish; [10]ʻ*ching ꜀ó ʻhai*, (the earth) contains the rivers and seas; COLL., [11]ʻ*ching siong*ʼ to add on, as counting fractions for whole numbers; ʻ*ching ꜀keng*, to move higher up, as on a seat.

ʻ拯 Chêng. To rescue, to pull out, as from a well; to deliver, to save; to raise up: [12]ʻ*ching keuʼ* to save; [13]ʻ*ching wong*ʼ to draw out, to rescue.

ʻ侲 Chang. A boy of ten or twelve years: [14]ʻ*ching ꜀tung*, boys who play at funerals.

ʻ賑 Chang. A largess, a bounty; to give, to relieve, to supply; rich, affluent, abundant: COM., [15]ʻ*ching chá*ʼ to give alms to the poor; COLL., ʻ*ching* ʻ*nü sek*꜇ ꜀*chiong*, aid you so as to "make you complete."

ʻ袗 Chang. Single thin garments, black silk worn in summer; embroidered garments: [16]꜀*tong ʻsü ʻching ꜀hi kʻek*꜇ in summer (wear) single grass-cloth.

ʻ軫 Chên. The boards of a carriage; the cross-board; to move; a carriage; cramped, disturbed, distressed; the last of the 28 constellations, *b. d. ē. g.* in Corvus; the pegs of a lute; [17]꜀*hü ʻching*, crooked, winding; distressed; [18]ʻ*ching niĕng*ʼ grieved in spirit.

ʻ殄 Chên. To terminate, to finish, to make an end of; to exterminate: [19]ʻ*ching chiok*꜇ to destroy utterly.

ʻ畛 Chên. To divide fields; to come before the idols; to announce the emperor's coming; to die; a motive.

ʻ診 Chên. To examine, to look at; to try, to verify: [20]ʻ*ching mek*꜇ to feel the pulse.

ʻ巹 Chên. A nuptial vase, the bride and groom pledge each other after exchanging them; they are often made of half a cocoa-nut, anciently were made of half a gourd or of metal; [21]*hak*꜇ ʻ*ching*, to exchange and pledge the nuptial cup.

ʻ井 Ching. A well; a deep pit; a field laid out regularly; to draw water; arranged, laid out in order: in the coll.

[1]枕 [3]繡 [5]靠 枕 動 河 [12]拯 [14]侲 [16]當 綌 念 脈
邊 枕 枕 [7]振 [9]振 海 救 童 暑 [17]紆 [19]殄 [21]合
[2]枕 [4]竹 [6]匟 起 興 [11]振 [13]拯 [15]賑 袗 軫 絕 巹
頭 枕 床 [8]振 [10]振 上 援 濟 絺 [18]軫 [20]診 ○

read ʻchang, q. v.: [1]ʻching ʻchwi, well-water; [2]chʻeʾ ʻching, a market-place; [3]chóʾ ʻching ˌkwang ˌtʻiéng, to look at the sky from a well—inexperienced, narrow-minded.

ʻ整 Chêng. To make even, to place evenly; to repair, to mend, to put in order; to make; to arrange, to adjust; to adorn, to make new, to trim up: [4]ʻching sok, to arrange, to bind in order; COM., [5]ʻching ˌchá, in order, trim; pretty, as a face or dress; [6]ʻching sëük, ˌï ˌkwang, "dress neatly and decorously," as for worship; [7]ʻching tongʾ to repair, to put in order.

ʻ𩸕 The roe or eggs of fish; the name of a fish.

鬒 Bushy, black hair; a fine head of black hair.

ʻ震 Tsʻêng. To shake, to quiver; to shiver; the 51st diagram, belongs to thunder; to shake, as by thunder; to quicken, as a fœtus; to awe, to impress; thundering, terrible, as a sound; dire, awful; to intimidate; to raise; to alarm: [9]ʻching ˌloi, rattling sound of thunder; [9]ʻching noʾ incensed; [10]ʻching tongʾ to quiver, agitated; [11]teʾ ʻching, an earthquake.

ʻ縝 Chên. Filaments from a cocoon; a thread; to tie; black: [12]ʻching mik, close, compact, as texture of cloth.

ʻ紾 To bind with cords; to turn, to twist; to revolve; a revolution; perverse, crabbed.

ʻ疹 Chêu. Pustules of any kind; eruptions, pimples; a cutaneous disease; sore lips: COM., [13]ˌhung ʻching, pustules from cold in the system.

ʻChing. A coll. euphonic prefix, as in [14]ʻching ʻchiong, to slap with the palm of the hand; [15]ʻching ʻchang, to cut off; ʻching ʻcheng, to clip off with shears.

ʻChing. A coll. word, as in [16]ˌtó ʻching, the back of a knife-blade; [17]ˌtʻü ˌtʻau ʻching, the part of a hoe above the handle; ˌtʻau ˌsë ʻching, the back of a comb.

秦 Chʻin. A kind of grain; a feudal state which occupied the region of the rivers *Wai* and *King*; a range of mountains in the south of Shensi: COM., [18]ˌsá ˌching, ancient feudal state (Shensi); [19]ˌching ˌtieu, the Tsin dynasty, B. C. 186-120; [20]ˌching ʻsü ˌhwong, "First Emperor" of the Tsin dynasty, who consolidated the Chinese empire B. C. 240.

螓 Chʻin. A small species of cicada; eggs of the mantis; a breeze or large blue-bottle fly: [21]ˌching ʻsiu, "breeze-head"—a handsome head.

ˌ情 Chʻing. The passions, reckoned to be seven; the feelings, the desires; temper, passion, affection; lust, concupiscence; the circumstances, the facts of a case; an

1 井水 2 市井 3 坐井觀天 4 整束 5 整齊 6 整肅衣冠 7 整頓 8 震雷 9 震怒 10 震動 11 地震 12 縝密 13 風疹 14 振掌 15 振斬 16 刀𩕳 17 鋤頭𩕳 18 西秦 19 秦朝 20 秦始皇 21 螓首

affair, a matter: com., [1]꜀ching ꜀ching, genuine feeling; ꜀ching ʻli, or ꜀ching ʻli siong꜄ according to facts, reasonable; ꜀sung ꜀ching, to act from mere feeling: [2]sik꜀ ꜀ching, the real facts; [3]ch'ek꜀ ꜀ching, the seven passions; [4]ʻkong ꜀ching, to act as a peace-maker; [5]꜀kang ꜀ching, a licentious disposition; ꜀ching ꜀iu, the facts or circumstances of a case; [6]꜀ching ꜀hing, appearance, state of affairs; [7]꜀ching hong꜄ fondness, as from mutual fitness; ꜀ching ꜀ing, intimates; [8]꜀ching hau꜄ close intimacy; [9]pok꜀ kĕüng꜄ ꜀ing ꜀ching, unnatural, outlandish; [10]꜀ing ꜀ching sié꜄ sëü꜄ "politeness and custom," as in making presents; ꜀ching miéng꜄ to regard tenderly the wishes of another; [11]ʻt'ó ꜀ching, to excite one's compassion.

晴 ꜀Ch'ing. The sky clearing up after a rain; the clear blue sky; the stars coming out; in the coll. ꜀sang, q. v.: [12]꜀t'iéng ꜀ching, the clear sky; ʻwang ꜀ching, clear sky at evening; ch'iok꜀ ꜀hu ꜀ching, the magpie's call promises clear weather.

꜀Ching. A coll. euphonic prefix, as in ꜀ching ꜀chĕng, to dash water on or against; ꜀ching ꜀chiüng, to spatter about, to rebound, as rain falling.

(53) Chio.

[The next six are interchangeably read chwo.]

朱 ꜀ A conifera with red heart-wood; vermilion; a cinnabar red; a surname: used for next in sense of dwarf: [13]꜀chio ꜀i, "red clothes," one of the attendants on the god of learning; com., [14]꜀chio ꜀tang, vermilion; [15]꜀chio ꜀hi, or ꜀chio ʻchü, or ꜀chio ꜀hu ʻchü, the celebrated commentator Chuhi, of the 12th century; [16]꜀yong ꜀chio, a philosopher who opposed the teachings of Mencius.

侏 ꜀Chu. Also read ꜀t'ü: a pigmy, a dwarf; a short pillar in the roof like the king-post: [17]꜀chio ꜀ü, a dwarf; the king-post.

茱 ꜀Chu. A warm peppery medicine: com., [18]꜀chio ꜀ü, hellebore.

硃 ꜀Chu. Cinnabar: com., [19]꜀chio ꜀sa, cinnabar ore; [20]꜀chio kwong꜄ essays of successful Küjin and Chinsz; ꜀chio ꜀p'ié, critiques in red; an imperial answer or rescript; ꜀ngüng ꜀chio, vermilion; ꜀chio ꜀tang, light red vermilion; ch'ek꜀ ꜀chio, finest vermilion; coll., ꜀chio tiäng꜄ or [21]꜀chio mëk꜀ red block-ink.

珠 ꜀Chu. A pearl; a bead; a necklace; bead-like; pearly; fine, excellent; in the coll. pox-pustules; round, plump, round and firm: com., [22]꜀ching ꜀chio, genuine pearls; ꜀chio ꜀kwang, a frontlet of pearls worn by females; wang꜄ ꜀chio, to barter in pearls; yâ꜄ ꜀ming ꜀chio, night-shining pearl; ꜀chio ꜀leng, "the beaded lily"—a female ornament; hak꜀ p'ek꜀ ꜀liêng ꜀chio, "united gems and strung pearls,"

---

[1]眞情 [2]實情 [3]七情 [4]講情 [5]姦情 [6]情形 [7]情分 [8]情厚 [9]不近人情 [10]人情世事 [11]討情 [12]天晴 [13]朱衣 [14]朱丹 [15]朱熹 [16]楊朱 [17]侏儒 [18]茱萸 [19]硃砂 [20]硃卷 [21]硃墨 [22]眞珠

emblems of connubial happiness; ˊ*tieu ˛chio*, court-beads; COLL., *˛chio ˛chio*, round and hard, as twisted rope; [1]*˛chio ˋma*, goddess of small-pox; [2]*˛chio toi'* ear-drops of pearl; [4]*˛chio piéng'* braid with bead-like edges; *mëk˒ ˋiu ˛chio*, has a pearl in his eye—clear-sighted, discriminating; *laiu' ˛chio*, beads made of silex, glass beads; [5]*ch'ok˒ ˛chio*, small-pox; *ˋchwi ˛chio*, chicken-pox; *lau' ˛hu kwa' so' ˛chio ˋka ˛chü ˛p'i*, "pearls strung on a tiger," false pity, as of a hypocrite.

祩 袾 Also read *˛t'ü:* to curse, to imprecate misfortunes upon one; a curse, an imprecation, an oath.

主 ˋ Chu. Read *ˋchü;* coll. *ˋchio:* interchangeably read *ˋchwo:* lord, master; a host; the chief, the head; a family, a household; to govern, to rule: [6]*ˋchio ˛nëng*, master; *˛ping ˋchio* guest and host; *ch'io' ˋchio*, owner of the house; [7]*taing' ˋchio*, shopman; [8]*˛hüng ˋchio*, a murderer; *ˋk'u ˋchio*, the person murdered; [9]*keu' ˋchio*, the Savior, the Lord Jesus; *˛ong ˋchio*, a benefactor; [10]*˛kung ˋchio*, a princess; [11]*ˋchio sëü'* a manager; *kwo' ˋchio*, a transfer, as of property; *ngiëk˒ ˋchio*, the proprietor; *ˋchio ˋchio*, every household; *ˋchio chaung'* chief occupant of a mausoleum; [12]*ˋchio e'* or *ˋchio ˛sing*, to control, to direct; *˛mó ˋchio e'* no help for it! *˛sing chó' ˋchio*, the mind is the ruler; [13]*má' ˋchio tek˒ e'* cannot control it; *ˋchio ˛choi*, to plan, to manage; *ˋchio cheng'* absolute control; [14]*chó' ˋchio*, to be master; *ˋchio ˋtung*, to inspirit, to encourage; [15]*ˋchio ho' ˋk'ó*, the two commissioners who preside at examinations for the Küjin degree; *o' ˋchio che'* marketable; *˛mó ˋchio che'* unsaleable.

[The next two are interchangeably read *chwo.*]

註 ˋ Chu. To define, to explain, to illustrate, to record, to write about; to give the meaning; annotations, emendations, a commentary, definitions, notes; in the coll. to decree, to destine: COM., *chio' che'* comments; [16]*chio' sek˒*, or *chio' siok˒*, notes, explanations; [17]*chio' saë'* the annotated classics; *˛t'iéng chio'* emendations, parallel readings; *chio' ˋngü*, the caption or first words of a written accusation; COLL., [18]*chio' tiäng'* to settle or determine, as by Heaven's decree; [19]*chio' seu' ˛si*, "ruler of longevity"—an attendant of the municipal guardian god; [20]*chio' ˛sang chio' ˋsi*, he determines life and death; *˛ing ˛yong ˛t'iéng chio' tiäng'* marriages are determined by Heaven.

鑄 ˋ Chu. To melt, to fuse metals; to cast, to coin: COM., *chio' ˋtiäng* to cast pans or kettles; [21]*chio' t'iék˒* cast-iron; *chio' p'au'* to cast cannon; *chio' ˛chiëng kwoh˒* a mint; COLL., *chio' wa'* or *chio' ˋla wa'* to coin talk, to make up a story.

[The next three are interchangeably read *chwo.*]

胙 ' Tso. Roasted flesh offered in sacrifices; to set up an altar to Ceres; to recom-

---

1朝珠 2珠媽 3珠墜 4珠辦 5出珠 6主仸 7店主 8凶主 9救主 10公主 11主事 12主意 13賣主的意 14做主 15主副考 16註釋 17註疏 18註定 19註壽司 20註生註死 21鑄鐵

pense, to reward; blessings, happiness; to bless; a seat, a place: [1]*chio*[2] *nük*, sacrificial flesh; *chio*[2] *keng*ʼ sacrificial flesh presented to condoling friends after funeral rites; [2]*chio*[2] ʻ*t'u*, to bestow land, as the emperor on a good officer; [3]*꜀t'iéng chio*[2] bestowed by Heaven; COLL., [4]*꜀pwong chio*[2] gifts of meats distributed among the friends at the conclusion of the third or seventh week of mourning.

祚[2] 祚[2] Tsu. Happiness derived from wealth or office; dignities, felicity; a year: [5]*hok, chio*[2] good fortune; [6]*꜀t'iéng chio*[2] *꜀ming taik*, Heaven blesses the virtuous; *꜀ngwong chio*[2] the first year, as of a reign; [7]ʻ*chiéng chio*[2] to succeed to the throne.

阼[2] Tsu. The steps on the east leading to the hall; landing at the head of the stairs where the host receives his guests: [8]*chio*[2] *꜀kai*, eastern steps where the master enters; ʻ*chiéng chio*[2] to ascend the steps.

(54) Chioh.

燭, 烛, Chio. Read *chëük,*; coll. *chioh,*: also interchangeably read *chwoh,*; the second is the vulgar form: a candle: [9]*lak, chioh,* wax-candles; [10]*꜀ngu ꜀iu chioh,* tallow-candles; [11]*ch'ai*ʼ *꜀iu chioh,* vegetable-oil candles; [12]*ngaing*[2] *꜀iu chioh,* hard candles of the *k'ëüng*[2] or tallow-tree; *꜀pong* (or *paung*[2]) *꜀sing chioh,* candles with stalk and pith wicking; *꜀tiéng ꜀sing chioh,* candles with cotton-wrapped wicks; *chioh, ꜀pwong* a wooden salver to lay candles on; [13]*꜀iu chioh, taing*ʼ oil and candle shop; *chioh, ꜀iu,* or *chioh, ꜀nü ꜀iu* candle-grease; [14]*chioh, ꜀sing,* candle-wick; *chioh,* ʻ*kó,* or *chioh, ꜀mëng,* the stalk wick of candles; *chioh, te*ʼ stumps of candles; ʻ*tiéng chioh,* to light candles; *chioh, lau*ʼ swaling or guttering of candles; [15]*꜀hiong chioh,* incense and candles; *chioh, sioh, ꜀teu,* one candle; ʻ*kang* ʻ*ma chioh,* torches carried in processions; [16]*chioh,* ʻ*tau,* a candlestick.

借, Chieh. Read *chiä*ʼ; coll. *chioh,*: to borrow; to lend; to ask for, to beg of: [17]*chioh, tai*[2] or *꜀nó chioh,* to borrow; *chioh, ꜀chiéng chó*[2] *chai*ʼ to get into debt; [18]*chioh, ꜀chiéng,* to borrow money; *chioh, haung*[2] a borrowed sum; *chioh, ꜀tó ꜀t'ai ꜀nëng,* to hire an assassin; *chioh, ꜀li,* to borrow; [19]*chioh, k'ó*ʼ to lend; *nóh, chioh, ꜀i,* lend him things; *chioh, má*[2] *꜀li,* can't borrow of him; *chioh, mwong*ʼ I beg to inquire; [20]*chioh, ꜀miăng,* to borrow a name; *siă*[2] *chioh,* thanks for the loan; *kaëng*[2] ʻ*nü chioh,* to borrow from you; [21]*chioh, sëük,* to beg a night's lodging; *chioh, ꜀ka ne*[2] *le*ʼ to borrow at 20 per cent per month; *chioh, ꜀pwo nak,* borrow to repay in nightly installments.

Chioh,. A coll. word, as in *chioh,* ʻ*hwi ꜀lëng,* to put a hand-stove under the clothes.

Chioh,. A coll. word, as in

[1]胙	[3]天	[5]福	明	[8]阼	[10]牛	油	燭	[14]燭	[16]燭	[18]借	[20]借
肉	胙	祚	德	階	油	燭	[13]油	心	斗	錢	名
[2]胙	[4]分	[7]天	[7]踐	[9]蠟	燭	[12]硬	燭	[15]香	[17]借	[19]借	[21]借
土	胙	祚	祚	燭	[11]菜	油	店	燭	貸	去	宿

chioh, *chioh*, *ˏchiong wang*² all alike, all just so.

嚼² Chio. Read *chiok*,; coll. *chioh*,: to eat, to chew, to masticate, to ruminate: ¹*chioh*, *ˏping ˏlong*, to chew beetle-nut; ²*chioh*, *'la e*² to chew and get the taste of; ³*chioh*, *lang*² to masticate; ⁴*'kong wa*² *chioh*, *chioh*, to speak cautiously.

(55) Chiok.

爵, Chiao. A cyanthus with three legs; a cup for libations; a metallic wine-cup; a bamboo wine-bottle; a degree of nobility, rank or station: used for *ch'iok*, small birds: ⁵*liék*, *chiok*, to discriminate ranks; COM., ⁶*ˏkwang chiok*, a degree of rank or nobility; ⁷*chiok*, *lük*, rank and income; ⁸*séü*' *chiok*, to bestow a title; ⁹*chiok*, *'chio*, titled lord, my noble lord! also applied to the *ˏsiăng ˏhwong* idol; ¹⁰*ˏping chiok*, decanter and goblets.

嚼, Chio. To eat, to chew, to bite, to craunch, to ruminate, to mumble, to masticate; a mouthful, a bite: ¹¹*ˏchu chiok*, to chew.

酌, Chao. To pour out wine, to fill a cup; a glass, *met.* wine, liquor; a dinner, a feast; to avail of, to choose the good and act upon it; to consult, to deliberate; to imitate, to adopt: ¹²*'sieu chiok*, to drink wine moderately; COM., ¹³*tói*' *chiok*, to drink together; ¹⁴*ˏching chiok*, to consider, to weigh; ¹⁵*chiok*, *liong*² or *chiok*, *ˏchoi*, to consider and decide; COLL., ¹⁶*chiok*, *tiăng*² to consider and settle; *'chiă tai*² *kié*' *'mwong chai*' *ˏching chiok*, *sioh*, *a*² consider the matter once more.

爝, Cho. A flambeau, a torch, a link; a lighted match burned at night; an arrangement for keeping a light during the night.

皭, Chio. A white color, pure, unsullied, clean; nice, clean-looking.

棁, A joist to support a plate or girder; a sort of king post.

著² **着**² Cho. To put on, as clothes; to cover over; to cause, to order, to commission one; after verbs it indicates effect or completion of the action; to stick to; to be, to be at, on, or in: in the coll. read *tioh*, q. v.: ¹⁷*ho*² *chiok*, joined to; ¹⁸*'na chiok*, seized; ¹⁹*'iu chiok*, true, real; attained; *ˏu chiok*, unreal, unattainable; *chiok*, *miéng*² sticks to the face; COM., ²⁰*chiok*, *kek*, urgent, hurried; ²¹*chiok*, *ˏmong*, distracted; *chiok*, *sik*, truly, really; *chiok*, *lok*, clear, certain, as a clue or trace of; ²²*chiok*, *e*² a fixed purpose or desire; *chiok*, *lik*, to exert one's self; COLL. *chiok*, *ˏi ˏsing siong*² to entrust to one; *chiok*, *'nü k'ó*' *paing*² I give you entire control of it.

絕² Chüeh. Interchangeably read *chwok*,: to interrupt a connection with, to cut off a thread; to interrupt, to

¹嚼梹榔 ²嚼喇味 ³嚼爛 ⁴講話嚼嚼 ⁵列爵 ⁶官爵 ⁷爵祿 ⁸賜爵 ⁹爵主 ¹⁰瓶爵 ¹¹咀嚼 ¹²小酌 ¹³對酌 ¹⁴斟酌 ¹⁵酌量 ¹⁶酌定 ¹⁷附著 ¹⁸拿著 ¹⁹有著 ²⁰著急 ²¹着忙 ²²着意

sunder, to break off, to terminate; to exterminate, to destroy utterly; to renounce, to abjure; to cross water, to overpass; shooting athwart, as meteors; a superlative, very, extremely, entirely, most; a stanza of four lines: COM., [1]*chiok, sëü'* posterity cut off; *chiok, 'chüng*, no seeds or germs—leaves no heirs; *chiok, 'ting*, the very top—as of a peak; [2]*chiok, kwo'* an inimitable sentence or stanza; [3]*ch'ek, chiok,* a stanza in sevens—heptameter verse; *chiok, saik,* very beautiful; [4]*pai' chiok,* utterly ruined; [5]*chiok, wong'* hopeless; [6]*chiok, ˏkau*, to break off friendship; [7]*chiok, mieu'* surpassingly excellent; [8]*chiok, ˏching*, no feeling, ungrateful: COLL., [9]*chiok, tio'* no road—resources all cut off; [10]*chiok, saung'* very exacting; *chiok, 'chio* a close-fisted fellow.

(56) Chiong.

章 ˏ Chang. A chapter, a section; a composition, an essay; a statement; rules, laws, regulations; a piece of music; clear, distinct, beautiful, manifest; a display; a grove; a metonic cycle: COM., [11]*ˏchiong 'chi*, the purport of a chapter or section; *yok, hwak, ˏsang ˏchiong*, "three contracts" of the emperor *ˏKö 'Chu* of the Han dynasty;—in the coll. a bargain, an agreement; [12]*ˏchiong ˏt'iäng*, regulations; a settled plan or mode; [13]*ˏtu ˏchiong*, a seal, a stamp; [14]*ˏchiong chiek,* chapter and verse; [15]*ˏung ˏchiong*, a literary composition, an essay; *ˏchiong kwo'* the sentences of a chapter or paragraph.

璋 ˏ Chang. An ornament or plaything, made of jade stone: [16]*ˏkie ˏchiong*, two kinds of stone ornaments borne at levees and sacrifices; [17]*liong' ˏchiong*, to bear a son.

彰 ˏ Chang. Luminous, beautiful, elegant; variegated; manifest; handsome plumage: [18]*ˏchiong ˏming*, or *ˏchieu ˏchiong*, illustrious; clearly stated; [19]*ˏchiong siéng'* to render illustrious the good—as by promotion; COM., [20]*ˏchiong hwa'* a district in the Taiwan prefecture, Formosa.

漳 ˏ Chang. Name of a river; a prefecture in Fookieu, near Amoy: COM., [21]*ˏchiong ˏchiu 'hu*, the Changchau prefecture; [22]*ˏchiong 'p'wo kaing'* a district in above prefecture; *ˏchiong ˏping*, rock-candy; also called in coll. *ˏt'ong ˏt'ong*; [23]*ˏchiong ˏüng*, a kind of velvet from Changchau.

將 ˏ Chiang. To take, to hold in the hand; sign of the future, shall, will, about to do; sign of the ablative, by, with; then, soon, presently; to help, to support, to nourish, to take care of, to accommodate; to use, to avail of; to go with, to escort, to accompany; to imitate; strong, stout; long, large; to receive and act upon, as orders; imbued with; to act, to advance, to increase, to make progress, to approach, to go towards a mark; to follow;

---

1 絶嗣 2 絶句 3 七絶 4 敗絶 5 絶望 6 絶交 7 絶妙 8 絶情 9 絶路 10 絶[illegible] 11 章旨 12 章程 13 圖章 14 章節 15 文章 16 圭璋 17 弄璋 18 彰明 19 彰善 20 彰化 21 漳州府 22 漳浦縣 23 漳絨

going, passing, as time; to conceal one's purpose: used in the coll. as *k'ek*, to mark the accusative or object of a succeeding verb; also in sense of near, nearly, about, like; how, in what way? why? wherefore? Also read *chiong'* q. v.: COM., [1]*,chiong ,lai*, hereafter; *,chiong ,hó 'i 'ch'ü*, how shall we manage it? [2]*,chiong ,kung sŭk, chói'* to atone for sin by merit; [3]*,chiong ,kung*, a general—applied to Tartar General of the city; COLL., *,chiong pwoh, 'hó*, nearly well, almost finished: *'mwong ,chiong chew' ,chiă k'ó'* just let it go at that! [4]*,chiong ch'ü'* about, nearly; [5]*,chiong wang'* thus, so; [6]*,chiong yong'* how? in what manner? [7]*,chiong ,ki*, or *,chiong yong' ,ki*, why? wherefore? [8]*,tang ,chiong chó' ,ni*, now how shall we manage it? [9]*,chiong kĕüng'* near, close at hand; *,chiong 'chiă nóh, ,tó k'ó'* take away this thing; [10]*,chiong ,sing 'pi ,sing*, to judge others by yourself; *,chiong ,kung pok, ha' 'ma*, "the general don't dismount"—a lock of which the key remains fast till the lock is shut; [11]*,chiong ch'ek, ,chiong paik*, "about 7 or 8"—nearly, as nearly spoiled, almost dead, &c.; [12]*,chiong ch'auk, chew' ch'auk*, it's wrong and let it go on so! *,chiong ,i ,t'u so' ,i huk*, "made his Budh with his clay"—equivalent of presents returned; bride dressed at expense of bridegroom, etc.

漿 ,Chiang. Pasty, half-fluid, thick; syrup, juice; pus or matter; broth boiled down thick; sometimes used for the next: COM., [13]*,chiong chaik*, the thin part of rice-starch; [14]*'chiu ,chiong*, wine, liquor; *tau' ho' ,chiong*, bean-curd whey; COLL., [15]*,t'u ,chiong*, mud, mire, slosh; *,t'au 'nó ,chiong*, the brains.

⿱將米 ,Chiang. An unauthorized character: starch, to starch; paste: COLL., [16]*,ku ,chiong*, flour-paste; *'mi ,chiong*, rice ground wet, rice-starch; *'sá ,chiong*, to wash and starch; *,chiong ,i ,siong*, to starch clothes; *,chiong ,cha*, the refuse of rice-starch; *mó' ,chiong*, to grind rice for starch; [17]*,ch'ang ,chiong*, common starch; *,chiong tói'* a starch-bag.

慞 ,Chang. Alarmed; apprehensive: *,chiong ,hwong*, terrified, a frightened look.

樟 ,Chang. The camphor (laurus camphora): *,chiong muk*, camphor-wood; COM., *,chiong 'nó*, gum-camphor; *,chiong ,ch'a*, camphor-wood.

鄣 ,Chang. A feudal state, now part of Tai-ngan-fu in Shantung; an ancient city in Kü, also in the modern Shantung.

螿 ,Chiang. A species of small cicada, or grasshopper, whose elytra are green.

麞 獐 ,Chang. A kind of chevrotain or gazelle, hornless and of elegant shape, and is said to appear when there is a good emperor on the throne: *,chiong hŭk*, ga-

[1]將來 贖罪 [4]將次 [6]將樣 [8]伶將 [9]將近 比心 將八 就錯 [14]酒漿 [16]糊⿱將米 [17]生⿱將米

[2]將功 [3]將軍 [5]將換 [7]將其 做呢 [10]將心 [11]將七 [12]將錯 [13]漿汁 [15]土漿 ○ ○

zelle and deer; [1]‚ngüng ‚chiong, a white gazelle.

嫜 Chang. A husband's parents, called ‚ku ‚chiong: [2]‚hing ‚chiong, a husband's brothers.

‚*Chiong*. A coll. word: to peep, to look at slyly: ‚t'au ‚chiong, to peep at slyly; ‚chiong ‚mwong p'ong' to peep through a door-crack; ‚chiong ‚nëng, to peer at people.

(The next four characters interchangeably read *chwong*.)

專 耑 Chuan. One, single, alone, undivided; bent on, to turn to one thing; to take upon one, to presume, to assume; selfwilled: [3]‚chiong ‘ch‘ü, only this; [4]‚chiong ek, to apply (the mind) to one thing; [5]pok, ‘kang ‚chiong, modest; [6]‚chiong ‚mwong, the single matter, the sole business; COM., [7]‚chiong ‚sing, or ‚chiong e' a single mind or purpose; [8]‚chiong ‚sing te' che' to have a fixed resolve; [9]chëü' ‚chiong, assuming, pertinacious; [10]‚chiong ‚kwong, or ‚chiong cheng' to have entire control; ‚t'iéng ha' ‚u ‚nang sëü' ‘chi p‘á' ‚sing pok, ‚chiong, nothing is difficult to the determined mind.

鷒 Chuan. Also read ‚t'wang: a bird: [11]‘kwang' ‚chiong, a bird, one says a species of jay.

鱄 Chuan. Also read ‚t'wang: a large fish, a pike? found in the lake Tungting.

磚 甎 Chuan. A brick, a tile; to cover with brick: COM., [12]‚chiong ngwa' bricks and tiles; [13]‚king ‚chiong, golden bricks—indicating wealth; [14]‚chiong ‚ch‘iong, a brick wall; [15]‚sieu ‚chiong, to burn bricks in the kiln; [16]‚p‘wo ‚chiong, to lay brick floors or pavement; [17]‚chiong ngiéng' a coarse ink-stone; [18]‚chiong ‚pwong, a large earthen vessel; COLL., ‚ëng ‚chiong, red bricks; ‘lié ‚chiong, to lay bricks; ‘tau ‘tá ‚chiong, a flat brick used for floors; ‚chiong ‚t'au, broken bricks.

掌 Chiang. The palm of the hand; the paw or sole of animals; a webbed foot; to grasp; to control, to rule; a control, a jurisdiction: COM., ‘ch‘iu ‘chiong (in coll. ‚pa ‘chiong), the palm of the hand; ‘chiong ‚sing yék, hot palm, as of a sick child; hak, ‘chiong, to clasp the hands, as in prayer; [19]‘chiong kau' to teach authoritatively, as college professors; [20]‘chiong ‘kwang, to control; [21]‘chiong so' or ‘chiong koi' to keep accounts; a clerk, a book-keeper; [22]‚siéng ‚ing ‘chiong, the genii-palm—a plant; ‘chiong siong' ‚ming ‚chio, a gem on the palm—i. e. precious, cherished; ‘chiong siéng' a large fan carried in processions; ‘chiong ‘ku, the drummer (in plays); ‘chiong ‚pwang, manager of a theatrical company; COLL., ‚ëng ‘chiong, a rosy palm—a lucky sign in palmistry; p‘ah, ‘ch‘iu ‘chiong, to strike the palms, to ferule one; ‘chiong ch‘oi' ‘p.i

[1]銀獐 [2]兄嫜 [3]專此 [4]專一 [5]不敢專 [6]專門 [7]專心 [8]專心致志 [9]自專 [10]專權 [11]鸛鷒 [12]磚瓦 [13]金磚 [14]磚墻 [15]燒磚 [16]鋪磚 [17]磚硯 [18]磚盆 [19]掌教 [20]掌管 [21]掌數 [22]仙人掌

(or ‘*p‘á*), to slap the cheek.

‘獎 Chiang. To exhort, to animate, to excite, to incite, to encourage; to laud, to praise, to commend; to vindicate, to give efficiency to; to set on, as dogs: [1]‘*chiong lá*² to stimulate one to effort; [2]‘*chiong siéng*² *hwak*, *auk*, to reward the good and punish the bad; [3]*‚pó* ‘*chiong*, to praise, to commend; COLL., [4]‘*chiong chong*’ excellent, perfectly upright.

‘蔣 Chiang. A surname; a place; sometimes used in coll. for this, thus: *‚ku* ‘*chiong*, a kind of aquatic grain; COLL., ‘*chiong* ‘*k‘wang*, or ‘*chiong* ‘*wang*, thus, in this manner.

‘槳 ‘桨 Chiang. An oar: *‚sĕng* ‘*chiong*, a pair of oars; COM., [5]‘*t‘aung*’ ‘*chiong*, to row; COLL., ‘*chiong sioh*, ‘*pa*, one oar.

‘鞝 Chiang. A kind of leather; to sew leather; to mend, as shoes: COM., [6]‘*chiong ‚á*, to mend shoes; COLL., ‘*chiong ‚p‘ui*, to patch with leather; [7]‘*chiong ‚á ‚sa ho*² a cobbler; ‘*chiong ‚á tang*’ a traveling cobbler's load.

醬’ Chiang. A sauce, pickle, brine, or condiment, made of salt and sugar, used in cooking; relishes, seasonings, like oilmen's stores; salted preparations: COM., [8]*‚tiéng chiong*’ sweet condiments; [9]*chiong*’ *‚hwong*, or *chiong*’ *‚hwong taing*’ a shop where condiments are sold; [10]*chiong*’ *e*² sauces, condiments; [11]*nük*, *chiong*’ pickled mince-meat; COLL., *tau*² *chiong*’ a bean-relish; *chiong*’ *wok*, preserved gourds; *chiong*’ ‘*king* ‘*king*, “pickled down close,” *met.*, plastered, daubed.

將’ Chiang. To take charge of troops, to lead troops into the field; to act as a general; a general, a leader: also read *‚chiong*, q. v.: COM., [12]*chiong*’ *‚kung*, a general; the Tartar General; [13]‘*u chiong*’ or [14]*chiong*’ *‚kwang*, military officers; *ho*’ *chiong*’ a lieutenant-general; [15]*chiong*’ *sói*’ general-in-chief; [16]*chiong*’ *‚tai*, a military observatory; [17]‘*ló chiong*’ a soldier; *‚ch‘ang chiong*’ a colonel or major; [18]*chiong*’ *‚ping*, to handle troops; [19]*ch‘ok*, *chiong*’ to go out to war, as a leader.

障’ Chang. To screen, to shade; to separate, to divide; to shut up, to include; to raise an embankment; a barricade, a trench, a fence; a screen, as of cloth; a dike; a terminus; an intervening distance: *‚chiă chiong*’ to shade, to cover over; [20]‘*pó chiong*’ to protect; a barrier; *chiong*’ *pié*² to obstruct the way.

瘴’ Chang. Malaria, pestilential vapors, pestiferous air: [21]*chiong*’ *lá*² an epidemic, a plague; COM., [22]*chiong*’ *k‘e*’ malaria; COLL., *pwok*, (or *pok*,) *chiong*’ a pestilence or distemper among animals—used as a curse; *pwok*, *chiong*’ *‚tü*, a hog dead from the distemper.

1獎勵	罰惡	4獎竣	6鞝鞋	司父	9醬園	11肉醬	18武將	15將帥	17老將	19出將	91瘴癘
2獎善	8褒獎	5盪槳	7鞝鞋	8甜醬	10醬味	12將軍	14將官	16將臺	18將兵	20保障	22瘴氣

瞕 Chang. A cataract growing over the eye: [1]'*chiong*' *ié*' a cataract.

(The next two characters interchangeably read *chwong*.)

全 Ch'uan. Complete, entire, unbroken, perfect; all, the whole; entirely; to complete, to finish, to perfect; to do all that is required: COM., [2]*chiong pe*' fully prepared; complete, as in virtues or graces; [3]*chiong* '*sü* *chiong* *chüng*, complete from beginning to end; [4]*chiong* *sing*, the whole heart; [5]*chiong* *neng*, almighty, plenipotentiary; [6]*sung* *chiong*, pure and entire; uniform, as a color; [7]*chiong* *ka*, all the family; [8]*sek*, *chiong*, perfect, faultless; [9]'*pó* *chiong*, to insure, to guarantee; '*liong* *chiong*, both complete; [10]*chiong* *chiä*' to trust wholly; [11]*sëü*' *chiong* *si*, "grants him an unmutilated corpse," *scil.* by suicide, to avoid being beheaded; [12]*chiong* *pwo*' a complete set, as of books; whole coffin-boards; [13]*chiong* *t'au*' extending the entire length; through and through, as water-soaked; *chiong* *t'aik*, a large folded card; COLL., *chiong* *paik*, *chiong* *kiäng*, he that knows all fears all; *chiong* *tói*' of a whole piece.

泉 **洤** Ch'uan. A fountain, a spring; the headwaters of streams; a department in Fookien: *yong* *chiong*, a deep fountain; [14]'*k'á* *chiong*, source of a stream; [15]*chiong* *pwo*' money—because it circulates; [16]'*kiu* *chiong*, Hades; COM., *chiong* '*chwi*, spring-water; [17]*chiong* *chiu* '*hu*, the Chinchew prefecture.

(57) Chiu.

周 Chou. Universal, complete, entire; to supply, to provide, to assist; plenty, enough, sufficient; to make a circuit, to surround, to environ; a famous dynasty of China, B. C. 1122–255; secret, subtle, fine; close together; a curve, a bend; to extend everywhere; honest, trustworthy; to the end, entirely: *chiu p'iéng*' all around, everywhere; COM., [18]*chiu* *chiong*, entire, complete; *chiu* *mik*, well done, as work; faultless, as politeness; *chiu* *chak*, all around, environing; [19]*chiu* *siong*, very minute, as in planning details; *chiu* *ui*, to surround; [20]*chiu* *tieu*, the Chow dynasty; *chiu* *chá*' to give alms; *tai*' *ing pok*, *chiu*, to treat a person indifferently; [21]*chiu* '*lé*, Rites of the Chow; *chiu* *kung*, the Duke of Chow, a son of Wan-wang, and brother of Wu-wang, who founded the Chow dynasty.

週 Chou. Interchanged with the last: to revolve, to circulate; to inform people; a year: [22]*chiu p'iéng*' everywhere; *chiu* *swoi*' a year, a birth-day anniversary; COM., *chiu* *chiong*, all complete; *chiu* *niéng*, the revolving year; anniversary of a death; *sieu* *chiu* *niéng*, to enact sacrificial rites.

[1]瞕翳 [2]全備 [3]全始全終 [4]全心 [5]全能 [6]純全 [7]全家 [8]十全 [9]保全 [10]全藉 [11]賜全屍 [12]全部 [13]全透 [14]溪泉 [15]泉布 [16]九泉 [17]泉州府 [18]周全 [19]周詳 [20]周朝 [21]周禮 [22]週遍

州 ˏChou. A district or department, less than a prefecture; a continent, a great division of the earth: [1]ˏchiu kong² the chiu district and the prefecture; COM., [2]ˏchiu p'wang² the magistrate of a chiu; [3]hok, ˏchiu, Foochow—the capital of Fookien; [4]ˏlüng ˏngang ˏchiu, department of Lungngan in S. W. part of Fookien; [5]ʻing ˏch'ung ˏchiu, department of Yungchun in southern part of Fookien; [6]ʻkiu ˏchiu wung² kwok, the nine continents, the world.

洲 ˏChou. A spot encircled by streams, as an island; alluvial tracts along margins of rivers; a place where men collect, a village: [7]ˏing ˏchiu, the island of the Genii; COM., [8]ˏchiu ˏpiéng, "the side of the island"—the "five points" of Foochow; COLL., [9]ˏtong ˏchiu, island of Chungchau between the bridges at Foochow; [10]ˏchiu ˏt'au, head of the island; [11]ˏchiu ˏch'eng, alluvial fields, made land.

舟 ˏChou. A boat, a junk, a ship, a vessel, a craft of any kind; to go in a boat; to transport, to carry in a vessel; a stand or holder for a cup; the 137th radical: [12]ˏchiu chiék, the propelling implements of a boat; COM., [13]ˏlüng ˏchiu, a dragon-boat, in coll. usually called ˏliong ˏsung.

侜 ˏChou. To cover over; to conceal, to hide, to shade; something stretched for a shade; to deceive.

稠 ˏChou. Grain growing thickly; thickly set, close together; crowded, dense: [14]ˏing ˏkü ˏchiu mik, dwellings crowded together; [15]sëü² muk, ˏchiu mik, a dense forest.

啁 ˏChou. Chirping or bickering of birds; to chirp, to bicker: [16]ˏchiu ˏchieu, the chirping of birds.

輈 ˏChou. A frame in front of a carriage, near which the driver sits; a kind of dashboard: [17]ˏliong ˏchiu, the beam or dashboard in front of a carriage.

輖 ˏChou. A heavily laden cart which is low in front; a heavy load; heavy.

賙 ˏChou. To bestow charity: [18]ˏsiong ˏchiu, to give alms; COM., ˏchiu chá² to relieve the indigent.

酒 ʻChiu. Spirits, liquor; distilled liquor, made from rice, samshoo; *met.* a feast, an entertainment; also used to designate beer, wine, and other liquors; to develope, as wine does the disposition: [19]chauk, ʻchiu, or yong² ʻchiu, to distil liquor; ˏt'iéng ʻchiu, dew; COM., ˏkau ˏpwoi ʻchiu, wine drunk by the bride and groom at the marriage ceremony; ʻchiu liong² capacity for drinking liquor; ʻchiu p'ek, one's disposition shown in his cups; ʻchiu ˏing, or ʻchiu aëng² earthen wine-jars; [20]ˏt'ang ʻchiu, or sié² ʻchiu, fond of liquor;

[1]州	[3]福	州	[6]九	[7]瀛	[9]中	[11]州	[13]龍	稠	稠	[17]樑	[19]作
郡	州	[5]永	州	洲	洲	田	舟	密	密	輈	酒
[2]州	[4]龍	春	萬	[8]洲	[10]洲	[12]舟	[14]人	[15]樹	[16]啁	[18]相	[20]貪
判	巖	州	國	邊	頭	楫	居	木	噍	賙	酒

[1]ʻlóʻchiu, old wine; [2]ʻchiu sik, a feast; [3]ʻchiu ʻiu, a boon companion; [4]ˏsieu ʻchiu, samshoo, whisky; [5]ʻchiu ˏping, or ʻchiu ˏhu, a wine-bottle; ʻchiu ʻchung, a small wine-cup; [6]ˏung ʻchiu, to brew liquor; [7]ʻchiu kʻoʼ a distillery; [8]ʻchiu ˏchiéng, or ʻchiu ˏchü, a fee, a douceur; [9]ʻchiu ˏtu, or ʻchiu ʻkwi, winebibbers, tipplers; COLL., sak, ʻchiu ˏhung, ravings of a drunkard; tioh ʻchiu ˏsa, to have a fit from intoxication; ʻchiu ʻing ʻkʻi, "commence drinking"—as at feasts; [10]siăh ʻchiu choiʼ drunk; ʻchiu wongʼ a wine-stain; ʻchiu kŏăk, a liquor-syphon; ʻchiu liăngʼ a forfeit to drink; paingʼ ʻchiu, to make a feast; ʻchiu ˏting, a large jar for carrying liquor; ʻchiu ˏtëng, tubes in wine-heaters.

ʻ*Chiu.* A coll. word, used for ʻsiu, to keep, to maintain: ʻchiu ʻkwa, or ʻchiu ʻkwa ˏchü ˏniong ˏnëng, one who maintains widowhood, a widow-woman: ʻchiu ˏsang ʻkwa, one whose husband is absent.

(58) Cho.

詛ʼ 呪ʼ Tsu. To curse, to imprecate; bad language, curses, imprecations: [11]choʼ cheuʼ to imprecate; COM., [12]choʼ maʼ to curse, to rail at; COLL., [13]choʼ chʻoiʼ to swear, to take oath; laungʼ choʼ to swear recklessly, to rave; [14]choʼ chengʼ chʻoiʼ to take a deep oath; choʼ chʻoiʼ ˏmó miăngʼ to swear away life—"may (I) die if it's not so"; choʼ ˏnëng ˏmó ʻkʻi ʻkó, to swear at people without rule—i. e., recklessly; choʼ ˏi chʻa ˏtʻau máʼ pwok, ʻyong, curse him as a block that can never sprout!

助ʼ Chu. To assist, to help, to aid, to strengthen; beneficial; to succor, to support: in the coll. read chaëʼ q. v.: [15]ˏpong choʼ to aid; COM., [16]hoʼ choʼ to succor; [17]choʼ ʻtang, to encourage, to embolden; [18]lok choʼ to help cheerfully; choʼ ek, piéʼ ˏchi lik, to lend a helping hand.

(59) Chó.

遭 Tsao. To encounter, to meet, to fall in with; to suffer, to endure; to occur, to happen; to cruise, to go about; to make a revolution; a season, a time, an occasion: [19]ˏchó ngëüʼ or ˏchó ˏhung, to meet, to happen; [20]ˏchó ʻpiéng, to degrade; COM., [21]ˏchó nangʼ to meet trials; [22]ˏchó ˏchai, or ˏchó ˏyong, to fall into calamity; COLL., ˏchó ˏi ʻchʻiu, fell into his hand—was injured by him; ˏchó hwaʼ a mere chance, fortunately.

ˏ*Chó.* A coll. word, as in ˏchó ˏngwong, senior wrangler at the Hanlin examinations; ˏchó ˏngwong ˏtié, a large pond outside the west gate of Foochow.

ʻ左 Tso. The left, the left hand; second, an assistant; to witness to, to prove, as a coadjutor; deflected, bad, depraved; to degrade, to reduce in rank; a surname: COM., [23]ʻchó ʻchʻiu, the left hand; chaiʼ ʻchó, on the left side; ʻchó ˏpiéng (coll. ʻchó ˏpeng), the left side; ˏsiong ʻchó, a mutual mistake; a

1 老	3 酒	5 酒	7 酒	9 酒	醉	罵	盡	16 護	18 樂	20 遭	22 遭
酒	友	瓶	庫	徒	11 詛	13 詛	嘴	助	助	貶	災
2 酒	4 燒	6 熅	8 酒	10 食	咒	嘴	15 幫	17 助	19 遭	21 遭	23 左
席	酒	酒	錢	酒	12 詛	14 詛	助	胆	遇	難	手

disagreement; to miss each other; [1]*chó tó'* a wrong road; false principles; [2]*chó ˏtong*, the chief of the two *óh*ˎ *ˏkwang* of a district; *'chó oe' ˏpung*, chambers on the left and right of the hall; COLL., [3]*'chó chak*ˎ petty officers.

早 *'Tsao.* The morning; early, soon; betimes, beforehand, previously; just commenced; then, presently: in the coll. read *'cha*, q. v.: [4]*'chó ˏsing*, the morning; [5]*'chó 'wang*, or *'chó mwo'* morning and evening; [6]*'chó bwang'* breakfast; [7]*'kik*ˎ *'chó*, early, forthwith; [8]*'chó swoi'* youth, the period of adolescence.

蚤 *'Tsao.* Used for the preceding: a flea; a sand-flea, or those produced in the sand; spokes entering the tire; in the coll. read *'chau*, q. v.

棗 朿 *'Tsao.* The fruit of the Canarium, or jujube tree; dates; the second character is the abbreviated form: COM., [9]*'kong' 'chó*, pressed dates without kernels; [10]*mik*ˎ *'chó*, sweet dates; [11]*ˏsong 'chó*, a kind of acid jujube plum; *'chó ˏkó*, sugared date-cakes; [12]*pah*ˎ *'chó*, the white date; COLL., [13]*'chó ˏt'au*, large dried dates; *'chó ˏná 'piăng*, cakes with date-stuffing.

'Chó. A coll. word, as in *'chó sioh*ˎ *'chó*, to rap with the knuckles; *ˏt'au k'á' ˏi 'chó sioh*ˎ *a'* give him a rap on the head with your knuckles.

做 *Tso'.* To do, to act, to perform the duties of; to build, to construct, to make, to create; to begin, to commence; to be, to become; used as the coll. of *chauk*ˎ and *ˏwi*: COLL., [14]*chó' che'* to write an agreement; *chó' uĕng'* to make a bustle; [15]*chó' tai'* or *chó' tai' kié'* or *chó' sĕü'* to work, to do business; *chó' ch'woi'* bold, bragging; [16]*chó' ˏhung*, a wind rising; fits, spasms; *chó' ˏkwang*, to be an officer; *chó' 'k'wang*, or *chó' ˏk'wang 'k'wang*, to "take on"—to scream and resist, as an unruly child; [17]*chó' má'* made for sale, as slop-goods; *chó' ˏch'a*, "to be a stick"—i. e., inflexible; *chó' ˏsang*, to cultivate mountain-land; *chó' 'ngang*, "to be eyes"—i. e., to oversee; *chó' yéng'* tired of doing; [18]*chó' ˏt'u*, a mason; [19]*chó' tói'* to make couplets; to contend with; *chó' 'pa hié'* to play at theatricals, as children do; to trifle, to pretend; [20]*chó' kwoh*ˎ to trick, to bait for; *chó' chá'* "to be dough"—a butt for imposition; [21]*chiăh, chó'* or *chiăh, chiăh, chó'* have just done it; *chó' sek*ˎ "celebrate the tens"—i. e., every *tenth* anniversay of one's birth; [22]*chó' 'chwi*, to soak in water, as rice to increase the quantity; to play in water, as a child; *chó' tau' ˏseng ˏhung*, the cold preceding the small-pox; *met.*, a fierce attitude; [23]*chó' hwoi'* to keep New Year's eve; [24]*tiăng' chó'* to contract for; *puk, miăng' chó'* to moil, to slave; *ng' ch'iong' chó'* not act like doing it; unwilling to do;

[1]左道 [2]左堂 [3]左雜 [4]早晨 [5]早晚 [6]早飯 [7]極早 [8]早歲 [9]貢棗 [10]蜜棗 [11]酸棗 [12]白棗 [13]棗頭 [14]做字 [15]做代 [16]做風 [17]做賣 [18]做土 [19]做對 [20]做局 [21]隻做 [22]做水 [23]做歲 [24]定做

'ch'ek, chó' paik, chó' to do helter-skelter.

佐' Tso. To assist, to help, to aid; a second, an assistant; a deputy, a substitute: [2]'ho' chó' to aid; [3]'i chó' ,t'iêng 'chü, to aid the emperor, as an officer does; COM., [4]'chó' 'liǎng, a major-general of Manchus or Monguls.

竈' Tsao. A furnace, a place for cooking; a kitchen range: in the coll. read chau' q. v.: [5]maing' ha' sëü' chó' offerings made to the kitchen deities in the 4th moon.

,曺 ,曹 Tsao. A sort of revising judge, a judge of appeals; a place where officers meet; a company, a class; denotes the plural of persons; a surname: [6]'i ,chó, you, your class; [7]',i ,chó, a group of children; COM., [8]lĕk, ,chó, the six Boards; [9],chó ch'ŏ' a famous general, A. D. 250; [10],t'iêng ,chó, heaven, the court of heaven; [11],kung ,chó, spirits, messengers.

,嘈 Tsao. Noise, clamor, hubbub; an outcry; to make a din, to vociferate: ,chó chak, to vociferate; the din of a crowd; COLL., [12]ló ,chó, a clamor; ,chó ,chó kieu' a hubbub.

,艚 Tsao. A small junk, a smack; a boat, a pinnace; pek, ,chó ,sung, a Canton sea-going junk.

,螬 Tsao. Maggots in ordure: ,chá ,chó, grubs found in filth.

,槽 Tsao. A trough, a log channelled out as a trough, a manger; a vat, a tub for liquor; a flexible wood; a sort of fruit; in the coll. read ,só, q. v.: [13]'ma ,chó, a horse-trough; [14]'chiu ,chó, a wine vat, a distillery.

,漕 Tsao. A mill-race, a sluice; a gulf, a gorge; a canal; to lead on, as water, to turn a water-course; to convey revenue to Peking: ,chó ong' to transport grain (to Peking); ,chó ,ó, the Grand Canal; COM., ,chó 'mi, or ,chó ,liong, grain-revenue of the Grand Canal; ,chó tok, the Superintendent of the Grand Canal.

,䐬 Tsao. Delicate, brittle; a rumbling in the stomach: used for the coll. as in ,chó ,t'au, the part above the thigh in a quarter of pork.

,Chó. A coll. word, as in ,chó chaĕk, a sense of emptiness in the stomach, as from eating bamboo-shoots, &c.

坐² Tso. To sit; to sit on the heels; sitting, remaining; a session; a seat, a place; to maintain, to hold; involved in, implicated; to sit in judgment on, to judge; to place, to set down; to kneel: used in coll. to buy up, as goods; to make up a loss; also in the coll. read sói² q. v.: [15]chó² ,tong, in court, occupying the magistrate's bench; [16]'hwang chó² returning on one's self, as a crime; [17]chó² ngwo² pok, ,ang, no rest sitting or sleeping; COM., chó² ,sang, or chó² ho² to live on an-

1 七做八做
2 護佐
3 以佐天子
4 佐領
5 孟夏祀竈
6 爾曹
7 兒曹
8 六曹
9 曹操
10 天曹
11 功曹
12 囉嘈
13 馬槽
14 酒槽 ○
15 坐堂 ○
16 反坐 ○
17 坐臥不安

other; to monopolize in trade; [1]'*chó[2] ,nang ,tieu paĕk*, back towards the south and front towards the north, as a house; [2]*chó[2] teng'* to continue in a place on guard, or at work; [3]*chó[2] chói[2]* involved in crime; COLL., *chó[2] 'peng*, itch on the buttocks; *chó[2] cheu'* to aid one in completing; *chó[2] k'ó'* to make up a loss—take it off your hands; *chó[2] hwo'* to lay in a stock of goods; *chó[2] chai'* burdened with debt; *chó[2] sióh, ,sang ,pung*, to sit idly and eat up your inheritance.

座[2] Tsó. A seat, a throne; a shrine, a pedestal; a classifier for temples, churches, towers, pagodas, hills, cities, moveable pavilions, &c.: [4]'*tá' chó[2]* the imperial star; [5]*'sā' chó[2]* four seats, as for a social party; COM., [6]*chó[2] oi[2]* a seat, a throne; [7]*paik, chó[2]* eight chairbearers; [8]*,kung chó[2] 'ié*, an armchair; '*wang chó[2]* the bottom of a bowl; [9]*,hiong ,lu chó[2]* the pedestal of an incense-vase; COLL., *sá' chó[2] kieu[2]* a sedan with four bearers; [10]*sioh, chó[2] ,siàng*, a walled city; [11]*siong[2] chó[2]* rites to the *o[2] kai[2]* in which the priests occupy high seats; '*chio chó[2]* the head priest in the ceremony.

皁[2] 皂[2] Tsao. A black color; underlings, lictors; low officers who execute commands; a stud of twelve horses; a manger or pen for horses; a tree whose seeds dye a dark color; grain not yet hardened: used for '*chó*, early: [12]*chó[2] pek,* black and white; COM., [13]*chó[2] lí[2]* or *chó[2] ,pwang*, lictors, policemen; *chó[2] ,hwang*, copperas; COLL., [14]*,i chó[2]* soap.

造[2] Tsao. To build, to erect; to make, to construct; to create, to begin, to commence; to act, to do; to record; also read *ch'ó'* q. v.: [15]*'sü chó[2]* to begin; [16]*,kiéng chó[2]* a horoscope for a male; *,k'ong chó[2]* horoscope for a female; COM., [17]*chó[2] ch'ah*, to record officially; [18]*ch'aung' chó[2]* to create; [19]*chó[2] chauk*, to fabricate; to repair, to patch up, as for sale; [20]*chó[2] hwa'* to form, to create.

(60) Chóh.

倅, Tsao. Read *chok,*; coll. *chóh*, persons employed to bury the neglected dead, and to act as coroners: [21]*'ngu chóh*, name commonly given to this class of persons; *a[2] chóh*, grasping, mean; *,wong chóh*, to bear false testimony.

Chóh,. A coll. word: to fill up, as holes and leaks; to stop, as an accuser by bribery; *chóh, kak,* to plug up tightly.

Chóh,. A coll. word, as in *chóh, ,ch'eng*, to farm on shares; *chóh, 'kwói 'chi ch'eu'* to rent fruit trees—to bargain beforehand for the fruit.

Chóh,. A coll. word: to throw down or away; to cast off; to throw aside as worthless: *chóh, lóh,* or *chóh, a[2]* to cast down; *chóh, tai[2]* to throw away; *chóh, te[2] ,tau*, to dash on the ground; *k'á' ,i chóh, ,piéng*, throw it aside, as grief, business, etc.

[1]坐	[2]坐	[4]帝	[6]座	[8]公	爐	城	白	皂	造	造	化
南	鎮	座	位	座	座	[11]上	[18]皂	[15]始	[17]造	[19]造	[21]仵
朝	[3]坐	[5]四	[7]八	椅	[10]一	座	隸	造	冊	作	倅
北	罪	座	座	[9]香	座	[12]皂	[14]胰	[16]乾	[18]創	[20]造	○

(61) Choi.

‚*Choi.* A coll. word; to gather, to crowd together: ‚*choi* ʻ*tó*, to push over by crowding against; ‚*choi* ʻ*mwang*, to fill with a crowd, to crowd a place.

醉 Tsui. Exhilarated with drink, intoxicated, fuddled, drunk; a debauch; fascinated, enchanted, devoted to, stupefied with; absorbed in, engrossed with: COM., [1]ʻ*chiu choi*ʼ intoxicated with liquor; [2]*choi*ʼ *e*ʼ tipsy; *choi*ʼ ʻ*pau* (coll. *choi*ʼ ʻ*pa*), drunk and full—a debauch; [3]‚*sing choi*ʼ fascinated with; *choi*ʼ ‚*ha*, salted prawns; [4]*choi*ʼ ʻ*ngang* ‚*mung* ‚*dung*, eyes dim from intoxication, muddled; [5]*choi*ʼ *hau*ʼ after intoxication, *scil.* people act in different ways; COLL., [6]‚*hong choi*ʼ intoxicated with smoking.

裁 Tsai. To cut out garments; to make clothes; to trim, to cut off; to moderate, to reduce, to diminish; to guess, to plan; to regulate, to adjust: COM., [7]‚*choi* ‚*chü*, to trim off books, as in binding; [8]‚*choi* ‚*i*, to cut out clothes; ‚*choi* ʻ*cheng*, to cut out; to adjust; to diminish, as the price; [9]‚*choi* ‚*p'ung*, to cut out and sew; [10]‚*choi* ‚*tó*, a paper-knife; [11]ʻ*chung* ‚*choi*, the examiner for the Chinsz degree; [12]‚*choi tok*‚ or *chiok*‚ ‚*choi*, to plan; [13]‚*choi* ʻ*keng*, to diminish; [14]‚*choi k'wok*‚ to reduce the number of men; COLL., ‚*choi ch'ioh*‚ a tailor's foot-measure; [15]ʻ*chio* ‚*choi*, to decide for yourself; *twai*ʼ ‚*choi*, cut out of whole cloth.

悴 Tsui. Sad, chagrined; downcast, sorry-looking, in which sense same as next: [16]*k'aung*ʼ *choi*ʼ sad, sorrowful.

顇 Tsui. Sick, lean and sallow, cadaverous: COM., [17]‚*ngang saik*‚ ‚*chieu choi*ʼ the visage wan and haggard.

萃 T'sui. Thick, tufted, like tussocks of grass; a sort of honeysuckle; to collect, to assemble, to flock together, to be with; a collection, a selection; rustling, as of bushes or apparel: [18]*koi*ʼ *choi*ʼ tufts of grass; clumps of trees; [19]‚*kung choi*ʼ a friendly gathering; [20]*choi*ʼ *chuk*‚ clansmen.

瘁 T'sui. Diseased, infirm, suffering; doleful, dumpish, indisposed; worn out, destroyed, ruined: [21]‚*ló choi*ʼ or ʻ*hwong choi*ʼ tired, fatigued.

啐 T'sui. Also read *chok*‚: to call out, to cry out in alarm; to hist, to call to; to taste, to eat, to craunch; to suck, noise of sucking.

淬 焠 T'sui. A thing to put out fire with, an extinguisher; to temper metals in water; to bring into contact with, as fire with water; the first also means to dip, to dye, to color; the second also means to burn.

睟 T'sui. The angles or canthi of the eye; a clear bright eye; clear, pure; to look directly at: [22]*choi*ʼ ‚*t'iéng*, the fifth heaven.

1 酒醉	3 心醉	朦朧	6 烟醉	8 裁衣	10 裁刀	12 裁度	14 裁缺	16 困悴	憔顇	19 羣萃	21 勞瘁
2 醉意	4 醉眼	5 醉後	7 裁書	9 裁縫	11 總裁	13 裁減	15 主裁	17 顏色	18 薈萃	20 萃族	22 睟天

誶3 Tsui. To rail at, to scold, to vilify, to abuse; to impeach, to accuse; petulant, angry: *kaiu3 choi3* to brawl, to rail at; [1]*'ling choi3* to disgrace one.

(62) Chói.

最' Tsui. To come together, to assemble; an adjective indicating the most important, the highest degree of; very, extremely, exceedingly; altogether; ability, as of an officer: COM., [2]*'chói' 'hó*, very good; [3]*'chói' yeu'* highly important; [4]*'chói' pok, ,k'ang*, utterly worthless; COLL., *chói' ,hwa ,ch'iā*, very wasteful; *chói' tĕk, hō' ,ing ,sing*, the malicious female heart; [5]*'chói' ,seng*, a long time ago, anciently; *chói' ,kiāng*, very timid.

晬' T'sui. Read *choi'*; coll. *chói'*: a full year of age: *,ma chói'* "clutch when a year old"—custom of placing implements before a child to see which it will first take; [6]*'siāng chói'* a full year old; [7]*'chói' 'pa*, or *chói' siong2* over a year old; [8]*sioh, chói' sioh, ,sang nik,* one year and one birth-day anniversary—i. e. three years of age, as the Chinese reckon; *chói' ne2* one year and two months old; [9]*'chói' 'kwi*, a year and how many months old?

罪 **辠**2 Tsui. A bamboo net for fish; to become entangled in the meshes of the law; a trespass, crime, sin, fault, offence; a violation of the laws of the land, or of decorum; to criminate, to regard as criminal; guilt, punishment, retribution; [10]*chói2 hwang2* or *chói2 ,ch'iu*, a culprit; COM., [11]*chói2 ,k'wi*, the chief culprit; [12]*hwang2 chói2* or *taik, chói2* to transgress, to sin; [13]*'sieu chói2* a trifling offence; [14]*neng2 chói2* to confess a fault; [15]*,tong chói2* to bear the penalty of sin; [16]*huk, chói2* to confess and submit to punishment; [17]*sük, chói2* to atone for sin; *te2 chói2* to punish offences; *chói2 auk,* wickedness; [18]*chói2 kwo'* or *chói2 ,k'iĕng,* transgressions, sins; *chói2 siong2 ,ka chói2* accumulated guilt; COLL., *chói2 taĕng2* or *chói2 twai2* a grievous sin; *mwong2 chói2* or *ch'ok, chói2* banished for crime; *'si chói2* a capital crime; *paing2 chói2* to inflict punishment.

(63) Chok.

卒, Tsu. One who executes orders; a lictor, a soldier; underlings, menials; to conclude, to end, to finish; to die; to the last, the very end; hastily, abruptly, urgently, in which sense also read *choi2*: *chok, ,yong*, abruptly; COM., *,ping chok,* a soldier; [19]*'sieu chok,* camp-followers; COLL., [20]*ngwoh, chok,* a turnkey, an under-jailer; [21]*chok, 'kiăng*, the "soldier" chess-pieces; a servant, one sent forward to do.

猝, T'suh. A dog rushing from a cover; abrupt; fierce, impetuous, precipitate; suddenly, hastily, hurriedly: [22]*,ch'ong chok,* impetuous; perplexed, harassed.

---

1 凌誶 2 最好 3 最要 4 最不堪 5 最前 6 成晬 7 晬把 8 一晬一生日 9 晬幾 10 罪犯 11 罪魁 12 犯罪 13 小罪 14 認罪 15 當罪 16 服罪 17 贖罪 18 罪過 19 小卒 20 獄卒 21 卒仔 22 倉猝

捽, Tso. To grasp, to clutch, to seize, as by the nape; to butt, to push; to pluck out: [1]*chok, ˏki hwak*, to clutch his hair.

昨, Tso. Yesterday; time past: recently: [2]*chok nik* yesterday: [3]*chok ˋngu*, yesterday-noon; [4]*chok yā*² last night.

怍, Tso. Ashamed, disconcerted, out of countenance; to blush, to redden; blushing, shame-faced: [5]*k'oi*' *chok*, ashamed.

酢, Tso. To pledge a host, to return health; to recompense, to return a compliment; a vessel for steaming food: [6]*ˏsiu chok*, host and guest pledging.

柞, Tso. A spinous tree of firm wood, whose new leaves appear as soon as the old ones fall; to root up trees, to fell trees; narrow, confined; a trap for catching beasts.

擢, Tso. To take out, to select, to raise, to promote; to employ in office; to reject, to extinguish, as good resolutions; to pull up, to extirpate: [7]*pak chok*, to promote good men to office.

濯, Cho. To wash, to rinse; to drink; large; fat, sleek, bright: [8]*chok chok*, sleek and fat; bare, as a mountain-top; bright; [9]*ˋsá chok*, to sprinkle; to cleanse, as the heart.

濁, Cho. Muddy, turbid, thick, foul, impure; vicious, profligate: [10] *hong*³ *chok*, mixed, ill-assorted; *met.*, bad company; COM., [11]*ˏch'ing chok*, clear and muddy; COLL., [12]*yéng*³ *chok*, confused, excessive, as ornament.

鑿 **鑿**, Tsao. A chisel, a punch; to cut, to chisel, to bore into; to grind or pound to powder; to dig, as a well; to open out, as a road; to puncture; to brand, to mark, as a thief; to act contrary to right principles: in the coll. read *ch'ĕk*, q. v.: [13]*tauk chok*, to chisel out; [14]*chok p'ek*, to dig through a partition; [15]*ˏch'iong chok*, to bore through; *met.*, to pervert right principles.

(64) Chong.

尊 **尊**, Tsun. Honorable, eminent; high, exalted, great; respected, noble; a term of respect, your; to respect, to revere, to dignify, to venerate; a vessel used for libations: COM., [16]*ˏchong hó*² (what is) your honorable name? [17]*ˏchong ˋtiong*, honored elders; [18]*ˏchong keng*³ or *ˏchong tëüng*² to revere; [19]*ˏchong koi*³ exalted, eminent; [20]*ˏchong ka*³ Sir! your honor! [21]*leng*² *ˏchong*, or *ˏchong ˏkung*, your father; [22]*ˏt'iéng ˏchong*, celestial, honorable ones—applied to Tauist idols.

遵, Tsun. To obey, to follow a superior; to comply with, to conform to; to act as required, to yield; to induce one to obey; obedience, acquiescence: [23]*ˏchong ˏsung*, to

[1]捽其髮〇 [2]昨日 [3]昨午 [4]昨夜 [5]愧怍 [6]酬酢 [7]拔擢 [8]濯濯 [9]洗濯 [10]混濁 [11]清濁 [12]豔濁 [13]琢鑿 [14]鑿壁 [15]穿鑿 [16]尊號 [17]尊長 [18]尊敬 [19]尊貴 [20]尊駕 [21]令尊 [22]天尊 [23]遵循

obey; [1]ʻkauk, ˏngi ʻling ˏchong, "let all tremblingly obey"—phrase at the end of edicts; COM., [2]ˏchong meng' to obey commands.

蹲 ˏTsun. To sit cross-legged or cuddled up, to sit on the heels; to make antics; to sit haughtily; to walk with measured steps; placed together, as scales of armor: [3]ˏchong ˏi, to sit haughtily.

樽 罇 ˏTsun. A vase for libations; a bottle, a decanter, a jar, a vase; the first also means luxuriant foliage: COM., [4]ʻchiu ˏchong, a wine vase; ˏkʻwi ˏchong, a feast given by a successful literary candidate; *chiĕk, ˏchong*, a feast given to a graduate by his friends.

臧 ˏTsang. Good, generous; virtuous, faithful; to scold slaves: [5]ˏchong hek, to berate slaves; ˏhó ĕüng' pok, ˏchong, in what respect is it not good?

粧 妝 ˏChuang. To adorn the head; ornamented, dressed, adorned; to dress, to rouge, to adorn, to beautify; to feign, to appear in a false guise: COM., [6]ˏchong sok, to make the toilet—as ladies do; [7]ʻsĕ ˏchong, to dress the hair; *tang'* ˏchong, moderately adorned; [8]ˏchong ˏtai, or ˏchong ˏtai tóh, a toilet-table; [9]ˏchong ˏliéng, a bride's dowry, trousseau; COLL., ˏchong lià' lià' or ˏchong chʻwoi' chʻwoi' finely dressed; [10]ˏchong chó' to assume to be, to feign; [11]ˏchong ʻta, to dress up, adorned; ˏhiong a' ˏchong, country-fashion.

羘 Chʻiang. A ram, a ewe; full, plenty; exuberant, as foliage.

賍 贓 ˏTsang. Booty, plunder, loot; stolen goods; pawned articles; to receive bribes; to suborn, to bribe; to hide, to conceal: COM., [12]ˏchong cheng' marks or proofs by which stolen property is recognized; [13]nak, ˏchong, to give a bribe; [14]chʻek, ˏchong, or ˏchong uk, booty, plunder; ˏchong ˏtang, an inventory of stolen articles; [15]ˏhung ˏchong pok, ˏming, an unequal division of the spoils; [16]taik, ˏchong, to receive bribes; ʻkwong ˏchong, to lay away pawned garments; [17]ʻmwang ˏchong, expiration of time on a pawned article.

裝 ˏChuang. To put into, as a bag; to store; to load, to stow in, to pack; to catch in, as rain; to receive, to contain; to send to, as a present; to bind, to tie on; to dress; style, dress, fashion: ˏchong sok, to tie up, as a bundle: COM., [18]ˏchong hwo' to pack away goods; [19]ˏchong ʻmwang, stowed full; [20]ˏming ˏtieu ˏchong, dress of the Ming dynasty; [21]ˏheng ˏchong, traveling clothes; siong' ˏchong, the upper parts of a garment; ʻnü ʻka ˏnang ˏchong, a female dressed in man's clothes; ˏchong ˏsiong, to pack in a box; to pack (paper) trunks (for the spirits at

1 各宜凜遵 2 遵命 3 蹲夷 4 酒罇 5 臧獲 6 粧束 7 梳粧 8 粧臺 9 粧奩 10 粧做 11 粧打 12 賍證 13 納賍 14 賊賍 15 分賍不明 16 得賍 17 滿賍 18 裝貨 19 裝滿 20 明朝裝 21 行裝 〇

a funeral); coll., ˏchong ˏhong, to put tobacco (in the pipe).

莊 ˏChuang. Plants growing rank or luxuriantly; sedate, serious, grave, stern; correct in conduct; adorned; a farmhouse; a barn, a grange; a cottage; a road; a surname: [1]ˏhiong ˏchong, (coll. ˏhiong ˏch'ong), a farmhouse, a village; [2]ˏchong ˏngiêng, stern; [3]saik, ˏchong, a false appearance.

庄 ˏChuang. A vulgar character sometimes used for the preceding: read ˏp'ang; coll. ˏchong: a large shop, a store: [4]'poo' ˏchong, a cotton-cloth store; [5]ˏchiêng ˏchong, a bank; [6]ˏchong ˏka, a customer; one of whom to borrow.

椿 ˏChuang. Read ˏch'ung; used in the Paik Ing for the coll. ˏchong: a sort, a kind; a classifier of affairs or incidents: [7]ˏchong ˏchong, sorts, kinds; ᶜchiă ˏchong, or [8]ᶜchiă ˏchong ˏt'au, this kind; [9]ᶜchi sioh, ˏchong ˏki tai' this particular affair.

鱒 ᶜTsun. A fish with red eyes and small scales like the roach. In Japan this character denotes the salmon: coll., [10]ᶜchong ˏmwang, the lamper-eel.

噂 ᶜTsun. Many persons conversing amicably; to talk pleasantly to one; unitedly, as a chorus: [11]ᶜchong tak, to flatter and then traduce.

撙 ᶜTsun. To restrain, to bring within limits; to hold the bridle-rein; to adjust, to regulate: [12]ᶜchong chiĕk, to regard order, to economize.

鑚 ᶜTsuan. Read ˏchwang; coll. ᶜchong, as in [13]ᶜchong pek, or ˏking ˏkong ᶜchong, a small diamond used for cutting glass.

吮 To suck, to draw the breast; to lick, as a sore: [14]chong' ˏŭng, or chong' ˏchü, to suck out an ulcer.

俊 **儁** Chün. Superior, remarkable, one of a thousand; to win, to overcome; to excel in wisdom, eminent, exalted; unusual, strange; in the coll., fine, splendid; attractive, agreeable; palatable: [15]chong' sëü' an eminent scholar; [16]chong' ᶜmi, good, excellent; com., [17]chong' seu' the purchased degree of kangseng; coll., [18]ᶜchiong chong' excelling in goodness; [19]ᶜyă chong' or cheng' chong' or chong' chiăh, chong' fine, most splendid! ᶜhó chong' excellent!

竣 Chün. To stop work, to finish, to complete a task; completed, done; to stand still; to wait aside, to retire; proud: [20]kó' chong' to report the completion of; com., [21]ˏwong chong' completed; [22]pó' chong' "reported done," finished, as a temple.

1鄉	3色	5錢	7椿	頭	其	11噂	13鑚	15俊	17俊	19野	21完
莊	莊	庄	椿	9只	代	沓	筆	士	秀	俊	竣
2莊	4布	6庄	8者	一	10鱒	12撙	14吮	16俊	18奬	20告	22報
嚴	庄	家	椿	椿	鰻	節	癰	美	俊	竣	竣

晙 Chŭn. To see, to look at; the name of a hero in the Han dynasty.

峻 **陖** Chŭn. High, lofty, steep, as mountains; impetuous, hasty; stern, severe, as one's temper; long, extended, large: ¹*chong*' '*hiéng*, high and precipitous; ²*ngiéng chong*' stern, exacting; *chong*' '*liǒng*, a lofty slope; ³*chong*' *kik*, *ũ*, *t'iéng*, towering to the skies; *met.*, exalted, as doctrine.

畯 Chŭn. A husbandman, a peasant, a rustic; an officer who superintended the fields; the god of husbandry; a district: ⁴*tiéng chong*' a superintendent of fields.

濬 Chŭn. Deep, profound, as water; to dig a channel, to deepen a water course; deep, serious, as reverence; abstruse, well-read; a district in Honan: ⁵*chong*' *tiék*, having deep wisdom.

浚 Chŭn. Interchanged with the preceding: deep, abstruse; reverential; to dig deep; necessary, should; to take out, to appropriate, as another's property: ⁶*chong*' '*ngó* '*i* *seng*, takes our property to nourish himself.

雋 Chŭn. Fat, fleshy, as a bird in season; an excellent scholar; racy, pleasant discourse: ⁷*chong*' '*nga*, elegant in style and sentiment, as an essay; ⁸*ing chong*' clever, excelling in intelligence.

駿 Chŭn. A stately horse; dignified, majestic; excelling; rapid; high, elevated: COM., *paik*, *chong*' or ⁹*paik*, *chong*' '*ma*, the eight fine horses—in ornamental work.

餕 Chŭn. Hot food; the fragments of a meal, or of an offering in worship: to eat the leavings: ¹⁰*chong*' *ũ*, the leavings: ¹¹*chong*' *hié*' the fragments distributed to the worshipers.

糉 **粽** Dumplings of glutinous rice, wrapped in leaves and eaten on the 5th day of the 5th moon: in the coll. read *chaěng*' q. v.

藏 T'sang. To store up, to lay by; to hoard, to treasure up; to contain; to conceal, to hide, to secrete; to gather, to accumulate: ¹²*ch'ing chong*, to hide closely; ¹³*chong k'é ũ' sing*, to equip with armor; *met.*, to have talent in reserve; COM., ¹⁴*chong chek*, to hoard large quantities; ¹⁵*chong liong*, or *chong ngwok*, *liong*, to lay up provisions for the month; ¹⁶'*ũng chong*, concealed, secret; COLL., ¹⁷*chong k'aung*' to lay by; to hide one's self; ¹⁸*chong te*' *ang*' to secrete in an underground vault; ¹⁹*chong sing hwa*' '*tau*, "hides the stars and transforms the Dipper"—tricky, scheming.

存 T'sun. To preserve, to defend from injury; alive, to exist; to lay by; to take care of, as of one's life; to inquire

¹峻險 ²峻極於天 ³嚴峻 ⁴田畯 ⁵濬哲 ⁶浚我以生 ⁷雋雅 ⁸英雋 ⁹八駿馬 ¹⁰餕餘 ¹¹餕惠 ¹²深藏 ¹³藏器於身 ¹⁴藏積 ¹⁵藏糧 ¹⁶隱藏 ¹⁷藏囥 ¹⁸藏地暗 ¹⁹藏星化斗

after, as one's health; to attend carefully to; COM., [1]꜂chong chieuʼ or ꜂chong ꜀kong, to keep fac-similes of bank-bills for proof; [2]꜂chong angʼ to reserve law-cases; COLL., ꜂chong ꜀sing ʻtié, to lay up in the mind; ꜂chong ʻchiă ꜂ngai ꜀sing, cherishes the wicked purpose; [3]꜂chong eʼ or ꜂chong ꜂chong eʼ to intend; ꜂chong chóʼ ngʼ ꜂chong chóʼ will you do it or not? ngʼ ꜂chong eʼ unexpected; ꜂chong auʼ have thought of the future; ꜂chong siăh, ʻchiă puongʼ intend to do this for a living.

(65) Chu.

租 ꜀Tsu. Rent in kind, rental, rent; to lease, to rent, to let; to hire; tribute, taxes: COM., ʻteʼ ꜀chu, land-rent; [5]꜀chu ʻpong, a rent-contract, a lease; [6]꜀chu yok, an agreement to rent; ʻié ꜀chu, seat-hire, as at theatres; [7]ʻpó ꜀chu, security for rent; [8]nak, ꜀chu, or tóiʼ ꜀chu, to pay rent; kʻiéngʼ ꜀chu, arrears of rent; [9]꜀chieu ꜀chu, or chʻok, ꜀chu, to offer to let—as in posted notices; ʻing ʻwong ꜀chu yok, a perpetual lease; [10]꜀tʻiu ꜀chu, a tax on rents; COLL., ꜀chu chʻioʼ or ꜀chu chʻioʼ teuʼ to rent a dwelling; ꜀chu pʻwoiʼ to hire bedding; ʻtʻó ꜀chu, to collect rent.

꜀Chu. A coll. word, as in ꜀chu waiʼ or ꜀chu waiʼ ʻnë, here, in this place.

祖 ʻTsu. A grandfather; a progenitor; ancestors; the founder of a family; ancestral temple; origin, beginning; the first, as of a family; to do like, to imitate a founder; accustomed to; to worship the wayside gods: COM., [11]ʻchu hoʼ grandfather and father, ancestry; [12]ʻchu ꜀chung, or ʻchu ꜀siéng, ancestors; [13]꜀cheng ʻchu, a great-grandfather; ꜀cheng ʻchu ʻpi, a great-grandmother; [14]꜀kó ʻchu, a great great-grandfather; ngwoiʼ ʻchu, and ngwoiʼ ʻchu ʻmu, maternal grandfather and grandmother; [15]ʻsü ʻchu, the first, as of a family—used for Adam and Eve; [16]tʻaiʼ ʻchu, the first emperor of the dynasty; [17]ʻchu ngiek, the ancestral estate; [18]ʻchu ꜀sü, an originator, an inventor; ꜀siéng ʻchu, a deceased grandfather; liéʼ ʻchu pok, liéʼ ꜀kʻiong, leaves the old home but does not forget his native tongue; COLL., [19]ʻchu chʻioʼ the old homestead; ʻchu tóiʼ siăh, ʻchiă puongʼ an employment perpetuated in a family.

阻 ʻChu. To hinder, to impede, to obstruct; to stop, to cause delay; to oppose, to prevent; grieved; dangerous; an impediment; a defile; to suspect, to doubt: [20]ʻhiéng ʻchu, obstructions by land and water; [21]ʻchu ꜀liu, to detain; [22]kʻwongʼ ʻchu, to coax and hinder; COM., [23]꜀lang ʻchu, to oppose, to stop; [24]ʻchu chek, to prevent, to block the way; ʻchu ʻchi, to hinder; COLL., ʻchu ʻü ꜂mó tek, ʻkʻi ꜀sing, prevented by rain from starting; ʻchu tek, teuʼ stopped him; ʻchu máʼ teuʼ could not prevent him.

沮 ʻTsu. Interchanged with the above: to stop, to prohibit; to pass over; to divulge; to destroy, to dis-

1 存照	3 存意	5 租榜	7 保租	9 招租	11 祖父	13 曾祖	15 始祖	17 祖業	19 祖厝	21 阻留	23 攔阻
2 存案	4 地租	6 租約	8 納租	10 抽租	12 祖宗	14 高祖	16 太祖	18 祖師	20 險阻	22 勸阻	24 阻截

福州方言拼音字典

comfit, to scare; ʻchu ʻchi, to quash, to intrigue against; [1]ʻchu te' obstructed. Read ˏchŭ: an affluent of the river Yang-Tsz, west of K'ing-chau-fu in Hupeh; an ancient district, now the extreme southwest of Shensi.

ʻ俎 ʻ爼 Tsu. A basin or bowl like a tripod, used in sacrifices: [2]ʻchu tau' a basin used in worship.

ʻ組 Tsu. A band, a fillet, a string, a tape for tying the dress or hair; a fringe or tuft of silk; to tie, to sew to: [3]ʻchu seu' cap strings; [4]ʻkai ʻchu ˏkwi ˏtiéng, to untie the cord and go home—to resign office.

ʻ咀 Tsu. Also read ˏchu: to taste, to bite; to chew in order to taste: [5]ʻchu chiok, to chew.

ʻ齟 Tsu. Irregular teeth, which do not interlock easily; discordant, as opinions, incongruous; to bite, to eat: [6]ʻchu ˏngu, teeth like saw-teeth; met., uncongenial.

ˏ鶵 Tsu. A chick, a fledgeling; the callow young of birds: [7]ʻsieu ˏchu, a fledgeling; [8]ʻyéng' ˏchu, young swallows.

ˏ岨 ˏ砠 Rocks covered with earth; cliffs. Read ʻchu, to obstruct, to hinder; an impediment; a defile.

ˏ蛆 Chu. Maggots in putrid flesh; fly-blows, eggs of flies: [9]siok, ˏchu, snow-worms, found in Sz-chuen. Read ˏchŭ, a centipede or millipede called [10]chek, ˏchŭ, that eats the brains of snakes.

ˏ殂 Tsu. To die; dead; a path to the grave: in the coll. dying, as fowls; gone! dead!—used to avoid the common term ʻsi: [11]ˏchu lok, to die like falling leaves: COLL., ˏchu ˏkié ʻkiăng, a dying chick; [12]ˏi ˏchu k'ó' ˏló, he's dead!

ˏ徂 Tsu. Interchanged with last: to go up; to proceed, to travel; to preserve, to lay up: [13]ˏchu ʻwong, to proceed; [14]ˏchu ˏching, to go forth to war.

(66) Chŭ.

ˏ書 Shu. A book, a volume; a record, a letter, a writing; documents, dispatches; to write; style of writing: [15]lĕk, ˏchŭ, the six styles of writing; COM., [16]ˏchŭ ʻping, an officer's correspondence; [17]ˏchŭ ˏking, the Shooking—Book of Records; [18]sëŭ' ˏchŭ, the Four Books; [19]ˏchŭ seng' or ˏchŭ chak, an epistle; ˏchŭ ka' book-shelves; [20]ˏchŭ paing' a writer in a government office; ˏchŭ ˏseng, a scholar—now applied to the character of "teacher" in plays; [21]ˏchŭ ʻngŭ, the language of books; mek, ˏchŭ, to re-write a book from memory; [22]ʻkong ˏchŭ, to discourse from a book, to preach; ˏchŭ ˏtung, boy waiters in schools; ˏchŭ ˏpau, a satchel for books; ˏchŭ ˏp'uí,

1沮滯 2俎豆 3組綬 4解組 歸田 5咀嚼 6齟齬 7小鶵 8燕鶵 9雪蛆 10蝍蛆 11殂落 12伊殂去囉 13徂往 14徂征 15六書 16書稟 17書經 18四書 19書信 20書辦 21書語 22講書

book-covers; [1]*ho'* ˛*chü*, a portfolio; [2]*ch'ó* ˛*chü*, or ˛*heng* ˛*chü*, a running-hand; ˛*k'au* ˛*chü*, an agreement in dividing an estate; [3]˛*t'ung* ˛*chü*, an almanac; COLL., ˛*chü t'ĕk*, ˛*t'au* '*lá k'ó*' learning reached only his head—a dull scholar; ˛*chü* ˛*tai*, a pedant, a mere book-worm; ˛*chü tah*, a pressing-block for books; ˛*i pok*, '*ló o*' ˛*chü kwong*' he is well read.

貲 ˛Tzu. Used for the next: a fine paid to redeem one's self; riches, wealth, property; to slander, to bear false witness: [4]˛*chü* ˛*chai*, property; [5]˛*ka* ˛*chü*, family possessions.

資 ˛Tzu. Property, riches, goods, things of value; necessaries, articles wanted; a fee, a douceur; a treat, a present; to take; to trust, to rely on; what belongs to one, what is natural, as disposition: [6]˛*chü hwo*' property, riches; COM., ˛*kwang* ˛*chü*, a teacher's salary; [7]*ngwok*, ˛*chü*, the monthly pay (of employés); [8]'*chiu* ˛*chü*, a douceur; *pek*, ˛*chü*, the pay of a writer or physician; [9]˛*chü* '*pwong*, capital; ˛*chü chek*, ability, intelligence; COLL., ˛*kĕng* ˛*chü*, wages.

咨 ˛Tzu. To deliberate, to plan, to consult; to state or ask in writing; a dispatch between equals in rank; to sigh, an interjection, ah! oh! [10]*wong*' ˛*chü*, to lament; [11]˛*chü* ˛*cheu*, to consult, as on official matters.

諮 ˛Tzu. Used for the last: to deliberate, to consult, to devise a way; to inquire about: [12]˛*chü* ˛*meu*, to plan.

姿 ˛Tzu. Manner, gait, form, carriage, air; beautiful, graceful; agreeable parts; natural endowments: [13]˛*hung* ˛*chü* a fine figure; [14]˛*t'iĕng* ˛*chü*, natural endowments; [15]˛*chü chek*, a beauty; natural ability.

儲 ˛ Also read ˛*sü*: to collect; to provide for need; furnished; to assist, to act as second to: [16]˛*tung* ˛*chü*, or ˛*chü* ˛*kung*, the heir-apparent.

諸 ˛Chu. To discriminate, to discuss; not one alone, all, several, many, every; in, respecting; a pronoun at the end of a sentence, or a word implying doubt; a sign of the dative, on, upon, to, from, at; it is often introduced to make rhythm; used in the coll. in the terms for woman and daughter: COM., [17]˛*chü* ˛*t'iĕng* ˛*pu sak*, all the celestial Budhs—24 in number; [18]˛*chü* ˛*hwang*, all, every; [19]˛*chü* ˛*heu*, a feudal prince or viceroy; [20]˛*chü oi*' all the persons, guests, or places; COLL., ˛*chü wa*' ˛*tu* '*hieu*, understands all that is said; [21]˛*chü* ˛*niong*, or ˛*chü* ˛*niong* ˛*nĕng*, a woman; ˛*chü* ˛*nĕng* '*kiong*, a daughter, a miss; [22]˛*chü* ˛*nĕng*, all those present.

疽 ˛Tsu. A deep-seated ulcer; a carbuncle or anthrax; in the coll. a kind of itch or rash: [23]'*tung* ˛*chü*, an ul-

[1]護書 [2]草書 [3]通書 [4]貲財 [5]家貲 [6]資貨 [7]月資 [8]酒資 [9]資本 [10]怨咨 [11]咨諏 [12]諮謀 [13]風姿 [14]天姿 [15]姿質 [16]東儲 [17]諸天菩薩 [18]諸凡 [19]諸侯 [20]諸位 [21]諸娘 [22]諸仈 [23]瘤疽

cerated wound; [1]chong' ˏchü, to suck a sore; COLL., [2]‛ch‘iu ˏchü, a rash on the hands; [3]ˏsang mah, ˏchü, to have "the wheat-rash"—during the harvest of the 3d moon.

髭 T‘zu. The mustaches, which the Chinese wear long; beautiful, good-looking.

疵 T‘zu. Malady, disease, infirmity; an imperfection, as a mole; a failing, a fault; an eccentricity: [4]‛sieu ˏchü, a trifling blemish, as in one's character; [5]ˏch‘wi ˏmó ˏkiu ˏchü, to magnify another's foibles.

趑 Tsu. To walk slowly, impeded in going: [6]ˏch‘ü ˏchü, hobbling, walking step by step.

粢 Tzu. A common name for grains and pulse; rice used in sacrifices, which must be of the best; a cake of glutinous rice: [7]ˏming ˏchü, clean cooked-rice; [8]ˏchü ˏsing, rice in vessels for sacrifice.

緇 Tzu. Dark colored silk or satin; the dark color of sediment; black: [9]ˏchü ˏi, dark clothes.

錙 Tzu. A weight equal to eight ˏt‘ü, or the third part of a tael—not now in use: [10]ˏchü ˏt‘ü, small weights; a mite.

餈 餈 Tzu. Unleavened cakes; pancakes, or dumplings made of rice-flour, called [11]‛hung ˏchü.

菑 甾 Tzu. Waste, untilled land: overgrown, jungly; to clear new or waste land; ground under cultivation one year; to open a road; to cut, to rend; a dead tree still standing; the end of the axle, in which sense used for next: [12]ˏchü ‛meu, to extirpate grass and weeds; cleared land.

輜 Tzu. End of the axle within the nave; treasure wagons, or such as carry arms and spoil; large wagons with places for sleeping and carrying stores; manure carts: [13]ˏchü ˏkü, baggage wagons; [14]ˏchü tëüng[2] traveling equipage, *impedimenta*.

茨 Tzu. To thatch; grass on a wall; a spinous trailing plant with a triangular seed; to collect: [15]ˏchü ˏku, the Caladium Sagittifolium, a species of Arum.

菹 Tzu. Pickled vegetables; melons, etc., salted; grass growing in marshes—sedge, rushes.

孳 Tzu. To bear, to produce; to suckle, to nourish, as animals; to grow; loving, affectionate, as mothers; unwearied, repeated, diligent, in which sense the same as the next: also read che[2] q. v.

孜 Tzu. Unwearied effort; diligent, persevering, untiring; self-denying, disinterested: [16]ˏchü ˏchü ˏui siéng[2] to labor unweariedly in doing good.

[1]吮疽 [2]手疽 [3]生麥疽 ○ [4]小疵 [5]吹毛求疵 ○ [6]趑趄 [7]明粢 ○ [8]粢盛 [9]緇衣 [10]錙銖 ○ [11]粉餈 [12]菑畝 [13]輜車 ○ [14]輜重 [15]茨菰 [16]孜孜爲善 ○

且 ‘Tzu. A phonetic particle used in the Shi King at the end of sentences, as an affirmative; this, that; many, as sacrificial vessels set in order; an ancient name of the 6th month: also read ‘ch‘iǎ, q. v.: [1]‘p‘i ‘ngó ˏsü ˏchü, not what I think of; [2]ˏpiêng taiu’ ‘iu ˏchü, many sacrificial vessels.

齊 ‘Chai. The lower parts of one's garments: also read ˏchá and ˏchai, q. v.: [3]niék, ˏchü ˏsing ˏtong, to hold up the robes and ascend to the audience-room.

訾 ‘Tzu. Also read ‘chié: to speak hastily or unadvisedly, to speak without thinking; to slander, to vilify; to think, to consult; to limit, to restrict; faulty, impertinent, disorderly: [4]ˏchü ngié’ to slander, to plot against.

苴 ‘Tsu. The female hemp plant; sackcloth; a rush, a sedge, used for sandals; coarse, unpolished: [5]‘pwo ˏchü, to repair defects; to correct, as bad essays.

淄 ‘Tzu. A river in the northeast of Shantung, flowing into the sea; a district in Shantung; a dark color.

睢 ‘Tzu. Also read ˏhwi: to raise the eyes, to stare at; to scowl, to look angrily; self-satisfied. Read ˏch‘wi, a river flowing into lake Hung-tseh in Kiangsu; a district of Kwei-teh in Honan.

胔 ‘T‘zu. Also read chĕü’: birds or beasts deficient in some member; monsters; abominable; old putrid bones having some flesh on: [6]ˏmai ˏchü, to bury putrid flesh.

觜 ‘Tsui. The 21st. zodiacal constellation in Orion's head; a large tortoise called [7]ˏchü ˏhié. Read ˏchwi, the horns of an owl; the crest, egret; to raise the crest on the head; to bristle up, to look incensed, to pout the lips in anger.

滋 ‘Tzu. Read ˏchü; coll., ˏchü: as in [8]ˏchü e’ a fine flavor, as of crabs.

子 ‘Tzu. A son, anciently it meant a child; a boy, a lad, a person; an heir, posterity, issue; interest on money; seeds of plants; a sage, a philosopher, a venerable and worthy man; Confucius; you! sir! a term of address somewhat like comrades; a degree of nobility, a viscount; the first of the 12 stems, denoted by the rat; the third watch—from 11 o'clock, P. M., to 1 o'clock, A. M.; the people in distinction from their prince; a spot, as of dirt, or on dice; added to nouns it often has a diminutive sense; the 39th radical: COM., [9]‘chü sek, a son; offspring; [10]ˏnang ‘chü, a son, a boy; [11]‘nü ‘chü, a daughter, a girl; [12]‘chü ˏsong ˏsi, guardian of posterity—a god of the municipal temple; [13]‘chü ˏsong ˏting, "posterity nails"—stuck in rice offered at graves, or on changing one's place of resi-

[1] 匪我思且 [2] 籩豆有且 [3] 攝齊升堂 [4] 訾議〇 [5] 補苴〇 [6] 埋胔〇 [7] 觜觿〇 [8] 滋味〇 [9] 子息〇 [10] 男子〇 [11] 女子 [12] 子孫 [13] 司子孫釘

dence; [1]*'tiong 'chŭ*, the eldest son; [2]*tek, 'chŭ*, children by the principal wife; [3]*sëŭ' 'chŭ*, an adopted son of the same surname; [4]*'chŭ 'nŭ*, sons and daughters; [5]*'chŭ tá'* younger sons and brothers; [6]*'chŭ 'ngu ˏsong ˏch'ŭng*, the hours *'chŭ* and *'ngu* (water and fire) conflict; *met.*, opposition in the destinies of two persons; [7]*'chŭ sá'* or *pwang' 'chŭ*, a son-in-law; [8]*t'ai' 'chŭ*, the heir apparent; [9]*ˏkung 'chŭ*, sons of the nobility; [10]*ˏing 'chŭ*, the sons of men—used for the Son of man, the Savior; *'k'ung 'chŭ*, or [11]*'k'ung ˏhu 'chŭ*, Confucius; [12]*ˏmi hok, 'chŭ*, a child born after the death of the father; *ngiék, 'chŭ*, a disobedient son; [13]*sié' 'chŭ*, anciently children of nobles, now of the gods; *'ngu 'chŭ ˏteng ˏk'wo*, five sons all Kŭjins; *'chŭ ˏsong ˏt'iong*, the two middle rafters of a roof; *ek, 'chŭ 'k'i ˏkó ˏleu*, one son raises the high tower, i. e. has talent.

ˋ仔 Tsu. To bear, to carry; to undertake, as an officer: [14]*'chŭ ˏkiéng tëŭng' eng'* able to sustain important offices; COM., [15]*'chŭ sá'* careful, discriminating.

ˋ耔 Also read *ˏchŭ*: to weed and hoe earth around the roots of plants, to hill.

ˋ煮 ˋ煑 Tsu. To boil in water, to stew, to steep, to decoct; to cook, to dress food; boiled, cooked: COM., [16]*'chŭ sŭk,* to cook thoroughly; *'chŭ ˏtiéng*, to boil with sweetening in; *ˏchiéng 'chŭ*, to fry and then stew; COLL., *'chŭ pwong'* to boil rice; *'chŭ lung'* to boil soft; *'chŭ mwoi' sŭk,* not boiled through; *'chŭ siáh,* to cook food; *ˏch'ung 'chŭ pah, ˏkong*, cooked without condiments; *'chŭ ˏhong*, to prepare opium for the pipe; *'chŭ 'chwi kak, 'tiăng*, boil water and it sticks to the pan; *met.*, unsettled, vexations.

ˋ主 Chu. A ruler, a lord, a master; the chief, the head; a host; to govern, to rule; to make one the head; certainly, undoubtedly, as a lord's behests: in the coll. read *'chio*, q. v.: [17]*'chŭ ˏkung*, or *'chŭ siong'* your highness! my lord! the emperor; [18]*'chŭ te'* to rule (the empire); [19]*ˏkung 'chŭ*, the daughters of the emperor; *ˏping 'chŭ*, guest and host; COM., [20]*ˏsing 'chŭ*, or *ˏsing 'chŭ ˏpá*, the ancestral tablet; *cheng' 'chŭ*, to place the tablet in the ancestral temple; COLL., *'teng 'chŭ*, to mark or dot the tablet—as done by an invited person of distinction.

ˋ拄 A prop, a post, to shore up; to pierce; to stick; to point at.

翥 Tsu. To fly upwards, to fly high; to soar like the phenix: *hong' 'chŭ*, the phenix flies high.

ˋ梓 Tzu. A sort of tree considered the best of all trees, is classed with the yew, cypress and cedar; to cut blocks for books; one's village: [21]*ˏsong 'chŭ*, mulberries and yews (planted by ancestors), hence one's birthplace; *'chŭ ch'iong'* a cabinet-maker; *'chŭ*

[1]長子 [2]嫡子 [3]嗣子 [4]子女 [5]子弟 [6]子午相冲 [7]子婿 [8]太子 [9]公子 [10]人子 [11]孔夫子 [12]遺腹子 [13]世子 [14]仔肩 [15]仔細 [16]煮熟 [17]主君 [18]主治 [19]公主 [20]神主 [21]桑梓

ˏtung tá' ˏkung, a title of the god of literature.

渚 ˋT'su. An affluent of the river Hwai, near Hoochow, in Honan; an islet; alluvion in a river: [1]ˏchiu ˋchŭ, an island.

楮 ˋCh'u. A mulberry (broussonetia papyfera) from the bark of which paper and cloth can be made: [2]p'iéng' ˋchŭ, a leaf of paper; ˋchŭ siéng ˏseng, a fine quality of paper.

麈 ˋ Sometimes read chēü': a large ruminant with a bushy tail (a yak?).

ˋChŭ. A coll. word: a brogue for ˋchwi, water.

慈 ˏT'zu. Maternal affection; love, kindness, mercy, compassion; gentle, soft, tender to; a mother: [3]ˏchŭ ˏngiéng, mother and father; [4]ˏing ˏchŭ, benevolent and merciful; com., [5]ˏka ˏchŭ, my mother; [6]ˏchŭ ˏp'i, compassionate; [7]ˏchŭ ˏp'i ˏui ˋpwong, compassion is the chief thing—a Budhist saying; [8]ˏchŭ ˏsing, kindhearted; [9]seng' ˏchŭ, of a kind disposition.

鷀 鸕 ˏT'zu. The fishing cormorant, the Phalacracorax; a wader, a kind of heron: [10]ˏlu ˏchŭ, the fishing cormorant; [11]lo' ˏchŭ, a white egret with pendent crest.

茲 ˏTzu. Herbs and shrubs growing in great abundance; a mat; an adjective, this, that; an adverb, now, the present; a conjunction, but, still: [12]ˏking ˏchŭ, the present.

滋 ˏTzu. Used for the last: sweet, pleasant, rich; humid, soft; to increase, to grow; to enrich; to moisten, to fertilize; to rise, to overflow; moisture, juices, sap; numerous, many: [13]ˏchŭ e' (coll. ˏchŭ e') a fine flavor; [14]ˏchŭ sēü' to get up a row; [15]ˏchŭ ˋpwo, to strengthen, as by tonics; com., [16]ˏchŭ ˏing kaung' ˋhwo, to nourish the vital secretions and depress the igneous principle, as by cooling food.

磁 ˏTzu. The loadstone; porcelain, chinaware: [17]ˏchŭ sik, ˋing ˏcheng, the loadstone attracts the needle; com., [18]ˏchŭ k'e' crockery, fine pottery; ˏyong ˏchŭ, foreign chinaware; coll., [19]ˏchŭ k'e' ˏhwi, pulverized porcelain.

鎡 ˏTzu. Also read ˏchŭ: a hoe, called [20]ˏchŭ ˏki, having a long, narrow blade.

孖 ˏTzu. Also read ˏchŭ: twins; to bear twins; to grow luxuriantly: read ma in Canton.

鼒 ˏTzu. Also read ˏchŭ: a small round tripod; a round lid or cover of a tripod.

(67) Chuí.

ˏChuí. A coll. word: an independent demonstrative pronoun, this: ˋchiā ˏchui, this, this thing; ˏchuí ˏtó k'ēük, ˏi, give this to him; ˏchuí ˏhó ch'ēü' ˋkong ˋk'i, how can this be told or explained!

[1]洲渚 [2]片楮 [3]慈嚴 [4]仁慈 [5]家慈 [6]慈悲 [7]慈悲爲本 [8]慈心 [9]性慈 [10]鸕鷀 [11]鷺鷥 [12]今茲 [13]滋味 [14]滋事 [15]滋補 [16]滋陰降火 [17]磁石引針 [18]磁器 [19]磁器灰 [20]鎡錤

(68) Chuk.

族 Tsu. A barb of a dart; to collect, to draw together, as a banner does; a clan, a tribe; a family, or kindred of the same surname; degrees of kin; a class, a kind: [1]*'chwi chuk,* aquatic animals; COM., [2]*,chung chuk,* of the same clan; [3]*chuk, 'tiong,* the chief of a clan; [4]*chuk, 'p'wo,* genealogical register of the clan; [5]*'koi' chuk,* a clan that produces officers; [6]*chuk, wong'* a flourishing clan; [7]*chuk, ,kang ,hing tá'* fellow-clansmen.

鏃 Tsu. The barb of a dart or arrow, iron head of a dart; sharp-pointed: [8]*'ch'i chuk,* or *chiéng' chuk,* the barb of an arrow.

簇 Tsu. Used for the last and the next: tufts of small bamboo; thick, luxuriant growth, as of trees or flowers; a mold for cakes.

蔟 Tsu. To collect, to crowd together; a crowd of people; a framework, or whisk, on which the silkworms spin their cocoons, called [9]*,chang chuk,*. Read *chau'* one of the notes in music.

鷟 Tsu. A phenix of a carnation color; a species of large duck near river banks.

(69) Chung.

宗 Tsung. An ancestral temple; an ancestral tablet; what is honored; to honor, to reverence; that to which men recur or resort; to revert to; the natural center; the origin or source of; a clan, those of the same surname: [10]*,t'iéng ,chung,* the celestial bodies; [11]*,chung ,ing 'hu,* Board of the imperial kindred; [12]*te' ,chung,* seas, rivers, mountains; [13]*hok, 'chiă ,chung ,chi,* students revere him (Confucius); *pai' 'chu ŭk, ,chung,* to disgrace one's ancestry; COM., [14]*,chung 'chu,* or *'chu ,chung,* ancestors; [15]*,chung mieu'* an ancestral temple; *,chung chuk,* fellow-clansmen; [16]*,chung ,hing,* senior kinsman!—a compellation; [17]*,chung tá'* I, your young kinsman.

悰 ,. To rejoice; pleasure, delight; to think over, to consider.

淙 ,. The noise of water; murmuring, flowing water; bubbling, as a fountain.

琮 Tsung. An ancient badge of princely dignity, eight or nine inches wide, octagonal, with a hole in it: [18]*p'ek, ,chung,* round and square gems, anciently worn by officers.

蹤 踪 Tsung. A vestige, a trace; a track, a footprint; to follow in the track of another: [19]*,p'eu ,chung,* straggling footsteps; *met.,* unsettled, vagrant; COM., *,chung chek,* a footprint; a trace, a clue to; [20]*,u ,chung ,u chek,* no clue whatever.

遚 Tsung. To recede, to retire; to act as if returning; to go back; to follow; a revolution of the moon; self-

---

[1] 水族 [2] 宗族 [3] 族長 [4] 族譜 [5] 貴族 [6] 族旺 [7] 族間兄弟 [8] 矢鏃 [9] [illegible]蔟 [10] 天宗 [11] 宗人府 [12] 地宗〇 [13] 學者宗之 [14] 宗祖 [15] 宗廟 [16] 宗兄 [17] 宗弟 [18] 璧琮 [19] 浮蹤 [20] 無蹤無跡

abashed, self-humiliated: [1]'ˎchung ˏsung, unable to advance; to shrink from, to desist.

ˏ罬 A kind of boiler; a run, a hank, as of hempen threads; to count; name of a place.

ˏ鬃 Tsung. A mane; ridge of bristles on a hog's neck; in the coll. read ˏchĕng, q. v.

ˏ縱 ˏ從 Tsung. Perpendicularly, downward; a meridian line; a vestige, a step; the first also read chĕüng' and the second ˏch'üng, ˏchüng, and chĕüng' q. v.

ˏ豵 Tsung. A pig six months or a year old; a pig, a shote; the last of a litter; a litter; met., many, numerous: [2]ˏchung ˏkiĕng, small and large pigs.

ˏ樅 A sort of tall thuja or yew, which furnishes timber; to beat, as a drum.

ˏ椶 ˏ棕 Tsung. A kind of gomati palm, the chamœrops, whose bracts furnish coir for ropes, mats, &c.; the coir from the borassus gomatus; a dark brown color, umber: in the coll. read ˏchĕng, q.v.

ˏChung. A coll. word: cold, shivering: kiăk, kiăk, ˏchung, or k'auk, k'auk, ˏchung, or ˏk'ong ˏk'ong ˏchung, in a great shiver and teeth chattering; 'k'i ˏchung, begin to shiver, scil. when cold weather commences.

'總 '揔 Tsung. To collect and tie up; to unite the whole; to combine or comprehend in one; all, altogether, the whole; still, nevertheless; a supervisor, one who controls all; a generic term; generally; in the coll. certainly, positively: com., [3]ek, 'chung, all in one; [5]'chung ˏkong, a summary, an outline; [7]'chung kĕüng' or kĕüng' 'chung, or [8]'chung kiĕk, the sum total; [9]'chung so' or 'chung p'wo' a general account book, a ledger; [10]'chung 'kwang, or [11]chung 'li, to have entire control of; [12]'chung tok, a viceroy; [13]ˏch'iĕng 'chung, a chiliarch, a colonel; [14]'chung ˏchoi, examiners for the Chinsz degree; COLL., [15]'lung 'chung, all, the whole; [16]'chung 'chung, wholly, certainly; [17]'chung 'mó, a model, a synopsis of; [18]'chung tioh, certainly, must; 'chung pwoh, chó' bent on doing; ˏi 'chung ˏli, he'll surely come; 'chung ˏt'au, the boss of a job; 'chung ˏmiăng, a general name or term.

'準 '准 Chun. To equalize, to fix, to adjust; to level, to measure; a rule, a gauge, a plumb, a line; even, exact, just; to run true, as a watch: [17]'chung chaik, a rule, a model; [18]ˏpieu 'chung, fixed, settled; COM., [19]'chung ˏt'i, the "many-handed" Budh; COLL., [20]'chung ˏt'au, the exact aim, as in archery; [21]ˏchŭng ˏkiăng á[2] 'chung má[2] 'chung, does the clock run right or not?

---

[1]逡巡 [2]豵豣 [3]一總 [4]總綱 [5]總共 [6]總結 [7]總數 [8]總管 [9]總理 [10]總督 [11]千總 [12]總裁 [13]隴總 [14]總總 [15]總樸 [16]總着 [17]準則 [18]標準 [19]準提 [20]準頭 [21]鐘行 儺準 賣準 ○

‘准 Chung. To permit, to approve; to hear or answer, as a prayer; to allow, to decide; to receive, as imperial orders on a certain day: COM., [1]pok, ‘chung (coll. ng꜆ ‘chung), not granted; [2]꜀p‘ié ‘chung, to approve officially; [3]‘chung pe꜆ to make ready; [4]‘chung ꜀ki ‘tó, to answer prayer, as God does; COLL. ‘chung sioh, siŭng꜆ ka꜆ granted on one throw of the divining blocks—one block with the obverse, the other with the reverse, side up.

‘Chung. A coll. word: to guess: ‘chung ‘chi, to guess dice, cash, or seeds, held in the hand; ‘chung me꜆ to guess riddles; ‘chung tioh, to guess correctly; ‘chung ꜀ting me꜆ to guess enigmas on lanterns—in the first month; k‘ëük, ‘nü ‘chung nioh, twai꜆ how many do you guess?

摏 榫 Read ‘sung in the dictionaries; to point a piece of wood and fit it into a hole; a tenon, a wooden spike.

‘傯 ‘偬 Ts‘ung. Poor and distressed; harassed, pressed: [5]꜀k‘ung ‘chung pok, ha꜆ worn out, harassed incessantly, distracted with cares.

꜀崇 Ts‘ung. Lofty, eminent; in the highest degree estimable and honorable; noble, exalted; worthy of worship; to adore, to praise, to extol; to revere; to collect, to fill: [6]꜀chung ꜀kó, very lofty; great, honorable; [7]꜀k‘ing ꜀chung ꜀t‘iéng tó꜆ to revere heavenly principles; ꜀chung ꜀tieu, the whole morning; [8]꜀chong ꜀chung, or ꜀chung tëüng꜆ to respect profoundly; COM., [9]꜀chung pai꜆ to worship; ꜀chung hong꜆ to obey reverently; [10]꜀chung ꜀ang, Chungan, a district in Kienning prefecture, celebrated for tea.

꜀叢 ꜀藂 Ts‘ung. A thicket, a bushy place; crowded, as trees; bushy; collected, assembled in numbers: ‘ch‘ó muk, ꜀chung, grass and trees crowded together; COM., [11]꜀chung ꜀ling, a thicket; [12]twai꜆ ꜀chung ꜀ling, a large monastery.

꜀潨 Smaller streams flowing into the main river—tributaries; the meeting of waters.

(70) Chŭng.

꜀鐘 Chung. A bell, a clock: COM., [13]꜀chŭng ‘ku, bells and drums; [14]꜀chŭng ꜀sang kang꜆ a temple of the ‘ngu tá꜆ at the ꜀Yong bridge, Foochow; [15]chëü꜆ ꜀ming ꜀chŭng, a clock; [16]꜀chŭng ‘pieu taing꜆ a clock and watch shop; taung꜆ ꜀chŭng, to ring or strike a bell; ꜀chŭng ‘hiong, the bell sounds; [17]꜀chŭng ꜀lau, a belfry; COLL., ‘kwi ‘teng ꜀chŭng, what o'clock is it?

꜀鍾 Chung. A measure equal to 64 or 100 ‘tau; a cup or goblet; to collect; to bestow, to confer; to repeat; heavy; gifted with, endowed; again, repeated: [18]꜀chŭng ai꜆ very dear, beloved; COM., sang꜆ ꜀chŭng, the surname ꜀Chŭng; [19]꜀chŭng ꜀ki, a god who

[1]不准 [2]批准 [3]准備 [4]准祈禱 [5]悾傯不暇 [6]崇高○ [7]欽崇天道 [8]尊崇 [9]崇拜 [10]崇安 [11]叢林 [12]大叢林 [13]鐘鼓 [14]鐘山澗 [15]自鳴鐘 [16]鐘錶店 [17]鐘樓 [18]鍾愛 [19]鍾馗

is said to extirpate evil spirits.

螽 ‘Tsung. A long-headed grasshopper; a species of locust: [1]‚*chüng* ‚*sü*, a green locust (truxalis).

舂 摏 ‚Chung. To beat with a pestle; to pound, to pulverize, to grind to powder: COM., [2]‚*chüng* ‘*mi*, to pound or hull rice in a mortar; COLL., [3]‚*chüng k‘o’* a stone mortar; ‚*chüng k‘o’ ‚t‘ui*, a pestle; ‚*chüng ch‘á’* to pound rice into flour; ‚*chüng* ‘*piéng*, to flatten by beating; ‚*kung* ‚*t‘au* ‚*chüng*, to beat with the fists.

終 ‚Chung. The end, termination, a finis; death; to end, to terminate; to end one's days; to the last; at length, finally: [4]‘*seng’* ‚*chüng*, to perform obsequies carefully; COM., [5]‘*siéng’* ‚*chüng*, a peaceful death; [6]‚*chüng* ‚*sing*, a lifetime; [7]‚*u* ‘*sü* ‚*u* ‚*chüng*, without beginning or end; ‚*chiong* ‘*sü* ‚*chiong* ‚*chüng*, complete from first to last; [8]‚*ling* ‚*chüng*, near death; ‚*chüng* ‘*kiu*, at last, finally; [9]‚*chüng* ‚*sing kiék‚ kwoh‚* to reap life's results—at death; [10]‚*chüng* ‚*sing twai’ sëü’* the great matter of life—i. e. marriage.

種 ‘Chung. A seed, a germ, a kernel; a sort, a kind, a class; that which sprouts: COM., [11]‚*tiong* ‘*chüng*, to transmit, to propagate; ‚*ong* ‘*chüng*, sprouts of grain; [12]‚*ngü* ‘*chüng*, little fishes; ‘*chüng* ‘*chüng*, sorts, kinds; [13]*chak‚* ‘*chüng*, mixed; illegitimate, a bastard; COLL. [14]‘*chüng* ‘*chi*, seed; *iê’* ‘*chüng*, to sow, to plant; *ch‘ioh‚* ‘*chüng*, seed-rice; *sioh‚* ‘*chüng loi’* of the same kind or species.

踵 ‘Chung. The heel; to follow one, to imitate, to go after one; to visit; to tread hard; to connect: [15]*chiék‚* ‘*chüng*, uninterruptedly.

煄 ‘Tsung. Fire burning up; to kindle, to burn: COM., [16]‘*hwi* ‘*chüng*, an ember or coal to kindle with.

瘇 腫 ‘Chung. To swell up, to tumefy; a swelling; inflated, swollen: COM., [17]‚*p‘eu* ‘*chüng*, swollen, inflated; ‚*wong* ‘*chüng*, jaundiced and puffed; [18]‘*chüng tiong’* dropsical; ‚*u* ‚*ming* ‘*chüng tuk‚* a sudden swelling or sore; COLL., *mëk‚ cheng’* ‘*chüng*, the eyes much swollen; ‘*chüng* ‘*k‘i* ‚*li*, to swell up, to bloat.

從 ‚Ts‘ung. To listen to, to follow, to comply with, to agree; to believe in; commencing from, place of origin; a preposition, through, by, from, in; since, whence; a way, a manner; compliance; a follower: also read ‚*ch‘üng* and *chëüng’* q. v.: ‚*chüng miéng’* to assent to one's face: COM., [19]‚*chüng meng’* to obey orders; ‚*chüng chëüng’* to follow the many; ‚*chüng piéng’* at convenience; [20]‚*chüng* ‚*kwong*, compulsory; [21]‚*chüng* ‚*chiéng*, formerly; ‚*chüng* ‘*ku* ‘*i* ‚*lai*, from former times to the present; ‚*chüng* ‘*ch‘ü haiu’* from this time on, henceforth; ‚*chüng* ‚*liong*, to reform, as a prostitute; *song’*

---

[1]螽斯 [2]摏米 [3]摏臼 [4]慎終 [5]善終 [6]終身 [7]無始無終 [8]臨終 [9]終身結局 [10]終身大事 [11]傳種 [12]魚種 [13]雜種 [14]種子 [15]接踵 [16]火煄 [17]浮腫 [18]腫脹 [19]從命 [20]從權 [21]從前

¸chŭng, to obey, to follow; [1]*chai^2 ¸ka ¸chŭng ho^2 ch'ok, ka^3 ¸chŭng ¸hu*, before marriage she obeys her father, after marriage her husband; COLL., [2]*¸chŭng ¸t'au ek, ne^3* item by item from the first; [3]*¸chŭng ¸sing chai^3 chó^3 ʻk'i*, to make over new again.

(71) Chwa.

抓 ʻChao. Read *ʻchau;* coll. *¸chwa:* to scratch, to titillate; to tear with claws; to grasp, to snatch, to clutch: [4]*¸chwa ¸pa ʻliăng*, to grasp by the collar; [5]*¸chwa ʻla ¸hong*, to mark or scratch in clutching; [6]*¸chwa má^2 tioh$_2$* fails to clutch it.

摣 ¸Ch'a. Read *¸cha;* used in the Paik Ing for the coll. *¸chwa:* to take; to pull, to draw, to drag; to pull out, to draw, as lots: the preceding character is commonly used instead of this: [7]*¸chwa ch'ok*, to pull out; [8]*¸chwa ¸ch'iéng*, to draw lots; [9]*¸chwa ¸pá*, to draw cards; [10]*¸chwa ¸k'ĕng*, to draw a bad card.

爪 ʻChao. Claws, talons, nails; to scratch, to claw; to take up with the fingers; an agent, a minion; the 87th radical: also read *ʻchau*, q. v.: [11]*ʻchwa ¸nga*, claws and teeth; *met.*, emissaries, assistants.

(72) Chwah.

Chwah$_2$ A coll. word: to vary from a model or standard; to err, to miss, to mistake: *yong^2 ʻchau chwah$_2$ k'ó^3* varies from the pattern; *kauk, chwah$_2$* a bone displaced, sprained.

(73) Chwai.

¸Chwai. A coll. word: to eat: *¸chwai kaing^3* accustomed to eat it; *¸chwai ʻpa*, or *¸chwai ʻpa ʻpa*, to eat heartily; *¸chwai má^2 k'ó^3* can't eat it all.

(74) Chwak.

攥 To grasp, to lay hold of; to take up with the hand.

繓 To bind, to tie; the lapping of a selvage, as in sewing.

(75) Chwang.

攢 ¸ Also read *chwang^3:* to collect, to assemble, to come together; to place a coffin in a dead house; poles and thatch to cover a coffin.

鑽 ¸Tsuan. An awl, a gimlet, an auger, a drill; to bore, to drill, to pierce, to perforate; *met.*, to worm yourself into, to investigate secrets; to pry into, as abstruse doctrines: [12]*¸chwang ¸chi ¸mi ¸kiéng*, the farther you bore the harder it is; *met.*, deep, abstruse; COM., [13]*¸chwang le^2* to toil for wealth, avaricious.

趲 ʻTsuan. Also read *chang^3:* to walk, to advance; to flee, to run away; to scatter, to put to flight; to hasten, to urge, to quicken, to press: [14]*ʻchwang pwo^4* to hasten one's steps.

纘 ʻTsuan. To connect things together, to continue, to carry on, to take up where another left off; to imitate, as virtues: [15]*ʻchwang sëü^2*

[1] 在家從父出嫁從夫 [2] 從頭一二 [3] 從新再做起 [4] 抓巴領 [5] 抓喇痕〇 [6] 抓賣着〇 [7] 摣出 [8] 摣籤 [9] 摣牌 [10] 摣空 [11] 爪牙 [12] 鑽之彌堅 [13] 鑽利 [14] 趲步 [15] 纘緒

or [1]‘chwang ˬsing, to carry on the work of a predecessor.

纂 ‘ Ts‘uan. Interchanged with the last: a kind of carnation band or cord, a red tassel or tape; to connect; to collate; to compile a work: [2]‘chwang ˬsiu, to collate, to examine and revise.

瓚 ‘ Tsuan. Also read chang’: a sort of stone scepter made with a cup, used in pouring out libations; a kind of bottle used in worship.

‘Chwang. A coll. word: full-fleshed, hearty, hale, stout.

賺 ’ Chuan. Huan. Read ‘kwang; coll. chwang’ in imitation of Foochow Mandarin: to profit, to make gain in trade: [3]chwang’ le’ to make gains; [4]ˬtó chwang’ ‘kwi ‘a ˬchiéng, gain a few cash more.

饌 ’ Chuan. To eat, to drink; to feed persons, to provide for; dressed food; delicacies, condiments, relishes: seng’ chwang’ a rich banquet; COM., [5]ˬngau chwang’ meats, delicacies.

撰 ’ Chuan. To regulate, to correct, to dispose in order; to grasp; to compose, to record; a statute, a rule; a received maxim; a business, an act; to edit, to revise books, to publish: [6]ˬsiu chwang’ to record; a title of the first Hanlin academician; [7]e’ chwang’ strange, marvelous; [8]chwang’ chié’ to compose works. Read saung’ to reckon. Read ‘song, to select, to commission.

譔 ’ Chuan. Used for the last: to admonish, to exhort by precepts; to communicate instruction: [9]chwang’ ˬung, to write essays; [10]chwang’ suk, to narrate.

(76) Chwi.

槌 ‘ Tsui. To beat anything with a piece of wood; a kind of hard wood.

顀 ‘ Tsui. Read ˬtwi; coll. ˬchwi: full, jutting out, prominent, as a forehead; full and rising in the middle, as the contents of a vessel: [11]ˬchwi ˬkeng, or ˬchwi ‘k‘i ˬli, rising, as leavened bread.

水 ‘ Chui. Water, liquids, fluids; fluid, running; clear, watery, limpid; aquatic; a stream, a river; a tide, the tide; a passage, the time of going by water from one place to another; danger by flood, inundation; the first of the five elements; a discount on coin or bullion; trivial, common, as water; easy, gentle, unstable; the 85th radical: COM., [12]‘ü ‘chwi, rain water; [13]‘chwi ‘k‘au, a town at the foot of the Min rapids; [14]‘chwi ‘hwo ˬhu, water-carriers and fire-kindlers; ‘chwi twai’ spring tides; [15]‘chwi ‘sieu, neap tides; [16]‘chwi ‘kieu, half-moon dumplings, stuffed and boiled; [17]‘chwi seng’ the nature of water; met., yielding, as said of bad women; [18]‘chwi ˬung, ripples; [19]song’ ‘chwi, to go with the tide; [20]‘chwi k‘auk, a puddle; [21]‘chwi

1 纘承 2 纂修 3 賺利 4 多賺幾個錢○ 5 殽饌 6 修撰 7 異撰 8 撰制 9 譔文 10 譔述 11 顀高 12 雨水 13 水口 14 水火夫 15 水小○ 16 水餃 17 水性 18 水紋 19 順水 20 水壑 21 水銀

,ngüng, quicksilver; [1]*'chwi ,lüng*, a fire-engine; [2]*'chwi ,siêng ,hwa*, the Narcissus; [3]*'chwoi 'hwo ,lu*, large pewter heaters used in liquor and barber shops; [4]*'chwi pwo'* the water-gate ward in Foochow suburbs; COLL., *'chwi ,hung*, the water is roiled; *'chwi p'wok,* scum on water; [5]*'chwi ,kié*, a frog; a flower of the 3d and 4th moons; *'chwi 'ma*, a water-spider; [6]*'chwi ,êng*, a pale red; [7]*'chwi p'au'* bubbles; [8]*'chwi p'a'* blisters; *,chu wai' 'chwi 't'u siăh, tek, tioh,* has become acclimated here; *chó' 'chwi*, watered, as rice to increase its bulk; to play in water, as a child; [9]*'chwi 'tong*, floodtide; [9]*'chwi p'wong'* ebb-tide; *'chwi t'auk*, or *'chwi tah,* water receding or drained off; *'chwi ,ch'au*, a naval review; *'chwi ,lau kiă'* water runs down; *met.*, to put the blame on subordinates; *'chwi 'ch'iêng ,ngü hiêng'* in shallows the fish appears; *met.*, known by plain facts.

(77) Chwo.

This syllable in its various tones is interchangeably read *Chio*, q. v.

(78) Chwoh.

This syllable in its various tones is interchangeably read *Chioh*, q.v.

(79) Chwoí.

贅, Chui. To plege, to pawn; an excrescence, a blemish; unsuitable; verbiage, tautology; connected with, hanging to, appended, as a postscript: [10]*chwoi' sá'* a son-in-law; [11]*chwoi' 'ngü*, tautology; [12]*ch'ok, chwoi'* to pawn, to pledge.

毳, The down on birds, the fine undergrowth of hair on animals; birds molting; furry, downy, soft, delicate; like felt, velvety: [13]*chwoi' 'miêng*, a felt hat; [14]*'hwo chwoi'* asbestos cloth; [15]*chwoi' mok,* a felt tent.

(80) Chwok.

(The next seven are interchangeably read *chiok.*)

茁, Chueh. Grass and plants just sprouting; fat, hearty, vigorous, as cattle: [16]*'ch'ó chwok, ,ki ,nga*, the plants have sprouted; *,ngiu ,yong chwok, chaung' 'tiong*, large fat cattle.

拙, Chueh. Stupid, dull; unskillful, unapt: [17]*'k'ieu chwok,* expertness and stupidity; COM., [18]*chwok, ,king*, the dull thorn, i. e. my wife: [19]*chwok, ,chai*, my poor abilities; COLL., *,i ,chai á' chwok, sioh, tek, 'kiăng*, his talent is rather inferior.

掇, Chueh. To pick up, to gather with the hand; to pluck, to seize, to lay hold on: [20]*chwok, sik,* to gather, to cull out.

(The next four also read *tiok.*)

啜, 歠, Chueh. To sob; to prate, to talk incessantly: to imbibe, to drink; to sip, to taste; to kiss: [21]*,liu chwok*, to gulp, to swill down; [22]*chwok, sëăk,* to drink congee; *met.*, poor, destitute.

剟, Chueh. To clip, to pare; to engrave; to mutilate, as culprits; to reject, to cast off:

[1]水龍 [2]水仙花 [3]水火爐 [4]水部 [5]水雞 [6]水紅 [7]水泡 [8]水濺 [9]水汐 [10]贅壻 [11]贅語 [12]出贅 [13]毳毧 [14]火毳 [15]毳幕 [16]草茁其芽 [17]巧拙 [18]拙荊 [19]拙才 [20]掇拾 [21]流啜 [22]啜菽

[1]'chwok, teng[2] to engrave and publish.

綴 Chueh. To join, to connect, to sew or tie together; to oversee royal robes; mixed, variegated; to stop, put an end to; fencers or posture-makers in ancient courts.

輟 Chueh. To stop, to desist from; a repaired carriage: [2]*hok, pok, chwok,* to study incessantly.

(81) Chwong.

This syllable in its various tones is interchangeably read *Chiong,* q. v.

(82) Ch'a.

差 Ch'a. A mistake, an error; mistaken, erroneous; to err, to differ, to miss the mark; difference, discrepancy; fault, excess; differing, unlike, unassorted: also read *ch'á* and *ch'i,* q. v.: COM., [3]*ch'a ch'auk,* error, mistake; used for death in coll. books; [4]*ch'a pok, tó,* nearly, almost; [5]*ch'a pok, 'teng,* unlike, of different sorts; [6]*hung hó pok, ch'a,* not the least error; COLL., [7]*ch'a tek, hwong*[2] a great difference; *ch'a sioh, pwo*[2] differs by one step—to vary slightly, a little too late; *ch'a sioh, 'hiéng,* a narrow escape from danger; *mó ch'a ié,* unchangeable, fixed.

叉 Ch'a. A fork in a road; a prong, a crotch; to cross or interlace the fingers: COM., [8]*ch'a 'ch'iu,* to interlace the fingers; [9]*t'iék, ch'a,* an iron fork; [10]*yá*[2] *ch'a,* evil spirits; COLL., *sang ch'a tio*[2] three diverging roads; [11]*sioh, kong sioh, ch'a,* a straight mark and a cross—error-marks in compositions; *ch'a má*[2] *tioh,* can't fork it.

扠 Ch'a. To fork out, to nip; to drive out, to pitch out, to strike.

杈 Ch'a. Used for the last: diverging branches of a tree; an instrument for catching fish; a prong for sticking mud-fish: [12]*ch'a ngü,* to fork fish; COM., [13]*ch'a t'iong*[2] a pronged stick; a long wooden fork; COLL., *aung*[2] *ch'a,* a long-handled prong, used in shops.

汊 岔 The first also read *ch'a*[2]: streams or roads diverging: [14]*sang ch'a lo*[2] *'k'eu,* a trivium; [15]*sang ch'a ó,* a river in Liautung.

瘥 Ch'a. Read *ch'ó;* coll. *ch'a:* to recover from sickness; convalescent, recovered; a slight ailment, a slight epidemic like the influenza: COM., [16]*'sau ch'a,* slightly better; COLL., *pang*[2] *á*[2] *ch'a,* the sickness has abated somewhat; *twai*[2] *ch'a,* much better; *chek, chiéng*[2] *'mwong ch'a,* steadily improving; *cheng*[2] *má*[2] *kiéng*[2] *ch'a,* no improvement in the disease.

炒 Ch'ao. To roast in a pan or boiler; to fry in fat or oil: COM., [17]*'ch'a ch'ai*[2] to fry vegetables in oil; [18]*'ch'a chau,* to fry with a seasoning of distiller's grains; COLL., *chiéng 'ch'a,* to fry and roast; *'ch'a 'mi,* or *'ch'a 'mi t'ong,* sug-

[1]剟定 [2]學不輟 [3]差錯〇 [4]差不多 [5]差不等 [6]分毫不差 [7]差的遠 [8]叉手 [9]鐵叉 [10]夜叉 [11]一杠一叉 [12]杈魚 [13]杈杖 [14]三岔路口 [15]三岔河 [16]稍瘥 [17]炒菜 [18]炒糟

ared rice roasted and formed into cakes; [1]*ch'a pwoi²* to heat and dry over a fire; *'ch'a ,chieu*, to roast and scorch, to toast thoroughly; *'ch'a ,kó ,pi*, to roast coffee; *'ch'a má² sŭk, ,kong má² lang²* fry it and it does not get done through, boil it and it does not become tender; *met.*, a blockhead.

吵 'Ch'ao. Read *'ch'au;* coll. *'ch'a:* to disturb, to annoy, to tease: [2]*'ch'a ,tiong*, to disturb a place of recreation; [3]*'ch'a 'ngu ,hiă*, to throw everything into confusion; [4]*p'ah, 'ch'a*, to cause trouble; [5]*k'ok, ,chu wai² 'ch'a 'ngwai*, you stay here and annoy me!

'Ch'a. A coll. word, as in *'ch'a ,seng*, or *'ch'a ,deng*, a short time since, a little while ago.

鈔 Ch'ao. Interchanged with *,ch'au* (to copy): a document, a government paper; a banknote, a receipt; paper money: COM., [6]*,chiéng ch'a'* (or *,chiéng p'ieu'*) government paper; [7]*pwang' ,ngŭng pwang' ch'a'* half in silver, half in paper; COLL., *ch'ek, ,siăng ,ngŭng ,sang ,siăng ch'a'* seven parts silver, three parts paper.

詫 Ch'a. To talk extravagantly, to vaunt; to deceive: [8]*,k'wa ch'a'* to boast; [9]*ch'a' nga²* startled; [10]*ch'a' e²* strange, in doubt.

吒 咤 Used for the last: to foam and sputter in anger; to talk angrily; to grumble: in the coll., to trouble, to interfere with: [11]*ch'ek, ch'a'* to rail at; COLL., [12]*p'ah, ch'a'* to disturb, to cause failures.

奼 Ch'a. A handsome girl, a beautiful unmarried young lady.

蜡 Ch'a. To bind up, to seal up; sealed up, as in winter; a sacrifice at the end of the year, when all things are sealed up by the cold.

柴 ,Ch'ai. Firewood, fuel, faggots; wood, brushwood; to stop up; to guard, to defend: COM., [13]*'t'ó ,ch'a*, to gather firewood; [14]*,ch'a ,tó*, a wood cleaver; [15]*,ch'a tang'* a picul of wood; [16]*,ch'a ,nga*, a wood broker; [17]*,ch'a ,hu*, a sudorific medicine; COLL., *p'wai' ,ch'a*, to split wood; *,ch'a kaik,* a sickle for cutting grass; *,ch'a ,t'au kioh,* blockheads, stupid workmen; [18]*,ch'a k'ah,* or *,ch'a 'chio k'ah,* wood dealers; *,ch'a 'hwi*, fuel; *,ch'a 'pa*, bundles of wood; *,ch'a 'tong*, a block to cut or pound on; *,ch'a p'woi'* chips, shavings; *,ch'a 'mi ,hu ,ch'á* "wood-and-rice husband and wife," *scil.* living together only while their stores last; *,ch'a kwok,* billets of wood; [19]*,ch'a ,ngü*, a wooden fish; *met.*, a blockhead.

瘵 ,Ch'ai. Thin, lean, emaciated, sick; *met.*, vicious, depraved; bad, spoiled, ruined: COLL., *,ch'a ngaing²* a kind of paralysis; [20]*,ch'a pe'* utterly vicious; ruined, as business; *cheng' 'yă ,ch'a*, a wasting disease; [21]*chó² ,ch'a*, to degenerate; to go on and spoil it; *mĕk, ,tu ,ch'a k'ó'* eyes fixed in death.

[1]炒	[3]吵	吵	吵	[7]半	[8]誇	[10]詫	[12]拍	[14]柴	[16]柴	[18]柴	[20]瘵
焙	五	[5]屈	我	銀	詫	異	吒	刀	牙	客	痺
[2]吵	鎛	只	[6]錢	半	[9]詫	[11]斥	[13]討	[15]柴	[17]柴	[19]柴	[21]坐
場	[4]拍	塊	鈔	鈔	訝	吒	柴	担	胡	魚	瘵

ₛ*Ch‘a.* A coll. prefix, as in ₛ*ch‘a* ₍*ch‘a*, forks; forked, transverse, crossed.

(83) Ch‘á.

妻 ₍Ch‘i. A wife, a partner, a spouse, a consort taken with legal ceremonies: [1]*‘ch‘ëü’* ₍*ch‘á*, to marry a wife; COM., [2]₍*hu* ₍*ch‘á*, husband and wife; [3]₍*ch‘á* ‘*chü*, wife and children; [4]*k‘aik*₎ ₍*ch‘á*, "destroys the wife"—as fortune-tellers say of a husband's adverse horoscope; [5]₍*ch‘á* ‘*chü hó*’ *hak*₎ a happy and united family; [6]₍*p‘au* ₍*ch‘a piék*₎ ‘*chü*, to leave wife and children, as when going on a journey; *t‘auk*₎ ₍*ch‘á kié*’ ‘*chü*, to entrust wife and children to another's care. Read *ch‘á*’; to give a daughter in marriage to one.

萋 ₍Ch‘i. Luxuriant foliage: ₍*ch‘á* ₍*ch‘á*, thick foliage; moving clouds; to exert one's self, as an officer does; [7]₍*ch‘á* ₍*chü*, cautious, reverential.

悽 ₍Ts‘au. Similar to the next: grieved, afflicted, sorrowful; suffering from hunger: [8]₍*ch‘á* ₍*ch‘á*, famishing; COM., [9]₍*ch‘á* ‘*ch‘ang*, or ₍*ch‘á* ‘*ch‘ang* ₍*ch‘á*, pitiable, distressing.

淒凄 ₍Ch‘i. Intense cold; bleak, cloudy, wintry, stormy, a cold wind; shivering, freezing; calamitous; afflicted, grieved: [10]₍*ku* ₍*ch‘á*, solitary, lonely; [11]₍*hung* ‘*ü* ₍*ch‘á* ₍*ch‘á*, sleety wind and rain; COM., [12]₍*ch‘á* ₌*liong*, or ₍*ch‘á* ₌*liong* ₍*ch‘á* ‘*ch‘ang*, pitiable, grievous; afflicted.

緀 ₍Ch‘i. The stripes, colored or plain, in silken fabrics; ornamented, blended colors and stripes.

棲栖 ₍Ch‘i. To roost, to perch, to nestle; to sojourn, to stay at; to reside, to settle down; to rest, to repose, at peace; a perch, a sleeping place, lodgings: [13]₍*ch‘á* ₍*seng*, a place to live, a home; [14]*chang*’ ₍*ch‘á*, temporary lodgings; COM., [15]₍*ch‘á* ₍*sing*, or ₍*ch‘á* ‘*chi*, or ₍*ch‘á póh*₎ a stopping place; COLL., ₌*mó tói*’ ₍*ch‘á póh*₎ no place to stay, no home.

差 ₍Ch‘a. Read ₍*ch‘ai* in the dictionaries; coll. ₍*ch‘á*: a messenger, a commissioner, an embassador, one sent to manage affairs; to send, to commission: also read ₍*ch‘a* and ₍*ch‘i*, q. v.: COM., [16]₍*k‘ing* ₍*ch‘á*, an imperial commissioner; [17]₌*meu* ₍*ch‘á*, to look out for business; [18]₍*tong* ₍*ch‘á*, to be a policeman; *chiék*₎ ₍*ch‘á*, the bearer of a memorial to the emperor; ₍*ch‘á* ‘*k‘iéng*, or [19]₍*ch‘á* ‘*sai*, to send, to commission; [20]₍*ch‘á* ₍*sung*, revenue cutters; ₍*ch‘á* ‘*lá*, a policeman's fees; ₌*ngwong* ₍*ch‘á* (coll. ₍*ch‘á yăh*₎ or ₍*ch‘á* ₌*nëng*), messengers, bailiffs; *paing*’ ₍*ch‘á*, to provide for officers while traveling; [21]₍*ch‘á* ₍*cha*, a police search.

糁 ‘Ts‘au. A vulgar character, used in the *Paik*₎ ₍*Ing* for coll. *ch‘á*’: flour made from rice: ‘*kwi ch‘á*’ rice flour for steamed dumplings; *t‘ai ch‘á*’ to sift rice flour; *ch‘á*’ ₍*chio*, coarse particles in pounded

[1]娶妻 [2]夫妻 [3]妻子 [4]尅妻 [5]妻子好合 [6]抛妻別了 [7]萋苴 [8]悽悽 [9]悽慘 [10]孤凄 [11]風雨凄凄 [12]凄凉 [13]棲生 [14]暫棲 [15]棲身 [16]欽差 [17]謀差 [18]當差 [19]差使 [20]差船 [21]差查

rice; *chʻá*ʾ *chʻá*ʾ *pah*꜀ as white as rice flour; ʻ*saĕng*ʾ *chʻá*ʾ a present of rice flour to a family in mourning; [2]꜀*hwoi chʻá*ʾ presents in return for rice-flour.

(84) Chʻaĕ.

⿱艹初ʾ Tsao. A vulgar character used in the *Paik*꜀ ꜀*Ing*; a kind of long gourd with a rough deep-green skin: COLL., [3]꜀*sié chʻaĕ*ʾ a long serpentine gourd; [4]*chʻaĕ*ʾ ꜀*nong*, gourd-pith—used as a medicine; *chʻaĕ*ʾ ʻ*mó*, seed-gourds; [5]*chʻaĕ*ʾ ꜀*pang*, a frame to trail gourd-vines on.

擦ʾ Chʻa. Read *chʻak*꜀; used for the coll. *chʻaĕ*ʾ: to rub with the hands or feet: [6]*chʻaĕ*ʾ ꜀*kwong* ꜀*kwong*, to rub smooth; [7]*chʻaĕ*ʾ ʻ*kʻi*, or *chʻaĕ*ʾ *kʻó*ʾ or *chʻaĕ*ʾ ꜀*mó*, to rub off; [8]*chʻaĕ*ʾ *má*² ʻ*kʻi*, can't rub it off.

*Chʻaĕ*ʾ A coll. word: to scold, to repel sternly: *chʻaĕ*ʾ ꜀*nĕng*, to scold people; *tói*ʾ *chʻaĕ*ʾ to rail at each other.

(85) Chʻaĕk.

軸꜀ Tsu. Read *tŭk*꜀; used in the *Paik*꜀ ꜀*Ing* for the coll. *chʻaĕk*꜀: a chart, a map; a hanging picture or drawing; pasteboard for maps, &c.: [9]*pwoi*ʾ *chʻaĕk*, to make pasteboard for charts; [10]*che*² *chʻaĕk*, a scroll with inscriptions; [11]*wa*² *chʻaĕk*, drawings, pictures; *chʻaĕk*꜀ ꜀*tʻau*, the lower roller of a chart; *chʻaĕk*꜀ *sioh*꜀ *hok*꜀ one map, one hanging picture; [12]ʻ*ku chʻaĕk*꜀ *má*² ꜀*kiăng*, old charts are not salable.

Chʻaĕk꜀. A coll. intensive particle, as in *chʻaĕk*, *chʻaĕk*, ꜀*sing*, or *chʻĕk*꜀ *chʻaĕk*, ꜀*sing*, quite fresh, span-new.

(86) Chʻaĕng.

諺ʾ Tsʻan. Read ꜀*chʻang*, used in the *Paik*꜀ ꜀*Ing* for the coll. *chʻaĕng*ʾ: to make another angry; to provoke; mutual recriminations: [13]*chʻaĕng*ʾ ʻ*kʻi* *chʻaĕng*ʾ angry recriminations.

*Chʻaĕng*ʾ. A coll. word, as in *chʻaĕng*ʾ ʻ*kʻi*, to bristle up, as hair; to rise, to flame up, as fire: ꜀*tʻau hwok*꜀ *chʻaĕng*ʾ ʻ*kʻi* ꜀*li*, the hair bristling; *kʻe*ʾ *chʻaĕng*ʾ *chʻaĕng*ʾ ʻ*kʻi*, steam rising; anger flaming up.

(87) Chʻah.

册꜀ Tsʻĕ. Read *chʻaik*꜀; coll. *chʻah*꜀: a slip, an inventory, a register, a list; a census-book; a patent or commission of nobility: [14]꜀*chü chʻah*, a register; books; [15]*hok*꜀ *chʻah*, to examine the official records; [16]*chai*ʾ *chʻah*, recorded; [17]*chaiu*ʾ ꜀*sieu chʻah*, revenue report to the emperor; [18]*chʻah*꜀ *kwong*ʾ documents, law-books; ꜀*kau tai*² *chʻah*, a transfer-paper; [19]*piéng*² ʻ*lang chʻah*, official list of literary candidates; [20]꜀*ting* ʻ*kʻeu chʻah*, a census of population; *chʻah*꜀ ꜀*hung*, a patent of nobility; a commission, as to appoint a king of Loochoo.

策꜀ Tsʻĕ. Read *chʻaik*꜀; coll. *chʻah*꜀: a book, an essay, writings: *ngo*² *tó*² *chʻah*, essays on the five themes at the 3d session of examina-

1送	3蛇	5⿱艹初	光	賣	10字	12古	13諺	册	册	18册	册
棲	⿱艹初	棚	7擦	起	軸	軸	起	15核	17奏	卷	20丁
2回	4⿱艹初	6擦	起	9褙	11畫	賣	諺	册	銷	19便	口
棲	瓤	光	8擦	軸	軸	行	14書	16載	册	覽	册

福州方言拼音字典

tions for Kŭjin—hence called [1]꜀sang ꜀tiong ch'ah꜆; [2]cheng꜄ ꜀tiâng ch'ah, the prize essay of the first Kŭjin, and list of graduates, as forwarded to Peking; [3]꜀hiong se꜄ ch'ah, essays at the 3d session of the provincial examinations; [4]꜀chŭ ch'ah, books; [5]tói꜄ ch'ah, to compare copies with the original essays; [6]mwong꜄ ch'ah, subjects for 3d session essays; [7]꜀taing꜆ se꜄ ch'ah, essays of the Chintsz at the examination before the emperor.

Ch'ah꜆. A coll. word, as in *ch'ah*, ꜂*k'i*, to raise up, to lift; to help one rise; *ch'ah* ꜀*keng*, to raise high.

Ch'ah꜆. A coll. word, as in *ch'ah*꜆ *ch'ih*꜆ almost, nearly, within a little: ꜂*wang* ꜀*tó* ꜂*ch'iu ch'ah*꜆ *ch'ih*꜆ *p'ah*꜆ *p'wai*꜄ carried the bowl in his hand and almost broke it.

(88) Ch'ai.

纔 ꜀Ts'ai. Read ꜀*ch'ai*; coll. ꜀*ch'ai*: now, just now; scarcely; used in imitation of the court dialect; the common colloquial is *chiâh*, q. v.: [8]꜀*ch'ai* ꜀*ch'ai*, just now; [9]꜀*ch'ai* ꜀*ch'ai k'ó*꜄ has just gone.

猜 ꜀Ts'ai. To guess, to conjecture, to doubt; to dislike, to abhor; to fear, to apprehend, lest: [10]꜀*teng* ꜀*ch'ai*, enigmas on lanterns; [11]꜀*ch'ai tok*꜆ to judge of; [12]꜀*ch'ai pok*꜆ *ch'ok*, inconceivable; COM., [13]꜀*ch'ai* ꜂*siong*, to suspect; ꜀*si* ꜀*ch'ai*, to "guess poetry"—by supplying the missing word; ꜀*ch'ai* ꜀*kung*, to "guess the fist," or number of extended fingers, morra—a drinking game; ꜀*ch'ai me*꜆ to guess a riddle; COLL., *k'ĕŭk*, ꜂*nŭ* ꜀*ch'ai*, for you to guess.

釵 ꜀Ch'ai. A broad hairpin; *met.*, females: COM., [14]꜀*ch'ai* ꜀*k'wang* ꜂*siu sek*, hairpins, rings, and head-ornaments in general; [15]꜀*hung* ꜀*ch'ai p'ó*꜄ *kiâng*꜄ to scatter the hairpins and break the mirrors; *met.*, a family broken up.

采 ꜂Ch'ai. Interchanged with the next three: to pluck, to choose, to take with the hand; variegated, adorned with colors; cities or lands allotted to officers for revenue; a surname: [16]꜂*ch'ai kwo*꜄ to select sentences; *pek*꜆ *seu*꜄ ꜂*ch'ai*, a white ground takes the colors; COM., [17]꜀*hwa* ꜂*ch'ai*, variegated, beautiful; [18]꜂*ngu* ꜂*ch'ai*, the five colors.

採 ꜂Ts'ai. To select, to pick, to pluck, to choose, to take with the hand: COM., [19]꜂*ch'ai* ꜂*mâ*, to buy up for government, as rice; ꜂*ch'ai* ꜀*leng*, or ꜂*ch'ai* ꜀*leng* ꜂*ku*, to collect money (as for the dragon-boat festival) by beating gongs, and drums; ꜂*ch'ai* ꜀*leng* ꜀*kó*, "songs of the Lotus," sung at the dragon-boat festival; ꜂*ch'ai* ꜀*ta*, to pick tea leaves.

寀 ꜂Ts'ai. Lands or cities allotted for the revenue of officers: ꜂*ch'ai te*꜆ territory set apart for grandees; ꜀*lieu* ꜂*ch'ai*, officers jointly ruling a circuit.

彩 ꜂Ts'ai. Variegated, ornamented with different colors, elegant, gay-colored; beautiful, as figures in silks and

[1]三場策 [2]進呈策 [3]鄉試策 [4]書策 [5]對策 [6]問策 [7]殿試策 [8]纔纔 [9]纔纔去 [10]燈猜 [11]猜度 [12]猜不出 [13]猜想 [14]釵環首飾 [15]分釵破鏡 [16]采句 [17]華采 [18]五采 [19]採買

gems; lucky, pleased: COM., [1]*,kwong 'ch'ai*, glossy, brilliant; [2]*'ch'ai wa'* painting in colors; [3]*'ch'ai saik,* variegated; COLL., *'ch'ai ch'ëü'* fine prospect, said of a flourishing family, festivities, &c.; *'ng' ,t'ëng pa'h, 'ngwai 'ch'ai ,t'au*, don't injure my good omen! *scil.* by uttering infelicitous words; *,hwa 'ch'ai*, a gift to a messenger; *'sieu 'ch'ai*, douceurs—as to waiters in eating houses; *hak, 'ch'ai*, to encore, to praise; *,k'wi 'ch'ai*, to commence any business; *mëk, 'ch'ai*, a good eye, discriminating taste.

'綵 Ts'ai. Interchanged with the last: variegated silks or satins; festoons, streamers: COM., [5]*'ch'ai ,tiu*, red silk for festoons; [6]*'ch'ai ,ki*, red silk banners borne before graduates and at funerals; [7]*'ch'ai pwo'* red cotton cloth; [8]*,lüng hong' 'ch'ai 'piäng*, presents of cakes before weddings; [9]*kiëk, 'ch'ai ,yong ,teng*, to wreathe festoons and light lanterns; COLL., *'ch'ai kaik,* festoons; *saëng' 'ch'ai*, to send silks and satins (to the betrothed); [10]*,sang ,cheng 'ch'ai kieu'* a three-storied ornamented sedan; *p'wak, 'ch'ai*, to wear silken scarfs, as graduates do.

'棌 Ts'ai. A sort of tree, the wood of which is hard and durable like that of the chestnut or locust.

'睬 Ts'ai. To pay attention to, to notice, to greet: [11]*pok, ,ch'iu* (or *,chieu*) *pok, 'ch'ai*, the cut direct, to pay no attention to.

菜' Ts'ai. Vegetables, edible herbs, greens; food, viands: [12]*ch'ai' saik,* an emaciated look; [13]*,su ch'ai'* vegetables: COM., [14]*ch'ai' ,hwong*, a garden of herbs; [15]*,chau ch'ai'* pickled vegetables; [16]*'hai ch'ai'* seaweed, limpets; [17]*'sieu ch'ai'* condiments of leaves and greens; COLL., *siäh, ch'ai'* to be a vegetarian; *ch'ai' ,t'au*, the turnip-radish; *ch'ai' 'chëng*, salted leaves of vegetables; *pah, ch'ai'* cabbage; *ch'ai' ,chai*, vegetable sprouts; *ch'ai' ,kang*, dried vegetables; *met.*, rumpled clothes; *ch'ai' ,t'ong pwong'* herb-soup and rice—thank-offering to the *a' kai'*; *ch'ai' huk,* "herb-Budh," i. e. a vegetarian; *ch'ai' ,pié*, or *ch'ai' ,pó ,pié*, the outer leaves of vegetables; *ch'ai' kwok,* vegetable stalks; *ch'ai' ,t'ëng ch'ai' 'lá 'si*, the vegetable worm perishes with the vegetable; *met.*, the sinner dies in his sins; *mwoi' siäh, ,sang nik, ch'ai' pwoh, 'siong siong' ,sá ,t'iéng*, expects to be deified before he has fasted three days.

蠆' Ts'ai. A bee; an insect having a sting; a kind of scorpion with a long tail: [18]*,p'ung ch'ai'* a bee; *ch'ai' 'mwi*, the sting of a bee.

蔡' Ts'ai. Grass, herbs, esculent herbs; a law, a rule; name of a feudal state, now Juning-fu in the southeast of Honan; a tortoise: *ch'ai' sëük,* a prince of the Chow dynasty.

纔 Ts'ai. An adverb of time; just now, near, at hand; shortly, presently, then, at once;

1光彩 2彩畫 3彩色 4体通 拍我 彩頭 5綵綢 6綵旗 7綵布 8龍鳳 綵餅 9結綵 燃燈 10三層 綵轎 11不睬 不睬 12菜色 13蔬菜 14菜園 15糟菜 16海菜 17小菜 18蜂蠆

scarcely, barely: in the coll. read *꜀ch'ai*, q. v.: [1]*꜀ch'ai ꜀lai*, just come; [2]*꜀ch'ai 'k'ó*, then it will do; [3]*꜀hwong ꜀ch'ai*, then, just now.

豺 Read *꜀chai*; coll. *꜀ch'ai*: a ravenous beast, a wolf or lynx: [4]*꜀ch'ai ꜀long*, a wolf; [5]*꜀ch'ai ꜀long ꜀sing ꜀kang*, a wolf's heart; *met.*, cruel.
꜀Ch'ai.

(89) Ch'aik.

側, Side, the side, on the side, lateral; to incline, to bow down, to bend; mean, perverted, low; rebellious, seditious; only one: in the coll. read *chaik*, q.v.: [6]*꜀sang ch'aik,* hill-side; *'tiéng 'tiong 'hwang ch'aik*, tossing to and fro, sleepless; [7]*ch'aik, muk,* to cast hateful glances at; [8]*ch'aik, 'ngi*, to incline the ear; [9]*'hwang ch'aik*, rebellious; COM., [10]*ch'aik, sek,* a concubine.
Ts'ê.

測, To fathom, to sound; to estimate, to measure; pure, clear, as varnish: COM., [11]*ch'aik, tok,* to fathom, to investigate; [12]*pok, ch'aik,* inscrutable, as a sudden death; [13]*ch'aik, che'* to dissect words—a species of divination.
Ts'ê.

惻, Secret grief; distress; to pity, to commiserate, to sympathize: in the coll. anger, envy: COM., [14]*ch'aik, 'ŭng*, tender-hearted, humane; [15]*'k'u ch'aik*, grieved; COLL., *ch'aik, ꜀sing*, or *ch'aik, ch'aik, ꜀sing*, displeasure; distressed, as by death of friends; *ch'aik, ꜀sing taĕng'* deep envy; *ch'aik, 'si ꜀nĕng*, "envious to death"—filled with envy; *꜀t'iê cheng' ch'aik*, to weep bitterly; *ch'aik, ꜀nĕng po' ch'ieu' ꜀nĕng ꜀kŭng*, to envy the rich and mock the poor.
Ts'ê.

莿, A thorn, a spike, a prickle; to prick, to pierce with a thorn.
Ts'ê.

策, A bamboo slip, such as books were once engraved on; a book, a writing; a stratagem, a plan, means, an expedient, a scheme; to whip, a switch, a whip; a divining slip: in the coll. read *ch'ah*, q.v.: [16]*꜀chü ch'aik*, books; COM., [17]*'kiê' ch'aik*, a scheme, a contrivance; [18]*꜀liong ch'aik*, a capital plan; [19]*hiong' ch'aik*, to submit a plan.
Ts'ê.

册, **冊**, A list, an inventory, a register; a census-book; a patent or commission of nobility; to choose, to plan, to contrive: in the coll. read *ch'ah*, q.v.: [20]*꜀chü ch'aik*, books; [21]*'sü ch'aik*, a historian.
Ts'ê.

栅, Posts of a stockade, a railing; a stockade: in the coll. read *chak,* q.v.: [22]*ch'aik, ꜀mwong*, street-gates.
Ts'ê.

拆, To break up or open, to split; to destroy, to pull down, to take away; to dissect, to take to pieces: [23]*ch'aik, eng'* to dismiss from office; *ch'aik, 'hwi*, to destroy; *ch'aik, ꜀k'ai*, to split, to open.
Ts'ê.

坼, To rive, to crack, to open, to burst open, as buds; split, riven, cracked: *kak, ch'aik*, the bursting of buds.
Ts'ê.

---

[1]纔來 [2]纔可 [3]方纔 [4]豺狼 [5]豺狼心肝 [6]山側 [7]側目 [8]側耳 [9]反側 [10]側室 [11]測度 [12]不測 [13]測字 [14]惻忍 [15]苦惻 [16]書策 [17]計策 [18]良策 [19]獻策 [20]書册 [21]史册 [22]栅門 [23]拆任

(90) Chʻaing.

讖ʾ Chʻien. To verify, to prove, to fulfill; a prognostic, an omen, a sign: COM., [1]*chʻaingʾ tieuʾ* a prophecy, an omen; [2]*chʻaingʾ ꜀chü*, a priest's fees; [3]*chʻaingʾ ʻngü*, prophetic sayings; COLL., *maĕngʾ chʻaingʾ* a prophetic dream; *chʻaingʾ ꜀ngai*, the omen is bad.

襯ʾ Tsʻen. Inner garments; to give, to assist, to patronize, to befriend; to give effect to, to illustrate, to show off; to match: COM., [4]*꜀pui chʻaingʾ* to illustrate by examples; [5]*chʻaingʾ ꜀sang*, long dresses worn by Manchu women and concubines; [6]*chʻaingʾ ꜀i*, or [7]*chʻaingʾ ꜀pó*, a Tauist's gown.

櫬ʾ Tsʻen. An inner coffin; to collect firewood. Read *kwangʾ* a bucket for drawing water.

倩ʾ Chʻien. Beautiful, good, comely, fair, personable, as youths; a pretty mouth, smiling; a daughter's husband; to borrow for a purpose, to serve an occasion: in the coll. read *chʻiăngʾ* q. v.: [8]*chʻaingʾ tai²* to employ a substitute, for, instead of; [9]*ʻmi chʻaingʾ* fine, beautiful.

蒨ʾ Chʻien. Used for the next: luxuriant herbage: fine growing grain; fresh, new; fine, illustrious.

茜ʾ Tsʻen. A plant, called [10]*chʻaingʾ ʻchʻó*, the root of which dyes red or madder; one sort gives the carnation color, once used to dye the imperial robes.

(91) Chʻaiu.

湊ʾ **凑**ʾ Tsʻou. To collect, to gather; to run together, to run into each other; a gathering on the water, as at a regatta; to go with, to enter together; a concurrence, as of circumstances; in the coll. to add to, to increase, to supply a deficiency: COLL., [11]*chʻaiuʾ ꜀chiĕng*, to add more cash; *chʻaiuʾ ʻking*, to add to one's troubles; *꜀tʻiĕng chʻaiuʾ* to add to; *chʻaiuʾ sioh꜆ chiŭh*, to add one more; *chʻaiuʾ ʻlá naungʾ* confusion worse confounded; [12]*chʻaiuʾ twang²* to increase the mortgage and sell off; *chʻaiuʾ soʾ* to make up the number; [13]*chʻaiuʾ poʾ* to grow richer and richer; *chak꜆ chʻaiuʾ* to add in at random.

(92) Chʻak.

察꜆ Tsʻa. To examine, to judge, to search out the truth, to observe closely, to look into all the particulars: COM., [14]*꜀cha chʻak*, to scrutinize; [15]*ʻsing chʻak*, to examine, as one's own heart; [16]*sáʾ chʻak*, to examine carefully; [17]*chʻak꜆ chʻok*, to ferret out; [18]*chʻak꜆ ꜀ching*, to investigate the circumstances of; [19]*chʻak꜆ twak꜆* to examiue and decide officially; [20]*angʾ chʻak꜆ ꜀si*, provincial judge; [21]*sek꜆ kauk꜆ chʻak*, to neglect to examine.

擦꜆ Chʻa. To rub with the hand; to rub hard: [22]*꜀mó chʻak*, to rub smooth.

扱꜆ Tsʻa. Wrongly used for the next: to take, to receive; to raise; to courtesy with the hands bowed to the

[1]讖兆 [3]讖語 [5]襯衫 [7]襯袍 [9]美倩 [11]湊錢 [12]湊斷 [14]查察 [16]細察 [18]察情 [20]按察 覺察

[2]讖資 [4]陪襯 [6]襯衣 [8]倩代 [10]茜草 ○ [13]湊富 [15]審察 [17]察出 [19]察奪 司 [21]失 [22]磨擦

ground; to tuck up the skirts.

插, 挿, Ch'a. To insert, to pierce, to set in, to stick into, to tuck in; to thrust into or through; to transplant; to set in a socket; to meddle, to interfere in, to help; an iron-pointed pole used for carrying sheaves or prying up clods, in which sense the next is used: COM., [1]ch'ak˒ ˓hwa, to insert flowers, as in a vase; [2]ch'ak˒ ˓liu, to stick willow boughs, as a charm at the ˓Ch'ing ˓ming festival; COLL., [3]ch'ak˒ ˓ch'ang, to stick up green twigs, as one does when leprous, to ward off the disease from his village; ch'ak˒ ˓ong, to set out rice shoots; [4]ch'ak˒ chioh, to stick up a candle; met., a boat going down stern foremost; ch'ak˒ ch'oi˒ to interrupt by talking; [5]ch'ak˒ ˓ch'ó má˒ ˓sing, "stick grass in the hair and sell one's self into slavery"—as the poor say when pressed for money; [6]ch'ak˒ pek˒ ˓nëng tai˒ to meddle in other people's business; ˓k'ing ch'ak˒ tai˒ willing to help.

鍤, Ch'a. Iron farming utensils, spades; a pointed pole to carry sheaves called [7]hó˒ ch'ak˒; a needle: used in the coll. for a flat hairpin ornamented with green swallow feathers: COLL., [8]ch'ak˒ ak˒ a hairpin casket.

臿, Ch'a. To pound off the husks of wheat; a pounder used in building earth walls: used for ch'ak˒ (to insert): [9]tëük˒ ch'ak˒ a pounder used in making earth walls, in the coll. called tëük˒ ˓ch'ü.

歃, Ch'a. To drink each other's blood in spirits; to bloody the lips—a form of oath: [10]ch'ak˒ hiék˒ to let blood and touch the lips with it—an oath of blood.

褔, Ch'a. Garments with a double border: COM., [11]ch'ak˒ kaëk˒ the pieces inserted at the sides where the skirts separate.

(93) Ch'ang.

參, 叅, Ts'an. To be concerned with; to join with for consultation, to advise, to give counsel to; to blend, to mix, to adulterate, to mix in, as inferior goods; to form one of three; to have an audience, to see one; to impeach, to report to the throne on other officers; confused, mixed, as colors; a deposition, an impeachment; the 20th constellation comprising the stars a, b, g, d, e, x, é, and k, in Orion: [12]˓ch'ang hiok˒ to wait upon a superior; [13]˓ch'ang ˓k'ó, to examine; COM., [14]˓ch'ang ˓meu, to plan, to scheme; [15]˓ch'ang pai˒ or [16]˓ch'ang kiéng˒ to visit a superior; [17]˓ch'ang chiong˒ a colonel; [18]˓ch'ang ˓ch'a pok˒ ˓chá, uneven, unassorted; [19]˓kwang ˓ch'ang, to depose from office; [20]˓ch'ang ˓wong, a degraded officer; COLL., [21]˓ch'ang ˓chwi, to add water; met., to talk covertly; ˓ch'ang taëng˒ to cool by adding cold water.

摻, Tsan. A delicate hand, a hand with tapering fingers; fine, tapering, small; to take up with the hand.

1 挿花 2 挿柳 3 挿青 4 挿燭 5 挿草賣身 6 挿別仈代 7 荷鍤 8 鍤盒 9 築臿 10 歃血 11 褔角 12 參謁 13 參考 14 參謀 15 參拜 16 參見 17 參將 18 參差不齊 19 官叅 20 叅員 21 叅水

篸 ꜀Ts'an. Bamboos varying in length; a pandean pipe; a hairpin.

驂 驂 ꜀Ts'an. Three horses abreast in a chariot; the horses outside the thills, called [1]꜀ch'ang ʻma; [2]tw'ak, ꜀ch'ang ꜀i chaing꜄ (Confucius) loosed the outside horse and gave it (to a poor man).

青 ꜀Ch'ing. Read ꜀ch'ing; coll. ꜀ch'ang: the color of nature, as the azure sky, or the green of growing plants; a green or blue tint; a dark color; wan, pale, sallow; [3]twai꜄ ꜀ch'ang, or ꜀ching ꜀ch'ang, dark, jet black; [4]꜀t'iéng ꜀ch'ang, a reddish black; [5]t'iék꜂ ꜀ch'ang, iron-gray; [6]꜀ch'ang kak꜂ a kind of green frog; [7]꜀ch'ang ʻkiăng, apricots; [8]꜀ch'ang ʻkwo, "the green fruit"—olives; ꜀ch'ang ꜀kŭng, "blue vein"—a fierce fellow; ꜀ch'ang ꜀lang, dark blue; [9]꜀ch'ang sioh꜂ porphyry; ꜀ch'ang ꜀ch'ang lioh꜂ lioh꜂ dark and greenish; ꜀ch'ang pok꜂ ꜀ch'ang ꜀lang pok꜂ ꜀lang, neither black nor blue; *met.*, as one neither decidedly wise nor silly; [10]꜀ch'ang ꜀i, "dark clothes"—a play-actor in female dress; ꜀ch'ang ꜀i siăng꜄ black silk thread; [11]꜀ch'ang pwo꜄ black cotton cloth; [12]꜀ch'ang ꜀wong, dark yellow, jaundiced.

生 ꜀Shĕng. Read ꜀seng; coll. ꜀ch'ang: raw, green, unripe; *met.*, ignorant, unskilled; a stranger: [13]꜀ch'ang ch'ek꜂ raw varnish; ꜀hwang ꜀ch'ang, "becomes more and more raw;" *met.*, at last unwilling; [14]꜀ch'ang siăh꜂ eaten raw; [15]ʻk'i ꜀ch'ang, to insult a stranger; [16]꜀ch'ang ʻleng, things raw and cold—*scil.* to be eaten sparingly; [17]꜀ch'ang ꜀t'au, "raw head"—one ignorant, yet assuming; ꜀ch'ang sŭk꜂ ꜀hong, uncured and cured tobacco; pwang꜄ ꜀ch'ang sŭk꜂ half raw and half ripe or cooked; [18]꜀ch'ang te꜄ a bulbous root—medicine for the blood; ꜀ch'ang ꜀kiăng, greatly frightened; ꜀ch'ang ʻch'iu, an unpracticed hand; ꜀ch'ang mwong꜄ taung꜄ green and silly, as in teasing one excessively.

青 ꜀Chĕng. Read ʻseng; coll. ꜀ch'ang, as in [19]꜀ch'ang ꜀mang, blind; ꜀ch'ang ꜀mang pó꜄ ʻmwo nai꜄ pwoh꜂ twai꜄ the blind in getting wives wish only for large ones; *met.*, to regard only size in choosing; ꜀ch'ang ꜀mang ꜀nëng ꜀k'ié hak꜂ ʻma, a blind man riding a blind horse; *met.*, to attempt hazardous feats.

慘 憏 ʻTs'an. Cruel, inhuman, hard-hearted; to be afflicted, pained, injured in mind; a superlative applied to sufferings, sad! lamentable! [20]ʻch'ang kok꜂ unfeeling, tyrannical; COM., [21]꜀ch'á ʻch'ang, most lamentable; [22]ʻch'ang ꜀siong, pained, deeply grieved; COLL., ꜀ch'á ꜀liong ꜀ch'á ʻch'ang, distressing, most pitiable; [23]ʻch'ang ʻló, alas! ʻch'ang ꜀mó ʻch'ang, is it not sad?

憯 ʻTs'an. Like the preceding: pained, feeling acutely, grieved, distressed; sickened from former suffering; already, formerly:

[1]驂馬 [2]脫驂 而贈 [3]大青 [4]天青 [5]鐵青 [6]青蛤 [7]青仔 [8]青果 [9]青石 [10]青衣 [11]青布 [12]青黃 [13]生漆 [14]生食 [15]欺生 [16]生冷 [17]生頭 [18]生地 [19]青盲 [20]慘酷 [21]悽慘 [22]慘傷 [23]慘咾

[1]*ch'ang t'ak*, to feel acutely.

醒 Sing. Read *sing*; coll. *ch'ang*, as in [2]*ch'ing ch'ang*, to awake, as from sleep or intoxication; [3]*pwak, ch'ang*, to arouse, to excite by appeal or instruction.

Ch'ang. A coll. word, as in *ch'ang ch'ang sing*, just new; fresh and fine, as clothes.

粲 Ts'an. Half a *tau* or peck; a meal; fine rice, rice flour; many, much; fine, excellent, beautiful, as woman;- to laugh, smiling; to examine; clear, bright; three girls together: [4]*pek, ch'ang* white rice, anciently culled as a punishment; [5]*ch'ang yong*, laughing; clear, pure; [6]*ch'ang ch'ang*, *i huk*, beautiful clothes.

燦 Ts'an. Bright, clear, resplendent: COM., *ch'ang lang* lustrous, brilliant; [7]*ch'ang lang kwong*, bright, luminous.

讖 懺 Ch'ien. The first read *ch'aing*; coll. *ch'ang*: to repent and confess; the prayers and incantations of Tauists and Budhists for the dead: COM., [8]*king ch'ang* prayers and confessions; [9]*pai ch'ang* to recite prayers, as employed priests do; [10]*ch'ang hwoi* to make penitent confession; [11]*ch'ang 'tau*, the worship of "Measure Mother" (guardian of children) on the 15th of the 8th moon; [12]*ch'ang ngwong* to regret (do away with) the vow—a ceremony enacted when a previous prayer has not been answered.

璨 Ts'an. A brilliant gem, the luster of gems: [13]*ch'oi ch'ang* pendent gems; *met.*, hanging flowers.

Ch'ang. A coll. word: strong, rude, fierce, eager, impetuous: *ch'ang ma* eager, venturesome; *ch'ang tek, 'heng*, very strong and bold; *ch'ang k'a ch'ang 'ch'iu*, strong feet and hands—to act rudely; *ch'ang ngu ch'ang 'ma*, (like) a fierce ox or horse.

(94) Ch'au.

抄 鈔 Ch'ao. To transcribe, to copy; to buy up, as forfeited goods; to confiscate, to sequestrate: in the coll. to beg, as priests do: the second also read *ch'a* q. v.: [14]*ch'au muk, ik, kwang*, confiscated to the government; COM., [15]*ch'au chü*, to transcribe a book; [16]*ch'au 'siă*, to copy; [17]*ch'au chong*, or [18]*ch'au taung* to buy forfeited goods at pawnshops; [19]*ch'au ka*, to confiscate household property; COLL., *ch'au hwa* to beg subscriptions, as Budhist priests do; *ch'au 'la 'tá*, to take a copy of; *'ch'iu ch'au k'woh, 'pwong*, a book of copied songs.

操 Ts'ao. Read, *ch'ŏ*; coll. *ch'au*: to practice, as troops, to train, to drill; anxious, solicitous: [20]*ch'au liéng* to drill; [21]*tëng ch'au*, a winter drill; *k'ang ch'au*, to review troops; *'chwi ch'au*, a naval review; *ch'au ping*, or

1 惺忪 2 青醒 3 撥醒 4 白粲 5 粲然 6 粲粲衣服 7 燦爛光 8 經懺 9 拜懺 10 懺悔 11 懺斗 12 懺願 13 璀璨 14 抄沒入官 15 抄書 16 抄寫 17 抄贓 18 抄當 19 抄家 20 操練 21 冬操

ˌ*ch'au* ʻ*yêng*, to drill troops; [1]ˌ*ch'au* ˌ*sing*, or ˌ*ch'au* ˌ*sing pah*ˌ *pok*ˌ anxious, careworn.

搊 ʻCh'iu. Read ˌ*ch'eu;* used in the *Paik*ˌ ˌ*Ing* for the coll. ˌ*ch'au:* to hold up the dress in walking; to overhaul, to examine: [2]*liong*ʻ *ch'iu* ˌ*ch'au* ˌ*i*, to hold up the dress with both hands; ʻ*ch'iu* ʻ*wong* ˌ*ch'au* ˌ*keng*, to push up the sleeves; [3]ˌ*ch'au chak*ˌ to raise and fasten (the skirts); [4]ˌ*ch'au naung*ʼ or ˌ*ch'au* ʻ*ngu* ˌ*hiâ*, to throw into utter confusion by overhauling.

草 艸 ʻTs'ao. Read ʻ*ch'ó;* coll. ʻ*ch'au:* grasses, herbs, plants with herbaceous stems, plants in general: [5]*ch'au tê*ʼ grassy lands; *met.*, disreputable places; *pek*ˌ ʻ*ch'au* ʻ*p'i*, to pull grass; *met.*, involved in trouble by others; [6]*cha* ʻ*ch'au*, straw of the first rice crop; ʻ*ch'au yoh*ˌ herb medicine; [7]ˌ*ling* ˌ*hiong* ʻ*ch'au*, a fragrant plant used in hair oil; ʻ*ch'au t'ak*, a straw bed; [8]*ch'au ch'aê*ʼ coarse, badly done, as needle-work, compositions, &c.; ʻ*ch'au* ʻ*li liâk*, straw slippers without heels; ʻ*ch'au* ˌ*pau*, a straw pouch; *met.*, a simpleton; [9]*ch'au* ˌ*á* ʻ*ma*, foot travelers; ʻ*ch'au* ˌ*á* ʻ*lá*, "straw-sandal fee"—to police going far; ʻ*ch'au* ˌ*nêng* ʻ*kiâng* ˌ*t'iâng yâ*ʼ *á*ʼ *pauk*ˌ ˌ*têng*, even a straw image hearing it would be excited as by inspiration.

吵 ʻCh'ao. To clamor, to wrangle; to annoy, to trouble, to tease; to interrupt one: in the coll. read ʻ*ch'a*, q.v.: COM., [10]*chauk*, ʻ*ch'au*, to trouble, as evil spirits do; [11]ʻ*ch'au* ʻ*yeu*, to annoy; ʻ*ch'au nau*ʼ to make a disturbance; COLL., ʻ*kê* ʻ*ch'au* (brogue *kaê*ʼ ʻ*ch'au*), to annoy one; ʻ*ch'au siâh*ˌ to tease for food; ʻ*ch'au* ˌ*nêng* ˌ*wong*, prince of teasers; ʻ*ch'au* ˌ*nang seu*ʼ hard to bear the annoyance.

臭 Ch'ou.ˀ Read *ch'eu*ʼ; coll. *ch'au*ʼ: effluvia, bad odor, putridity, stench; to stink, to smell, to rot; *met.*, vile, corrupt; disreputable, in bad odor: [12]*ch'au*ʼ *k'e*ʼ a stench; [13]*ch'au*ʼ *e*ʼ or *ch'au*ʼ ʻ*la e*ʼ a putrid scent; [14]*ch'au*ʼ *lang*ʼ or *ch'au*ʼ *ho*ʼ rotten; [15]*ch'au*ʼ ˌ*ch'ó*, or *ch'au*ʼ ˌ*sing* ˌ*ch'ó*, a fishy smell; *ch'au*ʼ ˌ*neng* ˌ*siêng*, the smell of milk; [16]*ch'au*ʼ *ma*ʼ to hoot, to rail at; *cheng*ʼ *ch'au*ʼ or *ch'au*ʼ ʻ*ngu seng*ʼ or [17]*ch'au*ʼ ʻ*ngu haing*ʼ an intolerable stench; [18]*ch'au*ʼ ˌ*miâng* ˌ*siâng*, a bad reputation; [19]*ch'au*ʼ ˌ*sing* ˌ*kang*, a corrupt heart; [20]*ch'au*ʼ *che*ʼ *ong*ʼ "bad-odor luck"—said in jest of one who succeeds with poor talents; *ch'au*ʼ ʻ*hwi* ˌ*ing*, smoked, as in being cooked; *ch'au*ʼ ˌ*kau k'auk*, *cheng*ʼ ʻ*si* ˌ*nêng*, even a filthy ditch may drown people: *met.*, it's dangerous to trifle even with trivial faults.

(95) Ch'auk.

錯 Ts'o.ˀ To wash or plate with gold; stripes, striæ, as in stones or fabrics; to file, to polish; to tattoo; a stone for grinding gems, &c.; to mistake, to err, to do wrong; to slip, erroneous; mixed, in disorder, confused; crossed, barred: also read *ch'o*ʼ q. v.:

[1]操心 [2]兩手 [3]搊衣 搊紮 [4]搊亂 [5]草地 [6]早草 [7]靈香草 [8]草莉 [9]草鞋馬 [10]作吵 [11]吵擾 [12]臭氣 [13]臭味 [14]臭爛 [15]臭鱢 [16]臭罵 [17]臭五杏 [18]臭名聲 [19]臭心肝 [20]臭字運

sëü' ˓*si ch‘auk*˒ ˓*heng*, the seasons rotate; COM., *sek*˒ *ch‘auk*˒ or *ch‘auk*˒ *ngwo*˒ to err, to mistake; [1]˓*ch‘a ch‘auk*˒ a mistake, an error; [2]*ch‘auk*˒ *chak*˒ mixed, miscellaneous; [3]*ch‘auk*˒*kwai*' to be offended by mistake; COLL., ‘*ch‘iong ch‘auk*˒ to err through haste, to do hurriedly.

蕞 蕝 Ts‘o. A sheaf of coarse sedge, as used for straining spirits through; to collect together; small, vile, insignificant, for which the first is commonly used.

撮 Ts‘o. To take a pinch with two or three fingers; a pinch, a pugil; to take up a little; to snatch; to bring together; a little; a measure of 256 grains: COM., [4]*ch‘auk*˒ *mó*˒ to snatch off one's cap; [5]*ch‘auk*˒ ˓*mó*, to pluck hair or feathers; COLL., [6]*ch‘auk*˒ ‘*k‘i*, to pluck up; *ch‘auk*˒ ˓*këng*, to hire additional workmen; *sioh*˒ ‘*pa sioh*˒ *ch‘auk*˒ *chek*˒ ˓*ki*, amassed by handfuls and pinches; *ch‘auk*˒ *sioh*˒ *kwo*' to select one sentence; *ch‘auk*˒ ˓*hwa*, to cull out here and there; *ch‘auk*˒ ˓*sa*, to pinch (the throat in order to cure) colic; *ch‘auk*˒ ˓*chiëng*, to borrow money; ˓*nó ch‘auk*˒ to borrow.

(96) Ch‘aung.

寸 Ts‘un. The Chinese inch, regarded as long as the middle joint of the finger, the tenth of a foot, and varies with the foot; a very little; the 41st radical: COM., [7]*ch‘aung*' *ek*˒ an inch and a tenth; [8]*ch‘aung*' *siong*˒ over an inch; [9]˓*hwong ch‘aung*' *lwang*˒ the mind confused; [10]*ch‘aung*' ˓*kwang ch‘ek*˒ the three locations of the pulse—a medical term; [11]*ch‘aung*' *mah*˒ only an inch of pulse—near death; [12]*ch‘aung*' ˓*ing*, an inch of time; COLL., *ch‘aung*' *ch‘aung*' ‘*pó*, mere bits precious—parsimonious; *ch‘aung*' ˓*king* ˓*nang* ‘*má ch‘aung*' ˓*kwong* ˓*ing*, with an inch of gold it is hard to buy an inch of time!

創 刱 Ch‘uang. To wound, to cut and injure, in which sense the first is also read ˓*ch‘ong*; to begin, to invent, to create, to found, to lay the foundation of; to reprove, to correct; the commencement, the first: [13]˓*ting ch‘aung*' to blame, to punish; COM., [14]*ch‘aung*' *chó*˒ to create; [15]*ch‘aung*' *sié*˒ to create the world; [16]*ch‘aung*' ‘*sü*, to begin; the commencement; *ch‘aung*' *ngiék*˒ ˓*üng e*˒ ‘*siu ngiék*˒ ˓*nang*, to make a fortune is easy, to keep it is difficult; [17]*ch‘aung*' *lié*˒ to establish a custom.

閂 Suan. Read ˓*song* or ˓*swang*; coll. *ch‘aung*': a cross-pin; a bar, a bolt; to bolt: [18]˓*hwang ch‘aung*' a cross-bar; *met.*, a sore on the abdomen; [19]˓*mwong ch‘aung*' a door-bolt [20]*ch‘aung*' ˓*mwong*, to bolt the door.

闖 Ch‘uang. A horse going out of a door; to thrust out the head; to appear suddenly, to bolt out; suddenly, abruptly, forcibly: COM., [21]*ch‘aung*' *tó*˒ to rush across the road, as before an officer when passing; [22]*ch‘aung*' ˓*wong* ˓*mwong*, to bolt by the gates of a yamun; *ch‘aung*' *kong*˒ or *ch‘aung*'

1差錯 2錯雜 3錯怪 4撮帽 5撮毛 6撮起 7寸一 8寸上 9方寸亂 10寸關尺 11寸脉 12寸陰 13懲創 14創造 15創世 16創始 17創例 18橫閂 19閂門 20閂門 21闖道 22闖轅門 ○

福州方言拼音字典

chiong' a rough, lawless fellow.

闖[2] Ch'uang. Read *ch'aung'*; coll. *ch'aung'*: to force one's way, to bolt ahead: [1]*ch'aung'* *'tié*, or *ch'aung'* *'tié k'ó'* to bolt into a place; *'mwong ch'aung' 'mwong ch'aung'* just push ahead! as when uncertain of the way; [2]*ngaung' ch'aung'* to rush about like a stupid fellow.

(97) Ch'e.

佽 Tz'u. Read *ch'ëü'*; coll. *ch'e'*: the bride's dowry, sent to the bridegroom's house a few days before marriage; a corpse: [3]*ₛngiăng ch'e'* to carry the dowry with a display; [4]*'chiĕk, ch'e'* to receive the dowry; [5]*ch'e' ₍tang,* list of the articles sent; *ch'e' p'ieu'* the carriers' tickets—as checks for their pay; [6]*kiĕng' ch'e'* to visit the corpse previous to its being encoffined.

⿰食也 Ch'ih. Read *ₛti;* used in the *Paik, ₍Ing* for the coll. *ch'e'*: to feed a child; to feed, as the parent bird its young; [7]*ch'e' ₛneng,* to feed with milk: [8]*ch'e' nié' 'kiăng,* to feed a child; [9]*ch'e' sioh, ch'ói'* give him a mouthful; [10]*ch'e' miéng'* to offer vermicelli (to the corpse in a sitting posture).

試 Chih. Read *sëü'*; coll. *ch'e'*: to try, to experiment, to test; to compare and find out; a test, a trial: [11]*c'he' k'ang'* to test and see; *ch'e' mwong'* or *ch'e' 'ang mwong'* to try with questions; [12]*ch'e' 'ch'iu taung'* to test one's skill; [13]*ch'e' sioh, ch'e'* to make a trial; *ch'e' ₍chong,* trial-toilet (of a bride); *ch'e' 'tiăng,* "try the pan"—the bride's essay at cooking when the husband's friends are invited.

⿰口妻 Ch'i. Read *ch'ói'*; used in the *Paik, ₍Ing* for the coll. *ch'e'* for which the last is commonly used: to try food, to taste: [14]*ch'e' siăh,* to taste food; [15]*ch'e' ₛsiong,* to test by tasting.

Ch'e'. A coll. euphonic prefix, as in *ch'e' ch'ié'* to stab, to kill, as a chicken; *ch'e' ch'ëü'* to look about.

市[2] Chih. A market place, a square or open place where people trade; a crowd, groups of marketmen; crowded, vulgar, billingsgate; marketable, salable; to buy, to trade in the market; to bid, to offer a price: [16]*ₛsieu ₛing këüng' ch'e'* low people frequent markets; COM., *ch'e' ka'* the market price; [17]*ₛmwong ch'e'* the regular shop-prices—in distinction from commission rates; [18]*ch'e' wong'* prosperous trade; *ch'e' pai'* (coll. *ch'e' ₛp'i*) dull trade; *'chwi ch'e'* the tide (which brings fish, etc.,) to market; the tide *serving; siong' ch'e'* opening of market; *t'ói' ch'e'* close of market; [19]*ch'e' 'king,* state of the market; COLL., *ch'e' ₛt'au,* a market place; *wa' ch'e' má' ₛmó ₛchiéng,* a brisk market but no profits.

⿰鼻疐[2] T'i. Read *te'*; coll. *ch'e'* as in *hak, ch'e'* to sneeze; [20]*ch'e' hak, 'kwi chiăh,* to sneeze a few times; *ch'e' hak, má' ch'ok,* unable to sneeze.

Ch'e'. A coll word: the obverse side of a cash; *ch'e' p'ok,*

[1]闖裡 [2]數闖 [3]迎佽 [4]接佽 [5]佽單 [6]見佽 [7]⿰食也乳 [8]⿰食也伲仔 [9]⿰食也一嘴 [10]⿰食也麵 [11]試看 [12]試手段 [13]試一試 [14]⿰口妻食 [15]⿰口妻嘗 [16]小人近市 [17]門市 [18]市旺 [19]市景 [20]⿰鼻疐喝幾使

the obverse and reverse sides; ꜁nong ch'e꜅ p'ok꜆ a game of twirling two cash and guessing heads or tails; ꜀sĕng ch'e꜅ both obverse sides up.

(98) Ch'ĕ.

初 ꜀Ch'u. Read ꜀ch'u; coll. ꜀ch'ĕ: the first, the beginning; incipient, at first: [1]꜀ch'ĕ ek꜆ the first day of the month; [2]꜀ch'ĕ ꜁t'au, the first few days of the month; [3]ch'ok꜆ ꜀ch'ĕ, the commencement of next month; [4]ngwok꜇ ꜀ch'ĕ, from the 1st to the 10th of the month; [5]꜀tong ꜀ch'ĕ, at the first, formerly; [6]꜀ch'ĕ ꜂kwi, what day of the first decade is it? [7]꜀ch'ĕ ek꜆ sek꜇ ngo꜅ the 1st and 15th days—are set days to burn incense to heaven and the gods; ꜀ch'ĕ sek꜇ ꜂tié, before the tenth; ꜀ch'ĕ sek꜇ ngié꜅ just after the tenth; ꜀ch'ĕ ꜂kau ne꜅ sek꜇ se꜄ the 9th and 24th—are fast days; ꜀ch'ĕ ꜀sang ꜀ch'ĕ se꜄ ꜁mi ꜁mó ngwok꜇ on the 3d and 4th it is eyebrow moon—new moon.

꜁Ch'ĕ. A coll. word: to scold harshly, to belch out a word or two in anger: ꜁ch'ĕ ꜂ngwai, you speak harshly to me! ꜁ch'ĕ kaing꜄ accustomed to scold.

(99) Ch'eh.

Ch'eh꜆. A coll. word, as in ch'eh꜆ k'ó꜄ to go fast, to run away; k'ĕük꜆ ꜀i ch'eh꜆ k'ó꜄ he has darted away from me; ꜁ch'i ch'eh꜆ to rush past; ch'eh꜆ ꜁mó, bolted! disappeared! ꜂mwang ꜀t'iéng ch'eh꜆ a kind of rocket; ꜂chwi ch'eh꜆ a squirt; ꜁ch'i ch'eh꜆ ch'óh꜇ ch'óh꜇ to rush to and fro.

(100) Ch'ek.

柒 七 Ch'i. The numeral seven; used in coll. as a superlative or intensive: COM., [8]ch'ek꜆ sek꜇ seventy; sek꜇ ch'ek꜆ seventeen; ch'ek꜆ ch'ek꜆ the seven sevenths—days of funeral rites for the dead; [9]ch'ek꜆ ꜂chü paik꜆ sá꜄ seven sons and eight sons-in-law—a numerous family; COLL., [10]ch'ek꜆ ꜂kong paik꜆ ꜂kong (or t'iăng꜄), to talk deceitfully; ch'ek꜆ chiăh꜆ seven (persons or things); ch'ek꜆ ꜂ka ꜁nĕng, seven persons; ch'ek꜆ ꜁ié paik꜆ ꜁ié, the tall and short devils—attendants of the ꜂ngu tá꜄; ch'ek꜆ ꜀t'ung paik꜆ k'ieu꜄ very quick to comprehend; ch'ek꜆ ꜁ki siong꜅ paik꜆ ꜁ki a꜅ (the mind confused) by many things; ch'ek꜆ ꜂pwo paik꜆ nak꜇ patched all over; taung꜅ ch'ek꜆ close of the 49 mourning days.

叱 Ch'a. To scold, to cry out to; to hoot at; to mention: [11]ch'ek꜆ ch'a꜄ to hoot at; [12]ch'ek꜆ ꜁ming ong꜅ ꜀ang, give my name and salutations—an epistolary phrase.

尺 Ch'ih. A cubit or Chinese foot of 10 ch'aung꜄: in the coll. read ch'ioh꜆ q. v.: [13]ch'ek꜆ ch'aung꜄ regular, proportioned; [14]꜀sang ch'ek꜆ kiéng꜄ a three-feet sword; ꜂chi ch'ek꜆ near, as to place; ch'ek꜆ hwok꜇ the looper or geometrical worm; [15]ch'ek꜆ ek꜆ ꜀chi ꜀chü, an epistle; [16]lĕk꜇ ch'ek꜆ ꜀chi ꜀ku, a minor reigning.

拭 Ch'ih. Read sek꜆; coll. ch'ek꜆: to wipe, to rub with a dry cloth: [17]hok꜆ ch'ek꜆ to dust and wipe; ch'ek꜆ mek꜇ ꜂chai, to wipe away tears;

[1]初一 [2]初頭 [3]出初 [4]月初 [5]當初 [6]初幾 [7]初一十五 [8]七十 [9]七子八壻 [10]七講八講 [11]叱咤 [12]叱名間安 [13]尺寸 [14]三尺劍 [15]尺一之書 [16]六尺之孤 [17]拂拭○

ch'ek, *'ié tóh*, to wipe chairs and tables; [1]*ch'ek*, *t'ah*, to wipe clean.

赤, Ch'ih. Carnation, purplish or light red, flesh color; naked, destitute, barren, poor; to redden; to denude; the 155th radical; in coll. read *ch'iăh*, q. v.: *ch'ek*, *saik*, carnation color; [2]*ch'ek*, *'chü*, an infant; the people; [3]*ch'ek*, *tó'* the equator; [4]*ch'ek*, *,sing*, sincere; COLL., *ch'ek*, *'pó ,tĕng 'ka chiăng' ,king*, bright brass counterfeits pure gold; *met.*, a hypocrite; *ch'ek*, *,tieu ,tieu*, nude, stripped to the waist.

漆, 桼, Ch'i. Varnish, lacquer, viscid or resinous juices that can be used in painting; to paint, to varnish; black, as lacquer; adhesive; exceedingly friendly, doating upon: [5]*,keu ch'ek*, *,siong ,lièng*, united as by glue and varnish—intimate friendship; COM., [6]*ch'ek*, *mièng'* varnish-paste—for stopping holes; [7]*,chio ch'ek*, red varnish; [8]*,iu ch'ek*, paint and varnish; [9]*ch'ek*, *'chwi*, the quality or gloss of varnish; COLL., *ch'ek*, *,sa hó'* a painter; *,ch'ang ch'ek*, raw varnish; *p'ah*, *ch'ek*, *'t'ĕng*, to close up the cracks of a coffin with varnish; *k'ĕük*, *ch'ek*, *ka'* poisoned by lacquer; *ch'ek*, *tek*, *'hó*, well varnished; *ch'ek*, *sioh*, *kwo'* to varnish one coat; *,t'oi ,kwong ch'ek*, highly polished varnishing.

膝, Ch'i. The knee, the patella; a long slender spear: [10]*ch'ek*, *há'* at the knee; *met.*, children; [11]*'pe' ch'ek*, *,nu ,ngang*, the knees and face of a slave—i. e., obsequious; COM., [12]*k'ok*, *ch'ek*, to bend the knee; [13]*hok*, *ch'ek*, stork's legs; *met.*, a long thin spear: in the coll. long-legged like a stork.

斥, Ch'ih. To exclude, to expel, to drive off, to send off; to scold at; to pry into; far-reaching, extending to, extensive; plenty; saltish land: [14]*,ming ch'ek*, or *tik*, *ch'ek*, to reprimand sternly; [15]*ping ch'ek*, to drive off; [16]*'chi ch'ek*, to point out one's faults; [17]*mièng' ch'ek*, to rebuke one to his face.

戚, Ch'i. Used for the second below: a sort of pole-ax; to compassionate, to pity; mournful, sorry; aroused, vexed; deformed, marked in any way; near, related to, dear to; relatives: *,hiu ch'ek*, *,siong ,kwang*, mutual sympathy; COM., [18]*,ch'ing ch'ek*, kindred; [19]*,hwong ,ch'ing kwok*, *ch'ek*, the imperial kindred; [20]*,ch'ing ,peng ch'ek*, *'iu*, kindred and friends; COLL., *'tié ,ch'ing ngwoi' ch'ek*, near and distant relatives; *,ch'ing ch'ek*, *twai' sá'* all of one's kindred.

慼, Ch'i. Used for the last; grief, sorrow; to be afflicted, sad, pained, mournful: *,iu ch'ek*, sad, afflicted.

鏚, Ch'i. A sort of pole-ax, a bill; an ornamental kind of ax carried in processions.

Ch'ek,. A coll. euphonic prefix, as in *ch'ek*, *ch'iok*, to drink; *ch'ek*, *ch'ak*, to insert: *ch'ek*, *ch'auk*, to pluck with the thumb and finger; *ch'ek*, *ch'iăk*, to rub, as clothes in washing; to

[1]拭漈 [2]赤子 [3]赤道 [4]赤心 [5]膠漆相聯 [6]漆麪 [7]硃漆 [8]油漆 [9]漆水 [10]膝下 [11]婢膝奴顏 [12]屈膝 [13]鶴膝 [14]明斥 [15]屏斥 [16]指斥 [17]面斥 [18]親戚 [19]皇親國戚 [20]親朋戚友

grate, to cut up fine, as vegetables.

賊 Tsê. Read *chek*, : coll. *ch'ek*,: a thief, a robber, a bandit, a highwayman; seditious, those who rise against the government, the enemy: a term of reproach: [1]*ch'ek*, *'p'i*, banditti; [2]*ch'ek* *'tong*, or *ch'ek*, *'hwo*, a band of thieves; *ch'ek*, *seu'* or [3]*ch'ek*, *,wo*, a den of thieves; [4]*'hai ch'ek*, a pirate; [5]*hwang ch'ek*, rebels; [6]*ch'ek*, *,t'au*, leader of thieves; [7]*pah*, *taung² ch'ek*, day-thieves; [8]*ch'ek*, *'chung kak*, a thief-catcher; [9]*niă'k*, *ch'ek*, *,ping ,chong*, to catch a thief by the articles stolen; *ch'ek*, *ch'oi' ch'ek*, *seng' 'chi*, a thief uttering an imperial edict; *met.*, he lies grandly! [10]*ch'ek*, *,pwi*, "thief's talent"—used in scolding a pilfering child; [11]*ch'ek*, *mĕk*, thief's eye; *met.*, keen eyesight; [12]*ch'ek*, *se² kek*, *,nĕng chó'* necessity makes thieves.

(101) Ch'ĕk.

鑿 Tsao. Read *chok*, ; coll. *ch'ĕk*,: a chisel, a punch; a cold chisel; to chisel: [13]*ch'ĕk*, *'kiăng*, a small chisel; [14]*,yéng ch'ĕk*, a gouge; *ch'ĕk*, *,hiă* (or *pauk*,), burst it in chiseling; [15]*ch'ĕk*, *t'au'* or *ch'ĕk*, *,t'ĕng t'au'* to chisel through; [16]*ch'ĕk*, *má² seu²* can't endure the chiseling—i. e., teasing, as of a child; *ch'ĕk*, *,t'iéng 'pwong 'ling*, able to chisel out the skies—has great ablity.

(102) Ch'eng.

橕 撐 Ch'êng. To prop, to shore up; to fasten open, as with a stretcher; to pole, to push off, to make a show; a fulcrum, a prop, a stay.

樘 Ch'êng. A branch stretching out; a fulcrum, a prop, a support, a slanting post; to pole a boat.

,Ch'eng. A coll. word: to murmur, to complain, to find fault: *,ch'eng ,i*, find fault with him; *,ch'eng ,ch'eng ,siăng*, teasing, as a child does; *,ch'eng ,hai ,hai*, to groan.

筅 Hsien. Read *'siéng*; coll. *'ch'eng*: a brush broom, a besom; a coarse bamboo brush for cleaning out pots and kettles; to sweep away: COM., [17]*ch'eng 'ch'iu*, a besom; [18]*ch'eng 'ch'iu ,sing*, a comet; COLL., *'tiăng 'ch'eng*, a brush to cleanse pans and pots; *'ch'eng k'ó'* to sweep away; *'ch'eng ,tong*, to clean house—in the 12th moon; *'ch'eng kwong'* to copy compositions carelessly—as examination-copyists do, unless feed by the students.

秤 Ch'êng. A steelyard: COM., *kwo' ch'eng'* to weigh it; *ch'eng' 'siu*, one who attends to the weighing, as at salt-houses; *ch'eng' ,cheng*, the pointer on the top of scales; [19]*,cheng ch'eng'* scales having a pointer; *'tau ch'eng'* the peck and scales, measure and weight; COLL., *ch'eng' 'kwang*, a steelyard bar; *ch'eng' ,hwa*, the notation of pounds and ounces on the bar; *ch'eng' ,t'ui*, the poise; *ch'eng' ,kau*, the hook; *ch'eng' nau²* the cord to hold by in weighing; *,pang ch'eng'* the common catty of 16 oz.; *twai² ch'eng'* the large catty of 18 or 20 oz.; *,iu ch'eng'* the oil catty of 17 8/10 oz.; *ek*, *paik*,

1賊匪 2賊黨 3賊窩 4海賊 5反賊 6賊頭 7白撞賊 8賊總甲 9拿賊憑贓 10賊胚 11賊目 12賊是急仈做〇 13鑿仔 14圓鑿 15鑿透 16鑿賣受 17筅箒 18筅箒星 19針秤

福州方言拼音字典

ch'eng' a catty of 20 or 21 oz.; *ˏting ˛pwang ch'eng'* a kind of steelyard used in fruit shops; *'kau' ch'eng'* full weight; *twai² ch'eng' ˏch'ing 'tié 'sieu ch'eng' ˏch'ing ch'ok,* to buy by the large pound and sell by the small.

稱 Ch'eng. Same as the preceeding: a steelyard; to weigh, to adjust; suitable, as one wishes; corresponding to, satisfied with: also read *ˏch'ing*, q.v.: ²*ˏsiong ch'eng'* suited to each other; ³*pok, ch'eng'* unsuitable, not fitted; ⁴*˛üng ch'eng'* to adjust, to regulate.

凊 Ching. Cold, as weather, the person, things; frigid: COM., ⁵*yék, ch'eng'* hot and cold; ⁶*ch'eng' ˏt'iéng,* winter; ⁷*oi' ch'eng'* (coll. *kiăng ch'eng'*) to fear the cold; ⁸*ch'eng' chek,* cold accumulated (in the system)—a medical term; COLL., *sói² ch'eng' 'ié,* "to occupy the cold chair"—rejected, not loved; *siăh, ch'eng' pwong'* to eat cold rice; *met.*, unusually early; *á² ch'eng' 'a má²* are you cold? *ch'eng' 'tiăng ch'eng' chau'* "cold kettle and hearth," destitute, desolate.

沁 Hsin. To sound, to fathom; *met.*, to comprehend; cold water; *met.*, to cool one's affections; a department in Shansi: ⁹*ch'eng' 'chwi,* a large affluent of the Yellow river; ¹⁰*ch'eng' ˏing ˏsing ˛pi,* to cool a person's affection.

Ch'eng'. A coll. euphonic prefix, as in *ch'eng' ch'iong'* to thread; *ch'eng' ch'ĕüng'* to insert, to join; *ch'eng' ch'aung'* to bolt; *ch'eng' ch'iăng'* to hire workmen; *ch'eng' ch'iéng'* to pierce; to join, as boards with bamboo pins; *ch'eng' ch'eng' ch'aëng' ch'aëng'* bristling of the hair; rising of rough flesh, as before an ague

田 T'ien. Read *˛tiéng;* coll. *˛ch'eng:* a field, a patch laid out in plats; land, a plantation, cultivated fields: ¹¹*˛ch'eng te²* cultivated lands; ¹²*˛ch'eng ˛hwong,* fields and gardens; ¹³*pwo' ˛ch'eng,* to set out rice-shoots; ¹⁴*˛ch'eng ˛loi ˛ung,* snail-shell striæ; *met.*, waving streaks in wood; eddies; ¹⁵*˛ch'eng k'ié'* land deeds; ¹⁶*˛ch'eng ˛ch'ing,* dikes between fields; *˛ch'eng ˏchu,* the rent of fields; ¹⁷*chó' ˛ch'eng,* to farm; ¹⁸*ˏhwong ˛ch'eng,* uncultivated fields; *˛ch'eng 'chio,* owner of lands; *ˏlung ˛niéng ˛ch'eng,* fields reaped in rotation—to support ancestral worship; *ˏchü ˛ch'eng,* fields for the support of a student; *˛ch'eng meng'* the chief ownership of land—which pays the taxes, etc.; *˛ch'eng ˏküng,* secondary proprietorship of one who rents and divides; ¹⁹*˛ch'eng 'kwi 'mu,* how many acres has the lot? *ˏkang ˛ch'eng ng² kau' só' 'chwi,* thirsty fields are insatiable; *met.*, the gains not enough to satisfy creditors.

蠶 蚕 Ts'an. Read *˛chang;* coll. *˛ch'eng;* the silk-worm, caterpillars which weave cocoons: ²⁰*˛ch'eng 'keng,* the silk worm; ²¹*˛ch'eng 'keng ˏsi,* cocoons; *˛ch'eng 'keng t'o' ˏsi* (or *'wong ˏsi*), the silkworm weaving silk; *'yong*

¹至秤 ²相稱 ³不稱 ⁴匀稱 ⁵熱凊 ⁶凊天 ⁷畏凊 ⁸凊積 ⁹沁水 ¹⁰沁人 心脾 ¹¹田地 ¹²田園 ¹³佈田 ¹⁴田螺紋 ¹⁵田契 ¹⁶田塍 ¹⁷做田 ¹⁸荒田 ¹⁹田幾畝 ²⁰蠶繭 ²¹蠶繭絲○

ₑch'eng 'keng, to rear silkworms; *ₑch'eng 'keng piêng' ₑngó*, silkworms change to moths; *ₑch'eng 'keng siăh, nioh,* the silkworm eats the leaves; *met.*, to eat greedily, a ravenous appetite; *ₑch'eng 'keng 'sai*, silkworm dirt—used medicinally for sore eyes.

Ch'eng². A coll. euphonic prefix, as in *ch'eng² ch'ong²* to twist, to wring, as clothes; *ch'eng² ch'iong²* to put up, as the boards of a shop-front, or the movable doors of shelves; to attach, as uppers to the soles of shoes.

(103) Ch'ëng.

葱 蔥 ʿ Ts'ung. Read *ₑch'ung*; coll. *ₑch'ëng*; onions: ¹*ₑch'ëng ₑchio*, onions cut up fine; ²*ₑch'ëng ₑt'au*, onion bulbs; *ₑch'ëng 'kiu saung²* onions, chives and garlic; ³*ₑch'ëng pah,* the stalk just above the bulb; a very light blue; ⁴*sang ₑch'ëng ₑhwa*, to sprinkle bits of onions in cooking; ⁵*ₑch'ëng ₑt'au ₑta*, decoction of onions and tea, used in measles and colds; ⁶*ₑch'ëng 'kwong*, onion-stalks; *met.*, things made hollow, as hairpins and ear pendants; *ₑch'ëng 'kwong chang²* a circular punch or chisel.

菖 ʿ Ch'ung. Read *ₑch'iong*; coll. *ₑch'ëng*, as in ⁷*ₑch'ëng ₑpwo*, sweet flag, used on doors as a charm, on the 1st day of the 5th moon; *'hang* ⁸*ₑch'ëng ₑpwo ₑhwa 'hang ₑtek ₑk'wi*, sweet flag rarely blooms; *met.*, a rarity, a wonder, as one strangely benevolent.

(104) Ch'eu.

搊 ʿ Ch'io. To seize, to take hold of with all the fingers; to rumple; to take, as the guitar.

篘 ʿ A strainer made of wicker or bamboo for straining spirits.

臭 ʾ Ch'ou. To track by the scent; effluvia, savor, smell, odor, stench, putridity; to rot, to stink; a bad name, disreputable: in the coll. read *ch'au'* q. v.: ⁹*ch'eu' ho²* putrid; spoiled; ¹⁰*ₑu ₑsing ₑu ch'eu'* without sound or smell—recondite, as principles; ¹¹*ₑmi ch'eu' wang² ₑniêng*, a bad name lasts forever; COM., ¹²*ₑhiong ch'eu' pok, ₑti*, can't tell fragrance from stench.

嗅 ʾ Ch'ou. To smell, to perceive odors, as a dog does; plaintive cry of birds.

糗 ʾ Ch'ou. Roasted or parched wheat or rice; coarsely pounded rice, like grits: ¹³*ch'eu' ₑliong*, food of dried grain: ¹⁴*ch'eu' ne'* parched rice-cakes.

趮 ʾ Ch'ou. To walk, to go, as if weary.

槺 ʾ Ch'au. A vulgar character, used in *Paik, ₑIng* for the coll. *ch'eu'*: wood, a tree; wooden; timber, lumber: ¹⁵*ch'eu' sioh, ₑtau*, a tree; ¹⁶*ch'eu' muk,* trees, woods: ¹⁷*ₑpa ch'eu'* to climb trees; *ch'eu' ₑsing*, silvan elves; *chiék, ch'eu'* to graft a tree; *ch'ói' ch'eu'* to fell trees; *ch'eu' laiu²* timber; *ch'eu' yéng²* a

¹葱珠 ²葱頭 ³葱白 ⁴散葱 花⁵葱頭茶 ⁶葱管 ⁷菖蒲 ⁸菖蒲花罕的開 ⁹臭腐 ¹⁰無聲無臭 ¹¹遺臭萬年 ¹²香臭不知 ¹³糗粮 ¹⁴糗餌 ¹⁵槺一株 ¹⁶槺木 ¹⁷爬槺〇

tree full of leaves and blossoms; *ch'eu' ˏku k'ó'* the tree decayed; *'ch'eu' kwok*, billets of wood; *ch'eu' nioh, tung² tioh, ˏt'au*, "(fears lest) a leaf may fall on his head"—wanting in boldness.

愁 Ch'ou. Mournful, sorry, sad, chagrined: COM., *ˏiu ˏch'eu*, sad; ²*ˏch'eu 'k'u*, grieved, distressed; ⁴*ˏch'eu mong²* dispirited; *ˏch'eu ˏmi*, a distressed look; ⁴*ˏsieu ˏch'eu*, to assuage grief.

(105) Ch'ëü.

娶 取 Ch'ü. To marry a woman with the legal ceremonies; a marriage; the 2d also read *'ch'ü*, q. v.: COM., ⁵*ka' ch'ëü'* betrothing daughters and taking wives; ⁶*ˏwong ch'ëü'* has married a wife; ⁷*ch'ëü' ˏch'á ch'ëü' taik, ch'ëü' ch'iék, ch'ëü' saik*, choose a wife for her virtues, a concubine for her beauty.

趣 Ch'ü. To run, to go, to advance quickly; to see what is pleasant and hasten to do it; to regard pleasurably; sprightly, playful, graceful; amusing, pleasing: ⁸*é' ch'ëü'* intention; ⁹*'chi ch'ëü'* the purport of; COM., ¹⁰*ch'ëü' hiong' pok, ˏtung*, dispositions differ; ¹¹*che' ch'ëü'* desire, purpose: ¹²*ˏching ch'ëü'* gratified, a relish for; COLL., *ó' ch'ëü'* remarkably amusing, novel; *ˏmó ch'ëü'* not worth seeing.

覷 覰 Hsien. To spy, to look at, to peep; to descry, to reconnoiter: COM., ¹³*'tói' ch'ëü'* to look at each other; COLL., ¹⁴*ch'ëü' ˏching*, to see correctly; ¹⁵*ch'ëü' ch'ëü'* to gaze at; *ch'ëü' 'chwi*, look at water; *met.*, to spy out beforehand, as thieves do; ¹⁶*ch'ëü' tio²* "looks at the road"—said of one gazing at the floor when near death; *ch'ëü' pah, pah*, look at nothing—helpless, hopeless; *k'ëük, ˏi ch'ëü' sioh, a² ng² 'hó 'yong*, if he gives you a look, you can't well exist! *ch'ëü' pang²* to visit a sick person; ¹⁷*këüng² ch'ëü'* near-sighted; *ch'ëü' ˏt'iéng siáh, pwong²* to trust to heaven for food.

佽 Tz'u. Light, nimble, sprightly; to help, to assist; to compare; for, instead: in the coll. read *ch'é'* q. v.: ¹⁸*ch'ëü' cho²* to aid, as by a gift of money.

次 Tz'u. Neither first nor last, medium, second in order; coming after, inferior, secondary; next, succeeding; to put in order; a halting place, an encampment; a resthouse, an inn; a shed, a stall; a mansion; a position, as of the stars; a time; a place, a station; to halt, to reach: *wok, ch'ëü'* to break the order; COM., ¹⁹*ch'ëü' sëü²* or *ch'ëü' tá²* order, arrangement; *só' ch'ëü'* several times; *ch'ó' ch'ëü'* hurried, impatient; ²⁰*ch'ëü' 'ch'ü*, the 2d class of merit: *ˏki ch'ëü'* the next in order; *ch'ëü' ˏnang*, the 2d son; COLL., *ch'ëü' pah*, second quality of white, as sugar, vermicelli, etc.; *ˏmiáng ch'ëü'* order of names; *ˏhúi ˏhúi ch'ëü' ch'ëü'* every time, repeatedly.

朿 Tz'u. The next is commonly used instead of this: a thorn, a prickle, a sliver, a sharp slit.

1 榠檝 2 愁苦 3 愁悶 4 消愁 5 嫁娶 6 完娶 7 娶妻 娶德 娶妾 娶色 8 意趣 9 旨趣 10 趣向 不同 11 志趣 12 情趣 13 對覷 14 覷眞 15 覷覷 16 覷路 17 近覷 18 佽助 19 次序 20 次取

刺' Tz'u. A thorn, a sting; to pierce, to prick, to thrust a sharp point into; to embroider; to brand, to tattoo; to cut into; a visiting card, because it was once cut in wood; to stab and kill; to spade up, as plants with a trowel; to pole a boat; to reprimand, to blame, to criticise; to lampoon; satire; to pry into, to overhear; to examine: [1]*ch'ëü' seu'* to embroider; [2]*mong ch'ëü'* a thorn; [3]*ch'ëü' 'sü*, the Prefect of a chau; COM., *ch'ëü' k'aik,* a concealed murderer.

處' Ch'u. A place, a spot; a circumstance, a condition; added to some nouns it often forms the concrete: also read *'ch'ü*, q. v.: [4]*hó ch'ëü'* where? COM., [5]*kauk, ch'ëü'* or *ch'ëü' ch'ëü'* everywhere; [6]*sëü' ch'ëü'* the four quarters; *sëü' ch'ëü' u mwong,* no way out; *met.*, in remediless straits; [7]*oi^2 ch'ëü'* a place; [8]*ch'ëü' 'sü*, the 14th solar term; [9]*ch'ëü' ch'ëü' kung 'chü ch'ëü' ch'ëü' 'sieu ing*, there are good and bad men everywhere; COLL., *ch'ek, ch'ëü' pié'* to run all about.

蠀' 蠀' Tzu. Insects that irritate the skin; a hairy, poisonous caterpillar, called [10]*mó ch'ëü'*.

(106) Ch'ëük.

觸, Chu. To gore, to push, as an ox; to excite, to oppose: [11]*kang ch'ëük,* excited, inspired by; COM., [12]*ch'ëük, hwang^2* to insult, to incur anger; [13]*ch'ëük, 'king seng ching,* feelings excited by the circumstances; *ch'ëük, muk, siong sing,* distressing to the sight and painful to the mind; COLL., *'yâ ch'ëük,* or *cheng^2 ch'ëük,* greatly distressd by.

歜, Cho. To be choked with anger, full of choler: COM., [14]*ch'ëük, no^2* made angry; COLL., *ch'ëük, 'si,* angry to death; *ch'ëük, 'pa,* filled with rage; *ch'ëük, pang^2* sick from excessive choler; *ch'ëük, soi,* or *ch'ëük, pi,* vexed, displeased at.

躅, Cho. To walk unsteadily: [15]*tik, ch'ëük,* irresolute, to walk unevenly; [16]*kwoh, ch'ëük,* to walk with short and halting steps.

促, Cho. To constrain; urgent, pressed upon; near, short, close, small; shortened, hampered: [17]*p'aik, ch'ëük,* very urgent; [18]*ch'ëük, hiék,* straitened; *ch'ëük, ch'ek,* knees to knees, as in sitting opposite.

浞, Chu. To soak, to steep in water; feces, dregs; in the coll. scurf on the hands, incrustations: COLL., *siong^2 ch'ëük,* incrusted, as dirty bowls; *ch'ëük, kak, kau^2* a thick crust adhering; *p'ah, pong^2 ch'ëük,* to chisel off urinary incrustations—for medicinal uses.

捉, Cho. To seize, to grasp, to gripe and hold, to catch: [19]*puo^2 ch'ëük,* to seize; [20]*ch'ëük, chek,* to catch thieves.

1 刺繡	3 刺史	5 各處	7 位處	9 處處	處處	10 毛蠀	12 觸犯	生情	15 躑躅	17 迫促	19 捕捉
2 芒刺	4 何處	6 四處	8 處暑	君子	小人	11 感觸	13 觸景	14 歜怒	16 跼躅	18 促狹	20 捉賊

蹴, Ts'u. Similar to the next two: to tread on, to press with the foot, to kick: ¹'ch'ëük, ‹yong, reverential.

蹙, Chu. Hurried, quick; uneasy, anxious, distressed; to tread on: ²kek, ch'ëük, hurried, urgent; COLL., ch'ëük, ‹nang kwo' the suspense hard to bear.

顣, Ts'u. To frown, to knit the brows: ³ch'ëük, ak, or ‹ping ch'ëük, to frown.

籗, A lifting-net for fish, made of fine bamboo net-work.

矗, Ch'u. High, eminent; equal, even, straight; to raise; luxuriant growth.

Ch'ëük,. A coll. word: to cut, to chisel or saw off: *ch'ëük, sioh, ‹kiéng*, "reduce an edge," as in making a tub smaller; *ch'ëük, 'toi*, to shorten, to reduce the length.

(107) Ch'ëüng.

銃, Ch'ung. A sort of hatchet; commonly used for bored iron; a gun, a blunderbuss, a ginjall, a pistol: COM., ⁴'*chio' ch'ëüng'* to cast guns; ⁵*ch'ëüng' ka'* gun carriages; ⁶'*ch'iu ch'ëüng'* small guns, pistols; ⁷*ch'ëüng' 'siu*, musketeers; ⁸'*sá ch'ëüng'* to clean or scale guns; COLL., *pong' ch'ëüng'* or *‹k'wi ch'ëüng'* to fire off guns; *ch'ëüng' sóh*, the fuse or trigger-cord.

[illegible], As in ⁹*tiok, ch'ëüng'* to come unasked: COLL., *ch'ëüng' 'lá siäh*, or ¹⁰*ch'ëüng' 'tiè ‹li siäh*, to invite one's self to eat; ¹¹*ch'ëüng' tóh*, to come unbidden to the table.

Ch'ëüng'. A coll. word; to insert, to put into its place: *ch'ëüng' pang'* to insert a handle; *ch'ëüng' ‹k'a tóh*, a table with movable legs; *ch'ëüng' kak*, or *ch'ëüng' taing'* to insert tightly.

Ch'ëüng'. A coll. word, as in *ch'ëüng' t'o'* to vomit from inhaling offensive odors; *ch'ëüng' tioh, ch'au' c'* to inhale stench.

Ch'ëüng'. A coll. word, as in *ch'ëüng' tioh*, to meet, to fall in with; *ch'ëüng' 'chiä 'king*, have met with this state of things; *ch'ëüng' 'ch'iu*, or *ch'ëüng' 'ch'ai* (spoken *‹ch'üng 'ch'iu*, &c.), to thrust in the hand and take at random.

(108) Ch'i.

癡 痴, Tz'u. Stupid, dull, inapt; foolish, silly, idiotic; lustful, hankering; out of his head, wandering: ¹²*‹ch'i ‹ching*, doting on; salacious; COM., ¹³*‹ch'i 'siong*, a silly thought; ¹⁴*‹ch'i hang'* or ¹⁵*‹ch'i ‹tai*, a dolt, a booby; ¹⁶*‹ch'i ‹sing wong' 'siong*, the (vain) hopes of the foolish; COLL., ¹⁷*‹ch'i ‹ch'i t'ëük, t'ëük*, to draw back sillily, as one peering and then avoiding; ¹⁸*‹ch'i ‹nang seng' kwo' 'k'ieu 'nü*, a stupid (but honest) man is better than a crafty woman.

¹蹴然 ²急蹙 ³顣頞 ⁴鑄銃 ⁵銃架 ⁶手銃 ⁷銃首 ⁸洗銃 ⁹[illegible] ¹⁰[illegible]入 梨[illegible] ¹¹[illegible]棹 ¹²癡情 ¹³癡想 ¹⁴癡漢 ¹⁵癡獃 ¹⁶癡心妄想 ¹⁷癡癡縮縮 ¹⁸癡男勝過巧女 ○

嗤 ‹Tz'u. Laughing, to laugh at, to ridicule: [1]chëü² ˛ch'i, to laugh at one's self, *scil.*, for blundering.

媸 ‹Tz'u. Ugly, unhandsome; a homely woman; lewd, worthless, foolish: [2]˛ngiêng ˛ch'i, pretty and homely.

蚩 ‹Tz'u. A worm; ignorant, stupid; unpolished, rustic; sincere; to impose on; to treat as if ignorant, to despise: [3]˛ch'i ˛ch'i, blunt, honest; [4]˛ch'i ˛mang, the uneducated people.

雌 ‹Tz'u. The female of birds, the hen; *met.*, weak: COM., ˛ch'i ˛hüng, female and male; *met.*, a pair; [5]˛ch'i ˛hüng ˛piêng, a pair of cudgels.

笞 ‹Ch'ih. To punish with a bamboo, to bastinado; to correct so as to reform; to scourge, to flog, to bamboo: [6]˛piêng ˛ch'i, to flog.

鴟 Ch'ih. A kind of owl or hawk: *met.*, as in [7]˛ch'i ˛tiong, to act unscrupulously; [8]kaĕk˛ ˛ch'i, or [9]˛ch'i ˛hieu, the horned owl.

差 ‹Ch'a. Uneven, projecting irregularly: also read ˛ch'a and ˛ch'á, q. v.: [10]˛ch'ang ˛ch'i, uneven, irregular.

‹Ch'i. A coll. word, as in ˛ch'i ʻk'i ˛li, ruffled, as feathers; ˛ch'i ch'ié² ch'ié² rough, uneven.

˛Ch'i. A coll. word: to snatch, to catch at, as the skirts of one running: ˛ch'i tek˛ tioh˛ caught, grasped; ˛ch'i má² tioh˛ can't catch him.

˛Ch'i. A coll. euphonic prefix, as in ˛ch'i ˛ch'iŭ, to twirl, to turn, as in a lathe; ˛ch'i ˛ch'ó, to twist, to roll between the hands.

齒 ʻCh'ih. The upper teeth; *met.*, the mouth, words; to speak of; age, years; sort, class, associates, equals; to commence; to sort, to class by the age; to record, to write in; the 211th radical: in the coll. ʻngai and ʻk'i, q. v.: [11]ʻch'i ˛nga, upper and lower teeth; [12]˛niêng ʻch'i, or [13]ʻch'i so² age, years old; [14]ʻch'i ʻtiong, elders; [15]pok˛ ʻch'i, not speak of him—he is worthless; COM., [16]këü² ʻch'i (coll. këü² ʻk'i), saw-teeth; [17]˛king ˛niêng ˛chong ʻch'i, what is your age this year?

矢 ʻChih. An arrow, a dart; swift as an arrow; direct, open; to set forth, to arrange; to swear, to vow; to display; to resolve, to form a purpose; to void ordure; the 111th radical: [18]ʻch'i sié² an oath; [19]˛ki tik˛ ˛ü ʻch'i, he is as straight as an arrow, i. e., blunt, honest; COM., [20]chiêng² ʻch'i, arrows; ˛küng ʻch'i, bow and arrow.

屎 ʻShi. Dung, ordure, excrement: in the coll. read ʻsai, q. v.: [21]ʻch'i ʻt'ung, a close stool. Read ˛hi: a sigh, a moan; a murmuring sound.

豕 ʻChih. A hog, a pig; the 152d radical: ʻk'eng ʻch'i, dogs and swine; hai² ʻch'i, (to confound) hai² with ʻch'i—to mistake words.

ʻCh'i. A coll. euphonic prefix, as in ʻch'i ʻch'a, to fire, as tea leaves; to roast, as coffee.

1 自嗤 2 妍媸 3 蚩蚩 4 蚩氓 5 雌雄鞭〇 6 鞭笞 7 鴟張 8 角鴟 9 鴟鴞 10 參差 11 齒牙 12 年齒 13 齒數 14 齒長 15 不齒 16 鋸齒 17 今年尊齒 18 矢誓 19 其直如矢 20 箭矢 21 屎桶

福州方言拼音字典

꜀Ch'i. A coll. euphonic prefix, as in *꜀ch'i ꜀ch'ë*, to hoot, to shout at angrily or contemptuously.

꜀Ch'i. A coll. word, as in *꜀ch'i ꜀li*, the fizzling sound of poor fire-crackers; *꜀ch'i ꜀li 'k'i ꜀li*, rough, bristling; *꜀ch'i ch'ié' ch'ié'* coarse, rough; disarranged; COM., *móh꜇ lóh꜇ 'chi kaëk꜇ ꜀ch'i ch'ié' ch'ié'* don't stay here and disarrange things.

(109) Ch'iă.

奢 Ch'ē. Wasteful, extravagant; to spread out, affluent: [1]*'kieu ꜀ch'iă ꜀ing ik꜇* pride, extravagance, licentiousness and laziness; COM., [2]*꜀ch'iă ꜀hwa*, gay, wasteful; [3]*꜀hwa ꜀ch'iă*, or *꜀ch'iă 'ch'ié*, extravagant, prodigal.

車 Ch'ē. Also read *꜀kü:* a chariot, a carriage, any vehicle, a cart; a machine for raising water into the fields; to roll or turn over; to turn about; to screw in; to turn, as in a lathe: COM., [4]*꜀t'ai ꜀ch'iă*, to draw a carriage; [5]*꜀ch'iă ꜀lung*, a wheel; [6]*꜀ch'iă ꜀hu*, a charioteer; [7]*꜀sung ꜀ch'iă*, boats and carriages, by water and land; [8]*'chwi ꜀ch'iă*, a water-raising machine: [9]*tak꜇ ꜀ch'iă*, to work this machine with the feet; [10]*'hwi ꜀lung ꜀ch'iă*, a locomotive, a railway car; [11]*꜀ch'iă kwo'* to turn it over; [12]*꜀ch'iă taing'* a turning shop; [13]*꜀ch'iă ngwoh꜇* to turn gems; [14]*꜀t'iéng ꜀ch'iă*, an elevator; COLL., [15]*꜀ch'iă pauk꜇* to exact exorbitant interest; *꜀ch'iă ꜀ch'iă ꜀yéng*, perfectly round; *꜀ch'iă ꜀ch'iă 'tiong*, to revolve; *꜀ch'iă 'tiong ꜀sing ꜀kiăng k'ó'* to turn and go away; *꜀ch'iă ꜀tié*, to raise water from a pond; *꜀ch'iă 'tié*, to screw in.

硨 Ch'ē. As in *꜀ch'iă ꜀kü*, a white stone of inferior quality, brought from India; [16]*꜀ch'iă ꜀kü 'ting*, the white-stone button—denotes the 6th official grade.

莗 Ch'ē. A plant called *꜀ch'iă ꜀chiéng*, a diuretic: COM., [17]*꜀ch'iă ꜀chiéng 'chi*, seeds of the same.

蛼 Ch'ē. As in [18]*꜀ch'iă ꜀ngó*, a large kind of mytilus; COLL., *꜀ch'iă ꜀ngó ch'oi'* mytilus-mouthed—i. e., taciturn; *꜀ch'iă ꜀ngó 'k'wi ꜀si*, "the mytilus gapes;" *met.*, at length he deigns to speak.

且 Ch'ieh. A conjunction, and, also; further, moreover, still; thus, so, yet; a word of doubt, if, should: COM., [19]*'keu 'ch'iă*, carelessly; *꜀ku 'ch'iă*, merely, for the time; *hëk꜇ 'ch'iă*, if, perhaps; *hwong' 'ch'iă*, still more; [20]*hëk꜇ 'ch'iă ꜀yong*, possibly so; [21]*꜀i 'ch'iă*, also; *'ch'iă 'hi*, joy to you! COLL., *'ch'iă maing'* by and by, presently; *'ch'iă mwong' sioh꜇ ꜀siăng*, just go and ask for once.

꜀Ch'iă. A coll. prefix, as in *꜀ch'iă ch'iă' 'kiăng*, small cymbals.

跅 Ch'ē. Diverging, branching off, a road parting; in the coll. diagonal, cris-cross: COLL., *ch'iă' ch'iă'* diagonally; *ch'iă' 'ngang*, cross-eyed, squinting; *ch'iă' ꜀teu* (coll. *ch'iă' 'leu*), strips of cloth cut bias.

[1]驕奢淫泆 [2]奢華 [3]花奢 [4]抬車 [5]車輪 [6]車夫 [7]船車 [8]水車 [9]踏車 [10]火輪車 [11]車過 [12]車店 [13]車玉 [14]天車 [15]車剝 [16]硨渠頂 [17]莗葥子 [18]蛼螯 [19]苟且 [20]或且然 [21]而且

Ch‘iă². A coll. word, as in *ch‘iă² ch‘iă²* the clattering sound of cymbals.

(110) Ch‘ĭăh.

赤, Ch‘ih. Read *ch‘ek,*; coll. *ch‘iăh,*: carnation, purplish, golden; flesh color; the color of any highly polished metal; naked, nude: [1]*ch‘iăh, ch‘iăh,* bright, burnished; [2]*,ĕng ch‘iăh,* a brilliant red; flushed, as the face; [3]*ch‘iăh, ,king,* burnished gold; [4]*ch‘iăh, ,sing lo² ‘t‘á*, naked; [5]*twai² ch‘iăh,* and *ne² ch‘iăh,* superior and inferior gilt; [6]*ch‘iăh, tak, tak,* or [7]*ch‘iăh, kwang² kwang²* very bright, as metallic surfaces; [8]*ch‘iăh, pau²* "red panther," a kind of strong, dark tobacco; [9]*kau² ch‘iăh,* the best gilding, as on paper; [10]*ch‘iăh, ‘kiăng ‘kwi,* malicious spirits that afflict children; [11]*ch‘iăh, ‘kiăng ‘kwi ,kié ,sieu t‘iék,* spirits infesting children are soon dispersed; *met.*, a narrow-minded person is satisfied with a trifle.

Ch‘iăh,. A coll. word, as in *ch‘iăh, che²* words branded or tattooed on the temples of banished criminals.

Ch‘iăh₂. A coll. word: to scoop from the bottom, as fruit in baskets; *ch‘iăh₂ ‘heng ‘heng,* to scoop up thoroughly; *ch‘iăh₂ ‘k‘i ,li k‘ang²* scoop up and see (if it is good).

(111) Ch‘iăk.

怓, Chi. Ancient form of the character for *kek,* (urgent)—used in the *Paik, ,Ing* for the coll. *ch‘iăk,*: fearful, timid, startled, palpitating: [12]*,kŭng á² ch‘iăk,* the veins throb; [13]*,sing ‘lá kiéng² ch‘ek, ch‘iăk, ch‘iăk,* to be startled, in a tremor.

Ch‘iăk,. A coll. word: to cut up fine, to mince, to grate; a coarse grater: *ch‘iăk, ch‘ói²* or *ch‘iăk, naung² naung²* to cut up fine; *ch‘iăk, ‘peng,* (black) wooden sticks beaten together in theaters by singing beggars; *ch‘iăk, ,hwang ,sü,* to grate potatoes for drying; *,hwang ,sü ch‘iăk,* a potato-grater.

Ch‘iăk,. A coll. word: to rub, as in washing clothes: *ch‘iăk, pah₂* to rub white.

Ch‘iăk,. A coll. word: to pluck, to twitch, to pull at, as the kite string: *ch‘iăk, ‘tong,* to break in twitching: *k‘ëük, ,i ch‘iăk, ‘chau,* he plucked himself away (from me); *ch‘iăk, ‘k‘i ch‘iăk,* tears himself away.

Ch‘iăk₂. A coll. word: to tread on, to trample: *ch‘iăk₂ ‘si,* to trample to death; *ch‘iăk₂ mauk,* to trample to a jelly; *ch‘iăk₂ t‘ak, ‘tá,* to tread the bottom out.

(112) Ch‘iăng.

,Ch‘iăng. A coll. word: a splinter, a sliver: *,ch‘iăng tóh₂* a sliver stuck (in the hand); *,ch‘iăng ,t‘ieu ‘k‘i,* to pick out a splinter.

‘請 Ch‘ing. Read *‘ch‘ing;* coll. *‘ch‘iăng*: to request, to ask courteously, to pray, to beg; to ask, as for orders; to invite, to bid, to engage; to confess: [14]*‘ch‘iăng ,hung ,teu,* to get the official seal to close (and protect) a place; [15]*‘ch‘iăng ‘chiu,* to invite to a feast; [16]*‘ch‘iăng t‘aik,* invitation-

[1]赤 [8]赤 露 [6]赤 慣 [9]厚 鬼 快 僻 見 [14]請 [15]請
赤 金 體 答 慣 赤 [11]赤 消 怓 戚 封 酒
[2]紅 [4]赤 [5]大 答 [8]赤 [10]赤 仔 撤 [13]心 怓 条 [16]請
赤 身 赤 [7]赤 豹 仔 鬼 [12]筋 禮 怓 〇 帖

cards; [1]'*ch'ăng sói*^{2} please sit; [2]'*ch'iăng piéng*^{2} please to consult your own convenience; [3]'*ch'iăng kiéng*' to beg an interview; '*ch'iăng* ˎ*ta*, please take some tea; [4]'*ch'iăng* ˎ*hwói* ˎ*mwoong*, to invite home—the parents' first invitation to a daughter after her marriage; '*ch'iăng* ˏ*t'iéng*, to ask for more; [5]'*ch'iăng* ˏ*hiong* '*hwói*, to get incense ashes (in bags) from temples; [6]'*ch'iăng leng*^{2} to ask for orders; [7]'*ch'iăng siong*' to get paper images (as of the '*Ngu tá*') to carry in procession; '*ch'iăng k'ah, ng*^{2} *chai*^{2} *sioh*, ˏ*sëng tëü*^{2} in inviting guests don't mind (providing) an extra pair of chop-sticks; [8]'*ch'iăng* ˏ*ang*, to salute, to present compliments; [9]'*ch'iăng chói*^{2} to confess an error; '*ch'iăng* ˏ*tëng* '*ch'iăng* ˏ*sá* ˎ*mó* '*ch'iăng tói*' *meng*' ˏ*ká*, invite from east and west but not from the opposite side of the street; *met.*, to admit strangers and exclude friends (from a part in any business).

'癬 Hsien. Read '*siéng:* coll. '*ch'iăng:* ring-worm: [10]ˏ*sang* '*ch'iăng*, to have ring-worm; [11]'*hwói* '*ch'iăng*, a reddish ring-worm: [12]'*kiu* '*ch'iăng* ˎ*sing lai*^{2} protracted ring-worm becomes leprosy.

'剗 '鏟 Ch'an. Read '*sang;* coll. '*ch'iăng:* to scoop, to lade up or out, as flour: [13]'*ch'iăng* ˏ*ki*, a scoop.

倩' Ch'ien. Read *ch'aing*'; coll. *ch'iăng*': to hire, to employ one to work for wages: [14]'*ch'iăng*' *tai*^{2} or *ch'iăng*' *chó*' to hire work done; [15]'*ch'iăng*' ˏ*kĕng*, or *ch'iăng*' *kioh*, or *ch'iăng*' ˎ*nëng* ˏ*kĕng*, to hire workmen; *ch'iăng*' '*sieu* ˏ*kĕng*, to hire for small jobs; *ch'iăng*' ˎ*tong* ˏ*kĕng*, to hire permanently; *ch'iăng*' ˎ*nëng* ˎ*t'ié* ˎ*ma* ˎ*mó mek*, '*chai*, hired mourners shed no tears—moral, what you wish done well, do yourself.

成 'Ch'êng. Read ˎ*sing;* coll. ˎ*ch'iăng:* to finish, to complete, as a job partly done: [16]*chó*' ˎ*ch'iăng*, to finish; [17]ˎ*ch'iăng ngié*^{2} to complete one's apprenticeship, as at a *second* shop; ˎ*ch'iăng* '*mwói*, or ˎ*ch'iăng* ˎ*wong*, ended, finished; [18]ˎ*ch'iăng miăng*^{2} to put an end to life, killed, as by additional ills; ˎ*ch'iăng twai*^{2} grown large; *chioh*, ˏ*hu* ˎ*ch'iăng* '*kiăng*, borrows (gets another) husband to rear her son.

Ch'iăng^2. A coll. word: an eel; a kind of reddish eel, called '*hwói ch'iăng*^{2} said to jump at the sight of fire and to be unfit for food.

(113) Ch'ié.

'吒 Ch'a. '尺 Ch'ih. Read *ch'ek*ˏ; coll. ˏ*ch'ié:* a note in music; the first also means to rail at, to scold: [19]ˏ*ch'ié* '*kwang*, a music school: [20]ˏ*ch'ié tang*' a load of musical instruments, as borne in idol processions; ˏ*ch'ié* ˏ*ch'ié* '*mó*, a vixen, a scolding woman; by *met.* applied also to men.

'侈 Ch'ih. Extravagant, profuse, large, superfluous, prodigal: [21]ˏ*kieu* '*ch'ié*, proud and showy; [22]'*ch'ié* ˎ*tang*, extrav-

1 請坐 2 請便 3 請見 4 請回門 5 請香火 6 請令 7 請相 8 請安 9 請罪 10 生癬 11 火癬 12 久癬成癩 13 剗箕 14 倩代 15 倩工 16 做成 17 成藝 18 成命 19 尺舘 20 尺担 21 驕侈 22 侈談

agant talk; COM., [22]꜀ch'iâ 'ch'ié, wasteful.

扯 撦 Ch'é. Also read 'ch'iâ: to tear open, to pull apart, to tear away; to drag, to pull up: [1]'ch'ié p'ó' to tear asunder; COLL., ꜀la 'ch'ié, to grasp, to embezzle; 'ch'ié p'wai' pĕk꜁ ꜀nĕng, to compel others to share the trouble or expense.

弛 Ch'ih. A bow unstrung; to let go the string of a bow, to relax, to cast off; injured, spoiled; easy, dissolute, unconcerned; [3]'ch'ié hwai' spoiled; [4]'ch'ié sang' scattered; COM., [5]hié' 'ch'ié, obsolete, effete, done away.

哆 Ch'ih. To gape, gaping; an open mouth, like a fish; large-lipped: [6]'ch'ié ꜀yong, sneering, disobedient.

'Ch'ié. A coll. word: to equalize: ꜀yeu 'ch'ié nioh꜁ wai' divides into what equal parts? 'ch'ié tek꜁ tik꜁ to come out even, as profits and losses; na' 'ch'ié tek꜁ 'pwong ꜀chiĕng tik꜁ comes out even, so as to save the capital only.

'Ch'ié. A coll. word, as in 'ch'ié 't'oi (or 'ch'oi), to half-kneel—a polite form, as in New Year's salutations.

幟 織 Chih. A fringe or border on a flag; a flag, a streamer or pennon, long and fringed; to tie or sew on fringes, as a signal: to signalize: [7]꜀ki ch'ié' flags; [8]'söü' ch'ié' to hoist a flag.

熾 戭 Chih. Flame, blaze, splendor; the glare of lights; to catch, to spread, as fire; *met.*, to rage, as lusts; numerous: COLL., ch'ié' nié' to spread, to catch, as fire; [9]ch'ié' 'hwi, to kindle, to catch fire; [10]ch'ié' 'k'i, to rise and burn, as lusts.

翄 翅 Tzu. Wings, fins: [11]'ching ch'ié' or 'kü ch'ié' to flap the wings; COM., [12]꜀ngü ch'ié' fins, the shark's fins; [13]ch'ié' ꜀seng, a superior kind of biche-de-mer.

饎 糦 Tzu. To cook or dress provisions; wine and food, victuals; millet used in sacrifice.

茦 莿 莿 Tzu. The first read ꜀chü, the second ch'aik, and ch'ëü', the third ch'ëü' and commonly used for the coll. ch'ié': thorns, briers, brambles; in a *met.* sense, to kill, as fowls; to excite feeling: COLL., [14]ch'ié' ch'ié' thorny, rough; [15]ch'ié' 'ch'au, briers; [16]ch'ié' ch'oi' the place stabbed, as of animals butchered; [17]ch'ié' pa' 'ch'au, thorns; [18]ch'ié' ꜀kié, to kill a chicken with a knife; [19]ch'ié' ch'ié' ꜀t'ui, "thorn-maul," wielded by the attendants of T'ai' ꜀sang, to beat the wicked in the next world; [20]ch'ié' ꜀ma tai' a species of small prickly caterpillar; *met.*, a dangerous fellow; ch'ié' mĕk꜁ or [21]ch'ié' mek꜁ ꜀chiu, it hurts the eyes—excites envy.

[1]扯破 [2]扯破 別仈 [3]弛壞 [4]弛散 [5]廢弛 [6]哆然 [7]旗幟 [8]樹幟 [9]熾火 [10]熾起 [11]振翅 [12]魚翅 [13]翅參 [14]莿莿 [15]莿草 [16]莿嘴 [17]莿霸 草 [18]莿雞 [19]莿 莿 [20]莿麻 鎚 帶 [21]莿目睛

栨 Tz'u. Read *chiék*, and *ch'ëü*ʾ; coll. *ch'ié*ʾ: the jams of a door, called ¹*ˏmwong ch'ié*ʾ or *t'aik, ch'ié*ʾ; ²*ch'ié*ʾ *ˏwai*, the jams are slanting; ³*ˏhwang ch'ié*ʾ the cross piece over a door-way; ⁴*tik, ch'ié*ʾ the side-pieces; *pŏh, ˏnëng ˏmwong ch'ié*ʾ *ˏpiéng*, to stop beside people's doors, as beggars do.

ˏCh'ié. A coll. word: to move heavy articles, to shove, to edge along; to veer, as the wind: *ˏch'ié chiăng*ʾ move it till it stands squarely; the sun approaching the summer solstice; *ˏch'ié ˏwai*, to move awry; the sun approaching the winter solstice; *ˏch'ié* ʿ*mi*, to shake rice to the middle of the sieve.

*Ch'ié*ʾ. A coll. word, the same as *ch'iă*ʾ: transverse, diagonally: *ch'ié*ʾ *ˏnia nói*ʾ somewhat diagonal.

(114) Ch'iék.

竊 窃 竊 Ch'ieh. To steal, to take slily; clandestine, underhand, privately; to regard privately, what you do yourself; I, my; when used alone, means I was there, it was my opinion, I did so: to have a place, to offer an opinion; unfit for; usurped, assumed; tinged, colored: ⁵*ˏt'eu ch'iék*, to steal; ⁶*ch'iék, ch'ieu*ʾ to laugh at secretly; ⁷*ch'iék, oi*ʾ to usurp an office; ⁸*ch'iék, ˏlang*, a light blue color; ⁹ʿ*ch'ü ch'iék*, ʿ*keu tó*ʾ rats and dogs steal—said of thievish people; *ch'iék, ˏung*, to hear by stealth.

切 Ch'ieh. To cut, to carve, to mince, to slice; to urge, to press; a superlative, very, vehement, earnest, eager; pressing, important, serious, momentous; the important parts, a resumé; sincere; all, the whole, entire; to feel, as the pulse; to express sounds by joining initials and finals, called ¹⁰*ch'iék, ˏing*: *ch'iék, sik*, sincerely; COM., ¹¹*ch'iék, ch'iék*, or *p'aik, ch'iék*, earnestly, pressingly; ¹²*ch'iék, wong*ʾ to hope for earnestly; ¹³ʿ*k'ong ch'iék, ˏki tŏ*, to pray fervently; ¹⁴*ek, ch'iék*, the whole; ¹⁵*ch'iék, ˏyeu*ʾ very important; ¹⁶*ch'iék, pok*, ʿ*k'ŏ ngwo*ʾ you must not delay; ¹⁷*ˏch'ing ch'iék*, intimate, as a friend; *ˏkwang ch'iék*, deeply impressed or charged, as with another's matter; ¹⁸*ch'iék*, ʿ*ch'i*, to gnash the teeth—deadly hate; *ch'iék, miéng*ʾ a kind of sliced vermicelli; COLL., *ch'iék, pŏh, pŏh*, to slice thin; *ˏsing* ʿ*yă ch'iék*, in deep earnest.

砌 Ch'i. A stone step; ornamented tiles laid for steps; to lay, as tiles; to place regularly, to fit in: ¹⁹*tëük, ch'iék*, to lay steps.

妾 Ch'ieh. A concubine, a secondary wife, one taken without the legal ceremonies; term by which ladies designate themselves: *ˏch'ing ˏing ch'iék, wak, ˏü ˏhu ˏing*, a man's concubine is called *ˏü ˏhu ˏing*; COM., ²⁰ʿ*má ch'iék*, to buy a concubine; *ch'iék, ˏsing* I, your handmaid; ²¹*chiéng*ʾ *ch'iék*, I, your lowly handmaid; ʿ*t'ung ch'iék*, or *ai*ʾ *ch'iék*, a beloved concubine.

¹門栨 ³横栨 ⁵偷竊 ⁷竊位 ⁹鼠竊 ¹⁰切音 ¹²切望 祈禱 ¹⁵切要 可誤 ¹⁸切齒 ²⁰買妾

²栨歪 ⁴直栨 ⁶竊笑 ⁸竊藍 狗盜 ¹¹切切 ¹³懇切 ¹⁴一切 ¹⁶切不 ¹⁷親切 ¹⁹築砌 ²¹賤妾

蠘 Ch'ieh.ˎ Read *chekˎ*; coll. *ch'iékˎ*: a large kind of crab with serrated claws and shell, the latter being more elongated than in the ˏ*sing*: [1]*ch'iékˎ ˏch'ang*, raw crabs, as sliced and seasoned; [2]*tongʼ ch'iékˎ*, crabs cut up and boiled; *hekˎ ch'iékˎ* crabs boiled whole; [3]*'mó ch'iékˎ* the female crab; *ch'iékˎ ˏkó*, red meat of the crab; [4]*ch'iékˎ 'yong*, crab-groins; [5]*ch'iékˎ ˏkeng*, a crab-stew; *ch'iékˎ p'angʼ* the crab is empty—has but little meat.

(115) Ch'iéng.

千 ˏCh'ien. A thousand; many, an indefinite number: COM., [6]ˏ*ch'iéng siongʼ* over a thousand; [7]ˏ*ch'iéng swoiʼ* (may the king live) a thousand years; your highness! [8]ˏ*ch'iéng cheʼ ˏung*, the thousand character classic; [9]ˏ*ch'iéng wangʼ* most certainly, by all means; ˏ*ch'iéng ˏking*, a thousand of gold, your daughter! ˏ*ch'iéng 'li 'ngang*, "the thousand *'li* eye"—an attendant of the goddess of seamen; [10]ˏ*ch'iéng 'li 'ma*, a courier; [11]ˏ*ch'iéng ˏmeu paik, kiéʼ* to scheme in every way; [12]ˏ*ch'iéng ˏsang wangʼ 'chwi*, very distant; ˏ*ch'iéng ˏniéng pok, 'sü ˏkwi*, the tortoise which does not die for a thousand years; *met.*, said jeeringly of a cuckold; *ek, ˏka 'pau 'nwang ˏch'iéng ˏka wongʼ* a thousand families hate the one rich family; COLL., ˏ*ch'iéng ˏking pok, ˏnó ˏié*, a thousand pounds can't move it; *met.*, unchangeable, inflexible; ˏ*ch'iéng ˏnëng maʼ* cursed by everybody.

仟 ˏCh'ien. The chief of a thousand men: [13]ˏ*ch'iéng paik, ˏchi taik*, to get a thousand or a hundred.

芊 ˏCh'ien. Exuberant foliage, flourishing vegetation; green-like jade: [14]ˏ*ch'iéng ˏch'iéng*, luxuriant.

阡 ˏCh'ien. A road leading north and south; a cross-way through the fields; a path to a grave: [15]ˏ*k'ai ˏch'iéng paik*, to dig up the roads betwen fields; *met.*, avaricious.

鮮 ˏHsien. Read *'siéng*; coll. ˏ*ch'iéng*: fresh, raw, as meat; fresh fish; bright, new, as colors; clean, pure; in good order: [16]*saik, 'chwi ˏch'iéng*, the colors are bright; [17]ˏ*ch'iéng ˏming*, fresh and bright; [18]ˏ*ch'iéng ˏngü*, or ˏ*ch'iéng hwoʼ* fresh fish; *ngʼ ˏch'iéng ch'ieuʼ* not bright, dull; ˏ*ch'iéng ˏhwa*, fresh flowers; ˏ*ch'iéng 'tieu ˏtieu*, or ˏ*ch'iéng kwangʼ kwangʼ* very fresh; ˏ*ch'iéng ch'aiʼ* fresh vegetables; ˏ*kwong ˏch'iéng*, clean and whole, in good order, as clothes.

蠘 虷 Ch'ien. Used for the coll. ˏ*ch'iéng*, as in ˏ*ha ˏch'iéng*, pickled prawns; [19]ˏ*ch'iéng ˏkang*, dried shrimps.

襁 ˏCh'ien. As in ˏ*p'iéng ˏch'iéng*, the motion of the dress in walking; garments shaken by the wind; in the coll., a kind of concealed stitch, to *fell*, in which sense often spoken *ch'iéngʼ*: ˏ*ch'iéng ˏcheng*, the concealed fell-stitch, as in facings of garments.

¹蠘	³㹚	⁵蠘	⁷千	文	里	百	萬	之	¹⁵開	水	¹⁸鮮
生	蠘	羹	歲	⁹千	馬	計	水	得	阡	鮮	魚
²炖	⁴蠘	⁶千	⁸千	萬	¹¹千	¹²千	¹³仟	¹⁴芊	陌	¹⁷鮮	¹⁹蠘
蠘	胦	上	字	¹⁰千	謀	山	佰	芊	¹⁶色	明	乾

遷迁 ˓Ch‘ien. To move, to remove, to place elsewhere; to ascend, to be promoted; to change, to transpose; to improve; to banish, to deport, to drive off: COM., [1]˓*ch‘iêng ˓ié*, to move; variable; [2]˓*ch‘iêng ˓kü*, to change one's residence; [3]˓*ch‘iêng siêng*ʼ ʻ*kai kwo*ʼ to improve, to reform; [4]˓*kwong* ʻ*king piêng*ʼ ˓*ch‘iêng*, (an unfavorable) change in the times; COLL., ˓*ch‘iêng cheu*ʼ done indifferently; ʻ*mwong* ˓*ch‘iêng cheu*ʼ *k‘á*ʼ ˓*i* ʻ*sai*, though poorly done, just accept (the article) from him!

躚 ˓Ch‘ien. As in ˓*p‘iêng* ˓*ch‘iêng*, to walk round and round, to whirl about; to writhe, to wriggle; to gesticulate, theatrical.

僉 ˓Ch‘ien. All, the whole; unanimous voice, the general opinion; a flail: COM., [5]˓*ch‘iêng* ˓*kung* ˓*tiăng*, a public document, as to state that an affair has been settled, &c.

憸 ˓Ch‘ien. Disputatious, skilled at argument; insidious, lying flattery: [6]˓*ch‘iêng* ˓*ing*, a flatterer; a disputatious person.

簽 ˓Ch‘ien. Slips of lettered bamboo, used for lots, for which the next is used; to subscribe, to write one's name, to append a signature; a kind of basket; the red slips of paper on the outside of envelopes: COM., [7]˓*ch‘iêng ak*˒ a kind of law-secretary in a yamun; [8]˓*ch‘iêng p‘wo*ʼ record of cases in a court; [9]*t‘aik*˒ ˓*ch‘iêng*, to stick the red slips of paper on envelopes; [10]*saëng*ʼ ˓*ch‘iêng*, to hand up a decision to the officer for approval; [11]˓*ch‘iêng* ˓*miăng*, to sign a name to a paper.

籤 ˓Ch‘ien. Similar to the last: a slip, a warrant, a permit, a ticket having the officer's name on it; lots before an idol; slips in cups before a judge, each slip denoting five blows; to probe, to bore through; sharp-pointed: COM., [12]˓*ch‘iêng p‘wo*, the written responses of idols—indicated by the "lots"; [13]*tëük*˒ ˓*ch‘iêng*, bamboo slips; [14]˓*ch‘iêng e*ʼ (coll.: ˓*ch‘iêng meng*ʼ), import of the lot; [16]˓*t‘iu* ˓*ch‘iêng*, to draw lots before idols; [16]ʻ*hwi* ˓*ch‘iêng*, an urgent warrant; [17]˓*ch‘iêng p‘wo*ʼ record of taxes.

箋 ˓Ch‘ien. Tablets or slips on which to make memoranda; a letter, a writing; note-paper with water-line or stamped pictures; writings handed to the monarch: COM., [18]˓*ch‘iêng* ʻ*chai*, fancy note-paper; [19]*lak*˒ ˓*ch‘iêng*, glazed billet-paper; ʻ*t‘u* ˓*ch‘iêng*, the domestic sort; [20]˓*su* ˓*ch‘iêng*, the Suchau sort; ʻ*ngu saik*˒ ˓*ch‘iêng*, fancy-colored varieties.

剗 ˓Ch‘ien. To cut, to pierce the throat; to part, to divide, to cut asunder.

戔 ˓Chien. Small, narrow, cramped; contracted, as one's mind: used for ˓*ch‘ang*, cruel.

孅 ˓Ch‘ien. Similar to the next: slender, sharp-pointed; acute; crafty, subtle: [21]˓*ch‘iêng yok*˒ delicate and weak.

1 遷移 2 遷居 3 遷善改過 4 光景變遷 5 僉公呈◯ 6 憸人 7 簽押 8 簽薄 9 帖簽 10 送簽 11 僉名 12 籤譜 13 竹籤 14 籤意 15 抽籤 16 火籤 17 籤簿 18 箋紙 19 蠟箋 20 蘇箋 21 孅弱

纖 摻 Ch'ien. Fine silk; small, delicate, like silken fibers; silk web with a white woof and black warp; niggardly, stingy: [1]*ch'iëng ˏhó*, trivial, a little; [2]*ˏch'iëng ˋsieu*, small, minute; [3]*ˏch'iëng ˏyeu*, a delicate waist.

殲 Ch'ien. To destroy utterly, to exterminate, to pierce, to kill.

鋟 Also read *ˏching* and *ˋch'ing*: to cut, to engrave; sharp pointed; a point, an awl; a graver.

韆 Ch'ien. To swing to and fro, to play on a whirligig: [4]*ˏch'iu ˏch'iëng*, a swing.

ˏCh'iëng. A coll. word: headforemost, prone, headlong: *ˏch'iëng lóh*, or *ˏt'au ˋting ˏch'iëng lóh, ˏdi*, to fall headlong.

ˏCh'iëng. A coll. word, as in *ˏch'iëng miëng*ˀ the city pronunciation for *ch'iëk, miëng*ˀ sliced vermicelli.

淺 Ch'ien. Shallow, not deep, superficial; light, as colors; easy, simple, as ideas; having few strokes, as characters; short-haired; flowing fast: COM., [5]*ˋch'iëng saik*, pale colors; [6]*ˋch'iëng ˏkau*, a slight acquaintance; [7]*ˋch'iëng pok*, (coll. *ˋch'iëng póh*,) thin, shallow, as soil, ideas, etc.; [8]*ˋch'iëng sauk*, scant, imperfect, as a composition; [9]*ˋch'iëng ˏlang*, a light blue; [10]*ˋch'iëng kiëng*ˀ *sek*, superficial knowledge; [11]*ˏngiong ˋch'iëng e*ˀ *ˏch'ing*, words simple, sense profound; [12]*ˋchwi ˋch'iëng sik, hiëng*ˀ the shallow water shows the stones—"murder will out."

闡 Ch'an. To open, to spread out, to enlarge from the original condition; manifest, clear, plain, to make plain: [13]*ˋch'iëng ˏming*, to explain clearly.

塹 Chan. The moat outside a wall, a fosse, a ditch, a sluice; to deepen, to dig out: [14]*ˏtoi ˏch'iong ˏteng ch'ieng*ˀ the falling wall fills the moat.

*Ch'iëng*ˀ. A coll. word: to stab, to prick, to pierce: *ch'iëng*ˀ *ˋsi*, to stab to death; *ch'ieng*ˀ *sioh, ˏtó*, to give a stab with a sword or knife.

槧 Chein. Boards for cutting books on; tablet for memoranda; tablets to be written on with a pencil.

*Ch'iëng*ˀ. A coll. word, as in *ch'iëng*ˀ *ch'iëng*ˀ few, not too much, just about the proper amount; *na*ˀ *ˋchiă ˋk'wang ch'iëng*ˀ *ch'iëng*ˀ *tioh*, only that much, just this medium.

*Ch'iëng*ˀ. A coll. word: bamboo pegs inserted in the edges of boards to unite them: *p'ah, ch'iëng*ˀ to unite by pegs.

ˏCh'iëng. A coll. word: the space between the extended arms; a fathom; to clutch and pull recklessly: *sioh, ˏch'iëng*, one fathom; *ˋnü ng*ˀ *ˏt'ëng ˏch'iëng*, you must not gripe and pull.

(116) Ch'ieu.

超 Ch'ao. To leap over, to trip, to hop across; to vault, to step over; to go before, to precede; to excel, to sur-

1 纖毫 2 纖小 3 纖腰 4 鞦韆 5 淺色○ 6 淺交○ 7 淺薄○ 8 淺率○ 9 淺藍○ 10 淺見識○ 11 言淺意深 12 水淺石現 13 闡明○ 14 隤牆塡塹

pass; to promote, to raise: in the coll., manifestation of sexual passion in animals; ˏch‘ieu ˏkung, to excel the crowd: COM., [1]ˏch‘ieu ˏsing, or [2]ˏch‘ieu pakˎ to raise, to deliver, as spirits in the ‘p‘wo toˀ rites: [3]ˏch‘ieu ˏseng, to grant life, to reprieve; COLL., ˏch‘ieu toˀ ˏnëng, to spirit people away (to heaven), as genii can; *met.*, to succor persons; [4]ˏch‘ieu ˏkié kaĕk, an excited chicken-cock; ‘yă ˏch‘ieu, excelling, very fine!

釗 ˏCh‘ao. Also read ˏchieu: to pare, to clip off; to see, to wait on; to encourage; distant.

鍫 鍬 ˏCh‘iu. An iron implement for turning the soil, a spade, a pick, a crow-bar; to dig deep.

ˏ*Ch‘ieu*. A coll. word: to hem: ˏch‘ieu ˏcheng, the hemming stitch; ˏch‘ieu ˏi ˏsiong, to hem garments.

‘**悄** Ch‘iao. Sad, downcast, sorrowful: [5]ˏiu ˏsing ‘ch‘ieu ‘ch‘ieu, sick at heart; sorrowing in secret.

‘**峭** Ch‘iao. Also read sieuˀ: a steep, abrupt hill; a cliff that obstructs the way; severe, strict, vehement: [6]‘ch‘ieu chiokˎ or [7]‘ch‘ieu p‘ekˎ a perpendicular cliff; [8]‘ch‘ieu tikˎ severe.

‘**俏** Siao. Like, as if, similar; handsome, pretty, beautiful, superior: [9]‘chongˀ ‘ch‘ieu, beautiful; [10]pokˎ ‘ch‘ieu, homely, unhandsome; [11]‘ch‘ieu ˏseng, lifelike, as the dress of actors, puppets, etc.; [12]máˀ ‘ch‘ieu, to show off one's beauty.

笑 咲 ˀ Siao. To laugh, to giggle, to be pleased; glad, joyful, smiling, laughing, pleasant, jolly; a smile; to laugh at, to ridicule: in the coll., light colors: COM., [13]ch‘ieuˀ ‘liéng (coll. ch‘ieuˀ mengˀ), a laughing face: [14]ˏhang ch‘ieuˀ smiling; [15]‘hó ch‘ieuˀ amusing, laughable; [16]ˏhi ˏhi ch‘ieuˀ to giggle; [17]kiéngˀ ch‘ieuˀ laughed at; [18]pe̍ˀ ˏing ‘t‘i ch‘ieuˀ to make yourself a laughing stock; COLL., [19]saikˎ ch‘ieuˀ the color is lightish; [20]ˏmong ch‘ieuˀ to jest, to make sport of; [21]ˏt‘au ch‘ieuˀ to laugh at secretly; ch‘ieuˀ ‘pa (or ‘tó), to laugh immoderately; ch‘ieuˀ mengˀ ‘hu, a smiling-faced tiger—one who hides a cruel heart under, &c.; ch‘ieuˀ ˏnëng ˏkŭng ch‘aikˎ ˏnëng poˀ to mock at the poor and envy the rich; ch‘ieuˀ ˏk‘iu (or ˏki ˏtiu ˏk‘iu, or ˏku ˏtu ˏk‘u, or ˏku ˏtung ˏch‘iong), to "laugh one's self into convulsive stooping"—split one's sides with laughter.

*Ch‘ieu*ˀ. A coll. word: to raise with a lever, to pry: ch‘ieuˀ siékˎ to break in prying; ch‘ieuˀ ˏsëng, to pry loose.

(117) Ch‘ih.

*Ch‘ih*ˎ. A coll. word, as in ch‘ihˎ ‘chau, to run away, to abscond; ch‘ihˎ ˏtëng ‘në k‘óˀ where has it run to? also used in the phrase ch‘ihˎ ch‘ihˎ ch‘uhˎ ch‘uhˎ the humming sound of low conversation.

[1]超	[3]超	公	悄	壁	俏	生	臉	笑	[17]見	恥	[20]玩
升	生	[5]憂	[6]峭	[8]峭	[10]不	[12]賣	[14]含	[16]嬉	笑	笑	笑
[2]超	[4]超	心	絕	直	俏	俏	笑	嬉	[18]被	[19]色	[21]偷
拔	雞	悄	[7]峭	[9]俊	[11]俏	[13]笑	[15]好	笑	人	笑	笑

Ch'ih꜇. A coll. euphonic prefix, as in *ch'ih꜇ ch'ioh꜇* or *ch'ih꜇ ch'ioh꜇ ch'ioh꜇* to tremble, as from fear.

Ch'ih꜇. A coll. word, as in *ch'ah꜇ ch'ih꜇* nearly, almost, within a very little.

Ch'ih꜇. A coll. imitation of the mandarin for eating, as in *ch'ih꜇ pok꜇ ꜂pau* can't satisfy his appetite, ravenous.

(118) Ch'ik.

Ch'ik꜇. A coll. euphonic prefix, as in *ch'ik꜇ ch'ĕk꜇* to chisel; *ch'ik꜇ ch'iăk꜇* or *ch'ik꜇ ch'ŭk꜇* to trample on; *ch'ik꜇ ch'ok꜇* to take a pinch of.

(119) Ch'ing.

青 ꜀Ch'ing. The color of nature, as the azure of the sky, or the green of growing plants; a very light green or blue tint; wan, fading away, pale; the 174th radical: in the coll. read *꜀ch'ang*, q.v.: [1]*꜀ch'ing ꜂ngang*, kindly, genial; [2]*lŭk꜇ ꜀ch'ing*, copperas; *꜀ch'ing lŭk꜇* lapis lazuli; [3]*꜁yong ꜀ch'ing*, smalts; COM., [4]*꜀ch'ing ꜁hung*, a blue cloud; [5]*꜀ch'ing ꜀ti'ĕng pek꜇ nik꜇* a clear, bright day; [6]*꜀ch'ing ꜀ch'ung*, or *꜀ch'ing ꜁niĕng*, youth, the time of youth; *꜀ch'ing ꜁leng ꜂chié*, a light purple.

蜻 ꜀Ch'ing. A dragon-fly which sips the water, called [7]*꜀ch'ing ꜁ting:* [8]*꜀ch'ing liĕk꜇* a species of cricket; *꜀ch'ing ꜁ling* a sort of dragonfly—one says *locust*.

清 ꜀Ch'ing. Pure, limpid, clear, unsullied; sharp-sighted; clean, incorruptible, right principled; clear, ringing, as a sound; to settle, to become clear; to settle an account; style of the present Manchu Dynasty of China, Manchu: COM., [9]*꜀ch'ing kiĕk*, or *꜀ch'ing chiăng꜄* pure, unsullied; [10]*꜀ch'ing tang꜄* weak, thin in consistence; light-colored; [11]*꜀ch'ing ꜀hiong*, fragrant, as flowers, a good reputation, etc.; [12]*꜀ch'ing tō꜄ ꜁ki*, flags carried before official sedans; [13]*꜀ch'ing ꜁ü ꜂chwi ꜁ming ꜁ü kiăng꜄* pure as water and clear as a mirror—unimpeachably chaste or honest; [14]*꜀ch'ing ꜁ming*, the festival of the tombs—in the 2d or 3d moon; [15]*꜀ch'ing ꜂ch'u*, or *꜀ch'ing ꜀ch'ing ꜂ch'u ꜂ch'u*, plain, intelligible, settled; [16]*꜀ch'ing ꜂chwi*, well-water; *꜀ch'ing ꜁liong*, clear and cool; cooling, as drinks; [17]*꜁teng ꜀ch'ing*, to make a final copy; *꜀ch'ing seu꜄* elegant in person; *꜀ch'ing ꜀chü*, writers in yamuns; *꜀ch'ing ch'iong꜄* one who only sings in plays; [18]*saung꜄ ꜀ch'ing*, to close up the account; COLL., *꜀ch'ing kŭk꜇* thin and thick, as fluids; *꜁ting ꜀ch'ing*, to clarify water; *pang꜄ ꜀ch'ing kiĕk*, scrupulously neat and cleanly.

深 ꜀Shĕn. Deep, profound, abstruse; ardent, as affection; well-read, learned; retired, far back, as an apartment; late at night; deep-tinted; an adverb, very, extremely, well; to secrete; a long robe: *꜀ch'ing ꜀yong*, an abyss, deep water; COM., [19]*꜀ch'ing ꜀kau*, intimate friendship; *꜀ch'ing ꜂ch'iĕng*, deep and shallow; [20]*꜀ch'ing ꜁chong*, to secrete, reticent, profound; *꜀ch'ing ꜀sang*, deep in (the recesses of) the mountains; *꜀kang ꜀ch'ing*, late in the night—

---

[1] 青眼 [2] 綠青 [3] 洋青 [4] 青雲 [5] 青天白日 [6] 青春 [7] 蜻蜓 [8] 蜻蜊 [9] 清潔 [10] 清淡 [11] 清香 [12] 清道旗 ○ [13] 清如水明如鏡 [14] 清明 [15] 清楚 [16] 清水 [17] 謄清 [18] 筭清 [19] 深交 [20] 深藏

福州方言拼音字典

toward morning; [1]ˌchʻing ʻwong, or ˌchʻing óʼ abstruse; [2]ˌchʻing sengʼ to believe implicitly; [3]ˌchʻing haiuʼ extremely generous; [4]ˌchʻing ˌchʻing chauk, ek, to make a profound obeisance; COLL., ngeʼ ˌchʻing, dull of hearing; ˌchʻing chiăh, ˌchʻing, very deep or profound.

稱 ʻChʻĕng. To weigh, to adjust by weight; to call, to name, to designate, to style; to say, to talk about; to compliment, to commend; to admire; to feign, to plead as an excuse; a designation, an appellation, a name: also read *chʻengʼ* q. v.: [5]ˌchʻing ʻhü, to extol, to concede one's goodness; COM., [6]ˌchʻing ˌhu, to style; termed, designated; [7]chĕüʼ ˌchʻing (coll. chĕʼ ˌchʻing), to praise or style one's self; [8]ˌchʻing ˌkŭng, to estimate by weight; COLL., ˌchʻing ˌkŭng pʻiék, a shallow bamboo basket to weigh in; ˌchʻing taĕngʼ mwiʼ ʻnü, sell it to you by weight; kʻĕăk, ˌnĕng ˌchʻing changʼ praised by others.

親 ˌChʻin. To love, to be attached to; liking, pleased with; near, intimate; near to, belonging to one's self, personal, myself; a relative, related to, having affinity; kindred, kin, kith; parents; a wife; affianced: COM., [9]ˌchʻing chʻek, kindred, relatives; [10]ˌchʻing ˌsu (coll. ˌchʻing ˌsĕ), near and distant relationship; [11]ˌchʻing ˌka, the families of a married couple; [12]ˌchʻing kĕüngʼ to be intimate with; [13]ngiéʼ ˌchʻing, adopted kindred; [14]ˌchʻing aiʼ to love, to cherish; [15]ˌchieu ˌchʻing, to introduce a husband; [16]lĕk, ˌchʻing, the six relations—father, mother, brother, sister, wife and children; [17]ˌchʻing ˌsing, one's self; [18]lengʼ ˌchʻing, your relative; siăʼ ˌchʻing, my relative; [19]ˌchʻing yĕk, or ˌchʻing haiuʼ warmly attached, as friends; [20]ˌchʻing ˌtong, or ˌchʻing ˌpung, descended from the same grandfather; [21]ˌchʻing ʻmu, mothers-in-law; ʻma ˌtʻau ˌchʻing, kindred of a paternal grandmother; ˌchʻing ˌka chĕŭk, pah, sister's husband's brothers; ˌchʻing ˌka keuʼ the wife's brothers—so called by the husband's relatives; COLL., chóʼ ˌchʻing, to betroth; [22]ʻtʻó ˌchʻing, to marry a wife; saĕngʼ ˌchʻing, to accompany the bride; tok, ˌchʻing, to take a bride by force; ˌchʻing ˌhiăng tiéʼ or ˌchʻing ʻchʻiu chĕük, own brothers.

ˌChʻing. A coll. word, as in ˌchʻing ʻchʻang to awake from sleep; aroused, attentive.

ˌChʻing. A coll. euphonic prefix, as in ˌchʻing ˌchʻiong, to dress; ˌchʻing ˌchʻang, to add more water, as in a pot of boiling water; ˌchʻing ˌchʻŭng, to pour on boiling water; ˌchʻing ˌchʻeng, to moan; to speak sternly.

寢 ʻChʻin. To sleep; rest, sleep; to rest, to desist, to repose; a back chamber, a bed chamber; an adytum in a temple; a retiring room in a palace; a dwelling house; a mausoleum, or house near a grave; [23]chengʼ ʻchʻing, the chief sleeping place; cheuʼ ʻchʻing, to go to sleep; ʻchʻing sek, a sleeping apartment; ancestral hall in a mansion; COM., ʻchʻing sik, pok, ˌang, no rest sleeping or eating.

1 深遠	3 深厚	作揖	6 稱呼	8 稱觔	10 親疎	12 親近	14 親愛	16 六親	18 令親	20 親堂	22 討親
2 深信	4 深深	5 稱許	7 自稱	9 親戚	11 親家	13 誼親	15 招親	17 親身	19 親熱	21 親母	23 正寢

'請 Ch'ing. To request; to ask courteosly, to pray, to beg; to request liberty to do; to ask, as for orders; to invite, to bid, to engage; to confess, to acknowledge; to inform: in the coll. read 'ch'iàng, q. v.: [1]'ch'ing hiok, to call and make inquiries; [2]'ch'ing ong' I beg to inquire; [3]'ch'ing chói' to apologize for a fault; [4]'keng' 'ch'ing, to invite respectfully; COM., [5]'pok, 'ch'ing chëü' ˏlai, he will come without an invitation.

'齔 Also read ch'aing': to shed the milk teeth, as children do; shedding or renewing the teeth.

'Ch'ing. A coll. word, as in 'ch'ing 'ch'ing, just so; exactly; 'ch'ing 'ch'ing 'hó, just right; just well or recovered; 'ch'ing 'ch'ing sük, just cooked through; just acquainted or skilled in.

'Ch'ing. A coll. euphonic prefix, as in 'ch'ing 'ch'iong, to rob; to act recklessly; 'ch'ing 'ch'eng, to sweep with a brush-broom; 'ch'ing 'ch'iàng, to invite, to request; 'ch'ing 'ch'iàng, to scoop, to lade out, as flour.

'Ch'ing. A coll. word: fresh, raw, as shell-fish not cooked through: 'chü k'ak, 'ch'ing, cooked too rare.

ˏ塍 ˏ塖 A dike, a ridge, or raised foot-path between fields: COM., [6]'mó' ˏch'ing, the ridge on the edge of mill-stones; [7]ˏt'u ˏch'ing, an earthen dike; COLL., ˏch'eng ˏch'ing ˏkü tek, 'chwi tó' 'li pooh, tek, ˏnëng, as field-dikes confine water, so doctrine binds people.

ˏCh'ing. A coll. word, as in ˏngau ˏch'ing, quarrelsome, stubborn.

ˏCh'ing. A coll. euphonic prefix, as in ˏch'ing ˏch'iong, to squat, to sit couchant; ˏch'ing ˏch'ong, to eat greedily; k'á' ˏnià nói' ˏch'ing ˏch'ong 'lá k'ó' hurry and stuff yourself! ˏch'ing ˏch'iàng, to finish; ˏch'ing ˏch'iëng, to grasp and pull at.

(120) Ch'io.

[The next three are interchangeably read ch'wo in the two different tones].

ˏCh'io. A coll. word: to turn round, as in marking or shaping; to turn, as screws, to screw: ˏch'io ˏkwong, to turn and make smooth; ˏch'io 'king, screw it tight; ˏch'io chiàng' to turn or screw straight; ˏch'io ˏch'io'tiong, turn it round and round.

ˏCh'io. A coll. word, as in ˏch'io ˏüng, or ˏch'io ˏung, a fruit that resembles the arbutus; ˏch'io ˏung ˏkang, dried arbutus; ˏch'io ˏung 'ting, a cap-knob like the arbutus.

厝' Ts'u. Read ch'auk, and ch'o'; used in the Paik, ˏIng for the coll. ch'io': a house, a dwelling, a residence: [8]'k'i ch'io' to build a house; [9]'ko' ch'io' an old house, a former residence; [10]'chu ch'io' the ancestral dwelling; [11]ch'io' ˏchu, the rent of a house; [12]twai' ch'io' a mansion; [13]ch'io' 'kiàng ch'io' ˏnié, small houses, shanties; [14]ch'io' chek, the ridge of a roof; [15]ch'io' ok, ch'ok, ˏchu, "a house to let"; [16]ch'io' 'chio, a house-owner; [17]teu' ch'io' to live

1請謁 2請問 3請罪 4敬請 5不請自來 6磨塍 ○ 7土塍 ○ 8起厝 9舊厝 10祖厝 11厝租 12大厝 13厝仔 厝伲 ○ 14厝脊 ○ 15厝屋出租 16厝主 17住厝

in a house; 'ch'io' 'tié, in the house; term for a wife; 'tiong ch'io' to return home; ³sioh, ch'io' ,nĕng, a whole family; ⁴ch'io' 'kwi lóh, how many suites of houses (separated by courts)? ch'io' nŭk, sá ² a dwelling having many apartments.

(121) Ch'ioh.

[The next four are interchangeably read ch'wok in the two different tones].

粟, Suh. Read sĕŭk,; coll. ch'ioh,: rice in the husk, unhulled rice, paddy: ⁴'mi ch'ioh, rice and paddy; ⁵ch'ioh, 'chŭng, seed-rice; ⁶ch'ioh, ,tiăng, a threshing and drying floor; ⁷ch'ioh, siăng² a paddy bin; ⁸ch'ioh, tong² stout bamboo mats set upright to inclose paddy; ⁹,ch'ong 'lá ch'ioh, granary-paddy; 'cha ch'ioh, and ¹⁰,wong ,chiéng ch'ioh, the 1st and 2d crops of rice; ¹¹p'ang' ch'ioh, blasted rice.

尺, Ch'ih. Read ch'ek,; coll. ch'ioh,: a cubit, the Chinese ft. of 10 inches: ¹²ch'ioh, siong² over a foot; ¹³ch'ioh, ch'aung' feet and inches—measured, proportioned; ¹⁴,liong ch'ioh, to measure by feet; ¹⁵k'woh, ch'ioh, a carpenter's square; ¹⁶,pang ch'ioh, or ,kung kau' ch'ioh, the common or standard foot: ¹⁷,ka ch'ioh, the domestic foot, also called ,á 'ló ch'ioh, (shoe-basket foot); ,choi ,p'ung ch'ioh, the tailor's foot—2 6/10 in. longer than the common; ,king ch'ioh, the Peking foot—about an inch longer than the common; t'iék, ch'ioh, an iron bar for beating thieves.

蓆, Hsi. Read sik,; coll. ch'ioh,: mat spread to sleep on: ¹⁸'ch'au ch'ioh, straw mats; ch'ioh, sioh, 'liăng, one piece of matting; 'chiéng ,t'au ch'ioh, a pillow mat-cover; ¹⁹,ch'ŭ ch'ioh, to spread mats.

Ch'ioh,. A coll. word: to start, startled; a sudden start; to toss about: ch'ioh, ,lieu 'kiăng, to toss about clams in cooking (so as to diffuse the seasoning); ch'ioh, sié ² ,iu, to diffuse the soy by tossing; ch'ioh, pwang' ,t'iéng ,keng, to toss half as high as the sky; greatly startled.

(122) Ch'iok.

雀, Ch'iao. A sparrow, a term for small birds like the finch or lark; a kind of cap; a sort of wheat: in the coll. read chiăh, q. v.: ²⁰,ma ch'iok, a sparrow; ,wong ch'iok, the goldfinch; ch'iok, yok, the sparrow hops; met., delighted with; ,mui ch'iok, almond trees and sparrows; com., ²¹'k'ung ch'iok, a peacock.

鵲, Ch'iao. A magpie, a jackdaw; a jay: ²²'hi ch'iok, (coll. ,k'a ch'ioh,) a magpie; ,u ch'iok, a raven; ch'iok, ,chau ,k'iu ,kŭ, the dove lives in the magpie's nest; met., a bride occupying her new home.

繳, 繁, Ch'iao. A string tied to an arrow to draw it back again: ,kŭng ch'iok, a bow and stringed arrow.

斫, Ch'io. To cut with a sword or knife; to amputate; to chop, to hew.

¹厝裏	仈厝	⁴米粟	⁶粟埕	⁸粟囤	粟	¹¹冇粟	¹³尺寸	¹⁵曲尺	¹⁷家尺	¹⁹舒蓆	²¹孔雀
²一厝	³幾落	⁵粟種	⁷粟樒	⁹倉禮	¹⁰黃占粟	¹²尺上	¹⁴量尺	¹⁶平尺	¹⁸草蓆	²⁰麻雀	²²喜鵲

爍, Chʻio. Light, bright, splendid, brilliant, refulgent; to shine; to polish, to burnish; to embellish; to forge metals: [1]chʻiok, chʻiok, brilliant; [2]chʻiok, ˏking ˏui eng˒ to forge metal for swords.

爝, Chio. A flambeau, a torch, a link; a lighted match burned at night—on an alarm.

灼, Chʻio. To burn, to singe, to cauterize with moxa; alarmed; clear, distinct; luxuriant, as flowers: [3]tó˒ chʻiok, fearful; [4]chʻiok, ngai˒ to burn the moxa; com., [5]chʻiok, kiéng˒ to perceive distinctly.

妁, Chʻio. A go-between—in making a marriage contract; a surname: [6]ˏmúi chʻiok, a match-maker.

勺, Chʻiao. A ladle, a spoon; a spoonful, a little; to bale or pour out; to adopt, to follow: [7]chʻiok, ʻing, to drink a little; [8]laiu˒ chʻiok, a cullender; [9]ek, chʻiok, ʻchwi ˏchi ˏtó, so much as a spoonful of water.

芍, Chʻio. The peony, also the dăhlia: com., [10]chʻiok, yoh, peony roots—a medicine; [11]pah, chʻiok, the white peony.

綽, Cho. Large, ample; slow, leisurely: com., [12]chʻiok, pok, faithless, dishonest; [13]chʻiok, hó˒ to nickname—both in a good and a bad sense; [14]chʻiok, chʻiok, ʻiu ˏü, overplus, more than enough—as of ability to do; coll., ʻyă chʻiok, or chʻiok, tek, ʻheng, very lively; pretentious.

鑠, Chʻio. To melt, to fuse, to forge; handsome, lustrous, as eyes; shining, as gold; brave, courageous; urged, impelled.

杓, Chʻio. A ladle; a beam for a bridge: [15]ˏpwi chʻiok, a dipper. Read ˏpieu, a pail-handle; the handle of the "Dipper"; to lead, to draw.

穛, Chʻiao. A city in the feudal state of Tsi, now a place in the Shantung province.

汋, Chʻiao. Also read chʻëük,: noise of dashing water; to lift up water with a ladle, to bale.

歠 啜, Chʻüeh. Read chiok,; coll. chʻiok,: interchangeably read chʻwok,: to drink, to sip, to imbibe by mouthfuls: [16]twai˒ chʻiok, a great drinker; [17]chʻiok, ˏkang ˏkang, sip it dry; chʻiok, sioh, chʻoi˒ to drink a mouthful.

(123) Chʻiong.

ˏ昌 Chʻang. Light of the sun; fine words; elegant, flourishing, prosperous, increasing in wealth or peace; powerful, effulgent; to increase, to illuminate any thing; good, rich, affluent: [18]ˏchʻiong tai˒ prosperous and powerful; [19]ˏchʻiong ˏming, splendid, fine, as an essay; com., [20]ˏchʻiong seng˒ flourishing, as having a numerous posterity; ˏung ˏchʻiong tá˒ ˏkung, the god of literature.

[1]爍爍 [2]爍金爲刃 [3]悼灼 [4]灼艾 [5]灼見 [6]媒妁 [7]勺飲 [8]漏勺 [9]一勺水之多 [10]芍藥 [11]白芍 [12]綽薄 [13]綽號 [14]綽綽有餘 [15]杯杓 [16]大啜 [17]啜乾乾 [18]昌大 [19]昌明 [20]昌盛

福州方言拼音字典

閶 ꜀Ch‘an. The door of heaven; a gate of the Soochow wall: [1]꜀ch‘iong hak꜁ the door of paradise—one says kept by Kwanti; a cool breeze.

猖 ꜀Ch‘ang. A herd of animals fleeing: COM., ꜀ch‘iong ꜀kwong, fierce, incontrollable; COLL., [2]꜀ch‘iong ch‘oi꜃ ‘yă siék꜁ has an ungovernable mouth and wild tongue.

鯧 ꜀Ch‘ang. As in [3]꜀ch‘iong ꜀ngü, the pomfret: COLL., ꜀ch‘iéng ꜀ch‘iong, fresh pomfret; [4]sŭk꜁ ꜀ch‘iong, cooked pomfrets—for sale.

娼 **倡** ꜀Ch‘ang. A singing woman, a prostitute, courtesan: COM., ꜀ch‘iong ho꜃ or [5]꜀ch‘iong ke꜃ a strumpet; [6]꜀ch‘iong ꜀iu lá꜃ chok꜁ (posterity of) prostitutes, play actors, lictors, and jailors (cannot compete for literary honors); COLL., chó꜃ ꜀ch‘iong, to be a courtesan.

鏘 ꜀Ch‘iang. Also read ꜀chiong: the sound of stones, bells and drums; a noise, a tinkling: [7]꜀k‘eng ꜀ch‘iong, the ring of stones or metals.

鎗 ꜀Ch‘iang. Interchanged with the last: sound of a bell; a kind of tripod or boiler; a wine boiler; a gun; a spear, a pike, a lance: [8]‘chiu ꜀ch‘iong, a wine-boiler, a still; COM., [9]꜀ch‘iong hwak, the art of handling the spear; [10]‘neu ꜀ch‘iong, a fowling piece; [11]꜀ch‘iong ꜀tó yoh꜁ plasters, etc., for spear and sword wounds; [12]꜀ch‘iong ‘ch‘iu, a spearman; *met.*, one employed surreptitiously to write an essay; COLL., [13]꜀ch‘iong t‘aĕk, to thrust with a spear.

槍 ꜀Ch‘iang. Interchanged with the last; a wooden spear sharp at both ends, a lance; to oppose, to withstand; to thrust at; to rush against.

蹌 ꜀Ch‘iang. To walk rapidly; to move toward a superior quickly; to gambol, to skip about.

蹡 ꜀Ch‘iang. Like the preceding; also read ꜀chiong: to move irregularly, to go across, to walk awry.

菖 ꜀Ch‘ang. The flag (Acorus): in the coll. read ꜀ch‘ĕng, q. v.: COM., [14]꜀ch‘iong ꜀pwo, sweet flag, used as a charm on doors in the 5th month, also as a decoction for driving away bed-bugs, etc.

村 ꜀Ts‘un. Read ꜀ch‘ong; coll. ꜀ch‘iong, as in [15]꜀ch‘iong ꜀lĕ, a country lout; [16]꜀ch‘iong ꜀lĕ ꜀pó, a country-woman.

[The next two are interchangeably read ch‘wong].

川 ꜀Ch‘uan. Mountain streams; perennial brooks: COM., [17]꜀ch‘iong ‘kwong, the Sz-chuen and Canton provinces; [18]꜀ch‘iong ‘kiéng and [19]꜀ch‘iong ‘hwong, two sorts of silk from Sz-chuen; [20]꜀ch‘iong ꜀liéng, a bitter herb from Sz-chuen—makes a cooling drink; [21]꜀ch‘iong ꜀kŭng, Sz-chuen tormentilla—used to purify the blood.

穿 ꜀Ch‘uan. A hole, an opening; to bore through, to perforate; to clothe, to put on; to string, as beads: in the coll., to stretch out, to extend (the

[1]閶闔 [2]猖嘴野舌 [3]鯧魚 [4]熟鯧 [5]娼妓 [6]娼優隸卒 [7]鏗鏘 [8]酒鎗 [9]鎗法 [10]鳥鎗 [11]鎗刀藥 [12]鎗手 [13]鎗刺 [14]菖蒲 [15]村驢 [16]村驢婆 [17]川廣 [18]川繭 [19]川紡 [20]川連 [21]川芎

hand): COM., [1]‚chiéng ‚ch'iong, the hole in Chinese cash; [2]‚ch'iong ‚cheng, to thread a needle; [3]‚ch'iong ‚sing (coll. ‚ch'iong ‚sing ‚peng), the abbreviated form of the 61st radical; [4]‚ch'iong ‚sang kak, the manis; COLL., ‚ch'iong ch'ĕk, "chisel a hole,"—i. e., get work to do; ‚ch'iong ‚ch'iong ʻtiong, going to and fro, unsettled; ʻch'iu ‚ch'iong tik, to stretch out the arm; ‚ch'iong ‚k'a ‚lĕ ʻtó, stretch the feet, then recline—get an inch and want an ell; ‚ch'iong ʻch'iu ‚mwo ‚t'iéng, extend the hand and touch the sky—a vaulting ambition.

搶 ʻ Ch'iang. Read ʻch'ong; coll. ʻch'iong: to take, to extort, to force away, to rob; to ravish; to snatch, to struggle for; sudden, abrupt, rude, grasping; a comet: [5]ʻch'iong tok, or ʻch'iong kiék, to plunder; [6]ʻeu ʻch'iong, to beat and rob; [7]ʻch'iong ʻhwi, to snatch from the flames; [8]ʻch'iong pah, to discover by quizzing; [9]ʻch'iong ‚chá, to "snatch the cakes offered," as spirits do; *met.*, to eat greedily; [10]ʻch'iong ʻcha ‚wong, finished early; [11]ʻch'iong ch'auk, to blunder, to do carelessly; ʻch'iong ‚chiéng ʻhu, the money-devouring tiger, as delineated in gambling hells; *met.*, a grasping, avaricious person.

喘 ʻ Ch'uan. Read ʻch'wang; coll. ʻch'iong, as in [12]ʻch'iong siong' to pant, to raise wind from the stomach; to rise, as the fetus in the womb.

敞 ʻ Ch'ang. A high terrace, or level spot, from which a good prospect opens up; high, conspicuous, open, displayed; to polish: [13]‚kó ʻch'iong tė' high, level ground; COM., [14]ʻch'iong liong' a fine situation, a good prospect; [15]‚k'wang ʻch'iong, broad, spacious.

惝 ʻ Ch'ang. Alarmed; frightened: [16]ʻch'iong ʻhwong, alarmed, apprehensive.

氅 ʻ Ch'ang. A shroud: [17]hok ʻch'iong, stork's feathers woven into clothes; a robe with wide sleeves and facings, worn in theaters, is so called.

廠 ʻ 厰 ʻ Ch'ang. A covered place not walled in; a shed or shanty for a work-shop; a building appropriated for a temporary use: COM., [18]‚chiéng ʻch'iong, a mint; [19]‚p'ung ʻch'iong, a matshed; [20]ʻk'i ʻch'iong, to build a shed; [21]ʻmi ʻch'iong, rice stands, i. e., for selling cheap in times of famine; ‚sung ʻch'iong, a shipbuilder's workshop; COLL., k'ëük, siáh ʻch'iong, a beggar's hovel.

昶 ʻ Ch'ang. Long days, a long period; bright; through, pervious, extended; filled: nik ʻch'iong, a long day.

唱 ʼ Ch'ang. To sing in recitative; to cry out, to give the word; to lead, to conduct, as singing; to crow: COM., ʻsieu ch'iong' singers of ditties; [22]ch'iong' ʻta, vocal and instrumental music; ‚ch'ing ch'iong' those who only sing (in plays); ‚hu ch'iong' ho' ‚sui, the

[1]錢穿 [2]穿針 [3]穿心 [4]穿山甲 [5]搶奪 [6]毆搶 [7]搶火 [8]搶白 [9]搶齋 [10]搶早完 [11]搶錯 [12]喘上 [13]高敞地 [14]敞亮 [15]寬敞 [16]惝怳 [17]鶴氅 [18]錢廠 [19]篷廠 [20]起廠 [21]米廠 [22]唱打〇

福州方言拼音字典

husband sings and the wife follows—connubial felicity; COLL., [1]'ch'iong' k'woh, to sing songs; ch'iong' sioh, ch'ok, to sing through one act; [2]'ch'iong' pwong' to offer rice to the corpse; ch'iong' ꜀leng ꜀hwa sau' to sing the lily-drawl, i. e., beggars' songs; ch'iong' tek, 'hó, well sung.

匠' Chiang. A workman, a mechanic, an artisan of any kind: [3]'k'ieu ch'iong' an expert workman; COM., [4]'muk, ch'iong' a carpenter, a joiner; [5]꜀t'u ch'iong' a mason; [6]'ch'iong' ꜀t'au, a head-workman, a boss.

倡' Ch'ang. To lead, to go before, to induce, or seduce; a leader, an example, a guide: also read ꜀ch'iong, q. v.: [7]'ch'iong' 'sü, to take the lead, to begin or invent; [8]'ch'iong' lwang' to head a riot; COLL., [9]'ch'iong' ch'ok, ꜀li, to lead, as in an enterprise; [10]ch'iong' sioh, teng' to lead a troop.

Ch'iong'. A coll. word: probably a corruption of ch'ëüng' to insert, as in ch'iong' ꜀t'au hié' "inserted-head play"—a play of puppets with movable heads.

[The next two are interchangeably read ch'wong].

釧' Ch'uan. A bracelet, an armlet, an amulet on the arm: [11]꜀king ch'iong' a gold bracelet.

串' Ch'uan. To string together, to connect; a string of; leagued or banded: COM., [12]ch'iong' ꜀t'ung, in league with; [13]ch'iong' ꜀meu, to form a cabal; [14]ch'iong' kwo' to pass a string through; [15]꜀hiong ch'iong' a string of fragrant beads; [16]꜀chiëng ch'iong' a string for cash.

牆 墻 ꜁ Ch'iang. A wall made of bricks, stones, or earth; a defense or wall: COM., [17]'hwi ꜁ch'iong, a fire-proof wall; [18]꜁ui ꜁ch'iong, to inclose by a wall; ꜁mwong ꜁ch'iong, a wall with a door in it; ꜁ch'iong 'peng, planks used in building adobie walls; [19]꜁hwang ꜁ch'iong, a cross wall; COLL., 'lié ꜁ch'iong, to build walls of brick or stone; ꜁ch'iong ꜀pung piăh, 'tó, walls slide and partitions fall; *met.*, a sudden calamity; ꜁ch'iong ꜁tong, a low wall; ꜁ch'iong ꜁t'au 'ting, on the top of the wall; ꜁ch'iong tio' 'hó, the line of wall is excellent; kah, sioh, ꜁t'ŭng ꜁ch'iong, to divide by a wall.

嬙 ꜁ Ch'iang. Female officers in the imperial harem: [20]peng' ꜁ch'iong, lady of the bed-chamber.

艢 檣 ꜁ Ch'iang. A mast, any mast or spar that supports the sails: [21]꜁sung ꜁ch'iong, ship-masts; ꜀hung ꜁ch'iong teng' 'ma, (like) sails and a cavalry-troop—rapid, to the point at once, as an essay.

薔 ꜁ Ch'iang. Also read saik,: a rose: [22]꜁ch'iong ꜁mi ꜀hwa, the cinnamon rose; ꜀tung ꜁ch'iong 'chü, a fruit that ripens in the 10th moon.

斨 Ch'iang. A sort of broad-ax; a pole-ax made square, a bill: ꜁sü ꜁ch'iong, a statesman in the days of Shun.

1 唱曲 2 唱飯 3 巧匠 4 木匠 5 土匠 6 匠頭 7 倡始 8 倡亂 9 倡出 梨 10 倡 一陣 11 金釧 12 串通 13 串謀 14 串過 15 香串 16 錢串 17 灰墻 18 圍墻 19 橫墻 20 嬪嬙 21 船艢 22 薔薇花 ○

戕 ˓Ch'iang. A spear, a wooden lance; a post; to maltreat, to rob, to wound, to kill: [1]*˓ch'iong chek˒* to maltreat and rob.

[The next two are interchangeably read *ch'wong*].

蹲 ˓Tun. Read *˓chong;* coll. *˓ch'iong:* to squat, to crouch, to sit on the heels; cuddled up: [2]*˓ch'iong kiăʼ* to squat low; [3]*˓ch'iong tiēʼ ˏtau,* to squat on the ground; *˓ku ˏtung ˓ch'iong,* to sit couchant.

˓Ch'iong. A coll. word, as in *˓ch'iong ˏhung,* to winnow in the wind; *˓ch'iong ch'ioh˒* to winnow paddy.

象ʼ Siang. An elephant; a figure, a form, an image, the shape things take; superstitious auguries or fancy, imagination, resemblance; a law; to imitate, pantomime: [4]*ʻsiong ch'iongʼ* an idea, illustration; COM., [5]*ch'iongʼ ˓nga,* ivory; [6]*ch'iongʼ ʻtang,* elephant's gall, used medicinally; [7]*ˏkwang ˏt'ieng ch'iongʼ* to look at the form of the heavens; COLL., *ch'iongʼ p'eʼ ˏkau ˏkau,* the proboscis is hooked; *met.,* applied to a beaked nose; [8]*ch'iongʼ ˓p'ui,* elephant's skin; a medicine; a name for India rubber in Canton.

像ʼ Hsiang. Interchanged with the preceding: like, similar; a figure, image, likeness; a statue, an idol; to resemble, to imitate: COM., [9]*˓hing ch'iongʼ* a form, an image; [10]*˓mwo ch'iongʼ* to limn, to copy; [11]*ʻngeu ch'iongʼ* or [12]*˓sing ch'iongʼ* an idol; COLL., [13]*ch'iongʼ yongʼ* or *ch'iongʼ kiéngʼ yongʼ* according to rule—right, excellent; *ngʼ ch'iongʼ ˓nĕng,* unmanly; *ngʼ ch'iongʼ saik˒* inferior color; *ch'iongʼ ˏtiă,* resembles his father; *ch'iongʼ kiéngʼ* to presume, to suppose; *ch'iongʼ chiăh˒ ch'iongʼ* very like to; *ngʼ ch'iongʼ chóʼ* to do contrarily, to blunder.

漎ʼ Siang. Also read *ʻtong;* a swift current; in the coll., to draw (water): [14]*ch'iongʼ yongʼ* the surging of water; COLL., [15]*ch'iongʼ ʻchui,* to draw water; *ch'iongʼ ˏta,* to draw out till dry; *ch'iongʼ sioh˒ p'wak˒* to draw a bucket of water; *ch'iongʼ sioh˒ ˏkong,* to draw a jar full.

鞝ʼ Chiang. Read *ʻchiong;* coll. *ch'iongʼ:* to place together, to insert; to fasten the uppers to the soles of shoes: [16]*ch'iongʼ ˓á,* to sole shoes; *ch'iongʼ t'ak˒ ʻpeng,* to insert the movable boards (in the front of a shop).

Ch'iongʼ. A coll. word, as in *ch'iongʼ ˓t'au,* to dress the bride's hair; *ch'iongʼ ˓t'au ch'ak˒* bridal pins of gold or silver—ornamented with beads; *ch'iongʼ ˓t'au ak˒* a casket of bridal presents.

(124) Ch'iu.

秋 ˓ **穐** ˓ Ch'iu. Autumn, harvest, the time of reaping; the return of the year; a year; autumnal; sorrowing, unhappy: COM., [17]*ˏch'iu ˏt'ieng,* or [18]*ˏch'iu kiéʼ* autumn; [19]*ˏch'iu ʻking,* autumn scenery; [20]*maingʼ ˏch'iu,* the seventh month; [21]*lik˒ ˏch'iu,* the beginning of autumn—13th solar term; [22]*ˏtüng ˏch'iu,* festival of the 8th moon, 15th day; *ˏch'iu ʻsing,* the autumn

---

[1]戕賊 [2]蹲下 [3]蹲地垗○ [4]想象 [5]象牙 [6]象胆 [7]觀天象 [8]象皮 [9]形像 [10]模像 [11]偶像 [12]神像 [13]像樣 [14]漎瀁 [15]漎水 [16]鞝鞋 [17]秋天 [18]秋季 [19]秋景 [20]孟秋 [21]立秋 [22]中秋○

assizes; ˏch'iu pó' "autumn reporter" (of Kŭjins graduating)—an attendant of the god of learning; ¹ˏch'iu ˏhung yă² ek, yă² 'leng ek, yă² at the autumnal equinox the nights become colder and colder; COLL., ˏch'iu haëng² glaring heat at the beginning of autumn; ˏloi p'ah, ˏch'iu twai² poang' ˏsiu, if it thunders on the first day of the lik, ˏch'iu term the harvest will be only a large half, i. e., meager.

僦 Ch'iu. Also read 'ch'ieu: malevolent; ill-natured: COM., ²'pok, ˏch'iu (or ˏchieu) pok, 'ch'ai, not to speak to, the cut direct.

揪 Ch'iu. To bind, to gather in sheaves; to collect, to assemble; to grasp, to clutch, to gripe.

楸 Ch'iu. A strong wood; the tree is like a yew or cypress: ³ˏch'iu ˏping, a chess-board.

啾 Ch'iu. The wail of infants, the hum of insects: ⁴ˏch'iu chek, the cry of infants; ⁵ˏch'iu ˏch'iu, chattering of birds; the tinkling, as of gems.

㵞 Ch'iu. Also read 'ch'ieu: to change the color of; to colly, to blacken, as with smoke.

鞦 Ch'iu. Traces of a carriage: ⁶ˏch'iu ˏch'iéng, a swing, a whirligig, a seesaw; COLL., ⁷p'ah, ˏch'iu ˏch'iéng, to turn the whirligig—a revolving toy of four paper men on projecting arms or axes.

鰍 鰌 Chiu. An eel, a mud or conger eel: ⁸ˏná ˏch'iu, a fresh water eel; COM., ⁹'hai ˏch'iu, a sea-dragon, myriads of miles long; met., in classic language, a long narrow boat.

鶖 Ch'iu. A long-legged bird like an adjutant, having red eyes and a bare neck; it is ravenous, hence met. applied to vicious persons.

湫 Ch'iu. A pond, a fish-pond, a pool; a small tributary of the Yellow River near Linhien, in Shansi; chilly, cool; mournful, to excite sad feelings; a narrow pass: ¹⁰ˏlüng ˏch'iu, a cascade, waterfall.

ˏCh'iu. A coll. word: whiskers, beard; the beard of some animals: ch'oi' ˏch'iu, whiskers, mustaches; ch'oi' ˏch'iu ˏhu, the whiskers covering the cheeks; ˏsüng ˏch'iu, pine leaves.

手 Shou. The hand, the arm; an autograph; handy, quick; to handle, to hold in the hand; met., a person, actions; the 64th radical: COM., ¹¹'ch'iu chëük, hands and feet; met., brethren; ¹²'ch'iu 'chiong, palm of the hand; ¹³'ch'iu pié' the arm; ¹⁴'ch'iu 'kwang, the fore-arm; ¹⁵tói' 'ch'iu, to work together; to lend a hand; handy, as an instrument; ¹⁶ˏtang 'ch'iu, single handed—to work alone; ¹⁷ˏking 'ch'iu, to have the management of; ¹⁸ha² 'ch'iu, to put the hands to, as to work, to seize one, etc.; ¹⁹'ch'iu ˏch'au, written, not printed; haiu² 'ch'iu, hereafter; 'ch'iu a² under one's control; 'ch'iu hwak, or 'ch'iu ˏmwong, or 'ch'iu taung² skill, art,

1秋 夜 2不 3楸 5啾 7拍 鰍 湫 掌 管 手 手
分 冷 揪 枰 啾 鞦 9海 11手 13手 15對 17經 19手
夜 一 不 4啾 6鞦 韆 鰍 足 臂 手 手 抄
一 夜 採 唧 韆 8泥 10龍 12手 14手 16單 18下 ○

dexterity; COLL., ‘ch‘iu ˏtang, the elbow; [1]‘ch‘iu ‘chai, the fingers; ‘ch‘iu chaik, joints of the arms and fingers; [2]‘ch‘iu mah, the wrist pulse; kak, ‘ch‘iu, working together, mutually suited; ‘ch‘iu ˏp‘a, a kind of hand-net; [3]‘ch‘iu ˏtong, long-armed; *met.*, avaricious, thievish; ‘ch‘iu chó’ t‘auk, done, finished; ‘ch‘iu ˏt‘au ‘toi, the hand short; *met.*, no work, no money; ‘ch‘iu kauk, chiéng² hands full of mischief; ‘ch‘iu ˏsing taëng² the "hand-force heavy"—noisy in working; ˏtó tëü² ‘ch‘iu (COM., twai² ‘ch‘iu), the right hand, that which holds the chopsticks; ˏtó ‘wang ‘ch‘iu (COM., ‘sieu ‘ch‘iu), the left hand, that which holds the bowl; [4]‘ch‘iu t‘ak, or ‘ch‘iu lóh, mittens; ‘ch‘iu ‘chiong ˏtong piăng’ ‘hwoi, fire emptied into the palm; *met.*, urgent; ‘ch‘iu meng’ yă² se² nük, ‘ch‘iu ‘tá yă² se² nük, it's flesh on the back, and it's flesh on the palm, of the hand; *met.*, to treat impartially.

‘醜 Ch‘ou. Ugly, deformed, ill-looking, vile, disagreeable, disgraceful, shameful; ashamed, shamefaced; to dislike, to hate; to compare; a group, a sort: [5]‘ch‘iu haing² disgraceful conduct; [6]ˏkung ‘ch‘iu, a gang of petty thieves; [7]‘ch‘iu loi² a vile set, vagabonds; COM., [8]‘ch‘iu ho² an ugly woman; [9]‘ch‘iu laiu² ugly, deformed; vile; [10]‘ch‘iu t‘ai’ a disagreeable gait; [11]‘ch‘iu sek, ho² ‘miéng pok, taik, kiéng’ ˏkung ˏku, a homely daughter-in-law can't avoid seeing her parents-in-law; *met.*, the culprit must appear before his parent or master.

帚 箒 ‘ Tsou. A besom, a broom; to sweep up dirt: [12]chek, ˏki ‘ch‘iu, holds duster and broom—term for a wife or concubine; COLL., [13]sau’ ‘ch‘iu, a broom; ‘ch‘eng ‘ch‘iu, a besom.

囚 紉 ˏ Ch‘iu. To imprison, to confine, to cage, to handcuff; a prisoner, a felon: COM., [14]ˏch‘iu hwang² (coll. ˏch‘iu ˏnëng), a criminal; [15]ˏkang ˏch‘iu, a prisoner; [16]ˏch‘iu ˏlëng, a cage for carrying criminals.

揪 ˏ Ch‘iu. Read ˏch‘iu; coll. ˏch‘iu: held, caught, bound, constrained; to pull towards one, as the branches of a tree: ˏch‘iu ‘king ‘king, tightly held, restrained: [17]móh, ˏch‘iu ‘ngwai, don't clutch me! [18]ˏch‘iu sioh, ˏtoi, gathered together.

ˏCh‘iu. A coll. word: thick, matted hair, disheveled hair.

ˏCh‘iu. A coll. word: wan, woebegone; ‘mu ˏnëng piéng’ ˏch‘iu, a certain person has become wan in his looks.

(125) Ch‘o.

醋’ Ts‘u. Vinegar, pickle, pickled: COM., [19]chiong’ ch‘o’ salt relishes and vinegar; COLL., ch‘o’ ‘mó ˏsong, as sour as the mother of vinegar! siăh, ch‘o’ to "drink vinegar"—jealous, as a wife; ch‘o’ aëng’ a vinegar jar; ch‘o’ ˏkŭng, animalcules in vinegar; ch‘o’ ˏsing taëng² deeply seated jealousy; ch‘o’ ˏp‘ang saëk, p‘wai’ "dash in pieces the vinegar jar"—used

[1]手指 [2]手脈 [3]手長 [4]手套 [5]醜行 [6]羣醜 [7]醜類 [8]醜婦 [9]醜陋 [10]醜態 [11]醜媳婦免不得見公姑 [12]執箕箒 [13]掃箒 [14]囚犯 [15]監囚 [16]囚籠 [17]莫揪我 [18]揪一堆 [19]醬醋

wholly in a *met.* sense for a raging fit of jealousy; *‹siéng ch'o' ‹tu ‹siong kwo'* have tasted both salt and vinegar; *met.*, have experienced all the bitter trials.

措' Ts'u. To place, to put into its place; to make known, to show abroad; to conceal, to set aside; to take at unawares; to use, to employ; to relinquish; arranged, well-ordered: [1]*ch'o' 'li*, or [2]*ch'o' ‹sié*, to adjust; [3]*ch'o' ‹sü*, an elegant phrase; [4]*‹u 'su ch'o' 'ch'iu chëük*, no place for the hands and feet—perplexed, distressed.

錯' Ts'o. Interchanged with the last: to place, to set down, to settle; to store up; to reject, to cast away: also read *ch'auk*, q. v.: [5]*'sià ch'o'* to throw aside; [6]*'kü tik‚ ch'o' ‹chü 'wong*, to promote the upright, and reject the perverse.

(126) Ch'ó.

‹操 Ts'ao. To take, to hold, to grasp; to manage, to exercise, to drill; expert, used to; to maintain, to restrain one's self, to moderate one's desires; a purpose, a design; a self-imposed rule; consistent, principled: in the coll. read *‹ch'au*, q. v.: COM., [7]*‹ch'ó ‹kwong*, to exercise authority; [8]*‹ch'ó 'siu*, or [9]*‹ch'ó ‹t'i*, to adhere to, as one's principles. Read *ch'ó'* as in [10]*chiék‚ ch'ó'* to maintain integrity.

‹搓 Ts'o. To twist by rubbing on the knee, to rub, or roll between the palms; to twist, as thread on the twisting apparatus: COM., [11]*‹ch'ó siàng'* to twist thread; COLL., *‹ch'ó ‹si*, and *‹ch'ó ‹wong*, to roll up the two kinds of rice-flour cakes into balls for the winter-solstice feast; *‹ch'ó ‹yéng*, to roll into a round shape; *met.*, to reconcile parties; *‹ch'ó 'chià tai' kié'* to settle this matter; *‹ch'ó ‹nó*, to adjust, as a difficulty between two; *‹ch'ó sóh‚ pwoh‚ ‹hung ‹t'ai*, "twist a rope to bind a tyfoon"—to attempt the impossible; [12]*‹ch'ó pwoh‚ ‹yéng niék‚ pwoh‚ 'piéng*, roll it nearly round, pinch it nearly flat; *met.*, one nearly succeeds in securing harmony, when another spoils all.

‹瘥 Ch'a. To recover from illness, convalescent; a slight ailment or epidemic, as the influenza: in the coll. read *‹ch'a*, q. v.

‹蹉 Ts'o. To pass by, to go over, to transgress, to slip, to err: [13]*‹ch'ó ‹tó*, to miss an opportunity.

‹艖 Ts'o. Also read *‹ch'a*: a skiff, a boat, a small vessel: [14]*'sieu ‹ch'ó*, a small boat.

‹瑳 Ts'o. Used for the next: a white, lustrous stone; fresh; beautiful, to look fascinating: [15]*'k'ieu ch'ieu' ‹chi ‹ch'ó*, a bewitching smile.

‹磋 Ts'o. To polish, to work on, to cut and polish; to work at, to make good, as an essay: [16]*ch'iék‚ ‹ch'ó*, to cut and polish; *met.*, to reform, to aid one in self-discipline; [17]*‹ü ch'iék‚ ‹ü ‹ch'ó*, like cutting and polishing (a gem), *scil.*, he improved himself.

---

[1] 措理 [2] 措施 [3] 措辭 [4] 無所措手足 [5] 捨錯 [6] 舉直錯諸枉 [7] 操權 [8] 操守 [9] 操持 [10] 節操 [11] 搓線 [12] 搓剁圓攝剁扁 [13] 蹉跎 [14] 小艖 [15] 巧笑之瑳 [16] 切磋 [17] 如切如磋

鱢 臊 Ts'ao. A fishy smell; strong, rank, reeking, as the scent of persons; *met.*, in the coll. lustful: COM., [1]*ˌngü ˌch'ó*, fishy scent; *met.*, fish; COLL., *ˌch'ó ˌtó*, fishy, briny; *ˌngü ˌch'ó tioh, ke²* (or *keng²*) you must avoid (eating) fish—as doctors say; *ch'au² ˌsing ˌch'ó*, the rank scent, as of persons or of a well dried up; [2]*ˌch'ó ˌsing*, or *ˌsing ˌch'ó*, lustful desire.

傞 Ts'o. The drunken frolics of a person in liquor: [3]*ˌch'ó ˌch'ó*, drunken antics.

嵯 Ts'o. Uneven hills: [4]*ˌch'ó ˌngó*, the inequalities of hills, undulating outlines of mountains.

璪 Ts'o. Pendants of precious stones or pearls hung like beads around the edge of a coronet.

藻 Ts'ao. A sort of striped aquatic grass (? a vallisneria) which ducks are very fond of; *met.*, to joy in, delighted with; fine, as an essay—in allusion to the variegated beauty of this grass: [5]*ˌung ˈch'ó*, two aquatic grasses, used in sacrifices; [6]*ˈch'ó ˈch'ai*, beautiful, variegated.

慅 Sao. Also read *ˌsó*: moved, aroused; sad; to afflict: [7]*ˈch'ó ˈch'ó*, toiling and suffering; [8]*ˌló ˌsing ˈch'ó ˌié*, ah, how wearied!

懆 Ts'ao. Chagrined, thoughtful, sad, vexed; covetous; affected by: [9]*ˈch'ó ˈch'ó*, chagrined, vexed. Read *ch'ó²* as in [10]*ˌchieu ch'ó²* distressed, bereft of peace.

草 艸 Ts'ao. Herbs, grass, plants with herbaceous stems; plants in general; hastily, carelessly; the running hand; a rough copy, the original draft; to cut grass, to mow; the 140th radical: in the coll. read *ˈch'au*, q. v.: [11]*ˈch'ó ˈyâ*, pertaining to the country, rustic; [12]*ˈch'ó ch'aung²* to make a model; COM., [13]*ˈch'ó muk*, plants; *paik, ˈch'ó*, all kinds of plants; *ˌkang ˈch'ó*, the "sweet herb"—licorice; [14]*ˈló ˈch'ó*, or [15]*ˈch'ó sauk*, or *ˈch'ó ˈch'ó*, hastily, carelessly; [16]*ˈch'ó che²* or *ˈch'ó ˌchü*, the running hand; [17]*ˈch'ó ˈkó*, first draft of a writing; [18]*ˈch'ó ˈchai* (usually *ˌch'u ˈchai* in the coll.), coarse paper; [19]*ˈch'ó ˌhwa*, flowers made of the pith of the *ˌt'ung ˈch'ó*.

焯 Ts'ao. A coll. character; a kind of barilla obtained from marine plants in Shantung; potash, pearlash, saleratus: [20]*ˈch'ó ˈchwi*, or *ˈch'ó ˌt'ong*, saleratus water; [21]*ˈch'ó lo²* a solution of potash; *ˈch'ó ˈtai*, residuum of barilla.

糙 Ts'ao. Coarse rice, paddy that has been hulled, but not cleaned; in the coll., darkish, unbleached: COM., [22]*ch'ó² ˈmi*, coarse or dark rice; COLL., *ch'ó² chá²* a coarse grass cloth; *ch'ó² pah*, a darkish white; *ch'ó² ˈchai*, darkish paper; *ch'ó² pah ˌt'ong*, a second quality of white sugar.

澡 Ts'ao. To bathe, to wash the person; to cleanse the heart, to reform: [23]*ˈsá ch'ó²* to bathe; *ch'ó² ˌsing ük, taik*, to perfect one's self in virtues.

---

1 魚臊 2 臊心 3 傞傞 4 嵯峨 5 繅藻 6 藻采 7 慅慅 慅分 8 勞心 9 懆懆 10 憔懆 11 草野 12 草創 13 草木 14 潦草 15 草索 16 草字 17 草稿 18 草紙 19 草花 20 焯水 21 焯滷 22 糙米 23 洗澡

挫' Ts'o. To break, to injure, to take off the edge; to humble, to oppress, to treat harshly; to trim, to file off, in which sense the same as next: [1]ch'ó' chiék, tried by afflictions; [2]pok, 'i ek, ˬhó ch'ó' ˏü ˬing, unwilling to put up with the slightest insult.

銼' T'so. An iron pan or boiler; a file, a rasp; to rasp, to file, to smooth off the sharp or rough points; to rub down.

剉' Ts'o. Used for the last: to cut, to lop off the corners and sharp points, to trim and prune; to cut up, to cut to pieces.

脞' Ts'o. To mince up meat; broken to bits, minced; small; to attend to trifles.

錯' Ts'o. Read ch'auk,; in the coll. ch'ó', probably in imitation of the coll. mandarin: a mistake, a fault, an error, a blunder: [3]pok, ch'ó' no mistake, right; [4]'k'ang' ch'ó' 'ngang, to see wrongly, the eye deceived; [5]'nü o' ch'ó' you err; [6]tai' kié' chó' ch'ó' to blunder in work.

造' Tsao. To go to, to arrive at, to advance, to enter; to contain; to complete; a prayer; hurried; also read chó' q. v.: [7]ch'ó' sëü' promotion of literary men; COM., [8]ch'ó' cheu' to complete; [9]ch'ó' 'kwang, to go to the school room; [10]ch'ó' 'hu, I'll go to your honorable mansion; [11]ch'ó' ch'ëü' flurried, agitated.

(127) Ch'óh.

Ch'óh,. A coll. word: to stab, to pierce, to thrust with the hand or a weapon; to stick, as with a pin; *met.*, to get employment, to rush about: *ch'óh, ˏt'ëng t'au'* to pierce through; *ch'óh, 'si*, to stab to death; *ú' ch'óh*, can bore in—can get work; *ˬmó nóh, k'ëük*, *'nü ch'óh*, nothing for you to gain out of me! *ˬch'i ch'ih, ch'óh, ch'óh*, to rush to and fro.

(128) Ch'oi.

'**崔** Ch'ui. Lofty, mountainous, rugged, as a hilly country; a surname: [12]ˏch'oi ˬngui, lofty, rocky peaks.

'**璀** Ts'ui. Also read 'ch'oi: the luster of a gem, a gem hanging down, as from the girdle.

'**催** Ts'ui. To urge, to press, to edge on; to importune, to hasten, as the payment of a debt; to reiterate; to hasten, as guests: in the coll. read ˏch'wi, q. v.: [13]ˏch'oi ch'ëük, to urge; [14]sëü' ˏch'oi, excuse us from (sending again) to urge—written on invitation cards.

'**漼** Ch'ui. Also read ˬch'oi: deep, clear water; tears trickling down; fresh, new, clean; spoiling, ruining; snow drifted; name of a stream.

'**髓** Sui. The marrow, medullary matter in bones: [15]ˏch'ing ik, kauk, 'ch'oi, (your kindness) penetrates to my very marrow; [16]chiok, ˬki 'ch'oi, sucked his marrow—i. e., was revenged; COM., [17]kauk, 'ch'oi, marrow.

---

[1]挫節 [2]不以一毫挫於人 [8]不錯 [4]看錯眼 [5]汝務錯 [6]代計做錯 [7]造士 [8]造就 [9]造舘 [10]造府 [11]造次 [12]崔巍 [18]催促 [14]賜催 [15]深入骨髓 [16]嚼其髓 [17]骨髓 ○

ʻ**揣** Ch'uai. To estimate, to calculate, to reckon; to try, to feel; to rub in order to ascertain, to detect: COM., [1]*ʻch'oi ˏmó*, to feel after, to search out the sense; [2]*ʻch'oi tokˎ* to investigate, to conjecture.

ʻ**惴** Tsui. Mournful; in straits, fearful: [3]*ʻch'oi ʻch'oi*, mourning, afraid; [4]*ʻch'oi këüˀ* anxious.

ʻ**嘬** Ts'ui. To gnaw, to masticate; to eat greedily, to bolt food.

ʻCh'oi. A coll. word: a chain, as worn on the neck by a criminal or a child: *t'iékˎ ʻch'oi*, an iron chain; *ˏngüng ʻch'oi*, a silver-chain necklace; *ʻch'oi tauˀ kaukˎ* to put a chain on the neck.

翠ˀ **翆**ˀ Ts'ui. The female of the king-fisher, the feathers of which are used in plumagery; the fleshy protuberance from which the tail of the bird grows: [5]*ʻhoi ˀ ch'oi ˀ* the male and female king-fisher; COM., [6]*ch'oi ˀ ˏmó*, feathers of the king-fisher; [7]*ch'oi ˀ ˏlang*, a purplish blue; COLL., *ch'oi ˀ ˏmó ʻcheu*, common name of the king-fisher; *ʻteng ch'oi ˀ* to ornament with its feathers.

嘴ˀ Tsui. The mouth, the beak, the bill of a bird; a spout, a nozzle; the edge of a knife, etc.; an aperture, an adit; to wrangle, to chatter, to talk much and impudently, to give lip: COM., [8]*ch'oi ˀ siékˎ* the tongue: [9]*ʻtói ˀ ch'oi ˀ* to speak face to face, to discuss; [10]*ˏtó ch'oi ˀ* the edge of a knife; [11]*ch'oi ˀ k'ak*, thirsty; [12]*ch'oi ˀ ˏtiéng*, honey-mouthed, affable; COLL., [13]*ch'oi ˀ siékˎ ʻkiáng*, the palate; *ch'oi ˀ ʻp'á*, the cheek; [14]*ch'oi ˀ k'iékˎ* a hare-lip; [15]*ch'oi ˀ ˏt'au waˀ* by-words, slang; [16]*k'aikˎ ch'oi ˀ ˏt'au*, abstemious; *ch'oi ˀ ʻma*, the gift of gab; *ch'oi ˀ t'ukˎ* (or *pongˀ*) dull, slow of speech; *pah, ch'oi ˀ* to open the mouth, to gape; [17]*ˏch'oi ˀ leˀ* clever in talk; *ch'oi ˀ ch'auˀ* a bad breath; railing; [18]*ch'oi ˀ siongˀ* your mouth itches (to eat)! [19]*ch'oi ˀ saikˎ* loss of appetite; *ch'oi ˀ ˏlang* (or *ˏt'ang*), remnants of food; [20]*ch'oi ˀ saungˀ* "reckon by mouth", i. e., without the abacus; *ch'oi ˀ ʻt'u ʻt'u*, to protrude the mouth, to pout; *ch'oi ˀ ˏp'ui k'ieuˀ k'ieuˀ* (the upper) lip curled; *ch'oi ˀ ʻkiáng ˏmié ˏmié*, critical, teasing; *ch'oi ˀ ʻtiê naingˀ ˏmi ˏtó ˏsing ˏkang ˏtó t'iéˀ ˏtó*, his mouth chants Budha, but his heart holds a razor!

摧 ˏTs'ui. To stop, to drive back, to repress; to overpower, to set down; to push upon, to thrust forward, to crowd against, to impel; to break, as the wind does trees; to reach; to put out, to extinguish, as a family: [21]*ˏch'oi ekˎ* to abate, to repress; [22]*ˏch'oi chiékˎ* to push against and break; *met.*, affected, disciplined by trial.

(129) Ch'ói.

碎ˀ Sui. To break in small pieces, to smash, to pound to bits, to comminute; bits, fragments, pieces, endings; petty, troublesome; disheartened, broken-down: COM., *ʻhung ch'ói ˀ* ground to powder; *ˏling ch'ói ˀ* bits, fragments;

---

1 揣摩 2 揣度 3 惴惴 4 惴懼 5 翡翠 6 翠毛 7 翠藍 8 嘴舌 9 對嘴 10 刀嘴 11 嘴渴 12 嘴甜 13 嘴舌仔 14 嘴[illegible] 15 嘴頭話 16 刻嘴頭〇 17 嘴利 18 嘴癢 19 嘴澀 20 嘴算 21 摧抑 22 摧折

[1]*ˈsó ch'ói'* fragmentary; *met.*, petty, troublesome; [2]*ch'ói' ˌkĕng,* odds and ends of work; [3]*ch'ói' so'* petty bills; [4]*ch'ói' ˈking,* bits of scenery, as delineated or embroidered; [5]*ch'ói' ĕüng*[2] for miscellaneous use; [6]*ch'ói' ˏngüng,* broken silver; COLL., *p'ah, ch'ói'* to smash, to break to pieces; *ch'ói' ˏchiéng chek, ˏkwong ˏchiéng,* to gather a large sum by driblets; *ch'ói' chó'* to do chores; *ch'ói' ˈkong ch'ói' t'iäng'* to prate about this and that petty concern; *ói' ch'ói' siäh*[2] (or *chioh*[2]) fond of constant nibbling.

剉 **莝** Ts'o. Read *ch'ó';* used in the *Paik, ˌIng* for the coll. *ch'ói':* to cut, to chop, to cut down, as trees: [7]*ch'ói' k'ó'* to cut off; [8]*ch'ói' ch'eu'* to fell trees; [9]*ch'ói' sioh*[2] *ngá*[2] to lop off a bough.

繀 Ts'ui. A spinning wheel, called [10]*ch'ói' ˏch'iă.*

(130) Ch'ok.

出 Ch'u. To go out, to issue, to proceed from, to manifest, according to the tenor of the following or preceding word; to eject, to put out; to surpass, to excel; an auxiliary verb, implying completion of an action; occasionally read *ch'oi'* with similar meaning: COM., [11]*ch'ok, ik,* out and in, ingress and egress; [12]*ch'ok, sié'* to be born; [13]*ch'ok, p'ieu'* to issue bank-bills; to issue a warrant; [14]*ch'ok, köi'* "produces honor" (in the family), as good sites do; [15]*ch'ok, ngié*[2] to complete an apprenticeship; [16]*ch'ok, laung*[2] oviparous; [17]*ch'ok, ˏsing,* to render personal service; to gain promotion; [18]*ch'ok, ˈsang,* the products of the soil; [19]*ch'ok, k'wok,* to enter upon office; *ch'ok, ch'oi'* to do the talking; [20]*ch'ok, chëüng'* to excel the crowd; [21]*ch'ok, ˏka,* to forsake the family—become a priest; [22]*ch'ok, ˏchiéng,* to pay money; *ch'ok, ˈpó,* to put forth the precious (pustules)—a polite phrase; [23]*ˈsiong pok, ch'ok,* inconceivable; COLL., *ch'ok, ˏküng,* to visit the privy; *ch'ok, ˏt'au,* to rise from poverty; *ch'ok, ˈk'au,* to put to sea; banished; *ch'ok, meng'* to be the responsible party; *ch'ok, ˏli,* to come forth; *ch'ok, lo*[2] "exudes brine"—said of a filthy garment: *ch'ok, ˏch'ë,* opening of the month; *ch'ok, ˏsang,* to make one's debut, to commence business, as young men; *ch'ok, pok,* original, self-originated, as ideas; *ch'ok, ˏnëng ˏseng,* to appear before people; *ˏt'au ch'ok, kaëk,* he has horns—beware of him!

炪 Ch'u. Read *chiok,;* used in the coll. for *ch'ok,:* to scorch, to cauterize, as with the mugwort or moxa punk: *ch'ok, ˏhung ˏmwong,* to scorch mosquitos (with a taper).

擉 Chu. Used in the *Paik, ˌIng* for the coll. *ch'ok*[2]*:* to take in the fingers, to take a pinch of: *ch'ok*[2] *sioh*[2] *ch'ok*[2] to take a pinch; *ch'ok*[2] *siäh*[2] let us take a pinch and eat—said by those eating at a friend's expense; *ch'ok*[2] *ˏwai,* to exact hush-money.

[1]鎖	[3]碎	[5]碎	[7]剉	[9]剉	車	世	貴	蛋	產	衆	錢
碎	數	用	去	一	[11]出	[13]出	[15]出	[17]出	[19]出	[21]出	[23]想
[2]碎	[4]碎	[6]碎	[8]剉	枝	入	票	藝	身	鈌	家	不
工	景	銀	樹	[10]繀	[12]出	[14]出	[16]出	[18]出	[20]出	[22]出	出

戳 Read *tauk*˒; coll. *ch'ok*˒: small seals or stamps, called [1]*'ch'ok*˒ *'kiăng*: [2]*p'ah*˒ *ch'ok*˒ to stamp.

(131) Ch'ong.

倉 ˓Ts'ang. A granary, a storehouse for rice or salt: a granary of the government: [3]˓*ch'ong 'ling*, a granary; [4]˓*ch'ong* ˓*mong*, fully occupied, distracted by cares; COM., [5]*'mi* ˓*ch'ong*, a rice granary; [6]˓*siĕng* ˓*ch'ong*, salt warehouses; [7]˓*ch'ong* ˓*ngó* (coll. ˓*ch'ong ch'io'*) a public granary; [8]˓*ch'ong 'chung*, a superintendent of granaries; [9]˓*ch'ong 'mi p'ieu'* tickets for drawing rice from the government granaries; [10]*hwak*˒ ˓*ch'ong*, to sell grain from the granary; [11]*ngié'* ˓*ch'ong*, a charity-granary—where rice is sold cheap in famine; COLL., ˓*ch'ong* ˓*seng*, localities of granaries and salt godowns; ˓*ch'ong 'mi pwong' lang' lĕk*˒ lade out the granary-rice which (is inferior and) boils to pieces; *met.*, to buy things or employ workmen without regard to quality.

蒼 ˓Ts'ang. Sometimes used for the last: hastily; the green tint of plants, the azure of the sky; flourishing, prospering; hoary, aged, old in service: [12]˓*ch'ong* ˓*t'iéng*, or ˓*k'üng* ˓*ch'ong*, azure sky, the firmament; [13]˓*ch'ong 'ló*, old, waning; an old man; *pek*˒ *hwak*˒ ˓*ch'ong* ˓*ngang*, a young-looking old man; COM., [14]˓*ch'ong* ˓*seng*, living things, the people; ˓*ch'ong suk*˒ a vegetable medicine—expels humors and bad exhalations.

瘡 ˓Ch'uang. An ulcerated wound, a sore, an ulcer; a boil, an eruption: [15]˓*ch'ong* ˓*i*, a wound; COM., ˓*ch'ong tuk*˒ the pus of sores; ˓*kang* ˓*ch'ong*, a dry sore; [16]*te'* ˓*ch'ong*, the piles; *saik*˒ ˓*ch'ong*, lice-sores; COLL., ˓*ch'ong hwak*˒ *sioh*˒ ˓*sing*, ulcers all over the body; ˓*ch'ong* ˓*sang siong' meng'* ulcers coming out on the face, as from licentiousness.

瑲 Ts'ang. Color of gems. Read ˓*ch'iong*, a musical sound; the jingling of stones.

滄 Ts'ang. Vast like the sea; name of a river and lake; a superior district in Tientsin-fu: [17]˓*ch'ong 'hai* ˓*chi liong'* capacity (to drink) like the sea.

村 ˓Ts'un. A hamlet, a village: ˓*sang* ˓*ch'ong*, a mountain hamlet; COM., [18]˓*hiong* ˓*ch'ong*, a village, the country; COLL., ˓*ch'ong* ˓*lĕ*, a rustic; ˓*ch'ong* ˓*lĕ* ˓*pó*, a country dame.

艙 Ts'ang. An unauthorized character, as in the coll. [19]˓*ch'ong 'tu*, compartments in a boat or ship; a hold; [20]˓*k'wi* ˓*ch'ong*, to break bulk; ˓*ch'ong 'peng* ˓*tu* ˓*mó*, the compartment-covers all gone.

窗 牕 窓 ˓Ch'uang. A window, an aperture to admit light; a sash, venetian blinds, a shutter; a school; a student: ˓*ch'ong* ˓*ngu*, a paper window; [21]˓*ch'ong ha'* at school, while at his studies; [22]˓*chü* ˓*ch'ong*, or ˓*kié* ˓*ch'ong*, a school-room; COM.,

---

1 戳仔 2 拍戳 3 倉廩 4 倉忙 5 米倉 6 鹽倉 7 倉厫 8 倉總 9 倉米票〇 10 發倉 11 義倉 12 蒼天 13 蒼老 14 蒼生 15 瘡痍 16 痔瘡 17 滄海之量 18 鄉村 19 艙堵 20 開艙 21 窗下 22 書窗

ˏtung ˏch'ong, or [1]ˏch'ong ˊiu, chums, fellow students; [2]sekˎ ˊchai ˏhung ˏch'ong, has studied painfully ten years—i. e., a long time.

鶬 Ch'uang. A kind of crane with ash-colored plumage and red cheeks: [3]ˏch'ong ˏkeng, mango-bird; [4]ˏch'ong kwak, the black crane.

ˊ忖 Ts'un. To guess, to judge, to surmise; to consider, to reflect on: [5]ˊch'ong tokˎ to conjecture; to reflect on.

ˊ愴 Ts'ang. Grief, sorrow: [6]ˏch'á ˊch'ong, to pity; grieved, distressed.

ˎ牀 ˎ床 Ch'uang. A bedstead; a couch, a settee; a suit of bed clothes; the boards which make the bedstead; a well-curb; a measure of 8 cubits: COM., [7]ˊtëük, ˎch'ong, a bamboo bedstead; [8]tukˎ soiˀ ˎch'ong, a single bedstead; [9]ˎch'ong ˏp'wo, bed and bedding; COLL., [10]ˎming ˎch'ong, a bedstead, a bed; ˎch'ong ˏkwang, the cross pieces; [11] ˎch'ong ˎtiu, a closet in the back frame; ˎch'ong ˏchiă ˏhung, the fenders; ˎch'ong ˎkung, a figured bed-valance; [12]k'aungˀ ˎch'ong, a couch, a settee; [13]ˎch'ong piăh, ˊtié, the backside of the bedstead; [14]takˎ ˎch'ong, a step in front of a bedstead; [15]ˏt'ieu ˎleu ˎch'ong, a kind of bedstead with front steps; [16]ˎmi ˎná ˎch'ong, "Budha-bedstead"—the common sort without steps and having curved feet.

ˎ鐘 T'ung. Read ˏtung; used in the Paik, ˏIng for the coll. ˎch'ong: to eat much; gluttonous—used opprobriously: [17]twaiˀ ˎch'ong, a glutton; [18]ˎch'ong ˊpa, eat your fill; [19]ˎch'ong pwongˀ stuff yourself with rice; [20]ˎch'ong chiéˀ eat and stuff; scil., and not work.

Ch'ongˀ. A coll. word: to wring, to wrench, to twist; to extort: ch'ongˀ ˏwang, wrench it crooked; ch'ongˀ ˏi ˏsiong, to wring out clothes; ˏt'an hwokˎ piéngˀ móh ˎch'ongˀ don't wrench his cue; ch'ongˀ ˎchiéng, to extort money.

(132) Ch'u.

ˏ初 Ch'u. To cut out garments; to begin, to commence; the first, the beginning; incipient, at first: in the coll. read ˏch'ë, q.v.: [21]ˏch'u ˏsing, the first thought; ˊsü ˏch'u, the beginning, at the first; COM., ˏch'u hokˎ to commence study; ˏch'u ˏch'u hwoiˀ to become acquainted with; ˏch'u ˏch'ëüˀ the first time; ˏch'u engˀ to enter on official life.

ˏ粗 ˏ麤 Ts'u. Coarse, uncleansed, dirty, as rice just threshed; large; open, coarse; rude, vulgar, boisterous, unpolished; gross, indecent; dirty; harsh, as a voice; partially, rudely: COM., ˏch'u euˀ coarse and fine; ˏch'u ˊlu, or ˏch'u sükˎ or ˏch'u ˎngwang (coll. ˏch'u ˎla), vulgar, unmannerly, as rustics; ˏch'u waˀ obscene language; COLL., ˏch'u ˎmang, rude, fierce; ˏch'u ˏp'wi, in the rough, the unfinished article; ˏch'u sauk, coarsely and hastily made; ˏch'u chóˀ to do rough work;

[1]窓友 寒窓 [4]鶬鴰 [6]悽愴 [8]獨睡牀 鋪牀 橱壁 壁裏 [15]挑樓牀 尼牀 [18]鐘飽 [20]鐘祭
[2]十載 [3]鶬鶊 [5]忖度 [7]竹牀 [9]牀 [10]眠牀 [11]牀 [12]匠牀 [13]牀 [14]踏牀 牀 [16]彌 [17]大鐘 [19]鐘飯 [21]初心

[1]ˏch'u ˏchong, a large, coarse female;[2]ˏch'u che² common words—such as the unlearned know; [3]ˏch'u ˏtié, the privy—a delicate phrase; [4]ˏch'u ˏsing twai² ʻtang, careless and bold; [5]ˏch'u pwong² tang² ch'ai² coarse rice and tasteless vegetables—a polite phrase used by a host; [6]ˏch'u ˏmi twai² ʻngang, shaggy eyebrows and large eyes.

楚 Ts'u. A coppice, a bramble bush; a thicket, a clump of trees; spinous; distinct, clear, orderly, well-done, properly finished; painful, sharp; a feudal state in the Chow Dynasty, now the chief part of Hunan and Hupeh: [7]t'ong² ʻch'u, or [8]ˏsing ʻch'u, painful, sharp suffering; [9]ˏwong ʻch'u, completed; COM., [10]ˏch'ing ʻch'u, clear, complete, finished or settled properly.

憷 Ts'u. Interchanged with the last, in the sense of painful, suffering.

礎 Ts'u. The stone base of a pillar or column; a pedestal, a plinth.

(133) Ch'ü.

趨 趍 Ch'ü. To hasten to one's place; to stride off, as in the presence of a superior; to run, to walk quickly: [11]ˏch'ü cheng² to hasten to the front; [12]ˏch'ü ˏch'iong, to advance quickly; [13]ˏch'ü ˏyéng ho² sié² run to the flame and stick to (the man of) influence—to be a parasite.

趑 趦 Ch'êu. Also read ˏchü: unable to advance from fear or disability; to go awry: [14]ˏchü ˏch'ü, impeded.

鶵 Ch'ü. Also read ˏchu: a chick or bird just out of the shell, and yet able to peck: [15]wang ˏch'ü, name of a southern bird.

芻 Chü. To cut grass; straw, hay, fodder: [16]ˏch'ü ˏngieu, to cut grass; [17]pe² ˏch'ü, a Budhist priest—in the Indian language; ˏseng ˏch'ü ek, sok, a bundle of green grass.

紓 Shu. Slow; remiss; insensibly, little by little; to free from or remove, as a calamity: [18]ˏch'ü nang² to free from evil; ˏch'ü ˏsü, slowly, carefully.

舒 Shu. To open out, to unroll, to expand, to make room; to disburden the mind: exhilarated; tranquil, at ease; lax, easy, remiss; slow, leisurely; in order; comfortable: in the coll., to lay, stretch, or spread out: [19]ˏch'ü ʻtiéng, to open out; ˏch'ü ˏsü, in order, slow, as a gait; COM., [20]ˏk'wang ˏch'ü, spacious, ample; ˏch'ü t'iong² joyous, exhilarated; ˏch'ü ˏtiong, roomy, spacious; COLL., ˏch'ü ˏming ˏch'ong, to spread the bed; ˏch'ü ʻtó, to lie flat, as culprits to be beaten; ˏch'ü meng² siong² to spread on the top of.

此 Tz'u. A pronoun and adverb; this, here, now; the last spoken of, the thing in hand: COM., ʻpi ʻch'ü, that

1 粗妝	3 粗池	大膽	淡菜	大眼	8 辛楚	10 淸楚	12 趨險	附勢	15 鵷鶵	17 苾芻	19 舒展
2 粗字	4 粗心	5 粗飯	6 粗眉	7 痛楚	9 完楚	11 趨進	13 趨炎	14 趄趦	16 芻蕘	18 紓難	20 寬舒

and this, there and here; [1]'ko' 'ch'ü, wherefore, consequently; [2]˛ing 'ch'ü, by, for, on account of; [3]'chi 'ch'ü, only this; [4]'chek, 'ch'ü, thus, then (it's so and so); [5]'chëü[2] 'ch'ü, from this time; 'k'i 'iu 'ch'ü 'li, how is there any reason in it? i. e., it cannot be right; [6]'pok˛ 'ch'ü chaik, 'pi, if not this, then that; if not now, then soon; [7]'ch'ü k'aik, this moment; 'ch'ü tó[2] ˛tüng ˛ing, (we) of this occupation; COLL., 'ch'ü 'king ng[2] 'pi 'hü 'king, this state (as of trade, etc.,) is not like that state.

'佌 Tz'u. Small, contracted, diminutive: [8]'ch'ü 'ch'ü, very small, minute.

'泚 Chü. Clear water; fresh, clean; name of a stream; also read 'sá, q. v.

'處 '處 Ch'u. To dwell, to reside; to be; to act; to occupy the place of; while in; to distinguish; to manage; to judge, to decide on; to attend to; to do what is proper; to adjust, to settle; to place: also read ch'ëü' q. v.: [9]'kü 'ch'ü, to reside, to dwell; COM., [10]'ch'ü te[2] to adjust, to set to rights; [11]˛tieu 'ch'ü, or 'ch'ü ˛hwo, to reconcile, to settle a dispute; [12]'ch'ü 'si, to visit with death; (I'll) kill (you); [13]'ch'ü 'chang, to behead; 'ch'ü ˛hung, to discriminate, as superiors in reference to faults of inferiors; [14]'ch'ü 'nü, a virgin; ˛chiong ˛hó 'i 'ch'ü, how shall we manage it? COLL., 'ch'ü sëü[2] ng[2] ˛siüng 'hwang pieng' ˛t'ieu ˛só, has not settled matters, but rather made more mischief!

'取 Ch'ü. To take, to lay hold on; to use; to exact; to seize on, to take away; to assume, to appropriate; to receive, to apply to one's use; to get, to induce, to bring upon; taken, applied, selected; also read ch'ëü', q. v.: [15]'ch'ü hwak, to imitate the pattern; 'ch'ü ˛chü, to rely on, to use for one's profit; [16]'ch'iék, 'ch'ü, to appropriate; COM., chëü[2] 'ch'ü, to bring on one's self; [17]'ch'ü e' to approve, pleased with; [18]'ch'ü 'k'ieu, to use cunning; [19]'ch'ü seng' to get credit, trusted; 'ch'ü 'pó, to get security or bail; COLL., ng[2] 'ch'ü e' dissatisfied with; 'ch'ü 'ngai, to extract a tooth.

'鼠 '鼡 Shu. A rat, a mouse, rodent animals in general; *met.*, timorous; thieving; skulking, lurking; a rascal, a mean fellow; the 208th radical: [20]'chwi 'ch'ü, a water rat; [21]˛hiong 'ch'ü, a muskrat; sik˛ 'ch'ü ˛chi ke' of ordinary abilities; COM., [22]'ló 'ch'ü, a rat; [23]˛chiéng 'ch'ü, moles (in coll. ˛ch'ang ˛mang 'ch'ü, blind rats); ˛tieu 'ch'ü, the marten or sable; 'ch'ü ˛chong ˛liong, rats hoard food; *met.*, be provident; COLL., 'ló 'ch'ü k'iák, a rat-trap; ˛ch'eng 'ch'ü, field rats; ˛hu 'ch'ü, a squirrel; 'ch'ü ch'ek˛ a pilferer, a petty thief.

癙 Sick from grief, a settled melancholy; moping, diseased by sorrow.

'攄 Chü. Read 'ch'u; used in the *Paik*, ˛*Ing* for coll. ˛ch'ü: an exclamation in driving animals, hoot! shoo! also a

[1]故此 [2]因此 [3]只此 [4]即此 [5]自此 [6]不此 則彼 [7]此刻 [8]佌佌 [9]居處 [10]處治 [11]調處 [12]處死 [13]處斬 [14]處女 [15]取法 [16]竊取 [17]取意 [18]取巧 [19]取信 [20]水鼠 [21]香鼠 [22]老鼠 [23]鼷鼠

word of contempt uttered with the middle finger thrust out.

(134) Ch'uh.

Ch'uh. A coll. word, as in *ch'ih, ch'ih, ch'uh, ch'uh*, a low sound as of two persons talking; *i 'hū 'tié ch'ih, ch'ih, ch'uh, ch'uh, má 'hieu tek, 'kong sié' nóh*, they are muttering there, I don't know what they are saying.

(135) Ch'uí.

箠 Read *sui;* coll *ch'uí:* bits of bamboo, a bamboo switch: [1]*ch'uí 'kiăng*, or [2]*ch'uí sá*, small switches; [3]*ch'uí hong*, stripes, marks; [4]*ch'uí t'au ch'ok, 'hó 'kiăng*, whipping makes a good child.

(136) Ch'uk.

Ch'uk. A coll. word: a superlative, as in *u ch'uk, ch'uk*, very black, very dark, as the night.

(137) Ch'ŭk.

Ch'ŭk. A coll; word: to tread, to trample; to destroy by treading on: *ch'ŭk, 'si*, to trample to death; *ch'ŭk, náh*, to indent by treading on; *ch'ŭk, taing* to trample down hard, as earth; *ch'ŭk, pang te* to tread level with the earth; *met.*, to break up and gut gamblers' dens, etc.; *ch'ŭk, k'a ch'ioh, 'tá*, trample under foot; *met.*, to oppress the weak.

(138) Ch'ung.

春 Ch'un. Spring; the beginning of the year; glad, joyous; wanton; wine, spirits; a man's name; *met.*, times, seasons, periods; budding, starting: COM., [5]*ch'ung t'iéng*, spring; *ch'ung chié'* spring sacrifices; [6]*ch'ung e'* vernal desire; *met.*, bawdy pictures; [7]*sing ch'ung*, early spring; [8]*maing' ch'ung*, the first month; [9]*lik, ch'ung*, opening of spring—the first of the twenty-four solar terms; [10]*ch'ung pó'* "the spring reporter (of literary success)"—name of an attendant of the god of learning; [11]*ch'ung ch'iu 'chó tiong'* Spring and Autumn Annals—a book of Confucius; COLL., [12]*ch'ung 'piăng*, a large kind of wafer cake; [13]*ngiăng ch'ung*, "meeting the spring"—an official street-procession, in which an earthen ox, called [14]*ch'ung ngu*, is borne; [15]*ch'ung t'iéng au' 'ná meng'* spring has a step mother's face, i. e., is changeable; *ch'ung sieu sioh, k'aik, tek, ch'iéng king*, a brief part of a spring-evening is worth a thousand of gold; *scil.*, to recreate in.

椿 杶 Ch'un. A long-lived tree resembling the banyan: [16]*ch'ung hiong*, the *ch'ung* tree and *hiong* shrub; *met.*, father and mother.

鰆 Ch'un. A salt water fish; it resembles the [17]*wong kwa*, and is called [18]*ch'ung 'chi*, in the Foochow colloquial.

驄 騘 Ts'ung. A dappled or iron-gray horse: [19]*ngu hwa ch'ung*, a pie-bald horse.

[1]箠仔 [2]箠擽 [3]箠痕 [4]箠頭出好仔〇 [5]春天 [6]春意 [7]新春 [8]孟春 [9]立春 [10]春報 [11]春秋左傳 [12]春餅 [13]迎春 [14]春牛 [15]春天後奶面 [16]椿萱 [17]黃瓜 [18]鰆子 [19]五花驄

蔥 Ts'ung. An onion; a kind of sword; a green color; wind or breath having vent; a thorough draft: in the coll. read ˛ch'ëng, q. v.: ˛ch'ung ˊling, the Karakorum Mt.'s.

悤 Ts'ung. Hurried, alarmed, agitated: [1]'no' k'e' ˛ch'ung ˛ch'ung, excited to anger, exasperated; [2]˛ch'ung ˛mong, precipitate.

璁 Ts'ung. A pebble or stone resembling a precious gem.

聰 聦 Ts'ung. Quick at hearing, astute, ready, quick-witted; to perceive clearly, to discriminate intelligently: [3]˛ch'ung ch'ak˒ to discriminate; [4]˛t'iéng ˛ch'ung, heaven-bestowed intelligence—said of the emperor; COM., [5]˛ch'ung ˛ming, clever, intelligent; [6]˛ch'ung ˛ming ˛ling le' clever and apt; [7]˛ch'ung ˛ming mok˒ kwo' tá' ˛wong, the cleverness (of others) can't exceed the emperor's! [8]˛ch'ung ˛ming ek˒ sié' 'mung 'tung ek˒ ˛si, clever all his life, stupid just this once; COLL., ˛ch'ung ˛ming ˛nëng, or ˛ch'ung ˛ming 'kiáng, a quick-witted person.

蠢 惷 Ch'ung. To crawl, to wriggle, as worms; to move, to stir; to do stupidly; foolish, simple; rude, unsubmissive: COM., [9]˛ngü 'ch'ung, simple.

睶 Ch'un. Large eyes: in the coll., drowsy, sleepy: COLL., [10]'ch'ung ˛ming, or [11]'ch'ung k'ó' sleepy, dozing; [12]'ch'ung sioh˒ k'aik˒ 'ku, to doze a spell; 'ch'ung sioh˒ 'ku ˛ming, to take a nap; 'ch'ung k'ó' ˛tu tek˒ (buy it) napping and it's worth all that!

(139) Ch'üng.

冲 沖 Ch'ung. Young, delicate; harmonious; deep, hollow; to mount upwards in the air; to agitate, to move; to rush, to dart, to strike against; to send, as letters; used in the coll. for steeping by pouring on hot water: [13]˛ch'üng tong' moved, excited by; COM., ˛ch'üng ˛t'iéng, to dart into the sky, as birds, dust, noise; [14]˛ch'üng p'ó' ruined (as business) by the happening (of an unlucky day, word or act); ˛ch'üng ˛t'iéng mó' ancient imperial cap with a peaked crown; k'e' tói' ˛ch'üng, mutually angered; ˛ch'üng 'hi, "has met joy"—said of a sick man who recovers on marrying; COLL., nau' ˛ch'üng ˛t'iéng, the outcry pierces the skies: ˛ch'üng ˛ta, to steep tea; ˛ch'üng ˛t'ong, or ˛ch'üng 'kung 'chwi, to pour boiling water on; ˛ch'üng yoh˒ to make a medicinal infusion.

种 Chu. Also read ˛t'üng: young grain, delicate, tender: [15]'eu' ˛ch'üng small and delicate.

盅 Also read ˛t'üng: a cup, a hollow vessel, generally small and covered: COM., [16]˛ta ˛ch'üng (coll. k'aing' ˛ch'üng), a kind of bowl or large cup, with the cover closely fitted to the rim.

從 Ts'ung. Easy, bland, complaisant, calm, gentle: also read ˛chung, ˛chüng, and chëüng' q.v.: COM., ˛ch'üng

---

1 怒氣悤悤 2 悤忙 3 聰察 4 天聰 5 聰明 6 聰明伶俐 7 聰明莫過帝王 8 聰明一世懵懂一時 9 愚蠢 10 睶眠 11 睶去 12 睶一刻古 13 冲動 14 冲破 15 幼种 16 茶盅

˛ŭng, or *˛ch‘ŭng ˛ch‘ŭng ˛ŭng ˛ŭng*, not hurried, easy, as one's manner; *˛ch‘ŭng hwang’* slow, not pressing; COLL., *˛ch‘ŭng ‘kwi nik˛* to allow a few days longer.

充 *˛*Ch‘ung. To fill, to satiate; to extend, to carry out, to continue; to act, to fill an office; to stop up, to stuff; sufficient; long, high; [1]*˛ch‘ŭng sik˛* stuffed solid; COM., [2]*˛ch‘ŭng chëŭng’* to distribute among all, as forfeits; [3]*˛ch‘ŭng ‘mwang*, filled; [4]*˛ch‘ŭng chëŭk˛* sufficient, in abundance, as wealth; [5]*˛ch‘ŭng ˛ki*, to satisfy hunger; COLL., [6]*˛ch‘ŭng sioh˛ ˛miăng*, to add another name, as of a partner; [7]*‘mwong’ ˛ch‘ŭng ˛kung*, banished to the colonies.

忡 *˛*Ch‘ung. Sorrowful, grieved: [8]*˛ch‘ŭng ˛ch‘ŭng*, distressed in mind.

㤝 *˛*Ch‘ung. The mind much moved; agitated, perturbed.

罿 *˛*Ch‘ung. Also read *˛tung*: a net for catching birds.

翀 *˛*Ch‘ung. To fly up high, to soar: [9]*‘che’ ‘k‘ŏ ˛ch‘ŭng ˛sieu*, heaven-aspiring ambition.

衝 *˛*Ch‘ung. A path, a crossway; to support; to move, to excite; to rise, to rush against, to overflow; abruptly; towards; a car: [10]*tai’ ˛ch‘ŭng*, a great road; COM., [11]*˛ch‘ŭng taung’* to meet suddenly, to come in conflict with; COLL., [12]*˛ch‘ŭng t‘au’* to go fully up to, as a sedan bearer to the opposite side before turning; [13]*˛ch‘ŭng taung’ ‘ma ˛t‘au*, to rush against the horse's head; *met.*, to come in conflict with a fierce fellow or some god (and receive injury).

(140) Ch‘wa.

簒 Ts‘uan. Read *ch‘wang’*; coll., *ch‘wa’*: to take away one's custom in business; to scheme, to plot against; to spoil the business of another, as by underselling: [14]*ch‘wa’ ˛li ch‘wa’ k‘ŏ’* mutually drawing away (each other's custom); [15]*ch‘wa’ kwo’ ˛peng*, draws (all the custom) to his side; [16]*ch‘wa’ te’ ˛hwong*, to get away another's place, as by slander.

Ch‘wa’. A coll. word: sudden distortions, pains which the Tauist priest professes to cure within 49 days: *ch‘wa’ ˛wai*, distorted, awry, as the limbs, mouth, &c., *ch‘wa’ ‘p‘iăng*, lame in the foot by distortion.

Ch‘wa’. A coll. word, as in *ch‘wa’ tŏ’* to take the wrong road,—to fall into sin, to become vicious.

(141) Ch‘wang.

餐 *˛*Ts‘un. **湌** *˛* **飱** Sun. The 3d properly read *˛song*, but classed with the others in the *Paik*, *˛Ing*: to swallow, to eat; a meal; a classifier of meals; to gather, to select; [17]*‘chó ˛ch‘wang*, breakfast; COM., [18]*sik˛ nik˛ ˛sang ˛ch‘wang*, three meals a day; *‘wang ˛ch‘wang*, supper.

[1] 充實 [2] 充衆 [3] 充滿 [4] 充足 [5] 充饑 [6] 充一名 [7] 個充軍 [8] 忡忡 [9] 志可翀霄 [10] 大衝 [11] 衝撞 [12] 衝透 [13] 衝撞馬頭 [14] 簒來簒去 [15] 簒過爿 [16] 簒地方 [17] 早餐 [18] 一日三餐

銓 ‘Ch‘üan. To weigh, to measure; to estimate the value of things; to choose according to merit or value; a carpenter's plane: [1]‘*ch‘wang* *heng*, steelyards, to weigh; *met.*, to estimate ability; [2]‘*ch‘wang* ‘*song*, to select, as good officers.

筌 ‘Ch‘üan. A crab-trap, a bamboo trap for fish, having a small entrance: [3]*taik*, *ngü* *wong* *ch‘wang*, to take the fish and forget the net; *met.*, ungrateful.

拴 ‘Ch‘uan. To select from, to pick out from with the hand.

詮 ‘Ch‘uan. To explain, to comment on; select sayings; to illustrate, to expound books; to discourse upon, to set forth and enforce.

跧 ‘ Stooping, creeping, bent down; to go along doubled over; decrepit; to kick.

痊 ‘Ch‘üan. Convalescent, recovered from sickness: [4]‘*ch‘wang* ‘*ü*, or [5]*peng*’ ‘*ch‘wang*, recovered from illness.

悛 ‘Ch‘üan. To stop; to change; next in order, to succeed: [6]‘*ch‘wang* ‘*kai*, to change.

湍 ‘Ch‘uan. Water gushing out; a rapid current: [7]*kek*, *liu* *wak*, *ch‘wang*, a rapid flow is called a torrent.

縓 ‘Ch‘uan. A reddish color; a pale yellow or carnation tint, made by once dyeing.

喘 ‘Ch‘uan. To pant, to wheeze, to gasp; breath, the life: [8]‘*ch‘wang ngik*, to gasp, to pant; [9]‘*ch‘wang sek*, the breath; COM., [10]‘*k‘e*’ ‘*ch‘wang*, to wheeze.

舛 ‘Ch‘uan. Erroneous; opposed; to contradict: the 136th radical: [11]‘*ch‘wang ch‘auk*, wrong, erroneous; [12]*meng*’ *tu* *tó* ‘*ch‘wang*, a bad destiny.

爨 Ts‘uan. A furnace, or cooking place; a mess, a table; to steam, to cook gently: [13]*ch‘ui ch‘wang*’ to steam, to cook; COM., [14]*tung ch‘wang*’ to eat at one table, as brothers before living separately; [15]*hung ch‘wang*’ to eat at separate tables.

穳 Ts‘uan. Read *ch‘wang*; coll. *ch‘wang*’; a spear, a javelin: [16]*tëak*, *kó ch‘wang*’ long bamboo-spears.

篡 Ts‘uan. To seize violently; to usurp, to turn traitor and seize the throne: used in the coll. for *ch‘wa*’ q. v.: [17]*ch‘wang*’ *ngik*, to rebel and seize by force; COM., [18]*ch‘wang*’ *oi*’ to usurp the throne.

攛 Ts‘uan. To fling away; to tempt, to seduce to evil; to get one to consent; [19]*ch‘wang*’ *chiok*, to entice, to inveigle.

竄 Ts‘uan. Used for the preceding: to sneak away, to hide, to skulk; to kill; to seduce; to fumigate; to secrete; petty, weak, pusillanimous: [20]*ch‘wang*’ *huk*, to hide away; ‘*ch‘ü ch‘wang*’ rats secrete them-

---

1銓 3得 4痊 6悛 曰 9喘 11舛 多 14同 16竹 17篡 19攛
衡 魚 愈 改 湍 息 錯 舛 爨 篙 逆 掇
2銓 忘 5病 7急 8喘 10氣 12命 13炊 15分 穳 18篡 20竄
選 筌 痊 流 逆 喘 途 爨 爨 〇 位 伏

selves; *met.*, pilferers skulking; *ₑtó ch'wang'* to run away.

(142) Ch'wi.

隹 ₑ Also read *ₑchwi*: a general name for birds with short tails; a species of pigeon or dove.

雖 ₑ Sui. A sort of gronnd lizard, an animal whose description resembles that of the proboscis-monkey; a dubitative particle, although, if, supposing, even if, though, allowing that; to push off; COM., [1]*ₑch'wi ₑyong*, although, albeit; COLL., *ₑch'wi ₑyong ₑchiong wang'* though it is so.

錐 ₑ Sui. An awl, a borer; a sharp pointed tool; the apex, the point; to bore; trifling: [2]*ₑmó ₑch'wi*, a pencil; [3]*ₑch'wi ₑtó ₑchi mwak*, (like) the points of awls and knives—small matters; [4]*ₑu lik, ₑch'wi ₑchi te'* no place to stick an awl—wretchedly poor.

騅 ₑ Ts'ui. A black horse with white spots: [5]*ₑu ₑch'wi 'ma*, the charger of Hang Yu of Tso.

推 ₑ T'ui To push away, to expel, to push from one; to abstain from; to shirk, to shift, to throw of, as responsibility; to refuse, to decline; to secede, to resign, to give up; to deny one's self; to examine closely, to infer; to select; to recommend: [6]*ₑch'wi ₑk'ai*, to push open; [7]*ₑch'wi ₑié*, to remove; [8]*ₑch'wi ₑsü*, to decline, to reject; [9]*ₑch'wi k'iok*, to refuse, to renounce; [10]*ₑch'wi t'auk*, or *ₑch'wi 'wi*, to shift from one's self to others; [11]*ₑsang ₑch'wi*, the three furrows plowed by the Emperor; [12]*ₑch'wi 'kü*, to recommend; [13]*ₑch'wi keu'* to scrutinize; [14]*ₑch'wi lauung'* to reason out, to infer.

綏 ₑ Sui. The traces of a carriage; reins; a hand strap to hold by in a coach; steady, quiet, tranquil: [15]*chek, ₑch'wi*, to hold the reins; [16]*ₑch'wi ₑang*, quiet, tranquil; [u]*ₑch'wi* to pacify, to quiet.

(143) Ch'wí.

炊 ₑ Ch'ui. To cook, to dress food: in the coll. restricted to steaming: COLL., [17]*ₑch'wí pwong'* to steam rice; *ₑch'wí ₑpau*, to steam bread; *ₑch'wí yék*, to heat by steaming; *ₑch'wí pwang' ₑsang* (or *ₑch'ang*) *sük*, steamed half done.

催 ₑ Ts'ui. Read *ₑch'oi*; coll. *ₑch'wí*: to urge, to press, to hasten; to dun, to importune for payment: [18]*ₑch'wí p'aik*, to urge greatly; [19]*ₑch'wí 'ch'iăng*, to press the invitation, as by sending a messenger for the guests; [20]*ₑch'wí 't'ó*, to dun urgently; [21]*ₑch'wí ₑsang*, to hasten parturition, as by medicine or by offerings to "Mother"; *ₑch'wí ₑseng 'sang*, parturition-powders; *ₑch'wí ₑchiéng ₑliong*, to dun for taxes; *ₑch'wí miăng' 'kwi*, you vexatious imp!

吹 歕 ₑ Ch'ui. To blow, as the wind or with the breath; to whistle, to puff; a blast, a gust; to play on a wind-instrument; COM., *ₑhung ₑch'wí*, the wind blows; *ₑch'wí ₑhung*,

[1]雖然 [2]毛錐 [3]錐刀之末 [4]無立錐之地 [5]烏騅馬 [6]推開 [7]推移 [8]推辭 [9]推却 [10]推托 [11]三推 [12]推舉 [13]推究 [14]推論 [15]執綏 [16]綏安 [17]炊飯 [18]催迫 [19]催請 [20]催討 [21]催生

exposure to wind—is bad for the sick; [1],*ch'wí ˌhü*, to praise, to recommend; [2]ˌ*ch'wí ˌking 'ku*, to play on instruments; a band of musicians; [3]ˌ*ch'wí ˌmó ˌkiu ˌchü*, to blow aside the hair to find a sore; *met.*, to pry into faults; COLL., ˌ*ch'wí ko'* old or faded by the wind; ˌ*ch'wí taĕng'* cooled by the wind.

ˌ*Ch'wí.* A coll. word; as in ˌ*ch'wí ˌkung*, to "guess fingers" a drinking game in which the loser must drink.

(144) Ch'wo.

[This word is interchangeably read *Ch'io*, q. v.]

(145) Ch'woh.

[This word is interchangeably read *Ch'ioh*, q. v.]

(146) Ch'woí.

脆' 脃' Ts'ui. Delicate, frail, easily broken, brittle, crackling, shivery, crumbling; crisp, light, as pastry-crust: in the coll., quick, spry; to make a swell, foppish: [4]ˌ*iu ch'woí'* pliant, flexible; COLL., [5]*song ch'woí'* quick, prompt; [6]*'k'á' ch'woí'* soon done or effected; [7]*ch'woí' ˌtiăng* (or ˌ*siăng*), fluent; constraining, authoritative; *ch'woí' ˌnĕng*, persons of influence; *'yă ch'woí'* very finely dressed; exceedingly prompt or successful; *ch'woí' 'tong ˌtong*, or *ch'woí' lang' ˌtong*, it's brittle and will snap in two; *met.*, applied to a foppish fellow.

(147) Ch'wok.

[This word is interchangeably read *Ch'iok*, q. v.]

(148) Ch'wong.

[This word is interchangeably read *Ch'iong*, q. v.]

(149) E.

意' Yi. The intention, will, purpose; thoughts, ideas; motive, inclination; sentiment, opinion; meaning of a word: COM., [8]*e' sëü'* idea, purport of; [9]ˌ*sing e'* intention, will; [10]*e' ngwoí'* beyond expectation; [11]*e' k'e' ˌsong ˌteu*, united in feeling; [12]*e' kiéng'* opinion, sentiment; [13]*'k'eu e'* purport of one's remarks; [14]*'iu e'* to have a purpose, intentionally; [15]*taik, e'* to get one's wish, gratified; [16]*hwoí' e'* to understand, to fathom, as a meaning; [17]*tĕüng' e'* satisfied with; [18]*pok, e'* unexpectedly; [19]ˌ*ü e'* according to one's wish; *met.*, a certain carved ornament—a symbol of luck; COLL., [20]*'ku e'* purposely—usually in a bad sense; [21]*ng' ˌchong e'* unexpected; *e' 'hó ng' chai' siăh*, the intention good, no matter about the feast (being poor).

臆' Yi. Used for the last: the breast, the pit of the stomach; the flesh on the breast; the heart, the bosom; the thoughts, opinions, feelings: ˌ*hüng e'* the breast; thoughts, desires.

薏' Yi. The seeds of the nelumbium; barley: *e' 'i*, pearl barley: COM., *e' 'mi*, pearl barley; *e' 'mi ˌt'ong*, barley broth; *e' 'mi ˌkŭng*, barley root—used medicinally to expel humors.

[1]吹噓 [2]吹京 鼓吹 [3]吹毛求 [4]柔脆 [5]爽脆 [6]快脆 [7]脆腥 [8]意思 [9]心意 [10]意外 [11]意氣相投 [12]意見 [13]口意 [14]有意 [15]得意 [16]會意 [17]中意 [18]不意 [19]如意 [20]故意 [21]怀存意

憶' Yi. To recall, to bring to mind, to recollect; to think upon, to reflect on: ¹e' niĕng² to think of; ²ˏhuí e' or ke' e' to recall, or bring to mind; ³ˏyeu e' to think of things long past.

億' Yi. Ten myriads, a lac, a hundred thousand; also a myriad, a hundred millions; innumerable; quiet, repose of mind; to supply and make quiet; to contrive, to calculate; to guess; to bet: ⁴e' tieu² ˏchi chĕūng' multitudes of people, all mankind; ⁵e' chaik, lĕū' tĕūng' plan, then you'll constantly succeed; COM., ⁶wang² e' myriads and lacs—in numeration.

檍' Yi. A tough wood, suitable for making bows, a sort of ash or alder.

衣' Yi. To clothe, to put on clothing, to wear clothes: also read ˏi, q. v.: ⁷e' ˏk'ing ˏkiu, to wear light fur-clothing; ⁸e' taik, ˏngiong, to clothe with virtuous words, i.e., to hear and embrace good doctrine.

扆' Yi. A silken screen used by the ancient emperors in the audience-chamber; it was ornamented with ax-heads.

瘞' Yi. A retired, obscure place; to bury, to inter; to sacrifice to those who have been buried, to streams, or to the moon; to hide.

矣' Yi. A final euphonic particle, denoting a plain statement, or the completion of the sense: ⁹ˏi ʿi e' finished, just that and nothing more.

未² Wei. Not yet, not now; denotes the sixth moon; the eighth of the "twelve branches", and symbolized by a sheep; time from 1 to 3 o'clock P. M.: COM., ¹⁰e² chiăng' 2 P. M.; ¹¹ʿngu e² ˏsi k'aik, time from from 11 A. M. to 3 P. M.; ¹²e² pek, ˏyong, not necessarily so, probably not; e² pok, ˏsiĕng ˏti, to foreknow without divination—often used facetiously; e² ˏhwong ʿsiu chiĕk, not yet married and maintaining chastity—as a girl who remains single after the death of her affianced.

味² Wei. Taste, flavor, seasoning, relish; a delicacy, a relish, a dainty; style or beauties of composition; to relish, to take pleasure in, to solace, to recreate in: ¹³ˏchŭ e² (coll. ˏchŭ e²) a fine relish; COM., ¹⁴ʿngu e² the five tastes, as sweet, bitter, etc.; a tonic medicine for the kidneys; ¹⁵ʿk'eu e² taste of the mouth; met., good to eat; ¹⁶k'e' e² the natural flavor; met., feelings; k'e' e² ˏteu hak, united in feeling; ˏti e² to discern tastes; met., to relish the beauties (of a book); ʿhai e² sea-relishes, i. e., fish; COLL., e² taĕng² or e² tiăng' a strong taste or scent; e² so' or e² tó² taste, flavor.

易² Yi. Easy, simple, plain, not hard to do, readily accomplished; negligent, remiss, disrespectful; to extirpate weeds, to dress a field: also read ik, q. v.: ¹⁷ˏnang e² difficult and easy; COM., ¹⁸ˏûng e² easy, not difficult; ¹⁹ˏk'ing e² to treat

---

1憶念 2回憶 3遙憶 4億兆之衆 5億則屢中 6萬億 7衣輕裘 8衣德言 9而已矣 10未正 11午未時刻 12未必然 13滋味 14五味 15口味 16氣味 17難易 18容易 19輕易

福州方言拼音字典

lightly, to contemn; [1]*‚ǔng ē² t'wak*, *'ch'iu*, easy rid out of hand, as salable goods.

異² Yi. Separated, foreign, of another country, different, diverse; admirable, unusual, strange, rare, extraordinary, bizarre; perverse, heterodox; to marvel at, to regard as different; to oppose: [2]*ē² ‚pang*, foreign countries; COM., [3]*ē² 'chŭng*, foreign kinds, as of plants; [4]*ē² ‚twang*, heterodox; [5]*ē² yong² 'hó*, remarkably good; [6]*ē² nik‚ 'pwo pó²* some future day I will requite (your kindness).

肄² Yi. To practice, to accustom one's self to, to be skilled in; to serve assiduously; sprouts of a stump: [7]*ē² ngiĕk‚* a resident graduate.

勩² Yi. Labor, distress, toil; afflictions, sufferings; to be weary; to endure, to labor in: [8]*mok‚ ‚ti 'ngó ē²* none know my trouble.

E². A coll. word: dirty, filthy: *tē² a² 'yă ē² ng² ‚t'ĕng sói²* the ground is very dirty, you must not sit on it.

E². A coll. euphonic prefix, as in *ē² wa²* to draw, to sketch.

(150) Ē.

呃 ‚ Read *‚i*, used in the *Paik‚ ‚Ing* for the coll. *‚ē*, as in *‚ē ‚kŭ*, the inarticulate noise or prattle of babes: *‚ē haĕ²* the cry of runners before the sedans of idols or officers; *chó² ‚ē haĕ²* to be a crier to clear the way.

呃 ‚ Read *‚i*; coll. *‚ē*, as in *‚ē ‚kŭ*, the same as *‚ē ‚kŭ*: *‚ē laĕh*, a hiccough, raising of wind after a full meal; *‚ē ‚ē*, used as a call, ho! halloo!

(151) Eh.

Eh‚. A coll. word, denoting pettishness or obstinacy: *eh, eh*, means I will! or I'll not! according to circumstances.

(152) Ek.

一 ‚ 壹 ‚ Yi. One; the first; the same; as one, alike; the whole, at once; a few; a, an; sincere, real, honest, perfect; to harmonize; to unite, to even, to make one or uniform; the first radical: in the coll. read *sioh‚* q. v.: COM., [9]*tá² ek‚* the first; [10]*ek‚ ‚sing*, with the whole mind; [11]*ek‚ 'chung*, or *ek‚ ch'iĕk‚* or *ek‚ k'ai²* all, the whole, wholly; [12]*hek‚ ek‚* fixed, uniform, as a rule; [13]*tuk‚ ek‚* the only one; [14]*ek‚ teng²* certain, settled; [15]*ek‚ ‚ka ‚ing*, one household; [16]*ek‚ tik‚* straight on, direct; [17]*ek‚ k'ē²* at one breath, i.e., without stopping; [18]*ek‚ 'hó*, it's the very best (thus); [19]*ek‚ hiong²* heretofore, habitually; *ek‚ ‚si ‚kang*, in a moment, suddenly; *ek‚ 'kŭ ek‚ tong²* in every act, the whole conduct; *‚hung ‚hung pok‚ ek‚* confused and disagreeing, as talkers; *ek‚ miĕng² ‚chi ‚kau*, just acquainted with; *ek‚ 'k'i saĕng² ‚hwang*, to pay up all at once; *ek‚ 'k'eu ka²* only one price, as asked or offered; *ek‚ ‚ngiong ke² ch'ok‚ sĕŭ² 'ma ‚nang ‚twi*, when a sentence has gone forth, a four-horse team can't catch it! COLL., *ek‚ ngó² ek‚ sek‚* "one five one ten"—all complete, as a narration; *ek‚ siăng²*

[1] 容易脫手 [2] 異邦 [3] 異種 [4] 異端 [5] 異樣 好異日補 [6] 報 [7] 肄業〇 [8] 莫知我勩 [9] 第一 [10] 一心 [11] 一總 [12] 畫一 [13] 獨一 [14] 一定 [15] 一家人〇 [16] 一直 [17] 一氣 [18] 一好 [19] 一向

,t'iĕng, a mere thread of sky—above a narrow court.

乙, Yi. Bent, curved, as a bud; the second of the ten stems, related to wood; second year in the cycle of 60 years; the 5th radical: [1]'t'ai' ek, the great first cause; [2]'kak, ek, the 1st and 2d of the 10 stems; *met.*, first and second, this and that, good and inferior.

鳦, Yi. The house-martin which has bluish plumage; the twitter of a swallow.

軋, Yi. Usually read *chak,*: the creaking roll of a wheel; a creaking, grating sound; punishment of the rack or wheel: [3]*ek, ek*, creaking of wheels.

揖, **讓**, To bring the hands before the breast and make a slight bow; a bow *a la Chinoise;* a salutation; to give way to, to cede, to resign, to yield; to bow in: [4]*ek, yong'* to yield to, to allow; [5]*'tiong ek*, to make a low bow; COM., [6]*,sang ek*, three bows; [7]*chauk, ek*, to make a respectful bow, to salute.

挹, Yi. Sometimes used for the last: to pour or bail out, to lade, to transfer liquids: [8]*ek, 'pi chĕü' ,chü*, to lade from that, and pour into this.

抑, Yi. A conjunction, or, either; moreover, further; to press down with the hand, to settle; to stop, to cause to desist, to keep back; to abate, to rule, to keep one's self-possession, to repress, to restrain; handsome: [9]*ek, ek*, slowly, reserved; [10]*ek, hĕk*, or, else, or perhaps; *ek, ok*, grieved; [11]*k'ok, ek*, to repress; [12]*ek, ,yong chĕü' ha'* humble, lowly-minded; [13]*ek, ek, ek, ,yong*, one low, one high—as musical sounds, now depressed, then elevated.

悒, Yi. Discontented, disquieted; looking sad, and feeling forlorn.

益, Yi. To pour in more, to augment, to increase; to benefit, to prosper, to advantage; advantageous, beneficial; full, superabundant; restorative, strengthening, as a tonic; more, in a higher degree; the 42d diagram: in the coll. read *yăh*, q. v.: [14]*,cheng ek*, to add to; [15]*,k'iĕng seu' ek*, the humble are prospered; COM., [16]*cheng' ek*, to advance and prosper; [17]*,u ek*, profitless; [18]*,hó ek*, of what advantage? how does it profit us? [19]*ek, 'mu ,kó*, a medicine used in pregnancy.

鎰, Yi. A piece of gold, in the Chou Dynasty weighing 30 taels; in the Han Dynasty, 24 taels; and in the days of Liang, 20 taels.

溢, Yi. Full even to overflowing; still, as a full vessel; to overflow, to run over; to spread abroad; a handful: [20]*,ing ek*, full to overflowing; *,yong ek*, overflowing; to spread, as one's fame; *'mwang ,i pok, ek*, full, yet not running over.

浥, Yi. Damp, dewy, moist, soaked through; to steep, to soak; water running down.

[1]太乙 [2]甲乙 [3]軋軋 [4]揖讓 [5]長揖 [6]三揖 [7]作揖 [8]挹彼注茲 [9]抑抑 [10]抑或 [11]屈抑 [12]抑然自下 [13]一抑一揚 [14]增益 [15]謙受益 [16]進益 [17]無益 [18]何益 [19]益母膏 [20]盈溢

鷁 Yi. The sea-eagle, or hawk, drawn on the bows or sterns of junks, to denote their swift sailing: ek꜆ ꜂siu, an eagle-head on the bows of junks.

嗌 Yi. The throat; to hiccough from impediment in the throat: [1]꜃ha꜅ ek꜆, to swallow. Read auk꜆: convulsive laughter.

唈 Yi. A sobbing, a catching of the breath: [2]꜀u ek꜆, a sigh, quick or asthmatic breathing.

邑 **阝** Yi. A city, a place where many people assemble; a domain, a feudal state, a principality; a fortified camp; a capital city; a district or its walled city; a stoppage of the breath; the 163d radical, contracted on the right of the primitive: [3]ek꜆ ꜂chai, a district magistrate; [4]꜀hung ek꜆, to appoint to a district magistracy—an ancient term; [5]꜀u ek꜆, to heave, to sigh; COM., [6]꜂siu ek꜆, the chief district of a prefecture.

Ek꜇. A coll. euphonic prefix, as in *ek꜆ ok꜆*, to bend; *ek꜆ ak꜆*, to repress, as quarrels; to insert, as dates; *ek꜆ wak꜆*, to scratch; *ek꜆ aik꜆*, to press with the hand.

(153) Eng.

鶯 ꜀Ying. The nightingale, or a gay species of thrush, that nestles on the willow and sings well; variegated plumes: [7]꜂iu ꜀eng ꜁ki ꜂ü, has variegated plumes; COM., [8]꜁wong ꜀eng, the mango bird—called in poetry [9]꜀ch'ung ꜀eng, the vernal thrush.

꜀Eng. A coll. word, for which the last character is sometimes used, as in *꜀eng sëük꜆*, the poppy; *꜀eng sëük꜆ ꜀hwa*, poppy flowers or capsules.

嚶 ꜀Ying. The harmonious singing of birds: [10]꜀eng ꜀eng, the carolings of birds; *met.*, mutual admonitions of friends.

嬰 ꜀Ying. Read ꜀ing in the dictionaries, but usually read ꜀eng in Foochow: an infant, a babe, a sucking child, a new-born girl; to rush against, to surround, to threaten; entangled, inclosed, hampered, restrained; female ornaments: [11]꜂kiu ꜀eng, a demon, a fire and water sprite; [12]ük꜇ ꜀eng ꜁tong, an orphan asylum; [13]꜀eng ꜁i, a suckling, a babe.

櫻 ꜀Ying. A cherry: [14]꜀eng ꜁t'ó, or [15]꜀chio ꜀eng, a red cherry; [16]꜀eng ꜁t'ó ꜂k'eu, cherry lips.

鸚 ꜀Ying. A parrot: [17]꜀eng ꜁loi, or [18]꜀eng ꜂u ꜁loi, the buccinum or nautilus shell—is like a parrot with its head on its breast; COLL., ꜀eng ꜀kó, the parrot; ꜀eng ꜀kó ka꜄ a parrot-perch; ꜀eng ꜀kó p'e꜄ parrot's nose; *met.*, a beaked nose.

薨 ꜀ The death of a prince or grandee; to die; many; fleet, prompt: [19]꜀chü ꜁heu ꜂sü wak꜇ ꜀eng, the death of a prince is called ꜀eng; [20]꜀eng ꜀eng, many; fleet, swift.

1 嗄嗌 2 嗚唈 3 邑宰 4 分邑 5 於邑 6 首邑 7 有鶯其羽 8 黃鶯 9 春鶯 10 嚶嚶 11 九嬰 12 育嬰堂 13 嬰兒 14 櫻桃 15 朱櫻 16 櫻桃口 17 鸚螺 18 鸚鵡螺 19 諸侯死曰薨 20 薨薨

訇 ˓Ying. Also read ˏheng: noise of drums or bells, clamor; the rushing of water; the din of loud voices: [1]˓p'eng ˓eng, a loud noise; ˓eng k'ai˒ rushing of waters; clang of bells.

渹 ˓Ying. Also read ˏheng: ˓eng ˓eng, the roaring of water over stones; the dashing of waves.

轟 ˓Hung. The rumbling of wheels; muttering of thunder; roaring of cannon; a buzzing, stunning noise: [1]˓loi ˓eng, the roar of thunder; [2]˓eng ˓eng, the rumbling of many carriage-wheels.

安 ˓Ngan. Read ˓ang; used in the coll. for ˓eng: to place, to put, to set, to lay on or down: [3]˓eng kiă˒ to place low; [4]˓eng nóh, to set things; (place) for setting things; [5]˓eng chiăng˒ place it straight; [6]˓eng ˓chi ˓tié, set it in here; [7]˓eng hiéng˒ hiéng˒ lay it in full view; [8]˓eng ˓lá ˓t'iăng ˓kang, waits vainly to hear the watches beat—a coarse expression applied to brothel-visitors; ˓eng ˓lá hiéng˒ sié˒ just staying in the world—said of a worthless fellow.

陰 ˓Yin. Read ˓ing; coll. ˓eng, as in [9]˓eng ˓u ˓t'iéng, a dark muggy atmosphere.

˓*Eng.* A coll. word: to touch, to tap, to strike lightly: ˓eng sioh˒ a˒ to give a touch; ˓eng ˓chiă ˓eng ˓chiă, touch! touch!

印˒ Yin. A seal, a stamp, an official signet; to seal, to stamp, to affix the credentials; to print, to take off an impression: COM., [10]˓k'ai eng˒ (coll. ˓k'wi eng˒) to open the seals—resume official business on the 20th day of the 1st month; [11]˓hung eng˒ to close the seals—on the 20th of the 12th month; [12]chiĕk˒ eng˒ to enter upon office; [13]kwo˒ eng˒ to transfer the seals of office; [14]eng˒ ˓chü, to print books; [15]eng˒ ˓hwa, to print flowers, as on cloth; [16]eng˒ ˓peng, printing blocks; eng˒ saik˒ a red pigment of oil and vermillion for stamping; pai˒ eng˒ to worship the seals; COLL., p'ah˒ o˒ eng˒ stamped, as dollars.

應˒ 譍˒ Ying. That which is proper and right, ought, should be, suitable—that which is likely to take place; to answer, to respond, to grant petitions; to fulfill, to come up to expectations, correspondent, answering to; correlative, proportionate, retributive; a lot, a number: also read ˓ing, q. v.: ˓tung ˓sing ˓siong eng˒ the echo answers; *met.*, people of the same tastes; COM., [17]eng˒ tói˒ to answer, a reply; eng˒ tak˒ or tak˒ eng˒ to answer, to respond; [18]chiĕk˒ eng˒ to entertain guests; to re-enforce, as in battle; eng˒ ˓hü, to promise, as superiors do; eng˒ ˓sing, to promise, to assent to, to permit; [19]eng˒ ˓siu, to pay civilities and make presents; [20]eng˒ ˓li, reasonable, proper; eng˒ ch'oi˒ to answer back—in anger; [21]eng˒ ˓kong, answered, saying; eng˒ ngiéng˒ fulfilled, answering to the prediction; COLL., ˓i má˒ eng˒ he can't or will not answer; eng˒ ˓kwang nioh˒ wai˒ amounts to how much? what is the sum total?

[1] 雷轟 [2] 轟轟 [3] 安下 [4] 安乇 [5] 安正 [6] 安只 [7] 安現現 [8] 安禮聽更 [9] 陰烏天〇 [10] 開印 [11] 封印 [12] 接印 [13] 過印 [14] 印書 [15] 印花 [16] 印板 [17] 應對 [18] 接應 [19] 應酬 [20] 應理 [21] 應講

福州方言拼音字典

瘞 Yin. A disease of the mind, grief, despondency; a settled melancholy.

蔭 蔭 Yin. To shade, to overshadow, to protect, to shelter; shade, shadow; shady, cool; the hereditary care of the state: COM., [1]*chiă eng*' to overshadow; [2]*pe*' *eng*' or [3]*eng*' *pe*' to shelter, to protect.

Eng'. A coll. euphonic prefix, as in *eng*' *ong*' to dip: *eng*' *aing*' to extinguish, as coals in a jar; *eng*' *aung*' to watch; *eng*' *yéng*' to engross; to insert, to patch, as with boards.

閒 Sien. Read *hang*; coll. *eng*: leisure, repose; idle, unemployed; indolent, empty, unoccupied, as a place: *mô eng*, no leisure, busy; [4]*eng nëng*, idle persons; [5]*te*' *eng*, the ground vacant; [6]*eng chiëng*, unemployed money; *eng chiëng*' idle and mischievous; [7]*eng si a*' leisure time, other than the special time; [8]*eng eng 'peng*, leisurely; [9]*eng chô*' *pah*, *chô*' to trifle, not doing one's task; *eng 'kong eng t'iàng*' to prate, talk of this and that; [10]*eng wa*' *hiu t'i*, don't introduce irrelevant talk; *eng 'kwang twai*' *pah*, *mô ch'oi*' *ch'iu*, idly trouble a husband's elder brother, because he has no mustaches! *met.*, to interpose in others' matters.

咏 詠 Yung. To sing or hum in a recitative, to chant or drawl out the words; music of birds: [11]*eng*' *si*, to sing hymns; [12]*eng*' *t'ang*' to sing and sigh, to hum plaintively.

泳 Yung. To walk under water; to dive and seek for things under the water; flowing, meandering: [13]*eng*' *chi iu chi*, to dive and sport in the water.

牣 Yung. Filled, stuffed, crammed, made solid; overflowed: [14]*u eng*' filled, crowded.

任 Jên. Sincere, worthy of trust, sure; friendship, confidence; trusted, relied on; trust, office, a responsibility; to bear, to sustain, to execute, to undertake, to be responsible: [15]*eng*' *ho*' to bear, to sustain; [16]*tuk*, *eng*' sole responsibility; [17]*seng*' *eng*' to trust one in a matter; *tëüng*' *eng*' a responsible trust; COM., *chaik*, *eng*' a trust, a charge; [18]*eng*' *e*' according to one's wish; *tô*' *eng*' to assume office; *ing eng*' *kó sing*, illustrious office, and steady promotion—a felicitous phrase.

恁 Jên. To consider, to think, to contemplate, to dwell upon with satisfaction; thus, in this manner.

賃 Lin. To rent, to lease, to hire, to charter—said of houses, furniture, vessels: [19]*chu eng*' to take on lease.

鵀 Jên. A bird with a crest, likened to a woman's headdress; perhaps it is a species of hoopoe.

刃 刄 Jên. A knife, a sword, a sharp weapon; the edge or point of a knife; sharp, strong; to cut, to kill: [20]*ping eng*' warlike weapons; *hung eng*' the edge or sharp point of.

[1]遮蔭 [2]庇蔭 [3]蔭庇 [4]閒人 [5]地閒 [6]閒錢 [7]閒時下 [8]閒閒板 [9]閒做白做 [10]閒話 休提 [11]咏詩 [12]咏嘆 [13]泳之游之 [14]於牣 [15]任負 [16]獨任 [17]信任 [18]任意 [19]租賃 [20]兵刃

妊[2] **姙**[2] Jên. Pregnant, with child: ʻeng[2] ük, to bear, to bring forth; ʻiu eng[2] to conceive; ,sü ,tʻai kwai' eng[2] illicit birth and strange conception; COM., [1]ʻ,hwai eng[2] pregnant; [3]eng[2] ho[2] a pregnant woman.

孕[2] Ying.

訒[2] Jên. Slow of speech, unready, hesitating so as not to speak unadvisedly; to stammer, to speak with difficulty; cautious remarks: [4],ing ʻchiä ,ki ,ngiong yä' eng[2] the words of the humane are spoken cautiously.

軔[2] Jên. To stop a carriage, to block a wheel; a chock, a catch; a length of eight cubits: [5]hwak, eng[2] to remove the catch; to unstop, to set agoing.

仞[2] Jên. A measure of eight cubits, or about ten English feet; to fathom, to measure the depth of; full, to fill.

韌[2] Jên. Soft and flexible, but tough or tenacious.

胤[2] Ying. A succession of descendants, a line of posterity, heirs; generations, ages; accustomed, practiced: [6]eng[2] sëü[2] descendants, posterity; [7]ʻing sek, chio' eng[2] to bestow official promotion on one's descendants in perpetuity.

Eng[2]. A coll. euphonic prefix, as in *eng[2] yong[2]* to move, as waves do: *eng[2] wang[2]* to change; to exchange; *eng[2] aung[2]* to rub; rubbed, daubed.

(154) **Ëng.**

,Ëng. A coll. word, as in *,ëng ngié[2]* ants: *,ëng ngié[2] ,wo,* an ant-nest; *,ëng ,ëng,* a centipede; *,ëng ,ëng ,kʻa,* a centipede's feet; *met.,* paper marked in a certain way—a kind of lottery, by which friends decide their respective contributions to an entertainment.

紅 ʻHung. Read *,hung;* coll. *,ëng:* a red color, reddish: [8]twai[2] ,ëng, a deep red; [9]ngüng ,ëng, a lightish red; [10],chau ,ëng, a dull red; [11],tʻó ,ëng, or *,mui ,ëng,* a peach or plum red; [12],ëng chʻiäh, a brilliant red; *,ëng chʻieu'* a lively red color; [13]o[2] ,ëng ,tʻau, has a reddish tinge; [14],ëng ,tang ,tang, or *,ëng liék, liék,* or *,ëng to' to'* intensely red; *,ngwong ,ëng ,kang,* dried *lichi* fruit; [15],ëng ,hwa, a red dye-stuff; *,ëng haik, mó[2]* the red and black caps, i. e., lictors; *,ëng ʻhung ʻkʻi pah, nük,* red cosmetics raise white flesh—sobriquet for a fair, fat man.

(155) **Eu.**

甌 ʻNgou. A bowl, a cup, a deep cup; a surname: *,tung ,eu,* ancient name of Fookien; COM., [16],ta ,eu, a tea cup; [17],tʻong ,eu, a kind of small bowl; [18],eu pwang' a cup full and a half; COLL., *,chʻüng ,eu,* a covered cup to make tea in.

漚 ʻNgou. Bubbles on the water, foam, froth, spume: [19],pʻeu ,eu floating foam. Read *aiu'* to soak, to macerate, to steep, to soften by soaking; [20]aiu' ,ma, to steep hemp.

[1]孕育 [2]懷孕 [3]孕婦 [4]仁者其言也訒 [5]發軔 [6]胤嗣 [7]永錫祚胤 [8]大紅 [9]銀紅 [10]糟紅 [11]桃紅 [12]紅赤 [13]有紅頭 [14]紅丹丹 [15]紅花 [16]茶甌 [17]湯甌 [18]甌半 [19]浮漚 [20]漚麻

福州方言拼音字典

鷗 Ngou. A gull: *pek꜆ ꜀eu*, or *꜀sa ꜀eu*, white gulls; *꜁hang ꜀eu*, a gull at rest; *꜁kung ꜀eu*, a flock of gulls.

꜀Eu. A coll. word: hungry: *pok꜆ 'ló ꜀eu*, the stomach empty, hungry; *꜀eu má' seu'* hungry beyond endurance, famishing.

謳 ꜀Ngou. To sing songs in recitative; a chant, a ballad, a ditty: [1]*꜀eu ꜀kó*, to sing songs; [2]*꜀eu ꜁nging*, to chant; [3]*siêng' ꜀eu*, fine chanting.

歐 ꜀Ngou. Used for the last and the next: to sing, to crow merrily; a surname: [4]*꜀eu ꜀tó*, an executioner's sword; [5]*꜀eu 'yǎ*, a celebrated sword-manufacturer of ancient times; COM., *꜀eu ꜁yong*, a surname.

嘔 'Ngou. Also read *꜀eu:* interchanged with the last two: to vomit, the noise of retching; to spit out; a child's prattle; to sing, to make a cheerful noise: in the coll. read *'au*, q. v.: [6]*'eu haik*, to spit blood; [7]*'eu t'o'* to vomit.

毆 'Ngou. To strike, to lash, to knock, to beat with a stick; to fight; to switch up, to drive on, to urge: [8]*taiu' 'eu*, to fight; [9]*'eu ŭk꜇*, to disgrace by beating; *꜀hŭng 'eu*, to cudgel ferociously; COM., [10]*'eu ꜀ch'á*, to beat the police; [11]*'eu ꜀siong*, to wound by inflicting blows.

幼' Yu. Young, tender, immature; small, youthful, under 16 years; in the coll., fine, as workmanship; delicate and tender, as meats, etc.: COM., [12]*꜁niêng eu'* young in years, juvenile; [13]*'ló eu'* old and young; [14]*'tiong eu'* the elder and younger; [15]*eu' ꜁tung*, a lad—applied to one entering the lists for Siu-tsai degree, while under 10 years; *eu' hok꜇ ꜀sŭ ꜀ti*, a youths' primary reader; COLL., *eu' naung'* sleek and soft, velvety; *eu' kiék꜆*, fine and of close texture.

又' Yu. An old form of the hand; a conjunction, more, also, further, moreover, and, and then, still again; in a higher degree; before a negative answers to but, still; the 29th radical: *eu' 'iu*, there are more; [16]*eu' ong'* to ask again; COM., [17]*eu' ꜀kiêng*, additional; *eu' sé' ek꜆*, *꜀hwang sié' kai'* (or *꜀kwong 'king*), there is still another state of things; COLL., *eu' eu' ꜀chiong wang'* yet again thus! *eu' eu' ek꜆ ꜁cheng ꜁cheng*, step by step over again—precisely the same as before.

褎' Yu. Elegantly dressed, embroidered garments; the blade of grain springing up; easy, quiet enjoyment, plenty. Read *seu'* a sleeve, a fur cuff.

右' Yu. The right hand, on the right; to honor, to give the precedence to, as the right was once the place of honor; to encourage, to aid, to support; high, honorable, noble; strong, violent, high-tempered; a second in rank or command: [18]*'chó' eu'* "to the right of your seat"—your honor! an epistolary phrase; COM., [19]*'chó eu'* left and right; [20]*eu' 'ch'iu*, or [21]*eu' ꜀peng 'ch'iu*, the right hand; [22]*'chó eu' ꜁ling*, one's neighbors on

[1]謳歌 [2]謳吟 [3]善謳 [4]歐刀 [5]歐冶 [6]嘔血 [7]嘔吐 [8]鬭毆 [9]毆辱 [10]毆差 [11]毆傷 [12]年幼 [13]老幼 [14]長幼 [15]幼童 [16]又問 [17]又兼 [18]座右 [19]左右 [20]右手 [21]右邊手 [22]左右鄰 〇

the left and right; *eu*[2] *꜀yâng*, the right camp or military division; *eu*[2] *꜀tong*, a district magistrate's assistant.

佑 祐[2] Yu. To aid, to help, to protect, to succor, to lend a hand to; divine protection, assistance, care, kindness of the gods; to protect, to shield, as the gods do: the first is commonly used in the sense of *divine*, as well as *human*, protection: [1]*pó eu*[2] to protect, to defend; [2]*eu*[2] *cho*[2] to aid; [3]*mek꜆ eu*[2] secret protection, as of the gods.

柚[2] Yu. A pumelo or shaddock (citrus decumana): [4]*eu*[2] *꜂chü*, the pumelo; [5]*kek꜆ eu*[2] mandarin-oranges and pumelos.

宥[2] Yu. Indulgent, to forbear with; lenient in punishing; to relax, to give scope to, to tolerate, to encourage; crimes of ignorance; a permanent benefit, a far-reaching advantage: [6]*eu*[2] *chói*[2] to remit punishment; [7]*꜀sang eu*[2] the three venial offences—sins of ignorance, accident, and thoughtlessness; [8]*꜀ngwong eu*[2] a mitigating circumstance; venial sin; [9]*꜂ki ꜀ui ꜀ngwong eu*[2] I beg you to regard it as venial.

侑[2] Yu. Used for the last: to encourage guests to eat (by music); to do the honors of the table; to urge to eat, to wait on: [10]*eu*[2] *sik꜆* to invite to eat; *eu*[2] *꜂chiu*, to offer wine.

囿[2] Yu. A park, an inclosure for animals; an aviary; a menagerie; a walled paddock; a limited acquaintance with; a superficial knowledge of; inclosed, confined, restrained: [11]*lëk꜆ eu*[2] a deer-park; [12]*꜀hwong eu*[2] gardens and parks.

鼬[2] Yu. A kind of weasel or ferret, of a yellowish color, which destroys rats; a polecat; the motion of hair or feathers: [13]*꜀pieu eu*[2] the feather floats.

Eu[2]. A coll. word: to glaze, glazed; the glazing of earthen ware: *o*[2] *eu*[2] is glazed; *p'wak꜆ eu*[2] to put on glazing, to glaze.

(156) Ëü.

Ëü[2]. A coll. word: on fire, burning without flame: *ëü*[2] *tioh꜆* caught fire, is burning; *ëü*[2] *꜀wong*, burnt up, consumed.

預[2] Yü. To prepare, to provide for, to get ready; beforehand, already; prepared for, provided, ready; to confer with: [14]*ëü*[2] *꜀ngiong*, a prediction; [15]*ëü*[2] *꜀ki*, or [16]*ëü*[2] *ke*[2] to anticipate, to long for; COM., [17]*ëü*[2] *꜀siéng* (coll. *ëü*[2] *꜀seng*), formerly, previously; [18]*ëü*[2] *꜂cha ꜂ta saung*[2] to plan beforehand; [19]*ëü*[2] *pe*[2] (coll. *ëü*[2] *paing*[2]), to get ready beforehand; [20]*ëü*[2] *꜀chié*, to prepay, as wages.

豫[2] Yü. Interchanged with the last: a large elephant; easy, contented, idle, indulgent, taking one's pleasure; a jaunt, an excursion: *ëü*[2] *tai*[2] lazy; [21]*꜀sü hwong*[2] *ëü*[2] *꜀hwong*, think of the evil in time and guard against it; *ha*[2] *ëü*[2] *꜀ch'ũng ꜀ũng*, easily and leisurely; COM., *꜀iu ëü*[2] monkey and elephant; *met.*, to suspect, suspicious, hesitating.

---

[1]保佑 [2]佑助 [3]默佑 [4]柚子 [5]橘柚 [6]宥罪 [7]三宥 [8]原宥 [9]祈爲原宥 [10]侑食 [11]鹿囿 [12]園囿 [13]彪鼬 [14]預言 [15]預期 [16]預記 [17]預先 [18]預早打算 [19]預備 [20]預支 [21]思患豫防

蕷² Yü. A tuber or esculent root, called [1]˓sü ëü^2 resembling the yam, but with a coarse fiber; it is used as a stomachic.

與² Yü. Together with, joined to, connected with, interested in: also read ‘ü and ˓ü, q. v.: [2]ëü^2 ˓meu, to consult with; [3]˓u ëü^2 unconnected with; [4]˓kang ëü^2 to interfere in, meddling; [5]*pok, taik,* ëü^2 unable to engage in; [6]ëü^2 ˓ti, to know as others do; [7]˓hó ëü^2 what connection with? COM., [8]ëü^2 hong^2 (coll. ëü^2 sioh$_2$ hong^2), to have, or contribute, a share; concerned in.

譽² Yü. To praise, to extol, to laud, to eulogize; to cajole, to flatter, to overpraise: [9]*seu*^{2} ëü^2 to receive praise; [10]*pok,* ˓*ngü* ˓*chi* ëü^2 unexpected praise; COM., [11]˓*ming* ëü^2 fame, reputation.

裕² Yü. Rich in clothes and chattels; to enrich, to leave to; plenty, superabundant; in excess, supererogation; liberal, generous: [12]˓*ch‘üng* ëü^2 full, in abundance; [13]ëü^2 *kwok,* to make the state prosperous; COM., [14]ëü^2 ˓*ngwong, pwo*^{2} superior Soochow cloth, marked ëü^2 ˓*ngwong.*

喻² Yü. To know, to understand the import of; to make known, to proclaim, to manifest, to declare; to instruct, to teach, to explain; to compare, to illustrate; instructed, manifested; instruction: [15]‘*hieu* ëü^2 to cause to know; to comprehend, as teaching; [16]‘*p‘i* ëü^2 to illustrate, to compare; [17]*siéng*^{2} ëü^2 qualified to instruct.

諭² Yü. Interchanged with the last: orders, commands, injunctions, edicts, official notifications; to signify, to proclaim (to the people), to order; to reprove; to compare, a comparison: ëü^2 *se*^{2} a proclamation; [18]ëü^2 ‘*chi,* or *siong*^{2} ëü^2 the emperor's command; ‘*ch‘iu* ëü^2 your letter; COM., ‘*hieu* ëü^2 to proclaim, to cause to know; ëü^2 *wa*^{2} official orders; [19]*kau*^{2} ëü^2 a district superintendent of the Siutsai.

Ëu^2. A coll. word: to wear away, to impair or diminish by constant attrition: ëü^2 *k‘ó*^{2} worn, attrite, rubbed, as a book, shoe, etc.

(157) Ëüh.

喐, Yü. Read ëük,; used in the *Paik,* ˓*Ing* for the coll. ëüh,: a sound in the throat; to blow, to pant, to wheeze: ëüh, ëüh, *kieu*^{2} (spoken rapidly ˓ü ˓ü *kieu*^{2}), a guttural sound, grunting, as of a pig.

(158) Ëük.

郁, Yü. An ancient region, now in the S.E. of Kansuh and S.W. of Shensi; an ancient town in Shantung; elegant, as an essay: [20]ëük, ëük, brilliant, gorgeous; [21]*hok,* ëük, fragrance.

彧, Yü. Used for the last: beautiful, colored, brilliant; elegant, said of a polished gentleman: [22]ëük, ëük, flourishing.

燠, Yü. Also read ó^2: warmth, heat, internal heat: ˓*hang* ëük, cold and heat;

1 薯蕷 2 與謀 3 無與 4 干與 5 不得與 6 與知 7 何與 8 與份 9 受譽 10 不虞之譽 11 名譽 12 充裕 13 裕國 14 裕源布 15 曉喻 16 譬喻 17 善喻 18 諭旨 19 教諭 20 郁郁 21 馥郁 22 彧彧

ʼ*ok*, *ĕük*, summer-heat; *ˏang ʻch'iă ĕük*, quiet and warm withal.

薁ˀ Yü. A sort of fruit like a plum, called ¹*ˏing ĕük*, or *ĕük*, ʻ*li*; some say a species of wild grape.

噢ˀ Yü. Sad, sorrowful; sadness, sorrow, grief: ³*ĕük*, *ˏi*, inward grief; ⁴*ĕük*, *ˏhau*, a moan, as of one in pain.

旭ˀ Yü. Read *hĕük*, in the dictionaries: the rising sun, the dawn: ⁵*ĕük*, *nik*, sun-rising; ⁶*ĕük*, *ĕük*, joy over success—applied to the *mean* man.

頊ˀ To carry the head in a serious manner, to conduct gravely; attentive, grave: ⁷*ĕük*, *ĕük*, to lose self-possession; ⁸*ˏchiong ĕük*, the emperor who succeeded Hwangti, B.C. 2513.

(159) Ĕüng.

湧ˀ **湧**ˀ Yung. Read ʻ*üng* in the dictionaries: water welling up in a spring; bubbling; rising up, protruding; an affluent of the Yang-tsz-kiang in the north of Hupeh: ⁹*ˏhüng ĕüng*ˀ water bubbling up; COM., ¹⁰*ĕüng*ˀ ʻ*k'i*, to well up, as a spring; ¹¹*ĕüng*ˀ *ch'ok*, (water) gushing forth; ¹²*ĕüng*ˀ *ˏchiong se*ˀ the bubbling spring monastery (at Kushan).

擁ˀ Yung. To embrace, to hold or clasp in the bosom; to carry in the arms; to tuck up the dress, as in running; to screen, as the face; to conceal from; to gather round, as a crowd, to push forward, to throng: ¹³*eu*ˀ *ĕüng*ˀ to embrace with the right arm; ¹⁴*haiu*ˀ *ĕüng*ˀ the criers in the rear of an officer; ¹⁵*ĕüng*ˀ *chëüng*ˀ followers, the rear-guard; ¹⁶*ĕüng*ˀ *pe*ˀ to screen; COM., *ĕüng*ˀ ʻ*chá*, to press; crowding, as in a full street.

壅ˀ Yung. To stop with earth, to close up, to dam; to obstruct, to hinder, to prevent; to heap earth about plants; to conceal from: *tó*² *lo*² *ĕüng*ˀ *saik*, the road is blocked up; ¹⁷*ĕüng*ˀ *ˏü siong*² *ˏung*, to prevent complaints from reaching the emperor.

齆ˀ Yung. A disease in the nose; a stoppage or catarrh in the nose.

用² Yung. To use, to employ, to serve of; to cause; use or exercise of a thing; use, efficiency; serviceable; using, availing of; by, with, by means of; commonly, generally; expenses, outlays; the 101st radical: COM., ¹⁸*kwok*, *ĕüng*² expenses of the government; ¹⁹*ĕüng*² *ˏhing*, to inflict punishment; ²⁰*k'e*² *ĕüng*² utensils, tools; *chiék*, *ĕüng*² to economize; *ĕüng*² *ˏping*, to employ troops; *ĕüng*² ʻ*pwong*, to employ capital; ²¹*ĕüng*² *sëü*² an employé, servant; *ĕüng*² *to*² for current expenses; *ĕüng*² ʻ*pwo*, to use strengthening (food); ²²ʻ*iu ĕüng*² useful; *ĕüng*² *ˏsing*, careful, heedful; *pok*, *tĕüng*² *ĕüng*² unfit, worthless; *ĕüng*² *cheng*² *ˏsing ˏki*, to exhaust the ingenuity of the mind on it; *ˏt'ung ˏheng ˏt'ung ĕüng*² current and used every-

---

1 鬱薁　2 蘡薁　3 噢咿　4 噢咻　5 旭日　6 旭旭　7 頊頊　8 顓頊　9 洶湧　10 湧起　11 湧出　12 湧泉寺　13 右擁　擁○　14 後擁　15 擁從　16 擁蔽　17 壅於上聞　18 國用　19 用刑　20 器用　21 用事　22 有用

where, as money; COLL., *má*[3] *ĕüng*ʼ *tek*꜆ *tioh*꜆ cannot apply it to this use; ʻ*sai ĕüng*ʼ to use, to employ; *ĕüng*ʼ ꜀*nĕng*, to employ men.

潤ʼ Jun. To moisten, to wet; to enrich, to fatten; to benefit; to increase; moist, damp; rich, fat; glossy, velvety, shining, sleek, in good liking: [1]*ĕüng*ʼ *tek*꜆ to enrich, to fertilize; [2]꜀*chü ĕüng*ʼ to moisten; [3]*long ĕüng*ʼ glossy, sleek; COM., [4]*ĕüng*ʼ ꜀*hwo*, moist and even, as the temperature of the body; [5]*ĕüng*ʼ *hié*ʼ an internal emollient for the lungs; [6]*ĕüng*ʼ *pek*꜆ "to moisten the pencil"—presents of eatables to one going to the examinations; COLL., ʻ*chiă* ꜀*tʻu* ʻ*yă ĕüng*ʼ this ground is very moist.

(160) Ha.

哈 ꜀ 嗬 ꜀ Ho. The 1st read *hak*꜆ and *hak*꜆; the 2d also read ʻ*ha*: used for the coll. ꜀*ha*, as in [7]꜀*ha* ꜀*ha chʻieu*ʼ noise of laughing; [8]꜀*ha* ꜀*ha* ꜀*ha twai*ʼ *chʻieu*ʼ a loud, hearty laugh.

*Ha*ʼ. A coll. word, used in answering to a call.

孝ʼ Hsiao. Read *hau*ʼ; used for the coll. *ha*ʼ: mourning, funereal: [9]*tai*ʼ *ha*ʼ to wear mourning; [10]*ha*ʼ *huk*꜆ mourning apparel; [11]*ha*ʼ ꜀*diéng*, a white cotton curtain hung before the coffin; [12]*ha*ʼ *tʻiong*ʼ the mourning staff—it is covered with white paper and carried by sons of the deceased; [13]*ha*ʼ ʻ*mwoang*, the period of mourning (27 months) ended.

霞 ꜀ Sia. Clouds tinged with red; vapor, smokiness: COM., [14]꜀*hung* ꜀*ha*, clouds and crimson vapor; [15]꜀*ha* ʻ*pʻwo kaing*ʼ the chief district of Fuhning prefecture; ꜀*ha* ʻ*pʻwo* ꜀*ká*, a street in Nantai (Foochow) at the north base of Great Temple Hill; [16]꜀*ha* ꜀*niong* ʻ*sang ho*ʼ two female idols in "*Bloody Pool*" temple; COLL., ꜀*ĕng* ꜀*ha*, crimson clouds; ꜀*ha* ꜀*ĕng*, lightish red.

瘕 ꜀ Hsia. A female complaint: [17]꜀*hong* ꜀*ha*, a scar, cicatrix. Read ʻ*ka*: chronic pain in the stomach: ꜀*ting* ʻ*ka*, intestinal concretions; ꜀*ngieu* ʻ*ka*, small worms in the intestines.

遐 ꜀ Hsia. Remote, distant from; why? what? [18]꜀*ha* ʻ*i*, far and near; ꜀*ha* ꜀*cheu*, distant retreats.

蝦 ꜀ 鰕 ꜀ Hsia. Small crustaceans; a shrimp, a prawn, a craw fish: the first is commonly used: COM., [19]ʻ*hai* ꜀*ha*, sea crawfish; ꜀*ha chiong*ʼ pickled shrimp relishes; ꜀*ha* ꜀*üng*, fresh shrimps minced and boiled; [20]꜀*ha* ꜀*ma*, a toad; COLL., ꜀*ha* ꜀*kʻu*, a long flat crustacean with short feelers; ꜀*kʻiu kaĕng*ʼ ꜀*ha* ꜀*kʻu sioh*꜆ *yong*ʼ cuddled up like a crustacean; ꜀*ha* ꜀*ing*, or ꜀*ha* ꜀*ning*, prawn meat; ꜀*ha* ꜀*chʻiu*, the feelers of a crawfish; ꜀*ha* ʻ*mi*, small shrimps dried; ꜀*ha chak*꜆ assorted prawns; ꜀*ha* ꜀*chʻiéng*, shrimps in pickle; ꜀*ha* ꜀*chiăng piék*꜆ *kwai*ʼ shrimp-sprites and turtle monsters; *met.*, weak, insignificant people; ꜀*ha* ꜀*ma* ʻ*siong*

---

[1] 潤澤 [2] 滋潤 [3] 朗潤 [4] 潤和 [5] 潤肺 [6] 潤筆 [7] 哈哈笑 [8] 哈哈哈大笑 [9] 帶孝 [10] 孝服 [11] 孝㡘 [12] 孝杖 [13] 孝滿 [14] 雲霞 [15] 霞浦縣〇 [16] 霞娘産婦 [17] 痕瘕 [18] 遐邇 [19] 海蝦 [20] 蝦蟆

siăh, *ˏt'iéng ˎngié*, a toad thinking to eat a wild goose; *met.*, one who attempts things beyond his ability.

瑕 ˎ Sia. A blemish in a gem; a crack, a flaw; a fault, a bad habit; distant, separated: [1]*ʻch'ek*, *ˎha*, carnation-colored gems; [2]*ˎha ˏchü*, a mistake, an inadvertence; [3]*pok*, *ʻnü ˎha ˏchü*, I do not consider you guilty.

ˎHa. A coll. word, as in *ˎha ʻtiăng*, soon, shortly, after awhile; *ˎha ʻtiăng k'ó*ˀ will go shortly; *ˏtang ˎmó ˎeng ˎha ʻtiăng siăh*, no leisure now, will eat soon.

下[2] Hsia. Below, down, bottom; inferior, mean, vulgar; next; to descend, to go down; to put, as the hand; to fall, as rain; to sprinkle, as powders: as a verb, often read *ʻa* in the Classics; in coll., read *a*[2] q. v.: COM., [4]*siong*[2] *ha*[2] above and below; [5]*ha*[2] *ˎping*, [6]*ha*[2] *k'ëü*ˀ and [7]*ha*[2] *ik*, the 5th, 7th, and 8th tones of the Foochow dialect; [8]*ha*[2] *ʻp'ing*, of an inferior class; [9]*ˎmwong ha*[2] pupils; *ha*[2] *ˏchieu laiu*[2] to sprinkle seasoning on; *k'aik*, *ha*[2] or *ʻngang ha*[2] at this instant; [10]*ha*[2] *ʻü*, to rain; *ha*[2] *ʻchüng*, to plant seeds; *met.*, to inoculate; [11]*kóh*, *ha*[2] or *ˏtai ha*[2] your excellency! *ha*[2] *ʻk'au ha*[2] *ngwong*[2] to utter vows, as in invoking curses on enemies before an idol; [12]*ha*[2] *k'e*ˀ to keep down the temper; *ha*[2] *ʻch'iu*, to put the hand to; to seize one; [13]*ha*[2] *pek*, to use the pen, to write; *pok*, *siong*[2] *pok*, *ha*[2] neither up nor down; *met.*, in straits, in a fix; COLL., *ha*[2] *lóh*, to put down into; a way of managing; *ˏtang o*ˀ *ha*[2] *lóh*, now there's a way to do it!

夏[2] Hsia. Summer; a mansion; clear; variegated; name of a dynasty: [14]*ˏtüng ha*[2] China; COM., [15]*ha*[2] *ˏt'iéng*, or *ha*[2] *kié*ˀ the summer season; [16]*ha*[2] *pwo*ˀ grass-cloth; *ha*[2] *ˏi*, summer clothes; [17]*ha*[2] *ˎtieu*, the Hia Dynasty (B. C. 2205–1766); [18]*lik*, *ha*[2] the 7th solar term, beginning of summer; *maing*[2] *ha*[2], *tëüng*[2] *ha*[2] and *kié*ˀ *ha*[2] the 4th, 5th, and 6th months; *ha*[2] *ʻkwi* steamed rice cakes—eaten at the *lik*, *ha*[2] term; COLL., *ha*[2] *che*ˀ *nik*, *ch'ok*, *ʻhwi*, at the summer solstice the sun emits fire—is very hot.

厦[2] Hsia. A mansion; a side room: [19]*tai*[2] *ha*[2] a spacious house; [20]*ˎhwa ha*[2] a showy mansion.

暇[2] Sia. Leisure, relaxation; self-indulgence; unoccupied: [21]*ˏhiu ha*[2] or *ha*[2] *ëü*[2] relaxation, ease; COM., *ˎhang ha*[2] at leisure; [22]*chëü*[2] *ko*ˀ *pok*, *ha*[2] no time to look after one's self.

Ha[2]. A coll. word: to transport, to convey; to carry from place to place in a boat or carriage: *ha*[2] *ʻmi*, to transport rice; *ha*[2] *sié*ˀ *nóh*, what are you transporting? *ha*[2] *ˎsung*, to convey (goods) by boat; *ha*[2] *sioh*, *sai*[2] to carry one boat load; *ha*[2] *kwo*ˀ *ʻhai*, to bring over the sea.

(161) Há.

ˏHá. A coll. word, expressing assent to another's statement, yes! it's so!

[1]赤瑕 [2]瑕疵 [3]不汝瑕疵 [4]上下 [5]下平 [6]下去 [7]下入 [8]下品 [9]門下 [10]下雨 [11]閣下 [12]下氣 [13]下筆 [14]中夏 [15]夏天 [16]夏布 [17]夏朝 [18]立夏 [19]大厦 [20]華厦 [21]休暇 [22]自顧不暇

福州方言拼音字典

ʻ睨 Ni. Read ʻngá; coll. ʻhá: to look aslant, or askance at; glancing the eyes: ʻhá móʼ to cast hateful glances at; [1]ʻhá ˓nëng, to leer at people; [2]ʻhá ˓sang ˓hwa, to stare till the eyes are dim; [3]piék˒ ʻhá laungʼ the turtle stares at its eggs; [4]˓mó ˓ngü ʻhá ʻlai, catching no fish he stares at his basket; *met.*, to pursue a less, in default of a greater, business.

Háʼ. A coll. word: an exclamation of grief or fear: *háʼ háʼ kieuʼ* sobbing, moaning.

˓Há. A coll. word, as in *˓há háh˒* a mocking, irritating tone; to sneer at; to make fun of; *˓há ˓há kieuʼ* sighing, sobbing, the same as *háʼ háʼ kieuʼ* q.v.

蟹ʼ 蠏ʼ Hsieh. Also read ʻhai and haiʼ: a crab: [5]˓pong háʼ crabs; com., [6]háʼ ˓keng, crab-soup; coll., [7]˓mó háʼ crabs with hairy claws; ˓mó háʼ ˓k'au k'eʼ hairy-clawed crabs and persimmons—said to be a poisonous dish breeding leprosy.

Háʼ. A coll. word: to sob, to cry, to whimper, as a child: *chaiʼ háʼ sioh˒ ˓siäng* (or *kwoʼ*) *ʻngwai cheuʼ p'ah˒* whimper once more, and I'll whip you!

Háʼ. A coll. word, as in *háʼ lóh˒ ˓li*, to settle or sag down, as the collar of a coat when unbuttoned; *háʼ háʼ tioh˒* settling, sagging down.

(162) Haë.

Haëʼ. A coll. word: to call out, to shout at, to vociferate, as before officers and idols: *chóʼ ˓ë haëʼ* to be a lictor or crier; a company of lictors; *haëʼ ʻhwang ˓t'iëng*, to cry loud enough to turn the heavens!

Haëʼ. A coll. word: to shame, to disgrace; to insult: *haëʼ ʻsieu ʻlá*, to shame one by drawing the fore-finger over the cheek and crying out *haëʼ*; *haëʼ ˓nëng ˓mó mengʼ ˓p'ú*, to reproach one for being shameless; *haëʼ haëʼ ˓t'ié ˓mu ˓wong*, shame! shame! you big cry-baby!

(163) Haëk.

蓄˒ Ch'u. Read hëük˒; coll. haëk˒: to collect, to get or buy for use: [8]haëk˒ peʼ to buy female slaves; [9]haëk˒ ngiék˒ to purchase property; [10]haëk˒ ˓nëng, or [11]haëk˒ ˓nëng ˓këng, to hire workmen; [12]haëk˒ ˓tong ˓këng (or chóʼ), to hire steady work; [13]haëk˒ ʻlá siäh˒ puongʼ employed to eat rice!—as said when workmen are lazy or too many.

(164) Haëng.

釁ʼ Hsing. Read hengʼ; coll. haëngʼ: a swelling on the person: [14]haëngʼ ʻk'i ˓li, to swell up; [15]haëngʼ ˓t'ong, puffed from (washing in) hot water, as a cut; [16]haëngʼ haëngʼ yék˒ an inflamed swelling; [17]haëngʼ hok˒ puffed into a small lump.

巷ʼ Hsiang. A lane, an alley; a street of dwellings: com., [18]˓küng haëngʼ the 2d of the "seven alleys" in the city of Foochow; [19]˓ká haëngʼ streets and alleys; ˓hwa ˓ká ʻliu haëngʼ "flower street and willow alley"—a locality of brothels; coll., ˓hëng haëngʼ alleys; haëngʼ ˓t'au, or

[1]睨仸 [2]睨生花 [3]鼈睨蛋 [4]毛魚睨籃 [5]螃蠏 [6]蠏羹 [7]毛蠏 [8]蓄婢 [9]蓄業 [10]蓄仸 [11]蓄仸工 [12]蓄長工 [18]蓄禮食飯 [14]釁起梨 [15]釁湯 [16]釁釁熱 [17]釁核 [18]宮巷 [19]街巷

haëngˀ ʻ*kʻau*, the entrance of an alley; *haëngˀ* ʻ*kiăng haëngˀ* ˏ*nié*, small alleys; *haëngˀ* ʻ*chieu kʻëük*ˎ *siăh*ˎ *sá*ˀ the alleys few, the beggars many; *met.*, little work with many to do it; supply small, demand great.

焮 [1] Hsien. Read ˏ*hüng*; coll. *haëngˀ*: to throw out heat; heat reflected or beating in, as through a window: [1]*haëngˀ haëngˀ yék*ˎ hot from the reflection; [2]*haëngˀ* ˏ*ta*, dried by the reflected heat; [3]*haëngˀ sük*ˎ matured by the warmth, as fruit; *haëngˀ* ˏ*niăng*, scorched yellow.

(165) Háh.

*Háh*ˎ. A coll. word, as in ˏ*há háh*ˎ to sneer at, to jeer; a sneering, mocking tone; to tease by saying ˏ*há háh*ˎ as to a crying child.

(166) Hai.

ʻ哈 Ho. To laugh and joke; to smile at, to ridicule; in the coll., an exclamation of surprise or astonishment.

ʻ海 Hai. The sea, ocean; the receptacle of rivers; maritime, marine: COM., [4]ʻ*hai* ˏ*yong*, an ocean; [5]*kwoˀ* ʻ*hai*, to cross the sea; [6]*chʻok*ˎ ʻ*hai*, to voyage; [7]ʻ*hai chʻek*ˎ pirates; [8]*seüˀ* ʻ*hai* ˏ*chi nói*ˀ within the four seas—i.e., the world; [9]ʻ*hai liongˀ* capacity like the sea; [10]ʻ*hai eˀ* marine delicacies; [11]ʻ*hai* ˏ*seng*, beche-de-mer; [12]ʻ*hai* ˏ*hwong* (spoken ʻ*hai* ˏ*wong*), the superintendent of maritime customs; [13]ʻ*hai ongˀ* transport-junks; [14]ʻ*hai* ˏ*kwang*, a port of entry, a custom house; [15]ʻ*hai* ˏ*lüng* ˏ*wong*, Neptune, god of rain; [16]*siongˀ* ʻ*hai*, Shanghai; *hok*ˎ ˏ*ü* ˏ*tung* ʻ*hai*, happiness like the east sea; COLL., [17]ʻ*hai kaëk*, "corners of the sea"—i.e., distant regions; ʻ*hai uaˀ* "sea talk"; *met.*, tales, yarns; ʻ*hai* ʻ*tá* ˏ*mwo* ˏ*cheng*, feeling for a needle on the bottom of the sea; *met.*, difficult, impracticable; ʻ*hai* ˏ*hwo siongˀ* the sea Budhist—a smooth-headed fish; ʻ*hai tʻaungˀ* a flood tide.

ʻ盒 ʻ榼 Ho. A wine vessel made of pewter; an amphora; earthen ones are sometimes so called: COM., [18]ʻ*chiu* ʻ*hai*, a wine vessel.

ʻ醢 Ho. Seasoned, minced meat, pickled in brine; the brine in which meat is pickled; to simmer: [19]ʻ*tʻang* ʻ*hai* ʻ*i chiéngˀ* to offer minced pickles in sacrifice.

喊ˀ Hai. To cry out, to bawl; in the coll., an exclamation of surprise, as on dropping something: [20]*hak*ˎ *haiˀ* to vociferate.

ˏ孩 Hai. An infant beginning to laugh; a child, children, youth; generally applied to boys: [21]ˏ*hai* ˏ*tʻüng*, insects; COM., ˏ*hai* ˏ*i*, a child, boys; COLL., ˏ*hai* ˏ*i kʻwaˀ* ˏ*leng*, boys treading on the lotus—as pictured on lanterns at New Year's; ˏ*hai* ˏ*kʻá* ˏ*pung*, "the boy-torrent has burst"—used in cursing noisy children.

ˏ頦 Hai. Bones of the chin; the chin: COLL., *pah*ˎ ˏ*hai*, the chin gapes; *met.*, you're lying! ˏ*hai pah*ˎ ˏ*hai tʻok*ˎ

[1]焮 乾 洋 海 海 量 參 運 龍 [17]海 [19]醢 [20]喝
焮 [3]焮 [5]過 [7]海 之 [10]海 [12]海 [14]海 王 角 醢 喊
熱 熟 海 賊 內 味 防 關 [16]上 [18]酒 以 [21]孩
[2]焮 [4]海 [6]出 [8]四 [9]海 [11]海 [13]海 [15]海 海 榼 薦 蟲

"your chin gapes and drops"—as said to a mendacious person. Read ˏ*kai;* ugly, ill-favored.

骸 ˏHai. Shin of the leg (tibia); bones of the human frame; bodily members: [1]ˏ*kŭng* ˏ*hai,* sinews and bones; [2]*lĕk*ˏ ˏ*hai,* the trunk, head, hands and feet; [3]ʻ*ngu* ˏ*kwang paik*ˏ ˏ*hai,* the five faculties and whole frame; COM., [4]ˏ*hai kauk*ˏ human bones, a skeleton.

諧 ˏHai. To harmonize, to agree, to pair; consenting; in concord, of one mind; to laugh at, to ridicule: [5]ˏ*hwi* ˏ*hai,* to ridicule; COM., [6]ˏ*hwo* ˏ*hai,* to harmonize; cordial, agreeing, as a married pair.

咳 ˏHai. The laugh or smile of a child; used in the coll. as an exclamation of surprise or pity, ah! alas! also a cry of burden-bearers. Read *k'ai*ʼ as in [7]*k'ai*ʼ *sau*ʼ to cough: [8]ˏ*kang k'ai*ʼ a dry, irritating cough.

硋 ˏHai. A coll. character: crockery: [9]ˏ*hai k'e*ʼ crockery-ware; [10]ˏ*hai* ˏ*yeu,* a pottery-kiln; ˏ*sieu* ˏ*hai,* to burn crockery; ˏ*hai kwang*ʼ an earthen pot.

亥^{2} Hai. A horary character, the 12th of the Branches, answering to boar: COM., [11]*hai*^{2} ˏ*tü,* the year "boar", as marking the time of one's birth; [12]*hai*^{2} ˏ*niéng,* years of the cycle containing this character; [13]*hai*^{2} *ngwok*ˏ the 10th month; [14]*hai*^{2} ˏ*si,* 9–11 o'clock, P.M.

閡^{2} Hai. Also read *ngai*^{2} in the dictionaries: to shut, to prevent entrance; stopped, hindered, obstructed: [15]*kaik*ˏ *hai*^{2} cut off from; *met.,* not comprehending; not agreeing in opinion.

械^{2} Hsieh. Military weapons; a spear, a bow; shackles, fetters: [16]ˏ*ki hai*^{2} a curious contrivance, delicate machinery; *met.,* cunning; COM., [17]*k'e*ʼ *hai*^{2} military weapons; COLL., *hai*^{2} *taiu*ʼ to be at feud, as two villages.

懈^{2} **解**^{2} Hsieh. Remiss, slow, negligent, inattentive; the 2nd also read ʻ*kai* and *ká*^{2} q.v.: [18]*sëük*ˏ *yá*^{2} ʻ*p'i hai*^{2} busy morning and night; COM., [19]*hai*^{2} *tai*^{2} lazily, slowly.

廨^{2} Hsieh. Read ʻ*kai* and *kai*ʼ in the dictionaries: a hall, suite of rooms: [20]ˏ*kung hai*^{2} a court, apartments.

獬^{2} Hsieh. A fabulous animal, called [21]*hai*^{2} *chai*^{2} the lion-unicorn, embroidered on the robes of censors and judges; *met.,* haughty, stern.

薤^{2} Hsieh. Chives, a kind of scallions which a person fasting is not allowed to eat: COLL., [22]*hai*^{2} *pah*ˏ chive-whites—i. e., the bulbs used medicinally.

㖷^{2} Hai. Also read *hai*ʼ: to cry out, to bawl; used in the coll. as a word of prohibition, stop that! you must not!

---

1 筋骸 2 六骸 3 五關百骸 4 骸骨 5 詼諧 6 和諧 7 咳嗽 8 乾咳 9 硋器 10 硋窰 11 亥猪 12 亥年 13 亥月 14 亥時 15 隔閡 16 機械 17 器械 18 夙夜匪懈 19 懈怠 20 公廨 21 獬豸 22 薤白

邂 ² Hsieh. Accidentally, a pleasant hap: *hai*² *haiu*² an unexpected meeting.

害 ² Hai. To injure, to hurt; to prejudice, to offend; to damage; noxious, calamitous; a sense or fear of, a feeling: COM., [1]*꜀chang hai*² to injure; [2]*꜀siong hai*² to wound, wounded; [3]*le*² *hai*² severe, hurtful, formidable; *met.*, stingy; [4]*꜀chai hai*² calamity; [5]*꜀hwong hai*² opposing and injurious, a risk; [6]*pie*² *hai*² to avoid calamity; [7]*tuk꜀ hai*² to poison; COLL., *hai*² *꜀ing hai*² *ʻki hai*² *che*² *꜀sing*, in injuring others you injure yourself; *hai*² *tek꜀ ʻch'ang*, to injure most grievously; *hai*² *꜀nëng p'ok꜀ ʻwang chiok꜀ sik꜀* to injure persons till their bowls are turned down (empty) and subsistence cut of. Read *hak꜀*: why not? how not?

(167) Haik.

血 ꜀ Hsieh. Read *hiek꜀*; coll. *haik꜀*: blood: [8]*haik꜀ mah꜀* blood and pulse; *met.*, race, stock; [9]*haik꜀ ꜀si*, small particles of blood; [10]*haik꜀ le*² dysentery; [11]*haik꜀ k'e*ʾ blood and breath—vigor, bodily stamina; [12]*k'e*ʾ *haik꜀ ꜀soi*, the constitution debilitated; [13]*ʻpwo haik꜀* to renew the blood (by tonics); [14]*këük꜀ haik꜀* coagulated blood; [15]*o*ʾ *haik꜀* effused blood, as in parturition; [16]*haik꜀ ʻpwong*, capital in trade; *haik꜀ ꜀tie*, the soft spot below the shoulder joint; *haik꜀ kwai*ʾ lumps of coagulated blood in the system; [17]*haik꜀ ꜀hu*, charms (written) in blood; *haik꜀ ꜀sang ꜀pung*, menstrual flooding; *haik꜀ ꜀ling ꜀ling*, profuse bleeding; *haik꜀ kang*² bloody sweat; *met.*, excessive toil.

黑 ꜀ Hei. Black, sooty; dark, obscure; cloudy, dull; *met.*, wicked, malicious: [18]*haik꜀ ʻchü*, dark moles on the skin; COM., [19]*haik꜀ ang*ʾ pitchy dark; *haik꜀ p'ieng*ʾ to deceive maliciously; [20]*haik꜀ yä*² night; *haik꜀ pek꜀ ꜀nang ꜀hung*, difficult to distinguish the bad from the good; COLL., *꜀sing ꜀kang haik꜀ saik꜀* black-hearted, malicious; *haik꜀ chiong*ʾ darkish purple.

赫 ꜀ Hê. Bright, splendid, luminous, like a fire or the sun; angry; to scorch, to glisten: [21]*haik꜀ no*² very angry; *haik꜀ haik꜀* fiery, as the sky in a drought; glorious, effulgent; COM., *ʻhieng haik꜀* brightly displayed, effulgent.

嚇 ꜀ Hsia. An angry tone; to threaten, to intimidate, to anger; scared, frightened: in the coll. read *hiah꜀*, q.v.: [22]*haik꜀ cha*ʾ to terrify by threats.

(168) Haing.

橫 ʾ Hêng. Perverse, obstinate, unreasonable; crabbed, cross-grained, mulish; disagreeing with others: also read *꜀hwang*, q.v.: [23]*haing*ʾ *ngik꜀* refractory, perverse; COM., *haing*ʾ *꜀heng*, to act unreasonably; headstrong; COLL., *haing*ʾ *haing*ʾ or *ʻyä haing*ʾ insufferably mulish.

莧 ʾ Hsien. An edible species of spinach, called *haing*ʾ *ch'ai*ʾ: COM., *haing*ʾ *ch'ai*ʾ *mieng*² spinach and vermicelli; *꜀hwang haing*ʾ a kind of spinach—used medicinally.

---

1 殘害 2 傷害 3 利害 4 災害 5 妨害 6 避害 7 毒害 8 血脉 9 血絲 10 血痢 11 血氣 12 氣血衰 13 補血 14 掬血 15 瘀血 16 血本 17 血符 18 黑子 19 黑暗 20 黑夜 21 赫怒 22 嚇詐 23 橫逆

荇 [2] Hsing. Also read haing2: an aquatic vegetable, a kind of duck-weed with white stalk and reddish leaf—used in wine to communicate a rich, delicate flavor.

幸 [2] Hsing. Fortunate, lucky, blessed; happily; an emperor reaching, or tarrying in, a place; to hope, to wait or long for; lucky in getting; to rejoice; to love, pleased: [1]'ke haing2 to hope for; [2]ˌhó haing2 how so lucky? COM., [3]pok, haing2 unlucky; [4]ˌka ˌmwong pok, haing2 a domestic misfortune—words used on cards, as at the death of the eldest son; COLL., haing2 tek, fortunately.

倖 [2] Hsing. Interchanged with the last: to obtain or avoid without merit or right; lucky, fortunate: [5]haing2 cheng2 undeservedly promoted; [6]haing2 neng2 to use flattery; COM., [7]'hieu haing2 a lucky hit, to get by a fortunate coincidence.

行 [2] Hsing. Actions, conduct: also read ˌheng and ˌhong, q. v.: COM., [8]taik, haing2 virtuous deeds; [9]'p'ing haing2 conduct, character; [10]ˌngiong haing2 words and acts; [11]ˌsing haing2 the disposition, intention, as good or bad; COLL., tuk, ˌsing ch'au2 haing2 a venomous heart and vile conduct; haing2 tëk, (his) acts (are) malicious.

杏 [2] Hsing. A kind of plum: COM., [12]haing2 ˌhwa ˌhiong sek, 'li, "the almond fragrance extends ten 'li"—a poetical phrase; [13]ˌngüng haing2 white almonds; one says, nuts of the Salisburia adiantifolia; [14]haing2 ˌing, almonds; [15]haing2 lok, ˌt'ong, an emulsion of almonds, rice, and sugar.

(169) Haiu.

候 [2] Hou. To wait; to inquire for; to wait on; to visit, to congratulate; to take care of; a time: COM., [16]'sëü haiu2 to wait upon, to serve; [17]ong2 haiu2 to inquire after, to send respects; haiu2 ka2 I wait for you, Sir! [18]ˌsi haiu2 time; haiu2 'song, to wait for selection or appointment; haiu2 'pwo 'hu, to wait for appointment, as prefect; haiu2 ˌchié, "waiting to redeem (our bills)"—a bank notice.

後 [2] Hou. After in time, late; behind; then, next; posterity, descendants: in the coll. read hau2 and au2 q.v.: COM., ˌchiëng haiu2 before and after; [19]haiu2 ˌlai, hereafter; [20]haiu2 ch'ëü2 the 2nd wife—after the death of the first; haiu2 hok, I, your pupil; haiu2 hwoi2 'iu ˌki, there'll be a time of meeting again; [21]haiu2 pwoi2 of the next class in age, juniors; kwo2 haiu2 after passing away—after death; COLL., haiu2 ˌpong, the next set or company; hereafter; haiu2 ˌsing, or haiu2 'ch'iu, afterwards; haiu2 t'óh, successors—scil., good or bad, as sons; ˌseng ˌnëng chó2 haiu2 ˌnëng ˌtiong, former people did so, and their successors perpetuate it.

堠 [2] Hou. A bank or tumulus, used to make fire signals on; milestones, a half or a whole league apart.

1 冀幸　2 何幸　3 不幸　4 家門不幸　5 倖進　6 倖佞　7 徼倖　8 德行　9 品行　10 言行　11 心行　12 杏花香十里　13 銀杏　14 杏仁　15 杏酪湯　16 伺候　17 問候　18 時候　19 後來　20 後娶　21 後輩

厚[2] Hou. Thick, large, substantial; liberal, generous, kind; well, very; faithful, intimate; well-flavored; rich, as soil; to esteem: COM., [1]*haiu*[2] *pok*˛ thick and thin, liberal and stingy; [2]*˛ing haiu*[2] kind, benevolent; [3]*˛ch'ing haiu*[2] intimate; [4]*haiu*[2] *tëüng*[2] grave, dignified; fat and heavy, as persons; [5]*haiu*[2] *tai*[2] to treat well; [6]*haiu*[2] *˛ong*, great favor; [7]*haiu*[2] *ē*[2] a rich flavor; [8]*haiu*[2] *ē*[2] a generous mind; [9]*haiu*[2] *p'auk*˒ a kind of medicinal bark; COLL., *haiu*[2] *haiu*[2] *saëng*[2] *'nü*, make you a liberal present; *haiu*[2] *pok*˛ *˛tu se*[2] *ē*[2] liberal or scant, still the *intention* is entirely (good).

后[2] Hou. A queen or empress; a prince or ruler; a tributary sovereign; behind: COM., [10]*˛hwong haiu*[2] the empress; [11]*˛hwong t'ai*[2] *haiu*[2] the empress dowager; [12]*t'ai*[2] *˛hwong t'ai*[2] *haiu*[2] the emperor's grandmother; [13]*haiu*[2] *'t'u*, gods of the land—worshiped on the left of the grave; [14]*˛t'iéng haiu*[2] or *˛t'iéng haiu*[2] *seng*[2] *'mu*, the Chinese Amphitrite—goddess of seamen.

逅[2] Hou. To meet unexpectedly; pleased, delighted to meet; unsettled: [15]*hai*[2] *haiu*[2] pleased to meet.

(170) Hak.

瞎˒ Hsia. Blind of one eye; wholly blind; *met.*, ignorant, uneducated: COM., [16]*hak*˒ *'chü*, a blind person; COLL., *hak*˒ *˛chü*, or *hak*˒ *'kiäng*, a blind man; *˛kwong hak*˒ the eyes open but sightless; *hak*˒ *kaë*[2] or *hak*˒ *nau*[2] to bawl, as a blind man—talking at random; *hak*˒ *˛chü ˛t'iäng ˛siäng*, the blind hear the voice; *met.*, to depend on information only; *hak*˒ *'kiäng k'e*[2] *mek*˛ *˛chiu ˛kwong*, the blind so angry that their eyes open; *met.*, a high degree of virtuous indignation.

喝˒ Ho. To call out loudly, to hoot, to shout at; to reprove, to reprimand; an angry hoot; a guttural, gurgling, choking sound: COM., [17]*hak*˒ *leng*[2] to shout the orders, as a leader in a mob; [18]*hak*˒ *laung*[2] *tai*[2] *˛sing*, the great god who hoots at the waves; *met.*, an outrageous scold; [19]*hak*˒ *'chwi ˛ngang*, gurgling-water rock—a spring near Kushan monastery; *hak*˒ *'chwi ˛sing ˛ping*, to congeal water into ice; *met.*, to succeed in every thing; [20]*hak*˒ *tó*[2] to clear the way, as lictors; *met.*, to bawl; COLL., *˛heng hak*˒ to reprove in a loud tone; *hak*˒ *nau*[2] *hak*˒ *kaë*[2] noisy vociferation; *hak*˒ *'ch'ai*, to applaud, to cry out "good! fine!" *hak*˒ *sioh*˛ *˛siäng ˛ngié piéng*[2] *chó*[2] *ak*˒ gave a hoot (loud enough) to change a goose into a duck; *met.*, to scare one out of his wits by hooting; *hak*˒ *˛toi*, to bargain for in the lump.

嗄˒ Hsia. Read *ha*[2]; used in the *Paik*˒ *˛Ing* for the coll. *hak*˒: the voice hoarse or broken; the sound of cracked earthen or metal ware: *˛siäng ˛ing hak*˒ the voice is hoarse; [21]*hak*˒ *˛siäng*, or *hak*˒ *hak*˒ *˛siäng*, a broken voice; a clattering, as of cracked metal.

[1]厚薄 [2]仁厚 [3]親厚 [4]厚重 [5]厚待 [6]厚恩 [7]厚味 [8]厚意 [9]厚朴 [10]皇后 [11]皇太后 [12]太皇太后 [13]后土 [14]天后 [15]邂逅 [16]瞎子 [17]喝令 [18]喝浪大神 [19]喝水巖 [20]喝道 [21]嗄聲

***Hak*,** A coll. word: to whet, to strop; also to sneeze; *₍tó hak*, *ʻkwi a'* strop the knife a few strokes; *hak, chʻe'* to sneeze; *chʻe' hak, ʻkwi chiăh,* to sneeze a few times.

合 Ho. 2 To unite, to join; to shut, to close; to collect, to convene; accordant to, agreeable, harmonious, suitable; a pair; the whole; united, together, with; a measure, about 1/10 of a *₍ching;* in the coll., to settle, to pay off a score; cheap, not dear; to break, to snap: [1]*₍tʻiĕng chauk, ₍chi hak*, marriages made in heaven; COM., [2]*₍chá hak*, joined together; [3]*hak ʻchiong,* to join the palms; [4]*hak ʻchiong ₍ká,* the street between opposite shops; [5]*hak kĕŭng'* all together, the sum total; [6]*hak ʻking,* shut or joined closely; *hak ₍ku,* a kind of child's cape; [7]*₍hwo hak* harmonious; [8]*hak ₍ngi,* suitable; [9]*hak ʻngang,* suiting the eyes, as spectacles do; [10]*hak chaung'* buried together; [11]*hak ₍sing,* of the same mind; [12]*hak sek,* "suits the pattern"—suitable, cheap; [13]*hak ₍ka,* all the family; [14]*hak chĕŭng' kwok,* the United States; COLL., *hak pwoi' tʻeng'* or *hak ₍chiĕng tʻeng'* to double one's capital by profits; *hak ₍chiĕng ʻkʻi ₍ka ek,* to double the capital and a tenth more; *hak ₍pwang,* a cheap lot of goods; *hak ₍chiĕng,* to break, snap asunder; *hak ₍chʻing,* to settle up; *hak ₍chiĕng ʻmwoi* to pay up the balance; *sioh hak* a pair; *hak ₍siĕng,* or *hiăk ₍siĕng,* hinges; *hak chʻioh,* a folding foot-measure; *hak tóh,* a pair of tables.

洽 Hsia. 2 Used for the last: to join pleasantly, to harmonize; united, blending; to instill into; imbued, pervaded with: [15]*₍ŭng hak* to blend, to mix; [16]*ʻpʻwo hak* pervading.

鞈 2 Also read *kak*: a knee-pad of leather; a sort of leathern sash or apron for soldiers.

闔 Ho. 2 A leaf of a door, a two-leaved door; all within doors, a family; to shut, to close; the whole, altogether; why not? [17]*hak pik* to shut and open; COM., [18]*hak ₍ka,* the whole family.

盍 Ho. 2 To cover over; to unite for a purpose; why not? *hak ₍kwi ₍hu ₍lai,* why not return home? [19]*hak kauk, ₍ngiong ʻi chė'* why do you not each reveal your wishes?

鶡 Ho. 2 The Tartar pheasant, which is gregarious and pugnacious—a symbol of courage: [20]*hak ₍kwang,* a helmet with plumes of pheasant's feathers; *hak tang'* a thrush that sings at night.

曷 Ho. 2 Why? why not? how? wherefore? to stop by an order; to intimidate, to hoot at: *hak kik,* where are its limits? limitless; *hak ₍ung ₍neng ₍lai,* how can you say he will come?

暍 Ho. 2 Also read *hiok,* in the dictionaries: warm, hot; injured by the sun's heat, a sun-stroke: COLL., *hak tioh nik ʻhwi,* struck by

[1]天作之合 [2]齊合 [3]合掌 [4]合掌街〇 [5]合共 [6]合緊 [7]和合 [8]合宜 [9]合眼 [10]合葬 [11]合心 [12]合式 [13]合家 [14]合衆國 [15]融洽 [16]溥洽 [17]闔闢 [18]闔家 [19]盍各言爾志 [20]鶡冠

the sun's heat; *móh, k'ó' nik, 'hwi 'lá hak,* don't go into the sun's heat and get a stroke!

嗑 Ho. Loquacious: [1]*'sié' hak,* one of the 64 diagrams.

褐 Ho. Short garments; poor, hempen clothes; woolen stuffs; stockings; a beggarly fellow: [3]*'e' hak,* to wear poor garments; [2]*'hak, ,hu,* a beggarly fellow; [4]*'sëü' hak,* menials, servants.

毼 Ho. A kind of twilled felt or haircloth from Shantung—used for cushions.

蝎 Ho. A scorpion; grubs found in decayed wood.

轄 Hsia. A linch-pin; the creaking of carriages; to regulate, to control; to guide the morals of society; to turn, to revolve: [5]*'kwang hak,* to govern.

顥 Ho. Hale, strong, robust, vigorous, sturdy: [6]*,heu hak,* to speak in a loud tone, to proclaim; [7]*'mwak, hak,* a flat nose and face; hale, robust.

(171) Hang.

酣 Han. Exhilarated, lively, cheerful; merry from wine, tipsy, half-drunk; jocund, riant, as nature: [8]*'chiu ,hang,* merry from wine; [9]*,hang chiéng'* excited in battle.

邯 Han. As in [10]*,tang ,hang,* a city of the ancient Han country in Hupeh. Read *,hang,* as in [11]*,hang ,tang,* a district of Kwang-ping prefecture in Chihli. Read *hang'* as in [12]*hang' tang'* full, abundant.

蚶 Han. A salt water cockle, a species of Arca or bivalve with furrowed shell, a small clam: COM., [13]*,chio ,hang,* a cockle with a smooth, dark shell; COLL., *,hang ,peng,* a dish of clams with one shell off; *,hang k'aëk,* clam shells.

憨 Han. Simple, foolish; an idiotic look: [14]*,ch'i ,hang,* or *,ngü ,hang,* silly, stupid.

,Hang. A coll. word, as in *,hang ,tiu,* a closet with two compartments for dishes and food.

罕 **罕** Han. Rare, few, scarce, seldom; a kind of flag; a net for birds or rabbits: [15]*'hang 'wong,* a bird-net; COM., [16]*'hang kiéng'* rarely seen; [17]*,hi 'hang,* or [18]*'hang 'iu,* scarce, rare; COLL., [19]*'hang 'kiáng,* rare child or children, as when born late and only one or a few in the family; *'hang tek, 'hang,* very scarce or seldom; [20]*'hang tek, ,li,* comes seldom.

悍 Han. An ardent, energetic disposition; fearless, violent; hasty, cruel: [21]*,kiong 'hang,* overbearing; [22]*'hang ho'* a violent woman; [23]*'hang chuk,* a fierce clan.

衎 Han. Pleased, contented; to be happy, joyous; credible, trustworthy, in which sense read *'k'ang* in the dictionaries.

1噬	2褐	5管	7頳	9酣	11邯	13蛛	15罕	17希	19罕	梨	22悍
嗑	夫	轄	顥	戰	鄲	蚶	網	罕	仔	21强	婦
3衣	4豎	6頷	8酒	10訮	12邯	14痴	16罕	18罕	20罕	悍	23悍
褐	褐	顥	酣	邯	淡	憨	見	有	的	〇	族

ʻ閈 Han. A gate; a gate of a village, ward, or street; a small wall; to shut: [1]ʻli ʻhang, a ward-gate.

ʻ豻 Han. Also read ˌkang: a kind of jackal found in the desert, but described rather as a fabulous beast. Read ngang² a village prison; [2]ˌpʻi ngang² a figure like a unicorn painted on prison doors; [3]ngang² ngük, a jail.

ʻ捍 Han. To grasp, to lift up; to ward off, to shield, to defend; to stop: [4]ʻhang woi² to guard; [5]ngü ˌchai ʻhang hwang² to guard against calamity and ward off troubles.

ʻ扞 Kan. Used for the last: to fend off; an obstacle, hindrance; to guard or escort; to environ: [6]ʻhang ˌkwang, to keep a pass; [7]ʻhang kaik, pok, ˌtʻung, impeded; conflicting, as ideas.

ʻ旰 Han. Sunset, evening: [8]ʻhang sik, a late evening meal; [9]hó² hó² ʻhang ʻhang, very light; abundant.

ʻ澣 Han. To wash clothes; to bathe, to purify one's self; a decade of days: [10]ʻhang chok, to wash, as clothes and cap-strings; [11]siong² ʻhang, the first decade of the month.

ʻ喊 Han. Angry cries; to call, to call for; to vociferate, to halloo after; to cry, to bawl: [12]ʻhang keu² to call for help; COM., [13]ʻhang kieu² to cry out, to bawl; [14]ʻhang ˌwong, to exclaim against false charges—as before magistrates.

ʻ僩 Hsien. Courageous, depending on one's self; martial, formidable, brave; liberal, magnanimous.

ʻ瞰 ʻ闞 Kan. To spy, to glance at; to bow down and look; to expect, to hope for; the 2nd also means a tiger's roar; *met.*, an angry tone, as in [15]ʻhang ˌü ˌhau ʻhu, he yells like a roaring tiger.

ʻ菡 Han. An unopened flower: [16]ʻhang ʻlang, the lotus flower—a poetical name.

ʻ鯇 The tench (Leuciscus idella) with dark green fins, spinous ventrals and dorsals.

ʻ撼 Han. Also read hang²: to move, to shake; shaking, trembling: [17]ˌhung ʻhang, shaken by the wind.

ʻ紺 Han. A violet color, a rose red, which the good man, it is said, does not wear.

漢ʼ Han. A large branch of the Yang-tsz river in Hupeh; a famous dynasty of China (B. C. 201–A. D. 260); Chinese; in the coll., personal appearance, form, stature: [18]ˌtʻieng hang² or ˌó hang² the milky way—in poetry called [19]ˌngüng hang² silvery river; COM., [20]ʻmwang hang² Manchus and Chinese; hang² ˌkung, naturalized bannermen; COLL., hang² ˌnëng, the Chinese; hang² ʻma, the form, stature; ngaing² hang² bold, reckless; ngaung² hang² or ˌchʻi hang² stupid; ʻló hang² I, an old man—used in plays; twai² hang² of great

1 里閈 2 豼豻 3 豻獄 4 捍衛 5 禦災捍患 6 扞關 7 扞格不通 8 旰食 9 皓皓旰旰 10 澣濯 11 上澣 12 喊救 13 喊叫 14 喊冤 15 闞如虓虎 16 菡萏 17 風撼 18 天漢 19 銀漢 20 滿漢

stature; *hang' liong[2] 'hó*, personable; *‚i hang' 'ma 'yă ‚keng*, he is very tall.

暵 Han. Also read *'hang*: dry, heated air; to dry; drying, parching.

熯 Han. Also read *siéng[2]*: much fire; to dry at the fire, to roast; to respect: [1]*hang' ‚kang*, roasted dry; [2]*'ngó 'k'ung hang' é'* I highly respect him.

Hang'. A coll. word: to think, to suppose, to consider, to regard as; also to give notice, to inform; to acknowledge, to confess; to ask, to request: *hang' tek*, to suppose; *hang' se[2] tié[2] ‚nĕng*, was thinking who it could be; *kaĕng[2] 'nü hang' 'lau*, I have already notified you; *hang' taik, chói[2]* or *hang' pok, se[2]* to confess a fault; *hang' k'aung[2]* inform (the dead) of going to sleep—i. e., to weep by the coffin before retiring; *hang' siă[2]* to express thanks; *hang' 'ch'iă 'hi*, to present joyous salutations, as women and rustics do; *hang' 'k'i taĕng[2]* to thank one for his trouble; *hang' 'nü k'á' 'ngwai chó'* request you to do it for me.

Hang'. A coll. word, as in the reduplicated form *hang' hang'* to be moderate, not persistent, not exacting; *hang' hang' 'mwong má[2] 'ngwai*, be easy (as to price) and just sell it to me.

閑 ‚Hsien. A bar, barrier, a fence; an inclosure, a fold or stable for horses; to close, to obstruct; to protect, to defend; to regulate by law; to forbid; to move about; large; accustomed, practiced: [3]*‚hwong ‚hang*, to guard against; [4]*‚hang ‚siă*, to repel evil influences; [5]*‚hang sik,* accustomed to.

咸 ‚Han. All, jointly, altogether; completely, totally; always; all around, reaching everywhere; concord, associated; hasty; a diagram: [6]*pok, ‚hang*, disagreeing; com., [7]*‚hang ‚hung*, the emperor Hien-fung (A. D. 1850-61).

閒 ‚Hsien. Leisure, repose, rest; indolent; unoccupied, empty: also read *‚kang*, q. v.: com., [8]*‚ang ‚hang*, repose, quiet; [9]*‚hang ha[2] chai[2] ‚ka*, at home unemployed; [10]*‚hang ‚ching*, feeling of leisure; [11]*‚iu 'ch'iu hó' ‚hang*, fond of idleness, lazy.

嫺 ‚Hsien. Skilled, accustomed to; loving leisure; elegant, refined: [12]*‚hang 'nga*, polished, elegant; com., [13]*‚hang sŭk,* versed in.

鷴 鷳 ‚Han. A kind of pheasant: com., [14]*pah, ‚hang*, the silver pheasant.

緘 ‚Chien. Cards for binding hampers; to close or bind up; to seal, to bind up crevices closely; used for *‚hang* (altogether): [15]*‚hung ‚hang* to seal, to close; [16]*nói[2] seng' ek, ‚hang*, the inclosed letter; [17]*ngŭk, ‚hang*, your esteemed favor.

---

[1] 熯乾 [2] 我孔熯矣 [3] 防閑 [4] 閑邪 [5] 閑習 [6] 不咸 [7] 咸豐 [8] 安閒 [9] 閒暇在家 ○ [10] 閒情 ○ [11] 遊手好閒 [12] 嫺雅 [13] 嫺熟 [14] 白鷴 [15] 封緘 [16] 內信一緘 ○ [17] 玉緘 ○

函 ˓Han. Used for the next: to contain, to infold, to comprehend in, to envelope; a letter or what is contained in an envelope, in which sense it is the same as the last; liberal, capacious: [1]˓hang kak˒ a coat of mail; COM., [2]˛pau ˓hang, to infold, to contain; magnanimous.

椷 梒 ˓Han. A cup, a wooden bowl; a casket, a case to hold things.

鹹 ˓Han. Saltish, as salt water; salted, preserved in brine; bitter: in the coll. read ˓keng, q. v.

含 唅 ˓Han. To hold something in the mouth; the mouth full; to contain; to cherish, to suffer, to put up with or tolerate; to restrain; to place gems in a corpse's mouth: in the coll., incomplete, confused; shabbily: COM., [3]˛pau ˓hang, to hold, to contain; to be lenient; [4]˓hang ch'ieu˒ to smile; [5]˓hang ˛wong, to endure false accusations; [6]˓hang hëük˒ to smother (resentments); COLL., [7]˓hang ˓t'ié, to be in tears; [8]˓hang ˓hang, incomplete, by halves; ˓hang ˓hu, or [9]˓hang hong˒ confusedly, anyhow; ˓hang ˓hë, at odds and ends, shabbily; ˓hang ˓ming ˓hang k'aung˒ half asleep; ˓hang ˓hu paik˒ to understand obscurely; [10]˓hang ang˒ ˛pwo, dusk, evening.

銜 ˓Han. Usually read ˓kang; coll. ˓hang, as in ˓hang ˓t'au, official rank, station; [11]˛i sié˒ nóh, ˓hang ˓t'au, what is his official rank?

憪 ˓Han. Also read ʻhang: composed, tranquil; pleased; liberal; affected, aroused, anxious for others: ˓hang ˓yong niéng˒ ngwoi˒ ˓ing ˛chi ʻiu ˛hi, aroused by considering others' faults.

諴 ˓Han. Union, harmony; to be accordant, united; sincere, cordial, hearty: [12]˓hang ˓hwo, to harmonize; [13]che˒ ˓hang ʻkang ˓sing, sincerity influences the gods.

鼾 ˓Han. Read hang˒; coll. ˓hang: to snore: [14]k'aung˒ ˓ngó ngó˒ ˓hang, to snore loudly in sleep.

韓 ˓Han. A fence about a well, a well-curb; a feudal state of the Chow dynasty; a surname.

涵 ˓Han. To sink in the water, submerged; to leak; marshy; to soak; to contain, capacious: [15]˓hang ˓t'ing, submerged; [16]˓hang ˓üng, to contain; enlarged, liberal; [17]˓hang ʻyong, to cherish, as virtues; kind, meek.

寒 ˓Han. Cold, wintry; shivering; poor, unsupplied, necessitous; my, mine; plain, simple: [18]swoi˒ ˓hang, or ˓hang ˛t'iéng, winter; [19]˓hang so˒ plain, unpretending; COM., [20]˓hang sik˒ the day before the ˛Ch'ing ˓ming festival, when, in former times, cold food was eat-

1 函甲 2 包函 3 包含 4 含笑 5 含冤 6 含蓄 7 含啼 8 含含 9 含混 10 含暗晡 11 伊世乇銜頭 12 諴和 13 至諴感神 14 睏哦哦鼾 15 涵沉 16 涵容 17 涵養 18 歲寒 19 寒素 20 寒食

en; ˛hang ˋsü, cold and heat; ˛hang ˋleng, shivering, cold; [1]ˏhung ˛hang, or ˛hang ˏsa, a cold; [2]ˊsi ˛hang, periodic colds, catarrhs; [3]˛hang ˛ü, a poor student; ˛hang ˏka, or ˛hang ˛mwong, my family; [4]˛hang ˏsing, the mind chilled (with fear), discouraged; [5]˛hang lo˒ "cold dews"—the 17th solar term; [6]˛hang k'e˒ ˏkwi seng² the cold has settled on the kidneys.

尷 ˛ An unsteady gait; embarrassed, irresolute: [7]˛hang kai˒ to walk awry; at a loss what to do.

˛Hang. A coll. word: to consume, to burn up; to heat, to boil: ˛hang t'au˒ to burn or heat through; ˛hang ˛tio, to burn coals in a furnace—on festive occasions; ˛hang ˏhiong, to burn fragrant wood; ˛hang laiu² to boil pig's food; to burn muck for manure; ˛hang ˋhwi ˏtoi, to burn a heap of refuse; ˛hang lai² a burning leprosy!—said to one carrying a hand-stove or wearing thick clothing in warm weather.

˛Hang. A coll. word, as in ˛hang ka˒ a bride's furniture; ˛hang ka˒ taing˒ a furnishing shop.

翰 ˛ Han. Usually read hang²; in coll. read ˛hang: [8]˛hang ˛ling yéng² or [9]˛hang ˛ling ˋkwang, the Imperial college.

翰² Han. A fabulous pheasant; to fly high; white; protracted, well-sustained; a plume or quill to write with; writings; a prop; the stump of a tree: [10]ˏchü hang² written with a pen; [11]hang² mëk² literary.

瀚² Han. The northern sea; met., wide, vast: [12]hong² hang² the troubled appearance of water; [13]hó² hang² vast, expansive.

憾² Han. To hate, to abhor; to murmur at; to feel indignant at, resentful; regretting, vexed: [14]wong˒ hang² to abhor; [15]pó² hang² to cherish anger.

陷² Han. To fall down or into, to sink; to descend into; overwhelmed, ruined; to involve another: [16]hang² nik² sunk, drowned; [17]hang² koi² a criminal's cage; [18]hang² seng² a pit for trapping animals; to fall into a trap; [19]hang² hai² to inveigle one; COLL., [20]˛siáng hang² the city-walls ruined.

䭞² Han. Not satisfied with eating, to eat too little.

餡² Hsien. Pastry; cakes stuffed with meat, sugar, dates, or other articles: in the coll. read ang² q. v.

銲² 釬² Han. Greaves on the arms; to solder; to hasten: in the coll. read ang² q. v.: [21]hang² yoh² soldering.

頷² Han. To contain in the mouth; sallow; the jaws, the chops; to shake the head: [22]ha² hang² the chin; hang² ha² ˏchio, the pearl under (the dragon's) chin.

[1]風寒 [2]時寒 [3]寒儒 [4]寒心 [5]寒露 [6]寒氣歸腎 [7]尷尬 [8]翰林院 [9]翰林館 [10]書翰 [11]翰墨 [12]混瀚 [13]浩瀚 [14]怨憾 [15]抱憾 [16]陷溺 [17]陷檻 [18]陷阱 [19]陷害 [20]城陷 [21]銲藥 [22]下頷

含² Han. Read ˏhang; used in the coll. for hang²: to close, to shut up; to close partially; to keep a fire by covering it with ashes: [1]ch'oi' hang² 'king 'king, mouth shut tight, as of a clam; [2]ˏmwong na' hang² 'lá, shut the doors partly—with the leaves overlapping.

(172) Hau.

哮 Hsiao. To howl, to bellow, to roar, as beasts when afraid or angry; to grunt, as swine; a loud call; to pant, to gasp: [3]ˏhau haik, enraged; [4]ˏpau ˏhau, to rave, to scold furiously; [5]ˏhau 'ch'wang, asthma; COLL., ˏhau ˏhau kieu' a howling, as of dogs.

虓 Hsiao. The scream or roar of a tiger; beside one's self with anger.

蒿 **薅** Ju. Read ˏkó; coll. ˏhau: to weed; to extirpate, as grass or weeds: [6]ˏhau 'ch'au, to pull grass, to weed.

吼 Kan. The cries of animals, especially of cattle and feline animals; met., to rave, to scold: [7]ˏsai 'hau, a lion roaring; met., as in [8]ˏó ˏtung ˏsai 'hau, a scolding wife, a shrew.

'Hau. A coll. word: to call one; to inform, to tell, to direct to do; also to bawl, to cry out, as in distress: 'hau ˏi ˏli, tell him to come; k'ó' 'hau, go and call him; 'hau ng² eng' calls and gets no answer; 'hau sioh₂ hiok, to call a-while; ˏsiáng 'hau ˏsiáng eng' to answer as soon as called; 'hau ˏli 'hau k'ó' to bawl back and forth, as two persons; 'hau keu' to cry for help; 'hau 'hwang ˏt'iéng, to bawl (loud enough) to turn the heavens; 'hau 'si 'hau wak₂ "cries dead and alive"—i. e., in great distress.

孝' Hsiao. Filial duty, obedience, respect to parents; mourning for parents: used in the coll. for ha' q. v.: COM., [9]hau' song² dutiful to parents; [10]hau' keng' to obey and revere; [11]hau' ˏsing, a filial disposition; [12]hau' ˏchü, filial duty and parental love; [13]hau' 'chü ˏhwong, portals in honor of filial piety; [14]pok₂ hau' unfilial; hau' ˏnang, a mourning son; [15]hau' ˏliéng, name for a Küjin graduate; [16]hau' ˏking, a classic on filial duties—one of the 13 ˏking; [17]hau' sing 'kang tong² ˏt'iéng te² the filial spirit moves heaven and earth!

鱟' **鱟** Hsiao. The horse-hoof or king crab; the Xiphosuræ or Limulus longispina: COLL., hau' 'ngiong, crab's groin; met., the human groins; hau' ˏkié, a crab-shell dipper; hau' k'uëk₂ siéng' fans curved like crab's shells; [18]hau' k'uëk₂ 'sang, foreign umbrellas—are so called; hau' hiäk₂ ˏmwong, venetian blinds; hau' ˏkié tó' ne' suk₂ 'mi ˏku, the crab-dipper on the contrary is baited (stuck over) with the glutinous rice paste; met., to get more (as presents) than one gave.

Hau'. A coll. word, as in the duplicate form hau' hau' round-shouldered; to bow in saluting one; ˏyeu ˏtó hau' hau' to make the loins bend—to bow respectfully.

1 嘴含緊緊 2 門那含禮 3 哮赫 4 咆哮 5 哮喘 6 薅草 7 獅吼 8 河東獅吼 9 孝順 10 孝敬 11 孝心 12 孝慈 13 孝子坊 14 不孝 15 孝廉 16 孝經 17 孝心感動天地 18 鱟殼傘

效^2 傚^2 Hsiao. To imitate, to learn, to copy; to verify; like, similar to; effectual, efficacious; an example; to exert one's self; to offer; effects, results: COM., [1]*hau^2 ngiéng^2* fulfilled; effectual; [2]*‚sing hau^2* wonderfully efficacious, as a medicine; [3]*hau^2 ‚iu*, to imitate a bad example; [4]*kiéng^2 hau^2* to be efficient, efficacious; [5]*hau^2 ŭng^2* a promoted dragoon, an aid-de-camp.

効^2 Hsiao. Used for the preceding: to toil, to labor; to follow a rule, to imitate; effects, results: COM., [6]*‚kung hau^2* meritorious effort; [7]*hau^2 lik‚* to exert one's self; [8]*hau^2 ‚ló*, to moil for others.

恔^2 Hsiao. Joy, hilarity; jovial, cheerful; pleased, as with others' company. Read ‛*kieu:* wise, intelligent.

校^2 Hsiao. A school, a college, as anciently called; an inclosure, a horse-pen: also read *kau^2* q. v.

後^2 Hou. Read *haiu^2;* coll. *hau^2*, as in [9]*hau^2 ‚sang*, young, youth, young persons from 16 to 30 years of age; *hau^2 ‚sang tiĕ^2* a licentious young scamp; [10]*hau^2 ‚sang ‚nĕng*, or *hau^2 ‚sang ‛kiăng*, or *hau^2 ‚sang ‚nĕng ‚nié*, young persons.

(173) Hauk.

摧 搕 Ho. The 1st read *k'auk*, the 2nd read *ak‚;* used in the *Paik*, *‚Ing* for the coll. *hauk‚*: to pound, to beat with a stick, to cudgel: [11]*k'ek‚ ‚hong ‚tĕng hauk*, to beat with a tobacco pipe; *hauk‚ lang^2 tĕük‚ ‚p'ié*, struck him two (a few) blows with the bamboo ferule; [12]*hauk‚ ch'ói^2* beat it to pieces; [13]*hauk‚ ‛chŭng*, swollen from a beating.

(174) Haung.

桁 Hsing. Read *‚heng;* used in the coll. for *haung^2:* a joist in a floor, a sleeper, a floor-beam: [14]*‚lau haung^2* or *‚lau ‚pang haung^2* upper floor beams; [15]*té^2 ‚pang haung^2* the joists of a lower floor; [16]*haung^2 ‛niong*, the floor joists are limber.

恨^2 Hên. Indignation, resentment; dislike, hatred, spite; to regret, vexed, sorry: [17]*‛k'ŏ haung^2* detestable; [18]*siok‚ haung^2* to gratify revenge; COM., [19]*‚hiéng haung^2* to hate; [20]*haung^2 ‚sing*, a resentful disposition; *haung^2 ‚sing taĕng^2* deep resentment; [21]*t'ong^2 haung^2* to have painful regrets; *haung^2 pok‚ taik‚* would that! O for! COLL., *haung^2 kau^2 ‛si*, to hate till death; *haung^2 ‚sang mŏh‚ haung^2 ‛si*, hate while living, not when dead—bury resentments in the grave.

項^2 Hsiang. Nape of the neck, that which rests on the pillow; great; a surname; often used for a species, class, sort, item, thing, article; in the coll., a sum, a deposit of money, funds: COM., [22]*haung^2 ‚tong*, the neck long, as of a goose or snake; *haung^2 ‛hu*, "neck tiger"—a virulent boil on the back of the neck; COLL., *chioh‚ haung^2* borrowed money; *‚kung haung^2* public funds; *haung^2 a^2* present resources, funds in hand; *k'iéng^2*

1效	3效	5效	7効	9後	仈	摧	䦳	棚	17可	19慊	21痛
驗	尤	用	力	生	11擭	12摧	14樓	桁	恨	恨	恨
2神	4見	6功	8効	10後	烟	碎	桁	16桁	18雪	20恨	22項
效	效	効	勞	生	筒	13摧	15地	軟	恨	心	長

*haung*² debts; *kauk, haung*² each sum or account of money.

行² Hang. Strong, powerful: usually read ˏ*heng* and *haing*² q.v.: [1]*haung*² *haung*² vigorous, strong and formidable.

(175) He.

懿' Hsi. Mild, virtuous, excellent, admirable; admired, as applied to women; the virtuous one—i.e., the empress: [2]*he*' ʻ*mi*, mild and excellent; [3]*he*' *hwang*² a virtuous exemplar—said of women; COM., [4]*he*' ʻ*chi*, Her Majesty's orders.

狒' Fu. Also read *hiĕ*': an animal of the monkey tribe, large and monstrous: [5]*he*' *he*' the orang-outang or chimpanzee.

亟' Chi. Frequently, repeatedly, again and again, repetition: usually read *kek*ˌ q.v.: [6]*he*' ˏ*ch'ing*, to praise or speak of repeatedly; [7]*he*' *koi*² to offer gifts frequently.

咥' Chih. To laugh out aloud, a loud laugh: [8]*he*' *he*' ˏ*yong*, the sound of hearty merriment: also read *tiék*ˌ to gnaw.

Hĕ'. A coll. euphonic prefix, as in *he*' *heü*' or *he*' *he*' *hĕü*' *hĕü*' to sob, sobbing, sighing; *he*' *ho*' or *he*' *ho*' *ho*' to sprinkle, as water with the hand; to spill or slatter, as food in eating; *he*' *hwa*' to burn (idol-paper).

Hĕ'. A coll. euphonic prefix, as in *he*' *haĕ*² to disgrace or shame another by drawing one's forefinger across the cheek and crying *haĕ*²! *haĕ*²!

(176) Hë.

[口靴] ˏHsueh. Read ˏ*k'wo*; used in the *Paik*, ˏ*Ing* for the coll. ˏ*hĕ*: to emit breath; heated, suffocated, as in a large crowd: [9]*k'e*' ˏ*hĕ ch'ok*, *k'ó*' the breath emitted; [10]*á*² ˏ*hĕ* ˏ*nĕng*, it suffocates people! as said of a crowd in a theater..

ˏ*Hĕ*. A coll. word: to eat, eaten, consumed: ˏ*hĕ* ʻ*kwoi* ʻ*wang*, to eat a few bowls full; ˏ*hĕ* ˏ*ch'ing* ʻ*ch'u*, all eaten up clean.

喉 ˏHou. Read ˏ*heu*; coll. ˏ*hĕ*, as in [11]ˏ*hĕ* ˏ*lĕng*, or [12]ˏ*hĕ* ˏ*lĕng* ʻ*kwong*, the windpipe, trachea; in common language, the throat: also read ˏ*hó* in the coll., q. v.: [13]ˏ*hĕ* ˏ*lĕng* ˏ*t'au*, or [14]ˏ*hĕ* ˏ*lĕng te*' the top of the throat—under the chin.

ˏ*Hĕ*. A coll. word: to blow or breathe upon, to emit the breath forcibly.

ˏ*Hĕ*. A coll. word: to steam, to dry by steaming after cooking; steam rising; to warm up, as food by steaming: ˏ*hĕ sŭk*ˌ steam it done: ˏ*hĕ yék*ˌ or ˏ*hĕ yék*ˌ *yék*ˌ to warm food; ˏ*hĕ* ˏ*sang p'au*' blistered by rising steam.

ˏ*Hĕ*. A coll. word, as in ˏ*hĕ me*² to cajole, to play the sycophant.

(177) Heh.

*Heh*ˌ. A coll. word: to sniff, to snuff up; to blow from the nose: *heh*ˌ ʻ*tié*, or *heh*ˌ ʻ*tié k'ó*' to snuff up, to draw into the nostrils; *heh*ˌ *ch'ok*ˌ ˏ*li*, blow it from the nose.

[1]行行 [2]懿美 [3]懿範 [4]懿旨 [5]狒狒 [6]亟稱 [7]亟餽 [8]咥咥然 [9]氣[口靴]出去 [10][亻鞋][口靴]仈 [11]喉嚨 [12]喉嚨管 [13]喉嚨頭 [14]喉嚨蒂

Heh,. A coll. euphonic prefix, as in *heh, hwah*, to sport, to play; to jest, to trifle.

(178) Hek.

翕, Hsi. To re-assemble, to unite, to collect; to rise up; to loll out the tongue; to revile, to slander: [1]*hek*, *ˌú yŏ*ʾ a concord of harmonies; [2]*hek*, *seu*[2] *ˌhu ˌsié*, to gather and to dispense.

熻, Hsi. Hot, burning; used in the coll. in the sense of to steam, to heat or cause fermentation by covering close; to smother, to "take a sweat", as under bedclothes: COLL., [3]*hek*, *pwong*[2] to cover and steam rice—after cooking it; [4]*hek*, *ˌhwang ˌsü*, to steam potatoes; [5]*hek*, *yék*, to cover and heat up; [6]*hek*, *ʿsi*, smothered to death; [7]*hek*, *ak*, *ʿkiăng*, to hatch ducklings by heat; [8]*hek*, *lai*[2] sweltering leprosy! said jocosely to one wearing thick clothes in hot weather.

闟, Hsi. Leaf of a door; a kind of lance with tassels, placed in chariots; a chariot so guarded; standing erect; settled.

歙, Hsi. To snuff up the nose; to draw in the breath; to gather, to collect: [9]*hek*, *ˌtiong*, to collect and to scatter; [10]*hek*, *hek*, a deep red.

潝, Hsi. The noise of flowing water; running, gurgling, murmuring, as torrents: [11]*hek*, *hek*, *ʿchié ʿchié*, to forsake duty and imitate bad examples.

洫, Hsieh. A water-course in fields; a moat; a sluice for water; overflowing.

淢, Same as the last. Read *mik*,: to flow rapidly; a current; water foaming and rising.

侐, Hsieh. Quiet, silent, peaceful; taciturn: [12]*hek*, *cheng*[2] peaceful, undisturbed.

奭, Shih. Read *sek*, in the dictionaries: to abound, to flourish, plentiful; to color up, to grow angry; flushed, crimsoned; a carnation or carmine color.

襫, Shih. Read *sek*, in the dictionaries: a rain cloak: [13]*pwak*, *hek*, an overcoat or cloak of leaves, worn by husbandmen.

肸, A sound spreading and reverberating; a buzz of flies; a soughing among trees; a report going abroad: [14]*hek*, *ˌhiong*, insects generated by dampness; [15]*pik*, *hek*, great, disproportional.

Hek,. A coll. euphonic prefix, as in *hek, hiék*, to heat or dry by a fire; *hek, hok*, to brush off; *hek, hak*, to hoot at; also to strop, as a knife or razor; *hek*, *hwak*, to give or pay out, to offer for sale; *hek, hauk*, to beat with a stick; *hek, haék*, to buy, as for one's use.

獲, Hu. A sort of wild beast; to take in hunting; to catch, as thieves; to get, to obtain, to receive; an opprobrious epithet for female slaves:

[1]翕如也 ○ [2]翕受敷施 [3]熻飯 ○ [4]熻番薯 [5]熻熱 [6]熻死 ○ [7]熻鴨仔 [8]熻癩 [9]歙張 ○ [10]歙赩 [11]潝潝訿訿 ○ [12]侐靜 [13]襏襫 ○ [14]肸蠁 ○ [15]佛肸 ○

[1]*hek$_2$ tó^2* to catch thieves; *ˏsiéng ˎnang haiu^2 hek$_2$* at first difficult, afterwards acquired, as knowledge; COM., [2]*hek$_2$ chói^2 ˏü ˏt'iéng ˎü 'su 'tó yă^2* if one sins against Heaven, there is no place for prayer—a saying of Confucius.

畫$_2$ Hua. To draw a line, to mark, to line off, to divide by a line; to paint, to sketch a picture; to devise, to draw a plan; a mark, a line: [3]*ek$_2$ hek$_2$* one stroke of a pencil; [4]*'chi hek$_2$* to trace with the finger; COM., [5]*hek$_2$ ek$_2$ pok$_2$ ne^2* "one mark, not two"—the prices are uniform; *che^2 hek$_2$* the strokes forming a character; COLL., [6]*nioh$_2$ wai^2 hek$_2$* how many strokes (in the character)? [7]*sek$_2$ ch'ek$_2$ hek$_2$* 17 strokes.

劃$_2$ Hua. To carve, to engrave, to cut with a graver; to cut glass; to cut open; a graver, a burin: [8]*hek$_2$ sëü^2* to attend to business; [9]*hek$_2$ ˏk'ai*, to split open; COM., [10]*k'aik$_2$ hek$_2$* to carve; *met.*, to shape, as one's ideas in composing.

澅$_2$ Hua. The name of a stream; the roaring of waves; sound of waves dashing against each other.

砉$_2$ Hua. The ripping sound heard in tearing off the skin, the sound of tearing flesh from the bones.

Hek$_2$. A coll. word, denoting cause, means, manner or instrument; with, by, in use of; to use, to employ, to make use of: also spoken *k'ek$_2$* q. v.: *hek$_2$ ˏtó*, with a knife; *hek$_2$ wa^2 hiăh$_2$ ˎnëng*, to threaten people with words; *hek$_2$ ˏchü ka^2 ˎnëng*, to teach people by books.

(179) **Hĕk.**

或$_2$ Huo. Uncertain, doubtful; perhaps, if, perchance, it may be so; a certain person, somebody; when repeated, it means either, or, this, that: *hëk$_2$ ˎing*, or [11]*hëk$_2$ 'chiă*, a certain person; [12]*hëk$_2$ wak$_2$* some one says; COM., [13]*hëk$_2$ 'ch'iă*, perhaps, probably; [14]*hëk$_2$ se^2 hëk$_2$ ˏhi*, either is or is not; COLL., [15]*hëk$_2$ ˎnëng*, a certain man, some one; [16]*hëk$_2$ sioh$_2$ pwang^2 ˎhúi*, perhaps half a time—i. e., very seldom. Read *mik$_2$*: a place that needs defence.

惑$_2$ Huo. To lead into error, to delude, to blind the mind; to excite doubt, to lead astray; to unsettle another's opinions; suspicion, doubt; deceived, blinded: COM., [17]*ˎyeu hëk$_2$* or *ˎmi hëk$_2$* to delude; *ˎngi hëk$_2$* to suspect, suspicious; *hëk$_2$ chëüng^2* to deceive the multitude.

斛$_2$ A measure equal to ten *'tau* or pecks, or to a picul of 100 catties; to measure grain.

趦$_2$ Read *haik$_2$*; used in the *Paik$_2$ ˏIng* for the coll. *hëk$_2$*: to pant, to puff, to gasp for breath: *k'e^2 hëk$_2$* panting; *cheng^2 hëk$_2$* or *'yă hëk$_2$* panting heavily; *hëk$_2$ sioh$_2$ hëk$_2$* to take a breathing spell; *hëk$_2$ ˎp'i ˎp'á*, sound of panting.

Hëk$_2$. A coll. word: to fuse metals, to smelt: *hëk$_2$ ˏking*, to smelt gold; *hëk$_2$ ˎngwong*

[1]獲盜 [2]獲罪於天無所禱也 [3]一畫 [4]指畫 [5]畫一不二 [6]筶壞畫 [7]十七畫 [8]劃事 [9]劃開 [10]刻劃 [11]或者 [12]或日 [13]或且 [14]或是或非 [15]或仏 [16]或一半回 [17]搖惑

'pó ˏhu, to fuse the ashes of idol-paper ingots—*scil.*, in order to extract the pewter.

(180) Heng.

亨 ˓Hêng. To pervade, to penetrate; good, successful: [1]ˏheng ˏka, excellent; [2]t'ai' ˏheng, great prosperity; COM., [3]ˏheng ˏt'ung, prosperous, successful.

哼 ˓Hêng. Foolish, frightened; in the coll., to vociferate, to speak harshly, to express dislike by vociferations: [4]ˏch'iong ˏheng, foolish and frightened; COLL., ˏheng hak, to scream at; heng ˏha ne' chiong' the two generals, ˏHeng and ˏHa—idols in the ˏSing ˏKwong monastery, near Black Rock hill, Foochow.

脝 ˓Hêng. A puffed belly: [5]ˏp'ang ˏheng, inflated, puffed up, as the belly with wind.

悻 ˓Hsing. As in 'heng 'heng, anger, hatred; greatly displeased, vexed; quarrelsome, pertinacious.

很 狠 ˓Hên. Read 'hong; coll. 'heng: a sign of the superlative, very, much, great, exceeding; stern, severe, harsh; grievous, painful: 'heng sá' very much; [6]'heng á' fully able; [7]'heng 'hó, very good, all the better; ˏtang 'heng ˏló, now we are at a sad pass! 'heng 'heng sié' or 'heng 'heng a' severely, harshly; [8]'heng 'hó pok, ˏkwo' incomparably good; 'heng 'k'ó 'iu, very well off, well-to-do in the world; pang' 'yá 'heng, very sick; [9]ˏhwang 'hi tek, 'heng, very much pleased; 'heng ˏsing, or 'heng 'heng ˏsing, harsh, unfeeling.

興' Hsing. To desire; to be moved, excited; an appetite, a passion, a desire; pleased, delighted with: also read ˏhing, q. v.: COM., [10]'k'i heng' the risings of desire; [11]ˏsi heng' poetical inspiration; [12]heng' 'tu, or 'tu heng' a passion for gaming; [13]heng' hwang' to call one to pleasure; to invite smilingly, as shopmen do; [14]heng' ˏp'ieu, lecherous; [15]ˏkó heng' a strong passion for; COLL., [16]p'ah, 'tong heng' or heng' ˏt'au p'uh, 'tong, the desire interrupted or thwarted.

逈' Hui. Void, waste, desert; distant, remote; to differ, to distinguish; also bright, lustrous: [17]heng' 'wong, remote; [18]heng' pok, ˏiu ˏing, very different from other men.

迥' Hui. Distant, remote; profound, vague; an abyss; to forbid.

Heng'. A coll. euphonic prefix, as in heng' hang' to tell, to report; heng' hiàng' or heng' tong' hiàng' vibrating, toppling; *met.*, uncertain, as to the issue.

行 ˓Hang. To go, to walk, to proceed; to act, to do, to direct; imports the action of the following verb; to appeal or transfer a case; a step, a road, a way, a path; the elements; a manner, a motion: also read haing' and ˏhong in the reading style, and ˏkiàng in the coll., q. v.: COM., [19]ˏheng ˏui, to do, to act; [20]ˏheng ˏi, to practice med-

[1]亨嘉 [2]泰亨 [3]亨通 [4]嗆哼 [5]膨脝 [6]狠僻 [7]狠好 [8]狠好不過 [9]歡喜的狠 [10]起興 [11]詩興 [12]興賭 [13]興喚 [14]興嫖 [15]高興 [16]拍斷興 [17]逈遠 [18]逈不由人 [19]行爲 [20]行醫○

ieine; [1]ˏheng ˏchü, a running hand; ˏheng ˏt'au, the dress, as being good or poor; [2]ˏheng 'lá, to salute in due form; [3]ˏheng ˏchong, a traveling dress—a short outside garment; [4]ˏheng ˏtai, the night lodgings of idols or officials; [5]ˏheng sek, lang^2 ˏhung, 2 *per cent.* interest a month; ˏheng 'cheu, to walk and run; *met.*, employed, as in official duties; [6]ˏheng sëü^2 or ˏheng paing^2 to transact business; [7]pwo^2 ˏheng, to go a-foot; [8]ˏheng siëng^2 to act virtuously; [9]ˏheng 'li, traveling baggage; ˏheng ngwok, ˏking, to have the menses; p'iëng^2 ˏheng, to go all around; [10]ngu ˏheng, the five elements; [11]ˏheng lok, ˏtu, picture of a person, a likeness; [12]ˏheng 'hó ˏsing, or ˏheng 'hó sëü^2 to be benevolent; COLL., ˏhu ˏheng laung^2 chó^2 to act as a rake or spendthrift. Read haung^2, as in haung^2 haung^2 ˏü yä^2 the appearance of great strength and energy.

桁 ˏHsing. The purlins of a roof; a plank to cross a rivulet; stocks for the feet; a clothes-horse: [13]ok, ˏheng, the purlins of a house.

衡 ˏHêng. A balance or thing to weigh with; to weigh; compared, adjusted; a balustrade; transverse; a yoke or strap on the head of cattle; the space under the eyebrows: [14]ˏheng ˏliong, to weigh and measure; *met.*, to estimate, as one's ability; [15]ˏkwong ˏheng, poise and scales; *met.*, accurate, definite; ˏki ˏheng, or ngük, ˏheng, a kind of armillary sphere; [16]ˏchung ˏheng, straight and transverse; COM., ˏheng ˏsang, name of a southern mountain.

恆 恒 ˏHêng. Constant, perpetual, regular; according to rule or law; to continue of the same mind, persevering: [17]ˏheng ˏsing, the mind constant, as in virtue; [18]ˏheng ˏsiong, perpetual; COM., ˏheng ˏsang, a mountain in the west of Chihli.

弘 ˏHêng. Twang of a bowstring; flapping of curtains; large, great; to enlarge, to act liberally: [19]ˏhang ˏheng, liberal, generous; ˏing ˏneng ˏheng tó^2 men can spread the doctrines.

宏 ˏHung. Used for the last; wide, extensive, ample, grand, as a prospect; the echoing noise of a wide hall: [20]ˏheng 'kwong, spacious; ˏheng 'wong, vast, extensive.

閎 ˏHêng. Gate of an alley; the bar of a gate; wide, spacious, vast and vacant: [21]hang ˏheng, the gate of an alley; [22]'kiu ˏheng, the gate of heaven.

蘅 ˏHêng. A fragrant plant, like mallows: to^2 ˏheng (?), sweet vernal grass; ˏhiong ˏheng, a fragrant plant.

珩 ˏHêng. A gem, anciently worn on the person as an ornament: pek, ˏheng, a white gem; ˏch'ung ˏheng, an azure-colored gem.

還 ˏHuan. Read ˏhwang; used in the coll. for ˏheng: to give back, to restore, to return; to pay back; to bid, to offer a price lower than

[1]行書 [2]行禮 [3]行裝 [4]行臺 [5]行息二分 [6]行事 [7]步行 [8]行善 [9]行李 [10]五行 [11]行樂圖 [12]行好心 [13]屋桁 [14]衡量 [15]權衡 [16]縱衡 [17]恆心 [18]恆常 [19]含弘 [20]宏廣 [21]閈閎 [22]九閎

that asked: same as ˏteng, q. v.: [1]ˏheng chai² to pay a debt; [2]ˏtó ˏheng ˏi, take and return it to him; [3]ˏheng ʻlau, returned; [4]ˏheng ka' to offer a lower price; [5]ˏheng ngwong² to pay vows; done as one wished; [6]ˏheng ˏch'ing, to give up a girl to be married; [7]ˏheng ʻpwong chëü² le' to repay principal by installments and stop reckoning interest: [8]ˏheng nioh, wai² how much do you bid? [9]ˏheng ˏch'ing ʻch'u, fully paid up.

ˏHeng. A coll. word: suspended, hanging down, as a cord; to bow or incline (the head): *ˏheng kiä²* or *ˏheng lóh, ˏli*, hanging down, dangling; *ˏheng kiä² ˏt'au*, to incline the head; *ˏheng ˏk'á tieu' kaëk*, drooping skirts and hitched up corners; *met.*, incomplete, not just the thing.

Heng². A coll. word: taciturn, reserved, incommunicative, silent, mum, of few words; to refuse to speak: *heng² heng²* taciturn; *tôi² heng²* both refusing to speak; *heng² ˏi chó²* keep silent and let him do as he pleases; *heng² tek, ʻheng*, very taciturn; *heng² heng² ʻk'eng ka² ʻsi ˏnëng*, the still dog bites people to death; *met.*, the reserved man is terrible when roused.

Heng². A coll. euphonic prefix, as in *heng² hwang²* to tie loosely; *heng² hang²* to keep a fire by covering with ashes.

(181) Hëng.

烘 ʻHung. Read *ˏhung*; coll. *ˏhëng*: to warm at a fire; to heat, to toast: [10]*ˏhëng ʻhwi*, to warm at the fire; [11]*ˏhëng ʻch'iu*, to warm one's hands; [12]*ˏhëng ˏpau*, to toast bread; [13]*ˏhëng ˏwang*, warped by fire; *ˏhëng ˏniäng*, burnt, scorched; [14]*ˏhëng k'ieu' ˏngau*, curled by the heat, as paper.

魟 ˏ Read *ˏkung* or *ˏhung*; coll. *ˏhëng*: a salt-water, scaleless fish—it is of a flat, circular shape, and sometimes has a yellowish tinge on the belly; found in the Foochow market: [15]*ˏwong ˏhëng*, a yellowish variety of this fish; [16]*ˏhëng ˏngü ʻsiong*, the *ˏhëng* salted and dried; [17]*ˏhëng ˏhëng e²* the *ˏhëng* flavor—applied to any fish partly spoiled.

ˏHëng. A coll. word: earnest, aroused, as by seeing what others effect: *ˏi ˏsing ʻlá á² ˏhëng*, his mind is aroused.

(182) Heu.

痚 ˏHou. Read *ˏhau* in the dictionaries: the asthma: COM., [18]*ˏheu chik,* or *ˏheu cheng'* disease of asthma; *ˏheu sau'* an asthmatic cough; *ˏheu ʻchü* (coll. *ˏheu ˏchü*) an asthmatic; COLL., *ˏheu ˏchü má² seu² tek, sau'* an asthmatic can't bear coughing; *met.*, one can't endure others' wickedness.

侯 ˏHou. A prince or feudal baron in ancient China; a marquis in modern days; pretty, handsome; but, unless; to receive happiness; a target for arrows; a surname: *ˏheu yong²* to avert evil and obtain good luck; COM., *ˏchü ˏheu*, a petty prince; *ˏheu ˏié*, my lord marquis; *ˏheu chiok*, title of marquis.

[1]還債 ○
[2]掏還伊 ○
[3]還了 [4]還價
[5]還願 [6]還親
[7]還本住利
[8]還箸壞 ○
[9]還清楚 [10]烘
火 [11]烘手 [12]烘
包 [13]烘彎 [14]烘
櫪交 [15]黃魟
[16]魟魚鯗 [17]魟
魟味 [18]痚疾

餱 ˏHou. Dry provisions, food prepared for a journey: [1]ˏheu ˏliong, dry provisions.

喉 ˏHou. The throat, the trachea: in the coll. read ˏhë and ˏhó, q. v.: [2]ˏheu ˏlëng, vulgarly either the windpipe or gullet; [3]ˏyéng ˏheu, the throat; COM., [4]ˈkiék ˏheu, Adam's apple; [5]ˏheu ˏngó, the quinsy; [6]ˏheu chëüˀ raw sores or inflammation of the throat.

篌 ˏHou. A musical instrument: [7]ˏkʻung ˏheu, a flat flute with 25 strings.

瘊 ˏHou. Pimples, pustules resulting from bad humors: [8]ˏheu ˈchü, a pustule.

婬 ˏHou. A female name; used in the coll. as an opprobrious epithet, applied to women; vile, wanton, adulterous: [9]ˏheu kaingˀ habitually lewd; ˏheu ˈkʻwang, or [10]ˏheu ˏheu siéˀ in a lewd way; [11]ˏheu ˏmó tiängˀ or ˏheu ˏtu ˏchʻiä, gadding about wantonly.

猴 ˏHou. A monkey, an ape: in the coll. read ˏkau, q. v.: [12]ˏmi ˏheu, a female monkey.

鍭 ˏHou. An arrow with an iron point and feathered shaft; the barb of a dart.

(183) Hëü.

煦ˀ Hsü. The genial warmth of the sun; hot, vivifying, nutritive; soothing, kind, gracious; to steam, to heat, to warm; to mature, to vivify; a red, warm color, carnation: [13]hëüˀ hëüˀ warm, genial; gracious; [14]ˏhwo hëüˀ genial, as weather; placid, kind.

呴ˀ Usually read ˏhü: to blow with the mouth; to speak well; used in the coll. in the sense of a rattling in the throat: COLL., hëüˀ hëüˀ kieuˀ a rattling sound in the throat, as from phlegm or asthmatic affections.

姁ˀ 嫗ˀ Chü. A mother; a dame, a matron: [15]ˈló hëüˀ an old woman; hëüˀ hëüˀ the fructifying effects of the sun.

饇ˀ To eat much, to gormandize; to give; gluttonous; satiated, filled, surfeited, loathing: [16]yéngˀ hëüˀ full fed, satiated.

酗ˀ Mad with drink, raving drunk, furious: [17]hëüˀ ˈchiu, delirium tremens.

(184) Hëüh.

*Hëüh*ˌ. A coll. word, as in hëühˌ ˈtié, to draw in the breath, as in wailing: hëühˌ hëühˌ kieuˀ a loud wailing, as of women for the dead.

(185) Hëük.

畜ˀ Chʻu. To rear, to feed, to raise; to domesticate, to herd; to cultivate; to restrain; to bear with; to obey; cattle, domestic animals; to gather, to hoard, in which sense the same as the next: [18]ˏseng hëükˌ domestic animals; [19]hëükˌ mukˌ to raise cattle; [20]hëükˌ chëüngˀ to

[1]餱糧 [2]喉嚨 [3]咽喉 [4]結喉 [5]喉蛾 [6]喉瘡 ○ [7]箜篌 [8]瘊子 [9]婬慣 [10]婬婬 [11]婬勢 婬毛定 [12]獼猴 ○ [13]煦煦 [14]和煦 [18]煦煦 ○ [15]老嫗 [16]饜飫 [17]酗酒 [18]牲畜 [19]畜牧 [20]畜衆

nourish the people; *ₑt'iéng ha²* *ₑsui hëük, ₑchi,* who in the world can bear with him! COM., *lëk₂ hëük,* the six domestic animals; *hëük, ₑseng,* you brute!

蓄, Ch'u. To collect, to accumulate, to hoard; to rear, to nourish; good vegetables: [1]*ₑchong hëük,* to hoard; [2]*hëük, lik₂* to reserve one's strength; [3]*'chi hëük,* fine vegetables; COM., [4]*chek, hëük,* to amass; [5]*hëük, e²* a purpose formed.

慉, Ch'u. To sustain, to encourage; to excite or treasure in the mind: [6]*hëük, 'yong,* to nourish; [7]*ung hëük,* treasured up, as virtue or learning; [8]*hëük, no²* to become angry, wrathful.

搐, Ch'u. To drag along, to pull by force, as one drags an ox; to shake rudely.

勗, 勖, To stimulate, to encourage, to stir up; to excite to effort, to animate.

(186) Hëüng.

釁, 衅, Hsin. To offer blood in sacrifice; to sprinkle sacrificial vessels with blood, to consecrate with blood, as temples; an offence, a wrong; a pretext, a cause of quarrel between nations; a presage, a token; to perfume one's self when worshiped, as an ancestor; to fumigate; to excite; a tiger's skin to wrap arms in: [9]*hëüng² 'ku,* to dedicate drums with blood; [10]*'k'ié hëüng²* to give cause of offence; COM., [11]*hëüng² k'ek,* a pretext for a quarrel; [12]*kiék, hëüng²* to be at feud with.

(187) Hi.

非 ₑFei. Not, negative; not so, opposite; not right, not good; false, bad, wrong; shameless, low; to slander, to reproach: [13]*ₑhi 'li,* unreasonable; [14]*ₑhi hwak,* unlawful; [15]*ₑhi yâ²* not so; [16]*ₑhi 'ch'ü ₑchi oi²* did not say (or mean) that; COM., [17]*sé² ₑhi,* yes and no, right and wrong; [18]*ₑhi 'ch'ü chaik, 'pi,* if not this then that; *ₑhi ₑngiong pok, ch'ok,* don't utter wrong words; *ₑhi ₑtung 'sieu 'k'ô,* not a trifling matter!

希 ₑHsi. Few, rare, seldom, infrequent; loose, not close or near; to hope, to wish, desirous; to scatter; to stop; to molt, as feathers; to shed, as hair: [19]*ₑhi wong²* to desire; COM., [20]*ₑhi 'hang,* scarce, few; *ₑhi ₑki,* rare, remarkable; COLL., *ₑhi haing²* how strange! unaccountable!

睎 ₑHsi. Used for the last; to look with longing, to hope earnestly; to remember kindly.

欷 ₑHsi. To sob, to catch the breath in weeping; to snore; timid: [21]*ₑhi ₑhü,* to sob and cry.

豨 Hsi. Name for pigs in Hunan; the noise of scampering pigs, grunting: [22]*ₑhung ₑhi,* a fabulous animal which protects against snakes; *ₑhi ₑling,* a medicinal root.

[1]藏蓄 [3]旨蓄 [5]蓄意 [7]蘊慉 [9]釁鼓 [11]釁隙 [13]非理 [15]非也 [17]是非 [18]非此則彼 [19]希望 [21]欷歔
[2]蓄力 [4]積蓄 [6]慉養 [8]慉怒 [10]啟釁 [12]結釁 [14]非法 [16]非此之謂 [20]希罕 [22]封豨

熺 熹 ꜀ Hsi. To heat, to roast or toast; hot, burning; light and heat together; abundant, pervading; day-break: com., [1]꜀Chio ꜀hi, a celebrated commentator on the *four books*—usually called ꜀Chio ‘chü.

熙 熈 ꜀ Hsi. Light, splendor, brightness; flourishing, glorious, prospering; extending, lasting, ample; dry, drying: [2]꜀hi ꜀hwo, prospering; [3]꜀hi ꜀ch‘ung ꜀ta, Hyson tea; [4]꜀hi ꜀tieu, a flourishing dynasty; com., [5]꜀k‘ong ꜀hi, the emperor Kang-hi, A. D. 1662–1723.

譆 ꜀ Hsi. The cry of one in pain or sorrow; sound of alarm or indignation, Oh! fie! grumbling; the muttering of spirits.

禧 ꜀ Hsi. Happy, lucky, blessed by the gods; to implore the gods: [6]꜀hung ꜀hi, great good luck; com., [7]꜀küng hó’ ꜀sing ꜀hi, "respectful congratulations on the new (year's) happiness"—written on cards.

稀 ꜀ Hsi. Open, wide apart, not close; loose, coarse, sleazy; thin, few; careless, remiss: [8]꜀hi ꜀su, bare, as leafless trees; com., [9]꜀ing ꜀seng ch‘ek, sek꜀ ‘ku ꜀lai ꜀hi, few men have ever reached the age of seventy; [10]꜀hi ꜀hi, open, apart; coarse, as cloth; coll., ꜀hi ꜀liăng, apart, not close; [11]‘yă ꜀hi sioh꜀ ꜀t‘au, very open or apart.

晞 Hsi. To dry, dried; day-break, bright.

俙 ꜀ Hsi. To counterfeit, simulated, pretending; like to; obscure, seen dimly: [12]ai’ ꜀hi, appearing as if.

絺 ꜀ Hsi. The fibers of hemp, used in making linen; fine hempen cloth: [13]꜀hi k‘ek, fine and coarse hempen cloth.

嬉 ꜀ Hsi. Pretty, handsome; pleasant sports, rambles; to play, to enjoy one's self: [14]꜀hi hié’ games of children; [15]꜀hi ꜀iu, a pleasure excursion; com., [16]꜀hi ch‘ieu’ playing and laughing.

妃 ꜀ Fei. A partner, a consort, a royal concubine; the wife of the heir apparent: [17]꜀küng ꜀hi, the imperial concubines; [18]꜀hi ꜀ping, a maid of honor.

姬 ꜀ Chi. The surname of Hwang-ti, also of the emperors of the Chow dynasty; a general term for the royal concubines, in which sense the same as the last; beautiful! noble women! (like Houri, Hebe), because of the fame of the Hi family.

嚱 ꜀ Hsi. The voice, sound of the breath emitted forcibly; a sigh.

嘻 ꜀ Hsi. The sound of mirth; agreeing, in harmony; pleased, delighted: coll., ꜀hi ꜀hi ch‘ieu’ to laugh pleasantly, the face lighted with smiles; ꜀hi ꜀li, to smile, to grin; ꜀hi ꜀hi ꜀hó ꜀hó, or ꜀hi ꜀hi ꜀hó ꜀hoi, a cooly's cry; ꜀hi ‘li ꜀hu ꜀tu (also spoken ꜀hi ‘li ꜀hu ꜀lu), carelessly, confusedly.

1朱	3熙	朝	禧	禧	生	來	11野	12僾	14嬉	16嬉	18妃
熹	春	5康	7恭	8稀	七	稀	稀	俙	戲	笑	嬪
2熙	茶	熙	賀	疏	十	10稀	一	13絺	15嬉	17宮	
和	4熙	6鴻	新	9人	古	稀	頭	綌	遊	妃	○

飛 ˏ Fei. To fly, to flit, flying; to go swiftly; soaring, lofty: used in the coll for ˏ*pwi*, q. v.: [1]ˏ*hi* ‘*neu*, or ˏ*hi* ˏ*k‘ing*, birds; [2]ˏ*hi* ˏ*lu*, a house on deck, a high cabin; [3]ˏ*hi* ˏ*liêng*, god of winds, Boreas; COM., [4]ˏ*hung* ˏ*hi p‘aĕk*ˎ *sang*ˀ frightened out of one's wits; [5]ˏ*hi* ˏ*sa* ‘*cheu sik*ˎ the dust flies and the stones run, as in a gale of wind; [6]ˏ*hi* ˏ*tó*, the flying dagger—in theatricals; ˏ*hi* ‘*hu* ˏ*ki*, the flying-tiger flag—borne before officers; [7]ˏ*hi pwak*ˎ ˏ*siéng* ˏ*sü*, the flying-cymbal priest—one of Budh's eighteen disciples; COLL., ˏ*hi* ˏ*siêng pôh*ˎ *piăh*ˎ can fly to the eaves and light on walls, as an expert thief.

羲 ˏ Hsi. Vapor; a name: COM., [8]*huk*ˎ ˏ*hi*, the traditional founder of the Chinese monarchy, Fohi—also called [9]ˏ*hi* ˏ*hwong*, the emperor Hsi.

犧 ˏ Hsi. A sacrificial animal of a uniform color; sheep, goats or oxen were used; spotless, pure: [10]ˏ*hi* ˏ*seng*, sacrificial animals.

僖 ˏ Hsi. Same as the next: to feel joy in; joyous, delighted; cautious, fearful of: [11]ˏ*hi lok*ˎ delighted.

喜 ‘ Hsi. Pleased, joyful; that which gives joy; to feel glad; to give joy to; to rejoice in, to like: COM., [12]‘*hi* ˏ*hwang*, or [13]ˏ*hwang* ‘*hi*, pleased, glad; [14]‘*kŭng* ‘*hi*, to congratulate in person, joy to you! [15]‘*hi sëü*ˀ or ‘*hi k‘eng*ˀ a joyful event; [16]‘*hi* ‘*chiu*, a feast; [17]‘*hi k‘e*ˀ a delighted look; [18]‘*hi* ˏ*king*, fees on festive occasions—paid to the village temple; COLL., *tai*ˀ ˏ*sing* ‘*hi*, pregnancy; ‘*hi* ˏ*sing taĕng*ˀ the joy-god stirs—i. e., the marriage is about to be consummated; ‘*hi chê*ˀ *lang*ˀ‘*a* ‘*k‘eu*, “the word ‘*hi* has two mouths in it”; *met.*, the two families quarreling about the marriage presents.

‘*Hi.* A coll. euphonic prefix, as in ‘*hi* ‘*hă*, to look askance, to look angrily at.

ˏ*Hi.* A coll. word or euphonic prefix, as in ˏ*hi* ˏ*hai*, sound of groaning; an ejaculation of burden bearers; ˏ*hi* ˏ*li* ‘*k‘i* ˏ*li*, to set up a laugh, to smile or grin; ˏ*hi* ˏ*hi* ˏ*ha* ˏ*ha*, indecent haste, as in eating; to speak low and fast, to mumble words.

(188) Hiă.

罅 鏬 ˏ Hu. The 1st is a vulgar character; the 2nd read *ha*ˀ and *ch‘a*ˀ; used in the *Paik*, ˏ*Ing* for the coll. ˏ*hiă*: to open, to crack open, as wood in drying; yawning, gaping; cleft; *met.*, lax, dissipated, foppish; to open, as a door; to straddle, to stride: [19]ˏ*hiă* ˏ*hiă* ˏ*k‘wi*, yawning; wide open, as doors; ˏ*pang* ˏ*hiă*, to stride; ˏ*hiă* ‘*hiă ch‘ieu*ˀ (also spoken ‘*hiă* ‘*hiă ch‘ieu*ˀ), to open the mouth wide and laugh immoderately; ‘*ngu* ˏ*hiă*, or ‘*ngu* ˏ*hiă lĕk*ˎ *leng*ˀ scattered, in utter confusion; ˏ*hiă liĕk*ˎ cracked, cleft; [20]ˏ*hiă lang*ˀ ˏ*peng*, yawning open, cleft in twain; ˏ*hiă ch‘oi*ˀ gaping mouth—i. e., dead, as a clam; ˏ*hiă* ˏ*pai*, “makes a spread”—foppish; ‘*chiă* ˏ*nëng* ‘*yă* ˏ*hiă*, this person is very dissipated.

---

[1] 飛鳥 飛廬 [3] 飛廉 [4] 魂飛魄散 [5] 飛沙走石 [6] 飛刀 [7] 飛鈸禪師 [8] 伏羲 [9] 羲皇 [10] 犧牲 [11] 僖樂 [12] 喜歡 [13] 歡喜 [14] 拱喜 [15] 喜事 [16] 喜酒 [17] 喜氣 [18] 喜金 [19] 罅罅開 [20] 罅二片

海上絲綢之路文獻集成 科技與文化编

福州方言拼音字典

‘*Hiă*. A coll. word: given to sport; idle, unemployed, to spend time in recreation: ‘*hiă kaing*’ habituated to idling; ‘*hiă sioh, hiok,* to sport awhile.

‘*Hiă*. A coll. word: that, that one, the other; the opposite of ‘*chiă* (this); also an intensive particle corresponding to *ne*^{2} (two), very, exceedingly, incessantly: ‘*hiă* ꜀*nĕng*, that person; ‘*hiă* ‘*t‘á*, or ‘*hiă* ‘*k‘wang*, that way, shape, or fashion; ‘*hiă* ꜀*huí*, or ‘*hiă nóh*, that time or thing! — an exclamation in trying to recall a thing to mind; ‘*hiă ma*’ *chiăh, se*^{2} *ma*’ such scolding is scolding indeed! ‘*hiă twai*^{2} *ne*^{2} *twai*^{2} very large! ‘*hiă kaĕ*’ *ne*^{2} *kaĕ*’ to cry out incessantly.

(189) **Hiăh.**

嚇 Hsia. Read *haik*,; coll. *hiăh*,: an angry tone, to threaten, to intimidate; frightened, intimidated: [1]*hiăh, ch‘a*’ to threaten, to browbeat; [2]*hiăh,* ‘*chau*, frightened away; [3]*twai*^{2} *wă*^{2} *hiăh,* ꜀*i*, to browbeat him with violent talk; [4]*hiăh,* ‘*si* ꜀*nĕng*, to frighten people to death with threats.

(190) **Hiăk.**

Hiăk,. A coll. word: to deceive, to impose upon, to delude; to cozen, to cheat: *hiăk,* ‘*hung*, to deceive; *hiăk, kwo*’ *siĕng*’ (or ꜀*peng*), to succeed in deluding; cheated, gulled.

Hiăk,. A coll. word: to fall, to topple over, to fall forward or backward; also to flap or move suddenly, as a door; *hiăk,* ‘*tó*, or *hiăk,* ‘*tó lóh*$_2$ ꜀*li*, to topple over flat; *hiăk, kwo*’ to flap over, as a leaf or a door.

Hiăk$_2$. A coll. word: to flap, as a bird's wings; to flutter, to flap in the wind; to raise or open, as things fast on one side; flapping, oscillating, as things pendent; throbbing, as the heart: *hiăk*$_2$ *hiăk*$_2$ oscillating; *hiăk*$_2$ ‘*k‘i*, to raise, as a trunk lid, or as a dog raises his ears; *hiăk*$_2$ *hiăk*$_2$ *kieu*’ the noise of things oscillating.

(191) **Hiăng.**

兄 ꜀Hsiung. Read ꜀*hing*; coll. ꜀*hiăng*: an elder brother; a senior, a superior; a term of respect: [5]꜀*hiăng tiĕ*^{2} or [6]꜀*hiăng tiĕ*^{2} ꜀*kó*, brothers; [7]꜀*hiăng tiĕ*^{2} *pwoi*’ friends; [8]꜀*pau* ꜀*hiăng*, own elder brother; [9]꜀*tong* ꜀*hiăng*, elder cousins-german; [10]*ngiĕ*^{2} ꜀*hiăng*, a foster-brother; a dear friend; also a woman's paramour; [11]꜀*hiăng* ‘*só*, elder brother's wife; [12]꜀*hiăng niong*^{2} *tiĕ*^{2} an older, yielding to a younger, brother; [13]꜀*hiăng tiĕ*^{2} ꜀*hung ch‘wang*’ (or ꜀*pwong chau*’), brothers cooking and living separately; [14]꜀*hiăng tiĕ*^{2} ꜀*chang* ꜀*ka* ‘*hwi*, brothers quarreling about the property.

꜀*Hiăng*. A coll. word: a rank smell, as of putrid fish; a stench, a fetid smell, an offensive odor: *ch‘au*’ ꜀*hiăng* ꜀*hiăng*, a stench; ꜀*hiăng* ꜀*hiăng e*^{2} a rancid smell.

Hiăng’. A coll. word: dangerous, perilous; a risk, a mere chance: *hiăng*’ *hiăng*’ *pauk*, very slight chances—*scil.*, of his recovery; *hiăng*’ *lóh*, to topple over, as one dozing in a chair.

1嚇叱 2嚇走

3大話嚇伊

4嚇死伙○

5兄弟○

6兄弟哥○

7兄弟輩○

8胞兄 9堂兄

10誼兄 11兄嫂

12兄讓弟○

13兄弟分爨

14兄弟爭家

伙○

(192) Hié.

廢' Fei. A house in ruins; to abandon, to throw aside, to destroy; to lose; to repudiate, to disinherit, to depose; to stop, to fail, to pass away; obsolete, null; spoiled, corrupt; useless, degraded: COM., [1]*꜀hwong hié'* to lie waste; abandoned; [2]*hié' ꜂ch'ie*, obsolete, intermitted; [3]*hié' ꜀ing*, cripples, infirm people; [4]*hié' ꜀si sek꜀ sëü'* time wasted and business failing; [5]*pwang' ꜀tu ꜀i hié'* to abandon it when half done; COLL., [6]*꜂chiă tai' má' hié' tek꜀ k'ó'* this matter cannot be set aside.

費' Fei. To spend, to use; to dissipate; to exert; expense, cost, trouble, outlay; waste; lavishing, squandering: COM., [6]*tong' hié'* or *hié' ꜀ŭng'* to spend money; [7]*꜀hwa hié'* to squander; [8]*p'ó' hié'* "a needless expense"–said politely by the guest or receiver of presents; [9]*chak꜀ hié'* miscellaneous expenses; *hié' lik꜀* to exert one's self; [10]*lo' hié'* traveling expenses; [11]*hié' cheng' ꜀sing ꜀ki*, to waste one's mental energies on; COLL., *hié' k'e'* spending breath on—troublesome, difficult to do.

戲' **戱**' Hsi. To fence, to play with weapons; to divert one's self, to sport; a play, a comedy, a theatrical exhibition: COM., [12]*꜀iu hié'* sports, games; [13]*hié' ꜀pang*, or *hié' ꜀tai*, a theatrical stage; [14]*hié' ꜂chŭ*, play-actors; [15]*hié' ꜂pong*, play-bills; *hié' ꜂pwong*, a list of plays; [16]*꜀tieu hié'* lewd dalliance; *hié' ꜀pung*, the "green room"; [17]*hié' tang'* a male actor dressed as a female; COLL., *hié' ꜀t'au ꜀kó*, head manager of a theater; *chó' hié'* to play, as actors; *hié' laĕng'* to make sport of, to annoy; *hié' siong' ꜀tiong*, the play has begun; *hié' ch'aung'* gadding about to theaters; *p'ah꜀ ꜀sing hié'* sporting, mischievous; *꜀pang ꜂kong hié'* plays in the colloquial; *hié' ch'ok꜀* the parts of a play; *hié' sioh꜀ ch'ok꜀* one part or act.

肺' Fei. The lungs; they are connected with *꜀king* (metal): *hié' ꜂hu*, the lungs; COM., [18]*꜀kang hié'* "liver and lungs"—as of goats sold in the market; *hié' ꜂kwong*, the bronchial tubes; [19]*hié' ꜀ló*, consumption of the lungs; *hié' ꜀chieu só'* the lungs dry and inflamed; *hié' ꜀siong ꜀hung*, cold in the lungs, bronchitis.

芾' Fei. Small: *pe' hié' ꜀kang ꜀tong*, a small sweet sorbus or service tree. Read *hok꜀* as in *hok꜀ hok꜀* luxuriant, umbrageous.

贔' Strong, robust, herculean, athletic: [20]*pe' hié'* energetic, strong to bear burdens.

奚 ꜀ Hsi. Why? how? a page to an officer; a waiting maid: [21]*chiu ꜀hié*, a waiting boy or maid; *꜀hié ꜂ch'ŭ*, how can you approve? *꜀hié pok꜀ k'ĕŭ' yă'* why do you not go?

徯 ꜀ Hsi. To wait for, to hope; a narrow pathway: *꜀hié keng'* a foot path.

---

[1]荒廢 [2]廢弛 [3]廢人 [4]廢時 失事而廢 [5]半途 [6]動費 [7]花費 [8]破費 [9]雜費 [10]路費 [11]費盡心機 [12]遊戲 [13]戲棚 [14]戲子 [15]戲榜 [16]調戲 [17]戲旦 [18]肝肺 [19]肺癆 [20]贔贔 [21]酒奚

蹊 ˏCh'i. A foot or bridle path, a narrow path; to penetrate through by-ways; to go where there is no road: [1]ˊsing ˏhié, made into a road.

鼷 ˏ A small meadow mouse, called [2]ˊngi ˏhié, or ˏkang ˊk'eu ˏhié, the sweet-mouthed rat; its bite is considered poisonous.

攜 擕 ˏHsieh. To lead by the hand, as a blind man or a child; to go with, to take along; to join, to lock arms; to carry, to take up from the ground; to leave: [3]ˏhié ˏt'i, to lead by the hand; [4]ˏhié ˊch'iu ˏtung ˏheng, to go hand in hand; [5]ˏhié ˏt'i, to take in the hand, to carry.

觿 ˏHsi. An ivory stiletto or horn bodkin, used for opening knots; anciently worn on the girdle; a kind of large tortoise: [6]pwoi² ˏhié, to tie the bodkin to the waist; [7]ch'oi² ˏhié, name of a star.

畦 ˏ A field of 50 ˊmu, or about 8 English acres; a plat of ground: [8]ˏhié ch'ai² kitchen vegetables. Read ˏkié, a low wall around a field.

惠² Hui. Kind, gracious, forbearing; benevolent, liberal, charitable; to show kindness to; give in charity; compliant; to give, to concede; to adorn; benefit, grace, charity, presents: [9]hié² ai² or ˏchü hié² compassionate kindness; [10]seu² hié² or ˏsing hié² to receive favors; [11]hié² kau² to teach kindly; COM., [12]ˏong hié² grace, mercy; [13]seng² hié² or haiu² hié² your great favor—an epistolary phrase; hié² ˏang kaing² a district of Chinchew prefecture.

蕙² Hui. A fragrant species of marshy orchid, like a *Hubernaria*, with many flowers on one stalk, called [14]ˏlang hié².

繐² Hui. Fine cloth or linen (from the west) of a loose texture, a kind of Decca muslin: [15]hié² ˏsiong, loose-textured cloth, anciently worn as mourning.

繫² Hsi. To tie, to bind; to continue; attached to, to think of; to retain, to hold: [16]ˏmi hié² to tie; [17]hié² ˏlieng, to follow, as results their causes; [18]hié² ˏsing, fixed in the mind; COM., [19]ˏkwang hié² important results, consequences involved.

係² Hsi. The substantive verb, to be, am, is; to connect, to continue; to succeed to, in which sense the same as the last and the next: ˊch'ü hié² this is (thus and so); [20]hié² se² ˏhó ko² what is the cause or matter?

系² Hsi. To connect, to tie, to continue; a succession: [21]ˏsiong hié² continuous; COM., [22]sié² hié² a genealogy, a family record.

慧² Hui. Intelligent, perspicacious, wise, clever; shrewd, quick-witted, subtle, ingenious, adroit, skillful:

1 成蹊 3 攜提 同行 6 佩觿 8 畦菜 10 受惠 12 恩惠 14 蘭蕙 16 維繫 18 繫心 20 係是 21 相系

2 䶊鼷 4 攜手 5 攜持 7 角觿 9 惠愛 11 惠教 13 盛惠 15 繐裳 17 繫聯 19 關繫 何故 22 世系

hó' ˏ*heng* ʻ*sieu hié'* desirous of appearing clever in some little matter; COM., [1]ʻ*te*' *hié'* wise, discerning; wisdom.

恚 Hui. Rage, anger; to hate, to dislike; irritated at, indignant, angry.

蟪 Hui. A species of beetle or cicada, called [2]ʻ*hié'* ˏ*ku*, living only half a year.

譓 Hui. To investigate, to discern; ingenious, full of plans and shifts; knowing, successful.

吠 Fei. Sound of a dog barking: [3]ʻ*k'eng hié'* or [4]ʻ*keu hié'* the dog barks.

(193) Hiék.

熁 Hsieh. Read *hiék,*; coll. *hiék,*: heat rising up, ascending heat; to warm, to heat; exposed to the fire, heated: [5]*hiék, siong'* heat rising up; [6]*hiék, tioh,* burnt; *hiék,* ˏ*ta*, dried; [7]*hiék,* ˏ*u*, blackened by the heat; [8]*hiék, sioh,* the loadstone.

血 Hsieh. Blood; the 143d radical: in the coll. read *haik,* q. v.: [9]*k'ek, hiék,* to weep tears of blood—written on funeral cards; [10]*te' hiék,* a species of madder.

俠 Chia. Generous, noble-minded, public-spirited, zealous for the right; bold, intrepid; to assist, to redress another's wrongs: [11]ˏ*hó hiék,* a hero; [12]*eng' hiék,* mutual sympathy; [13]*hiék, k'e'* noble-minded, intrepid; [14]*hiék, sëü'* or [15]*hiék, k'aik,* a bold advocate.

峽 Hsia. A mountain precipice; hills forming a gorge through which a stream of water forces its way: [16]*tieu' k'eng' hiék,* the Shauking gorge in Kwangtung province.

狹 Hsia. Narrow, strait; a contracted passage: *met.*, narrow-minded, mean: [17]ʻ*ch'iéng hiék,* shallow and narrow; [18]*hiék, ai'* a narrow pass; *met.*, mean; [19]ˏ*pi hiék,* low and contracted, mean.

挾 Hsia. To hold, to carry, to carry under the arm; to hold the string of a bow; to conceal; to store up; to hide in the bosom; to defend; to trust to, to depend on; to presume upon, overbearing, arrogant: used in the coll. for *keh,* q. v.: [20]*hiék,* ˏ*t'i*, to hold under the arm; to undertake; COM., [21]*hiék, chié'* to oppress arrogantly; COLL., *hiék,* ˏ*hiéng*, to cherish hatred; *kaéng'* ˏ*i hiék,* ˏ*hiéng*, is at feud with him.

脇 **脅** Hiseh. The sides of the body; the ribs, place under the arm; to gather; to intimidate, to reprimand; to take advantage of: *p'aik, hiék,* to intimidate; COM., [22]ʻ*chó hiék, eu' hiék,* the left and right side; *hiék, kauk,* the ribs; *hiék, a'* the side; COLL., *hiék, t'iáng'* side-ache.

穴 Hsüeh. A cave, formerly used for dwellings; a den, a cave, a hole, a grotto; underground cavities, graves; a lurking place for men or beasts; a sinus in the body; to bore or dig a hole, to dig through;

1 智慧 2 蟪蛄 3 犬吠 4 狗吠 5 熁上 6 熁着 7 熁烏 8 熁石 9 泣血 10 地血 11 豪俠 12 任俠 13 俠氣 14 俠士 15 俠客 16 肇慶峽 17 淺狹 ○ 18 狹隘 19 卑狹 20 挾持 21 挾制 22 左脅右脅

empty; the 116th radical: [1]‘*k‘ung hiék*, a hole, a den; *hiék* ꜀*kü*, to dwell in caverns; COM., [2]‘*mwo*’ *hiék*, graves, vaults; [3]‘*kek*, *hiék*, a lucky grave; *hiék*, *tó*² a good site, as of a grave; *met.*, a vital part of the system.

協 叶 Hsieh. Agreement, concord, union, harmony; mutual help; united, assistant, joint; to aid; submissive: COM., [4]꜀*tung* ꜀*sing hiék*, *lik*, to exert strength unitedly; [5]꜀*tüng hiék*, or *hiék*, ꜀*tai*, a brigadier; [6]*hiék*, ‘*liăng*, a brigadier-general of bannermen; [7]*hiék*, *pai*’ the second bridesmaid; [8]*hiék*, *paing*’ *tai*² *hok*, *sëü*’ assistants of a prime minister; *hiék*, *ong*’ rhyming, cadence.

勰 Hsieh. Harmony of sentiment; union of thought; a man's name.

頁 The head; the 181st radical, seldom used in classic writing; in the coll., the numeral for leaves of books or flowers, lobes of liver, etc.: COLL., [9]*hiék*, *so*’ the number of leaves; *hiék*, *so*’ *sioh*, *pah*, has 100 leaves; *hiék*, *pwang*’ a leaf and a half.

(194) Hiéng.

掀 Hsien. Read ꜀*hüng*; used in the *Paik*, ꜀*Ing* for the coll. ꜀*hiéng*: to lift up, to remove, as a cover, for which ‘*hwang* is more commonly used: [10]꜀*hiéng* ‘*k‘i*, or [11]꜀*hiéng* ꜀*k‘wi*, to uncover; ꜀*kwo kai*’ ꜀*hiéng* ‘*k‘i*, remove the skillet-cover; ꜀*hiéng* ‘*lá* ꜀*liăng*, uncover it and let it cool.

‘顯 ‘顕 Hsien. Light, manifest, apparent, conspicuous, clear; illustrious; glorious, effulgent; to make plain, to exhibit, to display; to render illustrious: [12]‘*hiéng* ‘*k‘ó*, "the illustrious finisher"—a deceased father; [13]‘*hiéng tëü*’ to manifest: COM., [14]‘*hiéng* ꜀*ming*, or ‘*hiéng hiéng*’ to make manifest; [15]‘*hiéng haik*, luminous, as a god's response; [16]‘*hiéng seng*’ clearly efficacious; [17]‘*hiéng tak*, distinguished, famous; [18]‘*hiéng* ‘*ch‘iu taung*’ to exhibit skill (in work or against an enemy); COLL., ‘*hiéng* ‘*la hiéng*’ made very clear.

‘幰 Hsien. A curtain drawn over or around a carriage to keep off the sun; the curtain of a sedan.

‘俔 To compare, compared to, like; to spy out, to explore; a weathercock: [19]*kang*’ ‘*hiéng*, a spy.

‘蜆 Hsien. General name of bivalve shells, but especially thin-shelled and lacustrine ones; sometimes applied to some hanging chrysalides: in the coll., ꜀*lieu* ‘*kiăng*, q. v.

‘晛 Yeu. Clear light, cloudless sunlight; the clear sun in winter melting the snow.

‘覞 Yeu. The eyes starting out; to see, to regard; to view slightly: [20]‘*hiéng* ‘*hiéng*, to look at; [21]‘*hiéng* ‘*wang*, good looking, pretty.

‘鋧 A small chisel, a sort of javelin; a hand-staff.

[1]孔穴 [2]墓穴 [3]吉穴 [4]同心協力 [5]中協 [6]協領 [7]協拜 [8]協辦大學士 [9]頁數 [10]掀起 [11]掀開 [12]顯考 [13]顯著 [14]顯明 [15]顯赫 [16]顯聖 [17]顯達 [18]顯手段 [19]間俔 [20]覞覞 [21]覞睆

APLH. DICT. 29

ʻ**險** Hsien. A precipice, an abyss; difficult, dangerous, hazardous; insecure, in danger; *met.*, corrupt, wicked: [1]*ˏkang ʻhiéng*, depraved; COM., [2]*ˏngui ʻhiéng*, dangerous, prejudicial; [3]*hiéng teʾ* a dangerous place; *met.*, the key of a position; COLL., [4]*ʻhiéng kwoʾ* or *ʻhiéng ʻla kwoʾ* to pass over danger, as of a serious illness; *pauk*, *ʻhiéng*, or *ʻhiéng pauk*, to risk the danger; *ˏtʻiéng ʻmwang teʾ ʻhiéng*, full of hazard, as walking on the verge of a precipice; *ʻhiéng ˏsié*, or *ʻhiéng ˏsié ˏsié*, almost, within a little; *ˏchʻa ʻhiéng ʻhiéng pwak*, came within a little of falling.

ʻ**玁** A dog with a long snout, a pointer used in hunting: [5]*ʻhiéng ʻüng*, name of a horde of Huns famous in the days of Confucius, so called from their savageness.

Hiéngʾ. A coll. word: to throw, to pitch, to toss; to fling away: *hiéngʾ kwoʾ* toss it over (here or there); *hengʾ hiéngʾ* pitch it away; *hiéngʾ ˏchʻa*, to toss bundles of wood; *hiéngʾ kiăʾ* or *hiéngʾ lŏh, kʻóʾ* fling it down.

Hiéngʾ. A coll. word, as in *hiéngʾ hiéngʾ* or *hiéngʾ hiéngʾ ˏhü*, dangerous, perilous, full of risk, as in standing, or placing things, close to a brink.

ˏ**賢** ˏ**賢** Hsien. Virtuous, wise, moral, worthy; excellent, superior in morals or in intellect; a term of laudation; to surpass; to praise, to call worthy: [6]*ˏhiéng ˏchai*, superior abilities; [7]*ˏhiéng ˏhiéng*, to value the virtuous; COM., [8]*ʻsengʾ ˏhiéng*, sages and philosophers; [9]*ˏhiéng ˏing*, a virtuous man, a philosopher—a class of men next to sages; [10]*ˏhiéng taik*, exalted virtue; [11]*ˏhiéng ˏchʻá*, a faithful wife; [12]*chʻek, sek, neʾ ˏhiéng*, the seventy-two disciples; COLL., *ˏhiéng hwoiʾ* "virtuous union"—a good wife is so called.

ˏ**嫌** Hsien. To dislike, to hold in contempt, to think meanly of; to loathe, to despise; prejudiced, suspicious; fastidious; jealous of: COM., [13]*ˏhiéng haungʾ* to hate; [14]*piéʾ ˏhiéng*, to avoid exciting suspicion; [15]*kʻeʾ ˏhiéng*, to dislike, to reject; COLL., *ˏhiéng laiuʾ* to be fastidious about things; *ˏhiéng ˏkang ˏhiéng kengʾ* "hates liver and gizzard"—dislikes this and that.

ˏ**懸** Hsüan. To suspend, to hang down; to be anxious, in suspense, undecided; anxiously; unlike: [16]*ˏhiéng chiok*, or [17]*ˏsiong ˏhiéng*, very unlike; COM., [18]*ˏhiéng ˏki*, the divining pen—usually called *ˏki pek*; [19]*ˏhiéng wongʾ* to look anxiously for; [20]*ˏhiéng ˏhü*, insecure, as one's footing; precarious, as affairs; COLL., *ˏhiéng ˏsing taiuʾ ʻtang*, the mind in great suspense; *ʻchiă taiʾ kiéʾ koʾ ˏhiéng ʻlá*, the matter still undecided.

ˏ**玄** Hsien. Dark, somber, blackish, like the deep sky; to manage; deep, still, silent; abstruse, profound; name of Kiaking; the 95th radical: COM., [21]*ˏhiéng táʾ* or [22]*ˏhiéng ˏtʻiéng siongʾ táʾ* the Shangti of the somber heavens; COLL., *ˏhiéng ˏtang*,

[1]奸險 [2]危險 [3]險地 [4]險過 [5]玁狁 [6]賢才 [7]賢賢 [8]聖賢 [9]賢人 [10]賢德 [11]賢妻 [12]七十二賢 [13]嫌恨 [14]避嫌 [15]棄嫌 [16]懸絕 [17]相懸 [18]懸乩 [19]懸望 [20]懸虛 [21]玄帝 [22]玄天上帝

a god supposed to act as porter in heaven.

泫 ˏHsien. Also read ʻhiéng: glistering dewdrops; pendent dewdrops; falling tears; deep flowing water, a wide sheet of water; name of a river in the south-west of Shansi.

弦 ˏHsien. The string of a bow; chord of an arc; the moon in quarter on the 8th and 23d days of the month; a beating pulse: [1]*ʻngu ˏhiéng*, a guitar with 5 strings; COM., [2]*ˏkŭng ˏhiéng*, the string of a bow; [3]*siong^{2} ˏhiéng*, and [4]*ʻha^{2} ˏhiéng*, first and last quarters of the moon; COLL., *ˏhiéng ʻtong*, a bow or lute string broken.

絃 ˏHsien. Silken strings of musical instruments: [5]*ˏhiéng ˏkó*, to play songs; [6]*ʻli ˏhiéng*, to tune the guitar; COM., [7]*ch'ek, ˏhiéng*, a seven-stringed fiddle; [8]*sŭk, ˏhiéng*, "join the guitar string"—a widower marrying his second wife.

眩 ˏHsien. Also read ʻ*hiéng:* confused vision, dizzy, wandering eyes; defective, squinting sight; confused, mixed, out of order; not discerning, mistaken.

蚿 ˏHsien. The Julus or gally worm, a sort of milleped, called [9]*ʻma ˏhiéng*, found in dry places; it is of a dark purple color and curls up when disturbed.

舷 ˏHsien. The side of a ship or boat, the gangway or bulwarks of a vessel: [10]*k'aiu^{2} ˏhiéng ˏi ˏkó*, to sing to the accompaniment of beating the junk's side.

衒 𧗳 ˏHsien. Also read ʻ*hiéng:* bragging, puffing, vaunting, boasting; to display for sale: [11]*ˏhiéng ngŭk, ˏkiu ˏsiu*, to offer a gem for sale; *met.*, seek a market for one's talents; [12]*chĕü^{2} ˏhiéng*, self-praise.

現^{2} Hsien. Used as a vulgar character for the next: luster of gems; to manifest, to appear; to display, to divulge, to show; apparent; to be seen now, plain, conspicuous, de facto; present: COM., [13]*hiéng^{2} ch'ok*, to become manifest; [14]*hiéng^{2} chai^{2}* now, at present; [15]*hiéng^{2} ˏhing*, to appear in real form; to show one's feelings; [16]*hiéng^{2} k'aik*, this instant; [17]*hiéng^{2} ˏchiéng*, ready money; [18]*hiéng^{2} ˏhwang*, current dollars; [19]*hiéng^{2} ʻli*, to pay (a bill) at once; [20]*hiéng^{2} ˏpwang*, the police now on duty; COLL., *hiéng^{2} sié^{2}* "a sight to the world"—the vicious going rapidly to ruin; *hiéng^{2} ˏsiăng*, or *hiéng^{2} ˏsiăng ˏsiăng*, ready, de facto; *hiéng^{2} ʻchiong tai^{2} ˏhu*, the great man with the ready palm—an epithet for beggars.

見^{2} Hsien. To appear, to be manifest; plain, open, revealed: [21]*ʻŭng hiéng^{2}* concealed and open, secret and revealed; COM., [22]*hwak, hiéng^{2}* to be manifest.

莧^{2} Hsien. Edible species of spinach, Artemisia and Chenopodium, distinguished by the adjectives prefixed: in the coll. read *haing^{2}* q. v.

---

[1] 五弦 [2] 弓弦 [3] 上弦 [4] 下弦 [5] 絃歌 [6] 理絃 [7] 七絃 [8] 續絃 [9] 馬蚿 [10] 扣舷而歌 [11] 衒玉求售 [12] 自衒 [13] 現出 [14] 現在 [15] 現形 [16] 現刻 [17] 現錢 [18] 現番 [19] 現理 [20] 現班 [21] 隱見 [22] 發見

(195) Hieu.

僥 ‹ Yao. False, hypocritical, deceitful: [1]‹hieu haingʾ to be wholly intent on gain; in coll., a lucky hit. Read ‹ngieu, as in [2]‹chieu ‹ngieu, a tribe of pigmies in the southwest, said to be three cubits high.

徼 ‹ Chiao. Also read ‹yeu: to ask, to seek, to beg, to solicit: [3]‹hieu hok, to pray for happiness; COM., [4]‹hieu haingʾ a lucky hit, a fortunate coincidence. Read kieuʾ in the dictionaries: to go round, to ward off; to assume; frontiers, limits: [5]‹iu kieuʾ a circuit-officer; [6]‹piéng kieuʾ the borders; [7]kieuʾ mieuʾ mysterious.

嘵 ‹ Hsiao. To dread, to apprehend; a tone of complaint, querulous: [8]‹hieu ‹hieu, apprehensive.

唻 ‹ Great; agitated, not at ease. Read ‹ch'ai: vulgar talk.

驍 ‹ Hsiao. A gentle horse; skillful at the game of throwing darts; strong, courageous; disinterested: [9]‹hieu ʻüng, valorous; [10]‹hieu ‹k'ié kauʾ an aid-de-camp among bannermen.

磽 ‹ Yao. Stony ground: [11]‹p'i ‹hieu, rich and poor soils.

澆 ‹ Yao. To sprinkle, to irrigate, to water; to dip; false, perfidious, ungrateful: COM., [12]‹hieu pok, false, hard-hearted; [13]‹hieu ‹lié, in a contrary way, perversely. Read ‹lieu: an eddy, a whirlpool.

枵 ‹ Hsiao. A hollow roof; hollow, empty, unfilled; famished, hungry: [14]‹hieu hok, an empty stomach; met., ignorant; [15]‹ngwong ‹hieu, a star in Aquarius.

梟 ‹ Hsiao. A kind of owl that eats its mother; met., strong, wicked; to hang up a criminal's head *in terrorem*: [16]‹hieu ‹keng, owl soup; [17]‹hieu kiongʾ or ‹hieu ʻüng, strong, unscrupulous; [18]‹hieu ‹t'ó, a winter peach; COM., ‹hieu ‹sing, ungrateful.

鴞 ‹ Hsiao. A horned, or barn owl, called [19]‹ch'i ‹hieu; a fabulous animal, called [20]‹pau ‹hieu, having a sheep's body and a man's face.

曉 ʻ Hsiao. Light, clear, in the morning; day-time; luminous, perspicuous, plainly stated, intelligible, apparent; to understand, to comprehend, to perceive: COM., [21]‹ming ʻhieu, to know clearly; [22]k'iéngʾ ‹hung ʻhieu, "wanting in perspicuity"—written as a critical note in essays; [23]ʻhieu ʻü or ʻhieu seʾ a proclamation for general information; COLL., ‹tu ʻhieu tek, know it fully; ʻhieu tek, ‹t'iáng, to understand what one hears; ʻhieu tek, siéʾ koʾ to understand worldly matters; ʻhieu tek, ʻlau, knew it already; ʻnü áʾ ʻhieu tek, máʾ do you understand or not?

(196) Hih.

Hih. A coll. euphonic prefix, as in hih, hwoh, to cheat, to deceive, to humbug.

[1]僥 [3]徼 [5]游 [7]徼 [9]驍 校 薄 腹 羹 桃 鴞 分
倖 福 徼 妙 勇 [11]肥 [13]澆 [15]元 [17]梟 [19]鴟 [21]明 曉
[2]僬 [4]徼 [6]邏 [8]嘵 [10]驍 磽 漓 枵 健 鴞 曉 [23]曉
僥 幸 徼 嘵 騎 [12]澆 [14]枵 [16]梟 [18]梟 [20]抱 [22]欠 諭

(197) **Hik.**

*Hik*₂. A coll. euphonic prefix, as in *hik*₂ *huk*₂ to fold up hastily and imperfectly; *hik*₂ *hak*₂ to shut, to close, as a fan.

(198) **Hing.**

興 ‘Hsing. To rise, to get up; to flourish; flourishing, prosperous; raised, elevated, promoted; to be in demand, fashionable; to move, to put in motion: also read *heng*˒ q. v.: [1] *‚hing ‚ping*, to march soldiers; COM., [2] *‚hing pai*˒ or *‚hing ‚soi*, to flourish and to decay; [3] *‚hing ‘k‘i*, to rise, to flourish; [4] *‚hing ‚chiong ‘ing tó*˒ the Tautai of Hinghwa, Chinchew, and Yungchun departments, Fookien; *‚hing ‘ku ‚sang pai*˒ *siok*₂ *‚hung*, "the Kushan monastery flourishes, the Siok Hung one decays"; *met*., said of new friendships, trade, etc., flourishing on the ruins of the old; [5] *‚hing wong*˒ flourishing, successful; [6] *‚hing hwa*˒ a department in Fookien; [7] *‚hing hwa*˒ *‚hiăng*, Hinghwaians; [8] *‚hing ‚kĕng*, to commence a work; [9] *‚si ‚hing*, fashionable; [10] *chauk*₂ *‚hing*, made over new, as a house; COLL., *‚hing ‚sang pai*˒ *lang*˒ the buyer (pays) three, and the seller two, *per cent*. (to the go-between).

兄 ‘Hsiung. An elder brother; a senior, a superior; a term of respect: in the coll. read *‚hiăng*, q. v.: COM., [11] *tai*˒ *‚hing*, or *‚hing ‘tiong*, elder brother, a superior; [12] *‚hing tá*˒ brothers; [13] *‚hing tá*˒ *‚ü ‘ch‘iu chëük*₂ brothers are like hands and feet; *‘pieu ‚hing tá*˒ male maternal cousins; also the sons of paternal aunts; [14] *‚pau ‚hing tá*˒ uterine brothers; [15] *‚tong ‚hing tá*˒ paternal cousins; *nói*˒ *‚hing tá*˒ wife's brothers; [16] *‚hing ‚tai*, exalted Sir! a term of respect in letters.

馨 ‘Hsiang. Odors perceived at a long distance: [17] *‚hing ‚hiong*, fumes of incense, savory; *met*., a wide reputation; *‚ming taik*₂ *‚mi ‚hing*, his illustrious virtues are fragrant.

歆 ‘Chin. To receive the savor of offering, to accept the fumes of incense; to enjoy food, to relish; to desire, to extol; to shake: *siong*˒ *tá*˒ *kü ‚hing*, Shangti receives our incense; [18] *‚hing siĕng*˒ to covet, to long for.

坰 ‘Chü. A desert or void place, a wild remote from towns; the edge of a forest: [19] *‚kau ‚hing*, tracts beyond towns, wilds.

駉 ‘Chü. A large, powerful horse; a pasture or paddock for horses: *‚hing ‚hing ‘meu ‘ma*, fine, robust stallions.

扃 ‘Chü. A door-bar, or latch outside of a door; to bolt or bar a door; a bar or frame in a chariot to hold weapons; an ear, a handle: [20] *‚hing ‚mwong*, to bolt the door. Read *‘keng:* to investigate fully.

‚Hing. A coll. euphonic prefix, as in *‚hing ‚heng*, to hoot at; *‚hing ‚hĕng*, to dry or warm at a fire; *‚hing ‚hwang*, to remove, as tiles from a roof.

詗 ‘Chü. Also read *heng*˒: to inform, to advise of; to spy, to pry into: *‚k‘ié ‘hing*,

[1] 興兵 [2] 興敗 [3] 興起 [4] 興泉永道 [5] 興旺 [6] 興化 [7] 興化兄 [8] 興工 [9] 時興 [10] 作興 [11] 大兄 [12] 兄弟 [13] 兄弟如手足 [14] 胞兄弟 [15] 堂兄弟 [16] 兄台 [17] 馨香 [18] 歆羨 [19] 郊坰 [20] 扃門

to search for information; *꜀tüng ‛hing*, a spy, informer.

‛*Hing*. A coll. euphonic prefix, as in *‛hing ‛hwang*, to turn over, as the leaves of a book; *‛hing ‛hiong*, just speak out (your price)!

侀 ꜀Hsing. Interchanged with the next: a thing perfectly formed; to form; a figure, a form, a body; a law, a statute, which should be fixed; perfect, fixed.

形 ꜀Hsing. Form, shape, figure, appearance, contour; material; bodily; manner, visage, air; site, aspect; a landscape; an apparition; to imitate, to give form to; to appear, to make manifest; to show, as the bones when lean: COM., [1]*꜀hing sié*ʾ the outline, as of scenery; [2]*꜀hing chaung*ʾ or *꜀hing yong*ʾ shape, form, appearance; [3]*꜀hing ch‛iong*ʾ a likeness, an image, as of a god; [4]*꜀hing ꜀ting ‛ku kwai*ʾ his visage is *outré;* [5]*꜀ngwong ꜀hing hiéng*ʾ *ch‛ok*, the original shape manifested; [6]*꜀hing chek*, form, appearance, a trace of; [7]*꜀hing saik*, the expression, looks; [8]*꜀hing chek*, or *꜀hing ‛t‛á*, bodily substance, the human form; [9]*꜀tu ꜀hing*, picture of a man; COLL., *꜀mó ꜀hing chek*, no clue, no traces of.

邢 ꜀Hsing. An ancient principality, now Hingtai district in the south-west of Chihli.

鉶 ꜀Hsing. An earthen vessel resembling a skillet or tripod, used to contain broth when sacrificing to ancestors.

型 ꜀Hsing. A mold of earth; an example, a formulary, an ensample; to mold; to be an example: [10]*‛tiéng ꜀hing*, a law, a precedent; [11]*꜀ngi ꜀hing*, a good example.

硎 ꜀Hsing. A whetstone; a square or oblong figure for sharpening tools; name of a valley.

刑 ꜀Hsing. Punishment by officers; to castigate; legal punishments torture; penal, criminal, as laws; inimical to, destructive of, said of one's destiny or of the elements; a law, a constant practice; to sacrifice victims: [12]*꜀ming ꜀hing*, to punish properly; COM., [13]*꜀ka ꜀hing*, or *tong*ʾ *꜀hing*, to punish; [14]*꜀hing hwak*, criminal laws, punishment; [15]*꜀hing ꜀pung*, the criminal office in a yamun; *‛ngu ꜀hing*, the five punishments; [16]*꜀hing hwak*, punishment; [17]*꜀hing pwo*ʾ Board of Punishments; [18]*꜀hing këü*ʾ instruments of torture; [19]*꜀hing k‛aik*, "punitive and destructive"—said of clashing fates among members of a family, producing sickness; [20]*꜀hing pwo*ʾ *꜀siong ꜀sü*, President of the Criminal Board.

眩 ꜀Hsüan. Read *꜀hiéng* and *‛hiéng;* coll. *꜀hing:* dizzy, confused, giddy, light-headed; to swim, as the head: [21]*꜀wong ꜀hing*, dizzy, giddy; *꜀t‛au ꜀hing*, light-headed; *꜀hing ꜀sung*, sea-sick; *꜀hing kieu*ʾ dizzy (from riding in) a sedan; *꜀hing ꜀hing ‛tiong*, reeling with dizziness.

陘 ꜀ A declivity in the contour of hills; an abrupt precipice; a defile, a ravine,

---

[1]形勢 [2]形狀 [3]形象 [4]形容古怪 [5]原形現出 [6]形跡 [7]形色 [8]形質 [9]圖形 [10]典型 [11]儀型 [12]明刑 [13]加刑 [14]刑法 [15]刑房 [16]刑罰 [17]刑部 [18]刑具 [19]刑尅 [20]刑部尚書 [21]昏眩

福州方言拼音字典

a gorge; a hob at the side of a furnace; a place in Hukwang.

Hing. A coll. euphonic prefix, as in *hing hang*, to burn, make a bonfire of; *hing heng*, to restore, to pay back; *hing heng heng*, hanging down, pendent.

(199) Hiok.

歇 Hsieh. To stop, to rest, to desist; to keep silence; to terminate, to discontinue, to appease: COM., [1]*hiok sek*, to discontinue, to rest; [2]*hiok k'e* to take a breathing-spell; [3]*hiok tang* to put down the load and rest; [4]*hiok sëük*, to lodge over night; [5]*hiok kié* to lay by for the season, as goods; COLL., [6]*hiok k'a*, to rest the feet (by sitting down); *hiok pwong taing* to stop at an inn; *mó hiok*, or *mó ting mó hiok*, without stopping, incessantly; *hiok tau* to rest at noon; *k'ó hiok*, "go rest"—a slang phrase, like "go to grass"; *hiok sioh hiok*, or *hiok sioh a* to stop awhile; *hiok sioh siäk*, or *hiok sioh k'aik 'ku*, to rest a spell.

蠍 Hsieh. A scorpion; used for scorpions in the classic and coll. Scriptures, as in Luke 10:19.

謁 To visit a superior or a gentleman; admitted to an audience; to signify to, to intimate; to state or declare, to inform by petition; a card: [7]*hiok kiéng* to visit a superior; [8]*hiok siä* a guest chamber.

(200) Hiong.

香 Hsiang. Fragrant, odoriferous, aromatic, sweet; incense; effluvia, or aroma; *met*., reputable, renowned, fragrant, as a name: COM., [9]*hiong 'ch'ó*, aromatic plants; [10]*hiong ku*, a fragrant mushroom; [11]*hiong loi*, a large species of univalve; [12]*hiong yong*, a kind of finger-lemon, the "Budh's hand"; [13]*t'ieng hiong*, "heavenly fragrance"—the Mowtan Camellia; [14]*hiong lu*, an incense vase, a censer; [15]*sieu hiong*, to burn incense; *hiong siäng* incense sticks; [16]*tëük hiong*, incense sticks with bamboo splints inside; *tong ung hiong*, incense sticks made without splints; *hiong 'hwi*, incense ashes—carried home from the temple after worshiping; *hiong 'ki tóh*, a censer stand; [17]*hiong 'këng*, Hongkong; COLL., *pe hiong*, to smell odors; *hiong kang*, bean-curd cakes, flavored with soy; [18]*hiong t'ak*, inferior incense in coils, used as night-burners; *hiong pui tü*, cakes of scented soap; *hiong tói* or *hiong pau*, small perfume bags, worn at the festival of the 5th month.

鄉 Hsiang. A village, a hamlet; the country; a ward, section of a town or city; five *chau*, or 12,500 houses, make a *hiong*; rude, country-like, rustic: [19]*hiong ki*, an old man titled by the Emperor; COM., [20]*hiong 'li*, village neighbors; [21]*hiong ch'ong*, a village; [22]*hiong 'tong*, an association, a society; [23]*hiong sing*, village gentry; [24]*hiong p'wai* the distribution of

[1]歇息 [2]歇氣 [3]歇擔 [4]歇宿 [5]歇季 [6]歇骹 [7]謁見 [8]謁舍 [9]香草 [10]香菰 [11]香螺 [12]香櫞 [13]天香 [14]香爐 [15]燒香 [16]竹香 [17]香港 [18]香塔 [19]鄉耆 [20]鄉里 [21]鄉村 [22]鄉黨 [23]鄉紳 [24]鄉派

ward business; *˛hiong ʻlô*, village elders; *˛hiong k'angʼ* the ward patrol; *pai*² *˛hiong*, a village of depraved morals; [1]*˛hiong seʼ* the provincial examinations for the Küjin degree; *˛hiong sŭk₂* village customs; *˛liêng ˛hiong*, a union of villages for defence; COLL., *˛hiong a*² the country; *˛hiong a*² *˛nĕng*, rustics; *˛hiong a*² *tio*² country roads; *˛hiong ʻmi ˛ch'ĕ ek₂ sek₂ ngo*² ward rice (contributed to temple keepers) on the 1st and 15th of the month. Read *hiongʼ*: facing, directed towards.

喧 ˛Hsüan. Clamor, hum, noise of talking; to vociferate: *˛hiong ˛hwa*, vociferation of a crowd; COM., [2]*kengʼ ʻchi ˛hiong ˛hwa*, noise is forbidden!

諠 ˛Hsüan. Interchanged with the last and the next: noise, vociferation; to forget; to impose on.

諼 ˛Hsüan. To impose on; false, deceitful; to forget: *˛hiong ˛wong*, to forget; [3]*chaʼ ˛hiong*, to deceive, to humbug.

暄 ˛Hsüan. A genial warmth, as of the sun in spring, a pleasant heat: [4]*˛hang ˛hiong*, cold and heat.

晅 ˛Hsüan. A bright, hot sun, the sun's heat; to dry, to parch: [5]*nik₂ ˛hiong ʻü ĕ̤ng*² warmed by the sun and moistened with rain.

萱 蘐 ˛Hsüan. The iris or fleur-de-lis, a plant used to dispel sorrow, also called [6]*lĕk₂ ˛ch'ĕng* (deer's onions); when worn on the person by a woman who desires a son, it is called *˛ngi ˛nang ʻch'ó*; *met.*, a mother; [7]*˛ch'ung ˛hiong*, father and mother; [8]*˛hiong ʻch'ó ˛wong ˛iu*, the iris dispels grief; [9]*˛hiong ˛tong*, a mother.

烜 ˛Hsüan. To dry at a fire; clear, brilliant, splendid; hot, to burn.

煊 ˛Hsüan. Warm, genial.

軒 ˛Hsüan. The hood of a car; a high-front chariot; a balcony, a low window; eaves; a study or library-room; laughing, playing; satisfied: [10]*˛hiong ˛ngong*, to carry the head high, a bold deportment; [11]*˛ngü ˛hiong*, a lady's carriage; [12]*˛hiong ˛hiong*, pleased, satisfied.

儇 ˛ Ingenious, expert, cunning; nimble; name of a country or tribe in primitive times.

晌 ˛Hsiang. Read *ʻsiong* in the dictionaries: noon, meridian: [13]*ʻhiong ʻngu*, midday.

響 响 ʻHsiang. Noise, clamor, fracas; a sound, echo, a ringing din: COM., [14]*ʻing ʻhiong*, shadow and echo; *met.*, a trace, an inkling of; [15]*ʻhiong k'eʼ* instruments of music; [16]*ʻhiong ˛ling*, small bells—like sleigh-bells; [17]*˛loi ʻhiong ˛t'iêng ha*² *˛ti*, when it thunders, all the world hears; *met.*, everybody hears the story; [18]*ʻhiong liong*² a clear sound; [19]*ʻhiong ˛kŭng*, "sounding bow"—a musical apparatus attached to a kite; COLL., *ʻhiong taĕ̤ng*² a rat-

1 鄉試 2 禁止 喧嘩 3 詐諼 4 寒暄 5 日晅 雨潤 6 鹿葱 7 椿萱 8 萱草 忘憂 9 萱堂 10 軒昂 11 魚軒 12 軒軒 13 晌午 14 影響 15 響器 16 響鈴 17 雷響 天下知〇 18 響亮 19 響弓

tling, a clatter; ‘*hiong* ‘*ma*, a name given to Shantung footpads; *p‘ah*, ‘*hiong* ‘*peng*, to inflict resounding (i. e. light) blows on culprits; ‘*hiong sioh*, ˛*siŭng*, it sounds, it reverberates.

‘**饗** Hsiang. To offer sacrifice; to feast a guest, to spread out a feast; a sacrifice, a banquet: [1]‘*hiong* ˛*ping*, to feast a guest; [2]‘*hiong sëü*’ to offer sacrifices.

‘**享** Hsiang. Used for the last: to offer up, to present to a god or superior; to enjoy, to receive an offering; a feast, repast: [3]‘*hiong ëüng*’ to enjoy the use of; COM., [4]‘*hiong seu*’ to enjoy long life; [5]‘*hiong hok*, to be happy, blessed.

‘**蠁** Hsiang. A worm that notices sounds; a silkworm (?): [6]‘*hek*, ‘*hiong*, insects bred in damp places, as mosquitos, etc.

珦’ Hsiang. Name of a precious stone; an ornament worn on the girdle.

向’ **嚮**’ Hsiang. Towards, facing, opposite to; thinking upon, inclined to; an intention; an object of study; time past, former, heretofore; a window or opening; points of the compass: [7]‘*e*’ *hiong*’ intention; COM., [8]˛*hwong hiong*’ or *hiong*’ ‘*siu*, the direction, bearing of; [9]*sëü*’ ˛*hwong hiong*’ the four points of the compass, everywhere; [10]*hiong*’ *paëk*, northerly; *hiong*’ *siong*’ facing upward; [11]*hiong*’ ˛*lai*, heretofore; [12]*hiong*’ *hau*’ hereafter; [13]*hiong*’ *nik*, ˛*ki*, a sunflower; *hiong*’ *siéng*’ inclined to good; [14]*hiong*’ *p‘ieu*’ bank bills stamped and made payable at another bank; COLL., *hiong*’ ˛*seng*, to advance.

曏’ Hsiang. Also read ‘*hiong*: a little while; suddenly; formerly.

餉’ Hsiang. Provisions for workmen and troops; taxes paid in kind to government; duties in general; to give or send food: [15]*hiong*’ ˛*tang*, a duty "chop"; COM., [16]˛*ping hiong*’ or ˛*liong hiong*’ soldiers' rations; [17]*hwak*, *hiong*’ to give out rations; [18]˛*chié hiong*’ to receive or pay rations; [19]*hiong*’ ˛*ngüng*, commissariat funds; [20]*cho*’ *hiong*’ contributions to aid government.

眴’ Hsien. Also read ˛*sung*: the eyes rolling, to move the eyes; to see indistinctly, dizzy; to appear fresh and clear: *hiong*’ *hwang*’ bright and clear, brilliant.

絢’ Hsüan. An ornamented wrapper for gems or seals; variegated, flowery, adorned; quick, rapid.

憲’ Hsien. A rule, a precept, a regulation; an example; governmental; a ruler, an officer of any rank from a prefect to a viceroy; to impose or publish laws, to govern; to follow closely; abundant; well-informed: [21]*hiong*’ ˛*chü*, the imperial calendar; [22]*hiong*’ *hiong*’ pleased, gratified; COM., [23]‘*hu hiong*’ the prefect; ‘*u hiong*’ the governor. Read ‘*hiéng*: bright, illustrious, as in ‘*hiéng* ‘*hiéng leng*’ *taik*, effulgent were his virtues!

[1]饗賓 [2]饗祀 [3]享用 [4]享壽 [5]享福 [6]肸蠁 [7]意向 [8]方向 [9]四方向 [10]向北 [11]向來 [12]向後 [13]向日葵 [14]向票 [15]餉單 [16]兵餉 [17]發餉 [18]支餉 [19]餉銀 [20]助餉 [21]憲書 [22]憲憲 [23]府憲

獻, 献, Hsien. To offer or present to a god, or a superior; to give or present to another (in polite language); to hand up to; an offering; intelligent: COM., [1]'hiong' *kĕüng*' to offer to idols; [2]'*hiong' pek*, to offer strips of mock-silk (by burning); [3]'*hiong' siong*' to offer up; [4]'*hiong' ch'aik*, to volunteer advice (to the government); [5]'*hiong' 'lá uk*, to present offerings; [6]'*hiong' ,kung*, to report merit.

讞, 谳, Hsien. Read *ngiĕk*, in the dictionaries: to consult on criminal cases; to judge or decide a case, to adjudge: [7]'*hiong' kĕük*, to examine a criminal case; [8]'*hiong' ngŭk*, to sentence; [9],*ch'iu hiong*' the autumnal assize.

(201) Hiu.

休, Hsiu. To cease, to rest from, to desist; to repudiate; a negative, don't, stop; good, excellent; to praise, to commend, to felicitate; to forgive, to let off: [10],*hiu ,ka*, excellent; [11],*hiu sek*, to desist; COM., [12]*wang*' *sëü*' *,hiu*, "every thing stops"—said when one dies; [13],*ngwong 'p'ing ,hiu te*' deprived of his office; [14],*hiu ,chü*, a bill of divorce; *,hiu t'eng*' *,pong ,ing laung*' *se*' *,hi*, don't listen to what bystanders say for or against!

幽, Yu. In a ravine or shady dell; dark, shady; solitary, secret, retired; far back, deep, hidden from view; obscure, mysterious; hades, the shades, the spirits in hades; to go or be sent into retirement, to rusticate: [15],*ch'ieu ,hiu*, to deliver spirits by masses; [16],*hiu ,ming*, the lower and upper worlds, spirits and men; [17],*hiu ang*' very dark; *,hiu p'ek*, solitary, as a place; *,hiu ,ch'iu*, an imprisoned culprit; COM., *,hiu 'nga*, retired and tasteful, as a room.

庥, Hsiu. Shade, shelter; protection, kindness from superiors; to protect, to sustain; a place for sheltering: [18],*sing ,hiu*, divine assistance; [19],*hung ,hiu*, great favor; [20],*hiu eng*' to protect, as the gods do.

咻, Hsiu. Also read ,*hau*: to call out, the confused noise of a crowd; a cry of pain, shrieks, moaning: *ó' ,hiu*, a moan of distress.

貅, 貅, Hsiu. A powerful beast, said to devour tigers: [21],*pi ,hiu*, a ferocious monster; *met.*, fierce, valiant, as troops.

髹, Hsiu. A fine war-steed, a high-spirited horse.

鵂, Hsiu. An owl, regarded as a bird of bad omen: [22],*ch'í ,hiu*, a horned owl.

朽, Hsiu. Also read '*hieu*: rotten wood; decayed, putrid, putrescent, rotten; failing, forgotten, out of mind: '*hiu muk*, *pok*, '*k'ó ,tieu*, rotten wood can't be carved; *met.*, a worthless scamp; ,*ming pok*, '*hiu*, an imperishable name; COM., '*hiu hwai*' ruined, destroyed; '*hiu lang*' or '*hiu po*' decayed, as wood.

[1]獻 [8]獻 [5]獻 功 獄 嘉 事 休 [15]超 [17]幽 [19]鴻 [21]貔
供 上 禮 [7]讞 [9]秋 [11]休 休 致 幽 暗 庥 貅
[2]獻 [4]獻 物 鞫 讞 息 [13]原 [14]休 [16]幽 [18]神 [20]庥 [22]鴟
帛 策 [6]獻 [8]讞 [10]休 [12]萬 品 書 明 庥 蔭 鵂

疞 Hsiu. Also read *'kieu:* sick, diseased; colic, griping pain in the bowels.

(202) Ho.

富 Fu. Rich; affluent, abundant; to provide, to enrich; weath, riches: in the coll. read *po'*, q. v.: COM., [1]*ho' koi' ˎping chiéng'* rich and poor, high and low; [2]*ho' koi' chai' ˎt'iëng*, riches and honor are from heaven; [3]*ho' chëük*, abundance, wealth; [4]*ho' ˎhó*, very wealthy; *ho' kwok, ˎkiong ˎping*, a rich country and brave soldiers.

副 Fu. To assist, to aid, to second; to investigate; an assistant, a substitute, a lieutenant, a vice, a deputy; an ancient head-dress; in the coll., a classifier for sets of certain things, as buttons, bowls, plates, cups, chop-sticks, bracelets, ear-rings, &c.: COM., [5]*'chiäng' ho'* principal and assistant; [6]*ho' 'li*, an assistant, a manager; [7]*ho' 'k'ó*, assistant examiner—in the provincial examinations for Küjin; [8]*ho' sai'* a deputy commissioner; [9]*ho' chiong'* a colonel; *ho' ˎié*, a compellation of low military officers; [10]*ho' 'pong*, under (Küjin) graduates; [11]*ho' 'chung ˎchoi*, a sub-examiner of Küjin at Peking; [12]*ho' koi'* a sub-clerk or vice-treasurer; COLL., *'wang sioh, ho'* a set of 10 bowls; *tëü' sioh, ho'* 10 pairs of chop-sticks; *sóh, sioh, ho'* a pair of bracelets.

付 Fu. To give, to deliver, to hand over: COM., [13]*ho' t'auk*, to charge with; [14]*ˎkau ho'* to deliver to; COLL., *ho' k'ëük, ˎi*, hand it over to him.

赴 Fu. To go to, to repair to, to hasten; to arrive at, to come: [15]*ho' kó'* to go and inform, to present a petition; [16]*ho' meng'* to obey an order; *ho' yok*, to engage to meet; COM., *ho' sik,* to go to a feast.

賻 Fu. To contribute towards defraying funeral expenses, to assist an interment by presenting articles.

訃 Pu. To announce the death of a parent or relative by the nearest mourner, on the 7th day; to go to: COM., [17]*ho' ˎing t'aik*, a card announcing the death of a parent and the commencement of funeral solemnities.

仆 Pu. To fall down, to fall to the earth; overthrown: *'yéng ho'* to fall down.

傅 Fu. To annex, to arrange; to lay on, as colors; to superintend; near; to arrive at; a tutor, a master; a workman; a surname: [18]*ˎsü ho'* a tutor, a master; COM., *ho' hwoi'* to imitate a bad example; in the coll., to do carelessly, anyhow; [19]*t'ai' 'chü t'ai' ho'* tutor of the heir-apparent.

賦 Fu. To exact, to levy, to collect, to require; taxes of money or military arms; tribute from fiefs; to give; to receive; to place in order; a meter of 4 and 6 feet in the lines: [20]*ho' swoi'* taxes, imposts; *ho' liëng'* to levy taxes;

[1]富貴貧賤 [2]富貴在天 [3]富足 [4]富豪 [5]正副 [6]副理 [7]副考 [8]副使 [9]副將 [10]副榜 [11]副總裁 [12]副櫃 [13]付託 [14]交付 [15]赴告 [16]赴命 [17]訃音帖 [18]師傅 [19]太子太傅 [20]賦稅

COM., *ˏsi ho'* regular poems and verses of 4s and 6s.

怤' (Fu.) To think upon with pleasure; pleased, gratified with, as a friend.

咐' (Fu.) To blow, to breathe; used in the coll. in the sense of to charge one with; to bid, to order, to instruct, to direct one how to do: COLL., [1]*ˏhing ho'* or *chĕük, ho'* to charge one.

Ho'. A coll. word: time enough for: *ho' ng^2 ho'* is there time enough or not? *ng^2 ho'* or *má^2 ho'* not time enough; *'kang 'king ˏkiăng cheu^2 ho'* walk quickly, then you'll have time enough.

Ho'. A coll. word: to sprinkle with the hand or a water pot, to dampen, to bedew: *ho' 'chwi*, to sprinkle with water; *ho' ˏsing 'lá*, sprinkled it on his body; *'chwi ˏtó ˏli ho'* bring water and sprinkle it; *ho' lang^2* to wet by sprinkling.

父^2 (Fu.) A father; a senior, an ancestor, an old man; the head, as of a family; a title applied to peasants or aged people; to rule, to act as a father; in a *met.* sense, kind, loving: COM., [2]*ho^2 'mu*, parents; [3]*ho^2 'chü*, father and son; [4]*ˏt'iĕng ho^2* Heavenly Father; [5]*ˏseng ho^2* own father; [6]*sĕü^2 ho^2* a foster-father; [7]*ˏka ho^2* my father; [8]*ho^2 ˏch'ing*, father—as used in epistles; [9]*'chu ho^2* grandfather and father; a grandfather; [10]*ˏsiéng ho^2* my late father; [11]*chĕük, ho^2* younger paternal uncle; [12]*ho^2 chai' 'chü ˏhwang*, the son pays his father's debts; [13]*ho^2 'mu hwoi^2* a charitable society to aid burials; COLL., *ˏsa ho^2* a teacher, a master, a skilled workman.

扶^2 (Fu.) Read *ˏhu*; used for the coll. *ho^2*: to support with the hands; to hold up, to sustain; to raise, to lift up: [14]*ho^2 'k'i*, help him to rise; [15]*ho^2 'ch'iu*, or *'ch'iu ˏtó ˏli ho^2* hold it up with your hands; [16]*ho^2 't'ĕng*, to support one in parturition.

輔^2 (Fu.) The rack or cheeks of a cart; end of the jaw-bones; to flank, to help, to second: *ho^2 chó'* to second; [17]*'sëü' ho^2* four stars near the north pole; a counsellor; COM., *ho^2 cho^2* to succor, to help.

婦^2 媍^2 (Fu.) A wife, a married woman, a female under subjection; a lady, a female; beautiful: COM., [18]*ho^2 'nü* (coll. *ho^2 'nü ˏnĕng*), women; *ho^2 tó^2* female duties; [19]*ˏhu ho^2* husband and wife; *ˏing ho^2* an adulteress; *sek, ho^2* a daughter-in-law; *tá^2 ho^2* a younger brother's wife; [20]*liĕk, ho^2* one that hangs herself at the death of her husband—a Chinese suttee; *'lang ho^2* lazy women; *met.*, fighting insects.

扈^2 (Hu.) Name of a country and of a bird; an officer; a retinue, a suite; to cover; a large, low hill; broad, extended: [21]*ˏsong ho^2* name of a bird; *met.*, a retiring scholar; *ho^2 ho^2* extensive; [22]*ho^2 chëüng^2* a retinue.

---

1 吩咐 2 父母 3 父子 4 天父 5 生父 6 嗣父 7 家父 8 父親 9 祖父 10 先父 11 叔父 12 父債 子還 13 父母會 14 扶起 15 扶手 16 扶〇 17 四輔 18 婦女 19 夫婦 20 烈婦 21 桑扈 22 扈從

負^2 Fu. To carry on the back or shoulder, to bear, a burden; to assume a duty; to rely, to depend on; to turn the back on, to disregard, to refuse; to be defeated, to fail; to owe; to slight, to be ungrateful: [1]*ˏku ho*^{2} ungrateful; disappointed; [2]*ho*^{2} *seng*ˀ to forfeit confidence; COM., [3]*ho*^{2} *chai*ˀ or *ho*^{2} *k'iéng*ˀ to owe, indebted; [4]*ho*^{2} *ˏong*, ungrateful for favors; [5]*ho*^{2} *ˏsing*, ungrateful; [6]*ho*^{2} *loi*^{2} involved in the crimes of others.

岵^2 Hu. A hill covered with trees and grass; some say a barren hill.

祜^2 K'u. Abundant happiness, the favor of Heaven: [7]*seu*ˀ *ˏt'iéng ˏchi ho*^{2} to receive the blessings of Heaven.

戶^2 Hu. To protect, to screen, to close upon; to stop further progress; a chamber door, an inner door; a one-leaved door; a hole, an opening; the nidus of larvæ; master of a family, ship, or shop; a person; people in a certain calling; a family, a household; the 63d radical: [8]*pok, ch'ok, ho*^{2} *ˏting*, does not go out of doors—a sedentary person; COM., [9]*ˏmwong ho*^{2} a door; [10]*ˏmwong ho*^{2} *'sieu ˏsing*, be careful of doors—i. e., guard against thieves; [11]*ho*^{2} *'k'eu*, the population; [12]*ho*^{2} *pwo*^{2} Board of Population and Revenue; [13]*ˏliong ho*^{2} taxes on landed property; COLL., *ho*^{2} *pwo*^{2} *ˏseng*, a ward of Chungchau Island, near the "Large Bridge", in Foochow.

戽^2 Hu. Also read *ho*ˀ: to bail out water; a bailing vessel: [14]*ho*^{2} *'teu*, a boat's bailing buckets or ladles.

怙^2 Ku. To rely on, to trust to, to depend upon; a father, a parent; a helper, a supporter: [15]*ho*^{2} *se*^{2} one's dependence—i. e., parents; [16]*sek, ho*^{2} to lose a father.

護^2 Hu. To aid, to deliver; to guard, to preserve, to save, to succor, to patronize; the flank of an army: COM., [17]*ho*^{2} *ka*ˀ an imperial escort; *ho*^{2} *ˏsing kiäng*ˀ "shield-mirror"—worn in plays; *ho*^{2} *ˏsing ˏhu*, "shield-charm"—i. e., the powerful aid of a patron; [18]*ho*^{2} *cho*^{2} to aid, to succor; *ho*^{2} *'li*, to hold an office temporarily; *ho*^{2} *ˏchü*, a portfolio; [19]*ho*^{2} *ˏhung*, "safely sealed"—two characters used on a latter-stamp.

蠖^2 Hu. Geometrical worms, which curl up and stretch out as they go; hampered, repressed, cowed down: [20]*ch'ek, ho*^{2} a worm, called the looper; to span with the thumb and fore-finger.

附^2 Fu. Near, about, approaching; to lean on; to follow; annexed, attached to, tributary, dependent; to join; supplement, appendix, inclosure: [21]*ˏi ho*^{2} to depend on; *kié*ˀ *ho*^{2} to intrust to, to send with; COM., *ho*^{2} *këüng*^{2} near, adjacent; *ho*^{2} *ˏkü*, to dwell near, as in a part of the same house; *ho*^{2} *chaung*ˀ to bury with other remains; *ho*^{2} *'chü*, a stimulating medicine.

---

1 辜負 2 負信 3 負債 4 負恩 5 負心 6 負累 7 受天之祜 8 不出戶庭 9 門戶 10 門戶小心 11 戶口 12 戶部 13 糧戶 14 戽斗 15 怙恃 16 失怙 17 護駕 18 護助 19 護封 20 尺蠖 21 依附

腐[2] Corrupted, carious, rotten, spoiled; pulverized; castrated: [1]ho[2] ˛hing, the punishment of castration; COM., [2]nŭk˛ ho[2] rotten meat; [3]ho[2] ˛ü (coll. ho[2] ˛ü ˛kó), a foolish pedant; [4]ho[2] lang[2] spoiled, as food; COLL., tau[2] ho[2] bean curd; ho[2] p'iêng[2] thin slices of curd; ho[2] ˛kang, dried bean curd.

祔[2] 禣[2] Fu. To sacrifice to ancestors in the hall; to inter in the same tomb: [5]ho[2] sik˛ to sacrifice to ancestors.

駙[2] Fu. Near; quick; to help: COM., [6]ho[2] 'ma, a son-in-law of the emperor.

鮒[2] Fu. A fresh-water fish resembling the perch, said to go in pairs or shoals, and to be faithful to each other; like the chek˛ ˛ngü, q. v.

互[2] Hu. Interlocking, like serrated edges, or cog-wheels fitting into each other; with, together, each to other, reciprocal, mutual, blended, interchangeable, responsive; a butcher's double hook: [7]˛kau ho[2] united; [8]ho[2] ˛siong ai' mutual love; [9]ho[2] uk˛ serrated, scaly.

沍[2] Closed up by the ice, ice-bound, frozen, congealed; a glazed, icy appearance.

(203) Hó.

呵 ˛ Read ˛ó; coll. ˛hó: a euphonic termination, as in singing songs: [10]˛hó ˛hó, sound of laughter.

好 ' Hao. Good, right, excellent, well; very; in the coll., an intensive adverb, both in a good and a bad sense, exceedingly, superlatively; done, thoroughly cooked; well, recovered from sickness: also read hó', q. v.: COM., [11]'hó e' a good intention; [12]'hó sëü[2] (coll. 'hó tai[2]), meritorious actions; [13]siong[2] 'hó, very good; [14]ek˛ 'hó, the best; capital! the very thing! [15]che' 'hó, very intimate friendship; [16]'hó ch'ieu' laughable, amusing; [17]'hó k'ang' pretty, beautiful; COLL., [18]'hó siăh˛ good to eat; [19]'hó 'ch'iu taung' fine skill or tact; yă' o' 'hó, passably good; [20]'hó miăng[2] good lot in life, a lucky state; 'hó 'kiăng pok˛ chai[2] ˛tó, a few good children are sufficient; [21]'hó 'tá, "good bottom"—i. e., wealthy; 'hó t'iék˛ pok˛ ˛king ˛sang ˛lu 'hwi, good iron is not passed thro' the furnace thrice; met., a good man does not need repeated reproof; [22]'hó 'heng, exceeding harsh or unfeeling; 'hó k'á' wak˛ in very good circumstances; 'hó tek˛ kik˛ extremely good; 'chü 'hó 'lau, cooked done; pang[2] 'hó, recovered from the sickness; 'hó ˛p'ung ng[2] 'ch'ai lok˛ te[2] ˛hwa, the good bee sips not a fallen flower; met., applied to one of high aims.

好' Hao. To love, to take pleasure in, fond of, to like, to desire, to wish for: also read 'hó, q. v.: hó' o' to like and to dislike; COM., chói' hó' greatly to wish for; [23]hó' hok˛ fond of study; hó' hak˛ domestic harmony; hó' ˛kó, aspiring; hó' saik˛ licentious, lewd; hó' 'chiu, a

[1]腐刑 [2]肉腐 [3]腐儒 [4]腐爛 [5]祔食 [6]駙馬 [7]交互 [8]互相 愛[9]互物 呵[10]呵 事[11]好意 [12]好上 [13]上好 [14]一好 [15]至好 [16]好笑 [17]好看 [18]好食 [19]好手段 [20]好命 [21]好底 [22]好狠 [23]好學

wine-bibber; *hó'* *sëü²* fond of meddling; COLL., *hó'* *siäh,* *'lang chó'* gormandizing and lazy.

耗 ' Hao. To diminish, consume or destroy through time or use; to spoil; to dissipate, to squander; to injure; to render void; vicious, bad: *,hü hó'* wasted, squandered; COM., [1]*hó' hié'* to spend, to expend largely; *chak, hó'* trifling expenses.

Hó'. A coll. word: an exclamation in answering to a call.

何 ‚ Ho. Which, who, what; how, wherefore; according to the sense of the context; a surname; to bear, to carry: also read *hó²*, q.v.: [2]*‚hó yă'* how? why? [3]*‚u ‚hó*, not long, a short time; COM., [4]*‚ü ‚hó*, how? in what way? *‚hó ‚ü*, how is it? how will it do? [5]*‚hó ko'* why? what is the reason? [6]*‚hó pek,* why must?—i. e., there's no necessity; [7]*‚hó 'teng ‚kang ‚nang*, how very difficult! *‚hó laung²* what matters it (between you and me)? *‚hó ‚hwong*, what hindrance!—i. e., it's of no consequence; *‚hó hwong'* how much more! much rather! *‚hó ‚ping ‚hó këü'* what evidence?—i. e., no proof whatever; COLL., *‚mó nai² ‚hó*, no resource, impossible; *‚hó che' ‚chiong wang²* how can it come to this!

荷 ‚ Ho. The lotus or Nelumbium; also applied to some Malvaceæ: also read *hó²*, q. v.: [8]*‚hó ‚hung*, a south wind; COM., [9]*‚hó ‚hwa*, the lotus; *‚hó ‚pau*, a purse carried at the girdle; [10]*pok, ‚hó*, mint, as spearmint, peppermint; COLL., *‚hó yék, ‚pau*, steamed flour cakes of the shape of lotus leaves.

豪 ‚ Hao. Used for the next: a porcupine with black, pointed quills; imperial—applied to H. M.'s herds and flocks; superior to others, eminent, excellent; martial, high-spirited, brave, a leader; excelling in mental qualities: COM., [11]*‚ing ‚hüng ‚hó kiék,* excelling in prowess, a hero; [12]*'t'u ‚hó*, a village brave; *‚hó k'e'* high-spirited; [13]*'ho' ‚hó*, wealthy and influential; [14]*‚hó ‚tü*, a porcupine.

毫 ‚ Hao. Long, fine hair; down; point of a pencil; atoms, motes, anything very minute; ten strands of silk; the ten-thousandth of a tael: [15]*‚hó ‚mó*, small hairs; [16]*‚hwi ‚hó*, to write; COM., *‚hó ‚lié*, or *‚si ‚hó*, a very little, a mote; [17]*‚hung ‚hó pok, ‚ch'a*, not the least error; COLL., *sioh, ‚si sioh, ‚hó ‚tu má² ‚ch'a*, differs not in the least.

壕 ‚ Hao. A city moat or ditch, a fosse: [18]*‚sing ‚hó*, a city ditch.

濠 ‚ Hao. Same as the last: the water in a fosse: [19]*‚hó siong²* on the bank of the moat.

蠔 ‚ Hao. An oyster: [20]*‚hó ‚sang*, an oyster bed.

譹 ‚ Hao. Used for the next: to call, to cry out, to implore; to groan: [21]*‚hu ‚hó*, to cry out, to call.

---

[1]耗費 [2]何也 [3]無何 [4]如何 [5]何故 [6]何必 [7]何等艱難 [8]荷風 [9]荷花 [10]薄荷 [11]英雄豪傑 [12]土豪 [13]富豪 [14]豪猪 [15]毫毛 [16]揮毫 [17]分毫不差 [18]城壕 [19]濠上 [20]蠔山 [21]呼譹

號 号 ˛ ˛ Hao. To roar, as a tiger, in which sense the same as the next; a cock's crow; to call aloud, to howl, to cry: also read *hóʾ*, q. v.: [1]*˛hu ˛hó*, to cry out; [2]*˛hó ˛t'iêng*, to implore Heaven.

嘷 ˛ Hao. Sometimes read *˛kó:* to roar and howl, as bears and tigers: [3]*˛hó ˛pau*, a howling.

喉 ˛ Hou. Read *˛heu;* coll. *˛hó*, as in [4]*˛hó ˛lĕng*, the windpipe, the throat; *˛hó ˛lĕng ˛t'au*, top of the throat; *˛hó ˛lĕng teʾ k'áʾ ˛nĕng ˛k'ang ʻking ʻking tioh*ˎ to clutch people tightly by the throat.

號 号ʾ Hao. Mark, designation, denomination; a "chop", label, name, epithet or style; sign of a shop; an order, verbal or written; a surname; signal, countersign; to name, to style, to designate, to mark: COM., [5]*˛chong hóʾ* or *taiʾ hóʾ* what is your honorable name? [6]*piék*ˎ *hóʾ* an additional name, as the virile style; [7]*kwok*ˎ *hóʾ* name of a dynasty; [8]*˛niêng hóʾ* name of the reign; [9]*hóʾ lengʾ* a mandate, a proclamation; [10]*cheʾ hóʾ* a mark; *hóʾ kwaʾ* a soldier's coat; [11]*hóʾ soʾ* the number of the marks, as on articles; [12]*waʾ hóʾ* to affix the signature; *ʻsiu hóʾ* the first, as to size, etc.; [13]*hóʾ p'auʾ* a signal-gun; *hóʾ ˛pung*, a recording office; [14]*hóʾ siăʾ* labeled cells in examination halls; COLL., *˛miăng hóʾ* a name or designation; *hóʾ ˛miăng*, or *hóʾ ʻla ˛miăng*, to name, to designate.

荷 何ʾ Ho. To bear, to sustain, to carry on the head or back, to carry on the shoulders: also read *˛hó*, q. v.: *hoʾ hóʾ* to carry on the back or shoulders; [15]*paik*ˎ *lŭk*ˎ *seʾ hóʾ* bears a hundred blessings.

賀ʾ Ho. To congratulate, felicitate at festivals or on happy events; to make presents, to reward; also *met.*, presents, to bear: COM., [16]*hóʾ ʻhi*, to congratulate; [17]*hóʾ ʻlá*, or *hóʾ kengʾ* congratulatory presents; [18]*hóʾ ˛niêng*, to offer New Year's salutations; *˛kŭng hóʾ* "respectful salutations", as written on presents; *hóʾ ʻmwang ngwok*ˎ to felicitate with presents when a child is a month old.

昊 皞ʾ Hao. White, a white color; a summer sun, a clear, luminous sky, for which the first is generally used: *hóʾ hóʾ* enlarged; self-possessed; [19]*hóʾ ˛t'iêng ˛king k'wok*ˎ the glorious heavens and golden palace (of Shangti).

顥 皓ʾ Hao. The light of heaven, luminous, like the clear sky; resplendent, bright, lustrous, glistering: [20]*t'aiʾ hóʾ* the firmament; [21]*hóʾ ʻsiu*, a hoary head; *sëŭʾ hóʾ* four gray beards (of the Han dynasty).

鎬ʾ Hao. A warming pan, a hand-stove; bright, lustrous; name of a place where Wu-wang had his capital, called [22]*hóʾ ˛king: hóʾ hóʾ ch'iok, ch'iok*, bright and splendid.

1呼號 3嘷咆 5尊號 7國號 9號令 11號數 13號炮 15百祿 16賀喜 18賀年 金闕 21皓首

2號天 4喉嚨 6別號 8年號 10字號 12畫號 14號舍 是荷 17賀禮 19昊天 20太皓 22鎬京

浩 Hao. Great, swelling waters; a watery expanse; immense, vast, affluent; an overplus, superabundant, enlarged, noble: [1]*hó˒ taung˒* or *hó˒ tai˒* vast, as the firmament.

灝 Hao. Extensive, as waters reaching to a distance; vast, boundless: [2]*hó˒ ʻkieu,* broad, like an expanse of water; [3]*˛siong ˛chü hó˒ hó˒* the books of the Shang dynasty (in import) are vast like the ocean.

(204) Hóh.

Hóh˒. A coll. word: to cook, or heat up, as cold food: *hóh˒ pwong˒* to warm up rice; *hóh˒ yék˒* to heat up; *hóh˒ ˛ta,* to heat, or fry, dry.

(205) Hoi.

˛Hoi. A coll. word: an exclamation of regret or surprise; the same as *˛oi,* q. v.: *˛hoi ˛ó,* Oh! Ah!

諱 Hui. To shun; to respect; to avoid mentioning, as sacred names or improper subjects; to hide; to muffle; name of a person in the ancestral hall: [4]*hoi˒ che˒* sacred names; *hoi˒ ˛ming pok˒ hoi˒ seng˒* names are sacred, but surnames are not; COM., [5]*ngëü˒ hoi˒* sacred name of the emperor; [6]*ke˒ hoi˒* to avoid using, as a sacred name; [7]*hwang˒ hoi˒* to trespass on forbidden subjects; [8]*˛chong hoi˒* the sacred name—*scil.,* of your deceased relative.

緯 Wei. The woof of cloth; degrees of latitude; cross, transverse lines; to weave, to entwine: *˛king hoi˒* warp and woof; [9]*ʻngu hoi˒* the five planets; [10]*te˒ hoi˒* geographical divisions; COM., *hoi˒ lik˒* a fringed ceremonial cap.

翡 A kingfisher, with beautiful plumage; the cock is called *hoi˒*, the hen *ch'oi˒*: COM., [11]*hoi˒ ch'oi˒ ngwoh˒* the chrysoprase.

˛Hoi. A coll. word, used in calling to a person: halloo! you there! the same as *˛oi,* q. v.

(206) Hok.

福 Fu. Happiness, felicity, good fortune; good, lucky; to bless; a blessing, divine prosperity; provided with all things; sacrificial meats; to store up; with: COM., [12]*hok˒ k'e˒* happiness; [13]*ʻhiong hok˒* to be happy; [14]*ʻngu hok˒* the five blessings—longevity, wealth and honor, peace, virtue, and a good death; [15]*hok˒ hong˒* a happy lot; *˛t'ó hok˒,* happy by your favor; [16]*hok˒ kiong˒* Fookien province; [17]*hok˒ ˛chiu,* Foochow; *hok˒ ˛ch'iäng kaing˒* the district of Fuhtsing in the Foochow prefecture; [18]*hwak˒ hok˒* to enjoy happiness—i. e., become fat; [19]*hok˒ lük˒ seu˒ ʻhi,* happiness, income, longevity, and joy (i. e., children); *hok˒ te˒ hok˒ ˛ing ˛mai* (coll. *˛lai*), the fortunate are buried in lucky grave sites; [20]*hok˒ taik˒ cheng˒ ˛sing,* the god of wealth, mammon; COLL., *hok˒ ˛chiu k'ah˒ tói˒ pwang˒ pah˒* Foochow traders halve the hundred—i. e., offer only half of the price demanded; *hok˒ k'e˒ ʻyä ʻhó,* or *ʻhó hok˒ k'e˒* "good luck"; *met.,* a fine, portly form.

---

[1]浩蕩 [2]灝漭 [3]商書灝灝 [4]諱字 [5]御諱 [6]忌諱 [7]犯諱 [8]尊諱 [9]五緯 [10]地緯 [11]翡翠玉 [12]福氣○ [13]享福 [14]五福 [15]福分 [16]福建 [17]福州 [18]發福 [19]福祿壽喜 [20]福德正神

楅, Also read *p'aik,*: a piece of wood on the horns of cattle to prevent their goring; a quiver for arrows.

輻, Fu. The spokes of a wheel: [1]*hok, chaiu'* to collect, as at a metropolis; converging, running together.

黻, Fu. Variegated, black and azure mixed; to embroider in colors; elegant, flowery, as writing; a variegated garment: [2]*hok, 'mieng*, an embroidered coronet.

拂, Fu. To brush, to wipe, to dust; to push away, to oppose, to expel; to contradict; perverse, disobedient; a kind of posture-making: [3]*hok, ,ing ,chi seng'* to thwart one's wishes; COM., [4]*hok, 'ie tóh*, to dust chairs and tables; [5]*hok, 'ch'iu*, a small dusting-broom; COLL., [6]*hok, ,ung ,ting*, to brush off dust; [7]*hok, t'ah*, to dust clean.

菖, An edible vegetable with white roots, of the size of the finger; it is found in Shantung.

茀, Fu. Brambles or luxuriant herbage concealing the path; happiness, luck; to screen; to clear away, to open: [8]*hok, lük,* happiness and official income; [9]*hok, k'wok, ,hung 'ch'ó*, to clear away the thick grass.

紼, Fu. Raveled silk; a screen; a trace to drag a bier: [10]*chek, hok,* to accompany a funeral.

紱, Fu. Used for the last two: a ribbon to hold a seal.

綍, Silken cords which are used to carry coffins; *met.*, fine, elegant, applied to the emperor's words: [11]*,lung hok,* eloquent, persuasive, as imperial sayings.

潑, Fu. Also read *hwak,*: cold; to open the sluices, to let water flow over fields, for purposes of irrigation: [12]*hok, taung'* to open the sluices.

祓, Fu. Clean, pure; to disperse, to drive off; to wash away; a sacrifice or baptism to obtain good: [13]*hok, ,tü,* to ward off (evil).

幅, Fu. A wide strip of cloth; a roll of paper or cloth; a selvedge or hem; a border or frontier; a classifier of maps, pictures, rolls, flags, walls, and strips of cloth; leg-wrappers: COM., [14]*,piéng hok,* a hem, a border; [15]*,chiong hok,* a whole strip; [16]*se' hok,* a set of four scrolls hung in halls; [17]*hok, pwang'* a strip and a half.

彿, Fu. Like, as if: [18]*'hwong hok,* resembling, appearing, seeming as if.

髴, Fu. Disheveled hair; head ornaments; like, nearly, applied to things.

弗, Fu. A negative; a term of deprecation; not, it should not be, not permissible;

1輻輳 2黻冕 3拂人之性 4拂椅棹 ○ 5拂手 6拂箒 塵 7拂潔 ○ 8茀祿 9茀蕨豐草 10執紼 11綸綍 13潑蕩 12祓除 ○ 14邊幅 15全幅 16四幅 ○ 17幅半 18彷彿

contrary, distorted: [1]*hok*, *ˏti*, not to know, ignorant of; [2]*hok*, *kik*, not to arrive at, to fail of.

蝠 Fu. A bat, called [3]*ʻpiéng hok*,—a term used in the coll. for the embroidered or painted figures of the bat.

蝮 Fu. An adder, cobra, or venomous serpent; a locust before it flies: [4]*hok*, *ˏsiè* (called in coll. *ʻngu tuk*, *ˏsiè*), a venomous serpent, a viper; [5]*hok*, *ʻwi*, a large snake.

怫 Fu. Dissatisfied, displeased, discontented: [6]*hok*, *ˏyong*, displeased; [7]*hok*, *ok*, vexed, disquieted.

馥 Fu. Fragrance, odors diffused around: [8]*hok*, *ëük*, a pleasant fragrance.

覆 Fu. To repeat; to and fro, back and forth; unstable, unsettled; to subvert, to overthrow, to defeat; to throw down, to upset, to prostrate; to judge, to inquire into carefully: also read *pʻaiu*, q.v.: [9]*ˏtiéng hok*, fallen down; *met.*, impoverished; reprobate; COM., [10]*ʻhwang hok*, to repeat; vacillating; [11]*hok*, *ʻkʻó*, to repeat an examination; [12]*ˏchiong ˏkung hok*, *muk*, the whole army annihilated.

複 Fu. A wadded or lined garment; doubled; the second: [13]*ˏtüng hok*, again, repeated; [14]*hok*, *tó*, a double road, one above and one below.

袯 Fu. A pad or covering for the knee. Read *pwak*,: a sort of tunic worn by foreigners.

腹 Fu. That which embraces; the belly, abdomen, bowels; the seat of the mind; the affections; rich, thick; intimate, dear; the earth: in the coll. read *pok*, q.v.: [15]*hok*, *ˏsing*, very dear, intimate; [16]*ˏmi hok*, a posthumous child; [17]*ʻku hok*, pot-bellied, dropsical; [17]*ʻtʻang hok*, a son-in-law.

鶴 Ho. A crane; an emblem of age; the name is applied to many of the waders: COM., [18]*hok*, *ʻliéng*, a paper sedan and crane, burnt on the last of the *seven-sevens* (funeral rites); [19]*hok*, *hwak*, *ˏtung ˏngang*, has gray hairs and a young face; *pah*, *hok*, a white egret; *hok*, *ˏsang*, a long dark cloth coat, worn by mounted attendants of officers; *hok*, *chʻek*, a crane's leg; *met.*, long-legged; *hok*, *ʻting*, crane-shaped button, worn by Siutsai and Kŭjin graduates.

鸒 Hsiao. The black bird, pie, or jay; small birds of this class which go in flocks.

學 **斈** Hsiao. To learn, to receive instruction; to practice; to imitate; learning, science, study, instruction, doctrines, tenets, school of; a college, a school-building; in the coll. read *óh*, q.v.: COM., [20]*hok*, *sik*, to study and learn; [21]*hok*, *sëü* doctors, academicians; [22]*ˏchʻu hok*, a freshman; *hok*, *ˏseng*, or *hok*, *ˏseng ˏkó*, a student, a

[1] 弗知 [2] 弗及 [3] 蝙蝠 [4] 蝮蛇 [5] 蝮虺 [6] 怫然 [7] 怫鬱 [8] 馥郁 [9] 顛覆 [10] 反覆 [11] 覆考 [12] 全軍覆沒 [13] 重複 [14] 複道 [15] 腹心 [16] 遺腹 [17] 坦腹 [18] 鶴輦 [19] 鶴髮童顏 [20] 學習 [21] 學士 [22] 初學

scholar; *hok,* ʻ*nü*, a female pupil; *hok, ˏtong*, a school-house; [3]ʻ*saung*ʼ *hok,* arithmetic; ʻ*sieu hok,* the primary lessons—a school book; [4]*hok, ˏtai*, or *hok, yéng*ʼ a literary chancellor; COLL., *hok, ong*ʼ *twai*ʼ of great learning; *hok, sëü*ʼ ʻ*ié*, a chair with carved arms and back.

翯 ʼ Hao. White, glistening plumes of birds; pure and white: [3]*pek,* ʻ*neu hok, hok,* a white bird with glistening plumes.

貉 ʼ Lo. Sometimes read *lok,*: a kind of animal allied to the fox; it burrows and sleeps much, has a sharp nose, and long pie-bald fur; a badger: [4]*hok, ˏkiu*, a fox-skin robe.

紇 ʼ Ho. The ends of silk cut off and hanging down: [5]*sëük, ˏliong hok,* the father of Confucius.

劾 ʼ To judge, to examine into, to search out; to keep in order; to punish; to prosecute or accuse one; to sentence: [6]*hok, sik,* to ascertain the facts; [7]*hok, paing*ʼ to revise a case; [8]*hok, chaiu*ʼ to accuse by memorial; COLL., *hok, sioh,* ʻ*pwong*, to send up a memorial accusing one.

核 覈 ʼ Hê. To investigate, to ascertain the facts; the real circumstances; truly, verily; to pare and carve; in the following senses the first is commonly used; the kernel or seed of fruits; the nucleus; a nodule; hard ganglions in flesh: [9]*hok, sik,* to investigate the facts; [10]ʻ*chung hok,* to search out a matter; [11]ʻ*kwo hok,* the kernels or seeds of fruit; COM., [12]*hok, ˏtʻó*, walnuts.

(207) **Hong.**

煙 烟 ˏ Yên. Read *yéng*; coll. *ˏhong*: tobacco; opium: [13]*ˏchʻang ˏhong*, raw tobacco—a yellow sort; [14]*sük, ˏhong*, cured tobacco; [15]*ˏking ˏsi ˏhong*, fine-cut tobacco; *kau*ʼ *ˏhong*, a kind of strong tobacco; [16]*ˏhong ˏpau*, a tobacco-pouch; *ˏhong ˏpau nak,* two bone or ivory pieces at the neck of the pouch; [17]ʻ*chʻa ˏhong*, to cure tobacco over the fire; ʻ*chwoi ˏhong*, a kind of tobacco smoked thro' water; [18]*ˏhong ˏtëng*, a tobacco or opium pipe; [19]*ˏhong këü*ʼ opium-smoking apparatus; [20]*ˏu ˏhong*, or *ˏyong ˏhong*, or *ˏa pʻiéng*ʼ *ˏhong*, opium; *ˏhong ˏtʻu*, crude opium in balls; *ˏhong ˏkó*, opium prepared for smoking; *ˏhong* ʻ*sai*, opium dregs; *ˏhong* ʻ*iu*, fellow opium-smokers; [21]*siáh, ˏhong*, to smoke tobacco or opium; ʻ*chʻiāng ˏhong*, please take a smoke; [22]*ˏhong* ʻ*kwang*, an opium-smoking den; *kaik, ˏhong*, to cure the habit of smoking; *ngiéng*ʼ *ˏhong*, or *ˏhong ngiéng*ʼ addicted to the use of opium.

ˏHong. A coll. word, as in *ˏhong ˏking*, inferior or imitation gold-leaf; *se*ʼ *ˏhong ˏking tʻaik, ˏki*, it is covered with imitation gold-leaf.

很 ʻ Hên. Disobedient, perverse, quarrelsome, revengeful; a superlative, very, much, excessive, in which sense read ʻ*heng* in the coll., q.v.;

[1]算 [3]白 [4]貉 紇 辦 實 核 煙 絲 [17]炒 [19]煙 [21]食
學 鳥 裘 [6]劾 [8]劾 [10]總 [12]核 [14]熟 煙 煙 具 煙
[2]學 翯 [5]叔 實 奏 核 桃 煙 [16]煙 [18]煙 [20]烏 [22]煙
臺 翯 梁 [7]劾 [9]核 [11]果 [13]生 [15]金 包 筒 烟 館

also used in the coll. for scowling, looking angrily at: COLL., ʻnü ꜀chiong wangʼ ʻhong ʻngwai, you scowl thus at me!

ʻ狠 Hĕn. Used for the last; the snarling of dogs; to bite, as pigs; quarrelsome, perverse; intractable: [1]ʻtaiuʼ ʻhong, to quarrel.

俸ʼ Salary of officers, stipend, emoluments, government allowance: COM., [2]hongʼ lŭk꜁ or hongʼ ꜀sing, official income; [3]hongʼ haiuʼ a fat salary; hongʼ ꜀sing ʻyong ꜀liĕng, a salary to promote probity.

訓ʼ Hsün. To instruct, to teach, to explain; a doctrine, a precept, a definition: COM., [4]ʻkauʼ hongʼ (coll. kaʼ hongʼ), to instruct; [5]hongʼ tó꜁ the second superintendent of education in a department; hongʼ ꜀mung ꜀chá, a school for children.

諷ʼ Fêng. To recite or rehearse in a musical tone; recitative; to ridicule, to satirize, to reprove by irony; metaphor, allusion: [6]hongʼ sëüngʼ to chant; [7]hongʼ chʻëüʼ to satirize, pointed irony; [8]hongʼ kangʼ to censure.

糞ʼ Fên. Ordure, dung, filth, muck, excrement; to manure: in the coll. read pongʼ, q. v.: [9]hongʼ ꜀ki ꜀tiéng, to manure the land.

奮ʼ Fên. To endeavor after; to excite, to rouse one's self; to spread abroad or reach to; to brush away; to lift; prompt, impetuous, rapid: [10]hongʼ ꜀hi, to spread the wings to fly; met., to put forth effort; COM., [11]hongʼ cheʼ to rouse one's energies.

꜂行 Hang. A row, a line, a column, as of characters; a series or order; a company of 25 men: also read ꜂heng and haingʼ, q. v.: [12]꜂hong liĕk꜁ to range in order; COM., [13]꜂hong ʻngu, a company of 25 men, military ranks; [14]꜂hong ʻngu chʻok꜁ ꜀sing, promoted from the ranks; [15]ngangʼ ꜂hong, wild geese (flying) in a row; met., the order or number in the series; COLL., ngangʼ ꜂hong tá꜁ ʻkwi, which number (of the brothers) are you?

꜂桁 Hsing. Read ꜂heng; used for the coll. prefix ꜂hong, as in [16]꜂hong haungʼ floor-beams (when spoken of collectively).

꜂杭 Hang. The capital of Chehkiang, famous for its silks; a square boat, a raft, in which sense used for the next: [17]꜀tʻiéng ꜂hong, the milky way; COM., [18]꜂hong ꜀chiu, Hangchau; [19]꜂hong siéngʼ Hangchau fans; [20]꜂hong ꜀cheng, a quilting needle; [21]꜂hong këŭk꜁ the Hangchau Aster or Chrysanthemum, used to flavor tea.

꜂航 Hang. A scow, a square boat for ferries; to sail, to navigate: [22]꜂chŭ ꜂hong, to pity and save—a Budhist phrase; ꜀tʻai ꜂hong, ladder and boats; met., to scale hills and cross seas.

---

[1]鬭狠 [3]俸厚 [5]訓導 [7]諷刺 [9]糞其田 [10]奮飛 [12]行列 [14]行伍出身 [15]雁行 [17]天杭 [19]杭扇 [21]杭菊

[2]俸祿 [4]教訓 [6]諷誦 [8]諷諫 [11]奮志 [13]行伍 [16]桁桁 [18]杭州 [20]杭針 [22]慈航

頏 ˏ To fly or dart down, as a bird; the neck, the throat.

吭 ˏ Hang. The neck or throat of a bird; an important pass into a country; to swallow.

痕 ˏ Hên. A scar, a cicatrix; a mark, a trace, a line; an itching; a flaw in glass or pearls, a crack in crockery-ware: COM., [1]'*chwi ˏhong*, a trace in water; *met.*, marks or seams in glass and gems; [2]ˏ*sing ˏhong*, a fresh mark; COLL., ˏ*hong ˏhong*, marks; ˏ*mó ˏhong ˏmó chiăh*, no marks whatever; ˏ*sung kwo*^{3} '*chwi ˏmó ˏhong*, the ship leaves no mark in the water; *met.*, no trace, no evidence of it.

降 ˏ Hsiang. To submit, to return to one's allegiance; to descend: also read *kaung*^{3}, q. v.: COM., [3]*huk*ˏ ˏ*hong*, or ˏ*hong huk*ˏ to submit to; [4]ˏ*hong ˏping*, troops surrendering; [5]ˏ*tau ˏhong*, to submit, as rebels; [6]ˏ*hong ˏchü*, or ˏ*hong 'pieu*, articles of submission.

防 ˏ Read ˏ*hwong;* coll. ˏ*hong:* to prepare, to guard against, to keep off: [7]ˏ*hong pe*^{3} or ˏ*tong ˏhong*, to be on one's guard against; [8]ˏ*hong ch'ek*ˏ to guard against thieves; ˏ*hong má*^{2} *teu*^{2} unable to ward off, or keep from.

鳳 ^{2} Fung. A fabulous bird; the male is called *hong*^{2} and the female ˏ*hwong;* the Chinese phenix; it seems to be a species of argus-pheasant; poetical title for the empress: COM., [9]*hong*^{2} ˏ*kwang*, a cap ornamented with phenixes—worn by brides; [10]*hong*^{2} ˏ*tié ˏchü yéng*^{2} the Phenix Lake College, Foochow; COLL., *hong*^{2} ˏ*hwong 'cheu pah*ˏ ˏ*pwang* ˏ*mó*, phenixes have a hundred kinds of feathers; *met.*, none whatever, wholly destitute—a play on the coll. ˏ*mó*, which means *feathers* and *none.*

奉 ^{2} Fêng. To receive respectfully in both hands; to receive from a superior, or offer to him; to approach respectfully, to revere; to obey, to follow: COM., [11]*hong*^{2} *sëü*^{2} to serve; [12]*hong*^{2} ˏ*sing*, to flatter; [13]*hong*^{2} *yong*^{2} to provide for one's parents; [14]*hong*^{2} '*chi*, to receive the imperial commands; [15]*hong*^{2} *kau*^{3} to embrace the doctrines (of a sect); [16]*hong*^{2} *hó*^{2} to offer congratulatory presents—an epistolary phrase; [17]*hong*^{2} *sëü*^{2} ˏ*hiong 'hwi*, to burn incense to; [18]*hong*^{2} ˏ*heng ko*^{3} *sëü*^{2} to follow the old (mode of doing), to imitate predecessors.

混 ^{2} Hun. A chaos of waters; roiled, turbid, muddy, as a torrent, foul; confused, indistinct; mixed, ill-assorted: COM., [19]*hong*^{2} *chak*ˏ mixed, promiscuous; ˏ*hang hong*^{2} or *hong*^{2} *tiong*^{2} confusedly, as in doing; [20]*hong*^{2} ˏ*tiéng*, crazy; COLL., ˏ*sing 'lá o*^{2} *nói*^{3} *hong*^{2} his mind is somewhat confused.

溷 ^{2} Hun. Used for the last: confused; dirty, turbid; unclean, as animals; filthy, foul, like a sewer; a privy: [21]*hong*^{2} *chok*ˏ foul, dirty; ˏ*hwang hong*^{2} a privy.

1 水痕 2 新痕 3 伏降 4 降兵 5 投降 6 降書 7 防備 8 防賊 9 鳳冠 10 鳳池書院 11 奉事 12 奉承 13 奉養 14 奉旨 15 奉教 16 奉賀 17 奉祀香火 18 奉行故事 19 混雜 20 混癲 21 溷濁

福州方言拼音字典

悤 慁[2] Tsung. To disgrace, to dishonor, to bring reproach on; grieved, ashamed, mortified; to distress, to excite, to trouble: [1]'hong[2] ,kung, to dishonor the prince.

分[2] 份[2] Fên. The 2d read ,ping, used for the coll. hong[2]: duty, the duties of an office or a situation; a part, a share, a portion, an interest in: the 1st also read ,hung, q. v.: [2],t'iéng hong[2] natural endowments; COM., chek, hong[2] duties of a position; [3]'pwong hong[2] one's own duty; [4]hong[2] teng[2] fixed, destined; [5]wok, hong[2] to go beyond one's proper sphere; [6]hong[2] ha[2] my, mine; hong[2] 'su ,tong ,ui, the duty that one ought to perform; hong[2] ngwoi[2] 'hó, superexcellent; COLL., o[2] hong[2] to have a share or concern in; ch'ok, sioh, hong[2] to contribute a share; hong[2] ,t'au, a share, a portion.

諢[2] Low jests, vulgar mirth, lewd allusions, scurrilous merriment: [7],iu hong[2] to trifle; [8]hong[2] ,i, a harlequin dress, a masquerade.

(208) Hu.

夫 ,Fu. To help, one who can assist; a scholar, a distinguished man; a man, a husband; a porter, a workman, a sedan-bearer; an exalted lady: also read ,hu, q. v.: COM., [9]t'iong[2] ,hu, a man, a husband; [10],hu ,ka, your husband; [11],hu ,ch'á, or ,hu ho[2] husband and wife; [12],hu ,ing, an officer's wife, your wife; ,ü ,hu ,ing, a concubine; [13]'ma ,hu, hostlers; ,ku ,hu, paternal aunt's husband; [14],hu sing 'chü sek, husband and children—in the language of fortune-tellers; COLL., [15],hu ,t'au, headman of porters or sedan-men; [16],hu 'kiăng, common porters, etc.; ,hu ,ing ,ná 'ná miăng[2] the lucky lot of her ladyship.

膚 ,Fu. The skin, the epidermis; the soft flesh; minced meat; pork; the breadth of four fingers; skin-deep, superficial; beautiful; large; to skin, to flay; to receive: [17],hu 't'á, the body; [18],ki ,hu, muscle, flesh; [19]hwak, ,hu, the scalp; COLL., [20],p'ui ,hu, the skin.

麩 䴸 Fu. Bran or husk of wheat; the refuse of hemp-seed or ground-nut, after the oil is expressed.

孚 ,Fu. To brood over, to hatch; accordant, agreement; belief, trust, confidence; calyx of a bud: [21],hu kak, the calyx, the coat of seeds germinating; [22],hu seng[2] veritable.

俘 ,Fu. To captivate, to capture, to take prisoners in war; a prisoner; spoil taken in battle: [23],hu ,ch'iu, a captive.

稃 Fu. The husk of grain; the capsule or pericarp of seed; the calyx.

郛 ,Fu. The outermost wall beyond the citadel; the suburbs; the purlieus of a city.

[1]悤君 [2]天分 [3]本分 [4]分定 [5]越分 [6]分下 [7]優諢 [8]諢衣 [9]丈夫 [10]夫家 [11]夫妻 [12]夫人 [13]馬夫 [14]夫星子息 [15]夫頭 [16]夫仔 [17]膚體 [18]肌膚 [19]髮膚 [20]皮膚 [21]孚甲 [22]孚信 [23]俘囚

莩 ‚Fu. The female hemp; the pellicle lining the culms of reeds; *met.*, related, a distant connection: [1]‚*ka* ‚*hu*, the white, medullary lining of some sedges; *met.*, distantly related, lightly esteemed.

桴 ‚Fu. A raft, a float of wood or bamboo; in the following senses read ‚*p'eu* in the dictionaries; a ridge-pole in a roof; a drumstick; a barrow to carry dirt: [2]‚*hu* ‚*sü*, (or [3]‚*p'eu* ‚*sü*), a screen, the inner doors opposite the main entrance; [4]‚*hu t'ang'* (or ‚*p'eu t'ang'*), light charcoal.

柎 ‚Fu. A stem or petiole; a calyx; a raft; lower bar of a railing; handle of a knife or bow; to wash in lye.

枹 Also read ‚*p'eu:* a drumstick. Read ‚*pau:* bushy, a thick, luxuriant growth of plants.

敷 ‚Fu. To spread out, to diffuse; to give; to issue an order, to promulgate, to announce, to show forth; to state to a superior: [5]‚*hu* ‚*sié*, to spread or promulgate, as laws; COM., [6]‚*hu ëüng'* sufficient for use; [7]*pok*, ‚*hu*, insufficient; [8]‚*hu yoh*, to apply a plaster.

痡 ‚Fu. Diseased; a wasting of strength, atrophy: [9]*tuk*, ‚*hu sëü'* '*hai*, to injure the whole empire, as by exactions.

砆 玞 ‚Fu. A stone resembling a gem, a false gem: [10]'*u* ‚*hu*, an inferior jade.

趺 To sit in audience or state, with the legs bent under one *á la Turque*, called [11]‚*ka* ‚*hu:* [12]‚*hu* ‚*hu* ‚*yong*, to make an obeisance, as females do.

跗 ‚Fu. The instep of the foot where sandals are tied; the toes: [13]‚*hu chëü'* over-alls worn by soldiers.

灰 ‚Hui. Read ‚*hwi;* coll. ‚*hu:* ashes: [14]'*hwi* ‚*hu*, ashes, cinders; [15]‚*hu laiu'* the ashes of pewter-foil paper.

呼 ‚Hu. Read ‚*hu:* used for the coll. ‚*hu*, as in [16]‚*hu hak*, or ‚*hu* ‚*hu hak*, *hak*, or [17]‚*hu tak*, *hak*, to blurt lies recklessly, to humbug; ‚*hu* ‚*hu kieu'* the buzz of insects' wings; the whistling of the wind.

‚*Hu.* A coll. word, as in ‚*hu wai'* or ‚*hu wai'* '*në*, there, in that place; see also in '*hŭ wai'*.

虎 'Hu. A tiger, the king of beasts; *met.*, brave, fierce; awful, violent: COM., [18]'*hu* '*chau*, tiger's claws; *met.*, tailor's shears; [19]'*hu* ‚*sing*, the tiger-crab; *met.*, an ugly face; [20]'*hu* ‚*tiu*, a tiger-trap; '*hu kauk*, ‚*kó*, tiger-bone salve; [21]'*hu pié'* tiger's arm—the right side of a grave; '*hu chiong'* a brave general; [22]'*hu* '*chang*, an executioner's block and knife, as carried in idol processions; '*ngu* '*hu*, the

1 葭莩 2 桴思 3 桴思 4 桴炭 5 敷施 6 敷用 7 不敷 8 敷藥 9 毒痡四海 10 碔砆 11 跏趺 12 趺趺然 13 跗注 14 火灰 15 灰料 16 呼喝 17 呼答喝 18 虎爪 19 虎蟳 20 虎椆 21 虎臂 22 虎斬

Five Tiger Mt's. south of Foochow; COLL., *lau' 'hu* (spoken *la' 'hu*), a tiger; *la' 'hu kwa' ꜀su ꜀chio*, a tiger wearing Suchow pearls; *met.*, feigned gentleness; *'hu ꜀tó ꜀tü*, a tiger carrying off a pig; *met.*, to carry a child on the back; *'hu ꜀t'au ꜀sié 'mwi*, a tiger's head and a snake's tail; *met.*, a fierce beginning and a cowardly ending.

'琥 Hu. A signet made of a veined stone like a tiger's skin: [1]*'hu ꜀hu*, a signet sent as a warrant, when soldiers were levied; COM., [2]*'hu p'aĕk꜇*, amber.

'滸 Hu. Also read *'hü:* the bank of a river, a descent or lawn sloping down to a stream; branch of the river Huai in Nganhwui.

'府 Fu. A store-house, a house; a record-office, a library, a treasury; the officer over them; a department or prefecture; a prefect: [3]*lĕk꜇ 'hu*, the six elements; COM., [4]*꜀kwang 'hu*, an officer; [5]*꜀hung 'hu*, a deputy-prefect; [6]*'hu 'k'ó*, prefectural examinations; [7]*siong' 'hu* and [8]*a' 'hu*, the upper and lower prefectures of Fookien; [9]*t'ai' 'hu*, his honor, the prefect; [10]*pwong 'hu*, our prefect; I, the prefect; [11]*'hu siong'* your house; [12]*hwi 'hu*, return to your home; COLL., *'hu pah꜇* the prefect's police—are so styled; *'hu 'lá po' ngwo' kaing' 'lá po' ngwo'* missed both at the prefect's and at the district magistrate's; *met.*, failed in both matters!

'俛 Same as the next: to stoop, to look down and consider; to condescend to. Read *'miéng:* to try earnestly, to exert one's self.

'俯 Fu. To stoop, to bow; to consider; to look down on, to condescend to; unequal: [13]*'hu huk꜇* to fall prostrate; [14]*'hu 'chung*, condescend to grant it; [15]*'hu 'siu*, to bow the head.

'腑 Fu. The inferior viscera: COM., [16]*chaung' 'hu*, the superior and inferior viscera; [17]*lĕk꜇ 'hu*, the stomach, gall, bladder, intestines, and secreting passages.

'父 Fu. A suffix of names, a title of respect and honor; to address respectfully; usually read *ho'*, q. v.: [18]*꜀ná 'hu*, the honorable *꜀Ná* (Confucius); [19]*siong' 'hu*, the eminent *Siong'* (coll. *꜀kiong t'ai' ꜀kung*) of the Chow.

'斧 Fu. A hatchet, an ax; to cut, to hack, to chop, to fell: [20]*'hu ꜀k'ó*, an ax-handle; [21]*'hu siok꜇* to criticise, to correct.

'釜 Fu. A boiler or caldron without feet; a measure, containing about 6¼ *'tau:* [22]*'hu chaing'* a boiler and rice-steamer; [23]*p'ó' 'hu ꜀t'ing ꜀chiu*, to break the skillets and sink the boats; *met.*, unavoidable, compulsory.

'簠 Hu. A sort of basket, square outside and round within, used to contain grain when worshiping, called *'hu 'kwi.*

1 琥符 2 琥珀 3 六府 4 官府 5 分府 6 府考 7 上府 8 下府 9 太府 10 本府 11 府上 12 囘府 13 俯伏 14 俯准 15 俯首 16 臟腑 17 六腑 18 尼父 19 尙父 20 斧柯 21 斧削 22 釜甑 23 破釜沉舟

ʻ**脯** Fu. Preserved or dried meat; flesh: [1]ʻ꜀siu ʻhu, or [2]ʻsok꜀ ʻhu, slices of dried meat, formerly sent to a teacher; teacher's salary; COM., [3]ʻlĕk꜀ ʻhu, dried venison.

ʻ**甫** Fu. Large; beautiful, good; numerous; great, eminent; to begin; I, myself; a term of respect in addressing one: [4]꜀chiong ʻhu, a cap worn by literati; [5]ʻhu ʻhu, much, numerous.

ʻ**黼** Fu. Black and white, diversified; embroidered, elegant dress: [6]ʻhu hok꜀ dresses anciently used in sacrifices, with black and white lines or embroidery resembling axes; elegant, as an essay.

꜂**胡** Hu. A dewlap; how; why, wherefore? dark, blackish; the Tartars, the Mongols or Huns; long, lasting, eternal; a spear; a surname; in the coll., careless, remiss, reckless; mendacious: [7]꜂hu ʻhung, a kind of rouge; [8]꜂hu ʻk'ó, an aged person; COM., [9]꜂hu ʻch'ü, a squirrel; COLL., [10]꜂hu ꜂tu, careless, remiss; [11]꜂hu ꜂heng laung꜄ chó꜄ to act recklessly; [12]꜂hu siok꜀ to lie, to talk ridiculously; ꜂hu ꜂ŭng pwo꜄ a fine Formosan fabric, made of woody fiber.

꜂**衚** A street in Peking is called [13]꜂hu ꜂tung; the term is mostly confined to the capital.

꜂**醐** Hu. A spirit fermented from mare's cream, called [14]꜂t'i ꜂hu; also butter, or oil of milk.

꜂**鶘** A sort of water bird, much dreaded by the fish: [15]꜂t'á ꜂hu, a bird like the pelican.

꜂**鬍** Hu. The beard: ꜂hu ꜂yĕng, the whiskers; COM., [16]꜂hu ʻchü (coll. ꜂hu ꜀chü), a whiskered person; [17]꜂hu ꜀sü, the beard on the chin; beard and whiskers; [18]꜂hu ꜂hu, long, curly beard.

꜂**楜** Hu. Pepper: COM., [19]꜂hu ꜀chieu, pepper; pah꜀ ꜂hu ꜀chieu, white pepper; ꜂hu ꜀chieu mwak꜀ ground pepper.

꜂**蝴** Hu. The papilionidæ: COM., [20]꜂hu tiĕk꜀ a butterfly; COLL., ꜂hu tiĕk꜀ ꜂t'au, the butterfly, as in embroidery; ꜂hu tiĕk꜀ taing꜄ "butterfly-shops"—shops on each side of a common passage.

꜂**湖** Hu. A lake: in the coll. read ꜂u, q. v.: COM., [21]꜂hu ʻkwong, the old province of Hukwang, now Hunan and Hupeh; [22]꜀kong ꜂hu, river and lake; *met.*, in the coll., beggars, jugglers, &c.; [23]ʻngu ꜂hu, the five lakes—the Poyang in Kiangsi, the Tungt'ing and Tsingt'sau in Hunan, and the Tai and Tanyang in Kiangsu; COLL., ꜂hu ꜂nang t'au꜄ kwo꜄ sëü꜄ ꜀ch'iong, Hunan thro' to Sz'chuen; *met.*, throughout—said of a long rent in clothes or houses; k'ang꜄ ꜂hu, a kind of game in playing cards.

꜂**瓠** Hu. Interchanged with the next: the bottle-gourd or gourd-squash: COM., ꜂hu ꜂lu, a bottle-gourd;

---

1 修脯 2 束脯 3 鹿脯 4 章甫 5 甫甫 6 黼黻 7 胡粉 8 胡考 9 胡鼠 10 胡塗 11 胡行亂做 12 胡說 13 衚衕 14 醍醐 15 鵜鶘 16 鬍子 17 鬍鬚 18 鬍鬍 19 楜椒 20 蝴蝶 21 湖廣 22 江湖 23 五湖

福州方言拼音字典

gourd (shaped); COLL., *ˏhu ˎlu ˏp'ieu*, spoons made of the halves of gourds.

葫 ˏHu. A gourd: COM., ¹*ˏhu ˏlu*, the bottle-gourd; ²*ˏhu saung*ˀ a large kind of garlic.

餬 ˏHu. Interchanged with the next: congee; to seek a living: COM., ³*ˏhu ˈk'eu*, to get a livelihood, a bare subsistence.

糊 ˏHu. Paste, gluten, thick porridge; to paste, to stick: in the coll., careless; confused, muddy; mendacious, reckless: in the coll. also read *ˏku*, q. v.: COLL., ⁴*ˏhu ˏtu*, careless, slovenly; ⁵*ˏhang ˏhu*, confusedly, any way; ⁶*ˏhu ˏtu ˏkwang*, a corrupt, reckless magistrate; *ˏhu ˏsá ˏsá*, shiftless, unreliable.

瑚 ˏHu. Coral: *ˏhu ˈliéng*, vases used in sacrifices; COM., ⁷*ˏsang ˏhu* (col. *ˏtang ˏhu*), coral.

鳧 鳬 ˏFu. A sheldrake or mallard; a wild duck with a crest; a small species, near the Yangtsz river, is called ⁸*ˈkwang ˏhu*, the crested duck; ⁹*ˏhu ˏi*, a wild duck or mallard.

夫 ˏFu. An initial particle, now, therefore, however: also read *ˏhu*, q. v.: ¹⁰*ˏhu ˏing ˈchiá*, now as to the benevolent man; ¹¹*ˈch'iá ˏhu*, moreover.

扶 ˏFu. To lend a hand, to aid, to help, to assist; to uphold, to protect: used for the coll. *hoˀ*, q. v.: ¹²*ˏhu choˀ* to assist; ¹³*ˏhu ˏngui*, to aid one in difficulty; COM., ¹⁴*ˏhu ˏt'i*, to uphold, to aid.

颫 ˏ A wind blowing down, called ¹⁵*ˏhu ˏyeu*: ¹⁶*ˏhu ˏhung*, a tempest.

鈇 ˏFu. A kind of hatchet or small ax.

芙 ˏFu. A flower: COM., ¹⁷*ˏhu ˏiùng*, the hibiscus mutabilis.

蚨 ˏFu. A species of cicada or dytiscus, called ¹⁸*ˏch'ing ˏhu*, supposed to be able to recover its young, and cause cash, rubbed with its eggs, to return to their owner; ¹⁹*ˏhu ˏsiéng*, a species of cicada.

狐 ˏHu. An animal that can change its form, or can be possessed; suspicious, mistrusting; a fox: ²⁰*ˏhu ˏkiu*, fox-skin furs; COM., ²¹*ˏhu ˏli*, a fox; ²²*ˏhu ˏsiéng*, a good fox-elf, worshiped as keeper of the official seals; ²³*ˏhu ˏngi*, to doubt, suspicious; *hwang*ˀ *ˏhu*, possessed by the fox-elf; *ˏhu ˈka ˈhu ˏwi*, the fox borrows the tiger's terror; *met.*, one who assumes a bold aspect; COLL., *ˏhu ˏli ˏma*, or *ˏhu ˏli ˏma ˏchiàng*, a fox-elf; *ˏhu ˏli ˈmwi ˈmwang teˀ ˏt'wa*, the fox-elf's tail dragged over all the ground; *met.*, one's bad deeds discovered.

弧 ˏHu. An arc in mathematics; curved, arched: *ˏtiong ˏhu*, to string a bow; *ˏhiéng ˏhu*, a bow suspended, as at the door on the birth of a son.

¹葫	³餬	⁵含	官	鳧	仁	¹²扶	¹⁴扶	¹⁶颫	¹⁸青	²⁰狐	²²狐
蘆	口	糊	⁷瑚	⁹鳧	者	助	持	風	蚨	裘	仙
²葫	⁴糊	⁶糊	珊	鷖	¹¹且	¹³扶	¹⁵颫	¹⁷芙	¹⁹蚨	²¹狐	²³狐
蒜	塗	塗	⁸冠	¹⁰夫	夫	危	颻	蓉	蟬	狸	疑

苻 ꜀Fu. A plant called ʻ*kwi muk*꜇ (devil's eye) from the red and round seeds it bears; a species of Hoya (?).

符 ꜀Fu. A tally made of two slips; a seal on two pieces; to correspond to; to testify, to agree with, to evidence; a spell or charm written for preventing evil or for a cure: [1]꜀*hu chiék*꜇ a tally of two slips; a pass or warrant; COM., [2]꜀*hu hak*꜇ to fit, to match; [3]*wa*ʾ ꜀*hu*, to draw a charm; [4]꜀*hu chieu*ʾ a written prayer or incantation; [5]꜀*hu ch'ah*꜇ manual of charms; COLL., [6]*pang*ʾ ꜀*hu*, sickness—a phrase of fortune-tellers; [7]꜀*hu tói*ʾ a bag containing charms—worn on the person; [8]꜀*hu* ʻ*chwi p'eng*ʾ *p'ong*ʾ to spirt charm-water from the mouth.

壺 ꜀Hu. A vase or pot, a cup, a tankard, a wine jug: [9]꜀*teu hu*, to throw arrows into the jar—an ancient game; COM., *chek*꜇ ꜀*hu*, to hold the tankard; COLL., *niă*ʾ ꜀*hu*, a chamber pot.

乎 ꜀Hu. An interrogative adverb; interjection of doubt, admiration, or inquiry, placed at the end of a sentence; after nouns, a sign of the vocative; after verbs, a preposition, in, towards, to, with, from, up to, in respect to, as, like; sign of the accusative; an expletive: [9]꜀*u* ꜀*hu*, how sad! how miserable! [10]ʻ*i e*ʾ ꜀*hu*, just that and nothing more—a closing phrase; [11]*pok*꜇ *ik*꜇ *lok*꜇ ꜀*hu*, is it not pleasing? [12]꜀*ti* ꜀*hu pok*꜇ ꜀*ti*, do you understand or not? [13]ʻ*k'ó* ꜀*hu*, will it answer?—i. e., it will not; ꜀*ki* ꜀*hu*, almost, perhaps; [14]ʻ*pó* ꜀*hu* ꜀*ming*, to protect the people; [15]*mok*꜇ ꜀*kó* ꜀*hu* ꜀*t'iéng*, nothing higher than heaven; ꜀*yong* ꜀*chai* ꜀*hu yă*ʾ are four final particles, used as the sense requires; COM., [16]꜀*chi* ꜀*hu yă*ʾ ʻ*chiă*, four particles in essays—spoken of by a critic as in excess.

呼 ꜀Hu. To breathe, an expiration; to call, to invoke: [17]꜀*u* ꜀*hu*, ah! alas! ꜀*hu* ꜀*hó*, to call out; COM., [18]꜀*ch'ing* ꜀*hu*, to address one by his title; compellation, address; ꜀*hu* ꜀*hung hwang*ʾ ʻ*ŭ*, to invoke wind and rain, as jugglers do; ꜀*hu ngek*, expiration and inspiration, breathing; COLL., ꜀*hu* ꜀*yeu hak*꜇ *lĕk*꜇ to call out "ace" (for the opponent) and "six" (for self).

嘑 ꜀Hu. Same as the preceding; also to hoot, to menace: [19]*tai*ʾ ꜀*hu*, to call out loudly; ꜀*hu tang*ʾ "call the morning," as a cock's crowing.

滹 ꜀Hu. A river in the South-west of Chihli, called ꜀*hu* ꜀*tó*, flowing into North lake, and thence into the Peiho above Tientsin.

꜀*Hu.* A coll. word, as in ꜀*hu* ꜀*siu* (sometimes spoken ꜀*hu* ꜀*diu*), a mud eel shorter than the common eel, of a dark yellowish color, and having a pointed head.

和 ꜀Ho. Read ꜀*hwo*; coll. ꜀*hu*, as in ꜀*hu siong*ʾ a Budhist priest; ꜀*hu siong*ʾ *se*ʾ a Budhist monastery: see also under ꜀*hwo*.

[1]符節 [2]符合 [3]畫符 [4]符咒 [5]符册 [6]病符 [7]符袋 [8]投壺 [9]於乎 [10]已矣乎 [11]不亦樂乎 [12]知乎不知 [13]可乎 [14]保乎民 [15]莫高乎天 [16]之乎也者 [17]嗚呼 [18]稱呼 [19]大嘑

(209) Hü.

虛 ‹Hsü. Empty, vacant; unsubstantial, unsatisfactory; void, vain, inane; humble, poor in spirit, pure; abstract contemplation, as understood by the Budhists; space, the void of the firmament; the constellation Aquarius: [1]*‹hü ‹k‘ung*, the firmament; COM., [2]*‹k‘ung ‹hü*, empty; [3]*‹hü ‹sing* (coll. *‹k‘iéng ‹hü*), humility; [4]*‘t‘á ‹hü*, the constitution weak; [5]*‹sing ‹hü*, fearful, timid; [6]*‹hü che²* particles, as adverbs, etc.; [7]*‹hü to²* to spend vainly (one's time); *‹hü ngiăh*, a deficient number or quantity; [8]*‹hü ‹kŭng*, "scant catty"—pound of 12 oz.; [9]*‹hü ‹ung*, vain forms or rites; *‹hü ‹ing ‹ching*, a hypocritical show of kindness; [10]*‹hü ‹tiong ‹sing sié²* to make a false display of one's state (or designs).

噓 ‹Hsü. To blow with the breath; respiration; to praise, to recommend: [11]*‹hü ngek*, breathing; COM., [12]*‹ch‘wi ‹hü*, to blow with the breath; *met.*, to speak a good word for; COLL., *‹hü ‹hü kieu²* sound of panting or of phlegm in the throat.

墟 Hsü. A mound; old mausolea, or burial-wastes; a deserted region, a wild; a place for fairs or markets, a fair: [13]*‹hü mwo²* a burial place; [14]*‹hü ‹tiong*, a place for fairs; [15]*‹kwi ‹hü*, to go to market.

歔 ‹Hsi. To rob; timid, fearful; breathing or sobbing, making a noise through the nose: [16]*‹hi ‹hü*, to sob, sobbing.

盱 ‹Yü. To stare, to open one's eyes at; to hope for, to gloat on; joyful: *‹hü ‹heng*, to stare at; [17]*‹chü ‹hü*, the joy of a mean man; a plain, homely appearance; *‹sung ‹hü*, pleased.

吁 ‹Yü. An interjection expressive of grief, distrust, or admiration: [18]*‹hü ‹chiă*, ah! alas!

冔 ‹Hsü. The crown worn in the Shang dynasty; it resembled a Cantab's cap in being flat on the top.

訏 ‹Hsü. To vaunt, to boast, to brag; false, boasting; great, big: [19]*‹hü ‹mwo*, excellent counsel or memorial, as on state affairs.

紆 ‹Yü. To stammer; slowly, leisurely; to wind or twist; bent, weak in the middle; a cord: [20]*‹hü hwang²* or *‹hü ‹sü*, slowly, leisurely; *‹hü k‘ŭk*, curved, pliant.

許 ‘Hsü. To grant, to allow, to let; to permit or acquiesce in, to accede to, to accord; to listen to and promise; to betroth or promise in marriage; to enter or advance; to flourish; an excess, more than, very; a surname; sometimes used in the coll. for the demonstrative pronoun *that*, also for the adverbs *so, thus:* COM., [21]*‘hü ngwong²* to vow; *‘sieu ‘hü*, a very little; *‘hü ‹ching ‹kung*, *‘Hü*, the true prince—a Tauist god; [22]*eng² ‘hü*, to promise; COLL., *‘hü chiăh*, that one; *‘hü wai²* there; [23]*‘hü tói²* (or *kaĕk*,), in

1 虛空　2 空虛　3 虛心　4 謙虛　5 心虛　6 虛字　7 虛度　8 虛斤　9 虛文　10 虛張聲勢　11 噓吸　12 吹噓　13 墟墓　14 墟場　15 歸墟　16 欷歔　17 睢盱　18 吁嗟　19 訏謨　20 紆緩　21 許願　22 應許　23 許塊

that place; ʻ*hü* ˛*si*, or ʻ*hü* ˛*seng nó*ʾ at that time; ʻ*hü* ˛*ong*, so long a time; ʻ*hü* ʻ*mang twai*ʾ so very large; ʻ*hü* ˛*peng*, on that side, in that direction; ʻ*hü* ʻ*tié*, in there.

ʻ詡 Hsü. Also read *hëü*ʾ: boasting talk; to display; to talk largely; energetic, bold, moderate: [1]˛*k*ʻ*wa* ʻ*hü*, to vaunt; [2]˛*yong* ʻ*hü*, to display, to spread abroad.

ʻ栩 Hsü. Also read *hëü*ʾ: a tree like the chestnut; it bears a black nut resembling an acorn; soft, flexible: ʻ*hü* ʻ*hü*, pleased, joyful.

(210) Huí.

˛回 ˛囘 Hui. To revolve, to turn round; to return back, to revert to; returning; repenting, changing the mind; crooked, deflected; a time, a turn; an effort; a chapter in a novel or book: COM., [3]˛*huí seng*ʾ (coll. ˛*huí* ˛*p*ʻ*ié*), to answer by letter; [4]˛*huí* ˛*ing*, "the reply"—an epistolary phrase; [5]˛*huí* ˛*ka*, to return home; [6]˛*huí lük*˛ a conflagration; a title of the god of fire; [7]˛*huí* ʻ*chü*, or ˛*huí* ˛*ngü*, to bring the ancestral tablet home after burial; [8]˛*huí* ˛*huí kau*ʾ Mohammedanism; [9]˛*huí pwo*ʾ to turn back; [10]˛*huí* ˛*nang*, to veer to the south, as a typhoon; [11]˛*huí* ʻ*ch*ʻ*iu*, "turn the hand"—i.e., to set down (the sedan); to return a blow; [12]ʻ*wang* ˛*huí*, to reconcile; [13]˛*huí* ˛*mwong*, the first visit to the bride's parents; [14]˛*lai* ˛*huí*, to come and go—i.e., to and fro, both ways; [15]˛*huí* ˛*sing* ʻ*tiong* *e*ʾ to change one's mind, to forgive; [16]˛*huí siok*˛ to repeat (teacher's) explanation, as pupils do; COLL., [17]ʻ*kwi* ˛*huí*, how many times? several times; ˛*huí* ˛*t*ʻ*au*, or [18]˛*huí* ʻ*tiong* ˛*t*ʻ*au*, to look back; *met.*, in a little while, soon; ˛*huí nong*ʾ to become damp; ˛*huí* ˛*ch*ʻ*ung*, "return of spring"—a poor man becoming prosperous; ˛*huí* ʻ*tiong* ˛*sing*, to turn round; ˛*huí sioh*˛ *saik*, to return one of the articles presented; ˛*huí* ˛*t*ʻ*au sak*, an injury coming on the injurer himself.

˛*Huí.* A coll. word, for which the last is sometimes used; an independent demonstrative pronoun, the correlate of ˛*chuí* (that); ˛*huí* ʻ*hó* ˛*chuí* ˛*ngai*, that good and this bad; ˛*huí ng*ʾ ʻ*pi* ˛*chuí*, that not comparable to this; ʻ*hiä* ˛*huí*, that! that there! an ejaculation in trying to recall a subject.

˛迴 ˛廻 Hui. Interchanged with the preceding character: to curve, to bend; to turn round; to double, as a fox: [19]˛*huí* ˛*k*ʻ*wang*, circling, as hills; COM., [20]˛*huí* ˛*long*, porches about a court; [21]˛*huí chieu*ʾ rooms on the front side of a court facing the house; [22]˛*huí pié*ʾ to avoid, to get out of the way—*scil.*, of an idol or officer.

˛痐 Hui. Long worms in the abdomen, the tape-worm.

˛徊 Hui. To pace to and fro, to go and return; to hover about: ˛*pai* ˛*huí*, irresolute, back and forth.

[1]誇	[3]回	[5]回	[7]回	教	南	回	回	意	回	[19]迴	[21]迴
詡	信	家	主	[9]回	[11]回	[13]回	[15]回	[16]回	[18]回	國	照
[2]揚	[4]回	[6]回	[8]回	步	手	門	心	說	轉	[20]迴	[22]迴
詡	音	祿	回	[10]回	[12]挽	[14]來	轉	[17]幾	頭	廊	避

福州方言拼音字典

洄 Hui. ₂ Water flowing round and round, an eddy, a whirlpool; name of a lake in Hupeh; indistinct, as eddying water: ₍huí ₍huí, indistinct, not perceived clearly; ¹₍ing ₍huí, an eddy, a whirlpool.

茴 Hui. ₂ Fennel or caraway seed, a small fragrant seed like dill; in the coll. read ₍p'uí, q.v.: ²₍huí ₍hiong, or ʻsieu ₍huí, fennel; ³tai² ₍huí, star anise-seed.

(211) Huk.

佛 髴 Fu. ₂ To see indistinctly, similitude; to turn aside, contrary, opposed, unreasonable; a bright appearance; Budha, the various Budhs: ⁴ʻhwong huk₂ seen indistinctly, resembling; COM., ⁵huk₂ kau² Budhism; ⁶huk₂ kauk₂ Budh's bone; met., a Budhist spirit or affinity in one; ⁷huk₂ tang² a load of Budhist idols and implements; ⁸huk₂ ʻchü, young Budhist novitiates; small images of Budh; ⁹huk₂ ₍song, a large red flower,(?)species of Hibiscus; ¹⁰huk₂ ʻch'iu ₍kang, finger-lemon—usually called ₍hiong ₍yong; ¹¹₍sang ʻpó huk₂ the three precious Budhs; ¹²ó ₍mi ₍tó huk₂ Amida Budha; ¹³₍mi ₍ná huk₂ (properly ₍mi lek₂ huk₂), the past Budh; ¹⁴huk₂ hwa² ʻiu ₍yong ₍ing, Budh transforms those having affinity with him; COLL., ¹⁵ch'ai² huk₂ a vegetarian.

伏 宓 Fu. ₂ To lie or fall prostrate; to humble, to subject, to oppress; to hide, to conceal; to brood; to acknowledge, to confess; to abscond; used as an adverb, meaning humbly, in my opinion: COM., ¹⁶huk₂ wong² to hope for—an epistolary phrase; ¹⁷huk₂ chói² to confess faults; ₍sang huk₂ midsummer, the dogdays; huk₂ ₍ping, soldiers in ambuscade; ¹⁸huk₂ sie² to assume a fixed shape, as things often bent; COLL., huk₂ tio² to lie in ambush by the road-side; ₍seng ₍mai huk₂ hiéng² ₍siáng, to plan well beforehand.

復 Fu. ₂ Again, reiterated, to do the second time; to return, to reply; to restore, to repay; to report to, to answer; to recall the spirit of one who died away from home: huk₂ ₍lai, to come again; ¹⁹huk₂ ₍siu, to take revenge; COM., ²⁰huk₂ meng² to report on a commission; huk₂ ₍ngwong, or huk₂ ʻtiong ₍ngwong chek₂ to regain former health; COLL., huk₂ ʻtiong ₍li, to revert, as a country to the original possessor. Read hok₂, as in ʻhwang hok₂ or ₍t'üng hok₂ repeated, again and again.

茯 Fu. ₂ China root (Smilax China), of which the best kinds are from Sz'chuen; COM., huk₂ ₍ling, China root; pah₂ huk₂ ₍ling, white China root; huk₂ ₍ling ₍kó, China root jelly.

袱 Fu. ₂ A square cloth-wrapper for inclosing things: COM., ₍pau huk₂ a wrapping cloth.

服 Fu. ₂ To use; to wait on, to serve; to submit, to yield to, to accord with; to cause to submit, to convince; accustom-

1 縈洄 2 茴香 3 大茴 4 彷彿 5 佛教 6 佛骨 7 佛擔 8 佛子 9 佛桑 10 佛手柑 11 三寶佛 12 阿彌陀佛 13 彌尼佛 14 佛化有緣人 15 菜佛 16 伏望 17 伏罪 18 伏勢 19 復讐 20 復命

ed to, acclimated; to think; to fold; to dress; garments, mourning apparel; a carriage cloth; a quiver; an affair: *‘k‘ok, huk,* to yield submissively; COM., [1]*‚i huk,* garments; [3]*‚sing huk,* to commence wearing mourning; [4]*huk, ‘mwang,* the period of mourning ended; [5]*huk, sëü’* to serve; [6]*huk, tuk,* to take poison; COLL., *huk, ‚sio,* vanquished; *huk, ‚i ‘kwang a’* submit to his rule.

Huk,. A coll. word, as in *huk, tuk,* gruff, rude, stern; hasty and cross, ill-natured, peevish; *cheng’ k‘ó’ huk, tuk,* exceedingly gruff.

(212) Hung.

風 ‚Fêng. Breath, spirit; passion; air-gusts, a gale, wind; haste, fleetness; manners, deportment, etiquette; institutes; administration, policy; fame; example, fashion; instruction, reformation; influence; disposition, temper; to affect by example; heat in animals: COM., [7]*‚liong ‚hung,* to take the air; [8]*‚hung laung’* or [9]*‚hung ‚p‘ó,* waves; [10]*‚hung e’* taste, flavor; [11]*‚hung ‚sing,* the human appearance; Æolus; [12]*‚hung ‘t‘u ‚ming ‚ching,* the manners and spirit of a people; [13]*‚hung sük,* customs, usages; *‚hung ‘king,* scenery, landscape; [14]*‚si ‚hung,* the winds of the season; [15]*‚hung ‚liu,* a wind-tumor; [16]*lo’ ‚hung,* to expose to the air; *met.,* to divulge a secret; *‚t‘ëng ‚hung,* a circulation of air; [17]*‚hung koi’* a bellows; [18]*‚hung ‚hung,* a cold; [19]*‚hung ‘chwi,* geomancy, the luck of a site; *‚hung ‚ch‘wi ‘liu,* the wind sways the willows; *met.,* applied to one who assents to every thing; *‚ié ‚hung ik, sük,* to change the customs; COLL., *p‘ah, ‚hung chó’ pó’* the wind blowing in heavy gusts; *‚hung ‚t‘ai,* a typhoon, hurricane; *‚hung ‚p‘ung,* sails; *‚hung ‚kwong,* brilliant, as funeral rites; *‚hung ‘chwi ‘mwi,* "luck's fag end"; *met.,* a boy hopelessly degenerate; *‚hung ‚siéng,* a fanningmill.

楓 ‚Fêng. The maple; also applied to the sycamore: [20]*‚tang ‚hung,* red maple; [21]*‚hung ‚sing,* the maple palace; *met.,* the emperor.

瘋 ‚Fêng. The leprosy, scrofula, and kindred diseases; insane, insensate; paralysis, palsy: COM., [22]*‚hung ‚tiéng,* lunatic, crazy; [23]*‚hung ‘niong,* a paralysis; *‚hung k‘e’* paralytic affections; *‚hung ‚kó,* plasters for the palsy: *‚hung tuk, ‚liu chëü’* scrofulous, or confluent, ulcers.

丰 ‚Fêng. Luxuriant; plump, good looking; easy, melodious; a round face: COM., *‚hung ‘ch‘ai,* a graceful gait; plump, as the face; *‚hung ‘nga,* elegant, as essays; *‚hung ‚sing,* a lively look; *‚hung ong’* fine harmony, as in music and and poetry.

峰 峯 ‚Fêng. The peak of a mountain; *met.,* a camel's hump: *‚hung ‚lwang,* peaks and ridges; COM., *‚chiéng ‚hung,* a bigh mountain-peak.

---

1 屈服 2 衣服 3 成服 4 服滿 5 服事 6 服毒 7 凉風 8 風浪 9 風波 10 風味 11 風神 12 風土民情 13 風俗 14 時風 15 風瘤 16 露風 17 風櫃 18 風寒 19 風水 20 丹楓 21 楓宸 22 瘋癲 23 瘋軟

福州方言拼音字典

鋒 ˓Fêng. The point of a weapon, a sharp point; the vanguard; turbulent; bristling, to rise up like spears: [1]ˏchiĕng ˓hung, the vanguard; COM., [2]pek˒ ˓hung, the point of a pencil.

烽 ˓Fêng. Fire-beacons, placed on hills to give notice of the enemy's approach: [3]˓hung ʻhwo, a beacon-fire.

吩 ˓Fên. Read ʻhung and hong˒ in the dictionaries; same as p'ong˒ (to spurt); in the coll. read ˓hung: to direct, to give orders to: [4]˓hung ho˒ or ˓hung no˒ to direct, to bid, to enjoin on; ˓hung ho˒ ˓hung tá˒ to charge straitly.

分 ˓Fên. To separate, to divide, to halve; to distribute, to apportion, to give; to partake with; a tenth in decimal notation; a candareen, tenth of a mace; the tenth of an inch: also read hong˒; in the coll. read ˓pwong, q. v.: COM., [5]˓hung ˏlié, or [6]˓hung piék˒ to separate, to part asunder, as friends; [7]˓hung piék˒ to discriminate, to distinguish; [8]˓hung sang˒ to scatter; [9]˓hung ˏming, clear, plain; [10]˓hung hwak˒ to portion out, as work, wages, &c.; sek˒ ˓hung, ten candareens; met., a superlative, very, perfectly; [11]˓hung pwang˒ one tenth and a half; [12]˓hung chau˒ to have separate kitchens; [13]˓hung ˓chong, to divide stolen goods; met., to divide into shares; [14]˓hung ʻhu, a deputy prefect; [15]˓hung ˏhó pok˒ ˓ch'a, not the least error; [16]˓hung ˏung pok˒ ʻch'ü, will not accept a cash (for services)! COLL., ˓hung ˏhó chiăh˒ che˒ ˓tu ˏmó, not the least, none whatever; ˓hung ch'uung˒ ˓tu lwang˒ k'ó˒ tenths and inches (met. the mind) utterly confused.

汾 ˓Fên. A river in Shansi, a branch of the Yellow river: ˓hung ˏyong ˏwong, name of a person in the Tang dynasty—synonym for happiness; [17]˓hung ˏyong ʻtiĕng hang˒ Fanyeung's king nodding his chin (because he did not know all his descendants); COM., [18]˓hung ʻchiu, Fanchou wine.

枌 ˓Fên. Also read ˏhung: a tree like the elm with white wood: [19]˓hung ˏü, the elm; met., the ancestral home.

紛 ˓Fên. Perplexed, confused, tangled; raveled; to mix up many things at once; hurry, bustle, clamor; a variegated ribbon: COM., [20]˓hung chak˒ mixed, confused; [21]˓hung lwang˒ (coll. ˓hung ˓hung laung˒), confused, as a crowd; perplexed, distracted; ˓hung ˓hung pok˒ ek˒ contradictory, as reports.

芬 ˓Fên. Budding, blossoming; the fragrance of plants or flowers; numerous; harmonious: ˓hung ˓hung, odoriferous; ˓hung ˓hwong, spreading fragrance.

氛 ˓Fên. Fume, vapor; shadowy signs, a will-o'-the-wisp, airy omens: auk˒ ˓hung, or ˓hung ˓ching, noxious vapors; ˓hung ˓ung, aerial influences; ʻhai ˓hung, marine vapors; met., pirates.

1 前鋒 2 筆鋒 3 [illegible] 4 吩咐 5 分離 6 分別 7 分別 8 分散 9 分明 10 分發 11 分半 12 分竈 13 分贓 14 分府 15 分毫不差 16 分文不取 17 汾陽點領 18 汾酒 19 枌榆 20 紛雜 21 紛亂

封 ˏFâng. The domain granted to princes; to heap up earth; great, affluent; to enrich; to invest nobles with rule, to appoint to office, to confer investiture; to give a title of nobility; to seal up, to close; an envelope, a classifier of letters: COM., [1]*ˏhung ˏkiong tai*ʼ *ˏsing*, the high provincial officers; [2]*teng*ʼ *ˏhung*, a rescript inclosed in boards, as a death warrant; [3]*ˏhung chaing*ʼ to bestow titles, as the emperor does; [4]*ʻngŭkˎ ˏhung*, rank conferred by Heaven; *nói*ʼ *seng*ʼ *ekˎ ˏhung*, one letter; [5]*ˏhung eng*ʼ to close the seals, as officers do on the 20th of the 12th month; [6]*ˏhung seng*ʼ (coll. *ˏhung ˏp'ié*), to seal a letter; [7]*ˏhung ˏsing tiong*ʼ the records of deification; *ˏhung ʻsó*, to shut up (a house); [8]*ˏhung ˏsung*, to impress boats; COLL., *ˏhung ˏmwang*, to (cure and) bind up eels with strings.

葑 ˏFâng. A species of turnip or rape: [9]*ˏhung ʻp'i*, rape and greens; *met.*, poor, trifling, as talent which is still available.

葷 ˏHun. Leeks, onions, strong-flavored vegetables; animal food: COM., [10]*ˏhung só*ʼ meat and vegetable diet; [11]*ˏhung é*ʼ the flavor of meats; COLL., *ˏhung ʻlá ˏsang ˏpwang ch'ai*ʼ *ch'ai*ʼ *ʻlá ˏsang ˏpwang ˏhung*, meats embrace three kinds of vegetables, and vegetables three kinds of meats.

焄 Vapor or steam; fumes from cooked vegetables, savory odors: [12]*ˏhung ˏkó*, steam from viands; odorous exhalations.

豐 ˏFâng. A full goblet; full, abundant, affluent, copious, exuberant; rich, fertile, prolific; talented: [13]*ˏhung ˏteng*, an abundant harvest; COM., [14]*ˏhung hau*ʼ generous, as a feast; wealthy; plump, fleshy; [15]*ˏhung ˏniêng*, a year of plenty; [16]*ˏhung ʻmwang*, abundant; full and plump, as the face; [17]*ˏhang ˏhung*, the emperor Hienfung.

酆 ˏFeng. The capital of Wan wang, now Huhien in Si-ngan-fu in Shensi: [18]*ˏhung ˏtu*, a district in Chung-chau in Sz'chuen, where the fire-wells occur—hence used as a synonym for hell or tophet.

棼 A fragrant wood burned for its perfume.

棼 ˏFâng. The beam or ridge-pole of a roof; confused, disordered, complicated; a hempen covering: [19]*té*ʼ *ˏsi ˏi ˏhung ˏchi*, to hatchel the silk and tangle it; *met.*, to complicate state affairs.

雰 ˏFên. A cold mist; hoar-frost; sleety rain: [20]*ʻü siokˎ ˏhung ˏhung*, drizzling rain and snow, sleet.

饙 餴 Rice half boiled; to steam rice after boiling: *ˏhung leu*ʼ rice boiled and steamed, food thoroughly dressed.

1封疆大臣 2釘封 3封贈 4玉封 5封印 6封信 7封神傳 8封船 9葑菲 10葷素 11葷味 12焄蒿 13豐登 14豐厚 15豐年 16豐滿 17咸豐 18酆都 19治絲而棼之 20雨雪雰雰

福州方言拼音字典

蚊 ʻFêng. Read ˓ung; coll. ˏhung, as in ˏhung ˓mwong, a mosquito; ˏhung ˓mwong tengʾ (or kaʾ), a mosquito bite; ˏhung ˓mwong ˓tëng, a medicated preparation in rolls, the smoke of which stupefies mosquitos; ˏhung ˓mwong ˓kiä, a "mosquito-cangue" — i. e., curtain; ˏhung ˓mwong chengʾ kauʾ the mosquitos are very thick.

ˏHung. A coll. word, as in ˏhung ˏhung angʾ evening twilight, dusk.

ʻ粉 Fêng. Rice broken to pieces; flour of any kind of grain; crushed, broken, comminuted, in fragments; pigment; to adorn; to whitewash, to color: COM., [1]ʻmi ʻhung, rice flour; [2]miëngʾ ʻhung, wheat flour; [3]ʻhung ˏkang, a kind of dry vermicelli; [4]ʻchwi ʻhung, moist vermicelli; [5]ʻhung pʻiëngʾ ˏkó, cakes of rice flour and sugar; [6]˓tu ʻhung, to powder, to whiten; [7]ʻhung ʻpeng, or [8]ʻhung ˓pá, a writing tablet—Chinese slate; [9]ʻhung chʻóiʾ or [10]ʻhung ʻhung chʻóiʾ smashed to shivers; [11]ʻü ʻhung, a drizzling, a falling mist; COLL., [12]ʻhung piäh, whitewashed walls; kʻáʾ ˏi ʻhung pah, ˓chiä, just whiten it over! [13]ʻhung ˓ëng, or ʻhung ʻhung ˓ëng ˓öng, a fair, rosy (face); ʻhung ˓deng, the small intestines of swine; lóh, sioh, mengʾ ʻhung, lose the powder from the whole face; met., to be ashamed.

ʻ扮 Fêng. To seize or hold with the hand; to move, to shake; in coll. books, also means to adorn, to deck: COLL., ʻta ʻhung, to dress out, to beautify.

ʻ僨 Fên. To fall prostrate, or on one's back; to overthrow, to ruin; to move, to shake, to agitate: [14]ʻhung sëüʾ to ruin an affair.

ʻ憤 Fên. Impatient desire, zeal, ardor; anger, violent feeling: [15]ʻhung ʻmwang (or mongʾ), vexed, chagrined; [16]hwak, ʻhung, ardent, zealous, as for study.

ʻ忿 Fên. Interchanged with the last; anger, indignation, resentment: ˏting ʻhung, to restrain anger; COM., [17]ʻhung noʾ or [18]ʻhung kʻeʾ anger, vexation; [19]ʻhung ʻhung pok, ˓ping, unappeased wrath.

ʻ鼢 A mole or field-rat, also called ʻyëng ʻchʻü, supposed to be a transformation of the butcher-bird.

ʻ哄 Hung. Hum of a crowd; singing, a commingling of voices; to intimidate by a loud voice; to cozen, to cheat, to beguile; to tempt, to deceive: COM., [20]ʻhung pʻiëngʾ to deceive; COLL., hiäk, ʻhung, to beguile, to cozen.

ʻ鬨 The voice of persons fighting; to quarrel, to wrangle, to fight.

ʻ汞 The ore of quicksilver, cinnabar; mercury, quicksilver: [21]˓sieu ˏtang liëngʾ ʻhung, to smelt cinnabar into quicksilver.

[1]米粉 [2]麵粉 [3]粉乾 [4]水粉 [5]粉片糕 [6]塗粉 [7]粉板 [8]粉牌 [9]粉碎 [10]粉粉碎 [11]雨粉 [12]粉壁 [13]粉紅 [14]僨事 [15]憤懣 [16]發憤 [17]忿怒 [18]忿氣 [19]忿忿不平 [20]哄騙 [21]燒鍊丹汞

恐 ʻK'ung. Read ʻk'ŭng; coll. ʻhung, as in ʻhung p'aʼ to fear lest; ʻhung p'aʼ ꜂i ĭʼ ꜀li, lest perchance he may come.

雲 ꜀Yün. Clouds, fog or mist on the hills; shaded, cloudy, numerous, like the clouds; a fructifying principle: ꜀hung ʻü, clouds and rain; *met.*, to copulate; [1]꜀hung ʻmu, mother o' pearl; [2]꜀hung hangʼ the milky way; COM., [3]꜀hung ꜀ling, or ꜀hung huk꜆ ꜀ling, Yunnan China root; [4]ʻk'i ꜀hung, clouds rising; [5]꜀hung ꜂chiă, or ꜀hung peʼ, or ꜀hung tauʼ covered by the clouds; [6]꜀hung oʼ a fog; [7]꜀hung ꜂t'ai, cloud-ladder; *met.*, literary promotion; [8]꜀p'eu ꜀hung, floating clouds; *met.*, uncertain, as wealth and honor; [9]꜀siong ꜀hung, propitious clouds; [10]꜀hung koiʼ the provinces of Yunnan and Kweichau; [11]꜀hung ʻpeng, a wooden block used to beat on in temples and yamuns.

紅 ꜀Hung. Red color, reddish, fiery, rosy, ruddy, as the complexion: used for ꜂kung (work); in the coll. read ꜀ĕng, q. v.: [12]꜀hung ꜂hwa, the Hibiscus rosa sinensis, or shoe-flower; [13]꜀hung ꜂tang, red lead; ʻnü ꜀hung, ladies' work; ꜀hung ʻü, "red rain"—(poetically) falling peach-blossoms; COM., [14]꜀hung haingʼ the red almond; ꜀hung ꜀ngang, a florid complexion; [15]꜀hung ʻhung ꜂ka ꜀ing, a painted beauty; COLL., ꜀hung ꜀ngang ꜂tŏ pok꜆ miăngʼ a rosy-faced (beauty) usually has bad luck—gets a poor husband.

馮 ꜀ A surname. Read ꜀ping: a horse running; to mount, to ascend; the sound of a hard wall; to trust, to rely on; boastful; dissatisfied.

鴻 ꜀Hung. A swan, a wild goose; *met.*, a letter-carrier, a postman; large, vast, profound; learned: [16]꜀hung piéngʼ to send a letter by one; [17]꜀hung ngangʼ a wild goose; ꜂hi ꜀hung, flying geese; *met.*, floating banners; [18]꜀hung ꜀mung, the primordial influence, or aura; the eastern horizon; COM., ꜀hung ꜀ong, great grace.

洪 ꜀Hung. Interchanged with the last: water rising; an inundation, a deluge, a torrent overflowing; great, vast, immense; a surname: [19]꜀hung ꜂hwong, a great waste, chaos; [20]꜀hung ʻchwi, a flood, the deluge of Yü; COM., ꜀hung ꜂sang ꜀kio, bridge over the Min 4 miles west of Foochow.

渾 ꜀Hun. A roaring, dashing torrent; the noise of many waters; turbid, roily, foul; polluted, sordid, dirty; great, confused, blended; the mass, the entire, the whole of: [21]꜀hung ꜂sing, the whole body; COM., ꜀hung ꜀hung, roiled; [22]꜀hung hwaʼ careless, doing without close scrutiny; [23]꜀hung ꜀sing (coll. ꜀hung ꜀siăng), suitable, fitting.

渢 ꜀ The noise of water, roaring of the waves. Read ꜀hwang, as in ꜀hwang ꜀hwang, floating; *met.*, an even, or well-modulated, sound.

潰 ꜀ Also read ꜂hung: a river overflowing and making streamlets; a river-bank; a river in Honan.

[1]雲母 [2]雲漢 [3]雲苓 [4]起雲 [5]雲遮 [6]雲霧 [7]雲梯 [8]浮雲 [9]祥雲 [10]雲貴 [11]雲板 [12]紅花 [13]紅丹 [14]紅杏 [15]紅粉佳人 [16]鴻便 [17]鴻雁 [18]鴻濛 [19]洪荒 [20]洪水 [21]渾身 [22]渾化 [23]渾成

虹 ˓Kung. Used for the next: a halo near the sun; colored vapor; the rainbow—all supposed to be an impure effluence of the sky: used for *kʻëüng*ʾ in the coll., q. v.: *˓hung ˓ngá*, a rainbow, colored vapors; ¹*˓hung ˓kio*, the arched rainbow—a poetic phrase.

訌 ˓Kung. To quarrel, to litigate; to injure, to denounce to officers; to involve others by speaking; domestic discords; a man's name.

焚 ˓Fên. To burn, to light, to set on fire; to kill, to destroy: in the coll. read *˓hang*, q. v.: ²*˓hung hwa*ʾ to burn up, as paper ingots before idols; *˓hung ˓hiong*, to burn incense; COM., *˓hung ˓chü ˓kʻang ˓ü*, to burn the books and throw the scholars into pits, as Tsin did.

墳 ˓Fên. A grave, a tomb, a tumulus; river-banks, an embankment; great, vast: *˓sang ˓hung*, heaven, earth, and man; COM., ³*˓hung mwo*ʾ a grave; *˓hung ˓sang*, hills covered with graves; *pai*ʾ *˓hung*, to worship at the tombs; ⁴*˓sang ˓hung ʻngu ʻtiéng*, name of an ancient book—now lost. Read *ʻhung:* a rich, loamy soil.

幩 ˓ Also read *ʻhung:* an ornament on the bit of a bridle.

蕡 ˓ Fruitful, flourishing plants; fragrant flowers growing together; string of a bow: ⁵*˓hung sik*, bearing much seed; ⁶*˓hung ʻchü*, hemp seed.

逢 ˓Fêng. To meet undesignedly, to fall in with, to run against; to occur; great, wide: COM., ⁷*˓hung ˓nging*, to meet and receive; *met.*, obsequious; ⁸*˓hung ˓si*, time of meeting with, seasonable; ⁹*˓hung ˓si le*ʾ *kʻe*ʾ opportunely and cleverly done, as an essay; ¹⁰*˓hung ˓niéng*, a propitious year; COLL., *˓hung ʻkwi*, set days; which are the set days? *˓hung ˓sang*, set days of threes—i. e., the 3d, 13th, and 23d of the month; *˓hung ˓ing ʻchi siok*, *˓sang ˓hung wa*ʾ on meeting people say only a little.

魂 **𩲡** ˓Hun. The soul, the spiritual part of the ghost, the ethereal manes which ascends: in Changloh, and some other brogues, spoken *˓hong:* ¹¹*sek, ˓hung*, to lose one's wits; COM., ¹²*˓sing ˓hung*, the spirit or mind; ¹³*˓sang ˓hung chʻek, pʻaëk*, the three ethereal, and seven animal, souls; ¹⁴*˓hwang ˓hung*, to revive, as one very sick; ¹⁵*˓ling ˓hung*, the soul, spiritual part of man; ¹⁶*˓chieu ˓hung*, to beckon (bring home) the soul (of one dying abroad); ¹⁷*˓hung ˓hi pʻaëk, sang*ʾ the souls flown and spirits scattered—frightened out of his wits; ¹⁸*˓hung pok, ho*ʾ *ʻtʻá*, the soul not cleaving to the body—a sudden fright; COLL., *˓hung pʻaëk, ˓kiäng ʻchau ʻkwong ˓tëng*, his souls (wits) frightened off to Canton!

餛 ˓ Sort of pork balls: ¹⁹*˓hung ˓tung*, pork balls seasoned with soy and onions, then rolled in flour and steamed.

1虹橋	3墳墓	五典	6蕡子	8逢時	利器	11失魂	13三魂	14還魂	16招魂	魄散	附體
2焚化	4三墳	5蕡實	7逢迎	9逢時	10逢年	12神魂	七魄	15靈魂	17魂飛	18魂不	19餛飩

(213) Hüng.

勳 Hsün. Loyal merit, meritorious; to acquire merit in the service of one's prince: [1]‚hŭng ‚ló, or [2]‚hŭng ngiĕk‚ merit in serving the state; [3]'kiong' ‚hŭng, to establish merit.

曛 Hsün. Twilight, the light reflected after sunset: [4]'sik‚ ‚hŭng, evening twilight; [5]‚siă ‚hŭng, reflected light.

昕 Hsün. The morn, the dawn, the sun rising in brightness: [6]'tai' ‚hŭng, early dawn.

昕 Hsün. Joy, rejoicing, pleased; to see indistinctly.

壎 塤 Hsün. An ancient musical instrument made of porcelain, with 8 holes about the size of a goose's egg, and blown at the apex.

烘 Hung. Also read ‚hung: the heat of fire rising up; a flash or flame; to dry at a fire: in the coll. read ‚hĕng, q. v.

熏 燻 Hsün. Smoke rising; steam, exhalations; to smoke, to fumigate; to heat, to parch; harmonious, agreeable; to becloud; distressed; evening: [7]‚hŭng ‚hŭng, agreeable; uneasy, fidgety; [8]‚hŭng sik‚ twilight; COLL., [9]'chiă ‚p'uí sé' ‚hŭng ‚ki, this skin is (dyed and) smoked.

焄 Like the last: fire rising; to heat; vapor or steam; fumes from cooked vegetables; savory odors: [10]‚hŭng ‚kó, steam from viands, odorous exhalations.

薰 Hsün. Fragrant plants, fragrance, as used in houses to expel demons; a savory smell; balmy, as a south wind: [11]‚nang ‚hŭng, or [12]‚hŭng ‚hung, the warm southern breezes.

醺 Hsün. Intoxicated, drunk; smelling of liquor: [13]'choi' ‚hŭng ‚hŭng, beastly drunk.

酗 酳 Hsuing. Analagous to the last, and properly read hĕŭ'; erroneously, but commonly, read ‚hŭng: mad with drink, ravingly drunk: COM., [14]‚hŭng 'chiu, infuriated with liquor, delirium tremens.

匈 獯 Hsuing. A tribe of aborigines, called [15]‚hŭng ük‚; they dwelt near Shensi; [16]‚hŭng ‚nu, the Huns, for which the first is mostly used.

凶 兇 Hsuing. Unfortunate, unlucky, unhappy, unpropitious, adverse; lugubrious, mournful; judgments of Heaven, calamity; malignant, cruel, bad, in which sense it is used for the next: [17]‚hŭng ‚niĕng, an unpropitious year; COM., [18]‚hŭng tieu' a bad omen; [19]‚hŭng seng' bad news; [20]‚hŭng huk‚ a mourning dress; [21]‚hŭng ‚tó kek‚ 'chieu, much bad, and little good, luck.

兇 Hsuing. Malevolent, cruel, inhuman; vicious, malignant; fearful, a cry of fear; COM.,

[1] 勳勞 [2] 勳業 [3] 建勳 [4] 夕曛 [5] 斜曛 [6] 大昕 [7] 熏熏 [8] 熏夕 [9] 者皮是熏其 [10] 焄蒿 [11] 南薰 [12] 薰風 [13] 醉醺醺 [14] 酗酒 [15] 獯鬻 [16] 匈奴 [17] 凶年 [18] 凶兆 [19] 凶信 [20] 凶服 [21] 凶多吉少

ˏhŭng hang' a fierce, cruel man; [1]ˏhŭng ʻch'iu, a murderer; ˏhŭng k'e' deadly weapons; ˏhŭng ˏt'ui pok, ʻta ch'ieu' ʻliéng, the deadly blow does not smite a smiling face; [2]ˏhŭng auk, wicked, truculent; ʻt'ing ˏhŭng, fierce, reckless; COLL., ˏhŭng ʻk'i ˏhŭng, very malicious.

洶 ˏ The bubbling of a spring, the noise of rapid waters; the sound of tumult: [3]ˏhŭng ʻŭng' gurgling of a fountain.

匈 ˏ **胸** ˏ **胷** ˏ Hsiung. The breast, the chest, the bosom; the mind, the heart, the feelings; the 1st character represents the breast inclosing the heart: [4]ˏhŭng ˏchong ʻking seu' literary, accomplished; [5]ˏhŭng ˏhwai, the feelings; COM., ˏhŭng ˏtong, the breast, as of fowls; [6]ˏhŭng ʻmwang, the chest puffed and hard—a medical phrase; COLL., ˏhŭng ˏseng, the bosom.

掀 Hsien. Also read ˏhiong: to raise, to lift up; to lay hold of, to pull out; high, lofty: used in the coll. for ˏhiĕng, q. v.: [7]ʻsiu ˏhŭng ˏhŭng, to raise the head high, as reptiles.

欣 ˏ **忻** ˏ Hsin. Joy, delight, happiness; gay, jolly, delighted; pleased at getting or doing something; laughing, merry: [8]ˏhŭng ˏhwang, pleased, delighted; [9]ˏhŭng ˏyong, with pleasure; ˏhŭng haing' in ecstasy over luck; [10]ˏhŭng oi' solaced.

纁 Hsün. A light red produced by a trine immersion in the dye; a scarlet tint: [11]ˏsang ik, ˏui ˏhŭng, three dips make a light red.

雄 ˏ Hsiung. A cock bird; masculine, male of small animals, birds, and insects; courageous, martial, brave, heroic; strong, rapid, energetic, bold: COM., [12]ˏch'i ˏhŭng, female and male; [13]ˏsing ˏhŭng, or ʻtang ˏhŭng, brave, heroic; [14]ˏkang ˏhŭng, unprincipled and ambitious; [15]ˏhŭng chaung' burly and strong, martial; [16]ˏhŭng ˏwong, or [17]ˏhŭng ˏwong ˏching, a mineral substance of a brick-red color from Loochoo—resembles sulphur; COLL., ˏkiăng ˏhŭng ˏniă nói' walk a little more rapidly; ˏhŭng ˏhŭng ʻch'iu, spry with the hands, to do quickly.

熊 ˏ Hsiung. A bear, the hibernating animal: [18]ˏhŭng ʻchiong, bear's palm—a delicacy; ˏhŭng ʻngi ˏsang, Bear-ear mountains—a range in Honan; COM., [19]ˏhŭng ʻtang, bear's gall—a medicine.

ˏHŭng. A coll. word: tight, taut, stretched; the opposite of nĕŭng' (slack): pek, ˏhŭng ˏhŭng tioh, pull it very tight.

(214) Hwa.

花 ˏ **華** ˏ **蘤** ˏ Hwa. A blossom, a flower; *met.*, pleasure, vice; variegated, ornamental, carved; to exaggerate: the 3d is the ancient form; the 2nd also read ˏhwa, q. v.: COM., [20]ˏhwa ˏpwong, a flower-pot; [21]ˏhwa ch'iong' (coll. ˏhwa ˏsa), a florist; ˏhwa ʻhoi,

[1]兇	[3]洶	錦	[6]胸	掀	然	入	雄	雄	黃	[18]熊	[20]花
手	湧	繡	滿	[8]欣	[10]欣	爲	[13]心	[15]雄	[17]雄	掌	盆
[2]兇	[4]胸	[5]胸	[7]首	歡	慰	纁	雄	壯	黃	[19]熊	[21]花
惡	存	懷	掀	[9]欣	[11]三	[12]雌	[14]奸	[16]雄	精	膽	匠

a flower bud; ꜀*hwa paing*^{2}, or ꜀*hwa p‘iéng*’ leaves of a flower; [1]‘*chai* ꜀*hwa*, to cultivate flowers; [2]꜀*hwa* ꜁*ki kwok*, the United States; ꜀*hwa* ꜀*ch‘iă*, wasteful, lavish; ꜀*hwa* ‘*ch‘ai*, a douceur; ꜀*hwa* ꜀*k‘wi* and ꜀*hwa siă*^{2} the opening and falling of flowers; ꜀*hwa* ꜁*chong*, a flower shop; [3]꜀*hwa tang*’ actors personating girls; [4]*pek*꜀ ꜀*hwa*, accomplished scholarship; ꜀*hwa* ‘*ch‘ó*, richly decorated with flowers; *met*., affable; *tai*’ ꜀*hwa*, to wear flowers; [5]꜀*hwa siăng*’ floss-silk; *ch‘eng*’ ꜀*hwa*, notation of pounds and ounces on steelyards; ꜀*hwa pwo*’ figured calico, chintz; [6]꜀*hwa hwoi*^{2} a lottery; [7]꜀*hwa* ꜀*seng*, peanuts; ꜀*hwa yong*^{2} flower patterns; [8]‘*ch‘ó* ꜀*hwa*, artificial flowers of pith; ꜀*hwa ch‘eu*’ fire-works like flowers and trees; *met*., fruitful, as a woman—term used by fortune-tellers; [9]꜀*t‘ang* ꜀*hwa laung*^{2} ‘*chü*, a profligate, a rake; COLL., *mek*$_2$ ꜀*chiu* ꜀*hwa*, dim eyesight; ꜀*hwa* ꜀*hwa sië*’ *kai*’ an extravagant age; ꜀*hwa sioh*$_2$ ꜁*pwo*, one flower; ꜀*hwa luk*$_2$ *lak*$_2$ or ꜀*hwa lok*꜀ *lok*꜀ flowers in profusion; ꜀*hwa* ‘*ku* ꜀*kung* and ꜀*hwa* ‘*ku* ꜁*pó*, male and female beggars from Nganhwui; ꜀*hwa pah*$_2$ spotted, speckled; ꜀*hwa meng*’ *k‘aĕk*꜀ a false face; ꜀*hwa* ꜁*ĕng* ‘*liu lioh*$_2$ gay colors, as of clothes; ꜀*hwa* ꜀*sang sek*$_2$ *paik*꜀ to rattle on in talking.

畫 ꜀Hua. Read *wa*^{2}; coll. ꜀*hwa*, as in ꜀*hwa* ꜁*mi*, a large yellowish hopping bird; [10]꜀*hwa* ꜁*mi t‘ieu*’ *ka*’ the ꜀*hwa* ꜁*mi* hops on to the cage-bars; *met*., restless, as a child.

化 Hua.’ To change, to influence so as to alter, to transform; to melt; to digest; to convert, to pass into metempsychosis; to create; to reform; to transmute, to barter, to exchange: COM., [10]*piéng*’ *hwa*’ to change, to reform; [11]꜀*sieu hwa*’ to digest (food); [12]*k‘wong*’ *hwa*’ to reform by exhortation; [13]*kang hwa*’ to transform—used for spiritual regeneration; [14]*kau*’ *hwa*’, or *hwa*’ *tó*^{2} to improve by instruction; [15]*hwa*’ ꜀*seng*, produced by metamorphosis, as insects and vermin; ꜁*hing hwa*’ a prefecture in Fookien; [16]*hwa*’ ꜁*ngwong* ‘*pó*, to burn mock-ingots (to idols); *hwa*’ ꜁*t‘ang* ꜁*wong*, pills for phlegm; [17]*hwa*’ *k‘e*’ ‘*sang*, powders to help the breathing; [18]*hwa*’ ꜀*chá*, to beg food, as priests do; [19]*hwa*’ ꜁*chiéng* ꜁*lu*, an urn for burning mock-money; *met*., a spendthrift; COLL., *kaĕng*’ *hwa*’ ‘*chai sioh*$_2$ *yong*^{2} like burning paper; *met*., to squander; *hwa*’ ꜁*mó*, or *hwa*’ *k‘ó*’ turned to nothing, burnt up, as paper; *chó*’ *hwa*’ by good luck, fortunately; ꜁*hung hwa*’, or ꜁*hung* ꜁*hung hwa*’ *hwa*’ careless, easy, indifferent.

華 蕐 ꜁Hua. The elegance of flowers; abundance of flowers, blooming, flowery; charming; ornamented, adorned; splendid, glorious; hoarheaded; a designation of China; to cut a melon in quarters: used for ꜀*hwa* (a flower), q. v.: [20]꜁*hwa* ‘*siu*, gray-headed; [21]꜁*yong* ꜁*hwa*, white-lead—a cosmetic; COM., ꜁*hwa lá*^{2} splendid, brilliant; ꜁*ing* ꜁*hwa*, glorious, glory; ꜀*ch‘iă* ꜁*hwa*, extravagant,

[1]栽花 [2]花旗國 [3]花旦 [4]筆花 [5]花線 [6]花會 [7]花生 [8]草花 [9]探花浪子 [10]變化 [11]消化 [12]勸化 [13]感化 [14]教化 [15]化生 [16]化元寶 [17]化氣散 [18]化齋 [19]化錢爐 [20]華首 [21]鉛華

prodigal, as of wealth; [1]꜀*hwa* ꜂*pieu*, a kind of honorary portico in front of a temple; [2]*pok*꜁ ꜀*hwa pok*꜁ *p'auk*꜁ neither gaudy nor plain, the just medium; [3]꜀*hwa tang*꜃ a god's birth-day; [4]꜀*hwa* ꜀*tó* ꜀*siéng*, the genius ꜀*Hwa* ꜀*tó* (of the Han dynasty); *met.*, a skillful doctor; [5]꜀*hwa* ꜀*kwong tai*꜃ *tá*꜃ his Effulgence, the great emperor—title of ꜂*ngu* ꜂*hiéng*, god of thieves.

樺 ꜀Hua. Also read ꜀*hwa*: a tree of whose resinous bark links are made, also used in making cups: [6]꜀*hwa chëük*꜁ a bark torch.

驊 ꜀Hua. A fine steed, a good horse; of eight steeds belonging to Muh-wang. B.C. 980, one was called [7]꜀*hwa* ꜀*liu* (Beauty).

嘩 譁 ꜀Hua. Clamor, noise, hubbub, vociferation: [8]꜀*hiong* ꜀*hwa*, a confused noise, as of a row; [9]꜀*hwa* ꜀*yong*, hurrah; COLL., [10]꜀*hwa* ꜀*hwa kieu*꜃ the rustling (of leaves), noise (of rain or running water).

划 ꜀Fa. A boat, a pinnace; to row a boat: [11]꜀*hwa* ꜂*chü*, a pinnace.

꜀*Hwa.* A coll. word: to estimate, to calculate: ꜀*hwa k'ang*꜃ calculate and see; ꜀*hwa* ꜂*pwong saung*꜃ *le*꜃ to estimate profits according to the original cost; ꜀*hwa chiäng*꜃ *ch'ëk*꜁ ꜀*wai*, to calculate straight and chisel out crooked; *met.*, to plan properly, but do it wrong; ꜀*hwa tek*꜁ *se*꜃ I reckon so, it's just so.

(215) Hwah.

Hwah꜁. A coll. word: to joke, to jest; to riot; vicious, dissolute, dissipated: *hwah*꜁ ꜀*ki* *wa*꜃ jesting; *móh*꜁ *hwah*꜁ don't jest; *k'ó*꜃ *hwah*꜁ to go on a spree; *p'ah*꜁ *hwah*꜁ to live riotously.

(216) Hwai.

꜀*Hwai.* A coll. word: to pass out of the mind; gone, ceased; relinquished, as a feeling of grief, resentment, &c.: ꜀*sing* ꜀*hwai*, or ꜀*hwai* ꜀*sing*, to pass out of mind: ꜂*chiü* ꜀*sing* ꜀*tu* ꜀*hwai k'ó*꜃ this feeling is all gone; ꜀*sing sëü*꜃ *má*꜃ ꜀*hwai*, can't get rid of the thought or feeling.

懷 怀 ꜀Huai. To cherish in the heart, to dwell on, to think of; to carry in the womb; to embrace, to favor; to comfort; to come to; to return; to put in the bosom, to store up, to lay by; to remember, to cherish, as ill will; wounded feelings; private, selfish; the heart the affections; kind thoughts of; the bosom, the lap: [12]꜀*si* ꜀*hwai*, poetical taste; [13]꜀*hwai taik*꜁ to meditate on virtue; COLL., [14]꜀*hwai niéng*꜃ to think of, to long for; [15]꜀*hwai eng*꜃, or ꜀*hwai* ꜀*t'ai*, pregnancy; [16]꜀*hwai pó*꜃ to carry in the bosom; [17]꜀*hwai* ꜂*ku*, a kind of small flat drum; ꜀*hwai hiék*꜁ *che*꜃ small fine-print books—are smuggled into the examination-hall; COLL., [18]꜀*hwai pó*꜃ ꜀*pi* ꜀*pa piék*꜁ *tieu*꜃ ꜀*tang*, clasp the guitar and play another tune; *met.*, to disagree and separate.

[1]華	不	[4]華	光	燭	嘩	嘩	[12]詩	[14]懷	[16]懷	[18]懷	別
表	朴	陀	大	[7]驊	[9]嘩	吽	懷	念	抱	抱	調
[2]不	[3]華	仙	帝	騮	然	[11]划	[13]懷	[15]懷	[17]懷	琵	彈
華	誕	[5]華	[6]樺	[8]喧	[10]嘩	子	德	孕	鼓	琶	○

淮 ˏHuai. A large affluent of the Yellow river, which (draining the provinces of Honan and Ngan-hwui) empties into it through the Hung-tsih lake; even, equable flow: COM., [1]*ˏhwai ˏsang*, a whitish wood—used medicinally as a tonic.

槐 ˏHuai. A species of Cassia (coll. *ˏhwai chʿeu*), resembling senna (Cassia sophora and Cassia alata); the yellow flowers are used as a dye: COM., [2]*ˏsang ˏhwai*, three cassia trees; *met.*, high statesmen; [3]*ˏhwai ˏhwa*, cassia flowers—a decoction of which gives the gold color to paper burnt before idols.

壞 孃 Huai. To spoil, to injure, to destroy, to ruin; broken down, fallen in ruins, dilapidated; ruined, injured; spoiled, rotten, useless: COM., [4]*ʿpʿó hwai*2 broken down; ruined, as a reputation; [5]*pai*2 *hwai*2 to destroy, to ruin; [6]*hwai*2 *sëü*2 to ruin one's affairs; [7]*ʿsong hwai*2 dilapidated, in ruins; [8]*ˏtiong hwai*2 the bowels diseased, as by chronic diarrhea; COLL., *ˏmiăng ˏsiăng hwai*2 *kʿó* his reputation ruined.

(217) Hwak.

法 灋 Fa. A rule, a law, usage; regulations, precepts; a punishment or legal infliction; an art; skill, industry; sect: COM., [9]*ʿli hwak*, reason and law, reasonable; [10]*hwak, to*2, or [11]*hwak, chié* rules, regulations; [12]*hwak, ˏka*, writer of accusations, a pettifogger; [13]*che*2 *hwak*, rules of writing; [14]*ˏtó hwak*, art of fencing; [15]*ʿchʿiu hwak*, handicraft, skill in; [16]*hwak, suk*, or *ˏsiéng hwak*, magic arts; [17]*kwok, hwak*, the laws of a country; [18]*hwak, ˏmwong*, a sect; *pok, hwak*, refractory; *ˏhwong hwak*, a way or mode (of doing); *hwak, ha*2 subject to a law or rule; *ˏu hwak, ʿkʿó te*2 incorrigible; *hwak, ʿma*, weights of large money-scales; *hwak, ˏteu*, the main-spring of a watch; COLL., *ˏmó hwak, tek*, unavoidable, necessitated.

發 Fa. To issue, to appear; to send forth, to germinate; to cause to go; to dispatch, to throw out; to ferment; to show forth, to manifest; *met.*, the spring and summer: COM., [19]*hwak, ˏsing*, to show pity, give in charity; [20]*hwak, leng*2 or *hwak, hó*2 to issue commands; [21]*hwak, pwo*2 to step forward; *met.*, to gain a degree; [22]*hwak, ʿsiong*, to make presents; [23]*hwak, ʿkʿi*, to prosper; to rise, as dough; [24]*hwak, ang*2 to publish the names of Siutsai graduates; *hwak, kang*2 to take a sweat (in fevers); *hwak, má*2 to offer for sale; *hwak, ˏchong*, to sell off pawned articles; *hwak, tʿiék*, to clear off, to get rid of; *ˏhung hwak*, to distribute, as wages or work; *hwak, sang*2 to show temper; *hwak, hok*, blessed—i. e., fat, corpulent; *hwak, ˏchai*, to grow rich; *ˏchá hwak*, "let us jointly prosper"—said in reply to the congratulatory phrase, *hwak, ˏchai*; COLL., *ˏting hwak, tek, sá*2 to have a numerous posterity; *hwak, chauk*, to sprout; to come out, as sores; to show (resentment); *hwak, kʿah*, to dis-

[1]淮山 [2]三槐 [3]槐花 [4]破壞 [5]敗壞 [6]壞事 [7]損壞 [8]腸壞 [9]理法 [10]法度 [11]法制 [12]法家 [13]字法 [14]刀法 [15]手法 [16]法術 [17]國法 [18]法門 [19]發心 [20]發令 [21]發步 [22]發賞 [23]發起 [24]發案

pose (of goods) to foreign traders; *hwak, ˏmui,* or *hwak, ˊp'u,* to become moldy.

髮 Fa. Hair of the head; *met.,* herbs, trees, moss: in the coll. read *hwok,* q.v.: [1]*haik, hwak,* black-haired, youth; [2]*pek₂ hwak,* white-haired, the aged; COM., [3]*ˏsü hwak,* beard and hair; [4]*hok₂ hwak,* crane's feathers; *met.,* gray-haired; [5]*hwak, kak,* "hair and nails"—applied to portions of these, as used in rites to recover the sick; [6]*ˏhó hwak, pok, ˏch'a,* not the least error.

伐 Fa. To destroy, to strike, to fight; to punish, to subdue, to desolate; to cut down; to brag; a meritorious deed; a go-between, to strike, as a bell or drum: [7]*hwak₂ chói*ˀ to punish crime; [8]*hwak₂ siéng*ˀ to boast of one's goodness; [9]*hwak₂ ˊku,* to beat a drum.

閥 Fa. A door on the left; meritorious services; to set forth one's services, in which sense same as the last: *hwak₂ yok,* the side doors of a gateway; worthy services.

筏 Fa. A bamboo raft, a large ship like a raft, an ark.

罰 Fa. A peccadillo, a crime: to punish, to castigate, to flog; to fine; a fine, a forfeit: COM., [10]*chaik, hwak₂* to punish; [11]*ˏhing hwak₂* punishment; [12]*hwak₂ ˏchiéng,* to fine; [13]*hwak₂ ˊchiu,* a forfeit of wine; [14]*hwak₂ hong*ˀ to mulct an officer's salary; *hwak₂ koi*ˀ *ˏhiong,* make him kneel (to his wife) while an incense stick burns—as in puppet plays.

乏 Fa. Want, destitution, deficiency, failure; without, deficient; to fail; to spoil, to injure; empty, poor; fatigued: [15]*ˏkûng hwak₂* or *ˏping hwak₂* indigent, beggared; COM., [16]*k'wok, hwak₂* destitute, in want.

猾 Hua. A boneless animal, said to get inside of tigers and gnaw them; crafty, tricky, deceitful, treacherous, lying; clever, artful, as children; to disturb, to cause trouble: [17]*ˊkieu hwak₂* traitorous, false; [18]*hwak₂ chek₂* a tricky rascal.

滑 Hua. Smooth, slippery; polished, glassy, glairy, soapy; sharp, knavish, oily; flattering, cunning; to disturb; used in the coll. for free, easy; also a mode of cooking: [19]*ˏkwong hwak₂* shining and smooth; COM., [20]*hwak₂ sioh₂* soapstone, a medicinal mineral of a whitish color; COLL., [21]*hwak₂ p'wak,* free, liberal (in the use of money); *hwak₂ ˏt'ong,* to cook in boiling water, as things rolled in flour.

(218) Hwang.

歡 **懽** Hwan. Joyous, jocund, glad, frolicsome, gleeful, merry; to rejoice, to be pleased with: COM., [22]*ˏhwang ˊhi,* glad, pleased; to like; [23]*ˊhi ˏhwang* (coll. *ˏhwang ˏhwang ˊhi ˊhi*), jubilant; COLL., *ˏhwang ˊhi ˏsong,* a happy funeral, as when the deceased has

1 黑髮 2 白髮 3 鬚髮 4 鶴髮 5 髮甲 6 毫髮不差 7 伐罪 8 伐善 9 伐鼓 10 責罰 11 刑罰 12 罰錢 13 罰酒 14 罰俸 15 窮乏 16 缺乏 17 狡猾 18 猾賊 19 光滑 20 滑石 21 滑潑 22 歡喜 23 喜歡

sons and grandsons; ˏhwang ʻhi ʻsi, ˏhwang ʻhi ˏmó miăng, ˏhwang ʻhi tek, ʻtʻeng, and ˏhwang ˏtʻiĕng ʻhi tĕ are phrases denoting excessive joy; ˏhwang ʻhi á ʻtʻieu to jump for joy.

燔 Fan. To roast meat for sacrifices: [1]ˏhwang chiă to roast, as meat and liver.

幡 ˏFan. A banner, a streamer with sentences on it, hung in a temple or carried in processions; a duster, a napkin; to move, to shake: [2]ˏhwang ˏgong, forthwith.

旛 Fan. Used for the last: a flag, a streamer; streamers in general: [3]ˏchʻing ˏhwang, or ˏhung ˏhwang, a banner borne at funerals.

番 ˏFan. A beast's footprint; a time, a turn, a repetition of; to reckon; to change; a tribe in the South, now applied to all foreigners; used in the coll. for a dollar: [4]ek, ˏhwang, once; [5]ˏliĕng ˏhwang, incessantly; COM., [6]ˏhwang ˏmang, barbarian; [7]ˏhwang kwok, foreign countries; [8]ˏhwang ˏsü, the sweet potato; ˏhwang ˏsung ʻpʻwo, ship-anchorage—a locality on the south bank of the Min; [9]ʻchʻü ˏhwang, this time, now; COLL., [10]ˏhwang ˏnĕng, (opprobriously ˏhwang ʻkiăng), foreigners; ˏkwong ˏhwang, or ˏchʻing ˏhwang, an unchopped dollar; ˏpʻung ˏtó ˏhwang, broken dollars; [11]ʻcheu ˏhwang, the Mexican dollar; ˏhwang ˏchiĕng ʻkiăng, fractions of the dollar; [12]kaĕk, ˏhwang, a quarter-dollar; [13]ˏtĕng ˏhwang, dollars alloyed with copper.

墦 ˏFan. A grave: [14]ˏhwang ˏkang, amid the graves; sepulchers.

蕃 ˏFan. Used for the next: plants growing luxuriantly; flourishing; plenty, many; to environ, to fence, to inclose: [15]ˏhwang ʻyĕng, plants growing luxuriantly; a numerous progeny.

藩 轓 ˏFan. A fence, a hedge; a boundary, a frontier; to inclose; to ward off, to protect; a cover for a chariot; a covered car, in which sense the 2nd is commonly used: [16]ˏhwang ˏlié, a fence, a wattle; [17]ˏhwang ˏping, a screen; *met.*, a statesman; [18]ˏti ˏyong chʻüŏk, ˏhwang, reckless—like a goat butting a fence; COM., [19]ˏhwang ˏtai, a title of the provincial treasurer.

籓 ˏFan. A dust basket or large sieve, called [20]ˏhwang ˏló; to hide, to cover, to shade.

蟠 ˏFan. The sow-bug or wood-louse, usually found under things left long on the ground: [21]ˏlüng ˏhwang ˏü ˏná, the dragon hides in the earth; *met.*, one unable to rise or gain rank.

膰 ˏFan. Meat roasted for sacrifice; remnants of a sacrifice sent to princes by the emperor: [22]ˏhwang nük, sacrificial meat dressed.

1 燔炙 2 幡然 3 青旛 4 一番 5 連番 6 番銀 7 番國 8 番薯 9 此番 10 番仸 11 烏番 12 角番 13 銅番 14 墦間 15 蕃衍 16 藩籬 17 藩屏 18 羝羊[illegible] 19 [illegible] 20 [illegible] 21 [illegible] 22 [illegible]

꜀讙 Fan. To bawl, to clamor, to vociferate, to cry out, to make a noise; pleased, delighted; name of an animal like a fox: used for ꜀*hwang* (glad, joyous): 1꜀*hwang* ꜁*ngó*, clamor, vociferation.

꜀貛 A male wolf; some say, a wild boar: ‘*keu* ꜀*hwang*, a species of jackal; ‘*hai* ꜀*hwang*, the Liautung muskrat; 2꜀*hwang* ‘*chü* ꜁*p‘i*, beaver skin.

꜀繙 Fan. To spread out; to agitate or wave, as the wind does a flag; to translate, to explain; loose, fluttering, as a flag.

꜀翻 Fan. To fly to and fro; to return, to change; to vacillate, fickle; to revise a case; to translate books, in which sense it is commonly used for the last: 3꜀*hwang ang*’ to rejudge a case; 4꜀*hwang hok*꜄ vacillating; COM., 5꜀*hwang ik*꜄ to translate (a book); 6꜀*hwang* ꜀*k‘iong*, or ꜀*hwang wa*’ to retract one's word; 7꜀*hwang* ꜀*küng*, to retract statements in court; COLL., ꜀*hwang chó*’ to do differently; ꜀*hwang* ꜀*siăng*, or ꜀*hwang* ‘*kong* ꜀*hwang t‘iăng*’ to take back a promise; ꜀*hwang* ‘*tiong* ꜁*peng*, to turn over, to invert.

꜀蹯 Fan. A paw of a plantigrade animal, as a badger: 8꜁*hüng* ꜀*hwang*, bear's paw—esteemed a delicacy.

‘反 Fan. To turn back; to turn, as the leaves of a book; to rebel, to be contrary; to combine against, opposed to; but, contrary, again; COM., 9‘*hwang hok*, repetition; changing; 10꜀*siong* ‘*hwang*, opposed to; opposite, as two meanings; 11‘*hwang* ‘*chiong*, to turn over the hand; *met.*, easily, readily; 12‘*hwang kwo*’ to turn over, as leaves; 13‘*hwang* ‘*pwong* ꜀*kwi* ꜁*ngwong*, to return to the original, as to principles of duty; 14‘*hwang hai*’ on the contrary it will be injurious; COLL., ‘*hwang* ‘*k‘i*, to remove, as tiles from a roof; 15*chó*’ ‘*hwang*, to rebel; 16*ka ĕ*’ ‘*hwang* ꜀*t‘iéng*, to scream loud enough to turn the sky over; ‘*hwang* ꜁*li hok*꜄ *k‘ó*’ "turn to and fro"—to vacillate; 17‘*hwang meng*’ the "reverse face"; *met.*, the opposite idea; to turn a cold shoulder to one.

‘返 Fan. To return, to come back, to go back: COM., 18‘*wong* ‘*hwang*, to go and return; difficult; ‘*hwang siă*’ to return to one's own house.

㤆’ Hasty, precipitate; a passionate disposition; to regret: 19*hwang*’ ꜀*sing*, to be sorry for.

飯’ Fan. Used in the coll. mandarin: cooked rice, a meal; to eat: 20*sik*꜄ *hwang*’ (coll. mand. *ch‘ih*꜄ *hwang*’), to take a meal; ‘*chó hwang*’ breakfast; ‘*a* · *hwang*’ the second meal (of the emperor).

喚’ Huan. To call to, to call out, to call for, to bid; to name: 21꜁*hu hwang*’ to call to; COM., 22꜁*miăng hwang*’ "her name is called"—as in the purchase-deed of a slave girl; COLL., *hwang*’ ꜀*i* ꜁*chá k‘ó*’ call him to go with; *hwang*’ ‘*tu*

1讙囂 2貛子皮 3翻案 4翻覆 5翻譯 6翻腔 7翻供 8熊蹯 9反覆 10相反 11反掌 12反過 13反本歸源 14反害 15做反 16呼反天 17反面 18往返 19㤆心 20食飯 21呼喚 22名喚

APLH. DICT. 35

pek, *꜀sio*, he who invites (another) to gamble will surely lose.

奐' Huan. Great; beautiful, handsome, variegated; leisurely, at ease; to take one's pleasure: [1]*'mi ꜀chai hwang' ꜁yong*, how excellent and beautiful!

煥' Huan. The brilliance of fire; refulgent, splendid: [2]*hwang' ꜁yong ek*, *꜀sing*, brilliant and all new; [3]*hwang' ꜁hu ꜁ki 'iu ꜁ung ꜀chiong*, how very fine and elegant!

梵' Fan. Name of a bonze; the country of Magadha, whence Budh came; the language of the Budhists, Pali, or Sanscrit: [4]*hwang' 'ngü*, Sanscrit; [5]*hwang' ꜀ing*, chanting of Budhist prayers; [6]*hwang' ꜁pung*, a cloister.

渙' Huan. A branch of the river Hwai in the east of Honan; to spread abroad, to expand, to dissipate; the 59th diagram, denoting dispersion: [7]*hwang' lang'* finely decorated.

汎' Fan. Used for the next: to float, driven by the wind; name of a river; broad, expansive: [8]*hwang' ai' chëüng'* to love the multitude.

泛' Fan. To float, to flow down; to transport; extensive; to spill over: [9]*꜁p'eu hwang'* to float; *met.*, vague, superficial; [10]*hwang' ꜀chiu*, to go in a boat; COLL., *hwang' lang'* shiftless; to do in a careless way.

氾' Fan. Used for the last two: to overflow; to float, to fluctuate; in motion, agitated: [11]*hwang' lang'* vast, as a deluge; [12]*hwang' hwang' pok*, *teng'* agitated and undecided.

販' Fan. To traffic, to deal in; to buy cheap and sell dear: COM., [13]*hwang' hwo'* to deal in goods; [14]*hwang' má'* (coll. *hwang' k'ó' má'*), to sell off (goods); [15]*hwang' ꜀sü ꜀siéng*, to carry on a contraband trade in salt; *hwang' má' ꜁ing 'k'eu*, to traffic in persons.

Hwang'. A coll. word: to act as a nurse, to suckle; to tend children: *hwang' ꜁neng*, to suckle; *꜁neng hwang'* and *꜀kang hwang'* wet and dry nurses; *hwang' nié' 'kiáng*, to suckle or tend children.

Hwang'. A coll. word, as in *hwang' pe'* to break wind—a vile phrase used to express contempt for what another says, as in *hwang' pe' wa'* and *hwang' 'nü pe'*.

還 ꜁Huan. To return, to revert, to come back; to restore, to give back, to repay; to regard, to look at, to give attention to; to look back; still, furthermore, even to this; now, forthwith, immediately: used in the coll. for *꜁heng* and *꜁teng*, q. v.: COM., [16]*꜁hwang 'ch'iu*, to strike back; [17]*꜁hwang ꜁yong*, or *꜁hwang ꜁hung*, to revive, as the sick; *꜀kau ꜁hwang ꜀ch'ing 'ch'ü*, to return or pay up in full; [18]*꜁hwang sük*, to return to common life; to become laymen, as priests do.

---

[1]美哉奐焉 [2]煥然一新 [3]煥乎其有文章 [4]梵語 [5]梵音 [6]梵房 [7]渙瀾 [8]汎愛衆 [9]浮泛 [10]泛舟 [11]氾濫 [12]氾氾不定 [13]販貨 [14]販賣 [15]販私鹽 [16]還手 [17]還陽 [18]還俗

福州方言拼音字典

繁 ꜀Fan. Much, numerous, many; confused, multitudinous; a variety of affairs; a saddle-girth, in which sense also read ꜀*pwang*: [1]꜀*hwang* ꜀*ung*, over-strained politeness; COM., [2]꜀*hwang* ʻ*kang*, much and little; [3]꜀*hwang chak*꜆ heterogeneous, as a crowd; confused in mind: [4]꜀*hwang* ꜀*hwa*, pomp, show; [5]꜀*ka* ʻ*k'eu hó*ˀ ꜀*hwang*, a numerous family.

蘩 ꜀Fan. A kind of southernwood or Artemisia, whose decoction is sprinkled on silkworm's eggs to hasten their hatching: [6]꜀*hwang* ꜀*kó*, a plant like celery—for pickling in winter.

凡 凢 ꜀Fan. All, everybody; common, vulgar, useful; generally, for the most part; the world: COM., [7]꜀*chü* ꜀*hwang*, all, every; [8]꜀*hwang* ʻ*su* ʻ*iu*, all that there is; [9]*tai*ˀ ꜀*hwang*, whatever, whoever; in general; [10]꜀*hwang* ꜀*kang*, the world; [11]꜀*sü* ꜀*hwang*, to think of the world, as bonzes relinquishing their vows; COLL., ꜀*hwang* ʻ*chung*, all, for the most part; ꜀*hwang sëü*ˀ *tioh*꜆ ꜀*sang* ꜀*sü*, in all matters think thrice.

煩 ꜀Fan. Troubled, annoyed, perplexed, heated; to trouble, to intrude on; troublesome, impertinent; grieved, sorry: COM., [12]꜀*hwang* ꜀*ló*, to trouble one; annoyed; [13]*sëü*ˀ ꜀*hwang*, much business perplexing one; [14]꜀*hwang* ʻ*nó*, troubled and anxious; [15]*pok*꜆ *nai*ˀ ꜀*hwang*, can't bear the trouble of; [16]꜀*hwang só*ˀ troubled and feverish; [17]꜀*hwang lik*꜆ to over-exert one's self, as after an illness.

橫 ꜀Hêng. A cross-bar; transverse, crosswise, athwart, across; perverse, grim, unreasonable; mulish, disagreeing from others; the narrowest width; unlucky, untimely, unfair; disrespectful; to cross, to go athwart: COM., [18]꜀*hwang tik*꜆ transverse and straight; [19]꜀*hwang* ꜀*sing* ꜀*hwang* ꜀*tong*, cross, perverse; ꜀*hwang* ꜀*liong*, to measure across; ꜀*hwang auk*, refractory; ꜀*hwang* ꜀*liong*, cross-beams; [20]꜀*hwang* ꜀*chai*, unjust gains; COLL., ꜀*hwang* ꜀*p'ié tóh*, or ꜀*hwang* ꜀*t'au tóh*, a long narrow table—as at the head of a hall; ꜀*hwang sau*ˀ a kind of flute; ꜀*hwang wah*꜆ the strokes of a Chinese character; ʻ*ta* ꜀*lang* ꜀*hwang*, across, athwart; ꜀*hwang* ꜀*yeu* and ꜀*hwang lak*꜆ the transverse strip and the boarding below the plastered portions of a room; ꜀*hwang* ʻ*kong* ꜀*hwang t'iàng*ˀ to prate unreasonably; ꜀*hwang* ʻ*mi* ʻ*chü* ꜀*mó pwong*ˀ "rice earned unjustly boils into no rice"—i. e., Heaven's curse is on injustice.

樊 ꜀Fan. A cage; a fence, a rail; ing; to cage, to confine-mixed: ꜀*hwang* ꜀*lëng*, a bird-cage, ꜀*hwang* ꜀*lié*, a fence, a wattle; ꜀*hwang* ꜀*yong* ꜀*ngau lwang*ˀ mixed and confused.

礬 ꜀Fan. Mineral salts, proper for painting or dyeing; alum; to dye with alum; to tan or cure (leather) in lime and copperas: COM., [21]*pah*꜆ ꜀*hwang*, alum; ꜀*hwang* ꜀*hu*, alum ash; ꜀*hwang sioh*꜆ alum shale;

[1] 繁文 [2] 繁簡 [3] 繁雜 [4] 繁華 [5] 家口浩繁 [6] 蘩蒿 [7] 諸凡 [8] 凡所有 [9] 大凡 [10] 凡間 [11] 思凡 [12] 煩勞 [13] 事煩 [14] 煩惱 [15] 不耐煩 [16] 煩燥 [17] 煩力 [18] 橫直 [19] 橫心橫腸 [20] 橫財 [21] 白礬

[1]꜀ch'ang ꜀hwang, blue copperas; ʻtang ꜀hwang, blue or green vitriol; [2]ʻchŏ꜅ ꜀hwang, sulphuret of iron, copperas used in dyeing black; COLL., ꜀ch'ang ꜀hwang, fresh (i. e. unburnt) alum; ꜀p'ŭi ꜀tŏ k'ŏ꜄ ꜀hwang, take the skin and dye it with alum; ꜀hwang ꜀p'ŭi taing꜄ a tanning shop.

桓 ꜀ Huan. A tree which produces hard black seeds used for beads; signboards placed between two boards before a hong; pillars before graves; posts to steady a coffin on trestles; title of defunct grandees: [3]꜀hwang ꜀hwang, a martial appearance; sorrowful; [4]꜀pwang ꜀hwang, to advance with difficulty; (coll.) intimate.

帆 ꜀ Fan. A sail of a boat or a ship: [5]pwo꜄ ꜀hwang, a canvas sail; [6]kwa꜄ ꜀hwang, to hoist sail.

黌 ꜀ An ancient college or gymnasium, A. D. 200, capable of accommodating 30,000 students: [7]꜀hwang ꜀küng, rooms for study near the Confucian temple—mostly disused in Foochow; [8]cheng꜄ ꜀hwang ꜀küng, to enter the college—be a Siutsai.

范꜅ Fan. Used for the next: herbs, grass; a bee or wasp; a surname: [9]hwang꜅ ꜀kwang, a bee's head.

範꜅ Fan. A rule, a guide; a custom, a usage; a mold, a pattern; to imitate: [10]꜀mwo hwang꜅ a pattern, an exemplar; [11]hwang꜅ ꜀ui, to preserve by good rules; [12]꜀hung hwang꜅ a popular custom.

幻꜄ Huan. A trick, a sleight of hand; magical arts, sorcery; apparitions, dreams, visions; false, deceptive; to delude: [13]piéng꜄ hwang꜅ magic arts; [14]hwang꜅ mong꜄ dreams, visions.

患꜅ Huan. Evil, trouble, distress, calamity, misfortune; grief, sorrow, affliction; sad, unhappy, vexed; distressing, fearful; to grieve, to sorrow for or with: [15]꜀iu hwang꜅ distress, affliction; [16]hwo꜅ hwang꜅ calamities; COM., [17]hwang꜅ nang꜅ misfortune, troubles.

宦꜅ Huan. One who serves, an officer, a servant of the crown: [18]꜀kwang hwang꜅ an officer; [19]꜀hiong hwang꜅ gentry; hwang꜅ sëü꜅ or hwang꜅ ꜀kwang, servants, as of the crown, eunuchs; COM., [20]hwang꜅ ꜀nong, salary, perquisites of office.

犯꜅ Fan. To rush against; to offend, to transgress, to violate, to invade; to resist, to oppose; a criminal, a culprit; to endure, to be possessed by: COM., [21]hwang꜅ hwak꜇, to violate law; [22]hwang꜅ ʻkwi, or hwang꜅ ꜀siă, possessed by a devil; [23]hwang꜅ chŏi꜅ to transgress; hwang꜅ siong꜄ to offend the higher authorities; hwang꜅ ꜀hung, an adverse wind; hwang꜅ hoi꜄ to violate sacred names; hwang꜅ ꜀ch'üng, to disagree with, opposed in views; hwang꜅ ke꜄, or hwang꜅

1 青礬 2 皂礬 3 桓桓 4 盤桓 5 布帆 6 掛帆 7 黌宮 8 進黌宮 9 范冠 ○ 10 模範 11 範圍 12 洪範 13 變幻 14 幻夢 15 憂患 16 禍患 17 患難 18 官宦 19 鄉宦 20 宦囊 21 犯法 22 犯鬼 23 犯罪

海上絲綢之路文獻集成 科技與文化编

ch‘ëük, to incur dislike or enmity; COLL., *hwang*꜅ *pang*꜅ taken sick; *hwang*꜅ *꜁nëng ch‘oi*꜄ offend people's mouths—i. e., provoke them to scold.

緩꜅ Huan. Slow, tardy, leisurely; careless, lax; easily, gradually, gently; to let things take their own way; to delay, to dawdle, to take matters easily; in the coll., to tie loosely: COM., [1]*hwang*꜅ *kek*꜆ *꜀siong chá*꜄ to help each other in emergencies; [2]*hwang*꜅ *꜀ping ꜀chi kié*꜄ to wait for reinforcements; *met.*, to gain by delay, as in matters of debt, &c.; [3]*꜁ti hwang*꜅ tardily, slowly; [4]*꜀k‘wang hwang*꜅ lenient, easy with, as in extending the time; COLL., *꜂mwong k‘á*꜄ *꜀i hwang*꜅ *sioh*꜆ *a*꜅ just tie it loosely; *hwang*꜅ *sioh*꜆ *pwo*꜅ wait a little.

豢꜅ To rear and feed domestic animals, to bait; to give presents to, to bribe, to allure with the hope of getting favor.

(219) Hwi.

輝 ꜀Hui. Brilliant, refulgent, glorious, like the sun; to glisten: [5]*꜀kwong ꜀hwi*, brilliant, glistering.

煇 ꜀Hui. Same as the last; luminous, splendid, like fire: [6]*taik*꜆ *꜀hwi*, illustrious virtue; [7]*꜀hwi ꜁hwong*, illuminated.

暉 ꜀Hui. Like the last two: effulgent, glorious, as the sun: [8]*꜁siă ꜀hwi*, slanting sunbeams; [9]*sik*꜆ *꜀hwi*, the evening sun.

揮 ꜀Hui. To sprinkle, to scatter, to throw away; to move, to shake; to animate; to be agitated; to point out, in which sense the same as the next: [10]*꜀hwi ꜁hó*, to flourish the pencil; [11]*꜀hwi ꜁k‘ing*, to play the lute; [12]*꜀hwi hwok*꜆ extravagant; [13]*꜂chi ꜀hwi*, a major in a Manchu corps; to point with the hand. Read *꜁hung*, as in [14]*꜁hung ꜁lung*, whole, unbroken.

撝 ꜀Hui. To rend open, to tear off; to point out; humble, unassuming: [15]*꜂chi ꜀hwi*, to point out, to direct; [16]*꜀hwi ꜁k‘iéng*, humble.

徽 ꜀Hui. Good, beautiful; a cord of three strands, a string; queenly garments; a kind of sash; a banner; the stops on a guitar: [17]*꜀hwi ꜀ing*, fine sounds; *met.*, female reputation; COM., [18]*꜀hwi ꜀chiu ꜂hu*, the Hwichau department in Nganhwui; [19]*꜀hwi mëk*꜆ Hwichau ink.

翬 ꜀Hui. To fly with noise; a kind of colored pheasant; colored, adorned: [20]*꜀hwi ꜀hwi*, to fly up and show the plumage; [21]*꜀hwi te*꜅ a variegated pheasant.

麾 ꜀Hui. A signal or marking flag; to make a signal, to motion to; quick, hasty: *꜀hwi ꜀keng*, to motion with the hand, as in giving orders; COM., *꜀hwi ha*꜅ your honor!—term applied to a military officer.

毀 ꜂Hui. To break down, to throw down, to level, as a house; ruined, destroyed, dilapidated, fallen; abolish-

---

1 緩急相濟 2 緩兵之計 3 遲緩 4 寬緩 5 光輝 6 德輝 7 煇煌 8 斜暉 9 夕暉 10 揮毫 11 揮琴 12 揮霍 13 指揮 14 揮掄 15 指撝 16 撝謙 17 徽音 18 徽州府 19 徽墨○ 20 翬翬 21 翬雉

ed, cast down; to vilify, to defame, to slander, in which sense same as the next; to deprecate calamities by prayer; to shed the teeth: COM., [1]'*hwi hwai*' ruined; [2]*chiék*, '*hwi*, to pull down, as an old house—term used in deeds; [3]'*hwi huk*, useless, as cripples; [4]'*hwi paung*' to backbite; COLL., '*hwi k'ó*' dilapidated; '*hwi ,nëng ,hung mwo*' to destroy (remove) people's graves.

譭 譤 Hui. To be angry with, to vituperate, to revile, to defame, to slander: COM., [5]'*hwi paung*' to vilify, to backbite.

燬 Hui. Fire; blazing, flaming; bright, splendid: [6],*sieu* '*hwi*, burned up.

(220) Hwí.

灰 Hui. Ashes, ashy; lime; to plaster; to give up one's purpose, disheartened: in the coll. read ,*hu*, q. v.: COM., [7],*hwói ,lu*, a limekiln; [8],*sieu ,hwói*, to burn lime; [9],*hwói* '*chwoi*, whitewash; [10],*ping ,long ,hwói*, the red lime eaten with betel-nut; ,*ngüng ,hwói*, ,*chio ,hwói*, and *mëk*, ,*hwói*, are three shades of ash color; [11],*hwói eng*' lime-stamp—used in marking goods; [12],*hwói* '*ch'ü kwa*' a coat of ash-colored rat skins; COLL., ,*niéng ,hwói chak*, '*k'au*, to plaster up an aperture; *ch'ó*' ,*hwói*, darkish lime; ,*hwói ,sié*, a small trowel; ,*hwói pidh*, a plastered partition; ,*hwói ,sing*, or ,*sing ,hwói*, discouraged, indifferent to.

悝 Hui. To jest, to ridicule, to laugh at; a name. Read '*li*: to pity; afflicted, sad; infirm, invalided.

恢 Hui. Read ,*k'wi* in the dictionaries: great, liberal, extensive; to enlarge: [13],*hwí huk*, to regain possession of; [14],*hwí ,hwí*, extensive, great.

詼 Hui. Read ,*k'wi* in the dictionaries: to play with, to laugh at: [15],*hwí ,chiu*, loud laughter; to ridicule; [16],*hwí ,hai*, to dally and sport with.

虺 Hui. Also read '*wi*: noise, a rattling, as of thunder; tired, jaded: ,*hwí ,hwí*, the sound of rumbling thunder; [17]'*ngó* '*ma ,hwí ,toi*, my horse is jaded.

火 Huo. Read '*hwo*; coll. '*hwí*: fire, flame; *met.*, quick, rapid, urgent; fiery, as the disposition: [18]'*hwí ,ing*, smoke; [19]'*hwí k'e*' heat, caloric; [20]'*hwí ,hu*, ashes; '*hwí* '*chüng*, or '*hwí mëk*, residuum of wood, embers; '*hwói yéng*' a flame; '*hwí ,hwa*, sparks; '*hwí tioh*, taken fire, lighted; [21],*sieu* '*hwói*, to burn; '*hwí ngó*' an oven; '*hwói ,tó*, a steel; '*hwói sioh*, flint; '*hwói ,muí*, a paper-lighter; *chëü*' ,*lai* '*hwói*, lucifer matches; '*hwí ngié*' tinder; *p'ah*, '*hwói*, to strike a light; '*hwói ,t'au*, a cook; '*hwí* '*t'oi*, smoked hams; [22]'*hwí yoh*, gunpowder; '*hwí sang*' a fiery temper; '*hwói p'ieu*' a hasty warrant; '*sieu ,sing* '*hwí chioh*, be careful of lighted candles! '*hwí*

[1]毀壞 [3]毀伏 [5]譭謗 [7]灰爐 [9]灰水 灰 [11]灰 鼠褂 [14]恢恢 [16]詼諧 虺隤 [19]火氣 [21]燒火

[2]折毀 [4]毀謗 [6]燒燬 [8]燒灰 [10]檳榔 印 [12]灰 [13]恢復 [15]詼啁 [17]我馬 [18]火烟 [20]火灰 [22]火藥

saik, color of fire—term used by smelters; [1]‘*hwi* ‚*k‘ing*, tongs; ‘*hwi* ‚*ch‘a*, a fireman's tongs; ‘*hwi* ‚*pa*, or ‘*hwi* ‘*ch‘iang*, a fire-shovel; ‘*hwi* ‘*pa*, a torch; crullers; [2]‘*hwi* ‘*kwong*, a bamboo blower—Chinese bellows; [3]‘*hwi tá*’ the god of fire; ‘*ing* ‘*hwi*, to catch, or set on fire; [4]‘*k‘i* ‘*hwi*, to kindle a fire; ‘*hwi* ‚*sieu pauk, pauk, kieu*’ the fire burns with a crackling; ‚*tau* ‘*hwi*, to leap into the flame, as insects; [5]‘*hwi* ‚*lung* ‚*sung*, a steamboat; [6]‘*hwi* ‚*sieu ch‘io*’ a conflagration; ‘*hwi yeu*’ fire-hawks—i. e., plunderers at a conflagration; *mëk*, *ch‘ok*, ‘*hwi*, eyes flashing fire.

‘伙 Huo. Read ‘*hwo;* coll. ‘*hwi*, as in [7]‚*ka* ‘*hwi*, household furniture, property: [9]‚*pwong* ‚*ka* ‘*hwi*, to divide property, as brothers do; [8]‘*hwi sik*, food, provisions; ‘*hwi sik*, ‚*lang*, a chow-chow basket.

‘夥 Huo. Read ‘*hwo;* coll. ‘*hwi*, as in [10]‘*hwi ke*’ or ‘*hwi e*’ a fellow-workman; ‘*hwi ke*’ ‚*këng*, workmen's wages.

(221) Hwo.

‘火 Huo. Fire, flame; to burn, to consume; heat, fever, feverish: in the coll. read ‘*hwi*, q. v.: COM., [11]‚*sing* ‘*hwo*, heart-fire; ‘*hwo ok*, fire pent; ‘*hwo tuk*, fire noxious; ‘*hwo só*’ fire parching; [12]‘*hwo wong*’ (or *tuai*’), fire excessive; [13]‘*hwo* ‚*ping* (or *t‘ói*’), fire abated—are all medical terms referring to "the igneous element" in the system.

‘伙 Huo. Perhaps an abbreviated form of the next; a messmate, a comrade, a companion: read in the coll. ‘*hwi*, q. v.: [14]‘*hwo* ‘*tiong*, the mate of a merchant ship—so called in Canton.

‘夥 Huo. A colleague, a comrade, accomplice, associate; many, numerous; a company, a party, band, society: in the coll. read ‘*hwi*, q. v.: [15]‘*hwo kié*’ (coll. ‘*hwo ke*’ or ‘*hwo e*’ or ‘*hwo e*’ ‚*kó*), partners, fellows; [16]‘*hwo p‘wang*’ associates, a company; *chëüng*’ ‘*hwo*, all the partners; COM., [17]*hak*, ‘*hwo*, joint partnership; COLL., ‘*hwo* ‘*lá chó*’ to work in company; ‘*hwo* ‘*lá* ‘*má*, to buy in partnership.

貨’ Huo. Goods, merchandize, commodities; to trade; to bribe: *hwo*’ ‘*wi*, bribes; COM., [18]*hwo*’ *uk*, goods; *hwo*’ *saik*, the quality of goods; *hwo*’ ‚*ching ka*’ *sik*, "the goods genuine and price true"—a shop sign; [19]‘*má* (or *paing*’ or *te*’) *hwo*’ to purchase goods, to buy stock; ‘*t‘u hwo*’ native goods; ‚*ngü hwo*’ fish; COLL., ‚*ngai hwo*’ bad goods; *hwo*’ ‚*tá*, or *hwo*’ *kiä*’ inferior goods; *hwo*’ *siäng*’ the goods (are) cheap.

‚禾 Huo. Sometimes used for the next; growing grain, especially paddy and wheat; grain, corn; the 115th radical: [20]‚*hwo mek*, paddy and wheat; [21]*ek*, ‚*hwo* ‚*seng* ‘*kiu soi*’ one stalk bears nine heads—in a good year.

1火	3火	5火	燒	9分	食	火	平	計	夥	貨	禾
鉗	帝	輪	厝	家	10夥	12火	14伙	16夥	18貨	20禾	生
2火	4起	船	7家	伙	計	旺	長	伴	物	麥	九
管	火	6火	伙	8伙	11心	13火	15夥	17合	19買	21一	穗

꜀和 ꜁咊 ꜀龢 Huo. Harmony, union, concord; agreement, peace after strife; mild, kindly; agreeing with, as medicine; inclined to; to agree, to be at peace, to unite, to harmonize; to go with, to join, to accompany; to conform to; in coll. mandarin, with, to: also read *hwo*² q. v.: [1]*꜀hwo ꜀hui*, harmony, as in music; cordial agreement; COM., [2]*꜀hwo k‘e*² or *꜀hwo song*² harmonious, agreeing; [3]*꜀hwo ‘nwang*, genial, as warmth or the weather; [4]*꜀hwo ‘hó*, or *꜀hwo ꜀ping*, or [5]*꜀hwo muk*₂ peaceable, on good terms; [6]*꜀hwo siong*² Budhist priests; [7]*‘kong ꜀hwo*, to exhort to peace; [8]*꜀hwo yok*, a treaty of peace, an agreement; COLL., [9]*꜀hwo yék*₂ or *꜀hwo ꜀hwo yék*₂ tepid, lukewarm; *꜀hwo ‘k‘eng ꜀song ka*² peaceable dogs biting each other; *met.*, two persons (instigated) to fight; *꜀hwo siong*² *má*² *chó*² *tek*, *‘mwo po*² *má*² *‘t‘ó tek*, can neither be a priest, nor marry a wife; *met.*, in straits—a dead lock.

꜀盉 Also read *hwo*²: used for the last and the next: to mix and season, as cooks do; dishes to mix food in.

和² Huo. To accord, to respond, as in singing; to conciliate; to mix up, to blend, as tastes: also read *꜀hwo*, q. v.: [10]*hwo*² *꜀si*, an antistrophe; to respond, as in refrains; [11]*‘kwa hwo*² a few voices in accord; *met.*, few agreeing or assenting; [12]*hwo*² *꜀keng*, to season soups; COLL., *hwo*² *sioh*₂ *‘siu*, to write a poem on the same theme (and compare with another's).

禍² Huo. Evil, misery, suffering; calamity, adversity, sorrow, judgment, woe, more especially when beyond one's control; unhappy, unfortunate; to curse, to injure; used in the coll. for rain, as dripping down: [13]*hwo*² *hwang*² adversity; COM., [14]*hwo*² *hai*² evil, misery; [15]*꜀chai hwo*² judgment, calamity; [16]*hwo*² *꜀kong*, the root of the evil; [17]*‘niă hwo*² to stir up trouble; [18]*hwo*² *pok*, *꜀tang ꜀heng*, calamities come not singly.

(222) Hwoh.

局₂ Read *kwoh*₂; coll. *hwoh*₂: to cheat, to deceive, to mislead, to entice: about as *kwoh*₂ q. v.: [19]*k‘ëük*, *꜀i hwoh*₂ *k‘ó*² deceived by him; *hwoh*₂ *k‘ó*² *‘tu*, enticed to gamble; *hwoh*₂ *kwo*² *꜀peng* (or *siéng*²), successfully deceived.

(223) Hwoi.

晦² Hui. Obscure, dark; night, the close of light; the last day of the month; misty, dim: [20]*hwoi*² *꜀ming*, obscure; COM., [21]*hwoi*² *k‘e*² lugubrious, unlucky.

誨² Hui. To teach, to instruct, to reiterate; to admonish, to give line upon line; to induce, to lead to, inviting: [22]*kau*² *hwoi*² to teach diligently.

1 和諧	3 和暖	5 和睦	7 講和	9 和熱	11 寡和	13 禍患	15 災禍	17 惹禍	單行	局去	21 晦氣
2 和氣	4 和好	6 和尚	8 和約	10 和詩	12 和羹	14 禍害	16 禍根	18 禍不	19 乞伊	20 晦明	22 教誨

福州方言拼音字典

悔 Hui. To repent, to change, to regret; vexed with one's self; to explain the diagrams: *hwoí' haung* vexed, remorseful; COM., *hwoí' 'kai*, or [1]*hwoí' chói' 'kai kwo'* to repent and amend; [2]*hwoí' ˏsing*, compunction; COLL., *t'ói' hwoí'* to regret, to repent; *hwoí' ˏtong ˏch'ē*, to regret having formerly done so.

歲 Sui. Read *swoí'*; coll. *hwoí'*: a year, the new year; a year of one's age, a year old according to Chinese reckoning—the year of birth being reckoned one: [3]*hwoí' so'* years of age; [4]*nioh, wai hwoí'* how many years old? [5]*'kwi hwoí'* how old (is the child)? *hwoí' sá'* young; [6]*hwoí' twai ˏnëng mwoí twai* the person is small for his age; *hwoí' pwong* New Year's rice, as offered to heaven and earth, and to the ancestral tablet; [7]*chó' hwoí'* (country brogue *ˏtiong hwoí'*) the feast on the last night of the year.

會 Hui. To collect, to assemble, to convoke, to bring or call together; to make a compact, to unite by agreement; a blending or joining; an association, a club, a society, a meeting, a cabal; a church, a congregation; a joint-stock-company; to meet, to visit; an opportunity, an occasion, a meeting; to let all know; to understand, to know: COM., [8]*hwoí chik,* to assemble; [9]*hwoí ngié* to meet for deliberation; *seng' hwoí* or [10]*kau' hwoí* a Christian church; *hwoí ˏsing*, or [11]*hwoí e'* or *hwoí ngwo'* to perceive, to comprehend [12]*hwoí 'iu*, fellow-members; *hwoí 'kwang*, a club-house, an exchange or guild-hall; [13]*hwoí tói* to pay money through bills of exchange; to pay through another, turn a debt; *hwoí pah*, a compellation of elder members; [14]*hwoí 'só*, wives of members; elder sisters in a church; *ˏki hwoí* an opportunity; *ˏsang hak, hwoí* the Triad society; *miéng hwoí* have (merely) met, slightly acquainted; [15]*pai' hwoí* to visit one; [16]*hwoí ˏk'wi*, Chinsz' graduates, from the 2nd to the 18th inclusive; *hwoí ˏch'ing 'chiu,* feast to a bride's relatives; COLL., [17]*hwoí tioh,* met, assembled; [18]*hwoí meng'* to meet face to face; *hwoí kwo' 'lau*, have met, as new friends; *ˏmó 'li hwoí* dull, stupid; *hwoí ˏt'au* and *hwoí ˏk'a*, the manager and members of a club.

繪 繢 Hui. To embroider, or adorn in colors; to paint, to draw, to sketch; also the thrums left in weaving; red colored threads: [19]*hwoí wa'* to sketch, to paint; [20]*hwoí ˏtu*, to draw plans or maps.

潰 Hui. To run in drops; to separate, to disperse; water flowing in a race-way; roaring surges; enraged, vehement: [21]*hwoí lwang'* enraged, as a mob; *hwoí pai* dispersed, broken, as troops.

匯 滙 Hui. Water gurgling and eddying, a whirlpool; the first also means a vessel or utensil: *sēü' ˏchü hwoí ˏch'ang*, the Four Books with all the comments.

1 悔罪改過 2 悔心 3 歲數 4 若干歲 5 幾歲 6 歲大仏昧大 7 做歲 8 會集 9 會議 10 教會 11 會意 12 會友 13 會兌 14 會嫂 15 拜會 16 會魁 17 會着 18 會面 19 繪畫 20 繪圖 21 潰亂

APLH. DICT. 37

闤[2] Hui. The outer gate of a market; the gate of a street leading to a market; a road: [1]꜀*k'wang hwoi*[2] a street gate.

讀[2] Hui. To stop in the middle, to stop suddenly; to understand; to deceive; to translate; to turn round, to arrange; to rouse, to call together.

瞶[2] Hui. Read *koi*[2] in the dictionaries: lack-luster eyes, a dull vision; eyes weak from the wind.

聵[2] Hui. To be deaf, born deaf: [2]꜀*lung hwoi*[2] entirely deaf.

憒[2] Hui. Troubled, moved, anxious, disturbed; stupid, lethargic: [3]*hwoi*[2] *hwoi*[2] or [4]꜀*hwong hwoi*[2] harassed, confused in mind.

頮[2] Hui. As in [5]*hwoi*[2] *mieng*[2] to wash the face.

(224) Hwok.

忽꜀ Hu. A single floss of silk; the smallest fraction in notation, a millionth; to forget, to disregard, to make light of; to extinguish; neglectful; suddenly, abruptly, unexpectedly, all at once: [6]꜀*k'ing hwok*꜀ to slight; COM., [7]*hwok*꜀ *liok*꜀ negligently, cursorily; [8]*hwok*꜀ ꜀*yong*, or [9]*hwok*꜀ ꜀*yong* ꜀*kang*, suddenly, abruptly; [10]꜀*lié* ꜀*hô* ꜀*si hwok*꜀ the smallest fractions in notation.

惚꜀ Hu. Minute; abstruse, inexplicable; that which dazzles or flutters the mind.

搃꜀ Ho. To clear away, to brush off dust; to take up refuse. Read *k'auk*꜀ to slap, to strike, to push.

擢꜀ Ho. To turn the hand back, to beckon, motion to one: [11]꜀*hwi hwok*꜀ extravagant.

笏꜀ Hu. A tablet of ivory, bamboo, gem, or wood, used at audiences in former times; designed for making memoranda, and afterward used as ornaments; they were held before the breast: [12]*chek*꜀ *hwok*꜀ to hold the tablet; COM., [13]꜀*nga hwok*꜀ an ivory tablet—used by Tauists, and in theatricals.

癨꜀ Ho. A violent distemper; disorder of the stomach, vomiting: [14]*hwok*꜀ *lwang*[2] vomiting and purging, cholera, bilious colic.

霍꜀ Ho. Used for the last: speed, celerity, agility; a surname; a range of mountains in Hupeh: [15]꜀*hwi hwok*꜀ aroused hastily, precipitate; [16]*hwok*꜀ ꜀*sang*, a mountain range in Hupeh—the Atlas of China.

藿꜀ Ho. Leaves of pulse, used as food; greens in general: [17]꜀*lá hwok*꜀ greens; COM., [18]*hwok*꜀ ꜀*hiong*, Betonica officinalis—used in colic and headache.

髮꜀ Fa. Read *hwak*꜀; coll. *hwok*꜀ as in ꜀*t'au hwok*꜀ the hair of the head.

攫[2] Ho. To seize, to take hold of, to grasp in the hand, to secure. Read *wa*[2] or

---

1 闤闠 2 聾聵 3 憒憒 4 昏憒 5 頮面 6 輕忽 7 忽畧 8 忽然 9 忽然間 10 釐毫絲忽 11 揮擢 12 執笏 13 牙笏 14 癨亂 15 揮霍 16 霍山 17 藜藿 18 藿香

福州方言拼音字典

hwa': a trap or snare for wild beasts. Read *ho'*: to spread abroad, to divide.

濩 Ho. Rain flowing in torrents; rushing streams; waters boiling and bubbling: [1]*ʻho' hwok*, a house with deep recesses. Read *ho'* as in *pwo' ho'* diffused, as doctrines.

穫 Ho. To cut grain, to reap the fields; a harvest, a reaping: [2]*‚chʻiu hwok*, the autumn harvest; [3]*ʻngié' hwok*, to reap grain.

䉙 Ho. A measure, a marking-line; to adjust by a line; to measure by a rod or line.

鑊 Ho. A large round pan or boiler without feet, called [4]*ʻtʻing hwok*; to bore, to chisel or engrave.

(225) Hwong.

方 ‚Fang. Square, cornered, angular; a place, a region, a side; manner, art, rule, means; correct, regular; then, thereupon, in that case, in consequence of; towards, to; like; to compare, to lay together; to possess; a prescription; a thin board; a written list of vassals: [5]*‚hwong ʻchʻiâ*, then, consequently; COM., [6]*sëü' ‚hwong*, the four points of the compass, everywhere; [7]*‚hwong hiong'* facing towards, the direction; [8]*te' ‚hwong*, a place, a situation, employment; [9]*ʻngu ‚hwong chak ʻchʻü*, resorted to from all quarters, as a central place; [10]*ʻpi ‚hwong*, to illustrate, as by parables; [11]*tai' ‚hwong*, liberal; [12]*‚hwong hwak*, the mode of doing; [13]*‚hwong ‚ui*, the circuit, the bounds of; *ʻkʻung ‚hwong ‚hing*, a name for copper cash; *‚hwong tëük*, "angular bamboo"—said to grow at [14]*‚Hwong ʻkwong ‚ngang* near Yungfuh; *‚heng ‚hwong piëng'* to do good, to bestow charity; *‚hwong tʻiong'* a Budhist monastery; *met.*, the abbot; COLL., *‚hwong chiâng'* squarely, in exact position; *‚hwong ‚tʻau ‚kʻwo*, square-toed boots.

坊 ‚Fang. A neighborhood; a street, a lane, an alley; a burg, a country house, a shop; an arched gateway, an honorary portal; used for *‚hwong* (to guard, to obstruct): COM., [15]*sioh ‚hwong*, a stone arch or gateway; [16]*‚chü ‚hwong*, a bookstore; [17]*chiék hau' ‚hwong*, portals to chaste and filial widows; [18]*paik seu' ‚hwong*, portal to a person (about) a hundred years old; COLL., [19]*kʻié' ‚hwong*, to erect an honorary portal.

芳 ‚Fang. Fragrant, odorous; *met.*, agreeable, pleasant; virtuous, excellent: [20]*‚kung ‚hwong*, a large collection of flowers; [21]*‚hwong ʻchi*, fragrant plants; COM., *‚liu ‚hwong paik sié'* to transmit a virtuous (reputation) to all coming time.

祊 ‚Fang. Also read *‚hwong*: a sacrifice to the manes within the gates of the ancestral hall; the area within the gateway; to sacrifice to the manes on two successive days.

枋 ‚Fang. A wood used by cartwrights and shipwrights; the white board used by fishermen to entice fish:

---

[1] 螻濩 [2] 秋穫 [3] 刈穫 [4] 鼎鑊 [5] 方且 [6] 四方 [7] 方向 [8] 地方 [9] 五方雜處 [10] 比方 [11] 大方 [12] 方法 [13] 方圓 [14] 方廣巖〇 [15] 石坊 [16] 書坊 [17] 節孝坊 [18] 百壽坊 [19] 豎坊 [20] 羣芳 [21] 芳芷

[1]˓su ˓hwong muk˒ a kind of logwood, sapanwood.

昏 ˓Hun. Used for the next: the sun setting, twilight, dusk; obscure, confused, dull; in disorder; to oblige to do: [2]˓hwong mwoi˒ confused, not discerning; [3]˓wong ˓hwong twilight; COM., [4]˓hwong ˓mi, in a stupor, unconscious; ˓sing ˓hwong, one just married.

婚 ˓Hun. Marriage; to take a wife: COM., [5]˓hwong ˓ing, nuptials; [6]˓hwong ‘lá, marriage etiquette; [7]˓hwong ˓chü (coll. twai˒ t‘aik˒), betrothal-contract; ˓hwong ˓nang ka˒ ‘nü, marriage of the sexes.

涽 ˓Hun. Unsettled, unstable, as water: [8]˓hwong ˓wong, the king of the Tsi state, about B. C. 300.

閽 ˓Hun. A porter; to shut the door at evening: [9]‘k‘aiu˒ ˓hwong, to visit the palace on matters of litigation; ˓hwong ˓ing, a door keeper, a eunuch who keeps the harem.

荒 ˓Huang. Used for the next: deserted, waste, wild, barren, unproductive; distant; jungle, heath; empty, uncultivated, void; unripe, blasted; a famine, a dearth; to overshadow: COM., [10]˓hwong ˓liong, deserted, gone to ruin; [11]˓hwong hié˒ waste, uncultivated; intermitted, as business; [12]˓hwong ˓su, at irregular intervals, as work; [13]˓hwong ‘yă, a desert, a waste; [14]˓ki ˓hwong, famine; COLL., [15]˓hwong ˓tong, incredible, random talk; ˓hwong ˓ch‘eng, uncultivated fields; ˓hwong ˓kié ng˒ oi˒ ˓ch‘ui ˓hwong ˓nĕng ng˒ oi˒ ˓p‘ui (or ˓mó meng˒ ˓p‘ui), a famished fowl does not fear the stick, so a hungry man has no shame (or fear of ridicule).

慌 㡆 ˓Huang. Fluttered, perturbed, confused; apprehensive, nervous; obscure: [16]˓hwong hwok˒ fluttered, nervous; COM., [17]˓hwong ˓mong, agitated, hurried; [18]˓hwong ˓chiong, apprehensive, precipitate; ˓hwong ˓chiong ‘k‘eng, a greedy dog; met., a rash, headlong person.

惛 怋 ˓Hun. Not discerning, stupid, dull; confused, forgetful.

衁 ˓Wang. Blood, the blood above the heart.

肓 ˓ A membrane, or part of the thorax above the heart; the vitals: [19]peng˒ ik˒ ˓kó ˓hwong, the disease reaches the vitals.

謊 諕 ˓Huang. To talk in sleep, incoherent; to lie, lying; raving: [20]˓hwong ˓ngiong, lies; [21]˓hwong mieu˒ fabulous, untrue.

訪 ‘Fang. To inquire, to search out; to inform one's self; to ask advice of, to consult, to deliberate: COM., [22]‘hwong ˓cha, to investigate; ‘hwong ang˒ to get information about a case, as through the police; ch‘ak˒ ‘hwong, to investigate officially; ‘hwong ‘iu, or ‘hwong

---

1 蘇枋木○ 2 昏昧 3 黃昏 4 昏迷 5 婚姻 6 婚禮 7 婚書 8 涽王 9 叩閽 10 荒涼 11 荒廢 12 荒疏 13 荒野 14 饑荒 15 荒唐 16 慌惚 17 慌忙 18 慌[illegible] 19 病入膏肓 20 謊言 21 謊謬 22 訪查

ˏkau, to seek friendly alliances, as by inquiry.

ʻ舫 Fang. A steersman, a pilot; a flat-boat, a raft; a galley of fifty men: [1]*ʻwa*ʾ *ʻhwong*, a carved or ornamented boat. Read *ˏhwong:* two vessels side by side, a double canoe.

ʻ紡 Fang. To spin, to twist into threads, to twine; lines, threads, cords; to suspend, to tie up: [2]*ʻhwong chek*, to spin, to weave; COM., [3]*ʻhwong ˏtiu*, reeled pongee; [4]*ʻhwong ˏtiu ˏsang*, a pongee robe.

ʻ彷 ʻ髣 Fang. Like, resembling; seen indistinctly, seeming, dreamy: [5]*ʻhwong ˏhwong*, timid, undecided; COM., [6]*ʻhwong hok*, somewhat like; COLL., *ʻhwong hok, ˏkiăng ˏchiă kwo*ʾ seen indistinctly as he passed by.

ʻ倣 ʻ仿 Fang. Used for the last: like to, seeming; to imitate, to copy; a model, a copy: [7]*ˏsiong ʻhwong*, much alike, similar; COM., [8]*ʻhwong yong*ʾ to copy the form or pattern; [9]*ˏmwo ʻhwong*, to follow the model; COLL., [10]*ʻhwong ˏi yong*ʾ imitate him; [11]*ʻhwong ʻchiă sek*, or *ʻhwong ʻchiă ʻp'wo*, follow this form or fashion.

ʻ恍 ʻ怳 Huang. Interchanged with *ˏhwong* (fluttered): wild, mad; fluttered, disturbed, unable to collect one's thoughts: [12]*ʻhwong hwok*, perturbed, half-crazy.

ʻ幌 Huang. A curtain, a screen for the light; an ancient ornament for the head.

ʻ貺 K'uang. Sometimes read *hwong*ʾ: to give, to bestow (said by the recipient): [13]*hie*ʾ *ʻhwong*, to give in kindness; [14]*haiu*ʾ *ʻhwong*, to bestow abundantly.

ʻ昉 Fang. The first light of the morning; clear, bright; *met.*, perspicuous, as an essay; to begin, the commencement; just at the time of, to occur, to happen.

ʻ況 K'uang. Cold water; to compare, comparison, illustration; to add to, to increase; a time; here; present, now: usually read *hwong*ʾ, q. v.: [15]*ˏking ʻhwong*, time, period; [16]*ʻhwong e*ʾ the state of the times.

放ʾ Fang. To reject; to let off, to let go; to extend, to liberate, to loose; to lay down; to indulge, to relax, to dissipate; to scatter; to open out; to accord: in the coll., a last; to stretch with a last; in the coll., also read *pong*ʾ, q. v.: [17]*hwong*ʾ *ʻtang*, daring, reckless; [18]*hwong*ʾ *te*ʾ to place; COM., [19]*hwong*ʾ *sĕü*ʾ dissolute, disorderly, impudent; [20]*hwong*ʾ *ˏkwong*, to emit light, as fire-flies; [21]*hwong*ʾ *kó*ʾ "open for accusation", as set days in a magistrate's court; [22]*hwong*ʾ *ˏseng*, let (animals) loose to live, as Budhists do; *hwong*ʾ *ˏseng hwoi*ʾ voluntary clubs (who buy animals) to "let them live"; COLL., *ˏá hwong*ʾ a shoe-last; *mó*ʾ *hwong*ʾ a cap-block; *hwong*ʾ *ˏá*, to stretch

1 畫舫 2 紡績 3 紡綢 4 紡綢 衫 5 彷徨〇 6 彷彿 7 相倣 8 倣樣 9 摹倣 10 倣伊樣 11 倣者式 12 恍惚 13 惠貺 14 厚貺 15 景況 16 況味 17 放膽 18 放置 19 放肆 20 放光 21 放告 22 放生

shoes; ʻhwongʼ twaiʼ (or ˏk'wang), stretched larger; hwongʼ pauk, burst in being stretched. Read ʻhwong: to imitate, to follow; to reach to; great, as in ʻhwong ˏhüng, great merit.

況 况 K'uang. More, moreover, further: sometimes read ʻhwong, q. v.: COM., [2]ʻking hwongʼ the times, one's prospects; [3]hwongʼ ʻch'iä, still more; [4]ˏhó hwongʼ how much more?

Hwongʼ. A coll. word: a boil: ˏsang hwongʼ to have boils; hwongʼ ˏsang sioh ˏsing, to have boils over the whole body; hwongʼ pauk, the boil has burst.

皇 ˏHuang. High, exalted, supreme, honorable, imperial; beautiful, fine, excellent; an autocrat, a monarch, a potentate, an emperor; Heaven; to act right; to go and come; quick, rapid: sometimes used in books for ˏhwong (the female phenix): [5]ˏhwong ʻk'ó and [6]ˏhwong ʻpi, deceased father and mother—now called [7]ˏsiéng ʻk'ó and [8]ˏsiéng ʻpi; COM., [9]ˏhwong táʼ the emperor; [10]ˏhwong haiuʼ the empress; [11]ˏhwong ˏch'ing, the Imperial Pure (dynasty)—used in the dates of tablets; [12]ˏhwong siongʼ His Imperial Majesty; [13]ˏhwong ˏhi, the imperial concubines; [14]ˏhwong ˏt'iéng haiuʼ ʻt'u, High Heaven and Earth; t'aiʼ siongʼ ˏhwong, the father of the emperor; ˏhwong ˏong, imperial favor; [15]ˏhwong ˏch'ing kwok ch'ek, the imperial kindred; ˏsang ˏhwong, the three emperors, Fu-hi, Shinnung, and Huangte; COLL., ˏhwong táʼ ch'oiʼ (or waʼ) k'ëük siäh ˏsing, "an emperor's mouth and a beggar's body"—he talks big but is dressed meanly! ˏhwong táʼ oʼ ˏchiéng máʼ ʻmá tek, wangʼ wangʼ swóiʼ the emperor has money but can't buy myriads of years to live.

喤 ˏHuang. To sob: ˏhwong ˏhwong, bitter crying, to wail, as a child; the harmony of drums and bells; [16]ˏhwong ak, clamor, hubbub.

徨 ˏHuang. Undecided, hesitating: [17]ʻhwong ˏhwong, or ˏpong ˏhwong, timid and irresolute; to go back and forth, as if one had lost his way.

凰 ˏHuang. The female of the phenix, a fabulous bird: hongʼ ˏkiu ˏhwong, the phenix seeks his mate; *met.*, marriage; COM., [18]hongʼ ˏhwong, the male and female phenixes.

遑 ˏHuang. Leisure, vacant time, disengaged; indifferent: [19]mok ʻkang hëk ˏhwong, does not dare to be idle; pok ˏhwong, busy, no leisure.

隍 ˏHuang. An empty ditch, a dry moat or fosse around a city; *met.*, the municipal guardian—an idol god: ˏsing ˏhwong, the city moat; COM., [20]ˏsiäng ˏhwong mieuʼ the palladium or municipal temple—in every walled, or district, city.

湟 ˏHuang. A river in Kansuh, a tributary of the Ta-t'ung and Yellow rivers, near Sining-fu; cold water; a turbulent torrent.

[1]放大 [2]景況 [3]況且 [4]何況 [5]皇考 [6]皇妣 [7]先考 [8]先妣 [9]皇帝 [10]皇后 [11]皇親 [12]皇上 [13]皇妃 [14]皇天后土 [15]皇親國戚 [16]喤呷 [17]彷徨 [18]鳳凰 [19]莫敢或遑 [20]城隍廟○

煌 ˓Huang. A great blaze; splendid, bright, luminous, glorious: [1]˓ming ˓sing ˓hwong ˓hwong, the brilliant stars; [2]˓hwi ˓hwong, effulgent.

惶 ˓Huang. Fear, apprehension, tremor; terror, dread, awe: [3]˓hwong ʻkʻüng, fearful; COLL., ˏkiăng ˓hwong, apprehensive, frightened.

蝗 ˓Huang. The locust: [4]˓hwong chaˀ the migratory locust—styled [5]˓hwong ˏchai, plague of locusts; [6]ang² ˓hwong, drought and locusts.

園 ˓Yüan. A garden, a yard, an orchard, an enclosure for flowers or vegetables; imperial sepulchers; used on shop signs in the sense of a fine establishment: [7]˓hwong eu² gardens and parks; COM., [8]chʻai² ˓hwong, a vegetable garden; [9]˓hwong ˏting, a gardener; [10]˓hwong ˓ting, a summer house; [11]˓hwong ˏchu, the rent of a garden; COLL., ˓hwong ong² a sort of garden-greens.

防 ˓Fang. A bank, a levee, a dike; a defense, a screen; to guard against, to keep off, to defend; to repress, to prohibit, to provide against: in the coll. read ˓hong, q. v.: COM., [12]˓hwong ʻtu, to guard, as soldiers; [13]˓hwong chʻek˒ to watch against thieves; [14]˓hwong pe² to be ready for, on one's guard; [15]˓hwong ʻsiu, to protect; [16]˓hwong ˏhung, medicine for flatulency; COLL., ˓hwong tek˒ ʻking, to keep strict watch; ˓hwong má² teu² unable to guard against or prevent.

妨 ˓Fang. An impediment, an obstacle, a hindrance; to injure: [17]˓hwong ngai² an obstacle; COM., [18]˓hwong hai² a troublesome, or dangerous, impediment; [19]˓hó ˓hwong, how can it obstruct or do harm! [20]pok˒ ˓hwong, or [21]˓u ˓hwong, no hindrance, harmless.

磺 ˓ Also read ˓wong in the dictionaries: the ore of metals; firm, strong; native sulphur: [22]˓tung ˓hwong, copper ore; COM., [23]˓liu ˓hwong, Loochoo sulphur.

魴 ˓Fang. The bream; a thin, broad fish of a greenish-white color, having small scales; its tail is said to turn red from fear or excessive exertion; a species of bream, common at Canton—is a foot long.

鰉 ˓Huang. The sturgeon; a species found in the river Yangtsz is of great size.

篁 ˓Huang. A species of bamboo with a white bark and joints close together; the wood is used for boats and musical reeds; a grove or cluster of bamboos.

˓*Hwong.* A coll. word, as in ˓hwong ˏswi, or ˓hwong ˏchʻwi, a medicinal herb (coriander?), a decoction of which is used to "bring out the measles."

˓*Hwong.* A coll. word: oppressed with cares, hurried: ˓hwong hĕk˒ panting with the hurry; ʻyă ˓hwong sioh˒ ˏlau, excessively driven indeed! chó² ˏma ˏma ˓hwong, distracted with many cares.

[1]明星煌煌 [2]輝煌 [3]惶恐 [4]蝗蚱 [5]蝗災 [6]旱蝗 [7]園囿 [8]菜園 [9]園丁 [10]園亭 [11]園租 [12]防堵 [13]防賊 [14]防備 [15]防守 [16]防風 [17]妨礙 [18]妨害 [19]何妨 [20]不妨 [21]無妨 [22]銅磺 [23]硫磺

遠 ʻYüan. Read ʻwong; coll. hwong²: distant, far off; a superlative, very, much, extremely: [1]ʻhwong² këüng² far and near; [2]ʻhwong² tio² a long road; hwong² tói² a remote place; lië² tek, hwong² far separated; ͵chʻa tek, hwong² very different from; nik, ʻchi ͵tong hwong² the days (seem) long, as from loneliness; [3]hwong² kʻang² to look at from a distance; ͵chʻa pok, ͵tó hwong² about the same distance, as two routes; hwong² hwong² ʻkong ʻkʻi ͵tʻau, to begin speaking at a distance (from the real point); hwong² tioh, ͵chʻiéng ʻli këüng² tioh, ͵ngang ͵seng, (search for it) a thousand miles off (yet find it) before your eyes.

(226) I.

衣 ͵Yi. Clothes, specially those for the body; a case or wrapper, a cover; the husk of cocoanuts; the 145th radical: also read e² q. v.: [4]pek, ͵i (coll. pah, ͵sing), students; COM., [5]͵i ͵siong, or [6]͵i huk, clothes; [7]ʻü ͵i, rain garments; [8]͵i ka² (also spoken ͵ü ka²) a clothes-horse; [9]͵i sik, clothing and food; ͵i tai² the umbilical cord; [10]͵i siäng² sewing-silk; [11]͵ming ͵i, pictures of garments on paper, burnt to the miserable dead; [12]seu² ͵i, a shroud; COLL., ͵i ͵siong ͵kʻá, the skirts; ͵i ͵siong pʻa² a lap made by holding up the skirt; ͵i ͵sang ͵lang ʻlü (or lëü²), the clothes ragged and dirty; [13]͵i ͵siong ͵chʻa chʻaung² ͵á ͵chʻa ͵hung, garments lacking (only) an inch, and shoes (only) a tenth—scil., do not fit well.

依 ͵Yi. To rely on, to trust to; to agree, to conform to; as, according to: [14]͵i ͵hi, like, similar; [15]͵i lai² to rely on; COM., ͵i ʻnü, as you like; [16]͵i ͵chüng, to conform to (his wishes).

伊 ͵Yi. He, she, it; an initial particle, only, because, that; a surname: [17]͵i ʻteng, they, them; COM., [18]͵i ʻüng, a famous statesman of the Shang dynasty, B. C. 1766; COLL., [19]͵i kauk, ͵nëng, they all; ͵i ʻchiä ͵nëng, that person; ͵i chó² ͵i se² he acts in his own peculiar way.

咿 喔 ͵Yi. To smile in bitterness, to moan: [20]auk, ͵i, a loud, forced laugh; ͵i ͵ngu, the hum (of children reading).

噫 ͵Yi. The tone of indignation, surprise, dissatisfaction; for shame! alas! groans, dolor; to belch; [21]͵i ͵hi, to sigh.

猗 ͵Yi. A fierce dog; extended, continuous; flourishing; to exclaim in praise, good! fine! an interjection; to add to, to depend on: ͵i ͵i, fine, flourishing.

犄 ͵Yi. Often read ʻkʻië: a kind of ox with diverging horns: also the same as the last: strong, fierce, as a dog; to display; long, extended; to rely, to depend on; an interjection, oh! ah!

洢 ͵Yi. Name of a river in Honan province, a branch of the river Loh; it runs through Sung-hien in Honan-fu.

[1]遠近 [2]遠路 [3]遠看 [4]白衣 [5]衣裳 [6]衣服 [7]雨衣 [8]衣架 [9]衣食 [10]衣線 [11]冥衣 [12]壽衣 [13]衣裳差寸鞋差分 [14]依稀 [15]依賴 [16]依從 [17]伊等 [18]伊尹 [19]伊各仈 [20]喔咿 [21]噫嘻

海上絲綢之路文獻集成 科技與文化编

漪 Yi. Ripples on water, the curling lines made by water in gentle motion.

醫 Yi. To heal, to cure; medical, medicine; in the coll. also used for *mwok*˒ q. v.: COM., [1]˛*i* ˛*seng*, a physician; [2]˛*i* ‘*kwang*, a dispensary, a hospital; [3]˛*i te*˒ to cure; [4]˛*kwang* ˛*i*, an officer's physician; [5]˛*sing* ˛*i*, a skillful physician; [6]˛*ŭng* ˛*i*, a quack, a charlatan; [7]˛*heng* ˛*i*, to practice medicine.

鷖 Yi. A blue and white duck, which frequents the seashore in flocks, and foretokens storms by flying inland; also said to fly to and fro with the tides.

阿 Ho. Read ˛*ó*; used for the coll. ˛*i*: a common appellative prefix: also read *ak*˒ q. v.: [8]˛*i* ˛*tiă*, father! [9]˛*i* ‘*ma*, grandma! [10]˛*i* ‘*chiă*, elder sister!

以 Yi. By, with; for, that; in order to, to the end that; a reason, the cause by which, using, taking; and; next, at, according to; preceded by ‘*su*, therefore, wherein, that by which, thereby; succeeded by ˛*ui*, deeming, to consider, to regard as; preceded by ˛*hó*, how? how could? often a sign of the accusative, from, to, in: [11]*pok*˒ ‘*i*, not deem or regard as; COM., [12]‘*k‘ó* ‘*i*, suitable, will answer; [13]‘*i* ˛*chiêng* (coll. ‘*i* ˛*seng*), formerly; [14]‘*i siong*˒ the preceding; ‘*ngwai* ‘*i ngwoi*˒ besides me; ‘*su* ‘*i* ˛*yong*, wherefore, wherein; [15]‘*i te*˒ so that; ‘*i* ‘*k‘eu ong*˒ ˛*sing*, "with the mouth ask the heart"—consult your own feelings.

苡 Yi. The purslane (Plantago): [16]*e*˒ ‘*i* (coll. *e*˒ ‘*mi*), pearl-barley.

薾 Luxuriant, growing rank; flourishing vegetation.

爾 尔 Urh. Thou, you, your; flourishing; a final particle, denoting that the subject is not of much consequence; also forms adverbs: [17]*sëük*˒ ‘*i*, suddenly; ‘*i* ‘*teng*, you all; [18]‘*nai* ‘*i*, it is thus, just so.

邇 Ürh. Near, next to, at hand; approaching both in time and place; to reach, to come towards, to approach: *mik*˒ ‘*i*, friendly; [19]‘*i* ˛*lai*, until now, near (in time).

倚 Yi. To rely on, to lean upon or against; trusting in, to depend on, to engage one to do; inclined, leaning; a fulcrum, a support: in the coll. read ‘*ai*, q. v.: [20]‘*i lai*˒ or ‘*i paung*˒ to depend on; [21]˛*p‘iêng* ‘*i*, partial.

輢 Yi. The sides of a chariot; place in a war-car where the weapons are placed.

已 Yi. At the beginning of a sentence, stopped, finished, just done, already, past; sign of the perfect; to terminate; to decline, to put away, to reject; as a final, excessive, no more: COM., [22]‘*i* ˛*king*, has, already has; [23]‘*i* ‘*wong*, past, done; [24]‘*i seng*˒ excessive, too

1醫生	3醫治	5神醫	7行醫	9阿媽	11不以	13以前	15以致	17倏爾	19邇來	21偏倚	23已往
2醫館	4官醫	6庸醫	8阿爹	10阿姐	12可以	14以上	16薏苡	18乃爾	20倚賴	22已經	24已甚

much: [1]'*i kwo*' *₍sing*, has past, is over, as a business.

'*I.* A coll. euphonic prefix, as in '*i* '*a*, to break in two; '*i* '*u*, to brandish, as the hands or weapons.

圯 ₍Yi. A bridge; the bank near a bridge; an embankment: also read '*ki*, q. v.

柂 杝 ₍Yi. Also read *₍ié* and '*ch'ié:* to split wood with the grain; to fall down; name of a wood used for inner coffins, on account of its durability.

栭 ₍Yi. A king-post or girder on the top of a pillar, to support the roof; a kind of chestnut; a fungus or Peziza, called [2]*₍chié ₍i.*

椸 ₍Yi. Also read *₍ié:* a clothes-horse: [3]*₍i ₍i*, a rack for clothes, which the sexes must not use together.

怡 ₍Yi. Harmony, concord; pleased with each other, as brothers and friends; joyful, satisfied: [4]*₍hing tá*' *₍i ₍i*, fraternal joys.

貽 ₍Yeh. Interchanged with the next: to confer, to bestow, to bequeath; to induce or bring on one's self; to cause: [5]*₍i ngwo*' to induce by an error; com., [6]*₍i hai*' *pok*, '*ch'iéng*, to injure deeply, as by a vicious example.

詒 ₍Yi. To hand down,. to bequeath, to leave to, to communicate to posterity; to present to; mutual deception; to ridicule; to act so as to be despised. Read *t'ai*': to defraud or insult. Read *₍tai:* weary; remiss, negligent.

訑 ₍Yeh. Also read *₍ié:* self-sufficient, assuming, arrogant; shallow-minded; to despise, to look down on, to insult; verbose, to brag.

夷 ₍Yi. Even, arranged; to equalize, to level; to wound, to kill; to cut grass; great, ample; to class, to sort; contented, pleased; remote, distant, foreign; a tribe in the west, now applied to all foreigners who do not speak Chinese, barbarians in the sense of the Greek *barbaroi:* [7]*₍i ₍siong*, to wound; [8]*₍i ₍ing*, or [9]*₍i tik*, a foreigner.

洟 ₍Yi. Mucus or a running from the nose: [10]*₍ung ₍i*, name of a marsh in Shansi.

洏 ₍Urh. Warm or hot water; flowing tears: [11]*₍liéng ₍i*, incessant weeping.

姨 ₍Yi. A wife's sister; maternal aunts: com., [12]'*mu ₍i*, a maternal aunt; [13]*₍i ₍hu*, maternal aunt's husband; husband of a wife's sister; [14]*₍i* '*ma*, and [15]*₍i ₍kung*, grandmother's sister and sister's husband; [16]*₍i ₍niong*, term for concubines.

痍 ₍Yi. A wound; an ulcer, a sore; to hurt, to injure; distressing to the mind, wounded in feeling.

而 ₍Urh. The whiskers; a copulative conjunction, and, also, together; and yet, even; a disjunctive, but, yet,

[1]已過身○ [2]芝栭 [3]衣椸 [4]兄弟怡怡 [5]貽悞 [6]貽害 不淺○ [7]夷傷○ [8]夷人○ [9]夷狄○ [10]温洟○ [11]漣洏 [12]母姨 [13]姨夫 [14]姨媽 [15]姨公 [16]姨娘

contrariwise; still, as; used for the person spoken to, thou; an initial particle; the 126th radical: [1]꜀i ꜀king ꜀i haiu' now and henceforth; [2]꜀i ʿi, a final phrase, denoting "that and nothing else"; COM., [3]꜀i ʿch'iä, moreover; [4]꜀i hwong' still further, much more.

咡 ꜀Urh. The sides or corners of the mouth; to close, or purse up, the mouth; to sip.

輀 ꜀ A funeral car, a hearse.

鮞 ꜀ The spawn, the young of fish.

虵 ꜀Yi. A wriggling gait; to stroll, to saunter: in the following senses, usually read ꜀sié; a snake, serpent, serpentine; subtle, malicious; the constellation Hydra.

迤 迆 ꜀ Also read ʿi and ꜀ié: to go by the side of the road: [5]꜀i ʿli, to walk sidewise, lounging.

兒 ꜀Urh. A boy, an infant, a male child; infantile, feeble; a suffix to nouns in the Court dialect: [6]꜀hai ꜀i, a boy; [7]꜀i ʿnü, children; COM., [8]ʿsieu ꜀i, my son; [9]꜀i hié' (like) child's play, as a thing done carelessly; [10]꜀i ꜀ta, cutch.

唲 ꜀Yi. Forced laughter, unwilling compliance; loquacious: in the coll. read ꜀ĕ and ꜀ĕ, q.v. Read ꜀wa: the prattle of children.

飴 ꜀Yi. Sweet cakes; sugared, sweet, pleasant; to feed: [11]꜀hang ꜀i, (like) taking a sugared cake in the mouth —so filial duty is pleasing to a parent.

頤 ꜀Yi. The chin, the sides of the mouth; one of the diagrams; to nourish, to feed: [12]꜀ki ꜀i, an old man who waits to be fed.

匜 ꜀Yi. A pitcher or goblet with a handle and spout; a water-pot or basin: [13]꜀chié ꜀i, wine and water pitchers.

彝 ꜀ A tripod or vase used in temples for libations; a constant rule or law, an invariable principle; constant, common: [14]꜀i ꜀siong, the (five) constant virtues; COM., [15]ʿu ꜀i ꜀sang, the Bohea hills.

(227) **Ié.**

椅 ʿYi. Also read ꜀i and ʿi in the dictionaries: a kind of hard wood, used in cabinet-work; a chair, a couch: COM., [16]꜀kung chó' ʿié, an arm-chair; [17]tik꜀ pwoi' ʿié, straight-backed chairs—without arms; [18]ʿié ꜀kwang, the rounds of a chair; [19]ʿié ük꜀ or [20]ʿié taing' a chair-cushion; COLL., ʿié ꜀t'au and ʿié ꜀teu, short and long benches; ʿié ʿkiäng, a small chair, a cricket; ʿma hok꜀ ʿié, a square stool; [21]ʿma chak꜀ ʿié, a folding chair; ꜀á ʿié "shoe-chair" —the chair occupied by ladies in dressing their feet; ʿié ʿkiäng ꜀teu, a sort of small mountain-sedan.

縊 ' The warp of cloth; to hang, to strangle one's self: ié' ʿsü, strangled to death.

---

[1]而今而後 [2]而巳 [3]而且 [4]而況 [5]迤邐 [6]孩兒 [7]兒女 [8]小兒 [9]兒戲 [10]兒茶 [11]含飴 [12]期頤 [13]巵匜 [14]彝常 [15]武彝山 [16]公座椅 [17]直背椅 [18]椅關 [19]椅褥 [20]椅墊 [21]馬刈椅

謚ʼ The results of conduct; a name or honorary title given after death; a posthumous title, an epitaph; a memoir or eulogy of the dead: [1]ʻiéʼ hwak, the rule or mode of bestowing posthumous titles.

殪ʼ To kill, to put to death, to exterminate; to overhang, to cover, to bury.

饐ʼ Used for the next: cooked rice spoiled by mold; a harsh, sour taste.

噎ʼ **咽**ʼ The second also read ꜀yéng: a stoppage in the throat; unable to swallow, choking; a hiccough, a sobbing.

曀ʼ Cloudy and windy; the sun obscured and almost hid by the clouds.

殪ʼ Poor, lean, meager; cadaverous, emaciated.

翳ʼ A feather fan or screen, a flabel; to screen, to intercept; to seclude from observation, to keep close; to repress; to destroy; an obscurity in the eyes; trees dying; a fabulous pheasant.

瞖ʼ Yi. A disease of the eye, a cataract, called [2]ʻchiongʼ iéʼ; COLL., [3]mek, ꜀chiu siongʼ iéʼ to have a cataract in the eye.

泄ʼ A tributary of the R. Hwai in Nganhwui; to disperse, to scatter, to spread abroad; easy, leisurely; many: [4]iéʼ iéʼ graceful, as a hawk's flight; many and busy, as workmen.

栘 ꜁ A species of bullace: [5]꜁ié ꜁yong, a kind of white willow found in Shantung.

移 ꜁ Yi. To transplant rice; to move, to transpose, to shift, to remove, to change the place or direction of; to transmit, to convey, as an infection; to migrate: COM., [6]꜁ié ꜀kʻwi, to move aside; [7]꜁ié ꜀si, to remove (the nuisance of) a corpse; [8]꜁ié ꜀ung, to forward an official dispatch; COLL., [9]꜁ié cheuʼ ʻhü kaëk, move it to that spot; [10]꜁ié sioh, hiongʼ to change the position of; [11]꜁ié ꜁yăng niăh, chʻek, move the camp so as to seize banditti.

扅 ꜁ The bar of a door, called [12]ʻyéng ꜁ié: [13]paik, ʻli ꜁hié ꜀chʻá ʻyéng ꜁ié ꜀pʻeng ꜀chʻi, Pehlihi's wife cooked a hen with the door-bar (from poverty).

貤 ꜁ Yeh. To remove; to advance, to reward the worthy: in the following senses usually read eʼ; a gradation, a series, as of steps, hills, weights, &c.; to rise, to superimpose: [14]꜁ié chaingʼ to confer honors, as on an officer or his parents; COM., [15]꜁ié ꜀hung, to ennoble (an officer's ancestors).

兮 ꜁ Also read ꜁hié: a poetical word, used as an exclamation of admiration or interrogation in the middle or at the end of a sentence; ah! oh! how! [16]haik, ꜁ié, how splendid!

[1]謚法 [2]瞕瞖 [3]目睭上瞖 [4]泄泄 [5]栘楊 [6]移開 [7]移戶 [8]移文 [9]移就許角 [10]移一嚮 [11]移營拿賊 [12]扊扅○ [13]百里奚妻扊扅烹雌 [14]貤贈 [15]貤封 [16]赫兮○

福州方言拼音字典

爺 Yi. A father, a sire; a title of respect given to officers and gentlemen: COM., [1]'pah ,ié, elder uncle; [2],kung ,ié, a duke, a title of the municipal god; [3]'kwang 'ló ,ié, the god of war; [4],wong ,ié, a prince royal; [5]ié ,mwong, an officer's household; [6],sü ,ié, a private secretary: COLL., twai' 'ló ,ié, your honor! —said to district magistrates, marine inspectors, &c.

嗜 Read sié'; used for the coll. ié', as in [7]ié' ch'oi' greedy mouth—said of one eating often or irregularly; [8]ié' ch'oi' ,chü ,niong, a greedy woman.

穓 Read choi'; used in the Paik, Ing for the coll. ié': to sow, to sprinkle, to scatter about: [9]ié' 'chüng, to sow seed; [10]ié' 'mwang ié' to scatter all over the ground; [11]ié' 'ngu 'chü, "sprinkle the five seeds or fruits"—on the bride's furniture to secure good luck.

夜 Yeh. Read yä'; sometimes used for the coll. ié', as in ié' ,ü, to work in the night; ié' sioh, ,kéng, to do a job of work by night.

(228) Ik.

易 Yi. The mutations or alternations in nature, as of the sun and moon; the theory of combinations and permutations exhibited by diagrams; to change, to exchange, to barter; a market: also read é', q.v.: COM., [12]maiu' ik, or ,kau ik, to trade; commerce, barter; [13]ik, ,king, the Yih King or Book of Changes; ,chiu ik, the Chow Book of Changes; [14],kung ,pang ,kau ik, to trade fairly.

昱 Yü. The light of the sun, the sun shining in its full strength: [15]ik, nik, to-morrow.

疫 Yü. A pestilence, a contagion, an epidemic, a distemper; a disease that has something supernatural in it: COM., [16],ung ik, a plague; ,ch'ung ,ung ha' ik, spring and summer contagions; [17],si ik, an epidemic.

煜 Yü. The brightness of fire; glorious, shining, blazing: the luster of a good name: [18]yéh, ik, flourishing.

熠 Yi. Brilliant, splendid, glistening, as a bird's plumage; to sparkle: [19]ik, yeu' shining, as fire-flies; refulgent.

翌 Yi. Interchanged with, and used for, the next in the phrase ik, nik, to-morrow; [20]ik, ,ming, bright, clear.

翼 Yi. The wings of a bird; sails of a ship; flanks of an army; side-horses; a counsellor; to assist, to support; to shelter, to brood over, to defend; to-morrow; leisure; cordial; vigorous, daring: ik, ik, respectful; flourishing, affluent; at ease; 'ü ik, wings; met., adherents; 'ku ik, to flap the wings.

翊 Yi. Like the last: wings; ready to fly; to help: ik, ik, respectful; ho' ik, an assistant, a counsellor.

1 伯爺 2 公爺 3 關老爺 ○ 4 王爺 5 爺們 6 師爺 7 嗜嘴 8 嗜嘴諸娘 9 穓種 10 穓滿 地 11 穓五子 12 貿易 13 易經 14 公平交易 15 昱日 16 瘟疫 17 時疫 18 曄煜 19 熠燿 20 翌明

液 Yi. Fluid secretions, as saliva, sweat, milk, pus, sap; thick dregs: *ngŭk ik* the pearly secretion—i. e., dew or pure water; [1]*ing ik* a continuous sound; COM., [2]*ching ik* secretions of the body.

泆 Yi. Overflowing waters, rising floods: [3]*ing ik* licentiousness, dissipation; [4]*taung ik* prodigal, as a spendthrift.

逸 Yi. To escape; to let loose; to retire, as into quiet; to run to excess; ease, leisure, idleness; to indulge one's ease or temper; kind, easy, careless about: [5]*ik ik* to move in regular order; COM., [6]*ang ik* quiet leisure; *ŭng ik* to retire from active life.

佚 Yi. Interchanged with the last: ease, leisure, repose, idleness; crime; luxury, voluptuousness; to omit, as a duty.

佾 Yi. The arranging of musicians; a player: *paik ik* a band of eight musicians; COM., [7]*ik seng*, a musician; those who wave plumes in the Confucian worship; graduates who could not be entered as Siutsai and are reserved.

亦 Yi. A conjunction, and, also, too, moreover; likewise, further: [8]*ik se* also is; [9]*ik ʻiu*, moreover; [10]*ik ʻkʻó*, also can or ought.

奕 Yi. Used for the next: large, great; abundant, flourishing; adorned, beautiful; in order; enduring, as generations, or a family: [11]*ik ik* sad, gloomy; [12]*ik yék* many ages, an old family.

弈 Yi. Confounded with the last: game of chess; handsome; a curtain: [13]*ik chʻiu*, the Philidor of China, B. C. 450; [14]*pauk ik* to play at chess.

役 Yi. Persons sent to guard the border; feudal or government service; to serve, to minister to; official underlings, hangers-on at offices, policemen; a servant; to put in rows: in the coll. read *yáh* q. v.: [15]*ik ik* incessant, as labor; [16]*sü ik* one sent on service, a servant; [17]*heng ik* to go abroad, as officials.

睪 Yi. To be on the lookout for, to spy, to peep; to be on the track for criminals; to lead on; to give, to bestow: [18]*ik ik* lively, pleased.

斁 Yi. To dislike, to put away, to discharge, to weary of; to put an end to, to finish; to suffice: [19]*u ik* not weary of, to like. Read *to'*: to besmear; to fall into ruins, destroyed; [20]*hó' to' ha' ʻtʻu*, to ruin the country.

譯 Yi. To explain, to make clear; to interpret, to translate; to make parties understand each other; to transfer from one language to another; to transcribe; an interpreter, a translator: [21]*tiong ik*, to interpret; COM., [22]*hwang ik* to translate.

---

[1]淫液 [2]精液 [3]淫泆 [4]蕩泆 [5]逸逸 [6]安逸 [7]佾生 [8]亦是 [9]亦有 [10]亦可 [11]奕奕 [12]奕葉 [13]弈秋 [14]博弈 [15]役役 [16]使役 [17]行役 [18]睪睪 [19]無斁 [20]耗斁下土 [21]傳譯 [22]翻譯

繹 Yi. $_2$ To draw out, to unravel, as silk; to get a clue; to state in order, to lay before, to explain, in which sense it is like the last; continued, unintermitted; long, great; at the last extreme; to exhaust, the utmost: [1]ʻ*kai ik*$_2$ to explain; [2]꜀*iu ik*$_2$ to unravel, get the clue to.

懌 Yi. $_2$ To like, to be pleased, to rejoice in, to have joy of; happy, pleased, contented.

掖 Yeh. $_2$ To throw one down; to support by the arm; side apartments, like retiring rooms: [3]꜀*hu ik*$_2$ to uphold; [4]*ik*$_2$ ꜀*ting*, side apartments of the imperial palace; [5]ʻ*iu ik*$_2$ to persuade, to induce one; ꜀*hung* (or ꜀*pʻung*) *ik*$_2$ a scholar's robes.

腋 Yi. $_2$ The armpit; the side; the part under the fore-legs of animals: *ik*$_2$ *ha*^{2} under the arms.

蜴 Yi. $_2$ A small species of spotted lizard or eft, called [6]ʻ*chʻó* ꜀*lüng* (grass-dragon); [7]*sek*, *ik*$_2$ a ground-lizard.

驛 Yi. $_2$ A post for the government, a place where couriers rest or exchange; a hostelry, a posthouse; a stage; a courier; to praise, to extol; uninterrupted, incessant: in the coll. read *yăh*$_2$ q. v.: [8]*lok*, *ik*$_2$ *pok*, *chiok*$_2$ incessantly, as persons passing; [9]*ik*$_2$ *chang*^{2} a post, a stage; [10]*ik*$_2$ ꜀*kwang*, the postmaster.

馹 Yi. $_2$ Interchanged with the last: a fleet horse, a racer: [11]*ik*$_2$ ʻ*ma*, a post-horse.

弋 Yi. $_2$ To shoot, as at birds flying; an arrow with a thread tied to it; to take, to seize; a perch, a roost; black; the 56th radical: [12]*ik*$_2$ ꜀*yong* ꜀*kong*, a river in the northeast of Kiangsi; [13]*ik*$_2$ *pok*, *ik*$_2$ *sëük*, do not shoot at a sleeping (bird).

杙 Yi. $_2$ A species of pear from Annam; a pillar, a stake or post to tie animals to.

入 Ju. $_2$ To enter, to go into, as a house; to penetrate; to become a member of; to enter a family; to recede from view; to receive, to take in; to put into; receipts, income; the 11th radical: used in the coll. for ʻ*tié*, q. v.: [14]*ik*$_2$ *hok*$_2$ to enter on one's studies; COM., [15]*chʻok*, *ik*$_2$ to go out and in; outlay and income; [16]*ik*$_2$ *lé*^{2} to pay part of the interest, as on a pawn-bill to obtain an extension of time; [17]*ik*$_2$ ꜀*siăng*, the two *entering* tones (4th and 8th); [18]*ik*$_2$ ꜀*chʻing*, entered in full,—i. e. the account all settled; [19]*ik*$_2$ *hau*^{2} *chʻok*, *tá*^{2} at home filial, abroad respectful to elders.

Ik$_2$. A coll. euphonic prefix, as in *ik*$_2$ *uk*$_2$ to throw away; to wave, as a flag; *ik*$_2$ *ok*$_2$ to sweep aside; *ik*$_2$ *yék*$_2$ to loosen by shaking, as a stake; *ik*$_2$ *yăk*$_2$ to fan.

---

[1]解繹 [2]紬繹 [3]扶掖 [4]掖庭 [5]誘掖 [6]草龍 [7]蜥蜴 [8]絡繹不絕 [9]驛站 [10]驛官 [11]馹馬 [12]弋陽江 ○ [13]弋不射宿 [14]入學 [15]出入 [16]入利 [17]入聲 [18]入清 [19]入孝出悌 ○

(229) Ing.

仍 ‹Jêng. As, according to; again, as before; in consequence of; just so, thus, like to, in imitation of: [1]‹*ing* ‹*yong*, or ‹*ing huk*‚ again, as before; COM., [2]‹*ing* ‹*ngwong* (coll. ‹*ing hwak*‚), still, yet, as before.

因 ‹Yin. A cause, a reason; to avail of, to take occasion; to follow, to comply with circumstances; because, on account of, for, wherefore; a participial form of the following verb, or an ablative absolute; an illative particle, then, next, so: [3]‹*ing* ‹*yong*, a latent cause, mutual sympathies; COM., [4]‹*yong* ‹*ing*, the cause, origin; [5]‹*ing oi*² on account of; [6]‹*ing* ʻ*kwo*, cause and effect; *met*., conduct and recompense, as absorption into Budh; [7]‹*ing* ʻ*chʻü*, on account of this, hence; [8]‹*ing hwo*² *taik*‚ *hok*‚ through calamity get happiness; ‹*ing* ‹*kang te*ʼ *meng*ʼ on account of the rape destroyed her own life—a phrase in law-suits; COLL., ‹*ing* ‹*chiong wang*ʼ hence, thus.

喑 ‹Yin. The wailing or incessant crying of children: ‹*ing* ʻ*a*, dumb from sobbing or grief.

音 ‹Yin. A sound, a noise; a tone, a musical note; the voice; a reply, a report, information, news; the 180th radical: COM., [9]‹*siăng* ‹*ing*, a sound, voice; [10]*paik*‚ ‹*ing*, the eight tones; a tonic Fookien dictionary; [11]ʻ*kwang* ‹*ing* and ʻ*tʻu* ‹*ing*, the mandarin and local pronunciations; [12]ʻ*ngu* ‹*ing*, the five musical notes; ‹*ing seng*ʼ *pok*‚ ‹*tʻung*, no intelligence has come; ‹*ti* ‹*ing*, to recognize a tune; *met*., to be on intimate terms; [13]‹*Kwang* ‹*Ing*, the goddess of mercy.

垔 堙 ‹Yin. To stop up, to close; to dam up, to turn water-courses; to raise an earth-work; the second also means an earthen mound, such as besiegers raise.

姻 婣 ‹Yin. Marriage, affinity; relationship on the female side, a bride: COM., [14]‹*hwong* ‹*ing*, betrothal, marriage; [15]*kiĕk*‚ ‹*ing*, to settle a marriage contract; [16]‹*ing* ‹*ka*, or ‹*ing* ‹*chʻing*, families related by marriage; the following phrases are used on letters and cards—[17]‹*ing* ‹*ka tá*² (commonly ‹*ing kwong*ʼ *tá*²) your relative's brother—said by uncles in addressing the father or uncles of the other family; [18]‹*ing* ‹*ngü tá*² your stupid relative—as the fathers-in-law style themselves.

攖 ‹Ying. To take in the hand; to press near, to run against, as a sword; to confuse; to assail; bold, audacious, provoking.

湮 ‹Yin. To dam up, to dike; to fall into the water, lost, drowned: [19]‹*ing muk*‚ sunk in the water, drowned.

烟 ‹Yin. Read ‹*yĕng;* coll. ‹*ing:* smoke: [20]ʻ*hwi* ‹*ing*, the smoke of a fire; [21]‹*hong* ‹*ing*, tobacco-smoke; ‹*ing* ‹*mang* ‹*mang*, very smoky, filled with smoke.

---

[1]仍然 [2]仍原 [3]因緣 [4]緣因 [5]因爲 [6]因果 [7]因此 [8]因禍得福 [9]聲音 [10]八音 [11]官音 [12]五音 [13]觀音 [14]婚姻 [15]結姻 [16]姻家 [17]姻家 [18]姻愚弟 [19]湮沒 [20]火烟 [21]燻烟 ○

愔 Yin. Harmonious; tranquil, peaceful, still: ˛ing ˛ing, agreeable; deep and solemn, as the music of a harp or organ.

應 Ying. That which is proper and right; suitable, agreeable to law and correct principles; ought, should: also read eng', q.v.: [1]˛ing ˛sü, should or must be; [2]˓chié ˛ing, should only be (thus); COM., [3]˛ing ˛kai, or [4]˛ing ˛tong, ought; COLL., ˛ing ˛kai ˛chiong wang' chó' this is the proper way to do.

膺 Ying. The breast, bosom; self, personally; to receive, to sustain, to assume responsibility; a girth, surcingle; stoppage of breath: [5]˛nang ˛ing tëüng' eng' hard to sustain a high office; [6]˛ing ëüng' a labored breathing.

瑛 Ying. The luster of gems, the polish of precious stones, as crystals: [7]˓chié ˛ing, rose quartz.

瓔 Ying. A fine pebble, like a gem; gems, or jewels for the neck: [8]˛ing ˛ngüng, a stone like the jade; [9]˛ing lok˛ a necklace of gems.

瘖 Yin. Dumb from disease, an ailment which produces dumbness; in pain, suffering: [10]˛ing ˓a, dumb; [11]˛ing ˛lung, dumb and deaf.

癭 Ying. The goiter; a ganglionic swelling on the neck; a wen, a tumor: [12]hiék˛ ˛ing, a bloody tumor; [13]˛küng ˛ing, a tumor with turgid veins; [14]k'e' ˛ing, a glandular swelling—which is aggravated by fits of passion.

禋 祵 Yin. Sincere worship, a pure sacrifice made to Heaven by the emperor: [15]˛ing sëü' an acceptable sacrifice; [16]˛ming ˛ing, pure worship.

罃 A vessel to keep fire in, an earthen jar with a long narrow neck.

罌 罌 Yin. Used for the preceding: a canister, a jar with a contracted mouth, a gallipot; an earthen pitcher: COM., [17]˓chiu ˛ing, a wine pitcher; [18]˛hai ˛ing, earthen gallipots.

甄 Yin. To mold, to model, to form in clay, a potter; met., to mold, as a ruler does the manners of the people; molded, transformed, influenced; to distinguish; plain, intelligible: [19]˛ing piék˛ ˛ing ˛chai, to discern men's abilities; [20]˛ing ˛tó sëü' loi' to train scholars.

氤 絪 Yin. The elements: ˛ing ˛ung, the genial influence of heaven and earth, the stimulus of nature which produces things; the 2d character is also applied to hemp.

纓 Ying. The tassel or fringe of a cap, the cord or throat-band to tie it with; the fringes or pendants on a bridle; tassels once worn on the breast: COM., ˛ing lik˛ a fringed ceremonial cap—worn in summer; lik˛ ˛ing, summer-cap fringes; haik˛ ˛ing, dark, mourn-

---

[1] 應須 [2] 祇應 [3] 應該 [4] 應當 [5] 難膺重任 [6] 膺壅 [7] 紫瑛 [8] 瓔琅 [9] 瓔珞 [10] 瘖瘂 [11] 瘖聾 [12] 血癭 [13] 筋癭 [14] 氣癭 [15] 禋祀 [16] 明禋 [17] 酒罌 [18] 硋罌 [19] 甄別人才 [20] 甄陶士類 〇

ing tassels; COLL., *ing sioh 'liu*, a set of cap-fringes.

英 Ying. Flowers without fruit; bloom, foliage; flourishing, luxuriant; excellent, superior, eminent, having fine talents; brave, noble-minded, virtuous; a tassel; an ancient state in the west of Nganhwui: [1]*'lok ing*, falling petals of flowers; [2]*ing hwa*, beautiful; English and Chinese; COM., [3]*ing hüng hó kiék*, brave, manly, heroic; [4]*ing hüng 'hó hang'* a mighty man, a hero; [5]*'tai' ing*, or [6]*ing kek le'* English, England; [7]*pah siōh ing*, quartz crystal; *'chié sik ing*, a bluish limestone.

蘡 Ying. Also read *eng*: a species of creeping plant, a vine called [8]*ing ëük*, resembling the wild grape.

茵 Yin. Thick mats used on floors; a padded mat or cushion in a carriage; tiger's skin cured to sit on; occurs in the term for wormwood: COM., [9]*ing ting*, or *ing ting kó*, wormwood; one says a medicinal plant like marjoram.

裀 Yin. Used for the last: a mattress; the lining of a garment; hems, plaits: [10]*'lwi ing liék 't'ing*, piled cushions and arranged pans (or dishes); *met.*, living in luxury.

闉 The gates of an inner city-wall; the wall inclosing them; to stop, to obstruct, to hem in; *met.*, poor, distressed, in straits: [11]*tüng ing*, the second or inner gate of a city.

陻 Yin. The sound of pestles in pounding mud-walls; numerous: *ing ing*, many, a great crowd.

陰 隂 Yin. Obscure, dark, somber, shady; the shades, hades; the lesser of the dual powers, the female or recipient in nature; matter quiescent; the inferior of two states or things in contrast, as the moon, earth, water, night, female, secret, private, shady, rear; to screen, to cover: [12]*hung ing*, or *ch'aung' ing*, a moment; [13]*t'ai' ing*, the moon; *ing 'ü*, dark and rainy; COM., [14]*ing yong*, the female and male principles in nature; *ing hung*, a departed spirit; [15]*ing 'hu*, or *ing kang*, hades; *ing ho'* or *ing mwong*, the female organs; [16]*ing ping*, "soldiers of hades"—spirits at the beck of the infernal gods; [17]*ing meu*, to scheme secretly; *ing taik*, or *ing k'ek*, private acts of benevolence; *ing cheng'* an internal ailment; an illness recurring in the afternoon; [18]*kwong ing*, time; [19]*ing hü*, or [20]*ing k'wi*, a female complaint; COLL., *ing yong meng'* a face of two colors, as the white and black face of the god *Ing yong si*; *met.*, the light and dark pieces of pork in a feast; *ing pok*, *ing yong pok*, *yong*, "neither *yin* nor *yang*"—undecided, at odds and ends.

駰 A piebald horse, spotted white and black, with brindled streaks.

---

[1] 落英 [2] 英華 [3] 英雄豪傑 [4] 英雄好漢 [5] 大英 [6] 英吉利 [7] 白石英 [8] 蘡薁 [9] 茵蔯 [10] 累裀列鼎 [11] 重闉 [12] 分陰 [13] 太陰 [14] 陰陽 [15] 陰府 [16] 陰兵 [17] 陰謀 [18] 光陰 [19] 陰虛 [20] 陰虧

福州方言拼音字典

鷹 'Ying. Accipitrine birds; the falcon, the hawk, the eagle, the owl: [1]'kaĕk, ,ing, the horned hawk; COM., [2],ing ,yong yéng' feast given to military Küjin graduates.

,Ing. A coll. euphonic prefix, as in ,ing ,ung, to sprinkle over; ,ing ,eng, to place, to set down; ,ing ,wang, crooked, winding, as a path; ,ing ,yéng, to cover, as the face with the hands.

'永 Yung. Water constantly flowing; perpetual, enduring; final, complete, as a cure; distant, long-continued, forever: COM., [3]'ing 'wong, or [4]'ing sié' forever; [5]'ing hok, the Yungfuh district in Foochow prefecture; [6]'ing ,ch'ung ,chiu, the Yungchau department in Fookien; [7]'ing twang' kak, ,teng, "vines cut off forever"—phrase in deeds, meaning *finally* conveyed, not redeemable; COLL., [8]'ing 'ku, (with a succeeding negative) never; 'ing 'ku má' hwak, ,chai, will never be rich; 'ing ,ch'ung ,pó ,lá, "(like the thin) Yungchau glass"—he's very irritable! Read eng': to recite, to chant.

'影 Ying. A shadow; a picture, an image of a thing; a vanishing appearance: in the coll. read 'ong, q. v: [9]'ing 'hiong, shadow and echo; *met.*, close attention, obedience; COM., [10]wa' 'ing ,tu ,hing, to draw a likeness, as of a thief in order to catch him; COLL., 'ing 'ong, a mere shadow or reflection—a clue, inkling of.

'引 Yin. To draw a bow; to precede, to lead on; to induce, to point out, to show; to introduce, to recommend, to bring one forward; to seduce, to influence to evil; confirmed, as a habit; to quote, as in proof; a halter for a cow; a prefatory notice; a fuse, a match; measure of 100 feet: [11]'ing ,küng, to draw a bow; COM., [12]'sieu 'ing, a short preface; [13]'ing tó' to lead, show the way; [14]'ing kiéng' to introduce to an audience with; [15]'ing cheng' to recommend; [16]'ing 'iu ,liong ,ka 'chü tá' to entice the sons of a virtuous family; [17]'ing 'hwí, to catch fire, combustible; COLL., 'ing 'niă ,t'au, a ringleader in mischief; 'ing tó' the main path (to a house); 'ing siăng' "leading thread"—to give one a clue to; 'ing tio'.,lüng, "the leading-dragon"—a blind man's staff.

'飲 Yin. To drink, to imbibe; to suck in, to draw in the breath; to rinse the mouth; drink, drinking; concealed, secret: see also the coll. words siăh, and ch'iok,: [18]'ing 'chiéng, a feast to one going on a journey; 'ing haung' to cherish hatred; COM., 'ing 'chwi ,ti ,ngwong, by drinking the water know the fountain; *met.*, to learn by experience, as trade-secrets. Read eng': to give to drink: eng' 'ma ,teu ,chiéng, watered his horse and threw down some cash.

'飪 Jên. To season and dress meats very thoroughly: [19],p'eng 'ing, to dress food; sek, 'ing pok, sik, meats poorly cooked (Confucius) would not eat.

[1]角	宴	世	春	葛	[9]影	圖	[12]小	[14]引	[16]引	子	[18]飲
鷹	[3]永	[5]永	州	藤	響	形	引	見	誘	弟	餞
[2]鷹	遠	福	[7]永	[8]永	[10]畫	[11]引	[13]引	[15]引	良	[17]引	[19]烹
揚	[4]永	[6]永	斷	古	影	弓	道	進	家	火	飪

ʻ矧 Chên. To stretch; still more, how much more; to grin broadly: [1]ʻ*ing wakˎ* to say further; [2]ʻ*ing ˏi ˏing e*ʼ how much more this man!

ʻ蚓 Yin. An earth-worm, the lumbricus: in the coll., *ˏka ʻkung*, q. v.: [3]*ˏkʻin ʻing*, the earth-worm, also called *ʻte^2 ˏlüng*, earth-dragon.

ʻ穎 Ying. A full head of grain; a spike of grain; the beard, awn; a sharp point, as of a pencil; an awl; a ring on a scabbard; a fine critical taste, in which sense the same as the next: [4]*sikˎ ʻing*, a full head of grain; [5]*tʻwakˎ ʻing*, to pierce through and protrude, as an awl through a bag; *met.*, of quick parts, clever.

ʻ頴 Ying. Clear; intelligent; literary, critical: [7]ʻ*ing ngwo*^{2} clever, having versatile talents.

ʻ衽 ʻ袵 Jên. A lappel or flap in front of a coat, buttoned under the right arm; the skirt; a single mat: [8]ʻ*chó ʻing*, the left flap and seam; [9]ʻ*liêng ʻing*, to put the hands together and bow, as females do.

ʻ荏 Jên. A kind of large, oily bean, like Windsor beans; gentle, kind-hearted: [10]*saikˎ lá^2 ˏi nói^2 ʻing*, stern-looking but kind in heart; [11]ʻ*ing ʻyéng*, to go and come, succession, as of day and night.

ʻ飲 A good taste, well flavored; to gormandize, to guzzle; well done, thoroughly cooked; mellow, ripe. Read *tiêng*ʼ: fine, excellent.

ʻ*Ing.* A coll. euphonic prefix, as in ʻ*ing ʻyong*, to nourish, to rear; ʻ*ing ʻang*, to shut a door, to close but not bolt it.

ˏ人 Jên. A man, a human being, a person; human, belonging to mankind; placed after nouns, a laborer, an artist, a person having a calling; the 9th radical: sometimes used for *ˏnëng* in the coll.: [12]*ˏnang ˏing*, a male; [13]ʻ*nü ˏing*, a female; [14]*ˏing ʻki*, others and self; [15]*ˏtüng ˏing*, a factor, a broker; COM., [16]ʻ*sieu ˏing*, a mean man; [17]*ˏsing ˏing*, to attain adult age—16 years old; [18]ʻ*tʻu ˏing*, aborigines; [19]*nói^2 ˏing*, my wife; [20]*ˏchong ˏhu ˏing*, your wife; *ˏing ʻchü*, sons; the Son of Man; *ˏka ˏing*, domestics, retainers; *ˏing ˏka*, families; *ˏing ukˎ* clay images, toys; *ˏing ˏngiong*, arsenic; [21]*ˏing ˏseng*, ginseng; *ˏing ˏsing ˏtʻiêng ʻli*, the mind (in accord with) celestial principles; *ˏing chëüng*ʼ *ˏhung ˏhung*, a confused crowd; *ˏing ˏui wang^2 ukˎ ˏchi ˏling*, man is the (most) intelligent of all beings; COLL., *ˏing ˏka chʻio*ʼ family residences, dwellings; *ˏing ˏtüng*, middle of the upper lip; *ˏing ˏtüng kʻieu*ʼ *kau*ʼ *pʻe*ʼ *má^2 siong^2 nè^2 sekˎ se*ʼ if one's upper lip curls up to the nose, he'll not reach the age of 24! *ˏing ˏsing pokˎ chëükˎ ˏsie ˏtʻong chʻiong^2* man's mind never satisfied (is like) a snake swallowing an elephant!

[1]矧曰 [2]矧伊 人矣 [3]蚯蚓 [4]地龍 [5]實穎 [6]脫穎 [7]頴悟 [8]左衽 [9]斂衽 [10]色厲而內荏 [11]荏苒 [12]男人 [13]女人 [14]人己 [15]中人 [16]小人 [17]成人 [18]土人 [19]內人 [20]尊夫人 [21]人參

仁 ˛Jên. Humanity, regard for others; fulfilling one's duty; benevolent, kind, considerate, merciful; with a negative, numb, insensible, paralyzed; the pupil of the eye; a kernel, a pit, a small seed: in the coll. read ˛ning, q.v.: [1]ʻch'ʻiu chĕük˛ pok˛ ˛ing, the hands and feet numb; COM., [2]˛ing ai˒ love, charity; [3]˛ing taik˛ kindness, benevolence; [4]˛ing haiu˒ trusty, faithful; [5]ʻpok˛ ˛ing, unfeeling, unkind; [6]ʻhaing˒ ˛ing, almonds; [7]˛ing ngié˒ ʻlá te˒ seng˒ humanity, rectitude, courtesy, wisdom, truth—are the five cardinal virtues.

盈 ˛Ying. A full vessel; full, completed, replenished, overflowing; fullness; arrogant, audacious; filling, increasing, as the moon; to overpass, stretching beyond, overplus: [8]ngwok˛ ˛ing, full moon; [9]˛ing k'wok˛ waxing and waning; [10]˛ing ʻmwang, full; complacent, conceited; [11]˛ing sauk˛ exceeding and deficient, as expenses and receipts; [12]chɔi˒ auk˛ kwang˒ ˛ing, his iniquities are full.

楹 ˛Ying. A column, as of a palace; a pillar that supports the roof; a prop, a support; in Canton, a tree with red heart-wood and grayish bark like the beech.

寅 ˛Yin. To reverence, to respect; a colleague, a fellow-officer; the third of the twelve branches, from 3 to 5 A.M.—belongs to wood and is denoted by a tiger: [13]˛ing ˛küng, to revere; COM., ˛ing ˛si ˛ch'ĕ, 3 A.M.; [14]˛tung ˛ing ˛kwang, fellow-officers.

夤 ˛Yin. Similar to the last: to respect; to advance, to gain promotion; a money-girdle; a colleague; far, distant: [15]˛ing ˛yong, to intrigue, to gain a cause by bribery; [16]˛ing yá˒ by night, evening.

壬 ˛Jên. The ninth of the ten stems, connected with water; great; to flatter, to adulate: [17]˛ing koi˒ the north—pertains to water.

任 ˛Jên. Sincere, worthy of trust, sure; friendship, confidence; trusted, relied on; to bear, to sustain: also read eng˒, q. v.

婬 ˛Jên. Interchanged with the next: luxurious, going about for amusement; theatrical, stage-plays; debauched, lewd, obscene, lascivious; to commit adultery.

淫 ˛Yin. The rising of water; to soak, to drench; to go to excess; to lust after; lewd, immoral, licentious; excess in calculations; great, as faults; to incroach; a long time: COM., [18]˛kang ˛ing, adultery, fornication; [19]˛ing lwang˒ lewdness, incest; [20]˛ing ho˒ an adulteress; ˛ing ˛hung, depraved manners (of a community); ˛ing ˛chü, obscene books; ˛ing haing˒ lewd conduct; ˛ing ˛ing ˛ch'á ʻnü (or ʻchü) ˛ch'á ʻnü (or ʻchü) ˛ing ˛ing, if one ravishes others' wives and daughters, others will ravish his.

1手足不仁
2仁愛 3仁德
4仁厚 5不仁
6杏仁 7仁義
禮智信 8月
盈 9盈闕 10盈
滿 11盈縮 12罪
惡貫盈 13寅
恭 14同寅官
15夤緣 16夤夜
17壬癸 18姦淫
19淫亂 20淫婦

APLH. DICT. 40

榮 ꜀Yung. Beams made of the [1]*ʻngu ꜀tung* tree; the turned-up corners of roofs; glory, fame, honor; splendid, glorious, beautiful, as flowers: COM., [3]*꜀ing ꜀kwong*, brilliant, as stars; [2]*꜀ing ꜀hwa ho*ʼ *koi*ʼ splendor, wealth, and honors; [4]*꜀ing yeu*^{2} glory, distinction; [5]*꜀ing ꜀chung yeu*^{2} *ʻchu*, to reflect honor on one's ancestry.

熒 ꜀Yung. The sparkling light, as of an illumination; dim, twinkling, shimmering; a doubtful, intermitting light; to illuminate: [6]*꜀ing ꜀tai*, a volcano; [7]*꜀ing ꜀ing*, shining faintly; [8]*꜀ing hĕk*꜁ *꜀sing*, a twinkling star.

瑩 ꜀Yung. Interchanged with the last: the color of gems, luster of pearls; bright, lustrous; intelligent: [9]*seu*ʼ *꜀ing*, a fine pebble like a gem; [10]*tʻeng*ʼ *꜀ing*, to hear indistinctly, to doubt, uncertain.

紖 ꜀ A cord, a single thread; to thread a needle; to tie together with threads.

紝 ꜀ Also read *eng*ʼ: threads used in weaving; to lay the warp; to weave, to make a fabric of silk or cloth: [11]*chek*꜁ *꜀ing*, to weave.

縈 ꜀Yung. To wind, to tie around; to roll up; to go around; confused, tangled: [12]*꜀ing ʻnau*, to twine about; tangled; [13]*꜀ing ꜀huí*, winding, as a path.

塋 ꜀Yung. A tomb, a cemetery, burial grounds: *꜀hung ꜀ing*, graves; [14]*꜀siéng ꜀ing*, the family cemetery.

嶸 ꜀Yung. Conspicuous, as a peak; high, mountainous; a high mountain: [15]*꜀cheng ꜀ing*, a high peak; *met.*, eminent, distinguished.

嬴 ꜀Ying. Erroneously used for the next: to bud, to expand, to shoot forth; to fill: [16]*꜀ing sauk*, to expand and contract; *꜀ing se*^{2} a famous beauty of the Chʻin state; [17]*ʻtiong ꜀ing*, summer.

贏 ꜀Ying. Gain, profits; abundance, overplus, superfluity; to win, to conquer, to excel: in the coll. read *꜀yăng*, q.v.: [18]*꜀ing ʻmwang*, abundance; *꜀ing ꜀ü*, overplus; *chiéng*ʼ *꜀ing*, to win a battle.

瀛 ꜀Ying. The broad ocean, the circuit of the seas; a place in Tsi, now Hokien-fu in Chihli: COM., [19]*꜀teng ꜀ing ꜀kio*, the bridge at the entrance of a provincial college; [20]*꜀ing ꜀kʻwang che*ʼ *liok*꜁ the Universal Geography—prepared by Gov. *꜀Sü kié*ʼ *꜀ü* of Foochow.

螢 ꜀Ying. A glow-worm, a fire-fly; luminous insects in wood; *꜀nong ꜀ing*, a fire-fly put in a (gauze or paper) case; *ho*^{2} *ʻchʻó ꜀ui ꜀ing*, rotten plants breed glow-worms.

瀅 ꜀Yin. Excessive showers; to rain for more than ten days: *꜀ing ʻü*, a long, drenching rain.

[1]梧	[2]榮	[4]榮	耀	[7]熒	星	瑩	繞	塋	縮	滿	[20]瀛
桐	華	耀	祖	熒	[9]琇	[11]織	[13]縈	[15]崢	[17]長	[19]登	寰
[3]榮	富	[5]榮	[6]熒	[8]熒	瑩	紝	絗	嶸	贏	瀛	志
光	貴	宗	臺	惑	[10]聽	[12]縈	[14]先	[16]贏	[18]贏	橋	略

營 ꜀Ying. To dwell in a market; to lay out, to measure; to plan, to scheme, to attend to business; to toil, to seek a livelihood; to erect, to build; a cantonment, a camp, an intrenchment; military; the infantry, troops of the line, the army: in the coll. read ꜀yăng, q.v.: [1]꜀king ꜀ing, to scheme, to seek a living; [2]꜀ing seng꜄ an outpost; [3]꜀ing ꜀seng, a livelihood; [4]꜀ing sek꜁ to build a house; a star near Aquila; [5]꜀ing ꜀meu, to trade.

꜀Ing. A coll. euphonic prefix, as in ꜀ing ꜀ŭng, to divide equally; ꜀ing ꜀wang, to take a circuit, to coil up, as reptiles; ꜀ing ꜀yéng, to collect (subscriptions); to assemble, as at a table, worship, etc.; ꜀ing ꜀ung, to sprinkle, as oil in a cooking-pan; ꜀ing ꜀yăng, to win, as in gaming.

(230) Iu.

憂 ꜀Yu. Sorrowful, grieved, mournful, sad; thoughtful, anxious; to think of with sorrow; to act so as to bring disgrace; grief from neglect or dispraise; low-spirited, melancholic, nervous; grieving for parents' death; sickness of pregnancy: [6]pok꜁ ꜀iu, not anxious, composed; [7]꜂ŭng ꜀iu, secret grief; COM., [8]꜀tang ꜀iu, to sympathize with, anxious about; [9]꜀iu ꜀ch'eu, or [10]꜀iu mong꜄ sad, dejected; [11]꜀ting ꜀iu, in mourning—as officers report to the emperor; [12]꜀iu lëü꜄ sorrowful and anxious.

懮 ꜀Yu. Also read ꜂iu: interchanged with the last: to take one's ease, relaxation from labor; grief; sad, sorrowing.

優 ꜀Yu. Abundant, extra, excessive, an overplus, supererogatory; satisfied, tranquil, joyous; leisurely, easy, unconcerned; to excel, more than able for, competent; to trifle, to play, to dally, to be on free terms with: [13]꜀i ꜀iu, cringing, obsequious; [14]꜀iu liok꜁ capable and incapable; [15]꜀iu ꜀iu ꜂iu ꜀ü, enough and more; [16]꜀iu ꜀ing, a comedian; COM., [17]꜀iu kong꜄ a grade above Siutsai—between the ꜂ling ꜀seng and pak꜁ kong꜄; COLL., [18]꜀iu ꜀iu chëü꜄ chai꜄ to saunter about at ease.

耰 ꜀Yu. A harrow to turn in the seed; to harrow in seed, to cover seed when sown.

麀 ꜀Yu. A doe, the female of the stag or of any other deer.

呦 ꜀Yu. The bleating or cry of deer: ꜀iu ꜀iu, the baying or bleating of deer.

友 ꜂Yu. A friend, a companion, an associate; attached to, fond of; to be friendly with, to unite cordially; to act as a friend, fraternal, hearty, friendly; friendship: [19]꜀lieu ꜂iu, fellow-officers; COM., [20]꜀peng ꜂iu (brogue ꜀pĕng ꜂iu), a friend; [21]hau꜄ ꜂iu, filial and fraternal love; [22]꜂iu ai꜄ brotherly regard; ꜂iu tó꜄ rules and duties of friendship; ꜂ló ꜂iu, an old friend; hwoi꜄ ꜂iu, a fellow-member; ꜂chiu nŭk꜁ ꜀peng ꜂iu, mercenary friends; leng꜄ ꜂iu, your friend.

[1]經營 [2]營汎 [3]營生 [4]營室 [5]營謀 [6]不憂 [7]隱憂 [8]擔憂 [9]憂愁 [10]憂悶 [11]丁憂 [12]憂慮 [13]伊優 [14]優劣 [15]優優有餘 [16]優人 [17]優貢 [18]優游自在 [19]僚友 [20]朋友 [21]孝友 [22]友愛

ʻ禸 Also read ˛iu: the step of a beast, the round marks of a paw in the ground; the tracks of wild animals; the 114th radical.

ʻ牖 Yu. A hole in a wall, a square window; a lattice with sliding doors; to lead on, to instruct, to bring up: [1]˛ch'ong ʻiu, or ho² ʻiu, a window; [2]ʻiu ˛ming, to instruct the people.

ʻ誘 Yu. To speak pleasantly to, to advise; to animate, to encourage; to allure, to entice, to draw on; to tempt, to mislead: [3]˛sung ˛sung siéng² ʻiu, to lead one to virtue; COM., [4]ʻing ʻiu, to entice, to lead one to evil; [5]ʻiu hĕk˛ to tempt, to seduce.

ʻ莠 Yu. Useless grass among grain, like the panic grass; tares, darnel, weeds; *met.*, the riffraff of society; vicious, mischievous: [6]ʻiu ˛ngiong, vile words; [7]˛long ʻiu, cheat, darnel.

ʻ卣 Yu. An ancient sacrificial vessel, made with a cover and a bail, to hold fragrant wine; it was placed in the center on the altar.

ʻ酉 Yu. Ripe, matured, finished; ripe, mellow, as grain for making spirits; elegant; satisfied; the 10th of the 12 branches, represented by a cock; the 164th radical: [8]ʻiu ngwok˛ the 8th moon; COM., [9]ʻiu ˛si, hour from 5 to 7 P. M.; [10]ʻiu ˛kie, the ʻiu hour-cock—term in divination; [11]ʻiu ˛si ʻmwi, about 7 P. M.

ʻ槱 Yu. To collect fuel to make a sacrificial pyre to Heaven.

ʻ有 Yu. To have, to possess; to be, to be in possession; often forms the past tense; in replies, is equivalent to yes, I have, it is; to attain, to get; farther, and, also, more, in addition: sometimes used for o² in the coll.: COM., [12]ʻiu ˛si, sometimes; [13]ʻiu aing² limited in amount; [14]ʻiu ëüng² useful; [15]ʻiu ˛sing, or ʻiu ė² purposely; [16]ʻiu ˛ü, overplus; [17]ʻiu ˛ming ˛u sik˛ the mere name without the reality; ʻiu ʻüng ˛u ˛meu, has strength but is no schemer; ʻiu ʻsü ˛u ˛chüng, a beginning without an end—left half done; [18]ʻiu ˛ngiong chai² ˛siéng, (just as) I said before.

ʻ黝 Yu. A dark green, a sort of invisible green; to smear and blacken.

˛蹂 Jou. To tread, as a beast; steps of animals, foot-tracks, traces; to tread over; to dampen grain to free it from the chaff; to winnow: [19]˛iu ʻchiéng, to trample; [20]˛iu leng² the trampling of animals; *met.*, devastated, as by rebels.

˛揉 Jou. Also read ʻiu; used for the next: to bend, to make pliable, to twist, to contort; to make wood supple by heat; to subdue, to bring under.

˛柔 Jou. Wood that is pliable, easy to bend; easy, flexible, not stiff; complaisant, condescending; compliant, meek, gentle, soft, mild,

[1]窓牖 [2]牖民 [3]循循善誘 [4]引誘 [5]誘惑 [6]莠言 [7]稂莠 [8]酉月 [9]酉時 [10]酉雞 [11]酉時尾 [12]有時○ [13]有限 [14]有用 [15]有心 [16]有餘 [17]有名無實 [18]有言在先 [19]蹂踐 [20]蹂躪

bland; fawning, flattering; tender, as budding plants; to show kindness, to be gentle with; to cause to submit, to subdue by kindness: [1]*˓iu ‛wong ˓ing*, to act kindly toward strangers from afar; COM., [2]*˓iu ‛niong*, gentle, yielding; [3]*˓iu yok˒* soft and weak; [4]*˓iu ˓ching*, complaisant feelings, as of a married couple.

蚘 ˓Yu. Used in the name [5]*‛ch‛i ˓iu*, a prince in the days of Hwangti. Read *˓hwi*: worms in the abdomen.

蝤 ˓Yu. The larvæ of a beetle: [6]*˓iu ˓chá*, long and white grubs which eat trees; *met.*, said of a graceful neck.

蝣 ˓Yu. Used with the last: ephemeridæ, flies which collect about offal: [7]*˓p‛eu ˓iu*, dung-flies.

斿 ˓Yu. The scollops on the edge or end of a flag; a fluttering of flags.

遊 ˓Yu. To ramble, to roam, to walk, to take a jaunt, to idle, to saunter; to travel incog., to go on a circuit; voyaging, traveling, absent: [8]*˓siéng ˓iu*, dead; COM., [9]*˓iu óh˒* go abroad to study, as the Siutsai do; [10]*˓iu taung˒* to vagabondize; [11]*˓iu ˓sang ngwang˒ ‛chwi*, to take excursions on the hills and water; [12]*˓iu ˓ká*, to saunter in the streets; [13]*˓iu ˓hung*, wandering ghosts; [14]*˓iu ‛ch‛iu hó˒ ˓hang*, idlers love leisure; [15]*ch‛ok˒ ˓iu*, an (idol) procession; [16]*˓iu kek˒* a lieutenant-colonel.

游 ˓Yu. Interchanged with the last: a tributary of the R. Hwai; to float, to drift, to swim; to travel, to rove, to go abroad; to go with the crowd; to take pleasure in, to enjoy one's self; satisfied, self-pleased, an air of content: [17]*˓iu ˓ming*, idle people.

滺 ˓Yu. Water flowing along with rapidity.

油 ˓Yu. A branch of the R. Pa, which flows into the Yangtsz east of Wuchang in Hupeh; oil, fluid grease; paint; oily, unctuous, fat, greasy; shining, sleek, glossy; easy, gliding; thick weather; cordial, agreeing; used as a verb; in the coll., to oil, to paint: COM., [18]*˓hwa ˓seng ˓iu*, peanut oil; *pok˒ ˓hó ˓iu*, essence of peppermint; [19]*˓iu ˓hwi*, putty; *˓iu pah˒* the whitest sort of lime; [20]*˓iu ch‛ek˒* paint and varnish; [21]*sioh˒ ˓iu*, petroleum; *‛meng ‛hwo ˓iu*, naphtha; *˓iu ˓ping*, an oil-can; *˓iu ˓tëng*, an oil-vessel made of a joint of bamboo; *˓iu ˓si*, the hair-spring of a watch; *˓iu ‛wang*, a pewter chandelier for burning oil; *˓iu lak˒ ˓hwa ‛hung*, oil, wax, flowers, and powder—necessary for a lady's toilet; COLL., *˓iu ne˒* stuck up with oil, greasy; *˓t‛ëng ˓iu*, wood-oil; *‛tiéng ˓iu*, to burn oil; *lóh˒ ˓iu ˓kwo*, to fall into the oil caldron (in hell); *˓iu ‛peng*, pork-fat, suet; *˓iu sioh˒ kwo˒* to paint one course; *˓iu ch‛oi˒ t‛ié˒ ˓tó ˓sing*, has an oily mouth and a razor heart.

[1]柔 軟 情 蠐 遊 蕩 水 魂 閒 擊 生 [20]油
遠 [3]柔 [5]蚩 [7]蜉 [9]遊 [11]遊 [12]遊 [14]遊 [15]出 [17]遊 油 漆
人 弱 蚘 蝣 學 山 街 手 遊 民 [19]油 [21]石
[2]柔 [4]柔 [6]蝤 [8]仙 [10]遊 玩 [18]遊 好 [16]遊 [18]花 灰 油

鮋 Yu. A small white fish, an eel (?): used for the coll., as in [1]iu ch'ié a fresh-water fish; the large ones are called chi ngü; [2]iu t'ëng, a small fish of a rank odor, abounding in fat.

[魚斿] Yu. A species of flat fish, with several antennæ, called in the coll. [3]iu ngü; sold in the markets in a dried form.

由 繇 Yu. The antecedents of a thing; a preposition, through, by, from; a way, a means; cause, instrument by which a thing is done; to serve of; from, or by permission of; to let, to permit, at liberty; to enter by; to pass through, as the hands of; to follow: [4]iu ch'ü, hence, therefore; [5]iu iu yong, gracefully, self-possessed; [6]ngwong iu, a cause; COM., [7]iu lai, heretofore, from the first; [8]iu t'iëng iu meng pok iu ing, it depends on Heaven and destiny, not on man; COLL., [9]iu chai nü, as you please, it rests with you; iu i hung, humor his whims; iu ngwai su ói as I desire; [10]mó lai iu, no reason for it; iu ch'ing kau së, from the near to the distant relatives—*scil.*, let your regards be portioned out.

郵 Yu. A post-house; a place for getting relays of horses and sending on dispatches; lodge for watching fields; to err, to mistake; very, exceedingly: [11]iu ik, a post-station.

酋 Yu. Spirits which have settled; wine after the fermentation is over; western regions; summer; to finish, to come to perfection; the end; valiant; accustomed to; a euphonic particle at the beginning of a sentence.

遒 Yu. To urge, to constrain, to press upon; a crowd, a throng; to exhaust, to carry to the utmost, to end, in which sense same as the last; brave, strong, unyielding; to bring together; to collect: [12]iu ing, a herald.

猶 Yu. Used for the next: a suspicious monkey; a lap-dog, a puppy; doubtful, suspecting; still, even; as if, like, alike, rather, same, resembling; thus, so: [13]iu ch'iä, still further; [14]iu yok, as if; [15]iu chü, a nephew; COM., [16]iu ëü pok kiok, doubting and undecided.

猷 Yu. A scheme, a plan; a drawing; to plot, to contrive; to draw, to make a likeness; a rule, a way, a mode of action; cheerful: [17]meu iu, a scheme; [18]ka iu, a fine plan.

蕕 Yu. A bad-smelling plant; stinking, fetid plants; the heavy smell of rotten wood.

蘨 Luxuriant, as vegetation, plants growing thick and abundantly.

1鮋趐 2鮋蟲 3鰟魚 4由此 5由由然 6原由 7由來 8由天由命不由人 9由在汝 10無來由 11郵驛 12遒人 13猶且 14猶若 15猶子 16猶豫不決 17謀猷 18嘉猷 ○

輶 ꜀Yu. A light carriage, like a curricle or chaise; light, trifling: [1]ʻtaik꜆ ꜀iu ꜀ñ ꜀mó, virtue light as a feather.

尤 ꜀Yu. Extraordinary, remarkable, exceeding; singular, strange; odd, differing; an adverb of comparison, very, excessively, still more; to exceed, to surpass; to dislike, to resent; a fault, a crime, in which sense same as the next: [2]꜀iu seng꜄ vastly more; [3]꜀iu e꜄ still more strange; [4]hau꜄ ꜀iu, to imitate, and exceed in, crime; [5]꜀iu uk꜆ a beautiful woman; [6]꜀iu ꜀ing, to hate people; ꜀k'iéng ꜀iu, a fault; ꜀ch'i ꜀iu, a prince in Hwangti's times; COM., ꜀iu ꜀k'á, a district of Yenping prefecture in Fookien.

訧 ꜀Yu. A fault, a crime, an error, wickedness; a man's name.

疣 ꜀Yu. An excrescence, a protuberance; a tumor, a swelling; ganglionic swellings on the neck: [7]ʻchwoi꜄ ꜀iu, an excrescence; *met.*, superfluities.

攸 ꜀Yu. To go on the water, to dart through the water; a place; a relative pronoun, who, what, that which; a euphonic particle; far, distant, long: [8]꜀iu ꜀yong, darting, as fish; *met.*, cheerfully; siong꜄ ꜀iu, to select a son-in-law; ꜀kung ʻchü ꜀iu ꜀heng, what the good man practices.

悠 ꜀Yu. To think of, to grieve for; discontented, mournful, sorry; boundless, remote; to go far; leisurely: [9]꜀iu ꜀iu, vast; perpetual; [10]꜀iu ʻkiu, a long time; ꜀iu ꜀chui, think about it!

(231) Ka.

嘉 ꜀Chia. Good, excellent; to praise, to commend, to eulogize; to make happy, to rejoice in: [11]ʻk'ó ꜀ka, commendable; [12]꜀ka ʻngeu, a happy union; COM., [13]꜀ka k'eng꜄ the emperor Kiaking, A. D. 1796–1821.

佳 ꜀Chia. Beautiful, fine, good of its kind, nice; excellence, goodness: COM., [14]꜀ka kwo꜄ a fine sentence; ꜀ka ꜀ing ꜀chai ʻchü, a beauty and a man of talent (married); [15]꜀ka ꜀ki, the happy time—a wedding; COLL., chauk꜆ ꜀ka, beautiful, fine.

加 ꜀Chia. To add to, to superadd, or place upon; to confer on; advanced, as officers are; to charge, as interest: COM., [16]꜀ka ʻkeng, to add and subtract, to increase and diminish; [17]꜀ka chói꜄ to increase guilt; [18]꜀ka k'wak꜆ to widen; [19]꜀ka ꜀kwang, to promote in office; [20]꜀ka ꜀sang, interest of 3 cash on 10 per month; [21]꜀ka tuëng꜄ increased weight, as of debt; [22]꜀ka ꜀cheng, or [23]꜀ka ꜀t'iéng, to add to, to increase; ꜀ka ek꜆ pwoi꜄ to duplicate; ꜀ka ka꜄ or ꜀ka ꜀chiéng, to add to the price, to offer more; COLL., ꜀ka pwoi꜄ auk, twice as wicked! ꜀ka ʻkeng cheu꜄ ꜀siäng ꜀hwa, (if the buyer) adds and (the seller) falls the bargain will be closed.

珈 ꜀ Gems on the hair-pin of a head-dress; a sort of brow-band or fillet.

1 德輶如毛　2 尤甚　3 尤異　4 效尤　5 尤物　6 尤人　7 贅疣　8 攸然　9 悠悠　10 悠久　11 可嘉　12 嘉偶　13 嘉慶　14 佳句　15 佳期　16 加減　17 加罪　18 加闊　19 加冠　20 加三　21 加重　22 加增　23 加添

家 ꜀Chia. What is within doors; a household, a family; a home, a dwelling; domestic, domesticated; title of a husband or master of a family; term applied to some dignitaries; the country, the government; to dwell, to live at; a sect, a profession or class; a suffix of nouns to denote persons: COM., 1꜀*ka kié*ʼ domestic expenses; 2꜀*ka loi*2 the burden of (supporting) the family; 3꜀*ka ngiék*꜁ property; *pai*2 ꜀*ka*, to squander a patrimony; 4*ch'ok*꜁ ꜀*ka*, to become a bonze or nun; 5*tó*2 ꜀*ka*, Tauists; 6꜀*i* ꜀*ka*, a physician; 7꜂*ü* ꜀*ka*, unprofessional practitioners; 8꜀*ka* ꜂*ing*, domestics, attendants; 9꜀*ka* ʻ*tiong*, the head of a family; 10*hak*꜁ ꜀*ka*, the whole family; 11*chëü*2 ꜀*ka*, self, myself; *tai*2 ꜀*ka*, all of us, you sirs! 12꜀*ka hoʼ* or ꜀*ka* ꜂*ngiéng*, my father; ꜀*ka paik*꜁ my elder uncle; ꜀*ka* ꜀*ku*, paternal aunts; ꜀*ch'ing* ꜀*ka*, fathers-in-law; COLL., ꜀*ka* ꜀*si*, utensils, tools; ꜀*ka* ꜂*hwo chó*ʼ made for family use—of superior quality.

麚 ꜀Chia. A buck, the male of deer: ʻ*kiu* ꜀*ka*, an elk with a short neck.

豭 猳 ꜀Chia. A boar, a local term for pig; hogs are called ꜀*ka* in Corea and Chihli.

葭 ꜀Chia. A bulrush or sedge; the Arundo, from the reeds of which musical pipes may be made: 13꜀*ka* ꜀*hu*, the white, medullary lining of sedges; *met.*, distantly related; lightly esteemed.

膠 ꜀Chiao. Read ꜀*keu*; coll. ꜀*ka*: glue, glutinous or adhesive jellies, viscid gums; to glue; glued or sticking together: 14ʻ*chwi* ꜀*ka*, glue; 15꜂*ngü* ꜀*ka*, isinglass; 16꜀*ó* ꜀*ka*, mule-skin jelly—used medicinally; ꜀*ka kak*꜁ to glue fast; *t'aung*ʼ ꜀*ka k'ó*ʼ the gluing has loosened.

交 ꜀Chiao. Read ꜀*kau*; sometimes used for the coll. ꜀*ka*, as in ꜀*ka hoʼ* to deliver or intrust to; 17꜀*ka k'ëük*꜁ ꜀*i*, deliver it to him; 18꜀*ka chëü*ʼ ꜀*pau*, a straw-bag to cook rice in; ꜀*ka* ꜂*ung ch'ioh*꜁ a kind of ornamented matting.

꜀*Ka.* A coll. word: to cut, to clip with shears: ꜀*ka* ꜀*tó*, shears; ꜀*ka* ꜀*tó* ʻ*kiăng*, small shears, scissors; ꜀*ka tói*ʼ ꜂*peng*, to cut into two parts.

꜀*Ka.* A coll. word, as in ꜀*ka* ꜀*lang* ꜀*k'i*, slanting, oblique, tilted, as a dilapidated house.

假 ʻChia. False, fictitious, illusive; feigned, hypocritical, unreal, simulated; a pretext, to pretend; supposing, if, because; to suppose, to instance; to borrow, to get an accommodation, to avail of; great: also read *ka*ʼ, q.v.: 19ʻ*ka* ꜂*ü*, if, for instance; 20ʻ*ka chiá*ʼ to borrow; in the coll., fictitious, as a story; COM., 21ʻ*ka* ʻ*ch'iu*, to borrow help, to do by proxy; 22ʻ*ka* ʻ*sü*, if, supposing that; ʻ*ka pok*꜁ *tá*2 to pretend not to have gained promotion, as ʻ*Sieu* ꜀*hwong* ꜀*k'ing* did; 23ʻ*ka* ʻ*hó*, hypocritical; ʻ*ka mó*2 to feign, to assume; ʻ*ka* ꜂*ch'iong*, a lath and plaster wall; ʻ*ka hwoʼ* spurious goods; COLL., ʻ*ka paik*꜁

1家計 3家業 5道家 7儒家 9家長 11自家 13葭莩 15魚膠 17交乞 注包 20假借 22假使
2家累 4出家 6醫家 8家人 10合家 12家父 14水膠 16阿膠 伊 18交 19假如 21假手 23假好

ching, to pretend to know the real facts; *'ka miäng'* a fictitious horoscope, as used in betrothals; *'ka che' ,sing ,t'au ,tó huk,* pretend to be extremely honest, yet steal a Budh! *met.*, a boastful, but false, claim to honesty.

絞 Chiao. Read *'kieu;* coll. *'ka:* to twist, to bind a cord about; to strangle with a cord: [1]*'ka 'king 'king tioh,* twist it about tightly; [2]*'ka 'chi,* an apparatus for twisting the strands in making a rope; [3]*'ka 'si,* to strangle to death.

'Ka. A coll. word, as in *'ka 'chau,* a flea.

'Ka. A coll. word, as in *'ka 'kě,* to annoy, to disturb, as by jabbering; obstinate; *,i 'chiä ,něng 'ka 'kě,* that man is perverse!

斝 斚 Chia. A three-legged goblet with an ear, and made of stone, holding six pints; it was used in the Shang dynasty: [4]*'k'wang 'ka haiu' sëü'* have washed the goblets and wait to converse (with you)—a phrase on invitation cards.

價 賈 Chia. The price or value of a thing; the 2nd, read *'ka,* is a surname; also read *'ku,* q. v.: COM., [5]*ka' ,chiěng,* the price; [6]*,sing ka'* one's name, reputation; [7]*,si ka'* the current price; [8]*'kong ka'* to ask (a high) price; [9]*pok, nê ka'* "not two prices"—used on signboards; [10]*,u ka' ,chi 'pó,* beyond price, invaluable; [11]*'k'i ka'* to raise the price; COLL., *ka' ,siäng,* the price demanded; *,lě ka' 'ma ka'* the value of an ass or horse; *met.*, an exorbitant price; [12]*lóh, ka'* or *t'ok, ka'* the price has fallen.

假 Chia. Leave of absence, a furlough: also read *'ka,* q.v.: COM., [13]*'kó' ka'* to apply for a furlough; [14]*,sieu ka'* expiration of a furlough; COLL., [15]*pong' ka'* to give a vacation; [16]*,k'wi ka'* to open shop at the close of the holidays (on the 5th of the 1st month); [17]*kó' pang' ka'* to ask for a furlough on account of sickness.

駕 Chia. A horse in the harness; to harness a carriage; a chariot for the sovereign's use; to drive or manage a horse; to sit in a carriage; to mount, to ascend; to embark, to go aboard; to avail of; a title of respect, as if addressing one in a chariot, sir, your honor: used in the coll. for divining-blocks: COM., [18]*ka' ,peng,* demise of the emperor; [19]*,chong ka'* or *,tai ka'* sir! your honor! [20]*seng' ka'* his majesty, his godship; *,sui ka'* followers of an officer or idol; *,ló ka'* I trouble you, sir! COLL., *ka' ,pwi,* divining-blocks; *,sang siäng' ka'* three lucky throws of the blocks; *'nü 'hó twai' ka'* you're very pompous indeed!

架 Chia. A stand; a press, a rack, a case; a dumb-waiter; an open frame on which things are placed; a scaffolding or frame-work; to lay on a frame; to fend, to ward off; used in the coll. as a classifier of bedsteads, closets, clocks, large money-scales, ladders, balustrades,

---

1 絞緊緊着 2 絞子 3 絞死 4 盥斝候敍 5 價錢 6 身價 7 時價 8 講價 9 不二價 10 無價之寶 11 起價 12 落價 13 告假 14 消假 15 放假 16 開假 17 告病假 18 駕崩 19 尊駕 20 聖駕

&c.: COM., [1]*'pek, ka'* a pencil-stand; [2]*'sek, che' ka'* a cross; [3]*,chü ka'* a book-case; [4]*,hwa ka'* a flower-stand; [5]*,i ka'* a clothes-horse; [6]*ka' 'k'i,* to raise, as a pole on forks; [7]*'tak, ka'* to erect a frame or scaffold; COLL., *meng' ka'* a wash-stand; *,ch'iong ka' kwo' k'ó'* to fend off with a spear.

檟 Chia. A shrub resembling the tea plant; its infusion was formerly used as a beverage.

嫁 Chia. To marry a husband; to send a bride to her husband's house; to cast imputations on another, to implicate: [8]*ka' hwo'* to bring evil on one; COM., [9]*ka' ch'ü'* to give in marriage and to marry; [10]*ka' ,chong,* a dowry; [11]*ch'ok, ka'* to become a bride; [12]*chüng' ka'* a slave-girl who goes with the bride; COLL., [13]*ka' sai'* or *ka' ,nüng k'ó'* married to a husband; *ka' ,kié t'eng' ,kié ,puó,* the hen flies with the cock—the wife follows the husband's fortunes.

稼 Chia. To sow or plant grain; *met.*, farming; the spike of grain; wild cerealia: [14]*ka' saik,* to sow and reap; [15]*hok, ka'* to learn husbandry.

教 Chiao. Read *kau';* coll. *ka':* to instruct, to teach, to show how: *ka' tó'* or [16]*ka' hong'* to instruct; [17]*ka' ,chü,* to teach (pupils) to read; [18]*ka' ,chá,* to teach school; *ka' ,tu tá' p'ah, ,sa ho'* teach an apprentice to strike his master; *met.*, the initiated injuring his teacher.

,Ka. A coll. word, as in *,ka 'kung,* the common earthworm.

,Ka. A coll. word, as in *,ka ,lau,* to roll about; *,ka ,lau ,hing,* the head swimming from dizziness.

,Ka. A coll. word, as in *,ka ,ka kieu'* a clamor of voices, the cawing of crows.

,Ka. A coll. word, as in *,ka lak, ,ch'a,* crossed, intersecting, as two sticks or lines.

咬 Yao. Read *'ngau;* used in the coll for *ka²:* to gnaw, to bite, to masticate, to chew, as a cud; to close the teeth firmly: [19]*ka² ,nga,* or *ka² 'ngai,* to gnash the teeth; [20]*,song ka²* to bite one another, as dogs; *ka² 'tong,* or *ka² taung²* to bite off; [21]*ka² sioh, ch'oi'* to bite off a mouthful, to give a bite.

(232) KÁ.

街 Chia. A street in a town, a thoroughfare, a market where people pass: COM., [22]*,ká ch'é'* a market-place; *,t'iéng ,ká,* streets near the imperial palace; *sek, ché' ,ká,* cross-streets; [23]*,ká tó'* a thoroughfare; *,ká so'* shop-accounts; COLL., *,ká ,tong,* a street; *,t'ung ,ká,* the whole street; *,ká ,t'au haéng' kaék,* heads of streets and corners of alleys—*scil.*, are noisy; *,pá ,ká,* displayed in the streets, as goods; *met.*, to sit in street-doors, as women do.

魨 Read *,tong;* used in the *Paik, ,Ing* for the coll. *,ká,* as in *,ká ,ngü,* a fish with a large belly, hence called

[1]筆架 [2]十字架 [3]書架 [4]花架 [5]衣架 [6]架起 [7]搭架 [8]嫁禍 [9]嫁娶 [10]嫁妝 [11]出嫁 [12]從嫁 [13]嫁使 [14]稼穡 [15]學稼 [16]教訓 [17]教書 [18]教齋 [19]咬牙 [20]相咬 [21]咬一嘴 [22]街市 [23]街道

twai² *pok*, *‚ká; met.*, a corpulent person.

‚Ká. A coll. word, as in *‚ká ‚ká kieu*ʼ (or *ká*ʼ *ká*ʼ *kieu*ʼ), to cry, as a child, to disturb others by loud talking.

ʻ解 Chieh. Read ʻ*kai;* coll. ʻ*ká:* to open, to loose, to untie, to unbind; to release, as one bound; to explain, to make plain, to comment; to dispel, as sorrow: [1]ʻ*ká* ʻ*pong*, to loose one's hands from behind his back; ʻ*ká ‚loi*, to untie a knot; [2]ʻ*ká ‚k*ʻ*wang*, or ʻ*ká ‚sëng*, to loosen, to relax; [3]ʻ*ká siok*, to explain; [4]ʻ*ká chio*ʼ to comment; annotations; ʻ*ká mong*² or [5]ʻ*ká ‚sing ‚chieu*, to dispel melancholy; [6]ʻ*k*ʻ*wong*ʼ ʻ*ká*, or ʻ*ká k*ʻ*wong*ʼ to persuade, to expostulate with; [7]ʻ*ká k*ʻ*ak*, to quench thirst; [8]ʻ*ká* ʻ*k*ʻ*au*, to avert threatened evil; [9]ʻ*ká má*² *‚k*ʻ*wi*, can't untie it.

解ʼ 觧ʼ Chieh. To forward, to transmit, to hand over to; to send under arrest; to exclude; to transfer an officer to another post: also read ʻ*kai* and *hai*², q. v.: COM., [10]*ká*ʼ *k*ʻ*wo*ʼ to pay in the salt-revenue; [11]*ká*ʼ *siong*² to send up for trial; [12]*ká*ʼ *‚kung ‚chong*, to forward the materiel of an army; [13]*ak*, *ká*ʼ a criminal's guard; [14]*ká*ʼ *‚ngwong*, first of the Kŭjin graduates.

疥ʼ 癬 Chieh. Read *kai*ʼ; coll. *ká*ʼ: the 2nd is a vulgar character: a kind of dry itch, called [15]*‚sai ká*ʼ—said to follow the common itch; [16]*‚sang ká*ʼ to have the itch—a country phrase.

廨ʼ Chieh. Read ʻ*kai* and *kai*ʼ in the dictionaries: a hall or suite of rooms in an officer's palace; an official hospice; rooms for subordinate officers, called [17]*‚kung ká*ʼ.

‚Ká. A coll. word, as in *‚ká* ʻ*ting*, or *‚ká* ʻ*teng*, or *‚ká* ʻ*ting sië*ʼ above, upon; aloft, in the upper story.

*Ká*². A coll. word, as in *ká*² *‚sung*, to tow a ship.

(233) Kaĕ.

呼ʼ Hu. Read *‚hu;* used in the coll. for *kaĕ*ʼ: to call out, to bawl, to cry out, to vociferate; to call out to: [18]ʻ*lá kaĕ*ʼ is calling out; [19]*mŏh*, *kaĕ*ʼ don't cry out; [20]*kaĕ*ʼ *kaĕ*ʼ *kieu*ʼ or *kaĕ*ʼ ʻ*hwang ‚t*ʻ*ièng*, to vociferate, to bawl; *kaĕ*ʼ *keu*ʼ to cry for help; [21]*kaĕ*ʼ *chó*ʼ ʻ*hwang*, to bawl (like) raising a rebellion; *kaĕ*ʼ *paik*, *‚kang ch*ʻ*io*ʼ *‚tu ‚t*ʻ*iăng kièng*ʼ to scream so as to be heard by (the people of) eight houses!

(234) Kaĕh.

Kaĕh,. A coll. word, as in *‚kĕ kaĕh*, to make a noise like one suffocated or strangled; to hiccough: *kaĕh*, *sioh*, *‚siăng*, to utter a choking sound; a suppressed cry, as of a fowl when seized.

(235) Kaĕk.

角ʼ Chiao. Read *kauk*, in the dictionaries, but commonly read *kaĕk*, in Foochow: a horn; to dispute, to test one's strength with another; to butt, to gore; horny, hard; a corner, a point, an angle; a protuberance or jutting out; a tuft

[1]解 [3]解 [5]解 解 口 [10]解 [12]解 [13]押 [15]沙 [17]公 [19]莫 叫
綁 說 心 [7]解 [9]解 課 軍 解 疥 廨 呼 [21]呼
[2]解 [4]解 焦 渴 賣 [11]解 裝 [14]解 [16]生 [18]禮 [20]呼 做
寬 註 [6]勸 [8]解 開 上 〇 元 疥 呼 呼 反

of hair; a headland, a cape; a wine-jar; wing of an army; one of the 28 constellations, *α* and *ε* in Virgo; the 148th radical: in the coll., a quarter, as of a dollar: [1]*ʻkaëk, ʻti,* to push with the horns; [2]*ʻchung kaëk,* tuft of hair worn before the age of puberty; [3]*ˌkung ˌung ek, kaëk,* an official dispatch; COM., [4]*ˌngu kaëk,* ox-horns; [5]*kaëk, ʻkʻeu,* to wrangle; [6]*ˌtʻiéng ˌpiéng ʻhai kaëk,* remote regions; COLL., *chʻio˒ kaëk,* corners of a house; *kaëk, ˌhwang,* a quarter-dollar piece; *se˒ kaëk,* square, four-cornered; *lĕk, kaëk,* hexagonal; *ˌsang ˌchiéng kaëk,* a corner, a projecting point; *ʻhü kĕk, kaëk,* in that corner.

雄, Hsiüng. Read *ˌhüng;* sometimes used in the coll. for *kaëk,:* a cock bird; masculine, male of certain animals and insects, as well as of birds: [7]*ʻmó kaëk,* female and male; [8]*ˌkié kaëk,* a chicken-cock, a rooster; [9]*ˌngu kaëk,* a bull; *ʻyong ˌtü kaëk,* (she) keeps a paramour.

(236) Kaëng.

Kaëng˒. A coll. word, as in *kaëng˒ kaëng˒* to bawl, to vociferate harshly; *kaëng˒ ʻkʻi kaëng˒* or *kaëng˒ ʻkʻi ˌhó ˌlĕng ˌkʻĕng,* to bawl at the top of one's voice.

共², Kung. Read *këüng˒;* coll. *kaëng²:* a preposition, with, by, to; for, in behalf of; with, in addition to; an adverb, as, like to: [10]*kaëng² ʻngwai ˌchá kʻó˒* go with me; *kaëng² ʻnü ʻkong,* I say to you; [11]*kaëng² ˌi tói˒ ʻchʻiu,* lend him a helping hand; *kaëng² ʻnü chó˒* do it for you; [12]*kaëng² ʻkiăng,* to tend a child; *kaëng² ˌchuí sioh, yong²* the same as this; *kaëng² ˌnĕng hung˒* to inform one; *kaëng² chʻoi˒ chioh, kwo˒* "borrow of the mouth"—to stint one's self in eating.

(237) Kah.

格, Ko. Read *kaik,;* coll. *kah,:* a pattern, a model, a rule; ruled lines placed under paper to write by: [13]*kah, sek,* one's bearing, mannerism; [14]*kaung˒ kah,* to humble one's self; [15]*ˌung kah,* a model for essays; *niăh, ʻchiă kah, sek,* to stand on one's dignity, pretentious; *kah, ʻngang ʻchai* (spoken *ʻkang ʻlang ʻchai*), paper ruled in squares.

隔, Ko. Read *kaik,;* coll. *kah,:* to separate or divide, as by a partition; to interpose; set apart, separated, sundered; next to, adjoining, neighboring: [16]*kah, piăh,* (usually spoken *ˌkang piăh,*), adjoining; *kah, taung˒* kept for a (subsequent) meal; [17]*kah, ˌmang,* to pass the night at; kept over night, as food; [18]*kah, sioh, nik,* interval of a day; [19]*kah, tek, hwong²* far removed, distant; *ˌing ˌyong na² kah, sioh, ˌtʻüng ʻchai,* the invisible and visible worlds are separated by only a thickness of paper.

Kah,. A coll. word: to test the weight, as by weighing with other scales: *kah, chʻeng˒* test the steelyards; *ˌtó kʻó˒ kah, kʻang˒ ˌchiă,* take it away and test it and see.

Kah,. A coll. word: mixed, interlocking: *kah, naung˒* interlaced confusedly, in a complete snarl.

[1]角抵 [2]總角 [3]公文一角 [4]牛角 [5]角口 [6]天邊海角 [7]雌雄 [8]雞雄 [9]牛雄 [10]共我齊去 [11]共伊對手 [12]共仔 [13]格式 [14]降格 [15]文格 [16]隔壁 [17]隔暝 [18]隔一日 [19]隔的遠

*Kah*₂. A coll. word: a close apartment in a boat; a bunch, a parcel, as of paper or books: *kah*₂ *meng*ʾ the top of the apartment.

*Kah*₂. A coll. word, as in *kah*₂ ʻ*k*ʻ*i*, to pry up or open; *kah*₂ ,*mwong*, to pry a door open; *kah*₂ *siék*₂ to break in two by prying.

*Kah*₂. A coll. word: distress, grief: *kah*₂ *sek*, to faint under great distress; *kah*₂ ,*tiéng*, crazed with grief; *á*ʾ *kah*₂ *pang*ʾ will grieve himself sick; *ang*ʾ *mang*ʾ *kah*₂ to grieve secretly.

*Kah*₂. A coll. word, as in *kah*₂ *meng*ʾ separated, estranged, as by a quarrel: *ng*ʾ ,*t*ʻ*ëng tioh*₂ *kah*₂ must not be offended—a polite phrase to a departing guest.

*Kah*₂. A coll. word, as in *sek*, *che*ʾ *kah*₂ transverse, crosswise, crossed, as two lines or sticks.

(238) **Káh.**

*Káh*₂. A coll. word: a rumbling and derangement of the bowels; to mutter, to feel angry: *pok*, ʻ*ló* ʻ*tié kih*₂ *kih*₂ *káh*₂ *káh*₂ the bowels in a very disordered state; ,*i* ,*sing* ʻ*lá ko*ʾ ʻ*lá káh*₂ ʻ*ngwai*, still vexed at me in his heart.

*Káh*₂. A coll. word; a brogue for *kek*₂: to carry under the arm; tight, small, contracted: *k*ʻ*á*ʾ ,*i káh*₂ *kwo*ʾ ,*li*, clasp him (the child) under the arm and bring him over here; *kóh*, *lóh*, *a*ʾ *k*ʻ*ak*, *káh*₂ (the garment) is too small under the arm.

(239) **Kai.**

皆 ,Chieh. All alike, uniform, things of the same sort; all, altogether; used after a recital of items, or nouns of multitude, as the sign of the plural: ¹,*kai* ʻ*iu*, all are or have; ²,*kai pok*, *kik*, none equal to, unequaled; ³,*kai* ,*yong*, all thus, all the same.

偕 ,Chieh. Used for the preceding: to accompany, to take along with one, as a parent takes his child; associated, in connection with; all at once, together: ⁴,*kai* ,*kai*, strong, robust; ⁵,*kai* ʻ*ló*, growing old together, as husband and wife; ⁶,*kai tá*ʾ with my younger brother—a phrase used on cards.

階 堦 ,Chieh. Steps, especially the stone ones at the door; the ascent to a hall, a flight of stairs; a grade, a degree, a rank; gradation; a source or cause of some evil; to rise, to emulate: ⁷,*kai ngek*, a step, gradation in office; ⁸,*kwang* ,*kai*, an official grade; ⁹,*kai* ʻ*siéng*, moss on stone steps; ¹⁰,*tai* ,*kai*, your house; ¹¹,*kai* ,*chiu*, a prefecture in Kansuh.

荄 ,Chieh. Roots; a kind of cress growing in marshes: ¹²,*kong* ,*kai*, the roots of plants.

喈 ,Chieh. The melody of birds; the sound of bells and drums, harmony heard at a distance; the soughing of the wind: ¹³,*kai* ,*kai*, birds singing.

---

1 皆有 2 皆不及 3 皆然 4 偕偕 5 偕老 6 偕弟 7 階級 8 官階 9 階蘚 10 台階 11 階州 12 根荄 13 喈喈

該 ꜀Kai. An agreement, an enlisting contract; to connect, to prepare, to arrange; fit, proper, just, what ought to be or is right; necessary, permissible, or convenient; deserving; full, abundant; the said, the, that, the aforesaid, the foregoing, what has been mentioned: [1]꜀*kai* ꜀*ing*, that man; COM., [2]꜀*kai* ꜀*tong*, or ꜀*ing* ꜀*kai*, ought, proper, just; [3]꜀*kai* '*kong*, ought to say it; COLL., [4]'*chiăng*' ꜀*kai*, just right or proper; *ng*' ꜀*kai*, ought not; [5]꜀*kai* '*si*, ought to die, an ejaculation, alas! dreadful! ꜀*kai* *tang*' in error! what a blunder! ꜀*mó* ꜀*kai* *chai*' uncertain, not to be depended on; ꜀*kai* ꜀*chó* '*chiă* *so*' ought to meet this fate.

垓 ꜀Kai. Interchanged with the next: a bank, a boundary, circuit, limit; to guard or re-enforce a frontier; a hundred millions: [6]꜀*kiêng* ꜀*kai*, the wide world; [7]꜀*chung* ꜀*kai*, high lands.

陔 ꜀Kai. Also read ꜀*hai*: a step, a grade, a succession, an order; a bank or terrace: [8]꜀*sang* ꜀*kai*, (an altar) with three terraces; [9]'*kiu* ꜀*kai*, the nine ascents; the imperial domain.

湝 ꜀Chieh. As in [10]꜀*kai* ꜀*kai*, the murmuring of streams flowing together; cold; incessant rain.

賅 ꜀ Unusual, strange, remarkable: [11]꜀*ki* ꜀*kai*, rare, uncommon.

꜀*Kai*. A coll. word, as in ꜀*kiê* ꜀*kai*, a fowl's crop; *tëük*꜀ ꜀*kai*, to stuff a chicken's crop—*scil.*, to make it weigh more; *twai*' ꜀*kai*, a large swelling on the front of one's neck; *söük*꜀ ꜀*kai*, a sluggish crop, one that does not digest.

改 'Kai. To change, to alter; to exchange; to reform, to do better; to correct, to amend, as a composition: in the coll. read '*kwi*, q.v.: COM., [12]'*kai* *yong*' or '*kai* *sek*꜀ to alter the form or pattern; [13]'*kai* *ka*' to marry another husband; [14]'*kai* *kwo*' to amend, to reform; [15]'*kai* ꜀*tu* *pek*꜀ *ngiék*꜀ to change one's employment; [16]'*kai* *piéng*' to to change, to do better; [17]'*kai* ꜀*ki*, to change the appointed time; [18]'*kai* *wang*' ꜀*mwong* ꜀*lü*, "alter the doors"—rise to a higher position.

解 'Chieh. To split a horn in two; to open, to take off, or apart; to cut up, to sever at the joints; to dissipate, to disperse; scattered; to explain, to narrate, to make plain, to comment; a commentary, a meaning, an explanation; to stop, to cease, to do away with the effects of; a trace: also read *ká*', and in the coll. '*kă*, q. v.: [19]'*kai* *t'wak*꜀ to let go, to escape from; COM., [20]*k'wong*' '*kai*, or '*kai* *k'wong*' to persuade, to restrain; *pok*꜀ '*kai*, can't discern (his purpose); [21]'*kai* ꜀*wong* *sek*꜀ *kiék*꜀ to relinquish false charges and settle the quarrel; '*kai* *tuk*꜀ to disperse bad humors.

[1]該人 [2]該當 [3]該講 [4]正該 [5]該死 [6]兼垓 [7]崇垓 [8]三陔 [9]九陔 [10]湝湝 [11]奇賅 [12]改樣 [13]改嫁 [14]改過 [15]改圖別業 [16]改變 [17]改期 [18]改換門閭 [19]解脫 [20]勸解 [21]解冤釋結

福州方言拼音字典

戒 ʼ Chieh. Interchanged with the next: a boundary, a limit; a region; to warn, to caution; to guard against; to inform or announce to; to beware of, to refrain from; to observe a regimen; to cure of the use of; injunctions, precepts, inhibitions: ¹ʻ*hwak*, *kai*ʼ to restrain by penalties; rules for a regimen; COM., ²*kai*ʼ ꜀*teu*, prohibitions; ³*kai*ʼ ʻ*chi*, a thumb-ring; ⁴*kai*ʼ *sak*꜀ avoid taking animal life; ⁵ʻ*king kai*ʼ to caution, to beware of; ⁶꜀*chai kai*ʼ *muk*꜁ *ük*꜁ "fast, abstain, bathe"—a notice posted on special occasions; ⁷*seu*ʼ *kai*ʼ "receive the injunctions"—Budhist initiation by a brand on the head; COLL., *kai*ʼ *a*ʼ *ch'ëü*ʼ beware of the second (offence); *kai*ʼ *ch'ioh*꜁ a ferule.

誡 ʼ Chieh. Rule of conduct, precepts, warnings, orders, injunctions; to deter by citing the penalty; to exhort to desist, to prohibit: *kó*ʼ *kai*ʼ to give good advice; COM., ⁸*sek*꜁ *kai*ʼ the Ten Commandments; ⁹*ting ek*꜁ *kai*ʼ *paik*꜁ rebuking one restrains a hundred; ¹⁰*tai*ʼ ꜀*ting* ʻ*sieu kai*ʼ grave offences are to be punished, trivial ones to be reproved.

悈 ʼ Chieh. To bid, to charge, to urge on one's attention. Read *kek*꜁: urgent. Read *k'aik*꜁: alarmed; self-willed, headstrong.

价 ʼ Chieh. Used for the next: one who serves, a waiting boy; great, good: COM., ¹¹*koi*ʼ *kai*ʼ your servant boy; ¹²ʻ*sieu kai*ʼ my valet.

介 ʼ Chieh. To assist, to attend upon; an attendant, a domestic, a valet, one who announces visitors; numeral of persons; for, because; great, good, firm, upright; a single animal, one alone; trifling, unimportant; a limit, frontier, border; conterminous, bordering on; the carapace of tortoises, &c.; armor, mail, a cuirass; to act, to represent: ¹³*ek*꜁ *kai*ʼ a single individual; ¹⁴꜀*ling kai*ʼ the scaly and shelly tribes; COM., ¹⁵*kai*ʼ *e*ʼ to take umbrage at, displeased through misapprehension.

尬 ʼ Chieh. To walk awry: ¹⁶꜀*kiëng kai*ʼ to walk irregularly and make no progress.

玠 ʼ Chieh. A kind of gem-tablet 12 inches long, in ancient times held in both hands when in the imperial presence.

蚧 ʼ Chieh. A red-spotted, scaly lizard, called ¹⁷*kak*꜁ *kai*ʼ found in damp places: used as an aphrodisiac medicine, also to expel bad humors.

芥 ʼ Chieh. The mustard plant: ¹⁸꜀*ch'iëng kai*ʼ small, trivial; COM., ¹⁹*kai*ʼ *ch'ai*ʼ the mustard plant; *kai*ʼ ꜀*lang ch'ai*ʼ a kind of coarse mustard—cultivated for greens; ²⁰*kai*ʼ *lak*꜁ or ²¹*kai*ʼ *mwak*꜁ ground mustard.

魪 ʼ Chieh. The sole fish, the plaice or flounder, also called ʻ*pi muk*꜁ ꜀*ngü*.

1 [illegible]
2 戒條
3 [illegible]
4 戒殺
5 [illegible]
6 [illegible]沐浴
7 受戒
8 十誡
9 懲一誡百
10 大懲小誡
11 貫价
12 小价
13 一介
14 鱗介
15 介意
16 尷尬
17 蛤蚧
18 纖芥
19 芥菜
20 芥辣
21 芥末

齘ʾ Chieh. Read *hai*ʾ in the dictionaries: to gnash the teeth; *met.*, furious, in a rage; the plates in mail armor.

疥ʾ Chieh. A scratch, a little sore, a scabbiness: *kak*, *kai*ʾ a scorbutic disease with scabs like scales; COM., [1]*kai*ʾ *ˌch'ong*, the itch—a refined term for *ˌkó ló*ʾ.

屆ʾ **届**ʾ Chieh. To reach to, to arrive at or tend towards in time or place; a limit, terminus, set time; the summit, the extreme point; unfortunately, unluckily: [2]*kai*ʾ *aing*ʾ expiration of the time; [3]*kai*ʾ *ˌki*, to come to the time, at the appointed time.

界ʾ Chieh. A division between fields, to mark separate ownership; a limit, boundary; frontier, terminus; to draw a line of separation, to limit; to sunder friends: COM., [4]*kai*ʾ *ˌpá*, landmarks; [5]*ˌkau kai*ʾ conterminous, adjoining; [6]*te*ʾ *kai*ʾ boundary of land; [7]*'a*ʾ *kai*ʾ the lower regions; *met.*, miserable ghosts; [8]*siong*ʾ *ˌtüng ha*ʾ *ˌsang kai*ʾ the upper, middle, and lower, worlds; [9]*sié*ʾ *kai*ʾ the world.

丐ʾ Kai. To ask alms, to demand, to beg; to give, to bestow: COM., [10]*k'ëük*, *kai*ʾ (coll. *k'ëük*, *siăh*,), a beggar; to beg; [11]*kai*ʾ *'siu*, king of the beggars.

葢ʾ **蓋**ʾ Kai. A kind of coarse grass used for thatch; a cover, a covering, a thatch, a roof; a canopy, a vault; to cover, to hide, to roof; to screen, to conceal literally and figuratively; to overshadow, to overtop; a conjunction, since, for, for that, now then: [12]*kai*ʾ *ˌing*, because that, since; COM., [13]*ˌkong kai*ʾ a jar-cover; [14]*ˌchiä kai*ʾ to cover, to overshadow; [15]*kai*ʾ *sié*ʾ *ˌu ˌsëng*, in all the world has no equal; [16]*'k'i kai*ʾ to build a house; COLL., [17]*kai*ʾ *'wang*, a covered bowl—also called *k'aing*ʾ *'wang*; [18]*ˌhwang kai*ʾ to remove and relay, as tiles on a roof; [19]*kai*ʾ *ˌt'au p'a*ʾ (or *ˌló*), a bridal veil; *kai*ʾ *sié*ʾ *ng*ʾ *tek*, wholly unappreciated in the world!—as one says ruefully.

犗ʾ A gelded ox; *met.*, strong, lusty, vigorous: [20]*kai*ʾ *ˌhing*, punishment of castration.

(240) Kaik.

隔ʾ **鬲**ʾ Ko. A partition, a bulkhead, something that stops the passage; a shelf; to obstruct, to intercept, to separate, to interpose, to hinder; separated, sundered; next to, neighboring: in the coll. read *kah*, and *ˌkang*, q. v.: COM., [21]*kaik*, *ˌch'iong*, a wall intervenes; *kaik*, *piék*, *ˌtó ˌniéng*, separated many years, as friends say on meeting; *kaik*, *'tu*, to divide into apartments; *kaik*, *twang*ʾ to cut off, to block, as a way.

---

1 疥瘡 2 屆限 3 屆期 4 界牌 5 交界 6 地界 7 下界 8 上中下三界 9 世界 10 乞丐 11 丐首 12 蓋因 13 缸蓋 14 遮蓋 15 蓋世無雙 16 起蓋 17 蓋碗 18 翻蓋 19 蓋頭帕 20 犗形 21 隔墻

鬲, Ko. A tripod, a kind of incense-caldron in temples; it contains about six ʻtau, or pecks; a heavy, earthen pot; to grasp, to take hold of; the 193d radical.

膈, Ko. The diaphragm, any thin membrane in bodies; the breast, the mind; a bell-frame: in the coll. read kʻaingʼ, q. v.: [1]kaik, mok, the midriff between the thorax and stomach; [2],hŭng kaik, the breast; COM., [3]kaik, sik, ,hwang oi[3] unable to eat and the stomach turned; [4]ʻlô ʻku kaik, ,sing ,siéng ,i pok, taik, consumption, dropsy, and inability to eat, even the genii can't cure!

挌, Ko. To strike, to box, to fight; to stop, to impede, to fend, to ward off; to repel, to beat back with the hand.

格, Ko. The spreading of branches; to come to, to reach; to examine, to sift or understand thoroughly; excellent, extraordinary; to influence, to cause; to attack; to change, to correct; to grow old; a mark, ruled lines to write by; a limit, a statute; a frame or stand; to advance, to rise; years having the "branch" ,ing in their cyclic name: in the coll. read kah, q. v.: [5],sing ,chi kaik, ,sü, a divine influence; [6]kaik, uk, to inquire into (the nature of) things; COM., [7]kaik, ngwoi[3] extraordinary, in excess of, beyond the usage or stipulation.

骼, The skeleton of a man or beast; the bones sticking out, lean.

革, Ko. The hides of animals after the hair is taken off; the human skin; to change, to put off, to renew, to molt; to cure or break off a habit; to degrade one from office; musical instruments of skin; defensive armor; leathern; a wing during molting; the 177th radical: COM., [8]kaik, chek, to deprive of office; [9]kaik, ,teu, a published dismissal; [10]kaik, ,a pʻiéngʼ to break off opium-smoking; COLL., [11]kaik, taung[3] ,kŭng, (the habit) broken off at the very roots; [12],chiéng ,liong kaik, his rations stopped; [13],miăng kaik, his name struck off—dismissed from the yamun.

緙, Ko. To piece, to seam; to form the woof, to weave.

翮, Ko. The quill or stem of a feather, a quill; interchanged with lik, meaning the hollow legs of a tripod: [14]hongʼ kaik, with rapid pinions; met., high resolves.

馘, 聝, To cut off the left ears, or the heads, as of prisoners, or those killed in battle; these were sent to court anciently as evidence of victory.

虢, The marks of a tiger's claws; gashes made in seizing its prey; a surname; the name of a state in the Tsin dynasty, now Yungyang district in the Kaifung prefecture, Honan.

結, Chieh. Read kiék, ; coll. kaik, : to tie, to fasten, to bind; tied, fixed: kaik, ,loi, to

[1]膈膜 [2]胸膈 [3]膈食翻胃 [4]癆蠱膈神仙醫不得 [5]神之格思 [6]格物〇 [7]格外〇 [8]革職〇 [9]革條 [10]革鴉片 [11]革斷筋 [12]錢糧革 [13]名 [14]革奮翮〇

tie a knot; [1]*kaik, taing'* to tie firmly; *kaik, 'si ˏloi,* to tie a dead (i. e. hard) knot; [2]*ch'ai kaik,* festoons; *kaik, 'ch'ai,* to festoon.

鍥 Ch'i. Read *kiĕk,*; coll. *kaik,*: a sickle, a reaping-hook, called also *ˏliĕng kaik,* and [3]*ˏliĕng ˏtó.*

(241) Kaing.

更 Kĕng. Read *ˏkeng;* in the coll. read *kaing'* and often used in epistles: a word of comparison, more, better, still, the more, the rather: [4]*kaing' 'hó,* the better; *kaing' kaing'* or [5]*ˏkeng kaing'* so much the more, the rather; [6]*kaing' ói'* to desire it all the more; [7]*kaing' ˏchié ˏlié,* to vary continually—becoming worse and worse; *kaing' ˏmó p'óh,* "the more without dregs"—said of one inveterately unprincipled.

慣 Kuan. Read *kwang';* coll. *kaing':* accustomed, addicted to, fixed in the habit of: [8]*kaing' sié'* habituated; [9]*chó' kaing'* used to doing it; [10]*ch'oi' 'kong kaing'* in the habit of talking so.

縣 Sien. A district, the fifth in order of territorial divisions; a district magistrate; the district city: COM., [11]*ˏti kaing'* a district magistrate; [12]*'siu kaing'* the principal district; [13]*ˏhung kaing'* or *kaing' ˏsing,* a deputy district magistrate; [14]*chek, ĕüng' kaing'* (graduates) appointed at once to the district magistracy; *ˏming kaing'* and [15]*au' ˏkwang kaing'* the two districts which embrace the city of Foochow; [16]*kaing' 'k'ó,* the district examinations. Read *ˏhiĕng,* and interchanged with *ˏhiĕng,* to hang up, to suspend.

(242) Kaiu.

搆 Kow. To drag, to pull; to scheme, to plot, to stir up, to implicate: [17]*kaiu' wong'* to contract a dislike for; [18]*kaiu' hwo'* to bring evil on one.

構 Kow. The truss of a roof; to roof over with beams; to construct; to unite, to join together; to copulate; finished, completed; to burst forth, to catch, as fire: [19]*kaiu' ˏching,* the procreative principle or action; COM., [20]*kiĕk, kaiu'* to contrive, as the plan of an essay.

購 Kow. To buy, to procure for sale; to barter; to hire one: [21]*kaiu' 'má,* or *kaiu' té'* to purchase, as goods for retail; *kaiu' siŏng'* to procure a clue to.

遘 Kow. Used for the next: to meet unexpectedly; to happen at, to bolt upon: *kaiu' nang'* to meet troubles.

覯 Kow. To meet with, to see suddenly; to occur, to happen; accidentally; to complete: *é' kaiu'* soon completed; to occur easily; soon caught, as a disease.

媾 Kow. To marry again, a second marriage; fondness, affection, love; to unite, sexual union: [22]*ˏhwong kaiu'* to marry again; *kaiu' hak,* or *ˏkau kaiu'* to cohabit.

---

[1]結 [3]鐮 [5]更 [7]更 勢 講 [12]首 [14]卽 官 [17]搆 [19]構 [21]購
有 刀 更 支 [9]做 慣 縣 用 縣 怨 精 買
[2]綵 [4]更 [6]更 離 慣 [11]知 [13]分 縣 [16]縣 [18]搆 [20]結 [22]婚
結 好 欲 [8]慣 [10]嘴 縣 縣 [15]侯 考 禍 構 媾

姤' Kow. Like the last: to meet with, to come in contact; the union of the sexes; the blending of the influences of heaven and earth.

垢' Kow. Dust grimed in, dirt, filth, scurf; impure, sordid, disgraceful: in the coll. read *'kau*, q. v.: [1]*,ting kaiu'* dirt; filthy, sordid.

詬' Kow. To shame, to disgrace one; to reproach, to taunt, to rail at; artful, unprincipled: [2]*no' kaiu'* to scold angrily; [3]*kaiu' choi'* to rail at, to abuse.

够' **夠'** Collected together; sufficient for use, enough; in excess, adequate, ample, filled up; completely, thoroughly.

彀' Kow. To stretch a bow to the full; archers, or bowmen; enough, full, in which sense used for the last: used in the coll. for *kau'*, q. v.: [4]*ik, kaiu'* to stretch a bow to its full power; COM., [5]*,neng kaiu'* and *pok, ,neng kaiu'* able and not able—used in imitation of the mandarin.

(243) **Kak.**

甲' Chia. The plumule or scaly covering of a growing seed; the budding of a plant; a sprout or bud; the first of the "ten stems"; *met.*, the first, number one, the head, excellent, the best—from the common use of the "stems" as ordinal numbers; to begin, to get the start of, to excel, to surpass; armor for the body, a cuirass, a corselet; military; applied to the hard, defensive coverings of animals, as the carapace of turtles, the elytra of beetles, the large scaly plates on some fishes; the finger-nails, &c.; graduates of the Chinsz degree: [6]*kak, ek,* the first and second of the "stems"—are used hypothetically for superior and inferior qualities, as of essays; [7]*lëk, kak,* the gravid uterus; COM., [8]*kak, 'siu,* one who heads a subscription; [9]*,k'wói kak,* armor; [10]*kak, 'chü,* the first of the "ten stems" and "twelve branches", used in combination to denote years; [11]*,ch'iong ,sang kak,* the manis; [12]*,sang 't'ing kak,* the three highest of the Chinsz graduates; COLL., [13]*kak, 'kiăng,* a kind of vest—when made with a pocket, called [14]*,ngüng kak,*; [15]*kak, ,t'au,* the head-man of porters (at a landing).

夾' Chia. To take or press under the arm; to carry secretly; to succor; assistants; to take up with pincers, to nip up; to squeeze, to press between two; doubled, lined: in the coll. read *kek,* q. v.: COM., [16]*kak, hak,* agreeing; [17]*kak, tai'* involved, as matters; [18]*kak, ,kung,* a double, or lined, petticoat; [19]*kak, 'peng,* joined boards, as in inferior coffins; [20]*kak, tëük, ,t'ó,* a flower like the peach, with leaves resembling the bamboo; COLL., *kak, la'* tricky, knavish; [21]*kak, mang'* a money-safe.

合' Ho. A measure containing about a gill; ten make a *,ching;* to collect, to join or come together; used in

---

[1] 塵垢 [2] 怒詬 [3] 詬誶 [4] 入彀 [5] 能彀 [6] 甲乙 [7] 六甲 [8] 甲首 [9] 盔甲 [10] 甲子 [11] 穿山甲 [12] 三鼎甲 [13] 甲仔 [14] 銀甲 [15] 甲頭 [16] 夾合 [17] 夾帶 [18] 夾裙 [19] 夾板 [20] 夾竹桃 [21] 夾幔 ○

the coll. to unite, to mix, to blend; to join, to sew seams: also read *hak*, q. v.: COLL., [1]*kak*, ʻ*pwong*, or [2]*kak*, ʻ*hwo*, to join partnership; [3]*kak*, *yoh*, ˓*wong*, to make pills; *kak*, *kóh*, to sew up sleeves; *kak*, *saik*, to visit prostitutes; *kak*, ˓*k*ʻ*a*, gambling partners; *kak*, ʻ*ch*ʻ*iu*, to work together, as those of equal skill can; [4]*kak*, *tek*, ʻ*hó*, or *kak*, *tek*, *lóh*, living together on good terms.

袷, Ho. A garment lined without wadding; doubled, lined; a neck-covering: [5]*kak*, ˓*sang*, a lined dress.

鴿, Ko. The Columbidae; a dove, a pigeon: [6]*yă kak*, a wild pigeon; COM., [7]*pah*, *kak*, (spoken *pah*, *tak*,), the domestic pigeon; COLL., *pong*ʼ *pah*, *kak*, (*tak*,) to let off pigeons.

蛤, Chia. Bivalve shells, thin and marked like a Tellina or Donax; a muscle, a cockle: [8]˓*sang kak*, a kind of striped frog; COM., [9]*kak*, ˓*kang*, dried muscles; [10]*kak*, ˓*li*, a yellowish kind of mollusk; COLL., *kak*, ʻ*niu*, the muscles of a cockle; *kak*, ˓*li p*ʻ*ong*ʼ to halve the edges of boards, as in floors.

蛺, Chia. A butterfly: [11]*kak*, *tiék*, a small butterfly or moth, like the cabbage, or sulphur, butterfly.

割, Ko. To cut, to gash, to hack; to wound, to injure; to cut in twain, to separate, to divide; to deduct, to take off: COM., [12]*kak*, *teu*ʼ to reap rice; [13]*kak*, *nük*, ˓*i* ˓*ch*ʻ*ong*, "cut out flesh (to patch and) heal an ulcer with"—to create a new want in supplying an old one; [14]*sá*ʼ *kak*, to flay alive; COLL., [15]*kak*, ʻ*tong*, or *kak*, *taung*ʼ to cut off; *kak*, ʻ*chai* ˓*tó*, a paper-cutting knife; [16]*kak*, ʻ*t*ʻ*ĕng*, to manufacture wooden pails; *kak*, *p*ʻ*ó*ʼ ˓*hwa* ˓*ăng*, "disfigured her fair face"—name of a play.

葛, Kuo. A creeping edible plant (the Dolichos tuberosus), of whose fibers a coarse yellow cloth is made; creepers; *met.*, relatives, posterity: COM., [17]ʻ*hung kak*, the mealy taro (Dolichos trilobus); [18]*kak*, ʻ*hung*, flour of the mealy taro; [19]˓*kwa kak*, melon and creeper; *met.*, relationship; [20]˓*chieu kak*, plantain grass-cloth; [21]*kak*, ˓*kong*, the *kak*, root—is a sudorific medicine.

轕, The rumbling of chariots rushing to battle; hasty, precipitate, violent motion: [22]˓*keu kak*, a rumbling, as of chariots; a confused melee.

詌, Read *hak*, and *hak*,; used for the coll. *kak*, as in *kak*, *kak*, *kieu*ʼ to talk constantly, loquacious, jabbering.

Kak,. A coll. word: to adhere, to stick, as paste; to stick fast; adhesive, tight in: *kak*, ˓*ku*, "paste sticking"; *met.*, confused, imperfectly done; illicit commerce; *kak*, *sak*, finally, at last (must do so); *kak*, *t*ʻ*iék*, *t*ʻ*iék*, *taing*ʼ immovably fixed; *sói*ʼ *má*ʼ *kak*, can't sit still; ˓*mô kak*, *siăh*, unimportant, trifling; *kak*, *taing*ʼ sticks to his

1 合本 2 合夥 3 合藥丸 4 合的好 5 袷衫 6 野鴿 7 白鴿 8 山蛤 9 蛤乾 10 蛤蜊 11 蛺蝶 12 割稻 13 割肉醫瘡 14 細割 15 割斷 16 割桶 17 粉葛 18 葛粉 19 瓜葛 20 蕉葛 21 葛根 22 轇轕

shop; *kak,* *ʻkau,* dirt hardened, as on the hands; *kak,* *siék,* an indistinct articulation; *ʻkong waʾ kak,* *ˌchau,* his talk is like sticking dregs—i. e., vile or useless; *kak,* *sioh,* *ˌwong,* stuck together into a ball; *kak,* *ˌngó,* contumacious, nonplussed.

Kak,. A coll. word: to be at or in: *kak,* *siongʾ sięʾ* is above; *kak,* *ʻchi ʻtie,* is in here; *kak,* *ʻchi ˌpeng,* is on this side.

(244) Kang.

干 ˌKan. A shield, a buckler; arms, defensive armor; what protects or fends off; bank of a stream; to seek, to try and obtain from, to procure; to provoke, to draw on one; to oppose, to offend, to break laws; offense, crime, guilt; incumbent, pertaining to, concerning, bringing results to one; trunk of some plants, a stem; a frontier; [1]*ˌkang ˌkʻwo,* arms; *met.,* war; [2]*ˌkang hwangʾ* to transgress, to incur guilt; [3]*yok, ˌkang,* how much? COM., [4]*ˌkang siék,* implication, concerned in; [5]*ˌkang chengʾ* to bear witness; [6]*ˌtʻiéng ˌkang,* the celestial stems—ten characters used in the cycle; [7]*ˌlang ˌkang,* a balustrade; COLL., *kaĕngʾ ʻngwai ˌmó ˌkang kwoʾ* it is no concern of mine.

ˌKang. A coll. word, for which the last is sometimes used: to force, to compel: *ˌkang ˌi chóʾ* compel him to do it.

竿 ˌKan. Culm of the bamboo; slender wooden things, as a rod, pole, cane, shaft, staff—often made of bamboo: COM., [8]*ʻtieuʾ ˌkang,* or [9]*ˌngü ˌkang,* a fishing-rod; [10]*tëük, ˌkang,* a bamboo pole.

玕 ˌKan. An inferior gem; a kind of coral: [11]*ˌlong ˌkang,* ornaments made of branching coral of the genus Isis.

肝 ˌKan. The liver; it belongs to the element *wood,* and rules the system; intimate, the feelings; a brown color, umber: COM., [12]*ˌtü ˌkang,* pig's liver; [13]*ˌkang kʻeʾ* the constitution, or state, of the liver; [14]*ˌkang ˌking chengʾ* disease of the liver; [15]*ˌkang muk, kʻaik, ʻtʻu,* "the liver *wood* repressing the *earth—i.e.,* stomach"—loss of appetite; [16]*ˌkang ˌtiong chʻaungʾ twangʾ* "liver and bowels cut into inches"—greatly distressed.

奸 ˌChien. Interchanged with the next: inordinate, unregulated desire; to violate decorum, to confuse propriety; to disobey; cunning cabals, plots; vicious, corrupt, selfish, malicious; clandestine; villainous, unprincipled, crafty, intriguing, traitorous; adulterous: COM., [17]*ˌkang ʻkʻieu,* crafty, wily; [18]*ˌkang ˌsing,* a traitorous officer; [19]*ˌkang sáʾ* a spy; *ˌkang ˌhüng,* to excel in cunning, a clever scamp; *ˌkang chaʾ* or *ˌkang ʻkwi,* false, fraudulent; *ˌkang chʻek,* you villain!

姦 ˌChien. Illicit intercourse, criminal connection, adultery; rape, incest; to deflower, to debauch: COM., [20]*ˌkang ˌing,* adultery, illicit commerce; *ˌkiong ˌkang,* rape; [21]*ˌkang*

[1]干戈 [2]干犯 [3]若干 [4]干涉 [5]干證 [6]天干 [7]欄干 [8]釣竿 [9]魚竿 [10]竹竿 [11]琅玕 [12]豬肝 [13]肝氣 [14]肝金症 [15]肝木尅土 [16]肝腸寸斷 [17]奸巧 ○ [18]奸臣 [19]奸細 [20]姦淫 [21]姦嬬

*ho*² an adulteress; *꜀kang ꜀ching ang*² a lawsuit about adultery; ¹*꜀kang ʻkwai*, to inveigle and seduce, to kidnap.

柑 ʻKan. The cooly orange (Citrus margarita): COM., ²*꜀hung ꜀kang*, "divide the orange"; *met.*, to share with others —an epistolary phrase; ³*huk*꜆ *ʻch'iu ꜀kang*, the finger-lemon—usually called *꜀hiong ꜀yong*.

杆 ʻKan. A wood like sandal wood or mulberry, good for spear-handles; a staff, a club; posts in a railing: COM., ⁴*꜀ki ꜀kang*, a flag-staff; ⁵*꜀ui ꜀kang*, a mast; COLL., *꜀ki ꜀kang kiek*꜆ the stone-posts which clasp and uphold a flag-staff.

乾 ʻKan. Dry, exhausted; to dry; *met.*, clean, entirely; all gone, wholly consumed: also read *꜀kiéng*, q. v.: COM., ⁶*꜀kang só*² parched, feverish; *꜀kang chiăng*² dry and clean; *met.*, all used up; ⁷*꜀kang sok*꜆ "dry salary"—i. e., a sinecure; ⁸*꜀kang saik*꜆ stoppage, as in eating dry things; *met.*, in a tight place, penniless; ⁹*꜀kang ʻkwo*, dried fruits; COLL., ¹⁰*꜀kang pwang*² mixed dry; *꜀kang ꜀pa ꜀pa*, roasted dry; *꜀kang ʻau*, a hard, dry retching; *꜀kang ʻta*, to contract for in "clean cash"—to pay in money (not in things).

更 ʻKêng. Read *꜀keng;* coll. *꜀kang:* the night-watches, of which there are five, commencing at about 7 P. M. and ending at 5. A. M.: ¹¹*ʻk'i ꜀kang*, to set the watch; ¹²*sioh*꜆ *꜀kang ꜀t'iêng*, one watch; *tiăng*² *꜀kang*, the first watch; ¹³*siong*² *꜀kang* and ¹⁴*a*² *꜀kang*, the early and late watches; ¹⁵*p'ah*꜆ *꜀kang*, to beat the watches; *꜀sung ꜀kang*, to go the rounds; *꜀kang ꜀hiong*, "watch-incense"—a night-burner placed near a coffin; *꜀kang ꜀tong maĕng*² *sá*² long nights make many dreams; *met.*, delay increases the risks.

粳 ʻKêng. Read *꜀keng* in the dictionaries: a superior kind of rice, slightly fragrant when cooked, called ¹⁶*꜀kang ʻmi;* it lacks the viscidity of the *suk*꜆ *ʻmi* (glutinous rice).

甘 ꜀Kan. Sweet, grateful, relishing to the taste, agreeable; pleased, happy; voluntary, willing; delightsome; specious, winning; the 99th radical: ¹⁷*꜀kang ʻchi*, pleasant food, such as is given to the aged; ¹⁸*꜀kang ꜀ling*, a timely rain; COM., ¹⁹*꜀kang chiá*² sugar-cane; *꜀kang ꜀ching*, a common porous plant resembling the cane; ²⁰*꜀kang ꜀sing*, or *꜀kang ngwong*² voluntary, willing; ²¹*꜀kang sëük*꜆ the province of Kansuh; ²²*꜀kang ꜀ló*, an ancient worthy who became minister at the age of 12; ²³*꜀kang ʻch'ó*, licorice root; COLL., *꜀kang ch'au*² *pok*꜆ *꜀kang lang*² to keep a thing till it spoils rather than give it away.

泔 ꜀Kan. Water in which rice has been washed; it is used for washing sores and for starch: in the coll. read *ʻang*, q. v.

¹姦拐 ²分柑 ³佛手柑 ⁴旗杆 ⁵桅杆 ⁶乾燥 ⁷乾束 ⁸乾塞 ⁹乾果 ¹⁰乾秤 ¹¹起更 ¹²一更天 ¹³上更 ¹⁴下更 ¹⁵拍更 ¹⁶粳米 ¹⁷甘旨 ¹⁸甘霖 ¹⁹甘櫨 ²⁰甘心 ²¹甘肅 ²²甘羅 ²³甘草

疳 ˓Kan. A disease of children, arising from imperfect digestion or bad treatment; progressive emaciation, atrophy: COM., [1]˓*kang* ˓*t'ëng*, worms in the ˓*kang* disease; [2]*pang*˒ ˓*kang*, atrophy; [3]˓*kang* ʻ*hwo* ˓*tung* ˓*ló*, consumption in children.

甘 ˓Kan. Licorice, much used in Chinese pharmacy; the root is called [4]˓*kang* ʻ*ch'ó*.

艱 ˓Chien. Hard, intractable soil; difficult, distressing; the origin of: COM., [5]˓*kang* ʻ*k'u*, miserable, wretched; [6]˓*kang* ˓*nang*, difficult; COLL., ˓*kang kai*˒ or ˓*kang ngai*˒ destitute, very poor; ˓*kang ngiék*˒ troublesome, as a sick or fretting child.

監 ˓Chien. To look down upon or into, as a god or an emperor does; to visit subjects; to look at, to require, to control by inspection; to superintend, to take charge of; an inspector, an overseer; in all which senses it is usually read *kang*˒, q. v.: a jail, a prison; to imprison; a halo: COM., [7]˓*kang* ˓*ló*, or [8]˓*kang ngwoh*˒ a prison; [9]˓*kang hwang*˒ or [10]˓*kang* ˓*ch'iu*, a prisoner; COLL., [11]˓*kwong* ˓*kang*, to imprison; [12]˓*kang* ʻ*tië*, in the prison.

閒 間 ˓Chien. A crevice; an interval, a space between; between, in the midst of, during, whilst, amongst; to allow, to make room for; to set apart; a classifier of buildings and rooms, for which the next is often used: also read *kang*˒, q. v.: COM., [13]*sié*˒ ˓*kang*, or [14]˓*hwang* ˓*kang*, this world; [15]˓*t'iéng tê*˒ ˓*kang*, in the world, on the earth; [16]˓*tüng* ˓*kang*, in the midst of; [17]˓*pung* ˓*kang*, a room, a chamber; [18]ʻ*k'ing k'aik*˒ ˓*chi* ˓*kang*, in a moment, a brief space.

棡 A vulgar character, commonly used in leases and deeds; a room, a chamber; a classifier of houses and apartments: COLL., [19]˓*sang* ˓*kang* ˓*pá*, three rooms abreast; *pah*˒ ʻ*pa* ˓*kang*, over a hundred houses; [20]˓*kang so*˒ the number of rooms; ˓*kang so*˒ *o*˒ ʻ*kwi* ˓*kang*, how many apartments are there?

隔 ˓Ko. Read *kaik*˒; coll. ˓*kang*, as in ˓*kang piäh*˒ *sié*˒ adjoining, neighboring; ˓*kang piäh*˒ *ch'io*˒ the next house.

˓*Kang*. A coll. word, as in ˓*kang* ˓*kang* ʻ*hó*, exactly right, just the thing.

簡 ʻChien. A slip of bamboo used formerly for making notes on; an official writing, documents; to abridge, to condense, to retrench; laconic, terse in style; to select, to distinguish, to choose from; to treat lightly, negligent, rude to; sincere; great, large; the sound of drums: ʻ*kang yeu*˒ the important points expressed in a terse style; [21]ʻ*kang chak*, a document, a dispatch; ʻ*kang lioh*˒ a resumé, synopsis; ʻ*kang mang*˒ to treat negligently; also used as a polite phrase; COM., ʻ*kang piéng*˒ at hand, spared (the trouble); ʻ*kang k'wok*, an office having but little

[1] 疳蟲 [2] 病疳 [3] 疳火童癆 [4] 甘草 [5] 艱苦 [6] 艱難 [7] 監牢 [8] 監獄 [9] 監犯 [10] 監囚 [11] 關監 [12] 監裏 [13] 世間 [14] 凡間 [15] 天地間 [16] 中間 [17] 房間 [18] 頃刻之間 [19] 三棡排 [20] 棡數 [21] 簡札

business; ‘*kang kiék*, or ‘*kang* ,*ming*, terse and clear; COLL., ‘*kang* ‘*sang*, to lessen, to reduce; sparing.

‘**柬** Chien. Often used for the preceding: to select, to sort; to reduce or abridge; a visiting card: ‘*kang t‘aik*, a visiting, or business, card.

‘**橄** Kan. The Chinese olive, the Canarium; it belongs to the genus Terebinthaceæ and resembles the real olive: COM., [1]‘*kang* ‘*lang* (spoken ‘*ka* ‘*lang*), olives; [2]‘*kang* ‘*lang sek*, olive-shaped; COLL., [3]‘*kang* ‘*lang* ‘*piâng*, olive-cakes, olives pressed and sweetened; [4]‘*kang* ,*chong*, a lady's toilet-case.

‘**敢** Kan. To walk up to and take; to dare, to have the hardihood, to venture; presuming, bold, rash, intrepid, saucy; to offend good manners; at the beginning of a sentence it answers to how, can: [5]‘*üng* ‘*kang*, bold, intrepid; COM., [6]‘*kang* ,*tong*, to venture to assume, as a trust; [7]*pok*, ‘*kang*, I dare not; [8]‘*k‘i* ‘*kang*, how can I presume—*scil.*, to receive such a compliment.

‘**感** Kan. To move the feelings, to excite; affected by, influenced physically or mentally: [9]‘*kang* ,*hwai*, to feel; feelings; COM., [10]‘*kang kek*, excited to gratitude; [11]‘*kang* ,*ong*, or [12]‘*kang taik*, grateful for favor; [13]‘*kang siâ*’ obliged for, thankful—the word *cumshaw* is a corruption of this phrase; [14]‘*kang tong*’ to influence, affected by; [15]‘*kang hwa*’ to improve, to convert; [16]‘*kang eng*’ to follow influential examples; to answer, as the gods are moved to do; [17]‘*kang mó*’ ,*hung* ,*hang*, to expose one's self to take a cold.

‘**鰔** Kan. A dusky green or purplish silure, the Pimelodus guttatus; it has jagged spines and is called [18],*hwa* ‘*kang*.

‘**秆** ‘**稈** Also read ‘*kung*: the stalks of grain, the straw of rice, stubble: [19],*hwo* ‘*kang*, straw of grain.

‘**赶** ‘**趕** Kan. To pursue, to run after; to hurry, to do quickly; to expel; to strive with, to emulate; busy, urged by, hastened, in a hurry: COM., [20]‘*kang kek*, hurried; COLL., [21]‘*kang* ‘*king*, quickly; ‘*kang kwo*’ ,*t‘au*, to excel by diligence; ‘*kang* ‘*kang* ,*kiâng*, to walk rapidly; [22]‘*kang* ‘*k‘ó*, to hurry to the examinations, as suttlers with their wares; ‘*kang k‘ó*’ ‘*si* (or ,*t‘ai*), in a hurry to get killed! an imprecation.

‘**哽** Kêng. Read ‘*keng*; coll. ‘*kang*: a stoppage in the throat, to choke, strangled: ,*t‘ang* ‘*kang*, suffocated by phlegm.

‘*Kang*. A coll. word: to cover, to spread over, to lay: ‘*kang ngwa*’ to lay tiles; ‘*kang mek*, lay them close together; ‘*kang p‘wói*’ to spread a comfortable over one.

‘*Kang*. A coll. word: to wipe with a wet cloth: ‘*kang* ‘*ü*, to wipe chairs; ‘*kang* ,*ta* ,*ta*, wipe it dry.

[1]橄欖 [2]橄欖式 [8]橄欖餅 [4]橄粧 [5]勇敢 [6]敢當 [7]不敢 [8]豈敢 [9]感懷 [10]感激 [11]感恩 [12]感德 [18]感謝 [14]感動 [15]感化 [16]感應 [17]感冒風寒 [18]花鰔 [19]禾秆 [20]趕急 [21]趕緊 [22]趕考

諫' Chien. To point out the right of a thing; to reprove, to remonstrate with; to testify against, to plead with a superior; to advise, to urge to reformation; remonstrance: [1]*kang' ˏchiong*, a memorial of censure or advice; [2]*kang' ˏsing*, a censor to His Majesty; [3]*'k'u kang'* to reprove earnestly; [4]*ˏkié kang'* to persuade by arguments; COM., [5]*tikˏ kang'* to reprove directly.

鑑' 鑒' Chien. Interchanged with the next: a tub in which the moon shines; a mirror, a speculum; an example, that by which one may take warning; term given to historical works; precept or admonition; to examine for purposes of approval; to audit or revise; to survey; to reflect light: [6]*kang' sekˏ* to perceive clearly; [7]*seng' kang'* the "sacred glance"—His Majesty's revision; [8]*ˏtai kang'* for you, sir, to see—an epistolary phrase; [9]*kang' ˏchiéng ˏkü*, to heed former examples.

監' Chien. To look at, to superintend, to oversee; to examine, to search into; to require, to control by inspection; to take charge of: also read *ˏkang*, q. v.: COM., [10]*kang' ch'ak*, to investigate; [11]*kang' ˏling*, to superintend (an examination); [12]*kang' tok*, an overseer, a bishop, as used in the Scriptures; [13]*kang' 'chang*, to conduct an execution; [14]*kang' yéng'* a college professor; *kang' ˏchá ˏwong*, a god who distributes cakes to ghosts; [15]*'t'ai' kang'* a eunuch; [16]*kang' ˏseng*, a purchased degree which entitles one to compete for the Küjin degree; [17]*ˏk'ing ˏt'iéng kang'* an astronomer royal.

幹' Kan. The trunk of a plant; the material of, the basis or original; capable, skillful; business, affairs; to do business, to attend to; a well-curb: also read *'kwang*, q. v.: [18]*sëü' kang'* an affair; COM., [19]*kang' sëü'* (coll. *kang' tai' ié'*), to attend to business; [20]*ˏneng kang'* ability.

閒' 間' Chien. To make a space between, to divide, to interrupt, to alternate; to interfere, to sunder, to part friends; to slander; a spy; far removed; vacant, unoccupied, as a road; to bear with, to allow; a mixed color, one varying from the standard color: also read *ˏkang*, q. v.: [21]*kang' twang'* broken off, intermitted; [22]*kang' k'ek*, to make an interstice; *met.*, to set at variance; [23]*'hwang kang'* to deceive an enemy, a spy; *kang' saikˏ* alternating colors.

癇' Read *ˏhang*; coll. *kang'*: spasms, convulsions in children, epilepsy, called *kang' ˏhung*; *ˏt'ang kang'* spasms caused by phlegm —said to produce idiocy.

澗' Chien. A stream in a valley, a mountain torrent: *kang' ˏchiong*, a mountain spring.

骭' Kan. The tibia; the ribs; applied to the bones of the body generally.

[1]諫章 [2]諫臣 [3]苦諫 [4]規諫 [5]直諫 [6]鑑識 [7]聖鑑 [8]台鑑 [9]鑑前車 [10]監察 [11]監臨 [12]監督 [13]監斬 [14]監院 [15]太監 [16]監生 [17]欽天監 [18]事幹 [19]幹事 [20]能幹 [21]間斷 [22]間隙 [23]反間

銜 ꜀ Hsien. Bit of a bridle; to hold in the mouth; to control, to guide one's self; to receive orders; affected by, moved, indignant; rank, position, title: in the coll. read ꜁hang, q. v.: [1]꜀kang haung꜄ to restrain one's anger; [2]꜀kang ꜀ong, affected by a favor; [3]꜀kang ꜀muí, to hold a gag in the mouth, as troops moving silently; COM., [4]꜁kwang ꜀kang, or chek꜁ ꜀kang, an official title.

啣 嗛 ꜀ ꜀ Han. Used for the last: to hold in the mouth; to receive, as a command: [5]꜀kang meng꜄ received your orders—said politely of a friend's request; COM., [6]꜀kang ꜂ch'au and [7]꜀kang ꜀chau, to carry grass to make nests; [8]꜀kang t'iék꜁ ꜀wong, to hold (red-hot) iron balls in the mouth (in hell)—used as an imprecation; COLL., [9]꜀kang ch'oi꜄ to hold in the mouth; [10]꜀kang ꜁sang ꜁kiéng, clings to the edge of the mountain, as the light of the setting sun.

嵌 ꜀ Also read ꜁k'ang and ꜁k'ang: a mountain cave; a hollow, a ravine; to inlay, to enchase, to set, as jewelry: [11]꜀kang ꜀ngang, a deep ravine.

꜀Kang. A coll. word: affected by the cold, chilled: ꜀kang ngaing꜄ stiff with cold; ꜀kang pang꜄ sick from exposure to cold; ꜀kang ꜂si, chilled to death; ꜀kang tioh꜁ affected by cold, as the cause of an illness.

汗꜄ Han. Sweat, perspiration; long, extended, as an expanse of water; bright: [12]hó꜄ kang꜄ bright and splendid; COM., [13]ch'ok꜁ kang꜄ (coll. ꜁lau kang꜄), to perspire; [14]kang꜄ ꜁kŭng, a sweat-napkin; [15]kang꜄ k'e꜄ the steam of reeking perspiration; [16]kang꜄ ꜁peng, a rash produced by (dried) sweat; COLL., kang꜄ t'au꜄ ꜁k'a, perspiration down to the feet, as in "taking a sweat"; kang꜄ ꜁lau kang꜄ t'ié꜄ a dripping perspiration; ꜀i ꜀siong tak꜁ kang꜄ the clothes sweated through.

(245) Kau.

交 ꜁ Chiao. To blend, to unite, to join; together, jointly; to deliver, or hand over to; to communicate with; to pay to; to exchange; joined to other verbs to denote their action; trade, barter, dealing; contiguous, conterminous; intercourse in society; a friend, friendship: used for the coll. ꜁ka, q. v.: COM., [17]꜁kau ꜁ka, to form friendships; ꜁kau ꜀peng ꜂iu, or [18]꜁kau ꜀peng kiék꜁ ꜂iu, intercourse of friends; [19]꜁kau chiék꜁ to be intimate with; [20]꜁kau ꜁ch'ing, very close friendship; [21]꜁kau ꜂ch'iu, hand-to-hand (fighting); [22]꜁kau ꜀pwang, to deliver to another, as a shop or an office; ꜁kau tai꜄ to hand over, to commit to; ꜂kwa ꜁kau, a limited circle of friends; chiok꜁ ꜁kau, to dissolve friendship; ꜁kau pai꜄ to salute each other, as the bride and groom in marriage; ꜁kau hong꜄ to pay over a share; to send a gift, as on festive occasions; ꜁kau ik꜁ trade; ꜁kau hak꜁ sexual intercourse; ꜁kau

[1]銜恨	[3]銜枚	[5]啣命	[7]啣巢	丸 [9]啣	山巔	[12]澔汗	[14]汗巾	[16]汗斑	[18]交朋	[19]交接	[21]交手
[2]銜恩	[4]官銜	[6]啣草	[8]啣鐵	嘴 [10]啣	[11]嵌巖	[13]出汗	[15]汗氣	[17]交家	結友	[20]交親	[22]交盤

ˌcheng, kind of *back* stitch; COLL., ˌkau ˌk‘a, to trip one up; ˌkau ˏteng, to return, to hand back to; ˌkau ˏung ch‘ioh, figured mats.

郊 ˌChiao. Waste or forest land, near or beyond the frontiers; waste common fifty ‘li from a city; imperial worship of heaven and earth at the solstices; to worship heaven and earth; the place where this worship was offered: [1]ˌkau ngwoi˒ remote wilds; COM., [2]ˌkau ˌt‘ieng, imperial sacrifices to heaven and earth.

茭 ˌ Dried grass, hay, fodder; a kind of cress growing in marshes; the flower is greenish white and the seeds are dark yellow.

蛟 ˌChiao. The dragon of thickets and morasses; the Chinese description answers nearly to the iguanodon: [3]ˌkau ˏlüng, a dragon like a boa.

鮫 ˌChiao. A sort of shark, whose skin furnishes shagreen: [4]ˌkau kaik, shagreen; [5]ˌkau ˏing, a mermaid—said to weep pearls.

溝 ˌKow. Read ˌkeu; coll. ˌkau: a drain, a gutter; a sewer, a ditch: [6]‘chwi ˌkau, or [7]ˌkau tio˒ a drain; [8]‘ch‘au˒ ˌkau k‘auk, a filthy ditch; [9]ˌkau sek, or [10]ˌkau má˒ ˌt‘èng, the gutter is obstructed.

勾 ˌKow. Read ˌkeu; coll. ˌkau: to bracket, to reject, as a sentence by inclosing it in brackets: [11]ˌkau k‘ó˒ bracketed, rejected.

鉤 ˌKow. Read ˌkeu; coll. ˌkau: a crooked iron, a hook; a barb, a fluke; bent, crooked; to hook: ˌkau ˌkau, hooked; [12]ˌkau ‘k‘i, or ˌkau siong˒ ˏli, to hook or fish up; ˌkau ˏlieng, or ˌkau ˏlieng ˌch‘iong, a bill-hook; [13]ˏngü ˌkau, a fish-hook.

九 ‘Chiu. Read ‘kiu; coll. ‘kau: nine; *met.*, many; the highest, since nine is a square number: [14]‘kau chiăh, nine persons or things; ‘kau ˏsiăng ‘kau, ninety-nine out of a hundred; *met.*, nearly done; [15]‘kau k‘aiu˒ or ‘kau chiék,(to pay) 90 on 100; [16]‘kau ‘ngu k‘aiu˒ 95 on 100; ‘kau ch‘ek, ninety-seven (out of a hundred); *met.*, nearly spoiled or worn out; [17]‘kau ˏt‘au ˏlüng, the nine-headed dragon—a sort of rocket; ‘kau ‘kau ˏhwang ˌkwi paik, sek˒ ek, nine times nine come to eighty-one—in abacus-reckoning; [18]‘kau ngwok˒ ‘kau, festival of the 9th day of the 9th moon—when kites are flown; [19]‘kau ˌching sek˒ ek, to˒ very precocious; [20]‘kau sai˒ a god worshiped by prostitutes.

垢 ‘Kow. Read kaiu˒; coll. ‘kau: an excretion on the surface of the body, scurf: ˏt‘au ‘kau, dandruff; ‘kau kang˒ incrusted perspiration.

詭 ‘ Read ‘kwi; used for the coll. ‘kau, as in ‘kau kwai˒ cunning, tricky; ‘kau kwai˒ tek, ‘heng, very crafty.

[1]郊	[3]蛟	[5]鮫	[7]溝	壑	賣	[12]鉤	[14]九	[16]九	頭	九	一
外	龍	人	路	[9]溝	通	起	隻	五	龍	[19]九	智
[2]郊	[4]鮫	[6]水	[8]臭	塞	[11]勾	[13]魚	[15]九	扣	[18]九	精	[20]九
天	革	溝	溝	[10]溝	去	鉤	扣	[17]九	月	十	使

教' Chiao. To instruct, to teach, to show how; to command, to order; precept, principle, rule; doctrines, tenets; a religious sect, a school or those who hold to the same opinions: in the coll. read *ka'*, q. v.: [1]*ch'ek, kau'* the seven precepts (on the social relations); COM., [2]*kau' ˌmwong*, a sect or school; [3]*ˌü tó' sek, ˌsang kau'* the three creeds, Confucianism, Tauism, and Budhism; [4]*siék, kau'* to open a school; [5]*kau' seu'* and *kau' ëü'* the superintendents of education in a *ʻhu* and a *kaing'* respectively; [6]*ˌtiong kau'* to propagate a creed; [7]*ˌka kau'* domestic instruction; [8]*ˌYâ ˌsu kau'* Protestantism; [9]*kau' sëü'* a teacher, a Christian minister; [10]*ˌt'iéng ʻchio kau'* Romanism; [11]*kau' ʻchio* (coll. *kau' ˌt'au*), the head of a sect, as the pope; [12]*kau' hong'* to teach, instruction; [13]*hong' kau'* to embrace a creed; [14]*ʻling kau'* I thankfully receive your instructions; COLL., *kau' sek,* a fencing-master; [14]*kau' ˌsü,* teacher of pugilism; [15]*ˌlë ʻma kau'* the ass-horse sect—term for Mohammedanism. Read *ˌkieu:* to cause, to induce or enable one to do.

酵' Chiao. Leaven, yeast; the residuum of distilled liquors: *ʻchiu kau'* barm cakes; COM., *ˌtü kau' chaik,* the feast of unleavened bread.

校' Chiao. Used for the next: stocks for the feet, in which prisoners are nightly secured; a lock-up; a pen for wild beasts; to examine, to compare things, to collate or revise books; to join battle, to fight: also read *hau'*, q. v.: [16]*kau' cheng'* or *kau' tói'* to correct for publication; COM., *ʻk'ó kau'* to examine, as military candidates.

較' Chiao. To compare, to measure strength, to try the accuracy of; generally speaking: also read *kauk,* q. v.: *kau' tëüng'* to compare weights; the heavier one; *kié' kau'* to estimate, to compare plans; [17]*kau' ˌliong,* or *kau' liong'* to measure, to discuss; COM., [18]*ʻpi kau'* to compare; COLL., *kié' kau'* to quarrel, to join issue with.

珓' Chiao. A pair of plano-convex stones, or blocks of split bamboo roots, tossed up to divine answers before idols; Area shells are also used: in the coll. termed *ka' ˌpwi,* q. v.: [19]*ˌing kau'* the blocks falling with both plain surfaces up; *ˌyong kau'* with both convex surfaces up; *seng' kau'* with one plain and one convex surface up, which is the most propitious.

窖' A receptacle or bin in the ground for storing grain, &c.; a cellar, a souterrain: *te' kau'* an underground store-room.

至' Chih. Read *che';* used in the coll. for *kau':* to come, to reach, to extend to; at, even, till, up to: [20]*kau' tói'* to arrive at one's destination; *kau' ʻchi,* to reach to this point; *pwoh, kau'* about to arrive; *kau' ˌtang,* till now; [21]*kau' ʻmwi,* at the last, finally; *kau' tek, sá'* an abundant supply (of goods) has come.

1七	3儒	教	授	教	9教	教	訓	師	16校	18比	20至
教	道	4設	6傳	8耶	士	11教	13奉	15驢	正	較	埗
2教	釋	教	教	穌	10天	主	教	馬	17較	19陰	21至
門	三	5教	7家	教	主	12教	14教	教	量	珓	尾

穀ˀ Kow. Read *kaiuˀ;* used for *kauˀ* in the coll.: enough, sufficient: ¹*o² kauˀ* there is enough; ²*kauˀ siăh₂ kauˀ ĕŭng²* enough to eat and meet expenses; ³*kauˀ eˀ* satisfied; *kauˀ ˈpwong*, the prime cost; *kauˀ ˌtĕng ˈnĕ*, enough where!—i. e., insufficient.

碍ˀ Read *ˌhau;* used in the *Paik, ˌIng* for the coll. *kauˀ*, as in ⁴*chiu kauˀ* a wine-measure containing about half a pint: ⁵*kauˀ twai²* the measure (at this shop) is large.

Kauˀ. A coll. word, for which the above character is used in the shops: a small earthen pot, called *ˌhai kauˀ*, having a spout and an ear-handle; *kauˀ ˈkiăng*, a little pot; in a *met.* sense, used as a low epithet; *ˌtĕng kauˀ* a copper pot with a straight handle and no spout.

猴 ˌHou. Read *ˌheu;* coll. *ˌkau:* a monkey: ⁶*ˌkau sangˀ* or *ˌkau pˈek*, a monkey's temper; *met.*, hasty, irritable; ⁷*ˌkau ˌtˈau ˈló ˈchˈŭ nge²* monkey's head and rat's ears; *met.*, ugly, ill-favored; ⁸*ˌkau nge² ˌpeng*, the monkey-ear radicals—the 163rd and 170th; *ˌkau pek₂ chaungˀ* a monkey drawing an awl; *met.*, difficulty, as in getting pay or borrowing; *ˌkau luk₂ tˈeu²* a monkey mounting a post—a toy; also an apparatus for raising, or lowering, lamps; ⁹*ˌkau hié² ˌsiăng ˌchˈiĕng ˈpwong*, "monkey tricks, a full thousand"; *met.*, full of wiles and annoying ways; *ˌtˈai ˌkié kaˀ ˌkau*, "kill a chicken to teach a monkey"; *met.*, to warn others by an act of severity.

厚² Hou. Read *haiu²;* coll. *kau²:* thick, not thin; *met.*, very superior; without shame: *kau²* or ¹⁰*kau² taung²* thick; ¹¹*kau² póh₂* thick and thin; ¹²*mengˀ ˌpˈuí cheng² kau²* or *kau² ˌpˈuí laĕ²* thick-skinned, brazen-faced; ¹³*kau² chˈiăh, ˌking*, very bright (superior) gold-leaf; *kau² ˈtá ˌá*, thick-soled shoes.

(246) Kauk.

各ˀ Ko. Each, every; various, separate, apart; calling to and being disregarded: in the coll., strange, odd, extraordinary: COM., ¹⁴*kauk, oi²* every place or person: ¹⁵*kauk, saik,* all colors; various kinds, as of goods; ¹⁶*kauk, chˈĕŭˀ* every-where; *kauk, ˈsiu ˈpwong hong²* let each perform his own duty; COLL., *kauk, yong²* every kind; strange, unusual; *kauk, chĕŭ² kauk,* each has his own business; *kauk, piék₂* strange, odd.

覺ˀ Chiao. Grand, exalted; correct, upright; to understand, to perceive; to notice, to advert to; wise, intelligent; awake, aroused to, conscious, to feel; to bring to light, to manifest: in the coll. read *kaĕk,* q. v: *ˌti kauk,* to know, to perceive; ¹⁷*kauk, ngwo²* aroused to a sense of; *hwak, kauk,* divulged; *kauk, ˌwong,* the wise king—i. e., Budh; *kauk, ˌló,* the Ghioro, surname of the reigning family in Manchu; COM., ¹⁸*ˌling kauk,* intelligent, shrewd.

埆ˀ Chiao. Rough land; hilly, rocky; poor land, like barrens; a rugged country.

---

¹務 穀 ⁴酒 ⁶猴 老 耳 成 叚 皮 赤 ¹⁵各 ¹⁷覺
穀 用 碍 性 鼠 爿 千 ¹¹厚 盡 金 色 悟
²穀 ³穀 ⁵碍 ⁷猴 耳 ⁹猴 本 薄 厚 ¹⁴各 ¹⁶各 ¹⁸靈
食 意 大 頭 ⁸猴 戲 ¹⁰厚 ¹²面 ¹³厚 位 處 覺

墽, Hsio. A crack in a jar or vessel. Read *hok*,: stiff clay, hard soil; bowlders on the tops of hills.

捔, Chiao. To seize and drag an animal by the horns; to push, to thrust at; to pierce, to stab.

桷, Chiao. A rafter or lath; the strips on which the tiles rest; a mallet; a handle; a tree in Kwangtung; its fruit is about the size of a hen's egg.

骨, Ku. The bones of bodies; whatever is hard and enclosed in something soft, as the ribs of leaves or the frame-work of certain things; the figure, the person; the 188th radical: COM., [1]*kauk*, *'ch'oi*, marrow; [2]*kauk*, *'keng*, the bones stiff; *met.*, unyielding, as an officer; [3]*,hai kauk*, a human skeleton; [4]*,siéng kauk*, has a fairy's bone—said of one's natural fitness to be divine; [5]*kauk*, *nük*, *,ch'ing*, blood relations; [6]*che' 'iu kauk*, *lik*, the words are vigorously written; *kauk*, *,pá*, dominoes; *kauk*, *sik*, (coll. *kauk*, *,t'au*) the dry bones of a skeleton; COLL., [7]*kauk*, *kah*, or *kauk*, *p'a'* the symmetry of the frame; [8]*kauk*, *pek*, *tik*, to crack the joints (of the fingers); [9]*chiéng' kauk*, *,t'au*, base dry bones—you impudent scamp! [10]*,ting ,lěng kauk*, the frame of a lantern.

鶻, A dark gray bird with a short tail; a species of turtle or wild pigeon; perhaps a francolin; also a kind of kite or glede; a sort of war-boat.

較, Chiao. The brazen horns used to support flag-staffs and spears; a boot in a car; to push with the horns; to contend, to wrangle: also read *kau'*, q. v.

斠, To adjust, to strike a measure, as of grain, salt, etc.: COLL., [11]*kauk*, *,pang*, to level the measure by scraping across the top with a stick.

刮, Kua. Read *kwak*,; coll. *kauk*,: to rub, to scrape, as with a knife: [12]*kauk*, *'tiăng*, to scrape (soot from) a pan bottom; [13]*kauk*, *sioh*, *,t'ũng*, to scrape off one thickness, to rub off the skin, as in falling; *kauk*, *'lē* (or *kaē'*) *,p'ui*, the skin bruised, as by a sprain; [14]*kauk*, *,chiong*, to rub starch, as on strips of cotton cloth.

(247) Kaung.

艮, Kên. Hard, firm; perverse, obstinate; a limit; to bound; the third of the eight diagrams; the 138th radical; often used in the shops for *,ngũng* (silver).

洚, Also read *,hung*: waters overflowing, an inundation; waters swelling over their banks and running in many directions.

絳, Chiang. A deep red, like the petals of the Hibiscus rosa-sinensis, a deep rose color: [15]*kaung' ,sung*, rosy lips; COM., [16]*kaung' ,t'ó*, a species of large peach.

降, Chiang. To descend, to come or fall down, as rain; to go down; to send down, to

1 骨髓 2 骨梗 3 骸骨 4 仙骨 5 骨肉親○ 6 字有骨力 7 骨格○ 8 骨拔直○ 9 賤骨頭○ 10 燈籠骨○ 11 斠平 12 刮鼎 13 刮一重○ 14 刮漿 15 絳唇 16 絳桃○

confer; to subject, to reduce to submission; to degrade: also read ˛hong, q. v.: COM., [1]ʻkaungʼ siéʼ to come into the world; [2]kaungʼ ˛seng, to become incarnate, as Jesus; [3]kaungʼ hok, to bless; [4]kaungʼ ˛ki, to write with the ˛ki pek, (divining pen); [5]˛song kaungʼ frost falling—the 18th solar term; [6]kaungʼ kaʼ the prices falling; [7]˛ming ˛sing angʼ kaungʼ apparent rise or gain, but real loss; [8]kaungʼ ngek, ˛liu eng² degraded in rank, but retaining one's office; [9]ha² kaungʼ to come down, as the gods; [10]kaungʼ ʻhwo, to reduce a fever; COLL., kaungʼ kiă² or kaungʼ lóh˛ ˛di, to descend; degraded.

鋼ʼ Kang. Read ˛kong in the dictionaries: iron assayed by fire; steel; hard, stiff, in which sense read ˛kong in Foochow: COM., [11]tʻiék, kaungʼ steel; kaungʼ chang² a steel-chisel.

槓ʼ Kuei. An unauthorized character: a case or set of boxes for carrying prsents in, borne by two persons; a pole for two to carry with; the poles of a sedan; a classifier of loads borne by two: COLL., [12]˛sang kaungʼ three loads; kaungʼ ˛cheng, the sections of a carrying-case; [13]˛kong kaungʼ to bear a case of presents; [14]kaungʼ ˛tang, a wooden carrying-stick, passed through holes in the top of the case; [15]kieu² kaungʼ sedan-poles; ˛seng kaungʼ and au² kaungʼ the fore and hinder ends of the poles; met., applied to the bearers.

(248) Ke.

記ʼ Chi. To remember, to recollect; to record, to register, to make a note of; a written record, history, memorial, account of; a style, a name; a mark, a signal; something to be remembered; used after the additional specific names of hongs and shops: COM., [16]keʼ chaiʼ to record; [17]keʼ soʼ to enter accounts; [18]keʼ niéng² to call to mind; [19]keʼ hóʼ a mark, designation; keʼ ˛chai, the faculty of memory; keʼ ˛sing (coll. keʼ ˛si), memory, recollection; COLL., [20]á² keʼ tek, can or do remember; [21]keʼ má² ˛ching, to remember imperfectly; má² keʼ tek, kʻóʼ forgotten; keʼ ˛chai ˛pang chiăng² a poor memory.

懻ʼ Chi. Violent, strong, overbearing: keʼ keʼ perverse, self-willed.

驥ʼ Chi. A horse of noble breed, great speed, and good points; a perfect horse: pek˛ keʼ a white carp—so called in Shantung; ho² keʼ ʻmwi, to tag on a steed's tail; met., to follow a man of influence to get promotion.

冀ʼ Chi. To desire, to expect, to hope for; desirous, eager: keʼ ˛chiu, a division of China in Yau's time, now corresponding to Shansi and part of Chihli; also a department in Chihli; keʼ haing² to wish for good luck; COM., keʼ wong² to hope for.

旣ʼ Chi. A slight repast; to exhaust; to lose; since, already, when; ended,

[1]降世 [2]降生 [3]降福 [4]降乩 [5]霜降 [6]降價 [7]明升暗降 [8]降級留任 [9]下降 [10]降火 [11]鐵鋼 [12]三槓 [13]扛槓 [14]槓擔 [15]轎槓 [16]記載 [17]記數 [18]記念 [19]記號 [20]能記 [21]記的 [21]記寶貫

finished; a sign of past time, and is placed before the verb: [1]*ke' chá'* finished; [2]*ke' 'wong*, past, gone; COM., [3]*ke' ,yong*, since, whereas; COLL., *ke' tek, se'* since it is, it being so.

覬' To hope for, to desire good fortune; lucky, fortunate; in the coll. read *'k'ai*, q. v.: [4]*'ke' ,ü*, or [5]*ke' ëü'* coveting, longing for.

Ke'. A coll. word, followed by *kieu'* or *yeu'*: unusual, in a different way: *ke' kieu'* (or *yeu'*) *siăh,* to eat or live peculiarly; *ke' kieu' 'kong*, to talk oddly.

Ke'. A coll. euphonic prefix, as in *ke' kieu'* to call; *ke' ka'* to erect a frame; *ke' kwa'* to suspend; *ke' kié'* to send; to leave, to deposit; *ke' këü'* to saw.

忌^2 Chi. To fear, to shun, to avoid; to hold in awe, or be cautious of; distasteful, to dislike trouble; to suspect; to hate; to have a superstitious dread of; COM., [6]*'ke*^{2} *,sing*, or [7]*'ke*^{2} *haung*^{2} to hate; [8]*'keng' ke*^{2} to refrain superstitiously, as from saying or doing what is distasteful; [9]*'to' ke*^{2} to envy, jealous of; [10]*,sieu ke*^{2} to keep the anniversary of a death; [11]*ke*^{2} *,sing*, the "dreadful hour", as the anniversary of an emperor's or relative's death; COLL., [12]*ke*^{2} *t'au' 'tá*, hate you forever!

惎^2 To poison; what is injurious, deadly, venomous; also to teach, to instruct, to institute.

技^2 Chi. Skillful, ingenious, inventive, expert, apt at making or contriving: COM., [13]*ke*^{2} *'ũng*, practiced in military drill; [14]*ke*^{2} *ngié*^{2} handy at work; the mechanic arts, trades; [15]*ke*^{2} *'k'ieu*, ingenious; hence finely finished.

伎^2 Chi. Interchanged with the last: ability, cleverness, talent, capacity: [16]*ke*^{2} *'liong*, artful, crafty; COM., [17]*ke*^{2} *'k'ieu*, ingenious, inventive. Read *,ki*: having six toes on a foot.

妓^2 Chi. A courtesan, a prostitute, a woman of ill-fame; a singing girl, one sent out to earn a living by singing and vice; *met.*, a fragrant plant said to cause oblivion: [18]*ke*^{2} *'kwang*, a brothel; COM., [19]*ke*^{2} *'nü*, or [20]*,ch'iong ke*^{2} a courtesan.

娍^2 Chi. Angry, enraged against; the anger or jealousy of a woman.

跽^2 Chi. To kneel low, to bow abjectly; awe-struck, filled with dread: [21]*,king ke*^{2} to kneel with folded hands, as before the emperor.

芰^2 Chi. A variety of the Trapa or water-caltrops, with three or four points; another variety is called *,ling*, q. v.: [22]*ke*^{2} *,hó*, Caltrops and Nelumbium.

***Ke*^{2}.** A coll. euphonic prefix, as in *ke*^{2} *ka*^{2} to bite; *ke*^{2} *kieu*^{2} to pry up, as heavy things.

1 旣濟 2 旣往 3 旣然 4 覬覦 5 覬礐 6 忌心 7 忌恨 8 禁忌 9 妬忌 10 燒忌 11 忌辰 12 忌透底 13 技勇 ○ 14 技藝 15 技巧 16 伎倆 17 伎巧 18 妓館 19 妓女 20 娼妓 21 擎跽 22 芰荷 ○

(249) Kĕ.

Kĕ. A coll. prefix, as in *kĕ kaĕh*, a noise caused by a stoppage in the throat; a hiccough; a suppressed cackle.

(250) Keh.

Keh. A coll. word: to thrust with a pointed instrument, to pierce: *keh 'tiĕ*, to thrust into; *keh sioh k'ĕng* (or *ch'iong*), to pierce a hole through; *keh sioh tó*, to give a stab with a knife or sword; *keh t'ĕng t'au* to pierce through.

(251) Kĕh.

Kĕh. A country brogue: to throw away; also about as *kaĕh*, a noise caused by an effort to clear the throat, hem! ahem!

(252) Kek.

吉 Chi. Felicitous; lucky, fortunate; gainful, advantageous, prosperous; happy, good, as indicating success or good luck; the first day of the month: COM., [1]'tai' kek, great luck—a felicitous phrase; [2]kek sing, a propitious star; [3]kek nik, a lucky day; [4]kek le' gainful; [5]kek hŭng, lucky and unlucky; [6]kek te' a lucky site, as for a grave.

佶 Chi. Exact, correct, upright; unwearied, firm, robust, strong and burly.

劼 Chi. To flay the skin from the face, to tattoo.

桔 Chi. Used for the next; the mandarin orange (citrus nobilis); an instrument for drawing water, consisting of a wheel or bucket worked by a pulley: COM., [7]'kek 'keng, a common medicine for coughs.

橘 Chü. The mandarin orange (citrus nobilis), of which there are several varieties: COM., [8]hok kek, (coll. [9]ĕng kek,), the Fookien mandarin orange; [10]king kek, a small, yellow orange—preserved in honey or sugar; COLL., [11]kek sieu, a wine made from oranges; [12]kek ĕng, orange peel—used medicinally for coughs; kek loi, small rough-coated oranges; kek p'au' large oranges; kek p'á' (or leng'), sections of an orange; [13]kek 'piăng 'ch'iong, a factory for pressing and preserving oranges; 'chwi 'tong kek, a species of small orange used ornamentally.

棘 Chi. A species of Rhamnus or Zizyphus, used for hedges; thorns, brambles, thickets; *met.*, troublesome affairs: used for kek, (a lance): [14]chung kek, a thicket; *met.*, a prison; COM., [15]king kek, thorny bushes.

襋 Chi. A collar of a coat, the part which envelops the neck.

給 Kei. To give to, to supply with, to provide what is necessary; abounding, to suffice; to give one an opportunity, hence to receive, or suffer from one; to be the recipient of: [16]k'eu kek, ready with a retort; COM., [17]kŭng kek,

[1]大吉 [2]吉星 [3]吉日 [4]吉利 [5]吉凶 [6]吉地 [7]桔梗 [8]福橘 [9]紅橘 [10]金橘 [11]橘燒 [12]橘紅 [13]橘餅廠 [14]叢棘 [15]荆棘 [16]口給 [17]供給

to furnish, as the proper food; [1]*kek*, *'siong*, to bestow rewards; *kek*, *'ting tai'* to confer an official button.

急, Chi. Hasty, impatient, urgent, pressing; anxious, solicitous; afflicted, unquiet; to urge, to expedite; deprived of every resource, at extremity; poor, wretched: COM., [2]*kó' kek*, to report pressing need, as an officer does; [3]*kek*, *siék*, a stammering tongue; [4]*kek*, *ëüng'* (coll. *kek*, *'sai*), urgent need of; [5]*kek*, *ˌling*, strangury; [6]*keu' kek*, to relieve the distressed; [7]*kek*, *sang'* or [8]*kek*, *k'e'* a hasty temper; COLL., [9]*kek*, *'si*, pressed to death—a sort of by-word; *'hwí ˌsieu ˌk'a ˌtang ko' má'* *kek*, fire burns his heels, yet he does not hurry—he's an incorrigible laggard; *ˌsing 'lá chiok*, *kek*, pressed in spirit; *kek*, *t'ieu' t'ieu'* fairly dancing from haste.

跲, Ch'ia. Also read *kiĕk*,: to stumble; to hesitate in speaking; for, instead of: *che' kek*, to fall, to stumble; [10]*ˌngiong ˌchiéng teng' chaik*, *pok*, *kek*, consider well your words, then you will not hesitate.

亟, C'hi. Haste, speed, in a hurry; prompt, ready; irascible, hasty; to hasten: [11]*kek*, *sok*, urgently; [12]*uk*, *kek*, be not hasty.

殛, Chi. To put to death, to punish capitally; to leave to perish.

戟, C'hi. A lance with three points; a kind of halberd with a crescent knife on one side; it is carried in processions for good luck: [13]*chek*, *kek*, *ˌlong*, ancient halberdiers; [14]*ˌsëng ˌchié kek*, the double-crescent halberd.

拮, Read *kiĕk*, in the dictionaries: occupied, laboring with hands and mouth; to claw at, to grasp and pull a plant with the hands; *met.*, to press upon: COM., [15]*kek*, *këü'* or [16]*kek*, *ˌkü*, perplexed and distressed from want of funds.

擊, Chi. To strike, to beat, to tap, or knock on; to rush upon or against, to charge, to attack or kill, as in battle: [17]*ˌkung kek*, to assault.

激, Chi. To impede and set back water, as rocks or dikes do in a current; a rapid place in a stream, made by an obstruction; to excite to gratitude or anger, to rouse the feelings; to stir up, to vex, to irritate; excitement, anger: [18]*'hung kek*, enraged; COM., [19]*'kang kek*, grateful for kindness; [20]*kek*, *ˌneng ˌseng piéng'* provocation will produce a change (in him for the worse); COLL., *kek*, *ˌnëng seu' k'e'* to excite persons to anger.

Kek,. A coll. euphonic prefix, as in *kek*, *kok*, or *kek*; *kek*, *kok*, *kok*, to wriggle, as worms; *kek*, *kiăk*, to turn away in displeasure; *kek*, *kauk*, to scrape; *kek*, *kak*, to cut; *kek*, *kaik*, to tie; to degrade; to break off a bad habit; *kek*, *këük*, to pin or run together; *kek*, *kiĕk*, to take with chopsticks or tongs.

[1]給賞 [2]告急 [3]急舌 [4]急用 [5]急痳 [6]救急 [7]急性 [8]急氣 [9]急死 [10]言定則不跲 [11]亟速 [12]勿亟 [13]執戟郎 [14]雙枝戟 [15]拮据 [16]拮据 [17]攻擊 [18]忿激 [19]感激 [20]激能生變

夾 Chia.[2] Read *kak,*; coll. *kek*$_2$: to press, as between two boards: [1]*kek*$_2$ *ʻpeng*, compressing-boards; [2]*ˏchü kek*$_2$ boards for pressing books; [3]*kek*$_2$ *ʻchai*, running sores between the fingers; [4]*kek*$_2$ *kongʼ* an instrument to torture the ankles; [5]*kek*$_2$ *ʻcheng*, large shears—for cutting silver; [6]*kek*$_2$ *sioh*$_2$ *ˏtoi*, pressed together; [7]*pʻieuʼ kʻëük, ˏnĕng kek*$_2$ *kʻóʼ* the bank-bills are kept by people (in their pocket-books) from circulation.

挾 Chia.[2] Read *hiék*$_2$; coll. *kek*$_2$: to clasp under the arm or between the legs; also to carry in the arms: *kek*$_2$ *kóh, lóh, a*[2] to carry under the arm; [8]*kek*$_2$ *nié*[2] *ʻkiăng*, to carry a child; [9]*kek*$_2$ *sioh*$_2$ *ˏpau*, to carry a bundle under the arm; *kek*$_2$ *ˏkʻa ˏpang a*[2] to place between the legs, as a hand-stove; to ride (a stick).

(253) Kĕk.

Kĕk$_2$. A coll. prefix, as in *kĕk*$_2$ *kaĕk,* a corner, an angle; *ˏi kʻok, tioh*$_2$ *ʻhü kĕk*$_2$ *kaĕk,* he's hid in that corner.

(254) Keng.

庚 ˏKêng. The seventh of the "ten stems"; to change, to alter; a way, a path; age, years; to restore; recompense; crosswise, transverse: [10]*ˏhu ˏkeng*, to ask charity; COM., [11]*ˏtiong ˏkeng*, the evening star; old, aged; [12]*ˏtung ˏkeng*, of the same age; [13]*ˏkeng tʻaik,* cards containing the record of births, etc., of two persons proposing to marry; [14]*ˏking ˏniéng ˏchong ˏkeng*, what is your age this year?—said to youth.

賡 Keng. To repeat a song; to encore a song or music; to join to; to continue: [15]*ˏkeng ˏkó*, to repeat a song.

鶊 ˏKêng. A bird called [16]*ˏchʻong ˏkeng*, with ash-colored plumage and black tail; a kind of magpie or perhaps a species of thrush.

更 ˏKêng. To change, to alter, to renew; substitution; emendation, reparation; a watch of the night, in which sense read *ˏkang* in the coll.: also read *kaingʼ*, q. v.: [17]*ˏkeng ˏsing*, to renew; COM., [18]*ˏkeng wang*[2] to change, to exchange; [19]*ˏkeng ʻkai*, to alter, to correct, as an essay; [20]*ˏkeng piéngʼ* to change, to fluctuate, as the state of the markets.

觥 ˏKuan. A large cyathiform goblet made of the born of the rhinoceros; a drinking cup; large, as a sheep; the sound of bells and musical stones.

耕 畊 ˏKêng. To plow, to cultivate fields; the period for plowing; *met.*, to labor; to be diligent in any occupation: *ˏkeng ˏhu*, a plowman, a farmer; *kʻwoʼ. ˏkeng*, to teach agriculture; *muk*$_2$ *ˏkeng*, to labor with the eyes, as physiognomists do; *siék*$_2$ *ˏkeng*, to teach for a living; COM., *ˏkeng chëüngʼ* to plow and plant, to till the ground.

羹 ˏKêng. A thick soup or broth; a savory porridge made of meat; a spoon or small

[1]夾板 [2]書夾 [3]夾指 [4]夾棍 [5]夾剪 [6]夾一堆 [7]票乞仫夾去 [8]挾伲仔 [9]挾一包 [10]呼庚 [11]長庚 [12]同庚 [13]庚帖 [14]今年尊庚 [15]賡歌 [16]鶬鶊 [17]更新 [18]更換 [19]更改 [20]更變

ladle: [1]'keng ˌt'ong, soups; [2]ˌhwo ˌkeng, a seasoned soup; *met.*, harmony produced by an able premier; [3]ˌtieu ˌkeng, to season soups; a soup-spoon.

肱 Kêng. The upper arm, the humerus; the arm: 'ku ˌkeng, legs and arms; *met.*, statesmen; [4]'k'ŭk, ˌkeng ˌi 'ching (or *cheng*') ˌchi, to double up the arm and pillow the head on it—said of the poor.

'亙 A limit, the extreme point; to fill, to extend everywhere; relics of antiquity: [5]''keng 'ku ê' ˌung, not heard of from the most ancient times.

'減 '减 Kêng. To diminish, to subtract, to take away part; to keep back, to contract, to abbreviate; to lighten, to retrench: COM., [6]'keng ˌk'ing, to lighten, as a load; [7]'keng ka' to lower the price; [8]'keng ˌsié ˌmi, to diminish a trifle; COLL., 'keng k'ak, sá' to reduce too much; 'keng 'k'eu chá' ˌseng, "diminish your food and help me live"—sung by beggars.

耿 Kêng. Large ears—reaching to the jaw-joint—thought to indicate nobility or long life; constant, firm, ingenuous, sincere; something sad impressed on the mind; restless, unquiet, melancholy: [9]'keng ˌkwong, to illumine, bright; [10]'keng kai' ingenuous, noble-minded; self-reliant; [11]ˌiu ˌsing 'keng 'keng, sad and disquieted.

'熲 Kêng. Used for the last; the light of fire: bright, shining, resplendent.

'褧 '絅 Keng. A garment without any lining, and of a plain color: the second read ˌhing, means to drag or lead one along rapidly.

'烱 Chün. To examine with a clear light; bright, clear, brilliant: [12]'keng 'keng, luminous, effulgent.

'梗 Kêng. A spinous tree like an elm; thorny, to prick, as a thorn; sickness; to ward off sickness; a résumé; to obstruct, to close; straight; strong, violent; a stem or petiole; in general, for the most part: [13]'keng tik, upright, honest; [14]'keng ˌngwang, rude and obstinate; [15]'keng k'ai' on the whole, generally speaking.

'哽 Kêng. Stoppage in the throat; hesitation in speech, from rage or impediment: in the coll. read 'kang, q. v.: [16]'keng ˌyéng, dumb, unable to speak, as from excessive grief.

'揀 Chün. To choose, to select, to discriminate; elected, chosen: COM., [17]'keng 'song, or [18]'keng tek, to select; [19]'keng ˌta, to sort tea; [20]'keng 'pwong, to select theatrical plays; COLL., 'keng ˌt'au, an inferior quality of tea; 'keng ˌlang (or ˌt'ang), or 'keng tiong' what remains after selecting; 'keng 'chio, to choose an employer, or a shop to patronize;

[1]羹湯 [2]和羹 [3]調羹 [4]曲肱而枕之 [5]亙古未聞 [6]減輕 [7]減價 [8]減些微 [9]耿光 [10]耿介 [11]憂心耿耿 [12]烱烱 [13]梗直 [14]梗頑 [15]梗槩 [16]哽咽 [17]揀選 [18]揀擇 [19]揀茶 [20]揀本

福州方言拼音字典

chui[1] ‘*nü* ‘*keng*, choose as you please; ‘*keng* ˛*pui* ‘*keng* ‘*seng*, "select fat or lean"—i. e., choose whichever you like!

‘綆 Keng. A well-rope: [1]*ngek*, ˛*ch'ing* ‘*keng* ‘*twang*, to draw deep water with a short rope; *met.*, to desire what is impracticable.

‘骾 ‘鯁 Keng. Fish bones; bones or anything sticking in the throat; *met.*, stiff, as a bone; decided, unyielding, blunt—applied to officers: [2]*kauk*, ‘*keng*, firm, unyielding; [3]˛*tüng* ‘*keng*, faithful.

敬’ Ching. Attentive, sedate, cautious; respectfully; to show respect to, to esteem, to honor; to venerate, to worship, to adore; to watch one's self; to apply the mind to: COM., [4]*keng*’ *e*’ reverential; [5]*keng*’ *oi*’ to stand in awe of; [6]*keng*’ *tüng*[2] to esteem highly; [7]*keng*’ *seng*’ *lioh*, a book on religion and morals; [8]*keng*’ ˛*pu sak*, to reverence idols; [9]*keng*’ ‘*tiong*, to revere superiors; [10]*keng*’ ˛*sang* ˛*pwi* to present three cups (of wine).

禁’ Ching. To prohibit, to guard against, to warn or forbid; to hinder, to restrain; forbidden, imperial; to regulate, to keep off; a kind of tray: COM., [11]*keng*’ ‘*tu*, to prohibit gambling; [12]*keng*’ *te*[2] forbidden ground, as the imperial palace; [13]*keng*’ *ke*[2] to "forbid dislikes", as infelicitous words, etc.; [14]*keng*’ ‘*chi*, to stop, to prevent; [15]*keng*’ ˛*teu*, prohibitory rules; [16]*hwang*[2] *keng*’ to violate a prohibition; [17]˛*k'wi keng*’ to remove restrictions; COLL., *keng*’ ‘*chi*, a jailer. Read ˛*king*: to bear, to endure; to overcome: *pok*, ˛*king*, unable to bear it.

噤’ Chin. To shut the mouth, to refrain from speaking, silent; unable to speak, as from lockjaw or other disease: used in the coll. for *keng*[2], q. v.

竟’ Ching. To exhaust, to finish; to examine fully; the end, the close; a confine, a termination, the utmost limit; then, at last, finally: [18]*keng*’ *nik*, a whole day; COM., [19]*pek*, *keng*’ after all, doubtless; *keng*’ ˛*yong*, finally; *keu*’ *keng*’ pushed to the utmost—certainly, entirely so.

鏡’ Ching. A mirror, a looking-glass; to reflect; bright, clear, luminous; to illustrate, to make plain: in the coll. read *kiăng*’, q. v.: COM., [20]*kó* ˛*tai* ˛*ming keng*’ (coll. *kiăng*’) a bright mirror on a high terrace; *met.*, an astute officer.

徑’ 俓’ Ching. A sideway, a path, a byway, a short cut; a bridle-path, a goat-path among hills; straight through, direct; the diameter; quick, prompt; to go, to pass by: *keng*’ ˛*ching*, straightforward; *chiék*, *keng*’ a short cut; *met.*, an easy method; COM., *lo*[2] *keng*’ (coll. *tio*[2] *keng*’), a path or road.

逕’ Chin. Interchanged with the last: a path, a by-way; to approach, to come near to; to pass by; to go up to: *tai*[2]

[1]汲深綆短 [2]骨骾 [3]忠骾 [4]敬意 [5]敬畏 [6]敬重 [7]敬信 [8]敬菩薩 [9]敬長 [10]敬三杯 [11]禁賭 [12]禁地 [13]禁忌 [14]禁止 [15]禁條 [16]犯禁 [17]開禁 [18]竟日 [19]畢竟 [20]高臺明鏡

₍siong keng' 'ting, very unlike, far apart.

勁 Chin. Read *keng'; coll. keng':* strong, brawny; the muscular strength, as of pugilists: *₍i o' keng'* he has fine muscle.

絹 Chuan. Read *'kiong;* used in the *Paik, ₍Ing* for the coll. *keng':* a kind of cheap silk-gauze, such as is used for the covers of lanterns.

Keng'. A coll. word: to cool hot things in water, as eggs, etc.

高 ₍Ko. Read *₍kó; coll. ₍keng:* high, lofty; tall, high in stature: [1]*₍keng twai'* tall and well-proportioned; *₍keng k'wa'* (or *kwa'*) high, as a house; long-legged, as fowls; [2]*₍keng hang'* a tall person; [3]*₍keng kiă'* high and low, uneven; about (so much); [4]*₍keng kiă' ₍sing*, partial; [5]*₍keng kwo' ₍t'au*, taller; [6]*na' o' ₍i ₍kiĕng ₍t'au ₍keng*, only up to his shoulder—he is a head taller.

鹹 ₍Sien. Read *₍hang; coll. ₍keng:* saltish, like sea-water; salted, preserved in brine: [7]*₍keng ₍ch'ó*, a salt-fish scent; [8]*₍keng lo'* brine, pickle; *₍keng p'wói'* salt condiments; [9]*₍keng e'* saltish taste; [10]*₍keng ₍song 'k'u lak, 'chiăng ₍tu ₍siong kwo' 'lau*, have tasted salt, sour, bitter, pungent, and fresh; *met.*, have experienced all kinds of ill fortune.

勁 Chin. Hard, firm, stiff; strong, robust, vigorous; unyielding, overbearing; indefatigable; used for the coll. *keng'*, q.v.: [11]*keng' tik*, well-matched enemies; [12]*₍kong keng'* firm, unyielding.

頸 Ching. The neck, specially the front of the neck, the throat; the back part is called *haung'*; also applied to the narrow part of things: [13]*'ung keng'* to cut the throat; [14]*'ung keng' ₍kau*, a very intimate friendship.

脛 踁 Ching. The leg-bone; the legs of birds and animals: [15]*kiok, keng'* the shank; *k'aiu' ₍ki keng'* (Confucius) hit his shins—to teach him to assume a respectful posture.

胻 Ling. A vulgar character, used in the *Paik, ₍Ing* for the coll. *keng':* the muscular stomach of fowls: [16]*ak, keng'* a duck's gizzard.

競 Ching. Violent, strong; emulous, pragmatic, bickering, testy, boisterous; to contend, to force, to struggle for; to drive off; great, abundant: [17]*₍cheng keng'* wrangling; *₍u keng' ₍sing*, unambitious.

妗 Ling. A sister-in-law on the wife's side: COM., *'mu keng'* a maternal uncle's wife; *keng' 'ma*, a grandmother's brother's wife—great aunt; *twai' keng'* and *sá' keng'* a wife's elder and younger brothers' wives. Read *₍chiĕng:* a pretty laugh.

噤 Chin. Read *keng'; coll. keng':* to shut the mouth; to refrain from speaking or eating; *keng' ch'oi'* to diet; *keng' 'k'eu le'* loss of appetite and dysentery.

[1]高 [3]高 心 [6]郇 頭 [8]鹹 [10]鹹 饕 了 勁 頸 [16]鴨
大 下 [5]高 務 高 滷 酸 都 [11]勁 [13]刎 交 胻
[2]高 [4]高 過 伊 [7]鹹 [9]鹹 苦 嘗 直 頸 [15]脚 [17]爭
漢 下 頭 肩 鮭 味 辣 過 [12]剛 [14]刎 踁 競

禁² Chin. Read *keng*²; used for the coll. *keng*²: to warn, to caution against; to impose superstitious restrictions: ¹*keng*² *꜀sang saiu*² to notify those whose birth-day characters ("conflict with the deceased"); ²*keng*² *꜀sang hong*² *꜀nëng*, to exclude strangers superstitiously, as at births and in times of sickness.

(255) Kĕng.

工 ꜀Kung. Read *꜀kung*; coll. *꜀kĕng*: labor, work, a day's work; craft, art, workmanship: ³*꜀kĕng ꜀hu*, or *꜀kĕng ꜀hu ʻkiăng*, or *꜀kĕng ꜀t'iăng*, work, skill; ⁴*꜀kĕng ꜀hu ꜀ta*, Congou tea; ⁵*p'ah꜁ ꜀kĕng*, work in beating (metals); ⁶*꜀tong ꜀kĕng*, constant occupation; ⁷*ʻta ꜀kĕng*, to engage by the job; ⁸*꜀siu ꜀kĕng*, to work by the day; ⁹*꜀kĕng ꜀chiĕng* (or *꜀chü*), wages; ¹⁰*꜀kĕng ngiĕ*² a craft, a trade; *꜀kĕng ꜀hu kiă*² his workmanship is inferior; ¹¹*꜀kĕng ꜀chiĕng chá*² barely (making) wages; ¹²*꜀kĕng che*² *꜀mó ʻt'u t'au*² the character *꜀kĕng* does not project above; *met.*, to earn small wages; *꜀kĕng ꜀hu ʻkiăng ʻyă lói*² the workmanship is excellent; *ch'ói*² *꜀kĕng*, jobs, chores; *sioh꜂ ꜀kĕng*, or *sioh꜂ ꜀kĕng sek꜂* a day's work.

江 ꜀Chiang. Read *꜀kong*; coll. *꜀kĕng*: a river: ¹³*twai*² *꜀kĕng*, a large or main stream; ¹⁴*꜀kĕng ꜀ó*, rivers and canals; ¹⁵*kwo*² *꜀kĕng*, to cross the river; ¹⁶*꜀tau ꜀kĕng*, to drown one's self; ¹⁷*꜀kĕng ꜀tong*, in the river; *꜀kĕng ʻchwi ꜀pwang ꜀li ʻsá má*² *꜀ch'ing*, bring river-water to wash it and still it is not clean—can't clear up the matter satisfactorily.

港 ʻChiang. Streams diverging, as one ascends a river; a passage for a ship, a reach, a frith, an estuary; a rivulet running into the sea; a cove: ¹⁸*p'wo ʻkĕng*, canals and streams; COM., ¹⁹*ʻkĕng ꜀mwong*, or *ʻkĕng ʻk'au*, the mouth of an estuary; ²⁰*꜀hiong ʻkĕng*, Hongkong; COLL., *ʻkĕng tio*² *chah*, the passage is narrow.

ʻKĕng. A coll. word: the male of quadrupeds: *ʻkĕng ʻmó*, the male and the female; *ʻkĕng ꜀tü*, a boar.

(256) Keu.

勾 **句** ꜀Kow. Sometimes interchanged with the next: to reject, to blot or strike out; to inveigle or entice; to mark off for punishment; crooked, hooked; *met.*, illegal, illicit, underhand; in the coll. read *꜀kau*, and *ʻkeu*, q.v.: *꜀keu kiok꜂*, to mark off for execution; COM., *꜀keu ʻing*, to entice; *꜀keu ꜀t'ung*, in collusion, as with thieves; *꜀keu ꜀sieu*, or *꜀keu ꜀tü*, to reject, to strike out, as from a list by brackets.

鈎 ꜀Kow. A crooked iron, a hook, a barb, a fluke; a sickle, a crooked sword, like a bill-hook; a clasp, a hasp; crooked, hooked; to hook, to drag along; to make hooked; to detain, to stop; to seduce, to tempt to do evil: in the coll. read *꜀kau*, q. v.

溝 ꜀Kow. A ditch, a drain, a sewer; a canal, a water-course in a field: in the coll. read *꜀kau*, q. v.: *꜀keu ꜀kü*, a sewer, a drain.

---

¹禁生肖 ²禁生混仸 ³工夫 ⁴工夫茶 ⁵拍工 ⁶長工 ⁷打工 ⁸修工 ⁹工錢 ¹⁰工藝 ¹¹工錢剩 ¹²工字毛凸透 ¹³大江 ¹⁴江河 ¹⁵過江 ¹⁶投江 ¹⁷江中 ¹⁸浦港 ¹⁹港門 ²⁰香港

篝 ꜀ Kow. A frame for fumigating or drying clothes by the fire: [1]꜂keu ꜁lĕng, a drying-frame.

韝 ꜀ Kow. A sort of leathern vambrace or defence for the arm, used by archers and called [2]pié꜄ ꜀keu, or siă꜄ ꜀keu.

轇 ꜀ Distant and indistinct, confused, intricate: [3]꜀keu kak꜇, a row of halberds; a confused mêlée.

嘐 ꜀ Chiao. The crowing of cocks; verbose, boastful, in which sense also read ꜀hieu: ꜀keu ꜀keu, bragging.

膠 ꜀ Chiao. Glue; glutinous or adhesive jellies, viscid gums; to glue; glued or sticking together, adhesive, compacted; obstinate, stupid, perverse, pertinacious, bigoted; to deceive; intimate, bound by friendship or pledge; sound of fishes: in the coll. read ꜀ka, q. v.: [4]꜀keu ch‘ek꜇, ꜁siong ꜁deu, united as by glue and varnish—very intimate; [5]꜀keu ꜁siong, a district or prefectural college.

勾 ꜂ Kow. Read ꜀keu; coll. ꜂keu, as in [6]꜂keu taung꜄ affairs, underhand doings: [7]꜂heu tek꜇, ꜂nü chó꜄ sié꜄ nóh꜇, ꜂keu taung꜄ how can I know what you are about!

枸 ꜂ Kow. A high tree shaped like the willow, with long sweetish seeds; probably a leguminosae: [8]꜂keu ꜂ki, a fruit allied to the medlar, used in ophthalmia, and as a tonic.

苟 ꜂ Kow. Grass, herbs, plants; devious, to the right or left; illicitly; inconsiderate, irregular, heedless; in any manner, carelessly; nevertheless, only; but, if, so: [9]pok꜇ ꜂keu, carefully, correctly; COM., [10]꜂keu ꜂ch‘iă, rudely, improperly, any how; [11]꜂keu hak꜇ illicit union, fornication.

狗 ꜂ Kow. A dog; little, contemptible, mean: [12]lak꜇ ꜂keu, a hunting-dog; [13]꜂keu hié꜄ a dog's bark; COM., [14]꜁long ꜁sing ꜂keu haing꜄ has a wolf's heart and a dog's ways! [15]꜂keu ꜂chü, you puppy! [16]꜂cheu ꜂keu, running-dogs—applied to waiters in low places.

笱 ꜂ Kow. A bamboo trap or weel for catching fish or shrimps; they are cylindrical and open at the end.

耇 ꜂ Kow. A face grimed with dirt and furrowed with age; very old, senile: [17]꜁wong ꜂keu, gray-haired, very aged; ꜁ki ꜂keu, the virtuous old man.

救 ꜄ Chiu. To assist, to rescue, to save, to liberate, to succor, to save from evil; to protect, to defend; to prohibit, to prevent from going wrong; to stop, to cause to cease; salvation, rescue; a tassel: COM., [18]keu꜄ nang꜄ to save from distress; keu꜄ yoh꜇ an efficacious medicine; keu꜄ wong꜄ to rescue; [19]keu꜄ chă꜄ to succor; keu꜄ ꜂hwi, to save from a fire; keu꜄ ꜀ping, a re-enforcement; keu꜄ sié꜄ ꜂chio, the Savior of the world; COLL., keu꜄ ꜁a keu꜄ ꜁a, save! save! keu꜄ ꜁sié keu꜄ ꜁t‘ĕng móh꜇ keu꜄

1篝籠	3轇轕	相投	6勾當	汝做	勾當	9不苟	11苟合	13狗吠	狗行	16走狗	18救難
2臂韝	4膠漆	5膠庠	7曉的	世乇	8枸杞	10苟且	12獵狗	14狼心	15狗子	17黃耇	19救濟

lang' *‚k'a* *‚nĕng*, save snakes and worms but not the biped man! — to be inhuman or ungrateful.

究' Chiu. To examine into, to search out, to inform one's self of; to push to the utmost; to devise, to scheme; finally, at last: COM., [1]*keu*' *ie*' to conduct an official examination; [3]*'kong keu*' to discuss, to examine the truth or merits of; [2]*keu*' *‚ki sik‚* on examination of the real facts; [4]*‚kŭng keu*' to investigate thoroughly; [5]*keu*' *keng*' finally.

宄' Chiu. Poor and sick; a chronic disease, a complaint which threatens death.

舅[2] Chiu. Maternal uncles: COM., [6]*‚niong keu*[2] a maternal uncle; [7]*keu*[2] *‚seng*, maternal uncles and nephews; [8]*twai*[2] *keu*[2] wife's elder brother; [9]*sá*' *keu*[2] wife's younger brother; [10]*keu*[2] *‚ku*, husband's father and mother; *keu*[2] *‚kung*, a maternal grandmother's brother—great uncle; [11]*keu*[2] *‚iê*, the maternal uncles—are so styled by servants and others.

舊[2] **旧**[2] Chiu. Old, worn out, not new or recent; formerly, anciently, before; venerable, venerated; passed away, defunct: in the coll. read *ko*[2], q. v.: COM., [12]*keu*[2] *‚kau*, an old friend; [13]*keu*[2] *‚ching*, former favor; [14]*keu*[2] *‚niêng*, last year; [15]*keu*[2] *chik‚* the old disease; [16]*keu*[2] *ngiê*[2] *‚nang* *‚wong*, it is hard to forget old friendships.

(257) Këü.

倨' Chü. Proud, haughty; a sans-souci carriage; a vain, self-confident gait; to stand or sit carelessly; strong: [17]*këü*' *ngô*[2] proud, haughty; *këü*' *mang*[2] impudent; [18]*këü*' *‚nga*, strong teeth, tusks.

遽' Chü. Hastily, urgently, instantly, suddenly, quickly; fleet, hurried, swift; agitated, trembling, fluttered; to forward, to send on, to transmit; an express, a post: [19]*kek‚* *këü*' hurried, urgent; *'k'ai këü*' agitated; *‚tiong këü*' *‚chi ik‚* a postman, courier.

據' Chü. To lay the hand on; to defend, to bar off; to maintain a place; to seize, to take possession of; to lean against, or on; to have form or substance; substantial, tangible; proof, testimony, evidence; relying on, according to, depending on, conformably to; it appears that: [20]*këü*' *siok‚* from what he says; [21]*këü*' *'hiĕng*, to guard a pass; COM., *këü*' *sik‚* according to the facts, truly; *'k'ó këü*' to search for evidence; *cheng*' *këü*' testimony; [22]*‚ping këü*' proof, evidence; COLL., *këü*' *'nü* *‚chiong wang*[2] *'kong*, according to what you say.

据' Chü. The grip of the hand between the thumb and fingers; a diseased hand; embarrassed; stiff-necked, prim, supercilious, imperturbable: COM., *kek‚* *këü*' straitened, distressed.

---

[1] 究治 [2] 究其實〇 [3] 講究 [4] 窮究 [5] 究竟 [6] 娘舅 [7] 舅甥 [8] 大舅 [9] 細舅 [10] 舅姑 [11] 舅爺 [12] 舊交 [13] 舊情 [14] 舊年 [15] 舊疾 [16] 舊義難忘 [17] 倨傲 [18] 倨牙 [19] 急遽 [20] 據說 [21] 據險 [22] 憑據

APLH. DICT. 45

拒' Chü. This and the next four characters are read *kĕü*' in the *Paik*, *,Ing:* to ward off with the hand; to stop, to obstruct, to withstand; to oppose a plan, to stand out against: COM., ¹'*k'aung*' *kĕü*' to resist, to oppose; ²*kĕü*' *chiok*, to renounce utterly; ³*kĕü*' '*siu*, to defend or protect one's self.

炬' Chü. A torch, made of reeds tied together, or of old bamboo cables cut up: ⁴'*hwo kĕü*' a lighted torch.

巨' Chü. The chief, the great one, the first of its sort; great, vast, very, mighty, large; how, in what manner? in which sense used for the next: ⁵*kĕü*' *wang*' myriads, innumerable; ⁶*kĕü*' *p'ek*, the thumb; ⁷*kĕü*' '*hai*, the vast sea; ⁸,*tiong* ,*k'ai kĕü*' '*k'eu*, to open the mouth wide.

詎' ,Chü. How, in what manner? often it implies the opposite of what is said; to reach to, to stop at; ignorant, as of a language: ⁹*kĕü*' *pok*, how not? is it not thus? ¹⁰*kĕü*' *e*' how could it have been thought of?—i. e., it was wholly unexpected.

鉅' Chü. Hard, as iron or steel, obdurate; great, chief; fierce, implacable: ¹¹*kĕü*' ,*kung*, a term for the emperor; ¹²*kĕü*' *ngiék*, or *kĕü*' *sĕü*' important matters.

鋸' Chü. A saw; to saw, to saw asunder; to divide, to reduce: COM., ¹³*kĕü*' '*ch'i* (coll. *kĕü*' '*k'i*), the teeth of a saw; ¹⁴*kĕü*' ,*k'ong*, saw-dust; ¹⁵*kĕü*' ,*ch'a*, to saw wood; ¹⁶'*ch'iu kĕü*' a hand-saw; COLL., ¹⁷*kĕü*' '*tong*, to saw off.

鐻' Chü. A frame for a bell or drum; a musical instrument of wood; an ancient table-utensil of gold or silver, in which sense also read ,*kü*.

秬' Chü. Also read '*kü*: a kind of black millet, of which spirits, used in libations, were anciently made.

距' Chü. A cock's spur; a dew-claw, a hallux; to go to, to reach; to oppose, to attack; to stand over against, opposite; to border on, conterminous; distance from or between; to skip or leap over; to stab back-handed: in the coll. read *kĕü*², q. v.: ¹⁸*kĕü*' *yok*, to leap, to skip.

踞' Chü. To squat, to sit on the feet; to sit in a rude, uncivil style: ¹⁹*kĕü*' *chó*² or ,*pwang kĕü*' to sit improperly; ²⁰,*ki kĕü*' to sit with the feet drawn up.

懼² **惧**² Chü. To fear, to dread, to stand in awe of; fearful, apprehensive: ²¹'*k'ung kĕü*² to fear, afraid lest; ²²*chiéng*' *kĕü*² to tremble with fear; ,*iu kĕü*² apprehensive; COM., *kĕü*² *nói*² to fear one's wife.

具² Chü. Prepared, ready; placed together orderly; to present, to furnish, to lay before; tools, implements: ,*ti* ,*ming pok, kĕü*² as you know the name, I do not insert it; COM., ²³*k'e*' *kĕü*² implements, tools;

¹抗拒 ²拒絶 ³拒守 ⁴火炬 ⁵巨萬 ⁶巨擘 ⁷巨海 ⁸張開巨口 ⁹詎不 ¹⁰詎意 ¹¹鉅公 ¹²鉅業 ¹³鋸齒 ¹⁴鋸糠 ¹⁵鋸柴 ¹⁶手鋸 ¹⁷鋸斷 ¹⁸距躍 ¹⁹踞坐 ²⁰箕踞 ²¹恐懼 ²²戰懼 ²³器具

福州方言拼音字典

[1]*'kĕü3 'ping*, "prepared petition"—words used as a heading; [2]*'ₛhing kĕü3* implements of torture; [3]*'kĕü3 t'iong3* a cane, a staff; [4]*'kĕü3 'ch'iu*, to hold in the hand, as a staff; COLL., *'lŏ kĕü3* an old man's staff.

俱3 Chü. Read *ₛkü*; coll. *kĕü3*, as in [5]*'kĕü3 ₛtŏ*, for the most part, usually so: [6]*'kĕü3 ₛchiong*, all complete, perfect; [7]*'ho3 'mu kĕü3 ₛchiong*, both parents still living.

埧3 Chü. A dike, an embankment, as to confine the waters of a freshet: [8]*'tĕük, kĕü3* to build a dike of earth.

颶3 **颶**3 A tempest, a hurricane; a typhoon, a cyclone, common in the Chinese seas: [9]*'kĕü3 'mu*, the first appearance, or signs, of a typhoon.

距3 Chü. Read *kĕü3*; coll. *kĕü3*, as in *ₛkiĕ kĕü3* a cock's spur; [10]*ₛk'a ₛsang kĕü3* its feet have grown spurs.

Kĕü3. A coll. word, as in *kĕü3 'hwi*, to strike a light, to light a match or paper-lighter; *kĕü3 tioh,* lighted.

(258) Kĕük.

菊, Chü. Syngenesious flowers, like the Aster, Chrysanthemum, Marigold: COM., [11]*kĕük, ₛhwa*, the China-aster—also called [12]*ₛch'iu kĕük*, and [13]*'wang3 swoi3 kĕük,*; [14]*ₛkang kĕük*, sweet aster—a cooling drink is made of its leaves; [15]*'siong kĕük*, to enjoy (the beauty) of asters; COLL., *'chwi 'tong kĕük*, (perhaps a corruption of *'chü ₛsong kĕük,*), "posterity-aster", a marigold.

匊, **掬**, Chü. To hold or grasp with both hands; a handful, the hand filled; the hollow of the hand; used in the coll. for collected, curdled, as blood; excited, angered: [16]*ek, kĕük,* a handful; [17]*ch'ieu3 ₛüng 'k'ŏ kĕük,* delighted, pleased with; COLL., [18]*kĕük, haik,* coagulated blood, as in wounds; *kĕük, ₛkwong*, irritated, as by disturbance.

鞠, Chü. Used for the next: a ball, a foot-ball of chaff; to bear, to bring up, to nourish, to train; to rule; a boy, a child; being, life; full, much; to bend the body; to investigate; to push to an extreme: [19]*kĕük, ₛküng*, to stoop; [20]*kĕük, ŭk,* to nourish.

鞫, Chü. To investigate a case judicially, to question a criminal, to get at the truth: [21]*seng3 kĕük,* or *'sing kĕük*, to inquire into and judge a case.

麴, Chü. Leaven, barm, the slime or mother which collects on liquors: *kĕük, ngiĕk,* barm-cakes; *ₛchau kĕük*, distiller's grains—made into a condiment.

顊, Chü. Read *uk,*; used in the *Paik, ₛIng* for the coll. *kĕük,*: to put a vessel in the water with the bottom downwards—to discover whether it leaks: *kĕük, 'si*, to drown by thrusting the head under water.

Kĕük,. A coll. word: to pin together with pins or needles; to run a seam.

1具稟 2刑具 3具杖 4具手 5俱多 6俱全 7父母俱全 8竹埧 9颶母 10胶生距 11菊花 12秋菊 13萬壽菊 14甘菊 15賞菊 16一匊 17笑容可掬 18掬血 19鞠躬 20鞠育 21訊鞫

(259) Kĕüng.

供[2] *Kung.* To place before, to offer or present to; to lay out, to arrange, as offerings to the gods: also read *˛kŭng*, q. v.: [1]*ʻsiĕk˛ kĕüngʾ* to arrange offerings; COM., [2]*kĕüngʾ hongʾ* to serve (the gods) with gifts; [3]*kĕüngʾ ˛ta*, to present tea; [4]*kĕüngʾ ˛kung ˛pŏ*, to offer to the ancestral tablets.

靳[2] Read *kĕüngʾ* in the dictionaries: the collar-strap of a harness; firm, vigorous, strong; to hold back, to restrain; to ridicule, to make odious; avaricious, parsimonious, sparing of; to take.

共[2] *Kung.* Generally, all, altogether, in all, collectively; in fine, in short, to sum up; with, and, together with; the same, alike; to include in, to live with: in the coll. read *kaĕngʾ*, q. v.: [5]*pok˛ kĕüngʾ taiʾ ˛tʻiĕng*, can't live under the same heaven (with him); COM., [6]*kĕüngʾ ʻchung*, or [7]*kĕüngʾ kiĕʾ* the whole amount; [8]*kĕüngʾ ˛chiĕng*, the total of a cash account; COLL., [9]*kĕüngʾ ˛sing*, the sum total; [10]*mwoiʾ kĕüngʾ sëüʾ* have had no dealings with him.

菫[2] *Chin.* Also read *˛kʻŭng:* tenacious clay, mud, yellow loam; adhesive; to smear, to lute; in these senses the next is generally employed. Read *ʻking:* a plant, also called [11]*˛u ˛tʻeu*, crow's head; [12]*king chʻaiʾ* the violet or pansy.

墐[2] *Chin.* To plaster or stop up with clay, to lute; to cover a corpse with earth, to inter; clay, argillaceous earth, mud; a way over a drain.

僅[2] *Chin.* Exactly, nothing wanting, nothing over; hardly, just missed, as an injury; scarcely, almost, a little short: [13]*kĕüngʾ ʻkʻŏ*, it will answer; [14]*kĕüngʾ ˛neng*, just able to.

廑[2] *Chin.* Also read *˛kʻŭng*, and is like the last; a cottage, a hut, a lodge; just enough, sufficient; partially, in a slight degree.

槿[2] *Chin.* Also read *ʻking:* a tree whose flowers blossom and decay in a day, perhaps a species of Malvaceæ; used figuratively for human glory, transient happiness; a handle.

殣[2] *Chin.* To die of starvation by the road-side; to cover a way-side corpse.

饉[2] *Chin.* A dearth or blasting of vegetables: [15]*˛ki kĕüngʾ* a famine of grains and vegetables.

近[2] *Chin.* Near, proximate, both in place and time; to touch, to approach; to bring near, to close upon, to urge; according to, like, familiar: [16]*hoʾ kĕüngʾ* near to; COM., [17]*˛chʻing kĕüngʾ* to be near one, intimate; [18]*kĕüngʾ piĕngʾ* conveniently near; [19]*kĕüngʾ ˛ka*, to stay at home—not travel far away; [20]*kĕüngʾ tŏʾ* consonant to reason; [21]*˛chiong kĕüngʾ* about to be; [22]*kĕüngʾ ˛lai*, or *kĕüngʾ ˛si*, recently; *kĕüngʾ mieuʾ ˛kʻi ˛sing*, "near the temple, slight the god"—familiarity breeds contempt;

[1]設供 [2]供奉 [3]供茶 [4]供公婆 [5]不共戴天 [6]共總 [7]共計 [8]共錢 [9]共成 [10]昧共事 [11]烏頭 [12]菫菜 [13]僅可 [14]僅能 [15]饑饉 [16]附近 [17]親近 [18]近便 [19]近家 [20]近道 [21]將近 [22]近來

kĕüngʼ seʼ (coll. *kĕüngʼ chʻĕüʼ* or *kĕüngʼ neʼ*) near-sighted.

覲ʼ Chin. To see, to have an audience with a superior, or the emperor; to look to the north—i. e., towards His Majesty; the autumnal audience: [1]*ˏtieu kĕüngʼ* introduced at court.

(260) **Ki.**

ˏ箕 Chi. A corn-fan, a winnowing-fan, a sieve; a refuse basket; to spread out like a fan; the long striæ on the finger's ends; part of Sagittarius, the 7th of the 28 constellations; *met.*, wind and rain, because this star forbodes them; a kind of wood used for quivers: [2]*ˏki ʻchʻiu*, dust-pan and broom; COLL., [3]*pwaiʼ ˏki*, a close sieve for throwing up grain to the wind; [4]*ʻpongʼ ˏki*, a mason's dirt-basket.

ˏ基 Chi. The foundation of a wall, a foundation, a rest, a basis; a beginning, a commencement, a starting-point; that on which a family or nation depends, fundamental; a patrimony, possession; farming utensils; a side apartment, an anteroom: COM., [5]*teʼ ˏki*, the foundation; [6]*ˏki ʻchi*, or *ˏki chóʼ* a foundation, a base; [7]*ˏki ngiékˎ* a patrimony, an inheritance; [8]*ˏteng ˏki*, to ascend the throne; [9]*ˏki chaungʼ* a strong foundation; COLL., *ˏki ˏpung kʻóʼ* the foundation has fallen.

期 Chʻi. A set time, a fixed period, a day agreed on; times, seasons; to meet; to expect, to wait for; to aim at; to engage to do: [10]*ˏkʻiéng ˏki*, to miss the time; [11]*ˏki ˏniéng*, a year; COM., [12]*ˏki ʻmwang*, the time is up; [13]*ˏki ʻmau*, set times, as in yamuns; [14]*ˏki pʻieuʼ* a promissory note; [15]*ˏki aingʼ* or *ˏki yok*, the time fixed or agreed upon; [16]*ˏki hukˎ* a year's mourning; COLL., *ˏki kauʼ* the set time has come.

ˏ朞 Chi. Interchanged with the last: an anniversary, full revolution of a year, 354 days: *ˏki ˏchi ˏsong*, a year of mourning; [17]*ˏki ng wokˎ* space of a month.

ˏ綦 A dark green or red, also a blue and gray color; variegated; shoe-strings; very, the utmost: [18]*ˏki ˏkŭng*, a grayish coiffure worn by girls; [19]*ˏki saik*, inquisitive, desiring to see novel things.

ˏ饑 Chi. Interchanged with the next: failure of the harvest, famine, scarcity of food: [20]*ˏki kĕüngʼ* a dearth of cereals and vegetables; COM., *ˏki ˏhwong*, a famine.

ˏ飢 Chi. Scarcity; hungry, famished; to starve, starving, necessitous: COM., [21]*ˏki ngóʼ* to starve; [22]*ˏki kʻak*, hunger and thirst; [23]*ˏki ˏhang ˏkau pʻaik*, distressed at once with hunger and cold; *ˏki ʻpau sek, ˏsi*, miss the times of hunger and fullness—i. e., to eat at irregular seasons.

ˏ幾 Chi. The springs of motion; subtle, hidden, mysterious; what is within, recondite; moderately, a little; dangerous; having stated periods, the proper time;

1 朝覲　2 箕帚　3 簸箕　4 糞箕　5 地基　6 基址　7 基業　8 登基　9 基壯　10 愆期　11 期年　12 期滿　13 期卯　14 期票　15 期限　16 期服　17 朞月　18 綦巾　19 綦色　20 饑饉　21 饑餓　22 饑渴　23 饑寒交迫

an omen, prognostic; to expect; to examine; a qualifying word, nearly, almost, about, rather, somewhat: also read ʻ*ki*, q. v.: ˏ*ki* ˏ*ki*, or ˏ*ki* ˏ*hu*, almost, at the point of; [1]ˏ*ki* ˏ*mi*, small, recondite; *sëü*ʼ ˏ*ki*, probably, yet for all that.

機 机 ˏChi. Used for the last: changes, permutations; the origin or spring of; the subtle influences of nature; the motive power in an operation; a machinery, a trap or hidden contrivance; stratagems, schemes; a loom: [2]ˏ*ki* ʻ*t'ü*, weaving implements; [3]ˏ*t'iéng* ˏ*ki*, the natural bent of a mind; [4]*sek*ˎ ˏ*ki*, to fail in a scheme—lose a battle; [5]ˏ*kung* ˏ*ki ch'ëü*ʼ the imperial council chamber; COM., [6]ˏ*ki* ˏ*pung*, a weaver's shop; [7]ˏ*ki* ˏ*meu*, to scheme, an artifice; [8]ˏ*ki* ˏ*kwang*, springs in a machine; *met.*, designs; [9]ˏ*ki mik*ˎ secret, undivulged; [10]ˏ*ki hwoi*ʼ an opportunity, occasion; COLL., [11]ˏ*ki pah*ˎ *chá*ʼ a fine white grass-cloth.

嘰 ˏChi. To eat sparingly; to sigh, to cry out: COLL., ˏ*ki* ˏ*ki kieu*ʼ to peep, as a chick; to mutter, as spirits are said to do.

璣 ˏChi. Pearls not perfectly round; a sort of armillary sphere, called [12]ˏ*siong* ˏ*ki*.

畿 ˏChi. An imperial park in ancient times, measuring a thousand ʻ*li* on each side, with the court in the center; a limit, a border; inside of a door, the threshold; the lands of princes: [13]ˏ*wong* ˏ*ki*, the imperial park or demesnes.

譏 ˏChi. To slander, to speak against; to ridicule, to mock, to satirize; to blame, to reprove, to remonstrate with; officious and contumelious speeches; to examine into, to test; machinations: [14]ˏ*ki sieu*ʼ (COM., ˏ*ki ch'ieu*ʼ), to jeer, to laugh at; [15]*ch'ëü*ʼ ˏ*ki*, to satirize or reprove covertly.

磯 ˏChi. Stones or rocks in a stream producing ripples; shallows, eddies; a stumbling-block; to impede, to rub, to grate against: [16]*tieu*ʼ ˏ*ngü* ˏ*ki*, a fishing-place.

蟣 ˏChi. A nit, a louse: ˏ*ki saik*ˎ lice. Read ˏ*ki*, and used for ˏ*ki*, a blood-sucker.

鐖 ˏChi. A barb, as of an arrow or fishhook: [17]ˏ*liéng* ˏ*ki*, a spring or catch in machinery.

錤 ˏChi. An iron implement like a hoe, called [18]ˏ*chü* ˏ*ki*, and having a long blade.

乩 ˏChi. To divine, to seek counsel of the gods; a kind of divination by writing in the sand with a twig of mulberry, willow, or peach: COM., [19]ˏ*ki pek*ˎ the divining pen; [20]ˏ*ki* ˏ*tong*, hall of divination; [21]ˏ*ki* ˏ*pwang*, a divining tray (containing sand); [22]*kaung*ʼ ˏ*ki*, to bring down the gods in divination.

肌 ˏChi. The flesh or firm muscle surrounding the bones: ˏ*ki* ˏ*hu*, muscle, solid flesh.

[1]幾微	[3]天機	[5]軍機	[6]機房	[8]機關	[10]機會	縳	畿	譏	[17]連鐖	[19]乩筆	[21]乩盤
						[12]璇	[14]譏	[16]釣			
[2]機杼	[4]失機	處○	[7]機謀	[9]機密	[11]機白	璣	誚	魚	[18]鎡錤	[20]乩堂	[22]降乩
						[13]王	[15]刺	磯			

臉 ʻChi. The flesh covering the jaws and cheek-bones; the cheeks.

˛Ki. A coll. euphonic prefix, as in *˛ki ˛ka*, to cut with shears; *˛ki ˛kau*, to hook up; to reject, as by bracketing words; *˛ki ˛kié*, to tie, to tether.

已 ʻChi. One's self, I, myself; self, added to pronouns; selfish, private, special; the 49th radical; to record; the 6th of the "stems", answering to earth: [1]*ʻki ˛sing*, own body, self; COM., [3]*chëü*ʾ *ʻki* (coll. *che*ʾ *˛ka*), one's self; [2]*˛ang hong*ʾ *ʻsiu ʻki*, to mind one's own affairs; [4]*oi*ʾ *ʻki ʻkʻi kiëng*ʾ to have a regard to one's private interests.

圯 ʻChi. To subvert, to destroy, as a city: also read *˛i*, q. v.: [5]*˛kʻing ʻki*, to overthrow, to cast down.

屺 ʻChʻi. A bleak, bare mountain, such as a hermit chooses; a high hill.

杞 ʻChi. A tree resembling the willow, called [6]*ʻkeu ʻki*; its fruit is like the medlar and used as a tonic; name of a state.

汜 ʻChi. Read *sëü*ʾ in the dictionaries: a branch diverging and afterward uniting again with the main stream: [7]*ʻki ʻchwi*, a river and town in Honan west of Kaifung.

紀 ʻChi. To sort silk threads; to arrange, to separate; to record, to narrate, to book, to ascertain and write; to rule, to govern; a history, annals, chronicles, narrative; a period of 12 years; a decimal or the completion of numbers; a foundation; a skein of 40 threads: [8]*˛kong ʻki*, to govern; COM., [9]*˛niëng ʻki*, a person's age; [10]*ʻki lioh*, to record, as an officer's merit; [11]*ʻki ˛kong hwak, to*ʾ outlines and method, as of an essay.

芑 ʻChi. A species of white millet: *ʻki chʻai*ʾ a vegetable like succory or wild endive, often cooked and eaten.

几 ʻChi. A bench or stool to lean on; a stand, a side-table; the 16th radical: [12]*ʻki ʻki*, tranquil; [13]*˛ung ʻki*, a writing table; COM., [14]*˛ta ʻki*, a teapoy; *˛hiong ʻki tóh*, a small stand for supporting the censer—used in private houses.

麂 ʻChi. A large kind of stag; also a small deer or antelope: COM., [15]*ʻki ˛pʻúi*, deer-skin; [16]*ʻki nük*, venison.

幾 ʻChi. Much or many; a part of, a few, several; an interrogative of quantity, how, how many, or much? also read *˛ki*, and in the coll. *ʻkwi*, q. v.: [17]*ʻki ˛tó*, or *ʻki ˛hó*, how many? [18]*ʻki ˛si*, when? [19]*˛u ʻki*, not much; [20]*ʻki ʻhü*, or [21]*ʻki kó*ʾ a few.

ʻKi. A coll. euphonic prefix, as in *ʻki ʻká*, to untie, to unravel; *ʻki ʻkwi*, to revise, as books; *ʻki ʻkieu*, to pry up; *ʻki ʻku*, to stir, as things in cooking; *ʻki ʻka*, to twist, as rope; to twist off, as fruit from a tree with a pronged stick.

[1]已身 [2]安分守己 [3]自己 [4]爲己起見 [5]傾圯 [6]枸杞 [7]汜水 [8]綱紀 [9]年紀 [10]紀錄 [11]紀綱法度 [12]几几 [13]文几 [14]茶几 [15]麂皮 [16]麂肉 [17]幾多 [18]幾時 [19]無幾 [20]幾許 [21]幾個

其 ꜀Ch'i. A relative or personal pronoun, referring to the person, place, or thing spoken of; he, his, she, her, it, its, they; there; an indefinite pronoun, wherever, whoever, the, that, the subject spoken of; used in the coll. to mark the possessive: [1]*꜀ki ꜀si*, that time; [2]*꜀ki ꜀ü*, as if, supposing; COM., [3]*꜀ki ꜀ü*, the rest; [4]*꜀ki ch'ëü*ʾ the second; [5]*꜀ki ꜀tüng pek, ʿiu ꜀yong ko*ʾ therein there must have been a cause; COLL., *꜀ki ꜀ki kó*ʾ *kó*ʾ every one, they all; [6]*lang*ʾ *꜀ki*, two, as of persons, cash, &c.; *꜀ki pwang*ʾ *꜀chiéng*, a cash and a half; *꜀ki ʿkau*, a cash and nine-tenths; [7]*꜀ki siong*ʾ or *꜀ki ꜀ling*, over a cash; *ʿngwai ꜀ki ch'io*ʾ my house; *꜀chui se*ʾ *tié*ʾ *꜀nëng ꜀ki*, whose is this?

碁 棊 棋 ꜀Chi. The game of chess: [8]*꜀kong ꜀ki*, a foundation; [9]*꜀ki kwoh*, a chess-board arranged for gaming: COM., [10]*ch'iong*ʾ *꜀ki*, a game of 32 men, invented by Wuwang, B. C. 1120; [11]*꜀ui ꜀ki*, a game of 360 men, half black and half white, invented by Yau, B. C. 2300; [12]*ha*ʾ *꜀ki*, to play chess; [13]*꜀ki ʿp'wo*, a manual of chess-playing; [14]*꜀ki ꜀pwang*, a chess-board; *꜀ki ʿchi*, chess-men; COLL., *꜀ki ꜀kiăng sioh, pwo*ʾ to make a move; *꜀ki ʿchi miéng*ʾ kind of wafer-cakes—offered to ancestral tablets in the 7th moon; *꜀ki ꜀pwang póh*, large square sheets of foil-paper—burnt to idols.

淇 ꜀Ch'i. A tributary of the Yellow river in Honan: [15]*꜀chiéng ʿpi ꜀ki ëük*, he looked on the banks of the *꜀Ki*.

沂 ꜀Ch'i. Name of a river in Shantung, flowing south into lake Lohma in Kiangsu, and thence into the sea.

圻 ꜀Ch'i. A border, a limit, confines: also used for *꜀ki* (the Imperial domains): [16]*꜀u ꜀ki*, boundless; [17]*꜀ki ʿhu*, a commander of the household guards.

頎 ꜀ Long, tall: *꜀ki ꜀ki*, elegant, graceful. Read *ʿk'ong*: earnest; pitiful, compassionate.

祈 ꜀Ch'i. To pray, to invoke, to supplicate the gods for happiness; to beg, to entreat, to request—in the language of courtesy: COM., [18]*꜀ki ʿtó*, or *꜀ki ꜀kiu*, to pray, to beseech (the gods); [19]*꜀ki sëü*ʾ to pray for a son; [20]*꜀ki ꜀kiu pek, eng*ʾ (the gods) will certainly answer prayer; *꜀ki ꜀hwa hwoi*ʾ to pray for (success in) lotteries; COLL., *꜀ki ꜀sang*, to pray for clear weather.

祺 ꜀Ch'i. Fortunate, lucky, felicitous; tranquil, composed, undisturbed: *꜀sing ꜀ki*, to be promoted—used as a complimentary phrase.

祇 ꜀ At rest, tranquil; to quiet, to console; much, large, great: used for *꜀ki* (the Imperial domain); sometimes confounded with *꜀chié* (to respect; but, only): *te*ʾ *꜀ki*, the divinity of the earth, who produces things—the Chinese Hecate or Cybele; *met.*, Earth, Terra.

1 其時 2 其如 3 其餘 4 其次 5 其中必有緣故 6 二其 7 其上 8 根棋 9 棋局 10 象棋 11 圍棋 12 下棋 13 棋譜 14 棋盤 15 瞻彼淇澳 16 無圻 17 圻父 18 祈禱 19 祈嗣 20 祈求必應

祁 ˏCh'i. Full, abundant, much; very, exceeding; large, great; slowly, leisurely, gently.

蜞 ˏCh'i. Used in names for leeches and land-crabs: in the coll. read ˏk'i, q. v.: [1]'*ma ˏki*, a leech; [2]ˏ*p'ang ˏki*, a species of small land-crab.

騏 ˏCh'i. A dappled horse, marked like a chess-board, a fine-looking horse.

麒 ˏCh'i. The Chinese unicorn—a fabulous animal: COM., [3]ˏ*ki ˏling*, the male and female unicorns; [4]ˏ*ki ˏling ˏch'iong*, a wall in front of yamuns with a unicorn-like quadruped, called ˏ*t'ang* (covet), drawn on it; [5]ˏ*ki ˏling kwo' ˏsang ˏlūng 'kung 'chwi*, the unicorn passes over the hills (scattering fire), but the sea-dragon stirs the water (and produces rain to quench it).

鶀 ˏ A small species of wild goose, perhaps a sheldrake.

旗 ˏCh'i. A flag, a standard, a banner with devices on it: COM., ˏ*ki hó*² a signal flag; [6]ˏ*ki tiong*' a frame-like banner borne before graduates; [7]ˏ*ki a*² Bannermen, Manchus or naturalized Chinese; [8]ˏ*hwa ˏki kwok*, the United States; [9]ˏ*ki ˏkang*, a flag-staff; [10]ˏ*ki ˏkang tëü*² fluted chopsticks; COLL., ˏ*ki a*² '*kiăng*, and ˏ*ki a*² '*kwai*, are epithets applied to Manchus; ˏ*ki a*² *k'ié*' '*nä ˏkang ˏma ˏma*, "a Manchu adopted mother (is called) dry nurse"—a play on the word ˏ*kang*, meaning I am quite dry and have no money for you.

旂 ˏCh'i. Used for the last: a flag, a banner; a pennon with bells or jingles attached to it.

耆 ˏCh'i. A sexagenarian, an old man; old, aged; a superior or elder; strong, violent; to adjust; a scar on a horse's back: [11]ˏ*sing ˏki*, gentry and elders; [12]ˏ*ki ngai*' a superior, a teacher; COM., [13]ˏ*ki 'ló*, the aged.

鬐 ˏ A horse's mane; the dorsal spines of fishes.

奇 ˏCh'i. Extraordinary, rare, surprising, out of the common way; monstrous, miraculous, unnatural; unexpected, strange, new, wonderful: also read ˏ*k'ié*, and in the coll. ˏ*k'iä*, q. v.: COM., [14]ˏ*ki tek*, strange, unusual; to wonder; [15]ˏ*ki kwai*' unnatural, rare; [16]ˏ*ki ngëü*² to meet with surprising luck; [17]ˏ*ki ˏmwong*, rare art, as in choosing lucky days; [18]ˏ*ki 'siong ˏt'iéng ˏk'ai*, strangely thinks that the heavens will open —expects wonders.

崎 ˏCh'i. A steep path among the mountains; a dangerous defile or precipice: [19]ˏ*ki ˏk'ü*, a rugged road across mountains.

岐 ˏCh'i. A hill with two peaks; a fork in a road; bicuspidate; a headland or cape; to branch off, to diverge; *met.*, ambiguous, as words or conduct: ˏ*ki lo*² diverging roads; *met.*, right and wrong, devious;

[1]螞蜞 [2]蟛蜞 [3]麒麟 [4]麒麟墻 [5]麒麟過山龍滾水 [6]旗帳 [7]旗下 [8]花旗國 [9]旗杆 [10]旗杆箸 [11]紳耆 [12]耆艾 [13]耆老 [14]奇特 [15]奇怪 [16]奇遇 [17]奇門 [18]奇想天開 [19]崎嶇

COLL., 'wa' 'kong 'liong ,ki, to speak with a double meaning, or differently to two different parties.

琦 ,Ch'i. A valuable stone; precious; a curiosity, a plaything, such as are got for presents or rarities; large, great: [2],ki ,ting, a rare stone; [8]'ngwang' ,ki, a plaything.

碕 ,Ch'i. A winding shore; a stone bridge; rugged, craggy.

畸 ,Ch'i. Land left after marking out a square field, odd parcels of land: [4],ki ,ling, odds and ends, overplus.

觭 ,Ch'i. Also read ,k'i and ,k'ié: one horn elevated and the other depressed; one, single; to obtain: [5],ki 'ngeu, single and double, odd and even.

萁 ,Ch'i. The stems or stalks of pulse; tendrils, as of vines and pulse; an edible plant like a fern: [6],ki 'ch'ó, an aquatic grass of which garments are woven.

葵 ,K'uei. A term for malvaceous plants, resembling the Malva, Geranium, Althea, Hibiscus, &c.: COM., [7],ki ,hwa, the Althea rosea; [8],ki ch'ai' an esculent mallows; [9]'hiong' nik, ,ki, the sunflower.

蘄 ,. A labiate plant, called [10],ki ngai', used in ulcers; bit of a bridle; to seek, to beg, to ask for.

芪 ,. A medicinal plant, called [11],wong ,ki, used for its tonic properties; a kind of lungwort.

疷 ,. Also read 'ti and ,chié: sick, diseased; sluggish action of the bowels, constipation.

軝 ,. The projecting part of an axle or center of a wheel, the nave or hub.

逵 ,K'uei. A road, a thoroughfare; a place where four ways meet: [12],t'ung ,ki, a main thoroughfare, from which branches diverge.

馗 ,K'uei. Interchanged with the last: the jaw-bones, the sides of the face; place where nine or many roads meet, a thoroughfare; name of a mushroom: [13]'kiu ,ki, a road diverging in nine directions; COM., [14],chüng ,ki, a man of the T'ang dynasty, now deified as a protector against devils—drawn clutching a sword and standing on one foot.

夔 ,. A monster like a dragon having only one leg; a strange, monstrous appearance; a statesman in the times of Shun; fearful, alarming.

魕 ,. A sprite, the demons of the south; a devil, devilish; applied in Canton to foreigners on account of their shrill voices.

,Ki. A coll. word, as in ,ki 'li ,ku ,lu, to mutter in an under tone; rattling sound of the bowels; ,ki ,li (or ,liu) ,k'iu, convulsed (with laughter); pinched (with cold).

,Ki. A coll. euphonic prefix, as in ,ki ,ku, to paste.

[1]話講兩岐 [2]琦珍 [3]玩琦 [4]畸畧 [5]觭偶 [6]萁草 [7]葵花 [8]葵菜 [9]向日葵 [10]蘄艾 [11]黄芪 [12]通逵 [13]九馗 [14]鐘馗

(261) **Kiă.**

迦 ‛Chia. This character and the next six are read ˏka in the dictionaries: used for *hai’* (to meet accidentally): COM., [1]‛*sek*, ˏ*kiă*, a country in the west; also used for Sakya, a name of Budh.

跏 ‛Chia. As in [2]ˏ*kiă* ˏ*hu*, or [3]ˏ*kiă* ˏ*hu*, to sit with the legs bent under one—a phrase in Budhist books.

茄 ‛Chia. The brinjal, egg-plant; also used for ˏ*hó* (the lotus): [4]ˏ*tiĕng* ˏ*kiă*, mad-apple, the nightshade, belladonna; [5]ˏ*hwang* ˏ*kiă*, tomatoes.

笳 ‛Chia. A kind of flageolet made of a reed, also called *pek*, *lek*,: [6]ˏ*p‘i* ˏ*kiă*, the plaintive flageolet.

袈 ‛Chia. A kind of sleazy camlet: COM., [7]ˏ*kiă* ˏ*sa*, a sort of stole or surplice—worn by Budhists.

伽 ‛Ch‘ieh. Also read ˏ*kiă*: a Budhist word; pertaining to Budh: [8]ˏ*cheng* ˏ*kiă*, Budhistic, a Budhist priest; COM., [9]ˏ*kiă* ˏ*lang*, name of a Budh.

枷 ‛Chia. A cangue worn around the neck, a wooden pillory in which criminals are exposed; to cangue, cangued: COM., [10]ˏ*kiă chaik*, (coll. ˏ*kiă p‘ah*,), to cangue and whip; [11]ˏ*kiă hwang’* a cangued culprit; [12]ˏ*kiă ngwong’* a vow to wear the cangue; [13]ˏ*kiă* ‛*sŏ ne’ chiong’* the cangue and the lock (chain) guards—are two idol attendants supposed to preside over these punishments; [14]ˏ*kiă* ˏ*hung*, the official superscription on a cangue; COLL., [15]ˏ*tó* ˏ*kiă*, to wear the cangue; [16]*muk*, *ch‘iong’ chó’* ˏ*kiă chĕ’* ˏ*kiă chĕ’* the carpenter makes the cangue and cangues himself; *met.*, to involve one's self while plotting against others.

Kiă’. A coll. word: low, not elevated; cheap, inferior, as goods: *kiă’ kiă’* low, placed low; *kiă’ hwo’* inferior goods; *kiă’* ˏ*chong*, an inferior quality; *kiă’* ˏ*ngüng*, adulterated silver; *kiă’ sioh*, ˏ*chong* (or *hó’*), one grade inferior; *kiă’ sioh*, ˏ*cheng*, a step lower.

(262) **Kiăk.**

Kiăk,. A coll. word: angry, displeased, dissatisfied; to turn away in a pet: *po’ kiăk*, again angry; *kiăk*, *k‘ó’* gone off displeased; *chai’* ˏ*i* ‛*mwong kiăk*, let him be huffy if he pleases! *kiăk*, *kiăk*, ‛*tiong*, to go about in a pet; *kek*, *kek*, *kiăk*, *kiăk*, petulant, in the sulks.

揵 Chien.’ Read ˏ*kiĕng*; used in the *Paik*, ˏ*Ing* for the coll. *kiăk*,: to carry on the shoulder, as a bag or a cooly's implements; *met.*, displeased, petulant, in which sense the same as the last: [17]*kiăk*, ˏ*kiĕng* ˏ*t‘au*, to carry on the shoulder; [18]*kiăk*, ‛*ch‘ai* ˏ*ki*, to bear banners; ˏ*tang* ˏ*lai kiăk*, *kioh*, or *kiăk*, ‛*peng* ˏ*tang sóh*, burden-bearers, coolies; [19]*kiăk*, ‛*k‘i kiăk*, to carry (the implements) easily; *met.*, to go off in a pet; *kiăk*, ‛*siong* ‛*pong*, to bear about a notice offering a reward.

---

1 釋迦 2 跏趺 3 跏趺 4 甜茄 5 番茄 6 悲笳 7 袈裟 8 僧伽 9 伽藍 10 枷責 11 枷犯 12 枷愿 13 枷鎖二將 14 枷封 15 搦枷 16 木匠做枷自枷自 17 揵肩頭 18 揵彩旗 19 揵起揵

(263) **Kiăng.**

驚 ‹Ching. Read *,king;* coll. *,kiăng:* to fear, to be afraid; perturbed, scared, frightened; to dread, to apprehend, apprehensive: [1]*,kiăng ,hwong,* or *,kiăng oi'* to fear; *,kiăng sek, k'ó'* insensible from fright; [2]*'ng' ,kiăng,* not afraid; [3]*,kiăng ,tiong,* afraid of the public gaze, bashful; [4]*,kiăng ,kŭng,* to dread poverty; [5]*,i ,kiăng ,nĕng ch'ieu'* he fears people will laugh at him; *,kiăng ,kiăng heng' heng'* fearful yet elated (with hope); *'ting ,kiăng ,nĕng,* frightful! horrid!

經 ‹Ching. Read *,king;* coll. *,kiăng:* the warp: [6]*,k'eng ,kiăng,* to stretch the warp-threads (on the loom).

'仔 Tsu. Read *'chü;* used for the coll. *'kiăng:* a son, a lad, a girl, children; a diminutive of persons and things; young fruit; used in opprobrious epithets: [7]*'kiăng ,nié,* one's children; [8]*twai^2 'kiăng,* the eldest son; [9]*nié^2 'kiăng ,kó,* children; *sá' 'kiăng,* a small child, an infant; [10]*k'ĕük, 'yong 'kiăng,* a foster-son; [11]*'kiăng nŭk, 'kiăng miăng^2 'kiăng ,sing ,kang,* children are one's flesh, life, and heart; [12]*'kiăng ,song,* posterity; *kiék, 'kiăng,* the setting of young fruit; *,tü 'kiăng,* a pig; [13]*,sung 'kiăng,* a sampan; *'p'ai 'kiăng,* vagabonds; *'kwong ,tĕng 'kiăng,* Cantonese.

鏡' Ching. Read *keng';* coll. *kiăng':* a mirror, a looking-glass: [14]*,tĕng kiăng'* a brass mirror; *kiăng' ka'* a mirror-frame; *chieu' ,sing kiăng'* a pier-glass; *'hwi kiăng'* a reflector; [15]*,ch'iĕng 'li kiăng'* a telescope; *p'ah, ,hwa kiăng'* a kaleidoscope; *kiăng' ,ping,* a mirror-case with drawers; [16]*'ngang kiăng'* spectacles; *kiăng' meng' ,ngăng,* a kind of sycee-silver.

行 ‹Hang. Read *,heng;* coll. *,kiăng:* to walk, to go, to proceed, to travel; to act, to enact; the movement, performance, as of actors; movable, portable; *met.*, to do evil, licentious: *,kiăng tak,* walking, going; *,kiăng 'lá,* to observe etiquette; [17]*maing^2 maing^2 ,kiăng,* walk slowly—a parting salutation; *,kiăng hai^2* the acting of stage-players; *,kiăng tio^2* to walk, to journey; *,kiăng ,piéng* (or *,k'wi*), to step aside; *,kiăng chau'* a portable furnace; *,kiăng ,pung,* the sexual act; *,kiăng ,si,* timely, in demand, as goods; *,kiăng 'mwong* (or *chak,*), to go the rounds; *,kiăng t'ok, au^2* to fall behind; [18]*,kiăng ,sié tio^2* to pursue a vicious course; *,kiăng t'uk, tio^2* to come to the blunt (end of the) path—i. e., in straits, distressed.

健^2 Chien. Read *kiong^2;* coll. *kiăng^2:* also spoken *k'iăng^2:* hale, hearty, lusty, vigorous in old age: *,k'ing kiăng^2* strong, hale, as an old man; *'mwong lau^2 'mwong kiăng^2* grows vigorous with age.

(264) **Kié.**

圭 ‹ 珪 ‹ Kuei. A scepter or baton made of stone, given to noblemen and princes as a sign of rank and used at levees; a measure equal to 64 grains, or what can be taken up in three fingers:

---

[1]驚惶 [2]怀驚 [3]驚場 [4]驚窮 [5]伊驚仈笑 [6]牽經 [7]仔伲 [8]大仔 [9]伲仔哥 [10]乞養仔 [11]仔肉仔命仔心仔肝 [12]仔孫 [13]船仔 [14]銅鏡 [15]千里鏡 [16]眼鏡 [17]慢慢行 [18]行邪路

pek, ˛kié, a white baton; [1]'t'u ˛kié, a gnomon.

刲 ˛ To cut open, to eviscerate; to pierce, to stab, to stick a knife into.

奎 ˛ Kuei. The stride of a man; the 15th of the 28 constellations, answering to parts of Andromeda and Pisces, and auspicious to students: COM., [2]˛kié ˛kwong kóh, a temple or shrine for worshiping the ˛k'wi ˛sing, god of literature.

跬 ˛ Ch'i. Also read 'k'ié: a single step, once lifting of the foot; a pace three feet in length; a double step, called pwo', is six feet in length.

閨 ˛ Kuei. A door round at the top and square at the bottom, like an ancient badge of office; the door separating the private, from the public, part of a house; the apartments of the women; unmarried females; women; female, lady-like, feminine: [3]kié seu' a talented lady; COM., [4]˛kié 'nü, a virgin, a young lady; [5]˛kié ˛mwong, door to the female apartments.

雞 鷄 ˛ Chi. The cock, the gallinæ; a chicken: COM., [6]˛kié kwoí' a cockscomb; also the cockscomb plant; [7]˛kié ˛kang, sodomy; [8]˛kié ˛mó hok, a feather-duster; COLL., ˛kié kaĕk, a cock; [9]˛kié 'kiăng, chickens; [10]˛kié ˛hing, loss of virility; [11]˛kié 'kwong, a kind of small pork-sausage; [12]˛kié kieu' cock-crowing; ˛kié ˛pa 'chau laĕ' (like) a hen scratching—coarsely done; [13]˛kié ˛t'au ak, chiong' "chicken-head" and "duck-general"—attendants of the 'ngu tá' idols; ˛kié tauk, ˛hang siék, ch'oi' the hen pecks at a clam and breaks its bill; *met.*, gets only the trouble for his pains.

階 ˛ Read ˛kai; coll. ˛kié, as in [14]˛kié chó' stone-steps; ˛kié chó' ˛cheng (or ˛t'ŭng), a flight of stone steps.

規 ˛ Kuei. A pair of compasses; a law, regulation, usage, custom; a rate for taking a farm; to rule men according to usage; to regulate, to plan; to line, or draw a line; disk of the sun or moon: ˛kié cheng' to regulate others; ngwok, pwang' ˛kié, the moon half full; COM., [15]˛kié 'kü, or [16]˛kié ˛mwo, usage, custom; [17]˛kié lié' or ˛kié ˛teu, rules, regulations; [18]˛chá ˛kié the rules of a school; [19]˛ong ˛kié, by-laws of a guild; [20]nik, ˛kié, a sun-dial.

羈 ˛ Ch'i. Used in Foochow for the next: a tavern, an inn; a halter, a bridle for a horse; a girl's tuft of hair, a coiffure; to bridle, to restrain; to regulate, to economize; to detain, to hinder: [21]˛kié 'lü, a caravansary; a wayfarer; [22]˛kié ˛liu, to stop at a hospice; detained, hindered.

羇 ˛ An inn, a hospice, a caravansary; to lodge: ˛kié k'aik, a sojourner; ˛kié 'lü, a traveler, a lodger.

醯 ˛ Hsi. Sour, an acid taste like vinegar: ˛kié chiong' pickled relishes; ˛kié 'hai, acid

[1] 土圭 [2] 奎光閣 [3] 閨秀 [4] 閨女 [5] 閨門 [6] 雞冠 [7] 雞姦 [8] 雞毛拂 [9] 雞仔 [10] 雞形 [11] 雞[illegible] [12] 雞叫 [13] 雞頭鴨將 [14] 階座 [15] 規矩 [16] 規模 [17] 規例 [18] 齋規 [19] 行規 [20] 日規 [21] 羈旅 [22] 羈留

condiments; [1]*‚kié ‚kié*, animalcules in vinegar.

枅 ‚ A cross-beam on posts to support a roof; the tie-beam of two pillars.

笄 ‚ Chia. A hair-pin, broad and bent, put on the back of the head at marriage; the coiffure; also applied to the cap first worn by young men; *met.*, the age of puberty: [2]*kwang' ‚kié*, to cap a young man; COM., [3]*kik‚ ‚kié*, to arrive at puberty, as girls.

‚Kié. A coll. word: to tie, to fasten; to tether, as animals; *met.*, to confine, as the mind: *‚kié k'o' tai'* to tie to the girdle; *‚kié ‚sing ‚piêng*, to suspend on the person; *‚kié ‚sing*, to fix the mind, as by giving one work to do; *‚kié 'lá taiu'* "tied and pitched down"—i. e., bound to, as by an engagement.

‚Kié. A coll. word: soon, quick; easily, rapidly: *‚kié twai'* to grow fast; *‚kié piêng' meng'* soon angry; *‚kié siong' ngié'* to learn easily how to do it; *‚kié á' ‚nang ‚ching*, easy to learn but hard to become thorough in; *‚kié 'pa ‚kié yéng'* soon filled and soon rejecting the food; *met.*, fickle, capricious.

計 ' Chi. A complete number, a deliberation in full assembly; to plan, to consider, to devise; to calculate, estimate, reckon, count, compute; stratagem, scheme, plot: COM., [4]*kié' ch'aik*, or [5]*kié' ‚meu*, a plan, a scheme; [6]*kié' kau'* to contend, to join issue with; [7]*kié' saung'* to reckon up; [8]*tai' kié'* a triennial examination of district magistrates; [9]*‚ka kié'* domestic expenses; [10]*'kwi kié'* a crafty scheme; [11]*sek‚ kié'* to reckon wrong.

桂 ' Kuei. The Cassia tree (Laurus Cassia and Cinnamomea); *met.*, literary reputation and honors: [12]*chiék‚ kié'* or [13]*‚p'ang kié'* to pluck a cassia twig—become a Küjin; COM., [14]*kié' ‚hwa*, the Olea fragrans; [15]*kié' ‚p'ui* cinnamon; [16]*ngwok‚ kié'* monthly rose, Rosa semperflorens; [17]*nük‚ kié'* fine cassia; [18]*póh‚ kié'* a common cassia; [19]*kié' ‚hwa ‚yong*, figured calico; [20]*kié' ho' 'li ‚tüng ‚wong*, stimulating pills of cassia and other ingredients.

繼 ' Chi. Connected threads; a line of succession in kindred; to continue, to enter on the duties or pursuits of others; to adopt; succeeding to, successively, to follow after: *kié' ngiék‚* a hereditary profession; COM., [21]*kié' 'mu*, a stepmother; [22]*kié' ch'ëü'* to take a second wife (after the death of the first); COLL., *kié' chioh‚* or *kié' 'hwi*, to finish by candle-light, as a play.

薊 ' Chi. A thistle, Carduus benedictus: *Kié' ‚chiu*, a district in the north of Chihli.

寄 ' Chi. To lodge, to remain awhile in a house; to confide in, to commit to, to trust in; to hand over, to deliver in charge; to send by, to transmit; to interpret; the east: *kié' t'auk*, to commit to;

[1]醯雞 [2]冠笄 [3]及笄 [4]計策 [5]計謀 [6]計較 [7]計算 [8]大計 [9]家計 [10]詭計 [11]失計 [12]折桂 [13]攀桂 [14]桂花 [15]桂皮 [16]月桂 [17]肉桂 [18]薄桂 [19]桂花洋 [20]桂附理中丸 [21]繼母 [22]繼娶

福州方言拼音字典

[1]kié' ˌseng, an epiphyte, a parasite; COM., [2]kié' seng' to send a letter or message; [3]kié' ˈmá, to send to buy; [4]kié' ˈk'eü seng' to send a verbal message; COLL., kié' k'ó' to send off; kié' ˈyong, to rear a child in a second husband's home; kié' ˌsiong, to send (paper) trunks (by one just deceased)—done by burning them; kié' ˈtiong ch'io' to send home.

季' Chi. Little, tender, junior, whatever is young and immature; the least or last of a series; a season, a quarter of a year: [5]maing' tëüng' kié' a series of three, as the three months of a season; [6]kié' sié' the last generation; a waning dynasty; COM., [7]sëü' kié' (coll. se' kié'), the four seasons; [8]ˌch'ung kié' spring; [9]kié' ˌch'ung, the 3rd month of spring; [10]kié' tói' paid quarterly; COLL., [11]siong' kié' and [12]a' kié' the former and latter half of the year—used somewhat indefinitely.

悸' Chi. Perturbed; agitation of the mind; to perturb; the edge or fringe of a belt or girdle: [13]ˌsing kié' the mind agitated.

罽' A seine for catching fish: [14]ˌlié kié' a kind of rug or carpet, made of felt or long hair.

鯕 ˌCh'i. Read ˌkié; used in the Paik, ˌIng for the coll. ˌkié: a kind of salted sea-fish; it is small, varying from one to four or five inches in length: [15]ˌung ˌt'i ˌkié, and [16]ˌt'i hok, ˌkié two varieties of ˌkié fish; ˌkwa ˈchi ˌkié, "pumpkin-seed ˌkié"—the smallest sort; ˌkié ˈtai, remnants of ˌkié fish.

(265) Kiék.

偈, Chieh. To exert one's strength; martial, vehement; to stop, to cease; a Budhist enigma: COM., [17]kiék, ˌngiong, or [18]kiék, ˈngü, the apothegms of Budhist books.

結, Chieh. A knot, a knob made of cord; a skein, a hank; to work or weave in knots, to knit; to tie, to fasten, to bind; to contract, to bind parties; stiff, as dry paste or dough; to set, as fruit; to induce, as ill-will; an agreement, bond, compact, engagement; united, banded together, engaged; tied, fixed: in the coll. read kaik, q. v.: COM., [19]kiék, ˌhwong, to betroth; [20]ngwok, kiék, a monthly settlement; [21]kiék, kwoh, final result, the issue of; [22]kiék, ˈkwo, to reap the fruits (of one's life); kiék, ˈwong, to knit nets; to weave webs, as spiders; kiék, wong' to to bear a grudge, at feud with; kiék, liék, fervent, earnest; kiék, pai' (or ngié'), to pledge friendship; kiék, ˈch'ó ˌkang ˌk'wang, "bind straw and bring a ring in the mouth"—an allusion to ancient fable, meaning I will requite your favor; COLL., kiék, ˈchi, to bear seed; kiék, sioh, pek, to cast an account.

纈, Chieh. To tie, to bind together pieces of silk in order to dye them.

絜, Chieh. Used for the next: pure, clear; a species of hemp. Read kiék,: a line, a rule; to bind; to bring within

[1]寄生 [2]寄信 [3]寄買 [4]寄口 信 [5]孟仲季 [6]季世 [7]四季 [8]春季 [9]季春 [10]季兌 [11]上季 [12]下季 [13]心悸 [14]氂罽 [15]鰯鮐 鯕 [16]鮐核鯕 [17]偈言 [18]偈語 [19]結婚 [20]月結 [21]結局 [22]結果

limits, as a river: ¹*kiék₎ tok₎* to adjust, to restrict by rule; ²*kiék₎ ʻkü*, to furnish a rule or model.

潔, Chieh. Limpid, pure, clear; untainted, above bribes, pure-minded; neat, trim clean, tidy; to purify, to cleanse, to correct: ³*₍liêng kiék₎* incorrupt, above bribes; COM., ⁴*kiék₎ chiāng*ʾ pure, undefiled; to cleanse; ⁵*₍ch'ing kiék₎* clean, as water; chaste, pure.

襭 結, Chieh. To take hold of a lappet or skirt; to put the skirt in the girdle, so as to hold something in it; to carry things in the skirt of the dress.

擷, Chieh. Used for the last: to carry any thing in the lap or bosom; to take with the fingers; to pluck, to select.

挈, Chieh. To lift, to raise from the ground; to suspend, to hold dangling; to adjust, to put in order: ⁶*₍t'i kiék₎* to lift and carry; *met.*, to recommend. Read *k'ié*ʾ: to write on tablets; deficient, exhausted.

揭, Chieh. To lift up, to lift or take off, as a hat or cover; to raise the dress; to take upon, to bear, to undertake; responsible for; to publish, or make known; a car drawn rapidly: ⁷*kiék₎ t'aik₎* to post a placard or pasquinade; ⁸*kiék₎ ₍tang*, a note of hand; ⁹*kiék₎ ʻhieu*, to publish, as a list of graduates; COM., ¹⁰*kiék₎ kai*ʾ to lift the (bridal) veil, as the bridegroom makes a feint of doing when married.

筴, Chia. To take up, as with chopsticks. Read *ch'aik₎*: to divine, as with bamboo sticks; also used for *ch'aik*, (bamboo slips; a plan, a scheme).

篋, Sia. Also read *k'iék₎*: a basket for sundries, a pannier: ¹¹*₍siong kiék₎* a long and narrow chest, a trunk; ¹²*₍chü kiék₎* a book-trunk.

碣, Chieh. Also read *kiék₎*: a round stone pillar with an inscription; an ignille or sharp projecting rock, as on the coast of Chihli near the Great Wall; the fluttering of birds: ¹³ *₍pi kiék₎* square and round stone pillars.

趨, To go away, to depart; martial, bold; a brave and valiant bearing.

莢, Chia. Pods of leguminous plants; legumes, including the seeds; an Acacia; a petiole sheath in grasses: ¹⁴*kiék₎ ₍chiéng*, a small coin of the Han dynasty, like the seeds of the elm; ¹⁵*₍ming kiék₎* a lucky plant—which grew in Yu's courtyard.

鋏, Chia. A frame for holding fused metal while casting; a sword: ¹⁶*₍tang kiék₎* to drum on the sword with the fingers.

鑷, Read *niék₎*; used for the coll. *kiék₎*: to take with tongs or pincers: *kiék₎ ₍mó ʻkwong*, to pluck out the pin-feathers; *kiék₎ niék₎* a pair of pincers, tweezers.

---

1 絜度 2 絜矩 3 廉潔 4 潔淨 5 清潔 6 提挈 7 揭帖 8 揭單 9 揭曉 10 揭蓋 11 箱篋 12 書篋 13 碑碣 14 莢錢 15 蓂莢 16 彈鋏

福州方言拼音字典

搘, Chi. Read *kiē*'; used in the *Paik*, *Ing* for the coll. *kiék*,: to take with chopsticks: [1]*kiék*, *sioh*, *tëü*' to take a morsel with chopsticks; [2]*kiék*, *k'ó*' *siăh*, take with the chopsticks and eat; *kiék*, *k'ó*' *p'woi*' to take of the condiments.

頰, Chia. The jaws, the sides of the face, the cheeks, utterance, articulation: [3]*hwang*' *kiék*, slow of speech; [4]*t'ó kiék*, rosy cheeks; COLL., [5]*u meng*' *kiék*, has dark cheeks.

刦, 刧, Chieh. To take by force, to snatch, to seize, to plunder, to rob; importunity, hurry; a Budhist period, a kulpa: COM., [6]*ch'iong kiék*, (coll. *p'ah*, *kiék*,) to rob; [7]*kiék*, *chai*' to plunder a stockade; [8]*kiék*, *hwong kong*' (coll. *kaung*'), to seize the imperial tribute.

盤, Chien. Read *pwang*, as in *hwak*, *pwang* (to sell goods to hucksters or retailers); used for the coll. *kiék*,, as in [9]*kiék*, *hwo*' to buy goods for retailing; [10]*kiék*, *ch'e*' the retail prices; [11]*kiék*, *k'ó*' *má*' buy them up and sell by retail.

傑, 杰, Chieh. Eminent in talents and virtue, a hero; proud, self-willed, opinionated; the second is also the name of a statesman ([12]*Ngoi*' *kiék*,), A. D. 956, in the days of the After Chow dynasty: COM., [13]*ing hüng hó kiék*, brave, heroic.

桀, Chieh. A hen-roost; courageous, excelling, gifted with great qualities, magnanimous; one of a thousand, a hero, in which sense used for the last; harsh, cruel, villainous, truculent; to lift, to carry: COM., [14]*kiék*, *teu*' the two wicked emperors, *Kiék*, *koi*' (the last monarch of the Hia, B. C. 1818), and *Teu*' *sing* (the last of the Shang, B. C. 1154).

竭, Chieh. To exhaust, to carry to the utmost; to sink away, wanting; defeated; to carry on the shoulder; exhausted power like that of the five elements, which are then succeeded by others: [15]*niéng soi lik*, *kiék*, aged and infirm; COM., [16]*kiék*, *lik*, to exert one's strength to the utmost; [17]*lik*, *kiék*, the strength exhausted; COLL., *po*' *taing*' *po*' *kiék*, very close and niggardly, as a mean employer.

(266) Kiéng.

鹼, Hsien. Also read *ngiéng*': salt, briny water; a kind of barilla obtained from marine plants in Shantung: COM., [18]*kiéng chwi*, lye, lixivium; [19]*kiéng t'ong*, hot lye.

幵, Level, even, equal; the hands lifted together; the name of a district.

豜, Chien. A pig three years old, a full grown hog; a hornless animal like a deer.

堅, Chien. Hard, solid, firm, durable; sound; stout, hale, robust; determined, persevering, constant, resolute, unwavering; to establish,

[1]搘一箸 [2]搘去食 [3]緩頰 [4]桃頰 [5]烏面頰 [6]搶刦 [7]刦寨 [8]刦皇貢 [9]盤貨 [10]盤市 [11]盤去賣 [12]魏杰 [13]英雄豪傑 [14]桀紂 [15]年衰力竭 [16]竭力 [17]力竭 [18]鹼水 [19]鹼湯 ○

to strengthen, to confirm; to harden, to congeal: [1]*˓kiéng chek˒* fixed in one's way; [2]*˓kiéng ˛nging*, stiffened; firm, resolute; compact, as a style; COM., [3]*˓kiéng ko’* solid, durable; unwavering; COLL., *˓kiéng ˓chong*, of fine, substantial quality; *‘yă ˓kiéng*, very strong, well-made.

肩 ˓Chien. The shoulder, the scapula; to take upon, to bear, to sustain; competent; firm; an animal three years old: [4]*‘sek˒ ˓kiéng*, to withdraw the shoulder, to desist; COM., [5]*˓kiéng ˓ting*, sores on the shoulder, as of coolies; [6]*˓kiéng pié’* fleshy part of the arm; [7]*˛pwang ˓kiéng*, trimming on the neck of a lady's dress; [8]*˓kiéng ˓t‘ieu ˓seng ‘li*, huckstering; COLL., [9]*˓kiéng ‘pong k‘wak˒* broad-shouldered; *met.*, has many influential friends; [10]*˓kiéng ‘tiu ˛kiéng*, shoulder to shoulder—crowded; *˓kiéng ˛t‘au k‘ëük˒ ˛nëng chó’ tio˒ ˛kiŏng*, the shoulder made a road for people to walk on; *met.*, over-ridden, imposed on by others.

兼 ˓Chien. A conjunction, moreover, together with, and, also, with, in addition to; equally, same; to attend to several things; to join, to connect together, connected: [11]*˓kiéng ˛ŭng*, to contain several; [12]*˓kiéng peng’* to coalesce; COM., [13]*˓kiéng p‘woi’* additional condiments; [14]*˓kiéng ‘sü*, to fill an additional office temporarily; COLL., *˓kiéng pek˒ nóh*, other things added; [15]*po’ ˓kiéng*, or *kaing’ ˓kiéng*, still more, in addition.

鰜 ˓Chien. A kind of sole, called [16]*‘pi muk˒ ˛ngü*, the paired-eye fish; it is said to have only one eye and to swim in pairs, clasped to each other.

鶼 ˓Chien. The spoonbill (Platalea major) Temm. and Schleg.; in Chinese books called [16]*‘pi ik˒ ‘neu*, the paired-wing bird, because having only one wing and one eye, it needs a mate to fly with.

蒹 ˓Chien. A marshy plant, a kind of sedge, called [17]*˓kiéng ˓ka*, which cattle fatten on.

縑 ˓Chien. A thick kind of lustring, woven close so as to shed rain; it is now called *‘kiong* and *kiong’*.

撿 ‘Chien. Interchanged with the next: to coerce, to repress; to gather and bind together; to inspect; to collect, to collate; to choose: [18]*‘kiéng sok˒* to restrain, to keep in subjection; COM., [19]*‘kiéng ‘tiéng*, to arrange carefully.

檢 ‘Chien. An envelope; a label or title put on a book; a model, a pattern, a rule; to examine; to assort, to arrange, to collate; to compose a book: COM., [20]*˛sung ‘kiéng*, the supervisor of a small district or township; [21]*˓seu ‘kiéng ˓kwang*, an officer who searches candidates on entering the examination-hall.

繭 ‘Chien. A cocoon; the silky pupæ of moths; the sound of gentle breathing: *˛chang ‘kiéng*, the silk-worm's co-

1 堅執	3 堅固	5 肩疔	7 盤肩	生理	闊 10 肩	11 兼容	13 兼配	15 仅兼	鳥 17 蒹	束 19 撿	檢 21 搜
2 堅凝	4 息肩	6 肩背	8 肩挑	9 肩膀	肘肩	12 兼併	14 兼署	16 比翼	葭 18 撿	點 20 巡	檢官

coon; COM., [1]'kiéng ꜀tiu, a sort of crape pongee; [2]꜀t'ing ꜀hiong'kiéng, a coarse, yellowish pongee; [3]'kiéng ꜀tiu ꜀á, pongee (mourning) shoes —also made of yellow nankeen. Read 'keng in the coll., as in ꜀ch'eng 'keng, silk-worms.

襇 'Chien. A plait, a fold; tucks, gathers: COLL., k'ak꜀ 'kiéng, to make plaits; pah꜀ 'kiéng ꜀kung, a skirt with many folds.

見 Chien.' To see, to look at, to notice, to perceive by the senses; to visit; an opinion, a mental view; seeing, observing, feeling, impressed by; used in forming reflective verbs, and denotes the passive voice and past time; the 147th radical: also read hiéng', q. v.: COM., [4]꜀kó kiéng' your opinion; [5]꜀siong kiéng' to see each other, an interview; [6]'k'ó kiéng' from which it can be seen; [7]kiéng' kwo' seen; [8]kiéng' ch'ieu' laughed at; [9]kiéng' sek꜀ knowledge; [10]ch'iok꜀ kiéng' clear discrimination; [11]kiéng' ꜀kwang, to see the officer—i. e., to go to law; [12]kiéng' 'hó, on good terms with; [13]kiéng' ꜀ch'a, better in health; [14]kiéng' chioh꜀ ꜀tó 'kwa, will borrow some of you—an epistolary phrase; kiéng' ꜀ang ꜀sü 'ma, see the saddle and think of the horse; met., to recollect by the law of association; COLL., kiéng' kaĕk꜀ to perceive; kiéng' ch'ëük꜀ angered, vexed; kiéng' meng' 'lá, a present to a visitor, as to a son-in-law; kiéng' tai' 'ma, an inquisitive woman; kiéng' ꜀chiéng cheu' ꜀ch'iong, crouches as soon as he sees money—sordidly covetous; kiéng' cheng' ꜀tó 'sieu ꜀nëng, of the many I have seen—scil., you are the worst!

劍 Chien.' A sword, a two-edged sword, a rapier: pwoi' kiéng' to wear a sword; [15]siék꜀ kiéng' ꜀sung ꜀ch'iong, tongue like a sword and lips like spears—cutting, sarcastic; COM., [16]'u kiéng' to fence; [17]꜀tó kiéng' swords; kiéng' ꜀tié, a pond near the examination-hall in Foochow; COLL., kiéng' sioh꜀ 'pa, one sword.

乾 ꜀Chien. Heaven, the power or agency of heaven; a sovereign; a father; the first diagram; enduring, stable, superior, strong; diligent, untiring: also read ꜀kang, q. v.: [18]'t'á ꜀kiéng, to embody heavenly principles—virtuous, as a prince; COM., ꜀kiéng ꜀lüng, the emperor Kienlung, A. D. 1736-1796; [19]꜀kiéng ꜀k'ong, the first and second diagrams—heaven and earth, father and mother, prince and minister; [20]꜀kiéng ꜀chü and [21]꜀k'ong ꜀chü, a boy's and girl's betrothal-cards.

墘 ꜀Ch'ien. A vulgar character: an edge, a border; a shore, a bank, a margin; eaves: ꜀kiéng ꜀kiéng, the edge of; ꜀kiéng kaĕk꜀ edges and corners; 'chwi ꜀kiéng, the water's side; 'k'au ꜀kiéng, the verge, border; ꜀siéng ꜀kiéng the eaves; ꜀kiéng ëü' k'ó' the edge worn off.

虔 ꜀Ch'ien. The firm step of a tiger; determined, inflexible, pertinacious; sincere, ingenuous; attentive, correct, pious, devout; to venerate, to respect; kind, beneficent;

[1]繭綢 [2]沉香繭 [3]繭綢鞋 [4]高見 [5]相見 [6]可見 [7]見過 [8]見笑 [9]見識 [10]灼見 [11]見官 [12]見好 [13]見瘥 [14]見借多寡 [15]舌劍脣鎗 [16]舞劍 [17]刀劍 [18]體乾 [19]乾坤 [20]乾書 [21]坤書

to take by force, to kill; a tiger killing his prey; a cleaving-block; trifling, unimportant: [1]ˏkiéng kó' to inform respectfully; [2]ˏkiéng keng' to revere; COM., [3]ˏkiéng ˏsing, sincere, devout; [4]ˏkiéng ˏsing ˏkiéng e' or ˏkiéng ˏkiéng ˏsing, the mind intently devout.

揵 ˏChien. Also read ˏkiong: to lift, to take up and carry on the shoulder: used for the coll. kiăk, q. v. Read ˋkiong: to raise; to close, to stop up; to establish a frontier.

騝 ˏChien. Also read ˏkiong: a dun or brown horse with a yellow back.

儉[2] Chien. Moderate, temperate, frugal, economical, sparing; close-fisted, stingy: [5]kiéng[2] saik, or kiéng[2] leng[2] stingy, niggardly; COM., [6]kiéng[2] ˋsang, economical; [7]kiéng[2] ëüng[2] or kiéng[2] kiéng[2] ëüng[2] to use sparingly; [8]chiék, kiéng[2] frugal, temperate; COLL., k'ak, kiéng[2] parsimonious, stingy; kiéng[2] kiéng[2] kau' ˋsai, enough for one's need by rigid economy.

(267) Kieu.

嬌 ˏChiao. Beautiful, comely, graceful; delicate, tender; dear, lovely; an affected, elegant, polished manner; a stylish figure or form; to cry or whine for; petted, spoiled: [9]ˏyeu ˏkieu, fascinating, like a siren; [10]Ak, ˏkieu, a famous beauty in the times of Wu-ti, B. C. 100; [11]ˏwong ˏkieu, the yellow beauty —i. e., wine; [12]ˏkieu k'aik, a son-in-law; COM., [13]ˏkieu ˋyong, to bring up tenderly—to wink at (a child's) vices; [14]ˏkieu ˏkieu, graceful, lovely; [15]ˏkieu ˏi ˏu hau' ˏkieu ˏch'á chauk, lwang' a petted son is unfilial and a petted wife makes trouble; COLL., [16]ˏkieu ˋkiăng, a dear, petted child; chó' ˏkieu, to whine and tease.

驕 ˏChiao. A stately horse, a wild, restive horse; proud, haughty, ungovernable; self-confident, conceited; to glory in, to disdain: [17]ˏkieu ˏch'ià ˏing ik, pride, waste, lewdness, and idleness; [18]ˏkieu chëü' ungovernable and vicious; COM., [19]ˏkieu ngó[2] proud, arrogant.

鷮 ˏChiao. A species of pheasant, called ˏkieu ˏkieu, perhaps from its clucking note; it has a long tail and is supposed by some to resemble the barred-tail or Rheeves' pheasant (syrmaticus).

ˋ晈 Chiao. To squint: ˋkieu ˋmau, to look askance; a side-glance, squinting.

ˋ皎 Chiao. Interchanged with the next: the brightness of the moon, splendor of the sun; clear, bright, effulgent; an immaculate, pure white: ˋkieu kiék, white and spotless.

ˋ皦 Chiao. White, lustrous, refulgent, like a bright gem: ˋkieu nik, a bright sun; ngwok, ch'ok, ˋkieu, the moon rising in brightness.

ˋ狡 Chiao. A little black poodle, found in the north; doublings of a fox; artful,

[1]虔告 [2]虔敬 [3]虔誠 [4]虔意 虔心 [5]儉嗇 [6]儉省 [7]儉用 [8]節儉 [9]妖嬌 [10]阿嬌 [11]黃嬌 [12]嬌客 [13]嬌養 [14]嬌嬌 [15]嬌兒 無孝 嬌妻 作亂 [16]嬌仔 [17]驕奢淫佚 [18]驕恣 [19]驕傲

crafty, specious, mendacious, deceitful; maddened, wild; cruel: [1]*ʻkieu kié*ʼ a tricky scheme; [2]*ʻkieu cha*ʼ mendacious; [3]*ʻkieu hwak*, or *ʻkieu kwai*ʼ deceitful, knavish; [4]*ʻkieu tʻo*ʼ the cunning rabbit; *met.*, a wily fellow; COM., [5]*ʻkieu auk*, crafty and overbearing.

姣 ʻ Chiao. Interchanged with the last: beautiful, winsome, pretty; flattering, artful, specious: [6]*ʻkieu me*ʼ pretty and captivating; *ʻkieu ʻhó*, handsome.

㽱 ʻ A colic, a violent pain in the bowels: used for *꜀kiu* in the coll., q. v.: COM., [7]*ʻkieu ꜀tong ꜀sa*, colic or cholera morbus; COLL., [8]*ʻkieu ꜀tong ʻkieu toʼ tʻiăng*ʼ griping pains in the bowels.

矯 ʻ Chiao. Interchanged with the next: straight; to straighten out; *met.*, to rectify, to correct what is wrong; bold, strong, martial; to simulate, deceitful, fraudulent; to usurp authority: [9]*ʻkieu cheng*ʼ to correct; [10]*ʻkieu ʻkiong*, to compel, to constrain; [11]*ʻkieu ꜀u*, to criminate falsely; [12]*ʻkieu tʻauk*, to act under false pretences; [13]*ʻkieu ꜀kiéng*, to seize by force, oppressive.

撟 ʻ Chiao. To raise the hand, to lift; firm, unyielding, violent; to straighten, to correct; false, deceitful; to take, to select; to bend by the application of fire; in the coll., to pry with a lever, to pry up or out: also read *kieu*ʼ in the coll., q. v.: COLL., [14]*ʻkieu ꜀kʻwi*, pry it away; *ʻkieu ʻkʻi ꜀li*, pry it up.

攪 ʻ Chiao. To stir up or about, to mix up; to beguile to evil; to disorder, to confuse; to trouble, to annoy, to incommode; to excite commotion: *ʻkieu ʻnau*, disordered, embroiled; [15]*ʻkieu lwang*ʼ to disorder, to make a commotion; COLL., [16]*ʻkieu ꜀soi*, frets himself lean; *ʻkieu ꜀ka ꜀chiăng*, a teasing, troublesome elf!

鉸 ʻ Chiao. Pivots on which a door turns; a hinge, a joint; a clamp, a hasp: [17]*꜀ting ʻkieu*, the pin, as of a hinge; [18]*ʻkieu ꜀tó*, or *ʻkieu ʻcheng*, shears. Read *kau*ʼ: to inlay metals.

餃 ʻ Read *kau*ʼ; used for the coll. *ʻkieu*: a small kind of dumpling with a stuffing of meat, sugar, turnip, etc.

絞 ʻ Chiao. To bind, to twist, to wrap about; to strangle; blunt, unceremonious; a sash, a girdle: [19]*ʻkieu chʻéü*ʼ to pick out others' faults; COM., [20]*ʻkieu ʻsi*, to execute by strangling; *ʻkieu ꜀kang hau*ʼ to await in prison the time of such execution.

繳 ʻ To wind about; a leg-wrapper; to hand to an officer; to deliver up, to return, to pay back: [21]*꜀wong ʻkieu*, paid up, settled; COM., [22]*ʻkieu ꜀kwang*, to deliver to an officer; *ʻkieu so*ʼ to render an account, as of money spent; *ʻkieu kwong*ʼ to hand in essays; COLL., *ʻkieu ꜀teng*, to return, to hand back; *ʻkieu kioh*, cooliage, porterage. Read *chʻiok*,: to tie a string to an arrow when shot.

---

1 狡計 2 狡詐 3 狡猾 4 狡兔 5 狡惡 6 姣媚 7 㽱腸痧 8 㽱腸㽱肚痛 9 矯正 10 矯强 11 矯誣 12 矯託 13 矯虔 14 撟開 15 攪亂 16 攪瘦 17 釘鉸 18 鉸刀 19 絞刺 20 絞死 21 完繳 22 繳官

ʻ蟜 *Chiao.* The writhings of a snake or dragon, to wriggle, to stretch one's self; a kind of ant.

ʻ蹻 *Chiao.* To raise the feet; to march, to prance; strong, martial, proud, valorous; to cut antics, as a successful fool; puffed up, delighted; unsettled: also read *kiok*, and *ˏk'ieu*, q. v.

叫ʼ 呌ʼ *Chiao.* To call, to send for, to call upon; to cry out; to name; to cause; to command, to tell to do; to persuade; named, called, termed: COM., [1]*kieuʼ keuʼ* to cry out for help; [2]*kieuʼ engʼ* call and answer; congruity, as of ideas in consecutive clauses; [3]*kieuʼ hwaʼ* to beg alms; COLL., [4]*kieuʼ ˏkang*, cock-crowing; *kieuʼ ʻhwang ˏt'iéng*, bawls (loud enough) to turn the sky; [5]*ˏnëng ʻlá kieuʼ ʻnŭ*, some one is calling you; [6]*ʻk'ëŭk, siăh, kieuʼ ˏká*, the beggars cry in the street; [7]*tiéʼ ˏnëng kieuʼ ʻnŭ chóʼ* who told you to do so? *kieuʼ ʻló siéʼ nóh, ˏmiăng*, by what name is it called? [8]*kieuʼ ʻcheu ˏt'ai ˏmó nŭk,* a singing bird when killed (furnishes) no meat; *met.*, a gabbler effects nothing.

嗷ʼ To cry out, to roar; a deep tone of voice: [9]*kieuʼ ˏtó*, suppressed weeping; [10]*kieuʼ kieuʼ* a deep tone; [11]*kieuʼ ˏhu*, to call out.

ˏ僑 *Chiao.* An inn, a lodging-place; a temporary sojourn; high: [12]*ˏkieu ˏkŭ*, to visit, to sojourn.

ˏ嶠 *Chiao.* A high sharp peak, where no water remains: [13]*ˏwong ˏkieu*, one of five lofty hills in Shantung where genii dwell.

ˏ喬 *Ch'iao.* Interchanged with the next in the *met.* sense for a father: high, stately, lofty; looking upward, aspiring, like the branches of a tree; curved, crooked; proud, discontented; a surname: [14]*ˏkieu muk,* stately trees—an order of plants in botany; [15]*ˏkieu ʻchŭ*, father and son; COM., [16]*ˏkieu ˏch'iéng ˏchi ʻhi*, congratulations on removing—a phrase written on presents to one removing to a new abode.

ˏ橋 *Chiao.* A bridge with high arches, planks laid across streams; a ferry-rope stretched over a river; a pulley-beam over a well; a viaduct; disobedient, disrespectful; a stately tree like a cypress or poplar; *met.*, a father: in the sense of a bridge read *ˏkio* in Foochow, q. v.: *ˏkieu ʻchŭ*, father and son.

ˏ蕎 *Chiao.* A kind of grain, called [17]*ˏkieu mek,*; buckwheat; the culm is reddish, it is two or three feet high, has white flowers, and is reaped in October.

轎ʼ *Chiao.* A sedan; formerly it denoted a covered chaise: COM., [18]*ˏhwa kieuʼ* a bridal sedan; *ˏming kieuʼ* an open sedan; *kieuʼ ʻkwang*, sedan-men's establishment; *kieuʼ ˏchiéng*, sedan-fare; *kieuʼ ˏchiă ˏyong*, sun-screens attached to a

[1]叫 [3]叫 [5]伙 [6]乞 [7]俤 做 毛 [10]嗷 [12]僑 [14]喬 [16]喬 [17]蕎
救 化 禮 食 伙 [8]叫 肉 嗷 居 木 遷 麥
[2]叫 [4]叫 叫 叫 叫 鳥 [9]嗷 [11]嗷 [13]員 [15]喬 之 [18]花
應 更 汝 街 汝 剖 咷 呼 嶠 梓 喜 轎

福州方言拼音字典

sedan; [1]*'kieu*^{2} *˛hu*, or *kieu*^{2} *˛pang*, sedan-bearers; [2]*kieu*^{2} *˛liéng*, curtains of a sedan; [3]*kwo*^{2} *˛sang kieu*^{2} a mountain-sedan—made long for reclining in; [4]*paik*$_2$ *chó*^{2} *kieu*^{2} a sedan with eight bearers; COLL., *˛t'wa 'tá kieu*^{2} a kind of large, heavy sedan; [5]*sói*^{2} *kieu*^{2} to ride in a sedan; [6]*kieu*^{2} *kaung*^{2} sedan-thills; *'yă kieu*^{2} sedans not belonging to a regular establishment; *kieu*^{2} *sioh*$_2$ *'pa* (or *'ting*), one sedan; [7]*kieu*^{2} *˛kong k'ó*^{2} *˛sieu*, sedans carried off and burnt!—said to one looking vainly for a sedan, and is an allusion to the custom of burning paper sedans for the dead; [8]*kieu*^{2} *˛ch'iă*, a kind of chair for a small child.

撟^2 Chiao. Read *'kieu;* used for the coll. *kieu*^{2}*:* to pry heavy things, to use force in prying: similar to *'kieu*, q. v.: [9]*kieu*^{2} *siek*$_2$ to break in prying.

(268) Kih.

Kih$_2$. A coll. word: to thrust, to pierce, as with the finger, or a sharp instrument: *kih*$_2$ *tioh*$_2$ pierced, perforated; *kih*$_2$ *má*^{2} *kwo*^{2} can't pierce it through; *kih*$_2$ *sioh*$_2$ *˛k'ĕng* (or *˛ch'iong*), to perforate; *kih*$_2$ *sioh*$_2$ *˛cheng*, to pierce with a needle.

Kih$_2$. A coll. euphonic prefix, as in *kih*$_2$ *kah*$_2$ to pry up; across, transverse, crosswise, as things thrown down promiscuously; *kih*$_2$ *kih*$_2$ *káh*$_2$ *káh*$_2$ a rumbling and derangement (of the bowels).

(269) Kik.

極$_2$ Chi. The ridge-pole of a roof; hence the utmost point, apex, place, verge, degree; sign of the superlative, very, exceedingly; the end, limit; to exhaust, to carry to the utmost, to reach to the end; to take; to let go a full-drawn bow; weary, exhausted: [10]*lĕk*$_2$ *kik*$_2$ zenith, nadir, and four quarters; the six calamities which befall men; [11]*paik*$_2$ *kik*$_2$ the eight cardinal and intermediate points; [12]*˛hwong kik*$_2$ the perfect limit—a fixed principle, as laid down by sages; COM., [13]*kik*$_2$ *˛ngui*, very dangerous; [14]*t'ai*^{2} *kik*$_2$ the great extreme—primordial principle or cause of things; [15]*paĕk*$_2$ *kik*$_2$ the north-pole, north-star; COLL., [16]*kik*$_2$ *o*^{2} *ch'ëü*^{2} very amusing! most admirable! [17]*kik*$_2$ *siăng*^{2} very cheap; [18]*kik*$_2$ *'chieu*, or *kik*$_2$ *'chieu 'chieu*, the very least—*scil.*, that will suffice; [19]*'k'u tek*$_2$ *kik*$_2$ the very extreme of misery.

及$_2$ Chi. As a verb, to effect, to reach to, to stretch or extend towards; to arrive at, to go to; to influence at a distance; to communicate, to connect; effected, completed, in which sense it is often a sign of the past tense; as a conjunction, and, with, also; at, about; to; concerning; much used with a negative to denote what is impracticable or unavailing: *˛chiong kik*$_2$ almost at or up to; *hwoi*^{2} *˛u kik*$_2$ too late for repentance; [20]*˛sing kik*$_2$ effected; COM., [21]*kik*$_2$ *tá*^{2} the three highest of the Hanlin degree; *kik*$_2$ *˛ting* and *kik*$_2$ *˛kié*, the age of puberty of boys and girls respectively—is 16 years; *kik*$_2$ *˛si*, at the time, seasonable, in season; *t'ai 'kwo* and *pok*$_2$

[1]轎夫 [2]轎簾 [3]過山轎 [4]八座轎 [5]坐轎 [6]轎槓 [7]轎扛去燒 [8]轎車 [9]撟折 [10]六極 [11]八極 [12]皇極 [13]極危 [14]太極 [15]北極 [16]極趣 [17]極賤 [18]極少 [19]苦的極 [20]成及 [21]及第

*kik*₂ to exceed and to fall short, superfluous and deficient.

*Kik*₂. A coll. euphonic prefix, as in *kik*₂ *kiăk*₂ or *kik*₂ *kik*₂ *kiăk*₂ *kiăk*₂ to bear on the shoulders, to carry easily, as a cooly's implements.

(270) King.

京 ˓Ching. Great, high, lofty; top of a mountain or hill; extensive; the capital or metropolis of a kingdom; ten millions: com., [1]*˓king ˓tu* (coll. *˓king ˓siăng*), a metropolis; [2]*paĕk*₂ *˓king*, Peking; [3]*˓king pó*ˀ the Peking Gazette; [4]*˓king sek*₂ the Peking mode; *˓king ˓ch'ang pwo*ˀ reddish-black cotton cloth; [5]*˓king ˋku*, musical instruments; [6]*˓king ˓k'iong* (coll. *˓king ˓p'iè*), the Peking mandarin; [7]*˓king k'ong*ˀ to impeach at the capital.

勍 ˓Ching. Strong, powerful, violent: [8]*˓king tik*₂ a powerful enemy.

黥 ˓Ching. To mark the face with black spots: [9]*mĕk*₂ *˓king*, to mark the face with ink; [10]*˓king miéng*ˀ to tattoo the faces (of criminals).

鯨 ˓Ching. A whale; the largest of the sea-monsters, fabled to be one thousand *ˋli* in length: [11]*˓king ˓ngü*, a whale; [12]*˓king ˓t'ong*, to swallow all, to swindle; [13]*˓k'ié ˓king ˋsiong ˓t'iéng*, to ride a whale to heaven, as Li-tai-peh did.

擎 ˓Ching. To raise with the hands, to elevate, to lift high: [14]*ek*₂ *chĕü*ˀ *˓king ˓t'iéng*, a column rising to heaven—a pillar of state, an able officer.

檠 ˓Ching. A stand for a lamp, or a wall-light; a frame to set a bow in when stringing it; also a stand for dishes: [15]*˓teng ˓king*, a stand for a wall-lamp.

驚 ˓Ching. A shy horse; to terrify, to frighten, to scare, to alarm; perturbed, alarmed, terrified, astonished: in the coll. read *˓kiăng*, q. v.: [16]*˓king ˋk'ai*, terrified; [17]*˓king ˓hwong*, frightened, alarmed; com., [18]*˓king tik*₂ "excited insects"—the 3d of the 24 solar terms; [19]*˓king tong*ˀ have disturbed you—a polite phrase; [20]*˓king ˓t'iéng tong*ˀ *te*ˀ alarms heaven and moves earth—said of a conspicuous act.

兢 ˓Ching. To fear; to forbear, to refrain; cautious: *chiéng*ˀ *˓king*, trembling; [21]*˓king ˓king*, wary, cautious, respectful; guarded, uneasy, watchful, anxious—according to the context.

涇 ˓Ching. A large tributary of the Yellow river in Shensi, whose waters are muddy; to flow through, pervious, joined by water; a fountain.

經 ˓Ching. The threads of a web, the warp; meridians of longitude; veins; the menses; to pass through, before, by, or across; a sign of past time; to weave or interlace; to manage, to regulate, to superintend; what is regular, right, or orderly; laws, canons; canonical books, standard works,

[1]京都 [2]北京 [3]京報 [4]京式 [5]京鼓 [6]京腔 [7]京控 [8]勍敵 [9]墨黥 [10]黥面 [11]鯨魚 [12]鯨吞 [13]騎鯨上天 [14]一柱擎天 [15]燈檠 [16]驚駭 [17]驚惶 [18]驚蟄 [19]驚動 [20]驚天動地 [21]兢兢

classics: [1]꜀king ‘sü, classics and histories; COM., [2]seng’ ꜀king, the Sacred Scriptures; [3]‘i ꜀king, has, already have; [4]꜀king kwo’ to pass by; [5]꜀king ‘ch‘iu, to pass through one's hands, done or managed by one; [6]꜀king ‘ki, an occupation; [7]꜀king ‘chwi, the menses; [8]꜀king lok꜆ the bloodvessels; [9]꜀king ‘li, to manage; [10]꜀king lik꜆ gone through with, done; a commissioner's assistant; ‘ngu ꜀king, the five classics; sek꜆ ꜀sang ꜀king, the thirteen classics; [11]꜀king hoi’ warp and woof; COLL., naing’ ꜀king, to chant prayers; ng’ se’ ꜁nu ꜀king ‘ch‘iu, it was not managed by me.

今 ꜀Chin. Now, presently, at this time, the present time: ꜀ü ꜀king, now; COM., [12]꜀king ꜁niéng (coll. ꜀king ꜁niéng ꜁mang), this year; [13]꜀king sié’ this world or age; [14]꜀king ꜀seng, the present life; ꜀king ‘ku ꜀ki ꜀kwang, rare scenes, modern and ancient—is the name of a book; ꜀king ꜀tieu pok꜆ ‘pó ꜁ming ꜀tieu sëü’ to-day cannot secure tomorrow's affairs; COLL., ꜀king tang’ or ꜀king tang’ nik꜆ to-day; ꜀king ꜀mwo, to-night; ꜀king tang’ ‘cha, this morning.

金 ꜀Chin. Metal; one of the five elements; gold, *par excellence* the metal; musical instruments of percussion; firm, strong, solid, hard; yellow, golden; a coin, a piece of money; during the Han dynasty, a catty of gold; precious, true, imperial; a surname; the 167th radical: COM., ꜀king muk꜆ ‘chwi ‘hwo ‘t‘u, metal, wood, water, fire, and earth—are the five elements; [15]꜁wong ꜀king, gold; [16]꜀ch‘iéng ꜀king, a thousand of gold; *met.*, your daughter; [17]꜀king ꜀sing, Venus; [18]꜀king póh꜆ gold-leaf; [19]꜀king ꜁leng, the golden lily—a lady's foot; [20]꜀king ꜁wong, golden-yellow; [21]꜀king ꜀ch‘iéng, a kind of gilt paper; [22]꜀king ꜀tang, an excellent pill; a book of essays; [23]꜀king k‘e’ head-ornaments of gold; ꜀king ꜀kong ꜀king, a Budhist classic; COLL., chëük꜆ ꜁siŭng ꜀king, pure gold; ꜀king ch‘iăh, ch‘iăh, a bright gold color; ꜀king ꜀king ꜁p‘au p‘au’ soap-bubbles; ꜀king ꜀k‘wo ꜀k‘wo, a term for money—taken from the three component parts of the character ꜁chiéng (cash).

鈞 ꜀Chün. Used for the next: a quarter of a stone or picul; a weight of 30 catties; a potter's lathe; to equalize, to harmonize; just; important: [24]tai’ ꜀king, or ꜁hung ꜀king, the great Framer or Wheel of events, heaven, nature; ꜀king ëü’ your wishes or orders—a polite phrase.

均 ꜀Chün. An instrument for molding pottery; equal, just, in similar parts; even, level, plane, flat; to equalize, to adjust; a musical instrument: ꜀king ꜁ping, to adjust properly; impartial, equal; ꜀king huk꜆ military garments; ꜁sing ꜀king, an ancient hall for study.

꜀King. A coll. word: to last long, enduring; good, as for use; able to bear or endure: ꜀king ꜁sieu, good to burn long; ꜀king ‘sai, good for use, will last long; ꜀king ꜀kang, able to bear the cold.

[1]經史 [2]聖經 [3]已經 [4]經過 [5]經手 [6]經紀 [7]經水 [8]經絡 [9]經理 [10]經歷 [11]經緯 [12]今年 [13]今世 [14]今生 [15]黃金 [16]千金 [17]金星 [18]金箔 [19]金蓮 [20]金黃 [21]金箋 [22]金丹 [23]金器 [24]大鈞

King. A coll. euphonic prefix, as in *king kong*, to carry between two.

景 Ching. Bright, clear sunlight, brilliant, illumined by the sun; a good site, a fine view, a prospect; the appearance, figure, aspect, or circumstances, of a place or thing; great, extensive; a resemblance, form, imagining, fancy; to look up to, or regard with affection; longing for; dress, apparel: [1]*ch'ing 'king*, neat and tasteful; [2]*'wang 'king*, the evening prospect; *met.*, old age; COM., [3]*kwong 'king*, or *'king hwong'* circumstances, prospects, as of trade; [4]*'king ch'iong'* the aspect of matters; [5]*si 'king*, signs of the time; [6]*'king te'* a vista, scenery, landscape; [7]*'hó 'king*, or *'king 'hó*, fine prospects, easy circumstances.

憬 Ching. To be excited upon, to give attention so as to understand; to seem remote, far, distant: [8]*'king kauk*, to perceive.

境 Ching. A limit, boundary, frontier, border; marches, confines; abode, place where one lives; a neighborhood, a district; state, condition of life, status: [9]*'king kai'* a boundary; [10]*song' 'king*, in good circumstances, favorably situated; [11]*sëü' 'king*, the four quarters; COM., [12]*'king siä'* a neighborhood-temple; [13]*'king hong'* fees paid to a temple.

謹 Ching. Diligent, careful, vigilant; serious, attentive; solemn, respectful; to venerate; to watch against sedulously, to consider, to heed: [14]*'king këü'* to send presents; COM., [15]*'king seng'* careful, cautious, circumspect.

警 儆 Ching. To warn, to caution, to enjoin; to threaten with a penalty; to forbid, to arouse, to urge to reform; to disturb, to alarm the secure: [16]*'king chëüng'* to warn the people; [17]*'king 'sing*, to examine and charge one's self; COM., [18]*'king kai'* to caution, to enjoin; [19]*'king kai' a' ch'ëü'* to warn against a repetition of.

錦 Chin. A kind of variegated silk, used in ornamental work; embroidered, worked or knit in colors; elegant, figurative, as a style; flowery, pictured: [20]*e' 'king*, clad in silks; *met.*, the gentry, official persons; COM., *'king tiu*, figured pongees; *'king seu'* embroidered, worked in colors; [21]*'king seu' ung chiong*, an elegant essay; *'king sing 'ó*, a lined silk tunic—worn by brides; *'king siong' t'iéng hwa*, add flowers to variegated silks; *met.*, to give to one already rich.

緊 Chin. To bind fast, to compress; a cord; urgent, strict; diligent, prompt, on the point of; in haste, pressing; strait, confined; rapid flow of water: COM., *'king 'king*, tight, fast; urgent, strict; [22]*'king kek*, very pressing; *'king yeu'* or *yeu' 'king*, important; *'king 'siu*, to guard strictly; COLL., *k'ak 'king*,

[1]清景 [2]晚景 [3]光景 [4]景象 [5]時景 [6]景致 [7]好景 [8]憬覺 [9]境界 [10]順境 [11]四境 [12]境社 [13]境份 [14]謹具 [15]謹慎 [16]警衆 [17]警省 [18]警戒 [19]警戒下次 [20]衣錦 [21]錦繡文章 [22]緊急

福州方言拼音字典

too tight, too close; *pwoh,* ʻ*king,* to tie tight; ʻ*king* ʻ*king siè*ʾ closely, tightly; ʻ*king* (or *kek,*) ʻ*chwi* ʻ*hó* ʻ*t'ó* ˌ*ngü,* swift water is a good place to catch fish in; *met.*, when business presses is just the time to make gain.

ʻ*King.* A coll. euphonic prefix, as in ʻ*king* ʻ*kong* to say, to tell, to speak of.

荆 ˓Ching. A bush found in Hunan, slender and lithe, formerly used for punishing criminals; there are several species; spinous, prickly; furze, brambles: [1]ˌ*king* ˌ*ch'á,* my wife; [2]ˌ*king kek,* thorny bushes, difficult; COM., [3]ʻ*chié* ˌ*king,* the crape myrtle; [4]ʻ*chiok,* ˌ*king* a stupid thorn—i. e., my wife; ˌ*King* ˌ*chiu* ʻ*hu,* a department in Hupeh; [5]ˌ*king kai*ʾ a medicinal plant used in colds.

敻 ˓ Far, distant, to go to a distance. Read *hiong*ʾ: to seek, to scheme for, to undertake, to try to obtain.

瓊 ˓Ch'iung. A red or carnation-colored gem; precious coral; small, pretty gems: COM., ˌ*king* ˌ*chiu* ʻ*hu,* the island of Hainan; [7]ˌ*king* ˌ*ling yéng*ʾ a feast given to the Chintsz' graduates; [8]ˌ*king* ˌ*hwa,* a rare flower—at which Sui-yang-ti looked (A. D. 605).

煢 ˓ 睘 ˓ 嬛 ˓Ch'iung The third also read ˌ*hiong:* alone, desolate, without brethren or protectors; downcast, sorrowing; the second also means to stare at fixedly, affrighted: [9]ˌ*king* ˌ*king,* downcast, dispirited; [10]ˌ*king tuk,* alone, solitary.

ˌ*King.* A coll. euphonic prefix, as in ˌ*king* ˌ*kong,* to bolt, to bar, and ˌ*king* ˌ*kong,* to boil thoroughly.

(271) Kio.

橋 ˓Ch'iao. A bridge of stone or planks; in the dictionaries read ˌ*kieu,* q. v.: [11]*ch'iok,* ˌ*kio,* the magpies' bridge (made for the meeting of *Chek,* ʻ*nü* and ˌ*Ngiu* ˌ*long*)—a fairy tale; COM., [12]ˌ*kio* ˌ*liong,* the wood or stone ties of a bridge; [13]ˌ*kio* ˌ*mwong,* the spans or arches; ˌ*kio* ˌ*lang,* the balustrades; [14]*wang*ʾ *seu*ʾ ˌ*kio,* bridge of myriad ages—name of the great bridge over the Min at Foochow; [15]ˌ*kio kwo*ʾ ˌ*tiu* ʻ*kwai,* after crossing the bridge throws away the staff; *met.*, ungrateful toward a benefactor; COLL., [16]*twai*ʾ ˌ*kio* ˌ*t'au,* head of the great bridge; [17]ˌ*p'u* ˌ*kio,* a floating bridge; [18]ˌ*kio* ʻ*tong,* the piers of a bridge.

蕎 ˓Ch'iao. Read ˌ*kieu;* coll. ˌ*kio,* as in [19]ˌ*kio mah,* buckwheat—is used medicinally in Foochow.

茄 ˓Chieh. Read ˌ*ka,* used in the *Paik,* ˌ*Ing* for the coll. ˌ*kio:* a name for [20]ʻ*chié ch'ai*ʾ the egg plant; also used with an indecent allusion.

(272) Kioh.

脚 Chioa. Read *kiok,;* used for the coll. *kioh,,* as in [21]*kioh, saik,* ability, skill; *met.*, laborers, workmen, coolies; *kioh,* ʻ*chieu,* or *kioh, saik,* ʻ*chieu,* few workmen; *kioh, saik,* ʻ*hó,* has good ability; *kioh, saik,*

1 荆妻 2 荆棘 3 紫荆 4 拙荆 5 荆芥 6 瓊州 府 7 瓊林宴 8 瓊花 9 煢煢 10 煢獨 11 鵲橋 12 橋梁 13 橋門 14 萬壽橋 15 橋過丟拐 16 大橋頭 17 浮橋 18 橋砧 19 蕎麥 20 紫菜 21 脚色

꜀ngai (or *kiă*꜄), inferior skill, as of actors.

(273) Kiok.

决 决 Chüeh. Name of a river; streams flowing different ways; to flow, to lead streams; to spread abroad; to decide, to pass sentence, to settle; to cut off; fixed, decided upon, certainly, positively, doubtless: [1]*kiok*, ꜀*ngi*, to decide doubtful points; [2]*kiok*, *chiok*, to renounce utterly; COM., [3]*kiok*, *e*꜄ to decide mentally; [4]*kiok*, ꜀*k'wo*, to determine the grades, as of the Siu-tsai before the Literary Chancellor; [5]*kiok*, *twang*꜄ *se*꜄ ꜀*hi*, to decide between the right and the wrong; [6]*kiok*, *pok*, *sik*, ꜀*ngiong*, positively will not eat (retract) my words!

潏 Water bubbling, as from a fountain; to gush forth; an islet or bank, formed by art in a stream; a river in Shansi. Read *ük*: water flowing along.

抉 Chüeh. To dig, to rake; to pluck out, to gouge; to twitch, to snatch; to press or pull, as a bow; to castrate: [7]*kiok*, ꜂*ngang*, to gouge out an eye; COM., [8]*kiok*, ꜀*tü*, to castrate swine, for which the usual coll. is ꜀*tong* ꜀*tü*.

鴃 鵙 Chüeh. The shrike or butcher-bird, called [9]*paik*, ꜀*lô*, it sings in the 7th moon and is said to eat its dam: [10]*kiok*, *siĕk*, a butcher-bird's tongue; *met.*, gibberish, as of southern people.

鴂 Chüeh. The tailor-bird, called [11]꜂*k'ieu ho*꜄ (the cunning woman) and other names; it sings at the equinoxes and marks the seasons.

玦 Chüeh. A broken or halved ring, formerly used to indicate breaking off all connection; a semicircle; an archer's ring; personal ornaments.

訣 Chüeh. Parting or dying words; to take leave, to depart; a farewell; an art, a rule, a precept; a mystery, a secret; abstruse doctrine; a trick, a sleight: [12]*kiok*, *piĕk*, to take a last farewell; [13]*pe*꜄ *kiok*, undivulged secrets; [14]*mek*, *kiok*, the doctrine of the pulse; [15]꜂*k'eu kiok*, art or skill in teaching; COLL., *kiok*, *tuiu*꜄ rules, methods in doing.

譎 Chü. Also read *k'iok*: feigned, counterfeited; false, hypocritical; to impose on, to gain an end by specious arts: [16]꜂*kwi kiok*, feigned, treacherous; [17]꜂*kieu kiok*, crafty.

屩 蹻 Chiao. Shoes or sandals made of twisted hemp cord; some say wooden shoes, or shoes with iron spikes in the soles: the second also read ꜂*kieu* and ꜀*k'ieu*, q. v.

脚 Chiao. The foot, but applied to the whole leg; *met.*, stable, based, firm; an art, a profession; capacity, skill, talent, in which sense read *kioh*, in the coll., q. v.: [18]꜂*ch'ek*, *kiok*, barefooted; [19]꜂*hô* ꜂*ch'iu kiok*, clever, handy; [20]*lo*꜄ *kiok*, to show the (cloven) foot; [21]*kiok*, *saik*, an art, ca-

[1]决疑 [2]决絶 [3]决意 [4]决科 [5]决斷是非 [6]决不食言 [7]抉眼 [8]抉猪 [9]伯勞 [10]鴃舌 [11]巧婦 [12]訣別 [13]秘訣 [14]脈訣 [15]口訣 [16]詭譎 [17]矯譎 [18]赤脚 [19]好手脚 [20]露脚 [21]脚色 〇

pacity, talent; COM., 'kek, ˎsi pó' huk, kiok, to clasp Budh's foot in distress; met., to look to a benefactor (only) when in straits.

觖, Chüeh. To hope or expect impatiently; to indulge in complaints, dissatisfied; to make known, to bring to light, as another's faults.

觼, 鐍, A ring with a tongue in it, a buckle, a hasp; part of a lock; a carriage ring for fastening the reins to, called ²kiok, nak,.

(274) Kiong.

姜 Chiang. The surname of the emperor Shinnung: COM., ³ˏkiong t'ai' ˏkung, a famous general, B. C. 1122—name used as a charm with the words 'chai' 'ch'ü (is here) added; ⁵maing' ˏkiong 'nü, a noted woman in the time of Chi-huang-ti, B. C. 246.

娟 Chüan. Beautiful, handsome, comely; slender, elegant; sprightly, pleasing; somber, distant: ˏsiéng ˏkiong, lady-like, graceful; ⁶ˏliéng ˏkiong, arched, crescent; ⁷piéng' ˏkiong, light and airy, buoyant.

羌 羗 Chiang. A tribe of aborigines in ancient Tangut, shepherd nomads belonging to the Scythian race; an initial particle, ah! strong, forcible; contrary, cross-purposes; neat, elegant.

蜎 Chüan. A large caterpillar; small red larvæ in stagnant water; the larvæ of mosquitoes; to disturb, to agitate, to stir up.

蜣 Chiang. Coleopterous bugs found in ordure: ⁸ˏkiong ˏlong, or ⁹kek, ˏkiong, the tumble-dung or ateuchus.

殭 Chiang. The white exuviæ of silkworm larvæ, called ¹⁰ˏkiong ˏchang—used medicinally.

蠲 Chüan. A worm produced in rotten grass or vegetables, a species of glow-worm; pure, bright, shining; to cleanse, to purify, to maintain purity; to illustrate, to manifest; to excuse from, to remit, as sums due to the government; speedily, quickly: ¹¹ˏkiong 'miéng, to remit, as taxes.

僵 Chiang. Used for the next: to throw down, prostrate; to bend over; to lie senseless.

殭 Chiang. Lying as if dead, senseless; prostrated, stretched out, as a corpse; stiff, rigid, yet uncorrupted: COM., ¹²ˏkiong ˏsi, a body seeming to be lifeless; ¹³ˏkiong ˏchang, the larvæ of silkworms.

橿 Chiang. The helve of a hoe, a hoe-handle; a durable wood, called ¹⁴wang' ˏniéng muk, used for the bars of carriages; ¹⁵ˏkiong ˏkiong, strong, vigorous, abundant.

薑 Chiang. Ginger: COM., ¹⁶paëk, ˏkiong, northern ginger—used medicinally; ¹⁷ˏwi ˏkiong, to roast ginger in the ashes; ¹⁸ˏt'ong ˏkiong, preserved ginger; ¹⁹p'au' ˏkiong, charred ginger; COLL., ²⁰ˏkiong 'mó, common name for ginger; ²¹ˏch'ang ˏkiong, raw ginger.

¹急時抱佛 脚²觼軜³姜 太公⁴在此 ⁵孟姜女⁶連 娟⁷便娟⁸蜣 蜋⁹蛣蜣¹⁰殭 蠶¹¹蠲免¹²殭 屍¹³殭蠶¹⁴萬 年木¹⁵橿橿 ¹⁶北薑¹⁷煨薑 ¹⁸糖薑¹⁹炮薑 ²⁰薑母²¹生薑

韁 ꜀Chiang. A bridle, a halter, made of silken or leather cords; the reins of a bridle: [1]*ʻma ꜀kiong*, a horse's bridle.

鞙 ꜀Chüan. A bridle, a crupper. Read *ʻkiong:* the traces of a harness; a scabbard: [2]*ʻkiong ʻkiong*, pendent, as gems; long, as fringes.

疆 ꜀Chiang. A boundary, limits, borders; to draw a limit, to bound: [3]*꜀kiong kaiʾ* a boundary; [4]*꜀kiong ꜀tiong*, a field of battle; [5]*chʻok꜀ ꜀kiong*, to emigrate; [6]*꜀u ꜀kiong*, boundless, infinite.

悁 ꜀Chüan. Irritated, angry, enraged; hasty, impetuous; grieved: [7]*ʻhung ꜀kiong*, angered; [8]*꜀kiong ꜀kiong*, careworn, sad.

涓 ꜀Chüan. A brook, a runlet, a small stream, which swells as it flows on; pure, clear; to cleanse, to purify; to select; to exclude; a river in Shantung: [9]*꜀kiong kek꜀*, to choose lucky days.

睊 ꜀Chüan. To look askance, to view with displeasure; mutual dislike: [10]*꜀kiong ꜀kiong*, to look reprovingly.

捐 ꜀Chüan. To reject, to throw away, to cast off; to disdain, to leave, to renounce; to contribute, to subscribe, as at a call from government; to buy office or title; to die of disease: [11]*꜀kiong kʻeʾ* to reject; COM., [12]*꜀kʻwi ꜀kiong*, to open a subscription for the government; [13]*꜀kiong ꜀pang*, purchased degrees or offices; [14]*꜀kiong ꜀hang*, or [15]*꜀kiong chek꜀*, to buy a title; [16]*꜀kiong ꜀tá*, to subscribe; [17]*꜀kiong haungʾ* the amount of a subscription; [18]*꜀kiong ʻmi*, to contribute rice; [19]*꜀kiong nak꜀ chʻok꜀ ꜀sing*, got his promotion by a subscription; *꜀kiong hiéngʾ engʾ* to buy immediate office.

鵑 ꜀Chüan. The cuckoo or a species of goat-sucker, which has the habit of laying its eggs in the nests of other birds: *toʾ ꜀kiong ꜀tʻá hiék꜀*, the cuckoo cries till blood (fills its eyes); COM., [20]*toʾ ꜀kiong*, the cuckoo; *toʾ ꜀kiong ꜀hwa*, the Azalea.

狷 獧 ʻChüan. To skip about, frisky, playful; hasty, quick, prompt; light-minded; a moderate, modest man of probity, but not talented; one who needs instruction.

罥 絹 ʻChüan. A gin, a snare; to take wild animals in a net or snare; the first also means to hang, to suspend; to tie, to bind with a cord.

强 彊 ʻChiang. To force, to constrain; to urge, to prevail on; by constraint or compulsion: also read *꜀kiong*, q. v.: [21]*꜀kʻeng ʻkiong*, forced, strained, as the construction of a phrase; COM., [22]*ʻkiong ꜀kiu*, to importune; *ʻkiong keʾ* to recall by effort of memory; [23]*ʻkiong ʻmiéng*, to constrain; COLL., *ʻkiong ꜀sing tangʾ* to force one's self to do; *ʻkiong siăh꜀ ꜀niă nŏiʾ* forcing one's self to eat a little.

蔃 ʻChʻiang. Name of a plant. Read *꜀kiong:* small roots; a lily; *꜀kiong suk꜀* the tuberose.

[1] 馬韁 [2] 鞙鞙 [3] 疆界 [4] 疆場 [5] 出疆 [6] 無疆 [7] 忿悁 [8] 悁悁 [9] 涓吉 [10] 睊睊 [11] 捐棄 [12] 開捐 [13] 捐班 [14] 捐銜 [15] 捐職 [16] 捐題 [17] 捐項 [18] 捐米 [19] 捐納出身 [20] 杜鵑 [21] 牽强 [22] 强求 [23] 强免

福州方言拼音字典

鏹 ʻ Ch'iang. A cord for threading cash; to string cash; a string of cash; a term for money or coin: [1]*pek*, ʻ*kiong*, the white coin, silver.

襁 ʻ Ch'iang. A swathing cloth to carry infants on the back; to carry pickback: [2]ʻ*kiong* ʻ*pó*, a cloth for strapping and carrying infants.

蹇 ʻ Ch'ien. Used for the next: lame, halt, weak in the legs; feeble, unable to work; difficult; disastrous, unhappy, unfortunate, afflicted; the 61st diagram, which denotes ill-luck; to pull up; crooked; lofty, proud: [3]*yéng* ʻ*kiong*, proud, haughty; pantomime; [4]*p'ó* ʻ*kiong*, lame, unfit for work; [5]*meng*ʼ ˏ*tu* ˏ*kwai* ʻ*kiong*, unfortunate in life, unlucky.

謇 ʻ Ch'ien. To beg, to pray, to supplicate, to beseech, to importune; to bring out one's words with difficulty; hard, difficult; honest, straightforward words: ʻ*kiong* ʻ*kiong*, good, honest advice; [6]ʻ*kiong ngauk*, faithful declarations.

絹 ʻ Chüan. Also read ˏ*kiong*: a thin cheap silk, used for linings, paintings, &c.; lustring, taffeta; bird-nets made of lustring; a target.

絹 ʼ Chüan. Read ʻ*kiong*; coll. *kiong*ʼ: a kind of silk of a loose texture, lustring; used for drawers or pantaloons: [7]*kiong*ʼ ˏ*sa*, a sort of gauze, lustring.

建 ʼ Chien. To establish, to confirm, as laws or institutions; to erect, to place, to set up, to constitute; to build: [8]*kiong*ʼ *chó*ˀ to build; [9]*kiong*ʼ *lik*, or *kiong*ʼ *te*ʼ to establish, to found; COM., [10]*kiong*ʼ ˏ*kung lik*, *ngiék*, to gain merit and establish one's fortune; [11]*hok*, *kiong*ʼ the Fookien province; [12]*kiong*ʼ *chieu*ʼ to institute sacrifices, as to spirits; [13]*ngwok*, *kiong*ʼ the luck of the month, as indicated by fortune-tellers.

毽 ʼ Chien. A kind of football or shuttlecock, made of cash and feathers: COM., [14]ˏ*p'ui kiong*ʼ a football with discs and tubular socket of leather; [15]*t'ek*, *kiong*ʼ to kick the football; COLL., *t'óh*, *kiong*ʼ to toss the shuttlecock.

强 **彊** ˏ Chiang. A black bug or weevil in rice; a strong bow; violent, headstrong, surly, firm; overbearing, boisterous, by force, regardless of right, obstinate; able-bodied, sturdy, brawny, strong, full grown; 40 years old; a remainder (in arithmetic); all years with the "stem" ˏ*ting* in their cyclic name: also read ʻ*kiong*, q. v.: COM., [16]ˏ*kiong kiék*, or ˏ*kiong* ʻ*ch'iong*, to plunder; [17]ˏ*kiong chaung*ʼ vigorous, hale; [18]ˏ*kiong pó*ˀ or ˏ*kiong auk*, violent, oppressive; [19]ˏ*kiong tó*ˀ a highwayman; [20]*chiă*ˀ ˏ*kiong*, to presume on one's strength; ˏ*kiong* ˏ*kang*, rape; ˏ*kiong* ˏ*sü tok*, *cheng*ʼ ʻ*li*, with violent words wrests truth—i. e., claims to be right; COLL., ˏ*kiong chioh*, to borrow forcibly; [21]ˏ*kiong* ˏ*t'au* ˏ*kiong* ʻ*nó*, with

[1]白鏹 [2]襁褓 [3]偃蹇 [4]跛蹇 [5]命途乖蹇 [6]謇諤 [7]絹紗 [8]建造 [9]建立 [10]建功立業 [11]福建 [12]建醮 [13]月建 [14]皮毽 [15]踢毽 [16]强刼 [17]强壯 [18]强暴 [19]强盜 [20]藉强 [21]强頭强腦

strong head and brains—i. e., headstrong, overbearing.

犍 ˓Chien. A castrated ox, a strong ox; a fabulous monster—half-man, half-leopard.

健² Chien. Strong, enduring, hard; hale, vigorous, healthy, robust; indefatigable, unwearied: in the coll. read *kiăng*² q.v.: *kiong*² *chaung*˒ vigorous, robust; ¹*'kiong*² *sëüng*² to go to law fearlessly, litigious; COM., ²*k'ong kiong*² hale, vigorous; COLL., ³*kiong*² *tek*˓ *'heng* (or *kik*˓), exceedingly vigorous, as an old man; ⁴*kiong*² *tek*˓ *kwo*˒ to endure (as cold) by one's constitutional vigor; to avoid by an inflexible will.

件² Chien. To divide, to partake; to separate; a classifier used to denote a particular article, subject, or affair; applied widely to food, dress, incidents, goods, things; a, an, one: in the coll. read *yong*² q. v.: ⁵*uk*˓ *kiong*² things; ⁶*sëü*² *kiong*² matters, affairs; ⁷*yok*˓ ˏ*kang kiong*² how many?

鍵² Chien. The bolt or key of a lock; a nave or hub; perverse, obstinate: ⁸*'kwang kiong*² a door-bolt or lock; ⁹*kiong*² *pié*² the two parts of a Chinese lock.

(275) Kiu.

[疒卉] [疒交] ˓Chieh. Read *'kieu*; used for the coll. ˏ*kiu*: bent, stooping, as when suffering intense pain; writhing with pain, as in colic or cholera morbus: ¹⁰ˏ*kiu* ˓*tong sau*˒ a cough with cramping of the bowels; *á*² ˏ*kiu* ˓*chiă* ˏ*kiu* ˓*chiă t'iăng*˒ to have a succession of cramping pains.

ˏ*Kiu*. A coll. word: to shorten, to contract, as cloth; shrunk, puckered, wrinkled: ˏ*kiu k'ó*˒ shrunk; *met.*, silent from bashfulness; ˏ*kiu 'tié*, to skulk, as rats; ˏ*kiu 'toi*, shortened, fulled, as cloth; ˏ*kiu nëük*, puckered; ˏ*kiu 'king*, shrunk compactly; to stick fast, as in riding pickback; ˏ*kiu sioh*˓ ˏ*toi*, to huddle together; ˏ*kiu sioh*˓ ˓*wong*, shrink into a ball—i. e., crouching, as from fear; ˏ*kiu* ˓*chiă t'ëük*˓ ˓*chiă*, drawing in its head, as a turtle.

久 'Chiu. A long time, enduring, lasting; to make or continue long: COM., ¹¹˓*tiong 'kiu*, or ¹²˓*tong 'kiu*, forever; ¹³˓*niëng 'kiu ngwok*˓ ˏ*ch'ing*, many years and months—a long time; ¹⁴*'kiu* ˓*ui*, long separated, as said on meeting a friend; ¹⁵*'kiu 'ü*, a protracted rain; ¹⁶*'kiu 'ngiong*, long regarded or esteemed, as one known by reputation; COLL., ¹⁷*'kiu pang*² ˓*siăng* ˓*long* ˏ*tüng*, one who is long sick becomes (himself) a doctor!

灸 'Chiu. To cauterize with moxa, or the dried leaves of the Artemisia, for which meaning see also *ko*˒ in the coll.: ¹⁸*ëüng*² *'hwo 'kiu*, the actual cautery.

羑 'Chiu. Read *'iu* in the dictionaries: right principles, reason; just, proper; to advance or lead on in rectitude: ¹⁹*'kiu 'li*, the place where Wan-wang was imprisoned.

¹健訟 ²康健 ³健的很 ⁴健的過 ⁵物件 ⁶事件 ⁷若干件 ⁸管鍵 ⁹鍵閉 ¹⁰[疒卉]腸嗽 ¹¹長久 ¹²長久 ¹³年久月深 ¹⁴久違 ¹⁵久雨 ¹⁶久仰 ¹⁷久病成郎中 ¹⁸用火灸 ¹⁹羑里

福州方言拼音字典

‘玖 Chiu. Used as the complex form of the next: a black gem, not of much value, perhaps black jasper.

‘九 ‘玖 Chiu. Nine; to collect together; *met.*, many, the highest, because nine is a square number: in the coll. read ‘*kau*, q. v.: [1]‘*kiu* ꜀*tüng*, the emperor's palace; [2]‘*kiu* ‘*kiu hak*꜇ *so*’ the multiplication table reaching to 81; COM., [3]‘*kiu* ꜀*kwi*, arithmetic; [4]‘*kiu* ꜁*ó*, the nine rivers (of China); ‘*kiu* ꜁*liêng* ꜀*k‘wang*, the nine interlocked rings—a puzzle; *met.*, several kites united to one string; [5]‘*kiu* ꜀*kong*, Kiukiang; [6]‘*kiu* ꜀*siêng* ꜀*sang*, hill of the nine genii—i. e., ꜀*Ü* ꜀*sang* in Foochow; [7]‘*kiu chuk*꜇ the nine grades of kindred; [8]꜁*tüng* ‘*kiu*, ninth day of the ninth moon; COLL., ‘*kiu chaik*꜇ ꜁*li*, a large squib emitting nine lights.

‘糾 ‘糺 Chiu. Also read ‘*kieu:* a threefold cord; to twist, to wind up; to combine, to collect; to examine, to bring to light; to inform; to raise, to elevate; to head a sedition; perverse: [9]‘*kiu* ‘*kiu*, wide apart, loose; [10]‘*mieu* ‘*kiu*, at ease, tranquil; [11]‘*kiu hak*꜇ ꜀*chi chëüng*’ a band of rebels.

‘赳 Chiu. Also read ‘*kieu:* to carry the head high, to move the head like a dragon; to act wisely and energetically: [12]‘*kiu* ‘*kiu*, brave, martial.

‘韮 ‘韭 Chiu. Scallions or chives, a salad onion; a plant that grows a long time from one root: COLL., [13]‘*kiu ch‘ai*’ ꜀*sang*, raw scallions —scalded with seasoning of soy, &c.; ‘*kiu ch‘ai*’ ꜀*pié*, chives-stem (shaped) as hair-pins; ‘*kiu ch‘ai*’ *miäng*꜄ *sioh*꜇ ꜁*tong chew*꜄ *kak*꜇ (like) a scallion's life, cut off as soon as grown—said of transient luck.

꜁求 Ch‘iu. To search for, to seek, to aim at; to beg, to ask, to supplicate; to wish for, ardently desirous of; to invite, to call out; to class with, or make like: COM., [14]꜁*ki* ꜁*kiu*, to pray, to supplicate; [15]꜁*kiu* ‘*k‘ong*, or [16]‘*k‘ong* ꜁*kiu*, to beg earnestly; [17]꜁*kiu* ꜀*k‘wang*, to entreat one's indulgence; [18]꜁*kiu hwa*’ to beg alms; [19]꜁*kiu chiêng*’ ꜀*chü*, to ask for a written recommendation; [20]꜁*kiu* ꜀*hwa hwoi*꜄ to pray for (success in) a lottery; ꜁*kiu* ꜁*ing pok*, ꜁*ü* ꜁*kiu* ‘*ki*, begging of others is not to be compared with begging of one's self—i. e., be self-reliant; COLL., ꜁*kiu cheng*꜄ ꜁*nëng*, to beg everybody; ꜁*kiu* ꜁*nëng* ꜁*t‘au ch‘ëü*’ ꜁*nëng meng*’ to entreat people and look in their faces—said of the dependent poor.

꜁俅 Ch‘iu. An ornamented cap; respectful, reverent: ꜁*kiu* ꜁*kiu*, grave and complaisant.

꜁捄 Ch‘iu. To put earth in a basket, to fill with earth; long and curved; to stop; to defend, to help.

[1]九	合	[4]九	[6]九	族	糾	合	赳	[14]祈	[16]懇	[18]求	書
重	數	河	仙	[8]重	[10]窈	之	[13]韭	求	求	化	[20]求
[2]九	[3]九	[5]九	山	九	糾	衆	菜	[15]求	[17]求	[19]求	花
九	歸	江	[7]九	[9]糾	[11]糾	[12]赳	生	懇	寬	薦	會

梂 ꜀Ch'iu. The cupule or cup of the acorn of the *lik*, tree; the haft of a chisel; a raft.

樛 ꜀ Also read ꜀*k'iu:* pendulous branches; to twist, to twine; laid transversely, athwart, across: [1]꜀*kiu* ꜀*liu*, to go wandering about.

裘 ꜀Ch'iu. Fur garments; furs after they are made up: [2]꜀*k'ing* ꜀*kiu*, fine fur garments.

毬 ꜀Ch'iu. A ball large enough to play with, made of wool or leather; a bladder-ball; a globe, a sphere: [3]*ta* ꜀*kiu*, or [4]*hié*꜄ ꜀*kiu*, to play ball; COM., [5]꜀*kiu* ꜀*ting*, globe-lanterns (in the 1st month); [6]꜀*kiu* ꜀*tiong*, a ball-alley; [7]*siok*, ꜀*kiu*, the snow-ball (flower).

球 ꜀Ch'iu. A sonorous jade stone, a gem made round; a ball, a globe, a sphere: COM., [8]꜀*t'iêng* ꜀*kiu*, a celestial globe; [9]*te*꜄ ꜀*kiu*, a terrestrial globe, the earth; [10]꜀*liu* ꜀*kiu*, Loochoo.

璆 ꜀ A sonorous gem, musical stones; a very precious, beautiful gem.

逑 ꜀Ch'iu. To collect, to gather together; to pair, to mate, to seek an alliance; a union, a marriage; pressing, urgent, in which sense used for the next: [11]*hó*꜄ ꜀*kiu*, to seek an alliance; [12]*hó*꜄ ꜀*kiu tiong*꜄ the Happy Union—name of a popular tale.

絿 ꜀Ch'iu. Hasty, quick, urgent, pressing; testy, petulant: [13]*pok, keng*꜄ *pok*, ꜀*kiu*, neither contentious nor hasty—remiss, easy with.

賕 ꜀Ch'iu. To swerve from the right, to seek in an illicit manner; to solicit by bribes; corrupted, bribed.

觩 ꜀Ch'iu. Crooked, like a rhinoceros' horn; a long horn; a bow made of horn; to relax a bow.

銶 ꜀Ch'iu. A kind of chisel, a stone-chisel; a single-headed axe or pick.

厹 叴 ꜀Ch'iu. Vapor ascending high; a kind of spear or halberd with three prongs.

艽 ꜀Chiu. Far, distant; a desert, a remote and barren waste; the lair of a wild beast: [14]꜀*kiu* *yâ*꜄, a howling wilderness; [15]꜀*kiu* ꜀*sau*, the burrows of a wild hog (? hyrax), which are found arranged in a regular form

頄 ꜀Chiu. The protuberance of the cheek-bones; thick.

鼽 ꜀ The nose stopped from the effects of a cold; a cold in the head, catarrh.

虯 虬 ꜀Ch'iu. A horned dragon; to wriggle, to writhe, as a snake; a quick, agitated movement: [16]꜀*kiu* ꜀*yéng*, a long, curly beard.

[1]樛流 [2]輕裘 [3]打毬 [4]戲毬 [5]毬燈 [6]毬場 [7]雪毬 [8]天球 [9]地球 [10]琉球 [11]好逑 [12]好逑傳 [13]不競不絿 [14]艽野 [15]艽脊 [16]虯髯

福州方言拼音字典

(276) Ko.

固ʾ Ku. Shut around, shut up; well-strengthened, fortified; impervious, solid; firm, constant; obstinate, pertinacious, fixed, determined; chronic, as disease; to defend; to render stable; assuredly, certainly, firmly; vulgar, rude, rustic: [1]koʾ ʻsiu, to maintain, to defend firmly; [2]koʾ eʾ willful; COM., [3]koʾ chek, pok, ꜀t'ung, obstinate and deaf to reason; [4]꜀kiéng koʾ stable, firm.

痼ʾ Ku. A chronic, incurable disease, such as leprosy, gout, &c.: [5]koʾ chik₂ a chronic malady.

錮ʾ Ku. To fuse copper or iron; to mend cracks, to stop up carefully; met., to bind, to prevent: [6]kengʾ koʾ to repress, to keep, as in banishment.

故ʾ Ku. A cause, an occasion, a pretext, that which effects or induces a result; a reason for, because, for, therefore, on that account, on purpose; that which was formerly, forgotten, neglected; old, long in possession; to die, to decease; a matter or affair: [7]koʾ ʻiu, an old friend; [8]tai² koʾ the "great death"—death of a parent; [9]piéngʾ koʾ an (important) change of affairs—said of sickness or death; COM., [10]ʻhó koʾ why? [11]꜀u koʾ causeless; [12]siéʾ koʾ affairs of the world; [13]꜀yong koʾ a reason, a cause; [14]koʾ ch'ü, therefore; [15]koʾ sëü² old affairs; met., ancient costumes, etc.

Koʾ. A coll. word, for which the last is sometimes used; a comparative, more, still more; an adverb, yet, still, again: koʾ ʻhó, better; koʾ o² yet have, have more; koʾ mwoi² not yet; koʾ ꜀chiong wang² again so; koʾ tek, ʻhó, luckily.

顧ʾ Ku. Used for the next: to turn the head and look; to look after, to attend to, to care for, to regard; considerate; to reflect on, to consider; consonant to, corresponding; to assist with one's counsel or business, to patronize; an initial word, but, on the contrary; a surname: COM., [16]chieuʾ koʾ to look after, to take care of; [17]pok, koʾ haiu² regardless of the future, improvident; [18]koʾ ꜀sing ꜀ming, to guard one's reputation; COLL., ng² koʾ to disregard; koʾ ʻla ch'oiʾ "care for the mouth"—get a living; koʾ tek, siáh, má² koʾ tek, sëüng² can care for food, not for clothes, as the poor.

雇 僱ʾ Ku. To rent, to hire, to engage for wages: tieu² koʾ to engage for wages; COM., [19]koʾ kieuʾ to engage a sedan; [20]koʾ ꜀kĕng, to hire workmen.

灸ʾ Tsai. Read ʻkiu; used in the Paik, ꜀Ing for the coll. koʾ: to cauterize, as with a moxa punk: koʾ lang² a running sore made by the cautery; [21]koʾ sioh, chaungʾ (or ch'aungʾ), to cauterize a spot; ha² ʻhwi koʾ the actual cautery.

舊² Chiu. Read keu²; coll. ko²: old, worn out, not new or recent; formerly, anciently,

[1]固守 [2]固意 [3]固執不通 [4]堅固 [5]痼疾 [6]禁錮 [7]故友 [8]大故 [9]變故 [10]何故 [11]無故 [12]世故 [13]緣故 [14]故此 [15]故事 [16]照顧 [17]不顧 [18]顧後聲名 [19]雇轎 [20]雇工 [21]灸一壯〇

before; long kept, of long standing: [1]ko꜄ to꜄ old, not new; [2]ko꜄ ʻtá, formerly; [3]ko꜄ chʻio꜄ the old house, former residence; [4]ko꜄ ʻchio kʻah꜇ an old customer—a shop phrase; ꜀i ꜁siong ôi꜄ ꜀sing ꜁nĕng ôi꜄ ko꜄ as to clothes, we want *new* ones, but as to men (employés) we want *old* ones.

(277) Kó.

蒿 ꜀Kao. Herbs higher than others; steam from plants; forms part of the names of different plants: [5]꜀tong ꜀kó, celery; COM., [6]꜀chʻing ꜀kó, wormwood.

薅 Ju. To weed, to pull up weeds: [7]꜀kó ʻchʻó, to weed out the grass.

高 ꜀Kao. High, lofty, elevated; eminent, exalted; loud; excellent, sublime, noble; a high degree; a periphrasis for *your* in direct address; old, advanced; a surname; the 189th radical: in the coll. read ꜀keng, q. v.: COM., [8]꜀kó kiéng꜄ your opinion; [9]꜀kó seu꜄ what is your age?—said to the aged; [10]꜀kó só꜄ dry, parched (ground); [11]꜀kó chieu꜄ a kind of large high lantern; [12]꜀teng ꜀kó, to ascend the hights—on the 9th day of the 9th moon; [13]꜀kó ꜁ming, intelligent; [14]꜀kó ꜀sing, to be promoted; [15]꜀kó ngó꜅ proud, arrogant; [16]꜀kó ʻchu, great-great grandfather; ꜀kó ꜁lí kwok꜇ Corea; COLL., ꜀kó ʻtá, the wooden heels (of ladies' shoes).

篙 ꜀Kao. A pole, a long stick to push boats with: COM., [17]tëük꜇ ꜀kó, a bamboo pole.

膏 ꜀Kao. Fat, grease, ointment; suet; rich food; glossy, greasy, unctuous; genial, fertilizing, fattening, rich; a jelly: [18]꜀kó tek꜇ grace, favor; [19]꜀kó ꜀hwong, the vitals, the parts beyond the reach of medicine; ꜀kó ꜀chié, unctuous, fat; COM., [20]꜀kó ʻhwo, government-allowance to students who write essays; ꜀kó yoh꜇ a medicinal plaster; [21]꜀kó ꜁liong ꜀sieu, a wine from Shantung; COLL., ꜀kó ꜁liong ꜁ĕng, a deep, dull read. Read kó꜄: to enrich, to fertilize, to fatten.

羔 ꜀Kao. A lamb, a kid: COM., [22]꜀kó ꜁yong, a lamb; haik꜇ ꜀kó, or ꜁u ꜀kó, black lambskin; COLL., pʻau꜄ ꜀kó, curly-haired lambskin.

糕 餻 Kao. The first is commonly used: unleavened cakes, pastry; dumplings of flour or arrowroot—baked when made of wheat flour, and steamed when made of rice flour, often with fruit mixed in: COM., ʻwang ꜀kó, cup-cakes; [23]ʻniong ꜀kó, pasty cake of rice flour and white sugar; ꜀kié laung꜅ ꜀kó, sponge-cake; ꜀kó ꜀tʻai, a flour sieve.

鼛 ꜀Kao. A drum, said to be 12 feet long, used in old times to encourage workmen.

歌 謌 ꜀Kao. To sing in a recitative, to chant with music accompanying; a song, a ballad: ꜀eu ꜀kó, to sing songs; ꜀kó ʻu, music and waving of plumes; COM., ꜀tung ꜁yeu ꜀kó, ballads, popular songs; chʻiong꜄ ꜀kó, to sing songs.

[1]舊	[3]舊	客	蒿	見	燥	高	陞	祖	澤	伙	[22]羔
度	厝	[5]塘	[7]薅	[9]高	[11]高	[13]高	[15]高	[17]竹	[19]膏	[21]膏	羊
[2]舊	[4]舊	蒿	草	壽	照	明	傲	篙	肓	粱	[23]軟
底	主	[6]青	[8]高	[10]高	[12]登	[14]高	[16]高	[18]膏	[20]膏	燒	糕

福州方言拼音字典

哥 ˓Ko. An elder brother; designation of the emperor's sons; a polite term for an elder or a stranger: in the coll., a term of respect applied to girls and boys: COM., 1ne' ˓kó, the 2d brother; 2twai' ˓kó, my elder brother; also a compellation for a stranger; 3ak˒ ˓kó, younger sons of the emperor—in the southern districts, term for boy; COLL., 4nié' ʻkiăng ˓kó, children; 5mwoi' ˓kó, his or your daughter; sister! Miss!

皐 ˓Kao. To inform, to call to, to announce; to drawl out, to whine; high, eminent; a bank, a marsh: 6˓kó ˓yeu, a celebrated officer of the Song dynasty; 7˓kó ˓kó, rude, uninformed.

槔 ˓Kao. A kind of tree: 8kek˒ ˓kó, a well-sweep.

櫜 ˓Kao. A bow-case or sheath; a case for armor, attached to a car; leathern wrapper for weapons.

嗃 ʻKao. Stern, severe and rigid; a sound of rejoicing; a noise, a clamor: 9ʻkó ʻkó, a harsh voice.

暠 ʻKao. Pure, clear and distinct; white, as applied to the hair.

藁 ʻKao. Interchanged with the next two: rotten wood; straw or thatch for huts; a draft or copy: 10˓ku ʻkó, dried, withered; COM., 11ʻkó ʻpwong, a medicine (? apium graveolens).

槁 ʻKao. Dry, rotten, as wood; a kind of tree, like the chestnut; others say it is like the tallow tree: 12ʻkó ˓ngü, dried fish.

稿 ʻKao. The culm of grain, straw; an original, the first draft of a writing; a sketch, a proof: COM., 13ʻch'ó ʻkó, a first draft; 14ʻkó ʻtá, a reserved draft, as of an official document; 15ʻkó ˓pung, a copyist's room; 16ʻkó ˓kung, the head-clerk in a military office; 17ʻkó chiăng' the draft and correct copy.

皜 ʻKao. White, gray and lustrous: ʻkó ʻkó, very white.

縞 ʻKao. Plain, white and fine silk; unornamented, simple; ʻkó so' plain, unadorned.

杲 ʻKao. The sun shining over trees; clear, bright; high, lofty: 18ʻkó ʻkó ch'ok˒ nik˒ the sun shining forth brightly.

箇 個 个 Ko'. A classifier, applied to human beings and to inanimate things of a round or compact form, periods of time, coins, schemes, &c.; an individual or thing; a pronoun, this, this one; used in Foochow in imitation of colloquial Mandarin, but the common classifier is chiăh, q. v.: 19ʻso' kó' a few, some; 20ʻchié kó' this one; 21ʻna kó' that one; COM., kó' kó' each, severally, all; 22ek˒ kó' one, single; COLL., kó' kó' ˓tu ʻchiă yong' all are of this sort—i. e., alike.

1二哥 2大哥 3阿哥 4伲仔哥 5妹哥○ 6皐陶 7皐皐 8桔槔 9嗃嗃 10枯藁 11藁本 12槁魚 13草稿 14稿底 15稿房 16稿公 17稿正 18杲杲出日 19數箇 20這箇 21那箇 22一箇

告' Kao. To accuse, to inform against, to impeach; to tell, to announce to a superior, to inform any one in courteous language; to ask, to request; to order: COM., [1]*kó' so'* to inform; [2]*kó' se'* (coll. *kó' che'*), a proclamation, an edict; [3]*ˎngwong kó'* the plaintiff; [4]*pe' kó'* the defendant; [5]*kó' chaung'* to accuse before a magistrate; [6]*kó' pok, hau'* to prosecute as unfilial; [7]*kó' ka'* to ask for a furlough; [8]*kó' ˎsü,* to take formal leave; [9]*kó' chói'* to admit a fault; [10]*kó' ang'* a lawsuit; [11]*kó' pah,* a plain notice, a placard.

誥' Kao. To order, to enjoin, to direct, to give commands, to signify one's wishes; a patent; a decoration: [12]*hong' kó'* to instruct; [13]*kó' t'ek,* letters patent; COM., [14]*kó' ˏhung,* or *kó' meng'* to confer rank, as on the parents or wife of an officer; [15]*kó' meng' ˏhu ˎing,* title of the wives of officers of the 1st and 2d grades.

ˎ瘑 Kao. Read *ʻkó;* coll. *ˎkó,* as in [16]*ˎkó ló'* the itch; [17]*ˏsang ˎkó ló'* to have the itch; *ˎkó ló' ˎsiu lóh, pok,* itch penetrating to the abdomen—produces bloating; *ˏkwong ˎmwong má' ˎkó ló' yoh,* sell itch-medicine with closed doors; *met.,* to trade in a private way.

ˎKó. A coll. word, as in *ˎkó ʻkiăng,* a viviparous fish resembling the shark; its meat is more delicate than that of the latter.

ˎKó. A coll. word, as in *ˎkó ˎló,* about the same as *ko' mwoi'* not yet, not so soon.

(278) Kóh.

閣, Ko. A door-screen; a long post, the posts of a door; a porch, a vestibule; a loft, an upper story or balcony; a gallery, a corridor; a safe or cupboard for eatables; *met.,* the assembled officers, the court; a safe or cupboard for eatables: [18]*kóh, ʻló,* a cabinet minister; [19]*kóh, tó'* a part of the constellation Cassiopeia; COM., [20]*nói' kóh,* the Inner Council; [21]*kóh, ha'* Your Excellency! Sir!

擱, Ko. An unauthorized character: to obstruct, to impede; delayed, hindered by difficulties; to run aground, as boats, in which sense *ˎk'ó* is more commonly used: COLL., *kóh, sioh, ʻpeng,* to defer a business; *k'ŭük, ʻü ˏtang kóh,* delayed by the rain; [22]*kóh, ʻch'iéng,* to ground on shallows.

袼, Read *lok,* and *kauk,;* coll. *kóh,:* the under seam of a sleeve: *kóh, lóh,* (or *lauk,*) *a'* under the arm, the armpit; *kóh, lóh, ˏwang,* the curvature of a garment under the arm.

Kóh,. A coll. word: to press, to stuff in, as condiment in cakes: *kóh, ʻpiăng,* to stuff cakes, to make sandwiches.

(279) Koi.

貴' Kuei. Honorable, noble, exalted, illustrious; dignified, worthy, good; your, thine, in direct address; dear,

1告訴 2告示 3原告 4被告 5告狀 6告不孝 7告假 8告辭 9告罪 10告案 11告白 12訓誥 13誥勅 14誥封 15誥命夫人 16瘑[疒老] 17生瘑[疒老] 18閣老 19閣道 20內閣 21閣下 22擱淺

high-priced; precious, valuable; to esteem, to honor, to desire, to make much of: COM., [1]'ho' koi' riches and honor; [2]koi' ˓chiu, the Kwaichow province; [3]koi' seng' your surname; [4]koi' ˓ing, the noble, the gentry, officials; [5]koi' chiéng' noble and mean; [6]koi' kaing' your district; Your Honor, the district magistrate; [7]koi' kang' your business; [8]koi' k'e' precious things—term applied to children; COLL., koi' siáng' dear and cheap; [9]koi' 'tá, costly stock—goods bought dear and not easily sold.

瑰' Kuei. A perfect pearl, which is lustrous by night; *met.*, rare, precious, admirable: ˓*king koi'* a kind of jasper; COM., [10]˓*muí koi'* the jasper; a species of red rose; [11]˓*muí koi'* '*chié*, a reddish brown.

癸' Kuei. The last of the ten stems, which with ˓*ing* belongs to the north and to water; supposed to represent water flowing to a center; to consider, to calculate: COM., [12]˓*t'iéng koi'* the menses, puberty.

˓*Koi.* A coll. word: the part of the dress over the breast; to place or carry in the bosom: ˓*koi* ˓*sing* '*tié*, to carry (a child) under one's garment: *k'aung'* ˓*koi* '*lá*, or ˓*koi* ˓*koi* '*lá*, to place in the bosom.

蕢' Kuei. A basket or hamper, made of bamboo or straw; a vegetable like the blite or strawberry-spinach, having a red stem; it resembles the [13]*haing' ch'ai'*; name o a hill.

匱' 櫃' Kuei. A case with doors, a chest, a press, a locker; the first also means exhausted, wearied out, to fail: [14]˓*king koi'* the state records; archives; COM., [15]˓*chiéng koi'* a money-safe; [16]˓*ch'ong koi'* a locker under a bedstead; [17]*koi* ˓*tiu*, locker and closet; COLL., [18]*koi'* ˓*t'au*, a counter; '*liéng koi'* a long box or chest on wheels.

餽' Kuei. About the same as the next: a term for sacrificing; to present to, to give, to offer; gifts of food.

饋' Kuei. Food, victuals, viands; presents of food; to prepare food; to attend to the kitchen; to offer food to any one: [19]*koi'* ˓*ing*, a king's baker.

跪' Kuei. To kneel, to bend the knee to the ground; the legs; a crab's leg: COM., [20]*koi' pai'* to kneel and worship; [21]*koi'* ˓*hiong*, to kneel holding incense in the hand; (obliged) to kneel while a stick of incense is burning, as an idle scholar; [22]˓*sang koi'* '*kiu k'aiu'* three kneelings and nine knockings (of the head), as in profound obeisance; *koi' liéng'* to kneel on chains—a mode of torture; COLL., *koi' sek*, knee pads; *koi' sioh*, *koi'* '*lá*, to perform an act of kneeling.

(280) **Kok.**

谷' Ku. Used erroneously for the next: a valley, a gulf, a ravine, with or without a stream; a channel for

[1]富貴 [2]貴州 [3]貴姓 [4]貴人 [5]貴賤 [6]貴縣 [7]貴幹 [8]貴器 [9]貴底 [10]玫瑰 [11]玫瑰紫○ [12]天癸 [13]莧菜 [14]金櫃 [15]錢櫃 [16]牀櫃 [17]櫃裯 [18]櫃頭 [19]饋人 [20]跪拜 [21]跪香 [22]三跪九叩

water between hills, the bed of a rivulet; an empty space; the east wind; to nourish, to sustain; difficulty, embarrassment; the 150th radical: *꜀hiu kok꜁* a sequestered valley; *꜀yong kok꜁* and *mwoi² kok꜁* the place of sunrise and sunset; COM., *꜀sang kok꜁* a valley, a ravine.

穀 穀, Ku. Grain, cereals, corn; real, substantial; good, excellent, virtuous; a succession, connected, to continue; living, alive; income, salary: ¹*kok꜁ tang²* a lucky day; ²*pok꜁ kok꜁* "the unworthy"—I, your humble servant; ³*paik꜁ kok꜁* all kinds of grain and vegetables; COM., ⁴*꜂ngu kok꜁* the common kinds of grain; ⁵*꜂mi kok꜁* rice, cereals in general; ⁶*kok꜁ ꜂ü*, the 6th of the 24 solar terms.

轂, Ku. The nave or hub of a wheel; *met.*, a wheel, a carriage: *꜀ch‘wi kok꜁* to push on the nave; *met.*, to recommend a person.

梏, Ku. Manacles, handcuffs; sedition; a neck-collar: ⁷*chek꜁ kok꜁* manacles and fetters; ⁸*kok꜁ ꜀wong*, to perish in a sedition.

牿, Ku. A shed, stable, or pen for cattle: ⁹*꜀tung ꜀ngiu kok꜁* a pen for calves.

鵠, Ku. A target, a bull's eye; an end or design; a little bird; the swan, also called ¹⁰*꜀t‘iêng ꜀ngô* (sky-goose); white, hoar, venerable, like an old man: ¹¹*kok꜁ lik*$_2$ to stand on the lookout, like a swan; ¹²*꜀hung kok꜁ ꜀chi che²* a lofty will, high aims—like the swan's flight; ¹³*kok꜁ hwak꜁* gray-haired.

嚳, To inform in haste; an urgent communication: ¹⁴*tá² kok꜁* the emperor Kuh—according to tradition, reigned B. C. 2435.

酷, Ku. Superior wine; ripe, as grain; hard-hearted, severe, inhuman, tyrannical; extremely, in a high degree: ¹⁵*kok꜁ lé²* a cruel, extortionate officer.

趉, Read *k‘wok꜁;* used in the *Paik꜁ ꜀Ing* for the coll. *kok꜁*, as in ¹⁶*kok꜁ ꜂chau*, or ¹⁷*kok꜁ kok꜁ ꜂chau*, to wriggle about and get away, as a worm; ¹⁸*kok꜁ kok꜁ ꜂tiong*, squirming about; restless, as a child.

Kok꜁. A coll. word, as in *kok꜁ ꜂k‘i*, or *kok꜁ ꜂k‘i ꜀li*, or *kok꜁ ꜂k‘i ꜀sing*, to rise up (from a seat); *kok꜁ tek꜁ ꜀ti*, to arise late (from bed).

滑, Hua. Read *hwak*$_2$*;* coll. *kok*$_2$*:* slippery, as a wet path: *kok*$_2$ *leu² leu²*, or ¹⁹*kok*$_2$ *chiăh꜁ kok*$_2$ very slippery; ²⁰*kok*$_2$ *꜂chau*, to slip away, as the foot; *kok*$_2$ *sioh*$_2$ *꜂tó*, to slip down.

(281) **Kong.**

缸, Kang. An earthenware jar, with or without glazing, in the coll. a kind of bowl: COM., *꜂mi ꜀kong*, rice-jars; *꜂chwi ꜀kong*, water-jars; COLL., *꜀p‘ung ꜀kong*, a slop-jar; *꜀lié ꜀p‘ui ꜀kong*, large glazed jars, used to contain rain-water; *twai² ꜀kong*, or *꜀kong ꜀pwong*, a large bowl.

---

¹穀旦 ²不穀 ³百穀 ⁴五穀 ⁵米穀 ⁶穀雨 ⁷桎梏 ⁸梏亡 ⁹童牛牿○ ¹⁰天鵝 ¹¹鵠立 ¹²鴻鵠之志 ¹³鵠髮 ¹⁴帝嚳 ¹⁵酷吏 ¹⁶趉走 ¹⁷趉趉走○ ¹⁸趉趉轉 ¹⁹滑隻滑 ²⁰滑走

釭 Kang. An iron tire on a tub; a sconce or globular shade, in which to hang lamps; the barb of an arrow: [1]˓*king* ˓*kong*, ornaments on wainscots, like the nave of a wheel.

豇 A kind of bean, called [2]˓*kong tau*˒; they are small and bent like kidneys, and have spotted eyes: COLL., ˓*kong tau*˒ *ang*˒ bean-stuffing for cakes; ˓*kong tau*˒ ʻ*kwi*, steamed cakes with bean-stuffing.

罡 Kang. A star: [3]˓*t'iëng* ˓*kong*, the seven stars in the constellation of the Great Bear, the Dipper—much used in charms.

扛 Kang. To carry between two; to bear burdens on a pole; to carry, as a sedan; to lift, as several persons do together: COM., [4]ʻ*tói*˒ ˓*kong*, carried by two; [5]˓*kong kieu*˒ to carry a sedan; COLL., ˓*kong mä*˒ ʻ*k'i*, can't carry it; [6]˓*kong* ˓*liêng* ˓*mai*, (expense of) bearing and interring (the dead).

杠 A cross-piece in the front of a bedstead; cross-bars in frames; a large beam over the doors of a wide room; a flag-staff; a ship's yards; the thills of a sedan; a foot-bridge: COM., [7]˓*kong* ˓*liong*, a long beam over doors; [8]˓*kong* ˓*liong* ˓*t'iäng*, a parlor so constructed.

根 Këng. Roots of plants; the origin, the beginning, root, bottom, foundation; fundamental; a classifier of trees: in the coll. read ˓*kũng*, q. v.: COM., [9]˓*kong* ʻ*pwong*, the source or original, as one's parents; [10]˓*kong* ˓*ngwong*, the origin, beginning; [11]˓*kong* ˓*ki*, the foundation; *met.*, constitution, as of a child; [12]˓*kong* ˓*ki chaüng*˒ has a vigorous constitution; [13]˓*kong* ʻ*tä*, the bottom, something to rest or depend upon; ˓*kong* ˓*ch'ing pok*, *p'a*˒ ˓*hung* ˓*yeu tong*˒ the roots are deep, no fear of the wind shaking it; *met.*, a good man need not fear slander.

江 Chiang. A river; *par excellence* the R. Yang-tsz, also called [14]*Tui*˒ ˓*kong* (the great river): in the coll. read ˓*këng*, q. v.: COM., [15]˓*kong* ˓*sang*, rivers and mountains, the empire; [16]˓*kong* ˓*su*, Kiangsu; [17]˓*kong* ˓*sä*, Kiangsi; [18]˓*Liëng* ˓*kong*, a district in the Foochow prefecture; COLL., [19]*ngie*˒ ˓*kong*, other provinces; [20]˓*kiäng* ˓*kong* ˓*hu*, itinerants from the rivers and lakes—term applied to fortune-tellers, jugglers, sellers of nostrums, &c.; ˓*kong* ˓*yeu chëu*˒ a large clam of which the muscles only are edible; *pai*˒ ˓*kong* ˓*sang*, "has ruined the empire"—wasted a patrimony.

肛 The colon, the large intestine; the anus: COM., [21]˓*kong* ˓*mwong*, the rectum; COLL., *t'ok*, ˓*kong*, protrusion of the rectum, the piles.

剛 Kang. Hard, solid, inflexible, unyielding, rigorous, firm; intrepid, enduring, valorous; an adverb of time; now, just now, recently: ˓*kong* ˓*hung*, just met with; [22]˓*kong kiong*˒ or ˓*kong* ˓*kiong*, strong, valorous, resolute; COM., ˓*kong tik*, firm in mind, upright;

1金釭 2豇豆 3天罡 4對扛 5扛轎 6扛連埋 7杠樑 8杠樑廳 9根本 10根原 11根基 12根基壯 13根底 14大江 15江山 16江蘇 17江西 18連江 19外江 20行江湖 21肛門 22剛鏹

²*ˏkong ˏiu ˏsiong chá'* severity tempered with kindness; ²*ˏking ˏkong*, the four gigantic guards in Budhist temples; *ˏking ˏkong sioh,* corundum, a diamond.

綱 ʻ Kang. The large rope to which a net is strung; a bond of society, an institution, a great principle: ³*ˏkong muk,* a synopsis; a book of history compiled by Chubi; ⁴*ˏkong ʻki*, a narrative, a series; ⁵*ˏkong ʻling*, a controlling principle; the argument of a book; COM., ⁶*ˏsang ˏkong*, three bonds—i. e., the relative duties of king, father, and husband; ⁷*ʻchung ˏkong*, the essence or origin of; ⁸*ˏkong kung'* a survey of dynasties, a history.

岡 ʻ Kang. The ridge, the watershed of hills; a summit, the culminating point: ⁹*ˏsang ˏkong*, the summit of a hill.

ˏKong. A coll. word, as in *ˏkong ˏchá*, to make offerings (to Confucius) in school in the 4th moon: *ˏkong ˏchá hong²* the shares contributed by scholars on the occasion.

講 ʻ Chiang. To converse, to talk, to say, to speak, to narrate; to explain, to unfold, to discourse or reason about, to propound, to preach; to investigate; to plan; to confer: talk, explanation: COM., ¹⁰*ʻkong wa²* to speak, to talk; ¹¹*ʻkong laung²* to discourse on; ¹²*ʻkong keu'* to investigate; ¹³*ʻkong ʻli*, to state the reason; ¹⁴*ʻkong ˏchü*, to explain books, to preach; ¹⁵*tik, ʻkong*, to speak frankly; COLL., *ʻkong ʻta*, or *ʻkong hwak*, conversational power; *ˏpang ʻkong hié'* a play in the patois; *p'ang' ʻkong*, to converse, to chat; *ʻyá ʻkong*, to lie; *ʻkong má² ch'ok*, unable to articulate; *ʻkong ʻchiu liăng'* to rhapsodize, or utter impromptu sentences at a feast; *ʻkong ˏt'iéng lói² té'* "says heaven and pounds earth"—to talk irrelevantly; *ʻkong lëk, ˏchiong*, "speaks the six chapters"—prates about everything.

貢' Kung. To offer tribute, to offer to a liege, to present; to pay taxes; tribute, taxes, or presents, given by inferiors or fiefs, as the peltry, gems, &c., of Tartar tribes, sent to Peking; *met.*, fine, of superior quality; to announce; offers of service—hence merit, worthy actions: COM., ¹⁶*cheng' kong'* to offer tribute; ¹⁷*kong' sai'* a tribute bearer; ¹⁸*kong' ˏseng*, Siutsai breveted as Küjin; ¹⁹*pak, kong'* Siutsai breveted by the governor; ²⁰*kong' taung²* a superior kind of satin; ²¹*kong' yéng²* the provincial examination-hall.

贛' Kun. Interchanged with the next; also read *ʻkang* and *kang'*: to give, to bestow; the prefecture of Kanchau in the southern part of Kiangsi.

灨' Kun. Also read *ʻkang* and *kang'*: the large river of Kiangsi flowing north into Poyang lake.

戇' Kun. Often read *maung'*: simple, stupid silly; rude, ignorant, doltish: ²²*ˏngü kong'* stupid, idiotic; ²³*ˏch'u kong'* rude, simple.

贑' Kun. A name for the seeds of the *é' ʻi*, pearl-barley. Read *ʻkang*: name of a plant.

¹剛柔相濟 ²金剛 ³綱目 ⁴綱紀 ⁵綱領 ⁶三綱 ⁷總綱 ⁸綱鑑 ⁹山岡 ¹⁰講話 ¹¹講論 ¹²講究 ¹³講理 ¹⁴講書 ¹⁵直講 ¹⁶進貢 ¹⁷貢使 ¹⁸貢生 ¹⁹拔貢 ²⁰貢緞 ²¹貢院 ²²愚戇 ²³粗戇

棍ˀ Kun. A round stick, a club; to bind up sticks; a sharper: ˈ*kongˀ* ˏ*sing*, spontaneously; COM., [2]ˏ*kwong kongˀ* a "bare-stick"—a scoundrel; [3]*teˀ kongˀ* the rowdies of the place; [4]ˈ*tu kongˀ* gamblers, blacklegs; [5]ˏ*ch'a kongˀ* a stick, a club; COLL., [6]ˏ*kung kongˀ* a club; [7]*p'ah, sioh, kongˀ* to give a blow with a club.

閂 ˏShan. Read ˏ*swang* in the dictionaries; coll. ˏ*kong*: a bar or beam for fastening a door: also read *ch'aungˀ* in the coll., q. v.: [8]ˏ*mwong* ˏ*kong*, a door-bar; [9]ˏ*hwang* ˏ*kong*, a cross-bar; [10]ˏ*kong* ˏ*mwong*, to bar a door; [11]ˏ*kong* ˈ*king* ˈ*king*, bar it tight.

ˏ*Kong*. A coll. word: to burn, to scald: ˈ*hwi* ˏ*kong*, burnt by the fire; ˏ*kong* ˏ*sang p'auˀ* burnt to a blister; ˏ*kong t'auk*, to burn and scald; *met.*, to startle, to excite intensely.

ˏ*Kong*. A coll. word: to cook thoroughly, to boil soft: ˏ*kong langˀ* or ˏ*kong mauk*, *k'óˀ* boiled to pieces; ˏ*kong chiongˀ* to cook with salt condiments.

ˏ*Kong*. A coll. word, as in ˏ*kong* ˏ*tieu* (or ˏ*sieu*) *pek*, *siék*, false or random talk.

郡ˀ Chün. An inhabited place, a principality, a small district, now applied to a prefecture: [12]ˈ*siu kongˀ* the chief prefecture in a province; [13]*kongˀ* ˈ*ma*, a prince's brother-in-law, or niece's husband.

(282) Ku.

刳 ˏK'u. Also read ˏ*k'u*: to cut open; to rip up, to kill; to cut or hew, as timber; to hollow out: [14]ˏ*ku muk*, to hollow out a tree; [15]ˏ*ku* ˏ*sing*, to make a clean breast.

孤 ˏKu. Fatherless, an orphan; desolate, alone, singular; unprotected; unequaled, solitary, applied by the emperor to himself; ungrateful, forgetting the kindness shown: [16]ˏ*ku* ˏ*ka*, I, the emperor; [17]ˏ*ku* ˈ*kwa*, or ˏ*ku* ˏ*tang*, alone, solitary; COM., [18]ˏ*ku* ˏ*sing*, or ˏ*ku tuk*, alone, no near kindred; [19]ˏ*ku* ˏ*hung*, a neglected, orbate spirit; [20]ˏ*ku* ˏ*ai* ˈ*chü*, an orphan; [21]ˏ*ku* ˏ*sá*, desolate and sorrowing; ˏ*ku siongˀ* one who keeps to himself, reserved; COLL., ˏ*ku* ˏ*t'au chiok*, ˈ*chüng*, solitary, and posterity all cut off!—an imprecation; ˏ*ku* ˈ*ló*, a leper.

菰 ˏKu. A water vegetable, the Caladium, cultivated for its tubers: ˏ*hu* ˏ*ku*, a sort of upland rice; [22]ˏ*ngiu* ˈ*ch'i* ˏ*ku*, the lycoperdon, puff-balls; COM., ˏ*hiong* ˏ*ku*, a small edible mushroom; ˏ*mó* ˏ*ku*, a mushroom brought from Tartary.

觚 ˏKu. A wine vase, used on sacrificial and festive occasions, holding two or three pints; a corner, square, angular; a law, a rule; a plan, a scheme; a sword-hilt: ˏ*ch'ó* ˏ*ku*, rash, inconsiderate.

柧 ˏKu. Interchanged with the last: a corner, angular; the cornice of a house: ˏ*ku* ˏ*ling*, the curvature of the peak, cornices.

枯 ˏK'u. Rotten wood; rotten, decayed, withered, doted; dry bogs: ˏ*ku* ˈ*kó*, decayed; emaciated, cadaverous; COLL., ˏ*ku* ˏ*ta*, withered;

[1]棍成 [2]光棍 [3]地棍 [4]賭棍 [5]柴棍 [6]棍棍 [7]拍一棍 [8]門閂 [9]橫閂 [10]閂門 [11]閂緊緊 [12]首郡 [13]郡馬 [14]刳木 [15]刳心 [16]孤家 [17]孤寡 [18]孤身 [19]孤魂 [20]孤哀子 [21]孤恓 [22]牛齒菰

˛ku muk˺ ˛hung ˛ch'ung po˺ pwok˺ ˛nga, when a dry tree meets the spring it buds again; *met.*, a poor man improving in his circumstances.

姑 ˛Ku. A polite term for females; a husband's mother is called *˛ku* by his wife; lenient, easy, lax, indulgent; just, merely, temporarily, for the time: [1]*˛kung ˛ku,* husband's father and mother; COM., [2]*˛ku ˛niang,* a young lady, Miss; also a married daughter; [3]*˛ku ˛ié,* compellation for a son-in-law; [4]*˛ku 'ná,* or *˛niong ˛ku,* or *˛ku ˛ma,* a paternal aunt; [5]*˛ku ˛hu,* or *˛ku t'iong˺* or *˛ku ˛tiă,* paternal uncles by marriage; [6]*˛ku ˛pó* and *˛ku ˛kung,* a grandfather's sister and sister's husband; [7]*˛ku t'ai˺* an officer's sister; [8]*˛ná ˛ku,* a Budhist nun; [9]*˛ku keu˺ 'pieu,* cousins, cousin-germans of different surnames; COLL., *twai˺ sá˺ ˛ku,* husband's sisters.

沽 ˛Ku. Name of a river in the Chinchew prefecture, Fookien; to contract bargains, to buy or sell, to trade; unworthy, trashy, anything coarse and inferior: [10]*˛ku ˛ming,* to buy a name, to purchase office; [11]*˛kung ˛ku,* the meritorious and unworthy.

酤 ˛Ku. Interchanged with the last: liquor just made and kept over night; to buy or trade in wines; a liquor shop: [12]*˛ku 'chiu,* to buy wine.

蛄 ˛Ku. A species of mole-cricket, called *˛leu ˛ku;* [13]*'hié˺ ˛ku,* a variety of the cicada.

辜 ˛Ku. A fault, a crime; sin, transgression, guilt; must, necessary, inevitably; to dissect sacrificial victims; to hinder, as in trade, to monopolize: [14]*˛ku ngwok˺* the 11th moon; [15]*˛ku kau˺* generally speaking; [16]*˛ku ho˺* ungrateful; COM., [17]*˛u ˛ku seu˺ loi˺* the guiltless involved by others.

骷 ˛K'u. The shoulder-blade; the thigh-bone; a skeleton: COM., [18]*˛ku ˛leu ˛kó,* the skeleton-song—showing the evils of prostitution.

鴣 ˛Ku. A partridge, called *chiă˺ ˛ku;* the Chinese description seems to include other birds of like habits and size.

˛Ku. A coll. word, as in *˛ku ˛ku kieu˺* the cooing of doves; their note is said to be *˛ku 'ku ko˺! ˛ku 'ku ko˺!*

罛 ˛Ku. A fishing-net, a large net dragged between boats; to fish.

罟 'Ku. Interchanged with the last: nets dragged along; a bird-net; *met.*, the net of the law: [19]*'wong 'ku,* a fish-ing-net; [20]*chói˺ 'ku,* the meshes of sin, involved in guilt.

股 胋 'Ku. The haunches, the upper part of the thigh, the rump; the leg; a strand of a cord; a spoke in a wheel; firm, stable; a division, a chapter or head, as of an essay; also used for a share, portion, quota, a classifier of shares: [21]*'ku ˛keng,* legs and arms; *met.*, statesmen; COM., [22]*˛sang 'ku,* made

[1]公姑 [2]姑娘 [3]姑爺 [4]姑奶 [5]姑夫 [6]姑婆 [7]姑太 [8]尼姑 [9]姑舅表 [10]沽名 [11]功沽 [12]酤酒 [13]螻蛄 [14]辜月 [15]辜較 [16]辜負 [17]無辜受累 [18]骷髏歌 [19]網罟 [20]罪罟 [21]股肱 [22]三股

of three strands, as cord; three shares; *paik*, 'ku, eight heads in an essay; [1]'*ku* ,*chiéng*, a common fund, the shares distributed in a yamun; COLL., ,*pwong* '*ku*, to distribute quotas; '*ku* ,*ch'iong*, or '*ku* ,*ch'iong* '*p'á*, the buttocks.

羖 Ku. A ram, or a black ewe, as the word was used in different periods; a parti-colored ram; a sheep, male or female, a full-grown sheep: [2]'*ngu* '*ku tai*', *hu*, the lord of the five sheepskins—a story of Pehlihi, B. C. 660.

'盬 Ku. A salt pond in or near Shantung; not lasting, badly made; to suck; temporary; hasty, hurried, confused.

'鹽 Ku. A vessel, a utensil: COM., [3],*ta* '*ku*, a tea-pot; [4],*têng* '*ku*, a brass kettle; COLL., '*ku* '*kiâng*, a small tea-pot.

'古 Ku. Ancient, that which has come down through ten *mouths;* remote, antique, old, from of old; antiquity, former; practiced in, accustomed: [5],*sang* '*ku*, the three periods of antiquity—times of Fohi, Wanwang, and Confucius, B. C. 2850, 1120, and 550; COM., [6]'*ku* '*ló*, old, antique; [7]'*ku* ,*king*, ancient and modern; [8]'*ku* '*cha* ,*si hau*' in ancient times; [9]'*ku wa*' antique paintings; [10]*chauk*, '*ku*, to die; [11]'*ku chek*, relics, sacred spots; [12]'*ku* '*ngü*, old sayings; [13]'*ku t'ó*' antique styles, as of dress; [14]'*ku* '*tung ngwang*' *uk*, antiques, curiosities; '*ku kwai*' odd, strange; tricky, knavish.

'嘏 Ku. Great, large; distant; strong, stable; great happiness, blessed, propitious, happy: [15]*chëük*, '*ku*, to bless, to implore blessings.

'估 Ku. To price, to estimate, to value; to guess, to reckon; price, value: [16],*t'ai* '*ku*, to raise the price; [17]'*ku kié*' to reckon, to appraise; COM., '*ku ka*' ,*chiêng*, to estimate the value, to set a price; COLL., '*ku k'ang*' *tek*, *nioh*, *wai*' ,*chiêng*, reckon and see what it is worth; '*ku* ,*siâng saik*, to estimate the quality or purity (of metals).

'牯 Ku. A cow, the female of kine; in some places used for the male of quadrupeds, usually of those domesticated.

'詁 Ku. To explain the words of the ancients by modern illustrations; to instruct: [18]'*ku hong*' to expound; notes, comments.

'蠱 Ku. Worms in the abdomen, which are thought to cause dropsy; a venomous worm, used to poison people; a slow poison; an unquiet ghost; to disturb, to stir up; suspicious; to trouble with doubts; to delude, to seduce, to beguile; the 18th diagram: [19]'*ku hëk*, to delude, to cozen; ,*yeu* '*ku*, to captivate, to bewitch, as elves are said to do; '*ku tuk*, poison; COM., '*ku tiong*' the dropsy.

'賈 Ku. A shopman, one who trades in a market; a resident tradesman; to trade, to traffic: also read *ka*', q. v.: [20],*siong* '*ku*, a merchant; [21]'*ku ch'e*' a market, a bazaar.

[1]股錢 [2]五羖大夫 [3]茶鹽 [4]銅鹽 [5]三古 [6]古老 [7]古今 [8]古早時候 [9]古話 [10]作古 [11]古蹟 [12]古語 [13]古套 [14]古董玩物 [15]祝嘏 [16]擡估 [17]估計 [18]詁訓 [19]蠱惑 [20]商賈 [21]賈市

ʻ**鼓** ʻ**鼔** Ku. A drum, skin instruments of music, once made of earthen; earthen seats or stands for flowers; a measure of about ten pecks; drum-shaped; to drum; to excite, encourage, arouse; to urge a fire; to soothe; a watch of the night; to play on a lute; the 207th radical: [1]*ʻku ʻchiong*, to clap the hands; [2]*ʻku ch'ŏ'* a great hubbub; [3]*ʻku hok*ˏ corpulent—said of people in the golden era of the emperor ˏYau; COM., [4]*ʻku ˏlau*, a drum-tower; [5]*ʻku ˏt'ui*, drumsticks; [6]*ʻwang ʻku*, the evening drum; [7]*ˏngü ʻku*, a fish tambourine—used by priests; [8]*ˏhwa ʻku*, a small, longish drum—used by itinerant musicians; [9]*ʻku ˏsang se²* the Kushan monastery; [10]*ʻku ʻch'iu*, or [11]*ʻku ˏpang*, a band of musicians; [12]*ʻku ngok*ˏ musical instruments; COLL., [13]*p'ah*ˏ *ʻku ʻpeng*, to beat instruments, as drums, etc.; [14]*ʻku ʻpeng sioh*ˏ *ho'* a set of such instruments; [15]*p'ah*ˏ *ˏkang ʻku*, to beat the watches.

ʻKu. A coll. word, for which the last is sometimes used: to stir up, to stir, as the contents of a vessel: *ʻku ˏlung*, to roil by stirring; *ʻku sang'* stirred and scattered, as a company by the intrusion of a wrangler; *ʻku t'aung' ˏch'ing*, made thin by stirring; *ʻku ʻchwi ˏnang ˏlung*, hard to roil the water by stirring it; *met.*, difficult to effect, as a matter attempted by one alone.

ʻ**瞽** Ku. Eyes without pupils, or which cannot see; blind; a musician, leader of an orchestra: [16]*ʻku muk*ˏ blind; [17]*ngëü² ʻku*, musicians of the palace: *ʻKu muk*ˏ father of the emperor Shun.

ʻ**故** Ku. Read *ko'*; used for the coll. *ʻku*, as in [18]*ʻku sëü²* antiquated matters, such as parades in antique costumes: [19]*ʻku e'* or [20]*ʻku ˏling e'* purposely and hypocritically.

ˏ**糊** ˏ**粘** Ku. Read *ˏhu*; coll. *ˏku*: paste, gluten; to paste, to stick: [21]*ˏku ˏchiong*, paste; *kak*ˏ *ˏku*, stuck with paste; *met.*, imperfectly done; an illicit connexion; *ˏku p'ŏh*, or *ˏku ˏking ˏngüng*, to paste foil-paper (in certain forms for idolatrous uses); *ˏku ʻchai ˏnó* (or *t'ak*ˏ), to paste paper-things, as images, boats, sedans, etc.; *ʻtiäng ˏpiéng ˏku*, a kind of rice crust (cooked) on the pan's sides (with seasoned soup).

ˏKu. A coll. word, as in *ˏku ˏchwi*, the turtle-dove; *ˏku ˏchwi mëk*ˏ "dove's eye"—a staple, a loop of iron or brass; *ˏku ˏchwi kieu' ˏku ʻku ko²* the dove sings *ˏku ʻku ko²*.

ˏKu. A coll. word, as in *ˏku ˏsai*, a kind of large shark.

ˏKu. A coll. word, as in *ˏku ˏlung ˏch'iong*, to squat; *ˏku tok*ˏ to wriggle; *ˏku ˏku lŏh*ˏ (or *kieu'*) noise in swallowing nice food; *ˏku ˏku kieu'* rumbling, as of the bowels; *ˏki ˏli ˏku ˏtu* (or *ˏlu*), muttering, grumbling.

(283) Kü.

ˏ**拘** Chü. To grasp with the hand, to detain, to grapple with, to stop; to restrain, to moderate, to repress; to hold, to adhere; obstinate-

[1]鼓掌 [2]鼓噪 [3]鼓腹 [4]鼓樓 [5]鼓槌 [6]晚鼓 [7]魚鼓 [8]花鼓 [9]鼓山寺 [10]鼓手 [11]鼓班 [12]鼓樂 [13]拍鼓板 [14]鼓板一副 [15]拍更鼓 [16]瞽目 [17]御瞽 [18]故事 [19]故意 [20]故心意 [21]糊漿

ly attached to, bigoted; to take, to receive; to hook; bent, crooked; to collect: COM., [1]*‚kü sok‚* to bind, as by fixed rules; [2]*‚kü chek‚* or *‚kü nái²* bigoted, set in one's opinion; [3]*‚kü ak‚* to take into custody; [4]*‚kü keng'* to imprison; [5]*‚kü ʻlá*, or *‚kü t'ó'* to be very ceremonious; [6]*pok‚ ‚kü*, not insist; no matter how or what; COLL., *móh‚ ‚kü*, don't insist, don't stand on ceremony; *pok‚ ‚kü nioh‚ wai²* without regard to the amount; *‚kü ‚ch'á ch'io'* in custody at a policeman's house.

琚 Chü. Ornamental gems hanging from a girdle, one on each side: [7]*‚king ‚kü*, precious ornaments, bijoutry; [8]*‚kü pwoi²* girdle-ornaments.

椐 Chü. A tree found in Honan, called [9]*‚kü koi²* used for whip-handles and walking-staves for old people.

居 Chü. To dwell, to stop at a place, to inhabit, to reside; to seat one's self, to remain stationary; to fill an office or station; to be acting, and is thus often a mere participial form of the next verb; to consist in; to hoard, to monopolize goods; to cease, to desist; retired, as from public life: [10]*‚kü ‚kwang*, to be in office; [11]*‚kü ‚song*, in mourning; [12]*ʻk'i ‚kü*, acting and quiescent; [13]*‚kü sëü²* a retired scholar; COM., [14]*‚song ‚kü*, a widow; [15]*‚kü chëü²* to reside, to live at; [16]*‚kü ‚ka*, to live in houses, families; [17]*‚ming ‚kü*, the people's homes; [18]*‚kü ‚ki*, (goods) kept to raise prices; [19]*‚kü ʻtiong*, to be the elder, as a brother; COLL., *‚kü ʻchwi*, water collected (in a place); *‚kü kek‚* hurried: *‚kü ‚tüng ‚tüng*, in the middle, middling, medium.

裾 Chü. The skirt of a robe, the tail of a coat: [20]*‚tiong ‚kü*, a long skirt or train. Read *këü':* proud, haughty.

車 Ch'ê. Chü. A wheeled barrow; a car, a cart, a carriage, a vehicle for carrying persons or goods; the jawbones; the 159th radical: also read *‚ch'iä*, q. v.: *ek‚ seng²* *‚kü*, one carriage; [21]*‚kung ‚kü*, a public office; [22]*hok‚ ho' ʻngu ‚kü*, rich in the lore of five cart-loads of books—i. e., very learned; COM., *‚kü ʻma p'a'* the chariot, horse, and gun—chessmen.

矩 ʻChü. A carpenter's square; a rule, law, usage, pattern; strict, exact; what is constant, uniform; an angle; to square, to adjust: *pok‚ ‚ü ʻkü*, (Confucius) did not overstep equity; [23]*kiék‚ ʻkü*, rules which influence others; COM., *‚kié ʻkü* (coll. *‚kwi ʻkü*), a rule, a usage.

踽 ʻChü. Also read *ʻngü:* a stately gait, independent, solitary; going alone, morose, unsociable: *ʻkü ʻkü ‚king ‚king*, to walk alone, unaccompanied, solitary.

舉 舁 ʻChü. To raise with the hands, to carry between two, to elevate; sometimes denotes the action of the next verb; to raise in public opinion, to introduce, to recommend; to venerate, to

---

1 拘束 2 拘執 3 拘押 4 拘禁 5 拘禮 6 不拘 7 瓊琚 8 琚珮 9 椐樻 10 居官 11 居喪 12 起居 13 居士 14 孀居 15 居住 16 居家 17 民居 18 居奇 19 居長 20 長裾 21 公車 22 學富五車 23 絜矩

rise in one's esteem; to speak of, to allude to, to extol, to praise; to advance, to promote; all, the whole number; to confiscate; an ancient weight of three taels: [1]‘*kü siê*’ mankind; COM., [2]*ˏkung ‘kü*, promoted or nominated by the public; [3]‘*kü chiéng*’ to recommend one; [4]‘*kü ˏheng*, to begin doing; [5]‘*kü tong*’ movements, actions; [6]‘*kü ‘chi*, deportment; [7]‘*kü ‘ch‘iu*, to raise the hand; [8]‘*kü ˏing*, or [8]‘*kü ‘chü*, a Küjin; [10]‘*kü ˏsing*, or ‘*kü e*’ to intend; [11]‘*kü ‘ngang ˏu ˏch‘ing*, "raise my eyes and (see) no relatives", as one says in a foreign land; ‘*kü ek, pok, ‘kü ne*’ "set forth the first, not the second"—have called one to do it and will not call another.

‘簴 The upright posts of a frame for a bell or drum: [12]‘*sung ‘kü*, a bell-frame.

‘蒟 A plant called [13]‘*kü chiong*’ when young and green; a kind of long pepper; its fruit is said to resemble the berries of the mulberry.

ˏ蕖 Ch‘ü. The water lily, called *ˏhó ˏhu ˏkü*; [14]*ch‘iok, yok, ˏhu ˏkü*, splendid as the lotus flower.

ˏ蘧 Ch‘ü. A kind of wild wheat, called [15]*ˏkü mek*; [16]*ˏkü ˏsu*, a mushroom; [17]*ˏkü ˏkü*, contented, satisfied.

ˏ籧 Ch‘ü. A coarse bamboo mat, used on floors, called *ˏkü ˏtü*; a deformity that prevents one's stooping; [18]*ˏkü ˏk‘wong*, a tray for silk-woms.

ˏ璩 Ch‘ü. A kind of ring; a surname, a man's name.

ˏ俱 Chü. All, altogether, at once; jointly, together with, both, the two; fully supplied, all right, prepared: in the coll. read *këü*’, q. v: [19]*ˏkü ˏchiong*, complete, perfect, entire; [20]*ˏkü pe*’ all prepared; *ˏkü se*’ all are (so).

ˏ渠 Chü. A drain, aqueduct, or gutter; a pool, pond, or cess-pool, into which a drain empties; great, ample, wide; gradual; pleased, laughing; a kind of armor; a district of Shunking-fu in Sz'chuen; a personal pronoun, he, she, it: *ˏkü ˏkü*, diligent, careful; *ˏhiong ˏkü*, laughing; [21]*ˏkü ho*’ ample, rich; *ˏkü ‘teng* (or *ˏnung*), they.

ˏ瞿 Ch‘ü. The frightened look of a bird; timid, fearful, apprehensive; to look at; to examine wildly or hurriedly; sparing, economical: [22]*ˏkü ˏyong*, alarmed. Also read *këü*’: careful, circumspect; *ˏliong sëü*’ *këü*’ *këü*’ a discreet, well-bred scholar.

ˏ臞 Ch‘ü. Thin, emaciated, poor, like a ghost; a lean, ghastly appearance.

ˏ磲 Chü. A kind of milky stone, resembling argentine, used for cap-knobs by officers of the 6th rank: COM., *ˏch‘ia ˏkü ‘ting*, a cap-knob of argentine.

[1]舉世 [2]公舉 [3]舉薦 [4]舉行 [5]舉動 [6]舉止 [7]舉手 [8]舉人 [9]舉予 [10]舉心 [11]舉眼無親 [12]簨簴 [13]蒟醬 [14]灼若芙蕖 [15]蘧麥 [16]蘧蔬 [17]蘧蘧 [18]籧篨 [19]俱全 [20]俱備 [21]渠富 [22]瞿然

鴝鶌 ꜂Ch'ü. A species of singing thrush or grackle, called [1]꜀kü ük꜇ or pek꜇ ꜀kó (? the Turdus violaceus); its plumage is black with a white spot on the secondaries: [2]꜀kü ꜂ngang, "thrush's eyes"—the spots seen in argillite inkstones.

衢 ꜂Ch'ü. A street, a broadway, a highway, a public road from which others diverge: [3]꜀t'ung ꜀kü, a thoroughfare; [4]꜀t'iéng ꜀kü, the equator; some say the Milky Way; *met.*, the Imperial presence.

(284) Kuh.

Kuh꜇. A coll. word: to dig at, to scoop strongly or forcibly: ꜂*wang kuh*꜇ *p'wai*꜄ broke the bowl in scooping with it.

(285) Kuk.

掘 Chüeh꜇. Used for the next: to dig into the ground, to excavate, to scoop, to open, to hollow out; to exhaust; to rise up alone: COM., [5]*kuk*꜇ ꜀*ch'ing*, to dig deep; [6]*kuk*꜇ ꜀*hwang* ꜁*sü*, to dig potatoes; COLL., *kuk*꜇ ꜂*k'i* ꜁*li*, to dig up; *kuk*꜇ ꜁*nëng mwo*꜄ ꜁*t'au*, "dig up people's graves"—*scil.*, you think me base enough to do even that!

崛 Chüeh꜇. Rising like a solitary peak; eminent, distinguished: COM., [7]*kuk*꜇ ꜂*k'i*, standing alone, distinguished, as the only one of a family who gains honors.

倔 Chüeh꜇. Obstinate, opinionated; willful, perverse: [8]*kuk*꜇ ꜀*kiong*, stubborn, refractory.

(286) Kük.

Kük꜇. A coll. word: thick, thickened, inspissated: ꜀*ch'ing kük*꜇, thin and thick; *kük*꜇ *kük*꜇ ꜂*ang*, thick rice-gruel; *kük*꜇ *chiäh*꜇ *kük*꜇ very thick.

(287) Kung.

公 ꜀Kung. The opposite of selfish or mean; common, public, universal; open, general; just, equitable, fair; male of animals; a duke; a lord, master, or head; a term of respect and dignity added to names of relationship: COM., [9]꜀*kung tó*꜄ or ꜀*kung* ꜁*pang*, just, fair; [10]꜂*ping* ꜀*kung*, to act justly; [11]꜀*kung* ꜀*sü*, public and private; [12]꜀*kung* ꜁*heu paik*꜇ ꜂*chü* ꜁*nang*, duke, marquis, earl, viscount, baron; [13]꜀*kung o*꜄ official business; [14]꜀*kung* ꜁*tong*, a court room; ꜀*kung ang*꜄ *tóh*, the magistrate's table; [15]꜀*kung* ꜂*su* (coll. ꜀*kung* ꜂*së*), a public place; [16]꜀*kung haung*꜄ a public fund; [17]꜀*kung* ꜁*üng* (coll. ꜀*kung* ꜀*t'ang*), to apportion equally, as a proposed subscription; [18]꜀*kung chëüng*꜄ the public, what is common to all; [19]꜀*kung* ꜁*ung*, a goverment dispatch; [20]꜀*chü* ꜀*kung*, you, gentlemen! [21]꜀*kung* ꜁*ié*, my lord duke—applied to the god ꜁*Siüng* ꜁*hwong* (municipal guardian); [22]꜀*kung* ꜂*chio*, the emperor's daughters; *ngié*꜄ ꜀*kung*, a maternal grandfather; ꜀*kung* ꜁*pó*, paternal ancestors —applied to their tablets; ꜀*kung pó*꜄ ꜀*sü* ꜁*siu*, to avenge a private quarrel through some public transaction; COLL., *lau*꜄ ꜀*kung* ꜂*ma*, husband and wife.

1鶌	3通	5掘	薯	强	公	侯	13公	15公	17公	19公	21公
鴝	衢	深	7崛	9公	11公	伯	務	所	匀	文	爺
2鶌	4天	6掘	起	道	私	子	14公	16公	18公	20諸	22公
眼	衢	番	8倔	10秉	12公	男	堂	項	衆	公	主

工 ˏKung. A laborer, workman, artisan, mechanic; labor, craft; art; an ornament requiring skill; a work; an officer; the 48th radical: in the coll. read ˏkëng, q. v.: [1]ˏkung ˏing, laborers; [2]paik, ˏkung, all kinds of work; [3]ˏchĭng ˏkung, fine work.

攻 ˏKung. To attack, to assault, to fight, to beat; to put in order; to work at, to apply diligently to; to rouse, to reprove for faults; to stimulate the energies or vital powers; urgency of desire in the heart, temptation; strong, enduring: [4]ˏkung ʻta, to fight; [5]ˏkung ˏchŭ, to study hard; [6]ˏkung ngŭk, to work gems; [7]ˏkau ˏkung, to join battle.

功 ˏKung. Actions deserving praise; honor; reward or merit; meritorious; virtuous, worthy; a good service, work, or affair; virtues of medicines: [8]ˏkung chek, or ˏkung liĕk, merit, earnest well-doing; [9]tai ˏkung, nine months' mourning, as for uncles; [10]ʻsieu ˏkung, five months' mourning, as for cousins; [11]ˏsing ˏkung, a finished work; [12]ˏu ˏkung, undeserving; [13]ˏkung hau efficacious, as medicine; laboriously wrought, as essays; COM., [14]ˏkung ˏló, merit; [15]ˏkung ˏming, fame, high rank; [16]ˏkung taik, meritorious deeds, as charitable subscriptions; [17]ˏkung taik, ˏsŭ, a temple where the tablets of the worthy are placed, a memorial temple; [18]ˏkung ˏló mó "cap of merit"—said facetiously to a hard worker.

蚣 ˏKung. An insect: [19]ˏngu ˏkung, the centipede, called in the coll. ˏëng ˏëng, q. v.

君 ˏChün. A chief, head of society; a prince, sovereign, or ruler; honorable, in high station, exalted; superior, wise, one who can influence others; a term of respect given to others, and used by all persons; to rule, to fulfill the duties of a sovereign: [20]ˏhu ˏkung, my husband; [21]sá ˏkung, my wife; ˏsiéng ˏkung, a deceased father; ʻhu ˏkung and t'ai ˏkung, father and mother—as used on ancestral tablets; [22]ˏkung ˏwong, or kwok, ˏkung, the sovereign, emperor; COM., ˏchong ˏkung, your father; ˏkung ˏlong, your son; ˏkung ʻchŭ, the princely man—the beau ideal of virtue; ˏkung ʻchŭ wong hain ˏhuí, the good man looks to the next time; *met.*, one who does a job well in hope of future employment.

軍 ˏChün. An army, a force of 12,500 men; the headquarters of a troop; an inclosure; military, warlike: [23]ˏkung ˏing (coll. ˏkung ˏyăng), a camp; ˏheng ˏkung, to move troops; COM., hang ˏkung, Chinese Bannermen; ˏkung ˏmwong, a general's marquee; chiong ˏkung, the Tartar-general; ˏkung ˏming ʻhu, a sub-prefect, a marine inspector—phrase borrowed from the Cantonese; ˏkung k'e military weapons; ˏkung ˏliong (or hiong), soldiers' pay; ˏkung ˏsŭ

[1]工人 [2]百工 [3]精工 [4]攻打 [5]攻書 [6]攻玉 [7]交攻 [8]功績 [9]大功 [10]小功 [11]成功 [12]無功 [13]功效 [14]功勞 [15]功名 [16]功德 [17]功德祠 [18]功勞帽 [19]蜈蚣 [20]夫君 [21]細君 [22]君王 [23]軍營

a military adviser; [1]*kung ki tai* [1] *sing*, the General Council of state; *kung ki 'ó* (or *kwa'*), a jacket with short sleeves—buttoning at the side; COLL., *tau kung*, to enlist; *mwong' ch'ũng kung*, banishment to the garrisons.

袞 衮 Kun. Imperial robes embroidered with dragons: [2]*kung 'miéng*, robes and crown—the imperial dress; [3]*kung 'kung*, pleasant to hear.

滾 滚 Kun. Water flowing in a rapid, bubbling manner; boiling, welling up; rolling, to roll about, to go off; commonly used in the sense of to boil, as water when heated: COLL., [4]*kung 'chwi* (or *t'ong*), boiling water; *'kung 'kung sié'* in a boiling state; *'kung t'ong p'a p'a 'kung*, the water boils violently; *'kung ch'iă lang' yék*, scalding hot; [5]*kung chiéng'* hasty, urgent; [6]*'kung 'nü ki tio'* go your way! begone! *yék 'kung lang'* hot and thoroughly cooked; *'mwang te' 'kung*, to roll all about, as a child; *p'ah 'kung 'tau*, to turn somersault.

鯀 Kun. A large fish; name of the father of Yü the Great, who lived B. C. 2200.

緄 Kun. A ribbon, a cord; to sew, to stitch together, to bind: [7]*kung tai'* an embroidered girdle.

栱 Kung. Read *'kũng*; coll. *'kung*, as in [8]*kung 'tau*, the projecting pieces and intervening blocks on the top of a post, which support a rafter; also used for a small, sour fruit or berry, found in the market in the 7th or 8th month.

羣 群 Ch'ün. A flock of three or more sheep; a herd; a concourse, a group, a multitude, a horde, a company; men of the same sort; friends, equals, companions, fellow-officers; a form of the plural number, to sort with, to agree with: [9]*kung seng*, all living; [10]*kung 'tong*, a company, messmates; [11]*kung kü*, to dwell together; COM., [12]*kung teng'* a group, a concourse; a flock, as of animals.

裙 Ch'ün. The plaited skirt of a lady's dress, sometimes elegantly embroidered; rim of a turtle's shell: [13]*tũng kung*, under skirts, petticoats; COM., [14]*tieu kung*, an embroidered apron worn at audiences; [15]*'ma kung*, a skirt worn by women when visiting a tribunal or temple; [16]*ui sing kung*, an apron; [17]*kung 'kiéng*, the plaits of a skirt; COLL., *kung kiăng'* the broad plait in the front of a skirt; *kung t'wa te'* the skirt draggles on the ground.

拳 Ch'üan. Read *kwong*; coll. *kung*: the hand doubled up, the fist; boxing, fisticuffs: [18]*kung t'au*, or *kung t'au 'mó*, the fist; [19]*kung hwak*, the art of pugilism; [20]*kung t'au pwo'* scientific passes of a pugilist; [21]*ch'wí kung*, to "guess fingers"—game of morra; *kung t'au k'a chiéng* (or *t'ek*), to fist and kick; *kung t'au p'woi'*

[1]軍機大臣 [2]衮冕 [3]衮衮 [4]滾水 [5]滾箭 [6]滾汝其路 [7]緄帶 [8]栱斗 [9]羣生 [10]羣黨 [11]羣居 [12]羣陣 [13]中裙 [14]朝裙 [15]馬裙 [16]圍身裙 [17]裙襉 [18]拳頭 [19]拳法 [20]拳頭步 [21]催拳

ˏtiăng ‛si ˏnĕng, to kill one by a glancing (chance) blow of the fist; paikˎ ˏkung ˏt‛au ‛hó ˏsong p‛ah, he who understands pugilism can fight well; met., the skilled readily do things.

(288) Kŭng.

弓 ˓Kung. A bow; archery; crescent, curved; a cover of a carriage; a measure of five or six feet, the length of a bow—fifty made a bowshot; to measure; the 57th radical: COM., [1]ˏkŭng chiéng' bow and arrows; [2]ˏkŭng ˏhiéng, a bowstring; [3]ˏkŭng ˏhwang, a bow inverting itself (in shooting); [4]ˏkŭng chiéng' ‛ch‛iu, archers; [5]ˏkŭng ˏtó sioh, trials in pulling bows, fencing, and lifting stones, as at military examinations; COLL., pekˎ ˏkŭng, or ˏk‛wi ˏkŭng, to pull a bow; ‛chiă ˏkŭng niohˎ waiˀ likˎ what is the strength (i. e. grade or power) of this bow.

芎 ˓Kung. Also read ˏk‛ŭng: a medicinal plant, the root of which resembles tormentilla; the best is from Sz'chuen; a decoction of it is used to purify the blood: COM., [6]ˏch‛iong ˏkŭng, the Sz'chuen variety of this plant.

躬 ˓Kung; One's person; personally, one's self: [7]këŭkˎ ˏkŭng, to bend the body—a respectful attitude; [8]teng' ˏkŭng, Ourself, the emperor; [9]ˏkŭng ˏch‛ing ˏki sëŭˀ to do a thing personally.

恭 ˓Kung. To respect, to behold with regard; to venerate by an outward serious deportment; respectful, complaisant, collected, courteous, affable in one's conduct; as an adjective, it often merely enforces the next word: [10]ˏkŭng hóˀ congratulatory presents; [11]ˏkŭng ˏing, the wife of an officer of the 4th rank; COM., [12]ˏkŭng keng' to respect, to venerate; COLL., ch‛ok, ˏkŭng, to visit the privy.

供 共 ˓Kung. To place before, to offer or present to; to lay out, to arrange; to supply with; to provide, to succor, to give; to confess, to give in evidence, to declare: the first also read këŭng' and the second këŭngˀ q. v.: [13]ˏkŭng chek, to assume an office; COM.; [14]‛k‛eu ˏkŭng, verbal evidence; [15]ke' ˏkŭng, to record testimony; [16]ˏkŭng ˏhwang, to retract a statement or confession; [17]ˏkŭng kek, to furnish; [18]ˏkŭng siéngˀ to provide food, as for a tutor or parent; ˏkŭng kek, ‛sĕ, an official butlery—at an examination-hall; COLL., ˏkŭng kek, mâˀ ‛k‛i, unable to support (him).

龔 ˓Kung. Interchanged with the last two: to give, to bestow; respectful, reverential. Read ‛kŭng: a surname.

宮 ˓Kung. A mansion, a building; now confined to the imperial residence, the palace; a wall; a temple; a district college; the first of the five notes in music; to castrate; to surround, the circuit of: [19]ˏkŭng taingˀ a palace; ‛piĕng lokˎ ‛leng ˏkŭng, degraded to the "cold palace"—said of a discarded wife or concubine; [20]‛siu ˏkŭng, a house-lizard; [21]ˏkŭng ‛ch‛ing, a seraglio; [22]ˏkŭng ˏhing, castration;

1弓	3弓	手	6川	8朕	其	11恭	13供	15記	17供	19宮	21宮
箭	翻	5弓	芎	躬	事	人	職	供	給	殿	寢
2弓	4弓	刀	7鞠	9躬	10恭	12恭	14口	16供	18供	20守	22宮
弦	箭	石	躬	親	賀	敬	供	翻	膳	宮	刑

COM., [1]꜀kŭng ꜀ngó, or ꜀kŭng ꜂nü, maids of honor; ꜀kŭng ꜂wong (coll. ꜀kŭng ꜂wong ꜂tié), the private apartments or imperial harem; ꜀kŭng ꜀ting, a kind of large, hexagonal lantern.

斤 觔 ꜀Chin. The second is an unauthorized character: to chop, to cut down; an ax, a hatchet; a test or machine for weighing; a catty of 16 taels or 1⅓ lb. av.; in Foochow, a pound varying from 12 to 21 oz., the standard being 16 oz. and about equal to the English pound: COM., [2]꜀kŭng sò꜄ or ꜀kŭng ꜂liong, the weight of; [3]꜀kŭng ek꜀, a pound and one ounce; [4]꜀kŭng ꜀siong꜄ over a pound; [5]꜀ch'ing ꜀kŭng, by weight; [6]꜂chëük꜀ ꜀kŭng, a full pound; [7]꜂hü ꜀kŭng, a pound of 12 oz—the weight of a pair of large candles; COLL., ꜀kŭng ꜀kié ꜂tau ꜂mi, (it requires) a peck of rice (to rear) a one-pound fowl; ng꜄ kau꜄ ꜀kŭng, "falls short of a pound"—said of a very bad boy. Read këüng꜄, as in këüng꜄ këüng꜄ to examine closely.

筋 ꜀Chin. A species of hard bamboo; a sinew, a tendon, a muscle; also the nerves and veins, as the Chinese do not distinguish accurately; sinewy, muscular, strong: COM., [8]lĕk꜀ ꜀kŭng, stag's sinews; [9]haik꜀ ꜀kŭng, veins; [10]꜀kŭng lik꜀ (coll. ꜀kŭng keng꜄), strength of muscle; [11]꜀kŭng ꜀sing, muscular vigor; met., the body, consistence of things; [12]꜀kŭng kauk꜀ pok꜀ ꜀ch'ü, the system in a disordered state; COLL., ꜀kŭng ꜀p'u, the veins prominent; ꜀kŭng ꜀k'iu, distorted veins, as in the aged.

根 ꜀Kĕn. Read ꜀kong; coll. ꜀kŭng: the roots of plants; met., the source, the origin, from the first; something to rest on, a foundation: [13]ch'eu꜄ ꜀kŭng, the root of a tree; ꜀kŭng te꜄ main root next to the trunk; ꜀kŭng ꜂tá, a support, as one's wealth; origin, source of.

跟 ꜀Kĕn. Read ꜀kong in the dictionaries: the heel; to follow at one's heels; to follow up, to pursue an inquiry; according to: COM., [14]꜀kŭng ꜀sui, to follow; attendants, followers; [15]꜀kŭng kieu꜄ a sedan-attendant; [16]꜀kŭng ꜀pang twai꜄ ꜀ié, an officer's personal attendant; [17]꜀kŭng ꜀sing ꜀pieng, to attach one's self to a person, as a disciple; COLL., [18]꜀kŭng ꜀i k'ó꜄ to follow him away; ꜀kŭng tio꜄ to follow after, as dogs do; ꜀kŭng ꜀p'iăng au꜄ or ꜀kŭng a꜄ ꜂tau, to follow on behind.

釿 ꜀Chin. Once used for ꜀kŭng (a catty), but now it usually means an adz or a plane for trimming and smoothing wood.

巾 ꜀Chin. A kerchief or cloth bonnet, anciently worn; a neckcloth; a napkin, a handkerchief; the 50th radical: COM., [19]꜂ch'iu ꜀kŭng, a towel, napkin; [20]kang꜄ ꜀kŭng, a handkerchief; [21]꜂wong ꜀kŭng, a kind of head-net or cap, as worn by bald women; kwoi꜄ ꜀kŭng, red coiffure-cord; k'ang꜄ ꜀kŭng, a fancy-napkin—worn at the girdle.

拱 ꜂Kung. To join the hands before the breast, as when bowing; to hold or take with

[1]宮娥 [2]斤數 [3]斤一 [4]斤上 [5]稱斤 [6]足斤 [7]虛斤 [8]鹿筋 [9]血筋 [10]筋力 [11]筋身 [12]筋骨不舒 [13]樹根 [14]跟隨 [15]跟轎 [16]跟班大爺 [17]跟身邊 [18]跟伊去 [19]手巾 [20]汗巾 [21]網巾

both hands; to encircle: ʻkŭng piék, to bow and part; COM., ¹ʻkŭngʻchʻiu, or ʻkŭngʻkŭngʻchʻiu, to salute by uniting the hands before the breast and moving them up and down; ²ʻkŭng ʻhi, joy to you! I congratulate you! ³kok, ˏsing ʻkŭng chieuʼ may happy stars shine around you!

栱 ʻKung. A post, prop, or pillar: used in the coll. for ʻkung, q. v.: COM., ⁴ʻkŭng ʻtau, the capital of a pillar, a kind of entablature of projecting timbers and square blocks, supporting the rafters.

鞏 ʻKung. To bind with thongs, to bind securely; firm, strong, well-secured, well-guarded against attack; to shrink or dry at the fire; a district in Honan-fu in Honan: ⁵ʻkŭng koʼ strong, securely guarded.

窮 ˏChʻiung Brought to the last degree; poor, exhausted, impoverished, destitute; poverty; the poor; the end, final termination; to make helpless or poor; to search thoroughly, to investigate to the bottom; to exhaust: ⁶ˏkŭng hwak, or ˏkŭng kʻaungʼ, destitute, without resources; ⁷ˏkŭng ˏtwi, to pursue everywhere; COM., ⁸ˏkŭng ʻkʻu, poor and miserable; ⁹ˏu ˏkŭng chengʼ exhaustless; ¹⁰ˏsang ˏkŭng ʻchwi chengʼ no path open; *met.*, no available resources; ¹¹ˏkŭng keuʼ to investigate thoroughly; COLL., ˏkŭng ʻkwi, poor devil! ˏkŭng ˏnĕng ʻyong ˏkieu ʻkiăng, the poor man (too) rears a spoiled child; ˏkŭng ˏkwang ˏkiong poʼ saiʼ a poor officer is better off than a rich man; ˏkŭng poʼ naiʼ ˏchʻa ak, ʻmó laungʼ poor and rich only differ a duck's egg; *met.*, the difference is trifling (and not worth grieving or striving about).

(289) Kwa.

瓜 ˏKua. General name for gourds, melons, cucumbers, brinjals, egg-plant, squash, &c. the 97th radical: ¹²ˏkwa tiék, ˏmiéng ˏmiéng, a numerous progeny; ˏkwa ˏhung, to divide like the carpels of a melon; COM., ¹³ˏkwa ʻchi, melon seeds; ¹⁴ˏking ˏkwa, a pumpkin; ¹⁵ˏsá ˏkwa, a water-melon; ¹⁶ˏchʻaiʼ ˏkwa, cucumbers; ¹⁷muk, ˏkwa, the papaw; a quince; ¹⁸ˏkwa paingʼ the sections of a melon; ¹⁹ˏkwa ˏleu, a wild gourd—used medicinally; ˏtĕng ˏkwa (coll. ʻkwong ˏkwa), a large, coarse squash; ˏkwa kak, "melons and creepers;" *met.*, involved; a liaison, collusion; COLL., ²⁰ˏkwa ʻchi mengʼ a longish, oval face.

ˏKwa. A coll. word: to catch, caught, as a sleeve on things in passing; ˏkwa tioh, caught; ˏi ˏsiong kʻĕük, tʻiék, ˏting ˏkwa pʻwaiʼ the clothes torn by catching on a nail.

篙 ʻKua. A spool on a stand, having sticks on the four corners and the spool in the center; hwok, ʻkwa, spindles for reeling silk.

剮 ʻKua. To cut a man in pieces, to punish by cutting off the flesh: COLL., ʻchiă chóiʼ ˏkai ˏtong wangʼ ʻkwa, this crime deserves (the punishment of) quartering; chʻóiʼ ʻkwa,

¹拱手 ²拱喜 ³福星拱照 ⁴栱斗 ⁵鞏固 ⁶窮乏 ⁷窮追 ⁸窮苦 ⁹無窮 ¹⁰盡山窮水 ¹¹盡窮究 ¹²瓜瓞綿綿 ¹³瓜子 ¹⁴金瓜 ¹⁵西瓜 ¹⁶菜瓜 ¹⁷木瓜 ¹⁸瓜瓣 ¹⁹瓜蔞 ²⁰瓜子面

cut (him) into bits!—sometimes used facetiously.

'寡 Kua. To distribute; few, little; seldom, unusual, rarely; alone; deficient, what is short; a widow; the regal We: [1],ku 'kwa, orphaned and widowed, left desolate; [2]'kwa ,ing, Ourself, I, the prince; 'kwa ,ung, little experience; COM., [3]'kwa hó' or 'kwa ,kü, a widow; [4]'siu 'kwa, to maintain widowhood; ,tó 'kwa, much or little, some; chiä' 'kwa, to presume on account of one's widowhood; 'kwa ük, of few desires, continent; 'kwa pok, tik, chëüng' the few can't resist the many.

卦' 卦' Kua. Divining lines or diagrams, invented by Fohi, to serve as an abacus by which to philosophize; first there were eight, then these were involved to sixty-four; to divine: [5]',chiéng kwa' to divine; COM., [6]'kwa' ,ngau, the lines of diagrams; [7]'kwa' ,chü, a divination-fee; COLL., [8]'pauk, kwa' to divine, as by a tortoise-shell; [9]'tauk, 'cheu kwa' to divine by birds picking up (oracular sentences); p'aung' ch'oi' kwa' to try luck by hearing a chance sentence (in the street); [10]'ma ,chiéng kwa' divination before a mounted clay or paper god.

挂' 掛' Kua. To suspend, to hang up; to dwell on or prolong; to divine by straws; to remember; to note, to enter in account; to distinguish; to lay aside; in suspense, anxious: [11]'kwa' 'ch'i, to be made the subject of conversation; [12]'tó' kwa' a small, green parrot; COM., [13]'kwa' lü' in suspense, anxious about; [14]'kwa' ,sing, or kwa' niéng' to bear in mind; [15]'kwa' ,chieu ,pá, to hang out a shop sign; [16]'kwa' ,sang, a kind of large bib—worn at feasts; kwa' k'iéng' to keep account of dues; COLL., kwa' sioh, pek, to make an entry.

褂' Kua. A jacket worn over the robe, having short and wide sleeves: COM., [17]'ma kwa' a riding-jacket, a sort of dress-sack; [18],pó kwa' robe and jacket; [19]hó' kwa' a soldier's sack; [20]t'ai' ,ping kwa' and taik, seng' kwa' military coats; ,kung ,ki kwa' a sort of sack with short sleeves.

罣' Kua. An impediment, a hindrance; to hinder, to obstruct; to fall into a snare: [21]kwa' ngai' an obstruction.

詿' Kua. To deceive, to cozen; to impose on; to cause one to fail, to disappoint, to disturb: kwa' ngwo' to mislead.

,Kwa. A coll. word: to clamor, to talk incessantly: ,kwa ,kwa kieu' to rattle on without let.

(290) Kwai.

'乖 Kuai. Perverse, obstinate, to turn the back on; cross-purposes; to contradict; strange, extravagant; cunning, crafty; used in the coll. in the sense of good, amiable, tractable; a lullaby, a word to soothe a babe: COM., [22],kwai 'k'ieu, knavish; ,kwai ,tiong, stubborn,

1孤寡 2寡人 3寡婦 4守寡 5占卦 6卦爻 7卦資 8卜卦 9啄鳥卦 10馬前卦 11掛齒 12倒掛 13掛慮 14掛心 15掛招牌 16掛衫 17馬褂 18袍褂 19號褂 20太平褂 21罣礙 22乖巧

cross-grained; [1]'*kwai p'ek*, a perverse temper; [2]*ong*' *₍tu ₍kwai* '*kiong*, one's destiny unlucky; COLL., [3]*₍kwai ₍kwai*, amiable! amiable! [4]'*cheng*' *₍kwai*, very good, tractable, as a child.

₍Kwai. A coll. word: old and hard, stringy, as vegetables: *₍kwai laĕ*' *luĕ*' very hard and stringy.

₍Kwai. A coll. word: to turn aside, to stop at, to call on one's way to another place: *₍kwai* '*tiong ch'io*' to call at one's house (before going elsewhere); *₍kwai* '*tiĕ ₍li*, call in; *₍kwai* '*ngwai siŭ*' *a*' call at my lowly abode.

'拐 Kuai. To deceive, to swindle, to gull; to seduce, to kidnap, to decoy in order to carry off; to entrap persons: COM., [5]'*kwai p'iéng*' to gull, to swindle; [6]'*kwai tai*' or [7]'*kwai* '*chü*, a kidnapper; COLL., [8]'*kwai k'ó má*' to decoy away and sell; '*kwai sioh*, *to*' to swindle out of a lot of money; [9]'*kwai ₍nëng lau*' '*ma*, to elope with a man's wife.

'柺 Kuai. An old man's staff or crutch, with a crooked top; in the coll. is also the name of a fighting-stick about two feet long, with a short handle inserted vertically near the end: COM., [10]'*kwai t'iong*' a staff.

'踝 Read *k'wa*'; used in the *Paik*, *₍Ing* for the coll. '*kwai*: an irregular gait; to shuffle, to limp: also read *₍kwai*, q. v.: '*kwai ₍chiă* '*kwai ₍chiă*, to go hobbling along.

怪' Kuai. Strange, marvellous, extraordinary; bizarre, supernatural, portentous, monstrous; rare, wonderful, curious; to deem strange, surprised at; also commonly used in the sense of to dislike, to be offended at, to bear a grudge against: COM., [11]*₍ki kwai*' strange, odd; [12]*₍yeu kwai*' an elf, hobgoblin; [13]'*kwi kwai*' trickish; [14]*chauk*, *kwai*' quick, intelligent, as a child; [15]*kwai*' *uk*, a monster, apparition; [16]*kwai*' '*ngwai*, offended at me; COLL., [17]*kwai*' *cheng*' *₍nëng*, has a grudge against everybody; [18]*kwai*' *₍siăng ₍p'iêng*, has a long list of grievances; [19]*móh*, *kiéng*' *kwai*' don't be offended.

₍踝 Read *k'wa*'; used for the coll. *₍kwai*; also spoken *kwai*' and same as '*kwai*, q. v.: an unequal, halting gait, as from habit or caused by a boil on the leg, or by a tight shoe.

₍Kwai. A coll. word, as in *₍kwai ₍t'au*, the end pieces of a coffin.

Kwai'. A coll. word: a trick, a malicious art, or method of injuring: '*sai kwai*' or *ha*' *kwai*' to use black art, to "deposit" someting hurtful, as house builders are superstitiously supposed to be able to do.

(291) Kwak.

佸, To unite all the parts, to include all; to collect or assemble; to reach, to arrive at: [20]*kwak*, *kwak*, united strength, tugging at.

括, Kua. To include, to inclose or embrace; to tie up, to envelop, to make into a

1乖	乖	4盡	6拐	8拐	仈	杖	怪	怪	我	18怪	見
癖	蹇	乖	帶	去	佬	11奇	13詭	15怪	17怪	成	怪
2運	3乖	5拐	7拐	賣	媽	怪	怪	物	盡	篇	20佸
塗	乖	騙	子	9拐	10拐	12妖	14作	16怪	仈	19莫	佸

bundle; to arrive at, to comprehend fully: *kwak, hwak,* to coil up the hair; *,nong kwak, sëü' 'hai,* he "bags the four seas"—i. e., knows everything, is very learned; COM., *,pau kwak,* to wrap up; to contain or embrace, as ideas in a sentence.

活, Huo. Water rushing along; the sound of water flowing rapidly: also read *wak,* q. v.: [1]*'mik, kwak,* a babbling stream; COLL., *kwak, kwak, kieu'* the croaking of frogs.

刮, Kua. To pare or scrape off, to abrade, to rub or rasp; to burnish; to even off grain; to rase; to erase; *met.*, to abate, as from a price; to extort, to squeeze: in the coll. read *kauk,* q. v.: [2]*kwak, siok,* to scrape; *met.*, to oppress, to cheapen; [3]*kwak, ,mó,* to rub, to grind; *kwak, kaiu'* to scrape off impurities, to polish, as gems; COLL., *kwak, kwak, kieu'* sound of scraping or rubbing, a grating sound.

聒, Kua. Kuo. To make a great clamor; to stun one with noise; importunate, noisy, bothering, distracting; to spoil an affair by much talk: [4]*kwak, 'ngi,* to din in one's ears; *kwak, kwak,* ignorant, stupid.

蛞, Huo. A kind of garden-slug, called [5]*kwak, ,ü,* also styled [6]*pik, t'á' ,t'üng,* or [7]*t'auk, ,t'ai ,t'üng,* eggs of a frog; [8]*kwak, ,leu,* the mole-cricket.

适, Kua. Fleet, hasty, quick; to hasten one; a man's name: [9]*Paik, kwak,* the name of a statesman in the days of Wan Wang.

鴰, Kua. A species of black crane, called [10]*,ch'ong kwak,;* it has red cheeks and nine feathers in its tail.

豁, Hua. An open valley; to penetrate through; to understand; liberal, magnanimous: [11]*kwak, tak,* perspicacious; [12]*kwak, ,yong,* intelligently; COM., [13]*kwak, 'mieng,* to remit, as a new emperor remits taxes.

欯, Read *kauk,;* used in the *Paik, ,Ing* for the coll. *kwak,* as in [14]*kwak, kwak, kieu'* a gurgling sound, the noise made in swallowing liquids; [15]*kwak, ,kang ,kang,* drink it dry, swallow it all.

Kwak,. A coll. word, as in *kwak, kwak, kieu'* a throbbing, as of the temples, or a large boil.

(292) Kwang.

官 ,Kuan. An officer of government; the magistrates, the authorities, rulers; a title of adulation or respect; the government collectively; an office belonging to government; a public court; official; business: COM., [16]*'ngu ,kwang,* media of the five senses—eyes, ears, nose, mouth, and eyebrows; [17]*,kwang 'hu,* or [18]*,kwang ,wong,* or *,kwang 'tiong,* officers, mandarins; [19]*,kwang ,ka,* official families; [20]*,ung 'u paik, ,kwang,* all the officers civil and military; [21]*'kieu ,kwang,* to deliver to an

---

[1]汩活 [2]刮削 [3]刮摩 [4]聒耳 [5]蛞蝓 [6]鼻涕蟲 [7]託胎蟲 [8]蛞螻 [9]伯适 [10]鶬鴰 [11]豁達 [12]豁然 [13]豁免 [14]欯欯叫 [15]欯乾乾 [16]五官 [17]官府 [18]官員 [19]官家 [20]文武百官 [21]繳官

officer; ꜀kwang sié' official power; [7]꜀kwang lik꜁ the official almanac; [2]꜀kwang ʻt'á (or yong'), official dignity—which is awe-inspiring; [3]꜀kwang wa' or ꜀kwang ꜀ing, the court dialect; [4]꜀t'iéng ꜀kwang sëü' hok꜁ may the ruler of heaven bless you! ꜀kwang ꜀sing hiéng' "the official star appears"—he will soon get an office; [5]꜀kwang ꜀hiu and [6]꜀sü ꜀hiu, the settlement (of quarrels) by law and privately; COLL., tioh꜁ p'ah꜁ ꜀kwang ꜀si, must refer the matter to the magistrate; ꜀kwang tio' a public road, highway; ꜀kwang twai' k'e' ʻsieu, "his office big but his mind little"—said of a stingy, rich man; ꜀kwang che' lang' ʻa ʻk'eu, the character ꜀kwang has two mouths; met., officers are double-tongued—i. e., decide as they are bribed to do; hwang' ꜀kwang ꜀hu, to fall into the clutches of the officer; lau' ꜀kwang, a husband's father.

倌 ʻ Kuan. The emperor's charioteer, the master of his carriages.

棺 ʻ Kuan. That which closes all affairs for this world, a coffin; the inner one when there are two; to encoffin, to close up: COM., [7]꜀kwang muk꜁ or [8]꜀kwang ꜀chai (spoken ꜀ch'ai), a coffin; [9]ong' ꜀kwang, to take a coffin home; [10]sié ꜀kwang, to give coffins in charity; ꜀kwang ꜀chai ʻpeng, coffin-boards; [11]꜀kwang kwoh꜁ ꜀i ꜀k'ing, inner and outer coffins, clothes, and shroud.

冠 ʻ Kuan. A conical cap or bonnet, a covering for the head; the comb of a cock; crest on the head of birds: also read kwang', q. v.: [12]꜀kwang ʻmiéng, a cap; [13]ʻmiéng ꜀kwang, take off your caps! [14]꜀ka ꜀kwang, to cap a young man; COM., [15]hong' ꜀kwang, "phenix-cap"—a bride's bonnet; [16]ngiáh꜁ ꜀kwang, a fillet worn by girls; t'ai' ʻchü ꜀kwang, a "prince-imperial hat"—a cap with a richly ornamented crown, worn by boys.

觀 覌 ʻ Kuan. To look at carefully, to see; to observe, to travel and see; to take a wide view of; to manifest; observed, manifested; appearance of, a sight, a spectacle; many: also read kwang', q. v.: [17]꜀ki ꜀kwang, a rare sight; COM., [18]꜀kwang wong' to look at, to observe; [19]꜀kwang ꜀chü, present of money to the bride's uncles; [20]꜀kwang ꜀kwong, to enter the literary examinations; sek꜁ ꜀kwang ꜀chiéng, to fail (in politeness) before the public gaze; ꜀kwang ꜀ing huk꜁ Kwanyin, the goddess of mercy; COLL., ꜀kwang ꜀seng ko' au' to look before and behind, as in carrying things.

鰥 ʻ Kuan. A large fish; a widower; an old man who has never been married; alone, single, unattended: [21]꜀kwang ꜀hu, a widower; [22]꜀kwang ꜀kü, to live alone; COM., ꜀kwang ʻkwa ꜀ku tuk꜁ widowers, widows, orphans, and those without posterity.

瘝 ʻ Kuan. Diseased, infirm, sick; incapable, incompetent for the discharge of duty: ꜀kwang ꜀kwang, an inefficient ruler.

[1]官曆 [3]官話 賜福 [6]私休 [8]棺材 [10]施棺 衣衾 [13]免冠 [15]鳳冠 [17]奇觀 [19]觀書 [21]鰥夫

[2]官體 [4]天官 [5]官休 [7]棺木 [9]運棺 [11]棺槨 [12]冠冕 [14]加冠 [16]額冠 [18]觀望 [20]觀光 [22]鰥居

꜀**關** **闗** **関** ꜀Kuan. To shut or bar a door; to stop up a doorway; to fasten, to fix, to stop a thing for a while; the cross-bar of a door; a gateway to a market; a frontier pass; a place where goods enter, a custom-house; a post-house; a limit, a line, a boundary, both literally and metaphorically; to bear upon, to effect, to have a relation to, to belong to, to concern; to allude to, to involve; consequences, results; to pass through or by the way of; to pierce, to penetrate; a surname: [1]꜀*sang* ꜀*kwang*, the "three passes"—ears, eyes, and mouth; [2]꜀*kwang* ꜀*tüng*, "within the pass"—a name for Shensi and the adjacent regions; COM., [3]꜀*kwang hiè*꜄ the consequences; [4]꜀*kwang* ꜀*sing*, to concern the mind, intent upon; [5]꜀*kwang sak*꜆ malign influences which affect children; [6]*kwo*’ ꜀*kwang*, "passing through the gate"—a ceremony in connection with the worship of "Mother" in behalf of children; [7]꜀*kwang* ‘*k‘au*, a pass where custom is paid, a custom-house; [8]‘*hai* ꜀*kwang*, the maritime customs; also used for the collector of customs at a port; [9]꜀*kwang* ꜀*chü*, written proposals to engage a tutor or secretary; *tah*꜆ ꜀*kwang*, is the coll. term for the present of money sent with the "proposals"; [10]꜀*kwang ngai*꜄ (coll. ꜀*kwang pwang*’), an obstacle, a difficulty in the way of; [11]꜀*kwang tá*꜄ the god of war—also styled [12]꜀*Kwang seng*’, ꜀*Kwang* ꜀*hu* ‘*chü*, and ꜀*Kwang* ‘*ló* ꜀*iè*; [13]꜀*kwang mah*꜆ the middle pulse in the wrist; ꜀*kwang siék*꜆ concern with implication.

‘**管** ‘**筦** Kuan. A little flute or flageolet; a reed, a tube; tubes to make pencils of; a classifier of fifes, flutes, pipes, quills, and tubular things; to rule, to govern, to control; to have the management or care of; to sway, to influence primarily: [14]‘*kwang kiéng*’ to see partially, as through a tube; COM., [15]‘*kwang* ‘*li*, or ‘*chiong* ‘*kwang*, to rule, to manage; [16]‘*kwang* ꜀*ka*, a major-domo, steward, butler; [17]‘*chung* ‘*kwang*, to superintend; [18]‘*kwang ang*’ to manage law-suits; [19]‘*kwang sok*꜆ to restrain; control, restraint; [20]‘*kwang a*꜄ subject to (his) rule; [21]‘*kwang* ꜀*kang*, a jailer; [22]‘*kwang sò*’ an accountant, a treasurer; *pek*꜆ ‘*kwang*, the tube or shaft of a pencil; COLL., *chek*꜆ ‘*kwang*, hence, then it is or must be—a kind of illative particle; ‘*kwang mâ*꜄ *teu*꜄ unmanageable; [23]‘*kwang* ꜀*eng tai*꜄ to interfere in others' matters.

‘**筦** Kuan. Used for the last: a string to suspend drums or bells; a pipe, a fife or like musical instruments; a shuttle; to rule, to supervise.

‘**菅** Kuan. Read ꜀*kang* in the dictionaries: a sort of rush, whose fibres after rotting are fit for making cords, thatch or mats; perhaps a kind of Phragmites.

‘**琯** Kuan. A tube of stone made into flutes; to polish metals; a gem-like pebble.

[1]三關 [2]關中 [3]關係 [4]關心 [5]關煞 [6]過關 [7]關口 [8]海關 [9]關書 [10]關礙 [11]關帝 [12]關聖 [13]關脈 [14]管見 [15]管理 [16]管家 [17]總管 [18]管案 [19]管束 [20]管下 [21]管監 [22]管數 [23]管閒事 ○

ʻ館 ʻ舘 Kuan. A hotel, an inn, a caravansery, a lodging or stopping place for travelers; a hall, or council-room, an exchange, or place for public consultations; an office, study, or counting-room, when they are built separately; a saloon; a room for any public purpose; a school-room: [1]*kʻaik, ʻkwang*, a tavern; [2]*ˏkʻai ʻkwang*, to open school; COM., [3]*ˏkung ʻkwang*, a government hall—where an officer lodges temporarily; [4]*ʻkwang teʼ* a post in a yamun as a secretary, a literary man's occupation; [5]*swoiʼ ʻkwang*, custom-house; [6]*ˏi ʻkwang*, a hospital; [7]*ʻkwang taingʼ* an eating-saloon, a restaurant; [8]*kieuʼ ʻkwang*, sedan-men's establishment; [9]*hwoiʼ ʻkwang*, a mercantile hall, an exchange; COLL., [10]*ˏa pʻiéngʼ ʻkwang*, or *ˏhong ʻkwang*, an opium-smoking den.

ʻ綰 Kuan. Bad, evil; to sew, to hem; to tie, to bind together; to make secure, to hold fast.

ʻ逭 Kuan. To run away, to escape from; to turn round, to step off; to revolve: [11]*hwak, pok, ʻkʻó ʻkwang*, he cannot escape the law.

痯 Kuan. Impotent, weak, worn out; sick from grief, disheartened by disappointment.

ʻ斡 Kuan. A handle, a winch; a grain-striker; to turn by a handle; to circulate, to move about: used for *ʻkwang* (to rule, to supervise).

ʻ榦 Kuan. The same as the last according to the dictionaries; used for the coll. *ʻkwang*: the trunk of a tree, the stems or stalks of plants: also read *kangʼ*, q. v.; COLL., [12]*chʻeuʼ ˏki ʻkwang*, the trunk of a tree.

冠ʼ Kuan. To cap a young man, at the age of twenty or at marriage—equivalent to putting on the *toga virilis;* the chief or head; able, superior: also read *ˏkwang*, q. v.: [13]*ʻüng kwangʼ ˏsang ˏkung*, the bravest capped in three armies—one promoted for courage; COM., [14]*kwangʼ ˏtiong*, to excel in the three martial tests; also to excel at the literary examinations; [15]*eʼ kwangʼ* not yet capped—said of students under 16 years competing at the examinations.

貫ʼ Kuan. A string of 1000 cash; to thread, to string upon, to run thread through, to connect; linked, joined to; to implicate, to involve; to penetrate, to go through; [16]*ek, kwangʼ ˏchiéng*, a string of cash; [17]*ˏü ˏloi kwangʼ ʻngi*, like thunder piercing the ear; COM., [18]*chik, kwangʼ* origin and parentage, as of students at the examinations; [19]*kwangʼ chʻiongʼ* to thread, to string upon; hence in a *met.* sense, connected, as ideas in a discourse or essay.

慣ʼ 摜ʼ Kuan. Accustomed to, experienced, practiced in; habitual, addicted to; the 2nd also means to take, to bear, to carry: the 1st used in the coll. for *kaingʼ*,

[1]客館 [2]開館 [3]公館 [4]館地 [5]稅館 [6]醫館 [7]館店 [8]轎館 [9]會館 [10]鴉片館 [11]法不可逭 [12]樹其榦 [13]勇冠三軍 [14]冠塲 [15]未冠 [16]一貫錢 [17]如雷貫耳 [18]籍貫 [19]貫串〇

福州方言拼音字典

q. v.: COM., *kwang' liéng'* drilled, practiced; [1]*kwang' 'chiă ˛ui ˛sü*, the practiced man is the teacher (of others); COLL., [2]*kwang' ˛t'au*, addicted to stealing; [3]*chó' kwang'* or *chó' tek˛ kwang'* accustomed to doing it.

觀 観 Kuan. A temple of Rationalists; a secluded cell or retreat, a hermitage; to point out, to make known: also read *˛kwang*, q. v.: [4]*˛lëu kwang'* a private gallery; COM., [5]*Tō' ˛sung kwang'* a Tauist monastery on the east end of Black Rock hill, Foochow.

鑵 礶 Kuan. An earthern pot for boiling things, having a handle and spout; a jar, a mug, a water-pot: COM., [6]*˛ta kwang'* a tea-pot or kettle; COLL., *˛kwang kwang'* earthen pots; *kwang' 'kiăng*, small pots or saucepans.

鸛 Kuan. A crane; two species of it are mentioned: [7]*pek˛ kwang'* the white crane; [8]*haik˛ kwang'* a crane having an ashy plumage and a black tail.

灌 Kuan. Used for the next: to pour out libations; to run or flow together, to flow towards; to discharge, to disembogue; to water, to moisten; to give one to drink; to collect; bushy trees; many, numerous; in the coll., to pour down one's throat, to force one to drink; to water (meat): [9]*kwang' chëü'* or [10]*kwang' k'ai'* to soak, to moisten; COLL., [11]*kwang' yoh˛* to pour medicine down the throat; [12]*kwang' choi' choi'* made him drunk; [13]*kwang' 'chwi*, watered, as pork; [14]*kwang' ˛siéng lo'* to fill with brine, as fish; [15]*kwang' ˛i ch'oi'* pour it into his mouth; [16]*kwang' 'chwi ang'* a lawsuit or accusation to squeeze money.

祼 Kuan. To pour out a libation on the ground to spirits; also to pour wine and offer it to guests: [17]*kwang' tiéng'* to offer a libation.

丱 Kuan. The two tufts made in dressing the hair of small children; the tuft on a girl's head is termed in the coll. *˛k'i ˛k'i kwoi'*, q. v.

˛Kwang. A coll. prefix, as in *˛kwang kwang'* earthen pots; *˛kwang kwang'* a bail, a handle, as of a basket.

扣 Read *k'wang'* and *˛siu* in the dictionaries; coll. *kwang'*: to carry by a bail or the like, to carry, as a bundle by the string; a bail, as of a bucket, pail, or basket: [19]*kwang' 'chwi*, to carry water (in buckets); [19]*kwang' ˛keng*, to lift high; [20]*˛kwang kwang'* a bail; *kwang' ak˛* a basket-like vessel of pewter; *kwang' 't'ëng*, a varnished bucket with a high bail.

(293) Kwi.

龜 亀 Kuei. The tortoise, the chief of mailed animals; also to advance; adorned, ornate; the 213th radical: *sié' ˛kwi*, the prognosticating tortoise—its carapace, divided into 28 plates on the edges, is used in divination; COM., *'chwi ˛kwi*, a water turtle;

[1]慣者爲師 [2]慣偷 [3]做慣 [4]樓觀 [5]道山觀 [6]茶鑵 ○ [7]白鸛 [8]黑鸛 [9]灌注 [10]灌溉 [11]灌藥 [12]灌醉醉 [13]灌水 [14]灌鹽滷 [15]灌伊嘴 [16]灌水案 [17]祼奠 [18]扣水 [19]扣高 [20]扣扣

‚kwi sek‚ tortoise-shaped; [1]*‚kwi pwoi'* a tortoise's back; *met.*, a sexagonal figure used ornamentally; *‚u ‚kwi* (coll. *‚t'ong ‚kwi*), a cuckold; COLL., *‚kwi ‚t'ó*, "turtle-peach"—a kind of cake having these figures and eaten as emblems of longevity; *‚kwi ʻpeng‚* tortoise shell pounded up and used medicinally; *‚king ‚kwi*, a species of beetle with a green back and of a greenish brown on the under part of the body.

歸 婦 ‚ Kuei. To return to the same place or state; to go or send back, to restore, to revert to; to terminate, to end; to belong to; to go home; to marry out; to send a present, to give, to promise; to unite, to assemble; a terminus *ad quem*; a home, a country, a native place; something to depend on, a refuge, a center; to divide fractional numbers: [2]*‚kwi ‚tiéng*, to return to one's fields—i. e., to resign office; COM., [3]*‚kwi ‚kwang*, to revert to the officer, as confiscated property; [4]*‚kwi ‚tü*, to add and reject (in reckoning on the abacus); [5]*twai² ‚kwi*, division; [6]*ʻsieu ‚kwi*, addition; [7]*‚kwi ‚pwang* (vulgarly called *‚pang ‚t'au cheng' sëü²*), the class of Chintsz' graduates awaiting official appointments; [8]*‚kwi ‚sing*, to fix the attention on; [9]*‚kwi cheng'* development of the real disease; [10]*‚kwi ‚t'iéng*, reverted to the heavens—deceased; [11]*‚kwi loi²* classified, arranged; [12]*‚tong ‚kwi*, a tonic medicine for the blood; [13]*‚kwi kiék‚* to compound (for a debt); COLL., [14]*o² ‚kwi tioh‚* has a place to go to; has a refuge or resource, as employment; [15]*‚kwi sioh‚ ‚t'au*, gathered together, as articles or items; *‚kwi ʻch'u ng² se² ‚kwi hang' ng² se²* "belongs neither to T'su nor Han"; *met.*, hard to say to whom the things belong.

皈 ‚ Fan. To conform to, to receive instruction, to comply with: COM., [16]*‚kwi ‚i ‚sang ʻpó*, to embrace (the tenets of) the three precious (Budhs).

飢 ‚ Chi. Read *‚ki*; coll. *‚kwi*, as in the expression *pok‚ʻló ‚kwi*, the belly empty, hungry.

‚Kwi. A coll. word, as in *‚kwi ʻkü*, usage, regulations; the same as *‚kié ʻkü*, q. v.

鬼 ʻ Kuei. A spirit of a dead person, manes, that to which the soul turns or reverts at death; a ghost, apparition, demon, spectre, phantasm, devil; a horrid-looking object; a miserable person, a wretch; applied by the Chinese to foreigners; the 194th radical: [17]*ʻkwi seu'* the 23d of the 28 constellations—stars *g. d. ē. th.* in Cancer: COM., [18]*ʻkwi ‚sing*, the spirits, gods; [19]*ʻkwi kwai'* hobgoblins; [20]*hwang² ʻkwi*, possessed by a demon; *ʻchwi ʻkwi*, ghost of a drowned man; [21]*‚wong ʻkwi*, the unavenged spirit of one murdered; *ʻkwi ʻhwi*, an ignis fatuus; *ʻkwi chok‚* (coll. *ʻkwi ʻkiäng*), imps; *ʻkwi kieu'* the plaintive cry of a ghost; *‚sang ‚sieu ʻkwi*, a mountain sprite which spirits things away; [22]*ʻsó ʻkwi*, a lock like

1 龜背 2 歸田 3 歸官 4 歸除 5 大歸 6 小歸 7 歸班 8 歸心 9 歸正 10 歸大 11 歸彙 12 當歸 13 歸結 14 務歸着 15 歸一頭 16 皈依三寶 17 鬼宿 18 鬼神 19 鬼怪 20 犯鬼 21 寃鬼 22 鎖鬼

a foreign door or drawer lock; [1]'*sang* '*kwi*, an umbrella-catch; [2]'*kwi* ˏ*mwong* ˏ*kwang*, the door of demons—entrance to hades; COLL., *pok*, ˏ*kang* '*kwi*, the ague demon; [3]ˏ*a p'iéng'* '*kwi*, a besotted opium-smoker; [4]ˏ*tong pang'* '*kwi* and [5]'*á paik*, '*kwi*, the tall and short devils—attendants of the '*ngu tá'* idols; [6]'*kwi niăh*, '*kwi*, "devil catch devil"—two rogues cheating each other; '*kwi laëng'* ˏ*nëng*, demons mock people, as by vain dreams.

'傀 Kuei. Great, strange, monstrous, as an eruption or meteor: used in the coll. for ˏ*k'wo*, q. v.: [7]'*kwi* '*lwi*, puppets, in the coll. ˏ*k'wo* '*loi*.

'宄 Kuei. Traitorous plans contrived outside of the court or country: [8]ˏ*kang* '*kwi*, domestic and foreign plots; banditti, villains.

'軌 Kuei. An axle, a rut; a trace, a vestige; an orbit, a path; a law, a rule; to imitate; treasonable plans against a country, in which sense same as the last: [9]*pok*, '*kwi*, unconformable; [10]'*kwi tó'* a constant path; to follow a rule or usage.

'匭 Kuei. A box, a casket, as for holding papers; to put in a box; to bind with cords.

'晷 Kuei. A gnomon, a dial; day-time, the day: [11]*nik*, '*kwi*, a sun-dial; [12]ˏ*hung* ˏ*kó kié'* '*kwi*, to prolong the day by burning candles.

'簋 Kuei. A dish for holding grain at sacrifices, once made round within and square without; a dish or platter: [13]'*hu* '*kwi*, square sacrificial vessels.

'垝 Kuei. A ruinous wall, one ready to fall; ruinous, dilapidated; to destroy, to demolish.

'詭 Kuei. To deceive, to cheat, to defraud; to blame, to censure; to oppose what is good; to vilify, to insult; bad, malicious, perverse; odd, strange: [14]'*kwi chá'* lying; [15]'*kwi é'* strange, incredible; COM., [16]'*kwi kwai'* (coll. '*kwi* '*chwi*), wily, tortuous, dishonest; [17]'*kwi kié'* ˏ*tó* ˏ*twang*, has many knavish tricks.

'幾 Chi. Read '*ki*; coll. '*kwi*: much or many of, a few; an interrogative of quantity, how? how many? [18]'*kwi chiăh*, a few, how many, as persons or things; '*kwi* '*a* ˏ*chiéng*, a few cash; '*kwi chiék*, or '*kwi chiék*, '*li*, a few tenths, as paid in compounding with creditors; [19]'*kwi* '*teng* ˏ*chüng*, what o'clock is it? '*kwi* ˏ*niéng* ˏ*seng*, several years ago; '*kwi sek*, *chiăh*, a few tens; '*kwi* ˏ*hui*, several times; '*kwi ch'oi'* how many mouths? how many in the family? '*kwi sié'* ˏ*mó mëk*, "for several ages without eyes"—as said of one who lacks judgment.

(294) Kwí.

'果 Kuo. Read '*kwo*; coll. '*kwí*, as in '*kwí* '*chi*, fruits; '*kwi* '*chi* ˏ*t'ang*, a fruit-stall; '*kwi* '*chi* ˏ*k'wong*,

[1]傘鬼 [2]鬼門關 [3]鴉片鬼 [4]長班鬼 [5]矮八鬼 [6]鬼拿鬼 [7]傀儡 [8]姦宄 [9]不軌 [10]軌道 [11]日晷 [12]焚膏繼晷 [13]簠簋 [14]詭詐 [15]詭異 [16]詭怪 [17]詭計多端 [18]幾隻 [19]幾點鐘

parcels of dried fruits—for offering to idols.

ʻ粿 Kuo. To cleanse rice; provisions of rice; in the coll., steamed rice-cakes; rice-cakes boiled in oil or fat: COLL., [1]ʻkwi ˛song, a rice-cake steamer; ʻkwi nëü' greasy rice-cakes; [2]˛tʻong ʻkwi, steamed cake of rice and red sugar; [3]ʻkau ˛tʻüng ʻkwi, rice-cake made in layers; [4]˛hwang ˛sü ʻkwi, steamed cakes of potato-flour.

ʻ改 Kai. Read ʻkai; coll. ʻkwi: to change, to alter the form of; to correct, to amend, as essays: [5]ʻkwi kʻó' altered; [6]ʻkwi che' to mend characters (wrongly written); [7]ʻkwi chiăng' to alter to the correct form; [8]ʻkwi ˛hwong, to change a medical prescription; [9]ʻkwi ˛si, to revise a poem

ʻKwi. A coll. word, as in ʻkwi chaĕng' to make three-cornered rice dumplings by wrapping in leaves.

(295) Kwo.

鍋 鍋 Kuo. A deep boiler for frying; sort of caldron for trying fat; a saucepan, a skillet; the rim or tire of a wheel: COM., [10]˛hai ˛kwo, earthen pots or basins—the same as pwak˛; [11]˛ngüng ˛kwo, a smelting pot, a crucible; COLL., ˛kwo ˛pa, crust adhering to a pan, as in boiling rice.

˛過 Kuo. To pass by; in the coll., too much, excessive; usually read kwo', q. v.: COLL., [12]ʻchü kʻak˛ ˛kwo, boiled too much; [13]˛kwo ˛siong, injured by excess, as of exertion or abstinence; [14]˛kwo só' too dry; exceedingly parched, as the system.

ʻ果 ʻ菓 Kuo. The 2d is commonly used for fruits; edible fruits, fruits containing seeds or kernels; to overcome, to surpass; results; to conclude; to see the end of; courageous, hardy; really, truly, indeed; perfection or nigban of the Budhists: in the coll. read ʻkwi, q. v.: [15]˛ing ʻkwo, cause and effect; the Budhist nigban; COM., [16]paik˛ʻkwo, all kinds of fruits; [17]˛king ʻkwo taing' a dried-fruit store; [18]kiĕk˛ ʻkwo, the setting of fruit; met., result or end of life, to die; [19]ʻkwo ʻpʻing, varieties of fruit (set before idols); [20]ʻkwo ˛yong, or ˛ü ʻkwo, certainly, truly; COLL., ʻkwo chong' truly excellent! ʻkwo ˛sa, deftly (done) indeed! [21]chiăng' ʻkwo, perfection, as in becoming a Budh or an immortal; ʻkwo ang' fruit-stuffing (in cakes).

ʻ蜾 Kuo. The solitary wasp or sphex, called [22]ʻkwo ʻlio, which brings the grubs of mulberry-caterpillars into its nests; these become young wasps, as the Chinese suppose. Read ʻlio: a kind of snail.

過' Kuo. To overpass, to exceed, to go beyond, to pass along; to pass, to spend, as time; beyond, further; to transgress, to violate propriety; an error, trespass, transgression; an imprudence, a sin of ignorance; denotes past time, the pluperfect; a sign of comparison, too, the more, rather,

[1]粿甑 [2]糖粿 [3]九重粿 [4]番薯粿 [5]改去 [6]改字 [7]改正 [8]改方 [9]改詩 [10]硋鍋 [11]銀鍋 [12]煑恰過 [13]過傷 [14]過燥 [15]因果 [16]八果 [17]京果店 [18]結果 [19]果品 [20]果然 [21]正果 [22]蜾蠃

much, great; in the coll., to do over, to repeat a process; a change or crisis in disease: also read *‚kwo*, q. v.: [1]*tai*^{2} *kwo'* and [2]*sieu kwo'* the 28th and 62d diagrams; COM., [3]*kwo' sié'* to die, deceased; [4]*‚nung kwo'* hard to pass by or over; [5]*t'ai' kwo'* too much, supererogatory; [6]*‚king kwo'* to pass by; [7]*kwo' ‘ngu*, past noon; [8]*kwo' k'e'* lost its essence or strength, as medicine; [9]*kwo' ‚tong*, to pass judicial investigation; [10]*kwo' hong*^{2} or *kwo' ‚ü*, excessive, superfluous; [11]*kwo' sek*, or *kwo' ngwo*^{2} a fault, transgression; COLL., [12]*kwo' ‚sing*, already past, done; [13]*kwo' ‘tiäng*, to cook or heat over in a pan; [14]*‘t'ó kwo' ‚mwong*, to take (a wife) to one's self; [15]*ko' kwo'* a comparative, the more, rather; [16]*sioh, kwo' ‚k'a*, when done, as soon as past; [17]*kwo' yoh*, to remove the taste of medicine (by eating sweet things); [18]*kwo' ch'eng'* to weigh again, as buyers do; *kwo' cheng'* a turn in a disease; [19]*k'ak, kwo'* too much, excessive; *kwo' t'óh*, to get rid of, as a slave-girl by selling her; *p'iéng' kwo' ‚peng* (or *‘ch'iu*), succeeded in cheating him; *kwo' ‘chio*, change of ownership; *kwo' oi*^{2} to go out or abroad; *kwo' kié'* an adopted (boy); *kwo' tio*^{2} to pass by; *kwo' ‚pwo*, to pass a night; *kwo' k'ieu'* "pass the aperture"—to manage a matter, as by getting security, etc.; *‚mó tek, kwo'* impassable; unable to continue (through the day), as one near death; *mó*^{2} *kwo' tek, e'* the feelings can't allow or bear it; *‚pang ‚pang kwo'* even tenor of one's way, as neither very good nor bad; *kwo' tek, ‘hai cheu' se' ‚siéng*, the sea once crossed, then it's fairy (land); *met.*, if one only succeeds (even with poor abilities) it's all well!

句' Chü. Read *kü'* in the dictionaries: a stop in reading, a comma; a period, a sentence; a phrase, an expression, a term, a word; a line in a stanza; a classifier of phrases: *‚chiong kwo'* the phrases of a section; [20]*kwo' tau*^{2} sentences; COM., [21]*kwo' hwak*, style or set order of clauses; [22]*kwo' kwo' tëüng' ‚k'wang*, the phrases all get circles—i. e., perfect marks; *met.*, your remarks are all perfectly correct; COLL., *‚i t'ëk, ‚mó kwo' hwak*, he reads incorrectly; *ng*^{2} *‚siäng kwo'* poorly composed, ungrammatical.

(296) Kwoh.

擴, K'uang. K'uo. To expand, to stretch a thing till it becomes large; *met.*, to enlarge the mind.

郭, Kuo. The suburbs of a city, a space about the gates inclosed by a wall to form a stronger defence; a surname.

廓, K'uo. To widen, to open out, to enlarge; great, wide, spacious, extended; to pare: *‚k'ai kwoh*, to enlarge.

椁, **槨,** Kuo. A box inclosing a coffin, an outer coffin; to measure: *sik, kwoh*, a sarcophagus; COM., *‚kwang kwoh*, the inner and outer coffins.

[1]大過 [2]小過 [3]過世 [4]難過 [5]太過 [6]經過 [7]過午 [8]過氣 [9]過堂 [10]過分 [11]過失 [12]過身 [13]過鼎 [14]討過門 [15]故過 [16]一過胶 [17]過藥 [18]過秤 [19]恰過 [20]句讀 [21]句法 [22]句句中圈

鞟 鞹 K'uo. A skin with the hair taken off, dressed or curried hides; red skins used in covering traveling carriages.

局 Chü. A square on a chess-board, a game of chess; *met.*, order, rank; contracted, coiled, bent, as the body; curling, as hair; mean, narrow, low-lived; look, aspect, bearing; an important establishment, a place that must be well-guarded, as a mint, a manufactory, an arsenal; also applied to large drug-stores; commonly used in the sense of to delude, to bait, to cozen; in the coll., complete, like the squares of a chess-board: [1]*kwoh ch'ëük*, cramped, confined; [2]*ek kwoh ki*, a game of chess; COM., [3]*kwoh sié* the position of a game; the peculiar arrangement (of an essay); [4]*kung chong kwoh*, an arsenal; [5]*chiëng kwoh*, or [6]*pó hok kwoh*, a mint; [7]*yoh kwoh*, a drug-shop; [8]*eng chü kwoh*, a printing establishment; [9]*cheng ngié chü kwoh*, an office for the revision of classic works; [10]*song miëng kwoh*, a kind of normal school to foster the silk and cotton manufactures; [11]*kwoh liong piéng ch'iëng*, of small capacity, mean-spirited; [12]*kwoh p'iëng* to gull one; COLL., [13]*o kwoh*, to have a nice place (and chance) for recreation, as at a friend's house; [14]*kah kwoh*, one's appearance, bearing; *kwoh chó* (or *tiong*) *tá lau*, have set a trap (for him); *tai kié mwoí siäng kwoh*, the the matter not yet completed.

跼 Chü. Bent, crooked, contracted; to bow the head, to stoop down, to humble one's self: [15]*kwong kwoh*, bent, cramped.

(297) Kwoí.

儈 Hui. Kuei. One who acts as a factor or broker to settle or enhance the price of goods: [16]*nga kwoí* or [17]*ch'e kwoí* a go-between in trade.

檜 Hui. Kuei. A durable kind of wood, a sort of juniper or cedar, the timber of which is suitable for coffins and ships; ornamented coffins; a kind of catapult; an ancient principality in Honan: COM., [18]*kwoí hiong*, the fragrance of juniper (burnt to idols).

劊 Kuei. To cut off, to amputate, to decapitate; to break asunder; to cut in two: COM., [19]*kwoí chü ch'iu*, an executioner; COLL., *kwoí chü ch'iu t'á t'ai*, "an executioner beheaded as substitute"; *met.*, to suffer, as a surety for the principal.

膾 鱠 Kuei. Hashed meat or fish; to cut small: *kwoí chiá* hashed and roasted; *kwoí chang*, the same as *ngüng ngü*, the silver fish, or white bait.

鱖 Kuei. A sort of ray or skate, whose flesh is like pork; a spotted fish like a bream: COM., *kwoí ngü siong*, dried bream.

噲 To swallow, to drink with avidity; voracious; the throat stopped; clamor of voices; name of a king: *kwoí kwoí* cheerful.

[1]局促 [2]一局棋 [3]局勢 [4]軍裝局 [5]錢局 [6]寶福局 [7]藥局 [8]印書局 [9]正誼書局 [10]桑棉局 [11]局量褊淺 [12]局騙 [13]務局 [14]格局 [15]蹺跼 [16]牙儈 [17]市儈 [18]檜香 [19]劊子手

福州方言拼音字典

澮 Hui. Kuei. A branch of the river Fan, in Shansi; a rill in a field, or pool for irrigating land; two streams joining: [1]*˛keu kwoi'* ditches and pools.

癐 A severe illness; very sick, debilitated, wasted. Read *˛wi*: to halloo, a clamor of voices.

獪 Kuei. Crafty, cunning, mischief-making: [2]*˛kieu kwoi'* crafty, fraudulent.

襘 Hui. The place where a girdle or a collar is fastened; a neck-string; a sash.

薈 Hui. Read *woi'*; coll. *kwoi'*, as in [3]*kwoi' 'ch'au*, a kind of grass, used for mats, also for strings to tie up goods in the shops; [4]*˛lu kwoi'* aloes.

蹶 Kuei. To move about; quick, spry, active, diligent; to play with the feet: also read *k'wok*, q. v.: [5]*˛liong sëü' kwoi' kwoi'* a good scholar is very diligent.

髻 Chi. Read *kie'* in the dictionaries: the coiffure of Chinese women: COM., [6]*'së kwoi'* to dress the hair; [7]*kwoi' ˛küng* (coll. *kwoi' sóh*,), coiffure-cord; [8]*kwoi' ˛ui*, a coiffure-band or frontlet (of silver); [9]*˛kwang ˛ing kwoi'* the Kwanyin knot; [10]*˛ngwong 'pó kwoi'* the ingot-shaped knot; [11]*kwoi' ˛sing ˛kwang*, ornamental center-piece of a coiffure; COLL., [12]*˛k'i ˛k'i kwoi'* tufts of hair on a girl's head; [13]*p'ok, p'ok, kwoi'* a kind of depressed knot; [14]*˛ch'eng ˛loi kwoi'* the spiral coiffure.

Kwoi'. A coll. word: to lean, to rest, as the hand or foot, on something: *kwoi' ˛p'iăng*, to lean the back (against a support); *˛k'a kwoi' 'ië 'lá*, to rest the feet on a chair.

(298) Kwok.

國 国 Kuo. A state, country, kingdom, empire; a nation, a people; a region; national, governmental: [15]*˛k'ai kwok,* to found a state; COM., [16]*kwok, ˛kung*, a sovereign; [17]*kwok, 'mu*, the empress; [18]*kwok, ˛ka*, the state; *tai' ˛ch'ing kwok,* the Manchu empire, China; [19]*pwong kwok,* native country; *kwok, ˛sü*, the emperor's adviser; [20]*kwok, ˛tieu*, a dynasty; *kwok, keu'* brothers of the empress; *kwok, 't'ong*, the national treasury; *kwok, ˛soi*, a waning empire; *kwok, ˛song*, mourning for an emperor; *chiéng' kwok,* the contending states, about B. C. 400-260; *kwok, ˛ka k'e' so'* an empire's destiny.

摑 Kuo. To strike with the hand, to box, to slap: *kwok, miéng'* to slap the face.

蟈 Kuo. A kind of small green frog, called *˛leu kwok,* having long thighs; COLL., *kwok, taëng'* (also spoken *kauk, taëng'*), a large brown or black toad which lives among rocks; it is cooked and eaten for its cooling properties.

幗 Kuo. A hempen cap or kerchief worn by women when mourning; a female

[1]溝澮 [2]狡獪 [3]薈草 [4]蘆薈 [5]良士蹶蹶 [6]梳髻 [7]髻巾 [8]髻圍 [9]觀音髻 [10]元寶髻 [11]髻心冠 [12]欹欹髻 [13]覆覆髻 [14]田螺髻 [15]開國 [16]國君 [17]國母 [18]國家 [19]本國 [20]國朝

head-dress: [1]ˏi ˏsiu ˏkäng kwokˎ, leaves (the act) as a legacy to make the kerchiefs (i. e. women) blush!

膕, Kuo. The hollow under the knee, the popliteal space: [2]kwokˎ k‘okˎ bow-legged.

蕨, Chueh. Read *k‘wok*ˎ; coll. *kwok*ˎ: an edible fern: [3]*kwok*ˎ ‘*hung*, farina made from the fern-root; the flour is used in the ‘*kwi* cakes, pork-balls, etc.

笏, Hu. Read *hwok*ˎ; used in shop-bills for the coll. *kwok*ˎ: a block or piece of ink: [4]*mĕk*$_{2}$ *sioh*$_{2}$ *kwok*ˎ one block of ink.

***Kwok*ˎ.** A coll. word: large, coarse, as thread and things in strips—the opposite of ‘*mieu* (fine): *k‘ak*ˎ *kwok*ˎ too coarse; *kwok*ˎ *tauk*ˎ tall and large (for his age).

***Kwok*$_{2}$.** A coll. word: a block, a piece of timber (sawed off); a section, a bit, a piece, as of thread or cord.

(299) Kwong.

光 ˏKuang. Light, splendor, luster; illustrious, brilliant, bright; honor, eclat, glory; *met.*, one's presence; naked, smooth, bare, bald; only, barely; to illuminate; to adorn; to reflect credit on: COM., [5]ˏ*kwong ang*^{2} light and dark; [6]ˏ*sing* ˏ*kwong*, effulgence of a god; [7]ˏ*kwong so*^{2} plain, without ornament; [8]*chauk*ˎ ˏ*kwong*, you make light (by your presence), as said to a guest; [9]ˏ*kwong* ‘*king*, the prospect, circumstances; [10]ˏ*kwong* ‘*ch‘ai*, or [11]ˏ*kwong* ˏ*siong*, splendid, gay; [12]ˏ*kwong* ˏ*kwong ëüng*^{2} *ëüng*^{2} bright and glossy; COLL., ˏ*kwong* ˏ*t‘ang* ˏ*t‘ang*, very bright, as the moon; *met.*, as plain as it can be! [13]ˏ*kwong kok*$_{2}$ slippery; [14]ˏ*kwong* ‘*piäng*, wheaten biscuits; [15]ˏ*t‘iĕng* ˏ*kwong* ‘*cha*, early dawn; ˏ*kwong pah*$_{2}$ *pah*$_{2}$ clearly, obviously; ˏ*kwong* ˏ*chiĕng*, smooth-looking, as good clothes; ˏ*kwong* ˏ*tang*, smooth, not rough; ˏ*kwong* ˏ*kwong* ˏ*sing*, the bare body—i. e., without dowry, portionless; [16]*ch‘ek*$_{2}$ ˏ*t‘au cheng*^{2} ˏ*kwong*, the thieves have made a clean sweep! *lang*^{2} ˏ*t‘au* ˏ*kwong*, from light to light, through the night, as a play.

洸 ˏKuang. Water sparkling in the sun; a river in Shansi; wide: ˏ*kwong* ˏ*kwong*, martial, threatening.

桄 ˏKuang. A kind of palm like the areca, called [17]ˏ*kwong* ˏ*long*, of which sedan-thills are made; a cut-water.

胱 ˏKuang. The bladder, called [18]ˏ*pong* ˏ*kwong*, the latter word referring to its breadth.

關 ˏKuan. Read ˏ*kwang*; coll. ˏ*kwong*: to inclose, to shut up, to include, to confine; to shut, as a door: [19]ˏ*kwong pwoh*$_{2}$ to inclose, to secure, as a yard; ˏ*kwong tai*^{2} to keep (a scholar) from his dinner; [20]ˏ*kwong* ˏ*kang*, to imprison; ˏ*kwong* ‘*sŏ* ˏ*mwong ho*^{2} to shut and lock the doors; ˏ*kwong* ˏ*tü*, to shut up pigs; ˏ*kwong* ˏ*mwong*, to shut a door.

[1] 貽羞巾幗 [2] 膕朏 [3] 蕨粉 [4] 墨一笏 [5] 光暗 [6] 神光 [7] 光素 [8] 作光 [9] 光景 [10] 光彩 [11] 光祥 [12] 光光潤潤 [13] 光滑 [14] 光餅 [15] 天光早 [16] 賊偷盡光 [17] 桄榔 [18] 膀胱 [19] 關縛 [20] 關監

‘捲 ‘卷 Chüan. To roll up in a scroll; spiral, crisped, curled, rolled up; to whirl about, to seize, to carry off; a classifier of things rolled up: the 2d also read *kwong’*, q. v.: [1]*’sik, ‘kwong*, to seize (the country or region); COM., [2]*‘kwong ,chong*, a pawn-shop depositary; [3]*‘kwong ‘k‘wong*, a depository for the dead, a vault; [4]*‘kwong ,chü*, ornamental scrolls; [5]*‘kwong ,loi ,hung*, a whirlwind; [6]*‘kwong ,lüng ,küng*, arches in walls; COLL., *‘kwong leu’* shavings; [7]*‘kwong ,chiéng*, rolls of glutinous rice (in thin crusts of bean-curd); [8]*‘kwong ,tëng chioh*, mold-candles.

‘廣 Kuang. Broad, extensive, wide, spacious; large, ample; to enlarge, to make broader or wider; to extend; to increase; to diffuse; a body of 15 chariots: used in the coll. for *‘k‘wong*, q. v.: [9]*‘kwong ,yong*, to publish widely; COM., [10]*‘kwong ,tëng*, Canton; [11]*‘kwong ,sá*, the Kwangsi province; [12]*‘kwong k‘aiu’* Canton buttons; [13]*‘kwong tai’* extensive, profound, as in learning or virtues; [14]*‘kwong k‘wak,* wide, spacious; *‘kwong ,kau*, wide circle of friends; COLL., [15]*‘kwong ,tëng ‘kiáng*, the Cantonese.

‘鑛 礦 Kuang. The ore of iron, lead, and other metals; minerals; the lode of metals, gems in the matrix: [16]*t‘iék, ‘kwong*, iron ore [17]*,king ‘kwong*, gold ore.

‘管 Kuan. Read *‘kwang;* coll. *‘kwong*, as in *‘chwi ‘kwong*, a water-dipper; [18]*‘mi ‘kwong*, a rice-measure—⅛ or ½ of a *,ching; ‘hwi ‘kwong*, a bamboo tube for blowing the fire; *‘chai ,mui ‘kwong*, an extinguisher for paper-lighters; *,hiong siáng’ ‘kwong*, an incense-stick holder.

‘Kwong. A coll. word, as in *‘kwong ,kwa*, a large kind of squash—the same as *,tëng ,kwa; ‘kwong ,kwa ,nong*, pulp of the squash.

卷’ 劵’ Chüan. A roll, a manuscript, a scroll, a book; a section, a division, a part of a book; ruled paper for essays; a classifier of books, Mss., &c.: also read *‘kwong*, q. v.: COM., [19]*kwong’ ‘chai*, essay-paper; [20]*,chü kwong’* books; *kwong’ ne’* Vol. II; [21]*mëk, kwong’* or *,chio kwong’* the essays of Küjin graduates; *lok, kwong’* rejected essays; COLL., *kwong’ kah*, ruled paper; *kwong’ tah*, a paper-weight; *,i ,chü kwong’ ‘hó*, he is well-read.

綣’ Ch‘üan Also read *‘kwong:* to bind; bound, as with silken cords: *‘k‘iéng kwong’* a friendly attachment, united, inseparable.

眷’ 睠’ Chüan. To love, to care for, to regard affectionately; those whom one loves; relatives, family, kindred; related to; gracious: *kwong’ ko’* to care for tenderly; *,ing kwong’ tá’* your relative by marriage—said to the paternal uncles of a married son or daughter; COM., [22]*,ka kwong’* or *kwong’ sük,* a family, one's household; *kwong’ liong’* to love tenderly; *,ch‘ing kwong’* relatives;

[1] 席卷 [2] 卷賍 [3] 卷壙 [4] 卷書 [5] 卷螺風 [6] 卷龍宮 [7] 卷館 [8] 廣筒燭 [9] 廣揚 [10] 廣東 [11] 廣西 [12] 廣釦 [13] 廣大 [14] 廣闊 [15] 廣東仔 [16] 鐵鑛 [17] 金鑛 [18] 米管 [19] 卷紙 [20] 書卷 [21] 墨卷 [22] 家眷

kwong꜄ ꜂*mi*, rice for family use—an allowance to soldiers. The 3d also read ꜀*kwong*, as in ꜀*kwong* ꜀*kwong*, to weep, to shed tears.

券꜄ (Ch'üan) A bond, deed, contract or agreement; each of the parties formerly retained one half; a book, a section; proof, evidence in deeds and contracts: *kwong*꜄ *yok*꜆, a bond; COM., *k'ié*꜄ *kwong*꜄ deeds, agreements.

桊꜄ To bore a cow's nose; a nose-ring or fastening: COLL., *kwong*꜄ *p'e*꜄ to ring an ox's nose.

權 ꜁Ch'uan The weight of the steelyard; a weight; to weigh; to balance, to equalize; to plan, to devise; power, authority, influence; influential; circumstances; position; meanwhile, for a time, temporary; contracted: [1]꜀*kwong* ꜀*ngi*, temporarily constrained; [2]꜀*kwong* ꜀*ü*, in the beginning; [3]꜀*kwong* ꜀*meu*, to plan at the instant, sagacious; COM., [4]꜀*kwong sié*꜄ or [5]꜀*kwong lik*꜆ influence, power; [6]꜀*ch'ó* ꜀*kwong*, to wield power; [7]꜀*ping* ꜀*kwong*, military authority; [8]꜀*chŭng* ꜀*kwong*, according to the exigency or circumstances; COLL., [9]꜀*kwong pang*꜄ power, authority.

顴 ꜁Ch'uan The cheek-bones: COM., [10]꜀*kwong kauk*, *twai*꜆ high cheek-bones; COLL., ꜀*kwong kauk*, *k'ié*꜄ *miăng*꜆ *ngaing*꜆ the projecting cheek-bones (of a wife indicate) a rigid lot (injurious to her husband).

鬈 ꜁Ch'uan A fine head of hair, curly hair: [11]꜀*ki* ꜀*ing* ꜂*mi* ꜂*ch'iŭ* ꜀*kwong*, the man is handsome and has fine hair.

惓 ꜁Ch'uan Careful, earnest, diligent; to stop, to desist: [12]꜀*kwong* ꜀*kwong*, earnest, intent on.

踡 ꜁ The limbs contracted; bent, doubled up: [13]꜀*kwong kwoh*꜆ stooping, crouching, as from cold.

拳 ꜁Ch'uan The hand doubled up, the fist; boxing, fisticuffs; strong, vigorous, athletic; to hold in the hand, to grasp: in the coll. read ꜀*kung*, q. v.: [14]꜀*kwong* ꜀*kwong*, to grasp, attached to; attentive, respectful.

狂 ꜁K'uang. Mad, crazed; raging, raving, wild, incoherent; hasty; unable to judge about matters, stolid; cruel, irascible; eccentric, enthusiastic, precipitate, rash, imprudent—often applied sneeringly to the acts of others; deranged, insane, delirious: COM., [15]꜀*tiéng* ꜀*kwong*, mad, crazy; [16]꜀*kwong* ꜀*hung*, a violent wind; [17]*hwak* ꜀*kwong*, raving, delirious; [18]꜀*kwong só*꜄ frivolous, light-minded; [19]꜀*kwong pó*꜆ fierce and oppressive; COLL., [20]꜀*kwong* ꜀*ming*, to talk wildly in sleep; [21]꜀*kwong* ꜀*kwong yék*꜆ burning with anger, ireful.

꜀*Kwong*. A coll. word: large, whole, unbroken, of a large denomination: ꜀*kwong p'ieu*꜄ large bank-bills; ꜀*kwong sò*꜄ a large, or wholesale, account; ꜀*kwong lak*꜆ whole grains, as rice

[1] 權宜 [2] 權輿 [3] 權謀 [4] 權勢 [5] 權力 [6] 操權 [7] 兵權 [8] 從權 [9] 權柄 [10] 顴骨大 [11] 其人美且鬈 [12] 惓惓 [13] 踡跼 [14] 拳拳 [15] 顛狂 [16] 狂風 [17] 發狂 [18] 狂躁 [19] 狂暴 [20] 狂眠 [21] 狂狂熱 ○

without broken kernels; *ˌkwong ho*' (or *ʻchio*), the large (wealthy) houses—*scil.*, which subscribe liberally.

ˌKwong. A coll. prefix, as in *ˌkwong ʻkwong*, bamboo tubes or cups; bits of bamboo, as for children's plays.

倦[1] Chüan. Tired, fatigued, wearied; to desist from labor: *k'aung' kwong'* wearied, jaded; *pok, ˌti yêng' kwong'* indefatigable; COM., [1]*ˌp'i kwong'* fagged out.

誑[2] K'uang. Read *kwong'* in the dictionaries: wild, incoherent talk; to deceive, to mislead, to lie to: *kwong' ˌngiong*, lying words; [2]*ˌk'i kwong'* to deceive.

逛[2] K'uang. Read *ʻkwong* and *kwong'* in the dictionaries: to wander about, to ramble, to go to and fro; to go abroad, to run away.

(300) **K'a.**

胶 Chiao. Read *ˌngau;* commonly used for the coll. *ˌk'a*, the foot: [3]*ˌk'a ʻt'oi*, the thigh; [4]*ˌk'a pok, ˌt'au*, the knee, the patella; [5]*ˌk'a ˌtĕng*, or [6]*ˌk'a ˌkwang*, the shin, the crural bone (tibia and fibula); [7]*ˌk'a ˌngu mĕk,* the ancles; *ˌk'a ˌtang*, or *ˌk'a au' ˌtang*, the heel; [8]*ˌk'a ʻpeng*, or [9]*ˌk'a ʻchiong ʻtá*, or *ˌk'a chioh, ʻtá*, the sole of the foot; [10]*ˌk'a ˌyeu*, the hollow, as of the bound feet of females; [11]*ˌk'a ʻchai*, the toes; *ˌk'a ʻchai kek,* spaces between the toes; [12]*ˌk'a kak,* toe-nails; [13]*p'iăng ˌk'a*, lame, halt; *lang' ˌk'a ˌliĕng* (or *ˌtiĕng*), a festering shin (bruise); [14]*ˌk'a pang'* a leg (of pork); [15]*ˌk'a pang' a'* the space between the legs; *ˌk'a siê'* manner of stepping, the tread; [16]*ˌk'a tak,* or *ˌk'a ch'iăk,* to tread, to trample; [17]*ˌk'a poo'* a step, pace; [18]*ˌk'a k'ô'* fetters; *ˌk'a ʻkiăng*, a footboy, lackey; *t'aung' ʻch'iĕng ˌk'a*, barefoot; *ˌk'a chai' mwoi' ʻmwang*, "the feet's debt not fully (paid)"—said ruefully by one going about.

ˌK'a. A coll. word, as in *ˌk'a ch'ioh,* the magpie; *ˌk'a ch'ioh, ˌwo*, a magpie's nest.

ʻK'a. A coll. word, as in *ʻk'a tak,* (*lak,*), to mend, to repair; to adjust, to clean up, as lamps; *ʻk'a lak, ʻié*, to mend chairs.

敲 Ch'iao. Read *ˌk'ieu;* used in the *Paik, ˌIng* for the coll. *k'a':* to beat, to pound, to knock: [19]*k'a' ʻsi*, to strike dead; [20]*k'a' ˌmwong*, to knock at a door; *k'a' ʻtié*, to drive in, as nails; *k'a' ch'ioh,* a sort of ferule, used by play-actors and street-readers.

(301) **K'á.**

溪 谿 Ch'i. A mountain stream; a pellucid pool among the hills; the source of a stream or river; a valley with a rivulet flowing through it: COM., [21]*ˌk'á ˌô*, streams and rivers; [22]*ˌk'á ʻchwi*, freshet-waters; *ˌk'á ˌsung*, the up-river boats; *ˌIu ˌk'á*, a district in the Yenping prefecture; COLL., *ˌk'á nak,* a bamboo tracking-rope.

[1]疲倦 [2]欺誑 [3]胶腿 [4]胶屈頭 [5]胶筒 [6]胶關 [7]胶牛目 [8]胶板 [9]胶掌底 [10]胶腰 [11]胶指 [12]胶甲 [13]跛胶 [14]胶柄 [15]胶柄下 [16]胶踏 [17]胶步 [18]胶靠 [19]敲死 [20]敲門 [21]溪河 [22]溪水

襟 ‚ Chin. Read ‚*k‘ing;* used for coll. ‚*k‘á:* the skirts of a garment, called [1]‚*i* ‚*siong* ‚*k‘á;* [2]‚*k‘á* ‚*piéng*, edges or openings of a skirt—where it is faced or lined; [3]*meng‘* ‚*seng* ‚*k‘á*, front skirts.

齟 ‚ Chü. Read ‘*chu;* used in the *Paik,* ‚*Ing* for the coll. ‚*k‘á:* to bite, to gnaw; *met.*, to take, to appropriate: [4]‚*k‘á kauk,* to gnaw bones; [5]‚*k‘á ‘cheng kak,* to bite the nails; [6]*k‘ëük,* ‚*i chiéng‘* ‚*k‘á k‘ó‘* he has appropriated (the article); [7]‚*k‘á ‘wang* ‚*kiéng*, "bite the bowl's edge"—merely get one's living, as an employé says.

快 ‘ K‘uai. Read *k‘wai‘;* coll. *k‘á‘:* quickly, speedily; to hurry, to make haste: [8]*k‘á‘* ‚*li*, to come quickly; *k‘á‘ ch‘woi‘* soon, very expeditiously; [9]*k‘á‘ k‘á‘* make haste! [10]*k‘á‘ ‘kang*, speedily; to pursue rapidly; [11]*k‘á‘ wak,* in easy, comfortable circumstances; [12]*k‘á‘ wak, siăh,* fine, good eating!

K‘á‘. A coll. word, as in *k‘á‘ á‘* (or ‚*k‘á á‘*) why? wherefore? *k‘á‘ á‘* ‚*chiong wang‘ chó‘* why do you so!

K‘á‘. A coll. word, used in the sense of *t‘á‘* for, in behalf of; of, from; about, concerning: *k‘á‘ ‘ngwai chó‘* do it for me; *k‘á‘* ‚*i ‘má* ‚*li*, buy it of him; *k‘á‘ ‘nü ‘siong*, think for or about you or your (matter).

(302) K‘aë.

K‘aë. A country brogue for *laë‘* to claw, to scratch, as a hen in the dirt.

(303) K‘aëk.

殼, **壳**, K‘o. Read *k‘auk,;* coll. *k‘aëk,:* the skin, shell, or covering of fruits or eggs; the shell or scale of mollusks; the exuviæ of snakes or chrysalides; bark, crust, or what covers: [13]*k‘aëk, sioh,* shell-fish; [14]*k‘aëk,* ‚*hwi*, shell-lime; [15]‚*p‘ui k‘aëk,* skins, shells; [16]‚*hwa meng‘ k‘aëk,* a mask; *t‘aung‘ k‘aëk,* to shed the skin, as a snake.

K‘aëk,. A coll. word, as in *k‘aëk, ch‘ëk,* to irritate, to provoke; *k‘aëk, lëk, ch‘ëk,* to cough, coughing, as from a stoppage in the throat.

(304) K‘aëng.

空 ‘ K‘ung. Read ‚*k‘ung;* used for the coll. *k‘aëng‘:* a void, an interstice, a blank space; a hole, an opening: *k‘aëng‘ laëng‘* an interval; [17]*k‘aëng‘ sioh,* ‚*hong*, one line left blank; [18]*k‘aëng‘ sioh, nik,* one day blank—fail to do or come one day.

K‘aëng‘. A coll. word; to claw, to scratch hard, as a place that itches; *met.*, to embezzle, to appropriate largely to private use: ‚*chiéng* ‚*tu k‘ëük,* ‚*i k‘aëng‘ ‘tu tói‘ ‘lá k‘ó‘* all the cash raked by him into his own pocket.

欬‘ K‘o. Read *k‘ai‘;* used for the coll. *k‘aëng‘*, as in *k‘aëng‘ sau‘* to cough, to hack; *k‘aëng‘ k‘aëng‘ sau‘* (or *kieu‘*), sound of constant hacking; *k‘aëng‘ ch‘ok, haik,* to cough blood.

1 衣裳襟 2 襟邊 3 面前襟 4 齟骨 5 齟指甲 6 乞伊佔齟去 7 齟碗墘 8 快來 9 快快 10 快赶 11 快活 12 快活食 13 殼石 14 殼灰 15 皮殼 16 花面殼 17 空一行 18 空一日○

福州方言拼音字典

(305) K'ah.

客 K'a. K'ĕ. Read *k'aik*,; coll. *k'ah*,: a guest, a visitor, a friend; a dealer; a customer; a foreign trader: [1]*nĕng k'ah*, a guest; [2]*chio k'ah*, shopman and customer; [3]*k'ah*, *siong*, or *k'ah*, *nĕng*, a foreign trader; *k'ah*, *ngĕü* (or *kwang*, or *taing*), an inn; *k'ah*, *kwang*, the visiting officers, as the Imperial examiners, or literary chancellor; *k'ah*, *t'iăng*, a parlor; *k'ah*, *ching*, or *k'ah*, *t'ó* politeness toward guests; [9]*k'ah*, *hwo* goods from other districts, foreign goods; [11]*tá k'ah*, teamen; [12]*nĕng k'ah*, *kiăng*, (our) little guests.

K'ah,. A coll. word, as in *k'ah*, *tieu*, or *k'ah*, *lieu*, (or *k'a tieu*), to play, to ramble, to recreate.

K'ah,. A coll. word, as in *k'ah*, *k'ah*, *kieu*, the chattering of magpies.

(306) K'áh.

K'áh,. A coll. word, as in *k'áh*, *k'áh*, *kieu* a sound, as of phlegm in the throat; *k'áh*, *sioh*, *siăng* *ngwai cheu* *p'ah*, utter a word and I'll whip!

(307) K'ai.

開 K'ai. To open, to unfold, to spread out; to institute, to begin, to commence, to start; to explain, to disclose, to reveal: in the coll. read *k'wi*, q. v.: [14]*k'ai hwak*, to distribute, as money; [15]*k'ai liĕk*, *ü chó*, "arranged on the left"—a phrase introducing items or names; [17]*k'ai tiĕng*, an open, cheerful look; com., [19]*k'ai chü*, present of money to a bride's uncles; [11]*k'ai chong*, a feast given by a graduate; [18]*k'ai sek*, to release; [19]*k'ai tiong chi hi*, congratulations to a friend on his opening a shop; *k'ai hwa sé* a Budhist monastery near the West Lake, Foochow; [20]*k'ai t'iĕng pik*, *tê* to form heaven and earth, the creation; *k'ai kwang ngiĕng* *si*, open the coffin and hold an inquest over the corpse; *met.*, excessively particular or captious.

揩 K'ai. To rub, to wipe: *k'ai pai*, to rush forward violently.

剴 K'ai. A sickle, a bill-hook; to cut; to move; to whet a knife; diligently, assiduously: *k'ai ch'iĕk*, *hieu ëü* fully make it known to you—a phrase in edicts.

塏 K'ai. A clear and elevated eminence: *song k'ai*, a high and pleasant location.

愷 豈 K'ai. Interchanged with the next: joyful, delighted, pleased; peaceful, contented; gentle, as a wind: the 2d also read *k'i*, q. v.: *paik*, *k'ai*, the eight excellent ones—sons of an ancient worthy: *k'ai tă* *kung chü*, a magnanimous officer; *k'ai tek*, kind and benevolent, gracious.

凱 K'ai. Victorious, triumphant; good, excellent; gentle, soothing; to celebrate a victory: *k'ai chiĕk*, to triumph; *k'ai siong*, to return triumphant from battle; *k'ai kó*, peans of victory; *k'ai hung*, southern zephyrs.

[1]伙客 [2]主客 [3]客商 [4]客伙 [5]客寓 [6]客官 [7]客廳 [8]客情 [9]客套 [10]客貨 [11]茶客 [12]伙客仔 [13]開發〇 [14]開列於左 [15]開展 [16]開書 [17]開樽 [18]開釋 [19]開張之喜 [20]開天闢地

覬 'K'ai. Read ke'; coll. 'k'ai, as in [1]'k'ai ĕü' to covet and appropriate; [2]'chiă nŏh, k'ĕük, ,i 'k'ai ĕü' k'ŏ' have let him covetously abstract the article from me!

'鎧 K'ai. A cuirass, a coat of mail; defensive armor; applied in a *met.*, sense to a priest's robe: [3]'k'ai kak, armor; [4]'siu 'k'ai, a helmet.

'闓 K'ai. To open, to loosen, to stretch out; to desire; also an archer's thumbring: [5]'k'ai ik, pleased; [6]'k'ai tek, a timely rain; *met.*, great benefits.

'楷 K'ai. A straight, graceful tree, which grew on Confucius' grave; a mold or model, a pattern; a rule, an example: [7]'mwo 'k'ai, a model, an exemplar; [8],tuang 'k'ai, correct or elegant writing; COM., [9]'k'ai ,chü, or [10]'k'ai che' the full, square form of character.

'駭 Hai. Also read 'hai: alarmed, frightened, terrified; apprehensive, afraid of; to scatter, to disperse; to beat drums, as to arouse an army: [11]'k'ai ngauk, amazed, astonished.

嘅' K'ai. Interchanged with the next: to sigh for, to lament: [12]k'ai' t'ang' to sigh, to grieve about.

愾' K'ai. To sigh, to groan; a long sigh; angry, enraged: [13]k'ai' haung' fierce anger, indignation.

慨' K'ai. The disappointment of a brave man; loyal, inflexible in virtue; noble, generous, magnanimous: [14]'k'ong k'ai' disinterested, generous; [15]'kang k'ai' moved by, commiserating.

憩' 愒' K'ai. Also read k'e'; the 2nd also read kiĕk,: to stop, to cease; to rest, to repose; also to covet; hasty, hurried.

槩' 概' K'ai. A striker to level grain; to even, to level, to adjust; a summing up, a resumé: [16]'k'e' k'ai' resolute, determined; COM., [17]tai' k'ai' generally speaking, on the whole, for the most part; [18]ek, k'ai' altogether, the whole of.

漑' K'ai. A river in Liautung; to wash or scour, as cooking utensils; to moisten; to roll on, as a torrent; to overflow, to inundate.

洎' Chi. To moisten, to fertilize; rich, fertile; to extend to. Read ke': the broth of boiled meats, soup, gravy.

塈' Ch'i. To daub, to plaster, to color walls; to stop holes and cracks in a wall; to collect; to cease, to rest, to take a breathing-spell.

暨' Ch'i. The sun peeping out; and, also, moreover, together with; the end, extreme; exactly, just at: [19]k'ai' ,king, just now; [20]k'ai' k'ai' daring, strenuous; [21]k'ai' kik, and, together with.

1覬	乞	去	4首	6闓	8端	10楷	12慨	14忼	16氣	18一	20暨
覦	伊	3鎧	鎧	澤	楷	字	嘆	慨	槩	槩	暨
2者	覬	甲	5闓	7模	9楷	11駭	13愾	15感	17大	19暨	21暨
乇	覦	〇	懌	楷	書	愕	恨	慨	槩	今	及

穊ˀ K'ai. Also read *kié*ˀ: to plant close in deep-plowed soil; plants set out close together, grain growing thickly.

欬ˀ K'ê. To cough, to belch; to hack, to hiccough; to call out in alarm: used in the coll. for *k'aěng*ˀ, q. v.: [1]*'kwong k'ai*ˀ to bawl out.

磕ˀ K'ê. Read *k'ak*, in the dictionaries: the sound of two stones striking together, the clatter of stones: in the coll. read *k'auk*, q. v.

(308) K'aik.

克, K'ê. To be able, superior to; to subdue, to overcome; to bear, to sustain, adequate to, overbearing: [2]*k'aik, 'ki*, to subdue self, to repress one's lusts or passions; [3]*k'aik, ˏtong*, to sustain; fit for; *ke*ˀ *k'aik*, envious and overbearing; COM., [4]*'k'aik, ˏk'ŭng k'aik, kiĕng*ˀ to be diligent and economical—as Yü the Great was.

剋, **尅**, K'ê. Interchanged with the last: to subdue, to overcome; to repress, to destroy, to exorcise; to insist on, urgent: in the coll. to deny self, to save by self-denial for the sake of others; also to stand close together, to crowd, to press, crowded: [5]*k'aik, ˏki*, a set time; COM., [6]*ˏseng k'aik*, to produce and destroy—said of the five elements; [7]*k'aik, chié*ˀ to suppress or subdue, as one "element" does another; [8]*k'aik, ˏsing chieu*ˀ a sacrifice (to expel) injurious demons; COLL., *k'aik, ngá*ˀ to save up by economizing; also to oppress, to force one; [9]*k'aik, ch'oi*ˀ *ˏt'au*, "deny the mouth"—to save in eating; [10]*k'aik, yĕk*, heated by the crowd; *cheng*ˀ *k'aik*, or *k'aik, ˏtu peu*ˀ very crowded.

刻ˎ K'ê. To cut, to carve, to chisel; to sculpture, to engrave; close, griping, cheating; insulting; ⅛ of a Chinese hour, 15 minutes; a little while: COM. [11]*k'aik, che*ˀ to cut characters; [12]*k'aik, che*ˀ *ch'iong*ˀ an engraver; [13]*k'aik, 'peng*, cut (on) blocks, engraved, not written; [14]*ˏsi k'aik*, constantly; [15]*'k'ing k'aik*, a short time; [16]*k'aik, ha*ˀ *ˏkwong 'king*, the present state or prospects; [17]*k'aik, chaik*, to oppress; [18]*k'aik, pok*, to cheat, fraudulent; insulting; COLL., *k'aik, pauk*, to break (blocks) in cutting; *met.*, to extort, to exact oppressively; [19]*sioh, k'aik, 'ku*, a little while.

客, K'ê. K'o. A guest, a friend; a stranger, a customer, a foreign dealer; foreign; a robber, a marauder; to lodge: in the coll. read *k'ah*, q. v.: [20]*ˏping k'aik*, guests; *'chŭ k'aik*, host and guest: *pó*ˀ *k'aik*, robbers; COM., *'wong k'aik*, strangers from afar.

喀, K'ê. The noise of retching; to expectorate violently, to hawk: *k'aik, sau*ˀ to hawk and cough.

[1]嚝	[3]克	克	[6]生	[8]尅	嘴	[11]刻	匠	刻	下	責	刻
欬	當	儉	尅	神	頭	字	[13]刻	[15]頃	光	[18]刻	古
[2]克	[4]克	[5]尅	[7]尅	煞	[10]尅	[12]刻	板	刻	景	薄	[20]賓
己	勤	期	制	[9]尅	熱	字	[14]時	[16]刻	[17]刻	[19]一	客

䁆' Yi. Read *yék,;* used in the *Paik*, *₍Ing* for the coll. *k'aik*,: to close, to shut, as the eyes: [1]*k'aik*, *mëk*, or [2]*'mek*, *₍chiu k'aik*, to shut the eyes; [3]*k'aik*, *'king 'king*, shut them tight.

(309) **K'aing.**

掯' K'ĕng. A word commonly used in criminal causes: to oppress, to extort from, to take by force; to hinder, to obstruct; oppressive, arbitrary: COM., [4]*k'aing' ka'* overbearing about the price; [5]*k'aing' sük*, to obstruct the redemption (of property), as a mortgagee does; COLL. *k'aing' 'si ₍kang 'tiŭ*, to cause death by rigid imprisonment.

膈' Kê. Read *kaik,;* coll. *k'aing':* the diaphragm, lower part of the chest: *k'aing' t'iăng'* pain in the chest.

K'aing'. A coll. word: to put on a cover, to cover, to close over; covered; *met*, to slap: *k'aing' mek*, to cover close; *k'aing' 'wang* or *k'aing' ₍ch'ŭng*, a bowl with the cover fitting close to the edge; *k'aing' sioh*, *'chiong*, to give one a slap (on the cheek).

(310) **K'aiu.**

叩' K'ou. Interchanged with the next: to strike, to tap, to knock upon; to prostrate one's self, to knock the head on the ground in worship, or when saluting a superior; to ask, to inquire; to investigate: [6]*k'aiu' 'siu*, the *kotow;* [7]*k'aiu' 'ping*, to petition humbly; COM., [8]*₍sang koi' 'kiu k'aiu'* three kneelings and nine knockings of the head—it is the highest act of of worship.

扣' K'ou. To beat, to rap, to knock; to lead a horse; to hook, to clasp, to buckle; to deduct, to discount; a reduction: used in the coll. for *k'a'* (to knock at a door): COM., [9]*k'aiu' ₍tü*, to deduct, to strike out, as from a list; [10]*'kau 'ngu k'aiu'* a reduction of 5 *per cent.*—i. e., 95 paid on 100; [11]*k'aiu' ₍t'au*, reduction, discount; [12]*k'aiu' pwo'* a kind of narrow cotton cloth; [13]*k'aiu' ₍këng ₍chiéng*, to cut wages; [14]*k'aiu' 'tá* (or *ch'iong'*), discount on a string of cash, the amount by which it falls short—the usual rate is 2 cash on 1000.

釦' K'ou. A gold or silver rim on vessels; to carve, to engrave; to make a noise, as by beating gongs; commonly used for buttons; to button, to hook, to clasp: COM., [15]*k'aiu' ₍mwong*, button-holes; [16]*k'aiu' siăng'* medium-sized silk thread; [17]*k'aiu' tai'* a girdle with a clasp or buckle; COLL., [18]*k'aiu' 'hó*, to button properly; *k'aiu' sioh*, *ho'* a set of (five) buttons; [19]*k'aiu' sioh*, *lak*, one button.

寇' K'ou. To rob, to plunder, to pillage; to riot, to do mischief; banditti, thieves, robbers, highwaymen, ladrones an enemy: cruel, tyrannical; [20]*k'aiu' chek*, outlaws, thieves; *'ch'ó k'aiu'* marauders; *'hai k'aiu'* pirates; *₍sü k'aiu'* a criminal judge.

[1]䁆目 [2]目睭䁆 [3]䁆緊緊 [4]掯價 [5]掯贖 [6]叩首 [7]叩稟 [8]三跪九叩 [9]扣除 [10]九五扣 [11]扣頭 [12]扣布 [13]扣工錢 [14]扣底 [15]釦門 [16]釦線 [17]釦帶 [18]釦好 [19]釦一粒 [20]寇賊 ○

簆' K'ou. The reed or slaie of a loom, a weaver's reed, made of bamboo.

蔻' K'ou. The nutmeg: COM., [1]'taiu' k'aiu' nutmegs—applied poetically to maidens; [2]'taiu' k'aiu' ,hwa, mace; [3]'nŭk, k'aiu' the best sort of nutmegs.

(311) K'ak.

渴, K'o. Dry, thirsty, to thirst; eager, longing for; anxious, desirous of (in a good sense): [4]'ung ,mui 'chi k'ak, hearing about apricots quenched their thirst—said of the soldiers of ,Chó ch'ó'; COM., [5]'ch'oi' k'ak, thirsty; [6],ki k'ak, hungry and thirsty; [7]'chi k'ak, to quench thirst.

恰, Ch'io. To apply the mind to; opportunely, seasonably, in good time; to the purpose, fitly, exactly, just right: [8]k'ak, sëü' very much alike; [9]k'ak, k'ak, the chirping of birds; COM., [10]k'ak, 'hó, opportunely, just right.

拾, Hsi. Read *sik,*; used for the coll. *k'ak,*: to collect, to gather, to pick up: [11]*k'ak, 'k'i,* to pick up; [12]*k'ak, ,ch'a p'woi'* to gather chips or shavings; [13]*k'ak, tioh, ,ngŭng,* to "pick up money"—get it luckily; [14]*k'ak, tioh, miăng'* to recover, as when near death; [15]*k'ak, 'k'i ,kiéng,* take it up and shoulder it; [16]*k'ak, ,i sioh, 'a 'ch'iu,* give him a lift, aid him (in his poverty); *k'ak, ,t'oi,* or [17]*k'ak, 'kiăng,* to perform the office of midwife.

K'ak,. A coll. word, like the last: to collect, as money, to get subscriptions; to take (a census); to assemble: *k'ak, hong'* to collect the quotas (for a village temple); *k'ak, hwoi'* to gather money for a (mutual-aid) club; *k'ak, ,ting 'k'eu,* to take the census of males and females; *k'ak, sioh, teng'* (or *,pong*), to assemble in a company.

掐, To pierce with the nails, to press or dig the nails into; to claw, to lacerate by clutching and clawing.

太, T'ai. Read *t'ai'*; sometimes used for the coll. *k'ak,*: a superlative, in excess, too, very, superfluous: [18]*k'ak, kwo'* over the proper amount or limit, excessive; [19]*k'ak, ,tong,* too long; *k'ak, chiéng'* very mean or low; *k'ak, siong' 'toi,* very much too short; *k'ak, 'chiong chong'* a very excellent man—one who is provident for his family; *k'ak, ,chiu mik,* excessively polite.

焀, Ho. Read *hak,* (fiery, flaming); used for the coll. *k'ak,*: to cook thoroughly, to boil soft: *k'ak, chëŭk,* to cook rice-gruel; *k'ak, ,mui lang'* to boil it very soft.

[illegible], K'o. To strike, to beat, to thump with the hand or foot: COLL., *k'ak, k'ak, kieu'* (or *'hiong*), sound of thumping.

1荳 花 梅 渴 渴 恰 起 18拾 着 肩 下 18太
蔻 8肉 止 6饑 8恰 10恰 12拾 着 命 16拾 手 過
2荳 蔻 渴 渴 似 好 柴 銀 15拾 伊 17拾 19太
蔻 4聞 5嘴 7止 9恰 11拾 配 14拾 起 一 仔 長

(312) K‘ang.

刋 K‘an. To cut, to carve, to pare; to engrave (blocks for printing); to erase or cut out from a block; to hew down, to fell: [1]꜀k‘ang k‘aik꜂ to engrave; [2]pok꜂ ꜀k‘ang, unmutilated; *met.*, imperishable, as the doctrines of a sage.

龕 ꜀K‘ang. Like a dragon; to contain, to hold, to receive; to excel, to overcome; a sound; a niche for tablets and images; a movable shrine: COM., [3]꜁pu sak꜂ ꜀k‘ang, an idol-shrine; [4]꜀kung ꜁pó ꜀k‘ang, an ancestral niche; COLL., ꜁k‘ang ꜀k‘ang, niches; ꜀k‘ang ‘kiăng or ꜁k‘ang ꜀k‘ang ‘kiăng, small shrines—sold as toys.

坑 ꜀K‘ang. A ditch, a trench, a hollow; a hole, cave, or pit, natural or artificial; a den, as for wild beasts; to excavate; to throw or fall into a pit, to involve, to ensnare: [5]꜀hung ꜀chü ꜀k‘ang ꜁ü, burned the books and threw the literati into pits—as the "First Emperor" did (B. C. 246); COM., [6]꜀sang ꜀k‘ang, a mountain-precipice or pit; [7]wang꜄ taung꜄ ꜀ch‘ing ꜀k‘ang, a deep abyss; COLL., [8]wang꜄ ꜁nëng ꜀k‘ang, a pit into which the bodies of beheaded criminals are thrown; [9]taung꜄ lóh꜂ ꜀k‘ang ‘lá, to fall into a pit.

堪 ꜀K‘ang. To sustain, to bear; to be able, adequate to, capable of; fit, worthy of: [10]꜀k‘ang ꜁ü, heaven and earth; [11]꜀k‘ang ꜁ü ꜀siéng ꜀seng, a geomancer; [12]꜀k‘ang eng꜄ able to bear a responsibility; COM., [13]pok꜂ ꜀k‘ang, unfit, unworthy.

嵁 ꜀K‘ang. Uneven, irregular; rocky, precipitous ledges: [14]꜀k‘ang ꜁ngang, a ledge, a cliff, a rugged summit.

戡 ꜀K‘ang. To stab, to pierce, to kill; to conquer, to subdue.

꜀*K‘ang*. A coll. word, as in ꜀*k‘ang* ꜀*k‘ang* ‘*hó*, just right, adequate, sufficient; ꜀*k‘ang* ꜀*k‘ang chiăng*꜄ ‘*lá* ‘*kong*, just as (I) was speaking (he came).

꜀*K‘ang*. A coll. word: to clutch, to clasp tightly: *tau*꜄ *kauk*, *k‘á*꜄ ꜀*i* ꜀*k‘ang* ‘*king* ‘*king tioh*꜂ clutch him tightly by the neck.

侃 ‘K‘ang. Plain, rigid, faithful, as in speaking; grave and unceremonious, as Confucious was in conversation: [15]‘k‘ang ‘k‘ang ꜁i ꜁tang, to speak perspicuously.

坎 埳 ‘K‘ang. A pit, a hole, a dangerous place; to dig a pit; to fall into snares or dangers; noise made in striking, a whack, a smack, a rap; also the noise of straining; one of the diagrams, belonging to water; a small vessel: COM., [16]‘k‘ang k‘ó꜄ "an uneven, rugged (path)"; *met.*, the difficulties of life; COLL., ‘*k‘ang seng*꜄ (or *t‘eng*꜄), the brainpan, the soft spot on the head of an infant.

欿 ‘K‘ang. Dissatisfied, discontented; sad, sorrowful. Read ꜀*t‘ang* or ꜀*k‘ang*: to covet, to desire.

砍 ‘K‘an. To chop, to fell, to cut down: COM., [17]‘k‘ang ‘tó, to fell (trees); ‘*k‘ang t‘iék*, ꜁*ü* ꜀*ná*, cuts iron like mud

1 刋刻 2 不刋 3 菩薩龕 4 公婆龕 5 焚書坑儒 6 山坑 7 萬丈深坑 8 萬仭坑 9 蕩落坑禮 10 堪輿 11 堪輿先生 12 堪任〇 13 不堪 14 嵁巖 15 侃侃而談 16 坎坷 17 砍倒

福州方言拼音字典

—i. e., is very sharp; COLL., 'k'ang tói' ˓tong, to cut in two; 'k'ang sioh˒ 'tó, to fell; to cleave, to cut down, as a thief or one's enemy.

'檻 K'an. A baluster, a lattice, the bars composing a lattice; a cage or den for wild beasts; to cage; a window: [1]k'ang 'k'ang, rumbling of carts; [2]k'ang ˓ch'iă, a cart with a felon's cage on it; COM., [3]k'ang ˓mwong, a window, a shutter; [4]k'ang ˓mwong ho' wooden sockets on which a window swings.

'艦 K'an. A war-junk, a man-of-war with strong bulwarks; a fortified house or inclosure on the deck: [5]chiéng' 'k'ang, a war-junk, a gun-boat.

'轗 K'an. Impeded, embarrassed: COM., [6]k'ang k'ó' uneven, rugged; met., bad luck, to lose money and be in trouble.

'K'ang. A coll. word, as in 'k'ang ˓peng, or 'k'ang ˓peng 'loi, bits of broken tiles; 'k'ang ˓peng tè' ground composed of broken tiles (mixed with earth).

看' K'an. Sometimes read ˓k'ang: to see, to behold, to view, to look at; to inspect, to examine; to regard, to esteem: COM., [7]k'ang' kiéng' to see, to notice; [8]téüng' k'ang' worth looking at; [9]k'ang' ˓ching, to see the true or real (state of); [10]k'ang' 'ma and [11]k'ang' kieu' show-horses and show-sedans, as in idol processions; [13]k'ang' p'wo' to serve as night-watchman of a ward; [13]k'ang' miăng' ˓kiĕng siong' to practice both fortune-telling and physiognomy; [14]k'ang' mah˒ to feel the pulse; [15]k'ang' ˓k'ing, to disesteem; [16]k'ang' 'kwang or ('siu), to guard, to keep; k'ang' p'ó' to penetrate; to to discover (the folly of); COLL., k'ang' ˓mó, look! see! attend! [17]k'ang' 'chwi, "look at the water"; met., to spy out beforehand, as thieves do; [18]k'ang' ˓nĕng tai' to treat persons with partiality; k'ang' má' ch'ok, can't see through or understand it; [19]k'ang' ˓t'iéng siăh˒ pwong' to look at Heaven and eat rice, —i. e., gain an honest living; k'ang' ng' siong' 'ngang, to regard with disfavor, to despise, as small gains.

瞯' K'an. To view, to observe narrowly, to watch one furtively. Read ˓hang: spots in the eyes, an eye with much white in it; the whites of the eyes showing in convulsions.

瞰' 闞' K'an. Also read 'hang: to spy, to glance at, to notice; to come down to examine; to hope for, to expect: the 2d read 'hang, means a tiger's roar, or an angry tone.

勘' K'an. Also read 'k'ang: to compare, to examine, to investigate; to judge, or ascertain facts, by going to the place; diligent: [20]k'ang' cheng' to rectify, to straighten; COM., [21]k'ang' ngiéng' to hold an inquest; tak˒ k'ang' to go and investigate.

[1]檻檻 [2]檻車 [3]檻門 [4]檻門戶 [5]戰艦 [6]轗軻 [7]看見 [8]中看 [9]看真 [10]看馬 [11]看轎 [12]看舖 [13]看命兼相 [14]看脈 [15]看輕 [16]看管 [17]看水 [18]看人待 [19]看天食飯 [20]勘正 [21]勘驗

磡' K'an. A cliff, a beetling crag; the covert under a projecting cliff.

(313) K'au.

꜀鬮 ꜀閹 Chiu. Read ꜀k'iu in the dictionaries: lots made of paper or wood; a lot, a ballot; to draw lots or tickets: [1]꜀k'au ꜀hung, to divide, as by the lot; COM., [2]꜀k'au ꜀chü, a record of the division of property; [3]꜀niéng ꜀k'au (coll. pek꜁ ꜀k'au), to draw lots; COLL., [4]꜀k'au chó' sioh꜁ ꜀ki, to prepare lots (for drawing).

꜀鏂 K'ou. Read ꜀eu; used in the Paik꜁ ꜀Ing for the coll. ꜀k'au: to dig, or scrape out, to rake or scrape up with the hand: [5]꜀k'au ꜀pa, an opium-pipe scraper.

꜀K'au. A coll. word: to mix, to mingle; confused, mixed, miscellaneous; *met.*, troublesome, difficult; to quarrel: *꜀k'au naung'* (or *laung'*), to mix confusedly, a medley; *꜀k'au tek꜁ ꜂chieu*, mixed in (too) little; *꜀k'au sioh꜁ ꜀toi*, mix together; *꜀k'au tah꜁*, to lap, to lay over, to "break the joints," as in laying courses of bricks; *so' mĕk꜁ ꜀k'au ꜀ma*, the accounts are confused.

꜀K'au. A coll. word: difficult, troublesome, involved, perplexing; quarrelsome, contending with; also to tack a boat, to put about: *꜀k'au k'e'* troublesome; to contend with; *꜀k'au hiong'* to tack ship; *met.*, to have a difficulty or quarrel with.

꜂口 K'ou. Read ꜂k'eu; coll. ꜂k'au: a mouth, entrance, opening; occurs in the terms for vows or imprecations before the gods: [6]꜀ké ꜂k'au, entrance to the street; [7]꜂hai ꜂k'au, passage to the sea; [8]꜀toi ꜂k'au, a hole, or small door, at the back of a prison (for removing dead prisoners); [9]꜀á ꜂k'au, the top of a shoe; [10]꜂k'au ꜀kiéng, the mouth, entrance; [11]꜂ch'iáng ꜂k'au, or [12]ha' ꜂k'au, to invoke curses (on an enemy); [13]꜂k'au ngwong' imprecation and vow; [14]꜀tó kau' ch'oi' ꜂k'au po' ꜀mó siáh꜁ (food) brought to the mouth and still not eat it; *met.*, a matter failing when near completion.

K'au'. A coll. word: a tone of displeasure, scolding, chiding: *k'au' sioh꜁ hiok꜁* to give a scolding, to berate, as mischievous children.

(314) K'auk.

壑꜁ K'o. A ditch, a pit; a fosse, a city-ditch; a valley, a gully, the bed of a torrent: [15]*tai' k'auk꜁* the ocean; [16]*꜀ngui ꜀ngang chiok꜁ k'auk꜁*, dangerous precipices and rugged gulches; COM., [17]*chwi k'auk꜁* or [18]*꜀kau k'auk꜁*, a small collection of water, a plash, a puddle.

涸꜁ K'o. Dry, dried up, exhausted: COLL., [19]*k'auk꜁ k'auk꜁ ꜀ta*, thoroughly dried; dry, as rice that has not been watered to increase the bulk.

榷꜁ Ch'io. A plank or piece of timber over a stream, a drawbridge where toll is paid; a species of Hovenia.

[1]鬮分 [2]鬮書 [3]捻鬮 [4]鬮做一其 [5]鏂爬 [6]街口 [7]海口 [8]堆口 [9]鞋口 [10]口墘 [11]請口 [12]下口 [13]口愿 [14]掏至嘴口伓毛食 [15]大壑 [16]危巖絕壑 [17]水壑 [18]溝壑 [19]涸涸乾

愨, K'o. To revere, to respect; awe, veneration; careful, attentive, vigilant, as one serving in a temple: [1]*k'auk*, *'siu*, to keep reverently.

慤, K'o. Like the last: careful, attentive; sincere, guileless; true, good-hearted, upright: [2]*ngwong'* *k'auk*, careful, diligent.

確, Ch'io. Hard, solid, firm; resolute, decided; truthful, sincere; really, indeed, certainly: [3]*pok*, *k'auk*, doubtful; COM., [4]*k'auk*, *tyong*, surely; [5]*tek*, *k'auk*, faithful; [6]*k'auk*, *sik*, or *k'auk*, *ching*, true, real, verily; COLL., [7]*k'auk*, *o'* *ping'* *këü'* truly there's evidence.

硞, Ch'i. Hard, stony; wearied, fagged out: *k'auk*, *k'auk*, *käng* *niëng*, wearied with labor the whole year.

磕 磕, K'o. Read *k'ai'*; coll. *k'auk*,: the clattering sound of stones; to "knock the head" before superiors; to thump, to knock: [8]*k'auk*, *t'au*, the *kotow* ceremony; [9]*k'auk*, *k'auk*, *su*, very crisp, as crust or cake; [10]*k'auk*, *á* *t'au*, "knock (your head) on (my) shoe-toes,"—*scil.*, and I can let you off—said contemptuously to an insolvent debtor; *k'auk*, *t'au p'ăh*, *ch'iéng*, to knock the head, kneeling on one knee.

殼 壳, K'o. The skin or covering of fruits or eggs; shell or scale of mollusks, snakes, or chrysalides; a bark, crust, or covering; an old hollow tree: in the coll. read *k'aük*, q. v.: COM., [11]*'chi* *k'auk*, the seeds of the *Hovenia dulcis*—used medicinally.

窟, Ch'ü. A hole in the ground, a receptacle, a chamber; burrows, caves in which the ancients dwelt: [12]*k'auk*, *sek*, an underground chamber; [13]*kieu t'o'* *sang* *k'auk*, a cunning rabbit has three holes.

郝, Ho. Name of a village in Tayuen prefecture, Shansi; a surname. Read *sek*, as in *sek*, *sek*, to plow, to till.

(315) K'aung.

伉', K'ang. Interchanged with the next: to oppose, inimical to; to mate, to match; to compare with; straight, direct: [14]*k'aung'* *lá'* a pair, husband and wife.

抗', K'ang. To lift, to raise with the hand; to obstruct, to oppose, to resist, to withstand; to screen, to shield; to save, to rescue: [15]*k'aung'* *ui*, to rebel against; COM., [16]*k'aung'* *këü'* to oppose, to resist; to refuse, as to pay taxes.

炕', K'ang. A wide couch or sofa, a raised sitting place, a divan; a sleeping place of brick, warmed underneath —used in the north: [17]*'hwo* *k'aung'* a fire-warmed bed; COM., [18]*k'aung'* *ch'ong*, a couch, a settee

1 愨守 2 愿慤 3 不確 4 確然 5 的確 6 確實 7 確有憑據 8 磕頭 9 磕磕酥 10 磕鞋頭 11 枳殼 12 窟室 13 狡兎三窟 14 伉儷 15 抗違 16 抗拒 17 火炕 18 炕床 ○

k‘aung’ ꜀ch‘ong tóh꜆ and *k‘aung’ ꜀ch‘ong ‘ki*, long and short stands set on a divan.

炕’ K‘ang. To roast, to broil; to dry, to toast; dry, dried up, a drought; to exterminate: *k‘aung’ ꜀ch‘ong*, a bed of brick, heated underneath; *k‘aung’ ‘hwo*, to dry before the fire; coals, embers.

困’ K‘uên. A house in ruins; confined, cramped, cribbed, hampered; weary, worn out, jaded; distressed, disheartened; poor, destitute, beggared; needy, in want; to weary, to weaken, to hinder or hamper influentially; addicted to, enslaved by; sorry, afflicted, mourning for; the 47th diagram: [1]*꜀kŭng k‘aung’* or *k‘aung’ ꜀kŭng*, impoverished, beggared; [2]*k‘aung’ hwok꜆* destitute, out of funds; [3]*pok꜆ ꜀ui‘chiu k‘aung’* not addicted to liquor; COM., [4]*k‘aung’ kwong’* jaded; [5]*k‘aung’ ‘k‘u*, distressed by want.

K‘aung’. A coll. word: to sleep, asleep: *k‘ó’ k‘aung’* to go to bed; *k‘aung’ tioh꜆* asleep; *k‘aung’ lóh꜆ ꜀ming*, gone to sleep, fast asleep; *k‘aung’ ꜀ch‘ing ‘ch‘ang*, to awake from sleep; *k‘aung’ tek꜆ ꜀ti*, to go late to bed; *k‘aung’ piăh꜆ ‘tié*, to sleep (on the side) next to the wall.

K‘aung’. A coll. word: to lay by, to store away: *k‘aung’ mek꜆* or *k‘aung’ ‘king ‘king*, to store away securely; *k‘aung’ ‘chu*, "you hide the obstruction"—you are too modest, as said politely to one declining wine, &c.; *k‘aung’ ꜀sing ꜀piéng*, to carry on the person.

K‘aung’. A coll. word: to knock, to thump heavily: *k‘aung’ p‘wai’* broken by a heavy thump; *tói’ k‘aung’* knocked heavily together.

(316) K‘e.

氣’ 气’ Ch‘i. The primordial substance from which all things emanate; vapor, exhalation, steam, fume; ether, air, halo; the breath; vital fluid, life, nervous principle which imparts substance; the spirit, temper, or feelings of men and things; the animal spirits; air, aspect, manner, bearing; influence, attraction; vehemence, courage, daring; an apparition; a semi-monthly term: COM., [6]*꜀t‘iéng k‘e’* the weather; [7]*k‘e’ sek꜆*, breathing, respiration; [8]*k‘e’ e’* vapor, fumes; flavor of; [9]*sek꜆ k‘e’* (coll. *nong’ k‘e’*), dampness; [10]*k‘e’ haik꜆*, robustness; [11]*k‘e’ saik꜆*, color, complexion; [12]*no’ k‘e’* anger; [13]*k‘e’ ꜀hü*, the system weak or debilitated; [14]*‘hó ong’ k‘e’* good luck; [15]*k‘e’ ‘kwong*, the windpipe; [16]*che’ k‘e’* energy, nerve; [17]*k‘e’ chiok꜆* (coll. *k‘e’ taung’*), dead; [18]*k‘e’ ch‘iong’* or *k‘e’ p‘aĕk꜆*, air, bearing; [19]*k‘e’ so’* luck, fate; [20]*k‘e’ ‘ü ꜀hiong ꜀ngong*, a bold, commanding presence; COLL., *ch‘au’ ꜀t‘u k‘e’* a foul, earthy scent, as after rain; *seu’ k‘e’* to get angry; *k‘e’ tĕük꜆*, or *k‘e’ ng’ song’* labored breathing; *k‘e’ piék꜆*, stifled, suffocated; *k‘e’ k‘e’* an angry appearance; *k‘e’ ‘si*, angry to death!

餼’ Ch‘i. An offering of live animals; grains, fruits, meats offered in sacrifice; a formal entertainment; [21]*sik꜆ ‘ling k‘e’* a stipend paid to *siutsai*.

1 窮困 2 困乏 3 不爲酒困 4 困倦 5 困苦 6 天氣 7 氣息 8 氣味 9 濕氣 10 氣血 11 氣色 12 怒氣 13 氣虛 14 好運氣 15 氣管 16 志氣 17 氣絶 18 氣象 19 氣數 20 氣宇軒昂 21 食廩餼

器' **噐**' Ch'i. A vessel, a vase, a dish; a tool, implement, instrument, utensil; capacity, ability; body, substance, as opposed to form or qualities: COM., [1]*k'e' kēü'* or [2]*k'e' ĕüng'* utensils, implements; [3]*'sieu k'e'* or *k'e' 'sieu,* mean, little-minded; close, stingy; [4]*ˏchü k'e'* porcelain-ware; [5]*ˏngüng k'e'* silver ornaments (for the head).

棄' Ch'hi. To reject, to cast off; to relinquish, to abandon; to refuse, to discard: [6]*ˏp'au k'e'* to throw away, to reject; COM., [7]*k'e' siē'* dead; [8]*k'e' ˏhiéng,* to dislike; [9]*k'e' ngiĕkˌ* to sell real estate; [10]*yéng' k'e'* to loathe; [11]*k'e' ˏch'ă 't'ung ch'iĕk,* to hate the wife and love the concubine; [12]*k'e' ˏsiă ˏkwi cheng'* "reject the corrupt and return to the correct"—to reform.

K'e'. A coll. euphonic prefix, as in *k'e' k'a'* to drive, as a stake; *k'e' k'iĕ'* (or *k'ŏ'*) to set upright.

柿' Hsi. Read *sëü'* in the dictionaries: the persimmon, Diospyros, or China-fig: COM., [13]*k'e' ˏwong,* a small dried persimmon (from Shantung); [14]*k'e' 'chŏ,* a date-like persimmon without pits; COLL. [15]*ˏkau k'e'* the monkey-persimmon—a wild, sour kind; [16]*k'e' 'piăng* persimmon-cakes—pressed and dried; [17]*ˏkau k'e' o' hokˌ* the monkey-persimmon has (large) pits; *met.,* said of a shrewd boy.

K'e'. A coll. euphonic prefix, as in *k'e' k'iĕ'* to stand, to rise and stand erect.

(317) K'ĕ.

ˏK'ĕ. A coll. word; the same as *ˏk'ü:* dull, stupid, unapt: *'yă ˏk'ĕ,* or *ˏk'ĕ tekˌ kikˌ* extremely dull.

(318) K'eh.

噱ˌ Ch'i. Read *k'iokˌ;* used in the *Paik, ˏIng* for the coll. *k'ehˌ:* to laugh immoderately: also used for *k'ihˌ* q.v.: *k'ehˌ siohˌ ˏsiăng,* a suppressed laugh; *k'ehˌ k'ehˌ ch'ieu'* to giggle, to titter.

K'ehˌ. A coll. euphonic prefix, as in *k'ehˌ k'wohˌ* crooked; *ˏing ˏwang k'ehˌ k'wohˌ* winding, as a path; *met.,* indirect, circumlocutory.

(319) K'ĕh.

K'ĕhˌ. A coll. word: sound made in clearing the throat; to heave or vomit slightly: *k'ĕhˌ ch'okˌ ˏli,* to raise and spit out, as phlegm; *k'ĕhˌ siohˌ ˏsiăng,* to clear the throat.

(320) K'ek.

泣ˌ Ch'i. To weep, to shed tears: [18]*k'okˌ k'ekˌ* to cry and sob; [19]*k'ekˌ hiĕkˌ* to weep blood—written on funeral cards.

湆ˌ Ch'i. Damp, moist, muddy: [20]*ekˌ k'ekˌ* dark and damp.

綌ˌ Ch'i. A sort of coarse hempen fabric, made of the Dolichos; anciently used for towels and kerchiefs: [21]*ˏhi k'ekˌ* fine and coarse hempen fabrics.

---

[1]器具 [2]器用 [3]小器 [4]磁器 [5]銀器 [6]抛棄 [7]棄世 [8]棄嫌 [9]棄業 [10]厭棄 [11]棄妻寵妾 [12]棄邪歸正 [13]柿丸 [14]柿棗 [15]猴柿 [16]柿餅 [17]猴柿有核 [18]哭泣 [19]泣血 [20]浥湆 [21]絺綌

隙, 隟, Ch'i. A hole or fissure in a wall; a crack, a chink, a crevice; a gap, an interstice; an interval of time, leisure; a pretext, an occasion or opening for variance: [1]*'k'ek, wong'* a feud, a quarrel; [2]*'kang' k'ek*, an interval: COM., [3]*'ₛsing k'ek*, to seek pretexts for a quarrel; [4]*'hëüng' k'ek*, an occasion for variance; COLL., [5]*'u' k'ek*, to have a quarrel with one.

隲, Tsü. Read *chek*, in the dictionaries: a stallion; to mount; to ascend; to raise, to elevate, to promote; to determine, to settle: [6]*'ₛing k'ek*, a benevolent act done secretly.

闃, Hsui. Also read *hek*, and *k'ik*,: still, as an unoccupied house; quiet, silent; alone, solitary: [7]*k'ek, chik*, still, quiet.

喫, Ch'i. Read *ngek*,; coll. *k'ek*,: to bear, to suffer, to endure: [8]*mã' k'ek, tek, k'ŏ'* can't endure it, unbearable; [9]*k'ek, ₛk'wi*, distress, suffering, in pain; [10]*mã' k'ek, tek*, slightly ill, indisposed; [11]*k'ek, chik*, hasty, irritable.

K'ek,. A coll. euphonic prefix, as in *k'ek, k'ak*, to pick up; *k'ek, k'iăk*, to pinch, to compress, as between two boards; to press, as tobacco, etc.

K'ek,. A coll. word, denoting cause, manner, or instrument; with, by, through; to use, to employ: the same as *hek*, q. v.: *k'ek, ₛchui*, take or use this (for the purpose); *k'ek, 'chiu 'ch'iăng ₛi*, invite him to a feast; *k'ek, nioh, wai'* take or use how much?

(331) K'eng.

牽, ₛCh'ien. To pull, to drag; to lead, as an ox by a cord; to guide, to induce, to influence, as the mind of another; to connect with, to deduce from; dragged into, held, as in suspense: used for the coll. *ₛk'eng*, q. v.: [12]*ₛk'eng 'ₛdiéng*, to connect, to implicate; COM., [13]*ₛk'eng 'ch'iu*, to take hold of hands; to grasp, to hold by, as a rope: [14]*ₛk'eng tik*, to pull straight; [15]*ₛk'eng ₛsi*, to stretch silk thread (in twisting); to make webs, as spiders; [16]*ₛk'eng ₛngu kwo' ₛlang*, lead an ox from the stall; COLL., [17]*ₛk'eng pek*, to pull along; [18]*ₛk'eng ₛsi ₛpeng*, the 120th radical.

牼, ₛK'ĕng. The shank bone of an ox: [19]*Song' ₛk'eng*, name of a person who lived in the time of Mencius.

莖, ₛChing. Read *ₛheng* in the dictionaries: the culm or stalk of herbs and shrubs; a stem, a twig; the hilt of a sword.

硜, ₛChing. The dull, heavy sound of stones, hard stones striking together; *ₛk'eng ₛk'eng*, jingling of stones; also the appearance of a mean, worthless man.

鏗, ₛChien. A ringing, metallic sound; to knock, to strike against, as sounding stones or glass: used for *ₛk'iăng*, *'k'iăng*, and *ₛk'iăng* in the coll. q. v.: *ₛk'eng ₛch'iong*, the jin-

---

1 隙怨 2 間隙 3 尋隙 4 釁隙 5 有隙 6 陰隲 7 闃寂 8 買喫的去 9 喫虧 10 賣喫的 ○ 11 喫疾 12 牽連 13 牽手 14 牽直 15 牽絲過欄 16 牽牛 17 牽拔 18 牽絲爿 ○ 19 宋牼 ○

gling of bangles; *꜀Chiêng ꜁k'eng*, a man who reached the fabulous age of 767 years.

꜂犬 Ch'üan A dog; the 94th radical: [1]*'k'eng 'ma ꜀chi pó'* humble service to requite favors; COM., [2]*'k'eng ꜀wo* (coll. *'k'eng seu'*), a dog's kennel; [3]*'k'eng ꜀sing ꜀kang*, (has) a dog's heart; [4]*'k'eng tak꜇ tai'* dog treading a pestle, as taught by beggars to do; [5]*꜀tiêng 'k'eng*, a mad dog; COLL. [6]*'k'eng kaëk*, and [7]*'keng 'mó*, bull and bitch; [8]*'k'eng 'kiăng*, dogs; [9]*'k'eng ꜀t'au ꜀li*, the dog-head pear—a hard species; [10]*'k'eng ꜀t'ong 'kiăng*, a full-grown pup; [11]*'k'eng ꜀t'au ngwong'* vow to the dog-headed god—as in seeking his aid against an enemy; *꜀k'eng 'k'eng lóh꜇ ꜀t'ong*, (like) dragging a dog into hot water—*scil.*, to persuade him to do such a thing; *'k'eng meng' kié' ꜀sang ꜀mó*, a dog's face soon grows hair; *met.*, said of those who soon settle their quarrels.

꜂畎 ꜂畂 Ch'üan. A ditch or channel between fields; a rill, a rivulet; to flow down; *met.*, diffused, as good instruction: [12]*'k'eng 'meu*, plats divided by rills.

꜂肯 ꜂肎 K'ĕn. To be willing, to assent, acquiescing; to allow, to permit: in the coll. read *'k'ing*, q. v.: [13]*pok꜇ 'k'eng*, unwilling, to refuse; [14]*'k'i 'k'eng*, how consent to?—i. e., unwilling. Read *'k'ai*: the attachment of the muscles to the bones.

慶꜄ Ch'ing. To congratulate, to bless, to approach with congratulatory presents or words; good, excellent; happy, blessed; path of rectitude, right principles; an initial particle, happily: COM., [15]*k'eng' hó'* to congratulate; [16]*꜁ping ꜀ang kek꜇ k'eng'* peaceful, lucky, and blessed; [17]*k'eng' 'siong ꜁ngwong ꜀sieu*, the joyous *꜁ngwong ꜀sieu* term (1st moon 11-15 days)—words inscribed on lanterns.

撳꜄ Ch'ing. To lay the hand on; to press down, to hold, to keep by a firm pressure.

㷫꜄ Ch'ing. To dry by a fire, to toast or roast; dried thoroughly.

磬꜄ Ch'ing. Ringing stones of prehnite or glass hung on frames—they are of various kinds; a musical instrument with a right angle, like a carpenter's square; hung up, suspended; to relax the reins: COM. [18]*k'eng' ꜀ting*, a lantern shaped like a *k'eng'*; *k'eng' ꜁pá*, a *k'eng'*-shaped ornament—worn by women and children; COLL. *k'eng' k'eng'* projecting, prominent, as one's forehead.

罄꜄ 磬꜄ Ch'ing. Formerly used for the last: an empty vessel; to exhaust, empty, exhausted; all, entirely; firm, strict: COM., *k'eng' ꜀k'ung*, empty, entirely gone or spent.

K'eng'. A coll. euphonic prefix, as in *k'eng' k'iăng'*, to nod the head; *k'eng' k'ang'* to look at; *k'eng' k'aung'* to store away.

---

[1]犬馬之報 [2]犬窩 [3]犬心肝 [4]犬踏碓 [5]癲犬 [6]犬公 [7]犬母 [8]犬仔 [9]犬頭梨 [10]犬豚仔 [11]犬頭願 [12]畎畝○ [13]不肯 [14]豈肯 [15]慶賀 [16]平安吉慶 [17]慶賞元宵 [18]磬燈

牽 ꜂Ch'ien. Read ꜀k'eng; used for the coll. ꜀k'eng: to clutch, to grasp and pull: ꜀k'eng 'king (or taing^{3}), to clutch tightly; móh$_{2}$ ꜀k'eng, don't clutch (so)! ꜀k'eng ꜀k'eng 'tiong, to grasp and pull about.

K'eng^{3}. A coll. euphonic prefix, as in k'eng^{3} k'iăng^{3} to shut together, as the leaves of a door; to gather together; to do in common; k'eng^{3} k'aung^{3} to strike against, to impinge.

(322) K'ĕng.

空 ꜀K'ung. Read ꜀k'ung; coll. ꜀k'ĕng: empty, void, vacant; hollow; in vain, vainly, to no purpose: [1]꜀k'ĕng ꜀k'ĕng, empty; in vain; [2]꜀k'ĕng tĕ^{2} vacant ground; [3]꜀k'ĕng 'ch'iu, empty-handed; [4]꜀k'ĕng ꜀lĕng, a hole; [5]꜀k'ĕng ꜀ngieu, vainly, uselessly; [6]꜀k'ĕng p'ang^{3} or ꜀k'ĕng p'ang^{3} ꜀sing, hollow; ꜀k'ĕng p'ang^{3} k'aĕk, an empty shell; *met.*, a weak constitution (though the frame seems robust); [7]꜀k'ĕng ꜀hwang 'hi, premature joy; ꜀k'ĕng ꜀lau ꜀lau, very empty, destitute; [8]꜀k'ĕng pok, seu^{2} ꜀kung ꜀t'au, "receive (a blow of) the fist on an empty stomach"—to suffer an unjust imputation.

꜀*K'ĕng*. A coll. word: a dry cough, a hacking: ꜀k'ĕng 'k'ĕng sau^{3} (same as in k'aĕng^{3}), to hack; sioh$_{2}$ nik$_{2}$ ꜀k'ĕng kau^{3} ang^{3} (or wang^{3}), to hack all the day long.

(323) K'eu.

彄 ꜀Ch'ü. A notch or catch at the end of a bow, in which the string is fastened; a ring.

摳 ꜀Ch'ü. Also read ꜀ch'eu: to lift up the dress, as in ascending a flight of steps; to feel for and take with the hand: ꜀k'eu ꜀i, to lift up the skirts.

口 'K'ou. The mouth; a door, an entrance or opening, a narrow passage into; a pass in the Great Wall; speech, utterance; a classifier of persons, swords, fill of pipes, draught of drinks, pans, betel-nuts in leaves, &c.; to say, to reiterate: in the coll. read 'k'au and ꜀k'eu, q. v.: [9]'ho^{2} 'k'eu, population: [10]꜀ing 'k'eu, persons, a family; COM., [11]'k'eu ꜀chai, ability in speaking, eloquence: [12]'k'eu kaĕk, good utterance, glibness; [13]'k'eu e^{3} (or k'e^{3}), the meaning of what one says; [14]'k'eu e^{2} taste, flavor; [15]'k'eu ꜀kŭng, verbal evidence, testimony; [16]'k'eu ꜀liong, provisions, rations; [17]'k'eu se^{2} ꜀sing ꜀hi, to speak hypocritically; [18]'k'eu ꜀ing (or 'ngü), dialect, tongue; [19]'k'eu ngwong^{2} wish, vow and imprecation, as against an enemy; [20]'k'eu siok$_{2}$ ꜀leng ꜀hwa, to utter words like lilies—i. e. sensible and complete; COLL., móh$_{2}$ 'k'eu siĕk$_{2}$ don't wrangle; 'tiăng sioh$_{2}$ 'k'eu, one cooking-pan; ꜀ping ꜀long sioh$_{2}$ 'k'eu, one piece of betelnut, as prepared for eating.

咎 Chiu^{3}. A fault, defect, error; crime, wickedness; a judgment, providential calamity; to blame, to reprehend, to criminate: ong^{3} ꜀hiu k'eu^{3} to consult (fortune-tellers) about luck; COLL., k'eu^{3} ꜀kwi tioh$_{2}$ ꜀i, the blame is chargeable on him.

---

[1] 空空 [2] 空地 [3] 空手 [4] 空籠 [5] 空喬 [6] 空冇 [7] 空歡喜 [8] 空腹受拳頭 [9] 戶口 [10] 人口 [11] 口才 [12] 口角 [13] 口意 [14] 口味 [15] 口供 [16] 口糧 [17] 口是心非 [18] 口音 [19] 口願 [20] 口說蓮花

偺' Chiu. Read 'kiu in the dictionaries; also read k'eu²: to destroy, to overthrow, to demolish; one says also used for I, myself.

疚' Chiu. This and next read keu' in the dictionaries: a chronic disease, protracted illness; grieved, dolorous (in connection with a negative), as in nói² ˏsing pok, k'eu' not grieved in mind about it—i. e. conscious of innocence.

廄' Chiu. A stable, a stall where horses are kept; the common term is 'ma ˏpung.

K'eu'. A coll. word: stiff, as thick, or well glazed paper, starched clothes, &c.; also stiff, tenacious, not soft, as rice cooked dry: má² k'eu' not stiff, limber; soft; k'eu' taung' stiff; tenacious; ˏi ˏsiong k'eu' k'eu' clothes (starched) stiff.

口 K'ou. Read 'k'eu; used for the coll. ˏk'eu, a ¹'sau' 'ngü, or coined word, meaning to eat: ²ˏk'eu 'pa, to eat till satisfied; ³ˏk'eu má² k'ó' can't eat it all up.

柩² Chiu. A corpse laid in a coffin; a coffin with the body in it: ⁴k'eu² ˏch'iâ, a hearse; ⁵song² k'eu² to accompany a funeral; com., ⁶ˏling k'eu² the encoffined corpse.

桕² Chiu. Read keu² in the dictionaries; in the coll. read kĕüng² q. v.: the tallow tree (Stillingia sebifera).

臼² Chiu. A mortar for pounding things, anciently a mere hole in the ground, afterwards made of wood or stone; to pound in a mortar: in the coll. read k'ó² q. v.: ⁷k'eu² 't'ü, mortar and pestle.

(324) K'ĕü.

去' Ch'ü. To go away, to depart; to separate, to part from, to become distinct; to go out, from, or through; to proceed, to advance, to pass on in a regular course; past, gone, former; the 3rd and 7th tones of the Foochow dialect; as a suffix, denotes the completion of the action in a preceding verb: also read 'k'ü; in the coll. read k'ó' q. v.: ⁸k'ĕü' sié' dead; ⁹kwo' k'ĕü' to go by, to pass away; ¹⁰k'ĕü' ˏniéng, last year; com., ¹¹siong² k'ĕü' and ¹²ha² k'ĕü' the 3rd and 7th tones, for which ¹³k'ĕü' ˏsiâng is the common term.

(325) K'ĕük.

乞, Ch'i. To beg, to ask alms; to request, to intreat, to implore: in the coll. to give, to bestow; also a sign of the passive, to let, to allow, to permit, to suffer: ¹⁴k'ĕük, sĕü' to beg one to give; ¹⁵huk, k'ĕük, to beg humbly; com., ¹⁶ˏkiu k'ĕük, to beg; ¹⁷k'ĕük, kai' (coll. k'ĕük, siâh,), a beggar; COLL., ¹⁸k'ĕük, 'ngwai, give it to me; ¹⁹k'ĕük, 'yong 'kiâng, a son given, or bought, to be reared (in one's family); ²⁰k'ĕük, siâh, ˏt'au, the chief or "king" of the beggars; k'ĕük, siâh, ng² kwo' lang² ˏch'a ˏkio, (even) a beggar will not cross a rotten wooden bridge; met., said of life which must not be exposed to peril; ²¹k'ĕük, ˏi p'ah, beaten by him; k'ĕük, ˏnĕng 'kong, talked about by people.

¹唒語 ²口飽 ³口賣去○ ⁴柩車 ⁵送柩 ⁶靈柩 ⁷臼杵 ⁸去世 ⁹過去 ¹⁰去年 ¹¹上去 ¹²下去 ¹³去聲 ¹⁴乞賜 ¹⁵伏乞 ¹⁶求乞 ¹⁷乞丐 ¹⁸乞我 ¹⁹乞養 仔 ²⁰乞食頭 ²¹乞伊拍○

曲, Ch'ü. Crooked, bent, carved, distorted; devious, tortuous, meandering; to wrong, to oppress; depraved, false, scheming; songs, ditties, sonnets; a silkworm tray: in the coll. read *k'wok*, q. v.: [1]*'k'ëük, tik,* crooked and straight, the right and wrong; [2]*,sü k'ëük,* tricky, underhand; [3]*k'ok, k'ëük,* crooked, bent; oppressed, kept in a low position; COM., [4]*'wi k'ëük,* grief, grievance; [5]*k'ëük, chiek,* "crooks and bends": *met.,* the arts and methods of trade; the reasons, exciting causes, as of a quarrel.

麴, 麯, Ch'ü. Read *këük,* in the dictionaries; dried ferment, leaven, barm: COM., [6]*k'ëük, ,oeong,* balls of leaven; [7]*,sing k'ëük,* a noted medicine for colds, etc., (from Chinchew); COLL., [8]*,ëng k'ëük,* a sort of yeasty preparation, used as a red dye.

(326) K'ëüng.

謽' Ch'iung. To talk, to question; verbose, prolix: used in the coll. for utterance, voice; drawl in singing: COLL., [9]*,tong k'ëüng'* drawling; [10]*'hó k'ëüng'* good utterance, excellent singing.

桕² Chiu. Read *k'eu²; coll. k'ëüng²:* the tallow tree, called [11]*k'ëüng² ch'eu':* [12]*k'ëüng² 'chi,* seeds of the tallow tree, from which the oil is expressed; [13]*k'ëüng² ,iu,* tallow-tree oil.

虹² Kang. Read *,hung;* used for coll. *k'ëüng²:* the rainbow: [14]*k'ëüng² tai'* a rainbow; [15]*'ngu saik, k'ëüng²* the five-colored bow; *k'ëüng² sioh, ,teu* (or *,hong*), one rainbow; *wak, sioh, k'ëüng²* to give a scratch with one's nails.

(327) K'i.

,欺 Ch'i. To impose upon, to cheat, to deceive; to deceive one's self; to fail in, to disappoint another; to ridicule, to revile, to upbraid: COM., [16]*,k'i ho²* to impose upon, to abuse; [17]*,k'i ,mwang,* or *,k'i p'iëng'* to cheat; [18]*,k'i ,sing,* to insult the gods; [19]*,k'i ,ping, tëüng² po'* to abuse the poor and respect the rich; [20]*,k'i ,sing,* self-deluded; to slight, to fail in (an engagement); COLL., *,k'i tek, 'tó,* to oppress or crush one; *,k'i lik,* to insult, to abuse; *,k'i ho² 'niong* (or *nuëng²*), to impose on the weak.

,僛 Ch'i. Tipsy, about to fall; to sport or reel like a sot; *,k'i ,k'i,* reeling, staggering.

,崎 Ch'i. Steep, dangerous, rugged, as mountain-paths; precipices, dangerous defiles: used for the coll. *k'ié'* q.: v. COM., *,k'i ,k'ü,* uneven, rugged; COLL., *,k'i ,k'i k'ieu² k'ieu²,* irregular, uneven, as a pavement.

,攲 ,敧 Ch'i. Inclined, not straight or upright, lateral; to take with nippers: [21]*,k'i k'e'* vessels easily upset; COM., [22]*,k'i ,sià* (coll. *k'i ,peng*), inclining; COLL., *,k'a ,lung ,k'i,* oblique, tilted, top-

---

[1]曲直 [2]私曲 [3]屈曲 [4]委曲 [5]曲折 [6]麴丸 [7]神麴 [8]紅麴 [9]長謽 [10]好謽 [11]桕椇 [12]桕子 [13]桕油 [14]虹帶 [15]五色虹〇 [16]欺負 [17]欺瞞 [18]欺神 [19]欺貧重富 [20]欺心 [21]攲器 [22]攲斜

pling; *,k'i 'tó ,peng*, or *,k'i sioh, ,peng*, inclined to one side; *met.*, partial; *,k'i ,k'i kwoi'* a knot or tuft of hair on a girl's head; *,k'i ,k'i k'woh, k'woh*, uneven and crooked, as roads.

踦 ,Ch'i. To stand on one foot; incomplete, defective; one, single, not double: *,k'i chiăh*, a single one; COLL., *,k'i ,k'i ,k'ieu ,k'ieu*, one foot lifted up, (to sit) cross-legged.

,K'i. A coll. euphonic prefix, as in *,k'i ,k'wi*, to open (doors); *,k'i ,k'u*, to bind with hoops, to hoop; *,k'i ,k'au*, to blend, to mix.

豈 'Ch'i. How! what! a particle implying a strong negative; with a negative, makes a strong affirmation; to desire; to advance, to ascend; to return victorious: also read *'k'ai*, q. v.: COM., [1]*'k'i pok, se'* how is it not! [2]*'k'i pok, ,ti*, how do I not know it! [3]*'k'i 'kang*, how dare!—a polite reply to a compliment; [4]*'k'i 'iu 'ch'ü 'li*, how is there such reason—i. e., it is wholly unreasonable.

起 'Ch'i. To rise, to arise, to stand up; to begin, to originate; to build; to make, to construct; to take, to undertake; to raise, to remove; beginning, commencement; before other verbs, denotes the beginning, and after them the completion, of an action: COM., [5]*'k'i ,sing*, to start on a journey; [6]*'k'i 'ch'iu*, to put the hand to, to begin; [7]*'k'i saik*, to introduce reforms, as a good officer does; [8]*'k'i sak*, to remove a malign influence; [9]*'k'i 'hwi*, to kindle a fire; [10]*'k'i ka'* to raise the prices; [11]*'k'i ,iu*, to remove a grease-spot; [12]*'k'i ,ch'ong*, to rise from a (sick) bed; [13]*'k'i 'kong*, the 3d section of an essay; [14]*'k'i kai'* (coll. *'k'i ch'io'*), to build a house; [15]*'k'i heng'* (or *,pi*), pleased, elated; COLL., [16]*'k'i ,li ,kiăng*, rise up and walk; *'k'i 'k'ang ,peng t'ak*, build a pagoda of broken tiles, as children do; *met.*, unsteady, fickle; *'k'i siăng'* beading, molding; *'k'i tek, 'cha*, rise early in the morning; *'k'i taĕng'* I'll trouble you! I have troubled you, thanks! *'k'i ,seng*, formerly, at first; *'k'i ,t'au 'k'i ek*, at the very start; *'k'i 'tó cheng'* relapses in a sickness; *'k'i pwang' ,lang ,ch'iăng*, half-built, as a house.

齒 'Ch'i. Read *'ch'i*; coll. *'k'i*: the upper teeth, the teeth; a tooth, a tine, a prong: [17]*'k'i chó'* the jaw; [18]*'k'i ,pau*, a gum-boil; *,kié pa' 'k'i*, harrow-teeth; *këü' 'k'i*, saw-teeth; *,t'au ,së siék, k'ó' sioh, 'k'i*, one tooth of the comb broken off; *'k'i t'iăng' chiăh, 'hieu tek, 'k'i t'iăng' ,nëng*, when one's tooth aches, he knows (how to pity) a person having the toothache; *met.*, the suffering can sympathize with sufferers.

'K'i. A coll. euphonic prefix, as in *'k'i 'k'wi*, to kneel, as before an idol.

蜞 碁 ,Ch'i. Read *,ki*; coll. *,k'i*: a leech: [19]*'ma ,k'i*, the leech; [20]*,lau ,k'i*, an edible worm of a greenish color—caught in rivers; [21]*'chwi ,k'i*, "water-leech"—a white, slimy

[1]豈	不	[4]豈	[5]起	[7]起	[9]起	[11]起	[13]起	[15]起	行	[18]齒	[20]流
不	知	有	身	色	火	油	講	興	[17]齒	包	蜞
是	[3]豈	此	[6]起	[8]起	[10]起	[12]起	[14]起	[16]起	座	[19]螞	[21]水
[2]豈	敢	理	手	煞	價	床	蓋	來	〇	蜞	蜞

worm, bred in moist places—sometimes called *hwo' ˛k'i; ˛p'ang ˛k'i*, a small land-crab.

鉗 鉆 Ch'ien. Read *˛k'ieng;* used for the coll. *˛k'i:* a kind of small clamp of iron or brass, used in mending glass or earthen ware; to fasten with clamps: ¹*˛k'i ˛kong*, to clamp jars; ²*˛k'i 'wang tang'* a bowl-mender's load (of stock and tools).

˛K'i. A coll. euphonic prefix, as in *˛k'i ˛k'ie*, to mount, to bestride.

(328) K'iă.

奇 Ch'i. Read *˛k'ie;* coll. *˛k'iă:* one, a single one; the odd numbers: also read *˛ki*, q. v.: ³*˛k'iă ˛k'iă*, odd numbers; ⁴*˛k'iă nik*, the odd days in a month; ⁵*sioh˛ ˛k'iă*, one, as of a pair of shoes, bracelets, earrings, &c.; ⁶*˛tang ˛k'iă*, an odd one.

跨 K'ua. Read *˛k'wa* and *k'wa';* used for the coll. *˛k'iă:* to treat insolently, to oppress, to be overbearing: ⁷*˛k'iă ˛nĕng*, to treat persons harshly; ⁸*˛k'iă tek˛ 'tó*, or *˛k'iă ˛i 'tó 'tó*, succeeded in crushing him; ⁹*˛k'iă ˛i má' tai'* can't get the mastery of him.

跨 K'ua. Read *˛k'wa* and *k'wa';* used for the coll. *˛k'iă:* to straddle, to bestride; on, across, astride: ¹⁰*˛k'iă pwoi'* bad luck, as from passing under what is regarded as unclean; ¹⁰*˛k'iă má' ˛keng* (or *twai'*) will be stunted in growth by being thus "bestrode"; ¹¹*˛k'iă ˛hong*, to write words on the line; *˛k'iă ˛k'a pang' a'* brought under one's legs, as in a fight.

(329) K'iăk.

谷 Ku. Read *kok˛;* used for the coll. *k'iăk˛* as in *˛sang k'iăk*, a gap or depression between hills; *˛sang 'hŭ 'tié o' 'la k'iăk˛ k'iăk*, there is a gap in the hills there; *k'iăk˛ k'iăk*, a gap, as in a road.

夻 Ku. Read *hak˛;* coll. *k'iăk˛:* to press, to squeeze; caught, as in a close place or in a door when shut; pinched, jammed: ¹²*k'iăk˛ 'si*, pinched to death; *k'iăk˛ ch'ói' ch'ói'* crushed into fragments; to cut, to mince, as medicinal herbs; *'ló 'ch'ü k'iăk*, a rat-trap; *k'iăk˛ ˛á 'tá*, to press shoe-soles; ¹³*k'iăk˛ cha'* crushed.

K'iăk˛. A coll. word: to deduct, to retain or keep back, as one's wages: *k'á' ˛i k'iăk˛ 'tiong ˛li*, get back (my pay) from him by deducting.

屐 Chi. Wooden-soled clogs, pattens: ¹⁴*muk˛ k'iăk˛* wooden overshoes—called in the coll. *˛ch'a ˛á* or *˛á t'ó'*.

𩚩 Read *'k'ang* and *˛k'ang;* used in the *Paik˛ ˛Ing* for the coll. *k'iăk˛* as in ¹⁵*k'iăk˛ k'iăk˛ sioh˛* a stone lying unevenly, a tilted stone.

K'iăk˛. A coll. word: to add, to put into, to mix in: *k'iăk˛ sioh˛ ˛toi*, to mix together; *k'iăk˛ ˛seu*, to mix evenly or uniformly; *k'iăk˛ ˛ngai ˛chiéng*, to mix in bad cash.

K'iăk˛. A coll. word: to prate, to jabber, verbose; to talk

¹鉆鋼 ²鉆碗擔 ³奇奇○ ⁴奇日 ⁵一奇 ⁶單奇 ⁷跨仸 ⁸跨的倒○ ⁹跨悖○ ¹⁰跨賣高○ ¹¹跨痕○ ¹²夻死○ ¹³夻迮○ ¹⁴木屐○ ¹⁵𩚩𩚩石○

incessantly without regard to the truth: *k'iăk꜁ kaing꜄ sié꜂* accustomed to prate recklessly; *꜀eng k'iăk꜁ pah꜁ k'iăk꜁* idle and mendacious jabber.

(330) K'iăng.

鏗 Chien. Read *꜀k'eng*; coll. *꜀k'iăng*, as in [1]*꜀k'iăng ꜀k'iăng kieu꜄* a ringing, or metallic sound; to rattle, to clatter.

꜀K'iăng, A coll. word, as in *꜀k'iăng ꜀k'iăng ꜀chung*, to tremble, to shiver, as from cold or fear.

꜂**鏗** Chien. Read *꜀k'eng*; coll. *꜂k'iăng*, as in *꜂k'iăng ꜂k'iăng kieu꜄* (same as *꜀k'iăng ꜀k'iăng kieu꜄*), a ringing, a clatter, as of metallic things; *꜂k'iăng ꜂k'iăng hwo꜄* poor or counterfeit goods, as alloyed articles of a head-dress; *met.*, a bad woman.

K'iăng꜄. A coll. word: to nod, to bow, to incline the head slightly: *k'iăng꜄ ꜀t'au* or *꜀t'au k'iăng꜄ k'iăng꜄* to bow the head.

鏗 ꜁Chien. Read *꜀k'eng*; coll. *꜁k'iăng*, as in *꜁k'iăng ꜁k'iăng kieu꜄* the ringing of metals; *met.*, to "make a din", to scold continuously; *꜁k'iăng ꜁k'iăng sau꜄* a hacking cough—the same as in *꜁k'eng*, q. v.

꜁K'iăng. A coll. word, as in *꜁k'iăng ꜁k'iăng ꜂chau*, to run away, to go off in a hurry.

K'iăng꜄. A coll. word: to bring together, to place edge to edge; to close, to shut to: *k'iăng꜄ ꜂lĕng*, or *k'iăng꜄ ꜂king*, to place close together; *k'iăng꜄ p'wai꜄* broken by knocking together, as two bowls; *꜀mwong k'iăng꜄ sioh꜁ a꜄* just close the door.

(331) K'ié.

奇 ꜀Chi. Odd, single; odd numbers; remainder, surplus: also read *꜀ki*; in the coll. read *꜀k'iă*, q. v.: [2]*꜀k'ié so꜄* odd numbers; [3]*꜀k'ié ꜀ling*, a surplus; COM., [4]*꜀k'ié ꜀k'ié*, something over, excess, surplus; COLL., [5]*꜀k'ié pwang꜄ ꜀peng*, an odd half-cash, as in a reckoning; [6]*꜀k'ié ꜂kwi ꜀hó*, odd few-tenths.

暌 ꜀K'uei. To oppose, the sun and moon in apposition; distant, separated from: [7]*꜀k'ié ꜀ui nik꜁ ꜂kiu*, a long time sundered, as friends.

稽 ꜀Chi. To examine into, to consult, to deliberate; to unite, to regulate; to stop, to detain; to reach to: [8]*꜀k'ié ꜀cha*, or [9]*꜀k'ié ꜂k'ó*, to examine, to investigate; [10]*꜂hwang ꜀sung ꜀siong ꜀k'ié*, mutual bickerings. Read *꜂k'ié*: to bow down: [11]*꜂k'ié ꜂siu*, or [12]*꜂k'ié ꜂song*, to bow the head to the ground.

窺 ꜀Kuei. To look furtively at, to spy, to peep at, as through a crevice; to observe, to take a view; a step, a pace: [13]*꜂kwang ꜀k'ié*, to look, as through a tube, to take a partial view of; [14]*꜀k'ié t'ang꜄* to spy out; [15]*꜀k'ié sëü꜄* to wait for, to observe.

闚 ꜀Kuei. Interchanged with the last: to peep under a door, to look through a crack; to glance at, to observe, to view partially: [16]*ch'iék꜁ ꜀k'ié*, to observe furtively.

---

1 鏗鏗叫 ○
2 奇數 3 奇零
4 奇奇 ○
5 奇半爿 ○
6 奇幾毫 ○
7 暌違日久
8 稽查 ○
9 稽考 ○
10 反唇相稽
11 稽首 12 稽顙
13 管窺 14 窺探
15 窺事 16 竊闚

'啟 啓 Ch'i. To open out, to explain, to make clear; to declare to, to inform a superior; to teach, to instruct; to reveal, to disclose, as by a revelation; to begin, as spring or summer; to divide, to distinguish; to engrave, to publish a book; the van or left wing of an army; clear sky after rain: [1]'*k'ié* ,*mung*, to teach the ignorant; [2]'*k'ié tik*, to point out the right way; [3]*eu*' '*k'ié* '*chiä*, a postscript; COM., [4]'*k'ié* '*chiä*, the informant, the writer—the opening phrase in a letter; [5],*ang* '*k'ié*, "open it calmly"—a superscription on letters; [6]'*k'ié chaiu*' to state by memorial; [7]'*k'ié* ,*ming* ,*sing*, "harbinger of light"—the morning star.

'棨 Ch'i. A signal, an ensign; a streamer on a lance, with characters inscribed on it, borne in state or sent with messengers,as their credentials; a check or passport of carved wood: [8]'*k'ié kek*, an ornamented lance, carried before kings and nobles.

'綮 Ch'i. A kind of silk; the cover of a spear-head; an ornamented and scolloped bandrol, borne by an escort or aid-de-camp. Read *k'eng*', as in [9]'*k'ai k'eng*' the attachment of the muscles and tendons.

'剞 Ch'i. Also read ,*ki*: a gouge, a crooked graver or burin: [10]'*k'ié k'wok*, a carving-gouge.

'掎 Ch'i. To draw to one side; to pull out anything by dragging with one foot; to display, to bring forth, to disclose.

'綺 Ch'i. A kind of open, figured silk, called [11]'*k'ié* ,*ló*, or ,*ló* '*k'ié*, used for summer dresses.

'錡 Ch'i. An iron pan or griddle, having feet; a stand for bows and other military armor, in which sense read *ngié*' in the dictionaries.

'跂 Ch'i. To raise the foot: the name of a country. Read ,*ki*: a foot with six toes; the crawling of insects. Read *k'ié*': same as the next, to stand erect, to stand on tiptoe and look at; to sit with the legs hanging down.

企' Ch'i. To stand erect: [12]*k'ié*' *wong*' to look for, to expect eagerly; COLL., [13]*k'ié*' ,*kó* and *k'ié*' *tá*' sodomites—used as terms of abuse.

契' Ch'i. An agreement, a contract, a bond, a deed; quippas were anciently used; to unite or compare the two parts of a check; mournful, distressed; frightened; a spit used in scorching tortoise-shells for divination; devoted to a god or person, adopted: also read *siék*, q. v.: [14],*chü k'ié*' documents; [15]*k'ié*' ,*tang*, a dynasty which ruled Northern China, A. D. 1118-1235, also styled the Golden Dynasty; COM., [16]*k'ié*' *kwong*' or [17]*k'ié*' *yok*, deeds;

[1]啟蒙 [2]啟直 [3]又啟者 [4]啟者 [5]安啟 [6]啟奏 [7]啟明星 ○ [8]棨戟 ○ [9]肯綮 ○ [10]剞劂 ○ [11]綺羅 ○ [12]企望 ○ [13]企哥 [14]書契 [15]契丹 [16]契券 [17]契約 ○

[1]*k'ié' chai' ˓ming pek,* plainly written in the deed; [2]*kiék, k'ié'* devoted, sworn to each other, as friends; [3]*k'ié' ˋnú,* an adopted mother, god-mother; COLL., [4]*˓ch'eng k'ié'* a deed conveying land; [5]*˓ëng k'ié'* "red deeds"—those officially stamped and taxed; *puh˒ k'ié'* a plain, or unstamped, deed; [6]*k'ié' ˓nié sai'* husband of an adopted daughter.

崎 Ch'i. Read *˓k'i;* used for the coll. *k'ié':* inclined, sloping, steep: *k'ak˒ k'ié'* too steep, very steep; *k'ié' ˋting,* or *ˋk'ang ˓peng k'ié'* (written *˓ang ˓ming k'ié'*) the eminence, or "broken-tile slope"—a locality north of Fish-market Bridge, Foochow.

竪 Shu. Read *sëü';* used for the coll. *k'ié':* to set upright, to erect, to stand on the end: [7]*k'ié' tik˒* set it up straight; [8]*k'ié' siéng'* to raise the sections of the frame (of a building); [9]*k'ié' ˓hwong,* to erect an honorary portal; *k'ié' ˋliăng,* an erect collar; [10]*k'ié' ˓hang ˓t'au,* to display one's official titles.

騎 Ch'i. To bestride, to mount, to ride horseback; to sit astride or crosswise, horse, cavalry: [11]*˓hi ˓k'ié,* light horse—used as the imperial body-guard in the Tang dynasty; *˓tang ˓k'ié,* to ride forth alone; COM., [12]*˓k'ié ˋma,* to ride a horse; *˓k'ié ˓sai, ˓k'ié ch'iong'* and *˓k'ié ˋhu,* riders of lion, elephant, and tiger, as certain gods are represented.

跬 Ch'i. Read *ˋk'ié ;* used in the *Paik, ˓Ing* for the coll. *k'ié ²:* to stand: [13]*k'ié ² ˋk'i,* to stand up; [14]*k'ié ² ˓sing,* a personal attendant or assistant; [15]*k'ié ² sié ²* "stand in or before the world"—to abide in widowhood; [16]*k'ié ² ˋtiăng,* a cook; [17]*k'ié ² ˓lëng,* to stand in a pillory, as a criminal till he starves to death; *k'ié ² ˓p'ó,* a military guard; [18]*k'ié ² taing'* employed in a shop; *k'ié ² sioh₂ ˋku,* to stand for (have) one share; *k'ié ² ˓k'a oi ² ch'ëü'* a standing-place; *met.,* means of livelihood; *k'ié ² ˋla ˋma sié ²* to assume a posture, as a pugilist or an archer; *met.,* applied to attitudes in talking.

(332) K'iék.

怯 Ch'ie. Fearful, timid, timorous, cowardly: [19]*˓sing k'iék,* weak-hearted; [20]*oi ² k'iék,* fearful, timid; COM., [21]*k'iék, ˋtang,* of little courage, pusillanimous.

愜 Ch'ie. Pleased in mind, gratified; cheerful, active, prompt, ready: [22]*k'iék, che'* satisfied; COM., *k'iék, e'* pleased, gratified.

慊 Ch'ie. Pleased, cheerful, contented, satisfied. Read *˓k'iéng:* angry, indignant; dissatisfied, discontented. Read *˓hiéng:* doubting, suspicious.

歉 Ch'ie. To eat insufficiently; deficient, scanty, as supplies; to covet, covetous, dissatisfied: *k'iék, swoi ²* year of dearth; *pó ² k'iék,* to feel deficiencies, not satisfied with.

1 契載明白　2 結契　3 契奶　4 田契　5 紅契　6 契女壻　7 豎直　8 豎搧　9 豎坊　10 豎銜頭　11 飛騎　12 騎馬　13 跬起　14 跬身　15 跬世　16 跬鼎　17 跬籠　18 跬店　19 心怯　20 畏怯　21 怯膽　22 愜志

缺 Ch'üeh. Read *k'wok,;* used for the coll. *k'iék,:* a flaw, a notch, a nick, as in a knife or pottery; wanting, defective: *k'iék, sioh, tói'* a bit wanting, nicked; *k'iék, 'ch'ó,* "too little saleratus—i. e. poor dough"—used only in a *met.* sense for one not trusty or competent; *k'iék, ch'oi'* a harelip; *k'iék, ,chü,* a harelipped person.

(333) K'iéng.

嗛 'Ch'ieng. Used for the next: humble, unassuming; the pouch in the mouths of monkeys and other animals; a bird's crop, the first stomach of ruminantia: also read *k'iék,* in the following senses; to dislike; a little, a deficiency: [1]*,k'iéng ,k'iéng,* a little; [2]*,k'iéng t'ói'* retiring, modest. Read *,kang:* to hold in the mouth.

謙 ,Ch'ieng. To revere, to show respect; respectful, yielding; lowly, humble, unassuming, modest, not self-sufficient: [3]*,k'iéng yong'* to yield, give way to; [4]*,k'iéng saung'* to yield complaisantly; [5]*,k'iéng ,hwo,* mild, placable; COM., [6]*,k'iéng ,pi,* or [7]*,k'iéng ,hü* (COLL. *,kü*), humble, unassuming.

愆 ,Ch'ieng. A fault, error, mistake, peccadillo; an excess, a crime; to exceed; a noxious disease: [8]*,k'iéng ,iu,* excess, crime; COM., [9]*'chói' ,k'iéng,* or [10]*,k'iéng kwo'* a transgression; [11]*,k'iéng ngiék,* crime (involving) retribution; COLL., [12]*,k'iéng taëng'* (or *twai'*), a grievous error; *,k'iéng ngiék, tek, k'ó'* have fallen into a penal sin!—a jocose phrase.

慳 ,Chieng. Also read *,k'eng:* saving, mean, stingy, niggardly; to be sparing of; [13]*,k'iéng leng'* stingy, parsimonious. Read *,hang:* experience of the aged.

汧 ,Ch'ien. Also read *,k'eng:* a tributary of the Wai in Shensi; water forming in pools, stagnant water, a marsh: [14]*,k'iéng ,yong,* a district in the West of Shensi.

搴 ,Ch'ien. Also read *,k'eng* and *'kiong:* to take, to seize; to pluck, as flowers; to extirpate: [15]*,k'iéng ,ki,* to capture a standard in battle.

褰 ,Ch'ien. Also read *,k'eng,* and *'kiong:* trowsers, drawers; shrunk, shriveled; to hold up the skirts in wading a stream.

騫 ,Ch'ien. A belt, a girth; a horse which excels in racing; a horse diseased in the belly; to suffer loss, injured, failing; to advance nimbly; a surname.

繾 'Ch'ien. United, attached: [16]*'k'iéng kwong'* intimate, inseparably attached, as friends.

譴 'Ch'ien. To question sternly, to blame, to reprimand; to rail at, to find fault with: [17]*'k'iéng no'* to speak angrily to; [18]*'k'iéng chaik,* to blame, to criminate.

遣 'Ch'ien. To send, to let go, to depute, to commision; to send into exile; to chase away, to expel; to present to: [19]*'k'iéng chói'* to

1 嗛嗛	3 謙讓	4 謙遜	5 謙和	6 謙卑	7 謙虛	9 罪愆	11 愆孽	13 慳吝	15 搴旗	17 譴怒	19 遣罪
2 嗛退	○	○	○	○	8 愆尤	10 愆過	12 愆重	14 汧陽	16 繾綣	18 譴責	○

福州方言拼音字典

exile for crime; 'k'iéng tük, to drive away; COM., ,ch'á 'k'iéng, to send on a mission or business.

欠' Ch'ien. To stretch and gape when weary; to owe; to be wanting, deficient in: [1]k'iéng' ,sing, to stretch one's self; COM., [2]k'iéng' ,ang, wanting in comfort—i. e., ill, indisposed; [3]k'iéng' chai' (or haung') to owe debts; [4]k'iéng' ho' a debtor; [5]k'iéng' k'wok, wanting, deficient in; [6]k'iéng' k'wo' to owe taxes, as salt-merchants; [7]k'iéng' ,pui, am wanting in attention—a phrase meaning please excuse my leaving you; COLL., 'chieu k'iéng' to owe but little; [8]k'iéng' ,chiéng tai' ,wong, "prince of debtors"—one getting deeply in debt; k'iéng' ch'ek, ,ká paik, haëng' "owes the seven streets and eight alleys"—in debt to everybody!

芡' Ch'ien. Read kiéng' in the dictionaries: a plant, also called fowl's head, whose leaf resembles the mallows; sometimes used for the coll. k'iéng' to stir, as flour in things while being cooked: COM., [9]k'iéng' sik, a medicinal herb—tonic for the stomach and kidneys; COLL., [10]k'iéng' 'hung, to stir flour in; k'iéng' ,niéng ,nó, stir (flour) in till it is thick and sticky.

岑 ,Ch'ing. A high, tapering peak, like an aiguille; a steep bank; a surname.

涔 ,Ch'in. Pure, crystal, limpid, as water; mountain rills; a fish-pool; to rear fish; to soak, to macerate; puddles after a rain: [11]'ü ,k'iéng ,k'iéng, heavy rains; [11],k'iéng loi' falling tears.

擒 ,Ch'in. To seize as a hawk does, to clutch, to grasp; to apprehend, to capture: [12],k'iéng 'na, or ,k'iéng ch'ëük, to seize; [13],seng ,k'iéng, to take alive; COM., [14],k'iéng 'ch'iu, to grasp with the hand; something to hold by, as in mounting a ladder; [15],k'iéng 'niu, to clutch, to collar; COLL., [16],k'iéng p'ah, to seize and beat; [17],k'iéng 'pwong, to get back one's capital; *met.*, (you intend) to get back the worth (of your presents)—said jocosely to a guest remaining long at a feast.

拑 ,Ch'ien Used for the next, as a verb, to pinch, to nip, to gripe; to hold or carry under the arm: [18],k'iéng 'k'eu, to shut the mouth, contumacious.

鉗 ,Ch'ien. To grasp with pincers, to gripe, to pinch; in Hunan, also means to rail at, to upbraid; pincers, nippers, forceps, tweezers, tongs; a kind of collar for slaves and culprits: in the coll. used for ,k'ing and ,k'i, q. v.: [19]t'iék, ,k'iéng, iron pincers or forceps; [20],k'iéng 'k'eu, to gag one.

鈐 ,Ch'ien. Used for the last: pincers, nippers; a kind of bolt or door-lock; also an axle of a wheel: [21],keu ,k'iéng, two stars in Scorpio, used in astrology; [22],k'iéng ke' a kind of stamp or seal, used by petty officers; COM., [23],k'iéng eng' to stamp edges, as of official documents or match bank-bills.

[1]欠身 [2]欠安 [3]欠債 [4]欠戶 [5]欠缺 [6]欠課 [7]欠陪 [8]欠錢大王 [9]芡實 [10]芡粉 [11]涔泪 [12]擒拿 [13]生擒 [14]擒手 [15]擒扭 [16]擒拍 [17]擒本 [18]拑口 [19]鐵鉗 [20]鉗口 [21]鉤鈐 [22]鈐記 [23]鈐印

箝 ꜀Ch'ien. Like the last two: a pair of pincers; to lock; *met.*, to forbid discussion: *꜀k'iéng 'ngü ꜀sieu ꜀chü*, to to interdict free speech and burn the books.

黚 ꜀Ch'ien. Black, as applied to the hair; a name of Kweichow province: [1]*꜀k'iéng ꜀lü*, black, as people's hair; [2]*꜀k'iéng 'siu*, "the black heads"—name given to the Chinese by the "First Emperor" from their black kerchiefs.

髡 ꜀Ch'ien. To remove criminals' hair, as a punishment; a wig made of such hair; a deep green or purple color.

(334) K'ieu.

撬 ꜀ To pry up, to raise with a lever.

敲 ꜀Ch'iao. To rap, to strike horizontally, to beat on one side with a club; a baton, a club: used in the coll. for *k'a'* q. v.: [3]*꜀k'ieu ꜀mwong*, to knock at a door.

蹻 ꜀Ch'iao. Same as the next; also read *꜀kieu:* to raise the feet in order to ascend: also read *'kieu* and *kiok*, q. v.

蹺 ꜀Ch'iao. To lift up the foot; to walk proudly, to prance; used in the coll. in the sense of tricky, taking advantage, as of another's necessities; indirect style of speech, to speak interrogatively in a tone implying the opposite sense: COLL., [4]*꜀k'ieu 'ta*, to take advantage of so as to injure; [5]*꜀k'ieu ꜀keng*, to lift the foot high; [6]*꜀i ꜀k'ieu 'ngwai*, he took advantage of me, as in exacting a high price; [7]*꜀k'ieu ꜀k'i ꜀ki wa'* indirect words, an interrogative phrase strongly implying the reverse idea; *tak꜁ ꜀k'ieu*, to wear the small ladies' shoes, as actors do; *met.*, to act vainly, presumptuous.

巧 'Ch'iao. Skillful, ingenious, clever, as an artisan; adroit, apt, handy, dexterous; subtile, wily, specious, crafty, deceitful; keen, shrewd, witty, pleasing; genius, ingenuity, talent: used in the COLL. for *k'ieu'*, q. v.: [8]*'k'ieu piéng'* specious in discussing; COM., [9]*꜀kang 'k'ieu*, wily, cheating; [10]*'k'ieu kiê'* a cunning scheme; [11]*'k'ieu ch'iong'* an ingenious artisan; [12]*'k'ieu cha'* fraudulent; [13]*'k'ieu ꜀ch'ä ꜀siong p'wang' chwok꜁ ꜀hu ꜀miéng*, a clever wife usually mates with a stupid husband.

豈 'Ch'i. Read *'k'i;* used for the COLL. *'k'ieu:* probably a corruption of *'k'i 'iu*, as in *'k'ieu 'ch'ü 'li*, how is there this doctrine!—i. e., it is unreasonable.

竅 Ch'iao.' A hole, pore, orifice, aperture; a cavity, a hollow, an interstice; *met.*, the mind, as intelligent or dull: [14]*'kiu k'ieu'* the nine passages of the body; COM., [15]*꜀ling k'ieu'* intelligence; [16]*꜀sing k'ieu'* the mind, intellect; [17]*ek꜁ k'ieu' pok꜁ ꜀t'ung*, "not a passage open"—i. e., is thoroughly stupid; COLL., *k'ieu' mä' ꜀t'ung*, not comprehending; *'chiä yoh꜁ ä' ꜀t'ung k'ieu'* the medicine has anastomatic qualities.

---

[1]黚黎 [2]黚首 [3]敲門 [4]蹺打 [5]蹺高 [6]伊蹺我 [7]蹺欺其話 [8]巧辯〇 [9]奸巧 [10]巧計 [11]巧匠 [12]巧詐 [13]巧妻常伴拙夫眠〇 [14]九竅 [15]靈竅 [16]心竅〇 [17]一竅不通

巧ʼ Ch'iao. Read ʻk'ieu; used for the coll. k'ieuʼ, as in k'ieuʼ mieuʼ skill, ingenuity; k'ieuʼ mieuʼ pok, ꜀tung, their talents are different.

趬ʼ Ch'iao. Read ꜀k'ieu; used for the coll. k'ieuʼ: turned or bent up, warped, twisted; bold, impudent, audacious, bragging: [1]k'ieuʼ ꜀ngan, warped, as a board; [2]k'ieuʼ ꜀k'a, the legs thrown up, as when one falls; [3]꜀tó tek, k'ieuʼ ꜀k'a, tripped up, made to fail in a business; k'ieuʼ ʻk'i k'ieuʼ or k'ieuʼ ꜀t'au k'ieuʼ ʻnó, a swaggering air; [4]k'ieuʼ ʻneng, the chest thrown stiffly out—said of a rascal's impudent gait; [5]k'ieuʼ ʻk'i ꜀t'ieng, to fall backwards with the face toward the sky.

鼽ʼ The nose turned up: COM., [6]k'ieuʼ p'eʼ a nose curving upward; kind of shoe with a single-corded, turned-up toe; p'eʼ k'ieuʼ k'ieuʼ tioh, his nose is curvated.

亮 Chʻiao. Read kieuʼ and k'ieuʼ; coll. ꜀k'ieu, as in [7]꜀k'ieu ꜀hü, uncertain as to the issue, not yet settled.

꜀**K'ieu.** A coll. word: well-dressed, a fine toilet, as of ladies: ꜀i ꜀chong ʻyă ꜀k'ieu, her toilet is very neat.

(335) K'ih.

噱, Read k'ioh,; used for the coll. k'ih,; similar to k'eh, q.v.: k'ih, sioh, ꜀siăng, to utter a giggling sound, to titter.

(336) K'ik.

檄, Chi. A tablet on which orders were anciently written; an official notification or summons; to give orders; in haste, urgent; a branchless tree: [8]꜀tiong k'ik, a sealed notice, a passport; [9]ʻü k'ik, a feathered (i. e., urgent) dispatch; COM., [10]k'ik, ꜀ung, an official summons or reprimand.

覡, A sorcerer, a wizard, a necromancer: [11]sengʼ ꜀u k'ik, to believe in witches and wizards.

詰, Chieh. To interrogate authoritatively, to demand of, to inquire into others' faults; to blame, to reprimand; to prohibit, to impose restrictions; to regulate, to reduce rebels to order: [12]k'ik, k'ŏk, cacophonous, harsh or intractable, as sounds; [13]꜀pwang k'ik, to examine rigidly; [14]k'ik, ꜀tieu, to-morrow morning.

頡, Chieh. Read kiĕk, in the dictionaries: a stiff or straight neck; to fly upwards; to rob, to plunder; to diminish, to exclude: [15]k'ik, hwak, difficult to do; involved or incorrect, artful, as one's language; COM., [16]꜀Ch'ong k'ik, name of the inventor of characters—in the times of Hwangte.

K'ik,. A coll. word: dried, shrunk, shriveled; lean and stunted, as a child: k'ik, ꜀chieu, seared and dried up, as by fire or solar heat.

K'ik,. A coll.word: to delay or hinder one, to put one off: k'ëük, ꜀i k'ik, chengʼ ꜀ong, delayed by him a very long time.

---

[1]趬淆 [2]趬骹 [3]掬澤 趬胶 [4]趬朧 [5]趬起 天鼽 [6]鼽鼻 〇 [7]亮亮 〇 [8]傳檄 〇 [9]羽檄 〇 [10]檄文 〇 [11]信巫覡 〇 [12]詰屈 〇 [13]盤詰 [14]詰朝 [15]頡滑 [16]蒼頡

K'ik,. A coll. euphonic prefix, as in *k'ik*, *k'ok*, to strike, to hit against; *k'ik*, *k'iăk*, to mix in (the bad with the good), as cash, goods, &c.; *k'ik*, *tuk*, *k'iăk*, to tip, tilting, as a stone or board.

(337) K'ing.

傾 ʻCh'ing The head leaning; inclined, lateral, aslant; falling, overturned; to subvert, to prostrate; wholly, entirely; to waste, to squander; to debate, to wrangle; to smelt, to assay, to purify metals: in the coll. read ‚*k'ing*, q. v.: [1]‚*k'ing* ʻ*tó*, to pour out; fallen, subverted; to convince or silence one; [2]‚*k'ing* ‚*sing yok*, *huk*, to submit cordially; [3]‚*k'ing* ʻ*ngi*, to incline the ear; [4]‚*k'ing* ‚*nong* ʻ*i chaing*ʾ gave him my whole purse; ‚*k'ing ch'aik*, inclined; ‚*k'ing* ʻ*ki*, overthrown, ruined; COM., ‚*k'ing* ‚*ka taung*ʾ ʻ*sang*, to ruin one's family and property; COLL., ‚*k'ing* ‚*pwong t'ó*ʾ *haik*, to vomit blood profusely—an excessive hemorrhage.

頃 ʻCh'ing. Read ʻ*k'ing*; coll. ‚*k'ing*, as in ‚*k'ing k'aik*, a little while; in a short time, very soon.

卿 ʻCh'ing. To revert towards, what men look up to; a noble, lord, grandee, high officer; term of respect addressed by a prince to his minister; [5]*lĕk*, ‚*k'ing*, the presidents of the six Boards; [6]‚*k'ing siong*ʾ a grandee, a prime minister; [7]‚*kung* ‚*k'ing*, nobles from 1st to 3rd ranks; [8]‚*k'ing* ‚*ka*, our ministers; [9]*ai*ʾ ‚*k'ing*, my wife.

欽 ʻCh'in. To stretch and yawn; to respect, to reverence, reverential; that which is revered; imperial, governmental; considered as from or by the emperor: [10]‚*k'ing t'ek*, letters-patent; COM., [11]‚*k'ing meng*ʾ a ukase; [12]‚*k'ing* ‚*ch'á*, an imperial envoy; [13]‚*k'ing* ʻ*teng* ‚*hang* ‚*ling*, to designate academicians; [14]‚*k'ing koi*ʾ valuable, precious; [15]‚*k'ing* ‚*t'iĕng kang*ʾ the imperial astronomers; [16]‚*k'ing* ‚*ka*, to confer an additional title.

嶔 Ch'in. High hills; the peaks of mountains; gaping, yawning: ‚*k'ing* ‚*nging*, a high, sharp peak.

矜 ʻChing. The haft of a pike or staff; to pity, to compassionate, to feel for; regretting, anxious for; to spare, regardful, careful of; to value, to esteem; bragging, boastful, conceited; to maintain one's self-respect; hazardous, dangerous: [17]‚*k'ing* ‚*i pok*, ‚*cheng*, to maintain one's dignity without wrangling; [18]‚*k'ing* ʻ*ming*, to pity; ‚*k'ing* ‚*ku sok*, ʻ*kwa*, to commiserate orphans and widows; ʻ*k'ó* ‚*k'ing* pitiable; COM., ‚*k'ing* ‚*k'wa*, to brag, boastful.

衾 ʻChing. A coverlet or large quilt, a single coverlet; a shroud: ‚*i* ‚*k'ing*, clothes and shroud for the dead; [22]ʻ*king* ‚*k'ing*, a figured quilt.

---

[1]傾倒 [2]傾心悅伏 [3]傾耳 [4]傾囊以贈 [5]六卿 [6]卿相 [7]公卿 [8]卿家 [9]愛卿 [10]欽勅 [11]欽命 [12]欽差 [13]欽點翰林 [14]欽貴 [15]欽天監 [16]欽加〇 [17]矜而不爭 [18]矜憫〇

衿 襟 Ching. The lapel or fold of a coat; a cord to fasten a lapel; a collar; to fasten, to tie with strings: [1]'k'ing ˛hwai, the bosom; [2]˛ch'ing ˛k'ing, the "green lapels"—Siutsai graduates; COM., [3]k'ing ˛hing tâ' those marrying sisters, brothers-in-law.

輕 Ch'ing. A light carriage; light, not heavy; small, paltry, frivolous; to disregard, to think lightly of, to disesteem, to slight; lightness, levity; dissipated: COM., [4]k'ing ˛seng, reckless of life, bold, audacious; [5]˛k'ing seng' credulous; [6]˛k'ing ˛kwong, frivolous, harum-scarum; [7]˛k'ing pok˛ disrespectful, shabby; [8]˛k'ing 'pwong tuëng' le' small capital and heavy profits; COLL., ˛k'ing 'sang, sparing, as of money or work expended; ˛k'ing ˛liong siâng' very cheap; ˛k'ing ˛üng e' easily, carelessly or superficially; ˛k'ing ˛p'ieu ˛p'ieu, very light; ˛k'ing ˛k'ing 'kiâng, lightly, in a slight degree; ˛k'ing ˛k'a ˛k'ing 'ch'iu, with light feet and hands, noiselessly. Read k'eng': quick, fast, with alacrity.

˛K'ing. A coll. euphonic prefix, as in ˛k'ing ˛k'wong, to place in a case, frame, or box; ˛k'ing ˛k'iâng, sound of metals or gems.

頃 Ch'ing. A hundred 'meu, about equivalent to 15.13 sq. acres, the largest of land measures; an instant, a moment, a glance: in the coll. read ˛k'ing, q. v.: [9]˛ngô 'k'ing, in a moment; [10]'k'ing yok˛ a glance at, as in reading cursorily; [11]'k'ing ˛ung, have just heard; COM., [12]'k'ing k'aik˛ or 'k'ing k'aik˛ ˛chi ˛kang, a very short time. Read ˛k'ing: the head inclined; a kind of basket; in epitaphs, means trembling, respectful: [13]˛k'ing ˛k'wong, a basket.

謦 Ch'ing. To cough slightly, to hack; sound of a hacking cough: [14]'k'ing k'ai' coughing; to speak smilingly.

肯 K'ĕng. Read 'k'eng; coll. 'k'ing: to assent, willing, acquiescing, permitting: [15]'k'ing chô' willing to do; [16]'k'ing t'ĕk˛ willing to study; [17]'k'ing kang' "willing to do"—free in spending money, more lavish than others; 'nü 'k'ing ng' 'k'ing, are you willing or not?

'K'ing. A coll. euphonic prefix, as in 'k'ing 'k'ong, to chop, to cut up, as meats; 'k'ing 'k'ang, to lop or cut off.

禽 Ch'in. The feathered and flying tribe, the class aves, birds; pregnant animals; to seize in battle: COM., [18]˛k'ing 'neu, birds; [19]˛k'ing seu' birds and beasts.

檎 Ch'in. A kind of Prunus: [20]˛ling ˛k'ing, a large kind of bullace, whose blossoms and fruit are red.

琴 Ch'in. A Chinese lute, having five or seven strings; its music used to control men's passions, hence, met., to restrain, to control one's self; also applied to foreign instruments, as the organ, piano, seraphine, melodeon, &c.: [21]˛hung ˛k'ing (coll. t'iĕk˛ 'ma), pieces of

1襟懷 2青衿 3襟兄弟 4輕生 5輕信 6輕狂 7輕薄 8輕本重利 9俄頃 10頃閱 11頃聞 12頃刻 13頃筐 14謦欬 15肯做 16肯讀 17肯幹 18禽鳥 19禽獸 20林檎 21風琴

metal or glass, hung up and jingled by the wind; COM., [1]*‚k'ing saik,* lutes and harps; [2]*‚k'ing ʻp'wo,* manual of instrumental music; [3]*‚k'ing ʻié,* a kind of long bench; [4]*‚yong ‚k'ing,* a music-box (coll. *paik, ‚ing ak,* the eight-tone box); [5]*‚k'ing ‚ki ‚chü waʼ* lute, chess, books, and paintings; [6]*‚k'ing ‚tong,* a district magistrate's hall; [7]*‚tang ‚k'ing,* to play the lute.

芩 ‚Ching. A kind of salt marsh-grass or sedge, a species of Salsola (?); the seeds are eaten by cattle: COM., [8]*‚wong ‚k'ing,* a yellow root like licorice—used for its cooling properties.

傾 ‚Ch'ing. Read *‚k'ing;* coll. *‚k'ing:* to pour, as from the spouts of vessels; to assay metals: [9]*‚k'ing ‚ta,* to pour tea; [10]*‚k'ing ʻch'iéng,* to "pour shallow"—i. e., not full, as one's wine-cup; [11]*‚k'ing ‚sieu,* or [12]*‚k'ing ‚ngüng,* to assay silver; *‚k'ing tiéngʼ ch'iok, ‚kang ‚ch'a ‚ka ek,* "pour full and drink it dry—makes a tenth more"—a bantering phrase at feasts.

鉗 ‚Ch'ien. Read *‚k'iéng;* coll. *‚k'ing,* as in *ʻhwi ‚k'ing,* a pair of tongs; *t'iék, ‚k'ing,* iron-tongs.

‚K'ing. A coll. word: a bear; same as *‚hüng,* q. v.: *‚k'ing ʻmó,* a female bear.

‚K'ing. A coll. euphonic prefix, as in *‚k'ing ‚k'iéng,* to grasp; *‚k'ing ‚k'wang,* to make circles; to go around; *‚k'ing ‚k'üng,* to gather in a bunch, to pile together; *‚k'ing ‚k'wong,* to take care of, as children, a shop, &c.

(338) K'iok.

却, 卻, Ch'io. To stop, to curb desires; to deny, to refuse, to decline doing or accepting; to retire, to go backwards; an adverbial particle, truly, really, certainly; preceded by *‚ch'wi* (though), it is a disjunctive, still, yet; also a particle, marking a turn in the discourse, now, then, then again: [13]*‚wong k'iok,* to forget; [14]*k'iok, ‚heng,* to walk backwards; [15]*k'iok, seʼ ‚ü ʻch'ü,* truly it is thus; [16]*‚ch'wi k'iok,* to decline, to refuse; [17]*ʻliu k'iok,* done and put away, or disposed of; *k'iok, siok,* we turn now to speak of; COM., [18]*‚ching pok, ʻk'ó k'iok,* the feelings make it impossible to refuse; COLL., *seʼ ‚i k'iok, ʻngwai,* it is he that rejects me—*scil.,* not I him.

孑, Chieh. A man without the right arm; alone, solitary, abandoned, orphaned; to come short, a remnant; behind, left; hale, strong; a kind of halberd: [19]*k'iok, k'iok,* alone, preeminent; larvae of musketos; [20]*‚keu k'iok,* a halberd; COM., *k'iok, ‚yong ek, ‚sing,* solitary, quite alone, as one without relatives.

矍, Ch'io. A frightened look, as of a bird; the fluttering, as of birds when caught; to look right and left, to glance about quickly; a wild look, a timid glance: [21]*k'iok, ‚yong,* alarmed; *k'iok, t'ek,* great,

1 琴瑟	3 琴椅	5 琴棋	6 琴堂	8 黄芩	10 傾淺	12 傾銀	14 却行	如此	17 了却	可却	20 鈎孑
2 琴譜	4 洋琴	書畫	7 彈琴	9 傾茶	11 傾銷	13 忘却	15 却是	16 推却	18 情不	19 孑孑	21 矍然

ly agitated; *k'iok, ch'iok,* active, as an old man.

攫 Ch'io. To clutch, to grasp, as with the claws or talons: [1]*k'iok, 'ch'ü,* to seize, to take forcibly.

躩 Ch'io. A short, measured step, as in ascending stairs; to walk gravely, as before superiors; to walk quickly: [2]*k'iok, pwo'* a quick, regular pace.

钁 Ch'io. A large hoe or mattock; a heavy pickax.

訐 Chi. Read *kiok,* in the dictionaries: to reprove one, to charge with a fault, to question about an accusation; to divulge, to bring to light, to reveal, to disclose secrets: [3]*'miêng' k'iok,* to reprimand personally; [4]*,kung k'iok,* to charge, to accuse one of; [5]*k'iok, ,ing 'twang ch'ëü'* to talk about people's faults.

劇 Ch'i. To increase, very, exceeding; miserable, distressing, very troublesome; to play, to sport, to gambol; a farce, a comedy, plays: [6]*'hië' k'iok,* to play; sports; [7]*'peng' k'iok,* a distressing illness.

謔 Nio. Also read *ngiok,:* to jest, to trifle with; to play, to sport; to mock, to ridicule, to make sport of: *k'iok, k'iok,* playful, pleased; [8]*'ch'ieu' k'iok,* to laugh at; [9]*'hië' k'iok,* to make sport of one.

(339) K'iong.

腔 Ch'iang. A hollow bone; hollow, empty, vacant; the flank of a horse; a tune, a style of reading or singing; a dialect, patois; swelled, puffed up; vain, ostentations, pedantic: [10]*,chong ,k'iong,* assuming, ostentatious; COM., [11]*'t'u ,k'iong,* the native dialect; [12]*,k'iong tieu'* the tone or tune in reading and singing; [13]*,k'iong taëng'* a heavy brogue; [14]*,ùng ,k'iong,* the "banian" (i. e., Foochow) dialect; [15]*,k'iong 'k'eu 'hó,* an excellent tone or style, as in reading and singing.

羫 Ch'iang. The ribs or skeleton of a sheep; a sheep's tendons. Read *k'ong':* dried mutton.

騿 Ch'iang A horse walking along, the gait of a horse.

,K'iong. A coll. word, as in *,k'iong e'* to have in mind, to intend, to purpose—the same as *,chong e'* q. v.: *,k'iong e' ,teng nioh, wai' ,chiêng,* how much cash do you intend to offer for it? *ng' ,k'iong e'* unexpected.

(340) K'iu.

丘 邱 坵 Ch'iu. The first is the proper name of Confucius, regarded too sacred for common use, for which the second is often substituted: a low hill, a mound, a tumulus; a hollow hill-top; a high place, or leveled hill for worshiping; a plat of land; to collect; great, empty: the 3d used for the coll. *,k'u,* q. v.: *,wong ,k'iu,* and

[1]攫取 ○ [2]躩步 ○ [3]面訐 ○ [4]攻訐 ○ [5]訐人短處 [6]戲劇 [7]病劇 [8]笑謔 [9]戲謔 [10]粧腔 [11]土腔 [12]腔調 ○ [13]腔重 ○ [14]榕腔 ○ [15]腔口好 ○

[1]*ˌhwong ˌk'iu*, round and square places for adoring heaven and earth; [2]*ˌsang ˌk'iu*, the three hills of the immortals; [3]*ˌk'iu 'lung*, a mound, tumuli, graves; [4]*ek, ˌk'iu ek, k'auk*, "one hillock and one pool"—a small locality or dwelling-place.

蚯 Ch'iu. An earthworm, called *ˌk'iu 'ing*, which makes humps in crawling; in the coll. *ˌka 'kung*, q. v.

鳩 Chiu. A pigeon, a wild dove, the turtle; to call together, to assemble; to rest, to dwell; in the coll. to collect, as money for public use: [5]*ˌpang ˌk'iu*, the pigeon; [6]*ˌk'iu ˌkü*, to dwell, as a bride in her new home; [7]*ˌk'iu chëü'* to assemble, to tranqilize; [8]*ˌk'iu t'iong'* an old man's staff; [9]*ˌk'iu ˌhing kok, miêng'* "a dove's form and a stork's face"; *met.*, lean, emaciated; COLL., [10]*ˌk'iu ˌchiêng*, to collect money; *ˌchiêng ˌk'iu chik, 'lëng*, to collect together the sums subscribed.

ˌK'iu. A coll. word: bent, curled, warped; torn, shabby, as clothes; poor, inferior, as workmanship, essays, etc.; distressed, miserable, impoverished, pinched by want: *ˌk'iu ˌk'iu*, warped, bent; *ˌk'iu 'toi*, shortened, contracted; *ˌk'iu t'ëük, k'ó'* bent and contracted, as a finger having a boil on it; *ˌnêng yong' ˌsang cheng' ˌk'iu*, one born much deformed; *che' 'siä tek, ˌk'iu*, the words badly written.

(341) K'o.

庫' K'u. A house for military carriages; an armory, an arsenal; a treasury, a storehouse, a magazine: COM., [11]*ˌch'ong k'o'* granary and treasury; [12]*puo' ˌsi k'o'* the provincial treasury; [13]*'chiu k'o'* a liquor-shop; [14]*'k'o' ˌngüng*, or [15]*k'o' haung'* funds in the treasury; [16]*k'o' ˌt'iäng* (coll. *k'o' twai' sai'*), a sub-treasurer; *k'o' lé'* a treasury-clerk; *'t'u k'o'* a store-room; *'hwi yoh, k'o'* a powder factory and magazine; *k'o' ˌtó*, or *k'o' ˌpang*, a weight in weighing silver, 100 oz. of which equal 102.4 oz. of the *ˌsing ngiê'*.

袴' 褲' K'u. The first also read *k'wa'*: a covering for the legs; drawers, breeches, trowsers: COM., [17]*t'ó' k'o'* overalls; [18]*kak, k'o'* lined drawers; COLL., [19]*k'o' 't'oi*, a sort of half-drawers, tied or buttoned at the waist; [20]*ˌpong 't'oi k'o'* drawers, trowsers; [21]*'lëng k'o'* a kind of trowsers worn by boatmen; *k'o' t'ak*, the dress-overalls of females; *sek, k'o'* an embroidered wrapper for a lady's ancle; *'chwi k'o'* and *k'o' ˌtong te'* short drawers, breeches; *ˌk'wi 'tau k'o'* a kind of open drawers—worn by small children; *k'o' sioh, ˌteu*, one pair of drawers.

臼' Chiu. Read *k'eu'*; coll. *k'o'*: a mortar: *sioh, k'o'* or *ˌchüng k'o'* a stone-mortar; *k'o' ˌt'ui*, a pestle; *sioh, tai' k'o'* small stone-mortars; *ˌmwong k'o'* a wooden door-socket; *t'ak, k'o'* hollow, depressed, like a mortar; *twai' 'chwi má' ˌlau sioh, ˌchüng k'o'* a freshet can't float off a stone mortar; *met.*, inflexible in purpose; secure in one's position, despite all calumny.

[1]方丘 [2]三丘 [3]丘壟 [4]一丘 一壑 [5]斑鳩 [6]鳩居 [7]鳩聚 [8]鳩杖 [9]鳩形 鵠面 [10]鳩錢 [11]倉庫 [12]布司 庫 [13]酒庫 [14]庫 銀 [15]庫項 [16]庫 廳 [17]套褲 [18]夾褲 [19]褲腿 [20]綁腿 腿褲 [21]攏褲

福州方言拼音字典

(342) K'ó.

尻 The lower end of the spine, the *os coxendicis;* the rump, the seat. ˎK'ao.

哿 Good, excellent, to commend; to be well off; to be able, can, may, might. ˊK'o.

柯 A helve, an ax-handle; a stem or stalk; a branch fit for a helve; a sort of javelin; a way, means, cause; a surname: [1] ˊ*hu* ˏ*k'ó*, helve of an ax; [2]*chek*, ˏ*k'ó*, to hold the helve (i. e., ax); *met.*, to be a match-maker. ˊK'o.

炣 Read ˊ*k'ó;* coll. ˏ*k'ó:* to cook thoroughly: [3]ˏ*k'ó lang*ˀ or ˏ*k'ó mauk*, to cook soft; [4]ˏ*k'ó tau*ˀ *ho*ˀ to cook bean-curd thoroughly. ˊK'o.

珂 A quartzose gem, of inferior value; a carnelian or whitish chalcedony, milky quartz; a sea conch, with a white nacre, used ornamentally: [5]ˏ*k'ó* ˏ*king*, a sort of metal; one says, pure gold. ˊK'o.

苛 Small plants; petty, troublesome, vexatious; small, minute, trifling; to vex, to trouble; to annoy, as a people by needless examinations; to blame, to reprove sharply: [6]ˏ*k'ó cheng*ˀ an oppressive government; [7]ˏ*k'ó chik*, a fatal disease; [8]ˏ*k'ó* ˊ*yong*, a slight itching; [9]ˏ*hwang* ˏ*k'ó*, troublesome; COM., [10]ˏ*k'ó* ˏ*kiu*, to importune; [11]ˏ*k'ó k'aik*, to be needlessly strict with, to harass; COLL., ˏ*i che*ˀ ˏ*ka* ˏ*k'ó k'aik*, he is strict with himself, close, parsimonious. ˊK'o.

軻 Wheels and axles connected with each other: also read *k'ó*ˀ q. v.: ˊ*k'ang* ˏ*k'ó*, a carriage dragging heavily; *met.*, impeded, hindered, disappointed; *maing*ˀ ˏ*k'ó*, surname and name of Mencius. ˊK'o.

ˏ*K'ó.* A coll. word, as in ˏ*k'ó tiẽ*ˀ or ˏ*k'ó tiẽ*ˀ *tai*ˀ why? wherefore?—about as *k'á*ˀ *á*ˀ q.v.

可 To be willing, to consent, to permit; can, may, could; able, free to do; fit, proper; worthy, competent; used interrogatively and by way of invitation, or to soften an order; forms verbal adjectives, or gerunds ending in able; [12]*pok*, ˊ*k'ó*, ought not, must not; [13]ˊ*k'ó* ˊ*p'eu*, will it do or not; [14]ˊ*iu* ˏ*hó pok*, ˊ*k'ó*, what forbids, why not? [15]ˊ*k'ó* ˊ*k'eu*, delicious to the taste; COM., [16]ˊ*k'ó ch'ieu*ˀ laughable; [17]ˊ*k'ó o*ˀ odious, disagreeable; [18]ˊ*k'ó* ˏ*ti*, or ˊ*k'ó kiéng*ˀ whence it can be seen or perceived; [19]ˊ*k'ó sek*, alas! how lamentable! [20]ˊ*k'ó* ˏ*ngi*, to doubt, be suspicious; [21]ˊ*sieu* ˊ*k'ó*, trifling, unimportant; [22]ˊ*k'ó* ˊ*pi*, to illustrate, by way of comparison; ˊ*k'ó* ˊ*i*, possible, it will answer; ˊ*k'ó* ˊ*i pok, pek*, it will do, no need (of anything farther); COLL., ˊ*k'ó* ˏ*leng*, to compassionate. ˊK'o.

拷 To grasp, to snatch violently; to beat, to torture in order to extort a confession: ˊ*k'ó* ˊ*ta*, to cudgel; ˊ*k'ó seng*ˀ to examine by torture. ˊK'ao.

[1]斧柯 [2]炣爛 腐[4]珂 [6]苛政 [8]苛癢 [10]苛求 [12]不可 [14]有何 [15]可口 [17]可惡 [19]可惜 [21]小可

[3]執柯 [4]炣豆 金〇 [7]苛疾 [9]煩苛 [11]苛刻 [13]可否 不可 [16]可笑 [18]可知 [20]可疑 [22]可比

ʻ**栲** K'ao. A tree yielding a gum used for varnish; a species of Dryandra? its wood is hard and whitish.

ʻ**考** K'ao. Old; a deceased father; complete, finished; to question, to examine; to beat, to strike: [1]ˏsiéng ʻk'ó, my departed father; COM., [2]ˏcha ʻk'ó, to examine; [3]ʻk'ó ch'ak, to investigate officially; [4]ʻk'ó seʾ examinations for the Siutsai degree; [5]ʻhu ʻk'ó, a prefectural examination; [6]ʻk'ó ʻu, military examinations; [7]ʻk'ó ˏchiéng ˏliong, to examine candidates for enlistment; [8]ʻk'ó ˏp'ié ʻsiu, the first of the Siutsai graduates; [9]ʻk'ó k'woʾ an examination three times a month; [10]swoíʾ ʻk'ó, and ˏk'wo ʻk'ó, the two examinations in the three years' term of the literary chancellor; [11]ʻk'ó ˏmi ˏchai, a trial-examination of the 3d class of Siutsai; ʻk'ó ngiêngʾ a triennial examination of officers; ʻk'ó këüʾ to examine evidence, as in books.

ʻ**攷** K'o. To examine, to search into, as one's qualifications, in which senses the same as the last: ʻk'ó ˏsing, decision as to one's official merits.

ʻ**舸** K'o. A large galley, or barge; a war vessel, called ʻk'ó ʻk'ang, in the ˏsang kwok, cheʾ (Annals of the Three States).

靠ʾ K'ao. To lean against; to rely on, to look to, to depend on another for aid; contrary, opposed to, rebelling against: in the coll. fetters: COM., [12]k'óʾ ʻching, a square pillow with rounded corners—used on couches; [13]k'óʾ ˏsang, against the hill side, as a grave; in *met.*, sense, to rely on a firm friend; [14]k'óʾ pwoíʾ (coll. k'óʾ ˏp'iàng), to lean the back against; COLL., [15]ʻai k'óʾ to rely or depend on; [16]k'óʾ ʻch'iu ʻpeng, a rest-board for the hands (in a sedan); k'óʾ ˏt'iéng siàh, pwongʾ "depend on Heaven and eat one's rice"—i. e., earn an honest living; k'óʾ tek, chëüʾ (or tieuʾ) he can be relied on; ˏk'a k'óʾ ʻch'iu k'óʾ fetters and manacles.

坷ʾ **軻**ʾ K'o. The first means rough, uneven, as a country or road; the 2d is also read ˏk'ó, q. v.: COM., [17]ʻk'ang k'óʾ rugged paths; *met.*, unsuccessful, unlucky; difficulties in life.

魺ʾ Ko. Read ˏhó and ʻk'ó; coll. k'óʾ: a kind of sea-fish, salted and dried, of which there are several varieties: [18]ˏwong nongʾ k'óʾ a small yellow sort; kak, ʻchü k'óʾ a kind having thick scales; pwoh, ˏp'uí k'óʾ flayed k'óʾ fish.

犒ʾ K'ao. To give extra pay, to reward: [19]k'óʾ ˏsü, to reward (victorious) troops; [20]k'óʾ ʻsiong, to confer bounties; [21]k'óʾ ˏngiu, bullocks given as a bounty.

去ʾ Ch'ü. Read k'ëüʾ; coll. k'óʾ: to go away, to depart, to separate; to go into, through, or out from; past, gone, former; as an adjunct, implies completion of action in the preceding verb: ch'ok, k'óʾ to go out; ʻtié k'óʾ to go into; ˏsü

[1]先考 [2]查考 [3]考察 [4]考試 [5]府考 [6]考武 [7]考錢糧 [8]考批首 [9]考課 [10]歲考 [11]考遺才 [12]靠枕 [13]靠山 [14]靠背 [15]倚靠 [16]靠手板 [17]坎坷 [18]黃韌魺 [19]犒師〇 [20]犒賞 [21]犒牛

海上絲綢之路文獻集成 科技與文化編

*má*ʾ *k'ó*ʾ can't decline or get rid of; [1]*k'ó* ꜀*chá*, to go to school; [2]*k'ó* ꜀*tó*, go and take it; *tek*, *tioh*, *k'ó*ʾ positively must go; ꜀*mó tek*, *k'ó*ʾ can't go; will not contain it; [3]*k'ó*ʾ ꜀*niéng*, or *k'ó*ʾ ꜀*niéng* ꜀*mang*, last year; [4]*k'ó*ʾ ʻ*ma siăh*, ꜀*chá*, gone to his grandmother's to eat ghosts' cakes—a coarse jest, used in the sense of gone away or dead.

磕 ꜀K'o. Read *k'ó*ʾ; coll. ꜀*k'ó*: to ground, to run aground, to strike the ground and remain fixed: ꜀*sung* ꜀*k'ó* ʻ*ch'iéng*, the boat has grounded on the shallows.

꜀*K'ó*. A coll. word like the last: to strike, to knock against an obstruction; also to defer, to put one off: ꜀*k'ó* ꜀*siong*, bruised by striking against; ꜀*k'ó lau*ʾ made leaky by a knock; ꜀*k'ó taiu*ʾ kept in suspense, delayed; ꜀*i* ꜀*k'ó* ʻ*ngwai*, he puts me off, keeps me waiting.

(343) K'oi.

꜀*K'oi*. A coll. word, as in ꜀*k'oi ié*ʾ why! wherefore!—about as *k'á*ʾ *á*ʾ and ꜀*k'ó tié*ʾ, q. v.; ꜀*k'oi ié*ʾ ꜀*chiong wang*ʾ why (do you) so!

愧 **媿**ʾ K'uei. Ashamed, abashed, disconcerted; bashful, shamefaced; contrite, conscience-smitten: [5]꜀*siu k'oi*ʾ or *k'oi*ʾ ʻ*t'i*, ashamed; [6]*k'oi*ʾ *hwoi*ʾ contrite, penitent; COM., [7]꜀*chang k'oi*ʾ feel ashamed—often said affectedly by one when praised; [8]ʻ*chĕü*ʾ *k'oi*ʾ abashed, mortified; [9]꜀*u k'oi*ʾ no shame, a sense of innocence.

(344) K'ok.

哭, K'o. To cry aloud, to lament with a loud voice; to wail, to groan, noise of excessive grief: [10]*t'ong*ʾ *k'ok*, to weep bitterly; [11]*k'ok*, ꜀*song*, to wail for the dead; [12]*k'ok*, *k'ek*, to cry and sob; [13]*k'ok*, ꜀*song t'iong*ʾ staff carried by a son at a funeral; COM., [14]*k'ok*, *yă*ʾ ꜀*u ek*, it is of no avail to lament (about it).

屈, Ch'ü. Bent, turned awry; to stoop, to crouch; to bow, to bend over, to kneel; to submit, as to necessity, to adapt one's self to circumstances; constrained, forced; grievance, wrong; affliction: [15]*k'ok*, *k'ĕük*, bent, crooked; [16]*k'ok*, ꜀*sing*, to crook and to straighten; [17]*k'ok*, *che*ʾ disappointed, grieved about; [18]*k'ok*, *huk*, or *k'ok*, *chiék*, to crouch meanly; *k'ok*, *ch'ek*, to kneel; [19]*k'ok*, ꜀*sing*, to bend the body; *met.*, to submit, as to suffering; COM., [20]*wong* *k'ok*, oppressed, ill-treated; [21]*k'ok*, *ka*ʾ you must stoop, Sir!—a polite form of invitation; COLL., *k'ok*, ʻ*chai o*ʾ *nioh*, ꜀*ong*, by count of the fingers how long has it been?

詘, Chueng. This and the next are like the preceding: to bend, to stoop; forced, constrained against one's will; a fold, a rumple, a a wrinkle; an impediment in the speech, stammering.

絀, Chueh. Also read *t'ok*,: crimson silk; to baste, to sew imperfectly; to bend, bent, constrained: used for *t'ok*, (to degrade). Also read *chiok*, as in ꜀*ing chiok*, to straight-

1 去齋 2 去掏 3 去年 4 去媽食穧 5 羞愧 6 愧悔 7 慚愧 8 自愧 9 無愧 10 痛哭 11 哭喪 12 哭泣 13 哭喪杖 14 哭也無益 15 屈曲〇 16 屈伸 17 屈志 18 屈伏 19 屈身 20 枉屈 21 屈駕

en out and bend: *met.*, opposite, up and down, unequal.

***K'ok*,**. A coll. word: to hide, to skulk, to conceal one's self; also to be in, or at, a place: *k'ok, mek$_2$ mek$_2$* to keep closely hid; *k'ok, 'ch'au p'ong'* to skulk in the straw; *k'ok, ˏtëng 'në*, hid where? *k'ok, sioh$_2$ ˏtoi*, to be together; *k'ok, a^2 'tá*, is down below; *á^2 k'ok, tek, lóh$_2$* can stay at, tolerable, as a place.

搕 K'o.$_2$ Read *ak*, in the dictionaries: to take; to strike, to knock, to touch lightly: COLL., *k'ok$_2$ tioh$_2$* impinged; *k'ok$_2$ náh$_2$* indented; *k'ok$_2$ sioh$_2$ a^2* gave it a knock; *k'ok$_2$ ˏhu*, a kind of game with cards; *'chiă ˏnëng má^2 k'ok$_2$ tek,* can't touch that person!—*scil.*, for he has such a quick temper.

磕 K'o.$_2$ Read *k'ai'*; coll. *k'ok$_2$*, as in *k'ok$_2$ k'ok$_2$ kieu'* the sound of stones struck together; a clatter, thumping, drumming, as of the hands or feet on things.

K'ok$_2$. A coll. word, as in *k'ok$_2$ k'ok$_2$ ˏchung*, to shake, to shiver, as from cold or fear.

K'ok$_2$. A coll. word, as in *k'ok$_2$ 'kiăng*, slaves—an opprobrious epithet; *ˏi chó^2 k'ok$_2$* he is a slave!

K'ok$_2$. A coll. word, as in *k'ok$_2$ k'ok$_2$* a kind of wooden drum, used by Tauists and Budhists; it has two carps (*'li ˏngü*) carved on it.

K'ok$_2$. A coll. prefix, as in *k'ok$_2$ k'auk,* a cavity or depression in the ground, with or without water; a hole, a pit, a plash, a puddle.

(345) K'ong.

坤 ˓K'un. K'uên. The 2d diagram: the earth, inferior or obsequious to heaven; hence applied to the moon, statesmen, wives, and whatever has a correlative superior (ˏkiéng); favorable, obedient, compliant: COM., [1]ˏkiéng ˏk'ong*, heaven and earth; [2]*ˏk'ong chó^2* a female's horoscope; [3]*ˏk'ong ˏchü*, a girl's betrothal contract—sent to the boy's family.

昆 ˓Kun, Kuên. The same, alike or comparable; together, with, at the same time; to take precedence, before; an elder brother; descendants: [4]*ˏk'ong ˏt'ūng*, all insects; [5]*hau^2 ˏk'ong*, descendants; COM., [6]*ˏk'ong tëüng^2* brothers; COLL., *ˏi ˏk'ong tëüng^2 o^2 sá^2* he has many brothers.

崑 ˓Kun, Kuên. The Kwanlun or Koulkun Mts., between the Desert of Gobi and Tibet, about lat. 35° N.; regarded by the Chinese as the abode of the mysterious and supernatural: in the coll. a symbol of longevity: COM., [7]*ˏk'ong ˏlong ˏsang*, the Kwanlun range; COLL., [8]*pai' ˏk'ong ˏlong 'tau*, to worship "the Kwanlun measure"—rites at the anniversary of one's birth.

焜 ˓Kun. Kuên. Also read *hong^2* in the dictionaries: fiery, bright, luminous; the flame of fire: [9]*ˏk'ong yeu^2* blazing; [10]*'hwo ˏk'ong ˏk'ong ˏi siong^2*

1 乾坤 ○ 2 坤造 ○ 3 坤書 ○ 4 昆蟲 ○ 5 後昆 ○ 6 昆仲 ○ 7 崑崙山 ○ 8 拜崑崙斗 ○ 9 焜耀 ○ 10 火焜焜而上烝 ○

,*ching*, the lambent flame curled upwards.

鯤 Kun. Kuên. The roe or spawn of fishes; a whale, leviathan, kraken: ,*k'ong hwa'* ,*ui* ,*peng*, the whale turns into a roc.

鵾 Kun. Kuên. A sort of gallinaceous bird, called ,*k'ong* ,*kie*, perhaps a heath-cock or jungle-fowl.

康 K'ang. Rest, repose, quiet; peaceful, blessed; good, excellent, delightful; a road or avenue: [1],*k'ong* ,*chong*, a fine level road; [2],*k'ong* ,*kiong*, hale, as an old man; [3],*k'ong* ,*ning*, health and tranquillity; COM., [4],*k'ong kiong'* strong, robust; [5],*k'ong* ,*hi* the emperor Kanghi, A. D. 1662—1723; [6],*k'ong* ,*hi che' 'tiêng*, Kanghi's dictionary; ,*k'ong mó'* a sort of wadded cap; COLL., ,*k'ong* ,*hi 'peng* (or *'mó*), the superior cash-coinage of Kanghi's reign.

糠 K'ang. The husk of grain, chaff, bran; poor, chaffy, despicable; troublesome, remiss: [7]*'pi* ,*k'ong*, chaff, refuse; *met.*, troublesome, petty; COM., [8],*ch'u* ,*k'ong*, husks; [9],*k'ong* ,*t'ai*, a grain-sieve; [10]*'këü'* ,*k'ong*, sawdust; COLL., ,*k'ong pwong'* bran (mixed in) boiled rice (to feed fowls); ,*k'ong 'yong* ,*tü 'mi 'yong* ,*nëng*, "chaff nourishes pigs and rice nourishes people"—part of a ditty.

亢 K'ang. The neck of a man; the throat of a bird. Read *k'aung'*: strong, overbearing; unbending; to oppose, to resist; to carry to an extreme, excess; to shelter, to protect; a star near Arcturus: [11],*siong k'aung'* alike domineering, are well matched.

髡 Kun. Kuên. The punishment of shaving the head, anciently inflicted on a prince's relatives; bald; a leafless tree.

,***K'ong.*** A coll. word, as in ,*k'ong sioh*, ,*siäng*, or ,*k'ong* ,*k'ong kieu'* to give a ringing, metallic sound.

墾 K'êng. To open new land, to plow, to cultivate; to act vigorously, energetic; to wound, to injure: [12]*'k'ong te'* new land; [13],*k'ai 'k'ong* (coll. ,*k'wi 'k'ong*), to clear land.

慷 K'ang. Noble, magnanimous: [14]*'k'ong k'ai'* liberal, high-minded; firm, unmoved by slander; disappointed, grieved, as at the faults of others.

懇 K'êng. To ask, to request, to beg; earnest, importunate; truly, sincerely: [15]*'k'ong kek*, to ask one to give; COM., [16]*'k'ong* ,*kiu*, to intreat, to importune; [17]*'k'ong* ,*ong keu' nang'* to beg one's favor to save from distress.

'K'ong. A coll. word: to chop or break to pieces, as things while being cooked in a pan: *'k'ong ch'ói'* to chop in pieces; *'k'ong* ,*kio*, to chop or break egg-plant, as with the edge of the ladle.

空 K'ung. To empty, to exhaust; empty, a deficiency: also read ,*k'ung*, q. v.: [18]*k'ong' hwak*, a deficit, defalca-

1 康莊 2 康强 3 康寧 4 康健 5 康熙 6 康熙字典 7 粃糠 8 粗糠 9 糠篩 10 鋸糠 11 相亢 12 墾地 13 開墾 14 慷慨〇 15 懇給〇 16 懇求〇 17 懇恩救難 18 空乏〇

tion; COM., [1] *˛k'wi k'ong'* a deficit, as of revenue paid to the imperial treasury; COLL., *ch'io' 'tié 'yă k'ong'* the family very short of funds; *t'ok˛ k'ong'* to fall behind in means.

控' K'ung. To draw, to pull, as a bow; to hold firmly, to check, to rein in; to inform a magistrate, to accuse, to impeach: [2] *'niék˛ k'ong'* to accuse falsely; COM., [3] *k'ong' kó'* to petition against; *wok˛ k'ong'* to petition the highest provincial officers directly; *siong' k'ong'* to send in an accusation.

鞚' K'ung. A bridle, the reins by which a horse is checked or reined in.

˛K'ong. A coll. word; to carry (on the shoulder); to bear, as a responsibility for another; to give bribes: *˛k'ong ˛kiéng ˛t'au*, to bear on the shoulder; *'ngwai k'á' ˛i ˛k'ong k'ó'* "I bear it for him"—as said by one acting as surety.

(346) K'u.

坵 Ch'iu. Read *˛k'iu;* used for the coll. *˛k'u*, as in *˛iu ˛k'u*, the residual substance of expressed oils, pomace; [4] *˛ta ˛k'u*, pomace of tea-nut oil—used as soap; [5] *tau' ˛k'u*, bean pomace—used as manure; *k'ëüng' ˛k'u*, pomace of the tallow-tree oil.

˛箍 Ku. A hoop; to hoop, to bind with hoops: COM., [6] *˛k'u pwak*, to hoop earthen basins; [7] *'t'ëng ˛k'u*, bucket-hoops; [8] *˛king ˛k'u*, gold head-band (of Rationalists)—used in plays; [9] *˛k'u 'pa*, or *˛k'u 'pa ˛ch'a*, bound bundles of wood; COLL., *˛k'u 't'ëng tang'* a block for driving hoops tight; *˛k'u pauk*, the hoops have burst.

˛古 Ku. Read *'ku;* coll. *˛k'u*, as in *˛K'u ˛ch'eng*, a district of the Foochow prefecture.

˛K'u. A coll. word: to call animals; to hum, to recite, to repeat: *˛k'u ˛kié*, to call fowls; *˛tü k'á' ˛i ˛k'u 'tié ˛li*, call in the pigs; *˛k'u paik˛ ˛ing*, or *˛k'u ˛pang chah*, to hum over words in the eight tones, as in making rhymes; *˛k'u 'ch'iăng*, to say prayers in a low tone; *˛k'u ˛nëng ˛kó yoh˛* a drawing-plaster.

˛K'u. A coll. word: sections, as of eels offered for sale: *chak˛ sioh˛ ˛k'u*, cut off a piece (of the eel); *chak˛ ˛k'u ˛mwang*, eels cut into sections.

'苦 K'u. A marshy plant, which becomes sweet when frozen; bitter, unpleasant to the taste; painful, grievous, troublesome; pressing, urgent; earnest, painstaking; as a verb, to dislike, to mortify, to feel grieved for: [10] *'k'u ˛sung*, to dislike sailing; COM., [11] *'k'u 'ch'u*, extreme grief; [12] *'k'u 'siu*, to maintain painfully; [13] *'k'u k'wok˛* a miserable (i.e., profitless) office; [14] *'k'u miăng'* a hard lot in life; [15] *'k'u k'wong'* to exhort earnestly; [16] *'k'u 'mwi*, a bitter taste left (in the mouth); [17] *'k'u nang'* afflictions; [18] *'k'u ˛seng*, bitter ginseng—an inferior sort; [19] *˛sing 'k'u*, wearied; COLL., [20] *'k'u 'lang*, bilious spittle; [21] *'k'u 'kiăng ch'ok˛ ˛sing*, a poor man rising to a place

[1] 虧空 [2] 揑控 [3] 控告 [4] 茶坵 [5] 豆坵 [6] 箍砵 [7] 桶箍 [8] 金箍 [9] 箍把 [10] 苦船 [11] 苦楚 [12] 苦守 [13] 苦缺 [14] 苦命 [15] 苦勸 [16] 苦尾 [17] 苦難 ○ [18] 苦參 ○ [19] 辛苦 [20] 苦灠 [21] 苦仔出身

of wealth and honor: [1]*k'u lo*꜄ *꜀keng*, as salt as brine; [2]*'k'u chai*꜄ *mwoi*꜄ *'mwang*, the debt of misery not yet fully paid; *'k'u ꜀pu na*꜄ *꜀sang 'k'u ꜀pu 'kiang*, the bitter gourd only yields a young, bitter gourd—proverb meaning like begets like.

꜀K'u. A coll. word, as in *꜀k'u sioh*꜆ *꜀wong*, shrunk into a bunch, as a cock after a fight.

(347) K'ü.

區 ꜀Ch'ü. Read *꜀eu* in the dictionaries: to hide, to conceal; a place for storing things; a hamlet, a dwelling, a small house or store-room; to sort, to classify, to fix a limit or bound; a line of division, a boundary; a measure of four pecks; a surname: [3]*꜀k'ü piek*꜆ to divide, to discriminate properly; *puk*꜆ *꜀k'ü*, to conceal; *꜀k'ü ꜀k'ü*, petty, trifling; one's own, as talents, opinions; *꜀k'ü ꜀k'ü ꜀chi ꜀sing*, one's private feelings.

嶇 ꜀Ch'ü. A rugged peak, a steep ascent, declivity; rugged, uneven: COM., *꜀k'i ꜀k'ü*, rough, as roads.

樞 ꜀Ch'ü. A sort of spinous tree; the pivot or socket of a door; the center, axle, that on which a thing turns; cardinal, fundamental, essential: [4]*꜀k'ü ꜀ki*, the hinge; *met.*, a controlling power, a superior man; [5]*꜀t'ieng ꜀k'ü*, the pole-star; [6]*꜀king ꜀k'ü*, the moon; *꜀k'ü 'niu*, the chief part, as that on which a machine works.

軀 ꜀Ch'ü. The body, the whole person: [7]*꜀sing ꜀k'ü*, or *꜀k'ü 't'á*, the body; *oi*꜄ *kwok*꜆ *꜀kiong ꜀k'ü*, to offer one's self for the state.

驅 敺 ꜀Ch'ü. A fleet horse; to run fast; to hunt, to drive beasts, as into an inclosure or pit; to lash, to switch; to urge, to exhort, to animate; to order into their proper place: [8]*꜀ti ꜀k'ü*, to whip up; [9]*꜀sieng ꜀k'ü*, the vanguard; [10]*haiu*꜄ *꜀k'ü*, the rear-guard; [11]*꜀k'ü ꜀tü*, to expel and destroy; COM., [12]*꜀k'ü tük*꜆ to drive away; [13]*꜀k'ü ꜀sia*, to expel noxious influences; [14]*꜀k'ü tük*꜆ *꜀hang ꜀ing*, "exclude idlers"—a notice.

駒 ꜀Chü. A colt under two years old; a fine colt; a pony, a small horse: [15]*꜀ch'ieng 'li ꜀k'ü*, a swift, young horse; *met.*, a sprightly lad; [16]*꜀lá ꜀k'ü*, name of a ballad.

劬 ꜀Chü. Read *꜀kü* in the dictionaries: labor, care, extreme solicitude, distress: [17]*꜀k'ü ꜀ló*, the toil and anxiety of parents; the pangs of childbirth.

痀 ꜀Chü. A crooked back, a curved spine: [18]*꜀k'ü ꜀leu*, a hunchback.

絇 ꜀Chü. Thread used in ornamenting the tops of shoes; embroidered figures on shoes: *꜀k'ü lëü*꜄ shoes with embroidered fronts.

朐 ꜀Chü. Read *꜀kü* in the dictionaries: pork cut in strips and dried in the wind: [19]*꜀k'ü 'hu*, jerked cutlets of pork.

[1]苦滷鹹 [2]苦債未滿 [3]區別 [4]樞機 ○ [5]天樞 [6]金樞 [7]身軀 [8]馳驅 [9]先驅 [10]後驅 [11]驅除 [12]驅逐 [13]驅邪 [14]驅逐閒人 [15]千里駒 [16]驪駒 ○ [17]劬勞 [18]痀瘻 [19]朐脯 ○

祛 (Ch'ü.) To avert evil by sacrifices; to dissipate noxious influences: ¹ˈk'ü ˌhong, to expel windy humors; ²ˈk'ü sang' to scatter; ˌk'ü ˌk'ü, strong, durable.

袪 (Ch'ü.) The sleeve of a coat, the cuff, wristband: an ornamented cuff; to bind, to wind round; to whisk the sleeve.

去 (Ch'ü.) To take away, to expel; to conceal, to stow away: also read k'ì' q. v.: ³ˈk'ü ok, to "expel badness"—reform the heart and life.

ˌ*K'ü.* A coll. word: slow to learn, dull, stupid: ˌk'ü tek ˈheng, very dull; mĕk₂ ˌchiu ˌk'ü, the eyes dull—i. e., not quick to perceive.

(348) K'uh.

K'uh₂. A coll. word, as in k'uh₂ k'uh₂ kien' the bubbling sound, as of boiling rice, etc.

(349) K'uk.

禿 (T'u.) Read t'uk₂; used in a like sense for the coll. k'uk₂: blunt, short, not reaching far enough: ⁴k'uk₂ ˈmui, a blunt end; ⁵k'ak₂ k'uk₂ too short, as a cord; tio' ˈyă k'uk₂ "the road very blunt"—in straits, penniless; ⁶ˈch'iu ˈchai k'uk₂ the (ends of the) fingers blunt or stubby.

(350) K'ung.

空 (Keung.) Empty, vacant, void, exhausted; at leisure; an opening or crevice; great, wide; the sky, firmament; poor, broken; the mind unoccupied, unprejudiced, able to perceive clearly; abstraction, as understood by Budhists; also read k'ong', and in the coll. ˌk'ëng, and k'aëng', q. v.: ⁷ˈt'ai' ˌk'ung, or ⁸ˌk'ung ˌtiong, the firmament, heaven; com., ⁹ˌk'ung ˌhü, exhausted, as a treasury or granary; ¹⁰ˌk'ung ˌu ˈsu ˈiu, wholly destitute. Read ˈk'ung: a hole, a cavity, an opening in the ground.

倥 (K'ung.) Ignorant, simple: ˌk'ung ˌtung, rude, ignorant; ¹¹ˌk'ung ˈchung, hurried by press of business, worn out.

悾 (K'ung.) Same as the last: ignorant, rustic; disheartened, as by ill luck; true, sincere: ˌk'ung ˌk'ung, simple.

崆 (K'ung.) A hill in Pingliang prefecture, Kansuh, called ¹²ˌk'ung ˌtung, the source of the river King: ˌk'ung ˌlung, a high hill.

箜 (K'ung.) A kind of flat lute with 25 strings, called ¹³ˌk'ung ˌheu; a basket.

ˌ*K'ung.* A coll. word: to turn up the earth with the snout, as swine: ˌk'ung ˌt'u, to root in the ground.

壼 (K'un. K'uĕn.) Corridors or passages between rooms for females in the palace: ¹⁴ˌkié ˈk'ung, a virtuous woman.

孔 (K'ung.) An opening, a hole, an orifice; a cave, a hollow; through; great, deep, excellent; a surname: ¹⁵ˈk'ung tŏ² a passage, thoroughfare; com., ¹⁶ˈk'ung ˈchü, or ¹⁷ˈk'ung ˌhu ˈchü, Confucius;

1 祛瘋 2 祛散 3 去惡 4 禿尾 5 恰禿 6 手指禿 7 太空 8 空中 9 空虛 10 空無所有 11 倥傯 12 崆峒 13 箜篌 14 閨壼 15 孔道 16 孔子 17 孔夫子

¹ᶜk‘ung ch‘iok, the peacock; ²ᶜk‘ung ꜀hwong ꜀hing, "square-hole brothers"—a term for cash in poems and epistles; COLL., ᶜk‘ung ᶜchü ngᶾ ꜀siu kah꜆ ꜀mang t‘aik, Confucius would not receive a card (of invitation) to be kept over night—used as a proverbial expression for the uncertainties of life; ᶜk‘ung auk, to be overbearing.

ᶜ**窘** Chün. Chiung. Afflicted, distressed; poor, in urgent need of; to distress, to harass; as formerly, still: ³ᶜk‘ung p‘aik, straitened.

ᶜ**悃** K‘un. K‘uên. Sincerity, singleness of heart; plain, simple, unadorned, as style: ᶜk‘ung p‘aik, sincere in feeling or aim; unadorned; ⁴ᶜk‘ung ꜀t‘ing, true, faithful.

ᶜ**捆** K‘un. K‘uên. Similar to the next: to arrange, to place together; to tie, to beat and bind; to work at; to make firm by pounding: ⁵ᶜk‘ung lëüᶾ to weave sandals.

ᶜ**綑** K‘un. K‘uên. To bind, to tie with cords, to fetter; to plait, to braid; to hem, to put on a band or fold; a border, as on a skirt for ornament: COM., ⁶ᶜk‘ung ꜀teu, strips, or tape, for binding and hems; ⁷ᶜk‘ung ᶜpong, to tie the hands behind the back; COLL., ᶜk‘ung ꜀á ᶜk‘au, to bind the tops of shoes; ᶜk‘ung sioh꜆ ᶜk‘ung, to bind in a bundle; ᶜk‘ung pwoh꜆ to tie, to bind; *met.*, cramped, distressed.

ᶜ**囷** Chün. Also read ꜀k‘ung and ꜀k‘üng: a round granary or receptacle for grain; a spiral, twisted; used for the coll. ꜀k‘üng, q. v.: ⁸꜀lung ᶜk‘ung, spiral, contorted as roots.

ᶜ**稇** Chün. To bind with cord; a bundle of rope; full, well provided: ⁹ᶜk‘ung chaiᶾ ꜀i ꜀kwi, to return home well laden—successful in business.

ᶜ**菌** Chün. A small kind of mushroom, regarded as pernicious to health: ¹⁰ᶜk‘ung kiéᶾ a sort of fine-quilled cassia.

ᶜ**閫** K‘un. K‘uên. A threshold; posts of a door; door of the female apartments; *met.*, females: ¹¹ᶜk‘ung nöiᶾ and ¹²ᶜk‘ung ngwoiᶾ within and without the palace, the court and country; COM., ¹³꜀tu ᶜk‘ung (or ¹⁴꜀tu ꜀si), a military officer of the 5th grade.

ᶜ**麕** Chün. Also read ꜀kung, or ꜀k‘ung: a name for deer, specially the antelope; *Antilope gutturosa?* the doe is hornless, and both the buck and doe are very timid.

꜀*K‘ung.* A coll. word: to coil, as rope; coiled, curled up; also bound, wound tightly: ꜀k‘ung ꜀yéng ꜀yéng, coiled up, as rope, a snake, &c.; ꜀k‘ung sioh꜆ ꜀wong, coiled into a bunch; ꜀k‘ung sioh꜆ ꜀toi, cuddled together, as animals.

(351) K‘üng.

꜀**穹** Ch‘iung. Lofty, vast and high, as the firmament; to exhaust; spacious, empty; very eminent; to stop, to obstruct: ¹⁵꜀k‘üng ꜀ch‘ong, the azure sky, empyrean;

¹孔雀 ²孔方兄 ³窘迫 ⁴悃愊 ⁵捆屨 ⁶綑條 ⁷綑綁 ⁸輪囷 ⁹稇載而歸 ¹⁰菌桂 ¹¹閫內 ¹²閫外 ¹³都閫 ¹⁴都司 ¹⁵穹蒼

[2],k'ŭng tèk, to stop up; [2],k'ŭng ,lŭng, lofty, eminent.

邛 'Ch'iung. An inferior department south-west of Chingtu-fu, Sz'chuen; name of a river; sick, infirm, wearied; troublesome.

筇 'Ch'iung. A species of bamboo; bamboos suitable for walking-sticks for old persons: [3]'tëŭk, ,k'ŭng, a bamboo-staff.

蛩 'Ch'iung. A fabulous animal like a griffin? a kind of locust, called [4]'hi ,k'ŭng: [5],k'ŭng ,nging, the locust's chirp; ,k'ŭng ,k'ŭng, sad about, concerned for.

銎 'Ch'iung. The eye of an ax or hammer: [6]'hu ,k'ŭng, the hole of an ax; ,k'ŭng ,k'ŭng, to strike at, to knock. Read ,hŭng: alarmed.

恐 恐 'K'ung. Apprehensive, suspicious, anxious about; alarmed, agitated; to fear lest, to suppose, to imagine; supposing, perhaps: in the coll. read 'hung, q. v.: [7]'k'ŭng këü' to dread; [8]pok, 'k'ŭng, quiet; COM., [9]'k'ŭng p'a' fearful of, apprehensive lest.

勤 'Ch'in. Diligent in duties, laborious, industrious; attentive to, sedulous: [10],k'ŭng ,wong, loyal, diligent in serving the prince; [11],k'ŭng lik, industrious; COM., [12],k'ŭng 'king, diligent; [13],k'ŭng 'k'u, painfully laborious, assiduous; [14],k'ŭng kiéng' 'k'i ,ka, to exalt one's family by diligence and economy; [15],k'ŭng 'iu ,kung hié' ,u ek, diligence has merit, play is profitless—two sentences near the close of the Three Character Classic.

懃 'Ch'in. Like the last: diligent, earnest: COM., [16],ŭng ,k'ŭng, anxious about duties; zealous, pressing on in spite of difficulties.

芹 'Ch'in. Celery or parsley; cress: [17]'chwi ,k'ŭng, water-cresses; 'ch'ai ,k'ŭng, to pluck the cress—i. e., become a Siutsai; COM., [18],k'ŭng ch'ai' celery.

囷 'Chün. Read 'k'ung, ,k'ung, and ,k'ŭng; used for the coll. ,k'ŭng: a stack, a pile, as of straw; a heap, as of wood, earth, or stones; to pile, to heap: sioh, ,k'ŭng, a stack, a pile; ,k'ŭng sioh, ,toi, to gather into a heap.

(352) K'wa.

夸 'K'ua. Also read k'wa'; interchanged with the next: great, prodigious; to brag, to vaunt; magniloquent; vain, conceited: ,k'wa ,p'i, servile, cringing.

誇 'K'ua. To talk largely, to boast, to brag; bragging, grandiloquent, arrogant, conceited; wide, ample, as a dress: [19],k'ing ,k'wa, to boast; COM., [20],k'wa 'k'eu (coll. ,k'wa ch'oi'), boastful, braggart; [21]'chëü' ,k'wa, self-laudation; COLL., ói' 'kong ,k'wa wa' fond of bragging; ,k'wa chiăh, ,k'wa, very boastful.

---

1 穹窒　2 穹窿　3 竹筇　4 飛蛩　5 蛩吟　6 斧銎　7 恐懼　8 不恐　9 恐怕　10 勤王　11 勤力　12 勤緊　13 勤苦　14 勤儉起家　15 勤有功戲無益　16 慇懃　17 水芹　18 芹菜　19 矜誇　20 誇口　21 自誇

姱 ˓K'ua. Good, neat, pretty; vain, conceited: [1]˓k'wa ˓siu, to act decorously; [2]˓k'wa chiék˒ fastidiously correct, finical.

跨˒ K'ua. Also read ˓k'wa: to bestride, to straddle, between the legs; to pass over, to encroach on; to surpass, to excel: used in the coll. for ˓k'iă and ˓k'iă, q. v.: k'wa˒ chó˒ (or chau˒), to excel, as a son his father; pok˒ k'wa˒ ˓ki kwok, not encroach on his territory; k'wa˒ wok˒ to excel; COLL., seu˒ ˓nĕng k'wa˒ a˒ domineered over by others.

胯˒ K'ua. Also read ˓k'wa and k'o˒: interchanged with the last: the thighs, space between the legs: [3]k'wa˒ ˓hu, one cowed or forced to submit; [4]seu˒ ˓ing k'wa˒ ha˒ ˓chi ĭk˒ shamed by being made to go between another's legs, or submit to him.

掛˒ Kua. Read kwa˒; used for the coll. k'wa˒ as in k'wa˒ so˒ or k'wa˒ sioh˒ pek˒ to take account, as of sales: k'ĕăk˒ ˓i k'wa˒ k'iéng˒ he is indebted as *per* account; k'wa˒ ˓la ˓mwi, to note a balance; k'wa˒ ˓hung ˓peng ˓lă, note it on the tablet or slate.

K'wa˒. A coll. word, as in k'wa˒ ˓ch'iéng, to run aground on shallows—same as k'ó ˓ch'iéng, q. v.

(353) **K'wai.**

夬 ˓K'uai. To pull or flow in different ways; different, parted, divided; absolute, certain, the 54th of the 64 diagrams.

蒯 ˓K'uai. A kind of rush or grass, used for making sandals, ropes, and mats; a surname: ˓k'wai ˓heu, cord wound on a sword's hilt.

塊˒ K'uai. Also read ˓k'wai in the dictionaries: a clod, a lump; a piece, fragment, fraction of; a classifier of lumps, dollars, and small flat things, such as boards, panes, slices; *met.*, stupid, doltish; sometimes used in imitation of the coll. mandarin: in the coll. read tói˒ q. v.: [5]tai˒ k'wai˒ heaven and earth, nature; [6]k'wai˒ ˓yong ˓u ˓ti, doltish and ignorant; [7]˓t'u k'wai˒ a clod of earth; COLL., ˓hwang ek˒ k'wai˒ one dollar.

快˒ K'uai. Glad, happy, cheerful, contented; pleasure, good health and spirits; quick, prompt, ready; alacrity; used in imitation of the coll. mandarin: in the coll. read k'ă˒ q. v.: [8]k'wai˒ ˓ma, a courier; [9]k'wai˒ ˓chü, chopsticks; COM., [10]k'wai˒ k'wai˒ make haste; [11]k'wai˒ ˓pang, lictors in yamuns; [12]˓song k'wai˒ well and happy; k'wai˒ ˓sing (or lok˒), pleased, joyful; [13]˓ma k'wai˒ an official thief-catcher; [14]k'wai˒ ˓ch'iu, aptly, adroitly; COLL., ng˒ ˓song k'wai˒ indisposed, out of sorts; k'wai˒ ˓sié, be a little spry!

(354) **K'wak.**

濶 闊˒ K'uo. Wide, broad; large, ample; far apart, distant; liberal; diligent; to enlarge, to widen: [15]˓su k'wak, long separated, as friends; COM., [16]k'wak˒ chah˒ wide and narrow; [17]˓kwong

---

[1]姱修 [2]姱節 [3]胯夫 [4]受人胯下之辱 [5]大塊無知 [6]塊然 ○ [7]土塊 [8]快馬 [9]快子 ○ [10]快快 ○ [11]快班 [12]爽快 [13]馬快 ○ [14]快手 [15]疎闊 [16]闊窄 [17]廣闊

ALPH. DICT. 59

k‘wak, extensive; *k‘wak*, *pwo*’ a kind of wide cotton-cloth; COLL., *k‘wak*, ‘*pai*, profuse and ostentatious, as in spending; *k‘wak*, *twai*² ample, capacious; *k‘wak*, *ch‘oi*’ ,*kong*, a wide-mouthed jar.

(355) K‘wang.

‘寬 K‘uang. Large, wide, spacious, ample; easy, indulgent; kind, clement, forgiving; slow; to relax, to enlarge, to widen: [1],*k‘wang chëüng*’ over-indulgent, conniving; COM., [2],*k‘wang* ,*ong*, gracious; [3],*k‘wang* ,*üng*, lenient, as toward a debtor or transgressor; [4],*k‘wang sëü*’ to forgive; [5],*k‘wang* ,*ch‘ü* (or ‘*ch‘iong*), spacious, roomy; [6],*k‘wang aing*² or ,*k‘wang hwang*² to allow a longer time; [7],*k‘wang* ‘*ing* ,*chiéng*, Loo Choo cash; [8],*k‘wang* ,*sing nai*² ‘*siu*, to exercise great forbearance; COLL., ,*k‘wang lauk*, *lauk*, very spacious; very large or loose, as a shoe; ,*k‘wang* ,*k‘wang* ‘*peng*, slow, not urgent.

‘欵 ‘款 K‘uang. Something desired; sincere, single-minded, true; to revere, to treat well; to knock at, to seek for; to reach; a record, memorandum; to enumerate; a numerative of articles, classes, affairs, etc.: [9]‘*tä* ‘*k‘wang*, to write an autograph; [10]‘*k‘wang* ,*liu*, to detain, as guests; COM., [11],*kwi* ‘*k‘wang*, to repay a loan; [12]‘*k‘wang tai*² to treat politely; [13]‘*k‘wang sek*, (or *sie*’, or *yong*²), a form, style, manner; [14],*sëng* ‘*k‘wang*, double marks, as the names of owner and writer, both inscribed on a fan or scroll; COLL., ‘*chiä* ‘*k‘wang*, this form or mode; *lóh*, ‘*k‘wang*, to append one's autograph; ,*i chó*’ ‘*la* ,*k‘wang* ‘*k‘wang*, he assumes a manner, acts in that fashion.

‘窾 K‘uang. An empty place; dry, dried up; hollow, as empty vessels; *met.*, uninformed, inexperienced, ignorant of: ‘*k‘wang kieu*’ a hole, hollow place; ‘*k‘wang* ‘*k‘ié*, uninformed.

‘盥 Kuan. To wash the hands, to wash before sacrificing: ‘*k‘wang* ‘*sá*, to wash, to perform ablutions.

‘*K‘wang*. A coll. word, as in ‘*k‘wang* ‘*k‘wang kieu*’, a clattering, as of tiles; rattling sound of thunder.

,圜 Huan. Complete, round, circular, a circle; to revolve, to circulate, to environ; to look alarmed, in which sense read ,*hwang* and ,*hwang* in the dictionaries: [15],*k‘wang sé*² ,*i* ‘*k‘i*, he started up and looked about; [16],*k‘wang hwak*, cash; [17],*k‘wang* ‘*t‘u*, a prison; COLL., ,*k‘wang* ,*k‘wang* ,*ui*, encircling, stretching around, as walls, hills; ,*k‘wang* ,*k‘wang* ,*kiéng*, the border on all sides; ,*k‘wang sioh*, ,*lau*, to go about once; ,*k‘wang p‘wai*’ a tonal mark at the corner of a character.

,環 Huan. Interchanged with the last: a ring, a circlet, a bracelet; to ring, to encircle: [18],*k‘wang pwoi*² girdle-jingles; [19],*k‘wang pó*² to embrace, to environ; COM., [20],*k‘wang tok*, circles and dots, to punctuate; [21],*k‘wang* ‘*mwang*, full

[1]寬縱 [2]寬恩 [3]寬容 [4]寬恕 [5]寬舒 [6]寬限 [7]寬永錢 [8]寬心耐守 [9]題欵 [10]欵留 ○ [11]歸欵 [12]欵待 [13]欵式 [14]雙欵 [15]圜視而起 [16]圜法 [17]圜土 [18]環佩 [19]環抱 [20]環點 [21]環滿

of circles, as a good essay so marked by the critic; *꜀k‘wang chak*, to circle, make a complete circuit; *꜀k‘wang ꜀k‘wang mó*² a kind of crownless cap—worn by Manchus; *ʻkiu ꜀liĕng ꜀k‘wang*, a chain-puzzle.

鐶 ꜀Huan. Like the last: a metal ring; a ring, a link: COM., *꜀mwong ꜀k‘wang*, a door-ring; [1]*ʻchi ꜀k‘wang*, a finger-ring; [2]*ch‘iu ꜀k‘wang*, bracelets.

鍰 ꜀Huan. Also read *꜀hwang*: a ring of iron; also a weight of six taels: *꜀tung ꜀k‘wang*, a brass ring for a door.

寰 ꜀Huan. The imperial domain; a wall about a palace; a circuit, a district: [3]*꜀k‘wang ʻn*, the world; [4]*꜀k‘wang nói*² the emperor's land.

闤 ꜀Huan. A market-place; the gate leading to it: [5]*꜀k‘wang hwoi*² the wall and gate of a market.

鬟 ꜀Huan. To dress the hair in rings on the crown, as anciently done; a tuft, a knob, a knot; the rounded crests of hills: [6]*kwoi*² *꜀k‘wang*, a lady's coiffure; [7]*꜀a ꜀k‘wang*, a slave-girl, maid-servant.

*K‘wang*². A coll. word: the heavy sound of gongs when struck: *꜀k‘wang k‘wang*² sound of a gong, clang! clang!

(356) K‘wi.

虧 K‘uei. Short breath, to pant; a failure, defect, deficiency, diminution; waning, as the moon; broken, injured: [8]*꜀k‘wi k‘wok*, deficiency; [9]*ngwok*₂ *ʻmwong chaik*, *꜀k‘wi*, the moon waxes and wanes; COM., [10]*꜀k‘wi k‘ong*² defalcation, arrearage; *꜀k‘wi ʻpwong*, loss of capital; *꜀k‘wi ꜀sing*, ingrate; COLL., *k‘ek*, *꜀k‘wi*, distress, suffering.

開 ꜂K‘ai. Read *꜀k‘ai*; coll. *꜀k‘wi*: to open, to unfold, to spread out; to begin, to commence, to institute; to enact, to perform, as rites; to explain, to disclose; to perceive clearly; to open, or clear, as new land; to dig out; to remove, do away with; to write, to make out, as shop-bills; to show (favor): [11]*꜀k‘wi ʻk‘i*, to open, to unfold; [12]*꜀k‘wi ʻch‘iu*, to begin to do; [13]*꜀k‘wi ka*² to open shop after the New-year festivities; [14]*꜀k‘wi ꜀hung*, to recommence animal diet; [15]*꜀k‘wi ʻk‘ong*, to clear new land; [16]*꜀k‘wi tó*² to clear the way, as before an officer's sedan; [17]*꜀k‘wi ꜀ch‘ú* to give (a school-boy) his first whipping; [18]*꜀k‘wi ꜀hwa*, to flower; [19]*꜀k‘wi ʻngang*, to "open the eyes", as of idols by certain rites; [20]*꜀k‘wi ꜀hwong*, to write a medical prescription; [21]*꜀k‘wi ꜀ong*, to show favor to; [22]*꜀k‘wi keng*² to remove a prohibition; [23]*꜀k‘wi ꜀t‘ĕng*, to perceive clearly; perspicuous, plain; *꜀k‘wi ꜀siŭng*, to speak out; *꜀k‘wi ʻká*, to explain; *꜀k‘wi ꜀t‘au*, or *꜀k‘wi ꜀sung*, to set sail; *꜀k‘wi tiing*² *꜀ka*, shopkeepers; *꜀k‘wi twai*² *꜀mwong pah*, *twai*² *ho*² "open the big doors"—i. e., let all know it, there's nothing to fear; *꜀k‘wi ʻchang k‘ëük*, *pek*₂ *꜀nëng siăh*, *ʻchwi*, "dig a well for others to drink the water;" *met.*, one has all the trouble and others reap the benefit.

---

1 指鐶　3 寰宇　5 闤闠　7 丫鬟　9 月滿則虧　10 虧空　12 開手　14 開葷　16 開道　18 開花　20 開方　22 開禁

2 手鐶　4 寰內　6 髻鬟　8 虧缺　11 開起　13 開假　15 開墾　17 開箠　19 開眼　21 開恩　23 開通

揆 ʻK'uei. Erroneously read ˏk'ui: to measure, to calculate; to guess, to surmise; to weigh in the mind, to consider how; to examine, to reason out: ʻk'wi tokˏ to estimate, to reason upon; paikˏ ʻk'wi, a general superintendent.

(357) K'wi.

盔 ˏK'uei. A basin, a porringer; a casque, a helmet, a defense for the head: COM., ˏk'wi kakˏ helmet and mail, armor; ˏk'wi mó' or ˏt'au ˏk'wi, a helmet or casque of iron plates.

魁 ˏK'uei. A star; the head, the chief; the first or highest in a class: COM., [1]ˏk'wi ˏsing, the north star—attendant of the god of Literature; [2]ˏk'wi ˏngu, lofty, as hills; met., high, tall in stature; [3]ˏk'wi ʻsiu, the first Kŭjin, or Chinsz', graduate; [4]ˏking ˏk'wi, from the 2nd to the 5th Kŭjin graduate; [5]ʻa ˏk'wi, from the 6th to the 12th; [6]ˏung ˏk'wi, from the 13th to the last of the class; [7]hwoi' ˏk'wi, from the 2nd to the 18th Chinsz' graduate; [8]ˏk'wi ˏngwong, the 2nd of the Kŭjin; COLL., ˏk'wi ˏpeng, the left part of the ˏk'wi character—a phrase used opprobriously for cunning, knavish; ˏk'wi ˏsing t'ekˏ ʻtau, the Star-god kicks the Dipper—is so represented.

ʻ𨇾 The same as koi' (to kneel); used in the *Paik, ˏIng* for the coll. ʻk'wi, to kneel in worshiping: [9]ʻk'wi pai' to kneel and worship; [10]ʻk'wi ˏpu satˏ, to kneel before idols; ʻk'wi ˏsang p'á' to kneel thrice with the head to the ground.

(358) K'wo.

戈 ˏKuo. Ko. A kind of halberd, with a cross bar used as a hook; a spear, a javelin: [11]ˏkang ˏk'wo, shields and spears; tong' ˏkang ˏk'wo, to take up arms, go to war; [12]ʻching ˏk'wo tai' tang' lay on their arms till morning.

科 ˏK'o. A root, the hollow culm of grain; empty, hollow, a vacuum; a rule; medical practice; a class, series, order, rank, gradation; a literary examination; to examine (and decide); in the coll. to reckon, to estimate, as prices: [13]ˏk'wo mukˏ a series, rank; [14]ˏk'wo ˏt'eu, bareheaded; COM., [15]ˏk'wo tá' examination for literary degrees; [16]ˏk'wo ˏtiong, the examinations for Kŭjin degree; ˏhiong ˏk'wo and hwoi' ˏk'wo, examinations for the grades of Kŭjin and Chinsz'; [17]ˏong ˏk'wo, an examination by (imperial) favor; [18]ˏk'wo kakˏ ch'okˏ ˏsing, official rank gained by literary success; [19]lŭkˏ ˏk'wo, the six departments in a yamun; [20]nói' ˏk'wo, internal practice, physic; [21]ngwoi' ˏk'wo, external practice, surgery; COLL., ˏk'wo ʻpwong, estimate the capital (and sell accordingly); tiohˏ ˏk'wo niohˏ wai' must reckon it how much? ˏk'wo mó' ch'okˏ can't judge how (the matter will turn out); ˏk'wo ʻtié ˏnia nói' reckon somewhat under (the price mentioned).

[1]魁星 [2]魁梧 [3]魁首 [4]經魁 [5]亞魁 [6]文魁 [7]會魁 [8]魁元 [9]𨇾拜 [10]𨇾菩 薩 [11]干戈 〇 [12]枕戈待旦 [13]科目 [14]科頭 [15]科第 [16]科場 [17]恩科 [18]科甲 出身 [19]六科 [20]內科 [21]外科

咼 A wry mouth, a mouth distorted naturally or by disease.
ˏKuo.

撾 To beat, as a bell with a stick: ˊˏk'wo ˋku, to beat drums.
ˏChua.

薖 簻 Grass, plants; wide and large; hungry, famished; a large whip, a switch, a lash, in which sense the 2nd is also read ˏchua.
ˏKuo.

靴 Boots: COM., ³ˏtaung' ˏk'wo, satin boots; ³ˏk'wo sek, boot-shape or fashion, as a kind of shoe is made; COLL., ˏk'wo hong' boot-tops; ⁴ˏk'wo ˋt'ëng, the inside of a boot-top; ⁵ˏchiëng p'e' ˏk'wo, sharp-toed boots; ˏpang ˏt'au ˏk'wo, boots with square toes.
ˏHsüeh.

刳 Read ˏku; used in the *Paik, ˏIng* for the coll. ˏk'wo: to cut, to clip, to pare off, to round; also to reap with a sickle: ˏk'wo ˏyéng, to cut round, as collars; ˏk'wo sioh, ˏkiéng, to pare off an edge.
ˏK'u.

傀 Read ˋkwi; coll. ˏk'wo, as in ˏk'wo ˋloi hié' puppet play; chó' ˏk'wo ˋloi, to hang one's self—a jesting phrase; ˏk'wo ˋloi ˏtüng ˏt'iu ngˀ ˋhó k'ung' "the puppets again pulled (i. e., played) don't look well;" *met.*, said of certain acts repeated, as begging.
ˏK'uei.

顆 A small head, lump, or clod; a numerative of things, as beads, pearls, shot: ⁶ek, ˋk'wo ˏchio, one bead; ⁷ˋki ˏtó ˋk'wo, how many of them?
ˋK'o.

課 To try, to essay; to deliberate, to plan; to lead on; an order, series; to advise, to exhort; a task, a lesson, an exercise, an example; literary pursuits: ⁸k'wo' ˏung, essays; ⁹swoi' k'wo' a tax, a duty; COM., ¹⁰ˏkung k'wo' literary work; ¹¹nik, k'wo' a daily task; ¹²ngwok, k'wo' monthly trials in composing; ¹³hwoi' k'wo' a literary club; ¹⁴ˋk'ó k'wo' to examine essays; ¹⁵ˏsiéng k'wo' or ¹⁶k'wo' ˏngüng, the duty levied on salt-merchants; ¹⁷k'wo' ˏch'á, the couriers of a salt-office.
K'o.

跔 Read ˏkü; used in the *Paik, ˏIng* for the coll. ˏk'wo, as in ˏk'wo ˏk'a, or ˏk'a ˏk'wo, one foot drawn up, to hop on one foot.
ˏCh'ü.

踒 Read ˏwo; used in the *Paik, ˏIng* for the coll. ˏk'wo, as in ˏk'wo ˏtoi siék, kauk, sprained leg and broken bone!—an imprecation; ˏk'wo ˋteu, strained, sprained; ˏk'a pouk, ˏk'wo, the foot sprained by a fall.
ˏWo.

(359) K'woh.

曲 Read k'ëük, ; coll. k'woh, : bent, crooked, twisting about, winding; a song, sonnet, ditty: k'woh, ch'ioh, a carpenter's square; k'woh, ˏtá ˋkiáng, boatmen, fishermen; ˏwang k'woh, or ˏk'i k'woh, crooked, winding; k'woh, ˏkié kaëk, "crooked cock"—said of one who is perverse or
Ch'ü.

¹撾鼓 ²緞靴 ³靴式 ⁴靴桶 ⁵尖鼻靴 ⁶一顆珠 ⁷幾多顆 ⁸課文 ⁹稅課 ¹⁰功課 ¹¹日課 ¹²月課 ¹³會課 ¹⁴考課 ¹⁵鹽課 ¹⁶課銀 ¹⁷課差

福州方言拼音字典

mischievous; *ch'iong' k'wok*, to sing songs; *k'wok, 'p'rong*, a song-book.

(360) K'wok.

亅, Chüeh. A hooked stroke; a hook, hooked; the barb of a weapon; a catch or mark; to mark off: *,keu k'wok*, to mark off criminals for execution, as done by the emperor at the autumnal assizes.

鈌 缺, Ch'üeh. Broken, defective or cracked, as a vessel; deficient, wanting, short; deficiency, defect; a vacancy in an office; a post, situation; duties of an office: COM., [1]*'kang k'wok*, an easy office; [2]*,hwang k'wok*, or [3]*yeu' k'wok*, an important office; [4]*k'wok, ch'ok*, a vacancy occurring; [5]*ch'ok, k'wok*, to fill a vacancy, get an office; [6]*k'iéng' k'wok*, deficient, failing; [7]*k'wok, hwak*, destitute; COLL., [8]*k'wok, ,pong*, deficient supply of goods; *k'wok, ,k'a*, want of requisite number of players, as in a game of cards; [9]*k'wok, 'chieu*, coming short, too few or little.

厥, Chüeh. A personal pronoun; he, she, it; his, hers, its; that, that one; short; to project stones; to bow: [10]*k'wok, 'mwi*, a stunted, bare tail; [11]*k'wok, kaëk*, to bow the head to the ground.

劂, Chüeh. A gouge, a chisel, a burin, used by carvers and carpenters: [12]*k'ié k'wok*, a graving tool.

橛, Chüeh. A post in the middle of a gateway; a stake, a pile; a stick, a piece of wood; the bit of a bridle; a drum-stick: in the coll. read *k'wok*, q. v.

獗, Chüeh. Rude, unruly: [13]*,ch'iong k'wok*, violent, ferocious, as robbers, or animals.

蕨, Chüeh. An edible fern, whose stalks are cooked for food when tender; supposed to resemble an *aspidium*, or the foot of a tortoise: in the coll. read *kwok*, q. v.: *k'wok, 'hung*, farina of fern-root.

蟨, Ch'üeh. An animal that is said to carry another; refers to some marsupial animal (?)

蹶, Ch'üeh. To stumble, to fall, to slip down; to fail in; prostrate; to leap, to jump: also read *kwoi'* q. v.: [14]*kiék, k'wok*, overthrown, subverted.

闕, Ch'üeh. A lookout above a gate; imperial; defective, wanting, lost; to err, to miss; faults, deficiencies; disrespectful: *k'wok, ,mwong*, His Majesty's palace; [15]*ngwok, k'wok*, the waning moon; [16]*k'wok, 'li*, a place in the south of Shantung, where Confucius taught; COM., [17]*k'wok, ,ing*, one of the three internal diseases ([18]*t'ai' ,ing*, [19]*sieu' ,ing*, and *kw'ok, ,ing*) "which are hard to cure", disease of the liver and kidneys.

1 簡鈌	3 要鈌	5 出鈌	7 鈌乏	9 鈌少	11 厥角	12 剞劂	13 猖獗	14 蹋蹶	15 月闕	16 闕里	18 太陰
2 煩鈌	4 鈌出	6 欠鈌	8 鈌尌	10 厥尾	○	○	○	○	○	17 闕陰	19 少陰

福州方言拼音字典

闋 K'uei. To shut the door, to close the office; to stop, to cease, to rest; done; end of a song: *huk*, *k'wok*, to take off mourning; *ngok*, *k'wok*, to stop the music.

橛 'Chüeh. Read *k'wok*,; coll. *k'wok*,: a block, a stick, a piece of wood: similar to *kwok*, q. v.: *këü' sioh*, *k'wok*, saw off a block.

(361) K'wong.

匡 'K'uang A vessel for containing rice; a square box, case, or frame; regular, square, rectangular; to frame, to place in a frame; to rectify, to reform; to assist, to deliver: in the coll. used for *k'wong'* q. v.: [1]*k'wong keu'* to save, to reform one; COM., [3]*mwong k'wong*, door-frames; [2]*k'wong mwong*, a door in a wall; [4]*k'wong sing*, to confine the mind, as of a child at study; COLL., [5]*k'wong kah*, or *k'wong tang'* ruled lines to write by; [6]*tau k'wong*, square ornamental frames or lanterns; *'kwi 'chi k'wong*, a kind of fruit-plate divided into sections; *k'wong sioh*, *toi*, to put (things) together in a box or frame; *k'wong mwong kiëk*, jambs of a wall-door.

劻 'K'uang Hasty, prompt, eager, zealous: [7]*k'wong siong*, urgent, hurried, an emergency.

眶 'K'uang Socket of the eye; the canthus: [8]*kó k'wong*, sunken eyes; COLL., *k'wong 'ngang twai'* "the eyes large;" *met.*, proud, aspiring; *k'wong 'ngang sái'* "the eyes small;" *met.*, of moderate desires, as in making small gains.

誆 'K'uang. Lying talk; to deceive, to swindle: COM., [9]*k'wong p'iéng'* to cheat, to defraud, to humbug; [10]*k'wong 'tu*, to entice one to gamble; COLL., [11]*k'wong t'ó'* a scheme to entrap one.

筐 'K'uang. A square basket; a basket without a cover: [12]*k'wong 'p'i*, baskets for sending presents in; [13]*k'wong ch'ong*, a bed, a couch.

圈 'Ch'üan. A coop, a pen for animals; an enclosure, a prison; *met.*, a trap, a snare: cups or bowls of bent wood; to encircle, to surround; a ring, a circle, a stop, a period, to mark or punctuate, in which senses *k'wang* is used in the coll.: COM., [14]*k'wong t'ó'* a gin, a snare; *met.*, a plot to entrap one.

棬 'Ch'üan. A wooden bowl or cup; vessels of bent wood: [15]*pwi k'wong*, cups and bowls.

壙 'K'uang. The vault or cavity of a tomb; a desert, a solitude: [16]*k'wong kung'* a wilderness; COM., [17]*mwo' 'k'wong*, vault of a grave; [18]*cheng' 'k'wong*, to envault (a coffin); [19]*hung 'k'wong*, to close a vault; COLL., [20]*k'wong seng chiê'* sacrifice in front of a grave.

纊 'K'uang. Raw cotton; the fibers of cotton, cotton in a silky state.

1匡救 2門匡 3匡門 4匡心 5匡格 6斗匡 7劻勷 8高眶 9誆騙 10誆賭 11誆套 ○ 12筐篚 ○ 13筐床 ○ 14圈套 15桮棬 16壙埌 17墓壙 18進壙 19封壙 20壙前祭 ○

ʻ曠 K'uang. Read *k'wong'*; coll. *'k'wong*, as in [1]*'k'wong 'yâ*, a wild, an uninhabited region.

ʻ廣 Kuang. Read *'kwong*; used for the coll. *'k'wong*, as in *'k'wong k'wak*, broad, spacious.

勸ʼ Ch'üan. To exhort, to advise, to admonish; to encourage, to stimulate; to acquiesce, to assent cheerfully: [2]*k'wong' 'miéng*, to incite one; COM., [3]*k'wong' ü'* to admonish officially; [4]*k'wong' hwa'* to reform by admonition; [5]*k'wong' ˌhwo*, to urge to peace; [6]*k'wong' ka'* to urge (a widow) to marry; [7]*k'wong' siéng'* to exhort to virtue; COLL., [8]*k'wong' 'kâ*, to advise (people) to settle (their quarrels); *k'wong' ˌkung móh, 'tu, se' ˌyâng ˌchiéng*, to persuade good folks not to gamble is winning money (for them).

曠ʼ K'uang. Clear, vacant, void, empty, waste; wide, distant, extended; long duration, ancient: in the coll. read *'k'wong*, q. v.: [9]*k'wong' ˌhu*, a bachelor; [10]*k'wong' 'wong*, ancient, remote; COM., [11]*k'wong' 'yâ*, a wild, a desert.

榥 Huang. Read *ˌheng*; used for the coll. *ˌk'wong*: a tub large at the top, a cask; a barrel, tierce, pipe, butt, hogshead; a wooden cistern: [12]*ˌk'wong 't'ëng*, large tubs; [13]*'chwi ˌk'wong*, a water-cistern; [14]*ˌk'wong 'tiàng*, a cooking pan surmounted by a wooden cylinder; [15]*miéng² 'hung sioh, ˌk'wong*, a barrel of flour.

ˌK'wong. A coll. prefix, as in *ˌk'wong ˌk'wong*, frames, as for doors; spaces marked off in a regular series.

ˌK'wong. A coll. word, as in the duplicated form *ˌk'wong ˌk'wong*, holes dug in the ground.

ˌK'wong. A coll. word: to govern, to rule, to manage; to oversee during another's absence: *ˌk'wong ˌchá*, to take charge of a school; *ˌk'wong ˌka*, to manage the household; *ˌmô ˌnëng ˌk'wong*, no one to take charge of.

匡² K'uang. Read *ˌk'wong*; used for the coll. *k'wong²*: squares, rectangular spaces; also the eye-socket, called *mek, ˌchiu k'wong²*: *k'wong² twai²* the spaces (are) large; *k'wong² kah*, (or *tang²*), paper ruled in squares, a writing-slip—same as *ˌk'wong kah*, q. v.

(362) La.

ˎ拉 La. Read *lak*₂; used for the coll. *ˌla*: to pull, to drag along; to pull or bend, as a bow; *met.*, to appropriate, to embezzle; imperfect, confused: *ˌla 'ch'ié*, or *ˌla ˌla 'ch'ié 'ch'ié*, to embezzle; *ˌla ˌi ˌchá k'ô'* pull him along with (you); *ˌli ˌla*, not clear, confused and wordy, as an essay.

ˌLa. A coll. word, as in *ˌla ˌcha*, foul, dirty, filthy.

ʻ喇 La. Read *lak*, and *lak*₂ in the dictionaries; used for the coll. *'la*: a particle like *'chiâ*, a, an, a certain one; *o² 'la ˌnëng*, there was a

[1]曠野 [2]勸勉 [3]勸諭 [4]勸化 [5]勸和 [6]勸嫁 [7]勸善 [8]勸解 [9]曠夫 [10]曠遠 [11]曠野 [12]榥桶 [13]水榥 [14]榥鼎 [15]麪粉一榥

man; ꜀*mó* ‘*la má*꜄ *chó*꜄ nothing that he can't do.

喇 La. Used for the coll. *la*꜄, as in *kak*꜆ *la*꜄ shuffling, tricky, artful, knavish.

俚 Li. Read ‘*li*; used in the *Paik*꜆ ꜀*Ing* for the coll. ꜀*la*: rustic, vulgar; rude, coarse; jesting, trifling; also sociable, affable, not reserved: ꜀*la sük*꜆ or ꜀*ch‘u* ꜀*la*, rustic in manners; ꜀*la* ꜀*li*, light, trifling; ꜀*ch‘u* ꜀*la* ‘*li*, coarse, as workmanship; ‘*yă* ꜀*la*, very sociable.

꜀*La*. A coll. word, as in ꜀*la* ‘*li*, a name for the ꜀*ch‘iong* ꜀*sang kak*꜆ the manis.

꜀*La*. A coll. prefix, as in ꜀*la* ꜀*lang kieu*꜄, a jingling, as of metals; ꜀*la* ꜀*la kieu*꜄ a rattling sound, as of things dragged on the ground; ꜀*la* ꜀*lĕng*, void, empty, as from want of food.

(363) Lá.

꜀*Lá*. A coll. word: to thrust the middle finger insultingly toward one who is speaking: ꜀*lá sioh*꜆ ꜀*lá*, or ꜀*lá sioh*꜆ *a*꜅ to make an insulting motion with the finger.

禮 礼 Li. Rites, ceremonies, acts that are suitable in serving the gods; propriety, etiquette, decorum, the rules of social life; good manners, politeness; worship, official obeisance; courtesy prompted by good feeling; offerings, gifts or presents required by usage: COM., [1]‘*lá so*꜄ or [2]‘*lá chiék*꜆ rules of decorum, politeness; [3]‘*lá mau*꜄ good manners; [4]‘*lá uk*꜆ presents; [5]‘*lá* ꜀*ngi*, the forms of propriety; *met*., gifts, offerings; [6]‘*lá puo*꜄ the Board of Rites; [7]*sœ̈ng*꜄ ‘*lá*, to send presents (to the bride before marriage); [8]*che*꜄ *kiéng*꜄ ‘*lá*, an introductory present to a superior; [9]꜀*chiu* ‘*lí*, [10]꜀*ngi* ‘*lá*, and [11]‘*lá ke*꜄ are three of "the thirteen classics"; [12]‘*lá pai*꜄ to worship; [13]꜀*u* ‘*lá*, impolite, rude; [14]*sek*꜆ ‘*lá* have failed in politeness—an apologetic phrase; [15]‘*lá* ꜀*seng*, a master of ceremonies —familiarly styled [16]‘*lá pah*꜆; [17]꜀*hung* ‘*lá*, meat offerings to the gods; COLL., ‘*lá* ꜀*tieu pá*꜄ bowing (before certain idols in the streets) with incense stuck in stools; ‘*lá* ꜀*seng* ꜀*i tié*꜅ "ceremony- master's younger brother"—i. e., ‘*lá* ‘*ting* (am waiting), an ironical phrase denoting refusal.

‘*Lá*. A coll. word, for which the last is often used in coll. books: before verbs, makes an active participial sense; after certain verbs, is euphonic or implies completion of the action; after nouns, means in, at, from, out of: *k‘ié*꜅ ‘*lá*, standing; ‘*lá* ‘*siong*, is thinking; *tioh*꜆ *ch‘io*꜄ ‘*lá*, is in the house; *chó*꜄ ‘*lá* ‘*lau*, done, have finished it; ‘*chwi* ‘*lá* ꜀*li* ‘*hwi* ‘*lá k‘ó*꜄ "comes from water, goes by fire"—to expend as fast as one earns; ꜀*lüng* ‘*lá wak*꜆ as spry as a dragon!

澧 Li. Name of a river flowing into Tungting Lake: [18]‘*Lá* ꜀*chiu*, an inferior prefecture in the north of Hunan; [19]‘*lá* ꜀*chiong*, an excellent fountain; *met*., wine.

1 禮數 2 禮節 3 禮貌 4 禮物 5 禮儀 6 禮部 7 送禮 8 贄見禮 9 周禮 10 儀禮 11 禮記 12 禮拜 13 無禮 14 失禮 15 禮生 16 禮伯 17 葷禮 18 澧州 19 澧泉

醴 Li. ʿ Interchanged with the last: sweet wine, newly distilled spirits; *met.*, sweet, excellent, as fountains or showers: [1] *ʿhiong ʿlá*, an imperial feast.

蠡 Li. ʿ A wood-borer, bugs which eat wood: *ˏp'ang ʿlá*, the name of a marsh; the middle portion of Poyang Lake, as marked in some maps. Read *ˏlié*: a calabash: *ʿi ˏlié ch'aikˎ ʿhai*, measure the ocean with a gourd — presumptuous ignorance.

Láʾ. A coll. word: to pass close to, to graze, as projectiles: *naʾ láʾ ˏchia kwoʾ* just grazed past him.

犁 犂 Li. ˏ A plow; to plow, to prepare ground for crops; just before dawn, daybreak; a piebald ox; forms part of the names of hordes of Huns: [2] *ˏlá ʿló*, old and wrinkled; stained, begrimed; [3] *ˏtang ˏlá*, hordes of Huns; COLL., [4] *ˏlá ˏch'eng*, to plow fields; *ˏlá ˏt'au*, or [5] *ˏlá ˏt'au t'iék*, a plowshare; *ˏlá máʾ tiohˎ paʾ yáʾ tiohˎ* if the plow can't reach it, the harrow can; *met.*, he will effect his object in some way; *ˏlá ʿsai ˏtü*, "use a pig to plow with;" *met.*, to insist doggedly.

ˏLá. A coll. word: to strike, to rub or brush against; to strand, as boats; to do toilsomely, to push one's way through, persevering, persistent: *ˏlá miängʾ* to have a hard lot, to toil at; *ˏlá ˏpa*, to do persistingly; *ˏlá kwoʾ* to press by; *ˏsung ˏlá ʿch'iéng*, the boat stranded on shallows; *ˏlá ˏlá ˏpang*, even, level, as a steelyard-bar in weighing.

瓈 Li. ˏ A precious stone, a gem: [6] *ˏp'ó ˏlá* (coll. *ˏpó ˏlá*), vitreous substances, glass.

藜 Li. ˏ A kind of herb; its leaves are eaten when young, and its stalks are suitable for canes: [7] *ˏlá t'iongʾ* a cane; [8] *chikˎ ˏlá*, a spinous plant used in ophthalmia; [9] *p'wóiʾ ˏlá*, spread forth, confused.

黎 Li. ˏ A kind of glutinous paste, used in making shoes; dark brown, black; many, numerous; interchanged with *ˏlá* (to plow) in the phrase [10] *ˏlá ˏming*, early dawn: [11] *ˏlá ˏming*, the black-haired people—the Chinese.

驪 Li. ˏ Also read *ˏlié*: a fleet horse, a charger; a black horse; to drive a span of horses: [12] *ˏlá kaʾ* a carriage and span; [13] *tóʾ ˏlá*, a swift steed.

鸝 Li. ˏ Read *ˏlié* in the dictionaries: a yellow bird, the [14] *ˏwong ˏlá*, or mango bird, of a dark yellow color.

厲 Li. ʾ Used for the next four: a whetstone; to rub, to grind, to sharpen; to begin, to commence; to excite, to stimulate, to discipline; stern, severe, majestic; violent, raging; cruel, tyrannical; ugly; dangerous, virulent, as disease; to ford streams: [15] *láʾ ʿkwi*, a fierce demon; [16] *láʾ ˏping*, to sharpen weapons; to animate

[1] 享醴 [2] 犂老 [3] 丹犂 [4] 犂田 [5] 犂頭鐵〇 [6] 玻瓈 [7] 藜杖 [8] 蒺藜 [9] 沛藜 [10] 黎明〇 [11] 黎民〇 [12] 驪駕〇 [13] 盜驪〇 [14] 黃鸝〇 [15] 厲鬼〇 [16] 厲兵〇

福州方言拼音字典

troops: ¹lá² ₍ming, to oppress the people; COM., ²₍ngiéng lá² stern and strict.

勵² Li. To exert strength; to arouse, to animate, to encourage, to urge to: COM., ³lá² che' to bend one's mind to, to do resolutely; ⁴'miéng lá² to urge, to rouse to effort.

濿² Li. Read lié² in the dictionaries: to cross a stream on stepping stones, to ford streams: ⁵₍ch'ing chaik₎ lá² if deep then use stepping stones.

癘² Li. Virulent ulcers, noisome sores, plague spots; a pestilence, epidemic; noxious vapors.

礪² Li, A coarse sandstone, a grindstone, whetstone for sharpening tools; to grind, to sharpen.

糲² Li. Unhulled rice, rice not cleansed; coarse food, rough fare: ⁶lá² sik₎ coarse food; ⁷₍ch'u lá² rough, plain, as one's fare.

蠣² Li. Read lié² in the dictionaries: a rock oyster, called ⁸meu lá²; the shell (lá² ₍pung) is used medicinally: used in the Paik₎ ₍Ing for the coll. tiē² q. v.

麗² Li. A stag walking and then stopping; an adjective of praise, elegant, graceful, adorned, good, fine, lovely, fair, beautiful, glorious; bright, flowery; luxurious, extravagant; to couple, a pair; attached, belonging to, relying on; to strike, to hit in shooting; a number; a small boat; a beam: ⁹lá² ₍p'i, two skins—anciently used as a symbol of union in marriage; ₍siong ho² lá² proportionate, as guilt and punishment; ¹⁰lá² ₍ch'ung, the bright, flowery spring; COM., ¹¹₍hwa lá² splendid, magnifical. Read ₍lá (in the dictionaries ₍lié), as in ¹²₍kó ₍lá kwok₎, Corea.

儷² Li. A pair, a couple, as husband and wife; mates, fellows, companions; and, together with: ¹³k'aung' lá² a match, a pair, conjugal union.

戾² Li. To stoop, to bend; curved, crooked, distorted; perverse, stubborn, rebellious; set, fixed, determined; criminal, guilty; to extend, to reach to: ¹⁴chói² lá² wicked; ¹⁵pó² lá² rebellious; tyrannical, fierce; ¹⁶₍yong ₍hi lá² ₍t'iéng, the kite soars to heaven.

盭² Like the last: perverse, intractable, to oppose; to bind so as to force out the blood; virulent, incurable; a plant which yields a green dye: ¹⁷lá² ₍hu, an unreasonable fellow; ¹⁸chek₎ lá² perverse, reckless, as thieves.

唳² Li. The chirping of birds: ¹⁹₍lieu lá² the scream of storks or herons; ²⁰₍leu lá² chirping, twittering.

捩² 棙² Li. A plectrum for thrumming a guitar; to thrum, to snap the strings; to twitch, to snap asunder; to guide as a helm.

¹厲民 ²嚴厲 ³勵志 ⁴勉勵 ⁵深則濿 ⁶糲食 ⁷粗糲 ⁸牡蠣 ⁹麗皮 ¹⁰麗春 ¹¹華麗 ¹²高麗國 ¹³伉儷 ¹⁴罪戾 ¹⁵暴戾 ¹⁶鳶飛戾天 ¹⁷盭夫 ¹⁸賊盭 ¹⁹嘹唳 ²⁰嘍唳

棣² Li. A sort of small plum, in size like the cherry; a wild cherry found in Shansi; piece of wood under a carriage.

隸² Li. Joined, attached, belonging to; official attendants, underlings; base, menial, as services; low, abject, vile, ignoble: [1]*'puk*, *lá²* servants, a suite; [2]*'tik*, *lá²* directly attached to, as the *ˏchiu* and *ˏt'ing* departments are under the control of officers above district magistrates; COM., [3]*'tik*, *lá²* *'seng*, the province of Chihli; [4]*'lá²* *ˏchü* or [5]*'lá²* *che'* the plain, square character; *chó²* *lá²* official runners, lictors; *lá²* *chok*, underlings.

(364) Laë.

鑢² Read *lëü'*; coll. *laë'*: a file, a rasp; to file; also to rub, to scour, to give polish to: *laë'* *ˏtong*, the file is dull; [6]*'laë'* *këü'* to file a saw; [7]*'laë'* *ˏtëng*, to scour brass; [8]*'laë'* *ˏkwong*, to polish, make bright or smooth; [9]*'laë'* *meng'* to rub the face, as with a cloth.

Laë². A coll. word: to claw, to scratch, to scrape or rake; to scrape, as rice into the mouth with chopsticks: *laë²* *sioh*, *ˏtoi*, to scrape together; *ˏpa laë²* to scratch, as a hen in the dirt.

(365) Laëk.

Laëk,. A coll. word: to become loose, loosened, parted, separated; to become tired of, to give up: *laëk*, *te'* stem dissevered, as of ripe fruit; *'p'i laëk*, *k'ó'* the scab has come off; *ˏling laëk*, to fall off, intermit gradually; *k'ëük*, *laëk*, to tire of, disgusted and giving up; *ˏmó tek*, *laëk*, can't stop or get rid of; *ˏk'a 'ch'iu laëk*, *laëk*, *ˏsong*, the feet and hands relaxed and aching, as from fatigue.

(366) Laëng.

Laëng'. A coll. word: an interval of time or space; a crack, crevice, interstice; to leave spaces or intervals; not doing, unemployed: *laëng'* *sioh*, *nik*, interval of one day; *laëng'* *hwong'* a wide interval; *laëng'* *p'ong'* an interstice; *laëng'* *k'aëng'* interval, vacant space; *'tiäng laëng'* to watch or wait for a leisure time; *laëng'* *'la tio'* to leave a road or passage-way.

衕² Tung. 衖² Hung. The first read *ˏtung* and *tong²*, the second read *haëng'*; used for the coll. *laëng²*: a narrow street, an alley—mostly narrower than a *haëng'*: *ˏlëng laëng²* a lane, alley; [10]*'tio²* *laëng²* a path, a passage to; [11]*'hwi ˏch'iong laëng²* a way between walls; [12]*'t'uk*, *ˏt'au laëng²* an alley shut at one end; [13]*ˏch'ong ˏt'au laëng²* spaces or passages at the two ends of a bed; [14]*'laëng²* *pang'* a straight passage, as in front of rooms.

弄² Lung. Read *liong²* or *lwong²*; coll. *laëng²*: to make sport of, to use badinage; to tease, to annoy, to trifle with; to make, to prepare, as dishes of food; to plan, to work for, or get by scheming: [15]*'hië' laëng²* or [16]*'chauk*, *laëng²* to trifle with, to annoy; *moh*, *laëng²* *ˏi*, don't tease him; [17]*'laëng²*

1 僕隸 2 直隸 3 直隸省 4 隸書 5 隸字 6 鑢鋸 7 鑢銅 8 鑢光 9 鑢面 10 路衕 11 火墻衕 12 禿頭衕 13 床頭衕 14 衕柄 15 戲弄 16 作弄 17 弄權

‚kwong, to have influence, as a favorite servant; [1]'laěng' pe' to cheat, to embezzle; [2]'laěng' sioh‚ k'wok‚ to scheme so as to get an office; [3]'laěng' pwong' to cook rice; [4]'laěng' 'k'ieu 'hwang ch'wok‚ scheme cleverly and have it turn out stupidly—to overreach one's self; [5]'laěng' 'nü ch'ek‚ ‚tiěng paik‚ 'tó, he fools you topsy-turvy most completely!

(367) Lai.

‚*Lai.* A coll. word, as in ‚*lai* ‚*tai*, filthy, dirty in person and dress; an untidy, seedy, appearance.

'[illegible] Lei. Lěi. Read '*lwi*; used in the *Paik‚ ‚Ing* for the coll. '*lai*: a small bamboo basket, called *těük‚ 'lai*, having a contracted top; it is worn by fishermen at the girdle for containing shell-fish, etc.: '*lai* '*kiǎng*, small fish-baskets.

瀨' Lai. Water flowing over sand; shallows in streams, rapids: COLL., *lai' 'yǎ* '*ch'iěng*, the rapid is very shallow.

Lai' A coll. word, similar to ‚*lá* and *lá'* as in *lai' kwo'* to graze, to rub or scrape past or over.

Lai' A coll. word: the opposite of *huk‚ tuk‚*; mild, amiable, not gruff, not morose: ‚*i chó' ‚mëng lai' lai' tioh‚* he is a very mild, pleasing person.

籟' Lai. A musical pipe with three tubes or reeds; a combination of pipes, as in an organ; a moaning or soughing noise: [6]‚*t'iěng lai'* a whirring in the air, whistling of the wind; [7]*těük‚ lai'* sough among the bamboos—a poetical phrase.

‚來 ‚来 Lai. To come, to reach, coming, arriving; to effect, to attain, to bring about, to induce; denotes the future or succession of time; after verbs, implies action or its completion; with a negative inserted between, expresses impracticability of the idea of the preceding verb; joined with *k'ëü'*, denotes coming and going, here and there, again and again; after the verbs '*k'i* and *ch'ok‚* it means to begin and expresses the commencement of the action of a previous verb: in the coll. read ‚*li*, q. v.: [8]'*siong pok‚ 'k'i* ‚*lai*, can not recall it; [9]*taik‚* ‚*lai*, have obtained it; COM., [10]‚*lai 'wong*, or '*wong* ‚*lai*, coming and going, intercourse with; [11]‚*lai* ‚*hui*, to and fro, both ways; [12]‚*chüng* ‚*lai*, hitherto; [13]*hau'* ‚*lai*, hereafter; [14]*këüng'* ‚*lai*, just now, recently; [15]‚*lai* ‚*song*, a great-great-great grandson; [16]‚*lai sié'* the future world or life; [17]‚*lai* ‚*iu*, the origin, cause; [18]‚*lai lik‚* the history, antecedent circumstances of; prestige, as of rank; [19]‚*lai e'* the object of one's coming; [20]‚*lai* ‚*lüng*, the coming dragon—a geomantic term; [21]‚*lai* ‚*sang k'ëü'* '*ngu*, three in and five out—to spend more than one gains; [22]‚*ngwong* ‚*lai*, originally, yes, so of course; COLL., ‚*lai* ‚*t'au*, immediate help or relief; ‚*lai tio'* a resource, an opening, as for one without employment. Read *lai'*: to meet, to receive kindly one coming.

[1]弄弊[2]弄一鈌[3]弄飯[4]弄巧反拙[5]弄汝七顛八倒[6]天籟[7]竹籟[8]想不起來[9]得來[10]來往[11]來回[12]從來[13]後來[14]近來[15]來孫[16]來世[17]來由[18]來歷[19]來意[20]來龍[21]來三去五[22]原來○

徠 ˎLai. Used for the last and the next: ˏ*chu* ˏ*lai*, name of a hill.

勑 ˎLai. To warn and encourage, to reward, to induce one to come: also read *t'ek*, q. v.

崍 ˎLai. A mountain in Sz'chuen, a peak of the Min Mts., near the confines of Shensi.

秾 ˎLai. A local name for wheat in Shantung.

箂 ˎLai. A species of bamboo; used for the coll. ˏ*lai*, a bamboo basket, a kind of basket mostly without bails: ˏ*lai tang*ˀ a cooly's two baskets; ˏ*lai ch'ioh*, ˋ*yong* ˏ*kăng* ˏ*kié*, a basket of paddy to rear a pound-fowl; *met.*, small gains at great expense.

萊 ˎLai. A thistle, wild herbs in waste places; sterile, untilled ground; to clear up jungle: [1]ˏ*tiéng* ˏ*lai*, a fallow, neglected fields; [2]ˏ*lai* ˋ*ch'ó*, an esculent sow-thistle; COM., [3]ˏ*p'ung* ˏ*lai* ˋ*tó*, the enchanted isles.

騋 ˎLai. A mare seven cubits high; a tall, strong horse: [4]ˏ*lai* ˋ*ping* ˏ*sang* ˏ*ch'iéng*, 3000 tall mares.

雷 ˎLei. Read ˏ*loi*; coll. ˏ*lai*: thunder: [5]ˏ*lai* ˏ*kung*, the god of thunder, thunder; [6]ˏ*lai p'ah*, ˋ*hwi* ˏ*sieu*, the thunder strikes and fire (lightning) burns; *met.*, hasty, urgent; [7]ˏ*lai p'ah*, *ch'ek*, *sié*ˀ ˏ*k'iéng*, the thunder smites (him for) the crimes of his seven transmigrations.

睞[2] Lai. The pupil of the eye distorted, to squint: [8]ˋ*miéng lai*[2] to glance sidewise; to look at earnestly.

癩[2] Lai. A virulent eruption, a chronic cutaneous disease; sores, blotches, scrofulous affections, itch, impetigo; specifically, the leprosy: [8]*lai*[2] ˏ*ch'ong*, ulcers, itch sores; COM., [9]*siong*[2] *lai*[2] (coll. *pang*[2] *lai*[2]), leprosy; [10]ˏ*kang lai*[2] dry leporsy; [11]ˏ*hwi lai*[2] the virulent, running leprosy; [12]*lai*[2] ˏ*t'ĕng*, leprosy-worms; [13]*kwo*ˀ *lai*[2] "the leprosy contagious;" *met.*, a troublesome affair shifted onto another.

瀨[2] Lai. To break, to destroy; fallen in ruins: ˏ*t'ü lai*[2] to curse one. Read ˋ*lang*: remiss in sacrificing.

藾[2] Lai. A water vegetable, a sort of duckweed, called ˏ*ping lai*[2]: to shade, to cover, shaded.

賴[2] **頼**[2] Lai. To depend, to lean on; to rely on, to confide in, to trust to; to get advantage, to profit one's self; to assume, to trump up; to calumniate, to accuse falsely; to blame, to charge on one who is innocent: COM., [14]ˏ*wong lai*[2] to defame; [15]ˏ*tu lai*[2] to criminate the guiltless; [16]ˏ*u lai*[2] ˏ*chi* ˏ*tu*, an unreliable fellow, a loafer, a suspicious chap; [17]*lai*[2] *ok*, to stick to a house; — *scil.*, and refuse to pay rent for it; [18]*lai*[2] *tiéng*[2] a usurping farmer, one in arrears for his field-rent;

1 田萊 2 萊草 3 蓬萊島 4 騋牝三千 5 雷公 6 雷拍火燒 7 雷拍七世慾 8 癩搶 9 上癩 10 乾癩 11 火癩 12 癩蟲 13 過癩 14 冤賴 15 圖賴 16 無賴之徒 17 賴屋 18 賴佃 ○

COLL., *lai*² *kwo*³ lean (on the table) farther along; *lai*² *tié*² *˛tau*, to lie sulkily on the ground; *lai*² *po*³ *˛kié ˋmó*, "a hen sitting (on eggs) inveterately"; *met.*, one careless in dress, a sloven; *ˋsi ˋsi pwoh˛ lai*² *ˋngwai*, persistently bent on criminating me.

賚² Lai. To confer, to bestow on an inferior; a reward, a largess: *lai*² *ˋtŭ*, to bestow, to grant; *ló*² *lai*² to reward for services.

(368) Laing.

*Laing*³. A coll. word, as in *˛pá laing*³ to turn the wrong side up, to invert; *met.*, to talk inconsistently, to contradict one's self: *˛i ch'oi*³ *á*² *˛pá laing*³ his talk is contradictory; *˛pá laing*³ *˛li ˛pá laing*³ *k'ó*³ to turn up and down; full of inconsistent (assertions).

(369) Laiu.

*Laiu*³. A coll. word, as in *laiu*³ *a*³ or *laiu*³ *lôh˛ k'ó*³ to slip, as a child from a chair; to slide, as one does in a sitting posture down a steep place.

廖² Liao. A man's name; a surname; the name of a state.

料² Liao. Read *lieu*² in the dictionaries: commonly read *laiu*² in the following senses; stuff, materials of which things are made; vitreous substances, glass; a mineral substance of which ornaments are made resembling *ngwoh*₂; ability, talent, cleverness, as of an employé; grain, provender; manure; to reckon, to consider, to suppose: also read *˛lieu* and *lieu*² q. v.: ¹*laiu*² *k'e*³ glass-ware, ware like *ngwoh*₂ (gems); ²*laiu*² *˛chio*, glass-beads; ³*˛sieu laiu*² ware of melted vitreous substances; ⁴*yoh*₂ *laiu*² materia medica; ⁵*ˋma laiu*² horses' provender; ⁶*˛chieu laiu*² spices; ⁷*˛ch'a laiu*² timber, lumber; ⁸*˛këng laiu*² work and materials; ⁹*laiu*² *to*² assortment of relishes; ¹⁰*laiu*² *ˋsiong*, to reckon, to suppose; COLL., ¹¹*ˋkwó ˋchi laiu*² dried fruits; ¹²*ch'ok˛ laiu*² to give out the strength, as things steeped; ¹³*sioh*₂ *laiu*² one lot of ingredients.

漏² Lou. To drip, to leak, to ooze out; a clepsydra; to forget, to lose, to let slip; to moisten, to bedew; to evade, to escape from; *met.*, to disclose, to divulge, to blab; a crack, an aperture, a leak: in the coll. read *lau*² and *lau*² q. v.: COM., ¹⁴*˛t'iëng ˛ki pok˛ ˋk'ó laiu*² *siék˛* you must not disclose celestial secrets;—i. e., don't predict such calamities; ¹⁵*˛sung tó*³ *˛kong ˛tüng ˋpwo laiu*² *˛ti*, when the boat has reached the middle of the river it is too late to stop the leak—an exhortation to prudence.

瘺² 瘻² Lou. A scrofulous swelling, as on the neck; an old sore, a running ulcer: ¹⁶*laiu*² *˛tüng*, an ulcer breeding worms; COLL., ¹⁷*laiu*² *ˋkwong*, the tubercles in piles; ¹⁸*˛sang ˋchiú laiu*² to have the piles.

¹料器 ²料珠 ³燒料 ⁴藥料 ⁵馬料 ⁶椒料 ⁷柴料 ⁸工料 ⁹料度 ¹⁰料想 ¹¹果子料〇 ¹²出料 ¹³一料 ¹⁴天機不可漏洩 ¹⁵船到江中補漏遲 ¹⁶瘺蟲 ¹⁷瘺管 ¹⁸生者瘺

陋[2] **Lou.** A strait, a narrow place; a vile, dirty residence; low, mean, rustic, vulgar; ugly, ill-favored; ignorant, uninformed, simple: *'laiu' liok,* mean, useless; [2]*,ku laiu'* lone, solitary; [3]*'ch'iu laiu'* ugly and deformed; [4]*'chai' laiu' haëng'* in a poor, narrow lane—where Yentzŭ lived; COLL., *laiu' auk, tek, 't'eng,* very mean and stingy.

(370) Lak.

襶 **La.** Read *lak,;* coll. *lak,* as in *lak, sak,* mean, shabby apparel; this phrase is not very commonly used.

Lak,. A coll. word: bald, bare; worn, rubbed off; peeled, flayed; all gone, stripped bare: *lak, ,t'au,* a bald head; *lak, ,chü,* or *lak, ,kó,* a bald person; *,p'ui lak, k'ó'* a fur (garment) worn bare; *lak, ,p'ui 'lo 'ch'ü,* (like) a scalded rat—i. e., worn off, rubbed bare; *lak, ,chü chó' ,hwo siong'* the bald man is a (ready-made) Budhist; *met.,* opportune, just the thing; *lak, ,chü siâh, k'iék, ,chü,* the bald living on the hare-lipped; *met.,* one beggar borrowing of another, etc.,; *lak, t'ak, cheng' ,kwong,* completely stripped, all gone.

Lak,. A coll. word: to move or slip up or down, as a string or ring which binds something: similar to *lak,* q. v.; *lak, kiă'* slip it down.

Lak,. A coll. word, as in *'k'a lak,* to repair, to mend; to adjust, put in order.

Lak,. A coll. word: to catch, as with a lasso or noose; *met.,* to entrap, to overreach, to injure by cunning: *k'ëük, ,nëng lak, k'ó'* insnared by others; *lak, ,i ,t'au 'lá,* noosed his head—i. e., entrapped him.

剌[2] **La.** Often confounded with *ch'ëü'* (to pierce): perverse, intractable, wicked; harsh, inhuman, unkind; to mangle, to lacerate: [5]*,kwai lak,* perverse; [6]*'pwak, lak,* the twang of a bowstring; [7]*'pak, lak,* noise of fish springing out of the water.

喇[2] **La.** To talk rapidly: in the coll. used for *'la* and *la'* q. v.: [8]*'hak, lak,* precipitate utterance; COLL., [9]*'lak,* (or *,la*) *,pa ,cheng,* the Lama of Tibet, a Lama-priest.

瘌[2] **La.** Inward pains, pain in the bones; bitter, painful: [10]*'lô lak,* an incurable disease; [11]*'t'ong' lak,* poisonous drugs.

揦[2] **La.** To turn over, to spread out, to extend; in the coll. to take off; to rub or scrape, as with the hand; to slip, to shove up or down: COLL., [12]*'lak, 'k'i,* to take off, as a ring from the finger; [13]*'ch'iu 'wong lak, ,keng,* to shove up the sleeve; [14]*'lak, k'ó'* scrape it away; *lak, ,kwong ,kwong tioh,* rub it smooth.

拉[2] **La.** To pull, to drag along, to induce one to go; to break, to destroy: used for the last in the coll. senses; in the coll. also read *,la,* q. v.: [15]*'lak, hiék,* to break one's ribs.

[1]陋劣 [2]孤陋 [3]醜陋 [4]在陋巷 [5]乖剌 [6]撥剌 [7]跋剌 [8]喝喇 [9]喇叭僧 [10]癆瘌 [11]痛瘌 [12]揦起 [13]手袖揦高 [14]揦去 [15]拉脅

粒$_2$ La. A kernel of rice or other grains; *met.*, food; a pellet, a numerative of small round things, as pearls, beads, grains, buttons, pebbles, etc.: [1]*lak*$_2$ *sik*$_2$ rice, food; COM., [2]*lak*$_2$ *so'* the number, as of seeds, grains, &c.; COLL., [3]*pwong'* *lak*$_2$ grains of cooked rice; *tiăh*$_2$ *tauing'* *lak*$_2$ all the fruit plucked off; *o'* *ˏch'eng* *tau'* *lak*$_2$ *twai'* as large as a field-bean.

擸$_2$ La. To hold and manage; to break off; in the coll. mixed, confused: *lak*$_2$ *lak*$_2$ noise of breaking, as of branches in a violent wind; COLL., [4]*lak*$_2$ *chak*$_2$ mixed, heterogeneous, odds and ends.

爉$_2$ La. Fiery, blazing; the crackling of flames; used in the coll. in a sense similar to *puk*$_2$ q. v.: COLL., [5]*lak*$_2$ *nük*$_2$ to smoke pork; *pong'* *'hwi* *ˏing* *'lü* *lak*$_2$ to cure in the smoke.

獵$_2$ Lieh. To hunt wild animals; the chase, gunning, fowling, hawking; to shake, to move; to get by experience, to pursue earnestly, as one's studies: [6]*siék*$_2$ *lak*$_2$ to wade and hunt (through books); COM., [7]*lak*$_2$ *ho'* huntsmen; [8]*ta lak*$_2$ to hunt; [9]*lak*$_2$ *'k'eng*, a hunting-dog.

腊$_2$ Read *sek*$_2$; used for the next in the following senses: dried meat; to sacrifice after the winter solstice; the 12th month: *lak*$_2$ *nük*$_2$ jerked meat.

臘$_2$ La. Dried meats; sacrifice after the winter solstice; to dry flesh: [10]*keu'* *lak*$_2$ the 12th moon of last year; [11]*lak*$_2$ *ngwok*$_2$ the 12th month; [12]*lak*$_2$ *paik*$_2$ the 8th of the 12th month—when meats should be cured.

蠟$_2$ La. Wax, bees-wax; waxy, waxed, glazed: COM., [13]*ˏwong* *lak*$_2$ yellow wax, bees-wax; [14]*pah*$_2$ *lak*$_2$ white wax—obtained from bugs on the [15]*lak*$_2$ *süü'* (wax-tree); [16]*lak*$_2$ *ˏch'iéng*, paper polished with a waxed stone, glazed paper; [17]*lak*$_2$ *ˏmúi*, a flower (Chimonanthus fragrans); COLL., [18]*lak*$_2$ *chioh*$_2$ wax-candles; *lak*$_2$ *'chwi*, a hawfinch (Coccothraustes melanura).

躐$_2$ Lieh. To tread, to stumble; to go out of the way, to stride or pass over, to overstep: [19]*lak*$_2$ *'teng*, to overstep (i. e., disregard) the regular order; [20]*siék*$_2$ *lak*$_2$ to travel over; *met.*, to acquire experience or knowledge.

鬣$_2$ Lieh. Also read *lek*$_2$: the bristles of a hog; a horse's mane; long pectorals or cirri of fish; stiff hair on animals' heads; stiff, bristly, hairy, bearded: in the coll. read *lĕk*, q. v.: *ˏkong* *lak*$_2$ a hog; *ˏtiong* *lak*$_2$ long beard.

鱲 Lieh. A common term for many fishes like the perch, having strong spinous dorsals.

1 粒食	3 飯粒	5 爉肉	7 獵戶	9 獵犬	11 臘月	12 臘八	13 黃蠟	14 白蠟	16 蠟箋	18 蠟燭	20 涉躐
2 粒數	4 擸揸	6 涉獵	8 打獵	10 舊臘	○	○	○	15 蠟樹	17 蠟梅	19 躐等	○

辣, 辢, La. Hot, as pepper; biting, piquant, pungent, sharp, acrid; used in the coll. in a *met.*, sense, severe, stringent, injurious, formidable: COM., [1]*lak*, *‚kiong*, ginger-root; [2]*kai' lak*, mustard; [3]*lak*, *‚chieu chiong'* strong pepper sauce; [4]*lak*, *ch'ai'* "hot vegetables"—i. e., the heart of mustard plants boiled up; COLL., *ch'au' lak*, *pak*, strongly scented; *met.*, unsavory, as one's name; *lak*, *chiăh*, *lak*, or *lak*, *kaĕng' kaĕng'* very biting or pungent; *'ch'iu 'yă lak*, has a very hot hand—is formidable in his plots.

涉, Shê. Read *siĕk*,; used for the coll. *lak*,: to pass through water, to ford, to wade across: [5]*lak*, *'chwi*, to wade in water; [6]*lak*, *kwo' ‚k'ă*, to wade a brook or stream; *'lu lak*, wet, sloppy.

Lak, A coll. word, as in *‚pa lak*, to give a twisting motion to, to turn, as a key in a lock; *‚pa lak*, *‚t'au*, to shake the head—unwilling, dissenting.

(371) Lang.

‚Lang. A coll. word: the sound of bells, a metallic sound; to clink, to tinkle: *‚lang ‚lang kieu'* to tinkle, tinkling.

'懶 Lan. Lazy, listless, remiss; indolent, averse, disinclined to do; sluggish, sleepy: COM., [7]*'lang tó'* lazy, indolent; [8]*'tio 'lang*, to shirk work; COLL., [9]*'lang ‚si*, lazy carcass, you lazy lout! [10]*'lang 'sang*, to slight work; [11]*'lang chó'* to idle, to laze; *'lang ch'ok*, *‚mwong*, indisposed to go abroad; *'lang laĕk*, to tire of, to stop and leave incomplete; *'lang lo'* foul, filthy, as one's dress.

'覽, '覧, Lan. To behold, to survey, to contemplate; to look at carefully, to see from a distance; to perceive, to understand: [12]*‚kwang 'lang*, to survey; [13]*ek*, *'lang*, at one view; [14]*pwok*, *'lang*, extensively read, learned.

'攬, '擥, Lan. To grasp, to carry firmly; to gather, to carry in both arms; to usurp, to monopolize, to hoard; grasping; in the coll. to clasp, to encircle with the arm and hold close to one's person: [15]*'lang 'ch'ü*, to take or seize all; COM., [16]*‚pau 'lang*, to engross, to monopolize; COLL., *k'ă' ‚i 'lang ‚sing 'lă*, hold him (the child) close to the person; *'lang k'wang* (or *‚sĕng*), to hold loosely in the arms.

'欖 Lan. The Canarium, or Chinese olive, called [17]*'kang 'lang*: [18]*pek*, *'lang*, the Canarium album; [19]*‚u 'lang*, Canarium pimela; COLL., *'ka 'lang*, olives; *'ka 'lang 'piăng*, olives pressed and sweetened; *mik*, *'kwo 'ka 'lang*, a kind of small, sweetish olive; *‚tă 'mó 'ka 'lang*, a large variety of olive.

'纜 Lan. Read *lang'* in the dictionaries; a rope, a hawser, a painter, a cable; to tie, to bind; to drag with a rope, to tow: [20]*'kai 'lang*, to loose the hawser, to weigh anchor.

[1] 辣薑 [2] 芥辣 [3] 辣椒醬 [4] 辣茶 [5] 涉水 [6] 涉過溪 [7] 懶惰 [8] 騃懶 [9] 懶尸 [10] 懶省 [11] 懶做 [12] 觀覽 [13] 一覽 [14] 博覽 [15] 攬取 [16] 包攬 [17] 橄欖 [18] 白欖 [19] 烏欖 [20] 解纜

萏 Tan. Mallows; budding flowers; variegated, flowery: [1]ˋhang ˊlang, the Hibiscus mutabilis.

ʻLang. A coll. word: spittle, saliva; the watering of the mouth; *ch'oi' ʻlang*, spittle; *p'oi' ʻlang*, to spit; *ʻlang p'wok*, frothy spittle; *ʻlang ˏchiă*, a child's bib, pinafore; *ʻlang ˏhu tói*² a long bib with pocket at the bottom; *ʻlang ˏhwa*, particles of spittle, as forced from the mouth in speaking; *ʻlang ˏt'ang*, phlegm; *ˏlau ʻlang*, to slabber, to drool; *ˏch'ing ʻlang*, watering of the mouth; *mâ*² *ˏsiu ʻlang*, can't stomach (such food).

Lang'. A coll. word, as in *ʻchiăng lang'* insipid, too fresh, as things not salted enough.

婪 ˏLan. Covetous, greedy of gain, extortionate; to covet, to desire, to long after: COM., [2]ˏt'ang ˏlang, avaricious, niggardly.

嵐 ˏLan. Vapor, cloudy mist on hill-tops, called [3]ˏsang ˏlang; [4]ˋk'ŏ ˏlang, a hill near Ta-yuen-fu in Shansi.

礛 ˏLan. As in [5]ˏlang ˏt'ang, thin and widely spread; in the coll. means large rocks, bowlders: COLL., [6]ˏlang ˏt'ang ˏlĕng (or ˏk'ĕng), caves in rocks.

籃 ˏLan. Baskets, usually with cross-handles and made of bamboo or rattan: [7]ˏlang ˏk'wong, baskets; COM., ʻch'ai' ˏlang, a vegetable-basket; [8]ˏtuong ˏlang, baskets which students carry to the examinations; [9]ˏsing ˏcheng ˏlang, a basket in parts or sections; COLL., [10]ˋhwi sik, ˏlang, a provision-basket.

藍 ˏLan. Used for the next: a plant used in dyeing blue; a surname: *ˏlang ˏtiĕng*, the Blue Field, a famous place near Si-ngan-fu in Shensi; COM., [11]ˏlang saik, a blue or indigo color; [12]ˏlang taing² native indigo; [13]ˏyong ˏlang, Prussian blue; *ʻch'iĕng ˏlang*, light blue; [14]ne² ˏlang, navy blue; [15]ˏkieu ˏlang, a fine, light indigo; [16]ˏlang ˏsang, a blue robe—worn by Siutsai graduates.

襤 ˏLan. A coverlet or covering; a single garment, one without collar, lining, or border; mean, ragged clothes: COM., [17]ˏlang ʻlü, or [18]ˏlang lëü² dirty, shabby, as raiment; COLL., ˏi ˏsang ˏlang ʻlü k'ëük, ˏnëng ˏk'i, one clad in tattered clothes is imposed on by others.

闌 ˏLan. Used for the next two: a door-screen; to screen, to seclude, to separate; late, evening; failing, fading; exhausted, finished; few, rare, scarce; in limited quantities, moderate: [19]ˏlang ik, to enter abruptly; [20]ˏmwong ˏlang, door-screens; [21]yâ² ˏlang, late in the night; [22]ˋchiu ˏlang, the wine nearly exhausted—the feast almost over; COLL., ˏlang tóh, ʻtá, leavings of a feast.

攔 ˏLan. To stop with the hand, to hinder, to prevent; to obstruct, to impede, to embarrass; to screen off, to separate: COM., [23]ˏchiă ˏlang, to screen from view; ˏlang

---

1 菡萏　2 貪婪　3 山嵐　4 岢嵐　5 礛深　6 礛倥　7 菜籃　8 塲籃　9 盛層籃　10 火食籃　11 藍色　12 藍靛　13 洋藍　14 二藍　15 嬌藍　16 藍衫　17 襤褸　18 襤褸　19 闌入　20 門闌　21 夜闌　22 酒闌　23 遮攔

˛ü, to stop an officer's sedan; [1]˛*lang kieu² tá²* ˛*diăng*, stopped the sedan and presented a petition; [2]˛*kwang* ˛*lang*, a hindrance, impediment; [3]˛*lang* ʻ*chu*, to hinder, to stop one; [4]ʻ*ch'iu* ˛*lang*, to restrain with the hand; COLL., ˛*lang* ˛*p'iăng k'ëük*, ˛*i p'ah*, *sioh*, *a²* beaten by him on the back; ˛*lang* ˛*t'au che² meng²* (mauled) on the head and face.

欄 ˛Lan. A balustrade, a railing, a row of bars below a window; a pen, a den for wild beasts; to cage, to shut up, to rail in: COM., [5]˛*lang* ˛*kang*, a railing; in the coll. also means dress-trimmings; [6]˛*tü* ˛*lang*, a pig-sty; [7]ʻ*ngu* ˛*lang*, a cow-pen; COLL., ˛*lang* ˛*tó*, a balustrade, a board-fence.

瀾 ˛Lan. Great, swelling waves, surges, waves rolling continuously; water in which rice has been washed: [8]˛*p'ó* ˛*lang*, rolling waves; [9]˛*lang kang²* long, far-reaching, as billows.

蘭 ˛Lan. A general name for gynandrous flowers, and some others with single or alternate flowers on a peduncle; also applied to a variety of woody and herbaceous plants; *met.*, fragrant, good, excellent; a surname: [10]*tieu²* ˛*lang*, an epidendrum or air-plant; [11]˛*lang* ˛*ngiong*, good words; [12]˛*lang* ˛*kang*, fine cloth; in the coll. dress-trimmings; COM., [13]*tek*, ˛*lang*, a flowerless shrub with jointed stems, used medicinally and for incense; [14]˛*lang* ˛*hwa*, a plant having lily-like leaves and bearing greenish white flowers, alternate on a common peduncle; [15]˛*chio* ˛*lang*, the Chloranthus inconspicuus; [16]*muk*, ˛*lang*, a tree bearing yellowish seed-like flowers, as the ˛*chio* ˛*lang*; other varieties of the ˛*lang* are ˛*kwang* ˛*ing*, the Kwanyin, *so²* ˛*sing*, the white-heart, and *pó² swoi²* harbinger-of-the-year, blooming in the 12th moon; [17]˛*hó* ˛*lang*, Holland; [18]*huk*, ˛*lang*, or *hwak*, ˛*lang*, France.

讕 ˛Lan. An unintelligible talk, gabble, gibberish: ˛*lang* ˛*dó*, jargon.

斕 ˛Lan. A mixture of colors on animals; mottled, speckled: ˛*pang* ˛*lang*, veined, striped, brindled.

躝 ˛Lan. To overstep, to leap or pass over; to excel, to surpass.

˛*Lang*. A coll. word, as in ˛*lang* ˛*ch'iăng*, excessive, much, increasing, worse and worse, as a quarrel, an illness, etc.,—similar to ˛*long pwoi²* q. v.

濫 Lan². A rising of water, a freshet; overflowing, inundating; to throw into the water, to soak; an excess, excessive, profuse, beyond bounds; intruding, encroaching on; loose, careless, irregular, lawless; in the coll. wet, moist, soaked with water: [19]˛*u lang²* no excess; COM., [20]*lang² kau*, to associate with the low-bred; [21]*lang²* ˛*hing*, illegal punishments; [22]*lang²* ʻ*tu*, excessively addicted to gambling; *lang²* ʻ*sieu*

[1]攔轎遞呈 [2]關攔 [3]攔阻 [4]手欄 [5]欄杆 [6]豬欄 [7]牛欄 [8]波瀾 [9]瀾汗 [10]吊蘭 [11]蘭言 [12]蘭千 ○ [13]澤蘭 [14]蘭花 [15]珠蘭 [16]木蘭 [17]荷蘭 [18]佛蘭 [19]無濫 [20]濫交 [21]濫刑 [22]濫賭

ing, low, mean fellows; COLL., *tě a² cheng² lang²* the ground is very wet; *lang² pwang²* or *lang² lě*, dirty, untidy, as in dress; *¹lang² hwang²* easy, careless, negligent; *lang² lěk*, "dip up indiscriminately"; *met.*, to buy up things good and bad; *²hang lang²* while yet moist or wet; *p'ah, lang²* to become wet, wetted.

爛² Lan. To cook thoroughly; boiled to shreds; rotten, corrupted, putrid; torn, tattered, worn out; broken, spoiled; bright, splendid; splendor, brightness: COM., *³chü lang²* to boil soft; *⁴ch'ang² lang²* brilliant, refulgent; *⁵lang² choi²* very drunk; COLL., *⁶po² lang²* rotten, decayed; *⁷lang² ch'ong*, a running sore; *⁸lang² chaëng²* (like) the pointed dumplings—i. e., very soft; running, festered, &c.; *⁹lang² měk, kiěng*, sore eyelids; *¹⁰lang² k'a liěng k'ok, mwong taing²* a sore shin (is sure to) knock against the threshold!

爤² Lan. Used for the last in the senses following; broken, destroyed, ruined, spoiled; rotten, corrupt; running, festering, mortified, as sores.

二² Erh. Read *ne²*; used for the coll. *lang²*: two: *¹¹lang² chiǎh*, or *lang² ki*, two persons or things; *lang² 'a nëng*, two persons; *lang² 'a sang*, twice three; *¹²lang² 'pa*, two bunches or bundles; two, as of certain implements having handles; *lang² t'au 'mwoi*, the two ends; *lang² 'a sang 'ch'iǎng ch'ok*, "two hills, please go out!"—a witty phrase referring to the character *ch'ok*, as composed of "two hills".

(372) Lau.

Lau. A coll. word: to lift, to draw up, as the skirts in walking; to appropriate fraudulently, to embezzle; to put in and take out soon, as in cooking slightly; to draw toward one, as in reaping with a sickle: see also in *la*: *lau keng*, lift (the skirt) high; *lau sioh, a²* or *lau sioh, 'kung*, give it a slight cooking; *lau sioh, to²* to embezzle an amount.

了 Liao. Read *'lieu*; coll. *'lau*: done, finished, completed; always, of course, spontaneously; after verbs, a sign of the past tense, have, has: *¹³chó² 'lau*, has done, finished; *¹⁴wong 'lau*, completed; all exhausted; *i 'lau 'lau chiong wang²* he always, or of course, will do just so.

溜² Liu. Read *leu²*; coll. *lau²*: to flow, to run out; to drop, as grains from a hole; to drink in; to pour, as melted lead in adulterating money; to put, to slip in slyly; to go about: *¹⁵lau² yong*, to adulterate with lead; *¹⁶lau² t'ong*, to drink broth; *¹⁷lau² tang*, or *lau² á tang*, to insert the cord at the heels (of girls' shoes); *lau² lau² sük*, thoroughly acquainted, glib, as in reading; *lau² sioh, lau*, to take a turn, to go about; *lau² 'ch'iu 'wong 'tiě*, slip it into the sleeve.

1 濫泛 2 還濫 3 煮爛 4 燦爛 5 爛醉 6 腐爛 7 爛瘡 8 爛粽 9 爛目墘 10 爛骹臁搕門閬 11 二隻 12 二把 13 做了 14 完了 15 溜鉛 16 溜湯 17 溜單

漏[2] Lou. Read *lau'*; coll. *lau'*: like the last; to drip, to ooze out; to overlook, to let slip, to miss: [1]*'lau' ˏk'au*, to overlook a lot or ballot; [2]*lau' so'* to miss entering into the account; [3]*lau' swoi'* to shirk toll, to smuggle; [4]*lau' ˏp'ieu*, a sort of skimmer; *lau' sioh, che'* to leave out a word; *lau' tek, sü'* much oozed out, or missed.

劉 ˏLiu. Read *ˏliu*; coll. *ˏlau*: a surname: [5]*ˏLau pe'* a famous general of the Three States—the prince *ˏLau-sieng-'chio*. A. D. 221; [6]*ˏlau 'hai tieu' ˏsieng*, Lauhai angling for the three-footed toad—a picture; *ˏlau 'kau 'ma neng' tang' sai'* Laukau's wife mistakes another for her husband; *ˏnek*, to mistake, take the wrong for the right one.

樓 ˏLou. Read *ˏleu*; coll. *ˏlau*: a loft; the upper floor or story; [7]*ˏlau ˏpang*, a wooden terrace on a roof; [8]*ˏlau 'ting* and [9]*ˏlau a'* the upper and lower stories, above and below; [10]*ˏlau ˏt'ai*, a ladder; [11]*ˏlau 'chang*, a sky-light; [12]*ˏlau koh*, a loft; [13]*'ku ˏlau*, the drum tower, as over South street, Foochow; *se' ˏchong ˏlau*, a dressing boudoir; *'chau 'ma ˏlau*, a veranda; *yong' ˏlau*, the north tower of Foochow; *ˏchung ˏlau*, a belfry; *ˏlau t'ak*, the floor crushed or fallen in.

流 ˏLiu. Read *ˏliu*; coll. *ˏlau*: to flow, as water; to drift, to float, to glide down; a time, once over: [14]*ˏlau kek*, to flow swiftly; [15]*'chwi ˏlau*, water flowing; [16]*ˏlau mek, 'chai*, to shed tears; *ˏlau p'e' 'chwi*, running of the nose; *ˏlau 'lang*, to slaver; *ˏlau pah, chok*, white urinary emissions; *lang' ˏlau*, twice over.

留 ˏLiu. Read *ˏliu*; coll. *ˏlau*: to detain, to stop, to stay; to retain, to keep back, to keep by one: *ˏlau ˏneng k'ah*, to stay a guest; [17]*ˏlau ka'* let me detain your honor! [18]*ˏlau ˏsiang*, keep the city-gate open, as awaiting the return of officers or idols; [19]*ˏlau ˏsü*, to leave whiskers unshorn; *ˏlau 'la 'mwi*, to leave a balance, as of debts, work, &c.; *ˏlau miang' k'ang' t'ai' ˏping*, to enjoy some prosperity (after a hard lot).

ˏLau. A coll. word, as in *ˏka ˏlau*, to roll about, as round things do; *ˏka ˏlau ˏhing*, dizziness of the head.

ˏLau. A coll. word: used with *sioh*, (one) as an emphatic suffix to adjectives; very, extremely, very much indeed: *'ya taeng' sioh, ˏlau*, exceedingly heavy, very weighty indeed.

老[2] 佬[2] Lao. The first read *'lo*, and the second *ˏlieu*; coll. *lau'*: old, aged, advanced in years; a term of respect, venerable; to die, dead, deceased—said of the aged and adults: [20]*lau' ˏneng*, an aged person; [21]*lau' ˏkung* and [22]*lau' 'ma*, husband and wife; *ˏlau lau'* old man, venerable Sir! *lau' ngwoi'* and *lau' tang'* the characters of old men and old women in plays; *lau' ˏsie*, a snake; *lau' heng'* old people's

[1]漏鬮 [2]漏數 [3]漏稅 [4]漏瓢 [5]劉備 [6]劉海 釣蟾 [7]樓棚 [8]樓頂 [9]樓下 [10]樓梯 [11]樓井 [12]樓閣 [13]鼓樓 [14]流急 [15]水流 [16]流目滓 ◯ [17]留駕 [18]留城 [19]留鬚 [20]佬伙 [21]佬公 [22]佬媽

whims; *lau*^{2} *yoh*$_{2}$ a species of hawk, a kite; *lau*^{2} *ch'eu*^{2} *ˌmó ˌküng*, old trees without roots; *met.*, old, infirm people; *lau*^{2} *miäng*^{2} *kuëng*^{1} *ˌi ˌp'ing* (or *ˌp'iäng*), will risk my old life in the contest with him; *lau*^{2} *pwoi*^{2} or *lau*^{2} *'mung 'tung*, old blockhead! *lau*^{2} *k'ó*^{3} deceased; *ˌliéng lau*^{2} in old age.

漏^{2} Loh. Read *laiu*^{2}; coll. *lau*^{2}: to leak, to run out; leaking, leaky: *lau*^{2} *'tá*, a leaky bottom, as of a tub; *lau*^{2} *'ch'iéng*, has leaked (till the water is) shallow; *ch'io*^{3} *lau*^{2} the house leaks; *ˌsing lau*^{2} to catch leaking water; *k'ak*$_{1}$ *lau*^{2} to arrange tiles so as to stop a leak.

(373) Lauk.

犖$^{>}$ Lo. Clear, open, manifest, patent: *tauk*$_{2}$ *lauk*$_{2}$ to excel; distinguished, preeminent; *lauk*$_{2}$ *lauk*$_{2}$ clearly understood. Read *lok*$_{2}$: a speckled or brindled cow.

Lauk$_{2}$. A coll word: to saunter; to put or fit in; to tread, as into mire or a hole; put in, fitted: *lauk*$_{2}$ *lauk*$_{2}$ to saunter about; *lauk*$_{2}$ *'tié*, to place, to thrust into; to slip, as the foot into a plash; *lauk*$_{2}$ *lauk*$_{2}$ *ˌsiéng*, rambling genii; *met.*, persons strolling about at leisure; *lauk*$_{2}$ *lauk*$_{2}$ *ˌk'wang*, large, fitting loosely, as shoes.

(374) Laung.

崙 崘$^{>}$ Lun. Read *ˌlung* and *ˌlong*; coll. *laung*$^{>}$: a mountain, a mountain ridge or slope; a classifier of hills and mountains: *'chi lang*^{2} *laung*$^{>}$ these two hills; [1]*ˌchiong ˌsang ˌchiong laung*$^{>}$ the whole hill or ridge, as bought for a grave-site.

晼$^{>}$ Lun. Read *k'aung*$^{>}$ in the dictionaries; coll. *laung*$^{>}$, as in *laung*$^{>}$ *laung*$^{>}$ to dry in the sun, as clothes; *pong*$^{>}$ *nik*$_{2}$ *ˌt'au 'lá laung*$^{>}$ *sioh*$_{2}$ *a*^{2} put it in the sun and dry it.

Laung$^{>}$. A coll. word: to open, to make trial; to rehearse, as in learning songs: *laung*$^{>}$ *tiing*$^{>}$ to open a new shop, to commence selling.

埌^{2} Lang. A tomb, a cemetery: [2]*ˌhwang laung*^{2} a burial place; [3]*'k'wong laung*^{2} a desert wild.

浪^{2} Lang. Waves, billows, surges; a drum; dissipated, dissolute, profligate; wasteful, extravagant; careless, unsettled; rude, impertinent, disrespectful: [4]*maing*^{2} *laung*^{2} reckless, rude, bragging; [5]*ngiok*$_{2}$ *laung*^{2} to mock, to ridicule; COM., [6]*ˌp'ó laung*^{2} or [7]*ˌhung laung*^{2} waves, billows; [8]*ˌu ˌhung 'k'i laung*^{2} waves raised without wind; *met.*, causeless trouble; [9]*laung*^{2} *taung*^{2} inconstant, vagabondish; [10]*laung*^{2} *'chü*, a spendthrift; [11]*laung*^{2} *ëüng*^{2}, wasteful; COLL., *'chang 'chwi má*^{2} *'k'i tek*$_{1}$ *laung*^{2} well-water can't raise waves; *met.*, incapable, without skill to effect a thing. Read *ˌlong*, as in [12]*ˌch'ong ˌlong*, a river in Shantung.

蛋^{2} Tan. Read *tang*$^{>}$ in the dictionaries: a tribe of the Miautsz'; an egg: COM., [13]*ˌkié laung*^{2} hens' eggs; [14]*laung*^{2} *ˌching* or [15]*laung*^{2} *pah*$_{2}$ the white of an egg; *laung*^{2}

[1] 全山全崙 [2] 墦埌 [3] 壙埌 [4] 孟浪 [5] 謔浪 [6] 波浪 [7] 風浪 [8] 無風起浪 [9] 浪蕩 [10] 浪子 [11] 浪用 [12] 滄浪 [13] 雞蛋 [14] 蛋精 [15] 蛋白

ˏ*wong*, the yelk; ¹*laung*² ˏ*kó*, sponge cakes; ²ˏ*hwa laung*² painted ducks' eggs—sent by a maternal grand-mother to a grand-child when a month old; COLL., ³ˏ*p'ui laung*² preserved eggs; ⁴*laung*² *móh*ˎ thin film inside of an egg-shell; ⁵*po*² *laung*² to hatch eggs; ⁶*laung*² ˏ*pi*, embryo eggs; *laung*² ˏ*pau*, eggs cooked in gravy, fried eggs; *laung*² *laung*² ˏ*kwong*, smooth and shining, glossy.

論² Lun. To discourse about, to consider and discuss; to think upon, to reason, to consult; a reasoning process, a full investigation and account of; counsel, delibera-tion, discourse; according to, by the; speaking of: ⁷ˊ*t'ó laung*² to search into, to investigate; COM., ⁸ˊ*kong laung*² to discourse upon; ⁹ˊ*pi laung*² to illustrate, an illustration, for instance; ¹⁰*yok*ˎ *laung*² if we admit, premising; ¹¹*laung*² *nik*ˎ by the day; ¹²ˊ*li laung*² to argue, to reason or remonstrate with one; ¹³ˏ*siong* ˏ*hang laung*² a medical book; COLL., ˏ*mó laung*² without regard to, no matter (how, what, how many, &c.); *laung*² ˊ*k'i* ˏ*li*, to speak of—a prefatory phrase; *laung*² ˊ*li á*² ˊ*sai tek*ˎ to judge from its reasonableness it will do. Read ˏ*lung*: to say directly or to the point, to discourse correctly and in order.

亂² 乱² Luan. Read *lwang*²; coll. *laung*²: to confuse, to disorder; confused, disordered, wrong; reckless, indiscriminate; anarchy, discord, insurrection, tumult: *laung*² ˏ*t'ai*, to slay indiscriminately; *laung*² ˏ*li*, to act recklessly, to go from bad to worse; *t'ié*² ˏ*nĕng laung*² to follow others in disorderly conduct; *laung*² ˊ*kong laung*² *t'iăng*² to lie, lying, mendacious; ˏ*hung* ˏ*hung laung*² confusion, anarchy.

(375) Le.

利² Li. Profitable, useful, advantageous, beneficial; happy, fortunate; gain, profit, interest on investments: also read *lé*² q. v.: COM., ¹⁴*pok*ˎ *le*² unlucky, not profitable; ¹⁵*ik*ˎ *le*² or *nak*ˎ *le*² to pay interest; ¹⁶*le*² *sek*ˎ or *le*² ˏ*chiĕng*, or ˏ*chiĕng le*² interest on money; ¹⁷ˊ*pwong le*² (coll. ˊ*mó le*²) principal and interest; *le*² ˊ*kwi* ˏ*hung*, what *per cent* interest a month? *le*² ˊ*chwi*, a urinative medicine; ¹⁸ˊ*chwi le*² deputy of a district magistrate or marine inspector; COLL., *le*² *yăh*, profit, advantage; ˏ*k'ing* ˊ*pwong taĕng*² *le*² small capital and large profits.

*Le*². A coll. euphonic prefix, as in *le*² *laĭ*² to file; *le*² *lĕŭ*² to saw off with a knife; *le*² *lié*² to cut, to slit open; *le*² *lói*² to bore.

利² Li. A sharp point or edge, keen-edged; acute, clever; address, fluency; greedy of gain, covetous; hurtful, formidable; to oblige, to benefit: also read *lé*² q. v.: ¹⁹*le*² ˊ*k'eu*, fluent speech; COM., ²⁰*le*² ˏ*tó*, a sharp knife; ²¹*le*² *hai*² formidable, hurtful; stingy; ²²ˏ*ming le*² (the pursuits of) literature and trade; ²³ˏ*chiĕng* ˏ*chai le*² avaricious, stingy; ˏ*kiu le*² to seek wealth.

1 蛋糕　2 花蛋　3 皮蛋　4 蛋膜　5 抱蛋　6 蛋脾　7 討論　8 講論　9 比論　10 若論　11 論日　12 理論　13 傷寒論　14 不利　15 入利　16 利息　17 本利　18 水利　19 利口　20 利刀　21 利害　22 名利　23 錢財利

俐[2] Li. Clever, cunning: COM., [1]ˏling le' clever; also trim, shapely, as the person; COLL., ˏchṳ́i wa' tek, ˏling le' this (map) is finely drawn; ˏmá le' expert, active.

痢[2] Li. A flux, a dysentery: COM., [2]le' cheng' (coll. ˏpang' le'), a dysentery; [3]haik, le' bloody flux, dysentery; [4]ˏhiu sek, le' a chronic diarrhea; [5]keng' ʻk'eu le' dysentery and loss of appetite; [6]ha' le' (coll. ˏau le'), a flux; COLL., [7]ˏhong le' flux from opium-smoking; ˏëng pah, le' the bloody and bloodless fluxes.

莉[2] Li. A flower highly prized by the Chinese, called mwak, (coll. mëk,) le' ˏhwa, the white jasmin; also the name of a popular song.

涖[2] **蒞**[2] **莅**[2] Li. Rushes, aquatic grasses; to come down, to descend towards, to arrive at; to enter on the duties of an office; the official seat or place; the first and second also mean water running down: [8]le' eng' to go to one's office; [9]le' ˏming, to govern the people; [10]le' sëü' to attend actively to business; [11]le' ˏkwang, official rule or conduct; le' le' sound of flowing water.

吏[2] Li. An officer; magistrates, rulers; a subordinate executive, as a deputy or secretary; to rule: COM., [12]ˏchü le' government writers; [13]le' pwo' Board of Civil Office; [14]le' ˏpung, department in a yamun which receives officers; [15]le' ˏwong, one who is promoted from the clerkship; [16]k'o' le' treasury-clerks; [17]ʻmwang le' term of clerkship completed.

Le'. A coll. euphonic prefix, as in le' ló' to go on a round of inspection; le' lai' to lean against; le' lói' to beat, as a drum or door; le' lieu' to stir, as things being cooked; le' lié' to withdraw; le' lëü' to strain, to filter; le' loi' to sort, to class.

(376) Lë.

ˏLë. A coll. word, as in ˏlë ʻtó, to recline at full length; ˏlë tik, tik, to stretch one's self out straight; ˏlë sioh, ʻtó, to fall down sprawling.

ʻ **魯** Lu. Read ʻlu; coll. ʻlë, as in ʻlë ʻlë, dull, obtuse; ʻlë ˏchṳ̈, a dull person.

驢 **馿** Lu. Read ˏlu; coll. ˏlë: an ass: [18]ˏlë ʻkëng, a jackass; [19]ˏlë ʻma kau' term for Mohammedanism; [20]ˏlë ˏmó wak, a kind of hair-stocking from Shantung; ˏlë ʻkiäng ng' kwo' chang' the ass will not pass the post-house; met., obstinate, decided, as not to give more; [21]ˏhiong ˏlë, a country clown—used derisively.

ˏLë. A coll. word: to project, to extend, to put forth: ˏlë ˏt'au, to thrust the head forward; ˏlë ˏt'au ʻlá k'ang' to put out the head to see; ʻch'iu ˏlë ˏtong kwo' ˏli ˏtó, reach the hand far out and take it.

ˏLë. A coll. word: to curse, to rail at, to blackguard: ˏlë póh, to revile scurrilously;

[1]伶俐 [2]痢症 [3]血痢 [4]休息痢 [5]噤口痢 [6]下痢 [7]煙痢 [8]涖任 [9]涖民 [10]涖事 [11]涖官 [12]書吏 [13]吏部 [14]吏房 [15]吏員 [16]庫吏 [17]滿吏 [18]驢牡 [19]驢馬教 [20]驢毛襪 [21]鄉驢 ○

ˌlë ˌnëng, to blackguard people; *ˌlë kwangˀ* to rail, as women do.

(377) Lek.

栗, Li. A chestnut; chestnut wood, often used for tablets; firm, solid, durable; severe, strict; to overpass; to exceed; to respect, to revere; full-grown grain: in the coll. read *lik*, q. v.: [1]*ˋchwi lek*, water-caltrops; [2]*lek ˌkai*, to pass over the steps, to trespass; [3]*sik lek*, ripe grain; [4]*ˌkʻwang lek*, mild and dignified.

慄, Li, Afraid, fearful, apprehensive, trembling: *lek, lek*, or [5]*chiëngˀ lek*, sorrowful, afflicted; [6]*ˌchai lek*, awe-struck.

凓, Li. Cold, frigid: [7]*lek, liëk*, a cold, piercing wind.

溧, Li. As in [8]*Lek, ˋchwi*, name of a river and district in Kiangsu, south of Nanking; [9]*lek, ˌchiu*, an island in the river Yangtsz'.

靂, Li. A clap, the roar of thunder: *pʻek, lek*, the splitting, crashing sound of thunder.

Lek,. A coll. word: scant, falling short, barely sufficing; similar to *ˋling*, q. v.: *lek, lek*, scantily, barely; *lek, ˌhung ˌhung*, a little scant; *lek, lek, oˀ tek, tioh*, will barely suffice.

Lek,. A coll. euphonic prefix, as in *lek, laëk*, loose, falling apart; weak, relaxed, as the hands and feet; tired of, giving up; *lek, lok*, at intervals, irregularly, as of persons passing, stars gradually appearing; *lek, lek, lok, lok*, moving about, rolling, as a puppet's eyes; *lok, lok, wak*, movable; ambiguous, as language.

勒, Lê. Lei. Lieh. A bridle-bit, a curb; a bridle, a headstall; to curb, to rein in, to restrain; to require, to oblige, to force to do; to vex, to exact, to extort; to cut in stone, to engrave; to bind, to tie up, to strangle: [10]*lek ˌhiu*, to require one to resign; COM., [11]*ˋma lek*, a horse's bit; [12]*lek ˋma*, to curb a horse; [13]*lek sauk*, to extort from; [14]*lek pʻaik*, to force, to insist on one's doing; [15]*lek chaˀ* to oppress in order to get money from; [16]*lek ˌpi*, to engrave on tablets; [17]*lek ˋsiä tʻöiˀ ˌhwong*, to compel one to give a written agreement annulling his betrothal-contract; COLL., [18]*ak, lek* to force by oppression; [19]*lek ˋsi*, to strangle to death—to oppress severely.

泐, Lieh. The veins of rocks; to split rocks according to the veins; to condense, to congeal; to write: [20]*lek ˌtʻang*, veined rocks; [21]*ˌming lengˀ lek*, my name is elsewhere written — phrase used instead of a signature.

扐, Li. To divine with 50 straws between the fingers; one thus describes the process—the 50 straws are reduced to 49 and divided into two parcels at hazard, from one of which a straw is

1 水栗 2 栗階 3 實栗 4 寬栗 5 戰慄 6 災慄 7 凓冽 8 溧水 9 溧洲 10 勒休 11 馬勒 12 勒馬 13 勒索 14 勒迫 15 勒詐 16 勒碑 17 勒寫退婚 18 押勒 19 勒死 20 泐潭〇 21 名另泐〇

taken and put by the little finger, and four others are then selected to put with it, the remainder of the parcel being distributed between the other two fingers; the other parcel is divided in the same manner on the other hand, and the lengths, of the two compared with the 64 diagrams to ascertain the luck; the word also means to bind.

芀$_2$ Li. A sort of rush or sedge; spines on plants; prickly, spinous: [1]*ʻtói ʾ miéngʾ lek*$_2$ the Gardenia spinosa; [2]*ʻló ʻchʻü lek*$_2$ a rough grass, the Spinifex squarrosus; [3]*ˏngiu ˏchié lek*$_2$ a medicine to check hemorrhage.

竻$_2$ A species of spinous, thorny bamboo, used for hedges; roots of bamboo, spines, thorns: COM., *tëük*$_2$ *lek*$_2$ *ˏsiéng*, salt heated in the *lek*$_2$ bamboo—used as a febrifuge and expectorant.

肋$_2$ Lieh. The ribs, the sides of the body: in the coll. read *lĕk*$_2$ q. v.: [4]*ʻhiĕk*$_2$ *lek*$_2$ the ribs; [5]*ˏkié lek*$_2$ hen's ribs—though having little meat, they are not to be thrown away; *met.*, said of an employment which is better than none. Read *ˏkŭng*: power of the muscles, sinews.

瘰$_2$ Li. Read *lik*$_2$; coll. *lek*$_2$: the scrofula, scrofulous sores on the neck below the ears, which sometimes induce a rigid deflexure of the head: *ˏsang lek*$_2$ to have scrofula; *lek*$_2$ *ˏhong*, scrofulous scars.

Lek$_2$. A coll. word: to draw, to pull: *lek*$_2$ *ʻking ʻking tioh*$_2$ pull it very tight.

(378) Lĕk.

六$_2$ 陸$_2$ Lu. Liu. The second read *lük*$_2$ in other senses; used as a complex form of the first: the cardinal number six: COM., [6]*sek*$_2$ *lĕk*$_2$ sixteen; *lĕk*$_2$ *lĕk*$_2$ thirty six; [7]*lĕk*$_2$ *hak*$_2$ six pairs or couples; the six points, north, south, east, west, zenith, nadir; the 12 horary characters in pairs; [8]*lĕk*$_2$ *sek*$_2$ *kak*$_2$ *ʻchü*, the cycle of 60 years; [9]*pai ʾ lĕk*$_2$ Saturday; [10]*lĕk*$_2$ *kaĕk*$_2$ hexagonal; [11]*lĕk*$_2$ *chiĕk*$_2$ six-tenths, as paid in compounding for a debt; [12]*lĕk*$_2$ *chiongʾ* the six assistants of the god *Tʻai ʾ ˏSang*—(in the coll.) *ˏtong ˏpang, ʻá paik*$_2$, *ˏkiă, ʻsó, ˏngu ˏtʻau, ʻma miéngʾ*; [13]*lĕk*$_2$ *ngwok*$_2$ *siok*$_2$ a kind of pear; [14]*lĕk*$_2$ *ek*$_2$ *ʻsang*, a cooling medicinal powder; COLL., [15]*lĕk*$_2$ *ˏĕng*, the six reds—red beans, used as dice with white ones in the streets; also a kind of wine; [16]*lĕk*$_2$ *mah*$_2$ *ngʾ ˏtieu ˏhwo*, the six pulses not composed—applied to one who is fearful or apprehensive.

磟$_2$ Read *lük*$_2$; coll. *lĕk*$_2$ as in *lĕk*$_2$ *tĕk*$_2$ a roller of stone or wood for leveling fields; *pʻah*$_2$ *lĕk*$_2$ *tĕk*$_2$ to use the roller; *ak*$_2$ *ʻmó ˏtʻang siăh*$_2$ *kʻëük*$_2$ *lĕk*$_2$ *tĕk*$_2$ *pʻah*$_2$ the duck coveting food is crushed by the roller; *met.*, one injuring himself by covetousness or gluttony.

[1]對面芀 [2]老鼠芀 [3]牛脂芀 [4]腦肋○ [5]雞肋○ [6]十六○ [7]六合 [8]六十 甲子 [9]拜六 [10]六角 [11]六折 [12]六將 [13]六月 雪 [14]六一散 [15]六紅 [16]六脈 不調和○

肋 Lieh.$_2$ Read *lek$_2$*; coll. *lĕk$_2$* as in *lĕk$_2$ ꜂teu kauk*, the ribs; *lĕk$_2$ ꜂teu*, the spare-ribs, as of pork or mutton.

鹿 Lu.$_2$ Read *lŭk$_2$*; coll. *lĕk$_2$*: a deer: [1]*lĕk$_2$ ꜂ĭing*, tips of deer's horns—used medicinally; [2]*lĕk$_2$ ꜂lu*, dried deer's meat: [3]*lĕk$_2$ ꜂kŭng*, deer-tendons; [4]*꜂muói ꜂hwa lĕk$_2$* the white-spotted, axis deer; [5]*lĕk$_2$ kaĕk, ꜂ka*, the viscous extract of deer's horns; [6]*lĕk$_2$ ꜂kĕng ꜂t'iăng*, magistrate of the *Lĕk$_2$ ꜂kĕng* district, Formosa.

鬣 Lieh.$_2$ Read *lak*, and *lek$_2$*; coll. *lĕk$_2$* as in *lĕk$_2$ ꜂chĕng*, a horse's mane.

Lĕk$_2$. A coll. word, as in *lĕk$_2$ ꜂chwi*, to wade, or walk about in the wet; *lĕk$_2$ ꜂ü ꜂tiong k'ó'* to wade home in the rain.

Lĕk$_2$. A coll. word: to dip up; to strain, to filter: *lĕk$_2$ ꜂p'ieu*, to dip duck-weed; *lĕk$_2$ pwong'* to lade rice (from the cooking-pan); *lang' lĕk$_2$* "scoop them up indiscriminately", as in buying or eating things, or employing persons.

Lĕk$_2$. A coll. word: to curse and rail, as women do: *lĕk$_2$ kaing'* in the habit of cursing.

Lĕk$_2$. A coll. word, as in *lĕk$_2$ p'ĕk$_2$* (falling of hail); used wholly in the *met.* sense of urgent, pressing, rapid; *lĕk$_2$ p'ĕk$_2$ ꜂kang kau'* to arrive and crowd in rapidly, as a multitude; *lĕk$_2$ p'ĕk$_2$ taung' lóh$_2$ ꜂li*, to rattle down like hail, as the rain or falling tiles.

(379) Leng.

꜁Leng. A coll. word, as in *꜁leng ꜁t'eng*, sated and indifferent to, as food, small gains, etc.

冷 冷 Lĕng. Cold, icy, chilly; indifferent to, frigid, cool, neglectful; still, quiet, clear: [7]*꜂leng ꜂ngung*, a cool, indifferent look; [8]*꜂hang ꜂leng*, cold, chilly; COM., [9]*꜁t'ieng ꜂leng*, chilly weather; [10]*꜁t'ong ꜂leng*, hot water cooled; [11]*꜂leng ch'ieu'* to smile coldly or sarcastically at; [12]*꜂leng tang'* distant, cool towards; insipid, tasteless, as books or employment: dull, as a place; [13]*꜂leng ꜁kŭng*, the still palace—for discarded wives; [14]*꜂leng ꜁ch'ing ꜁ch'ing*, still, quiet, lonely; [15]*꜂leng ꜂ngiong ꜂leng ꜂ngü*, cold, mocking words; [16]*꜁ing ꜂ching ꜂leng ꜂nwang*, men's feelings are very changeable; COLL., *꜁ch'ang ꜂leng*, (things eaten) raw and cold; *꜁k'a ꜂ch'iu k'wok$_2$ ꜂leng*, the limbs cold, as in severe sickness.

Leng'. A coll. word: a carpel, a lobe; a triangular section, natural or artificial, of round things, as fruit, etc.: *꜁kang sioh$_2$ leng'* a section of a cooly-orange; *kek$_2$ leng'* lobes of a mandarin orange; *met.*, the pieces composing the crown of a child's cap.

Leng'. A coll. euphonic prefix, as in *leng' lüng'*, to roll, rolling about; tossing about, as on one's bed; *leng' luung'* to make trial, to rehearse, as songs; to dry in the sun.

蓮 Lien. The lotus or nelumbium: COM., [17]*꜂leng ꜁hwa*, water-lily; [18]*꜂leng ꜂pung* (coll. *꜂leng ꜂p'ung*), the

[1]鹿茸 [2]鹿脯 [3]鹿筋 [4]梅花鹿 [5]鹿角膠 [6]鹿港廳 ○ [7]冷眼 [8]寒冷 [9]天冷 [10]湯冷 [11]冷笑 [12]冷淡 [13]冷宮 [14]冷清清 [15]冷言冷語 [16]人情冷暖 [17]蓮花 ○ [18]蓮房 ○

receptacle of the lotus; [1]ˏ*leng* ʻ*chi*, lotus-nuts; [2]ʻ*ch'ai* ˏ*leng*, to pluck the lotus; *met.*, to get contributions, as for a ʻ*Ngu tá*ʼ temple; [3]ˏ*king* ˏ*leng*, the golden lilies—i. e., a lady's feet; [4]ˏ*leng* ˏ*hwa chó*ʼ the lotus-seat—seat of a Budhist idol; [5]ˏ*leng* ˏ*pung k'aiu*ʼ lotus-shaped buttons; COLL., [6]ˏ*hai* ˏ*i* (or ˏ*ha* ˏ*i*) *kwang*ʼ ˏ*leng*, (picture of) a boy holding a lotus-flower and treading on a lotus-root; ˏ*leng* ˏ*hwa sau*ʼ a beggar's song; [7]ˏ*leng* ˏ*ngü*, a fish, perhaps a species of carp; [8]ˏ*leng* ʻ*ch'ó tói*ʼ a pair of the ˏ*leng* and ʻ*ch'ó* fish—i. e., one of each given as a present.

連 ˏ Lien. Read ˏ*lieng*; coll. ˏ*leng*, as in ˏ*leng* ˏ*kong kaing*ʼ the Lienkiang district of Foochow prefecture.

菱 ˏ Ling. Read ˏ*ling*; coll. ˏ*leng*, as in [9]ˏ*leng kaëk*ˏ water-caltrops, a three-horned aquatic vegetable; [10]ˏ*leng kaëk*ˏ ʻ*kwi*, small caltrops; [11]ˏ*leng kaëk*ˏ ʻ*kwi ch'ok*ˏ ˏ*chiéng*, small caltrops putting forth horns; *met.*, a child or a dolt attempting a great matter.

龍 ˏ Lung. Read ˏ*lüng*; coll. ˏ*leng*, as in [12]ˏ*leng* ʻ*keng*, the lungan or dragon's eye; ˏ*leng* ʻ*keng* ˏ*kó*, lungan-jelly; ˏ*leng* ʻ*keng hok*ˏ *k'ang*ʼ ˏ*nëng tai*² throw lungan-pits at different people differently; *met.*, use partiality—a play on the two coll. words *tai*² meaning respectively to throw and to treat.

憐 ˏ Lien. Read ˏ*ling*; coll. ˏ*leng*, as in ʻ*k'ó* ˏ*leng*, to pity, to compassionate; to show kindness or sympathy toward.

令 ² **令** ² Ling. Law, rule, orders; to command, to enjoin on, to warn against; a period of time, season; good, excellent, worthy; hence in direct address, your, your honored: used for *liâng*² in the coll. q. v.: [13]ˏ*si leng*² times and seasons; [14]*leng*² *taik*ˏ virtue, great excellence; [15]*kaing*² *leng*² a district magistrate; COM., [16]*meng*² *leng*² a command; [17]*hwak*ˏ *leng*² or *ch'ok*ˏ *leng*² to issue orders; [18]*leng*² ˏ*chong*, your father; *leng*² *cheng*ʼ your wife; *leng*² ˏ*long*, your son; *leng*² ʻ*t'ang*, your son-in-law; *leng*² *chiéng*ʼ a triangular warrant, as issued to patrols; a flag stuck in a criminal's ears; a warrant from an idol, as used to expel demons; *leng*² ˏ*pá*, an official tablet by which orders are conveyed. Read ˏ*ling*: to cause, to occasion; to serve of, to send: ʻ*sü* ˏ*ling*, to employ, to send one to do.

另 ² Ling. To be or dwell apart, separate, distinct, alone, particular, another; besides, furthermore; to cut open, to divide: COM., [19]*leng*² *ngwói*² besides, in addition; *leng*² *che*² by itself; *leng*² ˏ*kü*, to dwell apart; *leng*² ʻ*ngang*, to give special regard to; *leng*² *saung*ʼ to put in a separate account; *leng*² *nik*ˏ another day; *leng*² ʻ*chai* ʻ*k'i* ʻ*kó*, additional paper for rough drafts—*scil.*, must not be taken to the examinations.

---

[1]蓮子 [2]採蓮 [3]金蓮 [4]蓮花座 [5]蓮房鈕 [6]孩兒扣蓮 [7]蓮魚 [8]蓮草對 [9]菱角 [10]菱角鬼 [11]菱角鬼出尖 [12]龍眼 [13]時令 [14]令德 [15]縣令 [16]命令 [17]發令 [18]令尊 [19]另外 ○

吝 悋 恡 Lin. Avaricious, stingy, mean, sordid, sparing; to dislike, to part with, to spare; regretting, ashamed of: [1]'leng' saik, close, niggardly; [2]hwoi' leng' regretful, disconsolate; com., [3]'p'i leng' avaricious, sordid.

胷 Shĉn. Read seng'; coll. leng', as in leng' ,p'a, the scrotum; leng' hok, (or k'ok,) 'chi, the testicles.

藺 Lin. Also read neng': a rush suitable for making mats; a surname, name of a place: [4]'ma leng' the iris or fleur-de-lis; [5]leng' sik, stones on walls for casting down on an enemy.

躪 Lin. Also read neng': the rut of a wheel; to pass over, to run against or drive over one: [6],iu leng' to tread, to trample on.

(380) Lĕng.

,Lĕng. A coll. word, as in ,lĕng ,lié, a kind of screen, fixed in the center of the fronts of rooms; ,lĕng ,lié ,mwong, a screen with doors.

,Lĕng. A coll. word, as in ,lĕng ,lĕng, a cave, grotto; ,sang ,lĕng, a mountain cave; ,k'ĕ ,lĕng, a hole, orifice.

,Lĕng. A coll. word: a cool or chilly sensation: ,t'au kiéng' ,lĕng ,lĕng tioh, the head feels coolish (without the cap).

攏 Lung. Read 'lung; coll. 'lĕng: to cause to approach, to bring near, to draw close to; to gather together; *met.*, to open a negotiation: [7],kiŏng 'lĕng, to walk close to; [8],sung ,t'ang 'lĕng ngiăng' pole the boat close to the shore; [9]'lĕng sioh, ,toi to gather (things) together; [10]'lĕng ,tau or 'lĕng kĕŭng' to place close or near to; [11]'lĕng ,sing, to press near one, as in a fight; [12]'lĕng k'o' overalls—worn by boatmen; [13]'lĕng ,t'au hwok, to comb the hair in a knot, as girls about 16 years old; k'ó' 'lĕng ,i, go and negotiate with him.

籠 Lung. Read ,lung; coll. 'lĕng, as in tĕük, 'lĕng, or [14]'lĕng ,siong, a kind of bamboo box or chest: also read ,lĕng in the coll., q. v.

籠 Lung. Read ,lung; coll. ,lĕng: a cage, an open-work basket of bamboo: [15],kié ,lĕng tau' a movable hen-coop; [16]'cheu ,lĕng, a bird-cage; [17]'hwi ,lĕng, a hand-stove, consisting of a basket with an earthen pot holding coals; [18]pwoi' ,lĕng, a clothes-drying basket or frame of bamboo.

礱 Lung. Read ,lung; coll. ,lĕng: a hand-mill for hulling rice; to remove the husks, to hull, for which the last is commonly used: ,t'u ,lĕng, a hulling-mill; ,lĕng pié' the handle of a hulling-mill; ,lĕng ch'ioh, to hull paddy; ,lĕng k'o' hulling-mill and mortar.

嚨 Lung. Read ,lung; coll. ,lĕng, as in ,hó ,lĕng, or ,hĕ ,lĕng, the trachea; the throat; ,hó ,lĕng ,t'au (or te'), the top of the throat—under the chin.

---

1 吝嗇 2 悔吝 3 鄙吝 4 馬藺 5 藺石 6 蹂躪 7 行攏 8 船撑攏岸 ○ 9 攏一堆 ○ 10 攏垙 ○ 11 攏身 ○ 12 攏褌 13 攏頭髮 14 籠箱 15 雞籠罩 16 鳥籠 17 火籠 18 焙籠

櫳 Lung. Read ˏlung; coll. ˏlëng: a cage, a den; a wooden stockade or inclosure, as for animals: ˏch'iu ˏlëng, a cage for carrying prisoners; ˏkwong ˏlëng 'lá, shut up in a cage.

瓏 Lung. Read ˏlung; coll. ˏlëng: clear, translucent; met., discerning, perspicacious: [1]ˏt'ëng ˏlëng, translucent; [2]sëü' p'ek, ˏling ˏlëng, the four walls letting in the light—i. e., broken, dilapidated; ˏi pok, 'lò 'tié má[2] ˏt'ëng ˏlëng, his mind is not clear, he don't understand it.

聾 Lung. Read ˏlung; coll. ˏlëng: deaf, hard of hearing: [3]ˏlëng ˏchü, a deaf man; [4]nge[2] ˏlëng, deaf, deafness; [5]ˏt'iëng ˏlëng te[2] 'a, very deaf and dumb!—stupid, doltish; [6]ch'au' ˏlëng, you stupid fellow! ˏtiäng ˏlëng, half-deaf, as from disease in the ears; [7]ta' ˏlëng, to pretend to be deaf, to feign ignorance of.

ˏLëng. A coll. word, as in ˏlëng ˏt'au, to put out the head and peer at; ˏlëng sioh, a' take a stealthy look.

ˏLëng. A coll. word: to stir up, to excite: se[2] ˏi ˏlëng kwo' ˏli, it is he that stirred up (the quarrel).

(381) Leu.

蔞 Lou. Read ˏleu; coll. ˏleu: the leaf of the betel-pepper (Piper betle), called [8]ˏleu nioh[2].

ˏLeu. A coll. word, as in ˏleu ch'ok, ˏli, to thrust (food from the mouth) with the tongue, to reject food, as a babe does.

ˏLeu. A coll. word: to speak well, as of a child's fine health and looks—is regarded as unlucky and injurious: móh[2] ˏleu, don't speak in praise (of him)!

簍 Lou. Also read ˏleu, in the dictionaries: a bamboo basket or hamper: coll., [9]tëük, 'leu, an open-work bamboo basket; [10]t'ang' 'leu, a coal-basket; [11]'leu 'mi, hamper-rice—from the upper Min districts.

剾 K'ou. Read ˏeu; used in the Paik, ˏIng for the coll. 'leu: to dig into, to scoop out, to gouge, to excavate: [12]'leu ˏt'ëng t'au' to dig through, as a wall; [13]'leu ˏch'ing, to dig deep, as into the rotten part of fruit; [14]'leu sioh[2] ˏk'ëng, or 'leu ˏk'ëng k'aëng' dig a hole through.

'Leu. A coll. word: to lick, to taste with the end of the tongue: 'leu sioh[2] tek, take a little on the tongue; 'leu k'ang' take a lick and see.

'Leu. A coll. word: a strip, a slice, a piece; an incision, a stroke, a gash: 'chai sioh[2] 'leu, a strip of paper; ˏhwang 'leu, a tranverse slip, one made across the grain; ˏwa sioh[2] 'leu, to cut a gash; 'leu 'pwo, to cut out and insert, to patch.

溜 Liu. A river in Kwangsi; to flow, to issue forth; the eaves, a gutter under eaves; in the coll. to slide, to slip down; to slip out, as slippery things from the grasp; a fatal current on the Formosan

[1]通瓏 [2]四壁玲瓏 [3]聾子〇 [4]耳聾〇 [5]天聾地啞 [6]臭聾〇 [7]詐聾〇 [8]蔞葉〇 [9]竹簍〇 [10]炭簍〇 [11]簍米〇 [12]剾通透 [13]剾深 [14]剾一空

coast—said to carry junks away and detain them many years: [1]'ĭŭng' leu' the flow of water; COLL., [3]leu' k'ó' (or 'chau), to slip away, as an eel from the hand; [2]leu' sioh, 'tó, to slip down, catch a fall; [4]'kwong leu' shavings; [5]'kok, leu' slippery; hang' tek, 'nü lóh, leu' thought you had dropped into "the current"!—said to one who has been long absent.

擂' Liu. To take earth and daub it on, as in building walls; to spread out, to level with the hand. Read ,t'iu: to lead, to draw out.

籀' Liu. Read teu' in the dictionaries: the seal character, called [6]leu' ,ung, invented by [7]'Chou-t'ai-sz', the Great Historian.

婁 娄 ,Lou. Lü. The 16th zodiacal constellation; it is in the head of Aries; a surname: [8],Lié ,leu, an ancient worthy noted for his keenness of sight. Read lëü': to tie up an ox; troublesome, as a number; often, many; a mound; simple, stupid.

僂 ,Lou. A hunchback; stooping, bent over, curved: [9]pwoi' ,leu, humpbacked; [10]'ch'iu ,leu, a crooked hand or arm.

嘍 ,Lou. Talkative and troublesome; loquacity: used for ,liu in the coll. q. v.: [11],leu lá' chirping of birds; [12],liéng ,leu, loquacious; also troublesome, embarrassing; COM., [13],leu ,ló (coll. ,liu ,ló), a highwayman's fellows.

慺 ,Lou. Diligent; pleased, contented; joyous, gay: ,leu ,leu, sedulous; careful, respectful.

摟 ,Lou. To draw, to pull, to drag; to throw the arms about, to hug, to embrace; to carry off, to elope with: [14],leu pó' to embrace; ,leu 'ch'ü 'chü, to elope with a virgin.

樓 ,Lou. An upper story; a loft, a tower, a staging, an upper floor; in stories, storied; to assemble; a peak; used in the coll. for cheap, low in price: in the coll. read ,lau, q. v.: [15]wong' ,leu, a lookout tower; [16],hi ,leu, an ancient movable tower for spying into an enemy's citadel; [17],k'iéng ,leu, a lofty peak; COM., [18],kó ,leu, a high story or loft; [19],p'ung ,leu, a mat-covered hovel or lodge; ,leu ,tai, a staging, as for feats of pugilism; COLL., ,leu siáng' cheap; ,leu chiáh, ,leu, very cheap.

艛 ,Lou. A vessel, called pwoh, ,leu, having high stern galleries, or frames in stories.

蔞 ,Lou. An edible plant, called [20],leu ,kó, like the artemisia; it blooms early and its stalks are white; used to boil with fish to impart a pleasant flavor: in the coll. read ,leu, q. v.

貗 ,Lou. A sow in heat; also a certain wild beast: ,leu ,tü, a sow.

---

[1]湧溜 [2]溜去 [3]溜一倒○ [4]捲溜 [5]滑溜 [6]籀文 [7]周太史 [8]離婁○ [9]背僂○ [10]手僂 [11]嘍哰 [12]嗹嘍 [13]嘍囉 [14]摟抱 [15]望樓 [16]飛樓 [17]岑樓 [18]高樓○ [19]篷樓 [20]蔞蒿

螻 ˎ Lou. As in ¹ˏleu ˏku, the mole-cricket; a kind of ant; ²ˋt'u ˏleu, a fabulous four-horned goat; ³ˏleu kwok, a small, green frog.

髏 ˎ Lou. A skull without flesh and skin: ⁵tuk, ˏleu, the skull, upper bones of a skull; ⁴ˎku ˏleu, a dry skull, a skeleton.

餾 ² Liu. Read leu²; coll. leu²: to steam over in order to preserve from spoiling: ⁶leu² ˋkwi, to steam rice-cakes over.

Leu². A coll. word: quick, spry, swift, expeditious; sprightly, nimble: ˏkiang ˋyă leu² to walk very swiftly; ˏma ˋlá leu² as nimble as a cat.

Leu². A coll. word: to employ busily, to send to and fro on business, to weary one, as by onerous duties; to lead about, to exercise: leu² kaing² or leu² săk, accustomed to being wearily employed; leu² sioh, ˋtiong, (or ˏdau), sent on a round, as of errands; leu² ˋma, to exercise a horse; leu² yok, fagged out by imposed labor.

Leu². A coll. word: the first appearance or sprouting of a bud or shoot: ˏsing ˋyong chiăh, pwok, leu² the new bud has just sprouted.

(382) Lëü.

屢 屡 ˊ Lü. Often, many times, frequently, repeatedly; reiterated, continual; quick, prompt: ⁷lëü² chiéng² frequent battles; COM., ⁸lëü² ch'ëü² often, many times; COLL., ⁹ˏt'ëng lëü² (or nëü²), repetitious, as talk.

屨 ² Lü. Shoes or sandals, anciently made of coarse cloth: ¹⁰chek, lëü² to make sandals; ¹¹ˏp'i lëü² leather shoes (for winter).

窶 ² Chü. Poor, miserable; rude, rustic, unpolished, unceremonious; dwelling at ease, without ceremony: ¹²lëü² ˏping, rustic and poor; ¹³lëü² so² a defence for the head in carrying burdens.

縷 ² Lü. Lou. Fiber of hemp or silk not yet spun; a hank or knot; a forfeit of cloth: ¹⁴pwo² lëü² coarse cotton cloth; ¹⁵ek, lëü² ˏsi, a thread or knot of silk-floss; ¹⁶ˏteu ˏhung lëü² sek, to arrange and speak of points in order; ¹⁷kiék, lëü² a kind of grass.

褸 ² Lü. Also read ˋlü: torn, spoiled garments: in the coll. read lëü² q. v.: ¹⁸ˏlang lëü² a ragged, seedy garment; ¹⁹lëü² liék, torn and spoiled, as the clothes of the poor. Read ˏleu: the lappet of a coat.

鑢 ² Lü. A file, a rasp; a polishing tool; to file smooth, to polish, to give luster to; *met.*, to correct, to reform one's self; in the coll. to cut or saw off with a knife: also read lae² in the coll. q. v.: ²⁰ˏmó lëü² to polish; COLL., ²¹lëü² taung² or lëü² tói² ˏtong, to cut or saw in two with a knife; pong² ˋlá lëü² set to be sawed on — i. e., killed by inches, as said of one being gambled out of all his money.

¹螻蛄 ²土螻 ³螻蟈 ⁴髑髏 ⁵骷髏 ⁶餾粿 ⁷屢戰 ⁸屢次 ⁹重屢 ¹⁰織屨 ¹¹皮屨 ¹²窶貧 ¹³窶數 ¹⁴布縷 ¹⁵一縷絲 〇 ¹⁶條分縷析 ¹⁷結縷 ¹⁸襤褸 ¹⁹褸裂 ²⁰磨鑢 ²¹鑢斷 〇

慮[2] Lü. To think upon anxiously, to feel concern, to care about; to consider, to plan, to devise; to cogitate, to revolve in one's mind; concern, anxiety, doubt, suspicion: [1]*ˬsü lëü*[2] to think seriously of; [2]*ˬwong lëü*[2] not to particularize, to take a general view; COM., [3]*'kwa' lëü*[2] anxious about; [4]*'kwo' lëü*[2] to be needlessly concerned; [5]*'lëü*[2] *haiu*[2] to think of the future; [6]*ˬtó ˬngi ˬtó lëü*[2] full of doubts and cares; COLL., *lëü*[2] *ˬnĕng ˬtong lëü*[2] *ˬnĕng 'toi*, solicitous about others in everything.

濾[2] Lü. To filter, to strain liquids through cloths; to wash, to cleanse, to purify; in the coll, to wade about, to dabble in water: COM., [7]*'lëü*[2] *ˬchiong*, to strain starch; [8]*'lëü*[2] *ˬcha*, to separate the dregs by filtration; COLL., *lëü*[2] *'chwi*, to tramp about in water; *'ch'iu pong' 'hü 'tiĕ k'ŏ' lëü*[2] to dabble in it with the hands.

讁[2] Lü. False, deceitful; to deceive; a man's name, [9]*Chow-puh-lü* in the Sung dynasty.

褸[2] Lü. Read *'lü* and *lëü'*; coll. *lëü*[2], as in *ˬi ˬsang ˬlang lëü*[2] his clothes are mean and tattered.

(383) Li.

ˬLi. A coll. euphonic prefix, as in *ˬli ˬliu*, to throw away; *ˬli ˬlwa*, to grasp and pull, to clutch; to take greedily, as food; to filch, to embezzle; *ˬli ˬla*, or *ˬli ˬli ˬla ˬla*, to mix in, have connection with; much, miscellaneous, as talk; *ˬli ˬli ˬló ˬló*, indistinct, as one's speech near death; a confused jargon.

李 'Li. A plum, prune, apricot; to get ready for a journey; a surname: COM., [10]*ˬyéng ˬchiè 'li*, a red plum; [11]*ˬhu ˬing 'li*, a kind of blue or greenish plum; [12]*ˬheng 'li*, luggage; [13]*'Li pek*, a noted scholar of the T'ang dynasty; COLL., [14]*'li ˬkeng*, salted plums; [15]*'li p'wói'* and [16]*'li ˬkwi*, two preparations of preserved plums, halved, or sliced, and dried.

里 'Li. A residence, place of abode; a neighborhood, a village, originally of 25 or 50 families; a lane, a street, a place or court in a town; a measure of 360 paces, the Chinese mile; it varies in length, usually being (as computed by some) 1897½ English feet; the geographical *'li* is the 1/250 of a degree, or 1460.44 feet, or 1/10 of a French astronomical league; sad, mournful, alas! the 166th radical: [17]*ˬling 'li*, a neighborhood; COM., [18]*ˬhiong 'li*, a village; neighbors, townsmen; [19]*ˬch'iêng 'li 'ma*, a courier; [20]*sek*, *'li*, ten Chinese miles, one *p'wo'*; COLL., *'li 'pa tio*[2] distance of one *'li* and over.

俚 'Li. Rustic, vulgar, lowbred; gross, vile; to trust, to depend on; a trust, protection, dependence, resource: used for *ˬla* in the coll., q. v.: *ˬu 'li*, helpless; *'li sük*, rustic, vulgar; *'li ˬngiong*, low expressions; *'li 'chü*, a term for the people of Wuchou-fu, Kwangsi.

1 思慮	3 掛慮	5 慮後	多慮	8 濾渣	讁 10 腼	11 夫人	12 行李	14 李鹹	16 李龜	18 鄉里	馬 20 十
2 亡慮	4 過慮	6 多疑	7 濾漿	9 周不	脂李	李○	13 李白	15 李酡	17 鄰里	19 千里	里○

‘哩 Li, An expletive, a colloquial particle used at the end of a sentence; in Foochow it marks an interrogation, with the tone somewhat indefinite, as in *siê’ nóh*꜁ *‘li* (or *꜀li*), what is it?

‘娌 Li. As in *tŭk*꜁ *‘li*, brothers' wives, for which *‘mu ‘sing* is commonly used.

‘理 Li. To work gems according to their veins; to polish gems; the veins or striæ; style; to govern, to regulate; to rule, manage, adjust, or put to rights; reason in man, right principles, the natural rule of action, what is felt to be right or proper; the principle, power, mode, or rules, by which matter is kept in its essence: COM., [1]*꜀t‘iéng ‘li*, heavenly reason or principle—analogous to overruling Providence; [2]*tê’ ‘li*, geography; geomancy; [3]*꜀teu ‘li*, regulations; [4]*mah*꜁ *‘li*, the doctrine of the pulse; [5]*꜀ching ‘li*, natural feeling, as of gratitude; [6]*꜀lieu ‘li*, to regulate, to manage; [7]*pok*꜁ *‘li*, not to regard or treat well; [8]*‘li hwoi’* to comprehend; [9]*‘li sêü’* to attend to a matter; a manager; [10]*‘li hok*꜁ philosophical, sage-like; [11]*‘li so’* to settle accounts, pay debts; [12]*‘li hwak*, the right rule or mode; COLL., *‘li k‘éék*, his right is scant—is plainly in the wrong; *‘li ꜀teng ꜀i*, pay him (what is due); *‘li má’ ꜀k‘wi* (or *tik*꜁), can't bring it out straight—i. e., receipts fall short of expenses; *au’ ꜀mang ‘li*, opposed to reason, bad, wrong; *‘li ‘li*, only, constantly, invariably; *‘li chó’ sioh*꜁ *yong’* to do only one kind of work.

‘鯉 Li. The carp (Cyprinidae), the king of fishes and fabled to change into a dragon: [13]*꜀sëng ‘li*, an epistle; [14]*K‘ung ‘li*, the son of Confucius; COM., [15]*‘li ꜀ngü*, a carp; [16]*‘li ꜀ngü kak*, scales of a carp; *met.*, carving or embroidery like carp's scales; [17]*‘li ꜀ngü t‘ieu’ ꜀lüng ꜀mwong*, the carp leaps the dragon-gate; *met.*, to gain a literary degree.

‘履 Lü. A leather shoe; to put on shoes; to tread or walk on; *met.*, to act in a certain way, actions, conduct; a salary, living, subsistence, dependence: [18]*‘li ꜀ing*, to do humane acts; [19]*‘li ꜀heng*, to walk; the conduct; [20]*hok*, *‘li*, subsistence; [21]*꜀ü ‘li pok*꜁ *꜀ping*, like treading on thin ice; *met.*, need of caution; COM., *꜀chio ‘li ꜀á*, red shoes—such as worn by retired officers or those having honorary titles; *‘li lik*꜁ a record of good deeds; statement of one's antecedents (to a superior).

‘裏 ‘裡 Li. The inside of a garment, a lining; the inner surface of, inside, within; home: used for the coll. *‘tié*, q. v.: *‘pieu ‘li*, outside and inside; COLL., *‘li meng’* inside and outside, inner and outer surface; *‘li nëük*, the lining wrinkled; *꜀chiong t‘au’ ‘li*, the lining all of one material; *‘peng ‘tiong ‘li*, to turn the inside out.

‘*Li.* A coll. euphonic prefix, as in *‘li ‘leu*, to gouge, to cut or scoop out.

[1]天理 [2]地理 [3]條理 [4]脈理 [5]情理 [6]料理 [7]不理 [8]理會 [9]理事 [10]理學 [11]理數 [12]理法 [13]雙鯉 [14]孔鯉 [15]鯉魚 [16]鯉魚甲 [17]鯉魚跳龍門 [18]履仁 [19]履行 [20]福履 [21]如履薄冰

梩 ˏLi. A basket or hod for carrying earth; a spade or narrow mattock: ˏlui ˏli, a hod, dirt-basket.

梨 棃 ˏLi. A pear: tongʾ ˏli, the "cold pear"; *met.*, a face discolored with age; COM., [1]ˏtʻong ˏli, the native sugar-pear; [2]siok, ˏli and [3]ˏming ˏli, two varieties of russet pear from Shantung; [4]ˏmuí ˏwo ˏli, a kind of large, darkish pear; [5]ˏchʻiu pah, ˏli, the autumn-white — a clear-skinned sort; [6]ˏwong ˏli, the pine-apple; [7]ˏli ˏhwong ʻchü táʾ play-actors; COLL., chʻengʾ pwongʾ ˏli, the cold-rice pear—so called because it is dry and mellow like cooked rice; ˏli ˏsing kʻeʾ teʾ pear-heart and persimmon-stem; *met.*, small, trifling, worthless.

蜊 ˏLi. A sort of small yellowish clam, called kak, ˏli, found on the coast of Fookien; COLL., kak, ˏli pʻongʾ to halve the edges of boards in laying floors.

貍 狸 ˏLi. A name for small animals like the fox, raccoon, wild cat, &c.: [8]ˏma ˏli, a sort of wild cat; [9]ʻhai ˏli, a seal; [10]ˏhiong ˏli, the civet; [11]ˏngiu ʻmwí ˏli, the ox-tailed fox — a white-faced species; COM., [12]ˏhu ˏli, the fox; ˏhu ˏli ˏma, or ˏhu ˏli ˏma ˏchiăng, the fox-elf—i. e., the fox which can assume a human shape.

來 ˏLai. Read ˏlai; coll. ˏli: to come, to arrive, to reach; after verbs, implies completion of their action; in apposition with kʻóʾ (to go), denotes coming, here, again, &c.; after the particle tek, it expresses the practicability, and after the negative máʾ the impracticability, of the idea of the preceding verb; after ʻkʻi, it marks the beginning of an action: [13]ʻtié ˏli, to come in; to return, come back; ˏli ʻa mwoíʾ has he yet come or not? [14]ˏli ʻlau, has come; ˏli ˏló, come! arrived! [15]ʻkong ˏli, to speak out; [16]ˏtó ˏli, to bring; chóʾ máʾ ˏli, can't do it, impracticable; áʾ chóʾ tek, ˏli, practicable; [17]ʻchieu tek, ˏli, he rarely comes; ˏli kʻangʾ come and see; ˏli tek, ʻcha, to come early.

ˏLi. A coll. euphonic prefix, as in ˏli ˏlá, to plow; ˏli ˏloi, to gripe and twist with the fingers, as one's flesh; ˏli ˏló, to scald or cook hastily in boiling water; ˏli ˏlë, to rail at.

(384) Lia.

Liaʾ. A coll. word, as in liaʾ liaʾ or liaʾ sek, beautiful, elegant, as dress; ˏi ˏsiong ʻyă liaʾ the clothes are very pretty.

(385) Liăh.

𠜱 Read lik,; used in the Paik, ˏIng for the coll. liăh,: to tear, to rend apart; to slit open, to split, as with a knife; a rattling sound, as of bamboos dragged before idols: liăh, lóh, ˏli, split down, riven, as a wall; liăh, tóiʾ ˏpeng, split in two; liăh, liăh, kieuʾ sound of tearing; the rattling of bamboos.

靂 Li. Read lik,; coll. liăh,: the crashing sound of thunder: liăh, sioh, ˏsiăng,

1 糖梨 2 雪梨 3 榠梨 4 梅窩梨 5 秋白梨 6 黃梨 7 梨園子弟 ○ 8 貓貍 ○ 9 海貍 ○ 10 香貍 11 牛尾貍 12 狐貍 ○ 13 入來 14 來了 15 講來 16 掏來 17 少的來 ○

or ˏliă liăh ˏsioh, ˏsiŏng, a peal, a clap.

慈 A vulgar character used in the *Paik*, ˏ*Ing* for the coll. *liăh*, as in *tëük*, *liăh*, a large, round bamboo-tray to dry rice-flour on: *liăh*, *sioh*, *chiăh*, one tray.

(386) Liăk.

𤞚, Read *t'ak*,; used for the coll. *liăk*,: to lap, as a dog; the sound of lapping or gobbling up food: *liăk*, *liăk*, ˏ*kang*, licked dry, dried up, as a well or pond; *liăk*, *liăk*, *kieu'* a gobbling sound, as of pigs eating.

靸, Sa. Read *ngek*, and *sak*,; used in the *Paik*, ˏ*Ing* for the coll. *liăk*, as in *liăk*, ˏ*k'a*, slipshod; *p'ah*, *liăk*, ˏ*tang*, or *liăk*, *'tó* ˏ*tang*, to turn the quarters down at the heel; *liăk*, ˏ*á liăk*, to wear shoes slipshod; *liăk*, *liăk*, *kieu'* noise made by slipshod shoes.

Liăk,. A coll. word, as in *liăk*, *hiăk*, gaping open and hanging in strips, as timbers or plastering about to fall.

(387) Liăng.

ˏ*Liăng*. A coll. word, as in ˏ*liăng* ˏ*liăng*, cool, chilly, a feeling of chilliness; ˏ*sing 'lá kiĕng'* ˏ*liăng* ˏ*liăng tioh*, the body feels quite chilly.

ˏ*Liăng*. A coll. word: shrunk, as the staves of buckets, tubs, etc.: *'chiă 't'ĕng* ˏ*liăng*, this tub is shrunk.

'嶺 Ling. Read *'ling* in the dictionaries: a break or pass in a mountain where a road passes, a road over a peak; a ridge or chain of mountains: [1]ˏ*mui 'liăng*, the Plum ridge in the north of Kwangtung; com., [2]*paĕk*, *'liăng*, the North ridge—is a few miles north of Foochow; [3]*'liăng 'ting*, summit of a ridge; [4]*'liăng 'mi*, hill-rice, barley; coll., *'liăng 'tiĕ*, in the hills; [5]ˏ*pa* ˏ*sang wak*, *'liăng*, to clamber over mountains.

'襟 '領 Ling. Read *'ling*; coll. *'liăng*: a collar, a band or neck-cloth: [6]*tau' 'liăng*, a collar for the neck; [7]*'liăng* ˏ*wo*, the neck of a dress; [8]*k'ung 'liăng*, a collar-binding; [9]ˏ*p'ui 'liăng*, leather collars; [10]*k'ié' 'liăng*, a standing-collar; [11]ˏ*pwang 'liăng*, strip of trimming about the neck of a lady's dress; [12]*'liăng kak*, or [13]*'liăng t'ó'* a kind of vest to which a collar is sewed.

'領 Ling. Read *'ling*; coll. *'liăng*: to take, to receive from; to govern, to manage, to attend to; to head, to command, to lead: [14]*'liăng* ˏ*chiĕng*, to receive money; [15]ˏ*siu 'liăng*, to receive, take charge of; [16]*'kwang 'liăng*, to govern; [17]*'liăng* ˏ*ping*, to lead troops; [18]ˏ*tau 'liăng* to monopolize; [19]*chó' 'liăng*, a major-general of Manchus; [20]*tai' 'liăng*, to command, to head; [21]*'liăng chaung'* a receipt for government-money; [22]*'liăng sëü'* one who receives orders, a consul.

ˏ*Liăng*. A coll. word: to expose to the air in order to dry, to cool, as hot things: ˏ*liăng* ˏ*hwo*, to cool; ˏ*liăng ngaing'* to stiffen by drying; ˏ*liăng taĕng'* cool it in the air.

[1]梅嶺 [2]北嶺 [3]嶺頂 [4]嶺米 [5]爬山挖嶺 [6]脰領 [7]領[illegible] [8]綑領 [9]皮領 [10]豎領 [11]盤領 [12]領甲 [13]領套 [14]領銭 [15]收領 [16]管領 [17]領兵 [18]挽領 [19]佐領 [20]帶領 [21]領狀 [22]領事 ○

令 [1] Ling. Read *leng'*; used in the coll. for *liăng'*, as in [1]*chiu liăng'* a forfeit to drink wine, as in feasts.

(388) Lié.

'*Lié.* A coll. word: to lay, as bricks in building walls: '*lié* ˌ*chiong*, to lay bricks; '*lié* ˌ*ki*, to lay a foundation; '*lié chau'*, to build a kitchen-range.

罹 ' Li. Sadness, sorrow; to encounter, to incur; to meet, to happen on: [2]*paik, lié'* manifold griefs; [3]*lié'* ˌ*ki* ˌ*hüng hai'* have suffered malicious injury from him.

荔 ' Li. A fruit tree, the lichi (dimocarpus leche); a kind of flag having fibrous roots: in the coll read ˏ*lié*, q. v.: [4]*p'ek, lié'* a kind of fragrant flag.

詈 ' Li. To scold about, to blame or be angry with: [5]*lié' ma'* to rail at; [6]*lié' ük,* to disgrace by obloquy; [7]*lié' paung'* to blame covertly, to slander.

裂 ' Lieh. Read *liék,*; used for the coll. *lié'*: to cut apart, to slit; to tear straight, as paper after folding it: [8]*lié' 'chai,* to slit or tear paper; [9]*kak, lié'* ˌ*ki* ˏ*tá*, a theme composed of parts of consecutive sentences.

ˏ攡 Li. To stretch or open out, to spread forth, as wings; to set out, to place in order, to display.

ˏ漓 Li. Water dropping and soaking into the ground; the pattering of rain or hail; to instil by drops; thin, poor: [10]ˏ*ling* ˏ*lié*, sound of falling rain; [11]ˌ*hieu* ˏ*lié*, false, perverse.

ˏ璃 Li. A vitreous, translucent substance; glass, in the coll. ˌ*pó* ˏ*lá*, q. v.: ˏ*liu* ˏ*lié* ˌ*chio*, glass-beads; COLL., ˏ*lié* ˌ*p'uí* ˌ*kong*, large, flowery, glazed jars.

ˏ离 Li. Used for ˏ*lié* (a mountain elf); interchanged with the next: bright, clear, elegant; the 30th diagram.

ˏ離 Li. A yellow bird of a beautiful plumage; to leave, to part from; scattered, dispersed, absent, separated from; to divide, to cut in two; arranged, as in pairs; the 30th diagram; a mountain elf, a fairy: also read *lié'*, q. v.: [12]ˏ*lié* ˌ*ming*, the morning; [13]ˏ*lié* ˌ*song*, a sister's grandchild; [14]*pok,* ˏ*lié* ˌ*hi* '*neu*, (the parrot) is still nothing but a bird; COM., [15]ˏ*lié piék,* to part from, to leave, as friends; [16]ˏ*lié sang'* scattered, dispersed; [17]ˏ*lié* ˌ*chü*, a bill of divorcement; COLL., ˏ*lié* ˌ*hu*, widely astray, as doing improperly; ˏ*lié lié'* '*ch'iu*, to keep the hands off, to stand aloof, have nothing to do with; ˌ*pwong* ˏ*lié* ˌ*hwa*, the althea.

ˏ籬 Li. A bamboo hedge, called ˌ*hwang* ˏ*lié*; to fence, to inclose: COM., [18]ˏ*lié* ˌ*pa*, a wattle or fence of bamboo; COLL., [19]ˌ*chiá* ˏ*lié*, a bamboo-ladle, skimmer.

---

[1]酒令 [3]罹其 [4]蒔荔 [6]詈辱 [8]裂紙 其題 [11]澆漓 [13]離孫 飛鳥 [16]離散 [18]籬笆 [19]笊籬

[2]百罹 兇害 [5]詈罵 [7]詈謗 [9]割裂 [10]淋漓 [12]離明 [14]不離 [15]離別 [17]離書 ○ ○

黐 䵓 ꜀Li. To adhere, to attach to, to stick on; sticky, pasty, glutinous: ꜀lié ꜀keu, bird-lime.

縭 褵 ꜀Li. A sash, an ornamented girdle, put on a bride by her mother; a perfumed bridal veil; to sew shoes; also sharp, piercing, as a cold blast: kiék꜂ ꜀lié, has the girdle put on—is married.

螭 ꜀Li. A dragon without horns, or just molted; term applied to cruel men: [1]ch'ek꜂ ꜀lié, the female dragon; [2]lŭk꜂ ꜀lié ꜀ch'ung, the green-dragon horse—a fine steed.

魑 ꜀Li. A mountain elf or demon, a goblin, called [3]꜀lié mwoi꜄ supposed to be malicious.

謧 ꜀Li. Deceitful language; jests, jokes, sportive talk, bantering; to ridicule: [4]꜀lié ié꜄ verbose, exaggerated talk; not trustworthy.

醨 ꜀Li. Thin, poor spirits; weak liquor: [5]꜀lié lok꜂ the dregs of liquor.

嫠 ꜀Li. A woman whose husband is dead: [6]꜀lié ho꜄ a widow; [7]sok꜂ ꜀lié, to relieve or support a widow.

釐 厘 ꜀Li. Used for ꜂li (to govern): to rule, to regulate, to cause one to submit; the 1000th part of a tael, nominally equivalent to the coin called a cash; the second term in fractions, the hundredth, as of an inch; a grain, a very little; twins, a pair; to give, to bestow: [8]te꜄ ꜀lié, geomancy; [9]t'ek꜂ ꜀lié, paper made from sea-weed; COM., [10]꜀lié ꜂ting, a small money-steelyard; [11]꜀lié ꜀hó, a small fraction, a trifle; [12]꜀lié ꜀king, an extra local duty levied on goods; [13]sek꜂ ꜀chi ꜀hó ꜀lié ꜀ch'a ꜂i ꜀ch'iéng ꜂li, a trifling mistake makes a difference of a thousand miles!

荔 ꜀Li. Read lié꜄; coll. ꜀lié: a fruit tree, the lichi (dimocarpus leche), called ꜀lié ꜀chié ch'eu꜄: twai꜄ hok꜂ ꜀lié ꜀chié and cheu꜄ hok꜂ ꜀lié ꜀chié, the large-pitted and small-pitted sorts.

例 Li.[2] To compare, to classify, to adjust, to arrange; laws, by-laws, rules, regulations; the mode or custom; order, arrangement, disposition of: [14]chaik꜂ lié꜄ regulations, rules of the Boards; [15]꜂pi lié꜄ to compare together; COM., [16]luk꜂ lié꜄ laws; [17]sŭk꜂ lié꜄ custom, common practice; [18]lié꜄ keng꜄ forbidden by the rules; [19]lié꜄ hó꜄ or lié꜄ hié꜄ the ordinary expenditure, as in lawsuits, village-fees, &c.; [20]꜀sing lié꜄ to become a custom; COLL., ꜀tó lié꜄ to receive customary fees, as from dependents, unlicensed establishments, &c.; ꜀mó ꜂chiā lié꜄ there is no such rule.

砅[2] To cross a stream on stones; to lift the clothes in crossing streams.

離 Li.[2] To retire, to withdraw, to separate from, to leave; removed, withdrawn, distant, a certain interval from: also read ꜀lié, q. v.:

[1]赤螭 [2]緑螭 驄螭 [3]魑魅 〇 [4]謧詍 [5]醨酪 [6]嫠婦 [7]恤嫠 [8]地釐 [9]陟釐 [10]釐戥 [11]釐毫 [12]釐金 [13]失之 毫釐 差以 千里 [14]則例 [15]比例 [16]律例 [17]俗例 [18]例禁 [19]例耗 [20]成例

com., ¹lié ² ꜀ka, to leave home; ²wong² lié ² to keep aloof, as from bad men; COLL., ³lié ² ꜀k'wi, to separate, remove from; ⁴lié ² tó ² to go aside (and play), as a child not always staying by his mother; lié ² tek, hwong² far removed; lié ² sióh, ꜁peng, to yield one side of the way; lié ² ch'ioh, ꜂pa te² distant over one foot.

(389) Liék.

龍, Lung. Read ꜀lüng; used for the coll. liék, as in liék, (or liék,) miék,꜂ch'au, the dragon-tongue grass, a species of cactus (?), the juice of which is used on ladies' hair.

烈, Lieh. Read liék, : used for the coll. liék, : bright, glowing, fiery : [illegible] liék, liék, fiery-red, [illegible]es or the clouds at sunset; a bright red.

列, Lieh. ₂ To separate, to distinguish; to arrange in order, to dispose properly, to spread out; to state in order; files of soldiers; a rank, series, order; regularly, seriatim: ⁵liék, teng² troops in ranks; com., ⁶꜀pái liék, to set in order; ⁷liék, oi ² you, gentlemen! ⁸liék, kwok, a name given to the feudal states of China, B.C. 300-225; ⁹꜀teu liék, a set of rules; COLL., liék, ꜀k'wi, or liék, lang² ꜀peng, to separate, to dispose on two sides, as persons or things.

冽, Lieh. ₂ A cold air; cold, chilly: ꜀hung liék, a chilling wind; lek, liék, very cold.

栵, Lieh. ₂ Also read lié ²: a kind of wild chestnut, a hard, tough wood, used by cartwrights; trees growing in rows.

烈, Lieh. ₂ A raging fire; hot, flaming, burning, ardent; impetuous, energetic, daring; zealous, enthusiastic; fierce, cruel; faithful to principles, meritorious; excellent, eminent, dignified, majestic, imposing: used for liék, in the coll. q. v.: ¹⁰liék, sëü² a patriot; ¹¹liék, liék, sad, mournful; majestic; ¹²liék, ꜂chu, eminent ancestors; ¹³꜀tüng liék, zealous; com., ¹⁴liék, hó² or liék, ꜂nü, a chaste woman, one who hangs herself at the death of her husband; ¹⁵꜂hwi liék, fierce flames.

裂, Lieh. ₂ Remnants, the clippings of silk; to tear, to rend in two; to split, to crack open: used for the coll. lié ² q. v.: ¹⁶p'ó ² liék, to tear open; ¹⁷miék, liék, to destroy, to subvert, as principles or customs; COLL., liék, ꜀k'wi, or liék, ꜀hiä, rent asunder; pek, pek, liék, liék, seamed, marked with cracks, as crockery.

(390) Liéng.

斂, Lien. To gather in, as harvests; to receive, to collect; to hoard, to amass; to husband, sparing of; a hoard, ingathering: also read liéng² q. v.: ¹⁸꜀siu ꜂liéng, to gather in, to harvest; in the coll. careful, cautious, prudent; ¹⁹꜂liéng chëü² to collect; ²⁰꜂liéng ꜀chong, to hoard up.

1 離家 2 遠離 3 離開 4 離道 5 列陣 6 排列 7 列位 8 列國 9 條列 10 烈士 11 烈烈 ○ 12 烈祖 ○ 13 忠烈 ○ 14 烈婦 ○ 15 火烈 16 破裂 17 滅裂 18 收斂 19 斂聚 20 斂藏

‘瀲 Lien. Water overflowing; to overwhelm in the waves; the edge of waves: [1]‘liéng yéng’ brimful, running over; hwang’ ‘liéng, to float on the water.

‘臉 Lien. The cheek; the face; *met.*, one's reputation, honor: COM., [2]‘liéng miéng’ the face; *met.*, shamefacedness, modesty; [3]‚tiu ‘liéng, to feel ashamed; [4]‘ch‘ieu’ ‘liéng, a smiling face; [5]‚u ‘liéng, or pok‚ ko’ ‘liéng, shameless, brazen-faced; [6]‘liéng miéng’ ‚hó ‚chong, what has become of your shame! COLL., ‚lau ‘la ‘liéng k‘ëük‚ ‚i, leave him his face—don't wholly ruin his good name.

‘襝 Lien. To draw the hands into the sleeves: ‘liéng ‘ing, to sleeve the hands, a courtesy; ‘liéng ‘ing pai’ pays her respects—phrase on a lady's card.

‘摙 Lien. To bear, to carry in the hands; to remove, to transport, to convey, to take things to one: ‘liéng ‚ná, to carry earth, as insects in making their nests.

‘璉 Lien. Vases or chargers to hold grain at sacrifices in the ancestral hall, called ‚hu ‘liéng.

‘輦 Nien. A sort of barrow or hand-carriage, called ‘liéng ‚kü; the imperial chariot; *met.*, the court, the emperor; to draw, to take to; to transport, to convey: [7]‘liéng ha’ at court; [8]‘i ‚kü ‘liéng ‘mu, took his mother in the carriage; COM., [9]‘liéng koi’ a long box or safe on wheels; COLL., [10]‘liéng ‘chi, a wheel; rollers to move heavy things on; ‚i k‘ó’ ‘ngwai ‚tó ‚li chó’ ‘liéng ‘chi, he makes a roller of me—uses me as a drudge.

‘Liéng. A coll. word, like the next, but less frequently used: to turn; to revolve, to roll, as on wheels; to roll to and fro, as animals on the ground: ‘liéng ‚chio ‘ch‘iu ‘chi, small ornamental rings, finely braided and worn at the sides of a finger-ring.

Liéng’. A coll. word: to turn about, to revolve; to roll, as round things: liéng’ liéng’ ‘tiong, to roll to and fro; kieu’ liéng’ sioh‚ ‘tiong, turn the sedan round; liéng’ liéng’ ‘pó, gaming with the ‘pó ‘tau and ‘pó ‘chi; ‘kung ‘lung liéng’ to revolve incessantly; *met.*, persistent, pertinacious.

‚連 Lien. To connect, to continue, to join; reaching to, conjoined, contiguous, annexed; connection by marriage; a junction, a succession of; an adversative, connective particle at the beginning of a clause or sentence, and, also, even, with; a surname; in the coll. to occur suddenly, just at the time, unexpectedly: used for ‚leng in the coll. q. v.: [11]‚liéng ‚ing, allied by marriage; [12]‚liéng sek‚ tin ore; COM., [13]‚p‘i ‚liéng, connected, adjoining; [14]‚liéng chiek‚ to gain degrees at successive examinations; [15]‚liéng k‘aik‚ or [16]‚liéng puo’ at once, instantly; [17]‚liéng loi’ to involve; [18]‚liéng ‚kong, the district of Lienkiang in the Foo-

[1]瀲灩 [3]丢臉 [5]無臉 何存 [8]以車 [9]輦櫃 [10]輦杫 [11]連姻 [12]連錫 [14]連捷 [15]連刻 [17]連累

[2]臉面 [4]笑臉 [6]臉面 [7]輦下 輦母 ○ ○ ○ [13]毗連 ○ [16]連步 [18]連江

chow prefecture; [1]˓liéng ‛k‘eu eng˒ ˓sing, to assent as soon as asked; [2]˓liéng ‛pwong tai˒ le˒ both the principal and the interest; [3]˓liéng ˓sing ˓sang ngek˒, promoted three grades in succession; COLL., ko˒ ˓liéng or [4]po˒ ˓liéng, in addition to, besides; [5]˓liéng ˓si tai˒ a matter coming up suddenly; p‘ah˒ ˓liéng ˓k‘wang, successive firing of guns; ˓liéng meng˒ ˓tu ng˒ ‛sá, does not even wash his face.

漣 ˓Lien. Ripples on the water, a rippling appearance; name of a river; weeping: ˓ch‘ing ‛ch‘iă ˓liéng, pure and rippling; k‘ek˒ t‘á˒ ˓liéng ˓liéng, to shed tears incessantly.

濂 ˓Lien. A mountain stream falling in a sheet of water, a cascade; thin, poor.

廉 㢘 ˓Lien. On one side, a corner, angle of; economical, sparing, moderate; pure, disinterested, incorrupt; to examine: COM., [6]˓liéng ‛t‘i, modest, shamefaced, regardful of one's name; [7]˓u ˓liéng ‛t‘i, shameless, avaricious; [8]˓ch‘ing ˓liéng, incorruptible, as an officer; [9]hau˒ ˓liéng, filial and pure—applied to the literary Kŭjin; [10]‛yong ˓liéng, anti-extortion allowance to officers; [11]ka˒ ˓liéng, not high-priced.

幰 ˓Lien. A curtain; a screen of cloth, hung before doors: [12]˓mwong ˓liéng, a door-screen; [13]kieu˒ ˓liéng, sedan-curtains.

簾 ˓Lien. A screen or curtain of bamboo-splints: COM., [14]tĕük˒ ˓liéng, bamboo-blinds; [15]‛kwong ˓liéng, roll up the screen; [16]nói˒ ˓liéng ˓kwang, examiners of essays appointed by the governor.

磏 ˓Lien. A coarse sandstone, unfit for polishing; met., spurious, hypocritical; a red color: [17]˓liéng ˓ing, feigned kindness.

縑 ˓Lien. Fringes on flags; the embroidered quartering on a banner, on the inner edge near the staff.

臁 ˓Lien. The calf of the leg, the shin: COLL., ˓k‘a ˓liéng, the shin-bone; lang˒ ˓k‘a ˓liéng, a festered shin.

鐮 ˓Lien. A sickle, a reaping hook: COM., [18]˓liéng ˓tó (coll., ˓liéng kaik˒), a sickle.

鏈 ˓Lien. Unrefined lead or tin; connected, locked together, as by a chain.

鰱 ˓Lien. A species of carp, the Abramis bramula (?); the fish called ˓leng ˓ngü in Foochow (?), for which see under the word ˓leng (lotus).

奩 ˓Lien. A lady's dressing case, a toilet-box, a perfumery-case: COM., [19]˓chong ˓liéng, a bride's trousseau; ‛ch‘iŏng ˓kwang ˓liéng, please (come and) see the bridal outfit—words written on cards.

聯 ˓Lien. Connected, joined, as the ear to the head; to combine, to unite harmoniously, to assemble, to

[1]連	[2]連	[3]連	[4]仅	事	廉	[9]孝	[11]價	[13]轎	[15]捲	官	[18]鐮
口	本	陞	連	[6]廉	耻	廉	廉	幰	簾	[17]磏	刀
應	帶	三	[5]連	耻	[8]清	[10]養	[12]門	[14]竹	[16]內	仁	[19]粧
承	利	級	時	[7]無	廉	廉	幰	簾	簾	○	奩

associate; to join in a regular order; a distich, parallel aphorisms: COM., [1]ˌliéng ˌk'wong, distich-frames; [2]tói' ˌliéng, antithetical couplets on scrolls—hung up in houses; [3]so' ˌliéng, funeral couplets; [4]ˌch'ung ˌliéng, inscriptions on red paper at new year's; [5]ˌliéng kak, unions, an organization of families by tens; COLL., [6]t'eu^2 ˌliéng, flat or oval tablets on posts.

帘 ˌLien. A flag showing where wine is sold: [7]ˋchiu ˌliéng, a tavern-signboard; *met.*, a tavern.

楝^2 Lien. A tree bearing a sour berry, a species of cherry or bullace (?); the fruit is bell-shaped, and river-dragons are said to abhor it: COM., [8]ˋk'u liéng^2 ˋchi, the bitter liéng^2 berry—a medicine.

煉^2 Lien. Interchanged with the next: to fuse metals, to purify from dross; *met.*, to discipline, to test and perfect the character: COM., liéng^2 yoh, ˌwong, to make up pills; liéng^2 ˌtang, to refine pills; *met.*, to become immortal, as Tauists say.

鍊^2 Lien. To smelt ores, to refine and work metals; to forge; wrought, forged; the mutual action of the five elements; *met.*, to discipline; matured, disciplined, exercised; expert, skilled, practiced; a chain of any metal: [9]paik, liéng^2 thoroughly refined; [10]liéng^2 ˌching, well disciplined, perfect, as Tauists say; COM., [11]t'iék, liéng^2 an iron chain; [12]ˌsiu liéng^2 to practice austerity, to become religious; [13]kwa' liéng^2 bound with a chain on the neck; COLL., ˌtü ˋmó liéng^2 an iron cable; t'aung' liéng^2 to remove the chain—release the prisoner.

練^2 Lion. To boil silk, to soften its harshness by boiling; to try, to experiment on, to learn by practice; to drill, as troops; accustomed to, skilled; to select, to choose; white, shining, a whitish color; a piece of silk: [14]ˋkang liéng^2 to select veteran soldiers; [15]liéng^2 ˌi, mourning for a year or thirteen months; COM., [16]liéng^2 sük, experienced, mature; [17]ˌt'wang liéng^2 ward-organization and drill; [18]ˌch'au liéng^2 parade-drill; COLL., liéng^2 ˌkung ˌt'au, to practice in pugilism; kwang' liéng^2 accustomed, skilled in.

斂^2 Lien. To gather a harvest; to collect, to amass, to hoard; to extort money; avaricious, extortionate: also read ˋliéng, q. v.: [19]liéng^2 ˋchá, to harvest the ripe grain; [20]ˌsiu liéng^2 to gather, to harvest; chëü' liéng^2 to hoard up; to extort, as illegal duties.

殮^2 Lien. To dress a corpse, to lay out a body in all its clothes for the grave; the shroud, bandages of cloth or silk tied in knots about the seu^2 ˌi (grave-clothes): [21]ˌsiu liéng^2 or peng' liéng^2 to shroud and encoffin; COM., [22]liéng^2 këü^2 the shroud or bandages for the corpse; [23]ˌchiong liéng^2 and pwang' liéng^2 the complete, and the half, sets of bandages.

1 聯	3 素	5 聯	7 酒	子	10 鍊	12 修	14 簡	16 練	18 操	20 收	22 殮
匡	聯	甲	帘	9 百	精	鍊	練	熟	練	斂	具
2 對	4 春	6 柱	8 苦	鍊	11 鐵	13 掛	15 練	17 團	19 斂	21 收	23 全
聯	聯	聯	楝	〇	鍊	鍊	衣	練	穧	殮	殮

蘞 Lien. Also read ,lié'ng: a kind of creeper: pek, lié'ng² a drying or styptic medicine.

(391) Lieu.

了 Liao. A sign of the past tense, finished, done; to end, to finish, to conclude; settled, fixed, determined; intelligent, knowing; before a verb, it means very, wholly, entirely, clearly; it is much used in the court dialect: in the coll. read 'lau, q. v.: COM., 'lieu ,yong, or [1]'lieu ,yong ,ming pek, to understand very clearly; [2]'lieu pok, taik, excessive, incomparable, as in mischief, rudeness, etc.,; [3]pok, 'lieu, interminable; [4]'lieu kwoh, the matter completed; COLL., [5]'lieu lié² or 'lieu 'lieu lié² lié² all done, complete; comprehending clearly, perspicacious; 'lieu pok, taik, chiäng² (or ,wai), expert in mischief, full of knavery.

憭 Liao. Also read ,lieu: clever, keen, smart, discriminating; to reflect upon, to examine into: [6]'lieu lek, struck with alarm, agitated, greatly distressed.

瞭 Liao. A clear, bright eye; clear-sighted; to see far: [7],men 'chü 'lieu, the pupil of the eye clear.

蓼 Liao. An acrid herb, species of polygonum; met., sorrow, calamity: also read lük, q. v.: [8]'sieu 'lieu, a marsh-polygonum, smartweed.

窈 Yao. Read 'yeu; coll. 'lieu, as in 'lieu 't'ieu, beautiful; graceful, as a lady.

佬 Lao. Large, great: in the coll. read lau² q. v.

僚 Liao. An associate, a colleague; a companion; a fellow-officer; an equal, of the same rank; the same kind or class; to hold office and serve together: [9],kwang ,lieu, fellow-officers; the magistrates; [10],tung ,lieu, colleagues, of the same rank; [11]paik, ,lieu, the whole official corps. Read 'lieu: a good appearance, an easy manner.

寮 Liao. Interchanged with the last in the sense of a fellow-officer; fellow-students; a small window; to sit at the same window, or study in the same room: [12],lieu ,pung, a public office; [13],tung ,lieu ,chi 'iu, brother-officers.

寥 Liao. Empty, void, unoccupied; wide, vast; still, silent; solitary; [14]chik, ,lieu, vacant, solitary; [15],lieu lok, deserted; idle, not busied; COM., [16],lieu ,lieu ,u ,ki, reduced to a few, very little of.

蹘 Liao. To run; to escape, to go off, to hasten away; to cross the legs, to sit cross-legged.

憀 Liao. To trust, to confide in; to depend on as true or real; truly, really; anxious, impatient of, commiserating: [17],u ,lieu, no dependence, helpless.

---

1 了然明白 2 了不得〇 3 不了 4 了局 5 了離 6 憭慄 7 眸子瞭〇 8 小蓼 9 官僚 10 同僚 11 百僚 12 寮房 13 同寮之友 14 寂寥 15 寥落〇 16 寥寥無幾 17 無憀〇

福州方言拼音字典

聊 ˌLiao. Used for the last in the sense of to trust, to depend on; a ringing in the ears; an initial particle implying a diminution of, doubtful about, careless, anyhow, then: [1]ˌlieu ˌch'iu, ringing in the ears; [2]ˌu ˊi ˌlieu ˌseng, nothing to live on; [3]ˌlieu ˊü ˌchi ˌmeu, then let us consult.

嘹 ˌLiao. The cry of any creature: [4]ˌlieu liong' to listen to distant cries; to cry out, as in pain; in the coll. a clear sound, as of the voice or an instrument.

嫽 ˌLiao. A female name; to sport, to trifle, to play with; handsome, pretty: ˌlieu ˌlieu, name given to a maternal grandmother at Peking.

撩 ˌLiao. Like the last: to play with; to take hold of, to pull or stir about; to regulate, to wield, to manage; to provoke, to incite to evil, to seduce, to lead astray; in the coll. to trouble, to disturb, to annoy, to tease; light, frivolous: also read lieu' q. v.: [5]ˌlieu chiëng' to fight with long spears; coll., kó ˌlieu ˌi, go and excite him: ˌlieu süä' peak, ch'ié' to pull about in play, sport with mischievously; ˌlieu ˌpieu, light, frivolous.

燎 ˌLiao. Also read ˊlieu and lieu': to burn, to blaze; to set on fire; to enlighten, an illumination; torches set on stands to illuminate, links, fagots: [6]ˌmwong ˌlieu, a door-light; [7]ˌlieu ˌsing, fagots; [8]ˌlieu ˌü ˊchi ˊchiong, as plain as pointing to the palm.

獠 ˌLao. Also read lieu': to hunt by night with torches, as in deer-stalking: [9]lak, ˌlieu, hunting, a hunt.

繚 ˌLiao. To bind, to entwine, to wrap up; gyves, fetters; a sacrifice called [10]ˌlieu chié': [11]ˌlieu ˊnau, to entwine, to whirl into a ball. Read ˊlieu: to manage, to regulate.

遼 ˌLiao. Remote, distant, far off: [12]ˌlieu ˊwong, very distant; com., [13]ˌlieu ˌtëng and [14]ˌlieu ˌsá, East and West Liau, now Shingking; [15]ˌlieu ˌó, the river Liau in Manchuria.

鷯 ˌLiao. A small bird, like a wren or hedge-sparrow: ˌchieu ˌlieu, a sedge-wren which lives in marshy thickets.

膫 膋 ˌLiao. The fat about the intestines, fat taken from the bowels: [16]hiek, ˌlieu, blood and fat—also includes the marrow; coll., ˌlieu kau' your fat is thick — said facetiously to one wearing thin clothes in cold weather.

蜆 Hsien. Read ˊhiëng; used in the Paik, ˌIng for the coll. ˌlieu: a small bivalve, a clam: ˌlieu ˊkiëng, small clams; ˌlieu ˌtiëng, a clam-bed; ˌlieu k'uëk, ˊyeu ˊnü taing' k'wong ˌkang, even a clamshell will soon lade out your indigo-tub dry; met., gradual waste exhausts property.

料 ˌLiao. To oversee, to regulate, to manage, to dispose properly; to take a census; to pull; the clear sound of

1	2	3	4	5	6	7	8	9	10	11	12	13	14	15	16
聊啾	無聊以生	聊與之謀	嘹喨	撩戰	門燎	燎薪	燎如指掌	獵獠	繚祭	繚繞	遼遠	遼東	遼西	遼河	血膫

small drums: also read *lieu2* and *liu2* q. v.: *lieu ming*, to take the census of a people; *lieu hu ts'eu*, to pull the tiger's beard; COM., *lieu li*, to arrange, to manage.

Lieu. A coll. word: to cut to pieces, a mode of torture like flaying alive: *lieu si sá2 kak*, to execute by cutting to pieces.

料2 Liao. To judge, to measure, to estimate, to reckon, to calculate; in the following senses usually read *liu2*; stuff, materials; ability, cleverness, talent, as of an employé; grain, provender; manure: also read *lieu*, q. v.: COM., 1*lieu2 siong*, to judge, to estimate; 2*pok lieu2* (coll. *ng2 lieu2*), unexpected, sudden; 3*k'ing lieu2* to disparage, as for a trivial matter; COLL., *lieu2 má2 ch'ok*, or *má2 lieu2 tek ch'ok* incalculable, inscrutable.

撩2 Liao. To grasp, to catch, to take hold of; in the coll. to disturb, to molest, to interfere with; to stir, as things while cooking: also read *lieu*, q. v.: COLL., *lieu2 sük*, stir it till done; *móh lieu2* don't molest (the things), as said to a child.

療2 Liao. To cure diseases, to heal; to stop, to appease; medical practice: 4*lieu2 peng2* to cure an illness; 5*lieu2 ki*, to appease hunger.

Lieu2. A coll. word, as in *lieu2 lieu2* a sort of vegetable like garlic; it is salted and seasoned for food.

Lieu4. A coll. word, as in *lieu4 k'ieu2* curled stiff, rigid in death!

(392) Lik.

力2 Li. Strength, muscular power, brawn, nerve; the full use of an organ; force, vigor, spirit, mental energy; divine help; the material properties or strength of things; the stiffness of a bow; active, energetic, vigorous; a surname; the 19th radical: COM., 6*lü lik* strength, strong; 7*kêng lik* muscular energy; 8*lik liong2* capacity, aptitude; 9*lik k'é2* constitutional vigor; 10*ch'ok lik* or *ëüng2 lik* to exert one's self; 11*lik kü*, to recommend one strongly; 12*pek lik*, a nervous style; chaste penmanship; *ngang lik* keenness of eyesight; *lik kiong* (or *chüng2*), robust strength; 13*lik pok chüng sing*, one's strength unequal to his will; COLL., *tu mó k'wi lik* has no strength at all; *nioh wai2 lik* what is the stiffness (of this bow)?

立2 Li. To stand, to stand erect; to establish, to institute, to set up, to found, to perfect; to fix, to effect, to settle, to agree upon; to place in order, to arrange; the arrival of the time of; soon, speedily, at once; the 117th radical: 14*tuk lik* to stand alone, fixed, upright; COM., 15*lik ch'ung*, the first of the 24 solar terms, beginning of spring: 16*siék lik*, to establish; 17*sing lik* established (in life), as one arriving at maturity; 18*lik söü2* to adopt an heir; 19*lik che2*

1 料想 2 不料 3 輕料 4 療病 5 療饑 6 膂力 7 筋力 8 力量 9 力氣 10 出力 11 力舉 〇 12 筆力 〇 13 力不從心 14 獨立 15 立春 16 設立 〇 17 成立 〇 18 立嗣 19 立志

to resolve; *lik*$_2$ *ngiék*$_2$ to acquire property; to enter a profession or calling; *lik*$_2$ *‚sü* to found an ancestral temple; *lik*$_2$ *k'aik*$_2$ instantly; *lik*$_2$ *‚kung leng*^{2} *chaung*^{2} to make a military vow, as to destroy the enemy: *met.*, to contract under heavy penalties; COLL., *lik*$_2$ *tě*^{2} *'ch'ü 'si*, to kill on the spot; *lik*$_2$ *'ta lik*$_2$ *'si*, to die while being beaten.

苙$_2$ Li. A pen or inclosure, a basket for confining or carrying pigs; a medicinal plant, called *pek*$_2$ *lik*$_2$.

笠$_2$ Li. A rain hat, made of splints and leaves; a conical cap of braided straw; an open basket or hamper: COM., [1]*‚ing lik*$_2$ a ceremonial cap of finely woven straw or rattan; [2]*hoi*^{2} *lik*$_2$ a tasseled silk-hat; [3]*'ch'au lik*$_2$ a broad-brimmed straw hat; [4]*lik*$_2$ *tō*^{2} the inner ring or lining of a hat; COLL., *lik*$_2$ *k'aëk*, or *lik*$_2$ *‚t'ai*, the bodies of ceremonial hats; *lik*$_2$ *kwang*^{2} cap-strings; *'tau lik*$_2$ an umbrella-hat of bamboo splints and leaves.

栗$_2$ Li. Read *lek*$_2$; coll. *lik*$_2$ as in *lik*$_2$ *'chi*, a chestnut; *lik*$_2$ *'chi k'aëk*$_2$ chestnut-shells.

櫪$_2$ Li. A sort of oak, bearing edible acorns; a pen, a stable: [5]*‚chang lik*$_2$ frames for worms to weave cocoons on; [6]*'ma lik*$_2$ a stable; [7]*lik*$_2$ *‚sü*, to squeeze the fingers between sticks; thumb-screws.

櫟$_2$ Li. A kind of hard, tough oak, considered a useless wood, not even fit for fuel; in some places used as a depreciatory term for one's self; name of a bird.

曆$_2$ Li. The course of the spheres, a representation of the heavenly bodies; to calendar times and seasons; an almanac, for which the next is also used: [8]*lik*$_2$ *ch'iong*^{2} representation of the heavens; [9]*lik*$_2$ *hwak*$_2$ astronomy; COM., [10]*‚wong lik*$_2$ an almanac.

歷$_2$ Li. To pass by or over; to pass, as ages and generations; to pass through, to experience; to transgress, as the laws; arranged, in order, orderly; successive, next in order; disordered, confused; to extend, to exhaust; to say all; silent, retired; wide apart: [11]*lik*$_2$ *kō*^{2} to make a full statement; [12]*lik*$_2$ *'ch'i*, the teeth wide apart; [13]*lik*$_2$ *lwang*^{2} confused; [14]*lik*$_2$ *liéng*^{2} experienced in; COM., [15]*lik*$_2$ *tai*^{2} (coll. *lik*$_2$ *tói*^{2}), successive generations or ages; [16]*lik*$_2$ *‚niéng*, a series of years; [17]*lik*$_2$ *‚lai*, from the first till now; [18]*yok*$_2$ *lik*$_2$ to pass through, have experience of; [19]*'li lik*$_2$ a report of one's merit or antecedents.

瀝$_2$ Li. To drip, to fall in drops; a very little left in a cup: [20]*sek*$_2$ *lik*$_2$ sound of rain or hail; [21]*‚ü lik*$_2$ the dregs of a cup; [22]*lik*$_2$ *hiék*$_2$ to shed one's blood; [23]*lik*$_2$ *‚ching k'aiu*^{2} *'k'ong*, to petition humbly and sincerely; *tek*$_2$ *lik*$_2$ to drip, to drop.

[1]纓笠 [2]緯笠 [3]草笠 [4]笠套 [5]蠶櫪 [6]馬櫪 [7]櫪椺 [8]曆象 [9]曆法 [10]王曆 [11]歷告 [12]歷齒 [13]歷亂 [14]歷練 [15]歷代 [16]歷年 [17]歷來 [18]閱歷 [19]履歷 [20]淅瀝 [21]餘瀝 [22]瀝血 [23]瀝情叩懇

癧 Li. ₂ The scrofula: in the coll. read *lek*, q. v.: [1]*lio lik*, the king's evil, a scrofulous swelling on the neck.

磿 ₂ The noise of a stone: *lik, lik*, noise made by small stones; [2]*lik, sek*, name of a palace.

礫 Li. ₂ Small broken stones, pebbles, gravel, shingle, coarse sand: [3]*ngwa lik*, potsherds; [4]*wong lik*, a tree furnishing a yellow dye; [5]*tang lik*, ore of quicksilver, cinnabar.

躒 Li. ₂ To move, motion; a step, a pace: [6]*ki kė ek, lik, pok, neng ch'iéng pwo*, the finest steed can't by one step advance a thousand *li*; *met.*, the rites must be observed one by one. Read *lok*: to exceed, to surpass: [7]*tauk, lik*, extraordinary.

轢 Li. ₂ The path or track in which wheels move; to crush under wheels: [8]*lik, lik*, a rut made by wheels.

酈 ₂ Also read *lié* in the dictionaries: name of a place in the state of Lu, now comprised in the prefecture of Tangchau in Shantung; a surname.

*Lik*₂. A coll. euphonic prefix, as in *lik, lik, lok, lok*, scattered, sparse, as men coming at intervals; *lik, lak*, to rub off, as grain by drawing the head through the hand; to shove or draw off, as armlets.

(393) Ling.

鈴 Ling. Read *ling*; used for the coll. *ling*, as in *ling ling*, the tinkling of a bell; *met.*, a small bell, a hand-bell; *yeu ling ling*, ring the bell.

Ling. A coll. word, as in *ling ling*, or *ling ling*, a bit, remnant, piece left over.

Ling. A coll. euphonic prefix, as in *ling lang*, or *ling ling lang lang*, to swing to and fro; to vibrate, as a pendulum; *ling ling lang lang*, the ringing sound of metals and gems.

僯 Lin. Also read *ling*: to feel ashamed; abashed, humiliated; confounded, disconcerted.

稟 Pin. Ping. To give out grain; to provide food or money for, to give; to sustain, to nourish; also read *ping*, q. v.: [9]*k'ė ling*, to furnish food; [10]*ling meng*, to receive orders; [11]*ling ho*, received from heaven, as natural endowments.

凜 Lin. Ling. Intense cold; shivering with cold; an awe-inspiring manner; trembling, fearing, as in the presence of magistrates: *ling ling*, piercingly cold; awestruck; [12]*ling liek*, stern, terrific; com., [13]*wi hung ling ling*, terribly overawing.

懍 Lin. Fear, respect, awe, dread: *ling ling*, serious, afraid of, reverentially obedient to.

[1] 瘰癧　[2] 磿室　[3] 瓦礫○　[4] 黃礫○　[5] 丹礫○　[6] 騏驥一躒不能千步　[7] 卓躒○　[8] 轢轢○　[9] 餽稟○　[10] 稟命○　[11] 稟賦　[12] 凜冽　[13] 威風凜凜

‛廩 Lin. Ling. A government-granary; a corn-house, grange, depot for grain; to give to students, to dispense, as the college-allowance: [1]‚ch‛ong ‛ling, a granary; COM., [2]‛ling ‚seng, a stipendiary Siutsai; [3]‛pwo ‛ling, enrolled on the list of stipendiaries; [4]‛ling siéng² or ‛ling ‚liong, the stipend of a ‛ling ‚seng; [5]‛ling ‚á ‛pó, the two stipendiaries who act as sureties for an under-graduate.

‛領 Ling. The throat; the collar of a garment, a neck-ribbon or collar; to govern, to manage, to attend to; to take or receive, as orders or funds; to lead, to direct; to record: in the coll. read ‛liăng, q. v.: [6]‛ling seu² to receive; [7]‛ling keng² the throat; [8]‛ling seu² "collar and sleeve"—a leader, headman; COM., [9]‛ling kau' to receive instruction; [10]‛ling siā² received with thanks, as said in acknowledging presents; [11]‛ling e' "have received the intent"—said politely when the whole or most of a present is returned.

‛衿 Ling. The inside of a dress; a bridal robe; a band or neck-cloth, a collar.

‛*Ling*. A coll. word; scanty, barely sufficient: similar to *lek*, q. v.: ‛ling ‛ling, scant, yet sufficing; ‛ling ‛lìng ‚kiéng, just at the edge.

‛*Ling*. A coll. euphonic prefix, as in ‛ling ‛lang ‛lang, or ‛ling ‛ling ‛lang ‛lang, to throw the arms over another's shoulders, to embrace.

‚伶 Ling. To play the droll, to act the buffoon; musicians, posture-makers; apt, smart, clever; to employ one; alone, single: [12]‚ling ‚ing, a musician, buffoon; [13]‚ling ‚kwang, master of the musicians; [14]‛sü ‚ling, a servant; [15]‚ling ‚ting, alone, deserted; [16]‚ling le² clever; trim, good-looking; COLL., ‚ling le² mŏh₂ niăh₂ ‚kwong kong' the smart man is not equal to the scoundrel.

‚囹 Ling. A prison, a place inclosed by railing: [17]‚ling ‛ngü, a jail.

‚瓴 Ling. A long-necked jar or amphora having ears; the concave tiles used on roofs: [18]ĕüng' ‚ling, a water-jar; [19]‚ling tek, an amphora; large tiles.

‚翎 Ling. Feathers or wings, plumes; the feathers of an arrow; the tail-feathers of the peacock, &c., used in official caps: [20]chiéng' ‚ling, feather of an arrow; COM., [21]‚lang ‚ling (coll. ‛ch‛au ‚ling), a plain plume; [22]‚sĕng ‛ngang ‚hwa ‚ling, a two-eyed peacock's feather; ‚ling ‛kwong, the stone or metallic socket in which a plume is inserted.

‚聆 Ling. To hear, to listen, to attend to, to try sounds; to follow, to obey: ‚ling ‚ling, to comprehend; taik, ‚ling ‚ch‛ing hwoi' (happy) to hear your clear instructions; ‚ling sek, I understand it all—an epistolary phrase.

[1]倉廩 [2]廩生 [3]補廩 [4]廩餼 [5]廩挨保〇 [6]領受 [7]領頸 [8]領袖 [9]領教 [10]領謝 [11]領意 [12]伶人 [13]伶官 [14]使伶 [15]伶仃 [16]伶俐 [17]囹圄 [18]甕瓴 [19]瓴甋 [20]箭翎 [21]藍翎 [22]雙眼花翎

蛉 ꜀Ling. An insect; some say a grasshopper: [1]꜀*ming* ꜀*ling* an insect found on mulberry trees; *met.*, an adopted child; [2]꜀*ch'ing* ꜀*ling*, dragon-flies (Libellulidae)—called ꜀*ma* ꜀*hu* in the coll. q. v.

跉 ꜀Ling. To walk or saunter about: [3]꜀*ling* ꜀*ting*, to walk sidewise, to walk irregularly.

鈴 ꜀Ling. A small bell like a sleigh-bell; they are hung on horses' necks and on flags to announce approach: COM., [4]'*ma* ꜀*ling*, horse-bells, sleigh-bells; [5]*pang'* ꜀*ling*, bells with handles; [6]'*ma* ꜀*tau* ꜀*ling*, the capsules of lilies—used in pulmonary complaints; [7]꜀*king* ꜀*ling* '*chü*, a sort of medicinal nut—a specific for stomach-aches.

鴒 ꜀Ling. A small bird, the wagtail, called *chek*꜀ ꜀*ling*; some say a kind of titmouse; COM., [8]*paik*꜀ ꜀*ling*, a singing lark.

齡 ꜀Ling. The front teeth; *met.*, the age, years: [9]*hok*꜀ ꜀*ling*, storks' age—longevity; [10]꜀*ha* ꜀*ling*, old, gray-headed; [11]*mieu'* ꜀*ling*, young, under age.

苓 ꜀Ling. A kind of tonic medicine, the China root: [12]꜀*ling* '*ngi*, a sort of edible boletus or fungus; COM., [13]*huk*꜀ ꜀*ling*, China root; [14]꜀*hung* ꜀*ling*, the Yunnan root; [15]꜀*tü* ꜀*ling*, a dark, reddish sort of China root.

菱 ꜀Ling. An aquatic vegetable, the ꜀*ling* *kaĕk*, water-caltrops (trapa bicornis or tricornis), also called buffalo's horns: in the coll. read ꜀*leng*, q. v.: ꜀*ling* ꜀*hwa*, a poetical term for a mirror.

玲 ꜀Ling. The tinkling of gems: [16]꜀*lung* ꜀*ling*, a tinkling sound, as of gems or metals.

琳 ꜀Lin. A sort of precious stone, called [17]꜀*kiu* ꜀*ling*, perhaps a kind of prase-quartz.

璘 ꜀Lin. A veined appearance, like that of agate: [18]꜀*ling* ꜀*p'iéng*, streaked, variegated; ꜀*ling* ꜀*ping*, lustrous, chatoyant.

痳 ꜀Lin. A disease of the bladder or ureter; a strangury or dysury: COM., *haik*꜀ ꜀*ling*, bloody urine; *kek*꜀ ꜀*ling*, the gravel.

林 ꜀Lin. A clump of trees, a grove, a wood, a forest; a luxuriance, abundance of; a group, a company; one's native groves, home; a surname: [19]꜀*ling* ꜀*chüng*, a note in music; [20]*lük*꜀ ꜀*ling*, a mountain in Hupeh; *met.*, a den of thieves; ꜀*kwi* ꜀*ling* *ha'* to retire to one's home, as an officer; COM., [21]*ngëü'* ꜀*ling* ꜀*kung*, the Imperial Guard; [22]꜀*hang* ꜀*ling* *yéng'* the Hanlin college.

欞 ꜀Ling. A wooden lattice, window-bars; beams over doors; a plate under the eaves: ꜀*ling* '*k'ang*, a window having lattice or bars.

[1]螟蛉 [2]蜻蛉 [3]跉町 [4]馬鈴 [5]柄鈴 [6]馬兜鈴 [7]金鈴子 [8]百鴒 [9]鶴齡 [10]遐齡 [11]妙齡 [12]苓耳 [13]茯苓 [14]雲苓 [15]猪苓 [16]瓏玲 [17]球琳 [18]璘瑸 [19]林鐘 [20]綠林 [21]御林軍 [22]翰林院

棱 楞 Ling. Interchanged with the next: a square piece of timber; a corner, four-cornered; a beam in a temple-roof: [1]*ku ling*, the highest point of a house; [2]*mwo ling*, to aim at two objects, fickle, time-serving.

稜 Ling. An angle, a corner; a segment; a kind of rice, called *u ling;* a classifier of fields: [3]*ku ling*, angular; [4]*wi ling*, grand, awe-inspiring; *ki ling tiéng*, how many fields?

綾 Ling. Thin silk having a fine, glossy surface, thin satin; damask: COM., [5]*wong ling*, a thin, yellow silk; [6]*hwa ling*, damask; [7]*ü ling*, lastings; *pah ling liéng*, funeral aphorisms on white silk; [8]*ling lò p'ek taung* silks, gauzes, and satins.

陵 Ling. Interchanged with the next: a large mound, a barrow, a hillock; a cemetery, mausoleum; to insult, to desecrate; to invade, to usurp; to aim high, to aspire: [9]*k'iu ling*, a high mound or hill; [10]*pok ling chiék*, not act disorderly; COM., [11]*ling ti sá kak*, ignominiously cut to pieces —a punishment like quartering.

淩 Ling. An accumulation of ice, an ice-house; to insult, to disgrace, to dishonor, to put to shame; shameful, injurious; to advance, to have high aims: [12]*ling sek*, an ice-house; [13]*ling hung*, aspiring to the clouds, ambitious; [14]*k'i ling*, to abuse, to insult; COM., [15]*ling ük*, to disgrace; to deflower, to treat basely.

凌 Ling. To gallop over, to pass beyond; to tremble; a river in Kwangsi: [16]*ling lek*, trembling; *hwang 'hai ling sang*, to cross seas and mountains—to travel far.

潾 Lin. Name of a river; clear water, such as issues from rocks and runs among the hills.

淋 Lin. To water, to wet; to soak, to moisten; water dripping and running off: [17]*tai ü ling lié*, drenched by a heavy rain; *ling hwa*, to water flowers; COLL., *haik ling ling*, blood flowing profusely.

霖 Lin. Interchanged with the last: incessant rain, a timely rain of three days duration: [18]*ling ü*, continuous showers; *kang ling*, a good, seasonable rain.

零 Ling. The last drops of a shower, small rain; what is over, a fraction, residue, remainder; the excess of a round number; in numeration, means "and" or implies that one denomination is not used, a cypher: [19]*ling ting*, a solitary individual; *k'ié ling*, a surplus, residue; COM., [20]*ling sing* or *ling ch'ói* odd ends, fragments; *ling lok*, scattered, nearly all fallen off, as leaves; *sang 'liong ling paik hung*, 3 taels and 8 candareens; COLL., *sioh pah ling sang*, one hundred and three; *ling t'au k'ié 'mwi*, the odd amounts, something thrown in or not reckoned, as

1 柧棱 2 模棱 3 觚稜 4 威稜 5 黃綾 6 花綾 7 羽綾 8 綾羅 疋緞 9 丘陵 10 不陵節〇 11 陵遲細剮 12 淩室 13 淩雲 14 欺凌 15 凌辱 16 淩慄 17 大雨淋漓 18 霖雨 19 零丁 20 零星

cash, pounds, feet; *seʼ ʻteng ˏling*, a little past 4 o'clock.

靈 灵 ˏLing. A spirit, a soul, a mysterious, disembodied agency; a divine influence or energy; spiritual, incorporeal, subtle, ethereal, pervading; efficacious, miraculous, felicitous, able to act effectively on other powers; intelligent, discerning, penetrative; the type or most excellent of a class, as man of created things; ingenious; obscure; lucky, opportune, as a rain: *sëüʼ ˏling*, the four superior of all feathered, scaly, shelly, and hairy, beings—i. e., the phenix, dragon, tortoise, and unicorn; [1]*ˏling ˏki*, a curious contrivance; intelligent, astute; [2]*ˏsiéng ˏling*, one's ancestors; [3]*ˏing ˏling*, ghosts, the dead; [4]*ˏseng ˏling*, animated beings; [5]*ˏsang ˏling*, sun, moon, and stars; COM., [6]*ˏling ˏhung*, the human soul; [7]*ˏling kʻeuʼ* the coffin with the corpse in it; [8]*ˏling oiʼ* place of the spirit (of the deceased)—where his picture and chair are set; [9]*ˏmi ˏing wangʼ uk, ˏchi ˏling*, man is the most intelligent of all beings; [10]*ˏling ˏhu*, an efficacious charm; [11]*ˏling tongʼ* active, lively in mind; [12]*ˏling piéngʼ*, apt, ready, having tact; [13]*ˏling kʻieuʼ* "the mental apertures"—astute, perspicacious; [14]*ˏling engʼ* or [15]*ˏling hiéngʼ* a divine response; [16]*sengʼ ˏling*, the Holy Spirit, as used by some; COLL., *ˏling ʻkeu taiʼ ˏchiong ˏkung*, a dog-headed attendant of the god *ˏNgwong sôiʼ*; *ˏling ˏhiong ʻchʻau*, a fragrant plant used with hair-oil.

嶙 ˏLin. A precipice, lofty peaks of mountains: *ˏling ˏsung*, a lofty cliff, mountain hights.

憐 ˏLien. To pity, to compassionate, to have charity for, to sympathize with: in the coll. read *ˏleng*, q. v.: *ˏling sok*, to pity; COM., *ˏling ʻming* (coll. *ʻkʻô ˏleng*), to compassionate; *kiéngʼ ˏling*, to show pity toward; *ˏtung pengʼ ˏsiong ˏling*, those in the same distress sympathize with each other.

燐 粦 ˏLin. An ignis-fatuus, supposed to be an exhalation from the blood of murdered persons; shining, sparkling: *ʻkwi ʻhwo ˏling ˏling*, the devils' fires flash about; *ˏling ˏing*, the sparkling glow-worm.

磷 粼 ˏLin. Water purling among the stones; the clear water flowing over a rocky bottom: *ˏling ˏling*, clear, pure and sparkling. Read *lengʼ*: to rub thin; a thin stone, shingle, gravel.

遴 ˏLin. To choose, to select with care: *ˏling ʻsong*, to make a careful selection (of the talented). Read *lengʼ*: to walk with difficulty; covetous, grasping: *ˏtʻang lengʼ* to covet, niggardly.

驎 ˏLin. Also read *lengʼ*: a piebald horse; a horse having black lips: *ʻùng ˏling*, a piebald horse.

1 靈機 ○ 2 先靈 ○ 3 人靈 ○ 4 生靈 5 三靈 6 靈魂 7 靈柩 8 靈位 9 惟人萬物之靈 10 靈符 11 靈動 12 靈便 13 靈竅 14 靈應 ○ 15 靈現 ○ 16 聖靈 ○

鄰 隣 Lin. Near, neighboring, contiguous, proximate; connected, associated, assisting, as ministers do; a neighborhood of five families; neighbors: [1]*ling* '*li*, the neighbors; [2]*ling kwok*, adjacent countries; COM., [3]*ling këüng*' near to, in the vicinity of; [4]*ling ,kü*, or [5]*ling siă*' the next house, a house near by; COLL., '*wong ,ch'ing mŏh, niăh, këüng*' *ling*, a relative far off is not as good as a near neighbor.

轔 Lin. The rumbling of wheels, for which the last is also used; full, abundant; a threshold: *ling ling*, rumbling of chariot-wheels; [6]*ho*' *ling*, a doorway, threshold.

輘 Ling. The track or traces of; to follow the track, to run over: *ling lik*, the rut of a wheel; to crush under wheels.

臨 Lin. To look down upon, to superintend; to go to, to regard, to condescend, as superiors do; to descend, to visit, as with blessings or curses; at the point of, about to, to commence; during, when, at the time of meeting; makes the present gerundive; large, great; the 19th diagram: [7]'*chieu*' *ling*, to shine upon, to illumine; [8]*ling t'aik*, to imitate a writing; COM., [9]*ling ,hwang*, to descend into the world, as a god; [10]*ling ,ngui*, at the critical time (of death); [11]*ling ,chüng*, near decease, dying; [12]*kaung*' *ling*, to descend; the advent, as of Christ; [13]*ling ,si*, at the time; [14]*ling ,pwong*, time of parturition; [15]*ling cheng*' '*chi ,nang*, name of a book on diseases; [16]*ling* '*chwi* '*ná*, the Mother-goddess, guardian of children—a native of the southern suburbs of Foochow; [17]*ling ,ká* '*ch'iëng hëng*' at the street and in short alleys — *scil.*, one must speak low; COLL., [18]*ling ,mwong ,sang ,pwang siong*' on arriving look at matters all around, as said by a poor debtor to his creditor.

醽 Ling. Generous, rich spirits, made with great care, called *ling lük*.

羚 麢 Ling. A mountain sheep; an antelope or chamois: COM., [19]*ling ,yong kaëk*, and *ling ,yong ,chiëng*, chamois' horns and tips of the horns—used medicinally.

麟 Lin. The female unicorn; also used for *ling* (bright, clear): *ling* '*chi ,t'ing ,siong*, the unicorn's hoof brings luck; *met.*, an heir is born; COM., *,ki ,ling*, male and female unicorns; *,t'iëng sëü*' *ling ,i*, Heaven grant a fine child!

鯪 Ling. A species of carp, the Leuciscus or dace: *sik, ling*, name of a medicine; *ling* '*li*, the pangolin or manis—the Chinese say that it is transformed from a fish and grows as large as a kraken.

鱗 Lin. The scales of a fish; scaly animals, as fishes and snakes: *ling uk*, the scaly tribes; *ling kak*, scales.

[1]鄰里 [2]鄰國 [3]鄰近 [4]鄰居 [5]鄰舍 [6]戸轔 [7]照臨 [8]臨帖 [9]臨凡 [10]臨危 [11]臨終 [12]降臨 [13]臨時 [14]臨盆 [15]臨症指南 [16]臨水奶 [17]臨街淺巷 [18]臨門三般相 [19]羚羊角〇

(394) Lio.

[The next eight are interchangeably read *lwo*].

ʻ虜 Lu. To seize, to capture, to take prisoners in war; to take alive; captives, prisoners; a slave to, devoted to: [1]ʻ*lio liok*, to capture; [2]*siu* ˓*chiéng* ʻ*lio*, a slave to money.

ʻ擄 Lu. Interchanged with the last: to seize, to capture prisoners; to seize and detain persons as slaves, or for ransom: used for ʻ*lu* in the coll. q. v.: [3]ʻ*lio* ˓*ing*, to kidnap people.

ʻ蓏 Fruits ripening on the ground, those growing on vines and herbs, as melons, tomatoes, water-caltrops, etc.: [4]ʻ*kwo* ʻ*lio*, the two sorts of fruits—those borne on trees and those on vines or herbs.

ʻ裹 Kuo. To wind around, to bundle, to wrap up; to envelop; the capsule or receptacle of flowers, place where the fruit sets; anything wrapped up, a bundle: [5]ʻ*lio* ˓*liong*, to put up provisions for a journey; [6]˛*pau* ʻ*lio*, to wrap up; [7]ʻ*lio chëak*, to bind the feet, fettered.

ʻ裸 Lo. Naked, nude, bare-backed; the upper part of the person stripped; to strip, to make bare: [8]ʻ*lio* ˛*sing*, or [9]ʻ*lio* ˓*t'ing*, nude, stripped; [10]ʻ*lio* ˓*t'ŭng*, the naked insect; *met*., man.

ʻ瘰 Lo. Also read ʻ*lwi* in the dictionaries: the king's evil, called [11]ʻ*lio lik*; refers to scrofula only as it appears in the neck.

ʻ蠃 Lo. As in [12]ʻ*kwo* ʻ*lio*, the solitary wasp or sphex, which imprisons caterpillars in its nest and "makes them turn into wasps": also read ˓*loi*, q. v.

嚕ʻ Read ʻ*lio*; used for the coll. *lio*ʼ, as in ˓*lio lio*ʼ sound made in calling dogs; ʻ*yă* ʻ*kong cheu*ʼ *se*ʼ ˓*lio lio*ʼ if I am telling a lie, then I'm a dog!

(395) Lioh.

[The next three are interchangeably read *lwoh*].

緑 Lu. Lü. Read *lük*; coll. *lioh*: green color: *lioh* ˓*chi* ˓*chi*, or *lioh* ˓*p'ang* ˓*p'ang*, very green; ˓*p'ang* ˛*kwong lioh*, green (cloth) smoothed by the rolling-stone; [13]˛*tëng lioh*, winter-green—a common wood-dye used in cold weather; [14]˓*iu lioh*, to paint green; [15]*lioh tau*ʼ ˛*sieu*, spirits distilled from green beans; [16]*lioh* ˓*p'ui* ʻ*kang*, shoe-welts of green leather; ˓*tëng lioh* or *lioh* ˛*tang*, verdigris; [17]˓*yong lioh* French green; [18]*tai*ʼ *lioh mó*ʼ to wear a green cap—be a cuckold.

錄 Lu. Read *lük* in the dictionaries: a metallic luster or color; veins on a shell; to copy, to transcribe; to record, to register, make a note of; an order, a series, an index; the teeth: [19]*lioh chik*, record, as of a family; COM., [20]*lioh* ʻ*ch'ü*, to select, as the essays of candidates for a degree; [21]*lioh* ˓*mi*, to enter (the names of) de-

[1]虜掠 [2]守錢虜 [3]擄人〇 [4]果蓏 [5]裹糧 [6]包裹 [7]裹足 [8]裸身 [9]裸裎 [10]裸蟲 [11]瘰癧 [12]果蠃 [13]冬緑 [14]油緑 [15]緑豆燒 [16]緑皮簡 [17]洋緑 [18]戴緑帽 [19]錄集〇 [20]錄取 [21]錄遺

ferred Siutsai, as candidates for the Küjin degree; *ₒteng lioh₂* to copy (essays); *muk₂ lioh₂* an index; *ʻsá ₒwong lioh₂* a book on wounds and other causes of death—a coroner's manual; *má² lioh₂* to sell copied lists of graduates; *ₒngiong haing³ lioh₂* a record of words and acts; *lioh₂ ʻk'eu ₒküng*, to take minutes of evidence; COLL., *lioh₂ ch'ok₂ ₒli*, write it, copy it off.

斛 Read *liok₂*; used in the *Paik₂ ₒIng* for the coll. ₂ *lioh₂*: to strike, to level, as a measure; to wipe, to rub, to smooth with the hand: *lioh₂ ₒpang*, to level, make even; *lioh₂ ₒk'wi*, or *lioh₂ ₒpiéng*, to brush aside; *lioh₂ ₒt'au hwok₂* to smooth or comb the hair.

(396) Liok.

[The next three are interchangeably read *lwok*].

劣 Lieh. Infirm, weak, feeble; poor, humble, insignificant, a term used in a depreciating sense, as of one's own talents; a little, scarcely, barely; rustic, vile, rude, mean: [1]*liok₂ ₒsing*, depraved gentry; [2]*auk₂ liok₂* very bad; [3]*liok₂ ʻteng*, the inferior grade—Siutsai who cannot pass review; [4]*liok₂ ₒchai*, my poor talents; [5]*ₒiu liok₂* capable and incapable; [6]*liok₂ pok₂* poor, inadequate; [7]*liok₂ ʻmu* and [8]*liok₂ ʻsing*, the wives of brothers so style themselve in epistles.

埒 A low bank or wall, a mound; to mark or survey lands, and designate their limits; a mountain tarn, a pool; the same, alike, equal; a class: [9]*ʻma liok₂* a bridle-path; *ʻteng liok₂* the same sort; *ʻchwi liok₂* a tarn.

捋 Lieh. Lo. To grasp, to take or clasp with the fingers, to draw through the hand; to rub or stroke with the fingers: *liok₂ ʻch'ai*, to pluck; *liok₂ ʻü*, to milk.

掠 Liang. Lüo. To take by force, to rob, to plunder; to invade, to waste, as in making forays; to beat, to punish with a stick: *ₒch'au liok₂* to plunder, to filch; *ₒching liok₂* to invade, to make a plundering foray; *ʻpong liok₂* to bastinado.

畧 略 Lio. Lüo. To divide and mark fields; the limit, boundary; to plan, to contrive, to counsel together; astute, shrewd; to abridge, to diminish, as labor; a resumé, digest, abridgment of; in general, for the most part; a little, almost, about, rather; to slight, to disesteem; a path, a rule; to take, to seize; to offend, to transgress; to walk, to go; to sharpen: [10]*ₒking liok₂* to manage; [11]*ₒmeu liok₂* to contrive; clever at, forecasting; [12]*liok₂ te²* to enter, or pass through, a region; [13]*yeu³ liok₂* the important parts of; COM., [14]*tai² liok₂* or [15]*yok₂ liok₂* in general, about, for the most part; [16]*hwok₂ liok₂* cursorily; [17]*liok₂ ₒti ek₂ ne²* to understand a little about it; COLL., *liok₂ liok₂ ₒnié* (brogue *ₒlio ₒlio ₒnié*), a little, about, nearly.

1劣身 ○ 2惡劣 ○ 3劣等 ○ 4劣才 5優劣 6劣薄 7劣姆 8劣嬸 9馬埒 10經畧 11謀畧 12畧地 13要畧 14大畧 ○ 15約畧 ○ 16忽畧 ○ 17畧知一二

(397) Liong.

ʻ兩 ʻ両 Liang. Two, a couple, a pair; doubled, twice, again; a tael, a Chinese ounce, equal to 1⅓ oz. av., or 583⅓ qrs. tr.; the highest nominal money of China, worth about $1. 39, or 6s. 8d.: used for liongʾ (a car; a numerative of chariots): COM., [1]ˏngŭng ʻliong, silver money, ingots, sycee; [2]ʻliong yèngʾ the viceroy and governor; [3]ʻliong ˏhu, Hupeh and Hunan; [4]ʻliong ˏchiong, both complete; [5]ʻliong ʻlŏ, one's parents; [6]ʻliong kóʾ two; ʻliong soʾ reckoning by ounces; ʻliong piéngʾ convenient for both; ʻliong chŏʾ plaintiff and defendant; COLL., ˏsiăng ʻliong, a full ounce, about an ounce; ʻliong kaingʾ ʻniăng ʻkʻó, (students of) the two districts examined together; *met.*, things mixed and confused.

ʻ倆 Liang. Apt, clever at, skilled in: keʾ ʻliong, ingenious, cunning, expert.

ʻ魎 Liang. An elf or gnome, a sprite like a small child, called ʻwong ʻliong.

ˏ涼 ˏ凉 Liang. Cool, fresh; pleasant, refreshing; poor, meager, sparing; in need, straitened; distant, as manners: [7]ˏliong taik, superficial virtue; COM., [8]ˏliong ˏhung, a cool breeze; to take the air; [9]ˏchʻiu ˏliong, the coolness of autumn; [10]ˏchʻá ˏliong, pitiable; [11]ˏliong ˏchiu, a prefecture in Kansuh; [12]ˏliong ˏhung hwoiʾ a summer pleasure-party; COLL., ˏping ˏping ˏliong ˏliong, icy-cool, as fruits, bamboo-mats, etc.; máʾ chaiʾ tek, ˏliong, can't take cooling (medicines).

ˏ梁 Liang. A plank across a stream, a foot-bridge; a dam or piles to stop a current; a ridge-pole; a lintel, a beam, a stretcher; the fastening of a cap-knob; *met.*, the chief, principal; trustworthy: [13]ˏkiong ˏliong, atrocious, worthy of death; [14]tongʾ ˏliong, the main support; *met.*, an able minister; COM., [15]ˏkong ˏliong, a beam, a girder, as over front doors; [16]ˏkio ˏliong, the beams or ties of a bridge; COLL., ˏtong ˏliong, the ridge-pole; pʻeʾ ˏliong, bridge of the nose; ʻtʻĕng ˏliong, the center or movable part of bucket-bails.

ˏ樑 Liong. Used for the last: mast of a boat: COM., siongʾ ˏliong taiʾ kek, good luck to raising the ridge-pole—a sentence written on red paper and pasted on it.

ˏ粱 Lieng. Large-grained millet, a species of Holcus, of which there are yellow, green, and white, varieties: ˏlong ˏtung ˏliong, a term applied to weeds, tares, etc.; COM., ˏkó ˏliong ˏsieu, spirits distilled from the Barbadoes, or tall, millet.

ˏ糧 ˏ粮 Lieng. Food, provision, victuals; soldiers' pay, rations; land taxes: COM., [17]ʻmi ˏliong, rice; [18]ˏliong ˏchiéng, the land tax; [19]ˏchiéng ˏliong, taxes or their commutation; pay;

1 銀兩 ○ 2 兩院 ○ 3 兩湖 ○ 4 兩全 5 兩老 6 兩個 7 凉德 8 凉風 9 秋凉 10 凄凉 11 凉州 12 凉風會 ○ 13 強梁 14 棟梁 15 杠梁 16 橋梁 17 米糧 18 糧錢 19 錢糧 ○

[1]꜀liong ʻchʻó, food, victuals; [2]꜀liong chʻiong꜄ a receipt for payment of taxes; [3]chó꜄ ꜀liong and ꜀heng ꜀liong, home and traveling expenses; [4]꜀liong tó꜄ commissioner of the land-tax; ꜀u ꜀liong pok꜆ chĕü꜄ ꜀ping, can't keep soldiers without rations; COLL., siăh꜆ ꜀chiéng ꜀liong, to eat rations—in government pay, as soldiers.

良 ꜀Liang. Gentle, mild; benignant, liberal, kind-hearted; excellent of its kind, superior, perfect, valuable; a term of praise; loyal, obedient; able, capable; a long time: [5]꜀liong ꜀ing, my good-man; my good wife; [6]꜀liong yă꜄ late at night, past midnight; COM., [7]꜀liong ꜀sing, desiring to do right, a good conscience; [8]꜀liong ꜀ming, a loyal people; [9]꜀liong siéng꜄ or siéng꜄ ꜀liong, good, virtuous; [10]꜀sung ꜀liong, gentle, mild, docile; ꜀chüng ꜀liong, to become virtuous—i. e., forsake vice and marry a husband; ꜀liong ꜀kiong, galangal; COLL., ꜀mó ꜀liong ꜀sing, bad, unconscionable, oppressive; ꜀liong ꜀sing ꜀tʻiéng ʻli ʻtiăng ʻlá ꜀mó ʻmi, good and honest, but no rice in the pan—i. e., honest and poor.

量 ꜀Liang. To measure; to take counsel, to deliberate upon; to consider, to think about: also read liong꜄ q. v.: COM., [11]꜀liong ʻchung, to measure accurately; [12]꜀sü ꜀liong, to think of; [13]꜀song ꜀liong, to deliberate; COLL., ꜀liong tiéng꜄ to give full measure; ꜀liong chʻioh꜆ chʻaung꜄ to measure in feet and inches; ꜀liong ꜀ching kauk꜆ ʻtau, to measure the pints and strike the pecks—i. e., to retail, as rice, etc.

踉 ꜀Liang. To jump: tʻieu꜄ ꜀liong, to hop and dance about. Read ꜀long, as in ꜀long ꜀pong, to wish to go, ready to start.

龍 ꜀Lung. Read ꜀lüng; coll. ꜀liong, as in ꜀pa ꜀liong ꜀sung, to paddle the dragon-boats, as at the festival of the 5th moon; ꜀liong ꜀sung ʻku, the dragon-boat drums.

量꜄ Liang. To measure, to judge, to estimate; to consider, take account of; view of the mind, opinion, estimate; measure, capacity, limit, determinate point or quantity; a liberal mind, good feeling; generosity, magnanimity; ability to eat or drink: also read ꜀liong, q. v.: COM., [14]aing꜄ liong꜄ limited quantity; [15]to꜄ liong꜄ generosity, ability to bear or forgive; [16]pok꜆ chĕü꜄ liong꜄ to over-estimate one's self; COLL., liong꜄ liong꜄ to consider and judge; liong꜄ pok꜆ siăh꜆ ʻchwi, "calculate capacity to drink water"—to estimate one's ability to do a given thing.

亮꜄ Liang. Clear, bright, as the sun or moon; light, lustrous, illumined; transparent; trusting, believing in, in which sense used for the next; in the coll. clear, sonorous, as the voice: [17]꜀kwong liong꜄ bright, lustrous; [18]꜀tʻiéng liong꜄ daylight; COM., [19]ʻlieu liong꜄ discerning clearly; [20]liong꜄ ꜀sa, transparent gauze; [21]liong꜄ pʻau꜄ the

[1]糧草 [2]糧串 [3]坐糧 [4]糧道 [5]良人 [6]良夜 [7]良心 [8]良民 [9]良善 ○ [10]循良 ○ [11]量准 [12]思量 [13]商量 [14]限量 [15]度量 [16]不自量 [17]光亮 ○ [18]天亮 [19]了亮 [20]亮紗 [21]亮炮

morning gun: COLL., [1]*'liong^2 ˛ëng 'ting*, button of secondary-first grade; *˛siăng ˛ing 'yă liong^2* his voice is very clear; *liong^2 liong^2 meng^2* an open, honest face.

諒^2 Liang. To believe, to trust in, to accredit; faithful, veracious, sincere; to suppose, to conjecture; to think favorably of; to aid, to assist: [2]*'kang liong^2* faithful, trustworthy; COM., [3]*'liong^2 pek˛*, or [4]*'liong^2 ˛lai*, to regard as certain or quite probable; [5]*'t'á liong^2* or [6]*kiéng^2 liong^2* to think favorably of, make allowance for; *liong^2 ˛ching*, to take one's circumstances into account; COLL., *liong^2 pek˛ á^2 'k'ing*, think he will most probably be willing.

晾^2 Liang. To hang in the sun to dry; to dry in the sun: *sai^2 liong^2* to put in the sun to dry.

輛^2 Liang. A car, a carriage; a pair of wheels; a classifier of chariots: [7]*'paik˛ liong^2* a hundred chariots.

[The next three are interchangeably read *lwong*].

弄^2 Lung. Nung. Nou. To play with, to sport, to trifle and toy with; to use badinage, to treat disrespectfully; to feel, to handle, to do, to make: in the coll, read *laëng^2* q. v.: [8]*ngwang^2 liong^2* to play, to sport; [9]*liong^2 'ngwa*, to bear a daughter; COM., [10]*liong^2 'k'ieu 'hwang chwok˛* makes ingeniously but it turns out a stupid failure; COLL., *liong^2 'hó 'hó tioh˛* to practice thoroughly.

哢^2 Lung. The note or song of a bird, to chirp; singing, chirping.

戀^2 Lüan. To long for, to think of continually; to dote, to hanker for; ardent longing: [11]*liong^2 mwo^2* to cherish strong attachment for; [12]*liong^2 saik˛* lecherous; [13]*liong^2 liong^2 pok˛ 'siă*, loving tenderly and unable to part with.

(398) Liu.

'**丟** Tiu. Read *˛tiu*; used for the coll. *˛liu*: to throw away, to cast off; to leave undone, to give up; to run away from: *˛liu hwong^2* to throw far; *˛liu ˛piéng*, to fling aside; to throw up (a business); *˛liu 'chau*, has absconded.

˛Liu. A coll. word: pointed, tapering; *met.*, sharp, piercing, as a wind: *˛liu ˛liu*, sharp, pointed; *˛hung 'kiăng ˛liu ˛liu*, the breeze is piercing (to the thinly clad poor)!

'**柳** Liu. The willow; *met.*, pleasure, dissipation; crescent, arched, as the eyebrows; the 24th zodiacal constellation: [14]*'liu sëü^2* willow catkins; COM., [15]*ch'ak˛ 'liu*, to stick up willow-twigs, as at the *˛Ch'ing ˛ming* festival; [16]*˛hwa ˛ká 'liu haëng^2* streets in which brothels are located; [17]*'liu 'ló*, osier buckets; [18]*ngëü^2 'liu*, a species of tamarisk, a decoction of which is used to "bring out the measles"; COLL., *'liu nioh˛ ˛mi*, arched brows; *'liu ngá^2 p'ah˛ ˛nëng o^2 chôi^2* to strike persons with a willow-bough is a sin—

[1]亮紅頂○ [2]簡諒 [3]諒必 [4]諒來 [5]體諒 [6]見諒 [7]百輛 [8]玩弄 [9]弄瓦 [10]弄巧反拙 [11]戀慕 [12]戀色 [13]戀戀不捨 [14]柳絮 [15]插柳 [16]花街柳巷 [17]柳栳○ [18]御柳○

scil., because used by Tauists to expel imps.

絡 Liu. Every ten threads in a woof of cloth; twenty threads of silk; also used for a knot of thread of a hundred lengths; in the coll. a classifier of beards, lappets, and periwigs: COLL., *'chĕng sioh, 'liu*, one lappet, one false cue; *'ngu 'liu ,sü*, the five beards—fully bearded.

罶 Liu. A bamboo trap or net for catching fish and crabs, made somewhat like a seine.

劉 Liu. To kill, to slaughter; to arrange, to set in order, to lay out; a certain weapon, a kind of sword: in the coll. read *,lau*, q. v.

瀏 Liu. Deep, clear water; a strong, swift wind: [1]*,liu lê* the rustling sound of foliage; [2]*,liu ,yong*, a river in Hunan.

流 Liu. To flow, as water; flowing forth; to pass along, to go from one place to another; to spread, to be diffused; to shed, as tears; to shed (blood); to seek, to select; to beg, to entreat; to cast off restraint, to become vicious; a class, an order, a profession; the vicious, low people; roving, vagrant; shifting, floating; to be transported: in the coll. read *,lau*, q. v.: [3]*,liu ,ming*, vagrants; [4]*,liu loi'* to shed tears; [5]*'kiu ,liu*, the nine professions; [6]*'nü ,liu*, females; COM., [7]*,liu hwang'* those banished for crime; [8]*,lung ,liu*, to take turns in doing; [9]*,liu ,tung*, current, as good bills; [10]*,liu lok,* or [11]*,liu laung'* to wander, to vagabondize; [12]*,liu 'chwi p'wo'* a day-book; [13]*,liu ,niêng ong' k'e'* the luck of the current year; [14]*,liu 'hwo ,hung*, inflammatory rheumatism; COLL., *mwong' ,liu*, banishment, transportation.

琉 Liu. A pearl; a vitreous substance; glassy, shining: COM., [15]*,liu ,lié*, a vitreous substance; [16]*,liu ,kiu* (also spoken *,liu ,k'iu*), Loochoo; *,liu ,kwong*, small cups used for oil-lamps; [17]*,liu ,kiu 'kwang*, the Loochoo quarter in the suburbs of Foochow; COLL., *,liu ,kwong t'ek,* the brass or pewter frame of the oil-cup lamp; *,liu ,lié pok,* a clear, discerning mind.

旒 Liu. The narrow pendants of a flag, called *,ki tai'*; the pendants of a crown, hung before and behind.

硫 Liu. Sulphur: COM., [18]*,liu ,hwong* (spoken *,liu ,wong*) brimstone, flowers of sulphur.

留 畱 畄 Liu. To stop, to detain, as guests; to hold, to keep by one, to retain; to keep back; to delay, to procrastinate; slow, dilatory; a long time; a surname: in the coll. read *,lau*, q. v.: [19]*,ti ,liu*, to delay; [20]*,chiă ,liu*, a complimentary display in honor of a good officer; [21]*,liu piék,* a parting gift, keepsake; COM., *,liu eng'* to keep in office longer; *,liu liong'* tenderly attached to; *,siu*

[1]瀏莅 [2]瀏洋 [3]流民 [4]流淚 [5]九流 [6]女流 [7]流犯 [8]輪流 [9]流通 [10]流落 [11]流浪 [12]流水簿 [13]流年運氣 [14]流火瘋 [15]琉璃 [16]琉球 [17]琉球館〇 [18]硫磺 [19]遲留 [20]遮留 [21]留別

꜀liu, to take care of one left, as an orphan; *꜀liu ꜀sing* (or *꜀sing*, or *eʼ*), to keep in mind, to remember carefully.

榴 ꜀Liu. The pomegranate tree: COM., [1]*siohʼ ꜀liu*, the pomegranate; [2]*꜀hwang siohʼ ꜀liu*, the guava; COLL., *꜀liu ꜀ëng*, a pomegranate-red; *꜀hwang siohʼ ꜀liu má ʼ siongʼ tek*, *꜀sang kai ʼ tóh*, guavas can't be put (as offerings) on the tables of the gods; *met.*, applied to worthless persons.

[illegible] ꜀Liu. A kind of bamboo rat: [3]*chek*, *꜀liu*, a species of dog—famed for catching birds, etc.

瘤 ꜀Liu. A tumor, a swelling, a wen, an excrescence on the neck: COM., [4]*꜀hung ꜀liu*, a wind tumor; [5]*haik꜁ ꜀liu*, bloody tumors; [6]*kʻeʼ ꜀liu*, a swelling in the neck aggravated by gusts of anger; [7]*꜀cha ꜀liu*, a wen, a tumor.

遛 ꜀Liu. Lingering, detained on a journey: [8]*taiuʼ ꜀liu*, to loiter; making no progress, hindered.

騮 ꜀Liu. A chestnut or bay horse, with black mane and tail: [9]*ʻchié ꜀liu ʻma*, a sorrel horse with dark mane.

飀 ꜀Liu. The soughing of the wind: [10]*꜀seu ꜀liu*, sighing or whistling of the wind.

鶹 ꜀Liu. A species of owl, called *꜀liu ꜀lié*, or [11]*꜀liu lek*, and noted as a bird of bad omen—said to eat birds and mice.

嘍 ꜀Lou. Read *꜀leu;* coll. *꜀liu*, as in *꜀liu ꜀ló*, subordinate banditti, the band of a chief robber.

꜀Liu. A coll. word, as in *꜀liu ꜀ló*, girt, trim, ready for work.

(399) Lo.

露 Luʼ. Lou. Dew, mist which comes in drops and moistens all things; to bedew; to bless; to disclose, to divulge; to open, to exhibit, to make manifest; disclosed, apparent; nude, naked: [12]*paiʼ loʼ* exposed and frustrated; [13]*loʼ pwoʼ* general orders in an army; COM., [14]*loʼ ꜀tai*, the terrace (of a house); [15]*loʼ ꜀hung*, exposed to the air; [16]*pʻwak*, *loʼ* wet with the dews; [17]*loʼ ꜀ching*, a protruding eyeball; [18]*loʼ ʻtʻá*, nude, stripped; [19]*loʼ kauk*, "exposed bone"—i. e., an evil deed brought to light; COLL., *loʼ ʻla ꜀kʻa*, the feet uncovered; *꜀pʻau ꜀tʻau loʼ ʻliéng*, to show the face in public, as a lonely woman compelled to manage for herself.

滷 Luʼ. Read *ʻlu;* coll. *loʼ*: brine, pickle; briny, saltish: *loʼ chaik*, brine; [20]*꜀siéng loʼ* brine from salt; *꜀ha loʼ* relish of salted prawns; *loʼ hoʼ* brine-besprinkled; *met.*, shameful, scandalous.

潞 Luʼ. A river in Yunnan: COM., [21]*꜀Loʼ ꜀ang*, a department in the south-east of Shansi; [22]*loʼ ʻtong ꜀seng*, a sweet, tonic root from Lo-ang.

路 Luʼ. A road, a path, a way traveled over and made plain; a passage; *met.*, a way of action, duties; overthrown, destroyed;

1石 榴 瘤 瘤 遛 10颼 12敗 14露 16潑 18露 20鹽 22潞
榴 3執 5血 7渣 9紫 飀 露 臺 露 體 滷 黨
2番 [illegible] 瘤 瘤 騮 11鶹 13露 15露 17露 19露 21潞 參
石 4瘋 6氣 8逗 馬 鷅 布 風 睛 骨 安 ○

chief, principal, great; a carriage; a large gate: in the coll. read *tio*^{2} q. v.: *lŭk*^{2} *lo*^{2} land travel; COM., *lo*^{2} *keng*^{2} or *lo*^{2} *˳t'iŏng*, ways, roads; *lo*^{2} *˳teng*, way-lanterns—those hung in front of houses; *lo*^{2} *'ing*, an itinerary—also called *lo*^{2} *˳t'iŏng*.

璐^{2} Lu. Name of a gem: [1]*'pó lo*^{2} a valuable and beautiful gem.

簬^{2} Lu. A fine, lithe species of bamboo, good for making arrows.

鷺^{2} Lu. A long-legged bird, a heron: COM., [2]*˳chio lo*^{2} the red-headed crane—name of a song; [3]*pah˳ lo*^{2} a white egret-heron; COLL., *lo*^{2} *˳li* (or *˳si*), the fishing cormorant; *lo*^{2} *˳li p'aung*^{2} *tioh˳ t'iăk*, "the cormorant falls in with the otter"—rivalry, as in trade, conflicting interests.

賂^{2} Lu. To give money to one, to bribe, to corrupt; to leave; a sacrificial vessel; in the coll. to mock with vain promises, to deceive, to annoy: COM., [4]*'wi lo*^{2} to bribe, bribes; COLL., *'nŭ lo*^{2} *'ngwai*, you mock and disappoint me; *cheng*^{2} *k'ó*^{2} *lo*^{2} *siŏng*^{2} shamefully humbugging.

輅^{2} Lu. A large car, a state carriage; the traces of the harness; great, large: [5]*ngŭk˳ lo*^{2} the imperial chariot; [6]*lo*^{2} *'ch'ing*, a post-house for the emperor.

(400) Ló.

囉 ˓Lo. Read *˳ló*; coll. *˳ló*, as in *˳ló ˳só*, troublesome, annoying; *cheng*^{2} *k'ó*^{2} *˳ló ˳só*, exceedingly vexatious.

˳Ló. A coll. word: slow, dallying, putting off: *˳ló ˳ló 'peng*, or *˳ló ˳ló tioh˳* slack, negligent.

˳Ló. A coll. word, also spoken *'ló*: a euphonic particle, equivalent to commas and a period in a vocal enumeration of subjects or articles: *'ié ˳ló, tóh, ˳ló, ˳chü ˳ló*, chairs, tables, books.

老 ˓ Lao. Old, seventy years of age; used long, old, out of date; old at, skillful; aged, venerable; a term of respect and honor, prefixed to relationships and surnames, Mr., your; to grow old; the 125th radical: in the coll. read *lau*^{2} q. v.: COM., [7]*'ló yok˳* old and feeble; [8]*'ló 'mu*, my venerable mother; [9]*'ló eu*^{2} old and young; [10]*'ló ˳sing*, mature, like one having the experience of age; [11]*'ló 'ch'iu*, skilled at, practiced; [12]*'ló ˳ling*, Mr. Ling; [13]*'ló ˳tiă*, an officer; [14]*'ló ˳ié*, Sir, Your Honor; [15]*'ló ˳kung*, Lautsz', founder of the Tauist sect; [16]*'ló ˳pá*, one who arranges and drums in Tauist or Budhist rites; [17]*'ló sik˳* honest; COLL., [18]*'ló 'sieu*, a wife; [19]*'ló 'peng*, the master of a shop, the boss; [20]*˳ku 'ló*, a leper; *má*^{2} *tó*^{2} *'ló*, short-lived; can't continue long, as a poor business; [21]*'ló 'chio k'ah*, or *'ló ˳kau ˳kwang*, have traded (with him) long; *'ló ˳wa*, a crow, a raven.

1寶璐	3白鷺	5玉輅	7老弱	9老幼	11老手	13老爹	15老君	17老實	19老板	20孤老	21老主
2朱鷺	4賄賂	6輅寢	8老母	10老成	12老林	14老爺	16老排	18老小	○	○	客○

ʻ**筂** Lao. A basket; a bamboo pan or tray, curving up from the bottom: COM., ʻ*mi* ʻ*ló*, baskets in which rice is exposed for sale; ˓*á* ʻ*ló*, shoe-basket, lady's work-basket; ʻ*wong* ʻ*ló*, a market-basket; COLL., ˓*ló* ʻ*ló*, baskets; ʻ*ló* ˓*pwo*, a large bamboo-tray.

ʻ**囉** Lo. Read ˓*ló*; coll. ʻ*ló*: a particle following *kieu*ʾ or ˓*ch'ing* as in ˓*miáng kieu*ʾ ʻ*ló sié*ʾ *nóh*, by what name is he or it called?

ʻ**攞** Lo. To tear, to rend; to split asunder; to choose, to select.

ʻ**潦** Lao. Liao. A great rain; an inundation, a rushing torrent caused by rains; a collection of water; to soak, to macerate: [1]*heng* ʻ*ló*, water collected and running in a road, a torrent; [2]ʻ*ló* ʻ*tó*, self-reliant; rough, unmanerly; COM., [3]ʻ*ló* ʻ*ch'ó*, careless, remiss.

*Ló*ʾ. A coll. word: to expose to the sun or a fire, as things still damp; to dry thoroughly: *ló*ʾ ˓*i* ˓*siong*, to dry clothes.

˓**勞** ˓**劳** Lao. To toil, to labor, to exert one's self; to trouble one; toil, fatigue, hard service; distressed, anxious, careworn; exertion for others, worthy deeds, merit: also read *ló*ʾ q. v.: COM., [4]˓*ló* ʻ*k'u*, toilsome labor; [5]*k'ŭng* ˓*ló*, to be diligent; [6]˓*ló lok*˛ (coll. ˓*ló luk*˛), wearied and distracted; [7]˓*kung* ˓*ló*, merit; [8]˓*ló* ˓*sing hié*ʾ *lik*˛ careworn and fagged; [9]˓*ló tong*ʾ or [10]˓*tó* ˓*ló*, to trouble one (for a favor); [11]˓*ló ka*ʾ I trouble you, Sir! COLL., ˓*ló pwong*ʾ a hard (earned) livelihood; ˓*ló liéng*ʾ (or *tiéng*ʾ); to impose on, to harass one, as with arduous duties.

˓**癆** Lao. Wasting of the body, consumption, atrophy of the viscera; a pining away from care or grief; in Corea, a term for poisonous drugs: COM., [12]˓*ló cheng*ʾ (coll. ˓*ló pang*ʾ or *t'iék*˛ ˓*ló*), consumption, phthisis; COLL., ʻ*tié* ˓*ló*, has become a settled consumption.

˓**蟧** Lao. A kind of univalve shell-fish; also a small species of cicada, called ˓*tá* ˓*ló*.

˓**牢** Lao. An inclosure or stable for cattle, especially sacrificial animals, a corral; domestic animals; a granary; a prison, a jail; firm, secure, strong; to grasp firmly, to remember or know certainly: [13]*t'ai*ʾ ˓*ló*, an ox; [14]*sieu*ʾ ˓*ló*, a sheep; [15]˓*kiéng* ˓*ló*, firm, secure; [16]˓*ló ke*ʾ to remember well; [17]˓*ló* ˓*lung*, a cage; *met.*, a scheme to injure; COM., ˓*kang* ˓*ló*, or ˓*ló ngwoh*˛ a prison.

˓**羅** Lo. A spring-net for birds; a kind of dress-silk, woven like gauze; to spread out, to arrange in rows; a surname: [18]˓*tiong* ˓*ló*, to spread a net; *met.*, to borrow money; [19]*tai*ʾ ˓*ló*, the great canopy, heaven; COM., [20]˓*ló* ˓*king*, or ˓*ló* ˓*pwang*, a compass; [21]˓*ló hang*ʾ distinguished disciples of Budh, of whom 18 were personal; [22]˓*ló* ʻ*wong*, a fowler's net; *met.*, a

1 行潦 2 潦倒 3 潦草 4 勞苦 5 勤勞 6 勞碌 7 功勞 8 勞心 費力 9 勞動 10 多勞 11 勞駕 12 癆症 13 太牢 14 少牢 15 堅牢 16 牢記 17 牢籠 18 張羅 19 大羅 20 羅經 21 羅漢 22 羅網 ○

snare, the net of the law; [1] ˛ló siéng' a gauze-silk fan; [2] ˛ló ˛ngwong, the Loyuen district in Foochow prefecture; [3] ˛ló ˈma, Rome, Roman; COLL., [4] ˛ló ˈtá ˛sa, gauze for sieves; [5] ˛pá ˛ló hang' "Budh's disciples arranged"; met., persons sitting in a row.

囉 ˛Lo. A final sound in singing; the prattle of a child; in the coll. noise, clamor; also used as a final, emphatic particle: in the coll. read ˛ló and ˈló, q. v.: COLL., [6] ˛ló ˛chó a clamor, hubbub; [7] ˛liu ˛ló, banditti; ˛li ˛ló, has come; ˈhó ˛ló, good! well done! se' ˛ló, it's so, yes; ˛i k'ó' ˛ló ˛pá, has he gone?

欏 ˛Lo. A kind of tree growing in Hunan, which readily ignites: ˛ló lok˛ a fence made of stakes.

灑 ˛Lo. A river in Hunan, called Mik˛ ˛ló, in which Ch'ü yüan drowned himself; it flows into Tungting Lake.

籮 ˛Lo. Bamboo baskets, usually without covers or bails, used to contain fruit or grain; baskets with eared holes for cords to carry by.

蘿 ˛Lo. Parasitic plants, as dodder and convolvulus; the small stems of plants: [8] ˈkiék˛ ˛si ˛ló, the vines interlaced — marriage alliance, in allusion to the twining plants, [9] ˈt'o' ˛si and [10] ˈnü ˛ló; COM., [11] ˛ló puk˛ a carrot; a turnip-radish, termed in the coll. ch'ai' ˛t'au; [12] ˛wong ˛ló puk˛ the yellow carrot; COLL., ˛ëng ˛ló puk˛ red carrots; ˛ló puk˛ ch'ai' a mixed dish of turnips, etc.

鑼 ˛Lo. A gong; it is used in armies for wash-basin and boiler: COM., [13] ˛ló ˈku ˈpeng, gongs, drums, and rattling-sticks; [14] ˛ló ˛pwong, a brass wash-basin; COLL., [15] ˈkieu' ˛ló, [16] ˈeu ˛ló, and ˛cha ˛ló, the names of small gongs; [17] ˛ló pwak˛ a kind of small cymbal; [18] ˛ló kwang' kwo' ˛sang k'ó' p'ah˛ carry the gong over the hills to beat it; met., to make gain abroad or of strangers.

腡 ˛Lo. Also read ˛wo: lines in the palm of the hand, by which the Chinese pretend to divine one's fortune; the striae on the ends of the fingers.

醪 ˛Lao. The thick dregs of spirits; strong wines: ˛sung ˛ló, highly flavored spirits, generous wine.

騾 ˛Lo. A mule: COM., pah˛ ˛ló, a white mule; ˛k'ié ˛ló, to ride a mule.

㴲 ˛ Read yoh˛; used in the Paik˛ ˛Ing for the coll. ˛ló: to cook hastily in boiling water, to scald: ˛ló miéng' to scald vermicelli; ˛ló ˛kié, to scald a fowl (in order to pluck off the feathers).

˛Ló. A coll. word: a sort of bamboo or brass horn, curving up at the end, called ˛ló pa'; it is used at dragon-boat festivals and in processions in the first moon.

[1]羅扇 [2]羅源 [3]羅馬 [4]羅底 紗[5]排羅漢 [6]囉嘈 [7]嘍囉 [8]結絲蘿 ○ [9]兎絲 [10]女蘿 [11]蘿蔔 [12]黃蘿蔔 [13]鑼鼓板 [14]鑼盆 [15]叫鑼 [16]嘔鑼 [17]鑼鈸 [18]鑼扛過山去拍 ○

嫪[2] Lao. Also read ꜀*lō*: to hanker after, to dote on; lustful affection, concupiscence; also to envy, to be jealous: *liong*ʾ *lō*² to long, to lust for; *Lō*² *tuk*꜇ a paramour of the mother of Ch'in-shih-huang; hence a libertine.

勞[2] Lao. To reward labor, to note and recompense services; to commend, to encourage, to console: also read ꜀*lō*, q. v.: [1]*'oi*ʾ *lō*² to console.

撈[2] Lao. Also read ꜀*lō*: to dredge, to drag or fish for in the water; to grapple, to hook out: [2]*lō*² ꜀*si* ꜂*siu*, to drag for a corpse; COLL., [3]*kaëng*ʾ ꜂*chwi* ꜀*tüng* *lō*² *ngwok*꜇ *sioh*꜇ *yong*ʾ like hauling in the water for the moon—a bootless task.

澇[2] Lao. Also read ꜀*lō*, and similar to ꜂*lō* (a great rain): an inundation, a torrent, great floods; to steep, to macerate.

邏[2] Lo. To make a circuit, to spy, to inspect, as a guard does; a guard, a patrol; to inclose and screen, as mountains about a valley: [4]꜀*t'ing* *lō*² to guard, as a patrol; COM., [5]꜀*sung* *lō*² to patrol; [6]*lō*² ꜀*ká*, to go about the streets; COLL., *lō*² *lō*² ꜂*tiong*, to saunter about.

痨[2] Lao. Read ꜂*lō*; coll. *lō*², as in [7]꜀*kó* *lō*² the itch; ꜀*sang* ꜀*kó* *lō*² to have the itch.

*Lō*². A coll. word, as in *lō*² ꜀*mwong*, to shut and fasten a door.

*Lō*². A coll. word, as in *lō*² ꜀*pié*, a silver probe, used by coroners in examining a corpse.

(401) Lóh.

絡[2] Lo. Ch'üeh. Read *lok*꜇; used for the coll. *lóh*꜇: to put, as a box into a net of cords; a net, slings made of cords; a case, a cover: see also in *lóh*꜇: [8]꜂*sang* *lóh*꜇ an umbrella-case; [9]*ch'iu* *lóh*꜇ gloves, mittens; *lóh*꜇ ꜂*tié*, put it into (the sling or cover).

落[2] Lo. Lao. La. Read *lok*꜇; coll. *lóh*꜇: to fall, to descend; to tumble, to fall down; *met.*, to become bad, to degenerate, to decay; to set, as the sun; to place, to put in; at, in; a suite of rooms, a building, usually with front and back courts: [10]*taung*ʾ *lóh*꜇ to fall down, as things; [11]*lóh*꜇ *ch'io*ʾ in the house, at home; [12]*nik*꜇ *lóh*꜇ ꜀*sang*, sunset; [13]*lóh*꜇ *siok*꜇ to snow; [14]*lóh*꜇ ꜀*sung*, to take boat; [15]*p'ah*꜇ *lóh*꜇ ꜀*sing*, to produce abortion; [16]*lóh*꜇ *nioh*꜇ the falling of leaves; [17]*lóh*꜇ *ka*ʾ prices fallen; *met.*, a fallen reputation; [18]*lang*ʾ *lóh*꜇ two suites, two buildings; [19]*yék*꜇ *lóh*꜇ good and warm, as clothing; *pok*꜇ ꜀*ti* *ha*ʾ *lóh*꜇ wandered to parts unknown; *lóh*꜇ ꜂*tá*, originally, formerly; *lóh*꜇ ꜀*i* ꜀*k'wong* *t'ó*ʾ fell into his snare—cheated by him.

絡[2] Lo. Ch'üeh. Read *lok*꜇; used for the coll. *lóh*꜇: a net of cords, as used to send a present of caskets in: see also in *lóh*꜇: *lóh*꜇ *lóh*꜇ nets, slings; *ak*꜇ *lóh*꜇ box-nettings.

[1]慰勞 首 [3]共水中 撈月一樣 [4]偵邏 [5]巡邏 [6]邏街 [7]瘑痨 [8]傘絡 [9]手絡 [10]蕩落 [11]落厝 [12]日落山〇 [13]落雪 [14]落船 [15]拍落㛠〇 [16]落葉 [17]落價 [18]二落 [19]熱落

[2]撈屍

(402) Loi.

欙 Read ˏchwi; used in the *Paik*, ˏ*Ing* for the coll. ˏ*loi*: a knot in wood: ˏ*loi* ˏ*t'au*, a knot; ˏ*ch'a* ˏ*loi*, knots in wood; ˏ*loi* ˏ*loi*, knots, knotty.

纇 Lêi. Lei. Read *loi*²; used in the *Paik*, ˏ*Ing* for the coll. ˏ*loi*: knots in silk, thread, or cord: ˏ*loi* ˏ*t'au*, a knot; ˏ*loi kaik*, ˋ*king*, the knot tied tight; ˏ*loi p'ah*, *sioh*, *chiăh*, tie a knot; *p'ăh*, *kiék*, ˏ*loi*, knotted, tangled, as thread.

ˏ*Loi*. A coll. word: to strike, to beat: ˏ*loi sioh*, ˏ*kung* ˏ*t'au*, to give a blow with the fist.

ˏ*Loi*. A coll. word: used somewhat facetiously for gormandizing or stuffing with food: ˏ*loi* ˏ*wong*, all devoured; ˏ*loi* ˋ*pa* ˋ*pa*, has eaten to the full; ˏ*i cheng*² *â*² ˏ*loi*, he is very capable as an eater.

ˋ*Loi*. A coll. word, used in the country for *tiăh*, to pull, to pluck, as flowers or fruit: ˋ*loi sioh*, ˏ*pwo*, to pluck a flower.

雷 ˏLêi. Lei. Thunder; a deafening, thundering noise; to imitate, to do like; a surname: in the coll. read ˏ*lai*, q. v.: [1]ˏ*loi* ˋ*ku*, an octagonal drum; COM., [2]ˏ*loi* ˏ*kung*, Jupiter tonans, thunder; [3]ˏ*loi* ˋ*hwo*, a thunderbolt, lightning; [4]ˏ*loi aik*, killed with lightning; [5]ˏ*loi* ˋ*hiong*, sound of thunder; [6]ˏ*loi* ˏ*tĕng*, the same as another, alike, as two essays; [7]ˏ*ping te*² *ek*, ˏ*sing* ˏ*loi*, a clap of thunder on level ground—a sudden surprise; [8]ˏ*t'iĕng* ˏ*loi* ˋ*ta* ˋ*si*, may the thunder strike you dead!

擂 ˏLêi. Lei. To rub fine, to grind in a mortar, to triturate with pestles; *met.*, to oppress, to treat harshly: in the coll. read *lói*² q. v.

捩 ˏLi. Read *lá*²; used for the coll. ˏ*loi*: to grasp with the thumb and fingers, to pinch and twist: [9]ˏ*loi mek*, ˏ*chiu*, to pinch the eyelids, as of a stupid scholar; [10]ˏ*loi këük*, *haik*, to make the blood coagulate by pinching.

螺 蠃 ˏLo. A name of spiral univalves, like the Lymneus, Voluta, Helix, Murex, &c.; a conch; a volute; a screw; spiral, screw-like: the 2d also read ˋ*lio*, q. v.: COM., [11]ˏ*tié* ˏ*loi*, pond-snails: [12]ˏ*chio* ˏ*loi*, [13]ˋ*t'u* ˏ*loi*, [14]ˏ*wong* ˏ*loi*, [15]ˏ*hwa* ˏ*loi*, the bead, mud, yellow, and figured, univalves—are specimens of marine gasteropods; [16]ˏ*Loi* ˏ*chiu*, a town on the south Min channel: [17]ˏ*loi* ˏ*si*, a screw; [18]ˋ*hiong* ˏ*loi*, conches—used for horns; COLL., ˏ*ch'eng* ˏ*loi kwoi*² a spiral coiffure; ˏ*loi* ˋ*p'i* ˋ*ch'au*, a plant having a small, peltate, doubly crenate leaf, used medicinally for the itch.

罍 ˏLêi. Lei. A porcelain wine vase or goblet with looped ears, having clouds painted on it to denote its inexhaustibility; a large bowl or goblet used in sacrifices.

[1]雷鼓 [2]雷公 [3]雷火 [4]雷厄 [5]雷響 [6]雷同 [7]平地一聲雷 [8]天雷打死 [9]捩目睭 [10]捩搦血 [11]池螺 [12]珠螺 [13]土螺 [14]黃螺 [15]花螺 [16]螺洲 [17]螺絲 [18]響螺

˓*Loi.* A coll. word: the crown of the head; curved striae on the tips of the fingers: ˓*sĕ̤ng* ˓*loi*, a double crown; ˓*loi* ˓*wai*, the crown awry, or to one side; ʻ*ch*ʻ*iu* ʻ*chai* ʻ*kwi* ˓*loi*, a few finger-striae.

擂˒ Lôi. Lei. Interchanged with ˓*loi* (to grind): also read ˓*lui*, q. v.: to beat a drum or gong, to drum; to turn over stones: [1]*loi*˒ ʻ*ku*, to beat a reveille.

淚˒ 泪˒ Lei. Li. To shed tears, to weep, to cry; tears; grief, sorrow: [2]ʻ*ü loi*˒ to rain tears; [3]*loi*˒ ʻ*ngang*, weeping eyes; [4]˓*chio loi*˒ pearly tears; [5]*ha*˒ *loi*˒ or ˓*liu loi*˒ to weep; COLL., *mĕ̤k*˓ *loi*˒ matter in the corners of the eyes.

累˒ Lôi. Lei. To involve, to implicate, to compromise; to bring evil, as on posterity; to put an affair on another; involved, embarrassed, troubled with many affairs: also read ʻ*lwi*, q. v.: COM., [6]*tai*˒ *loi*˒ or [7]˓*liĕng loi*˒ to involve, to implicate; [8]˓*puá loi*˒ to suffer or make amends for another; COLL., *loi*˒ *tioh*˓ *pek*˓ ˓*nĕ̤ng*, to involve others; *loi*˒ ˓*twi* or *loi*˒ *t*ʻ*oi*˒ troublesome, perplexing; *lói*˒ *pa*˒ *loi*˒ ʻ*ná*, to involve one's parents in trouble.

纇˒ Lôi. Lei. Knots in silk thread; a flaw, a defect; confused; harsh, perverse, unmanageable: in the coll. used for ˓*loi*, q. v.: [9]˓*u loi*˒ no defect; [10]ʻ*hung loi*˒ morose and harsh.

彙˒ Lei. ʻHui. Wei. Like the next: a kind of hedgehog or porcupine; a class, a series; many of the same sort, a collection; to classify; dense, abundant: [11]*che*˒ *loi*˒ a dictionary; [12]*loi*˒ *chik*˓ to collect; COM., [13]*loi*˒ ˓*chü*, to arrange books; [14]*loi*˒ *teng*˒ to arrange and edit collections, as of essays; [15]*loi*˒ ˓*mwong loi*˒ to classify according to subjects.

類˒ 類˒ Lôi. Lei. Good, excellent, unselfish; a class, sort, kind, species; imperial sacrifice; to class with, to become one with: [16]*hĕ̤ŭk*˓ *loi*˒ domestic animals; [17]˓*tung loi*˒ of the same sort; [18]*siĕng*˒ *loi*˒ the good; [19]*loi*˒ ʻ*ngŏ* to become like me, one with us; COM., [20]*loi*˒ ʻ*tiĕng*, the book of collections—a work topically arranged; [21]˓*sang sek*˓ *lĕ̤k*˓ *loi*˒ the 36 classes, as of miserable ghosts in the ʻ*p*ʻ*wo to*˒ rites.

酹˒ Also read *liok*˓: to pour out a libation in worship: ʻ*i* ʻ*chiu loi*˒ *te*˒ to pour the wine on the ground.

(403) Lói.

錑˒ Lei. Read *loi*˒; coll. *lói*˒: to perforate, to bore, as with an awl or gimlet: *lói*˒ ʻ*la* ˓*k*ʻ*ĕng* ˓*k*ʻ*ĕng*, to bore a hole; *lói*˒ *sioh*˓ *chaung*˒ to make a hole with the awl.

擂˒ Lôi. Lei. Read ˓*loi*; coll. *lói*˒: to drum; to beat or pound with the fist: [22]*lói*˒ ʻ*ku*, to beat a drum; ˓*kung* ˓*t*ʻ*au lói*˒ to beat with the

[1]擂鼓 [2]雨淚 [3]淚眼 [4]珠淚 [5]下淚 [6]帶累 [7]連累 [8]賠累 [9]無纇 [10]忿纇 [11]字彙 [12]彙集 [13]彙書 [14]彙訂 [15]類門彙 [16]畜類 [17]同類 [18]善類 [19]類我 [20]類典 [21]三十六類 [22]擂鼓〇

福州方言拼音字典

fist; 'lói² t'ak, crushed, broken through by pounding.

耒² Lêi. Lei. The handle and beam of a plow, the plow—invented by Shin-nung; to plow; the 127th radical: lói² sëü¹ a plow; *met.*, agriculture.

銇² Lêi. Lei. To bore; also a plane: COLL., 'lói² chaung' an instrument for boring holes, the Chinese augur or gimlet—usually called ³,t'iëng ,pang lói², also ,pu luk, lói² and ,pa lak, lói².

Lói². A coll. word; used for ,li (to come): lói² ,ló, he has come.

(404) Lok.

碌 Lu. Liu. A green-colored stone, chrysoprase or malachite? stony, rocky; rough, uneven ground; small; laborious, toilsome; in the coll. to pass swiftly, as time; very, extremely: ⁴,iing lok, inefficient, worthless; ⁵lok, lok, rough, uneducated: COLL., ⁶lok, lok, kwo' to pass rapidly, as the days; lok, lok, ,u, very black.

角 用 Chiao. As in ⁷Lok, 'li ,siëng ,seng, one of four noted graybeards in the Han dynasty: usually read kaëk, q. v.

Lok,. A coll. word: to slip out of place, to slip, as a knot; to escape, to sneak away: lok, 'chau, to get away, to run off; lok, 'ch'iu, to slip from the hand; lok, k'o² "slipped from the mortar"; *met.*, has come out, divulged, as a secret, one's poverty, etc.

咯 Lo. To dispute; disputatious, contentious. Read kauk,: the cry of a cock or wild fowl.

烙² Lo. Lao. To burn, to burn in, to brand; a heated needle, a branding-iron; red-hot: ⁸p'au' lok, the ancient punishment of embracing a heated brass column.

絡² Lo. Ch'üeh. Hemp not yet macerated; silky cotton fiber, staple of cotton; continuous, joined; to bind, to tie around; to inclose, to wrap; slings, thread-nettings for boxes; the blood vessels: used for the coll. lóh, and lóh, q. v.: ⁹mek, lok, the pulse; ¹⁰,liëng lok, joined, continuous; COM., ¹¹,king lok, the blood vessels; ¹²,sing ,pau lok, the pericardium; ¹³kek, lok, (coll. kek, móh,), the inner pellicle of orange-peel.

酪² Lo. Lao. The thick part of milk, cream; dried milk, curds or liquors of mare's milk; fat, greasy, unctuous: COM., ¹⁴haing' lok, ,t'ong, a sweetened emulsion of almonds and rice.

落² Lo. Lao. La. Lu. The fall of leaves or rain; to fall, to tumble down, to fall into; to come down, to descend to or into; to let fall, to lay down; to put into, to enter, as items in accounts; the place to which one goes, the place of gathering; settled, fixed, arranged: in the coll. read lóh, q. v.: ,ch'ong lok, a village res-

¹檑埸〇 ²銇錐〇 ³天平銇〇 ⁴庸碌〇 ⁵碌碌〇 ⁶碌碌過〇 ⁷角里先生 ⁸炮烙 ⁹脈絡 ¹⁰連絡 ¹¹經絡 ¹²心包絡〇 ¹³橘絡〇 ¹⁴杏酪湯〇

idence; *tai² ˏhwong lok₂* term for five years of a cycle with *sëü²* in their name: COM., ¹*lok₂ ˏk'ung*, vain, profitless; ²*ˏling lok₂* fallen off, as leaves; ³*lok₂ pok₂* (coll. *lok₂ lá²* or *lok₂ säü²*), reduced in wealth, poor; ⁴*chiok₂ lok₂* fixed, certain, as a trace, a means; ⁵*lok₂ ˋch'ó ˏui k'aiu²* "fall into the grass and become a robber"—one compelled by poverty to steal.

樂₂ Lo. Yo. Yao. Pleasure, delight, joy; happiness, ease; mirth, gratulation; to rejoice, to delight in, to esteem a pleasure: also read *ngok₂* and *ngau²* q. v.: COM., ⁶*ˏang lok₂* peaceful and happy; ⁷*chauk₂ lok₂* to make merry; ⁸*ˏheng lok₂* portrait of a living person; ⁹*ˏtiong lok₂* (spoken *ˏtiong lóh₂*) the Changloh district in Foochow prefecture; ¹⁰*lok₂ e²* pleased, content.

濼₂ Lo. Name of a river in Shantung. Read *p'óh₂*: a bank; a large pool, an estuary.

洛₂ Lo. Lä. A river in Honan, a large tributary of the Yellow River; a dazzling glare from water: COM., ¹¹*lok₂ ˏyong*, the ancient Lohyang in Honan, capital of Fuhhi; ¹²*lok₂ ˏyong ˏkio*, a famous bridge near Chinchew.

駱₂ Lo. A white horse with a black mane; an ancient state near Annam or Cochin China: COM., ¹³*lok₂ ˏtó*, a camel.

雒₂ Lo. Interchanged with the last two: a kind of bird: ¹⁴*lok₂ lok₂ ˏyong*, timid, fearful.

(405) **Long.**

ˏLong. A coll. word: to pound, to knock against, to strike horizontally: *ˏlong ˏk'wi*, to knock open; *ˏlong sioh₂ ˏt'ui*, to give a blow (with the fist).

ˏLong. A coll. word, used at the close of an enumeration of articles or subjects, in the sense of &c., et cetera, and such like.

ˏLong. A coll. word, as in *ˏlong ˏlong ˏsi*, a kind of rice-ball, boiled and rolled in sugar and sesame-seeds.

ˋ朗 Lang. Clear, bright, lustrous, as the moon or sky; clearness; distinct, as utterance: in the coll. cool, coolish; thin, as gruel with only a few kernels of rice: ¹⁵*ˏming ˋlong*, clear, light; ¹⁶*ˋlong chieu²* ask your aid, blessed by you—a complimentary phrase in epistles; ¹⁷*ngwok₂ ˋlong*, moonshine; COM., ¹⁸*ˏsiăng ˏing ˋlong ˋlong*, the voice distinct; ¹⁹*ˋlong ˋlong ˏch'ing ˏch'ing*, bright and clear; thin, as gruel.

ˋ䄹 An unauthorised character used in the *Paik₂ ˏIng* for the coll. *ˋlong*: a garment worn next the person, a shirt, a tunic: ²⁰*ˋtoi ˋlong*, a shirt; *siăng² ˋlong*, a shirt or jacket of net-work; *tëük₂ ˋlong*, a shirt of netted bamboo-bugles; *ˋsieu seu² ˋlong*, a lady's tunic or under-garment; *ˏlong ˋlong*

¹落空 ²零落 ³落薄 ⁴着落 ⁵落草爲寇 ⁶安樂 ⁷作樂 ⁸行樂 ⁹長樂 ¹⁰樂意 ¹¹洛陽 ¹²洛陽橋 ¹³駱駝 ¹⁴雒雒然 ¹⁵明朗 ¹⁶朗照 ¹⁷月朗 ¹⁸聲音朗朗 ¹⁹朗朗清清 ²⁰短䄹

福州方言拼音字典

ₛt'ŭng kak꜀ kak꜀ only a shirt and a spencer—i. e., very poorly clad.

閬 ˋLang. Vacant, empty, unoccupied; wide, as a desert: ˋlong ˋlong, void, extensive; [1]ˋlong ˋwong, fairy land. Read laung²: a lofty door or gateway.

廊 ₛLang. Rooms or porches on the sides of the court; chambers adjoining the main house; covered passages in front of the hall, like galleries or corridors: [2]ₛlong ˋu, side galleries; [3]ₛlong mieu² ₛchai, great talents, as of statesmen; COM., [4]ₛhui ₛlong, porches on the sides of a court; [5]ˋliong ₛlong, side-rooms, as for offices in a yamun; COLL., [6]ˋch'ok꜀ ₛiu ₛlong, porches; ₛlong ˋtau, the anteroom of a chamber; ₛlong ₛt'au lauk꜀ ₛlong ˋmwoi, to saunter from end to end of a porch.

榔 根 ₛLang. A species of palm having an edible pith: [7]ˋkeu ₛlong, a Prunus found in Kwangtung; [8]ₛming ₛlong a rattle for driving fish into nets; COM., [9]ₛping ₛlong, the areca or betel-nut.

狼 ₛLang. A wolf or jackal, whose howl scares animals; met., cruel, truculent, oppressive: COM., [10]ₛchai ₛlong (coll. ₛch'ai ₛlong), a wolf; [11]ₛlong pwoi² involved, embarrassed; [12]ₛlong lě² cruel, oppressive; [13]ₛlong chik꜀ confused, scattered; met., in bad repute, as one's name; ₛlong ₛsing ˋkeu haing² a wolf's heart and dog's conduct—cruel, rapacious; COLL., ₛlong pwoi² k'ek꜀ ₛk'wi, in very great distress; ₛlong ₛki ch'ëüng² large cannon; ₛlong ˋch'eng, a pole supported on the crotches of two bamboos (for drying clothes).

郎 ₛLang. A place or summer-house in the Lu state; a term of respect for officials and others; a gentleman; a male: used for ₛnong in the coll. q. v.: [14]ₛlong ₛkung, my husband; COM., [15]ₛsing ₛlong, a bridegroom; [16]se² ₛlong, the vice-president of a Board; [17]leng² ₛlong (coll. ₛlong ₛchü), your son; COLL., ₛlong pa² (spoken ₛnong ma²), a father; ₛlong ₛtüng, a physician, a doctor.

瑯 琅 ₛLang. A precious stone: ₛlong ₛkang, coral, madrepore; ₛling ₛlong, the tinkling of gems; COM., ₛlong t'iong² a kind of long drum, shaped like an hour-glass.

鋃 Lang. Like the last: a long lock or clasp, called ₛlong ₛtong; a lock for the neck; met., something grievous to bear.

稂 ₛLang. Weeds in rice or any grain, darnel: ₛlong ˋiu, darnel, tare; COLL., ₛlong pok꜀ ₛlong seu² pok꜀ seu² neither darnel nor tares; met., good for nothing, worthless, as persons.

筤 ₛLang. Young bamboos, called [18]ₛch'ong ₛlong tüük꜀; a basket; an ornamented screen for a carriage.

[1]閬苑 [2]廊廡 [3]廊廟才○ [4]迴廊 [5]兩廊 [6]出遊廊○ [7]枸榔 [8]鳴榔 [9]檳榔 [10]豺狼 [11]狼狽○ [12]狼戾○ [13]狼藉○ [14]郎君 [15]新郎 [16]侍郎 [17]令郎 [18]蒼筤竹○

蒗 ꜁Lang. A kind of arundo, a sedge growing in marshes: [1]'꜀long taung' scammony or comfrey, whose seeds are said to craze people.

蜋 ꜁Lang. A mantis, called [2]꜀long ꜀long; met., ineffectual efforts; [3]꜀long ꜀long pwo' ꜀sieng, the mantis catches the cicada, (and the shrike catches the mantis). Read ꜀liong, as in [4]꜀kiong ꜀liong, the tumble-dung or pellet-beetle.

躴 ꜁Lang. As in [5]꜀long ꜀k'ong, tall in stature; COLL., ꜀long ꜀k'ong, large, bulky, unwieldy, cumbersome.

꜁Long. A coll. word, as in ꜀kó ꜀long, whole, entire; ꜀kó ꜀long ꜀teu, the whole piece, or strip.

꜁Long. A coll. word: to "overhand" in sewing; also a numerative of lengths of grass-cloth-nettle thread, each consisting of four or five separate threads.

(406) Lu.

꜀Lu. A coll. word: a noise made in calling dogs or hogs; similar to lio' q. v.

꜀Lu. A coll. word, as in ꜀lu ꜀t'i, to carry off things, to take them without leave.

魯 ꜂Lu. Blunt, dull, stupid, obtuse; a feudal state, now the province of Shantung; a surname: [6]'lu tong' dull in intellect; COM., [7]'lu kwok, the native country of Confucius; [8]'Lu ꜀pang, the patron of carpenters; [9]'Lu ꜀nang 'chü, name of an ancient worthy; met., a strict moralist: COLL., [10]'lu pek, a small bird of a changeable ash and green color; 'lu pek, ꜀sang ꜀ngiè laung' the 'lu pek, laying goose-eggs; met., a small thing producing great results.

櫓 艣 ꜂Lu. The scull on the stern of a boat; the first also means a great buckler of wood used on walls, also a high, movable tower: COM., [11]'yeu 'lu, to scull; COLL., [12]'lu k'ek, the scull-pivot; [13]'lu ꜀ch'ong the scull-socket; 'lu tai' or 'lu kwang' sóh, the scull-tie.

鹵 ꜂Lu. Salt, rock salt; salt lands, salt ponds or licks; a salt marsh, barren lands; rude, rough, uncivil; the 197th radical: [14]'lu pwo' order of the imperial cavalcade; [15]꜀sung 'lu, barren land; COM., [16]'lu ak, corned duck: [17]'lu chaik, pickle; [18]'lu ꜀hiong, spice for pickle; [19]'lu 'mong, or ꜀ch'u 'lu, rude, boorish; COLL., [20]'lu ang' a wager between students at an examination.

擄 ꜂Lu. Fierce, harsh, violent; to shake violently; to act in an arrogant manner.

擄 ꜂Lu. Read 'lio; coll. 'lu, as in 'lu 'ch'iong 'lu tok, to take violently—a phrase used chidingly to one taking things without leave.

'Lu. A coll. word, as in ꜀lu 'lu, or 'lu hā' a small yellowish or ash-colored crab; it is salted for the market.

廬 ꜁Lu. Lü. A thatched hovel, a hut, a cottage, a choltry by the roadside; a shed, a lodge in a field for workmen; a poor house, my

[1]蒗若 [2]蝗蜋 [3]蝗蜋捕蟬 [4]蜣蜋 [5]躴躿 [6]魯鈍 [7]魯國 [8]魯般 [9]魯男子 [10]魯鵖 ○ [11]搖櫓 ○ [12]櫓隙 [13]櫓床 [14]鹵簿 [15]淳鹵 [16]鹵鴨 [17]鹵汁 [18]鹵香 [19]鹵莽 [20]鹵案 ○

mean abode; to pass the night at: *pe*ˀ ꜀*lu*, my house; ꜀*tiéng* ꜀*lu*, a lodge in a field; ꜀*man* ꜀*lu*, a thatched shed.

籚 ꜀Lu. Interchanged with the last: a rush-like bamboo; a large covered basket; the handle of a spear; a prop: COM., [1]꜀*lu tëük*ꜙ the rush-bamboo; [2]꜀*lu* ʻ*kwang* ꜀*hu pek*, a superior kind of pencil.

盧 ꜀Lu. Interchanged with the last and the next two: a vessel for holding rice; a pan for fire; a grog-shop; a black color; used in the names of a sword, a spear, a bee, and a calabash; a kind of rush; a surname: [3]꜀*lu* ꜀*hu*, or ꜀*hu* ꜀*lu*, to laugh; ꜀*hu* ꜀*lu*, a calabash.

壚 ꜀Lu. Black, stiff clods, ground not yet harrowed; yellow earth: [4]ʻ*chiu* ꜀*lu*, a wine-shop; [5]꜀*wong* ꜀*lu*, the yellow clods—the grave, hades.

鑪 ꜀Lu. A vessel for spirits; a tavern; a furnace, a fire-place: [6]꜀*hwong* ꜀*lu*, a wine-vessel; [7]*hak*ꜙ ꜀*lu*, a long, slender arrow; [8]꜀*tong* ꜀*lu*, a shop where hot spirits are sold.

蘆 ꜀Lu. High rushes along river courses, rushes before they have flowered; reeds for repairing dikes: [9]꜀*lu* ʻ*wi*, rushes; COM., [10]꜀*lá* ꜀*lu*, hellebore; [11]꜀*lu kwoi*ˀ aloes; COLL., ꜀*lu* ʻ*ch'au ch'ioh*ꜙ rush-mats.

櫨 ꜀Lu. The blocks of wood between a post and the rafters; a queen-post; the peduncle of flowers: [12]꜀*lu kek*, the loquat or Chinese medlar (Eriobotrya Japonica); [13]꜀*kié* ꜀*lu*, tie-pieces supporting the rafters.

瀘 ꜀Lu. A river in the east of Kiangsi; an inferior prefecture in Sz'chuen on the R. Yangtsz': [14]꜀*Lu* ʻ*chwi*, tributary of the Yangtsz' in Sz'chuen.

爐 炉 ꜀Lu. A furnace, brazier, grate; a fire-place, a stove; a chafing-dish, a portable grate for coals; a censer: COM., [15]ʻ*hwi* ꜀*lu*, a fire-place; [16]꜀*hiong* ꜀*lu*, an incense-urn; [17]ʻ*ch'iu* ꜀*lu*, a brass hand-stove; [18]ʻ*chwi* ʻ*hwo* ꜀*lu*, a hot water urn, as in wine and barber shops; [19]꜀*lu chau*ˀ the furnaces—number of families, population; [20]꜀*lu a*ˀ *tá*ˀ ʻ*chü*, the disciple below the censer—i. e., the worshipper.

瓐 ꜀Lu. A kind of precious stone, a gem of a green color.

纑 ꜀Lu. A species of hemp; hempen threads; to hatchel flax or hemp, to make it ready for weaving.

臚 ꜀Lu. The skin; the abdomen; to arrange, to set in order, to spread out; to transmit, to convey, as orders; to hand down, to show, to intimate to: ꜀*lu liék*ꜙ to arrange; ꜀*lu* ꜀*ting*, to communicate, to state; COM., ꜀*hung* ꜀*lu sé*ˀ the Court of Ceremonies; ꜀*tiong* ꜀*lu*, the fourth among the Hanlin.

艫 ꜀Lu. A name for boats; the stem or stern of a vessel: *tük*ꜙ ꜀*lu*, a boat's stem and stern.

---

1 籚竹 2 籚管湖筆 3 盧胡 4 酒壚 5 黃壚 6 方鑪 7 鉀鑪 8 當鑪 9 蘆葦 10 藜蘆 ○ 11 蘆薈 12 櫨橘 13 枅櫨 14 瀘水 15 火爐 16 香爐 17 手爐 18 水火爐 19 爐灶 ○ 20 爐下弟子

轤 ˏLu. A windlass, a pulley, a snatch-block: in the coll. read ˏlü, q. v.: ¹ˋlük, ˏlu, pulley and rope for drawing things, a windlass.

驢 ˏLu. Lü. An ass: in the coll. read ˏlē, q. v.: ²ˋyâ ˏlu, the wild ass.

鱸 ˏLu. A term for the Labrax genus of fishes: ³pek, ˏlu, the white labrax, a perch; ⁴ˏlu kwoiˀ sliced or minced labrax; COM., ⁵ˏlu ˏngü, the white or spotted labrax.

顱 ˏLu. The skull of a man: ⁶ˏt'eu ˏlu, the skull of a human skeleton.

鸕 ˏLu. The fishing cormorant, called ⁷ˏlu ˏchü: in the coll. termed loˀ ˏsi, q. v.

(407) Lü.

呂 ˋLü. The back bone, the spine, as represented by the character; the *yin*, or flat, notes in music; a surname: ⁸lëk, ˋlü, the six flat notes; ⁹ˏsing ˋlü, loyal; COM., ¹⁰ˋlü ˏtung ˏping, one of the genii—patron of barbers; ¹¹ˋlü songˀ (coll. ˏlü songˀ) Spain; ˋsieu ˋlü songˀ Luzon or Manila.

侶 ˋLü. An associate, a fellow, a colleague; to accompany, to associate with: ¹²p'wangˀ ˋlü, a partner, companion; COM., ¹³kiék, ˋlü, to make up a party, form a company; ¹⁴ˏpong ˋlü, comrades, helpers.

筥 ˋLü. A round, osier basket, holding about half a peck of rice; four handfuls of grain or a sheaf: ¹⁵ˏkwong ˋlü, square and round baskets.

莒 ˋLü. A name for the taro in Shantung; name of a small ancient state in that province, now the superior district of Lüchou in Ichoufu.

旅 ˋLü. A battalion of 500 men; a stranger, a visitor, a guest, a lodger or sojourner; a company, many; to travel about; to sojourn, to lodge; an imperial sacrifice; a road, a way; to arrange in order; from abroad, foreign; self-planted or wild grain; the 56th diagram: ¹⁶ˏsiong ˋlü, or ¹⁷ˋlü k'aik, a traveling merchant; ¹⁸ˏheng ˋlü, a traveler; ¹⁹ˋlü ch'ëüˀ in order; ²⁰ˋlü taingˀ a lodging-house.

膂 ˋLü. The backbone, the spine: ²¹ˏsing ˋlü, heart and flesh; *met.*, a loyal minister; COM., ²²ˋlü lik, strong, strength.

ˋ*Lü.* A coll. word, as in ˋlü ch'ëüˀ often, constantly—probably a corruption of lëüˀ ch'ëü q. v.

櫚 ˏLü. A kind of palm, having sharp, pointed leaves: ˏlü muk, a fine-grained, red wood from Annam.

閭 ˏLü. The gate of a ward or village; a hamlet of 25 houses or families; a habitation; to dwell: ˏlü ˋli, a village-gate; ˏmwong ˏlü, a dwelling; COM., ˏLü ˏsang, the orthodox Tauist Mountain; ˏlü

¹轆轤 ²野驢 ³白鱸 ⁴鱸鱠 ⁵鱸魚 ⁶頭顱 ⁷鸕鶿 ⁸六呂 ⁹心呂 ¹⁰呂洞賓 ¹¹呂宋〇 ¹²伴侶 ¹³結侶 ¹⁴幫侶 ¹⁵筐筥 ¹⁶商旅 ¹⁷旅客 ¹⁸行旅 ¹⁹旅次 ²⁰旅店 ²¹心膂 ²²膂力〇

福州方言拼音字典

ˌsang hwak, *ʻchio*, the magician of Mt. Lü—who taught *ˌLing ʻchwi ʻná*.

轤 ˌLu. Read *ˌlu*, coll. *ˌlü*, as in *luk*ˌ *ˌlü*, a windlass; used in a *met.* sense, as in *luk*ˌ *ˌlü ˌki wa*ʾ ambiguous language.

(408) Lui.

擂 ˌLêi. Lei. To rub fine, to triturate with a pestle, to pulverize: also read *loi*ʾ q. v.: COM., [1]*ˌlui pwuk*, (or *ʻwang*), an earthen dish to grind paints or medicines in; [2]*ˌlui ˌngang laiu*ʾ to grind paints; COLL., *ˌlui eu*ʾ *eu*ʾ or *ˌlui mwak*ˌ *mwak*ˌ to grind fine.

縲 ˌLêi. Lei. A large rope; black ropes; to bind with cords, as criminals: [3]*ˌlui siék*, fetters, bonds.

纍 ˌLêi. Lei. Interchanged with the last: to join in a regular series, to concatenate; to place on, to superimpose; to involve, to entangle; to arrest, to detain, to bind a prisoner; to wind, to spread, as creepers; the hooks or ties of armor: [4]*ˌlui ˌsing*, a servant in bonds; [5]*ˌlui ˌlui*, discontented, forlorn; [6]*ˌlui hié*ʾ to bind with cords.

蔂 虆 ˌLêi. Lei. A kind of hod, a basket for carrying earth; creeping plants: [7]*ˌlui ˌli*, a hod or basket; [8]*ˌing ˌlui*, a basket full.

羸 ˌLêi. Lei. Lean, emaciated, meager; feeble, infirm, debilitated; caught in, entangled; turned over: [9]*ˌlui saiu*ʾ very lean; [10]*ˌlui ˌki kaëk*, caught by its horns; [11]*ˌlui hok*, turned bottom up.

ˌLui. A coll. word: worn by toil, fagged, wearied, careworn: *ˌlui lŏh*ˌ overworked, jaded; *ˌlui pang*ʾ made sick, as by toil or incessant care; *ˌlui ʻkwi nik*ˌ overburdened sevéral days.

(409) Luk.

律 Lü. ˌ A fixed law, a statute, an ordinance; a regulation, a command; a penal law; a military code; to divide, to adjust; to state, to declare, to record; to estimate the merits of; to trim the hair; the rules of versification; the *yang*, or sharped, notes in music; a stanza, a distich: [12]*lĕk*ˌ *luk*ˌ the six sharped notes; COM., [13]*luk*ˌ *hwak*, laws, penal statutes; [14]*luk*ˌ *kai*ʾ commandments; [15]*luk*ˌ *lié*ʾ the statutes, code of a country; [16]*luk*ˌ *hwak*ˌ *ˌnang ˌtó*, hard to escape the penalty of law.

率 Lü. ˌ A general number; the stretch, as of a bow; a seam or opening, as of the lapel in a garment; name of an office: also read *sauk*, q. v.

繂 Lü. ˌ A large bamboo rope or hawser for tracking boats; cords for lowering coffins, or for letting down into mines: in the coll. to raise or lower by cords; to climb up or descend, as by a pole, post, or rope: [17]*luk*ˌ *ʻnau*, cords for lowering a coffin; COLL., [18]*luk*ˌ *siong*ʾ to raise; to climb up; *luk*ˌ *kiä*ʾ to lower; *luk*ˌ *tʻeu*ʾ to climb a post; *luk*ˌ *kwo*ʾ *ˌchʻiong*, to climb over

[1]擂砵 [2]擂顏料 [3]縲絏 [4]纍臣 [5]纍纍 [6]纍繫 [7]蔂梩 [8]盈虆 [9]羸瘦 [10]羸其角 [11]羸覆 [12]六律 [13]律法 [14]律誡 [15]律例 [16]律法難逃 [17]繂繞 [18]繂上

a wall, as by a pole set against it; *luk, sóh,* a pulley-rope; *luk, 'piăng,* a pulley.

膔 Lü. The fat about the inwards of a sacrificial animal, anciently burnt in temples: *luk, ˛lieu,* the inside fat.

轆 Lu. Read *lük,*; coll. *luk,* as in *luk, ˛lü wa'* ambiguous language, double entente.

(410) Lük.

鹿 Lu. A stag, a deer, cervine animals; the 198th radical: in the coll. read *lĕk,* q. v.: [1] *˛iu lük,* a doe; com., [2] *lük, ˛ming yêng'* a feast to Küjin graduates at the governor's; [3] *˛tüng yêng' lük, ˛ming,* a second feast furnished them 60 years after the first.

摝 Lu. To move, to shake, to agitate; to shake, as a rattle, to ring: [4] *lük, tok,* to rattle a bell.

轆 Lu. The rut made by wheels; a wheel, a roller: in the coll. read *luk,* q. v.: [5] *lik, lük,* a wheel-rut; also spinning-wheel.

麓 Lu. The foot of a hill, a slope; a wooded declivity: [6] *lük, 'siu,* a forester; [7] *˛ling lük,* wooded places on hills.

簏 Lu. A high basket for inclosing fowls: [8] *˛chü lük,* a basket for books.

籙 Lu. A map or chart; ancient records, books: [9] *˛tu lük,* a chart; [10] *˛hu lük,* a written charm.

漉 Lu. A river in Chansha-fu in Hunan; to ooze out; clear water; water drained off: [11] *lük, chaik, 'swa te'* the dripping water sprinkles the ground.

祿 Lu. The emoluments of office, salary, income, pay; prosperity, enjoyment of good things; to enjoy an income; to salary: [12] *hong' lük,* salary; [13] *sik, lük,* pleasures of the table; [14] *˛kwong lük, se'* the Banqueting Office at Peking; com., [15] *˛huí lük,* god of fire, a conflagration; [16] *˛t'iêng pok, ˛seng ˛u lük, ˛chi ˛ing,* Heaven does not produce men without the means of living.

綠 Lu. Lü. Green color: in the coll. read *lioh,* q. v.: *lük, ˛i ˛long,* a rising man, one distinguished for his talents.

醁 Lu. A pleasant kind of spirits, called [17] *˛ling lük,* made with water from Lake Ling in Hunan.

騄 Lu. A famous steed, called [18] *lük, 'ngi,* belonging to the emperor Muh-wang of the Chow dynasty.

菉 Lu. A kind of plant or grass, called *lük, ük,* of which cloth may be made.

蓼 Liao. Long and large, as vegetation or grass: also read *'lieu,* q. v.: *lük, lük, 'chiă ˛ngó,* the long, large rush.

[1]麀鹿 [2]鹿鳴宴 [3]重宴鹿鳴 [4]摝鐸 [5]轣轆 [6]麓守 [7]林麓 [8]書簏 [9]圖籙 [10]符籙 [11]漉汁灑地 [12]俸祿 [13]食祿 [14]光祿寺 [15]回祿 [16]天不生無祿之人 [17]醽醁 [18]騄駬 ○

福州方言拼音字典

僇 Lu. ₂ Interchanged with the next: to disgrace, to put to shame, to injure; to act foolishly: [1]tai² lŭk₂ great disgrace.

戮 Lu. ₂ To kill, to slay, as in war or for crime, to massacre: to mangle, to disfigure or disgrace a corpse; to disgrace; to act shamefully: [2]sak₂ lŭk₂ to slaughter; [3]lŭk₂ ŭk₂ to disgrace; [4]lŭk₂ lik₂ united effort; COM., [5]lŭk₂ ˌsi, to treat a corpse barbarously.

稑穋 Lu. ₂ Late planted grain which ripens early in the season; that which ripens late though planted early is called ˌtŭng; the second, read ˌk'iu, means a species of grain.

陸 Lu. Lŭ. Liu. ₂ High, dry land, terra firma; land, as distinguished from water: used as the complex form of lĕk₂ (six): [6]ʻchwi lŭk₂ by water and land; [7]lŭk₂ ˌliê, mixed, confused; uneven; COM., [8]lŭk₂ sŭk₂ in succession, successively; COLL., [9]lŭk₂ tiô² land travel; [10]lŭk₂ tiô² ˌt'i tok₂ chief of the land forces, a major-general.

(411) Lung.

䁖 Lun. ˌ Read ʻkung and ʻlung; coll. ˌlung, as in mek₂ ˌchiu ˌlung ˌlung ʻtiong, the eyes rolling about.

ˌLung. A coll. word: to swing, to vibrate, to move to and fro, as things suspended; to go about busily, hurried, pressed: ˌlung tek₂ tioh₂ swung so as to hit; ˌlung nah₂ (or náh₂), to indent by swinging against; ˌlung ˌlung ʻtiong, to swing to and fro; to go about busily.

攏 Lung. ʻ Also read ˌlung: to grasp, to seize, to hold; to pull, to drag; to charge on, to attack; to bring close to, to collect; to exert one's self; to operate on, to act with; to effect an end: in the coll. read ʻlĕng, q. v.: [11]ʻlung hwak₂ to bind the hair; [12]au² ʻlung, to draw lots for drinking at feasts; [13]ʻlung liok₂ to plunder.

竉 Lung. ʻ Also read ˌlung and ʻlŭng: a hole, and aperture, a fissure or wide cleft; a den: [14]ʻk'ung ʻlung, a hole, an aperture.

壟 Lung. ʻ Also read ʻlŭng: a mound in a field, as for graves; a tumulus, tomb grave; to engross, to buy, up goods: [15]ˌk'iu ʻlung, a mound, a grave; [16]ʻlung twang² to engross, to speculate in.

隴 Lung. ʻ Also read ʻlŭng: an embankment, a dike to prevent the irruption of waters: used in the coll. phrase for all, the whole: [17]ʻLung ˌsá, an old name for the west of Shensi; [18]ʻlung ʻmeu, dikes and fields; COM., [19]taik₂ ʻlung wong² sŭk₂ having got Shensí he wants Sz'chuen; met., to covet something more or better; COLL., ʻlung ʻchung, all, entire, the whole; ʻlung ʻchung ˌli, all come; to take or buy all.

倫 Lun. Lŭn. ˌ Constant, regular, what is regarded as right and proper; a species, a class, an order, a sex; natural law, affinity, relationships; to choose, to distinguish:

[1]大僇 [2]殺戮 [3]戮辱 [4]戮力 [5]戮尸 [6]水陸 [7]陸離 [8]陸續 [9]陸路 [10]陸路提督 ○ [11]攏髮 [12]拗攏 [13]攏掠 [14]孔竉 [15]丘壟 [16]壟斷 [17]隴西 [18]隴畝 [19]得隴望蜀

[1]*₍lung loi*ʾ a class, as mankind; [2]*₍t'iéng ₍lung*, parents; [3]*₍lung ch'ëüʾ* a series; COM., [4]*'ngu ₍lung*, the five social relations; [5]*₍lung ₍siong*, the relations and constant virtues; [6]*'lwangʾ ₍lung*, to confuse or violate relationships, as by incest or other atrocious acts.

崙 ₅Lun. Lün. Also read *₍long*: a range of mountains, called [7]*₍k'ong ₍lung*, the Koulkun Mts. in Koko-nor: used for the coll. *laungʾ* q. v.

掄 ₅Lun. Lün. To choose, as fit persons for office; to select, to pick out; to connect, to join together: [8]*₍lung 'song*, to select, as suitable persons; [9]*₍lung ₍chai*, to select men of talent.

淪 ₅Lun. A ripple, an eddy, a whirl of waters; turbulent waters, chaos; to sink, engulfed, submerged, drowned; lost in perdition, damned: [10]*₍lung saungʾ* extinct, as a family or dynasty; [11]*₍lung lok₂* sunk in poverty and vice; COM., [12]*₍t'ing ₍lung*, engulfed; to sink into perdition.

綸 ₅Lun. Lün. Kuan. Silken threads or cords; to prepare raw silk for weaving; *met.*, to compare and classify, to adjust; to know: [13]*₍si ₍lung*, sorted silk; *met.*, fine thoughts; [14]*'mwang hok₂ ₍king ₍lung*, full of fine thoughts; [15]*₍lung ₍ing*, the silken sounds — His Majesty's words. Read *₍kwang*, as in *₍kwang ₍küng*, the cap of Kung-ming.

艙 ₅Lun. A kind of boat, called *₍lung ₍ü*; the bow-timbers of a vessel.

蜦 ₅Lun. The crawling of insects and reptiles; a large frog, said to eat snakes; some say, a kind of serpent.

輪 ₅Lun. Lün. A wheel with spokes; a wheel; a disc, a round surface; a round, a revolution, a circuit; to roll around, to rotate; great, large; also to do by turns; in rotation, by turns, a turn: [16]*'kwong ₍lung*, longitude and latitude, the expanse of a country; COM., [17]*₍ch'iä ₍lung*, a wheel; [18]*₍lung ₍hui*, transmigration; [19]*₍lung 'tiong* (coll. *₍lung wak₂*), circulating, as money or goods; [20]*chiewʾ ₍lung*, by turns, in rotation; [21]*₍lung nik₂* to rotate by the day; [22]*₍mwong ₍lung*, the axes of a Chinese door; *₍lung ₍liu k'angʾ 'siu*, to watch by turns; COLL., *₍lung tioh₂ 'ngwai*, my turn has come; *₍lung wangʾ t'ö* to take turns in work; *₍lung k'aiuʾ ₍mwong*, "rotation by the button holes"—i. e., regular turns, as in gaming, &c.

嚨 ₅Lung. The throat: in the coll. read *₍läng*, q. v.: [23]*₍heu ₍lung*, the gullet, the throat.

曨 ₅Lung. The rising sun obscured, the sun dimly seen: *₍tung ₍lung*, the break of day.

朧 ₅Lung. The moon just rising: *₍mung ₍lung*, obscure, dim, as a clouded moon or stained glass; *₍tung ₍lung*, the rising moon.

---

[1]倫類 [2]天倫 [3]倫次 [4]五倫 [5]倫常 [6]亂倫 [7]崑崙 [8]掄選 [9]掄材 [10]淪喪 [11]淪落 [12]沉淪 [13]絲綸 [14]滿腹經綸 [15]綸音 [16]經輪 [17]車輪 [18]輪迴 [19]輪轉 [20]照輪 [21]輪日 [22]門輪 [23]喉嚨

櫳 ˏLung. A stockade or wooden inclosure for animals; a prisoner's cage: in the coll. read ˏlĕ̈ng, q. v.: [1]ˏpung ˏlung, a barred or railed inclosure.

瀧 ˏLung. Also read ˏlüng: a pelting rain; moistened, soaked with rain; a stream in Kweiyang prefecture, Kweichau; a place in Loting-chou, Kwang-tung: [2]ˏlung tong˒ wet, moistened.

瓏 ˏLung. A dragon-shaped gem, used in deprecating drought: in the coll. read ˏlĕ̈ng, q. v.: [3]ˏling ˏlung, the tinkling of gems; the sighing of the wind; clear, bright.

礱 ˏLung. A mill for grinding; to grind grain; to rub, to grind down, to sharpen: in the coll. read ˏlĕ̈ng, q. v.: [4]ˏlung kok, to grind grain; [5]ˏlung ˏtó, to sharpen a knife; [6]ˏmó ˏlung, to grind; *met.*, to study hard.

籠 ˏLung. An open-work basket for holding earth or animals; a cage, a den; a quiver; to monopolize goods: in the coll. read ʻlĕ̈ng and ˏlĕ̈ng, q. v.: [7]ˏlung hwo˒ to buy up or monopolize goods; [8]ʻch'i ˏlung, a quiver.

聾 ˏLung. Deaf, hard of hearing; hidden, unperceived, as things covered up: in the coll. read ˏlĕ̈ng, q. v.: ˏch'i ˏlung, silly and deaf.

蘢 ˏLung. A species of water polygonum: [9]ˏmung ˏlung, overgrown with weeds, hidden, covered.

襱 ˏLung. A kind of leggings or overalls, worn by Chinese in the winter.

(412) Lüng.

龍 ˏLung. A dragon, the chief of scaly animals, supposed to have supernatural powers; the Chinese say there are several kinds of this animal, and its name is much used in geomancy; an emblem of imperial majesty and power, dragon-like, imperial; to pervade; budding forth; kind, gracious, harmonious; a fruit, the lungan or dragon's eye: used for ˏleng, ˏliong, and liĕk, in the coll. q. v.: [10]ˏsing ˏlüng, to take a wife; [11]ˏkau ˏlüng, the scaly dragon, one like a boa; COM., [12]ˏlüng ʻhu pié˒ arms of dragon and tiger—the left and right sides of a grave; [13]ˏlüng oi˒ the throne; [14]ˏlüng ˏmwong, the dragon-door—second door of the examination-hall; [15]ˏlüng kauk, dragon's bones; *met.*, strip of red silk or cloth between the "clothes" and "knotted shroud" of a corpse; [16]te˒ ˏlüng (coll. ˏka ʻkung), an earthworm; [17]ˏLüng ˏngang ˏchiu, an inferior prefecture in the south of Fookien; [18]ʻhai ˏlüng ˏwong, Neptune; [19]ʻu ˏlüng ˏting, to maneuver the dragon-lanterns; COLL., wak, ˏsiăng ˏlüng, as lively as a dragon, very agile; [20]ho˒ ʻch'iu ˏlüng, an assistant, accomplice; [21]ˏlüng hong˒ chioh, the bridal candles.

隆 ˏLung. Grand, eminent; overtopping, rising above, exalted, conspicuous; abundant, opulent, fertile; to

---

[1]房櫳 [2]瀧凍 [3]玲瓏 [4]礱穀 [5]礱刀 [6]磨礱 [7]籠貨 [8]矢籠 [9]蒙蘢 [10]乘龍 [11]蛟龍 [12]龍虎臂 [13]龍位 [14]龍門 [15]龍骨 [16]地龍 [17]龍巖州 [18]海龍王 [19]舞龍燈 [20]輔手龍 [21]龍鳳燭

exalt, to magnify, to glorify; to rise up; reverberating, as thunder; [1]'*ˎk'üng ˏlüng*, the azure expanse; [2]*ˏlüng seng*ˀ affluent; [3]*ˏlüng pok*ˎ thick and thin; *met.*, generous and mean; [4]*ˏlüng ˏtëng*, winter, cold season; COM., [5]*ˏkiéng ˏlüng*, the emperor Kienlung.

癃 ˏLung. Weak, old and infirm: *ˏlüng peng*ˀ diseased from age.

(413) Lwa.

ˏLwa. A coll. word: to pull, to draw, to drag, to pull down, as branches, for which *ˏla* is commonly used; a sort of embroidery, called *ˏlwa 'só*, in which successive loops made by one thread are stitched to the cloth by another.

(414) Lwang.

'卵 Luan. An egg; the roe of fish; the testicles: [6]*'lwang ˏseng*, oviparous; [7]*'lwang ik*ˎ to cherish, to bring up; [8]*'lwang 'chü*, testicles; [9]*sié*ˀ *ˏü hok*ˎ *'lwang*, a state of affairs like crushing eggs—i. e., perilous.

'怨 Also read *'lung:* to cut off corners, to go across; crosswise.

'孌 Luan. Handsome, beautiful, as a female; to love, to long for; to follow, to be attached to: [10]*'wang 'lwang*, elegant, graceful; [11]*ˏsü 'lwang*, to think of and long for.

孿 To bear twins; to suckle two children at once; to change: [12]*'lwang ˏseng*, twins.

'攣 Lüan. Also read *ˏlwang:* to bind, to connect, to tie together; to grasp and drag along; a contraction of the hands or feet by disease, bent, crooked: also used for *liong*ˀ to think of, to long for: [13]*'lwang ˏkü*, to take and bind; bound, contracted; [14]*ch'ek*ˎ *'lwang*, crooked legs.

臠 Lüan. To mince or cut meat into thin slices; jerked meat; a fish's stomach, the maw cut into strips: [15]*'lwang nük*ˎ sliced meat; *'lwang 'lwang*, a thin, lean appearance; *tai*ˀ *'lwang*, a fish's belly cut open.

ˏ巒 Luan. The vertex or peak of a hill; a pointed or conical summit: [16]*ˏngang ˏlwang*, a succession of high peaks; COM., [17]*leng*ˀ *ˏlwang* (coll. *leng*ˀ *ˏt'wang*), your wife's brothers; *ˏlwang ˏhing* and *ˏlwang tá*ˀ wife's elder and younger brothers—are epistolary appellations.

ˏ欒 Luan. A kind of tree, called [18]*ˏlwang ˏking*, having yellowish wood and red branches, used medicinally; a sort of gynandrous plant; the ends or corners of an angular bell; the appearance of bamboos, slender, graceful: [19]*ˏlwang ˏlwang*, poor, emaciated.

ˏ鑾 Luan. Lan. Little bells hung on imperial cars; imperial, royal: [20]*ˏlwang ˏling*, small bells; COM., [21]*ˏlwang ka*ˀ the emperor's car or chair; the imperial cortege; *met.*, a great idol's sedan; his godship;

1 穹隆 2 隆盛 3 隆薄 4 隆冬 5 乾隆 6 卵生 7 卵翼 8 卵子 9 勢如覆卵 10 婉孌 11 思孌 12 孿生 13 攣拘 14 膝攣 15 臠肉 16 巖巒 17 令巒 18 欒荊 19 欒欒 20 鑾鈴 21 鑾駕 ○ ○

福州方言拼音字典

[1]ˌking ˌlwang taing² the palace; [2]ˌlwang ʻch'iu (coll. ho² ˌlwang), the two persons who hold the divining pencil; [3]ˌhuí ˌlwang, His Majesty's return; also the re-installment of an idol.

鸞 ˌ Luan. Lan. Used for the last, because the bells were suspended from a phenix's bill: a fabulous bird, the phenix, the symbol of perfect beauty and grace; the cock is ˌlwang, the hen is ˌhwo: [4]ˌlwang ˌkié, the argus pheasant; [5]ˌlwang hong² ˌhwo ˌming, the phenixes sing in concert—a marriage; [6]ˌku ˌlwang ʻkwa seu² the solitary phenix and lone star—unmarried.

亂 ² 乱 ² Luan. Lan. To confuse, to disorder, to trouble; discord, insurrection, anarchy, civil commotion; in confusion, out of place, disarranged, raveled; to regulate, to put in order: in the coll. read laung² q. v.: [7]chauk, lwang² to rebel, to make riot; [8]lwang² ˌsing, an efficient officer; COM., [9]ʻhwang lwang² tumult, anarchy; [10]ʻyeu lwang² to make confusion, as banditti; [11]lwang² chak, mixed, miscellaneous, as a crowd or population.

(415) Lwi.

磊 ʻ Lêi. Lei. A heap of stones; to throw together, to pile up stones: [12]ʻlwi lok, regular, as a pile; met., intelligent, talented.

累 ʻ Lêi. Lei. Interchanged with lêü² (often): to bind, to tie together; to lay on, to heap up; often, repeatedly: also read loi² q. v.: [13]hié² ʻlwi, to bind; [14]ʻlwi ngwok, the few months past; COM., ʻlwi ʻlwi or [15]ʻlwi ch'ëü² repeatedly, constantly.

壘 ʻ Lêi. Lei. Used for the last: a military wall, ramparts, fortifications; to pile up, to lay on each other; a pile; graves in a row; often, reiterated; robust, vigorous: [16]ˌkung ʻlwi, an intrenched camp; [17]ʻlwi ʻlwang ˌchi ˌngui, danger as imminent as that of (breaking) a pile of eggs; [18]ʻlwi sik, to heap stones.

儡 ʻ Lêi. Lei. To injure, to destroy, to injure mutually, as in a fight: ʻkwi ʻlwi, puppets, automatons—in the coll. ˌk'wo ʻloi, q. v.

鸓 ʻ Lêi. Lei. A sort of flying squirrel, called [19]ʻlwi ʻch'ü, allied to the bat; they are supposed to possess medicinal properties.

藟 ʻ Lêi. Lei. A kind of melon or gourd, called [20]kak, ʻlwi; ˌch'iéng swoí² ʻlwi, a sort of vine or creeper.

蕊 ʻ 蘂 ʻ Jui. The stamens or pistils of flowers, the pointals; flowers in spikelets, opening successively; a leaf-bud; met., virginity: sik, ʻlwi, lichen; COM., ˌhwa ʻlwi, a flower-bud, pointals of blossoms; kiék, ʻlwi, to put forth buds; COLL., ʻlwi mwoí² ˌk'wi, the bud has not yet opened; ʻlwi sioh, lak, one bud; p'ah, ʻlwi, to bud; pwong² ʻlwi, rice when half-boiled.

[1]金鑾殿 ○ [2]鑾手 [3]回鑾 [4]鸞雞 [5]鸞鳳和鳴 [6]孤鸞寡宿 [7]作亂 [8]亂臣 [9]反亂 [10]擾亂 [11]亂雜 [12]磊落 [13]係累 [14]累月 [15]累次 [16]軍壘 [17]壘卯之危 [18]壘石 [19]鸓鼠 [20]葛藟

‘蕾 Lôi. Lei. A flower-bud; flowers partly opened, just beginning to bloom.

‘誄 Lôi. Lei. To write an epitaph, to eulogize the deceased; a eulogy: [1]‘lwi suk, to narrate one's virtues; [2]‘lwi ˏung, a eulogy, prayers burnt for the dead.

(416) Lwo.

[This word is interchangeably read *lio*, q. v.]

(417) Lwoh.

[This word is interchangeably read *lioh*, q. v.]

(418) Lwok.

[This word is interchangeably read *liok*, q. v.]

(419) Lwong.

[This word is interchangeably read *liong*, q. v.]

(420) Ma.

ˏ嬤 A common appellation for mother: COLL., *ˏma ˏma* or *ˏi ˏma*, mamma! mother!

ˏMa. A coll. word: to take with the hand, to grip, to grasp: *ˏma ‘king*, to grasp tightly; *ˏma chói*ʼ to take things when a full year old, as a child is allowed to do from a tray set before him; *ˏma sioh*ˎ *‘pa*, to grasp a bunch.

‘馬 Ma. A horse; warlike, spirited; cavalry; a posture, the right foot put forward; small posts in a house; surname; the 187th radical: [3]*ˏt‘iéng ‘ma*, Pegasus; COM., [4]‘*ma ˏping*, cavalry; [5]*ˏk‘ié ‘ma*, to mount a horse; [6]*ˏch‘iéng ‘li ‘ma*, a courier, an express; [7]‘*ma ˏang*, a saddle; [8]‘*ma kwa*ʼ a dress-sack, a jacket; [9]‘*ma k‘wai*ʼ the official thief-catcher; [10]‘*ma sié*ʼ a posture in archery or boxing; [11]‘*ma siong*ʼ on horseback; *met.*, at once, quick; also said of a good office; [12]‘*ma tó*ʼ a race-course; [13]‘*ma ˏpá*, notice borne by an avant-courier; [14]‘*ma ˏhu*, a hostler; [15]‘*ma ˏpung*, a stable; [16]‘*ma ‘ch‘iong*, a horse-shed; *met.*, place where able composers hire themselves to write essays for competitors; [17]‘*ma ˏtá seu*ʼ (coll. ‘*wong*), the Manchoo style of cuff; COLL., ‘*ma pau*ʼ a curry-comb; ‘*ma meng*ʼ a horse's face; *met.*, long-visaged; ‘*chau ‘ma ˏlau*, a veranda; ‘*ma ˏmó hiok*ˎ (to work like) a horse without rest; *twai*ʼ ‘*ma* and ‘*sieu ‘ma*, large and small sunken rocks; ‘*ma laung*ʼ large puffed balls, made of rice-starch and boiled in oil; ‘*ma ˏk‘a*, a fish like the mackerel.

‘媽 Ma. Mu. A mare; a dame; a grandmother; a female attendant; a mother, mamma, in which sense read *ˏma*: COM., [18]*ˏkung ‘ma*, paternal grandfather and grandmother; [19]‘*Ma ‘chu ˏpó*, the goddess of sailors; COLL., [20]*lau*ʼ ‘*ma*, a wife; [21]*ngié*ʼ ‘*ma*, maternal grandmother; *ˏi ‘ma* paternal grandmother; [22]*twai*ʼ ‘*ma*, paternal great-grandmother; ‘*ló twai*ʼ ‘*ma*, paternal great-great-grandmother; *p‘wang*ʼ *ˏpung ‘ma*, also called *ˏma ‘ma*, a bride's female attendant; ‘*ma ˏt‘au ˏch‘ing*, relatives of a paternal grandmother; ‘*chio ‘chū*

1 誄述 2 誄文 3 天馬 4 馬兵 5 騎馬 6 千里馬 7 馬鞍〇 8 馬褂 9 馬快 10 馬勢 11 馬上 12 馬道 13 馬牌 14 馬夫 15 馬房 16 馬厰 17 馬蹄袖 18 公媽 19 媽祖婆 20 佬媽 21 外媽 22 大媽

'*ma*, the master's wife, the mistress.

瑪 'Ma. The agate: COM., [1]'*ma* '*nó*, the cornelian or agate stone; it is used in rubbing and polishing articles when gilded.

碼 'Ma. Used for the last: weights for money; also used for the English yard: COM., [2]*hwak*, '*ma*, or ˬ*tó* '*ma*, weights; COLL., '*ma* '*chi*, abbreviated numerals; *p'ah*, '*ma* '*chi*, to use such numerals, as in accounts or to mark goods; *sioh*, '*ma*, one yard.

螞 'Ma. A leech: [3]'*ma* ˬ*wong* (coll. '*ma* ˬ*k'i*), a leech, blood-sucker; COLL., '*chwi* '*ma*, a kind of water-spider.

'*Ma*. A coll. word, as in '*ma* ˬ*tai* (or ˬ*lai*) ˬ*ié*, a species of large spider, which does not spin webs as common spiders do.

罵 嗎 Ma'. To scold; to rail at, to vilify, to abuse with vituperative words; to call vile names: [4]*ŭk*, *ma'* to vilify; COM., [5]'*cho'* *ma'* to curse; [6]ˬ*song ma'* to altercate; [7]*ma'* ˬ*hung ma'* '*ü*, to curse wind and rain; COLL., *ma' pwong²* to scold about one's food; *ma'* ˬ*nĕng ng²* '*sai* '*k'i* '*kó*, in scolding people, he has no need of (first) preparing a rough draught!

禡 Ma'. Sacrifices offered by an army, auguries to insure victory; worship on a march to the dii viae: *loi² ma'* sacrifices at home and abroad.

痳 ˬMa. Used in the south for the measles or chicken-pox; torpidity, paralysis, stagnation; numb, benumbed: in the coll. read ˬ*mwai*, q. v.: COM., [8]ˬ*ma* ˬ*hung*, leprosy; [9]ˬ*ma yoh*, benumbing applications, as in surgical practice; [10]ˬ*ma pe'* stagnated, as the blood from a sudden fright; *ch'oi' á²* ˬ*ma*, the mouth is torpid, as from eating unripe persimmons, etc.

麻 蔴 ˬMa. The second is unauthorized: hemp, the female plant; the linen of the Chinese, Cannabis; sackcloth, mourning apparel; a kind of drum; in the coll. mean, defrauding; troublesome; indistinct, not complete; lively, prompt; scarred, disfigured; the 200th radical: in the coll. read ˬ*mwai*, q. v.: [11]ˬ*sing hwang²* ˬ*ü* ˬ*ma*, the mind troubled like tangled hemp; COM., [12]ˬ*ma tëük*, a large species of bamboo; [13]ˬ*ma* '*sung*, edible bamboo shoots; [14]ˬ*ma* ˬ*wong*, a sudorific; COLL., ˬ*ma meng'* or *meng'* ˬ*ma* ˬ*chau* ˬ*chau*, the face pock-marked; ˬ*ma lak*, *hak*, pock-marked, bald, and blind; ˬ*ma le²* quick, prompt; ˬ*ma* ˬ*cha*, to insist perversely; troublesome; rough, incomplete; *a²* ˬ*ma tai²* fraudulent practices; ˬ*hwa* (or ˬ*hu*) '*li* ˬ*ma* ˬ*cha*, rough, rudely executed.

貓 猫 ˬMiao. Read ˬ*mieu* in the dictionaries: a cat, puss: COM., [15]'*yă* ˬ*ma*, a wild cat; [16]ˬ*ma* ˬ*á*, shoes with cats' heads figured on the toes; [17]ˬ*ma* '*ch'ü* ˬ*tung* ˬ*miéng*, the cat and rat sleeping together;

[1]瑪瑙 [2]砝碼 [3]螞蟥 ○ [4]辱罵 ○ [5]詛罵 [6]相罵 [7]罵風罵雨 [8]痳瘋 [9]痳藥 [10]痳痺 ○ [11]心亂如麻 [12]麻竹 [13]麻笋 [14]麻黃 [15]野猫 [16]猫鞋 [17]猫鼠同眠 ○

met., two parties in league, as a ruler and thieves; COLL., ˏ*ma* ʻ*kiăng*, a kitten, a cat; ʻ*hu* ˏ*peng* ˏ*ma*, tiger-striped cats; ˏ*t*ʻ*au siăh*ˎ ˏ*ma*, a thievish cat; ˏ*ma* ʻ*lá leu*ʾ as spry as a cat; ˏ*ma* ʻ*tiăng* ʻ*ch*ʻ*ü*, a cat watching for rats; ˏ*ma* ˏ*hung* ʻ*cheu*, an owl.

蟆 Ma. A striped frog: COM., [1]ʻ*ha* ˏ*ma*, the edible frog. Read *mok*ˎ: a sort of gnat.

ˏ*Ma.* A coll. word, as in ˏ*ma* ˏ*hu*, the dragon-fly.

ˏ*Ma.* A coll. word, as in ˏ*t*ʻ*ié* ˏ*ma*, to cry, to weep; ˏ*ma* ˏ*ma* ˏ*t*ʻ*ié* or ˏ*ma* ˏ*ma* ˏ*t*ʻ*ié*, to weep or sob convulsively.

(421) Má.

ʻ買 Mai. To buy, to purchase; to win, to obtain, as by bribes or presents: COM., [2]ʻ*má mâ*ʾ buying and selling, trade; [3]ˏ*kiong* ʻ*má*, to purchase arbitrarily, to exact a sale; [4]ʻ*má paing*ʾ a comprador, purveyor; [5]ʻ*má* ˏ*ming* ˏ*sing*, to win the people's hearts (by cunning); [6]ʻ*má twang*ʾ to buy finally or by an irredeemable bond; [7]ʻ*má chēük*ˎ ˏ*kwang* ʻ*hu*, to get official favor by bribery; COLL., [8]ʻ*má tio*ʾ to "buy (right of) way", as of highwaymen, or of demons by scattering mock-money before the coffin; [9]ʻ*má siăng*ʾ to hire persons to find a clue to; [10]*tau*ʾ ʻ*má*, a run of purchasers; [11]*sioh*ˎ *taing*ʾ ʻ*má*, bought at the same shop; *met.*, the same, alike, as two having a like design.

ˏ*Má.* A coll. word: to bend the body, to stoop, as in passing under something low: ˏ*má kiâ*ʾ or ˏ*má* ʻ*á*, to stoop low.

賣 Mai. To sell, to transfer or dispose of for money; to inveigle, to betray; to make game of; to show off, as one's charms: COM., [12]*ch*ʻ*ói*ʾ *mâ*ʾ to sell in small quantities; [13]*mâ*ʾ ˏ*sing*, to sell into slavery; COLL., [14]*mâ*ʾ *k*ʻ*ó*ʾ sold off; [15]*mâ*ʾ *tio*ʾ "sold the road" — said of one afraid to pass a yamun or a creditor's door; [16]ˏ*t*ʻ*ieu* ˏ*ch*ʻ*ëng mâ*ʾ *ch*ʻ*ai*ʾ to hawk vegetables, etc. (for a living); *mâ*ʾ *tek*ˎ *siăng*ʾ to sell cheap.

*Mâ.*ʾ A coll. word for which the last is often used: cannot, will not, is not; with *yong*ʾ, means not much, not very, only somewhat: *mâ*ʾ *â*ʾ can't, unable; *mâ*ʾ ʻ*toi*, not short, not too short; *mâ*ʾ *siăng*ʾ not efficacious, as an idol; *chó*ʾ *mâ*ʾ ˏ*li*, or *siăh*ˎ *mâ*ʾ ˏ*ta*, can't be done; *â*ʾ ʻ*a* *mâ*ʾ can or can't? will he or not? *mâ*ʾ ʻ*sai tek*ˎ will not do, must not; *mâ*ʾ *yong*ʾ *yék*ˎ not very hot, only a little warm; *mâ*ʾ *ke*ʾ ˏ*sing*, a poor memory, forgetting.

(422) Maĕk.

抹 Mo. Read *mwak*ˎ; coll. *maĕk*ˎ: to daub, to besmear, to stain; to rub or press on, to wet by rubbing: [17]*maĕk*ˎ ˏ*hwa*, spotted, stained; [18]*maĕk*ˎ ˏ*ta*, to make dry, as by repeated pressure of the fingers; *maĕk*ˎ ˏ*miăng*, "spots the name" — the mere name of; only a trifle of what was expected or promised; *ko*ʾ *ng*ʾ *kau*ʾ *maĕk*ˎ ʻ*lang*, not even enough to be wet with spittle — a very scant supply of food.

[1]蝦蟆 [2]買賣 [3]強買 [4]買辦 [5]買民心 [6]買斷 [7]買囑官府 [8]買路 [9]買線 [10]鬧買 [11]一店買 [12]碎賣 [13]賣身 [14]賣去 [15]賣路 [16]挑葱賣菜 [17]抹花 [18]抹乾

(423) **Maëng.**

夢' Mëng. Read *mong'*; coll. *maëng'*: a dream, a vision; *met.*, a vanity, vain hopes, something vague or visionary: 1*'ki maëng'* to pray for a revelation in dreams; 2*t'auk, maëng'* to see in dreams, spiritual vision; 3*'chó' maëng' k'ak, tioh, ,ngüng*, to dream of picking up silver — a day-dream, empty hopes; 4*'maëng' tieu'* the omens of a dream—a dream as prophetic of the future; *,siong maëng'* to interpret dreams; *'yă maëng'* vague dreams; *maëng' pok, ,siong*, the dream is unpropitious; *maëng' p'wo'* the dream-book—a manual on drawing lotteries.

縊 A character found in the *Paik*, *,Ing*: a fishing-net: COLL., 5*'maëng' sioh, ,t'iong* (or *sioh, chiáh,*), one net; 6*'ngü maëng'* a fish-net; 7*,p'a maëng'* to cast a net; 8*'maëng' tai'* a girdle made of a strip of an old net; also a long, flat fish caught with the net—in distinction from the *tieu' tai'* or angled girdle-fish; *ch'iăh, maëng'* to weave nets.

(424) **Mah.**

脈' Mai. Mo. Read *mek,*; coll. *mah,*: the pulse; the blood running in the veins, the circulation; a descent, line of succession: *haik, mah,* the circulation; descent, race or stock; *te' mah,* the geomantic forms and marks of the earth—supposed to influence the luck of places; 9*'ch'iu mah,* the pulse at the wrist; 10*k'ang' mah,* to feel the pulse; 11*mah, ,t'ing*, a low pulse; 12*mah, hwak,* (or *,p'eu* or *,hiéng*), the pulse unsteady or fluctuating; 13*mah, 'king* (or *kek,*), a quick pulse; 14*lëk, mah, ng' ,tieu ,hwo*, his six pulses are not equable—he is excited or uneasy; *mah, tio' chek, sioh, a'* to press on and stop the vital current (of an opponent in fighting).

麥' Mai. Mo. Read *mek,*; coll. *mah,*: wheat: *'sieu mah,* common winter wheat; *mah, ,p'wo*, wheat-bran; 15*'chëüng' mah,* to plant wheat; 16*mah, ,nga*, wheat-sprouts —used medicinally and in molasses-candy; 17*mah, pwong'* wheat cooked as rice; *mah, 'kó*, wheat-straw; 18*mah, ,chü*, a cutaneous eruption after small-pox, caused by eating wheaten food; *mah, koi' siah, 'piăng ch'ok, ,chiéng*, when wheat is dear, cake-eaters bear the expense; *met.*, the burden of high prices falls on the consumers; 19*,sang kaëk, mah,* buck-wheat; 20*twai' mah,* barley; *'mi mah,* a species of short-eared barley; *'kwi mah,* or *mah, 'kwi*, imp-wheat—i. e., wild oats.

(425) **Máh.**

咩' Mieh. Read *miéh,*; coll. *máh,*: the bleating of sheep and goats: *,yong máh,* a bleating; *met.*, a sheep, a goat; *máh, máh*, sound in calling goats; *máh, máh, ch'oi'* the mouth flat and sunken, as when toothless; *ch'oi' meh, meh, máh, máh, pwoh, ,t'ié*, his mouth flattens and he is about to cry!

Máh,. A coll. word: low, squat, low in stature, stocky; low, as a hill, a chair, etc.; flattened,

1祈夢 2托夢 3做夢拾著銀 4夢兆 5縊一張 6魚縊 7拋縊 8縊帶 9手脈 10看脈 11脈沉 12脈滑 13脈緊 14六脈伓調和 15種麥 16麥芽 17麥飯 18麥疽 19三角麥 20大麥

as the worn toe of a shoe; *máh,* *máh,* low, flattened; *'á máh,* low, not high, as a person, house, &c.

Máh,. A coll. word, as in *ch'au' ,kau máh,* a place made muddy by throwing water on it, a puddle, a plash.

(426) Mai.

'魅 Mei. Read *mwoí'*; used for the coll. *'mai*: a hobgoblin, a sprite said to come from old things: *nóh, piéng' 'mai,* things changing into sprites; *k'ëük, 'mai tah,* to have the nightmare; *met.,* unlucky; *'mai 'kwi,* mischievous imps.

'Mai. A coll. word: to fade, to decay; to become bad; spoiled, worthless, lost: *,hwa 'mai,* a flower not opening; *'chüng 'mai,* the seed has died (in the ground); *'mai ch'ih,* low and worthless; shabby, seedy; *,miăng ,siăng 'mai,* his reputation decayed, as said of a physician.

Mai'. A coll. word: worn, wearied out, as with waiting: *'t'ó mai'* wearied in a (fruitless) search for; *,tu 'ting mai' k'ó'* waited till I am all worn out!

,埋 Mai. Man. To bury, to inter; to put in the ground, to cover, to secrete, to conceal; to harbor, to cherish: in the coll. read *,mwai,* q. v.: [1]*,mai chaung'* to bury a corpse; [2]*,mai ,chong,* to secrete; [3]*,mai huk,* to lie in ambush; [4]*,mai wong'* to harbor resentment; [5]*,mai muk,* buried, not developed, as talents; [6]*,mai ,miăng,* a buried name, as said of one not gaining degree and rank.

,霾 Mai. Storms of wind and dust or sand; a sky clouded and dark from fog or dust: [7]*,mai hwoí'* smoky, foggy; [8]*,chüng ,hung 'ch'iă ,mai,* wind and clouds of sand all the day.

邁' Mai. To go away, to travel far; to wax old, senile, aged; to go beyond, to exceed, to surpass; vigorously, strenuously: [9]*,niéng mai'* or [10]*'ló mai'* old; [11]*nik, ngwok, ,ki mai'* the days and months pass away; [12]*mai' mai'* regardless, remiss; [13]*mai' 'chüng,* vigorous.

Mai'. A coll. word: to carry on the back or shoulder; *met.,* to owe, in debt: *mai' sek, che' ka'* to bear the cross; *mai' ,peng,* one-sided, inclined; *mai' chai'* to owe debts; *mai' mai' mai', mai' k'ó' k'ëük, ,tó tai'* "carry, carry, carry, carry you off and give you to the Tauist"—sung to a child.

(427) Maing.

孟' Mêng. The eldest, the first, senior; the first of the series, first month of the quarter; great, large, eminent; to begin, the commencement of; to use effort, to exert; a surname: [14]*maing' cheng'* to advance vigorously; [15]*maing' laung'* exaggeration, bragging; COM., [16]*maing' 'chü,* or [17]*maing' ,hu 'chü,* Mencius; [18]*maing' tëüng' kié'* the 1st, 2nd, and 3rd, of a series; [19]*maing' ,ch'ung,* the 1st month of Spring.

[1]埋葬 [2]埋藏 [3]埋伏 [4]埋怨 [5]埋沒 [6]埋名 [7]霾晦 [8]終風且霾 [9]年邁 [10]老邁 [11]日月其邁 [12]邁邁 [13]邁種 [14]孟晉 [15]孟浪 [16]孟子 [17]孟夫子〇 [18]孟仲季〇 [19]孟春〇

慢² Man. Read *mang²; coll. maing²:* slow, dilatory, leisurely, easy about: ¹*ˌti maing²* slow, tardy; ²*chó' tek, maing²* to do leisurely; ³*ˈch'iă maing² chó'* wait a while before doing it; ⁴*k'ak, maing²* too slow; ⁵*maing² maing² ˌkiăng,* to walk slowly; a good-bye to one going; *maing² ˌkiăng o² pwo²* make haste slowly, festina lente; *maing² maing² ˌngai,* to rest carefully, as a sore limb; to walk on slowly and painfully; *'ting ˌming tang' ˌló maing²* wait till to-morrow.

(428) Maiu.

懋² Mou. Interchanged with the next: to exert one's mind, force of moral purpose; full, abundant, luxuriant: *maiu² 'miéng,* to put forth effort; *taik, maiu²* strong in virtue.

茂² Mou. Mao. Exuberant foliage, rank, luxuriant; flourishing, thrifty, highly developed; a high rank, superior quality of; fine, elegant; to use effort, to endeavor; strong, vigorous; a group of five persons: ⁶*ˌyéng maiu²* cyclic years with the word *sok,* in; ⁷*maiu² seng²* exuberant, flourishing; ⁸*maiu² ˌchai,* fine talents; ⁹*seu' maiu²* rich, thrifty foliage; COLL., *kaĕng² ˌi 'yă maiu²* very intimate with him.

瞀² Mou. To look down intently at; to incline the head to see, as when the eyes are dim; indistinct vision; disheveled, as hair: ¹⁰*'ngang maiu²* the eyes dim; ¹¹*maiu² lwang²* confused, bewildered.

貿² Mou. Mao. To barter, to trade, to exchange; to do business, to carry on trade; commercial transactions; dim, obscure; ¹²*maiu² ik,* trade, commerce; *maiu² maiu²* dim vision.

(429) Mak.

帓₂ Read *mwak₂;* coll. *mak₂* as in ¹³*mak₂ ngiăh,* or ¹⁴*mak₂ ngiăh₂ mó'* a head-band or fillet, worn by elderly females; ¹⁵*mak₂ ngiăh₂ siék₂* the tongue-shaped piece on the center of the band; ¹⁶*mak₂ ngiăh₂ hong²* the bridal phenix-fillet, as used in plays.

(430) Mang.

ˌ脺 Read *ˌmang;* used in the *Paik, ˌIng* for the coll. *ˌmang,* as in *ˌmang to²* the inwards covered with fat; *met.,* dull in mind; ¹⁷*ˌmang ˌmung,* dull, stupid; *ˌi pok, 'ló 'lá o² nóh, ˌmang,* there's something covering his viscera—he is very stupid; *ˌmang mek₂* to cover close, as with a cover of cloth or paper; *ˌló kai' ˌmang,* incorrigibly stupid.

'猛 Mêng. Read *'meng;* coll. *'mang:* strong and active, quick, vigorous; hot, glowing, as fire: ¹⁸*'mang tak,* active, vigorous in doing; ¹⁹*'mang 'mang 'hwi,* a very hot fire; ²⁰*'mang 'mang sié'* quickly, vigorously; hot, glowing.

'蜢 Mêng. Read *'meng;* coll. *'mang,* as in *'ch'au 'mang,* a grass-hopper.

¹遲慢 ²做的 慢且慢做 ⁴恰慢 ⁵慢慢 ⁶閣茂 ⁷茂盛 ⁸茂才 ⁹秀茂 ¹⁰眼瞀 ¹¹瞀亂 ¹²貿易 ¹³帓額 ¹⁴帓額帽 ¹⁵帓額舌 ¹⁶帓額鳳 ¹⁷脺懞 ¹⁸猛答 ¹⁹猛猛火 ²⁰猛猛勢

'滿 Man. Read '*mwang;* coll. '*mang:* a corruption of '*mwang* (full, fully), following '*chi* or '*hü;* so very, so much: '*chi* '*mang* '*hó*, so very good; '*hü* '*mang* ˌ*keng*, so very high.

'*Mang.* A coll. word: a corruption of ˌ*mó* '*kang*, as in '*mang chó'* dare not do it.

Mang'. A coll. word: a corruption of ˌ*mó kang'* useless, worthless!

ˌ蒙 Mêng. Read ˌ*mung;* coll. ˌ*mang*, as in [1]ˌ*mang mwoi'* [2] (or *pwoi'*), dull of apprehension, simple, ignorant.

ˌ盲 Mêng. Mang. Blind from loss of the pupil or optic nerve, the eye sightless; blind in mind, obtuse, deceived: [2]ˌ*mang* ˌ*hung*, a swift or variable wind; [3]ˌ*mang* ˌ*sing*, an ignorant mind; COLL., ˌ*ch'ang* ˌ*mang*, blind; [4]*pwang'* *chiăh*, ˌ*mang*, half-blind, like sparrows at twilight.

ˌ氓 ˌ甿 Mêng. Read ˌ*meng* in the dictionaries: simple folk, country-people; vassals, fugitives from other countries: [5]ˌ*sing* ˌ*mang*, recent fugitives; [6]*kau'* ˌ*mang*, to teach rustics.

ˌ蝱 Mêng. A gadfly, a breeze; a fly or gnat that infests animals: [7]ˌ*ung* ˌ*mang*, mosquitos and gnats; [8]ˌ*hi* ˌ*mang*, a sort of arrow with three barbs.

ˌ蠻 Man. A very weak worm; the aboriginal tribes of the south; barbarians, those not reformed by Chinese civilization; external, outer, barbarous; fierce, savage, brutish, unreasonable; used in the coll. to jest, to joke, to make sport of: [9]ˌ*mang* ˌ*i*, barbarians; [10]ˌ*nang* ˌ*mang*, an old term for southern Chinese; COM., [11]ˌ*mang* '*li* ˌ*mang* *hwak*, barbarous principles, unreasonable and lawless; COLL., [12]*au'* ˌ*mang*, fierce, ungovernable; ˌ*ching chiăng'* ˌ*mang*, very fierce indeed; *ta'* *ta'* ˌ*mang*, to feign fierceness; [13]ˌ*mang* *ch'ieu'* or ˌ*mang* ˌ*mang ch'ieu' ch'ieu'* to jest, to laugh at.

ˌ尨 Mang. Interchanged with the next two: a shaggy dog; the long pelage of dogs; mixed, variegated, as furs: [14]ˌ*mang chak*ˏ mixed, confused.

ˌ厖 Mang. Large rocks; abundant, liberal; numerous; bulky; mixed, blended: [15]ˌ*tung* ˌ*mang*, abundant, affluent.

ˌ龐 P'an. A high house; filled full, abundant; mixed, confused; a surname: COM., [16]ˌ*Mang* '*t'ung*, a famous officer in the time of the Three States.

ˌ明 Ming. Read ˌ*ming;* coll. ˌ*mang*, as in [17]ˌ*mang* ˌ*niêng*, or ˌ*mang* ˌ*niêng* ˌ*mang*, next year; *au'* ˌ*niêng* ˌ*mang*, the year after next; ˌ*mang au'* ˌ*niêng*, next year or the year after; *k'ó'* ˌ*niêng* ˌ*mang*, last year; *sioh*ˏ ˌ*mang*, yesterday.

ˌ暝 Ming. Read ˌ*ming;* coll. ˌ*mang:* dark, obscure, night: [18]ˌ*mang ang'* dark night, it is very dark;

---

1 蒙昧 2 盲風 3 盲心 4 半隻 盲 5 新氓 6 教氓 7 蚊蝱 8 飛蝱 9 蠻夷 10 南蠻 11 蠻理 蠻法 12 拗蠻 13 蠻笑 14 尨雜 15 敦厖 16 龐統 17 明年 18 暝暗

¹ₛmang ₛpwo, or ₛmang ₛpwo ₛt'au, night; ₛmang ₛtong, the nights are long; nikₗ ₛmang, day and night; constantly.

ₛMang. A coll. word, like the last: evening, the evening meal: ₛmang chëükₗ, evening meal of rice-congee; siahₗ ₛmang, to eat supper.

鞔 ₛ Read ₛmwang; used in the Paikₗ ₛIng for the coll. ₛmang: to put on a cover, to close, to cover, as with leather, cloth, etc.; met., filled up, full to the brim: ²ₛmang ʻku, to cover a drum; met., brimful, flowing, as the wine-cup; ³ₛmang taing² cover it tight; ⁴ₛmang aëng² ch'oi² to close or seal up a jar's mouth.

曼² Man. Also read wang² in the dictionaries: long, lengthened, extended; good, fine, marked with fine lines; an adversative particle, no, not, not yet, do not: ⁵mang² ₛsü, good words; ⁶mang² siokₗ do not say.

墁² Man. Also read ₛmang and ₛmwang: to cover with earth, as a wall; to paint walls; ornaments on walls.

幔² Man. A curtain, a blind or screen; tapestry, silk hangings; to curtain off: ⁷tiong² mang² a screen; com., ⁸pwo² mang² a cloth curtain, an awning; ⁹mang² ₛt'iëng, to screen off the light or heat.

慢² Man. Interchanged with the next four: slow, leisurely; remiss, negligent ¹⁰pokₗ mang² not slow or remiss.

嫚² Man. To slight, to contemn, to despise; to insult, to disgrace, to treat contumeliously: ¹¹chiëng² mang² to insult arrogantly.

慢² Man. To be indifferent to, negligent, remiss, careless about; rude, disrespectful to, proud, supercilious; to contemn, to treat haughtily; slow, sluggish, dilatory; remiss, easy about: in the coll. read maing² q. v.: ¹²ngó² mang² proud, haughty; com., ¹³tai² mang² to treat with disrespect; ¹⁴ʻu mang² to insult, to blaspheme; ¹⁵mang² ₛsing, to contemn the gods.

漫² Man. Often used for the last: an expanse of water; to break bounds and destroy, as a flood; diffused, spreading, reaching everywhere, as water; to let go; loose, dissolute; vague, diffuse, as writing; the color of clouds; ¹⁶lang² mang² scattered, widely diffused; seng² mang² a slow or careless disposition; com., ¹⁷sang² mang² dispersed, scattered; diffuse, as an essay. Read ₛmang: a vast expanse, a broad sheet of water; to swell and spread, as floods.

謾² Man. To deceive a superior, unfaithful to a trust; slow, remiss, careless; to insult: ¹⁸ₛk'i mang² to deceive superiors; ¹⁹tai² mang² great disrespect, insult.

蔓² Man. Also read wang²: a sort of creeping plant, of which cloth may be made; one says, a kind of bean (Dolichos); vines, creep-

¹暝晡 ²鞔鼓 ³鞔冇 ⁴鞔甕 嘴 ⁵曼辭 ○ ⁶曼說 ⁷帳幔 ⁸布幔 ⁹幔天 ¹⁰不慢 ¹¹僭嫚 ¹²傲慢 ¹³怠慢 ¹⁴侮慢 ○ ¹⁵慢神 ¹⁶爛漫 ¹⁷散慢 ○ ¹⁸欺謾 ○ ¹⁹大謾 ○

ers; ʻto shoot forth, to ramify, as vines do; spreading, as vegetation; tangled, intricate, abstruse: used for ꜀*mwang* in the coll. q. v.: [1]ʻ*mang*ʼ *mang*ʼ to spread widely, perpetuated; [2]ʻ꜀*ngiong mang*ʼ to expatiate, diffuse, as style.

(431) Mau.

꜀*Mau.* A coll. word: to close the lips or mouth; still, silent, as from diffidence: ꜀*mau* ʻ*king* ʻ*king*, to close (the lips) firmly; *k*ʻ*ang*ʼ ꜀*nĕng cheü*ʼ ꜀*mau*, is silent as soon as he sees a person.

ʻ**卯** Mao. A horary character, the fourth of the "twelve branches"; belongs to wood and is referred to the rabbit; 5-7, A. M.; morning; a time, a set day, a term an installment; to bud, to blossom; luxuriant, flourishing: [3]ʻ*mau ngwok*, the 2d moon; [4]꜀*k*ʻ*ai* ʻ*mau*, to commence terms, as in offices; COM., [5]ʻ*mau* ꜀*si* (or *k*ʻ*aik*), 5-7, A. M.; [6]ʻ*mau chiăng*ʼ 6 o'clock; [7]ʻ*mau* ꜀*ki*, the 3d, 13th, 23d, 8th, 18th, and 28th, of the month, when papers are received by magistrates; set times when returns of taxes are made; [8]ʻ*teng* ʻ*mau*, to call the roll; [9]ʻ*pi* ʻ*mau*, to bamboo remiss policemen or recreant debtors; [10]꜀*t*ʻ*iéng* ꜀*kwong* ʻ*mau*, the light ʻ*mau* hours, as in summer; [11]ʻ*mau* ꜀*niéng* ʻ*mau ngwok*, the ʻ*mau* years and days—a long time, indefinitely protracted; [12]*ngwo*ʼ ʻ*mau*, to miss the set times, as the police failing to render the tax accounts; COLL., *á*ʼ ʻ*hieu tek*, ꜀*ing kaĕng*ʼ ʻ*mau*, does he know the ꜀*ing*, from the ʻ*mau*, hour?—i. e., don't know even that, is a numskull.

ʻ**昴** Mao. The eighteenth of the 28 constellations, answering to Pleiades; the constellation of the white tiger.

ʻ**茆** Mao. An aquatic vegetable like mallows; the leaves are large, thick, and smooth; also used for ꜀*mau*, reeds; high, rank grass.

ʻ*Mau.* A coll. word, like ꜀*mau*: to close or compress the lips; to take in the mouth, to close the mouth on what is taken; *met.*, to estimate, to judge, to calculate: ʻ*mau sioh*, *ch*ʻ*oi*ʼ to take a mouthful; ʻ*mwong* ʻ*mau k*ʻ*ang*ʼ ꜀*chiă* just calculate and see.

ʻ*Mau.* A coll. word; to turn or fold over, as the edge of; to clinch, as nails: ʻ*mau* ʻ*tié*, fold it in; ʻ*mau sioh*, ꜀*kiéng*, to turn an edge over.

꜀**矛** Mao. Miao. Mou. A hooked weapon, a spear, a lance; the 110th radical: [13]꜀*mau* ʻ*tong*, spears and shields; *met.*, a contradiction, opposing words; [14]꜀*t*ʻ*iéng* ꜀*mau*, star *B* in Bootes; [15]*chĕü*ʼ ꜀*siong* ꜀*mau* ʻ*tong*, to contradict one's self.

꜀**茅** Mao. Reeds, high rank grass, couch grass; grass used for thatching; a low palm like a Thrinax, or perhaps a scrub pine: COM., [16]꜀*mau* ʻ*ch*ʻ*au*, rush-thatch; [17]꜀*mau* ꜀*leu*, a thatched lodge (in fields); [18]꜀*mau* ꜀*sang*, the Mow hill—seat of heterodox Tauism; [19]꜀*mau* ꜀*sang* ꜀*siă hwak*, the

1 蔓蔓 2 言蔓 3 卯月 4 開卯 5 卯時 6 卯正 7 卯期 8 點卯 9 比卯 10 天光卯 11 卯年卯月 12 誤卯 13 矛盾 14 天矛 15 自相矛盾 16 茅草 17 茅樓〇 18 茅山〇 19 茅山邪法

国家出版基金项目
NATIONAL PUBLICATION FOUNDATION

海上絲綢之路文獻集成

總主編　陳支平　陳春聲

科技與文化編 91

主編　王揚宗　葉農

海峽出版發行集團
THE STRAITS PUBLISHING & DISTRIBUTING GROUP
福建人民出版社

本册目次

福州方言拼音字典［二］

（*An Alphabetic Dictionary of the Chinese Language in the Foochow Dialect*）

〔美〕麥利和（Robert Samuel Maclay） 摩嘉立（Caleb Cook Baldwin）編

corrupt magic of Mow hill; [1]*mau saik*, ignorance, mental darkness; [2]*pah mau kŭng*, roots of couch grass—used as a febrifuge and in hemorrhages.

蝥蟊 Mao. A grub which destroys the roots of grain, called [3]*mau chek*; [4]*pang mau*, cantharides, a beetle like Spanish-fly, used for blistering.

髳 Mao. Read *meu* in the dictionaries: an ancient state, situated in what is now the province of Sz'-chuen.

貌 Mao. The outward mien, aspect, manner, form, gait; the appearance, look, visage, countenance; in definitions, expresses the abstract quality of a thing; to draw a likeness: COM., [5]*ŭng mau* the form, figure; [6]*hó p'ing mau* an elegant form, personable; [7]*ngwoi mau* the outward appearance; [8]*ch'iu mau* ugly, homely; [9]*mi mau* handsome; [10]*siong mau* the countenance, appearance; [11]*lá mau* politeness, etiquette; COLL., [12]*mó mau* destitute of good looks, not attractive.

Mau. A coll. word, similar to *'mau*: to calculate, to make an estimate of: *mau k'ang* estimate and see; *mau 'la 'mó* (or *'tá*), to make a general calculation.

(432) Mauk.

Mauk. A coll. word: soft, tender; rotten, decayed, as fruit, paper; broken, worn till weak in texture, as clothes: *mauk, mauk*, or *mauk, k'ó* soft, as by cooking; rotted soft, reduced to a pulp; *mauk, mauk, sié* in a soft state; tender, seedy, as a garment.

(433) Maung.

𠯈 Read *mong*; used for the coll. *maung*: to eat, as the aged without teeth, to eat with the gums: *ch'oi maung chiă maung chiă*, the peculiar working of the mouth when thus eating.

Maung. A coll. word: flabby, flaccid, as the face; a puffed or bloated appearance: *meng maung maung tioh* the face is puffed and flaccid.

漭 Mang. Read *'mong*; coll. *maung*, as in [13]*maung yong*, a vast expanse, as of the waters of an inundation.

Maung. A coll. word: to feel after, to search or find out, as an unknown road; to make trial, as in a business whose profits are uncertain; also a mode, example, precedent, as in *k'ĕük, nĕng chó 'chu maung* (this is) a mode or example for others.

Maung. A coll. word: a signal-pole, erected on a reef or sunken rock; a float or buoy is called *t'aëng*.

(434) Me.

Me. A coll. euphonic prefix, as in *me ma* to scold, to rail at; *me mó* to pound, to beat.

[1]茅塞 [2]白茅根 [3]蝥賊 [4]螌蝥 [5]容貌 [6]好品貌 [7]外貌 [8]醜貌 [9]美貌 [10]相貌 [11]禮貌 [12]無貌 [13]漭洋

ALPH. DICT. 70.

媚^{2} Mei. Smiling, smirking, ogling; engaging, bewitching; to speak soft words to, to adulate, to flatter; blandishment, dalliance: [1]*˛kieu me*^{2} fascinating, bewitching; [2]*me*^{2} *t'ai*' a mincing, seductive gait; COM., [3]*'t'iêng me*^{2} to flatter; COLL., *˛hë me*^{2} to cajole, to toady.

寐^{2} Mei. To rest from labor, to sleep; sound sleep; sleepy-headed, stupid: [4]*ngwo*' *me*^{2} waking and sleeping; [5]*mong*' *me*^{2} to dream; [6]*sëük*, *˛hing yâ*^{2} *me*^{2} to rise early and go to bed late.

謎^{2} Mi. An enigma, a riddle, a double entente; to make an allusion, to puzzle by ambiguous words: [7]*me*^{2} *˛ung*, enigmas; COLL., [8]*chung me*^{2} to guess riddles; [9]*me*^{2} *'mó*, written enigmas; [10]*p'ah*, *˛ting me*^{2} to compose riddles for lanterns; *me*^{2} *'chung* (or *˛ch'ai*) *mâ*^{2} *tioh*$_{2}$ can't guess the riddle.

***Me*^{2}** A coll. word, as in *me*^{2} *'chwi*, to dive under water; *me*^{2} *˛t'au ˛siu*, to swim with the head under water.

***Me*^{2}** A coll. word: to go about and search, as for stolen things; to look for, to prospect; to examine, to study, as a lesson: *k'ó*' *me*^{2} *k'ang*' to go and prospect, as for a place to rent or buy; *me*^{2} *tioh*$_{2}$ or *me*^{2} *tek*, *tioh*$_{2}$ searched out, found; *me*^{2} *sioh*$_{2}$ *˛lau*, to make a search; to study over once.

***Me*^{2}** A coll. euphonic prefix, as in *me*^{2} *mó*^{2} to grind in a mill; *me*^{2} *mâ*^{2} to sell off.

(435) **Meh.**

***Meh*,.** A coll. word: to drink, to take a swallow: *meh*, *˛niâ nói*' to swallow a little; *meh*, *˛wong* (or *˛kang*), drink it all up; *meh*, *sioh*$_{2}$ *ch'oi*' to take a swallow.

***Meh*,.** A slight contraction of the muscles of the mouth: *meh*, *meh*, *'lá ch'ieu*' (or *'hó ch'ieu*'), to smile pleasantly; *meh*, *meh*, *máh*, *máh*, to contract or flatten (the mouth), as when about to cry.

(436) **Mek.**

***Mek*,.** A coll. euphonic prefix, as in *mek*, *mwak*, to rub, to rub on; to blot out; *mek*, *miăk*, to throw, or stick on, as mud; to splash, as wet and soft things in falling.

默$_{2}$ **嘿**$_{2}$ Mo. Dark, cloudy, somber; night; still, silent, retired; to meditate; memory, meditation; internal influence, inspiration; not at ease, dejected: [11]*mek*$_{2}$ *niêng*^{2} to meditate on; [12]*cheng*^{2} *mek*$_{2}$ still, retired; COM., [13]*mek*$_{2}$ *chëük*, to pray silently; [14]*mek*$_{2}$ *se*^{2} a spiritual communication, a revelation; [15]*mek*$_{2}$ *mek*$_{2}$ *˛u ˛ngiong*, not speak a single word; [16]*mek*$_{2}$ *˛chü*, to write from memory.

脉$_{2}$ **脈**$_{2}$ Mai. Mo. The pulse; the blood circulating in veins and arteries; *met.*, the current of thought, full idea of; lineage, descent, race, parentage: in the coll. read *mah*$_{2}$ q. v.: [17]*te*^{2} *mek*$_{2}$ geomantic marks on the earth, supposed to influence the

[1]嬌媚 [2]媚態 [3]諂媚 [4]寤寐 [5]夢寐 [6]夙興夜寐 [7]謎文 [8]準謎 [9]謎母 [10]拍燈謎 [11]默念 [12]靜默 [13]默祝 [14]默示 [15]默默無言 [16]默書 [17]地脈

luck of localities; subterranean springs; ʻek, *mek*$_2$ ꜀*siong* ꜀*sing*, unbroken succession, as of race or doctrine.

霢 $_2$ Mai. Mist, small rain: [2]*mek*$_2$ *muk*$_2$ fine rain, a drizzling rain which falls silently.

貊, 貉 $_2$ Mai. Sometimes used for the next: a tribe of northern barbarians near the *Tik*$_2$; still, silent, quiet, settled: the 2d also read *hok*$_2$ q. v.: [3]꜀*mang mek*$_2$ the Man and Meh barbarians.

貘 $_2$ Mo. A tapir, the Malacca tapir or a similar animal, of which many fabulous stories are told; it probably exists still in Yunnan.

驀 $_2$ Mai. Mo. To mount a horse; to jump, to leap over: [4]*mek*$_2$ *wok*$_2$ to leap over anything.

麥 $_2$ Mai. Mo. Wheat, grain with an awn, bearded grain; the 199th radical: in the coll. read *mah*$_2$ q. v.: [5]꜀*ch'u mek*$_2$ oats; [6]*tai*^{2} *mek*$_2$ barley; [7]ʻ*sëük*, *mek*$_2$ winter wheat; [8]*mek*$_2$ ꜀*ch'iu*, wheat harvest in the 4th moon.

目 $_2$ Mu. Read *muk*$_2$; coll. *mek*$_2$, as in [9]*mek*$_2$ ꜀*chiu*, the eye: also read *mëk*$_2$ in the coll. q. v.

密 $_2$ Mi. Read *mik*$_2$; coll. *mek*$_2$: thick, close together; still, covert, secret: [10]*mek*$_2$ *mek*$_2$ close together; secret, concealed; [11]*mek*$_2$ *saik*, secret, not openly; ꜀*chiă mă*^{2} *mek*$_2$ cannot cover it close; cannot conceal it.

(437) Mëk.

墨 $_2$ Mei. Mo. Read *mek*$_2$ in the dictionaries: ink; dark, obscure, black, as ink; *met.*, writings, letters; to brand with ink, to tattoo, as the face; a dejected countenance; a measure of five cubits: [12]꜀*ch'ing mëk*$_2$ sorrowful, dejected; [13]꜀*ung mëk*$_2$ literature; COM., [14]꜀*u mëk*$_2$ black ink, ink-marks; [15]꜀*king mëk*$_2$ or *ngëü*^{2} *mëk*$_2$ imperial ink; [16]*pek*, *mëk*$_2$ writing, penmanship; [17]꜀*ch'iu* ꜀*ngwong mëk*$_2$ a kind of inferior ink; [18]*mëk*$_2$ ꜀*t'ui*, ink in round sticks; [19]*mëk*$_2$ ꜀*hu*, a round cup for liquid ink, an ink-horn; [20]*mëk*$_2$ *kwong*ʼ a volume of select essays; [21]*mëk*$_2$ ꜀*hwi saik*, ash color; *mëk*$_2$ ꜀*ngü*, the cuttle-fish; COLL., *mëk*$_2$ ʻ*tau siăng*ʼ a carpenter's marking-line; *mëk*$_2$ ꜀*ngü pwong*ʼ the milt or roe of cuttle-fish; *mëk*$_2$ *sioh*$_2$ *kwok*, a cake of black ink.

纆 $_2$ Mo. Also read *mek*$_2$: a cord, a two-fold cord, a rope of two strands or twists; to bind, to cord up: ʻ*kiu mëk*$_2$ to wind up, to bind.

木 $_2$ Mu. Read *muk*$_2$; coll. *mëk*$_2$ as in [22]*mëk*$_2$ *ch'iong*ʼ or *mëk*$_2$ ꜀*sa ho*^{2} a carpenter.

茉 $_2$ Mo. Read *mwak*$_2$; coll. *mëk*$_2$ as in *mëk*$_2$ *le*^{2} (or *mek*$_2$ *le*^{2}) ꜀*hwa*, the jasmine; name of a song; *mëk*$_2$ *le*^{2} ꜀*kiu*, a bouquet of jasmines; *mëk*$_2$ *le*^{2} ꜀*ta*, tea flavored with jasmines.

1 一脈相承 2 霢霂 3 蠻貊 4 驀越 5 粗麥 6 大麥 7 宿麥 8 麥秋 9 目睭 10 密密 11 密塞 12 深墨 13 文墨 14 烏墨 15 京墨 16 筆墨 17 秋元墨 18 墨鎚 19 墨壺 20 墨卷 21 墨灰色 22 木匠

目 Mu. Read *muk,*; coll. *mĕk,*: the eye; a theme, a text: also read *mek,* in the coll. q. v.: [1]*mĕk, ˎchiu*, the eye; [2]*mĕk, ˎchiu ˏning* (or ‘*chi*), the pupil; the eyeball; *mĕk, t‘iăk,* the eyelashes; [3]*mĕk, ˏt‘ó*, upper surface of the eye; [4]*mĕk,* ‘*chai*, tears; [5]*mĕk, k‘wong’* socket of the eye; [6]*mĕk, ˏiu*, tears, as filling the eyes; [7]*ˏtá mĕk,* a theme; [8]*ˏku* ‘*chwi mĕk,* a staple, loop of metal; [9]*mĕk, ˏt‘au* ‘*ch‘iéng*, the inner corners of his eyes are shallow—covets things as soon as he sees them; *mĕk, ˎchiu ne’ ne’* near-sighted; *mĕk,* ‘*lá ˏmó ˏnĕng*, supercilious, conceited, as an upstart; *mĕk, ˎchiu ch‘iă’* ‘*ngang*, squint-eyed.

Mĕk, A coll. word, as in *mĕk, saik,* (or *mek, saik,*), a bed-bug; *mĕk, saik, cheng’ sá’* (or *kau’*), the bed-bugs are very many.

(438) Meng.

猛 Mêng. A strong, fierce dog; strong, resolute, determined, brave; stern, severe, rigid; cruel, inhuman; hot, as fire; sharp, cutting, as wind; to rouse, to inspirit: in the coll. read ‘*mang*, q. v.: [10]‘*meng liék,* ferocious; [11]‘*meng chiong’* a valiant general; *ˎhung* ‘*meng*, the wind is cutting; *ˎwi* ‘*meng*, majestic, stern; ‘*meng seng’* a violent temper.

蜢 Mêng. A grasshopper or locust, called *cha’* ‘*meng*: in the coll. read ‘*mang*, q. v.: ‘*ch‘ó* ‘*meng*, a grasshopper.

艋 Mêng. A small boat: *cha’* ‘*meng*, a pinnace, a gig or jolly-boat.

面 Mien. Read *miéng’*; coll. *meng’*: the face, visage, countenance; the front, top, surface; forwards, anterior, in front; the outside of; honor, character, shamefacedness: [12]*meng’ saik,* the complexion; [13]*meng’ mau’* (or *sié’*) the features, expression; [14]*meng’ ˏseng*, in front, before; in one's presence; [15]*meng’* ‘*p‘á*, the cheeks; [16]*ˏlang meng’* to one's face; *meng’* ‘*k‘ĕng*, "pores of the face"—the lineaments, features; [17]*meng’ tio’* the facial lines or surface; [18]*meng’ k‘aĕk,* a mask; [19]‘*li meng’* inside and outside; the lining and the exterior; [20]*meng’ lioh,* a green face; *met.*, dishonored, shamed; *ch‘au’ meng’* a disagreeable countenance; *pah, meng’* prostitutes; *kwok, che’ meng’* a face square, like the character *kwok,* (country); *che’ meng’* the plain purport of words, usus loquendi; *meng’ siong’* or *meng’* ‘*ting*, on the face or top of; *meng’ ˏseng* ‘*piăng*, present of cakes to a female guest; *meng’ ˏp‘uí cheng’ kau’* "skin of the face very thick"—destitute of honor, shameless.

Meng’. A coll. euphonic prefix, as in *meng’ mwong’* to ask, to interrogate; *meng’ maung’* to eat, as an old man without teeth.

盟 Mêng. Ming. An oath, anciently taken by smearing one's self with the blood of the victim; a contract, an agreement, alliance, compact; to swear, to bind one's self by oath before the gods; a chulkan or corps among the Mongols:

[1]目睭 [2]目䐗仁 [3]目桃 ○ [4]目滓 [5]目眶 [6]目油 [7]題目 [8]斑鳩目 ○ [9]目頭淺 ○ [10]猛烈 [11]猛將 [12]面色 [13]面貌 [14]面前 [15]面頰 [16]攔面 [17]面路 [18]面殼 ○ [19]裏面 [20]面綠

海上絲綢之路文獻集成 科技與文化编

福州方言拼音字典

[1]*ˏmeng sié*² to take an oath; [2]*ˏmeng ˏsing*, a solemn purpose, one that is guileless; COM., [3]*ˏmeng yok*, a sworn contract; [4]*ˏmeng ˏhing tá*² sworn friends.

萌 ˏMëng. The budding of plants; a sprout, a shoot; to bud, to germinate, to shoot forth; incipiency, first risings of; *met.*, the renewal of old evils or habits; to plow up: [5]*ˏmeng ˏnga* or *ˏmeng ngiék*₂ to germinate; [6]*keu*² *auk*, *huk*₂ *ˏmeng*, former bad tempers again rising.

命² Ming. To order, to command, to direct; a decree, an ordinance, a rescript, a direction; a polite request, an expressed wish; heaven, fate, destiny or lot in life; luck, fortune; nature, physical habits; the natural life of beings; living, animated creatures: in the coll. read *miäng*² q. v.: COM., [7]*ˏt'iéng meng*² the decree of heaven; [8]*meng*² *leng*² a command, an order; [9]*seng*² *meng*² life; [10]*meng*² *ang*² capital cases in law; [11]*hong*² *meng*² to receive orders; [12]*ˏwong meng*² *ˏchi ˏtu*, those subject to a death-warrant, fugitive desperadoes; [13]*sü ˏseng 'iu meng*² death and life are ordained; [14]*meng*² *pok*, *ˏhung ˏsi*, one's lot unseasonable—i. e., unlucky; COLL., *ˏwong meng*² *pié*² to run precipitately.

袂² Mei. Mi. Often read *me*²: a sleeve or cuff, a wide sleeve; to take hold of and open, to draw, as the arm from the sleeve: [15]*ˏhung meng*² to part sleeves—to take leave of; [16]*pa meng*² to seize the sleeves, as at meeeting.

鯩² A vulgar character, used for the coll. *meng*², as in [17]*meng*² *ˏngü*, a darkish sea-fish, resembling the *ˏwong ˏkwa*.

(439) Mëng.

ˏMëng. A coll. word: light and spongy, porous, soft: *ˏmëng ˏmëng*, spongy, soft; *ˏmëng ˏkó*, a light, steamed cake of rice-flour.

疹 ' Chên. Read *'ching;* used in the *Paik*, *ˏIng* for the coll. *'mëng:* the measles: [18]*ch'ok*, *'mëng*, to have the measles; [19]*tau*² *'mëng*, small-pox and measles; *'Mëng 'ma*, goddess of measles; *'mëng au*² after measles; *scil.*, the patient needs special care; *'mëng hwak*, *t'au*² the measles coming out fully.

蠓 ' Mêng. Read *'mung* and *ˏmung;* coll. *'mëng:* ephemera, sand-flies; small insects in wet places, gnats: *'mëng 'kiäng*, or *'mëng mwai*² (or *mai*²) gnats; *tuk*₂ *'mëng*, poisonous gnats; *ˏch'ang 'mëng*, greenish gnats that come before rain.

芒 ˏ Mang. Wang. Read *ˏmong;* coll. *ˏmëng:* a kind of plant like rush or straw; the stalks are used in the wicks of candles, and as whisk for brooms: *ˏmëng 'kó*, straws to which the wick is attached in candles; *ˏmëng sau*² a whisk-broom.

(440) Meu.

牡 ' Mou. Mu. The male of quadrupeds; sometimes applied to plants; a bolt of a door, the sliding part of a lock; a male screw; a piston: in

[1]盟誓 [2]盟心 [3]盟約 [4]盟兄弟 [5]萌芽 [6]舊惡復萌 [7]天命 [8]命令 [9]性命 [10]命案 [11]奉命 [12]亡命之徒 [13]死生由命 [14]命不逢時 [15]分袂 [16]把袂 [17]鯩魚 [18]出疹 [19]痘疹〇

the coll. read ʿmu, q. v.: [1]ʿp'ing ʿmeu, female and male, cow and bull; [2]ʿmeu ˏtang (coll. ʿmu ˏtang), the Mowtan peony; COM., [3]ʿmeu lá² the rock-oyster—its shells are used medicinally.

畝 畞 ʿMou. Mu. A Chinese acre, which has varied much at different eras; estimated at 260 pwo², it equals 733⅓ sq. yards, or 6.61 ʿmeu to an Eng. acre; met., fields, arable land: in the coll. read ʿmu, q. v.: [4]ˏt'iêng ʿmeu, fields and farms; swoi² ʿmeu, taxable fields.

謀 ˏMou. To make plans, to scheme, to devise, to contrive; to ponder, to deliberate about, to consult with; to plot, to cabal; a device, a scheme, a stratagem, an artifice: COM., [5]ˏmeu liok₂ or ˏmeu hek₂ a plan, a plot; [6]ˏmeu ˏseng or ˏmeu sik₂ to plan for a livelihood; [7]ˏtung ˏmeu, to conspire, to cabal; [8]ˏmeu hai² to plot against; [9]ˏt'ang ˏmeu, to scheme sordidly; [10]ˏmeu sëü² chai² ˏing, ˏsing sëü² chai² ˏt'iêng, man devises his ways but heaven completes them; COLL., [11]ˏmeu ˏnëng pwong² ʿwang, to scheme to get another's living or place; ˏmeu ˏt'iêng chó² ʿtiâng p'iêng² he plans to get the heavens for a pan-cover—i. e., is rash and grasping; ˏmeu kwo² ʿch'iu (or siêng²), to succeed in a plot.

牟 ˏMou. Used for the next: to low, to bellow; to take, to usurp, to encroach, to deprive of; to pass beyond, to surpass; to love, to like; to double; great; an earthen utensil; a Manchu surname: COM., ˏmeu ˏná huk₂ (coll. ˏmi ˏná huk₂), the past Budh.

麰 ˏMou. Early wheat; also barley: ˏlai ˏmeu, spring wheat; ˏmeu mek₂ barley, or barley and wheat.

侔 ˏMou. Even, equal, alike, of the same sort or class; to accord with: [12]ˏmeu ˏü ˏt'iêng, equal to Heaven; [13]pok₂ ˏsiong ˏmeu, unlike, discordant.

眸 ˏMou. The pupil of the eye; the eye: [14]ˏmeu ʿchü, the apple of the eye; [15]hó² ʿch'i ˏming ˏmeu, white teeth and bright eyes.

鍪 ˏMou. Also read ˏmau: an iron pan, a boiler; a kind of hat, turned up at the sides: [16]ˏteu ˏmeu, an ancient helmet with a flaring brim, worn by officers.

(441) Mi.

ˏMi. The mewing of cats: ˏmi ˏmi and ˏmi ʿkiâng are terms used in calling cats.

ˏMi. A coll. euphonic prefix, as in ˏmi ˏma, to grasp; ˏmi ˏmwo, or ˏmi ˏmwo ˏmwo, to touch, to feel of.

米 ʿMi. Husked or hulled rice; the small grains or seeds of plants; provisions of rice; the 119th radical: COM., [17]ʿmi kok₂ rice; [18]ʿmi ʿhung, rice flour; rice-vermicelli, also called ʿhung ˏkang; ʿmi saik₂ a yellowish white; ʿmi ˏliong koi² rice is dear; ˏha ʿmi, dried prawns; ʿmi ˏlai, a two-eared rice-basket; ʿcha ʿmi, and ˏsong ˏchiêng ʿmi, rice of the early and

[1]牝牡 [2]牡丹 [3]牡蠣 [4]田畝 [5]謀略 [6]謀生 [7]同謀 [8]謀害 [9]貪謀 [10]謀事在人成事在天 [11]謀人飯盌 [12]侔於天 [13]不相侔 [14]眸子 [15]皓齒明眸 [16]兜鍪 [17]米穀 [18]米粉

the late harvests; [1]ʻmi ˛chiong, rice ground wet; [2]suk˳ ʻmi, glutinous rice; COLL., ʻmi ˛pwo, or ˛pwo ʻmi, rice not cleansed, as that from Formosa; lak˳ ʻmi mwoi˒ ˛chiĕng ˛nga, not a grain of rice has yet wet my teeth—have not yet eaten; ʻsieu ʻmi, sago—so called in Foochow; ʻch'a ʻmi ˛hwa, popped or roasted rice.

ʻ美 ʻ媺 Mei. Sweet, delicious, well-flavored, savory; good, excellent; beautiful, handsome; happiness; to esteem, to delight in; to praise, to commend: [3]˛hwa ʻmi, elegant; [4]ʻmi lá˒ fine, as gems; COM., [5]ʻmi mieu˒ very excellent; divine, mysterious; [6]chang˒ ʻmi, to praise; [7]ʻmi ˛ing ˛tu, picture of a beauty; [8]ʻmi e˒ a fine idea—usually in a bad sense; [9]tai˒ ʻmi, American, the United States.

ʻ眯 Mei. Dust or motes in the eye, obscuring the vision. Read me˒: the nightmare, vulgarly called ʻmai tah, q. v.

ʻMi. A coll. euphonic prefix, as in ʻmi ʻmá, to buy; ʻmi ʻmau, to fold over, as an edge; to clinch (nails); to estimate.

˛眉 Mei. The eyebrows; old, aged: [10]ʻching ˛mi, the brink of a well; COM., [11]˛ngó ˛mi, arched eyebrows; [12]˛mi ˛mó ngwok˳ the moon crescent or waning; [11]wa˒ ˛mi, to paint the eyebrows; COLL., ˛mi ˛t'au k'ak˳ ʻkiĕng, the eyebrows contracted, rueful, sorrowful; ˛mi ˛mó kwa˒ ˛tü ʻtang, "the brows clothed in pig's gall"—a very doleful look; [13]˛hwa ˛mi, a greenish yellow, white-eyed thrush, a songster.

˛嵋 Mei. A famous peak, called [14]˛Ngó ˛mi, in Kiating-fu, Sz'chuen, near the Ta-tu river.

˛楣 Mei. The lintel of a door or window; the plate of a roof: COM., ˛mwong ˛mi, a lintel; met. a daughter; [15]˛hwang ˛mi, a cross-timber, as over large doors; ˛mwong ˛mi ʻch'ai, festoons over doors.

˛郿 Mei. A district city, south of the river Wei, in Fung-tsiang-fu, Shensi.

˛湄 Mei. The margin or brink of a stream; plants growing on the banks, tangled like a thicket.

˛溦 A slight shower of rain; a torrent flowing through a ravine.

˛濰 Wei. Name of a river near the Shantung promontory; a district on its banks.

˛瀰 Mi. Also read ʻmi and ʻni: a vast expanse of waters: ˛mi ˛mi, water flowing along: ʻmieu ˛mi, vast, boundless, as the ocean.

˛獼 Mi. A species of monkey: ˛mi ˛heu, a female monkey.

˛彌 Mi. A bow discharged; to shoot an arrow; to reach or pervade everywhere; full, universal, extensive; to terminate, to end; more,

1 米粟 ○ 3 秫米 ○
2 華美 ○
4 美麗 ○
5 美妙 ○
6 讚美 ○
7 美人圖 ○
8 美意 ○
9 大美 ○
10 井眉 11 蛾眉
12 眉毛月 ○
13 畫眉 ○
14 峨嵋 15 門楣

still more; long, distant: [1]*ˎmi ngwok*ˌ a month old; [2]*ˎmi ˏtó*, more; COM., [3]*ˎmi ˏp'ung*, to patch; *met.*, to cover over, to palliate; [4]*ˎmi ˋpwo*, to supply a deficiency; [5]*ˎmi ˏhung*, to seal, as the names of the writers before their essays are delivered to the examiners; [6]*ˎmi ˎná huk*ˌ the past Budh; *ˎmi ˎná ˎch'ong*, a kind of bedstead with curved feet.

帷 ˎWei. A curtain or cloth screen; a veil; a tent; an apron or skirt: [7]*ˎmi mok*ˌ a curtain; [8]*ˎmi pok*ˌ *pok*ˌ *ˏsiu*, the curtain became thin and (women) did not cultivate (modesty); COM., [9]*tiongˀ ˎmi*, a strip facing the top of a curtain.

唯 ˎWei. Used for the next two, as a conjunction: but, only; alone, simply, merely: also read ˋ*wi*, q. v.: [10]*ˎmi ˎt'iéng ˎui taiˀ* only Heaven is great.

惟 ˎWei. To think on, to consider, to plan; to have, to be, is, consists in; but, only; just, precisely: [11]*ˎmi ek*ˌ only one; COM., [12]*ˎmi tuk*ˌ but, only; [13]*ˎmi ˋiu*, only have or is; [14]*ˎmi ˋngó tuk*ˌ *ˏchong*, only I am honorable or great!

維 ˎWei. A carriage-curtain; to tie, to bind; attached, connected; to think on, to consider; a rope, a halter; a boat's painter; a net; a conjunction, but, only, only that; is, belongs to: [15]*ˎmi ˎsi*, at that time; [16]*ˏsü ˎmi*, to think, to ponder on; [17]*sëüˀ ˎmi*, the four cardinal virtues, propriety, right, integrity, and modesty; the four cardinal points; [18]*ˎmi hiéˀ* to tie up.

縻 ˎMi. A halter for an ox; to tie up, to tether, to fasten: *ˏkié ˎmi*, fastened, confined to a place.

糜 ˎMi. Rice-gruel, thin congee; dissolved, macerated, as by the action of fire or water; entirely, utterly: [19]*ˎmi chëük*ˌ rice-gruel; [20]*ˎmi langˀ* boiled to pieces; *met.*, oppressed, harrassed into rebellion; *ˎmi hiéˀ* to waste extravagantly.

醾 ˎMi. A spirit made from wheat, and drank from off the dregs; double-distilled spirits: COM., *ˏtu ˎmi ˏhwa*, a flower, probably the cinnamon-rose.

微 徵 ˎWei. Small, trifling, insignificant, mean; minute, delicate; in a slight degree, rather; hidden, concealed; obscure, recondite, abstruse; to fade, to decay, to diminish, to dwindle away; to repress, as grief; to hide away, to conceal; not, without, not having; an ulcer on the calf of the leg: *ˎmi sáˀ* or *sáˀ ˎmi*, small, fine; insignificant; *ˏching ˎmi*, subtle, recondite; COM., *ˎmi pok*ˌ (coll. *ˎmi mok*ˌ), petty, trifling, as gains; *ˎmi chiéngˀ* low, base, servile; *ˏsié ˎmi*, a little of, a trifle; *ˎmi ˎmi ch'ieuˀ* a passing smile; *ˎmi ˎmi ˋhwi*, a little fire; *ˎmi ˎmi ˋü*, a small, fine rain.

薇 ˎWei. A kind of pot-herb; herbs, table-vegetables: COM., *pah*ˌ *ˎmi*, swallow-

[1] 彌月 [2] 彌多 [3] 彌縫 [4] 彌補 [5] 彌封 [6] 彌尼佛 [7] 帷幕 [8] 帷薄不修 [9] 帳帷 [10] 唯天爲大 [11] 惟一 [12] 惟獨 [13] 惟有 [14] 惟我獨尊 [15] 維時 [16] 思維 [17] 四維 [18] 維系 [19] 糜粥 [20] 糜爛

wort, an asclepias; [1] ꜀ch'iong ꜀mi, or ꜀tu ꜀mi, the cinnamon-rose.

蘼 ꜀Mi. A sort of rose, called ꜀ch'iong ꜀mi, or ꜀tu ꜀mi, the cinnamon-rose, in which sense the same as the last.

迷 ꜀Mi. To deceive, to delude, to beguile; to charm, to bewitch; stupefied, bewildered, blinded, as by vicious allurements; charmed, ensnared by, stupidly attached to: [2] ꜀t'ing ꜀mi, enslaved, as by vice; COM., [3] ꜀mi hĕk꜁ to deceive; seduced; [4] ꜀hwong ꜀mi, in a stupor, insensible; [5] 'hwang꜄ ꜀mi ꜀hung, possessed by a siren or female demon; [6] ꜀mi ꜀hung teng꜄ a company of the bewitched, as in plays.

遺 ꜀Wei. I. To leave, as at death; to entail, to bequeath, to will; a will, testament; to leave, to forget, to lose; to emit, lose unconsciously; to omit, to retain, to keep back; a residue, surplus, leavings: [7] ꜀mi k'e꜄ to forsake, to cast away; [8] ꜀mi ꜀wong, forgotten; [9] 'sieu ꜀mi, to urinate; [10] ꜀mi 't'á, the body left—by my parents; COM., [11] ꜀mi meng꜄ a will; [12] ꜀mi ꜀tiong, handed down, as property or a profession; [13] 'chu ꜀mi, bequeathed by ancestors; [14] ꜀mi sek꜁ to lose; [15] ꜀mi ch'eu꜄ wang꜄ ꜀niéng, infamous a myriad of years-to-come; [16] ꜀mi pok꜁ 'chü, a posthumous child. Read me꜄, as in koi꜄ me꜄ to make presents, to give things.

壝 ꜀Wei. I. A low, mud wall, a low dike about an altar: ꜀mi ꜀küng, a house inclosed by a mud wall.

麋 ꜀Mi. A large species of deer, an elk, a stag: [17] ꜀mi lŭk꜁ a stag.

麛 ꜀ A fawn; the tender young of animals: [18] ꜀mi ꜀kiu, garments made of the furs of young animals.

꜀Mi. A coll. word: to incline, to bend the head, to stoop or crouch, as in passing under a low place: the same as ꜀má, q. v.: ꜀t'au ꜀mi kiă꜄ sioh꜁ tek꜁ 'kiăng, to bend the head down a little.

꜀Mi. A coll. euphonic prefix, as in ꜀mi ꜀mai (or ꜀mwai), to bury; ꜀mi ꜀má, to stoop; ꜀mi ꜀mwai, to grind, to whet.

(442) Miăk.

Miăk꜁. A coll. word: to smear, to plaster, to daub on, as by throwing mud; to fall with a splashing noise; met., to patch, as by sewing a piece of cloth over a rent; to fall to, or come on, a surety, as the payment of a debt: miăk꜁ ꜀ngai꜄ spoiled, as by a muddy splash; miăk꜁ 'ngwai ꜀sing siong꜄ has come on me (for liquidation); miăk꜁ lóh꜁ ꜀li, to fall splashing, as wet cloth, etc.

Miăk꜁. A coll. word: old and shabby, seedy, worn threadbare; weak, debilitated, prostrated by sickness: miăk꜁ miăk꜁ very weak, strength all gone; miăk꜁ miăk꜁ 'tó, to recline weak and exhausted; ꜀i ꜀siong sëüng꜄ 'yă miăk꜁ sioh꜁ ꜀lau, is wearing very shabby clothes indeed!

Miăk꜂. A coll. word: to strike with a stick, to beat, to cudgel: miăk꜂ sioh꜂ kong꜄ to beat with a club.

1 薔薇 2 沉迷 3 迷惑 4 惛迷 5 犯迷魂 6 迷魂陣 7 遺棄 8 遺忘 9 小遺 10 遺體 11 遺命 12 遺傳 13 祖遺 14 遺失 15 遺臭萬年 16 遺腹子 17 麋鹿 18 麛裘

Miăk, . A coll. word: to beat, to throb, as the heart: *miăk, miăk, taĕng*^{2} (or *kieu*ʼ), throbbing, palpitating.

(443) Miăng.

名 Ming. Read *꜀ming;* coll. *꜀miăng:* a name, an appellation; the given name, as distinguished from that of the family or clan; *met.*, a person; fame, reputation; eclat, merit, distinction, honor; to name, to designate: [1]*꜀miăng che*ʼ (or *hó*ʼ), name, designation; [2]*꜀miăng saik,* a name, as being well known; [3]*꜀miăng ꜀siăng,* reputation; [4]*꜀miăng ëü*^{2} distinction; [5]*꜀miăng muk,* (or *꜀tong*), the name, that by which a thing is called; [6]*ʻü ꜀miăng,* the infantile name; [7]*꜀hwa ꜀miăng,* a fictitious name, nickname; [8]*hong*^{2} *꜀miăng,* to forge a name; [9]*꜀miăng tʻaik,* (or *pʻiĕng*ʼ), a visiting-card; [10]*꜀miăng tek, ʻhó,* well-named; [11]*chʻok, ꜀miăng,* to appear, to act for (others); noted, famed; [12]*mwoi*^{2} *ʻyong ʻkiăng ꜀seng hó*^{2} *꜀miăng,* to name a child before it is born; *met.*, to say or do before-hand, to anticipate.

命 Ming. Read *meng*^{2}*;* coll. *miăng*^{2}*:* the natural life or being; fate, destiny, lot in life, as appointed by Heaven; fortune, luck: [13]*wak, miăng*^{2} one's natural life; [14]*miăng*^{2} *꜀küng,* life, as tenacious or surviving; [15]*sioh, ꜀teu miăng*^{2} a life; [16]*miăng*^{2} *pauk, chʻok,* to venture one's life in; [17]*miăng*^{2} *ong*^{2} a horoscope and its correlative, ruling character over five years; [18]*miăng*^{2} *kah,* the aspect of a horoscope; [19]*kʻang*ʼ *miăng*^{2} to tell fortunes; [20]*꜀lá miăng*^{2} to toil and struggle on; *miăng*^{2} *꜀ngai* (or *pok,* or *ʻkʻu*), a poor, wretched lot; *miăng*^{2} *tai*ʼ *koi*ʼ *꜀ing,* a horoscope which indicates honor or rank; *sioh, ꜀tʻau ꜀ma ʻkau ꜀teu miăng*^{2} a cat has nine lives; *cheng*ʼ *se*ʼ *꜀ung ꜀chiong, tëüng*ʼ *se*^{2} *miăng*^{2} the first degree is got by an essay, the second by destiny!

(444) Mié.

剫 Pʻi. Read *꜀pʻié;* used for the coll. *꜀mié:* to trim, to pare, as potatoes or sugar-cane; to whittle off by a motion of the knife outward: *꜀mié ꜀kwong,* to whittle smooth; *꜀mié sioh, ꜀tʻüng,* to pare off one film or thickness.

(445) Miéh.

乜 Mieh. Lieh. Read *ʻmiă* in the dictionaries, meaning oblique, squinting: in the coll. read *miéh,* what; the same as the coll. *sié*ʼ q. v.: *miéh, nóh,* what? *miéh, nóh, nóh,* what thing? *miéh, ꜀si haiu*ʼ what time? *kang*ʼ *miéh, tai*^{2} for what purpose (has he come)?

(446) Miék.

搣 Mieh. To strike with the hand; to pluck, to pull up or out; to push; to feel of: *꜀mó miék,* to rub, to feel of; in the coll. to toil, to drudge.

搣 Mieh. To beat, to strike: *miék, siék,* irregular, distorted, not square or exact.

[1]名字 [2]名色 [3]名聲 [4]名譽 [5]名目 [6]乳名 [7]花名 [8]混名 [9]名帖 [10]名的好 [11]出名 [12]未養仔先號名 [13]活命 [14]命根 [15]一條命 [16]命博出 [17]命運 [18]命格 [19]看命 [20]挈命 ◯

ˎ威 ˎ滅 Mieh. To destroy, as with fire, to extinguish; to finish, to exterminate, to cut off; to destroy utterly, to abolish: [1]*ˎchau miék*ˏ to extirpate, to rase to the ground, as rebels and their towns; COM., [2]*ˎtü miék*ˏ to destroy, to abolish; *miék*ˏ *ˎwong*, exterminated; [3]*pok*ˏ *ˎseng pok*ˏ *miék*ˏ fit neither to live nor perish—utterly worthless.

蔑ˏ Mieh. Interchanged with the last: to pare, to scrape thin; small, minute, worthless; not, without; to despise, to reject: [4]*miék*ˏ *ˎyong*, dull in vision, downcast; [5]*pok*ˏ *miék*ˏ not disregard or reject; [6]*miék*ˏ *ˎchü*, deserted, hopeless.

篾ˏ Mieh. The skin of the bamboo; reeds or bamboos split into slats; splints, as for hoops or baskets, splinters, lath-like slips; small, as the ends of twigs: COM., [7]*miék*ˏ *ˎnong*, the part of a splint next to the skin, inner splints; [8]*miék*ˏ *ˎk'u*, bamboo-hoops; [9]*ˎk'u ˊt'ĕng miék*ˏ splints for bucket-hoops; COLL., *miék*ˏ *nak*ˏ (or *ˎk'á nak*ˏ), a bamboo tow-line.

蠛ˏ Mieh. Sand-flies, ephemera about stagnant water or damp places, which light and heat destroy: *miék*ˏ *ˊmung*, gnats, ephemera.

衊ˏ Mieh. Blood, gore; the nose-bleed; to smear with filth, to defile: *ˎu miék*ˏ to smear with filth, to pollute; *met.*, to asperse, to defame.

齧ˏ Read *ngak*ˏ; used in the *Paik*ˏ *ˎIng* for the coll. *miék*ˏ to gnaw off, to strip, as meat from bones by gnawing.

(447) Miéng.

ˎMiéng. A coll. word, as in *ˎmiéng ˎmong*, or *ˎmiéng ˎmiéng ˎmong ˎmong*, adjusted, well arranged, in their proper places, as things; *tai*ˀ *ié*ˀ *chó*ˀ *tek*ˏ *ˎmiéng ˎmong*, the business all done properly.

ˊ免 Mien. To put away, to free from, to dispense with; to spare, to excuse, to forgive; to avoid, to evade, to escape from; avoided, escaped; to remove from office; as a negative, do not, no need of: [10]*ˊmiéng ˎkwang*, to take off a cap; COM., [11]*ˊmiéng chói*ˀ to pardon crime; to escape punishment; [12]*ˊmiéng ˎló*, spare the trouble, don't incommode yourself; [13]*sià*ˀ *ˊmiéng*, to forgive; *ˎnang ˊmiéng*, can't escape, as a penalty; [14]*ˊmiéng chiéng*ˀ *ˎpá*, a flag of truce, "the white feather"; COLL., *ˊmiéng tek*ˏ to avoid, lest, so that it may not; *má*ˀ *ˊmiéng tek*ˏ *k'ó*ˀ inexcusable, unavoidable; *ˊmiéng sioh*ˏ *ˎch'á*, to excuse from a police-duty; *met.*, to dispense with one's going to do.

ˊ冕 Mien. A crown or coronet; diadem of the Chow dynasty with pendants, made like a Cantab's cap: [15]*ˎkwang ˊmiéng*, a coronet; COM., [16]*ˊmiéng ˎliu ˎkwang*, the Chow diadem—cap worn by idols and in plays.

[1]剿滅 [2]除滅 [3]不生不滅 [4]蔑然 [5]不蔑 [6]蔑貲 [7]篾瓤 [8]篾箍 [9]箍桶篾 [10]免冠 [11]免罪 [12]免勞 [13]赦免 [14]免戰牌 [15]冠冕 [16]冕旒冠

‘娩 ‘挽 Mien. Wan. To bear children, to bring forth: the first also read ‘*wang*, q. v.: ˛*hung* ‘*miéng*, the act of bringing forth, parturition.

‘勉 Mien. To urge, to animate, to stimulate, to persuade one; to force one's self, to use effort; constrained, compelled, urged by circumstances: COM., ‘*miéng* ‘*kiong*, or ‘*kiong* ‘*miéng*, to force or constrain; unwillingly, by constraint; ‘*miéng lik*˛ to exert one's self, be diligent in; ‘*miéng lá*˒ to urge, to animate.

‘勔 Mien. Like the last: to excite, to stimulate, to urge one.

‘愐 Mien. To exert the mind; to recall; to think of, to consider, to reflect on.

‘緬 Mien. Interchanged with the last: fine silk thread; to imagine, to think of, to consider; absent, remote, distant; light, inconsiderable: [1]‘*miéng* ‘*siong*, or [2]‘*miéng* ˛*hwai*, to ponder; COM., [3]‘*miéng tiéng*˒ *kwok*˛ Burmah.

‘湎 Mien. Intoxicated, drunk, fuddled; addicted to, sunk in vice: [4]˛*t‘ing* ‘*miéng*, drowned in excess; [5]˛*liu* ‘*miéng*, wholly addicted to; [6]‘*miéng* ‘*chiu*, fuddled, constantly drunk.

‘沔 Mien. A lake near Hanyang in Hupeh; name of the R. Han near its mouth; the waters exuberant, overflowing the banks.

‘眄 Mien. To look askance; to glance the eyes, to ogle; to look fixedly at: [7]˛*siong* ‘*miéng*, to ogle each other; [8]˛*liu* ‘*miéng*, to look obliquely; ‘*miéng* ‘*miéng*, to look stupidly at.

‘*Miéng*. A coll. word: a corruption of *miéh*, as in ‘*miéng* ˛*miăng*, what name? what is the matter?

˛棉 Mien. The cotton plant, cotton; a cotton-comfortable: [9]*muk*˛ ˛*miéng*, the cotton tree (Bombax ceiba); COM., [10]˛*miéng* ˛*hwa*, raw cotton, cotton bowed or flocked; [11]˛*miéng* ‘*chai*, cotton paper; [12]˛*miéng* ˛*sa siăng*˒ cotton yarn or thread; [13]˛*tang* ˛*miéng*, to bow cotton; [14]˛*p‘wo* ˛*miéng*, to wad with cotton; [15]˛*miéng* ˛*yong*, a sheep; COLL., ˛*miéng p‘woi*˒ cotton-wadded bedclothes; ˛*miéng* ‘*tai*, the refuse in cotton; *p‘wai*˒ ˛*miéng chĕü*˒ refuse cotton-batting or bedding; *nik*˛ ˛*miéng*, to slip a cotton-bed into (its cover).

˛綿 ˛緜 Mien. Interchanged with the last; soft, cottony silk, as raw silk or floss; drawn out, extended, prolonged; uninterrupted, enduring, lasting; small, minute, weak; wound close or thick: [16]‘*niong* ˛*ü* ˛*miéng*, weak as floss: [17]˛*miéng* ˛*tiong*, perpetual; [18]˛*tiéng* ˛*miéng*, bound by

[1]緬想 [2]緬懷 [3]緬甸國 [4]沉湎 [5]流湎 [6]湎酒 [7]相眄 [8]流眄 [9]木棉 [10]棉花 [11]棉紙 [12]棉紗線 [13]彈棉 [14]鋪棉 [15]棉羊 [16]软如綿 [17]綿長 [18]纏綿

many ties, intimate; in the coll. protracted, as rain or a disease; COM., [1]ˌsi ˌmiéng, silk sheets—like cotton-batting; COLL., ˌmiéng ˌmiéng, soft and flexible; weak, relaxed.

眠 ˌ *Mien.* To close the eyes, as in sleep, to go to sleep; the sleep of animals and plants; a dim, confused vision: in the coll. read ˌming, q. v.: [2]ʻliu ˌmiéng, the sleep of the willow; [3]keng' sikˏ pokˏ ˌmiéng, a sleepless night; ˌngiu ˌmiéng te' sleeping cow's land—i. e., a lucky spot or site; ˌtiong ˌmiéng, the long sleep, death.

ˌ*Miéng*. A coll. word: to shave off; to pare, as fruit: ˌmiéng ʻli, to pare plums; ˌmiéng ˌk'a ˌneng, to shave off the hard skin of the feet.

面 ' *Mieu.* The face, the countenance, the visage; the front, the top or surface of; that which is anterior; a side, a face; the direction, points of compass; face to face, openly, in one's presence; to front, to turn the face to; to see or visit one; personally; honor, character, respectability, self-respect; a classifier of drums, gongs, and mirrors; the 176th radical: in the coll. read meng' q. v.: [4]pokˏ hokˏ miéng' ˌch'iong, he who does not study is as one who faces a wall—i. e., makes no progress: COM., [5]miéng' ëü' to give direct, verbal orders; [6]ʻt'á miéng' honor, respectability; [7]miéng' siéng' a familiar face; [8]sëü' ˌhwong paikˏ miéng' the eight points of the compass—in all directions; COLL., ˌlau siohˏ tekˏ pokˏ miéng' k'ëükˏ ʻngwai, leave me a little self-respect.

麪 ' **麵** ' *Mien.* Wheaten flour; vermicelli made of flour: COM., [9]miéng' ˌpau, vermicelli and small loaves, as presents; wheat bread; [10]miéng' p'ieu' tickets for vermicelli, as issued by the shops; [11]miéng' ʻhung (coll. miéng' mwokˏ or miéng' mokˏ), wheat flour; [12]ch'iékˏ miéng' and [13]sóhˏ miéng' the sliced and the thread-like kinds of vermicelli; COLL., miéng' ˌnëng ʻkiäng, dough images; miéng' siohˏ kaikˏ a knot of thread-vermicelli; miéng' siohˏ ʻp'iäng, a folded slice of vermicelli.

(448) Mieu.

杳 ʻ *Yao. Niao.* Obscure, as the sun setting behind trees, dark, dusk; distant and indistinct; profound, abstruse, not clearly perceived: nikˏ ʻmieu ʻmieu, the sun setting, evening; [14]ʻmieu ˌming, obscure, dull; profound; [15]ʻmieu ˌu ˌngiong, no word from him.

杪 ʻ *Miao.* A small branch or twig, the small end or point of a tree; the tapering end of a post; the limit, end of a season or year: [16]ˌling ʻmieu, skirts of a forest; swoi' ʻmieu, the close of the year; COLL., ʻmieu ʻmieu, fine, small, as thread—the opposite of kwokˏ; [17]ʻmieu miäng' the slender, fragile form (of a child); *met.*, fine, attenuated.

[1]絲綿 [2]柳眠 [3]竟夕不眠 [4]不學面牆 [5]面諭〇 [6]體面 [7]面善 [8]四方八面 [9]麪包〇 [10]麪票〇 [11]麪粉 [12]切麪 [13]索麪 [14]杳冥 [15]杳無言〇 [16]林杪 [17]杪命

‘渺 Miao. The boundless, indistinct, dazzling appearance of the ocean: *‘mieu ‘mieu*, vast, unfathomable; COM., [1]*‘mieu ˎmong*, or *‘mieu ‘mieu ˎmong ˎmong*, immense and indistinct; confounding, doubtful, scarcely susceptive of proof or belief.

‘眇 Miao. One eye small or wanting; a contracted, sunken eye; to glance, to look at with one eye, to examine minutely; small, trifling, minute, subtile, abstruse; to complete, the utmost, all, nothing beyond or better: [3]*ˏch‘ing ‘mieu*, mysterious; [2]*ˎmi ‘mieu*, minute; [4]*‘mieu muk*ˎ small eyes, near-sighted.

‘窅 Also read *‘yeu:* deep, hollow eyes; distant, remote, profound; vast, extensive: [5]*tieu*ˋ *‘mieu*, distant, profound. Also read *ˎmiêng*, as in [6]*ˎmiêng ˎyong*, chagrined, inconsolable.

‘藐 Miao. A plant yielding a purple dye, in which sense also read *mau*ˋ*;* small, little, petty; remote, distant; to slight, to look down upon, to regard contemptuously; proud, supercilious: [7]*‘mieu ‘wong*, distant; COM., [8]*‘mieu se*ˋ to slight, to regard with disdain.

‘邈 Miao. Interchanged with the last; deep, hidden, distant, mysterious; to look at from a distance: *‘mieu ‘mieu*, distant; sad, mournful; [9]*‘mieu pok*ˎ *‘k‘ó mwo*ˋ deep and unfathomable.

ˎ苗 Miao. The tender blade of grass or herbs, the shooting up of grain; progeny, descendants: [10]*ha*ˋ *ˎmieu*, the imperial summer hunt; [11]*ˎhwo ˎmieu*, paddy-sprouts; [12]*ˎmieu yo*ˋ posterity; [13]*ˎmieu ˎming* or [14]*ˎmieu ‘chü*, the Miau-tsz', aborigines of southern China; [15]*ˏlá ˎmieu*, prolific, many; COM., [16]*ˎmieu ˏch‘iêng*, small salted prawns.

ˎ描 Miao. To trace, to line, to design and sketch; to copy paintings or drawings: [17]*ˎmieu wa*ˋ to copy a drawing, to sketch; [18]*ˎmieu ˏking*, to make designs in gold; to gild, as china-ware.

ˎ貓 ˎ猫 Miao. Also read *ˎmau* in the dictionaries: a cat, a puss; the mewing of cats: in the coll. read *ˎma*, q. v.: [19]*chang*ˋ *ˎmieu*, a tiger-cat; a tiger shedding its hair.

ˎ錨 Mao. Also read *ˎmau:* an anchor; a grappling-iron: *ˏp‘au ˎmieu*, to cast anchor; *‘k‘i ˎmieu*, to weigh anchor.

ˎ繆 Miu. Read *ˎmiu* in the dictionaries: hempen threads bound around, to intertwine; *met.*, intimate, familiar, closely united by ties of friendship: [20]*ˏtiu ˎmieu*, wound about, intricate, closely united. Read *mieu*ˋ*:* erroneous, wrong. Read *ˏkiu:* mourning clothes, sack cloth: *ˏkiu ‘sü*, to strangle one's self. Read *muk*ˎ as in *ˏchieu muk*ˎ the order of precedence in the ancestral hall.

[1]渺茫 [2]深眇 [3]微眇 [4]眇目 [5]吊窅 [6]窅然 [7]藐遠 [8]藐視 [9]邈不可慕 [10]夏苗 ○ [11]禾苗 ○ [12]苗裔 ○ [13]苗民 [14]苗子 [15]黎苗 [16]苗蠘 [17]描畫 [18]描金 [19]貚猫 [20]綢繆

妙² Miao. Admirable of its kind, supremely good, excellent, capital, perfect; fine, wonderful; subtle, mysterious, incomprehensible, hard to fathom; spiritual, supernatural: ¹*mieu² ꜀niéng*, under age, a youth; COM., ²*'mi mieu²* admirable, perfect; ³*mieu² kiê²* a capital plan; ⁴*mieu² 'ch'iu*, skillful, as an artist, or a physician; ⁵*mieu² ꜀ing*, a strange, incomprehensible person; ⁶*'k'ieu² mieu²* capable, has genius; *pok꜀ mieu²* not fine, ordinary.

廟² 庙² Miao. A temple of idols, an ancestral hall or temple; the front hall of a palace: ⁷*mieu² 'ü*, a temple; *꜀long mieu² ꜀chi k'e²* a palace-utensil; *met.*, a rising man; COM., ⁸*mieu² chĕük꜀*, (coll. *k'ang² mieu²*), a temple curator, sexton; *mieu² hoi²* sacred names, as of the imperial ancestry; *꜀kwang tá² mieu²* the temple of Mars; COLL., *mieu² ꜀seng 'ma*, (like) horses (of clay) before temples—i. e., well appearing, but worthless; *mieu² 'tiê ꜀tü ꜀t'au*, pig's head (offered) in the temple; *met.*, already sold or betrothed, as a female slave.

謬² Miu. Lu. Niu. Read *meu²* in the dictionaries: extravagant words, as of fools; an error, mistake; to err, to mistake; to deceive, to defraud, to irritate, confound or mislead: ⁹*mieu² ꜀ngiong*, silly, extravagant gabble; ¹⁰*mieu² ngwo²* an error; COM., ¹¹*pwoi² mieu²* contrary, refractory; opposite, wrong, as the idea in an essay.

(449) Mih.

Mih꜀. A coll. word: to tread into, to sink, as the foot in mud: *꜀k'a mih꜀ 'tiê*, the foot steps or sinks into; *mih꜀ a²* or *mih꜀ lóh꜀* to sink down, as the foot in mire.

(450) Mik.

冖² 冪² Mi. To cover things with a cloth, to veil; a napkin to cover food with; the first is the 14th radical.

宓² Mi. At rest, still, quiet, silent; secret; to stop: COM., ¹²*꜀Ching mik꜀* a sage noted in the history of the Three States.

密² 宻² Mi. Thick, close together; fine, small, minute; hidden, secret, occult, retired; mysterious, profound; to stop, to rest; intimate, friendly: in the coll. read *mek꜀* q. v.: ¹³*pe² mik꜀* hidden, secret; ¹⁴*꜀ch'ing mik꜀* very intimate; ¹⁵*꜀ki mik꜀* a secret spring, hidden cause of; COM., ¹⁶*mik꜀ 'iu*, intimate friends; ¹⁷*mik꜀ chaiu²* to memorialize secretly; *꜀chiu mik꜀* complete, nothing wanting, as work, etiquette, etc.

謐² Mi. To speak in a low tone, to whisper; quiet discourse; still, silent; careful, attentive: ¹⁸*chik꜀ mik꜀* silent, still; ¹⁹*mik꜀ ꜀yong*, at rest, reposing.

滵² Mi. Full, overflowing, as waters; in the coll. overflowed, submerged, as by an inundation: COLL., *k'ĕük꜀ 'chwi mik꜀* covered

¹妙年 ²美妙 ³妙計 ⁴妙手 ⁵妙人 ⁶巧妙 ⁷廟宇 ⁸廟祝 ⁹謬言 ¹⁰謬誤 ¹¹背謬 ¹²秦宓 ¹³秘密 ¹⁴深密 ¹⁵機密 ¹⁶密友 ¹⁷密奏 ¹⁸寂謐 ¹⁹謐然

with the waters; *mik, kwo' ,t'au*, overflowing higher than one's head.

汨 Mi. Ku. As in [1]*Mik, ,ló ,yong* (coll. *Mik, ,ló ,kĕng*), a stream in Hunan, entering Tungt'ing Lake on the southeast, in which Ch'ü-yüan drowned himself. Read *kauk,*: to regulate; to open out, pervious; confused, mixed; to rise, to float; the noise of rising waves.

蜜 蜜 Mi. Honey, nectar; sugared, luscious, sweet; *met.*, honeyed, flattering: [2]*,p'ó ,ló mik,* the jack-fruit; COM., [3]*mik, ,p'ung*, the honey-bee; [4]*mik, 'chó*, sweet dates—boiled in sugar; [5]*mik, saik*, a yellowish color; COLL., [6]*mik, chiéng'* preserved in honey or sugar; [7]*mik, 'kwo 'ka 'lang*, a very fragrant olive from *,Ang ,ning ,k'á*; [8]*mik, ,ling ,king* (or *,k'ing*), a species of small apple; [9]*mik, chiéng' ,p'ié ,song*, "arsenic steeped in honey"—the flattering words of a scoundrel.

蜮 Yü. A marine animal, fabled to spurt sand at people, or bite their shadows, and so injure them; *met.*, a crafty, masked enemy: *,ui 'kwi ,ui mik,* plotting, traitorous.

域 Yü. A frontier, a boundary; a place, region, territory; lands, states; the borders of graves: [10]*,sá mik,* western regions, states beyond the western frontier; [11]*seng' mik,* Confucian groves; [12]*chiok, mik,* remote regions.

罭 Yü. A drag-net having nine sacs or bags woven in it: [13]*'kiu mik,* a drag-net for small fish.

緎 A seam in fur dresses; to sew fur garments; to stitch, to sew together.

閾 Yü. The threshold of the door, which is not to be trod on: [14]*,heng pok, 'li mik,* in walking don't tread on the threshold.

覔 覓 Mi. To go about and seek, to search for; to examine, to seek out, as quotations: [15]*mik, lo'* to look for the road; [16]*mik, kwo'* to search for quotations.

(451) Ming.

,Ming. A coll. word: to lie still, though unable to sleep; to keep quiet, to hush, to be silent about; to stop, to cease, as from lustful ways—used sarcastically: *'mwong ,ming ,ming*, just lie still, as said to a child.

,Ming. A coll. euphonic prefix, as in *,ming ,mang*, to cover, as a book with cloth, to put the cover on (a cotton bed).

'泯 Min. An expanse of water, watery; to flow off; exhausted, drained off; finished, destroyed; obscure, distant, confused: *'ming hwang'* in confusion, anarchy; *'ming muk,* utterly destroyed; *'ming 'ming*, obscure, indistinct.

'皿 Min. Ming. Dishes, vessels used in eating; a sort of dish or plate; the 108th radical: [17]*k'e' 'ming*, utensils used in

[1]汨羅淵〇 [2]波羅蜜〇 [3]蜜蜂 [4]蜜棗 [5]蜜色 [6]蜜浸 [7]蜜果橄欖 [8]蜜林檎〇 [9]蜜浸砒霜 [10]西域 [11]聖域 [12]絕域 [13]九罭 [14]行不履閾 [15]覓路 [16]覓句 [17]器皿〇

worship or eating; COM., [1]‘*king k‘e*’ ‘*ming*, a casket of gold head-ornaments.

‘**敏** Min. Active, quick; clever, smart, capable, skilled at; witty, of ready perception; serious, sedate, respectful, attentive; the great toe: [2]‘*ch‘ung* ‘*ming*, clever, of quick parts; [3]‘*ming* ‘*kiu*, to seek earnestly; [4]‘*ming* ‘*ü sëü*’ efficient, having executive skill; COM., [5]‘*ming chiék*’ ready, prompt, of quick perception.

‘**鰵** A salt-water fish; a fish like a perch, common at Macao, having dark brown spots, the Corvina catalea.

‘**閔** Min. Used for the next: mourners at the door; to mourn with, to commiserate, to feel for; sick at heart, as from grief or trouble; indisposed, sorrowing, grieved; to urge, to exert one's self: [6]‘*Ming* ‘*song*, a disciple of Confucius.

‘**憫** ‘**愍** Min. To pity, to compassionate, to mourn or feel concern for: [7]‘*ming* ‘*siong*, grieved, sorrowing for others; COM., [8]‘*ling* ‘*ming* (coll. ‘*k‘ó* ‘*leng*), to pity.

‘**暋** Min. Strong, robust; capable, able to do, having executive ability.

‘**茗** Ming. The young, tender leaves of the tea plant: [9]‘*hiong* ‘*ming*, fragrant tea; [10]‘*ching* ‘*hiong* ‘*ming*, a kind of white rose (Macartney's?).

‘**酩** Ming. A kind of liquor, called [11]‘*lá* ‘*ming*, made from glutinous rice and wheat: [12]‘*ming* ‘*ting*, very drunk, intoxicated.

‘**黽** ‘**黾** Min. Mêng. A kind of dark striped toad, sometimes called [13]‘*keng* ‘*ming*, or ‘*t‘u ak*, (earth-duck); to urge, to press on; to strive, to use great effort; forced beyond one's strength or inclination, by constraint, unwillingly; the 205th radical: [14]‘*ming* ‘*miéng*, to exert one's self, constrained to do.

‘*Ming.* A coll. euphonic prefix, as in ‘*ming* ‘*miéng*, to forgive: to avoid, to escape from.

‘**名** Ming. A name, that by which a person or thing is called; the given name, as distinguished from the surname; *met.*, a person, being; a designation, a title; fame, reputation, distinction, honor, éclat, credit, renown; literary or official merit; famed, noted, eminent, renowned; to name, to designate: in the coll. read ‘*miăng*, q. v.: [15]‘*sing* ‘*ming*, to obtain a reputation; COM., [16]‘*ming hong*’ relative duties; [17]‘*ming sëü*’ a distinguished scholar; [18]‘*ming* ‘*ka*, an illustrous family; [19]‘*ming lé*’ fame and wealth; [20]‘*kung* ‘*ming*, merit, reputation, official honors; ‘*ming* ‘*ing che*’ *va*’ the writing and painting of a famous artist.

‘**銘** Ming. To inscribe on the memory, to remember; to note, to keep a record of; to engrave, to carve on metal

1 金器皿 ○ 2 聰敏 3 敏求 ○ 4 敏於事 ○ 5 敏捷 6 閔損 7 憫傷 8 憐憫 9 香茗 10 眞香茗 11 醴酩 ○ 12 酩酊 13 耿黽 14 黽勉 15 成名 16 名分 17 名士 18 名家 19 名利 20 功名 ○

or stone; a record, book of precepts, guide for one's conduct: [1]ˏ*ming* ˏ*sing*, engraven on the mind; [2]ˏ*pi* ˏ*ming*, a stone tablet; COM., [3]ˏ*ming* ˏ*ching*, a eulogistic banner borne at funerals.

冥 ˏMing. Dark, obscure, dismal, doleful; deep, dark recesses; carvernous, gloomy, as night; the approach of night; the nether world, place of the shades, sheol, hades; uninformed, immature, as a child's mind: [4]ˊ*hiu* ˏ*ming*, lost to sight, the abode of spirits; [5]ˏ*ming* ˊ*hu*, or ˏ*ming* ˏ*kang*, limbo; [6]ˏ*ch'ing* ˏ*ming*, heaven; [7]ˏ*ming* ˏ*ngwang*, uninstructed, stupid; COM., [8]ˏ*ming* ˏ*i* ˏ*chiêng* ˊ*chai*, paper clothes and cash—burnt to wretched ghosts.

溟 ˏMing. The boundless ocean, the great deep; a drizzling rain; a fine mist, fog and clouds on hill-tops: ˏ*ming* ˊ*hai*, the deep, blue sea; ˏ*ming* ˏ*ming*, misty.

螟 ˏMing. An insect that devours grain and produces blight: COM., ˏ*ming* ˏ*ling*, a mulberry-caterpillar, which the sphex is said to adopt as its young; COLL., ˏ*ming* ˏ*ling* ˏ*ki* ˊ*kiâng*, an adopted son.

蓂 ˏMing. A lucky plant, called ˏ*ming kiék*, which grew in Yu's palace; its foliage followed the moon; probably a sort of bulb whose leaves alternately sprouted and died.

瞑 ˏMing. Also read ˊ*ming*: to close the eyes, as in death; a dull, indistinct vision: ˏ*ming* ˏ*ming*, obscure sight; ˏ*kang* ˏ*sing* ˏ*ming* *muk*ˎ to close the eyes cheerfully in death; ˏ*ming* ˏ*sing*, the blind statesman—epithet of Sz'kwang of Tsin, B. C. 540.

暝 ˏMing. The sun obscured; dark, obscure, the darkness of night: in the coll. read ˏ*mang*, q. v.

明 ˏMing. Mieh. Bright, clear, brilliant; plain, evident, open, manifest, patent, apparent; brightness, splendor; astute, intelligent, perspicacious; to distinguish, to understand clearly; to illustrate, shed light on, as by explanations: in the coll. used for ˏ*mang*, q. v.: COM., [9]ˏ*ming pek*ˎ plain, manifest; to understand clearly; [10]ˏ*hung* ˏ*ming*, plain, perspicuous; [11]ˏ*sing* ˏ*ming*, the gods, idols; [12]ˏ*ming* ˏ*tieu*, the Ming dynasty. A. D. 1368-1628; [13]ˏ*ming* ˏ*sing*, to show one's innocence, as by an oath before the gods; [14]ˊ*k'ié* ˏ*ming* ˏ*sing*, the morning star; [15]ˏ*ming* ˏ*t'iéng* (coll. ˏ*ming tang*'), to-morrow; [16]ˏ*ming* *kauk*ˎ ˏ*ting*, transparent horn-lanterns—made of sheep's horns; [17]ˏ*ming* ˊ*li*, to comprehend the reason or propriety of; [18]ˏ*sëng* ˊ*ngang pok*ˎ ˏ*ming*, blind in both eyes; [19]ˏ*ming* ˏ*ti ko' chauk*ˎ to do wrong knowingly; ˏ*lai* ˏ*ming* *k'ëü'* *pek*ˎ all clear and plain, all properly done; COLL., ˏ*ming* *t'eng'* *ang'* *siék*ˎ apparent gain, but actual loss, in trade.

旻 ˏMin. The autumnal sky, the period when leaves fall; to pity, to feel for, to sympathize with: ˏ*ming* ˏ*t'iéng*, autumn; *met.*, the clear expanse, sky.

[1] 銘心 [2] 碑銘 [3] 銘旌 [4] 幽冥 [5] 冥府 [6] 青冥 [7] 冥頑 [8] 冥衣錢紙 [9] 明白 [10] 分明 [11] 神明 [12] 明朝 [13] 明心 [14] 啟明星〇 [15] 明天 [16] 明角燈 [17] 明理〇 [18] 雙眼不明 [19] 明知故作

民 ꜀Min. The multitude, the people; subjects, embracing the uninstructed and those not in office: COM., [1]꜀*ming* ꜀*ka*, the people, subjects; [2]꜀*ming* ꜀*kü*, the dwellings of the people; [3]꜀*ngwang* ꜀*ming*, the canaille, ruffscuff; [4]꜂*má* ꜀*ming* ꜀*sing*, to steal the people's hearts; [5]꜀*ming* ꜀*ching*, the popular feeling or spirit; [6]꜀*ming* *chaung*꜄ class of policemen, followers, runners; [7]꜂*chü* ꜀*ming*, the people, you poor people; [8]꜀*ming* *hai*꜆ injurious to the public; [9]*séü*꜄ ꜀*ming*, the four classes of subjects; [10]꜀*liong* ꜀*ming*, loyal people; [11]꜀*ming* *piéng*꜄ the people changing—i. e., becoming rebellious; ꜀*ming* *chik*꜆ a registry, census.

岷 ꜀Min. A range of mountains in the north of Sz'chuen, a spur of the Pihling range, separating the valleys of the Yellow river and Yangtsz': ꜀*Ming* ꜀*këng*, a large tributary of the river Yangtsz'; ꜀*Ming* ꜀*chiu*, an inferior department of Kansuh.

珉 ꜀Min. A fine kind of stone, like alabaster or marble, but not classed as a gem: *pek*꜆ ꜀*ming*, a white pebble.

眠 ꜀Mien. Read ꜀*miéng*; coll. ꜀*ming*: to sleep; sleepy, drowsy, dozing: ꜀*ming* *nëü*꜄ drowsy; ꜀*ming* ꜀*ch'ong*, a bedstead; ꜀*ming* ꜀*á*, women's sleeping-shoes; ꜀*kwong* ꜀*ming*, to cry out in sleep; ꜂*ch'ung* ꜀*ming*, sleepy; ꜀*ngó* ꜀*ming*, to go without sleep; *k'aung*꜄ *lóh*꜆ ꜀*ming*. to fall asleep; *k'aung*꜄ *sioh*꜆ *kok*꜆ (or ꜂*ku*) ꜀*ming*, to take a short nap; ꜀*hang* ꜀*ming* ꜀*hang* *nëü*꜄ half-asleep.

緡 ꜀Min. A fishing-line; a string, a cord; to string, as cash; a string of cash; to give or use garments as bedding; abundant; grieved, pained: ꜀*ming* ꜀*chiéng*, a string of cash.

閩 ꜀Min. A species of serpent; the ancient name of Fookien; the river Min in this province: COM., [12]꜀*ming* *wok*꜆ the Fookien and Canton provinces; [13]꜀*ming* *chiék*꜆ the provinces of Fookien and Chehkiang; [14]꜀*ming* ꜂*seng*, the Min province—i. e., Fookien; [15]꜀*Ming* *kaing*꜄ the chief of the ten departments of the Foochow prefecture; [16]꜀*ming* ꜀*ang* *seng*꜄ (or *teng*꜄), a military post at the Mingan pass in the Min; COLL., ꜀*ming* *kaing*꜆ ꜀*seng* ꜀*kwong* ꜂*piàng*, "biscuits (made) in front of the Ming district magistrate's"; *met.*, things large and showy (but not superior).

鳴 ꜀Ming. The cry of a bird or animal, a crowing, a song, a buzz, a hum, a yell; sound, as of drums and other sonorous articles; to sound, to cause to emit sounds; birds calling to each other; to resound, as one's fame: [17]꜀*kié* ꜀*ming*, cock-crowing; [18]꜀*ming* ꜀*chüng*, to sound a bell; [19]꜀*ming* ꜀*wong*, to call for redress; COM., [20]꜀*ming* ꜀*ló*, to beat gongs; [21]꜂*chëü* ꜀*ming* ꜀*chüng*, a clock; ꜀*ku* ꜂*chiong* ꜀*nang* ꜀*ming*, it's hard to clap with one hand; *met.*, to need others' help.

[1]民家 [2]民居 [3]頑民 [4]買民心 [5]民情 [6]民壯 [7]子民 [8]民害 [9]四民 [10]良民 [11]民變 [12]閩粵 [13]閩浙 [14]閩省 [15]閩縣 [16]閩安汎 [17]鷄鳴 [18]鳴鐘 [19]鳴冤 [20]鳴鑼 [21]自鳴鐘

饅 Man. Read ˌmwang; coll. ˌming, as in ¹ˌming ˌt'au, steamed bread, leavened wheaten cakes or loaves — offered in piles of 36, or more, to hungry ghosts.

ˌMing. A coll. word, about the same as ˌmi: to incline the head, to stoop: ˌt'au ˌming kiä² sioh, tek, ʻkiäng, bend the head a little.

ˌMing. A coll. euphonic prefix, as in ˌming ˌmang, to cover, to stop with a cover, as of paper or cloth; ˌming ˌmiéng, to shave, to pare, as fruit.

(452) Mó.

ˌMó. A coll. word: to swell, to rise, to bunch, as from the bite of an insect; to jut, to protrude, to rise above the surface, as hillocks; a bunch, a swelling: sioh, ˌmó, a swelling; ˌmó sioh, tói² to jut or rise in a bunch; ˌmó ʻk'i ˌli, rising, swelling; sioh, ˌsing ˌtu se² ˌmó ˌmó, the person covered with small bunches (from bites).

ˌMó. A coll. word, borrowed from Shantung and equivalent to ˌpau, bread: ˌmó ˌmó, bread, loaves of bread; ˌmó ˌmó ˌpung, a pantry.

母 Mu. Read ʻmu; coll. ʻmó: a female, that which produces, the female of animals, met., principal, substance: ²ˌngu ʻmó, a cow; ³ˌkié ʻmó, a hen; ⁴ʻmó ch'iék, a large species of female crab; ⁵ʻmó kaëk, the female and male; ⁶la² ʻhu ʻmó, a tigress — a fierce woman; ⁷ʻmó siong² an effeminate appearance; ⁸ˌt'ong ʻmó, a barren woman; ⁹ʻmó le² principal and interest; ¹⁰ch'o² ʻmó, the mother in vinegar; ¹¹tai² ʻmó, or ¹²ʻchung ʻmó, the substance, an epitome.

拇 Mu. Mou. Read ʻmu; coll. ʻmó, as in twai² ʻmó (or ˌmó) ʻchai, the thumb; ˌk'a twai² ʻmó ʻchäi, the great toe.

Mó². A coll. word: to beat, to pound; to strike with a club: mó² ˌngai, to spoil by pounding; mó² ʻsi, to beat to death.

麽 Mo. Ma. Small, minute, delicate; a final interrogative in questions answered by yes or no; a particle expressing doubt, surprise, etc.; in the coll. the sound ˌpi is more common as a mark of interrogation: ˌyeu ˌmó, minute, small; seng² ˌmó (coll. sié² nóh,) what? ˌlai ʻlieu ˌmó, has he come? COLL., k'ang² ˌmó, lo! behold!

摩 Mo. To rub, to touch with the hand; to handle, to feel the texture of; to rub, to polish; to destroy: in the coll. read ˌmwo, q. v.: ¹³ʻhu ˌmó, to pat gently; ¹⁴ˌsiong ˌmó, to "rub each other"; met., to instruct or reprove mutually, as friends; ¹⁵ˌmó ˌsó, to feel of; to toy with; ¹⁶ˌmó t'aung² the operations of nature; ¹⁷ˌsieu ˌmó, to wear away, to destroy; COM., ¹⁸ʻch'oi ˌmó, to reflect on, search out the sense of.

磨 Mo. To grind, to sharpen by rubbing; to rub, to polish; met., to study, to examine closely; to afflict; afflicted, distressed, over-

¹饅頭 ²牛母 ³鷄母 ⁴母蠘 ⁵母雄 ⁶佬虎母 ⁷母相 ⁸槌母 ⁹母利 ¹⁰醋母 ¹¹大母 ¹²準母 ¹³拊摩 ¹⁴相摩 ¹⁵摩挱 ¹⁶摩盪 ¹⁷消摩 ¹⁸揣摩

come by trials: also read mó' and in the coll. ˏmwai, q. v.: [1]ˏmó lá' to examine, to study diligently; [2]ʻü tauk, ʻü ˏmó, like chiseling and grinding; *met.*, perfect, finished; thoroughness, as in learning; COM., [3]ˏmó nang' to be afflicted; to suffer from toilsome labor; [4]ˏmó miék, distressed; to waste, to destroy; [5]ˏmó liéng' to practice diligently, become skilled in.

[illegible] ˏ A bowl, a cup for water or tea; a drinking-vessel.

魔 ˏ Mo. A malignant spirit, a devil, a demon: [6]'soi' ˏmó, oppressed with sleep, drowsy and stupid; COM., [7]ˏmó ʻkwi, a devil, a demon; [8]ˏsiă ˏmó ʻkwi kwai' demons and frightful imps; [9]ʻchiu ˏmó, delirium tremens; [10]ˏsi ˏmó, poetic ravings.

劘 ˏ To cut, to dissect, to cut open; to pare off; to slice or divide up.

毛 ˏ Mao. The covering of brutes, hair, pelage, wool, fur; feathers, down; the nap of felt; herbage, covering of the earth; to strip off the hair; the 82nd radical; used in coll. books for no, not, none: [11]ˏiu ˏmó, a sheep; [12]ne' ˏmó, two sorts of hair—grayhaired; [13]pok, ˏmó ˏchi te' a wild, wilderness; COM., [14]ˏmó ʻü, hair, wool; feathers; [15]ʻü ˏmó, camlet; [16]ˏmó ˏku, a sort of edible mushroom; COLL., ˏmó ʻkwong, the barrel of a quill; pores in which hairs are located; ˏtü ˏmó ˏcheng, hog's bristles; ˏmó há' a kind of crab with hairy claws; ˏmó pang' an idiosyncrasy, a penchant, a vice, a failing; a flaw, a defect (in a thing); ˏmó ˏmó pang' free from failings; faultless, no flaws.

旄 ˏ Mao. A cow's tail, used as a signal in the army; also a squirrel or marten's tail on a spear or flag-staff: ˏkang ˏmó, the tail on a flag-staff.

酕 ˏ Intoxicated, drunk: ˏmó ˏtó, overcome with liquor, dead-drunk.

髦 ˏ Mao. The human hair; hair hanging over the forehead; tufts on a child's head, trimmed on each side; the long hairs; *met.*, eminent, courageous; [17]ʻliong ˏmó, the two tufts on an infant's head; [18]ˏmó sëü' an eminent scholar; [19]ʻchong' ˏmó, superior to others.

無 ˏ Wu. Read ˏu; used for the coll. ˏmó: not, no, none; without, destitute of, wanting; equivalent to the syllabic prefix *un* in certain English words: [20]ˏmó yeu' ʻking, unimportant; ˏmó ˏsing sëü' no heart for it; ˏmó hwak, tek, no resource, no help for it; o' ʻa ˏmó, have you or not, yes or no; ˏmó ʻtá, no property, poor; ˏmó nóh, ʻkong, nothing to say, ˏmó ʻchiă sëü' no such thing, entirely false; ˏmó ˏtang ˏtong, cannot; ˏmó meng' ashamed; ˏmó tói' (or nói') ʻmá, no place to buy it—not in the market; ˏmó tioh, or ˏmó tëü' not present: pʻah, ˏmó, lost; ˏmó kʻó' gone, disappeared; ˏmó niah, not equal or compara-

1 磨厲 2 如琢如磨 3 磨難 4 磨搣 5 磨鍊 6 睡魔 7 魔鬼 8 邪魔鬼怪 9 酒魔 10 詩魔 11 柔毛 12 二毛 13 不毛之地 14 毛羽 15 羽毛 16 毛菰 17 兩髦 18 髦士 19 俊髦 20 無要緊〇

ble to; ꜀mó ꜂chu, not to know clearly or definitely.

冒^2 冐^2 Mao. A head-covering; to go on blindly and rashly, to press heedlessly on; to assume, to feign, to presume; to usurp, to take upon one's self without authority; to venture on, to brave; rash, venturesome; to falsify, to counterfeit: [1]꜀t'ang mó^2 to covet and strive rashly for; [2]mó^2 chik꜆ to envy; COM., [3]꜂ka mó^2 to feign, to counterfeit; [4]mó^2 ꜀miăng, to assume a name; [5]mó^2 neng^2 to lay a false claim to; [6]mó^2 ꜂ü, indifferent to the rain; [7]mó^2 ꜂hiĕng, to brave danger; [8]mó^2 chik꜆ a false registration, as of a student's name, etc.

媢^2 Mao. To regard with ill-will, to envy, as another's prosperity; envy, jealousy: [9]mó^2 chik꜆ envy, hate; [10]mó^2 ho^2 a jealous woman.

帽^2 Mao. A hat, a cap, a turban, a covering for the head: COM., [11]꜀chiĕng mó^2 a felt cap; [12]kwok꜆ ꜀kung mó^2 an ancient ducal cap of a square form; [13]꜀hung mó^2 a kind of hood or winter-bonnet; [14]tai^2 mó^2 to wear a hat; [15]꜂wang mó^2 the bowl (i. e., common) cap; [16]mó^2 ꜂ting, a cap knob or button; ꜀k'wi mó^2 a helmet; COLL., ꜀ëng mó^2 a red-tasseled official cap; mó^2 ꜀t'au, a cap without tassels.

瑁^2 Mao. A sort of scepter, or badge of imperial authority: also read ngwoi^2 q. v.

磨^2 Mo. A quern, a hand-mill; a mill for grinding grain; to grind grain: also read ꜀mó, q. v.: COM., [17]mó^2 ꜀sing, the pivot of a quern; [18]꜀ai mó^2 to push the quern; [19]mó^2 ꜀cheng and [20]mó^2 ꜀pwang, the upper and nether millstones; [21]꜂chwi mó^2 a water-mill; [22]꜀ngu mó^2 a buffalo-mill; [23]mó^2 miĕng^2 ꜂hung, to grind wheat; mó^2 ꜀chiong, to grind rice wet, make rice-starch; COLL., ꜀tong mó^2 to dress or pick millstones; mó^2 ꜀cheng tah꜆ ꜀sing ꜀kang, "a millstone pressing the heart"—i. e., undisturbed, fearless.

芼^2 Mao. Overgrown with grass; herbage; to gather plants; vegetables in soups: mó^2 ꜀keng, meat-pottage; mó^2 ch'ai^2 pot-herbs, greens.

眊^2 Mao. An eye with a small iris; a dull eye, dim sight; stupid, bewildered: hwoi^2 mó^2 confused, perplexed.

耄^2 Mao. An old man of ninety years; old, senile, decrepit, in second childhood: ꜂ló mó^2 an aged person; ꜀soi mó^2 infirm and aged.

(453) Móh.

Móh꜆. A coll. word: to feel after, as in the dark; to say at a venture, to guess at: ꜂mwong móh, just say or guess; just feel after, as a road in the dark; móh꜆ tioh꜆ hit upon, guessed; ang^2 móh꜆ móh, very dark.

Móh꜆. A coll. word: a technical or coined term for 5, 50, 500, &c., as used by traders to indicate prices: móh꜆ móh, 55 cash.

[1]貪冒 [2]冒嫉 [3]假冒 [4]冒名 [5]冒認 [6]冒雨 [7]冒險 [8]冒籍 [9]媢嫉 [10]媢婦 [11]毡帽 [12]國公帽 [13]風帽 [14]戴帽 [15]碗帽 [16]帽頂 [17]磨心 [18]挨磨 [19]磨層 [20]磨盤 [21]水磨 [22]牛磨 [23]磨麩粉

膜 Mo. Read *mok*; coll. *móh*: the filmy skin between the flesh and epidermis, or between flesh and fat; the thin skin or peel inside the shells of eggs and rind of fruit: *móh móh* a thin film; [1]*sieu móh* the reed of the mouth-piece of a clarinet; [2]*laung móh* the film of eggs; [3]*kah sioh t'ũng móh* divided by a film; *met.*, not closely related.

莫 Mo. Mu. Read *mok*; coll. *móh*: a negative of prohibition or admonition, do not, must not, no need of: [4]*móh ch'ieu* don't laugh; [5]*móh kü*, don't insist, don't be ceremonious; *móh lieu i*, don't trouble him; [6]*móh niăh* (or *mó niăh*), not equal to, not as good as; *ko móh niăh ngwai yong* still not equal to my mode or style.

(454) Moi.

Moi. A coll. word, as in *moi moi* fine, drizzling, as rain; *ü moi* or *moi moi ü*, a drizzling rain, a mist; *moi lang* wet with mist.

(455) Mok.

Mok. A coll. word: a small, black gnat, sometimes called *mok chok*; *met.*, a worthless fellow; *mok* or *chwi mok*, infusoria, such as are generated in ponds.

Mok. A coll. word, as in *mok i*, fine sewing-silk.

莫 Mo. A negative of prohibition, do not, no need of; if, unless; preceding an adjective, it denotes the highest degree of, incomparable, nothing like; to plan; ample, great; thick, luxuriant; peace, tranquility: in the coll. read *móh*, q. v.: [7]*mok yok* or [8]*mok ü*, nothing like, incomparable, very proper; [9]*mok tai ü t'iéng*, there is nothing greater than heaven; [10]*mok hi*, it certainly is, unless (you) have; [11]*kwong mok* large, ample; com., [12]*mok pok se* it must have been, it probably was.

漠 Mo. Also read *mauk*: a sandy plain, moving sands; dry, clean; careless, indifferent to; arranged, spread out: [13]*tang mok* simple, retiring; *mok mok* vast; [14]*sauk mok* the northern desert, Shamo or Gobi; [15]*sa mok* (or *mauk*), a sandy plain, the desert of Shamo.

寞 Mo. Still, silent, as at night: com., [16]*chik mok* quiet and still, retired, solitary.

瘼 Mo. Sickness, disease; some say an itching complaint or eruption.

膜 Mo. The thin film or skin between the flesh and epidermis; any membrane or pellicle in plants or animals, as the cornea, mesentery, &c.; the thin peel inside of eggs, grasses and certain fruits; in the coll. read *móh* q. v.: *tëük mok* the inner peel of bamboo; *kũng mok* membranes in meat. Read *mwo*: to bow; to soothe by submitting, to kneel and receive.

鏌 Mo. A two-edged sword, called *mok yá*, celebrated in the Lieh-kwoh-chi.

[1]簫膜 [2]蛋膜 [3]隔一重膜 [4]莫笑 [5]莫拘 [6]莫拿〇 [7]莫若〇 [8]莫於 [9]莫大於天〇 [10]莫非 [11]庸莫 [12]莫不是〇 [13]淡漠〇 [14]朔漠〇 [15]沙漠 [16]寂寞

幕 Mo. Mu. A curtain, a screen, a canopy; a tent, a marquee; greaves, defences for the legs and shoulders; to cover; a private military secretary, a confidential clerk: [1]ˏmi mokˀ a screen; [2]mokˀ ˈhu, an encampment; a secretary's official rooms; [3]ˏiu mokˀ a secretary on a circuit; [4]lëkˀ mokˀ the universe; [5]mokˀ ˏping (com. mokˀ ˈiu), an officer's adviser or secretary.

(456) Mong.

ˏMong. A coll. word: a kind of grass, called ˏmong ˈch'au, gathered for fuel; ˏmong ekˀ (or kekˀ) a kind of candle with a single pith-wick attached to the ˏmëng ˈkó stalk—also termed t'ai' ekˀ by shopmen.

ˏMong. A coll. word, as in ˏmiéng ˏmong, or ˏmiéng ˏmiéng ˏmong ˏmong, all properly arranged, put in their places, as things.

ˏMong. A coll. word, as in ˏmong ˏmong or ˏmong ˏmong ˏhing, fluttered, distracted, harassed.

莽 莾 Mang. A dog in the grass; thick grass, weeds, underbrush; a plant noxious to fishes; indistinct, confused, tangled; rude, rustic, clownish: [6]ˈch'ó ˈmong, tangled, jungly; rude, boorish; [7]ˈch'ó mukˀ ˈmong ˈmong, a thick, tangled underbrush; COM., [8]ˈlu ˈmong, rough, impertinent.

蟒 Mang. The boa or anaconda, largest of serpents: [9]ˈmong ˏt'ăng, a species of caterpillar; COM., [10]ˈmong ˏsié, the boa; [11]ˈmong ˏpó, a court dress embroidered with boas; [12]ˈmong ˏkung, a skirt embroidered with boas or dragons.

夢 梦 Mêng. To dream, to see visions; a dream, a vision; a vanity; obscure, without evidence, visionary: in the coll. read maĕng' q. v.: [13]mong' tieu² prognostics of a dream; [14]mong' me² ˏchi sëü² a visionary affair; [15]ekˀ ˏtiong tai² mong' "one long dream"—i. e., this life, the world; COM., [16]mong' ˈsiong pokˀ tó' before one could dream or think—scil., it occurred.

懞 懵 Mêng. Dull, stupid, obscure, not intelligent; vexed, perturbed; grieved, sorrowful; ashamed: in the coll. read ˈmung, q. v.: mong' mong' ignorant, stupid.

忙 Mang. The mind distracted with cares, fluttered; busy, hurried, much occupied: COM., [17]ˏhwong ˏmong, hurried, perturbed; [18]ˏu sëü² ˏmong, to hurry about needlessly; ˏmong ˏtăng ˈch'ó ˈch'ó, to do superficially when in a hurry; COLL., ˏmong ˏmong ˈchau, to hurry to and fro, driven with work and cares.

砿 Mang. Name of a hill: ˏmong t'aukˀ (or taung'), a rocky mountain; COM., [19]ˏmong ˏsieu (or p'aukˀ ˏsieu), a kind of salt, like Epsom salts.

芒 Mang. Wang. The awn or beard of grain; the sharp, spinous points, as of grasses; any sharp point; close, crowded, great; fatigued: in the

[1]帷幕 [2]幕府 [3]遊幕 [4]六幕 [5]幕賓 [6]草莽 [7]草木莽莽 [8]鹵莽 [9]蟒蛀 [10]蟒蛇 [11]蟒袍 [12]蟒裙 [13]夢兆 [14]夢寐之事 [15]一場大夢 [16]夢想不到 [17]慌忙 [18]無事忙 [19]砿硝〇

福州方言拼音字典

coll. read ꜀*mĕng*, q. v.: [1] ꜀*kwong* ꜀*mong*, a gleam or flash of light; [2] ꜀*mong* ꜀*mong* ꜀*yong* ꜀*kwi*, excessively fatigued, he returned; COM., [3] ꜀*mong* ‛*chüng*, "bearded grain"—the 9th of the 24 solar terms; COLL., ꜀*mong* ‛*chüng taung*ʼ *hwo*ʼ ‛*hwi* ꜀*sieu* ꜀*ká*, in the ꜀*mong* ‛*chüng* term showers fall and the heat scorches the streets.

芒 ꜀Mang. The immense expanse of the ocean; confusing, dazzling; vast, indistinct, uncertain: [4] ꜀*ch‛ong* ꜀*mong*, vast, dreary, as a watery waste; COM., [5] ‛*mieu* ꜀*mong*, vast and indistinct, incapable of proof.

邙 ꜀Mang. Name of a hill and town, near the ancient capital Loyang.

鋩 ꜀Mang. The point or edge of a sword: ꜀*hung* ꜀*mong*, the edge of a knife or weapon.

悶ʼ 懣ʼ Mĕn. Sad, sorrowing, melancholic; chagrined, depressed in spirit; grieved, distressed, afflicted: COM., [6] ꜀*iu mong*ʼ or ‛*k‛u mong*ʼ grieved, sad, dejected; [7] *ok*꜀ *mong*ʼ vexed, unhappy; [8] *mong*ʼ *mong*ʼ *pok*꜀ *lok*꜀ disconsolate and joyless; COLL., ꜀*mang mong*ʼ discontented; *mong*ʼ ‛*si* ꜀*nĕng*, to grieve one's self to death.

*Mong*ʼ. A coll. word: to fry with a seasoning of oil, soy, etc.: *mong*ʼ *nük*꜀ to fry pork thus; *mong*ʼ ꜀*chau*, to fry (meats) with a seasoning made of distillers' grains.

(457) Mu.

‛母 Mu. A mother, she or that which produces; a female, the female of animals; *met.*, earth; the source of; large, superior: in the coll. read ‛*mó*, q. v.: [9] *sek*꜀ ‛*mu*, the ten stems; COM., [10] ‛*mu* ꜀*ch‛ing*, a mother; [11] ꜀*ch‛ing* ‛*mu*, husband's or wife's mother, the mothers-in-law; [12] *kié*ʼ ‛*mu*, a step-mother; [13] ‛*ü* ‛*mu*, a nurse, a foster-mother; [14] ‛*pwong* ꜀*seng* ‛*mu*, own mother; [15] ‛*mu keu*ʼ maternal uncles; [16] ꜀*tung ho*ʼ *ć*ʼ ‛*mu*, step brothers or sisters; [17] *kwok*꜀ ‛*mu*, the empress; [18] ꜀*t‛iĕng siong*ʼ *seng*ʼ ‛*mu*, Matsu, goddess of seamen; [19] *ho*ʼ ‛*mu* ꜀*kwang*, a district magistrate; ‛*chü* ‛*mu*, inferior and superior, small and large, as sorts of; *pwoi*ʼ ‛*mu*, a medicinal herb, used as an expectorant.

‛姆 ‛姥 Mu. A childless widow of fifty years, who can instruct others in female duties; a schoolmistress; an elder brother's wife is called ‛*mu* by her sisters-in-law: COM., ‛*mu* ‛*sing*, brothers' wives, sisters-in-law; *twai*ʼ ‛*mu*, wife of my husband's elder brother; ‛*mu* ꜀*pó*, wife of grandfather's elder brother, grand aunt-in-law.

‛拇 Mu. Mou. The thumb; the great toe: in the coll. read ‛*mó*, q. v.: *tai*ʼ ‛*mu*, the great toe; ꜀*piĕng* ‛*mu*, a double thumb or toe.

‛某 Mou. Mu. A certain time, place, person, or thing, used when the name is unknown or concealed, and in suppositive phrases; also for the

1光 然 4滄 6憂 8悶 9十 11親 13乳 母 父 母 母
芒 歸 茫 悶 悶 母 母 母 15母 異 18天 19父
2芒 3芒 5渺 7鬱 不 10母 12繼 14本 舅 母 上 母
芒 種 茫 悶 樂 親 母 生 16同 17國 聖 官

ALPH. DICT. 73

pronoun I: COM., [1]'mu nik, a certain day; [2]'mu ch'ëü' such a place; COLL., 'mu ,nëng, a certain person.

牡 Mou. Mu. Read 'meu; coll. 'mu, as in [3]'mu ,tang, the Mowtan peony; 'mu ,tang ,ta, the Mowtan camellia.

畝 Mou. Mu. Read 'meu; coll. 'mu: a Chinese acre, which has much varied in size; as now estimated, 6. 61 'mu equal an English acre: [4],ch'eng sioh, 'mu, an acre of arable land.

'Mu. A coll. word, as in 'mu liok, nearly, approximately; 'mu liok, nioh, wai' about how many or much?

(458) Muh.

Muh,. A coll. word: to strike, to beat with the fist, to pound, as something soft: muh, sioh, ,t'ui, to give a blow with the fist; muh, pwang' ,sang 'si, to beat half to death.

(459) Muí.

媒 Mei. One who negotiates marriages, a matchmaker, a go-between; the efficient agent or cause of an effect; to covet, to be officious: COM., [5]'siă' ,muí, to make presents to a matchmaker; [6],u ,muí pok, ,sing ,ch'ing, without go-betweens marriages can't be made; COLL., [7],muí ,nëng, a matchmaker; ,ch'iăng ,muí, to complete a marriage-contract (left unfinished by the former go-between); [8]'chó' ,muí, to act as a decoy at a gambling-place.

煤 Mei. Soot; coals, embers; coal, charcoal: COM., [9],muí t'ang' fossil or hard coal; [10]'chai ,muí, a paper match; [11]'hwi ,muí, embers; also paper-matches.

禖 Mou. Sacrifice or worship offered by an emperor to obtain a son and heir.

腜 Mou. To conceive, incipient conception; quickening: ,muí ,muí, fat, lusty, good-looking; [12],muí ,t'ai, to quicken in the womb.

脢 Mei. The flesh on the breast or between the heart and mouth; flesh by the back-bone.

梅 Mei. A plum, a prune, an apricot; the flowering almond: [13]'p'ieu ,muí, marriageable; [14],muí ,muí, dull, obscure; [15],muí 'ü, spring rains; COM., [16],muí ,hwa, the flowering almond; [17],song ,muí, pickled apricots; [18],muí ,hiong, almond-fragrance; met., a young female slave; [19],yong ,muí, (coll. ,ch'io ,ung), the Chinese tree-strawberry (a *Myrica*); COLL., ,muí ,ëng, a light red; ,muí sak, to chaffer, as a buyer does; ,muí ,hwa 'tiéng siék, (or 'piéng sik,) ,tang, a small yellow-coated pill (from Peking)—used on sores, &c.

枚 Mei. A shrub or stalk of a plant; a cane, a stick, a switch; a gag; a classifier, as of rings or the seeds of fruit; each, one of: [20],teu ,muí, branches and stems; ,kang ,muí, to hold a gag in the mouth; [21],ch'ai ,muí, to guess the fingers—game of morra.

[1]某日 [2]某處 [3]牡丹 [4]田一畝 [5]謝媒〇 [6]無媒不成 [7]媒人〇 [8]做媒 [9]煤炭 [10]紙煤 [11]火煤 [12]腜胎 [13]摽梅 [14]梅梅 [15]梅雨 [16]梅花 [17]酸梅 [18]梅香 [19]楊梅 [20]條枚 [21]猜枚

玫 ꜀Mei. A bright red stone, red coral: COM., [1]꜀muí koi꜄ red jasper; [2]꜀muí koi꜄ ꜀hwa, a kind of red rose.

鋂 ꜀Mei. A sort of large, double lock, a ring having in it two locks to bolt a door: [3]꜀tūng ꜀muí, a double lock.

莓 ꜀Mei. A kind of edible berry, like the raspberry, called [4]muk꜆ ꜀muí; moss: in the coll. read ꜂mwi, q. v.: [5]꜀muí ꜀t'ai, moss and lichens, as in damp places.

霉 ꜀Mei. Summer rains, damp weather; damp, moldy, mildewed; to mildew, spoiled by mold: COM., [6]꜀muí ꜂ü, incessant rains; [7]꜀muí ꜀t'iéng, damp, molding weather; COLL., ꜀muí mauk꜆ soft, rotten, spoiled by mildew.

꜀Muí. A coll. word, similar to máh꜆ in meaning, as in ch'au꜄ ꜀kau ꜀muí, a place where water is thrown, a filthy puddle.

꜀Muí. A coll. prefix, as in ꜀muí mwoi꜄ little sister! Miss!

(460) Muk.

木 Mu. ꜆ Wood, wooden; a tree; one of the five elements and eight sounds; plain, unpretending; stiff, honest, unbending; the 75th radical: in the coll. read mĕk꜆ q. v.: COM., [8]꜂ch'ó muk꜆ grasses and trees, plants; [9]muk꜆ laiu꜄ timber; [10]muk꜆ ꜀hiong, putchuck; one says starwort; [11]muk꜆ ꜀sing, the planet Jupiter; [12]꜀twang muk꜆ a surname, Mr. Twangmuk; [13]muk꜆ ch'iong꜄ a carpenter; [14]muk꜆ ꜂pwong ꜂chwi ꜀ngwong, "root and fountain"—one's ancestors; COLL., [15]꜂ch'eu꜄ muk꜆ trees; [16]꜂t'u so꜄ muk꜆ ꜀teu, images of clay and wood; met., a stupid fellow, a blockhead.

沐 Mu. Shu. ꜆ To wash the head, to cleanse and anoint the hair; to wash, to bathe; to enrich by kindness, to receive favor; favored, enriched; to rule kindly: COM., muk꜆ ꜀ong, to receive favor; [17]muk꜆ ük꜆ ꜀keng ꜀i, to wash, bathe, and change the clothes, as before an act of worship.

沒 殁 Mu. Mo. Mei. ꜆ To sink in water, to perish, fall into oblivion; to die, to finish one's course, dead, annihilated, gone; to exceed, to surpass, to transgress; to enrich one's self by swindling; a negative, not, without, nothing of, none at all, not the least: [18]muk꜆ ěüng꜄ useless; [19]muk꜆ ꜂iu, not to have, has none; [20]꜂ch'ok꜆ muk꜆ to come forth (and prowl) then skulk, as robbers, rats, etc.; muk꜆ sié꜄ (or ꜂ch'i) pok꜆ ꜀wong, till death I will not forget you; muk꜆ yoh꜆ myrrh; muk꜆ ꜀kwang, confiscated or appropriated by the officers; ꜀chiong ꜀ka hok꜆ muk꜆ the whole family has perished.

楘 ꜆ Ornamented bands of leather, put about a car to strengthen it.

鶩 Mu. ꜆ Mallards or wild ducks; a duck of any kind: ꜀ku muk꜆ a wild duck.

目 Mu. ꜆ The eye; met., the mind, mental perception; to eye, to look at; to designate, to quote or speak of, to

[1]玫瑰 [2]玫瑰花 [3]重鋂○ [4]木莓 [5]莓苔 [6]霉雨 [7]霉天 [8]草木 [9]木料 [10]木香 [11]木星 [12]端木 [13]木匠 [14]木本水源 [15]樹木 [16]土塑木雕 [17]沐浴更衣 [18]沒用 [19]沒有 [20]出沒

particularize; a director, a leader, the chief, the principal person; a list, a summary, an index; meshes of a net; squares on a chess-board; the 109th radical: in the coll. read *mek* and *mĕk* q. v.: [1]*teu muk* a list, summary; [2]*hwang muk* to turn against, unfriendly; [3]*k'wo muk* literary ranks above Siutsai; COM., [4]*muk ha* before the eyes, now; [5]*muk lioh* an index, table of contents; [6]*muk kek 'ngi ung*, to see with one's own eyes (or) hear by report; [7]*muk liêng chong 'chiă*, the honorable *Muk liêng*—an ancient worthy to whom vows are paid in puppet-shows.

苜 Mu. An herb: *muk sëük*, trefoil or clover on which cows and horses are fed.

睦 Mu. A kind eye; kind, benignant, harmonious, peaceful; harmony, concord among relatives; to make peace, to agree with: [8]*ch'ing muk* affectionate; COM., [9]*hwo muk* harmony, concord; *pok muk* discordant.

牧 Mu. To tend cattle, to pasture, to lead a flock to pasturage; a shepherd, a cowherd, a horse-keeper; to superintend, to watch over; ruler of a district, one in charge of a place; applied to religious teachers: [10]*muk ing* or *muk hu*, a herdman; [11]*pi 'i chëü muk* to be humble; [12]*muk ming*, to rule the people; *ui ming muk* to be a district magistrate; COM., [13]*muk sü*, an overseer, a shepherd; a pastor or christian minister.

穆 Mu. The fine appearance of grain; pleasing, handsome; majestic, inspiring respect and admiration; to please, to gratify; to revere; used in books for Mohammed: *muk muk* admirable, grand, royal; *chieu muk* order of precedence of ancestral tablets from left to right, as of grandfathers, fathers, sons—the *chieu* being always superior to *muk*.

霂 Mu. Small rain: [14]*mek muk* a fine, drizzling rain.

(461) Mung.

儚 Mêng. Read *meng* and *meng*; used in the *Paik Ing* for the coll. *mung*, as in [15]*mang mung*, dull, stupid; *mung mung tioh* a dull, confused look, as of one awaking from sleep.

濛 Mêng. Read *mung*; coll. *mung*, as in [16]*mung mung t'iêng*, dark, gloomy weather; *mang mang mung mung*, dark, dusky, as skies threatening rain; *mung mung t'iăng* a slight pain; *mung mung kek*, fretting, brooding over.

Mung. A coll. word, as in *mung 'king 'king*, to cover closely, to conceal, keep dark about.

Mung. A coll. word: to heat over: *mung pwong* to warm up cold rice.

懞 Mêng. Read *mong*; coll. *'mung*, as in [17]*'mung 'tung*, dull, not intelligent, confused in mind; [18]*'mung 'tung ong*

1條目 2反目 3科目 4目下 5目錄 6目擊 7目連 耳聞 尊者 8親睦 9和睦 10牧人 11卑以自牧 12牧民 13牧師 14霢霂 15朦儚 16濛濛天〇 17懞懂〇 18懞懂運〇

福州方言拼音字典

confused destiny, as of one always unlucky.

蠓 ꜂Mêng. Also read ꜁mung in the dictionaries: ephemera or sandflies, insects that fly over water: in the coll. read ꜂mĕng, q. v.: [1]miék꜆ ꜂mung, gnats.

蒙 ꜁Mêng. A kind of moss; ignorant, immature, as a child; dull, simple, beclouded, perceiving obscurely; a child, a pupil, a youth; to cover, to conceal from; to deceive, to cozen; to act rudely, rash, precipitate; thankful, obliged for, grateful for favors; the 4th of the 64 diagrams: in the coll. read ꜁mang, q. v.: [2]hong꜄ ꜁mung, to teach youth; [3]꜁hung ꜁mung, chaos; [4]꜀tó ꜁mung, many thanks, much obliged for; COM., [5]꜁mung mwói꜄ dull, ignorant; [6]꜁mung ꜀ong, to receive favors; [7]꜁mung hong꜄ confused, deceived; blended, mixed; [8]꜁mung pe꜄ to cover, to conceal; *met.*, tempted, seduced by; [9]꜁mung ꜂ku, the Mongols; COLL., [10]꜁mung kang꜄ yoh꜆ a medicinal powder, said to be used by thieves to stupefy sleepers.

矇 ꜁Mêng. Dim-sighted, weak eyes; unable to see clearly from a disease in the optic nerves, an amaurosis; ignorant of one's self, unlearned, untaught: [11]꜁mung ꜂seu, blind, as minstrels.

幪 ꜁Mêng. A covering; to screen off above; to shelter, as from sun or rain: [12]꜁ping ꜁mung, to screen; ꜁mung ꜁mung, abundant, luxuriant.

曚 ꜁Mêng. The sun obscured or not yet risen: ꜁mung ꜁lung, early in the morning, daybreak; COLL., ꜁mung ꜁lung ꜀tiéng ꜂tó, confused, jumbled, as the thoughts.

朦 ꜁Mêng. Similar to the last: the moon about to rise or set: [13]꜁mung ꜁lung, dim, obscure, as the moon beclouded or about to rise.

檬 ꜀Mêng. A tree like the cassia, having a yellow leaf; some say it resembles the ash: [14]꜁mung ꜂kwo, the mango, as some use the term.

濛 ꜁Mêng. Small, drizzling rain; misty, foggy: in the coll. read ꜀mung, q. v.: [15]꜁mung ꜁hung, or ꜁hung ꜁mung, vapors, primitive chaos.

艨 ꜁Mêng. A long, fast-sailing war-junk, called [16]꜁mung ꜁tung; a large sort of vessel.

饛 ꜁Mêng. A dish filled with food, hence an abundance of food, a plentiful table: [17]꜂iu ꜁mung ꜂kwi ꜀song, to have a repast on full dishes.

霥 ꜁Mêng. A small rain; fine drizzling showers: ꜁mung ꜁mung, incessant rains.

(462) **Mwai.**

Mwai꜄. A coll. word, about the same as *moi*꜄: a fine, drizzling rain or mist; wet or saturated with mist: *mwai*꜄ *mwai*꜄ ꜂*ü*, a fine rain; *mwai*꜄ *sioh*꜆ ꜀*sing*, the whole person wet with drizzle.

1 蠛蠓 2 訓蒙 3 鴻蒙 4 多蒙 5 蒙昧 6 蒙恩 7 蒙混 8 蒙蔽 9 蒙古 10 蒙汗藥 11 矇瞍〇 12 帡幪〇 13 曚曨〇 14 檬果〇 15 濛鴻〇 16 艨艟〇 17 有饛簋飧

埋 Mai. Man. Read ˛mai; coll. ˛mwai: to bury, to inter; to secrete, to conceal, to put under ground: [1]˛mwai chaung' to inter; [2]˛mwai huk˛ to lie in ambush; [3]wak˛ ˛mwai, to bury alive; [4]˛mwai muk˛ buried, undeveloped, as one's ability.

痳 Ma. Read ˛ma; coll. ˛mwai: a cutaneous, spotted disease, like the 'mëng (measles), but much less severe: [5]'ch'ok˛ ˛mwai, to have the ˛mwai eruption.

麻 蔴 Ma. Read ˛ma; coll. ˛mwai: hemp, the female plant; sackcloth, mourning apparel; hempen: [6]˛mwai pwo' hempen cloth; [7]˛p'ié ˛mwai, to wear mourning—term used in coll. books; [8]˛iu ˛mwai, the sesame; [9]˛mwai ˛iu, oil of sesame; [10]˛mwai ˛chié, a kind of doughnut, incrusted with sesame-seeds and boiled in fat or oil; [11]˛mwai se' ˛mwai tau' se' tau' "sesame is sesame and beans are beans"—to discriminate and perform accurately.

磨 Mo. Read ˛mó; coll. ˛mwai: to whet, to sharpen, to grind; to rub, to polish by rubbing: [12]˛mwai ˛tó, to whet a knife; [13]˛mwai mĕk˛ to grind ink (on the stone); [14]˛mwai ˛kwong, to polish; ˛mwai le' to sharpen; ˛mwai miăng' to toil, to druge.

(463) Mwak.

抹 Mo. To daub, to smear, to rub on; to color, to anoint; to rub out, to wipe clean, to sweep away all; to blot out, to erase, to obliterate: in the coll. read maĕk˛ q. v.: COM., [15]˛tu mwak˛ to blot out; [16]mwak˛ so' to cancel an account; [17]mwak˛ ˛yéng ˛chié, to apply rouge, as to the middle of the lower lip; COLL., mwak˛ sioh˛ ˛t'iong, to draw out a card; lau' yoh˛ mwak˛ ˛kie 'kiăng, the hawk swoops up the chicken.

沫 Mo. Ma. A branch of the river Yangtsz' in Sz'chuen; foam, bubbles on water; froth at the mouth, spittle: [18]˛yong mwak˛ froth, saliva; [19]'k'eu mwak˛ expectoration; [20]'t'o' mwak˛ to spit out, to sputter.

秣 Mo. Provender for cattle; to feed horses with straw, to give hay to cattle: [21]˛ch'ü mwak˛ provender, fodder.

末 Mo. The ends of branches, the outermost twigs; the end, the termination; the last of, the fag-end, the meanest the least important; opposite, of the origin or the root; small, weak; used for I, myself; far off, distant; the leavings, remnants, dust-powder, refuse of; the limbs; traders, as the least of the four classes: mwak˛ 'iu, no more of; mwak˛ chiong' I, the general; 'pwong mwak˛ origin and end; mwak˛ chik˛ the limbs diseased; ˛mi mwak˛ insignificant; COM., mwak˛ mwak˛ small particles, powdered; mwak˛ sié' "end of the world"—a waning dynasty; COLL., ˛ta nioh˛ mwak˛ remnants of tea leaves; tea-dust.

帓 A napkin, a handkerchief, a turban; a kind of sash: in the coll. read mak˛ q. v.:

[1]埋葬 [2]埋伏 [3]活埋 [4]埋沒 [5]出痳 [6]麻布 [7]披麻 [8]油麻 [9]麻油 [10]麻芝 [11]麻是麻豆是豆 [12]磨刀 [13]磨墨 [14]磨光 [15]塗抹 [16]抹數 [17]抹胭脂 [18]涎沫 [19]口沫 [20]沫吐 [21]芻秣 ○

COLL., 'mwak, ngiăh, a kind of head-band or fillet, worn by women.

茉 Mo. The jasmine, called [2]mwak, le' ,hwa, the Jasminum grandiflorum; name of a song: in the coll. read mĕk, q. v.

Mwak,. A coll. word, used by boatmen, as in *mwak*, 'tiong ,t'au, to turn about, as a ship anchored in the tide; *mwak*, p'wong' to swing with the ebb.

(464) Mwang.

'滿 '滿 Man. Full, filled up; replete, stuffed, surfeited; entire, all, complete, all that the subject includes; to fill, to abound, to suffice; finished, ended, as a set time; forms part of the name for Manchu: in the coll. read 'mang, q. v.: COM., [3],ch'üng 'mwang, or 'mwang cheük, full, filled, abundant; [4]'mwang ,sing, the whole mind or heart; [5]'mwang ,chiu, Manchu, Manchuria; [6]'mwang ,ki, the set time fully come; [7]'mwang hang' sik, a feast in which animals roasted whole are served up; [8],sing 'mwang e' cheük, satisfied, fully contented; 'mwang 'k'eu ,hu siok, his mouth is full of lies; COLL., 'mwang sié' or 'mwang tói' everywhere; 'chi 'mwang 'hó (usually spoken 'chi 'mang 'hó), so good, so very good; 'mwang ,sang ,ĕng, the red Azalea.

瞞 ,Man. A flat eye, one whose canthi are nearly level with the face; dull or half closed eyes, obscure vision; to blind, to deceive, to cheat; to conceal from, to impose on: [9]'ak, ,mwang, the infantile name of Tsao Tsa'o, A. D. 250; COM., [10],mwang p'iéng' to deceive; [11],chiă ,mwang, to conceal, to hide from; [12],mwang ,kwang móh, ,k'i ,kwang, deceive the officer, but don't insult him; COLL., [13]'che' ,mwang che' self-deception; [14],mó ,mwang ,t'iéng ,mó ,mwang te' not deceive Heaven and Earth—a form of strong asseveration.

璊 ,Man. A gem, a valuable stone of a reddish or carnation color.

蹣 ,Man. Also read ,pwang in the dictionaries: to walk lame, to move the feet irregularly in walking: [15],mwang ,ch'iong, to jump a wall.

蔓 ,Man. Read mang' and wang'; coll. ,mwang, as in ,mwang ,ching, a coarse vegetable, like the turnip; it has many fibrous roots, and its leaves are called ,mwang ,ching 'chĕng.

鏝 ,Man. A trowel: ,ná ,mwang, a plasterer's trowel; ,mwang ,hu term for a spear or halberd.

饅 ,Man. Steamed bread or wheaten loaves, leavened and light, called ,mwang ,t'eu, in the coll. ,ming ,t'au, q. v.

鰻 ,Man. An eel, called [16],mwang ,lai, like the conger eel, having large pectoral fins: COM., [17],lu ,mwang, a large kind of eel; [18],mwang ,ngü 'siong, eels salted and dried;

[1]帓頟 [2]茉莉 花[3]充滿〇 [4]滿心 [5]滿洲 [6]滿期 [7]滿漢 席[8]心滿意 足[9]阿瞞 [10]瞞騙 [11]遮瞞 [12]瞞官莫欺官 [13]自瞞自 [14]無瞞天無瞞地 [15]蹣墻 [16]饅[17]鱸鰻〇 鰻鱛

'*tang*' '*chwi* ˏ*mwang*, fresh water eels; COLL., ˏ*chong* (or *chaung*') ˏ*mwang*, a species of mud-eel; ˏ*mwang t'ié*' *kok*ˎ "the eel follows slipperily"; *met.*, to imitate readily.

(465) Mwí

ˏ*Mwi.* A coll. word: used to designate the daughters of a family in the order of ages: *twai*' ˏ*mwi*, *ne*' ˏ*mwi*, ˏ*sang* ˏ*mwi*, the first, second, and third daughters.

'每 Mei. Each, every, each one, all, any one; usually, always, constantly; although; to covet: COM., '*mwi* '*mwi*, always, constantly; [2]'*mwi* ˏ*hui* or [3]'*mwi ch'ü*' every time; [4]'*mwi ngwok*ˎ ˏ*ch'ë ek*, on the first day of every month.

'莓 Mei. Read ˏ*mui*; coll. '*mwi*, as in [5]'*mwi* ˏ*si*(or ˏ*li*) an aquatic vegetable, water-chestnuts —same as *pwok*ˎ ˏ*chú*, q. v.: '*mwi* ˏ*si* ˏ*kó*, cakes of water-chestnuts, grated and mixed with *kak*, '*hung*.

'尾 Wei. I. The tail of an animal; the end, extremity, termination of; the last, remnants, driblets; little things; the bottom, the hinder part of; a stern; a classifier of fishes; copulation of animals; the 6th of the 28 constellations: [6]'*só* '*mwi*, petty, trifling; [7]'*che*' '*mwi*, copulation of birds; COM., [8]'*mwi twai*' a rudder; [9]'*mwi* '*ch'iu*, afterwards, at last; [10]'*mwi tá*' *ne*' the second from the end; [11]'*pá* '*mwi*, to wag the tail; COLL., *wa*' '*mwi* ˏ*kiu k'ó*' to take back one's words; '*mwi* '*chai*, the little finger; *toi*' '*mwi*, at the end, finally; *o*' ˏ*t'au* ˏ*mó* '*mwi*, a beginning without end, incomplete; '*mwi* ˏ*pau te*' bottom of the spinal column; '*mwi* '*kiang* '*mwi* ˏ*ching* ˏ*chio*, "the last child is the last pearl"—the last one is the pet.

'浼 Mei. To defile, to foul, to stain, as with dirty water; used affectedly, to annoy, to request, to ask favors: [12]'*mwi t'auk*, to request one's kind offices. Read '*mieng*: to glide smoothly, as water.

'亹 Mên. Also read '*ni*: continued effort, unwearied, indefatigable; to do willingly: also read ˏ*mwong*, q. v.

(466) Mwo.

ˏ摸 Mo. ˏ捫 Men. The first read ˏ*mwo*, the second ˏ*mwong*; coll. ˏ*mwo*: to lay the hand on, to feel, to touch; to examine, or search for, with the hand; to rub, to soothe: ˏ*mwo tioh*ˎ touched, found by feeling; [13]*ang*' *ang*' ˏ*mwo*, dark, obscure; [14]ˏ*mwo* ˏ*u*, soiled by handling; [15]ˏ*mwo sük*ˎ skilled by practice in; [16]ˏ*sëng* '*ch'iu* ˏ*mwo* ˏ*t'iéng*, touches the sky with both hands—has a towering ambition; [17]ˏ*mwo sok*ˎ to stroke and soothe; ˏ*mwo mah*ˎ to feel the pulse.

'姆 A coll. character, used in the *Paik*, ˏ*Ing*: a wife: [18]'*mwo sai*' wife and husband; [19]'*mwo* '*kiang*, wife and children; ˏ*pwung ch'io*' *p'ah*, *taung*' ˏ*mwo*, in removing to a new abode lost his wife!

1淡水鰻○ 2每回 3每次 4每月初一 5莓蒔 6瑣尾 7孳尾 8尾舵 9尾手二 10尾第 11擺尾○ 12浼託 13暗暗 14摸烏○ 15摸熟 16雙手 摸天 17摸捞 18姆壻 19姆仔

墓² Mu. A tumulus, a mound, a barrow; a tomb, a grave, a sepulcher: COM., [1]mwo² té² sites of graves, a cemetery; [2]ˌhung mwo² graves; [3]'chié² mwo² or siong² mwo² to sacrifice at graves; [4]mwo² ˌpá, a grave-stone; [5]mwo² 'k'wong, the pit or vault of a tomb; [6]mwo² ˌtiăng, the level space before a grave: COLL., mwo² k'ah, one in charge of a grave.

嫫 ˌMo. The fourth concubine of Hwangti, B. C. 2600; plain, ordinary, ill-looking: COLL., kaĕng² ˌmwo 'mu sioh, yong² as ugly as dame ˌMwo.

模 ˌMo. A pattern, a model, a mold; a form, shape, or guide for imitation; a rule, a law: [7]ˌhing ˌmwo, a form, model; COM., [8]ˌmwo yong² a pattern; [9]ˌkié ˌmwo, a rule; manner, example; [10]ˌmwo ˌhu, obscure, illegible; COLL., [11]ˌnĕng ˌmwo, one's figure, as emaciated or seen dimly.

摹 ˌMo. Interchanged with the last: a rule, a pattern; to follow a pattern, to copy, to imitate, to sketch; to feel with the hand: [12]ˌmwo wa² to copy pictures, to sketch; COM., [13]ˌmwo 'hwong, to follow the pattern; [14]ˌmwo che² to take a copy or impression, as of graven words.

謨 ˌMo. Counsel, consultation, a matured plan; a rule, a settled course of action or conduct; to imitate: [15]ˌmeu ˌmwo, to devise plans. Used for ˌu (not), as in ˌmwo seng² not faithful, insincere.

ˌMwo. A coll. word, as in ˌmwo o² fog, mist; ˌmwo kau² a dense fog; ˌmwo lo² mist and dew, dew.

ˌMwo. A coll. word: dim, obscure, darkened, obscured: ˌmwo ˌmwo, obscure, as the weather, glass, etc.; ˌmwo ˌmwo ˌkwong, a dim light, day-break.

戊² Wu. The fifth of the ten stems, which answers to earth; a fortunate day; abundant, luxuriant.

慕² Mo. Mu. To think of with affection, to remember fondly; to long for, to hanker, to be fond of; to aspire, ambitious: [16]'ngiong mwo² to look up to, to revere: COM., [17]ˌsü mwo² or [18]'siong mwo² to think fondly of, to long for; [19]mwo² ˌming (or ˌmiăng), to aspire after fame.

募² Mu. To invite, to solicit, to call on people to do; to give bounties to, to enlist; a public invitation, a general call: [20]eng² mwo² to respond to a levy: COM., [21]ˌchieu mwo² to enlist, to levy; [22]mwo² 'üng, to enlist braves; [23]mwo² hwa² to beg alms, to get subscriptions, as priests do; [24]mwo² ˌyong, a general appeal or subscription.

暮² Mo. Mu. The evening, the sunset; decline of life; close of a period of time: ˌtieu mwo² morning and evening; nik, mwo² sunset; mwo² 'king, the state or prospects of the aged; COM., mwo² ˌniéng, evening of life, old age; ˌniéng ˌchăng swoi² mwo² close of the

[1]墓地 [2]墳墓 [3]祭墓 [4]墓牌 [5]墓壙 [6]墓埕 [7]形模 [8]模樣 [9]規模 [10]模糊 [11]人模 [12]摹畫 [13]摹倣 [14]摹字 [15]謀謨 [16]仰慕 [17]思慕 [18]想慕 [19]慕名 [20]應募 [21]招募 [22]募勇 [23]募化 [24]募緣

year; COLL., *mek*, *ˏchiu mwo*ʼ the eyes dim, dim-sighted.

瞙ʼ Read *mok*, *;* used in the *Paik*, *ˏIng* for the coll. *mwo*ʼ*: mwo*ʼ *mwo*ʼ dim, obscure; *ˏtʻiêng mwo*ʼ *mwo*ʼ *tioh*, the sky obscured.

(467) Mwoí.

妹ʼ Mei. A younger sister; one's daughter; a sister, a miss: [1]*ˏkwi mwoí*ʼ marriage of a girl; the 54th diagram; [2]*ngwoí*ʼ *mwoí*ʼ half-sisters; COM., [3]*ʻchiă mwoí*ʼ sisters; [4]*ˏpau mwoí*ʼ own sister; [5]*mwoí*ʼ *ˏhu*, younger sister's husband; [6]*ˏling mwoí*ʼ your sister; [7]*ʻpieu ʻchiă mwoí*ʼ female cousins; COLL., *ˏmuí mwoí*ʼ little sister! siss! *mwoí*ʼ *ˏkó* (or *ˏkwang*), his or your daughter, Miss.

沬ʼ Mei. Name of a stream; the name of a city of the ancient Wei state; dark, obscure.

韎ʼ Mei. A plant used in dyeing scarlet; a kind of leather covering for the knees, used by soldiers.

未ʼ Wei. Read *e*ʼ*;* used for the coll. *mwoí*ʼ*:* not yet, not now: [8]*mwoí*ʼ *ˏli*, has not yet come; *siăh*, *pwong*ʼ *ʻa mwoí*ʼ have you eaten rice yet? *mwoí*ʼ *pʻah*, *ˏseng kieu*ʼ cries out before he is whipped; *mwoí*ʼ *kau*ʼ *ˏki*, not yet come to the set time.

昧ʼ Mei. No sun, twilight, dull, dark, obscure, somber; not understanding, blind, ignorant; false, perfidious: [9]*mwoí*ʼ *ʻsong* and [10]*mwoí*ʼ *kok*, dawn and dusk; [11]*mô*ʼ *mwoí*ʼ rash, inconsiderate; COM., [12]*ˏmung mwoí*ʼ (coll. *ˏmang mwoí*ʼ), dull, ignorant.

魅ʼ Mei. An ogre, a demon-brute, which seduces and frightens people; supposed to have four legs and a human face: used in the coll. for *ʻmai*, q. v.: [13]*ˏliê mwoí*ʼ elves and ogres.

痗ʼ Also read *hwoí*ʼ*:* infirmity, disease induced by care or vexation; anxiety, distress of mind: [14]*ˏsing mwoí*ʼ sick at heart.

(468) Mwok.

醫ʼ I. Read *ˏi;* used for the coll. *mwok*, *:* to heal, to cure: [15]*mwok*, *pang*ʼ to heal disease; [16]*mwok*, *ʻhó ʻlau*, healed, cured.

Mwok, . A coll. word: to kill, to slaughter; to kill and dress: *mwok*, *ˏtü*, to slaughter hogs; *ˏkiê mwok*, *sioh*, *ˏtʻau*, to kill and dress a fowl.

(469) Mwong.

ʻ晚 Wan. Read *ʻwang;* used in *Paik*, *ˏIng* for the coll. *ʻmwong*, as in [17]*ʻmwong ˏtëng* (or *ˏkwang*), the second crop of rice—reaped in the 10th moon; [18]*ʻmwong teu*ʼ the second crop in the ear, or ready for the sickle.

ʻMwong. A coll. initial particle: just, merely, only, only just; the more, still more, increasingly; falsely, confusedly, in any way, no matter how: *ʻmwong ˏtʻiăng*, just listen; *ʻmwong ʻchieu*, the fewer, fewer and fewer; *ʻmwong po*ʼ increasingly rich; *ʻmwong kaĕ*ʼ

---

1 歸妹 2 外妹 3 姐妹 4 胞妹 5 妹夫 6 令妹 7 表姐妹〇 8 未來 9 昧爽 10 昧谷 11 冒昧 12 蒙昧 13 魑魅 14 心痗 15 醫病 16 醫好了〇 17 晚冬 18 晚稍

*ʻmwong k‘ó*ʼ the more (one) calls, the more (the other) goes off; *ʻmwong ʻkong*, just say or speak on; to lie; *ʻmwong chó*ʼ *ʻla wa*ʼ to make up a story.

們ʼ A coll. character: to ask, to inquire of or about; to search into, to investigate, to demand of; to convict and banish for crime: *ʻtioh*꜁ *mwong*ʼ you must ask; *꜀mó nóh*꜁ *mwong*ʼ nothing to inquire about; *ʻmwong mwong*ʼ just ask; *mwong*ʼ *taung*ʼ to interrogate sharply; to berate one; *mwong*ʼ *꜀i ʻt‘ó*, to ask or demand it from him; *mwong*ʼ *sioh*꜁ *꜀siăng*, to make an inquiry; [3]*mwong*ʼ *꜀tu*, to exile for three years; [3]*mwong*ʼ *꜀ch‘ŭng ꜀kung*, to banish to the garrisons; [4]*mwong*ʼ *chói*ʼ to exile for crime.

門 ꜀Mên. A door, a place of ingress and egress, a gate with two leaves, a gateway; *met.*, the household, family; an opening or entrance; a sect, a class, a profession; a classifier of cannon, etc.; the 169th radical: [5]*꜀i ꜀mwong*, the medical profession; COM., [6]*꜀mwong ho*ʼ or [7]*꜀mwong siéng*ʼ doors; [8]*꜀mwong ꜀mi*, a lintel; [9]*ch‘ok*꜁ *꜀mwong*, to go out, to go abroad; [10]*꜀mwong ꜀pau*, or [11]*꜀mwong ʻlă*, a present to the door-keeper; [12]*꜀mwong ꜀lau ꜀pung*, the porter's lodge; [13]*꜀mwong ꜀seng*, or [14]*꜀mwong ꜀tu*, a pupil, disciple; [15]*huk*꜁ *꜀mwong*, Budhism; [16]*꜀mwong siong*ʼ (coll. *꜀mwong ꜀t‘au*), an officer's servant, a major-domo; [17]*sëü*ʼ *ch‘ëü*ʼ *꜀u ꜀mwong*, no door in any quarter; *met.*, no resource, destitute and helpless; COLL., [18]*꜀mwong tak*꜁ a door hasp or ring; [19]*꜀mwong aing*ʼ (or *taing*ʼ) a threshold; [20]*꜀mwong tio*ʼ a door-way, passage; *p‘ah*꜁ *꜀mwong*, or [21]*k‘aiu*ʼ *꜀mwong*, to knock at a door; [22]*꜀mwong ʻk‘au*, or *꜀mwong ch‘oi*ʼ by the door, the entrance; *꜀mwong ꜀t‘au ʻchio*, a regular customer or employer; *ʻhwí tok*꜁ *sioh*꜁ *꜀mwong*, to light one light; *ch‘ëüng*ʼ *sioh*꜁ *꜀mwong*, one gun; *꜀mwong p‘ong*ʼ *k‘ang*ʼ*꜀nëng*, *k‘ang*ʼ *ʻpiéng*, look at a man through a door-crack, and he appears flat or thin; *met.*, to disparage one unjustly; *꜀mwong k‘iăk*꜁ or *꜀mwong ꜀lau k‘iăk*꜁ a porch-like covering over the outside of a gate.

們 ꜀Men. The sign of the plural of persons; fat, plump: *ʻngó ꜀mwong*, we, us; *꜀t‘a ꜀mwong*, they; COM., *꜀ié ꜀mwong*, official attendants, you, gentlemen!

亹 ꜀Mên. A narrow entrance like a door, where a stream or frith flows between hills: also read *ʻmwí*, q. v.

文 ꜀Wên. Read *꜀ung;* used for the coll. *꜀mwong*, as in *꜀mwong ꜀chü*, a goverment document, or official dispatch; *꜀mwong ꜀chü ꜀p‘ú* (or *tói*ʼ), an official envelope; *꜀p‘au ꜀mwong ꜀chü*, to bear dispatches.

(470) **Na.**

拿 ꜀**拏** Na. To lay hold of, to seize, to take; to arrest, to apprehend; *met.*, to get an idea of, to ascertain, to appreciate: in the coll.

[1]着	[3]們	罪	戶	楣	包	樓	[14]門	[16]門	無	[19]門	[21]釦
們	充	[5]醫	[7]門	[9]出	[11]門	房	徒	上	門	閬	門
[2]們	軍	門	楄	門	禮	[13]門	[15]佛	[17]四	[18]門	[20]門	[22]門
徒	[4]們	[6]門	[8]門	[10]門	[12]門	生	門	處	搭	路	口

read *niăh*, q. v.: [1]*'na ˌlai*, to bring; [2]*'na hek*, to arrest; [3]*'na ong'* to seize and interrogate; COM., [4]*'só 'na*, to arrest and chain (criminals).

'那 Na. Nai. No. Nôn. Nêng. A demonstrative and interrogative pronoun; an adverb of place; that, that one; then, there; which, what, where, how: also read *ˌnó*, q. v.: [5]*'na kó'* that one; [6]*'na ch'ü'* there; COM., [7]*'na 'iu*, how is there—i. e., there is not; [8]*'na 'li*, where? how? COLL., *'na 't'ó*, where find—not to be found, is none; *'na ˌpang*, a kind of fence or bar, on supports like an X, as used in front of temples; *met.*, to strut, to make a swell.

ˌNa. A coll. word: to evacuate, to void, as urine or excrement: *ˌna nieu'* to urinate; *'yă ˌna*, to have frequent or irregular stools; *ˌna le'* a dysentery, flux.

ˌNa. A coll. word: to measure with the thumb and middle finger extended: *sioh, ˌna*, one such measure or space; *ˌna k'ang' nioh, wai'* measure and see how much.

㑚² No. Read *ˌnó;* used for the coll. *na²*: but, only, simply, merely; if, but if: *na² ˌchui*, only this; *na² 'la 'nü*, only you (do thus)! *na² 'hó ˌchiong wong²* only well thus—this is best or will suffice; *na² ng² 'k'ing*, but if unwilling; *na² ˌmó*, if not or none.

Na². A coll. initial particle, as in *na² 'lá chó'* to do frequently; *na² paik, k'á'* instantly, expeditiously, at once.

(471) **NÁ.**

ˌNá. A coll. word: feminine, easy, flexible, as speech; slow, easy, as one's manner; dragging on, dilatory: *ˌná ˌná ˌhing*, a slow, easy manner; *ˌná sioh, hiok*, to put off a while, dilatorily.

'奶 '妳 '嬭 Nai. Read *'ni* and *'nai* in the dictionaries: the female breast; nipples, teats, udder; milk; common term for mother; a nurse: COM., [9]*'t'ai' 'ná*, an officer's mother; [10]*ˌniong 'ná*, mother; the goddess "mother", also called [11]*ˌLing 'chwi 'ná* and *T'ak, ˌting 'ná:* [12]*'ná ˌma*, a nurse; COLL., [13]*pa² 'ná*, parents; [14]*ˌmó pa² ˌmó 'ná*, orphaned; [15]*ˌpó 'ná*, a midwife; [16]*'chiă 'ná*, a father's concubine; [17]*au² 'ná*, a step-mother; [18]*ˌi 'ná*, mother! nurse! [19]*'ná 'ná*, an officer's wife, her ladyship; [20]*sieu' 'ná 'ná*, officer's daughter-in-law. Read *'nai*, as in *ˌwong 'nai*, to sleep in the day-time.

ˌ尼 Ni. To agree, to accord with; near, agreeing; a nun: also read *nek*, q. v.: COM., [21]*ˌná ˌku*, a Budhist nun; *ˌná ˌku ˌang*, a nunnery; *tëüng' ˌná*, name of Confucius.

ˌ呢 Ni. A twittering, a humming; to speak low, to murmur: also read *ˌni* q. v.: *ˌná ˌnang*, the twittering of swallows, incessant talking.

1拿來 2拿獲 3拿問 4鎖拿 5那个 6那處 7那有 8那裡 9太奶 10娘奶 11臨水奶 12奶嬤 13罷奶 14無罷無奶 15婆奶 16姐奶 17後奶 18阿奶 ○ 19奶奶 20少奶奶 21尼姑 ○

福州方言拼音字典

妮 ꜀Ni. A slave girl; also used in the term for a nun: COM., [1]꜀ná ꜀ku, a nun.

怩 ꜀Ni. Also read nek꜆: to blush, to redden, to color up; ashamed: nek꜆ (or ꜂niu) ꜀ná, to blush from shame.

泥 ꜀坭 ꜀埿 ꜀Ni. Mud, mire, dirt; earth, soil, clay, clods; dirty, miry; in the coll. to plaster, to daub on; soiled, dirtied, befouled; met., to defame, to asperse; to try to force, to press, to insist, as on one's buying a thing: also read ná² q. v.: [2]꜀tu ꜀ná, mud, mire; [3]꜂chié ꜀ná, a signet of purple clay, as anciently used; COLL., [4]꜀ná ꜀huéi, to plaster with lime; [5]꜀ná ꜀ku, to paste; [6]꜀ná p'iéng꜄ to press one trickishly, as to purchase things; ꜀ná má² kak꜆ the daubing will not stick; met., the slander misses its object; ꜀ná ꜀ná pwong² (or chëük꜆), thick rice-congee.

泥² Ni. To decide rigidly; fixed, inflexible, set, obstinate; pertinacious, bigoted; attached to, doting on; in the coll. similar to ꜀ná, to daub, to plaster; soiled, besmeared; to press one, to insist on his taking or buying: also read ꜀ná, q. v.: COM., [7]꜆kü ná² set in one's way, bigoted; COLL., ná² ꜀seu, to plaster evenly; [8]ná² ꜀pwang, a mason's mortar-board; [9]ná² ꜂mwang meng꜄ the face daubed all over; ná² ꜀nëng tih꜆ to force one's choice, to insist on his buying.

(472) Naë.

Naë². A coll. word: fat, obese, fleshy, corpulent: ꜀pui naë² naë² very corpulent.

(473) Naëng.

Naëng². A coll. word: soft, not hard, yielding, penetrable: ꜂yä naëng² very soft; ꜂niong naëng² pliable and soft, downy, as a bed; ke² naëng² the soft persimmon.

(474) Nah.

Nah꜆. A coll. word: to abate, to slacken, to stop, as rain: ꜂ü nah, the rain slackens; ꜂ü má² nah, the rain will not abate or cease.

凹 Wa. Yao. Yeh. Ao. Read ꜀au; used in the Paik, Ing for the coll. nah꜆: the opposite of ꜂t'u (to protrude); indented, sunken, concave; an indentation, a hollow, a cavity: the same as náh, q. v.: [10]tе² nah, a depression in the ground; [11]nah ꜂tié, sunken, indented; [12]nah ꜀yeu, a hollow waist; met., a depression, as in the ridge of a house or wall; [13]nah, t'ak, k'o² hollow as a mortar, indented, sunk in.

(475) Náh.

凹 Wa. Yao. Yeh. Ao. Read ꜀au; used for the coll. náh꜆: the same as the last, concave, sunken, indented; a hollow, a cavity: [14]꜂t'u náh, protruding and sunken; ꜂ti ꜂t'u ne² náh, uneven, as a surface; [15]꜂t'u ꜀ki ꜂t'u náh, ꜀ki náh, rough and irregular; [16]꜂t'u ch'oi² náh, p'e² the mouth pouting and nose depressed, as in anger.

1妮姑 2塗泥 3紫泥 4泥灰 5泥糊 6泥騙 7拘泥 8泥盤 9泥滿面〇 10地凹 11凹入 12凹腰 13凹塌 臼凹凹〇 14凸凹 15凸其凸凹 其凹 16凸嘴 凹鼻〇

Náh˒. A coll. word: dull, stupid, unintelligent: *náh*˒ ˛*pó*, a stupid woman; ˛*nang náh*˒ dull, blockish.

(476) Nai.

˛*Nai.* A coll. word, as in ˛*pui* ˛*nai* ˛*nai*, fat and plump, fleshy, corpulent.

ˋ乃 ˋ迺 Nai. An adversative conjunction, but, it may be; doubtless, forsooth; also, moreover; an illative particle, then, thereupon, till then, if, certainly, to wit, in which senses it often needs no rendering; also used for the substantive verb, to be, is; you, yours: [1]ˋ*nai yok*˒ but as to; [2]ˋ*nai* ˋ*k'ó*, then it will do; [3]ˋ*ch'ü* ˋ*nai*, this is.

柰² 奈² Nai. A kind of bullace or wild plum, sour yet edible; to occur, to meet with; a remedy, a resource; how, in what way? COM., [4]ˋ*li nai*² a kind of plum or bullace; [5]*nai*² ˛*hó*, what resource? [6]˛*u nai*² (coll. ˛*mó nai*² ˛*hó*), no help for it, irremediable; [7]*nai*² ˛*ó* ˛*kio*, a Tauist bridge over the Styx; *met.*, a very bad road.

耐² Nai. To shave the whiskers as a punishment; to bear with, to endure, to suffer, to forbear, to be patient with; patient, patience: COM., [8]ˋ*ŭng nai*² to bear patiently, to endure; [9]*nai*² ˛*sing*, a patient mind; [10]*nai*² ˋ*kiu*, to last long; [11]*nai*² ˛*hwang*, to bear trouble and trial; [12]*nai*² ˛*kĕng*, patient in work.

䨺² Dull, stupid, unacquainted with affairs: *nai*² *tai*² ignorant, doltish.

鼐² Nai. A metallic tripod of a great size, called *nai*² ˋ*t'ing*, having two ears.

*Nai*². A coll. word, as in ˛*nai* *nai*² a name given to beggars to frighten children; ˛*nai* *nai*² *pwoh*, ˛*li*, the beggars are coming!

(477) Naing.

踚ˀ Read *niĕk*˒; used in the *Paik*, ˛*Ing* for the coll. *naing*ˀ: to stand on the toes, tiptoe: [13]˛*k'a naing*ˀ ˋ*k'i*, to stand on the toes; *naing*ˀ ˋ*lá* ˛*kiăng*, to walk on tiptoe; *naing*ˀ ˛*k'a naing*ˀ ˋ*ch'iu*, on tiptoe and light-fingered, as a thief.

念² Nien. Read *niĕng*²; coll. *naing*²: to repeat memoriter; to read aloud, to chant in a set tone, to drone: [14]*naing*² ˛*king siăh*˒ *ch'ai*ˀ to say prayers and live on vegetable diet; [15]*naing*² *chieu*ˀ to recite spells; [16]*so*ˀ *naing*² to state in order, to tell; [17]ˋ*yă naing*² ˋ*yă ch'iong*ˀ to talk wildly, to prattle, as children; *naing*² *sioh*˒ ˛*lau*, to recite once.

(478) Naiu.

皺ˀ Chou. Read *chaiu*ˀ; coll. *naiu*ˀ: wrinkled, creased, corrugated; furrowed, contracted, frowning: [18]˛*mi* ˛*t'au naiu*ˀ ˋ*king* ˋ*king*, the brow rigidly wrinkled; ˛*i* ˛*siong naiu*ˀ the clothes wrinkled; *naiu*ˀ ˛*pa* ˛*pa*, creased, wrinkled up.

1 乃若 2 乃可 3 此乃 4 李柰 5 柰何 6 無柰 7 柰河橋○ 8 忍耐 9 耐心 10 耐久 11 耐煩 12 耐工 13 跂踚起 14 念經食菜 15 念咒○ 16 訴念 17 野念野唱 18 眉頭皺緊緊○

耨 2 Nou. A kind of spade or hoe for weeding; to weed, to clear ground of weeds; *met.*, to study and teach: [1]*'naiu' 'ch'ó*, to root out weeds; [2]*'pek, ,keng siék, naiu'* to plow with the pencil and dig with the tongue—to be a pedagogue.

(479) Nak.

吶 2 Reak *nok,;* coll. *nak,* as in *'só nak,* a musical pipe, a kind of copper clarinet or flageolet.

納 2 Na. Silk soaked in water, silken threads shrinking; to enter, to collect, to receive, to contain; to pay, to give to, to offer, as presents; in, within: [3]*nak, pe'* to present, as in homage; [4]*',üng nak,* to contain; liberal, generous in feeling; COM., [5]*nak, swoi'* to pay duties; [6]*nak, hwoi'* to pay one's share to a mutual-aid club; [7]*nak, 't'ung*, to take a concubine; [8]*nak, kang'* to purchase the degree of *kang' ,seng;* [9]*',siu nak,* to receive; [10]*seu' nak,* to embrace, as doctrines.

衲 2 Na. The garments of a priest, called *nak, ,i; met.*, a priest, a bonze; in the coll. to quilt or stitch together, as the pieces composing a shoe-sole; to overlay, to patch; mended, patched: [11]*'ló nak,* a priest; COLL., *nak, wak, 'tá*, to stitch stocking-soles; *nak, 'tá siäng'* thread for quilting soles; *ch'ek, 'pwo paik, nak,* all covered with patches.

軜 2 The reins of the inner span of a team of four horses: [12]*kiok, nak,* a carriage ring to which the reins are fastened.

鈉 2 Na. Also read *nok,:* to hammer iron, to beat it to a point; to sharpen wood, as for the handle of a chisel.

捺 2 Na. To press the hand heavily upon; a dash to the right in writing: [13]*p'iék, nak,* left and right strokes.

笝 2 Na. A rope of braided bamboo-splints, used in towing boats: COM., [14]*miék, nak,* a tow-line of splints; [15]*,k'á nak,* bamboo rope, as cut up and used for torches; COLL., [16]*pek, nak,* to pull the tow-line, to track a boat.

(480) Nang.

,Nang. A coll. word, as in *,nang náh,* simple, foolish, stupid; *,nang nong'* or *,nang naung'* confused in mind, obtuse.

'揇 Nan. To grasp with the hand; in the coll. to push away or out, as with the hand or foot; used for *,nang* in the coll. q. v.: COLL., [17]*'nang ,k'wi*, to push open; to push, as a boat from the shore; [18]*'nang 'k'i*, to push up, to raise, as a screen or shutter; [19]*'nang 'tó*, to push down.

'腩 Nan. Boiled flesh, dried meat; *'nang 'hu*, dried meat.

---

1 耨草 2 筆耕舌耨 3 納幣 4 容納 5 納稅 6 納會 7 納寵 8 納監 9 收納 10 受納 11 老衲 12 轂軜 13 撇捺 14 篾笝 15 溪笝 16 拔笝 17 揇開 18 揇起 19 揇倒

ˋ𢥞 To respect, to venerate; to fear, to be in awe of.

ˋ赧 Nan. To blush, to turn red in the face, to redden, to look ashamed: [1]*nang ˏngang*, a blushing face; [2]*ˋkoi ˋnang*, to blush with shame; *ˋnang ˋnang ˏyong*, abashed, as when caught in a mean act.

Nang'. A coll. word: to force one's self, as when weak or fagged; to arise or advance with difficulty, to drag one's self along: *nang' ˏkiĕ chó²* to toil up the stone-steps; *kiong² ˏsing nang'* to force one's self, as to labor, eat, &c.; *nang' mâ² ˋki*, unable to rise, as from weakness; *pˈih, nang'* hardly, laboriously.

ˏ南 Nan. The south; to face the south, to go southward; southern, austral: COM., [3]*ˏnang ˏking*, Nanking; [4]*ˏhu ˏnang*, Hunan; [5]*hiong' ˏnang*, facing the south; [6]*chó' ˏnang* (coll. *sói² ˏnang*), situate south, as the rear of a house; [7]*sá ˏnang*, south-west; [8]*chi ˏnang ˏkü*, a compass; [9]*ˏnang ˏtai* (coll. *ˏnang ˏtoi* or *ˏnang ˏnoi*), Nantai, the south suburbs of Foochow; [10]*a² ˏnang*, the southern districts, as Chinchew and Changchow; *ˏnang ˏu* (coll. *ˏnang ˏmó*), a Budhist term of respect, as in *ˏnang ˏmó ˏó ˏmi ˏt'ó huk,* O Amida Budh! *ˏhwo ˏnang*, to place the palms together—the Budhist style in worship; *pok, ˏnang pok, paĕk,* neither south nor north—unusual, odd, outré; *ˏnang ˏk'iong paĕk, tieu²* "southern brogues and northern tunes"; *met.*, a quarrel between two families.

ˏ喃 Nan. To chatter; to gabble, to talk incessantly: *ˏnü ˏnang*, incessant talking; the twittering of swallows.

ˏ諵 Nan. The noise of conversation, hum of voices; to mutter, to gabble: *ˏnang ˏnang*, incessant gabbling.

ˏ楠 枏 Nan. A kind of plum: COM., *ˏnang muk,* a hard, yellowish wood, suitable for furniture; *ˏnang muk, ˏküng*, a kind of *ˏnang* wood, having curled streaks or veins.

ˏ男 Nan. The male of the human species, a man; the lowest of the five ranks of nobility, a baron: COM., [11]*ˏnang ˋchü*, a male child, a man; [12]*ˏnang ˋchü hang'* one of a manly form and spirit; [13]*ˏnang ˋnü*, male and female, boys and girls; [14]*hau' ˏnang*, a filial son—so called after a parent's death; [15]*ˏnang ˏhung*, sodomy; [16]*ˏnang ˏing ˋnü siong'* an effeminate-looking man; [17]*ˏnang ˏkwang ˏing*, the male Kwanyin, as in a temple on *ˏü ˏsang*, Foochow; COLL., *ˏtung ˏnang ˋkiăng*, a young, unmarried man; *ˏmó ˏnang k'ó² ˋnü*, when one has no son, he depends on the daughter.

ˏ難 难 Nan. Hard, difficult, not easy or pleasant, grievous, irksome; often means cannot, impossible; to trouble, to distress, to make another do: also read *nang'* q. v.:

[1]赧顏 [2]愧赧 [3]南京 [4]湖南 [5]向南○ [6]坐南○ [7]西南 [8]指南車 [9]南臺○ [10]下南 [11]男子 [12]男子漢○ [13]男女○ [14]孝男 [15]男風 [16]男人女相 [17]男觀音○

COM., [1]˛kang ˛nang, difficult; [2]˛tʻieu ˛nang, to impose difficulties on one; [3]˛nang seuʼ intolerable; [4]ʻchengʼ tʻóiʼ ʻliong ˛nang, alike hard to advance or retreat, in a strait; [5]˛nang tóʼ hard to say; in the coll. an interrogative like ˛nó nóh, how? ˛nang ˛ui, to trouble, to burden; ˛nang ʻchʻiă, hard to bear, grievous; kaiʼ siéʼ ˛nang ˛sing, hard to find (the like) in all the world, peerless; COLL., ˛nang ˛wang, obstreperous and troublesome; wangʼ ˛pwang ʻkʻi ˛tʻau ˛nang, everything is difficult at the beginning.

蘭 ˛Lan. Read ˛lang; coll. ˛nang, as in ˛nang ʻchó, a species of date from Lanchou, Chehkiang.

楠 ˛Nan. Read ʻnang; used for the coll. ˛nang: to push with the hand or foot: ˛nang ˛hiă, or ˛nang ˛kʻwi, to push away or open; ˛nang ʻtó, to push down.

˛*Nang.* A coll. word, as in ˛nang ʻmwi ˛sing, a fire-fly or glow-worm.

難 Nan. ˛Nangʼ Trouble, adversity, calamity; difficulties, misfortune; to administer reproofs, to reprimand: also read ˛nang, q. v.: COM., ʻhwangʼ nangʼ afflictions, trials; [7]nangʼ ˛ming, distressed people—from other districts; [8]nangʼ ˛sing, a star boding calamities; [9]nangʼ ʻmwang, the measure of adversity full—*scil.*, then good fortune comes; [10]piéʼ nangʼ to avoid evil; [11]˛sung nangʼ to submit to sufferings and death; [12]ʻsang nangʼ death from childbirth; [13]˛mó nangʼ distressed, harassed.

(481) **Nau.**

撓 Nao. Read ʻnau; used for the coll. ˛nau: to grasp, to clutch with the fingers close together; to crumple by clutching; puckered, as the face: ˛nau ʻking ʻking, to clutch tightly; ˛nau sioh˛ ˛wong, crumpled into a ball; all puckered up; ˛nau chaiuʼ crumpled in the hand; ˛nau ˛nau, puckered.

撓 Nao. ʻ Also read ˛nau: to disturb, to disarrange; to trouble, to vex; to scratch; to twist, to wrench, to distort, to pervert: used for ˛nau in the coll. q. v.: [14]ʻnau lwangʼ seʼ ˛hi, to confound right and wrong; COM., [15]ʻnau ˛pau, an ancient crest or turban—now imitated in the costumes of certain idols.

繞 遶 Jao. ʻ To wind, to twine about; to be entangled in; to make the tour of, to go around; to compass, to environ: [16]˛tiéng ʻnau, to cord about; [17]˛ui ʻnau, to encircle; [18]ʻnau tóʼ to make a circuit.

橈 Jao. ˛ Crooked, bent, as a stick; distorted, tortuous; *met.*, perverted, prejudiced, unjust; to bend, to wrench, to break; slender, weak, lithe, flexible; to disperse, to scatter: [19]˛iu ˛nau, weak, feeble; [20]ʻwong ˛nau, distorted, bent; *met.*, to misrepresent, unjust in judgment. Read ˛ngieu or ˛nieu: a short oar.

[1]艱難 [2]挑難 [3]難受 [4]進退兩難 [5]難道 [6]患難 [7]難民 [8]難星 [9]難滿 [10]避難 ○ [11]殉難 [12]産難 [13]磨難 ○ [14]撓亂是非 [15]撓包 [16]纏繞 [17]圍繞 [18]繞道 [19]柔橈 [20]枉橈

鐃 ˏNao. A kind of cymbal, anciently used to stop the music in the army; the clang of martial instruments: [1]ˏ*nau* ˏ*kó*, martial songs; [2]ˏ*king* ˏ*nau*, military cymbals.

譊 ˏNao. To bawl out angrily; to argue loudly; noisy debate, contention, wrangling, disputing, as among sectaries: ˏ*nau* ˏ*nau*, noisy disputing; [3]ˏ*hiong* ˏ*nau*, to clamor.

詉 ˏ Noise, clamor, wrangling; a bother; unintelligible talk.

呶 ˏNao. Nu. Interchanged with the last two: a clamorous noise; vociferation, wrangling: [4]ˏ*hiong* ˏ*nau*, a clamor, uproar.

怓 ˏNu. Perturbation, confusion of mind; disordered, confused, beclouded: [5]ˏ*nau* *lwang*ʾ the mind bewildered; [6]ˏ*hwong* ˏ*nau*, confused, befogged.

峱 ˏ A mountain in the ancient state of Ch'i or Shantung.

硇 ˏ A natural salt from Tibet, called [7]ˏ*nau* ˏ*sa*, sal ammoniac.

ˏ*Nau*. A coll. word, as in ˏ*nau* ˏ*kung* (also spoken ˏ*na* ˏ*kung*), the sailor-hero, who is said to have introduced the Mings to Foochow; also styled *ho*ʾ *kwok*ˎ ˏ*kung*, Preserver of the State; ˏ*nau* ˏ*kung* *mieu*ʾ a temple of ˏ*Nau* ˏ*kung*—near Great Temple hill, Foochow.

鬧[2] **閙**[2] Nao. The noise and confusion of a fair or market; a noisy wrangling; a bustle, a great stir, as at a festival or funeral; hum, tumult, crowd; to scold, to rail, to make a great ado about; to embroil, to make a disturbance, to be obstreperous: COM., [8]*nau*ʾ *yék*ˎ a great stir, bustle; [9]*nau*ʾ ʿ*chiu*, a drinking carouse; [10]*nau*ʾ *ch'e*ʾ a lively market; COLL., [11]*nau*ʾ ʿ*a*, to bawl one's self dumb; [12]*nau*ʾ *p'wai*ʾ (the matter) divulged by a brawl; [13]*nau*ʾ *sioh*ˎ ˏ*tiong*, to make a stir or tumult.

淖[2] Nao. Name of a lake; mud, clay; muddy, miry; thoroughly wet. Read *chau*ʾ: harmonious. Read *ch'iok*, as in [14]*ch'iok*ˎ *yok*ˎ easy and graceful.

(482) Naung.

*Naung*ʾ. A coll. word: interlocked, tangled, as thread; confused, disordered, as the mind or affairs; confusion, disorder; anarchy, riot, rebellion: ˏ*hung* ˏ*hung* *naung*ʾ in great disorder; *naung*ʾ *pah*ˎ *chá*ʾ "tangled white hemp"; *met*., confused, as matters, or one's thoughts; *naung*ʾ ʿ*k'i* ˏ*li*, anarchy rising; ˏ*t'au* *hwok*ˎ *naung*ʾ the hair disheveled; hair for braiding false cues.

*Naung*ʾ. A coll. word: swelled, puffed, dropsical, bloated: *meng*ʾ *naung*ʾ the face bloated; ˏ*k'a* ʿ*ch'iu* *naung*ʾ feet and hands swelled.

---

[1] 鐃歌 [2] 金鐃 [3] 諠譊 [4] 喧呶 [5] 怓亂 [6] 惛怓 [7] 硇砂 [8] 鬧熱 [9] 鬧酒 [10] 鬧市 [11] 鬧啞 [12] 鬧破 [13] 鬧一場 [14] 淖約

Naung'. A coll. word, as in *naung*' *ˏli*, to wander or stray to a place; *naung*' *k'ó*' wandered off, as a child.

嫩² Tender, small, immature, not fully grown; weak, tender; fine, delicate; soft, supple: COM., [1]*ˋnaung*² *naung*² or [2]*ˋsá*' *naung*² small, delicate; [3]*ˋnaung*² *ne*' refined, as manners; fine, delicate, as workmanship; COLL., [4]*ˋnaung*² *ˋpiăng*, nice cakes; [5]*ˋnaung*² *ˏkĕng*, fine work; [6]*ˋnaung*² *sĕŭng*² for nice wear; *p'e*' *p'e*' *naung*² very small, delicate; [7]*ˋnaung*² *chiăh*, a small one.

Nên. Nun.

*Naung*². A coll. word, as in *naung*² *cheng*' a disease complicated and hard to cure, as consumption.

*Naung*². A coll. word: to ferment, to brew, to make spirituous liquors: *naung*² *ˋchiu*, to brew liquor.

(483) Ne.

咡' The corners of the mouth; sides of the mouth or space between the mouth and ear: [8]*p'ek*, *ne*' to whisper in one's ear.

弭' A bow unstrung and bent back; at ease, resting; to stop, to cease; to forget; to put down, to destroy: [9]*ne*' *tó*² *ˏang ˏliong*, to put down the seditious and quiet the loyal.

Mi.

餌' A kind of dumpling; pie, cakes, tidbits; a bait for fish; *met.*, an allurement, enticement, temptation; to bait, to tempt, to entice: COM., [10]*ˏngü ne*' a bait for fish; COLL., [11]*ˋpiăng ne*' flour-cakes, pasty; [12]*ne*' *ˏwong*, has nibbled it all away; [13]*siăh*, *twai*² *ne*' to seek large gains, as by an extensive business.

Erh.

Ne'. A coll. word, as in *ne*' *ne*' *mĕk*, the eye contracted, very near-sighted; *kĕŭng*² *ne*' near-sighted.

Ne'. A coll. word, to turn; to whirl one's self about, as a child in play: *ne*' *ne*' whirl! whirl!

二² 弍² 貳² Two; to bisect, to divide; to repeat, to reiterate; the third also means to help, to second; to suspect: the first used for the coll. *lang*² q. v.: COM., [14]*ne*² *sek*, twenty; [15]*ne*² *ngwok*, the second month; [16]*ne*² *paik*, two eights, sixteen; [17]*ne*² *ˏkó*, second brother—in common address, means brother, friend; COLL., [18]*sá*' *ne*² careful, cautious; [19]*sek*, *paik*, *nik*, *ne*² from 18 to 22, as said of marriageable virgins; [20]*ne*² *paik*, *ˏpang ˏkwong*, in the 2d and 8th months the days and nights are equal; *ne*² *ˏhwong ˏch'ing*, to marry again, as a widow; *ne*² *ˏhu*, a fiddle, a violin.

Erh.

樲' A species of wild jujube or date-plum; a stop for a wheel.

Erh.

膩² Grease, hardened fat; greasy, fat, gross; smooth, oily: *kaiu*' *ne*² dirty and greasy; COM., *ˏiu ne*² oily, greasy.

Ni.

[1]嫩嫩 [2]細嫩 [3]嫩膩 [4]嫩餅 [5]嫩工 [6]嫩穿 [7]嫩隻 [8]辟咡 [9]弭盜安良 [10]魚餌 [11]餅餌 [12]餌完 [13]食大餌 [14]二十〇 [15]二月 [16]二八 [17]二哥 [18]細二 [19]十八廿二 [20]二八平光

黐[1] Read ʻni; used in the Paik, ˏIng for the coll. *neˀ*: to stick, to adhere; adhesive, sticky, gluey, as oiled hair; ʻ*neˀ* ʻ*king*, to stick fast, to harden, as dirt or oil.

Neˀ. A coll. euphonic prefix, as in *neˀ náˀ* to daub, to besmear, as with oily hands.

(484) Nĕ.

ˏ*Nĕ*. A coll. word, similar to ˏ*nŭ*: inclined, awry: ˏ*nĕ k*ʻ*óˀ* out of perpendicular; ˏ*nĕ lóh*ˎ to fall over, to slip down.

ˏ*Nĕ*. A coll. word, the same as ˏ*ni*, as in ˏ*nĕ* ˏ*nĕ tioh*ˎ adhesive, sticky.

ʻ*Nĕ*. A coll. word: the sensation in eating very sour things, the teeth set on edge.

ˎ*Nĕ*. A coll. word, as in ʻ*lang* ˎ*nĕ*, thick spittle; *teˀ aˀ* ˏ*tu seˀ* ʻ*lang* ˎ*nĕ*, there's spittle all over the ground or floor.

(485) Nek.

尼ˀ Ni. To approach, to draw near, to be near; to stop; fixed, settled, determined: also read ˎ*ná*, q. v.

䁥 Ni. Small eyes.

*Nek*ˎ. A coll. word: perhaps a corruption of *tek*ˎ (a drop), as in *nek*ˎ *nek*ˎ or *nek*ˎ *nek*ˎ ʻ*kiăng*, a little, a very small quantity.

*Nek*ˎ. A coll. euphonic prefix, as in *nek*ˎ *nĕŭk*ˎ puckered, wrinkled; *nek*ˎ *niék*ˎ to take and press between the fingers, to work into a round shape; *nek*ˎ *niăk*ˎ to wink the eyes, to twinkle; to sparkle, as a fire-fly; also to speak irrelevantly.

(486) Neng.

ˏ*Neng*. A coll. word: hard lumps in the skin, indurated skin, as on the feet and palms of the hands; horn-like lumps, corns: ʻ*ch*ʻ*iu* ˏ*neng* and ˏ*k*ʻ*a* ˏ*neng*, hard skin on the hands and feet; ʻ*ló* ʻ*ch*ʻ*ü* ˏ*neng*, "rat-lumps"—term applied to hard lumps in the skin.

ˏ*Neng*. A coll. word, used for ˏ*neng*, as in ˏ*neng* ˏ*neng*, the mother's milk, the breast; *siăh*ˎ ˏ*neng* ˏ*neng*, to suck, to take the breast.

ˏ*Neng*. A coll. word: small in stature, delicate, attenuated: ˏ*neng* ˏ*neng*, or ˏ*neng sáˀ* slender and small.

ʻ朧 A coll. character found in the Paik, ˏIng: the loins or soft parts below the ribs: [2]ʻ*neng kaĕk*ˎ (or ˏ*piĕng*), the side under the ribs; [3]ʻ*neng pah*ˎ the loins "wrenched"; [4]ʻ*neng* ˎ*iu kek*ˎ *pauˀ* loin-fat instantly protruding; *met*., urgent, restive or impatient; *k*ʻ*ieuˀ* ʻ*neng*, to throw the chest out, to swagger, as a bully does.

Nengˀ. A coll. euphonic prefix, as in *nengˀ naungˀ* tangled, in disorder; disheveled; *nengˀ naingˀ* to walk on tiptoe; *nengˀ nangˀ* to stretch one's self up; to brace the body and push with force; *nengˀ naĕngˀ* or *nengˀ naĕngˀ naĕngˀ* soft, yielding; *nengˀ niongˀ* to move, as waves do; a

---

[1] 黐緊 [2] 朧角 [3] 朧擘 [4] 朧油急豹

○ ○ ○ ○ ○ ○ ○ ○

tremulous motion, as of the bed-clothes over a restless sleeper.

能 ꜀Nĕng. A sort of deer as large as a bear; power, ability, capacity; skill, talents; to be able, can, may; apt, able, competent: COM., [1]꜀neng kang꜄ ability; [2]꜀chai ꜀neng, talent, genius; [3]꜀neng kaiu꜄ and ꜂pok, ꜀neng kaiu꜄ able and unable, can and cannot; [5]pok, ꜀neng, unable, can't; [6]꜀tó ꜀neng, very competent, accomplished; [7]꜀neng siok, pok, ꜀neng ꜀heng, can talk but can't perform.

乳 ꜂Ju. Read ꜂ü; used for the coll. ꜀neng: milk; the breasts, an udder: [8]siăh, ꜀neng, to drink or suck milk; [9]꜀neng ꜀t'au, the nipple; full breasts, as after childbirth; [10]꜀ngu ꜀neng, cow's milk; [11]꜀ngu ꜀neng ꜀iu, butter; [12]꜀neng ꜀mwo, the breast of a male; [13]niĕk, ꜀neng, to milk; [14]ch'au꜄ ꜀neng ꜀siĕng, the strong scent of milk; [15]taung꜄ ꜀neng, to wean, weaned; [16]꜀neng ꜂chwi, (or chaik), milk; [17]꜀neng ꜂nă, or [18]꜀neng ꜀ma, a wet-nurse.

佞² Ning. Skilled in speech, eloquent, persuasive; artful, specious, insinuating; flattering; smart, ready in reply: [19]꜂t'iéng neng꜄ flattering, cringing; [20]pok, neng꜄ unready, slow of speech; [21]꜀kang neng꜄ false, treacherous in speech.

認² Jĕn. To recognize, to know well, to know again; to confess, to admit, to acknowledge; to distinguish, to discriminate between; a mark, criterion: COM., sek, neng꜄ to recognize, to identify; neng꜄ chói꜄ to confess guilt; mó꜄ neng꜄ (coll. ꜀pau neng꜄), to claim falsely; neng꜄ ꜀ching, to perceive truly or correctly; COLL., mă꜄ neng꜄ tek, can't recognize (him); chó꜄ ke꜄ neng꜄ to mark, to use as a criterion; k'á꜄ ꜀nĕng neng꜄ to be surety for one; to enter into recognizances; neng꜄ tang꜄ to mistake in recognition; to confess an error; neng꜄ p'ieu꜄ ng꜄ neng꜄ ꜀nĕng, (need only) recognize the bill or ticket, not the holder.

甯² A surname.

Neng꜄. A coll. euphonic prefix, as in neng꜄ niong꜄ to yield, give way to one; neng꜄ naing꜄ to chant or read over; neng꜄ niăng꜄ to flare, to flicker; to flash, as gunpowder.

(487) Nĕng.

꜂Nĕng. A coll. word: probably a brogue for ꜀nĕng, as in ꜂nĕng ꜀ka, I, we, us.

伩 ꜀ A coll. character: a man, a person, a human being; pertaining to mankind, human: ꜀nĕng ꜀nĕng, or kauk, ꜀nĕng, everybody; ꜂ngwai ꜀nĕng, we, us; tié꜄ ꜀nĕng, who? ꜀t'au ꜀nĕng, the head-man, the chief; ꜀nĕng ꜂kiăng, small images or pictures of persons; ꜀ĕng ꜀nĕng, a "red man"—i. e., a favorite; ꜀nĕng ꜀wong, the chief of a household; ꜀mó ꜀nĕng ꜀t'au, has no friends; twai꜄ ꜀nĕng, adults; the great, the noble; ꜀nĕng yok, weak in body; ꜀nĕng ꜀mwo, one's appearance, as thin or emaciated; ꜀nĕng k'aik, (or ꜀tó) ꜀nĕng,

[1]能幹 [2]才能 [3]能穀 [4]不能 穀[5]不能 [6]多能 [7]能說不能行 [8]食乳 [9]乳頭 [10]牛乳 [11]牛乳 [12]乳油 模乳 [13]攝乳 [14]臭乳糧 [15]斷乳 [16]乳水 [17]乳奶 [18]乳嬤 [19]諂佞 [20]不佞 [21]奸佞

men pressing men, a great crowd; *ˏnëng twai*² *ʻtang ʻsieu*, he is large but cowardly; *ˏnëng ʻkong ˏtʻiéng, ˏi ʻkong te*² one says heaven but he says earth—i. e., answers irrelevantly.

儂 ˏNung. Nëng. Read *ˏnung;* coll. *ˏnëng*, as in *ˏnëng ˏka*, I, myself, we; *ˏnëng ˏka kauk*, *ˏnëng*, we all, all of us.

膿 ˏNung. Read *ˏnung;* coll. *ˏnëng:* pus, matter in sores, matter from suppuration: [1]*ˏnëng chaik*, matter; [2]*ˏnëng haik*, bloody pus; [3]*kwang*ʾ *ˏnëng*, to come to a head, as a boil; [4]*ˏnëng ˏtʻau*, the core of a boil.

(488) Neu.

ˏNeu. A coll. word: to contract, to pucker, to shrivel, as a boil after breaking: *ˏneu ˏta*, dried up, shriveled, as fruit.

ˏNeu. A coll. word: pleasing, attractive, graceful: *ˏni ˏneu*, or *ˏneu ˏneu ˏhing*, a winning manner, as of a child.

ʻ鳥 Niao. Tiao. A bird, the general name for aves; the 196th radical: in the coll. used for *ʻcheu*, q. v.: [5]*ʻneu hwoi*² the beak of a bird; COM., [6]*ˏhi ʻneu*, a flying bird; [7]*ʻneu ˏchʻiong*, a fowling-piece; [8]*ˏhwa muk*₂ *ʻneu seu*ʾ (pictures of) flowers, trees, birds, and beasts.

ʻ蔦 Niao. A parasitic creeper like the ivy: [9]*ʻneu ˏló ˏchi ˏchʻing*, "union of creepers and vines"—related by marriage.

ʻ嫋 Niao. Read *ʻnieu;* coll. *ʻneu*, as in [10]*ʻneu ʻnó*, elegant, graceful, as a lady; [11]*ʻneu ʻnó tek*, *ʻheng*, extremely graceful.

*Neu*ʾ. A coll. word: to pinch; to pluck or nip off with the thumb-nail and forefinger; to pluck, as leaves or flowers: *neu*ʾ *ˏkŭng*, to pinch off the roots; *neu*ʾ *sioh*₂ *chaik*, to nip off a piece; *neu*ʾ *sioh*₂ *a*² to give a nip; *met.*, to bite, as a flea.

ˏNeu. A coll. word, as in *ˏneu ˏneu*, wrinkled or contracted, as the brow from anger, pain, grief, etc.

ˏNeu. A coll. word, as in *ˏneu ˏneu*, of medium consistence, as said of the stools after constipation.

(489) Nëŭ.

飫ʾ Read *ëŭ*ʾ and *hëŭ*ʾ; used in the *Paik*, *ˏIng* for the coll. *nëŭ*ʾ: a feeling of satiety, sated, surfeited, cloyed, as from eating fat things.

*Nëŭ*ʾ. A coll. word, as in *nëŭ*ʾ *nëŭ*ʾ drowsy, sleepy, half-conscious, as on being awaked from sleep; *nëŭ*ʾ *ʻking kʻaung*ʾ in a stupor, insensible, as in sickness.

(490) Nëŭk.

朒ˎ 肭ˎ The new moon seen in the east; to walk quickly; used in the coll. in the sense of weak, feeble; to sink down from weakness, to faint, to fall, as in a fit; crumpled, rough, corrugated, creased: COLL., [12]*nëŭk*, *chaik*, rough, indented; [13]*nëŭk*, *lóh*₂ *kʻó*ʾ to fall, as in a fit; [14]*ˏtʻŭng nëŭk*, repeated, carried forward, as an

[1]膿汁 [2]膿血 [3]灌膿 [4]膿頭 [5]鳥喙 [6]飛鳥 [7]鳥槍 ○ [8]花木鳥獸 [9]蔦蘿之親 [10]嫋娜 ○ [11]嫋娜的很 [12]朒節 ○ [13]朒落去 ○ [14]重朒 ○

old account; ʻnëük, sioh꜀ aʼ to sink down; *met.*, to fail, to suspend payment, as a bank; [2]ʻnëük, ʻtié, to fold or press in; [3]꜀chʻiong nëük꜀ a wall sinking and ready to fall.

(491) Nëüng.

*Nëüng*ʼ. A coll. word: the opposite of ʻ*king*, or ꜀*hüng;* slack, as a rope; slowly, leisurely; diminished, as a fire: *nëüng*ʼ *nëüng*ʼ slack, not tight; *nëüng*ʼ *sioh*꜀ *pwo*ʼ wait a little, take it leisurely.

(492) Ni.

꜀*Ni*. A coll. word, as in ꜀*ni* ꜀*ni*, or *á*ʼ ꜀*ni*, sticky, adhesive, as paste; ꜀*ni* ꜀*a* ꜀*chi*, to stick locusts—i. e., catch them with a pole having paste or glue on the end.

꜀*Ni*. A coll. euphonic prefix, as in ꜀*ni* ꜀*nü*, or ꜀*ni* ꜀*ni* ꜀*nü* ꜀*nü*, rickety, dilapidated; ꜀*ni* ꜀*nio*, the mincing gait of a lady; rickety; ꜀*ni* ꜀*nau*, to open and shut the hand, as an infant; to pilfer.

ʻ柅 Ni. A break to check or stop a carriage: to chock a wheel; trees growing luxuriantly: ʻ*ni* ʻ*ni*, exuberant foliage.

ʻ禰 Ni. An ancestral hall; a father's tablet in a temple: [4]꜀*kung* ʻ*ni*, a parent's tablet carried about.

ʻ*Ni*. A coll. euphonic prefix, as in ʻ*ni* ʻ*nó*, the mincing, elegant gait of a lady.

꜀呢꜀ Ni. A final interrogative particle; in the coll. used for woolens, broadcloths, etc.: also read ꜀*ná*, q. v.: COLL., [5]꜀*tang* ꜀*chiong* *chó*ʼ ꜀*ni*, now how shall we do or manage it? [6]꜀*lang* ꜀*ni* ꜀*pó*, a blue woolen robe; [7]꜀*ni* *meng*ʼ a woolen exterior; [8]꜀*ni* ʻ*ü*, woolens and camlets; [9]꜀*ni* ꜀*tʻau*, ends of woolens, the list or selvage.

꜀*Ni*. A coll. euphonic prefix, as in ꜀*ni* ꜀*ná*, to plaster, to daub; ꜀*ni* ꜀*nui*, to knead, as dough.

(493) Niă.

꜀*Niă*. A coll. word: shaky, rickety; unsteady, reeling: ꜀*nü* ꜀*niă*, shaky, unsteady; ʻ*chiu siăh*꜀ ꜀*niă* ꜀*niă*, to reel from intoxication.

꜀*Niă*. A coll. word, as in ꜀*niă* *nói*ʼ a little; ꜀*niă* *nói*ʼ ʻ*kiăng*, a very little, a mite.

ʻ惹 Jo. Jĕ. To stir up, to excite, to provoke, to irritate; to elicit; to induce, to bring down on one: COM., [10]ʻ*niă* *sëü*ʼ to make trouble; [11]ʻ*niă* *hwo*ʼ to induce calamity; [12]ʻ*ing* ʻ*niă*, to tempt, to excite: COLL., [13]ʻ*niă* ꜀*nëng* *seu*ʼ *kʻe*ʼ to provoke one to anger; [14]ʻ*niă* *kwo*ʼ ʻ*chʻiu*, to seduce (a woman); [15]*ng*ʼ ʻ*hó* ʻ*niă*, not well to provoke, don't touch him.

尿ʼ Niao. Sui. Read *nieu*ʼ; coll. *niă*ʼ as in [16]*niă*ʼ ꜀*hu*, a chamber-pot, a urinal; *niă*ʼ ꜀*hu* ꜀*siong* (or *ak*꜀), a box to contain a urinal, as in traveling.

*Niă*ʼ A coll. word: the same as ꜀*niă*, to reel, to stagger, as from intoxication; *niă*ʼ *niă*ʼ *tioh*꜀ unsteady, reeling.

[1]肭	[2]肭	[4]公	做	袍	[8]呢	[10]惹	[11]惹	[12]引	受	手	[16]尿
一	入	禰	呢	[7]呢	羽	事	禍	惹	氣	[15]怀	壺
下	[3]墻	[5]伶	[6]藍	面	[9]呢			[13]惹	[14]惹	好	
○	肭	將	呢	○	頭	○	○	伙	過	惹	○

(494) Niăh.

Niăh,. A coll. word: suddenly alarmed, startled, affrighted: *niăh*, *'k'i ,li*, startled; *niăh*, *,ch'ing 'ch'ang*, startled out of sleep; *niăh*, *pwang' ,t'iéng ,keng*, jumped half as high as the sky with alarm!

拿 Na. Read *'na;* coll. *niăh*,: to lay hold of, to seize, to arrest; to pull, as into the right position; to pinch, to manipulate; in a *met.*, sense, to take occasion, to avail of: [1]*niăh*, *ch'ek*, to catch a thief; [2]*niăh*, *tioh*, seized, caught; [3]*niăh*, *ka'* to hold for, or demand, a high price; [4]*niăh*, *chiăng'* pull it right or straight; [5]*niăh*, *,sa*, to manipulate one having the colic; [6]*,mó 'mwi k'ĕük*, *'nü niăh*, have done nothing that you can take hold of; [7]*niăh*, *kah*, to stand on one's digtiny, arrogant; [8]*niăh*, *'ch'iu*, adept, skilled in; [9]*niăh*, *,sié*, to ask a favor of one; [10]*niăh*, *,sing*, or *niăh*, *niăh*, *,sing*, careful, cautious; *niăh*, *,i 'twang*, to lay hold of one's fault (to his disadvantage.)

(495) Niăk.

Niăk,. A coll. word: to wink, to give the wink to; flashing, dazzling: *mek*, *,chiu kaĕng' ,i niăk*, *niăk*, gave him a wink of the eye; *nek*, *nek*, *niăk*, *niăk*, flashing, bespangled; *niăk*, *niăng'* the flash of lightning; *niăk*, *,li niăk*, *k'ó'* to place disorderly, to scatter about.

(496) Niăng.

'Niăng. A coll. word: to bring together, to combine; to unite, to mix, to mingle: *'niăng 'lĕng* or *'niăng sioh*, *,toi*, to put together, to unite in one; *'niăng 'k'ó*, to examine in one class, as students of different districts; *'niăng 'lá chó'* to do both at once.

Niăng'. A coll. word, as in *'niăng niăng'* or *niăng' niăng'* the lightning, flashes of lightning.

,Niăng. A coll. word: scorched, burnt, scorched yellow, as cloth.

Niăng². A coll. word, as in *niăng² niăng²* drunk, inebriated, intoxicated.

Niăng². A coll. word: the flickering or darting of flames: *niăng² 'k'i ,li*, to flame, to blaze up, as a house on fire.

(497) Nié.

,Nié. A coll. word, probably a corruption of *,niă*, as in *,nié nói'* a little, a small quantity.

伲 ,Ni. Read *'ni* (you); used for the coll. *,nié*: a final particle, meaning nearly, about, similar, not very different from; also used in the terms for children and son-in-law: [11]*'t'ó 'mó ,nié*, or [12]*yok*, *liok*, *,nié*, about, somewhat so or like to; [13]*,chiong ,nié*, thus, so; [14]*'kiăng ,nié*, one's children; [15]*,nié sai'* a son-in-law.

Nié². A coll. word, as in *nié² 'kiăng*, children; *nié² 'kiăng ,kó*, boys, children; *nié² 'kiăng ,t'ong*, a youth, a stripling; *nié² 'kiăng tai²* children's matters, as plays; *k'ĕük*, *nié² 'kiăng óh*, *yong²* an example for children to follow; *nié² 'kiăng ,yong*

[1]拿賊 [2]拿着 [3]拿價 [4]拿正 [5]拿痧 [6]無尾乞汝拿 [7]拿格 [8]拿手 [9]拿蛇 [10]拿心 [11]討拇伲 [12]約略伲 [13]將伲 [14]仔伲 [15]伲婿

ngiék, the child is a pest!—i. e., fretful and troublesome.

(498) Niék.

聶, Nieh. To incline the ear; to put the mouth to another's ear, to whisper, to lisp or mutter; whisperings; a surname: [1] '*niék*, '*hü*, to pledge, to promise.

囁, Nieh. An unbridled tongue; to backbite, to vilify; grumbling, scolding: [2] '*niék*, ˌ*sü*, chattering, querulous.

懾, Chê. To fear, to dread; to lose courage; subdued, downcast, disheartened.

捻, Nieh. Nien. To pinch or scrape together with the fingers, to take a pinch of; a pinch, a pugil: in the coll. read ˌ*niéng*, q. v.: [3] '*niék*, *ek*, *niék*, to take a pinch; [4] '*ek*, *niék*, ˌ*hung*, a "pinch of red"—i. e., the Mowtan flower.

攝, Nieh. To take, to collect, to gather; to direct, to manage, to adjust and control, to put in order; to act for others; skilled, capable of managing affairs for others; to pursue and seize; at a loss, puzzled, bewildered; also still, peaceful; in the coll. to grasp, to clutch; to pinch, to squeeze: COM., [5] ˌ*siu niék*, to collect; to nourish (one's energies); [6] '*niék*, '*li*, to act temporarily as a substitute; COLL., [7] *niék*, *kek*, to carry away under the arm; *met.*, to pilfer; [8] '*niék*, ˌ*neng*, to milk; [9] '*niék*, '*ch'iu*, to take hold of, to grasp, as a staff; *k'ük*, '*kwi niék*, clutched by a devil—*scil.*, so as to be stupid or reveal one's own guilt; [10] '*mwong niék*, '*mwong kieu*' the more you squeeze (a locust) the more he sings; *met.*, the more you check him the more he blabs.

躡, Nieh. To tread on; to mount, to ascend, to go up: [11] *niék*, ˌ*teng*, to ascend, to walk up.

鑷, Nieh. Pincers, forceps, pliers, tweezers for pulling out hairs; to take with pincers, to pull out; used for *kiék*, in the coll. q. v.: COLL., *kiék*, *niék*, or *niék*, *niék*, pincers, nippers; *chioh*, *niék*, a pair of snuffers.

籋, Nieh. Interchanged with the last two: to mount, to stride; pincers; a kind of small basket.

廿, Read *ik*, in the dictionaries; coll. *niék*,: a contraction of *ne*' *sek*, twenty; [12] *niék*, '*kau*, twenty-nine; [13] *niék*, *hwoi*' twenty years old; [14] *niék*, '*tié*, near the 20th of the month; *niék*, ˌ*chiéng*, 20 cash; [15] *niék*, *siong*' (or ˌ*ling*), over twenty. For similar uses of the character see in *nik*, and *niéng*'.

Niék,. A coll. word, as in *niék*, *niék*, narrow, contracted, as one's forehead; *k'ak*, *niék*, (made) too small or contracted.

揑, 捏, Nieh. To scratch together or collect with the fingers; to pinch, to work up with the fingers; *met.*, to fabricate, to trump up a story, to make a pretext to injure one: [16] ˌ*u niék*, to traduce;

1 聶	3 捻	4 一	5 收	7 攝	8 攝	9 攝	莽	11 躡	12 廿	14 廿	15 廿
許	一	捻	攝	挾	乳	手	叫	登	九	裡	上
2 囁	捻	紅	6 攝			10 莽			13 廿	廿	16 誣
嚅	○	○	理	○	○	攝	○	○	歲	○	揑

[1]'niék, k'ong' to make false charges against; COM., [2]'niék, ,sü, a trumped up story; [3]'niu niék, to fabricate; COLL., niék, 'la wa' to forge a story.

涅 Nieh. Name of a river; black mud in the water; to blacken, to soil, to muddy, to stick in the mud; *met.*, defiling: [4]niék, ,pwang, "the defiling platter"—a Budhist phrase for the world.

苶 Also read *niék,*: wearied out, fatigued, fagged, exhausted; also to forget: [5],soi niék, weak and worn out, unable to do duty.

(499) Niéng.

拈 捻 Nien. The 2d read *niék,*; coll. ,*niéng*: to take in the hand, to take up, to handle, to carry: COM., [6],niéng 'ch'iu, to take in the hand; something to hold by, a handle; [7],tó ,niéng, to take much or more; COLL., [8],niéng ,li, to bring; [9],t'au ,niéng, to abstract, to purloin; [10],niéng k'ëük, ,i, take and give it to him.

鮎 Nien. A silure or bull-head, a kind of mud fish with a greenish back; also described as a reptile like a siren, having two hands and four feet.

'撚 Nien. To hold between the fingers, to roll or work over by fingering; to toy with; to tread, to follow: [11]'niéng ,sü, to fondle the beard; [12]'niéng ,mó, to felt hair or wool.

'染 Jan. To dye, to tinge, to steep in a dye, to color; to taint, to catch, to be infected with; to pollute, to vitiate; to copy others' vices; soft, flexible, harmonious: [13]sik, 'niéng, to learn vicious habits; COM., [14]'niéng saik, to dye, to color; [15]'niéng taing' a dye-shop; 'niéng ,kong, dye-jars; ,tang 'niéng, to dye by sprinkling and brushing; [16],hwang hok, 'niéng, to re-dye; [17],tiong 'niéng, contagious, infectious.

年 Nien. A revolution of the seasons, a year; the years of one's life, age: COM., ,niéng ,niéng, yearly; [18],king ,niéng, this year; [19]keu' ,niéng, the old year; [20],hung ,niéng, a year of plenty; [21]'ló ,niéng, old, aged; [22],niéng 'ki, (coll. ,niéng hwoi') one's age; [23],niéng ,ching, prospects of the year or season; ,niéng keng' or ,niéng 'lá, new year's presents, as to employés: ,niéng ,keng paik, che' eight characters of the time of birth, used in the horoscope; COLL., k'ó' ,niéng ,mang, last year; ,mang ,niéng, or ,mang ,niéng ,mang, year after the next; chó' ,niéng, to keep the new year; ,pwong ,niéng, to perform idolatrous rites at the close of the year; ,niéng ,k'ing, young, inexperienced; ,niéng ,tau, or ,niéng ,piéng, or ,niéng ,mang, the close of the year; ,niéng ,chiong chaik, pwang' at the year's end (pay up) all, and at the festivals (of the 5th and 8th moons) the half (of one's debts); ,niéng ,mang nik, 'kwi (or se' 'kwi), past the 20th of the

[1]揑控 [2]揑詞 [3]扭揑 [4]涅盤 [5]衰苶 [6]拈手 [7]多拈 [8]拈來 [9]偷拈 [10]拈乞 伊拈 [11]撚鬚 [12]撚毛 [13]習染 [14]染色 [15]染店 [16]還覆染 [17]傳染 [18]今年 [19]舊年 [20]豐年 [21]老年 [22]年紀 [23]年情

12th moon—i. e., near the close of the year.

黏 粘 ꜀ ꜀ Nien. Paste; to paste, to stick up; viscid, sticky, glutinous; *met.*, to be attached to a person; COM., [1]*꜀niéng t‘aik*, to paste on, to stick up; COLL., [2]*꜀t‘ó ꜀niéng*, excessive, officious; [3]*꜀niéng sioh$_2$ ꜀toi*, to stick together; [4]*꜀niéng ꜀nó*, viscid, sticky; *met.*, attached, intimate with.

蜍 ꜀ A coll. character, found in the *Paik, ꜀Ing:* a very small, greenish bivalve, called [5]*꜀u ꜀niéng*, which appears in the markets during the summer.

廿 ^{2} Read *ik$_2$;* in the *Paik, ꜀Ing* read *niéng^2*, twenty: in the coll. used for *niék*, and *nik$_2$* (twenty), q. v.

念 ^{2} Nien. To consider, to reflect upon, to think of; to ponder, to dwell on with pleasure; to repeat memoriter; to chant in a set tone, to read loud; thoughts, reflections, intentions; remembrance; sometimes used for twenty, as in the dates of days of the month: in the coll. read *naing^2* q. v.: [6]*꜀hwai niéng^2* to bear in mind; COM., [7]*꜀sü niéng^2* to think of; [8]*‘ke’ niéng^2* to remember; [9]*‘kwa’ niéng^2* to charge one's mind with, to be in suspense; [10]*niéng^2 niéng^2 pok, ꜀wong*, a constant remembrance of; COLL., *niéng^2 ꜀t‘au*, thoughts, purposes; *niéng^2 tioh$_2$ ‘ngwai*, remember me; *niéng^2 ‘nü lau^2 ꜀nëng*, considering that you are an old man.

(500) Nieu.

‘嫋 ‘嬝 Niao. Delicate, as a girl; long and slender, waving, as willow-boughs; elegant, graceful; a hum, a continuous noise: in the coll. read *‘neu* and *꜀nio*, q. v.: *‘nieu ‘nieu*, curling upwards, as incense; delicate; COM., [11]*‘nieu ‘nó*, a mincing gait, graceful in movement and voice.

‘裊 Niao. Also read *‘neu:* an excellent horse, called *‘yeu ‘nieu*, or *‘mieu ‘nieu;* also to tie a horse with silk fringes.

Nieu’. A coll. word: to raise the eyes: *mek$_2$ ꜀chiu nieu’ ꜀keng*, to lift the eyes high, to look up.

嬈 ꜀ Jao. Also read *‘nieu:* pleasing, winsome, witty; fascinating, flattering; to disturb, to play tricks with: [12]*꜀kieu ꜀nieu*, agreeable, winning; [13]*‘kwi ꜀nieu*, ghosts that trouble people.

饒 ꜀ Jao. To spare, to acquit, to excuse, to forgive; liberal, indulgent; in the following senses usually read *꜀ngieu;* a plenty of food; ample, abundant, affluent, satisfied; an excess, overplus, leavings: COM., [14]*꜀nieu sëü’* to be indulgent, to forgive; [15]*ho’ ꜀nieu* (or *꜀ngieu*), abundant; [16]*꜀nieu ꜀ing pok, ‘kü ‘ch‘iu*, if you pardon a person, then don't raise your hand against him; COLL., [17]*꜀nieu sioh$_2$ ch‘ok$_2$* (or *chek$_2$*), to indulge with an additional act in theatricals; [18]*꜀nieu niong^2* to favor (as to price), to sell cheaper;

[1]粘貼 [2]拖粘 [3]粘一堆○ [4]黏黐 [5]烏蜍 [6]懷念 [7]思念 [8]記念 [9]掛念 [10]念念不忘 [11]嫋娜 [12]嬌嬈 [13]鬼嬈 [14]饒恕 [15]富饒 [61]饒人不畀手○ [17]饒一出○ [18]饒讓○

[1]*ˏnieu ˏnĕng miăng²* to spare one's life.

尿 ² Niao. Sui. Urine: used for *niă²* in the coll. q. v.: COM., [2]*nieu² kekˎ* urgent to urinate; COLL., [3]*ˏna nieu²* to urinate; [4]*nieu² ˏp'a*, the bladder; [5]*siĕ² nieu²* to urinate incontinently; [6]*ˏkau nieu²* ape's urine; *met.*, tricky, mischievous, as a child.

(501) Nih.

Nihˎ. A coll. word: the same as *mihˎ* to tread into, to sink, as the foot in mud: *ˏk'a nihˎ 'tiĕ*, the foot sinks in.

Nihˎ. A coll. euphonic prefix, as in *nihˎ nŏhˎ* to mix with the fingers; to feel of, as a fowl's crop; *nihˎ niăhˎ* to seize; to adjust by pulling into a proper position.

(502) Nik.

日 ² Jih. Jĕ. Shih. The sun; a day, days, time; daily; the emperor's day or reign; sorcerers: [7]*'chokˎ nikˎ* yesterday; COM., [8]*'nikˎ ˏt'au*, the sun: [9]*'nikˎ chieu²* a sun-shade, parasol; [10]*nikˎ sekˎ* a solar eclipse; [11]*nikˎ ĕŭng²* for daily use; [12]*nikˎ nikˎ 'iu*, a plant that blooms daily; [13]*leng² nikˎ* another day; [14]*nikˎ yă²* (coll. *nikˎ ˏmang*), day and night; [15]*ˏhŭng nikˎ* an unlucky day; [16]*nikˎ 'pwong*, Japan; [17]*nikˎ ch'okˎ*, sunrise; [18]*nikˎ ˏkiu ˏsang ˏch'wang yă² ˏkiu ek, sĕŭkˎ* one wants (only) three meals a day and one lodging at night, COLL., *nikˎ wong²* halo about the sun; *siohˎ nikˎ kau² ang²* (or *wang²*), the whole day; *nikˎ ˏtong*, day-time; *nikˎ 'chi*, days, time; *ˏking tang² nikˎ* to-day; *sŏhˎ nikˎ* day-before-yesterday; *au² nikˎ* day-after-to-morrow; *nŏhˎ au² nikˎ* the day after *au² nikˎ*; *nikˎ tau²* (or *chiăng²*), noon, midday; *nikˎ lŏhˎ ˏsang*, sunset.

暱 ² Ni. The sun approaching, time near at hand; to be near to, daily or familiar intercourse with.

匿 ² Ni. A large-bellied jar; to elude search, to abscond; to hide, to conceal, to secrete; hidden, clandestine; in the coll. to put into, to stuff, to press full: [19]*nikˎ ˏsong*, to conceal a parent's death and not wear mourning; [20]*nikˎ ˏming*, anonymous, pseudonymous; COM., [21]*ˏchong nikˎ* to hide, to secrete; COLL., *nikˎ mĕkˎ* to encoffin the corpse; *nikˎ nakˎ* to put in; to pay up, as rent or a quota; *nikˎ 'chiĕng ˏt'au*, to stuff pillows; *ˏtŏ ˏch'iong mă² nikˎ* "sword and spear can't penetrate"—hard, impenetrable.

䘌 ² The toothache; diseased or carious teeth.

惗 ² Ni. A feeling of shame, ashamed, mortified: *k'oi² nikˎ* to be ashamed.

惄 ² To hunger; to long for, to hunger after; sad, mournful; anxious thought or desire.

搦 ² Ni. To lay the hand on, to grasp, to catch hold of; to provoke, to excite, to arouse: *nikˎ chiĕng²* to provoke (an enemy) to battle.

[1]饒	急	脬	尿	頭	蝕	日	[14]日	[16]日	[18]日	夜	[19]匿	[21]藏
仈	[8]撒	[5]逝	[7]昨	[9]日	[11]日	有	夜	本	求	求	喪	匿
命	尿	尿	日	照	用	[18]另	[15]凶	[17]日	三	一	[20]匿	
[2]尿	[4]尿	[6]猴	[8]日	[10]日	[12]日	日	日	出	餐	宿	名	〇

福州方言拼音字典

溺 ˏ ₂ Ni. Niao. Yao. To sink, to drown one's self; to be drowned; to put under the water, to submerge; to stifle, to suffocate; *met.*, sunk in vice, lost to reproof, reprobate; greedy, fond of, given up to, inordinately attached to: used for *nieu*² (urine, to urinate): [1]*nik*₂ ʻ*chwi*, drowned, submerged; COM., [2]ˏ*tʻing nik*₂ to sink into; sunk, as in vice; [3]*nik*₂ ʻ*nü*, to drown daughters, infanticide; [4]*nik*₂ *ai*² *pok*₂ ˏ*ming*, a blind, indiscriminate love for, love-sick; *nik*₂ ˏ*ü* ʻ*chiu saik*₂ given to drink and licentiousness.

廿 ₂ Read *ik*₂; used for the coll. *nik*₂ a corruption of *ne*² *sek*₂ twenty: *nik*₂ *ek*₂ the 21st of the month; *nik*₂ ʻ*kau taung*² ˏ*sang sek*₂ the 29th (of a short month) is reckoned as the 30th; *nik*₂ (or ˏ*niéng*) ˏ*mang nik*₂ ʻ*kwi*, past the 20th of the 12th moon—near the end of the year. For similar uses of this character see in *niék*₂ and *niéng*².

(503) Ning.

ˏ*Ning*. A coll. euphonic prefix, as in ˏ*ning* ˏ*nung*, to murmur, to mutter; ˏ*ning* ˏ*niéng*, to take.

ʻ*Ning*. A coll. euphonic prefix, as in ʻ*ning* ʻ*niéng*, to dye; ʻ*ning* ʻ*niäng*, to mix, to mingle; ʻ*ning* ʻ*nang*, to push against with the hands or feet; ʻ*ning* ʻ*nong*, to warm, as wine; ʻ*ning* ʻ*niong* ʻ*niong*, limber, supple; weak.

寧 **甯** ˏ ˏ Ning. Nêng. Rest, repose, ease; quiet, tranquillity; to salute, to quiet, to bring or wish peace to; what one would prefer, to prefer; rather, better, preferable; a term of comparison, followed by a negative: [5]ˏ*kʻong* ˏ*ning*, peace, tranquillity; [6]ˏ*kwi* ˏ*ning*, a bride's first visit to her parents; COM., [7]ˏ*ning ngwong*² I prefer, I would rather; [8]ˏ*ning* ʻ*kʻó* better, rather; [9]ˏ*ning* ʻ*sü pok*₂ ˏ*chüng*, rather die than submit to; [10]*Kiong*² ˏ*ning*, and [11]*Hok*₂ ˏ*ning*, prefectures in the north of Fookien; [12]ˏ*ning* ˏ*pʻó*, Ningpo.

嚀 ˏ Ning. To bid, to order, to enjoin on, to reiterate orders: COM., [13]ˏ*ting* ˏ*ning*, to caution, to charge straitly.

擰 ˏ Ning. To pull, to haul, to upset, to tumble about: [14]ʻ*chʻong* ˏ*ning*, to throw into utter confusion.

濘 ˏ Ning. Also read *neng*²: muddy, miry: [15]ˏ*ná* ˏ*ning*, slimy and slippery, as roads after a rain.

獰 ˏ Ning. Hairy dogs; vicious, savage, fierce; clamor, like the baying of dogs.

仁 ˏ Jên. Read ˏ*ing*; coll. ˏ*ning*: the kernel, the meat of nuts; the pupil of the eye: [16]*hok*₂ ˏ*tʻó* ˏ*ning*, walnut-meat; [17]ˏ*kwa* ʻ*chi* ˏ*ning*, the kernel of a melon-seed; [18]*mĕk*₂ ˏ*ning*, or [19]*mek*₂ ˏ*chiu* ˏ*ning*, the pupil, the eyeball; [20]*pah*₂ ˏ*ning*, the sclerotica; ˏ*u* ˏ*ning*, iris and pupil.

ˏ*Ning*. A coll. euphonic prefix, as in ˏ*ning* ˏ*nang*, to push

[1]溺水 [2]沉溺 [3]溺女 [4]溺愛不明 [5]康寧 [6]歸寧 [7]寧願 [8]寧可 [9]寧死不從 [10]建寧 [11]福寧 [12]寧波 [13]叮嚀 [14]搶擰 [15]泥濘 [16]核桃仁 [17]瓜子仁 [18]目仁 [19]目睭仁 [20]白仁 仁○

with the hands or feet; ˛ning ˛nong, to twist with the fingers, to twirl, as a top.

(504) Nio.

嬝 Niao. Read ʻnieu; used in the Puik, ˛Ing for the coll. ˛nio: the tremulous, mincing gait of a lady; also to protract the time, to prolong, to delay: ˛nio ˛nio, or ˛ni ˛nio ˛nio, a mincing gait; ˛nio ˛ti, to spend time till it is late, belated; ˛nio ˛mó tek˛ ch'ok˛ he delays (in getting ready) and can't come out.

(505) Nioh.

葉 Yeh. Read yéh˛; coll. nioh˛: a leaf, the leaves of plants: [1]˛ta nioh˛ the tea leaf; [2]lóh˛ nioh˛ to shed leaves; [3]˛t'i nioh˛ dry leaves of a kind of bamboo; [4]nioh˛ yok˛ (or ʻyo), wilted leaves; nioh˛ cheng' yéng' the leaves very luxuriant and beautiful.

箬 Jo. Read yok˛; used for the coll. nioh˛ as in nioh˛ wai' how many? nioh˛ sá' how much or many? ʻnü nioh˛ wai' hwoi' how old are you? ˛sang nioh˛ yong' in what way? ˛i nioh˛ po' (or o') ʻlá, he is very rich! nioh˛ ˛ch'ing, how deep, is very deep.

(506) Niong.

軟 輭 Juan. Interchangeably read ʻnwong: moving softly, as muffled wheels; soft, tender, weak; limber, pliant, lithesome, yielding: COM., [5]ʻniong yok˛ weak, feeble; [6]˛hwo ʻniong, peaceable, conciliatory; [7]ʻniong ˛sing, a limber body—an idol having flexible joints and dressed in clothes; [8]ʻniong ʻniong sié' a gentle manner; feeble in influence; COLL., [9]ʻniong ʻch'oi, articles easily carried, as jewels and clothes; ʻniong nge' "limber-ears"—the crooked forms of the contracted 163d and 170th radicals; [10]p'iéng' ˛sing ʻniong, richly dressed; ʻniong yoh˛ limber, pliable; [11]ʻniong ʻpa, light refreshment, as tea; ʻniong ˛si ˛si, or ʻniong ˛si ˛pa, very limber; [12]ʻniong ˛yeu pek˛ kauk˛ to stretch one's limbs, as when fatigued; ʻniong chiăk˛ (or ch'iăk˛), bamboo mats on which paddy is dried.

煖 Nuan. Read ʻnwang; used for the coll. ʻniong (or ʻnwong), as in ʻniong kóh, the back part of a hall or temple, place of honor; ʻniong ˛wo (or ˛kwo), an earthen or metallic heater for warming food.

Niong'. A coll. word: to straighten or draw one's self up (so as to look out); to swell, to rise up, as things cooked; a waving, tremulous motion: niong' ʻk'i ˛li, to draw up, as the body; to rise, to boil up; neng' niong' or neng' neng' niong' niong' swelling, wavy, tremulous.

娘 Niang. A young lady, a girl, Miss; a mother; ladies: in the coll. read ˛nong, q. v.: COM., [13]˛niong ˛niong, the empress; a goddess; [14]˛niong ʻná, a mother; the goddess "Mother"; [15]˛niong ˛ku, paternal aunts; [16]˛niong ˛i, maternal aunts; [17]˛i ˛niong, concubines; [18]˛ié ˛niong, or ˛tiă ˛niong, father

1茶	3提	5軟	7軟	勢	10遍	11軟	拔	14娘	16娘	18爺
葉	葉	弱	身	9軟	身	飽	骨	奶	姨	娘
2落	4葉	6和	8軟	髓	軟	12軟	13娘	15娘	17姨	
葉	弱	軟	軟	○	○	腰	娘	姑	娘	○

and mother; [1]꜀*niong keu*꜄ and [2]꜀*niong keng*꜄ maternal uncles and their wives; [3]꜀*t'iéng haiu*꜄ ꜀*niong* ꜀*niong*, title of the goddess Matsu-po; COLL., ꜀*chü* ꜀*niong*, a female, a woman.

讓² Jang. Read *yong*꜄; coll. *niong*꜄: to yield, to give place to, to waive one's rights; yielding, courteous, complaisant: [4]*niong*꜄ *oi*꜄ to yield a place or office; [5]꜀*song niong*꜄ mutual concession; [6]*niong*꜄ ꜀*a*, yield! give way! [7]*niong*꜄ *sioh*꜆ ꜀*peng*, to yield one side, to stand aside; *niong*꜄ ꜀*i* ꜀*seng* ꜀*kiăng*, let him go before; *niong*꜄ *ch'oi*꜄ to let another eat it; *niong*꜄ ꜀*nëng* ꜀*sang* ꜀*hung mwoi*꜄ *saung*꜄ ꜀*ch'i*, yield to people three mites and you'll still not be regarded stupid.

(507) Niu.

꜀*Niu.* A coll. word: shriveled, puckered, as pasted paper when dried: ꜀*niu k'ó*꜄ wrinkled; ꜀*niu* ꜂*king*, puckered up close; drawn in tightly, as the toes to avoid slipping; ꜀*niu sioh*꜆ ꜀*toi*, shriveled into a bunch.

꜂恧 Also read *nek*꜆: similar to the next; a feeling of shame, abashed, ashamed: ꜀*chang* ꜂*niu*, mortified.

꜂忸 Niu. To be ashamed; habituated, accustomed to: ꜂*niu* ꜀*ná* (or *nek*꜆), to blush.

꜂狃 Niu. A dog that must be coaxed, proud, offish; familiar with, disrespectful; to approach; to repeat, to reiterate, accustomed, used to, in which senses interchanged with the last: [8]꜂*niu sik*꜆ practiced in.

꜂扭 Niu. To turn with the hand, to twist, to wrench, to wring; to collar, to seize one; to wriggle, to turn from side to side; twisted, contorted, cramped; *met.*, to fabricate, to trump up a story: COM., [9]꜂*niu* ꜂*ta*, to collar and beat; [10]꜂*niu niék*꜆ trumped up; [11]꜂*niu chaiu*꜄ to memorialize litigiously, as two enemies do; [12]꜂*niu* ꜂*king*, to twist tightly; [13]꜂*niu ch'ok*꜆ ꜀*ké*, to collar each other and go into the street.

꜂杻 Niu. A thick, bushy tree, like a prunus; it grows in marshes and its wood is good for bows; manacles: COM., [14]꜂*ch'iu* ꜂*niu*, handcuffs.

꜂紐 Niu. To knot, to braid into a knob; to tie, to bind; a knot or fastening that easily loosens; a point of junction, as the tie of a girdle: in the coll. used for ꜀*niu*, q. v.: COM., [15]*kwoi*꜄ ꜂*niu*, the hair twisted in a knot on the head; [16]꜂*niu* ꜀*hwa*, to make flowers.

꜂鈕 Niu. The knob of a seal; a button; a hilt; the process on which a thing turns or connects with another: [17]꜂*niu* ꜀*k'ü*, a pivot; *met.*, the Dipper; COM., [18]꜂*niu k'aiu*꜄ buttons—the characters so used on shop-signs; COLL., ꜀*niu* ꜂*niu*, the loops or eyes of buttons; junction of the muscle with the shell in shell-fish.

[1]娘舅 [2]娘妗 [3]天后娘娘 [4]讓位 [5]相讓 [6]讓吓 [7]讓一爿 [8]狃習○ [9]扭打 [10]扭揑 [11]扭奏 [12]扭緊 [13]扭出街○ [14]手杻 [15]髻紐 [16]紐花 [17]鈕樞 [18]鈕鉤○

衄 Niu. Also read *nek*,: to bleed at the nose, which is said to arise from fright; to be discomfited, a defeat, a rout.

禸 Jou. Also read *'iu* and *,iu*: the step of a brute, the round marks, as of a fox's paw; the 114th radical.

紐 Niu. Read *'niu*; coll. *,niu*: to twist, as the top of a bag to knot it; to grip, to grapple closely, as in play or a fight: [1]*,niu 'lau*, twisted and knotted; [2]*,niu sioh*, *,toi*, or [3]*,niu 'k'i ,li*, to clutch each other closely.

(508) No.

怒 Nu. Anger, ire, rage, passion, fury, indignation; spirit, energy, vigor, mettle; angry, indignant, getting into a passion: [4]*'pó*[2] *no*[2] cruel anger; [5]*,wi no*[2] sternness; COM., [6]*'hung no*[2] or [7]*'no*[2] *k'e*[2] anger, passion; [8]*no*[2] *k'e*[2] *,ch'ung ,t'iéng*, his wrath mounts to heaven; [9]*no*[2] *hwak*, *,ch'ung ,kwang*, his rage bristled his hair and lifted his cap.

No[2]. A coll. word: to raise food from the crop, as a bird does to feed its young: *no*[2] *ch'ok*, *,li*, throws up (its food).

(509) Nó.

娜 No. Agreeable, affable; genteel, elegant, as a lady's gait: *'ó 'nó*, handsome, graceful; COM., *'nieu 'nó* (coll. *'neu 'nó*), a genteel gait.

嫐 Analogous to the next: to play or dally with; lewd, wanton in behavior.

嬲 Niao. Nao. Also read *'nieu*: to pull about, to toy, to dally with; to play with women, lewd gambols.

惱 Nao. Vexed, annoyed, angered; to feel irritated, indignant, resentful: [10]*'nó haung*[2] irritated, indignant; COM., [11]*'ó 'nó*, vexed; [12]*,hwang 'nó*, troubled, disquieted.

瑙 碯 Nao. A precious stone of various kinds, as the cornelian, opal, fortification-agate, chalcedony; in the best sorts the striae resemble a horse's head: COM., [13]*'ma 'nó*, a cornelian.

腦 堖 Nao. The brain; soft, glossy, as marrow: COM., [14]*'nó ,chiong*, or [15]*,t'au 'nó*, the brain; [16]*'nó 'ch'oi*, brain and marrow; COLL., [17]*'nó tói*[2] the skull; [18]*,mó ,t'au ,mó 'nó*, "no head for", not able to comprehend, confused; *,lau p'e*[2] *'nó*, mucus flowing from the nose.

那 No. Na. Nai. Nên. Nêng. How? what? much; to end, to rest; peaceful, contented; a euphonic particle at the end of a sentence: also read *'na*, q. v.: *seu*[2] *hok*, *pok*, *,nó*, to receive a little happiness.

1 紐了 2 紐一 堆 3 紐起來 4 暴怒 5 威怒 6 忿怒 7 怒氣 8 怒氣冲天 9 怒髮冲冠 10 惱恨 11 懊惱 12 煩惱 13 瑪瑙 14 腦漿 15 頭腦 16 腦髓 17 腦袋 18 無頭無腦

福州方言拼音字典

挪 挼 ꜀ ꜀ No. To rub between the hands, to make round by rubbing; to move, to transfer; to misapply, as funds, to embezzle; to borrow of; used in a coll. term meaning how, why, wherefore: COM., ¹꜀nó ꜀iê or ²꜀nó ch'auk꜆ to loan temporarily; ³꜀ch'ó ꜀nó, to "round by rubbing"; *met.*, to settle an affair; ⁴꜀nó ꜀k'wang ch'auk꜆ kek꜆ to borrow from another's plenty to supply one's urgent need; COLL., ⁵꜀nó chioh꜆ to borrow of; ⁶꜀ku ꜂chai ꜀nó, to paste paper-toys; ⁷꜀choi ꜀nó, to compromise, to consult how; to bargain for (reduction in price); ⁸꜀nó chiāng꜄ to move or turn (a thing) straight; ꜀nó nóh꜆ an interrogative term implying the opposite idea, how, wherefore, how is it that; ꜂nü ꜀nó nóh, má꜄ ꜂hieu tek꜆ how do you not understand!

儺 ꜀ No. Soft, yielding; gentle, graceful, as one's step; to exorcise, to enact rites to expel pestilence, or the demons causing it: ꜀ó ꜀nó, delicate, genteel, graceful.

꜀Nó. A coll. word, as in ꜀nó e꜄ (probably a corruption of nok꜇ e꜄), a cheerful assent or approval.

懦 ² 愞 ² No. Infirm in purpose, timid, weak, cowardly, apprehensive: COM., ⁹nó² yok꜇ weak, feeble; ¹⁰꜀p'i nó² slow, dilatory.

糯 ² 稬 ² No. Glutinous rice, used in manufacturing distilled liquor; in the coll. heavy, inactive, as the stomach from eating cakes of glutinous rice: COLL., ꜂pa nó² sated, eaten to the full; ꜀t'au cheng꜄ nó² the head heavy and distressed.

(510) Noh.

Noh꜆. A coll. word, as in ꜀nu noh꜆ or noh꜆ noh꜆ the female mode of salutation, as before an idol; the hands are held close to the person and moved up and down.

(511) Nóh.

毛꜆ Used for the coll. nóh꜆: a thing, matter, substance; articles, goods; idols, things carried in procession: ¹¹꜀mó nóh꜆ nothing; ¹²sié꜄ nóh, or miéh꜆ nóh꜆ what thing? what? ¹³꜀chü nóh꜆ all, everything; ꜀sang nóh꜆ to have a cutaneous eruption; nóh꜆ ꜀t'au, things, goods; kauk꜆ ꜀t'au nóh꜆ "dry bones"—refuse, worthless things; ꜀ngiāng nóh꜆ to carry idols, etc., in procession; ꜀nó nóh꜆ why? how is it that? ꜀nó nóh꜆ ꜂sai ꜀kiáng, why need you fear?

Nóh꜆. A coll. word, as in nóh꜆ sóh꜆ nik꜇ day previous to day-before-yesterday, three days ago; nóh꜆ au꜄ nik꜇ three days hence.

Nóh꜇. A coll. word: to take and work over with the fingers, to finger, to fumble: nóh꜇ naiu꜄ to wrinkle by fingering; nóh꜇ ꜀seu, to mix evenly with the fingers, as ingredients.

¹挪移 ²挪撮 ³搓挪 ⁴挪寬 撮急 ⁵挪借 ⁶糊紙挪 ⁷裁挪 ⁸挪正 ⁹懦弱 ¹⁰疲懦 ¹¹毛毛 ¹²世毛 ¹³諸毛

海上絲綢之路文獻集成 科技與文化編

(512) Noi.

ˊ餒 Nei. Destitute of food, hungry, famished; putrid fish: [1]ˊnoi saik, a hungry look; COM., [2]ˊche˒ ˊnoi, depressed, discouraged.

Noi˒. A coll. word: to put away, to hide, to conceal, to secrete: *noi˒ ch'oi˒ ˊtiĕ*, put it in his mouth—has eaten it up; *noi˒ ˏk'wo ˊt'ĕng*, to secrete in the boot-tops; *noi˒ ˊch'iu ˊwong ˊtiĕ*, to hide in one's sleeve.

ˏ*Noi*. A coll. word, as in ˏ*noi ˊyeu* or ˏ*noi ˊchieu*, a vulgar term for the penis; *met.*, nothing! trifling!

(513) Nói.

內˒ Nei. Na. Within, inside, inner, internal, in; that which is within, the inclosed; the inwards; privy, personal, near to; family, domestic, private; amongst, in the midst of: [3]ˊ*ü nói*˒ the world; COM., [4]*nói*˒ *te*˒ the Inner Land, China; [5]*nói*˒ *kóh*ˏ the Privy Council; [6]*pok*ˏ *chai*˒ *nói*˒ not included, extra; [7]*nói*˒ *ngwoi*˒ inside and outside; [8]*nói*˒ ˏ*siong*, an internal injury; [9]*nói*˒ ˏ*chai*, mental ability, learning; [10]*chiĕng*˒ *nói*˒ or [11]*nói*˒ ˏ*ing*, my wife; [12]*nói*˒ *tik*ˏ a wife's nephew; [13]*nói*˒ ˏ*sing*, the heart, mind.

(514) Nok.

諾˒ 喏˒ No. An answer of approbation; a cheerful response, a nod, an assent: [14]*sĕük*ˏ ˏ*mung* ˏ*king nok*ˏ I early received your golden promise; [15]ˊ*hü nok*ˏ to assent, to grant; COM., [16]*nok*ˏ ˏ*yong* or [17]*nok*ˏ *e*˒ pleased, assenting; ˏ*i* ˊ*i* ˏ*king* ˊ*üng nok*ˏ he has granted it. The second read ˊ*niă* in the dictionaries: to speak respectfully: *ch'iong*˒ ˊ*niă*, a profound bow.

訥˒ 吶˒ No. To stammer, to stutter, to speak with difficulty; to be sparing of one's words, cautious; unready, embarrassed: the second used for *nak*ˏ in the coll. q. v.: [18]*ük*ˏ *nok*ˏ ˏ*ü* ˏ*ngiong*, he desired to restrain his words, was cautious in speech; *nok*ˏ *nok*ˏ to stammer, to stutter.

(515) Nong.

ˊ冗 ˊ宂 Jung. Also read ˊ*üng*: scattered, dispersed, gone home, off duty, as officers; a furlough-allowance; business, affairs, duties, occupation; confused, mixed; having no fixed abode, vagrant, wandering: [19]ˊ*nong* ˏ*kwang*, supernumerary officers; [20]ˊ*nong sik*ˏ a sinecure; [21]ˏ*hwang* ˊ*nong* or ˏ*hung* ˊ*nong*, much business; [22]ˏ*liu* ˊ*nong*, homeless people, vagrants; [23]ˊ*nong hiĕ*˒ needless expense; COM., *sük*ˏ ˊ*nong*, common matters; small, extra duties.

ˊ曩 Nang. Before, previous, in former times: ˊ*nong sek*ˏ anciently; ˊ*nong nik*ˏ a former day, lately.

氄 Also read ˏ*üng*: the fine feathers of birds, down; full of soft feathers: ˊ*nong* ˏ*mó*, down.

ˊ暖 Nuan. Read ˊ*nwang*; coll. ˊ*nong*: warm, mild, genial, as the weather: ˏ*t'iĕng* ˊ*nong*, the weather is mild; *pwang*˒ ˏ*hang pok*ˏ

[1]餒色 [2]志餒 [3]宇內 [4]內地 [5]內閣 [6]不在內 [7]內外 [8]內傷 [9]內才 [10]內賤 [11]內人 [12]內姪 [13]內心 [14]夙蒙金諾 [15]許諾 [16]諾然 [17]諾意 [18]欲訥於言 [19]冗官 [20]冗食 [21]煩冗 [22]流冗 [23]冗費

福州方言拼音字典

'*nong*, half-cold and not genial, fickle weather; *ˏch'ung 'nong* (or '*nwang*) *ˏhwa ˏhiong*, the mild spring (brings) fragrant flowers.

'暖 Nuan. Read '*nwang;* coll. '*nong:* to warm, to heat over; warming, heating: '*nong 'chiu*, to warm wine; '*nong yék*ˎ to heat up (food); '*nong ˏkwo* (or '*niong ˏkwo*), a heater, a vessel to warm food in.

'餪 Nuan. Read '*nwang;* coll. '*nong*, as in [1]'*nong seu*' (or '*niong seu*') a birthday feast, food presented to one by near relatives on the occasion.

戇' Kun. Read *kong'; used in the Paik, ˏIng* for the coll. *nong'* as in *ˏung nong'* or *ˏnang nong'* stupid, obtuse, blockish.

Nong'. A coll. word: moist, damp, humid: *nong' k'e'* damp vapors, dampness; *nong' ˏt'iéng*, a humid atmosphere; '*tiong nong'* to become damp, as from the south wind; *sëük*ˎ *nong'* damp, moist; *met.*, subject to the effects of dampness, as from sleeping in wet clothes.

ˏ囊 Nang. A bag, sack; a purse; *met.*, property, wealth: [2]*ˏheng ˏnong*, a traveling-bag; [3]*t'u ˏnong*, a cave, a hole; [4]*ˏk'ung ˏnong*, an empty purse—poor, penniless; [5]*ˏch'ing ˏnong*, the Green Bag—a work on geomancy; COM., [6]*ˏü ˏnong*, balance of money in a purse; *ˏp'ui ˏnong*, a leathern sack.

ˏ攮 Nang. Read '*nong;* coll. *ˏnong:* to twist between the thumb and fingers: [7]*ˏnong siăng'* to twist a thread; [8]*ˏnong yoh*ˎ *ˏwong*, to make pills by rolling in the fingers; [9]*ˏnong ˏyéng ˏyéng* (or *ˏchio ˏchio*), to twist or roll in a globular form; [10]*ˏnong 'chai 'ngiéng*, to make small paper-rolls; [11]*ˏnong p'ok*ˎ *ch'ieu'* or *ˏnong ch'e' p'ok*ˎ to twirl cash in gaming.

ˏ瓤 Jang. Read *ˏsiong;* coll. *ˏnong:* the pulp of a melon or squash; pith, pulp; the inner substance, as of bamboo or rattan; the second film, skin, or coat: [12]'*kwong ˏkwa ˏnong*, the pulp of a squash; [13]*tëük*ˎ *ˏnong*, the inner substance of bamboo; [14]*ˏnong kau'* the inner part is thick.

ˏ郎 Lang. Read *ˏlong;* coll. *ˏnong*, as in *ˏnong ma'* a father; *ˏnong ma' 'kiăng*, father and child.

ˏ娘 Niang. Read *ˏniong;* coll. *ˏnong*, as in *ˏnong 'ná*, a mother; the goddess "Mother"; *ˏnong 'ná siăng' 'pó ho' tié'* let "Mother" be efficacious and preserve my son!

閏' Jun. An intercalary month: COM., [15]*nong' ngwok*ˎ a month intercalated; [16]*nong' ˏniéng*, a year having an intercalary month; [17]*ˏniéng pok*ˎ *kié' nong'* (after one) year not reckon the intercalary month, as in paying monthly interest, etc.; COLL., *ngo' ˏniéng lang' 'tiong nong'* in five years two intercalary months.

[1]餪壽 [2]行囊 [3]土囊 [4]空囊 [5]青囊 [6]餘囊 [7]攮線 [8]攮藥丸 [9]攮圓圓 [10]攮紙撚〇 [11]攮覆笑〇 [12]廣瓜瓤〇 [13]竹瓤 [14]瓤厚 [15]閏月 [16]閏年 [17]年不計閏

韌 Jên. Read *engʾ;* used in the *Paik*, *ˏIng* for the coll. *nongʾ:* flexible, but tenacious; tough, as meat; *met.*, slow, dilatory: [1]*ˏpʻi nongʾ* slow, procrastinating; [2]*nongʾ ˏpʻui taiʾ* (like) a tough leathern girdle, incorrigibly slow or backward to do.

(516) Nu.

ˏNu. A coll. prefix, as in *ˏnu noh*, the female mode of salutation, as before idols; the hands are held together close to the person and moved up and down.

ʻ努 Nu. To exert one's self strenuously, to strive, to expend one's energies on; a desperate effort, energy, force: COM., *ʻnu likˏ* to exert strength, to strive for.

ʻ弩 Nu. A kind of ballista or cross-bow made with springs; it was contrived to shoot several arrows and set as a trap for animals: [3]*ʻnu ˏsü*, a corps of archers, employed in the Han dynasty; [4]*hwakˏ ʻnu*, to shoot a cross-bow; COM., [5]*ʻnu chiéngʾ* a small cross-bow, not now in use.

ˏ奴 Nu. A slave, a bondman, one bought with money and subjected to slavery; an abject, a term of contempt; slavish; used in Foochow for I, as in polite phrase or by inferiors: [6]*tëükˏ ˏnu*, a bamboo-pillow; COM., [7]*ˏnu pukˏ* a bondman; *ˏnu ˏchai* (coll. *ˏnu ˏchʻai*), a slave; I, your slave, as used by Manchus in addressing the emperor; [8]*ˏnu peʾ* male and female slaves; COLL., [9]*ˏnu kaukˏ ˏnëng*, we all, all of us.

ˏ㣽 Nu. Great strength; to exert one's self: [10]*ˏnu likˏ* to put forth one's utmost strength.

ˏ孥 ˏ帑 Nu. A child; my children; soft, tender, small and weak, that which needs soothing; a bird's tail: the 2d also read *ʻtʻong*, q. v.: [11]*ˏchʻá ˏnu*, wife and children.

ˏ駑 Nu. An old horse, a weak, broken down steed: [12]*ˏnu ˏtʻai*, a weak, old horse; *met.*, a term applied by statesmen to themselves.

(517) Nü.

ˏNü. A coll. word: leaning, slanting, as a poor house: *ˏnü ˏniä*, rickety, as a chair; *met.*, scolding back and forth, railing at each other.

ʻ女 Nü. Yü. A female, a woman; an unmarried girl, a daughter; female, feminine; the 10th of the 28 constellations, part of Aquarius; the 38th radical: [13]*siokˏ ˏi ʻnü*; a white cockatoo; COM., [14]*hoʾ ʻnü*, females, women; [15]*keʾ ʻnü*, prostitutes; [16]*ʻnü ˏliu*, the class of women; [17]*ʻnü ʻchü*, a maiden, a daughter; [18]*ʻnü ˏi*, I, your daughter; [19]*tikˏ ʻnü*, a brother's daughter, a niece; [20]*ˏsong ʻnü*, grand-daughter; [21]*ʻnü peʾ* a female slave; *ʻnü sáʾ* (coll. *ˏnié saiʾ*), a son-in-law; *ʻnü ˏkëng*, female work; *ʻnü hauʾ ˏking*, a classic on female duties;

[1] 疲韌 [2] 韌皮帶 [3] 弩師 ○ [4] 彀弩 [5] 弩箭 [6] 竹奴 [7] 奴僕 [8] 奴婢 [9] 奴各儂 [10] 㣽力 ○ [11] 妻孥 [12] 駑駘 [13] 雪衣女 ○ [14] 婦女 [15] 妓女 [16] 女流 [17] 女子 [18] 女兒 [19] 姪女 [20] 孫女 [21] 女婢

ʻnü ʻka ˛nang ˛chong, women dressed in men's clothes; *ʻnü siongʼ* an effeminate face and manner; COLL., *ʻnü mȧ² kwoʼ ˛chʻing ˛hu*, the woman's (leprosy) can't pass over to her husband. Read *nëüʼ* or *nëü²*: to give a daughter in marriage, to marry out one's daughter.

ʻ汝 Ju. ʻ你 Ni. ʻ女 The second personal pronoun, thou, you; thy, thine, your, yours; the first is also the name of a tributary of the river Hwai and of an inferior department in Honan: [1]*ʻnü ˛mwong*, you all; COM., [2]*ʻnü ʻngó*, you and I, both of us; COLL., [3]*ʻnü ˛nëng*, you, ye, *ʻnü ˛ki*, yours; *na² ʻla ʻnü*, only you (say or do thus); *ʻnü ek, hwak, ng² se² ˛nëng*, you surely are not a man, as said to an ingrate; *ʻnü chóʼ ʻnü chóʼ* attend to your own business! you will act in your own way!

˛Nü. A coll. prefix, as in *˛nü nëük*, (or *nük₂ nëük₂*), wrinkled, rumpled, as a sleeve shoved up; *met.*, to skulk, to squat out of sight.

(518) Nüh.

Nüh₂. A coll. word: similar to *nóh₂*; to press, to squeeze in the hand; to tread, as masons do the mud for plastering; *met.*, to roll or tumble in a bunch, as children in play: *nüh₂ pʻwaiʼ* to break by squeezing; *nüh₂ ho²* crumpled till it is all soft; *nüh₂ sioh₂ ˛toi*, squeezed into a bunch; tumbled together.

(519) Nuí.

˛挼 ˛捼 To rub and roll with the hand, to make round by rolling; in the coll. to knead; to rub, as clothes in washing; *met.*, to vex, to tease, to annoy; to weary, to bore one: COLL., [4]*˛nuí chȧ²* to knead dough; [5]*˛nuí chʻaiʼ* to rub (salt) in vegetables; [6]*˛wí ˛nuí*, to cast aside as worthless; *met.*, to ruin one's self; *˛nuí nóh₂* waste, refuse, useless remnants; *˛king ˛nuí nóh₂* he bears a teasing; [7]*˛nuí yok₂* tired from kneading; *met.*, fagged, as two at play; *˛nuí ʻyo*, soft, and flaccid from handling; *pongʼ ʻlá ˛nuí*, "set out to be kneaded", as said of one annoyed or of a quarrel to be settled by talk.

˛攔 Like the last: to rub between the hands, as in washing, to rumple; to push, to shake: [8]*˛hwang ˛nuí*, to rub, to rumple.

(520) Nük.

肉₂ Jou. Ju. The meat of animals, flesh; specifically applied to pork in Foochow; the pulp or meat of fruits and nuts; fat, fleshy; corporeal, fleshly; the 130th radical, contracted in composition: COM., [9]*˛tü nük₂* pork; [10]*˛yong nük₂* goat's meat, mutton; [11]*nük₂ ˛sing*, the body; [12]*nük₂ ˛wong*, pork-balls; [13]*nük₂ tóh₂* a butcher's stand; [14]*nük₂ ˛ting*, fat pork cut into small pieces; [15]*nük₂ ˛üng*, and [16]*nük₂ ˛si*, lean pork cooked and torn into shreds; [17]*˛chʻing kauk₂ nük₂* very nearly related; COLL., [18]*seng nük₂* lean pork; [19]*tang² chʻaiʼ nük₂* the

1 汝們　2 汝我　3 汝仏　4 挼劑　5 挼菜　6 擐挼　7 挼弱　8 煩攔　9 猪肉　10 羊肉　11 肉身　12 肉丸　13 肉桌　14 肉釘　15 肉絨　16 肉絲　17 親骨肉　18 瘠肉　19 淡菜肉

meat of a species of shell-fish; *˛kang ˛ta nük˛* and *'kwang' 'chwi nük˛* dry pork and water-blown pork; [2]*'nük˛ kóh˛ 'piăng*, a pork-and-biscuit sandwich; [3]*'nük˛ siong'* your flesh itches (for a whipping)! *nük˛ lang' chaik˛ 'lá 't'ó*, for soft-cooked pork one seeks (needs) gravy; *met.*, one must pay well for a good article. Read *eu'*: the rim or substantial part of copper cash; the hole is called *hó'*.

(521) Nung.

嚨 Nêng. Read *˛nung;* coll. *˛nung:* to speak in a low tone sullenly or in complaint, to murmur, to mutter, to grumble: *˛nung ˛nĕng*, to grumble at people; *˛ning ˛ning ˛nung ˛nung*, muttering; *˛nung ˛chü chak˛ kwak˛* to mutter incessantly.

˛Nung. A coll. word: to delay, to defer, to put off; late, slow, deferred: *chai' ˛nung sioh˛ k'aik˛ 'ku*, defer a little longer; *'chiü ˛t'iĕng ˛nung sioh˛ nik˛ ˛mó 'ü*, the sky or weather has passed the day without rain—*scil.*, though it has been threatening.

'忍 Jên. Read *'üng;* used for the coll. *'nung:* to repress anger or impatient feelings; to endure, to bear, to suffer patiently: [4]*'nung sang'* or [5]*'nung k'e'* a patient temper; *˛t'ong 'nung*, to keep down, to repress, as resentment; [6]*'nung sioh˛ kwo'* to suppress an (angry) utterance; *'nung ná' kwo'* insufferable, (the angry feeling) must have vent.

˛農 Nung. Nêng. To cultivate the ground, to dig and plow; to plant, to sow; agriculture: [7]*˛sang ˛nung*, the three kinds of husbandry—on the hills, marshes, and plains; COM., [8]*˛nung ˛hu*, a husbandman; [9]*˛nung ˛ka*, farmers; [10]*˛sing ˛nung*, the emperor Shinnung, who taught husbandry; [11]*k'wong' ˛nung*, to encourage agriculture, as the Emperor and officers do.

˛儂 Nung. Nêng. I, myself; in the coll. read *˛nĕng*, q. v.: [12]*˛ó ˛nung*, I, myself; *˛kü ˛nung*, he, himself.

˛濃 Nung. Nêng. Thick, inspissated, as liquids; spiced, seasoned; rich, strong, as infusions or flavors; heavy, as dew; kind, h e a r t y; nervous, terse, as style: in the coll. read *˛nüng*, q. v.: [13]*˛nung tang'* thick and thin; rich and weak; light and shade, as in pictures; *˛nung ˛nung*, heavy, as dew; [14]*˛nung soi'* deep sleep; [15]*˛nung pek˛* clear, heavy writing; COM., [16]*˛nung haiu'* a nervous, rich style.

˛穠 Nêng. Luxuriant, t h i c k, as growing grain: *˛nung mik˛* close set, exuberant, as shrubs, etc.

˛膿 Nung. Nêng. Pus, matter in boils and ulcers; a sloughing; to rot away, rotten, as stubble: in the coll. read *˛nĕng*, q. v.: *˛nung hiĕk˛* bloody pus.

˛醲 Nêng. Used for *˛nung* (thick, rich): strong, high-flavored: *˛nung 'chiu*, g o o d, generous wine.

[1]灌水肉 ○ [2]肉夾餅 ○ [3]肉癢 ○ [4]忍性 ○ [5]忍氣 ○ [6]忍一句 ○ [7]三農 [8]農夫 [9]農家 [10]神農 [11]勸農 [12]阿儂 [13]濃淡 [14]濃睡 [15]濃筆 [16]濃厚

福州方言拼音字典

(522) **Nūng.**

濃 ꜀Nung. Read ꜀nung; coll. ꜀nūng: thick, as a liquid; rich, strong, as an infusion; spiced, seasoned: [1]*꜀ta ꜀nūng*, the tea is strong; [2]*꜀nūng ꜀nūng mĕk꜆* thick ink; [3]*꜀nūng ꜀nūng ꜀iu*, highly seasoned with oil; *‘saik꜆ ꜀nūng*, a deep color, as of an infusion.

(523) **Nwa.**

Nwa². A coll. word: turned to one side, awry, deflected: *nwa² nwa²* awry, twisted; *nwa² tek꜆ sá²* much deflected; *‘chiă ꜀nĕng ‘yă nwa²* this person is far astray (from virtue); *꜀nū nwa²* to contend, to scold at each other.

(524) **Nwah.**

Nwah꜆. A coll. word: similar to the last; awry, twisted, sprained, wrenched out of place, as a bone in a sprained foot.

(525) **Nwang.**

‘暖 Nuan. Nan. The genial warmth of the sun; warm, agreeable, as the days of spring: in the coll. read *‘nong*, q. v.: [5]*nik꜆ ‘nwang*, warmth of the sun; [6]*‘nwang ꜀hung*, a genial breeze.

‘煖 Nuan. Nan. The warmth of fire; warm, soothing, agreeable, as a gentle fire; warmed; *met.*, warm, friendly, as the feelings; to warm in the sun or by a fire: in the coll. read *‘nong* and *‘niong*, q. v.: COM., [7]*‘nwang mó²* a wadded cap; [8]*‘nwang kóh꜆* the elevated place in the back of a hall or temple; [9]*꜀ung ‘nwang*, warm, genial; benign, soothing, as medicine; [10]*‘pau ‘nwang*, full and warm, well fed and clothed.

‘餪 Nuan. Food presented to superiors: in the coll. read *‘nong*, q. v.: [11]*‘nwang ong²* to present food; food presented, as to a superior; [12]*‘nwang ‘nü*, to send food to a daughter (three days after her marriage).

(526) **Nwo.**

[This word is interchangeably read *nio*, q. v.]

(527 **Nwoh.**

[This word is interchangeably read *nioh*, q. v.]

(528) **Nwoí.**

Nwoí². A coll. word: the cavity into which the tenon is fitted, a mortise; a socket: *nwoí² po²* the mortise rotted; *ch‘ĕūng² nwoí² ‘lá*, to insert (a tenon) in the mortise; *mwoí² lóh꜆ nwoí²* not yet entered the mortise or socket.

(529) **Nwong**

[This word is interchangeably read *niong*, q. v.]

(530) **Ng.**

伓² A coll. character; used for the strong nasal *ng²* which is not referable to the table of initial and final sounds; mostly placed before verbs in the sense of no, not, will not; before adjectives, it often answers to *un, dis, in;* between verbs repeated, it forms a question; repeated before succeeding verbs and adjectives, it means neither, nor: [13]*ng² ‘sai*, no need of, unnecessary; [14]*ng² eng²* he does not, or will not, answer; [15]*ng² tioh꜆* not done, done

1 茶濃	2 濃濃墨	3 濃濃油	4 色濃	6 暖風	8 煖閣	10 飽煖	12 餪女	14 伓應
○	○	○	5 日暖	7 煖帽	9 温煖	11 餪饆	13 伓使	15 伓着

wrongly; 'ng' kau' insufficient; ng' ˏt'ĕng, ought not, must not; [2]ng' chai' sié' in danger of, risk, hazard; ng' sié' not only (that or so much); chó' ng' chó' will you do it or not? ng' ˏchiong 'siong, not think so; ng' sé' po' 'kong, "is it not as one would say"—i. e., precisely so, of course just so; ng' ˏtong ng' 'toi, neither (too) long nor (too) short; ng' 'tiĕ ng' ch'ok, neither enters nor retires; ng' 'ngu sŭk, not well skilled in or acquainted with.

(531) Nga.

'雅 Ya. Elegant, correct; neat, genteel, decorous; also plain, simple, unadorned: [3]'nga tang' plain, yet neat; COM., [4]'nga te' elegant; correct, classic; fine, stylish; [5]sá' 'nga, genteel, decorous; [6]'nga tó' genteel employment, as of students; fine, as artist's work; [7]miéng' ˏsü pok, 'nga, to refuse openly would be indecorous—a sign on shops declining to sell on credit.

ˏ牙 Ya. The grinders, molars, double teeth; the teeth; a tooth-like process; toothed, jagged; ivory; a bud; commonly used for an agent, a broker; the 92d radical: COM., [8]ˏnga 'ch'i, the teeth; [9]twai' ˏnga, the grinders; [10]ˏnga hwok, an ivory tablet, anciently borne at audiences; [11]ch'iong' ˏnga, ivory; [12]ˏnga tĕü' ivory chop-sticks; [13]ˏnga hok, feasts to employés on the 2d and 16th of the month; [14]ˏnga ˏwong, a buff or salmon color; [15]ˏnga ˏkwang ngaing' the jaws stiff, as from a paroxysm of grief; COLL., ˏnga 'ch'i t'aĕk, a tooth-pick; ˏnga ˏsó ˏsĕng, "your jaws are loose"—said to a scolder; ˏnga ˏnĕng, a broker, commission-merchant; 'kwi 'chi ˏnga, a fruit-broker's.

ˏ芽 Ya. A germ, a plumule, a bud, a sprout; to bud, to sprout; the beginning, budding forth: [16]ˏmeng ˏnga, to bud; [17]hok, ˏnga, a seed-bud; COM., [18]hwak, ˏnga, (coll. pwok, ˏnga), to sprout; [19]ˏnga ˏchiéng, the tip of a bud; COLL., tau' ˏnga, bean-sprouts; mah, ˏnga, wheat-sprouts, used medicinally; ˏnga 'kiăng, a kind of tea.

ˏ齖 Ya. Irregular teeth: COLL., ˏnga 'ngá, to look crossly, sour, crabbed; ˏnga ngĕüng' (or ˏngai ngĕüng'), that which provokes, detestable; á' ˏnga ngĕüng' ˏnĕng, it will disgust people.

ˏ衙 Ya. The marquee of a general, distinguished by a standard; a court, a palace, an office, a tribunal, an official residence; the exercise of functions in a court: [20]'chó ˏnga, an early court; [21]ˏnga 'hu (or 'sü), an officer's residence; COM., [22]ˏnga ˏmwong, an office, a yamun; [23]nói' ˏnga, the private apartments of the yamun; 'pa ˏnga, an official door-keeper; ˏnga yăh, police, official attendants; siong' ˏnga ˏmwong an officer's visit to his superiors, as on set days of the month.

[1]伓殼 [2]伓在勢 [3]雅淡○ [4]雅緻 [5]細雅 [6]雅道 [7]面辭不雅 [8]牙齒 [9]大牙 [10]牙笏 [11]象牙 [12]牙筯 [13]牙福 [14]牙黃 [15]牙關硬○ [16]萌芽 [17]核芽 [18]發芽 [19]芽尖 [20]早衙 [21]衙府 [22]衙門 [23]內衙

研[2] Used for the coll. *nga*[2]*:* to polish by rubbing, to smooth, as with a stone or shell: *nga*[2] *˛kwong ˛kwong*, to rub smooth, to polish; [1]*nga*[2] *˛king*, silver articles gilded and polished with the agate; [2]*nga*[2] *˛loi*, a kind of shell used in polishing essay-paper; *nga*[2] *nga*[2] *kieu*ʾ a creaking, a grating sound.

訝[2] Ya. Interchanged with the next: to greet, to receive affably; to exclaim, to express surprise at: [3]*˛ch'ai nga*[2] to be suspicious of; [4]*˛chiă nga*[2] astonished.

迓[2] Ya. To go out and greet, to meet, to receive courteously: the 2d also read *ngëü*[2] q. v.: *˛nging nga*[2] to receive respectfully.

御[2] Yü.

(532) Ngá.

˛Ngá. A coll. word, as in *˛ngá sioh*ˌ *˛siăng*, to emit a creaking sound, as a door; *˛ngá ʻtié ˛ngá ch'ok*, to creak when one is going in and out; *˛ngá ˛ngá kieu*ʾ a low cry or wail, as of a child.

ʻ睨 I. To look aslant or askance at; to glance the eyes, as birds and beasts do; the sun declining or shining athwart: in the coll. read *ngá*[2] q. v.: [5]*ngá se*[2] to look askance; [6]*no*[2] *ʻngá*, an angry glance; COLL., *ʻp'á ʻngá*, to look askance at.

*Ngá*ʾ. A coll. word: to whine, to whimper, as a child: *ʻnü chai*ʾ *ngá*ʾ *sioh*ˌ *˛siăng ʻngwai cheu*[2] *p'ah*, you whimper once more and I'll whip.

˛倪 I. The young and delicate; small, weak, as children; to peep, to glance at; to benefit, to distinguish; an edge, the limit, verge of; a surname: [7]*˛twang ˛ngá*, exact, to the least point; origin, beginning; [8]*˛t'iéng ˛ngá*, the verge of heaven; [9]*ʻchó ˛ngá eu*[2] *˛ngá*, to glance left and right, to look about.

˛猊 I. A fabulous animal, called [10]*˛song ˛ngá*, like a lion; some say, a wild horse that travels 500 *ʻli* a day; used in the coll. in a *met.*, sense, as in *˛sá ˛ngá* or [11]*˛ngá tó*[2] unreasonable, overbearing or excessively strict.

˛輗 I. A cross-bar, to which animals are fastened in drawing a vehicle.

˛鯢 I. A hairy, marine animal, variously described by the Chinese; probably a species of seal or lamantin: *˛king ˛ngá*, the male and female whale; *met.*, a violent oppressor, like a Verres.

˛霓 I. A rainbow, specially the secondary one, called the female: [12]*˛hung ˛ngá*, the rainbow; [13]*ʻch'ai ˛ngá*, variegated; [14]*˛ting ˛ngá*, the rattling sound of thunder.

˛麑 A fawn; a lion-like animal, called *˛song ˛ngá*, which devours tigers; *˛ngá ˛kiu*, deer-skin garments.

1研金 2研螺 3猜訝 4嗟訝 5睨覘 6怒睨 7端倪 8天倪 9左倪右倪 10狻猊 11猊道 12虹霓 13彩霓 14霆霓

睨 I. Read ‘*ngá*; coll. *ngá*² as in ‘*p‘á ngá*² or *ngá*² *k‘ang*’ to examine closely, to scrutinize; *ngá*² ,*ching*, to identify or ascertain by close scrutiny; *ngá*² *má*² *ch‘ok*, can't see through it, inscrutable.

枝 Ch‘ih. Read ,*chié*; used for the coll. *ngá*²: a branch, a twig: ¹*ch‘eu*’*ngá*² branches of a tree; ²*ngá*² ,*sui* (or ,*heng*), the branches hang down; ,*kó* ,*long ngá*² the whole branch.

*Ngá*². A coll. word, as in *ngá*² *ngá*² *kieu*’ or ,*t‘ié ngá*² *ngá*² to cry and sob, as a child does.

(533) Ngah.

Ngah,. A coll. word, as in *ngah*, *ngah*, *kieu*’ a creaking sound, as of a bedstead, or the edges of boards rubbing against each other; ,*kiăng ngeh*, *ngeh*, *ngah*, *ngah*, creaks from being walked upon.

*Ngah*₂. A coll. word, as in *ngah*₂ *lah*₂ (or ,*nga lah*₂) *sioh*₂ ,*siăng*, it rattles, it makes a clattering sound; *ngih*₂ *lih*₂ *ngah*₂ *lah*₂ a rattling, as of tiles or things shaken by an earthquake.

*Ngah*₂. A coll. word: to stop, to block, to obstruct, so as to cause unevenness: *o*’ *nóh*, *ngah*₂ ‘*lá má*² *pong*’ *tek*, *lóh*₂ there is something that obstructs so that you can't set it down; ,*ngau ngah*₂ variance, cause of quarrel.

(534) Ngáh.

閼, Read *ngiăh*₂; used in the *Paik*, ,*Ing* for the coll. *ngáh*,: a harsh, grating sound, as of a door on its wooden sockets; also pinched, jammed, caught in a door when shut: ³,*mwong ngáh*, *sioh*₂ ,*siăng*, the door creaked harshly; ⁴‘*ch‘iu ngáh*, the hand jammed (in the door); ⁵*ngáh*, ‘*piéng*, squeezed flat.

Ngáh,. A coll. word: the creaking sound, as of a sedan or of a cooly's carrying stick and burden.

(535) Ngai.

捱 ‘Yai. Read ,*ngai*; used for the coll. ,*ngai*: to bear, to put up with, to endure; also to lean, to rest against: ⁶,*ngai* ,*ngai*, to endure, to bear trouble; ‘*mwong* ,*ngai* ,*chiă kwo*’ just bear and get along with it, as sickness or distress; ,*ngai má*² *kwo*’ can't endure it, intolerable; *lóh*₂ ‘*ié pwoi*’ ‘*lá* ,*ngai sioh*₂ *k‘aik*, ‘*ku*, lean against the back of the chair a while (to doze and rest).

‘齒 Ch‘ie. Read ‘*ch‘i*; used for the coll. ‘*ngai*: the teeth: ⁷‘*ngai chó*² the gums, the jaw; ⁸*pwok*, ‘*ngai*, to cut teeth; ⁹‘*ch‘ü* ‘*ngai*, to extract a tooth; ¹⁰‘*ngai cheu*’ the teeth are decayed; ¹¹‘*ngai t‘iăng*’ a toothache; ¹²‘*ngai* ,*ngŭng* (or ,*ŭng*), scurf on the teeth, tartar; ¹³‘*ngai sauk*, a tooth brush; ¹⁴*p‘ah*, *siék*₂ ‘*ngai*, "breaks a tooth"—does not talk to the point.

‘*Ngai*. A coll. word: to rest lightly on; to hold by the edge of: ‘*ngai sioh*₂ *tek*, ‘*kiăng*, to sit on a little, as the edge of a seat; lying close to the edge, as a beam.

¹楧枝 ²枝垂 ³門閼一聲 ⁴手閼○ ⁵閼扁○ ⁶捱捱○ ⁷齒座○ ⁸發齒○ ⁹取齒○ ¹⁰齒蛀○ ¹¹齒痛○ ¹²齒[illegible] ¹³齒刷 ¹⁴拍折齒○

艾ʾ **Ai.** Mugwort, artemisia, a plant from which the moxa is made; a term for labiate plants like mint or catnip; old, aged, fifty; to cherish, to quiet, to relax one's self: used for *ngie*ʾ in the coll. q. v.: [1]*pó ngai*ʾ to nourish; [2]*sieu*ʾ *ngai*ʾ a beautiful woman; [3]*ch'ak*, *ngai*ʾ to nail up mugwort on the 5th day of the 5th moon; [4]*sik*, *ngai*ʾ (like) plucking mint—easily done.

隘ʾ **Yai. Ai.** A pass, a defile; strait, narrow, confined; urgent, distressed; mean, illiberal; impeded, stopped, obstructed: *hiék*, *ngai*ʾ a narrow pass; *met.*, a contracted mind.

呆 獃 **Ai. Tai.** Foolish, silly, doltish; stupid, like a puppy; the first also means a kind of plum; used for the coll. *ngai*, bad, evil, wicked: COLL., [5]*ngai nĕng*, a bad man; [6]*ngai auk*, wicked; fierce, violent; [7]*ngai miăng*² a poor lot in life; [8]*ngai chai*ʾ "bad debt"; *met.*, a matter resulting unluckily; [9]*p'ah*, *ngai*, to break; broken, injured; *ngai ngëüng*² (or *nga ngëüng*²), that which offends, detestable, shameful; [10]*ngai t'iéng*, bad weather; [11]*chó*ʾ *tek*, *ngai*, poorly done or made; [12]*ngai tëük*, *ch'ok*, *'hó 'sung*, a bad bamboo yielding good shoots; *met.*, wicked parents having good children.

厓 崖 **Yai.** This and the next three also read *ngang*: the side of a hill; a high bank, cliff, ledge, precipice: [13]*ngai ngang*² a steep bank; *met.*, a discrepancy, disagreement of things or persons; [14]*Ngai chiu*, a district in Hainan.

捱 **Yai.** To lean against; to put off, to defer, to procrastinate; to lounge, to loiter, to trifle with: used for *ngai* in the coll. q. v.

涯 **Yai. Ya. I.** The banks of a stream, a shore, a beach; a limit: [15]*u ngai*, illimitable; [16]*seng ngai*, a business, occupation; [17]*ching ngai*, a wharf, a mart on a riverside; [18]*t'iéng ngai*, the horizon, distant regions.

睚 **Ai.** The outer corners of the eyes; to glance or stare, to look angrily at.

礙² **碍**² **Ai.** To hinder, to obstruct, to impede; to embarrass, to stop the way of, to oppose; to set a limit to; to let, to restrain, as the conscience does; to offend, to be an offense to; a hindrance, an impediment, obstruction; a restraint, an objection to: [19]*ngai*² *sik*, a stumbling-stone; COM., [20]*kwang ngai*² or *'chu ngai*² an obstacle, impediment; [21]*ngai*² *ching*, to be constrained by (another's) feelings or circumstances; COLL., *ngai*² *sié mi*, to infringe or trespass slightly on.

(536) Ngaing.

硬² **Ying.** Hard, not soft, solid; stiff, firm, not pliable; obstinate, perverse, inflexible; terse, strong, nervous, as style; to harden, to stiffen; a particle, denoting a settled

[1]保艾 [2]少艾 [3]插艾 [4]拾艾 [5]呆仈 [6]呆惡 [7]呆命 [8]呆債 [9]拍呆 [10]呆天 [11]做的呆 [12]呆竹出好笋 [13]崖岸 [14]崖洲 [15]無涯 [16]生涯 [17]津涯 [18]天涯 [19]礙石 [20]關礙 [21]礙情 ○

fact or purpose; surely, certainly, still, yet; indeed, only, must be: COM., [1]*ngaing*[2] *ˏsing*, a hard heart, a stubborn will; [2]*ngaing*[2] *tik*ˎ straight-forward, honest; [3]*ngaing*[2] *hang*ˀ a resolute person; [4]*ngaing*[2] *ˏlang*, to interpose or stop firmly; [5]*ngaing*[2] *sié*ˀ or [6]*ngaing*[2] *ˋch'iu*, power, prestige; COLL., *ngaing*[2] *ch'aing*ˀ stiff; *ngaing*[2] *laung*[2] strong, influential; *ngaing*[2] *ˏpang ˏpang* or *ngaing*[2] *k'wak*ˎ *k'wak*ˎ very hard or stiff, inflexible; *ngaing*[2] *k'aĕk*ˎ hard articles, as furniture, hardware, etc.; *ˏkiăng ngaing*[2] to use firmness, to carry a matter with a high hand; *ch'oi*ˀ *ngaing*[2] to talk bravely, as against feeling or conviction; *ngaing*[2] *ˏtiu ˏtiu*, stiff in death.

(537) Ngaiu.

*Ngaiu*ˀ. A coll. word, as in *ngaiu*ˀ *ˏtu ngaiu*ˀ (or *aiu*ˀ *ˏtu aiu*ˀ), the sound of horns, as used by the *ˏtó tai*[2] priests, toot! toot!

騳[2] A horse galloping wildly; to gallop in an irregular manner.

(538) Ngak.

愕ˎ To dismiss care; cheerful, contented, light-hearted: *ngak*ˎ *ˏyong*, happy, pleased.

戛ˎ Chia. A long spear, a lance; to spear, to lance; the jolting of a cart; rough, uneven, jolting; usual, as rules or ceremonies: *ngak*ˎ *ngak*ˎ rough, difficult; stammering.

秸ˎ Chi. The stalk or straw of grain; grain in the straw, or reaped with half of the stalk. Read *kek*ˎ: the cooing of doves.

鶂ˎ A goose; same as the *ek*ˎ or ship-bird; they are said to conceive by looking at each other; the cackling of geese, for which the usual coll. is *ngauk*ˎ *ngauk*ˎ *kieu*ˀ q. v.

齾ˎ 囓ˎ Ch'ih. To gnaw, to craunch: used for *ngiăk*ˎ and *miĕk*ˎ in the coll. q. v: *ngak*ˎ *kauk*ˎ to pick bones; *ngak*ˎ *ˏnga*, to grit the teeth; *ngak*ˎ *ngak*ˎ *kieu*ˀ or *ngak*ˎ *ngak*ˎ *kieu*ˀ the sound of gnawing.

(539) Ngang.

狺 Yin. Read *ˏang*; coll. *ˏngang*, as in *ˏngang ˏngang kieu*ˀ the growling or yelping of dogs; crying, bawling.

ˋ眼 Yen. The eye; a square, a space, a limit: [7]*ˏlŭng ˋngang* (coll. *ˏleng ˋkeng*) a fruit; the Dimocarpus, lungan or dragon's eye; COM., [8]*ˋngang ˏk'wo*, the treatment of eye-diseases; [9]*nŭk*ˎ *ˋngang*, a fleshly eye—unable to perceive goodness; [10]*tuk*ˎ *ˋngang ˏlŭng*, blind of one eye; [11]*ˋngang ˏk'wong twai*[2] "the eye-socket large"—proud, aspiring; [12]*tói*ˀ *ˋngang*, to suit the eye, as spectacles; [13]*hak*ˎ *ˋngang*, to fit the eyes; liked, approved; [14]*ˋngang lik*ˎ *ˋhó*, a good, keen eye; to see at a glance; [15]*ˏch'iéng ˋli ˋngang*, the far-seeing one—an attendant of Matsupo; [16]*ˋngang kiăng*ˀ spectacles; COLL.,

[1]硬心 [2]硬直 [3]硬漢 [4]硬攔 [5]硬勢○ [6]硬手○ [7]龍眼○ [8]眼科○ [9]肉眼○ [10]獨眼龍○ [11]眼眶大○ [12]對眼 [13]合眼 [14]眼力好 [15]千里眼 [16]眼鏡

[1]*chó*ʾ ʿ*ngang*, to be eyes (for others); [2]*ngang* ꜀*seng*, before the eyes.

唵 ꜀ To snore: ꜀*ngang mek*꜆ to be silent, to give no answer, as one who is sleepy; ꜀*ngang ngié*ʾ to breathe hard, or mutter, in one's sleep.

巖 岩 ꜀ ꜀ Yen. A high bank, a precipice; a rocky hill; lofty, dangerous: ꜀*ngang* ꜀*ngang* or ꜀*chang* ꜀*ngang*, very high and precipitous; [3]꜀*ngang* ꜀*long*, a hall, temple; COM., [4]꜀*ngang* ꜀*ta*, tea from ꜀*Chung* ꜀*ang* in *Kiong*ʾ ꜀*ning* prefecture, Fookien—also applied to some other good teas.

顏 ꜀ Yen. The space between the eyes and eyebrows; the countenance; color; hilly; a surname: [5]꜀*ngang* ꜀*üng*, the countenance; COM., [6]꜀*ngang saik*, color; [7]꜀*ngang laiu*ʾ coloring matter, pigments, paints; [8]꜀*Ngang* ꜀*huí* or [9]꜀*Ngang* ʿ*chü*, the chief disciple of Confucius; [10]꜀*chong* ꜀*ngang*, a term of respectful address, as in a letter; COLL., [11]꜀*ngang saik*, ꜀*ch'iéng ch'ieu*ʾ a fresh, bright color; ꜀*ngang saik*, *ko*ʾ *to*ʾ an old faded color.

嘫 ꜀ To snarl, to growl at each other, as dogs fighting: COLL., ꜀*ngang* ꜀*ngang kieu*ʾ a clamor of voices, loud wrangling.

꜀**Ngang.** A coll. word, as in ꜀*ngang* ꜀*leu*, the same as ꜀*hiong* ꜀*ü*, basil, garden-thyme, summer-savory.

喭ʾ Yen. Rude, rustic, unpolished, vulgar; blunt, unmannerly; to moan, to lament, to grieve excessively: also read *ngiêng*ʾ q. v.

岸ʾ An. The banks of a stream; a shore, a bank, a beach; an edge, a margin; a high cliff; steps of a palace; the end of a road; the aim, object, or goal; a country-prison; to exhibit, to show a front; a valorous, high-minded man: in the coll. read *ngiâng*ʾ q. v.: [12]*tó*ʾ *ngang*ʾ end of the road; [13]꜀*teng ngang*ʾ to land; [14]꜀*k'wí ngang*ʾ one eminent in virtue and valor.

雁 鴈ʾ ʾ Yen. The small kind of wild geese; a bird of passage, whose flight determines times; *met.*, in a series, in order, orderly; marriage ceremonies: [15]*ngang*ʾ ꜀*ngó*, a wild goose; [16]*tiêng*ʾ *ngang*ʾ to pour libations to the goose—a wedding rite emblematic of connubial felicity; [17]*ngang*ʾ *sai*ʾ a mountain-resort of wild geese; COM., [18]*ngang*ʾ ꜀*hong*, wild geese (flying) in a row; *met.*, brothers in the order of age; [19]*ngang*ʾ *t'ak*, ꜀*tá* ꜀*ming*, your name inscribed on the goose-pagoda— a complimentary phrase meaning "you'll gain your degree".

贗ʾ Yeu. False, not true or genuine; spurious, adulterated, as goods: ꜀*ching ngang*ʾ true and false, genuine and counterfeit.

1 做眼 2 眼前 3 巖廊 4 巖茶 5 顏容 6 顏色 7 顏料 8 顏回 9 顏子 10 尊顏 11 顏色鮮笑 12 道岸 〇 13 登岸 〇 14 魁岸 〇 15 雁鵝 16 奠雁 17 雁塞 18 雁行 19 雁塔題名

(540) Ngau.

虓 ꜀Chiao. Read ʻ*kieu;* used in the *Paik*, ꜀*Ing* for the coll. ꜀*ngau*, a tiger's howl: ꜀*ngau* ꜀*ngau kieu*ʼ to howl, to cry, as dogs and cats.

꜂咬 ꜂嚙 Chiao. Ao. To gnaw, to bite; to chew, to masticate, as a cud; to set the teeth firmly; to study, to con over, to ruminate upon: the first also read ꜀*kau*, the song of birds: in the coll. read ʻ*ngeu*, q. v.: COM., [1]ʻ*ngau siek*꜆ to gnaw the tongue (till it produces death); [2]ʻ*ngau* ꜀*nga ch*ʻ*iék*꜆ ʻ*ch*ʻ*i*, to gnash the teeth (in deadly hate).

*Ngau*ʼ. A coll. word: confused, jumbled, incorrect, as style in speaking or writing; gabble, jargon, brogue; obstinate, perverse: *ngau*ʼ *p*ʻ*ek*꜆ a perverse temper.

爻 ꜁Hsiao. Yao. To lay crosswise; blended, intermingled; to change, to imitate, as the changes of heaven and earth: the 89th radical: [3]꜁*ngau ch*ʻ*iong*ʼ aspect of the diagrams; COM., [4]*lĕk*꜆ ꜁*ngau*, diagrams with six blended lines—supposed to resemble the mutations of nature.

꜁肴 ꜁餚 Hsiao. Yao. Sacrificial meats in vases; dressed meats, viands, delicacies set out at a feast; to taste: COM., [5]ʻ*chiu* ꜁*ngau*, the viands of a feast; [6]꜁*ngau chwang*ʼ dressed meats, delicacies.

淆 ꜁Hsiao. Muddy water; mixed, confused; a river in Honan, tributary to the Yellow river: [7]꜁*ngau loang*ʼ in great disorder, as affairs; [8]*hong*ʼ ꜁*ngau*, turbid; mixed confusedly; COLL., [9]꜁*ngau tek*꜆ *sá*ʼ much confused, as cash accounts.

殽 ꜁Hsiao. Used for the last two: mixed, blended, jumbled together; mixed, as metals; bones and flesh mingled; a diet of pulse: [10]꜁*ngau liék*꜆ arranged, set in order.

崤 ꜁Hsiao. Name of a river; hills in the western part of Honan province.

꜁齩 Read ꜁*ngeu;* used for the coll. ꜁*ngau:* warped, twisted, as a board in seasoning; *met.*, perverted; fierce, obstinate: [11]*k*ʻ*ieu*ʼ ꜁*ngau*, twisted, warped; [12]꜁*ngau* ʻ*k*ʻ*i* ꜀*li*, bent up; [13]꜁*ngau* ʻ*ngá*, crabbed, obstinate in bearing; ꜁*ngau ngah*꜆ a difference, a variance; ꜀*i kaëng*ʼ ʻ*ngwai* *ó*ʼ *nói*ʼ ꜁*ngau ngah*꜆ there is a little disagreement between him and me.

꜁*Ngau*. A coll. word: numb, torpid, chill with cold: *k*ʻ*a* ʻ*ch*ʻ*iu* ꜁*ngau*, the feet and hands benumbed.

樂[2] Yao. Yo. Lo. Yüeh. To take pleasure in, to choose, to be fond of, to delight in: also read *lok*꜆ and *ngok*꜆ q .v.: [14]*ek*꜆ ʻ*chiá* ꜀*sang ngau*ʼ profitable are the three delights—propriety and music (i. e., accord), speaking of men's goodness,

[1]咬舌 [2]咬牙 切齒 [3]爻彖 [4]六爻 [5]酒餚 [6]餚饌 [7]淆亂 [8]混淆 [9]淆的 俉 [10]殽列 ○ [11]趬齩 ○ [12]齩起來 ○ [13]齩覫 ○ [14]益者三樂

and having many virtuous friends; COLL., *ngau² ʻchiă tai²* he takes pleasure in this matter.

藕 Ou. Read *ʻngeu* in the dictionaries: the roots of the nelumbium or water-lily: COM., *¹ngau² ꜀chiéng*, the first (tender) joint of lily-root; *²꜀tié ngau²* the pond lily-root; *³ngau² ʻhung*, flour made of lily-root; *⁴ngau² ꜀si*, the fine threads or filaments of the root; *⁵ngau² ꜀kó*, a comfit of lily-root-flour and sugar, made by scalding it; COLL., *⁶꜀ch'eng ngau²* roots of the field-lily; *⁷ngau² ꜀k'ĕng*, the small tubulous cavities in lily-roots; *⁸ngau² twang² ꜀si ꜀nang twang²* when the lily-root is broken, its filaments are still hard to break; *met.*, despite the quarrel, the bond of real attachment can't be sundered.

(541) Ngauk.

噩 O. Grave and serious; stern, rigid, severe; awe-struck, frightened: *⁹ngauk, mong²* an alarming dream; *¹⁰꜀king ngauk,* terrified.

咢 O. To strike with alarm; also the appearance of a high cap; the side of a sword; some say that the word, being composed of two mouths, denotes two persons singing responsively: *ngauk, ngauk,* words to the point.

愕 O. Surprised, astonished, amazed; to wonder at; opposed to, hindering, uncomplying: *¹¹ngauk, ꜀yong*, startled; COM., *¹²ch'auk, ngauk,* astonished at.

諤 諤 O. E. Blunt, straight-forward words; honest, faithful reproof; friendly advice: *ngauk, ngauk,* plain advice, as of a friend or minister.

鄂 O. Ao. Used for the last two: an ancient principality, now the province of Hupeh; also a name of Wuchang-fu; a limit, a boundary.

萼 O. The calyx or receptacle of a flower, called *¹³꜀hwa ngauk,*: in the coll. read *ngok,* q. v.

鱷 O. E. A crocodile, or gavial, said to have existed in Ch'ao-chou-fu, Kwangtung, and to have been exorcised by Han-yü; a term sometimes applied to rapacious officers and gentry: COM., *¹⁴ngauk, ꜀ngü*, a crocodile.

鶚 O. E. The ospray or fish-hawk; a good term for the genus Haliaetus: *¹⁵ngauk, lik,* to stand watching, as an ospray does; *¹⁶ngauk, chiéng²* promoted to be a Küjin.

鵝 Read *ngak,*; used for the coll. *ngauk,* as in *ngauk, ngauk, kieu²* the cackling of geese; *꜀hang ngauk, ngauk, kieu²* to snore loudly.

齶 Used for the coll. *ngauk,* as in *ngauk, ngauk, kieu²* noise made by the teeth in eating hard things, a crunching sound.

¹藕尖 ²池藕 ³藕粉 ⁴藕絲 ⁵藕糕 〇 ⁶田藕 〇 ⁷藕空 〇 ⁸藕斷絲斷難 ⁹噩夢 〇 ¹⁰驚噩 〇 ¹¹愕然 〇 ¹²錯愕 〇 ¹³花萼 ¹⁴鱷魚 ¹⁵鶚立 ¹⁶鶚薦

(542) **Ngaung.**

⿰黑欠[1] Read *ngak*, in the dictionaries; used in the *Paik*, ˏ*Ing* for the coll. *ngaung*²: dull, stupid, doltish; silly, foolish, not intelligent: *ta*² *ngaung*² to feign stupidity; ²*ngaung*² ˏ*lê*, a stupid ass—a country clown; ³*ngaung*² ʻ*siong*, to think stupidly; also applied affectedly to one's self; ³*ngaung*² ˏ*t'au ngaung*² ʻ*nó*, dull head and brains—very stupid; *ngaung*² *ch'aung*² to rush about stupidly.

(543) **Nge.**

*Nge*². A coll. euphonic prefix, as in *nge*² *ngó*² or *nge*² *nge*² *ngó*² *ngó*² to talk indistinctly; to murmur, to complain; *nge*² *ngëü*² a squeaking sound, as of a fiddle; to play the fiddle.

耳[2] Erh. Read ʻ*ngi*; coll. *nge*²: an ear, the organ of hearing; a handle, an ear, a small side-handle, as of a cup, pitcher, tub, pail, basket, etc.: ⁴*nge*² ʻ*kiăng*, an ear; ⁵*nge*² ˏ*tai*, the lobus or bottom of the external ear; ⁶*nge*² ˏ*k'ĕng* or ⁷*nge*² ˏ*mwong*, the opening at the bottom of the concha; ⁸*nge*² ˏ*t'iăng* or ⁹ˏ*t'iăng lŏh*ˎ *nge*² to hear with the ear; heard, listened to; ¹⁰*nge*² ˏ*lĕng*, deaf; ¹¹*nge*² ʻ*sai*, ear-wax; ¹²*k'ang*² *nge*² to dress the ears, as a barber does; ¹³*nge*² *chiéng*² an arrow (stuck through) the ear—a military punishment; *nge*²· ˏ*u*, a buzzing in the ear, as when partially deaf; ¹⁴*nge*² ˏ*piĕng* ˏ*hung*, (like) wind passing by the ear, as words unheeded; ¹⁵*nge*² *pó*² ˏ*sing*, "a spirit reporting to the ear"—to hear of secretly; ¹⁶*nge*² ˏ*p'uí* ʻ*niong*, "soft ear-skin"—i. e., very credulous; ¹⁷*nge*² ˏ*tai póh*ˎ his lobus is thin—he can't gain money; ¹⁸*nge*² ˏ*tieu* ˏ*sá*, to turn the ear toward the west—i. e., refuse to listen; *nge*² ˏ*pa* ˏ*sieu sek*, ear-pick and ear-brush; *nge*² *toi*² ear-pendants.

(544) **Ngë.**

ˏ*Ngë*. A coll. word, as in ˏ*ngë* ˏ*ngë tioh*ˎ about as ˏ*ngio* ˏ*ngio tioh*ˎ a grum look; grim, glum, sullen.

(545) **Ngeh.**

*Ngeh*ˎ. A coll. word, as in *ngeh*ˎ *sioh*ˎ ˏ*siăng*, to emit a grating sound, as the edges of boards rubbing against each other; *ngeh*ˎ *ngeh*ˎ *ngah*ˎ *ngah*ˎ creaking, grating.

(546) **Ngek.**

仡ˎ Ch'i. Strong, robust; martial, as the prancing of a steed; suddenly: *ngek*ˎ *ngek*ˎ large; valiant, warlike; *ngek*ˎ ˏ*yong*, ˏ*i ik*ˎ he entered abruptly.

伋ˎ Chi. Read *kek*, in the dictionaries: false, empty: ʻ*K'ung ngek*, name of the grandson of Confucius, author of the Chung-yung, or Doctrine of the Mean.

吸ˎ Chi. To draw in the breath, to inspire, to inhale; to imbibe, to suck in: *ngek*ˎ *ek*ˎ ʻ*k'eu k'e*² to take a long breath; COM., ˏ*hu ngek*ˎ expiration and inspiration.

---

[1] ⿰黑欠驢 [2] ⿰黑欠想 [3] ⿰黑欠頭⿰黑欠腦 [4] 耳仔 [5] 耳臺 [6] 耳空 [7] 耳門 [8] 耳聽 [9] 聽落耳 [10] 耳聾〇 [11] 耳屎 [12] 看耳 [13] 耳箭 [14] 耳邊風 [15] 耳報神 [16] 耳皮軟 [17] 耳臺薄〇 [18] 耳朝西〇

福州方言拼音字典

吃, Chi. Ch'i. Ch'ih. To eat, to swallow food; to stutter, to stammer, slow of speech: [1]'k'eu *ngek*, to eat or drink; [2]*ngek*, 'k'eu, to stammer; [3]*ngek*, ,*king*, startled, alarmed.

喫, Ch'ih. Interchanged with the last: to eat, to drink, to swallow; to suffer, to bear, to put up with: [4]*ngek*, '*king*, urgent, necessary; [5]*ngek*, ,*k'wi*, to swallow insults; harassed, troubled.

屹, Ch'i. An abrupt, isolated peak, with steep sides; the highest peak of a range.

岌, Chi. Similar to the last: a high hill, a slender peak in a range of hills; lofty, imminent, hazardous: *ngek*, *ngek*, high and dangerous.

扱, Chi. To take, to receive, to obtain; to lift, to raise; to tuck up, as the skirts; to courtesy with the hands pointing downward, as women do: also read *ch'ak*, q. v.

极, Chi. Panniers or pack-saddles, made of wood and used by muleteers.

汲, Chi. To draw water from a well; to draw, to drag, to lead, to draw out; incessant: [6]*ngek*, '*chwi*, to draw water; *ngek*, *ngek*, unremitting, as one's efforts; [7]*ngek*, '*ing*, to draw out.

笈, Chi. A box or satchel for carrying books: [8]*ho*' *ngek*, ,*chüng* ,*sü*, to take up the satchel and follow a teacher.

級, Chi. Threads arranged regularly; an order, a series, a gradation; steps, as of a stair-case, ladder, etc.; a degree, rank in office, grade of honorary merit; classed, sorted; a numerative of decapitated heads: [9]'*teng ngek*, gradation; [10],*kai ngek*, a step, rank; [11]'*siu ngek*, decapitated heads; COM., [12]'*p'ing ngek*, official grade or rank; [13],*ka* ,*sang ngek*, promoted three grades; [14]*kaung*' *ek*, *ngek*, degraded one rank.

訖, Chi. To stop, to cease, to close, to desist, to finish speaking; to clear off an account; to exhaust; to prohibit; to arrive at, to carry to the end, up to, until, in which senses the same as the next: [15]*ngek*, *tik*, to prohibit buying rice; [16],*siu ngek*, to collect the entire sum; [17],*ngiong ngek*, finished speaking.

迄, Ch'i. To come to, to reach, to arrive at; even, till, until, up to; finally, at last: [18]*ngek*, ,*king*, to this time, even till now; [19]*ngek*, *keng*' to the last, finally.

鈒, Also read *sak*,: a spear, a javelin; to engrave, to inlay on metal; to enchase, as the barbs of arrows.

靸, Sa. Also read *sak*,: children's shoes; a leathern shoe like a slipper; sandals such as the Chinese

1口	3吃	5喫	7汲	從	10階	12品	級	15訖	16收	17言	18迄
吃	驚	虧	引	師	級	級	14降	糴	訖	訖	今
2吃	4喫	6汲	8負	9等	11首	13加	一				19迄
口	緊	水	笈	級	級	三	級	○	○	○	竟

and Japanese wear: used for *liăk*, in the coll. q. v.

鬩, ,Hsi. Read *hek*, in the dictionaries: litigation, quarrels; bitter animosity, mutual and incessant strifes: [1]'*ngek, haung*^{2} reciprocal hate; [2]*,hing tá*^{2} *ngek, ,ü ,ch'iong*, brothers quarreling in the house.

Ngek,. A coll. euphonic prefix, as in *ngek,ngak*, a craunching sound, as of the teeth; *ngek, ngak*, or *ngek, ngauk*, the cackling of geese; *ngek, ngiăk*, to cut with shears, noise of shears in cutting; *ngek, ngiék*, to nip, to take with tongs or pincers.

(547) Ngeng.

,Ngeng. A coll. word: perhaps a corruption or imitation of *ngaing*^{2} (stiff), as in *,ngeng k'ó*^{2} stiffened in death, stark-dead.

Ngeng^2. A coll. euphonic prefix, as in *ngeng*^{2} *ngeng*^{2} *ngëüng*^{2} *ngëüng*^{2} apprehensive, dreading; afraid, as of meeting ghosts.

迎^2 Ying. To go out to meet, to go and receive in person: also read *,nging*, q. v.: com., [3]*,ch'ing ngeng*^{2} to receive in person, as anciently the bridegroom went to bring home his bride.

Ngeng^2. A coll. euphonic prefix, as in *ngeng*^{2} *ngiéng*^{2} to hold a coroner's inquest; to examine, as goods in order to levy duties.

(548) Ngeu.

'偶 Ou. A pair, a match; even, doubled, paired; a companion, a mate, a partner; to match, to pair, to unite, as in marriage; to mate, to accord, as friends: to fit, to harmonize; an image, an idol; to occur, to happen accidentally; incontinently, suddenly: [4]*'p'ek, 'ngeu*, a pair, a married couple; [5]*'p'woi*^{2} *'ngeu*, to mate; [6]*'ngeu hak*, matched, paired; [7]*'wong*^{2} *'ngeu*, an ill-sorted match; com., [8]*,ka 'ngeu*, a happy pair; [9]*'ngeu ,yong*, accidentally, by chance; [10]*'ngeu ngëü*^{2} to happen to meet; [11]*'ngeu ch'iong*^{2} images, idols; [12]*sek, 'ngeu*, has lost his mate, become a widower.

'耦 Ou. Two persons plowing; a double colter; a pair, an even number; a mate, a fellow; to pair, to match; to pervade; thorough, throughout: [13]*p'woi*^{2} *'ngeu*, to mate, to accompany one; [14]*'ngeu ,keng*, to plow together.

'咬 Chiao. Read *'ngau*; coll. *'ngeu*, as in [15]*'ngeu siék*, to gnaw the tongue, as a criminal does to kill himself.

(549) Ngëü.

Ngëü^2. A coll. word: to play a fiddle: *nge*^{2} *ngëü*^{2} to play the *ne*^{2} *,hu*, or fiddle; the sound of a fiddle.

寓^2 庽 Yü. To dwell, to lodge, to sojourn in; to attach to, to hang on; a lodging-place, a temporary abode, a house, a home; to pertain, to belong to; to borrow, as a metaphor; a hidden meaning: [16]*,liu ngëü*^{2} residents from other districts, not yet registered as citizens; [17]*ngëü*^{2} *,ngiong*, a metaphor, metonomy; com., [18]*chang*^{2} *ngëü*^{2} to lodge temporarily; [19]*kié*^{2} *ngëü*^{2} to sojourn, to lodge at; attached to, as a

[1]鬩恨 [2]兄弟 鬩於墻 ○ [3]親迎 ○ [4]匹偶 ○ [5]配偶 ○ [6]偶合 [7]怨偶 [8]佳偶 [9]偶然 [10]偶遇 [11]偶像 [12]失偶 [13]配耦 [14]耦耕 [15]咬舌 [16]流寓 [17]寓言 [18]暫寓 [19]寄寓

parasite; *ngĕü2 'su*, a lodging-place, a dwelling.

遇2 Yü. To meet, to fall in with, to come upon one; to occur, to happen, to befall; to receive, to treat, to entertain; happening, whenever: used for the coll. *p'aung2* q. v.: [1]*haiu2 ngĕü2* to treat well; COM., [2]*ngĕü2 piéng2* at one's convenience; [3]*ngĕü2 nang2* to encounter trouble; [4]*pok, ngĕü2* not to meet; unsuccessful, unlucky; [5]*ngĕü2 pok, ngĕü2* not sure of meeting or happening; [6]*ngĕü2 'king ,seng ,ching*, the meeting with (suggestive) circumstances excites the feelings; COLL., *ngĕü2 tioh,* to happen upon; *ngĕü2 tioh, ,t'au*, to find an opportunity; *ngĕü2 tioh, ,sing ,sang cheu2 k'ang' miăng2* gets his fortune told as soon as he falls in with a fortune-teller; *met.*, to buy this and that as soon as seen.

語2 Yü. I. To announce to, to tell, to inform; to warn, to caution against: also read *'ngü*, q. v.: *,ngu ngĕü2 'nü* or *,ngu 'ü ngĕü2* I tell you plainly.

御2 Yü. To drive horses, to act as charioteer; to govern, to control, to manage all; to rule, to break in or tame, as horses; a term applied to the emperor, imperial, royal; extending, pervading, as imperial power; rule, management; to wait upon, to help; to urge to drink, as one's guests: also read *nga2* q. v.: [7]*ngĕü2 ,kü*, to drive a chariot; [8]*ngĕü2 ,tĕng*, to bear (the cold of) winter; COM., [9]*ngĕü2 ka'* the emperor; [10]*ngĕü2 sĕü'* imperial gifts; [11]*ngĕü2 'sü*, censors; [12]*ngĕü2 ,chü ,ting*, a sort of pavilioned sedan in which the imperial grant of a title is borne; [13]*ngĕü2 ,ling ,kung*, the imperial body-guard; [14]*ngĕü2 ka' ,ch'ing ,ching*, the emperor going to war in person.

馭2 Yü. Interchanged with the last: to drive a chariot; to guide, to rule, to oversee; to rely on: [15]*ka' ngĕü2* to guide, as a chariot; to direct, to govern; [16]*,siéng ngĕü2* or [17]*ngĕü2 hok,* to ride to the genii, or to stride a stork—phrases for dying; [18]*ngĕü2 ,kung ,sing*, to oversee the crowd of officers.

(550) Ngĕüng.

慭' Also read *ngĕüng2*: to inquire, to ask respectfully; an initial particle, also, moreover; to force one's self; to wish, to desire; deficient; to wound; a laughing manner.

Ngĕüng'. A coll. word, as in *ngĕüng' ngĕüng'* or *ngeng' ngeng' ngĕüng' ngĕüng'* fearful, apprehensive; *,sing 'lá ngĕüng'* timid and irresolute; *p'ah, ngĕüng' ,t'au*, to have cause for apprehension, to be startled; *á2 ngĕüng' ,nĕng*, it will startle people, as when snakes are carried about by beggars.

Ngĕüng2. A coll. word, as in *,nga ngĕüng2* or *,ngai ngĕüng2* to excite unpleasant feeling, provoking, disgusting; *á2 ,ngai ngĕüng2 ,nĕng*, it will provoke people.

---

1 厚遇 2 遇便 3 遇難 4 不遇 5 遇不遇〇 6 遇景生情 7 御車 8 御冬 9 御駕 10 御賜 11 御史 12 御書亭 13 御林軍 14 御駕親征 15 駕馭〇 16 仙馭 17 馭鶴 18 馭羣臣〇

(551) **Ngi.**

꜀*Ngi.* A coll. euphonic prefix, as in ꜀*ngi* ꜀*li*, the singing, as of a kettle when the water is about to boil; ꜀*ngi* ꜀*li sioh*, ꜀*siăng*, a singing, a buzzing (in the ear); ꜀*ngi* ꜀*li* ꜀*ngu* ꜀*lu*, to mutter in a low tone; ꜀*ngi* ꜀*li* ꜀*ngó* ꜀*ló*, the buzzing, as of mosquitoes; ꜀*ngi* ꜀*nga*, or ꜀*ngi* ꜀*nga* ꜀*nga*, the sound of musical instruments—used jocosely for "piping up" in reference to a marriage or a graduate's procession; ꜀*ngi* ꜀*ngá*, or ꜀*ngi* ꜀*ngá* ꜀*ngá*, a squeaking, as of doors; the hum of conversation; ꜀*ngi* ꜀*ngá lang kwo* to lament two sentences (i. e., a little), as females do for a distant relative; ꜀*ngi* ꜀*ngiă*, or ꜀*ngi* ꜀*ngi* ꜀*ngiă* ꜀*ngiă*, diverging, as branches; scattered about.

儗 ʻI. Interchanged with the next: to compare, to assort; doubtful, suspicious of each other; to usurp. Read *hai*: stupid, foolish.

擬 ʻNi. I. To judge of, to estimate; to consider, to guess or conjecture; to decide after deliberation; form, figure; to compare; like, resembling; also to purpose, to intend: COM., ʻ*ngi tok*, to think on, to estimate; ʻ*ngi ngié* to conjecture and deliberate about; ʻ*ngi chaiu* to get up a memorial; ʻ*ngi chói* to judge criminal cases; ʻ*ngi* ꜀*tá*, to suppose a theme and write on it, as students do before examinations.

譺 ʻI. Interchanged with the last: to consult, to discuss, to deliberate; to decide upon; doubt, hesitation; to impose on: *miéng* ʻ*ngi*, to consult with one. Read *ngai*: foolish, doltish; to deceive.

薿 I. Luxuriant, growing rank; flourishing vegetation.

耳 ʻErh. The ear, organ of hearing; to perceive; the ears or small side-handles of things; a final euphonic or intensive particle, a particle to denote completion of the sense; the 128th radical: in the coll. read *nge* q. v.: ʻ*ngi sik*, to credit mere rumors; COM., ʻ*ngi* ꜀*ung*, heard by the ear, reported; ʻ*ngi* ꜀*ung pok*, ꜀*ü muk*, *kek*, hearsay is not equal to seeing; ʻ*ngi* ꜀*song*, a great-grandson's grandson; *song* ꜀*hung* ʻ*ngi*, quick of hearing—an attendant of the goddess Matsupo; COLL., ʻ*ngi muk*, *sá* "ears and eyes are many"—it is sure to be found out.

儀 ꜀I. The usages of society; a rule, a rite, a ceremony; decorum, etiquette; the external appearance or deportment; form, figure; what is proper, right, correct, regular, just; to study how to do, to imitate; the principles or powers of nature: ꜀*ngi* ꜀*üng*, the deportment; *liong* ꜀*ngi*, the dual principles; COM., ꜀*wi* ꜀*ngi*, dignified, imposing; ʻ*lá* ꜀*ngi*, forms, rites; ꜀*ngi* ꜀*mwong*, the door of ceremony—the 2d door of a yamun; *tiéng* ꜀*ngi*, or ꜀*hiong* ꜀*ngi*, or *chié* ꜀*ngi*, a present of money sent to mourners.

1 擬度　2 擬議　3 擬奏　4 擬罪　5 擬題　6 面擬　7 耳食　8 耳聞　9 耳聞不如目擊　10 耳孫　11 順風耳○　12 儀容　13 兩儀　14 威儀　15 禮儀　16 儀門○　17 奠儀　18 香儀　19 祭儀○

宜 ꜀I. Naturally reasonable, fit, suitable, proper, right; just, befitting; what ought or should be; harmonious, accordant; a form of the imperative mood or future tenses: used for ꜀ngié in the coll. q. v.: [1]'piéng' ꜀ngi, convenient; cheap; [2]꜀ing ꜀ngi, ought, necessary; COM., [3]hak꜁ ꜀ngi, suitable; [4]꜀ngi ꜀ing, title of a lady of the 5th rank; [5]꜀ngi ꜂t'ĕng, a chamber-vessel for women; [6]꜀ngi ꜀hing kwang' earthen teapots from ꜀Ngi ꜀hing district, Kiangsu.

疑 ꜀I. To doubt, to suspect; to hesitate, to surmise, to guess; suspicious, doubtful of; to dislike; perverse, corrupt: [7]꜀ngi sëü' doubtful, unsettled; COM., [8]꜂k'ó ꜀ngi, to doubt, to be suspicious; [9]꜀ngi ꜀nang, to apprehend difficulties; [10]pié' ꜀hiéng ꜀ngi, to refrain from suspicious acts; COLL., ꜀ngi ꜀sing taĕng' is very suspicious, full of doubts; ꜀ngi ꜀nĕng mŏh꜁ ĕüng', ĕüng' ꜀nĕng mŏh꜁ ꜀ngi, if you suspect a person, don't employ him; if you employ him, don't suspect him.

嶷 ꜀I. The name of a range, called ꜂kiu ꜀ngi, or Nine Mts., where the Emperor Shun was buried, said to be in Shansi; eminent, promising; to know; of quick parts, as children.

(552) Ngiă.

꜀Ngiă. A coll. word, as in ꜀ngiă ꜀ngiă or ꜀ngi ꜀ngiă, divergent, as roads, branches, etc.; ꜀ngiă ꜀k'wi, separating, diverging.

꜀Ngiă. A coll. word, as in ꜀ngiă ꜀ngiă, odd, uneven, what remains after a division.

꜀Ngiă. A coll. word, as in ꜀ngiă ꜀ngiă or ꜀ngiă ngauk꜁ doubting, hesitating; ꜀ngiă sioh꜁ hiok꜁ or ꜀ngiă pwang' nik꜁ to doubt a while; ꜀ch'iă ꜀ngiă or ch'auk꜁ ꜀ngiă, startled and doubting, as when a matter is first mentioned.

(553) Ngiăh.

額 O. E. The forehead; the front of; incessant; a fixed number or quantity; name of a place: [11]ngiăh꜁ ngiăh꜁ incessant, as the creaking of a chariot; [12]ngiăh꜁ ꜂song, the forehead; COM., [13]ngiăh꜁ so' the requisite number, full sum; [14]eng' ngiăh꜁ ought, should; [15]ngiăh꜁ ꜀t'au, the forehead; [16]꜀pá ngiăh꜁ an inscriptive tablet, as over the doors of graduates or officers; [17]ngiăh꜁ ngwoi' over the stipulated amount; also petty military officers, those without regular rank; [18]ngiăh꜁ mó' a broad fillet (of velvet), worn by matrons; [19]ngiăh꜁ chah꜁ (coll. kek꜁), a narrow forehead; COLL., ngiăh꜁ ꜀t'au k'eng' his forehead is protuberant; ꜀mó kau' ngiăh꜁ deficient in amount.

(554) Ngiăk.

齧 Ch'ih. Read ngak꜁; used for the coll. ngiăk꜁: to gnaw, to crunch: ngiăk꜁ ngiăk꜁ kieu' a craunching sound.

Ngiăk꜁. A coll. word: to cut with shears: ngek꜁ ngiăk꜁ to cut, to clip; noise of clipping; ngiăk꜁ ꜂toi, to cut off short; ngiăk꜁ tói' ꜀tong, cut it in two.

---

[1]便宜 [2]應宜 [3]合宜 [4]宜人 [5]宜桶 [6]宜興鑵 [7]疑似 [8]可疑 [9]疑難 [10]避嫌疑 [11]額額 [12]額顙 [13]額數 [14]應額 [15]額頭 [16]牌額 [17]額外 [18]額帽 [19]額窄

Ngiăk꜆. A coll. word: to raise, as the head, to look up: *ngiăk꜆ ꜂k'i ꜀t'au*, to lift up the head; *ngiăk꜆ ꜀keng*, to raise (the head) high.

Ngiăk꜆. A coll. word, as in *ngiăk꜆ ngiăk꜆ siong꜄* to itch, it itches very much.

(555) Ngiăng.

꜀Ngiăng. A coll. word: rough, bristling, as uncombed hair; sparse and rough, as hairs, leaves of plants, etc.: *꜀t'au hwok꜆ ꜀ngiăng ꜀ngiăng*, the hair is bristling; *꜀ngiăng ꜀ngiăng tioh꜆* sparse and rough.

Ngiăng꜄. A coll. word, as in *ngiăng꜄ ch'ok꜆ ꜀li*, toppling, leaning forward, as a closet, etc.

迎 ꜁Ying. Read *꜁nging;* coll. *꜁ngiăng:* to escort, to parade, to carry in procession: [1]*꜁ngiăng ꜁pu sak꜆* to parade Budhist idols; [2]*꜁ngiăng ꜀ch'ung*, procession to "meet the Spring"; [3]*꜁ngiăng hwoi꜄* idol processions of the guilds or companies; [4]*꜁ngiăng ꜀ch'ing*, to escort the bride; [5]*꜁ngiăng ꜀ká*, to parade through the streets, as a graduate does to visit his friends; [6]*꜁ngiăng ꜀song kaung꜄* a military parade in the 9th month.

꜁Ngiăng. A coll. word: rough, dry, not sleek, as the hair from want of oil; dry, as things eaten without liquids; dried, parched, lacking moisture.

岸꜅ An. Read *ngang꜅;* coll. *ngiăng꜅:* a shore, a bank, a beach; the margin of a brook, river or canal: [7]*ngiăng꜅ ꜂ting* or [8]*ngiăng꜅ siong꜅* on the bank, on shore; [9]*꜂liong ꜀peng ngiăng꜅* both banks; [10]*siong꜅ ngiăng꜅* to go ashore, to land; [11]*꜁mó ꜀sang ꜁mó ngiăng꜅* neither hill nor shore, boundless; *met.*, indistinct, not clear, as the way to effect an end.

(556) Ngiau.

꜀Ngiau. A coll. word, not referable to the table of final sounds: the mew of a cat; said playfully to a child and equivalent to bo-peep or peep-boo: *꜀ngiau ꜀ngiau*, peep! peep!

(557) Ngié.

艾꜄ Ai. Read *ngai꜄;* coll. *ngié꜄:* mugwort, artemisia, the plant from which the moxa is made; punk, tinder: [12]*ch'ak꜆ ngié꜄* to stick up mugwort (on the 5th day of the 5th moon); [13]*꜂hwoi ngié꜄* tinder; [14]*ngié꜄ ch'ai꜄* a vegetable with a leaf like the artemisia; [15]*ngié꜄ ꜂mó ꜀ta*, as dry as mugwort; [16]*ngié꜄ ꜁wong*, a pellet of mugwort, as burnt in cauterizing; [17]*pah꜆ ngié꜄* white artemisia, used to absorb and hold red ink for stamps or seals.

宜 ꜁I. Read *꜁ngi;* coll. *꜁ngié*, as in [18]*꜁peng ꜁ngié*, or *꜁ngié ꜁peng*, cheap, low in price.

鵝 ꜁O. E. Read *꜁ngó;* coll. *꜁ngié:* a goose: [19]*꜁ngié kaik꜆* a gander; [20]*꜁ngié ꜂kiăng*, goslings; *꜀t'ieng ꜁ngié* or *꜂yă ꜁ngié*, wild geese; *꜁ngié ꜁mó ꜂kwong*, goose-quills; *꜁ngié ꜂mwi ꜀chio*, the down about a goose's tail; *꜁ngié ꜂chiong ꜀hung*, films of skin, as peeling from the palms of the hands; *꜁ngié tói꜄ ngauk꜆* "goose against cackling

[1]迎菩薩〇 [2]迎春 [3]迎會 [4]迎親 [5]迎街 [6]迎霜降 [7]岸頂 [8]岸上 [9]兩邊岸上 [10]上岸 [11]無山無岸 [12]插艾 [13]火艾 [14]艾菜 [15]艾摶乾 [16]艾丸〇 [17]白艾 [18]便宜 [19]鵝雄 [20]鵝仔

(goose)"—two persons jabbering at each other.

乂^2 I. Used for the next: to cut grass; to rule, to manage, to regulate; able, clever, talented: *chong*' *ngié*^{2} capable, excelling; *ngié*^{2} *꜀ang*, at peace, as a country.

刈^2 I. To cut grass, to mow; to cut off, to kill, to exterminate: *ngié*^{2} *ʻch'ó*, to cut grass.

劓^2 To cut off the nose as a punishment; this torture is now quite disused and is virtually illegal.

義^2 I. Right, proper, fit, suitable; what which is just, conformable to what the heart feels to be right; equity, rectitude, righteousness, high moral feeling; superior, excellent, surpassing, virtuous; adopted, putative, supplied in place of, as an adopted father; common, free, public, as benevolent contributions, or an appropriation by government; patriotic, public-spirited; meaning, signification, definition; made up, composite, compounded: [1]*ngié*^{2} *mĕk꜇* composite ink; COM., [2]*ngié*^{2} *ʻli*, righteousness, rectitude; [3]*che*' *ngié*^{2} the meaning of a character; [4]*ngié*^{2} *꜀ch'ong*, a charity-granary; [5]*ngié*^{2} *hok꜇* (coll. *ngié*^{2} *óh꜇*), a free school; [6]*ngié*^{2} *꜁ing*, a righteous person; [7]*ngié*^{2} *puk꜇* a faithful slave; [8]*ngié*^{2} *ʻnü* (coll. *꜀a* *꜁t'au*), female slaves; [9]*ngié*^{2} *k'e*' right feeling, generous and kind; [10]*ngié*^{2} *꜁ming*, or [11]*ngié*^{2} *ʻüng*, patriotic volunteers; [12]*꜀Ka ngié*^{2} a district in Formosa; COLL., *k'ak*, *ngié*^{2} *hwoi*^{2} to raise money from a company of friends.

誼^2 I. Used for the last: suitable, fit, proper, right; friendly, acquainted; putative, supplied in place of, adopted: COM., [13]*ngié*^{2} *꜀ch'ing*, related by adoption; [14]*ngié*^{2} *ho*^{2} (coll. *ngié*^{2} *꜁nong ma*^{2}), an adopted father; [15]*ngié*^{2} *꜀hing tá*^{2} adopted brothers; [16]*ngié*^{2} *꜁i*, mother's adopted sister, maternal aunts by adoption; [17]*ngié*^{2} *mwoi*' an adopted younger sister; one's mistress, paramour.

詣^2 I. To meet, or wait for, one at a resting-place; to go in person, to advance, to repair to; to reach, to arrive at: *ch'ó*' *ngié*^{2} well learned, proficient.

議^2 I. To consult, to deliberate, to meet in council; to arrange, to decide on the best course; to choose, to select; deliberation, council; rules, laws: COM., [18]*ngié*^{2} *laung*^{2} to deliberate upon; [19]*꜀kung ngié*^{2} a public conference; *ngié*^{2} *꜀tang*, a schedule or fixed tariff (of prices); *ngié*^{2} *ka*' to consult and fix the prices.

艤^2 I. To turn a boat's head toward the shore; to bring a boat up to the bank.

蟻^2 I. An ant; a generic term for insects like the ant; sometimes used as a demeaning term by suppliants, as by the people when addressing their rulers; *met.*, the rabble, commonalty;

---

[1]義墨 [2]義理 [3]字義 [4]義倉 [5]義學 ○ [6]義人 ○ [7]義僕 ○ [8]義女 ○ [9]義氣 [10]義民 [11]義勇 [12]嘉義 [13]誼親 [14]誼父 [15]誼兄弟 ○ [16]誼姨 [17]誼妹 [18]議論 [19]公議

banditti, as assembled in numbers: [1]*ngié*[2] *'teng*, we; [2]*ngié*[2] *chik*, collected like ants, as banditti; COLL., [3]*,t'ëng ngié*[2] insects; *,ëng ngié*[2] the common red ant; *chó' pah, ngié*[2] to be a white ant—i. e., a go-between in buying property; *,ëng ngié*[2] *,wo*, (or *seu'*), an ant-nest; *,ëng ngié*[2] *,pá teng'* ants in troops or long lines.

毅[2] I. Firm, resolute, determined, bold, intrepid; forgetful of one's self, magnanimous; stern, wrathful; fortitude, power of endurance: [4]*ngié*[2] *,yong*, decided, resolute; *,kiong ngié*[2] intrepid, bold in the face of danger.

羿[2] I. A famous archer, called *Haiú' ngié*[2] who flourished about B. C. 1980.

藝[2] I. Ability, aptitude, skill or art in doing; a craft, an art, an occupation, an accomplishment; skilled in; to distinguish; to cultivate the arts: [5]*,ung ngié*[2] literary occupation; [6]*lëk, ngié*[2] the six accomplishments—ceremony, music, archery, horsemanship, writing, and arithmetic; COM., [7]*'u ngié*[2] military tactics; [8]*ch'iu ngié*[2] a handicraft; [9]*ngié*[2] *'pong*, an indenture; [10]*ngié*[2] *'mwang*, the term of apprenticeship completed; COLL., *óh, ngié*[2] or *óh, ,këng ngié*[2] to learn a trade.

蓺[2] Used for the last: to set out, to plant with the hand; to cultivate trees: *sëü*[2] *ngié*[2] to plant seeds.

外[2] Wai. Read *ngwoi*[2]; coll. *ngié*[2]: outside, without, beyond; out of doors, foreign, other; related by marriage, relatives of a wife: [11]*ngié*[2] *'tau*, or *ngié*[2] *'tau sié'*, or *ngié*[2] *hiong'* outside, without; [12]*,siàng ngié*[2] suburban; [13]*ngié*[2] *,piéng*, (the notation of pounds and ounces) on the outside of the steelyard; [14]*ngié*[2] *'seng*, other provinces; [15]*ngié*[2] *,ka*, the wife's family; [16]*ngié*[2] *,kung* and [17]*ngié*[2] *'ma*, maternal grandfather and grandmother; [18]*ngié*[2] *,seng* and [19]*ngié*[2] *,seng 'nü*, sister's sons and daughters, nephews and nieces; [20]*ngié*[2] *,seng ,song*, a daughter's son; [21]*ngié*[2] *,kong 'lá* (or *t'ó'*), the etiquette of other provinces; *ngié*[2] *,seng ,tó sëü*[2] *keú'* a nephew generally resembles his maternal uncle.

(558) Ngiék.

Ngiék,. A coll. word: perhaps a corruption of *kiék,*; to take hold or pull with pincers, tweezers, etc.: *ngiék, 'piéng*, flattened by a gripe of the pincers; *ngek, ngiék,* to take, as with tongs or nippers; *ngiék, má*[2] *'k'i*, can't pull it out.

業[2] Yeh. A beam to support a bell or drum; an office, occupation, profession, calling, pursuit, art, trade; estate, patrimony, property; a claim on account of merit; meritorious, deserving; past, done, finished: [22]*sëü*[2] *ngiék,* occupation; *,kung ngiék,* deserving; *ngiék, ,king*, or *ngiék, 'i*, done, past; COM., *,ka ngiék,* a family-estate; *ngiék, 'sang*, possessions,

1 蟻等 2 蟻集 3 蟲蟻 4 毅然 5 文藝 6 六藝 7 武藝 8 手藝 9 藝榜 10 藝滿 11 外斗 12 城外 13 外邊 14 外省 15 外家 16 外公 17 外媽 18 外甥 19 外甥女 20 外甥孫 21 外江禮 22 事業 ○

福州方言拼音字典

property; *ngiék*, *‚sü* and *seu'* *ngiék*, teacher and learner of letters or of an art; *ngiék*, *‚kwi* *‚ngwong* *'chio*, property reverting to the original owner.

鄴 Yeh. ₂ A part of the ancient Wei state, now embraced in the Linchang district of Changtê department in the north of Honan: *ngiék*, *ka'* the bookcase of prince Yeh or Li Pi—a complimentary term for a scholar's library.

孽 Yeh. Nieh. ₂ The son of a concubine; an illegitimate child, a bastard; *met.*, guilt, retribution, consequences or reward of crime; sorrow; clear, neat, ornate: *ngiék*, *ngiék*, neat, adorned; [1]*'sëü'* *ngiék*, son of a concubine; COM., [2]*‚k'iëng* *ngiék*, or [3]*'chói*[2] *ngiék*, consequences of sin, retribution; [4]*'chauk*, *ngiék*, to cause evil; *met.*, to commit suicide; [5]*ngiék*, *‚t'iéng*, bad weather, an unfavorable season; [6]*ngiék*, *'chü* or *ngiék*, *'chüng*, a child of infamy; a wicked son; [7]*ngiék*, *cha'* extortionate; [8]*ngiék*, *hëük*, an unruly beast; you brute! COLL., *‚kang ngiék*, to force, to press or trouble one; *ngiék*, *'si ‚nëng*, to vex one to death.

櫱 Yeh. ₂ The stock of a tree sprouting again, shoots from a stump: *‚meng ngiék*, suckers.

臬 Yeh. Nieh. ₂ A target; a law, rule, regulation; an administrator, a magistrate, a judge: COM., [9]*ngiék*, *‚si* (or *hiong'*), the provincial judge, addressed usually as [10]*ngiék*, *‚tai*; *ngiék*, *kiäng'* a large brass-mirror, carried in procession before an idol.

臲 Nieh. ₂ Uneasy, unquiet, restless: *ngiék*, *wok*, or *wok*, *ngiék*, disturbed, floating, moving about.

闑 Nieh. ₂ A threshold; a small post or pillar in a gateway; one says, the side door in an entrance.

(559) Ngiéng.

妍 ‚ Yen. Beautiful, pretty, elegant; witty, accomplished, talented; good, virtuous: *‚ch'i ‚ngiéng*, ugly and handsome.

研 ‚ Yen. To grind fine, to triturate, to pulverize; *met.*, to investigate: also read *ngiëng'* and in the coll. *'ngiéng*, q. v.: *‚ngiéng keu'* to examine thoroughly.

' 儼 Yen. To carry the head high; grave, dignified, commanding respect: *'ngiéng ‚yong*, grave, commanding; also consequential, taking on airs.

研 Yen. Read *‚ngiéng*; coll. *'ngiéng*: to rub, to triturate, to grind to powder; to roll, to roll out, as with a rolling-pin: [11]*'ngiéng ‚só*, a narrow, iron mortar in which drugs are ground; [12]*'ngiéng ‚t'ui*, a pestle; [13]*'ngiéng kong'* a wooden rolling-pin; [14]*'ngiéng sioh*, a stone-roller for smoothing cloth; [15]*'ngiéng ‚kwong*, to roll out smooth; [16]*'ngiéng mwak*, to pulverize; [17]*chai 'ngiëng*, small rolls or twists of paper.

[1]庶孽 [2]寃孽 [3]罪孽 [4]作孽 [5]孽天 [6]孽子 [7]孽詐 [8]孽畜 [9]臬司 [10]臬臺 [11]研槽 [12]研槌 [13]研棍 [14]研石 [15]研光 [16]研末 [17]紙研

硯 研 ' Yen. A Chinese ink-stone: the 2d also read ‚ngiéng and in the coll. ‘ngiéng, q. v.: [1]ngiéng' ‚hing, a fellow-student; [2]ngiéng' ‚tiéng, to get a living by the pencil; COM., [3]‘t‘u ngiéng' an earthen ink-stone; ‚ngüng ‚chio ngiéng' an ink-stone for red ink; ‚twang sioh‚ ngiéng' a superior kind of ink-stone; ngiéng' ‚tié, a cavity for water in the ink-stone.

癮 ' Yin. Read ‘üng; used for the coll, ngiéng': addicted to, confirmed in a habit, besotted, victimized: [4]‚a p‘iéng' ngiéng' confirmed in opium-smoking; [5]siong' ngiéng' the habit just become fixed; [6]kwo' ngiéng' the longing (for the pipe) satiated; ngiéng' ‚t‘au taëng[2] the hankering excessive, fully victimized; ‘chiu ngiéng' addicted to drinking liquor.

嚴 ‚ Yen. Stern, severe, strict; rigid, austere, cold, reserved; majestic, dignified, grave, solemn, reverential; inducing respect, awe-inspiring; epithet of a father; a night watch or guard; a surname: [7]kai' ‚ngiéng, to guard, to prepare defences against; COM., [8]‚ka ‚ngiéng, my father; [9]‚siéng ‚ngiéng, a deceased father; [10]‚wi ‚ngiéng, stern, majestic; [11]‚ngiéng keng' to forbid strictly; [12]‚ngiéng sok‚ or ‚ngiéng ‘king, strict, rigid.

巖 ‚ Yen. A shelter, a breastwork for archers or spearmen; to oppose, to fend off.

閻 ‚ Yen. The gate of a ward or village, called ‚lü ‚ngiéng; a lane, an alley; to be influenced, to receive advice; fine, beautiful, as long robes; a surname: COM., [13]‚ngiéng ‚ló ‚t‘iéng ‘chü, or [14]‚ngiéng ‚ló ‚wong, the emperor or king of hades, judge in the invisible world; specifically applied to the judge in the 5th of the 10 halls.

唁 喭 [2] Yen. To mourn with another over the loss of a country; to visit and comfort the bereaved; to condole with one degraded in rank: the 2d also read ngang[2] q. v.: [15]tieu' ngiéng[2] to condole with those bereaved.

彥 [2] Yen. Accomplished, talented, virtuous and learned, as a scholar: [16]chong' ngiéng[2] eminent, excelling.

諺 [2] Yen. A proverb, common saying, a tradition; a blunt speech: ngiéng[2] ‘ngü, a vulgar saying.

驗 騐 [2] Yen. To examine officially in order to identify, to discover proof, to verify; to witness before officers; proved by experience or trial; proof, evidence, testimony; fulfillment, verification: COM., [17]‚cha ngiéng[2] or ‘k‘ó ngiéng[2] to investigate officially; [18]hau' ngiéng[2] fulfilled; efficacious; [19]ngiéng[2] ‚si, to examine a corpse, as coroners do; [20]ngiéng[2] hwo' to examine goods (for the duty); COLL., [21]ngiéng[2] t‘ói' to examine marks left by a thief; ngiéng[2] ‚mó ‚siong, to hold an inquest and find no wounds (on the corpse).

1硯兄 2硯田 3土硯 4鴉片癮 5上癮○ 6過癮 7戒嚴 8家嚴 9先嚴 10威嚴 11嚴禁 12嚴束 13閻羅天子 14閻羅王 15弔唁○ 16俊彥 17查驗 18效驗 19驗屍 20驗貨 21驗退

釅 $_2$ Yen. Pickle, vinegar; sour, sharp, as spirits or vinegar highly rectified.

(560) Ngieu.

堯 Yao. Earth heaped up; high, lofty, eminent in worth: COM., [1]*ngieu song'* the emperors Yao and Shun, B. C. 2357 and 2255.

蕘 Yao. Grass, turf, stubble, rushes or twigs, used for fuel: *ch'ü ngieu*, light fuel for kindling.

翹 Ch'iao. Long tail-feathers; a kind of flag adorned with feathers; to raise the tail; to lift the head, to look up; to elevate, to excite; high, raised; imminent, dangerous; distant: [2]*ngieu ngieu*, thick and high, as trees; in danger, as a house about to fall; [3]*ngieu 'siu*, to raise the head; COM., [4]*lièng ngieu*, a medicinal plant, used as a febrifuge.

饒 Jao. Abundance of food; full, ample, abundant, affluent; an overplus, excess, superfluity; the leavings; a surname: also read *nieu*, q. v.: [5]*ho' ngieu*, affluent; [6]*hung ngieu*, abounding in, ample.

Ngieu. A coll. word: a sort of coined term, similar to *chu;* gone! dead!

(561) Ngih.

Ngih$_2$. A coll. euphonic prefix, as in *ngih*$_2$ *lih*$_2$ *ngah*$_2$ *lah*$_2$ a rattling, as of tiles or things by a sudden concussion.

(562) Ngik.

逆 $_2$ Ni. To resist, to disobey; to go out against, to withstand, to encounter; opposing, rebellious, seditious, refractory; contrary, contumacious; against one, adverse, as wind or tide; to receive; to report on; to calculate or reckon on, to know beforehand: [7]*ngik*$_2$ *so'* to reckon or know beforehand; [8]*ngik*$_2$ *meng*^{2} to receive orders; COM., [9]*pwoi*^{2} *ngik*$_2$ to oppose, to rebel against; [10]*ngik*$_2$ *hung*, a contrary wind; [11]*cheng' ngik*$_2$ an incurable disease; [12]*'ngu ngik*$_2$ refractory, willful; [13]*ngik*$_2$ *lai song*^{2} *seu*^{2} when adversity comes, bear it meekly.

⿰口逆 $_2$ Ni. To throw up, to vomit, to puke: [14]*'eu ngik*$_2$ to vomit, to disgorge.

凝 $_2$ Ning. Ying. Read *nging;* coll. *ngik*$_2$: to freeze, to congeal; to coagulate, to become solid; frozen, stiffened: [15]*ngik*$_2$ *kiék*, to freeze or congeal; to coagulate; [16]*ngik*$_2$ *taĕng'* to thicken and cool, as lard, gravy, etc.; [17]*'chwi ngik*$_2$ the water is frozen; [18]*haik*$_2$ *ngik*$_2$ coagulated blood.

鶂 $_2$ The medallion pheasant (Tragopan satyrus), called *t'o' seu*^{2} *'neu*, the bird that ejects the comb, and [19]*'king nong*, the elegant bag.

虉 $_2$ Small plants of different colors, grass having ribbon-like marks.

Ngik$_2$. A coll. euphonic prefix, as in *ngik*$_2$ *ngok*$_2$ *ngok*$_2$ or *ngik*$_2$ *ngik*$_2$ *ngok*$_2$ *ngok*$_2$ to raise the

[1] 堯舜 [2] 翹翹 [3] 翹首 [4] 連翹 [5] 富饒 [6] 豐饒 [7] 逆數 [8] 逆命 [9] 悖逆 [10] 逆風 [11] 症逆 [12] 忤逆 [13] 逆來順受 [14] 嘔⿰口逆 [15] 凝結 [16] 凝凍 [17] 水凝 [18] 血凝 [19] 錦囊

head, to lift the head and look, as birds, turtles, snakes, etc.

(563) Nging.

ʻ*Nging*. A coll. euphonic prefix, as in ʻ*nging* ʻ*ngiéng*, to roll, to crush or roll out, as with a rolling-stick; to triturate, as with a pestle.

吟 唫 ˛ Yin. To hum, to chant, to sing; to recite, to repeat quickly, to say over; to sigh, to moan, to groan; a mournful voice: [1]˛*nging eng*ʾ to chant, to recite; [2]˛*liéng* ˛*nging*, a concert; COM., [3]˛*nging* ˛*ngó*, to hum, to say over; [4]˛*nging* ˛*si chauk, tói*ʾ to recite verses and compose distichs. The 2d also read *keng*ʾ: shut, closed, as the mouth; congealed, torpid, dormant.

凝 ˛ Ning. Ying. To freeze, to congeal, to turn into ice; to coagulate; frozen, stiffened; fixed, finished, settled, determined; collected, abundant: in the coll. read *ngik*˛ q. v.: [5]˛*nging kiék*˛ to congeal; [6]˛*nging* ˛*sing* ʻ*wong chéü*ʾ to look far with a fixed gaze; COM., ˛*nging* ˛*hi*, much happiness —a felicitous phrase stuck up in houses.

迎 ˛ Ying. To go out to meet, to receive, as a guest; to occur, to happen, to meet with; to calculate, as astronomers calculate days; a reception, meeting, interview: also read *ngeng*ʾ and in the coll. ˛*ngiăng*, q. v.: [7]˛*hung* ˛*nging*, to try to please, to flatter; COM., [8]˛*nging chiék*˛ to greet, to receive, as guests; [9]*sek*˛ ˛*nging*, to miss a visit, to fail to receive one; [10]˛*nging* ˛*kwang chiék*˛ *saing*ʾ to receive and accompany officers, as the subordinate officers do.

垠 ˛ Yin. Read ˛*ngŭng*; coll. ˛*nging*: a bank, a ridge; a raised path by a stream or pond: [11]˛*nging* ˛*pung k'ó*ʾ the bank has burst and fallen.

˛*Nging*. A coll. euphonic prefix, as in ˛*nging* ˛*ngiăng*, to parade, to carry in procession, as idols, a bride's furniture, &c.

(564) Ngio.

˛*Ngio*. A coll. word, about the same as ˛*ngē*, as in ˛*ngio* ˛*ngio tioh*˛ glum, sullen; a fixed, grum look, as of one displeased or indifferent.

(565) Ngioh.

Ngioh˛. A coll. word, as in *ngioh*˛ *ngioh*˛ to raise the head and look; ˛*t'au ngioh*˛ *sioh*˛ *a*ʾ to lift and slightly move the head, as in token of assent.

Ngioh˛. A coll. word, similar to *ngiăk*˛ as in *ngioh*˛ ˛*keng*, to raise the head high, as for another to look into one's mouth or at one's throat.

(566) Ngiok.

虐 ˛ Nio. To tyrannize over, to oppress, to maltreat; cruel, harsh, unfeeling, inhuman; calamity: [12]˛*chang ngiok*˛ to ravage, to devastate; [13]*ngiok*˛ ˛*ming*, to oppress the people; [14]*tai*ʾ *ngiok*˛ great calamities; COM., [15]*pó*ʾ *ngiok*˛ cruel, oppressive.

[1]吟咏 [2]聯吟 [3]吟哦 [4]吟詩作對 ○ [5]凝結 ○ [6]凝神遠注 [7]逢迎 ○ [8]迎接 [9]失迎 [10]迎官接送 [11]垠崩去 ○ [12]殘虐 ○ [13]虐民 ○ [14]大虐 [15]暴虐

瘧 ₂ Nio. A fever, fever and ague; febrile complaints: [1]ʻngiok₂ chik₂ or [2]ʻngiok₂ chengʾ an intermittent or remittent fever; [3]ʻping ngiok₂ ague fits; [4]ʻmeu ngiok₂ feverish fits; [5]꜀hang ngiok₂ a fever preceded by chills.

(567) Ngiong.

ʻ仰 Yang. To look upwards; to look to a superior, to respect, to regard highly; to look forward, to expect, to long for; to think of kindly; to transmit orders, to command an inferior; to rely, to trust, to wait on; a surname; in the coll. thin boards for ceilings, &c.: [6]ʻngiong wongʾ to long for; [7]ʻngiong ꜀i ꜀sü ꜀chi, in a brown study, thinking intently about; COM., [8]ʻngiong mwoʾ to look to with great desire; [9]ʻkiu ʻngiong, have long thought (of you); [10]ʻngiong ʻpeng, ceiling-boards; [11]ʻtóʾ ʻngiong, a ceiling; [12]ʻlauʾ ʻngiong, the "dripping boards"—the thin boards on which the tiles are laid.

ʻ巘 Yen. Also read ꜀ngiong and hiongʾ: the summit or peak of a hill, likened to a boiler or jar.

言 ꜀ Yen. Nien. Yüan. Words, speech, talk, language; a sentence, an expression; to say, to speak, to discourse; to address, to speak to; to express an opinion; a word, an order; the 149th radical: [13]꜀ngiong ꜀ngiong, high and large; [14]ʻp'iéngʾ ꜀ngiong, one sentence; COM., [15]꜀ngiong ʻngü, words, conversation; [16]꜀ngiong haingʾ words and acts; [17]꜀ngiong ꜀kwang, censors; [18]ʻk'ieu ꜀ngiong, artful talk; [19]sik₂ ꜀ngiong, to eat one's words, to retract; [20]pok₂ ꜀sing ꜀ngiong, interminable words, a long story (to tell all about it); [21]꜀ngiong ꜀sang ʻngü seʾ loquacious, babbling; ꜀ing ꜀ngiong, arsenic.

(568) Ngiu.

牛 ꜀ Niu. Yu. An ox, a cow; oxen, kine; the 9th of the 28 constellations; the 93d radical: in the coll. read ꜀ngu, q. v.: COM., ꜀ngiu ꜀wong, ox-bezoar; ꜀ngiu ch'ek, ox-knees—a medicinal plant, described as growing like grain; ʻYéng paik₂ ꜀ngiu, a noted disciple of Confucius; ꜀ngiu ꜀long chek₂ ʻnü, the herdsman and female weaver—stars in Aquarius and Lyra (?), emblematic of connubial union.

(569) Ngo.

五 ₂ 伍 ₂ 乄 ₂ Wu. Read ʻngu; coll. ngoʾ: five: sek₂ ngoʾ fifteen; ngoʾ sek₂ fifty; ngoʾ ngwok₂ ngoʾ the 5th day of the 5th moon; nik₂ ngoʾ the 25th day of a month; paiʾ ngoʾ Friday; ꜀i ngoʾ fifth brother; ngoʾ t'euʾ ch'ioʾ a house five posts (deep); ngoʾ ꜀ch'iéng tieuʾ 5,000,000 of cash; ngoʾ tóiʾ ꜀tung ꜀tong, five cotemporary generations in a family.

(570) Ngó.

ʻ我 Wo. O. E. The first personal pronoun, I, my, mine, me; we, our, ours, us; often used emphatically in the plural: in the coll. read ʻngwai, q. v.: ʻngó ꜀mwong, or ʻngó ʻteng, we; chaiʾ ʻngó, it

[1]瘧疾 [2]瘧症 [3]牝瘧 [4]牡瘧 [5]寒瘧 [6]仰望 [7]仰而思之 [8]仰慕 [9]久仰 [10]仰板 [11]倒仰 [12]溜仰 [13]言言 [14]片言 [15]言語 [16]言行 [17]言官 [18]巧言 [19]食言 [20]不勝言 [21]言

三語四〇

pertains to me; ˛u ˋngó, be not selfish; ˋngó ˏchiu ˏkung, our lord Chow.

ˋ傲 Ao. Read ngó² used for the coll. ˋngó, as in ˋngó ˋngó tioh˛ proud, supercilious, as in not replying to a question.

*Ngó*ˀ. A coll. word, as in ngóˀ ngóˀ kieuˀ railing at, saying insulting words to or about one; ˏhang ngóˀ ngóˀ kieuˀ to snore loudly.

*Ngó*ˀ. A coll. word: to throw back, as the head in sleeping; to bend or turn up the foot: ngóˀ ˋk'i ˏli, to lift the head and fall asleep; ˏk'a ˛tó ngóˀ ˋk'i sioh˛ tek˛ ˋkiăng, turn up the foot a little.

*Ngó*ˀ. A coll. word: the sound made in calling geese; the cackling of a goose.

˛俄 O. A moment, momentarily; in haste, suddenly; about to fall, falling: ¹˛ngó ˛yong, suddenly; ˛ngó ˋk'ing, an instant, a while; COM., ²˛ngó ˛ló ˛sŭ, Russia.

˛娥 O. E. Good, excellent: COM., ³ˏkŭng ˛ngó, maids of honor; ⁴˛siong ˛ngó, the goddess of the moon, the Chinese Diana.

˛峩 O. High, lofty, as mountains: ˛ngó ˛ngó, high, grand; *met.*, a commanding presence; COM., ⁵˛Ngó ˛mi ˏsang, a noted peak in Sz'chuen, near the junction of the Tatu and Min rivers.

˛莪 O. A plant having edible stalks like celery; the tender stalks of plants.

˛哦 O. E. To chant, to sing, to say over, to rehearse in recitative, to hum to one's self: COM., ⁶˛nging ˛ngó, to hum, as in reciting poetry.

˛嗷 Ao. A loud cry, a wailing, a clamor, as of one begging food; noise, hubbub, as from many voices; the cry of birds: ⁷˛chó ˛ngó, hum of voices; mournful song of birds; COLL., ⁸tiongˀ ˛ngó, has an expanded throat, as said of a liar or railer; kak˛ ˛ngó, or ˛ngó kek˛ your throat is stopped—you can't say a word more; ⁹˛ngó ˛ngó kieuˀ the clamor of a multitude.

˛囂 Ao. Hsiao. Also read ˏhieu: to vociferate, to make a noise; hum, clamor, as of a market; a complaining tone, murmuring: ˛ngó ˛ngó, clamorous; satisfied, complaisant.

˛敖 Ao. To saunter, to ramble; long, protracted, prolix: ¹⁰˛ngó ˛ngó, elongated; pleased, gratified; COLL., ¹¹˛ngó yăˀ to stay up all night; ¹²˛ngó ˛ming ˛siăng twaiˀ pangˀ to spend sleepless nights causes severe illness. Read ngó²: proud, haughty.

˛廒 Ao. A large receptacle for grain: COM., ¹³ˏch'ong ˛ngó, a granary, such as farmers have.

¹俄然 ²俄羅斯 ³宮娥 ⁴嫦娥 ⁵峩眉山 ⁶吟哦 ⁷嘈嗷 ⁸脹嗷 ⁹嗷嗷叫 ¹⁰敖敖 ¹¹敖夜 ¹²敖眠成大病 ¹³倉廒

摮 ꜂Ao. To strike so as to move; to shake, to rattle, to joggle.

熬 ꜂Ao. To boil in water; to simmer, to distill, to brew, to decoct; to boil in water in another vessel: COM., [1]꜂ngó ꜀t'ong, to make a decoction of; [2]꜂ngó ꜂iu, to try out fat; to purify oils, as painters do; [3]꜂ngó yoh꜆ to decoct medicine; [4]꜂ngó ꜀kó, to make a jelly.

獒 ꜂Ao. A large, sagacious dog, said to be four feet high and able to speak; perhaps refers to the Tibetan mastiff; a fierce dog.

璈 ꜂Ao. A sort of musical instrument of metal or stone, which makes a jingling noise.

𢁳 ꜂Ao. The stem or cut-water of a vessel; the lowest timber in the hull.

遨 ꜂Ao. Also read ngó꜆: to saunter, to ramble, to travel about for pleasure: [5]꜂ngó ꜂iu, to stroll about; [6]꜂ngó ꜀hi, to attend shows, to ramble for diversion.

驁 ꜂Ao. Also read ngó꜆: a spirited, vicious horse; stubborn, indomitable, regardless of consequences: [7]tai꜆ ꜂ngó, remiss and rude; [8]kiék꜆ ꜂ngó or ꜂ngó kiék꜆ resolute; also proud, overbearing; [9]꜂ngó ꜂yong pok꜆ ko꜄ reckless as to consequences.

鼇 鰲 ꜂Ao. A kraken or whale, a great sea-monster, fabled to carry the mountain P'êng Lai on its back: COM., [10]꜂ngó ꜂ngü, a species of Scorpaena; [11]꜂ngó ꜀hung ꜀chü yéng꜄ a college in the south-east section of Foochow; [12]꜂ngó ꜀sang, a "whale-hill"—paper toys of mountains, caves, etc., as on anniversaries of the emperor's birth; [13]tuk꜆ chiéng꜄ ꜂ngó ꜂t'eu, "perched on the whale's head"—to attain the highest literary rank.

螯 ꜂Ao. The large claws of a crab or lobster, called [14]há꜆ ꜂ngó: COM., [15]꜀ch'iâ ꜂ngó, a large species of mytilus.

蛾 ꜂O. E. I. The silkworm moth, called [16]꜂chang ꜂ngó; moths, millers, which fly at night; also used for the quinsy: COM., [17]'hwi ꜂ngó, millers; [18]꜂ngó ꜂mi, handsome, arched eyebrows; [19]꜂ngó ꜂mi ngwok꜆ the new moon; [20]꜂heu ꜂ngó, or ꜂t'ang ꜂ngó, inflammation in the throat, quinsy; a swelling on one side is called ꜀tang ꜂ngó, on both sides, ꜀sĕng ꜂ngó.

鵞 鵝 ꜂O. E. A goose; also large, aquatic birds with habits like those of geese: in the coll. read ꜂ngié, q. v.: ꜀t'iéng ꜂ngó, a crane; ꜂tong ꜂ngó, a pelican; k'ié꜄ ꜂ngó, a penguin; 'yă ꜂ngó, wild geese.

鷔 ꜂Ao. Also read ngó꜆: an infelicitous bird, said to resemble the owl and asemble in deserts: ꜂woong ꜂ngó, a

[1]熬湯 [2]熬油 [3]熬藥 [4]熬膏 [5]遨遊 [6]遨嬉 [7]大驁 [8]桀驁 [9]驁然不顧 [10]鼇魚 [11]鼇峰書院 [12]鼇山 [13]獨占鼇頭 [14]蟹螯 [15]蛼螯 [16]蠶蛾 [17]火蛾 [18]蛾眉 [19]蛾眉月 [20]喉蛾○

bird of ill omen, with a human face.

翱 ꜀Ao. To fly like a hawk, to skim, to float in the air: [1]꜀ngó ꜀siong, to wheel, to soar to and fro.

鏖 ꜀Ao. Read ꜀ó in the dictionaries: a sort of pan; to kill, to slay, to slaughter, to exterminate; to fight with a reckless disregard of death.

鼉 ꜀T'o. A species of dragon, or large iguana, whose skin was used for covering drums: [2]꜀ngó ꜂ku ꜀p'ung ꜀p'ung, the drums rattling.

꜀Ngó. A coll. word, as in ꜀ngó ꜂ngá, a fierce, proud look, a defiant air—similar to ꜀ngau ꜂ngá, q. v.

꜀Ngó. A coll. word: to bend, to turn up, as in ꜀k'a ꜀ngó ló² ꜂k'i, turn up the foot.

傲² Ao. Proud, arrogant, haughty; uncivil, neglectful; pride, hauteur; to treat rudely; to defy proudly, to brave: used for ꜂ngó in the coll. q. v.: [3]ngó² mang² to treat insolently; COM., [4]꜀kieu ngó² or [5]꜀kó ngó² proud, haughty; [6]ngó² k'e² an arrogant spirit; twai² ngó² great pride, excessive hauteur.

鏊² Ao. An iron pot or pan to bake in; to bake, to heat and dry in an oven: COM., [7]ngó² ꜀lu, an earthen baker, an oven; COLL., [8]ngó² ꜂tiăng, a baking-pan, with flat bottom and a cover on which coals are placed; ngó² twai² sŭk, to bake thoroughly; yĕk, kaĕng² ꜂hwi ngó² sioh, yong² as hot as a heated oven.

餓² O. E. Hungry, faint from want of food; starved, famished; to fast, to go without food: COM., [9]꜀ki ngó² to starve: [10]ngó² tó² ꜀hwong ꜂kwi, famished ghosts, as those served with offerings in the ꜂p'wo to² rites; [11]ngó² ꜂tó, to fall down from starvation; COLL., [12]ngó² pok, hungry; [13]ngó² taung² to go without a meal; [14]ngó² ꜂si ꜀nĕng ꜀pa, starved to death, a mere human crust!—as one says when destitute of employment.

奡² Lofty, proud, haughty; assuming, overbearing; name of a man mentioned in the Lun-yü, who rowed boats on land.

(571) Ngoh.

Ngoh,. A coll. word: to cut, to slice off; also a sound as of scraping, rubbing, etc.: ngoh, sioh, ꜀tó, to give a stroke with a knife; ngoh, ngoh, kieu² a sound, as of rubbing hard things, or of rats gnawing.

(572) Ngoi.

僞² Wei. False, deceitful, hypocritical; spurious, counterfeit, not genuine, surreptitious; to deceive: [15]chauk, ngoi² to act falsely; [16]cha² ngoi² fraudulent, deceitful; [17]꜀tá ngoi² impure, counterfeit, as money; [18]ngoi² kwok, a rebel state.

魏² Wei. High, eminent, lofty, as a mountain; a surname; one of the Three States, including the modern Honan, over which Ts'ao-

1 翱翔　2 鼉鼓　逢逢　3 傲慢　4 驕傲　5 高傲　6 傲氣　7 鏊爐　8 鏊鼎　9 饑餓　10 餓道　荒鬼　11 餓倒　12 餓腹　13 餓頓　14 餓死　仈疤　15 作僞　16 詐僞　17 低僞　18 僞國　○

ts'ao ruled, A. D. 250; also one of the contending states, B. C. 450, now comprised in Shansi.

(573) Ngok.

岳 Yo. ₂ Used for the next: a lofty mountain: COM., [1]'ngok₂ ho' or ngok₂ tiong' (coll. ₍tiong ₍nĕng), a wife's father; [2]ngok₂ 'mu, (coll. 'tiong 'nâ), a wife's mother; [3]₍siĕng ngok₂ my deceased father-in-law; [4]'leng' ngok₂ your wife's father.

嶽 Yüeh. Yao. Yo. Yü. ₂ A high peak; the principal mountains of China: COM., [5]₍tung ngok₂ (coll. ₍tĕng ôh₂), a temple of the god T'ai' ₍Sang, outside the east gate of Foochow; [6]'ngu ngok₂ the five principal peaks worshiped by the Chinese, viz., [7]₍tung ngok₂ in Shantung, [8]₍sâ ngok₂ in Shensi south of the capital; [9]₍nang ngok₂ in Hunan near the center, [10]paĕk₂ ngok₂ in the south-west of Chihli, and [11]₍tŭng ngok₂ in the west of Honan near the Yellow river; each of these has other names.

鸑 Yo. ₂ A kind of large eagle, or phenix, called ngok₂ chuk₂ an emblem of marriage.

樂 Yao. Yo Lo. Yüeh. ₂ Music, one of the six arts; instruments of music; *met.*, the refinement, or elegancies, of life: also read lok₂ and ngau' q. v.: [12]chauk₂ ngok₂ to play on instruments; COM., [13]ngok₂ k'e' musical instruments; [14]'lá ngok₂ politeness and music; [15]ngok₂ ₍seng, musicians, as employed in the worship of civil and military sages; [16]'yĭng ngok₂ musical practice or rehearsal.

蕚 O. ₂ Read ngauk₂: coll. ngok₂: a bud of flowers, fruits, etc.: pwok₂ ngok₂ to put forth buds, to bud, to sprout.

Ngok₂. A coll. word, as in ngok₂ 'k'i, to raise the head (to look); ngik₂ ngik₂ ngok₂ ngok₂ to keep raising the head (and peering about), as a person, a bird, a turtle.

(574) Ngong.

卬 ₍ Ang. Great, high; dear, high-priced; strenuous effort; to lift the head, attitude of expectation; the pronoun I, as used by females and sometimes by males: [17]₍tá ₍ngong, low and high; [18]e' 'k'ong k'ai' ₍i chĕū' ₍ngong, to exert one's self with noble aims.

昂 ₍ Ang. Similar to the last: to rise, as the sun; to issue forth; to raise, to elevate; tall, lofty, stately, imposing; costly, dear in price: [19]₍ngong 'siu, to carry the head high; [20]₍ngong koi' dear, exorbitant; [21]₍hiong ₍ngong, an erect, portly gait; ₍ngong ₍ngong, stately, as a horse's gait; *met.*, noble, princely.

駒 ₍ Ang. A horse that carries its head high; a horse with a white belly: ₍ngong ₍ngong, a horse startled or enraged, a prancing steed.

₍*Ngong*. A coll. word, as in ₍ngong ₍ngong kieu' a loud din, a clamor of voices.

[1]岳父 [2]岳母 [3]先岳 [4]令岳 [5]東嶽 [6]五嶽 [7]東嶽 [8]西嶽 [9]南嶽 [10]北嶽 [11]中嶽 [12]作樂 [13]樂器 [14]禮樂 [15]樂生 [16]演樂 [17]低卬 [18]意慷慨而自卬 [19]昂首 [20]昂貴 [21]軒昂 ○

(575) Ngu.

ˏNgu. A coll. word, as in *ˏngu ˏlu* (or *ˏngu ˏlu*), to mutter in a low tone; *ˏngu ˏngu kieu'* a low, dull sound, as of a rice-hulling machine; *ˏngi ˏli ˏngu ˏlu*, a low, muttering sound, a hum, a buzz.

'五 '伍 '𠄡 Wu. The second is the complex, and the third the contracted form: five; a perfect number denoting all, as virtues, tastes, elements, planets, colors, grains, human relations, viscera, ranks of nobility, points of the compass, night watches, etc.: in the coll. read *ngo'* q. v.: COM., [1]*'ngu kok*, all kinds of grain; [2]*'ngu tá'* the five emperors, gods over plagues; [3]*'ngu saik*, the five colors; [4]*'ngu ˏing*, the five notes, viz., [5]*ˏküng*, *ˏsiong*, *kaëk*, *'ti*, and *'ü*; [6]*'ngu 'kwi ˏwong ˏsiu*, "enmity of five devils"—a deadly quarrel; [7]*'Ngu 'hiéng ˏkung*, a god of thieves; COLL., [8]*'ngu ˏhiǎ*, or *'ngu lié' ˏhwong sang'* scattered in utter confusion; [9]*'ngu haing' ch'au'* an excessive stench; [10]*'ngu ˏk'iéng tek*, *k'ó'* or *'ngu tá' tek*, *k'ó'* alas! dreadful! *'ngu ˏt'ü ˏchiéng twai' ˏk'ëng*, the Han cash have large holes; *met.*, loud voices in talking.

'伍 Wu. A file of five soldiers, ranks, squads; a company; a friend, comrade, fellow, companion; to associate with; a surname: [11]*ˏsiu 'ü ˏui 'ngu*, ashamed to be in his company; COM., [12]*ˏhong 'ngu*, or *toi' 'ngu*, rank and file, platoons; [13]*ˏyǎng 'ngu ch'ok*, *ˏsing*, promoted from the ranks.

'仵 Wu. Sometimes used for the last: an equal in rank; a match, an opponent: COLL., [14]*'ngu chóh*, coroners, those employed by magistrates to hold inquests; [15]*'ngu ˏchü*, common undertakers, who bury the friendless dead; *'ngu ˏchü ch'ük*, may the undertaker tread you down!

'午 Wu. The seventh of "the twelve stems or branches", answers to fire and the horse; time from 11 A. M. to 1 P. M.; noon, midday; to cross, to oppose; crosswise, transverse; the south, as marked on the compass: COM., [16]*ˏtwang 'ngu*, festival of the dragon-boats in the 5th moon; *siong' 'ngu*, and *ha' 'ngu*, (coll. *siong' tau'* and *a' tau'*), forenoon and afternoon; *'ngu yá'* from noon to midnight, as plays; *'ngu këüng'* the noon-offering, as to Budh in the *'p'wo to'* rites; *'ngu ˏsi ˏleng*, a kind of small, white lily, which blooms at midday; *'ngu ˏtieu ˏmwong*, the south gate of the palace; COLL., [22]*ˏtong 'ngu*, or *chiǎng' 'ngu*, midday, noon.

'忤 Wu. To oppose, to go counter, to cross another's wishes; set in opinion; untoward, obstinate, willful; seditious, disobedient: *'ngu 'ngu*, displeased; COM., *'ngu ngik*, obstinate, rebellious.

'迕 Wu. Interchanged with the last: to meet, to fall in with; to go contrary, to oppose, to resist; athwart,

[1]五穀 [2]五帝 [3]五色 [4]五音 [5]宮商角徵羽 [6]五鬼冤仇 [7]五顯公 [8]五鏬 [9]五𠳐 ... [10]五𠸶的 [11]去羞與為伍 [12]行伍〇 [13]營伍出身 [14]仵作 [15]仵子

福州方言拼音字典

contrary; confused, mixed, disordered: ʻngu ʻchi, to oppose the imperial will; ˏsiong ʻngu, to meet together, a rencontre; ch'auk, ʻngu, confused, mixed up.

ʻNgu. A coll. word: used in combination with ng² (not), in about the same sense as má² yong² not very or much, imperfectly; ng² ʻngu paik, not very well acquainted with; ng² ʻngu ch'iong² not much like to, imperfectly resembling.

吳 ˏWu. Loquacious, bragging; to boast, to talk largely; one of the Three States in the east of China; a surname: ¹pok, ˏngu pok, ngó² neither clamorous nor haughty; COM., ²ˏngu ˏü, a medicinal plant, bearing a small, black, acrid seed.

蜈 ˏWu. As in ˏngu ˏkung, the centipede; ˏngu ˏkung ʻch'ó, a shrub whose branches somewhat resemble a centipede.

吾 ˏWu. A personal pronoun, I, my; we, us; to resist, to keep off, to guard: ³ˏngu ʻteng, we, us, we all; ⁴ˏngu pwoi² we of this class; COM., ˏngu söü² pek, my business is completed; ˏngu tó² ˏtüng ˏing, all here of our trade or profession.

梧 ˏWu. Name of a tree, having wood of a fine, even grain, suitable for making lutes; a slanting post; opposed to; in the coll. an apparatus for righting buildings, consisting of an upright timber, lever, and fulcrum; to right, to shore up: ⁵ˏchié ˏngu, upright and slanting posts; ⁶ʻk'wi ˏngu, a portly form; COM., ⁷ˏngu ˏtung, the Eleococcus oleifera, or Dryandra cordifolia of Thunberg; the fall of its leaf denotes autumn; COLL., ˏngu ch'io² to shore up a house; ˏngu chiăng² to right, to make it erect.

鼯 ˏWu. The flying squirrel, called ˏngu ʻch'ü; also styled ˏhi ˏseng, because it is supposed to bring forth on the wing.

齬 ˏWu. Also read ˏngü: awry, distorted, crooked, ill-arranged, as teeth: ʻchu ˏngu, the teeth uneven; met., contradictory, uncongenial.

牾 ˏWu. A wild animal, perhaps a sort of deer; to oppose, to come in conflict with; stubborn, obstinate.

牛 ˏNiu. Yu. Read ˏngiu; coll. ˏngu: an ox, a cow, oxen, kine: ⁸ˏngu ʻkĕng, a bull; ⁹ˏngu ʻmó, a cow; ¹⁰ˏngu ʻkiăng, a calf; ¹¹ˏwong ˏngu, the "yellow" or common cow; ¹²ʻchwi ˏngu, the water-ox, buffalo; ¹³ˏngu mó² a mill worked by bullock-power; ¹⁴ˏngu ˏneng, cow's milk; ¹⁵ˏngu ˏneng ˏkó, cheese; ¹⁶ˏngu ˏwong ˏwong, pills of ox-bezoar; ¹⁷ˏngu nŭk ˏpa, pieces of dried beef, as offered to ʻtau ʻmu, or Measure-mother, on the fifteenth of the 8th moon; ¹⁸ˏNgu ˏt'au ʻMa miéng² the ox-headed and horse-faced—attendants of the gods T'ai² ˏsang and ˏSiăng ˏhwong;

¹不吳不傲 ²吳茰 ³吾等 ⁴吾輩 ⁵枝梧 ⁶魁梧 ⁷梧桐 ⁸牛雄 ⁹牛母 ¹⁰牛仔 ¹¹黃牛 ¹²水牛 ¹³牛磨 ¹⁴牛乳 ¹⁵牛乳膏 ¹⁶牛黃丸 ¹⁷牛肉疤〇 ¹⁸牛頭馬面

¹‚*ngu kah*, or ‚*ngu kah*‚ ‚*tang*, an ox-yoke.

(576) Ngü.

ʻ俁 Persons with large features; a large, imposing appearance.

ʻ麌 Yü. The male of deer, a buck; to herd together: ‚*iu lük*‚ ʻ*ngü* ʻ*ngü*, the does and stags in a herd.

ʻ禦 Yü. To oppose, to withstand, to resist; to stop, to forbid, to cause one to desist; to sacrifice: ²ʻ*hang* ʻ*ngü*, to fend off, to guard against; ³ʻ*ngü* ‚*ki*, to satisfy hunger; COM., ⁴ʻ*tói*ʾ ʻ*ngü*, to stand on mutual defence, to stop fighting and eye each other.

ʻ圉 Yü. A groom, a stable-boy, a hostler; to oppose, to defend; a frontier, the borders; a prison: ⁵ʻ*ngü* ‚*ing*, a hostler; ʻ*ngü* ʻ*ngü*, stationary, as a fish when first placed in the water; ⁶ʻ*siu* ʻ*ngü*, to guard the borders.

ʻ圄 Yü. Wu. A prison; to confine, to imprison, to detain: ‚*ling* ʻ*ngü*, a prison, a lock-up.

ʻ敔 Wu. An instrument shaped like a tiger, struck to stop the music; to stop, to keep the time, as in music: *chëük*‚ ʻ*ngü*, instruments to start and stop the music.

ʻ語 Yü. I. To talk, to say, to discourse; to converse with, to discuss; to set forth, to explain; speech, words, language; an expression, a sentence, a phrase: also read *ngëü*ʾ q. v.: ⁷ʻ*tiong* ʻ*ngü*, a word that gives a turn to the sense; COM., ⁸*laung*ʾ ʻ*ngü*, the Conversations of Confucius; ⁹‚*ngiong* ʻ*ngü*, words, talk; ¹⁰*wa*ʾ ʻ*ngü pok*, ‚*tung*, their language or dialects unlike; ¹¹*sük*‚ ʻ*ngü wa*ʾ a vulgar phrase, a saying or proverb; ‚*ngiong* ʻ*ngü pok*‚ *saung*ʾ the language not conciliatory, contentious words.

ʻ鋙 Wu. Not suiting, unmatched, unfitted for each other, as a round handle in a square hole: ‚*t'ü* ʻ*ngü*, uncongenial, forced. Read ‚*ngu*, as in ¹²‚*K'ong* ‚*ngu*, name of a hill, which produces a superior metal for swords.

ʻ*Ngü*. A coll. word: to calculate, to intend, to have a purpose: ‚*sing* ʻ*lá* ʻ*ngü* ‚*ki*, had it in mind to do.

‚魚 Yü. A fish, the fishy tribes; fishy; the 195th radical: ¹³‚*ngü* ‚*chü*, a letter; COM., ¹⁴‚*tié* ‚*ngü*, pond-fish; ¹⁵*tieu*ʾ ‚*ngü*, to angle for fish; ¹⁶‚*ngü* ʻ*chüng*, small fish for propagating the stock; ¹⁷‚*ngü tö*ʾ fish-maws; ¹⁸‚*ngü hwo*ʾ a lot of fish, as in the markets; ¹⁹‚*ngü ne*ʾ a fish-bait; ²⁰ʻ*t'ó* ‚*ngü*, to fish, as with nets; ²¹‚*ngü* ʻ*siong*, dried salt-fish; ²²‚*ngü* ‚*liong*, a large beam; *to*ʾ ‚*ngü*, a book-moth; COLL., ‚*ngü* ‚*ch'i*, the gills of a fish; ‚*ngü* ‚*ka*, isinglass; ‚*ngü pah*‚ darkish white; ‚*ngü* ‚*pong* ʻ*chwi* ʻ*chwi* ‚*pong* ‚*ngü*, fish help water, water helps fish; *met*., to be mutually helpful or dependent.

¹牛軛 ²扞禦 ³禦饑 ⁴對禦 ⁵圉人 ⁶守圉 ⁷轉語 ⁸論語 ⁹言語不同 ¹⁰話語 ¹¹俗語話 ¹²錕鋙 ○ ¹³魚書 ¹⁴池魚 ¹⁵釣魚 ¹⁶魚種 ¹⁷魚肚 ¹⁸魚貨 ¹⁹魚餌 ²⁰討魚 ²¹魚鯗 ²²魚樑

福州方言拼音字典

漁 ꜀Yü. To fish; to seize, to take indiscriminately; immoderate, promiscuous: ꜀ngū saik꜀, inordinate lust; ꜀ngū ꜀ki lé꜄ a selfish greed for gain; COM., ꜀ngū ꜀ung, an old fisherman, as represented in plays and pictures.

禺 ꜀Yü. A term for quadrumanes, especially gibbons; the incipient development of things; the hour from 9 to 11, A. M. called ꜀ngū ꜀tūng.

喁 ꜀Yü. Yung. Also read ꜀ngūng: the motion of a fish's mouth in breathing, the gasping of a fish; response in singing.

嵎 ꜀Yü. A mountain where the sun rises: ꜀ngū ꜀i, the land of the sun, the orient.

愚 ꜀Yü. The capacity of a monkey; simple, dull, stupid, silly; rude, uninstructed, confounding right and wrong, unwise; used for I, your humble, as at the end of a letter: [1]꜀ngū chwok꜀, stupid, unskilled; [2]yok꜀ ꜀ngū, to seem foolish, but really wise; [3]꜀hiong ꜀ngū, rustics, clowns; [4]꜀ngū ꜀ming, the common people, the canaille; COM., [5]꜀ngū ꜀ch'ung, dull, ignorant; [6]꜀ngū kiéng꜄ in my humble opinion; [7]꜀ngū ꜀hing, your humble servant, as said by a senior.

隅 ꜀Yü. A corner, an angle; a nook, a secluded spot; a cove, a bay, an inlet; a small part, a portion; accurate, rigid, like a corner: [8]꜀hai ꜀ngū, a lagoon; ꜀ngū chó꜄ to sit at one corner; ꜀liéng ꜀ngū, strict, incorrupt; ek꜀ ꜀ngū ꜀chi te꜄ a parcel of land.

娛 ꜀Yü. To please or divert one's self or others; joyous, delighted; pleasure, relaxation, diversion: ꜀hwang ꜀ngū, delight; COM., [9]hié꜄ ꜀ch'ai ꜀ngū ꜀ch'ing, played with colored cloths to amuse his mother—said of the aged ꜀Ló ꜀lai ꜀chū.

虞 ꜀Yü. A fabulous, benign, white and black tiger, called ꜀cheu ꜀ngū, said to have appeared in Wan Wang's day; to consider, to be anxious about, to provide for; ready, prepared, vigilant; to expect; to aid, to help; to choose, to select; pleased; a mishap, an impediment, an accident: [10]꜀su ꜀ngū, remiss, unguarded; [11]꜀ngū ꜀ing, a warden of the imperial parks and ponds; [12]꜀u ꜀ngū, nothing to fear; COM., [13]pok꜀ ꜀ngū, a mishap, an unforeseen accident; [14]꜀ngū song꜄ reign of the emperor Shun.

꜀Ngū. A coll. word, as in ꜀ngū lëū꜄ the rattling sound of phlegm.

(577) Nguh.

Nguh꜆. A coll. word: to make rude, imperfect strokes with the pencil; composed and written crudely: ꜂nü che꜄ á꜄ ꜂siā ꜂chiā ꜂k'wang ꜂mwong nguh꜆ your words written in that fashion—just scribbled off!

(578) Ngui.

危 ꜀Wei. High, precipitous; imminent, hazardous, dangerous; unsteady, uneasy, as a position; not upright,

[1]愚拙 [2]若愚 [3]鄉愚 [4]愚民 [5]愚蠢 [6]愚見 [7]愚兄 [8]海隅 [9]戲彩娛親 [10]疏虞 [11]虞人 [12]無虞 [13]不虞 [14]虞舜

inclined; seriously ill, near death; critical, perilous, in danger of; to endanger, to rush into danger; the 12th of the 28 constellations comprising *α* Aquarius and *ε*, *ο* Pegasus: [1]*꜀ngui ꜀ngiong*, words of warning; COM., [2]*꜀ngui ‘hiéng*, hazardous, perilous; [3]*꜀ling ꜀ngui*, in a critical state, near dissolution; [4]*꜀ngui cheng’* a dangerous disease; [5]*꜀ngui kek꜁* imminently critical; [6]*꜀ngui chai² tang’ sik꜁* in immediate danger day and night, as of starvation.

巍 嵬 ꜀Wei. High, elevated, lofty and alone, as a detached peak; sublime, exalted, conspicious, as one's virtues: *꜀ngui ꜀ngui ꜀hu*, how eminent! how grand! *꜀ch‘oi ꜀ngui*, lofty, sublime.

(579) Ngük.

玉 Yü.꜁ A gem, a precious stone, a mineral fit for the lapidary; gemmeous, pearly; to complete, to perfect; valuable, precious; lovely, admirable; the best, of the highest grade, perfect, as applied to gods and emperors; happily, pleasantly; your, your precious or noble; the 96th radical: in the coll. read *ngwoh꜁* q. v.: [7]*ngük꜁ sik꜁* jade, prehnite; [8]*ngük꜁ ꜀sing*, to complete; [9]*ngük꜁ sik꜁* sumptuous fare; [10]*ngük꜁ keng’* the moon; [11]*ngük꜁ ‘t‘á*, your precious self; COM., [12]*ngük꜁ ‘tiéng*, open (this letter) yourself; [13]*ngük꜁ ꜀hwong*, the Pearly Emperor, supreme god of Tauists: *ngük꜁ ꜀sang kang’* a temple of the *‘ngu tá’* or five emperors, Foochow.

獄 Yü.꜁ A prison, a jail; hard, firm, harsh: in the coll. read *ngwoh꜁* q. v: [14]*sëüng’ ngük꜁* to litigate; [15]*ngük꜁ chok꜁* a turnkey; *twang’ ngük꜁* to decide criminal cases, jail-delivery; *wok꜁ ngük꜁* to break jail.

(580) Ngüng.

銀 ꜀Yin. 艮 ꜀Kên. Silver; money; the name of a place: the 2d, often used for the 1st in the sense of silver, is properly read *kaung’* q. v.: COM., [16]*꜀ngüng ꜀chiéng*, silver and cash, money; [17]*‘chwi ꜀ngüng*, quicksilver; [18]*꜀ngüng ‘chwi*, the difference in value of different kinds of silver; *꜀ngüng saik꜁* the fineness or quality of silver; *꜀hwa ꜀piéng ꜀ngüng*, flower-edged, or milled, silver—a term for Spanish dollars; *꜀ngüng ꜀kwo*, a crucible; [19]*꜀ngüng ꜀ó*, the milky way; [20]*꜀ngüng ꜀si*, fine silver wire; [21]*꜀ngüng sieu’* a round wooden case for transporting silver; [22]*꜀ngüng ꜀ngü*, the silver-fish, the White-bait; *꜀ngüng t‘aik꜁ ꜀king*, silver articles gilded; COLL., *kiá’ ꜀ngüng*, inferior silver; *꜀ngüng ‘só kwang²* a silver neck-locket; *꜀ngüng ‘chai kak꜁* finger-sheaths of silver, worn by brides; *꜀ngüng se² pah꜁ mek꜁ ꜀chiu ‘chi se² ꜀u*, silver is white, and the pupil of the eye is black—a proverb meaning beware of him, he's watching keenly to cheat you.

垠 ꜀Yin. A bank; a limit, a boundary: in the coll. read *꜀nging*, q. v.: *꜀u ꜀ngüng*, unlimited; *‘kiu ꜀ngüng*, the limits of heaven.

[1]危言 [2]危險 [3]臨危 [4]危症 [5]危急 [6]危在旦夕 [7]玉石 [8]玉成 [9]玉食 [10]玉鏡 [11]玉體 [12]玉展 [13]玉皇 [14]訟獄 [15]獄卒 [16]銀錢 [17]水銀 [18]銀水 [19]銀河 [20]銀絲 [21]銀鞘 [22]銀魚 ○

琨 ꜂Yin. A precious stone, a pebble nearly resembling the jade stone; a stone marked with veins.

嚚 ꜂Ying. The sound of conversation; dull, stupid; to utter incredible words: [1]*ho*꜄ *꜁ngwang ꜀mu ꜁ngŭng*, the father obstinate and the mother stupid.

狺 ꜂Yin. Chin. To bark and fight, as dogs do: *꜀meng ꜀k'eng ꜁ngŭng ꜁ngŭng*, fierce dogs fighting together.

誾 ꜂Yin. To reprove gently; to speak kindly to; pleasant, agreeable, respectful: *꜁ngŭng ꜁ngŭng*, affable, conciliatory.

顒 ꜂ A large head; correct, dignified, portly and imposing; a presence that is commanding, yet benign.

꜁Ngŭng. A coll. word, as in *꜁ngŭng laung*꜄ (also spoken *꜁ngŭ laung*꜄), salted duck's eggs.

(581) Ngwa.

瓦 ꜀ Wa. A tile; a generic term for earthen ware, pottery; the 98th radical: in the coll. read *ngwa*꜄ q. v.: [2]*liong*꜄ *꜀ngwa ꜁chi k'eng*꜄ the joy of having a daughter born; [3]*꜀ngwa ꜀kai*, dispersed, disentangled.

瓦꜄ Wa. Read *꜀ngwa*; coll. *ngwa*꜄: earthen tiles for roofs and walls: [4]*ngwa*꜄ *꜁só*, the lower, or concave, rows of tiles in a roof; [5]*ngwa*꜄ *꜁tĕng*, narrow tiles, as used on the caps of walls; [6]*ngwa*꜄ *p'iĕng*꜄ pieces of tiles; [7]*ngwa*꜄ *꜁yeu*, a tilery; [8]*ngwa*꜄ *꜁tó*, a tool for breaking and shaping tiles; [9]*ch'io*꜄ *ngwa*꜄ *꜀ting*, the tiled roof of a house; [10]*꜀kang ngwa*꜄ to lay tiles; [11]*ngwa*꜄ *꜀hwang ꜀k'i*, to remove tiles (from a roof).

(582) Ngwah.

楇 Read *hwak*꜆; used in the *Paik*꜆ *꜁Ing* for the coll. *ngwah*꜆: the noise of bones, as of the limbs when suddenly moved: *ngwah*꜆ *sioh*꜆ *꜁siăng*, to give a rattling sound, as bones; *ngeh*꜆ *ngeh*꜆ *ngwah*꜆ *ngwah*꜆ to snap and crack, as a pugilist's limbs.

Ngwah꜆. A coll. word, as in *ngwah*꜆ *laung*꜄ to jest, to make sport of; *꜀nŭ ngwah*꜆ *kw'ai*꜄ *꜀lá*, you jest with much gusto; *ngwah*꜆ *sioh*꜆ *taung*꜄ *k'wai*꜄ to joke and tease a while.

(583) Ngwai.

我 ꜀ Wu. O. E. Read *꜀ngó*; coll. *꜀ngwai*: the first person, I, my, mine, me; we, our, ours, us: *꜀ngwai ꜁ki*, mine; [12]*꜀ngwai kauk*꜆ *꜁nĕng*, we, all of us; [13]*꜀ngwai kiĕng*꜄ I perceive, I suppose; [14]*꜁ch'ing ꜀nŭ ꜀na ꜀ngwai*, to say "you" and "I", to talk impertinently.

(584) Ngwak.

齰 Read *k'ik*꜆; used in the *Paik*꜆ *꜁Ing* for the coll. *ngwak*꜆ as in *ngwak*꜆ *ngwak*꜆ *kieu*꜄ a grinding sound of the teeth; a grating noise, as in scraping something hard.

---

[1] 父頑母嚚 [2] 弄瓦之慶 [3] 瓦解○ [4] 瓦槽○ [5] 瓦筒○ [6] 瓦片 [7] 瓦窰 [8] 瓦刀 [9] 厝頂瓦 [10] 蓋瓦○ [11] 瓦反起 [12] 我各人○ [13] 我見○ [14] 稱汝荅我

(585) Ngwang.

刓 园 ꜀ ꜂ Wan. Also read ꜂*ngwong:* to cut off the corners, to pare off, to round; to remove asperities, to equalize, to trim, to smooth: ꜂*ngwang kaĕk*, to clip or rub off corners.

頑 ꜂ Wan. Simple, stupid, dull; immovable, impassible; obstinate, mulish; to push with the head, to butt; unruly, mischievous; lascivious, lusting: [1]꜂*ngwang* ꜂*p'i*, doltish, incapable; [2]꜀*t'ieu* ꜂*ngwang* (coll. ꜀*tieu* ꜂*ngwang*), mulish, captious and perverse; [3]꜂*ngwang* ꜂*tung*, sodomy; COM., [4]꜂*ngwang chauk*, naughty, mischievous; [5]꜂*ngwang* ꜂*tu*, an unruly scholar or apprentice; COLL., [6]꜂*ngwang* ꜂*t'au* ꜂*ngwang* ꜀*nó*, doggedly perverse; very naughty, full of mischief.

玩[2] Wan. Gems to play with, playthings; to play, to sport, to dally with; to trifle, to toy with, to delight in; to ramble about, to divert one's self: [7]*ngwang*[2] ꜀*king*, to enjoy scenery; COM., [8]꜂*iu ngwang*[2] or *ngwang*[2] ꜀*swa*, to ramble and recreate; [9]*ngwang*[2] *uk*, toys, delectable things; COLL., *ngwang*[2] *ngĕü*[2] (or *ĕü*[2]), good to sport with; one who is odd, amusing, or witty.

翫[2] Wan. Similar to the last: to be versed or perfect in; to study till weary of; to do or look at till one is sated.

(586) Ngwi.

꜀***Ngwi.*** A coll. word: the first person, I, we, us, as spoken, instead of ꜀*ngwai*, by natives of the Changloh district, Fookien.

(587) Ngwo.

姽 ꜀ Handsome, excellent, good; weak, slender, delicate: ꜀*wo* ꜀*ngwo*, beautiful, delicate.

囮 ꜂ To translate a foreign speech, to interpret the cries of birds and beasts; to improve, to transform; to decoy, to inveigle; a decoy or stool-pigeon, also called ꜀*neu* ꜂*mui*.

訛 ꜂ Wo. O. E. A fabulous animal supposed to be able to speak and lie; to change speech, to falsify; to promulge error; false, deceitful, lying; to rouse, to move; an ignis fatuus, called [10]꜂*ngwo* ꜀*hwo:* [11]꜂*ngwo* ꜂*ngiong*, idle stories; [12]꜀*i* ꜂*ngwo* ꜂*tiong* ꜂*ngwo*, to retail idle talk, to transmit error.

譌 ꜂ Interchanged with the last: idle rumors, vain and foolish stories, deceptive talk.

啎[2] Wu. To oppose, to run against; rebellious, disobedient; obstinate; undutiful, as to parents.

晤[2] Wu. Light, clear, lustrous; intelligent, perceiving what another says; to be present, to meet with; to explain, to make clear: [13]*miéng*[2] *ngwo*[2] a personal interview; [14]*ngwo*[2] *tói*[2] face to face, op-

---

[1] 頑疲 [2] 刁頑 [3] 頑童 [4] 頑作 [5] 頑徒 ○ [6] 頑頭頑腦 [7] 玩景 ○ [8] 遊玩 ○ [9] 玩物 ○ [10] 訛火 [11] 訛言 [12] 以訛傳訛 [13] 面晤 [15] 晤對

posite; *ngwo*[2] *ˎkó*, to sing in harmony.

誤[2] 悮[2] Wu. To err, to miss, to fail; to deceive, to mislead; to hinder by a mistake; in error, wrong, misled; false, erroneous: COM., [1]*'sek*, *ngwo*[2] to miss, to fail to do; [3]*ngwo*[2] *ˏch'á*, to neglect official business; [3]*ngwo*[2] *ˏsiong*, to wound accidentally; [4]*kwo*[3] *ngwo*[2] or *ch'auk*, *ngwo*[2] an error, a mistake, a fault; [5]*ngwo*[2] *ˏki*, or *ngwo*[2] *'mau*, to fail in time; [6]*ngwo*[2] *seng*[3] mistaken trust; COLL., [7]*ngwo*[2] *chó*[3] to do accidentally; *ngwo*[2] *ˏnëng*, to "fail persons", to leave them helpless, as one does by his death; *ngwo*[2] *tek*, *'ch'ang*, has failed (his family) lamentably!

悟[2] Wo. To arouse one's self so as to perceive clearly; aware of, alive to, noticing, discerning: [8]*'sing* *ngwo*[2] to arouse one's self, to awaken; [9]*kauk*, *ngwo*[2] to catch the idea; [10]*chëü*[2] *ngwo*[2] to bethink one's self; COM., [11]*hwoí*[2] *ngwo*[2] to apprehend, to get a perception of.

寤[2] Wu. Interchanged with the last: to awake from sleep: *ngwo*[2] *me*[2] waking and sleeping.

卧[2] 臥[2] Wo. To rest from work, as servants do; to cease for a while, to intermit care and toil; to go to bed, to recline, to sleep, to doze; to be changed, as one's spirits in sleep: [12]*ngwo*[2] *ˏpung*, a bedroom; [13]*ngwo*[2] *sek*, to rest, to repose; [14]*chó*[2] *ngwo*[2] *pok*, *ˏning*, no ease sitting or lying; [15]*ˏkó ngwo*[2] to "sleep high"—let the world wag; *'ngiong ngwo*[2] to sleep on one's back.

遻[2] To meet with; to be startled by meeting suddenly; obstinate, opposed to, untoward; rebellious, disobedient; to run counter to, to cross another's wishes.

(588) Ngwoh.

玉[2] Yü. Read *ngük*[2]; coll. *ngwoh*[2]: a mineral fit for the lapidary, gems, precious stones; valuable, precious, beautiful, like gems: [16]*ngwoh*[2] *k'e*[3] articles made of precious stones; [17]*ngwoh*[2] *ˏchang*, stone hair-pins; [18]*ngwoh*[2] *ˏpá*, gemmeous ornaments, worn on the person; [19]*ngwoh*[2] *'së*, the imperial seal; [20]*ngwoh*[2] *ˏp'uí*, rough, unfinished gems; [21]*ngwoh*[2] *ˏt'i ˏtó*, the stone-knife-holder, a female ornament for the head; *ngwoh*[2] *ˏsëng ˏliéng ˏk'wang*, stone ear-rings linked in pairs.

獄[2] Yü. Read *ngük*[2]; coll. *ngwoh*[2]: a prison, a jail: *ngwoh*[2] *ˏkwang*, the governor or keeper of a prison, as the *pwo*[3] *ˏt'iäng* and *ˏking ˏt'iäng*, of districts and prefectures are; *ngwoh*[2] *chok*, an under-jailer, a turnkey; *lóh*[2] *të*[3] *ngwoh*[2] to go to hell.

(589) Ngwoí.

外[2] Wai. Outside, without, beyond; another, other, foreign, strange, from abroad; besides, moreover; to reject, to exclude, to put aside; relations by marriage, the wife's relatives: in the coll.

1失誤 3誤傷 5誤期 7誤做 9覺悟 11會悟 13臥息 不寧 16玉器 18玉牌 20玉皮 21玉提刀
2誤差 4過誤 6誤信 8省悟 10自悟 12臥房 14坐臥 15高臥 17玉簪 19玉璽 〇 〇

read *ngié*2 q. v.: COM., [1]*ngwoí*2 *miéng*2 the exterior, the outside; [2]*ngwoí*2 ꜀*kwang*, the provincial officers; [3]*ngwoí*2 ꜀*song*, a daughter's son, a grandson; [4]*ngwoí*2 *mau*2 one's appearance; [5]*ngwoí*2 *kwok*꜀ foreign countries; [6]*ngwoí*2 ꜁*chai*, extra talent—knowledge other than that of books; [7]*'e*2 *ngwoí*2 unexpectedly; [8]*'i ngwoí*2 besides, exclusive of; [9]*ngwoí*2 *'chwi*, from abroad, from other parts, as goods.

瑁2 **Mao.** Read *mwoí*2 in the dictionaries: tortoise-shell, called *tai*2 *ngwoí*2; a mottled, reddish brown and yellowish color: also read *mó*2 q. v.: COM., *tai*2 *ngwoí*2 the tortoise-shell of commerce; *tai*2 *ngwoí*2 ꜁*ma*, a tortoise-shell cat.

(590) Ngwok.

月 **Yüeh.**2 The moon; a moon, a lunar month; monthly; *met.*, round, circular, like the moon; the 74th radical: [10]*ngwok*2 ꜁*lung*, the moon's disk; COM., [11]*ngwok*2 *ngwok*2 monthly; [12]*ngwok*2 *yǎ*2 moonlight nights; [13]*ngwok*2 *sek*꜀ an eclipse of the moon; [14]*'mwang ngwok*2 a month after marriage or childbirth; [15]*ngwok*2 *kiék*꜀ a monthly estimate; [16]*ngwok*2 *twai*2 a month of 30 days; [17]*ngwok*2 *'sieu*, a month of 29 days; [18]*ngwok*2 ꜀*king*, the menses; [19]*song*2 *ngwok*2 the end of pregnancy; *ngwok*2 *pwang*2 the middle of the month; *ngwok*2 *ha*2 *'ló*, term for marriage-brokers; COLL., *ngwok*2 *pah*꜀ a pale, bluish color; *ngwok*2 ꜁*yéng*, full moon; *ngwok*2 *k'iék*꜀ the moon waning; *ngwok*2 *wong*2 a halo about the moon; ꜀*chiáng ngwok*2 the first month; *sioh*2 *a*2 *ngwok*2 *nik*2 one month; *ngwok*2 ꜀*peng* ꜀*tië*, semicircular ponds; *chó*2 *ngwok*2 *le*2 (or ꜀*tong*), to observe a regimen for a month after confinement.

跀 **Yüeh.**2 To cut off the feet; to maim, to distort; distorted: *ngwok*2 ꜁*ing chëök*꜀ to cut off a person's feet.

(591) Ngwong.

原 ꜁**Yüan.** A high, level space, a plateau, a terrace; a waste, a common; the origin, source, root, foundation, beginning; natural, innate; the true state, the proper condition of; originally, primarily; indeed, really, truly; to examine, to trace to the source; to repeat; a repetition, a second, another, again; to forgive, to remit: also read *ngwong*2 q. v.: [20]꜀*tüng* ꜁*ngwong*, Honan; also applied by extension to China; COM., [21]꜁*ngwong 'pwong*, the origin, the original, as ancestors; [22]꜁*ngwong* ꜁*iu*, the causes of; [23]꜁*ngwong chik*2 the family-seat, one's native place; ꜁*ngwong pe*2 *kó*2 plaintiff and defendant; [24]꜁*ngwong 'chio*, the first owner, the proprietor; ꜁*ngwong* ꜁*ching*, extenuating circumstances; ꜁*ngwong 'ch'iu*, the principal, not a substitute; ꜁*ngwong sié*2 *pok*꜀ *tong*2 don't stir it, leave it (undone) just as it was; COLL., ꜁*ngwong* ꜀*pong*, the original lot, genuine goods; ꜁*ngwong 'cha 'cha*, or ꜁*ngwong 'tá 'tá*, in the beginning, the most ancient times; ꜁*ngwong* ꜁*lai se*2 ꜀*chiong wang*2 "so from the

---

[1]外面 [2]外官 [3]外孫 [4]外貌 [5]外國 [6]外才 [7]意外 [8]以外 [9]外水 [10]月輪 [11]月月 [12]月夜 [13]月蝕 [14]滿月 [15]月結 [16]月大 [17]月小 [18]月經 [19]順月 [20]中原 [21]原本 [22]原由 [23]原籍 [24]原主

福州方言拼音字典

first"—i. e., really so; ꜀ngwong ꜀ta ꜀ngwong taing^2 the genuine, dry and hard—i. e., rice not wet to increase its bulk.

源 ꜁Yüan. A spring, a fountain; source, origin, in which sense it is like the last: [1]꜁ngwong ꜁chiong, a fountain; [2]꜁ngwong ʻwong ꜁liu ꜁tiong, flowing from a far source—alluding to ancestry; COM., [3]꜁ngwong ꜀tʻau, a spring, head-waters; [4]ʻing ʻchwi ꜀sü ꜁ngwong, when you drink think of the fountain—never forget a benefactor; [5]꜁ngwong ꜁ngwong ꜁i ꜁lai, to come incessantly, as customers.

嫄 ꜁Yüan. A woman, named [6]꜀Kiong ꜁ngwong, ancestress of Wan-wang and Duke Chow.

螈 ꜁ A species of small lizard, called ꜁ing ꜁ngwong: ꜁ngwong ꜁chang, wild silkworms, which produce no silk.

騵 ꜁Yüan. A bay horse with a white belly.

元 ꜁Yüan. The origin, the commencement, the first cause; the first, the head, the chief; chief, principal, original, primary: COM., [7]꜁ngwong ʻsü, the beginning, first cause; [8]꜁ngwong kʻeʼ the original, vital principle; stamina, constitution; [9]꜁ngwong ꜀tieu, the Mongolian dynasty, A. D. 1280—1368; [10]꜁ngwong ꜀song, a great-great-grandson; [11]꜁ngwong tung^2 new-year's day; [12]꜁ngwong ꜁niéng, the first year of a reign; [13]꜁ngwong pʻwoiʼ (or pʻengʼ) the first or principal wife; [14]꜁ngwong ʻpó, ingots of pure silver; paper-ingots, as burnt to idols; [15]siong^2 ꜁ngwong, [16]꜀tüng ꜁ngwong, and [17]ha^2 ꜁ngwong, festivals on the 15th of the 1st, 7th, and 10th moons; [18]kâ^2 ꜁ngwong, [19]hwoi^2 ꜁ngwong, and [20]chaung^2 ꜁ngwong, the senior wranglers at examinations for the Küjin, Chinsz', and Hanlin, degrees; COLL., ꜁ngwong ꜀éng, dried lichi fruit.

芫 ꜁Yüan. A noxious plant, whose flowers kill fish; hemlock?

袁 𧝝 ꜁Yüan. Long robes; a surname: also read ꜁wong, q. v.: ꜁Ngwong ꜀chiu, a prefecture in the west of Kiangsi.

黿 ꜁Yüan. A fabulous tortoise, made at the creation of heaven and earth: ꜁ngwong piék, a tortoise ten feet in diameter; COM., ꜁ngwong ꜁ngó ꜀kau ꜁lüng, the great tortoise, whale, iguanodon, and dragon.

愿^2 原^2 Yüan. The first of the two often used for the next in the sense of vowing; careful, attentive; good, moral, virtuous; sincere, faithful; devout, reverential: the 2d also read ꜁ngwong, q. v.: COM., [21]ʻhü ngwong^2 to make vows, as in distress; ꜀kiâ ngwong^2 a vow to wear the cangue.

1 源泉 2 源遠流傳 3 源頭 4 飲水思源 5 源源而來 6 姜嫄 7 元始 8 元氣 9 元朝 10 元孫 11 元旦 12 元年 13 元配 14 元寶 15 上元 16 中元 17 下元 18 解元 19 會元 20 狀元 21 許愿

願 Yüan. A large head; to stretch the neck in looking; to hope, to expect, to long for; to wish, to desire; to vow; the object of desire, a wish; a vow; a conscientious promise; each, every: COM., [1]꜀kang ngwong² to be willing, to consent or submit willingly to; [2]꜀sing ꜀kang e' ngwong² a willing spirit; [3]ngwong² che² a written agreement; [4]꜀ching ngwong² to prefer, I would rather; [5]꜀sing ꜂su ngwong² the heart's desire; COLL., [6]ng² ngwong² not willing; [7]꜂k'eu ꜀t'au ngwong² a hasty, thoughtless imprecation; ꜂hü ꜀hu ꜂hü ngwong² to utter vows, as before idols.

(592) O.

惡 Wu. O. ' To hate, to loathe; detestable, abominable; to be ashamed: also read ꜀u and auk, q. v.: [8]o' auk, to hate evil; [9]꜀siu o' shamefaced; ashamed, as to do wrong; COLL., cheng² ꜂k'ó o' very detestable.

塢 Wu. ' A dike, a low rampart; barracks; a fortified camp or place; in the coll. a safe place for boats; a yard or dock where boats are made or repaired: COLL., ꜂tié o' ꜂tié, to enter the cove or dock; [10]꜀sung o' a dry or wet dock; [11]o' ꜂mwi, a ward in the suburbs of Foochow; [12]kieu² o' a sedanmen's establishment.

汙 污 Wu. ' Foul, muddy, as stagnant water; impure, obscene, lewd; to defile, to stain; to debauch: also read ꜀u, q. v.: COM., [13]o' woi' filthy, defiled; COLL., p'ah, o' to become filthy; morally defiled; o' sioh, ꜀wong, a spot, a stain, as on clothes.

瘀 Yü. ' Read ǘ' in the dictionaries: blood settled in a wound or sore, extravasated blood; the blood of parturition, lochial discharges: COLL., o' haik, ng² ꜂k'ó ' ꜀sing nük, má² ꜀sang, if the settled blood is not removed, new flesh will not grow—if the evil is not put away, the good will not be attained.

O'. A coll. word: a share, part, portion, as reserved for one: ꜀chiéng o' a portion of money; o² ꜂chiă o' tioh, ꜂lá, there is a share reserved.

務 Wu. ² To apply the mind to, to use earnest effort, to exert one's self; duty, business, affairs; important, must: [14]sëü² o² one's business; [15]o² ꜂pwong, the important duties; o² ꜂pwong ngiék, to attend to one's own business; [16]o² yeu' very important; [17]꜀kung o² public business; COM., [18]o² pek, indispensable; [19]o² ngwoi² mere show, external accomplishments.

騖 Wu. ² A good horse; to gallop; to run precipitately; violent: [20]꜀ti o² to gallop; to rush headlong.

婺 Wu. ² Name of a star in Capricornus, called [21]o² ꜂nü; [22]o² ho² a woman who maintains her widowhood.

霧 Wu. ² Fog, mist, vapor from the ground, foul exhalations: COM., ꜀hung o² clouds and mist.

1 甘願 2 心甘意願 3 願字 4 情願 5 心所願 6 怀願 7 口頭願 8 惡惡 9 羞惡 10 船塢 11 塢尾 12 轎塢 13 汙穢 14 事務 15 務本 16 務要 17 公務 18 務必 19 務外 20 馳騖 21 婺女 22 婺婦

有 Yu. Read ʻiu; used for the coll. o': to have, to possess; to be, to exist; yes, I have, I did, it is; forms the past tense, has, have; and, in addition: o' ʻa ‚mó? o' ‚a, are there any? yes; [1]ʻyong' yong' ‚tu o' there are all sorts; [2]o' aing' limited; [3]o' pang' sick; [4]o' hwak‚ to have skill or magic art, to have the means of doing; [5]o' ch'ëü' amusing, entertaining, as a show; [6]o' ‚sing ʻhi, pregnant; o' k'e' k'ëük‚ ʻnü seu' I'll anger you—*scil.*, if you refuse compliance; o' wa' ʻkong, to have something to say; to wrangle; [7]o' ‚sing sié' or o' ‚tang ‚tong, can; o' ‚t'au ‚mó ʻmwi, incomplete, unfinished; o' siăh‚ o' tiong' has enough to eat and more; o' ʻhü ‚mó siă' to vow but not thank (the gods); *met.*, to promise but not pay; o' ‚sang ‚mó lang' or o' ch'ek‚ ‚mó paik‚ incomplete, deficient, as said of men or things; o' k'aëng' ‚mó nói' chaung' a hole, but no such thing as creeping into it—a way of relief, but prevented from using it.

(593) Ŏ.

熝 Warm; to warm, to roast, to cook in ashes; to boil, to stew.

炣 Ho. Used in the coll. for the preceding: to cook, to stew; to leave things to simmer over the fire: chak‚ ‚ó, to stew up fragments; ‚ó lang' to stew soft.

痾 O. K'o. Disease, severe sickness; sickness of children from fright; convulsions: [8]ʻk'eu ‚ó, sores about the mouth.

呵 Ho. Wo. To blame, to reprimand, to scold; to be angry with; sound of laughter: also read ‚ó, q. v.

訶 Ho. Used for the preceding: to speak sharply, to speak in a loud and angry tone; to blame, to reprimand.

猗 I. A fierce, strong dog; extended, continuous; beautiful, flourishing; an exclamation, good! fine! to add to; to depend on.

阿 A. E. O. Wo. A mound, an undulating ridge; a river-bank; inclined, tilted; prejudiced; near to; to lean against, to rest on; a beam; to answer, to assent; to yield to one's whims, to flatter, to wheedle; who? what? an exclamation, O! alas! a disjunctive in questions, equivalent to "or" when condition or choice is implied; also a final particle in answers and exclamations, when it is spoken ‚ó, or ó'; but in the coll. ‚a, and a' are more common; also used for ak‚ and ‚i in the coll. q. v.: [9]‚ó ‚sui, who? COM., [10]‚ó ‚mi ‚t'ó huk‚ Amida Budha, often used by bonzes as a devout or polite salutation; COLL., [11]‚ó ‚ka, mule-skin glue or jelly—a famous medicine.

屙 To void excrements; in the coll. to void incontinently: COLL., ‚ó ʻsai ‚ó nieu' to void excrement and urine, as a child while asleep.

‚O. A coll. word: hard, difficult; inconvenient, impolitic: ‚ó chó' hard to do; ʻchiă

[1] 件件都有 [2] 有限○ [3] 有病○ [4] 有法○ [5] 有趣○ [6] 有娠喜○ [7] 有身勢○ [8] 口痾 [9] 阿誰 [10] 阿彌陀佛 [11] 阿膠○

*wa*² *,ó 'kong*, difficult or impolitic to say that!

'襖 Ao. An outer garment, a robe, a gown, a jacket: COM., [1]*,tong 'ó*, a long robe; [2]*,mieng 'ó*, a cotton-wadded gown or jacket; [3]*'ó k'o'* gown and drawers; COLL., [4]*'ó ,lung*, a common garment worn over a robe, an overall.

'懊 Ao. Vexed, angry; to regret; avaricious: [5]*'ó haung*² to hate; COM., [6]*'ó 'nó*, vexed, irritated; COLL., *'ó 'nó ,ki tai*² a vexatious matter.

'娿 '妸 As in *'ó 'nó*, weak, delicate: the graceful gait of a woman. Read *,ó*: undecided.

澳' 澚' Ao. Yü. This and the next three also read *ŭk,*: a bay, a deep bight, an inlet: [7]*ó' ,mwong*, Macao: COM., [8]*ó' ,t'au*, a busy landing or wharf; [9]*ó' ,kio*, and [10]*ó' ,mwong ,kio*, names of two bridges in Foochow.

墺' Ao. Interchanged with the last and the next; a square plat of ground; flat, open ground, as a plateau; a bay, an inlet.

隩' Ao. A bay, an inlet, a cove; a steep cliff, a bank: [11]*ó' 'ŭng*, to secrete: [12]*ó' ,chong*, to store up.

奧' Ao. The south-west corner of a house; retired, deep, remote; recondite, mysterious; to collect, to mix, to be thick: COM., [13]*,ch'ing ó'* deep, abstruse; [14]*ó' mieu*² mysterious, hard to understand.

,呵 Ho. Wo. To interrogate; also to blame, to reprimand; in the coll. a tone of assent, exclamation of surprise, O! Ah! also read *,ó*, q. v.: COLL., *,ó ,ó kieu*² to assent readily, O, yes!

,河 Ho. A river, the Yellow river by way of eminence; a canal, a moat; a wine-vessel: COM., [15]*,t'ieng ,ó*, the Milky Way; [16]*,wong ,ó*, the Yellow river; [17]*,ó 'hai*, rivers and seas; *,ó tok*, or [18]*,ó ,kung 'chung tok*, superintendent of the Yellow river; [19]*,ó ,nang*, Honan; COLL., *,ó ngiáng*² a canal-bank.

啊² A. A lulling sound, a lullaby; a tone of surprise or anger; an exclamation on apprehending the meaning, or when another catches the idea and does a thing properly; COLL., *ó*² *ó*² ah! yes, that's it!

(594) Óh.

Óh,. A coll. word: wise, discreet; clever, sharp, shrewd: *óh, lóh*, wise, shrewd; *óh, chiáh, óh*, very clever, quick of apprehension: *óh, ,nëng tiáh, pah, 'mi ngaung*² *,nëng 'chü lang*² *pwong*² the wise buy white rice, the fools boil wet rice—i. e., wise men are truly economical, while fools are not.

1 長襖 2 棉襖 3 襖褲 4 襖輪 5 懊恨 6 懊惱 7 澳門 8 澳頭 9 澳橋 10 澳門橋 11 隩隱 ○ 12 隩藏 ○ 13 深奧 14 奧妙 15 天河 16 黃河 17 河海 18 河工總督 ○ 19 河南 ○

福州方言拼音字典

學 Read *hok*, ; coll. *ŏh*, : to learn, to practice, to imitate : [1]*ŏh*, *yong*² to imitate a pattern ; [2]*ŏh*, *kung* *t'au*, to learn pugilism ; [3]*ŏh*, *nĕng ch'oi*ʾ to imitate one's words, to learn bad language from others ; [4]*ŏh*, *ngiĕ*² to learn a trade ; [5]*ŏh*, *kwang*, a superintendent of the Siutsai of a prefecture or district, also styled [6]*ŏh*, *sü*, or *ŏh*, *'lŏ* *sü* ; [7]*ŏh*, *seng*, the Siutsai under charge of a superintendent ; [8]*ŏh*, *'teu* (or *mwong* *'teu*), a servant of official business at a superintendent's.

Hsiao. Hsio. Hsüo. Hsüeh.

Ŏh, . A coll. word : as, according to : *ŏh*, *chiong wang*² in this manner, thus, then.

Ŏh, . A coll. word : to tell, to inform against : *ŏh*, *kaĕng*² *sing sang 'kong*, to tell the teacher ; *k'ŏ*ʾ *ŏh*, to go and tell.

(595) Oi.

唉 Read *ai* ; used for the coll. *oi*, as in *oi ŏ* ! an ejaculation of regret or surprise, ah ! oh !

Ai.

畏ʾ To fear, to venerate, to stand in awe of ; to respect, to dread ; to dislike ; fear, awe, devotion, submission : [9]*oi*ʾ *kĕü*² fear, apprehension ; [10]*oi*ʾ *sauk*, shrinking, cowardly ; COM., [11]*oi*ʾ *'siu oi*ʾ *'mwi*, afraid of beginning and end —to dread an undertaking ; [12]*oi*ʾ *sĕü*² afraid of trouble ; [13]*oi*ʾ *ch'eng*² to dread the cold ; COLL., *oi*ʾ *'sieu 'lă* or *oi*ʾ *ch'iu*, bashful, sensitive to shame.

Wei.

慰ʾ To soothe, to console, to comfort ; to pacify, to tranquilize : [14]*oi*ʾ *ong*² a visit of condolence ; [15]*tieu*ʾ *oi*ʾ to mourn, as with the friends of the dead ; COM., [16]*ang oi*ʾ to comfort, to console.

Wei. Yü.

熨ʾ As in *tuk*, *oi*ʾ or [17]*oi*ʾ *t'aik*, to apply plasters to sores : also read *ok*, q. v.

Yü. Yün.

蔚ʾ A sort of southern wood ; luxuriant, rank growth, thick foliage ; finely veined, close-grained, as wood ; numerous, as population : in the coll. read *woi*ʾ q. v. : [18]*ung oi*ʾ deep and close veins ; [19]*seu*ʾ *oi*ʾ beautiful, flourishing.

Wei.

尉ʾ To press smooth ; to tranquilize ; tranquil, at ease, quietly settled ; military officers : [20]*ting oi*ʾ an ancient officer of the palace ; [21]*t'ai*ʾ *oi*ʾ an officer like the modern lieutenant-general ; COM., *hung k'iĕ oi*ʾ the title of a *'siu pe*² or major.

Wei. Yü.

螱ʾ The perfect ant having wings, hence called *hi oi*ʾ the winged ant.

Oi. A coll. word : an exclamation used to call the attention, halloo !

位² To sit erect, as in a gateway ; a place, a seat ; a throne ; a trust, dignity, situation ; to enthrone, to begin to reign ; right, proper, correct ; established ; the room or place occupied by a thing ; a numerative of persons, gentle-

Wei.

[1]學樣 [2]學拳頭 [3]學人嘴 [4]學藝 [5]學官 [6]學師 [7]學生 [8]學斗 [9]畏懼 [10]畏縮 [11]畏首畏尾 [12]畏事 [13]畏凊 [14]慰問 [15]弔慰 [16]安慰 [17]熨貼 [18]文蔚 [19]秀蔚 [20]廷尉 [21]太尉 ○

men: [1]˛lŭng oi² the dragon-seat—imperial throne; [2]sek˛ oi² dethroned; [3]˛teng oi² to ascend the throne; COM., [4]˛sing oi² shrine of an idol; [5]˛sang oi² ek˛ 't'á, three persons in one essence, triune, the Trinity; [6]liék˛ oi²! Sirs! gentlemen! [7]'te' oi² a place, a position; twai² oi² a high seat—place of honor; COLL., sói² oi² reigning, a reign; pek˛ oi² or pek˛ oi² ch'ëü' another place.

胃 膶 Wei. ² The stomach; the 17th zodiacal constellation, three large stars in Musca Borealis: COM., [8]˛pi oi² the stomach; [9]oi² mah˛ the pulse in the right wrist; [10]oi² 'hwo seng² excess of the igneous principle in the stomach—a morbid stomach; [11]k'ëü' oi² 'hwo, to cool the blood, to correct bad humors; kaik˛ sik˛ ˛hwang oi² it turns the stomach; COLL., ˛pi oi² mwoi² ˛k'wi, to have no appetite.

謂 Wei. ² To address, to inform, to speak to; to announce, to report to; to say, to speak of; to send with a message; designates, refers to, is termed: [12]'iu oi² something to be said for it, commendable, excusable; [13]˛u oi² inexcusable; nothing in its favor, of no use; [14]oi² ˛chi wak˛ addressing him, said; [15]oi² ˛chi, it means, it is called; [16]˛hó oi² what is it called? how is it explained?

喟 Wei. ² To lament, to sigh, to groan, as from regret: oi² ˛yong ˛i t'ang' to sigh deeply, to groan.

渭 Wei. ² A tributary of the Yellow River, flowing through Shensi, famous for its turbid waters; the roaring of waves, hurrying, as a torrent; disquieted, perplexed.

猬 蝟 Wei. ² A hedgehog like a rat in size, perhaps a species of tenrec; its spines said to be forked, and its skin stomachic.

爲 Wei. ² For because, wherefore; a motive, a reason; in behalf of, to help, to aid; to take one's part; a sign of the passive, to receive, to suffer; reputed, reckoned, is esteemed; also read ˛ui, q. v.: [17]oi² ˛hó, why? [18]'iu oi² to have a reason or motive for; ˛u oi² unnecessary, quite useless; COM., [19]˛ing oi² because, on account of; [20]oi² kwok˛ ˛kiu ˛hiéng, to seek wise men for the good of the state—sentence over the gate of the provincial examination-hall: COLL., oi² 'mwo oi² 'kiăng, in behalf of wife and children.

(596) Ói.

欲 Yü. ³ Read ük˛; used for the coll. ói³: to wish for, to desire; to like, to be fond of: ói³ tih˛ to wish for; ói³ siăh˛ to wish to eat; ói³ tih˛ sá² to desire much or many; ói³ ˛pá ˛tiong (or ˛liong), fond of making a show; ói³ ˛p'ieu, addicted to licentiousness.

Ói³. A coll. word: an exclamation used in answering to a call, ay!

---

[1]龍位 [2]失位 [3]登位 [4]神位 [5]三位一體 [6]列位 [7]地位 [8]脾胃 [9]胃脈 [10]胃火盛 [11]去胃火 [12]有謂 [13]無謂 [14]謂之曰 [15]謂之〇 [16]何謂 [17]爲何 [18]有爲 [19]因爲 [20]爲國求賢

(597) **Ok.**

鬱, 欝, Yü. Fragrant herbs used in offerings; bushy, thick, luxuriant; irritated, vexed; the feelings suppressed; anxious, careworn; mildewed, putrid: [1]*'ok, ,tŏ,* deeply anxious about; [2]*ok, t'iong'* an herb used in offerings; COM., [3]*ok, kiĕk,* a settled feeling, as of grief or vexation; [4]*ok, mong*[2] deep melancholy; *ok, ok, pok, lok*$_2$ unmitigated grief; *k'e' ok,* smothered feeling; sick from vexation; *,Sing ,tu* and *Ok, 'lwi* (or *Ok,luk*$_2$) the names of two door-divinities—written on doors as charms to keep out evil spirits; *ok, ,chieu,* a lily-like plant, the leaves of which, boiled in wine, are applied to sprains.

熨, Yü. Yün. A smoothing-iron, a flat iron containing coals; to iron, to push or rub, as in ironing: also read *oi'* q. v.: COLL., [5]*ok, 'tau,* a flat-iron; [6]*ok, ,i ,siong,* to iron clothes; [7]*ok, huk*$_2$ *siĕ'* to iron into a fixed shape.

爩, Yü. Smoke; smoke issuing forth.

𢹬, Yü. To bend; twisted, bent: COM., *ok, tik*$_2$ to bend out straight; *ok, ,wang,* to crook, to twist; COLL., *ok, siĕk*$_2$ to break by bending.

屋, Wu. A house, a dwelling; a building; the covering of a carriage: *ok, chek,* the ridge of a roof; [8]*ok, siă'* habitations; COLL., [9]*ch'io' ok,* a house; [10]*ch'io' ok ch'ok, ,chu,* a house to let.

剭, Also read *auk,*: to put to death privately, to execute one in a retired place or private house.

Ok$_2$. A coll. word: to sweep, to brush aside: *ok*$_2$ *,ta,* sweep it dry; *ok*$_2$ *,piĕng,* to sweep to one side.

Ok$_2$. A coll. word: to edge along, to pass gradually on: *ok*$_2$ *,chiă kwo'* to pass along in a sitting posture, as decrepit beggars; *met.*, to shirk payment; to endure patiently; *ok*$_2$ *ĕü*[2] worn away, as a seat by friction; *ok*$_2$ *,kă k'ĕük, siăh*$_2$ beggars going through the street in a sitting posture: *ok*$_2$ *sok*$_2$ to delay, to dally; to lessen by degrees; to hang about, as one does for employment.

(598) **Ong.**

恩, En. Favor, kindness, grace; benefits, obligations; imperial favor; kind, charitable; to favor, to oblige; to love, to be partial to; private, concealed: COM., [11]*seu*[2] *,ong,* to receive favor; [12]*,ong tëüng*[2] *,ü ,sang,* favor great as a mountain; [13]*,ong taik,* kindness, benevolence; [14]*,ong ai*[2] love, grace; conjugal affection; [15]*,ong 'tiĕng,* or [16]*,ong hiĕ*[2] or *,ong tek*$_2$ grace, beneficence; [17]*,ong ,ing,* a benefactor; [18]*,ong ,k'wang,* liberal, magnanimous; [19]*,ong ,k'wo,* an extra examination for the Küjin degree by imperial favor; [20]*,wong ,ong* and *ho*[2] *,ong,* ungrateful; [21]*'kang ,ong,* to feel grateful;

[1]鬱陶 [2]鬱悒 [3]鬱結 [4]鬱悶 [5]熨斗 [6]熨衣裳 [7]熨伏勢 [8]屋舍 [9]厝屋 [10]厝屋出租 [11]受恩 [12]恩重如山 [13]恩德 [14]恩愛 [15]恩典 [16]恩惠 [17]恩人 [18]恩寬 [19]恩科 [20]忘恩 [21]感恩

[1]˓k'wi ˓ong, to show favor, easy with, indulgent.

秧 Yang. Also read ˓yong: the blade of grain; shoots, young rice-plants: COM., [2]˓ong ʻchŭng, rice-plants, sprouts for transplanting.

ʻ影 Ying. Read ʻing: coll. ʻong: a shadow; overshadowing, protecting: [3]ʻong hiéˀ shadowy, indistinct; [4]ʻong kaˀ credit, ability to aid; ʻong kaˀ taĕngˀ his influence is weighty; [5]ʻong ˓siă, an oblique shadow.

揾ˀ 搵ˀ Wên. En. To place the hand on; to dip in the water; to immerse, as in a dye or any liquid: COLL., ongˀ langˀ to wet by dipping; [6]ongˀ ch'oˀ to dip in vinegar.

愠ˀ Wên. Suppressed anger; indignant, wrathy: [7]ongˀ noˀ angry; [8]ongˀ saik, flushed with anger; [9]˓ing pok, ˓ti ˓i pok, ongˀ not feel angry at others' want of just appreciation.

醞ˀ Wên. Fermented spirit, liquor fermented by white and red ferment, the latter imparting a rich red color: [10]ongˀ chik, able to endure; liberally educated, genteel.

蕹ˀ Wêng. Read ˓ung and ʻung; coll. ongˀ as in ongˀ ch'aiˀ name of a vegetable, greens.

˓行 Hang. Hsing. Read ˓heng; coll. ˓ong: a hong, a warehouse, a godown; a large shop, a wholesale establishment: ˓ong hoˀ or ˓ong ˓ka, hongs; [11]˓ta ˓ong, a tea-hong; [12]ngiéˀ ˓ong, the deliberations of a guild; ˓ong ˓kié, the regulations of a hong; [13]˓ong ʻiu or ˓ong ˓tŭng ʻiu, fellow tradesmen, those of the same guild; [14]˓ong ˓ching ˓t'ĕng ˓t'ĕng ˓kwong, thoroughly acquainted with the current prices; [15]˓ong táˀ a "class term," the distinctive name of those of the same generation in a family or clan—derived from eulogistic sentences in ancestral halls (when the clan has such) and used as prefixes or suffixes in the names of the individuals of the clan; [16]pwong ˓sing miéh, chéˀ ˓ong táˀ what is your class-term? ˓nu ˓cheng chéˀ ˓ong táˀ my class-term is ˓Cheng.

˓Ong. A coll. word: a long time; lasting, enduring, continuing long: chengˀ ˓ong, a very long time; ʻchi ˓ong or ʻchi ʻmang ˓ong, thus long!

˓Ong. A coll. word, as in ˓sai ˓ong, a sandy beach — the same as ˓sai ˓hong, q. v.

運ˀ Yün. To revolve, to turn, to move in a circuit; to go in an orbit, to gyrate; the course of nature; to travel around; to transport; a revolution, a period of 5 years; constant use; to adapt to use; length from north to south; turn, chance, calculations and conjunctions in a horoscope; luck, lot, a run, times: [17]˓t'iéng ongˀ motions of the heavens; *met.*, dynastic changes; COM., [18]ongˀ tongˀ revolutions in nature; to move, to go about; ongˀ ˓kwang, to carry a coffin home; ongˀ ˓liong,

[1]開恩 [2]秧種 [3]影戲 [4]影駕 [5]影斜 [6]揾醋 [7]愠怒 [8]愠色 [9]人不知而不愠 [10]醞藉 [11]茶行 [12]議行 [13]行友 [14]行情通通光〇 [15]行第 [16]本身也字行第 [17]天運 [18]運動

to transport soldiers' rations; [1]ong² so² destiny, fate, allotment; [2]che² ong² one's horoscope; che² ong² song² a lucky conjunction; [3]꜀si ong² times, stated lot; ꜂ong² k'e² or ong² ꜀tu, one's luck, run, times; [5]kwo² ong² to come to a new horoscope period of 5 years; [6]ch'ok꜆ ong² to reach a happy turn, to become prosperous; [7]ong² ëüng² to adapt to its use; the usage of (words); COLL., sioh꜆ che² ong² ngo² ꜀niéng, a horoscopic period is five years; á² ꜂hieu tek꜆ ong² ëüng² to know the proper use, as of a character.

問² Mên. To demand, to exact; to ask, to search into, to inquire of or about; to examine a case, to convict, to give sentence; to clear up doubts; a command, order, mandate: [8]ong² ꜀ang or ong² haiu² to inquire after another's health; [9]ong² nang² to ask an explanation of difficulties, to put hard questions; [10]ong² che² to ascertain the lineage — as of a girl, when betrothing; [11]ong² ꜀kung, transported to the garrisons for crime; [12]ong² ꜂k'iéng, exiled to the colonies; COM., [13]ong² tak꜆ question and answer; a dialogue, a catechism; [14]꜂i ꜂k'eu ong² ꜀sing, consult your own mind or feelings; ong² ꜀sing ꜀hó ꜂ǜng, ask yourself how harsh (your treatment is).

韻² 韵² Yün. Sounds rhyming in their tones; two even, or two oblique, tones; rhyme; the rhyming word; a line of poetry; a harmony, a chord: COM., [15]꜀ing ong² a chord; [16]ak꜆ ong² to make a rhyme; [17]hiék꜆ ong² rhyming; [18]꜀ping ong² rhymes in the even tones; [19]chah꜆ ong² rhymes in the oblique tones; [20]꜀si ong² a book of rhyming characters; COLL., ꜂chau ong² failing to rhyme, discordant.

紊² Wên. Tangled, as thread; confused, intricate, involved; to embroil, to confuse: pok꜆ ꜀ǜng ong² to disallow confusion—as in human relations.

汶² Wên. A river in Shantung, flowing west into the Grand Canal, near Wênshang hsien: ong² ong² contumely, disgrace.

暈² Yün. A halo round the sun or moon; the obscurity of a fog; dense, thick; to condense: in the coll. read wong² q. v.: ngwok꜆ ong² halo round the moon.

鄆² Yün. A city in ancient Lu, now the district of Yünch'êng in Shantung; a village in Shansi.

(599) Pa.

巴 ꜀ Pa. An ancient principality in the southeastern part of Sz'chuen; a sign of the optative, O that! would, would that! [21]꜀Pa sük꜆ a name still applied to Sz'chuen; [22]꜀Pa ꜀ling, a district in Hunan; [23]꜀pa ꜀sié, a python; COM., ꜀pa ꜀tiong, a lottery-rendezvous—usually called ꜀hwa hwoi² ꜀tiong; ꜀pa pok꜆ taik꜆ or ꜀pa pok꜆ ꜀neng kaiu² O that I had! how greatly I desire! COLL., ꜀pa kiék꜆ to strive to gain favor, to flatter; ꜀pa ꜂chiong,

[1]運數 [2]字運 [3]時運 [4]運氣 [5]過運 [6]出運 [7]運用 [8]問安 [9]問難 [10]問字 [11]問軍 [12]問遣 [13]問答 [14]以口問心 [15]音韻 [16]押韻 [17]叶韻 [18]平韻 [19]仄韻 [20]詩韻 [21]巴蜀 [22]巴陵 [23]巴蛇

the palm of the hand ; ˏˏ*pa* ʻ*kiăng töh*, small lotteries.

吧 ʻPa. Dumb; large mouthed; the babbling of infants: ʻ*a* ˏ*pa*, dumb; [1]ˏ*pa* ˏ*nga*, to open the mouth wide.

疤 ˏPa. A disease of the joints; a scar, a cicatrix; in the coll. a hard crust: COM., [2]ˏ*pa* ˏ*hong*, mark of a wound; a scar, a cicatrix; COLL., ˏ*pa* ʻ*niu*, a raised scar; ʻ*tiăng* ˏ*pa*, the crust formed in a cooking-pan; *pwong*ʾ ˏ*pa*, crust of boiled rice.

羓 ˏPa. A sort of dried meat: COLL., [3]ˏ*ngu nŭk*ˎ ˏ*pa*, strips of dried beef, as offered to "Measure-mother".

豝 ˏPa. A sow; a two-year old hog; a large hog; dried meat, in which sense interchanged with the preceding.

舥 Pa. A floating bridge; it is usually made of boats.

葩 ˏPʻa. The flower or blossom of a plant, corol, inflorescence; flowery, elegant, as an essay: ˏ*hang* ˏ*pa*, an unopened flower.

芭 ˏPa. The banana, the plantain: COM., [4]ˏ*pa* ˏ*chieu* ʻ*kwo*, plantains; ˏ*pa* ˏ*chieu* ˏ*ping*, plantain-shaped vases: [5]ˏ*pa tau*ʾ a leguminous plant having strong, cathartic properties, the croton tiglium.

笆 ˏPa. A spinous species of bamboo: COM., [6]ˏ*lie* ˏ*pa*, a fence of bamboo-wattles.

鈀 ˏPa. A war chariot; the defense or guard of a chariot; a drag, a five-toothed harrow, or rake; also the long, sharp point of an arrow: in the coll. read ˏ*pa*, q. v.

把 ʻPa. To hold, to grasp, to seize; to take for the purpose of using; a numerative of things held in the hand, as a fan, a knife, an umbrella; also of a bundle, handful, faggot, &c.; used in the Court dialect in the sense of with, a cause; to consider or regard as, having, for; the sign of the accusative of the following noun: COM., [7]ʻ*pa* ˏ*tʻi*, to hold fast, to keep securely; [8]ʻ*pa* ʻ*siu*, to keep, to maintain; [9]ʻ*hwi* ʻ*pa*, a torch; [10]ˏ*chʻa* ʻ*pa*, bundles of wood; [11]ʻ*pa* ʻ*chung*, a centurion, an ensign; [12]ʻ*pa* ˏ*nga*, a bailiff or sergeant in a yamun: [13]ʻ*pa* ˏ*mwong*, a door-keeper; [14]ʻ*pa hié*ʾ juggler's tricks, sleights of hand; COLL., *sioh*ˎ ʻ*pa* ˏ*tó*, a knife, a sword; *pʻah*ˎ ʻ*pa sek*ˎ a mountebank, a posture-maker; *met.*, one who is adroit in money-making; [15]ʻ*pa pang*ʾ "grasp the handle", to have something to hold by, proof, evidence; ˏ*sing* ˏ*kang* ʻ*pa tiăng*ʾ *tiăng*ʾ to keep the mind unmoved; ˏ*ma sioh*ˎ ʻ*pa kang*ʾ "catch a sweat"—to undertake what is difficult or hazardous.

飽 ʻPao. Read ʻ*pau*; coll. ʻ*pa*: full, satisfied, sated: [16]*siăh*ˎ ʻ*pa* ʻ*lau*, have eaten enough; [17]ʻ*pa nëŭ*ʾ sated, as with fat things; [18]ʻ*pa yéng*ʾ satisfied, desire fully gratified; ʻ*pa* ˏ*leng*, cloyed, rejecting food, as a child does; ʻ*pa pok*, a full stomach.

---

[1]吧呀 [2]疤痕 [3]牛肉羓 [4]芭蕉果 [5]芭豆 [6]籬笆 [7]把持 [8]把守 [9]火把 [10]柴把 [11]把總 [12]把衙 [13]把門 [14]把戲 [15]把柄 [16]食飽了 [17]飽飫 [18]飽厭

‘*Pa*. A coll. word, as in ‘*pa* ‘*lang* ‘*ku*, a small hand-drum with one or two pellets attached, which are caused to strike the drum by a rapid motion of the hand; it is used by those who peddle small articles in exchange for old rags, &c.

‘*Pa*. A coll. word: a prefix equivalent to how, and implying a negative: ‘*pa tak*, ‘*k‘ing*, how can he assent! — he will of course be unwilling.

‘*Pa*. A coll. word: over, excess: *pah*, ‘*pa* ˌ*chiéng*, a hundred cash and over; *sek*$_2$ ‘*pa nik*$_2$ over ten days.

‘*Pa*. A coll. word, for which the next, read ‘*pa*, may be used: a target, the bull's eye: *sioh*$_2$ *tioh*$_2$ ‘*pa* ‘*lá*, to hit the target (with the arrow); *chiéng*’ *sioh*$_2$ *má*^{2} *kau*’ ‘*pa*, the discharged arrow does not reach the mark.

弝’ Pa. The part of the bow grasped by the hand.

霸’ Pa. **伯’** Pai. Po. To reign by terror and force; to incroach upon, to usurp; a tyrant, a usurper: [1]*pa*’ ˌ*wong*, a valiant prince or leader; the 2d also read *paik*, q. v.: COM., [2]‘*ngu pa*’ the five superior princes, who engrossed power in the Chow dynasty; [3]*pa*’ *tô*^{2} to rule by force; overbearing; [4]*pa*’ *chiéng*’ to incroach on, to infringe upon another's rights; [5]ˌ*kiong pa*’ to usurp violently; COLL., *pa*’ ‘*king* ‘*king*, to seize and hold persistently.

灞’ Pa. A small tributary of the Wai river near Si-ngan-fu in Shensi.

欛’ Pa. The handle or hilt of a sword or knife: [6]*pa*’ *peng*’ a handle; *met*., authority, way of acting.

壩’ **垻’** Pa. An embankment or pier to restrain waters; name of many towns on the Yellow River, so called from their position near levees: COM., [7]‘*tëük*, *pa*’ to build levees; COLL., *chôh*, *pa*’ to fill broken places in levees; [8]*pa*’ *pauk*, the levee has burst.

靶’ Pa. The reins; the part of the reins or bridle held by the hand; the dashboard of a carriage.

***Pa*’.** A coll. word, as in ˌ*pa pa*’ ‘*cheu*, or ˌ*hwang* ˌ*pa pa*’ a species of black bird, a grackle or minor; the natives clip its tongue and teach it to talk; ˌ*pa pa*’ ‘*cheu t‘ié*’ ˌ*nëng* ˌ*siâng*, the grackle imitates the human voice.

***Pa*’.** A coll. word, as in ˌ*pa pa*’ the penis.

ˌ鈀 Pa. Read ˌ*pa*; coll. ˌ*pa*: a trident: ˌ*pa tak*, a sort of rake or hoe, having five iron teeth.

ˌ笆 Pa. A rake; COLL., ˌ*pa chá*’ a kind of bamboo rake, the teeth of which are bent by heating.

---

1 霸王 2 五霸 3 霸道 ○ 4 霸占 ○ 5 强霸 ○ 6 欛柄 ○ 7 築壩 8 壩剝

杷 ˛Pa. P'a. A beetle, or heavy hoe, to break clods and level fields; a rake to collect straw: COM., *˛pi ˛pa*, the loquat (Eriobotrya japonica), a common fruit.

琶 ˛P'a. A guitar: COM., [1]*˛pi ˛pa*, the Chinese guitar; it is pear-shaped and has four strings.

爬 ˛P'a. To scratch; to crawl, to creep; to rake up, to claw; to climb, to clamber; a scratcher; a pick: COM., [2]*˛pa ˛ch'iong*, to climb a wall; *met.*, to cut out a go-between, get his place and fees surreptitiously; [3]*˛pa ˛siâng*, to climb a city wall; COLL., [4]*˛pa siong²* to scratch an itching place; [5]*˛pa pwong²* to eat rice with chopsticks; [6]*˛pa ˊk'i ˛li*, to rise after a fall; [7]*˛pa ˛sai ˛ka*, to appropriate to private use, to embezzle; [8]*˛pa ˛t'au wak, nge²* to scratch the head and ears, as in thinking.

扒 ˛P'a. To pull, to pluck up; to break, to divide; in the coll. interchanged with the last: COLL., *˛pa siék,* (or *tiék,*), paddles, as of a dragon-boat; *˛pa pong² tó²* to rake up refuse; *˛pa ˊpó*, to rake for valuables, as amid ruins; *ˊpiéng ˛pa*, a flat pin, or head-ornament.

˛Pa. A coll. word, as in *˛pa lak, ˛t'au*, to shake the head, as in refusing; *˛pa lak, ˛sai*, the hair disheveled; *ˊsó ˛sié ˛pa lak, sioh, a²* give the key a turn.

˛Pa. A coll. prefix, as in *˛pa pa²* the penis; *˛pa pa² ˊcheu*, the grackle or minor; *˛pa pah*, uncle!—a familiar compellation in addressing elders.

˛Pa. A coll. word, as in *a² ˛pa*, the chin—the same as *a² ˛hai*, q. v.

罷² Pa. To suffice, to cease from, to break off; to finish, to quash; to strike for higher wages; enough, no more; a final particle, meaning that will do; used in the coll. term for father: also read *˛p'i*, q. v.: [9]*pa² ˊlieu*, enough! stop at that! [10]*pa² ˊch'iu*, to stop work; COM., [11]*pa² chek, ˛ui ˛ming*, to be dismissed from office and become a citizen; [12]*pa² ch'e²* to shut the shops, as in a panic; [13]*pa² ˊk'ó*, to stop the examinations, as when the students refuse to attend; COLL., *pa² ˛ló pa² ˛ló*, enough! that will do! *pa² ˛i k'ó²* away with him! be quit of him! *pa² ˊná*, parents; *˛long pa²* (spoken *˛nong ma²*), father.

爸² Pa. Read *ˊpó;* may be used in the coll. for *pa²* as in [14]*pa² ˊná*, father and mother, parents; *ak, pa²* father!—a term used by southern people.

耙² P'a. Also read *pa²*: a harrow with one row of teeth, guided by a handle: COLL., [15]*pa² ˛ch'eng*, to harrow the fields; *˛kié pa²* or [16]*˛kiâ pa²* a harrow; *˛kié pa² ˊk'i*, harrow-teeth.

跁² P'a. To walk irresolutely; to squat, to crouch, to sit cross-legged; to creep, to crawl, as children, in which sense the same as *˛pa* in the coll.: [17]*pa² ˛k'i*, a dwarf.

[1]琵琶 [2]爬墻 [3]爬城 [4]爬癢 [5]爬飯 [6]爬起來 [7]爬私家 [8]爬頭挖耳 [9]罷了 [10]罷手 [11]罷職為民 [12]罷市 [13]罷考 [14]爸奶 [15]耙田 [16]枷耙 [17]跁跂

(600) **Pá.**

睥 ʿPi. Read *pe*ʾ; used for the coll. *ˏpá*, as in [1] *ˏpá ˏsá* (or *ˏpá ˏsá*), also *ˏpá ˏlá ˏsá* and *ˏpá ˏlá ˏsié*, to look askance, to turn and look; *ˏpá ʿlá* (or *ʿleng*) *ʿngá*, to leer, to look angrily from the corner of the eye.

ʿ擺 Pai. Read *ʿpai*; used for the coll. *ʿpá*, as in *ʿpá ʿpá*, or *ʿpi ʿpá*, to strut, to swagger; to wag, to whisk: *ˏyeu ʿpá*, a swaggering gait; *ʿpá ˏli ʿpá kʻóʾ* to strut to and fro; *ˏyeu ˏtʻau ʿpá ʿmwí*, to shake the head and wag the tail—a strutting coxcomb; *ʿpá ˏngüng ˏiu*, to dip in melted silver, to give (an article) a silver-wash.

*Pá*ʾ. A coll. word: a corruption of *pai*ʾ (to worship), as in *ʿlá ˏtieu pá*ʾ the ceremony of bowing, as before certain idols in a street-procession.

牌 ˏPʻai. A shield, a buckler; a signboard; a tablet, memorandum; a government-notice; a warrant, a passport, a port-clearance; a medal, a token, a mittimus, a writ; dominoes, playing-cards: COM., [2] *ʿhwí ˏpá*, an express; [3] *ˏpá ˏhwong*, a portal, a sort of wooden gateway — marking limits in the streets, before yamuns, &c.; [4] *ˏsing ʿchü ˏpá* (coll. *ˏpá tʻóʾ*) the ancestral tablet; [5] *ˏyeu ˏpá*, a policeman's pass or token — worn at the girdle; [6] *ˏpá pʻieu*ʾ a warrant to arrest; [7] *ʿsiong ˏngüng ˏpá*, a silver-medal, as a reward to soldiers; [8] *ˏpá ngiăh*ˎ (coll. *ˏpá ʿpeng*) tablets, as in temples and over the doors of graduates; [9] *ˏting ˏpá*, rattan-shields; [10] *ˏchieu ˏpá*, a signboard; [11] *kauk*ˎ *ˏpá*, dominoes; [12] *ʿchai ˏpá*, playing-cards; [13] *ˏpá ˏhwa*, lists of students at the examinations; COLL., *pʻah*ˎ *ˏpá*, to play cards; *ʿchai ˏpá sioh*ˎ *ho*ʾ a set of cards.

棑 ˏPʻai. Read *ˏpai*; coll. *ˏpá*: a float, a raft: *chʻeu*ʾ *ˏpá*, a raft of timber; *lo*ʾ *ˏsi ˏpá*, a fishing-cormorant float.

排 ˏPʻai. To arrange in order, to place properly; to make a show; to push open; a row; a set out: COM., [14] *ˏpá liék*ˎ or [15] *ˏpá siék*ˎ to arrange; [16] *ˏpá ka*ʾ an imperial display or cortege; *met.*, to display one's self, to appear important; [17] *ˏpá tó*ʾ an official retinue; [18] *ˏpá nang*ʾ *ʿkai ˏhung*, to settle people's difficulties; [19] *ˏpá pwo*ʾ or *ˏpá ʿta*, to set in order; [20] *ˏpá ˏtiong*, or *ˏpá ˏliong*; to dress and show one's self, make a swell; [21] *ˏpá teng*ʾ or *ˏpá toi*ʾ military ranks, files of soldiers; [22] *ˏpá tóh*ˎ or *ˏpá ʿchang töü*ʾ to lay a table; *ˏpá kauk*ˎ the ribs, as of pork; COLL., *ˏpá ko*ʾ to become old, as by long standing; *ˏpá ˏhong*, the order of ages, as of brothers; *ˏpá ˏpá ʿli liăh*ˎ to sit closely in a row.

誹 ˏPʻai. Read *ʿpʻi* and *ˏpai*; coll. *ˏpá*, as in *ˏpá paung*ʾ to slander, to backbite — the same as *ˏpai paung*ʾ q. v.

---

1 睥西 2 火牌 3 牌坊 4 神主牌 5 腰牌 6 牌票 7 賞銀牌 8 牌額 9 籐牌 10 招牌 11 骨牌 12 紙牌 13 牌花 14 排列 15 排設 16 排駕 17 排道 18 排難解紛 19 排布 20 排場 21 排陣 22 排桌

叭 Pa. Read *paik*, or *p'aik*,; used for the coll. *pá*: a final particle like *mó*, in questions answered by yes or no: *tang k'ó' pá*, now shall we go?

Pá. A coll. word, as in *pá 'leng*, or *pá 'leng p'ok*, to invert, to turn over; *pá laing'* to reverse or invert; to contradict one's self.

(601) Paëk.

北 Pei. Po. Pu. The north; to be conquered, to flee; to oppose, perverse: [1]*'pai' paĕk*, defeated; COM., [2]*paĕk, hwong* or [3]*paĕk, sié'* or [4]*paĕk, piĕng*, the northern regions, a north direction; [5]*paĕk, king*, Peking; [6]*paĕk, 'tau*, the Dipper; [7]*paĕk, siong'* to go to (the examinations at) Peking; [8]*paĕk, kik*, the north pole; [9]*paĕk, 'k'au ngwoi'* beyond the Great Wall; [10]*paĕk, 'ngu 'seng*, the five northern provinces; [11]*sá paĕk*, north-west; COLL., *paĕk, mah*, northern wheat — used medicinally; *paĕk, k'ah*, traders from the north; *paĕk, ka tiong p'ah, 'kung 'tau*, you'll turn somersault at the north execution-ground — used as an imprecation.

(602) Pah.

百 Pai. Po. Read *paik*,; coll. *pah*,: a hundred: [12]*pah, sang'* the hundred surnames—the people: [13]*pah, hwoi'* "hundred years old" *met.*, to die, as applied to the aged; [14]*pah, nik*, the hundred days—funeral rites 100 days after decease; *pah, 'pa*, or [15]*pah, siong'* or *sioh, pah, ling*, over a hundred; [16]*pah, ka sang'* a book of surnames; [17]*sioh, pah, wang'* a million.

伯 Pai. Po. Read *paik*,; coll. *pah*,: a father's elder brother, an uncle; a senior, an elder, a superior: [18]*chĕük, pah*, paternal uncles; [19]*ek, pah*, eldest paternal uncle; uncle! a familiar compellation; [20]*pah, kung*, a grandfather's eldest brother, great uncle; [21]*twai' pah*, and *pah, 'ang*, a husband's elder brother and elder brother's wife.

柏 Pai. Po. Read *paik*,; coll. *pah*, as in *'piĕng pah*, the juniper; the arbor vitae.

擘 Pai. Po. Read *p'ek*,; used for the coll. *pah*,: to open, to break apart, to break into pieces; [22]*pah, p'wai'* to break up; *pah, naung'* to break small, to comminute; *pah, lang' peng*, to break in two; *k'iĕng pah*, to clutch and pull at, as children do; *pah, mwong pah, ho'* to keep opening and shutting the doors.

Pah,. A coll. word: to tie, to fasten together; also in other senses, as below: *pah, kauk*, to fasten together frame-work, as of kites or lanterns; *pah, 'chai yeu'* to make paper-kites; *pah, ch'oi'* to gape; *pah, hai*, to "drop the chin"—i. e., to bawl, to scream; *pah, nang'* to toil, to drudge.

澤 Chai. Tsĕ. A coll. word, as in *pah, mieu* (read *Tĕk, mieu*), the name of a village beyond the south channel of the Min, where

[1]敗北 [2]北方 [3]北勢 [4]北邊 [5]北京 [6]北斗 [7]北上 [8]北極 [9]北口外 [10]北五省 [11]西北 [12]百姓 [13]百歲 [14]百日 [15]百上 [16]百家姓 [17]一百萬 [18]叔伯 [19]一伯 [20]伯公 [21]大伯 [22]擘破

福州方言拼音字典

the worship of the god [1]*Ngu ʻhiěng ˏkung* originated.

白 Pai. Po. Read *pek₂*; coll. *pah₂*: a white color; an unlucky hue, pertaining to mourning; disinterested, freely; vain, fruitless; only, merely: [2]*pah₂ ch'á' ch'á'* very white; *pah₂ liă' liă'* very pale, as one's face; [3]*pah₂ ˏmong ˏmong*, whitish and somber, dusky, hazy; [4]*pah₂ tak*, a dove, a pigeon; [5]*pah₂ meng'* a white face—a prostitute; *met.*, one who makes a dear purchase; [6]*pah₂ ˏnĕng*, an albino; [7]*pah₂ ʻchü*, to boil it without seasoning; [8]*păh₂ siăh₂* to eat gratuitously; to eat a single dish without condiments; *pah₂ che'* words used for the sound, not the sense; *pah₂ che' ˏsi*, a rythmical coll. satire, a pasquinade; *pah₂ pah₂ chó'* to do vainly or without profit; *pah₂ lo'* "white dew"—the 15th solar term; *pah₂ siĕng' ˏt'u*, a fine white clay used in plaster, cement, and porcelain; *pah₂ pah₂ ch'ĕü' ˏchiă kwo'* only looked at it and passed on—unable to buy it; *ʻk'eu pah₂* the spoken parts of a play; *kó' pah₂* a notice; *pah₂ ˏting* (or *ˏsing*), one without a degree, a commoner.

(603) Pai.

擺 Pai. To spread out, to expose, to arrange; to move, to shake; to strut, to swagger; to turn, as a rudder in steering: in the coll. read *ʻpá*, q. v.: *ʻpai pwo'* to spread out, to arrange; COM., [9]*yeu ʻpai*, to strut and swing the hands; [10]*ʻpai ʻch'iu*, the arms of a grave; in the coll. to stride so as to turn, as the leading sedanman calls out to his fellow; COLL., *ʻpai twai'* turn to the right; *ʻpai ʻsieu*, turn to the left.

捭 Interchanged with the last: to throw down; to strike the hands together; to ruin, to destroy.

誹 Fei. Read *ˏpai*; coll. *ʻpai*, as in [11]*ʻpai paung'* to slander, to backbite; [12]*ʻpai ch'e' ʻkwi*, one who spoils a sale by officious talk.

跛 Po. Read *ʻp'ó*; used for the coll. *ʻpai*, in imitation of coll. mandarin: lame in the feet, crippled: [13]*ʻpai ˏchü*, a cripple.

ʻPai. A coll. word, as in *ʻpai pwói'* unlucky, unfortunate, as in health, trade, &c.

拜 Pai. To bow, to show honor to; to make an act of courtesy, obeisance, or worship; to worship religiously; to visit, to salute; a visit, salaam, obeisance; to salute as a superior: [14]*pai' ʻhwong*, to pay a visit; [15]*pai' hó'* to congratulate one; COM., [16]*tong' ʻsiu pai'* "with respectful salutations"—a phrase on cards; [17]*pai' ʻpwong* or [18]*pai' chiek*, to bow to the memorial, as done before transmitting it; [19]*ʻlá pai'* to pay divine honors; worship, reverence; [20]*ˏhuí pai'* to return a visit; [21]*pai' t'auk*, to intrust one to do; *pai' hwói'* official visits, as between those of the same rank; *pai' ˏtong*, to "worship in the hall"—to bow to heaven, earth, and ancestors, as the

[1]五顯公 [2]白茈 樓樓 [3]白茈 茈 [4]白鴿 ○ [5]白面 [6]白仸 [7]白煮 [8]白食 [9]搖擺 [10]擺手 [11]誹謗 [12]誹市 鬼 [13]跛子 [14]拜 訪 [15]拜賀 [16]頓 首 拜 [17]拜本 [18]拜摺 [19]禮拜 [20]回拜 [21]拜託

ALPH. DICT. 84

bride and groom do; 'pai' siong' a prime minister; *met.*, prime, capital, as a full, round price; COLL., pai' 'nü chó' ,sing ,sang, I salute you as my teacher! pai' 'pa, to swear to be brothers, to vow lasting friendship.

湃 P'ai. The sound of a torrent or dashing waves: ,p'ang pai' the roar of waters.

徘 ,P'ai. To walk about, to run to and fro: ,pai ,hui, to walk back and forth irresolutely.

俳 ,P'ai. Used for the last: to walk irresolutely; dissipation: ,pai ,iu, amusements; plays, shows, sports.

排 ,P'ai. To place, to dispose, to arrange in order; to make a show; to shove, to push; a row, a rank, a file: in the coll. read ,pá, q. v.: ,pai 'chá, to push and elbow.

棑 ,P'ai. A raft, a float: in the coll. read ,pá, q. v. Read pai': the name of a tree; a thwart piece of wood at the stern of a boat.

誹 ,Fei. To speak against, to slander, to defame, to backbite: in the coll. read 'pai and ,pá, q. v.: COM., ,pai paung' to slander.

粺 Pai. Good, white rice, hulled and thoroughly cleansed by pounding.

稗 Pai. Tares, cockle; a noxious weed having a small grain and resembling rice; *met.*, hypocrites, dissemblers; used for p'á' in the coll. q. v.: pai' 'ch'ó, darnel; pai' siok, vicious novels; pai' hwang' a huckster.

憊 Pei. Debilitated, weak, exhausted: ,p'i pai' to suffer from total loss of strength.

唄 A term in Budhist books for praise; to laud, the sound of reciting prayers.

敗 Pai. To subvert, to destroy; defeated in battle; broken, ruined, spoiled, as affairs or things; corrupt, tainted: COM., 'ek, pai' ,tu té' a complete loss, or wreck, as of property; a total rout; pai' hwai' ruined, wrecked; pai' 'liu ,chang ,hwa, "a ruined willow and faded flower"; *met.*, lost beauty or chastity; pai' chiong' a defeated general; pai' heng' pleasure spoiled, as by interruption; lóh, pai' ruined, wasted; COLL., pai' ,ong ,ching, to derange prices, as by underselling; pai' 'mwoi 'kiäng, a son who makes a final wreck, a spendthrift, scape-grace; pai' t'ah, t'ah, to make "a clean sweep," to ruin utterly.

(604) Paik.

百 Pai. Po. A hundred; a round number, the whole of a class or sort; many, numerous, all: in the coll. read pah, q. v.: COM., paik, 'ch'ó, all kinds of grasses; paik, ,pwang, all sorts of; paik, hak, ,hwa, the lily; paik, hak, 'hung, arrowroot; paik, seu' ,tu, a scroll with a hundred, or more, forms of the

1拜相 2徘徊 3俳優 4誹謗 5稗草 6稗說 7稗販 8疲憊 9一敗塗地 10敗壞 11敗柳殘花 12敗將 13敗興 14落敗 15敗行情 16敗尾仔 17百草 18百般 19百合花 20百合粉

word *seu'* —presented on birthday-anniversaries; *paik, sĕü' tai' kek,* great luck in every thing! [1]*paik, hwak, paik, tëüng'* a hundred shots a hundred hits—always successful; [2]*paik, ,u ek, sek,* not a miss in a hundred times—makes no blunders.

佰 Pai. Used for the last: a hundred men; a string of a hundred cash: *paik, ,hu 'tiong,* a centurion.

伯 Pai. Po. A father's elder brother, an uncle; a senior, an elder, a superior; the third in order of nobility, an earl: also read *pa'* and in the coll. *pah,* q. v.: [3]*paik, tëüng'* brothers; [4]*paik, chëük,* paternal uncles; [5]*,hung ,sing 'ü paik,* the gods of Wind and Rain; COM., [6]*paik, ho'* and [7]*paik, 'mu,* a paternal elder uncle and uncle's wife; [8]*paik, chiok,* an earldom.

栢 柏 Pai. Po. The cypress, the cedar; great, large; to urge, to impel: in the coll. read *pah,* q. v.: [9]*'piéng paik,* the juniper (Cupressus thyoides); the arbor vitae; [10]*paik, ,hi,* a heroine of the Yuen dynasty—styled in the coll. *pah, ,kié 'sieu 'chiă* (White-fowl-sister), because "a favorite white fowl jumped with her into a well to commit suicide".

陌 Mai. A raised path between fields; a road or street through a market: [11]*,ká paik,* a market-street; [12]*paik, lo' ,ing,* "a person on the road"—one who is disagreeable, a friend treated coldly.

八 捌 Pa. Eight; the 12th radical; the second is the complicated form, and also means to divide, to break open, to rend; a ripping sound: COM., [13]*tá' paik,* the eighth; [14]*sek, paik,* eighteen; [15]*paik, ,ing,* the eight tones; the eight musical sounds; [15]*paik, ,ing ak,* a music-box; [16]*paik, ,tó,* to divide, to share—alluding to the composition of the character *,hung* (to divide); [17]*paik, 'ma,* the winner in a game of dominoes; [18]*paik, che'* the eight characters (of one's horoscope); COLL., *paik, kak,* the eight united (pieces of a coffin); *paik, 'a lĕk,* forty-eight; *,tong paik, haik,* a knave, a scoundrel; *paik, che' ,k'a,* the feet turned out like the word "eight", as in walking; *paik, 'ku sóh, t'eng' siăh,* to earn a living as a cooly or huckster.

仈 Pa. Used for the coll. *paik,:* to know, to understand; to be aware of, to be acquainted with: [19]*paik, tio'* to know a road; *paik, ng' paik,* do you know it or not? are you acquainted or not? [20]*paik, che'* to know how to read; *paik, ,tiong,* to learn by report; *paik, kiéng'* experience; *paik, che' pah,* you're a reader, eh! *paik, ,i se' ,sui,* I know who he is!—a phrase expressing strong dislike; *paik, ,lié 'ting ,mó ,ngüng ,ch'ing,* "understand the scales, but have no silver to weigh"—wholly destitute of funds; *paik, ,cheng,* a term denoting the past tense, has, have.

1 百發百中　2 百無一失　3 伯仲　4 伯叔　5 風神雨伯　6 伯父　7 伯母　8 伯爵　9 扁栢　10 栢姬　11 街陌　12 陌路人　13 第八　14 十八　15 八音匣　16 八刀　17 八馬　18 八字　19 仈路　20 仈字

(605) Paing.

Paing'. A coll. word: similar to *'peng;* to invert, to turn over; to rock, to roll: *paing' 'tiong ꜀peng*, to turn the other side up; to turn and show the back of the head, as a bride standing to be gazed at; *paing' sioh₂ 'tiong*, to turn a thing over, or the other side outward; *peng' paing' paing'* to roll, as a boat does.

瓣² Pan. P'an. Read *piéng²* in the dictionaries: the carpel or divisions of melons, etc.: COM., [1] *꜀hwa paing²* a petal, a flower-leaf; [2] *꜀kwa paing²* the sections of a melon or pumpkin.

辦² Pan. To manage, to dispose; to attend to; to prepare, to provide; to depute; to transact business, as a factor: also read *piéng²* q. v.: COM., [3] *paing² 'li*, to manage; [4] *'pe² paing²* to prepare, to provide for; [5] *꜀chü paing²* an official scribe; [6] *paing² ang'* to manage a lawsuit; [7] *paing² chói²* to condemn, to give sentence; [8] *'má paing²* a comprador or steward; [9] *paing² ꜀ch'á*, to provide for officers on a journey; [10] *paing² hwo'* to contract for goods; [11] *paing² 'hó* or [12] *paing² 't'io taung'* to manage properly; well done; *paing² 'chiu*, to prepare an entertainment.

(606) Pak.

烢, Ch'a. Read *ch'a';* used in the *Paik, ꜀Ing* for the coll. *pak,:* the crackling or snapping of fire: *pak, 'k'i ꜀li*, to snap up; *pak, pak, kieu'* a crackling sound.

叭, Read *paik,;* used in the *Paik, ꜀Ing* for the coll. *pak,:* the chirping of birds: *pak, pak, 'cheu*, "a chattering bird;" *met.*, a talkative person; *pak, pak, kieu'* an incessant clatter of voices.

Pak, A coll. word: the sound of thread breaking: *pak, pak, 'tong*, to snap in two, as thread.

Pak, A coll. word: a brogue for *pwak,* as in *pak, 'ma*, a pickpocket.

煖₂ The heat of fire, hot air ascending; used for the coll. *pak₂:* to smoke a pipe; the sound made in smoking, called *pak, ꜀chiă pak, ꜀chiă.*

援₂ 拔₂ Pa. To pull up, to eradicate, to pull up by the roots; to pull or select out; to destroy, to extirpate; to storm a city; to elevate, to promote; quickly; eminent above one's fellows; the barb of an arrow: in the coll read *pek₂* q. v.: [13] *pak₂ choi²* to surpass one's associates; COM., [14] *pak₂ kong'* a selected Siutsai; [15] *꜀t'i pak₂* to advance, to bring one forward.

鈸₂ Po. A small bell like a sleigh-bell, used by priests in chanting idolatrous services; cymbols of various sizes: in the coll. read *pwak₂* q. v.

跋₂ Po. To travel by land: to walk through grass; to draggle, to trudge along; to stumble; the bottom of

[1] 花瓣 [2] 瓜瓣 [3] 辦理 [4] 備辦 [5] 書辦 [6] 辦案 [7] 辦罪 [8] 買辦 [9] 辦差 [10] 辦貨 [11] 辦好 [12] 辦妥 當 [13] 拔萃 [14] 拔貢 [15] 持拔

海上絲綢之路文獻集成 科技與文化編

a candle; addenda of a second edition; the heel; the root, the foundation, handle of: used for the coll. *pwak*$_2$ q. v.: [1]*'pak*$_2$ *siék*$_2$ to travel by land and water, a toilsome journey; COLL., *lak*$_2$ *pak*$_2$ an intensive, meaning very bad, poorly done, stinking, offensive, according to the context.

茇 **茇**$_2$ The roots of grass, stubble: [2]*pak*$_2$ *siá'* a thatched hut. Read *pwak*$_2$ as in [3]*'pek*$_2$ *'pwak*$_2$ a small, spicy berry, cubeb.

魃$_2$ Pa. Po. The demon of drought, called *ang' pak*$_2$; represented in Formosa with a mouth like a bird and many eyes on the head and hands, having a fiery red sash across the shoulder, and as fleet as the wind.

Pak$_2$ A coll. word, as in *pak*$_2$ *꜀kau*, resin.

(607) Pang.

꜀般 Pan. Similar to the next two: a boat returning: to move, to remove; to distribute, to divide among: also read *꜀pwang*, q. v.

꜀頒 Pan. To confer upon, to give, to distribute among all; to bestow, as a king does; to publish abroad; circulating everywhere; gray, grisly: [4]*꜀pang 'siong*, to distribute rewards; [5]*꜀pang chieu'* to publish imperial orders; COM., [6]*꜀pang ꜀heng ꜀t'iéng a'* to publish to the world.

꜀班 Pan. To confer, to distribute, as rewards or places; to circulate everywhere; to place in a series; an order, rank, series, grade; a class of persons; a turn, a numerative of groups or classes; a manager; variegated, striped, in which sense the same as the next: also read *꜀pwang*, q. v.: [7]*꜀pang pek*$_2$ grayhaired, grisly; COM., [8]*꜀pang 'kwang* or *꜀pang ꜀pung*, a room where prisoners are kept till time of trial; [9]*'chó' ꜀pang*, a lictor, a torturer; [10]*k'wai' ꜀pang*, an official messenger; [11]*꜀tiong ꜀pang*, official attendants in constant employ; [12]*siong' ꜀pang*, to take one's turn; [13]*hié' ꜀pang*, a company of play-actors; [14]*'Lu ꜀pang*, the patron of carpenters; COLL., *'Lu ꜀pang meng' ꜀seng liäng' ꜀tó 'p'wo*, to wield an ax before Lopan—to assume skill before superiors.

꜀斑 Pan. Variegated, striped, mixed: used for the coll. *꜀peng*, q. v.: *꜀pang ꜀lang*, streaked and colored; COM., [15]*꜀pang 'teng*, spotted; [16]*꜀pang tëük*$_2$ a species of spotted bamboo.

꜀斒 Pan. Variegated, streaked, as agate: *꜀pang ꜀lang*, of mixed colors, veined.

꜀瘢 Pan. P'an. A scar, cicatrix; darkish pimples, marks, pits on the skin: *꜀ch'ong ꜀pang*, a scar, mark of a sore.

꜀螌 Pan. A poisonous, striped fly; it is found on pulse: *꜀pang ꜀meu*, any blistering fly, cantharides.

1 跋涉 2 茇舍 3 蓽茇 4 頒賞 5 頒詔 6 頒行天下 7 班白 8 班館 9 皂班 10 快班 11 長班 12 上班 13 戲班 14 魯班 15 斑點 16 斑竹

邦 ‘Pang. A feudal state, a fief, a principality; to confer the rule of a state on one: [1]ˌpang kwok, a country; [2]ˌpang ˌka, the state, the nation; [3]ˌpang ˌkung, a feudal prince.

ˌ*Pang.* A coll. word: to open, to separate, to spread apart: ˌpang ˌk‘wi, to spread apart, as curtains or the feet; ˌpang ˌhiă, to make a gap between; ˌk‘a ˌpang ˌpang, to spread the feet apart, as a small child in walking.

ˌ*Pang.* A coll. word, as in ˌpang pong² slow, heavy in one's movements; dull, stupid: ˌpang ˌpang taëng² pompous, puffed with conceit; ˌpang á² liëk₂ or ˌpang á² p‘wai² you'll burst yourself! you'll collapse!

板 ‘Pan. A board, a plank, deal; a plate of any kind; a page, wooden blocks for books; a flat stick, used as an instrument of punishment; a stroke of the stick or bamboo; obstinate, doltish; castanets; a stretch of wall; a register: in the coll. read ‘peng, q. v.: [4]‘pang te² stupid, doltish; COM., [5]‘ku ‘pang, "old boards"—antiquated, old fogyish.

版 ‘Pan. Interchanged with the last; a schedule, a register; a mace, a baton, insignia of office; boards, planks used in building mud walls; to divide: [6]‘pang ˌtu or [7]‘pang chik₂ a census, registration of the people; [8]ˌteu ‘pang k‘e² ˌkwang, to throw down the mace and give up the office.

昄 ‘Pan. Interchanged with the last in the sense of a register or census: great; extremely: ‘pang ˌchiong, the sun very bright.

坂 ‘Fan. A bank, a ridge; a slope near the water; a hillock: [9]ˌp‘ó ‘pang, a dyke, a mole, a levee.

柄 Ping.’ Read peng²; coll. pang²: a handle, a haft; the root, the source; *met.*, authority, influence: [10]ˌkwong pang² power, authority; [11]‘pa pang² to "grasp the handle"—to have proof; pang² p‘ah₂ siëk₂ the handle is broken.

棚 ˌP‘ëng. A scaffolding, a stage; a framework or trellis; a hut, a shed of mats or bamboos; a covering, an awning: COM., [12]ˌliong ˌpang, an awning; [13]tak₂ ˌpang, to erect a staging; [14]hié² ˌpang, a theatrical stage; [15]ˌhwa ˌpang, a flower-trellis.

平 ˌP‘ing. Read ˌping; coll. ˌpang: even, level, uniform, plain; the same, equal; colloquial; just, right; common, usual; *met.*, tranquil, peaceful: ˌpang ‘tiăng, level and smooth; [16]ˌkung ˌpang, just, equitable; [17]ˌpang tio² a level road; [18]ˌpang ˌsiong, common, usual; [19]ˌpang ˌyong ˌch‘iëng ‘ch‘ó, a level country; ˌpang wa² the patois, colloquial; ˌpang tik₂ straight; ˌpang ‘tá, a flat bottom; ˌpang chiăng² ordinary, inferior in quality; ˌpang p‘ek₂ to stop even, to cry quits; ˌpang tak₂ evenly adjusted, all right; ˌpang paik₂ consumed, gone; ˌpang ˌk‘a, the

[1]邦國 [2]邦家 [3]邦君 [4]板滯 [5]古板 [6]版圖 [7]版籍 [8]投版棄官 [9]坡坂 [10]權柄 [11]把柄 [12]凉棚 [13]搭棚 [14]戲棚 [15]花棚 [16]公平 [17]平路 [18]平常 [19]平洋芊草

large footed (class of women); *꜀pang ꜁t'au ꜀chieng*, even money, as a full hundred, thousand, &c.; *꜀pang ꜀pang twai*² equal in size; *꜀pang 'kong hié*³ a colloquial play; *꜀pang 'tu ꜀pang taiu*² a fair game, to deal fairly; *꜀pang 'chwi 'sai ꜀pang ꜀sung*, "sail a steady boat on smooth water"; *met.*, straight forward, honest.

病² Ping. Read *peng*²; coll. *pang*²: sickness, illness, disease; malady, infirmity; *met.*, defect, fault, sin: ¹*p'wai*³ *pang*² sick, ill; ²*pang*² *cheng*² diseases; ³*pang*² *t'iăng*² sickness and pain; *pang*² *na*² *tiong*² *'la k'aĕk*꜀ wasted to a shadow by illness; *pang*² *tó*³ *puk*꜀ a relapse; *꜀sang ꜀ch'ong pang*² *ká*³ to have bad sores (all over one); *pok*꜀ *꜀kang pang*² ague and fever; *pang*² *'kwi*, the demon of disease; sick imp, as said facetiously; *pang*² *꜀kong*, the root of the disease; *pang*² *t'auk*꜀ *'t'á*, the system recovered from a sickness; *pang*² *꜀chiéng ꜀ló*, a passion for money-making; *'nü mek*꜀ *꜀chiu pang*² *꜀wong k'ó*³ *꜀ló*, your eyes are jaundiced!—i. e., you are prejudiced and falsely impute wrong; *꜀mó pang*² a defect, fault; a moral failing; *꜀mó ꜀mó pang*² no defect, blameless.

(608) Pau.

꜀包 Pao. To wrap around, to enwrap, to infold, to inclose; to contain, to embrace, to be included in; to be patient; to undertake, to contract; to manage a whole matter, to monopolize; to assume all the risks for a consideration; to promise, to warrant, to insure; a bale, a bundle, a wrapper, a roll; used in the coll. for bread: COM., ⁴*꜀pau kwak*꜀ to embrace, to contain; ⁵*꜀pau huk*꜀ (coll. *꜀pa huk*꜀), a bundle or parcel, a knapsack; ⁶*꜀pau ꜀kiéng*, to bind or cover the edge; ⁷*꜀pau ꜀ngüng*, to plate with silver; ⁸*꜀pau chai*² *nói*² included, embraced in; ⁹*꜀pau wang*² to engage to exchange an article (if not good); ¹⁰*꜀pau 'lang*, to monopolize; to assume risks (for the specified fees); ¹¹*꜀pau ꜀chong*, to harbor, as a criminal; ¹²*꜀pau ꜀hang*, patient, forbearing; COLL., *p'ah*꜀ *꜀pau*, to wrap up, to mat or make into a bundle; *꜀pau cheu*³ warranted to be small-pitted lichi; *꜀pau 'liăng*, to assume the whole management of; *꜀pau ꜀tiong*, to contract for a job; *꜀pau 'chio*, the responsible head, as of a theatrical company; *꜀pau chá*² dough; *꜀pau ꜀pui*, yeast; *꜀pau ꜀wong*, a sort of boiled rice-dumpling.

'飽 Pao. To eat enough; fed, satiated; pleased as with flattery: in the coll. read *'pa*, q. v.: ¹³*꜀ki 'pau sek*꜀ *꜀si*, to take meals irregularly; COM., ¹⁴*'pau 'nwang*, fed and clothed; ¹⁵*'pau hok*꜀ very learned.

豹³ Pao. A leopard, a panther, ounce, or other wild spotted felinæ; spotted: ¹⁶*꜀kó ꜀kiu pau*³ *sek*꜀ a lambskin robe with leopard-skin facings; COLL., *pau*³ *꜀t'au ꜀hwang 'ngang*, has a panther's head and fierce eyes; *ch'iăh*꜀ *pau*³ "red panther"—a kind of dark tobacco.

趵³ P'ao. To run and jump, to leap, to gambol. Read *pauk*꜀: to strike the feet

¹破病 ²病症 ³病痛 ⁴包括 ⁵包袱 ⁶包墘 ⁷包銀 ⁸包在内 ⁹包換 ¹⁰包攬 ¹¹包藏 ¹²包函 ¹³饑飽失時 ¹⁴飽煖 ¹⁵飽學 ¹⁶羔裘豹飾

against anything; the sound of the feet striking together.

胞' Pao. An angry look: COLL., *pau' pau'* the eyes large and protruding; *mek˒ ˏchiu ˓pau pau'* (or *˓pau lau'* or *˓ku 'lung pau'*), a fierce, angry glare of the eyes.

Pau'. A coll. word, similar to *pou':* to appear, to come out; to have in addition, additional: *po' pau' sioh˒ yong' ˓ki tai'* another matter coming up; *po' pau' sioh˒ 'chio ch'ok˒ ˓li˒* another creditor making his appearance.

Pau'. A coll. word: to burst, to break out; bulging, protruding: *pau' ch'ok˒ ˓li˒* to burst, to bulge out, as wood from the force of a wedge, or of a nail driven too near the edge.

˓胞 Pao. P'ao. The placenta; uterine, brotherly, near, own, of the same parents: [1]*˓pau ˓i*, the after-birth; COM., [2]*˓pau ˏhing tá'* (coll. *˓pau ˏhiăng tiĕ'*) own brothers; [3]*˓pau 'só*, the wife of an own elder brother; [4]*˓pau tik˒* the sons of own brothers, nephews; [5]*˓pau ˏku*, father's own sisters, paternal aunts; [6]*˓pau 'chiă mwoi'* own sisters.

˓炰 Pao. To boast and swagger: sometimes used for the next, also for *p'au'* a gun. Read *p'au':* to wrap up and roast, to roast in the ashes.

˓咆 P'ao. To roar, as a tiger or bear; to bluster: [7]*˓pau ˏhau*, to roar as a tiger; angry blustering.

˓鮑 Pao. Also read *p'au':* a kind of dried fish; salted or pickled fish; stinking, rank fish; a surname: in the coll. read *p'au'* q. v.: [8]*˓ū ik˒ ˓pau ˓ngü ˏchi sëü'* like entering a salt fish market — so the society of the vicious soon blunts the moral perceptions.

˓匏 P'ao. A species of bitter gourd, formerly used for musical and drinking utensils; a calabash, a gurglet or gourd-like vessel: *˓pau ˏkwa*, a gourd; the name of a star.

˓苞 Pao. Also read *ˏpau:* rushes used in making mats and sandals; rank, luxuriant; presents wrapped in leaves; a stem, the trunk of a mulberry: [9]*hiĕ' ˓ū ˏpau ˏsong*, tied to the mulberry trunk; *met.*, stable, secure; *˓pau ˏchū*, presents wrapped up, bribes.

˓庖 P'ao. A slaughter-house; a kitchen, a public cook-house: [10]*˓pau ˓ing*, a cook, a butcher; [11]*˓Pau ˏhi sé'* name of the inventor of cookery; [12]*tai' ˓pau pok˒ ˓ing*, a large kitchen not filled; *met.*, sparing, frugal.

˓刨 Pao. P'ao. A plane; to plane, to shave, to smooth.

˓鞄 A currier, a leather-dresser.

---

[1]胞衣 [2]胞兄弟 [3]胞嫂 ○ [4]胞姪 ○ [5]胞姑 ○ [6]胞姐妹 ○ [7]咆哮 ○ [8]如入鮑魚之肆 [9]繫于苞桑 [10]庖人 [11]庖犧氏 ○ [12]大庖不盈

皰 Pao. Read *p'au'*; coll. *pau'*: to thump, to strike with the knuckle of a bent finger: *p'ah, sioh, pau'* to give a thump with the knuckle; *tói' pau'* to strike knuckle against knuckle.

鉋 Pao. Read *p'au'* and *꜀pau*; coll. *pau'* as in *ʻma pau'* a curry-comb; *pau' ʻma*, to curry a horse: *pau' sauk,* to curry and brush.

Pau'. A coll. word: to peck at, to fight with the bill; also to tread, to cover, as a cock: *pau' sioh, ch'oi'* to give a stroke with the beak; *pau' ʻsi*, pecked to death, as a cock in a fight; *pe' pau'* to tread, to feather.

(609) Pauk.

爆 Pao. The crackling noise of fire: also read *puk,* q. v.: COLL., [1]*pauk, sioh, ꜀siăng*, to give a crackling sound; *pauk, pauk, kieu'* crackling, snapping; *pauk, ꜀tĕng*, inspired by a god; *met.*, excited, angry; [2]*pauk, ꜀t'ong* or *pauk, ʻchwi*, disputing, caviling about this and that.

襮 A red collar worn outside of the dress at court or at sacrifices: *ʻpieu pauk,* to show outside; external, outward.

膊 Po. A slice of meat, a collop, dried slices; the shoulder, the upper arm; to slice; to flay and mangle, as a carcass; the sound of striking, a clinking, as of stones: in the coll. read *ʻpong*, q. v.: [3]*꜀kiĕng pauk,* the shoulder.

駁 Po. A piebald-horse; mixed, impure; to dispute, to contradict, to oppose; to find fault with, to criticise; to tranship; also used in the sense of to change, to exchange: used for the coll. *p'auk,* q. v.: [4]*꜀p'ié pauk,* to reverse the decision of a lower court; COM., [5]*pauk, ʻk'eu*, to dispute, to contradict; COLL., *pauk, wang'* to exchange, to barter; *pauk, ꜀hwang*, to change dollars; *pauk, ꜀hui* or *pauk, ꜀teng*, to send back and exchange (an article); *ch'iăng' pauk, sai'* to hire boats to tranship a cargo.

博 Po. Ample, extended, spacious; general, universal; intelligent, versed in, well informed; to barter; to game, as at chess: [6]*lĕk, pauk,* to play dice; [7]*pauk, ʻlang*, well-informed; [8]*pauk, sĕü'* a learned scholar, a doctor; COM., [9]*pauk, hok,* learned, well-read; [10]*pauk, ʻku ꜀tiu*, a cabinet of curiosities; [11]*ʻtu pauk,* to gamble; COLL., [12]*pauk, miăng' ꜀p'au*, to run rapidly, a break-neck race; *pauk, miăng' kaë'* to cry out lustily; *pauk, tá'* to "try for a degree"; *met.*, to hasten, to press on; *pauk, ʻta*, a fine, promising chance.

剝 Po. Pao. To flay, to peel, to skin; to strike with force; to split off; to diminish; to let fall; to extort, to oppress; the 23d diagram; in the coll. to burst, to split asunder, riven: also used for the coll. *pwoh,* q. v.: COLL., *pauk, ꜀k'wi* (or *꜀hiă*), burst open; *pauk, ꜀nĕng*, pus from a burst (boil);

1	2	3	4	5	6	7	8	9	10	11	12
爆一聲	爆湯	肩膊	批駁	駁口	六博	博覽	博士	博學	博古橱	賭博	博命跑
○	○	○	○	○	○	○	○	○	○	○	○

ALPH. DICT. 85

pauk, *ch'oi*' to open the mouth, as shell-fish when spoiled or cooked; *pauk*, *'kiéng*, to open a coffin and hold an inquest on the corpse; *pauk*, *siok*, injured, as the system by imprudence; injuring, causing loss; [1]*pauk*, *tiék*, fallen, unfortunate, in reduced circumstances.

卜, Pu. Read *pok*,; coll. *pauk*, as in [1]*pauk*, *kwa*' to tell fortunes by rattling cash in a tortoise shell; *pauk*, *sioh*, *kwa*' to try one's luck at a diviner's; *pauk*, *'ma ,chiéng kwa*' to divine by "the revolving horseman"; *met.*, to dispute, to contradict everything.

搏, Po. To lay hold of, to seize, to take; to play on an instrument; to fight, to strike: [2]*pauk*, *chek*, to seize; [3]*pauk*, *kek*, to strike.

鎛, Po. A kind of hoe; a bell, the thwart piece from which a large bell is suspended: *pauk*, *,ling*, the brazen ornaments on a bell-frame.

礴, To fill up, to cram: *,pong pauk*, filled, stopped up; diffused, as the air; mixed, in confusion; a vast number.

(610) Paung.

謗, Pang. P'ang. To detract, to vilify, to slander: COM., [4]*hwi paung*' or [5]*,pai paung*' to backbite, to speak evil of.

傍, Pang. P'ang. Near, by; placed or standing near a thing; to lean or depend on: also read *,pong*, and in the coll. *p'aung*' q. v.: *,i paung*' to rely on; COM., [6]*paung*' *,ch'iong*, by the wall; COLL., *paung*' *'mó*, a guide or rule; a pattern to work by; *paung*' *,nëng ,mwong ch'ié*' to lean on another's door-post; *met.*, poor and dependent.

徬, P'ang. To run by the side of a cart or carriage: [7]*paung*' *,hwong*, perturbed, agitated.

棒, Pang. Also read *p'aung*': a stick, club, staff, cudgel; to beat, to cudgel: *,tong ,t'eu ek*, *paung*' a rap on the pate.

Paung'. A coll. word, also spoken *p'aung*': the report of a gun: *paung*' *sioh*, *,siäng*, to give a sound, to boom, bang!

(611) Pe.

痺 痹, Pi. Rheumatism, weakness or paralysis of the limbs; numbness, attributed to wind, cold, or dampness: COM., [8]*ch'iu pe*' the hands benumbed; COLL., *,k'a ,kiäng ,tu pe*' *k'ó*' the feet numb from walking; *ch'eng*' *pe*' a chilly sensation.

庇, Pi. P'i. To shelter, to cover; to afford protection; to lodge one: in the coll. read *'pi*, q. v.: [9]*pó pe*' to shield, to protect; COM., [10]*pe*' *eu*' or *pe*' *eng*' to protect, as the gods do.

蔽, Pi. Brushwood, small plants; minute, delicate; to hide, to keep back; to shade, to screen, to cover, to conceal; to embrace, to include in; obscured: [11]*,sü ük*, *ko*' *pe*'

---

1 卜卦 2 搏執 3 搏擊 4 毀謗 5 誹謗 6 傍墻 7 徬徨 8 手痺 9 保庇 10 庇佑 11 私慾固蔽

○ ○ ○ ○ ○ ○ ○ ○ ○ ○

his lusts stifled (his conscience); [1]*chëük*ˎ *ʻi pe*ˀ *ˏku*, it fully atones for his crimes; COM., [2]*ˏchiä pe*ˀ to hide from view; to keep secret; [3]*ˏmung pe*ˀ to conceal from, to deceive or beguile.

秘 祕ˀ Pi. Abstruse, secret, mysterious; inspired; inexplicable: [4]*pe*ˀ *ˏtiong*, mysteriously communicated; [5]*pe*ˀ *mik*ˎ undivulged; [6]*pe*ˀ *kiok*ˎ a secret art or trick, an undivulged mode of doing.

箅ˀ Pi. Used for the coll. *pe*ˀ: a steaming-rack, made of bamboo splints, such as is used over boiling water in a common cooking-pan; [7]*pwong*ˀ *ˏsong pe*ˀ a rack (in the bottom) of a rice-steamer.

疿ˀ Fei. Small boils, or ulcers, pimples, sores from heat: [8]*yék*ˎ *pe*ˀ or [9]*chó*ˀ *pe*ˀ prickly heat, called *poi*ˀ in the coll. q. v.

泌ˀ Pi. To flow, to rush, as from a fountain; flowing between banks, a torrent; a river in the S. W. of Honan, a branch of the Han: [10]*ˏheng pe*ˀ a place of dignified retirement.

沸ˀ Fei. Fu. To bubble, as a spring or boiling water. Read *hok*ˎ: to sprinkle. Read *pʻwoi*ˀ as in [11]*pʻwoi*ˀ *oi*ˀ disturbed, dissatisfied.

閟ˀ Pi. A closed door; to shut, to secrete; to skulk; hidden, concealed; deep, profound, occult; spiritual; careful, attentive: [12]*ˏchʻing pe*ˀ occult; [13]*pe*ˀ *nik*ˎ to hide, to skulk; [14]*pe*ˀ *ˏling*, to "shut the coffin," to decline farther visits of condolence.

苾 Pi. Occasionally read *pik*ˎ: fragrant, odoriferous; perfume of flowers: [15]*pe*ˀ *ˏhung*, a fragrant scent, as of savory food. Read *piék*ˎ: a pot-herb.

毖ˀ Pi. Careful, attentive, heedful; labor, fatigue; painstaking, laborious; water flowing from a spring: [16]*ˏu pe*ˀ *ˏü sok*, not dreading fatigue and danger, as soldiers.

駜ˀ Pi. Sometimes read *pik*ˎ: a strong horse, a horse well-fed and robust.

賁ˀ Pi. Pên. To adorn, to ornament; variegated, as herbage; the 22d diagram, relating to fire: also read *ˏpwong*, q. v.

潷ˀ Pi. Read *pek*ˎ; used for the coll. *pe*ˀ: to drain, to draw off, to decant, as liquids: *pe*ˀ *ˏta*, to drain dry, to draw it all off.

*Pe*ˀ. A coll. euphonic prefix, as in *pe*ˀ *pwai*ˀ to winnow; *pe*ˀ *pwo*ˀ to set out (rice plants); *pe*ˀ *pié*ˀ to run, to hasten.

敝ˀ Pi. Tattered, bad, spoiled; vile, abject; ruined, injured, as clothes; to stop, to cover; the language of politeness or affectation, my, our, your humble: COM., [17]*pe*ˀ *ʻiu*, my friend; [18]*pe*ˀ *ˏhiong*, your humble servant's village; [19]*pe*ˀ *taing*ˀ my poor shop; [20]*pe*ˀ *ngiék*ˎ *ˏsü*, my teacher.

[1]足以蔽辜 [2]遮蔽 [3]蒙蔽 [4]秘傳 [5]秘密 [6]秘訣 [7]飯甑箅 [8]熱疿○ [9]痤疿 [10]衡泌 [11]沸渭 [12]深閟 [13]閟匿 [14]閟壼 [15]苾芬 [16]無毖于恤 [17]敝友 [18]敝鄉 [19]敝店 [20]敝業師○

弊 2 **獘** 2 Pi. Analogous to the above; ruined, spoiled; distressed, fatigued, reduced to extremities; corrupt, vicious, tricky, fraudulent; deteriorated, debased, as coin; used for my, our: [1]*chauk‚ pe*2 or [2]*ʻu pe*2 to impose on, to hoodwink; COLL., [3]*laëng*2 *pe*2 to deceive, to obtain fraudulently; *ʻchi ʻtié o*2 *pe*2 *pang*2 *ʻma chai* ʼ there's some deception about it perhaps!

斃 2 Pi. To fall prostrate, to fall down dead; a violent death; to ruin, to kill, to slaughter.

幣 2 Pi. Full pieces of silk, silks; things given as presents; riches, wealth; pearls and gems, gold, copper—are three kinds of *pe*2: *pe*2 *pek‚* pieces of silk, presents in general; *‚p'i pe*2 rich furs.

備 2 **俻** 2 Pei. To prepare, to provide, to make ready; to guard against; prepared, complete, ready; sufficient; entirely, all: [3]*chëük‚ pe*2 enough provided; [4]*pe*2 *lik‚ ‚kang ‚ngui*, has experienced trouble; COM., [5]*ëü*2 *pe*2 or *pe*2 *paing*2 to prepare, to make ready.

婢 2 Pei. Pi. A maid-servant, a female slave, a slave-girl, one bought or condemned to servitude: [6]*‚kwang pe*2 condemned women; [7]*‚nu pe*2 slaves; COM., [8]*pe*2 *ʻnü*, a female slave; a handmaid—applied by women to themselves.

媲 2 To couple with, to pair, to marry; equal, paired, matched: [9]*pe*2 *ʻmi*, alike pretty.

篦 2 A rake or toothed net for catching crabs; a single, or double, fine-toothed comb; to comb; to lead or draw: COLL., [10]*pe*2 *‚sě*, a fine-toothed comb; [11]*pe*2 *‚t'au hwok‚* to comb the hair with a fine comb; *pe*2 *‚t'au ʻkau*, to comb out dandruff.

狴 2 Pi. A wild beast, called *pe*2 *ngang*2; a jail, a prison.

陛 2 Pi. To ascend steps; the steps of the throne; ascent to a palace or into court: [12]*pe*2 *kiéng*2 to have an audience; [13]*pe*2 *ha*2 Your Majesty, (we who are) before the throne.

比 2 Pi. P'i. To harmonize, to equal; even, equal, regular, uniform; near, intimate; party-spirited, clannish; close, secret; to reach, to attain to; the 8th of the 64 diagrams: also read *ʻpi*, q. v.: *pe*2 *pe*2 constantly; [14]*‚ó pe*2 selfish, partisan.

畀 2 **畁** 2 Pi. To grant, to confer, to give, to bestow; to distribute among; a man's name.

睥 2 **睤** 2 Pi. To peer, to look about: in the coll. read *‚pá*, and *ʻp'á*, q.v.: [15]*pe*2 *ʻngá*, to look askance; also the parapets and embrasures of a wall.

---

1 作弊 ○
2 弄弊 ○
3 足備 ○
4 備歷艱危
5 預備 ○
6 官婢 ○
7 奴婢 ○
8 婢女 ○
9 媲美
10 篦梳
11 篦頭髮 ○
12 陛見
13 陛下
14 阿比
15 睥睨

被[1] Pei. To reach, to add to; to cover over, to protect; to suffer, a sign of the passive, for which the coll. equivalent is *sew*ʾ or *k'ëük,*; by, from, of: in the coll. read *p'woi*ʾ q. v.: ¹*pe*ʾ *hai*ʾ injured; ²*pe*ʾ *këü*ʾ all ready; ³*pe*ʾ *loi*ʾ involved, implicated; COM., ⁴*pe*ʾ *kó*ʾ the defendant in a lawsuit.

詖[2] P'i. Also read ,*p'i*: to dispute; to flatter, to adulate; specious debate in order to flatter and win over: ⁵*pe*ʾ ,*sü*, flattering words.

貱[2] P'i. To add to, to augment; to benefit, to take from one and confer on another: ⁶*e*ʾ *pe*ʾ to increase in order, gradation.

贔[2] Pi. Pei. Also read *pe*ʾ: strong, robust, like a tortoise which can bear great weights.

*Pe*ʾ. A coll. word: to smell, to scent: *pe*ʾ *k'ang*ʾ to test by smelling; *pe*ʾ ,*hiong*, to scent the fragrance.

*Pe*ʾ. A coll. euphonic prefix, as in *pe*ʾ *pó*ʾ to embrace, to carry in the arms; *pe*ʾ *pwoi*ʾ to dry over a fire; *pe*ʾ *poi*ʾ to bark, as dogs.

(612) Pĕ.

,*Pĕ*. A coll. word: vain, fruitless: ,*pĕ k'ó*ʾ it has come to nothing, a complete failure!

,*Pĕ*. A coll. word: to emit suddenly and forcibly, to spirt out; ,*pĕ ch'ok*, ,*li*, to spout forth, as a liquid; ,*pĕ* ,*pĕ sià*ʾ an urgent stool.

,*Pĕ*. A coll. word: to shake, to flap, to flutter: ,*pĕ lĕk*, *sik*, to flap the wings.

(613) Peh.

Peh,. A coll. word: to spirt, to squirt, to pop out; to spout, as liquid from a crevice: *peh*, ʿ*mwang nói*ʾ to spirt all about, as spittle; *peh*, *sioh*, ,*sing*, spirted over the whole person.

Peh,. A coll. euphonic prefix, as in *peh*, *pah*, to break into pieces; *peh*, *póh*, to curse, to revile; *peh*, *pwoh*, to flay; to strip off.

(614) Pek.

筆 笔, Pi. The Chinese pencil, a small brush, a pen, a stylus; to write, to compose; *met.*, writing, penmanship, drawing; composition, style: ⁷*t'iĕk*, *pek*, the "iron pen"—*scil.*, which does not flatter, as in writing the archives of the land; ⁸,*ung pek*, ,*hung*, a small sharp-peaked pagoda—to secure literary fame for a place; COM., ⁹*pek*, ,*tĕng*, a pen-cup; ¹⁰*pek*, *ka*ʾ a pen-rack; ¹¹*pek*, ,*ch'ong*, a grooved pen-stand to lay pens on; ¹²*pek*, ,*hung*, the fine point of a pen; ¹³ʿ*niong* (or ʿ*chwi*) *pek*, and ¹⁴*ngaing*ʾ *pek*, soft and hard pencils—those kept moist and those not; ¹⁵*tai*ʾ *pek*, to act as scribe; ¹⁶*pek*, ʿ*kwang*, a pen-shaft or handle; ¹⁷*pek*, *hwak*, rules of penmanship; *met.*, rules and style of composition; ¹⁸*pek*, *chek*, or *pek*, *sié*ʾ penmanship, one's pecu-

¹被害 ²被具 ³被累 ⁴被告 ⁵詖辭 ⁶貤貱 ⁷鐵筆 ⁸文筆峰 ⁹筆筒 ¹⁰筆架 ¹¹筆床 ¹²筆鋒 ¹³軟筆 ¹⁴硬筆 ¹⁵代筆 ¹⁶筆管 ¹⁷筆法 ¹⁸筆跡

liar handwriting; [1]pek, ˏchü, a writer's pay; a physician's fees; [2]pek, t'aik, sek, the clerks of the Six Boards at Peking; COLL., pek, 'kwong t'ak, a pen-sheath; pek, kauk, one's handwriting, as being firm or easy; pek, taung² k'á² facility in composing and writing.

阦 Pi. A fissure, a rent in the ground; in the coll. to crack, cracked; a crack, rent, fissure; COLL., pek, ˏhiă, or pek, liĕk, cracked open; pek, sioh, swoi² has a crack in it.

煏 Pi. To roast, to fry or try out: COLL., [3]pek, ˏiu, to try out the fat of meats; [4]pek, pauk, or pek, pek, pauk, pauk, to crackle, as fire; to snap out, as oil from meat when fried.

迫 逼 Pi. Read p'aik, ; coll. pek, : to oppress, to harass, to abuse, to reduce to straits: [5]pek, ˏsang, to "press to the hill"—drive one to extremities; [6]pek, 'si, to drive one to commit suicide.

必 Pi. Certain, fixed, absolute; necessarily, must; decided, determined on: [7]pek, yeu² indispensable; [8]pek, hiê² it certainly is; [9]pek, taik, will doubtless obtain; COM., [10]pok, pek, not necessitated or certain; [11]ë² pek, not quite certain, not positively so; [12]ˏhó pek, what necessity? why must it be? [13]pek, teng² ˏü e² it will certainly be as one wishes —a play on the names of "pen", ingot" and the ˏü e² or "luck-ornament", which are painted or carved on various things to secure luck.

畢 Pi. To finish, to conclude; completed, ended, over; the last, the end; all, entirely; the 19th zodiacal constellation, comprising the Hyades; a sort of fork or spit used in sacrifices; an iron under a carriage; a document, writings: [14]'i pek, done, finished; [15]pek, che² all came; [16]ˏkung sëü² pek, the public matters completed; COM., [17]pek, ˏing, the marriage consummated; [18]pek, keng² at last, finally.

蓽 Pi. Used for the next: a kind of pulse: [19]pek, puak, long peppers.

篳 Pi. A wicket; an inclosure hedged in, made of osiers or bamboo; a wood cart: [20]pek, ˏmwong, a wicker-gate; met., a poor man's cot; [21]pek, lek, a flageolet.

嗶 Pi. Fragrant; to talk sweetly, sweet words: used for the coll. p'ek, q. v.

韠 Pi. A sort of apron; leathern pads for the knees in kneeling.

蹕 Pi. To warn persons off the road, to yield the way to the sovereign; an imperial journey; to stop, to halt: [22]'king pek, to bid people to halt or retire.

觱 A sort of horn, called pek, lek, blown by the Tartars to frighten horses; to issue, to pour out:

[1]筆資 [2]筆帖式 [3]煏油 煏爆 [5]迫山 [6]迫死 [7]必要 [8]必係 [9]必得 [10]不必 [11]未必 [12]何必 [13]必定如意 [14]已畢 [15]畢至 [16]公事畢 [17]畢姻 [18]畢竟 [19]蓽茇 [20]篳門 [21]篳篥 [22]警蹕

福州方言拼音字典

[1]*pek, hok,* water flowing from a fountain; [2]*pek, hwak,* a cold wind.

Pek,. A coll euphonic prefix, as in *pek, pauk,* to change (money); to return, as a present; also to snap, to crackle, as fire.

白 ₂ Pai. Po. White, a mourning color, immaculate; bright, as moonlight; explicit, plain, manifest; free, disinterested; the white part of a thing; to explain, to make clear; the 106th radical: in the coll. read *pah,* q. v.: [3]*pek, ,ting,* a commoner, one of no rank, or literary degree; [4]*pek, tai'* fluor albus, leucorrhoea; [5]*pek, chok,* lues venerea; COM., [6]*,ch'ing ,ti'éng pek, nik,* in open day, in broad daylight; [7]*,ming pek,* clear, intelligible; to understand clearly; [8]*pek, ,i tai' séü'* the white-draped Kwanyin; [9]*pek, 'ch'iu ,sing ,ka,* to rise in life by one's own efforts.

帛 ₂ Pai. Plain silk, taffety; a present of silk; wealth; rolls of white paper to represent silk, offered to Confucius; paper on bamboo frames, offered to the dead in funeral rites: [10]*,chai pek,* wealth, property.

拔 ₂ Pa. Read *pak,;* coll. *pek,:* to pull; to pull up, to eradicate; to draw out, to extend; to pay out: [11]*pek, ,k'au,* to draw lots; [12]*pek, ,p'ung,* to raise a sail; *pek, siăng'* to "pull the string"—to annoy, to humbug; [13]*pek, chaik,* to grow by joints, as a bamboo; *met.,* the growth of a child; [14]*,kwong ,sieu pek, siék,* to be a great liar; [15]*pek, nak,* to tow a boat; [16]*pek, 'pwong,* to use one's capital; [17]*pek, ,chiéng,* to pay out money; [18]*pek, hek,* to be constantly paying out; [19]*pek, tek, tik,* enough to meet expenses; *pek, ,ló t'ói'* to remove (a corpse) through a hole in the prison-walls; *pek, 'k'i ,tang,* to draw up the heel of the shoe.

別 ₂ Pieh. Read *piék,;* coll. *pek,:* other, another, different: *pek, chiăh,* or *pek, ,ki,* another one; *pek, sang'* a different surname; *pek, tói'* or *pek, oi' ch'éü'* another place; *pek, oi' siăh, pwong'* to eat elsewhere—to be banished; *pek, ,nëng ,k'a t'ek, 'k'eng,* to kick a dog with another person's foot—to injure one through another.

(615) Peng.

斑 ‹ Pan. Read *,pang;* used for the coll. *,peng,* as in *,peng k'ó'* mildewed; *siong' ,peng,* mildewed; spotted, as the face; *'hu ,peng,* striped as a tigers's skin; striped (cloth).

崩 ‹ Pêng. The fall or slide of a mountain; to fall in ruins; to fall from a high estate or position; the demise of an emperor: used for the coll. *,pung,* q. v.: *,sang ,peng te' liék,* the mountain fallen and the earth rent—a great ruin; *ka' ,peng,* the emperor is dead.

繃 綳 ‹ Pêng. To bind, to tie, to fasten; a bandage, a cloth for carrying an infant pickapack.

[1]濊沸 [2]濊發 [3]白丁 [4]白癩 [5]白濁 [6]青天白日 [7]明白 [8]白衣大士 [9]白手成家 [10]財帛 [11]拔鬮 [12]拔篷 [13]拔節 [14]講謝拔舌 [15]拔箇 [16]拔本 [18]拔錢 [17]拔穫 [19]拔的直 ○

板 Pan. Read *'pang;* coll. *'peng:* a board, a plank; a plate of iron or any metal; a page, a printing block; the bamboo, an instrument of punishment; strokes of the bamboo; castanets; tablets: [1]*'peng laiu'* boards; [2]*t'iék, 'peng,* iron plates; [3]*peng ,p'wo,* a bedstead of boards (laid on benches); [4]*peng t'aiu'* a plank-crossing (over a stream); [5]*peng lak,* boarding on the sides of a room; [6]*peng ,pang,* a board-floor; [7]*ch'iăk, 'peng,* castanets; [8]*kek, 'peng,* and *,k'wang 'peng,* quick and slow-measure in castanet-playing: [9]*kek, 'peng,* boards to hold or support things; *twai' 'peng* and *'sieu 'peng,* the large and small bamboos (to beat culprits with); *p'ah, se' sek, 'peng,* to inflict forty blows; *eng' 'peng,* printing-blocks; *k'aik, 'peng ,ki,* printed, not written; *,sang 'peng,* a sampan or small boat.

'Peng. A coll. word, for which the last may be used; to invert, to turn over: *'peng 'tiong, ,peng,* to turn the other side up; *'peng 'tiong 'li,* to turn inside out; *'peng 'tiong p'ok,* to turn the face of a thing down, as bowls, etc.; *'peng 'tiong ,sing,* to turn the body, to turn about; *'peng 'ku,* to play cat's cradle; *'peng ,tong 'peng to'* to retch violently; *,chiéng k'ëük, ,i 'peng k'ó'* cheated out of money by him.

扁 Pien. P'ien. Read *'piéng;* coll. *'peng,* as in *'peng ,tang,* a cooly's carrying-stick; [10]*'peng ,tang sóh,* the carrying stick and ropes; *'peng ,tang ,tó,* the edge of the stick, as used in a fight; *'peng ,tang p'ah, 'tó ek, ché' ,pang,* the carrying stick has fallen as flat as the character "one"; *met.,* a prosperous man reduced by poverty to the level of others.

匾 Pien. Read *'piéng;* coll. *'peng,* as in [11]*'peng ngiăh,* or *,pá 'peng,* a door tablet, as of Kūjin, and in temples.

'Peng. A coll. word: a corruption of *paik, ng'* as in *'peng paik, 'ngwai,* do you know me or not?

迸 Pêng. To be dispersed; to flee; expelled, driven away; to wander, to idle about.

幷 并 並 竝 Ping. Two standing or going together, dual; also, and, with, moreover, together; even with, united; to compare together; to copulate: [12]*peng' ,hi,* not at all, by no means; [13]*peng' lik,* two standing together; [14]*peng' ,t'ong,* to seize or usurp all; [15]*peng' tëüng'* equally heavy; COM., [16]*peng' 'ch'iă,* also, moreover; COLL., *peng' ,mó 'chiă tai'* there was no such affair, it was not so at all; *peng' ,t'au ,leng,* two lotus flowers on one stem—an emblem of the marriage relation.

併 Ping. Used for the last: equal, even, on a line with; to make one, reduce to a uniform size or likeness; to expose, to be regardless of: used for the coll. *piăng'* and *,p'ing,* q. v.: *peng' këü'* opposed to; [17]*peng' meng'* to expose life, as in battle.

[1]板料 [2]鐵板 [3]板鋪 [4]板透 [5]板拉 [6]板棚 [7]切板 [8]急板 [9]挾板 [10]扁擔索 [11]匾額 [12]並非 [13]並立 [14]并吞 [15]并重 [16]並且 [17]併命

儐 Pin. Interchanged with the next: to receive a guest ceremoniously; to honor, to worship, to revere; to arrange; to enter, to go in: ¹'peng' siong' a master of ceremonies.

擯 Pin. P'in. To eject forcibly, to expel, to drive off; to receive guests; an officer sent to the frontier to receive an envoy: ²'peng' tŭk, to drive away.

嬪 Pin. P'in. Also read ,ping: a woman, a lady; a concubine or maid of honor; to marry out; a deceased wife: ³,hi peng' ladies of the palace; 'peng' ho² his late wife; ⁴peng' ,yong, much, many.

殯 Pin. To enshroud and encoffin a corpse; to attend a funeral, to carry out and inter: ⁶song' peng' to accompany a burial; ⁷peng' lièng² to enshroud and encoffin; ⁸ch'ok, peng' to bear forth to bury.

鬢 鬂 Pin. The hair on the sides of the face, the points of hair back of the temples; the sides of the face; curls, tresses; whiskers: ⁹,hung peng' the hair puffed out; COM., ¹⁰peng' ,hwa, flowers worn on the sides of the head; COLL., peng' ,k'a, the hair by the temples.

柄 Ping. Also read 'ping: a haft, a handle; the root, the source; met., authority, power, influence, control: in the coll. read pang' q. v.: ¹¹'pa peng' to hold by the handle; to have power or influence.

摒 To expel, to banish, to drive off, to reject.

Peng'. A coll. euphonic prefix, as in peng' pong' to let go; peng' paing' to rock to and fro; to contradict one's self; peng' 'tung paing' to rock, as boats do.

朋 P'ĕng. ,A friend, an associate, an equal; a fellow-student, acquaintance; to join, to associate with; a pair of wine cups: ¹²,peng 'tong, a clique or cabal, a party in the state; COM., ¹³,peng 'iu, a friend; ,peng 'iu tó² the laws of friendship; ¹⁴,peng 'iu ,ch'ing ,ka, friends related by the marriage of children; ,peng 'iu ,hiăng tié² friends loving as brothers; COLL., ,peng ,hiăng ,hong, a kind of dark tobacco.

硼 P'ĕng. ,As in ,peng ,sa (coll. ,pĕng ,sa), borax, the subborate of soda. Read ,p'eng: the name of a stone.

爿 ,Read ,ch'iong; used in the Paik, ,Ing for the coll. ,peng: a side, a part, one of two parts or halves: pwang' ,peng, the half of; sioh, tói² ,peng, to cut in two parts.

便 Pien. P'ien. ,Read ,piĕng; coll. ,peng, as in ¹⁵,peng ,ngié, cheap, low in price; ¹⁶,peng ,ngié 'mă, to buy cheaply; ,peng ,ngié ,kŭng, poor by buying cheap, as one

¹儐相 ²擯逐 ³妃嬪 ⁴嬪婦 ⁵嬪然 ⁶送殯 ⁷殯殮 ⁸出殯 ⁹雲鬢 ¹⁰鬢花 ¹¹把柄 ¹²朋黨 ¹³朋友 ¹⁴朋友親家 ¹⁵便宜 ¹⁶便宜買

buying what he does not need; [1]ˎpeng ˎngié ˏkung tô² siǎng² at a cheap and fair price.

鵬 ˎP'eng. A monstrous bird like the Arabian roc, fabled to be changed from the kraken: COLL., tai² ˎpeng ʿcheu, the great roc, as represented in plays.

ˎPeng. A coll. prefix, as in ˎpeng paing² to prepare, to make ready; ˎpeng ʿpeng, pieces of board; ˎpeng ʿpeng ch'öi² (or ˏkô), blocks, as for a child's play.

病 Ping.² Sickness, disease; infirmity, malady; vice, vicious; a defect, a fault; grief, sorrow, affliction; damaged, injured; to hate, to dislike; to distress, to disgrace: in the coll. read pang² q. v.: [2]chik₂ peng² diseases; [3]peng² ʿü, convalescent, well; [4]peng² kwok₂ ˏyong ˎming, to injure the state and the people.

(616) Pëng

ˏPëng. A coll. word, also spoken ˏp'ëng: a kind of gong, protuberant in the center like a cymbal: ˏpëng ˏpëng kieu² the ringing sound of the ˏpëng.

ʿPëng. A coll. word, as in ʿpeng ʿpëng ch'iǎ² (or ʿp'ëng ʿp'ëng ch'iǎ²), a kind of cymbal used by priests, so called from its peculiar sound.

硼 ˎP'ëng. Read ˎpeng; coll. ˎpëng, as in [5]ˎpëng ˎsa, natural borax, sub-borate of soda.

ˎPëng. A coll. word: to kick, to thrust out the foot with the sole foremost: ˎpëng sioh₂ ˏk'a, to give a kick.

ˎPëng. A coll. word: to belch forth, to utter with violence: ˎpëng sioh₂ kwo² to belch out a sentence, as in breaking the silence with a curse or harsh word.

ˎPëng. A coll. word, as in ˎpëng ˎpëng ʿku, a bamboo drum, covered only at one end and used by a certain class of beggars; ˎpëng ˎpëng ʿku p'ah₂ siong² ˏli, to "beat the bamboo drum from below"—a short man cursing a tall one.

(617) Peu.

Peu². A coll. word, as in peu² k'ô² to burst out, to leave the former position, as a row of cash pressed unevenly at the ends; *met.*, to fail, to come to nothing, as an agreement or business.

Peu². A coll. word: to issue, to appear: peu² sioh₂ chiǎh₂ another one appears, as coming in unexpectedly for a share; peu² sioh₂ lak₂ to come out, as a boil or sore.

(618) Pi.

萆薢 ˏPi. A medicinal plant, called [6]ˏpi ˏkai, used as a diuretic: COM., [7]ˏpi ˎmwai ˎiu, castor oil—is used in red stamping-ink.

碑 ˏPei. A pillar to which victims were formerly tied; stone tablets: [8]ˏpi ˎung, an epitaph, inscription; [9]ʿk'eu ˏpi chai² tô² has a mouth-tablet on all the road—praised by people everywhere; COM., [10]sioh₂ ˏpi, a stone *in memoriam*; [11]mwo² ˏpi, a grave-stone.

1 便宜公道 賤 ○ 2 疾病 ○ 3 病瘉 ○ 4 病國殃民 5 硼砂 ○ 6 萆薢 ○ 7 萆蔴油 ○ 8 碑文 ○ 9 口碑載道 10 石碑 11 墓碑

卑 ‚Pei. Base, low, vulgar, mean, inferior, menial, contemptible; humble, respectful; to humble, to abase: [1]*‚pi laiu*^{3} vulgar, low; poor and mean, as a house; [2]*‚chong ‚pi*, noble and plebeian; [3]*‚pi ‚pi pok, chëük, tó*^{3} too trifling to be mentioned; COM., [4]*‚pi chek,* I, the magistrate.

俾 ‛Pei. Also read *pe*^{3} or *pe*^{2}*:* to give, to benefit; to cause, to enable; to send, to employ; to follow, to accord; to let, to allow; as a conjunction, that, so that, to the end that: [5]*sauk, ‚pi*, to accord; [6]*‚pi ‛ngá*, to squint, to look askance.

裨 ‛Pei. To assist, to supply deficiencies, to reinforce; useful to, beneficial; to hand over, to enable or allow one to do; small, inferior, as caps worn by lords in worship: [7]*‚pi ‛pwo*, to assist; [8]*tai*^{3} *‛iu ‚pi ek,* of great benefit.

埤 ‛Pei. A low wall; to add to, to augment; attached to; thick, liberal, abundant. Read *pe*^{3}*:* low, damp: [9]*pe*^{3} *sek,* damp, marshy ground.

陴 ‛P‘i. Also read *‚pi:* a parapet or breastwork, in which embrasures are made; to aid, to benefit: [10]*siu ‚pi*, an officer who guards the walls.

鼙 ‛P‘i. A kind of drum or cymbal, borne on horseback and sounded in battle near the general; to drum.

庳 ‛Pei. Low, as a house or palace; mean, humble, unpretending; short; the nose. Read *‛pi*, as in [11]*‛Iu ‛pi*, the name of a principality which the brother of Shun governed.

屄 ‛Pi. The female organs, the vulva.

‚Pi. A coll. word; used for *pek*$_2$*:* to pull, to draw, to take out: *‚pi sioh*$_2$ *‚teu*, pull out one thread or strip; *‚pi ‚t‘au hwok,* to pull one's hair; *‚pi se*^{3} *pah, ‚chiĕng k‘ëük, ‚i,* take 400 cash and give to him.

‚Pi. A coll. word, as in *‚pi ‚pi ‛hiong*, the sound of a whistle; hence a whistle, such as children use.

‚Pi. A coll. euphonic prefix, as in *‚pi ‚pau*, to wrap up; *‚pi ‚pó*, to soothe, to coax.

比 ‛Pi. P‘i. To compare, to judge of; to sort, to classify; to equal, to correspond to; to select; a comparison, an illustration; an allegory: also read *pe*^{3} q. v.: [12]*‛pi ‛t‘á*, metaphor, allegory—a term used in poetry; COM., [13]*‛pi kau*^{3} to compare, to illustrate; [14]*‛pi ëü*^{3} or [15]*‛pi ‚hwong* or [16]*‛pi laung*^{2} to institute a comparison; for the sake of illustration; [17]*‛pi yong*^{2} to use as a pattern; COLL., *‛pi p‘iăng*^{2} to compare; *‛pi ‚nu ‛siong*, in my opinion; *‛pi pa*^{3} hold it up and brag about it, as children do; *‛pi ‚ch‘á*, to bamboo policemen; *‛pi sioh*$_2$ *‛pi*, to give one a bambooing.

庇 ‛Pi. P‘i. Read *pe*^{3}*;* coll. *‛pi*, as in *‛pi eu*^{3} or *‛pi eng*^{3} to protect, to care for, as the gods do.

[1]卑陋 [2]尊卑 [3]卑卑不足 道[4]卑職〇 [5]率俾〇 [6]俾倪〇 [7]裨補〇 [8]大有裨益 [9]埤濕[10]守陴 [11]有庳[12]比體 [13]比較[14]比喻 [15]比方[16]比論 [17]比樣〇

海上絲綢之路文獻集成 科技與文化編

ʻ妣 Pi. Pʻi A deceased mother: [1]ʻkʻó ʻpi, deceased parents; COM., [2]ˏka ʻpi, my paternal grandmother; [3]ˏsiéng ʻpi, a deceased paternal grandmother; [4]leng ʻpi, your paternal grandmother.

ʻ仳 Pi. To part, to take leave of, to separate from. Read ˎpi, as in ˎpi ˏhwi (or ˏchʻwi), plain, homely, as a woman.

ʻ粃 Pi. Grain that does not mature; chorion, immature seed; chaffy grain; tares: [5]ʻpi ˏkʻong, chaff, husks. Read ˎpi: ignorant, uninformed.

ʻ匕 Pi. A spoon or ladle, a spoon with which sacrifices are taken out; a sort of stiletto or dagger; the 21st radical: [6]ʻpi tëü chopsticks.

ʻ彼 Pi. Pei. A distributive pronoun, the correlate of ʻchʻü (this); that, the other, the opposite, the further of two; to exclude, to leave out: ʻpi ˏchai ʻpi ˏchai, he, indeed! he, indeed! COM., [7]ʻpi ˎsi, at that time; [8]ʻpi ʻchʻü, that and this, then and now, there and here.

ʻ指 Chih. Read ʻchi; coll. ʻpi: to point with the finger; to designate, to refer to: ʻpi ʻpi, to point at; ʻpi tié ˎnëng, to whom does he refer?

ʻPi. A coll. euphonic prefix, as in ʻpi ʻpwi, to rake and search, as for a thing dropped among shavings; ʻpi ʻpá, to strut, to swagger.

ˎ脾 Pʻi. The stomach, the internal tunic which digests food; the digestion, the appetite; the temper; to stop: COM., [9]ˎpi oi the stomach; [10]ˎpi kʻeʼ "gastric effluence"—i. e., the temper; [11]ˎpi ˏchʻing, a delicate stomach; [12]ˏkʻwi ˎpi, to excite the appetite, as with bitters; [13]ˎpi ʻtʻu hqiu a good digestion; COLL., [14]ˎpi tʻiàng a stomach-ache; [15]ˎpi ˏhwa ˏniéng ˏpiéng, away with your schemes! Read ʻpi; fat, full, abundant.

ˎ膍 Pʻi. Used for the last: the stomach or tripe of a cow; thick, substantial, abundant: ˎpi ˏchʻi, the entrails of birds; ˎpi ˏchá, the human navel.

ˎ貔 Also read ˎpʻi: a species of leopard from Liautung; some say a spotted bear or badger: ˎpi ˏhiu, a flag with a leopard on it; *met.*, valiant, as troops.

ˎ琵 Pʻi. A musical instrument; name of a scaleless fish; to push with the hand: COM., [16]ˎpi ˎpa, the guitar or viol, pear-shaped and having four strings: [17]ˎwong ˎliéng chʻeu ˏmwi ˎtang ˎpi ˎpa, to play the guitar in the top of the bitter Huang lien tree—to be joyful in sorrows.

ˎ枇 Pʻi. A fruit: COM., [18]ˎpi ˎpa, the loquat, medlar (Eriobotrya japonica): [19]ˎpi ˎpa nioh loquat leaves, used in coughs; ˏsang ngwok ˎpi ˎpa chʻok ʻhó sié the loquat comes in the 3d month at the right time (when there are no other fruits); *met.*, to get a place

1 考妣 2 家妣 3 先妣 4 令妣 5 粃糠 6 匕箸 7 彼時 8 彼此 9 脾胃 10 脾氣 11 脾清 12 開脾 13 脾土厚〇 14 脾痛 15 脾花 16 拈邊琵琶 17 黃連樸尾彈琵琶 18 枇杷 19 枇杷葉

or position before others. Read *'pi:* forks to lift victims from the boiler. Read *pe':* a fine-toothed comb.

蚍 A large species of ant, called [1]*ₛpi ₛp'eu;* a flower of a reddish color, like a hibiscus.

毗 Also read *ₛp'i:* contiguous, as fields; clear, manifest; liberal, kind; to treat kindly, to assist; thick, substantial; cringing, obsequious: [2]*ₛk'wa ₛpi,* servile; COM., *ₛpi ₛliéng,* (coll. *ₛp'i ₛliéng*), adjoining, as fields or houses.
P'i.

躴 躴 The body pliant; lithe, lissome; fulsome, cringing: *ₛk'wa ₛpi,* to bow and cringe, servile, flattering.

ₛPi. A coll. word, as in *ₛpi ₛpa tau' kiék,* the common name for a bat.

ₛPi. A coll. word: to add water, as to fat in a pan to make gravy: *ₛpi 'tié,* add (some water) in.

ₛPi. A coll. euphonic prefix, as in *ₛpi ₛpa,* to rake up; *ₛpi ₛpa 'chau,* to creep away, to jump up and run off; *ₛpi ₛpá,* to arrange.

(619) Piăh.

壁 Read *p'ek,;* coll. *piăh,:* a partition wall, a wall of lath and plaster, called *ₛt'u piăh,* or *ₛhwi piăh,:* [3]*chieu' piăh, ₛch'iong,* a curtain-wall before a yamun, an opposite wall; [4]*piăh, ₛpung,* the boarding below the plastering of a partition; [5]*piăh, ₛtó,* the small wooden pieces with which the laths are interlaced; [6]*piăh, sioh, 'tu,* a section of lath wall; *ₛkang piăh,* neighboring, the next door.
Pi.

(620) Piăk.

Piăk,. A coll. word, also spoken *p'iăk,* and *piăk,:* to slap, to strike with the palm; to clap the hands: *piăk, sioh, 'chiong,* to give one a slap; *piăk, ch'oi' 'p'á,* to slap the cheek.

Piăk,. A coll. word: to splash, to spatter, as water thrown out.

Piăk,. A coll. word, also spoken *p'iăk,* and *p'iăk,:* to tread, to walk about with wet or bare feet; *piăk, piăk, 'tiong,* to keep treading about (so as to stain the floor): *piăk, 'tié piăk, ch'ok,* to tread in and out.

(621) Piăng.

餅 Read *'ping;* coll. *'piăng:* a cake, a biscuit, pastry made of flour, water and fat: [7]*ₛkwong 'piăng,* biscuit; [8]*ₛsieu 'piăng,* a kind of cake sprinkled with sesame; [9]*naung' 'piăng,* nice cakes—a general term for the more expensive sorts; [10]*'piăng ang'* the stuffing of cakes, as sugar, pork, etc.; [11]*ₛchiéng 'piăng,* fried cakes, fritters; [12]*'chwi ₛching 'piăng,* crystal cake—made with stuffing of fat pork and white sugar.
Ping.

Piăng'. A coll. word, for which the next may be used: to pour, to pour out, to cast away; to mould, to cast: *piăng' kwo' 'wang,* to pour into a bowl; *piăng' chaik, 'tá,* to give

[1]蚍蜉 [2]夸毗 [3]照壁墻 [4]壁枋 [5]壁㓞 [6]壁一堵 [7]光餅 [8]燒餅 [9]嫩餅 [10]餅餡 [11]煎餅 [12]水晶餅

○ ○ ○ ○ ○ ○ ○ ○ ○ ○ ○ ○

away the leavings, as to beggars; *piáng' ˏking*, to cast gold; *piăng' taing'* to sell off old things to a broker.

併' Ping. Read *peng'*; used for the coll. *piăng'*: to reckon, to cast up; to unite, to bring together: [1]*piăng' so'* to foot up an account; [2]*piăng' ˏpá*, to place together, as chairs side by side; [3]*piăng' ˏhiong*, feuds and fights between villages.

ˏ閛 Read *ˏp'eng*; used for the coll. *ˏpiăng* (or *piăng²*): a noise, as of the slamming of doors; a thumping, a pounding: *ˏpiăng sioh, ˏsiăng*, a thump, a slam; *ˏpiăng ˏpiăng kieu'* a constant noise, as of doors, etc.

(622) Pié.

ˏ鎞 Pi. The iron colter of a plow; the barb of an arrow; a probe with a barbed point: COM., [4]*ˏngŭng ˏpié* (coll. *ló² ˏpié*), a silver probe, used by coroners to detect the presence of poison.

ˏPié. A coll. word: the leaf of a vegetable, called *ch'ai' ˏpié*; *a² póh, ˏpié*, the lower leaves of vegetables; *'piéng ˏpié*, bracelets having a flat surface.

ˏPié. A coll. word: to add to, to enlarge: *ˏpié k'wak*, to widen by adding a piece; *ˏpié 'ch'iu 'wong*, to widen a sleeve; *ˏpié sioh, hok*, to add a breadth of cloth.

臂' Pei. The fore-arm, the cubit; the arm; the shoulder or leg of a slaughtered animal; the power or strength of an arm: [5]*pié' chiék*, the elbow-joint; [6]*'hwang pié'* to throw the arm backwards; [7]*'cho² ek, pié' ˏchi lik*, to lend a hand, to help; COM., [8]*ˏkiéng pié'* the upper-arm, humerus; *'ch'iu pié'* the arm; [9]*'hu pié'* the tiger's arm—right side of a grave; COLL., *pié' ˏsong 'nĕ*, the arm aching from fatigue; *pié' t'aung' k'ó'* dislocation of the shoulder-joint.

轡' P'ei. The reins attached to a headstall or bridle: *chek, pié'* to grasp the reins, to hold a horse.

Pié' A coll. word: to run, to go quickly: *pié' pié' 'chau*, to run away; *pié' yok*, jaded by running; *pié' tek, ˏhĕ ˏp'i ˏp'á*, to run till one pants.

避² Pi. Pei. To flee from, to escape, to avoid, to shun, to shirk; to stand aside, to withdraw; to hide, to abscond: [10]*pié² chai'* to avoid creditors; [11]*pié² sié'* or *pié² te'* to go into privacy; COM., [12]*ˏtó pié'* to flee from, to abscond; *pié² ka'* flight of the emperor; [13]*ˏhuá pié'* "stand aside"—written on staves carried before magistrates and idols; [14]*pié² ˏchai* or *pié² nang'* to shun distress; *pié² 'sü*, to escape hot weather; [15]*pié² ˏhiéng*, to avoid suspicion; [16]*pié² 'ngang hwak*, (coll. *piéng' 'ma hwak*,), a sleight of hand, juggler's tricks; *pié² ˏsing ˏhu*, a charm to make one's self invisible.

[1]併數 [2]併排 [3]併鄉 [4]銀鎞 [5]臂節 [6]反臂 [7]助一臂之力 [8]肩臂 [9]虎臂 [10]避債 [11]避世 [12]逃避 [13]迴避 [14]避災 [15]避嫌 [16]避眼法

閉ˀ Pi. To shut a door; to shut out, to exclude; to screen, to shade; to store, to lay up; to stop; obstructed, closed: [1]*pié*ˀ *ˏmwong*, to close the door—to go into privacy; [2]*pié*ˀ *ˏking*, obstruction of the menses; *pié*ˀ *pié*ˀ full, abundant; [3]*pié*ˀ *saik*ˎ stopped up; [4]*ˋk'ié pié*ˀ commencement of autumn and winter.

(623) Piék.

鼈 鱉ˎ Pieh. A turtle, said to hear with its eyes; marine cheloniæ; the stars Corona Australis: *nak*ˎ *piék*ˎ a kind of turtle unable to retract its head; com., [5]*ˋhwi piék*ˎ a water turtle red under the body; [6]*piék*ˎ *k'aĕk*ˎ turtle shells.

鷩ˎ A species of pheasant or francolin, called [7]*piék*ˎ *te*ˀ like the gold pheasant; it is said to be fond of seeing its own reflection in the water.

蹩ˎ Pieh. Lame, halt, hobbling; club-footed: [8]*piék*ˎ *chëük*ˎ lame; coll., *piék*ˎ *piék*ˎ club-footed; *piék*ˎ *ˏwang*, the foot bent or deflected; coll., *ˏk'a piék*ˎ *ˋlá sôi*ˀ to sit with one foot across the knee.

撇ˎ To strike, to beat; to brush away; to pierce; used in the *Paik*ˎ *ˏIng* for the coll. *piék*ˎ to turn over, to roll up: [9]*piék*ˎ *ˋch'iu ˋwong*, to roll up the sleeves; [10]*piék*ˎ *sioh*ˎ *ˏkiéng*, to turn over an edge, as a hem.

別ˎ Pieh. To separate, to distinguish: also read *piék*ˎ q. v.: com., [11]*ˏhung piék*ˎ or [12]*piéng*ˀ *piék*ˎ to distinguish, to discriminate; [13]*ˏhung piék*ˎ *ˏching ˋka*, to distinguish between true and false.

別ˎ Pieh. To leave, to recede from, to go off; a separation, a parting; different, another: also read *piék*ˎ and in the coll. *pek*ˎ q. v.: [14]*ˋkó*ˀ *piék*ˎ to announce one's leaving; [15]*piék*ˎ *ngiék*ˎ to change one's calling; com., [16]*piék*ˎ *ˏlié*, or [17]*ˏlié piék*ˎ to depart from, to leave, as one's friends; [18]*piék*ˎ *k'e*ˀ *ch'ok*ˎ *ˏka*, to forsake one's family and become a Bonze; [19]*piék*ˎ *ˏseng ˏchié chiék*ˎ "grow another branch"—to change to something different.

(624) Piéng.

邊ˏ Pien. The side; an edge, a bank; a border, frontiers, confines, boundary: [20]*ˏpiéng ˏkiong*, the boundary, the frontiers: *ˏpiéng ngwoi*ˀ beyond the frontier; com., *ˏhwa ˏpiéng*, an embroidered edge or border; milled, as a dollar; *ˏsing ˏpiéng*, at one's side; *ˋhai ˏpiéng*, the seaside; *ˏt'iéng ˏpiéng*, the horizon; distant; *ˏpiéng kaĕk*ˎ a corner, a by-place; *ˏpiéng ˏmwong*, a side-door; *ˏpong ˏpiéng*, the side, at the side; coll., *ˋtié ˏpiéng*, inside.

籩ˏ Pien. A bamboo basket, called *ˏpiéng taiu*ˀ made like a dish and used to contain offerings of fruits: *ˏpiéng ˏing*, one who brings the salver at sacrifices.

---

[1]閉門 [2]閉經 [3]閉塞 [4]啟閉 [5]火鼈 [6]鼈殼 [7]鷩雉 [8]蹩足 [9]撇手袖 [10]撇一墘 [11]分別 [12]辯別 [13]分別眞假 [14]告別 [15]別業 [16]別離 [17]離別 [18]別棄出家 [19]別生枝節 [20]邊疆

筽 ʻPien. A bamboo cart or barrow used for transporting earth.

鞭 ꜀Pien. A whip, a lash; a cut or lash of a whip; an iron cudgel; to whip, to flog: [1]꜀piéng ʻta or ꜀piéng tʻak꜆ to flog; COM., [2]ʻma ꜀piéng, a horsewhip; [3]tʻiék꜆ ꜀piéng, an iron bludgeon; COLL., [4]꜀pʻui ꜀piéng, a lictor's lash; ꜀piéng ꜀pʻah, to whip.

鯿 鯾 ꜀Pien. A bream (Abramis bramula); one or two species are reared by the Chinese: COM., [5]꜀piéng ꜀ngü, the bream.

扁 ʻPien. Pʻien. Flat, low, not globular; used for the next in the sense of tablet: also used for ʻpeng in the coll. q. v.: COM., [6]ʻpiéng ꜀sing, the character for heart (in distinction from [7]꜀tong ꜀sing, the character for body); [8]ʻpiéng kʻaiuʾ flat buttons; [9]ʻpiéng ak꜆ a round flat box for containing presents; [10]ʻpiéng ak꜆ flat duck—preserved in saltpetre; [11]ʻpiéng pah, the juniper; the arbor vitae; [12]ʻpiéng sik꜆ a sort of meat dumplings; COLL., ʻpiéng ʻpiéng chʻoiʾ flattened mouth, as of a child about to cry. Read ꜀pʻiéng: a small boat.

匾 ʻPien. Analogous to the last: flat, thin; a slice; honorary or votive tablets: in the coll. read ʻpeng, q. v.: [13]ʻpiéng ngiâh꜆ (coll. ʻpeng ngiâh꜆ or ꜀pá ʻpeng), a tablet, as over a graduate's door; votive tablets in temples.

蝙 ʻPien. Also read ꜀piéng: a bat, called [14]ʻpiéng hok꜆; ꜀siéng ʻchʻü, the fairy rat—the bat; in the coll. the terms yâʾ yéngʾ (night-swallow) and ꜀pi ꜀pa tauʾ kiék꜆ are common: COM., ʻpiéng hok꜆ ꜀tʻau, the figure of a bat, as on the toes of shoes; ʻpiéng hok꜆ seuʾ the bat and word "longevity," as in embroidery.

惼 ʻPien. Hasty, narrow-minded; mean, covetous; pusillanimous.

褊 ʻPien. Interchanged with the last: cramped, contracted, narrow; petty, small, strait, as territory, garments, or the mind: [15]ʻpiéng ʻsieu, small, mean; ʻpiéng laiuʾ cramped and mean; ʻpiéng ꜀sing, hasty, fearful.

貶 ʻPien. To dispraise, to censure; to criticise; to diminish; to degrade: [16]꜀pó ʻpiéng, to praise and blame, as a critic; [17]ʻpiéng chaik꜆ to censure and degrade; COLL., ʻpiéng kʻóʾ degraded.

窆 ʻ To bury, to put the coffin into the grave: ʻpiéng kʻeʾ implements used in interments.

變 Pien.ʾ To change, to alter; to transform, to metamorphose; a change, a mutation in being or condition; a turn of affairs, a revolution in the state; a calamity, a judgment from Heaven: [18]꜀tʻiéng piéngʾ providential calamity; [19]pʻaik꜆ piéngʾ to excite to revolt

[1]鞭打 [2]馬鞭 [3]鐵鞭 [4]皮鞭 [5]鯿魚 [6]扁心 [7]長身 [8]扁鈕 [9]扁盒 [10]扁鴨 [11]扁栢 [12]扁食 [13]匾額 [14]蝙蝠 [15]褊小 [16]褒貶 [17]貶謫 [18]天變 [19]迫變 ○

by oppression; COM., ¹piéng˒ ˏkeng or ²piéng˒ ˏch'iéng or ³piéng˒ wang˒ to change, to alter; ⁴piéng˒ hwa˒ a change in nature or substance; to change by moral influence; a metamorphosis, as of elves; ⁵piéng˒ saik, to change or lose color; ⁶ˋtiong piéng˒ to change, to assume another aspect, as an affair; cheng˒ piéng˒ a change in a disease; ˋkai piéng˒ to reform; to alter; piéng˒ ˏt'ung, to have versatile talents; COLL., piéng˒ ˋsi, change at death—as in the mind, disposition, etc; piéng˒ ˏchiăng, metamorphosed to elves, as animals by long discipline; piéng˒ meng˒ change of countenance—displeased; piéng˒ ˏmó k'ó˒ gone, lost, has disappeared; piéng˒ ˋma hié˒ or piéng˒ ˋma hwak, sleights of hand, juggler's tricks.

胼 ˏ Also read ˏping: the hard skin of a laborer's hand; hard, firm, callous, indurated; also loose, flabby skin and flesh.

駢 ˏ Also read ˏping: a span of horses; a redundance, superfluity, overplus; to arrive together; to associate, to join together, to clan: ˏpiéng ˋmu, a double thumb.

便 ˏ Pien. P'ien. To investigate, to discuss; easy, graceful; adulatory, flattering; full, well-read, learned; accustomed, habituated: also read piéng² and in the coll. ˏpeng, q. v.: ˏpiéng p'ek, to flatter; ˏpiéng ˏpiéng, to discuss; COM., ˋsieu ˏpiéng, to urinate; twai² ˏpiéng, to go to stool; COLL., ˏsing mwoi² ˏpiéng, the mind not yet accustomed to; chó˒ ˏpiéng k'ó˒ accustomed to doing it.

緶 ˏ Pien. Also read ˏp'iéng: to join flaxen threads; to sew, to seam; to connect, to bind; also to lift up one's garments.

便 ² Pien. P'ien. To put one at ease; to accord with; rest, convenience; convenient, opportune, advantageous; ready, at hand, at pleasure; an adverb, then, so, thus; forthwith, just as; that is: also read ˏpiéng, q. v.: ⁷piéng² ˏang, at leisure, otium; ⁸piéng² se² it is just so, that is; ⁹piéng² chiék, quick, ready at; handy, good to use, as a fine implement; COM., ¹⁰song² piéng² to embrace an opportunity; ¹¹taik, piéng² at one's convenience; ¹²ˏsui piéng² as you please, when convenient; ¹³ˏheng ˏhwong piéng² to do deeds of benevolence; ¹⁴piéng² kek, convenient, handy; ¹⁵piéng² kiéng˒ you will then see at once (that it is so); COLL., piéng² tëü² (dispose) your chopsticks at convenience—i. e., don't wait till I finish eating; piéng² ˋié, convenient seats; ng² piéng² not ready; inconvenient; piéng² ˏsing, (go) just as you are—without change of dress.

辨 ² Pien. To separate, to divide, to distinguish, to discriminate; to inquire into, to learn by investigation; the frame of a bedstead; an ancient land-measure: also used for p'iéng˒ (pervading) and

¹變更 ²變遷 ³變換 ⁴變化 ⁵變色 ⁶轉變 ⁷便安 ⁸便是 ⁹便捷 ¹⁰順便 ¹¹得便 ¹²隨便 ¹³行方便 ¹⁴便急 ¹⁵便見

○ ○ ○ ○ ○ ○ ○ ○ ○ ○

ʻ*piéng* (to censure): ˏ*hung piéngʼ* to distinguish, to explain; COM., [1]*piéngʼ piékˏ*, to discriminate.

辯ʼ Pien. Pan. Analogous to the last: to distinguish, to examine minutely; to set in order; to review, to criticise; to insinuate; to debate, to discuss, to wrangle, to contend; artful, specious: also read *paingʼ* q. v.: [2]ˏ*cheng piéngʼ* to wrangle; [3]ˏ*mi piéngʼ* to insinuate; an innuendo; [4]*piéngʼ teʼ* to regulate; COM., [5]*piéngʼ laungʼ* to debate, to discuss; [6]*piéngʼ paukˏ*, to dispute, to contradict; [7]*piéngʼ* ˏ*ming* (or ˏ*ch'ing* ʻ*ch'u*), to argue or discriminate clearly; ʻ*k'eu* ˏ*neng siékˏ piéngʼ* able in argument.

辮ʼ Pien. To plait, to braid, to twist, to intertwine; a cue: [8]*ta piéngʼ* to braid a cue; COM., [9]*piéngʼ siángʼ* silk-braid; COLL., ˏ*piéng piéngʼ* or ˏ*t'au hwokˏ piéngʼ* the cue; *p'ahˏ piéngʼ* or *piéngʼ* ˏ*t'au hwokˏ*, to braid the cue; *p'ahˏ* ʻ*chwi piéngʼ* to braid the cue loosely; ˏ*lau* ˏ*piéng piéngʼ* or ˏ*lau* ˏ*chiéng piéngʼ* to leave (the hair) for the cue, as when boys are first shaved; ˏ*t'au hwokˏ piéngʼ* ʻ*niu* ʻ*lá*, to wind the cue round the head.

卞ʼ Pien. To go quickly; swift, quick, hurried; a rule, a law; name of a district; a surname: *piéngʼ kek*, perturbed.

忭ʼ Pien. To be pleased; delighted, gay, joyous; jubilant, exhilarated.

汴ʼ Pien. A stream in Hupeh, a branch of the river Han: [10]*Piéngʼ* ˏ*liong*, the former name of K'aifung in Honan.

弁ʼ Pien. A leathern casque or helmet; a ceremonial bonnet used in the Chow dynasty; military officers; quick, alarmed, trembling; to strike with the hand: also read ˏ*pwang*, q. v.: ˏ*wong piéngʼ* civil and military officers.

拚ʼ P'ing. Pang. To put the hand on, to grasp; to reject, to throw away; to brush aside: often read ˏ*p'ing*, q. v.

艑ʼ A flat-bottomed boat, a scow; a shallop, used in Eastern China.

625) **Pieu.**

ˏ標 Piao. The topmost branch, the opposite of the root; a signal, a signal-post; a spear; *met.*, a command or division of troops; a signboard; a ticket, a card; a warrant, a mittimus; to raise a signal; to post a card or notice; to write, to inscribe in; to note, to insert, as additional clauses, etc; to appear, to show; high, conspicuous; fine, handsome: [11]*kiongʼ* ˏ*pieu*, to raise a signal; [12]ˏ*pieu* ʻ*chung*, to set an example: COM., [13]ˏ*pieu teʼ* fine, beautiful, pretty; [14]ˏ*pieu* ˏ*teu*, a ticket, a notice or card of prices; [15]*t'aikˏ* ˏ*pieu*, to post a notice; [16]ˏ*pieu* ˏ*miáng cheʼ* to inscribe a name; [17]*tokˏ* ˏ*pieu* and [18]ʻ*u* ˏ*pieu*, the divisions of the viceroy and governor; *ch'akˏ* ˏ*pieu*, to hoist a

1 辨別 2 爭辯 3 微辯 4 辯治 5 辯論 6 辯駁 7 辯明 8 打辮 9 辮綫 10 汴梁 11 建標 12 標準 13 標戳 14 標條 15 貼標 16 標名字 17 督標 18 撫標

signal; to stick up a card of prices; ˏpieu ˏtiong, a cockpit, a place where birds fight; COLL., tokˎ ˏpieu to get the prize, as a successful dragon-boat.

幖 ʻ Piao. A streamer, a pendant on the staff above the flag: COM., [1]ˏpieu taiˀ a tag or tab; the silk tags on the robes of brides, officers and graduates.

滮 ʻ Piao. The name of a river; a flowing stream, water running north: used for the coll. ˏpiu, q. v.: [2]ˏpieu ˏtié, a flowing pool.

瀌 ʻ The noise of sleet; the falling of rain and snow: [3]ʻü siok, ˏpieu ˏpieu, rain and snow falling abundantly.

麃 ʻ Piao. P'ao. To hoe up weeds; feathers that change color, as the feathers of the ptarmigan: ˏpieu ˏpieu, a martial appearance.

膔 Piao. Full of flesh, fat, gross: [4]ˏchié ˏpieu, fat and full, obese.

鑣 Piao. A bridle-bit: ˏpieu ˏpieu, full, abundant; in numbers, as a stud of horses.

儦 ʻ Piao. A company of men, a group, a crowd; herds in motion; crowds passing along.

彪 ʻ Piao. A small beast, striped like a tiger; a tiger's stripes; veins, streaks; ornate, elegant: [5]ˏpieu ˏping, ornate, as literary style.

髟 ʻ Piao. Long hairs, locks hanging down the face; the 190th radical: ˏtiong hwak, ˏpieu ˏpieu, long bushy hair.

猋 ʻ Piao. Dogs running about; also a violent wind rushing upwards: ˏpieu ˏhung, a whirlwind.

表 ʻ Piao. The outer or upper garments; external; beyond the borders; to show, to manifest; a guide, a signal; a statement sent to the emperor; a permit, a manifest; relations of a different surname, cousins; a watch: [6]ʻpieu ʻli ˏü ek, the inside and outside alike; ʻpieu ʻpieu, lofty, conspicuous; COM., [7]ˏsi ˏsing ʻpieu, a watch; [8]ʻpieu ˏchiong, a statement to the Emperor; [9]chengˀ ʻpieu, to make a statement, as to the Pearly Emperor by burning it; [10]ʻpieu ˏming, to show, to manifest; [11]ʻpieu ʻli ʻó, a lined, bridal robe; [12]ʻpieu ˏch'ing, relations of another surname, maternal relations; [13]ʻpieu ˏhing tá² maternal cousins; [14]ʻpieu tikˎ sons of a maternal cousin, second cousins; [15]ʻpieu sangˀ ˏhung ˏhang, to cure a cold.

婊 ʻ Piao. A woman's name; used in the coll. in the sense of a strumpet, as in the expressions ʻpieu ʻkiăng, a bastard; [16]ʻpieu ʻchü ˏtiong, a brothel.

褾 ʻ Piao. A lady's neckerchief, a sort of comforter; to paste papers, to make pasteboard, to mount scrolls or pictures: COM., [17]ʻpieu pwoiˀ

1 幖帶 2 滮池 3 雨雪瀌瀌 4 脂膔 5 彪彬 6 表裏如一 7 時辰表〇 8 表章 9 進表 10 表明 11 表裏襖 12 表親〇 13 表兄弟〇 14 表姪 15 表散風寒 16 婊子塲 17 褾褙〇

to paper, as a wall; to mount maps, etc; *'pieu pwoi' ch'iong'* a paper-hanger.

(626) Pih.

Pih₂. A coll. word: to pop, to spirt, to squirt out: *pih₂ cheng' ₍keng*, to spirt very high; *pih₂ leh₂ sioh₂ ₍siăng*, a squirting sound, pop! *pih₂ lih₂ puh₂ luh₂* to clatter, as books falling; *pih₂ leh₂ puh₂ loh₂* or *pih₂ peh₂ puh₂ poh₂* a splashing sound, as of things falling into water.

Pih₂. A coll. euphonic prefix, as in *pih₂ pwoh₂* to tie up, to bind; *pih₂ puh₂* a noiseless blow, as of the fist on the clothes.

(627) Pik.

闢₂ P'i. To burst forth, to open, to expand; to disclose, to appear; to develop, as nature; to avoid, to shun: [1]*'ek₂ hak₂ ek₂ pik₂* an opening and a shutting; culmination and decline, as of states; [2]*₍ch'u pik₂ te' ₍hwong*, to occupy new land; COM., [3]*₍k'ai pik₂ ₍t'iéng te'* or *₍k'ai ₍t'iéng pik₂ te'* to spread abroad the heavens and the earth, creation.

鼻₂ Pi. The nose, nasal; to bore the nose; the 209th radical; *met.*, the first, the original: in the coll. read *p'e'* q. v.: *pik₂ 'chu*, the first ancestor in a genealogy; *'hwang pik₂* an adder.

佖₂ Pi. Also read *pe'*: used for the next; grave, dignified, majestic; full, filled with; a man's name.

怭₂ Pi. Also read *pe'*: to act rudely or disrespectfully, as when one is muddled with liquor.

愎₂ Pi. P'i. Perverse, self-willed, pertinacious; wicked, disobedient.

弼₂ Pi. To aid, to assist, as statesmen do; a sort of splice or support on a bow; perverse, opposing:

拂₂ Fu. the 2d also read *hok₂* q. v.: [4]*'ho' pik₂* ministers, assistants; [5]*₍liong pik₂* a good minister.

甓₂ P'i. A large kind of tile, in which lines are made, and which is partly covered by other tiles when laid.

Pik₂. A coll. euphonic prefix, as in *pik₂ pek₂* to draw, to pull, to pull out.

(628) Ping.

兵 ₍Ping. Arms, weapons; a soldier, troops, forces, armies; military, martial, pertaining to war; to fight, to use arms: [6]*₍tiong ₍ping*, long arms, as spears and muskets; [7]*'twang ₍ping*, short arms, as swords and daggers; COM., [8]*₍ping k'e'* arms, military weapons; [9]*₍ping hiong'* soldiers' pay, rations; [10]*₍ping ₍ting* or [11]*₍ping sū'* a soldier; [12]*₍ping ₍sung*, a man-of-war; [13]*₍ping hwak₂* military tactics; [14]*₍ping ₍kwong*, military power; [15]*₍ping 'ma*, infantry and cavalry; [16]*'ma ₍ping*, cavalry; [17]*pwo' ₍ping*, infantry; [18]*₍ping pwo'* the Board of War; [19]*₍ping ₍pung*, the military office, as at a district magis-

[1] 一闔一闢 [2] 初闢地方 [3] 開闢天地 [4] 輔弼 [5] 良弼 [6] 長兵 [7] 短兵 [8] 兵器 [9] 兵餉 [10] 兵丁 [11] 兵士 [12] 兵船 [13] 兵法 [14] 兵權 [15] 兵馬 [16] 馬兵 [17] 步兵 [18] 兵部 [19] 兵房

trate's; [1]huk꜆ ꜀ping, an ambush; [2]keu꜄ ꜀ping, troops succoring others, a reinforcement; [3]꜂kwang ꜀ping, government troops; [4]꜀chieu ꜀ping ꜂má ꜂ma, to enlist soldiers and buy horses; [5]꜀tong ꜀ping, to be a soldier; [6]꜀tó ꜀ping, arms, equipments; ꜂k‘i ꜀ping ꜀kau chiéng꜄ to raise troops and go to war; ꜂hwí ꜀ping, firemen.

冰 氷 ꜀Ping. Ice; icy, cold, as ice; frozen; clear, pure; to freeze: [7]꜀ping sek, an ice-house; [8]꜀ping ꜁t‘ong, sugar-candy, rock-candy; [9]꜀ping ꜀ch‘ing ngŭk꜆ kiĕk꜆ clear as ice and pure as a gem—chaste, virtuous; ꜀ping ꜀ki ngŭk꜆ chek꜆ a clear skin and faultless form; *met.*, bright and beautiful, as flowers; COM., ꜀ping p‘iéng꜄ Baroos camphor; ꜀ping ꜁ing, a go-between, match-maker; ꜀chiong ꜀ping or ꜀ping ꜁t‘ong, rock-candy; COLL., ꜀ping ꜀song taĕng꜄ or ꜀ping ꜀song lang꜄ taĕng꜄ as cold as ice and frost.

檳 梹 ꜀Ping. The arecà or betel-nut, called ꜀ping ꜁long; COM., [10]꜀ping ꜁long ꜁pwang, a betel-nut plate; a pewter tray on which the nut is exposed for sale; COLL., ꜀ping ꜁long ꜂chi, pieces of betel-nut; ꜀ping ꜁long sioh꜆ ꜂k‘eu, a chew of betel-nut.

賓 賔 ꜀Pin. A guest, a visitor; to receive a guest, to act as the host; to submit, to come under civilizing influences: [11]꜀ping k‘aik꜆ a visitor; [12]꜀ping ꜁peng, a friend; [13]꜀sá ꜀ping, a domestic tutor; [14]sëü꜄ ꜂hai ꜀ping huk꜆ the whole country submitted; COM., [15]꜀ping ꜂chü ꜂lá, rules of politeness for guest and host.

濱 ꜀Pin. The bank of a stream, the brink, shore, margin; near, adjoining, contiguous to; to outlie, to border on: ꜂hai ꜀ping, the sea-shore.

浜 ꜀ A sluice or creek into which boats are run; a sort of dock for repairing boats.

繽 ꜀Pin. P‘in. Mixed, blended, as colored silks; numerous, confused: ꜀ping ꜀ping, blended, as colors in silks or bouquets; ꜀ping ꜀hung, many, confused.

蠙 ꜀Pin. As in ꜀ping ꜀chio, a pearl; the term may refer to those found in fresh water.

彬 斌 ꜀Pin. A due mixture of plainness and ornament; well-contrasted: ꜀ping ꜀ping, elegant and neat, but not gaudy; ꜁ung chek꜆ ꜀ping ꜀ping, elegance and simplicity in harmony.

豳 邠 ꜀Pin. The name of an ancient state in the south of Shensi, ruled by the family of Chow before they gained the throne, B. C. 1134.

掤 ꜀ A case for arrows, a quiver; to put the hand on the quiver so that the arrows may not drop out.

꜀*Ping.* A coll. euphonic prefix, as in ꜀ping ꜀pong, to aid, to help; ꜀ping ꜀pang, or ꜀ping

[1]伏兵 [2]救兵 [3]官兵 [4]招兵買馬 [5]當兵 [6]刀兵 [7]冰室 [8]冰糖 [9]冰清玉潔 [10]檳榔盤 [11]賓客○ [12]賓朋 [13]西賓 [14]四海賓服 [15]賓主禮○

‹ping ‹pang ‹pang, to spread the feet apart, as a child learning to walk.

‘禀 ‘稟 Pin. Ping. To state to a superior verbally or in writing; to inform a higher officer; to receive an order in course of duty or after inquiry; to receive from heaven; endowments, disposition; to petition, to ask for; a petition, a statement: also read ‘ling, q. v.: [1]‘ping hok, to reply to a superior; [2]‘ping meng’ to ask leave to do; to report on orders received; [3]kĕü’ ‘ping, a prepared petition; [4]‘ping ka’ to petition for a furlough; [5]‹chü ‘ping or [6]‘k‘e’ ‘ping, the natural temper, one's talents; COM., [7]kó’ ‘ping, to inform and petition a superior; [8]‘ping t‘aik, the card of a lower officer; an official statement to a superior; [9]‘ping tó’ to inform a superior of one's arrival; [10]‘ping ‹ang or ‘ping kiéng’ to visit a superior; [11]‘tá’ ‘ping, to present a petition.

‘秉 Ping. A handful of grain; an ancient dry measure equal to 16 hĕk, or 160 ‘tau; to seize, to grasp, to lay hold of; to maintain, to uphold: [12]‘ping taik, to adhere to virtue; [13]‘ping chĕük, tai’ tang’ to hold a light watching for the dawn; COM., [14]‘ping ‹kung ‹heng sĕü’ to act justly.

‘箳 Ping. A carriage curtain or screen, a wagon-covering: COM., ‘ping ‹liéng, a bamboo screen or curtain—usually called tĕük, ‹liéng.

‘餅 Ping. A cake, a biscuit; dumplings; a general name for pastry of flour, water and fat: in the coll. read ‘piăng, q. v.

‘丙 Ping. The third of the ten stems; a fish's tail: ‘ping ‹ting, the 3d and 4th of the stems, which belong to fire and the south, and hence mean bright; [15]‹ch‘ing ‘ping, heaven; [16]‹ing ‘ping chó’ hiong’ facing the south, as a house or grave; COM., [17]‘ping k‘e’ wong’ the igneous element prevalent—i. e., he has a warm physical temperament.

‘炳 ‘昺 Ping. The light of fire; bright, clear, as daylight; luminous, perspicuous, as style.

‘怲 Ping. Sad, sorrowful; grieved, deeply afflicted: [18]‹iu ‹sing ‘ping ‘ping, a mournful spirit, sorrowing.

‘邴 Ping. A city in the ancient principality of Sung; also one in that of Ching, in the east of China: ‘ping ‘ping, harmonious, agreeable.

‘牝 P‘in. The female of birds and beasts; also applied to plants: [19]‘ping ‘meu, male and female; ‘ping ‹kié ‹sü ‹sing, the hen rules the morning—the wife governs.

‘鞞 A scabbard, called ‘ping ‘p‘ung. Read pe’: a kind of drum, used as an accompaniment in music; to help.

1 稟覆 2 稟命 3 具稟 4 稟假 5 資稟 6 氣稟 7 告稟 8 稟帖 9 稟到 10 稟安 11 遞稟 12 秉德 13 秉燭待旦 14 秉公行事 15 青丙 16 壬丙 17 坐向丙 丙氣 18 旺 憂心怲 怲 19 牝牡 ○

臏 ‘ Pin. The knee-pan, the patella; the skin; to cut off the leg, as a punishment: COM., ˛Song ‘ping, a worthy so mutilated by ˛Mang ˛kiong at the close of the Chow dynasty.

‘*Ping.* A coll. euphonic prefix, as in ‘*ping* ‘*peng*, to turn over, to invert; to invert; to rock, as a boat does; ‘*ping* ‘*pong*, the splashing of water.

平 ˛ P‘ing. Even, level, uniform; just, upright; fair, equitable, as a price; usual, common, daily; tranquil, peaceful, undisturbed; to pacify, to tranquilize, to subdue; to adjust, to harmonize; plenty; a plain: in the coll. read ˛*pang*, q. v.: [1]˛*ping* ˛*hwo*, at peace, tranquil; [2]˛*ping* ˛*ming*, dawn; [3]˛*ping huk*˛ to subdue; COM., [4]‘*t‘ai*’ ˛*ping*, a state of peace; [5]˛*ping so*’ or [6]˛*ping nik*˛ ˛*kang*, heretofore, usually, daily; [7]˛*ping* ˛*ang*, well and happy, free from trouble; [8]˛*ping cheng*’ peace and quiet; a calm, as after a storm; [9]˛*ping chah*˛ ˛*siâng*, the even and the deflected tones; COLL., ˛*ping* ˛*ang ne*’ *che*’ *tek*˛ ˛*ch‘iéng* ˛*king*, the two words ˛*ping* and ˛*ang* are worth a thousand of gold!

抨 ˛ Ping. To grasp, to hold; to raise up. Read ˛*p‘eng*: to cause, to occasion; to follow.

泙 ˛ P‘ing. A valley; a cave on the seashore, where the waves rush in; name of a stream: ˛*ping* ˛*ping*, the roaring of surges.

苹 ˛ P‘ing. Used for the next: a sort of edible celery or cress, called ˛*ping* ˛*lai*, of which deer are fond; it has straight stalks and whitish leaves: ˛*ping* ˛*ping*, grassy, herbaceous.

萍 ˛ P‘ing. A kind of duckweed, a floating plant grown in fishponds, a species of Azolla; *met.*, busy, wandering about: [10]˛*ping* ‘*chwi* ˛*siong* ˛*hung*, to meet, as floating duckweed—i. e., accidentally; [11]˛*ping* ˛*chung* ˛*u teng*’ to have no fixed abode, as travelers.

枰 ˛ P‘ing. A sort of wood, suitable for tables and stools; made plain and smooth; a chess-table; *met.*, a game of chess.

蘋 ˛ P‘in. An apple: [12]˛*ping* ˛*pó*, the Sterculia balanghas, an edible fruit; COM., [13]˛*ping* ‘*kwo*, a kind of apple, brought from Shantung.

頻 ˛ Pin. P‘in. Urgent, pressing; precipitate, urged, hurried; continually, incessantly; the margin of a stream: [14]˛*ping* ˛*lai*, to come incessantly; [15]˛*ing* ˛*ping*, the areca-nut; [16]˛*ping* ˛*niéng*, these few years past.

顰 ˛ Pin. P‘in. To smile, to simper and giggle; to knit the brows, to frown: [17]*hau*’ ˛*ping*, a poor imitation, as one says of his own writing, etc.: [18]˛*Tung* ˛*sié hau*’ ˛*ping*, Tungshih's miserable attempt to imitate (the beautiful Hsishih)—which only made her look uglier

1 平和 2 平明 3 平服 4 太平 5 平素 6 平日間 7 平安 8 平靜 9 平仄聲 10 萍水相逢 11 萍踪無定 12 蘋婆 13 蘋果 14 頻來 15 仁頻 16 頻年 17 效顰 18 東施效顰

蘋 ꜀Pin. P'in. P'ing, An aquatic plant, a large kind of Lemna or duckweed; it bears a white flower and was anciently used in sacrifices.

馮 ꜀Fêng. A horse running; to mount, to ascend; the sound of a hard wall; dissatisfied, angry; to rely on; boastful. Read ꜀*hung:* a surname.

凴 憑 凭 ꜀P'ing. A stand for a valuable stone; to lean on; to trust to, to rely on; to act in accordance with, to obey; as, according to; proof, evidence: COM., [1]꜀*ping kĕü*꜄ proof; [2]꜂*k'eu siok*꜆ ꜀*u* ꜀*ping*, mere woods are no proof; [3]꜀*ung* ꜀*ping*, an officer's commission; [4]꜀*ping yong*꜅ a model; according to the pattern; [5]꜀*ping sik*꜆ ꜂*kong*, to speak truly; [6]꜀*ping* ꜁*t'iéng twang*꜄ as Heaven decides it; [7]꜀*ping p'ieu*꜄ ꜁*chié* ꜀*chiéng*, to cash a note or bank-bill.

屏 ꜀Ping. P'ing. A wall inside a doorway as a screen; a screen; to screen, to cover, to keep out of view: [8]꜀*ping hang*꜅ servants, those who protect the state, as the emperor and magistrates; [9]꜀*ping e*꜄ a god of rain; COM., [10]꜀*ping* ꜁*hung*, a door-screen; also an aquatic plant, called ꜁*hwong* ꜁*hung;* [11]*ch'ak*꜆ ꜀*ping* ꜀*mwong*, the small doors of a fixed screen; [12]꜀*ui* ꜀*ping*, a folding-screen; [13]*kiăng*꜄ ꜀*ping*, a pier-glass in a standing frame; [14]꜀*ping* ꜁*hung kiăng*꜄ pictures on glass slid into frames; [15]꜀*Ping* ꜀*nang kaing*꜅ a district of the Foochow prefecture. Read ꜂*ping:* to expel, to scatter; to reject; to spoil, as robbers; to retire, to withdraw.

貧 ꜀P'in. Poor, destitute; indigent, impoverished, penniless: [16]꜀*ping* ꜀*hang*, wretchedly poor; [17]꜁*ang* ꜀*ping*, contentedly poor; COM., [18]꜀*ping* ꜀*kŭng*, poor, destitute; [19]꜀*ping chiéng*꜅ poor and lowly, ignoble; ꜀*ping* ꜀*kŭng* ꜂*k'u* ꜂*ch'u*, poor and distressed; ꜀*ping peng*꜅ ꜁*kau* ꜁*ka*, poverty and sickness combined; ꜀*ping* ꜁*cheng*, I, a poor priest.

瓶 缾 ꜀P'ing. A vessel to draw water; a steaming utensil; a vase, a jar, a cruet, a vessel with tubular neck and small mouth; a phial, a bottle: COM., ꜁*hwa* ꜀*ping*, a flower-vase; ꜂*chiu* ꜀*ping*, a wine-jug; ꜀*ping chiok*꜆ a wine-jug and goblet, used in oblations; ꜀*ping* ꜂*kwo*, flower-vase and (plate of) fruit.

帡 ꜀P'ing. Also read ꜁*ping* and ꜂*ping:* a side-screen; a covering, a canopy, a curtain: ꜀*ping* ꜀*mwong*, curtains, awnings.

凭 ꜀Ping. P'ing. To lean upon or against; to depend on, to trust to, to confide in: ꜀*ping* ꜀*lang*, to lean on the railing.

꜀*Ping.* A coll. euphonic prefix, as in ꜀*ping* ꜀*pong*, or ꜀*ping* ꜀*pong* ꜀*pong*, a report, as of fire-crackers, bang! ꜀*ping* ꜀*piăng*, or ꜀*ping* ꜀*ping* ꜀*piăng* ꜀*piăng*, the noise, as of doors slamming.

[1]憑據 [2]口說無憑 [3]文憑 [4]憑樣 [5]憑實講 [6]憑天斷 [7]憑票支錢 [8]屏翰 [9]屏翳 [10]屏風 [11]插屏門 [12]圍屏〇 [13]鏡屏 [14]屏風鏡 [15]屏南縣 [16]貧寒 [17]安貧 [18]貧窮 [19]貧賤

(629) Piu.

滮 Piao. Read ,pieu: water flowing, a stream running north: used for the coll. ,piu, to spirt, to spout forth: ,piu ch'ok, to spirt out; ,piu cheng² ,tong, to spirt out in a long stream.

(630) Po.

富³ Fu. Read ho³; coll. po³: rich, wealthy: ¹po³ ,nĕng, a rich man; ²po³ ho³ a wealthy family; po³ ,tu p'ak, overflowing with wealth.

菢³ Pao. Read pó³; coll. po³: to brood, to incubate, to cover, as a bird broods over her eggs, to hatch; a hatch, a brood: ³po³ luung³ to hatch eggs; po³ ak, 'kiăng, to hatch ducklings; ⁴po³ sioh, po³ to hatch a brood; ⁵ch'ok, po³ hatched out.

腐³ Fu. Read ho³; coll. po³: to rot, to decay: po³ lang³ decayed, rotten, as wood; 'ang po³ to rot or decay.

仸³ A coll. character: and, also, moreover, again, further; both, the same, at the same time; before a negative, but, still, yet; combined with a negative, neither, nor: ⁶po³ ,kiéng, and, in addition; ⁷po³ ,li, to come again; ⁸po³ se³ it yet is; ⁹po³ ,t'ié po³ ch'ieu³ to cry and laugh at the same time; ¹⁰po³ ,chau po³ chiong³ both sauce and pickle; met., to go to extremes; excessive, supererogatory; ¹¹po³ ch'ek, po³ paik, both seven and eight—both this and that, extreme, exorbitant.

(631) Pó.

褒 褎 ,Pao. Long garments or skirts; to proclaim the excellence or merits of; to praise, to extol, to laud, to commend, as virtuous deeds: ¹²,pó 'chiong, to praise; ¹³,pó 'piéng, to praise and to censure; COM., ¹⁴,pó 'mi (coll. ,pó 'pi), to extol; COLL., ¹⁵,pó ,nĕng ,hwang 'hi, to please one by praising him.

鄱 ,P'o. A district in Kiangsi, called ,pó ,yong; COM., ¹⁶,pó ,yong ,hu, the Poyang Lake in the north of Kiangsi.

皤 ,Po. P'o. White, plain; gray, white-haired, as the aged; silvery hair turning gray; a white belly; abundant, affluent.

坡 ,P'o. Read ,p'ó; coll. ,pó: a mound, a hill, a hillock: ,t'u ,pó, a mound of earth; ,pang ,pó, a hill with a level top.

玻 ,Po. P'o. Read ,p'ó; coll. ,pó, as in ,pó ,lá, a vitreous substance, glass; ,pó ,lá ,ting, a glass lantern; ,pó ,lá p'iéng³ panes of glass; ,pó ,lá 'chai, a kind of clear, smooth paper.

,Pó. A coll. word: a corruption of the next, as in ,pó ho³ to protect, to guard or bless, as the gods do.

1 富仸
2 富戶
3 菢蛋
4 菢一菢
5 出菢
6 仸兼
7 仸梨
8 仸是
9 仸啼仸笑
10 仸糟仸醬
11 仸七仸八
12 褒獎
13 褒貶
14 褒美
15 褒仸歡喜
16 鄱陽湖

‘保 Pao. To protect, to preserve, to guard; to feed, to nourish; to warrant, to guaranty, to secure, to be surety for; a protector, a guardian; a bail, a surety; an advocate, a mediator: [1]*‘ing ‘pó ˓u ˓ngü*, forever kept from injury; COM., [2]*‘pó ho²* to protect, as the gods do; [3]*‘pó ‘kü*, or *‘pó chiéng’* to recommend another; [4]*‘pó neng²* (coll. *chó² ‘pó*), to be surety for; *‘pó ˓pieu* or *‘pó ka’* to defend, take one's part; [5]*‘pó ˓chié* or *‘pó p‘ieu’* to be security for the payment of a bond; [6]*‘pó tëüng² ˓sing ‘t‘á*, to take care of the health; [7]*‘pó ˓sing ˓hu*, a charm to guard the person; [8]*té² ‘pó*, or *‘pó ‘tiong*, or *‘pó ‘tiong ˓kung*, a village constable; [9]*‘pó kak*, a union for mutual protection, as in a ward or village; [10]*˓tüng ‘pó*, a mediator; *liéng ˓k‘wang ‘pó*, mutual security, or several persons being security for one; *˓kung ‘pó*, a stamped certificate, given to students by the *Ôh˒ ˓kwang*.

‘堡 Pao. P‘u. A low wall or breastwork; a battery, a fort; a post or small fortified town; a citadel in the country: *‘pó chiong’* a military post, a barrier.

‘葆 Pao. Interchanged with the last and the next: luxuriant herbage, thick, bushy; sprouts of mulberry and other trees; to cover, to shade, as trees; even, level; to store up; a wild leguminous vegetable. Read *˓pó*: wide, broad.

‘褓 Pao. A swaddling-cloth: in the coll. read *pó²* q. v.: *‘kiong ‘pó*, a clout; a swathe to carry an infant on the back.

‘寶 Pao. Precious, valuable, as gems; value, worth; a term of respect; to regard as precious or felicitous, to esteem, to value; noble, honorable; *met.*, the great seal, the throne: [11]*˓ting ‘pó*, jewels, trinkets; [12]*˓teng tai² ‘pó*, to ascend the throne; COM., [13]*‘pó pwói’* precious, costly; [14]*‘pó ˓wong*, large, dried lungans; [15]*‘pó taing’* your shop; [16]*‘pó ˓kwang* and *‘pó ne²* the proprietors of a gambling establishment; [17]*‘pó ˓tiong*, a gaming establishment; [18]*‘pó chó²* an idol's seat; [19]*paik˒ ‘pó*, "the eight precious"—certain silver ornaments on a child's cap; [20]*wang² ‘pó ˓chiong ˓chü*, a book of plays, &c.; *˓u ka’ ˓chi ‘pó*, priceless; *kwok˒ ‘pó*, or *˓t‘ung ‘pó*, the precious metals; COLL., *paik˒ ‘pó*, to know the merits or value of; *ch‘aung’ ch‘aung’ ‘pó*, trifling things esteemed precious; *‘pó ‘tau* and *‘pó ‘chi*, the two blocks (one within the other) of the apparatus used in the *liéng’ liéng’ ‘pó* gaming.

‘鴇 Pao. A kind of wild goose, having spotted plumage, and flying in flocks; it is described as without a hind toe.

報’ Paó. To recompense, to requite for benefits or injuries, to avenge; a retribution, a reward, a recompense; to tell, to state, to inform; to report; a messenger;

---

[1]永保無虞 [2]保護 [3]保舉 [4]保認 [5]保支 [6]保重身體 [7]保身符 [8]地保 [9]保甲 [10]中保 [11]珍寶 [12]登大寶 [13]寶貝 [14]寶圓 [15]寶店 [16]寶官 [17]寶場 [18]寶座 [19]八寶 [20]萬寶全書

a report, an advertisement, a gazette; to debauch superiors: [1]꜀*ing pó*ʾ and [2]꜂*yong pó*ʾ secret and open requital; [3]*nik*꜀ *pó*ʾ a daily Court Circular; also the official business circulars, issued by magistrates; COM., [4]*pó*ʾ *tak*꜀ to recompense; [5]*pó*ʾ *eng*ʾ a reward or recompense; retribution; [6]*pó*ʾ *seng*ʾ to give intelligence of; [7]*pó*ʾ *chong*ʾ finished, all completed; [8]*pó*ʾ ʻ*hwói*, to inform (the officers) of a conflagration; [9]*pó*ʾ ꜂*siu*, to take revenge; [10]*pó*ʾ ꜀*kwang*, to inform a magistrate; [11]*pó*ʾ ꜀*ong*, to requite a favor; [12]*pó*ʾ *swoi*ʾ to report for toll (at a custom house); [13]*pó*ʾ *ko*ʾ to report a death; [14]*pó*ʾ ꜀*ting* ꜀*iu*, to report the death of one's parent, as an officer does; ꜂*tʻi* ꜂*tong pó*ʾ intelligence by official courier; [15]꜀*king pó*ʾ the Peking Gazette.

播ʾ Po. To sow seed; to disseminate, to scatter; to publish, to divulge; to throw aside, to reject; to dupe, to befool; to shake; in the coll. to give alms: also used for the coll. *pwo*ʾ q. v.: [16]*pó*ʾ ʻ*chüng*, to sow seed; [17]*pó*ʾ ꜂*yong*, to promulge; to winnow grain; *pó*ʾ *liong*ʾ to dupe; COLL., *pó*ʾ *sié*ʾ to give alms—a term used by beggars.

颶ʾ **颶**ʾ Chü. Read *këüʾ*; used for the coll. *pó*ʾ: a furious wind without rain: *pʻah*꜀ ꜀*hung chó*ʾ *pó*ʾ a storm of wind, a violent gust of wind; ʻ*kʻi pó*ʾ or *hwak*꜀ *pó*ʾ a gust rising.

簸ʾ Po. A winnowing fan, called *pó*ʾ ꜀*ki*; to fan grain in the wind: in the coll. read *pwai*ʾ q. v.

꜂**婆** Pʻo. An old woman, a wife; a dame, a gammer, a granny; matronly; much used by Budhists in the sense of immortality: [18]꜀*siu* ꜀*seng* ꜂*pó*, a midwife; COM., [19]꜂*pó* ꜀*kwang* ꜂*pó* ʻ*chiá*, the thirty six attendants of ꜂*Ling* ʻ*chwi* ʻ*ná* (the guardian of children); [20]꜂*múi* ꜂*pó*, an old match-maker; [21]꜀*kung* ꜂*pó*, male and female ancestors; [22]*sá*ʾ ꜂*pó*, a concubine; *twai*ʾ ꜂*pó*, the principal wife; COLL., *lau*ʾ ꜂*pó* (or *lau*ʾ ꜂*pʻó*), a wife—an imitation of the term in the Court dialect; ꜂*pó* ꜂*pó* or *lau*ʾ ꜂*pó* ꜂*pó*, an old lady; ꜀*i* ꜂*pó*, old lady! Madam! *kʻwoh*꜀ ꜂*tá* ꜂*pó*, a boat-woman; a strumpet; ꜂*pó* ʻ*ná*, a midwife; ꜂*Pó* ʻ*ná* ꜀*sang*, a slight eminence in the suburbs of Foochow.

꜂**蔢** Pʻo. Luxuriant vegetation: ꜂*pó* ꜀*só* or ꜂*pó* ꜂*pó* ꜀*só* ꜀*só*, an exuberant growth; COLL., ꜂*pó* ꜀*pó*, peppermint; ꜂*pó* ꜀*pó* ʻ*kwói*, steamed rice-cakes, flavored with peppermint—eaten in the ꜀*chʻing* ꜂*ming* festival.

꜂**袍** Pʻao. A robe, a court dress, a long garment of ceremony; a gown single or quilted; the front skirts: ꜂*tung* ꜂*pó*, compeers; *chiéng*ʾ ꜂*pó*, defensive armor, mail; COM., *tó*ʾ ꜂*pó*, a Tauist's robe; ꜂*pʻúi* ꜂*pó*, a fur robe; ʻ*mong* ꜂*pó*, a court dress embroidered with boas or dragons; *kak*꜀ ꜂*pó*, a double or quilted robe; ꜂*pó* ꜂*lung*, an overall, worn to preserve the robe; *kak*꜀ ꜂*pó twang*ʾ *ngié*ʾ to break friendship.

[1]陰報 [2]陽報 [3]日報 [4]報答 [5]報應 [6]報信 [7]報竣 [8]報火 [9]報仇 [10]報官 [11]報恩 [12]報稅 [13]報故 [14]報丁 憂[15]京報 [16]播種 [17]播揚 [18]收生婆 [19]婆官 婆姐 [20]媒婆 [21]公婆 [22]細婆

ˏ*Pó.* A coll. word, as in ˏ*pó ˏló ch'ó'* disquieted, disturbed and anxious.

抱 Pao. To infold, to contain; to carry in the arms, to embosom, to embrace, to grasp; to encircle; to feel, to cherish in the mind; to adhere to; the lap, the bosom: [1]*ˏhwai pó* to carry in the bosom, as a babe; [2]*pó hauug ek, ˏseng*, to cherish anger to the end of life; [3]*chai pó* in the lap; [4]*pó hang* to feel regret: COM., [5]*pó wong* to cherish enmity; [6]*pó kó* to accuse, or conduct a suit for the plaintiff; [7]*pó pok, ˏping*, aroused, as on witnessing a cruel act; COLL., *pó ˏchiéng ʻchwi*, to lose the discount, to allow a premium on; *pó ˏsing ˏsiéng*, pleased with a new thing; *pó ʻkiáng pó ˏsong*, he has sons and grandsons—is a happy man; *pó ˏma má ka ʻch'ü*, a carried cat can't bite the rat—one must be left to act freely.

菢 勽 Pao. To cover, as a bird her eggs, to brood, to incubate: in the coll. read *po* q. v.

暴 Pao. P'ao. The fierce rays of the sun, scorching; cruel, violent; to strike with the hand; to grasp; boisterous, stormy, as a wind; suddenly, abruptly; to display, to manifest: [8]*pó ʻü*, a violent rain; [9]*ˏhwang pó* overbearing, outrageous; [10]*pó no* violently angry; *pó pó* suddenly; COM., [11]*pó ngiok,* oppressive, as an officer; [12]*pó lá* perverse; fierce, cruel.

爆 Pao. Sad, melancholy, sorrowful: COLL., *pó lok,* toilsome, full of trouble, as one's life.

褓 Pao. Read ʻ*pó*; coll. *pó* as in *pó ˏkung*, a clout, a swaddling cloth; a swathe to carry a child on the back.

Pó. A coll. word, as in *po cha* at first, just at first, on the instant; *pó cha ˏt'iang*, on first hearing; *pó cha ch'eng ch'eng ʻsi ˏnëng, pó cha po ˏk'i ho ˏnëng*, when the weather first becomes cold it freezes one to death, so when one first becomes rich he treats persons overbearingly.

(632) Poh.

Poh,. A coll. word, as in *poh, poh, kieu* or ˏ*pu poh, kieu* a sound, as in breaking wind.

(633) Póh.

Póh,. A coll. word: to rail, to curse at, to abuse a person by using vile language about his relatives: *póh, ˏnëng*, to curse people; ˏ*p'ieu póh*, or ˏ*lë póh*, to blackguard, to revile.

箔 Po. Also read *pok,* and used for the next: a curtain, a door-screen; foil of tin or gold; idolatrous paper covered with tinfoil: COLL., *póh, ˏch'ang* and *póh, ˏking*, tin or pewter foil; *p'ah, sek, póh,* or *p'ah, póh, ˏch'ang*, to beat out pewter-foil.

[1]懷抱 [2]抱恨一生 [3]在抱 [4]抱憾 [5]抱怨 [6]抱告 [7]抱不平 [8]暴雨 [9]橫暴 [10]暴怒 [11]暴虐 [12]暴厲

○ ○ ○ ○ ○ ○ ○ ○ ○ ○ ○

鉑 Po. Gold-leaf; foil of tin, brass, or other metals: [1]*ˌking póh* gold-leaf.

泊 Po. Also read *pok*: the glare of water; ripples; to stop; still, unoccupied; to anchor, to moor: [2]*tang póh* wholly unemployed; COM., [3]*póh ˌsung*, to anchor or moor a boat; COLL., *póh o' 'lá*, to anchor in the cove.

舶 Po. A large junk; a ship, a vessel suitable for crossing seas: [4]*'hai póh*, a large junk or ship.

樸 Pu. Read *puk*; used in the *Paik, ˌIng* for the coll. *póh*: to rent, to bargain, as for the fruits of trees or gardens: [5]*póh ˌchu*, to engage or hire previously; [6]*póh ˌp'ung*, to bargain for the swill; [7]*póh ˌngü ˌtié*, to rent a fish-pond.

薄 Po. Pao. Read *pok*; coll. *póh*: thin, not thick: *póh lóh*, (or *tóh*,), thin, thinness; *'ting póh* very thin; *póh ch'woi'* a kind of thin flour cake; *ˌk'a ˌp'uí ˌkiäng póh*, the skin of my feet worn thin—by coming so often.

Póh. A coll. word: to roost, to perch, as birds: *ˌch'á póh*, or *ˌtau póh*, to stay at; *met.*, to depend on one; *póh ˌnëng ˌmwong ch'ié' ˌpiéng*, to lean on people's door-posts—depend on them for aid; *póh piäh, há'* the "wall-perching crab"—a wall-fixture for candles.

(634) Poi.

痱 Read *pe'*; used in the *Paik, ˌIng* for the coll. *poi'*: the prickly heat: [8]*ˌsang poi'* to have the prickly heat; [9]*poi' siong* the itching sensation of prickly heat.

吠 Fei. Read *hié'*; used in the *Paik, ˌIng* for the coll. *poi'*: to bark: *'k'eng poi'* the dog barks—used as an abusive term, you yelping cur! *poi' 'hwang ˌt'iéng*, to bark furiously; *'yä poi'* to bark wildly—i. e., without cause.

(635) Pok.

不 Pu. Fou. Po. Pou. An adverb, no, not, usually qualifies verbs and adjectives; before the latter it answers to *un*, *dis*, *in*; repeated with *taik*, or *'k'ó*, it forms an affirmation; following another negative, it strengthens the affirmation; before *ˌü* or *yok*, it negatives the comparison; after *'k'i*, it makes an affirmative question; placed between a verb repeated, it forms a question; repeated before verbs and some adjectives, it answers to neither, nor: the coll. equivalent is *ng'* q. v.: [10]*pok, yok, k'ëü'* rather go, better to go; COM., [11]*'k'i pok, se'* how is it not? it is so; [12]*pok, haing'* unlucky; [13]*pok, kik,* to fail to reach, deficient; [14]*pok, 'lá*, impolite; [15]*pok, tek,* or *pok, tuk,* or *pok,*

1 金鉑 2 淡泊 3 泊船 4 海舶 5 樸租 6 樸泔 7 樸魚池 8 生痱 9 痱癢 10 不若去 11 豈不是 12 不幸 13 不及 14 不禮 15 不特

'*chi*, not only, not simply; [1]*pok*, '*lieu*, can't get done with, can't get rid of; [2]*pok*, ˛*sing k'e*' worthless, defective, as men or things; [3]*pok*, *chai*' not here—dead; [4]*pok*, *chá' sëü*' the business can't be completed; [5]*pok*, *taik*, '*i*, necessary, unavoidable; [6]*pok*, *taik*, *pok*, '*kong*, must say it; [7]*pok*, *laung*' or *pok*, ˛*kü*, without regard to, no matter which or what; [8]*pok*, ˛*nang pok*, *paëk*, "neither south nor north" —neither the one thing nor the other, incomplete, incongruous.

卜 Pu. To divine by rattling cash in a tortoise's shell; to guess, to conjecture; divination, sortilege; to give; the 25th radical: in the coll. read *pauk*, q. v.: *pok*, *kwa*' to divine; ˛*chiéng pok*, to draw lots, to prognosticate in any way.

腹 Fu. Read *hok*,; coll. *pok*, as in *pok*, '*ló*, the belly, the abdomen, the bowels; the seat of the mind; the affections: [9]*pok*, ˛*tong*, the intestines; [10]*pok*, ˛*sai*, the navel; *pok*, '*ló* '*tié*, in the abdomen; in the mind; *pok*, '*ló t'iàng*' the belly-ache; *pok*, '*ló* ˛*ku*, a kind of female necromancer; *pok*, '*ló* ˛*kwi* (or ˛*eu*), hungry; *pok*, '*ló* ˛*küng ch'ieu*' ˛*k'iu*, the muscles of the abdomen convulsed with laughter; *pok*, '*tié* ˛*ming*, the mind clear; ˛*sing pok*, near, esteemed and trusted; *pok*, '*ló* '*tié* ˛*ha* ˛*ma* '*kiàng* ˛*toi* ˛*sang*, "the mind full of little toads"—very clever, precocious.

***Pok*,.** A coll. word: to gather, to scrape up and gather in the arms; the quantity gathered: *pok*, ˛*tu*, to gather up dirt; *pok*, *sioh*, *pok*, to gather a quantity or the arms full.

***Pok*,** A coll. word, as in *pok*, ˛*kang*, or *pók*, ˛*kang pang*' the ague and fever.

***Pok*,.** A coll. word, as in *pok*, *chiong*' (or *pwok*, *chiong*'), a pestilential disease, a plague or distemper among animals; also used as a curse: *pok*, *chiong*' ˛*tü*, a hog having the distemper.

薄 Po. Trees standing singly, no brushwood; thin, subtile; slight; poor, bad, unfortunate, unlucky; light, few; careless, vain; to slight, cold, inattentive to, impolite; stingy; a screen, a curtain; a thin leaf, a pellicle: in the coll. read *póh*, q. v.: [11]˛*ing* ˛*ting* ˛*tang pok*, to have few descendants; com., [12]*pok*, ˛*ching* ˛*long*, an unfeeling husband; [13]*pok*, ˛*ch'ing*, distant relationship; [14]*lok*, *pok*, reduced to extreme poverty; [15]*pok*, '*li*, or *pok*, *pok*, *e*' to be mean or stingy, as in presents; also affectedly, my poor feast or presents; [16]*pok*, ˛*hó* ˛*iu*, the essence of peppermint. Read *p'aik*,: to near, to approach.

亳 Po. A place in Honan, the capital in the early period of the Shang dynasty: [17]*Pok*, ˛*chiu*, a department in the north-west of Nganhwui.

[1]不了 [2]不成器 [3]不在○ [4]不濟事 [5]不得已 [6]不得不講 [7]不論 [8]不南不北 [9]腹腸 [10]腹臍 [11]人丁單薄 [12]薄情郎○ [13]薄親 [14]落薄 [15]薄禮 [16]薄荷油 [17]亳州○

福州方言拼音字典

(636) Pong.

幇 幫 幚 ʿPang. To bind the edge of a shoe; a binder, a support; to take a part or share in; to lend a hand, to assist; to succor, to defend; in the coll. a lot of goods; a picking of tea: COM., [1],pong chai[3] to aid, to help; [2],pong ʻmó, a guide or rule to work by; [3],pong ,ch'á, an assistant policeman; [4],pong ʻlü, a company, a club; ,pong tak, to take passage on a boat with others; [5],pong t'aik, to make up a deficiency; ,pong siéng to get a share in the (wind of another's) fan; to go shares in a partition between shops; ,pong ,ngiong, to speak a good word for one; ,pong ʻch'iu, to lend a helping hand; COLL., ,t'au ,pong ,tá, the first picking of tea; ,pong sioh ʻku, to take a subsidiary share in a business; ʻchi sioh ,pong ,ki hwoʼ this lot of goods.

垹 An elf or sprite, coming out of the ground; it is greedy to eat and has no fingers.

梆 ʿPang. The name of a tree; a wooden cylinder used in offices to call people; a watchman's rattle, called in coll. p'ok p'ok ʻkwong, q. v.: COLL., ,pong ,pong ʻku, a long drum slender in the middle, as the ,long t'iongʼ; a sort of one-headed drum used by begging-musicians.

榜 榜 ʿPang. To propel a boat; a fleet; to bamboo criminals; a slip, a splinter of wood; a rule for selecting graduates of the second and third degrees; a list of successful Küjin or Chinsz'; famed, celebrated: [6],king ʻpong, or [7],lüng ʻhu ʻpong, the official list of graduates; [8],pieu ʻpong, celebrated; COM., [9],tung ʻpong tëüngʼ fellow-graduates; [10]ʻliong ʻpong ch'ok, ,sing, a Chinsz' entering upon office; [11]ʻpong ,ung, an official notice, as inviting aid against rebels; also a notice of the ,kung taik, or ʻp'wo toʼ rites; [12]ʻpong ʻngang (coll. ʻpó ʻngang), the second on the list of Chinsz'; [13]hwak, ʻpong, to post up the list of graduates; [14]ʻhó ʻpong kaʼ a firm attitude in archery; ʻpong yongʼ an example; ,chu ʻpong, a lease. Read ,p'ang: a support put on a bow.

搒 挷 ʿPang. To cover, to screen from view; to propel a boat; a boatman; the 2d also used for ,pong (an elf). Read ,pong: to beat, to pound.

綁 ʿPang. To bind, to tie with cords, to tie the hands behind the back; in the coll. a pair of drawers or overalls, in which sense also read ʻpwong, q. v.: ,sëng ʻpong, to loosen the bonds; COM., pwoi[2] ʻpong, to tie the hands behind the back; ʻpong ch'ek, to tie a thief; siongʼ ʻpong, bound, as a criminal for execution; COLL., ʻpong ʻt'oi, a pair of overalls or leggings; ʻpong ʻt'oi k'oʼ full drawers, drawers lined or wadded for winter-wear.

[1]幇助 [2]幇㑹 [3]幇差 [4]幇侶 [5]幇貼 [6]金榜 [7]龍虎榜〇 [8]標榜〇 [9]同榜中〇 [10]兩榜出身 [11]榜文 [12]榜眼 [13]發榜〇 [14]好榜架〇

膊 ʻ Po. Read *pauk,*; coll. *ʻpong*, as in *,kiéng ʻpong*, the shoulders; *ʻpong k'wak,* the shoulders broad; *met.*, to have many friends; *ʻpong chah,* narrow-shouldered—having few friends.

髈 ʻ Pang. P'ang. The pelvis, the hip-bone, the bones of the groin.

滂 ʻ P'ang. Read *,pong*; used for the coll. *ʻpong*, as in [1]*ʻpong ʻpong kieu'* (or *ʻp'ong ʻp'ong kieu'*) the splashing sound of water; *ʻpong ʻpong ,ch'ing,* thin, having but few grains in, as rice-gruel.

放 ' Fang. Read *hwong'*; coll. *pong'*: to dismiss, to let go, to loose, to liberate; to fire off; to issue, to invest; to set, to place, to put down: [1]*pong' k'ó'* to release; [2]*pong' ch'ok, ,li,* to set things out, as from a closet; [3]*pong' ,sang,* to let go alive; [4]*pong' ʻch'iu,* to relax the grasp; to relinquish a work; [5]*pong' ,tong,* to let out long, as a string; [6]*pong' ʻchai yeu'* to fly a kite; *pong' pong' ,sing,* to dismiss anxiety; [7]*pong' tau'* to dismiss for dinner, as a school; [8]*pong' t'aik,* to issue cards of invitation; [9]*pong' chai'* to invest money; *pong' ch'ëüng'* to fire off guns; *pong' ʻchi,* to deposit the eggs, to spawn, as fish.

糞 ' Fên. Read *hong'*; coll. *pong'*: ordure; filth, muck; excrement, dung; refuse, sweepings; *met.*, vile, bad, wicked: [10]*pong' ʻt'ëng,* a dung-bucket; [11]*pong' p'woi'* a crust of ordure; *met.*, used as a term of abuse; [12]*pong' ,tié* or *pong' hĕk,* a manure-pit or cistern, as in fields; [13]*pong' ,k'ang ch'io'* a privy; [14]*pong' ,k'ang ,ku,* the goddess of privies; *pong' ,mwong ʻk'au,* the anus; *pong' tó'* dirt, sweepings; *pong' tó' ,toi,* a heap of refuse.

畚 ' P'ên. Read *ʻpwong*; used in the *Paik, ,Ing* for the coll. *pong'* as in *pong' ,ki,* a shallow bamboo basket, a mason's hod; *pong' ʻtau,* a dust-pan.

旁 ʿ P'ang. Large, extensive; the side; at or by the side of; lateral, sidewise: [15]*ʿpong hong'* marginal comments; [16]*,ki ʿpong,* a three-forked road; COM., [17]*ʿpong ,piéng,* the side, at the side; COLL., *ʿpong ,sing chioh,* candles made with a pith-wick at the side of the *,mëng ʻkó* stalk.

傍 ʿ Pang. P'ang. Same as the last in the sense of the side, at the side; at, near, by: also read *paung'* and in the coll. *p'aung'* q. v.: COM., *ʿpong ,ing,* a by-stander; *ʿpong ,kwang ʻchiă ,ming,* a looker-on sees (the matter) clearly.

滂 ʿ P'ang. Also read *,p'ong*: a great rain; the noise of rain; the roar of a torrent: used for the coll. *ʻpong,* q. v.: *ʿpong ,yong,* vast, extensive; [18]*ʿpong p'woi'* a flood; flooded; [19]*ʿpong ,tó tai' ʻü* (coll. *,p'ó ,tó twai' ʻü*), a heavy rain.

1. 放去
2. 放出來
3. 放生
4. 放手
5. 放長
6. 放紙鷂
7. 放午
8. 放帖
9. 放債
10. 糞桶
11. 糞殼
12. 糞湍
13. 糞坑厝
14. 糞坑姑
15. 旁訓
16. 歧旁
17. 旁邊
18. 滂沛
19. 滂沱大雨

福州方言拼音字典

膀 ꜀P'ang. The ribs; the region of the groin: ꜀pong ꜀kwong, the bladder; [1]꜀pong ꜀kwong kiék, yék꜆ inflammation of the bladder.

㥿 ꜀P'ang. Timid, alarmed, afraid: ꜀pong ꜀hwong, fearful, apprehensive.

磅 ꜀P'ang. The noise of stones falling: in the coll. read ꜀p'ong, q. v.: ꜀p'eng ꜀pong, the crash of falling rocks; COLL., ꜀ping ꜀pong, a loud sound, the report (of fire-crackers).

螃 ꜀P'ang. A crab, a sea-crab: ꜀pong hâ² a species of swimming or sea-shore crab.

蹺 ꜀P'ang. To go quickly, to rush forward; to appear as if about to go.

鈍² Tun. T'un. Read tong²; used in the Paik, ꜀Ing for the coll. pong²: dull, slow, stupid, obtuse: pong² chiăh, pong² or pong² ꜀chi che² excessively stupid; pong² ꜀chai 'chü, a dull scholar; ꜀pang pong² slow, as in walking.

(637) Pu.

꜀*Pu.* A coll. word, as in ꜀pu ꜀pu kieu² the sound of blowing; a purling or gurgling sound, as in smoking the water tobacco-pipe.

꜀*Pu.* A coll. word, as in ꜀pu (or ꜀pu) ꜀sung tong² a sudden tremor, as over the body.

菩 ꜀P'u. P'ai. A kind of tree, called ꜀pu ꜀t'i, brought from Magadha, India; [2]꜀pu ꜀t'i sak, ꜀sui, a Budhist term, meaning grateful; COM., [3]꜀pu sak, a contracted form of the last, a Budhist demigod, a deified hero, an idol; [4]꜀pu sak, ꜀k'ang, an idol-shrine or niche; [5]wak, ꜀pu sak, a very efficacious Budh; [6]tai² ꜀chü tai² ꜀p'i ꜀pu sak, the very compassionate Budha—Kwanyin. Read ꜀pùi: grass, herbage, thatch, a small mat. Read p'aiu²: a fragrant plant.

瓠 ꜀Hu. Read ꜀hu; coll. ꜀pu: a gourd, the bottle-gourd or gourd-squash, a calabash: ꜀pu te² the stem of a gourd; *met.*, a small cue; ꜀pu ꜀p'ieu, spoons made of gourds; ꜀pu ꜀pang, a frame on which gourds are grown.

葡 ꜀P'u. Read ꜀pwo; coll. ꜀pu, as in [7]꜀pu ꜀tó, grapes; [8]꜀pu ꜀tó 'chié, grape-color, purple; [9]꜀pu ꜀tó ꜀kang, dried grapes, raisins.

蒲 ꜀P'u. Read ꜀pwo; coll. ꜀pu: a kind of rush: ꜀pu ꜀pau, rush-wrapping; [10]꜀pu ꜀t'wang, round or square rush-mats; [11]꜀pu siéng² a palm-leaf fan.

꜀*Pu.* A coll. word, as in ꜀pu ꜀sing, a house-fly; ꜀king ꜀pu ꜀sing, a bottle-fly; *met.*, applied to one making vain pretensions; ꜀pu ꜀sing 'hu, a spider which jumps on flies; ꜀pu ꜀sing 'sai, fly-dirt; *met.*, pimples, freckles; ꜀pu ꜀sing p'e² k'ëük, siăh꜆ nge² has a fly's nose and a beggar's ears—i. e., has a

[1] 膀胱結熱 [2] 菩提薩埵 [3] 菩薩 ○ [4] 菩薩龕 ○ [5] 活菩薩 ○ [6] 大慈大悲菩薩 ○ [7] 葡萄 [8] 葡萄紫 [9] 葡萄乾 [10] 蒲團 [11] 蒲扇

keen scent, is quick to hear all about it.

ₛPu. A coll. word; similar to *ₒpu*, as in *ₛpu ₒtu*, noise in blowing a fire; a gurgling sound, as in smoking the water-pipe; *ₛpu ₒtu ch'ok*, *ₒli*, to throw out, as the food in laughing; to blurt out, as words.

ₛPu. A coll. word: to bake or roast in the ashes: *ₛpu sŭkₗ* to roast till well done; *ₛpu tiéᵓ ₛpwo*, to roast oysters in the shell.

ₛPu. A coll. word, as in *ₛpu ₒtung ₒsai*, the hair disheveled.

ₛPu. A coll. word, as in *ₛpu ₛpwang sóiᵓ* to sit with the limbs bent and crossed, as a foreign tailor, or a Bonze in meditation.

(638) Puh.

Puhₗ. A coll. word, as in *pihₗ puhₗ* the sound of a stroke on soft things; *puhₗ siohₗ ₒt'ui*, to give a blow with the fist; *puhₗ siohₗ ₒsiăng*, the sound, as of an arrow on a target.

(639) Pui.

肥 ₛFei. Read *ₛp'i;* coll. *ₛpui:* fat, oily; rich, fertile; fleshy: ¹*ₛpui ʿchwi*, fat, fleshy; ²*ₛpui twaiᵓ* fat and large; ³*ₛpui chóᵓ* the fat layers of pork (under the lean part); *ₛpui ₒnai ₒnai* or *ₛpui naĕᵓ naĕᵓ* very corpulent; *ₛpui teᵓ* fertile land; *ₛpui ₒtu pek* obese; *ₛpui ʿseng*, the fat and lean (of meat); *ₛpui ₒtŭ ʿkwo*, "the fat-pig fruit", a kind of fruit with a thick skin, containing two or three nuts; macerated and made into balls, it is used as coarse soap and called *ₛpui ₒtŭ ₛwong*.

ₛPui. A coll. word, equivalent to *kauᵓ:* leaven, yeast: *hwak*, *ₛpui*, leavened; *ₒpau ₛpui*, yeast.

(640) Puí.

賠 ₛP'ei. To make up a loss, to indemnify; to restore, to supply a deficit; to confess: ⁴*ₛpuí ₛhwang*, to restore, to repay; COM., ⁵*ₛpuí ₛchiéng*, to indemnify by paying money; ⁶*ₛpuí ₛchiéng hwoᵓ* goods that sell below cost; ⁷*ₛpuí ʿpwo* or *ₛpuí taingᵓ* to make up a deficit; ⁸*ₛpuí waᵓ* or *ₛpuí pok, seᵓ* to confess a wrong; ⁹*ₛpuí ch'oiᵓ ₛpuí siékₗ* to act as an advocate for one.

培 ₛP'ei. To add earth to, to heap mold or manure about plants; to till; to nourish, to assist; to add energy to; to dam up: COM., ¹⁰*ₒchai ₛpuí*, to plant and till; *met.*, to instruct, to train up; ¹¹*ₛpuí ʿyong*, to invigorate; to fertilize, to manure, as plants; ¹²*ₛpuí ʿyong ₛngwong k'eᵓ* to invigorate one's constitution.

陪 ₛP'ei. Analogous to the last; to add mold to; to assist, to aid; to accompany, to fellowship; to attend upon; to double, to match; attached to, subordinate; to fill: ¹³*ₛpuí ₛsing*, subordinate ministers, as feudal princes style themselves; COM., ¹⁴*k'iéngᵓ ₛpuí*, owe my company—i. e., excuse my leaving you; ¹⁵*ₛpuí chóᵓ* (coll. *ₛpuí sóiᵓ*), to sit with a guest; ¹⁶*ₛpuí ch'ieuᵓ* to laugh with one;

¹肥水	³肥座	⁴賠還	⁵賠錢	⁶賠錢貨	⁷賠補	⁸賠話	賠舌	¹¹培養	¹²培養元氣	¹³陪臣	¹⁵陪坐
²肥大	○	○	○	○	○	⁹賠嘴	¹⁰栽培	○	○	¹⁴欠陪	¹⁶陪笑

福州方言拼音字典

[1]*,pui pai'* to return salutations; [2]*,pui p'wang'* to bear one company.

(641) Puk.

僕 Pu. P'o. To follow, to serve; a vassal, a retainer; a slave, a menial, a servant; a charioteer; a disciple; I, your servant; to belong to; hidden, secret: [3]*,ka puk* domestics; *'puk pe'* male and female servants; *'puk lá'* menials, criers before an officer; [5]*puk puk ,hung ,ting,* troublesome matters, toil, drudgery; COM., [7]*,nu puk* a slave, a male servant.

幞 P'u. A kerchief for the head; a sort of military hood; the skirts trimmed off.

蹼 P'u. The web of geese and other water-fowl; web-footed.

濮 Name of a river; a large kind of bamboo with the joints a foot apart; a district in Shantung, called *Puk ,chiu;* a drum in Corean language: COM., *puk yéng'* a thin silk fabric from *Puk ,chiu.*

瀑 Pu. Pao. Water rushing down precipices, a cascade: *puk pwo'* a cataract; *puk pwo' ,hiéng ,chiong,* a cascade appearing as a hanging fountain. Read *pó':* a heavy rain.

暴 Pao. P'ao. To sun, to dry in the sun; to manifest; to proclaim: [8]*ek nik puk ,chi, sek nik ,hang ,chi,* "one day in the sun and ten days in the cold"—(a prince) one day with good counsellors and ten days with bad ones.

曝 Pao. Same as the last and mostly used in the sense of to dry, to sun: in the coll. read *p'woh,* q. v.

爆 Pao. To burn, to canterize; to snap, to burst from heat; to dry by the fire; hot, crackling; in the coll. to fumigate; blackened with smoke: also read *pauk,* q. v.: COLL., [9]*kwa' chau' ,mi ,t'au puk,* to smoke over a furnace, as meat; [10]*'hwi ,ing puk ,u,* blackened by the smoke; *puk ,hwa yong'* to make pictures of flowers by fumigation.

轂 Hu. A large goblet; to exhaust; thin, poor; a hoof; the top of the foot; harsh, unkind: [11]*puk sok,* trembling from fear, as animals when pursued.

匐 P'u. To fall prostrate: *,pwo puk,* to crawl, as children do, or as persons prostrating themselves before the emperor; [12]*,pwo puk 'wong keu'* to hasten to relieve (a friend).

葍 P'u. A fragrant white flower, called *'tang puk:* COM., [13]*,ló puk,* a term for edible, spindle-shaped roots, as beets, radishes, parsnips, but specifically applied to carrots; COLL., *,ló puk 'chĕng,* carrot-leaves.

(642) Pung.

崩 Pĕng. Read *,peng;* coll. *,pung:* the fall or sliding of a mountain, to cave in; to fall into ruins:

[1]陪拜 [2]陪伴 [3]家僕 [4]僕婢 [5]僕隷 風塵 [6]僕僕 [7]奴僕 [8]一日暴之 十日寒之 [9]掛灶眉頭 [10]爆火烟爆 [11]烏轂觫○ [12]匍匐往救 [13]蘿葍○

[1]꜀pung ʻtó, to fall, as a wall; [2]꜀pung tʻak, to fall and settle; caved in, as a grave; ꜀pung sioh, kʻiăk, fallen so as to make a gap; haik, ꜀sang ꜀pung, a copious hemorrhage, flooding.

枋 ꜀Fang. Read ꜀hwong; used in the Paik, ꜀Ing for the coll. ꜀pung, as in ꜀yeu ꜀pung, the boarding below the plastered walls in Chinese houses; piăh, ꜀pung, (partitions of) lath-walls and boarding.

房 ꜀Fang. A room, a chamber; a house; an office, a department of an office; one living in the same room; a branch or line of a family; the sexual act; a calyx; a quiver; a sacrificial vessel; a bee's nest; the 4th of the 28 constellations, Scorpio: COM., [3]꜀pung ok, a house; [4]꜀pung ꜀kang, rooms; [5]꜀pung sĕŭk, lodgings; [6]꜀mwong ꜀pung, an anteroom; [7]lĕk, ꜀pung, the six departments of an office (lé, hoʼ, ʻlá, ꜀ping, ꜀hing, ꜀kung); [8]꜀pung sĕŭʼ the sexual act; [9]꜀pung ʻtiong, the head of the branch of a family; [10]pʻwangʼ ꜀pung, a bride's attendant; [11]hiéʼ ꜀pung, the greenroom; [12]꜀pʻiéng ꜀pung, a concubine; [13]꜀yăng ꜀pung, a camp; COLL., ꜀kiăng ꜀pung, sexual intercourse; ꜀pung ʻtʻĕng, a wooden chamber-vessel; ꜀pung ʻtié, a bed-chamber; ꜀pung ꜀seng pok, tʻiăngʼ (or ꜀puí ꜀neng pok, tʻiăngʼ), the custom of sending money and food to the bride's parents after marriage.

縫 ꜀Fêng. Read ꜀pʻung; coll. ꜀pung, as in ꜀pung kʻaiuʼ ꜀mwong, to work button-holes.

꜀Pung. A coll. word: to blow with the mouth: ꜀pung ꜀tĕng, a blow-pipe; ꜀pung kwoʼ to blow out (a light); ꜀pung ʻhwi, to blow a fire; ꜀pung ꜀tü ꜀pʻa, to inflate a hog's bladder; ꜀pung ꜀king ꜀king ꜀pʻau pʻauʼ to make soap-bubbles; ꜀pung ꜀hung, to blow on or into; met., to whisper, to tell tales about one.

(643) Pwai.

簸ʼ Po. Read pòʼ; coll. pwaiʼ: a winnowing-fan; to fan grain in the wind: pwaiʼ ꜀ki, a bamboo basket or tray to winnow grain; pwaiʼ ʻmi, to fan rice; pwaiʼ ꜀ki ʻku, the winnowing-fan (beaten as) a drum by women cursing when things are stolen; pwaiʼ ꜀ki ꜀sing, the god of the fan.

(644) Pwak.

撥 Po. Pa. Pu. To spread out, to arrange; to distribute, to allot, to dispose; to detach, as troops; to expel, to abolish; to rid, to exclude; to dissipate, to scatter, as clouds; to flirt, as a fan; the fluttering of a dress; the ropes of a hearse; to draw a bow; the recoil of a bow; in the coll. to stir up, to excite, to arouse; to move, as with a stick: [14]pwak, ꜀kŭng, to pull a bow; COM.. [15]pwak, ꜀chʻá, to detach police; [16]pwak, ʻma, a pickpocket; [17]pwak, ꜀liong ʻchʻó, to give out rations; [18]pwak, ꜀kʻai ꜀hung ʻuʼ kiéngʼ ꜀chʻing ꜀tʻiéng, to "scatter

[1]崩倒 [2]崩塌 [3]房屋 [4]房間 [5]房宿 [6]門房 [7]六房 [8]房事 [9]房長 [10]件房 [11]戲房 [12]偏房 [13]營房 [14]撥弓 [15]撥差〇 [16]撥馬〇 [17]撥糧草〇 [18]撥開雲霧見青天〇

the fog and see clear sky"—to get relief from distress; COLL., *pwak,* *'ch'ang,* to arouse, to excite one to duty; *pwak, so'* to "turn" an account—to pay a creditor through a debtor; *pwak,* *,kwong,* to increase the light by raising (the wick); COLL., *pwak,* *,mwong ch'aung'* to pick a lock or bolt; *pwak,* *,teng ,i,* take and return it to him.

襏, A rain-garment, made of leaves or coarse cloth: *pwak, hek,* a rain cloak or overcoat.

鉢, Po. An open dish, usually earthen; a narrow-mouthed dish, used by Bonzes: [1]*,tiong ,i pwak,* to hand down the robe and dish—to leave, as one's profession to a disciple or a son; COM., [2]*pwak, ,pwong,* a priest's dish or basin.

鈸, Po. Read *pak,;* coll. *pwak,:* a kind of cymbal with a bulging center: *twai' pwak,* large cymbals; *pwak, 'kiăng,* small cymbals; *ne' pwak,* cymbals of a medium size.

跋, Po. Read *pak,;* used for the coll. *pwak,* as in *pwak, hiék,* toilsome, laborious.

跌, Tieh. Tsai. Read *tiĕk,;* used for the coll. *pwak,:* to stumble and fall, to fall down: [3]*pwak, 'tó,* to fall; [4]*pwak, 'si,* to fall dead—an imprecation; [5]*pwak, 'ta,* agile movements, the movements of actors; [6]*pwak, saĕk,* very troublesome, difficult to effect; *pwak, 'kiăng ,k'ang,* "fall into a children's ditch"—to have many children.

Pwak,. A coll. word: to estimate dimensions, to measure with a rule, &c.: *pwak, k'ang'* measure it and see.

(645) Pwang.

般 Pan. A sort, a manner, a kind, a way: also read *,pang,* q. v.: [7]*,tó ,pwang,* many kinds; [8]*ek, ,pwang,* the same as, similar to; COM., [9]*sek, paik, ,pwang 'u ngié' yong' yong' ,kai ,neng,* the eighteen kinds of military drill, he can do them all; *met.,* to have manifold ability, very clever. Read *,pwang:* a large boat; ease, pleasure. Read *pwak,* and used by Budhists in the sense of wise, intelligent.

'搬 Pan. Su. To remove, to move, to transport; to bicker, to tell tales: COM., [10]*,pwang ,ié,* to remove; [11]*,pwang ,só,* to instigate, to excite to evil; COLL., [12]*,pwang 'hwi,* to move from a burning house; [13]*,pwang ch'io'* to remove, to change residence; *,sang 'a ngwok, nik, ,pwang ,tang,* the allowance of three months' free rent to the lessee for expenses of moving.

'班 Pan. An order, rank, series; a class, a company, as of actors, police, attendants: in the same senses also read *,pang,* q. v.: COM., [14]*,ung ,pwang,* and [15]*'u ,pwang,* the civil and military classes; [16]*,lung ,pwang,* to serve in turn, as policemen.

---

[1]傳衣鉢〇 [2]鉢盆 [3]跌倒 [4]跌死 [5]跌打 [6]跌摔 [7]多般 [8]一般 [9]十八般武藝樣樣皆能〇 [10]搬移 [11]搬唆 [12]搬火 [13]搬厝 [14]文班 [15]武班 [16]輪班〇

半' Pan. To divide in two; a half, a moiety; a piece, a portion of: COM., [1]'pwang' p'iĕng' half a slice; [2]'pwang' k'aik, a while; [3]'pwang' ,sing, half of the person, the bust; [4]'pwang' ,siĕng, "half-fairy"—one endowed with genius or prescience; [5]'pwang' ,nang 'nü, a hermaphrodite; [6]'pwang' ,sang ,ta, the "half-hill-tea"; [7]'pwang' chiĕk, ,sang, a coat or gown in two parts of different material united in the middle; [8]'pwang' ,heng 'ch'ó, a half-running hand in writing; [9]'pwang' ,nang pok, paĕk, "half south, yet not north"—incomplete, not wholly good or bad; COLL., pwang' ,mang, midnight; pwang' ,tong ,yeu, the middle, as of a pole or wall; pwang' meng' 'chü, a half-son—i. e., a son-in-law; pwang' ,p'u ,t'eng, half-floating and half-sinking, as one only partially successful in trade; pwang' tio' 'mwo, a temporary wife; pwang' ,lang ,ch'iăng, half-done, unfinished; pwang' 'a ngwok, nik, half-a-month.

Pwang'. A coll. word, as in ,kwang pwang' an obstacle, a hindrance, a difficulty in the way of; ,mó nóh, ,kwang pwang' nothing to hinder.

Pwang'. A coll. word: to annoy, to tease: móh, pwang' ,i, don't tease him; ,mó k'ok, ,mó pwang' I did not touch or annoy (the child).

盤 槃 ,P'an. A plate, a platter; a tray, a dish, a trencher; curved, coiled up; to examine, to investigate; to transfer, to transport; in the coll. to be together; to copy; to take an inventory of; to buy goods; exorbitant, wholesale: used for the coll. kiĕk, q. v.: COM., [10],pwang 'wang, plates and bowls; [11],pwang 'kwo, a plate of artificial fruit; [12],pwang ch'ai' dishes of food; [13],pwang ,cha, to examine into; [14],pwang k'ik, ,kang 'p'i, to search vagabonds—words on small flags as at the city gates; [15],pwang ong' to transport, as salt from the salt-houses; [16],pwang 'ku, P'anku, the first man; [17],pwang ,chiĕng, or [18],pwang hié' traveling expenses; COLL., ,pwang ,chü, to copy a book; ,pwang taing' to take an inventory of shop (goods); ,pwang kiĕk, to buy goods for retailing; ,pwang saung' an exorbitant estimate, as for interest; hwak, ,pwang, to sell at wholesale, as to hucksters; ,pwang ,hwang, to company together; ,pwang pauk, or ,pwang ch'oi' to debate, to dispute; ,tó ,pwang, to borrow capital; 'chio ,pwang, to manage, as a superintendent.

槃 ,P'an. Used for the last: a tray, a waiter; a tub, a wash-basin; to rejoice; to revolve or turn around: [19],pwang lok, to rejoice; [20],pwang ,ting, to revolve so as not to advance.

磐 ,P'an. A large rock, a foundation-stone: ,pwang sik, ,chi ,ang, peaceful as if settled on a rock; ,pwang

[1]半片 [2]半刻 [3]半身 [4]半仙 [5]半男女 [6]半山茶 [7]半樓衫 [8]半行草 [9]半南不北 [10]盤碗 [11]盤果 [12]盤菜 [13]盤査 [14]盤詰奸匪 [15]盤運 [16]盤古 [17]盤錢 [18]盤費 [19]槃樂 [20]槃停

˓nga, an unbroken series; incessant, as incursions of bandits.

鞶 ˓P'an. A large, leathern girdle; an ornamented sash; *met.*, a purse: [1]*˓pwang tai'* a leathern belt.

[般/足] ˓ To curl up the legs, to sit crosslegged: [2]*˓pwang ch'ek˓ ˓i chó'* to sit with the feet bent under one.

[足般] ˓ To walk lame; to jump a wall, in which sense the same as *˓mwang*, q. v.

胖 P'ang. Fat, corpulent, gross, obese, as one at ease; the half of a carcass; a slice, the collops on the ribs: [3]*˓sing 'kwong 't'á ˓pwang*, good-natured and fat.

弁 ˓Pien. To rejoice, to be glad: also read *piéng'* q. v. [4]*˓sieu ˓pwang*, name of an ode in the Shih King.

絆' Pan. A kind of lasso, a rope to catch or trip horses' legs; to hamper, to restrict; an obligation; in the coll. to brush away, to strike with limber things, as a rope's end: [5]*˓ing ngié' ˓chi ˓kié pwang'* the obligations of benevolence and rectitude; COM., [6]*˓tiéng pwang'* entangled, tripped, as by an obstruction; *met.*, involved, obscure; COLL., *pwang' 'ma sóh*, a rope for tripping horses' feet; *pwang' ˓hung ˓mwong*, to brush away musquitoes.

[米半]' Pan. Things mixed or harmonizing; in the coll. to mix in, to sprinkle spices or seasoning, as on cooked vegetables: COLL., *pwang' kai' lak˓* to season with mustard; [7]*'˓kang pwang'* "dry-mixed", as a dish of seasoned vermicelli without broth.

叛' Pan. P'an. Pang. To revolt, to rebel; to desert a government: [8]*pwang' ngik˓* rebellion; [9]*˓lié pwang'* to disavow a government's authority.

(646) **Pwí.**

杯 盃 桮 Pei. A cup, a glass, a goblet, a drinking-bowl; in the coll. divining-blocks: COM., [10]*˓ta ˓pwí*, a tea-cup; [11]*keng' ˓sang ˓pwí 'chiu*, to offer three cups of wine; [12]*˓pwí ˓pwang 'chang*, a (silver) salver and goblet—given to Küjin graduates at the Governor's feast; [13]*˓kau ˓pwí 'chang*, "the united goblets"—cups united by silk cord at a bridal; COLL., [14]*˓pwí t'óh*, the small salver of a wine-cup; [15]*'ka' ˓pwí*, the divining-blocks, used before idols; [16]*mwong' ˓pwí*, to inquire by the blocks.

˓Pwí. A coll. word: to fly, to flit; to go swiftly; flying: *˓pwí k'ó'* has flown away; *˓pwí 'cheu*, birds; *˓pwí ˓t'èng*, winged insects; *˓pwí ˓siéng*, projecting eaves, at the ends of a roof; *˓pwí 'k'au*, winged imps, such as go about tormenting folks; *˓pwí ˓chai*, an incidental calamity, as coming from another source; *˓king ˓kié 'kiâng 'mwang ˓t'iéng ˓pwí*, golden chicks flying through all the sky—as seems to the sight when one is dizzy or falls heavily.

[1]鞶帶 [2][般/足]膝而坐 [3]心廣體胖 [4]小弁 [5]仁義之羈絆 [6]纏絆 [7]乾[米半] [8]叛逆 [9]離叛 [10]茶杯 [11]敬三杯酒 [12]杯盤盞 [13]交杯盞 [14]杯托 〇 [15]珓杯 〇 [16]問杯 〇

ʻ掘 P'ei. Read *pwoi*²; used in the *Paik*, ˏ*Ing* for the coll. ʻ*pwí*: to dig for, to rake or scratch open; *met.*, to instruct: [1]ʻ*pwí ch'ok*, to rake out, as from a heap of rubbish; ʻ*pwí pwak*ˎ to instruct, to enlighten one's mind.

(647) Pwo.

ˏ晡 Pu. Time from three to five P. M.; the afternoon, the sun declining; in the coll. night: COM., [2]*pwang*ʼ ˏ*pwo*, the middle of the afternoon, about 4 P. M.; [3]ˏ*pwo* ˏ*si* ʻ*ü*, afternoon showers, summer gusts; COLL., [4]ˏ*hang pwang*ʼ (or *ang*ʼ) ˏ*pwo*, dusk; ˏ*mang* ˏ*pwo*, or ˏ*pwo* ˏ*si* ˏ*t'au*, the night-time; ˏ*pwo* ˏ*pwo*, every night; ˏ*pwo nak*ˎ to repay (borrowed money with interest) by nightly installments.

ʻ補 ʻ緖 Pu. To repair, to mend; to restore, to close a breach; to complete, to make up a deficiency; to aid, to assist; to recruit, as the body; a supplement, addenda; a term for a thousand millions: [5]ʻ*pwo huk*ˎ an embroidered official robe; COM., [6]ʻ*pwo* ˏ*i* ˏ*siong*, to mend clothes; [7]ʻ*pwo* ˏ*ngüng*, to patch up dollars; [8]ʻ*pwo* ˏ*ngüng* ʻ*chwi*, to make up the discount; [9]ʻ*pwo* ˏ*pi*, to strengthen the digestion; [10]ʻ*pwo yoh*ˎ to recruit with medicine; [11]ʻ*pwo k'wok*, to supply a deficiency, to fill a breach; [12]ʻ*pwo k'o*ʼ to supply a deficit in the treasury; *met.*, to contribute idol-paper to a temple; [13]ʻ*pwo ch'iong*ʼ (or ʻ*tá*) to supply (the odd cash) in strings of cash; [14]ʻ*pwo pó*ʼ to requite favor; COLL., ʻ*pwo má*² *tik*ˎ short of funds to meet liabilities; *siäh*ˎ ʻ*pwo*, to eat nourishing food; ˏ*tai* ʻ*pwo*, to patch.

布ʼ Pu. Cloth of cotton or hemp, nankeen, grasscloth, etc.: to spread out, to arrange; to diffuse, to publish; to infer; to worship the stars; a spring, a [illegible] in the coll. a numerative of [illegible] needles: [15]*pwo*ʼ *hwo*ʼ [illegible] coin; [16]*pwo*ʼ ˏ*i*, "cotton-cl[illegible] the common people; [17]*pwo*ʼ *sié*ʼ to disburse in charity; COM., [18]*pwo*ʼ *p'ek*, cotton piece-goods; [19]ˏ*yong pwo*ʼ foreign cotton-cloth; [20]ˏ*siä* ˏ*ung pwo*ʼ drillings; [21]ʻ*chié* ˏ*hwa pwo*ʼ nankeen; *chá*ʼ *pwo*ʼ grasscloth; ˏ*king* ˏ*ch'ang pwo*ʼ reddish blue nankeen; ˏ*iu pwo*ʼ oil-cloth; ˏ*hwa pwo*ʼ chintzes; ˏ*mwai pwo*ʼ hempen cloth; *pwo*ʼ *mang*² or *pwo*ʼ ˏ*p'ung*, a cotton screen or awning; *pwo*ʼ ˏ*üng*, or *pwo*ʼ ˏ*mó*, the nap of cotton cloth; *pwo*ʼ ˏ*si*, or *pwo*ʼ *cheng*ʼ ˏ*si*, a provincial treasurer; COLL., *pwo*ʼ ʻ*kiäng*, narrow cotton goods; *pwo*ʼ *sié*² the coarse threads or lines on cotton cloth; *twai*² *pwo*ʼ and *né*ʼ *pwo*ʼ large and second sized (needles).

佈ʼ Pu. Used for the last and the next: to publish; on all sides, reaching, extending everywhere: *pwo*ʼ *kó*ʼ to publish abroad; *pwo*ʼ *tó*ʼ to arrange; to place, as soldiers to guard a position.

捬ʼ Pu. Also read ˏ*p'wo*: to loosen, to open out, to expand, to extend; to disperse, to scatter; to strike: *pwo*ʼ *p'iéng*ʼ scattered all about.

[1]掘出 [2]半晡 [3]晡時雨 [4]含半晡 [5]補服 [6]補衣裳 [7]補銀 [8]補銀水 [9]補脾 [10]補藥 [11]補缺 [12]補庫 [13]補串 [14]補報 [15]布貨 [16]布衣 [17]布[illegible] [18]布疋 [19][illegible] [20][illegible]

怖ʼ Pu. Afraid, frightened, alarmed; to frighten, to cause fear; dread, terror, as on account of crime: [1]*ˏking pwo*ʼ alarmed.

播ʼ Po. Read *pó*ʼ; used for the coll. *pwo*ʼ as in [2]*pwo*ʼ *ˏch'eng*, to set out (rice plants) in the fields; [3]*pwo*ʼ *sioh*ˏ *ʻmu*, to plant a *mou* or acre; [4]*pwo*ʼ *ˏtau*, bunches of plants for transplanting.

ˏ蒲 P'u. Interchanged with the next: a water rush or sedge, used for mats and sandals, the cat-tail reed; the sweet flag (acorus gramineus): read *ˏpu* in the coll. q. v.: *ˏpwo kiéng*ʼ the sword-like leaves of the flag, hung as charms over doors; [5]*ˏpwo chiék*, the "flag-festival"—the 5th of the 5th moon; [6]*ˏpwo ˏkung ˏing*, the dandelion; COM., [7]*ˏpwo ˏt'wang*, rush-mats; COLL., *ˏmi ˏpwo* or *ʻhai ˏpwo*, the imported rice.

ˏ莆 P'u. The sweet flag: COM., [8]*ˏpwo ˏtiéng*, a district of the Hinghwa prefecture in Fookien.

ˏ葡 P'u. The grape: read *ˏpu* in the coll. q. v.: COM., [9]*ˏpwo ˏtó ch'eu*ʼ a grape-vine; [10]*ˏpwo ˏtó ʻchiu*, grape-wine; *ˏpwo ˏtó ʻchié*, purple.

ˏ匍 P'u. To lie prostrate; to crawl, as a child does; to strive for, to exert one's self: [11]*ˏpwo puk*ˏ to go on the hands and knees.

ˏ逋 To flee, to abscond; to suspend, to hang; to owe the government, to be a defaulter; a peculator: [12]*ˏpwo ho*[2] debts; [13]*ˏpwo ˏtó*, to escape from arrest.

ˏ餔 Pu. P'u. An afternoon meal or tiffin; to eat; thick rice-gruel: also used for *pwo*[2] (to feed infants).

鯆 A species of ray or skate that "stings with its tail"; its appearance is said to indicate rainy weather.

ˏPwo. A coll. word: a numerative of flowers: *ˏhwa sioh*ˏ *ˏpwo*, one flower; *ˏpwo so*ʼ or *ˏpwo ˏt'au*, a number of flowers.

ˏPwo. A coll. word: used for *ˏpung*, as in *tié*[2] *ˏpwo*, oysters in the shell; *tié*[2] *ˏpwo k'aïk*, the shells of oysters.

步[2] Pu. To walk, to go afoot, to step; a step, a pace, a stride; to go slowly; to travel in a barrow or sedan; a measure of about five feet; the span or length of a bow, used in land measure, called [14]*ˏkung pwo*[2]; infantry; a way, a manner; a mischievous demon which injures men and animals; a jetty, a landing, for which the next is more used: [15]*pwo*[2] *ˏheng*, to go afoot; [16]*ˏt'iéng pwo*[2] the ways of heaven; [17]*pwo*[2] *ʻli pok*ˏ *ˏchiéng*, my step is slow—i. e., I am old and can't serve the state; COM., [18]*pwo*[2] *pwo*[2] *ˏkó ˏsing*, to rise gradually in office; [19]*pwo*[2] *ˏping*, footmen, infantry; *ʻma pwo*[2] *chiéng*ʼ horse and foot archery; [20]*pwo*[2] *so*ʼ

[1]驚怖 [2]播田 [3]播一畝 [4]播株 [5]蒲節 [6]蒲公英 [7]蒲團 [8]莆田 [9]葡萄棋 [10]葡萄酒 [11]匍匐 [12]逋負 [13]逋逃 [14]弓步 [15]步行 [16]天步 [17]步履不前 [18]步步高陞 [19]步兵 [20]步數

steps; [1]*'t'ói pwo* to retire; *pwo pwo ˏliu ˏsing*, careful in everything; [2]*pwo chëüng* an idol's attendants; COLL., *ˏi ˏkiăng ó pwo so* he is a fast or steady walker; *met.*, he works systematically; *maing sioh, pwo* stop! wait a little! *pwo taiu* the step or movement, as of actors or sedanmen; *ˏch'iă 'tiong pwo* as soon as one can turn, in a little while.

埠 埔 Pu. Fou. The 2d is unauthorized: a port, a landing, a mart on the sea side: COM., [3]*pwo ˏt'au*, a commercial town; a mart, as where salt is collected.

捕 Pu. To seize, to pursue and capture; to watch for, to set a watch in order to arrest; to chase, to hunt; to angle for: [4]*pwo ˏngü* to angle for fish; [5]*pwo ˏhung ch'ŭük, 'ing*, to chase the wind and catch shadows—a vain search; COM., [6]*pwo ch'ek,* to watch for thieves; [7]*pwo ˏnga* or *pwo ˏt'iăng*, subordinate officers who make arrests—their office is near the district magistrate's; [8]*pwo ˏnga ˏch'á*, the police of a *pwo ˏnga*; COLL., *pwo sioh, hiok,* to watch a while (for thieves); *pwo tĕk, 'king*, to keep a strict watch.

哺 Pu. Also read *ˏpwo*: to feed an infant, as with a spoon; to mumble food for a child; to chew, to masticate; to give to eat; a mouthful: *'ü pwo* to feed with milk, to suckle; *t'o pwo* to spit out the food.

部 Pu. The sum, the totality, collective or general amount of; a general control, jurisdiction; a class, a tribe; a genus, as in natural history; the elements; the radicals of the Chinese language; classification of the stars; a bureau, a Board; a public court; a division of a book larger than a *kwong*; a classifier of books; a horde, a tribe, a clan; to divide, to spread abroad: [9]*'ngu pwo* the five elements; [10]*ˏhwi pwo* Mohammedan tribes; COM., [11]*lĕk, pwo* the six Boards, (*Lé, Ho, 'Lá, ˏPing, ˏHing, ˏKung*); [12]*ché pwo* the radicals; [13]*pwo chiong* officers under a general; [14]*pwo sŭk,* the officers composing a Board; [15]*pwo chieu* a commission or letters-patent issued by a Board; [16]*pwo ˏtong* and [17]*pwo yéng* titles of a viceroy and a provincial governor; [18]*'Chwi pwo* the water-gate suburb of Foochow.

蔀 Pu. A luxuriant plant; a plant eaten by fish, called [19]*ˏch'ü pwo*; a screen, an awning; a period of 72 years: [20]*pwo ok,* a mat house, a hut.

Pwo. A coll. word: a country brogue, as in *pwo lo* (or *su* or *to*), equivalent to *sioh, yong* as used in comparisons; *kaĕng ˏsié pwo lo* like to a serpent.

(648) **Pwoh.**

剝 Po. Pao. Read *pauk,*; coll. *pwoh,*: to flay, to peel, to skin, to exfoliate, to stripe off, as skin, bark, the clothes,

---

1 退步 2 步從 3 埠頭 4 捕魚 5 捕風捉影 6 捕賊 7 捕衙 8 捕衙差 ○ 9 五部 10 回部 11 六部 ○ 12 字部 13 部將 14 部屬 15 部照 16 部堂 17 部院 18 水部 19 蔀蔀 20 蔀屋 ○

福州方言拼音字典

etc.; also used for will, shall, about to; nearly; bent on, resolved: [1]*pwoh, ꜀p'uí*, to skin; [2]*pwoh, ꜂i ꜀siong*, to strip the clothes (from one); *pwoh, ꜀kwong ꜀kwong*, to strip bare; [3]*pwoh, ꜀t'au ꜀p'uí*, "bald pate!"—i. e., a Bonze; [4]*pwoh, ꜀p'uí ꜀tu*, to gamble away one's clothes; *꜀chiong pwoh*, will, about to; *pwoh, ꜀li*, about to come, will come soon; *pwoh, sük*, nearly ripe; almost done or cooked through; *pwoh, ꜀chiong wang*² bent on (do ng) so.

縛 Po. ₂ To bind, to tie up; to fasten baggage on a cart; to roll up; a roll: COM., [5]*pwoh*₂ *so'*₂, a limit or fixed, binding rule; impeded circulation (in the system); [6]*pwoh*₂ *tai'* to tie the girdle; COLL., [7]*pwoh*₂ *pe'* to make racks for rice-steamers; [8]*pwoh*₂ *꜀k'a ꜀t'oi*, to bind things on the thigh, as a widow at her second marriage taking things to her new home; *pwoh*₂ *sioh*₂ *'pa*, to tie up a bundle or bunch.

(649) Pwoí.

輩 輩 Pei. ' A hundred chariots make a *pwoí'*; chariots in line; a phalanx, a company; a class, an order, a generation; alike; kinds, sorts; to compare, to class; a sign of the plural of pronouns: [9]*'ngó pwoí'* we, our class; [10]*꜀chong pwoí'* you all—a polite phrase; COM., [11]*꜀chiéng pwoí'* seniors—a polite compellation of the aged; [12]*꜀tiong pwoí'* seniors; [13]*꜀tung pwoí'* (coll. *꜀pang pwoí'* or *꜀pang ꜀kiéng pwoí'*), of the same class or generation; [14]*wang pwoí'* or *haiu*² *pwoí'* juniors.

貝 Pei. ' Tortoise shell; also other fine sea-shells; cowries used as money before the time of Ch'in Shih-huangti, B. C. 246; a conch; jewels, riches, money, valuables; precious, valuable; name of a silk; the 154th radical: [15]*pwoí' 'king*, rich silks or dresses; [16]*pwoí' lek*₂ a Manchu title of nobility; COM., [17]*'pó pwoí'* precious; [18]*꜀kwi pwoí'* tortoise shell; ornamental work, figured as shells.

萛 Pei. ' Name of a plant: COM., *pwoí' 'mu*, a medicinal herb, the seeds of which are used as an expectorant.

根 Pei. ' A high tree, called *pwoí' ꜀tó*, growing in India and Burmah, of whose bark books are made; perhaps the talipot palm.

褙 Pei. ' Ancient long garments; used in the *Puik, ꜀Ing* for the coll. *pwoí'*; to paste paper together, to paper, as walls; to mount maps and pictures: COLL., [19]*pieu pwoí'* to paper walls; to mount scrolls, etc.; [20]*pwoí' 'chai*, to paste paper on; [21]*pwoí' ꜀liéng*, to make scrolls: [22]*pwoí' póh*₂ to paste the foil on idol-paper; *pwoí' pidh*, to paper walls; *pwoí' tak*, a kind of jacket, or vest.

背 Pei. ' The back, the back part; behind, rear, opposite of face or front; may be applied to the cover of a book, roof of a house, etc.; rays of the sun; north side of a hall; aged; secret-

[1] 剝皮 [2] 剝衣裳 [3] 剝頭皮 [4] 剝皮賭 [5] 縛束 [6] 縛帶 [7] 縛箅 [8] 縛股腿 [9] 我輩 [10] 尊輩 [11] 前輩 [12] 長輩 [13] 同輩 [14] 晚輩 [15] 貝錦 [16] 貝勒 [17] 寶貝 [18] 龜貝 [19] 裱褙 [20] 褙紙 [21] 褙聯 [22] 褙箔

ly: also read *pwoi*² q. v.: ¹*pwoi*² *chek*, the back; ²*hiong*² *pwoi*² front and rear; ³*ˌt'ai pwoi*² aged, growing old; COLL., ⁴*pwoi*² *au*² or *pwoi*² *te*² behind the back; secretly, clandestinely; *pwoi*² *au*² *'ch'iu*, "hand behind the back"—double-dealing; to slander or injure secretly; *p'ah*, *pwoi*² *ˌhwa*, to beat a woman on the thighs at a yamun; *ˌsang pwoi*² to have a carbuncle or anthrax on the back.

背² Pei. To turn the back on; to oppose, to disobey; to recite memoriter; the opposite, the reverse; in the coll. to put on the back, to saddle: also read *pwoi*² q. v.: COM., ⁵*ˌui pwoi*² to oppose, to rebel against; ⁶*hwang pwoi*² the opposite, reverse of what it should be; ⁷*pwoi*² *'pong*, the hands tied behind the back; ⁸*pwoi*² *ˌchü*, to recite with the back to the teacher; ⁹*pwoi*² *'ch'iu*, the hand casting its shadow on; COLL., *pwoi*² *'ong*, to throw a shadow back (on a thing).

悖² Pei. Pu. 誖² Analogous to the preceding: copious and confused; perverse, contrary, contumacious; to rebel, to oppose: COM., ¹⁰*pwoi*² *ngik*, to oppose; ¹¹*pwoi*² *k'e*² opposing fortune, infelicitous.

蓓² A flower bud; an opening blossom, termed *ˌsing 'yong* in the coll.

倍² Pei. To double, to multiply; answers to fold; repeated; to rebel, to oppose; low, vulgar: COM., ¹²*ˌka pwoi*² to double, to increase; ¹³*hak*, *pwoi*² or ¹⁴*ˌsëng pwoi*² twofold. Read *ˌpui*: the name of a hill.

佩² Pei. P'ei. Things worn on the girdle, pendants, girdle ornaments; to gird about one, to wear on the girdle; to keep by one; *met.*, to remember: ¹⁵*pwoi*² *huk*, *pok*, *ˌwong*, "gird on my clothes and not forget"—I'll never forget (your kindness); COM., ¹⁶*pwoi*² *ˌtó*, to wear a dagger or sword; ¹⁷*pwoi*² *ˌsing*, to gird on one's person.

珮² Pei. P'ei. Girdle ornaments, gems worn by women on their persons; tinkling stones hung in the wind.

焙² Pei. To dry by or over a fire: COM., ¹⁸*pwoi*² *ˌta*, to dry tea; ¹⁹*pwoi*² *sük*, thoroughly dried; ²⁰*pwoi*² *ˌlëng*, a large drying-basket of bamboo; ²¹*pwoi*² *ˌhwa ˌseng*, to cure peanuts by drying or toasting.

狽² Pei. An animal said to be of the wolf species, perhaps like the kangaroo; having short fore or hind legs, so that one rides the other to make progress: COM., ²²*ˌlong pwoi*² the name of this animal; *met.*, an embarrassed condition; much, excessively involved, as by many crimes; COLL., *ˌi chó*² *'yä ˌlong pwoi*² he does very wickedly; *'mwong piéng*² *'mwong ˌlong pwoi*² to become worse and worse; *'pai pwoi*² unlucky.

¹背脊 ²向背 ³台背 ⁴背後 ⁵違背 ⁶反背 ⁷背綁 ⁸背書 ⁹背手 ¹⁰悖逆 ¹¹悖氣 ¹²加倍 ¹³合倍 ¹⁴雙倍 ¹⁵佩服不忘 ¹⁶佩刀 ¹⁷佩身 ¹⁸焙茶 ¹⁹焙熟 ²⁰焙籠 ²¹焙花生 ²²狼狽〇

邶[2] Name of a city or small region in the Shang dynasty: [1]'pwoi' ,hung, the name of an ode in the Book of Odes.

(650) Pwok.

Pwok, A coll. word: to germinate, to bud; to sprout, to shoot forth; to manifest, to show; to contract, as mold: *pwok, ngok,* or *pwok, ,nga* or *pwok, 'yong,* to bud, to sprout; *pwok, 'ch'au,* grass springing up; *pwok, 'lwi,* to grow a leaf-bud; *pwok, ,mó,* to grow hair, as a fledgeling; *pwok, 'ngai,* to cut teeth; *pwok, 'p'u,* to become moldy; *pwok, ,hung ,mó,* to have a rash, as from a cold or wine-bibbing; *pwok, ,kwong,* to get into a violent rage; *pwok, chiong'* (or *pok, chiong'*), to have the distemper, as swine.

餑 Po. [2] Used in the coll. for flour, as in [2]*'mieng' pwok,* (or *mok,*); wheat flour.

浡 P'o. [2] To bubble up, as a spring; to shoot up, as plants; copious, abundant; sudden: [3]*pwok, kiok,* gurgling, bubbling; [4]*,pong pwok,* disturbed, vexed; [5]*pwok, 'li 'hai,* name of a southern sea, the seas of Sooloo and Celebes?

荸 P'o. [2] The water chestnut, called [6]*pwok, ,chá;* the Eleocharis tuberosis, an edible tuber; in the coll. termed *'mwi ,si,* q. v.

孛 [2] Interchanged with the next: to shoot up suddenly, as plants; disobedient, stubborn, intractable: [7]*pwok, ,sing,* a comet.

勃 P'o. Pu. [2] To change countenance; fluttered, confused, disconcerted; to arrange hastily: [8]*pwok, ,yong,* suddenly, furiously.

(651) Pwong.

分 Fên. Read *,hung;* coll. *,pwong:* to divide, to distribute; to separate: [9]*,pwong tuung'* or *,pwong lié'* to divide (the property) and separate, as brothers do; [10]*,pwong suëng'* to distribute presents; [11]*,pwong 'ku,* to divide into shares; [12]*tói' ,pwong,* to share with each other; [13]*,pwong ,chü,* to distribute books; [14]*,pwong ,ka 'hwói* or *,pwong ,ka ,chai,* to divide the property; *,pwong twai' ,pwong sá'* or [15]*,pwong ,tüng ,pwong ,sá,* to divide among all.

奔 Pên. Cattle frightened and scattering; to walk fast or flee, to run away in confusion; to elope or marry informally; to be busy, to toil and drudge; fagged out: [16]*,ing ,pwong,* or [17]*,sü ,pwong,* a clandestine marriage; [18]*,pwong ,ti,* to hasten, as a courier; urged, pressed; COM., [19]*,pwong ,p'ó* (coll, *,pwong ,p'ó ,ló luk,*), toiling, overwhelmed with cares; COLL., [20]*,pwong ,lié,* the althea—perhaps so called because used for a *,lié ,pa,* or hedge-fence.

---

[1] 邶風 [2] 麫餑 [3] 浡潏 [4] 滂浡 [5] 浡里海〇 [6] 荸薺 [7] 孛星 [8] 勃然 [9] 分斷 [10] 分送 [11] 分股 [12] 對分 [13] 分書 [14] 分家伙〇 [15] 分東分西 [16] 淫奔 [17] 私奔 [18] 奔馳〇 [19] 奔波 [20] 奔離

賁 ꜀Pên. Pi. Strenuous, valorous, as in serving one's prince: also read *pe'* q. v.: [1]*'hu ꜀pwong*, to serve with energy. Read *'hung:* full of rage; defeated, as troops. Read *꜀hung:* large, as a drum; a tortoise with three feet.

本 'Pên. The root of a tree or plant; the origin, source, root, cause of; the beginning or fundamental part of; proper to, special; capital, principal; native, one's own; I, my, our, own; this, the present; a numerative of books and documents, a volume: COM., [2]*'pwong ꜀chiéng*, capital in trade; [3]*'pwong le'* principal and interest; [4]*ch'ok꜀ 'pwong*, to advance capital; [5]*'pwong ꜀sing*, I, self, own; [6]*'pwong seng' kek꜀* his temper is hasty; [7]*'pwong ꜀niéng*, this year; [8]*'pwong kwok꜀*, one's native land; [9]*'pwong te' wa'* the patois; [10]*'pwong 'hu*, I, the prefect; our prefect; [11]*'ch'iu 'pwong*, a visiting-card sent to a superior; [12]*siong' 'pwong*, to present a petition; [13]*'pwong ꜀lai* or *'pwong tá*, originally, naturally; [14]*'pwong saik꜀*, the original color; *met.*, one's own ability; [15]*'pwong 'ling* or [16]*'pwong sëü'* ability, talent, genius; [17]*'pwong ꜀seng hô'* an own father; COLL., *'pwong ꜀nëng*, the principal, not an agent; *k'꜀oh, 'pwong*, a book of theatrical plays; *꜀pwong 'pwong 'tiu ꜀pwong 'pwong*, the sales offset the capital, no profits; *'pwong ꜀sang ꜀ngu na' sië'꜀ 'pwong ꜀sang 'ch'au*, "the ox eats only the grass of his native hills"; *met.*, to succeed only in one's own sphere, or native place.

笨 'Pên. The inner part of bamboo; coarse, inferior; stupid, ignorant.

畚 'Pên. A basket for containing grass, earth, or refuse; a provision-basket; also a spade or shovel: used for the coll. *pong'* q. v.

綁 'Pang. Read *'pong;* used for the coll. *'pwong*, as in [18]*'pwong 't'oi*, a sort of overalls or leggings, tied at the bottom and extending to the thighs; *'pwong 't'oi k'o'* full overalls or drawers; *'pwong 't'oi lai'* remnants of cloth fit for overalls.

盆 ꜀Pên. Basins, pots of earthen; wash-basins of brass, etc.: COM., [19]*꜀hwa ꜀pwong*, flower-pots; [20]*꜀pwong 'king*, flower-pots ornamented with scenery; [21]*꜀pwong ꜀mui*, a species of almond grown in pots; [22]*꜀pwong ꜀lang*, pot-hyacinths; *꜀pwong ꜀ngü*, fish reared in jars, gold and silver fish; *꜀ling ꜀pwong*, a child-birth; *꜀hai ꜀i ꜀pwong*, a small bathing-tub for children; *'chiong ꜀pwong*, department-clerks in pawnshops; *pwak꜀ ꜀pwong*, to fall into a pot—blundering, constantly making mistakes; *꜀chiong ꜀pwong* (or *꜀chiong ꜀ló* or *꜀chiong ꜀ló pwak꜀*), large earthen basins.

飯 飰 Fan. Read *hwang';* coll. *pwong':* cooked rice; a meal: *pwong' 'mi*, rice for cooking, the kinds used in ordinary meals; *pwong' chëük꜀*, rice-congee; *pwong' ꜀wong* (or *pwong' 'mô*),

[1]虎賁 [2]本錢 [3]本利 [4]出本 [5]本身 [6]本性急 [7]本年 [8]本國 [9]本地話 [10]本府 [11]手本 [12]上本 [13]本來 [14]本色 [15]本領 [16]本事 [17]本生父 [18]綁腿〇 [19]花盆 [20]盆景 [21]盆梅 [22]盆蘭

rice-balls; [1]*'sioh, taung' pwong'* a meal of rice; *met.*, a while; [2]*pwong' ,pau* (or *,ka chëü' ,pau*), grass bags to boil rice in; [3]*pwong' ,song*, a rice-steamer; [4]*pwong' luk,* grains of cooked rice; [5]*siăh, pwong' ,lé mwoi'* have you eaten yet? [6]*pwong' tuing'* an eating-house; [7]*'siăh, pwong' ,t'iăng*, a dining-room; [8]*pwong' ,t'eu*, rice turned sour; [9]*,k'wi pwong'* to spread the repast—term used in high families; [10]*pwong' ch'ai'* a common or inferior entertainment; [11]*'chü pwong'* to cook rice; [12]*'cha pwong'* breakfast; [13]*piéng' pwong'* the ordinary meal, as for a friend when he happens in; [14]*pwong' liong'* one's capacity for eating; [15]*pwong' taĕng'* the temples; [16]*pwong' ,sié kauk,* the shoulder-blade; *pwong' má' 'hieu tek, 'mi 'chü*, does not know that rice is the grain boiled—an ignoramus, a ninny.

(652) P'a.

抛 'P'ao. Read *,p'au;* coll. *,p'a*, as in [17]*,p'a teng'* to drop anchor; [18]*,p'a maĕng'* to cast a net; *ó' ,p'a*, to get a draught (of fish); *met.*, to have in abundance—no fear of want; *'chi sioh, maĕng' ,p'a tek, sá'* this (throw of the) net has caught many.

脬 'P'ao. Read *,p'au;* coll. *,p'a*, as in [19]*leng' ,p'a*, the scrotum; [20]*nieu' ,p'a*, the bladder; [21]*,tü ,p'a*, a hog's bladder.

,P'a. A coll. word, as in *,p'a a' 'tau k'ó'* to withdraw by a back way, to go around, as to catch a thief or avoid meeting a person; *,tó ,p'a sioh, liéng' 'tiong*, made an extra circuit.

,P'a. A coll. word, as in *,p'a ,p'a 'kung*, to bubble up, as boiling water.

帕 帊 P'a'. A kerchief or veil for the head; a stomacher for children; the first (read *mang'* or *mak,*) also means a turban or silk fillet anciently worn by soldiers; the second also means a roll of silk, a wrapper, a bundle of clothes: COM., *'ch'iu p'a'* a handkerchief; *,t'au p'a'* a fillet worn by elderly females.

怕 P'a'. To fear, to dread; to apprehend, to suppose as likely to occur: *'k'ai p'a'* to dread; COM., *pok, p'a'* not to fear; *p'a' 'chi p'a'* only fear that; *,t'ang ,seng p'a' 'sü*, to covet life and dread death; *'k'üng p'a'* (coll. *'hung p'a'*), to fear lest, lest perchance.

P'a'. A coll. word: the skirt raised to receive things, a lap, lappet; to put or hold things in a lap: *p'a' tioh, 'ó p'a'* to place in the lappet of the coat; *,i ,siong ,k'á ,tó ,li p'a'* to make a lap of the skirt of the dress.

P'a'. A coll. word, as in *'ch'wi p'a'* a water-blister, as from being pinched or burnt.

(653) P'á.

䀗 'Pi. Read *pé';* used for the coll. *'p'á*, as in *'p'á 'ngá*, to look askance at; *'p'á ngá'* to scrutinize, to examine closely.

[1]一頓飯 [2]飯包 [3]飯甑 [4]飯粒 [5]食飯囉昧 [6]飯店 [7]食飯廳 [8]飯餿 [9]開飯 [10]飯菜 [11]煮飯 [12]早飯 [13]便飯 [14]飯量 [15]飯洞 [16]飯匙骨 [17]抛碇 [18]抛緪 [19]腎脬 [20]尿脬 [21]猪脬 ○

稗' Pai. Read *pai*'; used for the coll. *p'á*': a noxious weed resembling rice and producing small seeds; cockle, darnel, tares: *ó*[1] *p'á*' *cheng*[2] *sá*' there are many tares.

***P'á*'.** A coll. word: a carpel, lobe, section, as of an orange or pomelo.

***P'á*'.** A coll. word: probably a corruption of *pai*' (to worship); a numerative of kneelings or acts of homage: '*k'wi* *lang*[2] *p'á*' to kneel twice.

***꜀P'á*.** A coll. word, as in *꜀p'á* *꜀p'á kieu*' short, quick breathing, as of a sick child or one carrying a burden.

***꜀P'á*.** A coll. word, as in *꜀wong* *꜀p'á*, a species of toad.

(654) P'aĕk.

魄꜀ P'o. T'o. The animal soul, which partakes of the *yin*, or inferior principle of nature; it is termed *chok*꜀ (gross) as distinguished form the *꜀hung* which is *꜀ch'ing* (pure); the faculties of the senses; the animal spirits in distinction from the rational; form, figure, manner; the dark disk of the moon: [1]*ching p'aĕk*꜀ vigor of the senses; [2]*lok*꜀ *p'aĕk*꜀ poor and destitute, disheartened; [3]*꜀seng p'aĕk*꜀ the waning of the moon; COM., [4]*꜀sang ꜀hung ch'ek*꜀ *p'aĕk*꜀ the three souls and seven spirits of a man—the latter are said to give energy to the limbs and bodily senses.

珀꜀ P'o. Amber, of which there are red, yellow, and streaked, varieties: COM., [5]*꜀hu* *p'aĕk*꜀ the common term for amber.

迫꜀ P'o. **逼**꜀ Pi. Read *p'aik*꜀; coll. *p'aĕk*꜀: to oppress, to harass, to abuse; to crowd, to press upon; urgent, pressing: [6]*kek*꜀ *p'aĕk*꜀ urgent, in straits; [7]*p'aĕk*꜀ *tăk*꜀ to persecute; [8]*p'aĕk*꜀ '*si*, to ill-use so as to cause death; [9]*p'aĕk*꜀ *tek*꜀ '*king*, very pressing; [10]*k'ĕăk*꜀ '*hwo p'aĕk*꜀ to be affected by fever in the system.

***P'aĕk*꜀.** A coll. word, as in *p'aĕk*꜀ *p'aĕk*꜀ to apply powders, as to a running sore.

(655) P'aĕng.

⿰月放' Pang. Read *p'aung*'; used for the coll. *p'aĕng*': to swell, to rise, as yeast, cotton, etc.: [11]*p'aĕng*' *twai*' to rise high; light, spongy; '*chiă ꜀miĕng* '*yă p'aĕng*' this cotton-coverlet is very soft and loose; *꜀ch'wi p'aĕng*' to steam (the dough) till it rises—a superstitious custom, as on the 5th or 7th day of an attack of small-pox.

(656) P'ah.

拍꜀ P'o. To pat, to caress, to tap with the hand; to beat, to strike, to smite: [12]*p'ah*꜀ '*ch'iu*, or [13]*p'ah*꜀ '*chiong*, to clap the hands; [14]*hak*꜀ *p'ah*꜀ to accord, to rhyme.

***P'ah*꜀.** A coll. word of wide signification, for which the last is commonly used; to be, to become; to do, to effect, to enact; to beat, to strike; to break; to fight; also used in other senses, as in phrases following: *p'ah*꜀ '*ta*, mock fighting, as in plays; *p'ah*꜀

1 精魄 2 落魄 3 生魄 4 三魂七魄 5 琥珀 6 急迫 7 迫逐 8 迫死 9 迫的緊 10 乞火迫 11 ⿰月放大 12 拍手 13 拍掌 14 合拍

p'wai' broken; *p'ah, kieu'* to bring a sedan; *p'ah, pok, ˏkang,* to have the ague; *p'ah, t'iĕk, ˏsa ho'* a blacksmith; *p'ah, hak,* to conspire; *p'ah, chak,* jest, ribaldry; *p'ah, ˏch'iéng,* to kneel on one knee; *p'ah, ˏtong,* lasting, forever; *p'ah, ch'ĕüng'* to fire guns; *p'ah, tiong'* to war; *p'ah, ˏkiu,* to play ball; *p'ah, ʻmi,* to buy up rice; *p'ah, ka'* to ask and settle the price; *p'ah, ˏyăng,* to gain the victory in a fight; *p'ah, ˏhwa,* soiled, blotted; *p'ah, ʻkung ʻtau,* to turn a somersault; *p'ah, ˏkwang ˏsi,* to accuse before a magistrate; *p'ah, ʻtiong ˏt'au,* to turn end for end; *p'ah, ʻtong,* to break or snap in two, as threads; *p'ah, chaung'* a crooked stick with a spike, used for making holes; *p'ah, taung'* to let fall; to miss, to pass over; *p'ah, ˏmó,* lost; *p'ah, lak,* the sexual act of birds or insects; *p'ah, ˏi tá' ek, ʻhó,* to set him down as the very best.

(657) P'áh.

P'áh,. A coll. word; to sit or throw one's self down carelessly: *p'áh, tié' ˏtau,* to sit on the ground, as a child; *p'áh, ˏla ˏcha,* to sit in the dirt; *p'áh, sioh, ˏtoi sói'* to sit together, to crowd together on a seat.

(658) P'ai.

ʻP'ai. A coll. word; low, mean; shabby, seedy: *ʻp'ai ʻkiăng,* a vagabond, a worthless scamp; *ʻyă ʻp'ai,* very mean; shabby, as clothes; *ʻp'ai ˏsing k'e'* shameful, mean, as a person or act.

(659) P'aik.

逼, 偪, Pi. To ill-use, to oppress, to harass, to force; to approach near, to crowd, to press upon; near, pressing, urgent: in the coll. read *p'aĕk,* and *pek,* q. v.: [1]*sĕü' p'aik, ˏu nai'* a matter pressing and no resource—i. e., necessitated, obliged to do.

迫, 廹, Po. Used for the last: to urge, to insist upon; to vex, to press, to reduce to straits; to compel arbitrarily; near, urgent, pressing: in the coll. read *p'aĕk,* and *pek,* q. v.: COM., [2]*p'aik, ka'* to force (a widow) to marry; [3]*p'aik, kĕüng'* to press near; imminent; [4]*p'aik, ch'iĕk,* very urgent, importunate; [5]*p'aik, chai' ˏling ˏmwong,* the duns have reached his door, as in the 12th moon; COLL., [6]*p'aik, miăng'* or *p'aik, ʻsi ˏnĕng,* to oppress one so that he commits suicide; [7]*p'aik, lóh, ʻhai,* to force (people) to the sea—compel them by oppression to become pirates; [8]*ˏch'wi p'aik,* to urge, to hurry; to dun one.

(660) P'aiu.

覆, Fu. Fou. Also read *haiu':* to cover, to overshadow; to brood, as a hen: also read *hok,* q. v.: [9]*ʻneu p'aiu' ik, ˏchi,* the bird covers it with her wings; [10]*ˏt'iĕng p'aiu' te' chai'* the heaven covers and earth sustains.

---

1 事逼無奈 2 迫嫁○ 3 迫近○ 4 迫切○ 5 迫債臨門 6 迫命○ 7 迫落海○ 8 催迫○ 9 鳥覆翼之 10 天覆地載

阜 **𨸏** Fou. A mound or hill of earth; great, high, large; fat, full, complete, abundant; the 170th radical: [1]*ˏhung p'aiu'* abundant, as harvests; [2]*ˏhiong p'aiu'* the fragrant mound—a Budhist temple.

蜱 Fou. A kind of grasshopper or cricket: [3]*p'aiu' ˏchüng*, a sort of green locust.

掊 Interchanged with the next: to grasp, to take to one's self; to collect, to exact; to extract salt from sea-water: also read *'p'eu*, q. v.: [4]*p'aiu' k'aikˎ* to exact rigorously, as duties.

裒 Pao. Also read *ˏp'eu*: to collect; to reduce, to diminish; many, numerous: [5]*p'aiu' ˏtó ek, 'kwa*, to diminish the surplus and add to the deficiency—aid the poor by taking from the rich.

(661) P'ak.

P'ak₂. A coll. word: to bubble, to rise and overflow: *p'ak₂ 'k'i ˏli*, bubbling up; *tiéng' p'ak₂* brimful; *p'ak₂ ˏlau k'ó'* full and running over.

(662) P'ang.

攀 **扳** P'an. Also read *ˏp'wang*: to lead, to drag, to pull towards one; to climb, to pull one's self up; to drag into, to implicate: [6]*ˏp'ang 'ch'iu*, to lead by the hand; [7]*ˏküng ˏp'ang*, to denounce, to inform against; [8]*ˏp'ang 'ch'ié*, to implicate; [9]*'kang ˏp'ang ˏtai ka'* I presume to drag you, Sir (to my house); COLL., *ˏp'ang 'nü má' 'k'i*, I can't presume to associate with you—sometimes used satirically; *ˏp'ang ˏi chó' ˏwo ˏka*, to implicate him as a receiver of stolen goods.

眅 Pan. An eye showing much of the white, a turned up or distorted eye: [10]*ˏp'ang ˏching*, a cataract.

潘 P'an. Read *ˏp'wang* in the dictionaries: dirt on the face; water in which rice has been washed; a surname; a river in Yung-yang district- Honan.

ˏP'ang. A coll. word: to divide, to distribute; to equalize; to pay off; to separate: *ˏp'ang hwak*, to disburse; *ˏp'ang ˏp'wo*, to equalize, to apportion; *ˏp'ang so'* or *ˏp'ang chai'* to pay debts; *ˏp'ang ˏmó ˏseng ˏp'ang ˏmó au'* not enough to meet all demands.

ˏP'ang. A coll. word, as in *ˏp'ang ˏp'ang ˏěng aěng'* gallipots, jars of all sizes; *met.*, a medley of things.

丼 Used for the coll. *ˏp'ang*: the splash of a bucket in a well: *ˏp'ang sioh₂ ˏsiǎng 'hiong*, the reverberation of a bucket on the water.

冇 A coll. character: empty, open, hollow; light, porous, loose-grained: [11]*p'ang' ˏch'a*, porous wood; [12]*ˏk'ěng p'ang'* hollow, empty; [13]*p'ang' ˏsing*, the hollow heart, as of a tree; [14]*p'ang' ch'ioh*, blasted rice; [15]*p'ang' 'kong*, to chat; [16]*p'ang' ˏtang*, chitchat; aimless talk; [17]*p'ang' ˏchau ˏchau*, very porous; exceedingly vain,

1 豐阜 2 香阜 3 蜱螽 4 掊克 5 裒多益寡 6 攀手 7 供攀 8 攀扯 9 敢攀台駕 10 眅睛 11 冇柴 12 空冇 13 冇心 14 冇粟 15 冇講 16 冇談 17 冇糟糟

as talk; ¹ʻp'angʼ ˏp'ung ˏwo, as hollow as a bee's nest! p'angʼ ʻkong kwohˎ mere talk, tentative words.

彭 ˏP'êng The beating of a drum; a chariot-scythe; to journey; a road; abundant, numerous; unceasing; a river and districts in Sz'chuen: ˏp'ang ʻlá, the west side of the Poyang lake; COM., ²ˏP'ang ʻchu, a noted officer in the era of the Shang, said to have died on the 12th of the 6th month, aged 800 years; COLL., ˏp'ang ʻchu ˏpó ˏt'ié ʻyă ch'aikˎ "Madam Pang cries bitterly"—said when it rains on the 12th of the 6th month.

蟛 ˏP'êng. Small land-crabs: COM., ³ˏp'ang ˏki (coll. ˏk'i), a small crab, found in rice fields; ⁴ˏp'ang ˏki kĕük, the Crab-aster; COLL., ˏp'ang ʻngai, or ˏp'ang ʻhai, sea-shore crabs having longer claws than the ˏp'ang ˏk'i; ⁵ˏp'ang ch'iékˎ the large male crab with elliptical shell: ˏĕng ʻkĕng ˏp'ang ˏk'i, a small crab having red claws.

膨 ˏP'êng. The belly puffed and swollen: ⁶ˏp'ang ˏheng, the belly much distended; COLL., pokˎ ʻló ˏp'ang ˏp'ang tiongʼ a distended belly, flatulency.

澎 ˏP'êng. The noise of dashing waters: COM., ⁷ˏp'ang ˏhu ʻtó, the Pescadore Islands off the west coast of Formosa; ⁸ˏp'ang ˏhu ˏt'iăng, the magistrate of the Pescadore district.

評 ˏP'ing. To discuss the merits of, to discourse, to deliberate; to fix fairly, to dispose, to arrange; to criticise, to revise for publication: COM., ⁹ˏp'ang laungʼ to discourse about, to discuss the merits of; ¹⁰ˏp'ié ˏp'ang, to make critical notes, to review a book; COLL., ˏp'ang langʼ a reunion or party to which each person contributes his share of the expense.

砰 ˏP'êng. Read ˏp'eng; used for the coll, ˏp'ang: to roll out cloth, to press cloth with a roller: ¹¹ˏp'ang siohˎ stone cloth-rollers, consisting of upper and nether stones; ¹²ˏp'ang ˏkwong, to roll cloth smooth.

ˏP'ang. A coll. word, as in ˏp'angˏp'angʻk'i, to ascend, to rise densely, as smoke or dust.

ˏP'ang. A coll. word, as in ˏp'ang ˏp'ang chiéngʼ in a tremor, shivering.

搒 P'êng. Read ˏp'eng and p'angʼ; used in the Paikˎ ˏIng for the coll. p'angʼ, but seldom heard in Foochow patois: a loud thump, a heavy knock: p'angʼ siohˎ ˏsiăng, the clang of a gong, or booming of a gun.

(663) P'au.

拋 ˏP'ao. To fling, to throw down; to reject, to cast off; to toss up: in the coll. read ˏp'a, q. v.: ¹³ˏp'au ˏmieu, to anchor; ¹⁴ˏp'au k'eʼ to reject, to abandon; ˏp'au ˏkü, a balista; COM., ¹⁵ˏp'au ˏch'á piékˎ ʻchü, to leave wife and children (and go abroad).

¹有蜂窩〇 ²彭祖 ³蟛蜞 ⁴蟛蜞菊〇 ⁵蟛蠘〇 ⁶膨脝〇 ⁷澎湖島〇 ⁸澎湖廳〇 ⁹評論〇 ¹⁰批評〇 ¹¹砰石 ¹²砰光 ¹³拋錨 ¹⁴拋棄 ¹⁵拋妻別子

枹 ‹ Fou. Read ˏ*hu;* used for the coll. ˏ*p'au:* a pomelo: [1] ˏ*p'au* ʻ*wang*, bowls made of pomelo-rinds; ˏ*p'au* ʻ*kiăng* ˏ*ta*, tea impregnated with the flavor of the pomelo—by enclosing it in pomelo rind and exposing it to the air.

泡 ʾ P'ao. Read ˏ*p'au* in the dictionaries: a bubble, froth, spoon-drift, spume; name of a river; to dip, to steep in; to add water to: in the coll. read *p'au*ʾ q. v.: COLL., [2] *p'au*ʾ ʻ*chwi siăh*, to eat it with an infusion of water; *p'au*ʾ ʻ*piéng sik*, to season pork-dumplings with gravy. Read ˏ*pau:* full, copious, abundant: ˏ*pau* ˏ*pau*, the flow and murmuring sound of water.

炮 ʾ P'ao. To bake or roast in ashes, to wrap up and roast; to fire or roast in a pan; to boil water; a gun, a cannon, in which sense used for the next: COM., [3] *p'au*ʾ *chiéʾ* to roast, as medicines in a pan; [4] *p'au*ʾ *ho*ʾ to toast slices of the Rhamnus; COLL., [5] *p'au*ʾ ˏ*ta*, to boil water for tea; [6] *p'au*ʾ ʻ*kung* ˏ*t'ong* or *p'au*ʾ ʻ*kung* ʻ*chwi*, to boil water; [7] ˏ*sieu* ʻ*hwi* *p'au*ʾ to burn the wood-pile on the evening of the 30th of the 12th moon.

砲 ʾ **礟** P'ao. The ancient balista or catapult; a cannon, a great gun; fire-works: [8] ˏ*ming* ˏ*ló* ˏ*sing* *p'au*ʾ a salute of gongs and guns; COM., [9] *p'au*ʾ ˏ*tai*, a fort, a battery; [10] *p'au*ʾ *ka*ʾ a gun-carriage; [11] *p'au*ʾ ˏ*mwong*, a touch-hole; [12] *p'au*ʾ ʻ*chi*, a cannon-ball; [13] *p'au*ʾ ʻ*ch'iu*, a gunner; [14] ʻ*sá* *p'au*ʾ to scale guns; [15] ˏ*liéng* ˏ*k'wang* *p'au*ʾ or ˏ*liéng* ˏ*siăng* *p'au*ʾ or *paik*, ʻ*chü* *p'au*ʾ strings of fire-crackers; COLL., *pong*ʾ *p'au*ʾ to fire cannon; *p'au*ʾ ʻ*hiong* ˏ*sang* ˏ*siăng*, three reports of cannon; *p'au*ʾ *liong*ʾ a large kind of fire-cracker.

橐 ʾ P'ao. Used for the coll. *p'au*ʾ: swollen, puffed; to expand, to grow large: also read *p'au*ʾ in the coll. q. v.: *p'au*ʾ *p'au*ʾ puffed up, as a boil; ˏ*hwa* ˏ*k'wi* ʻ*yă* *p'au*ʾ the flower has opened very large.

*P'au*ʾ. A coll. word, as in *p'au*ʾ *kieu*ʾ a ceremony to "secure ˏ*i sik*, (clothes and food)" to the bride's family, when she enters her sedan—fruits and various useful articles are placed in a red coverlet held by the corners, and "good words" said over them by the bride's maid; *p'au*ʾ *tiong*ʾ a like ceremony at the bridegroom's on the day preceding.

跑 ˏ P'ao. To run, to gallop; to prance, to gambol; to paw the ground; to ride rapidly, as a courier; to dispatch: COM., [16] ˏ*p'au* *chang*ʾ to post, to travel swiftly; [17] ˏ*p'au* ʻ*ma*, to gallop; COLL., [18] ˏ*p'au* ˏ*mwong* ˏ*chü*, to dispatch an official document; [19] ˏ*p'au* ʻ*chau* or ˏ*p'au* *taĕng*ʾ to run, to go on errands; [20] ˏ*p'au* ˏ*ká*, a traveling agent; ˏ*p'au* *yok*, jaded from running about.

鮑 ʾ Pao. Read ˏ*pau;* coll. *p'au*ʾ as in *p'au*ʾ ˏ*ngü*, a species of salted fish from Loochoo.

[1]枹碗 [2]泡水 食[3]炮製 [4]炮 附[5]炮茶 [6]炮 滾湯 [7]燒火 炮[8]鳴鑼升 砲[9]砲臺 [10]砲架 [11]砲門 [12]砲子 [13]砲手 [14]洗砲 [15]連環砲 [16]跑站 [17]跑馬 [18]跑門書 [19]跑走 [20]跑街 〇

皰[2] Read p'au'; coll. p'au[2] as in ꜀p'au p'au[2] a blister on the skin; [1]p'au[2] pauk꜀ the blister has burst.

泡[2] P'ao. Read p'au'; coll. p'au[2]: a bubble, water-bubbles, soap-bubbles: [2]'chwi p'au[2] water-bubbles.

橐[2] P'ao. Read p'au'; used for the coll. p'au[2]: large, the largest; the head, the chief: [3]kek꜀ p'au[2] the largest oranges (of the lot); 'nü pwoh꜀ chó' ꜀p'au p'au[2] you wish to be chief, eh!

雹[2] Pao. Read pauk꜀ in the dictionaries: hail; to hail: in the coll. read p'ĕk꜀ q. v.

(664) P'auk.

撲꜀ 朴꜀ P'o. P'u. To lean, to recline against; to pat, to brush; to strike, to flog; to impinge, to rush against; to flap, to flutter: [4]p'auk꜀ ik꜀ to flap the wings; [5]p'auk꜀ miék꜀ to puff out, as a light; met., in the coll. to suppress or stop, as a quarrel; COLL., [6]p'auk꜀ p'e' ꜀hiong, fragrance striking the nose, very fragrant.

駁꜀ Po. Read pauk꜀; coll. p'auk꜀ as in p'auk꜀ chak꜀ mixed, miscellaneous; met., confused in mind, distracted.

嚗꜀ Po. Read pauk꜀; coll. p'auk꜀: to expand the mouth; to mouth, to take in the mouth: p'auk꜀ sioh꜀ ch'oi' to bite or take a mouthful, as a dog; p'auk꜀ p'auk꜀ ꜀pó, a blind fortune teller's rattle; met., empty, eaten out, hollow, as wood.

樸꜀ P'o. P'u. Hard, fine-grained wood; unwrought wood; unfinished, as a vessel; the substance of, the body without ornament or gloss; plain, unadorned, simple, sincere: [7]p'auk꜀ so' ꜀hung ꜀kiéng, plain and unadorned, yet strong; COM., [8]p'auk꜀ sik꜀ plain, rustic, unpolished.

朴꜀ P'o. The bark of a tree; also used for the preceding in the sense of plain, sincere: COM., [9]'hau' p'auk꜀ or ꜀ch'iong p'auk꜀ a medicinal bark from Sz'-chuen; [10]p'auk꜀ ꜀sieu, the sulphate of soda; Epsom salts.

仆꜀ Fou. To fall prostrate: also read ho' q. v.: [11]꜀tiéng p'auk꜀ or p'auk꜀ 'tó, to fall down flat; [12]꜀kiong p'auk꜀ to fall stiff, as if dead.

璞꜀ P'o. An unpolished stone; the crust of a gem, gems in the ore: [13]p'auk꜀ ngük꜀ an unwrought gem.

(665) P'aung.

胖' P'ang. Fat, obese: ꜀p'i p'aung' corpulent, lusty; [14]p'aung' tiong' swollen, puffed.

蚌[2] Pang. Pêng. P'êng. A bivalve (Uniones), a muscle like the oyster, large and thick-shelled; the pearl oyster: COM., [15]'ló p'aung[2] ꜀séng ꜀chio, the old oyster has a pearl, as said when an old man has a child.

傍[2] Pang. P'ang. Read ꜀pong and paung[2]; coll. p'aung[2]: to be at, on, or in: p'aung[2] 'chi ꜀peng, it is on this side.

1 皰剝 2 水泡 3 橘橐 4 撲翼 5 撲滅 6 撲鼻香 7 樸素渾堅 8 樸實 9 厚朴 10 朴硝 11 顛仆 12 僵仆 13 璞玉 14 胖脹 15 老蚌生珠

遇[2] Yü. Read *ngü'n²*: used for the coll. *p'aung²*: to meet, to come upon; to hit upon, to occur, to happen: [1]*p'aung² tioh,* to meet, to happen on; *p'aung² tioh, ˬt'au,* a rare hit; [2]*p'aung² chó ˀ hwa'* or *p'aung² ˬsi tó ˀ* to hit on the lucky time; [3]*p'aung² 'ch'iu,* as they come to hand, not to cull out, or select; [4]*p'aung² ˬmwong,* "at the very door"—the time has come, just now.

P'aung². A coll. word, for which the last may be used: to run upon; to strike, to bump or knock against: *p'aung² náh,* indented by a knock; *p'aung² ˬting,* bumped against a nail — have incurred his anger, as a servant says.

(666) P'e.

鼻ˀ Pi. Read *pik,*; coll. *p'e'*: the nose, nasal; mucus; *met.*, skill, cleverness; a point, an end: [5]*p'e' ˬliong,* the bridge of the nose; [6]*p'e' ˬk'ëng,* the nostrils; [7]*p'e' 'sai,* or *p'e' ˬnë,* thick mucus from the nose; [8]*p'e' 'chwi,* watery mucus, as in the snuffles; [9]*p'e' ˬk'ëng ˬk'a,* the alar cartilages of the nose; [10]*p'e' ˬt'au ˬsa,* influenza in the nose; [11]*ˬeng ˬkó p'e'* a parrot-beak nose — a Roman nose; [12]*p'e' ˬhong,* snuff; [13]*p'e' tok, tok,* to pat the nose with the finger—a challenge to fight; *p'e' p'ah, sioh, chiăh,* to make a fastening, as at the end of a seam; *p'e' ˬtong kwo' tóh,* has a nose longer than a table—too clever to be cheated; *ˬsëng p'e'* double-corded toes, as of shoes; *ˬsang p'e'* the end of a hill.

齂ˀ Also read *p'e²*: the noise of hard breathing; to pant, to have a labored breathing.

屁ˀ Pi. P'i. To break wind: in the coll. read *p'oi* ˀ q. v.: *p'e' 'ku,* the haunches, the posteriors; COLL., *p'e' nóh,* nothing! *ˬp'i p'e' tai*ˀ nothing of any consequence; *p'e' nóh, 'kong,* he said nothing, had nothing to say.

嬖ˀ Also read *'p'i*: a familiar, a favorite, a vile but beloved person; partial to, blinded in favor of; depraved, lecherous: [14]*p'e' ch'iék,* a favorite concubine; [15]*p'e' haing²* or [16]*p'e' ˬtung,* a catamite.

(667) P'ë.

ˬP'ë. A coll. word, sometimes used for *p'ëk,* very, exceedingly: *ˬp'ë ˬp'ë yék,* very hot! piping hot!

ˬP'ë. A coll. word, as in *ˬp'ë ˬp'ë ˬsiăng,* a broken voice, a voice wanting in clearness and volume.

(668) P'eh.

P'eh,. A coll. euphonic prefix, as in *p'eh, p'ah,* to beat, to strike.

(669) P'ek.

匹, P'i. A pair; one of a pair; a mate, a partner; to unite, to match and pair; a classifier of horses and fledgelings: [17]*ek, p'ek, ˬchu,* a fledgeling; [18]*p'ek, ˬhu,* a solitary man, one without relatives; COM., [19]*p'ek, p'woi*ˀ to mate, to marry; [20]*p'ek, 'ma ˬtung ˬch'iong,* a solitary spearman on horseback—without company, journeying alone.

[1]遇 化 門 空 水 [10]鼻 哥 [13]鼻 妾 童 [18]匹 [20]匹
著 [3]遇 [5]鼻 [7]鼻 [9]鼻 頭 鼻 點 [15]嬖 [17]一 夫 馬
[2]遇 手 梁 屎 空 痧 [12]鼻 點 倖 匹 [19]匹 單
造 [4]遇 [6]鼻 [8]鼻 胶 [11]鸚 烟 [14]嬖 [16]嬖 雛 配 鎗

福州方言拼音字典

疋, P'i. A classifier of cloths, woolens and silks, the; 103d radical: COLL., [1]*siok,* *p'ek,* one piece of cloth; [2]*p'ek,* *t'au,* piece goods, a roll of silk, &c.

霹, P'i. A clap of thunder: [3]*p'ek,* *lek,* a crash, a splitting clap, a sharp peal; a crashing noise; the rumbling of wheels.

癖, P'i. Indigestion, a morbid appetite; a penchant, a fancy, partiality for; one's natural disposition: [4]*ka p'ek,* costiveness; [5]*p'ek,* *chik,* indigestion; COM., [6]*t'ang p'ek,* accumulation of phlegm, as from excessive wine-bibbing; [7]*p'ek,* *e'* or *pe'k,* *seng'* or *p'ek,* *k'e'* the natural bent or disposition; [8]*p'ek,* *au'* a stubborn disposition; [9]*p'ek,* *e'* *kwai* *tiong,* a perverse, unamiable spirit; [10]*chiă* *ngu* *o'* *p'ek,* this ox has temper.

璧, Pi. A badge of office, made round to represent heaven, with a square hole in the centre to represent Earth, used in ancient Chinese courts; the *kié* and *p'ek,* were a sort of letters-patent; to decline: [10]*hwang p'ek,* to return presents; [11]*p'ek,* *siā'* declined with thanks, as written on a card in returning a present.

壁, Pi. A mud wall; plastered partitions; a screen, an obstruction, a military defense; a steep ridge; the 14th zodiacal constellation, *g* in Pegasus, and *a* in Andromeda: read *piăh,* in the coll. q, v.: [12]*ka* *tu* *p'ek,* *lik,* only bare walls, a poor family; [13]*miêng'* *p'ek,* to face the wall —i. e., to study hard.

僻, P'i. Pei. Mean, low, vulgar; depraved, licentious; partial, prejudiced; private, retired, secluded: in the coll. read *p'iăh,* q. v.: [14]*p'iéng p'ek,* depraved; out of the way, retired; [15]*p'ek,* *cheng'* secluded and quiet, [16]*hwong' p'ek,* dissolute.

辟, P'i. Pi. Used for the last, also for *pik,* (to open, to expand): a prince, a ruler; heaven; a law, rule, example; to perceive; clear, distinct; to punish; punishment; to kill; depraved, partial: used for the coll. *p'iăh,* q. v.: [17]*tai' p'ek,* a severe punishment, death; [18]*p'ek,* *ming,* nominal; false pretences; [19]*hwong p'ek,* a title applied by a wife to her husband in worshiping his manes.

劈, P'i. To split, to rive, to cut open; to rend, to tear asunder: [20]*p'ek,* *liék,* to cut or tear open.

躃, Pi. Unable to walk, lame; upset, overthrown, prostrate.

襞, The seam joining two pieces of leather; clothes folded: *p'ek,* *chek,* plaits or folds in a skirt; the gathers in a dress.

擗, P'i. Also read *pik,*; interchanged with the next: to open, to break off; to beat the breast; to

1 一疋 2 疋頭 3 霹靂 4 瘕癖 5 癖疾 6 痰癖 7 癖意 8 癖拗 9 癖意乖張 10 反璧 11 璧謝 12 家徒壁立 13 面壁 14 偏僻 15 僻靜 16 放僻 17 大辟 18 辟名 19 皇辟 ○ 20 劈裂 ○

bend the knee, to bow: [1]p'ek, ʻŭng k'ok, k'ek, to beat the breast, stamp the feet, and wail.

擘 P'i. Also read p'aik,: to break asunder, to part, to divide into pieces: used for *pah*, in the coll. q. v.: [2]*kĕŭ*ʼ *p'ek*, the thumb; *met.*, the principal person; [3]*ʻwang p'ek*, to draw a bow.

碧 Pi. A valuable, translucent stone, like prase or jade; some are greenish, and others blue, like the deep sea: [4]*p'ek*, *‚hung*, the azure clouds; [5]*p'ek*, *sĕŭ*ʼ a coralline tree, fabled to grow in the Kwan-lun mountains.

嗶 Pi. Read *pek*,; used for the coll. *p'ek*, as in [6]*p'ek*, *‚chié*, a kind of coarse, twilled, woolen cloth.

P'ek,. A coll. euphonic prefix, as in *p'ek*, *p'auk*, to eat, as dogs do; *p'ek*, *p'iăk*, to throw or dash out, as water; *p'ek*, *p'wak*, to scatter, to sprinkle on.

(670) P'ĕk.

雹 Po. Pao. Read *p'au*ʼ; coll. *p'ĕk*,: hail: *lŏh*, *p'ĕk*, to hail.

P'ĕk,. A coll. word: hot: *p'ĕk*, *p'ĕk*, *yék*, very warm, hot, piping hot—the same as in *‚p'ĕ*, q. v.

(671) P'eng.

烹 ‚P'êng. To boil, to stew; to decoct: [7]*‚p'eng ‚ta*, to boil water for tea; [8]*‚p'eng ‚yong*, to stew mutton; com., [9]*‚p'eng tieu*ʼ the art of cookery, to cook professionally.

伻 ‚P'êng. To order, to send on a message; to conduct, to convoy: a messenger; according, following, agreeing to.

聘 P'ing. To ask, to inquire of; to make inquiries of a suzerain through an envoy, to request, to invite with a present, as to take office; to request the services of a teacher; to negotiate a marriage, to espouse, to betroth; to engage a partner: [10]*p'eng*ʼ *ʻch'ing*, to invite, as a teacher or official adviser; com., [11]*p'eng*ʼ *‚king*, a present in money to the bride's parents; [12]*p'eng*ʼ *ʻlá*, marriage-presents; presents to one invited to office; [13]*p'eng*ʼ *p'woi*ʼ matched, mated, as by destiny; to be a partner in a work.

娉 P'ing. Used for the last: to inquire, to request or invite with a present; elegant, graceful, in which sense also read *‚p'ing*: [14]*p'eng*ʼ *‚ting*, a lady-like deportment.

騁 P'ing. To run swiftly; to fly in a direct course, as when defeated: [15]*‚ti p'eng*ʼ to ride swiftly, as a courier; [16]*p'eng*ʼ *‚hwai*, pleased, elated.

*P'eng*ʼ. A coll. euphonic prefix, as in *p'eng*ʼ *p'wang*ʼ to investigate and decide (a case); *p'eng*ʼ *p'ang*ʼ *ʻking ʻkong*, to chat.

[1] 擗踊哭泣 [2] 巨擘 [3] 挽擘 [4] 碧雲 [5] 碧樹 [6] 嗶吱 [7] 烹茶 [8] 烹羊 [9] 烹調 [10] 聘請 [11] 聘金 [12] 聘禮 [13] 聘配 [14] 娉婷 [15] 馳騁 [16] 騁懷

*P'eng*³. A coll. euphonic prefix, as in *p'eng*³ *p'iăng*³ the slamming of doors; *p'eng*³ *p'aung*³ to knock, strike against; *p'eng*³ *p'iăng*³ to compare two articles.

(672) P'ĕng.

ₛP'ĕng. A coll. word, as in *ₛp'ĕng ₛp'ĕng ʿk'i*, vapor or steam rising; *met.*, growing prosperity.

(673) P'eu.

ʿ缶 Fou. P'i. Earthenware vessels; a jar, a vessel for containing wine; a measure of capacity; a jar to drum on in order to keep time: *ʿngwa ʿp'eu*, earthenware.

ʿ芣 Fou. Also read *ₛp'eu*: the plantago or plantain leaf, called *ʿp'eu ʿi*.

ʿ否 Fou. Pi. P'i. Not so, ought not; at the end of a sentence, it makes a negative interrogation; else, whether, otherwise, or not: also read *ʿp'i*, q. v.: ¹*ʿk'ŏ ʿp'eu*, will it do, or not? ²*se*² *ʿp'eu*, is it so? ³*wak*₂ *ʿp'eu*, it is not; ⁴*ₛcheng ʿp'eu*, has it occurred or not?

ʿ剖 Pao. P'ou. To cut in two; to split, to divide, to halve; to judge, to decide; to expose, to lay open: ⁵*ʿp'eu p'wang*³ to judge and decide; COM., ⁶*ʿp'eu ₛming* or *ʿp'eu pek*₂ to state clearly, to make manifest, as one's innocence.

ʿ掊 Also read *ₛp'eu*: to collect, to add to; to grasp, to take hold of; to exact rigorously, as duties: also read *p'aiu*³ q. v.

ₛ浮 Fou. Fu. To float, to drift; to overflow, to exceed, to inundate; past time; fleeting; light, unsteady; unreal, vapory; rising, floating, as vapors; many and violent, as waters: used for the coll. *ₛp'u*, q. v.: *ₛp'eu ₛp'eu*, light, vain; much; ⁷*ₛp'eu hwang*³ to float; vague; ⁸*ₛp'eu ₛngiong*, unmeaning words, mere compliments; ⁹*ₛp'eu sik*₂ pumice; ¹⁰*ₛp'eu ₛseng*, the living; COM., ¹¹*ₛk'ing ₛp'eu* or *ₛp'eu sŏ*³ fickle, unsteady; ¹²*ₛp'eu ngiăh*₂ a false number or reckoning; ¹³*ₛhü ₛp'eu*, void, unreal.

ₛ蜉 Fou. A large ant, called *ₛpi ₛp'eu*; ¹⁴*ₛp'eu ₛiu*, an ephemera, produced from muck.

ₛ罦 Fou. A rabbit-net: *ₛp'eu ₛsü*, a sort of wooden screen outside of a door or a window.

ₛ吥 To draw in the breath, to inhale, to inspire.

ₛ紑 New silken garments; elegant, lustrous.

ₛ抔 Also read *ʿp'eu*: to take in both hands, as water or grain; a handful: ¹⁵*ek*₂ *ₛp'eu ʿt'u*, a handful of earth.

¹可否 ²是否 ³曰否 ⁴曾否 ⁵剖判 ⁶剖明 ⁷浮泛 ⁸浮言 ⁹浮石 ¹⁰浮生 ¹¹輕浮 ¹²浮額 ¹³虛浮 ¹⁴蜉蝣 ¹⁵一抔土

○ ○ ○ ○ ○ ○ ○ ○

(674) P'i.

悲 ‹Pei. Compassion, deep feeling without tears; sympathy, grief; to feel for, to commiserate; tragic, as a play: [1]꜀p'i ꜀ai, to lament; [2]꜀p'i ꜀chai, ah! alas! woe worth! com., [3]꜀chü ꜀p'i, pity, compassion; [4]꜀p'i ꜀siong, grief, wounded feelings.

丕 P'ei. Often read ꜂p'i: great, grand, distinguished; first, chief; to offer up, to present to; to receive: [5]꜀p'i ꜂chü, the eldest son.

伾 Also read ꜂p'i: strong, robust; valiant; many, a multitude: [6]Tai[2] ꜀p'i, a mountain in Honan.

狉 Also read ꜀p'i: a fox's cub: [7]꜀p'i ꜀li, a young fox.

駓 Also read ꜀p'i: a speckled, white and yellow horse, a bright chestnut horse: ꜀p'i ꜀p'i, pressing, hurrying along.

騑 Fei. A horse three years old; the two outside of a team of four horses: ꜀p'i ꜀p'i, the regular march of horses.

緋 Fei. Red or crimson-colored silk: [8]꜀p'i ꜀pó, a crimson robe.

裶 Long, trailing dresses; to lift the skirt: [9]꜀p'i ꜀i, to hold up the dress.

扉 Fei. The leaf of a door; a wooden, two-leaved door; *met.*, a rustic house.

蜚 Fei. A stinking bug which infests clothes and grain; a fabulous animal, like an ox, whose appearance is ominous of pestilence.

霏 Fei. Rain and snow, a pelting sleet, driven by the wind and filling the air.

꜀P'i. A coll. euphonic prefix, as in ꜀p'i ꜀p'wo, to spread out; to lay, as a stone road; ꜀p'i ꜀p'ié, to whittle, to sharpen, to point.

痞 P'i. Pain or disease in the bowels; stoppage, costiveness, constipated; weak, feeble; dizzy; used for the coll. ꜂p'i, a scab, scabbiness: [10]tau[2] ꜂p'i, scabs of the small-pox; luék꜆ ꜂p'i, or [11]t'aung꜄ ꜂p'i, to shed a scab; [12]kiék꜆ ꜂p'i, a scab forming; ꜂chiă ꜂p'i na[2] kak꜆ "the scab still sticks"; *met.*, his bad name will continue to follow him.

否 Fou. Pi. P'i. To bar the way, to hinder, to interrupt; closed, shut up; bad, vile, wicked, as mankind; the 12th diagram: also read ꜂p'eu, q. v.: [13]꜂p'i saik, impeded, blocked up; [14]꜂p'i kik꜆ ꜂t'ai[2] ꜀lai, it is so bad that it must soon be better.

譬 P'i. Often read p'e[3]: to compare, to make comparisons or illustrations; to understand; a simile, a parable, an illustration: [15]꜂p'i ĕü[2] (coll. ꜂pi ĕü[2]), to illustrate by comparison; [16]꜂p'i ꜀ü, or ꜂p'i yok꜆ just like, for instance as; [17]꜂ch'ü ꜂p'i pok꜆ ꜂wong, to use a common illustration.

1悲哀 2悲哉 3慈悲 4悲傷 5丕子 6大伾 7狉貍 8緋袍 9裶衣 10瘟痞 11脫痞○ 12結痞○ 13否塞○ 14否極泰來 15譬諭○ 16譬如○ 17取譬不遠

ʻ**鄙** Pi. P'i. A frontier town, a small place; a town of 500 houses; five ʻp'i towns make one *hsien* or district; a border, a frontier; low, rustic, vile, mean; to despise, to contemn: [1]ʻ*p'i laiu*ʾ vulgar, low; mean, dilapidated, as a house; [2]˛*piĕng* ʻ*p'i*, the frontiers; COM., [3]ʻ*p'i pok*˛ to treat meanly; [4]ʻ*p'i ch'ieu*ʾ to despise and ridicule; [5]ʻ*p'i leng*ʾ stingy, niggardly; COLL., ʻ*nü* ˛*chiong wang*ʾ *chŏ*ʾ *á*ʾ *k'ëük*˛ ˛*nĕng* ʻ*p'i*, if you do so people will despise you.

ʻ**菲** Fei. A red, marshy plant; pot-herbs, greens; sparing, frugal; fragrant; mixed, blended; beautiful, variegated; straw sandals: [6]ʻ*p'i pok*˛ poor, of no value, shabby; [7]ʻ*p'i uk*˛ (only) a mean thing, as one says affectedly of his present; [8]ʻ*p'i keng*ʾ "my poor respects" — written on a present of money. Read ˛*p'i*, as in ˛*hwong* ˛*p'i*, exuberant vegetation.

ʻ**匪** Fei. A square bamboo-box; a graceful gait; the regular march of horses; not right, illegal; banditti, vagabonds: [9]ʻ*p'i saik*˛ variegated; [10]ʻ*p'i* ʻ*tong*, a band of villains; COM., [11]ʻ*p'i* ˛*tu* or ʻ*p'i loi*ʾ thieves, vagabonds. Read ˛*hung*: to distribute, as a prince does.

ʻ**斐** Fei. Elegant, graceful, polished, adorned, as actions or essays: [12]ʻ*p'i* ʻ*mi*, pleasing; [13]ʻ*p'i* ˛*yong* ˛*sing* ˛*chiong*, an ornate and finished composition.

ʻ**靡** Mi. Spread abroad, dispersed, overturned; scattered, defeated, put to flight, as troops; poured out; profuse, showy; extravagant display, luxury; not, without, not having; to involve, to implicate: ʻ*p'i* ʻ*p'i*, slow; small, insignificant, private; [14]ʻ*ch'ie* ʻ*p'i*, extravagant; [15]ʻ*p'i nik*˛ *pok*˛ ˛*sü*, not a day without thinking.

ʻ**悱** Fei. Hesitating, embarrassed, unable to express one's ideas.

棐 ʻ**榧** Fei. Used for the next: a kind of cabinet-wood with lines, suitable for furniture; a piece of wood tied to a bow at the grasp to strengthen it; to aid, to assist; to lean on: [16]ʻ*p'i* ʻ*chü*, a long nut like the hazel, found in Shantung.

ʻ**篚** Fei. A round, bamboo basket; square ones are called ˛*k'wong*.

˛**疲** P'i. ˛**罷** Pa. Fatigued, wearied, exhausted; inability, loss of strength; in the coll. slow, sluggish; the 2d also read *pa*ʾ q. v.: [17]˛*p'i* ˛*nu*, worn out, as a statesman says of himself; [18]˛*p'i* ˛*nang*, tiresome and difficult, as an office; COM., [19]˛*p'i kwong*ʾ wearied, jaded; COLL., ˛*p'i nŏ*ʾ or ˛*p'i* ˛*p'i tieu*ʾ or ˛*p'i* ˛*p'i nong*ʾ *nong*ʾ slow, sluggish in working.

˛**皮** P'i. The skin, the undressed hide; tanned hides, leather; leathern, leathery; furs; bark, peel; wrap-

1鄙陋	3鄙薄	5鄙吝	6菲薄	7菲物	9匪色	11匪徒	13斐然	14侈靡	不思	17疲駑	19疲倦
2邊鄙	4鄙笑	○	○	8菲敬	10匪黨	12斐美	成章	15靡日	16榧子	18疲難	○

pers, as for goods, the tare; to skin; to cover, as skin does; the 107th radical: in the coll. read *ˏp'ui*, q. v.: [1]*ˏp'i ˏhu*, the skin; [2]*ˏp'i pe'* money, presents; [3]*'tĕüng' ˏp'i*, grave and plain; [4]*ˏp'i ˏheu*, a target.

肥 ˏFei. Fat, oily, greasy; fleshy, corpulent; rich, fertile; to fatten, to profit; to unite and form one source: in the coll. read *ˏpui*, q. v.: [5]*ˏp'i 'tong*, fat, as a pig; [6]*ˏp'i chek*, fertile and barren; [7]*ch'aik, ˏp'i*, to whip one's horse.

腓 ˏFei. The calf of the leg; sick, diseased; changed, altered; to shun, to avoid, to flee from.

淝 ˏFei. A river in Nganhwui, flowing into Lake Ch'ao by Luchou-fu; diverging, as streams from a common source.

羆 ˏPi. P'i. Pei. A large species of bear; a grisly bear, found in Liautung: [8]*ˏhüng ˏp'i*, a bear—when dreamed of, is ominous of the birth of a son.

ˏP'i. A coll. word, as in *ˏp'i ˏp'i kieu'* or *ˏp'i ˏp'á ˏp'a*, to pant, to breathe hard and quick.

ˏP'i. A coll. euphonic prefix, as in *ˏp'i ˏp'au*, to run, to scamper.

(675) P'iă.

'跛 Po. Read *'p'ó*; coll. *'p'iă*, as in [9]*'p'iă ˏwai*, to tread obliquely; [10]*'p'iă ˏk'a*, to tread the foot to one side; [11]*'p'iă kaing'* or *'p'iă kaing' sié'* in the habit of treading on one side of the heel.

ˏP'iă. A coll. word: inclined, oblique: *ˏp'iă ˏp'iă*, slanting, not plumb: *ˏp'iă tio'* a depraved course, licentious practice.

ˏP'iă. A coll. word: to shun, to avoid: *ˏp'iă k'ó'* and *ˏp'iă 'chau*, to run away, as from creditors or the police.

ˏP'iă. A coll. word: poor, inferior, damaged: *ˏp'iă ˏp'iă hwo'* inferior goods.

(676) P'iăh.

僻ˎ P'i. Pei. Read *p'ek,*; coll. *p'iăh,*: to step to one side, to get out of the way of another: *p'iăh, p'iăh,* or *ˏpiĕng p'iăh,* retired, a by-place; [12]*p'iăh, cheng'* retired and quiet; [13]*p'iăh, 'chau*, to run away; [14]*p'iăh, ˏpiĕng* or *p'iăh, sioh, ˏpeng*, to step to one side.

辟ˎ Pi. P'i. Read *p'ek,*; used for the coll. *p'iăh,* as in *p'iăh, ˏsiă*, to expel or avert malign influences, as with charms.

P'iăh,. A coll. word, as in *ˏt'u p'iăh,* mud-flats left by the ebb of the tide; *ˏsai p'iăh,* sand-flats.

(677) P'iăk.

潑ˎ P'o. Read *p'wak,*; used for the coll. *p'iăk,*: to throw from a vessel: *p'iăk, sioh, ˏsing*, spattered over the the whole person.

P'iăk,. A coll. word, used for *hiăk,* as in *p'iăk, lóh,* to topple over, as a wall; *p'iăk, kwo' k'ó'* it fell over the other way.

[1]皮膚 [2]皮幣 [3]重皮 [4]皮侯 [5]肥腯 [6]肥瘠 [7]策肥 [8]熊羆 [9]跛歪 [10]跛胶 [11]跛慣 [12]僻靜 [13]僻走 [14]僻邊

P'iăk,. A coll. word: even, exactly corresponding, as accounts: *p'iăk, k'ó'* balanced, squared; *p'iăk, so'* the accounts balanced; *p'iăk, tek, tik,* just even —neither one owing the other.

P'iăk,. A coll. word: to throb, as the heart or the temples: *p'iăk, p'iăk, 'tiong*, to throb or palpitate incessantly; *p'iăk, 'k'i p'iăk,* a continuous throbbing.

P'iăk,. A coll. word: to slap: *p'iăk, sioh, ,siăng*, the sound of slapping or of a thing falling.

(678) P'iăng.

拚 Pang. P'ing. Read *piéng'* in the dictionaries; often read *,p'ing;* coll. *,p'iăng:* to contend, to strive together: [1]*,p'iăng 'la ,sio ,yăng*, to strive for the mastery, to decide by a fight or lawsuit who is to rule, etc.

,P'iăng. A coll. word, used for *pwoi':* the back; behind, rear, the back part, the opposite of the face or front: *,p'iăng au'* behind the back, the back; *,p'iăng chek, kauk,* the vertebral column; *,p'iăng ,p'ui kau'* the skin of the back thick; *met.*, rich, wealthy; *,p'iăng ,p'ui k'á' ,i ,mwo ,mwo*, pat the skin of his back—wheedle him to give money; *,p'iăng p'ok,* humpbacked; *,p'iăng 'tiu ,p'iăng*, back to back—making a united effort.

跛 Po. Read *'p'ó;* used for the coll. *'p'iăng:* lame: [2]*'p'iăng ,k'a*, maimed, crippled in the feet; [3]*'p'iăng ,chü*, a cripple.

'P'iăng. A coll. word: a large spot or stain, as of grease on clothes; a patch, a broken place, as in plastering; a numerative of folded pieces of vermicelli: *miéng' sioh, 'p'iăng*, one fold of vermicelli.

'P'iăng. A coll. word, as in *'p'iăng 'p'iăng kieu'* a rattling sound, the clatter as of crockery.

'P'iăng. A coll. word: to spill: *'p'iăng ,wong*, all spilled out.

閛 Read *,p'eng;* used in the *Paik, ,Ing* for the coll. *,p'iăng* (or *p'iăng'*): similar to *,piăng* (and *piăng'*), but with the meaning intensified; the slamming of doors; a violent pounding or thumping.

P'iăng'. A coll. word, analogous to *k'iăng':* to unite, to place together: *p'iăng' 'king* or *p'iăng' 'lĕng*, to bring close together.

P'iăng'. A coll. word: to compare, to place in juxtaposition, so as to compare together: *'pi p'iăng'* to compare, to illustrate; *p'iăng' 'chi twai'* as large as this; *p'iăng' 'chiă yong'* after this sort or fashion.

(679) P'ié.

批 P'i. To strike with the hand; to push away, to turn round; to pare, to scrape off; to revise, to criticise, to animadvert; to assist; to give an official reply, to post a case at the door of an office; the notice of a case; a comment, a gloss: COM., [4]*,p'ié ,p'ang*, to criti-

[1]拚喇輸贏 [2]跛胶 ○ [3]跛子 ○ [4]批評 ○

cise, to add critical notes, as to an essay; [1]꜀p'ié ꜂ngü, or ꜀p'ié se꜄ to post a case, the notice of a case posted at an office; [2] p'ié ꜂hung, to grant a petition; [3]꜀p'ié pauk꜇, to return a petition ungranted; COLL., tĕük꜇ ꜀p'ié, a bamboo stick or ferule; ꜀ch'ui ꜀p'ié, a switch.

꜀P'ié. A coll. word, for which the last may be used: a letter, an epistle: ꜀p'ié seng꜄ or ꜀p'ié chak꜇, a letter; ꜀p'ié tói꜄ (or ꜀p'ui), a letter-envelop; ꜀p'ié sioh꜇ ꜀hung, one letter; ꜀p'ié meng꜄ the superscription; ꜂sia ꜀p'ié, ꜀hung ꜀p'ié, and kie꜄ ꜀p'ié, to write, seal, and send a letter.

披 ꜀P'i. To hold on one side; to open, to spread out, to extend; to unroll; to rive, to break; to throw on, as a cloak; to cast off clothes; to oppose; disheveled: [4]꜀p'ié ꜂lang, to turn the leaves and read; [5]꜀p'ié ꜀sing tai꜄ ngwok꜇, to don the stars and put on the moon—to travel by night; COM., [6]꜀p'ié ꜀hung, a large cape or cloak; [7]꜀p'ié ꜀kiéng (or ꜀ui ꜀kiéng), a sort of tasseled cape, as worn by brides; [8]꜀p'ié p'wai꜄ to distribute to others, as money to be used for a common object; [9]꜀p'ié ꜀t'au sak꜇ hwak꜇ the hair all disheveled.

㓟 ꜀P'i. To trim, to hew, to pare off; to peel, to flay: COLL., ꜀p'ié ꜀p'ui, to pare off the skin, or bark; ꜀p'ié chiá꜄ to pare sugar-cane; ꜀p'ié ꜀k'a ꜀neng, to trim of the hard skin of the feet.

磇 砒 ꜀P'i. An ore of arsenic, realgar, red sulphuret of arsenic: COM., [10]꜀p'ié ꜀song, arsenic, commonly called seng꜄ or ꜀ing ꜀ngiong.

(680) P'iék.

丿 P'ieh. A stroke from right to left in writing; the 4th radical.

撆 撇 P'ieh꜇ To tap, to strike lightly; to brush along, to wipe; to divide; to skim off; to pull, to lead, to drag; gently, somewhat, a modicum; the stroke to the left in Chinese characters; in the coll. a light, bamboo basket to weigh in: COM., [11]p'iék꜇ siü꜄ a roof sloping one way, as on the sides of a court; met., mustaches, also called ne꜄ p'iék꜇ ꜀sü; [12]p'iék꜇ ꜀iu, to skim off the fat; met., to learn surreptitiously another's art; COLL., [13]chó꜄ tai꜄ p'iék꜇ t'auk꜇ to do up a business properly; [14]p'iék꜇ ꜀k'wi or p'iék꜇ k'ó꜄ to set aside or dismiss (a matter); [15]p'iék꜇ ꜀ngüng ꜀iu, "skim off a film of silver"—a business that is not lucrative; p'iék꜇ ꜂chwi p'iék꜇ to throw (shells) so as to skim the water; ꜀chiéng ꜀tó p'ah꜇ ꜂chwi p'iék꜇ to take money and make it skip over the water—i. e., to waste it; ꜀ch'ing ꜀küng p'iék꜇ a weighing-basket.

瞥 P'ieh꜇ To glance at, to look at slightly; just perceived: [16]p'iék꜇ kiéng꜄ a hasty glance.

[1]批語 [2]批准 [3]批駁 ○ [4]披覽 [5]披星戴月 ○ [6]披風 ○ [7]披肩 ○ [8]披派 [9]披頭撇髮 [10]磇霜 [11]撆樹 [12]撆油 [13]做事撆托 [14]撆開 [15]撆銀油 [16]瞥見 ○

福州方言拼音字典

劈, To pare, to whittle, to sharpen to a point; to deliver a blow with a sword: COLL., *p'iék, 'toi,* to whittle off short; [1]*p'iék, sioh, ˌtó,* to give a stroke with a sword; [2]*ek, ˌtó p'iék, trang'* to cleave off with a blow—have nothing to do with it; [3]*p'iék, ngek,* to behead—term used jestingly.
P'ieh.

P'iék,. A coll. word, as in *p'iék, sŭk,* a strange, outre custom; a style different from the prevailing mode: *p'iék, sŭk, tek, kik,* excessively odd.

(681) P'iéng.

ˌ篇 Slips of bamboo, anciently used for books; a leaf of a book, a section; books, publications; a species of edible red-skinned bamboo: [4]*ek, ˌp'iéng,* one leaf; COM., [5]*ˌp'iéng sik,* a section or chapter, as in the Book of Odes; [6]*ˌchiong ˌp'ieng,* a whole section.
P'ien.

ˌ偏 Inclined, lateral; a side, at or by the side; partial, bent on having, longing for; depraved, selfish; a half; 25 chariots; fifty men: [7]*ˌp'iéng ai'* partiality; [8]*ˌp'iéng kiéng'* prejudiced; [9]*ˌp'iéng chek,* to be opinionated; [10]*ˌp'iéng ˌsŭ,* selfish; COM., [11]*ˌp'iéng p'ek,* a perverted will; [12]*ˌp'iéng ˌpung,* a concubine; [13]*ˌp'iéng ˌkŭng,* an Imperial concubine; COLL., *ˌkiăng ˌp'iéng ˌmwong,* "go in a side-door"; *met.,* to follow evil ways, dissolute; *ˌp'iéng ˌpeng,* inclined; partial; *ˌp'iéng ˌp'iéng pwoh, chó'* perversely bent on doing; *ˌp'iéng 'lieu, ˌp'iéng ˌló,* and *ˌp'iéng kwo' 'lieu,* expressions borrowed from the Court dialect, meaning have eaten, have taken my meal.
P'ien.

ˌ編 A cord to tie ancient bamboo-books; to arrange materials for a book; to string things on a cord; to compose; records, books; to twist, to plait; a kind of turban: [14]*kang ˌp'iéng,* a book; [15]*ˌp'iéng ˌniéng,* annals; [16]*ˌp'iéng ˌsiu,* a reviser of books—the lowest title in the Hanlin; COM., [17]*ˌp'iéng ˌchŭ,* to compose a book; *ˌp'iéng 'sieu siok,* or [18]*ˌp'iéng ˌping wa'* to compose novels.
Pien.

ˌ㾫 A paralysis, a palsy on one side: COM., *ˌp'iéng ˌhung,* a palsy.
P'ien.

ˌ翩 To fly swiftly; to hurry to and fro; a bustle and running, as at a parade; hovering, fluttering, as pennons: *ˌp'iéng ˌp'iéng,* flying about.
P'ien.

片' A thin and small thing, a leaf, slip, splinter, strip, bit, chip, fragment; a short time; a petal; to split, to slice, to divide; a half, a section of; the 91st radical: [19]*p'iéng' ˌhang,* a note, a chit; [20]*p'iéng' ˌngiong,* a word or sentence; [21]*ch'iék, p'iéng'* to slice up; COM., [22]*p'iéng' ˌsi,* a while; *p'iéng' ˌtang,* or *ˌtang p'iéng'* visiting-cards; *p'iéng' nŭk,* slices of pork; *ngwa' p'iéng'* pieces of broken tiles; COLL., *p'iéng' ˌsieu,* to slice up an animal roasted whole; *p'iéng' 'chai chiăh, che'*
P'ien.

[1]劈一刀 [2]一刀劈斷 [3]劈級 [4]一篇 [5]篇席 [6]全篇 [7]偏愛 [8]偏見 [9]偏執 [10]偏私 [11]偏僻 [12]偏房 [13]偏宮 [14]簡編 [15]編年 [16]編修 [17]編書 [18]編平話 [19]片緘 [20]片言 [21]切片 [22]片時

꜀tu ꜀mó, "not a slip of paper or word"—no evidence of; no lawsuits, etc.; *꜀hung ꜀ling p'iéng'* wafer-cakes of rice flour and China root.

騙 騗 P'ien. To mount a horse; to take advantage of, to delude, to deceive, to cheat, to lie to: [1]*p'iéng' kwoh,* a plan to cheat; COM., [2]*haik, p'iéng'* to impose on one most grossly; [3]*k'i p'iéng'* or [4]*hung p'iéng'* to delude, to cheat; COLL., [5]*p'iéng' ꜀nĕng ꜀chiéng*, to cheat one of money; *p'iéng' ꜀nĕng 'kiăng*, "a child who deludes one"—as said of a child dying early; *p'iéng' ch'oi'* to cheat the mouth, as by eating cheap things.

遍 徧 Pien. Universal, all around, pervading; the entire, the whole; to make a circuit; a visit, a walk: [6]*p'iéng' kwok,* throughout the whole land; [7]*ek, p'iéng'* (in the Court dialect) a visit, a walk, a trip; COM., [8]*p'iéng' ꜀sing*, the whole person; [9]*'p'wo p'iéng'* universal, pervading; COM., [10]*p'iéng' ꜀sing 'niong*, "the whole person limber" —dressed in silks and satins; *p'iéng' ꜀sang p'iéng' 'yă ꜀tu o'* "are both in hill and country" — everywhere, in all places, all about.

(682) P'ieu.

飄 P'iao. A spiral gust, a whirlwind; a brisk gale; noise of the wind; blown or swayed by the wind; a light, easy manner; vain, frivolous; to fall: [11]*꜀p'ieu ꜀ling*, the falling of leaves; COM., [12]*꜀p'ieu ꜀hü* (coll. *꜀p'ieu ꜀hü*), empty, not substantial; [13]*꜀p'ieu ꜀liu*, floating about; roving; [14]*꜀p'ieu taung'* to wander about, to vagabondize; [15]*꜀p'ieu ꜀yong kwo' 'hai*, sailed or blown over the sea.

漂 P'iao. Analogous to the last: to float, to be moved by the wind or waves; cold, dismal: also read *p'ieu'* q. v.: *꜀p'ieu ꜀p'ieu*, floating, soaring aloft; COM., [16]*꜀p'ieu ꜀liu laung' 'chü*, a dissipated person; COLL., *꜀k'ing ꜀p'ieu ꜀p'ieu*, very light; trifling, frivolous.

嘌 P'iao. Without rule, irregular; a carriage thundering along, swift: [17]*꜀p'ieu ch'iong'* to sing loose songs.

螵 P'iao. A chrysalis: [18]*꜀song ꜀p'ieu ꜀sieu*, chrysalides of insects which have a woolly envelop, as the mantis; *'hai ꜀p'ieu ꜀sieu*, a cuttle-fish.

鏢 The end or mouth of a scabbard, covered with copper and ornamented; the point of a knife.

縹 P'iao. Also read *p'ieu'*: a sort of fine blue silk; blue, azure, greenish: *'p'ieu 'p'ieu*, buoyant, light and floating; [19]*p'ek, 'p'ieu*, amethystine, cerulean; [20]*ch'oi' 'p'ieu*, leek green; *'p'ieu 'mieu*, floating in the air, as the genii.

剽 P'iao. To strike, to stab; to pierce, to puncture; to cut off; to rob, to plunder;

[1]騙局 [2]黑騙 [3]欺騙 [4]哄騙 [5]騙伙錢 [6]遍國 [7]一遍 [8]遍身 [9]普遍 [10]遍身軟 [11]飄零 [12]飄虛 [13]飄流 [14]飄蕩 [15]飄洋過海 [16]漂流浪子 [17]嘌唱 [18]桑螵蛸 [19]碧縹 [20]翠縹 〇

福州方言拼音字典

nimble, swift: [1]‘p‘ieu ꜀ch‘iong, a spear, a dart; [2]‘p‘ieu liok꜁ to rob; [3]‘p‘ieu ch‘iék, to purloin, to plagiarize. Read ꜀p‘ieu: a medium-sized bell, giving an acute sound.

‘摽 Piao. To beat the breast, to lay the hand on the heart; to strike, to smite; to fall, as leaves; to beckon, to signalize; the point of a sword: [4]‘p‘ieu ꜀ki, to make a signal to.

‘莩 殍 P‘iao. Also read ‘p‘eu: famished, dying of hunger; to rot and fall, as trees: [5]ngŏ’ ‘p‘ieu, starved to death.

票’ P‘iao. Also used for ꜀pieu (a ticket): to rise or fly swiftly; a signal by fire; light, soaring as a pennant; a warrant, a mittimus; a note, a bill; a ticket, a passport: COM., [6]‘taung’ p‘ieu’ a pawn-ticket; [7]꜀chiéng p‘ieu’ a bank-bill; a bank-note payable in cash; [8]p‘ieu’ ꜀kong, fac-similes or tallies of bank bills—to detect counterfeits; [9]p‘ieu’ ꜀teu, a shin-plaster, temporary issues of small value; [10]p‘ieu’ këü’ or ‘ch‘iu p‘ieu’ a bond, a promissory note; [11]ch‘ok꜁ p‘ieu’ to issue a warrant; to issue bank-notes; [12]p‘ieu’ chiék, a leathern pocket-book; [13]kwong’ p‘ieu’ a ticket to get blanks for compositions—at the examinations; [14]‘tiong p‘ieu’ to renew a bond; COLL., ‘kung p‘ieu’ to run on a bank.

漂’ P‘iao. To bleach, to whiten: also read ꜀p‘ieu, q. v.: COM., [15]p‘ieu’ pwo’ to bleach cotton cloth; [16]p‘ieu’ pah꜁ to bleach.

驃’ Also read ꜀pieu: a cream-colored horse; a spirited, fleet steed: [17]p‘ieu’ ꜀k‘ié, a general-in-chief.

鰾’ Piao. P‘iao. A fish's sound or air-bladder: COM., [18]꜀ngü p‘ieu’ the sound, from which fish-glue is made.

꜀薸 P‘iao. Duckweed—an aquatic plant like a Riccia, floating on fish ponds: COLL., ꜀p‘ieu ‘mó, large duckweed; ꜀p‘ieu ‘kiăng, small duckweed.

꜀瓢 P‘iao. A calabash; a drinking vessel of gourd, a dipper; in the coll. a spoon: [19]ek꜁ ꜀p‘ieu ‘ing, only a gourd full (of soup) to drink—which satisfied Yentzu; COM., [20]꜀yă ꜀p‘ieu, a coccoa-nut dipper, also called ꜀yă ‘wang; COLL., [21]꜀p‘ieu ꜀keng (or ꜀peng), a soup-spoon—also called hok꜁ ꜀p‘ieu (a crane-spoon).

꜀嫖 Piao. Light, trifling: wanton, lascivious; given to lewdness; to go a whoring: [22]hó’ ꜀p‘ieu, addicted to lewdness; COM., [23]꜀p‘ieu yéng’ a brothel—commonly termed ‘pieu ‘chü ꜀tiong; COLL., ꜀p‘ieu k‘ah, a fornicator; ꜀p‘ieu ‘tu ‘ing ꜀a p‘iéng’ ꜀kung ꜀t‘au ꜀ch‘ié, whoredom, gaming, drinking, opium-smoking, boxing, and playing instruments—are all vices; ꜀p‘ieu póh, to blackguard, to revile.

(683) P‘ih.

P‘ih꜁. A coll. word: to dart nimbly, as a rat; to hop away, as insects: p‘ih꜁ ‘chau (or ch‘ok꜁), to dart off, as rats or pigs.

1 剽鎗 2 剽掠 3 剽竊 4 摽旗 5 餓殍 6 當票 7 錢票 8 票根 9 票條 10 票據 11 出票 12 票摺 13 卷票 14 轉票 15 漂布 16 漂白 17 驃騎 18 魚鰾 19 一瓢飲〇 20 椰瓢 21 瓢羹 22 好嫖 23 嫖院

P'ih. A coll. word, as in *p'ih sioh, kwo'* to throw out a word (to one's face); *á' k'ëük, nëng p'ih* will have people blirt at you.

P'ih. A coll. word, as in *p'ih 'mui*, a blunted end, as of a needle or awl.

(684) P'ik.

P'ik. A coll. euphonic prefix, as in *p'ik p'iák* to throb, to palpitate; the pattering sound of bare feet, or walking in the wet; *p'ik p'ok* to beat, to pound; *p'ik lik p'ok lok*, a rattling sound, as of cash falling.

(685) P'ing.

拚 P'ing. Pang. To risk, to jeopardize, to peril: also read *piéng'* and in the coll. *p'iáng*, q. v.: COM., [1]*p'ing miáng'* to peril life; [2]*p'ing miáng' p'au*, to run recklessly; *p'ing miáng' 'kang*, to pursue rapidly, to go in hot haste.

併 Ping. Read *peng'*; used for the coll. *p'ing*: to fit, to adjust; to calculate, to consider how: [3]*p'ing siong'* to fit in, to adjust, as the parts of; [4]*p'ing p'woi'* to adjust properly; to engage, as a suitable partner; [5]*p'ing 'hwo*, to engage partners.

P'ing. A coll. euphonic prefix, as in *p'ing p'ang*, to apportion, to divide equally, as shares.

品 P'in. A class, a series, a grade, a degree; one sort out of a variety; an official rank or standing; a rule, law, guide, example; actions, conduct; an article, one of a sort; a delicacy, a rare dish; to classify, to rank, to arrange; temperament: [6]*p'ing chiëk*, the deportment, as conformed to the rites; [7]*kwo 'p'ing*, sorts of fruit; [8]*siong' 'p'ing*, superior, the best quality; [9]*p'ing uk*, things, articles; COM., [10]*kik 'p'ing*, the highest rank; [11]*kiu 'p'ing*, the nine official ranks, divided into *chiáng'* and *chëáng'* chief and secondary; [12]*p'ing mau'* countenance, expression; [13]*p'ing haing'* actions, conduct; [14]*p'ing ngek*, an official grade; [15]*p'ing kah*, the deportment or carriage, one's natural ways; [16]*p'ing 'wang*, a kind of large, fine bowl.

'P'ing. A coll. euphonic prefix, as in *'p'ing 'p'ong*, or *'p'ing 'p'ing 'p'ong 'p'ong*, the sound of water when agitated: *'p'ing 'p'iáng* or *'p'ing 'tung 'p'iáng*, to surge, to roll, as waves or as water in a vessel; also a swaying or unsteady gait.

P'ing. A coll. euphonic prefix, as in *p'ing p'iáng*, or *p'ing p'ing p'iáng p'iáng*, a loud noise, as of the slamming of doors; *p'ing p'ong*, or *p'ing p'ing p'ong p'ong*, a loud thumping; a report, as of firecrackers, bang!

P'ing. A coll. word: equal, balancing; even; to smooth, to make level: *p'ing p'ek*, equal, even; balancing, as accounts; *p'ing p'ang*, to make level; *p'ing p'ing tong*, of equal lengths.

(686) P'o.

P'o'. A coll. word: jutting above the surface, protuberant, convex, bulging out: *p'o' 'k'i li*, raised, protruding.

[1]拚命 [2]拚命跑 [3]併上 [4]併配 [5]併夥 [6]品節 [7]果品 [8]上品 [9]品物 [10]極品 [11]九品 [12]品貌 [13]品行 [14]品級 [15]品格 [16]品碗

P‘o’. A coll. word: a kind of convex bamboo cover for rice-steamers, etc., called *p‘o’ ‘ló.*

(687) P‘ó.

‹波 Po. A wave, a ripple; moved, agitated; moistened; a glance; bright, glossy; to flow, to communicate; old, aged: [1]*‹king ‹p‘ó*, the bright moon; [2]*‹ong ‹p‘ó*, to confer favor; [3]*‹ü ‹p‘ó*, remnants; [4]*‹p‘ó ‹ping laung’ cheng’* smooth water; COM., [5]*‹p‘ó laung’* waves, billows.

‹菠 Po. A vegetable from abroad, a coarse wintergreens, called [6]*‹p‘ó ‹ling*, or *‹hung ‹küng ch‘ai’* the red-rooted greens; in the coll. *‹p‘wo ‹ling*, q. v.

‹碆 Stones that may be used for arrow-heads; perhaps a sort of obsidian.

‹坡 P‘o. A hill, a mound, the side of a hill; a pile or tumulus thrown up: in the coll. read *‹pó*, q. v.: [7]*‹p‘ó ‘pang*, a bank, an embankment by a river; COM., [8]*‹sang ‹p‘ó*, a mound; COLL., [9]*k‘ié’ ‹p‘ó*, a military guard or escort.

‹陂 Pei. Also read *‹p‘i*; interchanged with the last, also with the next in the sense of uneven: a bank, a side; to bank in, to inclose and drain: [10]*‹p‘ó ‹tié*, a pool.

‹陁 Uneven, as roads; the sides of a road: [11]*‹p‘ó ‹tó*, irregular, not level.

‹P‘ó. A coll. word, as in *‹p‘ó ‹tó twai’ ‘ü*, a heavy rain, rain falling in torrents.

‘頗 P‘o. The head inclined; deflected, leaning; uneven; an excess; considerable, somewhat, a little; doubtful: used for the coll. *‘p‘wo*, q. v.: [12]*‘p‘ó ‘hó*, pretty well, will answer; [13]*‘p‘ó ‹tó*, rather much; COM., [14]*‘p‘ó song’*, *‘p‘ó ‹ka*, and *‘p‘ó ‘t‘io*, passable, pretty good—written on essays as critical notes; *‘p‘ó ‘p‘ó* somewhat, a little, in some degree.

‘跛 Po. Lame, halt in the feet; impotent, crippled; to walk lame, to go or stand on one foot; to loll: in the coll. *‘pai*, *‘p‘iă*, and *‘p‘iăng*, q. v.: *‘p‘ó kiok*, lame.

‘叵 ‘回 P‘o. A negative, the reverse of *‘k‘ó* (can or will do); can not, ought not, will not do; do not; then, forthwith: [15]*‘p‘ó seng’* unworthy of belief; [16]*‘p‘ó ch‘aik*, unfathomable; [17]*‘p‘ó ‹ló*, a wine-cup.

破’ P‘o. To rend, to break, to rive, to split, to rip open; broken, torn, ragged; injured, spoiled; ruined, defeated; stormed, occupied by force; to detect, to lay bare a scheme; to see through a plot; in the coll. read *p‘wai’* q. v.: [18]*p‘ó’ hwai’* destroyed, spoiled; [19]*p‘ó’ liék* riven; [20]*p‘ó’ pai’* defeated; COM., [21]*p‘ó’ ‹yong* and [22]*p‘ó’ ‹sing*, the first sexual acts of males and females; [23]*k‘ang’ p‘ó’* to see through, to penetrate, as a design; *p‘ó’ ‹chai*, to waste property; *p‘ó’ hié’* to spend, to squander; *p‘ó’ té’ nguoh*, to "open hell"—to deliver spirits, as in the *pai’*

1 金波　2 恩波　3 餘波　4 波平 浪靜　5 波浪　6 菠蔆　7 坡坂　8 山坡　9 跬坡　10 陂池　11 陂陀　12 頗好　13 頗多　14 頗順　15 叵信　16 叵測　17 叵羅　18 破壞　19 破裂　20 破敗　21 破陽　22 破身　23 看破

ch'ang' rites; *p'ó' ˏka taung' 'sang,* to ruin family and property by dissipation; *p'ó' siong'* a marred face; maimed, defective in person; COLL., *'p'ó' ˏnĕng ˏing ˏyong ch'ek, sié' ˏk'iĕng,* one who breaks up negotiations for betrothal will suffer for his guilt to seven generations.

(688) P'oh.

P'oh,. A coll. word, as in *p'oh, sioh, ˏsiăng,* a sound, as of an arrow striking the target, or of one falling on the ground.

(689) P'ŏh.

粕, P'o. The grains of liquor; in the coll. the hard, fibrous part, as of sugar-cane, fruits, etc., rejected in eating: *²ˏchau p'ŏh,* sediment floating in a vat; dregs, grounds; *³ˏcha p'ŏh,* sediments, refuse.

(690) P'oi.

屁' P'i. Read *p'e'*; coll. *p'oi'*: foul wind: *pong' p'oi'* to break wind.

呸' P'i. Read *p'ek,*; used in the *Paik, ˏIng* for the coll. *p'oi'*: to spit: *⁴p'oi' 'lang,* to void spittle; *⁵p'oi' haik,* to spit blood; *⁶p'oi' sioh, ˏk'ŭng,* to spit a puddle.

(691) P'ok.

覆, Fu. Read *hok,*; coll. *p'ok,*: to invert, to turn the top or face of a thing down: *⁷p'ok, 'chiong* (or *'ch'iong*) *saĕk, sioh, 't6,* to fall headlong violently; *⁸p'ok, 'wang chiok, sik,* to invert his bowl and cut off his means of living, as by drawing off his customers; *⁹ˏnong p'ok, ch'ieu'* a mode of gambling by twirling and matching cash; *¹⁰p'ok, ˏsó,* the inverted tiles, those laid with the concave side down; *p'ah, p'ok,* to turn over, to upset; *¹¹p'ok, 'tiăng,* the convex top of a grave.

P'ok,. A coll. word: to bend, to incline, as the head or body: *ˏt'au p'ok, kiă'* to bow the head; *p'ok, kak,* round-shouldered.

浡 ² Read *pwok,*; used in the *Paik, ˏIng* for the coll. *p'ok,* as in *p'ok, sioh, ˏsiăng,* a noise, a sound, as of things set down or of wood when struck.

梆 ² Pang. Read *ˏpong*; used for the coll. *p'ok,* as in *p'ok, p'ok,* the sound of a watchman's rattle; *p'ok, p'ok, 'kwong,* a watchman's rattle; *p'ok, ˏsang p'ok,* to beat three beats.

P'ok,. A coll. word, as in *p'ok, p'ok, t'ieu'* (the mind) trembling with fear.

P'ok,. A coll. word, as in *p'ok, 'long sioh, ˏsiăng,* a sound, as of a stone thrown into the water, splash! *p'ok, ˏlong,* a dull, heavy sound.

P'ok,. A coll. word, as in *p'ik, p'ok,* to beat, to pound: *k'á' ˏi p'ok, sioh, ˏt'ui,* give him one blow.

(692) P'ong.

ˏ斛 P'ang. Also read *ˏpong*: abundant, an overflowing measure: COLL., *ˏp'ong chiăh, ˏp'ong,* superabundant, profuse, bountiful, as a feast.

¹破仈姻緣 七世愆〇 ²猜粕 ³渣粕 ⁴呸漶〇 ⁵呸血〇 ⁶呸一囷〇 ⁷覆掌捽一 倒〇 ⁸覆碗絶食 ⁹擇覆笑〇 ¹⁰覆槽〇 ¹¹覆鼎〇

雱 霶 P'ang. Also read ₛpong, and interchanged with ₛpong (a great rain); a storm of sleet; abundance of snow, the noise of a driving storm: [1] ₍p'ong ₛtó, a heavy rain; [2] ₍p'ong p'woi' a vast expanse of waters, a flood.

ʻ丼 A character used in the Paik, ₍Ing for the coll. ʻp'ong, as in ʻp'ong sioh, ₍siăng (or ₍p'ong sioh, ₍siăng), a sound, as of a thing dropped into a well; similar to ₍p'ang, q. v.

噴' P'ên. To expel the breath forcibly, to hoot, to spurt; to snort; to breathe hard through the nose: [3] p'ong' k'e' to snort and rave; a breathing or aspirate; com., [4] p'ong' ʻchwi, to spurt water; [5] p'ong' ʻchwi ₍hwa, to spurt water, as over clothes; [6] p'ong' ₍hu ʻchwi, to sprinkle charm-water, as in exorcisms. Read ʻhung: the sound of breathing: ʻhung t'e' to sneeze.

馩' Read ʻp'ung; used for the coll. p'ong', as in p'ong' p'ong' ₍hiong, very fragrant; p'ong' p'e' ₍hiong (or p'auk, p'e' ₍hiong), fragrance striking the olfactory nerves—very odoriferous.

P'ong'. A coll. word: a crack, a crevice, an interstice: ₛp'ung p'ong' cracks; p'ong' ₍hong, a seam or crack, as in a wall; p'ong' ₍hi, a wide crack; p'ong' swoi' a seam in a garment.

P'ong'. A coll. word: the space between the toes or fingers: ʻch'iu ʻchai p'ong' (same as ʻch'iu ʻchai kek,) space between the fingers.

ₛ磅 P'ang. Read ₛpong; coll. ₛp'ong: the noise of stones falling: ₛp'ong sioh, ₛsiăng, a loud thump; ₛp'ong ₛp'ong kieu' (or ₛpong ₛpong kieu'), a dull, heavy sound, loud thumping, as on a floor.

(693) P'u.

ʻ醭 Read p'auk,; used in the Paik, ₍Ing for the coll. ʻp'u: mold, mildew: [7] ʻp'u ₍hwa, a whitish mold, as on food or clothing; mildewed; [8] ʻp'u k'e' or ʻp'u e' or ch'au' ʻp'u, a moldy scent; ʻp'u ʻp'u saik, an old, faded color; [9] ₍sang ʻp'u pah, ₍si (or pah, ne') ₛmó, all covered with mold.

ₛ浮 Fu. Fou. Read ₛp'eu; coll. ₛp'u: to float, to drift; floating; protuberant, raised, in relief: [10] ₛp'u ʻtu, raised panel-work; [11] ₛp'u ₍hwa, flowers in relief; [12] ₛp'u ₍kio, a floating bridge; [13] ₛp'u lo' rising, swelling; [14] ₛp'u ₛtiong, gaming to help a needy friend by allowing him a percentage of the winnings; [15] ₛp'u ʻma, a wire support for wicks in the ₛliu ₍kwong lamps; ₛp'u ₛp'u tioh, weak, relaxed, as the system after illness.

ₛ烰 Fou. Read ₛp'eu; coll. ₛp'u: to boil or fry in oil or fat: [16] ₛp'u chak, to boil in oil; [17] ₛp'u ʻpiăng, doughnuts; [18] ₛp'u ʻkieu, stuffed cakes boiled in oil; [19] ₛp'u ₛngü, to fry fish.

---

1 雱沱　2 雱沛　3 噴氣　4 噴水　5 噴水花〇　6 噴符水〇　7 醭花　8 醭氣　9 生醭白絲毛　10 浮堵〇　11 浮花　12 浮橋　13 浮露　14 浮塲　15 浮馬　16 烰炸　17 烰餅　18 烰餃　19 烰魚〇

(694) P'uh.

P'uh. A coll. word: a swollen appearance, as of spoiled food: *p'uh*, *ngai k'ó* puffed and spoiled.

P'uh. A coll. word, about the same as *puh* as in *p'ih p'uh* a noiseless blow, sound of a blow on soft things.

(695) P'ui.

P'ui. A coll. word: to spurt, to eject forcibly from the mouth; a sound expressing dislike or contempt.

(696) P'uí.

茴 Hui. Read *húi*; coll. *p'úi*, as in *p'úi hiong*, fennel, caraway seed, specifically termed *sieu p'úi hiong*.

皮 P'i. Read *p'i*; coll. *p'úi*: the skin; a hide; leather, leathern; furs; bark, peel; shameless: [1] *p'úi hu*, the skin; [2] *p'úi móh*, the cuticle; [3] *p'úi nong*, the inner parts of an undressed hide; [4] *p'úi 'ó*, a fur jacket; [5] *p'úi laung* duck's eggs cured by a coating of saltpetre, ashes, &c.; [6] *p'úi 'ch'au* or *p'úi hwo* furs; [7] *p'úi 't'ëng*, furs not made up; *'nü meng p'úi cheng kau* you are very shameless; *p'úi pau kauk*, very lean, emaciated; [8] *p'úi meng* the outside, merely external; [9] *p'úi tó k'ó hwang*, to take hides and tan or cure them; *kauk, 'lë p'úi*, to bruise or rub off the skin.

裴 P'ei. A long robe; a surname; also used for *pai*, to go and fro, to walk irresolutely: COM., *sang p'úi*, surnamed *P'úi*.

(697) P'ung.

蠭 蜂 Fêng. Bees, wasps, hornets: COM., [10] *mik p'ung*, the honey-bee; [11] *wong p'ung*, a hornet; [12] *tong yeu p'ung*, a wasp; [13] *p'ung cheng*, a bee's sting; [14] *p'ung teng* the bee stings; [15] *p'ung tiu*, a bee-hive; [16] *p'ung wo* or *p'ung seu* a bee's nest; [17] *p'ung 'ch'ai hwa*, the bee sips flowers; [18] *p'ung 'hwang ch'ek laung* the bees revolting and thieves tumultuous—a rebellion; an angry quarrel; noisy sport.

P'ung. A coll. word, as in *p'ung 'chwi*, swill; *p'ung 't'ëng*, a swill-pail; *p'ung só*, a swill-trough; *'mi p'ung*, the rinsings of rice.

捧 Fêng. P'êng. To offer with both hands; to receive or hold in both hands; to scoop up in the hand; a handful, a double-handful; in the coll. read *p'ung*, q. v.: [19] *'p'ung t'uk* to hold and read; COLL., *'p'ung 'chwi siáh* to scoop up water to drink; *'p'ung sioh 'p'ung*, to scoop up a double-handful.

琫 Pêng. Ornaments of gold, gems, or metal, on the scabbard or hilt of a sword; an emperor has gems, a prince has gold.

唪 𡂿 Fêng. A loud, boisterous laugh; great merriment: the 2d also means the vines of a melon yielding much fruit.

1 皮膚 2 皮膜 3 皮瓤 4 皮襖 5 皮蛋 6 皮草 7 皮桶 8 皮面 9 皮掏去韃 10 蜜蜂 11 黃蜂 12 長腰蜂〇 13 蜂針 14 蜂釘 15 蜂櫥 16 蜂窩 17 蜂採花〇 18 蜂反賊亂 19 捧讀〇

福州方言拼音字典

'莑 Pêng. P'êug. Grass growing luxuriantly; grassy, herbaceous: [1]'p'ung 'p'ung, abundant, luxuriant, laden with fruit.

'紡 Fang. Read 'hwong; used in the *Paik*, ˏ*Ing* for the coll. 'p'ung: to spin or twist thread with a twisting machine or hand-reel, called 'p'ung ˏch'ia; [2]'p'ung ˏmiéng ˏsa, to twist cotton-yarn.

ˏ帆 ˏ帆 Fan. A sail of mats or canvas: COM., [3]ˏhung ˏp'ung, sails; [4]ˏch'iă ˏp'ung, to hoist sail by windlass; [5]tiong ˏp'ung, to shift a sail, to wear ship; [6]ˏk'au ˏp'ung, (or ˏk'au hiong'), to tack.

ˏ芃 P'êng. Luxuriant herbage, grassy, flourishing; bushy, as the tail of a fox or squirrel: ˏp'ung ˏp'ung, abundant, as a field of grain.

ˏ蓬 P'êng. A species of flag or rush; a medicinal plant growing among hemp; tangled, disorderly, a jungle; disheveled; waving, as grass in the wind; a malign star: COM., [7]ˏp'ung ˏlai, a district in Shantung; [8]ˏp'ung ˏlai 'tó, the fairy islands, the abode of genii.

ˏ篷 ˏ篷 ˏ篷 P'êng. Mats of bamboo leaves and woven splints, used for sails, boat-covers, etc.: COM., [9]ˏhung ˏp'ung, a sail; [10]ˏp'ung ˏleu, a mat-lodge or hovel; [11]ˏp'ung 'ch'iong, a mat shed; [12]pwo' ˏp'ung, a cloth awning; COLL., [13]ˏp'ung sioh, 'liăng, one mat.

ˏ𡏖 Flying dust; dust blown about by the wind: ˏp'ung ˏp'ung 'k'i (or ˏpung ˏpung 'k'i), to rise, as dust or vapor.

ˏ逢 Fêng. P'ang. The sound of a drum: also read ˏhung, q. v.: ˏngó 'ku ˏp'ung ˏp'ung, the drums rattling.

ˏ縫 Fêng. To sew, to stitch: in the coll. read ˏpung, q. v.: [14]ˏp'ung ˏi, to sew garments; COM., [15]ˏchoi ˏp'ung, to cut out and sew, to be a tailor. Read p'ong': the seam of a garment.

ˏ鬔 ˏ鬔 Fêng. P'êng. The hair in disorder, disheveled hair: [16]ˏp'ung ˏsung, the hair uncombed and tangled.

ˏ捧 Fêng. P'éng. Read 'p'ung; coll. ˏp'ung: to offer with both hands; to bring, as dishes of food to the table, to serve up: [17]ˏp'ung pwong' to serve up the rice; [18]ˏp'ung ˏta ˏchong ˏhong, to offer tea and pipes; [19]ˏp'ung ˏtó ˏhwang, chopped dollars.

ˏ*P'ung*. A coll. word; the same as ˏp'ó, q. v.: ˏp'ung ˏtó twai' 'ü, a very heavy rain, the rain falling in torrents.

(698) P'wai.

破' P'o. Read p'ó'; coll. p'wai': to break, to split, to rend, to rive, to rip; broken, torn, ragged, spoiled, injured: [20]p'ah, p'wai' to

1蓁蓁 紗 4車 6闊 8蓬 鎥 厰 一 15裁 17捧 裝 畨
2紡 3風 帆 帆 萊 10篷 12布 領 縫 飯 烟 20拍
綿 帆 5轉 7蓬 島 樓 篷 14縫 16鬔 18捧 19捧 破
○ 帆 萊 9風 11篷 13篷 衣 鬆 茶 捣 ○

break; broken; [1]*p‘wai’ lang’* tattered, as clothes; running, as a sore; [2]*p‘wai’ leng’* to divide into segments; parted, as a forehead by a vertical indentation; [3]*p‘wai’ leng’ ‘k‘eng*, a dog with a white streak down the forehead; *met.*, a fellow who will prove an injury to one; [4]*p‘wai’ meng’* "split face"—detected, well known, as a thief; [5]*p‘wai’ tëük*, to split bamboo; [6]*p‘wai’ pwo’* cotton rags; *p‘wai’ ‘kiăng* or *pw‘ai’ ˎtá*, the first two sentences of an essay; *p‘wai’ ˎló ˏsiăng*, a shattered voice; *p‘wai’ pwo’ ˏsiéng*, old-rags-fairy—i. e., a penniless vagabond; *p‘wai’ ‘ngu ˏhiă* or *p‘wai’ ˏcha ˏli*, much broken; wholly spoiled; *ˏkiăng p‘wai’ ‘tang*, frightened (enough) to burst his gall-bladder! [7]*p‘wai’ ‘wang cho’ ch‘oi’* to break a bowl and swear, as before an idol; [8]*p‘wai’ lai² seu’ ˏchoi*, a knavish Siutsai.

派 洂 P‘ai. To branch, as a stream; to ramify, to branch off; a line or branch of posterity; to distribute, to give to each one; to appoint, to assign to places: COM., [9]*p‘wai’ chek, sëü²* to assign his office to each; [10]*ˏhiong p‘wai’* the apportionment of village-dues (for idol worship); [11]*ˏkwang p‘wai’* an official levy, as for expenses of street-gates, &c.; [12]*p‘wai’ ‘wi ˏwong*, to appoint a deputy; [13]*ek, p‘wai’ te² ˏhwong*, a strip of land; COLL., *p‘wai’ ‘chwi*, to lead off water, as in fields; *p‘wai’ tau’* or *p‘wai’ ˏtong tau’* midday, noon.

紕 P‘ai. Raveled silk; in the coll. to part, to divide; to separate into threads; COLL., [14]*p‘wai’ ˏhwa siăng’* to separate floss, as for embroidering; *p‘wai’ ˏt‘au hwok*, to part the hair.

𣎵 Strips of hemp-bark; in the coll. to separate the fibers, as of grass-cloth nettle, or of hemp for making ropes: COLL., [15]*p‘wai’ ˏmwai p‘iéng’* to part hemp-fibers.

(699) P‘wak.

潑 P‘o. To sprinkle, to throw water about; to drip, to ooze; a shower; to write boldly; a foot, in the Corean language: used for the coll. *p‘iăk*, q. v.: [16]*ˏnung p‘wak*, characters written with heavy strokes; COM., [17]*p‘wak, ‘chwi*, to throw water on, to irrigate; [18]*p‘wak, laiu²* to sprinkle manure; *p‘wak, ho²* or *p‘wak, chiéng²* an adulteress; a brazen-faced woman; *wak, p‘wak,* lively, enheartened; *p‘wak, lai²* to beg impudently, to squeeze by threats; COLL., *p‘wak, chioh,* to coat candles red—by pouring melted wax with an infusion of *‘chié ‘ch‘ó*; *‘ü p‘wak, ‘tié ˏli*, the rain beats in.

P‘wak,. A coll. word: to stride, to straddle, to step over; a step, a pace: *p‘wak, kwo’* to step over, as a threshold; *ˏk‘a p‘wak,* steps, stepping; *p‘wak, sioh, pwo²* to take a step—to gain a degree.

P‘wak,. A coll. word: to throw or hang, as a garment over a chair or a clothes-horse;

[1]破爛 [2]破稜 [3]破稜犬 [4]破面 [5]破竹 [6]破布 [7]破碗詛嘴 [8]破賴秀才 [9]派執事 [10]鄉派 [11]官派 [12]派委員〇 [13]一派地方 [14]紕花線 [15]𣎵麻片 [16]潑潑 [17]潑水 [18]潑料

福州方言拼音字典

p'wak, *kiëng* *t'au*, carry it over the shoulder; *p'wak*, *'ch'ai*, to wear a red silk sash, as Siutsai graduates do.

P'wak. A coll. word, as in *p'wak*, *'t'ëng*, a well-bucket; *p'wak*, *'t'ëng sóh*, a well-bucket rope.

(700) P'wang.

拌 Pan. Also read *pwang* and *p'wang'*: to reject, to cast off; to cut off, to divide, to distinguish.

磻 P'an. Also read *p'ang*: a mountain stream in the west of Shensi, a tributary of the river Wei: COM., [1]*p'wang* *k'á*, the stream P'an—in which [2]*Kiong t'ai' kung* angled.

判 P'an. Pang. To divide, to halve; to distinguish, to judge, to decide, to sentence; to join two parts; to marry; also to scatter, to dissolve: [3]*p'ié p'wang'* to give an official decision; COM., [4]*p'wang' ang'* to pass judgment on a case; [5]*p'wang' twang'* to judge and decide; [6]*p'wang' kwang*, (coll. *p'ang' kwang*), a judge, recorder — applied to the attendants of the god *Siāng hwòng*; [7]*tung p'wang'* a syndic, the magistrate in an inferior department.

泮 P'an. Pang. A semicircular pond near the colleges of princes, called in coll. *ngwok*, *peng* *tié*, or half-moon ponds; a stream in Shantung, near Ta-ngan-fu; to dissolve, to scatter: [8]*p'wang' tié*, the college-pool: COM., [9]*p'wang' kūng*, a prefectural college; [10]*p'wang' ngwong*, the first of the Siutsai graduates; COLL., [11]*tié p'wang' kūng*, or *'tié p'wang' 'chwi*, to enter college—to become a Siutsai.

頖 Interchanged with the last: to break, to scatter; the colleges of the princes.

盼 P'an. Pang. The white and black of the eye clearly distinguished; a beautiful eye; to look about: [12]*p'wang' wong'* to look for, to expect.

伴 Pan. An associate, a comrade, a companion; to follow, to attend on, to keep one company: [13]*tung p'wang'* a fellow, an equal; COM., [14]*p'wang' teng'* to bear one company; [15]*p'wang' 'k'ó*, to "go in with the crowd" to an examination—a phrase used affectedly; [16]*p'wang' ling*, to keep the spirit company, as a son sleeping by a father's coffin; [17]*p'wang' 'tu*, to stand by and tell others in gambling; [18]*p'wang' pung* or *p'wang' pung 'ma*, a bride's attendant; COLL., [19]*p'wang' nëng kwo' sié'* (merely) keep people company through the world, as the poor say.

畔 Pan. A division or path between fields, a landmark: in the following senses also read *pwang'*; to separate from, to revolt; to transgress the rules for ceremonial dress: *keng 'chiă yong' p'wang'* the farmers yield the landmarks.

[1] 磻溪 [2] 姜太公 [3] 批判 [4] 判案 [5] 判斷 [6] 判官 [7] 通判 [8] 泮池 [9] 泮宮 [10] 泮元 [11] 入泮 入泮宮 [12] 盼望 [13] 同伴 [14] 伴陣 [15] 伴考 [16] 伴靈 [17] 伴賭 [18] 伴房 [19] 伴仈過世

(701 P'wi.

胚 肧 P'i. An embryo; a foetus one month old; an unformed mass, any thing unfinished; vapors, clouds not condensed: [1]*,p'wi ,t'ai*, pregnant; COLL., [2]*,p'wi p'aĕk*, native talent; *,p'wi p'aĕk, 'hó*, good natural ability; [3]*,sing ,p'wi twai'* he has a large body.

坯 坏 P'ei. A hillock rebuilt, a mound; unburnt pottery; to plaster up a seam or crack; a rough block; crude, unformed, in the rough: COM., [4]*'chai ,p'wi*, thick paper or pasteboard, as for lining or stiffening; [5]*'tēū' ,p'wi*, chop-sticks in the rough, common unpainted ones; COLL., *pwoi' ,p'wi*, to make pasteboard.

(702) P'wo.

鋪 P'u. To spread out, to extend, to arrange; to lay, as a pavement; to make known, to pervade; a disease, ill; a door-ring, or knocker: also read *p'woʾ* q. v.: COM., [6]*,p'wo sioh*, to pave with stones; [7]*,p'wo 'peng*, bed-boards; [8]*,p'wo kai'* bedding; [9]*,p'wo ,pá* or *,p'wo sēū'* to arrange in order; [10]*,p'wo ,p'ang*, to divide, to apportion; *,p'wo té' 't'ang* or *,p'wo té' 'king*, carpets spread on the floor; [11]*,p'wo ,chiéng kaik, 'ch'ai*, to spread rugs and hang up festoons, as on festive occasions; COLL., [12]*,p'wo tio'* to pave roads; [13]*,p'wo ,pang*, or *,p'wo ,pang 'tiāng*, to lay even or level; [14]*,p'wo 'peng ,pang*, to lay a board-floor; *p'ah, ,p'wo*, to arrange the bed-boards.

䟽 The prints of a horse's feet, hoof-marks.

麩 Fu. Read *,hu;* used in the *Paik, ,Ing* for the coll. *,p'wo*, as in *mah, ,p'wo*, the bran or husk of wheat.

菠 Po. Read *,p'ó;* coll. *,p'wo*, as in *,p'wo ,ling ch'ai'* a sort of coarse winter-greens, also called *,ĕng 'kūng ch'ai'* the red-rooted greens.

圃 Pu. A vegetable-garden, an orchard; *met.*, a gardener: [15]*,nung 'p'wo*, a small farmer; [16]*'ló 'p'wo*, a gardener; [17]*,hwong 'p'wo*, a garden.

浦 P'u. A bank, a margin or brink of a lake or river; a creek, an inlet or stream running into a larger one: [18]*'P'wo ,siāng*, a district of Kien ning-fu in Fookien; [19]*,Hwang ,sung 'p'wo*, the anchorage for foreign vessels in the south suburbs of Foochow.

溥 P'u. Used for the next: large, great, extensive, pervading; everywhere: [20]*'p'wo pauk*, vast, as the sea. Read *pok,:* to smear, to bedaub.

普 P'u. The sun obscured or undistinguished; daylight everywhere; great; all, universal, pervading, as the light; everywhere: *'p'wo chá' chēūng' ,seng*, to relieve or save all the living, as Budhists

---

1 胚胎 2 胚皖 3 身胚大○ 4 紙坯 5 箸坯 6 鋪石 7 鋪板 8 鋪蓋 9 鋪排 10 鋪頒 11 鋪氈結綵 12 鋪路 13 鋪平 14 鋪板棚 15 農圃○ 16 老圃 17 園圃 18 浦城 19 番船浦 20 溥博○

say: COM., [1]'p'wo p'iěng' or 'p'wo p'wai' everywhere, universally diffused; [2]'p'wo ꜀t'iěng a² under the whole heavens, the world; [3]'p'wo ꜀ang ꜀hu, paper-charms, named after the Budha 'P'wo-꜀ang; [4]'p'wo ꜀tó ꜀ngang, the Puto Islands near Chusan; [5]'p'wo to² rites to get souls out of hell.

'**譜** Pu. P'u. A list, a record; a treatise on any art; a register, a chronicle, a genealogical table; a biography; to inscribe, to insert; to arrange; to pertain or belong to; in the coll. rule, system, method, routine: [6]lik꜀ 'p'wo, historical annals; [7]'p'wo hiě² a genealogy; COM., [8]chuk꜀ 'p'wo, a clan-genealogy; [9]꜀ka 'p'wo, a family record; [10]꜀ki 'p'wo, a treatise on chess; COLL., [11]꜀c'hiě 'p'wo, a music book; [12]'p'wo tio² rule, routine; ꜀i o² 'p'wo, he is systematic; ꜀mó 'p'wo tio² no system or method.

'**頗** P'o. Read 'p'ó; used for the coll. 'p'wo: about, almost: 'p'wo 'p'wo 'mwong k'ó' let it go at that, it will do pretty well.

'**斧** Fu. Read 'hu; used for the coll. 'p'wo, as in [13]'p'wo ꜀t'au, an ax, a hatchet: [14]'p'wo ꜀t'au 'ching, and [15]'p'wo ꜀t'au ch'oi' the back and the edge of an ax.

'**補** Pu. Read 'pwo; coll. 'p'wo: the square, embroidered pieces on the front and back of a coat or robe: 'p'wo sioh꜀ ho' a set (i. e., two) of such pieces; 'p'wo kwa' a robe with the embroidered squares.

鋪' **舖**' P'u. The second character is altered from the first: a shop; a ward, a district; the first also read ꜀p'wo, q. v.: COM., [16]p'wo' nói² in the ward; [17]p'wo' ho² the shops of a ward; [18]p'wo' ꜀ka, a customer, a small shop that buys of a larger one; [19]p'wo' ꜀seng 'ting, a ward in the suburbs of Foochow; [20]ló p'wo' an old establishment; p'wo' ꜀t'au kieu² the sedans of a regular stand.

P'wo'. A coll. word: to prepare and smuggle in an essay: p'wo' 'ch'iong, a smuggling office, as temporarily hired near an examination hall; ꜀i sė² p'ah꜀ p'wo' he got his essay by smuggling.

꜀P'wo. A coll. word: to help, to say a good word for, to give one a lift; to be indulgent, as in accepting work though inferior: ꜀p'wo t'óh꜀ to help, to say a word for; to employ, as a poor workman; ngaing² ꜀p'wo siong² to force one's self and take the article; to carry it through though it will be poorly done; ꜀p'wo sioh꜀ kwo' to speak a good word for one.

꜀P'wo. A coll. word, as in ꜀p'wo ꜀p'wo or ꜀p'wo ꜀p'wo sié' light, slight, as the pressure of the hand; to do a thing gently.

簿² Pu. Read pwo² in the dictionaries and often spoken pwo²: a register, a tablet; a book for notes, memoranda or accounts; an ivory tablet used by officers at imperial audiences; to record: ꜀teng p'wo² to enter in the record or account; COM.,

---

[1]普遍 [2]普天下 [3]普庵符 [4]普陀巖○ [5]普度 [6]立譜 [7]譜系 [8]族譜 [9]家譜 [10]棋譜 [11]吡譜 [12]譜路 [13]斧頭 [14]斧頭頂 [15]斧頭嘴 [16]舖內 [17]舖戶 [18]舖家 [19]舖前頂 [20]老舖○

¹*so' p'wo'* an account-book; ²*siong' p'wo'* (or *siong' so'*), to enter in account; ³*nik, ke' p'wo'* a diary; ⁴*'che' p'wo'* a copy-book; ⁵*'chio p'wo'* a keeper of records in courts, a Hanlin of the 7th or 8th rank; *hwoi' p'wo'* the records of a company, society, or club; ⁶*'hwa p'wo'* a pattern book, as of embroidery-patterns; COLL., *,nëng 'kiáng p'wo'* a picture-book of persons, plays, etc.

(703) P'woh.

曝 Pao. Read *puk,*; coll. *p'woh,*: to sun, to scorch, to dry in the sun: ⁷*p'woh, ch'au'* spoiled by exposure to the sun; ⁸*p'woh, yok,* (or *'yo*), wilted in the sun; ⁹*p'woh, nik, t'au,* or *p'woh, laung'* to expose to the sun; ¹⁰*p'woh, 'siong,* to dry fish; ¹¹*p'woh, ,ngau* or *p'woh, k'ieu' ,ngau,* curled, warped, as by solar heat.

(704) P'woi.

配 P'ei. The color of liquor; a fellow, an equal; united, agreeing; to mate, to match, to pair, to unite, as in marriage; to copulate; to equal, to compare; comparable; in the coll. to hire; to purchase and forward goods; the condiments of a meal: ¹²*pok, p'woi'* no match, ill assorted; ¹³*,hwong p'woi'* to marry; COM., ¹⁴*p'woi' tói'* or *p'woi' hak,* to join, to match; mating; ¹⁵*p'woi' 'hiong seng' mieu'* to occupy the second rank in the sage's temple; COLL., *p'woi' ,sung,* to hire a suitable boat, as to transport goods; *p'woi' hwo'* to purchase and ship goods, to fill an order for goods; *p'woi' pwong'* to serve as condiments for the meal of rice; *p'woi' sik,* or *p'woi' 'ch'au,* viands, relishes; *,ch'a p'woi'* shavings; *'wang p'woi'* fragments of broken bowls.

沛 P'ei. A river in Liautung and in Kiangsu; humid, showery; copious, abundant; moving, increasing, expanding; to run, to flow; to dam up water for irrigating land; laid prostrate; suddenly: ¹⁶*,tiéng p'woi'* all in disorder; ¹⁷*,pong p'woi'* wet, flooded; ¹⁸*p'woi' ,yong,* suddenly, in an overwhelming manner.

霈 P'ei. A heavy rain, copious showers; to flow, as water; wet, sloppy: ¹⁹*,p'ong p'woi'* very rainy, rain in torrents.

旆 Also read *pwoi'*: a pennon, a streamer on a staff above the large flag: *p'woi' p'woi'* streaming and flapping, as pennons.

被 Pei. Read *pe'*; coll. *p'woi'*: a coverlet, a blanket; a quilt or covering for a bed; ²⁰*p'woi' ,tang,* a sheet, a counterpane or single covering; ²¹*kak, p'woi'* a double coverlet (without the cotton); ²²*p'woi' 't'ëng,* the open part of the coverlet; *p'woi' aëng'* (or *t'aëng'*) a quilt folded, in which one ensconces himself; *p'woi' sioh, ,ch'ong,* one comfortable; *p'woi' ,p'wo ,tong,* in bed, abed.

P'woi'. A coll. word: to consult, to deliberate, to consider: *p'woi' 'pi,* to consider, to

¹數簿 ²上簿 ³日記簿 ⁴字簿 ⁵主簿 ⁶花簿 ⁷曝臭 ⁸曝弱 ⁹曝日頭 ¹⁰曝鯗 ¹¹曝翹 ¹²不配 ¹³婚配 ¹⁴配對 ¹⁵配享聖廟 ¹⁶顛沛 ¹⁷滂沛 ¹⁸沛然 ¹⁹雱霈 ²⁰被單 ²¹夾被 ²²被桶

福州方言拼音字典

consult about; *p‘woi* ꜄ *꜁nó*, to contrive, to plan, as ways and means; *p‘woi* ꜄ *꜁hwong*, a medical consultation.

(705) P‘wok.

渤 ꜄ Po. Read *pwok꜄*; used for the coll. *p‘wok꜄*: scum, froth: [1]*chwi p‘wok꜄* froth of water; [2]*꜂lang p‘wok꜄* white frothy spittle; *꜂pwong꜄ p‘wok꜄* the scum of boiling rice; *p‘wok꜄ p‘ak꜄ ch‘ok꜄ ꜁li*, scum bubbling out, as from under a cover.

(706) P‘wong.

汐 ꜄ Hsi. Read *sik꜄*; used in the *Puik꜄ ꜀Ing* for the coll. *p‘wong꜄*: the ebbing of the tide: *‘chwi p‘wong꜄* the tide is ebbing; [4]*‘p‘wong꜄ ‘ch‘iĕng*, ebbed till it is shallow; *p‘wong꜄ ꜀kang*, (or *tah꜄*), ebbed all dry.

(707) Sa.

沙 ꜀ Sha. Sand, gravel; pebbles; sandy, gritty; granulated, comminuted; small and sweet, as fruit; in the coll. ready, skillful at: read *꜀sai* in the coll. q. v.: [5]*꜁liu ꜀sa*, shifting sands; [6]*꜀sa mok꜄* a sandy desert, as of Shamo or Gobi; [7]*꜀sa ꜁mwong*, a Budhist priest; also defined diligent conduct; [8]*꜀sa ꜁li*, a russet pear; COM., [9]*꜀Sa kaing꜄* a district of Yenping-fu in Fookien; COLL., *꜀sa chiăh꜄ ꜀sa*, ready at, doing easily and well.

砂 ꜀ Sha. Used for the last in the sense of pebbles, sand: COM., [10]*꜀chio ꜀sa*, cinnabar; [11]*꜀sa ꜁ing*, the seeds of a certain fruit used to aid digestion; [12]*꜁pĕng ꜀sa*, borax.

紗 ꜀ Sha. Thin silk, gauze; gauzy; fibers, thread: COM., [13]*꜀sa ꜁ló*, two kinds of gauze, of which the former is the thinner; [14]*꜀sa ꜁ting*, a gauze lantern; [15]*꜀sa mó꜄ ꜁yĕng ‘liăng*, the gauze cap and round collar of the Ming dynasty; [16]*chaiu꜄ ꜀sa*, crape; [17]*‘ü ꜀sa*, bombazine, camlet; [18]*꜁miĕng ꜀sa siăng꜄* cotton-thread; COLL., *꜀t‘ai ꜁lĕng ꜀sa*, gauze for sieves.

痧 ꜀ A coll. character: sudden, griping pains in the bowels, colic; cholera-morbus: [19]*꜀sa chik꜄* a colic; *tioh꜄ ꜀sa*, to have the colic; *tioh꜄ ꜁mi ꜀sa*, a fit of insensibility from colic; [20]*꜁hang ꜀sa*, or *꜀hung ꜁hang ꜀sa*, a severe cold; [21]*‘kung to꜄ ꜀sa*, a griping colic; *kauk꜄ ꜀sa*, to scrape one having colic (with a cash dipped in oil).

桬 ꜀ The name of a fine wood, called [22]*꜀sa ꜁tong*, brought from Tibet; it bears a red blossom and fruit like a plum.

裟 ꜀ Sha. A stole or surplice: COM., *꜁kiă ꜀sa*, a priest's robe.

師 ꜀ Shih. 司 ꜀ Ssu. Read *꜀sü*; used for the coll. *꜀sa*, as in *꜀sa ho꜄* a teacher or professor; a skilled workman, one practiced in a profession, trade, or art.

Sa꜄. A coll. word: a vulgar term for the sexual act, used in railing at one.

꜁Sa. A coll. word: to tie with a cord; a knot: *wak꜄*

[1]木渤 [2]瀾渤 [3]飯渤 [4]汐淺 [5]流沙 [6]沙漠 [7]沙門 [8]沙梨 [9]沙縣 [10]硃砂 [11]砂仁 [12]硼砂 [13]紗羅 [14]紗燈 [15]紗帽圓領 [16]綢紗 [17]羽紗 [18]棉紗線 [19]痧疾 [20]寒痧 [21]滾肚痧 [22]桬棠

˓*sa*, a slipping knot; ʻ*si* ˓*sa*, a tight knot; ʻ*hói* ʻ*kwong* ˓*sa*, the "bellows-knot"—a knot with the cord rove through a bamboo-bellows-tube to tie an animal with.

˓*Sa*. A coll. word, as in ˓*sa* ˓*la*, the rustling of grass; ˓*sa* ˓*la kieu*ʾ a pattering, as of rain; ˓*sa lah*˒ a sudden noise, a rattling sound; ˓*sa* ˓*sa kieu*ʾ a rattling, as of things drawn about by rats.

(708) Sá.

西 ˓ Hsi. The west; in divination belongs to metal; western, foreign, European, American; used in names of places; heaven, in the language of Budhists; in a *met*., sense, that, there: COM., [1]˓*sá* ˓*yong*, the western ocean, western countries; [2]˓*sá* ˓*tʻiéng*, the western heavens, the Budhist Paradise; [3]˓*sá* ˓*hu* (or ˓*u*), the west lake—in the suburbs of Foochow; [4]˓*sá chaung*ʾ Tibet; [5]˓*sá* ˓*iu ké*ʾ a book of tales about ˓*Tong* ˓*sang chaung*ʾ journeying westward to get the Budhist books; [6]˓*sá chieu*ʾ a west exposure to the sun's rays; [7]˓*Sá* ˓*sié*, a famous beauty of ancient times; [8]˓*sá* ˓*nang*, and [9]˓*sá paĕk*˒ S. W. and N. W.; COLL., [10]˓*sá tio*ʾ the west road—the upper Min region; [11]˓*tĕng sioh*˒ *chʻoi*ʾ ˓*sá sioh*˒ *kwo*ʾ a mouth here and a sentence there—everybody has something to say.

恓 ˓ Hsi. Angry, frowning; vexed; sad, much grieved: [12]˓*sá* ˓*hwong*, troubled, sorry; COM., [13]˓*ku* ˓*sá*, solitary and wretched.

粞 ˓ Hsi. Bruised rice; the rice left in a mortar, broken to dust after hulling.

犀 ˓ Hsi. A rhinoceros, called [14]˓*sa* ˓*ngiu*; several varieties are enumerated with the horn in different positions about the head; good sword-metal; the carpels of a melon: [15]˓*sing* ʻ*iu* ˓*ling* ˓*sá*, a discriminating mind; COM., [16]˓*sá kaĕk*˒ a rhinoceros' horn; ˓*sá* ˓*ngiu wong*ʾ *ngwok*˒ ˓*kʻĕng hié*ʾ ˓*pi* ˓*hwa*, "a rhinoceros wishing in vain for the moon"—to wish for what is not attainable.

樨 ˓ Hsi. A diminutive sort of the Olea fragrans, called *muk*˒ ˓*sá*, bearing reddish flowers; the name often occurs in poetry.

˓*Sá*. A coll. word: dryness or hoarseness of the throat, as after much talking: ˓*hó* ˓*lĕng* ˓*sá* ˓*sá tioh*˒ the throat very dry.

˓*Sá*. A coll. word: rank, rancid, as old lard: *siong*ʾ ˓*sá* (or ˓*chié*), to become rancid; ʻ*kʻu* ʻ*lá* ˓*sá*, bitter and rank, very bitter.

洗 ʻ Hsi. Hsien. To wash the feet; to purify, to clean; to cleanse morally; a washing vessel; in the coll. purging, cathartic; to sponge out of; to shuffle; to dash down; to tease, to annoy: [17]ʻ*sá ŭk*˒ to bathe; [18]˓*ka* ˓*ping* ˓*ú* ʻ*sá*, as poor as though all washed out; [19]ʻ*sá* ʻ*ma*, name of an office in the Hanlin; ʻ*sá* ˓*sing*, to wash one's self; ʻ*sá* ˓*tʻong*, to bathe in warm water; ʻ*sá tʻói*ʾ *saik*˒ to wash out

1西洋 2西天 3西湖 4西藏 5西遊記 6西照 7西施 8西南 9西北 10西路 11東一嘴西一句 12恓惶 13孤恓 14犀牛 15心有靈犀 16犀角 17洗浴 18家貧如洗 19洗馬 ○

the color; [1]'sá p'au' (coll. 'sá ˛long ˛ki), to scale guns; [2]'sá ˛sang tang' the ceremony of washing a child —on the third day after birth; COLL., 'sá taung' to wash and rinse; 'sá ˛pwang, to wash plates; *met.*, to "sponge" a treat out of one; 'sá ˛pá, to shuffle cards; 'sá ˛pang té' to dash things on the ground in anger; 'sá ˛tong 'sá tó' a violent purgative; *móh˛ p'ah˛ 'sá*, don't tease me.

洒 Sha. Shai. 'To wash, to wipe off; *met.*, to avenge a wrong, to wipe off a reproach, as by the death of one's enemy: also read 'swa, q. v.

泚 'Perspiration; to perspire, to sweat on the forehead: also read 'ch'ü, q. v.

葸 Hsi. 'Afraid, fearful, terrified; craven, dispirited, cast down; timid, backward, bashful; thrown off one's guard: [3]'oi' 'sá, abashed.

蓰 Hsi. 'Also read ˛sü: name of an herb; to quintuple; fivefold.

躧 屣 Hsi. 'Straw sandals, slippers, grass shoes, as worn by posture-makers; to go barefoot: [4]'k'e' ˛ü pé' 'sá, to renounce like a pair of old sandals, as the world or one disliked.

徙 Hsi. 'To move, to remove; to change, as one's abode; to be exiled; transported by royal authority; to exceed or overpass, as time: [5]'sá siéng' to become good, to reform; [6]˛ch'iéng 'sá, to change one's abode; [7]'sá ngwok˛ to overpass the month.

纚 Li. 'A sort of silk cap or kerchief for the head, a turban; a hair-band; a kind of gauze with square figures; the strings of a cap; to bind together or upon; neatly connected; a crowd passing; floating banners.

釃 Shai. 'To decant and strain liquors; to pour out a libation; to divide, as streams of water: [8]'sá 'chiu, to pour off spirits.

枲 Hsi. 'A plant, allied to hemp in its fibers, and used for weaving into cloth; fine linen or grasscloth.

璽 Hsi. 'The royal signet, the imperial seal; the great seal of the state: in the coll. read 'sĕ, q. v.

細 Hsi. Fine, small, minute; small and delicate, neatly made; petty, trifling, unimportant; careful, attentive; thoroughly: COM., [9]sá' naung' small in size; [10]sá' ˛sing or 'chü sá' very careful or attentive; [11]sá' ˛cha, to examine minutely; [12]sá' 'nga, small and delicate, as a person; [13]sá' ˛pó or sá' 'chiă, a concubine; [14]sá' kak˛ to kill by cutting to pieces; [15]sá' muk˛ taing' a furniture-shop; COLL., [16]sá' 'kiăng, a young child, a babe; [17]sá' ne' to be careful; [18]sá' kah˛ a small kind, or breed, as of fowls; [19]'á sá' low in stature, as a child, a plant; [20]sá' ˛siăng, a low voice.

1洗炮 2洗三旦 3畏葸 ○ 4棄如敝屣 5徙善 6遷徙 7徙月 8釃酒 9細嫩 10細心 11細查 12細雅 13細婆 14細割 15細木店 ○ 16細仔 17細膩 18細格 19矮細 20細聲 ○

Sá'. A coll. word, similar to the last: young, younger; inferiority in rank or degree of relationship; my, our: *sá' ˏku*, a husband's younger sister; *sá' ʻsing*, husband's younger brother's wife; *sá' keu'* a wife's younger brother; *sá' sioh, hwoi'* a year younger; *sá' sioh, pwang'* younger by one half, only half as old.

壻 婿 Hsü. A son-in-law; a husband sometimes so called: used for the coll. *sai'* q. v.: [1]*chü sá'* or [2]*nü sá'* a son-in-law; [3]*ˏhieng sá'* a worthy son-in-law.

狻 Suan. Read *ˏsong*; used for the coll. *ˏsá*: a fabulous animal, called [4]*ˏsá ˏngá*, like a lion, or (as some say) like a horse; *met.*, overbearing; particular, strict; hard to please, as a customer; exacting, as a seller; [5]*ˏsá ˏngá p'aung' tioh, ˏsai*, the *ˏsá ˏngá* encountering the lion; *met.*, one strict person finding his match in another.

佮 A coll. character: many, much: *sá' ʻchieu*, many and few; much and little; *cheng' sá'* very many or much; *sá' wa'* or *sá' ch'oi'* talkative; *ko' sá'* more; *sá' ˏsing sëü'* many thoughts—fearful; doubting, incredulous.

(709) Saĕ.

疏 Shu. To state distinctly to a superior; a statement to the emperor; a plain record; forms of prayer, as recited and burnt to idols: also read *ˏsu*, q. v.: [6]*ʻchaiu' saĕ'* to present a statement; COM., [7]*saĕ' ke'* a written prayer, burnt to an idol; COLL., [8]*kaĕng' chiék, saĕ' sioh, yong'* like a priest receiving written prayers, as said of one greedily taking money.

Saĕ'. A coll. word: to beat one on the buttocks: *k'á' ˏi ˏch'ü ʻlá saĕ'* stretch him (on the floor) and beat him; *saĕ' ʻkwi sek, ʻpeng,* to beat one a few tens of blows of the bamboo.

(710) Saĕk.

摔 Shuai. Read *sauk,*; coll. *saĕk,*: to slap with the hand, to strike violently; to thresh grain, as on the *teu' ˏk'wong* or threshing-frame; to knock things about, to dash down in anger: [9]*saĕk, p'wai'* to dash to pieces; [10]*saĕk, teu'* to thresh rice; [11]*saĕk, sioh, ʻchiong,* to give a slap with the hand; [12]*saĕk, ʻwang saĕk, tiék,* to dash down bowls and plates in a rage; *saĕk, sioh, ʻtó,* to catch a violent fall.

(711) Saĕng.

送 Sung. Read *song'*; coll. *saĕng'*: to send presents, to give, to present to; to accompany, to go with; to see a guest out; a present, a gift: [13]*song' ˏhung ˏsiong saĕng'* may prosperous breezes attend you! [14]*saĕng' ʻlá uk,* to make presents; [15]*saĕng' chói'* to make presents when a child is a year old; [16]*saĕng' ˏch'ing,* to accompany the bride, as a few of her male relatives do; [17]*saĕng' sek, lak,* to to make presents (to a bride)

---

[1]子壻 [2]女壻 [3]賢壻 [4]狻猊 [5]狻猊遇着獅 [6]奏疏 [7]疏記 [8]共接疏一樣 [9]摔破 [10]摔稻 [11]摔一掌 [12]摔碗摔碟 [13]順風相送 [14]送禮物 [15]送晬 [16]送親 [17]送十號〇

ten days after marriage; [1]*saĕng*' *sŭng*' *pek*, to "give something to bedew the pencil"—presents to a Siutsai before the examinations; [2]*saĕng*' '*chŭ* ˛*pó* ˏ*kwang*, the ladies who give children—attendants of ˛*Ling* '*chwi* '*ná*; *saĕng*' '*lí* or *saĕng*' '*ch'ai*, to send bridal presents; *saĕng*' *chaung*' to attend a burial; *saĕng*' *k'ah*, to escort a guest out.

宋 ˀ Sung. Read *song*'; coll. *saĕng*': a surname: [3]*saĕng*' ˏ*tieu*, the Sung dynasty, A. D. 970—1280; [4]*saĕng*' '*t'á che*' the square, flat character, introduced in the Sung dynasty.

(712) Sah.

Sah˛. A coll. word, as in *sah*˛ *sioh*˛ ˏ*siăng*, a low, sudden sound, slight knock, rattling.

(713) Sáh.

Sáh˛. A coll. word: the motion of a sedan in riding: *sáh*˛ *sáh*˛ seesaw! up and down!

(714) Sai.

沙 ˛ Sha. Read ˏ*sa*; coll. ˏ*sai*: sand, gravel, pebbles: ˏ*sai te*' sandy ground; [5]ˏ*sai* ˛*hong* (or ˛*ong*), a sand beach; *ngwah*, *ngwah*, *kieu*' ˏ*tu se*' ˏ*sai*, a very grating sound and all gritty (in chewing).

鯊 ˛ Sha. Read ˏ*sa* in the dictionaries: the shark, so called from its rough skin: COM., [6]ˏ*sai* ˛*ngŭ*, a shark; [7]˛*lá* ˛*t'au* ˏ*sai*, the plow-share or shovel-nosed shark; [8]'*hu* ˛*t'au* ˏ*sai*, a kind of spotted shark; ˏ*sai* ˛*ngŭ* ˛*p'ui*, shark-skin—used for polishing; COLL., ˛*ku* ˏ*sai*, a large shark, having fine-flavored flesh; [9]'˛*ching* ˛*wong* ˏ*sai*, a shark with hexagonal spots.

師 ˛ Shih. Read ˏ*sŭ*; coll. ˏ*sai*: a master, a teacher, an instructor; one skilled in an art: [10]ˏ*sai* ˏ*kung*, a Tauist magician or acrobat, who mounts a ladder of knives, goes through fire, &c.; [11]ˏ*sai* ˏ*hiăng*, *tie*' those taught by the same master, fellow-apprentices, or priests.

獅 ˛ Shih. Read ˏ*sŭ* in the dictionaries; a lion; a dog that whelps two pups: COM., [12]ˏ*sai* '*k'eng*, a small shaggy dog, used as a pet; [13]ˏ*sai mó*' a child's cap adorned with a lion's face; [14]ˏ*sai* '*chŭ* ˛*leu*, a tower with three lions couchant, in South street, Foochow; [15]'*u* ˏ*sai*, to play masked lions; COLL., ˛*pu* ˏ*tung* ˏ*sai*, (the hair) all disheveled; [16]ˏ*sai* ˛*t'au paik*, *kwa*' *meng*' a lion's head and eight-diagram face—ugly, ill-favored; *p'ah*, ˏ*sai* '*pa*, to parade a mock-lion, as in processions.

嘶 ˛ Ssu. The neighing of a horse; to belch, to hiccough; a hoarse, broken noise; a crashing or clattering sound: ˏ*sai suk*, a furious onslaught, the din of battle.

顋 腮 ˛ Sai. The lower part of the face, the chops, the sides of the jaws; the cheeks: COLL., ˏ*sai* ˏ*sai* ˛*t'au* ˛*hing*, ˏ*sai* ˏ*sai* '*chiu chŏi*' cheek, cheek, head dizzy! cheek, cheek, drunk with wine! a lullaby sung while holding a child's head and rocking it to and fro; ˏ*sang* ˛*tong* ˏ*sai*, to have long (swollen) cheeks, the mumps?

[1]送潤筆 [2]送子婆官 [3]宋朝 [4]宋體字 [5]沙痕 [6]鯊魚 [7]犁頭鯊 [8]虎頭鯊 [9]泰王鯊 [10]師公 [11]師兄弟 [12]獅犬 [13]獅帽 [14]獅子樓 [15]舞獅○ [16]獅頭八卦面○

鰓 Sai. The gills of a fish, the bones supporting the gills. Read *'sá*, as in *'sá 'sá*, alarmed.

鰓 Sai. Also read *˛sü:* the bony marrow or column in horns; the burr at the base of an antler; the soft, velvety covering of antlers.

毸 Sai. Also read *˛sü:* to extend the wings, to spread the wings, as if about to fly; the graceful gambolings of a phenix.

鬛 Also read *˛sü:* a long beard; bushy whiskers.

私 Ssu. Read *˛sü;* coll. *˛sai*, as in [1]*˛sai ˛ka*, private, one's own, as surplus gain; *˛sai ˛ka tai*² one's private affair.

屎 屄 Shi. Read *'ch'i;* coll. *'sai:* ordure, dung, excrement: [2]*'sai nieu*² ordure and urine; [3]*'sai ˛k'ang*, a term for a privy, used by southern people; [4]*'sié*² *'sai*, an involuntary stool; [5]*'sai pwo*' a diaper, a swathing-cloth; [6]*˛na 'sai*, to have a stool; [7]*kwang*² *˛tü 'sai 'ló*, a street-scavenger.

駛 使 Shih. Read *'sü;* used for the coll. *'sai:* to order, to send, to commission one; to use, to employ; to cause, to occasion; need, expense, use; answering the purpose, fit: [8]*'sai ëüng*² to use, to expend; an outlay; [9]*'sai ˛chiëng*, to expend money; *'sai ˛nëng k'ó*' to send one; [10]*'sai ch'oi*' a servant; [11]*'sai hwang*' to employ a magician, as to expel evil spirits from the sick; [12]*'sai hwak˛ twai*² the expense heavy, as of a feast; [13]*'sai ˛chiëng ˛sa hu*² a spendthrift; *'sai heng*² sulky, pouting; [14]*'sai 'ch'iu*, to use a hand—to employ an agent, as for menial duties; [15]*'sai ang*' *˛cheng*, to use "the dark needle"—to injure secretly; [16]*'sai sang*' angry; *á*² *'sai tek*, it will answer, that will do; *ng*² *'sai*, no occasion for, need not; [17]*'sai ˛sung*, to row or sail a boat.

壻 Hsü, Hsi. Read *sá';* coll. *sai*' as in *˛nié sai*' a son-in-law.

使 Shih. Read *sëü';* used for the coll. *sai':* a husband: [18]*mwo sai*' wife and husband; [19]*'Kau sai*' a god worshiped by prostitutes; [20]*ne*² *sai*' a woman's paramour; *˛kwang ˛kwang ˛sai sai*' officers, the noble and wealthy; *paik, ng*² *paik, lau*² *sai*' don't you know me, the old bruiser, as a braggart says tapping his nose with his finger.

殺 Sha. Shai. To clip, to shear; to pare off, to reduce; to descend, to bend or come down to effect an object; to cover with hair or feathers; something placed under a corpse: also read *sak*, q. v.

---

[1]私家 [2]屎尿 [3]屎坑 [4]逝屎 [5]屎布 [6]撒屎 [7]扣猪屎箬 [8]使用 [9]使錢 [10]使嘴 [11]使喚 [12]使伐大〇 [13]使錢師傅 [14]使手 [15]使暗針 [16]使性〇 [17]駛船 [18]奴使 [19]九使 [20]二使

晒' **曬**, Shai. To expose to the sun's heat, to dry in the sun: *sai*' *,i*, to sun clothes; [1]*'sai*' *,kang*, to dry by the sun's heat.

塞' Sai. Sĕ. A limit, a border; the passes of a country: also read *saik*, q. v.: *ch'ok, sai*' to pass over the border, as the heroine *,Wong ,chieu ,kung* did; [2]*sai*' *ngwoi*' beyond the frontier.

臍 ,Ch'i. Read *,chá;* used in the *Paik, ,Ing* for the coll. *,sai*, as in *pok, ,sai*, the navel; *,sai eng*' a navel-pad or bandage (for new-born infants).

,Sai. A coll. word: to set in a vacant place, to occupy, to obstruct: *,sai 'hiâ oi*' *ch'ëü*' place it there; *'ié ,sai ,chu wai*' *sói*' place the chair here and sit; you have set yourself down here in the way!

祀' Ssu. Read *sëü*'; coll. *sai*': to establish or set, as an idol in its place with religious rites; to set up to worship: [3]*sai*' *huk*, to set up a Budh or any god; [4]*sai*' *siâng*' *k'ó*' established and become efficacious, as from long use.

儎' Tsai. Read *chai*'; used for the coll. *sai*': a boat-load: [5]*'kwi sai*' how many boat-loads? [6]*sang sai*' three boat-loads; [7]*há*' *sai*' to freight, to bear freight.

(715) Saik.

色, Shê. Sĕ. Shai. The shades of color, or expression, in the countenance; the appearance, form, manner; color, hue, tint; the quality, kind, description of; beauty, radiance; lust, sexual pleasure; the 139th radical: [8]*kwok, saik*, the beautiful women of a country; [9]*'nó*' *saik*, an angry face; [10]*'king saik*, landscape, scenery; [11]*cheng*' *saik*, a sedate manner; COM., [12]*,ngang saik*, color; [13]*saik, k'e*', *saik, 'chwi* and *saik, tek*, the hue, quality of; [14]*chak, saik*, various sorts; [15]*'ngu saik*, the five colors, azure, black, white, yellow, red; [16]*,siâng saik*, the degree of purity, as of metals; [17]*'hiêng saik*, a clear color; *met.*, work well-done; [18]*'hi saik*, a joyful look; [19]*saik, ch'ieu*' a bright, lively color; [20]*ch'ai saik*, colors, colored, as a painting; [21]*swoi*' *saik*, to contest with dice, as in the *,yeu hwoi*'; [22]*t'ói*' *saik*, to lose the color, faded out; [23]*k'ang*' *'hwi saik*, to watch the color in fusing metals; *saik, 'ch'iéng* (or *tang*'), a light color; *ch'ok, saik*, fine, well made or done; *,t'ang saik*, or *hó*' *saik*, lustful, libidinous; *'nü saik*, venery; *saik, pok, ,mi ,ing ,ing chëü*' *,mi*, it is not beauty that beguiles men, they beguile themselves; COLL., *'au 'au saik*, an old, faded color.

塞, Sai. Sĕ. To fill, to stop up, to close; to prevent, to obstruct; stopped up; true, sincere; unintelligent, stupid; an important pass in a country: also read *sai*' and in the

1 晒乾 2 塞外 3 祀佛 4 祀聖 5 去幾儎 6 三儎 7 下儎 8 國色 9 怒色 10 景色 11 正色 12 顏色 13 色氣 色雜 14 雜色 15 五色 16 成色 17 顯色 18 喜色 19 色笑 20 彩色 21 賽色 22 退色 23 看火色

coll. *sek*, q. v.: COLL., ¹*saik*, *ʻtiē*, to stuff in, to stop; ²*saik*, *ˌnëng ch'oi'* to "stop one's mouth", as by a bribe; ³*saik*, *ʻngai p'ong'* (only) fills the interstices between the teeth—not enough to eat; *ch'oi' ʻk'au saik*, *k'ŏ'* the opening or mouth stopped up.

虱 蝨 ˌ *Sě.* A louse: ⁴*t'ieu' saik*, (coll. *ʻka ʻchau*), a flea; ⁵*keu saik*, dog-ticks; COM., ⁶*ˌngu saik*, an ox-tick; ⁷*ˌtü saik*, swine-ticks: ⁸*saik*, *ʻmŏ*, a louse; ⁹*saik*, *lang'* nits; ¹⁰*saik*, *ˌch'ong*, lice-sores—on the head from uncleanness; ¹¹*mĕk*, *saik*, bed bugs; COLL., *saik*, *ˌk'ong*, small lice.

瑟 ˌ *Shê.* A kind of harpsichord or psaltery, with silken strings; numerous; stern, haughty, dignified; elegantly: *saik*, *saik*, the humming of the wind; COM., ¹²*ˌk'ing saik*, lutes and harps; ¹³*ˌk'ing saik*, *ˌtieu ˌhwo*, lutes and harps in concord—conjugal union.

澀 澁 濇 ˌ *Sě. Shê.* Rippled, as the surface of water; dry, harsh; rough, rugged; the name of a bamboo: COM., *saik*, *saik*, harsh in taste; rough, not glossy, as cake in which too little lard has been used; dry and smarting, as the eyes.

嗇 ˌ *Sě.* The harvest, the crops; to be fond of, to desire and accumulate; to begrudge; frugal, sparing; mean, stingy, avaricious, parsimonious: ¹⁴*saik*, *ˌhu*, a farmer; ¹⁵*leng' saik*, niggardly.

穡 ˌ *Sě.* Interchanged with the last: to reap, to gather a harvest; grain ready for the sickle; careful, not wasteful: ¹⁶*ka' saik*, sowing and reaping, husbandry.

(716) Saiu.

瘦 ˀ *Shou. Sou.* Lean, lank, emaciated; poor, thin, as from sickness: ¹⁷*kauk*, *saiu' ˌü ˌch'a*, his bones stick out like sticks; COM., ¹⁸*ˌsoi saiu'* lean, wasted away; *saiu' ˌchi che'* very lank, extremely emaciated; ¹⁹*meng' saiu'* thin-visaged.

肖 ˀ *Hsiao.* Read *sieu'*; coll. *saiu'*: the twelve animals, supposed to resemble the twelve branches (*te' ˌchiē*), and used to designate the year of one's birth, hence called *ˌsang saiu'*; they are the rat, ox, tiger, rabbit, dragon, serpent, horse, goat, ape, fowl, dog, and hog: *ʻnü saiu' siē' nŏh*, *ʻ saiu' ˌkau*, what is your animal (year)? the ape (year); *saiu' ˌsiē ˌtŏ ˌsing sŏi'* one born in the serpent (year) is much given to doubts and perplexity.

漱 ˀ *Sou.* To rinse the mouth; to wash out, to scour; to purify, to correct; to gnaw: ²⁰*saiu' ʻk'wang*, to wash; ²¹*saiu' ʻk'eu*, to rinse the mouth.

欶 嗽 ˀ Also read *sauk*, and *sok*, : to suck; to draw in the breath, to inhale, to inspire; also to cough, to eructate.

¹塞入 ²塞仈 ³嚐塞齒縫 ⁴跳虱 ⁵狗虱 ⁶牛虱 ⁷猪虱 ⁸虱㚢 ⁹虱蛋 ¹⁰虱瘡 ¹¹木虱 ¹²琴瑟 ¹³琴瑟調和 ¹⁴嗇夫 ¹⁵吝嗇 ¹⁶稼穡 ¹⁷骨瘦如柴 ¹⁸衰瘦 ¹⁹面瘦 ²⁰漱盥 ²¹漱口

(717) Sak.

殺, Sha. Shai. To kill, to slay, to murder; to wound with murderous intent; to die from famine; destroyed or forgotten; killed, as by frost; to hunt and kill game; to cut grass; furious, murderous; to brush, to sweep away, to exterminate; name of an arrow or lance: also read *sai'* q. v.: [1]*'sak, ꜀t'eu*, to decapitate; COM., [2]*sak, ꜀seng*, to kill animals; [3]*sak, 'ch'iu*, a headsman, executioner; [4]*sak, sak, ꜀sing*, a murderous intent, deadly hate; a loathing, as for a bad habit; [5]*ch'ek, sak,* the seven degrees of manslaughter; *met.*, a bad man, a cheat, a rascal; COLL., [6]*meng' tai' sak, k'e'* his face wears a furious aspect; [7]*sak, sioh, teng'* an onslaught, a fight.

煞, Sha. Analogous to the preceding, of which it is the vulgar form: to injure, to kill; to strike with a noxious influence; baleful, malign, noxious; to end, to cease; the end, the last: COM., [8]*sak, k'e'* deadly vapors; a baleful influence; [9]*sak, ꜀sing,* a malign spirit or effluence; [10]*sak, ꜀sing,* a baleful star; [11]*sak, kaëk,* the malign influence, under which one is born; unlucky, as a site; [12]*꜀hung 'chwi hwang' sak, kuëk,* the geomancy is affected by a malign influence; [13]*sak, 'mwi,* the end, termination; [14]*sak, kwoh,* (coll. *sak, kwah,*) the finale, completion, as of a job; [15]*sak, 'ch'iu,* to stop doing; [16]*sak, sik,* true, real, actual.

𢵧, To strike a backhanded blow; to rub off; to sweep away: *mwak, sak,* to wipe off.

撒, Sa. To scatter, to disperse, to throw about; to set loose: [17]*suk, 'chüng,* to sow seed; [18]*sak, p'wak,* to waste, as property: COM., [19]*sak, lai'* to implicate by magnifying a fault—to press one, to "squeeze" money; *꜀p'ié ꜀t'au sak, hwak,* the hair disheveled; *sak, ꜀chieu laiu'* to sprinkle spices on; COLL., *sak, 'yá,* abandoned, profligate; rude, impudent.

鎩, Sha. Also read *sai':* a long spear or halberd; to clip, as the wings of a bird to prevent it from flying.

霎, Sha. A slight shower; a drizzling, passing rain; momentarily: *sak, ꜀yong,* suddenly; COM., *sak, ꜀si ꜀kung,* in a moment, on a sudden.

翣, Sha. Feathers used to adorn coffins; a flabellum or great fan, painted with feathers and flowers, and anciently borne behind the sovereign.

辣, An acrid taste: *sak, lak,* hot, biting; *met.*, in the coll. very severe, harsh and authoritative in manner.

剎, Ch'a. A pillar, a shaft, as in Budhist temples; a Budhist monastery; a tope or pagoda-like monument over the ashes of a priest: *'pó sak,* your monastery.

---

[1]殺頭 [2]殺生 [3]殺手 [4]殺殺心 [5]七殺〇 [6]面帶殺氣 [7]殺一陣〇 [8]煞氣 [9]煞神 [10]煞星 [11]煞角 [12]風水犯煞角 [13]煞尾〇 [14]煞局 [15]煞手 [16]煞實 [17]撒種 [18]撒潑 [19]撒賴

薩 ‚Sa. A religious word, introduced by Budhists; it means to see everything, to help, to assist; also a surname: COM., [1]‚*pu sak*, a Budhist deity, an idol, an image—the term is a contraction of Bodisat, a candidate for a Budhaship.

颯 ‚Sa. Li. The sound of wind, a gust, a blast; sudden, rushing, as the wind: *sak*, *sak*, rushing and whistling; [2]‚*soi sak*, decaying, declining, growing old.

*Sak*₂. A coll. word; to boil in water, to seethe; to boil food without seasoning or condiments: *sak*₂ *pwong*ʾ ‚*t'ong*, to heat or boil cooked rice in water; *pah*₂ *sak*₂ ‚*kie*, a boiled fowl, one boiled without sauce; *sak*₂ *sük*₂ ʻ*k'eng* ‚*t'au*, a well-boiled dog's head; *met.*, one constantly laughing.

*Sak*₂. A coll. word, as in *ka*ʾ *sak*₂ (or *ka*ʾ *lak*₂), a roach, a cockroach; *sak*₂ ʻ*mó*, large roaches; ʻ*chwi sak*₂ a kind of black edible bug or winged insect.

(718) Sang.

三 叁 參 川 ‚San. Sa. Three; thrice; the third: COM., [3]ʻ*tá*ʾ ‚*sang*, the third; [4]ʻ*chai*ʾ ‚*sang*, repeatedly; [5]‚*sang* ‚*lang*, the third or lightest shade of blue; [6]‚*sang kai*ʾ the three worlds; [7]‚*sang* ‚*hwa*, a set of actors—actors with painted faces, clowns, buffoons; [7]‚*sang* ʻ*peng t'aung*ʾ a sampan; *met.*, one who limps; [8]‚*sang kaëk*, ‚*kiéng*, the shoulder thrust forward, as of one who pushes his way in a crowd; [9]‚*sang kak*, *laiu*ʾ a cement of earth, sand, and lime; [10]‚*sang lëk*₂ ʻ*kau*, three-six-nine, set days of a month having the figures 3, 6, and 9 in—seldom, infrequent; [11]‚*sang* ‚*seng*, the three sacrificial animals, pig, ox, and goat; [12]‚*sang* ‚*niéng hau*ʾ three years' mourning for parents; [13]‚*sang* ‚*si*, the three commissioners—provincial treasurer, judge, and salt-commissioner; [14]*pok*₂ ‚*sang pok*₂ *se*ʾ neither three nor four—unsuitable, worthless; [15]‚*sang ch'aung*ʾ *k'e*ʾ "three inches of breath"—dying; COLL., ‚*sang* ‚*pa lang*ʾ *laë*ʾ "rake it in quick"—eat quick (and come); ‚*sang* ‚*sang lëk*₂ ʻ*hai sioh*₂ *hong*ʾ ‚*ch'eng*, (Fookien is) three parts mountain, six parts sea, and only one part fields; ‚*sang sek*₂ *lëk*₂ ʻ*wu*, a miserable shirk. Read *sang*ʾ: to do thrice, to reiterate: *sang*ʾ ‚*sü*, to think thrice, to consider deliberately.

山 ‚Shan. A hill, a mountain; heights, mountain ranges; wild, waste; *met.*, graves; the 46th radical: [16]*ik*₂ ‚*sang*, to retire to private life; [17]‚*sang* ‚*k'ing*, wild fowl; COM., [18]‚*sang* ʻ*ting*, the top of a hill; [19]‚*sang* ‚*hung*, a peak; [20]‚*sang laung*ʾ hills, a group of mountains; ‚*sang chai*ʾ robbers' den in the mountains; ‚*sang* ‚*sieu*, a hill demon who spirits away things; ‚*sang* ‚*yong*, a goat; ‚*sang* ‚*tëng*, Shantung; ‚*sang* ‚*lang chiong*ʾ *k'e*ʾ malaria from forests or dank places; ‚*sang* ‚*kó* ‚*hwong tá*ʾ

[1] 菩薩 [2] 衰颯 [3] 第三 [4] 再三 [5] 三藍 [6] 三界 [7] 三板盪 [8] 三角肩 [9] 三夾料 [10] 三六九 [11] 三牲 [12] 三年孝 [13] 三司 [14] 不三不四 [15] 三寸氣 [16] 入山 [17] 山禽 [18] 山頂 [19] 山峰 [20] 山崙

'*wong*, the hills high and the emperor distant, as said of the lawless living at a distance from the magistrates; COLL., ‹*sang* '*tié*, in or among the hills; ‹*sang k'iăk*, a mountain gorge; ‹*sang* ‹*tü p'aung*' *tioh*, ‹*ing* ‹*ka* ‹*p'ung*, "a wild hog finding house-swill"—a poor man catching a windfall.

生 ‹Shêng. Read ‹*seng*; coll. ‹*sang*: to bear, to beget; to produce, to bring forth; to grow; life, living; born, birth: [1]‹*sang* '*kiăng*, to beget children, to bear young; [2]‹*sang ch'ok*, *sié*' born; [3]‹*sing* ‹*sang*, a teacher, Sir, Mr.; ‹*Ting* ‹*sing* ‹*sang*, Mr. Ting: [4]*pai*' ‹*sang nik*, to congratulate one on the anniversary of his birth; [5]‹*sang laung*' to lay eggs; [6]‹*sang* ‹*ch'ong*, to have ulcers; [7]‹*sang* ‹*t'ĕng*, to breed worms; ‹*sang* ‹*sing*, to rust; [8]‹*sang tek*, '*hó*, beautiful; [9]‹*sang hong*' strange, unknown; ‹*sang leu*' (or *teu*'), slow, tardily.

彡 ‹Shan. Feathers, long hairs, used ornamentally; to adorn with feathers; the 59th radical; a kind of yellow fish, called ‹*wong* ‹*sang*, having small scales.

杉 ‹Shan. Sha. Fir, pine: COM., [10]‹*sang muk*, or ‹*sang* ‹*ch'a*, a species of soft pine, used for building and furniture; [11]‹*sang* ‹*ch'a tóh*, a pine table.

衫 ‹Shan. A jacket, a spencer, a coat; an under-shirt; clothes: [12]‹*i* ‹*sang*, garments; COM., [13]‹*tong* ‹*sang*, a robe, toga; COLL., ‹*sang* ‹*tong*, '*ch'iu* '*wong* '*toi*, a long robe with short sleeves; *met.*, deficient, not just the thing; hard to be kept secret.

刪 ‹Shan. To pare off; to expunge, to correct, to amend and settle the text: [14]‹*sang* '*kai*, to reject and alter; [15]‹*sang k'ëü*' to expunge, as bad phraseology.

姍 ‹Shan. This and the next two sometimes read ‹*tang*: good, fair, beautiful; also to ridicule, to make sport of: [16]‹*sang ch'ieu*' to laugh at.

珊 ‹Shan. Coral, of which there are red and green varieties: often read ‹*tang*, q. v.: ‹*sang* ‹*hu*, (coll. ‹*tang* ‹*hu*), coral, which may be worked into ornaments; [17]‹*sang* ‹*hu sëü*' branched coral; ‹*lang* ‹*sang*, scattered, as fallen flowers.

跚 ‹Shan. Unable to advance; to walk lame, to hobble, to halt, in which senses interchanged with the last two: ‹*mwang* ‹*sang*, to halt, to make poor progress.

芟 ‹ To cut grass, to mow; to cut herbs; to root out; a large reaping-hook, a scythe.

潸 ‹Shan. To weep, to cry bitterly; tears flowing: ‹*sang* ‹*yong k'ek*, *ha*' tears streaming down from the eyes.

‹ 產 ‹ 産 Ch'an. To produce, to grow; to bear, to beget; a birth, parturition; the productions of a country; natives; an estate, a patrimony; occupation, livelihood; a

[1]生仔 [2]生出世 [3]先生○ [4]拜生日○ [5]生蛋 [6]生瘡 [7]生蟲 [8]生的好 [9]生混○ [10]杉木 [11]杉柴桌 [12]衣衫○ [13]長衫 [14]刪改 [15]刪去○ [16]姍笑○ [17]珊瑚樹○

three-holed flageolet: [1]ʻsieu ʻsang, an abortion; COM., [2]ˏka ʻsang, family possessions; [3]ʻtʻu ʻsang, productions of the soil; [4]ʻchʻok ʻsang, the products of a place; [5]ʻsang ˏmwong, the vagina; [6]ʻsang nangʼ death from child-birth; [7]nangʼ ʻsang, protracted parturition, as from wrong presentations; [8]hoʼ ʻsang, a midwife, as written on signs or cards; [9]ngiékˎ ʻsang, property, an estate; [10]ˏkʻing ˏka taungʼ ʻsang, the family estate all lost.

ʻ嵼 Tortuous paths among the mountains: ʻkiong ʻsang, crooked, winding, as paths.

ʻ剷 ʻ刬 Interchanged with the next: to pare off, to trim, as iron; to smooth, to level off.

ʻ鏟 Ch'an. A thin metal plate; a plane, an iron shaving-tool; to cut and pare; to level.

ʻ繖 ʻ傘 San. To shade from rain or sun; an umbrella, a parasol: COM., [11]ˏliong ʻsang, the official umbrella, a canopy carried before high officials; [12]ʻü ʻsang, an umbrella; [13]wangʼ ˏming ʻsang, a canopy presented to an officer by the people; COLL., [14]ʻsang lóhˎ an umbrella-case; ʻsang ˏkʻwi ʻkʻi, to open an umbrella.

ʻ省 Sheng. Hsing. Read ʻseng; coll. ʻsang: economical, frugal, sparing: [15]ʻsang chiékˎ or [16]ʻsang kiéngʼ economical; [17]ʻsang ˏchieng, to use money sparingly; ʻsang siohˎ chʻoiʼ one mouth less to fill; ʻsang sĕûʼ to avoid getting into trouble.

ʻ散 San. A medicinal powder; the name of a song; miscellaneous; various, odds and ends; common, ordinary: in the coll. to scatter, to sprinkle, as powders: also read sangʼ q. v.: [18]ʻsang ˏkung, a day-laborer; COM., [19]ˏtang ˏkó ˏwong ʻsang, nostrums, plasters, pills, and powders; COLL., ʻsang siohˎ tekˎ ʻkiâng, to sprinkle a little on; ʻsang ˏtʻong (or ˏtʻai ˏtʻong), red sugar in a sifted form.

散ʼ San. To scatter, as by the wind; to separate, to dissipate; to spread abroad; to disband, to disperse, to break up; to distribute; a wine vessel, an amphora; a measure equal to five ˏching; empty, vague, as talk; dissipated: also read ʻsang, q. v.: [20]pwoʼ sangʼ ˏliu ˏngiong, to spread false reports; ˏhang sangʼ leisure; COM., pwakˎ sangʼ to distribute or post, as troops; sungʼ ˏchá, to dismiss school, as at the end of the year; ˏka sangʼ ˏing ˏwong, the family scattered and dead; sangʼ hwangʼ scattered and confused, all gone, as one's spirits; sangʼ ˏpwang, to disperse a company, to retire, as attendants at the close of their term; hwakˎ sangʼ to dissipate, as a cold, boils, &c.; sangʼ chʻaiʼ a temple-feast; sangʼ ˏkó ʻhwo, to distribute prize-money for compositions; COLL., ˏchiéng pʻahˎ sangʼ the cash all scattered, as by the snapping of the string.

1 小產 2 家產 3 土產 4 出產 5 產門 6 產難 7 難產 8 扶產 9 業產 10 傾家蕩產 11 涼傘 12 雨傘 13 萬民傘 14 傘紛〇 15 省節 16 省儉 17 省錢 18 散工 19 丹膏丸散 20 布散謠言

福州方言拼音字典

姓 Hsing. Read *seng'*; coll. *sang'*: the surname, the name of a family or clan: [1]*ₑsĕng chê' sang'* a double surname; [2]*'pah, sang'* the people; [3]*ₑi sang' miĕh,* what is his surname? *paik, ₑi sang' miĕh, ₑmiăng ₑsui,* I know his surname and name! — an expression of contempt.

性 Hsing. Read *seng'*; coll. *sang'*: the natural disposition, temper, spirit: [4]*sang' nai'* a patient disposition; [5]*sang' ₑchü,* a kind, compassionate spirit; [6]*sang' ₑkong,* an inflexible temper; *ₑi sang' 'ting kek,* his temper is very hasty.

疝 Shan. Griping pains, wind in the stomach; swelling of the testicles: [7]*sang' k'e'* stricture in the bladder; [8]*ₑsing sang'* angina pectoris; [9]*ĕüng' sang'* inflammation of the testes.

汕 Shan. Fish sporting in the water; to snare fish in a wicker-net; the name of a river in Corea; a bar in a river—perhaps a local use of the word: COM., [10]*sang' ₑt'au,* Swatow.

訕 Shan. To rail at, to scold; to slander, to traduce, to vilify: [11]*sang' ch'ieu'* to mock; [12]*kang' ₑi ₑu sang'* reprove but do not scold.

糤 饊 San. Also read *'sang*: rice boiled till it separates; cakes fried in fat till dry: [13]*sang' hwang'* boiled rice.

晴 'Ch'ing. Read *ₑching*; used in the *Paik, ₑIng* for the coll. *ₑsang*: the sky clearing up after rain: [14]*ₑt'iĕng ₑsang,* the sky clear, fair weather; *ₑsang sioh, nik,* clear for one day.

Sang'. A coll. word: to be silent, not to speak: *sang' sang' mŏh, chŏ' ₑsiăng,* be still, don't talk! *sang' năh,* quiet, of few words, not noisy.

(719) Sau.

梢 'Shao. A twig, the top of a tree, the end of a branch; small, slender; small sticks for fuel; a rudder or tiller; a steersman, a sailor; to knock a thing off; a farming tool; a flag; a staff used in pantomimes: [15]*ₑsau 'chü,* sailors; COM., [16]*ₑsau ₑkung,* a steersman; COLL., [17]*ₑsau ₑtiong twai' hang'* tall and portly.

弰 'Shao. A bow discharging the arrow; the ends or tips of a bow.

莦 'Shao. A coarse weed or grass, of which wild boars make their lairs, like houses in form. Read *ₑsieu*: the roots of grass.

ₑSau. A coll. word: to glance at: *ₑsau sioh, a'* to glance, to take a look at; *ₑkwang ₑsau,* to inspect, to look about, as at night.

'Sau. A coll. word, analogous to the preceding: *'sau sioh, a'* merely glance at it—and instantly understand, as said of a person of talent.

1 雙字姓 2 百姓 3 伊姓乜 4 性耐 5 性慈 6 性剛 7 疝氣 8 心疝 9 湧疝 10 汕頭 11 訕笑 12 諫而無訕 13 饊飯 14 天晴 15 梢子 16 梢公 17 梢長大漢

稍 ‘ Shao. A thing developing gradually; a granary; government stores; a ration of grain; slowly, by degrees, gradually; slightly, partially: [1]*sau ‘sieu*, rather small; [2]*sau ‘k‘ó*, does pretty well, tolerable; [3]*sau ‘iu pok, hak,* it does not quite suit; COM., *‘sau ‘sau*, a little, slightly, in some degree.

哨 ’ Shao. Ch‘iao. A distorted mouth, as of a jug; to patrol, to go about and inspect; a guard-boat, a revenue-cutter: [4]*sau’ t‘ang’* a spy; COM., [5]*sau’ ꜀sung*, revenue-boats to suppress smuggling; [6]*sau’ ‘chung*, the chief of the revenue-police; [7]*chwi sau’* and [8]*ngiăng’ sau’* water and land revenue-guards; [9]*chó sau’ eu’ sau’* the left and right guards or divisions of a camp; COLL., [10]*ch‘ok, sau’ huk, tio’* to place pickets; [11]*sau’ ‘chi*, the tongue in the mouth-piece of a wind instrument; [12]*sau’ ‘ngü*, a coined word or phrase, private terms, as for prices; ꜀*Ch‘ong* ꜀*seng sau’* the peculiar coinage of the granary locality in the city—consists in fanciful uses and combinations of the initials and finals. Read *sieu’*: verbose, gabbling; a guard station to suppress banditti; to disallow.

艄 ’ Shao. Analogous to the preceding: the stern of a boat; a fast sailing, armed boat; guard or revenue vessels: COM., [13]*sau’* ꜀*sung*, a revenue boat; [14]*tok, sau’* the superintendent of a guard-station; [15]꜀*siéng sau’* the guards of a salt department, who suppress smuggling.

瘶嗽 ’ Sou. To cough; to raise phlegm; a cough: COM., [16]꜀*t‘ang sau’* to raise phlegm; COLL., *k‘aĕng’ sau’* a hacking cough; [17]*lau’ sau’* a cough common in old age; *kaiu’* ꜀*tong sau’* a violent, racking cough, (?) whooping-cough.

掃 ’ Sao. Read *‘swa*; coll. *sau’*: to sweep, to brush; to sweep and clean up; to dampen ardor: [18]*sau’ ch‘io’* to sweep the house; *sau’ ‘ch‘iu*, a broom; *sau’ pong’ tó’* to sweep up dirt; *sau’ ‘ch‘iu* ꜀*mĕng*, broom-whisk; *sau’ ‘ch‘iu* ꜀*t‘ui*, (or ꜀*tong*), the stump of an old broom; *p‘ah, sau’ heng’* to dampen ardor, to dash one's hopes; *sau’* ꜀*pi*, to reprove one to his face, to tantalize and disappoint him; [19]*sau’* ꜀*lang*, to paint a blue ground.

(720) Sauk.

刷㕞 , Shua. A brush, a scraper; to brush, to scrape, to scrub; to cleanse; to print: ꜀*k‘ang sauk*, to cut blocks and print; [20]*sauk, ‘t‘i*, to wipe off the disgrace; COM., [21]꜀*á sauk*, a shoe-brush; *sauk,* ꜀*á*, to brush shoes; ꜀*chĕng sauk*, a coir-brush; *pau’ sauk*, to curry and brush (a horse); COLL., *sauk, sauk, ‘kiăng*, a small brush.

率 , Shuai. A bird-net; to follow, to cause to follow; to conform to; to head, to lead, to conduct, to take the command of; prompt, act-

---

1 稍小 2 稍可 3 稍有不合 4 哨探 5 哨船 6 哨總 7 水哨 8 岸哨 9 左哨右哨 10 出哨伏路 11 哨子 12 哨語 13 艄船 14 督艄 15 鹽艄 16 痰瘶 17 佬瘶 18 掃厝 19 掃藍 20 刷恥 21 鞋刷

福州方言拼音字典

ive; suddenly, hastily; generally, for the most part, in the gross; a mark, a guide; a leader, a ruler: also read *luk*, q. v.: [1]'*i* '*ch'ü* ,*ui* *sauk*, let this be a pattern; [2]'*pieu* *sauk*, a leader; an example; a sample; [8]'*tai*' *sauk*, for the most part; [4]'*sauk*, ,*yong*, suddenly; COM., [5]'*ch'ó* *sauk*, carelessly, anyhow; [6]'*sauk*, *chëüng*' to lead a multitude, to raise a mob against; *sauk*, *seng*' to conform to the nature or circumstances of; [7]'*sauk*, '*liäng*, to lead, to command (troops).

蟀, So. A cricket: COM., *sek*, *sauk*, the hearth or house cricket; COLL., *sek*, *sauk*, ,*lëng*, a cricket-cage—made of a joint of bamboo.

㪣, So. To smear, to daub over; to lay on with a brush, to whitewash, to paste over: COLL., [8]*sauk*, *piäh*, to whitewash walls: [9]*sauk*, ,*chiong*, to starch with a brush, as cloths; *sauk*, *pah*, '*hung*, to whiten, as a shoe-sole; [10]*sauk*, ,*hwi* '*chwi*, to whitewash with lime.

朔, So. The new moon; the first day of the month; to begin, a beginning; the north: [11]*cheng*' *sauk*, new year's day; [12]*sauk*, *nik*, the first day of the month; COM., [13]*sauk*, *wong*' ,*sieu* ,*hiong*, to burn incense on the 1st and 15th of the month.

槊, So. A great spear, 18 feet long, such as Ts'ao Ts'ao wielded: ,*ki* *sauk*, a game of chess.

矟, Same as the last; a long spear, used on horseback; also a harpoon or fish-spear.

索, 繂, So. Stalks from whose fibers cords are made; a string, a cord, a rope; to bind; to get, to obtain; to pull out, to select; to search, to seek for, to inquire into, to study or investigate; that which binds; a precept, a law, a rule, an obligation; uneasy, disquieted: used for the coll. *sóh*, q. v.: *sauk*, *sauk*, uneasy, apprehensive.

摉, So. To feel for, to seek after; to take, to obtain; to select: ,*mwo* *sauk*, to feel with the hand; *met.*, to search for truth.

縮, So. Shu. To draw in, to contract; confused, disordered; to collect again; to coil or curl up, as snakes; to creep, as into a hole; to retract, to draw back or cease from; to strain, as wine; puckered, shortened, shrunk; tangled, snarled; upright, straight; retiring, diffident: used for the coll. *t'ëük*, q. v.: [14]*chëüng*' *sauk*, remiss, disorderly; [15]*t'ói*' *sauk*, to withdraw.

蹜, So. Shu. Sometimes read *sëük*,: to walk mincingly, to shuffle along; to walk carefully, as in a narrow path.

帥, Shuai. To lead on, to conduct; also to follow, to comply; to collect; a napkin at the girdle: also read *sói*' q. v.: [16]*sauk*, ,*sü*, to lead troops.

[1]以此爲率 [2]表率 [3]大率 [4]率然 [5]草率 [6]率衆 [7]率領 [8]㪣壁 [9]㪣漿 [10]㪣灰水 [11]正朔 [12]朔日 [13]朔望燒香 [14]縱縮 [15]退縮 [16]帥師

數 ˀ So. Shu. Shuo. In a dilemma, hurried, fluttered; repeated, frequent; close; numerous, troublesome: also read *so*ˀ q. v.: [1]*ˏhwang sauk*ˎ reiterated, troublesome, as affairs.

謖 ˀ Su. To arise hastily; to collect, to draw together; to draw up, as the sleeves: *sauk*ˎ *sauk*ˎ to stand erect; a stern, decided manner; [2]*sauk*ˎ *ˏyong*, to unite; to draw, as the dress about one.

(721) Saung.

算 ˀ **筭** ˀ Suan. A counting board, an abacus; to reckon, to cipher, to calculate; to estimate, to regard; to plan, to plot, to scheme; numbers; a plan, a scheme; a slip of bamboo to keep the reckoning, as in games: COM., [3]*saung*ˀ *ˏpwang*, an abacus; [4]*saung*ˀ *kié*ˀ to plot, to scheme against; [5]*saung*ˀ *ˊta*, to scheme; [6]*ˊta saung*ˀ to plan, to consider; [7]*saung*ˀ *so*ˀ to reckon accounts; [8]*ˏu so*ˀ *saung*ˀ innumerable; [9]*chiok*ˎ *saung*ˀ to reckon to the last cash, close-fisted; [10]*saung*ˀ *k'wa*ˀ to reckon a part as a whole, as years of age; [11]*saung*ˀ *chëük*ˎ to reckon full (years); [12]*saung*ˀ *hwak*ˎ arithmetic, skill in numbers; [13]*hak*ˎ *saung*ˀ to reckon items into one sum; cheap; COLL., [14]*saung*ˀ *miäng*ˀ *ˏsing ˏsang*, or *ˏch'ang ˏmang saung*ˀ a blind fortune-teller; *ˏpwang saung*ˀ to monopolize, as profits; to exact high rates; to cheapen, as labor when work is scarce; *ˏt'au hwok*ˎ *k'ëük*ˎ *ˏi saung*ˀ *lak*ˎ he has reckoned the hair all off my head—got every cash in settling.

蒜 ˀ Suan. Garlic, chives: COM., [15]*saung*ˀ *ˏt'au*, garlic bulbs; [16]*saung*ˀ *chiong*ˀ garlic sauce, pickled with soy; [17]*ˏch'ëng ˊkiu hai*ˀ *saung*ˀ onions, scallions, chives, and garlic—are excluded from a vegetarian's diet; COLL., *saung*ˀ *p'á*ˀ sections of garlic bulbs.

遜 ˀ Hsün, Sun. Complaisant, yielding, conciliatory; humble, meek, mild; respectful, obsequious; to venerate, to yield obedience: [18]*saung*ˀ *yong*ˀ to give place, to yield respectfully; [19]*ˏk'iéng saung*ˀ to yield humbly to, retiring.

巽 ˀ **巺** ˀ Hsün. Sun. Interchanged with the last: a stand or support; to grasp and place firmly; to select; to enter, to ingratiate; the 8th of the 8, or 57th of the 64, diagrams; it relates to wind, and denotes mildness; bland, mild, gentle, insinuating: [20]*saung*ˀ *song*ˀ mild, yielding.

喪 ˀ **丧** ˀ Sang. To lose, to fail to obtain; to pass into obscurity; lost, ruined; forgotten, out of mind; to cease, to die; failure: also read *ˏsong*, q. v.: [21]*saung*ˀ *ˏming*, blind; *saung*ˀ *kwok*ˎ to lose a kingdom; COM., *ˏing ˏchai saung*ˀ *meng*ˀ lost his life in getting a fortune.

*Saung*ˀ. A coll. word: to strangle with a cord: *saung*ˀ *ˊsi*, to kill by strangling; *saung*ˀ *ˊking*,

---

1 煩數 2 謖然 3 算盤 4 算計 5 算打 6 打算 7 算數 8 無數算 9 絕算 10 算跨 11 算足 12 算法 13 合算 14 算命先生 15 蒜頭 16 蒜醬 17 葱韭薤蒜 18 遜讓 19 謙遜 20 巽順 21 喪明 ○

to draw the cord tight so as to strangle.

(722) Se.

四' 肆' 乂' Ssu. Read *söü'; coll. se'*: four, the fourth; *met.*, everywhere: the second is the complex, and the third the abbreviated, form: [1]*se' chiăh,* or *se' 'a*, four of certain things; *se' a' 'kau*, thirty six; [2]*se' kaëk, sek, lëk, hëk,* "four corners and sixteen measures"—square, cubical; *met.*, strict, precise; [3]*se' kié'* the four seasons; [4]*se' 'a ngwok, nik,* four months; [5]*se' ,k'a ,pa*, to crawl on four legs —I'm a dog (if what I say is not true); [6]*se' ,hwong paik, miëng'* universal, extensive; [7]*se' ,k'a se' 'ch'iu pek, tik, tik,* stretched in death; [8]*se' pok, ch'iong'* does nothing properly.

試' Shih. Read *söü'; coll. se'* as in *'k'ó se'* examinations for the Siutsai degree.

Se'. A coll. euphonic prefix, as in *se' sié'* connected, attached, added on.

是' Shih. Right, straight, direct; what the mind approves; the substantive verb to be, is, am, are; this, that, these, those: [9]*se' nik,* that day, then; [10]*yok, se'* if it is so; [11]*se' pek,* certainly; [12]*se' 'i,* therefore, by this means; COM., *pok, se'* (coll. *ng' se'*) not so, no; *se' ,hi,* right and wrong; *'k'eu se' ,sing ,hi,* to say but not mean; *chëü' se'* self-conceited; *,pwi pok, se'* to confess a wrong; *se' se'* there truly is or should be; *se' sié'* in the right shape or form, it fits so; COLL., *se' ,i chó'* it was he that did it; *se' ,sing tioh, pai' se' chá' tioh, ,nui,* if a god, worship him; if dough, knead him—treat him according to his character (so as to get his money).

諟' Shih. Anciently used for the last: to be, is; right, proper; correct principle; to examine, to judge.

寺' 閣' Ssu. Shih. An official residence; chambers for officers about a court; an office, a hall; chamberlains, eunuchs; a Budhist temple or monastery: [13]*se' ,mwong,* Budhists; *tai' 'li se'* the Court of Appeal at Peking; [14]*se' ,ing* or *nói' se'* eunuchs; COM., [15]*se' yéng'* a Budhist monastery; *Eüng' ,chiong se'* name of the Kushan monastery, near Foochow; *pah, t'ak, se'* the White Pagoda monastery in Foochow.

峙' A high, isolated peak; to provide; provided, supplied, as with provisions: *,küng se'* to prepare, as public stores.

侍' Shih. To receive the orders of a superior; to follow, to attend; near to, waiting on, at the side of, as servants or officers near their superiors: [16]*se' woi'* officers of the Imperial guards, household guards; *se' t'uk, hok, söü'* academicians; *huk, se'* to wait on; COM., [17]*se' ,long,* Vice President of a Board; a provincial governor.

---

[1]四隻 [2]四角十六斛 [3]四季 [6]四個月日 [5]四胶爬 [6]四方八面 [7]四胶四手拔直直 [8]四不象 [9]是日 [10]若是 [11]必是 [12]是以 [13]寺門 [14]寺人 [15]寺院 [16]侍衛 [17]侍郎

恃² Shih. Ch'ih. To lean upon, to trust to, to rely on; to look to for protection or help; to presume on, assuming; dull, unintelligent; used in the *met.* sense for a mother: ¹*ho*² *se*² parents; ²꜀*i se*² to rely on; ³*se*² *sié*² to presume on one's power or station; ⁴*se*² ꜂*ch'iu chëük*꜀ to depend on one's hands and feet —i. e., on brothers.

視² **眎**² Shih. To see, to observe, to inspect, to examine; to notice and imitate; to treat, to behave toward; to regard and compare; to cause to be seen, to view as: ⁵꜀*siă se*² to look aslant at; ⁶*k'ang*² *se*² to inspect, to look at; COM., ⁷*këüng*² *se*² near-sighted.

示² **亓**² Shih. To show, to declare; to make known, as Heaven's will; to instruct, to admonish, as the people; an edict; a prognostic, revelation, sign, as from heaven; a polite phrase in letters; the 113th radical: ⁸*ch'ok*꜀ *se*² to issue an edict; ⁹꜀*huí se*² to return an answer; ¹⁰*hong*² *se*² to teach one; COM., ¹¹*kó*² *se*² a proclamation; ¹²*se*² *chëüng*² to admonish the people—as by an execution, etc.; ¹³*se*² ꜀*ti*, inform me—an epistolary phrase; ¹⁴꜂*chi se*² to point out, to direct one. Read ꜀*ki*: the same as ꜀*ki* (a spirit).

氏² Shih. A family, a clan; a sect; appended to names, it denotes females; a family name; an ancient honorary title; the 83d radical: ¹⁵*sek*꜀ *se*² the Budhists; COM., ¹⁶꜀*ngu se*² Madame ꜀*Ngu*; ꜀*ting* ꜀*ling se*² or ꜀*ting* ꜀*mwong* ꜀*ling se*² Mrs. ꜀*Ting* ꜀*Ling*—the ꜀*Ting* being her husband's, and the ꜀*Ling* her father's, surname.

(723) Së.

梳 ꜀ Shu. Read ꜀*su* in the dictionaries; coll. ꜀*së*: a comb; to comb, to dress the hair: ¹⁷꜀*t'au* ꜀*së*, a coarse comb; ¹⁸*pe*² ꜀*së*, a fine-toothed comb; *ch'iong*² ꜀*nga* ꜀*së*, an ivory comb; ꜀*së* ꜀*chong*, to make the toilet, as a lady does; ꜀*së kwoí*² to dress the hair in a coiffure; ꜀*së* ꜀*piëng piëng*² to dress the cue; ¹⁹꜀*së* ꜀*t'au* ꜂*sá meng*² to comb the hair and wash the face.

疏 **踈** ꜀ Shu. Read ꜀*su*; coll. ꜀*së*: open, wide apart, coarse; sleazy; distant in relationship: ꜀*së* ꜀*së*, open, separated; remotely related; ²⁰꜀*ch'ing* ꜀*së*, near and distant relationships; ²¹꜀*së* ꜀*pung* ꜀*hiăng tié*² male relatives of the same surname, but distantly related.

黍 ꜂ Shu. Read ꜂*sü*; coll. ꜂*së*: paniceled millet: ꜂*së sau*² brooms made of millet-tops.

所 ꜂ So. Su. Shu. Read ꜂*su*; coll. ꜂*së*: a place: ꜀*kung* ꜂*së*, a public place, a hall; ꜂*së siék*꜀ ꜀*tëng* ꜂*në*, where's the place for meeting?

璽 ꜂ Hsi. Read ꜂*sá*; coll. ꜂*së*: as in *ngwoh*꜁ ꜂*së*, the imperial seal.

꜀*Së*. A coll. word: slanting, projecting, leaning over, as the front of a house: ꜀*së ch'ok*꜀ ꜀*li*, to jut out, to lean over; ꜂*ngai*

¹怙恃 ²依恃 ³恃勢 ⁴恃手足 ⁵邪視○ ⁶看視 ⁷近視 ⁸出示 ⁹回示 ¹⁰訓示 ¹¹告示 ¹²示衆 ¹³示知 ¹⁴指示 ¹⁵釋氏 ¹⁶吳氏 ¹⁷頭梳 ¹⁸餚梳 ¹⁹梳頭洗面 ²⁰親疏 ²¹疏房兄弟

꜀sĕ ꜀sĕ, the teeth uneven and projecting.

꜀*Sĕ*. A coll. word: a superlative used for emphasis, as in ꜀*sĕ* ꜀*sĕ lau*ʾ very leaky.

꜀*Sĕ*. A coll. word: to impose on by fraud, as in selling poor articles: ꜀*ngai hwo*ʾ ꜀*sĕ* ꜀*nĕng*, to palm off bad goods on persons; *k'ëük*꜀ ꜀*nĕng* ꜀*sĕ*, to be swindled by persons; ꜀*sĕ má*ʾ *kwo*ʾ *siéng*ʾ to fail to take one in.

(724) Seh.

Seh꜀. A coll. euphonic prefix, as in *seh*꜀ *sëüh*꜀ to suck, to draw into the mouth quickly; *seh*꜀ *sóh*꜀ to suck, as blood, milk, etc.; *seh*꜀ *sioh*꜀ to slice, to cut up.

Seh꜀. A coll. word, as in ꜀*si seh*꜀ to hiss, to whiz, to whir, as an arrow or a rocket; ꜀*si seh*꜀ *sioh*꜀ ꜀*siăng*, to make a hissing sound; ꜀*si seh*꜀ ꜀*chiă kwo*ʾ to pass whizzing by.

(725) Sek.

惜꜀ Hsi. To pity, to compassionate; to love, to regard; to regret; to be careful of, sparing; parsimonious, close, stingy: [1]*leng*ʾ *sek*꜀ niggardly, griping; [2]*sek*꜀ ꜀*kwong* ꜀*ing*, careful of time; [3]*t'ong*ʾ *sek*꜀ to feel deeply for; COM., [4]ʿ*k'ó sek*꜀ lamentable, sad, alas! [5]*ai*ʾ *sek*꜀ to love, to regard; [6]*keng*ʾ *sek*꜀ *che*ʾ ʿ*chai*, to take a reverent care of written or printed paper.

悉꜀ Hsi. To comprehend fully and thoroughly; the complete knowledge of; altogether, entire; fully, completely, all; both, united: [7]*sek*꜀ ꜀*ti*, to know fully; [8]꜀*ch'ing sek*꜀ ꜀*ki* ꜀*siong*, to comprehend perfectly in all its minute details.

息꜀ Hsi. One expiration and inspiration, a breath, a gasp; to breathe; to sigh; to stop, to rest, to repose; progeny, offspring; to bud, to sprout, as in spring; usury, interest, profits; to toil, to labor; to obstruct, to stop up; a moment, a breath: [9]*t'ai*ʾ *sek*꜀ a long sigh; [10]*sek*꜀ *no*ʾ pacified; COM., [11]*k'e*ʾ *sek*꜀ breathing; a bad odor; [12]ʿ*chü sek*꜀ one's children; [13]*sek*꜀ ꜀*sü*, or ꜀*hwo sek*꜀ a statement of amicable settlement, as handed in to a magistrate; [14]*le*ʾ *sek*꜀ interest; [15]*ch'ok*꜀ *sek*꜀ to pay interest, to make profit; [16]꜀*ang sek*꜀ ꜀*hiong*, gum benzoin; *seng*ʾ *sek*꜀ the news, intelligence.

媳꜀ Hsi. The wife of a son or grandson: used for the coll. ꜀*sing*, q. v.: COM., [17]*sek*꜀ *ho*ʾ (coll. ꜀*sing mo*ʾ), a daughter-in-law; [18]꜀*song sek*꜀ a grandson's wife.

熄꜀ Hsi. To cover a fire with ashes; to put out a fire; to quash, to extinguish: *sek*꜀ *chëük*꜀ to extinguish a candle.

煬꜀ Dry. Read *ik*꜀: bright, as flames; clear, brilliant, splendid.

濕 溼꜀ Shih. The second is an erroneous form: damp, wet, humid; hurried; disappointed, sad, dejected: [19]꜀*hung sek*꜀ rheumatism; [20]*sok*꜀ *sek*꜀ impetuous; COM., [21]*sek*꜀ *k'e*ʾ

[1]悋	陰	惜	惜	知	詳	怒	息	息	息	[18]孫	[20]束
惜	[3]痛	[5]愛	字	[8]深	[9]太	[11]氣	[13]息	[15]出	香	媳	濕
[2]惜	惜	惜	紙	悉	息	息	辭	息	[17]媳	[19]瘋	[21]濕
光	[4]可	[6]敬	[7]悉	其	[10]息	[12]子	[14]利	[16]安	婦	濕	氣

dampness, humid exhalations; [1]*'sek, ,seng*, insects generated in water; [2]*'sek, 'chwi*, wet, damaged by wet, as goods.

隰, Hsi. Low, marshy land; wet meadows at the base of hills; a marsh, a fen, a morass.

失, Shih. To lose, to drop, to mislay; to fail, to omit; to err, to miss the road; to forget, to leave behind; to slip, to let slip; a failure, a fault: [3]*sek, 'lieu*, lost; [4]*sek, kauk*, to fail to perceive; COM., [5]*sek, ,ngiong*, lapsus linguæ; [6]*sek, 'chwi*, dropped in the water; damaged by water, as goods; [7]*sek, ,nging*, I missed your call; [8]*sek, tó*² stolen; *sek, 'chio*, the loser; [9]*sek, 'ch'iu*, slipped out of the hand—and lost; a blow by mistake; [10]*sek, sĕü*² to neglect business, to do a thing wrongly; [11]*sek, keng'* or *sek, 'lá*, I fail in politeness, as a host says; *sek, 'kiéng 'tiéng*, to be careless; *sek, k'ieu'* stupid, obtuse; COLL., *,kiăng sek, k'ó'* to faint from fear.

室, Shih. A house, a dwelling-place; a room; a wife; one's kindred, a family: to marry; a cavern; the 13th of the 28 constellations, *a* and *b* in Pegasus: [12]*cheng' sek*, and *ch'aik, sek*, wife and concubine; [13]*seu² sek*, a marriage; [14]*,ka sek*, a family; COM., [15]*sek, ,tüng*, my wife, a term used in writing; [16]*,ta sek*, tea-houses—used on sign-boards.

釋, Shih. To unloose, to relax; to free, to let go; to acquit, to forgive; to open out, to explain; to put from one; to melt; to dissipate, as ice in the sun; to make soft, to soak; to submit; Budhism: [17]*sek, ,hui*, to return from exile; [18]*sek, haung²* to banish resentment; [19]*,k'ai sek*, to settle and dismiss (a lawsuit); COM., *sek, hwong'* to let go, as from prison; *sek, ,kiă ,meu ,ná*, Sakyamuni (Budha)—a Sanscrit term; *sek, ,ka*, or *,sek ,mwong*, Budhists; *sek, kau'* Budhism.

錫, Hsi. An alloy resembling white copper; its constituents vary according to required uses; tin, block-tin; pewter of lead and tin; to bestow; a sort of fine linen: [20]*sek, hok*, to confer happiness; *sek, t'iong²* an abbot's crosier; COM., [21]*sek, k'e'* pewter utensils; *sek, 'ku*, a pewter teapot; a pewter saucepan or salver; *sek, tong²* a pewter cooking vessel with an inner cylinder; *sek, póh,* pewter foil.

識, Shih. Chih. To know, to learn, to recognize; to be acquainted with; experienced, versed, skilled in: [22]*neng² sek*, to recognize; acquainted with; [23]*che' sek*, to know thoroughly; COM., *,ti sek*, judgment, discretion; *sek, p'ó' ,ki ,kwang*, to penetrate one's schemes; *sek, che² ,liong*, the pay of a scribe in a military office.

昔, Hsi. Dried meats; formerly, anciently, of old, a long time ago; the previous, former; a night: *sek, ,si*, in former times; *ek, sek*, the whole night; [24]*sek, 'chiă*, former-

---

1 濕生　2 濕水　3 失了　4 失覺　5 失言　6 失水　7 失迎　8 失盜　9 失手　10 失事　11 失敬　12 正室　13 受室　14 家室　15 室中　16 茶室　17 釋囘　18 釋恨　19 開釋　20 錫福　21 錫器　22 認識　23 至識　24 昔者

福州方言拼音字典

ly; [1]*ˎking sek, pok, ˏtung*, it is not now as it was formerly.

腊, Hsi. A long time; extreme; hasty, quick, speedy; to put down, to lay aside; dried meat, in which sense used for *lak,* q. v.

踖, To stride, to step across; to straddle over: also read *chek,* q. v.

飾, 飭, Shih. To paint, to adorn, to dress up, to ornament; to wipe or rub; to pretend, to gloss over; to excuse; harmony, concord in music; to dress a victim for sacrifice; head-ornaments; an ornamented cuff, binding, or facing; a collar; weapons: [2]*hung sek,* to whitewash; to gloss over; [3]*ˏsiu sek,* to adorn; COM., [4]*siu sek,* (coll. *ch'iu sek,*), head-ornaments; [5]*ˏchong sek,* (coll. *ˏchong sok,*), to attend to one's toilet, to dress or trick out; *sek, ˏsü* or *'yéng sek,* fiction, feigned words.

蟋, Hsi. A cricket: COM., [6]*sek, sauk,* a house-cricket; COLL., *p'ah, sek, sauk,* to fight crickets.

蝕, Shih. Also read *sik,:* to corrode, to injure gradually; eaten by worms; to encroach on, to eclipse: COM., [7]*nik, sek,* a solar eclipse; [8]*ngwok, sek,* a lunar eclipse.

螫, Shih. Also read *siă':* a sting; to sting; to poison; the poison of a sting; venemous; troublesome: [9]*ˏsing sek,* a virulent poison, malignant.

蜥, Hsi. A ground lizard, called [10]*sek, ik,;* it is livid like a chameleon.

栻, Shih. A kind of tree, anciently used in divination and sorcery.

析, Hsi. To split up wood; to separate, to discriminate; to solve doubts: [11]*sek, ˏsing,* to split firewood; [12]*sek, ié'* a rainbow; *'p'eu sek,* to discriminate.

淅, Hsi. To wash and scour rice; the water in which rice has been washed: [13]*sek, lik,* the pattering of rain or hail; [14]*Sek, ˏch'iong,* a district in the south-west of Honan.

晳, 晰, Hsi. Clear, bright, brilliant; to distinguish, to discriminate, to discern clearly.

式, Shih. A form or shape; fashion, style, mode, manner; a rule, a law; an example or precedent; to imitate, to copy after; to respect, to reverence, to honor; an initial particle, Oh! a cross-bar in a carriage, for which the next is used: COM., [15]*yong' sek,* form, fashion, style of; [16]*hak, sek,* to correspond to the pattern; *met.,* suitable, cheap; [17]*'k'wang sek,* form, shape; manner.

軾, Shih. The front bar or board of a carriage or sedan to lean on, as when bowing to others, termed in the

[1]今昔不同 [2]粉飾 [3]修飾 [4]首飾 [5]粧飾 [6]蟋蟀 [7]日蝕 [8]月蝕 [9]辛螫 [10]蜥蜴 [11]析薪 [12]析翳 [13]淅瀝 [14]淅川 [15]樣式 [16]合式 [17]款式

coll. *k'ó'* *'ch'iu* *'peng* or leaning-board.

拭, 栻, To rub with a cloth, to wipe, to clean up; to brush away; to wash sheep: in the coll. read *ch'ek,* q. v.: *hok, sek,* to dust.

舄, Hsi. The sole of a shoe; thick, wooden soles; clogs, pattens, to preserve the feet from dampness; great, large: used for *ch'iok,* (a magpie); also for *sek,* as in *sek, 'lu,* salt, barren land.

適, Shih. Ti. To proceed, to advance; to go to, to reach, to arrive at; to go to her husband's house, as a bride; to pass over a long way; to occur, to happen; to suit, to accord with; to follow; happening suddenly, just now, presently, recently; usual, common; pleased; good, suitable; coming to pass, accomplished; in the west of China, means to supply vacancies, as in an army: [1]*sek, ˏyong,* suddenly; [2]*sek, ˏlai,* has just come; [3]*sek, ˏking,* just now, recently; [4]*sek, ˏchüng,* to follow or adhere to, as a party; [5]*e' sek, ˏka,* not yet married.

塞, Sai. Sĕ. Read *saik,*; coll. *sek,*: to stop an aperture; to fill, to stuff, to close; also a stopple, a stopper: *sek, 'king,* to stop tightly; *sek, 'tié,* stuff it in.

Sek,. A coll. euphonic prefix, as in *sek, sauk,* to brush; *sek, saĕk,* to dash, to throw down violently; to thresh out (grain).

十 [1], 拾 [2], Shih. Ten; wholly; perfect, complete; the 24th radical: the second is the complex form: COM., [6]*sek, ˏchiong,* or *sek, ˏpwang ˏchiong,* complete, entire; [7]*sek, pok, ˏchiong,* very defective, full of blemishes; [8]*sek, ˏsiăng,* pure, fine, as metals; [9]*sek, ˏhung,* entire, the whole; very, exceedingly; [10]*sek, saung'* to reckon accurately; [11]*sek, wong'* the ten hatreds—name of a book of songs; [12]*sek, sek, chëük,* full, complete; [13]*sek, che' ka'* the cross; [14]*sek, che' ˏká,* a cross street; [15]*sek, auk, 'kwi,* the ghost of one who dies an unnatural or violent death; COLL., [16]*p'ah, sek, ˏhwang,* to be an amateur musician; [17]*sek, hong' sioh,* one out of ten; *sek, o' paik, 'kau,* eight or nine out of ten—nearly completed or settled.

(726) Sĕk.

Sĕk,. A coll. word: to shake, to agitate; *met.,* to experience (toil or hardship): *sĕk, ˏch'iéng,* to shake the lots (before an idol); *ˏt'au sĕk, ˏwong ˏhing,* dizzy from the motion, as of a boat or sedan; *mwoi' sĕk, kwo'* have not yet passed the ordeal.

(727) Seng.

生, Shêng. To bear, to produce; to live; to excite, to cause to grow; life, living; born, birth; raw, unripe; strange, unacquainted; the 100th radical: read *ˏsang* and *ˏch'ang* in the coll. q. v.: [18]*ˏseng ngiék,* a calling, an employment; [19]*t'auk, ˏseng,* metempsychosis; [20]*'iu ˏseng,* friends; *ˏch'ong ˏseng,* the

[1]適然 [2]適來 [3]適今 [4]適從 [5]未適家 [6]十全 [7]十不全 [8]十成 [9]十分 [10]十算 [11]十怨 [12]十十足 [13]十字架 [14]十字街 [15]十惡鬼 [16]拍十歡 [17]十分一 [18]生業 [19]託生 [20]友生

people ; [1]ʻ*pek*‚ ‚*seng*, or ‚*seng* ‚*ping*, the whole life ; COM., [2]ʻ*hok*‚ ‚*seng* or ‚*mwong* ‚*seng*, a pupil, scholar, disciple ; [3]‚*siéng* ‚*seng*, a teacher ; [4]ʻ*sieu* ‚*seng*, young gentleman—a character in plays ; ‚*seng tang*ʼ ʻ*tʻiu mwak*‚ *chiăng*ʼ the general names of characters in plays ; [5]‚*king* ‚*seng*, and ‚*lai* ‚*seng*, the present and future states of existence ; [6]*chëüng*ʼ ‚*seng*, all living beings, animals ; [7]‚*seng kʻe*ʼ vitality ; to get angry ; ‚*seng* ‚*sing*, to have a (bad) heart, as in cheating a partner; ‚*seng sëü*ʼ to make trouble; ‚*seng* ‚*sing* (or ‚*siăng*), natural, not artificial ; [8]‚*seng kʻaik*‚ to produce and destroy, as applied to the five elements in fortune telling ; [9]‚*seng* ‚*küng* (or *mó*ʼ), cap of the Ming dynasty—now worn in plays ; [10]‚*seng* ʻ*li*, or [11]‚*seng e*ʼ trade ; [12]‚*seng* ‚*ki* ʻ*sang*, medicinal powders to grow solid flesh in sores ; ‚*seng* ‚*lié* ʻ*sü piék*‚ separations in life and death.

甡 ‚Shêng. A multitude standing or going together, as animals : ‚*seng* ‚*seng* ‚*ki lŭk*‚ how numerous are the deer !

甥 ‚Shêng. A sister's or daughter's children ; a son-in-law : [13]‚*seng keu*ʼ son-in-law and wife's father ; [14]ʻ*kwang* ‚*seng*, a son-in-law ; COM., [15]*ngié*ʼ ‚*seng*, and [16]*ngié*ʼ ‚*seng* ʻ*nü*, a sister's children, nephews and nieces ; *ngié*ʼ ‚*seng* ‚*song*, children of a nephew or niece ; also a daughter's children ; *ngié*ʼ ‚*seng* ‚*song sá*ʼ a sister's son-in-law; ‚*seng* ‚*ié* ‚*niong*, compellation of a sister's son's wife ; ‚*seng lik*‚ *keu*ʼ *sëü*ʼ to adopt a sister's son.

笙 ‚Shêng. A musical instrument of the organ kind, consisting of 13 reeds inserted in a bulb ; small, slender : [17]‚*seng* ‚*kó*, to play and sing ; *met.*, delight ; COM., [18]‚*seng* ‚*sieu* ʻ*ku ngok*‚ the organ, flageolet, drum, and all sorts of musical instruments.

牲 ‚Shêng. Sacrificial animals, cattle : [19]‚*seng* ʻ*kʻeu*, cattle, draught animals ; ‚*hi* ‚*seng*, sacrificial animals : COM., [20]‚*sang* ‚*seng*, the three victims or sacrificial meats, pig, ox, and goat, or fowl, fish, and pork ; *lëk*‚ ‚*seng*, the six kinds of animals, horses, kine, sheep, fowls, dogs, and swine—in the coll. termed *lëk*‚ *hëük*‚.

先 ‚Hsien. Read ‚*siéng*; coll. ‚*seng* : before, first ; previous ; early, formerly : ‚*seng kau*ʼ to arrive first ; ‚*seng au*ʼ ʻ*chʻiu*, before or after (the set time) ; ‚*seng au*ʼ *pwo*ʼ he left just before you came ; ‚*seng* ‚*tiéng haiu*ʼ ʻ*kʻu*, first sweet then bitter —first rich then poor ; ‚*seng* ʻ*sieu* ‚*ing haiu*ʼ ‚*kang* ʻ*chü*, "first the mean man then the good man"— first make the bargain then stick to it.

參 ‚Shên. Tsên. Tsʻên. Tsʻan. A medicinal root, the Panax quinquefolia, ginseng ; also applied to a variety of roots having tonic properties ; the 21st zodiacal constellation : also read ‚*chʻang*, q. v. : COM., [21]‚*ing* ‚*seng*, ginseng ; ‚*kó* ‚*lá* ‚*seng*, and ‚*king* ‚*seng*, Corean ginseng ; ‚*seng* ‚*sü*, ginseng rootlets ; [22]ʻ*hai* ‚*seng*, beche-de-mer ; ‚*yong* ‚*seng*,

[1]畢	[3]先	[5]今	[7]生	[9]生	[11]生	散	甥	甥	[18]笙	[19]牲	[21]人
生	生	生	氣	巾	意	[13]甥	[15]外	女	簫	口	參
[2]學	[4]小	[6]衆	[8]生	[10]生	[12]生	舅	甥	[17]笙	鼓	[20]三	[22]海
生	生	生	尅	理	肌	[14]館	[16]外	歌	樂	牲	參

or ‘*ku* ‚*kĕng* ‚*seng*, ‘*tong* ‚*seng*, *t‘ai*’ *kik*, ‚*seng*, *hok*, ‚*seng*, ‚*ngwong* ‚*seng*, ‚*sa* ‚*seng*, and ‚*tang* ‚*seng*, are other varieties of ‚*seng*; COLL., ‚*seng tong*² a vessel for decocting ginseng.

滲 ‘ Shên. To drip, to ooze out; also to steep: [1]‚*seng lŭk*, to ooze out; ‚*seng* ‚*liĕ*, flowing along; ‚*ling* ‚*seng*, just fledged.

槮 ‘ Shên. Used for the next: stakes set up to catch fish; trees in winter, leafless trees looking tall and bare.

罧 ‘ A trap for fishes, made by covering a hole with sticks and gathering the fish caught in it at low water.

森 ‘ Sên. Shên. Shêng. The Melia Azedarak, or Pride of India; thickly wooded, overgrown, forest-like; somber, densely shaded; severe, as laws; to plant trees: [2]‚*seng* ‚*ngiéng*, majestic, stern, rigorous.

省 ‘ Shêng. Hsing. To diminish, to abridge, to lessen; frugal, sparing; within the palace, a spot guarded for officers; a province: also read ‘*sing* and in the coll. ‘*sang*, q. v.: [3]‘*seng* ‚*ung*, a terse phrase; COM., [4]*sek*, *paik*, ‘*seng*, the 18 provinces of China Proper; [5]*hok*, *kiong*’ ‘*seng*, the province of Fookien; [6]‘*seng* ‚*siăng tëüng*² *te*’ the provincial capital, an important place; [7]‘*seng* ‚*pieu*, of the provincial flag, city troops.

眚 ‘ Shêng. Interchanged with the preceding in the sense of to lessen or diminish, and with the next in the sense of emaciated; a film, staphyloma obscuring the sight; a disease caused by a demon; a fault, a crime; a calamity.

瘠 ‘ Shêng. Lean, thin, emaciated; in the coll. the lean part of meat: [8]‘*seng nŭk*, lean pork.

信 ’ Hsin. Sincere, faithful; truthful, unsuspicious; one who keeps his word, as the two parts of the character indicate; sincerity; faith, belief; to believe, to trust, to follow; a seal or stamp; a letter; two nights' lodging; an envoy, a messenger; arsenic, also called ‚*ing* ‚*ngiong*, from the composition of the character: *eng*’ *seng*’ a seal; COM., [9]*seng*’ *sik*, sincere, worthy of trust; [10]*seng*’ *taik*, sincerity; faith; [11]*seng*’ ‚*Yă* ‚*Su*, to believe in Jesus; [12]*seng*’ *sek*, the news; [13]‚*ing seng*’ news, intelligence; [14]*sek*, *seng*’ to forfeit confidence, to break one's word; [15]‘*ch‘ŭ seng*’ to take his word for it; *nói*² *seng*’ the inclosed letter; [16]‚*hŭng seng*’ a letter containing bad news, as of a death; [17]‘*t‘ó* ‚*huí seng*’ to get an answer to a letter; COLL., [18]*má*² *seng*’ *tek*, *kwo*’ or *má*² *seng*’ *tek*, ‚*sing*, can't believe it; [19]‚*p‘ié seng*’ a letter.

勝 ’ Shêng. To conquer, to win, to beat, to get the victory; superior, the best, excelling; to add; a female head-dress, representing flowers and called [20]‚*hwa seng*’ or

1滲 3省 省 6省 7省 9信 11信 息 信 信 18賣 19批
漉 文 5福 城 標 實 耶 13音 15取 17討 信 信
2森 4十 建 重 8瘠 10信 穌 信 信 回 的 20花
嚴 八 省 地 肉 德 12信 14失 16凶 信 過 勝

ʻ*chʻai seng*ʾ formerly worn on the 7th of the 1st moon: also read *꜀sing*, q. v.: [1]*sengʾ tiong*ʾ to get a victory; [2]*hóʾ sengʾ* to love pre-eminence; COM., [3]*taik꜀ seng*ʾ victorious; *sengʾ pai*ʾ victory and defeat, winning and losing; COLL., *pʻah꜀ sengʾ tiong*ʾ to gain a victory.

聖 圣 ʾ Shêng. Intuitively wise and good, having universal knowledge, the highest style of intellectual and moral power; perfect; sacred, holy; sage; imperial: read *siǎng*ʾ in the coll. q. v.: [4]*sengʾ* ʻ*chü*, or *sengʾ* ꜀*tʻiêng* ʻ*chü*, the emperor; COM., [5]*sengʾ* ꜀*wong*, the sage kings, as Yau, Shun and others; [6]*sengʾ* ꜀*ing*, the Sage, Confucius; [7]*sengʾ* ꜀*hiêng* ꜀*ing*, sages and philosophers; [8]*sengʾ* ꜀*ing mieu*ʾ a Confucian temple; *sengʾ* ꜀*mwong tá*ʾ ʻ*chü*, Confucius' disciples; [9]*sengʾ* ʻ*chi*, the Imperial will; [10]*sengʾ* ꜀*ing* ꜀*king*, the sage's classic, a book for children; ʻ*a sengʾ* the second sage, Mencius; *chiéʾ sengʾ* to sacrifice to the sage; *sengʾ* ꜀*sing*, *sengʾ* ꜀*king*, and *sengʾ nik꜀* the Holy Spirit, the Bible, and the Sabbath.

姓 ʾ Hsing. A surname, a patronymic, the name of the clan or family; a clan; to bear a son: in the coll. read *sang*ʾ q. v.: *sengʾ se*ʾ a surname, as of a sept; [11]*paik꜀ sengʾ* the people; COM., [12]*koiʾ sengʾ* (what is) your honorable surname?

性 ʾ Hsing. The nature and principles given by heaven, the natural faculties; innate qualities; the natural disposition, temper, and spirit: in the coll. read *sang*ʾ q. v.: [13]*sengʾ chwok꜀* dull in learning; [14]꜀*tʻiêng sengʾ* natural ability, native genius; COM., [15]*sengʾ* ꜀*ching*, temper, disposition; [16]*pʻek꜀ sengʾ* one's natural temper or spirit; [17]*sengʾ sóʾ* a hasty temper; [18]*sengʾ yék꜀* of a heating quality, as pepper; *sengʾ meng*ʾ life, existence.

汛 ʾ Hsin. Hsün. To sprinkle; the appearance of water, watery, wet; speedy, quick, as the wind or a courier; a military station, a guard-house: [19]*sengʾ* ʻ*swa*, to sprinkle and sweep; COM., *sengʾ te*ʾ a guard-house; ꜀*tong sengʾ* a station, a stage between stations, equal to ten ʻ*li;* ꜀*tong* ꜀*chiu sengʾ* the fort or military post on Tong-chiu island in the Min.

迅 ʾ Hsin. Hsün. Swift, quick, hasty, fleet; to hasten, to go speedily; a wolf's cub: [20]*sengʾ sok꜀* quick, speedy; *sengʾ* ꜀*loi pok꜀ kik꜀* ʻ*yéng* ʻ*ngi*, a quick clap gives no time to stop one's ears—quick, as a word and a blow.

訊 ʾ Hsin. Hsün. To inquire, to search out, to investigate; to try, to interrogate judicially; an examination; to inform against, to accuse; to direct; to agitate; to wrangle, to bicker: [21]*sengʾ ong*ʾ to question judicially; *ongʾ sengʾ* to salute, to make a bow to; [22]*chek꜀ seng*ʾ to catch another's words; to seize and question; also a bearer of dispatches; *sengʾ chik꜀* to cure diseases.

---

[1]勝仗 [2]好勝 [3]得勝 [4]聖主 [5]聖王 [6]聖人 [7]聖賢人 [8]聖人廟 [9]聖旨 [10]聖人經○ [11]百姓 [12]貴姓 [13]性拙 [14]天性 [15]性情 [16]癖性 [17]性燥 [18]性熱 [19]汛洒 [20]迅速 [21]訊問 [22]執訊

囟 顖 Hsing. The sinciput; the place on an infant's head where the skull unites: ¹*seng*ˀ *ˌmwong*, the fontanel; COLL., ²*k'ang seng*ˀ (or *t'eng*ˀ), the brainpan, soft spot on an infant's head.

*Seng*ˀ. A coll. euphonic prefix, as in *seng*ˀ *saung*ˀ to count, to reckon: *seng*ˀ *saĕng*ˀ to make presents; *seng*ˀ *siong*ˀ to look, to glance at; *seng*ˀ *siĕng*ˀ to salt, to pickle.

前 ˁCh'ien. Read *ˌchiĕng*; used for the coll. *ˌseng*: before, in front of; in the presence of; previously, formerly: ³*chai*² *ˌseng*, before, then; ⁴*ˌseng ˌpong* or *ˌseng ch'ëü*ˀ or *ˌseng ˌhui* or *ˌseng tó*ˀ the former time, the previous occasion; ⁵*ˌseng ˁkwi nik*, a few days ago; ⁶*ˌseng au*² before and behind; ⁷*ˌseng ˁch'iu*, previously; ⁸*ˌseng au*² *ˁch'iu*, just before or after; ⁹*ˌseng ˌt'iāng*, "former road"—a former literary degree; ¹⁰*ˌseng sié*ˀ *ˌhu ˌch'á*, (they were) husband and wife in a former life; *ˌseng au*² (used for *ˌsi haiu*²) time, period; *ˁchiă ˌseng au*² at this time.

盛 Shêng. Ch'êng. Abundant, affluent, exuberant; flourishing, blooming, prosperous; a surname; used in complimentary phrases: also read *ˌsing*, q. v.: ¹¹*seng*² *ˌching*, your great kindness; ¹²*seng*² *ˌsoi*, to flourish and decay, as empires; COM., ¹³*seng*² *ˌking*, Shingking, Moukden; *seng*² *ha*² the excessive heat of summer.

甚 Shên. Social delights; excessive pleasure; very, extremely, in the highest degree: ¹⁴*ˁt'ai*ˀ *seng*² excessive; ¹⁵*ˁi seng*² has reached the highest pitch; *pek*, *ˁiu seng*² *ˌyong*, there is even worse than this; ¹⁶*seng*² *ˁhó*, very good; COLL., *seng*² *ˌmó ˌtung ˌsi*, what is it? —a phrase in imitation of the Court dialect.

葚 椹 Shên. The berries of the mulberry, called *ˌsong seng*²; the 2d, read *ˌt'ing*, means a kind of ax; a staff.

腎 Hsien. The kidneys, said to be connected with water and to preside over strength, one of the five viscera; the kidneys of beasts are called *ˌyeu*; the gizzard of fowls (called *keng*² in the coll.); to lead; hard, firm: used for *leng*² in the coll. q. v.: ¹⁷*nôi*² *seng*² the kidneys; ¹⁸*ngwói*² *seng*² the testes; ¹⁹*seng*² *ˌnong*, the scrotum: COM., ²⁰*seng*² *k'e*ˀ *wong*² the kidneys in a healthy state; *seng*² *ˁchwi chëük*, the semen abundant—indicates vigor.

乘 Shêng. Ch'êng. A numerative of chariots; a carriage, a chariot; a span of horses, a team of four horses: also read *ˌsing*, q. v.

剩 賸 Shêng. The 2d also read *eng*²: a remainder, residue, overplus; fragments, leavings, in which senses *tiong*² is the coll. equivalent; not only; to retain, to keep back: ²¹*ˁiu seng*² there is

¹囟門 ²砍囟 ³在前 ⁴前番 ⁵前幾日 ⁶前後 ⁷前手 ⁸後前手 前程 ¹⁰前世夫妻 ¹¹盛情 ¹²盛衰 ¹³盛京 ¹⁴太甚 ¹⁵已甚 ¹⁶甚好 ¹⁷內腎 ¹⁸外腎 ¹⁹腎囊 ²⁰腎氣旺 ²¹有剩〇

something over; COM., ˏū seng[2] the remainder, what is over.

阱穽[2] Ching. A pit, a pitfall, a hole to catch beasts in; to fall into: hang[2] seng[2] to tumble into a pit.

慎[2] 愼[2] Shên. To be careful, to act seriously; attentive, diligent, cautious; sincere; still, quiet; to consider intently: [1]seng[2] tëüng[2] circumspect; [2]pok, seng[2] heedless; COM., [3]king seng[2] careful, attentive.

Seng[2]. A coll. euphonic prefix, as in seng[2] sëüng[2] to put on one's clothes; seng[2] siong[2] to enter an account, as in a ledger.

(728) Sĕng.

ˏ雙 双 Shuang. A pair, a brace, a couple, two; a match, an equal, mates; to mate, to go with; five acres of land: COM., [4]ˏsĕng ˏch'ing, both parents; [5]ˏsĕng ˏchiong, both parents living; [6]ˏsĕng 'hi, the character 'hi (joy) written double, as on bridal sedans, etc.; [7]ˏsĕng ˏsang, twins; [8]ˏsĕng nik, the even days of a month; [9]ˏsĕng ˏloi, a double crown—on the head; [10]ˏsĕng pwoi[2] two-fold; [11]ˏsĕng kwoi[2] ˏting, a double-headed nail; COLL., [12]ˏsĕng ˏk'iă 'ma, to "ride double"—a double use, or meaning; ˏsĕng 'ch'iu niăh, tioh, lang[2] ˏt'au ˏmwang, to seize two eels with the hands; *met.*, to undertake two employments at once.

ˏ鬆 Sung. Read ˏsung; coll. ˏsĕng: relaxed, loose, slack; not strict; easy, not anxious; loose, straight and smooth, not tangled, as the hair: [13]ˏsĕng ˏsĕng, loose, slack; not urgent; [14]pwoh, tek, ˏsĕng, tied loosely; [15]ˏsing 'yă ˏsĕng, the mind very easy about it; [16]ˏsĕng taĕng[2] in funds, moneyed; in very good health or spirits.

'Sĕng. A coll. word: to push or shake violently: 'sĕng ch'ok, to push open the door and get out; 'sĕng sioh, a[2] give it a shaking; 'sĕng ˏwong ˏhing, dizzy from being shaken; móh, 'sing 'sĕng 'sĕng, don't joggle so!

(729) Seu.

ˏ搜 捜 Sou. To search, as the police do; to throw about in searching; to investigate, to search or find out; to inquire into the meaning of, to examine a book; swift; to assemble: COM., [17]ˏseu ˏsing, to search, as for secreted things; [18]ˏseu ch'ek, to search a thief; [19]ˏseu 'kiĕng or ˏseu ˏsing, to search the person; [20]ˏseu ˏchong, to search for stolen goods; COLL., ˏseu ˏsing wak, k'aĕng[2] he is a sharp searcher.

ˏ颼 Sou. The sound of the wind; windy, chilly: [21]ˏseu ˏseu, a blast, a gust.

ˏ艘 Sou. Also read ˏsieu and ˏsó: a general term for vessels, a boat, a junk, a ship; [22]ˏseu chiék, a boat and oars.

[1]慎重 [2]不慎 [3]謹慎 [4]雙親 [5]雙全 [6]雙喜 [7]雙生 [8]雙日 [9]雙螺 [10]雙倍 [11]雙鬐釘 [12]雙跨馬 [13]鬆鬆 [14]縛的鬆 [15]心野鬆 [16]鬆動 [17]搜尋 [18]搜賊 [19]搜撿 [20]搜贓 [21]颼颼 [22]艘楫

廋 ʻSou. Interchanged with the next: to hide, to conceal; to hide away.

㛐 ʻSou. Also read ʻseu: to secrete, to conceal; to search, as a house for hidden things; to examine into; crafty: [1]ʻseu ˛kiu, to seek.

蒐 ʻSou. A plant used in dyeing red; it may be a Rubia or madder; one says, perhaps a sort of Rumex; the spring hunt, when pregnant animals are not killed; to assemble for a hunt; to hide, to screen.

筲 ʻShao. A basket, a hamper to carry grain in: [2]ʻteu ˛seu ˛chi ˛ing, a man of the peck and hamper—a rustic, one who only knows about eating.

˛*Seu.* A coll. word: to mix in, as water with flour to make dough: ˛*seu ch'á'* to mix rice flour; ˛*seu* ˛*t'u* ˛*chiong*, to make mortar.

˛*Seu.* A coll. word: similar to ˛*si*; each, every one, severally: ˛*seu sioh*, *chiăh*, one by one; ˛*seu sioh*, ʻ*chio*, family by family.

叟 傻 ʻSou. An old man, a senior, a venerable person, Sire! [3]ʻ*ló* ʻ*seu*, venerable Sir! Read ˛*seu*, as in ˛*seu* ˛*seu*, the sound of washing rice, in which sense the same as the next.

溲 ʻSou. To steep in water, to soak, to macerate; to infuse, to soak meal in flour. Read ˛*seu*: the sound of scouring rice; to dilute wine; to urinate; full, abundant: [4]ʻ˛*seu* ˛*piéng*, to urinate.

瞍 ʻSou. Blind, sightless, as an eye without a pupil: [5]ʻ*ku* ʻ*seu*, blind Sou, the name of Shun's father.

藪 ʻSou. A large, marshy preserve, in which game is kept and fish reared; a thicket; fat, rich, profitable. Read *so'*: a measure of 16 ʻ*tau*: [6]*'lëü' so'* a sort of pad for carrying burdens on the head.

ʻ*Seu.* A coll. word, analogous to ʻ*teu*: to strike with a limber thing, to whip, to switch: ʻ*seu má'* *tioh*, failed to hit; ʻ*seu sioh*, ˛*piéng*, to give a stroke with a whip.

ʻ*Seu.* A coll. word: a stripe, a scratch; a crack, a split, a rent: *k'ëüng' sioh*, ʻ*seu*, a scratch, as on the face; *pek*, *sioh*, ʻ*seu*, a split, cracked.

秀 Hsiu. *seu'* Sometimes interchanged with the next: grain flowering and in seed; gay, splendid, beautiful; to flourish; elegant, adorned; fair, comely; accomplished; the first, the best: [7]*seu' k'e'* elegant in manners; beautiful, as a landscape; [8]*taik*, ˛*t'iéng té'* ˛*chi seu'* (man is) the best in heaven and earth; com., [9]*seu' maiu'* green and charming, as fields; [10]*seu'* ˛*chai* (coll. *seu'* ˛*choi*), "accomplished talent"—a Siutsai graduate; [11]*chong' seu'* excellent, virtuous; a fine person; [12]˛*ch'ing seu'* finely chiseled, as the features; clear and perfect, as gems, flowers, etc.

1 廋求 2 斗筲之人 3 老叟 4 溲便 5 瞽瞍 6 寠藪 7 秀氣 8 得天地之秀 9 秀茂 10 秀才 11 俊秀 12 清秀

繡 **綉**ʾ To embroider, to adorn with colored silks; ornamented, worked; to embellish, to variegate; to illustrate with prints; in the coll. to mend rents, to darn: [1]*seuʾ ˓küng*, an embroidered handkerchief or scarf; COM., [2]*˓mieu ˓lüng seuʾ hong²* to embroider dragons and phenixes; *met.*, to write fine essays; to take needless pains, as in coarse work; COM., [3]*seuʾ ˓hwa*, to embroider flowers; [4]*seuʾ ˓lüng ˓pó*, to embroider a robe with dragons; COLL., [5]*seuʾ ʻpwo*, to darn; [6]*˓pá seuʾ tóh*, to keep a darning table or stand (in the street); [7]*seuʾ ʻpwo ʻkʻi ˓iu*, to darn, and remove grease spots.
Hsiu.

琇ʾ A pretty gem or colored stone; pebbles which may be used for ear-drops.
Hsiu.

鏽 **銹**ʾ The rust of iron, steel, tin, etc.: oxides: [8]*ʻkeng seuʾ* the dull, green tarnish on mirrors.
Hsiu.

獸ʾ A beast, a hairy brute; quadrupeds, wild animals: COM., [9]*˓kʻing seuʾ* birds and beasts; [10]*ʻyă seuʾ* wild beasts; [11]*˓ing miéng² seuʾ ˓sing*, a human face and a brute's heart—cruel, ferocious; *ʻngu seuʾ* the five animals, tiger, panther, lion, elephant, and unicorn.
Shou.

Seuʾ. A coll. word: the nest of a bird; a lair, a kennel, a sleeping place of domestic animals.

宿ʾ A constellation, the stars: also read *söük*, q. v.: COM., [12]*ne² sek˓ paik˓ seuʾ* the 28 zodiacal constellations; [13]*˓sing seuʾ* stars.
Hsü. Hsiu. Su.

首ʾ To confess a crime; to acknowledge, to take upon one's self; to place at the head: also read *ʻsiu*, q. v.: COM., [14]*chʻok˓ seuʾ* to lodge information, to inform against.
Shou.

狩ʾ A hunting dog; to hunt in winter on grounds burnt over: [15]*˓sung seuʾ* an imperial tour of inspection.
Shou.

˓Seu. A coll. word: constantly, frequently, habitually: *˓seu ˓seu chóʾ* to do constantly; *˓seu tek˓ ëüng²* in constant use; *˓tó ˓seu*, more frequently.

˓Seu. A coll. word: pure, unmixed, uniform; medium in size or quality; smaller: *˓seu ˓seu pwo²* even, regular steps; *˓seu ˓seu twai²* of the same uniform size; *˓tüng ˓tüng ˓seu ˓seu*, medium, as quality of cloth; *˓seu ˓niă nóiʾ* a little smaller; *˓seu sioh˓ hó²* (or *˓chong*), a size smaller.

壽² Age, longevity, long life; *met.*, birthday of the aged; the dead: [16]*˓tiong seu²* aged; [17]*˓tüng seu²* medium old age, about 70 years; COM., [18]*seu² ˓ngwong*, or [19]*seu² soʾ* one's life, length of life; *seu² tangʾ* a birthday anniversary; *paiʾ seu²* to congratulate one on his birthday; *seu² ˓sing*, a portrait, the head of which is painted when the person is 40 or 50
Shou.

1 繡	繡	4 繡	補	7 繡	8 鏡	10 野	獸	八	14 出	16 長	18 壽
巾	鳳	龍	6 排	補	鏽	獸	心	宿	首	壽	元
2 描	3 繡	袍	繡	起	9 禽	11 人	12 二	13 星	15 巡	17 中	19 壽
龍	花	5 繡	棹	油	獸	面	十	宿	狩	壽	數

years old, and the body after death; [1]*seu*[2] *ˏi*, grave-clothes; [2]*seu*[2] *ʻpeng*, coffin-boards; [3]*ˏkó seu*[2] what is your age?—said to those advanced in life; [4]*ˏsiong seu*[2] a birthday anniversary between the tens; [5]*siong*[2] *seu*[2] to enter the class of the aged—a woman at 40, a man at 50, years of age; [6]*Seu*[2] *ˏning*, a district of the Fuhning prefecture in Fookien.

受[2] Shou. To receive, to accept of; to continue, to succeed, to inherit; a form of the passive, to bear, to endure, to suffer; susceptible of; a charge, a trust: COM., [7]*pok, ʻkang seu*[2] I dare not accept it—a polite phrase; *ʻiu hok, pok, ˏti seu*[2] *ëüng*[2] to have happiness and not know how to use it; [8]*seu*[2] *kaiʼ* to receive the precepts or inhibitions—become a Bonze; [9]*seu*[2] *kauʼ* to be instructed, docile; [10]*seu*[2] *ˏsiong*, injured, bruised; [11]*seu*[2] *kʻeʼ* to become angry; [12]*seu*[2] *chóiʼ* or *seu*[2] *ˏhing*, to be punished; [13]*seu*[2] *ʻkʻu*, to suffer; COLL., *seu*[2] *ˏnëng chiék, chiéʼ* (or *ˏkʻwa a*[2]), to be subject to another's control; *seu*[2] *sioh, pok, kʻeʼ* to have a fit of passion; *má*[2] *seu*[2] *tek, kʻóʼ* can't endure it.

授[2] Shou. To give, to communicate, to deliver to: *seu*[2] *seu*[2] receiving and giving; COM., *ˏtiong seu*[2] to impart, as instruction.

綬[2] Shou. The cord to which a seal is attached; a bag for a seal; cord of a tent or curtain; the ties of knee-pads.

袖[2] **褎**[2] Hsiu. The sleeve, the cuff; to put into the sleeve: the 1st used for the coll. *ʻwong* and the 2d also read *eu*[2] q. v.: [14]*ʻling seu*[2] "collar and sleeve"—a chief, one who commands; COM., [15]*seu*[2] *ʻkʻau*, a cuff, folded over and shaped like a horse's hoof; *seu*[2] *ʻchʻiu ˏpong ˏkwang*, to fold the hands and look on.

岫[2] Hsiu. A cave or den in a hill; a gorge, a defile, a ravine.

(730) **Sëü.**

思ʼ Ssu. To be anxious; to have pure intentions, pure-minded: also read *ˏsü*, q. v.: COM., [16]*eʼ sëüʼ* thoughts, intentions; idea, purport; COLL., [17]*ng*[2] *ʻhó eʼ sëüʼ* disreputable, ashamed, put to the blush.

恕ʼ Shu. Benevolent, indulgent, gracious; to excuse others, to treat others as one wishes to be treated; to pardon; to bear with; sympathizing: [18]*ˏtüng sëüʼ* sincere and forgiving, kind-hearted; COM., *ˏnieu sëüʼ* to be indulgent, to excuse; *ˏkʻwang sëüʼ* lenient, not very strict.

庶ʼ Shu. A multitude, many, the people; all; near, nearly, about so; fat and sleek; a concubine: [19]*sëüʼ uk,* all things; *ˏlá sëüʼ* or *sëüʼ ˏming*, the people; [20]*sëüʼ ˏki*, or *sëüʼ ˏhu*, almost, probably; COM., *sëüʼ ʻmu*, the concubine, as the children of the first wife call her; *sëüʼ ʻchü*, or *sëüʼ ˏnang*, sons of a concubine; [22]*sëüʼ kek, sëüʼ* a Hanlin graduate.

[1]壽	[3]高	[5]上	[7]不	戒	傷	罪	袖	思	思	物	母
衣	壽	壽	敢	[9]受	[11]受	[13]受	[15]袖	[17]伓	[18]忠	[20]庶	[22]庶
[2]壽	[4]常	[6]壽	受	教	氣	苦	口	好	恕	幾	吉
板	壽	甯	[8]受	[10]受	[12]受	[14]領	[16]意	意	[19]庶	[21]庶	士

試' Shih. To use; to try, to essay, to test, to experiment; to compare and find out; to examine, as literary graduates; a trial, a test: used for the coll. *ch'e'* and *se'* q. v.: [1]*'siong sëü'* to taste, to test, to try; [2]*'t'ang' sëü'* to make trial of; [3]*sëü' ,tiong*, (coll. *,k'wo ,tiong*), an examination for Küjin; COM., [4]*sëü' ëüng'* employed on trial, as Chinsz' graduates holding the office of district magistrate.

使' Shih. A messenger; one sent with presents to inquire; an agent: also read *'sü* and in the coll. *sai'* q. v.: [5]*ch'ok, sëü'* an envoy, one sent on official business; [6]*sëü' ,sing*, a legate, a commissioner; COM., [7]*sëü' 'chiä*, one sent; also used for angels; [8]*,hu sëü'* the messengers of an idol.

泗' Ssu. Mucus, snivel; a large feeder of the Grand Canal near Yenchou-fu, Shantung: *t'á' sëü' ,pong ,tó*, tears and snivel flowing profusely; COM., [9]*sëü' ,chiu huk,* a Budh worshiped in shrines at street-corners.

駟' Ssu. A team of four horses abreast: [10]*sëü' 'ma ,kü*, a chariot and four; [11]*,t'iéng sëü'* the stars *b, o, p, r*, in Scorpio; *sëü' seng'* a war-chariot; COM., *sëü' 'ma ,nang ,twi*, hard to catch a four-horse team; *met.*, what's said can't be unsaid—hence be careful.

四' **肆**' **乂**' Ssu. Four; everywhere; the second is the complex, and the third the abbreviated, form: in the coll. read *se'* q. v.: COM., [12]*sëü' ,hwong*, or *sëü' ch'ëü'* the four points, everywhere; [13]*sëü' ,chü*, the Four Books; [14]*sëü' ,ch'iong*, Sz'chuen; *sëü' ,chié*, the legs and arms; [15]*sëü' tai ' ,king ,kong*, the rulers of the four quarters—gigantic guards in the front of Budhist temples; *sëü' kwo' lük, ,liéng*, very ready or fluent in speech; *sëü' 'ma pwoh, ,tá*, the four horses' hoofs tied together; *met.*, strict conditions; *sëü' ,t'ung paik, tak,* has versatile talents, knows everything.

肆' Ssu. To expand, to spread out; to exert to the utmost; great, large; reckless, excessive, abandoned, dissolute, unrestrained; position of the heavenly bodies; to decline, to refuse; to arrange as goods; a shop, a market-place; to expose, as the bodies of executed criminals; abruptly; just now: [16]*'chiu sëü'* a wine-shop; *sëü' ,yong*, to arrange a feast; *ch'e' sëü'* a market, bazaar; COM., [17]*hwong' sëü'* disorderly, profligate.

賜' **賜**' Ssu. Tz'u. To confer, to bestow, as a superior or the Emperor does; an imperial grant; a favor, a benefit: [18]*sëü' muk,* to let one look at; [19]*,sing sëü'* to receive a favor; COM., [20]*,k'ing sëü'* an imperial gift; [21]*,t'iéng ,kwang sëü' hok,* may the celestial powers send blessings; *sëü' 'ting*

1嘗試 2探試 3試場 4試用 5出使 6使臣 7使者 8符使 9泗洲佛 10駟馬車 11天駟 12四方 13四書 14四川 15四大金剛 16酒肆 17放肆 18賜目 19承賜 20欽賜 21天官賜福

tai to bestow the button; [1]*sëü pek* to give a piece of silk, as to a condemned officer to hang himself with.

絮 Hsü. Nü. Poor, coarse silk; refuse silk or cotton, left after the best is gathered; to mix, to mingle, to compound; to repeat, to reiterate, verbose; pendent: [2]*sëü ngü*, tautology; *t'ó t'ó sëü sëü* loquacious, jabbering; [3]*liu sëü* catkins of the willow.

弒 Shih. To murder a superior, as a king or father: [4]*sëü ho* a parricide; [5]*sëü kung*, a regicide.

戍 Shu. This character must be distinguished from *sok* (the 11th of the 12 branches): to guard frontiers; to defend against incursions; a sort of military punishment imposed on exiles; soldiers on guard: [6]*sëü piëng*, to guard a frontier.

Sëü. A coll. word, as in *t'ëng sëü* eaten or perforated by insects, as fruit, clothes, wood; *sëü sioh k'ëng*, a hole eaten in it.

士 Shih. A learned man a doctor, a scholar; an appellative of men in general, gentlemen; soldiers, officers, statesmen; a manager, a superintendent; the 33d radical: [7]*tai hok sëü* ministers of state; [8]*sëü chok*, a soldier; [9]*kü sëü* a private scholar; [10]*sëü chü*, teachers, literati; COM., [11]*ming sëü* a good scholar; [12]*cheng sëü* a doctor—the 3d literary degree; *tai sëü taing* a temple to Kwan yin; [13]*sëü nung kung siong*, literati, husbandmen, artisans, merchants.

仕 Shih. To act as a magistrate, to serve, to fill a station or an office; an officer: [14]*ch'ok sëü* to assume office; [15]*te sëü* to resign a public station; *sëü hwang chi ka*, an honorable family.

食 Shih. Ssu. To give food to, to feed; to bring up, to rear, to nourish; food, provisions: also read *sik* q. v.

飼 飤 Ssu. Interchanged with the last: to set food before, to give to eat; to nourish, to rear, as animals; food, provisions, eatables.

笥 Ssu. A vessel to contain rice or clothes, a basket, a hamper: [16]*chü sëü* a portable book and writing-case; [17]*hok sëü* learned, well read.

伺 Ssu. Tz'u. To wait upon, to wait for; to spy, to examine closely: COM., [18]*sëü hau* to attend, to wait upon; [19]*sëü chiu*, to wait (on guests) at a feast.

嗣 Ssu. To connect, as in a family line; to adopt; to inherit; children, posterity, heirs; an adopted heir; to practice, to learn; hereafter, till: [20]*sëü hau* hereafter; *kié sëü* an adopted heir; [21]*sëü oi* to succeed to the throne; COM., [22]*hau sëü* descendants; *lik sëü* to adopt an heir; *chiok sëü* a family cut off or failing; *u*

1 賜帛 2 絮語 3 柳絮 4 弒父 5 弒君 6 戍邊 7 大學士〇 8 士卒 9 居士 10 士子 11 名士 12 進士 13 士農工商 14 出仕 15 致仕 16 書笥 17 學笥 18 伺候 19 伺酒 20 嗣後 21 嗣位 22 後嗣

sĕü² *₍tang*, an orbate altar—small temple or shrine built by a larger one; ¹*sĕü² ho²* adopted father.

祀² Ssu. To sacrifice to gods, devils, or departed spirits; sacrifical; a year; like, as if: in the coll. read *sai²* q. v.: ²*sĕü² ʿchu*, to worship ancestors; ³*₍ngwong sĕü²* the first year of a reign; COM., ⁴*sĕü² ʿtiĕng*, sacrificial rites; ⁵*₍u sĕü²* no descendant.

巳² Ssu. The sixth of the 12 branches or horary characters, denoted by a snake, 9—11, A. M.: COM., ⁶*sĕü² ₍ch'ĕ*, or *sĕü² ₍si ₍ch'ĕ*, 9 A. M.; ⁷*sĕü² chiăng²* 10 A. M.

澍² Shu. Moistened, well watered; to fertilize by rains; timely rain; rushing waters.

樹² 樹² 尌² Shu. A tree, plants that grow erect, plants in general; to plant; to set up, to establish, to place a screen, in which sense the next is more commonly used: ⁸*sĕü² ʿchü*, the heir-apparent of a feudatory; ⁹*sĕü² ₍ling*, a grove, a forest; ¹⁰*sĕü² muk₎* trees; COM., ¹¹*ʿku sĕü²* an old tree.

豎² 竪² Shu. To erect, to set up, to plant; to raise on one end, to set upright; to fix, to establish; chaste, upright, correct, principled; a lad, a waiting boy; a mean, low person: ¹²*nói² sĕü²* eunuchs; ¹³*muk₎ sĕü²* a herd boy; ¹⁴*sĕü² ʿchü*, menials.

藇² Hsü. Good, mellow, pleasant, as liquor. Read *₍ü*: a kind of fragrant plant.

鱮² Hsü. The tench or roach; a large species of carp, found in Kiangsu.

嶼² 嶼² Hsü. Yü. An island; an islet or rising land surrounded by water; detached hills near a shore: COM., ¹⁵*ʿku laung² sĕü²* the island of Kulangsu near Amoy.

似² 佀² Ssu. Shih. Like, alike, similar; as, as if, as it were, resembling, seeming; to have the aspect of: ¹⁶*sĕü² pok₎ sĕü²* is it like or not? ¹⁷*sĕü² se² ₍i ₍hi*, appearing right, but still wrong; COM., ¹⁸*₍siong sĕü²* to be alike, to resemble each other.

姒² Ssu. The wife of an elder brother: ¹⁹*sĕü² tá²* sisters-in-law; ²⁰*sĕü² ho²* an old lady; *t'ai² sĕü²* the wife of Wan Wang.

耜² Ssu. A plowshare; the part of a plow that enters the ground, a colter; a plow.

俟² 竢² Ssu. To wait, to stay; to wait upon; to look for, to expect; to prepare for; until, expecting: ²¹*sĕü² ha² ngwok₎* till next month.

涘² Ssu. The banks of a stream; the shores or mouths of rivers.

¹嗣父 ²祀祖 ³元祀 ⁴祀典 ⁵無祀 ⁶巳初 ⁷巳正 ⁸樹子 ⁹樹林 ¹⁰樹木 ¹¹古樹 ¹²內豎 ¹³牧豎 ¹⁴豎子 ¹⁵鼓浪嶼 ¹⁶似不似 ¹⁷似是而非 ¹⁸相似 ¹⁹姒娣 ²⁰姒婦 ²¹俟下月 ○

緒 Hsü. The end of the thread in a cocoon; the clue or beginning of a ball; a thread, a hint, a clue; the commencement; the rule or guide to what follows; the course of events; what is handed down, a calling, a patrimony; to examine, to perfect what another began; to succeed, as to an office: [1]ˌ*t'eu sëü'* the beginning, first principles; [2]*sëü'* ˌ*ü*, a remnant, addenda, fag end; [3]ˌ*ki sëü'* a patrimony.

事 Shih. An affair, a matter, a concern; business, occupation, pursuit, service; an action, anything done; to serve, to obey; to manage an affair: COM., [4]*chek, sëü'* to occupy a station; a manager; a deacon; [5]*sëü' sik,* the facts of an affair or narrative; [6]*sëü'* ˌ*ching*, the circumstances; an affair; [7]*sëü'* ˋ*kang*, but little business; [8]ˌ*ka sëü'* domestic affairs; [9]ˌ*seng sëü'* to breed trouble; [10]*taung' sëü'* to regard as important; *sëü' pok,* ˌ*mwoang* ˌ*ching*, there can be no deception as to the real truth; COLL., *ng' chié' sëü'* not much, a very trifling amount.

序 Hsü. Eastern and western walls; an order, a series; the order of precedence, to follow in order; a preface, an exordium; a school, a college; an asylum for the aged: [11]ˋ*tiong eu'* ˋ*iu sëü'* the rule of precedence among seniors and juniors; [12]COM., *sëü'* ˌ*t'au*, a preface; [13]*sëü'* ˋ*ch'i*, according to ages; [14]ˋ*ch'ëü' sëü'* in order, seriatim.

敘 叙 敍 Hsü. Like the preceding: to arrange, to set in order; series, order, rank; to converse, to discourse about: [15]*sëü'* ˌ*tang*, to converse, to chat; [16]*ngié' sëü'* to deliberate about (rewards); [17]ˌ*t'iëng sëü'* the five social relations; COM., *sëü' sio'* a "thank-feast," as for those who made presents, but could not come on the set day.

(731) Sëüh.

Sëüh,. A coll. word: to suck, to draw into the mouth: *sëüh,* ˋ*tiê*, to suck into (the mouth); *sëüh, sëüh, kieu'* noise made in thus eating.

(732) Sëük.

蓿 Su. A grass for cattle: [18]*muk, sëük,* a sort of clover, grown for fodder.

宿 Su. Hsü. Hsiu. Used for the next in the sense of early: a halting place every thirty ˋ*li*; a lodging place; a night's rest, a lodging; to lodge, to sojourn; former, old, continued; in the coll. moldy, sour, turned, musty, as food; rotted, as manure; spoiled, water-soaked: also read *seu'* q. v.: [19]*sëük, wong'* to cherish hatred for; [20]*sëük,* ˌ*siu*, old enemies; COM., [21]*sëük, sik,* stoppage of food, food indigested; COLL., *sëük, sioh,* ˌ*pwo*, to stay a night; to put to soak over night; *sëük, pong'* to rot manure; [22]*sëük,* ˋ*chwi*, water-soaked, as goods; [23]*sëük, po'* rotted, moldy; *sëük, sëük, e'* a musty smell.

1 頭緒 2 緒餘 3 基緒 4 執事 5 事實 6 事情 7 事簡 8 家事 9 生事 10 當事 11 長幼有序 12 序頭 13 序齒 14 次序 15 敍談 16 議叙 17 天敍 18 苜蓿 19 宿怨 20 宿仇 21 宿食 22 宿水 23 宿腐

福州方言拼音字典

夙, Su. Hsü. Early in the morning, the early dawn; morn, morning; early: [1]*'sëük, yâ'* morn and eve, early and late.

肅, Su. Respectful, reverential; still, awed; fear, caution; to recede, to retire respectfully; severe, majestic; to receive guests politely; hasty, rapid: [2]*'ngiéng sëük,* dignified, awe-inspiring; [3]*sëük, sëük,* quick; decorous, respectful; COM., [4]*,twang sëük, pai'* my respectful salutations — words used on a lady's card of invitation; [5]*sëük, cheng' ,hui pié'* stand aside reverently—words in temples and on staves borne before idols and officers. Read *seu':* pure, clear; reverential.

驌, Su. A famous charger, called [6]*sëük, ,song,* the Bucephalus of ancient Chinese history.

倏 倐, Shu. A sudden change, on a sudden, abruptly, quickly: [7]*sëük, hwok,* hastily, unexpectedly.

俶, Shu. To begin; to do, to act, to perform; good, excellent; also to repair, to arrange, to put in order.

淑, Shu. Interchanged with the last in the sense of good, excellent; clear, limpid; correct, virtuous: [8]*sëük, ,ing,* a virtuous man; a wife of an officer of the 3d class; [9]*sëük, taik,* female virtue; [10]*sëük, k'e'* fine, balmy weather, as in spring.

菽, Ssu. A general term for pulse, the edible kinds of pulse; [11]*sëük, 'chwi ,sing ,hwang,* with pulse and water please (one's parents), as the poor do.

踧, Shu. To walk with circumspection: [12]*sëük, sek,* (or *chek,*), to walk carefully. Read *tik,:* to walk along, as on smooth ground.

叔, Shu. To collect, to amass, to hoard; a father's younger brother, an uncle; a respectful term for those who are older, for acquaintances, and for strangers casually met; a wife calls her husband's younger brother *sëük,:* in the coll. read *chëük,* q. v.: [13]*sëük, tik,* uncles and nephews; [14]*'ló sëük,* a father's old friend; [15]*sëük, ,tai,* a family friend; [16]*'sieu sëük,* a husband's younger brother; [17]*sëük, ho'* and *sëük, 'mu,* junior paternal uncle and his wife.

粟, Su. Hsü. A general name for glumaceous grain; rice in the husk; also the seed of panic grass; rent in kind, tithes: [18]*,t'ü sëük,* produce of public fields paid as tax; [19]*ok, sëük,* household taxes; COLL., *,eng sëük, ,hwa,* the poppy.

Sëük,. A coll. word: to become old, aged, old-looking; mature, fully ripe, as grain: *pwang' 'ló sëük,* middle-aged, about 40 years old; *,sang tek, sëük,* old-looking, prematurely old.

---

[1]夙夜 [2]嚴肅 [3]肅肅 [4]端肅 拜 [5]肅靜迴 避 [6]驌驦〇 [7]倏忽 [8]淑人 [9]淑德 [10]淑氣 [11]菽水承歡 [12]踧踖 [13]叔姪 [14]老叔 [15]叔臺 [16]小叔 [17]叔父 [18]鋤粟〇 [19]屋粟〇

(733) Sëüng.

訟[1] Sung. Interchanged with the next: to contend in court, to litigate, to demand justice; litigation, pleadings, legal strife; law cases; to sing, to chant; the 6th of the 64 diagrams: [1]*sëüng² ˏsü*, an indictment; [2]*ˏcheng sëüng²* disputes, wranglings; [3]*t'eng' sëüng²* to hear a case; [4]*sek, sëüng²* to settle or quash a case; *chëü² sëüng²* self reproach.

誦[2] Sung. To hum, to recite over; recitative, chanting, as priests; to read in a humming tone; to dispute, to calumniate: [5]*sëüng² ˏking*, to chant a liturgy; [6]*sëüng² t'uk,* to recite in a singing tone; [7]*pwói² sëüng²* to say memoriter.

頌[2] Sung. The face, the countenance; easy, free, public; to praise publicly, to proclaim one's virtues, to eulogize; name of a musical instrument like the *k'eng'*: *sëüng² ˏki taik,* to eulogize his virtues; [8]*sëüng² chang'* to laud.

Sëüng². A coll. word: to put on, to dress, to clothe; to wear: *sëüng² ˏi ˏsiong,* to put on clothes; *sëüng² k'aung' ˏi ˏsiong,* night-clothes; *sëüng² tai'* to wear clothes and cap; *sëüng² seü² ˏi,* to dress a corpse; *ˏmó sëüng²* nothing to wear.

(734) Si.

司 Ssu. A manager, a commissioner, an officer: to control, to rule, to manage, to supervise; a township, a subdivision of a *kaing²* or district: also read *ˏsü* and in the coll. *ˏsa,* q. v.: COM., [9]*'pwo' ˏsi,* the provincial treasurer; [10]*'ang' ˏsi,* the criminal judge; [11]*ˏt'ung cheng' ˏsi,* Court of Representation or Memorials at Peking; [12]*ˏsung 'kiéng ˏsi,* a township-judge; [13]*'iu ˏsi,* judges, magistrates; COLL., *p'ah, ˏkwang ˏsi,* to go to law; *ˏsi sau'* used for *'pa 'chung,* a centurion.

伺 飼 To ruminate, to chew the cud.

尸 Shih. A corpse, for which the next is commonly used; an image, an effigy; useless like a statue, making a sinecure of; to arrange; to order, to preside over; the 44th radical: [14]*ˏsi oi² so' ˏch'wong,* to neglect the office but get the pay.

屍 Shih. A dead body, a corpse laid out: COM., [15]*ˏsing ˏsi,* or *'si ˏsi,* or [16]*ˏsi 'siu,* a corpse; *ˏsi ˏhai,* a skeleton, corpse; *ngiéng² ˏsi,* to hold an inquest; [17]*chioh, ˏsi ˏhwang ˏhung,* "borrow another corpse and come to life"—as one who revives when apparently dead; [18]*ˏié ˏsi ˏtu lai²* to implicate one by laying a corpse at his door; COLL., *ˏsi ˏhai pó² lo'* to expose a corpse to the sun and dew.

鳲 Shih. The wood pigeon, or turtle dove, called [19]*ˏsi ˏk'iu,* but more commonly [20]*ˏpang ˏk'iu.*

1 訟詞　2 爭訟　3 聽訟　4 息訟　5 誦經　6 誦讀　7 背誦　8 頌贊　9 布司　10 按司　11 通政司　12 巡檢司　13 有司　14 尸位素餐　15 身屍　16 屍首　17 借屍還魂　18 移屍圖賴　19 鳲鳩　20 斑鳩

絲 ‚**絲** Ssu. Silk as made by the silk-worm, raw silk; silken, flossy; silk in general; fine, small, minute; a hundredth part, as of a cash; stringed instruments of music: [1]*‚si tëük*, *ʻkwang ‚hiéng*, stringed and wind instruments; COM., [2]*‚hu ‚si*, Kiangsu silk; [3]*tʻu ‚si*, native silk; [4]*‚si pwoʼ* or *‚si ‚kiäng pwoʼ hoiʼ* a fabric, of which the warp is silk, and the woof, cotton; [5]*‚si ‚miéng*, silk-batting; [6]*‚tëng ‚si*, fine copper wire; [7]*‚iu ‚si*, the hair-spring of a watch; COLL., *‚si tek*, *ʻkiäng*, a little; *‚si ‚hó ‚mó tangʼ* not the least error.

蓍 Shih. A sort of labiate plant like milfoil or verbena, anciently used in divination; its stalks also served for hair-pins.

‚**詩** Shih. The feelings expressed in set words, poetry, verse, rhymes; an ode, a poem, a hymn; to hold, to receive: [8]*‚si ‚ing*, a poet; COM., [9]*‚si ‚king*, the Book of Odes; [10]*‚nging ‚si*, to hum verses; to make poetry; [11]*‚tá ‚si*, to write verses impromptu; [12]*‚si ongʼ* rhyme; *‚si ‚ung cheʼ* poems, essays and penmanship—in which students should be versed; [13]*‚si ‚chü*, the books of Odes and Records; the classics; COLL., *‚si pah*, a bard.

‚Si. A coll. euphonic prefix, as in *‚si ‚só ‚só* (or *‚si ‚só ‚só*), to move the bill about, as a duck eating in the water; to move the eyes about; to turn the head and peer.

ʻ**死** Ssu. Read *ʻsü;* coll. *ʻsi:* to die, to decease; death, dying; deadly, fatal; dangerous, desperate; fearless, to the death; pale, ghastly: [14]*ʻsi ‚si*, a corpse; *ʻsi tioh, ‚nĕng*, there is a death (in the family); [15]*ʻsi chiok*, all died off; *ʻsi chiäh*, *ʻsi*, very bad! a desperate strait! [16]*ʻsi ‚sing*, with intense desire, resolved to; *ʻchiä ‚sing ʻsi kʻóʼ* the desire all gone, as to gamble, etc.; *pwangʼ ‚sang ʻsi*, half dead, as one dangerously ill; *ʻsi tioʼ* a fatal course, as a vicious life; [17]*ʻsi hwoʼ* unsalable goods; *‚i mengʼ saik*, *ʻsi pah*, his complexion is deadly pale; *ʻsi ‚sié wak*, *ʻmwi*, "a dead snake with a live tail"—not fully settled up, still likely to trouble one, as debts, etc.; *pʻah*, *ʻsi ‚loi*, to tie a hard knot; *ʻngwai ʻsi chʻëük*, *‚i* (or *‚hiéng ‚i*), I hate him with deadly hate.

ʻSi. A coll. euphonic prefix, as in *ʻsi ʻsó*, to lock; *ʻsi ʻsá*, to wash.

‚**時** Shih. Time, a period; an hour, a Chinese hour; a season or quarter of a year; an opportunity; proper, convenient, in time; to time rightly; to be, is, this; to see, to observe; at the beginning of a sentence, then, at that time; after a verb, as, while, during: [18]*sëüʼ ‚si*, the four seasons; COM., *pok*, *taik*, *‚si*, an unsuitable time; [19]*sek, neʼ ‚si ‚sing*, twelve hours, a day and night; [20]*‚si haiuʼ* time; [21]*‚tong ‚si*, at that time; *‚tʻiéng ‚si*, weather; *‚si sek*, or *‚si yongʼ* or *‚si ‚hing*, the fashion, fashionable; [22]*‚si ʻkwo*,

[1]絲竹管絃
[2]湖絲 [3]土絲
[4]絲布 [5]絲綿
[6]銅絲 [7]油絲
[8]詩人 [9]詩經
[10]吟詩 [11]題詩
[12]詩韻 [13]詩書
[14]死屍 [15]死絕
[16]死心 [17]死貨
[18]四時 [19]十二
時辰 [20]時候
[21]當時 [22]時果

fruits of the season; [1]*wong* ꜀*si*, formerly; [2]꜀*si cheng*꜄ a pestilence, an epidemic; [3]꜀*si k'aik*꜆ incessantly; constantly; ꜀*si tó*꜄ *ch'ok*꜆ to become lucky; [4]꜀*si* ꜀*sing paik*꜆ *che*꜄ the eight words from which one's horoscope is calculated; COLL., ꜀*mô* ꜀*si*, unlucky; ꜀*si* ꜀*si* ꜀*hwang k'aik*꜆ *k'aik*꜆ *piéng*꜄ very fickle, vacillating.

塒 ꜀Shih. A hen-roost, made by excavating a place in a wall and inserting sticks for roosting on.

蒔 ꜀Shih. Anise or dill, called ꜀*si* ꜀*ló* ꜂*chü*; COLL., [5]꜀*mwi* ꜀*si* (or ꜀*li*), an aquatic vegetable, the water-chestnut. Read *se*꜄: to erect, to set up; to set out, to plant, to transplant.

鰣 ꜀Shih. A fish like the shad, which enters the rivers from the ocean in May, and returns in September: in the coll. read ꜀*chi*, q. v.

糘 ꜀Shih. A coll. character: cakes of glutinous rice, eaten at the winter solstice: ꜀*si* ꜀*pa*, dried cakes of glutinous rice; ꜀*si t'eng*꜄ *yék*꜆ ꜂*kwi t'eng*꜄ ꜀*ch'iéng* (or *naëng*꜄), rice cakes (must be eaten) when hot, steamed cakes when fresh or soft; *met.*, to do at once, act promptly.

꜀*Si.* A coll. word: gradually, by degrees: ꜀*si sioh*꜆ *nik*꜆ day after day; ꜀*si sioh*꜆ ꜀*si lang*꜄ by degrees; ꜀*si* ꜀*niă nói*꜄ by little and little; ꜀*si* ꜀*sié* ꜀*sié*, to walk slowly and feebly.

꜀*Si.* A coll. euphonic prefix, as in ꜀*si* ꜀*si* ꜀*sa* ꜀*sa*, a rattling, a rustling sound, as of creeping insects, or dry leaves in the wind.

(735) Siă.

賒 賖 Shê. To buy or sell on credit; slow, remiss; distant; to defer: [6]꜀*siă tiong*꜄ credits: COM., [7]꜀*siă so*꜄ on credit; [8]꜀*t'ang* ꜀*siă koi*꜄ ꜂*mâ*, he who covets buying on credit buys dear; COLL., [9]*k'ĕük*꜆ ꜀*nĕng* ꜀*siă k'iéng*꜄ persons owe me on credit; ꜀*siă* ꜀*ki wa*꜄ a surmise, a supposition.

鉈 ꜀ A short spear or lance.

꜂寫 ꜂寫 Hsieh. To write, to copy; to make out, as accounts; to draw, to paint; to remove, to subvert, to put aside; to quiet or compose the mind; to cast, as images; to leak, to spill: COM., [10]꜂*siă che*꜄ to write; [11]꜀*ch'au* ꜂*siă*, to copy; [12]꜂*siă e*꜄ to draw an outline; [13]꜂*siă* ꜂*ch'iu*, a writer; [14]꜂*siă* ꜂*ch'ó che*꜄ to write a running hand; [15]꜂*siă* ꜀*sung* ꜀*ong*, a commission-office for hiring boats; COLL., *ch'iăng*꜄ *t'aik*꜆ ꜂*siă*, or *ch'iăng*꜄ ꜀*pong* ꜂*siă*, to hire a writer; [16]꜂*siă* ꜀*p'ié*, to write a letter; [17]꜂*siă tek*꜆ ꜀*ngai*, written badly.

꜂炧 Also read ꜂*tó*: the snuff of a candle; the expiring wick of a lamp; alike, resembling.

꜂捨 Shê. To let go, to part with, to relinquish; to leave, to abandon; to renounce; to sacrifice one's self, as for the state; to bestow,

---

[1]往時 [2]時症 [3]時刻 [4]時辰 八字 [5]莓蒔 [6]賒賬 [7]賒數 [8]貪賒貫買 [9]乞伙賒欠 [10]寫字 [11]抄寫 [12]寫意 [13]寫手 [14]寫草字〇 [15]寫船行〇 [16]寫批〇 [17]寫的呆〇

福州方言拼音字典

to give alms: ¹'sia 'sü ˬwong ˬseng, ready to die and forgetful of life; COM., ²'siă sié' to give in charity; ³'siă ˬsing, to give up one's self, as to be a Bonze; ⁴ˬYă ˬSu 'siă miăng' Jesus gave his life; COLL., 'nü á' 'siă tek, 'chiă ˬsing, you can bear to do so! má' 'siă tek, ˬchiéng, stingy, miserly.

'舍 Shê. To stop, to halt, to rest; to lodge, to dwell; used for the preceding in the sense of to part with, to relinquish: also read siă' q. v.

舍' Shê. A lodging in a market; a rest; a stage of 30 'li; a hospice; a booth, a cottage; lodgings; my, as applied to junior relatives: also read 'siă, q. v.: COM., ⁵ˬpung siă' rooms, apartments; siă' tik, my nephew; ⁶siă' tá' my younger brother; ⁷siă' ˬing, or siă' ˬing ˬkó, the sons of the goddess "Mother" or ˬLing 'chwi 'ná; siă' ˬing mieu' a temple of the same; ⁸siă' le' 'chü, Budhist relics.

赦' Shê. To forgive, to pardon, to excuse; to let go, to remit, to reprieve; pardon, amnesty: COM., ⁹siă' 'miéng, to forgive; ¹⁰siă' chói' to pardon sins; ˬt'iéng siă' nik, the days when "Heaven forgives", as marked in calendars; twai' siă' ˬt'iéng a' a general anmesty; siă' ˬchiéng ˬliong, to remit the taxes.

鉘' 卸' Hsieh. To lay off, as clothes or armor; to lay aside, to relinquish; to vacate, as an office; to land cargo; in the coll. to sell, as a lot of goods: COM., ¹¹siă' sëü' to throw up a business, to leave one's calling; siă' eng' to relinquish the seals, give up an office; ¹²siă' ˬkiéng, or siă' tang' to put down a load; COLL., siă' hwo' to sell off goods.

瀉' 潟' Hsieh. To drain land; to leak, to ooze; a diarrhea, a flux, looseness of the bowels; to purge: ¹³siék, siă' to leak out; involuntary purging in small quantities; ¹⁴siă' to' dysentery; COM., ¹⁵pang' siă' diarrhea; pang' t'o' siă' cholera; siă' yoh, a purgative; 'chwi siă' a watery stool; COLL., siă' 'kwi ˬhúi, how many movements have you had? siă' yok, weak from diarrhea.

ˬ邪 Hsieh. Deflected; swerving from rectitude, depraved, vicious; corrupting, obscene, filthy; specious, false, deluding; illegal, heretical, unacknowledged by the state or the classics: ¹⁶ˬkang ˬsiă, illicit, licentious, depraved; COM., ˬsiă kau' heretical doctrines; ¹⁷ˬsing ˬsiă, the mind depraved; ¹⁷ˬsiă hwak, or ˬsiă suk, tricks, philters; arts emanating from ¹⁸ˬMau ˬsang; ˬsiă ˬpó, countrywomen from the hills north-west of Foochow—do not intermarry with other classes; ¹⁹ˬsiă 'kwi, or ˬsiă ˬmó, evil spirits, devils; ²⁰'k'e' ˬsiă ˬkwi cheng' to forsake the wrong and turn to the correct, to reform.

¹捨死忘生 ²捨施 ³捨身 ⁴耶穌捨命 ⁵房舍 ⁶舍弟 ⁷舍人 ⁸舍利 子 ⁹赦免〇 ¹⁰赦罪 ¹¹卸事 ¹²卸肩 ¹³泄瀉 ¹⁴瀉肚 ¹⁵病瀉 ¹⁶奸邪 ¹⁷邪法 ¹⁸茅山 ¹⁹邪鬼 ²⁰棄邪歸正

斜 ˏ Hsieh. Hsia. Sometimes used for the preceding: distorted, not straight, aslant, oblique, crisscross; scattered, unsettled: [1]*ˎsiă ˎyong*, the afternoon sun; COM., *nikˏ ˎtʻau ˎsiă*, the sun is declining; [2]*ˎsiă ˎsá*, slants to the west, as the sun; [3]*ˎsiă ˎtó*, a knife with an oblique edge—for cutting in angles; [4]*ˎsiă ˎung pwoˀ* drillings; COLL., *ʻchʻioˀ ˎsiă*, the house leans over.

社² Shê. The god of a locality, a tutelary deity, the lares rustici; sacrifices to the gods of the land and grain; altars of the same; a hamlet embracing anciently 25 houses; a society, a company: [5]*siă² nikˏ* two festivals for worshiping the lares—occurring about the beginning of spring and autumn; [6]*ˎtiéng siă²* a hamlet of 10 or 25 houses; a field-altar; COM., [7]*siă² chekˏ ˎsing*, gods of the land and grain, worshiped by the sovereign—their altars are without roofs; [8]*ʻngu ʻpó chʻekˏ siă²* the five *ʻpó* streets and seven temples or shrines—on the south of Great Temple Hill in the suburbs of Foochow.

射² Shê. Shih. Yeh. I. To shoot with a bow; to cheat, to counterfeit; to implicate; to glance, to dart, as rays of light; to issue forth, as evil influences; an ancient officer, a fugleman or drill-sergeant: in the coll. read *siohˏ* q. v.: [9]*lwang² siă²* to shoot wide of the mark; [10]*siă² le²* to counterfeit one's mark and undersell him, to gain by fraud; [11]*ʻing siă²* to implicate, to cast the blame on one; COLL., *pʻahˏ siă²* to practice archery. Read *ikˏ* or *toˀ*: to dislike, to loathe.

麝² Shé. The musk deer of Sz'-chuen and Tibet: COM., *siă² ˎhiong*, musk.

榭² Hsieh. A terrace with trees about it, an arbor; a place for storing musical instruments and sacrificial vessels; a keep, a turret or high lookout; a military school or fencing-room.

謝² Shieh. To decline, to withdraw, to go away; to resign, as office; to fade, as flowers; to inform; to thank, to show gratitude, as by presents; to confess, to excuse one's self: COM., [12]*ʻling siă²* and *pʻekˏ siă²* to receive and decline presents—words written on cards; [13]*ˎsiu siă²* to requite in kind, as by presents; [14]*ˎtó siă²* many thanks, thank you; [15]*ʻkang siă²* to feel grateful; [16]*siă² chôi²* to confess a sin; [17]*siă² tieu²* to thank mourners and decline calls—words posted on the door, as after the feast of the 2nd seventh day; [18]*siă² pwo²* to thank mourners or guests for their calls; [19]*siă² ʻü*, to return thanks for rain; [20]*siă² ngwong²* to pay a vow, to make a thank-offering; [21]*ˎhwa siă²* the flower has faded; COLL., [22]*siă² chioh*, thanks for the loan; *hang² ˎtó siă²* to express thanks.

(736) Siăh.

𠜲 (**鍻**) Read *ʻhiéng;* used in the *Paikˏ ˏIng* for the coll. *siăhˏ*: to shave with a knife, to sharpen by shaving thin; to scrape, to

1 斜陽	3 斜刀	5 社日	7 社稷	8 五保	9 亂射	11 影射	13 酬謝	15 感謝	17 謝弔	19 謝雨	21 花謝
2 斜西	4 層斜	6 田社	神○	七社	10 射利	12 領謝	14 多謝	16 謝罪	18 謝步	20 謝願	22 謝借

福州方言拼音字典

scale off: *siăhˎ ˏtó*, to shave a knife or sword; *siăhˎ ˏling*, to scale fish; *siăhˎ ˏkó ʻtá*, to make wooden heels, as for ladies' shoes; *siăhˎ siohˎ ˏtʻüng*, to shave off a film or shaving.

食 Shih. Read *sikˎ*; coll. *siăhˎ*: to eat, to drink; to smoke: [1]*siăhˎ pwongʼ* to eat rice, to take a meal; [2]*siăhˎ yéngʼ* sated with food; *siăhˎ sikˎ lükˎ* to live luxuriously; [3]*siăhˎ ˏliong*, to eat cold or cooling things; *met.*, to take up a matter which does not concern one; [4]*ˏsong siăhˎ* to join, to fit; to weld; *siăhˎ oʼ ʻpwo*, strengthening food; *siăhˎ ˏkʻwi*, a poor job, as when materials are high and wages low; *siăhˎ ˏlang siăhˎ tiongʼ* remnants of food, leavings; *siăhˎ likˎ* fatigued, jaded; [5]*siăhˎ ˏtong ˏchá*, to use vegetable diet for life; [6]*siăhˎ ʻsai ĕüngʼ* current expenses; *siăhˎ kwoʼ ngeʼ* to eat or take more than one's share; *siăhˎ ʻsi ˏnëng*, fatal to life, deadly, as poison; *siăhˎ cheʼ ˏka*, to find one's own food, as a hired man; [7]*siăhˎ ˏi*, the food furnished by him (as well as pay); *siăhˎ máʼ ˏta* or *siăhˎ máʼ ˏli*, cannot do it; *siăhˎ ʻpa ˏteng*, sated with food; *met.*, a full run of business; *kaëngʼ siăhˎ ˏta siohˎ yongʼ* like drinking tea—easily done.

(737) Siăk.

瞔 Read *sakˎ*; used in the *Paikˎ ˏIng* for the coll. *siăkˎ*: similar to *tʻiăkˎ*; to blink, to wink: *siăkˎ ˏchiă cheuʼ ˏmó*, gone in a twinkling, suddenly disappeared; *mĕkˎ siăkˎ* (or *tʻiăkˎ*), the eyelashes.

Siăkˎ. A coll. word: to shake, to make a rattling sound: *siăkˎ siăkˎ kieuʼ* to give a rattling sound; *sikˎ sikˎ siăkˎ siăkˎ* to clatter, to rattle.

(738) Siăng.

聲 声 Shêng. Read *ˏsing*; coll. *ˏsiăng*: a voice; a tone in speaking or music; the tones of Chinese words; a word, a sentence; a sound or noise: [8]*ˏsiăng ˏing*, a voice, a sound; [9]*ˏsiăng ʻmwi*, a final sound, a drawling tone; [10]*ˏping chahˎ ˏsiăng*, the two even and six deflected tones; *ˏsiăng ˏkʻwi* and *ˏsiăng hakˎ* a clear and a hoarse voice; [11]*ˏsiăng ʻa*, the voice low or broken, as from long speaking; [12]*ˏkʻing ˏsiăng sáʼ ʻngü*, to speak in a low tone; [13]*ˏsiăng ʻkʻeu*, the peculiar tone or quality of the voice, as in singing; *ˏsiăng ˏing ʻneu ʻnó*, a delicate voice; [14]*ˏmiăng ˏsiăng*, fame, reputation; [15]*ˏmwong ˏsiăng*, the noise of doors; *ˏi ˏsiăng ʻkʻëng ngʼ ʻhó ˏtʻiăng*, his utterance is bad to hear or very harsh.

ʻSiăng. A coll. word: perhaps a corruption of *ʻchʻang*; sad, pitiable; ah! alas! what a pity! *áʼ ʻsiăng*, or *ˏkai ʻsiăng*, oh! alas! *ʻsiăng chiăh*, *ʻsiăng*, very lamentable!

線 綫 Hsien. ʼ Thread of silk, hemp, or cotton; sewing silk or thread; a fine cord; a line, beading, molding; a clue, a trace; a spy; a mere remnant, as of a family, an orphan: COM., [16]*siăngʼ taingʼ* a thread shop; [17]*ˏsi siăngʼ* silk thread; *ˏmiĕng ˏsa*

---

[1] 食飯 [2] 食厭 [3] 食凉 [4] 相食 [5] 食長齋〇 [6] 食使用〇 [7] 食伊 [8] 聲音 [9] 聲尾 [10] 平仄聲 [11] 聲啞〇 [12] 輕聲細語 [13] 聲口 [14] 名聲 [15] 門聲〇 [16] 線店〇 [17] 絲線〇

siăng' cotton thread; [1]*ᶜi siăng'* and *ᶜsó siăng'* fine and coarse silk-thread; [2]*ᶜsiăng' ᶜkwong,* a spool; [3]*ᶜhwa siăng'* floss silk; *ᶜk'i siăng'* molding, beading; [4]*ᶜhiong siăng'* an incense-stick; [5]*ᶜsiăng' miéng'* a kind of flour vermicelli; [6]*ᶜsiăng' hié'* a puppet-play; *ᶜu ᶜcheng pok, ᶜing siăng'* can't sew without a needle; *met.*, can't effect a thing without means; COLL., *siăng' sioh, ᶜchi,* a skein of thread; *siăng' swoi'* a seam; *chó' siăng' sóh,* to be a spy, one who tries to find a clue to a matter; [7]*pek, siăng'* to mislead, to humbug; *ᶜnü pek, siăng' ᶜngwai,* you deceived me, you failed to meet your engagement.

聖 Shêng. Read *seng';* coll. *siăng':* propitious, favoring, efficacious, able to protect, as a god: *má' siăng'* unpropitious; *siăng' chiăh, siăng'* extremely propitious; [8]*siăng' ka'* a lucky throw of the divining blocks—falling with one round and one flat side up.

城 ᶜCh'êng. Read *ᶜsing;* coll. *ᶜsiăng:* a walled city; a capital of a province, prefecture, or district; a city wall: *ᶜseng ᶜsiăng,* the provincial capital; *sioh, chó' ᶜsiăng,* a city; [9]*ᶜsiăng ᶜting,* the top of a city wall; [10]*ᶜsiăng ᶜlau,* a tower on the wall; *ᶜsiăng ᶜtié,* a city-moat; *ᶜtié ᶜsiăng,* to go into the city; *ᶜsiăng ᶜsiu ᶜyăng,* the city-guards; [11]*ᶜsiăng ᶜhwong,* the municipal god—provincial guardian; *ᶜsiăng ᶜtié ᶜting ᶜlêng, ᶜhiong a' kauk,* city-lanterns made with country-frames; *met.*, a countryman living in the city, but still rustic in manners.

成 ᶜCh'eng. Read *ᶜsing;* coll. *ᶜsiăng:* to finish, to complete; to effect one's part; to make or bring about; to become, perfect, completed; whole, entire, full; a tenth; used to denote the quality, as of metals, wood, etc.: [12]"*ᶜsiăng ᶜhwa,* to "complete the flower"—to close a bargain, to effect a matter; *paik, ᶜsiăng ᶜta,* eighth-tenths dry, as fire-wood; *ng' ᶜsiăng ᶜnêng,* not be a man, not capable, not honest, &c.; [13]*ᶜsiăng pah,* a full hundred; *ᶜsiăng ᶜtoi ᶜsang,* a whole heap—a large number or amount; *ᶜsiăng pó' ᶜui,* as large round as the span of the arms; *ᶜsiăng ᶜnêng ᶜkeng,* as high as a man; [14]*ᶜsiăng pang' ᶜsiăng t'iăng'* it will end in a disease, or much pain; [15]*hiéng' ᶜsiăng kwo'* an extant phrase.

㯌 A coll. character, used in the *Paik, ᶜIng:* a large bin, a grain-receptacle: *siăng' ᶜcheng,* the stories of a bin.

賤 Chien. Read *chiéng';* used in the *Paik, ᶜIng* for the coll. *siăng':* cheap, low in price: *siăng' siăng'* very cheap; [16]*ka' ᶜchiéng siăng'* the price is low; [17]*siăng' ᶜli siăng' k'ó'* bought cheap and sold cheap.

(739) Sié.

些 ᶜHsieh. A little, few, small in number; trifling, unimportant; partly, rather, somewhat; in the court dialect, this, these; also a word of comparison: [18]*k'wai' ᶜsié,* quicker; [19]*ᶜchié ᶜsié,* this, these; [20]*ᶜsié ᶜsiu,*

1 衣線 2 花線 3 線捲 4 香線 5 線麪 6 線戲 7 拔線 8 聖𥳑 9 城頂 10 城樓 11 城隍 12 成花 13 成百 14 成病 成痛 15 現成 句 16 價錢賤 17 賤來賤去 18 快些 19 這些 20 些少 ○

a little, few; COM., [1]ˌ*sié* ˌ*sü* or ˌ*sié* ˌ*mi*, a trifling amount; COLL., ˌ*sié* ˌ*sü* *yă*^{2} *se*^{2} *e*' though only a trifle, it was (given) with good intent; ˌ*sié* ˌ*mi* ʻ*kiăng*, a mere bit.

施 ˌ Shih. A banner unfurled; expanded, spread out; to confer, to relieve, to bestow in charity; to permit; to grant, to allow to be done; to use, to add to; moving slowly; in the coll. to scatter, to drop: also read *sié*' q. v.: ˌ*sié* ˌ*sié*, slow, hesitating; pleased, happy; [2]ˌ*sié* ʻ*siá*, to give, to aid; [3]ˌ*sié* ˌ*heng*, to allow; to dispense, to perform; COM., [4]ˌ*sié* ˌ*ong*, to bestow favors, to show kindness; COLL., *p'ah*ˏ ˌ*sié*, to scatter, as grains, seeds, etc.; [5]ˌ*sié* ʻ*mwang* *te*^{2} scattered all about. Read ʻ*ch'ié:* to relax, to cast off. Read *e*^{2}*:* to remove, to transfer, to change.

絁 纚 ˌ Coarse threads used in weaving; fine and coarse sorts of silks, as sarcenets.

ʻ**暆** Read ˌ*ié;* used in the *Paik*ˏ ˌ*Ing* for the coll. ʻ*sié:* the course of the sun, the motion of the sun's shadow; *met.*, in the coll. to move by degrees: COLL., [6]ʻ*sié* *siong*' *k'ó*' rising, as the shadow on a wall in the P. M.; to move up, as a heavy article; to push, to shove up; ʻ*sié* *kwo*' ˌ*li*, move it gradually this way.

施' Shih. To give, to relieve, to bestow charitably: also read ˌ*sié*, q. v.: COM., [7]*sié*' *chá*' to give in charity; [8]*sié*' *saĕng*' to bestow gratuitously; [9]*sié*' ʻ*chio*, one who gives, as to a temple; *sié*' ˌ*kwang*, to give a coffin; [10]*sié*' *chéük*ˏ to distribute congee, as in a famine; *sié*' *siong*^{2} *chó*^{2} to offer (to orbate spirits) in the *siong*^{2} *chó*^{2} rites.

世 丗' Shih. The world, mankind; an age, a generation, the space of thirty years; times, life, experience in life; hereditary: COM., *sié*' *sié*' ages, forever; [11]*k'e*' *sié*' or *kwo*' *sié*' to die; *ch'ok*ˏ *sié*' to be born; [12]ˌ*king sié*' and ˌ*lai sié*' the present and future world or life; [13]*ch'aung*' *sié*' ʻ*i* ˌ*lai*, from the creation to the present time; [14]*sié*' ˌ*ka*, an old family, one that follows the hereditary calling; [15]*sié*' ˌ*hing*, a friend's brother or son; ˌ*sang sié*' ˌ*i*, a medical profession continued in the 3d generation; [16]*sié*' *sük*ˏ the customs of the world; [17]*sié*' ˌ*kang*, the world; *sié*' ʻ*chü*, the sons of the idol gods, [18]ʻ*Ngu tá*' and [19]ˌ*Siang* ˌ*hwong*; *sié*' ˌ*ching* *pok*ˏ the world has no feeling; [20]*sié*' *tói*^{2} ages, generations; [21]*sié*' *sëü*^{2} or *sié*' *ko*' worldly affairs; *sié*' ʻ*mwi*, bad times; *pié*^{2} *sié*' to retire from active life; *pwang*' *sié*' from 30 to 40 years old; COLL., *sioh*ˏ *sié*' ˌ*nĕng*, to the very end of life.

Sié'. A coll. word, for which the last is commonly used in coll. books, as in [22]*sié*' *nóh*ˏ (or ˌ*sié* *nóh*ˏ), what? what is it? *sié*' *nóh*,

---

[1]些須 [2]施捨 [3]施行 [4]施恩 [5]施滿地 [6]暆上去 [7]施濟 [8]施送 [9]施主 [10]施粥 [11]棄世 [12]今世 [13]創世以來 [14]世家 [15]世兄 [16]世俗 [17]世間 [18]五帝 [19]城隍 [20]世代 [21]世事 [22]世毛

˛miăng, what name? what is the matter? siéˀ nóh˛ nóh˛ what things? ²ˀsiéˀ nóh˛ ˛k'iéng, what crime—*scil.*, was he guilty of in his former state of existence.

貰ˀ Shih. Shê. To get on trust, to purchase on credit; to borrow; to show lenity, as to criminals: ²siéˀ siăˀ to remit, to pardon.

勢 埶ˀ Shih. Authority, influence, power; station, rank, dignity; splendor; strength; virility, the testes; the exterior, the figure; the aspect, state, or condition of: ³siéˀ oi² station, authority; ⁴kak˛ siéˀ to castrate; COM., siéˀ ˛t'au or siéˀ miéng² or ⁵siéˀ lik˛ power, influence; ⁶chiăˀ siéˀ to rely on one's station or influence—to injure others; ⁷siéˀ leˀ to play the sycophant, greedy of small gains; ˛hing siéˀ form, figure, appearance; ˛hung siéˀ course of the wind; ⁸teˀ siéˀ configuration of the ground; k'angˀ siéˀ to have regard to circumstances; ⁹huk˛ siéˀ set, fixed in a certain shape; ˛chai siéˀ lik˛ ˛sang ˛pwang ˛chiong, wealth, station, power, he has all three complete.

Siéˀ. A coll. word: to add to, to piece out; to connect, to attach to the end of; to follow, to succeed one in a work: siéˀ ˛t'au, to piece out the end; siéˀ k'wak˛ to widen by piecing; siéˀ lóh˛ to add on to; continuous; siéˀ sioh˛ chaik˛ to add one section or piece.

蛇 ˛ Shê. A snake, a serpent; serpentine, crooked; malicious, treacherous, subtile; the constellation Hydra: ¹⁰˛sié ˋi ˋngang t'engˀ the snake hears with its eyes; ˛lüng ˛sié tongˀ dragons and snakes moving; *met.*, fine penmanship; COM., ˛long ˛sié tengˀ the long-serpent-evolution—in strategy; ¹¹˛sié ˛chiăng, a snake-elf; ¹²˛sié ˋtang, snake's gall—a medicine; waˀ ˛sié ˛t'iéng chëük˛ to "paint a snake with feet"— superfluous, supererogatory; ¹³˛sing ˛sié, a god incarnate in a snake; COLL., lauˀ ˛sié, a snake; ˛ch'ang tëük˛ ˛sié a green-colored snake; ¹⁴˛sié sóh˛ to talk as another does, to chime in; to hoax, humbugging talk; ˛sié lóh˛ tëük˛ ˛têng chaik˛ chaik˛ ˛nang, a snake in a bamboo tube impeded by every joint; *met.*, a succession of difficulties; ˛sang ˛sié ˛t'au, to have a whitlow. Read ˛i: crooked; to squirm.

匙 ˛ Shih. Ch'ih. A key; a spoon: COM., ¹⁵ˋsó ˛sié, a key; ¹⁶˛ta ˛sié, a small brass or silver spoon; COLL., ˋsó ˛sié ˛pa lak˛ sioh˛ aˀ give the key a turn.

啻² Shih. Only; to stop at: ¹⁷pok˛ sié² not only, more than; ¹⁸˛hó sié² ˛ch'iéng wangˀ how can it stop at ten millions! ¹⁹pok˛ sié² hoˀ ˋmu, more (grateful) than to one's father and mother.

嗜² Shih. To delight in, to relish; to indulge the animal desires; to gormandize; greedy for, addicted to: ²⁰sié² hóˀ to love, to relish; sié² sik˛ fond of eating; COM., sié²

---

¹世毛䘏〇 ²貰赦 ⁸勢位 ⁴割勢 ⁵勢力 ⁶藉勢 ⁷勢利 ⁸地勢 ⁹伏勢 ¹⁰蛇以眼聽 ¹¹蛇精 ¹²蛇膽 ¹³神蛇 ¹⁴蛇索 ¹⁵鎖匙 ¹⁶茶匙 ¹⁷不啻 ¹⁸何啻千萬 ¹⁹不啻父母 ²⁰嗜好

ʻ*chiu*, addicted to wine; [1]*sié* [2] ʻ*tu*, fond of gaming.

噬 [2] Shih. To bite, to gnaw at, to devour; grief, sorrow; reaching to: [2]*sié* [2] ˏ*chá*, to bite one's own navel; *met.*, to attempt impossibilities; [3]*sié* [2] *hak*ˎ name of the 21st diagram, denoting punishment.

筮 [2] Shih. To divine, as with straws or slips of milfoil; the most efficacious are from Confucius' grave; to plan, to decide.

誓 [2] Shih. To swear, to take an oath, to bind one's self; to vow, to promise solemnly; an oath, an adjuration; careful, to caution; to order, to issue special injunctions; to receive a superior's command; to espouse clandestinely: [4]*hwak*ˎ *sié* [2] to swear; [5]*sié* [2] *yok*ˎ to promise with an oath; COM., [6]*siék*ˎ *sié* [2] to confirm by oath; [7]*sié* [2] *ngwong*[2] to vow or resolve solemnly; COLL., *sié* [2] *ngwong*[2] *ng*[2] *siăh*ˎ ʻ*chiă pwong*[2] I vow not to continue this business for a living.

逝 [2] Shih. To depart, to go away, to pass away; to go into oblivion, to leave this life, to die; used for the coll. to void or discharge involuntarily: [8]ˏ*tiong sié* [2] gone forever; [9]*sié* [2] ʻ*chiă* ˏ*ü* ˏ*sü*, the dead are like this (flowing water); COLL., *sié* [2] ʻ*sai sié* [2] *nieu*[2] to make involuntary discharges, as in sleep.

豉 [2] Shih. Salted eatables, as beans, etc., dried and used as relishes: [10]ʻ*ch*ʻ*ó sié* [2] a sort of leek; COM., [11]*sié* [2] ˏ*iu*, soy; [12]ˏ*iu sié* [2] soy-beans or residual grains; [13]*tau*[2] *sié* [2] ˏ*kiong*, a sauce of salted beans and ginger; [14]*sié* [2] ˏ*iu* ʻ*ch*ʻ*iong*, a soy-factory.

(740) Siék.

榤 Hsieh. I. An instrument for adjusting a bow. Read *ié* [2]: an oar.

紲 Hsieh. To tie, to fasten, to bind; to put in fetters; tied, bound; a bridle, a halter; a frame to keep a bow in shape.

絏 Hsieh. Interchanged with the last: bonds, fetters; to halter, to tether, to tie, as animals: [15]ˏ*lai siék*ˎ to fetter, to bind with cords.

洩泄 Hsieh. I. To leak, to ooze out; to divulge, as secrets; to rest, to desist from; to diminish; dissipated, exhausted; a stream in Chehkiang: the 2d also read *ié* [2] q. v.: [16]*laiu*[2] *siék*ˎ ˏ*ki* ˏ*kwang*, to divulge the whole scheme; COM., [17]*siék*ˎ ˏ*ching*, to emit semen; [18]*mong*[2] (or *maëng*[2]) *siék*ˎ nocturnal emissions; [19]*siék*ˎ ʻ*ngü*, to talk wildly, as in a delirium; [20]*siék*ˎ *k*ʻ*e*[2] "lost the scent"; *met.*, to lose future prospects, as a child by being treated as an officer—a superstitious notion. Read *ié* [2]: loose, scattered.

*Siék*ˎ. A coll. word, for which the last may be used: to disappear unaccountably, to spirit away: *k*ʻ*ëük*ˎ ʻ*kwi siék*ˎ *k*ʻ*ó* [2] spirited away; *siék*ˎ *pwong*[2] *k*ʻ*e*[2] to consume the essence of the rice, as ghosts are supposed to do.

---

1 嗜賭 2 噬臍 3 噬嗑 4 發誓 5 誓約 6 設誓 7 誓願 8 長逝 9 逝者如斯 10 草豉 11 豉油 12 油豉 13 豆豉薑 14 豉油廠 15 縲絏 16 漏洩機關 17 洩精 18 夢洩 19 洩語 20 洩氣 ○

揳, Hsieh. To rub off, to wipe over: [1]*miék‚ siék‚* not square, angular, irregular, cornerwise.

挈, Hsieh. Ch'i. Distressed, suffering; wide, parted; separated, as from friends; to carve, to cut off: also read *k'ié'* q. v.

設, Shê. To institute, to found, to establish; to place, to set up, to build; to suppose; large; a band of soldiers, a cantonment: [2]*‚p'wo siék‚* to set in order; [3]*siék‚ kau'* or *siék‚ tiong'* to establish a school; COM., [4]*siék‚ lik‚* to institute, to establish; [5]*siék‚ ngié' óh‚* to open a free school; [6]*siék‚ kié'* to form a plot or plan; [7]*siék‚ ‘sü,* if, supposing that; [8]*siék‚ ‚sü,* to improvise words, to make up a story; [9]*siék‚ hwak‚* to devise means; [10]*siék‚ ‚ping ‘pa ‘siu,* to place soldiers on guard.

燮 **爕**, Hsieh. To dress or mature by fire; in concord, harmonious; united, friendly; [11]*siék‚ ‘li,* to regulate kindly; [12]*siék‚ ‘li ‚ing ‚yong,* to rule in accord with *yin* and *yang*, or earth and heaven, as officers should do; [13]*siék‚ ‘iu,* friendly.

屑, Hsieh. Pure, clear; diligent, laborious; attentive, respectful, observant; to regard, to take pains for; to reduce to powder; minute; broken bits, crumbs, fragments; in the coll. poor, mean, scanty, as presents or a feast: [14]*siék‚ siék‚* unsettled; [15]*‘só siék‚* petty, vexatious, trifling; COM., [16]*pok‚ siék‚* to disregard, to view as not deserving a thought; COLL., *siék‚ ‚chi che'* very mean or scanty.

屧, Hsieh. The lining or stuffing of a shoe; a patten: [17]*‘hiong siék‚ ‚long,* the Clattering Patten Corridor — name of an ancient story.

薛, Hsieh. Hsüeh. A plant, a sort of Malaxis, called [18]*siék‚ ‚só;* a feudal state, the present Yenchau-fu in Shantung; a surname.

媟, Hsieh. Interchanged with the next: to outrage, to insult females; to lust after, to act lewdly toward.

褻, Hsieh. Undress, dishabille; ordinary or dirty clothes; rags, tatters; filthy, impure; to revile, to blaspheme; to treat disrespectfully, as gods or great men: [19]*siék‚ mang'* insulting in words or conduct; COM., [20]*siék‚ tuk‚* to profane the gods; to treat one insultingly; [21]*siék‚ ‚i,* in undress, without one's coat on, as when a friend calls unexpectedly.

暬, Dark, obscure; female attendants; also the same as the last, to insult, to despise, to treat shamefully.

Siék‚. A coll. word, a corruption of *se' sek‚* forty; *siék‚ hwoi'* forty years old; *siék‚ ek‚* forty one; *siék‚ ne' ‚sang,* forty two or three.

舌, Shê. The tongue; the clapper of a bell; the bent end of a clasp; the rim of a target; talkative, wordy;

[1] 搣揳 [2] 鋪設 [3] 設教 [4] 設立 [5] 設義學 [6] 設計 [7] 設使 [8] 設辭 [9] 設法 [10] 設兵把守 [11] 燮理 [12] 燮理陰陽 [13] 燮友 [14] 屑屑 [15] 瑣屑 [16] 不屑 [17] 響屧廊 [18] 薛莎 [19] 褻慢 [20] 褻瀆 [21] 褻衣

福州方言拼音字典

the 135th radical: [1]ʻsiék, ˏkeng, "plow with the tongue"—to teach; COM., [2]ʻchʻoiʼ siék, the tongue; [3]siék, ˏtʻau ngaingʼ the organs of speech rigid, as from age; [4]ʻtwai ʼ siék, a thick, indistinct articulation; [5]ʻkek, siék, to stutter, to stammer; [6]ʻpaik, siék, the hundred-tongued—name of a mocking-bird; COLL., ʻkʻeng siék, ˏá, shoes with cording on the toes like a dog's tongue; kaĕngʼ ˏi ʻkʻeu siék, to quarrel with him; siék, ʻkiăng, the palate.

涉 Shĕ. ₂ To wade across, to ford; *met.*, to pass through (the world); to spend (time); to pore over, to investigate, as books; to become versed in; to involve, to implicate, to have a tendency to: [7]siék, sié ʼ to pass through the world; [8]siék, lak, to wade and hunt (through books); COM., ˏkang siék, or ˏkwang siék, implication; involved, concerned in.

折 Shĕ. Chĕ. Cho. ₂ Read chiék,; used in the *Paik, ˏIng* for the coll. siék,: to break, to part, to snap in two; to lose in trade: siék, sioh, ngáʼ a branch broken off; [9]ʻpʻah, siék, to break in two; [10]siék, ʻpwong, to sell below the prime cost; [11]siék, tʻengʼ to lose and gain; [12]siék, chʻoiʼ to talk in vain, lost words; ˏkʻwo ˏkʻa siék, ʻchʻiu, a short leg and stiff arm; siék, ʻla ˏkʻa ˏkiăng, or siék, sioh, ˏlau ˏkʻa, to "walk with a broken leg"—fail in the object of going.

(741) Siéng.

羶 ˏShan. The rank odor of goats; frouzy, fetid, rank; sheep's fat, mutton tallow: COM., [13]ˏsiéng eʼ a rank smell, frouzy; COLL., chʻauʼ ˏsiéng, rank, fetid; chʻauʼ ˏneng ˏsiéng, has the strong scent of milk, as a babe's mouth—a term used in reproving a child's forwardness.

仙 ˏHsien. An immortal, an old man who never dies; a fairy, a genius; to become immortal; elysium, hades: [14]ˏsiéng ˏiu, to ramble in elysium—to die; COM., [15]ˏsiéng ˏtang, the elixir of immortality; *met.*, said of an excellent recipe; ˏkwi lük, neʼ ˏsiéng ˏka, the "turtle-stag-two-genii-glue"—name of a strengthening medicine; [16]ˏsiéng ʻking (or kaiʼ), elysium; [17]paik, ˏsiéng, the eight genii, ʻLü ˏtung ˏping, ʻLi tʻiék, ʻkwai, Hangʼ ˏchüng ˏlié, ˏChŏ kwok, keuʼ, ˏLang ʻchʻai ˏhwo, ˏTiong ʻkwo ʻló, ˏHang ˏsiong ʻchü, ˏHó ˏsiéng ˏku (who is a female); [18]ˏsiéng kauk, has fairy's bones—said of one peculiar in appearance; [19]ˏSiéng ˏiu kaingʼ a district of Hinghwa prefecture, Fookien; [20]hongʼ ˏsiéng, the impatiens; ˏsing ˏsiéng, the immortals, the genii; COLL., ˏsiéng ˏka paik, sóh, rogues, scoundrels.

僊 ˏHsien. Used for the preceding: a genius, an immortal; to frisk: [21]ˏsiéng ˏsiéng, to dance and waltz.

躚 ˏHsien. As in [22]ˏpʻiéng ˏsiéng, to whirl, as dervishes do, to wriggle; to walk round and round.

[1]舌耕 [2]嘴舌 [3]舌頭硬 [4]大舌 [5]急舌 [6]百舌 [7]涉世 [8]涉獵 [9]拍折 [10]折本 [11]折趁 [12]折嘴 [13]羶味 [14]仙遊 [15]仙丹 [16]仙境 [17]八仙 [18]仙骨 [19]仙遊縣 [20]鳳仙 [21]僊僊 [22]蹁躚 ○

褼 ‘Hsien. To dress: ¹‘piêng ‘siêng, clad, dressed, having clothes on.

先 ‘Hsien. To precede, to go first; to begin, in the first place; previous, before, early, formerly; past, gone before; late, deceased, ancient: in the coll. read ‚seng and ‚sing, q. v.: ²‚cheng ‚siêng, to strive to be first; COM., ³‚siêng ‚seng, a teacher; a physician; Sir, Mr.; ⁴‚siêng hau² before and after, in time or place; ⁵‚siêng ‘ch‘iu, before, previous; ⁶‚siêng tă² the late emperor; ⁷‚siêng ‚ti, a prophet; ⁸‚siêng ‚ing, ancestors; ⁹‚siêng ho² my late father: ‚siêng tôi² ‚chu hau² chêŭ² ok, first pay the rent due, then occupy the house. Read siêng²: to lead the way; to put first; to assume the precedence.

𥐨 ‘Hsien. A fine pebble, a stone inferior to a gem, such as red jasper or rose quartz.

煽 ‘Shan. Read siêng²; used for the coll. ‚siêng: to fan grain, to cleanse by fanning: ¹⁰‚hung ‚siêng, a fanning-mill; ‚tô ‚hung ‚siêng ‘lá k‘ô² ‚siêng, take it to the mill and fan it.

鮮 ‘Hsien. A live or fresh fish; fresh, raw, as meat; bright, new, as colors; clean, pure, in good order: also read ‘siêng and in the coll. ‚ch‘iêng, q. v.: ¹¹‚siêng ‚hwa, fresh flowers; ¹²‚siêng ‚ming, new and bright, as goods; COM., ¹³‚sing ‚siêng, fresh, new, as things newly made.

鮮 尟 ‘Hsien. Few, rare, seldom; complete, finished: the first also read ‚siêng, q. v.: ¹⁴‘siêng ‘sieu, very few; ¹⁵‚t‘iêng ha² ‘siêng e² few such in the world.

廯 ‘Hsien. A granary for storing rice: ¹⁶‘ling ‘siêng, a storehouse for grain.

癬 ‘Hsien. Tetter, ringworm; scrofulous diseases, scab, scald-head: used for ‘ch‘iêng in the coll. q. v.: ¹⁷kai² ‘siêng, scab, scorbutic complaints.

蘚 ‘Hsien. Moss, confervæ growing in damp places: ¹⁸‚t‘ai ‘siêng, green moss, as on tiles and walls.

閃 ‘Shan. To peep out of a door, to step out suddenly; a sudden and brief appearance; to shun, to evade; to glisten, to flash, as the lightning; to move about, to squirm, to wriggle; flashing, glittering; adulatory; in the coll. a sprain, an acute, lancinating pain; a crook in timber; to defer, to let a business rest: ¹⁹‘siêng tiêng² a flash of lightning; ²⁰‘siêng ‚k‘ai, to turn aside, to avoid; COLL., ²¹‘siêng ‚peng, a crook, a deflection, as in split timber; ‘siêng sioh₂ ‘peng, to let (the matter) rest a while, put it off; ‚yeu ‘siêng, a sprain or stitch in the side.

陝 ‘Shan. The region west of the Yellow river, now the province of Shensi, called ²²‘siêng ‚sá; COM., ²³‘siêng ‚kang, the provinces of

1 褊褼 2 爭先 3 先生 4 先後 5 先手 6 先帝 7 先知 8 先人 9 先父 10 風煽 11 鮮花 12 鮮明 13 新鮮 14 鮮少 15 天下鮮矣 16 廩廯 17 疥癬 18 苔蘚 19 閃電 20 閃開 21 閃爿 22 陝西 23 陝甘

Shensi and Kansuh. Also read *hak*: narrow.

燹 Hsien. A fire, fiery; fire on the moors, a signal fire, a beacon.

'僎 Also read *chwang*: to arrange, to number; the governor at a village feast; utensils, household gear.

'獮 Hsien. To kill; deleterious influences; the autumnal hunt taken by ancient emperors, which was also a kind of judicial progress through the land.

'毨 Hsien. To molt, to renew the hair or feathers; sleek, glossy, as newly molted birds.

'跣 Hsien. To walk without shoes, barefooted: [1]*siĕng chĕük*, naked feet. Read *siĕng*, as in [2]*p'iĕng siĕng*, to walk round, to whirl, to wriggle about.

'銑 Hsieh. The luster of metals; bright, lustrous, burnished; a small chisel; cold, chilly; not harmonious, disagreeing; the corners of an oblong bell; clamps on the ends of bows.

扇' Shan. Leaves of a door; a fan, a screen; to fan, to move to and fro; in the coll. a section of the frame of a building, a bent: [3]*chĕü siĕng* to fan itself, as said of a fly or butterfly; COLL., [4]*t'wang siĕng* round fans, usually of silk painted or embroidered; [5]*pah siĕng* white paper fans; [6]*chiong siĕng* a large, fan-like tablet, carried before officers, idols, and brides; [7]*siĕng kauk*, the frame or ribs of a fan; COLL., [8]*siĕng meng* (or *nioh*), the paper covering the frame; [9]*siĕng tŏi* a fan-case; [10]*siĕng ngiong*, the pin or rivet fastening the ends of the ribs; *yák siĕng* to fan; [11]*p'ah siĕng* to fan as an attendant does; [12]*siĕng sioh 'pa*, a fan; [13]*k'iĕ siĕng* to raise a bent.

搧' Shan. To strike with a fan or the hand; to fan, to brush off.

煽' Shan. A fierce fire; to fan a flame, to make a blaze; *met.*, to excite people, to stir up sedition: used for the coll. *siĕng*, q. v.: [14]*siĕng hĕk ing sing*, to incite people's minds, as to rebellion.

磶' Shan. To work and polish gems; a name for a jeweler.

謆' Shan. To talk speciously, to seduce or delude by fair speeches; to circumvent others and effect one's plans.

騸' Shan. To geld a horse; to castrate: [15]*siĕng 'ma*, a gelding; [16]*siĕng sĕü* to graft trees.

霰' Hsien. Snow and sleet falling, a storm of sleet; freezing rain; stars: [17]*siĕng ná*, an expelled nun.

醃' Yen. 醶' The 1st read *yĕng*; the 2d read *ch'ing* and used in the *Paik, Ing* for the coll. *siĕng*: to salt, to lay in brine; salted, pickled, corned: [18]*siĕng nük* to salt pork; [19]*siĕng tiĕ* cured

1 跣足 2 蹁跣 3 自扇 4 團扇 5 白扇 6 掌扇 7 扇骨 8 扇面 9 扇袋 10 扇仰 11 拍扇 12 扇一 把 13 豎扇〇 14 煽惑人心 15 騸馬 16 騸樹 17 霰尼〇 18 醃肉〇 19 醃𩵚〇

oysters; *siéng' k'ak, ˏkeng*, too highly salted; *siéng' ʻsi*, killed by salting, as clams, small fish, etc.

鹽 塩 ˏ Yen. Salt; to salt; name of a song, a lake, a hill, and an ancient state: [1]*ʻu ˏsiéng*, an ancient heroine who was homely but good; COM., [2]*ˏsiéng tó'* or *ˏsiéng hwak, tó'* the salt-commissioner; [3]*ˏsiéng ˏsiong*, a salt-merchant, manager of the salt-monopoly; [4]*ˏsiéng ʻkwang*, a salt-merchant's office; [5]*ˏsiéng k'wo'* the duty on salt; [6]*ˏsiéng ˏching*, lumps of salt; [7]*ˏsiéng lo'* brine; [8]*ˏsiéng ʻmi*, salt and rice — scattered about as charms; *ˏsiéng ˏtiong*, salt-yards; COLL., *ˏsiéng aěng' che' ˏsang ˏt'ěng*, the salt-jar has itself bred worms—a quarrelsome family; *ˏsiéng ch'o' mwoí' ˏsiong tioh*, has not yet tasted salt and vinegar—no experience of trials.

儃 ˏ Also read *ʻtang* and *tang'*: figure, air, manner, appearance: [9]*ˏsiéng ˏhui*, irresolute, hesitating whether to go on. Read *siéng'*: to abdicate, to resign to another.

澶 ˏ Shan. Still water; a river in the state of Sung, called [10]*ˏSiéng ˏyong*. Read *tang'*: slow, indolent; to give way to; distant.

蟬 ˏ Shan. Ch'an. The cicada or broad locust, called [11]*ˏtieu ˏsiéng*; to join, to connect: [12]*ˏch'iu ˏsiéng*, the autumn locust—a poetical term; [13]*ˏsiéng peng'* the hair in puffs on the temples; *ˏsiéng ˏyong*, to join; COM., [14]*ˏsiéng t'ói'* the exuviæ of a cicada; [15]*ˏsiéng ˏt'au*, the cicada-figure, as on the toes of shoes; *ˏsiéng kwoí'* the locust-coiffure. Read *siéng'*, as in *ʻwang siéng'* to squirm about.

禪 ˏ Shan. Ch'an. Tan. To sit and meditate, as Budhists do; abstraction: COM., [16]*ˏsiéng ˏtong*, the hall of contemplation; [17]*ˏsiéng t'iong'* a priest's wand; *ˏsiéng ˏsū*, a priest, an abbot; COLL., *sói' ˏsiéng*, to sit in deep meditation, as priests do. Read *siéng'*: to level a place for sacrificing; to abdicate, to resign the throne to another family, as Trajan and Yau did.

嬋 ˏ Beautiful, graceful, bewitching, as a woman: [18]*ˏsiéng ˏkiong*, elegant, as flowers or waving bamboos; *ˏsiéng ˏliéng*, relatives.

蟾 ˏ Shan. Ch'an. A striped toad, called [19]*ˏsiéng ˏtū* or *ˏsiéng ˏchū*, fabled to be in the moon; *met.*, the moon, a month; [20]*ˏsiéng ˏkwong*, moonlight; [21]*ˏsiéng ˏkūng*, the lunar palace, Diana's hall, the moon.

簷 檐 ˏ Yen. The eaves, the projecting part of a roof: used for the coll. *ˏsing*, q. v.: COM., [22]*ˏsiéng ˏchiéng* (coll. *ˏsing ˏkiéng*), the eaves; [23]*ˏsiéng ˏchiéng ʻná ʻmu*, the female spirit of the eaves; COLL., *ˏsiéng ˏkiéng lau' tek, k'auk*, the eaves drip and wear cavities; *met.*, said of one who is steady and trusty.

1 無鹽 2 鹽道 3 鹽商 4 鹽館 5 鹽課 6 鹽精 7 鹽滷 8 鹽米 9 儃佪 10 澶淵 11 蜩蟬 12 秋蟬 13 蟬鬢 14 蟬退 15 蟬頭 16 禪堂 17 禪杖 18 嬋娟 19 蟾蜍 20 蟾光 21 蟾宮 22 簷前 23 簷前奶母

暹 ˬ Hsien. Read ˬt'iĕng in the dictionaries: the increasing light and splendor of the sun; advancing, rising: COM., [1]ˬ*siéng ˬló kwook*, Siam, a word probably corrupted from Hsien through the Portuguese language.

單^2 Shan. Tan. Also read ˬ*siéng* in the dictionaries: according to De Guignes, a famous chief of the Huns, called [2]*Siéng*^{2} ˬ*ü*, B. C. 25; wide, vast, as deserts: also read ˬ*tang*, q. v.

善^2 Shan. Good, excellent; wise, virtuous; meek, gentle, docile; great, eminent; clever, expert, good at, dexterous; much, in a high degree; a term of approbation, well! good! to expedite, to do a thing well; to approve, to admire: [3]*siéng*^{2} *taik*, virtue; [4]'*pok*, *siéng*^{2} bad, vicious; unskillful; COM., [5]*siéng*^{2} ˬ*ing*, a good, virtuous man; [6]*siéng*^{2} ˬ*chüng*, a good end, a peaceful death; [7]*hó*' *siéng*^{2} to delight in doing good; [8]*miéng*^{2} *siéng*^{2} acquainted with one; *siéng*^{2} ˬ*liong*, good and gentle; *siéng*^{2} *auk*, *tó*' ˬ*t'eu* ˬ*chüng* '*iu pó*' good and evil will finally be recompensed.

墡^2 Shan. White earth, a whitish clay used for plastering walls.

蟮^2 Shan. An earthworm, called [9]ˬ*wong siéng*^{2} or '*wang siéng*^{2}.

鱔 鱓^2 Shan. A kind of eel, similar to the *ch'iăng*^{2}: [10]ˬ*sié siéng*^{2} a species of spotted, yellow and black eel; COM., [11]*siéng*^{2} ˬ*ngü*, an eel.

繕^2 Shan. To mend, to patch, to prepare, to put in order; to furbish, as weapons; to copy, to correct and state properly on paper; a scrivener: [12]*siéng*^{2} *lioh*, to transcribe; [13]ˬ*ching siéng*^{2} to put in order; [14]*siéng*^{2} '*siă*, to copy, to write out, as in offices.

饍 膳^2 Shan. Provisions, prepared food; viands, delicacies: [15]'*chó siéng*^{2} breakfast; [16]*siéng*^{2} ˬ*hu*, the court butler; COM., [17]ˬ*küng siéng*^{2} to furnish food, as to a tutor; [18]ˬ*sĕng siéng*^{2} to furnish a double portion, as to a tutor and his son; [19]'*yong siéng*^{2} the share for (a parent's) support.

羨 羡^2 Hsien. To desire, to covet, to long for; a remainder, an excess; to estimate higher than others, to laud: [20]ˬ*hing siéng*^{2} or ˬ*hüng siéng*^{2} to expect joyfully; [21]ˬ*ch'ing siéng*^{2} to praise; [22]*siéng*^{2} ˬ*ü*, a surplus. Read ˬ*yong*: the path leading down to a tomb.

擅^2 Shan. To do as one pleases; to assume, to usurp; to take the responsibility of acting; willful, dogged, pertinacious; arbitrarily, illegally; despotic, presumptuous: [23]*siéng*^{2} ˬ*tiong*, to manage ably; *siéng*^{2} ˬ*kwong*, to usurp authority; *siéng*^{2} ˬ*heng*, to act without or-

---

1 暹羅國 ○ 2 單于 3 善德 4 不善 5 善人 6 善終 7 好善 8 面善 9 蝹蟮 10 蛇鱔 11 鱔魚 12 繕錄 13 征繕 14 繕寫 15 早饍 16 饍夫 17 供饍 18 雙饍 19 養饍 20 興羨 21 稱羨 22 羨餘 23 擅長

ders; ‚chüong siĕng² to take on one, to assume.

贍 ² Shan. To lend aid, to give to, to supply; plentiful, sufficient, liberal: ‘k‘ŭng pok, siĕng² I fear there is not enough for a supply.

(742) Sieu.

燒 ‚ Shao. To burn; to light, to set fire to; to burn moors over; to fry, to roast; fired, distilled, as spirits: COM., [1]‚sieu ‘hwi, to kindle; to burn in the fire; [2]‚sieu hwa² to burn up; [3]hwak, ‚sieu, to have a fever; [4]‚sieu ngwa² to burn tiles; [5]‚sieu ‘chiu, ardent spirits; [6]‚sang ‚sieu, "thrice distilled", samshoo; COLL., ‚sieu tioh, ignited; ‚sieu ‚t‘ong, to heat water; ‚sieu k‘ó² to roast; ‚sieu ‚hiong ‘tiĕng chioh, to burn incense and light candles (to idols); ‚sieu ‚sang ke² and ‚sieu ‘si ke² to burn (mock money) on anniversaries of births and deaths; ‚sieu ‚hiong p‘ah, ‘tó huk, "burn incense and knock over the Budh"—to do a thing carelessly.

熽 ‚ Hsiao. To burn, to scorch; parched, dried up.

蕭 ‚ Hsiao. A plant, bitter like rue; a district in Soochow prefecture; a surname: [7]‚sieu ‘hu, a sort of pruning hook; [8]‚sieu se² a Budhist monastery; [9]‚sieu ‚sieu, neighing; [10]‚sieu ‚yong, agitated, troubled; COM., [11]‚sieu ‚teu, lonely, desolate; poor, impoverished.

簫 ‚ Hsiao. The pandean or orphic pipes; a sort of flute, a musical reed; the ends of a bow: COM., [12]‚sieu ‘kwong, a flute; [13]‚sieu móh, a reed or flap over the hole of a flute; [14]‚ch‘wi ‚sieu, to blow a flute.

彇 ‚ Hsiao. The ends or tapering points of a bow.

瀟 ‚ Hsiao. Stormy, wind and rain; clear, as water; a river in Yunnan, a tributary of the Pearl River; also a branch of the river Siang in Hunan: ‚sieu ‚sieu, a driving rain; [15]‚sieu ‘swa, neat, fine looking, as a person; pleasant, as a place.

蠨 ‚ Hsiao. A sort of long-legged spider or crane-fly (tipula), called [16]‚sieu ‚sieu; the name is applied to several long-legged insects.

蛸 ‚ Hsiao. A kind of long-legged spider or tipula, called ‚sieu ‚sieu; a caterpillar, called [17]‚song ‚p‘ieu ‚sieu, having a woolly envelop, and found on mulberry trees; [18]hai ‚p‘ieu ‚sieu, a cuttle fish.

消 ‚ Hsiao. To melt, to thaw, to liquefy; to lessen, to diminish, to annul; used up, consumed, exhausted; spent, as time; to allay, to quench, as thirst; to digest; diminished, dissipated; sold out, salable, in demand: [19]‚sieu yĕk, to abate a fever; COM., [20]‚sieu sang² dispersed; reduced, as a boil; [21]‚sieu hwa² to digest; [22]‚sieu sek, news; in the coll. an ear-brush; [23]‚sieu ‚chai, to remove calamities;

1 燒火	3 發燒	5 燒酒	7 蕭斧	9 蕭蕭	11 蕭條	13 簫膜	15 瀟灑	17 桑螵	螵蛸	20 消散	22 消息
2 燒化	4 燒瓦	6 三燒	8 蕭寺	10 蕭然	12 簫管	14 吹簫	16 蠨蛸	蛸 18 海	19 消熱	21 消化	23 消災

福州方言拼音字典

[1]ₒsieu ₒtü or ₒsieu miéks to destroy, to exterminate; [2]ₒsieu ₒmó, wasted, as money; ₒsieu ₒch'eu 'ká mong² to dissipate one's melancholy; COLL., 'chiá hwo' o² nói' sieu ₒt'au, these goods are tolerably salable.

銷 Hsiao. Analogous to the preceding: to fuse, to melt metals; to dissolve, to dissipate; to spend, to finish, to exhaust; deficient, wanting, as in politeness; small, attenuated, as the voice; also a kind of spade: [3]ₒsieu ₒking, to fuse metals; [4]ₒsieu 'hwi, to dissolve, to destroy what is useless; COM., [5]ₒk'ing ₒsieu, to run metal in molds; [6]ₒsieu ka' to report one's self after a furlough; [7]ₒsieu ang' to decide a case in court; to settle a case amicably; [8]paing² chaiu' ₒsieu, to prepare an account of taxes or revenue to forward to the emperor.

ₒ霄 Hsiao. The highest region of the a i r, the empyrean; misty snow which melts as it falls; a haze, vapor, fleecy c l o u d s: [9]ₒch'ing ₒsieu, the pure vapors, heaven; [10]ₒhung ₒsieu, fleecy c l o u d s; [11]ₒch'ûng ₒsieu, vapors ascending; [12]ₒsieu siok, half melted snow.

ₒ宵 Hsiao. N i g h t, the n i g h t; dark; to travel by night; few, small: [13]ₒsieu ₒheng, the glow-worm; C O M., [14]ₒt'ung ₒsieu, throughout the night; a kind of red candle; [15]ₒngwong ₒsieu, the full moon of the 1st month, the feast of lanterns (11th to the 15th day); [16]ₒngwong ₒsieu ₒwong, feast-of-lanterns balls, made of glutinous rice with stuffing of pork, etc.

ₒ硝 Hsiao. Nitre, s a l t p e t r e, of which seven kinds are enumerated; saline incrustations in rocks: COM., [17]ₒsieu 'ch'iong, a saltpetre factory; [18]ₒsieu ₒhwong, salt-petre; [19]p'auk, ₒsieu, epsom salts; ₒsiéng ₒsieu, saline incrustations, settlings of brine.

ₒ綃 Hsiao. Raw or unworked silk, plain silk fabrics; the woof of silk in weaving; a yard for suspending a s a i l: [20]ₒkau ₒsieu, a kind of byssus. Read ₒsau: to comb the hair in a tuft.

ₒ逍 Hsiao. To saunter about, to roam in joyance, as the immortals: COM., [21]ₒsieu ₒyeu chëü² chai² to ramble at ease and in fine spirits.

ₒ翛 The sound of wings; the molting of birds, the feathers rubbed off: [22]ₒsieu ₒyong, suddenly, hastily, impromptu; ₒsieu ₒsieu, a rushing of wings; molted, rubbed off.

ₒSieu. A coll. word, as in ₒsieu mai² small bread-cakes with stuffing in, cooked by steaming.

'羞 Hsiu. Read ₒsiu; coll. 'sieu, as in 'sieu 'lá, shame, ashamed; 'sieu 'lá ₒnëng, a shameless f e l l o w; má² 'hieu tek, 'sieu 'lá, shameless, brazen faced.

'小 Hsiao. Small, l i t t l e; petty, mean, trifling; narrow, contracted; my, our; inferior; y o u n g; subtile,

[1]消除 [2]消磨 [3]銷金 [4]銷毀 [5]傾銷 [6]銷假 [7]銷案 [8]辦銷奏 銷霄 [9]清霄 [10]雲霄 霄 [11]冲霄 [12]霄霄 霄 [13]宵行 [14]通宵 [15]元宵 [16]元宵丸 宵 [17]硝廠 [18]硝磺 [19]朴硝 [20]鮫綃 [21]逍遊自在 [22]翛然

minute; to disesteem; the 42d radical: COM., [1]'sieu ˌsing, careful; [2]'sieu 'chwi, urine; [3]'sieu ˌing, a mean, unprincipled man; 'sieu 'chü, a young child; my pupil; 'sieu ˌi, my son; [4]'sieu ˌkĕng, small work, jobs, as of assistants of regular workmen; [5]'sieu ch'ek, a pilferer; [6]'sieu 'k'ó, unimportant, trifling in amount; [7]'sieu 'chŭng, Souchong tea; 'sieu ˌteng ˌk'wo, to gain the small degree—i. e., to get married; COLL., 'sieu ˌnĕng, my humble self; 'sieu ˌnĕng 'kiăng, a girl, an unmarried daughter; 'sieu 'kwong, the shrill cry of fowls, falsetto.

'少 Shao. Little, few; briefly, rarely, seldom; in a slight degree; wanting, insufficient; to owe; to disparage, to defame: also read sieu' and in the coll. 'chieu, q. v.: [8]'sieu 'twang, inadequate, a limited supply of; [9]che' 'sieu, very few; [10]'sieu k'iéng' to owe; COM., [11]ˌtó 'sieu, how many? 'sieu pok, 'miéng, quite unavoidable.

'篠 Hsiao. A small kind of bamboo, which is very firm and smooth, and suitable for making arrows and small organs.

少' Shao. Young in years, juvenile; a youth; to assist, to second: also read 'sieu, q. v.: sieu' 'chü, the youngest son; [12]'ló sieu' the old and the young; COM., [13]sieu' ˌniéng, young in years; [14]eu' sieu' tender, delicate; sieu' ˌié, a young gentleman; sieu' sieu' smallish; sparse and neat, as flowers; tender, just budded.

嘯' Hsiao. A whistling sound, as of a swift wind; a sharp, hissing sound, as of steam let off; to whistle; to roar, to scream: [15]'hu sieu' a tiger's roar; [16]ˌkó sieu' the sound of singing songs; [17]siéng' sieu' good at whistling.

肖' Hsiao. To assimilate, to imitate, to be like; a relationship, as between parent and child—said to be proved by their blood readily mingling in a cup; like, resembling, alike; small, dwindling, deteriorating; scattered, lost: in the coll. read saiu' q. v.: [18]sieu' 'chü, a good son; COM., [19]p'aik, sieu' very similar, closely resembling; [20]pok, sieu' inferior, degenerate, as a son.

鞘' Shao. Ch'iao. A case, a sheath, the scabbard of a sword: ˌping pok, lié' sieu' arms not leaving their sheaths—a time of peace; COM., [21]ˌtó sieu' the sheath of a knife or sword. Read ˌsau: a whip.

誚' Hsiao. Ch'iao. To blame, to reprehend; to ridicule, to speak harshly or sarcastically to: used for chieu' (to scold), q. v.: [22]ˌki sieu' to satirize.

ˌ韶 Shao. An ancient musical instrument; the music of Shun; to connect, to continue; the harmony of voices; mild, gentle: [23]ˌSieu ˌchiu 'hu, a department in the north of Kwangtung.

---

[1]小心 [2]小水 [3]小人 [4]小工 [5]小賊 [6]小可 [7]小種 [8]少短 [9]至少 [10]少欠 [11]多少 [12]老少 [13]少年 [14]幼少 [15]虎嘯 [16]歌嘯 [17]善嘯 [18]肖子 [19]迫肖 [20]不肖 [21]刀鞘 [22]譏誚 [23]韶州府○

軺 ꜀ A small carriage, a one-horse cart or chaise.

齠 ꜀ T'iao. To shed teeth; young, in childhood: [1]꜀*sieu* ʻ*ch'ing*, to get the new teeth; [2]꜀*sieu* ꜀*niêng*, a young child.

迢 ꜀ T'iao. To go far; distant, remote, far away: [3]꜀*sieu* ꜀*iu*, far, remote; [4]꜀*ch'iêng* ʻ*li* ꜀*sieu* ꜀*sieu*, thousands of miles away.

髫 ꜀ T'iao. The hair of a child hanging down, ringlets: [5]꜀*sieu* ꜀*niêng*, young; ꜀*sieu* ꜀*sieu*, falling tufts.

꜀*Sieu*. A coll. word: to seesaw, to have a reciprocating motion, as a sedan, or bridge of planks: ꜀*sieu siék*$_{2}$ broken by a violent shaking; ꜀*kau* ꜀*sieu*, "a monkey's motions"—fickle, vacillating.

召^{2} Chao. Used for the next in the sense of a surname and name of a place: also read *tieu*^{2} q. v.

邵^{2} **郘**^{2} Shao. High, eminent in virtue and character; a surname; a city of the ancient Tsin; to animate, to stimulate to effort: [6]꜀*niêng* ꜁*kó taik*꜀ *sieu*^{2} aged and highly virtuous; COM., [7]*Sieu*^{2} ʻ*u* ʻ*hu*, a department in the N. W. of Fookien.

劭^{2} Shao. To exert one's self; to stimulate one; beauty, excellence: [8]*sieu*^{2} ꜀*nung*, to encourage husbandmen.

紹^{2} Shao. To connect, to tie; to succeed to, to hand down, as a trade; to imitate one's predecessors: [9]*kai*ʾ *sieu*^{2} an agent or assistant; [10]*sieu*^{2} ꜁*ki* ꜀*kiu*, to follow a father's business; COM., [11]*sieu*^{2} ꜁*hing*, a department in Chehkiang, famous for silks, etc.; [12]*sieu*^{2} ꜁*hing ch'o*ʾ Sieuhing vinegar; COLL., *sieu*^{2} ꜁*hing* ʻ*chio*, Sieuhing bean-curd. Read ꜀*sieu*: slow, dilatory.

Sieu^{2}. A coll. word: to be fond of, to desire greatly; greedy, addicted to: *sieu*^{2} *siăh*$_{2}$ given to appetite; *sieu*^{2} *sëüng*^{2} fond of dress; *sieu*^{2} ꜀*nëng* ʻ*hó*, pleased with another's good conduct; ꜁*t'ang sieu*^{2} to regard admiringly, to desire to equal.

Sieu^{2}. A coll. word, as in ꜀*ngü sieu*^{2} a white conglomerate substance, like pancreas or sweetbread, as found in the *pah*$_{2}$ *lik*$_{2}$ fish.

(743) Sik.

襲$_{2}$ Hsi. A double garment, lined robes, a court dress; a suit; a robe fastened on the left side; united, collected, repeated; to invade, to make a foray into; to receive, to inherit; hereditary, descending in a family: [13]*sie*ʾ *sik*$_{2}$ hereditary; [14]*sik*$_{2}$ *eng*ʾ hereditary protection and pension, as for the merit of ancestors; [15]*sié*ʾ *sik*$_{2}$ ʻ*chü chiok*, a hereditary baronetcy.

什$_{2}$ Shih. A file of ten men, two ranks of five; various, sundry: [16]*sik*$_{2}$ *uk*$_{2}$ things, articles; [17]꜀*p'ieng sik*$_{2}$ paragraphs, books; [18]*sik*$_{2}$ *k'e*ʾ

[1]齠齔 [2]齠年 [3]迢遙 [4]千里迢迢 [5]髫年 [6]年高德邵 [7]邵武府 [8]劭農 [9]介紹 [10]紹箕裘 [11]紹興 [12]紹興醋 ○ [13]世襲 [14]襲蔭 [15]世襲子爵 [16]什物 ○ [17]篇什 [18]什器

chattels, utensils; [1]'sik ˏmó (in the court dialect *shih mo*), what?

值 Ch'ih. To happen, to occur, to meet with: also read *tik*, and in the coll. *tek* and *tih*, q. v.: [2]'*sek*, *sik* it happened; [3]ˏ*siong sik* to meet with.

埴 Shih. Adhesive clay: [4]ˏ*t'wang sik* to mold in clay; [5]'*chaik*, *sik* to feel one's way with a stick.

殖 Shih. To plant, to enrich; to grow, to flourish, to fatten; to amass, as riches; to appoint, to found, to establish: [6]*sik*, *hwo*' to amass, greedy of gain; [7]ˏ*hung sik* to appoint to office.

植 Ch'ih. Shih. To plant, to set up; to transplant, to set out; erect, upright, as trees; to lean on; a beater or mallet; a post to hang silk on: *sik*, ˏ*ki t'iong* leaned on his staff; [8]'*ho*' *sik* door-posts.

稙 Grain planted early, the first crop; to sow in good time; the first wife.

夕 Hsi. The evening, dusk; late; the last day, as of a year; out of the perpendicular; the 36th radical: [9]ˏ*tieu sik* morning and evening; [10]ˏ*tü sik* last day of the year; [11]ˏ*king sik* this evening.

穸 Hsi. A dark chamber in a tomb, a vault, a niche or recess in a sepulcher; dark, obscure, as night: [12]ˏ*tung sik* the tomb.

汐 Hsi. The evening tide, high tide at sunset; the name of a stream.

湜 Shih. Pure, limpid water, through which the bottom can be seen; sincere, pure-minded; to maintain correctly and firmly.

席 Hsi. Interchanged with the next: a mat to sleep on; a table, a repast; to spread out; ample, wide, large or flowing, as a garment: [13]ˏ*yong sik* a feast; [14]ˏ*tung sik* a fellow-guest; [15]ˏ*sü sik* a teacher; [16]*siék*, *sik* to spread a feast; COM., [17]'*chiu sik* a banquet.

蓆 Hsi. A mat, as of rush or rattan; a mat spread to eat on; a meal, a repast, a table; to spread, to lay out, as mats; large and wide, as robes; to depend on; to aid, to assist; pliable, as one's disposition; rest, quiet: used for the coll. *ch'ioh*, q. v.

食 Shih. To take food, to eat; to drink; to smoke; to undo, to retract; to receive, to enjoy; to befool, to delude; the 184th radical: also read *söü*' and in the coll. *siáh*, q. v.: [18]*muk*, *sik* to look at wistfully; ornamental dishes; 'ngi *sik*, *pok*, *hwa*' to hear and not understand; [19]*hiék*, *sik* to sacrifice; COM., [20]ˏ*hang sik* the day before the ˏ*ch'ing* ˏ*ming*, or 5th of the 24 solar terms; [21]'*ing sik* to drink and eat; [22]'*hwi sik* daily food, provisions; [23]ˏ*i sik* clothing and food; [24]*sik*, ˏ*lang*, a provision-basket; *chiék*, *sik* an extra allowance of

1 什麽	3 相值	5 擿埴	7 封殖	9 朝夕	11 今夕	13 筵席	15 師席	17 酒席	19 血食	21 飲食	23 衣食
2 適值	4 摶埴	6 殖貨	8 戶植	10 除夕	12 窀穸	14 同席	16 設席	18 目食	20 寒食	22 伙食	24 食籃

cash for food; 'sik, ,t'ëng, worms in the bowels; ³kaik, sik, indigestible; dyspepsia; COLL., 'nü siáh, sik, lük, you are on salary!—reproof of a glutton. Read sek,: an eclipse.

石 Shih. ² A stone, a rock; stony, rocky; petrified, ringing stones; hard, firm, decided; a stone, a dry and liquid measure, varying at different times; a measure of 10 'tau or pecks; a weight of 100—120 catties; an aerolite; in a met., sense, barren, as a womb; the 112th radical: in the coll. read sioh, q. v.

碩 Shih. ² Great, fat, corpulent; to fill; full, replete; ripe, mature; met., eminent in talents, high-minded.

鼫 Shih. ² A burrowing rodent, which destroys grain; a species of field mouse, or dormouse.

習 Hsi. ² The continued flight of birds; to repeat, to practice; accustomed, skilled in; use, custom, habit, reiteration; to review, as the lessons of 6 days: ³sik, sük, versed, mature; ⁴sik, liéng' practice; COM., ⁵sik, kwang' chëü' ,yong, practice makes it natural; COLL., ,i k'e' sik, ,ngai, his habits are bad.

翼 Yi. I. ² Read ik,; coll. sik,: a wing: ⁶,cheu sik, birds' wings; ⁷sik, 'pong, the shoulder of a wing.

慴 ² To lie prostrate; timid, alarmed, cowardly: the same as chiék, q. v.: sik, huk, to lie down flat, to succumb; ⁸,ching sik, to be alarmed.

熠 I. ² Bright, brilliant, splendid; to glisten, to sparkle: ⁹sik, yeu' refulgent, shining, as fire-flies.

槢 ² A hard, solid wood, durable timber: ¹⁰sik, muk, a sort of hard wood.

霫 ² A heavy shower, rainy; ancient tribes of northerners near Corea or Manchuria, spoken of during the T'ang dynasty and sometimes called Chüyen, Wujomu, and Huangshui.

拾 Shih. ² To gather, to collect with the hand; to dispose in order, to arrange; a sort of armlet, or defence for the arm: sometimes used, but erroneously, for siék, (to ford): also read sek, and used for k'ak, in the coll. q. v.: COM., ¹¹,siu sik, to gather up, to put in order; met., to manage one, to plague or take revenge on him.

實 寔 实 Shih. ² Real, solid; full, stuffed; settled, compact, as ground; true, sincere, honest; fixed, as a price; to fill, to cram; fruit of plants; results, effects; the reality, the facts of: ¹²,kung sik, military stores: COM., ¹³sik, ,hü, true and false, substantial and empty; ¹⁴sik, seng' to believe truly; credible; ¹⁵sik, chai' (coll. sik, lóh,) truly,

¹食蟲 ²腸食 ³習熟 ⁴習練 ⁵習慣自然 ⁶鳥翼 ⁷翼膊 ⁸震慴 ⁹熠燿 ¹⁰槢木 ¹¹收拾 ¹²軍實 ¹³實虛 ¹⁴實信 ¹⁵實在

really, indeed; [1]*lô sik*$_2$ honest; kind, tame, as an animal; *sik*$_2$ *k‘wok*$_2$ "the real vacancy"—a permanent appointment; *te*^{3} *sik*$_2$ the ground settled or solid; [2]*sik*$_2$ *këü*^{3} true evidence, good proof; *kiék*$_2$ *sik*$_2$ to set, as fruit; to bear fruit; [3]*sik*$_2$ *taik*$_2$ net gain; [4]*sik*$_2$ *sëü*^{3} a fact, a reality; *sik*$_2$ *,sing sik*$_2$ *e*^{3} real intent, heartily; *sik*$_2$*hek*$_2$ *,ching ,chong*, he is the real thief; COLL., *sak*$_2$ *sik*$_2$ or *sak*$_2$ *sak*$_2$ *sik*$_2$ most positively it is.

Sik$_2$. A coll. euphonic prefix, as in *sik*$_2$ *siok*$_2$ to run about, to whirl about, as boys in play; *sik*$_2$ *sak*$_2$ to boil things; *sik*$_2$ *sok*$_2$ to rub gently; to paint; *sik*$_2$ *siék*$_2$ to break in two; *sik*$_2$ *sëk*$_2$ to shake to and fro.

(744) Sing.

身 *,* Shên. The body, the trunk; *met.*, the main part of a thing, the hull of a ship; I, myself, one's self; the 158th radical: COM., [5]*‘chüng ,sing*, the whole lifetime; [6]*,sing ‘t‘á*, or *nük*$_2$ *,sing*, (coll. *,sing ,tá*), the body; [7]*,sing ,si*, a corpse; *,sing sié*^{3} personal bearing; presence, authority; [8]*,sing hong*^{3} one's calling; body, substance, stamina; *,sing haiu*^{3} after death; *,sing ,ka*, self and family; [9]*,sing ,piéng*, by or with one; *kwo*^{3} *,sing*, all past, done; *pwang*^{3} *,sing*, half of the person, the bust; [10]*‘pwong ,sing*, one's self; *,ch‘ing ,sing*, personally, in person; [11]*ch‘ok*$_2$ *,sing*, to enter on life, to establish one's self in business; COLL., *sioh*$_2$ *,sing t‘iäng*^{3} the whole body in pain; *,sing ,p‘wi*, the bodily frame, as to size, &c.; *o*^{3} *,sing sié*^{3} and *,mó ,sing sié*^{3} can and cannot.

娠 孕 *,* Shên. The fœtus; to be pregnant: COM., [12]*,sing ‘hi*, or *tai*^{3} *,sing*, pregnant; COLL., [13]*lóh*$_2$ *,sing*, an abortion, a miscarriage; *p‘ah*$_2$ *lóh*$_2$ *,sing*, to produce abortion.

媳 *,* Hsi. Read *sek*$_2$; used for the coll. *,sing*, as in *,sing mo*^{3} a daughter-in-law, a bride; *,sing mo*^{3} *‘kiäng*, a girl betrothed in infancy and reared in the family of her future husband.

心 忄 小 *,* Hsin. The physical heart; the mind, the understanding; the heart, the affections, the will; *met.*, the center, the inside of; intention, desire, aim; origin or source; the 5th of the 28 constellations, answering to Antares, *s* and *t* in Scorpio; the 61st radical: [14]*,t‘iéng ,sing*, the zenith; *,sing ché*^{3} *,kó*, ambitious; high-toned feeling; COM., [15]*‘piéng ,sing*, the character for "heart" in distinction from [16]*,tong ,sing*, the character for "body;" [17]*nói*^{3} *,sing* (coll. *,sing ‘tié*), in the heart, the heart, the mind; [18]*,sing sang*^{3} the disposition; [19]*,sing ,kang*, heart and liver; *met.*, the affections, the heart; [20]*,sing e*^{3} thought, intention; *,sing ,sü ,ngiong haing*^{3} the thoughts, words, and actions; [21]*,sing suk*$_2$ one's principles; [22]*,liong ,sing*, a good heart, conscience; *,sing k‘ieu*^{3} the mental apertures, clever, astute; *,sing ,hü*, timid, apprehensive; [23]*,sing chak*$_2$ confused, distracted; [24]*,sü ,sing*, private, selfish; *,sing te*^{3} the mind or intellect,

1 老實 3 實得 5 終身 7 身尸 9 身邊 11 出身 13 落娠 15 扁心 17 內心 19 心肝 21 心術 23 心雜
2 實據 4 實事 6 身體 8 身分 10 本身 12 娠喜 14 天心 16 長身 18 心性 20 心意 22 良心 24 私心

perceptive power; [1],sing ,tiéng, the heart, the mind as to moral quality of goodness, etc.; [2],sing 'si, the mind dead to an object; ngaing' ,sing, a stubborn will; [3],sing ,chieu, distressed in mind; COLL., ,sing 'pa tiăng' to keep the mind at ease; not to fear; o' ,sing chó' to have a heart to do; ,mó ,sing sëü' no heart for it; ng' kwo' ,sing, can't endure the thought of, can't have the heart to; p'ang' ,sing, or p'aëng' ,sing, hollow, decayed inside; ,sing ,mó tioh, ,kang, absent-minded.

沁 'Hsin. A large affluent of the Yellow river, and an inferior department in S. E. Shansi. Read 'sing: to sound, to fathom, to try the depth of water; *met.*, to comprehend.

星 ,Hsing. A star, a planet; a meteor; a spark; dots, points; miscellaneous, scattered; quick, shooting; the 25th zodiacal constellation: [4],heng ,sing, planets; [5],king ,sing, fixed stars; ,sing ,sing, stars; ,sing sang' scattered as stars, sprinkled about; ,sing ,sing, numerous, starry; silvery hairs; COM., [6]'ngu ,sing, the 5 planets, viz., [7]'chwi ,sing, Mercury, [8],king ,sing, Venus, [9]'hwo ,sing, Mars, [10]muk, ,sing, Jupiter, and [11]'t'u ,sing, Saturn; [12],sing seu' constellations; [13],sing toi' a star falling, a meteor, an aerolite; ,liu ,sing 'ma, a camp spy; [14]ch'ek, ,sing, the Pleiades; ch'ek, ,sing 'ná, a patroness of children; 'hó ,sing seu' (born under) a lucky star! 'mwang ,t'iéng ,sing, a small yellow aster; *met.*, spotted, as firs; figured, as the sewed soles of shoes.

猩 ,Hsing. Shêng. A species of ape, called ,sing ,sing, found in Yunnan; fabled to weep as a child and to be able to talk; it is probably a species of chimpanzee.

腥 ,Hsing. Small tumors on the body, about as large as grains of rice; measly flesh; raw meat; rancid, strong, stinking, frouzy; the smell of fresh meat: ,sing ,ngü, raw fish; COM., [15],sing ,ch'ó, rank, stinking, fishy.

勝 ,Shêng. To bear, to sustain; able to assume, adequate to, worthy of; to raise, to elevate: also read seng' q. v.: pok, ,sing, the highest degree of, not surpassable; [16]pok, ,sing ,ki eng' unequal to the office; COM., [17]pok, 'k'ó ,sing ,ngiong, cannot all be told!

醒 ,Hsing. Also read 'sing: to recover from intoxication, to become sober; to awake, to arouse or bestir one's self; incited, stirred up, awakened: used for the coll. 'ch'ang, q. v.: [18]choi' ,sing, to recover from a debauch; [19],sing sié' to arouse the age; [20],sing kauk, to attend to and comprehend.

鋥 ,Hsing. Also spoken ,ching: the coating of iron, rust; tarnish: COM., [21],sang ,sing, to rust; [22],tó ,sing, rust on a knife.

升 ,Shêng. A dry measure, containing ten *kak*, and once made to hold a catty of rice, a Chinese pint; a

[1]心田	[3]心焦	[5]經星	[7]水星	[9]火星	[11]土星	[13]星墜	[15]腥臊	其任	勝言	[19]醒世	[21]生鋥
[2]心死	[4]行星	[6]五星	[8]金星	[10]木星	[12]星宿	[14]七星	[16]不勝	[17]不可	[18]醉醒	[20]醒覺	[22]刀鋥

skein of 80 threads; the 46th diagram, denoting advancement; to advance, to rise in office; to ascend; to complete, to accumulate: in the coll. read *꜀ching*, q. v.: [1]'*nik*꜁ *꜀sing*, the sun rising; COM., [2]*꜀sing kaung*ʾ to ascend and descend; [3]*꜀sing꜀t'iĕng*, to ascend to heaven, as a god does.

陞 ꜀Shêng. Same as the preceding in the following meanings; to ascend, as stairs; to rise, to advance; promoted in office: COM., [4]*꜀sing ꜀kwang ꜀tu*, catalogues of those holding office; [5]*꜀sing siong*ʾ to ascend; to take a higher seat; [6]*꜀sing kaung*ʾ to promote and to degrade; [7]*kó ꜀sing*, to rise in office, promotion; [8]*꜀liĕng ꜀sing ꜀sang ngek*, to rise three grades successively; COLL., [9]*꜀sing 'k'i*, to raise (the poles)—so that one may enter or leave the sedan.

昇 ꜀Shêng. To rise, to ascend, as the sun; peaceful, tranquil: [10]*꜀sing ꜀ping*, peaceful, as a time of plenty and prosperity.

先 ꜀Hsien. Read *꜀siĕng*; coll. *꜀sing*, as in *꜀sing ꜀sang*, a teacher; Sir, Mr.; a physician; *꜀sing ꜀sang 'mu*, or *꜀sing ꜀sang ꜀niong*, a teacher's wife, lady, Mrs.

詵 ꜀Shên. To converse with, to inquire, to ask information; the opinion of the multitude: *꜀sing ꜀sing*, a crowd, a multitude conversing.

侁駪 ꜀Shên. A multitude of men and horses; a large crowd: *꜀sing ꜀sing*, a multitude in motion, the noise and tramp of a crowd.

騂 ꜀Hsing. A bay or sorrel horse; a yellowish or reddish brown color: [11]*꜀sing ꜀ngiu*, a red or yellowish cow; *꜀sing ꜀sing*, well adjusted, as bows.

辛 ꜀Hsin. Pungent, sharp, piquant; acrid, bitter; *met.*, grievous, bitter, sad, toilsome; the 8th of the ten stems, used in astronomical divisions of time; the 160th radical: [12]*꜀sing ĕ*ʾ an acrid taste; COM., [13]*꜀sing 'k'u*, distressed; wearied, fagged; COLL., *꜀sing ꜀song móh꜁ k'ŏ*ʾ *tio*ʾ *꜀t'au ꜀t'iĕ*, when in distress don't go to the street to weep—*scil.*, for you'll get no sympathy.

莘 ꜀Hsin. ꜀Shên. A marshy plant, like sweet-flag or the asarum; long: *꜀sing ꜀sing*, numerous; [14]*꜀sing 'yâ*, marshy land; [15]*꜀Sing kaing*ʾ a district in the west of Shantung.

新 ꜀Hsin. To cut and gather wood; new, fresh; the latest, the best; to renew, to improve, to increase, add to; occurs in many names of places: [16]*taik꜁ hwa*ʾ *nik꜁ ꜀sing*, his virtues daily renovate others, as said of a good ruler; [17]*꜀sing p'aiu*ʾ a new port; Singapore; COM., [18]*꜀sing ꜀siĕng*, new and fresh; [19]*꜀sing yong*ʾ a new fashion; [20]*꜀sing ch'aung*ʾ newly invented; *꜀sing*

---

[1]日升 [2]升降 [3]升天 [4]陞官圖 [5]陞上 [6]陞降 [7]高陞 [8]連陞三級 [9]陞起 [10]昇平 [11]騂牛 [12]辛味 [13]辛苦 [14]莘野 [15]莘縣 [16]德化日新 [17]新埠○ [18]新鮮 [19]新樣 [20]新創○

,hwong, just married; [1],sing ,long and [2],sing ,ing, the bridegroom and bride; ,sing ,mwo, a new coinage; ,sing ,ung 'chai, a newspaper; ,sing ,kwang tó' eng' the new officer just entering on his office; COLL., ,sing ko' new and old; ,sing siong' nóh, a new invoice of goods; ,sing ,li, or ,sing kau' just come, newly arrived, as a person.

薪 ‚Hsin. Firewood, fuel; brambles; to collect fuel: [3],sing 'ch'ó, grass for fuel; [4]ho' ,sing, to carry faggots.

聲 声 ‚Shêng. A sound, a noise; a voice, a tone; music; verbally; fame, reputation; to declare, to publish; to praise; to exhibit, to make an example of: in the coll. read siáng, q. v.: [5],sing kau' to give verbal instruction; [6],hung ,sing, the spirit and manners of the age; a report; COM., [7],sing ka' one's credit, a parade of talents or influence; [8],sing k'e' harmony, congeniality of spirit; ,sing ,ming ,long chik, an infamous reputation.

申 ‚Shên. To extend; to stretch out, to stretch, as from fatigue; to state, to explain; to reiterate; again, repeated; the 9th of the 12 stems, the hour from 3 to 5 P. M. ruled by the ape: ,sing ,sing ,ü ,ü at ease, composed; [9],sing t'ek, to charge straitly; COM., [10],sing ,si, or ,sing k'aik, or ,sing ,kau, the 9th hour; [11],sing ,ming, to state clearly; [12],sing 'chwi, a premium on silver; [13]p'ieu' sing, the premium on a bank-bill.

伸 ‚Shên. Analogous to the preceding: to straighten, to stretch out; to state, to elucidate a matter; to stretch and yawn; to right, to redress, to vindicate the innocent; redressed, righted: [14],sing 'ch'iu, to extend the hand; [15]k'ieng' ,sing, to stretch and yawn; [16],sing ,ung, a statement; [17],sing suk, to extend and to contract; COM., [18],sing ,wong, to redress a wrong.

呻 ‚Shên. To groan, to lament; to hum, to chant: [19],sing ,nging, to recite, as poems or books.

紳 ‚Shên. A sash, a large girdle with ornamented ends; to gird; those who may wear sashes, the gentry: [20],sing sê' or ,sing ,k'ing, the gentry and graduates; COM., [21],hiong ,sing, the gentry; cheng' ,sing lioh, a record of civil and military officers, the Red Book.

,Sing. A coll. euphonic prefix, as in ,sing ,song, to bolt, to shove a bolt; ,sing ,siong, to inlay, to insert, to set, as glass.

省 'Shêng. Hsing. To look narrowly at, to examine, to inspect; to discriminate; to awaken; watchful; a fault: also read 'seng, q. v.: 'sing 'sing, uneasy, disquieted; [22]nói' 'sing, to examine the heart; [23]'sing ,ch'ing, to visit one's parents, as an officer does; COM., [24]'sing ch'ak, (also spoken 'seng ch'ak,) to examine.

[1]新郎 [2]新人 [3]薪草 [4]負薪 [5]聲教 [6]風聲 [7]聲價 [8]聲氣 [9]申飭 [10]申時 [11]申明 [12]申水 [13]票申 [14]伸手 [15]欠伸 [16]伸文 [17]伸縮 [18]伸冤 [19]呻吟 [20]紳士 [21]鄉紳 [22]內省 [23]省親 [24]省察

‘惺 ‘[忄省] Hsing. The first also read ,*sing:* intelligent, comprehending; still, tranquil, as a night; passionless: [1]‘*sing ngwo*’ to recall, to awaken to a sense of.

‘蜃 Shên. A large kind of cockle: [2]‘*sing ,kau* or [3]‘*sing ,leu*, a large snake, fabled to produce cities, houses, &c., with its breath; [4]‘*sing t‘ang*’ charcoal of burnt cockle-shells. Read *seng*’ as in [5]*seng*’ *,kiong*, the Mirage Land, as Loochoo people call their country.

‘淰 Shên. Also read ‘*niéng:* muddy, thick, turbid; water flowing; an implement for dredging mud: [6]‘*sing ‘siéng*, the flowing of water.

‘沈 Shên. Interchanged with the the next in the sense of gravy: an ancient state; a surname: also read ,*t‘ing*, q. v.

‘瀋 Shên. Juice, gravy. Read *seng*’: to put water in a vessel; a vessel to pour from.

‘審 Shên. To investigate, to search into; to discern, to discriminate; to judge, as a magistrate; a bundle of plumes or feathers for arrows: [7]‘*sing ong*’ or [8]‘*sing seng*’ a judicial inquiry; [9]‘*sing keu*’ to examine (a case) minutely; COM., [10]‘*sing ,si*, a judge; [11]‘*sing ang*’ to try a case; [12]‘*sing p‘wang*’ (or *twang*’), to judge, to decide a case; [13]‘*tieu*’ ‘*sing*, to summon (a prisoner) to court; COLL., ‘*sing sioh*, *,tong*, to hold one session on a case.

‘嬸 Shên. The wife of a father's younger brother: ‘*mu* and ‘*sing*, are terms by which the wives of older and younger brothers call each other respectively: COM., [14]‘*sing ,pó*, the wife of a grandfather's younger brother; [15]‘*sé*’ ‘*sing*, the wife of my husband's younger brother; [16],*ch‘ing ,ka ‘sing*, the wife of the younger brother of a sister's husband; COLL., ,*i* ‘*sing*, a compellation of women, younger than one's self, called *ak*, ‘*sing* in southern districts.

‘稔 Shên. Read ‘*ing* in the dictionaries: ripe grain; matured, abundant; a season or harvest, a year; accumulated: [17]‘*sing ,nieng*, an abundant year; [18]‘*sing ŏk*, mature in wickedness.

‘諗 Shên. To consider maturely, to consult about; to reprove, to reprehend; to announce one's views; to go into a deep or abyss.

‘哂 Shên. To smile, to laugh at with slight disapproval; to seem pleased: [19]‘*sing nak*, to receive smilingly; [20],*hu ‘chü ‘sing ,chi*, the master smiled at him.

‘*Sing.* A coll. euphonic prefix, as in ‘*sing ‘siong*, to bestow rewards; ‘*sing ‘sĕng*, to shake to and fro; ‘*sing ‘sang*, to sprinkle powders; ‘*sing ‘siong*, to think of, to consider.

辰 Ch‘en. To produce motion; the heavenly bodies, which mark time; a Chinese hour, the twelfth

[1]惺悟 [2]蜃蛟 [3]蜃樓 [4]蜃炭 [5]蜃疆 [6]淰潤 [7]審問 [8]審訊 [9]審究 [10]審司 [11]審案 [12]審判 [13]吊審 [14]嬸婆 [15]細嬸〇 [16]親家嬸〇 [17]稔年〇 [18]稔惡 [19]哂納 [20]夫子哂之

of a day; the hour from 7 to 9 A. M., the 5th of the 12 branches, ruled by the dragon; times, seasons; the 161st radical: [1]꜀*chung* ꜀*sing*, a divining book; [2]*pok*꜀ ꜀*sing*, ill-starred, unlucky; [3]꜀*hwa* ꜀*sing ngwok*꜀ *sik*꜀ the time of blooming flowers and moonlight nights; COM., [4]꜀*si* ꜀*sing*, a Chinese hour; ꜀*sing* ꜀*si chiăng*꜄ 8 A. M.; ꜀*si* ꜀*sing* ꜂*chŭng*, a clock; ꜀*si* ꜀*sing* ꜂*pieu*, a watch.

宸 ꜀Ch'ên. A secret chamber, an emperor's retired apartment: [5]꜂*hung* ꜀*sing*, the maple palace; *met.*, the emperor.

晨 ꜀Ch'ên. The sun beaming forth in the morning; day, dawn; clear, bright: [6]꜀*sing sik*꜀ morn and eve; [7]꜂*chó* ꜀*sing*, early dawn; [8]꜀*sing* ꜂*hung*, a bird of prey of the hawk species; ꜀*sing* ꜂*hwong teng*꜄ ꜂*seng*, to inquire after parents' health morning and night.

晟 ꜀ Also read *seng*꜄: the full brightness of the sun; light, effulgence, splendor.

成 ꜀Ch'êng. To finish, to perfect, to effect; to become; to fulfill one's duty; to assist, to aid in effecting; to adjust, to pacify, to tranquillize; good, entire, whole; full, overflowing; repeated, doubled; a rest, a complete piece of music; a tenth; a field ten ꜂*li* square; a district in Kansuh: used for the coll. ꜀*siăng* and ꜀*ch'iăng*, q. v.: [9]꜀*sing* ꜂*kung*, to achieve merit; COM., [10]꜀*sing cheu*꜄ effected, done; [11]꜂*seng* ꜀*sing*, natural, spontaneous; [12]꜀*sing huk*꜀ to put on mourning the 7th day after a decease; [13]꜀*sing k'e*꜄ a perfect man; one skilled in gaining a competence; [14]꜀*sing* ꜂*ting*, of age, 16 years old; [15]꜀*sing* ꜂*ch'ing*, married; in the coll. the first sexual commerce; ꜀*sing pai*꜄ ꜂*iu so*꜄ success and failure are fated; ꜀*sing* ꜂*ka lik*꜀ *ngiék*꜀ to build up a family and property; COLL., ꜀*sing* ꜀*heng*, an agent, a factor, a broker.

誠 ꜀Ch'êng. Sincere, true, honest, guileless; perfect in virtue; unmixed; as an adverb, really, verily: COM., [16]꜀*sing sik*꜀ sincere, truthful; [17]꜂*kiéng* ꜀*sing chai*꜄ *pai*꜄ devoutly repeat the worship, as Tauists say in chanting prayers.

城 ꜀Ch'êng. A walled city, a citadel; the walls of a city; a provincial capital; a sepulcher, a burial place; to mend, to repair; completed, done: in the coll. read ꜀*siăng*, q. v.: [18]꜀*ü chó*꜄ ꜀*ch'eu* ꜀*sing*, like sitting in a mournful city—in great distress.

郕 ꜀ The name of an ancient feudal state, lying in the present Shantung province.

盛 ꜀Ch'êng. Shêng. Rice in a vessel for offering; a cup, a vessel; to receive, to contain in a vessel; in full costume, court dress; perfected, completed: also read *seng*꜄ q. v.: [19]*ek*꜀ ꜀*sing* ꜂*chiu*, one vessel of wine; [20]꜀*sing huk*꜀ in full dress; COM., ꜀*sing* ꜂*lang*, a large basket, like a chow-chow basket—used to convey offerings to graves, etc.

燖 ꜀ Warm, hot; to steep or boil in broth, to make a broth of.

---

[1]叢辰 [2]不成 [3]花辰月夕 [4]時辰 [5]楓宸 [6]晨夕 [7]早晨 [8]晨風 [9]成功 [10]成就 [11]生成 [12]成服 [13]成器 [14]成丁 [15]成親 [16]誠實 [17]虔誠再拜 [18]如坐愁城 [19]一盛酒 [20]盛服○

尋 尋 (Hsin. Hsün.) To seek, to search for; to investigate; to use, to employ; to connect with; usual, ordinary; unexpectedly, suddenly; for a long time; a measure of eight cubits: [1] *,sing ik,* to investigate; [2] *,sing ,sü,* to study; COM., [3] *,sing 't'ó,* to search for; [4] *,sing ,siong,* usually, commonly; [5] *,sing sëü'* to seek an occasion, as to quarrel, meddlesome; COLL., *,sing ,k'ieu,* to pick flaws, to find fault; [6] *,sing mú' tioh,* can't find it.

澠 ('Shing. Ch'ëng.) The name of a river in the state of Tsi (now Shantung), a branch of the Tsing-shwui.

繩 繩 (Shing.) A cord, a line, a rope; a line stretched taut; to mark by a line; to adjust; to connect, to continue, to succeed; to cause to conform; to restrain and warn; to praise: [7] *'chung ,sing,* to make exact; *,sing ,sing,* many, continuous; [8] *ch'ek, ,sing hië' chëük,* to bind the foot with a red cord—to betroth.

蠅 (Ying.) A house-fly; *met.*, a busybody, a turbulent fellow: [9] *,kang ,sing,* name of a famous archer; [10] *,sing ,t'eu ,mi le'* gains as petty as a fly's head; COLL., *,pu ,sing,* the common house-fly; *,king ,pu ,sing,* a gold-colored fly.

蟳 (Hsin.) A species of crab having a round shell, while the shell of the *ch'iék,* is oval: [11] *,ch'ing ,sing,* a large, green crab; COM., [12] *,sing ,keng,* crab-soup: COLL., *,sing 'pi há' ,ch'a tek, sá'* the *,sing* crab is very different from the *há'*; *met.*, said of a person or thing very superior to another.

鱘 The sturgeon.

鱏 An enormous fish having a long snout, found in the Yang-tsz', probably a sturgeon; it is said to be eight feet long and to weigh 1000 lbs.

鐔 The guard on the hilt of a sword; a dirk, a dagger. Read *,t'ang:* the edge of a sword.

神 (Shên.) Any invisible, spiritual power or cause, operating by its own subtile energies and causing things to develop; that which is inscrutable, mysterious, or supernatural; the soul of the *yang* principle; a spirit, the human spirit or mind; any spiritual intelligence, a worshiped spirit, a god, a divinity; the manes, spirits of the dead; a genius, an elf, a sprite; the essence, or essential idea, as of a composition or discourse; life, animation, vigor, physical energy, animal spirits; used by some for God, by others for the Spirit: [13] *,sing ,ling,* spiritual; intellectual; [14] *,sing ,sü,* the thoughts; [15] *,sing ,hung,* the spiritual soul; [16] *,sing mieu'* divinely excellent; [17] *,t'ieng te' ,chi ,sing,* the spirits of heaven and earth; COM., [18] *,sing ,ming ,pu sak,* gods and Budhs, a common term for idol gods; [19] *,sing tó'* Tauist

1 尋繹 2 尋思 3 尋討 4 尋常 5 尋事 6 尋覓着 7 準繩 ⊙ 8 赤繩繫足 9 甘蠅 10 蠅頭微利 11 青蟳 12 蟳羹 13 神靈 14 神思 15 神魂 16 神妙 17 天地之神 18 神明菩薩 19 神道

deities; ʻkoung˺ ˳sing, to bring down the gods, as by libations or burning charms; [2]˳sing ˏkung, and ˳sing ʻma, male and female conjurers; [3]˳siä ˳sing, spirits whose worship is not legalized; evil spirits, demons; ˏka ˳sing, lares, ancestral divinities; [4]˳sing ʻchü, or ˳sing ʻchü ˏpài, the ancestral tablet; [5]˳sing oi˺ the seat of an idol; the place where the names of ancestral divinities are written; [6]ˏang ˳sing, to set an idol in its place; ˳sing mieu˺ an idol temple; [7]˳sing ch'iong˺ an image, idol; [8]˳sing ˏsiëng, genii; ˳sing ˳hang, the title of a god or promoted spirit; ˳sing ˏch'á ʻkwi ʻk'iëng, sent by a god or spirit, as said of a medicine proving efficacious; [9]ˏching ˳sing, or ˳sing k'e˺ the animal spirits, natural vigor or energy; ˳sing k'e˺ pok˳ chëük˳ deficiency of vigor, weak, languid; [10]ˏliu ˳sing, careful; ˏló ˳sing, you have wearied yourself (for me)—a polite phrase; ëüng˺ ˳sing, to give the mind to; [11]seng˺ ˳sing, inscrutably intelligent; the Holy Spirit; [12]˳sing ʻli mah˳ hwak, the essential idea, reasoning, consecutiveness, and style (of an essay); [13]˳sing k'ëük˳ a superior medicine for cold and indigestion (from ˳Chiong ˏchiu); COLL., ˳sing ˏsieng yü˺ ü˺ p'ah˳ tauung˺ kiëng˺ even genii sometimes drop their swords; *met.*, one will sometimes make mistakes.

臣 ˳Ch'ên. A servant, one in subjection; a minister of a prince, an officer; to serve the state; the 131st radical: [14]˳sing huk˳ to submit; pok˳ ˳sing, an unfaithful minister; COM., [15]˳sing ʻchü, a minister, an officer; ˏtüng ˳sing, a loyal minister; [16]˳chang ˳sing, an intriguing politician; ˏkung ˳sing, prince and minister.

承 ˳Ch'êng. To receive, to accept; to succeed to an office; to accept a trust, to undertake, to receive orders; to sustain; to stop, to impede; to assist, to second, to act as deputy, in which sense it is interchanged with the next; in the coll. to catch in a vessel, as leaking water: [17]sik˳ ˳sing, the stone base of a pillar; COM., ˳sing ˏching, I received your kind favor; [18]˳sing ʻliäng or ˳sing seu˺ to receive in charge, to act as an agent; [19]˳sing ˏch'á, a deputy; ˳sing tëüng˺ ˏsong, son of the eldest son, who represents the family after the father's decease; [20]hong˺ ˳sing, to flatter; COLL., ˳sing ʻchwi, to catch water; ˳sing ʻü kau˺ to catch leaking rain-water.

丞 ˳Ch'êng. To aid, to assist; a second, a coadjutor, a deputy: [21]˳sing siong˺ a prime minister, so styled in the Ch'in dynasty, now [22]ʻchai siong˺ COM., kaing˺ ˳sing, the deputy of a district magistrate.

乘 ˳Ch'êng. Shêng. To ascend a carriage; to mount, to ride in a chariot; to avail of, to embrace an opportunity, to take advantage of; to plan, to calculate; to regulate, to put in order; to multiply; to add, as on the abacus: also read seng˺ q. v.: [23]˳sing ˏhung, to mount a cloud; ˳sing lwang˺

1 降神 2 神公 3 邪神 4 神主 5 神位 6 安神 7 神像 8 神仙 9 精神 10 留神 11 聖神 12 神理 脉法 13 神麯 14 臣服 15 臣子 16 讒臣 17 石承 18 承領 19 承差 20 奉承 21 丞相 22 宰相 23 乘雲

ʻch'iong twak, to avail of a state of anarchy to plunder.

䰒 A huge kettle or boiler, having a large top and small bottom; also quick, nimble.

簷 Yen. Read ,siêng; coll. ,sing: as in ,sing ,kiêng, the edge of a roof, the eaves: ,sing ,kiêng a under the eaves.

,Sing. A coll. euphonic prefix, as in ,sing ,sang, clear weather; ,sing ,sung, to go about and inspect; ,sing ,siong ,siong, to wriggle, to creep, as worms.

(745) Sio.

[This word is interchangeably read swo.]

輸 Shu. Read ,sü; coll. ,sio: to lose, to be beaten; overcome, vanquished, discomfited: ,sio ,yăng, to lose and to win; to be beaten and to conquer; ,sio meng appearance of losing, as in a game; ,sio ,chieng, to lose money in a game; ,sio yék, or ,sio ,kwong, hot or crazy to play, as one after losing; ,sio sioh, teng to lose a battle; ʻtu ,sio, to bet, to lay a wager; ,sio sioh, ,tong, to lose a lawsuit.

Sio. A coll. word: to spread under; to lay down, as a cloth or paper, in order to put things on it: sio a ʻtá, to spread below; sio sioh, ,t'ăng, spread down one thickness of it.

(746) Sioh.

[This word is interchangeably read swoh.]

削 Hsiao. Read siok,; coll. sioh,: to cut, to mince, to carve, to slice up: sioh, ʻtong, or sioh, toung to cut it off; sioh, sioh, p'iêng to cut off one slice; sioh, ch'ói mince it up; sioh, ka to beat one down to a low price.

射 Shê. Read sia; coll. sioh,: to shoot an arrow; to dart, as rays; to send forth, as evil influences; to point at, or overlook, as the peak of a roof pointing toward the opposite house—deemed unlucky: sioh, chiêng to shoot an arrow; sioh, ʻcheu, to shoot birds with arrows; sioh, pwo chiêng foot archery; sioh, te ,kiu, to shoot at a three-cornered ball from horseback; sioh, má kau ʻpa, not reach the target in shooting.

石 Shih. Read sik,; coll. sioh, a stone, a rock, a mineral; stony, petrified; a musical stone; a dry and liquid measure of 120 catties, or about 160 lbs. avoirdupois, but varying at different times; also a measure of two ,hu, or about 11 ʻtau: sioh, ,t'au or sioh, ,t'au ʻmó, a stone that can be taken in the hand, small stones; sioh, buung roundish stones, pebbles; sioh, ʻpeng, a stone slab; sioh, ʻtong, a stone pillar; sioh, te stony ground; a paved floor; ʻhwi sioh, a flint; ,tó sioh, a whetstone; sioh, kak, rough, sharp stones—to throw at an enemy from a city wall; sioh, ,hwi, lime made from limestone; sioh, ,kó, gypsum; sioh, ,hwa, moss on rocks; sioh, ,ch'ang, a dark gray color; sioh, ʻnü, a barren woman; sioh, k'ia ʻná, "stone-pressed-mother"—the name of a goddess, a patroness

1 簷墘下 2 輸贏 3 輸面 4 輸錢 5 輸熱 6 輸一陣 7 賭輸 8 輸一堂 9 削斷 10 削價 11 射箭 12 射鳥 13 射步箭 14 射地球 15 石蛋 16 石頭 17 石板 18 火石 19 刀石 20 石灰 21 石花

福州方言拼音字典

of children; [1]'hiĕk, sioh, a magnet; [2]pah, sioh, white granite; ,ch'ang sioh, dark granite; [3],tu ,tu (or sü) sioh, agalmatolite, used for cutting seals and fancy articles—called seu' ,sang sik, on sign-boards; [4],ch'eng sioh, the field-stone, an agalmatolite; [5],hung ,nang sioh, Yunnan marble; sioh, koi' a kind of stinking bug or winged insect.

一 Yi. I. Read ek,; coll. sioh,: the numeral one; the same, alike; a, an; the whole; *met.*, sincere, real, perfect; single, only one, each, one by one; at once, as soon as: [6]sioh, chiăh, one, as of persons or things; [7]sioh, 'a 'chai, one finger—when held up, is used to designate prices, as one ten, one hundred; [8]sioh, a' once; a while; [9]sioh, tŏi' one piece, one lump; one dollar; [10]sioh, ch'ok, one act or scene of a play; sioh, twai' pwang' the larger half; [11]sioh, ,sing ĕ' of the same mind; [12]sioh, kwo' once over; ng' sioh, yong' unlike; [13]sioh, tek, 'kiăng, a small quantity; [14]sioh, ,lau 'chwi, one tide; sioh, ,pi ,ti, a bunch, as of grapes; sioh, 'cha ,seng, a while ago; sioh, ,k'iă ,tiă sioh, ,k'iă 'nă, "one is papa, the other mamma"—they are not mates; sioh, 'a ,chiĕng lĕk, 'a che' "a cash has six words on it"; *met.*, he is very close-fisted; sioh, chiăh, pwang' ,kŭng, sioh, ,ki paik, 'liong, one is a half pound, the other is 8 oz.—they are both alike bad, as two quarrelsome fellows.

Sioh,. A coll. word, as in sioh, ,mang, yesterday; sioh, ,mang ,pwo, last night; sioh, ,mang pwang' ,pwo, last evening.

Sioh,. A coll. word: similar to ch'ioh, to start, to spring, to leap up, as to reach a high object: sioh, kwo' to leap over or forward; sioh, pwang' ,t'iĕng ,keng, to spring half as high as the sky.

(747) Siok.

[This word is interchangeably read swok.]

削 Hsiao. Hsio. Hsüeh. To cut, to pare, to shave, to scrape off; to erase; to deprive of rank or title, to despoil, to seize another's territory; weak, debilitated; a graving tool, an erasing knife, now called [15],chü ,tŏ: in the coll. read sioh, q. v.: [16]siok, chek, to degrade in rank; 'kai siok, to correct by erasing; siok, hwak, ,ui ,nă, to shave the head and become a nun.

雪 Hsüeh. Snow; to whiten, to blanch; to wipe, to rub off; to wash clean; snowy, white; to wipe out, as a disgrace, to clear one's self; to revenge: [17]siok, 't'i, to revenge disgrace; siok, ,hwa lĕk, ch'ok, hexagonal snow-flakes—sign of a bountiful harvest; COM., [18]siok, tŭng' a cool grotto; [19]siok, ,kiu, the snow-ball, a large white flower; siok, siok, pah, snowy white; ha' siok, or lŏh, siok, to snow; [20]siok, p'iĕng' white wafer-cakes; siok, haung' pŏ' ,siu, to gratify hate by revenge; siok, 'chwi ,p'eng ,ta ,t'iĕng siong' ĕ' tea made with snow-water has a celestial flavor.

[1]熁石 [2]白石 [3]圖書石 [4]田石 [5]雲南石 [6]一隻 [7]一個指 [8]一下〇 [9]一塊 [10]一出 [11]一心意〇 [12]一句 [13]一滴仔 [14]一流水 [15]書刀 [16]削職 [17]雪恥 [18]雪洞 [19]雪球 [20]雪片

說 Shuo. Shui. Sa. To say, to talk, to converse; to tell, to narrate, to discourse about; to explain, to describe, to unfold a meaning; speech, talk: also read *swoi'* q. v.: [1]*siok, ,ti*, to tell, to inform; *siok, ,ing se' ,hi*, to talk scandal; COM., [2]*'kă siok*, to explain the sense of; [3]*'sieu siok*, a novel; [4]*,siă siok*, an obscene book; *siok, p'ó' ,ki ,kwong*, to expose one's specious designs; *lik, siok, tĕü' ,chü*, to prepare and publish books.

Siok. A coll. word: to go about, to run to and fro: *siok, siok, siok*, to go the rounds, as in marketing; *,k'wong ,k'wong siok*, to circle about, as in play; *'mwo siok*, to hang about a wife, as one just married; *siok, cheng'* or *siok, chuk*, to take a complete circuit.

(748) Siong.

襄 Hsiang. To disrobe in order to plow; to effect, to accomplish; to animate, to assist; to remove, to clear away; upper, superior; successful, as in war or founding a state; an equipage: [5]*,Siong ,yong*, a prefecture in the north of Hupeh; [6]*,siong chang'* to encourage by praise.

鑲 Hsiang. To inlay, to enchase, to let in; to coat or plate with metal; to set, to insert, as a gem, glass, etc.; to connect, to clamp, to mortice on; bordered, as by another color: COM., [7]*,siong ,pó ,li*, to set glass; [8]*,siong ,hwa ,piéng*, to make an ornamented border; *siong ,wong ,ki*, a bordered yellow banner; [9]*,siong ngwoh*, to inlay with precious stones.

驤 Hsiang. A horse having the right hind leg white; a spirited horse; to gallop; to elevate; to go far: [10]*,teng ,siong*, or *,siong ,teng*, to canter.

瀼 Jang. Wet with dew, dew falling; running, sparkling water; also turbid streams of water; a river in the east of Sz'chuen: [11]*,ling lo' ,siong ,siong*, a heavy dew.

鬤 Also read *'yong*: the hair in great confusion; uncombed, tangled, disheveled.

勷 Hsiang. In great haste, pressing, urgent: [12]*,k'wong ,siong*, hurried.

觴 Shang. A horn, a cup, a goblet; a bumper; a feast, a banquet; to give to drink: [13]*te' ,siong*, or *kiĕk, ,siong*, to prepare a feast; [14]*,ch'ing ,siong*, to take wine with; [15]*cheng' siong*, to offer the goblet; [16]*lang' ,siong*, to overrun, to exceed.

傷 Shang. To wound, to bruise, to injure; a wound, a hurt; to grieve; to distress one; to waste, as property; to exhaust, as strength; sad, mourning; injured, chagrined, wounded in feeling: COM., [17]*,siong ,hung pai' sŭk*, depraved and ruinous customs; [18]*,siong ,hong*, the mark of a wound; [19]*,siong 'song*, injured, hurt; [20]*,siong hai'* to injure; [21]*,siong hiĕ'* an affection

1 說知	3 小說	5 襄陽	7 鑲玻	花邊	10 騰驤	瀼瀼	13 治觴	15 晉觴	17 傷風	18 傷痕	20 傷害
2 解說	4 邪說	6 襄贊	璃 8 鑲	9 鑲玉	11 零露	12 劻勷	14 稱觴	16 濫觴	敗俗	19 傷損	21 傷[illegible]

福州方言拼音字典

of the lungs; [1]*siong hung*, to take cold; [2]*siong 'pwong*, impairs the capital—to sell so low; *siong sing*, grieved; [3]*ang' siong*, an internal injury; *ngiéng' siong*, to inspect wounds, as officers do; [4]*siong sing*, dispirited, wearied; COLL., *siong taung'* injured in one's interests, a losing business.

殤 Shang. To die before puberty; an untimely death, as of one under 19 years of age: *kwok, siong*, a soldier killed in battle; [5]*ka' siong*, to wed the effigy of a betrothed husband dying before marriage.

相 Hsiang. To examine, to inspect; to blend with; mutual, reciprocal; by turns, interchangeably, from one to another; often denotes a reflective form of the verb; substance or essence, not the accidents: also read *siong'* and in the coll. *song*, q. v.: [6]*siong 'ü*, together, intimate; [7]*siong sëü'* similar, somewhat alike; COM., [8]*siong këüng'* near, contiguous; [9]*siong 'chó*, to miss each other; [10]*siong taik*, on good terms; COLL., *mó siong kang*, vain, worthless.

箱 Hsiang. A box, a chest, a trunk of leather, wood, or bamboo; a coffer, a casket; the boot of a carriage: COM., [11]*chëng siong*, a palmcoir trunk; [12]*siong 'lëng*, a traveling chest, or box, of bamboo; *'chai siong*, paper boxes (to burn to the dead); [13]*siong tiu*, a closet for placing trunks; [14]*p'ui siong ka'* a case or stand for leathern trunks; a half-closet with space above for a trunk; [15]*k'wi siong*, to open the boxes—to dress for a theatrical play; *'piéng siong*, a low trunk; *met.*, one fond of attending his wife on visits, as her trunk does.

廂 Hsiang. A side chamber, rooms on each side of the hall, called [16]*tung sá siong*, the east and west apartments.

湘 Hsiang. A large tributary of the Yangtsz' in Hunan; also name of a lake and of three districts in Hunan; to cook, to roast: [17]*siong hi*, a spotted kind of bamboo, named after Shun's princess.

緗 Hsiang. Silk of a light yellow, like the budding leaves of the mulberry: [18]*'p'ieu siong*, blue and yellow, as silks.

商 謪 Shang. To consult, to deliberate, to devise, to arrange; a merchant, a trader, a dealer from abroad; to trade; the 2d of the five musical notes; a short time before sunrise or after sunset; an ancient dynasty: used for the coll. *song*, q. v.: [19]*siong 'lü*, a merchant from abroad; COM., [20]*k'ah, siong*, a trader from abroad; [21]*siéng siong*, a licensed salt-merchant; [22]*siong tiu*, the Shang dynasty, B. C. 1766-1122.

上 Shang. To ascend, to go up; to go, as to court; to insert, to write in; to advance; to hand up; to esteem highly, to exalt, to honor: also read *siong'* q. v.

1 傷風 2 傷本 3 暗傷 4 傷神 5 嫁殤 6 相與 7 相似 8 相近 9 相左 10 相得 11 椶箱 12 箱籠 13 箱棡 14 皮箱架 15 開箱○ 16 東西廂○ 17 湘妃 18 縹緗 19 商旅 20 客商 21 鹽商 22 商朝

ALPH. DICT. 103

ʻ鮝 Hsiang. Dried fish: COM., [1]ˏ*ngü* ʻ*siong*, a common term for dried fish; [2]ˏ*mwang* ʻ*siong*, dried eels.

ʻ賞 Shang. To give to an inferior; to confer, to bestow; to grant, as heaven does; to give a largess or bounty, to reward; to celebrate, to praise, to congratulate, to exhort; to rejoice or delight in: [3]ʻ*siong lai*ˀ or ʻ*siong kek*, to reward; ʻ*k'ó*ˀ ʻ*siong*, to give largesses, as to troops; COM., [4]ʻ*siong sëü*ˀ a reward; ʻ*siong kak*, and [5]ʻ*siong* ʻ*pong*, official and private notices offering rewards; [7]ʻ*siong* ˏ*hung*, a present, a douceur; ʻ*siong* ˏ*niéng*, new-year's largesses; ʻ*siong hwak*, to reward and to punish; ʻ*siong* ˏ*hwa*, to enjoy flowers.

ʻ想 Hsiang. To think, to consider, to reflect upon; to plan; to hope, to expect, to desire; a thought, an idea: ʻ*siong ik*, ˏ*sing*, immersed in thought, in a reverie; COM., ˏ*sü* ʻ*siong*, to think; ʻ*siong* ʻ*siong*, to consider, to reflect; ʻ*siong* ˏ*t'au*, a conception, a notion; [8]*mong*ˀ ʻ*siong pok*, *tó*ˀ could not have dreamed it (to be practicable)! ˏ*k'ëng* ʻ*siong*, a vain idea; [9]ʻ*siong mwo*ˀ to think of with strong desire; COLL., ʻ*siong saung*ˀ *kié*ˀ ˏ*nëng*, to think how to circumvent another; ʻ*siong* ʻ*k'i*, to recollect; ˏ*sing* ʻ*lá* ʻ*siong*, or [10]ʻ*siong* ˏ*sing sëü*ˀ the mind engaged in thought.

相ˀ Hsiang. To assist, to help, to support; a prime minister; to select, to choose; to regulate, to direct; to lead, as one blind; to observe times; to receive an envoy; physiognomy and palmistry; a name for the 7th month; small stars near *d* in Ursa Major: also read ˏ*siong*, q. v.: [11]*siong*ˀ ʻ*chiá*, leader of a blind man; COM., [12]ʻ*chai siong*ˀ or *pai*ˀ *siong*ˀ a prime minister; *siong*ˀ ˏ*këng*, noble Sir! *ne*ˀ *siong*ˀ noble second Sir!—addressed to the second brother; [13]*siong*ˀ *mau*ˀ the face, physiognomy; [14]ʻ*k'ang*ˀ *siong*ˀ to tell fortunes by the lines of the face; [15]*siong*ˀ *koi*ˀ and *siong*ˀ *chiéng*ˀ noble and ignoble faces, as indicating the fortune; *siong*ˀ *siong*ˀ to inspect, to scan; COLL., *siong*ˀ ˏ*ching* ˏ*ching*, to observe the true state of; *siong*ˀ *sëü*ˀ ˏ*pó* and *siong*ˀ *sëü*ˀ *pok*, ʻ*ló* ˏ*ku*, female fortune tellers and ventriloquists; *ng*ˀ ʻ*hó k'ang*ˀ *siong*ˀ does not look well.

ˏ常 Shang. Ch'ang. Usual, common, ordinary; constant, long continued, habitual; a rule, a law; a spear 16 cubits long; the name of a banner: [16]ˏ*siong huk*, ordinary dress; [17]ˏ*siong piéng*ˀ constant and changeable; COM., ʻ*ngu* ˏ*siong*, the five constant virtues; ˏ*siong* ˏ*siong*, or ˏ*si* ˏ*siong*, or ˏ*siong* ˏ*si*, always, constantly; ˏ*hi* ˏ*siong*, unusual; [18]ˏ*kü* ˏ*siong*, for the most part, generally; [19]*chieu*ˀ ˏ*siong* or [20]ˏ*ang* ˏ*siong*, as usual, customary; ˏ*siong* ˏ*ing*, one of ordinary capacity; ʻ*hwang hok*, ˏ*u* ˏ*siong*, constantly changing; [21]ˏ*siong* ˏ*kié* or ˏ*siong lié*ˀ a standing regulation.

ˏ嫦 Ch'ang. The goddess of the moon, called [22]ˏ*siong* ˏ*ngó*; COM., ˏ*siong* ˏ*ngó* ʻ*nü*, Diana; *met.*, a beautiful lady.

---

1 魚鮝 2 鰻鮝 3 賞賚 4 犒賞 5 賞賜 6 賞榜 7 賞封 8 夢想 9 想慕 不到 10 想心事 11 相者 12 宰相 13 相貌 14 看相 15 相貴 16 常服 17 常變 18 居常 19 照常 20 安常 21 常規 22 嫦娥

裳 ˛Shang. The lower garments, the skirt, petticoats: COM., ¹ˊi ˛siong, the dress, clothes, garments.

嘗 嚐 甞 ˛Ch'ang. To taste, to test by tasting; to try, to essay, to prove; before, formerly, a sign of past time prefixed to verbs; the autumnal sacrifices, as to ancestors: ²˛siong ˛ung, I have heard; COLL., ˊch'e' ˛siong, to test by tasting; ˛siong k'ang' sie' nóh, e' taste and see what is the flavor; ˛siong pwong' "just tasted the rice"—to keep one's place only a short time.

鱨 ˛Ch'ang. A sort of flying gurnet, called ˛yong ˛wong hiék˛ the yellow-cheeked flier; it has orbital spines and mailed cheeks.

償 ˛Ch'ang. To restore, to make amends; restitution; to pay, to forfeit, to suffer a penalty: ⁴sěük, ngwong' ˛nang ˛siong, hard to fulfill the former desire, as an old man to gain a degree; COM., ⁵˛siong miăng' to forfeit one's life; ⁶k'iéng' chai' ˛siong ˛chiéng, he who owes a debt must pay the money; ⁷ti ˛siong, to forfeit, as life.

痒 ˛Yang. Shên. Also read ˛yong; a sore, a wound, an ulcer: also read ˊyong, q. v.: COLL., ˛siong ˛siong, a tickling sensation, as when a part is scratched; á' ˛siong, to feel the titillation, it tickles; ⁸kiăng ˛siong, afraid of being tickled; ˛siong sěü' the poison of insects, a slight irritation from poisonous bites.

庠 ˛Hsiang. An asylum for the aged in ancient times; a village school, a college, a gymnasium; to teach: ⁹˛siong ˛seng, a Siutsai; ¹⁰ik˛ ˛siong, to become a Siutsai.

祥 ˛Hsiang. Sometimes used for the next: happiness, felicity, fortune, good luck; an omen, a sign, a prognostic: ¹¹˛ting ˛siong, a happy sign; excellent; COM., ¹²˛siong soi' auspicious, a lucky omen; ¹³kek˛ ˛siong ˛ü e' good fortune according to one's wish; ¹⁴pok˛ ˛siong, unlucky; ˊsieu ˛siong and tai' ˛siong, the sacrifices to ancestors at the end of one and two years of mourning.

詳 ˛Hsiang. To examine carefully; to learn and report to superiors; to reason and discourse upon; to narrate minutely, to state circumstances; the details, the facts; fully, minutely: ¹⁵˛siong sek, a clear, intelligible statement; ¹⁶˛siong ˛ming, to explain clearly; COM., ¹⁷˛siong sá' minutely, particularly; ¹⁸˛siong ˛ung, an official report to a superior; COLL., ¹⁹˛siong maĕng' to interpret a dream. Read ˛yong: false, hypocritical.

翔 ˛Hsiang. To soar, to hover over, to fly to and fro; to look back; stern, severe; dignified: ²⁰˛hui ˛siong, to turn and look regretfully, as at one's native village.

1 衣裳 2 嘗聞 3 試嘗 4 夙願 5 難償 6 償命 7 欠債 8 償錢 9 抵償 10 鰷痒 11 庠生 12 入庠 13 禎祥 14 祥瑞 15 吉祥 16 如意 17 不祥 18 詳悉 19 詳明 20 詳細 21 詳文 22 詳夢 23 迴翔 ○

遄 ꜀Ch'uan. To go and come often; to walk rapidly; haste, speed.

[The next four are interchangeably read *swong*.]

旋 ꜀Hsüan. Hsüen. 還 ꜀Huan. To wave a flag as a signal; motion of soldiers' legs in marching; to pursue, to follow about; to revolve, to go in an orbit; to return to the same point; curling, as waves; quick, ready; then, forthwith, afterwards; in the coll. to creep; to climb, to trail: the second also read *꜀hwang*, q. v.: [1]*꜀siong ꜀hiong*, to return to one's village; [2]*꜀siong ꜀lung*, to revolve, as the moon; [3]*꜀siong ꜀hung*, a whirlwind; COLL., *꜀siong ꜀siong ꜀tiong*, to go around, to creep about, as fleas; [4]*꜀siong ꜀ting*, a vine, creepers; [5]*꜀siong ꜀pung*, to climb the frame or trellis.

璿 ꜀ 璇 ꜀Hsüan. Hsüen. A beautiful gem, called [6]*꜀siong koi꜄*—an ornament worn by ancient kings; [7]*꜀siong ꜀ki*, an armillary sphere or planetarium, by which the motions of stars were anciently noted.

漩 ꜀Hsüan. A small whirlpool, or circling eddy, an eddying fountain.

鏇 ꜀ A pewter vessel, into which hot water is put to warm the wine, a wine-heater; a pulley.

上 [2] Shang. Above, up, on, upon; the top of; high; ancient; before in time; excellent, superior, the best; noble, exalted; supreme, the highest, as the emperor; to rise, to ascend: also read *꜂siong*, q. v.: COM., *siong[2] ha[2]* above and below, up and down; [8]*siong[2] lŏh꜆* to ascend and descend; [9]*siong[2] ꜀t'iéng*, to go to heaven; *꜀t'iéng siong[2]* in heaven, in the sky; [10]*ché siong[2]* the highest, supreme, as God; [11]*꜀hwong siong[2]* the Emperor; [12]*siong[2] seu[2]* to be aged, to reach the age of 50; *siong[2] ꜀chá*, to enter school, as at the beginning of a term; [13]*siong[2] ꜂ku*, high antiquity; [14]*siong[2] ꜂ch'iu*, formerly, before; [15]*siong[2] ꜀hiéng*, and *a[2] ꜀hiéng*, the 1st and 3d quarters of the moon; [16]*siong[2] ꜂ngu* (coll. *siong[2] tau[2]*), forenoon; [17]*꜀sing siong[2]* on one's person; *siong[2] sié꜄* above; [18]*siong[2] ꜀ung*, the preceding context; *siong[2] ꜂hó*, the very best quality; *꜂pi siong[2] pok, chëük, ꜂pi ha[2] ꜂iu ꜀ü*, medium, in moderate circumstances; [19]*꜀chieu siong[2] ꜀mwong*, to invite one to be a son-in-law; [20]*siong[2] ꜂ma chié꜄* offerings to the dead when encoffined; COLL., *siong[2] meng[2]* the face, upper surface; *siong[2] a[2] ꜂chi sá[2]* about that much or many.

尙 [2] Shang. Used for the preceding in the sense of high, noble; to add to, to honor, to adorn; to esteem, to value, to boast; to rule, to direct—used in official titles; to get a princess for a wife; still, yet, nevertheless; answers to *꜀ch'wi* (although) in the preceding part of a sentence; probably, perhaps: *siong[2] ꜂iu*, there is still some; [21]*siong[2] ꜂ch'iă*, still, yet; *siong[2] ꜂k'ó*, perhaps it will answer; [22]*siong[2] ꜂ch'i*, noble on account of age; COM., [23]*꜀hwo siong[2]* Bonzes; *siong[2]*

[1]旋鄉 [2]旋輪 [3]旋風 [4]旋藤 [5]旋棚 [6]璿瑰 [7]璿璣 [8]上落 [9]上天 [10]至上 [11]皇上 [12]上壽 [13]上古 [14]上手 [15]上弦 [16]上午 [17]身上 [18]上文 [19]招上門 [20]上馬祭 [21]尙且 [22]尙齒 [23]和尙

‚chü (spoken ‚sü), the President of a Board; [1]'Siong' ‚sü ‚kung, a famous marine god—much worshiped in the suburbs of Foochow.

癢 Yang. Read 'yong; used for the coll. siong': to itch; an itching place: cheng' siong' or siong' tek‚ 'heng, it itches intensely; ‚pa siong' to scratch an itching place.

(749) Siu.

收 収 Shou. To take, to receive; to collect, to gather, to harvest; to seize, to bind, to imprison; to desist, to conclude; an ancient hat made to receive the hair; a cross bar in the back of a carriage; to be annoyed, or affected by, a sign of the passive: com., [2]‚siu sik‚ to gather up, to arrange; met., to trouble or take revenge on; [3]‚siu ‚kang, to imprison; [4]‚siu taing' to shut up shop; ‚siu so' to collect accounts; [5]‚siu ‚ping, to recall troops; [6]‚siu ‚sing, a harvest; [7]‚siu ‚tĕng, to reap; ‚siu lié' to gather fees, as on licenses or government land; [8]‚siu ‚pwang, to close up business; coll., [9]‚siu lang' saik‚ to retain two parts (of a present); ‚siu ‚sang, to reform, to stop a course of life; ‚siu k'ó' to put away, to lay by; ‚siu 'tié, to receive. Read seu': an abundant harvest.

修 Hsiu. To adorn, to renew; to mend, to repair; to clean, to put in order; to regulate; to cultivate, to exercise, as the heart; to practice or study, as virtue: [10]‚siu sek‚ to adorn; to polish, as an essay; [11]‚siu ‚chü, to write a letter; [12]'kiong ‚siu, a go-between, matchmaker; [13]‚siu ‚king, a teacher's stipend; com., [14]‚siu 'li, to regulate, to repair; ‚siu 'pwo, to mend, as clothes; [15]‚siu liéng' to refine, as one's nature by austerities; ‚siu ‚sing siăh‚ ch'ai' to cultivate virtue and be a vegetarian; coll., ‚siu ‚kio ‚p'wo tio' to repair bridges and make roads; ‚siu ‚k'a ‚neng, to trim the callous parts of the feet.

羞 Hsiu. Used for the next: viands, savory food; to offer up, to present or send in; to feel ashamed, to blush; ashamed, conscious of guilt, feeling unworthy; modest, bashful: in the coll. read 'sieu, q. v.: [16]‚siu ŭk‚ to feel insulted; [17]‚siu k'oi' shamefaced; [18]‚siu 't'i, ashamed; ‚hang ‚siu, to blush; [19]‚siu o' ashamed of one's self.

饈 Shiu. Viands, delicacies, savory; to offer food: [20]‚ch'iéng ‚siu paik‚ é' all sorts of viands.

首 Shou. The head, the chief, the most important part; a leader, a chief; the chief heads of a subject; first, foremost; kinds, sorts; a classifier of stanzas of poetry; beginning, source; to place in the van; to manifest, to display; the hilt of a sword; the 185th radical: also read seu', q. v.: 'siu ‚siéng, the first; [21]‚ŭng 'siu, the general, as

[1] 尙書公〇 [2] 收拾 [3] 收監 [4] 收店 [5] 收兵 [6] 收成 [7] 收冬 [8] 收盤 [9] 收二色 [10] 修飾 [11] 修書 [12] 蹇修 [13] 修金 [14] 修理 [15] 修煉 [16] 羞辱 [17] 羞愧 [18] 羞恥 [19] 羞惡 [20] 千饈百味 [21] 戎首〇

of an invading army; [1]*,hong 'siu*, to draw up troops in line; COM., [2]*'siu 'hu*, the chief prefecture; [3]*,p'ié 'siu*, the first of a class of Siutsai graduates; [4]*'chang 'siu*, to decapitate; [5]*'tong' 'siu pai'* "respectfully bows the head"—written on a present; *'siu sek*, (coll. *'ch'iu sek,*), female head ornaments.

'守 Shou. To hold fast, to keep, to maintain; to guard, to protect; to supervise, to watch; steadfast: *'siu wong'* to guard and watch, as against thieves; COM., [6]*'siu pe'* a major; *'siu 'siu*, guard it, keep it; [7]*'siu chak,* or *'siu chak, 'k'au*, to guard a pass or station; [8]*,hwong 'siu*, to keep strict watch; *'siu yă'* or *'siu ,kang*, to watch at night; *,siăng 'siu*, the city-garrison; [9]*'siu 'kwa* or *'siu chiék*, to remain in widowhood; [10]*'siu ha'* to wear mourning; [11]*'siu hong'* or *'siu 'pwong hong'* to perform one's duties; [12]*'siu ,sing*, to preserve the health, to avoid vices. Read *seu'*: any thing guarded, a charge, a post.

,酬 ,酧 Ch'ou. To pledge a guest; to recompense, to make a return: *,siu ,ping*, to pledge guests; [13]*,siu chok,* pledging, as host and guest do; [14]*,siu tak,* to recompense, to respond; [15]*,siu ngwong'* to make a thank-offering; COM., *,siu siá'* to return thanks, as by presents; *,siu chai'* to "pay the debt" — to requite parents by obedience.

,讐 ,讎 ,仇 Ch'ou. Used for the last: to oppose; to hate, to dislike; to resent, to revenge, to take vengeance; enmity; an enemy, a rival, an opponent; to rail at, to recriminate; to requite, to recompense; to collate, to verify by a correspondence of parts; a pair; a sort, a class; the third also means proud, and is sometimes read *,kiu* in the sense of to unite; a pair, a match: *,siu 'k'eu*, to rail at, to slander; [16]*,siu k'ek,* a feud, variance; COM., *,siu ,ing* or [17]*,siu tik,* an enemy; *,siu wong'* or *,siu hëüng'* (coll. *,siu këüng'*) hatred, resentment; *pó' ,siu*, to take revenge; [18]*'t'ó pó' ,siu*, to seek revenge; [19]*kiék, ,siu*, to be at feud with.

,犨 Ch'ou. A white ox; the lowing or snorting of a cow; to issue, to proceed from.

,售 Shou. Also read *'siu*, and in the dictionaries *seu'*: to sell, to dispose of by sale; to restore, to pay back: *,siu ka'* the price of an article sold; [20]*,sieu ,siu*, the consumption of goods by selling; COM., [21]*hwak, ,siu*, offered for sale—a term used on signboards.

,泅 Hsiu. To swim: COM., [22]*,siu 'chwi*, to swim in the water; *,siu kwo' ,këng*, to swim over the river; COLL., *á' me' á' ,siu*, can dive and swim; *met.*, expert in trade; *,mi ,t'au ,siu 'si 'kiáng t'aë'* (the two modes of) swimming on the face and on the back.

[1]行首 [2]首府 [3]披首 [4]斬首 [5]頓首拜 [6]守備 [7]守卡 [8]防守 [9]守寡 [10]守孝 [11]守分 [12]守身 [13]酬酢 [14]酬答 [15]酬願 [16]仇隙 [17]仇敵 [18]討報仇 [19]結仇 [20]鎖售 [21]發售 [22]泅水 ○

(750) So.

數 數 数 Shu. So. Shuo. An account, a list; a shop-bill; to count up, to enumerate; a number, several, a few; lot, destiny, fate; to blame, to find fault: also read *sauk*, q. v.: COM., [1]*so' mëk*, the number, account; [2]*ˌu so'* innumerable; *so' ˌtang*, a bill, shop-bill; a list, catalogue; [3]*so' p'wo'* an account-book; [4]*ch'ó so'* or *ˌliu ˈchwi so'* a blotter, waste-book; [5]*ˈchung so'* a ledger; *k'iéng' so'* to owe a bill; *ˈt'ó so'* or *ˌsiu so'* to collect debts; *ˈsi so'* dead (unliquidated) accounts; [6]*so' ˌpung*, a book-keeper's office; [7]*so' ˌniéng*, a few years; *ˌt'iéng so'* Heaven's decree; *so' ˌnang ˌtó*, hard to escape one's destiny, as to die; COLL., *so' ˌma ˌcha*, confused accounts; *p'ok, so'* insolvent; *ˌhwang ˌhung so'* "resuscitated accounts, as when payment is again exacted; *ˌp'ang so'* or *ˌheng so'* to pay up debts. Read *ˈsu*: to count, to enumerate; to recapitulate, as one's faults; to find fault, to blame.

訴 愬 Su. To state, to inform, to announce, to tell; to accuse, to inform against; to reply to an accusation; a defense; to defame, to detract; calumny: the 2d read *sauk*, to fear, alarmed; COM., [8]*kó' so'* to relate, to inform; [9]*so' ˌtiäng*, a reply to an accusation; [10]*so' ˌküng*, testimony before a magistrate; [11]*so' ˌwong*, to state one's wrongs; COLL., [12]*so' naing'* to tell, to narrate; *so' ˌpá*, to tell the history of, as in a play.

遡 溯 泝 Su. The 1st used for the preceding in the sense of to accuse; to go against the current, to meet or go against; formerly; towards, to revert to: *so' ˌhui*, to go against the stream; *so' ˌiu*, to go with the tide.

塑 㙑 Su. To shape, to mold in a certain form; to model in clay, to make idols; molded: COM., [13]*so' ch'iong'* to mold images; [14]*so' huk,* to mold a Budh, to make clay idols; [15]*ˈt'u so' muk, ˌteu*, molded clay and carved wood, as idols; *met.*, stupid, doltish; COLL., *so' sioh, ˌsing* (or *ˌting*), to mold one idol.

素 Su. So. White cloth or silk; plain, unadorned, wanting lively colors; white and coarse, as mourning apparel; empty, all gone; simple in dress or manners; the original state, formerly, usually, as at first; dubious, hesitating: also read *sauk*, q. v.: [16]*p'auk, so'* plain, simple; *so' che'* or [17]*so' seng'* natural disposition, bent; COM., [18]*ˌping so'* formerly; habitually; [19]*so' ˌsiong*, usually; [20]*so' mó'* a mourning cap; [21]*ˌkü so'* to wear mourning; [22]*so' ch'ai'* vegetable diet; *ˌkwong so'* plain, unadorned; *so' ˌtiu*, plain silks, those not red; COLL., [23]*pah, so'* plain, blank, as blank parts of tin-foil paper; *so' ˈch'iu ˌk'ëng ˌk'ëng*, empty-handed, as one making his own fortune.

1 數目	3 數簿	5 總數	7 數年	9 訴呈	11 訴冤	13 塑像	15 土塑	16 樸素	18 平素	20 素帽	22 素菜
2 無數	4 草數	6 數房	8 告訴	10 訴供	12 訴念	14 塑佛	木雕	17 素性	19 素常	21 居素	23 白素

愫 Su. Sincere, honest, guileless; to have real intentions, or purposes.

(751) Só.

梭 ‹So. A shuttle; swift, as a shuttle; to move to and fro, as a shuttle: [1]‹p'au ‹só, to throw the shuttle; [2]‹ngü ‹só, a fish darting through the water; COM., [3]nik, ngwok, ‹ü ‹só, the days and months (pass) like a shuttle. Read *chong'*: the name of a kind of wood.

唆 ‹So. Tsun. To prattle, to answer each other, as children; to incite, to instigate; to importune: [4]‹sü ‹só, to provoke to evil; COM., [5]‹t'ieu ‹só, to instigate; to sow discord; [6]‹só sëü' to excite trouble; [7]‹só sëüng' to be litigious—language of courts; COLL., [8]‹ló ‹só, troublesome, vexatious.

娑 ‹So. To frisk, to gambol, to dance about; to trip, to skip; to lounge, to sit at ease; to play with the dress; idle, negligent, dissolute: [9]‹pó ‹só, to play antics, to frisk.

莏 ‹So. Abundant, luxuriant, as vegetation: ‹pó ‹só, flourishing; [10]‹só ‹pó, the roots of plants.

莎 ‹So. A triquetrous plant with hairy roots, called [11]‹heu ‹só, a sort of cyperus; to rub in the fingers, in which sense used for the next. Read ‹sa, as in [12]‹sa ‹kié, a species of cricket.

挱 ‹So. To feel, to rub in the hand: [13]‹mó ‹só, to finger, to take in the hand and play with.

睃 ‹So. To peep, to peer about, to steal a glance at: COLL., [14]‹só ‹só 'tiong, to look about furtively.

搔 ‹Sao. To scratch, to scrape with the nails; to feel of, to rub gently, to titillate; to set at variance. Read *'chwa*: the nails, the claws.

鰠 ‹Sao. A fish like a sturgeon; in Canton, a sort of bream; it is said to indicate the approach of armies by its motions.

騷 ‹Sao. To rub down a horse; to move, to agitate, to disturb, to annoy; perturbed, sad, mournful; lame; sorrow, trial, distress: [15]‹só ‹ing, a bard; [16]‹hung ‹só, bewitching, winsome; [17]‹lié ‹só, Dissipation of Sorrows—a poem; [18]‹ló ‹só, grieved, distressed; [19]‹só sak, fluttering loose in the wind; [20]‹só 'yeu, to harrass.

颾 ‹Sao. The sound of the wind.

臊 ‹Sao. Rancid, rank, as putrid meat; strong, reeking; the scent of goats: also read ‹ch'ó, q. v.: [21]‹kó ‹só, rancid fat; [22]‹sing ‹só, rank, strong, fetid.

繅 ‹Sao. To reel silk from cocoons; a piece of variegated silk to place a gem or seal on.

---

1 拋梭　2 魚梭　3 日月如梭　4 使唆　5 挑唆　6 唆事　7 唆訟　8 囉唆　9 婆娑　10 莏蔢　11 侯莏　12 莎雞　18 摩挱　14 睃睃轉○　15 騷人　16 風騷　17 離騷　18 牢騷　19 騷殺　20 騷擾　21 膏臊　22 腥臊

‚Sǒ. A coll. word: a sharp, pungent taste, to smart: *chʻoi’ siĕk‚ ‘mwi ‚sǒ ‚sǒ ‘tiong*, the end of the tongue smarts, as from touching pepper.

‚Sǒ. A coll. word: to eat, as ducks and other broad-billed fowls do; to move the bill about to get the food.

‚Sǒ. A coll. word: to darn, to mend by darning.

‘嫂 Sao. An elder brother's wife, a sister-in-law; madam! my good woman! [1]*‚ku ‘sǒ*, sisters-in-law; COM., [2]*‚hiĕng ‘sǒ*, an elder brother's wife; *‘kwa ‘sǒ*, an elder brother's widow; *‘twai’ ‘sǒ* and *ne’ ‘sǒ*, wives of the first and second brothers; [4]*‚ka ‘sǒ*, my elder brother's wife; [5]*‘sǒ chĕ̤k, pok‚ ‚tʻung ong’* one's wife and younger brother must not be familiar; [6]*‘pieu ‘sǒ*, aunt's daughter-in-law; madam! COLL., *‚i ‘sǒ*, good woman!

‘掃 Sao. To sweep, to brush away; to sweep and clean up; a broom, a besom; to dampen, as one's ardor or hopes; to clear off, to rid: also read *‘swa* and in the coll. *sau’* q. v.

‘鎖 ‘鎖 So. A lock; to lock; to fetter; to knit the brows, to frown; chains or rings for locking: [7]*‚king ‘sǒ kak‚*, chain armor; [8]*‚chʻeu ‚mi ‘sǒ pok‚ ‚kʻai*, the brows rigidly contracted; COM., *‘sǒ ‚mwong*, to lock a door; [9]*‘sǒ ‚sié*, a key; [10]*‚hung ‘sǒ*, to seal and close, as a broken bank; [11]*‘kʻieu ‘sǒ*, an ingeniously contrived lock; COLL., [12]*pʻang’ ‘sǒ*, an "empty lock"—one whose springs are spoiled and which can be opened without a key; *‚mi ‚tʻau ‘sǒ ‘lá*, his brows are knit! *‘sǒ ‚chʻiu*, the springs of a common Chinese lock; *chiong’ ‚kung ‘kwang ‘sǒ ‚sié*, the (Tartar) general holds the keys; *met.*, one who has a special charge or control; *‘sǒ nak‚* a sort of pipe, a clarinet.

‘Sǒ. A coll. word, for which the last may be used: a sort of interlaced stitching, to work a binding of such stitches: *‘sǒ ‘kʻau*, to bind edges, as the tops of shoes; *‘sǒ pʻe’* to stitch shoe-toes; *‘sǒ siăng’* silk thread for binding.

‘瑣 瑣 So. The fragments of gems; the tinkling of gems or precious stones; minute, small; low, petty, trifling; fine, delicate, tender, small; annoying, vexatious, troublesome; connected: [13]*‚hwang ‘sǒ*, vexatious; [14]*‘sǒ ‚liĕng*, connected; [15]*‘sǒ ‘mwi*, small, delicate; COLL., *‘sǒ chʻói’ ‚ki tai’* petty affairs.

‘鮹 Sao. A roundish sack-like fish; it is salted, and termed in the coll. *‘sǒ ‘kwong*.

燥’ Sao. Dry, scorched, chapped; to dry by the fire; fierce, fiery: [16]*sǒ’ liĕk‚* fierce, raging, as fire or one's temper; COM., [17]*‚kang sǒ’* dry, parched; [18]*‚hung ‚kǒ uk‚ sǒ’* the wind high and things inflammable—a caution in official placards; [19]*sǒ’ kʻe’* a dry atmosphere; *‚kǒ*

[1]姑嫂 [2]兄嫂 [3]大嫂 [4]家嫂 [5]嫂叔不通間 [6]表嫂 [7]金鎖甲 [8]愁眉鎖不開〇 [9]鎖匙 [10]封鎖 [11]巧鎖 [12]冇鎖 [13]煩瑣 [14]瑣連 [15]瑣尾 [16]燥烈 [17]乾燥 [18]風高物燥 [19]燥氣

só' high and dry, as a locality; [1]*'só' kang'* to absorb sweat; [2]*'só' 'hwo*, parching heat (in the system); COLL., *só' ˏta*, to dry by absorbing (the moisture); *só' 'lang*, to absorb the saliva, as dry cakes do; *só' pong'* constipated.

譟' Sao. The noise and vociferations of a crowd; a clamor, a disturbance, a hubbub: [3]*'ku só' ˏi 'k'i*, to beat drums and make a clamor.

噪' Sao. Also read *ch'ó'*: the singing of many birds, a loud chirping; to cry, to bawl; the hum of men's voices.

躁' Sao. To go quickly; hasty, precipitate, heedless; fierce, oppressive; dried by heat and so light as to be easily blown away: [4]*ˏkieu só'* wanton and oppressive; [5]*ˏp'eu só'* light, unsteady, fickle.

槽 ˏTs'ao. Read *ˏchó*; coll. *ˏsó*: a trough, a log channeled out; a manger: [6]*'chwi ˏsó*, an eaves-trough; *ˏp'ung' ˏsó*, a swill-trough; [7]*'ma ˏsó*, a manger; [8]*'p'ok ˏsó*, and *k'ieu' ˏsó*, tiles with convex and concave sides up; *sioh ˏsó*, a stone receptacle for fish or rock-scenery.

(752) Sóh.

索, So. Se. Read *sauk,*; coll. *sóh,*: a rope, a cord, a line, a string: [9]*'ch'au sóh*, cord of the stalks of grass; [10]*ˏchĕng sóh*, palm-coir ropes; *ˏchiéng kwong' sóh*, cord to string cash on; *p'ah, sóh*, to twist rope; *ˏtong paik, sóh*, one who lives by his wits, a loafer.

嗽, Read *ch'ëük,*; used in the *Paik, ˏIng* for the coll. *sóh,*: to suck, to draw into the mouth; to cup; to "extract wind" with the cup: *sóh, ˏnĕng*, to draw out the pus, as a plaster does; *sóh, ch'oi'* to suck with the mouth; *sóh, haik,'ma ˏk'i*, a leech, a blood-sucker; *met.*, one who cheats another out of money; *sóh, ˏt'au aĕng' 'tio ˏngüng hwak, ˏchai 'iu aing'* like money put into a (small) cupping-cup, so are gains limited in amount.

鐲, Cho. Used commonly in the sense of bracelets, anklets: COM., [11]*'ch'iu sóh,* a bracelet; *k'a sóh,* anklets; [12]*ˏngüng sóh,* silver bracelets; COLL., [13]*sóh, 'kiăng*, small bracelets. Read *chok,*: small bells, used for army signals.

Sóh,. A coll. word, as in *sóh, nik,* day before yesterday; *sóh, ˏniéng* or *sóh, ˏniéng ˏmang*, the year before last.

(753) Soi.

衰 Shui. Shuai. To fade, as a garment; old, worn out; weak, debilitated, dwindled; adverse, failing, unprosperous; to decay, to lessen, to decline; small, weak, minute: [14]*ˏsoi sié'* a vicious age; [15]*ˏsoi mwo'* the evening of life; COM., [16]*ˏsoi ˏsoi*, lean, emaciated; [17]*ˏsoi k'é'* unprosperous; [18]*ˏsoi yok,* debilitated; [19]*ˏsoi ˏmi*, failing, wasting away; [20]*ˏsoi oi'* an unlucky place or seat, as in a game; COLL., *ˏsoi k'iăk, k'iăk,* very lank and lean; [21]*ˏsoi ˏloi*, a

1 燥汗 2 燥火 3 鼓譟而起 4 驕躁 5 浮躁 6 水槽 7 馬槽 8 覆槽 9 草索 10 椶索 11 手鐲 12 銀鐲 13 鐲仔 14 衰世 15 衰暮 16 衰衰 17 衰氣 18 衰弱 19 衰微 20 衰位 21 衰螺 ○ ○

small, tapering snail; *met.*, a bitter taste; [1]*ˌsoi ˌloi ˋmwi*, always unlucky.

蓑 ˓So. Read *ˌsó* in the dictionaries: a rain cloak of bamboo or palm leaves; pendent, hanging loose, as flowers; to cover, to thatch, to screen from rain: [2]*ˌsoi lik*, a rain cloak and hat.

縗 ˓Ts'ui. A mourning badge, worn on the breast; the unhemmed, frayed edges of mourning clothes, called [3]*chang ˌsoi*; the feathers on a heron's head.

榱 ˓Ts'ui. A row of curved rafters, called [4]*ˌsoi ˌtá*, which project from the plate in imperial buildings: [5]*ˌhwa ˌsoi*, an ornamented beam or plate.

粹ˀ Sui. Good, unmixed grain; pure, alike, uniform, unadulterated; also used for *ch'ói*ˀ (broken into bits): [6]*ˌsung soi*ˀ pure, unmixed.

睡ˀ Shui. To sleep; to doze, to nod and snooze, as in a chair: [7]*ˋta soi*ˀ to sleep; *ˌch'ing soi*ˀ a deep sleep; [8]*soi*ˀ *ˋsing*, to wake up.

穗ˀ Sui. An ear of corn, a spike of wheat or any grain; the heads of grasses; a spikelet, a tufted ear; elegant, graceful: [9]*ek, ˌhwo ˋkiu soi*ˀ *ˋteu ˋmi ˌsang ˌung*, nine heads on a stalk, and a peck of rice for three cash!—a felicitous phrase for a time of plenty; COM., *soi*ˀ *kiék, sik*, the heads have kernels set; COLL., *soi*ˀ *pek, p'ang*ˀ empty heads of grain.

繸ˀ Sui. A fringe, a tassel, any bordering of threads: COM., [10]*mó*ˀ *soi*ˀ the fringe on a cap; [11]*siàng*ˀ *soi*ˀ a thread-tassel; [12]*ˌchio soi*ˀ a bead-fringe, as on a head-dress; COLL., *soi*ˀ *sioh, ˌt'ó*, one tassel. Read *soi*ˀ: a string for attaching ornaments to a girdle.

祟ˀ Sui. Calamities, judgments from heaven or the gods, which men are impotent to avert: [13]*kwai*ˀ *soi*ˀ a monstrous calamity.

ˌSoi. A coll. word, as in *yok, ˌsoi*, weary of, disappointed, dispirited, as from poor success in a pursuit; *lóh, ˌsoi*, wasted, emaciated.

遂ˀ Sui. To go through, to effect, to complete; to follow, to accord with; to comply, to yield, not to oppose or hinder; next, after that, then, forthwith, finally; a moor; also a canal or sluice for irrigation: [14]*soi*ˀ *e*ˀ or [15]*soi*ˀ *ngwong*ˀ according with one's wishes; [16]*pok, soi*ˀ *ˌki ük*, discouraged his request; [17]*pok, taik, soi*ˀ *ˌsing*, to be disappointed in one's hopes.

瑞ˀ Shui. Jui. A stone signet, or sign of authority, given to a feudatory; a sign, a token; a happy omen or prognostic; auspicious, felicitous: COM., *ˌing soi*ˀ *ˌniéng ˌhung*, men fortunate and the year abundant—a sentence used on doors; [18]*ˌsiong soi*ˀ an auspicious sign; felicitous; *soi*ˀ *ˋtiéng kwok*, Sweden, as sometimes called.

1衰螺尾 2蓑笠 3斬縗 4榱題 5華榱 6純粹 7打睡 8睡醒 9一禾九穗三文斗米 10帽繸 11線繸 12珠繸 13怪祟 14遂意 15遂願 16不遂其欲 17不得遂心 18祥瑞

璲² Sui. A gem hung on the girdle; it is supposed to have lucky qualities.

燧² Sui. A speculum for setting fire to things, a sun-glass; also a wooden implement for igniting by friction: ¹*Soi*² *ˌing se*² the Chinese Prometheus; ²*ʻhwo soi*² a match.

邃² Sui. Deep, far back, distant; in the rear, as a back apartment; poor, exhausted.

穟² Sui. The fine appearance of growing grain: *soi*² *soi*² smiling fields of grain.

襚² A shroud; to present grave-clothes or an equivalent in money; also apparel presented to friends: *soi*² *ˌi*, grave-clothes.

(754). Sói.

帥ˀ Shuai. A general, a leader, a commander; to lead, to take the chief command: also read *sauk*, q. v.: COM., ³*ʻchiong*ˀ *sói*ˀ a general; ⁴*ˌngwong sói*ˀ a generalissimo; ⁵*ʻpwong sói*ˀ I, the general; ⁶*ʻchio sói*ˀ our general; ⁷*kwa*ˀ *sói*ˀ to wear the seal of a general; COLL., ⁸*ˌngwong sói*ˀ *kiék*, the magic (attitude) of the god *ˌTiéng ˌngwong sói*ˀ (with two fingers extended); *met.*, a term used in offering prices, as two, two tens, two hundreds.

坐² Tso. Read *chó*²; coll. *sói*²: to sit, to be seated; to sit in judgment; to sit, as Budhists do: *sói*² *sói*² to sit; just sit! ⁹*ch'iăng sói*² please be seated; ¹⁰*sói*² *oi*² to take places, as at a feast; ¹¹*sói*² *tóh*, to sit at table; ¹²*sói*² *ˌtong*, to sit in judgment; *sói*² *ˌtong ˌkang*, perpetual imprisonment; ¹³*sói*² *hiong*ˀ the position, as of a grave; ¹⁴*sói*² *ˌchá*, to be a schoolmaster; ¹⁵*sói*² *ˌsiéng*, to sit and meditate, as Budhist priests; ¹⁶*sói*² *ˌsang*, to buy up mountain products, as paper, bamboo sprouts, etc.; *sói*² *sioh*, *ʻtó*, to fall backwards; *sói*² *ʻlá siăh*, to live without working; *ˌmó ˌchiéng sói*² *ˌtong ʻtu*, no cash and yet occupy the middle stateroom; *met.*, as one claiming the best gratis.

(755) Sok.

束ˀ Su. Shu. To tie up, to bind in a bundle; to coerce, to control, to restrain; a sheaf, a bundle, as of five pieces of cloth, ten pieces of dried meat, or fifty arrows: COM., ¹⁷*sok*, *ˌsiu*, or ¹⁸*sok*, *ˌking*, a teacher's stipend; ¹⁹*ʻkwang sok*, to restrain those under one; *yok*, *sok*, to bind by contract.

觫ˀ Su. To move suddenly, to tremble, to start; trembling, affrighted: ²⁰*puk*, *sok*, terribly frightened, as animals when pursued.

餗ˀ Su. The cooked contents of a boiler or kettle; dressed food.

速ˀ Su. Used for the next in the sense of mean: fleet, quick, hurried; precipitately, hastily; to call, to invite; the tracks of deer: ²¹*sok*, *sok*, quickly; also estranged, friendless; ²²*ʻhwo sok*, rapid as flames, with utmost haste; COM.,

¹燧人氏〇 ²火燧 ³將帥 ⁴元帥 ⁵本帥 ⁶主帥 ⁷掛帥 ⁸元帥訣〇 ⁹請坐 ¹⁰坐位 ¹¹坐棹 ¹²坐堂 ¹³坐向 ¹⁴坐齋 ¹⁵坐禪 ¹⁶坐山 ¹⁷束修 ¹⁸束金 ¹⁹[illegible]束 ²⁰[illegible]觫 ²¹[illegible] ²²火速

[1]*sok, ngŭk*, hasten your precious steps, and [2]*sok, kaung'* descend soon—terms used on cards of invitation; [3]*sok, pó'* *,si*, a god who reports speedily.

蔌, Culinary vegetables, herbs, legumes; poor, mean: *sok, sok*, low, mean; the wind whistling by.

遬, Also read *sëük,*: to step briskly; to dispatch, to expedite, to hurry through with; alert, active, speedy; attentive, respectful.

簌, A sieve; to sift out; showering down, as autumnal leaves in the wind; thick, close, luxuriant.

樕, A small tree, a sapling, a shrub: [4]*'p'auk, sok*, small trees, as suitable for posts.

恤, 卹, 䘏, Hsü. Hsüeh. To feel for, to pity, to commiserate; to love, to feel attachment to; affection, pity, sympathy, sorrow for: [5]*'t'á sok*, to pity and assist; [6]*sok, ,ling*, to compassionate; [7]*sok, 'kwa*, to relieve widows; [8]*'ching sok*, to give alms to; [9]*'u sok*, to soothe.

戌, Hsü. This must be distinguished from *sëü'* (to guard frontiers): the 11th of the 12 branches, denoted by a dog; the fall of the year, the fading of plants in autumn: [10]*sok, ngwok*, the 9th moon; COM., *sok, ,si*, or *sok, k'aik*, 7—9, P. M.; [11]*sok, chiăng'* 8 P. M.

抄 So. Read *,só*; used in the *Paik, ,Ing* for the coll. *sok,*: to stoke, to rub gently with the hand: *sok, sok*, to stroke; [12]*,mwo sok*, to stroke gently, to soothe by stroking; *sok, sioh, a'* give it a gentle rubbing.

Sok,. A coll. word: to smear, to paint: *sok, ,lang*, to paint a blue color.

(756) Song.

桑 Sang. The mulberry tree; *met.*, peaceful retirement: [13]*,song 'chü*, one's native village; [14]*,song ,tüng ,chi yok*, illicit intercourse; COM., [15]*,song ,chié*, and *,song pah*, mulberry twigs and root-bark, used for medicine; [16]*,song kié' ,seng*, an epiphyte, growing on the mulberry; COLL., *,song ,tai* (or *,lai*), the berry or fruit of the mulberry; *,song ,p'úi ,miéng*, or *,song ,p'úi 'chai*, mulberry-bark paper—is dark-colored and of a firm texture.

孫 Sun. A grandchild; what grows again, or is reproduced; a surname: COM., [17]*,cheng ,song*, [18]*,ngwong ,song*, and [19]*,lai ,song*, the three generations after "grandson"; [20]*,kung ,song*, grandfather and grandson; *,song 'nü*, a granddaughter; [21]*ngwoi' ,song*, (coll. *ngié' ,seng ,song*), a daughter's son; *,song sá'* (or *sai'*), a granddaughter's husband; *ngié' ,seng ,song sái'* a son-in-law's son-in-law. Read *saung'*: mild, complaisant.

[1]速玉 [2]速降 [3]速報司〇 [4]樸樕 [5]體恤 [6]恤憐 [7]恤寡 [8]賑恤 [9]撫恤 [10]戌月 [11]戌正 [12]摸抄 [13]桑梓 [14]桑中之約 [15]桑枝 [16]桑寄生〇 [17]曾孫 [18]元孫 [19]來孫 [20]公孫 [21]外孫

蓀 ꜀Sun. A species of fragrant herb, like the sweet flag: [1]*'k'á ꜀song*, an aquatic plant, a kind of iris?

猻 ꜀Sun. A monkey: [2]*꜀heu ꜀song*, a species of small monkey.

相 ꜀Hsiang. Read *꜀siong;* coll. *꜀song:* mutually, reciprocally; by turns, interchangeably: [3]*꜀song 'hó*, on good terms; [4]*꜀song ꜀hwo*, agreeing, in accord, at peace; [5]*꜀song niong'* mutually yielding; *꜀song p'ah꜀* to fight together: [6]*꜀song siăh꜀* adhering, joining; welded; *꜀song ꜀k'iă*, to strive to get the advantage of each other; [7]*꜀song ꜀tĕng*, alike; *꜀song 'chĕ*, or *꜀song ꜀ch'a tio'* to take different roads, so as to miss one another.

商 ꜀Shang. Read *꜀siong;* coll. *꜀song*, as in [8]*꜀song ꜀liong*, to consult, to deliberate.

霜 ꜀Shuang. Congealed dew, or vapor, hoar-frost, rime; frigid, cold; grave: [9]*'chiĕk, ch'ŏ' ꜀ping ꜀song*, as chaste as ice and frost—on monuments to widows; [10]*꜀song ꜀wi*, stern, majestic; COM., [11]*꜀song siok*, frost and snow; *lŏh꜀ ꜀song*, a fall of frost, frosty; [12]*꜀song kaung'* the 18th of the 24 terms—usually in October and November; COLL., *꜀eng ꜀song*, dark, chilly weather after frost.

礵 ꜀Shuang. An unauthorized character, used for the last in the term for arsenic: COM., [13]*꜀p'ié ꜀song*, arsenic, usually called *seng'*.

孀 ꜀Shuang. A widow, called [14]*꜀song ho'*; [15]*꜀ku ꜀song*, orphans and widows; a lone widow; COM., [16]*꜀song ꜀kü* (coll. *꜀song ꜀kü ꜀nĕng*), a widow.

驦 驌 Shuang. A famous Bucephalus, called [17]*sĕŭk꜀ ꜀song*, belonging to *Kwoh꜀ p'auk꜀* of the Chin dynasty.

酸 ꜀Suan. Sour, acid, sharp, tart; harsh, irritating, distressing; grieved, afflicted; a loitering gait, as from debility; also occurs in names of a bird and wood: [18]*꜀song 'kwo*, pickles; COM., [19]*꜀sing ꜀song*, grieved, sympathizing; *꜀song e'* a sour or acid taste; *꜀song 'mwí*, a sour taste left; [20]*꜀song ꜀muí ngau'* pickled apricot and (sugared) lily-root — a cooling drink; *꜀song 'chó ꜀kó*, sour-date jelly; COLL., *ch'o' 'mó ꜀song*, as sour as the mother-of-vinegar; *꜀song keu' leu'* very acid.

䨳 ꜀ A slight shower.

痠 ꜀Suan. In pain; aching, as from fatigue: *꜀song sik꜀* a sort of stone; COM., [21]*'ch'iu ꜀song 'niong*, the hands aching and weak; COLL., *꜀song 'nĕ*, aching, as from toil; *mek꜀ ꜀chiu ꜀song saik꜀* the eyes smart.

朘 ꜀Hsüan. The genitals of an infant; shriveled, as flesh; puckered, contracted; to lessen, to diminish, to reduce by oppression.

[1]溪蓀 [2]猴猻 [3]相好 [4]相和 [5]相讓 [6]相食 [7]相同 [8]商量 [9]節操冰霜 [10]霜威 [11]霜雪 [12]霜降 [13]砒礵 [14]孀婦 [15]孤孀 [16]孀居 [17]驌驦 [18]酸果 [19]心酸 [20]酸梅藕〇 [21]手痠軟〇

喪 喪 ‹ *Sang.* To mourn for the dead; funereal; mourning; a funeral; mourning apparel: also read *saung'*: q. v.: [1]*‹song huk*, a mourning dress; [2]*‹kü ‹song*, or *‹siu ‹song*, to mourn for parents three years; COM., [3]*ch‹ok ‹song*, to inter; [4]*‹k‹wi ‹song*, to institute funeral rites; [5]*kwok ‹song*, mourning for the emperor; [6]*‹song ‹mwong tieu' k‹aik*, the names of two imps—who must be appeased in times of sickness.

宣 ‹ *Hsüan. Hsüen.* To proclaim, to publish, to promulge by authority; to pervade, to extend, to spread everywhere; to expand, to revolve, to circulate, as the winds; extended, expansive, manifested; to summon, as rulers do; slow; beginning to be bald: *‹song ‹tiong*, to promulge; [7]*‹song tieu'* to summon, as to court; *pok ‹song*, not to say more—an epistolary phrase; *‹song t‹uk siong' ëü'* to read aloud the emperor's orders; COM., [8]*‹song ‹lu*, a kind of censer—named from [9]*‹Song taik*, of the Ming dynasty.

瑄 ‹ A jade stone, six inches long, anciently held in the hands by princes as insignia.

飧 ‹ *Sun.* Water put in rice to soften or separate the grains; prepared food, a meal, in which sense used for *‹ch‹wang*, q. v.: [10]*siëk ‹song*, to arrange a meal; [11]*te' ‹song*, to give food to one.

‹Song. A coll. word: to bolt, to bar a door; to shove a bolt; a small bolt, a peg or catch: *‹song ‹tié*, to push a bolt in; *‹song ‹king*, bolt it fast; *ang' ‹song*, a secret catch.

損 ‹ *Sun.* To diminish, to lessen; to injure, to damage; to wound; to lose; to reprove, to blame, as a critic does; detrimental; damage, bad luck; the 41st diagram: *‹song pai'* ruined; *‹mwang ‹chieu ‹song*, riches invite misfortune; [12]*‹song sük* poor and good crops; COM., *‹siong ‹song*, wounded; [13]*‹song hwai'* (coll. *p‹wai' ‹song*), ruined, dilapidated, as a house; [14]*‹song hai'* to injure, hurtful; [15]*‹song ‹ting*, to lose a member of the family by death; [16]*‹song cheng'* a wasting disease; [17]*‹song ‹ing le' ‹ki*, to injure others in order to benefit one's self; *‹t‹iéng ‹niéng ‹song*, the harvest has failed.

選 ‹ *Hsüan.* To choose, to select, to elect; to cull, to pick out; to select men for office; to dance in a circle; a moment; one hundred thousand; timid, apprehensive: [18]*‹song tek* to choose; [19]*‹song ‹kang*, or *‹sieu ‹song*, an instant; COM., *‹song ‹küng ‹nü*, to select girls for the harem; [20]*‹keng ‹song*, to pick out, to elect; [21]*‹song chiong'* to select a leader. Read *saung'*: to reckon: also used for *saung'* yielding; [22]*saung' nó'* weak, vacillating.

爽 爽 ‹ *Shuang.* To admit the light; light, cheerful, pleasant; easy, comfortable, healthy, vigorous; noble; impetuous, forcible; to fail, to miss; error, defect:

1 喪服	3 出喪	5 國喪	弔客	8 宣爐	10 設飧	12 損熟	14 損害	16 損症	利己	19 選間	21 選將
2 居喪	4 開喪	6 喪門	7 宣召	9 宣德	11 致飧	13 損壞	15 損丁	17 損人	18 選擇	20 揀選	22 選懦

'ˌch'ing 'song, pure and clear; ²'song yok, to fail in an engagement; ³'song sek, to lose, to miss; ⁴mwoi ² 'song, early dawn; COM., ⁵'song 'k'eu, palatable; ⁶'song k'wai ² in good health and spirits; COLL., ⁷'song ch'woi ² quick, ready.

'礎 Sang. The stone base or plinth of a pillar: COM., ⁸'song ˌpwang, or 'song sioh, the base of a post (under the t'eu ˌchio, or carved plinth).

'顙 Sang. The forehead, the front of the head: ⁹'kwong 'song, a broad or high forehead; ¹⁰'k'iê 'song, to bow the head.

舜' Shun. An ancient monarch, called ¹¹ˌNgü song' B. C. 2255; in posthumous titles, it means sage, holy, intelligent: COM., ¹²song' tá ' or tá ' song' the emperor Shun.

橓 蕣' Shun. A plant, also called ¹³muk, kĕüng ² whose flowers bloom in the morning and fade at night—an emblem of what is fading and transitory.

瞤' Also read ˌsung: to blink the eyes, the sparkling of the eyes, as when pleased; a nervous twitching of one's eyes.

宋' Sung. To dwell, to reside; a dwelling; a feudal state lying in the prefecture of Kueitô in the east of Honan; name of a famous dynasty, A. D. 970-1280; also a shorter one, A. D. 420-477: in the coll. read saĕng' q. v.

送 送' Sung. To give, to present, to send presents; to go or send with; to accompany, to escort, to go with; to see a guest out; a present, a gift: in the coll. read saĕng' q. v.: ¹⁴ˌt'ü song' to implicate one another, as criminals; ¹⁵chĕüng' song' skilled in archery.

Song'. A coll. word, as in song' song' to do readily as others say; raw, verdant, credulous, like a greenhorn; song' song' ˌkŭng ˌi k'ó ' has verdantly followed him away.

'甑 Tsêng. Ching. Read chaing'; used in the Paik, ˌIng for the coll. ˌsong: a wooden rice-steamer, called pwong' ˌsong; ˌsong tak, a steaming-cylinder, placed over the grating in a pan; ¹⁶'kwi ˌsong, a rice-cake steamer; ¹⁷ˌch'wi ˌsong, a steamer with a fixed grate or rack in the bottom.

ˌSong. A coll. word: to smart; a pungent, local pain; to cause to smart: á ² ˌsong, it prickles, it smarts; á ² ˌsong ˌsiĕng, it will make one smart.

順² Shun. To accord with, to agree to, to follow; to obey, to comply, to acquiesce, to yield; harmonizing, compliant, agreeable; convenient, what one can readily do; at hand, to avail of; fair, as the wind or tide; flowing, rhythmical, as a style; free, easy, as penmanship: ¹⁸paik, song² agreeing in every respect; ¹⁹ˌkwi song² to return to obedience; COM., ²⁰song² 'li, to conform to reason or propriety; ²¹song² le² prospering; song² ngwok,

¹清爽 ²爽約 ³爽失 ⁴昧爽 ⁵爽口 ⁶爽快 ⁷爽脆 ⁸磉磐 ⁹廣顙 ¹⁰稽顙 ¹¹虞舜 ¹²舜帝 ¹³木槿 ¹⁴株送 ¹⁵縱送 ¹⁶粿甑 ¹⁷炊甑 ¹⁸百順 ¹⁹歸順 ²⁰順理 ²¹順利 ○ ○ ○

according to the month, as time of parturition; *song' ꜀ki chëü'* *꜀yong*, according to the natural state of; [1]*song' che'* to trace over the copy (in learning to write); [2]*song' 'k'eu*, palatable, as mellow wine; *song' pièng'* at convenience; [3]*'hau' song'* filial; *song' ꜀t'au song' e'* to yield ready obedience; *song' ꜀hung song' 'chwi*, with wind and tide; [4]*'song' ꜀hung ꜀siong song'* may favoring gales attend you! [5]*Song' te'* the first emperor of the Great Pure dynasty.

(757) Su.

酥 Su. A preparation of curd; butter, as made at the north; tender, crisp, flaky, short, as crust: [6]*꜀su ꜀iu*, butter, ghee—also called *'ma ꜀sü ꜀kó*; [7]*꜀tu ꜀su*, mulled or medicated wine; a medicine; COM., [8]*꜀su ꜀kó*, flour cake sliced up; COLL., *꜀su chiāh꜀ ꜀su*, very crisp; *꜀sieu 'piāng ꜀kwong 'piāng ꜀iu chak꜀ 'kwi 'yā ꜀su*, cakes, biscuits and crullers, very crisp (for sale)! —a street cry.

穌 甦 Su. To collect grain; to take; to cease, to take rest, to enjoy ease; to resuscitate, to revive, as persons rescued from the water; to live again, to rise from the dead; a resurrection: [9]*꜀su lëk꜀* the Sooloo isles; COM., [10]*꜀yā ꜀su*, Jesus.

蘇 蘓 Su. Used for the last and the next: a sort of sage or clary; to take; to revive, cheerful, happy; to cease, to rest; a surname; to agitate: COM., [11]*'chié ꜀su*, sweet basil; [12]*꜀su hak꜀ ꜀iu*, storax; [13]*꜀su ꜀chiu*, Soochow, the capital of Kiangsu; *꜀su mëk꜀ ꜀ch'a*, sapan or Brazil wood; [14]*꜀su ꜀hong ꜀chiu*, Soochow and Hangchow; *꜀su ꜀chiu 'mi ꜀ing*, a Soochow beauty; COLL., *꜀su 'kwong ꜀pong*, Soochow and Canton goods. Read *so'*: to meet, to come in conflict with.

廝 Su. As in *꜀tio ꜀su*, a monastery, a convent, a nunnery; also a kind of wine, which is said to expel humors from the system when drunk on the 1st day of the first moon.

蔬 Su. A general term for vegetables and edible herbs: [15]*꜀ka ꜀su*, rice; [16]*꜀su ch'ai'* greens; *꜀su sëü'* a meal of herbs.

疏 疎 蹠 踈 Su. Used for the last: open, wide apart, coarse; sleazy, as cloth; remiss, careless, lax; easy, free, generous; sundered, distant, distantly related; to divide, to partition; to part with; to regulate; to engrave, to carve; to paint, to delineate; to discard; to spread out, to enlarge; large, full, ample: also read *saë'* and in the coll. *꜀së*, q. v.: [17]*꜀hu ꜀su*, luxuriant, as leaves; [18]*꜀su ꜀ngü*, remiss, negligent; COM., [19]*꜀ch'ing ꜀su*, near and distant relationships; [20]*hwong' ꜀su*, to leave off for a long time, out of practice; *꜀su ꜀t'ung*, to open, to make permeable; *꜀su k'e'* (coll. *꜀su ꜀pa*), generous, free, as with money; [21]*꜀su ꜀chai tëüng' ngié'* generous and kind in aiding; *꜀ing*

[1] 順字 [2] 順口 [3] 孝順 [4] 順風相送 [5] 順治 [6] 酥油 [7] 酴酥 [8] 酥糕 [9] 穌六 [10] 耶穌 [11] 紫蘇 [12] 蘇合油 [13] 蘇州 [14] 蘇杭州 [15] 嘉蔬 [16] 蔬菜 [17] 扶疏 [18] 疏虞 [19] 親疏 [20] 放疏 [21] 疏財重義

tė² ˏseng ˏsu, the people and place strange (to a traveller).

ʿ所 ʿ𪐴 So. Su. Shu. Shuo. The sound of cutting wood; a place, a spot; a classifier of houses and parcels of ground; a town or post; the means or cause by which; a relative pronoun, that which, what, in which sense it precedes the verb and noun: in the coll. read *ʿsė*, q. v.: ¹*ok, ek, ʿsu*, one house; ²*ch'ëü² ʿsu*, the locality of; ³*ki ʿsu*, how many places? COM., ⁴*su chai²* a place; *ˏkung ʿsu*, a place of public meeting; ⁵*ˏu ʿsu pok, ˏti*, omniscient; *ʿsu ʿiu*, whatever, all that there is; ⁶*ʿsu ʿi ˏyong*, wherefore, whence, the cause for which; ⁷*ˏu ʿsu pok, ˏk'iéng*, faulty in all things; *ʿsu ik, pok, ˏhu ʿsu ch'ok*, the receipts fall short of the expenses; *taik, ʿsu*, to get a situation.

(758) Sü.

ˏ師 Shih. A company, an assemblage; part of an army, a legion of 2500 men, troops; to call out and lead troops; a metropolis; a chief, a leader, a general; a master, a professor, one skilled in; a patron; a sage, a pattern to others; to teach; to imitate; used in names of gods of wind, rain, and thunder; the 7th of the 64 diagrams: used for the coll. *ˏsa* and *ˏsai*, q. v.: ⁸*ˏking ˏsü*, the capital; *ˏsiéng ˏsü*, ancient sages; ⁹*ˏsü ˏseng*, teacher and scholar; COM., ¹⁰*ʿchu ˏsü*, the original teacher or founder of an art, the patron; *ʿchwi ˏsü*, marines; ¹¹*wa² ˏsü*, an artist; ¹²*ˏsü ˏié*, an officer's private secretary; ¹³*ˏsü ʿmu* and *ˏsü ˏku*, compellations of a teacher's wife and sister; ¹⁴*wang² sié² ˏsü ʿpieu*, the pattern of 10,000 ages—i. e., Confucius.

ˏ篩 Shai. A huge bamboo, used for boats; a utensil for separating the fine from the gross particles, a sieve: usually read *ˏt'ai*, q. v.

ˏ螄 Shih. Ssŭ. A spiral shell or helix, called *ˏloi ˏsü*; crenulated shells.

ˏ獅 Shih. A lion; also a dog that whelps two pups: usually read *ˏsai*, q. v.

ˏ思 Ssŭ. To think, to consider, to reflect; to wish or desire; to commiserate; an auxiliary euphonic particle at the beginning or end of a sentence: also read *sëü²* q. v.: COM., ¹⁵*ˏsü ʿsiong*, or ¹⁶*ˏsü ˏliong*, to think, to reflect on; *ˏsü niéng²* to consider, to think of; ¹⁷*ˏsü lëü²* to be anxious; *ˏsing ˏsü*, one's thoughts; ¹⁸*ˏsü ˏchiéng lëü² hau²* to think anxiously about everything; *sang² ˏsü ˏi hau² ˏheng*, to think thrice (i. e., deliberately) and then act.

ˏ罳 Ssŭ. A screen before a door: ¹⁹*ˏp'eu ˏsü*, a sort of vestibule or screen before an entrance.

ˏ偲 Ssŭ. To urge, to stir up; to reprove, to admonish, as friends do; to excite one's self to duty. Read *ˏsai*: a large beard.

¹屋一所 ²處所 ³幾所 ⁴所在 ⁵無所不知 ⁶所以 ⁷無所不然 ⁸京師 ⁹師生 ¹⁰祖師 ¹¹畫師 ¹²師爺 ¹³師母 ¹⁴萬世師表 ¹⁵思想 ¹⁶思量 ¹⁷思慮 ¹⁸思前慮後 ¹⁹罘罳

偲 ꜀Ssŭ. The mind not decided, unsettled, uncertain: [1]ch'iék, ch'iék, ꜀sü ꜀sü, to blame, to reprove earnestly, as friends do mutually.

楒 ꜀Ssü. A tree having hard-grained wood, called [2]꜀siong ꜀sü, the Abrus precatorius, whose red fruit is hard and durable like beans.

颸 ꜀ A cool breeze: [3]꜀cheng ꜀sü, a high wind.

緦 ꜀Ssü. A coarse sort of grass-cloth or hempen fabric, used as half-mourning for distant relatives; flaxen, hempen: [4]꜀sü ꜀ma huk꜀ light mourning, worn three months.

繻 ꜀ Also read ꜀ü: fine, variegated silk; silk woven close; the selvage or frayed edge of cloth, a loose fringe or raveled border.

需 ꜀Hsü. To be stopped by rain; compelled to stop; to doubt, to hesitate; to search for; necessary, required, must; the 5th of the 64 diagrams, pertaining to water: [5]kek꜀ ꜀sü, needed at once; [6]꜀sü ëüng꜄ wanted for use. Read ꜀ü: flexible. Read ꜂niong: weak, delicate.

嚅 ꜀Ju. Chattering, the indistinct hum of conversation; also to restrain the expression of one's views: [7]niék꜀ ꜀sü, chattering, querulous.

濡 ꜀Ju. Also read ꜀ü: to steep, to immerse, to soak; to moisten; wet, damp; thick, viscid; fresh, glossy; at ease, tranquil; to urinate; patient, enduring; dregs, sediment; a river in the east of Kwangsi: [8]꜀chiëng ꜀sü, soaked; [9]꜀sü ꜂üng, patient; [10]꜀sü tê꜄ stopped, obstructed, flowing slowly.

湑 ꜀Hsü. To settle and flavor wine by an infusion of herbs; to steep in liquor; to make manifest, to show the figure through; full, supplied; rich, as a dress.

胥 ꜀Hsü. Crabs minced and pickled; to help; to wait, to expect; mutually, all, altogether; a final particle; to store, to accumulate, to have ready: [11]lê꜄ ꜀sü, a clerk in a yamun, termed [12]꜀chü paing꜄ in the coll.

糈 ꜀Hsü. Fine rice, as an offering to the gods; food, rations, a government salary, official income.

私 ꜀Ssŭ. Private, own, personal, peculiar; selfish, illiberal; secret, clandestine, treasonable; sisters call each other's husbands ꜀sü; contraband, illicit; plebeian, all below the Emperor; to consider, to regard; urine: in the coll. read ꜀sai, q. v.: com., [13]꜀sü a꜄ private, one's own; secret; [14]꜀siëng ꜀kung haiu꜄ ꜀sü, public before private interest; [15]꜀sü ꜀t'ung, illicit; illegal or treasonable intercourse; [16]꜀sü chio꜄ counterfeit coinage; [17]꜀sü taung꜄ taing꜄ an unlicensed pawnshop; [18]꜀sü ꜀sung, smuggling-boats; [19]꜀sü chiëng꜄ ꜀kwang tê꜄

---

[1]切切偲偲 [2]相楒 [3]曾颸 [4]緦麻服○ [5]急需 [6]需用 [7]囁嚅 [8]沾濡 [9]濡忍 [10]濡滯 [11]吏胥 [12]書辦 [13]私下 [14]先公後私 [15]私通 [16]私鑄 [17]私當店 [18]私船○ [19]私佔官地

to appropriate public lands; [1]꜀sü ük꜁ lusts; ꜀sü ꜀sing, or [2]꜀sü eʼ partial, unjust; COLL., ꜀sü ʻlú sioh꜁ ꜀pau꜁ a present given secretly (as a bribe).

須 湏 ꜀Hsü. The second form is erroneous, but commonly used: the beard about the mouth and chin; the cirri of fish; to wait for, to expect; slow; must, ought; what is required, necessary, requisite; of service, good for use; a buckler; a surname; occurs in names of a star, a plant, a vegetable, and a bird: [3]꜀sü ꜀ü, a moment, a while; [4]pek꜁ ꜀sü, absolutely required; ꜀u ꜀sü, needless; [5]꜀chüng ꜀sü, always necessary; [6]꜀sü ꜀tong ꜀hó chóiʼ what punishment ought he to receive? COM., [7]꜀sié ꜀sü, a small amount, a trifle.

鬚 ꜀Hsü. The hair on the chin, the beard; the whiskers of animals; bearded, hairy: ꜀hwa ꜀sü, the stamens of flowers; COM., ꜀lau ꜀sü, to wear a beard; ꜀hu ꜀sü, the beard on the cheeks, whiskers; ꜀sü hwak꜁ ꜀hwa pah꜁ the beard and hair half gray; [8]pʻiék꜁ ꜀sü, mustaches.

輸 輸 ꜀Shu. To suffer defeat, to lose, to be beaten; to exhaust; ruined, decayed; to submit, to make presents, to send in tribute; a present, an offering; the skirt, the part of a garment which falls down behind: in the coll. read ꜀sio, q. v.: [9]꜀sü nak꜁ to pay a tax; ʻta ꜀sü, beaten, discomfited; [10]꜀kiong ꜀sü, to subscribe to the government.

司 ꜀Ssu. To preside, to rule, to control, to manage; an officer, a manager or commissioner; a township, a subdivision of a district: also read ꜀si and in the coll. ꜀sa, q. v.: [11]kauk꜁ ʻiu ʻsu ꜀sü, each has his own business.

斯 ꜀Ssŭ. To split with an ax; to rive, to rend, to separate; this, that, these, those; forthwith, then; presently, in a moment; literary, genteel; mean, low, inferior; a euphonic particle: [12]꜀sü sēüʼ this affair; [13]꜀sü ꜀sü, forthwith; COM., [14]꜀sü ꜀ung, literary, polished, the literati; ꜀sü ꜀sü ꜀ung ꜀ung, very scholarly; genteel, decorous; [15]꜀sü ꜀ung ʻswa teʼ a literary man dragged in the dirt—i. e., dishonored or abused; [16]꜀pʻó ꜀sü kwok꜁ Persia.

澌 ꜀Ssŭ. Also read ꜀sai: to immerse; to melt and disappear; the water exhausted, dried up, run out: also used for ꜀sai (to neigh): ꜀sü miék꜁ lost in the water.

撕 ꜀Ssŭ. Also read ꜀sai: to rend, to rive, to pull apart; to direct attention to; to rouse up, to put one on his guard: [17]꜀tʻi ꜀sü, to point out, to direct one, as in study.

廝 厮 廝 ꜀Ssŭ. To employ; one employed, a servant, a waiter, an attendant, a menial; a camp-follower, a forager or a woodcutter; to feed, to care for one; scattered, broken; in confusion, a mêlée: [18]ʻsieu ꜀sü, a servant boy; [19]꜀sü ꜀tu, followers,

[1]私慾 [2]私意 [3]須臾 [4]必須 [5]終須 [6]須當何罪 [7]些須 [8]撇鬚 [9]輸納 [10]捐輸 [11]各有所司 [12]斯事 [13]斯須 [14]斯文 [15]斯文掃地 [16]波斯國○ [17]提撕 [18]小廝 [19]廝徒○

privates, soldiers; ˏsü ʻyong chok, camp-followers.

ˏSü. A coll. word, as in, ˏsü ˏsü, vain, puffed, a stuck-up air.

ʻ暑 Shu. Summer heat, the sun's heat; hot weather: [1]ʻsü ˏt'iéng, the dog days; com., [2]ʻsü k'eʾ solar heat, heat in the system—a medical term; [3]ʻsü ˎsiâ, a malign influence of heat; seuʾ ʻsü, affected by the sun; [4]ʻpiéʾ ʻsü, to escape the heat.

ʻ曙 Shu. Bright, clear; the dawn of day, sunrise; open, manifest.

ʻ署 Shu. A public court, an office, a tribunal; to appoint to an office; acting, substituted, holding an office temporarily: [5]ˏnga ʻsü, or [6]ˏkwang ʻsü, a magistrate's office, a yamun; com., [7]ʻsü ʻli, to oversee or act temporarily for; ʻsü sëüʾ the business of an acting officer; [8]ʻsü engʾ a seal or office held temporarily.

ʻ駛 ʻ駃 Shih. A horse running; fleet, swift; promptly, speedily, in haste, unceremoniously; to sail a vessel: in the coll. read ʻsai, q. v.

ʻ使 Shih. To order, to command; to use, to employ, to send, to commission; to cause, to effect, to occasion; use, service, expense: also read sëüʾ and in the coll. ʻsai, q. v.: [9]ʻsü ik, to employ; a servant; [10]ʻsü hwangʾ to call, to have at one's beck; [11]t'engʾ ʻsü, to be in waiting.

ʻ史 Shih. A historian, an annalist; a history, registers, chronicles, annals: [12]kwok ʻsü, archives, historical records; [13]ʻsü ˏkwang, a historiographer; [14]ʻchó ʻsü and euʾ ʻsü, the two court-historians; com., [15]ngëüʾ ʻsü, censors; ʻsü ˏchü or [16]ʻsü keʾ history, annals; sek ˏsang ˏking neʾ sek ek ʻsü, the 13 classics and 21 histories—one versed in them is a learned man.

ʻ始 Shih. The beginning, the commencement, origin; to begin; at the commencement of a sentence, it often means then, at that time, it was: [17]ʻsü ˏch'u, the beginning, at the first; com., [18]ch'aungʾ ʻsü, invention; [19]ʻk'i ʻsü, or ˏnguong ʻsü, in the beginning; [20]ʻsü ʻchu, one's first ancestors; ʻsü ˏchüng, beginning and end. Read sëüʾ: to begin, to originate.

ʻ黍 Shu. Millet, the panicled millet, Milium nigricans; the 202d radical: in the coll. read ʻsë, q. v.: [21]kaëk ʻsü, a preparation of millet or glutinous rice in bamboo leaves, made on the 5th of the 5th moon—in the coll. termed chaëngʾ q. v.

ʻ死 Ssu. To die; the end of life; the death of the young; dying, dissolution; pale, deadly, ghastly; mortal, dangerous; fearless, to the death; urgent, intense: in the coll. read ʻsi, q. v.: ʻsü ʻsiu, to maintain fearlessly; [22]seʾ ʻsü ˏü ˏkwi, to regard dying as going home; com., [23]ʻsü piék separation by death; ˏseng ʻsü pok ˏming, not

[1]暑天 [2]暑氣 [3]暑邪 [4]避暑 [5]衙署 [6]官署 [7]署理 [8]署印 [9]使役 [10]使喚 [11]駛使 [12]國史 [13]史官 [14]左史 [15]御史 [16]史記 [17]始初 [18]創始 [19]起始 [20]始祖 [21]角黍 [22]視死如歸 [23]死別

known whether he is living or dead; [1]'*sü ꜀seng 'ìn meng'* death and life are appointed (by Heaven).

諝 (Hsü.) To know, to possess learning and talents; sage, learned, scholarly: *cha' 'sü*, cunning, deceitful.

醑 (Hsü.) To strain wine, to clarify spirits; the dregs, lees; pure liquor, good wine.

薯 (Shu.) An esculent root, or tuber; the yam: COM., *꜀sü ' sü'* a tuber like the yam; it is white and bitter, and used as a stomachic; *꜀sü ꜀long*, the root of a sort of creeper, used for dyeing brown or red; [2]*꜀sü 'hung*, yam flour; [3]*꜀hwang ꜀sü*, sweet potatoes; [4]*꜀hwang ꜀sü 'mi*, potatoes coarsely grated and dried; [5]*꜀hwang ꜀sü ꜀seng*, a preparation of small potatoes dried; [6]*꜀hwang ꜀sü ꜀sieu*, light spirits made from potatoes; COLL., *꜀sü ꜀t'ong k'äk꜀* (or *꜀k'an*) *wo' chaik꜀* yam broth mixed with taro juice; *met.*, an indiscriminate mingling of men or things.

祠 (Tz'u. Ssu.) To sacrifice to ancestors in the spring; a family shrine, an ancestral temple; to get a blessing: COM., [7]*꜀sü ꜀tong*, an ancestral temple; [8]*chiék꜀ hau' ꜀sü*, a temple for the tablets of those who have remained in widowhood; [9]*꜀sü ꜀ting*, the keeper of an ancestral temple; [10]*꜀sü nôi' ꜀ting*, an expectorant compounded of orange peel and other ingredients; COLL., *꜀sü ꜀tong 'ku che' ꜀ku lôi'* the ancestral temple's drum beats itself!—a quarreling household.

詞 (Tz'u. Ssu.) To tell the thoughts, to speak, to say; a word, a sentence; a term, a phrase, an expression; a writing, an accusation; to ask, to request; to accuse: [11]*꜀ung ꜀sü*, writings; [12]*꜀sü tieu'* a meter, a measure, as in poems; *꜀sü ꜀ling*, the Hanlin Academy; COM., [13]*'mwang 'chai ꜀p'eu ꜀sü*, the paper (accusation) is full of lies; *꜀kiong ꜀sü tok꜀ cheng' 'li*, to wrest truth by violent talk; [14]*꜀sü pok꜀ tak꜀ e'* the expression does not convey the sense.

辭 辤 (Tz'u. Ssu.) Similar to the last: an expression, a word; a particle, or part of speech; language, phraseology; to decline with thanks; to resign, to leave, to take leave of; to dismiss, to send away: *t'ang' 'ngü ꜀sü*, an interjection; COM., [15]*siék꜀ ꜀sü* or *t'auk꜀ ꜀sü*, to decline on false pretences; *꜀sü 'kwang*, to resign a place, as secretary or teacher; *꜀sü piék꜀* or [16]*꜀sü ꜀heng*, to bid adieu on commencing a journey; [17]*꜀sü sié'* to die; *꜀u niék꜀ pok꜀ ꜀sing ꜀sü*, without trumped-up stories an accusation is not complete! COLL., [18]*꜀sü ng' kiéng'* to decline seeing a visitor; *꜀sü pwong'* to "intermit the meals (for the dead)"—a ceremony on the last (i. e. 49th) day of funeral rites.

殊 (Shu.) To kill, to slay, to slaughter; to cut off, to exterminate; to wound; to distinguish; unlike, differing; to exceed; a sign

[1]死生有命 [2]薯粉 [3]番薯 [4]番薯米 [5]番薯蔘 [6]番薯燒 [7]祠堂 [8]節孝祠 [9]祠丁 [10]祠內陳 [11]文詞 [12]詞調 [13]滿紙浮詞 [14]詞不達意 [15]設辭 [16]辭行 [17]辭世 [18]辭伓見

of the superlative: [1]꜀niêng ꜀sü ch'ek꜆ sek꜆ just past 70 years of age; [2]꜀sü saik꜆ surpassingly beautiful.

殳 ꜀Shu. To kill with a weapon; a long spear or pole; the handle of a spear; the 79th radical.

徐 ꜀Hsü. Grave, serious; majestic, dignified; slowly, leisurely; to walk in a slow, dignified manner: ꜀sü ꜀sü, grave, tranquil, as a gait; [3]꜀sü pwo꜄ to walk gracefully.

(759) Sui.

隨 ꜀Sui. Ts'ui. To follow, to accord with; to yield, to comply obediently; to permit or let; suiting; according to, as, like, as one may or can; wherever; forthwith, soon; the 17th of the 64 diagrams; the toes of the feet; a feudal state, now Suichou in the N. E. of Hupeh: [4]꜀sui chek꜆ immediately; COM., ꜀sui ꜂ch'iu, to suit the hand, as it is convenient to do; [5]꜀sui piêng꜄ at convenience; [6]꜀sui tai꜄ to take along with one; [7]꜀kâng ꜀sui, to follow; attendants; [8]꜀sui ꜂k'eu, to answer or say readily; ꜀sui haiu꜄ afterwards; [9]꜀sui ch'ëü꜄ everywhere; [10]꜀sui e꜄ as one pleases; [11]꜀sui ꜀si eng꜄ piêng꜄ to make changes to suit occasions.

隋 ꜀Sui. T'o. A dynasty, A. D. 590–620, followed by the T'ang. Read tó꜄: to fall; scattered, dissipated; lazy, indolent. Read ꜂t'io: to rend flesh; to part a sacrifice.

陲 ꜀Ch'ui. A border, a limit, a boundary; a hanging precipice, hazardous.

垂 垂 ꜀Chui. To hang down, to suspend, to let fall; to drop, as the hands; to hand down from ancient times; to spread abroad; to bow, to regard condescendingly; suspended, hanging down; nearly, almost, near to; a boundary; the place near the main door: [12]꜀piêng ꜀sui, a frontier; [13]꜀sui ꜂lò, near old age; [14]꜀sui ꜀ngui, imminent; [15]꜀sui kò꜄ to regard kindly; COLL., ꜀sui ꜀sui, suspended, hanging down; ꜀sui kiä꜄ or ꜀sui lóh꜆ ꜀li, to droop, as the limbs of trees.

誰 ꜀Shui. Who? what person? whose? whom? [16]꜀sui ꜀ing, who? [17]꜀sui ꜀hó, what, what matters it? [18]se꜄ ꜀sui, who is it?

꜂Sui. A coll. word: similar to ꜀si in the phrase ꜀si ꜀niä nòi꜄; gradually, little by little: ꜀sui ꜂chieu ꜀t'iêng and ꜀sui ꜂chieu ꜂keng, to add and take out gradually, or little by little.

(760) Suk.

朮 术 Shu꜆ Chu꜆ A glutinous grain; also a bitter herb, like a Sonchus, used as a medicine: COLL., [19]pah꜆ suk꜆ the white bitterish root; [20]꜀tiêng suk꜆ or ꜀tëng suk꜆ the "sweet" root — it leaves a bitter taste in the mouth.

秫 Shu꜆ A species of glutinous grain, millet, used to distil spirits: [21]꜀tang suk꜆ red millet; COM., [22]suk꜆ ꜂mi, a sort

1 年殊	2 殊色	4 隨卽	6 隨帶	8 隨口	10 隨意	應變	13 垂老	15 垂顧	17 誰何	19 白朮	21 丹秫
七十	3 徐步	5 隨便	7 跟隨	9 隨處	11 隨時	12 邊垂	14 垂危	16 誰人	18 是誰	20 甜朮	22 秫米

of glutinous rice; [1] *˓tang suk*$_2$ the early glutinous rice, reaped in the 6th month after a "single" season's growth; *˓tĕng suk*$_2$ the winter variety, harvested in the 10th month; *suk*$_2$ *ˋmi chŏ̤uk*$_2$ a congee of glutinous rice.

述 Shu. Su. $_2$ To follow another, to comply with; to imitate, to practice what another has invented; to tell, to narrate, to recite; to compile, to arrange the materials of a work; to revise books; to publish; to set forth one's rank or office: [2] *˓siu suk*$_2$ to revise a work; [3] *hoˀ chauk*$_2$ *ˋchü suk*$_2$ the father invented and the son practiced it; COLL., *suk*$_2$ *ˋchia waˀ* to narrate what was said.

術 Shu. Su. $_2$ Sometimes used for the last: a path through grain; a road in a city, a path; a way of doing things; an art, an artifice, a trick; a plan, a contrivance, a device; a mystery, a rule or art; something magical or demoniacal, black art; a profession, a craft, a trade: [4] *hok*$_2$ *suk*$_2$ the rules, or art, of study; [5] *suk*$_2$ *sĕ̤ü*ˀ a conjurer; *suk*$_2$ *soˀ* all kinds of magic arts; COM., [6] *˓sing suk*$_2$ *pok*$_2$ *˓twang*, his designs are not honest; [7] *hwak*$_2$ *suk*$_2$ magic art, conjuring; [8] *˓sià suk*$_2$ heterodox magic, black art. Read *soiˀ*: a district containing 12,500 families.

(761) Sŭk.

蜀 Shu. $_2$ A worm, a sort of caterpillar, like the silk-worm; a sacrificial tripod: [9] *lŭk*$_2$ *sŭk*$_2$ the onager? a zebra? [10] *˓Pa sŭk*$_2$ one of the three states into which China was divided, A. D. 220; a name still applied to Sz'chuen.

蠋 Chu. $_2$ Also read *ch'ĕ̤ŭk*$_2$: the large, green caterpillar of the sphinx moth, called [11] *tik*$_2$ *sŭk*$_2$ and found on pulse.

藚 Su. $_2$ A marshy, climbing plant, having leaves like purslane, also called cow's lips; one says it is commonly termed [12] *tek*$_2$ *siaˀ*.

續 Su. Hsü. $_2$ To continue, to join on; to keep up, to carry on the succession; to piece, to tie together; following, continuously; to carry on what another has begun: [13] *twangˀ sŭk*$_2$ intermitted, by spells, as work; [14] *sŭk*$_2$ *ch'ĕ̤üˀ* to marry a second wife; [15] *sĕ̤üˀ sŭk*$_2$ family succession; COM., [16] *lŭk*$_2$ *sŭk*$_2$ successively, one after another; [17] *sŭk*$_2$ *˓hiĕng*, to "join the guitar-string"—take a second wife.

贖 Shu. $_2$ To ransom, to redeem; to give a pledge or security; to compound for punishment, to commute by paying a fine; to atone for by merit: *ˋlio ˓ing lek*$_2$ *sŭk*$_2$ to seize and hold men for ransom; COM., [18] *sŭk*$_2$ *˓hui*, (coll. *sŭk*$_2$ *ˋtiong ˓li*), to redeem, to get back, as property by paying the mortgage; [19] *sŭk*$_2$ *chŏiˀ* to atone for sin; [20] *sŭk*$_2$ *˓sing*, to ransom one; to redeem, as slaves; [21] *sŭk*$_2$ *taungˀ* to redeem a pawn; [22] *ˋch'ü sŭk*$_2$ the clerk who receives payment for pawns; COLL., *sŭk*$_2$ *˓ch'eng*, to redeem a field.

---

[1] 單秫 [2] 修述 [3] 父作子述 [4] 學術 [5] 術士 [6] 心術不端 [7] 法術 [8] 邪術 [9] 鹿蜀 [10] 巴蜀 [11] [illegible]蠋 [12] 澤瀉 [13] 斷續 [14] 續娶 [15] 嗣續 [16] 陸續 [17] 續絃 [18] 贖回 [19] 贖罪 [20] 贖身 [21] 贖當 [22] 取贖

孰 Shu. $_2$ To take a bait; a crop, a harvest; ripe, plentiful; to examine; who? what? *sük$_2$ pok$_2$ ‘k‘ó ‘üng yâ’* what would he not bear to do!

熟 Shu. $_2$ Ripe, mellow; well done, well cooked; thorough, perfect at; skilled, ready, experienced; intimate, on friendly terms; soft, pliable, as silk; cured, as tobacco; sound, deep, as sleep; a crop: COM., [1]*ˌsing sük$_2$* ripe; *sük$_2$ ‘ch‘iu*, handy, skilled in; [2]*sük$_2$ ˌhong*, cured tobacco; *sük$_2$ ch‘ek$_2$* a thief acquainted with a place; COLL., *pwang’ ˌch‘ang sük$_2$* half-cooked; [3]*sük$_2$ sük$_2$ sük$_2$ má^2 koi’ nük$_2$* most thoroughly acquainted yet sells me his pork dear!

塾 Shu. $_2$ A room by a gate; a vestibule, an anteroom; rooms to study in, a place for teaching, a domestic school: *ˌka sük$_2$* or [4]*ˌmung sük$_2$* a private school.

俗 Su. Hsü. $_2$ What pertains to common people; ordinary, common, rude; vulgar, unpolished, as manners; low, rough, ungenteel; the laity: [5]*ˌting sük$_2$* worldly pursuits; COM., [6]*ˌhung sük$_2$* or *ˌhiong sük$_2$* the manners or customs of a place; [7]*ˌhwang sük$_2$* to return to common life, as a priest or nun; [8]*sük$_2$ sëü^2* the routine of life, the prevailing customs; [9]*sük$_2$ k‘e’* common, ordinary, as a sight or play; [10]*sük$_2$ ˌing*, plebeians; [11]*sük$_2$ ‘ngü wa^2* proverbs, sayings; [12]*ˌsiong ˌhung pai^2 sük$_2$* to corrupt the manners, as by a vicious life.

屬 / 属 Shu. ^{2} Attached to, as an animal's tail, connected with; to belong to; pertaining to, depending on; allied, related, of kin; degrees of relationship; subject, as subordinates are; a sort, a rank; is, actual, existing; to revise, to compose: [13]*sik$_2$ sük$_2$* it really is; COM., [14]*kwong’ sük$_2$* or *ˌka sük$_2$* family relatives; [15]*ha^2 sük$_2$* underlings, official subordinates; [16]*sük$_2$ kwok$_2$* colonies, tributary states; *ˌch‘ing sük$_2$* kindred; [17]*ˌung ‘u pok$_2$ ‘t‘ung sük$_2$* civil and military are of different sorts; *met.*, yours and mine are different matters; COLL., *se^2 sük$_2$ tié^2 ˌnëng*, to whom does it pertain or belong? Read *chëük$_2$*: to entrust, to give in charge; to collect; respectful.

(762) Sung.

嵩 / 崧 ˏSung. The central and highest of the five great mountains—in Honan; a lofty mountain; elevated, eminent, as a statesman: COM., [18]*ˌsung ˌsang*, the Sung mountain; also an idol's name; *ˌsung ˌsang kung’* the temple of *ˌSung ˌsang*.

鬆 ˏSung. Disheveled hair, shaggy, undressed hair; confused, disordered; to relax, to let go; to unloose, to cast off; loose, flabby; spongy, soft, as cakes; slack, easy, indulgent; not urgent or important; at ease, not anxious: in the coll. read *ˌsëng*, q. v.

1 成熟　2 熟煙　3 熟熟熟賣貴肉　4 蒙塾　5 塵俗　6 風俗　7 還俗　8 俗事　9 俗氣　10 俗人　11 俗語話○　12 傷風敗俗　13 實屬　14 眷屬　15 下屬　16 屬國　17 文武不統屬　18 嵩山○

詢 'Hsün. To ask about, to inquire; investigation, inquiry; to consult, to deliberate; to inform one's self: [1]'*sung ong*' to inquire about; [2]'*sung* ˌ*meu*, to deliberate, to plan.

峋 'Hsün. Also read ˌ*sung*: [3]'*ling* ˌ*sung*, hills rising over hills; deep ravines among mountains.

洵 'Hsün. To sob, to weep convulsively; far, remote, distant; true, faithful; a branch of the Han in the south of Shensi, at whose mouth stands the town of Hsün-yang.

珣 'Hsün. Also read ˌ*sung*: a kind of gem from Liautung, of which there are three varieties; a sort of utensil.

徇 狥 'Hsün. Used for the next: all around, pervading; to go or extend everywhere; to inspect or consider in all aspects; to make, to cause; quick, in haste; to follow, to comply; somewhat, generally: [4]'*sung ngié*' to follow right principles.

殉 'Hsün. To bury the living with the dead, as anciently, though rarely, done; to comply, to follow; to seek, to pursue an object immoderately; engrossed in, given up to, greedy for: [5]'*sung chaung*' to bury the living with the dead; [6]'*sung saik*, addicted to lust; COM., [7]'*sung* ˌ*ching*, to act according to feeling, as in releasing a culprit; [8]'*sung nang*' to risk suffering.

'筍 '笋 Hsün. Sun. The young, edible shoots of bamboo; conical, pointed, like a bamboo shoot; a tenon, a dovetail; a cross bar on which bells are hung, in which sense used for the next: COM., [9]*tĕük*, '*sung*, bamboo shoots; [10]'*sung* ˌ*kang*, dried shoots; [11]'*sung* ˌ*si*, shoots sliced and pickled; [12]'*sung* ˌ*ūng*, the outer films of shoots (fresh or pickled); [13]ˌ*tĕng* '*sung*, the winter-shoots; [14]'*sung laung*' short, thick shoots; COLL., [15]'*sung* ˌ*kau*, a bug like a beetle, that infests bamboos; [16]'*sung chiăh*, *ch'ok*, ˌ*chiéng*, the bamboo shoot has just sprouted—just commencing life, as a young man; [17]'*sung k'aek*, *chó*' *mó*', ˌ*wang* ˌ*wang* ˌ*nié*, the bark of a bamboo shoot curved just right to make a cap of! *met.*, to happen just as one wished. Read *chong*': a bamboo sledge. Read ˌ*sung*: a fine, flexible sort of bamboo for making mats.

'栒 '簨 Hsün. The cross piece on which bells and drums are suspended in temples; the name of a tree and a district; a sort of utensil.

'恂 Hsün. Also read ˌ*sung*: true, sincere, conscientious; respectful, devoted; pleased; also to exert a good influence; fearful: [18]'*sung lek*, standing in awe of; [19]ˌ*t'ing* '*sung*, faithful.

---

1 詢問 2 詢謀 3 嶙峋 4 徇義 5 殉葬 6 殉色 7 殉情 8 殉難 9 竹筍 10 筍乾 11 筍絲 12 筍蓊 13 冬筍 14 筍蛋 15 筍猴 16 筍隻出尖 17 筍殼做帽彎彎倔 18 恂慄 ○ 19 悅恂 ○

ʻ**悚** Sung. Ch'u. Fearful, agitated, swayed by hope or fear: [1]ʻ*sung* ˏ*yong*, on the *qui vive*, excited; COM., [2]ʻ*sung lek*, at once, quick, prompt, as in paying or promising.

ʻ**竦** Sung. To stand stiffly; reverent, respectful; to exalt, to elevate one; roused, excited; horrified, the flesh creeping from fear: [3]ʻ*sung lik*ˎ to stand in a formal posture; [4]ʻ*sung tong*ˀ agitated.

ʻ**聳** Sung. Tsung. Interchanged with the last two: to be born deaf, entirely deaf; to excite, to animate, to urge on; to respect; astonished, alarmed; high, elevated: [5]ʻ*sung t'eng*ˀ astonished in hearing it; [6]ˏ*kó* ʻ*sung*, lofty; [7]ʻ*sung* ˏ*ing ngé*ˀ *muk*ˎ to startle people's ears and eyes.

ʻ**慫** Tsung. Ts'ung. To alarm, to arouse, as by a remonstrance or warning: [8]ʻ*sung* ʻ*ũng*, to excite, to stimulate.

ʻ**㩳** To hold, to seize; to push; to stretch one's self out: [9]ʻ*sung* ˏ*sing*, to stand erect.

ʻ**瞬** Shun. To roll the eyes about; to dart, to look; a glance: [10]ʻ*sung sek*, or *ek*ˎ ʻ*sung* ˏ*chi* ˏ*kang*, in a twinkling, instantly.

ˏ**船** ˏ**舡** Ch'uan. A boat, a junk, a ship, a vessel; a revenue cutter, a barque; a saucer; a sort of mortar; the collar of a coat: COM., [11]*to*ˀ ˏ*sung*, a passage-boat; ˏ*ping* ˏ*sung*, a man-of-war; ˏ*yong* ˏ*sung*, a sea-going vessel, a ship; [12]ʻ*hwi* ˏ*lung* ˏ*sung*, or [13]ˏ*ch'iă* ˏ*sung*, a steamer; ˏ*sung* ˏ*t'au*, the bow; ˏ*sung* ʻ*mwi*, the stern; [14]ˏ*sung* ˏ*sing*, a hull, a hulk; ˏ*sung* ʻ*tu*, or [15]ˏ*sung* ˏ*ch'ong*, a boat's compartments, state-rooms; ʻ*t'ó* ˏ*sung*, to hire a boat; [16]*tak*ˎ ˏ*sung*, to take passage; *siong*ˀ ˏ*sung*, to go aboard; also to go ashore; [17]ˏ*sung* ˏ*ka*, boatmen, a crew; ˏ*sung chai*ˀ the fare, passage-money; ˏ*sung* ˏ*pá*, a boat's license; [18]ˏ*hung* ˏ*sung*, to impress boats or junks; [19]ˏ*sung* ˏ*ch'iă* ˏ*lai* ʻ*wong*, traveling by water; COLL., *sioh*ˎ ˏ*teu* ˏ*sung*, one boat, one vessel; ˏ*sung* ˏ*k'wi* ˏ*t'au*, to weigh anchor; ˏ*sung kwo*ˀ ʻ*chwi* ˏ*mó* ˏ*hong*, a boat crossing the water leaves no trace—said of matters without tangible proof; ˏ*kiăng* ˏ*sung* ʻ*chau* ʻ*ma* ˏ*sang* ˏ*hung miăng*ˀ only three chances (out of ten) for safety in boats and on horseback; ˏ*sung* ʻ*sai* ʻ*lĕng ngiăng*ˀ to work a vessel up to the shore.

ˏ**揗** Hsün. To feel, to stroke, to pat; to soothe, to encourage; to sympathize with.

ˏ**循** Hsün. To follow a leader; to accord, to comply with; to revolve; to perambulate, to go about and examine; good, easy, docile; leisurely; to soothe; to state, to explain: [20]ʻ*u* ˏ*sung*, to soothe, to encourage; ˏ*sung* ˏ*sung*, in order, gradually; COM., [21]ˏ*sung sok*, yielding to control; ˏ*sung* ˏ*liong*, docile, meek, gentle; ˏ*sung* ʻ*li*, to follow reason; ˏ*sung* ˏ*kié tó*ˀ ʻ*kü*, to obey the rules;

1 悚然 2 悚慄 3 竦立 4 竦動 5 聳聽 6 高聳 7 聳人耳目 8 慫慂 9 㩳身 10 瞬息 11 渡船 12 火輪船〇 13 車船 14 船身 15 船艙 16 搭船 17 船家 18 封船 19 船車來往 20 撫循 21 循束

¹*t'iĕng tü'* *sung* *k'wang*, the course of heaven's laws as to prosperity and adversity.

馴 *Hsün.* A tame, well-trained horse; gentle, docile, yielding; kind, amiable, harmless; to tame; to acquire gradually: ²*nga sung*, elegant, as diction; ³*sung huk*, docile, obedient; com., *sung liong*, gentle, mild, good-natured.

紃 *Hsün.* A silk tassel; fine, silken cords, bindings, ornaments; a rule, model, pattern: ⁴*sung ch'ak*, to examine.

純 *Shun.* Pure silk; pure, unmingled, uniform; all, the whole, perfect, entire; great; fine, the best; simple, single, guileless; a measure of 15 feet: ⁵*sung hau'* honest, upright; ⁶*sung ek*, uniform throughout, singleness of purpose; ⁷*sung sük*, versed in, experienced; com., ⁸*sung chiong*, uniform and entire; ⁹*sung saik*, a pure color. Read *'chung*: a fringe, selvage. Read *tong*: to tie in a bundle.

唇 脣 *Shun. Ch'un.* The lips: ¹⁰*chio sung*, vermillion lips; com., ¹¹*sung 'ch'i siong i*, lips and teeth mutually dependent—mutually dependent, as persons; ¹²*sung hung 'ch'i pek*, ruby lips and white teeth; ¹³*sung wong 'ch'i hang*, when the lips are gone, the teeth are cold; *met.*, destitute, nothing to rely on.

漘 *Shun.* The high banks of a stream, a beach, a brink, a margin; a shore by deep water.

淳 *Shun.* Pure, clear, limpid; honest, true; to sprinkle, to wash, to cleanse; war-chariots; saltish, barren land: *sung sung*, floating, rippling; ¹⁴*hung sük sung hau'* his manners are plain and correct.

醇 *Shun.* Rich, generous, pleasant, as wine; good and thick, as syrups; pure, single, as one's motives; liberal, magnanimous; careful, attentive; clear, healthy, as the complexion; subtile, seminal, essential: ¹⁵*sung 'chiu*, generous wine; ¹⁶*sung hau'* liberal; *sung 'king*, observant.

犉 *Shun.* A yellow bullock with black lips; an ox seven feet high, suitable for a sacrifice.

鶉 *Shun. Ch'un.* A quail, called ¹⁷*ang sung*, which the Chinese say is transformed from rats or toads: *sung i*, poor raiment, like a quail's short, shabby tail.

旬 *Hsün.* A decade of days or years; the whole of, complete, finished, as a number; used in one of the periods of mourning; in the coll. to review lessons on the tenth day: ¹⁸*sung swoi'* a complete year; com., *siong' sung*, *tüng sung*, and *ha' sung*, the first, second, and third decades of a month; *lĕk sung seu' 'k'ó*, a father deceased 60 years of age—term used on lanterns; ¹⁹*lĕk sung*, mourning rites on the 60th day.

---

1 天道循環 2 雅馴 3 馴伏 4 紃察 5 純厚 6 純一 7 純熟 8 純全 9 純色 10 朱唇 11 唇齒相依 12 唇紅齒白 13 唇亡齒寒 14 風俗淳厚 15 醇酒 16 醇厚 17 鵪鶉 18 旬歲 19 六旬

福州方言拼音字典

荀 ꜀Hsün. Sometimes read ʻ*sung:* a plant bearing a yellow flower and red fruit, said to fatten those eating it; a surname; a feudal state, in which sense used for the next.

郇 ꜀Hsün. A feudal state in the Chow dynasty, now Pu-chou-fu in the south-west of Shansi with the adjacent region.

巡 廵 ꜀Hsün. To go on a circuit, to go the rounds, to cruise; to examine what is being done, to take a tour of inspection: [1]꜀*sung sau*ʼ to cruise, as a guard-boat does; COM., [2]꜀*sung* ꜀*kang*, to serve as a watchman; [3]꜀*sung yă*[2] to go on a round of inspection at night; [4]꜀*sung lô*[2] to go on a circuit; ꜀*sung* ʻ*hai*, to cruise at sea; [5]꜀*sung* ʻ*u*, the provincial governor—is so styled; [6]꜀*sung pwo*ʼ the special aids (of high officers); [7]꜀*sung* ꜀*ká ngĕü*[2] ʻ*sü*, imperial street-inspectors—applied jocosely to beggars; [8]꜀*sung* ꜀*hwong kwoh*꜇ place of consultation for the public defence; [9]꜀*sung* ʻ*chwi* (coll. ꜀*sung* ꜀*ch*ʻ*eng*), to inspect the watering of fields.

蕁 ꜀Shun. A kind of aquatic vegetable or cress, eaten in summer; thick rushes; plants growing bushy.

(763) Sŭng.

松 ꜀Sung. The fir or pine tree; an emblem of longevity: ꜀*sŭng* ꜀*kong* ʻ*hu*, the Sungkiang prefecture, in which Shanghai is; COM., [10]꜀*sŭng pah*, the pine; ꜀*sŭng pah*, ꜀*hwa* (coll. ʻ*lai*), pine-cones; [11]꜀*sŭng tëük*, ꜀*mui* ꜀*sang* ʻ*iu*, three friends (are like) the fir, bamboo, and plum; COLL., ꜀*sŭng* ꜀*miŭng*, or ꜀*sŭng* ꜀*miŭng lek*꜇ pitch-pine; [12]꜀*sŭng* ꜀*mô* ꜀*ch*ʻ*iu*, pine leaves.

淞 ꜀Sung. The name of a river in Kiangsu, for which the last is also used.

榕 ꜀Yung. Jung. Read ꜀*ŭng;* coll. ꜀*sŭng:* the bastard banian, the Indian fig, called [13]꜀*sŭng ch*ʻ*eu*ʼ; [14]꜀*sŭng ch*ʻ*eu*ʼ ꜀*sü*, the pendent rootlets of the banian; ꜀*sŭng ch*ʻ*eu*ʼ ꜀*k*ʻ*ĕng ch*ʻ*ok*, *siĕ*ʼ born from the hollow of a banian tree; *met.*, to be unfilial.

(764) Swa.

耍 ʻShua. Sha. To play, to sport, to amuse; to trifle with; to exercise, as in fencing; play, jollity, games; in the coll. easy, remiss; bold, swaggering: [15]꜀*chiĕng* ʻ*swa*, expert at, clever; COM., [16]꜀*iu* ʻ*swa*, to ramble about; [17]*ngwang*[2] ʻ*swa*, to play, to sport; COLL., [18]*k*ʻ*ô*ʼ ʻ*swa*, to go on a ramble; ʻ*nü* ʻ*chi* ʻ*mang* ʻ*swa*, you are so free and reckless! [19]ʻ*swa* ʻ*swa tioh*꜇ free and easy; reckless, as in using money.

灑 洒 ʻSha. Shai. To sprinkle; to scatter, as the wind scatters leaves; to divide; to cast, as a hook for fish; high, deep; steep, as a bank; alarmed, shivering, in a tremor: the 2d also read ʻ*sá*, q. v.

掃 ʻSao. To sweep, to brush; to clean and sweep up; a broom, a besom; to damp-

[1]巡哨 [2]巡更 [3]巡夜 [4]巡邏 [5]巡撫 [6]巡捕 [7]巡街御史 [8]巡防局 [9]巡水 [10]松柏 [11]松竹梅三友 [12]松毛鬚 [13]榕樸 [14]榕樸鬚 [15]尖耍 [16]遊耍 [17]玩耍 [18]去耍 [19]耍耍着○

en, to interrupt, as one's pleasure; to rid, to clear off: also read ʻsó and in the coll. *sau*ʼ q. v.: [1]*ta ʻswa*, to sweep; [2]*swa ˏtü ˏkang ʻtong*, to dismiss traitors (from court); COM., [2]*swa heng*ʼ to interrupt one's pleasure, to chill one's hopes.

ʻ埽 Sao. Also read ʻ*só;* used for the last; to sweep the ground, to clean up; a dike, an embankment, a dam made of bamboos and earth.

*Swa*ʼ. A coll. word: the same as *ch*ʻ*wa*ʼ*;* a sudden pain; contraction or distortion of the limbs, said to be caused by a *swa*ʼ ʻ*mwi*, or malign influence; *k*ʻ*ëük*, ˏ*hung swa*ʼ *swa*ʼ a sudden affection caused by malign influence of wind.

(765) Swai.

ʻ*Swai*. A country brogue, sometimes used for ʻ*sai*, to use, to employ.

(766) Swang.

ʻ孿 Lüan. Read *swang*ʼ in the dictionaries; usually read ʻ*lwang*, q. v.: to bear twins; to suckle two children at once; to change.

(767) Swi.

ʻ荽 Sui. Also read ˏ*ch*ʻ*wi:* a plant, called [4]ˏ*hu* ˏ*swi*, the coriander or caraway.

ʻ*Swi*. A coll. word; also spoken ʻ*swi* or ʻ*soi* by some: perhaps a contracted form of *sioh*ˌ ʻ*k*ʻ*i*, all, the whole lot: ʻ*swi k*ʻ*ó*ʼ let all go, take the whole lot; ʻ*swi má*ʼ to sell off all at once.

(768) Swo.

[This word is interchangeably read *sio*, q. v.]

(769) Swoh.

[This word is interchangeably read *sioh*, q. v.]

(770) Swoí.

彗ʼ Sui. Sao. Also read *woi*ʼ*:* the same as the next in the sense of a brush-broom, a besom: [5]*swoí*ʼ ˏ*sing* (or *woi*ʼ ˏ*sing*), a broom-star —i. e., a comet, commonly called [6]*ch*ʻ*eng* ʻ*ch*ʻ*iu* ˏ*sing*, q. v.

篲ʼ Sui. A besom, a broom made of bamboo-twigs, used for sweeping the fields: [7]*ëüng*ʼ *swoí*ʼ to use the broom, to sweep.

稅ʼ Shui. Rent; taxes in kind, impost; duties on goods; toll, customs; to bequeath; to stop, to rest; to halt, as at a post-house: [8]*swoí*ʼ *le*ʼ a custom-house officer or clerk; [9]*swoí*ʼ *ngiăh*ˌ the fixed rates of duties; COM., [10]*pó*ʼ *swoí*ʼ to report and pay toll or duty; [11]ˏ*siu swoí*ʼ to receive custom; [12]ˏ*yong swoí*ʼ foreign customs, customs on imports; [13]*swoí*ʼ *taung*ʼ a licensed pawn-shop; [14]*swoí*ʼ *k*ʻ*ié*ʼ to pay a tax on a deed, to get a deed stamped and registered; [15]*swoí*ʼ ʻ*kwang* (or ʻ*k*ʻ*au*,), a custom house. Read *t*ʻ*wak*ˌ*:* to release. Read *yok*ˌ*:* pleased.

說ʼ Shuo. Shui. Sé. Interchanged with the preceding in the sense of to release and to be pleased; to persuade to a course; to urge, to incite to; to plead by specious arguments: also read *siok*, q. v.:

[1]打掃 [2]掃除 [3]奸黨 掃興 [4]胡荽 [5]彗星 [6]箒帚星 〇 [7]擁篲 [8]稅吏 [9]稅額 〇 [10]報稅 〇 [11]收稅 〇 [12]洋稅 〇 [13]稅當 〇 [14]稅契 〇 [15]稅館 〇

福州方言拼音字典

'[1],iu swoi' to go about and incite others; COM., '[2]swoi' k'aik, (or siok, k'aik,), a pleader, a specious talker.

帨' Tui. A handkerchief or napkin hung at the girdle: '[3],kŭng swoi' a napkin.

蜕' T'ui. The exuviæ or skin, cast off by snakes, crabs, locusts, &c.: '[4],siéng swoi' the cast skin of a cicada.

賽' Sai. To recompense, to make a return; to emulate, to match; to contest for, as in plays, etc.; to make a show, as in processions; to announce an offering: '[5]swoi' ,teng, to show lanterns, as on the 15th of the 1st moon; COM., '[6]swoi' saik, to throw dice for the stakes, as in the dice-shaking or mutual-aid club; '[7]swoi' ,yang, to emulate, to see who excels; '[8]swoi' ,tai, to emulate in theatricals, as two companies in succession; COLL., '[9]tau' swoi' to contest for the victory.

歲' 嵗' 歳 Sui. To pass over; a year of one's age; age, years, revolution of the seasons; a harvest: in the coll. read hwoi' q. v.: [10]swoi' ch'ëü' the characters for the cyclic year; [11]chaung' swoi' robust, sinewy; [12]ak, swoi' a new-year's present; [13]k'aik, swoi' last year; COM., [14]wang' wang' swoi' may His Majesty live forever! [15]t'ai' swoi' a clay image, the Chinese Cybele, carried in procession to "meet the Spring"; also a period of 1728 years; [16]swoi' swoi' ,ping ,ang, prosperous every year!

Swoi'. A coll. word: a seam, a crack: siăng' swoi' a seam; swoi' pauk, the seam is ripped; pek, swoi' a crack, as in bamboo; t'iëng' 'tië sioh, swoi' sew it (the width of) a seam farther in.

Swoi'. A coll. word: something on which to found a claim, an antecedent, a precedent: ,i o' swoi' he has a claim or precedent, as said of one who has already received alms from another.

(771) Swok.

[This word is interchangeably read siok, q. v.]

(772) Swong.

[This word is interchangeably read siong, q. v.]

(773) Ta.

,Ta. A coll. word: dry, not wet, not moist: ,ta ,sëng, dry and mellow, very dry; ,ta só' parched; ,ta ,chieu, scorched, as things in being cooked; dried up, shriveled, as the face; ,kang ,ta, dry, not watered, as pork; ,hëng ,ta, to dry at a fire; ,ta k'auk, k'auk, or k'auk, k'auk, ,ta, thoroughly dry; ,ta tó' the net profit.

,Ta. A coll. word, as in ,ta a' where?

'打 Ta. To strike, to beat; to pound, to knock; to attack, to fight; to cause to fight; a blow, punishment by blows; to play with or on; as an auxiliary before verbs, denotes simple action, or marks present time; by, in, at, through: [17]'ta 'sü, killed; COM., [18]'ta 'yeu, I have troubled you! [19]'ta ,këng, to

[1]遊說 [2]說客 [3]巾帨 [4]蟬蛻 [5]賽燈 [6]賽色 [7]賽贏 [8]賽臺 [9]鬥賽 [10]歲次 [11]壯歲 [12]壓歲 [13]客歲 [14]萬歲萬萬歲 [15]太歲〇 [16]歲歲平安 [17]打死〇 [18]打擾〇 [19]打工〇

job out work; [2]*ta siăh*₂ to do a job and board one's self; [3]*ta ꜀t‘au*, the boss, the one who contracts for work; beggars' headman; [4]*ta lak*₂ to hunt game; [4]*ta saung*’ or ‘*ta* ‘*tiéng*, to reckon, to calculate; ‘*ta hwak*, to distribute, to apportion, to assign; ‘*ta t‘eng*’ *seng*’ *sek*, to go and learn the news; ‘*ta t‘iék*, wrought iron; COLL., ‘*ta ꜀lang ꜀hwang*, crosswise, athwart; ‘*ta ꜀tiong hwo*’ things ready made, not made to order—are inferior; ‘*ta sóh*, to twist rope; ‘*ta sau*’ to sweep; a sweeper.

‘**踔** Read ‘*tó;* used in the *Paik*, ꜀*Ing* for the coll. ‘*ta*, as in ‘*ta ta*’ to walk unsteadily, to toddle, as a child learning to walk.

醡’ Cha. Read *cha*’; coll. *ta*’: a wine or oil press; to express or separate spirits: [5]‘*chiu ta*’ a wine press; [6]*ta*’ ‘*chiu*, to express wine; *ta*’ *tói*’ a bag for expressing the juice.

Ta’. A coll. word: to feign, to counterfeit; feigning, pretending: *ta*’ *k‘aung*’ to feign sleep; *ta*’ *ta*’ *sié*’ feignedly; *ta*’ *ngaung*’ to pretend to be stupid; *ta*’ *meng*’ *maung*’ a feigning manner or look; *ta*’ *chó*’ *ta*’ ꜀*la* ꜀*li*, to feign in mere sport, as children do.

꜀**茶** Ch‘a. The infusion of tea; a tea, teas: COM., [7]*siăh*₂ ꜀*ta*, to drink tea; [8]꜀*ta ꜀hwa*, the Camellia; [9]꜀*ta* ‘*chi*, nuts of the tea-oil tree; [10]‘*kĕŭng*’ ꜀*ta*, to furnish tea, as scholars at school; [11]꜀*ta* ‘*piăng*, tea pressed into cakes; [12]꜀*ta sik*₂ a sort of cruller boiled in oil; [13]꜀*ta* ꜀*ong*, a tea-hong; ꜀*ta* ‘*kwang taing*’ a restaurant; [14]꜀*ta* ꜀*sŭ*, a tea-taster; [15]꜀*ta saik*, the quality of tea; [16]꜀*ta* ꜀*pwang*, a tea-tray; ꜀*ta* ‘*ki*, a teapoy; ꜀*ta* ꜀*pwi*, or ꜀*ta* ꜀*eu*, a tea-cup; ꜀*ta* ꜀*sung* (or ꜀*lung*), a long tea-saucer; [17]꜀*ta* ꜀*pó*, a tea-pot; COLL., ꜀*ta nioh*₂ the tea-leaf, teas; ꜀*ta nioh*₂ ꜀*ing*, a tea caddy or canister; ꜀*ch‘u* ꜀*ta* ꜀*pó*, large coarse tea-leaves — also called ‘*mwang t‘iéng* ꜀*pwi*.

(774) TÁ.

‘**低** Ti. Also read ꜀*ti:* to bend down, to droop; to incline, as the head; low, down, as to place; low, as the voice; cheap; low, humble; common: [18]꜀*kó* ꜀*tá*, high and low; [19]꜀*tá* ꜀*ngong*, to look down and up—low and high, as prices; [20]꜀*tá* ꜀*sing*, in a low voice; COM., *ka*’ ꜀*tá*, the price is cheap.

‘**底** Ti. Read ‘*ti;* coll. ‘*tá:* the base, the bottom; below, beneath, under; the bottom, the remnant; a foundation, property, wealth on which to depend; a copy, first draft; [21]*a*’ ‘*tá*, below, underneath; *kau*’ ‘*tá* ‘*tá*, to the very bottom; [22]*t‘au*’ ‘*tá*, to the very last, forever; ꜀*i o*’ ‘*tá*, he has money, "is well-to-do"; [23]‘*tá tio*’ (or ꜀*nong*) ‘*yă kau*’ very opulent; ꜀*mó* ‘*tá* ꜀*k‘ang*, a bottomless pit; *met.*, gluttonous, voracious; ꜀*kó* ‘*tá*, wooden heels, as of ladies' shoes; wooden-soled shoes; ꜀*lau* ‘*tá chó*’ ‘*tá*, keep it for a copy.

[1]打食 [2]打頭 [3]打獵 [4]打算 [5]酒醡 [6]醡酒 [7]食茶 [8]茶花 [9]茶子 [10]供茶 [11]茶餅 [12]茶食 [13]茶行 [14]茶師 [15]茶色 [16]茶盤 [17]茶婆 [18]高低 [19]低昂 [20]低聲 [21]下底 [22]透底 [23]底路野厚

福州方言拼音字典

抵 Ti. Read ʻti; coll, ʻtá: to oppose, to resist, to stop, to ward off; to sustain, to bear the responsibility of, to take the blame: [1]ʻtá tik, to oppose, to meet a foe; [2]ʻtá ˎtong, to bear a responsibility; [3]ʻtá sak, to ward off malign influences; ʻchʻiu ʻtá, to fend, or parry with the hand; ʻtá má' teu' unable to ward off.

帝 Ti. One who judges, a ruler of the nations; one whose virtue is like that of heaven, heaven's vicegerent; a sovereign, a prince, a potentate, an emperor; applied to several deities denoting supremacy in their peculiar attributes: tá' hau' an empress; COM., [4]ˎhwong tá' an emperor; ˎhwong tá' oi' the imperial throne; [6]ˎkwang tá' Mars; [7]ʻHwi tá' the god of fire; [8]ˎung ˎchʻiong tá' ˎkung, Apollo; [9]ʻsiong tá' the Supreme Ruler; used for God; [10]tá' ˎwong, a sovereign; [11]ʻngu tá' the five emperors before Yü, the Great, B. C. 2597—2255; gods over plagues; [12]tá' ˎsing, the star of the Emperor's destiny.

諦 Ti. To examine, to scrutinize, to judge: [13]ʻsing tá' to examine and decide a case; [14]tá' se' to determine, as the qualities of things.

螮蝃 Ti. Small insects, as ephemera, generated in the air; the rainbow is said to be made of them: [15]tá' tong' the rainbow. The 1st read tai': a snake. The 2d read chiok,: a spider.

蹄 Ti. A hoof; *met.*, horses; the feet of pachydermatæ, solidungula and ruminantia; to kick, a hare-trap; a leg of pork or mutton: COM., [16]ʻma ˏtá, a horse's hoof; [17]ˎtü ˏtá, a leg of pork; COLL., ˏseng ˏtá, a fore-leg; ˏtá ˎwo, a round of pork, a cut near the body; ˏtá ʻkʻa pang' the leg-part of a round; ʻmä ˏtá ʻwong, a hoof-shaped cuff.

鵜 Ti. Read ˏtʻá in the dictionaries; an aquatic fowl, called [18]ˏtá ˎhu, a kind of gregarious pelican, having a red bill and plumage like an owl's.

媞 Ti. At ease; elegant: [19]ˏtá ˏtá, fascinating, as ˎSá ˏsi was. Read se': a mother.

瑅 Ti. Also read ˏtʻi: the name of a gem, called [20]ˏtá ˏtong.

睼 Ti. Also read ˏtʻi: to go out and see; to sit and look at; to survey from a distance.

蝭 Ti. Name of an insect: [21]ˏtá ló, a species of cicada.

鞮 Also read ˏtá: leathern shoes; plain shoes, those without figured toes: [22]ˏtá lëü' plain, mourning shoes.

騠 Ti. Also read ˏtʻi: a fine, frisking horse; [23]kiok, ˏtá, a nimble palfrey.

[1]抵敵 [2]抵當 [3]抵煞 [4]帝后 [5]皇帝 [6]關帝 [7]火帝 [8]文昌帝君 [9]上帝 [10]帝王 [11]五帝 [12]帝星 [13]審諦 [14]諦視 [15]螮蝀 [16]馬蹄 [17]猪蹄 [18]鵜鶘 [19]媞媞 [20]瑅瑭 [21]蝭蟧 [22]鞮屨 [23]駃騠

題 Ti. The forehead, the head; the important part of; a theme, a subject for writing; a preface; the title of a book; to discuss one's merits, to praise; to compose, to write; to subscribe: com., [1] ˓*tá mĕk*˒ a theme, a text; *met.*, authority for; [2] ˓*ch'ok*˒ ˓*tá*, to give out themes; [3] *p'wai*ˀ ˓*tá*, the exordium of an essay; [4] ˓*sing* ˓*tá*, the amplification of the subject; [5] ˓*tá* ˓*si*, to compose poems; [6] ˓*tá* ˓*chiĕng*, to subscribe money; [7] ˓*tá* ˓*yong*, to subscribe, as to the ˓*p'wo to*ˀ rites; ˓*tá* ˓*kwang*, a written engagement with a tutor; *pok*˒ ˓*tá*, or *mang*ˀ ˓*tá*, we defer this point—a term used in novels; coll., *t'eng*ˀ ˓*nĕng* ˓*tá tieu*ˀ to be at one's beck, to be servant of all work; ˓*sieu* ˓*tá twai*ˀ *chŏ*ˀ to make too much of a small matter. Read *tá*ˀ: to notice, to look at.

鯷 Also read ˓*i*: a sort of cottus or bull-head with protruding eyes; sour things found in a fish's stomach.

弟² Ti. To bind with leathern cords; to rise by degrees, in order, consecutive; a younger brother; to act as becomes a younger brother; a junior, a scholar: in the coll. read *tié*ˀ q. v.: [8] ˓*nü tá*ˀ a younger sister; [9] *pok*˒ *tá*ˀ disrespectful to elder brothers or superiors; com., [10] ˓*hing tá*ˀ brothers; [11] *tá*ˀ ˓*chü*, pupils; your disciple! as said in addressing a god; [12] *hau*ˀ *tá*ˀ filial and deferential; [13] *tá*ˀ *ho*ˀ a younger brother's wife; [14] *sià*ˀ *tá*ˀ my younger brother; [15] *tá*ˀ *tik*˒ younger brothers and nephews; *ngié*ˀ ˓*hing tá*ˀ sworn to be brothers.

悌² Ti. T'i. Used as a verb for the above: to act as younger brothers should, to be brotherly; respectful, reverent to superiors or elders.

娣² Ti. A younger sister: [16] *tá*ˀ *sĕü*ˀ sisters-in-law; [17] *tá*ˀ *ho*ˀ a younger brother's wife.

睇² Ti. To glance at, to view slightly, to look with the eye half closed.

第² Ti. To wind in an ascending order; a series, an order, a rank, a gradation; forms the ordinal numbers; a literary degree; a mansion; but, yet, merely: [18] *ch'ĕü*ˀ *tá*ˀ rank, order; [19] *tá*ˀ *t'ek*˒ an officer's mansion; [20] *kik*˒ *tá*ˀ a doctorate, a Hanlin; com., [21] *pok*˒ *tá*ˀ did not gain his degree; *tá*ˀ *ek*˒ ˓*hó*, prime, the best; [22] *tá*ˀ ˓*kwi*, which one in order? *tá*ˀ *ngo*ˀ ˓*pwong*, the 5th volume.

苐² T'i. Used for the last as a conjunction, but, yet, only; name of a plant: [23] *pok*˒ *tá*ˀ a double surname.

禘² Ti. A quinquennial sacrifice to the manes of an emperor's predecessors; the worship of one's royal ancestors.

締² Ti. A tight or indissoluble knot; to tie tightly; to fasten, to close: [24] *tá*ˀ ˓*kau* inseparably united, as friends, or a couple when married.

[1] 題目 [2] 出題 [3] 破題 [4] 承題 [5] 題詩 [6] 題錢 [7] 題緣 [8] 女弟 [9] 不弟 [10] 兄弟 [11] 弟子 [12] 孝弟 [13] 弟婦 [14] 舍弟 [15] 弟侄 [16] 娣姒 [17] 娣婦 [18] 次第 [19] 第宅 [20] 及第 [21] 不第 [22] 第幾 [23] 不苐 [24] 締交

福州方言拼音字典

杕^{2} Ti. To stand alone, as a tree; single, solitary; luxuriant, flourishing. Read ˈtó: a small scull or tiller to steer with.

遞^{2} 遰^{2} Ti. To transmit, to send on, to pass from one to another; to hand up or in; to alternate, to exchange; distant; for, instead of: [1]ˏtiong tá^{2} to send on, as by post; [2]ˏsieu tá^{2} distant, to go far; COM., [3]tá^{2} ˏniéng, in successive years; [4]tá^{2} ˏtiàng, to present an accusation or statement; [5]tá^{2} ˈchung, the petition granted; [6]tá^{2} ˏta, to offer tea, as to gods in a procession; [7]tá^{2} chiéngˀ ˏchü, to send a written challenge; [8]tá^{2} ngëü^{2} chaungˀ to appeal to the emperor. Read taiˀ: to twine, to twist around.

Tá^{2}. A coll. word: to cover, to spread over; to screen, to veil, to shade: tá^{2} ˏhung, to screen from the wind; tá^{2} angˀ to darken by covering or veiling; tá^{2} ˏung ˏting, to screen from the dust.

(775) Taë.

苧^{2} Ch'u. Read ˈt'ü; coll. taë^{2}: the grasscloth nettle; its fiber is used for cords and cloth: [9]taë^{2} taingˀ a grasscloth shop; [10]taë^{2} siàngˀ thread made of grass-cloth-nettle.

(776) Taëk.

捔ˏ Chiao. Read ˈch'ü and ch'ëük,; used in the *Paik, ˏIng* for the coll. taëk,: to poke, to gore, to push, as an ox; to press, or crush, with the thumb-nail; to count, to tell over, as cash with the thumb; exact, precise, corresponding, as a date: [11]taëk, ˈsi, to gore to death; taëk, saik, ˈmó, to crack lice; [12]taëk, k'angˀ count (the cash) with the thumb and see (how many); taëk, taëk, ˏki, at the precise time.

罩ˀ Read tauˀ; used in the *Paik, ˏIng* for the coll. taëk,: to shut up, to cover, as fowls; a coop: [13]ˏkié taëk, (or ˏkié ˏlëng tauˀ), a movable bamboo-coop for covering over fowls; [14]taëk, ˏkié, to coop fowls; [15]tiàng taëk, a high pan-cover; [16]tek, tek, taëk, taëk, to put heads close together, as two men in earnest conversation.

Taëk,. A coll. word, similar to ngëü^{2} or p'aungˀ: to meet, to fall in with, to come upon one: taëk, tek, tioh, met him; taëk, má^{2} tioh, failed to meet him; taëk, tioh, ˏngai ˏnëng, to fall in with bad people.

Taëk,. A coll. word, as in ˏchiéng taëk, (or laëk,) a savings-box.

(777) Taëng.

凍ˀ Tung. Read tongˀ; coll. taëngˀ: cold, cooled, as applied to things: [17]taëngˀ nóh, cold things, as food; [18]ˈch'iu chengˀ taëngˀ my hands are very cold; [19]ˏliàng taëngˀ to cool by exposing to the air; [20]taëngˀ ˏping ˏping, icy-cold; ˈang na^{2} ˈmwong taëngˀ yä^{2} ˏniéng ˏnó, even though the gruel cools it is still thick; *met.*, though so bad, he is still your brother or friend.

---

[1]傳遞 [2]迢遞 [3]遞年 [4]遞呈 [5]遞准 [6]遞茶 [7]遞薦書 [8]遞御狀 [9]苧店 [10]苧線 ○ [11]捔死 [12]捔看 [13]雞罩 [14]罩雞 [15]鼎罩 [16]的的罩罩 [17]凍毛 [18]手盡凍 [19]凉凍 [20]凍冰冰

棟 Tung. Read *tong'*; coll. *taĕng'*: the main supports in houses: [1]*taĕng' t'eu'* (or *taung' t'eu'*), the central or main posts; [2]*taĕng' ˏliong*, or *taĕng' ˏang*, beams, joists.

重 Chung. Ch'ung. Read *tëüng'*; coll. *taĕng'*: heavy, weighty; severe, heinous; strong, harsh, as words; important, momentous; to regard, to esteem highly, to give importance to: *taĕng' tai'* hard work; toil; *taĕng' wa'* harsh words; [3]*ˏi chói' 'yá taĕng'* his crime is heinous; *o' nioh, taĕng'* how heavy is it? [4]*k'ang' taĕng'* to view as important; *taĕng' le' ˏch'iă pauk,* to take exorbitant interest, as widows do; *'lang ˏchü ˏtang taĕng' tang'* lazy louts carry heavy loads—to avoid going twice.

動 Tung. Read *tong'*; coll. *taĕng'*: to move, as the hands; motion, movement, action: [5]*taĕng' ˏk'a taĕng' 'ch'iu*, to move feet and hands—to go and do; *teng' taĕng'* to move, to be agitated; *te' teng' taĕng'* an earthquake; [6]*'kieu' ˏi má' taĕng'* I call him but he'll not move! [7]*'k'i taĕng'* thanks for your trouble! *ng' 'k'i taĕng'* no thanks needed! no trouble! [8]*'hiong taĕng'* a noise, a clatter, as of crockery.

洞 Tung. Read *tong'*; coll. *taĕng'*: a cave, a grotto; *met.*, a delightful spot: [9]*taĕng' 'k'au*, the cave's mouth; *ˏhwa ˏting siok, taĕng'* flower pavilions and cool grots; [10]*ˏsiéng taĕng'* a fairy's grot; *met.*, a fine spot.

(778) Tah.

壓 Ya. Read *ak*, used for the coll. *tah,*: to press upon, to crush, to press, as with weights; to compress, to reduce to a certain form by pressure; to repress, as fear; to stay (the foot), to wait; to stake, to pledge, to put at hazard in games; to adopt; an encumbrance: [11]*tah, 'si*, crushed to death; [12]*tah, huk,* to press into a required shape; [13]*tah, ˏkiăng*, to quiet, as old people and children with tea or food; a red patch on an infant's clothes, as a charm; [14]*tah, kieu'* to put additional weight on a sedan; [15]*tah, 'pó*, to stake money in certain games; [16]*tah, ˏhwa hwoi'* to try luck at a lottery; *tah, má' tioh,* to lose one's stake; *tah, ch'io' chek,* to "press the ridge-pole"—an encumbrance, as an unmarried girl; [17]*tah, ˏhwa ch'eu'* to adopt a daughter; *tah, 't'ëng 'kiăng*, the encumbrance of a widow's children (when she marries again); [18]*tah, koi'* to "press the counter"—a fee for a license, as to sell salt; *tah, sioh, pwo'* to wait a while; [19]*'ló hwoi' tah, tah,* let (the procession of) the venerable company halt!—used in a *met.* sense for wait! slow! be easy!

Tah,. A coll. word, as in *tah, lóh,* to dishonor, to bring reproach on, to disgrace, as a wicked son does his parents.

擇 Tsê. Chai. Read *tek,*; coll. *tah,*: to choose, as lucky days: *tah, nik, 'chi*, to choose a lucky day; *tah, nik, ˏká*, the lucky-day-street—a street in Foochow where

1 棟柱 2 棟樑 3 伊罪野重 4 看重 5 動跤動手 6 呌伊賣動 7 起動 8 響動 9 洞口 10 仙洞 11 壓死 12 壓伏 13 壓驚 14 壓轎 15 壓寶 16 壓花會 17 壓花模 18 壓櫃 19 老會壓壓

are many "lucky-day" shops or offices.

宅 Tsĕ. Chai. Read *t'ek*, ; coll. *tah*, : sometimes occurs in names of places; as in [1]*₍sang sek*, *lĕk*, *tah*, the 36 villages (on the island between the Min channels in the district [2]*Hong*' *₍kong* '*li*, spoken *₍Ong ₍ong* '*tié* or *₍Ong ₍kong* '*tié*).

Tah,. A coll. word: to heat, to keep warm; dried, wholly run off, as the tide: *tah*, *₍t'ong*, to heat water; *tah*, *pwong*' to keep the rice warm; *p'wong*' *tah*, to ebb all dry.

(779) Táh.

Táh,. A coll. word, the same as *tih*, : to stammer, to stutter: *táh*, *má*' *ch'ok*, stutters and can't get the words out! *táh*, *pwang*' *sá*' *nik*, stammers half-a-day!

(780) Tai.

獃 Tai. Ai. 懛 Used in the *Paik*, *₍Ing* for the coll. *₍tai* : the first also read *₍ngai*, q. v.: stupid, ignorant; silly; dirty, slovenly: [3]'*cheng*' *₍tai*, excessively stupid; [4]*₍chü ₍tai*, a pedant, a bookworm, one who is ignorant of common things; *₍lai ₍tai*, dirty, slovenly; [5]*₍tai siong*' a stupid face.

₍Tai. A coll. word: what? why? *₍tai* '*sai*, what need? what's the use of it? *₍tai* '*sai ₍chiong wang*' why so! why do so!

₍Tai. A coll. word: a kind of millet, yielding a reddish or yellowish grain: '*k'eng* '*mwi* *₍tai*, and *ak*, *₍k'a ₍tai*, the dog-tailed and duck-footed kinds—so called from the shape of the heads.

歹 歺 Tai. Bad, evil, vicious, perverse; the 78th radical: [6]*pok*, *₍ti* '*hó* '*tai*, not know good from bad; [7]*₍ui ₍hi chauk*, '*tai*, to make confusion and evil; COM., [8]'*tai sëü*' a bad business, a wicked act.

滓 Tzü. Read '*chai*; used in the *Paik*, *₍Ing* for the coll. '*tai* : residuum, refuse; dregs, sediment; settlings, as in a water jar: [9]'*tai p'óh*, (or *₍cha p'ok*,), residuum or refuse.

帶 帯 Tai. A sash, a girdle; a scarf, a tape, a ribbon; a bandage, a compress; a belt, a region of country; to carry, to take along with one; to pilot, to conduct, to lead, to guide; belonging to, implicated; in the coll. a little, somewhat, slightly: COM., [10]*wak*, *tai*' garters; [11]*₍pieu tai*' a silk tag or tab, as on caps or robes; silk pendants, as votive offerings to idols; [12]*₍k'a tai*' the bandages on ladies' feet; [13]*k'aiu*' *tai*' to clasp a girdle; [14]*₍i tai*' the umbilical cord; *ek*, *tai*' the whole region (of country); [15]*tai*' *₍ping*, to lead troops; [16]*tai*' *loi*' to implicate; [17]*tai*' *₍sing*, pregnancy; COLL., *tai*' *₍li*, to bring with one; [18]*tai*' *ch'oi*' to speak of by the way; *tai*' *tio*' to conduct, to guide one; *pwok*, *₍ĕng tai*' "wears a red girdle"—said of one who enjoys favors, as the relative of a headman; *tai*' '*ch'ó*, ambiguous, as a reproof; [19]*tai*' *₍mang tai*' *ch'ieu*' in a jesting manner;

[1]三十六宅 [2]鳳岡裡〇 [3]盡獃 [4]書獃 [5]獃相 [6]不知好歹 [7]爲非作歹 [8]歹事 [9]滓粕 [10]韈帶 [11]幖帶 [12]骹帶 [13]扣帶 [14]衣帶 [15]帶兵 [16]帶累 [17]帶身 [18]帶嘴 [19]帶蠻帶笑

ko' tioh, tai' *ˎwong*, it should be somewhat more yellow.

戴' Tai. To carry or wear on the head; to bear, to sustain; to have over one, as the sky; to meet, to happen: COM., [1]*'pok, këüng' tai'* *ˏt'iéng*, the same sky shall not cover us; [2]*'tang tai'* to undertake for; [3]*tai' ˏhwa*, to wear flowers; *tai' mó'* to put on a cap; [4]*tai' ha'* to wear mourning; COLL., *tai' 'ngang kiöng'* to wear spectacles.

碓' Tui. A pestle, a beater to pound in a mortar, a foot-pestle; to pound in a mortar; a beat of a pestle: COM., [5]*'chwi tai'* or *ˏch'iă tai'* pestles moved by water power; [6]*tai' 'mi*, to pound rice. Read *ˏtoi:* a bank, a heap.

炱 ˎ The soot from fire, smoky soot; flying ashes and cinders.

台 ˎT'ai. High, exalted, eminent, noble; your honor; venerable: [7]*'ló ho' ˎtai*, our district magistrate; [8]*ˎtai ka'* eminent Sir! [9]*ˏhing ˎtai*, noble brother! your honor! Read *ˏt'ai:* a surname; name of a star: *ˏsang ˏt'ai*, three double stars in Ursa Major. Read *ˎi:* I, myself; grateful, pleased; to rejoice; to nourish.

臺 ˎ 臺 ˎT'ai. Interchanged with the preceding: a high square terrace, a platform, a staging; a gallery; an open terrace, an observatory, a lookout over a gate; a fort; a compellation; a title of officers; a menial; a servant: [10]*hiong' ˎtai*, a censor, a magistrate; COM., [11]*ˎtai ka'* noble Sir! [12]*ˎtai kóh*, a frame on which children are carried, as in processions of the goddess "Mother"; [13]*hié' ˎtai*, a theatrical stage; [14]*nau' ˎtai*, to beat instruments before a play; [15]*cheng' ˏhiong ˎtai*, the terrace of incense-offering, as on the summit of Black-rock Hill, Foochow; [16]*lo' ˎtai*, an open terrace, as on a house-top; *chié' ˎtai*, *'u ˎtai*, *ˏhwang ˎtai*, and *hok, ˎtai*, Viceroy, Governor, Treasurer, and Literary Chancellor; [17]*ˎtai ˏwang* (coll. *ˎtai ˎwang*), Formosa; *ˎtai 'mi*, Formosan rice; *wang' ˎtai*, to change or relieve Formosan (soldiers); [18]*p'au' ˎtai*, a fort; COLL., [19]*tioh, ˎtai 'ting 'lá 'u*, performing on the stage; *met.*, to be engaged in trade, making gain.

檯 ˎT'ai. The name of a tree; also interchanged with the last; a staging, a platform, a terrace.

薹 ˎT'ai. A sedge, called [20]*ˎhung ˎtai*, which grows in damp places; a culinary vegetable.

䲦 ˎ Read *nai'*; used in the *Paik*, *ˏIng* for the coll. *ˎtai*: a small worm bred in rice.

ˎTai. A coll. word, as in *ˎtai ˏka*, or *ˎtai ˏka 'ná*, a husband's mother; *lau' ˏkwang* and *ˎtai ˏka*, a husband's father and mother.

ˎTai. A coll. word: to put in, to insert a piece, to patch; to mend, as with cloth, wood, or metal; *met.*, to throw in, as a word to settle a matter: *ˎtai 'pwo*,

---

1 不共戴天 2 擔戴 3 戴花 4 戴孝 5 水碓 6 碓米 7 老父台 8 台駕○ 9 兄台 10 憲臺 11 臺駕 12 臺閣 18 戲臺 14 鬧臺 15 進香臺 16 露臺 17 臺灣 18 炮臺 19 着臺頂禮舞 20 [illegible]臺

to patch; ˌtai ʻpwo ˌmó niāh, ˌngwong ˌhong, a patch is not equal to the original stuff—the indemnity not as good as the article itself; ˌtai sioh, kʻwoʼ to settle by a final sentence.

大^2 Ta. Tai. To. Chua. Large, great, grand; extensive, long; important, prominent; fat, plump; as a superlative, very, much; to enlarge, to grow large; to exceed; the 37th radical: in the coll. read twai^2 q. v.: [1]tai^2 ˌkong, the main string of a net; hence the chief, the most important; [2]tai^2 ˌchʻiéng, the great thousand—the world; [3]tai^2 aing^2 the great limit — death; COM., [4]tai^2 ˌka, all, we all, you all; tai^2 ˌhwang, all, whoever, whatever; [5]tai^2 yok, or tai^2 liok, generally, for the most part; [6]tai^2 kwoh, or tai^2 ʻtʻá, the main part, mostly; [7]tui^2 tó^2 just, fair as to price; [8]tai^2 ˌwong, rhubarb; tai^2 kek, great luck; [9]tai^2 hok, the Great Learning—one of the Four Books; tai^2 ˌtung ʻsieu é^2 slightly different.

逮^2 隶^2 Tai. To follow after; to be at, to reach to, to come into contact with; equal to a duty; the root or origin; the 171st radical: sēak, yā pok, tai^2 unable to come up to them by day or night; tai^2 tai^2 pleasing, harmonious; ʻu che é^2 tai^2 to have the will but not the ability.

逮^2 迨^2 Tai. An adverb of time, till, until, to, unto: [10]tai^2 kik, even to; [11]tai^2 ˌking, until this time.

埭^2 Tai. A dam; a lock or inclined plane on rivers and canals, where boats are passed by a windlass: [12]tai^2 kaik, the scale of transit charges at a lock.

靆^2 Tai. Dark, obscure, cloudy: [13]ai^2 tai^2 obscure, as when clouds cover the sun.

代^2 Tai. A generation, an age; to change, for, instead of; in the place of one, a substitute; delegated, deputed: in the coll. read tói^2 q. v.: [14]sié^2 tai^2 an age; [15]ʻngu tai^2 the Five Dynasties, A. D. 907-959; lik, tai^2 successive generations or reigns; [16]ʻngu tai^2 ˌtung ˌtong, five generations living at once; COM., [17]tai^2 tʻá^2 instead of, to act as a substitute; tai^2 paing^2 to manage for one; [18]tai^2 pek, the writer, the amanuensis or clerk; tai^2 neng^2 to be surety for.

玳^2 Tai. Tortoise shell: COM., [19]tai^2 ngwoi^2 the tortoise-shell of commerce—used in ornamental work.

岱^2 Tai. The most eastern of the five mountains of China, the high peak in Shangtung, also called [20]tʻai^2 ˌsang, or Great Mountain.

貸^2 Tai. Tʻai. To lend, to loan on interest; to intrust to another; to give, to confer; to pardon, to release; also to borrow: [21]ˌpong tai^2 to borrow for another; ˌchʻa tai^2 to vary from a rule; [22]tēing^2 chaik, pok, tai^2 to punish severely and not pardon; COM., kó^2 tai^2 ˌu ˌmwong, to inquire and find no

1 大綱	3 大限	5 大約	7 大道	9 大學	11 迨今	13 靉靆	15 五代	同堂	18 代筆	20 泰山	22 重責
2 大千	4 大家	6 大局	8 大黄	10 逮及	12 埭格	14 世代	16 五代	17 代替	19 玳瑁	21 旁貸	不貸

way of borrowing; COLL., [1]'*chioh, tai'* to borrow.

黛^2 Tai. To mark or blacken the eyebrows; to shave off the eyebrows and make black marks instead: [2]*ˎch'ing tai'* an invisible green.

袋^2 Tai. A bag, a sack; a case or cover to inclose things; a purse, a pocket; a satchel: in the coll. read *tói'* q. v.

待^2 Tai. To wait for, to expect, to wait upon; to await, to provide against; to treat, to behave to: [3]*teng tai'* to "wait for one; [4]*tai' ka'* "wait for the price"—i. e., till invited to office, as Confucius said; COM., [5]*k'ang' tai'* to treat well or ill; [6]*chiék, eng' tai' k'ah,* to entertain guests; COLL., *tai' ˎnĕng ˎngai,* to treat persons ill.

怠^2 Tai. Careless, negligent, remiss; lazy, indolent; inattentive, wanting in courtesy: [7]*tai' tó'* indolent; [8]*tai' hwang'* slow, sluggish; COM., [9]*hai' tai'* remiss, lazy; *tai' mang'* to treat disrespectfully; COLL., *'chi ˎpong ˎnu tai' mang'* this time I have failed in courtesy.

殆^2 Tai. Used for the last in the sense of lazy; imminent, perilous, dangerous; to expose, to hazard; near, familiar, approaching; to begin, about to do; nearly at, on the limits, almost: [10]*ˎheng tai'* to run into danger; [11]*ˎngui tai'* hazardous; [12]*tai' kik,* nearly, about.

Tai^2. A coll. word: to throw, to cast away, to reject: *tai' k'ó'* to throw away; *tai' ka'* to sell cheap, as in competition; *tai' ˎtĕng,* to cast into the (money) tube — gather the tithings, as from the members of a guild.

Tai^2. A coll. word: a matter, a business: *sié' nóh, tai' kié'* (or *ié'*), what business? what's the matter? *chó' tai'* to do work.

Tai^2. A coll. word, as in *tai' ˎtong,* in the middle, the midst; *tai' ˎtong ˎtong,* in the very center.

(781) Taik.

淂, Tê. Used erroneously for the next: the appearance of water; water; humid, watery.

得, Tê. Tei. To get, to obtain, to attain, to acquire; to have, to be or become; to wish, to desire; as an auxiliary, may, can; able to be done; after a verb, expresses completion of action, for which sense *tek,* is used in the coll.; in the coll. slyly, secretly: COM., [13]*taik, pang'* to be sick; [14]*taik, e'* pleased with; [15]*ˎsiong taik,* mutually agreeable; [16]*taik, 't'á,* to be just, as in bargains; [17]*taik, ˎtŭng,* medium, fair, as a price; [18]*taik, 'ma,* to become a cavalry-soldier; [19]*taik, chói'* to sin against, to offend; [20]*taik, tê lê* to have a lucrative place (for trade); [21]*pok, taik, 'i,* remediless, must be so; *pok, taik, pok, 'kong,* can't help speaking of; COLL., *taik, taik,* or [22]*ˎt'au taik,* secretly; *taik, taik, ˎhwang 'hi,* secretly rejoiced; *taik, ˎki taik, sek, ˎki sek,* there must be gainers and losers.

[1]借貸 [2]青黛 [3]等待 [4]待價 [5]看待 [6]接應待客 [7]怠惰 [8]怠緩 [9]懈怠 [10]行殆 [11]危殆 [12]殆及 [13]得病 [14]得意 [15]相得 [16]得體 [17]得中 [18]得馬 [19]得罪 [20]得地利 [21]不得已 [22]偷得

德 悳 Tĕ. Virtue, moral excellence; favor, beneficence; the virtue, quality, or efficacy of; to be affected by favors, grateful; to increase; happy: COM., [1]'sëü' taik, the four (female) virtues; [2]taik, haing[2] virtuous actions; [3]'kang ,ong 'kang taik, grateful for favors; [4]'kung taik, meritorious acts; certain rites for the dead; [4]'song taik, to impair virtue, as by vice; Taik, hwa' a district of Yungchun prefecture, Fookien; taik, cheng' ,kio, a bridge in Foochow; COLL., ,mó taik, haing[2] vicious, immoral, wicked.

(782) Taing.

店 Tien. A place to put goods in, a shop, a stand; an eating-house, an inn: COM., [5]taing' ,t'au, a shop; [6]'k'ah, taing' a tavern, caravansary; [7]'mi taing' a rice-shop; [8]taing' k'ó' the treasure-room, a strong apartment back of the front shop; [9]taing' 'chio, or taing' ,ka, a shopkeeper; [10],siu taing' to shut shop; 'tó taing' a shop failing; hiok, taing' to put up at an inn; COLL., laung' taing' to open a new shop; pwong[2] taing' an eating-house.

凳 櫈 Têng. A bench, a stool, a form, a seat without a back: [11],tiong taing' a long bench; [12]'pang taing' a wooden stool.

蹬 Têng. Also read taing': to step, to tread; to miss a step: [13],cheng taing' wearied, exhausted; at one's wits' end, in despair.

鐙 Têng. Also read taing': COM., [14]'ma taing' a stirrup. Read ,teng: a dish, a sacrificial vessel; formerly used for ,teng, a lamp, a candlestick.

鄧 Têng. A surname; an ancient feudal state, now a district of Nanyang-fu in Honan.

殿 Tien. A lofty hall, the imperial hall of audience; a palace; a temple, the main hall of a temple: COM., [15],king ,lwang taing[2] the palace, the audience chamber; [16],hwong tá' taing[2] the emperor's temple—where his tablet is worshiped; tai[2] ,hüng 'pó taing[2] the "large precious hall" in Budhist temples; [17]taing[2] ha[2] a title of the crown-prince; the imperial kindred; [18]taing[2] se[2] the examination for Hanlin degrees. Read tiéng': the rear of an army, to bring up the rear of flying troops; fixed; inferior merit.

靛 Tien. Indigo, an indigo color; to dye blue: COLL., [19]taing[2] ,k'wong, an indigo-tub; taing[2] ,hwa (or p'wok,), scum on native indigo.

墊 Tien. Read tiéng'; coll. taing[2]: a cushion, a large mat; to bear the burden of, to pay for another; to place under, to wedge, to use blocking: [20],pui taing[2] to stand surety, as in paying another's debt; [21]taing[2] ,tong, to bear all the burden or brunt of; [22]pai' taing[2] a cushion to kneel on in worship; 'ié taing[2] a chair-cushion; [23]taing[2] 'hó, to block up properly; taing[2]

[1]四德 [2]德行 [3]功德 [4]損德 [5]店頭 [6]客店 [7]米店 [8]店庫 [9]店主 [10]收店 [11]長凳 [12]板凳 [13]躓蹬 [14]馬鐙 [15]金鑾殿 [16]皇帝殿 [17]殿下 [18]殿試 [19]靛樘 [20]賠墊 [21]墊當 [22]拜墊 [23]墊好

'*tá*, "propping at the bottom"—vegetables in a dish under the meat.

㡳' Read *aing*'; coll. *taing*' as in [1]˓*mwong taing*' the threshold of a door.

有' A coll. character: firm, solid, durable; hard, not soft; stupid, obtuse: [2]*cheng*' *taing*' very hard; [3]*taing*' *tó*' firm, strongly made; [4]*taing*' ˓*ch'a*, hard wood; [5]*taing*' *t'ang*' hard-wood charcoal: [6]*taing*' ˓*sing*, the hard center of anything; obtuse, dull; *taing*' ˓*ch'a kong*' a hard-wood stick or club.

(783) Taiu.

鬥 鬭 鬪 閗' To fight, to wrangle, to squabble; to contest, to compete for, to strive for the precedence; to contend, to debate sharply: in the coll. read *tau*' q. v.: [7]˓*cheng taiu*' to fight; a brawl; *taiu*' *hwak*, competitive arts or tricks; COM., [8]*taiu*' *k'e*' bellicose, pugnacious; [9]*taiu*' *ch'oi*' to wrangle; *taiu*' '*eu ang*' lawsuits about brawls; COLL., [10]*kai*' *taiu*' to fight with weapons.
Tou.

吊' Read *tieu*'; coll. *taiu*': to hang down; suspended, as from a ceiling; to hang one's self; to let down, to lower by cords: ˓*tu* ˓*tu taiu*' suspended; [11]*taiu*' *ch'ek*, to hang a thief (by the hands); *taiu*' *lóh*, *k'ó*' to lower, as by a cord; [12]*taiu*' '*si*, to hang one's self; [13]*taiu*' *sóh*, a suicide's rope; [14]*taiu*' '*kwi*, the ghost of a suicide—supposed to tempt others to the same crime; [15]*taiu*' ˓*siàng*, to scale the city wall by a cord; *taiu*' *pwoi*' inverted tile-work, as to cover joints on roofs.
Tiao.

竇' A hole, an aperture; a den, a burrow, a cavern; a drain, an aqueduct; to dig through, to burrow; to lead off, to drain: [16]'*keu taiu*' a dog's kennel; [17]*taiu*' *hiék*, a hole, a burrow; [18]'*chwi taiu*' a drain, a channel for water.
Tou.

讀' A sentence, a period or full stop in reading: also read *t'uk*, q. v.: [19]*kwo*' *taiu*' periods and sentences; punctuated, as a writing.
Tu. Tou.

豆' A trencher, a platter; sacrificial dishes; an ancient weight equal to 16 grains of millet, and the 144th of a tael; beans, pulse, for which the usual sound is *tau*' q. v.: [20]˓*piéng taiu*' a sacrificial vessel; [21]*muk*, *taiu*' a wooden trencher. Read '*teu*: a peck; to measure.
Tou.

荳' Used for the preceding: peas, beans, legumes, for which *tau*' is the common term: COM., [22]*taiu*' *k'aiu*' nutmeg.
Tou.

篠' A bamboo basket, used by farmers to carry hay or muck; grain sprouting; [23]*hó*' *taiu*' to carry a basket.
T'iao.

逗' To detain; to stop, to delay, to loiter; to remain without leave, to skulk about in order to avoid: [24]*taiu*' ˓*liu*, to loiter, to skulk.
Tou.

1 門㡳	3 有道	5 有炭	7 爭鬥	9 鬥嘴	11 吊賊	13 吊索	15 吊城	17 竇穴	19 句讀	21 木豆	23 荷篠
2 盡有	4 有柴	6 有心	8 鬥氣	10 械鬥	12 吊死	14 吊鬼	16 狗竇	18 水竇	20 籩豆	22 荳蔻	24 逗遛

Taiuʾ. A coll. word: to cast, to pitch, to throw in a level position, as in the game of pitching cash; *taiuʾ ˏchiéng*, to pitch cash; *taiuʾ ˏsang pʻok*, to pitch and get three reverse sides up; *taiuʾ má² ʻkiong*, throw it down and it does not ring, as a bad dollar.

(784) **Tak.**

答, 荅, Ta. A bamboo-rope to track boats; to reply, to answer, to rejoin; an answer, an echo; to recompense; to sustain, to feel an obligation; agreeable, suitable, corresponding; coarse: [1]*tak, pwoʾ* coarse cloth; COM., [2]*tak, siă² ˏhung ˏong*, to recompense your great favor—words on votive tablets to the gods; [3]*ong² tak,* question and answer; [4]*tak, engʾ* to reply; [5]*tak, ʻlá*, to respond to the politeness, as relatives of the dead do by beginning to wail when friends call to condole with them; [6]*ʻsu ong² ˏhi ʻsu tak,* an inappropriate reply to a question; COLL., [7]*tak, ʻkʻeu*, a mere taste—only a small part of the debt received; *tak, tak, ʻkʻeu*, to take a little in the mouth, to taste.

荅, Ta. The contracted form of the last: a kind of pulse; to bear, to sustain, to assume: [8]*ˏkü tak*, a sort of chevaux-de-frise; [9]*chaʾ tak,* ox-bezoar.

嗒, Ta. To sip, to taste, to lick. Read *tʻak,*: to forget, to to lose one's self-possession, in a flurry; to throw off care: [10]*tʻak, ˏyong yok, saungʾ* bewildered, as from grief.

搭, 搭, Ta. To strike, to smite; to lodge at, to become a guest; to add to; joining on, attached; to erect, to build up, to construct; to hang, to suspend; to take passage; to avail of an opportunity, as to send goods; in the coll. to save, to rescue; to take shares in: COM., [11]*tak, kaʾ* to make a frame or stand; [12]*tak, hiéʾ ˏtai,* to put up a theatrical stage; [13]*tak, ˏsung,* to take passage on a boat; [14]*tak, hwoʾ* to send goods (by boat); [15]*tak, chʻengʾ* or *tak, chʻengʾ ˏtʻau,* to put more on the scales in weighing; *tak, ʻié tak, tóh,* to smite chairs and tables (in a rage); COLL., *kʻáʾ ˏnu tak, kʻóʾ* take it along for me; *tak, keuʾ* to save, to deliver; *tak, sioh, ʻku,* to take a share (in business). Read *tʻak,*: to touch, to rub gently, to handle.

Tak,. A coll. word, for which the last may be used: to fit closely, as a joint; to suit, to agree precisely; literal, exact, as a definition or translation: *ʻyă tak,* fitting closely; [16]*tak, chiéngʾ* to adjust the arrow (to the string); [17]*tak, tói²* a cash-bag, made of cloth with an opening in the center; *tak, kangʾ* perspiration coming through one's clothes.

妲, Ta. Also read *tangʾ*: occurs in the name [18]*Tak, ʻki,* or Tanki, the infamous concubine of the tyrant Chau-sin, B. C. 1130; *met.*, a vile woman.

組, Read *tengʾ*; used in the *Paik, ˏIng* for the coll. *tak,*: to baste, to sew slightly: [19]*tak, ˏi ˏsiong*, to

---

[1]答 鴻 [4]答 [6]所 答 荅 然 架 [13]搭 [15]搭 [17]搭 [19]組
布 恩 應 問 [7]答 [9]鮓 若 [12]搭 船 秤 袋 衣
[2]答 [3]問 [5]答 非 口 荅 喪 戲 [14]搭 [16]搭 [18]妲 裳
謝 答 禮 所 [8]湜 [10]嗒 [11]搭 臺 貨 箭 已 ○

baste clothes, to take a tuck in a garment; *tak, siăng'* basting-thread.

鍚 A hook, a grapnel; to hook, to draw up with a hook; a strap, or clasp of a door: COM., [1]*ʻtak, ˏkau,* a hook, as on the end of a boat-pole; [2]*ˏmwong tak,* a door-clasp of iron, or brass; COLL., *tak, tioh,* hooked up; fastened, latched; *ˏmwong tak, sioh, a'* just latch the door.

撻 噠 Ta. Read *tak,;* coll. *tak,* as in [3]*tak, ˏchü,* a name for the Tartars; [4]*tak, ˏpó ˏchong,* the Manchoo female costume; the dress of the small-footed Chinese women, as worn by the large-footed; [5]*tak, ʻkiăng ʻka ʻmwang ˏchiu,* "a Tartar pretending to be a Manchoo"—said of one who uses a foreign costume, etc.

踏 Ta. To step, to tread; to trample on; to take measured steps in singing: [6]*chiêng tak,* to trample on; COM., [7]*tak, ʻtau,* a footstool; steps, stairs; [8]*tak, ʻpeng,* a step attached to the front of a bed; [9]*tak, tai'* a pestle or beater, worked with the foot; [10]*tak, ˏmwong,* to kick a door open; [11]*tak, ˏk'a,* to tread on; something to rest the foot on; [12]*tak, kieu' ˏá,* bridal shoes; COLL., *tak, hai'* the step of an actor; *tak, tio'* to "tread the path" — to pave one's way in a business; *tak, ˏk'a chioh, ʻtá,* to trample under foot; to impose on, to abuse; *sioh, ˏk'a tak, ʻliong ˏsung ˏpong,* one foot treading on the edges of two boats; *met.,* to attempt two things at once.

遝 Ta. Many, abundant; mixed, repeated: [13]*chak, tak,* things mixed up, a medley.

達 Ta. Open, pervious, permeable; to pervade, to permeate, to extend all about; to see through, to perceive clearly, as a subject; intelligent; intelligible; to penetrate, as water; to transfer to, to give or hand over to; to promote, to advance; to spring, as plants; all, every, universal; suitable, fit: used for the coll. *tak,* q.v.: [14]*siong' tak,* rising, as in fame or honor; also to inform the throne; [15]*tak, ˏing,* a shrewd man; [16]*chiêng' tak,* to introduce, to recommend; COM., [17]*ˏt'ung tak,* to understand fully; ready, intelligent; [18]*hwak, tak,* rising, prosperous.

蓬 Ta. The name of a plant: [19]*ˏchieu tak,* the plantain.

沓 Ta. Water rippling or bubbling up; prattling, jabbering; joined, united; to pile up; covetous, greedy; rash, blindfold, foolhardy; slow, leisurely, remiss.

鼛 Ta. The sound of a drum: COLL., *tak, tak,* or *tak, tak, ʻku,* a low, one-headed drum, also called *ˏch'ing ʻku,* or the clear drum; *tak, tak,* is also a small toy drum and drummer on wheels.

(785) Tang.

丹 Tan. A carnation color; red; *met.,* sincere; a medicine, a remedy, a prescription: [20]*ek, p'iêng' ˏtang ˏsing,* wholly sincere, devoted,

[1]鍚鈎 [2]門鍚 [3]撻子 [4]撻婆粧 [5]撻仔假滿洲 [6]踐踏 [7]踏斗 [8]踏板 [9]踏碓 [10]踏門 [11]踏跤 [12]踏轎鞋 [13]雜遝〇 [14]上達 [15]達人 [16]薦達 [17]通達 [18]發達 [19]蕉蓬 [20]一片丹心

福州方言拼音字典

loyal; COM., [1]‚tang ‚sa, vermillion, cinnabar ore; [2]‚tang ‚hwong, a good recipe; [3]‚tang ‚p‘ui, a medicinal bark—to reduce flatulence; [4]‚tang kié’ the red-hearted cassia; [5]‚tang ‘tá, a yellowish earth, used in paints; ‚sing ‚siéng liéng[2] ‚tang, the genii distill medicines; *met.*, said of an excellent recipe; [6]‚tang ‚tiéng, the lower part of the abdomen—source of strength, as in voice.

珊珊 ‚Shan. ‚San. Coral: also read ‚sang, q. v.: ‚tang ‚tang, the jingling sound, as of girdle ornaments; COM., [7]‚tang ‚hu, coral; ‚tang ‚hu ‘ting, a red coral button, the highest in rank; ‚tang ‚hu söü[2] branched coral; ‚tang ‚hu ‚chio, coral beads.

跚 ‚Shan. To walk as if lame, to halt, to hobble; unable to advance, making slow progress: properly read ‚sang, q. v.

聃聑 ‚Tan. Dull of hearing; a man's name; [8]‘Ló ‚tang, commonly called [9]‘Ló ‚kung, or [10]‘Ló ‘chü, the founder of Tauism or Rationalism.

耽躭 ‚Tan. Also read ‚t‘ing, and interchanged with the next: long ears, the ears hanging down—a mark of wisdom; addicted to pleasure; to delight in.

眈 ‚Tan. Also read ‚t‘ing: to look at and yet think of something else; lustful, given to pleasure; to look about, as tigers while eating: [11]‚tang ‚tang, a fierce, grand look, as of a tiger.

單单 ‚Tan. ‚Shan. Single, one, alone, solitary, isolated; a single garment; only, simply; wholly, entirely; exhausted, poor, thin, bad; around, pervading; a bill, a receipt; a check, an agreement: the 1st also read siéng[2] q. v.: COM., [12]‚tang ‚tang, or ‚tang chiăh, single, the only one; [13]‚tang ‚t‘üng, a single thickness; [14]‚tang ‘ch‘iu, single-handed, working alone; [15]‚tang pok, poor, thin; few, reduced, as a family; [16]‚tang ‚sing ‚kó, a bachelor, one who has no family; [17]‚ku ‚tang, orphaned; isolated; [18]hwo’ ‚tang, an invoice of goods; [19]‚k‘wi ‚tang, to make out a bill; [20]‚ti ‚tang, a circular, a note of information; [21]siă[2] ‚tang, a note of thanks (for presents); COLL., ‚tang tëük, ng[2] ‚siăng ‚pá, a single bamboo can't make a row; *met.*, to need others' help to succeed well; ‚tang ‚hwang ‚só ‘kong wa[2] to talk unreasonably; ‚tang ‘tiu ‚tang, one to one (in a fight).

殫 ‚Tan. Also read ‘tang: to carry to the utmost; the extreme, last stage of; exhausted: [22]‚tang lik, the whole strength.

襌 ‚Tan. A single garment, one having no lining: [23]‚tang ‚i, a single, inner garment.

嘽 ‚Tan. To breathe hard, to pant; to rejoice; asthmatic, broken-winded, as a horse; slow, easy; full, many: ‚tang ‚tang, many; vigorous.

---

[1]丹沙 [2]丹方 [3]丹皮 [4]丹桂 [5]丹底 [6]丹田 [7]珊瑚 [8]老聃 [9]老君 [10]老子 [11]眈眈 [12]單單 [13]單重 [14]單手 [15]單薄 [16]單身哥 [17]孤單〇 [18]貨單 [19]開單 [20]知單 [21]謝單 [22]殫力 [23]襌衣

簞 ˓Tan. Tien. A small, round basket of bamboo or rush, for holding rice; a calabash: ¹ʻek, ˓tang sëü² a basket of rice; ²˓tang tëük˒ a kind of bamboo, having large leaves and long joints.

鄲 ˓Tan. A region in the south of Chihli province, now the district of Hantan in Kwangping prefecture.

擔 担 ˓Tan. To carry on the ends of a stick across the shoulders; to bear, to sustain a responsibility; to be security for; in the coll. to delay, delayed: also read tang˒ q. v.: COM., ³˓tang tang˒ to carry a load; ⁴ʻpeng ˓tang, a carrying-stick or yoke; ⁵˓tang ˓kĕng, cooliage; ⁶˓tang ˓sing, to act as security; ⁷˓tang ˓iu, to be anxious about, solicitous; ⁸˓tang ˓tong, to be responsible for; COLL., o² ˓tang ˓tong and ˓mó ˓tang ˓tong, can and cannot; ˓tang tek˒ ʻkʻi, pong˒ tek˒ ʻtó, can carry a load and set it down; met., able to do it without trouble; ˓tang kóh, delayed, retarded; ˓tang kóh˒ nik˒ ʻchi, days wasted by delay. Read siéng²: to borrow; false, pretending.

儋 ˓Tan. Interchanged with the last: to bear, to carry; a load of two piculs of grain; a large town in the northwest of Hainan Island: ⁹˓ka ˓u ˓tang sik˒ no food in the house, destitute.

佮 A coll. character: now, the present time: ¹⁰˓tang cheu² kʻó˒ to go immediately; ¹¹kau² ˓tang, till now; ¹²˓tang ˓ki ˓nĕng, the men of the present time.

湛 ˓Chan. Given to pleasure, indulging to excess: also read ˓tʻing, q. v.: Read ʻtang: a northern affluent of the Yellow river near Shansi; to sink into; to soak, to immerse; to plunge in; deep, limpid, still; clear, calm; liberal.

˓Tang. A coll. word: on the contrary, by contraries; reversely, backwards: ˓tang tó˒ on the contrary, wrongly, reversely; ˓tang tó˒ chó˒ to do the wrong thing first; ˓tang tó˒ ˓tʻau, the wrong end first.

˓Tang. A coll. word, as in ʻchʻiu ˓tang, the elbow; ˓kʻa ˓tang, or ˓kʻa au² ˓tang, the heel; ʻchʻiu ˓tang ˓tung, to knock with the elbow.

膽 胆 ʻTan. The gall, the gall-bladder; courage, bravery; fortitude; to rub, as the down from fruit: COM., ¹³˓kang ʻtang, the liver and gall; met., the very heart; very intimate; ¹⁴twai² ʻtang, great courage; ¹⁵ʻtang kʻe˒ a courageous spirit; ¹⁶ʻtang ʻsieu, cowardly, timid; ¹⁷ʻtang ˓hang, his bravery has died out; ¹⁸ʻtang ˓hwang, vitriol; COLL., ˓kiáng pʻwai˒ ʻtang, scared enough to split his gall-bladder!

癉 ʻTan. Also read tang˒: disease from overwork; fatigued, wearied; ulceration, sores; erysipelas; a disease of children, like the piles or strangury: ¹⁹ʻtang auk, to vex the wicked; COM., ²⁰meng² siong² ˓wong ʻtang,

¹一簞食〇 ²簞竹 ³擔担 ⁴板擔 ⁵擔工 ⁶擔承 ⁷擔憂 ⁸擔當 ⁹家無儋食 ¹⁰佮就 ¹¹至佮 ¹²佮其伙 ¹³肝膽 ¹⁴大膽 ¹⁵膽氣 ¹⁶膽小 ¹⁷膽寒 ¹⁸膽礬 ¹⁹癉惡 ²⁰面上黃癉

the jaundice appearing on the face.

ʻ紞 Tan. Fringes on the border of a coronet to cover the ears; flaps or pendants on caps; sound of a drum.

ʻ亶 Tan. True, sincere; to trust; plentiful, abundant; name of a far country beyond the sea.

ʻ*Tang*. A coll. word, often, frequently, constantly: ʻ*tang* ʻ*tang* ˏ*chiong wang*ˀ repeatedly so; ʻ*tang* ʻ*tang chʻeng*ˀ constantly cold, as the weather.

但ʼ Tan. But, only, simply; whenever, as soon as; exposed, unrestrained; adds force to the beginning of a clause: [1]ʻ*kʻi tang*ʼ how only; [2]*pok*ˎ *tang*ʼ not simply; [3]*tang*ʼ ˏ*hwang*ˏ but, however, whoever; COM., [4]*tang*ʼ *ngwong*ˀ only wish that! would that!

旦ʼ Tan. Sun-rising, the morning, dawn; light, clear, bright; men who act as females in plays; anciently used for ˏ*sing*, a spirit, a god: [5]*tang*ʼ *sik*ˎ morning and evening; [6]ˏ*ngwong tang*ʼ new year's day; [7]*sauk*ˎ *tang*ʼ the 1st day of a month; [8]*ek*ˎ *tang*ʼ in a morning, instantly; COM., [9]ʻ*sieu tang*ʼ actors in female dress; [10]ʻ*u tang*ʼ the character of a female warrior in plays; [11]ˏ*hwa tang*ʼ actors who personate girls; [12]*paik*ˎ ˏ*mang tang*ʼ the eight actors—on horseback in certain idol processions.

笪 Ta. Also read ʻ*tang*: to strike, to brush away; a small basket; bamboo mats for a roof. Read *tʻak*ˎ: the heavens suddenly becoming dark.

擔ʼ 担 Tan. A burden, a load carried at the ends of a stick across the shoulder; a load of 100 catties, a picul; in the coll. a numerative of carrying-ropes: also read ˏ*tang*, q. v.: COM., [13]*taëng*ˀ *tang*ʼ a heavy load; [14]ˏ*lai tang*ʼ a load carried in baskets; a pair of carrying-baskets and stick; [15]*chiék*ˎ *tang*ʼ to go and relieve one of his load; COLL., [16]ˏ*chëng sóh*ˎ *sioh*ˎ *tang*ʼ a set of palm-coir ropes, a hank of two such ropes.

誕ʼ 誔 Tan. To talk wildly, to boast, to brag; incoherent, fabulous, idle, nonsensical; to enlarge, to magnify; great, vast; to bear, to nourish, to bring up: [17]*hwong*ʼ *tang*ʼ to lie, to brag; [18]*tang*ʼ ʻ*chü* to bear a son; [19]ˏ*sing tang*ʼ a god's birthday.

蛋ʼ Tan. An egg; a tribe of the Miautsz': commonly read *laung*ʼ q. v.

***Tang*ʼ.** A coll. word: to force, to exert the muscles violently, as in speaking; to strain, as at stool: *tang*ʼ ʻ*kʻi* ˏ*hó* ˏ*lëng* ˏ*kʻëng nau*ˀ to strain one's windpipe by outcries.

***Tang*ʼ.** A coll. word: to spread, to extend, to enlarge, as a spot of grease or ink on paper; a copy-slip placed under and showing through the paper, called *che*ˀ *tang*ʼ; *tang*ʼ *twai*ˀ the spot much enlarged; *tang*ʼ ˏ*tʻëng tʻau*ʼ it has wet through; ˏ*kʻwong tang*ʼ

---

[1] 豈但 [2] 不但 [3] 但凡 [4] 但願 [5] 旦夕 [6] 元旦 [7] 朔旦 [8] 一旦 [9] 小旦 [10] 武旦 [11] 花旦 [12] 八蠻旦 ○ [13] 重擔 ○ [14] 棶擔 ○ [15] 接擔 ○ [16] 棕索一擔 [17] 放誕 [18] 誕子 [19] 神誕 ○

a ruled form, as placed under paper to write by.

談 ꜁T'an. To converse; to discuss, to talk about; to prate, to cavil, to dispute; talk, chit-chat: [1]'*mi* ꜁*tang*, pleasant talk; [2]꜁*hang* ꜁*tang*, chit-chat; [3]'*ch'iu* ꜁*tang*, to play chess; COM., [4]*kong ch'ieu'* ꜁*tang*, to laugh and chat; to jest; [5]꜁*tang* ꜁*king pauk*, '*ku*, to converse about things ancient and modern; [6]꜁*tang laung'* to discourse about.

餤 ꜁T'an. To serve up food; to bait, to allure with a bait; to eat, to devour; cakes with flesh rolled in, a sandwich.

壇 ꜁T'an. An altar of sacrifice, an altar before idols and shrines; a terrace or high place for worship; an arena, a public hall: [7]꜁*ung* ꜁*tang*, a hall for literary meetings; COM., [8]*siă' chek*, ꜁*tang*, an altar to Ceres; [9]꜁*t'iéng tê'* ꜁*tang*, an altar or terrace to heaven and earth; [10]꜁*pá* ꜁*tang*, to arrange an altar; COLL., *chiék*, *sioh*, ꜁*tang*, to have charge of an altar-service.

檀 ꜁T'an. A hard, tough wood, suitable for axles; sandal-wood: in the coll. read ꜁*t'ang*, q. v.

꜁*Tang*. A coll. word; to shine, the reflection of the sun's rays; to dart, as rays of light; to expose in the sun; to place so as to show through, as a copy-slip: ꜁*tó k'ó'* ꜁*tang* ꜁*tang*, take and put it in the sun; ꜁*tang* '*tié* ꜁*li*, to shine into; ꜁*tang k'ang'* to hold to the light and examine; ꜁*tang* '*ong*, a shadow cast on to; ꜁*tang che' tang'* (or *t'aik*,) to place a copy-slip under (thin paper) to write by.

彈 弹 ꜁Tan. T'an. To fillip, to snap with the fingers; to thrum, to play on stringed instruments; to snap, to bow or whip, as cotton; to accuse, to report against: also read *tang'* q. v.: [11]꜁*tang* '*chi*, to snap the fingers; COM., [12]꜁*tang* ꜁*k'ing*, to play on lutes, etc.; [13]꜁*tang* '*niéng*, to dye by sprinkling; [14]꜁*tang* ꜁*miéng*, to bow cotton; [15]꜁*tang* ꜁*t'ui*, a bowing-stick; *met.*, to pound each other, as in a quarrel; ꜁*tang ak*, to subdue, to subject; [16]꜁*tang* '*hung siăng'* to mark with a marking-line, as tailors do.

彈' Tan. T'an. A ball, a pellet, a bullet; to shoot with a pellet-bow; any thing small, a plat of ground: also read ꜁*tang*, q. v.: [17]'*kwi tang'* injurious meteorological phenomena, malarious influences; COM., [18]*tang'* '*chi*, or *tang'* ꜁*wong*, a pellet; COLL., *tang' ch'ok*, *k'ó'* shot out from a pellet-bow; ꜁*hwang tang' tik*, *tang'* to cross-question, to harass with words.

僤' Tan. Sincere, in earnest, the whole heart engaged; hasty, urgent: [19]*tang' no'* heavy wrath. Read *siéng'*: to move about, to disturb.

憚' Tan. To dread trouble or pain; sore, fatigued; fearful, apprehensive: [20]꜁*u kê' tang'* not fear any one, disrespectful, reckless; *pok*, *tang'* '*kai*, not dread (the trouble of) reforming.

[1]美談 [2]閒談 [3]手談 [4]講笑談 [5]談今博古 [6]談論 [7]文壇 [8]社稷壇 [9]天地壇 [10]排壇 [11]彈指 [12]彈琴 [13]彈染 [14]彈棉 [15]彈槌 [16]彈粉線 [17]鬼彈 [18]彈子 彈丸 [19]僤怒 [20]無忌憚

鄭[2] Chèng. A feudal state in the Chau dynasty, now the prefecture of Kaifung in Honan: COM., [1]*tang*[2] *tëüng*[2] earnest, diligent; respectful.

啖[2] 啗[2] 噉[2] Tan. To eat, to taste; to chew, to masticate and swallow; to entice, to hold out baits, to allure; a bite, a morsel, a swallow; wild, incoherent.

淡[2] 澹[2] Tan. Fresh, tasteless, flat, insipid; thin, weak, watery, the opposite of *ˏnüng;* light, as color; dull, as trade; heartless, indifferent to; strange, distant, as a friend; the 2d also means still, tranquil, as water; agitated, as the mind: COM., [2]*tang*[2] *sié*[2] a soy somewhat fresh; [3]*tang*[2] *saikˎ* a light color; [4]*tang*[2] *ˏchong*, to use light cosmetics; [5]*ʻleng tang*[2] indifferent to; insipid; few, reduced, as a family; dull, as a market; [6]*tang*[2] *ʻchwi*, Tamshui in Formosa; COLL., [7]*tang*[2] *ˏta ʻch'iăng tang*[2] *k'ahˎ* to treat distant guests to weak tea, as sometimes said jocosely by the host.

Tang[2]. A coll. word: to err, to mistake; an error, a fault; wrong, erroneous: *ˏmó tang*[2] no error, right; *ʻnü o*[2] *tang*[2] you are in fault; *tang*[2] *tio*[2] the wrong road; *met.*, a vicious course; *tang*[2] *ʻlau tang*[2] *ˏch'iăng*, wrong already and finish it wrong!

Tang[2]. A coll. word: a cooper's block to drive down hoops with; to drive hoops: *tang*[2] *tang*[2] *siohˎ lang*[2] *a*[2] to give (the hoop) one or two (more) blows.

(786) Tau.

兠 ˏ兜 ˏ兜 ˏ Tou. Also read *ˏteu:* a sort of helmet or morion; helmet-shaped; to incite, to provoke; in the coll. at, by, near in time or place; to fit closely: COM., [8]*ˏtau ˏmau*, an iron or brass helmet; [9]*tëükˎ ˏtau ˏmau*, a helmet-shaped bamboo hat; COLL., [10]*chaikˎ ˏtau*, near the time of a festival; [11]*ˏnang ˏmwong ˏtau*, at the south gate; [12]*ˏtau takˎ* fitting closely, as a sheath.

㨮 ˏ Tou. Also read *ˏteu:* to strike, to grasp, to seize; to scheme after, to engross, to monopolize; to criticise, to correct; in the coll. to draw, to bring near to; to befriend, to care for; to tuck, to press, to fold under: [13]*ˏtau ʻlang*, to grasp after, to engross; COM., [14]*ˏtau ʻliăng*, to get commissions; to monopolize, as trade; COLL., [15]*p'woi*[2] *ˏtau ʻtié*, to tuck the quilt under; [16]*ˏtau ˏsing ˏpiéng*, to bring near to one's self; to befriend, as an orphan; [17]*ˏtau ˏmwong ˏt'au*, to get people's custom; *ˏtau ʻtiong ʻma ˏt'au*, to turn a horse's head.

株 ˏ Chu. Read *ˏt'ü;* coll. *ˏtau:* the classifier of posts, pillars, trees, round timbers, etc.: [18]*siohˎ ˏtau ch'eu*[2] a tree: [19]*siohˎ ˏtau t'eu*[2] a post.

1鄭重 2淡豉 3淡色 4淡粧 5冷淡 6淡水 7淡茶請淡客 8兜鍪 9竹兜鍪 10節兜 11南門兜 12兜搭 13㨮攬 14㨮領 15被㨮裏 16㨮身邊 17㨮門頭 18一株樹 19一株柱

斗 Tou. T‘ou. Read *‘teu;* coll. *‘tau:* a dry measure of 10 *꜀ching* or pints, but varying in size; vessels like pecks: [1]*꜀kwang ‘tau,* the legal peck, containing about 15 pounds; [2]*‘mi ‘tau,* the common rice-peck; [3]*꜀ch‘ong ‘tau,* the granary-peck, containing 6½ catties, and measuring $1\frac{1}{32}$ gallons; [4]*tau ek,* those who measure rice at public granaries; [5]*‘tau lik,* a broad-brimmed rain-hat of bamboo splints and leaves; [6]*‘tau ꜀lang,* a storied basket; [7]*‘tau aëng’* a sort of small earthen jar with a large mouth; [8]*tak, ‘tau,* a foot-stool; steps, stairs.

‘Tau. A coll. word: to shake, as clothes; also to count, to reckon up: *‘tau ‘tau,* shake it; *‘tau ꜀ung ꜀ting,* to shake out the dust; *‘tau so’* to reckon the account, as of a day's gains.

罩 Chao. A kind of basket to catch mud-fish by covering them; to cover; a shade, a cover: COM., [9]*꜀ting tau’* a lamp-globe; a screen or cover for lamps; [10]*kieu’ tau’* a sedan-cover; *꜀kwang ꜀ch‘ai tau’* a pall of cloth of simple or mixed colors; *꜀kié ꜀lĕng tau’* a movable bamboo coop for covering over fowls; *tau’ kwo’ ꜀t‘au,* to cover the head, as with the bedclothes.

鬥 Tou. Read *taiu’;* coll. *tau’:* to strive for superiority, to compete, to contest: [11]*tau’ k‘á’* to compete in speed; [12]*tau’ k‘e’* a spirit of competition; [13]*tau’ ngaing’* to contend stiffly, as in law suits; *tau’ ꜀sio ꜀yăng,* to strive for superiority in; *tau’ ꜀liong ꜀sung,* to race dragon-boats.

Tau’. A coll. word: midday, noon; *met.,* dinner: *nik, ꜀t‘au tau’* the sun at the meridian, 12 M.; *siong’ tau’* and *a’ tau’* forenoon and afternoon; *p‘wai’ tau’* mid-day, in the heat of the day; *tau’ siäh, ‘lau,* have eaten dinner.

骰 Shai. Formerly used for *‘ku* (the thigh): dice, called [14]*꜀tau ‘chi:* COM., [15]*꜀tau saik,* the numbers on dice; [16]*꜀tau ꜀ka,* the keeper of a gambling den; [17]*꜀tau ꜀pwong,* a dice bowl, set in a clay mold; [18]*꜀yeu ꜀tau,* to shake the dice; COLL., *꜀tau ‘chi twai’* as large as a die; *꜀tau ꜀ka ꜀kiĕng ‘tu ꜀sio ‘nü ꜀mó ‘chu,* if the gaming-house keeper joins in the game, it is not clear whether he loses or not!

投 T‘ou. Read *꜀teu;* coll., *꜀tau:* to throw, to cast down, to reject; to drop, to fall into; to go to, to engage one to do, to intrust; to submit; to throw one's self on another; to report, to inform; to lodge information against: *꜀tau ꜀i ‘lá,* to throw one's self on him for support; [19]*꜀tau tó’* to report one's arrival; [20]*꜀tau ꜀kung,* or *꜀tau ꜀yăng,* to enlist; [21]*꜀tau ꜀hong,* to return to allegiance; [22]*꜀tau sëük,* to beg a night's lodging; [23]*꜀tau póh,* to cleave to, to depend on, as an orphan does; [24]*꜀tau ꜀t‘ai,* preternatural conception in the womb; *꜀tau ‘pó ‘tiong,* to inform the constable; *꜀tau ꜀tĕng ꜀tau ꜀sá,* to tell east and west—tell everybody;

1 官斗 2 米斗 3 倉斗 4 斗乙 5 斗笠 6 斗籃 7 斗甕 8 踏斗 9 燈罩 10 轎罩 11 鬥快 12 鬥氣 13 鬥硬 14 骰子 15 骰色 16 骰家 17 骰盆 18 搖骰 19 投到 20 投軍 21 投降 22 投泊 23 投宿 24 投胎

ˌtau ˌmwong ˌchü, to send in an official document.

ˈ*Tau.* A coll. word, corrupted from *ˌta* (tea), as in *ˌtau ˈkwang taingˈ* a restaurant.

豆 荳 [2] Tou. Beans, peas, legumes: also read *taiu*[2] q. v.: COM., [1]*ˌking tau*[2] peas; [2]*ˌkong tau*[2] a sort of white bean with spotted eyes; [3]*ˌch'ang tau*[2] or *tau*[2] *ˌch'ang,* green pot-beans; [4]*tau*[2] *kiek,* the long-pod, or string, bean; [5]*tau*[2] *sië*[2] salt-bean relish; [6]*tau*[2] *ho*[2] bean curd; [7]*tau*[2]*ˌkang* (coll. *tau*[2] *ˌkwang*), cakes of bean curd; [8]*tau*[2] *ˌnga,* bean sprouts, made by covering so as to heat or ferment; *tau*[2] *ho*[2] *tëu*[2] "curd-chopsticks"—the film from the surface of the curd made into rolls; *tau*[2] *ho*[2] *ˈpeng,* a bean-curd press; COLL., *ˌch'eng tau*[2] or *ˌch'iëng tau*[2] the common field-bean; *tau*[2] *ˌpeng tau*[2] *lengˈ* crushed beans; *tau*[2] *ˈchio,* fermented bean-relish.

痘 [2] Tou. The small-pox: COM., [9]*tau*[2] *ˈma,* the goddess of small-pox; [10]*chëungˈ tau*[2] to inoculate; [11]*ˌyong tau*[2] the foreign vaccine-virus; [12]*tau*[2] *ˌchiong,* the virus of a pustule; *tau*[2] *siong*[2] *ˌchiong,* the pustules suppurating; [13]*ch'ok, tau*[2] to have the small-pox; COLL., *tau*[2] *ˌseng ˈmëng haiu*[2] before the pox and after the measles — are critical periods.

脰 [2] Tou. Read *taiu*[2]; coll. *tau*[2] as in [14]*tau*[2] *kauk,* the neck; [15]*tau*[2] *ˈliäng,* the collar or neck of a garment; *tau*[2] *kauk, t'ëük,* to contract the neck; a short neck.

(787) **Tauk.**

啄 ˌ Cho. To peck; to pick up, as grain with the bill; to eat, as fowls do: [16]*pauk, tauk,* to knock at a door; COLL., *tauk, sioh, ˈch'oiˈ* to pick up a bill full; to peck at; *tauk, ˈcheu,* a game with cards in which each takes three at a time; *tauk, ˈcheu kwaˈ* to divine by the pecking of birds; *tauk, cheuˈ* to peck through the shell, as chicks do.

琢 ˌ Cho. To work gems; to cut, carve, and dress stones; to choose: [17]*ˌtung tauk,* to select; [18]*tauk, ˌmo,* to carve and polish; COM., [19]*ngük, pok, tauk, pok, ˌsing k'eˈ* if the gem is unwrought, it will not become a useful ornament; *met.,* the duty of diligence in study, etc.; [20]*ˌteu tauk,* to cut and dress, as gems.

拯 ˌ Cho. To beat, to strike; to push, to shove; to carve, as letters; to peck, to pierce; the noise of rapping.

涿 ˌ Cho. To fall in drops, to drop, to trickle down; to strike on the water; a stream and district south-west of Peking.

椓 ˌ Cho. To pound on wood, to bang; to castrate, as a punishment: [21]*tauk, ˌchi ˌteng ˌteng,* to strike with repeated blows.

卓 ˌ Cho. Firm, stable; high, eminent, surpassing the multitude, exalted above others; lofty and pro-

[1] 金豆 [2] 豇豆 [3] 青豆 [4] 豆結 [5] 豆豉 [6] 豆腐 [7] 豆乾 [8] 豆芽 [9] 痘媽 [10] 種痘 [11] 洋痘 [12] 痘漿 [13] 出痘 [14] 脰骨 [15] 脰領 [16] 剝啄 [17] 敎琢 [18] 琢磨 [19] 玉不琢不成器 [20] 雕琢 [21] 椓之丁丁

found; to establish, to erect: also read *tóh*, q. v.: [1]*ˌch'ieu tauk*ˌ pre-eminent; [2]*tauk*ˌ *wok*ˌ *ˌing ˌkung*, to excel the whole crowd; [3]*tauk*ˌ *lik*ˌ to erect, to set upright; [4]*tauk*ˌ *é'* meritorious, as said of officers at the quinquennial trial; COLL., *tauk*ˌ *chiŏng'* (a concubine) promoted to be the chief wife.

倬, Cho. Great, large, lofty; extensive; bright; to show, to manifest.

踔, Ch'ao. Also read *tau'*: to tread on; to stretch forward in running; to jump over, to leap far and high; to walk lamely; very long, distant; unusual, irregular.

斲, 斵, Cho. To cut, to hack; to hew, to chop; to rive or split; to hash, to mince; to carve, to engrave.

*Tauk*ˌ. A coll. word: to take up, to lift, to carry with both hands: *tauk*ˌ *'k'i*, to take it up; *tauk*ˌ *'ié*, to carry a chair; *tauk*ˌ *chiŏng'* to take and place properly.

(788) Taung.

當', Tang. To pawn, to pledge; to consider, to regard as, to use as; reputed as; for, instead of, as; a basis, foundation; safely, securely, properly; honest, trusty: also read *ˌtong*, q. v.: COM., [5]*'swoi' taung'* and [6]*ˌsü taung'* licensed and unlicensed pawnbrokers; [7]*taung' taing'* a pawnshop; [8]*taung' ˌt'au*, articles pawned; [9]*taung' ˌi ˌsiong*, to pawn clothes; [10]*taung' p'ieu'* a pawn-ticket; [11]*sük*ˌ *taung'* or *'t'ó taung'* to redeem a pawn; [12]*'ch'au taung'* to trouble a pawnbroker, as by clamoring for high rates; [13]*taung' ˌch'ĕng*, to "regard as only an onion"; *met.*, to slight, to treat lightly; [14]*taung' ˌta*, in the place of tea; [15]*'ung taung'* secure, safe; COLL., *taung' taing' 't'ĕng*, the apartments of a pawnshop; *taung' taung'* in place of a regular meal; *chó' taung'* a pledge, guarantee; *ng' taung' ˌi chó' wa'* don't regard what he says!

擋', Tang. To impede, to obstruct, to resist; to screen; in the coll. to hold upright and let fall, to jolt, to jounce things on the ends: [16]*taung' ˌpang*, to make the ends even by jouncing; [17]*taung' t'ak*ˌ *'tá*, to jounce out the bottom; [18]*taung' ˌp'wo 'peng*, to jounce bed-boards on their ends; [19]*taung' mek*ˌ *saik*ˌ to jolt out the bed-bugs.

頓', Tun. Read *tong'*; used for the coll. *taung'*: a portion of food taken at one time, a meal, a repast; *met.*, a spell, a while: [20]*sioh*ˌ *taung' pwong'* one meal of rice; *sioh*ˌ *nik*ˌ *ˌsang taung'* three meals a day; *k'ah*ˌ *ˌlieu sioh*ˌ *taung' k'wai'* to play or divert one's self a while.

Taung'. A coll. word: to insert a piece, to patch: *taung' ˌkiĕng*, to patch the shoulder; *taung' sioh*ˌ *tói'* to insert a piece.

[1]超卓 [2]卓越 人羣 [3]卓立 [4]卓異 [5]稅當 [6]私當 [7]當店 [8]當頭 [9]當衣 裳 [10]當票 ○ [11]贖當 [12]吵當 [13]當葱 [14]當茶 [15]穩當 [16]擋平 [17]擋塌底 [18]擋 鋪板 [19]擋木 虱 [20]一頓飯

福州方言拼音字典

段 段 Tuan. To push away; a part, a piece, a fragment, a section; a piece of silk; a numerative of sections, pieces, affairs, plats, etc.; skill, workmanship: *ek, taung* a plat of land, a spot; COM., [1] *'pek, taung* skill in writing, penmanship; *'hó 'ch'iu taung* good skill, workmanship.

緞 緞 Tuan. Glossy silk; satin: COM., [2] *,tiu taung* silks and satins; *,tiu taung taing* a silk mercer's; [3] *,hwa taung* brocade; [4] *,kwong taung* plain satins; [5] *kong taung* satins of the best quality; [6] *taung ,k'wo,* satin boots; *'ch'au taung* sleazy satin.

煅 Tuan. The heel of a shoe; also a shoe-lining.

遁 遯 Tun. To run away, to hide one's self; to skulk; to disappear unaccountably; to retire, as into privacy; the 33d diagram: [7] *'üng taung* to retire to private life; COLL., [8] *taung ,ch'ang,* "escaped alive" — to disappear unaccountably, as frogs from a jar tightly covered.

撞 Chuang. Read *,tung* and *tong*; coll. *taung*: to pound, to strike violently, to thump; to dash against; to meet accidentally or abruptly; to intrude; *met.,* to cheat, to swindle: [9] *taung 'tó,* to knock over; [10] *taung t'ak,* to knock out; [11] *taung 'tié,* to go in abruptly, to intrude; *taung ,chüng,* to pound bells (in worship); [12] *pah, taung ch'ek,* a thief who goes in on a pretence; *,chieu ,yeu taung p'iéng* to over reach, to swindle; *taung muk, ,chüng,* to "beat the wooden bell" —to claim the pay on pretence of having rendered the service.

斷 Tuan. Read *twang*; coll. *taung*: to interrupt, to stop; broken off, discontinued; clean, free from: [13] *taung ,ch'ang* (or *,ch'iăng*), to stop coming, fail to appear; [14] *taung tio* "the road cut off"; *met.,* to break off intercourse, as friends; [15] *taung ,ong,* long discontinued; [16] *taung k'e* to die; [17] *taung ,neng,* to wean; *taung ,sang 'yong,* to cease bearing; *taung 'teng o* without a spot; quite new, as clothes; [18] *taung ch'ek,* the last of the seven funeral rites, the 49th day.

逿 T'ang. To miss, to err; to slip, to fall; in the coll. to let fall, to drop; to rain: COLL., [19] *taung k'ó* dropped, lost; *taung ,mó,* lost, gone! [20] *taung lang* to fall and become wet; [21] *p'ah, taung* to let fall; [22] *taung 'ü,* to rain; [23] *taung hwo* or *taung ,pwo ,si 'ü,* a summer shower or gust; *taung lóh, ,li,* to fall down, as things; *taung sioh, chak,* a rain, a shower; *taung ,i 'tiăng 'lá,* to drop into his frying-pan; in a *met.* sense, to stop and eat with him; also to fall into his toils.

碭 Tang. Also read *t'auk,*: a variegated stone, a stone with streaks or veins through it; to exceed, to overrun, to pass by; an excess: [24] *taung ,sang,* a district in the west of Kiangsu.

[1] 筆段 [2] 綢緞 [3] 花緞 [4] 光緞 [5] 貢緞 [6] 緞靴 [7] 隱遁 [8] 遁生 [9] 撞倒 [10] 撞塌 [11] 撞入 [12] 撞賊 [13] 斷生 [14] 斷路 [15] 斷久 [16] 斷氣 [17] 斷乳 [18] 斷七 [19] 逿去 [20] 逿濫 [21] 拍逿 [22] 逿雨 [23] 逿禍 [24] 碭山

湯[2] 宕[2] Tang. Tang. T'ang. The 2d also read *t'aung'*: large, vast, magnificent; slow, leisurely; agitated, shaking, ready to run over; vagrant, unsettled; dissolute, extravagant; to squander, to run riot, to waste wantonly; the 2d also means a house like a cave: [1]*hwong' taung'* careless, profligate; [2]*taung' taung'* vast and deep, vague; to overturn, as the laws or regulations.

盪[2] Tang. T'ang. A washing tub; disturbed, moved about; large, great; depraved: also read *t'aung'*, q. v.: [3]*tik, taung'* to shake things, as in washing; [4]*taung' taung'* licentious; [5]*t'ien' taung'* in a panic; COM., [6]*sá taung'* to wash and rinse; COLL., *,kó taung'* (or *taung'*), to rinse.

丈[2] Chang. Read *tiong'*; coll. *taung'*: ten feet in common measure, about equal to 117½ English inches: [7]*taung' ek, ne'* 11 or 12 feet; [8]*taung' siong'* over 10 feet; [9]*taung' ,kó*, a measuring-pole.

(789) Te.

蒂' 蔕' 蔕' Ti. The peduncle or footstalk of flowers; the stem of leaves or fruit; what fruit hangs by; *met.*, unfounded: COM., [10]*,hó te'* stems of lily-leaves — the infusion used as a cooling drink; [11]*peng' te' ,leng*, a double-flowered lotus; COLL., [12]*,ti te'* a stem; [13]*,pu te'* a gourd-stem; *met.*, the tuft of hair on the side of a child's head; *siang' te'* remnants of threads, as left in sewing. Read *tai'*: the roots of plants; [14]*tai' kai'* prickles, motes, trifles.

智' 知' Chih. Wisdom, understanding; knowledge, judgment, discretion; wise, intelligent; able, clever, shrewd: the 2d also read *,ti*, q. v.: [15]*te' ,ngü*, clever and stupid; [16]*siong' te'* superior wisdom; [17]*te' 'üng*, wise and brave; COM., [18]*te' hié'* wisdom, intelligence.

致' Chih. Sometimes used for the next: to go; unto, leading, tending to; to visit; to invite, to induce, to lead on; to intimate to, to inform; to regulate, to order, to manage; to resign a place; to venture, to risk, to hazard; to investigate; the form, appearance of; a causative before verbs, to cause one to do; that, in order to; an object, an end, a tendency; to exert, to carry to the utmost; very, extremely; thoroughly; secret, close, subtile: [19]*ek, te'* a single aim; *te' sëü'* to resign an office; *te' meng'* to risk life for; COM., [20]*te' e'* or *te' te' e'* to intimate, to signify by a nod; to bow slightly.

緻' Chih. Fine, close, as texture; soft, delicate; handsome; to mend clothes; torn, tattered: COM., [21]*,pieu te'* fine, elegant, pretty.

置' Chih. To establish, to found, to set up; to appoint; to place, to arrange; to lay aside; to decide, to judge; to punish; to purchase for one's own use: [22]*te' ,sing ,u te'* no place to hide, ashamed; failing in

1放 3滌 5跳 7丈 上 蒂 12蒂 14蒂 16上 18智 20致 22置
蕩 盪 盪 一 9丈 11並 蒂 芥 智 慧 意 身
2蕩 4盪 6洗 二 篙 蒂 13瓠 15智 17智 19一 21標 無
蕩 盪 盪 8丈 10荷 蓮 蒂 愚 勇 致 緻 地

one's plans, destitute; COM., ʻte' hwoʼ to buy goods, lay in a fresh stock; COLL., te' má ʻk'i, not rich enough to buy it; te' má cheng' can't finish the purchases!—scil., for there are so many things that must be got.

寘 實 Chih. Like the last: to place, to set down; to receive; to stop; to put aside, to reject: ʻang te' to put by securely.

Te'. A coll. word: to poke, to butt, to push with the head; to raise, as with the head and hands: te' ch'ok, to push and get out; te' siong' to raise with the head and hands; te' má ʻk'i, can't raise it, as a very heavy article.

地 Ti. The earth, the globe, the ground; one of the three powers; a place, a site, a situation, a spot; terrestrial, earthy; the foundation of; the ground, the first color in painting; only, merely: COM., ʻte' ʻt'u, the ground, the soil; ʻte' k'e' the quality of soils; te' ˏsoi, the ground barren; ʻte' le' products of the ground; advantages of a locality; strategic points; ʻte' ˏlüng, an earth-worm; ʻˏsing te' the mind, perceptive power; ʻte' ʻchio, a landlord; ʻpwong te' native; ˏü te' a remnant of land; met., a resource, something reserved for the future; te' kong' the bully of the place; te' ˏloi, a mine, or underground infernal-machine; te' ʻpeng, the bottom-board of a coffin; te' a' on the ground; te' ʻli, geomancy; te' oi' or te' ˏtiong, a place, a locality; Te' chaung' ˏwong, a deified Buddhist, named Muk, ˏlieng; COLL., te' kang' (or ang'), an underground store-room; te' ˏt'au, on the ground; p'ah, te' to prime in painting; te' ˏt'au ˏsing, the local deity; met., a chief, a leader.

治 Chih. Ch'ih. A stream in the east of Shantung; to rule, to govern, to regulate; to manage; to oversee; to heal; to form, to construct; to try causes; talented, as in ruling; good government; the capital, the seat of government; the retired chambers of Tauists: ˏping te' general tranquility; COM., ˏtung te' the style of the emperor T'ung-chih, A. D. 1862; ʻli te' to manage, to arrange for; ʻch'ü te' to punish a criminal; te' ˏt'ieng a' to rule the empire; te' chói' to inflict punishment; ˏi te' to cure; te' pang' to heal a sickness; ˏu hwak, ʻk'ó te' no way of managing him. Read ˏti: to initiate rule, to set about regulating.

滯 Chih. Water impeded; to obstruct, to stop; a hindrance, a stoppage: to congeal, to condense, any obstruction in the system, indigestible: te' chëü' a stoppage; te' k'e' an inactive mind; COM., te' te' obstructed, met., a dull, heavy look; k'e' te' stoppage of secretions; ˏnging te' congealed, hardened; chek, te' a fit of indigestion; met., goods accumulating, dull trade. Read che': discordant.

1 置貨 2 安寘 3 地土 4 地主(?) 5 地利 6 地瓏 7 心地 8 地主 9 本地 10 地根 11 地雷 12 地板 13 地理 14 平治 15 同治 16 理治 17 處治 18 治罪 19 醫治 20 治病 21 滯住 22 滯氣 23 氣滯 24 積滯

稺[2] 穉[2] 稚[2] Chih. Young grain or that which ripens late; small, delicate; young, tender; also self-conceited, haughty: [1]ˌtung te² or te² ʻchü, a youngster, a boy; [2]te² k'e² childish, immature, delicate.

雉[2] Chih. Wild fowl, of which there are said to be 40 kinds; pheasants, francolins; to rule, to regulate; an embrasure on a wall; fragrant herbs: [3]te² tiék, parapet-walls; [4]te² ˌmwong, the south door of a seraglio; COM., [5]te² ˌkié, a pheasant; te² ˌkié ˌmó, pheasant's feathers—worn by military actors in plays.

痔[2] Chih. The piles; to gnaw, as insects: COM., [6]te² ˌch'ong, ulcers of the anus, piles; [7]ʻnói ² te² and [8]ʻngwoi ² te² the internal and external, or bleeding and blind, piles.

彘[2] Chih. A sow, a pig: [9]ˌing te² a corpse cut into pieces—allusion to a speech of a princess of the Han dynasty.

Te². A coll. euphonic prefix, as in te² tai² to throw away; te² tá² to screen; te² tieu² to set in order, to assign, as workmen to their tasks.

(790) Tĕ.

ˌ*Tĕ.* A coll. word: used for ʻsi, to die; ˌtĕ k'ó² dead! he is dead!

ˌ*Tĕ.* A coll. word: an exclamation, as in directing another's attention, there! there it is!

(791) Tek.

的, Ti. Clear, bright; true, real, authenticated; an important circumstance; a target, the bull's eye; a spot appearing distinctly; after nouns and pronouns, a sign of the possessive; after adjectives, implies personality, quality, or comparison; in the coll. used for must, positively, certainly; after verbs, it is a euphonic particle and denotes completion of the action; after ʻchieu and ˌtó, makes an adverbial sense: [10]ʻsieu tek, the little one, I, your servant! [11]ʻngó tek, mine; [12]kĕüng² tek, the nearer; COM., [13]tek, pek, one's own handwriting; [14]tek, ʻch'iu, with his own hand, he managed it; [15]tek, taung² trustworthy; [16]tek, tĕüng² good, reliable; [17]tek, yeu² important; [18]tek, sik, or tek, k'auk, true, fully substantiated; honest, trusty; COLL., [19]tek, lik, aiding, helping in emergencies; tek, ˌnĕng t'iăng² loved, esteemed by others; ʻhó tek, sá² much better; ʻkong tek, k'á² to speak rapidly; á² ʻhieu tek, to know it; mă² k'ang² tek, kiéng² can't see it, invisible; [20]tek, se² it certainly is; tek, tek, o² must be or have; [21]tek, tioh, must, positively, absolutely; [22]ʻchieu tek, ˌli, to come seldom; ˌtó tek, ˌli, to come often.

靮, Ti. A bridle: [23]chek, ˌkié tek, to hold the reins.

桎, Chih. Also read tik, and chek,: stocks of wood or iron, fetters, gyves; to manacle; to pierce; a spike, a thorn; to stop, to close; a thing

[1]童稺 [2]穉氣 [3]雉堞 [4]雉門 [5]雉雞 [6]痔瘡 [7]內痔 [8]外痔 [9]人彘 [10]小的 [11]我的 [12]近的 [13]的筆 [14]的手 [15]的當 [16]的重 [17]的要 [18]的實 [19]的力 [20]的是 [21]的着 [22]少的 梨 [23]執轡靮

to clog wheels: [1]*tek*, *kok*, fetters and manacles; [2]*tek*, *hak*, a linchpin; *met.*, a guide, one who controls, a censor of manners.

挃, Also read *tiék*: to cut grain; the noise of reaping; to strike, to beat with the fist.

窒, Chih. To close, to stop, as a mouth or opening; to hamper; the moon in opposition: [3]*tek*, *ngai* hindrances, obstructions.

嫡, Ti. The first or wedded wife, a consort: [4]*tek*, *sek*, the wife; COM., [5]*tek*, *ʻchü*, children of the wife; [6]*tek*, *ʻmu*, the wife-mother, as related to a concubine's children; [7]*tek*, *ˏchʻing*, or *tek*, *tek*, *ˏchʻing*, blood relations; [8]*tek*, *ˏchiong sëü* *pwang* (children of) the wife have whole, (those of) a concubine have half, shares.

滴, Ti. To drop, to drip, to ooze; a drop; *met.*, a very little: [9]*tek*, *lik*, to fall by drops; COM., [10]*tek*, *ʻchwi*, eaves; beads worn on a bride's forehead; COLL., *tek*, *sioh*, *tek*, to drop a drop; [11]*sioh*, *tek*, *ʻkiáng*, a little; *sioh*, *tek*, *ˏtu ˏmó*, not the least particle, not a bit; *mek*, *ʻchai tek*, *tek*, *lóh*, tears falling; *tek*, *tek*, *ˏking*, a squib which emits yellowish globules of fire.

甋, Ti. A tile: [12]*ˏling tek*, a large tile; a jar or amphora with ears on the neck.

鏑, Ti. The point of an arrow or dart; a barb, a sharp point: [13]*ˏming tek*, a whizzing arrow.

蹢, Ti. The hoof of a beast, especially of a pig or horse; to go over to, to join a party. Read *tik*: to stop the foot: [14]*tik* *chʻëük*, uneasy, irresolute, not knowing what to do.

Tek,. A coll. word: to seize firmly, to gripe: *tek*, *ʻking* *ʻking*, to grasp tightly, as the reins, or a cue.

Tek,. A coll. euphonic prefix, as in *tek*, *tak*, to baste; to paste together; to erect, as a staging; to latch, to hook; to attach, as grappling irons; *tek*, *tauk*, to carry with both hands; *tek*, *taëk*, to cover over; *tek*, *tok*, to dot, to punctuate; to light, as a lamp.

值, Chih. Read *sik*, and *tik*; coll. *tek*: the price, cost, worth of; to cost, to be worth: [15]*tek*, *ˏchiéng*, it's worth money, dear; *tek*, *ng* *tek*, is it worth (so much) or not? [16]*tek*, *nioh*, *wai* what is it worth? [17]*ʻting tek*, well worth—cheap at that.

擇, Chai. Tsê. To choose, to select, to prefer: in the coll. read *tah*, q. v.: [18]*tek*, *ˏkau*, to select associates; COM., [19]*tek*, *kek*, to choose lucky days—words on fortune-tellers' signs; [20]*keng tek*, to select; [21]*tek*, *ˏhiéng*, to choose a good one, as a child for adoption; *tek*, *sá* to select a son-in-law.

1 桎梏 2 桎鎋 3 窒礙 4 嫡室 5 嫡子 6 嫡母 7 嫡親 8 嫡全庶半 9 滴瀝 10 滴水 11 一滴仔 12 瓴甋 ○ 13 鳴鏑 14 蹢躅 15 值錢 16 值䓂壞 17 頂值 18 擇交 19 擇吉 20 揀擇 21 擇賢 ○

澤 Chai. Tsê. ₂ A marsh, a fen, a bog, a pool; to moisten, to soften, to enrich, to fertilize; to anoint, to cause to shine; to favor, to benefit, to show kindness; favor, kindness; to make to grow; rich, fertile; redolent, as with fragrance: [1]ʻü tek$_2$ moistened by rain; [2]ŭng' tek$_2$ to enrich; moist and fresh; [3]tek$_2$ siăʼ a marshy plant like purslane; COM., [4]ˏong tek$_2$ favor, beneficence.

Tek$_2$. A coll. word, for which the last may be used: to drip, to drain, to draw off, to filter: *tek$_2$ ˏta*, drained dry; *tek$_2$ ʻmi*, to dip up rice with a filtering-dipper; *tek$_2$ tek$_2$ lŏh$_2$* dripping down.

特 Tʻĕ. ₂ The male of beasts; a single bullock; a victim; an animal three years old; a team of four; to pair, to mate, to match; to stand forth alone; single, solitary, alone, insulated; only, specially, of set purpose: [5]*tek$_2$ ˏseng*, an ox for sacrifice; COM., [6]*tek$_2$ ü'* a special edict; [7]*tek$_2$ e'* or *tek$_2$ tik$_2$* with special design or purpose; [8]*tek$_2$ che' ˏtʻung ˏti*, I write specially to inform you.

(792) Tŏk.

毒 Tu. ₂ Read *tuk$_2$*; coll. *tĕk$_2$*: a poison, a bane; noxious, venemous; cruel, malevolent, baneful; to hate, to injure: [9]*tĕk$_2$ yoh$_2$* a bane; violent remedies; [10]*chʻoiʼ tĕk$_2$* malicious talk; [11]*tĕk$_2$ ˏsing*, cruel, malevolent; [12]*tĕk$_2$ ʻmĕng*, noxious gnats.

Tĕk$_2$. A coll. prefix, as in *tĕk$_2$ taĕk$_2$* a cover; to cover, to coop up.

Tĕk$_2$. A coll. corruption of *tek$_2$* as in *tĕk$_2$ e'* and *tĕk$_2$ tik$_2$* specially, purposely.

(793) Teng.

登 ˏTêng. To ascend; to advance, to go up higher; to begin, to start, as on a journey; to gain a degree; to record, to note; to become perfect; complete; ripened; at once, as soon: [13]*ˏteng ˏsi*, immediately; [14]*ˏhung ˏteng*, abundant, as harvests; [15]*ˏteng ˏteng*, responsive, as voices; [16]*ˏteng chik$_2$* to take a census; COM., [17]*ʻngu ʻchü ˏteng ˏkʻwo*, to have five sons all graduates; [18]*ˏteng ˏsang toʼ ʻchwi*, to climb hills and cross rivers—to travel; *ˏteng ˏtai paiʼ chiongʼ* to mount the stage and receive the appointment of general; COLL., *ˏteng ˏkó pongʼ ʻchai yeuʼ* to ascend heights and fly kites—on the 9th of the 9th moon. Read *taingʼ*: to tread on.

燈 灯 ˏTêng. A lamp; a lantern; *met.*, moral light, the precepts of Budh: in the coll. read *ˏting* and *ˏtiéng*, q. v.: [19]*ˏteng ʻchʻó*, the Scirpus capsularis, Lour., a pith used for wicks; [20]*ˏteng ˏngó*, a miller, a moth.

簦 ˏTêng. A bamboo mat or covering, such as hucksters use to keep off the rain; a sort of umbrella.

䔲 ˏTêng. Name of a plant: [21]*ˏking ˏteng*, a kind of golden rod or hypericum.

ˏTeng. A coll. word: to prick, to bruise, as the foot by treading on things; *met.*, to in-

---

[1] 雨澤 [2] 潤澤 [3] 澤瀉 [4] 恩澤 [5] 特牲 [6] 特諭 [7] 特意 [8] 特字 通知 [9] 毒藥 [10] 嘴毒 [11] 毒心 [12] 毒蠓 [13] 登時 [14] 豐登 [15] 登登 [16] 登籍 [17] 五子 登科 [18] 登山 渡水 [19] 燈草 [20] 燈蛾 [21] 金䔲

jure: ˏ*teng tóh*ˎ to bruise, as the foot; ʻ*kong wu*ˀ ˏ*teng tóh*ˎ ʻ*ngwai*, he injured me by what he said.

ʻ**等** Têng. A class, kind, degree, sort, species; the same, like, equal; a grade, a rank; to wait, to attend; a sign of the plural; to compare: used for the coll. ʻ*ting*, q. v.: [1]ʻ*teng ngek*, official grade; ʻ*teng haiu*ˀ to wait for; [2]ʻ*teng loi*ˀ sorts, classes; [3]ʻ*teng* ˏ*ing*, or ʻ*teng* ˏ*iu*, such like causes or circumstances; [4]ʻ*ngó* ʻ*teng*, we, us; ʻ*i* ʻ*teng*, you all; COM., *siong*ˀ ˏ*tüng ha*ˀ ˏ*sang* ʻ*teng*, the three classes, upper, middle, and lower; *ek*ˎ ʻ*teng*, the first class of; *pok*ˎ ʻ*teng*, or *chak*ˎ *pok*ˎ ʻ*teng*, different, unlike; mixed kinds.

ʻ**點** Tien. Read ʻ*tiéng*; coll. ʻ*teng*: a dot, a black spot; a stain, spotted; the stroke of a clock, an hour; to count, to reckon, to look over and see that a number is complete; to call a roll; to detail, to draft, as troops; to appoint; to discover, to bring to light: [5]ʻ*teng o*ˀ a spot, a stain; [6]ʻ*kwi* ʻ*teng* ˏ*chüng*, what o'clock is it? [7]*lang*ˀ ʻ*teng kwo*ˀ past two o'clock; ʻ*teng kwo*ˀ to count over; [8]ʻ*teng saung*ˀ to reckon, to count up; [9]ʻ*teng hwa*ˀ metamorphoses, as of Budhas and elves; [10]ʻ*teng p'ó*ˀ to detect and expose (a fault); [11]ʻ*teng* ˏ*ping*, to detail troops; [12]ʻ*teng ka*ˀ to take an inventory of goods, as on re-opening shop in the 1st month; [13]ʻ*teng* ˏ*miâng*, to call the roll; ʻ*teng t'iék*ˎ ˏ*sing* ˏ*king*, can turn iron into gold! — has superior talent.

ʻ**典** Tien. Read ʻ*tiéng*; coll. ʻ*teng*: to mortgage: [14]ʻ*teng taung*ˀ to mortgage and pawn; to pawn; [15]ʻ*teng ngiék*ˎ to mortgage property; [16]ʻ*teng k'ié*ˀ a mortgage; ʻ*teng kwo*ˀ ʻ*chio*, mortgaged to another person; ʻ*teng* ʻ*chio*, the mortgagee; *ch'ok*ˎ ʻ*teng*, to mortgage; ʻ*teng k'ié*ˀ *mwoi*ˀ *twang*ˀ only mortgaged, not sold—hence redeemable.

矴ˀ **碇**ˀ Ting. Ballast; a stone used for an anchor; in the coll. an anchor, a grapnel: COLL., [17]*teng*ˀ *sóh*ˎ an anchor-cable; [18]ˏ*p'a teng*ˀ to cast anchor; [19]ʻ*k'i teng*ˀ to weigh anchor; [20]*p'ah*ˎ *teng*ˀ to anchor, to moor.

定ˀ **頂**ˀ Ting. The forehead, the front of anything; to capitalize by placing a character higher in the line: the 1st also read *teng*ˀ q. v.: ˏ*tá teng*ˀ the forehead, the front of.

鎮ˀ **鎭**ˀ Chên. To press down; to repress, to keep in subjection; to pacify; to quell, to overrule evil influences, as hills do; to guard, to protect; a mart, an entrepôt; in the coll. paper-ingots: [21]*teng*ˀ *ak*ˎ to quell disturbances; COM., [22]*teng*ˀ ʻ*siu*, to guard, as a frontier; *teng*ˀ ˏ*tai*, a brigadier; [23]*ch'e*ˀ *teng*ˀ a market, a busy mart; COLL., *teng*ˀ *k'o*ˀ to "keep the treasury" — the first ingot which is put in and retained for luck; paper ingots in idolatry; *teng*ˀ *tiâng*ˀ ˏ*mó tek*ˎ *kwo*ˀ *oi*ˀ to be confined to a place or employment, to be "a fixture".

1 等級 2 等類 3 等因 4 我等 5 點汚 6 幾點鐘 7 二點過 8 點算 9 點化 10 點破 11 點兵 12 點架 13 點名 14 典當 15 典業 16 典契 17 矴索 18 抛矴 19 起矴 20 拍矴 21 鎮壓 22 鎮守 23 市鎮

釘 Ting. To nail, to fasten with nails; to bind, as books: in the coll. to sting, as bees; severe, as blows: also read ,ting, q. v.: COM., [1]teng' ,ting, to drive a nail; [2]teng' ,chü, to bind books; [3]teng' 'si, to kill by nailing fast; [4]teng' 'peng ,pang, to lay a floor; COLL., [5],p'ung teng' the bee stings; [6]p'ah, 'yă teng' to strike heavy blows, to beat severely.

Teng'. A coll. word, for which the last may be used: to stitch: [7]teng' ,á, to stitch shoes round the tops and on the toes; [8]teng' tek, ,ch'u, coarsely stitched or seamed.

訂 Ting. To revise, to criticise; to edit, to collate; to arrange, to adjust, as taxes; to settle the terms, to make an agreement; to fix upon, as a day; to delay: [9]kau' teng' to collate and edit a work; COM., [10]'loi [2] teng' to make a collection; a collection, as of model essays; [11]teng' yok, to enter into an agreement.

Teng'. A coll. word: strong, high flavored, as infusions; deep, as colors: ,ta k'ak, teng' the tea is too strong; teng' ,lang, a deep blue; teng' ,t'ó ,ĕng, a deep peach-red.

Teng'. A coll. euphonic prefix, as in teng' taung' to pawn; to jolt, to jounce up and down.

澄 ,Teng. Ch'êng. Still water; pure, clear, limpid: [12],teng ,ch'ing, very limpid; still, quiet, as a place.

瞪 ,Teng. To look straight at, to fix the eye on, to gaze, to stare: [13],teng se' to gaze at.

棖 ,Teng. The side posts of a door; to follow; a staff: [14],teng chĕü' to cause one to comply.

疼 ,T'êng. A pain, an ache; acute pain; used by some in the sense of affection, extreme regard for: [15],teng t'ong' severe pain, as in the bowels.

滕 ,T'êng. Water spurting and dashing about; to mouth words, to brag; vacant, empty; a feudal state, now the district of T'êng in Shantung.

螣 ,T'êng. A flying serpent, fabled to rise to the clouds and cause rain.

騰 ,T'êng. To leap, as a horse; to run, to gallop; to mount up, to ascend: COM., [16],teng ,hung ka' o' to mount to the clouds and ride the mist, as said of Budhs and fairies.

謄 ,T'êng. To copy, to transcribe: COM., [17],teng lioh, to copy out; [18],teng lioh, 'ch'iu, the copyists of essays at examinations; [19],teng lioh, ,kwang, a superintendent of copyists; [20],teng ,wong, written on yellow paper.

塡 ,Tien. T'ien. To stop, to fill up; to make up a deficiency, to add to; to pay; to forfeit, as life; flowing, confluent; complying; a rumbling, as of drums: also read ,tiéng,

[1]釘	[3]釘	棚	野	[8]釘	訂	[11]訂	[13]瞪	[15]疼	騰	[18]謄	錄
釘	死	[5]蜂	釘	的	[10]彙	約	視	痛	霧	錄	官
[2]釘	[4]釘	釘	[7]釘	粗	訂	[12]澄	[14]棖	[16]騰	[17]謄	手	[20]謄
書	板	[6]拍	鞋	[9]校	〇	清	柱	雲	錄	[19]謄	黃

q. v.: COM., [1]ˏ*teng* ʻ*mwang*, filled up, entirely stopped; [2]ˏ*teng* ʻ*siă*, to fill blanks in writing; ˏ*teng piéngˀ* ʻ*lang*, to note in the schedule or register, as a student's name and antecedents; [3]ˏ*teng* ˏ*kĕng*, to fill the river; *met.*, hope you'll be drowned! COLL., ˏ*teng* ʻ*mai*, to spoil a sale, as by depreciating the goods. Read ˏ*ting:* to fix, to settle. Read ˏ*ting:* a long time. Read ʻ*tiéng:* exhausted, diseased; liberal.

還 ʻHuan. Read ˏ*hwang;* used for the coll. ˏ*teng:* to repay, to cancel a debt; to restore, to give back, as a borrowed article: [4]ˏ*teng chaiˀ* to pay a debt; [5]ˏ*teng* ʻ*pwong chĕüˀ léˀ* to pay principal (by installments) without interest; [6]ˏ*teng* ʻ*ngwai*, to pay me; to return it to me; [7]ˏ*teng kaˀ* to offer one a lower price; ˏ*teng* ˏ*ch'ing*, to let a daughter go to be married; ˏ*teng soˀ mĕkˏ* to settle an account.

定ˀ Ting. Settled, fixed; tranquil, secure; surely, certainly; positively, absolutely; to set, to fix, to settle on; to bring to a state of rest; to decide, to determine, to adjust: also read *tengˀ* q. v.: [8]ˏ*ang tengˀ* at rest; [9]*tengˀ* ˏ*yong*, absolutely; COM., [10]*pekˏ tengˀ* it must be; [11]*ekˏ tengˀ* positively; [12]*tengˀ* ˏ*sing*, to quiet the mind; [13]*tengˀ p'engˀ* to agree definitely on a betrothal; [14]*ikˏ tengˀ* in a trance, abstracted, as Budhists; COLL., *tengˀ* ˏ*chü*, to recite by reading, not repeating memoriter.

綻ˀ Chan. A rent seam; to rip, to tear; a hint, an inkling: [15]*tengˀ liékˏ* to rip seams; COM., [16]*p'óˀ tengˀ* to hint a matter, to divulge inadvertently.

錠ˀ Ting. A salver or trencher with feet, used in sacrifices; an alloy of tin or tutenag; an ingot, a shoe of bullion, in which sense read *tiăngˀ* in the coll. q. v.

陣ˀ Chên. 陳ˀ Ch'ên. A rank, a battalion, a file of soldiers; an army; a company, a flock; to marshal, to place in ranks; a while, transitory; a gust, a shower; a spell, as of pain: the 2d also read ˏ*ting*, q. v.: [17]*pwoˀ tengˀ* to marshal columns; COM., [18]ˏ*pá tengˀ* to post troops; in rank, in file; [19]*chiéngˀ tengˀ* an army in battle; [20]*paiˀ tengˀ* a defeated army; [21]*tengˀ* ˏ*wong*, to die in battle; [22]*tengˀ siéˀ* the ranks, files; COLL., *siohˏ* ˏ*kung tengˀ* a company, a squad; a flock, a herd; ˏ*hung siohˏ tengˀ* a gust of wind; *siohˏ tengˀ kwoˀ siohˏ tengˀ t'iăngˀ* successive pains, as in parturition; *chóˀ tengˀ* to bear (one) company.

朕ˀ 朕ˀ Chên. Chêng. Shên. Anciently used for I; now used only by the Emperor, We, Ourself: [23]*tengˀ tieuˀ* subtile, recondite; incipient springs of action.

Tengˀ. A coll. word: to place or set in, as a cup of tea in water to cool it: ˏ*tó tengˀ siohˏ aˀ* take and set it in (the water).

[1]塡滿 [2]塡寫 [3]塡江 [4]還債 [5]還本住利 [6]還我 [7]還價 [8]安定 [9]定然 [10]必定 [11]一定 [12]定心 [13]定聘 [14]入定 [15]綻裂 [16]破綻 [17]布陣 [18]排陣 [19]戰陣 [20]敗陣 [21]陣亡 [22]陣勢 [23]朕兆

*Teng*ʾ. A coll. euphonic prefix, as in *tengʾ taĕngʾ* to move; shaken, agitated; *tengʾ taungʾ* to fall down, to drop, as rain; *tengʾ tangʾ* to drive hoops, as a cooper does.

(794) Tëng.

冬 ꜀Tung. The winter season; the close, the end; to store up: [1]*꜁chang ꜀tëng*, the 12th month; COM., [2]*꜀tëng ꜀t'au*, the beginning of winter; harvest in the 10th month; [3]*꜀tëng* [4]*꜀t'iéng*, or *꜀tëng kiéʾ* the winter season; [4]*꜀tëng cheʾ* the winter solstice—22d solar term; *꜀tëng chaik꜀*, *꜀mang haʾ cheʾ nik꜀* the night of the winter, and day of the summer, solstice—are the longest; COLL., *꜀tëng chaik꜀ ch'áʾ wangʾ ꜀t'ong ꜀wong*, to barter the solstice rice-flour for boiled dumplings; *met.*, to gain nothing by the process; *꜀tëng ꜂chi*, chilblains.

佟 ꜀T'ung. A surname: [5]*꜀Tai ꜀tëng*, a famous sorcerer in the Han dynasty.

東 ꜀Tung. Read *꜀tung;* coll. *꜀tëng:* the east; *met.*, this, this one; here: [6]*꜀tëng ꜀hwong* or [7]*꜀tëng siéʾ* the east quarter; [8]*꜀tëng paĕk꜀*, north-east; [9]*꜀tëng óh꜀* a title of the god *T'aiʾ ꜀sang;* *꜀tëng ꜂tó ꜀sá ꜀wai*, to lounge here and there; *꜀tëng ꜀t'wa ꜀sá pek꜀* or *꜀tëng ꜂ch'iăng ꜀sá ꜀ch'wi*, pulled here and there, pressed with invitations from different parties; *꜀tëng ꜂t'ó ꜀ló ꜀sá ꜂t'ó ꜂ku*, the east demands gongs and the west demands drums—dunned by many creditors.

꜀Tëng. A coll. word, as in *꜀tëng ꜂nĕ* (brogue *꜂tëng ꜂nĕ*), where? whither? whence? how? *꜀tëng ꜂nĕ ꜀li*, whence did you come? *꜀tëng ꜂nĕ seʾ ꜀chiong wangʾ* how is it thus!—it is not so; *꜀tëng ꜂nĕ ꜀nĕng*, whence is he? what is his native place?

同 ꜁T'ung. Read *꜁tung;* coll. *꜁tëng:* the same, alike, agreeing; of the same place or age; together, fellow, associate: [10]*꜁tëng yongʾ* the same sort; [11]*꜁tëng hwoiʾ* of the same age; [12]*꜁tëng hóʾ* the same mark, of the same stamp or quality, as goods; [13]*꜁tëng ꜀hiong*, fellow-citizens; [14]*꜁tëng ꜀k'wo*, fellow graduates or Kŭjin.

筒 ꜁T'ung. Read *꜁tung;* coll. *꜁tëng:* a tube, a pipe, a hollow cylinder; a tubular cup: [15]*hóʾ ꜁tëng*, a trumpet; [16]*꜀ing ꜁tëng*, or *꜀yéng ꜁tëng*, a chimney, a flue; [17]*꜀hong ꜁tëng*, a tobacco-pipe; [18]*pek꜀ ꜁tëng*, a pencil-cup; [19]*꜁iu ꜁tëng*, an oil-receiver—made of a joint of bamboo; [20]*꜀hwa ꜁tëng*, a kaleidoscope.

銅 ꜁T'ung. Read *꜁tung* in the dictionaries: copper, brass, called the red metal; of copper, brazen: COM., [21]*꜁tëng taingʾ* a coppersmith's; *꜁tëng k'eʾ* brass or copper utensils; *꜁tëng hooʾ* "brass goods"—counterfeit head-gear; *pah꜀ ꜁tëng*, white copper, tutenag; [22]*꜁wong ꜁tëng*, brass; [23]*꜁tëng lioh꜀* verdigris; [24]*꜁tëng ꜁chiéng*, cash; *꜁tëng yék꜀* "brass leaves"—the round bits of gilt paper in the flowers of a graduate's cap; *꜁tëng ꜀sing t'iék꜀ kauk꜀* an iron constitu-

[1]殘冬 [2]冬頭 [3]冬天 [4]冬至 [5]臺佟 [6]東方 [7]東勢 [8]東北 [9]東嶽 [10]同樣 [11]同歲 [12]同號 [13]同鄉 [14]同科 [15]號筒 [16]烟筒 [17]煙筒 [18]筆筒 [19]油筒 [20]花筒 [21]銅店 [22]黃銅 [23]銅綠 [24]銅錢

tion; COLL., ꜀tĕng ch'au' smells coppery—said of one who buys office.

僮 (꜀T'ung.) Read ꜀tung; used for the coll. ꜀tĕng, as in [1]꜀tĕng ʻchi, or ꜀tĕng ꜀sing, a medium, one who pretends to inspiration; [2]ho' ꜀tĕng, and [3]꜀tĕng ꜀t'au, those who support the ꜀tĕng ʻchi, and invoke the god; [4]p'ah꜀ lóh꜀ ꜀tĕng, to enact the above ceremony; [5]꜀tĕng ꜀t'au ꜀ki ʻmwoi, the beginning of the ꜀tĕng, and the end of the ꜀ki, (ceremonies)—are efficacious or important.

(795) Teu.

兜 (꜀Tou.) A kind of helmet, a morion; shaped like a helmet; to excite, to irritate; to doubt: commonly read ꜀tau, q. v.

㨮 (꜀Tou.) To correct, to criticise; to clip, to cut off; to grasp; to strike; to scheme after, to engross: commonly read ꜀tau, q. v.

篼 (꜀Tou.) Also read ꜀tau: a trough, or pail, for giving a horse drink; a light mountain-sedan: COM., [6]꜀teu kieu' or [7]kwo' ꜀sang ꜀teu, a mountain chair, or light traveling sedan; [8]꜀teu ꜀hu, the bearers; COLL., ʻié ʻkiáng ꜀teu, a small, uncovered chair, having a stick attached by cords to rest the feet on.

雕 (꜀Tiao.) Read ꜀tieu; coll. ꜀teu: to engrave, to cut figures on, to carve; to polish, as an essay; ornamented: [9]꜀teu k'aik꜀, to carve, to cut, as characters; [10]꜀teu tauk꜀, to cut gems; *met.*, to elaborate, as an essay; [11]꜀teu ꜀tó, an engraving-tool; [12]꜀teu ꜀hwa, to adorn with carvings; [13]꜀teu tek꜀, ʻhó, well-engraved; [14]꜀teu sioh꜀ ꜀pwo, to carve a flower; ꜀teu so' ꜀sing ch'iong' to carve and mold idol-images.

꜀Teu. A coll. word: bitterish, harsh in taste: ꜀teu ʻmwi, a bitter taste left (in the mouth); ʻk'u ꜀teu ꜀teu, very bitter.

斗 (Tou. T'ou.) ʻA dry measure of ten ʻching or pints—varies in size; vessels like pecks; the 8th of the 28 constellations; the 68th radical; a wine-vessel: in the coll. read ʻtau, q. v.: COM., [15]paĕk꜀ ʻteu, the Dipper, Ursa Major—rules life; [16]꜀nang ʻteu, the southern polar star—rules death; [17]ʻteu ʻmu, "Peck-mother" — a guardian of children till they are 16 years old; ʻteu ʻmi ꜀sang ꜀ung, a peck of rice for three cash—used as a felicitous phrase; COLL., ʻteu ʻtang, with great boldness, to presume—a polite, deprecatory phrase.

抖 (ʻTou.) To take, to raise, to lift up; to arouse: COM., [18]ʻteu ʻseu ꜀ching ꜀sing, to rouse up one's spirits.

枓 (ʻTou.) The capital, the square block on the top of a pillar. Read ʻchü: a long-handled ladle.

蚪 (ʻTou.) A tadpole: [19]ʻteu ꜀ung, the tadpole head or style; an ancient form of character.

[1]僮子 [2]護僮 [3]僮頭 [4]拍落僮 [5]僮頭乩尾 [6]篼轎 [7]過山篼 [8]篼夫 [9]雕刻 [10]雕琢 [11]雕刀 [12]雕花 [13]雕的好 [14]雕一朵 [15]北斗 [16]南斗 [17]斗母 [18]抖擻精神 [19]蚪文 ○

福州方言拼音字典

糾 'Tou. Also read *'t'eu:* a sort of yellow silk; to announce, to inform; to accuse, to blame or warn.

陡 'Tou. Used in the *Paik, ,Ing* for suddenly; COM., [1]*'teu ,yong ,kang*, suddenly, quickly, unexpectedly.

'Teu. A coll. word: to strike with something limber, to whip, to switch, to lash; pendent: *'teu má' tioh,* failed to hit it; *'teu meng' ,seng,* hanging down in front, as the ends of strings; *'ti 'teu 'teu,* hanging in tatters.

'Teu. A coll. word: to tremble, to shiver, to quake, as with fear: *'teu 'teu chiéng'* in a tremor, trembling.

投 ,T'ou. To throw, to cast down; to reject; to give, to present; to receive; to take away, to remove; to engage to do, to commission, to intrust to; to cast one's self on another, to go to; suiting, agreeing; to cover; to raffle or bid for: in the coll. read *,tau,* q. v.: [2]*,teu ,ki 'su hó'* to like what he likes, sycophantic; [3]*chëü' ,teu ,ló 'wong,* fell into his own snare; COM., [4]*,teu hak,* unanimous, agreeing; [5]*,teu ,ki,* corresponding, suiting, as words pleasing the listener; [6]*k'e' ang' ,teu ,ming,* to reject the dark and come to the light; *met.,* to reform.

條 ,T'iao. A twig, a small branch; applied to certain things that are long and slender; a numerative of long things, as chains, threads, strings, spires of grass, worms, streams, streets, hairs, boats, towels, needles, chopsticks; a bill, an item,. an article, a section, a theme; a law, a rule: COM., [7]*'liu ,teu,* a narrow map or hanging scroll; [8]*,teu pwang'* a piece and a half; [9]*,teu ,teu,* all the items; [10]*,pieu ,teu,* a notice, a posted slip; [11]*,kié ,teu,* regulations; [12]*,teu 'li,* reason, reasonable; [13]*hwak, ,teu,* the mainspring of a watch; COLL., [14]*ek, ,teu ,lüng,* a continuous thread, not spliced; *siáng' sioh, ,teu,* one thread; *,teu ,teu o' 'li,* it is all reasonable; [15]*,teu tik,* a corruption of *,tieu tik,* all right; honest, straightforward. Read *,t'ieu,* as in [16]*,t'ieu lok,* the fall of leaves.

鰷 ,T'iao. A long, slender fish, called [17]*pah, ,teu,* a species of Thrissa?

鞗 ,T'iao. A pair of leathern reins; a bridle.

苕 ,Chao. A kind of edible plant, growing in the summer; a reed or rush, whose tops are fit for brooms: [18]*,ling ,teu,* a marshy plant, whose juice dyes the hair black; *,teu ,teu,* high, lofty.

調 ,Tiao. ,T'iao. Read *,tieu;* coll. *,teu:* to blend ingredients, to compound, to mix in; to spice: [19]*,teu ,siong,* to season with salt; [20]*,teu pwong'* to mix (ingredients) in rice; *,teu hwak, hwak,* to mix it of a ropy consistence.

1陡	其	投	合	暗	條	條	條	條	15條	17白	19調
然	所	羅	5投	投	8條	10標	12條	14一	直	鰷	鹽
間	好	網	機	明	半	條	理	條	16條	18陵	20調
2投	3自	4投	6棄	7挪	9條	11規	13法	龍	落	苕	飯

ˏ*Teu.* A coll. word, analogous to ˊ*teu:* to beat, to castigate, to whip, as with a stick: ˏ*teu* ˊ*heng* ˊ*heng*, to whip severely.

宙² Chou. To contain, as the earth does; the whole period from ancient times to the present, all ages: [1]ˊ*ü teu*ˋ the universe.

胄² Chou. Often confounded with the next: a helmet, a morion: [2]ˊ*kak*ˎ *teu*ˋ cuirass and helmet.

冑² Chou. Posterity, descendants: [3]ˊ*sie*ˋ *teu*ˋ generations of men; [4]*teu*ˋ ˊ*chü*, the eldest son; [5]ˊ*yo*ˋ *teu*ˋ posterity.

稻² The grain of rice in the ear, the ripe grain; rent, taxes: COM., [6]*teu*ˋ *sük*ˎ rice ripened; [7]*teu*ˋ ˊ*kó*, rice stalks; [8]*teu*ˋ *ch'ok*ˎ *soi*ˋ the rice has headed; [9]*kak*ˎ *teu*ˋ to reap rice; COLL., [10]*saëk*ˎ *teu*ˋ to thresh rice; [11]*teu*ˋ ˏ*k'wong* and [12]*teu*ˋ ˊ*ma*, frames or stands on which rice is threshed—the former is used in the fields, the latter at home.

酎² New spirits, liquor thrice distilled; pure, strong wine; rich, mellow spirits, used in ancestral temples.

紂² Chou. Used for the next: a crupper; a silk trace; used in epitaphs for cruel, unjust, as applied to emperors or officers: COM., [13]*teu*ˋ ˏ*wong*, the infamous prince, Chousin, who ended the Shang dynasty.

[革紂]² Chou. A crupper; also a horse's bridle.

*Teu*ˋ. A coll. word: to dwell, to reside, to live in or at; also a suffix having the force of able at the end of some English words: *teu*ˋ *ch'io*ˋ to live in a house; ˏ*tĕng* ˊ*nĕ teu*ˋ where do you reside? *teu*ˋ *sük*ˎ or *teu*ˋ *kaing*ˋ accustomed to or acquainted by long residence; ˏ*eng teu*ˋ to stay at home with nothing to do; ˏ*tong mă*ˋ *teu*ˋ intolerable; ˊ*kwang â*ˋ *teu*ˋ can be governed, manageable.

(796) Tĕü.

著² Chu. Cho. Chao. Chè. To manifest, to set forth; clear, conspicuous; to narrate, to compose and publish books; to settle; a porch: also read *chiok*ˎ q. v.: [14]*tĕü*ˋ ˏ*ming* or ˏ*ming tĕü*ˋ an illustrious name, famed; [15]ˊ*hiĕng tĕü*ˋ to manifest; [16]*tĕü*ˋ *suk*ˎ to write a narrative; COM., [17]*tĕü*ˋ ˏ*chü lik*ˎ *siok*ˎ to compose a book.

箸² 筯² Chu. Chopsticks: COM., [18]ˏ*nga tĕü*ˋ ivory chopsticks; [19]*tĕü*ˋ ˏ*p'wi*, chopsticks in the rough, common unpainted ones; [20]ˏ*ki* ˏ*kang tĕü*ˋ chopsticks rounded like a flagstaff; [21]*tĕü*ˋ ˏ*tĕng* and (coll.) *tĕü*ˋ *laĕng*ˋ (or *taĕng*ˋ), two sorts of cups for holding chopsticks; ˏ*chio tĕü*ˋ red painted chopsticks; COLL., *tĕü*ˋ *sioh*ˎ ˏ*k'iă*, one chopstick.

*Tĕü*ˋ. A coll. word, used in the sense of *tioh*ˎ: to be at or in a place, present; *tĕü*ˋ ˏ*mó*

---

1 宇宙 2 甲胄 3 世胄 4 胄子 5 裔胄 6 稻熟 7 稻稿 8 稻出穗 9 割稻 ○ 10 摔稻 11 稻楻 12 稻馬 13 紂王 14 著名 15 顯著 16 著述 17 著書立說 18 牙筯 19 筯坯 20 旗杆筯 21 筯筒 ○

*tëü*² is he present or not? *tëü*² *꜀tëng* ʻ*nē*, where is he or it?

(797) Tëük.

竹 Chu. The bamboo; one of the eight musical notes: ¹*tëük*, *choi*² *nik*, the 13th day of the 5th month; ²*tëük*, *꜀wong*, tabasheer; COM., ³*tëük*, ʻ*sung*, bamboo sprouts; ⁴*tëük*, *chaik*, the joints of the bamboo; ⁵*tëük*, *꜀si*, bamboo shavings, as for calking, etc.; ⁶*tëük*, *꜀ü*, (or *꜀üng*), the outer coat of the bamboo—contains silex and is used as a medicine; ⁷*tëük*, *mŏh*, the inner pellicle of bamboo—used for flute-stops; ⁸*tëük*, *꜀kó*, poles for propelling boats; ⁹*tëük*, *꜀t*ʻ*au ꜀mau*, a sort of bamboo helmet; ¹⁰*tëük*, *lek*, *꜀siéng*, salted sap of the *lek*, bamboo—a febrifuge; COLL., ¹¹*tëük*, *꜀p*ʻ*ié*, a bamboo stick for punishing children.

竺 Chu. A kind of bamboo; a surname and name of a country: COM., ¹²*꜀t*ʻ*iéng tëük*, *kwok*, India, the land where Budh was born.

筑 Chu. A sort of bamboo dulcimer having 13 cords; also to collect, to gather up.

築 築 Chu. To pound earth as in making pavements of cement; to make adobe bricks; to pile and beat earth solid; to flap the wings; to incite, to urge one; a dwelling: ¹³*ch*ʻ*wi tëük*, to urge, to prompt; COM., ¹⁴*tëük*, *꜀ch*ʻ*iong*, to make a wall of earth by pounding it between two sets of boards; COLL., *tëük*, *꜀t*ʻ*u ꜀tong*, to make adobe bricks; *tëük*, *꜀sang kak*, ʻ*t*ʻ*u*, to make a cement pavement; COLL., *tëük*, *꜀kai*, to stuff a fowl's crop; *tëük*, ʻ*ch*ʻ*ü*, a pounder used in making mud walls. Read *tük*, : a pestle with a handle.

*T*ʻ*ëük*,. A coll. word, about the same as *kek*, to stir up, to excite, as to anger: ʻ*tiu tëük*, to excite, to move one to do.

*T*ʻ*ëük*,. A coll. word: to reckon without the abacus, to sum up mentally: *tëük*, *siong*² to reckon up; *ch*ʻ*oi*² *tëük*, to reckon with the mouth or mentally.

(798) Tëüng.

中 Chung. Ch'ung. To hit the center; struck, hit; to attain, to accomplish; fit, suitable, exact: also read *꜀tüng*, q. v.: COM., ¹⁵*tëüng*² *é*² to suit one's wish, to like, pleased with; ¹⁶*tëüng*² *ëüng*² (coll. *tëüng*² ʻ*sai*), fit for use; ¹⁷*tëüng*² *siäh*, good to eat; ¹⁸*tëüng*² *꜀hung*, palsied; ¹⁹*tik*, *tëüng*² to have an apoplectic fit; ²⁰*tëüng*² ʻ*kü*, to become a Küjin; ²¹*tëüng*² *kié*² entrapped; COLL., *ng*² *tëüng*² *tih*, not desirable, wholly worthless, as men or things; *tëüng*² *sioh*, *chiéng*² to hit (the mark) with an arrow.

仲 Chung. Ch'ung. The second of three; the second brother; the second month of a season; a musical instrument: ²²*paik*, *tëüng*² two brothers; *tëüng*² *꜀ná*, name of Confucius, who was the second brother; COM., *꜀k*ʻ*ong tëüng*² brothers; *tëüng*² *ha*² the 5th month.

¹竹醉日 ²竹黃 ³竹筍 ⁴竹節 ⁵竹絲 ⁶竹菇 ⁷竹膜 ⁸竹篙 ⁹竹頭鍪 ¹⁰竹瀝鹽 ¹¹竹披 ¹²天竺國 ¹³推築 ¹⁴築牆 ¹⁵中意 ¹⁶中用 ¹⁷中食 ¹⁸中風 ¹⁹直中 ²⁰中舉 ²¹中計 ²²伯仲

重ʼ Chung. Ch'ung. Heavy; important, momentous; severe, heinous; respectable, grave, decorous; to attach importance to; expresses a superlative degree of: also read ˏtüng, and in the coll. taĕngʼ and ˏt'üng, q. v.: [1]ʻsengʼ tĕüngʼ careful, grave; COM., [2]chĕüʼ tĕüngʼ self-respect; [3]tĕüngʼ ĕüngʼ to employ one in weighty matters; [4]tĕüngʼ ngiéʼ to give importance to right; [5]ʻung tĕüngʼ steady, trusty; [6]tĕüngʼ hoʼ ˏk'i ˏping, to court the rich and despise the poor.

(799) Ti.

ˏ知 Chih. To know, to understand; to perceive, to apprehend; acquainted with; to be intimate, as a friend, an associate; to inform; knowledge, prudence; ruling, as applied to certain magistrates: also read teʼ q. v.: COM., [7]ˏu ˏti, ignorant; [8]ˏti sek, knowledge, understanding; [9]ˏti tóʼ to understand; [10]ˏti kauk, to perceive, to notice; [11]ˏt'ung ˏti, to tell, to inform; [12]ˏti chĕük, contented; [13]ˏu ʻsu pok, ˏti, omniscient; ˏti k'ah, or ˏti k'ah, ˏsü, those who receive guests, as at a monastery; [14]ˏti ˏing, or ˏti ˏsing, intimate, as friends; [15]ˏti ʻhu, a prefect; [16]eʼ pok, ˏsiéng ˏti, to know without resorting to divination; COLL., ˏti ʻsi ˏp'ang ˏk'i ngʼ ʻsai ch'iéngʼ a crab that knows how to die needs no stabbing; *met.*, one conscious of his guilt need not be charged with it.

ˏ蜘 Chih. A plant, affodile: COM., ˏti ʻmu, affodile, used as an expectorant.

ˏ胝 Ti. Also read ˏchiĕ: thick, indurated skin, as on the hands; to grow callous; corns on the feet.

ˏ*Ti.* A coll. word: hanging, suspended: ˏti ˏtu ˏtu, or ˏti ˏti ˏtu ˏtu, hanging all about, as things from a ceiling.

ˏ*Ti.* A coll. word: a corruption of tiĕʼ which? what? ˏti sioh, chiăh, which one?

ˏ*Ti.* A coll. word, as in sioh, ˏti ˏti, very little of, a mere mite; sioh, ˏpi ˏti (or ˏt'i), a bunch, a cluster.

ʻ氐 Ti. To arrive at; reaching, arriving at; to return or revert to; the origin; radical, fundamental; low, as in price; base, inferior; a lodging place for the night; the 3d of the 28 constellations, *a*, *b*, *g*, and *i* in Libra: [17]ʻti ʻsiu, to bow the head; [18]ʻti ˏing, the people of a certain country, described as mermaids.

ʻ牴 Ti. To push with the horns, to gore; to come in contact with, to oppose: [19]taiʼ ʻti, generally speaking; [20]kaĕk, ʻti, to butt and gore; mixed music.

ʻ邸 Ti. The place where feudatories lodged at the capital; a hotel, a lodging-house; a court or royal residence; the bottom, the basis or support; a stand for a scepter; a screen outside a door; to reach, to arrive at: [21]ʻlü ʻti, an inn; ʻti ˏking, to reach the capital.

[1]慎重 [3]重用 [5]穩重 欺貧 [8]知識 [10]知覺 [12]知足 不知 [15]知府 先知 [18]氐人 [20]角牴

[2]自重 [4]重義 [6]重富 [7]無知 [9]知道 [11]通知 [13]無所 [14]知音 [16]未卜 [17]氐首 [19]大牴 [21]旅邸

ʻ**抵** Ti. To oppose, to resist; to stop, to ward off, to rush against; to sustain, to bear the blame; to offend, to transgress; to forfeit; to reach, extending, up to; equal in value, to pay an equivalent: in the coll. read ʻ*tá*, q. v.: [1]*tai*ʾ ʻ*ti*, for the most part; COM., [2]ʻ*ti* ˏ*tong*, to sustain or bear the blame of; [3]*tói*ʾ ʻ*ti*, to barter, to exchange; [4]ʻ*ti* ˏ*siong*, to atone for, to forfeit, as one's life; [5]ʻ*ti chai*ʾ or ʻ*ti so*ʾ to pay a debt with an equivalent; COLL., ʻ*ti* ʻ*la kek*, to meet a pressing exigency, as by borrowing; ʻ*ti tek*, *tik*ˏ to make both ends meet, to cancel outlays by gains; ʻ*ti má*ʾ ˏ*kʻwi*, unable to meet all expenses.

ʻ**柢** Ti. The trunk of a tree, the part near the ground; the root, the foundation: [6]ˏ*kong* ʻ*ti*, the root; the origin, foundation.

ʻ**砥** Ti. A grindstone, a mill-stone; a hone or whetstone; level, smoothed; *met.*, to polish one's conduct, as by regarding rules: [7]ʻ*ti lá*ʾ a grindstone; to reform one's self.

ʻ**詆** Ti. To scold, to blame; to charge falsely; to vilify: [8]ʻ*ti paung*ʾ or ʻ*ti* ʻ*u*, to slander, to defame; [9]ʻ*chʻiu* ʻ*ti*, to vilify.

ʻ**軧** Ti. The back part of a large carriage; the nave or hub of an axle, projecting beyond the wheel.

ʻ**弤** Ti. The famous bow of the emperor Shun; a red bow; a bow with ornamental carvings on it.

ʻ**舐** Ti. To lick; to lap; to take up with the proboscis.

ʻ**底** ʻ**底** Ti. To dwell at the foot of a mountain; the base, bottom, foundation; below, beneath, at the bottom; a first copy; sediment, remnant; to stop at, to reach the bottom; to impede, to obstruct; low, menial, as a servant; but, only: in the coll. read ʻ*tá*, q. v.: [10]ˏ*u* ʻ*ti*, bottomless; [11]ʻ*sieu* ʻ*ti*, attendants; COLL., [12]ʻ*ti* ʻ*chi*, the antecedents of, a clue to; [13]ˏ*mó* ʻ*ti* ʻ*chi*, no antecedents or clue to; no bottom to—no way of counting the articles, because so many.

ʻ**褫** Chʻih. To take off clothes, to denude, to disrobe; to take away insignia; a fringe: [14]ʻ*ti kaik*, to degrade; [15]ʻ*ti* ˏ*chiĕng*, plush, felt.

ʻ*Ti.* A coll. euphonic prefix, as in ʻ*ti* ʻ*tau*, to shake things; ʻ*ti* ʻ*teu* ʻ*teu*, suspended, hanging in shreds or tatters; ʻ*ti* ʻ*tó*, or ʻ*ti* ʻ*ti* ʻ*tó* ʻ*tó*, to recline, to lie down.

羝 ˏTi. Read ˏ*ti* in the dictionaries; a ram three years old; a ram, a buck, a he-goat.

蚳 ˏTi. The eggs or larvae of ants: [16]ˏ*lung* ˏ*ti*, a fabulous animal, described as a horned pig.

---

[1] 大抵 [2] 抵當 [3] 對抵 [4] 抵償 [5] 抵債 [6] 根柢 [7] 砥礪 [8] 詆謗 [9] 醜詆 [10] 無底 [11] 小底 [12] 底止 [13] 無底止 [14] 褫革 [15] 褫氈 [16] 蠪蚳

坻 ˓Ti. An islet; a bank or ledge in a stream; an embankment; to bank in, to stop: [1]*ʻpang ˓ti*, a bank, a levee.

墀 ˓Ch'ih. A porch, a portico; a vestibule or piazza at the top of steps; a slightly elevated walk between the gate and the palace: [2]*˓tang ˓ti*, the vermillion porch or avenue—the emperor's palace.

遲 ˓Ch'ih. To delay, to walk leisurely; slow, dilatory; late, tardy; to procrastinate; hesitating: [3]*˓ch'ă ˓ti*, to lodge at, to stop and wait for; [4]*˓ti te²* impeded; COM., [5]*˓ti ˓yong* or *˓ti hwang²* (coll. *˓ti maing²*), late, tardy; [6]*˓ti ʻcha*, late and early: [7]*˓ti ˓ngi pok, kiok,* hesitating and unable to decide; [8]*˓ti ˓sang nik,* after three days; COLL., *t'ŏi² hwoi² k'ak, ˓ti*, to repent too late; *˓li tek, ˓ti*, to come late. Read *te²:* to wait for.

馳 ˓Ch'ih. Also read *˓t'i:* to ride rapidly, to gallop, as couriers; to go fast; a fleet horse; far, spread abroad: [9]*˓ti tŏ²*; the middle road, that one over which the emperor travels.

˓Ti. A coll. euphonic prefix, as in *˓ti ˓tui*, to beat, to hammer; *˓ti ˓teu*, to mix, to stir in; *˓ti ˓tau*, to inform, to tell, as one's grievances; *˓ti ˓tu*, to plaster; *˓ti ˓tŏ*, to take.

(800) Tiă.

爹 ˓Tieh. A father: *˓tiă ˓tiă*, papa! COM., [10]*˓tiă ʻná*, father and mother; [11]*ʻlŏ ˓tiă*, his Honor, the officer; COLL., [12]*˓i ˓tiă*, papa! *˓tiă ˓mŏ ˓ch'ing ʻná ˓mŏ ch'ek,* not related to him either on father's or mother's side; *˓tiă o² ʻná o² ˓mŏ niăh, che² o²* papa and mamma's having (money) is not like having it one's self!

˓Tiă. A coll. word; weak, debilitated, drooping; dull, lifeless, as poor eyes; *˓tiă ˓tiă*, or *ʻyă ˓tiă*, very weak; *mek, ˓chiu ˓tiă ˓tiă*, his eyes are dull and leaden.

(801) Tiăh.

摘 Chai. Tsê. Read *chaik,;* used for the coll. *tiăh,:* to lay hold of; to pick, to pluck, to cull; [13]*tiăh, ˓hwa*, to pluck flowers; [14]*tiăh, ˓ta*, or *tiăh, ˓ta nioh,* to pick tea; [15]*tiăh, eng²* to take away (an officer's) seal; [16]*tiăh, ˓kŭng*, "nip the root"—nip it in the bud, as a youth's vice.

糴 Ti. Read *tik,;* coll. *tiăh,:* to buy, to lay in a supply, as of rice: [17]*tiăh, ʻmi*, to buy rice; [18]*tiăh, tau²* to purchase beans; [19]*tiăh, ˓ki ʻkiăng*, a purchased boy; [20]*tiăh, p'ang² ch'ioh,* to buy blighted rice; *met.*, to buy poor cash to mix with the good, as bankers do.

Tiăh,. A coll. word: to throw dice, called *tiăh, ˓tau;* *tiăh, laung²* to throw for eggs; *tiăh, ˓nĕng ʻkiăng*, to throw for toy-images; *tiăh, ˓chŏ ˓ngwong ˓t'iu,*

1	3	5	7	8	9	11	13	15	17	19	20
坂坻	棲遲	遲 6延	遲疑	遲三	馳道	老爹	摘花	摘印	糴米	糴其	糴有
2 丹墀	4 遲滯	遲早	不決	日〇	10 爹奶	12 阿爹	14 摘茶	16 摘根	18 糴豆	仔〇	粟〇

a game with bamboo slips, inscribed with literary grades.

(802) Tiăk.

Tiăk, A coll. word: to cheat, to overreach, to cozen: *tiăk, kwo' 'ch'iu* (or *siĕng'*), to succeed in cheating one; *tik, tiăk,* or *hak, tiăk,* to humbug by crying up one's goods.

Tiăk,. A coll. word: to expose to, to let the wind blow on; borne by the wind, as perfume; *tiăk, taĕng'* to cool by exposure to the wind; *tiăk, p'e'* to scent it; *,hiong k'e' tiăk, kwo' ,li,* the fragrance wafted over to one.

(803) Tiăng.

偵 Chĕng. Ch'ĕng. Read *,t'ing;* coll. *'tiăng:* to spy; to lie in wait, to watch for: [1]*'tiăng ch'ek,* to watch for thieves; [2]*'tiăng k'aĕng'* (or *laĕng'*), a brief respite in watching; *met.*, an interval of leisure; *'tiăng 'tiăng ,hŭ,* the watch intermitted, off one's guard; *,ma 'tiăng 'ch'ü,* a cat watching rats; *met.*, to do or act on the sly, as when the master is out.

鼎 鼏 Ting. Read *'t'ing;* coll. *'tiăng:* a frying pan of brass or iron: [3]*'tiăng chau'* pans and furnaces; [4]*'tiăng ,muo,* molds for casting pans; [5]*'tiăng ,sai,* the center of a pan's bottom on the outside; [6]*'tiăng kah,* a steaming-grate; [7]*'tiăng p'iĕng'* a flat pan-cover; [8]*'tiăng 't'ĕ* (or *ch'iăh,*), a small shovel for turning things in cooking; [9]*kauk, 'tiăng,* to scrape pan-bottoms; [10]*'tiăng ,piĕng kŏh,* cakes steamed on the pan's side; [11]*p'ok, 'tiăng,* the convex top of a grave; *'tiăng ,piĕng ,ku ,ung 'la cheu' sŭk,* rice-batter on the pan's side cooks through as soon as thrown on; *met.*, very sociable, soon acquainted.

Tiăng'. A coll. word: strong, intense, as a scent; intensely fragrant: *e' 'yă tiăng'* the scent is very strong.

呈 Ch'ĕng. Also spoken *,t'iăng:* a statement, a plea; a written accusation; to present a statement; to show, to set forth, to petition: also read *,t'ing*, q. v.: com., [12]*,tiăng ,sü,* a written statement; [13]*,tiăng ,ki,* the set days for sending in petitions—the 3d, 13th, 23d, 8th, 18th, 28th of the month; [14]*,tiăng ,kwang keu' te'* to petition a magistrate to investigate and decide; [15]*'tá' ,tiăng,* to present a petition; [16]*,ch'iĕng ,tiăng,* a united petition or accusation.

埕 Ch'ĕng. An unauthorized character, used for the coll. *,tiăng:* an area, a space before a house: [17]*,k'ĕng ,tiăng*, or *,t'u ,tiăng,* a plat; [18]*pong' tó' ,tiăng,* ground where refuse is thrown; [19]*p'woh, ch'ioh, ,tiăng,* an area for drying grain.

,Tiăng. A coll. word: to fall on, to crush; knocked, banged; to pour in, to add to; to give a hint; also to rebound, to bounce; to splash; to fall from concussion: *,tiăng 'si,* crushed to death; *,tiăng tioh, ,t'au,* to get a thump on the head; *,tiăng 'chwi,*

[1]偵賊 [2]偵空 [3]鼎灶 [4]鼎模 [5]鼎臍 [6]鼎格 [7]鼎片 [8]鼎鏟 [9]刮鼎 [10]鼎邊 擱 [11]覆鼎○ [12]呈詞 [13]呈期 [14]呈官究治 [15]遞呈○ [16]簽呈○ [17]空埕 [18]糞倒埕 [19]曝粟埕

to add water; to water, as swill or milk; ꜀tiăng ꜀siăng, to give a hint in words; to give a broad hint, as in dismissing a bore; tó꜄ ꜀tiăng ꜀siăng, an echo; ꜀tiăng ꜂k'i ꜀li, to rebound; to splash, as rain; tó꜄ ꜀tiăng ꜀tung, to fall and rebound.

꜀Tiăng. A coll. word: a peg, a pin or nail for hanging things on: k'a꜄ ꜀tiăng, to drive in a peg; taiu꜄ ꜀tiăng, to "hang by a peg", as one says who has no place to sleep.

定² Ting. Read teng²; coll. tiăng²: steady, fixed; really, surely, absolutely; brought to a state of rest; to fix, to settle on, to adjust; tranquil, serene, peaceful: [1]꜀mó tiăng² or ꜀mó tiăng² tioh꜁ uncertain; [2]tiăng² ꜀chiéng, bargain-money; [3]tiăng² hwo꜄ to contract for goods; [4]tiăng² ngiăh꜁ a fixed amount; tiăng² ꜀t'ëng, a lazy lout; tiăng² chó꜄ to engage to do or make; tiăng² tiăng² sié꜄ in a fixed form; fast, held still; tah꜁ tiăng² to settle a betrothal; tiăng² tiăng² óh, clever without parade or show; ꜀siu tiăng² to receive bargain-money; pauk꜁ tiăng² to return bargain-money; tiăng² ꜀kang p'au꜄ the signal gun of the 1st watch; ꜀sing ꜂pa tiăng² tiăng² tioh꜁ keep your mind at rest!

錠² Ting. Read teng²; coll. tiăng²: an ingot, a shoe of bullion: [5]꜀ngwong ꜂pó tiăng² an ingot of sycee; a door-button; paper-ingots to burn to gods; [6]sek꜁ ꜂liong tiăng² a ten-ounce ingot; [7]꜂chié ꜀king tiăng² a medical preparation for sores.

(804) Tié.

入 ꜂ Ju. Erh. Read ik꜁; used for the coll. ꜂tié: to go in, to enter; to enter (and remain), to become a member of; entrance: [8]꜂tié k'ó꜄ to go in; [9]꜂tié ch'ok, in and out, ingress and egress; [10]꜂tié ꜂ch'iu, got, obtained; [11]꜂hó ꜂tié ꜂k'eu, good to eat; [12]꜂tié yéng² to enter the lazaretto, as a leper; [13]꜂tié ꜀siăng, to go into the city; [14]꜂tié ꜀tiong, to attend the examinations for Küjin.

裡 ꜂ 裏 ꜂ Li. Read ꜂li; coll. ꜂tié: similar to the last; in, within, inside; nearly related: ꜂tié tié꜄ in, within; [15]꜂tié ngié² within and without; [16]꜂ch'io꜄ ꜂tié, in the house; a term for wife; [17]꜂tié ꜂ma ngié² ꜂ma, paternal and maternal grandmothers; ꜂tié eng꜄ ngwoi² hak꜁ treasonable intercourse with outside (enemies).

池 ꜀ Ch'ih. A pond, a pool, a tank; a moat, a ditch, a fosse; stagnant water; the ornamental cover of a coffin: [18]꜀tung ꜀tié, the heart; [19]ngük꜁ ꜀tié, the kidneys; ꜀ch'a ꜀tié, flying, fluttering; [20]꜀tié ꜀tong, a fish-pool; COM., ꜀ngü ꜀tié, a fish-pond; ꜀tié ꜀chu, the rent of a pond; ngau² ꜀tié, a lotus-pond; ꜀tié ꜀loi, a fresh water snail with a greenish shell. Read ꜀tó: diverging streams.

篪 ꜀ Ch'ih. A bamboo musical pipe, a sort of seven-holed flute; its sound resembles the wailing of children: ꜀hüng ꜀tié, the eight-holed and

---

[1]無定 [2]定錢 [3]定貨 [4]定額 [5]元寶錠 [6]十兩錠 [7]紫金錠 [8]入去 [9]入出 [10]入手 [11]好入口 [12]入院 [13]入城 [14]入場 [15]裡外 [16]厝裡 [17]裡媽外媽 [18]中池 [19]玉池 [20]池塘

seven-holed instruments (played together); *met.*, fraternal love.

꜀Tié. A coll. word, as in *mek꜀ ꜀chiu ꜀tié ꜀tié*, the eyes dull and heavy— about the same as in *꜀tiă*, q. v.

弟 Ti. Read *tá*²; coll. *tié*²: a younger brother; a boy, a lad; a junior, used as a compellation: [1]*꜀hiăng tié*² brothers; [3]*sá*² *tié*² a lad; *꜀tié tié*² or [3]*꜀i tié*² my boy! my lad! *tié*² *꜀ing*, or [4]*tié*² *꜀sing mo*² a younger brother's wife; *tié*² *ma*² *꜀hiăng siong*² *꜀kwang ꜀t'iăng*, a younger brother, railing at an elder one, must be taken to the magistrate!

蠣 Li. Read *lá*²; coll. *tié*²: an oyster: [5]*tié*² *꜀pwo*, oysters in the shell; [6]*tié*² *꜀kang*, dried oyster-meat; [7]*tié*² *piăng* and [8]*꜀pau tié*² two sorts of oyster-fritters; [9]*sioh꜀ tié*² a marine shell-fish, like an oyster.

*Tié*². A coll. word: an interrogative pronoun, qualifying the following noun, which, what, whose; whoever, whatever; preceded by *꜀k'ó*, why? wherefore? *tié*² *꜀nĕng*, who? *tié*² *꜀nĕng* *tié*, at whose house? *tié*² *oi*² *꜀nĕng*, what place is he from? *tié*² *sioh꜀ chiăh*, which one? *ngwai o*² *tié*² *tio*² *꜀ngai*, in what matter am I bad? *꜀k'ó tié*² or *꜀k'ó tié*² *tai*² wherefore? why so?

*Tié*². A coll. corruption of *te*² (ground), as in *tié*² *꜀tau*, on the ground.

(805) Tiék.

哲 喆 Chên. Wise, sage, intelligent, perspicacious; to know intuitively; versed in, fully aware of: [10]*꜀ming tiék꜀* to understand clearly; [11]*pok꜀ tiék꜀* dull, slow in apprehending.

蜇 Chê. The sting of insects, any part of them which inflicts a poisonous wound.

Tiék꜀. A coll. word: dishonored, disgraced, put to shame: *tiék꜀ k'ó*² or *tiék꜀ ꜂ku*, to be disgraced, in ignominy; *tiék꜀ pauk꜀* or *pauk꜀ tiék꜀* reduced in estate, ruined by misfortune.

咥 Tieh. To bite, to gnaw. Read *he*²: to laugh aloud: [12]*he*² *he*² *꜀yong*, the sound of merriment, boisterous laughter.

喋 Tieh. T'ieh. To talk readily; fluent, loquacious; the flowing of blood; to taste blood: *tiék꜀ tiék꜀* verbose, talkative, wordy.

牒 Tieh. A block or tablet for writing on; a certificate, a diploma; a record, a genealogical register; official instructions or dispatches: [13]*tó*² *tiék꜀* a priest's certificate, which entitles him to three days' lodging; [14]*ngŭk꜀ tiék꜀* a royal genealogy; [15]*p'wo tiék꜀* family records; [16]*꜀ung tiék꜀* or *tiék꜀ ꜀ung*, a government dispatch.

[1] 兄弟 [2] 細弟 [3] 阿弟 ○ [4] 弟媳 婦 ○ [5] 蠣房 ○ [6] 蠣乾 ○ [7] 蠣餅 ○ [8] 包蠣 [9] 石蠣 [10] 明哲 [11] 不哲 [12] 咥咥然 ○ [13] 道牒 ○ [14] 玉牒 ○ [15] 譜牒 [16] 文牒

諜$_2$ Tieh. Interchanged with the last two: to spy, to intrigue, to sound others' views; to tamper with soldiers of the opposite side; a prepared statement, a minute of, chronicles: [1]*'kang' tiĕk*$_2$ a spy or secret agent.

垤$_2$ Tieh. A hillock, high ground; an ant-hill; a cavern: [2]*ˏk'iu tiĕk*$_2$ mounds, hillocks.

堞$_2$ Tieh. A parapet with embrasures, a battlement; to surround with parapets.

揲$_2$ Tieh. Also read *siĕk*$_2$ and *siĕk*$_2$ in the dictionaries: to hold, to grasp; to take up and count, to estimate; to take the divining reeds or straws.

渫$_2$ Tieh. Also read *siĕk*, and *siĕk*$_2$: to exclude; to clean a well; to scatter, to disperse; to stop and rest, to cease; to disclose; through, pervious; to leak; foul, dirty; to defile, to disgrace; waves surging on.

帙$_2$ Tieh. A cover for a book; a book-wrapper; a small bag, a satchel; to arrange, to put in order: [3]*'kwong' tiĕk*$_2$ a book-envelope.

秩$_2$ Also read *tik*$_2$: order, succession; in a series, regular; to dispose in order; to multiply; an office, a post, a station; usual, constant; acquainted, versed in, wise; clear, as teaching; a decennium: [4]*lŭk*$_2$ *tiĕk*$_2$ official salary; [5]*ˏi ˏpang tiĕk*$_2$ according to the order of rank.

袠$_2$ Interchanged with the last two: a covering or wrapper for a book, a satchel; a decennium, or period of 10 years; to pierce with a needle, to stitch: [6]*ˏpwoang tiĕk*$_2$ a satchel.

瓞$_2$ Tieh. Young melons, those just set; small cucumbers, gherkins: [7]*ˏkwa tiĕk*$_2$ large and small melons; *met.*, children and grandchildren, posterity.

疊曡叠$_2$ Tieh. To pile up, to make a heap; to repeat, to reiterate; to add to; to fold, to double; a fold, a doubling; alarmed, trembling with fear: in the coll. read *t'ak*$_2$ q. v.: [8]*ˏtŭng tiĕk*$_2$ to pile up, to reiterate; [9]*tiĕk*$_2$ *ch'ëü'* repeated, as visits.

碟$_2$ Tieh. Read *siĕk*$_2$ (to curry leather); in the coll. read *tiĕk*$_2$: a small plate, a saucer: [10]*tiĕk*$_2$ *'kiăng*, a saucer, a cup-plate; [11]*sek*$_2$ *nĕ' tiĕk*$_2$ the twelve small plates—containing seeds, fruit, etc., for the first course; [12]*'wang tiĕk*$_2$ bowls and small plates; [13]*ˏch'a tiĕk*$_2$ lacquered plates; [14]*'siong tiĕk*$_2$ a douceur to a cook.

絰$_2$ Tieh. Mourning badges of coarse cloth, worn on the head and waist, mourning scarfs: [15]*piĕng' tiĕk*$_2$ a cap with a mourning badge.

耋$_2$ Tieh. Seventy or eighty years of age, an octogenarian; old, infirm; hard-featured, as the aged are.

---

1 間諜 2 丘垤 3 卷帙 4 祿秩 5 依班秩 6 縏袠 7 瓜瓞 8 重疊 9 疊次 10 碟仔 11 十二碟 12 碗碟 13 茶碟 14 賞碟 15 弁絰

蛭^2 Tieh. A leech, of which several kinds are enumerated: [1]*'chwi tiék$_2$* a leech, a blood-sucker.

蝶^2 Tieh. T'ieh. A butterfly: COM., [2]*ˌhu tiék$_2$* a butterfly; [3]*tiék$_2$ kié'* the butterfly-shaped cassia; [4]*ˌhu tiék$_2$ ˌt'au*, an embroidered butterfly; *ˌhu tiék$_2$ 'ch'ai ˌhwa*, the butterfly sips the flower.

艓^2 Tieh. A small boat, a punt, such as poor people use.

蹀^2 Tieh. To move the feet, to step, to walk along; to stamp with the foot.

跌^2 Tieh. To kick out, to slip, to stumble and fall; to pass or jump over; to walk quickly: used for the coll. *t'iék$_2$* and *pwak$_2$* q. v.: [5]*tiék$_2$ chëuk$_2$*, to lose one's footing.

迭^2 軼^2 Tieh. To change, to alternate; reciprocal, alternating; to change places; rotation; to rush out suddenly: [6]*tiék$_2$ ˌhing tiék$_2$ hié'* now rising and then declining.

轍^2 Chê. Ch'ê. The rut of a wheel: [7]*k'auk$_2$ tiék$_2$* a dry rut; *met.*, in great straits; [8]*ˌing tó' ˌchiéng tiék$_2$* to go in the old rut—to act badly again.

輒^2 輙^2 Chê. Shê. The sides of a carriage, where arms are placed; suddenly, abruptly; unceremonious, without leave; a kind of disease of the feet: [9]*tiék$_2$ ˌyong*, directly, forthwith.

韘^2 A thumb-ring, an archer's thimble of stone or ivory, commonly called *ˌpang 'chí*, in the coll.

(806) Tiéng.

甛 甜 餂 ˌ T'ien. Sweet in taste; pleasant, agreeable, savory; good, excellent; *met.*, smooth, honeyed, as words: the 3d also read *'t'iéng*, q. v.: [10]*ˌtiéng soi'* sweet sleep; COM., [11]*ˌtiéng ˌngiong mük$_2$ 'ngü*, smooth, deceitful words; [12]*ˌtiéng song'* mellow, as wine; *ˌtiéng ˌt'au*, sweetness; *ˌtiéng 'mwi*, a sweet taste left; [13]*ˌtiéng chiong'* a sort of bean-relish.

癲 瘨 ˌ Tien. Deranged, crazed, insane; foolish, confused in mind; insanity, as shown by silliness and giggling; mad, raving, frantic; fits, convulsions; to act as if crazy, to act wildly: COM., [14]*ˌtiéng ˌkwong*, raving mad; [15]*ˌtiéng ˌchü*, a madman; [16]*ˌtiéng ˌsing*, the demon of insanity; [17]*ˌtiéng k'e'* incipient madness; [18]*ˌtiéng 'k'eng 'mó*, a mad slut; *met.*, a bad woman; [19]*ˌtiéng ˌhing ˌtiéng chaung'* you act as if crazy! COLL., *ˌtiéng ˌp'a*, wild, confused, incoherent; *ta' ˌtiéng*, to feign insanity.

顚 ˌ Tien. Sometimes used for the preceding: the top, the apex, summit; the head, beginning of; to fall down; to upset, to subvert; overthrown, destroyed: *ˌtiéng 'tó*, inverted, turned upside down; *ˌtiéng p'auk$_2$* to fall, to topple over; *ˌtiéng mwak$_2$* beginning and end. Read *ˌtiéng*, as in *ˌtiéng*

---

[1] 水蛭 [2] 蝴蝶 [3] 蝶桂 [4] 蝴蝶頭 [5] 跌足 [6] 迭興迭廢 [7] 涸轍 [8] 仍蹈前轍 [9] 輒然 [10] 甜睡 [11] 甜言蜜語 [12] 甜順 [13] 甜醬 [14] 癲狂 [15] 癲子 [16] 癲神 [17] 癲氣 [18] 癲犬嫲 [19] 癲形癲狀

,tiéng, singly devoted to; sorrowful.

巔 ‘Tien. The summits of hills, the apex or highest peak of a mountain.

蹎 ‘Tien. To trip, to stumble, to fall: [1]*,tiéng p‘auk*, to slip and fall down.

驞 ‘Tien. A horse with a white spot on his forehead.

燈 ‘Têng. Read *,teng;* used for the coll. *,tiêng*, as in *,tiéng ,sing*, a wick; [2]*,tiêng ,sing ‘ch‘au*, a pith used for wicks, the scirpus capsularis; [3]*,tiéng ,sing tuung‘ t‘iong² këü²* to use a wick for a staff—to depend on one beyond his ability; *,tiéng ,sing chô‘ ‘ku ,t‘ui naung² naung² p‘ah*, to use a wick for a drumstick and beat lightly—to do by piecemeal, afraid to make large ventures; also to harry, to annoy one with much work.

典 ‘Tien. A classic, a standard work, a canon, a ritual; a code, statutes; documents, records; a law, a constant rule; to rule, to control, to have charge of; to mortgage: in the coll. read *‘teng*, q. v.: [4]*‘tiêng ‘siu*, to keep, to have control of; [5]*‘tiéng ,chiong*, classics; [6]*‘tiéng chik,* books, documents; COM., [7]*‘che‘ ‘tiéng*, a dictionary; [8]*‘ku ‘tiéng*, ancient records; [9]*‘tiéng ko‘* (it is quoted) from the standards; [10]*,ong ‘tiéng*, favor, grace.

淟 ‘T‘ien. Foul, dirty, muddy; to sink in the water: [11]*‘tiéng ‘niéng*, filthy, muddy.

腆 ‘T‘ien. Also read *‘t‘iéng:* an abundance; much, plentiful, enough: good, excellent; rich, thick, as food; to forget; a long time: [12]*pok, ‘tiéng*, deficient, not worth receiving; [13]*,u pok, ‘tiéng*, by no means unsavory.

點 黙 点 ‘Tien. A dot, a spot; stained, spotted; an hour, the stroke of a clock; to designate; to detail, to draft, as troops; to count, to reckon, to prick off, as in calling the roll; a comma, a point in punctuation; to italicise with dots; to blot out, to mark for correction; to disgrace one's self; to nod in assent; to light, as lamps; a luncheon: in the coll. read *‘teng*, q. v.: [14]*ek, ‘tiéng*, a dot, a point; a little; COM., [15]*‘chi ‘tiéng*, to direct, to show to one; [16]*‘tiéng ,sing*, a tiffin; [17]*‘tiéng ‘hwi*, to light a fire; [18]*‘tiéng ,lang* (coll. *‘tiéng ,t‘ang*), burnt wholly or in part, as a candle; [19]*‘tiéng ‘hwi ,si*, at candle-lighting; *‘tiéng t‘au‘ yâ* will burn all night; [20]*‘tiéng ‘chwi ,u ,kau*, not intimate in the least; COLL., *‘tiéng ,sing châ²* just enough to buy tiffin with—a mere trifle. Read *‘tó:* grass and leaves decaying.

展 ‘Chan. To unroll, to open out; to arrange and examine; to expand, to stretch out; to judge of; true, sincere; a cheerful look: *,ch‘ü ‘tiéng*,

---

1 蹎仆　2 燈心草　3 燈心當杖具　4 典守　5 典章　6 典籍　7 字典　8 古典　9 典故　10 恩典　11 淟涊　12 不腆　13 無不腆　14 一點　15 指點　16 點心　17 點火　18 點闌　19 點火時　20 點水無交

to open or spread out; 'tiéng ˌmi, open brows—a pleasant look; COM., 'tiéng aing' to extend the time; ˏsiu 'tiéng, receive and open—used in the inscriptions of letters.

碾 ' Chan. A roller for smoothing fields, or clearing grain of the husk; an iron roller: also used for 'ngiéng (to grind, to triturate).

輾 ' Chan. Ch'én. Nien. To roll, to turn over half way: [1]'tiéng 'tiong 'hwang ch'aik, to turn back and forth, as on the bed; *met.*, to ponder; COM., [2]'tiéng 'tiong, to go to and fro, to pass the time here and there. Read tiéng': a water-mill.

皽 ' Loose skin, the epidermis or scurf skin; a scab; to separate, to tear off, as a scab. Read 'tang: the skin of the face diseased.

玷 ' Tien. A flaw or spot in a gem; a defect; chipped, spotted; *met.*, to disgrace one's self or family: COM., [3]'tiéng' ūk, ho' 'mu, to disgrace one's parents; [4]'p'ó' tiéng' chipped, spotted, as a gem; *met.*, to have faults; COLL., [5]tiéng' sioh, tói' it has a flaw, is spotted; ˏi ˏmó p'ah, tiéng' he is free from vices or faults.

瑱 ' T'ien. A gem worn in the ear, an ear-ring; the name of a gem; the blending of ornament and splendor.

阽 ' Also read ˏchiéng: dangerous, as a tottering wall; harsh, disagreeable, as a sound: [6]'tiéng' ˏngui, in great peril, as one on the edge of a precipice.

坫 ' Tien. A sort of earthen stand or tea-board, used by princes in meeting to make treaties; a buffet, a cupboard; a screen in a doorway: [7]'hwang tiéng' to invert the cups on the stand.

墊 ' Tien. To put down, to place on; to fall down, to sink into; engrossed with; merged in; to pay money, to make up, as for another: in the coll. read taing' q. v.

簟 ' Tien. Tan. A fine slender sort of bamboo; fine bamboo mats, elegantly woven with flowers.

田 ˏ T'ien. A field; plats of land, cultivated fields; to plant grain; arranged in order, like cultivated plats; the 102d radical; to plant, to cultivate, to hunt, in which senses used for the next: in the coll. read ˏch'eng, q. v.: [8]ching ˏtiéng, well-field—an ancient division of land into 9 parcels, the center one being cultivated for the prince; [9]chik, ˏtiéng, the field plowed by the Emperor; [10]ˏtong ˏtiéng, land occupied by soldiers; [11]ˏtiéng ho' the crown-tax; [12]ˏchü ˏtiéng, fields rented to support scholars; *met.*, a scholar's inkstone; COM., [13]ˏtang ˏtiéng, the lower part of the abdomen—source of a strong, sonorous voice; [14]ˏsing ˏtiéng, the mind, the natural disposition, as being good or kind.

1 碾轉反側 2 輾轉 3 玷辱父母 ○ 4 破玷 ○ 5 玷一塊 ○ 6 阽危 ○ 7 反坫 ○ 8 井田 ○ 9 籍田 ○ 10 屯田 ○ 11 田賦 12 書田 13 丹田 14 心田

福州方言拼音字典

畋 ʻT'ien. To level land and prepare it for cultivation, to till, to cultivate; also to hunt, to fish: [1]꜀tiéng lak꜀ to go on a hunt.

填 ꜀Tien. T'ien. To fill up, to fill in; to supply a deficiency; to add to; to pay; to forfeit, as life; flowing along; a rumbling, as of drums; noted for, characteristic of, as said of officers; to exhaust; liberal; a long time: commonly read ꜀teng, q. v.

滇 ꜀Tien. Full, abundant: [2]꜀tiéng ʻmiéng, a wide expanse of water. Read ꜀tiéng: tribes of Laos near Yunnan: [3]꜀tiéng ꜀tié, a lake in the east of Yunnan; ʻku ꜀tiéng, a name for Yunnan.

磌 ꜀Tien. The noise of falling stones or rocks; the stone base of a pillar.

闐 ꜀Tien. T'ien. To fill up, to stuff; full, abundant; a noise, a sound: ꜀tiéng ꜀tiéng, the rattling of drums; rumbling of carriages; [4]꜀tiéng ꜀mwong, to fill the door, as a crowd.

廛 ꜀Ch'an. Ground allotted to one serf; a shop, a bazaar or market: [5]꜀tiéng ch'e[2] or ch'e[2] ꜀tiéng, a bazaar; [6]꜀tiéng sëü[2] a shop.

纏 ꜀Ch'an. To wind around, to bind; to wrap, to swathe, to bandage; entwined; *met.*, to involve, to molest, to implicate: [7]꜀tiéng ʻnau, to convolve, to cord; *met.*, to implicate; COM., [8]꜀tiéng ꜀miéng, bound by many ties; in the coll. protracted, as rain or sickness; [9]꜀tiéng ꜀k'a, compressed feet—a small-footed woman; [10]꜀tiéng pwang[2] caught, tripped up, as by a rope; involved, obscure, as one's words; COLL., [11]꜀tiéng nau[2] wound, twisted, as the hook-cord of a steelyard; *met.*, indistinct, involved, as words or acts; ꜀tiéng ꜀tiéng siok꜀ staying, hanging about; [12]꜀tiéng ꜀yeu ꜀sié, herpes, shingles; [13]꜀tiéng ꜀nëng ꜀k'a pwang[2] ꜀nëng ʻch'iu, to "fetter people's feet and hands"—in one's way, as children.

躔 ꜀Ch'an. To tread, to walk on; to go in order, to follow; to turn in an orbit; a course, an orbit; a trodden path, a track: [14]chek꜀ ꜀tiéng, a foot-print, a vestige; [15]꜀tiéng to[2] an orbit.

佃[2] Tien. Also read ꜀tiéng: to till, to cultivate fields; to farm on shares; to hunt; an ancient carriage: [16]tiéng[2] ꜀hu, or tiéng[2] ꜀ting, a husbandman; [17]꜀sing tiéng[2] to till on shares; COM., [18]tiéng[2] ho[2] a plowman, one who farms on shares; COLL., [19]kiu tiéng[2] ꜀siöng ngiék꜀ ʻchio, to become the proprietor by tilling long on shares—said of claims founded on long possession.

甸[2] Tien. The royal domain, extending 500 ʻli around the capital; land measuring 64 square roods, which furnished a war chariot, three men-at-arms, and 71 soldiers; to plow, to cultivate; to extend; frontier lands: tiéng[2] ꜀ing, royal foresters.

[1]畋獵 [2]滇瀰 [3]滇池 [4]闐門 [5]廛市 [6]廛肆 [7]纏繞 [8]纏綿 [9]纏跤 [10]纏絆 [11]纏鬧 [12]纏腰蛇 [13]纏仈跤絆仈手○ [14]跡躔 [15]躔度 [16]佃夫 [17]承佃 [18]佃戶 [19]久佃成業主○

蜔[2] Tien. Inlaid shell-work, inlaid figured work: [1]꜀loi tiéngᵓ lacquered ware having shells and figures inlaid.

鈿[2] Tien. T'ien. Also read ꜀tiéng: flowers, inlaid work in gold, nacre or feathers for a head-dress; also used for bracelets of the best kinds: COM., [2]꜀ch'ai tiéngᵓ hairpins and bracelets; [3]꜀king tiéngᵓ gold bracelets; COLL., [4]꜀yéng ᶜkwang tiéngᵓ bracelets having a round surface.

奠[2] Tien. Fixed, settled, as mountains, and streams; to offer sacrifices and libations to gods; to place, to lay down: COM., [5]chiéᵓ tiéngᵓ to offer in sacrifice; sacrifices and libations; [6]tiéngᵓ ᶜchiu, to pour out libations; [7]tiéngᵓ ꜀ngi, "respectfully presents a gift"—as written on a present to friends of the deceased.

電[2] Tien. Lightning; electricity: [8]꜀loi tiéngᵓ thunder and lightning; [9]꜀tiàng tiéngᵓ "respectfully presented to your glance"—an epistolary phrase; [10]ᶜsiéng tiéngᵓ a flash of lightning; COM., [11]tiéngᵓ ᶜmu, the goddess of lightning.

*Tiéng*ᵓ. A coll. word: full, up to the brim: *tiéng*ᵓ *tiéng*ᵓ brimful; ᶜ*tio tiéng*ᵓ *tiéng*ᵓ filled full; *k'ak*, *tiéng*ᵓ *ă*ᵓ *p'ak*, too full, it will overflow.

(807) Tieu.

刁 ꜀ Tiao. Read ꜀t'ieu; coll. ꜀tieu: perverse, rebellious, reckless; to make difficulties, to insist perversely; exacting: ꜀tieu ꜀ngwang, perverse, reckless, overbearing; ꜀tieu ꜀nu, a rebellious slave; ꜀tieu ꜀nang, exact unreasonably, to oppress; to object, to bring up difficulties.

啁 ꜀ Tiao. Talkative, verbose; the chirping of birds: used for ꜀chau (to deride); also read ꜀chiu, q. v.: [12]꜀tieu ꜀keu, loquacious.

琱 ꜀ Tiao. To work gems, to cut and engrave precious stones; a pebble like a gem: [13]꜀tieu tauk, to polish gems.

凋 ꜀ Tiao. To fade and fall, as the sere leaf; injured, exhausted: ꜀tieu ꜀ling, fallen and faded, dying, as plants; [14]꜀tieu siàᵓ fading, withered, as flowers.

雕 彫 ꜀ Tiao. To cut, to engrave, to carve figures; *met.*, to polish, as essays; to tattoo; ornamented, engraved; the first also means a kind of hawk, a sparrow: in the coll. read ꜀teu, q. v.: [15]꜀tieu k'aik, to engrave.

鵰 ꜀ Tiao. A species of eagle or lammergeir, a large bird of prey, whose presence is said to make other birds cast their feathers.

蜩 ꜀ T'iao. A cicada or broad locust: [16]꜀tieu kak, the cast skin or exuviae of the cicada.

朝 ꜀ Chao. Ch'ao. The dawn, morning; early: also read ꜀tieu, q. v: [17]꜀tieu ᶜwang, morning and evening; [18]ek, ꜀tieu, in a morning, quickly; ꜀tieu ꜀tieu, every morning; [19]꜀tieu ꜀siéng, Corea.

---

[1] 螺蜔 [2] 釵鈿 [3] 金鈿 [4] 圓管鈿 [5] 祭奠 [6] 奠酒 [7] 奠儀 [8] 雷電 [9] 呈電 [10] 閃電 [11] 電母 [12] 啁嘐 [13] 琱琢 [14] 凋謝 [15] 雕刻 [16] 蜩甲 [17] 朝晚 [18] 一朝 [19] 朝鮮

貂 ‚ Tiao. The marten or sable, called ‚*tieu* ‘*ch‘ü*: [1]‘*keu* ‘*mwi sŭk*, ‚*tieu*, a dog's tail tacked to a sable—incongruous, as when an unlearned man holds office; COM., [2]‚*tieu* ‚*p‘uí*, marten furs; [3]‚*tieu* ‘*mwi*, fur tails, worn by military officers; [4]‚*tieu* ‚*hó* ‘*k‘ai*, a pencil of marten hair.

‚*Tieu*. A coll. word, as in ‚*tieu* ‚*mieu*, lively, playful, as a child.

咮 ’ Chu. The bill of a bird; to peck with the bill; the twittering of birds. Read ‚*chio*: loquacious, chattering, as birds.

弔 ’ **吊** ’ Tiao. To condole with mourners; to visit mourners and worship the deceased; to compassionate, to sympathize with; condolence; to suspend, to hang up; to order a rehearing of a case: in the coll. read *taiu’* q. v.: COM., [5]*tieu’ ang’* to order a second trial; [6]*tieu’* ‚*song*, or *chauk*, *tieu’* to condole and wail over the dead; [7]*siă’ tieu’* to decline visits—a notice posted after funeral rites; [8]‚*k‘wi tieu’* to prepare for a funeral; [9]*tieu’ t‘aik*, the visitor's card—on white paper; [10]*tieu’ ch‘ok*, ‚*kang*, to bring one out of prison (for trial); [11]*tieu’* ‘*sing*, to summon parties to a trial; COLL., ‚*ié* *tieu’* loose, not tight in, as a tooth or nail.

Tieu’. A coll. word, for which the last may be used: to draw, to produce suppuration, as digestives do; to stretch, as furs in making robes; *tieu’* ‚*kó*, a digestive plaster; *tieu’* ‚*siong*, to extract (the pain of) a wound; *tieu’* ‚*p‘uí*, to make fur garments.

綁 ’ To bind or confine a person; to tie things; to suspend, to hang up.

晝 ’ Chou. A day, the daytime, daylight: [12]*tieu’ yă’* day and night, incessantly; [13]*pek*, *tieu’* in broad daylight, openly.

釣 ’ Tiao. Shao. To fish, to angle; a fishhook; to bait, to set a trap for one; to use, as a means; to fish, to seek after, as praise: COM., [14]‚*ngü tieu’* or *tieu’* ‚*kau*, a fish-hook; [15]*tieu’ ne’* a bait; [16]*tieu’* ‚*ha*, to angle for prawns; [17]*tieu’* ‚*ngü*, to angle for fish—a game at cards with three players in the set.

Tieu’. A coll. word, used for ‚*ch‘iéng*, a thousand cash; ‚*chiéng sioh*, *pah*, *tieu’* a hundred thousand cash.

朝 ‚ **鼂** ‚ Chao. Ch‘ao. To attend an audience, as ministers; to go to court, to show fealty, as nobles or princes; an audience, the imperial presence; the court, the palace, to enter the court, to hold an audience; a dynasty; courtly, pertaining to the court, as dress; in the coll. towards, fronting, facing: the 2d read *tieu’* is a surname and name of a district: also read ‚*tieu*, q. v.: [18]*se’* ‚*tieu*, H. I. M. entering court; [19]‚*tieu kong’* to present tribute; COM., [20]‚*tieu kiéng’* to see the em-

1 狗尾續貂 2 貂皮 3 貂尾 4 貂毫楷 ○ 5 弔案 6 弔喪 7 謝弔 8 開弔 9 弔帖 10 弔出監 11 弔審 ○ 12 晝夜 13 白晝 14 魚釣 15 釣餌 16 釣蝦 17 釣魚 18 覲朝 19 朝貢 20 朝見 ○

peror; [1]꜀*tieu* ꜀*ting*, the court; His Majesty; [2]꜀*tieu hó*꜄ the Imperial title; [3]꜀*tieu tói*꜄ a dynasty; [4]꜂*chó* ꜀*tieu*, the morning audience; [5]꜀*tieu huk*꜇ (or ꜀*i*), a court dress; [6]꜀*tieu* ꜀*siéng*, Corea—usually called ꜀*kó* ꜀*lá kwok*꜇; ꜀*tieu* ꜀*ting* ꜀*kwang* ꜀*ká*, public roads; COLL., ꜀*tieu ch'ok*꜇ facing outward; ꜀*tieu siong*꜄ turned upward; ꜀*tieu* ꜀*nang sói*꜄ *paĕk*꜇ fronting south with the back to the north, as a house; ꜀*tieu* ꜂*ong*, shaded, shadowed.

潮 ꜀ Ch'ao. The morning tide; a flood tide; damp: [7]*song*꜄ ꜀*tieu*, to go with the tide; ꜀*tieu sek*꜇ moist; COM., ꜀*tieu twai*꜄ spring tides; [8]꜀*Tieu* ꜀*chiu*, a prefecture in the east of Kwangtung; ꜀*tieu* ꜀*lang*, a blue color; COLL., ꜀*tieu* ꜂*tong* ꜂*chwi*, the flood tide.

惆 ꜀ To suffer failure; frustrated, disappointed: ꜀*tieu tiong*꜄ sad, vexed, sick at heart.

調 ꜀ Tiao. T'iao. To harmonise, to blend; to mix, to compound, as medicines; to season, to spice; to adjust, to make up differences between parties; to attend to one's health; to tune, as an instrument; to regulate, to modulate; to combine properly, as initials and finals, to spell words; to laugh at, to deceive: also read *tieu*꜄ q. v.: [9]꜀*tieu ch'ieu*꜄ to ridicule; COM., [10]꜀*tieu* ꜀*ing*, to harmonize sounds; [11]꜀*tieu e*꜄ to spice; [12]꜀*tieu* ꜀*hwo*, moderate, regulated, as the air, temperature, sounds, health; [13]꜀*tieu t'iong*꜄ well and happy, joyous; [14]꜀*tieu* ꜂*yong*, to nurse one's self; [15]꜀*tieu te*꜄ to heal, to cure; ꜀*tieu* ꜀*ting*, to settle a quarrel, to be a mediator; ꜀*tieu* ꜂*ch'ü*, to manage or settle, as lawsuits; COLL., ꜀*tieu tik*꜇ (or ꜀*teu tik*꜇) straight, proper; honest, outspoken.

調² Tiao. T'iao. A tune, a song, a ballad; tones in vocal and instrumental music; to select; to move, to change about; to change places; to transfer, as officers; to seek, to ask: also read ꜀*tieu*, q. v.: COM., [16]꜀*k'iong tieu*꜄ a ditty, a ballad; [17]*tieu*꜄ ꜂*sü*, to hold an office temporarily; [18]꜀*tieu to*꜄ to depute, to change (agents) about; to arrange or move things about; *tieu*꜄ *oi*꜄ to change one's place, as at a gaming table.

召² Chao. To summon, to cite, to order one to come; to dispatch, to send, as officers to their posts: also read *sieu*꜄ q. v.: COM., [19]*tieu*꜄ *kiéng*꜄ to call to court; [20]*tieu*꜄ *oi*꜄ to seat guests (at a feast); *tieu*꜄ ꜂*kwi* (coll. *tieu*꜄ ꜂*ch'üng*), to call ghosts to eat, as priests do; *tieu*꜄ *pek*꜇ ꜂*seng*, to send (an officer) to another province.

兆² Chao. A prognostic, an omen; an altar; the ground of a tomb; one million: [21]*e*꜄ *tieu*꜄ myriads; [22]*tieu*꜄ ꜀*ming*, millions of men, the people; [23]*kek*꜇ *tieu*꜄ a lucky omen; COM., ꜂*hó tieu*꜄ a good omen; ꜀*hüng tieu*꜄ an unpropitious sign; [24]*pai*꜄ *tieu*꜄ "prognostic of ruin"—said of vicious children.

1 朝廷 2 朝號 3 朝代 4 早朝 5 朝服 6 朝鮮 7 順潮 8 潮州 9 調笑 10 調音 11 調味 12 調和 13 調暢 14 調養 15 調治 16 腔調 17 調署 18 調度 19 召見 20 召位 21 億兆 22 兆民 23 吉兆 24 敗兆

旐[2] **Chao.** A banner with dragons and tortoises on it, to represent some superstitious idea: [1]*tieu*² *₍hwang*, banners and scrolls, as borne at a father's funeral.

肇[2] **Chao.** To strike; to begin, to institute or lay the foundation of; to devise; to rectify; to extend; capable, intelligent: [2]*tieu*² *k'eng*² a department west of Canton, once the provincial capital.

趙[2] **Chao.** To hasten to; to announce to a suzerain, to pay court to one's feudal lord; a long time; a few; a surname; a feudal state in the south of Shansi and Chihli.

(808) Tih.

値[2] **Chih.** Read *sik*$_2$ and *tik*$_2$; used for the coll. *tih*$_2$: to wish, to desire: [3]*tih*$_2$ *ng*² *tih*$_2$ wish it or not? [4]*ngwai pwoh*, *tih*$_2$ I wish for it; [5]*bi*² *tih*$_2$ to desire, to want; [6]*tih*$_2$ *sie*² *nóh*$_2$ what do you wish? [7]*tih*$_2$ *tek*$_2$ *k'ó*² want it all—will take or buy all of it.

***Tih*$_2$.** A coll. euphonic prefix, as in *tih*$_2$ *tiăh*$_2$ to buy (rice); *tih*$_2$ *tuh*$_2$ to pierce; to thrust, as the middle finger toward one insultingly.

***Tih*$_2$.** A coll. word: to stutter, to stammer: same as *chih*$_2$ q. v.: *tih*$_2$ *má*² *ch'ok*$_2$ stuttering and unable to enunciate; *tih*$_2$ *pwang*² *₍seng* (or *sá*²) *nik*$_2$ he stammers half-a-day!

(809) Tik.

直[2] **Chih.** Used for the next in the sense of worth, value: to look ahead; straight, not crooked; honest, true, upright; blunt, outspoken; just, exact; to proceed, to go direct; to rectify, to straighten; suitable, proper; to wait upon; but, only, merely; purposely: COM., [8]*tik*$_2$ *lá*² Chihli; [9]*tek*$_2$ *tik*$_2$ purposely; [10]*tik*$_2$ *tó*² right principles; COLL., [11]*tik*$_2$ *₍nĕng*, a blunt, honest man; [12]*ek*$_2$ *tik*$_2$ *₍kiăng*, to walk straight on; [13]*pek*$_2$ *tik*$_2$ to stretch out, to straighten; *móh*$_2$ *seng*² *tik*$_2$ *₍tăng tik*$_2$ don't believe everything that is strongly asserted; *tik*$_2$ *₍kĕ laĕng*² very blunt, boorish; to blab, as a child; *tik*$_2$ *₍teu*, the rib-pieces (of pork); *₍t'au hwok*, *p'ah*, *₍tiu ₍tiu tik*$_2$ her hair knocked out straight (in a quarrel).

値[2] **Chih.** To take, to hold; to manage; the price, value, worth: also read *sik*$_2$ and in the coll. *tek*$_2$ and *tih*$_2$ q. v.: COM., [14]*tik*$_2$ *nik*$_2$ to serve in turn (in a yamun); [15]*tik*$_2$ *nik*$_2$ *₍hu sëü*² attendants of a god, serving in rotation—called *₍hu sëü*² because their services are engaged by burning the *₍hu* or charms; [16]*tik*$_2$ *₍tong*, those who serve in turn in yamuns, as scribes or interpreters.

姪[2] 侄[2] **Chih.** A brother's children: COM., [17]*tik*$_2$ *₍i*, a nephew; [18]*tik*$_2$ *'nü*, a brother's daughter, a niece; [19]*ngwoi*² *tik*$_2$ a wife's nephews; [20]*leng*² *tik*$_2$ your nephew; *tik*$_2$ *sá*² husband of a brother's daughter; *tik*$_2$ *₍song*, sons of a nephew;

[1]旐	[3]値	剢	[6]値	的	[9]特	[11]直	行	[14]値	待	[17]姪	[19]外
旛	伓	値	世	去	直	仈	[13]拔	日	使	兒	姪
[2]肇	値	[5]欲	毛	[8]直	[10]直	[12]一	直	[15]値	[16]値	[18]姪	[20]令
慶	[4]我	値	[7]値	隸	道	直	⊙	日	堂	女	姪

tik${}_2$ *ho*^{2} a nephew's wife; ${}_{\varsigma}$*niéng tik*${}_2$ sons of alumni of the same year; *'ngü tik*${}_2$ your foolish nephew! — used in writing to a senior.

擲 ${}_2$ Chih. Jêng. To throw down; to cast away, to reject; to waste, as one's time: [1]*'tik*${}_2$ *k'e*^{2} to discard; [2]*'tik*${}_2$ ${}_{\varsigma}$*hwang*, to return disdainfully; [3]*'hü tik*${}_2$ to waste, as time.

⿰虫鄭 ${}_2$ Chih. A large green caterpillar, called [4]*'tik*${}_2$ *sŭk*${}_2$ or *tik*${}_2$ *ch'ŭk*${}_2$ which feeds on pulse.

躑 ${}_2$ Chih. To go back and forth; impeded, embarrassed, undecided: [5]*'tik*${}_2$ *ch'ŭk*${}_2$ unable to advance, irresolute.

敵 ${}_2$ Ti. A foe, an enemy; a competitor, an antagonist; equal, matched; to oppose, to fight against; to compete, to contest: used for the coll. *t'ik*${}_2$ q. v.: [6]*'tik*${}_2$ ${}_{\varsigma}$*ping*, the enemy's forces; com., [7]*'tói' tik*${}_2$ to oppose each other; [8]*'tik*${}_2$ *'ch'iu*, a competitor; [9]*'tik*${}_2$ *kwok*${}_2$ rival nations; [10]${}_{\varsigma}$*siu tik*${}_2$ an enemy; [11]*'tái tik*${}_2$ to oppose, to withstand.

滌 ${}_2$ Ti. To wash, to rinse, to cleanse vessels; to purify; to reform, as the heart; to dilute spirits; a place for domestic animals, a stable, a stall: *tik*${}_2$ *tik*${}_2$ a dry, warm atmosphere; hot breezes.

翟 ${}_2$ Ti. Chai. The Tartar pheasant; garments adorned with feathers; a bunch of feathers waved at sacrifices; an ancient state, now Yen-gan-fu in Shensi: [12]*'eu*^{2} *'ch'iu 'ping tik*${}_2$ their right hands held the feathers.

糴 ${}_2$ Ti. To buy rice, to lay in a stock, as of rice or other grain; to wash rice; swift, speedy: in the coll. read *tiăh*${}_2$ q. v.: [13]*ak*${}_2$ *tik*${}_2$ to forbid buying up grain.

籊 ${}_2$ Ti. Long, tapering bamboos; rods cut off at the points and suitable for fishing-poles.

笛 ${}_2$ Ti. **篴** ${}_2$ Ti. Chu. A flute, a fife; a flageolet having seven holes: the 2d read *tŭk*${}_2$ is the name of a bamboo: [14]${}_{\varsigma}$*sêng tik*${}_2$ a double flute; com., [15]${}_{\varsigma}$*ch'ui tik*${}_2$ to play on the flageolet.

迪 ${}_2$ **廸** ${}_2$ Ti. To tread in the path of another, to follow; to go to, to arrive at; to advance, as in knowledge; to get, to obtain; to show the way, to teach, to direct; the right way: [16]*tik*${}_2$ *kek*${}_2$ to get luck, to be happy; [17]${}_{\varsigma}$*iu tik*${}_2$ to admonish, to direct one aright; [18]*'k'ié tik*${}_2$ to open a way, to set a good example.

狄 ${}_2$ Ti. Used for the next: name of Scythian tribes on the north in the deserts; a stag, a large deer; musical officers.

逖 ${}_2$ Ti. Far, distant, remote; to put away; to go to a distance: [19]*tik*${}_2$ *tik*${}_2$ earnest, eager, as to succeed in life.

---

1 擲棄　3 盧擲　5 躑躅　7 對敵　9 敵國　11 抵敵　秉翟　14 雙笛　16 迪吉　17 由迪　18 啟迪　19 逖逖

2 擲還　⿰虫鄭蠋　6 敵兵　8 敵手　10 仇敵　12 右手　13 遏糴　15 吹笛　○　○　○　○

荻 *Ti.* A delicate, aquatic plant, having white fragrant flowers; a sort of arrow-leaf: [1] *˛lu tik˛* a tall species of arundo.

蟄 *Chê. Chih.* To hide in a quiet place; to burrow, to go into holes and become torpid, as insects: COM., [2] *˛king tik˛* the "excited insects"— name of the 3d of the 24 solar terms, about March 5th to 20th.

覿 *Ti.* Two persons seeing each other, to have an audience: [3] *tik˛ mièng˒* to see face to face; [4] *˛sü tik˛* a private interview.

Tik˛. A coll. euphonic prefix, as in *tik˛ tük˛* to pursue; to urge on; *tik˛ tok˛* to snatch, to rob.

(810) Ting.

丁 *Ting.* A sting; a peg; a wooden pin; the 4th of the ten stems, it belongs to fire; an individual; an adult, robust; to bear, to sustain office; to order, in which sense the same as the next: [5] *˛ling ˛ting*, lonely; COM., [6] *˛sing ˛ting*, of age, 16 years old; [7] *hwak˛ ˛ting*, or [8] *ch'ok˛ ˛ting*, lucky, as a grave which secures posterity; [9] *˛ting ˊk'eu*, (the census of) males and females; [10] *˛ting ˛iu*, mourning for a parent; *siong˒ ˛ting*, *˛tüng ˛ting*, and *ˊmwi ˛ting*, the set days of sacrifice in the three decades of the month; [11] *˛ting ˛hiong*, cloves; [12] *pah˛ ˛ting*, an undergraduate; [13] *˛ting che˒ ˛ká*, the corner where a side-street ends; COLL., *˛ting ˛hiong k'ó˒* the clove *k'ó˒* — a small sea-fish; *ˊkĕng ˛ting ˛hiong* and *ˊmó ˛ting ˛hiong*, the male and female cloves.

叮 *Ting.* To bid, to charge one: COM., [14] *˛ting ˛ning chëük˛ ho˒* to bid, to enjoin straitly on one; [15] *˛ting sek˛ p'ieu˒* to warn banks (not to accept) lost bills—if presented by strangers; COLL., *˛sung ˛ting lang˒ chai˒* or *˛ting ˊló chai˒* (or *taiu˒*), to charge repeatedly and strictly.

仃 行 *Ting.* Alone: *˛ling ˛ting*, solitary; [16] *˛ling ˛ting ˛yong*, the bay of Lintin, south of the Bogue; COLL., *˛ku ˛ting ˛ting*, entirely alone, by himself or itself.

燈 灯 *Têng.* Read *˛teng*; coll. *˛ting*: a lamp, a lantern; *met.*, laws of Budh: [17] *˛ting ˊma*, a lamp; [18] *˛ting ˛lĕng*, a lantern; [19] *˛ting ˊchang*, the oil cup of a common lamp; [20] *˛ting ˛pang*, an illuminated stage, as on the Emperor's birthday; *˛ting ˛t'ieu*, the stick by which a lantern is borne; *˛ting kauk˛* the frames or ribs of lanterns; *˛ting ˛lĕng kwang˒* (or *t'ek˛*), the bow over which the frame or body is placed; *˛ting ˛lĕng ˛ki*, the frame or body of a lantern; *˛ting ˊma pwak˛* a wick-mover; [21] *˛küng ˛ting*, bridal lanterns; *˛liu ˛lié ˛ting*, transparent lanterns, as those made of sheep's horns.

玎 *Ting.* The sound of a stone when struck, the noise of jingling stones: *˛ting ˛ling*, the tinkling of gems.

1 蘆荻 2 驚蟄 3 覿面 4 私覿 5 巠丁 6 成丁 7 發丁 8 出丁 9 丁口 10 丁憂 11 丁香 12 白丁 13 丁字街〇 14 叮嚀囑咐 15 叮失票 16 伶仃洋 17 燈馬 18 燈籠 19 燈盞 20 燈棚 21 宮燈

珍 ꜀Chên. Read ꜀*ching* in the dictionaries: valuable, precious, excellent; important, rare, noble; to prize, to esteem; a rarity; delicacies: [1]ʻ*chiong siong*ʼ ꜀*ting*, a pearl in the palm—a daughter; ꜀*ting* ʻ*pó*, precious; COM., [2]꜀*ting* (or ꜀*ching*) ꜀*chio*, pearls; [4]꜀*ting tëüng*ʼ to esteem, to take care of; ꜀*ting* ꜀*siu paik*꜆ *e*ʼ all sorts of delicacies.

釘 ꜀Ting. A nail, a pin, a peg; a brad, a spike: also read *teng*ʼ q. v.: COM., [5]ʻ*t'iěk*꜆ ꜀*ting*, iron nails; [6]ʻ*tëük*꜆ ꜀*ting*, a bamboo nail; [7]꜀*sëng kwoi*ʼ ꜀*ting*, a double-headed nail; COLL., ꜀*ting* ꜀*k'iëng*, an iron bar and ring for drawing nails; *siáng*ʼ ꜀*ting*, the ends of threads in a ripped seam.

疔 ꜀Ting. Ulcers, of which there are enumerated 13 kinds; a bubo, a chancre, syphilis sores: [8]꜀*ting* ꜀*ch'ong*, an ulcer; COM., [9]꜀*sang* ꜀*ting*, to have ulcers; ʻ*hwi* ꜀*ting*, burning pimples, tetter.

癥 Chêng. Obstinate constipation; colic caused by obstruction in the bowels: [10]꜀*ting* ʻ*ka*, an intestinal concretion, obstruction with griping pains.

徵 ꜀Chêng. Chih. To cite, to summon; to testify, to witness; to verify; to act, to set in motion; complete; to seek, to inquire after; to collect, as taxes; to raise troops; proof, evidence, fulfillment: [11]꜀*ting tieu*ʼ to summon; [12]ʻ*iu* ꜀*ting*, proved, verified; ꜀*ting* ʻ꜀*ping*, to enlist troops; ꜀*u* ꜀*ting*, no proof of; ꜀*ting p'eng*ʼ to induce by presents; ꜀*ting ngiëng*ʼ accomplished.

懲 ꜀Ch'êng. To curb, to repress; to warn, to reprove, to reprimand; a caution, a warning, a lesson: [13]꜀*ting te*ʼ to govern strictly; [14]*pok*꜆ ꜀*ting*, an admonitory hint.

窨 ꜀Chan. A coll. character, found in the *Paik*꜆ ꜀*Ing*: to deposit temporarily, as coffins: [15]꜀*ting ch'io*ʼ a dead-house for depositing coffins.

貞 ꜀Chên. Chêng. To divine, as with cash and turtle shells; chaste, virtuous; pure, correct; uncorrupted in principles and morals: COM., [16]꜀*ting* ʻ*nü*, a chaste maiden; [17]꜀*ting chiëk*, or ꜀*ting* ʻ*siu*, chaste, as a widow; [18]꜀*ping* ꜀*ting ngük*꜆ *kiëk*꜆ chaste and pure, as ice and gems.

楨 ꜀Chên. Chêng. A hard wood, a species of fir: [19]ʻ*nü* ꜀*ting*, a conifer growing on Taishan in Shantung; [20]꜀*ting kang*ʼ planks used in making mud walls, termed in the coll. ꜀*ch'iong* ʻ*peng*.

禎 ꜀Chên. Chêng. A good omen; lucky, favoring, auspicious: [21]꜀*ting* ꜀*siong*, a happy sign; good, excellent.

꜀*Ting*. A coll. word, as in ꜀*ting* ʻ*peng*, a kitchen chopping-block.

꜀*Ting*. A coll. word: midday, as in ꜀*ting* ʻ*hwi pwong*ʼ a midday meal, as for those conducting idolatrous processions.

1掌	2珍	4珍	6竹	釘	9生	11徵	13懲	15窨	17貞	玉	20楨
上	寶	重	釘	8疔	疔	召	治	厝	節	潔	皸
珍	3珍	5鐵	7雙	瘡	10癥	12有	14薄	16貞	18氷	19女	21禎
○	珠	釘	鬠	○	瘕	徵	懲	女	貞	楨	祥

,Ting. A coll. euphonic prefix, as in *,ting ,tung*, to tarry; *,ting ,tung*, to swing, to knock against; *,ting ,tong*, to sweep into a dust-pan.

'頂 Ting. The top, the summit, the peak, the crown; an official ball or button, worn on the top of the cap; to carry on the head or top of; to substitute, to take the place of another; a classifier of caps and sedans; in the coll. a superlative, very, extremely: also used for the coll. *'t'ing*, q. v.: COM., [1]*'ting ,t'au*, to the very top (of the column)—no blank spaces; in the coll. to be surety for; [2]*'ting tai'* to wear an official button; [3]*'ting t'á'* to act as a substitute; [4]*'ting ,miàng*, to answer to another's name, as at examinations; [5]*'ting ,t'iéng lik, te'* to stand on the earth and reach heaven—very talented; COLL., *'ting ,chiêng*, very sharp, pointed; *met.*, clever; *'ting siong'* the very best; *'ting 'ma*, horsemen attending officers or idols; *'ting ,tó*, best ardent spirits; *'ting pok, ,k'ang*, very unworthy, worthless.

'酊 Ting. Intoxicated, drunk: [6]*'ming 'ting*, stupefied with liquor, dead drunk.

'戥 Têng. A small steelyard: COM., [7]*,lié 'ting*, small scales for weighing money and silk.

'等 Têng. Read *'teng*; coll. *'ting*: to wait, to delay: *'ting 'ting*, wait! [8]*'ting ,mwong*, to keep the door unlocked for one (at night); *'ting sioh, siâk, 'ku*, or *'ting sioh, sieu'* wait a while; *'ting 'chwi ,nang 'tong*, the tide rises slowly while one waits for it! *met.*, hard to wait, as for one's pay.

'Ting. A coll. euphonic prefix, as in *'ting 'teng*, to count, to reckon up.

,亭 T'ing. A portico, a pavilion, a dome supported on pillars; a shed or rest-house for travelers; the same, equal; straight; to stop, to rest at: [9]*,ting 'ngu*, noon: COM., [10]*,ta ,ting*, the tea-pavilion; [11]*,liong ,ting*, a summer-house.

,停 T'ing. To rest, to stop, to cease; to delay; fixed, arranged: used for the coll. *,t'ing*, q. v.: COM., [12]*,ting pwo'* to stop walking; [13]*,ting ,kĕng*, to stop work: [14]*,ting ,i*, detention of the placenta; [15]*,ting ,chié*, to suspend specie payments; [16]*,ting te'* a stoppage, as indigestion; COLL., *,ting ,ló sak, 'ku*, gong and drum (of priests) ceased beating; *met.*, no trade; *,mó ,ting ,mó hiok*, incessantly.

,渟 T'ing. Water stopping, stagnant, as a pool in a stream; low banks, flats along a stream.

,婷 T'ing. Handsome, pretty: [17]*'p'eng' ,ting*, graceful, as a lady.

,埕 An unauthorized character; an amphora, an earthern, pear-shaped jar without handles, for carrying wine: COLL., [18]*,ting ,p'ang pwak, aĕng'* earthen

1 頂頭 2 頂戴 3 頂替 4 頂名 5 頂天立地 6 酩酊 7 釐戥 8 等門 ○ 9 亭午 10 茶亭 11 凉亭 ○ 12 停步 13 停工 14 停衣 ○ 15 停支 16 停滯 17 娉婷 ○ 18 埕磻砵甕

jars of various sorts—are needed for domestic use.

塵 ˓Ch'ên. Dust, particles; effluvia, atoms, molecules; *met.*, the world, worldly customs and vices; traces: [1]˓*ting ˓ai*, dust; [2]˓*ting sié*˒ or ˓*hung ˓ting*, the world; [3]˓*ting sŭk*˒ worldly customs; [4]*hain*˒ ˓*ting*, traces, impress, as of one's example after death; COLL., ˓*ung ˓ting*, dust.

澄 ˓Têng. Read ˓*teng;* coll. ˓*ting:* still, clear, limpid; to settle and become clear: [5]˓*ting ˓ch'ing*, settled, limpid; [6]˓*ting* ʻ*tá*˒ settled to the bottom.

廷 廷 T'ing. A court, a hall where audiences are held; even, correct, straight, regular: COM., [7]˓*tieu ˓ting*, the court; *met.*, His Majesty, the Emperor.

庭 T'ing. An open court in a palace, a vestibule before a hall; a hall; straight: [8]˓*ka ˓ting*, a domestic hall; domestic, pertaining to the family; [9]˓*ting hong*˒ parental instruction; [10]ʻ*mwang ˓ting ˓ü ch'e*˒ the vestibule is like a fair, as a statesman's when besieged by applicants.

蜓 T'ing. The libellula, or dragonfly, called ˓*ch'ing ˓ting*, in the coll. ˓*ma ˓hu*, q. v. Read ʻ*tiêng*, as in ʻ*yêng* ʻ*tiêng*, a kind of lizard.

霆 T'ing. The sound of thunder: ˓*loi ˓ting*, the rumbling of thunder; ˓*loi ˓ting ˓chi no*˒ thundering wrath, as of a king.

籐 T'êng. Read ˓*teng* in the dictionaries; interchanged with the next: vines, creepers; specifically the rattan; a district in the east of Kwangsi: COM., [11]˓*ting ˓nong*, the inner substance of rattan; [12]*k'wá ˓ting*, large rattan, as for binding the tops of posts; [13]˓*ting* ʻ*ié*, cane-bottomed chairs; [14]˓*ting ˓pú*, a rattan shield; [15]*ch'iong*˒ ˓*ting*, to make cane-work; [16]˓*ting ˓ch'ong ˓k'wong*, a rattan bed-bottom.

藤 T'êng. Read ˓*teng* in the dictionaries: creepers, trailing plants: COM., [17]˓*ting ˓wong*, or ˓*teng ˓wong*, gamboge; COLL., ˓*siong ˓ting*, a creeper; to climb, as vines; ˓*king ˓kwa* ʻ*tong ˓ting*, the pumpkin drops from the stem; *met.*, to fall, as things or persons.

陳 Ch'ên. To arrange, to set in order, to spread out; to state, to narrate, to tell; to memorialize; old, a long time; many, all; the passage before a hall; a feudal state near the present capital of Honan; a surname: also read *teng*˒ q. v.: [18]˓*ting siék*, to arrange; COM., [19]˓*ting ˓p'ui*, dried orange peel—used medicinally; [20]˓*p'wo ˓ting* ʻ*king tiong*˒ quilts and fine curtains, as spread on bridal furniture in a procession; ˓*ting ˓ling ˓t'iêng a*˒ *pwang*˒ half of the empire has the surnames ˓*Ting* and ˓*Ling*.

蔯 Ch'ên. A medicinal herb, good for rheumatism: COM., [21]˓*ing ˓ting*, wormwood; one says a plant like origanum.

---

1 塵埃 2 塵世 3 塵俗 4 後塵 5 澄清 6 澄底 7 朝廷 8 家庭 9 庭訓 10 滿庭如市 11 籐瓤 12 魁籐 13 籐椅 14 籐牌 15 串籐 16 籐床匡 17 藤黄 18 陳設 19 陳皮 20 鋪陳錦帳 21 茵陳○

‚Ting. A coll. euphonic prefix, as in *‚ting ‚tang*, to snap the fingers; to play on a stringed instrument; *‚ting ‚tong*, to stamp with the feet.

(811) Tio.

[This word is interchangeably read *two*.]

‘垜 ‘垛 To. A target; side-apartments, as for schoolrooms: *siǎ’ ‘tio*, a target for arrows.

‘躲 To. The body; to shun, to evade; to slip off, to hide, to conceal one's self: [1]*‘tio nik‚*, to skulk; COM., [2]*‘tio pié’* to evade; [3]*‘tio chai’* to abscond from creditors; [4]*‘tio ‘ü*, to shun the rain; [5]*‘tio ‚ing ‚ching*, to avoid making presents; COLL., *‘tio sioh‚ ‚kiéng*, to rest from a burden; *‘tio sioh‚ hiok‚* (or *k‘e’*), to take a breathing spell; *‘tio ‘siéng* (or *‘tiéng*), to dodge, to avoid or escape from.

‘貯 Chu. Read *‘t‘ü*; used for the coll. *‘tio*: to contain, to hold; contained in: *‘tio nóh‚ ‘sai*, used to contain things; *‘tio p‘ak‚* full and running over; *‘tio tak‚ p‘e’* so full as to touch the nose (in eating); *‘tio ‘chwi*, to hold water.

‚屠 T‘u. To cut open, to rend, to rip up; to kill, to butcher animals: COM., [6]*‚tio ho’* a butcher; [7]*keng’ ‚tio*, to prohibit butchering animals; [8]*‚k‘wi ‚tio*, to remove the prohibition to butcher.

‚廚 ‚厨 Ch‘u. A kitchen, a cook-room; a slaughter-house; a case, a drawer; a quiver: COM., [9]*‚tio ‘chiu*, a feast prepared by a professional cook; [10]*‚tio taing’* a public cooking-shop; [11]*‚tio ‚pung*, a kitchen; [12]*‘siong ‚tio*, to give douceurs to cooks; *‚pong ‚tio*, a cook's mate, a scullion.

路’ Lu. Read *lo’*; used for the coll. *tio’*: a road, a path, a way; *met.*, a course of action: [13]*tio’ keng’* (or *‚t‘iǎng*), a road, a course; [14]*siong’ tio’* and [15]*a’ tio’* the upper and lower roads or districts from Foochow; [16]*‘má tio’ ‚chiéng*, black mail; cash to buy the (ghost's) path; *‚kiǎng tang’ tio’* to take the wrong road, to lead a vicious life; [17]*tio’ hwong’* a long way or journey; [18]*chioh‚ mwong’ tio’* to inquire the way; [19]*tio’ ‚tong*, in the way, on the road; [20]*tio’ ‚t‘au* (or *‘k‘au*), a public place, a busy mart; *‚sang hong’ tio’* a strange road; *tio’ ‘lú ‚pang, siǎng’ ‘lá tik‚*, as plain as a road and straight as a thread—plain, easily done; *tio’ siǎng’* road-threads—paths hard to trace; [21]*song’ tio’* by or on the way (do the errand for me).

Tio’. A coll. word, analogous to *‘tio*; to shirk, to do lazily; *tio’ ‚këng*, to shirk work; *tio’ kwo’ nik‚*, to laze through the day.

(812) Tioh.

[This word is interchangeably read *twoh*.]

貯‚ Chu. Read *‘t‘ü*; used for the coll. *tioh‚*: to put, as into a vessel; to cause to contain: *nóh‚ tioh‚ ‘chi ‘tié*, put

[1]躲匿 [2]躲避 [3]躲債 [4]躲雨 [5]躲人情〇 [6]屠戶 [7]禁屠 [8]開屠 [9]廚酒 [10]廚店 [11]廚房 [12]賞廚 [13]路徑 [14]上路 [15]下路 [16]買路錢〇 [17]路遠 [18]借問路 [19]路中〇 [20]路頭 [21]順路

the things into this; *tioh, tiēng*² fill it up; *tioh, sioh*, *'wang*, to fill a bowl full.

Tioh,. A country brogue for *,niéng* or *,tó*, to take: *k'ĕūk, ,i tioh, k'ó*² it was taken away by him.

灼 Read *ch'iok*,; used in the *Paik*, *,Ing* for the coll. *tioh*,: to kindle, kindled; *met.*, to excite to anger: ¹*tioh*, *'k'i ,li*, kindled, lighted; *'hwi má*² *tioh*, the fire will not kindle; *'nū á*² *'hwi tioh*, *,nëng*, you will provoke people!

着 Cho. Read *chiok*,; coll. *tioh*,: to be at or in, to be present; ought, must; also marks the completion of an act: *tioh*, *,mó tioh*, is he here or not? *tioh*, *ch'io*' *'tié*, in the house; ²*tioh*, *p'ah*, must beat him; ³*tioh*, *t'ek*, to stumble; ⁴*t'ó tek*, *tioh*, have found it; ⁵*mwoi*² *k'ó*² *tioh*, have never gone there; *tek*, *tioh*, must, positively, absolutely; *hwoi*² *tioh*, to meet with; met, assembled; *ng*² *tioh*, *,ki tai*² wrong doing, bad conduct.

Tioh,. A coll. word, for which the last may be used: to have, seized, taken with; to hit a mark: *tioh*, *,sa*, to have violent pain in the bowels, the gripes; *tioh*, *,ming ,sa*, a colic accompanied with stupor; *tioh*, *sioh*, *chiéng*' to hit the target with an arrow; *tioh*, *mah*, to "hit the pulse"—used only in a *met.*, sense, as in *k'ĕūk*, *'ngwai 'kong tioh*, *mah*, he was hit exactly by what I said (and shamed or miffed by it).

(813) Tiok.

[This word is interchangeably read *twok*, q. v.]

(814) Tiong.

張 Chang. To draw a bow; to extend, to spread out, to open; to draw up, as a list, to state; to grow, to increase; the 26th zodiacal constellation; a classifier of things spread out, as a chair, a table, paper, for which the coll. is *,t'iong*, q. v.: COM., ⁶*,tiong ,k'wi*, to open out, as a shutter hinged at the top; ⁷*,tiong tau*' to cover; *met.*, to make a show, to arrange so as to look well; ⁸*,tiong ,lá*, to rig a plow; COLL., ⁹*,mó 'chio ,tiong*, no way to manage it; ¹⁰*,tiong ,sang mó*² *k'ĕūk*, *'li se*' *tai*² to put Chang-san's cap on Li-ssŭ—incongruous, unsuitable. Read *tiong*': to boast, to make a display.

[The next two are interchangeably read *twong*.]

轉 Chuan. Chuai. To turn, to revolve, to circulate; to change, to shift, to pass over to another; to do by proxy; to carry, to transmit; to transport, as goods; to return, to go back: ¹¹*'tiong 'ngang*, in a twinkling; COM., ¹²*'tiong ,hung*, the wind veers; ¹³*'tiong 'ping*, to petition by proxy; ¹⁴*'tiong kié*' to transmit at second-hand; ¹⁵*'tiong p'ieu*' to give a new bill or bond; ¹⁶*'tiong saēng*' to give away a present; ¹⁷*'tiong ,sū*, to change one's mind; ¹⁸*'tiong cheng*' the turn in a disease, past the crisis; ¹⁹*'tiong ong*² to transmit goods; a lucky change; *'tiong ,siāng*, the

¹灼起梨〇 ²着柏 ³着踢 ⁴討的着 ⁵昧去着 ⁶張開 ⁷張罩 ⁸張犂 ⁹無主張 ¹⁰張三帽乞李四戴 ¹¹轉眼 ¹²轉風 ¹³轉禀 ¹⁴轉寄 ¹⁵轉票 ¹⁶轉送 ¹⁷轉思 ¹⁸轉症 ¹⁹轉運

change in the voice (at puberty); [1]ʻtiong ˏwang, to turn a corner; [2]ʻtiong siéʼ or ʻtiong ˏlung ˏhúi, metempsychosis; [3]ʻtiong ˏlung kauk, a ball-and-socket joint; COLL., ʻtiong ˏwang pwoak, kaĕk, the turns and corners; *met.*, the twists and turns of a business; ʻtiong kʻóʼ or ʻtiong chʻioʼ to return home; ʻtiong tauʼ to go home to dinner; ʻtiong sioh, ʻpeng, to change and say or do something else; ʻtiong taĕngʼ to move about, to take exercise.

ʻ**囀** Chuan. The singing of birds; warbling notes, delicate modulations of sound: [4]ˏeng ʻtiong, the nightingale's song.

ʻ**長** Chang. Ch'ang. Senior, older; greater, superior; to excel, to advance, to prosper; to increase, to grow; to exalt, to think highly of: COM., [5]ˏka ʻtiong, a paterfamilias; [6]ʻtiong pwoiʼ of the senior class, seniors; [7]ʻtiong ʻchü, (or ˏnang), the oldest son; [8]ʻtiong ʻló, elders, presbyters; [9]ʻtiong ˏpung, the family of the oldest brother; [10]ˏsang ʻtiong, the president of a college; [11]ˏseng ʻtiong, to grow; to be born and brought up; [12]ʻtiong ʻchü ʻtiong ˏsong, the eldest son of an eldest son; COLL., ʻtiong twaiʼ to grow in age and size; ˏnu ʻchʻi ʻtiong ʻnü ˏsang hwoiʼ I am three years older than you, as said by the aged; ʻtiong ˏtʻau ˏtʻoi, the first-born.

ʻ**丈** Chang. Read tiong²: coll. ʻtiong, as in ʻtiong ʻná, a wife's mother.

帳ʼ Chang. A curtain, a screen; a tent, an awning; to extend, to stretch out; *met.*, a house, an abode; to estimate, as an account; the reasons of; an account, for which the next is also used: [13]siék, tiongʼ to become a teacher; COM., [14]hongʼ tiongʼ confused, incoherent; [15]ˏyang tiongʼ or tiongʼ ˏpung, (coll. tiongʼ ˏpʻung), a military tent; [16]chiongʼ ˏkung tiongʼ a large awning, as over a court; [17]tiongʼ ˏmi, the upper facing of a bed-curtain; tiongʼ ˏtʻó, the cords and tassels of a curtain.

賬ʼ Chang. An unauthorized character: an account, a bill, a charge in account: COM., [18]tiongʼ ˏpung, a counting-room; the office where accounts are kept at marriages or funerals; [19]tó tiongʼ to fail on account of (unpaid) bills.

漲ʼ Chang. Also read ˏtiong and ʻtiong in the dictionaries: a large sheet of water, an inundation; to rise higher and higher, to overflow; the southern sea.

脹ʼ Chang. A swelling of the abdomen; a swelling or protruding; dropsy, dropsical: COM., [20]ku tiongʼ a swelling of the abdomen; [21]tiongʼ ˏhung, flatulency; COLL., kʻaĕngʼ tiongʼ a swelling of the side; siăh, tiongʼ ˏpʻiăng, eats till his back swells out! pok, ʻló tiongʼ the belly puffed; tiongʼ soʼ to swell the account—to charge interest on credit sales. Read ˏtiong: the intestines.

---

1 轉彎 2 轉世 3 轉輪骨〇 4 鶯囀 5 家長 6 長輩 7 長子 8 長老 9 長房 10 山長 11 生長 12 長子長孫 13 設帳 14 混帳 15 營帳 16 將軍帳 17 帳眉〇 18 賬房 19 倒賬 20 蠱脹 21 脹風

ALPH. DICT. 114

Tiongʼ. A coll. word: to alter, to change, to become different: *tiongʼ saik꜁* to change color; *tiongʼ pah꜁* to turn white; *tiongʼ pek꜁ pangʼ* to change to another disease; *piéngʼ tiongʼ* to change or pawn for ready money.

場 場 ꜀Ch'ang. An area, a lot, a level space; a sacrificial ground; a threshing place; an arena; a class, a company of; a classifier of certain affairs; in the coll. a job of work: [1]*꜀ung ꜀tiong*, a literary resort; com., [2]*ʻk'wo ꜀tiong*, the examination for the Küjin degree; [3]*ʻu ꜀tiong*, a place for martial exercises; [4]*꜀tiong peʼ* tricks at examinations; *꜀pieu ʻchü ꜀tiong*, a brothel; coll., *kaʼ ꜀tiong*, a parade ground; a place of execution; *chiék꜁ sioh꜁ ꜀tiong*, to get a job of work; *chóʼ ꜀tiong*, to perform a service, as a priest does.

腸 ꜀Ch'ang. The intestines; the bowels; *met.*, the feelings, affections: in the coll. read *꜀tong*, q. v.: *꜀u ꜀tiong ꜀kung ʻchü*, a crab; com., [5]*꜀tiong ꜀hung*, foul wind; *꜀tiong kiék꜁* (or *sóʼ*), constipation.

長 ꜀Chang. Ch'ang. Long in time or distance; constantly; always, continuous; good at, skilled, practiced; to excel: in the coll. read *꜀tong*, q. v.: [6]*꜀tiong ʻwong*, enduring; [7]*꜀tiong ꜀seng*, long life; [8]*ek꜁ ꜀u ʻsu ꜀tiong*, changeful, not persevering; com., [9]*꜀tiong ʻkiu*, a long time, lasting; [10]*꜀tiong ʻtwang*, long and short, the length; *met.*, a turn in matters, something unfavorable; [11]*꜀tiong ꜀ch'ung ꜀hwa*, a rose; [12]*꜀Tiong lóh꜁* a district of the Foochow prefecture; coll., *naʼ oʼ ʻla ꜀tiong ʻtwang ꜀chiong ʻchio eʼ* should trouble (as sickness) come, how shall we manage.

萇 ꜀Ch'ang. A sort of fruit, the carambola (averrhoa), commonly called *꜀yong ꜀t'ó*, or sheep's peach.

[The next two are interchangeably read *twong*.]

團 ꜀T'uan. Read *꜀t'wang*; used for the coll. *꜀tiong*, as in *꜀tiong ꜀tiong*, to form a circle, a reunion; united, as a family: [13]*hwoiʼ ꜀tiong ꜀tiong*, to meet (and shake the dumplings), as a family on the eve of the winter festival; *꜀hu ꜀ch'á ꜀tiong ꜀tiong*, the intimate union of husband and wife—a felicitous phrase.

傳 ꜀Chuan. Ch'uan. To transmit, to hand down, to perpetuate; to publish, to propagate; to deliver orders; to transfer, to move; to narrate: also read *tiongʼ* q. v.: [14]*꜀tiong ꜀ung*, to tell, to inform; com., [15]*꜀tiong tóʼ* to publish a doctrine; [16]*꜀tiong seuʼ* to deliver, to communicate; [17]*꜀tiong ʻniéng*, to give a disease to, infectious; [18]*꜀tiong waʼ* to interpret, an interpreter; [19]*꜀tiong ꜀liu*, handed down, as a trade or art; [20]*꜀tiong ꜀ló*, to give an alarm by beating gongs; [21]*꜀tiong ꜀ka*, to perpetuate in the family, as a trade; *꜀tiong ꜀sing*, to bring out a life-like expression, as in painting a likeness; *꜀yong ꜀tiong*, to publish, to spread abroad; *꜀tiong ʻchüng*, to propagate a species; *꜀tiong chiüngʼ ꜀sing*, to bring the principals (before a

1 文場 2 科場 3 武場 4 場弊 5 腸風 6 長遠 7 長生 8 一無所長 9 長久 10 長短 11 長春花 12 長樂 13 會團團 14 傳聞 15 傳道 16 傳授 17 傳染 18 傳話 19 傳流 20 傳鑼 21 傳家 ○

magistrate); ₍tiong ₍ka ʻpó, to transmit the family jewels.

丈 [1] Chang. Read tiong²; used for the coll. ₍tiong, as in ₍tiong ₍nëng, a husband's father-in-law.

₍Tiong. A coll. word, used for ʻwong, past, former: ₍tiong nik₂ former days; ₍tiong ₍húi, a former occasion.

傳 [2] Chuan. Ch'uan. Interchangeably read twong²: the moral instructions of wise men; narratives, chronicles, traditions; in the coll. to move, to stir; to hand from one to another, to pass things: also read ₍tiong, q. v.: COM., [1]ʻchó tiong² the chronicles of Tso, in Confucius' Spring and Autumn; [2]₍hung ₍sing tiong² annals of deification of gods—name of a book of stories; COLL., [3]tiong² ch'ok, to pass things out; [4]ʻnü ʻmwong tiong² k'a tiong² ʻch'iu, do stir your limbs (and help)!

丈 [2] 丈 [2] Chang. A measure of ten feet or cubits; to measure; an elder, a senior: used for the coll. ʻtiong, ₍tiong, and taung² q. v.: [5]ʻtiong² ₍hu, a husband; [6]ʻngok₂ tiong² a wife's father; [6]ʻtai² tiong² ₍hu, a great man, one who is capable; [7]₍hwong tiong² a Budhist monastery; met., the abbot.

仗 [2] Chang. To rely, to lean on, to look up to, to depend on; a sharp weapon; to fight: [8]seng² tiong² a victory; [9]ʻta tiong² to fight, at war; [10]ʻngiong tiong² to look to for aid; [11]ʻi tiong² to trust to; COM., [12]₍chiong tiong² (coll. ₍chiong t'iong²), to depend on wholly.

[The next two are interchangeably read twong.]

篆 [2] Chuan. A kind of ancient character, called from its use the seal character; to engrave such characters; ornaments on bells: COM., [13]tiong² ₍chü (or che²), seal characters; [14]ʻt'iék₂ siáng² tiong² a seal character with thread-like strokes; COLL., ₍yéng tiong² the rounded seal character.

瑑 [2] Chuan. An ancient ornament like a seal character, on the top of the tablets held as badges by officers and princes.

Tiong². A coll. word: a residue, remainder, overplus; fragments: [15]tiong² ʻtá, leavings, remnants; tiong² ʻla ʻmwó, a balance remaining, as of a debt; ko² ó² tiong² there is still some left.

(815) Tiu.

丟 ₍ Tiu. To throw away; to reject, to cast off, to rid, to be relieved of; to lay aside, to leave undone: used for the coll. ₍liu, q. v.: [15]₍tiu pok₂ ha² cannot get rid of; COM., [16]₍tiu ʻliéng, to dishonor, to ruin one's good name; [17]₍tiu ₍k'wi k'e² kak₂ to throw away helmet and mail; met., ruined in one's business; COLL., [18]₍tiu saëk₂ to dash it down; [19]₍tiu sioh₂ ʻpeng, to throw aside, as work in a strike, &c.; ʻtó ₍tiu ₍tiu tik₂ to lie stretched out.

[1]左傳 [2]封神傳 [3]傳出 [4]汝夫丈 [5]岳丈○ [6]大丈夫 [7]方丈 [8]勝仗 [9]打仗 [10]仰仗 [11]倚仗 [12]全仗○ [13]篆書 [14]鐵線篆 [15]丟不下 [16]丟臉 [17]丟盔棄甲 [18]丟摔 [19]丟一板○

'**肘** Chou. The fore-arm; the elbow, the wrist; to take by the wrist; a joint or quarter of meat; a measure of one and a half or two cubits: [1]*'ch'iu 'tiu*, the wrist; [2]*'tiu ik,* arms and sides; *met.*, near relatives.

'*Tiu.* A coll. word: to prop, to shore; a support, a prop; to offset, to meet; to place by, up to; *met.*, to oppose, to answer, to overthrow in argument: *,mwong 'tiu*, a door-prop; *'tiu piăh,* to prop partitions; to place by the wall; *'tiu t'á'* to be a substitute; *'tiu 'tó*, to prop so as to push over; *met.*, to beat in argument; *'tiu ,i ch'oi'* to answer him with fit words; *'tiu kek,* to meet an emergency; *'tiu p'e'* up to one's nose, as a full bowl of rice in eating; *nge' 'tiu 'lá ,t'iăng*, to incline the ear to hear; *'tiu tiăng'* to stick to, to stay at a place; *'tiu tëük,* to stir up, to excite one to do.

'*Tiu.* A coll. word: to happen, to occur; suiting, meeting; just at the time of: *'tiu 'tiu 'hó*, happens just right; *'tiu 'tiu ,lí*, has just come; *'tiu 'tiu 'chiă ,si hau'* in the nick of time.

,**櫉** ,**橱** The first means a sort of hard wood like rosewood, and (read *cheu'*) a pole for poling boats; the second is a vulgar form; both used in the coll. for a closet: COLL., *,hang ,tiu*, a cupboard; [3]*,chü ,tiu*, a bookcase; small closets; [4]*pauk, 'ku ,tiu*, a cabinet; [5]*yoh, ,tiu*, a medicine-case; *met.*, one who takes much medicine; *,tiu hiăk,* the brass straps of closet-doors to pull by; [6]*,tiu ,t'au 'ting*, on the top of the closet.

,**綢** Ch'ou. Silks in general; pongee, lustring; to bind, to wrap round; to hang with ornaments; thick, close: COM., [7]*,tiu taung'* silks and satins; [8]*,ning ,tiu*, fine pongee; [9]*'hwong ,tiu*, reeled pongee, mostly of a bluish white color; [10]*,miĕng ,tiu*, a cottony silk fabric from Soochow; [11]*'kiĕng ,tiu*, crape pongee, coarse serge; [12]*,su ,tiu*, Soochow silks; COLL., [13]*,tiu ,hong*, a needle for quilting silk. Read *,t'ó:* silk wrapped about a flag-staff.

,**紬** Ch'ou. The same as the last in the sense of silk: to draw out and arrange threads for weaving; *met.*, to investigate first causes, to arrange subjects: [14]*,tiu chek,* to prepare threads for weaving. Read *,tu:* a clue.

,**裯** Ch'ou. To cover, as with bedclothes; a single coverlet; a bed-curtain; an undershirt. Read *,tó:* the sleeve of a coat.

(816) To.

妒' **妬**' Tu. Jealous, as a wife; envious, having ill-will towards: [15]*to' ho'* a jealous woman; COM., [16]*chik, to'* or [17]*to' ke'* jealous, envious; [18]*to' ,sing taĕng'* a feeling of deep jealousy or envy.

1 手肘 2 肘腋 3 書櫥 4 博古櫥 5 藥櫥 6 櫥頭頂 7 綢緞 8 寧綢 9 紡綢 10 綿綢 11 繭綢 12 蘇綢 13 綢杭 14 紬織 15 妒婦 16 嫉妒 17 妒忌 18 妒心重

蠹' **蠧**' Tu. Small worms or grubs in wood; the tinea, book-worms; weevil-grubs: in the coll. read ʻ*tu*, q. v.: [1]꜀*nga to*' extortionate police.

哇' Read ʻ*chü*; used in the *Paik*, ꜀*Ing* for the coll. *to*' as in [2]*to*' *to*' a noise made in calling fowls; ꜀*tu to*' a noise in calling fowls; also a term for fowls.

To'. A coll. word: clever, expert: *sek*, ꜀*ching* ʻ*kau to*' "ten-true-nine-clever"—thoroughly expert at.

杜² Tu. A sort of pear; to stop, to obstruct, to restrict; a surname: [3]*to*² *chiok*, to block the way, to stop; [4]*to*² ꜀*ing*, a fibrous grass for making cords; COM., [5]*to*² *tëüng*² a yellowish pear-wood; [6]*to*² ꜀*kiong*, a cuckoo or goat-sucker; COLL., ꜀*yeu t'iăng*' ꜀*ch'iong* ꜀*küng*, ꜀*t'au t'iăng*' *to*² *tëüng*² (use) the Sz'-chuen root for side-ache and the *to*² for headache.

肚² Tu. The belly, abdomen; the stomach; the mind, intellect: used for the coll. ʻ*tu*, q. v.: COM., [7]꜀*tü to*² pig's stomach; [8]꜀*tong to*² the bowels; COLL., [9]*kwo*' ꜀*tong kwo*' *to*² "for the bowels and belly"—eatables, which should be promptly paid for; ʻ*peng* ꜀*tong* ʻ*peng to*² to turn the stomach, nauseated; ʻ*si* ꜀*ma* ꜀*tong* ʻ*si* ꜀*ma to*² a dead cat's intestines; *met.*, dirt, filth; dull, stupid; [10]*sëük*, *to*² to "lodge" and clog the stomach, as a meal taken just before going to bed.

度² Tu. To. Interchanged with the next: to arrange, to spread out; a measure; a rule, a regulation; a limit; degrees of latitude and longitude; to pass, as time; endurance: also read *tok*, q. v.: [11]꜀*u to*² unlimited; [12]꜀*tiéng to*² an orbit; COM., [13]*to*² *tiék*, a priest's certificate; passports for souls—sheets burnt at the [14]ʻ*p'wo to*² rites; [15]*hwak*, *to*² regulations; [16]*to*² *so*' rule, method in doing; *to*² *liong*² *twai*² of great endurance, very generous and forbearing; [17]*to*² ꜀*seng*, or *to*² *miăng*² to gain a livelihood; [18]꜀*ch'ieu to*² to get souls out of hell; ʻ*p'wo to*² rites to release souls from limbo; *to*² *nik*, ꜀*ü* ꜀*niéng*, to pass days as years—i. e. tediously.

渡² Tu. To cross a stream; to ford; to go through, extending through; a passage boat: COM., [19]*to*² ꜀*këng*, to cross a river; [20]*to*² ꜀*sung*, a passage-boat; *to*² ꜀*sung* ꜀*t'au*, a ferry; [21]*to*² *chai*² ferriage; *A*² *to*² a remote southern suburb of Foochow.

鍍² Tu. To gild, to wash with gold; specifically to plate with gold: COM., [22]*to*² ꜀*king*, to plate with gold; ʻ*kwong* ꜀*tëng to*² Canton gold-plating; *to*² ꜀*king sóh*, gold-plated bracelets.

*To*². A coll. word, as in *to*² *taing*² a sort of lizard-like reptile; it is cooked with rice and administered to children having marasmus; *to*² *taing*² ꜀*mó* ꜀*k'a sioh*, *taëng*² ꜀*sié*, "a footless lizard belongs to the same den as snakes"; *met.*, only differing slightly.

1 牙蠧	3 杜絕	5 杜仲	7 猪肚	9 過腸	10 宿肚	12 躔度	14 普度	16 度數	17 度生	19 渡江	21 渡儎
2 哇哇	4 杜棠	6 杜鵑	8 腸肚	過肚	11 無度	13 度牒	15 法度	〇	18 超度	20 渡船	22 鍍金

(817) Tó.

刀 ˏTao. A knife; a one-edged sword; a dagger, a poniard; a rapier; a knife-shaped coin of the Han dynasty; a small-boat, a canoe; a classifier of quires of paper of various sizes, for which the coll. is *ˏt'ó*, q. v.; the 18th radical: COM., [1]*ˏtó ch'oiʼ* the edge of a knife; [2]*ˏtó ˏhung* (or *ˏchiéng*), the point of the blade; [3]*t'ièʼ ˏtó*, a razor; [4]*ch'aiʼ ˏtó* or *ˏtio ˏtó*, a cleaver; [5]*ˏtó sioh*, a whet-stone; [6]*ˏYong ˏtó*, foreign knives; *ˏtó sieuʼ* a scabbard; *ˏtó ˏping*, weapons; *leʼ ˏtó*, a sharp knife; COLL., *ˏtó sioh ʻpa*, one knife; *ˏka ˏtó*, shears, scissors; *ˏtó ʻkiăng*, a small knife, a pen-knife; *p'ah ˏtó ˏhwa*, to practice fencing; *ˏtó ʻching* (or *ˏp'iăng*), the back of a knife-blade; *ˏtó tauʼ* the knife-bean—a large kind, so called from the shape of the pod.

忉 ˏTao. Sad, sorrowful, grieved: [7]*ˏsing ˏyong ˏtó ˏtó*, the heart bursting with grief.

舠 Tao. A long, narrow boat, a punt; a full cargo of 300 *hĕk* or 20 tons.

多 ˏTo. Many, much; more; a superlative, very, too, much, excessive; to beg, to want, to crave more; to add; to admire, to praise: [8]*ʻki ˏtó*, how many? COM., [9]*ˏtó lĕüʼ* very anxious; [10]*ˏtó ˏngi*, doubting, suspicious; [11]*ˏtó sĕüʼ* much trouble, mischief; [12]*ˏtó siăʼ* many thanks! [13]*ˏsang ˏtó*, the three many—i. e. sons, prosperity, and old age; *ˏtó ʻkong*, to say too much; *ˏtó ˏü*, excessive; *ʻlü ˏtó ˏing pek chaʼ* the too polite are certainly deceitful! *ˏtó ʻkwa*, much or little, somewhat; COLL., *ˏtó tek ˏtó*, mostly, for the most part; *ˏtó ˏnĕng ˏhiéng*, many hate him.

島 ʻTao. A sea-island: [14]*ʻtó sĕüʼ* islands, islets; COM., *ˏp'ung ˏlai ʻtó*, fairy isles; [15]*ʻhai ʻtó*, islands in the sea.

擣 搗 ʻTao. To beat, to pound; to beat, as clothes; to construct, to make solid, as walls; to lean on, to comply with; to collect: [16]*ʻtó ˏi*, to beat clothes in washing.

禱 ʻTao. To pray, to supplicate the gods; to beg, to request in courteous phrase: [17]*seʼ ʻtó*, I request—a phrase at the end of letters; COM., [18]*ˏki ʻtó*, to pray; *ˏki ʻtó ˏung*, a written prayer; [19]*ʻtó kóʼ* to inform (the gods).

倒 ʻTao. To fall down; to lie down, to recline; to invert, subverted, destroyed, in ruins; an adverb, yet, indeed: also read *tóʼ* in the coll. q. v.: [20]*ˏtiéng ʻtó*, subverted; deranged, confused in mind; [21]*chiok ʻtó*, to laugh immoderately; COM., [22]*ʻtó hwaiʼ* ruined, in ruins; [23]*ʻtó ongʼ* unlucky; *ʻtó taingʼ* to fail, as a shop; *ʻtó p'ieuʼ* unredeemable bank-notes; *ʻtó ˏch'ong*, confined to the bed by illness; COLL., *p'ah ʻtó*, to knock over; fallen, knocked down; *ʻtó tiăngʼ* (or *ʻtiéng*), fixed, constant, as at a place or employment; *ʻtó chiăʼ* falling sugar-canes; *met.*, many dying, banks failing, etc.

1 刀嘴　2 刀鋒　3 剃刀　4 菜刀　5 刀石　6 洋刀　7 心焉忉忉　8 幾多　9 多慮　10 多疑　11 多事　12 多謝　13 三多　14 島嶼　15 海島　16 擣衣　17 是禱　18 祈禱　19 禱告　20 顛倒　21 絕倒　22 倒壞　23 倒運

福州方言拼音字典

倒 Tao. Read 'tó; coll. tó': reversed, opposite, on the contrary; to empty, to throw out: p'ah, tó' 'kong, to use words contrary to one's real meaning; [1]tang tó' on the contrary; tang tó' t'au, the wrong end first; [2]tó' t'ié' to shave reversely; [3]tó' ngai, on the contrary it's worse; [4]tó' t'ói' to recede, to go backward; tó' k'ié lë, to bestride an ass backward—to "put the cart before the horse"; tó' ing kang' steam on the under side, as of a pot-cover; tó' yă' se' after all it is so; tó' pong' tó' to throw away refuse; tó' tieu t'iăng, a room back of a second court and facing the main hall.

到 Tao. To arrive; to reach, to extend to; to go to; up, at, up to; still, yet, on the contrary; sign of the past tense; complete: [5]tó' 'lieu, has arrived; COM., [6]tó' 'tá, after all, at last; finally; [7]chiu tó' complete, perfect in all respects; [8]tó' ch'ëü' everywhere; [9]tó' eng' to arrive at one's office, as a new officer; [10]tó' 'pa, to hit the target; [11]pok, tó' has not come—not present, as at roll-call.

他 T'a. Interchanged with the next; also read t'a, q. v.: Read t'ó: a man's name; [12]ŭng kung chi t'ó, a general in the time of Mencius.

佗 T'o. Used for the next: to carry on the back: [13]tó pwoi' to bear on the back; humpbacked; [14]wi tó, elegant, genteel; COLL., tó k'ié' 'ma, to carry astride the shoulders.

馱 To. T'o. A horse carrying a burden; to carry on horseback, to load a horse: [15]ho' tó, to carry a pack; a pack-horse or mule; COM., [16]Ui tó, (spoken ui nó), the wand-bearer or guard—an idol standing back of Mi ná huk, in the front temple.

駝 T'o. A camel; to bear burdens, as animals: COM., [17]lok, tó, a camel; COLL., 'ung tó p'iăng, humpbacked, a hunchback.

咷 T'ao. To cry, to bawl: [18]hó tó, screaming, bawling; [19]kieu' tó, to sob incessantly, as a child.

檮 T'ao. A block of wood, a useless stick; stupid, ignorant; an auspicious animal: [20]tó wok, perverse, dogged; the annals of the Ch'u state; also a noted bandit mentioned in the Spring and Autumn annals.

沱 T'o. Streams diverging; a branch, a tributary; a heavy rain: [21]pong tó, rain in torrents; falling tears.

淘 T'ao. To wash and scour, to wash, as rice; to sift or move about in washing; to search for and cleanse, as gold dust: [22]tó sa, to wash out the sand; tó tó, water flowing gently on.

濤 T'ao. Waves, billows, waves rolling and dashing violently: [23]p'ó tó, billows.

1 單倒 2 倒喇 3 倒呆 4 倒退 5 到了 6 到底 7 周到 8 到處 9 到任 10 到靶 11 不到 12 尹公之他 13 佗背 14 委佗 15 負馱 16 韋馱 17 駱駝 18 號咷 19 呌咷 20 檮杌 21 滂沱 22 淘沙 23 波濤

紽 ,
Silk threads, as spun or woven; a skein of silk; a hank of floss; silken tassels, as used to ornament furs.

綯 ,T'ao.
To braid or twist, as cords; to bind; a twisted string, a cord: [1]'sauk, ,tó, to twist ropes.

翿 ,T'ao.
To cover with feathers; a feather flag or fan, used by actors.

痑 ,
Sickness, ailments, disease; one says to have a diseased spine, a humpback.

砣 ,
A stone roller; also the game called "flying bricks".

𦍩 ,T'o.
A fabulous animal like a sheep, having four ears and nine tails.

詑 ,T'o.
To deceive, to impose on, to insult; light, trickish; lying and boastful. Read ,i, as in ,i ,i, self-satisfied.

舵 柁 ,To.
Also read 'tó: a helm, a rudder: in the coll. read twai' q. v.: [2],tó ,kung, a helmsman.

萄 ,T'ao.
The vine: com., [3],pwo ,tó, grapes; [4],pwo ,tó 'chié, a purple color.

跎 ,T'o.
To slip, to miss: [5],ch'ó ,tó, to trip or stumble, as in ascending; to miss a good chance, to lose an opportunity.

逃 迯 ,T'ao.
To flee, to escape; to abscond, to desert; to elude search: [6],tó hok, to play truant; [7]'kwai ,tó, to kidnap, to abduct; [8],tó ,ing, a deserter, a fugitive; com., [9],tó 'chau, to run away; [10],tó pié' to elude; [11],tó ,ping, a deserter; [12],tó hwang' an escaped prisoner; [13],tó nang' to escape calamity, as by migration.

酡 ,T'o.
The face flushed with wine: [14],tó ,ngang, red in the face, rubicund, flushed.

醄 ,T'ao.
Tipsy, drunk, intoxicated: [15],mó ,tó, overcome with liquor, reeling.

鋾 ,T'ao.
Blunt, dull; used as a term for a kind of scales: com., [16],t'iéng ,pang ,tó, large scales for weighing silver; [17],tó 'ma or [18],tó 'chi, the weights of the same.

裪 ,T'ao.
The end of the sleeve, the cuff; it is often shaped like a horse's hoof and embroidered.

鞀 ,T'ao.
The wooden part of a drum. Read ,iu: a drum.

陀 ,T'o.
Precipitous, steep, dangerous; a Budhist word: [19],p'ó ,tó, uneven, rugged, as a path along a cliff; fading, decaying; com., [20]'p'wo ,tó ,sang, the island of Pooto near Chusan.

[1] 索綯 [2] 舵公 [3] 葡萄 [4] 葡萄紫 [5] 蹉跎 ○ [6] 逃學 [7] 拐逃 [8] 逃人 [9] 逃走 [10] 逃避 [11] 逃兵 [12] 逃犯 [13] 逃難 [14] 酡顏 [15] 酕醄 [16] 天平鋾 ○ [17] 鋾碼 [18] 鋾子 [19] 陂陀 ○ [20] 普陀山 ○

福州方言拼音字典

꜀陶 ꜀匋 T'ao. An earthen vessel, pottery; a furnace for burning earthenware, a kiln; to nourish; to be pleased, exhilarated; to give vent to the feelings; right, correct; a surname: [1]꜀*tó* ꜀*ing*, a potter; [2]꜀*tó* ꜀*ũng*, to melt; to reform, to transform; [3]*ok*꜆ ꜀*tó*, mournful, vexed, distressed. The first read ꜀*yeu*, as in ꜀*yeu* ꜀*yeu*, pleased, satisfied; [4]꜀*Kó* ꜀*yeu*, a celebrated minister of Shun.

꜀鼗 ꜀鞉 T'ao. A hand-drum with two buttons or pellets tied to strings, twirled by peddlers in the streets; it is termed in the coll. ꜂*pa* ꜂*lang* ꜂*ku*, q. v.

꜀鮀 T'o. A kind of water gavial, which burrows in the sand; one says, also a species of dogfish or lamprey.

꜀掏 T'ao. Used for the coll. ꜀*tó*, to take in the hand; to lift, to raise; to carry: [5]꜀*tó* ꜀*li*, to bring; [6]꜀*tó k'ó*꜄ to take away; [7]꜀*tó* ꜀*pwang*, to borrow money for carrying on a business; [8]꜀*tó* ꜀*lëng piè*꜄ to tug at a hulling-machine handle; *met.*, disappointed, shamed by labor lost; ꜀*tó tëü*꜅ ꜀*chiă p'e*꜄ to cover the nose with the chop-sticks—a vain effort at concealment; ꜀*tó taĕng*꜅ to have credit, able to borrow.

꜀道 Tao. Read *tó*꜅; coll. ꜀*tó*, as in [9]꜀*tó tai*꜅ a class of lay Tauists or secular priests: ꜀*tó tai*꜅ *p'ah*꜆ ꜂*si* ꜀*tó tai*꜅ ꜀*siăng*, kill the priest and still his is a priest's voice; *met.*, to stick to an assertion, to persist, as in a wrong.

꜀*Tó*. A coll. word, as in ꜀*tó tek*꜆ to injure, to spoil, to waste; to tease, to trouble, to annoy; to misuse: ꜀*tó tek*꜆ ꜀*nëng*, to annoy one, to injure, as by deception; ꜀*tó tek*꜆ *nóh*, to spoil or waste things; ꜀*tó tek*꜆ ꜂*chiă* ꜀*kwong* ꜂*king*, to ruin one's prospects.

道꜅ Tao. A path, a way, a road, a thoroughfare; a course, a zone; reason, doctrine, principle; the Reason of the Tauist sect; a cause, a reason for; to follow, to accord; to lead, to direct, to teach, in which sense it is like the next; to speak, to say, to talk; by, from, by means of; a classifier of edicts and dispatches: in the coll. read ꜀*tó*, q. v.: [10]*tó*꜅ *lo*꜅ a road, a way; [11]*siok*꜆ *tó*꜅ to say; COM., [12]*tó*꜅ ꜂*li*, doctrine, reason, what is right and proper; [13]*tó*꜅ ꜀*ing*, a Tauist priest; [14]*tó*꜅ *sëü*꜅ or *tó*꜅ ꜀*kung* (coll. ꜀*tó tai*꜅), lay Tauists or secular priests; [15]*tó*꜅ ꜀*tai*, an intendant of circuit; [16]꜀*si tó*꜅ commissioners and intendants; [17]*tó*꜅ *kau*꜄ Tauism; *tó*꜅ ꜂*ki* ꜀*si*, the superintendent of the lay priests; *tó*꜅ ꜂*li* ꜀*ch'ing* ꜂*wong*, abstruse doctrine; [18]*taik*꜆ *tó*꜅ to attain nigban; [19]꜀*wong tó*꜅ the royal road, what is perfect or just; [20]꜀*kung tó*꜅ just, equitable; *chëü*꜅ ꜂*ku tó*꜅ the proverb saith; [21]*tó*꜅ ꜀*t'au*, a wharf, a landing; *tó*꜅ ꜀*sang kwang*꜄ the temple of Reason's hill, Foochow; *tó*꜅ ꜀*pó*, a surplice; *pa*꜄ *tó*꜅ tyrannical; [22]꜂*ma tó*꜅ the race-course of a parade ground; [23]*ch'ek*꜆ *tó*꜅ the equator; *tó*꜅ *taik*꜆ virtue; COLL., *tó*꜅ ꜂*li*

1 陶人 2 陶鎔 3 鬱陶 4 皇陶 5 掏梨 6 掏去 7 掏盤 8 掏礱臂 9 道大〇 10 道路 11 說道 12 道理 13 道人 14 道士 15 道臺 16 司道 17 道教 18 得道 19 王道 20 公道 21 道頭 22 馬道 23 赤道

pwoh, *tek*, *‚nĕng*, reason constrains people.

導[2] Tao. To lead, to conduct, to point out the way; to teach, to direct; to regulate: COM., [1]*‘ing tó*[2] to instruct, to guide one, as to virtue; [2]*‚k‘wi tó*[2] to teach one first principles; [3]*hong*[2] *tó*[2] a district professor, teacher of the Siutsai; *‚hiong tó*[2] *‚kwang*, a village guide — one who formerly led troops to seize banditti.

悼[2] Tao. Wounded in mind, grieved; afflicted, distressed; to grieve for, to pity, as an ignorant offender; to fear; an early death: [4]*tó*[2] *‚wong*, to grieve over the death (of relatives).

惰[2] 墮[2] To. Indolent, lazy, spiritless; flagging, drooping; rude, impolite: the 2d also read *toi*[2] q. v.: [5]*tai*[2] *tó*[2] indolent; careless, remiss; COM., [6]*‘lang tó*[2] lazy, loitering.

隋[2] An undulating range of hills; hills having sharp peaks and intervening hollows.

盗[2] 盜[2] Tao. To covet and take by fraud or force; to rob; a highwayman, a robber, a footpad; a pirate; to embezzle, to abstract, to appropriate others' property: [7]*tó*[2] *‚ming*, to get a good name falsely; [8]*‘sieu tó*[2] a pilferer; COM., [9]*‘hai ‚yong tai*[2] *tó*[2] a sea-rover, a pirate; you great pirate! COLL., *tó*[2] *ch‘ek*, *‚p‘ung ‘k‘i*, thieves swarming like bees; *‘chwi ‘hwo tó*[2] *‚tu ng*[2] *‚kiăng*, no fear of freshets, conflagrations, and thieves, as a safe residence.

稻[2] Tao. Rice in the plant, paddy; rice, as cultivated in the south: [10]*lŭk*, *tó*[2] upland rice; [11]*‘chó tó*[2] the early rice.

蹈[2] Tao. To step, to walk; to tread under foot, to trample on; to violate; trodden, as a path: [12]*‘ch‘iu ‘u chŭŭk*, *tó*[2] to move the hands and feet, gesticulation; [13]*‚kó tó*[2] to go far; to retire into privacy.

Tó[2]. A coll. word, used for *hó*[2] as in *tó*[2] *‘hi*, to congratulate, to give a present on a joyous occasion.

(818) Tóh.

卓, Cho. A surname: also read *tauk*, q. v.

棹, 桌, Cho. Read *tauk*, in the dictionaries; coll. *tóh*,: a table; a stand: the 1st also read *chau*[2] q. v.: [14]*tóh*, *‘kiăng*, a small table; [15]*ngwok*, *tóh*, round or semicircular tables; [16]*paik*, *‚sieng tóh*, a square table, which seats eight guests; [17]*‘sieu ‚yeu tóh*, an oblong table; [18]*‚hwang ‚t‘au tóh*, a long narrow table, as for idols and flowers in a hall; [19]*k‘aung*[2] *‚ch‘ong tóh*, or *‘Mwang ‚Chiu tóh*, a low stand on a dais; [20]*tóh*, *tau*[2] a table-covering; *tóh*, *‚kung*, a table-valance.

Tóh,. A coll. word: to prick; also to nip, to strip off, as roots and poor leaves of vege-

1引導 2開導 3訓導 4悼亡 5怠惰 6懶惰 7盜名 8小盜 9海洋大盜 10陸稻 11早稻 12手舞足蹈 13高蹈 14棹仔 15月棹 16八仙棹 17小腰棹 18橫頭棹 19匠床棹 20棹圍

tables in cooking: *tôhˌ siohˌ ˏcheng*, to give a prick with a needle.

(819) Toi.

堆 ʻ Tui. Tsui. A heap, a mass; mounds, piles, as of earth: a multitude, a crowd; to heap, to pile; to accumulate; to put aside; a guard-house, called [1]*ˏkwang ˏtoi*; COLL., [2]*siohˌ ˏtoi*, together; [3]*ˏt'u ˏtoi*, a heap of earth; [4]*ch'au ˏtoi*, a pile of straw or grass; *ˏtoi siohˌ ˏtoi* (or *ˏk'ŭng*), to pile in a heap; [5]*ˏsiăng ˏtoi ˏsang* (or *seʼ*), a great number, a crowd; a large quantity of; [6]*ˏtoi ʻk'au*, a shrine outside a prison wall; the hole by which dead prisoners are removed; [7]*pongʼ tóʼ ˏtoi*, a heap of refuse.

ˏToi. A coll. word: where? how? *ˏtoi k'óʼ* whither has he gone? where did you go? *ˏtoi ʻhieu* (or *ˏchong*), how could I know it?

短 ʻ Tuan. Read *ʻtwang*; coll. *ʻtoi*: short, not long; brief, contracted; to fall short, a lack, a deficiency; a balance against: *ʻtoi niăh*, short, too short; [8]*ʻtoi chekˌ* a brief section, a short scene (in plays); [9]*ʻtoi miăngʼ siongʼ* a physiognomy indicating short life; *ʻtoi niohˌ waiʼ* how much too short? [10]*ˏtong ʻtoi*, long and short, a difference, as in an account; *ʻtoi ʻtoi ˏk'a*, very short feet (of a lady).

䢒 ʼ Read *ʻtoi*; coll. *toiʼ*: to pull strongly; to hold fast, as by a rope; to tow: [11]*toiʼ aʼ* (or *kiăʼ*) *k'óʼ* to drag down; [12]*ˏsung ʻkiăng toiʼ twaiʼ ˏsung ʻlă ˏkiăng*, a small boat towed by a large boat.

懟 ʼ **憝** ʼ Tui. To be displeased with; to hate, to abhor; disliking, angry at; inimical, hostile: [18]*wongʼ toiʼ* to hate, to have spite towards; *ˏngwong auk, taiʼ toiʼ* great hatred to the chief criminal.

隤 ˏ **穨** ˏ Tui. To fall in ruins; overthrown, prostrate, ruined; lost, irremediably injured; to involve in ruin; to cause to fall, to push over; obedient, complying; soft, yielding: [14]*ˏhwi ˏtoi*, jaded, as an old horse.

頹 ˏ **頽** ˏ T'ui. Interchanged with the preceding: the jaws; a bald head; a violent gust, a hurricane; to rush, to flow down; to fall, to slide, as a mountain; yielding, obedient: [15]*ˏtoi ˏyong*, compliant; [16]*ˏtoi tôʼ* lazy; [17]*ngŭkˌ ˏsang ˏtoi*, a drunkard reeling; COM., [18] *ˏsoi ˏtoi* or *ˏtoi paiʼ* infirm, wasted.

魋 ˏ T'ui. A marvelous animal like a bear, having short yellow hair. Read *ˏt'ui*: the hair bound in a knot, as a Tauist's.

ˏToi. A coll. word, as in *ˏtoi tikˌ* specially, purposely—the same as *tekˌ tikˌ* q. v.

隋 ² To. To fall into ruin; fallen, dilapidated, destroyed; poor, reduced, decayed; to sag, to hang down; to flow down, as tears; disused,

---

1官堆 2一堆 3土堆 4草堆 5成堆山 6堆口 7糞倒堆 8短截 9短命相 10長短○ 11䢒下去 12船仔䢒大船 禮行 18怨懟 14魋隤 15頹然 16頹惰 17玉山頹 18衰頹○

effete, worn out: also read *tó*ˀ q. v.: [1]*toi*ˀ *loi*ˀ tears flowing down; [2]*ngwok*, *toi*ˀ the setting moon; [3]*toi*ˀ *lok*, to fall down; fallen, poor, reduced.

墜ˀ Chui. To fall, to tumble; to topple, to fall over; prodigal, wasteful; in the coll. to let down by a cord; to hang a weight on; to mark, as prices; at, after; to sink, to settle: COM., [4]*toi*ˀ *꜀t'ai*, an abortion, a miscarriage; *toi*ˀ *te*ˀ *ngwoh*, to fall into hell; [5]*toi*ˀ *꜀wang*, bent by a suspended weight; COLL., *toi*ˀ *lóh*, *k'ó*ʼ to let it down; *tói*ˀ *ʻmwi ꜀li*, to come last; *toi*ˀ *ʻla ʻma ʻchi*, to mark prices in abbreviated numerals.

隊ˀ Tui. Same as the last: to fall, to slide from a high place; to slip down; a group, a company, a crowd; a flock, a herd; a rank, a file; 100 men: [6]*ek*, *toi*ˀ a group, a flock; [7]*꜀ping toi*ˀ a file or detachment of troops; COM., [8]*toi*ˀ *ʻngu*, files, platoons; [9]*꜀pá toi*ˀ to dress ranks. Read *soi*ˀ: a dangerous pass in a mountain.

隧ˀ Tui. Also read *soi*ˀ; interchanged with the last two: a path to a tomb, an underground way; a common road, a path, a lane; also to turn, to revolve: [10]*toi*ˀ *tó*ˀ a way, a road.

縋ˀ Chui. A cord, a rope; to suspend or let down by a cord: COLL., [11]*toi*ˀ *lóh*, to let down, as into a well; *toi*ˀ *꜀yong ʻchi*, to carry weights of lead, as on the feet in practicing at jumping.

(820) Tói.

對ʼ **对**ʼ Tui. To answer, to reply to; to suit, to agree with, to correspond; fronting, opposite to; to pair, to match; a pair; opposed, inimical; sign of the dative: COM., [12]*tói*ʼ *che*ˀ to compare (copied) words (with the original); [13]*tói*ʼ *p'wo*ˀ a book of antithetical phrases, as written out by a pupil; [14]*tói*ʼ *che*ˀ to confront accuser with accused; [15]*tói*ʼ *ʻch'iu*, to lend a helping hand; [16]*tói*ʼ *meng*ˀ opposite, face to face; [17]*tói*ʼ *swoi*ˀ to emulate, as two processions; [18]*tói*ʼ *ʻk'eu*, palatable; [19]*tói*ʼ *taëng*ˀ equal in weight; *꜀liéng tói*ʼ corresponding phrases on scrolls; [20]*tói*ʼ *꜀t'au*, opposed, inimical; *tói*ʼ *ch'oi*ʼ *ʻkong*, to speak face to face; *tói*ʼ *hak*, agreeing, matching; *tói*ʼ *꜀t'au ꜀hung*, a head wind; COLL., *tói*ʼ *꜀t'iéng hwong*ˀ very distant; [21]*tói*ʼ *꜀peng*, in two parts or halves; *tói*ʼ *ʻtá*, to fit the sole to, to sole shoes; *tói*ʼ *heng*ˀ both keep mum; *ek*, *tói*ʼ *꜀ka lak*, *꜀su*, both of the same stamp, as being dull, sluggish, &c.

塊ʼ K'uai. K'uei. Read *ʻk'wai* and *k'wai*ʼ; coll. *tói*ʼ: a clod, a lump; a piece, a fraction of; a numerative of pieces, bits, slices, places, plats, &c.: [22]*tói*ʼ *pwang*ˀ a piece and a half; a dollar and a half; *sioh*, *tói*ʼ *꜀t'u*, a lump of earth; *sioh*, *tói*ʼ *te*ˀ a piece of land; *꜀kó ꜀long tói*ʼ a whole piece; [23]*ʻmwang tói*ˀ (or *nói*ˀ), every where; *꜀mó tói*ʼ *k'ié*ˀ

[1]墜淚 [2]月墜 [3]墜落 [4]墜胎 [5]墜彎 [6]一隊 [7]兵隊 [8]隊伍 [9]牌隊 [10]隧道 [11]縋落 [12]對字 [13]對簿 [14]對質 [15]對手 [16]對面 [17]對賽 [18]對口 [19]對重 [20]對頭 [21]對爿 [22]塊半 [23]滿塊 ○

no place to stand; ʻcheu ˛hwang ˛sang tói' three Mexican dollars.

兌' Tui. Read tói²; coll. tói': analogous to the next; to barter, to give an equivalent; to pay over, to discharge a debt: [1]ʻtói' ˛ngüng, to barter silver; [2]ʻtói' ˛chu, to pay rent; pwang' ˛niéng tói' to pay in half-yearly installments; [3]kié' tói' paid in quarterly installments; [4]ʻtói' ka' to pay off a debt.

兌² 兊² Tui. To exchange, to barter; to give an equivalent, to weigh against; collected; permeable, straight through; satisfied, pleased with; the 58th diagram: in the coll. read tói' q. v.: COM., [5]tói² wang² (or pauk,), to exchange, as coin or jewels; [6]tói² ˛ngüng, to weigh or exchange silver; [7]tói² hwoi² to turn a debt, pay through one who owes; hwói² tói² kwoh, an office for the sale of bills of exchange or credit.

駾² A horse going rapidly: [8]tói² tok, to bolt, to rush out suddenly.

代² Tai. Read tai²; coll. tói²: a generation, an age: tói² tói² successive generations; [9]sié' tói² ages of the world, generations; [10]hau² tói² succeeding generations, posterity.

袋² Tai. Read tai²; coll. tói²: a bag, a sack; a case; a purse or pocket; [11]˛toi tói² a bag; [12]tak, tói² a sort of money-sack with an opening in the middle; [13]˛mwai tói² a hempen sack; [14]tói² ˛kong, a cord across the bottom of bags; ʻtu ˛peng tói² the pocket at the bottom of the ʻtu ˛peng; [15]˛küng chiéng' tói² a quiver; ʻchiu ˛nong pwong' tói² a wine-bibber and glutton.

(821) Tok.

督, Tu. To lead, to conduct, to command; to examine; to urge, to incite; to warn, to reprove; to set in order, to correct; a general, an overseer; the middle; sore eyes: [16]˛ka tok, the eldest son; tok, sauk, to head, to lead; COM., [17]ʻchung tok, the Viceroy; [18]tok, ʻu, Viceroy and Governor; tok, ˛ping twai² ˛ngwong sói² a generalissimo; [19]tok, ʻli, to direct, to superintend; [20]tok, ˛këng, to oversee work; [21]tok, teng² to lead battalions.

篤, Tu. True, sincere, simple, earnest; firm, stable, strong; pure, unmixed; kind, liberal; to augment; to attach importance to, to regard seriously; severe, as diseases; a sick horse; used as a superlative: [22]tok, sik, true and sincere, trustworthy; tok, hok, diligent in study; [23]tok, seng' to believe sincerely; peng² tok, dangerously ill; tok, ˛heng, to do vigorously, to apply the whole mind to.

Tok,. A coll. word: to point, to dot, to mark with the pencil or tip of the finger; to dip in; to punctuate; to prick in; to light: tok, sioh, tok, to make a dot; tok, ˛chü, to punctuate a writing; tok, má² lóh, can't be marked off, is ungrammatical; tok, ʻch'ó, to prick saleratus in (green persimmons); tok, ˛siéng ka² ˛kiong, to dip in salt and gnaw

1 兌銀 2 兌租 3 季兌 4 兌價 5 兌換 6 兌銀 7 兌會 8 駾突 9 世代 10 後代 11 袋袋 12 搭袋 13 蔴袋 14 袋綱 15 弓箭袋〇 16 家督 17 總督 18 督撫 19 督理 20 督工 21 督陣 22 篤實 23 篤信

ginger—too poor to buy savory food; *tok, siok, chiāh,* to light one, as a match or lamp; *sek, tok,* a soldering-iron.

凸 Tu. Tieh. Any thing that juts above the surface, as a wen, a swelling, a hillock; a tenon; convex, protuberant; used for the coll. *ʻt'u,* q. v.

突 宊 Tu. T'u. Abruptly, furiously; to rush out, to bolt; to offend, to insult; inconsiderate; to pierce, to make a hole; blunt, bald; to guard a door; a vicious horse: [1] *ˌch'ūng tok,* to rush against; [2] *tok, ˌŭ ˌki ˌlai,* to come upon suddenly; COM., [3] *tok, ˌyong ˌkang,* suddenly, abruptly. Read *tiēk,*: a dog issuing from his hole; slippery.

㸚 Tu. To offend by pride; rude, insulting, arrogant: [4] *ˌtong tok,* insufferably proud, haughty in manner and speech.

堗 Tu. The door of a furnace or kitchen range, the place where the fire is put.

奪 To. Read *twak,*; coll. *tok,*: to take forcibly; to rob, to plunder; to snatch, to gain hardly, get by hook and crook: [5] *ch'iong tok,* to rob; [6] *tok, ˌpieu,* to get the prize, as at a boat-race; [7] *tok, ˌhui,* to get back, to recover; [8] *tok, siāh,* to get one's livelihood hardly; [9] *tok, ʻpwong,* to realize only the capital invested; [10] *tok, ˌhung ʻtiong tëük,* to get back the soul (of the sick) by turning a bamboo, as a *ˌsai ˌkung* pretends to do.

度 Tu. To. To guess, to conjecture; to estimate, to reckon, to calculate; to throw in, as into a caisson; to throw, as dirt between planks in making walls: also read *to²* q. v.: [11] *ˌch'ai tok,* to judge of, to guess; COM., [12] *ˌch'oi tok,* to conceive, to seek the sense of; [13] *tok, ʻk'i ʻli,* I conceive the state of the case to be—an initial phrase in talking.

鐸 To. A bell or cymbal, used to convey orders in an army; *met.,* one who arouses the age: [14] *muk, tok,* a sort of rattle or bell with a wooden clapper; [15] *ˌhung tok,* wind jingles.

(822) Tong.

櫄 Tang. A wooden bench, bed, or couch; the name of a tree. Read *taung²*: the purlines or transverse beams of a roof.

璫 Tang. An ear-ring, pendants, drops; ornaments or jewels worn on the head: [16] *ˌting ˌtong,* jingles hung in the wind; [17] *ˌking ˌlong ˌtong,* bells, jingles.

鐺 Tang. Ch'ĕng. Interchanged with the last: the sound of a drum: [18] *ˌlong ˌtong,* a clasp, a lock for the neck; *met.,* something hard to bear.

當 Tang. A proper value set on a field; suitable, proper, opportune, just; adequate, equal to; to mate, to match;

[1] 冲突 ○ [2] 突如其來 [3] 突然間 ○ [4] 僖㸚 [5] 搶奪 [6] 奪標 [7] 奪回 [8] 奪食 [9] 奪本 [10] 奪魂轉竹 [11] 猜度 [12] 㨮度 [13] 度起理 ○ [14] 木鐸 [15] 風鐸 [16] 玎璫 [17] 金璫 瑲 [18] 鋃鐺 ○

福州方言拼音字典

to bear, to take the responsibility; to meet, to occur; at the time of, when; the present participle; to manage, to superintend, to mete out justly; to oppose, to withstand; to protect; to act as, to be: also read *taung'* q. v.: COM., [1]*ˌing ˌtong*, or *ˌkai ˌtong*, ought, is proper; [2]*ˌtong ˌching*, true; [3]*ˌtong chói'* to bear guilt or punishment; [4]*pok, ˌtong*, can't bear (such honor)! [5]*ˌnang ˌtong*, hard to bear; [6]*ˌtong ˌping*, to be a soldier; [7]*ˌtong ˌhong*, to be on one's guard; [8]*ˌtong ˌsi*, or *ˌtong a'* at that time; *ˌtong ˌka 'li kié'* to be the head and manager of a family; [9]*ˌtong ang' chek*, to be a thief-catcher; [10]*ˌtong ˌt'iéng*, toward the open sky; [11]*ˌtong ˌkwi*, a medicine for the blood; COLL., *ˌtong mâ' teu'* can't endure it, as pain; *ˌtong ˌsiéng ˌka paik, sóh*, to be a bully, a shameless bruiser or villain; *ˌtong meng' ˌch'ang 'chwi*, to add in water before one; *met.*, to disparage one before another person.

襠 *ˌ*Tang. A sort of waistcoat or wrapper: [12]*k'o' ˌtong*, a pair of breeches; [13]*ˌkung ˌtong*, the waistband of trowsers; [14]*seu' ˌtong*, an embroidered cover.

鈍 Tun. T'un. Read *tong'*; coll. *ˌtong*: dull, as a knife: [15]*ˌtong tek*, *'heng*, very dull; [16]*ˌtong ˌtó tói' le' 'ch'iu*, a dull knife in a skillful hand — *scil.*, does the work though difficult.

中 *ˌ*Chung. Ch'ung. Read *ˌtüng*; coll. *ˌtong*: the middle, center; the heart, the core of: *ˌtong ˌtong* or [17]*tai' ˌtong*, in the middle; *tai' ˌtong ˌtong*, in the very midst; [18]*ˌtong ˌsing*, the heart, the core; *ˌtong ˌtong chiâng' chiâng'* exactly straight, not oblique; [19]*ˌTong ˌchiu*, an islet between the Min bridges, Foochow.

墩 *ˌ*Tun. Read *ˌtung*; coll. *ˌtong*: a numerative of villages; a prop: *sioh, ˌtong*, a village; [20]*p'ah, ˌtong*, to place props; *ˌtó ˌtong 'tiu sioh, a'* take props and prop it.

ˌTong. A coll. word: to sweep into, to take up in: *ˌtong pong' 'tau*, to sweep into the dustpan; *ˌtong k'ó' tó'* sweep it up and throw it away.

ˌTong. A coll. word: to emasculate, to geld, to castrate: *ˌtong ˌtü*, to castrate a boar; *ˌtong ˌkié*, to geld a cock.

ˌTong. A coll. word: to trap, to entrap: *ˌtong 'cheu*, to snare birds; *ˌtong ˌngü*, to catch fish; *ˌtong 'ló 'ch'ü*, to trap rats.

ˌTong. A coll. word: to renew with the chisel, to pick: *ˌtong mó'* to pick mill-stones.

ˌTong. A coll. word: to take turns, to serve in rotation: *ˌtong ˌt'au*, or *ˌtong hok, 'siu*, to take one's turn in superintending, as a temple and yearly processions; *ˌtong ˌniéng*, the yearly turn, as to reap the ancestral field; *ˌtong nik,* to serve in daily rotation, as in offices.

盾 'Tun. Shun. A shield, a buckler; to scamper away, to hide, to skulk: [21]*ˌmau 'tong*, contradictory views or statements.

1 應當 2 當真 3 當罪 4 不當 5 難當 6 當兵 7 當防 8 當時 9 當暗緝〇 10 當天 11 當歸 12 袴襠 13 褌襠 14 繡襠 15 鈍的很 16 鈍刀對利手 17 大中 18 中心 19 中洲 20 拍墩 21 矛盾

‘楯 Shun. A railing, a balustrade, a parapet; a sort of shield or defence used by posture-makers; to raise the eye; a hearse: [1]*,lang ‘tong*, a balustrade.

‘腯 Tun. Obese, fat; full and fat, plump; to drag the feet in walking: [2]*,p‘i ‘tong*, very fat, as a pig.

‘砧 Read *,t‘ing;* coll. *‘tong:* a block of wood or stone; an anvil: [3]*sioh, ‘tong*, a stone-seat; a stone pillar or base; [4]*k‘ié ‘ ‘tong*, one who cuts (idol paper) on a block; [5]*t‘iék, ‘tong*, an anvil.

‘擋 Tang. To strike; to impede, to obstruct, to resist, to stop; to cover, to screen; to push along; a company, a cabal, in which sense used for the next: COM., [6]*‘tong ka’* to stop the chariot—i. e. to take a visitor's card instead of his visit.

‘黨 ‘党 Tang. Not a few; a village of 500 houses; a cabal, faction, league, brotherhood; a seditious junto; to club, to form a conspiracy; to assist in evil; associates; intelligent, to bring to mind; a place, a time; partial; to involve: [7]*‘p‘i ‘tong*, banditti, villains, vagabonds; [8]*‘tong cheng’* a village-chief; [9]*‘tong ‘ü*, adherents of a faction, intriguers; [10]*,peng ‘tong*, a brotherhood, a faction; COM., [11]*kiék, ‘tong*, to form a cabal; [12]*‘tong twai’* the gang is a large one.

‘讜 ‘說 Tang. Right, forcible words, honest speech, faithful advice: [13]*‘tong laung’* to advise, to exhort, as to virtue.

‘斷 Tuan. Read *twang’;* coll. *‘tong:* to snap, to break in two; snapped, broken, shivered; *met.*, arrested, stopped, deprived of: [14]*p‘ah, ‘tong*, snapped in two; [15]*‘tong chek,* severed, as a procession; *‘tong kwok,* broken in two, as a stone slab; [16]*‘tong ,sai*, to cut the umbilical cord; [17]*‘tong ,kŭng*, parted at the root; *met.*, arrested in a vicious course.

‘Tong. A coll. word: the rising of the tide: *‘chwi ‘tong*, or *,tieu ‘tong ‘chwi*, the flood-tide; *‘tong paik,* the tide risen eight tenths; *‘tong tiĕng’* full tide.

‘Tong. A coll. word: to indulge one, to permit wrongfully; also to gain, to increase; to grow, as new flesh; *‘tong ,i*, give him the reins, let him do as he will; *‘tong nŭk,* to become fleshy; *‘tong ,sing nŭk,* to grow new flesh, as under a scab; *‘tong ‘k‘i ,ching ,sing*, to regain one's spirits, joyous; *‘tong ‘nü ,mwong ,hung*, it raises your family reputation.

‘Tong. A coll. word: to buy, as piece-goods: *‘tong pwo’* to purchase cotton cloth; *‘tong sioh, p‘ek,* to buy one piece (of cloth or silk).

凍’ Tung. Cold, freezing, icy; to freeze, to congeal; to cool: in the coll. read *taĕng’* q. v.: COLL., [18]*,pu ,sung tong’* a shiver, a

[1]欄楯 [3]石砧 [5]鐵砧 [7]匪黨 [9]黨羽 [11]結黨 [13]讜論 [15]斷截 [17]斷根○ [18]箁鬆凍○

[2]肥腯 [4]跬砧 [6]擋駕 [8]黨正 [10]朋黨 [12]黨大 [14]拍斷 [16]斷臍

sudden tremor, as over one's body.

棟 Tung. The main supports in a house, posts, joists, columns; a pillar of the state; the four corners of an outer coffin; name of a tree: in the coll. read *taëng'* q. v.: [1]*'ok, tong'* the rafters, the plate; [2]*tong' ˛liong ˛chi ˛chai*, ability to uphold a state.

蝀 Tung. The rainbow, called [3]*'tá' tong'*; it is supposed to be made of insects.

囤 Tun. A large hamper, a bin for rice; specifically, a thick bamboo-mat to hold grain; it is united at the ends and placed upright on the floor: COM., [4]*tong' chek,* to hoard grain; COLL., *sioh, tong' 'mi*, a bin of rice.

頓 頔 Tun. To bow the head, to fall before, to bow with the head to the ground; to salute respectfully; an inn, a resting-place; to stop, to rest; to adjust, to put in order; to part with; to haste; to reject, to injure; a meal, a spell, the time of a meal, for which the coll. is *taung'* q. v.: COM.,[5]*'tong' 'siu pai'* with respectful salutations—a phrase on cards; [6]*'ching tong'* to adjust, to repair, or put in order; COLL., *tong' 'tong*, a stone to which a culprit is fastened; *˛tang tong'* delayed, kept waiting; *tong' ˛hu wai'* stops or waits there; *tong' sioh, a'* to pause, to rest the voice on a word.

屯 T'un. Chun. To collect and station troops, to bring under one control: also read *˛tung*, q. v.: [7]*˛tong ˛ping*, troops at a station, where they till the land; [8]*˛tong ˛tiéng*, fields allotted to soldiers; [9]*˛hung ˛tong yeu' hai'* to detail troops to important posts.

傭 搪 T'ang. Wayward, disobedient, willful; to spread, to stretch out: [10]*˛tong tok,* abrupt, brusk; rude, froward, wanting in humility; [11]*˛tong saik,* to stop one's mouth, to answer a charge, as with feigned words.

唐 T'ang. To boast, bragging, gasconade; the path to an ancestral temple; name of a dynasty, A. D. 620—904: COM., [12]*˛hwong ˛tong*, exaggeration; [13]*˛tong ˛chü*, tales of the T'ang dynasty; *˛tong ˛ming ˛hwong ˛yeu ngwok, ˛kŭng*, the Emperor Ming of the T'ang visits the moon-palace—a play; COLL., [14]*˛tong ˛pwo*, a male; a husband; [15]*˛tong ˛pwo ˛nëng*, a male, a man; *˛tong ˛pwo 'kiáng*, a male child, a boy, a son; [16]*˛tong ˛nëng*, a Chinese.

塘 T'ang. A pool, a tank, a fishpond; a stagnant pool; a numerative of leagues or military stations: [17]*˛tié ˛tong*, a pond; [18]*˛tong ˛kó*, celery; COM., [19]*˛tong seng'* a guard-house, the officer of a station; [20]*˛pá ˛tong*, guard-houses at intervals of ten *'li* or a league.

螗 T'ang. As in [21]*˛tieu ˛tong*, a species of cicada or broad locust.

[1]屋 之 [4]囤 拜 兵 屯 傑 唐 哺 [16]唐 [18]塘 [20]牌
棟 才 積 [6]整 [8]屯 要 [11]傭 [13]唐 [15]唐 仈 蒿 塘
[2]棟 [3]蝃 [5]頓 頓 田 害 塞 書 哺 [17]池 [19]塘 [21]蜩
樑 蝀 首 [7]屯 [9]分 [10]傭 [12]謊 [14]唐 仈 塘 汎 螗

螳 ꜀T'ang. A mantis: [1]꜀tong ꜀tong, the praying mantis.

堂 ꜀T'ang. A hall, a mansion; a palace; a temple; a court-room; a public establishment; the chief hall of a house; a presiding magistrate; illustrious, exalted; just, upright, perfect; an elevated plateau; a family designation; distant relatives of the same clan; a classifier of trials: [2]꜀kó ꜀tong, parents; [3]꜂hung ꜀tong, a general laugh; [4]꜀tieu ꜀tong, an audience-chamber; COM., [5]hok꜆ ꜀tong, a school, a seminary; [6]chiáng꜄ ꜀tong, title of a district magistrate; [7]꜂chó ꜀tong, and [8]꜀eu꜄ ꜀tong, superintendents of the Siutsai; ꜀kwang ꜀tong ꜀ting, the court-room of a yamun; [9]leng꜄ ꜀tong, your mother; [10]꜀ming lung ꜀tong, a literary hall by a Confucian temple; [11]꜀tong ꜂lá, presents to police; [12]꜀t'ieng ꜀tong, heaven, paradise; ꜀tong ꜀tong ꜀nang ꜂chü hung꜄ a man of talent and integrity; ꜀tong ꜀hing tá꜄ and ꜀tong ꜂chiá mwói꜄ paternal uncle's sons and daughters, cousins; [13]꜀tong hó꜄ distinctive name of a family or clan; COLL., ꜂sing sioh꜆ ꜀tong, to hold one session of court; sói꜄ ꜀kwang ꜀ing ꜀tong, sits in Kwan-yin's hall — sticks close to his wife.

棠 ꜀T'ang. A species of sorbus or service, the wood of which is suitable for junks; the side boards of a cart: [14]꜀tong lá꜄ the sorbus and plum; *met.*, brothers; [15]꜀ch'iu ꜂hai ꜀tong, the Cydonia Japonica?

瞠 ꜀T'ang. Often read ꜀t'ong: to look straight forward; to stare, to gaze at.

鏜 ꜀T'ang. Also read ꜀t'ong: the sound of bells and drums, a drumming; to bore through and bind with iron.

餹 餳 ꜀T'ang. Sugar, candy; sugared, preserved in sugar: in the coll. read ꜀t'ong, q. v.

膛 ꜀T'ang. Fat, fleshy, corpulent: COM., [16]꜀hüng ꜀tong, the bosom, the breast, as of a fowl.

腸 ꜀Ch'ang. Read ꜀tiong; coll. ꜀tong: the intestines: [17]꜀tong to꜄ the bowels; [18]twai꜄ ꜀tong and [19]꜂sieu ꜀tong, the large and small intestines.

臀 ꜀T'un. The buttocks, seat, nates; the rump; the lower side, bottom; a man's name.

豚 豘 ꜀T'un. A pig, a porker, a sucking-pig, small pigs; to drag the feet; dragged, draggled: [20]꜀tong ꜀tá, a small leg of pork, pettitoes; [21]꜀ó ꜀tong, a porpoise.

長 ꜀Chang. ꜀Ch'ang. Read ꜀tiong; coll. ꜀tong: long in time or dimension; far off; regular, constant; protracted, long continued; more, over, exceeding; drawn out, drawling: ꜀tong ꜀long or ꜀tong ꜀tong sié꜄ long, longish; [22]꜀tong te꜄ ꜀t'wa, long and trailing, as a dress; ꜀tong

1 螳螂　2 高堂　3 哄堂　4 朝堂　5 學堂　6 正堂　7 左堂　8 右堂　9 令堂　10 明倫堂　11 堂禮〇　12 天堂　13 堂號　14 棠棣　15 秋海棠　16 胸膛　17 腸肚　18 大腸　19 小腸　20 豚蹄　21 河豚　22 長地拖

福州方言拼音字典

*miâng*² (or *seu*²), long life; ¹*ˌtong ʻtoi*, long and short, the difference, as in length, accounts, &c.; ²*ˌtong pek*ˌ a long sword—wielded with both hands; ³*ˌtong ëüng*² to expend (so much) more; ⁴*ˌtong ˌkëng*, steady employment; *ˌtong kʻe*² *lik*ˌ long-winded; *ˌtong ˌkʻa lëk*ˌ a long-paced stag; *met.*, one who takes long steps; ⁵*ˌtong ʻkiu*, a long time, lasting; ⁶*ˌtong pang*² *ʻkwi*, the tall imps—attendants of the *ʻngu tá*² and some other idols; *ˌtong ˌtong ˌsiâng*, a drawling voice.

ˌTong. A coll. word: to stamp, set down the foot forcibly: *ˌtong tʻieu*² to stamp and jump up and down, as in a rage; *ˌtong tʻak*, to stamp (a thing) through or out; *ˌkʻa ˌtong sioh*ˌ *a*² to give a stamp with the foot.

動² Tung. To move, to excite, to agitate; to revolve, to come forth, as the spring; to put the hand to, to begin; to move, or influence the mind; excited, surprised; restless, irritated; motion: in the coll. read *taëng*² q. v.: *tong*² *ˌsing*, agitated in mind; ⁷*tong*² *chauk*ˌ to make; work; COM., *ˌheng tong*² *ʻkü ʻchi*, actions, conduct; ⁸*tong*² *kʻe*² irritated, angry; ⁹*ʻkang tong*² to influence, as the Spirit does; ¹⁰*tong*² *ˌhing*, to inflict torture; ¹¹*ʻwong tong*² to trifle, to do thoughtlessly; ¹²*ʻhwo tong*² lustful feelings; *tong*² *pok*ˌ *tong*² restless, hasty; at once, on the instant; *tong*² *ˌtó ˌping*, to initiate war; *tong*² *ʻchʻiu*, to put the hands to, to begin; ¹³*tong*² *cheng*² a stir, commencement of preparations.

慟² Tung. Tʻung. The feelings deeply moved, excessively grieved, greatly excited: ¹⁴*ˌai tong*² extremely distressed; ¹⁵*ˌsing tong*² grieved in spirit.

挏² Tung. Also read *ˌtung*: to lead, to draw; to beat, to churn, to bring butter from milk: ¹⁶*tong*² *ʻma*, an officer who attended to the preparation of quass.

𦪒² Tung. The boards of a boat, timber used in building boats.

洞² Tung. To flow rapidly; a swift current; a den, a cave, a grotto; a dell, a gorge, a ravine; deep, profound, deep and clear; to understand, to perceive clearly; thoroughly acquainted with: in the coll. read *taëng*² and *ˌtung*, q. v.: ¹⁷*tong*² *sek*ˌ to know fully; ¹⁸*tong*² *ˌpung* (coll. *ˌtung ˌpung*) a bridal chamber; COM., ¹⁹*tong*² *ˌting ˌhu*, the Tungtʻing lake in Hunan.

沌² Tun. Mixed, confused, chaotic, undeveloped; the rush of waters: ²⁰*kong*² *tong*² chaos, without form; also the name of one of four bad men in the time of Shun.

炖² Tun. Read *ˌtung*; coll. *tong*²: to heat or cook in an inner tube or vessel: ²¹*tong*² *yék*ˌ to warm up; ²²*tong*² *pwong*² to cook rice, as in a vessel set in a pan of water; ²³*tong*² *lang*² to cook soft.

鈍² Tun. Tʻun. Blunt, dull, the edge turned; witless, obtuse, stupid: used for the coll. *ˌtong* and *pong*² q. v.

¹長短 ²長白 ³長用 ⁴長工 ⁵長久 ⁶長柄鬼 ⁷動作 ⁸動氣 ⁹感動 ¹⁰動刑 ¹¹妄動 ¹²火動 ¹³動靜 ¹⁴哀慟 ¹⁵心慟 ¹⁶挏馬 ¹⁷洞悉 ¹⁸洞房 ¹⁹洞庭湖 ²⁰混沌 ²¹炖熱 ²²炖飯 ²³炖爛

衕 [2] Tung. T'ung. As in [1]ʻˏhu tongʼ a name for a lane or street in Peking; the term is probably confined to the capital.

鼟 鼕 [2] T'ung. The 2d read ˏtung; the 1st used in the Paik, ˏIng for the coll. tongʼ as in tongʼ tongʼ the noise of drums.

(823) Tu.

都 ˏTu. Tou. A metropolis, the capital; the site of an imperial temple; a fief granted to princes, a city whose revenues were given to statesmen; the sub-divisions of a hsien, tax-districts; the empire; full, abundant; fine, excellent; to dwell; all, general, the whole number; in the coll. all, wholly, altogether; both, either one, in either way: [2]ˏtu tok, the commander of the Imperial armies; [3]ˏking ˏtu, the capital; COM., [4]ˏtu ʻtʻung, a major-general of the Tartars; [5]ˏtu ˏsi, or ˏtu ʻkʻung, a military officer of the 5th rank; [6]ˏtu chʻak, yéngʼ the Board of censors or inspectors; COLL., [7]ˏtu ˏsing, a carpenter; ˏtu ʻhó, all good, either will do; ˏtu ˏmó, none at all; ˏtu seʼ ʻnü chóʼ it's all your doing; ˏtu ʻsai tek, any way will answer.

闍 ˏTu. A double door in a city gate; a tower or watchman's turret over the gateway. Read ˏsié, as in [8]ˏsié ˏmi, to burn the body of a priest, cremation of Budhists.

ˏ*Tu.* A coll. word, as in ˏtu ˏtu taiuʼ suspended, as from a ceiling; ˏti ˏtu, or ˏti ˏti ˏtu ˏtu, or ˏti ˏti ˏtu ˏtu, hanging all about.

堵 ʻTu. A wall; 50 cubits of wall; to obstruct, to shut, to wall off the way to, to guard; a suspended bell; settled, tranquil, at peace; in the coll. a section, as of wall; a panel, a compartment, an apartment: [9]ʻtu ngëüʼ to guard; [10]ˏó ʻtu, an old term for coin, pelf; [11]ˏang ʻtu, tranquil; COLL., [12]ʻtu mengʼ the top of a compartment or stateroom; ʻtu ʻtiė ʻtʻó siăh, to hunt for food in the cabins, as rats; *met.*, gamblers; ʻchek, chóʼ langʼ ʻtu, to divide into two apartments.

睹 覩 ʻTu. To see, to view, to observe; perceived, observed: [13]ʻtu uk, ˏhwai ˏing, to remember one by looking at a memento; ʻtu uk, ˏsiong ˏsing, grief on looking at relics (of departed friends).

賭 ʻTu. To gamble, to play, to game; to stake, to wager, to bet; gaming: COM., [14]ʻtu pauk, gaming; [15]ʻtu ˏchiéng ˏtiong, a gambling-place; [16]ʻtu ˏsio, to lose the game; to wager; [17]ʻtu chengʼ kinds of gambling, games; [18]ʻtu kongʼ or ʻtu ˏchiéng ʻkwi, a gambler, a blackleg; [19]ʻtu ˏka ʻhwi, to gamble away property; COLL., ʻtu ˏchiéng áʼ piéngʼ siongʼ laiʼ yāʼ oʼ yoh, if a gambler can reform, then too is there a medicine for leprosy!

肚 ʻTu. Read toʼ; coll. ʻtu, as in [20]ʻtu ˏpeng, a sort of half-waistcoat or vest, worn in front and fastened by

1 衚衕　2 都督　3 京都　4 都統　5 都司　6 都察院　7 都成○　8 闍維　9 堵御　10 阿堵　11 安堵　12 堵面　13 睹物懷人　14 賭博　15 賭錢場○　16 賭輸　17 賭症　18 賭棍　19 賭家伙　20 肚肀○

cords about the neck and waist; *‘tu ˏpeng tai’* and *‘tu ˏpeng ˏk‘wang*, its cords and rings; *‘tu ˏpeng tói’* or *‘tu tói’* the pocket at its bottom; *ˏui ‘tu*, a leathern pocket, worn by police and low people.

蠹 ‘Tu. Read *to’*; coll. *‘tu*, as in [1]*‘tu ˏngü*, the tinea or book-worm.

‘Tu. A coll. word, about the same as *‘tiu*: to happen, to chance, just as; just right: *‘tu ‘tu ‘hó*, to happen well or exactly right; *‘tu tek, tioh*, happened, hit upon; *‘tu ‘tu ch‘ok, ˏing ˏseng*, at this very juncture comes out the *ˏing ˏseng* (lottery-name for the day); *met.*, to chance, inopportune, as rain when one has no umbrella.

圖 圕 啚 ˏT‘u. A map, a drawing, a chart, a diagram; to sketch, to delineate; to plan, to scheme; to plot, to intrigue; to calculate; to wish, to desire earnestly: [2]*ˏtu chik*, books and drawings; [3]*‘pang ˏtu*, a census; COM., [4]*ˏtu ˏmeu*, to plot, to intrigue; [5]*ˏtu le’* to scheme for gain; [6]*ˏtu lai’* to charge, to blame unjustly; [7]*te’ ‘li ˏtu*, geographical maps; [8]*ˏtu ˏch‘á*, a tax-gatherer; [9]*ˏtu ˏchiong*, a private seal.

徒 ˏT‘u. To go afoot; a footman, a soldier; a disciple; a multitude; a clan, cabal; vile fellows, banditti, ruffians; servants in offices; empty, vain, futile; simply, only, barely; to transport for three years: [10]*ˏtu ˏyong*, in vain; [11]*ˏtu pwo’* to foot it; COM., [12]*ˏtu té’* a disciple, a learner, an apprentice; [13]*ˏmwong ˏtu*, disciples; [14]*ˏtu chói’* transported for crime; *ˏtu ˏló ˏu ek*, useless trouble; [15]*‘p‘i ˏtu*, banditti, roughs; COLL., [13]*mwong’ ˏtu*, to exile for three years.

塗 塗 ˏTu. ˏT‘u. Mud, clay; miry roads; to daub, to besmear, to dirty; to plaster, to whitewash; to blot out, to efface, to erase; to fill, to stop up; thick, stupid; liberal: [16]*ˏná ˏtu*, mud, dirt; COM., [17]*ˏtu mwak*, to blot out; [18]*ˏtu ‘kai*, to strike out and alter; [19]*ˏtu ˏhwi*, to plaster with lime; [20]*ˏtu yoh*, to rub on ointment; *ˏtu ‘hung wa’ ˏmi*, to use cosmetics and paint the brows; COLL., *ˏhu ˏtu ˏkwang*, a stupid, reckless magistrate.

涂 ˏT‘u. Name of a stream in Shantung, flowing into the gulf of Pechihli: [21]*ˏtu ngwok*, the 12th month; *ˏtu ˏtu*, a heavy dew.

途 ˏT‘u. Interchanged with the last two: a road, a path, a way; *met.*, a pursuit, a mode; destiny: [22]*lo’ ˏtu*, a road; COM., *ˏkŭng ˏtu*, way to poverty—a poor employment; *pwang’ ˏtu ˏi hié’* to stop half way, give up a pursuit; *ong’ ˏtu*, the course of one's luck; *‘kai ˏtu piék, ngiék*, to change to another employment.

梌 梚 ˏT‘u. A variety of pine: COM., [23]*ˏtu muk*, or *ˏtu ˏch‘u*, fine hard pine, used in furniture. Read *ˏt‘u*: sharp-pointed, thorny.

---

1 蠹魚　2 圖籍　3 版圖　4 圖謀　5 圖利　6 圖賴　7 地理圖○　8 圖差　9 圖章　10 徒然　11 徒步　12 徒弟　13 門徒　14 徒罪　15 僩徒　16 泥塗　17 塗抹　18 塗改　19 塗灰　20 塗藥　21 涂月　22 路途　23 梌木

稌 ꜀T'u. Also read *to²*: a kind of glutinous rice or millet, growing in marshy ground.

酴 ꜀T'u. The sediment of spirits, the lees, the dregs; the ferment put into wine: [1]*꜀tu ꜀mi*, double-distilled liquor, a kind of gin.

鵌 ꜀T'u. A bird that burrows with marmots or rats; the description of its habits assimilates it to the burrowing owl.

駼 ꜀T'u. The name of a place in the north whence horses are brought: [2]*꜀tó ꜀tu*, a gentle, well-trained horse.

荼 ꜀T'u. A bitter herb, perhaps a sort of colt's foot, Tussilago; *met.*, wretched, miserable: [3]*꜀tu ꜀mau*, a flowering rush; lithe, graceful, as a girl; [4]*꜀tu tuk*, bitter trials; COM., [5]*꜀tu ꜀mi ꜀hwa*, the cinnamon rose; *꜀Sing ꜀tu* and *Ok꜀ ꜂lwi*, two gods, whose names are written on doors as a charm.

薔 ꜀Ch'iang. A rose: also read *꜀ch'iong*, q. v.: COM., [6]*꜀tu ꜀mi*, the cinnamon rose—mentioned in songs. Read *saik꜀*: an aquatic vegetable.

瘏 ꜀T'u. Sick, diseased, as an animal; worn out by travel: [7]*꜂ma ꜀tu*, a jaded horse.

(824) Tü.

猪 ꜀Chu. A hog, swine: COM., [8]*꜀tü ꜂mó*, a sow; *met.*, large, coarse; [9]*꜂yong ꜀tü*, to raise swine; [10]*꜀tü ꜀p'a*, a pig's bladder; [11]*꜀tü ꜀iu*, lard; [12]*꜀tü nük꜀*, pork; [13]*꜀tü ꜀tá*, a leg of pork; [14]*꜀tü ꜀lung*, a pig-sty; [15]*꜀tü ꜀ling*, a species of China-root—a urinative; COLL., *꜀tü ꜀t'ong*, a shote, a porket; [16]*꜀tü ꜀t'au chiong꜄* the mumps—perhaps the same as *꜀sang ꜀tong ꜀sai*; *꜀tü ꜀k'a hwoi²* a club to buy pigs cheap, as for new year's; *꜀tü paik꜀ kú꜄* a pig-mouthed worthy; *met.*, one who pouts in anger; [17]*꜀tü ꜂mó ꜀cheng*, coarse needles; *꜀tü ꜂mó lièng꜄* an iron cable; *꜀tü ꜀p'iăng aung² aung² o꜄ ꜀iu*, just stroke a pig's back and you get grease—a little flattery will win some of his money.

瀦 ꜀Chu. Also read *꜀chü*: a place where water settles, a pool, a reservoir.

誅 ꜀Chu. Also read *꜀t'ü*: to inquire judicially; to punish, to destroy, to slay, to execute; to blame, to reprimand; to involve in guilt: [18]*꜀tü miék꜀* to exterminate; *꜀t'iéng ꜀tü*, divine or imperial infliction; [19]*꜀ching ꜀tü*, to punish rebellious states.

滁 ꜀Ch'u. A city in the east of Nganhwui; a stream flowing into the river Yangtsz' between Nanking and Ichêng.

篨 ꜀Ch'u. A mat rolled up: [20]*꜀kü ꜀tü*, a coarse mat; *met.*, an ailment that prevents stooping, hunchbacked.

蜍 ꜀Ch'u. As in [21]*꜀siéng ꜀tü*, a striped toad, a common toad, termed in the coll. *꜀ha ꜀ma*, q. v.

[1] 酴醾 [2] 騊駼 [3] 荼茅 [4] 荼毒 [5] 荼蘼花○ [6] 薔薇 [7] 馬瘏 [8] 猪母 [9] 養猪 [10] 猪脬 [11] 猪油 [12] 猪肉 [13] 猪蹄 [14] 猪欄 [15] 猪苓 [16] 猪頭齉○ [17] 猪母針○ [18] 誅滅 [19] 征誅 [20] 籧篨 [21] 蟾蜍

福州方言拼音字典

除 ꜀Ch'u. Steps to a hall; a vestibule, space between a door and inner screen; to exclude, to remove, to except; to reject, to destroy; to deduct, to divide; exclusive of; to cure, to heal; to exchange: [1]꜀*tü* ꜀*kwang*, to exchange one's office, promoted; COM., [2]꜀*tü* ꜂*k'i*, to deduct; [3]꜂*kwi* ꜀*tü*, to add and subtract; to multiply and divide; [4]꜀*tü miek*꜄ to destroy, to exterminate; [5]꜀*tü hai*꜆ to destroy what is hurtful, as thieves; [6]꜀*tü* ꜀*hi*, excepting that, unless; ꜀*tü* ꜀*siu ngwoi*꜆ after deducting what has been received; ꜀*tü* ꜀*chiéng pok*꜄ *keu*꜅ not inquire into the past (of your errors); COLL., ꜀*tü t'ah*꜄ *t'ah*꜄ to make a clean sweep of; ꜀*tü* ꜀*p'ui t'iăh*꜄ *kauk*꜄ to deduct the tare or refuse.

躇 ꜀Ch'u. The feet entangled; perplexed: also read ꜀*t'ü*, q. v.: COM., [7]꜀*t'iu* ꜀*tü*, embarrassed, hesitating, at a loss how to proceed.

躕 ꜀Ch'u. Also read ꜀*t'ü*: hindered, unable to advance: [8]꜀*t'i* ꜀*tü*, impeded, stopped, involved.

(825) Tuh.

㧻꜆ T'u. Read *t'uk*꜆; coll. *tuh*꜆: to stab, to perforate, to pierce: [9]*tuh*꜆ *p'wai*꜅ to break by thrusting; *tuh*꜆ ꜀*t'ëng t'au*꜅ to perforate.

(826) Tui.

搥 ꜀Ch'ui. To beat, to pound, to strike; to hammer out: also read ꜀*t'ui*, q. v.: COLL., [10]꜀*tui* ꜀*k'a* ꜂*t'oi*, to beat the thighs—*scil.*, in order to relieve pain; [11]꜀*tui* ꜀*king pòh*꜆ to beat gold-leaf; ꜀*tui* ꜀*mwong p'ah*꜄ *ho*꜆ to pound on the doors.

(827) Tuk.

毒꜆ Tu. A poison, a bane; poisonous, noxious, venomous; injurious, hurtful; cruel, malignant, malicious; to hate, to abhor; to poison; to injure; also painful, grievous; to rule: in the coll. read *tëk*꜆ q. v.: [12]꜀*liu tuk*꜆ a lasting injury; COM., [13]*huk*꜆ *tuk*꜆ poisoned; [14]*tuk*꜆ *yoh*꜆ a poison; [15]*tuk*꜆ *k'e*꜅ noxious vapors or humors; [16]*tuk*꜆ ꜂*ch'iu*, a malicious villain; ꜂*i tuk*꜆ ꜂*kung tuk*꜆ to neutralize one poison with another; [17]꜀*ch'ong tuk*꜆ venereal ulcers; [18]꜀*sing tuk*꜆ cruel, malicious; *tuk*꜆ *sak*꜄ ꜀*ch'ing* ꜀*hu*, to poison one's own husband.

纛꜆ Tu. Tao. A standard, a large banner of feathers, hair, or silk; a flag borne before the coffin at funerals: COM., [19]*twai*꜆ *tuk*꜆ a large banner; [20]*tuk*꜆ ꜀*ki*, the main standard of an army.

獨꜆ Tu. Alone, solitary; single, one's self; only; widowed, childless; a species of baboon: [21]*tuk*꜆ ꜂*chü*, an only child; [22]*tuk*꜆ *eng*꜆ to bear a responsibility alone; COM., [23]*tuk*꜆ *ek*꜄ one only; *tuk*꜆ *soi*꜆ ꜀*ch'ong*, a single bedstead of the larger pattern; *tuk*꜆ *kiok*꜄ *tóh*꜄ a one-footed or center table; *tuk*꜆ *chiéng*꜅ ꜀*ngó* ꜀*t'eu*, to usurp the whale's head—get the first degree at Peking; ꜀*tang* ꜀*mwong tuk*꜆ *ch'e*꜅ the only shop that sells (the article).

1 除官 2 除起 3 歸除 4 除滅 5 除害 6 除非 7 躊躇 8 踟躕 9 㧻破 10 搥骹腿 11 搥金箔 12 流毒 13 服毒 14 毒藥 15 毒氣 16 毒手 17 瘡毒 18 心毒 19 大纛 20 纛旗 21 獨子 22 獨任 23 獨一

韇 Tu. A sheath for a bow; a case or covering to preserve bows.

匵 櫝 Tu. Also read *chëük*, and *sük*,: a case, a covering, as for tablets: a scabbard; a drawer, a casket, a receptacle for books; a coffin: [1]*'ung tuk*, *ˌi ˌchong*, to lay by carefully, as gems.

殰 Tu. To die in the womb; an untimely birth, an abortion.

瀆 瀆 Tu. A drain, a sluice, a sewer; a river which drains the land; foul, muddy; the first only is used in the following senses; to profane, to insult; to despise, to treat rudely; to bother, to annoy, as by reiteration: [2]*ˌkeu tuk*, a sewer, a ditch; [3]*sëü' tuk*, the four sluices, the Yangtsz', the Yellow, the Huai and the Chi rivers; [4]*'tuk*, *t'eng'* to annoy by reiterating; you bother my ears, as magistrates say; COM., [5]*siëk*, *tuk*, to blaspheme, to insult a superior.

牘 Tu. Tablets to write on, blocks for books; books, documents, registers; a sort of musical instrument, a bamboo beaten to keep time: [6]*ch'ek*, *tuk*, a card, a note, a brief; a tablet; [7]*'ang' tuk*, law cases, a record of precedents in law.

犢 Tu. A calf, a heifer; a sacrificial victim: [8]*'ló ˌngiu 'ti tuk*, an old cow licks her calf —emblem of parental love.

讟 Tu. To be grieved; discontented, dissatisfied, seditious; complaints, reviling, murmuring, as against rulers: [9]*'paung' tuk*, to slander, to vilify.

(828) Tŭk.

妯 Chu. Chou. Two sisters-in-law call each other [10]*tŭk*, *'li*, in Foochow termed [11]*'mu 'sing*. Read *ˌt'iu*: to move about; disquieted, agitated in mind.

軸 Chu. Chou. The ends of an axle; a pivot, center of motion; the roller of a map; the woof frame-work; a picture or map; scrolls inscribed with words; weak, unable to walk: [12]*ˌkiéng tŭk*, to turn, to revolve; COM., [13]*ˌliéng tŭk*, narrow and wide scrolls; [14]*seu' tŭk*, scrolls inscribed with the word *seu'* or *hok*, given as birthday presents; *tŭk*, *ka'* (a present in money of) the value of a scroll; COLL., [15]*tŭk*, *sioh*, *hok*, one map or scroll.

逐 Chu. To expel, to drive out, to order away; to pursue; to press, to urge on, as a marriage; to take up in order, as topics; sincere, earnest; successive: [16]*tŭk*, *tŭk*, in earnest; COM., [17]*tŭk*, *'kwi*, to exorcise demons; [18]*tŭk*, *ˌch'ing*, to urge marriage, as the parents or guardians do; [19]*tŭk*, *nik*, day by day, daily; [20]*tŭk*, *ˌkié*, to fray fowls; *tŭk*, *ˌkung 'ta teng'* to press on in crowds; COLL., *tŭk*, *tŭk*, *'tiong*, to chase all about; [21]*tŭk*, *pah*, *tak*, to fly pigeons; *má' tŭk*, *tek*, *tioh*, can't overtake him.

[1]韇匵而藏 [2]溝瀆 [8]四瀆 [4]瀆聽 [5]褻瀆 [6]尺牘 [7]案牘 [8]老牛舐犢 [9]謗讟 [10]妯娌 [11]姆嬸 [12]乾軸 [18]聯軸 [14]壽軸 [15]軸一幅 [16]逐逐 [17]逐鬼 [18]逐親 [19]逐日 [20]逐雞 [21]逐白鴿

蓪 Noxious weeds, weeds hard to root out, as the dock or thistles.

(829) **Tung.**

東 ꜀Tung. The east; the place of honor; the host; a master, a friend: in the coll. read ꜀tĕng, q. v.: COM., [1]꜀tung ꜀hwong, the east; [2]꜀tung ꜀nang, south-east; [3]꜀tung ꜀ka, the host; the master, head of an establishment; [4]'koi' ꜀tung, your employer; [5]꜀tung tó꜄ a host; [6]꜀tung ꜀kŭng, the seraglio; [7]꜀tung ꜀si, a thing—a phrase borrowed from the Court dialect; COLL., [8]'ngwai chó' ꜀tung, I'll be host (and furnish the feast).

哼 ꜀Tun. Verbose, garrulous; the breath; talk, speech: [9]꜀tung ꜀tung, to reiterate; heavy and slow, as a carriage.

諄 ꜀Chun. Ch'un. To inculcate, to inform fully; to reiterate an admonition; really, in earnest; pure, unmixed: [10]꜀tung ꜀tung ꜀ngiong ꜀chi, to make plain and impress on one.

焞 ꜀Tun. A dull fire, not bright; darkened, as stars by the sun; a torch to burn a tortoise-shell, as in divination. Read ꜀sung: bright, fiery, blazing; the color of fire.

燉 ꜀Tun. T'un. A raging fire, a blaze; the color of fire; fiery, lurid.

墩 ꜀Tun. A hillock on a plain; a heap, a mound, a tumulus, a barrow: in the coll. read ꜀tong, q. v.

敦 ꜀Tun. Interchanged with the next: angry, enraged; to revile; full, great, substantial; liberal, generous; simple, honest; to deem important; to urge, to impel to do; who? [11]꜀tung hau' tá꜄ to lay stress on filial and fraternal duties; [12]꜀tung hau꜄ honest, faithful; [13]꜀tung 'ch'ing, to invite cordially.

惇 ꜀Tun. Chun. Liberal, kind; true, generous feeling; to regard as important, to strive for: [14]꜀tung hau꜄ true, faithful.

屯 ꜀Tun. Chun. Incipient vegetation, budding, as plants; difficult to proceed; pressed together, thick; sparing; the 3d of the 64 diagrams: also read ꜀tong, q. v.

迍 ꜀T'un. To make no progress: [15]꜀tung ꜀chiéng, unable to advance; *met.*, unlucky, unsuccessful.

窀 ꜀Chun. To bury, to inter: [16]꜀tung sik꜄ a grave, a vault; to put into a vault.

肫 ꜀T'un. The cheeks, the bones of the face; earnest, sincere, honest; pieces of dried meat: [17]꜀tung ꜀tung ꜀ki ꜀ing, sincere in his benevolence.

飩 ꜀T'un. Often read tong꜄: a sort of flour cake with meat in: [18]꜀hung ꜀tung, pork balls seasoned, then rolled in flour and steamed.

꜀*Tung.* A coll. word: to knock, to strike against: ꜀tung 'tó, to knock over.

---

1 東方　2 東南　3 東家　4 貫東　5 東道　6 東宮　7 東西　8 我做東　9 哼哼○　10 諄諄言之　11 敦孝弟○　12 敦厚　13 敦請　14 惇厚　15 迍邅　16 窀穸　17 肫肫其仁　18 餛飩

ˏ*Tung*. A coll. word: to delay, to detain: ˏ*tung* ˏ*ti*, kept back, delayed; ˏ*ting* ˏ*tung*, to tarry; ˏ*ch'ang* ˏ*tung*, delayed a long time.

董 ʻTung. To rule correctly, to influence, to train one; to manage, to superintend; to clap the hands; firm, solid; to hold firmly, to store safely; the roots of the nelumbium: [1]ʻ*tung* ʻ*siu*, a chief, a superintendent; COM., [2]ʻ*tung sëü*ʾ or ʻ*tung* ʻ*li*, to rule, to manage, as a committee does; [3]ʻ*ku* ʻ*tung*, curiosities, antiques.

懂 懂 ʻTung. The mind confused, disturbed, so as not to perceive clearly: COLL., [4]ʻ*mung* ʻ*tung*, dull, bewildered in mind; [5]ʻ*mung* ʻ*tung ong*ʾ a confused destiny, always unlucky.

同 仝 ˏT'ung. Together, all, united; with, and; the same, like, agreeing; in or of the same, as class, place, time, etc.; to unite, to harmonize; to assemble; a sort of wine cup: in the coll. read ˏ*tëng*, q. v.: [6]ˏ*tung che*ʾ of the same aim or pursuit; [7]ˏ*tung* ˏ*lieu*, fellow-officers; COM., [8]ˏ*tung* ˏ*kü*, living in the same house; [9]ˏ*loi* ˏ*tung*, identical; [10]*pok*ˏ ˏ*tung*, different; [11]ˏ*tung tó*ʾ of the same occupation; ˏ*tung* ˏ*ti*, a sub-prefect; ˏ*tung* ˏ*sing hak*ˏ *e*ʾ to agree in mind; ˏ*tung ho*ʾ *e*ʾ ʻ*mu*, of the same father but different mothers; COLL., ˏ*tung p'ah*, ˏ*t'iéng a*ʾ together assault the empire; *met.*, to succeed, as partners in trade.

峒 ˏT'ung. A den, a cavern in a hill; uneven: [12]ˏ*k'ung* ˏ*tung*, a hill in Pingling department, Kansuh, the source of the King river.

桐 ˏT'ung. The oil-seed tree, Eleococcus oleifera: in the coll. read ˏ*t'ëng*, q. v.: [13]ˏ*tung sëü*ʾ the Jatropha curcas, or oil tree; [14]ˏ*tung yék*ˏ ˏ*ti* ˏ*ch'iu*, the leaves of the ˏ*Tung* recognize autumn — by shedding one; COM., [15]ˏ*ngu* ˏ*tung ch'eu*ʾ a species of ˏ*Tung*, suitable for musical instruments. Read ˏ*t'ung*: to remove lightly.

洞 ˏTung. Read *tong*ʾ; coll. ˏ*tung*, as in [16]ˏ*tung* ˏ*pung*, a bridal chamber; ˏ*tung* ˏ*pung* ˏ*hwa chioh*, the flowery candles of the bridal chamber.

筩 筒 ˏT'ung. A tube, a hollow cylinder, a pipe; a tubular cup or measure: the 2d used for the coll. ˏ*tëng*, q. v.: [17]*siá*ʾ ˏ*tung*, a species of slender bamboo.

鮦 ˏ. A species of silure, or mud-fish; it is small, and resembles a blenny.

童 ˏT'ung. A boy, a lad, an unmarried youth; a slave boy; a student, a bachelor; a girl, a virgin; chaste, undefiled; fresh, fair, youthful; bare, as a hill-top; luxuriant: [18]ˏ*tung puk*ˏ a young slave; [19]*muk*ˏ ˏ*tung*, a herd-boy; [20]ˏ*tung* ˏ*ngang*, a fresh complexion, as of the aged; [21]ˏ*sing* ˏ*tung*, at puberty, the age of 16; ˏ*tung* ˏ*mung*, youthful inex-

[1]董首 [2]董事 [3]古董 [4]懵懂 [5]懵懂運〇 [6]同志 [7]同僚 [8]同居 [9]雷同 [10]不同 [11]同道 [12]崆峒 [13]桐樹 [14]桐葉知秋 [15]梧桐楱〇 [16]洞房 [17]射筒 [18]童僕 [19]牧童 [20]童顏 [21]成童

perience, a child; COM., [1]꜀tung ꜀seng, a student, a candidate for the Siutsai degree; [2]꜀tung ‘chü, wooden images of children—used in prayers to "Mother"; [3]꜀tung ꜀yeu ꜀kó, satirical ballads, anciently sung by boys in the streets; [4]꜀tung tè² ꜀si haiu² in the time of youth; [5]꜀tung ‘seu ꜀u ꜀k‘i, we don't cheat young or old—a phrase on shopmen's cards; COLL., [6]꜀tung ꜀nang ‘kiăng, a bachelor, one unmarried at the age of 30 or 40.

僮 ꜀T‘ung. A slave girl or boy, a servant; a concubine; a boy, a lad; rude, doltish, ignorant: used for the coll. ꜀tĕng, q. v.: [7]‘ka ꜀tung, a house-boy, or waiter; [8]꜀chü ꜀tung, a serving lad in a school.

幢 ꜀● A screen or curtain for a carriage; an embroidered scroll, streamers hung from the roof in temples.

憧 ꜀Ch‘uang. Disturbed in mind, hesitating, undecided, irresolute: [9]꜀tung ꜀tung, wavering. Read ꜀chüng: silly, stupid.

曈 ꜀T‘ung. The sun about to rise: [10]꜀tung ꜀lung, the sun still obscured, or below the horizon, the break of day.

橦 ꜀T‘ung. A tree in Yunnan, from whose blossoms cloth can be made, ? the cotton tree; a piece of squared timber.

潼 ꜀T‘ung. The name of several streams; a tributary of the Yellow river in Shensi, near the Great Bend: [11]꜀tung ꜀kwang, a town and pass on this stream.

瞳 ꜀T‘ung. The pupil of the eye; to stare at; a vacant look: [12]꜀tung ‘chü, the pupil.

撞 ꜀Chuang. Also read tong²: to beat, to thump, to pound; to strike against, to run or dash suddenly upon, to strike accidentally or abruptly: in the coll. read taung² q. v.

罿 ꜀ A kind of trap or frame to take birds: also read ꜀ch‘üng, q. v.

艟 ꜀T‘ung. A long and swift boat used in fighting, called [13]꜀mung ꜀tung, and like a revenue cutter.

穜 ꜀T‘ung. Also read ꜀tüng: late, autumnal grain; grain planted early, but ripening late; the late planted, but early ripening, is called lük꜀ q. v.

彤 ꜀T‘ung. A red color; red, rosy, as the cheeks: [14]꜀tung ‘kwang, a red pencil.

鼕 ꜀T‘ung. The noise or beating of drums: used for the coll. tong² q. v.

(830) Tüng.

中 ꜀Chung. Ch‘ung. The middle, the center; uniform, medium, as size; half, in the middle of; in, within; exact, complete, right: also read tëüng² and in the coll. ꜀tong, q. v.: [15]꜀tüng ‘chi, half done, incomplete; [16]꜀tüng ꜀hing, flourishing in the middle, as a dynasty; COM., ꜀tüng

[1]童生 [2]童子 [3]童謠歌〇 [4]童穉時候 [5]童叟無欺 [6]童男仔〇 [7]家僮 [8]書僮 [9]憧憧 [10]曈曨 [11]潼關 [12]瞳子 [13]艨艟 [14]彤管 [15]中止 [16]中興

kwok, China; [1]*ˏing ˏtüng*, the suture of the lip; [2]*ˏtüng ˏkang*, inside, in the midst; [3]*ˏtüng ˏniéng*, middle aged, about 40; [4]*ˏtüng ʻpó*, a mediator—applied to Christ; [5]*ˏtüng ˏi*, women's drawers; *ˏtüng ʻwang*, medium-sized bowls; [6]*ˏtüng ˏtong*, title of a prime minister; [7]*ˏtüng ˏyong*, the middle; [8]*ˏtüng ˏchai*, of moderate ability, mediocre; COLL., *ˏtüng ˏtüng*, or *ˏtüng ˏseu*, or *ˏtüng ˏtüng ˏseu ˏseu*, medium, as size or quality.

忠 ˏChung. Faithful, loyal, patriotic; reverent; true, honest, upright, sincere; unselfish, devoted: *ˏtüng ˏsing ʻkeng ʻkeng*, true, faithful; COM., [9]*ˏtüng ngiéʼ* faithful, having integrity; [10]*ˏtüng ˏsing*, a loyal minister; [11]*ˏtüng tikˏ* faithful and straightforward; *ˏtüng haiuʼ ʻló sikˏ* sincere and honest.

衷 ˏChung. Inner garments; the heart; sincere, upright; rectitude, equity; the midst, middle; a full knowledge of: [12]*pokˏ ˏtüng*, insincere; [13]*ˏtüng ˏtiong*, the feelings.

重 ˏChung. Ch'ung. To add, to duplicate; to repeat, to reiterate; to pile up: also read *tëüngʼ* and in the coll. *ˏt'üng* and *taëngʼ* q. v.: *ˏtüng ˏtüng*, a succession, as of peaks; [14]*ˏtüng tiékˏ* increased, piled up; [15]*ˏtüng ˏui*, to surround; COM., [16]*ˏtüng hokˏ* to duplicate, to repeat; *ˏtüng ʻching ˏkié ˏteu*, to remodel rules; [17]*ˏtüng ˏsing*, to renew, to reform; [18]*ˏtüng ˏhu*, (will marry) a second husband, as diviners say; [19]*ˏtüng ˏyong*, "the double-odd"—festival of the ninth of the 9th moon; *ˏtüng ˏhwong ʻkai kaʼ* to marry again, as widows do.

ˏTüng. A coll. word: used in the sense of *ˏchüng*, from, whence, commencing from: *ˏtüng ʻch'ü*, from this (time); *ˏtüng ʻtá kauʼ mengʼ* from the bottom to the top.

(831) Twa.

ˏTwa. A coll. word: to shake about, as grain in a tray, to bring the chaff to the top: *ˏtwa siohˏ aʼ* give it a shaking up; *ˏtwa ʻmi*, to sift rice.

(832) Twai.

大 [1] Ta. Tai. To. Chua. Read *taiʼ*; coll. *twaiʼ*: large, big, great; senior, the eldest; old, noble; the chief, important; a superlative, much, very, exceeding; to grow large: *twaiʼ chiáh*, a large one; *twaiʼ ʻló tóiʼ* or *twaiʼ ʻló p'okˏ* a very large piece; [20]*twaiʼ kahˏ* a large sort, as of fowls; [21]*twaiʼ ˏpó*, the chief wife; [22]*twaiʼ aingʼ* the great limit—death; *twaiʼ ʻhó*, thoroughly done or cooked; wholly recovered (from sickness); entirely well; *twaiʼ ˏpeng ʻch'iu*, the right hand; [23]*twaiʼ séʼ* large and small, one's near relatives; *ˏkié twaiʼ* to grow fast; *twaiʼ ˏli twaiʼ k'óʼ* to gain and expend largely; *twaiʼ ˏnang ʻsieu ʻnü*, old and young of both sexes (in the family); *chóʼ twaiʼ ʻchwi*, a freshet; *ˏmó twaiʼ pokˏ séʼ* irreverent to seniors; [24]*twaiʼ ˏié*, the great sires or sirs—the official attendants or managers in a yamun;

---

[1] 人中 [2] 中間 [3] 中年 [4] 中保 [5] 中衣 [6] 中堂 [7] 中央 [8] 中才 [9] 忠義 [10] 忠臣 [11] 忠直 [12] 不衷 [13] 衷腸 [14] 重疊 [15] 重圍 [16] 重複 [17] 重新 [18] 重夫 [19] 重陽 [20] 大格 [21] 大婆 [22] 大限 [23] 大細 [24] 大爺

*twai*² ‘*kiăng*, the oldest son; *twai*² ꜀*sing mo*² the oldest son's wife.

舵² 柁² To. Read ꜀*tó* and ‘*tó*; coll. *twai*²: a rudder, a steering-oar, called ¹‘*mwi twai*²; ²*twai* ꜀*kung*, a helmsman; ³*twai* ‘*ná*, or *k‘ie*² *twai*² a helm, a rudder; ⁴꜀*niêng twai*² to take the helm, to steer; *twai*² ꜀*nga*, the handle of a rudder; ⁵꜀*pwang twai*² to put the helm to starboard; ⁶꜀*á twai*² to port the helm.

(833) Twak.

奪₂ To. To seize, to take by force, to rob; to oppress, to fleece; to obtain, as a prize; to deprive of rank; to criticize, to lop off; a narrow path: in the coll. read *tok*₂ q. v.: ⁷*twak*₂ ꜀*k‘wói*, to gain one of the first grades, as of Küjin; ꜀*kwong* ‘*ch‘ai twak*₂ *muk*₂ its elegance ravished the eyes.

(834) Twang.

端 ꜀ Tuan. Straight, correct, upright; decent, grave, decorous, proper; commencing, springing forth; the origin, the first principle, the originating cause; a numerative of matters, subjects, and pieces of silk; a length of 18 cubits: *chek*₂ ꜀*ki* ‘*liong* ꜀*twang*, to hold both ends, to attend to all; ⁸꜀*twang* ꜀*ngá*, the beginning, the clue to; COM., ⁹꜀*twang* ꜀*chong*, correct, decorous; ¹⁰꜀*twang chiăng*² upright, well-principled; ¹¹꜀*twang* ‘*ngu*, festival of the 5th of the 5th month; ¹²꜀*twang sioh*₂ a superior dark or greenish stone (for inkstands).

‘短 Tuan. Short, not long; contracted; to shorten, to curtail; to come short; failings, shortcomings, defects, faults: in the coll. read ‘*toi*, q. v.: ¹³‘*twang kiéng*² wanting in experience; ¹⁴*k‘é*² ‘*twang*, short-winded; ¹⁵‘*twang* ꜀*heng*, rude behavior; COM., ¹⁶‘*twang ch‘ëü*² shortcomings, faults; ¹⁷‘*twang ngiăh*₂ deficient in quantity; ¹⁸‘*twang kié*² (driven to) extremities, as a suicide; ¹⁹‘*twang ko*² to hire for short stages, as in journeying; COLL., *niăh*₂ ꜀*i* ‘*twang*, to lay hold of one's shortcomings; ‘*twang* ‘*chieu*, still owing, in arrears.

斷² Tuan. To decide, to settle; to judge and determine a case; to give an opinion; surely, decidedly, positively: also read *twang*² q. v.: COM., ²⁰*twang*² *ang*² to decide a lawsuit; *twang*² *kek*₂ ꜀*hüng*, to determine the lucky and unlucky, as diviners do; ²¹*kiok*₂ *twang*² to decide, to resolve how to do; COLL., *twang*² *twang*² *ng*² ‘*k‘ing*, decidedly unwilling; *twang*² *hak*₂ ꜀*mó twang*² ꜀*lié*, decided for union not separation, as a matrimonial lawsuit.

斷² Tuan. To divide, to cut asunder; cut, broken, split, snapped; broken off, interrupted, as intercourse: also read *twang*² and in the coll. *taung*² and ‘*tong*, q. v.: ²³*twang*² ꜀*tiong*, cut to the heart, greatly distressed; ²³*pok*₂ *twang*² uninterrupted; COM., ²⁴*twang*² *pié*² severed her arm, as the chaste

1 尾舵	3 撥奶	5 撥舵	7 奪魁	9 端莊	11 端午	13 短見	15 短行	17 短額	19 短僱	21 決斷	23 不斷
2 舵公	4 拈舵	6 挨舵	8 端倪	10 端正	12 端石	14 氣短	16 短處	18 短計	20 斷案	22 斷腸	24 斷臂

woman did—a play; *twang*[1] *ˌki kau*' *ˋchü*, she broke the loom to teach her son (diligence in study); [2]*twang*' *k'ie*' final deed of sale, an unredeemable bond.

(835) Twi.

追 Chui. To pursue, to chase, to follow after; to come up with, to overtake, to catch; to expel; to sue, to dun; to seek out, to trace back; to reflect on, to look back on, retrospective; to go with, to escort: [2]*ˌtwi keu*' to investigate fully; [3]*ˌtwi e*' or [4]*ˌtwi ˌsü*, to recall and reflect on, to think of something past; COM., [5]*ˌtwi ˌping*, soldiers in pursuit; [6]*ˌtwi ˌchong*, to go in search of stolen goods; [7]*ˌtwi chai*' or [8]*ˌtwi ˌchieng chai*' to dun; COLL., [9]*ˌtwi má*' *tioh*, cannot overtake him; [10]*ˌtwi ˋking ˋking*, to give sharp chase to.

肭 Read *ˌtwi* in the *Paik*, *ˌIng*, but correctly read *ˋtoi*: to pull with all one's strength: in the coll. read *toi*' q. v.

(836) Two.

[This word is interchangeably read *tio*, q. v.]

(837) Twoh.

[This word is interchangeably read *tioh*, q. v.]

(838) Twok.

[This word is interchangeably read *tiok*.]

惙 Cho. Chüeh. This and the next three also read *chiok*, or *chwok*: sad, sorrowful; the mind disquieted or unsettled; wearied, panting: [11]*twok, twok*, sad in heart, disquieted.

畷 Chüeh. A way or road between raised banks in a field: [12]*ˋching twok*, paths or roads through the open country.

裰 Ch'o. Chui. To. As in [13]*ˋpwo twok*, to repair old garments.

諁 Chüeh. To talk incessantly; talkative, loquacious.

(839) Twong.

[This word is interchangeably read *tiong*, q. v.]

(840) T'a.

他 它 T'a. A personal pronoun; he, she; him, her, it; they, them; that, the other; another: [14]*ˌt'a ˌm wong*, they; [15]*ˌt'a tek*, his, hers; [16]*ˌt'a ˌing*, that person, another; [17]*ˌt'a nik*, another day.

ˌT'a. A coll. word, as in *ˌt'a ˌna*, in fine circumstances, showy, in grand style.

ˌT'a. A coll. word: to row or work a boat against: *ˌt'a ˌhung ch'ok*, to work out against the wind; *ˌt'a ˋtong*, to propel against the flood-tide.

鮓 蚱 Cha. Tsê. Read *cha*'; coll. *t'a*': a sort of Medusa or sea-blubber: [18]*t'a*' *ˌp'ui*, [19]*t'a*' *ˌk'a*, and [20]*t'a*' *ˌnong*, the skin, feet, and stomach, of a Medusa; [21]*twai*' *ˌpwo t'a*' a big sea-blubber; *met.*, a booby, a stupid fellow; *t'a*' *ˌmó mëk*, *ˌha chó*' *mëk*, the Medusa has no eyes, shrimps are its eyes—the inexperienced or dull aided by the clever.

[1]斷契 [2]追究 [3]追憶 [4]追思 [5]追兵 [6]追賊 [7]追債 [8]追錢 債[9]追實着 [10]追緊緊〇 [11]惙惙 [12]畛畷 [13]補裰 [14]他們 [15]他的 [16]他人 [17]他日 [18]鮓皮 [19]蚱胶 [20]蚱纇 [21]大蒲蚱〇

福州方言拼音字典

(841) T'á.

體 ʻ T'i. The body, the corporeal substance, the whole person; a body, a trunk; a body of officers; real, essential, substantial, the essentials of; decorous, becoming, decent, proper; respectable, reputable; to realize, to embody, to carry out another's views; to join, to unite closely; related; to partition; to receive courteously: [1]ʻ*t'á sok*, to pity; [2]ʻ*t'á sek*, decorum, propriety; COM., [3]*ʻek*, ʻ*t'á*, the whole; the same, alike; [4]*nŭk*, ʻ*t'á*, or ˏ*sing* ʻ*t'á*, the body; [5]*paik*, ʻ*t'á*, all the bodily members; [6]ʻ*t'á* ʻ*t'ung*, decorum; [7]ʻ*t'á t'ai*ˀ bearing, gait, carriage; [8]ʻ*pwong* ʻ*t'á*, the original form; originally, physically; [9]ʻ*t'á k'e*ˀ *chaung*ˀ vigorous health; [10]ʻ*t'á t'aik*, to embody, to realize; COLL., [11]ʻ*t'á* ˏ*nëng e*ˀ to carry out a person's idea or intention; ʻ*t'á* ˉ*siong*ˀ ʻ*t'á kiă*² must please both great and small, as a servant; *t'auk*, ʻ*t'á*, to recover from sickness.

替 ˀ T'i. To change, to substitute, to put another instead of; to abolish, to set aside; to wait, to stop; for, instead of, in behalf; a sign of the dative, also of the accusative: [12]*tai*² *t'á*ˀ for, in behalf of; [13]ˏ*u t'á*ˀ unfailing, unchanging; COM., [14]*t'á*ˀ ˏ*sing*, a substitute; COLL., [15]*t'á*ˀ ˏ*kiėng*, to carry a burden for another; *t'á*ˀ ˏ*nëng* ˏ*sang t'á*ˀ ˏ*nëng* ʻ*si*, to live and die for another—constant and faithful; *t'á*ˀ ˏ*i* ˏ*i te*² or *t'á*ˀ ˏ*i mwook*₂ to heal him; *t'á*ˀ ʻ*si* ʻ*kwi* ˏ*chang che*ˀ *k'e*ˀ to maintain the resolution (of widowhood) for a deceased husband; [16]*t'á*ˀ *siăh*₂ to be a substitute at a feast.

匾 ˀ **楴** ˀ T'i. The 2d is unauthorized: thin, flat; in the coll. a drawer, as of a table or closet: [17]ʻ*piěng t'á*ˀ flat; COLL., [18]*t'á*ˀ *pek*₂ the knob, or brass-piece to pull a drawer by; *k'aung*ˀ *t'á*ˀ ʻ*lá*, to put away in the drawer.

綈 ˀ T'i. Thick, glossy silk; lustrous silk or satin, made into robes and given as presents; a coat, a pelisse.

涕 ˀ **鼶** T'i. To cry, to weep, to shed tears; tears: [19]*t'á*ˀ *k'ek*, or *k'ek*, *t'á*ˀ to weep and lament; [20]*t'á*ˀ *sëŭ*ˀ profuse weeping.

捇 ˀ T'i. To cast away, to reject, to discard; also to take, to grasp; a kind of hairpin to secure the hair in a knot.

啼 ˏ **嗁** ˏ T'i. To weep, to bewail; to howl and cry; to crow, to coo; the cry of birds; to scream, as apes and parrots: in the coll. read ˏ*t'ié*, q. v.: [21]ˏ*t'á k'ok*, to weep and lament; [22]ˏ*kié* ˏ*t'á*, a cock's crow; ˏ*kié lwang*² ˏ*t'á*, a general crowing, as at dawn.

稊 ˏ **稗** ˏ T'i. Tares, weeds like rice that bear small seeds, and are not readily distinguished from the rice; cockle in rice fields; also shoots on trunks of willow: [23]ˏ*t'á pai*² tares.

1 體恤 2 體式 3 一體 4 肉體 5 百體 6 體統 7 體態 8 本體 9 體氣壯 10 體貼 11 體仈意 12 代替 13 無替 14 替身 15 替肩 16 替食 17 匾匾 18 匾扳 19 涕泣 20 涕泗 21 啼哭 22 鷄啼 23 稊稗

荑 ꜀ Plants just budding, new sprouts; weeds, tares. Read ꜀*i*: to cut grass: [1]*'sing ꜀i ꜀hwa*, the Magnolia purpurea.

霬 ꜀ A cessation of rain, the sky clearing up, fair weather.

鶇 ꜀ T'i. A sort of pheasant: [2]*꜀t'á ꜀hu*, a species of pelican. Read ꜀*i*, as in [3]*꜀i ꜀iu*, a flying squirrel.

꜀T'á. A coll. word: usual, ordinary, medium: *꜀t'á ꜀t'á ꜀siâng*, an even, ordinary tone of voice, monotonous; *꜀t'á ꜀t'á ꜀pwo'* a medium gait; *꜀t'á ꜀t'á pang'* ailing, not getting better or worse; *꜀t'á ꜀t'á tieu'* a tune on the medium pitch; *met.*, in tolerable circumstances; *lok꜀ ꜀t'á*, failing, reduced.

(842) T'aë.

T'aë'. A coll. word: to push with the feet; to kick off: *t'aë' p'woi'* to kick off the bed clothes (in sleep); *t'aë' ꜀k'wi*, to push it away with the feet.

(843) T'aëk.

劏 A vulgar character used in the *Paik*, *꜀Ing* for the coll. *t'aëk*꜀: to thrust with a knife, to pierce, to stab: [4]*t'aëk꜀ sioh꜀ ꜀tó*, to give a stab, or thrust; [5]*t'aëk꜀ 'si*, to stab to death; [6]*t'aëk꜀ p'wai'* to break by thrusting at; *met.*, to inform against, to expose one; [7]*꜀t'ieu t'aëk꜀* to instigate, to edge on.

T'aëk꜀. A coll. word, as in *꜀t'au t'aëk꜀* a kind of two-pronged hair-pin, worn by country women.

(844) T'aëng.

澄 Read ꜀*teng*; used in the *Paik*, *꜀Ing* for the coll. *t'aëng'*: to be carried away by a flood or freshet; soaked, saturated; a passage from the main stream: [8]*t'aëng' 'tó*, swept down (as houses) by a freshet; [9]*t'aëng' ꜀pang te'* leveled to the ground by the flood; [10]*t'aëng' lóh꜀ 'hai*, swept out to sea; [11]*siong' t'aëng'* the upper passage, as that leading to Changloh opposite Pagoda Anchorage; [12]*'chwi kwang' 'yâ t'aëng'* completely saturated with water, as watered pork.

T'aëng'. A coll. word: idle, dissipated; light, frivolous, not to be depended on; also completed, all done, off one's hands: *'chiâ ꜀nëng 'yâ t'aëng' sioh꜀ ꜀lau*, that man is very trifling and untrustworthy indeed; *nik꜀ ꜀mang chó', chó' má' t'aëng'* work at it day and night, and can't get through with it!

T'aëng'. A floating mark or signal, a buoy, as to indicate shoals and rocks: *꜀p'u t'aëng'* floats, buoys.

T'aëng'. A coll. word; to excite, to instigate, to edge on: *t'aëng' sioh꜀ kwo'* to instigate by a word; *t'aëng' ꜀nëng ꜀song p'ah꜀* to edge on persons to fight; *ng' ꜀t'ëng t'aëng'* must not instigate (to a quarrel).

(845) T'ah.

T'ah꜀. A coll. word: clean, pure; untainted, clean in a moral sense; honest, not making gain of one; all gone, lost, or stolen: *t'ah꜀ kaik꜀* clean; *má' t'ah꜀*,

1 莘荑花 ○ 2 鶇鶘 8 鶇鸇 4 劏一刀 ○ 5 劏死 6 劏破 7 挑劏 8 澄倒 9 澄平地 ○ 10 澄落海 ○ 11 上澄 ○ 12 水灌野澄

海上絲綢之路文獻集成 科技與文化编

福州方言拼音字典

t'ah, sold all out; *t'aung' t'ah, t'ah*, stripped naked; *ngwoh*, *'lá t'ah*, as pure as a gem.

(846) T'ai.

篩 Shai. Read *‚sü* in the dictionaries: a sieve; to sift, to pass through a sieve: [1]*‚hwa ‚t'ai ngwook*, *'ing*, the flowers sift the moon's light; com., [2]*'mi ‚t'ai*, a rice-sieve; [3]*‚t'ai 'mi*, to sift rice; [4]*‚k'ong ‚t'ai*, a chaff-sifter, used after the rice has been hulled and pounded; [5]*‚t'ai ‚lĕng*, a sieve; coll., *‚t'ai ‚lĕng t'ak*, the wooden rim of a sieve; *‚t'ai ch'á' 'ü*, a mizzling rain.

擡 枱 T'ai. To raise, to lift; to carry, as a sedan; to move, to agitate: com., [6]*‚kó ‚t'ai ‚si ka'* to raise the current price; [7]*‚t'ai 'kü* (or *'ü*), to recommend one; to give (a shop) one's custom; [8]*‚t'ai ‚ch'iă*, to drive a chariot, a charioteer; coll., *‚t'ai ‚á liák*, slipshod; *‚t'ai ‚ló t'ói'* to remove (a corpse) by a hole in the prison-wall; *‚t'ai 'k'eng lóh*, *‚t'ong*, (like) dragging a dog into hot water—*scil.*, to get you to work.

胎 T'ai. The womb; a pregnant womb, pregnancy; congenital; to begin; to rebel against, to abscond; a pearl: in the coll. read *‚t'oi*, q. v.: [9]*sik*, *‚t'ai*, a barren womb; com., [10]*‚hwai ‚t'ai*, pregnant; [11]*‚t'ai k'e'* the state of pregnancy; [12]*taik*, *‚t'ai*, to become pregnant; [13]*‚t'ai ‚seng*, viviparous; [14]*‚t'ai ‚i*, the placenta; [15]*‚t'ai tuk*, (coll. *‚t'oi tuk*,) bad humors from birth, as in a child; coll., *siék*, *‚t'ai*, a white, furred tongue; *‚t'ai taung'* or *‚t'ai ak*, to pawn or mortgage, as to a wealthy man.

駘 T'ai. A weak, jaded horse; a miserable hack, a worthless nag: [16]*‚t'ai taung'* wide, expanding, as said of the opening spring.

苔 T'ai. Moss, lichens, confervae, small plants on rocks and in damp places; mossy, moss-grown: in the coll, read *‚t'i*, q. v.: [17]*‚t'ai 'siéng*, mosses; [18]*‚ch'ing ‚t'ai*, green mold, fucus on water.

邰 An ancient feudal state, comprising the modern district of Wukung in the Chienchou department in the center of Shensi.

梯 T'i. A ladder; stairs, steps; *met.*, a means to an end; to lean upon: *‚t'ai ‚hung pwo' ngwook*, to mount to the clouds and climb to the moon—ambitious, aspiring; com., [19]*‚lau ‚t'ai*, a ladder; [20]*‚t'ai ‚cheng*, the rounds of a ladder; *'ch'iu ‚t'ai*, a hand-ladder—sticks driven in a wall to ascend by; [21]*pwo' ‚t'ai*, a rope-ladder of cotton cloth; *‚ch'ing ‚hung ‚t'ai*, the azure-cloud-ladder—degree, rank, promotion; *siong' ‚tó ‚t'ai*, to mount the sword-ladder, as Tauist magicians do.

嚎 T'ai. Read *‚tai*; used for the coll. *'t'ai*: fine, as a voice in speaking another tongue: *‚i ‚kwang wa' 'kong 'yá 't'ai*, he speaks Mandarin most admirably.

1 花篩月影　2 米篩　3 篩米　4 糠篩　5 篩籠　6 高擡時價　7 擡舉　8 枱車　9 石胎　10 懷胎　11 胎氣　12 得胎　13 胎生　14 胎衣　15 胎毒　16 駘蕩　17 苔蘚　18 青苔　19 樓梯　20 梯層　21 布梯　○

太 **夳** T'ai. T'ui. Large, very great; too, very, excessive; wide, extensive; a title of honor; smooth, slippery: COM., *t'ai kik* the Great Extreme, first cause or origin; *t'ai ek ching ing*, name of a Tauist star-god; *t'ai ping* general peace; a fanciful name for ducks' eggs; *t'ai hau* the emperor's mother; *t'ai chü*, the crown-prince; *t'ai tó*, too much; *t'ai kwo* and *pok kik* excessive and insufficient; *t'ai 'ló* and *t'ai 'ná*, an officer's father and mother; *t'ai siong* the chief, the head of the family; *t'ai t'ai* (spoken *t'ai t'ai*), an officer's wife, her ladyship! *'ló t'ai t'ai* a compellation for an officer's mother.

泰 T'ai. Interchanged with the preceding: great, exalted, honorable; extreme, extravagant; pervading, universal; peaceful; the 11th diagram: *kwok t'ai ming ang*, the country prospering and the people at peace; COM., *t'ai sang*, a famous mountain in Shantung; an idol god, emperor of the world of spirits; *t'ai sang* and *t'ai 'chwi*, terms applied to a wife's parents.

汰 T'ai. Slippery; excessive, overflowing, as waters; to wash, to rinse, to cleanse: *sa t'ai* to scour with sand; *ch'iă t'ai* extravagant; incontinent, lustful.

態 T'ai. Form, figure; one's habit, gait, air, bearing, motions; the expression of an idea; a configuration, circumstance, state: *kieu t'ai* hauteur; *me t'ai* a seductive manner, ogling; *sié t'ai yéng liong*, the world's warmth and coolness—i. e. the fickleness of its love; COM., *t'á t'ai* air, gait.

T'ai. A coll. word, used for *t'eng* as in *t'ai tio* to go by road, to travel by land; *'mwong t'ai chiă k'ó* just let it go, don't quarrel about it!

刣 Read *chüng*; used for the coll. *t'ai*: to kill, to slaughter; to behead, to execute a criminal; *met.*, a gambling term: *t'ai t'au*, to behead; *t'ai 'si*, to kill; *t'ai ch'ek* to kill a thief; to shave one's head, as said jocosely; *t'ai nëng pong 'hwói*, murder and arson; *t'ai 'kiăng chëüng kwa*, to kill a boy and plant a melon—a juggler's trick; *kak k'a t'ai i*, to plot together to cheat him or win all his money; *t'ai t'au seng e o nëng chó* there are those (willing to) conduct a trade that ruins others!

(847) T'aik.

帖 T'ieh. A written scroll; a writing, a document; a note, a billet, a visiting-card; a copy-slip; fixed, settled: COM., *pai t'aik* a visiting-card; *t'aik t'au*, proposals for a betrothal; *chiong t'aik*, a card of several folds; *t'aik nük* note of invitation to a feast; *t'aik sek ch'ing hu*, styles of address in cards—a manual on the subject; *pó wong t'aik*, or *ho ing t'aik*, a note informing one of a death; COLL., *pong t'aik*, to send cards

1 太極 2 太平 3 太后 4 太子 5 太多 6 太上 7 國泰民安 8 泰山 9 泰山 10 泰水 11 沙汰 12 奢汰 13 驕態 14 媚態 15 體態 16 刣頭 17 刣死 18 刣賊 19 拜帖 20 帖頭 21 全帖 22 帖肉 23 赦帖

of invitation; *t'aikˎ ngeʼ* a slip with name on, as at the top of a funeral card.

貼, T'ieh. To leave or give in pledge; to cover over; to post, to paste up or on; to gild; to apply, as plasters; to supply a deficiency, to add to; to help, to assist; to lean on, attached: [1]*t'aikˎ ˏsing,* attached to one, as a servant; COM., [2]*t'á t'aikˎ* to carry out another's views; [3]*t'aikˎ ˏking,* to lay on gold-leaf; [4]*t'aikˎ pahˎ* to paste up white paper, as in mourning; [5]*t'aikˎ ˏpieu,* to post notices, as of articles for sale; [6]*t'aikˎ ʻsiä,* an assistant-scribe; *t'aikˎ ˏkó yohˎ* to apply plasters; [7]*t'aikˎ ˏchiéng,* to pay extra.

怗, T'ieh. Still, quiet, peaceable; resigned, submissive: [8]*t'aikˎ hukˎ* to be resigned. Read *ˏchiéng,* as in [9]*ˏchiéng teʼ* discordant, broken, as sounds.

忒, T'ai. T'ĕ. T'ui. To change, to alter; to doubt, to suspect; to err; an error or excess; very, extremely: [10]*pokˎ t'aikˎ* no doubt, no mistake; *hóʼ ˏt'iéng pokˎ t'aikˎ* High Heaven errs not.

慝, T'ĕ. Wicked, filthy, lewd, dissolute; secret vice; a depraved heart; malicious; to act the hypocrite, to gloss over vice; sunk in vice; the moon seen after sunrise: [11]*ʻüngˎ t'aikˎ* to hide one's wickedness; [12]*ˏkang t'aikˎ* profligate, licentious; [13]*ˏsiu t'aikˎ* to reform one's evil ways.

(848) T'aing.

T'aingʼ. A coll. word: jutting, protuberant, convex, bulging out: *t'aingʼ pokˎ* big-bellied; *met.*, a molding, raised work, as in panels; *t'aingʼ ʻtu,* a panel, a section in relievo; *t'aingʼ ch'okˎ ˏli,* protuberant; *ˏsing ˏkang t'aingʼ t'aingʼ* the chest prominent.

(849) T'aiu.

透, T'ou. Read *t'auʼ;* coll. *t'aiuʼ:* a plank, or narrow wooden bridge; as a verb, to manage, as one does with limited means: [14]*t'aiuʼ ʻpeng,* a plank, as from a boat to the shore; [15]*peng t'aiuʼ* a foot-bridge; [16]*ˏch'ü t'aiuʼ* or *p'ahˎ t'aiuʼ* to place a walking-plank; *t'aiuʼ ˏchiä kwoʼ* to pass a time of want, as by economy or borrowing.

(850) T'ak.

塔, 墖, T'a. The sound of things falling; a pile of earth; a pagoda, a tower: COM., [17]*ngangʼ t'akˎ* the wild-goose pagoda, on which a literary aspirant inscribed his name; [18]*pahˎ t'akˎ* and [19]*siohˎ t'akˎ* the White and Stone Pagodas in Foochow; [20]*ˏló* (or *ˏmó*) *ˏsing t'akˎ* the marshaled stars' pagoda—the Pagoda Anchorage in the Min; *ʻtiéng t'akˎ* to illuminate the pagodas—in the 8th month; [21]*t'akˎ ˏting ʻná,* the goddess "Mother" at *T'akˎ ˏting* in the suburbs of Foochow.

塌, T'a. Low ground, ground settling; to sink, to settle down, to fall in ruins; a first plowing: COLL., [22]*t'akˎ siohˎ ˏk'ëng,* a hole made

1 貼身 2 體貼 3 貼金 4 貼白 5 貼標 6 貼寫 7 貼錢 8 怗服 9 怗滯 10 不忒 11 隱慝 12 姦慝 13 修慝 14 透板 15 板透 16 舒透 17 雁塔 18 白塔 19 石塔 20 羅星塔 21 塔亭奶 22 塌一⿱穴土〇

by settling; [1]'*t'ak*ˎ *k'o*' caved in, like a mortar; [2]'*chauk*ˎ *t'ak*ˎ or '*chau t'ak*, to spoil or ruin, to waste things.

搨ˎ Ta. To lay the hand on, to feel; to make a fac-simile by transfer; a copy, a counterpart: [3]'*keu*' *t'ak*ˎ an old copy or fac-simile.

*T'ak*ˎ. A coll. word, for which the last may be used: to cover, to sheathe, to put in a sheath; to wear; a sheath, as of a pencil; an over-sleeve: *t'ak*ˎ *lŏh*ˎ (or '*tié*), to sheathe, as a pencil; *pek*ˎ *t'ak*ˎ or *pek*ˎ '*kwong t'ak*ˎ a pencil-sheath; '*ch'iu* '*wong t'ak*ˎ an over-sleeve; '*hó* ˏ*ki* ˏ*i* ˏ*siong na*' '*hó t'ak*ˎ *t'ak*ˎ it's best to wear your good clothes only occasionally.

榻ˎ **橡**ˎ T'a. A long, narrow bedstead, a wooden couch: [4]ˏ*ch'ong t'ak*ˎ a bed; [5]*ha*' *t'ak*ˎ to let down the bed—a story of Hsü Tzu in the After Han dynasty.

漯ˎ T'a. Name of a stream in Shensi; also an ancient district in that region: [6]'*hëük*ˎ *t'ak*ˎ waters accumulating and rushing on.

撻ˎ Ta. T'a. To beat, to whip, to flog, to chastise, to castigate; a slap, a blow; swift, rapid; the center of a bow.

闥ˎ T'a. A door, an inside door; a screen; the door of a harem; in the coll. movable boards, as in a shop's front: [7]ˏ*pung t'ak*ˎ a bed-chamber; [8]ˏ*pai t'ak*ˎ to open a door; COLL., [9]*t'ak*ˎ '*peng*, the movable boards for closing the front of a shop; [10]ˏ*k'wi t'ak*ˎ '*peng*, to open shop; *ch'ëüng*' *t'ak*ˎ '*peng*, to shut shop.

怛ˎ Ta. Moved, affected; sad, grieved, distressed; alarmed, agitated; wearied, burdened, as with trials; to pity, to commiserate.

疊ˎ **疊**ˎ Tieh. Read *tiĕk*ˎ; used in the *Paik*ˎ ˏ*Ing* for the coll. *t'ak*ˎ to pile up or on, to make a heap, to heap up; to make thick; *met.*, to multiply, as accusations against one in court: [11]*t'ak*ˎ '*k'i* ˏ*li*, to pile up; [12]ˏ*t'üng t'ak*ˎ to heap one on another; [13]*t'ak*ˎ ˏ*á* '*tá*, to make thick shoe-soles; [14]*t'ak*ˎ ˏ*ch'a*, to pile wood; [15]*t'ak*ˎ *kauk*ˎ to "pack the bones"—a firm, compact posture (in pugilism); [16]*t'ak*ˎ ˏ*p'au* ˏ*hwa*, to make "the pomelo-flower"—a kind of open tiling on walls.

*T'ak*ˎ. A coll. word: the sound of water dropping, called *t'ak*ˎ *t'ak*ˎ '*hiong* or *t'ak*ˎ *t'ak*ˎ *kieu*'.

(851) T'ang.

貪 ˏ T'an. To covet, to desire inordinately; avaricious, greedy; ambitious of; in the coll. to praise, to be pleased with one; also the quadruped like a unicorn, drawn on the screen-wall before offices to caution officials against the sin of bribery: [17]ˏ*t'ang* ˏ*chong*, to desire bribes; COM., [18]ˏ*t'ang* ˏ*sing*, a covetous disposition; [19]ˏ*t'ang* ˏ*lang*, covetous, niggardly; [20]ˏ*t'ang* '*siong*, to think greedily about; [21]ˏ*t'ang* ˏ*t'au*, the object or motive

1 搨白　2 作搨　3 舊搨　4 床榻　5 下榻　6 滄漯　7 房闥　8 排闥　9 闔板　10 開闔板　11 疊起梨　12 重疊　13 疊鞋底　14 疊柴〇　15 疊骨　16 疊袍花　17 貪贓〇　18 貪心　19 貪婪　20 貪想　21 貪頭

of desire; [1]*ˌt'ang saik*, or *ˌt'ang ˌhwa*, lustful, libidinous; [2]*ˌt'ang siăh*, gluttonous; [3]*ˌt'ang ˌchai*, avaricious; COLL., *ˌt'ang sieu'* to regard with admiration; *ˌt'ang ˌchiĕng ka' lau' sai'* to marry (a daughter) to an old man because rich; *met.*, to act recklessly as to future results; *ˌt'ang che' kaĕng' ˌping sioh yong' 'siă*, the character for "covet" is written like the one for "poor" — a caution against covetousness; *ˌt'ang lau'* to age fast, to look old.

灘 ˌT'an. A rapid, a torrent rushing through a rocky pass: [4]*ˌt'ang ˌt'eu*, the head of the rapids; [5]*ˌt'ang ˌsü*, a pilot through rapids; [6]*ˌch'ing ˌt'ang*, a deep torrent.

癱 ˌT'an. A contraction of the muscles; numbness of the tendons: [7]*ˌhung ˌt'ang*, palsy, paralysis.

探 ˌT'an. Also read *t'ang'*: to feel or search for; to examine, to investigate, to explore; to try, to essay; to go to make inquiries, to spy out; to visit: [8]*ˌt'ang sëü'* to try, to test; COM., [9]*ˌt'ang 'ma*, a spy; [10]*ˌt'ang pó'* to spy out and report; *ˌt'ang t'eng'* to obtain news of; [11]*ˌt'ang ˌhwa*, the third on the list of Hanlin doctors; *ˌt'ang 'k'eu e'* to learn one's mind by prying questions.

攤 ˌT'an. To open, to spread out; to gesture; a stand or stall on which things are placed for sale; to pay in installments; to share, to divide amongst; slow, remiss; to defer, to prorogue: COM., [12]*ˌpá ˌt'ang*, to set out a street-stall; [13]*ˌsang 'ku ˌt'ang*, to divide into three shares; [14]*ˌt'ang ka'* to strut; to make a mere show, as of wealth; [15]*ˌt'ang ˌk'a 'u 'ch'iu*, to flourish the feet and hands; [16]*ˌt'ang ˌtiong*, a gambling place; [17]*ˌtau ˌt'ang* and [18]*ˌchiĕng ˌt'ang*, modes of gambling with dice and cash; COLL., *ˌt'ang pah*, to make a show of plenty; *ˌt'ang k'ó' ˌpui*, to make up a loss or debt by paying shares.

撐 橕 ˌCh'êng. To prop, to shore up; to separate, to open out; to push off, to pole, as a boat: a fulcrum, a prop, a stay: in the coll. read *t'ang'* q. v.: [19]*ˌt'ang to'* to pole over a ferry; *met.*, to intrigue for friends; COM., [20]*ˌt'ang ˌsung*, to pole a boat; *ˌt'ang ˌsung ik ch'e'* to pole boats into the market, as during a freshet.

嗿 'T'an. The noise, as of many eating, the hum of a full table; craunching, grinding of the jaws.

坦 'T'an. Plain, level, broad and even; quiet, composed, tranquil; a son-in-law: [21]*'t'ang ˌyong*, gratified; *'li tô' 't'ang 't'ang*, a fine, level road; COM., *leng' 't'ang*, your son-in-law.

袒 'T'an. To shove up the sleeves, to bare the arm; bare, next to the skin; to disclose: [22]*nŭk 't'ang*, bared, as the breast; *'chó 't'ang*, to help one when in the wrong.

禫 'T'an. A sacrifice to the manes of parents at the end of 27 months, which is termed the three years mourning:

---

1 貪色 2 貪食 3 貪財 4 灘頭 5 灘師 6 深灘 7 瘋癱 8 探試 9 探馬 10 探報 11 探花 12 排攤 13 三股攤〇 14 攤架 15 攤股舞手 16 攤場 17 骰攤 18 錢攤 19 撐渡 20 撐船 21 坦然 22 肉袒

COM., [1]*ˊt'ang huk*ˎ the lighter mourning, worn from the 25th to the 27th months inclusive.

ˋ髧 Tan. Long hair, the hair falling on the forehead or cheeks; a child's curls, tresses; also ornamental fringes, as of a cap.

ˋ醓 Tan. Brine, gravy; the serous juice oozing from meats: [2]*ˋt'ang ˋhai*, salted meats, preserved delicacies.

ˋ毯 T'an. A hair rug, or bed mat, a coarse ratteen or serge: COM., [3]*ˏchiêng ˋt'ang*, felted woolen rugs and hair mats; COLL., [4]*ˋt'ang sioh*ˎ *ˋliăng*, one piece of hair-matting; [5]*ˋt'ang sioh*ˎ *ˏch'ong*, one hair bed-mat.

ˋ菼 T'an. Also read *ˋlang*: rushes just sprouting; marshy plants; a reed or sedge suitable for brooms.

撐ˀ Ch'êng. Read *ˏt'ang*; coll. *t'ang*ˀ: to prop, to support; to raise, as a shutter with a stick; to stretch, to distend: [6]*t'ang*ˀ *ˋk'i*, to raise up, as a shutter or screen; [7]*t'ang*ˀ *twai*ˀ distended, expanded by something underneath; [8]*t'ang*ˀ *ˏch'ŭng*, a shutter with hinges at the top.

炭ˀ T'an. Charred wood, charcoal; coals of any kind: *ˏseng ˏming ˏtu t'ang*ˀ the people down-trodden, as by officers; COM., [9]*p'ang*ˀ *t'ang*ˀ and [10]*taing*ˀ *t'ang*ˀ soft and hard wood coals; [11]*ˏmui t'ang*ˀ fossil coal; [12]*t'ang*ˀ *mwak*ˎ coal-dust; [13]*t'ang*ˀ *aëng*ˀ a coal-extinguishing jar.

嘆ˀ 歎 T'an. To sigh, to moan, to groan; a musical expiration; to laud, to admire: [14]*t'ang*ˀ *sek*ˎ a deep sigh; [15]*t'ang*ˀ *siêng*ˀ to admire; COM., [16]*t'ang*ˀ *k'e*ˀ to sigh; a moan, a groan; COLL., *t'ang*ˀ *sioh*ˎ *ˏsiăng k'e*ˀ to fetch a sigh.

*T'ang*ˀ. A coll. word: to rival, to compete in trade; to get the custom by under-selling another: *t'ang*ˀ *ˏnëng ˏseng e*ˀ to to get people's trade by underselling them; *tói*ˀ *t'ang*ˀ to compete with each other in trade.

ˏ覃 T'an. To extend, to reach, to arrive at; great, extensive: [17]*ˏt'ang ˏong*, royal favor.

ˏ譚 T'an. Used for *ˏtang* (to converse): to discuss, to talk about; large, extensive; to boast; to manifest; an ancient feudal state, east of Tsinan-fu in Shantung; in the coll. to try one with words, to put tentative questions: COLL., [18]*ˏt'ang sioh*ˎ *ˏsiăng*, to try with a word — and see what he'll say; *ˏt'ang ˏi sié*ˀ *nóh*ˎ *e*ˀ *sëü*ˀ try him and see what his idea is.

ˏ潭 T'an. Name of a river; a placid expanse of water with deep holes; deep, limpid: COM., [19]*ˏt'ang ˋchwi*, deep, clear water; [20]*ˏt'ang ˋhu*, profound Sir! — a term used in letters; [21]*ˏt'ang kiăng*ˀ *ˋlá ˏch'ing*, (the water) as clear as a mirror.

ˏ燂 T'an. Also read *ˏchiêng* and *ˏsing*: to burn in the fire; to scorch, to put in the blaze; to warm, to boil; warm, hot; *met.*, distressed.

---

1 禫服 2 醓醢 3 毡毯 4 毯一領 5 毯一床 6 撐起 7 撐大 8 撐冲 9 冇炭 10 冇炭 11 煤炭 12 炭末 13 炭甕 14 嘆息 15 嘆美 16 嘆氣 17 覃恩 18 譚一聲〇 19 潭水 20 潭府 21 潭鏡禮清

壜 ˓ 墰 ˓ T'an. An earthen vase to contain spirits, a wine jar: COM., [1]ᶜchiu ˓t'ang, a jar for holding wine.

曇 ˓ T'an. Clouds extending over the heavens: ˓t'ang ˓t'ang, the sky overcast, a lowering sky.

痰 ˓ T'an. Phlegm, mucus from the lungs: COM., [2]˓t'ang ᶜing, thin phlegm; [3]˓t'ang sau˒ cough with phlegm; [4]˓t'ang kiĕk˒ a gathering of phlegm; [5]˓t'ang ˓pwong, a spittoon; [6]˓t'ang loi² you are troubled with phlegm; *met.*, dull, stupid; *hwa˒ ˓t'ang*, an expectorant; ˓t'ang ˓mi ˓sing k'ieu˒ phlegm has closed the mental apertures — a medical phrase; COLL., ˓t'ang p'wok˒ frothy phlegm.

檀 ˓ T'an. Read ˓tang; coll. ˓t'ang: a tough wood fit for axles; sandal wood: [7]˓t'ang ˓hiong ˓ch'a, sandal wood for incense; [8]ᶜchié ˓t'ang ˓ch'a, red sandal wood, rosewood; [9]˓t'ang sok˒ ˓hiong, the ˓t'ang and sok, woods, as burnt to idols.

⿱穴淡 ˓ T'an. As in [10]˓lang ˓t'ang, thin and spread widely; in the coll. large rocks; COLL., [11]˓lang ˓t'ang sioh² large, dark rocks, bowlders; [12]ᶜhung ˓t'ang, brittle stone, a sandstone, used in making crockery.

˓*T'ang*. A coll. word, as in ˓*t'ang t'aik*, a mischievous fish, like a bull-head cat-fish, "one of which sort is found in every pond"; *met.*, a troubler, a mischief-maker, as in a shop, or school.

(852) T'au.

偷 ˓ T'ou. Read ˓t'eu; coll. ˓t'au: to steal, to pilfer; to obtain unfairly; secretly, stealthily, underhand: [13]˓t'au ch'ok, to go out slyly; [14]˓t'au tuik˒ privately, clandestinely; [15]˓t'au ˓tó, to steal; [16]˓t'au ᶜchau, to steal off; ˓t'au ˓chiong, to peer, to look furtively at; [17]˓t'au niĕk˒ kek˒ to pilfer; [18]˓t'au cheng˒ ˓kwong, has stolen everything; [19]˓t'au ᶜtio ˓chá, to play truant from school; ˓t'au siăh² pwo² to learn an art by seeing others do; ᶜmá ˓ma ˓t'au pó² ᶜk'eng, buy a cat, but steal a dog —*scil.*, if you want good ones.

ᶜ*T'au*. A coll. word: to loosen, to open out, to unravel, to disentangle; to blow, as the nose; intelligent, well-informed; well, free from illness: ᶜt'au p'e˒ to blow the nose; ᶜt'au ˓sëng, to loosen, to unravel; ᶜt'au sang˒ or ᶜt'au laĕk˒ to separate; loose, untwisted, as the cue; ᶜt'au ˓tieu tik˒ to straighten out; ᶜt'au t'óh˒ (or lóh˒), well, not sick; well-informed; ng² ᶜt'au t'óh˒ indisposed; ignorant; ᶜt'au sioh² t'aik˒ to get relief by a dose (of medicine).

透˒ T'ou. To pass over, to proceed; to pass through, to permeate; to penetrate, as light; through, throughout; reaching, extending to; to comprehend thoroughly; alarmed: used for the coll. t'aiu˒ q.v.: COM., [20]˓chiong t'au˒ the same

1 酒壜 2 痰飲 3 痰嗽 4 痰結 5 痰盆 6 痰累 7 檀香柴 8 紫檀柴 9 檀束香 10 濫⿱穴淡 11 濫⿱穴淡石 12 粉⿱穴淡 13 偷出 14 偷得 15 偷掏 16 偷走 17 偷捻挾 18 偷盡光 19 偷躲齋 20 全透

throughout, as a dress; [1]*ˏt'ĕng t'auʼ* through, permeable; [2]*t'auʼ ʻtá*, to the last, forever; [3]*t'auʼ nik*ˎ throughout the day; [4]*t'auʼ t'iĕk*ˎ to understand fully; COLL., *mwoiʼ t'auʼ ˏhwang*, not yet full grown, as a duck's feathers and wings; *t'auʼ ˏhong ˏtĕng*, to clean a tobacco pipe with a wire; *t'auʼ ʻtá t'auʼ mengʼ* (the same) from top to bottom, no sham.

T'auʼ. A coll. word: to blow strong or fresh: *ˏhung ʻyâ t'auʼ* the wind blows very strong.

T'auʼ. A coll. word: to poison: *t'auʼ ʻsi*, to poison to death; *t'auʼ ʻló ʻch'ü*, to poison rats.

T'auʼ. A coll. word: to decoy, to kidnap; to induce, to allure one, as a workman by the offer of higher wages: *t'auʼ t'auʼ* (or *lauʼ*) a kidnapper; *t'auʼ k'óʼ máʼ* to kidnap and sell.

頭 ˏT'ou. Read *ˏt'eu;* coll. *ˏt'au:* the head; the first, best, chief; the end, the large end of a thing; the beginning of; a classifier of animals, birds, fish, reptiles; occurs in the names of round things, as in [5]*sioh*ˎ *ˏt'au*, a stone; [6]*ˏt'au ˏseng*, in front; [7]*ˏt'au ˏhui*, or *ˏt'au ˏpong*, the first time; [8]*ˏt'au ʻnó*, the brains; *ˏt'au ʻwang kauk*, the skull; [9]*ˏt'au ˏka*, or *ˏt'au ˏnĕng*, or *ˏt'au ʻnó ˏkó*, the principal, the head man; [10]*ˏtong ˏt'au*, to be the manager; *ˏk'wi ˏt'au*, to start, as a boat; *ˏt'au ˏnĕ ʻnĕ*, at the head or top of; [11]*sioh*ˎ *ˏt'au*, one end of; one party, as in a marriage contract; [12]*ʻhü ˏt'au*, in that direction; [13]*ˏt'au ʻchwi*, "first water"—the first, as a picking of flowers, etc.; *ˏt'au ʻting teʼ* the top or crown of the head; *ˏt'au ʻting ˏtong*, above one's head; [14]*ˏt'au ʻkau*, dandruff; *p'ah*ˎ *chiĕk*ˎ *ˏt'au*, to compound (with creditors); [15]*ch'ok*ˎ *ˏt'au*, to be a leader; successful, rising; *kwoʼ ˏt'au*, too much, in excess; *ˏt'au ʻwang kauk*ˎ *ˏk'wi ˏhwa*, "the skull blossoms"; *met.*, a shock, stunning, as a fall or blow; [16]*ˏt'au paiʼ* a kind of small candle; [17]*siàngʼ ˏt'au*, bits or remnants of thread, as in sewing.

ˏT'au. A coll. word, for which the last is often used, as in *ˏt'au ˏsang*, a brute, an animal; domestic animals, specifically quadrupeds.

(853) T'auk.

託 T'o. To charge with, to intrust to; to engage one to do, to commission; to trust, to depend, to rely on; to give as an excuse, to use as a pretext: COM., [18]*t'auk*ˎ *koʼ* or *t'auk*ˎ *ˏsü*, to make an excuse in declining; [19]*hoʼ t'auk*ˎ to entrust to, to commission; [20]*paiʼ t'auk*ˎ to request as a favor; [21]*t'auk*ˎ *siéʼ* to rely on another's influence, as in law-suits; COLL., *t'auk*ˎ *ˏi chóʼ* to engage him to do it; [22]*t'auk*ˎ *maĕngʼ* to receive communications in dreams, as from gods or ghosts; *t'auk*ˎ *ˏsang ˏyong seʼ* to engage several persons to aid.

托 T'o. Used erroneously for the last: to take, to bear on the hand, to carry on the palm: in the coll. read *t'óh*, q. v.: [23]*t'auk*ˎ *ʻchü*, or [24]*t'auk*ˎ *ˏpwang*, a tray, a waiter;

[1]通透 [2]透底 [3]透日 [4]透徹 [5]石頭 [6]頭前 [7]頭囘 [8]頭腦 [9]頭家 [10]當頭 [11]一頭 [12]許頭 [13]頭水 [14]頭垢 [15]出頭 [16]頭拜 [17]線頭 [18]託故 [19]付託 [20]拜託 [21]託勢 [22]託夢 [23]托子 [24]托盤

lok, *t'auk*, or *t'auk*, *lok*, discouraging, not favorable, as the times.

拓, T'o. To receive in the hand; also to push away; to take up, to collect, in which sense read *chiă'* or *chiăh*, in the dictionaries.

柝, T'o. A watchman's rattle or stick, on which he beats; to beat the watches: '*kek*, *t'auk*, to strike the hours.

橐, T'o. A bag or sack open at both ends; a sort of purse worn on the waist; a potter's implement: [2] *'ₒnong t'auk*, bags and sacks.

驝, T'o. A camel having one hump: [3] *t'auk*, *ₒtó* (coll. *lok*, *ₒtó*), the Bactrian camel, a camel.

籜, T'o. The sheath of the bamboo, the envelop which covers the joints; name of a plant.

蘀, T'o. Withered, fallen, as leaves; rotten, dead, as trees or the bark of plants.

脫, T'o. T'u. Read *t'wak*, ; coll. *t'auk*,: to escape from, to evade, to get rid of; to recover from sickness: [4] *t'auk*, *ₒtó*, to escape from; [5] *t'auk*, *ₒsing*, to slip away, to shirk; [6] *t'auk*, *'ch'iu*, to get rid of, as old goods; [7] *t'auk*, *'t'á*, well, recovered from illness; [8] *t'auk*, *ₒsing wang' 't'á*, a radical change in the system, as by tonics.

飥, T'o. As in *'ping t'auk*, a bun of wheaten flour, wheaten cakes.

T'auk,. A coll. word: to pour boiling water on; to steep, to scald: *t'auk*, *ₒta*, to steep tea; *t'auk*, *ₒch'ŭng ₒta*, to make tea in cups, as for guests; *t'auk*, *ₒchiong*, to prepare starch; *t'auk*, *'si*, to scald to death, as bed bugs; *t'auk*, *ch'ok*, *laiu'* to draw out the strength, as of tea.

(854) T'aung.

盪, Tang. T'ang. To push a boat on the land: in the coll. to row, to propel with oars: also read *taung'* q. v.: COLL., [9] *t'aung' 'chiong*, to ply the oars; [10] *t'aung' ₒsung*, to row a boat; [11] *t'aung' cheng'* to make progress by rowing.

脫, T'o. T'u. Read *t'wak*,; coll. *t'aung'* and used for the next: to undress, to strip; to take off, as the shoes; to shed, to cast, as animals their skins; to molt; to bone; to remove, as the pits of fruit: [12] *t'aung' k'aĕk*, to shed the skin; [13] *t'aung' ₒmó*, to molt; [14] *t'aung' kauk*, to bone, as fowls; to remove the ribs, or frame of; [15] *t'aung' ₒk'wang k'aiu'* buttons with movable rings; *t'aung' ₒch'ing t'aung' kŏh*, precipitated, become thin and watery, as gruel; *t'aung' t'ah*, *t'ah*, stripped naked.

褪, T'un. Read *t'ŏi'*; coll. *t'aung'*: to undress, to disrobe: [16] *t'aung' ₒi ₒsiong*, to undress; [17] *t'aung' piĕng'* stripped, as a debtor or gambler of his clothes; *t'aung' t'aung' sĕŭng' sĕŭng'* taking off and putting on, as one's clothes in changes of weather.

---

1 擊柝　2 囊橐　3 驝駝　4 脫逃　5 脫身　6 脫手　7 脫體　換體　8 脫身　9 盪槳　10 盪船　11 盪進　12 脫殼　13 脫毛　14 脫骨　15 脫環鈕　16 褪衣裳　17 褪變

T'aung'. A coll. word: to put into boiling water; to boil slightly, to scald: *t'aung' ˏch'iă ˏngó*, to scald the mytilus or large clam; *t'aung' ˏhiă*, boil them till they gape open; *t'aung' k'ak, ˓heng*, scalded too much.

T'aung'. A coll. word: to heat over, to warm up cooked food; also to exercise, to renew practice, as in study or music: *t'aung' yék*, to heat or warm up; *t'aung' pwong'* to warm up the rice; *t'aung' ˏta*, to heat (cold) tea.

(855) T'e.

䟡' Ti. Hindered, impeded, embarrassed; prevented from doing or advancing; to hinder, to obstruct; the stem or stalk of fruit; to remove a stalk; to unravel embroidery; to slink away, as a dog does.

嚏 Ti. T'i. To sneeze; sneezing: [1]*p'ong' t'e'* or *˓hung t'e'* to sneeze; [2]*ˏkiu t'e'* to sneeze from catching cold.

懥 T'i. Irritated, vexed, angry; hatred: [3]*hung t'e'* greatly enraged.

T'e'. A coll. euphonic prefix, as in *t'e' t'ié'* to shave; *t'e' t'ieu'* to dance; *t'e' t'o'* to vomit; *t'e' t'aĕ'* to kick off (the bed-clothes).

(856) T'ë.

ˏT'ë. A coll. word: sloping, inclined, slanting; to slide, to slip down, as on a slope: *ˏt'ë ˏt'ë*, slanting; *ˏt'ë ˏt'ë sioh*, an inclined stone (walk); *ˏt'ë lóh ˏli*, to slide down; *ˏt'ë sioh ˓tó*, to slip and catch a fall.

ˏT'ë. A coll. word: to stretch one's self, to lie at full length: *ˏt'ë tik tik*, or *ˏt'ë ˏt'ë tik*, to lie stretched at full length.

˓鏟 Ch'an. Read *˓sang;* used for the coll. *˓t'ë:* to shell off, to scale: [4]*˓t'ë piăh*, to scale plastered walls, as with a chisel or like instrument; [5]*˓t'ë ˓k'i*, or *˓t'ë k'ó* to shell it off; [6]*tiăng ˓t'ë* (or *ch'iăh*), a sort of small shovel for scaling, or turning things in a pan.

(857) T'eh.

T'eh,. A coll. euphonic prefix, as in *t'eh t'iăh*, to strip, to tear off or down; *t'eh t'óh*, to bear or support, as on the palm of the hand.

(858) T'ek.

勅, 敕, 勑, Ch'ih. An imperial order or prohibition; a special ordinance, precepts, admonitions; a charter, a commission: the 3d also read *ˏlai*, q. v.: COM., [7]*t'ek ˏhung*, a special title, preferment; [8]*t'ek ˏchü*, letters-patent; [9]*t'ek leng'* a command; a special order, as from a god—written on charms; [10]*t'ek chaing'* to bestow honors on one's deceased parents; [11]*t'ek ˏhu*, to write a charm.

飭, 飾, Ch'ih. Sometimes confounded with *sek*, (to paint, to adorn): to repair, to strengthen; to adjust, to arrange and regulate; to enjoin on, to direct, to

[1] 噴嚏 [2] 勼嚏 [3] 忿懥 [4] 鏟壁 [5] 鏟起 [6] 鼎鏟 [7] 勅封 [8] 勅書 [9] 勅令 [10] 勅贈 [11] 勅符 ○

command; firm, compact; ready, prepared; careful, reverent: [1]'t'ek, ,ch'á, to send on public service; [2],sing t'ek, to charge strictly; [3]t'ek, leng' to order, to command.

裼, T'i. To push up the sleeves, to bare the arm and breast; a sort of vest or waistcoat: [4]'t'ang t'ek, to expose the bosom; to bare one's arm, as to fight; [5]t'ek, ,kiu, to turn a fur garment.

惕, T'i. Regard, respect; grieved, sorrowful; quick, diligent, careful not to offend: t'ek, t'ek, to love; loving, affectionate.

踢, T'i. To kick: COM., [6]t'ek, kiong' to kick the shuttle-cock; [7],k'wi ,sing t'ek, 'tau, Boötes kicking the Dipper—a picture; COLL., p'ah, ,k'wi t'ek, to kick like a Boötes, as said of a good pugilist; 't'ek, sioh, ,k'a, to give a kick. Read ch'iok,: hurried, alarmed.

剔, T'i. To cut the flesh from the bones; to scrape off, to pick and cleanse; to dig out: COM., [8],t'ieu t'ek, to find fault, to criticise and reject.

陟, Chih. To ascend, to assume a higher office: promoted, advanced; to mount, to go up, to advance, to proceed to: [9]t'ek, 'lang, to behold from on high; [10]t'ek, kaung' promotion and degradation.

倜, T'i. Free, easy, unrestrained: [11]t'ek, 't'ong, freedom of manner, a fine, noble bearing.

鷩, An aquatic bird, a gay-colored bird with a crest; a hoopoo?

T'ek,. A coll. euphonic prefix, as in t'ek, t'aĕk, to stab; t'ek, t'ĕük, to draw back, to skulk; t'ek, t'auk, to commission; to pour boiling water on, to scald; t'ek, t'ak, to cover, to sheathe.

宅, Chai. Tsĕ. A dwelling, a residence, a mansion; a grave; to reside, to settle; to conform to; a place, a station, an office: used for the coll. tah, q. v.: [12],ka t'ek, a residence; [13],tiĕng t'ek, fields and houses; [14]tieu' t'ek, to divine for a grave; [15],ing t'ek, a grave; ancestral halls or shrines.

(859) T'ĕk.

讀, Tu. Tou. Read t'uk,; coll. t'ĕk,: to read aloud; to read attentively, to study; to recite, to chant: [16]t'ĕk, ,chü, to read a book, to study; [17]t'ĕk, ,t'ung, well read, thorough in scholarship; [18]t'ĕk, ho' to chant metres of 4s and 6s; t'ĕk, má' lóh, a faulty construction; t'ĕk, ,chü ,nĕng, scholars, literati; [19]t'ĕk, yă' ,chü, to study at night; t'ĕk, ,hwang ,ch'ang, to read crudely; immature, not thorough in study.

(860) T'eng.

蟶, Read ,t'ing; coll. ,t'eng: a bivalve, the razor-sheath or solen: [20],t'eng 'niu, the muscles of a solen; [21],t'eng ,k'a, a solen's feet; met., the two tabs of silk braid at the end of a cue; [22],t'eng ,kang, dried solen meat; ,t'eng tieu' (or lieu'), also called

---

[1]飭差 [2]申飭 [3]飭令 [4]袒裼 [5]裼裘 [6]踢毽 [7]魁星踢斗 [8]挑剔 [9]陟覽 [10]陟降 [11]倜儻 [12]家宅 [13]田宅 [14]兆宅 [15]陰宅 [16]讀書 [17]讀通 [18]讀賦 [19]讀夜書 [20]蟶鈕〇 [21]蟶骹 [22]蟶乾

'*ka* ˎ*lau* ˎ*ki*, a hash of solen meat, pork, eggs, and onions; COLL., ˏ*t'eng* ˎ*peng*, solen seasoned and fried on one shell; ˏ*t'eng* ˎ*tiâng*, place for planting solen, solen-beds.

'*T'eng*. A coll. word: the same as '*ch'ang* or '*siâng*; an interjection, alas! sad! pitiful!

很 Hên. Read '*hong*; coll. '*t'eng*: perhaps a corruption of '*heng*; a superlative, very, extremely: [1]ˎ*ngai tek*, '*t'eng*, very bad; *hai*ˀ '*ngwai* '*yâ* '*t'eng*, he greatly injured me.

'*T'eng*. A coll. word: prominent, protuberant: probably a corruption of *t'aing*ˀ q. v.: '*t'eng* ˏ*hûng*, a full, prominent bosom.

聽 聽 听 T'ing. Also read ˏ*t'ing*: to hear; to hearken, to listen to; still, quiet so as to hear; to accord with, to comply; to receive and obey orders; to decide cases; to tarry, to wait for: in the coll. read ˏ*t'iâng*, q. v.: [2]*t'eng*ˀ *sëûng*ˀ to hear and decide cases; [3]ˎ*tûng t'eng*ˀ hard of hearing; COM., [4]*t'eng*ˀ ˏ*ch'â*, a servant, a messenger in an office; [5]*t'eng*ˀ *haiu*ˀ to wait, to attend on; [6]*t'eng*ˀ ˎ*ping*, to accord; subject to one's control, as property bought or rented; [7]*t'eng*ˀ ˏ*ki chëû*ˀ ˎ*yong*, as it may naturally happen; [8]*t'eng*ˀ '*song t'eng*ˀ *tieu*ˀ to be at a master's bidding; [9]*t'eng*ˀ ˎ*chûng* ˎ*ki piëng*ˀ according to one's convenience.

趁 Ch'ên. Nien. 趂 Ch'ên. To follow, to come up behind; to walk hastily up to; to avail of, to embrace an opportunity; at the time; by, through: [10]*t'eng*ˀ *sië*ˀ to avail of the chance; COM., [11]*t'eng*ˀ ˏ*ki hwoi*ˀ to embrace the opportunity; COLL., [12]*t'eng*ˀ *yëk*ˎ *k'â*ˀ *k'ô*ˀ *siâh*ˎ go quickly and eat it while hot; [13]*t'eng*ˀ ˎ*t'au hwok*ˎ ˏ*ch'ang*, while her hair is still black—*scil.*, a widow should marry; [14]*t'eng*ˀ '*cha* ˏ*li*, to come early; [15]*t'eng*ˀ *tio*ˀ by the road, by land; *t'eng*ˀ ˏ*chu wai*ˀ *k'ô*ˀ to pass here, to go by this way. Read ˎ*ting*: to pass, to step over.

疢 Ch'ên. A fever, febrile complaint; a delicate appetite. Read '*ching*: the same as '*ching* (pustules), q. v.

賺 Chuan. Read '*kwang*; used for the coll. *t'eng*ˀ: to gain in trade, to make profit: also read *chwang*ˀ in the coll. q. v.: [16]*t'eng*ˀ *siâh*ˎ to earn a living; [16]*t'eng*ˀ *le*ˀ to get interest on; [17]*t'eng*ˀ ˏ*kêng* ˏ*chiëng*, to earn wages; *t'eng*ˀ *twai*ˀ ˏ*chiëng*, to get large profits; *t'eng*ˀ *ô*ˀ '*hwi sik*ˎ *châ*ˀ to earn only enough to eat; *t'eng*ˀ *siâh*ˎ *t'eng*ˀ *k'ah*ˎ ˏ*lieu*, got his food and recreation besides, as a servant attending his master to a feast.

*T'eng*ˀ. A coll. euphonic prefix, as in *t'eng*ˀ *t'ang*ˀ to push out and up, to raise, as an awning; *t'eng*ˀ ˏ*t'ung t'ang*ˀ to assume a defiant attitude; *t'eng*ˀ *t'aung*ˀ to undress; to take off, as a door from the hinges; *t'eng*ˀ *t'aëng*ˀ swept away by a freshet.

[1]呆的很○ [2]聽訟 [3]重聽 [4]聽差 [5]聽候 [6]聽憑 [7]聽其自然 [8]聽調聽遣 [9]聽勢 [10]趁機會 [11]趁熱快去食 [12]趁頭髮靑 [13]趁早梨 [14]趁路 [15]聽食 [16]聽利 [17]聽工錢

沉 ꜀Ch‘ên. Read ꜀t‘ing; coll. ꜀t‘eng: to sink; sunk, immersed; low, settled, depressed: [1]꜀t‘eng ‘tá, to sink to the bottom; [2]꜀t‘eng ꜀só, a hollow, a depression; the concave side up, as tiles; [3]tak꜁ ꜀t‘eng, trod down, as a weak floor.

T‘eng’. A coll. word: even, equal in size; uniform, of the same size throughout, as timber: *t‘eng’ t‘eng’* alike, of about the same size; *‘yă t‘eng’* very uniform.

T‘eng’. A coll. euphonic prefix, as in *t‘eng’ t‘aĕng’* to instigate, to edge on; *t‘eng’ t‘iong’* to pass things from one to another; *t‘eng’ t‘aung’* to heat over; to resume practice, as of music or study.

(861) T‘ĕng.

通 ꜀T‘ung. Read ꜀t‘ung; coll. ꜀t‘ĕng: pervious, permeable; open to, open throughout, extending through; to see clearly; understanding, comprehending, intelligent; clear, translucent; all, complete, thorough; to breathe, to give vent to: [4]꜀t‘ĕng t‘au’ open, extending through; ꜀kau má’ ꜀t‘ĕng, the drain is stopped; [5]꜀t‘ĕng ꜀t‘iéng, open to the air or sky; [6]꜀t‘ĕng ‘yă, a wide, open space; [7]꜀t‘ĕng ‘yă ꜀t‘ĕng ꜀yong, a broad expanse; *met.*, to speak irrelevantly; [8]꜀t‘ĕng ch‘ai’ or ꜀t‘ĕng ꜀hung, to begin to feed a child with animal food; the latter also means to resume the ordinary, after the vegetable, diet; *hwo’ má’* ꜀t‘ĕng, the goods are not salable; [9]꜀t‘ĕng ꜀lĕng, translucent, as glass; ꜀t‘ĕng ꜀t‘ĕng ꜀kwong, light, clear; *met.*, to know thoroughly, as customs, prices; [10]꜀ling k‘ieu’ ꜀k‘wi ꜀t‘ĕng, the intellectual pores open—clever, knowing; ꜀t‘ĕng ꜀t‘ĕng tik꜁ prostrate, stretched at full length.

꜀*T‘ĕng*. A coll. word, for which the preceding character is often used: ought, must: ꜀t‘ĕng ng’ ꜀t‘ĕng, ought to or not? ꜀t‘ĕng k‘ang’ ought to see?—you must not look at it.

桶 ‘T‘ung. A square vessel containing six ꜀ching; a tub; a pail, a bucket: COM., [11]‘chwi ‘t‘ĕng, large water-pails; [12]꜀k‘a ‘t‘ĕng, a wash-tub; [13]‘ma ‘t‘ĕng, a wooden chamber-vessel; [14]‘t‘ĕng sioh꜁ varnished tubs, etc.,—as on signboards; [15]hok꜁ ‘t‘ĕng, a pail or tub to "contain malaria" in the ch‘ok꜁ ‘hai ceremony; [16]‘t‘ĕng ꜀liong, the movable center-piece of a bucket-bail; COLL., ‘t‘ĕng p‘wói’ bucket-staves; ꜀kau ‘t‘ĕng, a small pail; ‘t‘ĕng ꜀pwang, a sort of large tray or waiter.

‘*T‘ĕng*. A coll. word: perhaps a corruption of ꜀t‘ĕng, as in ‘t‘ĕng ꜀siéng’ a door set open, an open window; ‘t‘ĕng ‘t‘ĕng tik꜁ straight out, at full length.

‘*T‘ĕng*. A country brogue, as in ‘t‘ĕng ‘cha, early, formerly, a while ago.

蟲 虫 ꜀Ch‘ung. Read ꜀t‘ŭng; coll. ꜀t‘ĕng: worms; insects in general: [17]꜀t‘ĕng laung’ the eggs of insects; [18]‘mi ꜀t‘ĕng, worms bred in rice grains; [19]꜀t‘ĕng ngiê’ insects; [20]lai’ ꜀t‘ĕng, worms in leprous sores.

1 沉底 3 踏沉 5 通天 7 通野 8 通菜 10 靈竅 11 水桶 13 馬桶 15 福桶 17 蟲蛋 19 蟲蟻

2 沉槽 4 通透 6 通野 通洋 9 通瓏 開通 12 胶桶 14 桶石 16 桶梁 18 米蟲 20 癩蟲

桐 ꜀T'ung. Read ꜀*tung;* coll. ꜀*t'ëng:* a tree producing oily seeds, called [1]*꜀t'ëng ch'eu*'; [2]*꜀t'ëng ꜀iu*, wood-oil; [3]*꜀t'ëng ꜀iu ꜀hwi*, a putty of wood-oil and lime; *꜀t'ëng ꜀iu aëng*' '*tio ꜀t'ëng ꜀iu*, the wood-oil pot contains wood-oil; *met.*, each is suited to his own occupation.

(862) T'eu.

偷 ꜀T'ou. To steal, to pilfer; to obtain by pretexts; remiss, c a r e l e s s, disrespectful; privately; stealthily, clandestinely: in the coll. read ꜀*t'au*, q. v.: [4]'*keu ꜀t'eu*, a petty theft; [5]*꜀t'eu pok*꜀, careless, disrespectful; lax, depraved, as the customs of a place; ꜀*t'eu ꜀seng*, to save one's life dishonorably; COM., [6]*꜀t'eu ꜀hiong ch'iék*꜀ *ngük*꜀, to act as a libertine—a phrase used in novels.

鍮 ꜀T'ou. An ore like gold, which forms an amalgam with quicksilver; it is perhaps gold quartz, and is said to come from Persia.

꜀*T'eu.* A coll. word: turned, soured, spoiled: *pwong*' ꜀*t'eu*, the rice is spoiled; *ch'au*' ꜀*t'eu*, sour and stinking.

꜀*T'eu.* A coll. word: weak, infirm, debilitated.

T'eu'. A coll. word: to exchange, to substitute a bad, for a good, article: *t'eu*' *k'ó*' exchanged; *t'eu*' ꜀*pau*, to exchange surreptitiously, as in marrying off girls; *t'eu*' '*ka*, to substitute a different one; *t'eu*' *taung*' to pawn another article in exchange.

頭 ꜀T'ou. The head; the chief, the principal; the top or front; the end, one end of; the first, the best; the beginning of a matter; a numerative of acts, or affairs; as a suffix, it merely makes a dissyllable, or indicates a roundish form like a head: in the coll. read ꜀*t'au*, q. v.

柱² Chu. Read *chëü*²; coll. *t'eu*²: a post, a pillar, an upright support: [7]*sioh*꜀ *t'eu*² a stone pillar; *t'eu*² '*ma twai*² the posts (of the house) are large; [8]*t'eu*² ꜀*chio*, a plinth, a carved base; [9]*ngo*² *t'eu*² five posts (deep), as a house; [10]*t'eu*² *e*² the two divisions of a theme or section in an essay.

(863) T'ëük.

縮꜄ So. Shu. Read *sauk*꜀; used for the coll. *t'ëük*꜀: to withdraw, to retract, to pull back; to contract, to shorten, as a worm does: [11]*t'ëük*꜀ '*toi*, to shorten itself; [12]*t'ëük*꜀ '*chau*, to recede, to s h u n observation; [13]*t'ëük*꜀ '*ch'iu*, to draw the hand, as into the sleeve; [14]*t'ëük*꜀ ꜀*t'au* ꜀*kwi*, "a tortoise drawing in its head"—a person who has a short neck.

(864) T'i.

黐 ꜀Ch'ih. To attach, to stick to; sticky, glutinous, pasty; viscous, stringy, r o p y: also read ꜀*lié*, q. v.: COM., [15]꜀*t'i* ꜀*niéng*, sticking; ꜀*t'i* ꜀*t'i*, sticky, p a s t y; COLL., ꜀*t'i* '*mwang nói*² sticking all about, as salted-snail pickle.

蜘 ꜀Chih. Read ꜀*ti* in the dictionaries: a spider, the araneidæ: COM., [16]꜀*t'i* ꜀*t'ü*, a spider of the web-weaving sort;

[1] 桐楔 [2] 桐油 [3] 桐油灰 [4] 狗偷 [5] 偷薄 [6] 偷香竊玉 [7] 石柱 [8] 柱珠 [9] 五柱 [10] 柱意 [11] 縮短 [12] 縮走 [13] 縮手 [14] 縮頭龜 [15] 黐黏 [16] 蜘蛛

海上絲綢之路文獻集成 科技與文化編

福州方言拼音字典

ˏt'i ˏt'ü ˏsi (or ʻwong), cobwebs; ˏt'i ˏt'ü ˏchiăng, a spider-elf; COLL., ˏt'i ˏt'ü ˏmang, a spider's web; *met.*, the thread-netting on the top of a sedan.

ˏ*T'i.* A coll. word: to take without leave, to appropriate; to pull along accidentally, as a thing adhering: ˏlu ˏt'i, to appropriate, to pilfer; siăngʾ k'ëük, ˏi ˏt'i ˏsing ʻlá, has carried off the thread sticking to his person.

ˏ*T'i.* A coll. euphonic prefix, as in ˏt'i ˏt'wa, to pull, to drag; ˏt'i ˏt'ieu, to raise, as on the point of a stick; to pick out, as a splinter; ˏt'i ˏt'oi, to refuse, to decline; to plane.

ʻ恥 ʻ耻 Ch'ih. To feel ashamed; to blush; shamed, disgraced, humbled, chagrined: [1]ˏmung ʻt'i, covered with disgrace; [2]ˏsiu ʻt'i, ashamed, shame; [3]ˏu ʻt'i ˏchi ˏtu, a brazen-faced rascal; [4]ʻt'i ch'ieuʾ to laugh at and shame one.

ʻ*T'i.* A coll. euphonic prefix, as in ʻt'i ʻt'ié, to rend; ʻt'i ʻt'ë, to scale, to shell off, as plaster from walls; ʻt'i ʻt'u, to hand to; to take and put away; ʻt'i ʻt'au, to shake, give it a shaking.

ˏ持 Ch'ih. To grasp, to lay hold of; to keep, to maintain; to manage, to direct firmly: [6]ˏkung ˏt'i, a vessel for drawing water; [7]chek, ˏt'i, to take in the hand; COM., [8]ʻpa ˏt'i, to keep, to control; [9]ˏt'i ʻsiu, to maintain; [9]ˏt'i ˏsing, to keep one's self from vice; [10]ˏhu ˏt'i, to aid; [11]ˏt'i ˏka kieʾ to manage domestic matters, to plan for the expenses; COLL., ˏt'i ˏt'wa ˏt'wa, to drag, to pull; long, draggling; drawling; ˏt'i mâʾ ˏk'wi, unable to meet the expenses.

ˏ提 Ti. T'i. To lift in the hand, to take up; to hold, to carry; to help, to bring forward, to patronize; to bring before a magistrate; a sort of drum or sounding tube; to throw away: [12]ˏt'i ˏhwong, to watch; [13]ˏt'i ˏhié, to lead by the hand; ˏpu ˏt'i, the right way or principle—a Budhist phrase; [14]ˏt'i ˏhing, the criminal judge of a province; COM., [15]ˏt'i tok, a major-general; [16]ˏchwi ˏsü ˏt'i tok, an admiral; [17]ˏt'i ˏtong, a courier; [18]ˏt'i tieuʾ an overseer of students at examinations; [19]ˏt'i ˏlu, a censer—carried before idols and high officers; ˏt'i ˏtó, a kind of knife; *met.*, knife-shaped lanterns and head ornaments; ˏt'i ˏt'au, characters elevated at the head of a column; ˏt'i pak, to assist, to help one.

ˏ堤 Ti. T'i. A bank, a dike, a levee; to stop, to fill with earth; to settle or place firmly; to guard, to prepare against, to set up a barrier.

ˏ隄 Ti. Interchanged with the last: a fence, a limit, a ridge, a barrier; to dike off; bridged over; a way made to cross on: [20]ˏt'i ˏhwong, a barrier, as against floods; [21]ˏt'i ngangʾ a diked bank or shore.

[1]蒙恥 [2]羞恥 [3]無恥之徒 [4]恥笑 [5]軍持 [6]執持 [7]把持 [8]持守 [9]持身 [10]扶持 [11]持家 計 [12]提防 〇 [13]提携 [14]提刑 [15]提督 [16]水師提督 [17]提塘 [18]提調 [19]提爐 [20]隄防 [21]隄岸

醍 ꜀T'i. Pure, clear liquor, reddish spirits; the essential oil of milk; a liquor refined from the coagulum of butter, elaine: [1]꜀*t'i* ꜀*hu*, the unctuous liquor from cream or butter; *met.*, the beneficent temper of Budha.

踟 ꜀Ch'ih. Irresolute, undecided: ꜀*t'i* ꜀*tü*, embarrassed, unable to advance, going on and then returning.

苔 ꜀T'ai. Read ꜀*t'ai*; coll. ꜀*t'i*: moss, lichen: [2]꜀*t'i ch'ai*꜄ sea-moss; [3]꜀*ch'ang* ꜀*t'i*, green moss, rock moss.

篪 ꜀T'i. A species of bamboo: COLL., [4]꜀*t'i t'óh*, the bark of bamboo shoots—dried and used in shoe-soles.

鮐 ꜀T'ai. Read ꜀*t'ai*; used for the coll. ꜀*t'i*, as in [5]꜀*ung* ꜀*t'i*, a small sea-fish, valued for its tonic qualities; [6]꜀*ung* ꜀*t'i* ꜀*kié* and [7]꜀*t'i hok*꜁ ꜀*kié*, two kinds of small, salted seafish.

꜀*T'i*. A coll. word, as in *sioh*꜁ ꜀*pi* ꜀*t'i*, a bunch, as of grapes—the same as in ꜀*ti*, q. v.

꜀*T'i*. A coll. euphonic prefix, as in ꜀*t'i* ꜀*t'ai*, to kill; ꜀*t'i* ꜀*t'ié*, to cry; ꜀*t'i* ꜀*t'ieu*, to select, to cull out.

(865) T'iăh.

拆 Chê. Shê. Cho. Read *ch'aik*꜁; used for the coll. *t'iăh*꜁: to pull down, to tear in pieces; to peel, to strip off; to remove, to separate; to open; *met.*, to abase, to disgrace, to dishonor: [8]*t'iăh*, *ch'io*꜄ to tear down a house; [9]*t'iăh*, ꜀*k'wi* (or *sang*꜄), to open, as a package; [10]*t'iăh*, ꜀*pang tē*꜄ to raze to the ground; [11]*t'iăh*, *po*꜄ to separate a brood from the hen; [12]*t'iăh*, ꜀*năng* ꜂*liĕng miĕng*꜄ (or ꜀*sing ka*꜄), to dishonor, to abase one; [13]*t'iăh*, ꜀*tĕng* ꜀*ch'iong* ꜂*pwo* ꜀*sá piăh*, to tear away the east wall to fill in the west partition—to pay debts by borrowing.

(866) T'iăk.

獺 T'a. The otter: COM., [14]꜀*sang t'iăk*, a beaver, a fresh-water otter; [15]꜂*hai t'iăk*, a seal; *t'iăk*, ꜀*p'uá* ꜂*liăng*, a seal-skin collar; *t'iăk*, ꜀*sai*, a thin flat fish, like a flounder or halibut.

T'iăk꜁. A coll. word: to wink: *mĕk*꜁ *t'iăk*, the eye-lashes; *mek*꜁ ꜀*chiu t'iăk*, to wink the eyes.

(867) T'iăng.

聽 ꜀T'ing. Read *t'eng*꜄; coll. ꜀*t'iăng*: to hear, to listen; to understand; to hearken to, to obey, to comply: [16]*ng*꜄ ꜀*t'iăng kiĕng*꜄ did not hear; ꜀*t'iăng mă*꜄ *ch'ok*, can't understand what I hear; ꜂*hó* ꜀*t'iăng*, pleasant to hear; ꜂*ngwai* ꜂*kong* ꜂*nü* ꜀*t'iăng*, let me tell you; ꜀*t'iăng ch'oi*꜄ to obey orders.

廳 ꜀T'ing. Read ꜀*t'ing* in the dictionaries: a hall, a parlor, a drawing-room: COM., [17]꜀*kwang* ꜀*t'iăng*, a room for officers' meetings, as at parade; [18]꜀*t'iăng* ꜀*tong*, the central hall or reception-room; *k'ah*, ꜀*t'iăng*, a parlor; ꜀*t'iăng* ꜀*piĕng* ꜀*pung*, side-rooms.

---

[1] 醍醐 [2] 苔菜 [3] 青苔 [4] 篪籜 [5] 鰨鮐 [6] 鰨鮐鮭 [7] 鮐核鮭 [8] 拆厝 [9] 拆開 [10] 拆平地〇 [11] 拆拖 [12] 拆拖臉面 [13] 拆東墻補西壁 [14] 山獺 [15] 海獺 [16] 怀聽見〇 [17] 官廳 [18] 廳中

揁 ' Tien. Read *'tiĕng;* used in the *Paik*, *ˏIng* for the coll. *'t'iăng:* to push with the hand: [1]*'t'iăng 'tó*, to push over; [2]*'t'iăng ˏk'wi*, to push open or aside; [3]*'t'iăng kwo' oi'* to push one along on a seat; [4]*'t'iăng chai'* to stave off (payment of) a debt; *'t'iăng laëkˎ* to decline and get rid of.

痛 ' T'ung. Read *t'ong'*; coll. *t'iăng':* to ache, to be in pain; a pain, an ache, a twinge: *ā' t'iăng'* it aches, it hurts; [5]*ˏt'au t'iăng'* a headache; *pokˎ 'ló t'iăng'* the belly-ache.

愛 ' Ai. Read *ai';* used for the coll. *t'iăng':* to love, to feel attachment for, to take delight in; love, regard, affection: [6]*t'iăng' nikˎ* or *t'iăng' taëng'* (or *naëng'*), to be very fond of; [7]*'hó t'iăng'* lovely, amiable; [8]*ng' 'hó t'iăng'* cross, unamiable; *t'iăng' nóhˎ* to love things—i. e. sparing or careful in using them; *tekˎ ˏnëng t'iăng'* to win others' love.

程 ˏCh'êng. A road, a path, a journey; rules, regulations; a limit, a measure; *met.*, a task, a course or period of duty: also read *ˏt'ing*, q. v.: COM., [9]*ˏchiong ˏt'iăng*, rules, regulations; the articles, as of a treaty; [10]*ˏT'iăng 'chü*, a disciple of Chuhi; COLL., [11]*tio' ˏt'iăng*, a road, a journey; one's course in life.

(868) T'ié.

'T'ié. A coll. word: to tear, to rend, to pull apart: *'t'ié pahˎ*, to tear into pieces; *'t'ié 'chai*, to tear paper; *'t'ié pahˎ meng' ˏp'uí*, to dishonor, to insult one.

剃鬀 ' T'i. To shave: COM., [12]*t'ié' ˏt'au*, to shave the head; [13]*t'ié' ˏtó*, a razor; *t'ié' ˏt'au tang'* a traveling barber's apparatus; COLL., [14]*ˏt'au hwokˎ t'ié' chó' ˏhwo siong'* to shave off the hair and become a Bonze.

薙 ' T'i. Interchanged with the last: to shave. Read *t'á':* to root out grass and weeds, to clear off land; underbrush. Read *te'* as in *ˏsing te'* (or *ˏsing ˏi*), the magnolia purpurea—probably the same as *mukˎ pekˎ* in the coll.

T'ié'. A coll. word: to follow on; to avail of; to do something extra or miscellaneous, as at the end of a main job: *t'ié' 'mwi au'* to follow after others; *t'ié' 'ch'iu chó'* to do while one's hand is in; *t'ié' ˏpong*, to let it go in with the main lot; *t'ié' ka'* to buy at the same price that others did; *t'ié' ˏnëng ˏsiăng*, to repeat after one.

T'ié'. A coll. word, also spoken *tié':* to trickle, as water: *t'ié' lóhˎ* or *t'ié' t'ié' lóhˎ* to trickle down.

啼 ˏ T'i. Read *ˏt'á;* coll. *ˏt'ié:* to cry, to weep; to bewail, to lament, to mourn for: [15]*ˏt'ié ˏma*, to cry; [16]*ˏt'ié tekˎ ch'aikˎ* to weep bitterly; [17]*ˏt'ié ˏma ch'ieu'* to smile amid tears; [18]*ˏt'ié 'kiăng*, to mourn for a (deceased) child; [19]*ˏt'ié yă' ˏu ekˎ*, no use in crying about it; [20]*ˏma ˏma ˏt'ié*, to weep convulsively.

---

[1]揁倒 [2]揁開 [3]揁過位 [4]揁債 [5]頭痛 [6]愛溺 [7]好愛 [8]伓好愛 [9]章程 [10]程子 [11]路程 [12]剃頭 [13]剃刀 [14]頭髮剃做和尚 [15]啼嘛 [16]啼的惻○ [17]啼嘛笑 [18]啼仔 [19]啼也無益 [20]嘛嘛啼

(869) T'iék.

鐵, 鉄, T'ieh. Iron, called *haik*, *˛king*, the black metal; made of iron; firm, decided, irreversible; firm, well-knit, as one's frame; hard, unfeeling: COM., [1]*t'iék*, *k'e'* iron utensils; [2]*˛yong t'iék*, sheet-tin; [3]*t'iék*, *siăng'* iron wire; [4]*t'iék*, *˛teu*, rod-iron; [5]*t'iék*, *hang'* one having a firmly set frame; [6]*t'iék*, *sik*, in very sooth, positively; [7]*t'iék*, *˛kwang ˛ing*, an iron Kwanyin—a dark beauty; [8]*t'iék*, *pek*, *˛u ˛pó*, the iron pencil is without flattery, as a fortune-teller says; COLL., *t'iék*, *sau'* *ʻch'iu*, the iron broom—is a dangerous element in a girl's horoscope; *t'iék*, *ch'eu'* the sago-palm; *t'iék*, *ʻkang*, an iron cudgel; *t'iék*, *ch'ioh*, *˛mwai ˛siăng ˛cheng* (even) an iron cudgel may be ground into a needle; *met.*, perseverance effects wonders.

徹, Ch'ê. Pervious, pervading; to penetrate; all, entire, throughout; a thoroughfare; to remove; intelligent, perspicacious; to skin, to peel; to destroy; to cultivate: [9]*t'iék*, *chwang²* to remove food; [10]*˛t'ung t'iék*, to discern clearly; COM., [11]*t'iék*, *˛tiong*, the breaking up of a literary examination; [12]*t'iék*, *ʻtá*, to the very end of; COLL., [13]*t'iék*, *yă'* *˛mó hak*, *ʻngang*, did not close my eyes through the whole night!

撤, Ch'ê. Analogous to the preceding in some senses: to send away, to remove; to recall; to set one aside; to take off, to flay: [14]*t'iék*, *˛hui*, to recall an officer; COLL. [15]*t'iék*, *k'ó'* to remove things, as at the end of a feast; to remove, as a shed or booth.

澈, Ch'ê. Read *tiék*, in the dictionaries: pure and limpid, as water; clear, pellucid; water dried up in its channel: [16]*˛teng t'iék*, pure in principle, pure-minded.

餮, T'ieh. Greedy in eating, gluttonous: [17]*˛t'ó t'iék*, greedy, avaricious; an emblem of avarice—a monster drawn as a head without a body.

跌, T'ieh. Read *tiék*,; coll. *t'iék*,: as in [18]*t'iék*, *ʻta yoh*, medicine for bruises and stripes.

T'iék₂. A coll. word: lean, wasted, emaciated from disease: *t'iék₂ t'iék₂* much wasted; *t'iék₂ ˛ló*, the consumption; *t'iék₂ ˛ló ˛kié*, a fowl wasted with disease; *t'iék₂ ˛ló ʻkwi*, a lank ghost!

(870) T'iéng.

天, 靝, T'ien. The highest and greatest of things; the heaven, the sky, the air; the empyrean, firmament; a day; a season; the ages; the weather; heavenly, celestial; the superior powers, the Supreme; Providence, Nature; the over-ruling power, Heaven; *met.*, the Emperor; to regard or honor as heaven; in the coll. with *te²* (earth) gives a superlative or emphatic form to a phrase: COM., [19]*˛t'iéng te² ˛ing*, heaven, earth, man—the three powers; [20]*˛t'iéng ʻchŭ*, the emperor; *˛t'iéng a²* the

1 鐵器 2 洋鐵 3 鐵線 4 鐵條 5 鐵漢 6 鐵實 7 鐵觀音 8 鐵筆無褒 9 徹饌 10 通徹 11 徹場 12 徹底 13 徹夜無合眼 14 徹回 15 撤去 16 澄澈 17 饕餮 18 跌打藥 19 天地人 20 天子

empire; the world; [1] *ˌt'iéng ˌtong*, in the open air; [2] *ˌt'iéng ˌtong*, paradise, heaven; [3] *ˌt'iéng säü'* angels; [4] *ˌt'iéng so'* (or *e'*), the will of Heaven, destiny; *ˌt'ieng k'e'* vapors; air, weather; [5] *'hó ˌt'iéng*, fair weather; [6] *ˌt'iéng kaung'* to descend from heaven; an advent, as of Jesus; [7] *ˌt'iéng ˌung*, astronomy; [8] *ˌt'iéng 'chang*, the open court of a building; [9] *ˌt'iéng koi'* the menses; [10] *ˌt'iéng 'keu*, the sky-dog—said to devour children; [11] *ˌt'iéng 'peng*, the top-board of a coffin; [12] *ˌt'iéng ˌkwong 'cha*, day-break, early in the morning; [13] *ˌch'ung ˌt'iéng*, Spring; [14] *ˌt'iéng ˌhwa*, small-pox; [15] *ˌt'iéng ˌseng chëü' ˌyong*, natural, spontaneous; original, as gifts or talents; [16] *hwang' ˌt'iéng ˌteu*, to transgress heaven's laws; [17] *ˌt'iéng 'li ˌliong ˌsing*, the natural rule of rectitude, conscience; COLL., *ˌt'iéng ˌsang*, clear weather; *ˌt'iéng miéng' hang'* a tall person; *ˌt'iéng ˌpang ˌcheng*, the pointer of a pair of scales; *met.*, the spot below the sternum; *ˌt'iéng ˌpang te' ˌpang*, very level; very correct (colloquial); *ˌt'iéng ˌpang te' ˌkeng*, very high or lofty.

添 T'ien. To add to, to increase, to put in more; additional, extra: COM., *ˌka ˌt'iéng*, to add more; [18] *ˌt'iéng ch'eng'* to give good weight; *ˌt'iéng ˌhwa ˌt'iéng 'ch'ai*, to give an extra douceur; *ˌt'iéng ˌting hwak, kak*, to bear a son who is to get preferment—a felicitous phrase; COLL., *ˌt'iéng 'la ˌhiong ˌlu ˌtó 'la 'kwi*, an extra censer makes an extra demon (to worship); *met.*, an additional matter or person creates extra trouble and expense.

'忝 T'ien. Ashamed, humiliated; disgraced, dishonored; to become conscious of guilt; to bring reproach on: [19] *ˌu 't'iéng*, no disgrace; COM., *'t'iéng kwong'* I, your humble friend—used by a lady in writing to her equal; *se' 't'iéng kwong'* and *'wang 't'iéng kwong'* the same as used by elders and juniors.

'舔 T'ien. To draw the tongue over, to lick anything with the tongue.

'餂 T'ien. To take with a hook; to entrap, as by specious talk: also read *ˌtiéng*, q. v.: *'i ˌngiong 't'iéng ˌchi*, to catch them with words.

'諂 Ch'an. To flatter, to cajole; to give gods or men worship or praise not due to them; pleasing, gratifying to the eye or ear; adulation, sycophancy: [20] *'t'iéng ˌü*, to flatter; *'t'iéng ch'ieu'* to smirk and cajole one; COM., [21] *'t'iéng me'* to flatter, to fawn on.

'㥏 T'ien. Bashful, ashamed; to blush from shame, to feel disgraced.

'靦 '覥 T'ien. Analogous to the last: a blushing face; to redden, to grow red, as from shame or a sense of insult.

[1]天	[3]天	[5]好	[7]天	[9]天	[11]天	早	花	然	[17]天	[18]添	[20]諂
中	使	天	文	癸	板	[13]春	[15]天	[16]犯	理	秤	諛
[2]天	[4]天	[6]天	[8]天	[10]天	[12]天	天	生	天	良	[19]無	[21]諂
堂	數	降	井	狗	光	[14]天	自	條	心	忝	媚

T'iéng'. A coll. word: to sew, to join with stitches: *'pwo t'iéng'* to patch and sew, to mend; *t'iéng' ,á nge'* to put on a heel-strap; *t'iéng' ,hi,* to take long stitches; *t'iéng' sioh, ,cheng,* to take a stitch or two, as to mend a small rent.

恬 T'ien. Peaceful, still, tranquil, contented; to pass a tranquil life: [1]*,t'iéng cheng'* at rest, quiet, composed.

湉 T'ien. Water flowing noiselessly, a gentle stream: [2]*'chiéng ,t'iéng,* to glide smoothly along.

鮋 A coll. character: a darkish white pond-fish, called [3]*,t'iéng laung'*.

,T'iéng. A coll. word: to fatten, as fowls by cooping them and stuffing their crops; shut up and fattened; fat, good and solid, as meat; also, medium, uniform in size: *,t'iéng ak,* fattened ducks; *,t'iéng ,pui ,pui,* to fatten; *,t'iéng ,t'ieng twai'* of a uniform size; *'chiä tói' so' cheng' ,t'iéng,* these pieces (of meat) are capital!—language of the markets.

(871) T'ieu.

刁 Tiao. The original form of the character for *,tó* (a knife): wicked, perverse; seditious, artful, intriguing, caballing: in the coll. read *,tieu,* q. v.: [4]*,t'ieu ,hung,* depraved manners, seditious cabals; [5]*,t'ieu ,t'ieu,* lightly moved by the wind; [6]*,t'ieu ,mang,* violent, barbarous.

佻 Tiao. T'iao. Yao. Weak, young and tender; unable to travel far; light and trifling; to be envious of others; to assume, to appropriate to one's self.

𠜱 Tiao. To pare, to scrape, to cut off.

挑 T'iao. To carry on the shoulder, or the end of a stick; to raise, to lift; to remove or pick out, as a splinter from the hand; to move, to stir, to separate things; to select out of; to stir up, to provoke, to instigate; to breed trouble; to sew, to embroider; to lead; to trifle, to dally with; frivolous; quickly; a spoon: in the coll. read *,t'ieu,* q. v.: [7]*,t'ieu tang'* (coll. *,tang tang'*), to carry a load with a cooly-stick; [8]*,t'ieu 'ing,* to lead, as in mischief; [9]*,t'ieu ,hu,* a porter; COM., [10]*,t'ieu ,só,* (coll. *,t'ieu t'aëk,*), to instigate; [11]*,t'ieu sëü' ,seng ,hi,* to stir up evil; [12]*,t'ieu ,ting,* to carry a lantern at the end of a stick; [13]*,t'ieu ,hwa,* to embroider flowers; [14]*,t'ieu ek, 'teng,* to select graduates for district magistrates; COLL., [15]*,kiéng ,t'ieu 'má má'* to peddle, a huckster; [16]*,t'ieu ch'ié'* (or *,ch'iäng*), to pick out a splinter; [17]*,t'ieu 't'u ,peng,* the abbreviated form of the 32d radical.

恌 T'iao. Mournful, sorry, grieved; to disesteem, to fail to treat kindly.

祧 T'iao. To move or replace ancestral tablets; the ancestral hall: [18]*'siu ,t'ieu,* to guard the lares.

1 恬靜 2 瀞湉 3 鮋蛋 4 刁風 5 刁刁 6 刁蠻 7 挑擔 8 挑引 9 挑夫 10 挑唆 11 挑事生非 12 挑燈 13 挑花 14 挑一等○ 15 有挑買賣 16 挑刺 17 挑土才 18 守祧○

窕 ‘ Tiao. Deep, profound, having apartments extending far back, as a house; handsome, elegant; reserved, lady-like: [1]*yeu ‘t'ieu*, still, tranquil; gentle and easy, beautiful, as a lady.

糶 ’ T'iao. To sell grain: COM., [2]*‘ch'ok, t'ieu’* to sell out, to dispose of (grain); [3]*t'ieu’ ‘mi*, to sell rice.

眺 ’ T'iao. To look aslant; to peer, to glance furtively; to look far: [4]*t'ieu’ wong’* to look forward to, to gaze at.

跳, **趒** ’ T'iao. To leap, to jump, to skip; to dance, to hop about; to beat, to palpitate, as the heart; to shoot, as sprouts: COM., [5]*t'ieu’ t'ieu’ ‚ngü*, the frisker—name of a small fish; [6]*‚sing ‚kang t'ieu’* the heart beating, as from fear; [7]*t'ieu’ kwo’ ‚ch'iong*, to leap a wall; [8]*t'ieu’ ‚lüng ‚mwong*, to leap the dragon's gate—to gain literary and official honors; also applied to officers hastening to the examination-hall; COLL., [9]*siong’ t'ieu’ ‚chai a’ t'ieu’ ‘hi*, the twitching of the upper (eyelid) is (an omen of) wealth; that of the lower, of joy; *t'ieu’ t'ieu’ ‘tiong*, to hop or skip about. Read *tieu’*: to walk along.

覜 ’ T'iao. High officers sent by princes to visit the court; to send envoys; to have an audience. Read *‘hu*: to bend the head, to incline the ear; to look closely at any thing: [10]*hu ‘siu*, to hang one's head and skulk away.

挑 ‘ T'iao. Read *‚t'ieu*; coll. *‚t'ieu*: to choose, to select: [11]*‚t'ieu ‘hó ‚ki*, to select good ones; [12]*‚t'ieu ‘song*, to cull out; [13]*‚t'ieu ‚këng ‚hu*, to choose good workmen; [14]*‚t'ieu ‚küng ‚sing*, to select men of muscle; [15]*‚t'ieu ‘p'ing mau’* to choose fine-looking persons.

(872) T'ih.

T'ih₂. A coll. euphonic prefix, as in *t'ih₂ t'uh₂* to pierce, to thrust, as the finger through paper—about as in *tih₂* q. v.

(873) T'ik.

敵 ₂ Ti. Read *tik₂*; used for the coll. *t'ik₂*: to control, to manage, as family expenses; to strive, to compete with, to match, as in a fight: [16]*t'ik₂ ‚ka kié’* to manage family expenses; *t'ik₂ má’ ‚k'wi*, unable to meet (expenses); unable to fight (so many); [17]*t'ik₂ ‚ing ‚ching*, to "meet persons' feelings"—to make presents, as at festivities; *‚i á’ t'ik₂ tek₂ ‘kwi chiáh₂ kwo’* he can oppose and overcome several.

T'ik₂. A coll. word: to comb out straight, to hatchel; to bone; to pull out: *t'ik₂ ‘chëng*, to comb a false cue; *t'ik₂ ‚chëng*, to hatchel palm-coir; *t'ik₂ kauk₂* to bone, as fish or fowl; *t'ik₂ ch'ok₂ ‚li*, to extract, as a book from a pile; *pe’ ‚së t'ik₂* a comb-cleaner; *t'ik₂ ‚t'au hwok₂ naung’* to comb out snarled hair (to make cues of).

T'ik₂. A coll. euphonic prefix, as in *t'ik₂ t'ak₂* to pile up; *t'ik₂ t'ëk₂* to study; *t'ik₂ t'ak₂* the sound of falling drops; *t'ik₂ t'ok₂* to fall, as prices.

1 窈窕 2 出糶 3 糶米 4 眺望 5 跳跳魚 6 心肝跳 7 跳過牆 8 跳龍門 9 上跳財下跳喜 10 覜首 11 挑好其 12 挑選 13 挑工夫 14 挑筋身 15 挑品貌 16 敵家計 17 敵人情

(874) T'ing.

偵 ˓Chêng. Ch'êng. A spy, a scout, commonly termed ¹˓t'ang ˊma, q. v.: to inquire, to spy, to reconnoiter: ²˓iu ˓t'ing, or ³˓t'ing sëü² a spy.

赬 Ch'êng. A carnation or pink color; to dye red; cloth dyed twice over; to become red by fatigue, as said of fishes' tails; *met.*, distressing toil which flushes one.

廳 ˓T'ing. A hall, a parlor, a drawing room; a court: commonly read ˓t'iáng, q. v.

檉 ˓Ch'êng. A water-willow having a reddish bark, supposed by its waving to indicate rain: COM., ⁴˓t'ing ˓ch'a, the wood of the same, used in cabinet-work.

汀 ˓T'ing. Water with level shores; a low bank: a prefecture in the south-west of Fookien: COM., ⁵˓t'ing ˓chiong ˓lüng tō² the Tautai of T'ingchou, Changchou, and Lungyen prefectures in Fookien. Read *t'eng²*: unable to gain one's wish, as a degree.

湛 ˓Chan. To imbue, to moisten, to wet; also an excess, as of pleasure: also read ˓tang, q. v.: ⁶˓t'ing ˓ong, imbued with favor; ⁷˓t'ing lok₂ excessive delight.

煁 ˓ Also read ˓sing: a portable furnace; a three cornered stove, used to warm apartments.

琛 Ch'ên. A beautiful stone; something precious, a treasure: ⁸˓t'iéng ˓t'ing, gems of nature, natural curiosities.

砧 碪 ˓Chên. A stone to beat clothes on; a chopping block, an anvil, for which the coll. words are ˓ting and ˊtong, q. v.: ⁹˓t'ing ˊt'ü, a stone and pestle for washing clothes; ¹⁰kó ˓t'ing, a stone to beat plants on.

酖 ˓Chên. Interchanged with the next: given to wine, exhilarated by liquor; spirits impregnated with poison, a poisonous drink: ¹¹˓t'ing ˓ü ˊchiu, given to wine.

鴆 Chên. A bird that eats snakes; the drawing of it is like the secretary; venemous, deadly, virulent, poisonous: ¹²˓t'ing ˊchiu, poisoned wine; ¹³˓t'ing tuk₂ a deadly poison.

忱 訦 諶 ˓Shên. True, sincere, trustworthy; faithful, devoted; to speak honestly; the last is a man's name, also the name of a small state during the Han dynasty.

˓T'ing. A coll. euphonic prefix, as in ˓t'ing ˓t'ang, to open out; *met.*, to strut, as a fop; ˓t'ing ˓t'ëng, to open; to clean out, as drains; to sell off cheap, to get rid, as of old goods; ˓t'ing ˓t'ong, to swallow.

¹探馬 ²游偵 ³偵伺 ⁴檉柴 ⁵汀漳龍道 ⁶湛恩 ⁷湛樂 ⁸天琛 ⁹砧杵 ¹⁰槖砧 ¹¹酖於酒 ¹²鴆酒 ¹³鴆毒 ○ ○

‘挻 Ting. T'ing. To pluck, to pull out, to draw forth; to hold firmly; to relax, to enlarge; to lead out; straight; to stand forth, to bolt, to rush out: [1]‘*t‘ing* ꜀*hüng* (coll ‘*t‘eng* ꜀*hüng*), a prominent chest; COM., [2]‘*t‘ing* ꜀*sing*, to assume, to take upon one's self to do.

‘脡 T'ing. Meat or fish salted and dried in the sun; jerked meat.

‘梃 T'ing. A single branch or stick; a staff, a club: [3]*chiè*' ‘*t‘ing*, to brandish a club.

‘艇 ‘艇 T'ing. A boat, a punt, a barge; a canoe, a long narrow boat, in the coll. [4]꜀*ma* ‘*lang* ꜀*sung*: COM., [5]‘*t‘ing* ꜀*sung*, a Cantonese piratical craft.

‘鋌 T'ing. Iron or copper ore; the barb of an arrow; empty, hollow, all gone, entirely exhausted.

‘頲 T'ing. A narrow head; straight, upright; straight, direct, as a road.

‘町 Ting. Waste land; a dike, a raised footway between fields; a piece of ground by a house; ground leveled, as for a terrace or altar.

‘頂 Ting. Read ‘*ting*; coll. ‘*t‘ing*: to carry on the head; to support on the palm or foot; [6]‘*t‘ing* ꜀*t‘au*, to carry on the head; to be surety for; [7]‘*t‘ing* ‘*ch‘iu*, or [8]‘*t‘ing* ꜀*pa* ‘*chiong* ꜀*tong*, to carry on the palm; [9]‘*t‘ing* ꜀*kong*, to support (and whirl) jars on the feet, as jugglers do; [10]‘*t‘ing* ꜀*cheng*, a thimble.

‘鼎 ‘鼑 ‘鐤 Ting. A tripod, a caldron; a three-legged pan; firm, safe, secure; to fix, to establish; *met.*, the state; to tie up a boat; the 50th diagram; the 206th radical: in the coll. read ‘*tiăng*, q. v.: [11]‘*t‘ing lik*꜆ to establish, as a new dynasty; [12]꜀*ch‘ung* ꜀*ch‘iu* ‘*t‘ing seng*' in the prime of life; [13]‘*t‘ing chëük*, a tripod; *met.*, the Three States, A. D. 170; COM., [14]꜀*sang* ‘*t‘ing kak*, the highest three of the Hanlin.

‘逞 Ch'êng. To put one's self forward; confident, presuming; hasty, precipitate, rash; pleased with; to extend, to exhaust: [15]*pok*꜆ ‘*t‘ing*, displeased; careless, regardless; COM., [16]‘*t‘ing* ꜀*kung*, or [17]‘*t‘ing* ꜀*kung* ꜀*lô*, to be eager in works of merit, to claim the praise of.

‘郢 Ch'êng. The capital of the feudal state of Tso, now the district city of Kiangling in the north of Hupeh.

‘*T‘ing*. A coll. euphonic prefix, as in ‘*t‘ing* ‘*t‘iăng*, to push away; to refuse, to decline.

‘呈 Ch'êng. A statement, a plea of a case; to present a petition or statement; to state, to set forth; to show, to explain, to discover: usually read ꜀*tiăng*, q. v.: [18]*cheng*' ꜀*t‘ing*,

[1]挺胸 [2]挺身 [3]制挺 [4]猫覽船 [5]艇船〇 [6]頂頭 [7]頂手 [8]頂巴掌中 [9]頂缸 [10]頂針 [11]鼎立 [12]春秋鼎盛 [13]鼎足 [14]三鼎甲 [15]不逞 [16]逞功 [17]逞功勞 [18]進呈

to memorialize; [1]ˌt'ing siong' to present (a petition) to a superior.

程 ˏCh'êng. The hundredth part of a ch'aung' or inch; a portion; a percentage; a rule, a regulation; a pattern; a limit, a period; an order or series; a measure, an allowance; to rule; to measure, to estimate; a road, a journey; to travel: also read ˌ*t'iăng*, q. v.: [2]'*k'i* ˌ*t'ing*, to begin a journey; [3]ˌ*t'ing so'* a decimal part, percentage; [4]ˌ*t'ing sek*, a form, a model; [5]*ek*, ˌ*t'ing*, one tenth; [6]*pok*, ˌ*t'ing* ˌ*ki lik*, I underrated his strength.

裎 ˏCh'êng. The upper part of the body, as in a nude state; to disrobe; also a girdle: [7]'*lio* ˌ*t'ing*, naked, nude.

酲 ˏCh'êng. To drink liquor till one is sick; stupefied, only half-sober and ashamed of being drunk; the feelings after a drinking spree.

沉 沈 ˏCh'ên. To sink, to immerse; sunk in the water; lost, ruined; to quash, as a law case; a lake; muddy, confused; deep, as colors: the 2d also read '*sing* and the 1st read ˌ*t'eng* in the coll. q. v.: [8]ˌ*t'ing tëüng'* very sick; [9]ˌ*t'ing* ˌ*mi*, stupefied, besotted; [10]ˌ*t'ing muk*, lost in the water; COM., [11]ˌ*t'ing nik*, to secrete; to embezzle; besotted, sunk in vice; [12]ˌ*t'ing* ˌ*lung*, sunk, lost; to go to perdition; [13]ˌ*t'ing* ˌ*wong*, the grievance sunk—no redress at law; [14]ˌ*t'ing nik*, *kwok*, '*pó*, to embezzle the Emperor's treasures; [15]ˌ*t'ing* ˌ*hiong*, aloes; a dark yellow or ash color.

霃 ˏCh'ên. Dark, cloudy, darkness continuing long; dull, the threatening appearance of the sky.

停 ˏT'ing. Read ˌ*ting*; coll. ˌ*t'ing*: safe, well-arranged; quiet, correct; honest, trusty: [16]ˌ*t'ing cheng'* well-behaved, correct, not gadding about; [17]ˌ*t'ing taung'* safe, trustworthy; [18]ˌ*t'ing* '*t'io*, right, all proper, in good order.

ˌ*T'ing*. A coll. word: even, equal, uniform: ˌ*t'ing* ˌ*t'ing* ˌ*pang*, even, as the ends of sticks; ˌ*t'ing* ˌ*t'ing sá'* in equal quantities; *taung'* ˌ*t'ing*, to jounce even.

ˌ*T'ing*. A coll. euphonic prefix, as in ˌ*t'ing* ˌ*t'ŭng*, to pile up.

(875) T'io.

[This word is interchangeably read *t'wo*.]

妥 'T'o. Safe, secure; settled, fixed; quiet, at ease; properly arranged: COM., [19]'*t'io t'aik*, settled, secured; [20]'*t'io taung'* or '*t'io* '*t'io taung' taung'* all right, safe, secure; honest, trusty; COLL., '*t'io taung'* ˌ*nëng*, a trusty person.

朶 朵 'To. Pendent branches; a numerative of flowers; to move; to take with the hand, to lead; the east and west wings of a temple: [21]ˌ*hwa* '*t'io*, flowers, bouquets; [22]'*ngi* '*t'io*, the ear; '*t'io* ˌ*i*, the chops.

[1]呈上 [3]程數 [5]一程 其力 [8]沉重 [10]沉沒 [12]沉淪 [14]沉匿 [15]沉香 [17]停當 [19]妥貼 [21]花朵

[2]起程 [4]程式 [6]不程 [7]裸裎 [9]沉迷 [11]沉溺 [13]沉冤 國寶 [16]停靜 [18]停妥 [20]妥當 [22]耳朵

剢 'To. Read *tó'* in the dictionaries: to cut fine, to chop up, to hash, to mince, as meat.

𡑞 'To. Firm ground; hard, compact earth, clods, lumps.

(876) T'iong.

張 ꜀Chang. Read ꜀*tiong;* coll. ꜀*t'iong:* a numerative of things spread out, as a chair, a table, paper: [1]'*chai sioh*꜆ ꜀*t'iong*, a sheet of paper; [2]'꜀*t'iong* ꜀*t'iong*, every sheet; [3]'꜀*t'iong so'* the number of sheets, chairs, &c.

倀' Chang. Also read ꜀*tiong:* to grope, to wander blindly about; carelessly, madly, crazily; to fall down: [4]'*t'iong'* '*kwi*, the ghost of one eaten by a tiger; *met.*, a person who entices others to evil.

悵' Chang. Ch'ang. Vexed, disappointed: [5]'*t'iong' wong'* sick at heart from disappointed hopes.

韔' Ch'ang. A case for a bow; to place a bow in its case.

昶' Ch'ang. A long day; to permeate, through, extended; long, remote, in which senses interchanged with the next: also read '*ch'iong*, q. v.

暢' Ch'ang. The inner feelings or qualities developed; joyous, elated, in high spirits; hilarity, joy; to permeate, spreading, filling; long, remote: [6]'*t'iong' ngwok*꜆ the 11th month; [7]'*t'iong' tak*꜆ permeating; COM., [8]'*t'iong' e'* (or *k'e'*), joyous, elated; [9]'꜀*tieu t'iong'* well and happy; [10]'*t'iong'* '*tang*, very bold, presumptuous.

鬯' Ch'ang. Millet and fragrant herbs, as infused in wine for sacrifices; mixed sacrificial wine: [11]'*kěü' t'iong'* fragrant spirits of black millet; [12]'*chü t'iong'* one who prepares the libations.

T'iong'. A coll. word: to disseminate, to tell, to spread a report: *t'iong' kauk*꜆ *ch'ěü'* (or *se' sié'* or *ch'ek*꜆ *ch'ěü'*), to spread reports everywhere; ꜀*yong t'iong'* to disseminate, to report; *t'iong' sioh*꜆ ꜀*těng*, reported a whole season—i. e. a long time; *t'iong'* ꜀*tu* ꜀*p'u*, widely told, fully reported.

椽 ꜀Ch'uan. Interchangeably read ꜀*t'wong:* a round beam to support a roof or heavy eaves; specifically the rafters on which the tiling is laid; sometimes used in writing as a classifier of houses: COM., [13]꜀*t'iong laiu'* materials for rafters.

杖' Chang. Read *tiong'* in the dictionaries: a cane, a staff; a club; a mourning-staff carried by the oldest son of the deceased: [14]꜀*ch'i t'iong'* or ꜀*t'ai t'iong'* to bamboo; [15]'*mwang t'iong'* to inflict the full number of strokes; [16]'*t'iong'* ꜀*ü* ꜀*hiong*, a village sexagenarian; COM., [17]꜀*siéng t'iong'* a crosier; *met.*, a sort of hair-pin with a Budh's hand, worn by aged women; [18]'*kwai t'iong'* a staff, a cane; [19]'*t'iong'* ꜀*hwa*, the

[1]紙一張〇 [2]張張 [3]張數 [4]倀鬼 [5]悵望 [6]暢月 [7]暢達 [8]暢意 [9]調暢 [10]暢膽〇 [11]秬鬯 [12]主鬯 [13]椽料 [14]笞杖 [15]滿杖〇 [16]杖於鄉〇 [17]禪杖 [18]枴杖 [19]杖花〇

passes made in brandishing clubs; COLL., ꜀*t‘iong t‘iong*’ a club, a stick, a cane; ꜀*tong t‘iong*’ or *ha*’ *ch‘e*’ *t‘iong*’ a mourning-staff.

T‘iong’. A coll. word, analogous to *tiong*’: to move or pass things; to bear, as a message; to stir about, to work: *t‘iong*’ ꜀*piĕng*, move them aside; *t‘iong*’ *sie*’ *sëü*’ to keep up worldly customs, marriages, births, festivals; *t‘iong*’ *wa*’ to covey a statement or message; *siăh*꜀ ꜀*nĕng mwong*’ *k‘ă*’ ꜀*nĕng t‘iong*’ must work for one whose rice you eat.

(877) T‘iu.

抽 ꜀Ch‘ou. To take from, to deduct; to reject; to take dividends; to select, to draw out; to levy, to tax, to assess; to take tenths, to tithe; to raise water, to pump; to utter: COM., [1]꜀*t‘iu* ꜀*ch‘iĕng*, to draw lots (before idols); [2]꜀*t‘iu* ꜀*chu*, to levy a tax on rents; [3]꜀*t‘iu swoi*’ to levy duty; [4]꜀*t‘iu* ꜀*ting*, to draft militia; [5]꜀*t‘iu* ꜀*t‘au*, to deduct a percentage; [6]꜀*ka ek*꜀ ꜀*t‘iu*, to take a tenth; COLL., ꜀*t‘iu* ꜀*t‘iu*, slender and tall; [7]꜀*t‘iu sie*’ to miss threads in weaving; [8]꜀*t‘iu* ꜀*k‘wo* ‘*loi*, to play puppets; *met.*, to hang one's self.

瘳 ꜀Ch‘ou. To cure; curable; healed, convalescent: [9]*k‘wok*꜀ *chik*꜀ *pok*꜀ ꜀*t‘iu*, his disease was incurable.

丑 ‘Ch‘ou, The second of the 12 horary characters, from 1 to 3, A. M. denoted by an ox; in the coll. the 2d class of fools or buffoons in theatricals: COM., [10]‘*t‘iu* ꜀*si*, 1 to 3 A. M.; [11]‘*t‘iu chiăng*’ 2 A. M.; COLL., [12]‘*t‘iu ne*’ a second-grade buffoon; [13]‘*t‘iu* ꜀*hing* ‘*t‘iu chaung*’ he acts like the fool!

儔 ꜀Ch‘ou. Used for the next: a party, a company of four; a mate, a companion; fellows, comrades, friends; a class; to aid, to sympathize: [14]꜀*t‘iu loi*’ a class, a concourse; [15]꜀*t‘iu* ‘*lü*, a comrade, a mate.

疇 ꜀Ch‘ou. To plow, to till, to cultivate; a tilled field; a field of hemp; in time past, formerly; a sort, a class; who? what? [16]꜀*t‘iu sek*, formerly.

幬 ꜀Ch‘ou. A single curtain, the curtain of a carriage; a leathern screen. Read ‘*tó*: a canopy; to screen, to cover, as the sky does: [17]*p‘aiu*’ ‘*tó*, to overspread, to canopy.

籌 ꜀Ch‘ou. To calculate, to reckon; to plan, to scheme, to devise; a lot; a reed; a tally, bamboo slips or checks, carried by porters: [18]꜀*t‘iu* ‘*ch‘i*, wands thrown into a jar, a kind of game; [19]꜀*t‘iu ch‘aik*, a plan, a stratagem; [20]*ong*’ ꜀*t‘iu*, to plan, as a campaign; COM., ꜀*t‘iu* ‘*ma*, bamboo slips used in gaming, also for small weights; [21]꜀*t‘iu hek*꜀ to plan, to scheme; COLL., ꜀*chó* ꜀*ngwong* ꜀*t‘iu*, a game with slips marked with literary degrees; ꜀*t‘iu* ‘*keng* ‘*song*, to select, as in making purchases; ꜀*pwong* ꜀*t‘iu*, to issue checks (to porters).

1抽籤 2抽租 3抽稅 4抽丁 5抽頭 6加一抽 7抽系 8抽傀儡 9厥疾不瘳 10丑時 11丑正 12丑二 13丑形丑狀 14儔類 15儔侶 16疇昔 17覆幬 18籌矢 19籌策 20運籌 21籌畫

譸 ‚Ch'ou. Also read ‚chiu; used for the last: able and quick to reply; irregular, hurried, bustling; to deceive: [1]‚t'iu ‚tiong ‚ui hwang' to delude with specious arts.

躊 ‚Ch'ou. Embarrassed: COM., [2]‚t'iu ‚t'ü pok, kiok, irresolute, unable to decide.

颼 ‚ A gentle, rustling wind, a cool breeze. Read ‚tó: a strong wind.

(878) T'o.

兎 兔 T'u. A rabbit: COM., [3]yă t'o' a hare; [4]t'o' ‚mó pek, rabbit-hair pencils; [5]t'o' ‚chüng 'mi, a rabbit pounding rice (in the moon)—a toy; COLL., t'o' 'kĕng and t'o' 'mó, the male and female rabbits.

菟 T'u. A medicinal plant like sesamum, called [6]t'o' ‚si; COM., [7]t'o' ‚si 'chü, seeds of the same, used in kidney complaints. Read ‚tu, as in ‚u ‚tu, the name for a tiger in the Ts'u state.

吐 T'u. To vomit, to spew; to spit out; to blossom; to speak out, to disclose; to confess; to spin silk, as silkworms: [8]t'o' siék, to thrust out the tongue, as in surprise; COM., [9]pang' t'o' siă' vomiting and purging, the cholera; [10]t'o' haik, to spit blood, hemorrhage of the lungs; [11]t'o' ‚si, to spin silk, as the silk-worm does; COLL., ‚t'ong ‚t'ong t'o' t'o' swallowing and vomiting; *met.*, to tell hesitatingly; *pwoh, ‚hwang pwoh,* t'o' the stomach nauseated; t'o' ‚si, to protrude the flesh, as clams and snails do; t'o' sik, ‚t'ĕng, to vomit worms.

(879) T'ó.

叨 ‚Tao. T'ao. Tĕ. To desire food; to covet, to long for, as honors; inordinately desirous, addicted to; to feel deeply grateful for; ashamed to receive, as feeling unworthy of: [12]‚t'ó ‚mung, very thankful for, much obliged; [13]‚t'ó ‚kwong, have enjoyed your countenance; desirous of your kind favor; [14]‚t'ang ‚t'ó, greedy of, addicted to, as lust; COM., [15]‚t'ó hok, blessed with your favor!

刀 ‚Tao. Read ‚tó; coll. ‚t'ó: a classifier of Chinese quires or parcels of paper, in which the number of sheets varies widely according to the kind of paper: [16]sioh, ‚t'ó, a quire or parcel.

拖 拕 ‚T'o. To pull, to drag; to draw, to draggle; to protract, to defer, to put off; to lead by the hand; to involve, to implicate: in the coll. read ‚t'wa and ‚t'wa, q. v.: [17]‚t'ó ‚nă tai' 'chwi, to draggle in mud and water; *met.*, turbid, inflated, as a style; [18]‚t'ó loi' involved, as in danger; COM., [19]‚t'ó ‚niĕng, to stick to; excessive, persistent, as in doing or saying.

滔 ‚T'ao. Waters rising and swelling; to inundate; to rush impetuously, as waters; rude, disrespectful to superiors; branch of the Han

1譸	2躊	3野	筆	6菟	子	吐	11吐	13叨	15叨	17拖	18拖
張	躇	兎	5兎	絲	8吐	瀉	絲	光	福	泥	累
爲	不	4兎	搗	7菟	舌	10吐	12叨	14貪	16一	帶	19拖
幻	决	毛	米	絲	9病	血	蒙	叨	刀	水	粘

in Shensi: [1]ˏt'ó ˏt'ó pok, twong² to flow incessantly; COM., ˏt'ó ˏt'iéng twai² swells to the heavens, as a flood or freshet. Read ˏtó: to collect.

慆 ˏT'ao. To rejoice, to be pleased; an excess of joy; indulgent, excessive; to suspect, to doubt; to treat disrespectfully; a long time: [2]ˏt'ó ˏsing, reckless, insolent; ˏt'ó ˏt'ó pok, ˏkwi, not return for a long time.

縚 絛 ˏT'ao. Sometimes used for the next: a plaited cord or sash; a fringe, a silk tassel: [3]ta ˏt'ó, to braid fringes; COM., [4]ˏt'ó soi² tassels; tiong² ˏt'ó, curtain-tassels.

韜 弢 ˏT'ao. A case for a bow; a sheath, a scabbard, a covering for weapons; a vantbrace; just, righteous; liberal: [5]ˏt'ó liok, military plans, tactics.

饕 ˏT'ao. Greedy, voracious, gluttonous; to gormandize; grasping, rapacious: ˏt'ang ˏt'ó, or ˏt'ó t'iék, avaricious and gluttonous.

討 ʻT'ao. To rule, to manage; to fight, to attack enemies; to punish criminals; to kill, to destroy rebels; to seek, to investigate; to beg, to ask for; to induce, to bring on one's self; mixed; used variously in the coll. according to subject: [7]ʻt'ó chói² to punish for crime; COM., [8]ʻt'ó yéng² to excite dislike; [9]ʻt'ó ˏchiêng, to beg money, to dun; [10]ʻt'ó pó² ˏsiu, to seek revenge; [11]ʻt'ó siah, to beg food; to partake of sacrifices, as ghosts do; [12]ʻt'ó ˏtĕng, to beg rice or cash in the 11th month; [13]ʻt'ó ˏngû, to fish, as with a net; [14]ʻt'ó seng² to ask for news; [15]ʻt'ó sié² to have regard to the state or circumstances of; COLL., ʻt'ó chai² ʻkiâng, you little dunner, as said to a teasing child; met., a child dying young after much care and expense; ʻt'ó ˏwong ˏhung, to consult ghosts; ʻt'ó ˏpi e² to humor one's whims; compliant; ʻt'ó ʻtiê, careful; backward, reticent; ʻt'ó tio² k'ĕûk, ˏk'a ˏkiâng, to seek more road to travel—to overdo, supererogatory; ʻt'ó ˏch'ing, or ʻt'ó lau² ʻma, to marry a wife; ʻt'ó ne² ˏhwong, or ʻt'ó sioh, ch'ok, to marry a widow; ʻt'ó ʻcha pwong² to prepare breakfast.

ʻT'ó. A coll. word, used for ʻp'ó: about, just at; somewhat, slightly: ʻt'ó ʻt'ó or ʻt'ó ʻmó, just, nearly; ʻt'ó ʻmó ʻchiâ ˏsi haiu² about this time; ʻt'ó ʻmó paik, slightly acquainted with.

套 T'ao². Large and wide, what envelopes; to enwrap; to superadd; a wrapper, a case, an envelope; included, of general use or application; met., a snare, a trap; a cave; a classifier of suits and sets: [16]t'wak, t'ó² to eschew customs and fashions; [17]ˏó t'ó² the Great Bend in the Yellow river; [18]ˏt'ung t'ó² of general use; COM., [19]t'ó² ˏsang, an under-coat; [20]t'ó² k'o² overalls; [21]t'ó² ˏkiêng, shoulder-lining; [22]ˏchiong t'ó² a complete suit; a full set, as of implements; wang² t'ó² a change of clothes; t'ó² ˏung or t'ó² ʻngû, polite

[1]滔滔不斷 [2]慆心 [3]打縚 [4]縚繸 [5]韜畧 [6]貪饕 [7]討罪 [8]討厭 [9]討錢 [10]討報仇 [11]討食 [12]討冬 [13]討魚 [14]討信 [15]討勢 [16]脫套 [17]河套 [18]通套 [19]套衫 [20]套褲 [21]套肩 [22]全套

phrases or compliments; *ˏk'wong t'ó'* a snare, wiles, devices; COLL., *t'ó' ˏi wa'* to draw him out (by indirect questions); *t'ó' mŭ' ch'ok*, can't draw him out; *t'ó' ˏi taing'* (or *t'ói' ˏi taing'*) an old clothes' broker's; *t'ó' 'tiĕ tiĕ'* to line partially or patch inside.

唾 T'o. T'u. To spit; spittle, saliva: *t'ó' mwak*, phlegm; *t'ó' ˏhu*, a spittoon; *t'ó' miéng'* to spit in one's face.

桃 逃 T'ao. A peach: [1]*ˏt'ó se'* a sword-cutler; [2]*ˏt'ó ˏt'ŭng*, "peach-bug"—the wren; COM., [3]*kaung' ˏt'ó*, a kind of large, red peach; [4]*ˏt'ó ˏhwong*, a peach orchard; [5]*kak, tëŭk, ˏt'ó*, the oleander; [6]*hok, ˏt'ó*, walnuts; [7]*ˏyong ˏt'ó*, carambola; [8]*ˏt'ó ˏhu*, the peach charm—red paper hung on doors; [9]*p'ek, ˏt'ó' hwa*, the jade-peach flower—a play; COLL., *ˏt'ó ˏĕng*, peach red; *ˏt'ó ˏhwa ˏtiéng*, lascivious, lustful; *ˏt'ó ˏpau*, steamed dumplings tinged red; *ˏt'ó ˏpeng 'li leng'* sections of peaches and plums; *met.*, certain rocks on Black Rock Hill, Foochow; *ˏt'ó ˏt'ó 'kiŭng*, a knot of hair, as on a child's head.

(880) T'oh.

T'oh,. A coll. word: to pierce, to thrust through: *t'oh, kwo' k'ó'* to give a thrust at; *t'oh, ˏt'ĕng t'au'* to pierce through.

(881) T'óh.

托 T'o. Read *t'auk,*; coll. *t'óh,*: to bear, to carry on the palm, or shoulder: [10]*t'óh, 'ch'iu*, or *t'óh, ˏpa 'chiong ˏtong*, to bear on the palm of the hand; [11]*t'óh, ˏkiĕng ˏt'au 'ting*, to shoulder things; [12]*t'óh, ˏkiu*, to toss a ball on the palm; *t'óh, 'nŭ k'ó'* I pass it to you—i.e. let you have it, sell it to you; [13]*ˏt'u t'óh*, a mason's mortar-board.

T'óh,. A coll. word also spoken *lóh*, as in *'t'au t'óh*,(or *lóh*,), well, not sick; perceiving clearly; *ng' 't'au t'óh*, indisposed; dull, ignorant.

(882) T'oi.

推 T'ui. Read *ˏch'wi*; coll. *ˏt'oi*: to refuse, to decline; to shift, to throw off responsibility; to put the blame on another; to plane: [14]*ˏt'oi ˏsŭ*, or *ˏt'oi 't'iŭng*, to decline, to refuse; [15]*ˏt'oi ˏi ˏsing siong'* to shift it off, charge the blame on him; [16]*ˏt'oi ˏtó*, a plane; [17]*ˏt'oi ˏkwong ch'ek*, highly polished varnishing.

胎 T'ai. Read *ˏt'ai*; coll. *ˏt'oi*: the womb; the fetus: [18]*ˏt'au ˏt'oi*, the first-born; *ne' ˏt'oi*, the second-born; *ˏt'oi tuk*, bad humors or tetter sores from birth.

腿 T'ui. The thigh, the ham: COM., [19]*ˏsu 't'oi*, Soochow hams; [20]*hwi 't'oi*, a cured ham; *twai' 't'oi*, the thigh-piece; *'sieu 't'oi*, the leg; COLL., *'t'oi 'chi*, the lean meat of the thigh in pork; *pang' 't'oi*, a common term for leprosy; *ˏk'a 't'oi pwak, ˏch'ŭng*, the thigh sprained by a fall.

硾 Ch'ui. Read *t'oi'*; coll. *t'oi'*: heavy, weighty, weighing down; to make heavy by adding weights; dull, captious; troublesome to deal

[1]桃氏 [2]桃蟲 [3]絳桃 [4]桃園 [5]夾竹桃 [6]核桃 [7]羊桃 [8]桃符 [9]碧桃花 [10]托手 [11]托肩頭 [12]托毬 [13]土托 [14]推辭 [15]推伊身上 [16]推刀 [17]推光漆 [18]頭胎 [19]蘇腿 [20]火腿

with; *t'oi' t'oi'* heavy, as an iron ball, or fruit on the tree; *t'oi' mong'* not clear, captious; *t'oi' mong' tai'* a troublesome affair.

'T'oi. A coll. prefix, as in *,t'oi t'ói'* a hole, a burrow.

硾 磓 Ch'ui. Used in the *Paik*, *,Ing* and analogous to *toi*: to attach a weight, to weight, as the end of timber in sawing; hanging, dragging down; sagged, loaded: the first read *t'oi'* in the coll. q. v.: COLL., *t'oi' mâ' ,kiăng*, loaded, weighted, (as the pockets, or a fowl's foot with a drag) and unable to walk.

(883) T'ói.

退 T'ui. To retire, to withdraw, to recede; to decline, to refuse; to excuse one's self; yielding, complaisant: [1]*t'ói' yong'* to yield to one; [2]*t'ói' sauk,* to shrink, to back out; COM., [3]*t'ói' ,pang*, attendants retiring from court; [4]*t'ói' ka'* to withdraw an offer, to offer less for; [5]*t'ói' saik,* to lose the color, to fade; [6]*t'ói' ch'e'* the close of a fair or market; [7]*,siéng t'ói'* the exuviæ of cicadas — used medicinally; [8]*t'ói' ,hwong*, to break a betrothal; [9]*t'ói' hwoi'* to regret, to repent; [10]*t'ói' ,sü* (or *'siong*), to reconsider, to think over; [11]*t'ói' yék,* (or *,hwo*), the fever abated; COLL., [12]*t'ói' k'ó'* to retire; [13]*t'ói' ,tëng*, the god has retired, the inspiration past; [14]*t'ói' ,si hwo'* goods or fruits past the season—are inferior; *t'ói' sioh, pwo'* to recede a step; *met.*, to desist a while, as from a quarrel.

褪 T'un. To undress, to disrobe; to fade and fall, as flowers: in the coll. read *t'aung'* q. v.

T'ói'. A coll. word: a hole, a den, a burrow: *,t'oi t'ói'* a hole; *,k'wi t'ói'* to dig a hole through, as thieves do; *siăh, seng' 'ló 'ch'ü 'chau ,mó t'ói'* the rat that eats arsenic has no hole to run to; *met.*, there's now no resource or escape for the rogue!

(884) T'ok.

黜 Ch'u. To blame and degrade, to put out of office; to expel: [15]*t'ok, t'ek,* to degrade and to promote; [16]*t'ok, t'ói'* to cashier or expel from office; [17]*,sang t'ok,* thrice degraded as *'Liu hu' hié'* was; *ük, t'ok,* disgraced and degraded.

絀 Ch'u. Used for the last: crimson silk; to sew, to stitch; to baste, to sew imperfectly; bent, constrained, obstructed: also read *k'ok,* q. v.: [18]*,ing t'ok,* (or *,ing chiok,*), to straighten and bend; *met.*, to appear and to retire; opposite, unequal.

怵 Ch'u. To fear, to dread; fear, terror; mad, wild; to tempt, to entice, as by hope of profit; enticed, allured: [19]*t'ok, t'ek,* timorous.

沰 Read *t'auk,*; used in the *Paik*, *,Ing* for the coll. *t'ok,*: to subside, to ebb, as the tide; [20]*'chwi t'ok,* the water has lowered; *t'ok, 'kwi ch'aung'* fallen a few inches.

1 退讓 2 退縮 3 退班 4 退價 5 退色 6 退市 7 蟬退 8 退婚 9 退悔 10 退思 11 退熱 12 退去 13 退僮 14 退時貨 15 黜陟 ○ 16 黜退 17 三黜 18 盈絀 19 怵惕 20 水沰 ○

T'ok. A coll. word: to lose flesh; to place or write lower; to fall, as prices; to fall behind; to protrude, gaping: *t'ok, ,hing,* emaciated, sunken, as the face; *t'ok, au'* to fall behind; *t'ok, ka'* the price has fallen; *t'ok, sioh, ,tong,* a long way behind; low in purse; *t'ok, ,tang,* the heel (of a shoe) slipping; *t'ok, ,kong* (or *chaung'*) protrusion of the rectum; *t'ok, ,hai k'ó'* the gaping *k'ó'*—a small, dried fish; *,t'ai t'ok,* to annoy one by delay.

(885) T'ong.

吞 (,T'un.) To swallow, to gulp; to devour, to bolt; to grasp, to seize, to appropriate, to engross, to usurp; to merge together: [1]*,t'ong p'iéng'* to defraud; [2]*,t'ong peng'* to engross all; COM., [3]*,t'ong ,king,* to swallow gold-leaf; [4]*,t'ong yoh, ,wong,* to take pills; COLL., *,t'ong 'tié* (or *lóh,*), to swallow down; [5]*,t'ong 'nung,* to suppress resentment; [6]*,t'ong 'lang mwong' ,sing ,kang,* swallow your spittle and ask your heart—consult your own conscience.

湯 (,T'ang.) Hot water; soup, broth; rain from passing clouds: COM., [7]*,t'ong k'e'* steam; [8]*'kung ,t'ong,* boiling water; [9]*,t'ong ,mwong,* the Hot Water gate of Foochow; [10]*,t'ong ,tié,* hot springs; [11]*,t'ong ,t'au,* the boiling place of the spring; a medicinal recipe; [12]*,t'ong yoh,* a medicinal decoction; [13]*nük, ,t'ong,* pork soup; [14]*,t'ong ,wong,* dumplings of rice flour, stuffed with peanut and sugar; [15]*,t'ong ,hu,* a hot water pot with an inner cylinder. Read *t'aung':* to bathe or rinse in hot water. Read *taung':* dissolute. Read *,siong:* to flow, as waves.

倘 儻 ('T'ang.) If, should, supposing, perhaps; suddenly, unexpectedly: [16]*'t'ong ,lai ,chi uk,* what comes unexpectedly, as sudden gains.

帑 ('T'ang.) A treasury, a repository of precious metals and cloths: also read *,nu,* q. v.: [17]*'hu 't'ong,* a treasury; COM., [18]*kwok, 't'ong,* the national treasury; *'t'ong haung'* the government share or stock, as in licensed pawnshops.

'T'ong. A coll. word: fat, corpulent, pursy: *,pui ,pui 't'ong 't'ong,* very corpulent, as said of a person.

痛 (T'ung'.) A disease giving pain; a pain, an ache; an acute feeling; distressed, miserable; to feel pity, to commiserate; very, extremely: in the coll. read *t'iáng'* q. v: [19]*,ai t'ong'* deeply grieved, distressed; [20]*t'ong' 'ing,* to drink to excess; [21]*t'ong' 'k'u,* deep grief or sorrow; COM., *t'ong' ,sing,* grieved in mind; *t'ong' haung'* to abhor, to detest; to regret bitterly.

糖 餹 (,T'ang.) Read *,tong;* coll. *,t'ong:* sugar; sugared things, candy; sweetened with sugar: *,t'ong ,t'ong* (same as *,chiong ,ping*), rock-candy; *,t'ong 'peng,* red sugar in cakes; *,hwa ,seng ,t'ong,* peanut candy;

---

[1]吞騙 [2]吞併 [3]吞金 [4]吞藥丸 [5]吞忍 [6]吞瀧儭心肝 [7]湯氣 [8]滾湯 [9]湯門 [10]湯池 [11]湯頭 [12]湯藥 [13]肉湯 [14]湯丸 [15]湯壺之物 [16]倘來 [17]府帑 [18]國帑 [19]哀痛 [20]痛飲 [21]痛苦

[1]ˏ*pwong kiék*, ˏ*t'ong*, clarified cone-sugar ; [2]*ch'ó' pah*ˌ ˏ*t'ong*, darkish white sugar : [3]ˏ*t'ong ang*² stuffing of sugar, as in cakes ; [4]ˏ*t'ong* ˈ*kwi*, steamed sweet-cake of rice—also called ˏ*niéng* ˏ*kó* ; [5]ˏ*t'ong* ˏ*wong*, lump-sugar from Formosa ; [6]ˏ*t'ong* ˈ*chwi*, molasses ; [7]ˏ*t'ong* ˈ*kwo*, sugared fruits, sweetmeats ; ˏ*t'ong huk*ˌ a sugar Budh ; *met.*, a giggler ; [8]ˏ*kwi* ˏ*t'ong*, a cuckold.

𥝱 ˏT'un. Read ˏ*tong;* used in the *Paik*, ˏ*Ing* for the coll. ˏ*t'ong* : between puberty and manhood, half-grown ; medium in size and age : *nié*² ˈ*kiăng* ˏ*t'ong*, a large boy, a stripling ; ˏ*tü* ˏ*t'ong*, a shote ; ˏ*kié* ˏ*t'ong* ˈ*kiăng*, a young cock ; a pullet.

ˏ*T'ong.* A coll. word : alike, equal in size : ˏ*t'ong* ˏ*t'ong*, or ˏ*t'ong* ˏ*t'ong twai*² of the same size.

鼕² Read ˏ*tung;* used in the *Paik*, ˏ*Ing* for the coll. *t'ong*² as in *t'ong*² *t'ong*² the sound of drums—the same as *tong*² q. v.

*T'ong*². A coll. word : short and thick, as a person or a stick : ˈ*á paik*ˌ *t'ong*² low and thick, stout.

(886) T'u.

凸 ˈTu. Tieh. Read *tok*ˌ ; used in the *Paik*, ˏ*Ing* for the coll. ˈ*t'u:* jutting, projecting ; protuberant, in relief : [9]ˈ*t'u náh*, projections and depressions ; [10]ˈ*t'u ch'oi*² *náh*ˌ *p'e*² a pouting mouth and flattened nose—is displeased.

ˈ*T'u.* A coll. word, analogous to the last : to extend, to stretch out, as the hand ; to thrust in, to put away, as in a drawer : ˈ*t'u* ˏ*t'au*, to put out the head (to look) ; ˈ*t'u siék*ˌ to thrust out the tongue ; ˈ*t'u k'ëük*ˌ ˏ*i*, hand it to him.

土 ˈTu. T'u. Earth, ground, soil ; the last of the five elements ; a place, a region ; lands, possessions, patrimony ; a clayey, sallow, or dingy, color ; earthy ; local, peculiar, native : in the coll, read ˏ*t'u*, q. v. : [11]*ko*² ˈ*t'u*, one's native place ; COM., [12]ˈ*t'u* ˏ*k'iong* (or *wa*²), a patois ; [13]ˈ*t'u* ˏ*si*, native silk ; [14]ˈ*t'u* ˈ*niéng*, home or native dyed ; [15]ˈ*t'u* ˈ*sang*, the productions of a place ; [16]ˈ*t'u* ˈ*p'i*, local banditti ; [17]*p'ó*² ˈ*t'u*, to open ground, as on a new site ; [18]ˈ*t'u* ˏ*sing*, the terminalia ; [19]ˏ*kwi* ˈ*t'u*, to return to dust, to die ; [20]ˈ*t'u* ˏ*ing*, the natives ; [21]ˈ*chwi* ˈ*t'u*, the climate of a place ; ˈ*t'u* ˏ*sing*, Mercury ; ˈ*t'u te*² ˏ*kung*, god of the land, much worshiped by shopmen ; COLL., ˈ*t'u* ˈ*ngang*, a poor eye, as of one unskilled in judging qualities ; ˈ*t'u* ˏ*ing* ˏ*seng*, native ginseng—i. e. potatoes ; ˈ*t'u* ˏ*mai* ˏ*toi*, tumuli, graves without monuments ; ˈ*chwi* ˈ*t'u siăh*ˌ *má*² *tioh*ˌ can't become acclimated.

土 ˏTu. T'u. Read ˈ*t'u;* coll. ˏ*t'u* : earth, soil, clay, mud : ˏ*t'u* ˈ*hung*, fine earth, dust ; ˏ*t'u te*² an earthen floor ; ˏ*t'u* ˏ*toi*, a mound ; ˏ*t'u ch'iong*² or ˏ*t'u* ˏ*sa ho*² a mason ; ˈ*t'u* ˈ*kau*, settlings of dirt ; [22]ˏ*t'u* ˏ*tang*, inferior cinnabar ; ˏ*t'u piăh*,

[1]盆結糖 [2]糙白糖 [3]糖餡 [4]糖粿 [5]糖丸 [6]糖水 [7]糖果 [8]龜糖 [9]凸凹 [10]凸嘴凹鼻 [11]故土 [12]土腔 [13]土絲 [14]土染 [15]土產 [16]土匪 [17]破土 [18]土神 [19]歸土 [20]土人 [21]水土 [22]土丹

福州方言拼音字典

a lath and plaster wall; [1] ˏa p'iéngˀ ˏt'u, crude opium; [2] ˏt'u t'óh, a mason's mortar-board; [3] ˏt'u ˏmieu, salted shrimps; [4] ˏt'u ˏma, a clay cat, as on roofs; *met.*, a stupid fellow; [5] ˏt'u ˏiu or ˏt'u ˏmúi ˏchiong, soft mud, slush; ˏt'u ˏt'u saik, sallow, dingy; [6] ˏt'u ˏmieu ongˀ ch'oˀ ˏka ch'ek, paik, siék, to dip shrimps in vinegar and lose 7 or 8 tenths; *met.*, to lose heavily in trade.

(887) T'ü.

侏 ˏChu. Sometimes read ˏchio: a pigmy; *met.*, low, short: [7] ˏt'ü ˏü, a dwarf; a short pillar in a roof, like a king-post.

姝 ˏCh'u. Read ˏk'ü in the dictionaries: beautiful, handsome, as a woman; a fine scholar; to adorn as a female; weak, fearful, timorous: [8] ˏt'ü saik, a pretty woman.

株 ˏChu. The trunk of a tree; a bole, a stem, a stalk; a numerative of trees; low down, the lowest place: used for the coll. ˏtau, q. v.: [9] ˏt'ü ˋsiu, confined in a low position, kept in obscurity; ˏt'ü ˏü, a short pillar or post; a dwarf.

洙 ˏChu. A small stream flowing northward from T'ai Shan into the river Ssŭ.

蛛 ˏChu. A spider: COM., [10] ˏt'i ˏt'ü, the spider that weaves webs; [11] ˏt'i ˏt'ü ˋwong, a spider's web; COLL., [12] ˏt'i ˏt'ü ˏmang, a web; *met.*, the thread netting on a sedan; [13] pek, kaˀ siongˀ ˏt'i ˏt'ü, his pen-stand covered with cobwebs, as said of doctors or fortune-tellers without custom.

邾 ˏChu. A feudal state, now the Tsau district in the south of Shantung; ˋsieu ˏt'ü was a principality lying south of it.

銖 ˏChu. A small weight or ancient silver coin, estimated as equal to 100 grains of millet; 24 ˏt'ü made a tael; farthings, trifles, small matters; blunt, dull: COLL., [14] ˋngu ˏt'ü ˏchiéng twaiˀ ˏk'ĕng, the ˋngu ˏt'ü (or Han) cash had large holes; *met.*, a loud voice in talking.

宁 ˋChu. The porch or space between the gate and the screen; to accumulate.

佇 竚 ˋChu. ˋCh'u. To stand a long time; to stand and wait, to look for: [15] ˋt'ü lik, to stand up; [16] ˋt'ü wongˀ to be expecting, to long for.

抒 ˋCh'u. To decant, to drain off liquids; to strain; to scoop, to take out; to explain, to lay open one's mind; to disburden, to relieve, as the feelings.

杼 ˋCh'u. A shuttle; long; thin, as a wheel; a kind of chestnut: ˋmwang ˋt'ü ˏking ˏlung, learned as a full shuttle; COLL., huk ˏmó ˋt'ü, a wand to subdue demons, as the wand of the god ˏUi ˏnó. Read ˋsü: a water-trough.

[1] 鴉片土〇 [2] 土托 [3] 土苗 [4] 土貓 [5] 土油 [6] 土苗搵醋加七八折 [7] 侏儒 [8] 姝色 [9] 株守 [10] 蜘蛛 [11] 蜘蛛網 [12] 蜘蛛幔 [13] 筆架上蜘蛛 [14] 五銖錢大空 [15] 佇立 [16] 佇望

'杵 Ch'u. A wooden pestle; a beater, a pestle: [1]'k'eu² 't'ü, mortar and pestle.

'紵 '紵 Ch'u. A coarse kind of hemp for making cloth; a coarse covering; the 2d is the contracted form; the 1st is the private name of Hien-fung: [2],hi 't'ü, fine and coarse sorts of hemp.

'羜 Ch'u. A lamb five months old: [3],p'i 't'ü, a fat lamb.

'苧 Ch'u. The Bœhmeria Tenacissima, the grasscloth nettle: in the coll. read *taë²* q. v.

'貯 Chu. To accumulate, to hoard, to store up; a hoard, a treasure: used for the coll. *'tio* and *tioh,* q. v.: [4]*t'ü chek,* or *chek,* *'t'ü,* to accumulate; [5],*chong* 't'ü, to store up.

,鋤 ,鉏 Ch'u. A hoe, a mattock; to hoe, to cultivate, to assist a growth: used for the coll. ,*t'ui,* q. v.: COM., [6],*t'ü* ,*t'au* (also spoken ,*t'ui* ,*t'au*), a hoe; [7],*t'ü* ,*hwong,* to hoe a garden; [8],*t'ü* *'ch'au,* to hoe up grass.

,躇 Ch'u. Embarrassed, hesitating, perplexed: also read ,*tü,* q. v.: COM., [9],*t'iu* ,*t'ü,* hesitating, doubtful how to proceed.

(888) T'uh.

搋, T'u. Read *t'uk,*; coll. *t'uh,*: analogous to *tuh,*; to thrust at, to pierce, as with a pointed instrument; *met.*, to tell about, to inform against: *t'uh,* *p'wai²* to break by piercing; *met.*, a matter revealed; *k'ó² t'uh,* ,*i,* go and inform against him.

(889) T'ui.

,搥 Ch'ui. To strike, to beat, as bells; to throw, as stones; in the coll. a blow, as with the fist; a classifier of blows: also read ,*tui,* q. v.: COLL., [10],*t'ui* *lik,* the weight or force of a blow; *muh,* *sioh,* ,*t'ui,* to give a blow with the fist; ,*t'ui* *'ma* *'yă* *teng²* a very heavy blow; ,*t'ui* *taing²* a pounded cushion; *met.*, one who is the butt or mark for all the blows.

,槌 ,椎 Ch'ui. To beat, to knock; a beater, a club; a pestle, a mallet; a bludgeon; the 1st also means to reject; a stand for silk-worms: COM., [11],*ch'a* ,*t'ui,* a maul, a wooden pestle; [12]*ku* ,*t'ui,* drumsticks.

,錘 ,鎚 Chui. A steelyard weight, a pestle, a hammer; to beat, to pound; to dress gems: COM., *'mi* ,*t'ui,* a rice-pestle; [13]*t'iék,* ,*t'ui,* a hammer; [14]*ch'eng²* ,*t'ui,* the poise of a steelyard; [15],*liu* ,*sing* ,*t'ui,* a slung-shot; COLL., [16]*t'iék,* ,*t'ui* *tói²* *t'iék,* *'tong,* hammer against anvil; *met.*, two fierce fellows fighting.

,鋤 Ch'u. Read ,*t'ü;* coll. ,*t'ui,* as in ,*t'ui* ,*t'au,* a hoe—same as ,*t'ü* ,*t'au,* q. v.

(890) T'uk.

禿, T'u. Bald, the hair gone; blunt, bare, fallen off, as leaves; the bald-pated, as

---

1 臼杵 2 絺紵 3 肥羜 4 貯積 5 藏貯 6 鋤頭 7 鋤園 8 鋤草 9 躊躇 10 搥力 11 柴槌 12 鼓槌 13 鐵鎚 14 秤錘 15 流星鎚〇 16 鐵鎚對鐵砧〇

a Budhist priest: [1]‛t‘uk, ˓küng, to let the cap fall off; COM., [2]‛t‘uk, te‛ "blunt twig"; *met.*, end of a road, extreme limit, as of time; [3]‛t‘uk, *pek*, a worn-out pencil; [4]‛t‘uk, ˓t‘au *haëng*‛ an alley ending (at a wall); [5]‛t‘uk, ˓lu, bald ass — an epithet applied to Budhists.

T‘uk. A coll. word, for which the last may be used: a superlative, very, e x t r e m e l y: *t‘uk, chong*‛ very e x c e l l e n t; ˓*kiäng t‘uk, tio*‛ walked to the very end of the road—one's resources exhausted, p e n n i l e s s; *t‘uk* ‛*tiu* ˓*ngai*, very bad indeed!

鵚 T‘u. The bald-headed crane: *t‘uk*, ˓*ch‘iu*, a sort of adjutant or buzzard.

讀 Tu. Tou. To read aloud, to recite, to chant; to read carefully, to study; a reader; also to select: also read *taiu*‛ and in the coll. *t‘ëk*, q. v.: [6]‛t‘uk, ‛*lä*, am reading the ritual —a notice to decline visits while mourning for parents; [7]*pai*‛ *t‘uk*, have respectfully perused it, as said by one who has examined another's essay.

黷 Tu. Often read *tuk*,: to soil, to dirty, to blacken; dirty, filthy, soiled, stained; to annoy, to insult: [8]*siék*, *t‘uk*, to treat rudely, to outrage.

(891) T‘ung.

通 ˓T‘ung. To go through, to perceive, to see clearly; to inform, to make known to; to communicate with, to have friendly dealings; pervious, permeable, pervading; prosperous, successful; intelligent, learned; clear, transparent; perspicuous, as style; current, circulating everywhere; all, the whole; complete, general; illicit, adulterous; uniform in color; a beat of a drum, report of a gun; a draft of wind: in the coll. read ˓*t‘ëng*, q. v.: [9]˓*t‘ung che*‛ a general topography, statistics; [10]‛*ku* ‛*ta* ˓*sang* ˓*t‘ung*, three beats of a drum; COM., [11]*pok*, ˓*t‘ung*, not thorough, as a scholar; [12]˓*t‘ung tak*, to perceive clearly, very perspicacious; [13]˓*t‘ung* ˓*ming*, clear in thought; transparent, as glass; [14]˓*t‘ung* ˓*ti*, to inform one; [15]˓*t‘ung ch‘ek*, to hold commuication with thieves; [16]˓*t‘ung* ˓*ching*, kind, liberal feeling; [17]˓*t‘ung* ˓*heng*, current, as coin or doctrine; [18]˓*t‘ung* *sëü*‛ an interpreter, a linguist; [19]˓*t‘ung* ˓*chü*, an almanac; ˓*t‘ung* ˓*t‘iéng a*‛ the world, the whole empire; ˓*t‘ung* ˓*t‘iéng* ‛*hieu*, knows every thing!—a universal genius; ˓*t‘ung* ˓*kwang* ‛*sang*, a medicinal powder to arouse the system—is taken by snuffing.

蓪 ˓T‘ung. A medicinal plant, called [20]˓*t‘ung* ‛*ch‘ó*; the pith, sliced into sheets, is erroneously called rice-paper; it is also used in artificial flowers, pillows, and shoe-soles.

侗 ˓T‘ung. Also read ˓*tung*: plain, r u d e, ignorant, without learning or ability: [21]˓*k‘ung* ˓*t‘ung*, an ignorant boy.

恫 ˓T‘ung. Also read *tong*‛: pained, distressed; to groan, moaning from pain: [22]‛*c h u n g* ˓*t‘ung*, disappointed.

[1]禿巾 [2]禿蒂 [3]禿筆 [4]禿頭巷 [5]禿驢 [6]讀禮 [7]拜讀 [8]褻黷 [9]通志 [10]鼓打三通〇 [11]不通 [12]通達 [13]通明 [14]通知 [15]通賊 [16]通情 [17]通行 [18]通事 [19]通書 [20]蓪草 [21]倥侗 [22]憁恫

痌 ʻT'ung. Interchanged with the last: in pain, aching, distressed. Read ꜀*tung:* an ulcer breaking.

冢 ʻChung. Same as the next in the sense of a grave, a mound; the summit of a hill; first, the eldest, great, honorable: [1]*ʻt'ung ʻchü*, the eldest son; [2]*ʻt'ung ʻchai*, a prime minister; high cabinet ministers.

塚 ʻChung. A grave, a tomb, a tumulus, sepulchers: [3]*꜀hwong ʻt'ung*, a deserted, unlucky grave.

寵 寵 ʻCh'ung. Grace, favor; love, affection, tender regard; to prefer, to esteem, to delight in: also read *ʻt'ŭng*, q. v.: COM., [4]*ʻt'ung ai'* to love ardently; [5]*ʻt'ung ꜀ch'á pwoi' ʻmu*, to love a wife and oppose a mother; [6]*ʻk'e' ꜀ch'á ʻt'ung ch'iék*, to reject the wife and love the concubine; [7]*taik, ʻt'ung*, to win the love, as of a husband or parent.

捅 ʻT'ung. To advance, to lead onward; also to beat, to strike.

桶 ʻT'ung. A tub, a cask; a pail, a bucket; also a case or square wooden vessel: in the coll. read *ʻt'ĕng*, q. v.

畽 ʻ Also read *ʻchŭng:* wild land near towns; tracts where deer and other wild animals range, paths of beasts.

統 ʻT'ung. The origin, beginning; the head, chief; a thread; *met.*, a clue, a hint, the first of a subject; the whole, general, sum total of; to rule, to control: [8]*ʻchung ʻt'ung*, the whole, entirety; in fine, all; [9]*ek, ʻt'ung ꜀ó ꜀sang*, the empire under a single government; COM., [10]*ʻt'ung kēūng'* (coll. *ʻt'ung piăng'*), the sum total; [11]*ʻt'ung ʻliăng*, a general control; [12]*ʻt'ung ʻkwang*, to take chief command of; COLL., *ng' ꜀siăng ʻt'á ʻt'ung*, not trim, slovenly; careless, indecorous.

(892) T'ŭng.

寵 ʻCh'ung. Grace, favor, kindness; love, tender regard; the favor of superiors; to prefer, to esteem: also read *ʻt'ung*, q. v.

蟲 虫 ꜀Ch'ung. A general term for coleopterous and crustaceous insects; small animals that creep, hairy or naked insects; usually applied to insects and worms: in the coll. read *꜀t'ĕng*, q. v.: [13]*paik, ꜀t'ŭng*, insects in general.

重 ꜀Chung. Ch'ung. Read ꜀*tüng;* coll. ꜀*t'ŭng:* to double, to duplicate, again, repeated; a thickness, a classifier of thicknesses: [14]*꜀t'ŭng hok*, doubled, repeated, two at once; [15]*꜀t'ŭng nëū'* repetitious in talking; [16]*꜀t'ŭng k'eng'* to keep a second birthday, as on the intercalary month; [17]*꜀t'ŭng nëūk*, folded, crumpled; [18]*꜀t'ŭng t'ak,* or *꜀t'ŭng tah, ꜀t'ŭng*, to pile up; [19]*lang' ꜀t'ŭng*, two thicknesses; *꜀t'ŭng ʻkang*, to take a fresh cold; [20]*꜀t'ŭng ʻkong ꜀t'ŭng t'iăng'* to say over and over.

(893) T'wa.

拖 ꜀T'o. Read ꜀*t'ó;* coll. ꜀*t'wa:* to draw, to drag, to pull along; to draggle; to in-

1 冢子 2 冢宰 3 荒塚 4 寵愛 5 寵妻背母 6 棄妻寵妾 7 得寵 8 總統 9 一統河山 10 統共 11 統領 12 統管 13 百蟲 14 重複 15 重飫 16 重慶 17 重肭 18 重疊 19 二重 20 重講重論

volve: ꜀*t'wa pek*꜇ to protract, to do slowly; [1]꜀*t'wa k'iéng*ʼ to continue in debt; [2]꜀*t'wa* ʻ*ch'iu*, to pull by the hand; [3]꜀*t'wa loi*ʼ to implicate; [4]꜀*t'wa t'oi*ʼ a hinderance, a drag on one; [5]꜀*t'wa* ʻ*tá kieu*ʼ a sort of large sedan.

拖 ꜁T'o. Read ꜀*t'ó;* coll. ꜀*t'wa:* like the last; to defer, to put off; tedious, prolonged, protracted: ꜁*t'wa kwo*ʼ *nik*꜇ to defer from day to day; ꜁*t'wa* ꜁*t'wa pang*ʼ protracted illness; ꜁*t'wa ch'ok*꜇ *pang*ʼ to turn into a serious illness, as a slight ailment; ꜁*t'wa* ꜁*t'wa pwo*ʼ a slow gait.

(894) T'wak.

脱, 脫, T'o. T'u. Thin, emaciated; wasted, spoiled, dissolving; to reject, to remove; to avoid, to escape, to evade; to shed or cast, as a skin; if, perhaps; to put off, as clothes: in the coll. read *t'auk*, and ʻ*t'aung*ʼ q. v.: [6]*t'wak*꜇ *liok*꜇ to abridge; slightly, carelessly; [7]*t'wak*꜇ ꜁*p'i*, to cast the skin, to peel off; COM., [8]*t'wak*꜇ ꜀*sing*, to slip out from, to evade, as punishment; [9]*t'wak*꜇ *lié*ʼ to get rid of, to escape. Read *yok*꜇*:* to look fresh and well, as insects which have cast their skins.

(895) T'wang.

彖ʼ T'uan. A pig running or walking; a hedgehog: [10]*t'wang*ʼ ꜁*sü*, the explanation of the *kwa*ʼ or diagrams.

踹ʼ To tread on with the heel, to stamp, to trample; the heel.

腶ʼ T'uan. To cure meats with spices and dry them: [11]*t'wang*ʼ ꜀*siu*, spiced meat dried.

鍛ʼ 煅ʼ Tuan. To forge, to heat and hammer metals; to found, to cast; to work upon, to elaborate; practiced, experienced, matured: [12]*t'wang*ʼ *liéng*ʼ thoroughly versed or skilled in.

團 ꜁T'uan. A globular mass, a lump, an agglomeration; round, globular; united, harmonious; assembled, collected after long separation; to surround, to inclose; to heap, to mass together; rounded, as figures; a numerative of lumps, collections, and round things: in the coll. read ꜀*tiong*, q. v.: [13]꜁*t'wang kiék*꜇ connected, blended; [14]꜁*t'wang chëü*ʼ assembled, as friends; COM., [15]꜁*t'wang* ꜀*wong*, circular; full, as the moon; united, meeting, as a family; [16]꜁*t'wang siéng*ʼ a round-framed fan; [17]꜁*t'wang pai*ʼ to meet and salute, as about the table of offerings on new year's day; [18]꜁*t'wang liéng*ʼ *kwoh*꜇ a drill-room; [19]*ek*꜇ ꜁*t'wang* ꜀*hwo k'e*ʼ a harmonious spirit; *met.*, a felicitous term for the rounded figure of a child on cakes, scrolls, lanterns, etc.

慱 ꜁T'uan. Mental labor, sorrow, grief; painful, grievous.

摶 ꜁T'uan. To turn with the hand; to make round, to roll into a ball; to push together, to unite in one; to roll and pat with the hand.

1 拖欠　2 拖手　3 拖累　4 拖硾　5 拖底轎　6 脱略　7 脱皮　8 脱身　9 脱離　10 彖辭　11 腶脩　12 鍛鍊　13 團結　14 團聚　15 團圓　16 團扇　17 團拜　18 團練局　19 一團和氣

漙 ꜀T'uan. Dew in great abundance, a heavy dew; a river in Shantung.

剸 ꜀T'uan. To cut up; to mutilate, to cut into pieces, as a criminal.

(896) T'wo.

[This word is interchangeably read *t'io*, q. v.]

(897) T'wong.

[This word is interchangeably read *t'iong*, q. v.]

(898) U.

圬 ꜀ **杇** ꜀ Wu. To daub on, to plaster, as walls; to adorn walls, to stucco: ¹꜀*u* ꜀*ing*, a plasterer, a bricklayer.

杇 ꜀Wu. A trowel for plastering walls; to plaster, to daub on mortar.

洿 ꜀Wu. A pool; muddy, standing water; filthy, unclean, dirty; to scoop out earth; deep water: ²꜀*u* ꜀*tié*, a pond; ³꜀*u* ꜂*niéng*, to defile, to stain.

汚 ꜀ **汙** ꜀Wu. Interchanged with the last: stagnant water; foul, dirty; impure, unclean physically and morally; obscene, vile, depraved; to insult, to defile, to debauch; low, muddy fields; drudgery: also read *o*꜄ q. v.: ⁴꜀*u ŭk*꜇ to insult, to debauch; ⁵꜀*u* ꜂*niéng*, to stain; ⁶꜀*tung* ꜀*liu hak*꜇ ꜀*u*, to herd with the vulgar; COM., ⁷꜀*u wói*꜄ filthy, impure; defiled. Read ꜀*wa*: to dig into the ground.

惡 ꜀Wu. O. An exclamation of regret, why, how! alas! also read *o*꜄ and *auk*꜇ q. v.: ⁸꜀*u sé*꜄ ꜀*hó* ꜀*ngiong yă*꜄ ah, what words are these!

巫 ꜀Wu. Read ꜀*u* in the dictionaries: to perform incantations; a sorceress, a witch, an enchantress; sorcery, magic: ⁹*nü* ꜀*u*, a sorceress; ¹⁰꜀*nang* ꜀*u*, a wizard, a sorcerer; ¹¹꜀*u sük*꜇ magic arts; ¹²꜀*U* ꜀*sang*, a mountain and district in K'ueichou department, Sz'chuen.

誣 ꜀Wu. To invent, to affirm what is unreal; to deceive; to accuse falsely, to inculpate; to slander, to calumniate; false, visionary, superstitious: ¹³꜀*u niék*꜇ to trump up, to use mere pretences; ¹⁴꜀*u lai*꜄ to calumniate or charge unjustly; COM., ¹⁵꜀*u kó*꜄ to accuse falsely.

烏 ꜀Wu. Used for the next: a crow, noted for being filial; filial; dark, black, inky; to blacken; an interrogative particle, implying a negative, how? what? ¹⁶꜀*u* ꜀*a* (coll. ꜂*ló* ꜀*wa*) a crow; ¹⁷꜀*u* ꜀*sü yoh*꜇ a hair-dye; ¹⁸꜀*u* ꜂*iu*, how is there? none, all gone; ¹⁹꜀*king* ꜀*u*, the golden crow—in the sun; ²⁰꜀*sang chĕük*꜇ ꜀*u*, the three-legged crow; *met.*, the sun; COM., ꜀*u muk*꜇ black wood, ebony; ꜀*u* ꜀*kwi*, a black tortoise; *met.*, a cuckold; mudded beggars in the 12th month; ꜀*u* ꜀*yéng*, soot; lamp black; ꜀*u* ꜀*hong*, opium; ꜀*u* ꜀*tu*, thick, heavy strokes in writing; ꜀*u* ꜂*teng*, spots, freckles; ꜀*u ang*꜄ dark, darkness; ꜀*u hak*꜇ ꜀*chi chëüng*꜄ lawless fellows,

¹圬人 ²洿池 ³洿染 ⁴污辱 ⁵汚染 ⁶同流合污 ⁷污穢 ⁸惡是何言也 ⁹女巫〇 ¹⁰男巫 ¹¹巫俗 ¹²巫山 ¹³誣捏 ¹⁴誣賴 ¹⁵誣告 ¹⁶烏鴉 ¹⁷烏鬚藥 ¹⁸烏有 ¹⁹金烏 ²⁰三足烏

as the Triads; [1]‚u sioh, ‚sang, Black Rock Hill, Foochow; COLL., [2]‚u ‚niêng, a small, greenish clam; [3]‚u k‘ik, a species of small black-bird; ‚u lok, ‚u or ‚u lok, lok, or ‚u t‘ok, t‘ok, very dark, black as the ace of spades; ‚u lok, ‘kwi, you black imp! a black man, a negro; ‚u che‘ siong‘ pah, ‘chai, black words on white paper—clear evidence, as a written contract; ‚u ‚tü tói‘ pah, ‚yong, a black pig vis-à-vis with a white goat; *met.*, incompatible, incongruous.

於 ‚Yü. **嗚** ‚Wu. An interjection; a note of surprise or wonder; to sigh, to lament, ah! alas! the 1st also read ‚ü, q. v.: ‚i ‚u, sobbing; COM., [4]‚u ‚hu ‚ai ‚chai, alas! lamentable! a phrase used in funeral eulogies.

鄔 ‚Wu. An ancient city in the west of Shansi, near the Yellow river.

迂 ‚Yü. Also read ‚ü: far, distant, remote; wide, spacious; vague, wide of the mark; bent, distorted, loose; to deprave; to avoid: [5]‚u k‘wak, vague, baseless; [6]‚u ‘kiu, a long time, enduring.

侮 ‘Wu. **侮** ‘Hu. To insult, to treat rudely, to despise; to ridicule, to burlesque; to trifle, to make sport of; disrespect: [7]ak, ‘u, to contemn; COM., [8]‘u mang‘ to insult, to treat contemptuously.

儛 ‘Wu. Interchanged with the next: to skip and dance; to excite: [9]‚Tieu ‘u ‚sang, a mountain in Shantung.

舞 ‘Wu. To posture, to play minuet-dancing; to gesture, to brandish; to dance about; sleight of hand, pantomime, fencing, etc.: COM., [10]‘u ‚tó, to flourish swords, to fence; [11]‘u ngok, to wave pheasants' tails with music—in Confucian worship; [12]‘u hié‘ to brandish weapons in plays; [13]‘u tong‘ to wave, to flourish; [14]‘u ‚lüng ‚ting, to parade the dragon-lanterns—at new year's; COLL., [15]‚kau ‘u t‘iong‘ monkeys flourishing sticks; ‘u ‘u ‘tiong, moving about, restless; ‘u ‚sai p‘wói‘ to parade the lion-blanket (figure of a lion); *met.*, to fling one's self about in a passion.

撫 ‘ **撨** ‘Fu. To soothe, to tranquilize; to pat, to stroke with the hand; to hold, to keep down; to control, to manage; to cherish, to provide for; to comfort one; hasty; to strike, to thrum, as a lute: [16]‘u ‚ing, to lay the hand on the breast; COM., [17]‘u ‘yong, to nourish, to rear up; [18]‘u yiêng‘ or ‘u ‚tai, the provincial Governor; [19]‘u ‚pieu, a Governor's troops—termed [20]‘u ‘chó and [21]‘u eu‘ the governor's left and right (divisions); COLL., ‘u yiêng‘ pah, a compellation for the Governor's police.

拊 ‘Fu. Used for the last: to lay the hand on; to pat, to strike gently; to soothe, to quiet; the handle of an instrument.

弣 ‘Fu. The middle of a bow, the place where it is grasped by the hand.

---

[1]烏石山 [2]烏蛉 [3]烏鵖 [4]嗚乎哀哉 [5]迂闊 [6]迂久 [7]狎侮 [8]侮慢 [9]朝儛山 [10]舞刀 [11]舞樂 [12]舞戲 [13]舞動 [14]舞龍燈 [15]猴舞杖 [16]撫膺 [17]撫養 [18]撫院 [19]撫標 [20]撫左 [21]撫右

‘廡 Wu. Side apartments or galleries; a porch, a lodge, a portico or corridor near the gate; a large house. Read ˛u, as in [1]ˏhwang ˛u, luxuriant foliage.

‘憮 Wu. To caress, to soothe, to comfort; an expression of mingled love and regret; [2]‘u ˛yong, alas for you! sad! Read ˛hu: large, great; proud.

‘甒 Wu. A jar holding five ˏching or pints; it is large in the middle and has a flat bottom.

‘膴 Wu. As in ‘u ‘u, fat, good-looking; thick, substantial, fine. Read ˛u and ˏhu: meat dried without bones, as used in sacrifices; also a law, a rule or pattern.

‘武 Wu. Military, martial, warlike; strong, brave, audacious; to suppress anarchy; dignified, majestic; a trace, a footstep; to connect with: [3]‘u ‘ŭng, brave and strong; [4]‘u ˏhu, a hero, a soldier; COM., [5]‘U chaik, ˏt‘iéng, an infamous empress, A. D. 640, a courtesan; [6]˛ung ‘u, civil and military; [7]k‘e’ ˛ung cheu² ‘u, to abandon civil pursuits for military; [8]‘u ˏkwang, military officers; [9]‘u seng’ a military sage, as the god of war ˏKwang tâ’; [10]‘u ngié² military arts; ‘u ‘ta, to use weapons, as in play or drill; [11]‘u ˛tung ˏseng, a military student, a cadet; [12]‘u ˛i ˛ngang ˏta, tea from the Bohea hills.

‘碔 Wu. A stone, called ‘u ˏhu, having a fine grain, but not classed with gems.

‘鵡 Wu. A parrot of a large size, called ˏeng ‘u; a species of macaw.

‘U. A coll. word, as in ‘u a² an infant’s cry.

毋 ˛Wu. Interchanged with the next: a prohibitive negative; do not, don’t; an interrogative particle; the 80th radical: chó² ˏhu ˏchïong ˛u, may I sit or not? COM., ˛u ˛ŭng ngié² no need to deliberate—it is all settled or decided.

無 无 ˛Wu. Not, none, not existing; destitute of, without, wanting: used for the coll. ˛mó, q. v.: COM., [13]˛u ˏti, without knowledge, brutish; [14]˛u ˏsing, unintentional, without design; [15]˛u so’ innumerable; [16]˛u ˏhwong, unimportant; [17]˛u sëü² no business, no farther trouble; [18]˛u ko’ causeless; [19]˛u ˏki, a little, a trifle; [20]˛u ˏhwa ‘kwo, the fig; ˛u ‘su pok, che’ going to extremes, wholly reckless; ˛u hwak, ˛u ˏt‘iéng, lawless; ˛u ˛tŭng ˏseng ‘iu, to bring something from nothing, as wealth from small capital; COLL., ˛u ˏsung pok, se’ neither 3 nor 4—neither one thing nor another, incongruous; ˛u ˛tu lai² exacting, pressing.

蕪 ˛Wu. Overgrown with weeds, a rank growth: ˛u woi’ covered with rank, dirty weeds; ˏhwong ˛u, grassy, uncultivated.

---

1 蕃廡 2 憮然 3 武勇 4 武夫 5 武則天〇 6 文武 7 棄文就武 8 武官 9 武聖 10 武藝 11 武童生 12 武彝巖茶 13 無知 14 無心 15 無數 16 無妨 17 無事 18 無故 19 無幾 20 無花果

湖 ꜀Hu. Read ꜀*hu;* coll. ꜀*u*, a lake: [1]꜀*sá* ꜀*u*, the west lake, in the western suburbs of Foochow.

꜀*U.* A coll. word: a buzzing in the ear, as when diseased: ꜀*u* ꜀*u kieuʼ* it buzzes, it rings.

(899) Ŭ.

於 扵 于 ꜀Yü. A preposition, a relative particle; in, at, on; by, with, through; at the beginning of a sentence, it means respecting, as to; often points out an accusative; sometimes makes a passive form of the verb; forms the comparative degree, than, more than; the last also means to go, to talk large; an exclamation, oh! also great, extensive, in which sense read ꜀*hü:* the 1st also read ꜀*u*, q. v.: [2]꜀*ü seʼ* thus; [3]꜀*ü* ꜀*king*, at this time; [4]꜀*ü* ʻ*chʻü*, here; [5]*cheʼ* ꜀*ü cheʼ siéngʼ* to attain to the highest good; *ongʼ* ꜀*ü* ʻ*ngó*, he asked me; *liék*꜇ ꜀*ü* ʻ*chó*, stated on the left or below; [6]*mok*꜇ *taiʼ* ꜀*ü* ꜀*tʻiéng*, nothing greater than Heaven; ʻ*sü* ꜀*ü* ꜀*tó*, to die by the sword; [7]꜀*ü* ꜀*chiá*, oh! ah! com., [8]꜀*ü* ꜀*sing* ꜀*hó* ꜀*ang*, how can you have peace of mind! [9]꜀*Ŭ* ꜀*sang*, a hill in the south quarter of Foochow.

淤 ꜀Yü. Also read *ëüʼ:* a deposit of mud and weeds in a stream: a foul, sedgy bank rising in the water; full, satiated.

竽 ꜀Yü. Also read ꜀*hü:* a kind of organ, having 36 tubes or pipes, of different lengths, meeting in a bulb; it led the choir, and hence was called *tóʼ* ꜀*ü*, the thieving-organ.

꜀*Ŭ.* A coll word: rich and proud: ʻ*yä* ꜀*ü sioh*꜇ ꜀*lau*, makes a great parade of his money! a big swell!

꜀*Ŭ.* A coll. word, as in ꜀*ü* ꜀*ü kieuʼ* to squeak, to squeal, to grunt, as a pig—same as in *ëüh*, q. v.

乳 ʻJu. The breasts, the nipple; an udder; milk; soft, tender; to nurse, to suckle; to suck the breast: used for the coll. ꜀*neng*, q. v.: [10]ʻ*ü pwoʼ* to nurse, to feed, as with a spoon; [11]ʻ*ü* ʻ*chü*, to suckle an infant; [12]꜀*yong* ꜀*kó koiʼ* ʻ*ü*, a lamb kneels to suck—symbol of filial piety; com., [13]ʻ*ü* ʻ*mu* (coll. ꜀*neng* ʻ*nä*), a wet-nurse; [14]ʻ*ü* ꜀*miäng*, the infantile name; [15]ʻ*ü* ꜀*hiong*, olibanum.

予 ʻYü. To give, to grant, to bestow, to confer: also read ꜀*ü*, q. v.: [16]*sëüʼ* ʻ*ü*, to confer on one, to bestow.

宇 ʻYü. The sides of a roof; to cover, as the eaves do; to shelter, as birds; to regard, to protect; wide, extensive, on every side; the canopy of the heavens, the world: [17]ʻ*ü nöiʼ* in the universe; [18]ʻ*ü teuʼ* the world, the universe; [19]*tongʼ* ʻ*ü*, a roof, a house; [20]꜀*ing* ʻ*ü*, his kindness protects.

窳 ʻYü. A defect, a flaw, as in a vase; defective, weak, feeble; sick, invalid; idle, vicious; listless, slothful; a puddle; foul, filthy.

[1]西湖 [2]於是 [3]於今 [4]於此 [5]至於至善 [6]莫大於天 [7]于嗟 [8]於心何安 [9]于山 [10]乳哺 [11]乳子 [12]羊羔跪乳 [13]乳母 [14]乳名 [15]乳香 [16]賜予 [17]宇内 [18]宇宙 [19]棟宇 [20]仁宇

ʻ**庾** Yü. A receptacle for grain in a field, a place to stack grain; a pile, a stack; ample, abundant, affluent: [1]*tai*ʾ *ʻü ʻliáng*, the Great Stack Mts., or Meiling, between Kwangtung and Kiangsi.

ʻ**瘐** Yü. In pain, suffering; sick, diseased; melancholy, sadness; disappointed; to die from cold and hunger in prison.

ʻ**愈 瘉** Yü. To surpass, to overcome, to prevail; to advance, to add; to increase, more, better, still more; to cure; to get well, getting well, convalescent, healed: [2]*peng*ʾ *ʻü*, the sickness cured; [3]*ˏiu ˏsing ʻü ʻü*, to lament more and more; COM., [4]*ʻü ˏtó ʻü miau*ʾ the more there is the more admirable!

ʻ**禹** Yü. The name of an insect; to expand; expanded, loose, easy: [5]*Tai*ʾ *ʻü*, the founder of the Hsia dynasty, B. C. 2205.

ʻ**瑀** Yü. A pebble resembling a gem or precious stone.

ʻ**羽** Yü. The long quill-feathers of birds, feathers; wings, plumes; feathered, made of feathers; a feather-banner or signal; quick, flying; the 5th of the 5 musical notes; a sort of plume held by posture-makers; the 124th radical: [6]*ʻü loi*ʾ birds; COM., [7]*ʻü ˏmó*, camlets; *ʻü ˏsa*, a thin camlet; [8]*ʻü ˏling*, lastings; *ˏHó ˏlang ʻü*, Dutch camlets—also called [9]*ʻü taung*ʾ or *ʻü ˏmó taung*ʾ; [10]*ʻü ik*ˎ *e*ʾ *ˏsing*, feathers and wings not yet grown; *met.*, has not yet attained its full strength, as a rebellion.

ʻ**與 ʻ与** Yü. A class, a company, a band, a confederation; to consort, to join together, to be on good terms; good, agreeable; a preposition, with, by, to; a conjunction, and, together; a disjunctive when repeated, either, or; as, like, as if; followed by *ˏning*, denotes comparison; to give, to grant, to bestow; to transfer, to concede to; to promise; to permit, to allow; to wait, to delay; to use, to employ; sometimes marks the dative before, and a transitive sense after, verbs: also read *ˏü* and *ü*ʾ q. v.: [11]*ʻtong ʻü*, a clan, confederates; *ˏsiong ʻü*, on friendly terms; [12]*pok*ˎ *ʻngó ʻü*, make no use of me; *ˏsong ʻü ˏki e*ʾ *yʻ ˏning ch'ek*ˎ in mourning grief is better than show; COM., [13]*ʻü kwok*ˎ *ˏtung ˏhiu*, to end or perish with the dynasty.

ʻ**雨** Yü. Condensed vapor falling, rain; a rain, a shower; to come thick and fast as rain; the 173d radical: [14]*ʻch'i sik*ˎ *ʻü ha*ʾ the darts and stones rained fiercely; [15]*chik*ˎ *ʻü*, a dashing shower; COM., *ˏtiu ʻü*, a long rain; *ʻü ʻchwi*, rain-water; [16]*ʻü lo*ʾ rain and dew; *ˏmi ˏmi ʻü*, fine rain; [17]*ha*ʾ *ʻü*, (coll. *taung*ʾ *ʻü*), to rain; COLL., *ʻü moi*ʾ or *ʻü ˏhwa*, or *ʻü ʻkiáng*, fine, drizzling rain; *ʻü p'iák*ˎ *ʻtié ˏli*, the rain beats in; *ʻü nah*ˎ the rain has slacked; *kwo*ʾ *ˏhung ʻü*, a

1 大庾嶺〇 2 病愈 3 憂心愈愈 4 愈多愈妙 5 大禹 6 羽類 7 羽毛 8 羽綾 9 羽緞 10 羽翼未成 11 黨與 12 不我與 13 與國同休 14 矢石雨下 15 疾雨〇 16 雨露 17 下雨

passing shower. Read *ĕüʼ* or *ĕüʼ:* to rain.

予 余 ꜀Yü. Erh. As a personal pronoun, I, we, ourself, ourselves; written in humble style in small size and deflected form by the side; the 2d is a surname and distinguished from the next by being termed from its parts [1]*꜀ing ꜀hwo* (coll. [2]*꜀ing seʼ*); it also means the 4th month: the first also read *ʻü*, q. v.

兪 俞 ꜀Yü. To answer, to respond; tone of assent, yes, well, very good, quite so; also a surname and distinguished from the preceding by the term [3]*꜀ing chaik꜁*: [4]*꜀ü ʻüng*, to promise, to assent; *꜀ü ꜀ü*, mild and respectful.

畬 ꜀Yü. A field after two years' tillage; some say three years'; to till, to cultivate. Read *꜀siă* or *꜀chʻiă:* something to bring fire, tinder.

餘 ꜀Yü. Remnants of food, leavings; a remnant, residue, surplus; a remainder; superabundant, supererogatory: COM., [5]*꜀ü sengʼ* the rest, what is left; [6]*꜀tó ꜀ü*, or *ʻiu ꜀ü*, more than enough; [7]*꜀ü ꜀chang*, worthless scraps; *꜀ü teʼ* a vacant spot; *met.*, something reserved, as in a quarrel some ground left for future friendship; [8]*꜀ki ꜀ü*, overplus; [9]*꜀ü ꜀nong*, the overplus of proceeds; *꜀ü aʼ* what remains; *ngoʼ nik꜁ ꜀ü*, five days' grace; COLL., *꜀ü tiongʼ* the remnant; *꜀ü ꜀yeu pooʼ oʼ kʻwak꜁ ꜀mó ꜀tong*, the *꜀ü ꜀yeu* cotton-cloth is broad but short; *met.*, to begin with a flourish and end in a failure.

儒 ꜀Ju. A scholar, a philosopher; learned men, the literati; learned, scholarly: [10]*꜀ü sĕüʼ* scholars; [11]*꜀hang ꜀ü*, an indigent scholar; [12]*꜀ü hok꜁* (coll. *óh꜁ ꜀kwang*), a superintendent of Siutsai; COM., [13]*꜀ü ʻchiă* or *꜀ü ʻchiă ꜀ka*, the literary class; [14]*꜀ü ʻnga*, genteel, elegant; [15]*꜀ü kauʼ* Confucianism; [16]*꜀ü ꜀ka*, an independent artisan, doctor, &c., one not belonging to the regular guild or profession; *꜀ü ꜀ka hiéʼ* theatricals by an amateur troupe.

伃 妤 ꜀Yü. Good, excellent: [17]*chiék꜁ ꜀ü*, a kind of female chamberlain in the palace, in the Tʻang dynasty.

如 ꜀Ju. A conjunction, as, according to; like, as if; if, perhaps; at the beginning of a sentence, means as to, as regards, like as; following adjectives, denotes manner, appearance, also adds emphasis to the meaning: [18]*꜀ü yok꜁* as if; [19]*꜀ü ꜀king*, now; COM., *꜀ü ʻchʻü*, thus; [20]*꜀ü ʻchʻü ʻteng loiʼ* this sort of (low) fellows; [21]*꜀hó ꜀ü*, how is it? how will it do? *꜀ü seʼ* thus, then; *꜀u ꜀ü*, not like, not as well as; [22]*꜀ü ʻkwo*, truly, verily, indeed; [23]*꜀ü ꜀siong*, as usual; *꜀ü ꜀hu ꜀ing*, your lady (concubine); *꜀ü ꜀ngü taik꜁ ʻchwi*, as fish getting water—*scil.*, so is it to get a good servant or wife; *ʻhwang* (or *tóʼ*) *pok꜁ ꜀ü*, but it's nothing like, or as good as.

1 人禾　2 人示　3 人則　4 兪允　5 餘剩　6 多餘　7 餘殘　8 其餘　9 餘囊　10 儒士　11 寒儒　12 儒學　13 儒者　14 儒雅　15 儒教　16 儒家　17 婕妤　18 如若　19 如今　20 如此等類　21 何如　22 如果　23 如常

孺 ꜀Ju. Also read ꜂ü: an infant at the breast, a suckling; attached to, intimate; a surname: [1]꜀ü ꜂chü, an infant, a child; [2]꜀ü ꜀ing, the wife of an officer of the 7th rank.

愉 ꜀Yü. A happy, contented air; pleased, delighted; willingly, joyfully; satisfied, gratified: [3]꜀ü *saik*, a happy countenance; [4]꜀ü ꜀ü, pleased, gratified.

榆 ꜀Yü. The elm, of which there are reckoned ten varieties: [5]꜀*song* ꜀ü, mulberry and elm; *met.*, evening, the evening of life, old age; COM., [6]꜀ü ꜀*kang*, elm-berries? — an expectorant.

楰 ꜀Yü. A species of tree, whose wood is tough in dry, and brittle in wet, weather.

樗 ꜀Yü. A tree having a shining bark and fetid leaves, whose wood is fit only for the fire, a sort of smilax? [7]꜀ü *lik*₂ ordinary material; *met.*, useless, as an officer calls himself.

雩 ꜀Yü. Name of a sacrifice, offered to secure rain; to pray for rain. Read *ü*²: the rainbow.

洳 ꜀Ju. The name of a stream; to imbibe, to soak in, to become moist: [8]꜂*chu* ꜀ü, watery, soaked through.

渝 ꜀Yü. To become muddy, as a stream; to deteriorate, to grow worse; the name of a district and several rivers; a stream near the east end of the Great Wall.

臾 ꜀Yü. A brief time, a moment: [9]꜀*sü* ꜀ü, in a little while, presently. Read *koi*²: a basket to contain grass.

舁 ꜀Yü. To raise with both hands, to bear aloft; to sustain with all the strength.

與 歟 ꜀Yü. A final particle, indicating surprise or admiration; an interrogative or dubitative particle; a sign of the vocative; to breathe freely; easy, dignified; the first also read ꜂ü and *ü*² q. v.: [10]꜂*k'ó pok, seng*² ꜀ü, must we not be careful? [11]꜀*ki* ꜀*ui* ꜀*ing* ꜀*chi* ꜂*pwong* ꜀ü, is not this (filial piety) the root of benevolence.

輿 ꜀Yü. The body of a cart; a chariot; a barrow; to hold, to sustain, to bear, as the earth does; a substratum, a foundation; the beginning of; a term for the earth; many, numerous: [12]꜀*sing* ꜀ü, the equipage, etc., of the emperor; [13]꜀ü ꜀*ing*, a carriage-maker; [14]꜀*k'ang* ꜀ü, heaven and earth, geomancy; [15]*té*² ꜀ü ꜀*tu*, a map of the earth or a country.

鸒 ꜀Yü. A black bird, the pie or jay; small birds of this kind that assemble in flocks.

旟 ꜀Yü. Banners adorned with paintings of birds, used to animate soldiers; to display, to wave.

---

[1]孺子 [2]孺人 [3]愉色 [4]愉愉 [5]桑榆 [6]榆甘 [7]樗櫟 [8]沮洳 [9]須臾 [10]可不慎歟 [11]其爲仁之本與 [12]乘輿 [13]輿人 [14]堪輿○ [15]地輿圖○

福州方言拼音字典

瑜 瑜 ꜀Yü. The luster of gems; a beautiful stone; *met.*, virtue, excellence: [1]*ʿking ꜀ü*, a fine gem; [2]*꜀ü ꜀ha*, excellencies and defects.

茹 ꜀Ju. Ku. Also read *ʿü:* roots intertwisted; joined by the roots; tangled, interlaced: to take, to receive; to eat and drink greedily, to gobble down; to conjecture; soft, pliant, flexible; dried, putrid, as herbs; things dying of themselves: *꜀ü ꜀ngü*, putrid fish; [3]*pak₂ ꜀mau ꜀liéng ꜀ü*, to pluck up the couch grass with the roots.

萸 ꜀Yü. A kind of pepper, called *꜀chio ꜀ü;* it is a bitter, umbelliferous seed, prescribed as an alterative.

腴 ꜀Yü. Fat on the belly; fat, corpulent, soft and flabby; rich, fertile; the belly; the entrails, as of dogs and pigs: [4]*꜀pʻi ꜀ü*, fat; [5]*꜀kó ꜀ü*, fertile, as land.

諛 ꜀Yü. To flatter, to praise, to adulate; to caress; adulation; one who flatters, a sycophant: [6]*ʿtʻiéng ꜀ü*, to flatter; [7]*꜀ó ꜀ü*, to cajole, to wheedle; [8]*꜀ü saik₂*, a simpering, ogling look.

譽 ꜀Yü. To praise, to laud, to extol; to overpraise, to eulogize extravagantly; to flatter one: also read *ëü²* q. v.: [9]*miéng² ꜀ü ꜀ing*, to flatter people to their face; [10]*꜀chʻing ꜀ü*, to praise excessively; [11]*꜀ü ʻchʻü*, to receive praise with delight.

蝓 ꜀Yü. A garden slug, a limax, called [12]*ˎié ꜀ü;* some say a kind of garden spider.

蠕 ꜀Ju. Sometimes read *꜀sü:* to crawl, to wriggle along, as snakes and worms; the name of a horde of Huns.

窬 ꜀Yü. A small door made in a wall or a partition; a small door cut in a large gate; to make an opening in, to bore a hole: [13]*꜀chʻiong ꜀ü*, to cut through a wall, as thieves do.

覦 ꜀Yü. Also read *ëü²:* to wish earnestly, to desire, to covet: [14]*ke² ꜀ü*, to long for.

踰 逾 ꜀Yü. Yüeh. To pass over, to cross; to overstep, to advance, to go beyond; to exceed a limit; to pass by, as time: [15]*꜀ü ngwok₂* to pass over the month; [16]*꜀ü wok₂* to overstep; [17]*꜀ü aing²* to exceed the limit or mark.

(900) Üh.

Üh₂. A coll. word: to rise, to get up, as from the floor: *üh₂ ʻkʻi* or *üh₂ ʻkʻi ꜀li*, to rise, spring up; *üh₂ ʻlá chai² ʻlá*, up! jump up! as said to a child.

(901) Ui.

桅 ꜀Wei. The mast of a vessel: COM., [18]*꜀ui ꜀kang*, a mast; [19]*twai² ꜀ui*, the mainmast; *꜀ui ꜀kang sóh*, a rope to raise a sail; [20]*꜀ui ʻmwi*, masthead; [21]*꜀ui ꜀pwang*, the tops in a foreign ship; COLL., [22]*kʻié² ꜀ui*, to raise or step the mast. Read *ʻkwi:* a yellow wood to dye with; a javelin.

[1]瑾瑜 [2]瑜瑕 [3]拔茅連茹 [4]肥腴 [5]膏腴 [6]諂諛 [7]阿諛 [8]諛色 [9]面譽人 [10]稱譽〇 [11]譽處 [12]蝘蝓 [13]穿窬 [14]覬覦 [15]踰月 [16]踰越 [17]踰限 [18]桅杆 [19]大桅 [20]桅尾 [21]桅盤 [22]豎桅

爲 為 ˏWei. To do, to effect; to act, to make; a substantive verb; to cause; to manage, to administer; to esteem, to consider as: also read *oi²* q. v.: [1]*ˏui ˏkwang*, to be a magistrate; *ʻsu ˏui*, that which is done; [2]*ˏhó ˏui*, will do what? *ʻi ʻka ˏui ˏching*, to reckon the false as the true; COM., [3]*ˏui ʻpwong*, (this) is the chief thing; [4]*ˏheng ˏui*, to do, acts, doings; *ˏui siéng²* to do good; [5]*ˏui chaik*, or *ˏui aing²* (this) is the limit, as to time, expense, etc.; [6]*ˏui hai² pok, ʻch'iéng*, it will be very injurious; *ˏhó sëü² pok, ʻk'ó ˏui*, then what will he not do—will be ready for any thing bad!

韋 ˏWei. Tanned leather, also soft leather; leathern straps or thongs; perverse, refractory, rebellious; a surname; the 178th radical: [7]*ˏi ˏui*, harmonious, in concord; [8]*ˏui piéng²* a leathern casque; COM., [9]*ˏUi ˏtó* (coll. *ˏUi ˏnó*), name of a Budhist god, the wand-bearer—stands in the front temple, back of *ˏMi ˏná huk,*.

圍 ˏWei. To surround, to inclose; to limit, to circumscribe; to hem in, to invest, to besiege; to encircle, as animals in hunting; confined, as metals in molds; a snare, an inclosure; a dam, an embankment about fields; a circumference; half a cubit: [10]*ˏui k'aung²* to besiege; [11]*ʻta ˏui*, to drive (animals) into a circle; COM., *ˏk'wang ˏui*, encircling; *ˏui ˏch'iong*, to inclose with a wall; *ˏui ch'ok,* to carry the inclosure farther out; *ˏui ˏping*, soldiers besieging; [12]*ˏui ˏkiéng*, a bride's embroidered cape; [13]*ˏui ˏping*, a set of ornamental, folding screens; [14]*ˏui ˏngü ˏk'wong ʻtu*, to inveigle a simpleton to game; COLL., *sioh, pó² ˏui twai²* as large as one can span with his arms; [15]*ˏui tiék,* fan-shaped dessert-cups, as arranged on a circular tray.

幃 ˏWei. A single curtain; a perfume-bag: [16]*ˏhiong ˏui*, the iris-curtain or apartment; *met.*, a mother; [17]*ˏchü ˏui*, the loving curtain—a mother.

褘 ˏWei. Interchanged with the last: a lady's perfume-bag; a covering for the knees, an apron; chaste, elegant, beautiful. Read *ˏhwi*: a queen's embroidered robe, worn at sacrifices.

違 ˏWei. To oppose, to disobey, to rebel, to give no heed to; to leave, to vacate, as an office; to shun, to avoid; perverse, seditious, contumelious: [18]*ˏi ˏui*, undetermined; *ˏyong hong² ˏing ˏui*, to agree to one's face and disobey behind his back; *ˏui ˏhwo*, indisposed, ill; COM., *ˏui lié²* to transgress rules; [19]*ˏu ˏui tek, se²* do not disobey this special edict; *ˏui pwoi²* to turn the back on, to rebel against; *ˏui aing²* to transgress the limit, as of time.

闈 ˏWei. The door of a harem; side doors of the palace; the examination hall: [20]*ˏhiong ˏui*, or *ˏch'iu ˏui*, the examination for Küjin; [21]*hwoi² ˏui*, or *ˏch'ung ˏui*, the

1爲官 3爲本 5爲則 不淺 8韋弁 10圍困 12圍肩 14圍愚 15圍碟 17慈幃 19毋違 20鄉闈

2何爲 4行爲 6爲害 7依韋 9韋馱 11打圍 13圍屏 誑賭 16香幃 18依違 特示 21會闈

examination for Chinsz'; *ik*$_2$ *꜀ui*, to enter the examination; *꜀ui mĕk*$_2$ the essays of graduates.

(902) **Uk.**

勿 Wu. ^{2} A negative, not, do not; a banner at temples: *uk*$_2$ *uk*$_2$ in haste, ardently desirous of; COM., [1]*꜀hi ꜂lá uk*$_2$ *꜀ngiong*, do not utter what is impolite or indecorous.

沕 Wu. ^{2} As in *uk*$_2$ *muk*$_2$ deep, abstruse; inexhaustible. Read *mik*$_2$: small, minute, recondite; a particle of dust, an atom.

物 Wu. ^{2} A thing, a substance; an article, goods; a matter, a business; creatures, beings; a class, a sort; to distinguish things, as by color, &c.; to know thoroughly: [2]*uk*$_2$ *yong*^{2} things; [3]*uk*$_2$ *loi*^{2} sorts of things; [4]*uk*$_2$ *꜂sang*, natural productions; COM., [5]*hwo*^{3} *uk*$_2$ merchandise; [6]*꜀seng uk*$_2$ living things; [7]*wang*^{2} *uk*$_2$ all things; [8]*꜂ku ꜂tung ngwang*^{2} *uk*$_2$ antiques and toys; *꜀ing uk*$_2$ *꜀hwa ꜂neu*, men, flowers, birds, as in pictures or sketches.

Uk$_2$. A coll. word: to toss, to cast, to pitch things: *uk*$_2$ *kwo*^{3} *꜀ch'iong*, to toss over the wall; *uk*$_2$ *꜀liu ꜀sing ꜀t'ui*, to play with iron balls; *uk*$_2$ *꜀liu ꜀kwong ꜀t'ui*, to wave lanterns—in the first of the 1st month; *uk*$_2$ *tioh*$_2$ *tioh*$_2$ shake it till well kindled, as a torch.

(903) **Ŭk.**

欲 Yü. ^{2} Interchanged with the next: to breathe after, to wish, to long for; to covet, to seek ardently; to love; desires, aims, aspirations; inclinations; about to be, ready to, on the point of: used for the coll. *ói*^{2} q. v.: [9]*ngwong*^{2} *ŭk*$_2$ to wish; [10]*꜀sui ꜀sing ꜂su ŭk*$_2$ just what one desires; *uk*$_2$ *ŭk*$_2$ desire or lust for (other) things; COM., *ŭk*$_2$ *꜀ti ꜀t'iéng ɑ*^{2} *sëü*^{2} *꜀sü t'uk*$_2$ *꜂ku ꜀ing ꜀chü*, if one would know worldly affairs he must read the ancients.

慾 Yü. ^{2} Inordinate desire, lust, appetite, concupiscence; lustful, lascivious, licentious: [11]*sié*^{2} *ŭk*$_2$ inordinate passion or desire; [12]*ŭk*$_2$ *꜂hwo*, raging lust; COM., [13]*ŭk*$_2$ *꜂siong*, wanton thoughts; [14]*saik*$_2$ *ŭk*$_2$ sexual lust; [15]*꜀sü ŭk*$_2$ selfish aims, one's lusts; [16]*꜂kwa ŭk*$_2$ *꜀tó ꜀seng ꜂chü*, continence secures a numerous progeny.

浴 Yü. ^{2} To wash the body, to bathe; to perform an ablution; to cleanse, to purify and correct the mind; to fly up and down, to warp, as birds and insects do: [17]*muk*$_2$ *ŭk*$_2$ to wash face and body, to bathe; COM., *ŭk*$_2$ *꜀a ꜀tié* (coll. *꜂ló ꜀wa k'auk*$_2$), crows' bath-pools—small basins of water among the rocks of Black Rock Hill, Foochow; [18]*꜀chai kai*^{3} *muk*$_2$ *ŭk*$_2$ fast, abstain, cleanse—a notice posted in streets on idols' days; *ŭk*$_2$ *꜀pwong sak*$_2$ a malign influence of the bath-tub—which must be exorcised before the 3d day's washing of the infant.

溽 Ju. ^{2} Damp, moist, wet; moist and hot, reeking; rich, savory, as food; name of a stream: *pok*$_2$ *ŭk*$_2$ poor, meager, as food;

[1] 非禮勿言 [2] 物件 [3] 物類 [4] 物產 [5] 貨物 [6] 生物 [7] 萬物 [8] 古董玩物 [9] 願欲 [10] 隨心所欲 [11] 嗜慾 [12] 慾火 [13] 慾想 [14] 色慾 [15] 私慾 [16] 寡慾多生子 [17] 沐浴 [18] 齋戒沐浴○

ˌling ˌu pok, ük, woods are always dank.

辱 ₂ Ju. To put to shame, to disgrace, to dishonor, to bring reproach on; to insult, to rail at; to defile, to corrupt, to debauch; degraded, disgraced, shamed: [1]*ük, ˌsing,* to defile the person—do menial offices; [2]*k'ok, ük,* to submit to ignominy; [3]*ˈt'i ük,* shamed, put to shame; [4]*ˌing ük,* glory and shame; [5]*ˈung ük, ˌt'eu ˌseng,* to save one's life dishonorably; COM., [6]*ˌling ük,* to disgrace; to debauch.

蓐 ₂ Ju. Grass again springing up; shoots, sprouts; a rush for making mats; a frame for silk-worms: [7]*ˈma ük,* straw for horses' beds; [8]*ük, ˌsiu,* the harvest of the 7th moon.

褥 ₂ Ju. A stuffed mat, a mattress; a cushion, a wadded seat; a thick, felt cover: COM., [9]*ˈma ˌang ük,* a saddle-cushion; [10]*p'woi² ük,* coverlet and mattress; [11]*ˌmiéng ük,* a cotton-stuffed mattress; [12]*tóh, ük,* a felt table-cover; [13]*ˌp'ui ük,* a leathern mat, used on beds. Read *nó':* a child's dress.

縟 ₂ Ju. Adorned with colors, variegated; pretty, gay, elegant; to adorn; much ornament.

繘 ₂ Yü. A rope for drawing water, a well-rope.

遹 ₂ Yü. To comply with, to follow, to obey; to narrate; an initial particle.

霱 ₂ Yü. Clouds of many colors; auspicious clouds, those that are tricolored.

驈 ₂ Yü. A black horse, having white hind quarters.

鷸 ₂ Yü. An aquatic bird which knows the time of rain, perhaps a kind of kingfisher; it has red legs and yellowish streaks; to fly swiftly, to dart, as the kingfisher on its prey: [14]*ük, p'aung² ˌsiong ˌt'i,* the kingfisher and oyster catch each other—then the fisherman profits.

鴥 ₂ Yü. A species of singing thrush or grackle, called *ˌkü ük,* or *paik, ˌkó.*

聿 ₂ Yü. A style, a writing implement, a pencil; to obey, to follow; to declare, to narrate; an initial word, then, forthwith, accordingly; the 129th radical.

毓 ₂ Yü. Same as the next: to nurture, to rear, to raise; to educate, to train a child to virtue; abundant: [15]*ük, ˌling,* to give birth to a fine son; COM., *ük, ˌling ˌküng,* a temple to the goddess "Mother".

育 ₂ Yü. To bear; to nourish, to bring up, to support; to train children to virtuous habits; to cause to grow, to produce: [16]*ük, taik,* to cultivate virtue; [17]*ük, ˈtiong,* to cause to grow; [18]*hwak, ük, wang² ük,* to produce and rear all things, as God does; COM., [19]*ˈyong ük,* to

---

[1]辱身 [2]屈辱 [3]恥辱 [4]榮辱 [5]忍辱偷生 [6]凌辱 [7]馬蓐 [8]蓐收 [9]馬鞍褥 [10]被褥 ○ [11]棉褥 [12]桌褥 [13]皮褥 ○ [14]鷸蚌相持 [15]毓麟 [16]育德 [17]育長 [18]發育萬物 [19]養育

rear, to support; *ŭk₂ ˏeng ˏtong*, or *ˊyong ŭk₂ ˏtong*, a foundling asylum.

鬻 Yü. Used for the last; to nourish; to sell: COM., [1]*ŭk₂ ˏchʻá nik₂ ˊnü*, to sell wives and drown daughters. Read *kĕük₂*: to nourish; young, tender. Read *chĕük₂*: congee, gruel, for which the upper half of the character is used in the coll. q. v.

(904) Ung.

氳 Yün. Vapor; the genial life-giving principles of nature; procreative aura: [2]*ˏing ˏung*, the influence of heaven and earth which begets things.

緼 Yün. Interchanged with the last: raveled silk; confused; a deep red or purple color: also read *ˊung*, q. v.: [3]*ˏhung ˏung*, raveled, in confusion; full, abundant.

温 Wĕn. Wu. A river and district in Honan; warm, tepid, genial, temperate; mild, kind, gentle; bland, soothing; to revive, as affection; to know thoroughly, matured, versed in; to review, to study over: [4]*ˏung ˊpau*, clothed and filled; [5]*sieu sëü ˏhang ˏung*, to chat about matters, to talk of old times; COM., [6]*ˏung ˏiu*, soft, gentle, yielding; [7]*ˏung ˏhwo*, gentle; tepid; mild, as the weather; [8]*ˏung ˏchü*, to review lessons, specifically a three days' review; [9]*ˏung sik₂* review of six days' lessons; [10]*ˏung sük₂ sük₂* to review thoroughly.

熅 Wĕn. A smothered fire, smoke without a blaze; a genial warmth; vapor, warm steam; in the coll. to boil or heat, as in [11]*ˏung ˊchiu*, to heat wine in jars—the end of the distilling process. Read *ˊung*: to stretch things by heat.

瘟 瘟 Wĕn. A pestilence, an epidemic disease; a slight pain, giddiness: COM., [12]*ˏung ik₂* a plague, distemper; [13]*ˏung pang²* sick with the plague; [14]*ˏung ik₂ ˏtiong ˊnieng*, the plague is infectious; [15]*ˏung pwo² ˊchio ˊchai*, rulers of the pestilence—term applied to the *ˊNgu tá²* idols; COLL., *pwok₂ ˏung*, you'll have the plague—an execration. Read *uk₂*: sorrow, sadness.

鰫 As in the coll. *ˏung ˏtʻi*, a species of small sea-fish; *ˏung ˏtʻi ˏkié*, the salted *ˏung ˏtʻi*, as found in the markets; *ˏung ˏtʻi lo²* the brine of the *ˏung ˏtʻi*.

翁 Wĕng. Plumage on the neck, the neck-feathers; flying about; a term of honor, a venerable man, a graybeard: [16]*ˏung ˏku*, a husband's father and mother; [17]*ˏchong ˏung*, your respected father; [18]*ˏing ˏung*, the fathers of wedded children—so term each other in letters and cards; [19]*pek₂ ˏtʻeu ˏung*, a white-headed thrush; an old man; *ˏung tëüng²* human images of stone before officer's graves.

嗡 Wĕng. To low, to bellow; the lowing of cattle; the hum of insects.

[1]鬻妻溺女 [2]氤氳 [3]紛緼 [4]温飽 [5]少敘寒温 [6]温柔 [7]温和 [8]温書 [9]温習 [10]温熟熟 [11]熅酒 [12]瘟疫 [13]瘟病 [14]瘟疫傳染 [15]瘟部主宰 [16]翁姑 [17]尊翁 [18]姻翁 [19]白頭翁

ALPH. DICT. 124

˓*Ung.* A coll. word, as in ˓*ung nong*ʾ or ˓*ung* ˓*sung*, dull, stupid; ˓*ung nong*ʾ *k'e*ʾ ʻ*k'i* ˓*hwa* ˓*kwong*, the stupid fellow emits a flash (of genius)! ˓*ngai* ˓*chiéng* ʻ*sai* *tà*ʾ *cheng*ʾ ˓*ung nong*ʾ ʻ*si mà*ʾ ˓*wong*, bad cash get used up, but dolts never all die off!

ʻ**塕** Wêng. Read ʻ*ung*; used in the *Paik*, ˓*Ing* for the coll. ˓*ung*: to sprinkle, sprinkled: [1]˓*ung* ˓*ting*, dust; ˓*ung* ˓*ting* *seu*ʾ a dirty hole — a room filled with dust; ˓*ung* ˓*ting* ˓*pung* ˓*pung* ʻ*k'i*, dust rising; [2]˓*ung sioh*˳ *tóh*, the whole table covered with dust; ʻ*hwi* ˓*hu* ˓*ung mek*˳ ˓*chiu* ʻ*lá*, to sprinkle ashes in the eyes.

ʻ**刎** Wên. To cut one's own throat: [3]ʻ*ung keng*ʾ ˓*kau*, clasp-neck friendship — close friends; COM., [4]ʻ*ung* ʻ*si*, to commit suicide by cutting the throat.

ʻ**吻** Wên. The corners of the mouth; the lips; *met.*, speech, talk: [5]*chiék*˳ ʻ*ung*, to join the lips, to kiss; [6]ʻ*t'o*ʾ ˓*sung* ʻ*ung*, to pout the lips; [7]ʻ*k'eu* ʻ*ung*, one's peculiar talk or meaning — phrase used in novels.

ʻ**脗** Wên. To blend in one; joined, united, intermingled: [8]ʻ*ung hak*˳ joined, blended harmoniously.

ʻ**惲** Yün. Liberal, kind, magnanimous; to deliberate, to devise a plan.

ʻ**殞** Yün. Interchanged with the next in the sense of to fall: to die, to become extinct, to fail, to perish: [9]ʻ*ung miék*˳ to become extinct, as a family; [10]ʻ*ung meng*ʾ to die.

ʻ**隕** ʻ**磒** Yün. To fall from a height; to roll, to crash down; to fall, to fail, to perish, to go into ruin: [11]˓*sing* ʻ*ung* ˓*ü* ʻ*ü*, the stars fell like rain; [12]ʻ*ung t'á*ʾ to shed tears.

ʻ**穩** ʻ**穏** Wên. To tread out grain; safe, secure; well-placed, settled, fixed, immovable; sure, trusty, firm, constant; assured, implicit; to rest, to place securely: [13]ʻ*ung* ˓*pó* (coll. ˓*pó* ʻ*ná*), a midwife; COM., [14]ʻ*ung taung*ʾ safe, free from risks; [15]˓*ang* ʻ*ung*, settled, fixed securely; [16]ʻ*ung* ˓*ü t'ai*ʾ ˓*sang*, as safe as T'aishan (mountain); [17]ʻ*ung tëüng*ʾ steady, constant, not light and trifling; COLL., ʻ*ung* ʻ*ung* ˓*siàng*, safely effected; ʻ*ung chiáh*˳ ʻ*ung*, very secure, fully assured.

ʻ**媼** Wên. Also read ˓*ung*: an old woman, a dame; a term for mother; the spirits of the earth: [18]ʻ*ló* ʻ*ung*, or [19]ʻ*ung* ˓*pó*, an old dame. Read *uk*˳ as in *uk*˳ *nak*˳ a fat child.

ʻ**縕** Yün. Hempen; deep, abstruse, as doctrines: also read ˓*ung*, q. v.: ʻ*ung* ˓*pó*, a hempen robe; a tattered gown.

ʻ**薀** Yün. Wên. An aquatic plant; collected, as duckweed; heaped up, as plants are when out; luxuriant; collected,

[1]塕塵 [2]塕一棹 [3]刎頸交 [4]刎死 [5]接吻 [6]吐唇吻 [7]口吻 [8]脗合 [9]殞滅 [10]殞命 [11]星隕如雨 [12]隕涕 [13]穩婆 [14]穩當 [15]安穩 [16]穩如泰山〇 [17]穩重〇 [18]老媼 [19]媼婆

assembled; to hoard; deep, profound, as learning: *ʻung kiék*, oppressed in mind, displeased; *ʻung ʻch'ó*, clumpy, tussocky grass.

韞 ʻYün. An orange color; a case for a bow; the inside or lining; to store up, to conceal, to guard carefully.

ʻ*Ung.* A coll. word, as in *ʻung ˏp'iǎng*, hump-backed.

文 ˓Wên. Strokes, lines, marks; veins, spots, bands, striæ; variegated, colored, ornate; symmetrical lines or colors; chaste; genteel, elegant, stylish; extraneous, as ornaments; letters, literature; literary and official or civil; scholarly, accomplished, learned; a dispatch; a classifier of coins; the 67th radical: used for the coll. *ˏmwong*, q. v.: [1]*˓teu ˓ung*, to deliver a dispatch; [2]*˓ung pok˒ ˏka ʻtiéng*, the composition is faultless; COM., [3]*ek˒ ˓ung*, one cash; [4]*˓ung ˏchiong*, a composition, an essay; [5]*˓ung hwak˒*, rules of writing, grammar; [6]*ˏsü ˓ung*, a literary man; [7]*˓ung ʻli*, style, tenor of an essay; [8]*˓ngwong ˓ung*, the original text; [9]*pak˒ ˓ung*, the simple text; [10]*˓ung k'e˒* the spirit of a composition; genteel; [11]*˓ung ʻnga*, neat, elegant; [12]*˓ung ˏhung*, the literary atmosphere or fame of a place; [13]*˓ung mĕk˒*, literature; model essays; [14]*˓ung seng˒ ʻu seng˒* Confucius and Kuanti; [15]*˓ung ˏch'iong tà˒ ˏkung*, god of learning; *˓ung ˏpung sëü˒ ʻpó*, writing apparatus; *˓ung pok˒ ˓sing ʻu pok˒ cheu˒* an adept neither in civil nor military affairs, can neither learn nor work; *ˏhü ˓ung*, false, mere fables; empty forms; COLL., *˓ung ˓ung pwo˒* step by step, to keep step, as sedanmen; *˓ung ˓ung chaiu˒ chaiu˒* excessively polite, affected gentility; *˓ung tang˒* a superior sort of pomelo. Read *ong˒*: to hide, to gloss over.

抆 ˓Wên. Also read *ʻung:* to rub, to feel, to smooth with the hand; to wipe or dry by rubbing: *˓ung loi˒* to wipe away tears.

紋 ˓Wên. A pattern or figures in weaving; marks, seams in wood; lines in carving and drawing; the lines on the palm of the hand: COM., [16]*˓siă ˓ung pwo˒* cotton drills; *chaiu˒ ˏsa ˓ung*, crapes; [17]*ˏhwa ˓ung*, carved, flowered; [18]*˓ung ˓ngüng*, pure silver, sycee; [19]*ʻch'iu ˓ung*, lines on the palms; *ʻchwi ˓ung*, ripples on water; *tik˒ ˓ung* and *ˏhwang ˓ung*, with and across the grain; *pok˒ twang˒ ˓ung*, straight, connected figures, as in carving; *wang˒ che˒ ˓ung*, an ancient form of *wang˒* (myriad)—used ornamentally.

蚊 ˓Wên. A musquito, a gnat: used for the coll. *ˏhung*, q. v.: *˓ung ʻchü*, a fruit, resembling the mespilus or medlar.

鮫 ˓Wên. The name of a fish, having small scales and brilliant spots, a Sparus?

云 ˓Yün. To say, to declare; said, spoken of; to turn, to move around; abundant: [20]*˓hu pok˒ ˓ung*, why not say so? *˓ung ˓ung*, what was spoken of, this and that;

---

[1]投文 [2]文不加點 [3]一文 [4]文章 [5]文法 [6]斯文 [7]文理 [8]原文 [9]白文 [10]文氣 [11]文雅 [12]文風 [13]文墨 [14]文聖武聖 [15]文昌帝君 [16]斜紋布 [17]花紋 [18]紋銀 [19]手紋 [20]胡不云

etc., &c.; plentiful; ʻku ʻngü ˏung, the old saying is; COM., ˏung söü² or ˏung ˏung ˏchi söü² the matter spoken of; ˏung haung² the amount mentioned, the sum said (to be due).

紜 ˏYün. Raveled, confused, tangled; mixed up, embroiled: ¹ˏhungˏung, all in confusion.

耘 ˏYün. To weed ground, to clear away what is noxious; to rid fields of grass and weeds.

芸 ˏYün. Used for the last; a fragrant herb like rue; its leaves are said to keep insects out of mats and books: ²ˏung ˏhiong, a perfume, like benzoin or sandarac; ³ˏung ˏch'ong, a study, a library; ⁴ˏung ˏseng, grass in abundance; *met.*, the people.

聞 ˏWên. To hear, to perceive by the ear, to learn by report; to state to, to inform; fame, news, a report; to scent, to smell: ⁵t'eng² ˏung, to hear; ˏtiong ˏung, to publish a report; a tradition; ⁶pok, ʻüng ˏung, distressing to hear, most heart-rending; ⁷pik, ˏung, to smell; COM., ⁸ˏhung ˏung, a report; ⁹ngi ˏung, heard by the ear, reported; ¹⁰ˏsing ˏung, news; ¹¹ˏsing ˏung ʻchai, a newspaper, a gazette. Read ong²: the place to which the voice reaches; character, fame; leng² ong² your fair name.

(905) Ŭng.

殷 ˏYin. Used for the next: the highest degree of, full, flourishing, great, many, complete, perfect; a full band; a name for part of the Shang dynasty, B. C. 1401—1137: ¹²ˏŬng ˏchiu ˏchi kiê² the era of the last of the Shang and first of the Chow; COM., ¹³ˏüng sik, ho² or ˏüng sik, ˏchi ˏka, a wealthy family. Read ʻüng, as in ʻüng ʻüng, abundant.

慇 ˏYin. Sorrowing, depressed in spirit, melancholy: ˏüng ˏüng, grieved, sorrowful; COM., ¹⁴ˏüng ˏk'üng, very careful, anxiously diligent.

灉 ˏYung. A side sluice or waste-weir, which receives the overflow of the Yellow river.

雍 邕 ˏYung. The 1st is more commonly used; used for the next: harmony of sounds; union, concord, agreeing; to assist, to protect; collected, crowded together: COM., ¹⁵ˏüng ˏhwo, harmonious; mild, genial, equable, as temperature; ¹⁶ˏüng cheng² the Emperor Yungching, A. D. 1723; ¹⁷ˏüng cheng² söü² a kang² ˏseng purchased degree. Read üüng²: to guard against freshets.

雝 ˏYung. Similar to the last: a kind of sparrow, called ˏüng ˏkü; ˏüng ˏüng, the cry of wild geese; the harmonious song of birds; ¹⁸ˏüngˏhwo, harmonious, agreeable.

廱 ˏYung. In concord, harmonious: ¹⁹p'ek, ˏüng, a college or gymnasium, where government pupils were taught.

癰 ˏYung. A swelling, a boil, a sore; an ulcer, an abscess; a running sore: ²⁰pwoi² ˏüng, a carbuncle on the

¹紛紜 ²芸香 ³芸窓 ⁴芸生 ⁵聽聞 ⁶不忍聞 ⁷鼻聞 ⁸風聞 ⁹耳聞 ¹⁰新聞 ¹¹新聞紙 ¹²殷周之季 ¹³殷實戶 ¹⁴慇懃 ¹⁵雍和 ¹⁶雍正 ¹⁷雍正進士 ¹⁸雝和 ¹⁹辟廱 ²⁰背癰

back; *chong'* *ˏüng*, to suck a sore—a lickspittle; *ˏüng ˏchü*, a deep, sluggish ulcer.

臃 ʻYung. Also read *ëüng'*: to swell; puffed, swollen: *ˏüng ʻchüng*, to swell up, as the flesh; swollen, pursy.

饔 ʻYung. Dressed food; to prepare food; an early meal, breakfast: [1]*ˏüng ˏing*, a cook; [2]*ˏüng ˏch'wang*, breakfast and supper; [3]*ˏüng ˏch'wang pok, kie'* the meals not continuing—too poor to have regular meals.

允 ʻ**允** ʻYün. Jun. Yu. To permit, to assent, to promise, to accede to; allowed, permitted; really, truly, honestly, sincerely: [4]*ʻüng ʻchung*, to grant, granted it; [5]*eng' ʻüng*, permission given; [6]*pok, ʻüng*, not allowed; [7]*ʻüng yok,* sincere; COM., *ʻüng nok,* to assent readily to.

狁 ʻYün. A tribe of Huns or Scythians, called [8]*ʻHiéng ʻüng*, who troubled the emperors of the Chow dynasty.

尹 ʻYin. To hold, to rule, to govern; to advance; true, faithful; a surname: [9]*ʻüng chié'* dried meat for sacrifices; [10]*ʻhu ʻüng*, the mayor of Peking; COM., [11]*ˏI ʻüng*, a famous statesman of the Shang dynasty, who died B. C. 1713.

忍 ʻJên. To bear, to endure, to suffer patiently; patience, endurance; able to sustain, fortitude; wrathful, hard, harsh, severe, hardhearted: used for *ʻnung* in the coll. q. v.: [12]*ˏhang ʻüng*, to curb or repress feeling; COM., [13]*ʻüng nai'* patient; [14]*ʻüng k'e' ˏt'ong ˏsing*, to curb resentment and refrain from speaking; [15]*ʻüng ük, pó' ˏsiu*, to bear disgrace in order to take revenge; *ˏüng ˏsing hai' ʻli*, severity violates reason; COLL., *ʻüng má' kwo'* unable to endure it.

涊 ʻJên. A stream in the south-east of Shansi. Read *ʻniéng*: dirty water; muddy, filthy; scurf from perspiration; beastly drunk.

甬 ʻYung. Bursting, budding, as plants; bubbling, as a fountain; a measure of ten *ʻtau* or pecks; common, constant: *ʻüng tó'* a raised path to the hall, a covered way, as for the emperor.

俑 ʻYung. A human puppet with springs; an effigy formerly buried with the dead: *chauk, ʻüng*, an inventor of what is injurious.

勇 ʻYung. Ying. Strong, brawny; brave, fearless, intrepid, daring; courage; to advance boldly, to resist manfully: [16]*ʻüng ʻmeng*, valorous; [17]*tai' ʻüng* true bravery; [18]*ʻsieu ʻüng*, false courage, mere passion; [19]*ʻüng sëü'* a hero; [20]*ʻüng ʻkang*, rash; [21]*hong' ʻüng*, ardent courage, impetuosity; COM., *ʻüng lik,* very strong, vigorous; *ˏhiong ʻüng*, village braves; *ʻüng pok, ʻk'ó ˏtong*, irresistibly brave; *ʻiu ʻüng ˏu ˏmeu*, is brave, but no tactician!

慂 ʻYung. To urge, to inspirit; *ʻsung ʻüng*, to exhort, to stir up or instigate one.

---

[1] 饔人 [2] 饔飧 [3] 饔餐不繼 [4] 允准 [5] 應允 [6] 不允 [7] 允若 [8] 玁狁 [9] 尹祭 [10] 府尹 [11] 伊尹 [12] 含忍 [13] 忍耐 [14] 忍氣吞聲 [15] 忍辱報仇 [16] 勇猛 [17] 大勇 [18] 小勇 [19] 勇士 [20] 勇敢 [21] [illegible]勇

蛹 Yung. ʻ The chrysalis of the silkworm; a pupa, an aurelia: *ʻkiéng ʻüng*, the chrysalis in a cocoon; *ʻtʻu ʻüng*, a singing grub.

衕 Yung. ʻ A lane, an alley in a town; a path leading to a stairway: *ʻüng tóʾ* a street or way.

踴 踊 Yung. ʻ To jump, to leap for joy, to exult; to stamp, to leap in an excited manner: [1]*ʻüng yok,* to skip for joy; [2]*pʻek, ʻüng*, to beat the breast and stamp for sorrow.

隱 隠 㐆 Yin. ʻ Small, minute; secret; covered, hidden, put away; retired; privacy, in private life; obscure, abstruse; to retire, to withdraw; fixed, settled; in pain, sad, sorry; to pity, to compassionate; to hang the head, as embarrassed; abundant: [3]*ʻüng ˏchong*, to hide, to secrete; [4]*ʻüng ʻngü*, ambiguous words, innuendo; [5]*ʻüng ˏmi*, abstruse; [6]*ʻüng söü²* a retired officer; [7]*ʻüng muk,* obscure, unknown; to hide, as from arrest; *ʻüng ʻüng*, troubled; full, abundant; COM., [8]*ʻüng ˏkü*, to retire to private life.

癮 Yin. ʻ A pimple, a boil, an eruption, blisters: used for the coll. *ngiéng²* q. v.: *ʻüng ʻching*, small sores, pustules.

檃 Yin. ʻ The hidden framework of a roof; an instrument for adjusting things: *ʻüng kwak*, machines for straightening and squaring wood.

匀 Yün. ˏ Equal, even, alike, equally; to divide alike, to equalize; few, a little: [9]*ˏking ˏüng*, divided equally; COLL., *ˏüng ˏseu*, to apportion evenly; *ˏüng ˏsang aʾ* or [10]*ˏüng ˏsang hongʾ* to divide into three equal parts.

畇 Yün. ˏ Land laid out in plats or fields for cultivation; to till land.

筠 Yün. ˏ The tough skin of the bamboo, called *tëük, ˏüng*, which contains silex.

戎 Jung. ˏ A weapon, arms, warlike implements; soldiers; military; a war chariot; large, great; thou, you; to assist; to pluck out; an ancient region in the N. W. of Yunnan: [11]*ʻngu ˏüng*, the five kinds of weapons; [12]*ˏüng ˏping*, military weapons; soldiers; [13]*ˏüng ˏhong*, troops in line, the army; [14]*ˏngwong ˏüng*, a general; [15]*ek, ˏüng ˏi*, (as easy as putting on) a suit of armor; [16]*ˏüng tik,* tribes in Turfan.

絨 Jung. ˏ Fine cloth; sometimes used for woolens; floss, fine silk; velvet; the nap of cloth; *met.*, down, fine hair, feathers; the down or egret of plants: [17]*ʻsieu ˏüng*, flannel; [18]*taiʾ ˏüng*, broadcloth; [19]*ˏsiä ˏüng*, kerseymere; COM., [20]*ʻcheng ˏüng*, a thick sort of velvet; [21]*ˏüng siüngʾ* floss; [22]*chak, ˏüng*, to make artificial flowers of velvet; [23]*ˏüng cheʾ* words of velvet, as on scrolls; *ˏüng ˏkié*, or *ˏüng ˏmó ˏkié*, a

1 踴躍 2 擗踊 3 隱藏 4 隱語 5 隱微 6 隱士 7 隱沒 8 隱居 9 均匀 10 匀三 11 五戎 12 戎戎 13 兵戎 14 元戎 15 一戎衣 16 戎狄 17 小絨 18 大絨 19 斜絨 20 剪絨 21 絨線 22 紮絨 23 絨字

species of fowl with a velvety coat of white feathers.

容 ˛Jung. Yung. Feeling or manner in receiving; to receive kindly; to bear with, to tolerate; to suffer, to allow one in; face, countenance, looks, air, manner; easy, unconstrained; perfumed amulets; a screen, as for archers; [1]˛*hang* ˛*ŭng*, to contain; patient, generous; [2]˛*hwa* ˛*ŭng*, pretty, as a girl; [3]*ch'ieu'* ˛*ŭng*, simpering, smirking; [4]*sek*˛ ˛*ŭng*, to blush, disconcerted; COM., [5]˛*ŭng mau'* the face, figure, form; [6]'*hi* ˛*ŭng*, a portrait; [7]˛*ŭng mau'* '*ching* ˛*chá*, a pretty face; [8]˛*k'wang* ˛*ŭng* or ˛*ŭng sëŭ'* to be lenient, indulgent; [9]˛*ŭng chëŭng'* ˛*sŭ ŭk*˛ to give the rein to lusts; [10]˛*t'ung* ˛*ŭng*, to treat generously; [11]˛*ŭng e'* easy, not hard; ˛*ch'ŭng* ˛*ŭng* '*kwi nik*˛ to allow a few days more; COLL., *ng'* ˛*ŭng* ˛*i*, not suffer him to.

榕 ˛Jung. Yung. The bastard banian (ficus indicus), called [12]˛*sŭng ch'eu'* in the coll. q. v.: it is worshiped for longevity and sometimes has shrines built among its branches: COM., [13]˛*ŭng* ˛*siăng*, the banian-city, Foochow; [14]˛*ŭng* ˛*k'iong*, the Foochow patois.

溶 ˛Jung. Yung. Full and flowing gently, as water between its banks; to fill; an easy, leisurely manner.

蓉 ˛Jung. Yung The Hibiscus: COM., ˛*hu* ˛*ŭng*, the hibiscus mutabilis.

茸 ˛Jung. Plants growing thick and luxuriantly; collected, thick together: ˛*mung* ˛*ŭng*, confused; indistinct utterance: COM., *lëk*˛ ˛*ŭng*, hartshorn; ˛*ŭng p'iëng'* the shavings of deer's horn.

鎔 ˛Jung. Yung. To smelt, to fuse metals; to cast, to forge; a mold or matrix in which metal is cast; die for coining; to influence, to transform, as by doctrine: used for the coll. ˛*yong*, q. v.: ˛*ŭng hwa'* to melt, to fuse.

鏞 ˛Yung. A large bell.

庸 ˛Yung. To employ, as servants; constant, usual, ordinary; meritorious; toilsome, laborious; harmonious; kind, cordial, accommodating; rude, plebeian; taxes, revenue: [15]˛*ŭng* ˛*hu sŭk*˛ '*chŭ*, common people; [16]˛*ŭng* ˛*ing*, a mediocre; [17]˛*u* ˛*ŭng*, no need of, unnecessary; [18]˛*ŭng* ˛*chai*, ordinary talent; [19]˛*ping* ˛*ŭng*, common, inferior; ˛*teng* ˛*ŭng*, to attain office; COM., ˛*tŭng* ˛*ŭng*, the Doctrine of the Mean—one of the Four Books.

傭 ˛Yung. To hire, to engage one's self to work, to serve for wages; hired, employed; in the following senses, read ˛*chŭng* and '*chŭng* in the dictionaries; equal, impartial; of the same rank; to treat alike; to use, to do: [20]˛*ka* ˛*ŭng*, domestics; *mâ'* *ch'ai'* ˛*ŭng*, a green-grocer; COM., [21]˛*ŭng* ˛*këng*, engaged as a laborer.

[1] 涵容 [2] 花容 [3] 笑容 [4] 失容 [5] 容貌 [6] 喜容 [7] 容貌 整齊 [8] 寬容 [9] 容縱 私慾 [10] 通容 [11] 容易 [12] 榕樸 [13] 榕城 [14] 榕腔 [15] 庸夫俗子 [16] 庸人 [17] 毋庸 [18] 庸才 [19] 平庸 [20] 家傭 [21] 傭工

墉 ꜀Yung. A wall, a rampart; a redoubt, a small citadel; a mud wall; to build adobe walls; the northern wall of a hall.

慵 ꜀Yung, Jung. Lazy, indolent; dilatory, remiss, careless: [1]*꜁su ꜀üng*, lazy, negligent.

鄘 ꜀Yung. The capital of Chowsin, B. C. 1154; a small feudatory of the Chow dynasty, now the Weihui prefecture in the N. E. of Honan; a place among the southern barbarians.

彤 ꜀Yung. A daily or continual sacrifice, as to ancestors; to worship or sacrifice daily: [2]*꜀Üng ꜀ngü se꜄* a concubine of Hwangti. Read *꜀t'ing:* a boat sailing along.

融 蝠 ꜀Yung. Jung. The steam of melted things, vapor rising; melted, liquefied; blending, mixing, harmonizing; high and large; clear, bright, intelligent: [3]*꜀üng ꜀hwo*, blending; genial, as temperature; [4]*꜀üng hwoi꜄ kwang꜄ ꜀t'ung*, to comprehend fully, well versed in it.

(906) Wa.

劃 ꜀Hua. Ho. Read *hek꜆;* used for the coll. *꜀wa:* to mark or cut with a knife; to cut open; to cut glass: [5]*꜀wa ꜂pwo*, to cut out (an old piece) and insert(a new one), to revise or counterfeit, as by changing a word; [6]*꜀wa sioh꜆ tói꜄* to cut off a piece; [7]*꜀wa pok꜆ ꜀tong*, to rip open the intestines.

呱 ꜀Kua. Ku. Also read *꜀ku:* to cry out, as children do, to babble: [8]*꜀wa ꜀wa ꜀i k'ek꜆* to cry and scream: COLL., *꜀wa ꜀wa*, to utter inarticulate sounds; to babble, as a child in play with the hand on the mouth.

哇 ꜀Wa. Words of flattery, affected sounds; wanton, lascivious music; to spue, to vomit, to retch; to whine, to drone.

娃 ꜀Wa. A beautiful woman, a pretty girl, a beauty. Read *꜀ki:* deep sunken, as the eyes.

蛙 鼃 ꜀Wa. Wai. A frog, green and striped, with a line down the back; also wanton sounds: [9]*no꜄ ꜀wa*, the enraged frog, as mentioned in an ancient story; [10]*꜂ching ꜂ti ꜀wa*, a frog in a well; *met.*, inexperienced.

搲 ꜀Wa. To clutch, to grasp and haul; to claw, to scratch into pieces; to grapple, to grab at; to seize a handful of.

窊 ꜀Wa. A depression, a cavity, a puddle, a low muddy spot; the bottom of water; a hoof-print: [11]*꜀wa ꜀lüng*, low and high; contemptible and exalted.

窪 ꜀Wa. A deep ditch; a puddle, dirty water collected, as in footsteps; also deep, clear water: [12]*꜂ti ꜀wa*, a low spot or puddle.

騧 ꜀Kua. A yellowish or cream-colored horse with a black mouth: [13]*Kié꜄ ꜀wa*, one of eight brothers, an able

---

[1]疏慵○ [2]彤魚氏○ [3]融和 [4]融會貫通 [5]劃補 [6]劃一塊○ [7]劃腹腸○ [8]呱呱而泣 [9]怒蛙 [10]井底蛙 [11]窊隆○ [12]低窪 [13]季騧

statesman in the Chow dynasty.

ʻ *Wa.* A coll. word: to turn aside, to call at on one's way: *ʻwa ˏpiéng*, to go aside, to avoid; *ʻwa ʻmu ˏnëng chʻioʼ* to stop at a certain person's house; *ˏá ʻwa*, to loiter about, to stop here and there; *ʻwa tak,* to borrow everywhere and not return or pay back; *ˏhwa hwoïʼ ˏsang sek, lëk, ʻwa*, the lottery has 36 changes; *met.*, uncertain, indefinite.

Waʼ. A coll. word: brisk, flourishing, as trade: *waʼ chiăh, waʼ* very busy, as a market; *waʼ chʻeʼ máʼ ˏmó ˏchiéng*, a brisk trade, but no profits.

划 ˏ Hua. Read *ˏhwa;* coll. *ˏwa:* to sweep, to brush aside, as with the hand; to paddle: *ˏwa ˏkʻwi*, to brush aside; *ˏpa siék, ˏtó ʻchwi ʻlú ˏwa*, put the paddles in the water and paddle away!

話ʼ Hua. Words, discourse; speech, language; to talk, to converse; to tell, to narrate; able to speak well; to clamor; to put to shame; to regulate: COM., [1]*ʻkong waʼ* to speak, to talk; [2]*waʼ ˏtʻau*, initial phrases, by-words; [3]*ˏpui waʼ* to confess one's wrong; [4]*ʻtʻu waʼ* or *ˏpang waʼ* the colloquial; [5]*waʼ eʼ* the import of what is said; [6]*waʼ siok,* it is said—a phrase in colloquial books; [7]*ˏtó waʼ* (coll. *ˏtó waʼ ˏsó*), talkative; [8]*ʻtwaiʼ waʼ* bragging; [9]*ˏhui waʼ* to return a verbal answer; COLL., *waʼ ˏkʻa* or *waʼ pʻongʼ* a clue or inkling from one's words; [10]*waʼ ʻkong ˏhang ˏhu*, to talk confusedly; *ˏkwang waʼ ngʼ kauʼ ʻtʻu ˏkʻiong chʻaiʼ* if you don't know enough of the mandarin, eke out with the patois.

畫ʼ 畫ʼ 画ʼ Hua. Ho. To draw, to mark; to paint pictures; to map, to mark out a plan of; a picture, a drawing, a painting: the 2d also read *hek,* q. v.: COM., [11]*waʼ ˏsü*, one who sketches or paints, an artist; [12]*waʼ chʻiongʼ* a worker in stucco or plaster figures, as on walls; [13]*tangʼ waʼ* and *ʻchʻai waʼ* ink sketches and colored paintings; [14]*waʼ hóʼ* or [15]*waʼ ˏhwa ak,* to sign one's private mark or designation; [16]*waʼ ʻmi ˏing*, to paint a beauty; [17]*waʼ ʻing ˏtu ˏhing*, to sketch the picture, as of a thief or a runaway; [18]*waʼ ʻpiăng ˏnang ˏchʻüng ˏki*, picturing out cakes can not satisfy hunger; *met.*, a pressing need, insufficient, unreliable; COLL., *sioh, hok, waʼ* a picture.

(907) **Wah.**

豰, Read *huk,;* used in the *Paik, ˏIng* for the coll. *wah,:* to grunt, as swine: *wah, wah, kieuʼ* to grunt, to squeal; *ˏwa wah,* grunting; the sound used in calling pigs; *met.*, a hog, a pig.

畫, Hua. Ho. Read *hek,;* coll. *wah,:* a mark, a line; strokes of the pencil; to mark, to draw a line, to line off: [19]*wah, sioh, wah,* to make one mark or stroke; *wah, sioh, ˏhwang*, to make a horizontal stroke; *wah, ʻla yongʼ* to

[1]講話 [2]話頭 [3]賠話 [4]土話 [5]話意 [6]話說 [7]多話 [8]大話 [9]回話 [10]話講 含糊 [11]畫師 [12]畫匠 [13]淡畫 [14]畫號 [15]畫花押 [16]畫美人 [17]畫影圖形 [18]畫餅難充饑 [19]畫一畫

sketch a pattern of; *wah₂ sioh₂ pek,* to make a mark with the pencil; *ih₂ wah₂* to make strokes; to write hastily, to scribble off.

(908) Wai.

歪 ꜀Wai. Out of perpendicular, aslant, awry, askew; crooked, distorted; wicked, depraved; as a verb in the coll. to extort from, to squeeze one: COM., ¹꜀*wai* ꜁*sià*, depraved, corrupt; ²꜀*wai ch'oi'* a wry mouth; COLL., ³꜀*wai pwang'* ꜀*peng* (or ꜁*peng*), aslant on one side, as a house; COLL., ⁴꜀*wai* ꜀*t'au* ꜀*wai* ꜂*nó*, "wry head and brains"; *met.*, very crooked, all askew; ꜀*wai* ꜁*nëng* ꜀*chiéng*, to squeeze money, as by threats or false pretences; to shirk a debt rascally; ꜀*wai sioh₂ to'* (or *tiong'*), to extort a sum (of money).

꜀*Wai.* A coll. word: a country brogue for ꜀*ai*, as in ꜀*wai* ꜀*a*, or ꜀*wai* ꜁*ó*, (or *wai'* ꜀*a* and *wai'* ꜁*ó*), an exclamation of wonder, astonishment, etc.; ꜀*wai a'* a term of intense astonishment, ah, most wonderful!

(909) Wak.

窊 Wa. To hollow out a cavity in the ground, to feel in a hole; a hole, a deep hollow, as in a hill; large and hollow.

挖 Wa. To dig out, to excavate; to gouge, to scoop out, to dredge; to scratch: COM., ⁵*wak*, ꜁*mwong*, to scratch or claw the door; ⁶*wak, ngau'* to dig up lotus roots with the hand; ⁷*wak, nük₂* ꜀*i* ꜀*ch'ong*, to gouge out flesh to heal an ulcer; *met.*, to have only the labor for the pains, to borrow of one to pay to another; COLL., *wak,* ꜀*seu*, to search everywhere; *wak, k'aëng'* to "dig a hole"; *met.*, very, excessively, as in *wak, k'aëng'* ꜀*ki* ꜁*ngai*, very bad, exceedingly wicked! *wak, sioh₂ meng'* the whole face scratched; ꜁*pa* ꜀*t'au wak, nge'* to scratch the head and ears, as in deep thought.

曰 Yüeh. ² To speak, to say, to declare; to speak of, to denominate; called, termed, designated; the 73d radical: also read *wok,* q. v.: ⁸*tói' wak₂* he answered, saying; ⁹*chü wak₂* Confucius said; ¹⁰*ek, wak₂* one says; one is called, as in a list.

活 Huo, Ho. ² A river in the southeast of Shansi; living, moving; life, motion; lively, active, bustling; cheerful; to vivify: also read *kwak,* q. v.: ¹¹*wak, kie'* an employment, means of living; ¹²*pok,* ꜀*ti* ꜂*sü wak₂* careless of life; heedless, unconcerned, as children; COM., ¹³*wak₂ miàng'* life; ¹⁴*wak₂ tong'* sprightly, quick, handy; ¹⁵*wak₂ taëng'* lively, free and easy, good, as one's credit, trade, or improved prospects; ¹⁶*wak₂* ꜂*pó*, available treasure, as money; ¹⁷*wak₂ che'* a verb; ¹⁸*wak₂ huk₂* a living Budh, the Lama; *met.*, a prognosticator, one shrewd at guessing; also tame, kind; ¹⁹*wak₂ t'wak,* active, bustling; also quick in perception; easy, flowing, as one's style; COLL., ²⁰*k'a' wak₂* lively, in good health and spirits; *wak₂ t'ieu' t'ieu'* spry, stirring; ꜂*nü* ꜂*yà*

1 歪斜 2 歪嘴 3 歪半爿〇 4 歪頭歪腦 5 挖門 6 挖藕 7 挖肉醫瘡 8 對曰 9 子曰 10 一曰 11 活計 12 不知死活 13 活命 14 活動 15 活動 16 活寶 17 活字 18 活佛 19 活脫 20 快活

wak, you are very smart, as said to a braggart; *po' wak*, to revive, as plants or one near death; resurrection.

襪 韤 Wa. Stockings, socks, hose: COM., [1]*,tang wak*, stockings of a single thickness; [2]*kak, wak*, lined hose; [3]*,miéng wak*, quilted socks; [4]*wak, tai'* garters; [5]*wak, ,kong*, a loop on the bottom of a stocking to suspend by; COLL., *wak, kiék*, the "cheeks" or side pieces on the foot of a stocking; *wak, hong'* the legs of stockings; *wak, 't'ëng*, the inside of the legs, as for thrusting things into.

(910) Wang.

彎 ,Wan. To draw a bow; to bend, to curve; bent, bowed, curved; to turn: [6]*,wang ,küng*, to draw the bow; COM., *,wang ,wang*, bent, crooked; [7]*,wang ,tó*, a wood-cleaver; COLL., *,wang ch'ong'* crooked, twisted; *met.*, a business not well done; *'tiong ,wang ,t'au*, the place to turn, the corner; *'a ,wang*, to bend, to make crooked; *,wang 'tié*, to turn and enter, as a street.

灣 ,Wan. A curved shore; a cove, a bay; a low beach; to anchor, to moor; an anchorage: used for the coll. *,wang*, q. v.: [8]*,sa ,wang*, a low, sandy beach; COM., [9]*,tai ,wang* (coll. *,tai ,wang*), Formosa.

挽 'Wan. To draw a bow; to lead, to conduct; to take, to carry in the hand; to bring back, to restore to a good state: [10]*'wang ,toi ,hung*, to reform degenerate manners; *'wang k'eu'* to lay the hand on the bier, as anciently done; to drag a hearse; COM., [11]*'wang ,huí* or *'wang 'tiong*, to reform, to bring again to a good state; [12]*'wang ,huí ,t'iéng e'* to induce Heaven's favorable will; COLL., *'wang ,t'au hwok,* to wind the cue (about the head).

輓 'Wan. Similar to the last: to pull, to drag, as a carriage or hearse; the cords to draw a bier: *'wang ,kó*, songs of the hearse-men; COM., *'wang ,liéng*, funeral scrolls, as hung in the hall.

晚 'Wan. Decline of the sun, evening, night; *met.*, late in life; late, tardy, afterwards: used for the coll. *'mwong*, q. v.: [13]*yä' 'wang*, late at night; [14]*'wang ,niéng*, aged; [15]*'wang ,hwo*, the last crop of rice; [16]*hwoi' ,chi 'i 'wang*, too late to repent; COM., [17]*'wang 'ku*, the evening drum; [18]*'wang 'king*, evening prospect; *met.*, the condition of the aged; [19]*'wang pwoi'* juniors; [20]*'wang ,seng*, I, your junior; *'wang 'chü*, the child of one's old age; *'cha 'wang*, morning and evening; *'wang ,ch'wang*, supper; *,siong kiéng' haung' 'wang*, I deeply regret that I did not know you before.

捥 腕 'Wan. The wrist; to grasp with the hand, to grasp and twist, to wrench; to seize and carry: [21]*'ch'iu 'wang* (coll. *'ch'iu 'kwang*), the wrist, the fore-arm.

---

[1]單襪 [2]夾襪 [3]棉襪 [4]襪帶 [5]襪根 [6]彎弓 [7]彎刀 [8]沙灣 [9]臺灣 [10]挽頹風 [11]挽回〇 [12]挽回天意 [13]夜晚 [14]晚年 [15]晚禾 [16]悔之已晚 [17]晚鼓 [18]晚景 [19]晚輩 [20]晚生 [21]手腕

ʻ剜 Wan. Wa. To pare, to cut off; to scrape: ¹ʻ*wang nŭk*, ˏ*i* ˏ*ch'ong*, to cut out a piece of flesh to cure a boil—to cause the greater injury or trouble.

ʻ婉 Yüan. ʻ娩 Wan. Mien. Docile, yielding, obedient; soft, winning, complaisant; youthful, beautiful: the 2d also read ʻ*miéng*, q. v.: ²ʻ*wi* ʻ*wang*, soft and winning, easy, gentle; ³ʻ*wang* ˏ*ŭng*, kind and obliging.

ʻ宛 Yüan. Wan. To screen one's self in the grass; to yield, obliging, accommodating, in which senses the same as the preceding: ⁴ʻ*wang* ˏ*yong*, as if, according to; ⁵ʻ*wang* ʻ*tiong*, to accommodate one's self to circumstances; the warbling of birds, harmonious music. Read ʻ*wong*: small, delicate.

ʻ惋 Yüan. To be alarmed and irritated; to dislike, to hate, to be dissatisfied with.

ʻ琬 Yüan. A round or oval tablet or scepter of jade or gem, given to princes—emblematic of perfect virtue and harmony.

ʻ碗 ʻ盌 ʻ椀 Wan. A bowl, a dish; a bowlful: COM., ⁶ʻ*wang ch'ai*ʼ dishes of food; ⁷ʻ*wang* ˏ*kó*, steamed bread-cakes of rice-batter; ⁸ʻ*wang* ˏ*kong*, a sort of large bowl; ⁹ˏ*k'wo* ˏ*tiong* ʻ*wang*, the bowls used (by students) at examinations—are of a small size; COLL., ¹⁰*pwong*ʼ ʻ*wang*, bowls to eat rice from; ʻ*wang* ˏ*peng* ˏ*hu*, pulverized crockery; ¹¹*p'wai*ʼ ʻ*wang chó*ʼ *ch'oi*ʼ to break a bowl and take an oath.

ʻ菀 Yüan. Yü. Also read *ok*ˎ: luxuriant, abundant, flourishing: also used for ʻ*wong* (a pasture, a park): ¹²ʻ*chié* ʻ*wang*, a red, tough root, used as an expectorant.

ʻ莞 Huan. Kuan. To seem pleased: ¹³ʻ*wang* ʻ*i*, to smile, to look pleased. Read ˏ*hwang*: a species of coarse grass for weaving into mats. Read ʻ*kwang*, as in ¹⁴ˏ*Tung* ʻ*kwang*, a district in Kwangtung east of the Pearl river, near the Bogue.

ʻ浣 Huan. Read ʻ*ngwang* in the dictionaries: to cleanse in water, to wash; to bathe; a decade of days: ¹⁵ʻ*wang* ˏ*i*, to wash one's clothes; COM., ¹⁶*siong*ʼ ʻ*wang*, ¹⁷ˏ*tŭng* ʻ*wang*, and ¹⁸*ha*ʼ ʻ*wang*, the three decades of a month—terms used in letters.

ʻ睆 Wan. Read ʻ*ngwang* in the dictionaries: bright, brilliant, as a star; true, real; large, lustrous, rolling, as the eyes; nicely pared, made smooth and neat; finely molded; to look about, to see clearly; to soothe, to coax, to wheedle.

ʻ綄 Huan. To wrap around, to tie up, to bind. Read ˏ*hwang*: a vane, a weather-cock.

1 剜肉	2 委婉	4 宛然	6 碗菜	8 碗缸	9 科場	10 飯碗	詛嘴	13 莞爾	15 浣衣	17 中浣	18 下浣
醫瘡	3 婉容	5 宛轉	7 碗糕	○	碗○	11 破碗	12 紫菀	14 東莞	16 上浣	○	○

綰 ʻ Wan. Like the last: to tie, to fasten, to bind; to hold, to keep securely; to sew, to hem; bad, evil: also read ʻ*kwang*, q. v.

玩 ˛ Wan. Read *ngwang*^{2}; used for the coll. ˛*wang*: to ramble: [1]˛*wang* ʻ*swa*, to recreate, to divert one's self; [2]*kʻó*˒ ˛*wang*, to go rambling; ˛*wang chak*˒ roving all about; ˛*wang sioh*$_2$ ˛*lau*, to take a ramble.

灣 ˛ Wan. Read ˛*wang*; coll. ˛*wang*: a turn, a curve or bend, as in a river: ˛*wang* ʻ*tiê* ˛*chiu* ˛*piéng*, the names of two localities on the north bank of the Min; ˛*tai* ˛*wang*, Formosa.

換^2 **換**^{2} Huan. To change, to exchange; to commute, to interchange; to barter; to move from one place to another: COM., [3]*wang*^{2} *tʻá*˒ to act as a substitute, to work in another's place; [4]*wang*^{2} ʻ*chʻiu*, to change to the other hand; to get other workmen; [5]*wang*^{2} ˛*mwong*, to change to another employment; [6]*wang*^{2} *siăh*$_2$ to work for one's food only; [7]*tói*˒ *wang*^{2} to barter; [8]*wang*^{2} ˛*hwang*, to exchange dollars; [9]*wang*^{2} ˛*i* ˛*siong*, to change one's dress; [10]ʻ*kai wang*^{2} to alter, to make in another form or style; [11]*wang*^{2} *tʻaik*˒ ˛*hing tá*^{2} sworn friends; [12]˛*king pok*˒ *wang*^{2} "for gold not change it"—name of a variety of Chinese pencil; also a medicine made of old excrement; COLL., *wang*^{2} *kwo*˒ ˛*peng*, to change to the other side; to change, as shoes from one foot to the other.

萬^2 **万**^{2} Wan. Bees swarming in numbers; a myriad, ten thousand, the highest number commonly used in notation; all, many, an indefinite, large number; as a superlative, very, wholly, great, exalted: *wang*^{2} ʻ*u*, a kind of posture-making; COM., [13]˛*chʻiéng wang*^{2} a thousand myriads, ten millions; *met.*, most positively; [14]*wang*^{2} *ek*˒ one in a myriad, a mere chance, a bare possibility; [15]*wang*^{2} *kwok*˒ all countries; [16]*wang*^{2} *seu*^{2} the emperor's birthday; [17]*wang*^{2} *haing*^{2} a myriad lucks—an epistolary phrase; [18]*wang*^{2} *swoi*˒ ˛*ié*, the sire of a myriad years—the emperor; [19]*wang*^{2} ˛*niéng* ˛*sūng*, a species of long-lived dwarf-fir; *met.*, a dwarf; *wang*^{2} *pok*˒ ʻ*kʻó*, positively ought not; *wang*^{2} ˛*u ek*˒ *sek*˒ "in a myriad not lose one"—no failure, all coming out right; *wang*^{2} *pok*˒ *taik*˒ ʻ*i*, it must be, no help for it; *wang*^{2} *pok*˒ *kik*$_2$ *ek*˒ not one can equal him; ˛*chʻiéng* ˛*chʻiéng wang*^{2} *wang*^{2} an innumerable multitude; COLL., *sioh*$_2$ *wang*^{2} 10,000; *sioh*$_2$ *pah*˒ *wang*^{2} one million.

卍^2 Wan. The Indian figure Swastica, called "the myriad character": COM., [20]*wang*^{2} *ché*^{2} ˛*ung*, a sort of Vitruvian scroll of this figure, as in window lattices, or as stamped on paper.

(911) Wi.

威 ˛ Wei. Majesty, official dignity, rigid composure; state, pomp; august, grave; intimidating, overawing: ˛*wi*

---

1 玩耍 2 去玩 3 換替 4 換手 5 換門 6 換食 7 兌換 8 換番 9 換衣裳〇 10 改換 11 換帖兄弟 12 金不換 13 千萬〇 14 萬一 15 萬國 16 萬壽 17 萬幸 18 萬歲爺〇 19 萬年松〇 20 卍字文〇

‘*meng*, ferocious; COM., [1]˛*wi ˛hung*, a majestic bearing, dignity; [2]˛*wi ˛ngiéng*, stern and severe, awe-inspiring; [3]*tiéng ˛wi*, to make a display of power; [4]˛*wi ˛ling ‘hiĕng eng’* grandly efficacious and clearly responsive, as a god; [5]˛*wi ˛ling ˛kung*, a title of ˛*Siŭng ˛hwong*, the municipal guardian; COLL., [6]˛*mó ˛wi*, has no dignity or sternness, as a teacher; ˛*seng ‘tiéng ‘la ˛wi k‘ëŭk*, ‘*nŭ k‘ang’* will first show you my awful power (then you will tremble)!

˛***Wi.*** A coll. word, but rarely used: an exclamation denoting surprise, and uttered with the hands thrown out excitedly.

葳 ˛Wei. Flourishing, luxuriant; full, abundant: ˛*wi ˛wi*, a plant like knot grass, whose roots are sudorific.

蕤 ‘Jui. Pendent twigs or branches, weeping plants, fringed flowers; pendent ends or fringes, as of cap-bands; a flag: [7]˛*wi ˛ping*, a musical note; the 5th moon; ‘*wi ˛wi*, the knot grass, used medicinally.

緌 ˛Wei. Also read ˛*ch‘wi*: the tassel or fringe on a cap; the lappets or throat-bands of caps; female head-pendants; a cow's tail tied on the end of a pole, as a standard.

逶 ˛Wei. Also read ‘*wi*: to walk awry, to reel in walking; crooked, tortuous: [8]˛*wi ˛i*, to reel; to swagger, to strut.

桵 ‘ A low thorny tree or bush, producing fruit like an ear-pendant; a hazel-nut or filbert?

卉 ‘Hui. A general term for plants; herbs, plants, vegetables: [9]‘*wi muk*˛ herbs and trees, plants.

唯 ‘Wei. To answer smartly, to echo, as in answering; an answer in the affirmative, yes! also read ˛*mi*, q. v.: ‘*wi ‘wi*, aye, aye! yes, yes! [10]‘*wi ˛i ‘k‘i*, to answer and come quickly.

虺 Hui. A large snake, with a huge head and small neck: also read ˛*hwi*, q. v.: [11]‘*chwi ‘wi*, a sea-serpent; [12]*kok*˛ ‘*wi*, an adder, a large snake; [13]˛*wong ‘wi*, an enormous serpent; [14]*Tŭng*’ ‘*wi*, a noted statesman of the Shang dynasty.

偉 ‘Wei. Great, rare, extraordinary: [15]*chong*’ ‘*wi*, a brave man, a hero; [16]˛*ki ‘wi*, remarkable, curious.

煒 ‘Wei. A blazing fire; light, bright, glowing; a flaming red color; lurid, brilliant, as flames.

瑋 ‘Wei. A red-colored gem; a rarity, precious things, curious gems.

韡 ‘Wei. Full of leaves and flowers, luxuriant, flourishing; showy, splendid.

韙 ‘Wei. Right, correct, proper; to show the right, to throw light on a subject: [17]*pok*˛ ‘*wi*, an impropriety.

[1]威風 [2]威嚴 [3]展威 [4]威靈顯應 [5]威靈公 [6]無威 [7]蕤賓 [8]逶迤 [9]卉木 [10]唯而起 [11]水虺 [12]蝮虺 [13]王虺 [14]仲虺 [15]傀偉 [16]奇偉 [17]不韙

福州方言拼音字典

‘葦 Wei. A large sedge, a reed, a rush: [1]꜀lu ‘wi, sedge, grass used for tying things; [2]ek, ‘wi ꜀hong ꜀chi, crossed (the stream) on one reed.

‘薳 Wei. Yüan. Also read ꜀wi: grass, plants, herbs; a surname: also read ‘wong, q. v.

‘萎 Wei. Leaves falling; dried, withered, blasted, wilted; rotten, decayed, dying: [3]‘wi lok, plants withering; ‘wi ꜀wi, knot grass; a sort of creeping plant, whose roots are used medicinally.

‘委 Wei. To bend under a burden; to bear, to sustain, as an office; to belong to; to send away, to reject; to commit to, to trouble one with; to depute, to delegate; deputed, commissioned on public service; a government storehouse; a wrong, an injustice; the end, the last; indeed, truly: [4]꜀twang ‘wi, robes of ceremony; [5]꜀ngwong ‘wi, first to last, the circumstances; [6]‘wi ꜀chi, to reject it; [7]hong‘ ‘wi, to receive orders, deputed; [8]‘wi eng‘ to bear office; COM., [9]‘wi ꜀wong, a deputed officer; [10]‘wi ꜀pá, the commission or warrant; [11]ngwoi‘ ‘wi, petty military officers (promoted from the cavalry); COLL., [12]‘wi ꜀i k‘ó‘ paing‘ to depute him to manage it; ‘wi k‘ëük, ‘chi sioh, ꜀huí, (bear) the grievance this once! ‘wi sik, ‘kong ꜀li, speak out truly!

‘痿 Wei. Also read ꜀wi: a paralysis of the limbs, caused by dampness; rheumatism, numbness of the extremities; weak, lame, crippled, impotent: [13]‘wi pe‘ a paralysis; [14]꜀ing ‘wi, or [15]꜀yong ‘wi, loss of virility.

‘諉 Wei. To involve, to implicate, to lay the blame on others; to apologize and decline repeatedly; to shirk the trouble, to entrust, to give to another to do: [16]꜀ch‘wi ‘wi, to decline, to excuse one's self evasively; [17]‘wi t‘auk, to entrust, to lay on another.

‘餧 Wei. To feed, to give provender to: [18]‘wi sëü‘ to feed; [19]‘wi ꜀ngiu, to feed oxen. Read ‘noi: hungry; putrid fish.

(912) Wí.

倭 Wei. Wo. Yielding: ꜀wi ꜀ti, to come from a distance: also read ꜀wo, q. v.

偎 Wei. To love, attached to, fond of: ꜀wi ꜀ying, to love one devotedly.

喂 Wei. Read ꜀wi in the dictionaries: to fear, to be alarmed; to feed, to give provender, to tend: COM., [20]꜀wi ‘ma (also spoken ꜀wi ‘ma), to feed a horse.

椳 Wei. The projections on the top and bottom of a door, the hinges or pivots on which it turns.

煨 Wei. The fire in a chafing dish; to heat things in a fire; to roast, to cook in embers or ashes: [21]꜀tong ꜀wí, embers, hot ashes for roasting in; COM., [22]꜀wi ꜀kiong, to roast ginger root in ashes; ꜀wi ꜀chieu, scorched or charred in

1 蘆葦 2 一葦航之 3 萎落 4 端委 5 原委 6 委之 7 奉委 8 委任 9 委員 10 委牌 11 外委 12 委伊去辦 13 痿痺 14 陰痿 15 陽痿 16 推諉 17 諉託 18 餧飼 19 餧牛 20 喂馬 21 煻煨 22 煨薑

roasting; COLL., ,wí mwoi'[1] sŭk, not yet roasted done; ,wí 'hwi ,lĕng, to cover (coals) in a hand-stove; to use the hand-stove under (the bed-clothes). Read ok,: a collection of burning coals.

,Wi. A coll. word, like the preceding: to bury, to cover, to secrete; to keep secret: ,wí ,t'u 'tié, to bury or hide in the ground; ,wí 'king 'king, to secrete safely; to keep a matter secret; ,wí ,nui, or ,wí ,wí ,nui ,nui, to spend (money) needlessly; ,wí ,wí aik, aik, to slight in doing, press (the work) through in any way; ,wí ,p'wo, to skulk under the bed-clothes, as in cold mornings.

猥 'Wei. The barking of dogs; a slut that whelps three pups; many, accumulated; mixed, ill assorted; vile, low; rustic; bent, distorted: [1],pi ,wí, low, vulgar; [2]'chak, ,wí, mixed.

隈 渨 ,Wei. A bend or cove in a shore; a winding stream; to sink; the 2d also means foul, dirty: [3]'ó ,wí, a deep bay, a sinuous shore.

洧 'Wei. Occurs in the names of several streams; a small branch of the Han in K'aifêng fu, Honan, at which there was a ford.

賄 'Hui. Wealth, riches; cloths and silks, as constituting one's wealth; to give to others, specifically to bribe; bribes, hush-money: [4]'wí song' to make presents, as a bribe; [5]'wí lo' a bribe; to bribe; [6]'wí chŏk, to bribe; COM., [7]'sêu' 'wí, to take bribes; [8]'wí lo' ,kung ,heng, bribing is a general practice.

鮪 'Wei. A kind of sturgeon of a greenish color, with a small sharp head: [9],wong 'wí, a large species of sturgeon.

(913) Wo.

窠 ,K'o. Read ,k'wo in the dictionaries: empty; a hollow place; a nest in a cave or hollow; a roost of pheasants.

窩 ,Wo. Huo. To dwell in caves; a hole, a grot; a nest on the ground; a bird's nest; a lonely dwelling; met., a den, a rendezvous of robbers: to harbor thieves, to receive plunder; in the coll. convex, arched: used for the coll. 'wo, q. v.: COM., [10],sing ,wo, the hollow on the breast-bone; [11]'cheu ,wo, a bird's nest; [12]ch'ek, ,wo, a den of thieves; [13],wo ,chong, to harbor, to secrete, as thieves or stolen goods; [14],wo ,ka, or [15],wo 'chio, a receiver of plunder; COLL., [16],wo ,cheng, to round (the heads of) needles; ,wo ,wo, convex, swelling out, bulging; [17],wo mek, close from wind, cozy; [18],wo yék, comfortable and convenient, as connected apartments; [19],sing 'lie ,wo, shooting stars.

媧 ,Kua. The Chinese Pandora, called [20]'nü ,wo, who is said to have repaired the heavens; some say she was Eve, others deny that she

---

[1] 卑猥 [2] 雜猥 [3] 隩隈 [4] 賄送 [5] 賄賂 [6] 賄囑 [7] 受賄 [8] 賄賂公行 [9] 紆籲 [10] 心窩 ○ [11] 鳥窩 [12] 賊窩 [13] 窩藏 [14] 窩家 [15] 窩主 ○ [16] 窩針 [17] 窩密 [18] 窩熱 [19] 星離窩 [20] 女媧 ○

福州方言拼音字典

was a woman: COM., ʻnü ˏwo seʼ liéngʼ sioh, ʻpwo ˏtʻiéng, Madam Nü-kwa melted stones to repair the heavens.

渦 ˏWo. Read ˏkʻwo in the dictionaries: an eddy, a whirlpool; a branch of the Huai, which rises in Honan, and flows S. E. into it at Huai-Yüan city, Nganhwui.

萵 ˏWo. A kind of vegetable, called [1]ˏwo kěʼ wild endive, succory, chiccory; lettuce, salad: COLL., [2]ˏwo ˏpu, a kind of smooth-skinned gourd; ˏwo ˏpu ˏtʻoi, a gourd-rind shaver; ˏwo ʻpa chʻaiʼ a kind of spring greens of a bitterish taste; ˏwo ʻsung, the heart of the stalks of such greens, preserved in sugar and ˏchau or red ferment.

蝸 Kua. A snail; a garden slug; poor, low huts, or hovels: [3]ˏwo ˏngiu, a snail, a helix; ˏwo siáʼ a snail-shell of a house.

倭 ˏWo. Wei. Japan: also read ˏwí, q. v.: [4]ˏwo ˏing, the Japanese; [5]ˏwo kʻaiuʼ Japanese marauders; COLL., [6]ˏwo tak, pirates from "the eastern sea" who infested the coasts of Fookien at the close of the Ming dynasty.

ʻ婐 Slender, delicate; a maid servant, a waiting woman: [7]ʻwo ʻngwo, slender and delicate, elegant, as a female.

ʻ窩 Wo. Huo. Used for the coll. ʻwo, as in ʻwo ˏhung, to shelter or screen from the wind; ʻwo sioh, ˏtoi, to huddle together.

盂 ˏYü. Read ˏü in the dictionaries; also read ˏwo, but commonly ˏwo: a basin of wood or metal; a clap-dish, a vessel to contain food or liquids: [8]pwak, ˏwo, a priest's magic basin—commonly called [9]pwak, ˏpwong; COM., [10]ˏwo ˏlang sengʼ hwoiʼ the All-souls festival in the first half of the 7th moon, also at other times in private houses.

芋 Yü. The taro (arum aquaticum): COLL., [11]woʼ ˏtʻau, large taros; [12]woʼ laungʼ small taros; [13]woʼ ˏtʻau ˏting, large round lanterns in the first month; [14]woʼ ʻkwi, steamed cake of taro and rice-starch—sliced up and boiled in oil; [15]woʼ ˏná, taro-pudding, seasoned with sugar and lard; [16]woʼ ˏwang, taro tops, as fed to swine; ngʼ chʻiongʼ ˏló puk, ngʼ chʻiongʼ woʼ neither like carrots nor taros; met., neither one thing nor another, shapeless.

(914) Woh.

沃 Wo. Wu. Read auk,; used for the coll. woh,: to water, to irrigate; wet, moistened, as with rain: [17]woh, chʻaiʼ to water vegetables; [18]kʻeük, ʻü woh, langʼ got wet by the rain; [19]woh, pwongʼ to moisten one's rice, as with tea or broth; [20]woh, siéʼ ˏiu, to sprinkle soy on; woh, sioh, ˏsing, got thoroughly drenched.

1萵苣 2萵瓠 3蝸牛 4倭人 5倭寇 6倭㑩 7婐妠 8鉢盂 9鉢盆 10盂蘭 勝會 11芋頭 12芋蛋 13芋頭 燈 14芋粿 〇 15芋泥 16芋盤 17沃菜 18乞雨 沃 沃濫 19沃飯 20沃豉 油 〇

(915) **Woï.**

嚖ʾ Hui. A low, clear sound; clear and harmonious, as flutes: *woï*ʾ *woï*ʾ *꜀yong*, a sweet melody, as in a concert of instruments.

噦ʾ Hui. Yüeh. A rising of wind or breath; to belch, to eructate; to retch; wind on the stomach; the deep, retired parts of a mansion: *woï*ʾ *woï*ʾ the voices of birds, tinkling of bells, rumbling of a carriage.

濊ʾ Wei. Deep and vast, as an abyss; great, rich, as favors; dirty, turbid; a river in Honan: [1]*꜀wong woï*ʾ many; numerous.

穢ʾ Wei. Weeds or plants growing in disorder; foul, dirty, filthy; lewd, obscene; licentious; to defile, to debauch: [2]*꜀u woï*ʾ overrun with weeds; [3]*꜀sang woï*ʾ to weed; [4]*woï*ʾ *lwang*ʾ lewd disorder; COM., [5]*꜀u woï*ʾ unclean, dirty; morally defiled; [6]*woï*ʾ *k'e*ʾ stench, effluvia; [7]*woï*ʾ *chok*$_2$ filthy, noisome; [8]*woï*ʾ *haik*, menstruous blood; [9]*woï*ʾ *꜀pung*, the lying-in room; [10]*p'ó*ʾ *woï*ʾ to lustrate, as a house after a death; COLL., *t'ie*ʾ *woï*ʾ *hwok*, to shave an infant's head (a month after birth).

翽ʾ Hui. The sound of flying, the clapping of wings, the rushing noise made by a flock of birds; also many, numerous, abundant.

薈ʾ Hui. Kuei. A species of leek or garlic; to overspread, to cover; to screen, to hide, to shelter; to ward off; to rise, as clouds or vapor: used for the coll. *kwoï*ʾ q. v.

蔚ʾ Wei. Yü. Read *oï*ʾ; coll. *woï*ʾ as in *woï*ʾ *woï*ʾ growing luxuriantly, a rank growth; dense foliage.

衛$_2$ **衞**$_2$ Wei. To accompany and protect, to escort; to guard, to defend; to check, as enemies; a military station, an outpost, a frontier town; an ancient feudal state in the south of the modern Chihli: [11]*ho*ʾ *woï*ʾ to protect; [12]*hang woï*ʾ to oppose, to guard against; [13]*woï*ʾ *꜀seng ꜀pó*, a midwife; [14]*se*ʾ *woï*ʾ the imperial guards; COM., [15]*woï*ʾ *'siu pe*ʾ a captain; [16]*woï*ʾ *꜀seng*, life-preserving, as opium-pills; [17]*woï*ʾ *haëng*ʾ a street near the Examination Hall in Foochow.

(916) **Wok.**

兀$_2$ Wu. High and level at the top, a height; to cut off the feet, as a penalty; an interjection, oh! ah! [18]*wok*$_2$ *'chiá*, the maimed; [19]*wok*$_2$ *tek*, alas! how, what!—a theatrical term.

屼$_2$ Wu. Also read *hwok*$_2$: the bare, arid peak of a mountain: [20]*ngu wok*$_2$ a five-peaked mountain in the Chien-wei district in Sz'-chuen.

卼$_2$ Wu. Dangerous, perilous; agitated, disquieted: [21]*ngiék*$_2$ *wok*$_2$ unsteady, as on a giddy height; disturbed, moving about.

---

1 汪濊 2 蕪穢 3 芟穢 4 穢亂 5 汚穢 6 穢氣 7 穢濁 8 穢血 9 穢房 10 破穢 11 護衛 12 捍衛 13 衛生婆 14 侍衛 15 衛守備 16 衛生 17 衛巷 18 兀者 19 兀的 20 五屼 21 鯢卼

抓 Wu.$_2$ To move about, to sway to and fro; to disturb, to shake, to joggle; disquieted, inconstant.

杌 Wu.$_2$ Interchanged with the last two: a stump or trunk without branches; a shoot, a sprout; unsettled, disturbed, discontented: [1]*'tó wok$_2$* perverse; a noted bandit mentioned in the Ch'un Ch'iu; the annals of the Ch'u state.

軏 Yüeh.$_2$ The bar across the front of a carriage by which it is drawn.

刖 Yüeh.$_2$ To cut off the feet at the ankles; to mutilate, to disable from walking.

曰 Yüeh.$_2$ A euphonic initial particle, to direct the attention; now, now then, see, observe: also read *wak$_2$* q. v.: [2]*wok$_2$ yok$_2$* a euphonic term, as used at the commencement of the Shooking.

粵 Yüeh.$_2$ An initial particle, to draw the attention to, now, see, observe, in which senses interchanged with the preceding; in, at; an old name for the south of the Meiling in Kwangtung: [3]*wok$_2$ 'hai ˏkwang*, the hoppo of Canton; COM., [4]*wok$_2$ ˏtung*, the Kwangtung province; [5]*'liong wok$_2$* Kwangtung and Kwangsi; [6]*wok$_2$ 'p'i*, Cantonese thieves.

越 Yüeh.$_2$ To pass over, to overstep; to surpass, to excel; to trespass on, to transgress, to violate, as the rules; to lose, to waste, to scatter; to spread abroad, to publish; far, distant, remote; a sign of the comparative, more; vague, wide of the mark; a hole in a lute; an ancient feudal state in the east of Chehkiang: [7]*wok$_2$ ˏnang*, one of the names of Annam; [8]*wok$_2$ ˏyong*, to publish; [9]*wok$_2$ 'lé*, to overstep propriety; [10]*wok$_2$ oi^3* to usurp a place; COM., [11]*wok$_2$ ˏkang*, or [12]*wok$_2$ ˏch'iong*, to escape from prison; [13]*wok$_2$ ˏkie*, to break the regulations; [14]*wok$_2$ hó^3* to take another cell covertly at the examinations; [15]*wok$_2$ ˏti wok$_2$ 'hó*, the later the better; [16]*Wok$_2$ ˏsang*, a hill in Foochow near the north gate; [17]*Wok$_2$ ˏwong*, a hero of the Han dynasty, worshiped at Foochow.

𧄼 Used in the *Paik$_2$ ˏIng* for the coll. *wok$_2$*: a species of smooth-skinned gourd, like the cucumber or the *ch'aë^3*.

鉞 戉 Yüeh.$_2$ A crescent-like battle-ax; a lictor's ax, as a sign of authority; the star *e* in Gemini and *ps* in Capricorn: *'hu wok$_2$* a long-handled ax.

(917) Wong.

ˏ寃 ˏ冤 Yüan. To force one to crouch; to injure, to abuse, to oppress; wrong, oppression, ill-usage; a grudge, resentment; to implicate, to charge unjustly: [18]*ˏhang ˏwong* or *ˏkang ˏwong*, to bear a grudge, to cherish resentment; COM., [19]*ˏwong k'ok$_2$* or *ˏwong 'wong* (coll. *ˏwong 'kong*), to accuse falsely; [20]*ˏwong ˏk'ieng*, injury, wrong, sudden evil, mishap

[1] 檮杌 [2] 曰若 [3] 粵海關 [4] 粵東 [5] 兩粵 [6] 粵匪 [7] 越南 [8] 越然 [9] 越禮 [10] 越位 [11] 越監 [12] 越墻 [13] 越規 [14] 越號 越好 [15] 越遲 [16] 越山 [17] 越王 [18] 含冤 [19] 冤屈 ○ [20] 冤枉 ○

—regarded as penalty of crime in a former state; [1]*,wong ,siu*, grudge, enmity; [2]*,wong ,ka*, to quarrel, at feud, as brothers; [3]*,wong ,hung* (or *'kwi*), the ghost of the murdered; [4]*,sing ,wong*, to redress a wrong; [5]*'sá ,wong lioh,* "avenge-wrong-manual"—a book used by coroners and criminal judges; [6]*,wong 'sü ,siâng*, the abode in hades of those who have died by wrong; COLL., *,wong chóh*, to charge falsely, to libel.

尢 *Wang.* Having crooked legs, lame, deformed; a hunchback; short and contorted; the 43d radical.

尪 *Wang.* Interchanged with the last: lame, crooked legs; sick, weak, feeble; one who is sick and deformed or emaciated.

汪 *Wang.* Deep and wide; an expanse of water, a lake, a pool; still and clear; vast, large, capacious; the southern sea; a surname: [7]*,wong ,yong*, the vast ocean; [8]*loi' ,wong ,wong*, deep tears in the eyes, tears flowing profusely.

眢 The pupil of the eye injured; the eye not clear; sunken eyes; a well without water.

鴛 *Yüan.* The drake of the mandarin duck: COM., *,wong ,yong*, the mandarin drake and duck (Anas galericulata), an emblem of conjugal love; *met.*, a pair, specifically of nuptial things; [9]*,wong ,yong ,miêng*, a pair of coverlets in one cover; [10]*,wong ,yong piêng'* braid of two colors; [11]*,wong ,yong ,leng*, a pair of ducks, and red and white lilies, as in paintings, etc.

鵷 *Yüan.* A curious bird, perhaps the peacock or Tartar pheasant; it is also described as a phenix found in the south.

,Wong. A coll. word, as in *,wong tiong'* confused, not perceiving clearly, stupid and not knowing how to do it.

,Wong. A coll. word, as in *,wong ,hing*, a dizziness, dizzy; *,wong ,wong 'tiong*, to swim with dizziness, as the head; *,wong ,t'au laëk, 'nó*, excessively dizzy.

往 徃 *Wang.* To go, to depart; to send by, to send, as a present; past, formerly; frequently: [12]*,hó 'wong*, where are you going? [13]*'wong 'ku*, anciently; COM., [14]*,u 'wong pok, le'* makes profit everywhere and in everything; [15]*,lai 'wong*, going and coming, both ways; friendly intercourse, visits; [16]*'wong nik,* formerly; [17]*'wong ,húi*, the former occasion; [18]*'wong ,king ,kiu ,ming*, to go to the capital to get a degree, as Küjin do; COLL., *'wong 'wong ,chiong wang'* constantly so.

枉 *Wang.* To rule tyrannically, to force, to oppress; bent, crooked, distorted; illegal, unjust; needlessly, of no use whatever: [19]*'wong ka'* bend or humble yourself (to come)—a polite phrase; *'wong ,kü ,ing sié'* to live in the world to no purpose; COM., *,wong 'wong*, or *'wong k'ok*, to accuse unjustly; *'wong*

[1]冤仇 [2]冤家 [3]冤魂 [4]伸冤 [5]洗冤錄 [6]冤死城 [7]汪洋 [8]淚汪汪 [9]鴛鴦綿 [10]鴛鴦辮 [11]鴛鴦蓮 [12]何往 [13]往古 [14]無往不利 [15]來往 [16]往日 [17]往回 [18]往京求名 [19]枉駕

hiĕ' *‚sing* *‚ki*, to lose all one's labor.

‘罔 Wang. Used for the next; a net, entrapped, deceived; stopped, hindered; to impose on, to accuse falsely; deceitful; not, none, nothing; without: *‘wong ‘ku*, nets for hunting and fishing; *‘wong kiéng'* saw nothing of it.

‘網 Wang. A net for fowling or fishing; a net, a web; *met.*, that which binds or restrains, as the law; to net, to catch; to involve, to entangle, to implicate; a haul of a net; in the coll. to twist, to wind: ¹*‘wong ‚ngü*, to catch fish; ²*‚t‘iéng ‘wong*, the government of Heaven, Providence, fate; COM., ³*‘wong ‚küng*, a net-cap, as worn by actors or bald-headed women; ⁴*‚t‘i ‚t‘ü ‘wong*, a spider's web; ⁵*‚t‘iéng ‚ló te' ‘wong*, in a *met.* sense, a close, strong place or apartment; a prison, hades; a net-trap for rats; COLL., ⁶*‘wong ‚kiu*, to wind into a ball; ⁷*‘wong ‚si*, to wind silk; to spin cocoons, as silkworms do; *‘wong ‘ló*, a sort of bamboo market-basket.

‘惘 Wang. Flurried, excited so as to neglect duty: *‘wong ‚yong*, irresolute, not knowing what to do.

‘輞 Wang. A felly, a band or tire about a wheel; the emperor's hunting car had double rims.

‘魍 Wang. A sprite, a gnome, sprites dwelling among rocks and trees: *‘wong ‘liong*, a water-elf, an undine.

‘苑 Yüan. A pasture, a paddock; a park; a palace; occurs in the names of a constellation, a country, and a district: ⁸*nói' ‘wong*, a palace; COM., ⁹*‚küng ‘wong* (coll. *‚küng ‘wong ‘tié*), the imperial apartments, the harem.

‘薳 Yüan. Wei. A kind of medicinal herb, called *‘wong che'*. Also read *‘wi*, q. v.

‘遠 ‘逺 Yüan. Distant, remote, far off, in time or place; to regard as distant: also read *wong'* q. v.: ¹⁰*‘wong k‘aik*, a friend from afar; ¹¹*‘wong ‘ku*, in remote antiquity; ¹²*‚yeu ‘wong*, very far; ¹³*‚niéng ‚ing sié' ‘wong*, many years since, ages ago; COM., ¹⁴*‘ing ‘wong*, eternal, for ever; ¹⁵*‘wong lëü'* to lay plans for the future; ¹⁶*‘wong lié' ‚t‘a ‚hwong*, to "remove to other parts", as said of a bad friend, or in exorcising demons; COLL., ¹⁷*‘wong ‘wang*, troublesome, inconvenient, difficult; *‘wong ‚ch‘ing ‚mó niăh, këüng' ‚ling*, a relative far off is not comparable to a near neighbor!

‘阮 Yüan. Juan. Read *‘ngwang* in the dictionaries: name of a hill; a feudal state in the days of Wan-wang, in the S. E. of the present Kansuh.

‘袖 Hsiu. Read *seu'*; used for the coll. *‘wong*, as in ¹⁸*‘ch‘iu ‘wong*, a sleeve; *‘wong ‚t‘au* (or *‘mwi*), the end of the sleeve; ¹⁹*‘ch‘iu ‘wong lóh*, sleeve-covers.

¹網魚 ²天網
³網巾 ⁴蜘蛛
網 ⁵天羅地
網 ⁶網球○
⁷網絲 ⁸內苑
⁹宮苑 ¹⁰遠客
¹¹遠古 ¹²遙遠
¹³年湮世遠
¹⁴永遠 ¹⁵遠慮
¹⁶遠離他方
¹⁷遠挽 ¹⁸手袖
¹⁹手袖絡○

怨 ʼ Yüan. To hate, to be inimical, hating; to dislike; to feel resentment; an injustice, a wrong, a cause of hate; to murmur, to repine at; ill-will, malice; ashamed of, regretting: [1]*wongʼ ˏngiong*, bitter words; COM., [2]*wongʼ haungʼ* to hate; [3]*wongʼ kʻeʼ* resentment, hatred; malice; [4]*wongʼ miăngʼ* to repine at one's lot; [5]*chʻekˎ wongʼ* a thief's regret, as at poor luck; [6]*sekˎ wongʼ* the ten dislikes — a song; [7]*wongʼ kʻeʼ ˏchʻŭng ˏtʻiéng*, hate rising up to heaven! [8]*ˏmai wongʼ* to harbor ill-will; *wongʼ tʻangʼ* to murmur at, grumbling. Read *ˏhwi*: to accumulate, to hoard up.

丸 ˏ Huan. A pellet, a small ball; a bullet; pills: *ˏtang ˏwong*, a bullet; *met.*, a very small plot of land; COM., [9]*yohˎ ˏwong*, a pill; [10]*lakˎ ˏwong*, wax-coated pills; [11]*ˏtʻong ˏwong*, small dumplings of rice flour, with stuffing of peanut and sugar; *ˏu ˏmuí ˏwong*, balls of black plum and sugar; COLL., *kiékˎ ˏwong*, to form into lumps, lumpy.

紈 ˏ Huan. Read *ˏhwang* in the dictionaries: a plain, white sarcenet; plain, simple, not figured; fine, close, white, as silk: *ˏwong siéngʼ* silk fans; *ˏping ˏwong*, cloth woven fine and strong.

芄 ˏ Huan. A creeping plant, called *ˏwong ˏlang*, of which mats may be made; it is fragrant, and perhaps is an orchis.

亡 ˏ **亾** ˏ Wang. Used for the next, also for *ˏu* (no, not): lost, gone; destroyed, exterminated; dead, forgotten; to flee, to escape; a fugitive: [12]*ˏtó ˏwong*, to flee away; [13]*ˏwong ˏing*, a fugitive, a refugee; one dead; [14]*ˏwong koʼ* deceased; [15]*eʼ ˏwong ˏing*, the one not yet dead, as a widow styles herself; COM., [16]*ˏwong kwoʼ* or *ʻsi ˏwong*, dead; *ˏwong ˏhung*, a ghost; *ˏka sangʼ ˏing ˏwong*, the family utterly extinct; COLL., *ˏwong mengʼ* "at risk of life", hasty, precipitate; *ˏwong mengʼ siăhˎ* to bolt one's food; *ˏwong ˏnëng ˏsing*, a paper image to represent the dead, as in the *paiʼ chʻangʼ* rites.

忘 ˏ Wang. To escape the mind, to forget; to neglect, to disregard; inattentive: [17]*ˏwong ˏching*, ingrate, unfriendly; [18]*siéngʼ ˏwong*, absent-minded, forgetful; [19]*hwokˎ ˏwong*, negligent; [20]*chóʼ ˏwong*, to sit in vacant thought; COM., *ˏwong keʼ* to forget; *ˏwong ˏong pwoiʼ ngiéʼ* a miserable ingrate; *ˏwong paik*, one destitute of the eight virtues, a wretch; COLL., *ˏwong paik, laungʼ* you brute! *ˏwong paik, ˏtʻau*, an epithet given to a brothel-keeper.

員 ˏ Yüan. Yün. A numerative of round things, as dollars, and of officers; round, a round thing; to circulate, to extend all around: [21]*ˏkwang ˏwong*, officers, grandees; [22]*ekˎ ˏwong ˏkwang*, an officer; *hokˎ ˏwong*, the area, as of a state; *ˏwong ˏchʻá*, policemen; COM., *hukˎ ˏhwang ekˎ ˏwong*, (good for) one

1 怨言 2 怨恨 3 怨氣 4 怨命 5 賊怨 6 十怨 7 怨氣冲天 8 埋怨 9 藥丸 10 蠟丸 11 湯丸 12 逃亡 13 亡人 14 亡故 15 未亡人 16 亡過 17 忘情 18 善忘 19 忽忘 20 坐忘 21 官員 22 一員官

dollar (or 7 mace of ꜀p'ung ꜀tó silver), as stamped on a dollar bill; ꜁seng ꜀wong, a Siutsai; ꜀wong ngwoi꜄ a clerk in Tribunals at Peking; *met.*, the rich, the great, as styled in plays and coll. books.

圓 ꜀Yüan. Round; a circle; a ball, a sphere, a round lump, a clod, in which senses analogous to the preceding; to make round, to clip off the corners of; to interpret, as dreams: in the coll. read ꜀yéng, q. v.: [1]꜂hwong ꜀wong, square and round; [2]꜀wong mong꜄ to interpret a dream; COM., [3]꜀t'wang ꜀wong, a complete circle, as a family; the full moon; [4]hak꜇ ꜀wong, two lungans (dragon's eyes) on one stem; COLL., [5]꜀wong ꜂tiong, rounded, complete, as one's talk, or a thing well-done.

完 ꜀Wan. Yüan. To finish, to complete; done, finished; satisfactorily completed, well and thoroughly done; wholly, entirely, perfectly: COM., [6]꜀wong ꜀chiong, all completed; [7]꜂kong ꜀wong, done speaking; [8]꜀wong chong꜄ finished, as a job; [9]꜀wong ꜁p'iéng, to finish an essay; [10]꜀wong ꜀liong, or ꜀wong ꜀chiéng ꜀liong, to pay land-tax; COLL., ꜁tu ꜂sai ꜀wong, all used up, wholly expended.

爰 ꜀Yüan. Often read wong꜄: to lead to another subject; an illative word, hence, therefore; at, in, up to; even to, arriving at; to deduce; to remove, to change; sad, lamentable: ꜀wong ꜀wong, slowly.

援 ꜀Yüan. To take by the hand; to draw forth, to pull or pluck out; to lead forward: also read wong꜄ q. v.: ꜀wong ꜂ing, to lead on; ꜁p'ang ꜀wong, to combine for mutual help.

湲 ꜀Yüan. Water flowing or drawn off; the purling noise of a rapid current.

猨猿 ꜀Yüan. A monkey, the Simiadæ or Lemuridæ: haik꜇ ꜀wong and pek꜇ ꜀wong, black and white monkeys; ꜁t'ung pié꜄ ꜀wong, a monkey that stretches out one arm as it shortens the other.

黃 ꜀Huang. Yellow, ocherous, a clay color; the imperial color; hurried; the 201st radical: [11]꜀wong ꜂k'eu, an infant; [12]꜀wong hwak꜇ an old man; [13]꜁ch'ong ꜀wong, hasty, impetuous; COM., [14]꜀wong tó꜄ the ecliptic; [15]꜀wong tó꜄ kek꜇ nik꜇ a lucky day; [16]꜀wong ꜁sa, a yellowish haze or vapor—sign of wind and rain; [17]꜀wong ꜀ó, the Yellow river; [18]tai꜄ ꜀wong, rhubarb; [19]꜁kiong ꜀wong, turmeric; ꜀wong pah꜇ a yellow dye-wood; [20]꜀wong ꜀ki, lungwort, used for asthma; [21]꜀wong ꜀li, a pine-apple; [22]꜀wong ꜁king te꜄ an expensive location, as on a business-street; ꜀wong ꜀yong muk꜇ a sort of box-wood; ꜀wong ꜀liéng, a very bitter, yellow herb, used for its cooling properties; ꜀wong ꜀lüng ꜀pó, an Imperial robe; ꜀wong ꜁chiéng ꜂mi, rice of the late harvest; COLL., ꜀wong ꜀na ꜀na, or ꜀wong lak꜇ lak꜇ a deep yellow; ꜀wong ꜀p'ó, a

1 方圓 2 圓夢 3 團圓 4 合圓 5 圓轉 6 完全 7 講完 8 完竣 9 完篇 10 完糧 11 黃口 12 黃髮 13 蒼黃 14 黃道 15 黃道吉日 16 黃沙 17 黃河 18 大黃 19 薑黃 20 黃芪 21 黃梨 22 黃金地〇

small, yellowish toad; ˓*wong* ˓*liéng* ‘*k‘u* ‘*lang*, spittle as bitter as the herb ˓*wong* ˓*liéng;* ˓*wong* ‘*chăng p‘ang*’ *p‘uh*˒ a yellowish, bloated look.

璜 ˓Huang. A gem shaped like a semicircle, called a half-signet and hung at the girdle.

獚 ˓Huang. A species of dog; a dog.

癀 ˓Huang. The jaundice, icterus: COM., [1]˓*wong* ‘*tang*, the jaundice; the term also includes some forms of dropsy.

簧 ˓Huang. The tongue in the mouth of an organ; the mouth-piece of the ˏ*seng* or reed-organ; the reed of a flageolet: ˓*seng* ˓*wong*, an organ with its pipes; ˓*wong* ‘*ku*, to deceive by specious talk.

潢 ˓Huang. A pool, a lake without an outlet; water bright and sparkling, deep and clear water; the Sira-muren river, flowing into the Gulf of Chihli: [2]ˏ*t‘iéng* ˓*wong ek*, *p‘wai*’ of the same imperial generation. Read ‘*wong*: to dye paper.

洹 ˓Yüan. The name of a small branch of the river Wei in the N. E. of Honan, near Changtê-fu: ˓*wong* ˓*wong*, flowing along; [3]ˏ*ná* ˓*wong*, a certain state of existence —a Budhist term.

垣 ˓Yüan. A low wall, as inclosing a yard; to guard, to protect, as a wall does: [4]˓*ü* ˓*wong*, to leap a wall.

袁 ˓Yüan. Long robes; a prefecture in the west of Kiangsi; a surname, commonly spoken ˓*ngwong*, q. v.

轅 ˓Yüan. The cross-bars in front of a chariot; the thills or shaft; the side gates of the court of a yamun, or temple; gateways to a general's marquee: [5]ˏ*hiong* ˓*wong*, a constellation of 12 stars in *Leo*, a designation of the Yellow Emperor; COM., [6]ˏ*tëng* ˓*wong* ˓*mwong* and [7]ˏ*sí* ˓*wong* ˓*mwong*, the east and west gates of a yamun or temple; also gateways over a street where a great idol stops; [8]˓*wong* ˓*mwong pó*’ a provincial court circular—publishes names of degree-men and purchased ranks; [9]˓*wong* ˓*mwong* ˏ*kwang*, the gate-keeper of a yamun.

王 ˓Wang. A king, a sovereign, a ruler; a title of emperors before the Tsin dynasty; lords, princes; imperial uncles and brothers; royal, lordly, princely: also read *wong*’ q. v.: [10]˓*wong ho*’ deceased grandfathers; [11]ˏ*hwang* ˓*wong*, Tartar chiefs; [12]*hwak*˒ ˓*wong* or [13]*ch‘iong*’ ˓*wong*, Budha; COM., [14]*kwok*˒ ˓*wong*, a king, a prince, a ruler; [15]ˏ*hung* ˓*wong*, one who rules by imperial investiture; [16]˓*wong leng*’ an imperial rescript, as to order an execution; [17]˓*wong tô*’ the royal road, what is just and honorable; [18]*Tai*’ ˓*wong*, the great king—god of the land or place; [19]˓*Wong* ‘*sing* ˏ*ti*, the chief who subdued the Min country (Fookien); COLL., [20]*twai*’ *siáh*˒ ˓*wong*, a large eater;

[1]癀癉 [2]天潢一派 [3]泥洹 [4]踰垣 [5]軒轅 [6]東轅門 [7]西轅門 [8]轅門報 [9]轅門官 [10]王父 [11]番王 [12]法王 [13]象王 [14]國王 [15]封王 [16]王令 [17]王道 [18]大王 [19]王審知 [20]大食王

ₑwong lik, a coll. term for *ₑt'ung ₑchü*, an almanac.

王² Wang. To reign, to govern, as a king; to rule justly; full, abundant, plentiful: also read *ₑwong*, q. v.: ¹*wong² ₑt'iéng ha²* to rule the empire.

旺² Wang. The sun appearing in splendor, to brighten into full day; prospering, brilliant, flourishing: ²*chaung² wong²* strong and lusty; COM., ³*ₑhing wong²* to flourish; ⁴*ₑsoi wong²* to fail and to prosper; losing and winning; ⁵*wong² tê²* a good locality; a lucky spot, as for a grave; ⁶*ₑting ₑchai 'liong wong²* prosperous both in family and in purse.

暈² Yün. Read *ong²*; coll. *wong²*: a halo; a spot, a stain: ⁷*nik₂ wong²* a halo about the sun; *wong² twai²* a large stain; *ₑwong wong²* a spot, spotted; ⁸*'chiu wong²* the stain of wine.

望² Wang. To hope, to expect, to anticipate; to look at or towards; to go straight on without looking back; to stare, to gaze fixedly; a hope, an expectation; fronting, opposite, as the moon in opposition; the full moon; sacrifices, as to hills and streams: ⁹*ₑu 'su wong²* hopeless; ¹⁰*chaik₂ wong²* to reprove and hope for (one's reformation); COM., ¹¹*wong² ₑt'au*, a hope or expectation; ¹²*suuk₂ wong²* the 1st and 15th of the moon; ¹³*ₑming wong²* a good reputation; ¹⁴*'ai wong²* to hope, to expect confidently; ¹⁵*ₑkwang wong² pok₂ ₑchiéng*, to look on but not go to (one's help); COLL., *mek₂ ₑchiu wong² ₑsang ₑhwa*, one's eyes dim from waiting and looking for; *wong²* ¹⁶*'nü ₑtoi ₑsang tai²* hope many things from or about you!

妄² Wang. Disorderly, irregular; false, vain, wild, absurd; reckless, abandoned, immoral: sometimes used for *ₑhwang* (all): ¹⁶*ₑu wong²* the 25th diagram; unimportant; ¹⁷*wong² ₑui*, unseemly conduct; *wong² cheng²* to testify falsely, perjury; ¹⁸*wong² tang² pok₂ ₑking*, mere fables and not found in the books; COM., *wong² 'siong*, an absurd thought, as of becoming rich or famous. Read *ₑwong*, to cease to be, not existing.

媛² Yüan. A beauty, one like Venus or Hebe; beautiful, winning, attracting many admirers: *sëük₂ wong²* a chaste, pretty woman. Read *ₑwong*, as in *ₑsiéng ₑwong*, to draw, to attract, as beauty does.

援² Yüan. To assist, to save, to rescue, to deliver: also read *ₑwong*, q. v.: COM., ¹⁹*keu² wong²* to come to the rescue, to save, to deliver.

瑗² Yüan. A ring made of precious stone or gem, a signet with a large hole in it; it was borne by ancient kings or princes at audiences in token of their friendship.

迋² Wang. To go about; to deceive; to fear: ²⁰*'sü wong²* to send one; *ₑhung wong² wong²* his spirit was greatly terrified.

¹王天下 ²壯旺 ³興旺 ⁴衰旺 ⁵旺地 ⁶丁財兩旺 ⁷日暈 ⁸酒暈 ⁹無所望 ¹⁰責望 ¹¹望頭 ¹²朔望 ¹³名望 ¹⁴倚望 ¹⁵觀望不前 ¹⁶無妄 ¹⁷妄爲 ¹⁸妄誕不經 ¹⁹救援 ²⁰使迋

遠[1] *Yüan.* To separate, to keep at a distance; to rid, to be free from: also read *'wong*, q. v.: COM., *'wong^2 lié^2* to separate, to remove from; COLL., [2]*,ngai ,nëng wong^2 lié^2* may you be rid of bad people—phrase used in prayers by priests.

(918) Yă.

呀 *Ya. A. Hsia.* Read *,ha* and *,nga*; coll. *,yă*: to gape, to open the mouth wide in astonishment, an exclamation of wonder (with the hands thrown up).

'冶 *Yeh.* To fuse metals, to melt, to smelt; to compound or alloy; a smelter, a founder; meretricious, bedizened: [3]*'yă ,ūng,* a soft, bewitching countenance or air; [4]*,yeu 'yă,* bedizened and mincing, as a woman.

'墅 *Shu.* A separate residence; a cottage; a garden-lodge; a shed in a field; a hamlet: [5]*piék, 'yă,* a separate dwelling, a country house.

'野 *Yeh.* Used for the last: wastes outside of a city; a common, a wilderness, a moor; a desert; wild, savage, untamed; uncultivated, as grass and plants; rude, rustic, ill-mannered; roving, vicious: [6]*,kau 'yă,* a moor; [7]*'yă ,ngü,* a forester; [8]*'yă e^2* wild game; COM., [9]*k'wong 'yă,* or *k'wong^2 'yă,* a wild, a desert; [10]*'yă 'seu^2* wild beasts: [11]*'yă 'kwi,* roving ghosts, orbate spirits or those having no relatives to offer sacrifices to them; [12]*'yă 'sü,* novels; COLL., [13]*'yă ,miëng,* or *'yă 'kiăng,* a vagabond, a vicious fellow; [14]*'yă ,siëng paik, sóh,* a rogue, a scamp; [15]*'yă hwo^2* miserable baggage—a bad woman.

'Yă. A coll. word, for which the last character is often used: confused, disorderly, without regard to forms; false, lying; also a superlative, very, extremely: *'yă siăh,* to eat indiscriminately, careless in one's diet; *'yă maëng^2* confused or vain dreams; *'yă 'kong,* or *'yă k'iăk,* to talk at random, to lie; *,yă poi^2* you lying cur! *'yă ,ch'ong 'yă chië^2* a glutton, a mere beefeater; *'yă siăng^2* very cheap; *'yă 'heng,* very bad or wicked; in a bad fix, desperate, as an affair; *'yă a^2 chóh,* very mean or niggardly; *'yă taik, e^2* well pleased, it just suits my wish.

'Yă. A coll. word, followed by *o^2* (to have, to be): slightly, partially, somewhat, tolerably, adequately, what will answer: *'yă o^2 'hó,* somewhat good, pretty well; *'yă o^2 á^2* pretty well able to; *'yă o^2 sŭk,* tolerably well-cooked.

'Yă. A coll. word: to reject, to throw from the mouth, as a child does its food: *'yă ch'ok, ,li,* to spue it out, to reject it.

也' *Yeh.* A final euphonic particle, used to close the idea and round the period; after a proper name, makes the vocative; as a connective, and, also, even, further, likewise; before a negative, it makes a question or implies an alternative; before *se^2* (to be, is), it intensifies the meaning; repeated

[1] 遠離 遠離 [4] 妖冶 [6] 郊野 [8] 野味 [10] 野獸 [12] 野史 [14] 野仙八索 [15] 野貨

[2] 呆仸 [3] 冶容 [5] 別墅 [7] 野虞 [9] 曠野 [11] 野鬼 [13] 野仸 ○

with ‘*iu* (to have), it means also, too, likewise; often used after verbs to arrest the attention: used for the coll. *yă*² q. v.: ¹‘*yă*’ ꜀*cheng*, already; ²‘*se*² ꜀*hó* *yă*’ what is it? what is meant? ³*ek*, *yă*’ the same, just alike; ⁴‘*k‘ó* ꜀*ti* *yă*’ it can (thus) be known, (from which) it is perceived; ⁵*é*² ꜀*chi* ‘*iu* *yă*’ there's no such thing! ⁶꜀*sing* *yă*’ *pok*, ꜀*ti*, even the spirits don't know it!

呀 ꜀Ya. Read ꜀*ha* and ꜀*nga*; coll. ꜀*yă*: an exclamation, as in mock fights; ah, here's at you!

椰 梛 ꜀Yeh. The cocoanut: ⁷꜀*yă* ꜀*hwa* ‘*chiu*, cocoanut wine; COM., ꜀*yă* ‘*chi*, a cocoanut; cocoanut beads, as on the neck-string of a ‘*tu* ꜀*peng*; ⁸꜀*yă* ꜀*p‘ieu*, or ꜀*yă* ‘*wang*, cocoanut dippers, made of the shell halved.

耶 邪 ꜀Yeh. ꜀Ya. An appellation of a father; an interrogative particle at the end of a sentence, often in regimen with ‘*k‘i* (how); a kind of two-edged sword, in which sense used for the next: ⁹‘*u* ꜀*yă*, low ground; ¹⁰‘*k‘i* ‘*iu* *se*² ꜀*yă*, how is it so? ¹¹꜀*hó* ꜀*yă*, what is the meaning (of the above)? COM., ¹²꜀*Yă* ꜀*su*, Jesus; ¹³꜀*Yă* ꜀*su* *kau*’ Protestant christianity.

鋣 ꜀Yeh. A famous two-edged claymore, called *mok*, ꜀*yă*, from the name of its maker's wife.

琊 ꜀Yeh. A place, called ꜀*Long* ꜀*yă*, in the Shantung promontory, now a part of the Ch‘ingchou prefecture; ꜀*long* ꜀*yă* ꜀*tai*, the Langyeh terrace.

꜀*Yă*. A coll. word, as in ꜀*yă* ꜀*leng*, excessive, extreme, as excessively annoying, wicked, mischievous, etc.; ‘*ting* *sak*, ‘*yă* ‘*ting* ꜀*yă* ꜀*leng*, very rude or insolent; excessively vicious, abandoned; ꜀*yă* ꜀*i* ꜀*tiéng*, sickish-sweet.

夜² Yeh. After the sun's setting, after daylight, night; late at night: ¹⁴*chok*, *yă*² last night; ¹⁵*yă*² ꜀*tai*, the night terrace—the grave; COM., ¹⁶*tieu*’ *yă*² or *nik*, *yă*² day and night; ¹⁷*yă*² ꜀*heng*, abroad late at night; ‘*ngu* *yă*² (plays) in the afternoon and night; *t‘iék*, *yă*² or *t‘au*’ *yă*² throughout the whole night; ¹⁸꜀*cha* *yă*² a night-patrol; *hwang*² *yă*² to violate night regulations; *yă*² ꜀*ming* ꜀*chio*, the carbuncle; *yă*² ꜀*lai* ꜀*hiong*, Pergularia odoratissima; *yă*² ‘*ngang*, has night-eyes, as said of a thief; COLL., ꜀*ngó* *yă*² to stay up through the night.

也² Yeh. Read *yă*’; used for the coll. *yă*²: and, also, too, moreover; also is, is too; when repeated, it is a correlative, both, and: *yă*² ‘*hó*, also good or well, it too is good; *yă*² ꜀*chiong* *chó*’ also do thus; *yă*² *o*² ꜀*kĭng* *yă*² *o*² *pó*’ there are both rich and poor.

(919) Yăh.

益 Yi. I. Read *ek*,; coll. *yăh*,: to benefit, to profit, to advantage; beneficial, advantageous: *o*² *yăh*, profitable, beneficial; ¹⁹*le*’ *yăh*, benefit, gain, advantage; *yăh*, *mëk*, (medicine) good for the

¹也曾 ²是何 | 也 ³一 也 ⁴可 | 知也 ⁵未之 | 有也 ⁶神也 | 不知 ⁷椰花 | 酒 ⁸椰瓢 ⁹汙 | ¹⁰耶豈有是 | ¹¹耶何 ¹²耶耶 | ¹³穌耶穌教 | ¹⁴昨夜 ¹⁵夜臺 | ¹⁶晝夜 ¹⁷夜行 | ¹⁸查夜 ¹⁹利益

eyes; ¹'*yăh*, *cheng*' ꜀*nëng*, to benefit the multitude.

役 Yi. I. Read *ik*꜀; coll. *yah*꜀: a policeman, a runner, an official underling: ²꜀*ch'á yăh*꜀ a police-runner; ³*yăh*꜀ *k'ie*' the purchase-deed of a policeman's place; ⁴*yăh*꜀ *k'wok*꜀ the post of policeman or writer; ⁵*yăk*꜀ *sioh*꜀ ꜀*miăng*, one police-runner.

驛 Yi. I. Read *ik*꜀; coll. *yăh*꜀: a post for government-couriers, a hostelry, a post-house; a stage of a post-route: ⁶*yăh*꜀ ꜀*hu*, a courier; ⁷*yăh*꜀ *chang*' a stage, a post; a posthouse; ⁸*tai*' *yăh*꜀ '*ma*, has post horse's (luck)—a divining phrase, indicating a life of toil.

(920) Yăk.

Yăk꜀. A coll. word, analogous to *hiăk*꜀: inverted, turned over; puffed, blown out: *yăk*꜀ *kwo*' turned over, as a leaf by a sudden puff; blown or puffed out; *k'ëăk*꜀ ꜀*hung yăk*꜀ *kwo*' turned over by the wind; puffed out.

Yăk꜀. A coll. word: to beckon with the hand; to motion, to signal to, to call by beckoning: *yăk*꜀ '*ch'iu*, to beckon with the hand; *yăk*꜀ ꜀*nëng* ꜀*li*, to beckon one to come.

Yăk꜀. A coll. word, like the last: to use the fan, to fan: *yăk*꜀ *siëng*' to use a fan; *yăk*꜀ '*hwi*, to fan the fire; *yăk*꜀ *tiong*' ꜀*hung*, you'll contract flatulency by fanning (so hard)! *yăk*꜀ *tioh*꜀ *tioh*꜀ to fan it till well-kindled.

(921) Yăng.

꜀*Yăng*. A coll. word: about the same as ꜀*hiăng*, as in ꜀*yăng* ꜀*yăng* *ë*' a fetid or rancid scent; *ch'au*' ꜀*yăng* ꜀*yăng*, a very offensive odor, a stench.

'*Yăng*. A coll. word: to receive, to get, to contract by exposure; *met*., brought, conveyed, as news: '*yăng* ꜀*hung*, to take cold by exposure to the wind; '*yăng* *ă*' ꜀*täng* '*kang*, exposure will cause a fresh cold; ꜀*mó* ꜀*hung* '*yăng*, no report brought, no intelligence (to verify it).

'*Yăng*. A coll. word: efficacious, operating, as medicine: *o*' '*yăng* ꜀*mó* '*yăng*, is it efficacious or not?

映' Ying. Read *yong*'; used for the coll. *yăng*': to expose to the sun or one's gaze; to show, to let one see: ⁹*yăng*' *k'ang*' to give him a glimpse of it; ꜀*tó nik*꜀ ꜀*t'au* '*li* *yăng*' *sioh*꜀ *ă*' take and expose it to the sun a while.

꜀**營** Ying. Read ꜀*ing*; coll. ꜀*yăng*: a camp, a cantonment, an intrenchment, a pitched camp; an army: ¹⁰꜀*kung* ꜀*yăng*, the army; ¹¹꜀*yăng* ꜀*puăng*, a camp; ¹²*tie* ꜀*yăng*, to enlist; ¹³*chak*꜀ ꜀*yăng*, to encamp; ¹⁴꜀*yăng* '*ngu* (or '*u* ꜀*yăng*) *ch'ok*꜀ ꜀*sing*, promoted from the ranks; ¹⁵꜀*yăng* *hiong*' rations, wages.

꜀**贏** Ying. Read ꜀*ing*; coll. ꜀*yăng*: to gain, to win, as in a game or lawsuit; to beat, to conquer, to excel: ¹⁶꜀*sio* ꜀*yăng*, to lose and win; to bet, to wager; ¹⁷꜀*yăng* ꜀*chiëng*, to win money in gaming; ¹⁸*pau* ꜀*yăng*,

---

¹益盡仈○ ²差役 ³役契 ⁴役缺 ⁵役一名 ⁶驛夫 ⁷驛站 ⁸帶驛馬 ⁹映看 ¹⁰軍營 ¹¹營盤 ¹²入營 ¹³扎營 ¹⁴營伍出身 ¹⁵營餉 ¹⁶輸贏 ¹⁷贏錢 ¹⁸包贏○

to warrant one's winning; *꜀yăng sioh꜆ teng'* to win a battle; *꜀yăng meng'* a prospect of winning or gaining.

꜀*Yăng*. A coll. word: to extend, to spread, as grass in growing; to spread, as a rash, the itch, or other cutaneous eruption: *꜀yăng ʻmwang tŏi'* to spread everywhere; *꜀yăng sioh꜆ ꜀sing,* to spread over the whole person; *ʻmwong ꜀yăng ʻmwong sá'* to spread more and more.

Yăng'. A coll. word: bright, shining, shiny; lustrous, glittering: *yăng' yăng' ꜀kwong,* very bright, as paint or metals; *á' yăng'* it is shiny; *ʻk'i yăng'* to emit gleams, lustrous.

(922) Yék.

曄꜆ Yeh. The flash of lightning; the splendor of the sun: *yék꜆ yék꜆* full, abundant; light, clear.

燁꜆ 爗꜆ Yeh. The light of fire, a great blaze; bright, blazing; the 2d is the form used for the personal name of the emperor Kanghi.

饁꜆ Yeh. Provisions for a journey; to supply with food, to carry food, as to workmen in the fields: [1]*yék꜆ seu'* to sacrifice animals, as at the borders to the spirits of the four quarters.

熱꜇ 爇꜇ Jê. Jo. Warm, hot; ardent, warm-hearted; feverish; to heat, to warm food: COM., [2]*yék꜇ k'e'* hot air, caloric; [3]*yék꜇ ch'eng'* hot and cold; [4]*hwak꜆ yék꜇* feverish; [5]*꜁hwang yék꜇* excited and feverish, nervous; [6]*꜁hwo ꜁hwo yék꜇* lukewarm, tepid; [7]*yék꜇ tuk꜆* hot humors, appearing in boils, etc.; [8]*yék꜇ ꜀sing,* zealous; [9]*nau' yék꜇* a bustle, a great stir; [10]*꜀ch'ing yék꜇* warmly attached, very intimate; [11]*yék꜇ pang'* or *yék꜇ cheng'* a fever, a kind of epidemic disease; [12]*yék꜇ ꜀ó,* Jêho, a summer residence of the Emperor, N. E. of Peking; COLL., *yék꜇ siăh꜇ ꜀wong,* small bowls, used to contain warm viands at a feast; *yék꜇ se' ꜀kung chĕŭng' ch'eng' se' ꜀sai ꜀ka,* heat is common property but cold is personal (to the poorly clad).

楪꜇ Yeh. A window; also occurs in the name of a district. Read *siék꜆*: a thin plate or leaf. Read *tiék꜆*: a bed-mat.

葉꜇ Yeh. Shê. The leaves of plants; a leaf of a book; the thin plates of metal, foil; an age, ages, posterity; to collect: used for the coll. *nioh꜇* q. v.: [13]*꜀tŭng yék꜇* the middle age, as of a dynasty; [14]*ek꜆ yék꜇ ꜀p'iéng ꜀chiu*—a flat punt, a mere skiff; [15]*paik꜆ yék꜇* the manyplus of oxen, tripe; COM., [16]*yék꜇ ʻchü,* fine gold-leaf; [17]*yék꜇ lok꜇ ꜀kwi ꜀kong,* leaves fall and revert to the root; *met.*, all should recognize and honor their ancestry; [18]*꜀k'ai ꜀chié hwak꜆ yék꜇* to branch and leaf; *met.*, to have posterity. Read *yék꜆*: the name of a district.

鍱꜇ Yeh. A ring or knob; the point of an arrow; metal plates, as for plate-armor.

Yék꜇. A coll. word: to shake, to loosen, to extract by shaking to and fro: *yék꜇ t'iék꜆ ꜀ting,*

[1]饁獻 [2]熱氣 [3]熱淸 [4]發熱 [5]煩熱 [6]和和 熱〇 [7]熱毒 [8]熱心 [9]鬧熱 [10]親熱 [11]熱病 [12]熱河 [13]中葉 [14]一葉扁舟 [15]百葉 [16]葉子 [17]葉落歸根 [18]開枝發葉

to pull out a nail; *yék*˛ *ʻngai*, to extract a (loose) tooth; *yék*˛ *ʻtó*, to shake down; *yék*˛ *˛i kok*˛ *ʻkʻi*, to arouse him by shaking.

(923) Yéng.

咽 ʻ ˛ Yen. Yeh. The throat, the esophagus, in distinction from *˛heu*, the windpipe; a narrow passage, a pass: COM., [1]*˛yéng ˛heu*, the throat; [2]*˛yéng ˛heu ʻsu chái*ʾ an important pass, the key of a position. Read *ʻyéng*: to swallow. Read *yék*˛: a stoppage of breath. Read *˛ing*: the roll of drums.

胭 ˛ Yen. Interchanged with the last: to swallow; the throat; a cosmetic: COM., *˛yéng ˛heu*, the throat; a gorge, a pass; [3]*˛yéng ˛chié*, rouge; [4]*˛yéng ˛chié ʻli*, a species of red plum.

烟 煙 ˛ Yen. Smoke; mist, vapor; tobacco or opium, because they are smoked: in the coll. read *˛ing* and *˛hong*, q. v.: [5]*˛yéng ˛chʻiong*, an opium-pipe; COM., [6]*ʻkwi ˛yéng* (or *˛ing*), smoke; [7]*˛u ˛yéng*, soot, lamp-black; [8]*˛yéng ˛téng*, a chimney, a flue; [9]*˛yong ˛yéng*, foreign smoke—i. e. opium; [10]*˛wong ˛yéng*, sulphur squibs, as on the 5th of the 5th moon; [11]*˛yéng ˛hwa ˛leu*, a brothel; COLL., *˛téng ˛iu ˛yéng*, the smoke or soot of wood-oil.

奄 ˛ Yen. Also read *ʻyéng*: to detain awhile; to remain; to cover, to conceal; a surplus, an excess; hastily, suddenly; a place in Shantung: [12]*˛yéng ˛kwang*, to survey long; [13]*˛yéng ʻiu séüʾ ˛hwong*, he suddenly obtained the whole region.

崦 ˛ Yen. Also read *ʻyéng*: a mountain in the West, called [14]*˛yéng ˛chü*, fabled to contain a cave or fountain where the sun went at night.

俺 ˛ Yen. Also read *ʻyéng*: the mind exercised upon; to love; desirous, willing: [15]*˛yéng ˛chʻiéng*, restless, unsteady; disputing, loquacious.

掩 ˛ Yen. Read *ʻyéng*; coll. *˛yéng*: to cover, to hide, to screen, as with the hands; *met.*, to suppress, to prevent: [16]*˛yéng mengʾ* to cover one's face; [17]*˛yéng ngéʾ* to stop the ears; [18]*˛yéng ˛nëng chʻoiʾ* to stop people's mouths—to prevent scandal; *˛yéng ˛hung ˛yéng taiʾ mëk*˛ blind-man's buff.

淹 ˛ Yen. To soak, to saturate; to sink; the margin of a stream; to stay, to be detained: [19]*˛yéng muk*˛ to drown and spoil in water; *˛yéng ʻkiu*, or *˛yéng ˛liu*, to tarry long.

腌 ˛ Yen. Also read *ʻyéng* and *yék*˛: to salt flesh; salted or pickled meat: used for the coll. *˛ang*, q. v.

醃 ˛ Yen. To lay in salt, to preserve by salting; pickle, brine for preserving fish: used for the coll. *siéngʾ* q. v.

閹 ˛ Yen. To castrate, to geld; one who guards the door of the harem, a eunuch: [20]*˛yéng hwangʾ* or *˛yéng séüʾ* eunuchs of the palace.

[1]咽喉 [2]咽喉所在 [3]胭脂 [4]胭脂李 [5]烟鎗 [6]火烟 [7]烏烟 [8]烟筒 [9]洋烟 [10]黃烟 [11]烟花樓 [12]奄觀 [13]奄有四方 [14]崦嵫 [15]俺愉 [16]掩面 [17]掩耳 [18]掩仈嘴○ [19]淹沒 [20]閹宦

'蚦 '蚺 Jan. A large snake, said to be eatable; its fangs are said to be five or six inches long, and its gall is considered a cure for consumption.

'髯 Jan. Also read 'yéng: the whiskers, hair on the cheeks near the ears; the beard: [1]'mi ,yéng ,kung, the lord of the handsome whiskers — i. e. Kuanti, god of war.

'兗 Yen. As in [2]'yéng ,chiu, the Yenchou department in the Shantung province.

'剡 Yen. Sharpened, pointed; to sharpen; to cut off; to rise up; light, brilliant.

'扊 Yen. Sometimes read ,yéng: the transverse bar, called [3]'yéng ,ié, which bars a gate inside—in the coll. termed ,mwong ,kong, q. v.

'琰 Yen. A gem of great luster, often set on the top of tablets; it was held by ministers or by envoys, when commissioned to punish refractory princes; bright, luminous; part of the name of the emperor Kiaking.

'冉 Jan. To advance; slowly, gradually; weak and feeble, pliant: [4]'Yéng 'iu, a disciple of Confucius.

'苒 Jan. Luxuriant, tender herbage; by turns, alternately, successively: [5]'ing 'yéng, going and coming, alternating, as day and night.

'偃 Yen. To lie down, to recline, to repose; to cease, to desist; to fall down, prostrated: [6]'yéng ngwo' to lie down to sleep; [7]'yéng sek, to cease or rest from; [8]'yéng 'kiong, impeded, unlucky; undecided; proud, lofty; [9]'yéng ,tü, low, marshy ground.

'蝘 Yen. A species of cicada, called [10],tong 'yéng and other names; [11]'yéng 'tiéng, a house lizard, which is livid and harmless.

'鰋 Yen. A kind of white-headed silure or mud-fish, which feeds at the bottom of the water.

'鼴 Yen. A mole, called [12],lá 'ch'ü or plow-rat, and [13]'üng 'ch'ü, or the secret rat; also a fabulous, ox-like animal, said to lie in rivers.

'堰 Yen. A dam, a dike; to dam off water; to stop, to arrest.

'揜 Yen. To cover with earth, to bury in the ground.

'掩 Yen. To shade, to cover over, to conceal from view; to shut; to insert, as a board; to stroke with the hand, to soothe, to console; to surprise, to take at unawares: in the coll. read ,yéng, q. v.: [14]'yéng ,mwong, to shut a door; [15]'yéng 'ch'iu, to hide disgrace; com., [16]'yéng 'peng, to insert a board, to board over; [17]'yéng sek, to conceal, to hide or cover up (a matter);

1 美髯公 ○ 2 兗州 3 扊扅 4 冉有 5 荏苒 6 偃臥 7 偃息 8 偃蹇 9 偃猪 10 螗蝘 11 蝘蜓 12 犂鼠 13 隱鼠 14 掩門 15 掩醜 16 掩板 17 掩飾

[1]ʻyéng ʻngi tō' ꜂ling, to cover his ears to steal the bell—hard to circumvent him, like "belling a cat"; [2]꜂chiă ʻyéng, to hide, to keep secret; COLL., mă' ꜂chiă ʻyéng tek, k'ó' can't be kept secret.

ʻ弇 Yen. To cover over, to shade, to obscure; to hide, as an occultation does; to turn inwards; a vase with a small mouth and large belly: [3]ʻyéng ꜂tŭng, a narrow pass among hills; [4]ʻyéng nik the sun obscured, as by clouds.

ʻ渰 Yen. The appearance of clouds and rain; to soak, to cause to vegetate, as rain does.

ʻ演 Yen. A stream flowing far; to pass through, permeating; to lead on, extended, ample; to bedew, to moisten; to practice, to exercise, to drill: [5]ʻwang ʻyéng, eddies; COM., [6]ʻyéng hié' to perform theatrical plays; [7]꜂ch'au ʻyéng, (or ꜂ch'au liéng'), to drill troops.

ʻ衍 ʻ衍 Yen. To inundate, to overflow; to spread out, to amplify; much, wide, far; elegant, handsome; prolix, diffuse, turgid; plains at the base of hills: [8]꜂iu ʻyéng, to ramble; [9]꜂sa ʻyéng, a sand-spit; mang' ʻyéng, interminable; COM., [10]꜂hu ʻyéng, diffuse, as style.

ʻ靨 Yen. Yeh. Also read yék,: spots, pimples on the face; beautiful, handsome: [11]ʻyéng ho' the cheeks, the jaws.

ʻ魘 Yen. To be troubled in one's sleep, disturbed by dreams; to have the nightmare.

ʻ黶 Yen. Black pimples, hair moles, black spots on the face or the body.

宴' 讌' Yen. Rest, ease; festivity, merriment; a feast, an entertainment: [12]yéng' lok, joyful; COM., [13]yéng' hwoi' joyous assemblies, as of genii; yéng' hié' a feast and theatricals; [14]sié k, yéng' or ꜂pá yéng' to spread a feast, as to idols; [15]꜂ing ꜂yong yéng' a feast given to military Kŭjin graduates; COLL., yéng' sioh, chó' a feast prepared, an entertainment.

燕' Yen. Used for the preceding: a feast; to rest; still, peaceful; a swallow, a martin; to disgrace; a shuttlecock, played with the foot, called kiong' in Foochow: [16]yéng' ꜂kü, to live at ease; [17]yéng' ꜂peng, to disgrace one's friends; COM., [18]yéng' ꜂wo, edible bird's nest; [19]yéng' ꜂wong, pork balls in flour crusts; yéng' ʻchü ꜂kang ꜂ná ꜂k'ung hié' lik, the swallow wastes its strength in carrying mud (for its nest), met., to have children who become vicious or die early. Read ꜂yéng: the ancient name of a state, now the province of Chihli, and still often applied to it and the metropolis.

厭' Yen. To dislike, to reject, to loathe, to feel disgust; filled, satisfied; satiated, cloyed, sated: [20]hok, pok, yéng' not weary of study; COM., [21]yéng' k'é' to loathe and reject; [22]yéng' ꜂hwang, to dislike trouble, annoyed; COLL.,

[1]掩耳盜鈴 [2]遮掩 [3]弇中 [4]弇日 [5]渦演 [6]演戲 [7]操演 [8]遊衍 [9]沙衍 [10]敷衍 [11]靨輔 [12]宴樂 [13]宴會 [14]設宴 [15]鷹揚宴 [16]燕居 [17]燕朋 [18]燕窩 [19]燕丸 [20]學不厭 [21]厭棄 [22]厭煩

福州方言拼音字典

[1]*yéng' chiéng'* or *yéng' ˛ngwang*, to reject with disgust as worthless; *k'ah˓ ˛tieu yéng'* tired of play; *siăh˓ mά' yéng'* does not cloy the appetite. Read *˛yéng:* peaceful, tranquil. Read *'yéng:* to conceal, to screen. Read *yék˓:* wet, damp. Read *ak˓:* to press down, to subdue; compressed, straitened.

饜 Yen. The same as the last: to eat to repletion; satisfied, satiated; loathing, feeling distaste for: *yéng' hëü'* surfeited.

Yéng'. A coll. word: to take all, to engross; to appropriate, to assume unfairly; to keep, to retain for one's own use; also to insert, as a piece of board, in which sense the same as *'yéng*, q. v.: *yéng' oi'* to keep a seat, have it reserved; *yéng' 'lá chó'* to monopolize work; *yéng' 'lá 'kong*, to keep the floor, not allow others to speak.

炎 Yen. Fire blazing up, flame; a fire spreading; hot, burning; luminous, brilliant: [2]*˛yéng siong'* to flame up; [3]*˛yéng ˛t'iéng*, the south quarter; [4]*˛yéng tá'* the emperor Shinnung; COM., [5]*˛yéng yék˓* the severe heat of summer; [6]*'sié' t'ai' ˛yéng ˛liong*, the world's ways are inconstant, friends are fickle. Read *˛tang:* to discriminate, to reason well.

圓 Yüan. Read *˛wong;* coll. *˛yéng:* round, circular; to gather, to collect, to assemble: [7]*˛yéng ˛k'wang*, a ring; [8]*˛yéng seu'* the character for longevity in a round form, as on scrolls; [9]*˛yéng ˛pung*, to marry a girl reared in the family; *˛yéng ˛yéng* or [10]*˛yéng 'tiăng*, very round, circular, spherical; [11]*˛yéng ˛si*, hemispherical ingots; [12]*˛yéng ˛chiéng*, to collect money; *˛yéng 'lëng*, or *˛yéng sioh˓ ˛toi*, to collect together, as persons or things; *˛yéng ˛chio ˛chio*, round as a pearl, globular; [13]*˛yéng 'tiăng tói' se' kaĕk˓ ˛song*, a round pan with a square steamer on; *met.*, not matching, incongruous.

焰 **燄** Yen. The same as *˛yéng* (fire blazing up): a flame, a blaze; bright, shining; brilliant, luminous: [14]*˛kwong yéng'* brilliant; luminous, clear, as an essay; COM., [15]*'hwi yéng'* the flame of fire; [16]*yéng' 'k'eu*, rites and offerings to ghosts, as in All-souls' festivals.

艷 **豔** **豓** Yen. Beautiful, tall and handsome; captivating, voluptuous; pretty, brilliant, as flowers; full, plump, as a face; luxurious, dissipated: [17]*˛kieu yéng'* brilliant, gay, as flowers, colors, faces; COM., [18]*saik˓ yéng'* the color gay; [19]*yéng' lé'* pretty, elegant; [20]*˛hwa muk˓ yéng'* the beauty of flowers and plants.

灩 Yen. As in *'liéng yéng'* agitated, as water; brimful, overflowing, running out.

院 Yüan. A walled inclosure, a court-yard; a public establishment; an office, a court, a hall; a college, a monastery, a hospital; a

1 厭賤 2 炎上 3 炎天 4 炎帝 5 炎熱 6 世態炎涼 7 圓環 8 圓壽 9 圓房 10 圓鼎 11 圓絲 12 圓錢 13 圓鼎對四角甑 14 光焰 15 火焰 16 焰口 17 嬌艷 18 色艷 19 艷麗 20 花木艷○

body of officers, attendants; used in titles of high officers; firm, strong: [1]ₑ*tu ch'ak, yéng*ᵓ the censorate; COM., [2]*'kong' yéng*ᵓ a provincial examination-hall; [3]*ch'ak, yéng*ᵓ the magnate — a character in plays; [4]*yéng*ᵓ *'k'ó*, examination for the Siutsai degree; [5]*hok, yéng*ᵓ a literary chancellor; [6]ₑ*chü yéng*ᵓ a college; COLL., [7]ₑ*ku 'ló yéng*ᵓ a lazaretto.

(924) Yeu.

幺 么 ₑYao. Small, tender, as a new-born child; the last pig of a litter; the ace face of a dice; a ballad, called *lëk*, ₑ*yeu*; small, diminutive; small things: ₑ*yeu* ₑ*tong*, the runt; COM., ₑ*yeu ne*ᵓ ₑ*sang*, the faces of a dice from one to three—a kind of game with three dice.

吆 ₑYao. A sound, a noise.

喓 ₑYao. The singing of insects in the grass; a humming or chirping, as of grass-hoppers, &c.

要 ₑYao. To adjust, to make an agreement with; to seek, to importune; to examine, to scrutinize, to search out the facts; to call, to convoke, to assemble: also read *yeu*ᵓ q. v.: *'kiu* ₑ*yeu*, long agreed to or settled.

腰 ₑYao. The loins, the waist, the lumbar region, parts between the ribs and pelvis; *met.*, the middle of a thing: [8]*chiék*, ₑ*yeu*, to bend the loins—i. e. to bow to one; COM., [9]ₑ*yeu kauk*, the haunch-bone; [10]ₑ*yeu 'niong*, supple loins; COLL., [11]ₑ*yeu 'chi*, or ₑ*yeu* ₑ*sing 'chi*, the two loin-pieces, sirloin; [12]*pwang*ᵓ ₑ*tong* ₑ*yeu*, the middle, as of a beam or a wall; [13]ₑ*yeu 'siéng* (or *chwah*,) a wrench or stitch in the side; [14]ₑ*yeu* ₑ*piêng p'au*ᵓ Indian corn; ₑ*yeu* ₑ*piêng o*ᵓ *nóh*, he has things at the girdle—has money or means.

葽 ₑYao. Grass, herbage; a vigorous, luxuriant vegetation; also a wide or distant prospect: *seu*ᵓ ₑ*yeu*, the blooming herbage.

邀 ₑYao. To cover, to conceal; to send for, to invite; to wish, to seek, to try to obtain; to stop, to obstruct; to salute: [15]ₑ*chieu*ᵓ ₑ*yeu*, to call, to invite; [16]*pwang tó*ᵓ ₑ*yeu* ₑ*chi*, stopped him in the midst of the way; [17]ₑ*yeu 'ch'ing*, to invite; COM.,[18]ₑ*hü* ₑ*yeu*, my poor invitation or feast.

ₑ*Yeu.* A coll. word, for which the last character may be used: to lead, to conduct, to show the way to: ₑ*yeu 'ch'iu*, to lead by the hand; ₑ*yeu* ₑ*i* ₑ*chá k'ó* to take him along; ₑ*yeu tio*ᵓ to lead the way, to conduct one.

妖 ₑYao. Beautiful, enchanting, bewitching; odd, strange, unusual; ominous, unnatural, monstrous, lusus naturæ; magical, heretical, contrary to doctrine or usage; a phantom, a metamorphosis, a sprite; to flatter, to enchant: [19]ₑ*yeu* ₑ*ngiong*, enticing words; COM.,[20]ₑ*yeu ngiék*, a prodigy, some-

[1]都察院 ○ [2]貢院 [3]察院 [4]院考 [5]學院 [6]書院 [7]孤老院 [8]折腰 ○ [9]腰骨 [10]腰軟 [11]腰子 [12]半中腰 [13]腰閃 [14]腰邊褰 [15]招邀 [16]半道邀之 [17]邀請 [18]虛邀 [19]妖言 [20]妖孽

thing ominous of evil; mischievous sprite! as said to a child; ꜀yeu kwai꜄ or ꜀yeu ꜀mó, a monster, an elf; a being capable of metamorphosis; ꜀yeu hwak꜀ or ꜀yeu suk꜀ the tricks of elves.

夭 ꜂ Yao. Pleasing, attractive, winning; small, delicate; luxuriant, as vegetation; calamitous: also read ꜂yeu, q. v.: [1]꜀t'ó ꜀yeu, peach blossoms; *met*., the time of nuptials.

夭 殀 ꜂ Yao. To die early, short-lived; a premature death, a judgment, a calamity; to kill children: the 1st also read ꜀yeu, q. v.: [2]꜂yeu seu꜄ early death and long life; [3]꜂yeu chiĕk꜀ to die young; COM., [4]꜂yeu siong꜄ a physiognomy indicating an early death, as said of one having a short chin.

擾 擾 ꜂ Jao. To give trouble, to incommode, to embarrass, to annoy; to confuse, to disorder; to infest, as banditti do; to breed, to rear; domestic animals; to soothe, to tranquilize: [5]lĕk꜀ ꜂yeu, the six domestic animals—the same as lĕk꜀ hĕük꜀ q. v.: COM., [6]꜂yeu lwang꜄ to disorder, to produce anarchy; [7]꜂yeu hai꜄ te꜄ ꜀hwong, to infest and devastate a region; [8]꜂ch'au ꜂yeu, to trouble, to annoy.

窈 ꜂ Yao. Also read ꜂mieu: deep and far, obscure, still, profound; retired, reserved: used for the coll. ꜂lieu, q. v.: [9]꜂yeu ꜂t'ieu, at leisure, tranquil; gentle, quiet; handsome, as a lady.

舀 舀 ꜂ Yao. To change a liquid from one vessel to another; to lade, to bail, to dip out: COM., [10]꜂yeu ꜂chwi, to lade water; COLL., [11]꜂yeu k'ó꜄ siăh꜀ to dip it up and eat it.

鷕 ꜂ Yao. The cry or cackling of the female pheasant, as when calling for its mate.

要 ꜄ Yao. To want, to wish, to desire, to require; what is requisite, important, essential, urgent, necessary; a compend, an epitome, abstract: also read ꜀yeu, q. v.: [12]yeu꜄ tó꜄ the essential principles; [13]꜀p'iĕng yeu꜄ must have it, will not be refused; COM., [14]ch'auk꜀ yeu꜄ a compend, an abridgment; [15]yeu꜄ ꜂king or ꜂king yeu꜄ important; [16]yeu꜄ ĕüng꜄ useful, needed; COLL., [17]yeu꜄ ꜂king ꜀nĕng, the important man—the main-stay of a family.

姚 ꜁ Yao. The descendants of Shun; a surname; beautiful, elegant. Read t'ieu꜄: light, airy.

傜 ꜁ Yao. To serve as a vassal; feudal labor of serfs, vassalage, villenage; [18]꜁yeu ik꜀ labor given by fiefs.

愮 ꜁ Yao. Sad, troubled; distressed and having no one to disburden to; depraved; tempted, deceived. Read yeu꜄: to adjust, to set to rights.

搖 ꜁ Yao. Also read yeu꜄: to shake, to move, to wave; to wag, as the head; agitated, disturbed; to make: [19]꜁hu ꜁yeu, a violent wind; [20]꜀sü ꜁yeu, a moment; COM., [21]꜁yeu tong꜄ to

[1]桃夭 [2]殀壽 [3]殀折 [4]殀相 [5]六擾 [6]擾亂 [7]擾害地方 [8]吵擾 [9]窈窕 [10]舀水 [11]舀去食 [12]要道 [13]偏要 [14]撮要 [15]要緊 [16]要用 [17]要緊人 [18]傜役 [19]扶搖 [20]須搖 [21]搖動

move, to disturb; to agitate (a matter); [1]ˏ*yeu* ˏ*t'au*, to shake the head, as a sign of dissent; [2]ˏ*yeu* ʻ*mwi k'ëük*, ˏ*ling*, "wag the tail and beg pity"—to act the sycophant; [3]ˏ*yeu* ʻ*lu*, to scull; [4]ˏ*yeu hwoi*ʾ to shake (dice in order to draw one's share) at a mutual-aid club; COLL., [5]ˏ*yeu* ˏ*chiéng ch'eu*ʾ to shake "the cash-branch", as beggars do at new-year's.

猺 ˏYao. A kind of wild beast: [6]ˏ*yeu* ˏ*ming*, a tribe of the Miautsz' mountaineers in Lienchou and vicinity, supposed by the Cantonese to have tails.

瑤 ˏYao. A precious gem: [7]ˏ*yeu* ˏ*kwong*, a star in Ursa Major; [8]ˏ*yeu* ˏ*ch'iéng*, your gemmy epistle—a complimentary term.

窰 窯 ˏYao. A kiln for burning tiles and bricks; a pottery: [9]ʻ*chëü*ʾ *p'ó*ʾ ˏ*yeu*, to live in old kilns, vagrant; COM., [10]*ngwa*ʾ ˏ*yeu*, a brick kiln; ʻ*wang* ˏ*yeu*, a pottery.

蘨 ˏYao. Plants growing thickly; abundant, luxuriant, as vegetation.

繇 ˏYu. Used for the last and the next: luxuriant; to follow; a song, a ballad; to exact service of the people: [11]ˏ*yeu ik*ˀ service, vassalage; used for ˏ*iu*, to wander, to rove; for ˏ*iu*, to go far, remote, to walk leisurely; also for ˏ*tó* (when read ˏ*yeu*), as in [12]ˏ*Kó* ˏ*yeu*, a noted minister of Shun: also used for ˏ*iu* (by, from), q. v.

謠 ˏYao. A song, a ballad, rustic ditties; to vilify, to satirize in songs: [13]ˏ*kó* ˏ*yeu*, ballads; COM., [14]ˏ*tung* ˏ*yeu*, or ˏ*tung* ˏ*yeu* ˏ*kó*, ditties, popular songs; [15]ˏ*yeu hëk*ˀ to lure, to tempt; ˏ*yeu* ˏ*ngiong hëk*ˀ *chëüng*ʾ to deceive the multitude with idle tales.

遙 遥 ˏYao. Far, distant, far off, remote in place: [16]ˏ*yeu* ʻ*wong*, a long way off; COM., ˏ*sieu* ˏ*yeu chëü*ʾ *chai*ʾ to ramble leisurely, to rove about in fine spirits.

颻 ˏYao. The wind shaking things, as a flag; fluttering, floating on the breeze, waving in the wind; also a high wind: [17]ˏ*yeu yé*ʾ waving in the wind.

軺 ˏYao. A small carriage: also read ˏ*sieu*, q. v.: [18]ˏ*yeu* ˏ*kü*, a one-horse chaise or cart.

曜 [2] Yao. Yüeh. The effulgence or light of the sun: [19]*ch'ek*ˀ *yeu*ʾ the seven lights—i. e. sun, moon, and five planets.

燿 耀 [2] Yao. Yüeh. Same as the preceding; the 2d is more commonly used: to shine upon, to illumine; to dart rays; luminous, effulgent; glorious, splendid: COM., [20]ˏ*kwong yeu*ʾ bright, resplendent; [21]ˏ*ing yeu*ʾ glory, distinction; to render illustrious; ˏ*ing* ˏ*chung yeu*ʾ ʻ*chu*, to immortalize one's ancestors, as by good deeds.

鷂 [2] Yao. A hawk, a kite of variegated plumage: COM., ʻ*chai yeu*ʾ a paper-kite;

[1]搖頭 [2]搖尾乞憐 [3]搖櫓 [4]搖會 [5]搖錢樹 [6]猺民〇 [7]瑶光 [8]瑶箋 [9]住破窰〇 [10]瓦窰 [11]繇役 [12]皐繇 [13]歌謠 [14]童謠 [15]謠惑 [16]遙遠 [17]颻曳 [18]軺車 [19]七曜 [20]光耀 [21]榮耀

COLL., *pah*, *tak*, *k'ŭŭk*, *yeu²* *p'ah*, the dove struck (swooped up) by the hawk. Read ˌ*yeu*, as in ˌ*yeu te²* a species of large pheasant, like the medallion pheasant.

(925) Yo.

'*Yo.* A coll. word: weak, feeble, drooping, as from sickness or fatigue; wilted, withered, as plants: '*yo* '*yo* or '*yo ch'ioh*, weak, exhausted; '*yo* ˌ*lau* ˌ*lau*, limpsy, not stiff; extremely feeble; all wilted down.

曳² I. Used for the next: to trail, to drag after one; to saunter, to walk leisurely; to take by the hand: [1]ˌ*yeu yo²* fluttering, waving in the wind; *yo² yo²* an easy, sauntering gait.

拽² Yeh. Hsieh. Chuai. Also read *siĕk*,: to trail, to drag the feet along the ground; to take hold of one's hand.

睿² **叡**² Jui. Wei. Perspicacious, of superior discernment, wise, astute; the divine intelligence ascribed to sages; keen, shrewd, knowing: [2]*yo² seng²* wise, sapient, sage-like; [3]*yo² te²* wise, intelligent; intuitive perception.

汭² Jui. A branch of the river King in the east of Kansuh, near the town of Hwating; the junction of two rivers; the windings of streams; the north of a stream: [4]ˌ*sa yo²* the edge of a sand-spit.

蚋² **蜹**² Jui. A gnat, a mosquito; also a venemous snake: [5]ˌ*ung yo²* mosquitoes and gnats; [6]ˌ*sing yo²* flies and gnats, as gathering in swarms over the water.

芮 Jui. Rocky plants, short alpine herbs; shooting forth, budding, as plants; fine, small, delicate; a bank, a brink; a feudal state, now Juich'êng in the S. W. of Shansi.

裔² I. The skirt of a robe; the lower border; a border, an extreme point, frontiers; posterity, descendants: [7]*yo² yo²* walking, flying about; [8]ˌ*mieu yo²* posterity; [9]*tek*, *yo²* direct descendants; COM., [10]*haiu² yo²* one's posterity.

⿰氵裔² I. Rough, troubled water: [11]ˌ*ŭng yo²* a broad expanse of water; *met.*, many, multitudinous, as people.

銳² Jui. Tui. Wei. Sharp-pointed, lanceolate; acute, peaked, conical; ardent, zealous; valiant, courageous; keen, cunning, quick-witted; small, trifling, insignificant, as a fault: [12]*yo² le²* sharp, as an edge; [13]'*k'eu yo²* talkative, cunning in speech, detracting; [14]*yo²* '*ming*, keen, quick, ready; [15]*yo²* ˌ*sü*, valiant troops; [16]*yo² che²* a resolute will; valiant and eager, as for battle; COM., [17]*yo² k'e²* a zealous spirit; valiant; earnest, studious, as a learner.

(926) Yoh.

Yoh,. A coll. word, as in *yoh*, *yoh*, or ˌ*yo yoh*, to

1 飄曳 2 睿聖 3 睿智 4 沙汭 5 蚊蚋 6 蠅蚋 7 裔裔 8 苗裔 9 嫡裔 10 後裔 11 溶⿰氵裔 12 銳利 13 口銳 14 銳敏 15 銳師 16 銳志 17 銳氣 ○

calculate, to make a rough estimate of; *yoh,* *k'ang'* to calculate and see (how much); *yoh,* *'la 'mó,* to make a rough estimate of the amount.

藥 葯 Yo. Yao. Yüeh. Medicinal herbs; materia medica, medicines, physic; drugs, compounds, preparations; to administer medicine, to heal; medical, healing: the 2d read *tek,* also means to bind, to entwine: COM., [1]*,kung ,sing yoh,* a preparation of medicinal ingredients; [2]*yoh, ,chai,* medicines; [3]*yoh, seng'* the nature or properties of medicine; [4]*yoh, 'hung,* or [5]*yoh, 'sang,* powders; [6]*yoh, ,wong,* pills; [7]*yoh, 'chiu,* medicated spirits; [8]*yoh, ,hwong,* a medical prescription; [9]*'ló 'ch'ü yoh,* ratsbane; [10]*yoh, 'ing,* a disguise with the dose; [11]*chiě' yoh,, kak, yoh,* and [12]*,ngó yoh,* to prepare, mix, and decoct drugs; COLL., [13]*yoh, k'e' ,kiàng,* the operation of a dose; [14]*yoh, sioh, t'aik,* or *yoh, sioh, huk,* a dose of physic; [15]*ch'auk, yoh,* to buy medicine; [16]*yoh, chak,* a drug-cutter. The second character read *yok,* : the leaves of angelica or *pah, 'chi.*

瀹 Yo. Yüeh. To soak, to wash and cleanse; to boil, to dress, to cook in soup; boiling, bubbling: [17]*,su yoh,* to open and clean, as a drain; [18]*,t'ang yoh,* agitated, as water.

禴 Yo. Yüeh. Sacrifices offered in the spring; a poor, mean sacrifice.

籲 龥 Yo. Yü. Also read *ëü'*: to cry out in supplication, to invoke, to implore, to importune: [19]*,hu yoh,* to call on; [20]*'k'ong yoh,* to invoke earnestly; *yoh, siong' tá'* to invoke the Supreme Ruler.

鑰 Yo. Yao. Yüeh. Used for the next: a lock, a bolt or catch: to go in, to enter: [21]*'só yoh,* a lock; [22]*ho' yoh,* a door-lock; COLL., *,mwong yoh, sioh, a'* to give the bolt a push and fasten the door.

龠 籥 Yo. Yüeh. Used for the last: a musical reed or pipe with three or more holes, resembling a flageolet; a measure of 1200 grains of millet; two such measures make a *hak,* or gill.

Yoh, . A coll. word, as in *yoh, ,t'ai,* or *yoh, ,t'ai ch'eu'* an instrument consisting of an upright axis with lights turned by a pole or lever "to light the spirit" of a deceased parent; *,pwang yoh, ,t'ai,* to turn this instrument, as the eldest son or a married daughter does; *yoh, ,t'ai ka'* the priest's fee for chanting prayers on the occasion.

Yoh, . A coll. word, as in *lau' yoh,* a large species of hawk or kite: *lau' yoh, mwak, ,kiě 'kiàng,* the hawk swoops up the chick.

(927) **Yok.**

約 Yo. Yao. Yüeh. To bind with a cord; to agree, to contract; to restrict, to retrench, to economize; to bind by rules, to cause to submit, to restrain, to control; to

1 君臣藥 2 藥材 3 藥性 4 藥粉 5 藥散 6 藥丸 7 藥酒 8 藥方 9 老鼠藥 10 藥引 11 製藥 12 熬藥 13 藥氣行 14 藥一貼 15 撮藥 16 藥閘 17 疏瀹 18 潭瀹 19 呼籲 20 懇籲 21 鎖鑰 22 戶鑰

stoop, to bend down; an agreement, a promise, a contract; a treaty, a compact; an association, as of streets or guilds; a neighborhood; poor, reduced; brief, condensed; briefly, compendiously; to divide, as in arithmetic: [1]*yok, seng*ʼ a sworn engagement; [2]*‚tieu ‚ū ʻiu yok,* tides are like compacts—i. e. trustworthy; COM., [3]*yok, che*^{3} a written contract; [4]*‚ming yok,* a plain agreement; [5]*yok, ka*ʼ the price agreed on; [6]*yok, ‚tang,* a bill of sale, a contract; a list or scale (of prices), as settled by a guild; [7]*hak$_2$ yok,* to make an agreement; [8]*yok, liok$_2$* or *tai^2 yok,* in general, for the most part; [9]*pok, yok, ‚i ‚tung,* to agree or to meet undesignedly; [10]*yok, hwak,* the terms or rules of a compact; [11]*yok, sok,* to bind by contract; restraint, control, as over inferiors.

閱, Yüeh. To examine, to inspect, to take an account of, to look and see that all is right; to review, as troops; to pass through, to have experience of; to compare, to read, to criticise; to admit of, to permit: [12]*yok, ‚chʻau,* to review troops; [13]*yok, kwong*ʼ to revise or criticise an essay; COM., [14]*yok, lik$_2$* to have experience, as in worldly matters.

弱, Jo. Read *yok$_2$;* coll. *yok,:* weak, jaded, worn, fatigued; to lose one's desire for, to be discouraged, disheartened: *yok, ‚mó lik$_2$* the strength wasted with fatigue; *yok, ‚pi,* or *yok, ‚pai,* to lose heart, to become disinclined to *kʻah, ‚tieu yok,* tired with play; *chóʼ nioh$_2$ yok,* to work till very jaded.

悅$_2$ Yüeh. 說$_2$ Yüeh. Shuo. Shui. Sê. To feel happy, contented; pleased, gratified, delighted; to agree, to submit gladly: the 2d also read *siok,* and *swoiʼ* q. v.: [15]*ʻhi yok$_2$* gratified; [16]*yok$_2$ muk$_2$* to please the eye; COM., [17]*yok$_2$ e*ʼ pleased, delighted; *yok$_2$ ʻnü ‚sing e*ʼ I (do it) so as to please you.

弱$_2$ 弱$_2$ Jo. Jao. Ni. Niao. Weak, feeble, debilitated, languishing; delicate, fragile, slender; ruined, destroyed, lost, gone: used for the coll. *yok,* q. v.: [18]*yok$_2$ chek,* a weak constitution, a woman; weak, thin, as in substance; *yok$_2$ ʻnü,* my young daughter; [19]*yok$_2$ kwang*ʼ a young man; COM., [20]*‚soi yok$_2$* emaciated and weak; *yok$_2$ kang^2* to perspire from weakness.

蒻$_2$ Jo. A sort of rush like a flag, of whose tender plants mats may be woven: [21]*ʻkü yok$_2$* a culinary vegetable, a sort of yam.

若$_2$ Jo. Jê. Yo. Yao. To gather plants; to accord with, to yield to, to follow; a conjunction, if, perhaps, supposing that; as, like, according to; it points out the distinct subjects spoken of, as to; also denotes the second personal pronoun, thou, you; used as a euphonic particle: [22]*pok, yok$_2$* or *‚u yok$_2$* not like or equal to, not as good as; *sük$_2$ yok$_2$* which is the

[1]約信	有約	[4]明約	[6]約單	[8]約畧	而同	[11]約束	[13]閱卷	[15]喜悅	[17]悅意	[19]弱冠	[21]蒟蒻
[2]潮如	[3]約字	[5]約價	[7]合約	[9]不約	[10]約法	[12]閱操	[14]閱歷	[16]悅目	[18]弱質	[20]衰弱	[22]不若

better? [1]ʻyokˎ ˏü, if, since, it seems; [2]yokˎ chěüʼ ˏhó ˏlai, whence did you come? [3]yokˎ wakˎ it was said, one says; [4]ˏsiong yokˎ similar, probably; [5]yokˎ ʻchʻü yokˎ ʻpi, as to these and those; [6]ˏpwang yokˎ wise, intelligent—a Budhist term; COM., [7]yokˎ ʻsü, or [8]yokˎ ˏhwang, if, supposing that; [9]yokˎ laungʼ if we speak of, in regard to.

箬ˎ Jo. The cuticle of the bamboo; a kind of southern grass (Arundo?), whose broad leaves are made into hats or shoe-soles, or used to line tea-chests: used for the coll. *niohˎ* q. v.

鄀ˎ Jo. A feudal state, now I-chʻêng district in Hsiang-yang-fu, in the north of Hupeh.

躍ˎ Yo. Yüeh. To leap, to jump, to hop; to leap for joy; to frisk, to sport, to gambol: [10]tʻieuʼ yokˎ to jump about; [11]ˏngü yokˎ ˏlüng ˏmwong, the fish (carp) leaps the dragon-gate—rapid advancement.

(928) Yong.

央 ˏYang. In the midst, the center, the middle of; the half; wide, ample, extensive; to finish; to end; a fine, fresh appearance; commonly used in the sense of to request as a favor, to solicit or trouble one to do: [12]yâʼ ēʼ ˏyong, the night not yet past; COM., [13]ˏtüng ˏyong, the center, middle of; [14]ˏyong tʻaukˎ to trouble one with a commission; COLL., [15]ˏyong ˏmuí ˏnëng, to commission a match-maker; ˏmó nóiʼ ˏyong, no one whom I can solicit or beg to do it.

殃 **祆** ˏYang. Punishment, calamity; a visitation, a divine judgment, a retribution; ruin, misfortune; to punish; unluckily: [16]chikˎ ˏyong, fatal sickness; [17]ˏtʻiéng ˏyong, divine retribution; COM., [18]ˏchai ˏyong, calamities, judgments.

泱 ˏYang. Moving cloud or vapor; swift, rapid, as a torrent; vast, wide; agitated: ˏyong ˏyong, vast, as a sea; violent, as wind.

淵 Yüan. An eddy, a whirpool; a deep pool; a deep, an abyss, a vortex, a gulf: [19]ˏchʻing ˏyong, a deep abyss, the vast deep; ˏtʻiéng ˏyong ˏsiong kaikˎ as far apart as the sky and the abyss; ˏyong ˏyong, a concert of drums.

鴦 ˏYang. The female of the mandarin duck: [20]ˏwong ˏyong, a yellow macaw; some say, the mango bird; COM., ˏwong ˏyong, the male and female mandarin duck; *met.*, a pair, as in ˏwong ˏyong ʻching, a pair of bridal pillows.

鳶 ˏYüan. A kite or sparrow-hawk; its scream indicates wind and storm: ˏhung ˏyong, or ʻchai ˏyong, a paper-kite.

焉 ˏYen. An initial interrogative particle, implying a negative answer, how, what: also read ˏyong, q. v.: ˏyong ˏti, how can one know? ˏyong ˏneng, how can, how able to? ˏyong taikˎ pokˎ ʻkong, how

1 若如 2 若自何來 3 若曰 4 相若 5 若此若彼 6 般若 7 若使 8 若凡 9 若論 10 跳躍 11 魚躍龍門 12 夜未央 13 中央 14 央託 15 央媒仸 16 疾殃 17 天殃 18 災殃 19 深淵 20 鴛鴦

can one not say it? one must say or speak of it.

嫣 Yen. Hsien. Handsome, beautiful; the smile of beauty, a gracious smile; also to connect.

ʻ蔫 Yen. Not fresh, corrupt, rotten, putrid, stinking, as flesh: COM., [1]˓ngü ˓yong, the fish not fresh; [2]˓yong ˓yong ĕʾ a stench, as of spoiled meat. Read yéngʾ: decayed plants.

ʻ攘 Jang. Also read ˓yong: to push, to drive off violently; to steal, to seize and appropriate to one's self, as strayed animals; to refuse, to reject; to stop, to exclude: also read yongʾ q. v.: [3]˓yong ˓yong, to appropriate a stray sheep. Read ʻyong: to confound, to embroil: [4]ʻyeu ʻyong, to throw into disorder.

ʻ壤 Jang. Nang. Soft, loamy soil; mold, earth, soil; land, region, place; a hill, a mound; good, amiable, as a child; confused, in disorder: [5]kaiʾ ʻyong, cover and ground—heaven and earth; [6]auk, ʻyong, a rich soil; [7]ngiēʾ ʻyong, an ant-hill; [8]nôiʾ ʻyong, and [9]ngwoiʾ ʻyong, the inner and outer limbs, as in an eclipse; [10]kek, ʻyong, an ancient game.

ʻ穰 Jang. Also read ˓siong: the culm or stalk of grain; luxuriant, as fields of grain; abundant, plentiful, fruitful: [11]hok, ʻyong, the blessing of plenty, great prosperity.

ʻ養 Yang. To feed, to nourish, to rear, to bring up; to support, to maintain, as the indigent; to tame, to improve, as breeds; to cultivate, as plants; to care for one's health, to take relaxation, to rest; to improve, as one's heart; food, aliment; a cook: as used for the next, to itch: also read yongʾ q. v.: [12]ʻyong chăʾ yéngʾ a hospital, an infirmary; COM., [13]ʻyong wak, to support life, to nourish; [14]ʻu ʻyong, to nourish or rear up; [15]ʻyong ˓sing, to cultivate the heart; [16]ʻyong siéngʾ a portion of property reserved for the support of parents; [17]ʻyong ˓ngü, to breed fish; [18]ʻyong sŭk, to tame, to domesticate; [19]ʻyong ŭk, ˓tong, a foundling-asylum; COLL., [20]ʻyong ʻkiăng, or [21]˓tʻiéng ʻyong, to bear children; ʻyong sioh, poʾ to hatch a brood, to have a litter; ʻyong ˓i sioh, sieʾ mengʾ to support him his whole life-time.

ʻYong. A coll. word, as in ˓sing ʻyong, a new bud or sprout; ˓sing ʻyong chiăh, pwok, leuʾ the new bud has just sprouted.

ʻ癢 ʻ癢 Yang. ʻ痒 Yang. Shên. The 3d also read ˓yong: to itch; a sore, an itching, a desire to scratch: the 1st used for the coll. siongʾ and the 3d also read ˓siong, q. v.: [22]˓sŏ ʻyong, to scratch an itching place; pok, ˓kwang tʻongʾ ʻyong, does not involve the least pain, of no more account than a scratch.

ʻ抰 Yang. To beat, as with a carriage strap; to beat, to whip with a strap.

---

[1] 魚蔫 [2] 蔫蔫味 [3] 攘攘羊〇 [4] 擾攘 [5] 盖壤 [6] 沃壤 [7] 蟻壤 [8] 內壤 [9] 外壤 [10] 擊壤 [11] 福穰 [12] 養濟院 [13] 養活 [14] 撫養 [15] 養心 [16] 養饍 [17] 養魚 [18] 養熟 [19] 養育堂 [20] 養仔 [21] 添養 [22] 搔癢

怏' Yang. Discontented, uneasy, restive, insubmissive: *yong' yong' ˏsing*, fastidious, disgusted; *yong' ˏyong*, conceited, supercilious.

恙' Yang. A vegetable-worm that gnaws men's hearts; sad, sorrowful; grief, melancholy, low spirits; a disease, sickness; ailment, indisposition, complaints: [1]*'piék, ˏlai ˏu yong'* have you been well since we parted?—an epistolary phrase; COM., [2]*'koi' yong'* your ailment; [3]*'chiéng' yong'* my complaint.

映' **暎**' Ying. The sun past the meridian; to shine, to reflect, as images; the sunlight; a glare, a bright light; to gleam, to glimmer; an image, a reflection; bright, clear, apparent, manifest: used for the coll. *yăng'* q. v.: [4]*'yong' nik,* clear sunlight; COM., [5]*'yĕng yong'* to shimmer, a glimmering of light, as from water in motion; [6]*'tó' yong'* reflected light.

盎' Yang. A vessel for containing wine or water, a sort of basin or tureen; an earthen vessel, which was struck in regulating music; full, abundant: *ˏt'ong yong'* a soup tureen; *'ngwa yong'* an earthen basin.

鞅' Yang. Ornaments or trappings on a bridle; a rope to tie an ox, a halter; to tie, to halter; a trace to draw a cart; fierce, violent: *yong' 'chiong*, fluttered, embarrassed, as by a burden; harassed by cares.

羊 ˏYang. A sheep, a goat; a gazelle, a chamois; to saunter, to roam at one's ease: COM., [7]*ˏmiéng ˏyong*, a sheep; [8]*ˏsang ˏyong*, a goat; [9]*ˏling ˏyong*, an antelope, an argali, whose horns are used medicinally; [10]*ˏyong 'ku*, a ram; [11]*ˏyong 'mó*, a ewe; [12]*ˏkó ˏyong*, (coll. [13]*ˏyong 'kiăng*), a lamb, a kid; [14]*ˏyong ˏchié,* mutton-suet; [15]*ˏyong nük,* mutton, goat's meat; [16]*ˏyong hwang'* a sheep-dealer; [17]*ˏyong ˏt'ó*, the carambola; COLL., [18]*k'aung' ˏyong mĕk,* to sleep with sheep's eyes — i. e. with the eyes partly open; [19]*ˏyong ˏhing*, a swoon, a fainting-fit; [20]*ˏyong 'kiăng t'á' p'ah*, the kid beaten instead — one who is beaten as a substitute for the real culprit.

佯 ˏYang. To pretend, to feign, to simulate; false, unreal, pretended; a pretense, a feint, a ruse, a dodge: [21]*ˏyong pok, ˏti,* to pretend not to know; *ˏyong ˏkwong*, to feign madness.

徉 ˏYang. To ramble, to rove about; to stray off, to wander: *'hwong ˏyong*, or *ˏsiong ˏyong*, to ramble, to stroll about.

洋 ˏYang. The sea, the ocean; vast, broad, extensive; water overflowing; from beyond the sea, foreign, western, European; two streams in the north of Shantung, also one in Kansuh; in the coll. a wide expanse of fields, a cultivated plain: [22]*ˏyong ek,* to overflow, inundating; to extend widely, as one's fame; COM., [23]*hai ˏyong*, seas,

---

1 別來無恙 2 貴恙 3 賤恙 4 映日 5 掩映 6 倒映 7 綿羊 8 山羊 9 羚羊 10 羊羖 11 羊母 12 羔羊 13 羊仔 14 羊脂 15 羊肉 16 羊販 17 羊桃 18 睡羊目 19 羊眩 20 羊仔替拍 21 佯不知 22 洋溢 23 海洋

oceans; [1]꜀yong ꜀sung, a sea-going junk, a ship; [2]ʻchʻok, ꜀yong, to cross the sea, as for trade; [3]꜀yong yĕngʼ a sort of bean-vermicelli, which dissolves like gelatine; [4]꜀sá ꜀yong kiăngʼ portable dioramas; [5]꜀yong ʻchü ꜀kĕng, the river Yang-tsz'; [6]꜀yong ꜀tio, a kind of brasier, used in the middle of a room; [7]꜀yong ꜀siong, a foreign merchant; COLL., ꜀yong mengʼ the face of the sea; an expanse of fields; ꜀yong ꜀chʻang, ultramarine or prussian blue, ferro-cyanate of potash.

沿 ꜀ **沿** ꜀ Yen. To follow a stream, to travel along a shore; to sail with; to follow, to comply with, to conform, as to others' wishes; to make a tour, to go through a circuit; accommodating, obsequious; continuous, successive: ꜀yong ꜀kong, to follow the (windings of) rivers; ꜀hung sük꜀ ꜀siong ꜀yong, the custom has been perpetuated; ꜀yong ꜀tu, the circuit of a journey.

鉛 ꜀ Yüan. Yen. Chʻien. Lead, the ꜀chʻing ꜀king, or blue metal; leaden: [8]haik꜀ ꜀yong, or haik꜀ sek꜀ common lead; [9]꜀yong ʻhung, ceruse, white lead; COM., [10]꜀yong ʻchi, a leaden ball or bullet; a term applied to cannon balls and shot; [11]꜀yong cheʼ words or characters engraved on lead, foreign type; [12]ʻpwo ꜀yong, to patch with lead, as broken dollars; [13]꜀yong ꜀teu, bar-lead, pig-lead; [14]꜀yong tʻiĕk, tin-plate, sheet-tin; COLL., lauʼ ꜀yong, to pour in melted lead, to adulterate with lead, as dollars; ꜀yong ʻchi, (or [15]sek, lak꜀) the blanks on which type is cut.

鎔 ʻ Yung. Jung. Read ꜀üng; used in the Paik, ꜀Ing for the coll. ꜀yong: to smelt, to melt, to fuse metals: ꜀yong kʻŏʼ melted; ꜀yong ꜀ngüng, to fuse silver.

瘍 ꜀ Yang. A wound, a sore, an ulcer; sore, wounded; a sore head.

揚 ꜀ Yang. To rise, to dash, as the waves; to spread out, to extend, to display; to open, as the eyebrows; to elevate, as the voice; to scatter, to winnow; to stir up, to excite the feelings of one; to divulge, to report; to publish, to make famous; to bluster, to make a show of: [16]ek꜀ ꜀yong, low and high, as musical notes; ʻhai pok꜀ ꜀yong ꜀pʻŏ, no waves on the sea—all was peace (in Wan Wang's time); ꜀ing ꜀yong, (like) a fluttering eagle—i. e. brave; [17]pŏʼ ꜀yong, to publish; COM., [18]꜀yong ꜀tiong, to spread abroad, to divulge; [19]꜀yong ʻu ꜀yong ꜀wi, to bluster, to assume an attitude of authority; ʻchi pwoʼ ꜀yong ꜀sing, stop and call out! a term on common placards; [20]꜀yong kʻeʼ or ꜀yong eʼ pleased, delighted; ꜀yong ꜀yong taik꜀ eʼ to obtain fully one's wish; COLL., ꜀yong tʻiongʼ to spread a report, to tell everywhere.

颺 ꜀ Yang. Similar to the last: blown about by the wind; whirled, driven, tossed; sailing along; winnowed: pŏʼ ꜀yong, to winnow grain; ꜀yong ꜀ngiong, loud, hasty words.

暘 ꜀ Yang. The sun rising; a clear bright sun; dry, serene, as weather; to dry in the

1洋船 2出洋 3洋燕 4西洋鏡 5洋子江 6洋厨 7洋商 8黑鉛 9鉛粉 10鉛子 11鉛字 12補鉛 13鉛條 14鉛鐵 15錫粒 16抑揚 17播揚 18揚傳 19揚武揚威 20揚氣

sun: *꜀yong kok꜀*, the place of sunrising, the orient.

楊 ꜀Yang. Used in the names of the willow and some other trees: [1]*꜀yong sëüᵓ* a sort of banian, ficus religiosus; COM., [2]*꜀yong ᶜliu*, the willow; [3]*꜀yong ꜀mui*, a tree yielding a fruit like the a r b u t u s; [4]*꜀yong ꜀mui ꜀ch'ong*, a bubo; [5]*꜀yong ꜀t'ó*, the carambola, also called *꜀yong ꜀t'ó*, sheep's peach; [6]*꜀yong ꜀chiu ch'eᵓ* "the Yangchou market-place"—a term applied to the 36 paper-shops, as burnt in the *ᶜp'wo toᵓ* rites.

陽 ꜀Yang. Lofty and clear, manifest, splendid; the superior of the dual powers in nature, as heaven, the sun, day, male; matter in motion, the purer and more subtle parts of matter, from which were evolved spirits, gods, and the human soul; the superior of two things in contrast, as the north bank of a stream, the front, light; open, openly; the male member, virility; the 10th moon; to i n j u r e: [7]*꜀ch'ing ꜀yong*, pure, subtile; [8]*꜀yong ꜀yong*, ornate, polished, as language; [9]*꜀hung ꜀yong*, hamadryads; [10]*꜀ch'ing ꜀y o n g*, the spring; [11]*sik꜀ ꜀yong*, evening; COM., [12]*꜀ing ꜀yong*, the dual powers; [13]*t'aiᵓ ꜀yong*, the sun; [14]*꜀twang ꜀yong*, the 5th of the 5th moon; [15]*꜀yong siéᵓ* or *꜀yong ꜀kang*, the world; *꜀yong uk꜀* the virile member; *chaungᵓ ꜀yong*, an aphrodisiac; *꜀yong k'eᵓ wongᵓ* the male principle predominant, many men; *꜀hui ꜀yong*, to revive, as when near death; *kek꜀ keuᵓ ꜀hui ꜀yong*, to save life in extremity, as a cholera-medicine; *꜀yong siéᵓ pok꜀ ꜀ti ꜀ing siéᵓ sëüᵓ* this world does not know the other world's affairs.

煬 ꜀Yang. To fuse, to refine, to assay: to melt and refine, as wax. Read *yongᵓ*: to roast, to scorch, to warm or dry at the fire; opposite a fire; hot, blazing, fiery.

焉 ꜀Yen. A final particle, an adverb denoting an affirmation and completion of the sense; a euphonic particle, giving emphasis to the previous word: also read *꜀yong*, q. v.: *ᶜi ꜀yong ꜀chai*, is it done? is it already settled? [16]*꜀ü ꜀t'iéng ꜀yong*, as it is in heaven.

然 ꜀Jan. Sometimes used for the next: to burn, to simmer; to assent to, to comply; used as a final particle, yes, truly, so, verily, certainly; as a disjunctive introducing another statement, but, then, if so then; used as the sign of adverbs: [17]*choiᵓ ꜀yong*, suddenly; [18]*eᵓ pek꜀ ꜀yong*, not certainly so, probably not; [19]*꜀yong yáᵓ* just so; COM., [20]*ᶜkwo ꜀yong*, a kind of chimpanzee; truly, surely; [21]*chëüᵓ ꜀yong*, or *chëüᵓ chëüᵓ ꜀yong ꜀yong*, spontaneously, of course; *chëüᵓ ꜀yong ꜀i ꜀yong*, spontaneous, self-existent, underived, as God; *꜀yong hauᵓ* afterwards, then.

燃 ꜀Jan. To burn, to fire; to boil, to decoct: *꜀yong ꜀sieu*, to catch fire, to burn; a conflagration; *꜀yong ꜀mi ꜀chi kek꜀* so imminent as to burn the eyebrows—very urgent or pressing; dangerous; COM.,

[1]楊樹 [2]楊柳 [3]楊梅 [4]楊梅瘡 [5]楊桃 [6]楊州市 [7]清陽 [8]陽陽 [9]雲陽 [10]青陽 [11]夕陽 [12]陰陽 [13]太陽 [14]端陽 [15]陽世 [16]如天焉 [17]卒然 [18][illegible] [19][illegible] [20]果然 [21][illegible]

福州方言拼音字典

kiék꜀, ʻch'ai ꜀yong ꜀teng, to hang festoons and light lamps, as on a god's birthday; COLL., *꜀yong ëüʼ* to smoulder; *met.*, to waste away gradually; diminished, used up.

延 ꜀Yen. To go far; protracted, prolonged; long, slow, dilatory; distant; to extend far, to spread, as a creeping plant; to advance, to enter; to reach, to arrive at; to call, to invite; spread out, arranged; to involve another: [1]*꜀yong ꜀ti*, slow; [2]*꜀ch'iéng ꜀yong*, to delay, to protract; [3]*꜀yong ꜀ping*, to invite guests; COM., [4]*꜀á ꜀yong*, to put off, to procrastinate; [5]*꜀yong ꜀ping ʻhu*, the Yenping department in Fookien.

埏 ꜀Yen. Shan. The limit of a piece of land, the border, the boundary; the path to a grave: *paik꜀ ꜀yong*, the eight points of the compass, all around, everywhere.

涎 ꜀Nien. The watering of the mouth, saliva, the spittle; sometimes written for the coll. *ʻlang*: *꜀yong mwak꜀*, froth, saliva. Read *siéng^2* as in *꜀i siéng^2* connected, succeeding; *ʻmiéng siéng^2* water flowing.

筵 ꜀Yen. A bamboo mat; a mat spread to eat on, as anciently done; a spread table; *met.*, a feast, a banquet: [6]*꜀yong sik꜀* or *꜀yong yéngʼ* a feast, an entertainment; [7]*ʻsëüʼ ꜀yong*, to spread a banquet; [8]*꜀king ꜀yong*, the hall where the Emperor meets the academicians; COM., [9]*ʻhi ꜀yong*, the joyous feast—a phrase on wedding-cards.

緣 緣 ꜀Yüan. Yen. A binding, a trimming or facing, as on the collar or sleeves of a dress; to accord, to harmonize with something previously existing; intimacy, sympathy due to some hidden influence, as fate or providence, an affinity, a connection; union, marriage; a circumstance, a reason, a cause; for, because, since, therefore; to comply with; to climb: used for the coll. *yong^2* q. v.: [10]*꜀ing ꜀yong*, connected; to intrigue, to use bribery; [11]*꜀yong muk꜀ ꜀kiu ꜀ngü*, to climb a tree to catch a fish—a useless search; COM., [12]*꜀yong koʼ* or *꜀yong ꜀ing*, a cause, a reason; [13]*꜀yong ꜀hó*, why? wherefore? [14]*꜀yong ꜀iu*, the source or originating cause; [15]*꜀yong hong^2* natural affinity or connection; [16]*꜀ing ꜀yong*, marriage; [17]*꜀liong ꜀yong ꜀t'iéng teng^2* happy unions are decreed by Heaven; [18]*꜀tá ꜀yong*, to subscribe for public purposes; [19]*hwaʼ ꜀yong*, to beg fees, as priests do; [20]*꜀yong hong^2 ʻch'iéng*, the affinity was shallow, as said when one of the married pair dies early.

件^2 Chien. Read *kiong^2* in the dictionaries: a classifier of wide application, an article, an affair, a subject, a thing, a commodity, an article of dress, etc.; answers to a, an, one: COM., [21]*yong^2 soʼ* the number of articles; COLL., *꜀i ꜀siong sioh꜀ yong^2* one garment; *ʻchi sioh꜀ yong^2* this one; *na^2 ʻkwi yong^2* only a few; *yong^2 yong^2 ꜀tu á^2* can do everything.

[1]延遲 [2]遷延 [3]延賓 [4]挨延 [5]延平府 [6]筵席 [7]肆筵 [8]經筵 [9]喜筵 [10]貪緣 [11]緣木求魚 [12]緣故 [13]緣何 [14]緣由 [15]緣分 [16]姻緣 [17]良緣天定 [18]題緣 [19]化緣 [20]緣分淺 [21]件數

養² Yang. To provide for, to support, to maintain, as one's parents: also read *'yong*, q. v.: [1]*'yong*² *,ch'ing*, to support one's parents; [2]*'küng yong*² to provide for; COM., [3]*'hong*² *yong*² to nourish, to provide, as for parents; *kó*³ *yong*² to report (resignation of office) to take care of one's parents.

樣² Yang. A rule, a pattern; the form, shape, style, fashion; a way, a mode, a manner; *met.*, a guide, an example: COM., [4]*yong*² *sek*, the shape, the contour; mode, sample, pattern; [5]*,mwo yong*² a mode or pattern, an exemplar; [6]*wang*² *,sing yong*² to change to a new fashion; COLL., *,chiong*² *yong*² how, in what manner? *,chiong yong*² *,ki*, why? how? *,sang nioh, yong*² what sort or manner? *óh, ,i yong*² to imitate him; *ng*² *ch'iong*² *yong*² not like things, shapeless, unsuitable; poor, mean, as said affectedly of presents.

漾² **瀁**² Yang. A river in the south of Kansuh; agitated water, the motion of waves; waves, ripples; long, vast, extensive; deep: [7]*,yeu yong*² roughened into waves; in the coll. to agitate or talk about, to expose, to make known; COLL., [8]*yong*² *,k'wi*, separated by the motion of the water, as boats; [9]*yong*² *,hung*, turbid or roiled by being disturbed; [10]*yong*² *t'aung*³ *,ch'ing*, cleared by being shaken, made to settle, as thin congee. The second read *'yong*, as in [11]*'kwong 'yong*, vast, as an expanse of water.

攘² Jang. To yield, to give place to; to cede, to waive, as one's rights, in which senses the same as the next: also read *,yong*, q. v.

讓² Jang. To give up, to waive, to recede, as from one's rights; to yield, to give place to; to prefer others to one's self; yielding, retiring, courteous, complaisant; humble, lowly; also to reprove, to recriminate: used for the coll. *niong*² q. v.: [12]*,k'iéng yong*² humble; [13]*t'ói*³ *yong*² retiring; [14]*'lá yong*² courteous, complaisant.

禳² Jang. Read *,yong* and *,siong* in the dictionaries: to make offerings and pray in order to avert calamity, to deprecate evil: [15]*yong*² *,sing*, to pray to one's star; COM., [16]*'chie yong*² or *t'ói*³ *yong*² to avert evil by offerings; [17]*yong*² *,chai*, to deprecate calamity; [18]*yong*² *t'ai*³ *swoi*³ to sacrifice to the Chinese Cybele or Great Cycle.

釀² Jang. To make liquor from boiled rice with yeast cakes, to brew wine or rice spirits; *met.*, to breed trouble, to foment, as sedition: [19]*yong*² *'chiu*, to distill spirits; [20]*yong*² *,sing tai*² *hwo*² to provoke great calamity, as by trivial intermeddling.

緣² Yüan. Read *,yong*; used in the *Paik*, *,Ing* for the coll. *yong*²: to put on a binding or border; to trim or ornament an edge, as with braid, or with thread or foil of gold, silver, or brass: *yong*² *sioh*, *,kiéng*, to trim an edge, to make an ornamental border.

---

1 養親 2 供養 3 奉養 4 樣式 5 模樣 6 換新樣 7 搖漾 ○ 8 漾開 9 漾渾 10 漾盪清 11 廣瀁 ○ 12 謙讓 13 退讓 14 禮讓 15 禳星 16 祭禳 17 禳災 18 禳太歲 19 釀酒 ○ 20 釀成大禍

Note. This list is designed to introduce a few additional uses of characters, and some additional Romanized words and phrases. All the characters given in the list, except the two under sections (342) and (804), have appeared as leading characters in the body of the dictionary. The figures marked with an asterisk (*) indicate syllables that now appear for the first time.

(2*) Aë.

Aë. A coll. word, similar to *꜀ë;* used as a familiar call, ho! halloo! ho, you there!

(26) Chang.

站² Chan. Used in the coll. for the full time, amount, value: ¹*kau' chang'* to come to the set time, as for taking the meal; ²*mwoi' kau' chang'* has not yet reached the time, amount, full value, etc.

(31) Chë.

‛Chë. A coll. word: to miss, to fail to meet: *꜀song ‛chë,* to miss each other, as by taking different roads, or one coming after the other has left.

(38) Chëü.

絮' Hsü. Read *sëü';* coll. *chëü'* as in ³*p‛wai' ꜀miëng chëü'* refuse cotton-batting or bedding.

(41) Chi.

‛枳 Chih. Used for the coll. *‛chi;* a numerative of skeins, and of small bunches, as of coarse paper, flowers, coiffure-cord, incense-sticks, etc.

(46) Chié.

Chié'. A coll. word, as in *ng² chié' sëü²* not much, a very little, a trifling amount.

(65) Chu.

‛Chu. A coll. word, as in *o' ‛chu,* to have a clear perception of; *꜀mó ‛chu,* not to know clearly or definitely.

(88) Ch‛ai.

才 ꜂Ts‛ai. Read *꜀chai;* coll. *꜀ch‛ai,* as in ⁴*꜀nu ꜀ch‛ai,* a slave, a bondman.

材 ꜂Ts‛ai. Read *꜀chai;* coll. *꜀ch‛ai,* as in ⁵*꜀kwang ꜀ch‛ai,* a coffin.

(116) Ch‛ieu.

‛釗 Ch‛ao. Used in the coll. for an iron testing probe, called ⁶*t‛iék,꜀ch‛ieu;*⁷*꜀t‛ong꜀ch‛ieu,* a probe for testing sugar.

(131) Ch‛ong.

꜂床 Ch‛uang. Used in the coll. as the numerative of sheets, blankets, etc.: ⁸*꜀miéng sioh,꜀ch‛ong,* one cotton comfortable.

(139) Ch‛üng.

꜀Ch‛üng. A coll. word: to wrench, to sprain, as the foot or hand: *꜀k‛a pwak,꜀ch‛üng,* the foot sprained by a fall.

(207) Hong.

Hong'. A coll. word, as in *wak, hong'* the leg of a stocking; *꜀k‛wo hong'* the leg of a boot.

(208) Hu.

꜀Hu. A coll. word: the sound of the wind: *꜀hung ꜀hu ꜀hu kieu'* the wind whistling.

(221) Hwo.

禍² Huo. Used in the coll. for rain, a gust, a shower: ⁹*taung² hwo'* to rain, as in summer; a fall of rain, a shower; ¹⁰*hwo' lau' tek,* a dripping of rain (from the eaves).

---

¹至站 ○ ²昧至站 ○ ³破棉絮 ○ ⁴奴才 ○ ⁵棺材 ○ ⁶鐵釗 ○ ⁷糖釗 ○ ⁸棉一床 ○ ⁹蕩禍 ○ ¹⁰禍漏滴 ○

(227*) **Ih.**

Ih,. A coll. euphonic prefix, as in *ih, wah,* to mark, to make strokes; *met.*, to write quickly; '*mwong ih, wah, sioh, a*' just scribble it off, as one says when waiting impatiently for a letter.

(231) **Ka.**

個 Ko. Read *kó*'; coll. '*ka*, also spoken '*a*, as in [1]'*sioh*, '*ka* ,*chiéng* or *sioh*, '*a* ,*chiéng*, one cash; [2]'*lang*' '*a* ,*nĕng*, two persons.

(235) **Kaĕk.**

覺 Chiao. Read *kauk*,; coll. *kaĕk*,: to perceive, to observe, to be aware of: [5]'*ng*' *kaĕk*, or [4]'*ng*' ,*chai kaĕk*, not perceiving, not aware of; [3]'*kiéng*' *kaĕk*, to perceive, to notice or take cognizance of.

(239) **Kai.**

再 Tsai. Read *chai*'; coll. *kai*': a second time, again, repeated: [6]*kai*' *chó*' to do again, to repeat the act.

(240) **Kaik.**

結 Chieh. Read *kiék*,; coll. *kaik*,: a numerative of skeins or knots, as of thread and vermicelli: [7]'*miéng*' *sioh*, *kaik*, one knot of thread-vermicelli.

潔 Chieh. Read *kiék*,; coll. *kaik*, as in *t'ah, kaik*, clean, pure in a physical or moral sense.

(243) **Kak.**

Kak,. A coll. word, as in *ng*' *kak*, ,*kŭng*, displeased, miffed; dissatisfied, unwilling; ,*i* ,*mó miéh*, *nóh*, *kak*, ,*kŭng*, he is not very well pleased about it!

(255) **Kĕng.**

公 Kung. Read ,*kung*; coll. ,*kĕng*, as in [8]*siong*' ,*kĕng*, a compellation for Sir, or Respected Sir; [9]*twai*' *siong*' ,*kĕng*, [10]*ne*' *siong*' ,*kĕng*, [11],*sang siong*' ,*kĕng*, compellations for the first, second, and third, brothers.

(265) **Kiék.**

頰 Chia. Used for the coll. in a *met.* sense, as in [12]*wak*, *kiék*, the "cheeks" or outside pieces on the foot of a stocking.

(288) **Kŭng.**

,*Kŭng*. A coll. word, as in *ng*' *kak*, ,*kŭng*, miffed, displeased, dissatisfied.

(289) **Kwa.**

桂 Kua. A numerative of things that are strung or suspended, as beads, keys, fire-crackers, etc.

(290) **Kwai.**

怪 Kuai. As in the coll. phrase, [13]*kwai*' *tek*, *se*' why, it is just so! what you say explains the matter!—about as ,*hwa tek*, *se*' q. v.

(292) **Kwang.**

管 Kuan. Used for the coll. '*kwang*, as in [14]'*ch'iu* '*kwang*, the wrist, the fore-arm.

(300) **K'a.**

股 Chiao. Used in the coll. as a numerative for one of a pair of things, as shoes, stockings, bracelets, etc.: the same as ,*k'iá*, q. v.: [15]*wak*, *sioh*, ,*k'a*, one stocking.

---

1 一個錢 2 二個伙 5 伓覺 4 伓哉覺 ○ 3 見覺 6 再做 7 麪一結 ○ 8 相公 9 大相公 10 二相公 11 三相公 ○ 12 襪頰 13 怪的是 14 手管 ○ 15 襪一股 ○

(342) K'ó.

熇ʾ Used for the coll. *k'óʾ* in the phrase [1]*ˏsieu k'óʾ* to roast meat, as on a spit or iron bars.

(350) K'ung.

ʿ綑 Used in the coll. as a numerative of packages of paper, and of rolls or solid bunches, as of bedding, cloth, rope, etc.
K'un.
K'uen.

(367) Lai.

ʿLai. A coll. word, as in [2]*ˏsüng pahˏ ʿlai*, the conical fruit of the pine tree, pine-cones.

(387) Liăng.

ʿ領 Read *ʿling;* coll. *ʿliăng:* used as the numerative of mats, carpets, etc.: [3]*ch'iohˏ ˏsang ʿliăng*, three pieces of matting.
Ling.

(392) Lik.

力ˏ As in the coll. phrase [4]*likˏ lóhˏ* active and ready in doing, as work not properly in one's province; also means in good health, not ailing.
Li.

(426) Mai.

ʿMai. A coll. word, as in *ˏteng ʿmai*, to undervalue or disparage, as another's goods; to spoil the sale by disparaging remarks.

(430) Mang.

ʿ慢 Read *mangʾ;* used for the coll. *ˏmang*, as in [4]*ˏt'i ˏt'ü ˏmang*, a spider's web; *met.*, the thread-netting on the top of a sedan.
Man.

(467) Mwoi.

昧ˏ Used in coll. books for *mwoiˏ* not yet: [5]*ˏi mwoiˏ k'óʾ* he has not yet gone.
Mei.

(494) Niăh.

拿ˏ Read *ʿna;* used for the coll. *niăhˏ* as in [6]*ˏmó hwakˏ niăhˏ ˏi ˏai*, or *ˏmó niăhˏ ˏi ˏai*, no way of managing or compelling him to; no way of doing it! impossible!
Na.

(513) Nói.

塊ʾ Read *tóiʾ;* coll. *nóiʾ* as in [7]*ʿmwang nóiʾ* everywhere; [8]*ˏmó nóiʾ ʿchau*, no place to run to, no way of escape.
K'uai.

Nóiʾ. A coll. word, probably a contraction of *ˏniă nóiʾ* as in *maingʾ nóiʾ k'óʾ* (or *maingʾ naiʾ k'óʾ*), delay going a little, don't go just yet.

(555) Ngiăng.

ʿNgiăng. A coll. corruption of *ʿngăng* (eye), as in *ʿngiăng ngiăngʾ* (i. e. *ʿngăng kiăngʾ*), glasses for the eyes, spectacles.

(592) O.

務ˏ Used in coll. books for *oˏ* to have; to be, is, it is; has, have: [9]*oˏ aingˏ* to have a limit, limited; [10]*oˏ ch'ëüʾ* amusing; [11]*oˏ ˏtang ˏtong*, is able, can.
Wu.

(593) Ó.

ˏÓ. A coll. word, as in *ˏó ˏchiéng*, to beg or tease for, to try to get the little that another has—a term used reprovingly or peevishly by the one importuned.

ˏÓ. A coll. word: to boil slowly, to stew; to mix and stew, as remnants: *ˏó langˏ langˏ tiohˏ* or *ˏó maukˏ maukˏ tiohˏ* to boil soft, to stew all to pieces; *ˏó siohˏ ˏtoi*, to huddle together, as children or gamblers.

---

[1] 燒熇 ○ [2] 蘦三領 ○ [3] 力落 ○ [4] 蜘蛛幔 ○ [5] 伊昧去 ○ [6] 毛法拿伊 ○ 唉 ○ [7] 滿塊 ○ [8] 毛塊走 ○ [9] 務限 ○ [10] 務趣 ○ [11] 務擔當 ○

(607) Pang.
꜀*Pang.* A coll. word, as in ꜀*pang* ‘*chi*, a ring worn on the thumb; an archer's thumb-ring, made of bone.

(609) Pauk.
爆 Pao. Used for the coll. *pauk*꜀, to fry quick and crisp or hard in oil, as a fowl, duck, piece of pork, etc.

(615) Peng.
邊 Pien. Read ꜀*pieng;* coll. ꜀*peng*, as in [1]‘*twai*² ꜀*peng*, or [2]‘*twai*² ꜀*peng* ‘*ch‘iu*, on the right hand or side; [3]‘*sieu* ꜀*peng*, or [4]‘*sieu* ꜀*peng* ‘*ch‘iu*, on the left hand.

(618) Pi.
꜀*Pi.* A coll. word, as in *sioh*꜁ ꜀*pi* ꜀*ti* (or ꜀*t‘i*), a bunch, a cluster, as of grapes.

(630) Po.
葩 Pao. Read *pŏ*²; coll. *po*²: a litter, as of cubs, whelps, pigs, kittens, etc.

(636) Pong.
幇 Pang. Used in the coll. for a time or season, as in [5]‘*chi* ꜀*pong*, at this time; [6]*a*² ꜀*pong*, next time, hereafter.

(702) P‘wo.
鋪 P‘u. Used for the coll. *p‘wo*² a numerative of Chinese leagues: [7]*sioh*꜁ *p‘wo*² one league or ten ‘*li*.

(742) Sieu.
*Sieu*². A coll. word, as in *sioh*꜁ *sieu*² a while—the same as *sioh*꜁ *siăk*꜁ ‘*ku*, or *sioh*꜁ *k‘aik*꜁ ‘*ku;* ‘*ting sioh*꜁ *sieu*² wait a while.

(744) Sing.
身 Shĕn. Also spoken ꜀*ting:* used as a numerative of idols and ancestral tablets: COLL., [8]꜀*pu sak*꜁ *sioh*꜁ ꜀*sing*, one idol.

(755) Sok.
束 Su. Shu. The name of a light-colored wood, burnt in idolatrous worship with the ꜀*t‘ang* or sandal-wood; it is said to (‘*ing* ‘*hwi*) kindle the sandal-wood: COLL., [9]꜀*t‘ang sok*꜁ ꜀*hiong*, the ꜀*t‘ang* and *sok*, incense-woods.

(770) Swoi.
*Swoi*². A coll. word: a channel made by a plow, a furrow: ꜀*lá sioh*꜁ *swoi*² to plow a furrow.

(780) Tai.
*Tai*². A coll. word: to cast away; used in the coll. for the death of a child, gone, dead!

(786) Tau.
‘*Tau.* A coll. suffix, as in ꜀*seng* ‘*tau*, or ꜀*seng* ‘*tau sie*² before, in front; *a*² ‘*tau*, behind, after, in the rear.

(804) Tié.
俤² A coll. character, used for the interrogative *tié*² as qualifying the following noun: which, what, whose; whoever, whatever; preceded by ꜀*k‘ŏ*, why, wherefore? [10]*tié*² ꜀*nĕng*, what person? who? [11]*tié*² *sioh*꜁ *chiăh*, which one? [12]꜀*k‘ŏ tié*² or [13]꜀*k‘ŏ tié*² *tai*² wherefore? why thus?

(822) Tong.
‘党 Tang. Used in the coll. as a numerative of packages, as of 1000 sheets of incense-paper, several ꜀*t‘ŏ* or quires of paper, etc.

(876) T‘iong.
杖² Chang. Used in the coll. as a numerative for stalks of sugar-cane: [14]*chiá*² *sioh*꜁ *t‘iong*² one stalk of sugar-cane.

---

1 大邊 ○ 2 大邊手 ○ 3 小邊 4 小邊手 5 只幇 6 下幇 7 一鋪 ○ 8 菩薩一身 9 檀束香 ○ 10 俤仈 ○ 11 俤一隻 ○ 12 靠俤 ○ 13 靠俤代 ○ 14 蔗一杖 ○

LIST OF THE 214 RADICALS;

With their sounds in the Foochow dialect, and one or more of their leading significations, as found in Kaughi's Dictionary. The sign ‡ marks the Radicals mostly used in combination; the contracted forms are always found in combination.

——— :O: ———

I STROKE.

- 一 1. *Ek*, One, unity.
- 丨 2. ʻ*Kung*. ‡ A stroke.
- 丶 3. ʻ*Chü*. ‡ A point.
- 丿 4. *Pʻiék*, ‡ A left stroke.
- 乙 5. *Ek*, One, curved.
- 亅 6. *Kʻwok*, ‡ Hooked.

II STROKES.

- 二 7. *Nè* Two.
- 亠 8. ˏ*Tʻeu*. ‡ A cover.
- 人 亻 9. ˏ*Ing*. Man.
- 儿 10. ˏ*Ing*. ‡ A man walking.
- 入 11. *Ik*$_2$ To enter.
- 八 12. *Paik*, Eight.
- 冂 13. ˏ*Hing*. ‡ A limit.
- 冖 14. *Mik*$_2$ ‡ To cover.
- 冫 15. ˏ*Ping*. ‡ Ice, cold.
- 几 16. ʻ*Ki*. A table.
- 凵 17. ʻ*Kʻang*. ‡ A receptacle.
- 刀 刂 18. ˏ*Tŏ*. A knife.
- 力 19. *Lik*$_2$ Strength.
- 勹 20. ˏ*Pau*. ‡ To infold.
- 匕 21. ʻ*Pi*. ‡ A spoon.
- 匚 22. ˏ*Hwong*. ‡ A chest.
- 匸 23. ʻ*Hi*. ‡ To conceal.
- 十 24. *Sek*$_2$ Ten.
- 卜 25. *Pok*, To divine.
- 卩 㔾 26. *Chiék*, ‡ A joint, a knot.
- 厂 27. *Hang*ʾ ‡ A shelter.
- 厶 28. ˏ*Sü*. ‡ Selfish, deflected.
- 又 29. *Eu*ʾ Moreover.

III STROKES.

- 口 30. ʻ*Kʻeu*. Mouth, orifice.
- 囗 31. ˏ*Ui*. ‡ To inclose.
- 土 32. ʻ*Tʻu*. Ground, earth.
- 士 33. *Sëü*ʾ A scholar.
- 夂 34. ˏ*Chüng*. ‡ To follow.
- 夊 35. ˏ*Soi*. ‡ To walk slowly.
- 夕 36. *Sik*, Evening.
- 大 37. *Tai*ʾ Large.
- 女 38. ʻ*Nü*. Female.
- 子 39. ʻ*Chü*. A child.
- 宀 40. ˏ*Miéng*. ‡ A cover.
- 寸 41. *Chʻaung*ʾ An inch.
- 小 42. ʻ*Sieu*. Small.
- 尢 尣 兀 尤 43. ˏ*Wong*. ‡ Distorted, lame.
- 尸 44. ˏ*Si*. A corpse.
- 屮 45. *Tʻiék*, ‡ A sprout.
- 山 46. ˏ*Sang*. Mountain.
- 川 巛 巜 47. ˏ*Chʻiong*. A stream.
- 工 48. ˏ*Kung*. Work.
- 己 49. ʻ*Ki*. One's self.
- 巾 50. ˏ*Küng*. A napkin.
- 干 51. ˏ*Kang*. A shield.
- 幺 52. ˏ*Yeu*. Small.
- 广 53. ʻ*Yéng*. ‡ Shelter, roof.
- 廴 54. ʻ*Ing*. ‡ A journey.
- 廾 55. ʻ*Küng*. ‡ To join hands.
- 弋 56. *Ik*$_2$ An arrow.
- 弓 57. ˏ*Küng*. A bow.
- 彐 彑 58. *Kié*ʾ ‡ A swine's head.
- 彡 59. ˏ*Sang*. ‡ Feathers, hair.
- 彳 60. *Tʻek*, ‡ A short step.

IV STROKES.

- 心 忄 ⺗ 61. ˏ*Sing*. The heart.
- 戈 62. ˏ*Kʻwo*. A spear.
- 戶 63. *Ho*ʾ A door.
- 手 扌 64. ʻ*Chʻiu*. A hand.
- 支 65. ˏ*Chié*. A branch.
- 攴 攵 66. *Pʻauk*, ‡ A blow.

文 67. ꜀Ung. Letters.
斗 68. ‘Teu. A measure.
斤 69. ꜀Küng. A catty.
方 70. ꜀Hwong. Square.
无 旡 71. ꜀U. ‡ Not, wanting.
日 72. Nik꜃ The sun.
曰 73. Wak꜃ To speak.
月 74. Ngwok꜃ The moon.
木 75. Muk꜃ Wood.
欠 76. K‘iéng’ To owe.
止 77. ‘Chi. To stop.
歹 歺 78. ‘Tai. Evil.
殳 79. ꜀Sü. ‡ Weapons.
毋 80. ꜀U. Do not.
比 81. ‘Pi. To compare.
毛 82. ꜀Mó. Hair.
氏 83. Se’ A family.
气 84. K‘e’ ‡ Breath.
水 氵 氺 85. ‘Chwi. Water.
火 灬 86. ‘Hwo. Fire.
爪 爫 87. ‘Cha. Claws.
父 88. Ho’ A father.
爻 89. ꜀Ngau. ‡ To blend.
爿 90. ꜀Peng. ‡ A couch.
片 91. P‘iéng’ A splinter.
牙 92. ꜀Nga. Teeth.
牛 93. ꜀Ngiu. A cow.
犬 犭 94. ‘K‘eng. A dog.

V STROKES.

玄 95. ꜀Hiéng. Somber.
玉 王 96. Ngük꜃ A gem.
瓜 97. ꜀Kwa. A melon.
瓦 98. ‘Ngwa. Earthen tiles.
甘 99. ‘Kang. Sweet.
生 100. ꜀Seng. To produce.
用 101. Eüng’ To use.
田 102. ꜀Tiéng. A field.
疋 103. P‘ek꜃ A roll, a piece.
疒 104. ꜀Ch‘ong. ‡ Diseased.
癶 105. Pwak꜃ ‡ To straddle.
白 106. Pek꜃ White.
皮 107. ꜀P‘i. Skin.
皿 108. ‘Ming. A dish.
目 罒 109. Muk꜃ The eye.
矛 110. ꜀Mau. A spear.
矢 111. ‘Ch‘i. An arrow.
石 112. Sik꜃ A stone.
示 礻 113. Se’ To admonish.
禸 114. ‘Niu. ‡ Print of a claw.
禾 115. ꜀Hwo. Grain.
穴 116. Hiék꜃ A cave.
立 117. Lik꜃ To stand.

VI STROKES.

竹 118. Tëük꜃ Bamboo.
米 119. ‘Mi. Rice.
糸 120. ꜀Si. ‡ Silk.
缶 121. ‘P‘eu. Crockery.
网 罒 罓 122. ‘Wong. ‡ A net.
羊 123. ꜀Yong. A sheep.
羽 124. ‘Ü. Feathers.
老 125. ‘Ló. Aged.
而 126. ꜀I. And, still.
耒 127. Lói’ A plough.
耳 128. ‘Ngi. The ear.
聿 129. Ük꜃ ‡ A pencil.
肉 月 130. Nük꜃ Flesh.
臣 131. ꜀Sing. A minister.
自 132. Chëü’ Self, from.
至 133. Che’ To extend to.
臼 134. K‘eu’ A mortar.
舌 135. Siék꜃ The tongue.
舛 136. ‘Ch‘wang. Error.
舟 137. ꜀Chiu. A boat.
艮 138. Kaung’ ‡ Perverse.
色 139. Saik꜃ Color.
艸 艹 140. ‘Ch‘ó. Shrubs.
虍 141. ꜀Hu. ‡ A tiger.
虫 142. ꜀T‘üng. Reptiles.
血 143. Hiék꜃ Blood.
行 144. ꜀Heng. To walk, to do.

海上絲綢之路文獻集成 科技與文化編

衣 衤 145. ‚*I.* Clothing.

襾 西 146. ‚*Sá.* To cover, the west.

VII STROKES.

見 147. *Kiéngʼ* To see.

角 148. *Kauk,* A horn.

言 149. ‚*Ngiong.* Words.

谷 150. *Kok,* A valley.

豆 151. *Taiuʼ* Pulse, beans.

豕 152. ʻ*Chʻi.* Swine.

豸 153. *Chaiʼ* Reptiles.

貝 154. *Pwoíʼ* Pearls, precious.

赤 155. *Chʻek,* Flesh color, bright.

走 156. ʻ*Cheu.* To run.

足 157. *Chëük,* The foot.

身 158. ‚*Sing.* The body.

車 159. ‚*Kü.* A carriage.

辛 160. ‚*Sing.* Bitter.

辰 161. ‚*Sing.* Time.

辵 辶 162. *Chʻiok,* ‡ Motion.

邑 阝 163. *Ek,* A city. [placed on the right.]

酉 164. ʻ*Iu.* Ripe, spirits.

釆 165. *Piéngʼ* ‡ To separate, to cull.

里 166. ʻ*Li.* A mile.

VIII STROKES.

金 167. ‚*King.* Metal, gold.

長 镸 168. ‚*Tiong.* Long, old.

門 169. ‚*Mwong.* A door.

阜 阝 170. *Pʻaiuʼ* ‡ A mound. [Placed on the left.]

隶 171. *Taiʼ* ‡ To extend to.

隹 172. ‚*Chwi.* ‡ Fowls.

雨 173. ʻ*Ü* Rain.

青 174. ‚*Chʻing.* Green, azure, dark.

非 175. ‚*Hi.* Not, wrong.

IX STROKES.

面 176. *Miéngʼ* The face.

革 177. *Kaik,* Skin, hide.

韋 178. ‚*Ui.* To oppose.

韭 179. ʻ*Kiu.* Leeks.

音 180. ‚*Ing.* Sound.

頁 181. *Hiék,* The head, a leaf.

風 182. ‚*Hung.* Wind.

飛 183. ‚*Hi.* To fly.

食 184. *Sik,* To eat.

首 185. ʻ*Siu.* The head.

香 186. ‚*Hiong.* Incense.

X STROKES.

馬 187. ʻ*Ma.* A horse.

骨 188. *Kauk,* Bones.

高 189. ‚*Kó.* High.

髟 190. ‚*Pieu.* ‡ Long hair.

鬥 191. *Taiuʼ* ‡ To quarrel.

鬯 192. *Tʻiongʼ* Fragrant wine.

鬲 193. *Kaik,* A tripod, urn.

鬼 194. ʻ*Kwi.* A demon.

XI STROKES.

魚 195. ‚*Ngü.* Fish.

鳥 196. ʻ*Neu.* A bird.

鹵 197. ʻ*Lu.* Salt.

鹿 198. *Lük,* A deer.

麥 199. *Mek,* Wheat.

麻 200. ‚*Ma.* Hemp.

XII STROKES.

黃 201. ‚*Wong.* Yellow.

黍 202. ʻ*Sü.* Millet.

黑 203. *Haik,* Black.

黹 204. ʻ*Chi.* To sew.

XIII STROKES.

黽 205. ʻ*Ming.* A frog.

鼎 206. ʻ*Tʻing.* A tripod, pan.

鼓 207. ʻ*Ku.* A drum.

鼠 208. ʻ*Chʻü.* A mouse, rat.

XIV STROKES.

鼻 209. *Pik,* The nose.

齊 210. ‚*Chá.* Even, correct.

XV STROKES.

齒 211. ʻ*Chʻi.* The teeth.

XVI STROKES.

龍 212. ‚*Lüng.* A dragon.

龜 213. ‚*Kwi.* A tortoise.

XVII STROKES.

龠 214. *Yoh,* A pipe, flute.

In the following index the characters contained in this dictionary are distributed under their respective radicals, and are grouped according to the number of strokes they contain, characters having the same number of strokes being placed in one group. The figures immediately on the right of each character indicate the page of the dictionary on which it is found. The figure in brackets at the right of the radical indicates its number in the List of Radicals: the small figures on the extreme right in each column indicate the number of strokes in the group of characters immediately below.

1 一
2 丨
3 丶
4 丿
5 乙

6 亅 7 二 8 亠 9 人

9 人

ALPH. DICT. 131.

海上絲綢之路文獻集成 科技與文化編

30 口

海上絲綢之路文獻集成 科技與文化編

32 土 33 士 34 夂 35 夊 36 夕 37 大

37 大

38 女

女 (38)

福州方言拼音字典

61 心忄⺗

61 心 忄 㣺

悰	115	惇	909	慍	638	愷	405	慧	219
悽	124	惙	914	愉	960	愾	406	憂	295
惑	209	愛	9 5 933	惼	668	慊	425	慣	310 392
悻	210	惻	128	愈 愈	958	愧	437	慨	406
惠	219	惨	131	愎	672	愿	631	愨	413
惛	276	愁	141	惺 㥉	790	㥬	685	慶	417
惚	274	惴	168	想	798	慎 愼	755	慱	953
㥏	935	意	179	愢	815	愬	803	慳	426
惎	324	惶	279	惰	894	愫	804	憀	488
惧	334	愔	289	慄	10 470	態	918	慢	529 531
悸	347	感	316	慇	968	慷	11 439	慕	565
惓	402	惲	966	慈	114	慾	963	慪	584
惟	540	愒	406	㥯	969	慺	476	慰	635
悶	557	愜	425	慅	166	慵	972	憑	676
惄	584	愆	426	愮	999	慮	478	慫	823
悲	710	愐	544	愴	171	慙 慚	33	慝	919
悱	711	愍	549	慉	214	慴 慴	72 785	慟	903
惜	747	惹	579	慁 㥪	243	慞	93	憎	12 46
悳	837	惱	588	慌	276	慘	131	憔	81
惆	876	愞	589	慆	944	慼	137	憮	956
惕	927	愕	603					憯	131
悼	894	愚	625						

福州方言拼音字典

61 心忄⺗
62 戈
63 戶

64 手 扌

海上絲綢之路文獻集成 科技與文化編

64 手 扌
65 支
66 攴 攵
67 文

曰 (73)

月 (74)

75 木 76 欠 77 止

海上絲綢之路文獻集成 科技與文化编

福州方言拼音字典

水氵氺

福州方言拼音字典

85 水氵氺

85 水 氵 氺 86 火 灬

海上絲綢之路文獻集成 科技與文化編

86 火 灬

93 牛 牜 94 犬 犭 95 玄 96 玉 王

96 玉 王

海上絲綢之路文獻集成 科技與文化編

102 田
103 疋
104 疒

104 疒
105 癶
106 白
107 皮
108 皿
109 目 罒

海上絲綢之路文獻集成 科技與文化编

—

米 (119)

120 糸
121 缶
122 网 罒 㓁
123 羊

福州方言拼音字典

140 艸 艹

海上絲綢之路文獻集成 科技與文化编

福州方言拼音字典

140 艸 艹

140 艸 艹 141 虍 142 虫

福州方言拼音字典

143 血
144 行
145 衣 衤

149 言

149 言

149 言
150 谷
151 豆
152 豕
153 豸
154 貝

162 辵 辶

167 金

福州方言拼音字典

福州方言拼音字典

178 韋
179 韭
180 音
181 頁
182 風

183 飛
184 食
185 首
186 香
187 馬

190 髟
191 門
192 鬯
193 鬲
194 鬼
195 魚

海上絲綢之路文獻集成　科技與文化編

福州方言拼音字典

The following corrections can be readily made by the student in the body of the dictionary with a Chinese pencil.

1. In the Chinese and English text.

——:o:——

Page		col.		line				
Page 45,	2d	col.	11th	line	for	euphonic prefix	read	word
„ 106,	1st	„	35th	„	„	eel.	„	eel ?
„ 112,	2d	„	8th	„	„	21st	„	20th
„ 131,	1st	„	7th	„	„	*꜀i*	„	*꜁i*
„ 138,	1st	„	15th	„	„	*niăk꜇*	„	*niăh꜇*
„ 140,	1st	„	20th	„	„	*saung꜄*	„	*saung꜅*
„	„	„	37th	„		strike out the word		*꜂hang*
„ 189,	2d	„	14th	„	„	*ĕü꜄*	read	*ĕü꜄*
„ 207,	1st	„	31st	„	„	*heü꜅*	„	*hĕü꜅*
„ 236,	2d	„	25th	„	„	first	„	second
„ 250,	2d	„	19th	„	„	(that)	„	(this)
„ 258,	1st	„	19th	„	„	holes about	„	holes; it is about
„ 267,	2d	„	23d	„	„	*꜀hwang*	„	*꜁hwang*
„ 322,	2d	„	26th	„	„	third	„	fourth
„ 336,	1st	„			„	董 and 墐	„	堇 and 墐
„ 337,	1st	„	1st	„	„	*ch'ĕü꜄*	„	*ch'ĕü꜅*
„ 344,	2d	„	2d	„	„	*p'ah꜆*	„	*pah꜆*
„ 363,	1st	„	17th	„	„	61st	„	39th
„ 369,	1st	„	20th	„	„	Song dynasty	„	emperor *Song꜅* or Shun
„ 381,	1st	„	3d	„	„	*pek꜇*	read	*paik꜆*
„ 383,	2d	„			„	裾	„	裙
„ 394,	1st	„	4th	„	„	*꜁t'ong ꜀kwi*	„	*꜀kwi ꜁t'ong*
„ 411,	2d	„			„	瞰	„	矙
„ 470,	1st	„			„	漂	„	溧
„ 497,	2d	„	1st	„	„	*꜀pwong*	„	*꜁pwong*
„ 523,	1st	„	36th	„		after q. v.:	insert	COM.,
„ 564,	2d	„	41st	„	„	*꜁mwo*	„	*꜂mwo*
„ 660,	1st	„	28th	„	„	*꜂tiong꜆*	„	*꜂tiong*
„ 726,	2d	„	24th	„		after one:	insert	COM.,
„ 730,	2d	„	39th	„		„ out;	„	COM.,

Page 731,	1st col.		the character	徙	in some of the copies erroneously printed		徒
„ 749,	2d „			for	晣	read	晰
„ 805,	2d „			„	鮹	„	鯖
„ 848,	1st „			„	斵	„	斲
„ 859,	2d „	14th line		„	*'ching*	„	*ˏching*
„ 937,	2d „	36th „	„		*hwok,*	„	*hwk*
„ 992,	(caption) change the 2d				YĂK	to	YANG
„ 1012,	1st col. 30th line for				*kaih,*	read	*kaik*

2. In the Chinese phrases at foot of page.

Page	45,	*No.*	17,	for	會	read	會
„	92,	„	16,	„	漳	„	璋
„	„	„	22,	„	溥	„	浦
„	123,	„	11,	„	斥	„	叱
„	144,	„	3,	„	蚔	„	蚊
„	169,	„	1,	„	鎖	„	瑣
„	227,	„	12,	„	椽	„	櫞
„	228,	„	4,	„	寒	„	塞
„	283,	„	11,	„	貽	„	飴
„	307,	„	14,	„	隣	„	鱗
„	324,	„	5,	„	礜	„	鼠
„	335,	„	8,	„	竹	„	築
„	424,	„	2,	„	直	„	迠
„	454,	„	9,	„	沛	„	配
„	470,	„	6,	„	災	„	齊
„	528,	„	15, the chararcter		論	in some of the copies erroneously printed	浪
„	581,	„	14, strike out the 2d				廿
„	609,	„	8,	for	凝	read	凝
„	715,	„	5,	„	席	„	什

Page	736,	for	20,	for	嗷	read	滶
,,	,,	,,	21,	,,	噭	,,	激
,,	750,	,,	5,	,,	末	,,	未
,,	766,	,,	6,	,,	賑	,,	賬
,,	771,	,,	1,	,,	狽	,,	須
,,	791,	,,	2,	,,	成	,,	辰
,,	802,	,,	20,	,,	鎖	,,	銷
,,	803,	,,	16,	,,	樸	,,	樸
,,	892,	,,	16,	,,	醄	,,	鋾

3. In the Index of Characters.

Page	1018,	1st	col.	under		181	insert	795
,,	,,	1st	,,	insert	与	958	[under 3	strokes]
,,	1019,	1st	,,	,,		575	,,	465
,,	1038,	2d	,,	insert	彊	418	[under 11	strokes]
,,	1043,	5th	,,	under		571	insert	573
,,	1056,	5th	,,	for		852	read	825
,,	1066,	3d	,,	strike out	袷	312		

4. In the Introduction.

Page xviii, last col. 15th line from the top of the Table, for *p'ong* read *p'wong*.

——————:o:——————